GRANGER'S INDEX TO POETRY

GRANGER'S INDEX TO POETRY

SIXTH EDITION, COMPLETELY REVISED AND ENLARGED, INDEXING ANTHOLOGIES PUBLISHED THROUGH DECEMBER 31, 1970

EDITED BY WILLIAM JAMES SMITH

COLUMBIA UNIVERSITY PRESS
NEW YORK AND LONDON 1973

GRANGER'S INDEX TO POETRY

SIXTH EDITION, COMPLETELY REVISED AND ENLARGED

ISBN 0-231-03641-8

PRINTED IN THE UNITED STATES OF AMERICA

3106 Columbia University Press 3-14-73

Library of Congress Cataloging in Publication Data

Granger, Edith.
Granger's index to poetry.
First ed. published in 1904 under title: Index to poetry and recitations.
1. English poetry—Indexes. 2. Poetry—Indexes. I. Smith, William James, 1918- ed. II. Title. III. Title: Index to poetry.
PN1021.G7 1973 808.81'0016 73-4186
ISBN 0-231-03641-8

PREFACE

GRANGER'S INDEX TO POETRY was first drafted as an informal reference work at the turn of the century by P. W. Coussens in the offices of A. C. McClurg & Co. in Chicago. The manuscript was edited by Edith Granger of the McClurg Co. and first appeared in book form in 1904, as a guide to anthologized poetry and "recitations." GRANGER'S has since become a standard reference work for all but the very smallest libraries. The editing and publication of the work was taken over by Columbia University Press in 1945. Recitations—and all prose works—were dropped from the listing, title and first lines were combined into a single alphabetical list, and the Subject Index was greatly expanded. Otherwise the format and purpose of the book remain substantially unchanged—to assist the reader in identifying and locating poems or selections from poems which have appeared in the most generally accessible anthologies. Each entry in the Title and First Line Index is followed by alphabetical symbols of the anthologies in which the work appears. A Key to Symbols will be found at the front of the book.

In preparation for this Sixth Edition of GRANGER'S a questionnaire was sent to hundreds of reference librarians throughout the United States and Canada, requesting their advice and recommendations on features of the book. The response to the questionnaire was large (almost 75%) and gratifyingly enthusiastic. Notable was the near unanimity on the usefulness of the Subject Index. We have, accordingly, continued the expansion of this portion of the book. The present Subject Index itemizes poems under nearly five thousand subject categories, including such "timely" topics as Ecology and Women's Liberation.

A word on the use of the Subject Index: The subject indexing of poetry is, at best, a parlous task; the general rule is: the better the poem, the more difficult its classification under an arbitrary subject heading. We have tried to avoid the more obvious pitfalls of subject assignment, but we have included a number of somewhat doubtful subject classifications on the theory that the individual can make his own judgment as to the suitability of our suggestions. Some subjects, of course, such as Love, are so universally a theme of poetry that we have made no effort to include individual poems, but have instead in the Subject Index referred readers to anthologies devoted to the subject. Librarians may also wish to remind users of the Subject Index that the Title and First Line Index may very well serve as a supplementary subject index—though titles are frequently deceptive in this respect. The Subject Index may additionally be useful in the identification of poems when neither the title, author, nor first line is known.

The Sixth Edition of GRANGER'S indexes a total of 514 volumes of anthologized poetry. Some of these are new editions of standard works which have proved so popular over the years that both the new edition and the earlier ones have been included (as the Palgrave series), with a distinctive symbol for each edition. The present edition includes the bulk of those anthologies which appeared in the Fifth Edition and the 1967 Supplement. Eliminated have been a number of out-of-print or less durably popular works which are not likely to be found in today's average small library. One hundred and fourteen new volumes, or new editions of older works, have been indexed for the first time. For those editions which have been retained the symbols used earlier have also been retained. New symbols have been assigned works included for the first time. No new symbol duplicates any used previously.

Notable in the present edition—and partially again in response to our questionnaire—is the inclusion of a number of volumes of Negro poetry. Emphasis too has been placed on the inclusion of representative volumes of contemporary and *avant garde* poetry which have proliferated during the past decade.

An accompanying page lists most of the members of the staff of Columbia University Press whose arduous, and ardent, endeavors have contributed to the making of the present volume—the selection, marking and checking of the anthologies, typing, filing and editing of the hundreds of thousands of cards which make up the manuscript of GRANGER'S. It is impossible, unfortunately, to name the innumerable librarians, scholars, amateurs of poetry—and some of the poets themselves—who have contributed in greater or lesser degree to the solution of such problems as source and attribution of various poems, but their assistance is gratefully acknowledged.

Special thanks are due the Libraries of Columbia University for facilitating our work by lending us many volumes for extended periods of time, and to the New York Public Library for the use of its collections.

William F. Bernhardt, Editor of the Fifth Edition of GRANGER'S, may be said to have laid the basis for the present edition of the work by his patient accumulation over the years of information on anthologies for possible inclusion in the current work, and he made his time generously available for consultation on the details of organization and editing.

William H. Harris, Editor of the Columbia Encyclopedia, initiated the collection of anthologies for this edition and supervised the early stages of the work. Production and design of the book was under the direction of Gerard Mayers, head of the Production Department for the Press. Particular thanks are due to Kathryn E. Pearcy, who proofread the entire volume in its complicated computer print-out form.

To all those, named and unnamed, who contributed with patience and meticulousness and good humor to an arduous task, the editor is grateful.

December 16, 1972 W. J. S.

CONTENTS

PREFACE	V
EXPLANATORY NOTES	X
ABBREVIATIONS	XI
KEY TO SYMBOLS	XIII
TITLE AND FIRST LINE INDEX	I
AUTHOR INDEX	1663
SUBJECT INDEX	2029

EXPLANATORY NOTES

Each of the approximately 500 volumes of poetry indexed in GRANGER'S is referred to by a short alphabetical abbreviation. These abbreviations, or symbols, are listed after the appropriate entries in the Title and First Line Index and mean that the relevant poem appears in that anthology. The complete title of the work and the essential publishing information can be found in the Key to Symbols at the front of the book.

The Author Index and the Subject Index are designed to be used in connection with the Title and First Line Index. A poem identified by title in the Author or Subject Index should be checked in the Title and First Line Index for the anthologies in which it appears.

Titles and first lines are arranged in one alphabetical listing in the Title and First Line Index. Titles are distinguished by initial capital letters on the important words. All first line entries are followed by the title of the poem, if there is a title. When the title and first line of a poem are identical, or nearly so, only the title is listed.

Indented listings below a title entry have the following significance: A single indentation indicates a *selection* from the above work; double indentation, within parentheses, signifies a *variant* title as used in the anthologies that follow.

Mother Goose rhymes are listed by first line only, rather than by the numerous arbitrary titles assigned to them by anthologists.

Generic title entries, such as Ode, Song, Sonnet, are followed by the first line in quotes for ease of identification. Such entries, of course, may also be located by first line listing.

Titles and first lines beginning with "O" and "Oh" are filed as though all were spelled "O." In a few instances words with variant spellings such as "honor" and "honour" are filed as though all followed standard American spelling. Names beginning "Mac," "Mc," and "M' " are filed as if all were spelled "Mac."

Chinese and old-style Japanese names in the Author Index are alphabeted, following standard practice, in uninverted form. Modern Japanese names, however, are inverted in the Western manner for filing purposes.

ABBREVIATIONS

abr.	abridged
ad.	adapted
add.	additional
arr.	arranged
at.	attributed
Bk.	book
br.	brief
c.	copyright
ch.	chapter
comp.	compiled *or* compiler
comps.	compilers
cond.	condensed
diff.	different
Eng.	English
fr.	from
frag.	fragment
incl.	included *or* including
introd.	introduction *or* introductory
ll.	lines
Mid.	Middle
misc.	miscellaneous
mod.	modernized *or* modern
N.T.	New Testament
O.T.	Old Testament
orig.	original
par.	paraphrase *or* paraphrased
pr.	prose
prol.	prologue
pseud.	pseudonym
Pt.	part
rev.	revised
sc.	scene
Sec.	section
sel.	selection
sels.	selections
sl.	slightly
st.	stanza
sts.	stanzas
tr.	translator, translation, *or* translated
trs.	translators *or* translations
var.	various
vers.	version *or* versions
wr.	wrong *or* wrongly

KEY TO SYMBOLS

Note: The date or number of an edition given in parentheses after a symbol in the TITLE AND FIRST LINE INDEX [e.g., MoBrPo (1962 ed.), HBV (8th ed.), OBEV (1st ed.), OBEV (new ed.)] indicates that the poem appears in that particular edition only.

AA — American Anthology, An, 1787–1900. *Edmund Clarence Stedman, ed.* (c.1900) Houghton Mifflin Company

ABF — American Ballads and Folk Songs. *John A. Lomax and Alan Lomax, comps.* (1934, reissue, 1946) The Macmillan Company

ACP — Anthology of Catholic Poets, An. *Shane Leslie, ed.* (1926, rev. ed., 1953) The Macmillan Company, *later pub. by* The Newman Press

ACV — Anthology of Commonwealth Verse, An. *Margaret J. O'Donnell, ed.* (c.1963) Blackie & Son Limited

ALV — Anthology of Light Verse, An. *Louis Kronenberger, ed.* (c.1935) The Modern Library

AmePo — American Poets, The, 1800–1900. *Edwin H. Cady, ed.* (c.1966) Scott, Foresman and Company

AmFN — America Forever New. *Sara Brewton and John E. Brewton, comps.* (c.1968) Thomas Y. Crowell Company

AmLP — American Lyric Poems; from Colonial Times to the Present. *Elder Olson, ed.* (c.1964) Appleton-Century-Crofts

AmNP — American Negro Poetry. *Arna Bontemps, ed.* (c.1963) Hill and Wang

AmP — American Poetry (American Literary Forms). *Karl Shapiro, ed.* (c.1960) Thomas Y. Crowell Company

AmPC — American Poems; a Contemporary Collection. *Jascha Kessler, ed.* (c.1964) Southern Illinois University Press

AmPP — American Poetry and Prose. *Norman Foerster, ed.* (3d ed., c.1947; 4th ed., c.1957; 5th ed., c.1970) Houghton Mifflin Company

AmSS — American Sea Songs and Chanteys. *Frank Shay, ed.* (c.1948) W. W. Norton & Company. Edition of 1924, published by Doubleday, Doran & Company, had title Iron Men and Wooden Ships

AnAmPo — Anthology of American Poetry, An. *Alfred Kreymborg, ed.* (2d rev. ed., 1941) Tudor Publishing Company

AnAnS 1-2 — Anchor Anthology of Seventeenth Century Verse, The. Vol. I, *Louis L. Martz, ed.;* Vol. II, *Richard S. Sylvester, ed.* (c.1969) Doubleday Anchor Books

AnEnPo Anthology for the Enjoyment of Poetry. *Max Eastman, ed.* (1939) Charles Scribner's Sons

AnFE Anthology of Famous English and American Poetry, An. *William Rose Benét and Conrad Aiken, eds.* (c.1945) The Modern Library

AnIL Anthology of Irish Literature, An. *David H. Greene, ed.* (c.1954) The Modern Library

AnIV Anthology of Irish Verse, An. *Padraic Colum, ed.* (Rev. ed., 1948) Liveright Publishing Corporation

AnNE Anthology of the New England Poets, An; from Colonial Times to the Present Day. *Louis Untermeyer, ed.* (c.1948) Random House

AnNZ Anthology of New Zealand Verse, An. *Robert Chapman and Jonathan Bennett, comps.* (1956) Oxford University Press

AnOE Anthology of Old English Poetry, An. *Charles W. Kennedy, tr.* (1960) Oxford University Press

ANYP Anthology of New York Poets, An. *Ron Padgett and David Shapiro, eds.* (c.1970) Random House

AP American Poetry. *Gay Wilson Allen, Walter B. Rideout, and James K. Robinson, eds.* (c.1965) Harper & Row

APA American Poetry, 1671–1928. *Conrad Aiken, ed.* (c.1929) The Modern Library. Revised edition of 1944 has title A Comprehensive Anthology of American Poetry. *See* CoAnAm

AS American Songbag, The. *Carl Sandburg, comp.* (c.1927, reissue, 1936) Harcourt, Brace and Company

AtBAP Atlantic Book of British and American Poetry, The. *Edith Sitwell, ed.* (c.1958) Little, Brown & Company

ATP Approaches to Poetry. *Walter Blair and W. K. Chandler, eds.* (1935, 2d ed., c.1953) D. Appleton–Century Company, *later pub. by* Appleton-Century-Crofts

AWP Anthology of World Poetry, An. *Mark Van Doren, ed.* (Rev. and enl. ed., 1936) Reynal & Hitchcock

BaBo Ballad Book, The. *MacEdward Leach, ed.* (1955) Harper & Brothers

BALP Black American Literature: Poetry. *Darwin T. Turner, ed.* (c.1969) Charles E. Merrill Publishing Company

BANP Book of American Negro Poetry, The. *James Weldon Johnson, ed.* (Rev. ed., 1931) Harcourt, Brace and Company

BBGG Beastly Boys and Ghastly Girls. *William Cole, ed.* (c.1964) The World Publishing Company

BBV Boy's Book of Verse, The. *Helen Dean Fish, comp.* (1923, rev. ed., 1951) Frederick A. Stokes Company, *later pub. by* J. B. Lippincott Company

BEL Book of English Literature, A. *Franklyn Bliss Snyder and Robert Grant Martin, eds.* (3rd ed., 1933) The Macmillan Company

BeLS Best Loved Story Poems. *Walter E. Thwing, ed.* (c.1941, reissue, 1948) Garden City Publishing Company

BePJ Beautiful Poems on Jesus. *Basil Miller, comp.* (1948) Beacon Hill Press

BF Black Fire; an Anthology of Afro-American Writing. *LeRoi Jones and Larry Neal, eds.* (c.1968) William Morrow & Company

BFSS Ballads and Folk Songs of the Southwest; More than 600 Titles, Melodies, and Texts Collected in Oklahoma. *Ethel Moore and Chauncey O. Moore, comps.* (c.1964) University of Oklahoma Press

BiCB Birthday Candles Burning Bright; a Treasury of Birthday Poetry. *Sara Brewton and John E. Brewton, eds.* (c.1960) The Macmillan Company

BiS Bird Songs. *Gwendolyn Reed, comp.* (1969) Atheneum

BLPA Best Loved Poems of the American People, The. *Hazel Felleman, ed.* (1936) Garden City Publishing Company

BLRP Best Loved Religious Poems, The. *James Gilchrist Lawson, comp.* (1933) Fleming H. Revell Company

BoAN 1–2 Books of American Negro Spirituals, The; including The Book of American Negro Spirituals and The Second Book of Negro Spirituals. *James Weldon Johnson, ed.* (c.1925, 1926, 2 vols. in 1, 1940, reissue, 1944) The Viking Press

BoAu Book of Australian and New Zealand Verse, A. *Walter Murdoch, ed.* (Rev. ed., 1945, reissue, 1949) Oxford University Press. Edition of 1918 had title The Oxford Book of Australasian Verse

BoAV Book of Australian Verse, A. *Judith Wright, ed.* (1956) Oxford University Press

BoC Book of Comfort, A; an Anthology. *Elizabeth Goudge, ed.* (c. 1964) Coward-McCann

BoChLi Book of Children's Literature, A. *Lillian Hollowell, ed.* (c.1939, 2d ed., c.1950) Rinehart & Company

BOHV Book of Humorous Verse, The. *Carolyn Wells, comp.* (Rev. and enl. ed., 1934, reissue, 1947) Garden City Publishing Company

BoLiVe Book of Living Verse, The. *Louis Untermeyer, ed.* (Rev. ed., c.1939, new [rev.] ed., c.1945) Harcourt, Brace and Company

BOLo Black Out Loud. *Arnold Adoff, ed.* (c.1970) The Macmillan Company

BoLP Book of Love Poems, A. *William Cole, ed.* (c.1965) The Viking Press

BoNaP Book of Nature Poems, A. *William Cole, comp.* (c.1969) The Viking Press

BoPe Book of Peace, A. *Elizabeth Goudge, ed.* (c.1967) Coward-McCann

BoSA Book of South African Verse, A. *Guy Butler, comp.* (1959) Oxford University Press

BoTP Book of a Thousand Poems, The. *Jeannie Murray MacBain, ed.* (1942) Evans Brothers

BoW Book of the Winter, A. *Edith Sitwell, comp.* (c.1951) The Vanguard Press

BP Black Poetry. *Dudley Randall, ed.* (c.1969) Broadside Press

BrPo British Poetry 1880–1920; Edwardian Voices. *Paul L. Wiley and Harold Orel, eds.* (c.1969) Appleton-Century Crofts

BrR Bridled with Rainbows. *Sara Brewton and John E. Brewton, eds.* (1949) The Macmillan Company

BuBa Bundle of Ballads, A. *Ruth Manning-Sanders, comp.* (c.1959) J. B. Lippincott Company

BWP Beginning with Poems. *Reuben A. Brower, Anne D. Ferry, and David Kalstone, eds.* (c.1966) W. W. Norton & Company

CABA College Anthology of British and American Verse, The. *A. Kent Hieatt and William Park, eds.* (1964) Allyn and Bacon

CABL Collins Albatross Book of Longer Poems; English and American Poetry from the Fourteenth Century to the Present Day. *Edwin Morgan, ed.* (c.1963) William Collins Sons & Company

CAD City in All Directions. *Arnold Adoff, ed.* (c.1969) The Macmillan Company

CaFP Case for Poetry, The; a Critical Anthology. *Frederick L. Gwynn, Ralph W. Condee, and Arthur O. Lewis, Jr., eds.* (2d ed., c.1965) Prentice-Hall

CaP Canadian Poetry in English (Canadian Literature Series). *Bliss Carman, Lorne Pierce, and V. B. Rhodenizer, eds.* (Rev. and enl. ed., c.1954) The Ryerson Press

CavP Cavalier Poets, The. *Robin Skelton, ed.* (1970) Oxford University Press

CAW Catholic Anthology, The. *Thomas Walsh, ed.* (Rev. ed., 1932, reissue, 1939) The Macmillan Company

CBEP Cassell Book of English Poetry, The. *James Reeves, ed.* (c.1965) Harper & Row

CBV College Book of Verse, A. *C. F. Main, ed.* (c.1970) Wadsworth Publishing Company

CDC Caroling Dusk; an Anthology of Verse by Negro Poets. *Countee Cullen, ed.* (1927) Harper & Brothers

CenHV Century of Humorous Verse, A, 1850–1950 (Everyman's Library). *Roger Lancelyn Green, ed.* (1959) E. P. Dutton & Company

CEP Collection of English Poems, A, 1660–1800. *Ronald S. Crane, ed.* (1932) Harper & Brothers

CH Come Hither. *Walter de la Mare, comp.* (Rev. ed., 1928, new ed., 1948, 3d ed., 1957) Alfred A. Knopf

ChBR Christmas Bells Are Ringing; a Treasury of Christmas Poetry. *Sara Brewton and John E. Brewton, eds.* (c.1951) The Macmillan Company

ChER Choice of English Romantic Poetry, A. *Stephen Spender, ed.* (1947) The Dial Press

ChIP Christ in Poetry. *Thomas Curtis Clark and Hazel Davis Clark, eds.* (c.1952) Association Press

ChMP Chatto Book of Modern Poetry, The, 1915–1955. *C. Day Lewis and John Lehmann, eds.* (New ed., 1959) Chatto & Windus

ChrBoLe Christmas Book of Legends and Stories, The. *Elva Sophronia Smith and Alice Isabel Hazeltine, eds.* (c.1944) Lothrop, Lee & Shepard Company

ChTr Cherry-Tree, The. *Geoffrey Grigson, comp.* (c.1959) Phoenix House

CIV Cat in Verse, The. *Carolyn Wells and Louella D. Everett, comps.* (1935) Little, Brown & Company

CLWM Come Live with Me; Five Centuries of Romantic Poetry. *Charles Norman, ed.* (c.1966) David McKay Company

CMoP Chief Modern Poets of England and America. *Gerald D. Sanders, John H. Nelson, and M. L. Rosenthal, eds.* (1962, 4th ed.) The Macmillan Company

CoAnAm Comprehensive Anthology of American Poetry, A. *Conrad Aiken, ed.* (c.1944) The Modern Library. Edition of 1929 had title American Poetry, 1671–1928. *See* APA

CoAP Contemporary American Poets, The; American Poetry since 1940. *Mark Strand, ed.* (c.1969) World Publishing Company

CoBA College Book of American Literature, A. *Milton Ellis, and others, eds.* (2d ed., c.1949) American Book Company

CoBE College Book of English Literature. *James Edward Tobin, and others, comps.* (c.1949) American Book Company

CoBMV College Book of Modern Verse, A. *James K. Robinson and Walter B. Rideout, eds.* (c.1958) Row, Peterson and Company

CoMu Common Muse, The; an Anthology of Popular British Ballad Poetry, XVth–XXth Century. *Vivian de Sola Pinto and Allan Edwin Rodway, eds.* (1957) Philosophical Library

CoPo Controversy of Poets, A; an Anthology of Contemporary American Poetry. *Paris Leary and Robert Kelly, eds.* (c.1965) Doubleday & Company

CoSo Cowboy Songs and Other Frontier Ballads. *John A. Lomax and Alan Lomax, eds.* (Rev. and enl. ed., 1938, reissue, 1948) The Macmillan Company

CrMA Criterion Book of Modern American Verse, The. *W. H. Auden, ed.* (c.1956) Criterion Books

CTC Confucius to Cummings; an Anthology of Poetry. *Ezra Pound and Marcella Spann, eds.* (c.1964) New Directions

DD Days and Deeds; a Book of Verse. *Burton Egbert Stevenson and Elizabeth B. Stevenson, comps.* (1931) Doubleday, Doran & Company

DiPo Dimensions of Poetry, The; a Critical Anthology. *James E. Miller, Jr., and Bernice Slote, eds.* (c.1962) Dodd, Mead & Company

DTC Dylan Thomas's Choice; an Anthology of Verse Spoken by Dylan Thomas. *Ralph Maud and Aneirin Talfan Davies, eds.* (c.1963) New Directions

DTo Dark Tower, The; Nineteenth Century Narrative Poems. *Dairine Coffey, comp.* (1967) Atheneum

EaLo Earth Is the Lord's, The; Poems of the Spirit. *Helen Plotz, comp.* (c.1965) Thomas Y. Crowell Company

EG English Galaxy of Shorter Poems, The. *Gerald Bullett, ed.* (1934) The Macmillan Company

EiCL Eighteenth Century English Literature. *Geoffrey Tillotson, Paul Fussell, Jr., and Marshall Waingrow, eds.* (c.1969) Harcourt, Brace & World

EiCP Eighteenth-Century Poetry. *Patricia Meyer Spacks, ed.* (c.1964) Prentice-Hall

EiPP Eighteenth Century Poetry and Prose. *Louis I. Bredvold, Alan D. McKillop, and Lois Whitney, eds.* (2d ed., c.1956) The Ronald Press Company

ElL Elizabethan Lyrics. *Norman Ault, ed.* (3d ed., c.1949) William Sloane Associates. Paperback edition of 1960 published by G. P. Putnam's Sons

ELP English Lyric Poems, 1500–1900. *C. Day Lewis, ed.* (c.1961) Appleton-Century-Crofts

ELU Eight Lines and Under. *William Cole, ed.* (c.1967) The Macmillan Company

EnL English Literature; a College Anthology. *Donald B. Clark, Leon T. Dickinson, Charles M. Hudson, and George B. Pace, eds.* (c.1960) The Macmillan Company

EnLi 1–2 English Literature and Its Backgrounds, Vols. I-II. *Bernard D. N. Grebanier and Stith Thompson, eds.* (c.1939) *Bernard D. Grebanier, Samuel Middlebrook, Stith Thompson, and William Watt, eds.* (Rev. ed., c.1949) The Dryden Press

EnLit English Literature; a Period Anthology. *Albert C. Baugh and George William McClelland, eds.* (c.1954) Appleton-Century-Crofts

EnLoPo English Love Poems. *John Betjeman and Geoffrey Taylor, comps.* (1957) Faber and Faber

EnPE English Poetry of the Mid and Late Eighteenth Century; an Historical Anthology. *Ricardo Quintana and Alvin Whitley, eds.* (1963) Alfred A. Knopf

EnPo English Poetry 1400–1580. *William Tydeman, ed.* (c.1970) Barnes & Noble

EnRePo English Renaissance Poetry; a Collection of Shorter Poems from Skelton to Jonson. *John Williams, ed.* (c.1963) Doubleday & Company

EnRP English Romantic Poetry and Prose. *Russell Noyes, ed.* (1956) Oxford University Press

EnSB English and Scottish Ballads (The Poetry Bookshelf). *Robert Graves, ed.* (1957) The Macmillan Company

EP English Poetry 1550–1660. *Fred Inglis, ed.* (c.1965) Methuen & Company

EPN English Poetry of the Nineteenth Century. *G. R. Elliott and Norman Foerster, eds.* (1923, reissue, 1954) The Macmillan Company

ERoP 1–2 English Romantic Poetry, Vols. I–II. *Harold Bloom, ed.* (c.1963) Doubleday Anchor Books

ErPo Erotic Poetry; the Lyrics, Ballads, Idyls, and Epics of Love—Classical to Contemporary. *William Cole, ed.* (1963) Random House

ESPB English and Scottish Popular Ballads. *Helen Child Sargent and George Lyman Kittredge, eds., from the collection of Francis James Child.* (c.1904, 1932, reissue, 1947) Houghton Mifflin Company

EtS Eternal Sea, The; an Anthology of Sea Poetry. *W. M. Williamson, ed.* (c.1946) Coward-McCann

EvOK Everybody Ought to Know. *Ogden Nash, ed.* (c.1961) J. B. Lippincott Company

ExPo Exploring Poetry. *M. L. Rosenthal and A. J. M. Smith, eds.* (c.1955) The Macmillan Company

FaBoBe Family Book of Best Loved Poems, The. *David L. George, ed.* (c.1952) Hanover House

FaBoCh Faber Book of Children's Verse, The. *Janet Adam Smith, comp.* (1953) Faber and Faber

FaBoEn Faber Book of English Verse, The. *John Hayward, ed.* (1958) Faber and Faber

FaBoMo Faber Book of Modern Verse, The. *Michael Roberts, ed.* (2d ed., 1951, with a supplement of poems chosen by Anne Ridler) Faber and Faber

FaBoTw Faber Book of Twentieth Century Verse, The; an Anthology of Verse in Britain, 1900–1950. *John Heath-Stubbs and David Wright, eds.* (1953) Faber and Faber

FaBV Family Book of Verse, The. *Lewis Gannett, ed.* (c.1961) Harper & Row

FaChP Favorite Christian Poems. *Donald T. Kauffman, ed.* (c.1969) Fleming H. Revell Company

FaFP Family Album of Favorite Poems, The. *P. Edward Ernest, ed.* (c.1959) Grosset & Dunlap

FaPL Famous Poems and the Little-known Stories behind Them. *Ralph L. Woods, ed.* (c.1961) Hawthorn Books

FaPON Favorite Poems Old and New. *Helen Ferris, ed.* (c.1957) Doubleday & Company

FCP Five Courtier Poets of the English Renaissance. *Robert M. Bender, ed.* (1967) Washington Square Press

FiBHP Fireside Book of Humorous Poetry, The. *William Cole, ed.* (1959) Simon and Schuster

FiMAP Fifteen Modern American Poets. *George P. Elliott, ed.* (c.1956) Rinehart & Company

FiP Fifteen Poets; Chaucer to Arnold. (1941) Oxford University Press

FiSC Fire and Sleet and Candlelight. *August Derleth, ed.* (1961) Arkham House

FlW Flock of Words, A. *David Mackay, ed.* (c.1969) Harcourt, Brace & World

FOL From Other Lands. *Al Hine, ed.* (c.1969) J. B. Lippincott Company

ForPo Form of Poetry, The. *Thomas R. Arp, ed.* (c.1966) The Macmillan Company

FosPo Forms of Poetry. *James L. Calderwood and Harold F. Toliver, eds.* (c.1968) Prentice-Hall

FRC First Reader of Contemporary American Poetry, A. *Patrick Gleeson, ed.* (c.1969) Charles E. Merrill Publishing Company

FTB Four & Twenty Blackbirds. *Helen Dean Fish, ed.* (1937) Frederick A. Stokes Company, *later pub. by* J. B. Lippincott Company

GaP Gaily We Parade. *John E. Brewton, comp.* (c.1940, reissue, 1944) The Macmillan Company

GBV Girl's Book of Verse, The. *Mary Gould Davis, comp.* (1922, rev. ed., 1952) Frederick A. Stokes Company, *later pub. by* J. B. Lippincott Company

GFA Golden Flute, The. *Alice Hubbard and Adeline Babbitt, comps.* (c.1932) The John Day Company

GN Golden Numbers. *Kate Douglas Wiggin and Nora Archibald Smith, eds.* (1902) Doubleday, Doran & Company

GoBC Golden Book of Catholic Poetry, The. *Alfred Noyes, ed.* (c.1946) J. B. Lippincott Company

GoJo Golden Journey, The; Poems for Young People. *Louise Bogan and William Jay Smith, comps.* (c.1965) Reilly & Lee

GoSl Golden Slippers; an Anthology of Negro Poetry for Young Readers. *Arna Bontemps, comp.* (4th ed., c.1941) Harper & Brothers

GoTL Golden Treasury of Longer Poems, The (Everyman's Library). *Ernest Rhys, ed.* (1939, rev. ed., 1949) J. M. Dent & Sons

GoTP Golden Treasury of Poetry, The. *Louis Untermeyer, ed.* (c.1959) Golden Press

GoTS Golden Treasury of Scottish Poetry, The. *Hugh MacDiarmid, ed.* (1941) The Macmillan Company

GoYe Golden Year, The; the Poetry Society of America Anthology, 1910–1960. *Melville Cane, John Farrar, and Louise Townsend Nicholl, eds.* (1960) The Fine Editions Press

GSP Great Story-Poems. *Theodoric Jones, comp.* (c.1966) Hart Publishing Company

GTBS Golden Treasury of the Best Songs and Lyrical Poems in the English Language. *Francis Palgrave, comp.* (1929) Oxford University Press

GTBS-D Golden Treasury of the Best Songs and Lyrical Poems in the English Language, The. *Francis Turner Palgrave, comp. With additional poems selected by C. Day Lewis.* (1954) William Collins Sons & Company

GTBS-P Golden Treasury of the Best Songs & Lyrical Poems in the English Language. The. *Francis Turner Palgrave, comp. With a fifth book selected by John Press.* (c.1964) Oxford University Press

GTBS-W F. T. Palgrave's The Golden Treasury of the Best Songs and Lyrical Poems (A Mentor Book). *Revised and enlarged by Oscar Williams.* (c.1953) The New American Library

GTSE Golden Treasury (Everyman's Library). *Francis T. Palgrave, comp.* (1934) E. P. Dutton & Company

GTSL Golden Treasury of Songs and Lyrics, The. *Francis T. Palgrave, comp.* (Rev. and enl. ed., 2 vols. in 1, 1928, reissue, 1944). The Macmillan Company

HaMV Harrap Book of Modern Verse, The (Harrap's Modern English Series). *Maurice Wollman and Kathleen B. Parker, comps.* (1959) George G. Harrap & Company

HBMV Home Book of Modern Verse, The. *Burton Egbert Stevenson, ed.* (1925, 2d ed., c.1953) Henry Holt and Company

HBV Home Book of Verse, The. *Burton Egbert Stevenson, ed.* (6th ed. c.1926, 8th ed., c.1949, 2 vols.) Henry Holt and Company

HBVY Home Book of Verse for Young Folks, The. *Burton Egbert Stevenson, ed.* (Rev. and enl. ed., 1929) Henry Holt and Company

HH Highdays and Holidays. *Florence Adams and Elizabeth McCarrick, comps.* (1927) E. P. Dutton & Company

HoPM How Does a Poem Mean? (An Introduction to Literature, Part III). *John Ciardi, ed.* (c.1959) Houghton Mifflin Company

HT Here and There; 100 Poems about Places. *Elinor Parker, ed.* (c.1967) Thomas Y. Crowell Company

HW High Wedlock Then Be Honoured. *Virginia Tufte, ed.* (c.1970) The Viking Press

HYE Holding Your Eight Hands. *Edward Lucie-Smith, ed.* (c.1969) Doubleday & Company

IDB I Am the Darker Brother. *Arnold Adoff, ed.* (c.1968) The Macmillan Company

IHA I Hear America Singing. *Ruth Barnes, comp.* (1937) John C. Winston Company

ILP Introduction to Literature: Poems. *Lynn Altenbernd and Leslie L. Lewis, eds.* (c.1963) The Macmillan Company

ImOP Imagination's Other Place; Poems of Science and Mathematics. *Helen Plotz, comp.* (c.1955) Thomas Y. Crowell Company

InMe Innocent Merriment; an Anthology of Light Verse. *Franklin P. Adams, comp.* (c.1942) McGraw-Hill Book Company

InP Introduction to Poetry, An. *Jay B. Hubbell and John O. Beaty, eds.* (Rev. ed., c.1936, reissue, 1949) The Macmillan Company

InPo Introduction to Poetry. *Mark Van Doren, ed.* (c.1951) William Sloane Associates, *later pub. by* The Dryden Press

InvP Invitation to Poetry; a Round of Poems from John Skelton to Dylan Thomas. *Lloyd Frankenberg, ed.* (1956) Doubleday & Company

IrPN Irish Poets of the Nineteenth Century (The Muses' Library). *Geoffrey Taylor, ed.* (c.1951) Harvard University Press.

ISi I Sing of a Maiden; the Mary Book of Verse. *Sister M. Thérèse, ed.* (1947) The Macmillan Company

JAWP Junior Anthology of World Poetry, A. *Mark Van Doren and Garibaldi M. Lapolla, eds.* (1929) Albert & Charles Boni. *Same as* WBP

JKCP Joyce Kilmer's Anthology of Catholic Poets. *Joyce Kilmer, ed.* (New ed., 1926, reissue, 1939) Liveright Publishing Corporation. *With a new supplement by James Edward Tobin.* (c.1955) Doubleday & Company (Image Books). Edition of 1917 had title Dreams and Images; an Anthology of Catholic Poetry

Kal Kaleidoscope; Poems by American Negro Poets. *Robert Hayden, ed.* (c.1967) Harcourt, Brace & World

KiLC Kings, Lords, & Commons; an Anthology from the Irish. *Frank O'Connor, ed. and tr.* (1959) Alfred A. Knopf

LaA Late Augustans, The; Longer Poems of the Later Eighteenth Century (The Poetry Bookshelf). *Donald Davie, ed.* (c.1958) The Macmillan Company

LaNeLa Lays of the New Land; Stories of Some American Poets and Their Work. *Charlie May Simon, ed.* (c.1943) E. P. Dutton & Company

LBN Little Book of Necessary Nonsense, A. *Burges Johnson, comp.* (1929) Harper & Brothers

LHV Little Book of American Humorous Verse, A. *T. A. Daly, comp.* (1926) David McKay Company

LiBL Little Book of Limericks, The. *H. I. Brock, comp.* (c.1947) Duell, Sloan and Pearce

LiPo Lincoln and the Poets. *William W. Betts, Jr., ed.* (c.1965) University of Pittsburgh Press

LiTA Little Treasury of American Poetry, A. *Oscar Williams, ed.* (1948) Charles Scribner's Sons

LiTB Little Treasury of British Poetry, A. *Oscar Williams, ed.* (1951) Charles Scribner's Sons

LiTG Little Treasury of Great Poetry, A. English and American. *Oscar Williams, ed.* (1947) Charles Scribner's Sons

LiTL Little Treasury of Love Poems, A. *John Holmes, ed.* (1950) Charles Scribner's Sons

LiTM Little Treasury of Modern Poetry, A, English and American. *Oscar Williams, ed.* (1946, rev. ed., c.1950; 3rd ed., 1970) Charles Scribner's Sons

LiTW Little Treasury of World Poetry, A. *Hubert Creekmore, ed.* (1952) Charles Scribner's Sons

LO Love. *Walter de la Mare, ed.* (1946) William Morrow & Company

LoBV London Book of English Verse, The. *Herbert Read and Bonamy Dobrée, comps.* (1949, 2d rev. ed., 1952) The Macmillan Company

LoEn Love's Enchantment; Story Poems and Ballads. *Helen Ferris, comp.* (c.1944) Doubleday, Doran & Company

LoGBV Looking Glass Book of Verse, The. *Janet Adam Smith, comp.* (c.1959) Looking Glass Library. Revised edition of FaBoCh

LOW Lean Out of the Window; an Anthology of Modern Poetry. *Sara Hannum and Gwendolyn E. Reed, comps.* (1965) Atheneum

MaC Magic Circle, The; Stories and People in Poetry. *Louis Untermeyer, ed.* (c.1952) Harcourt, Brace and Company

MaMe Major Metaphysical Poets of the Seventeenth Century, The. *Edwin Honig and Oscar Williams, eds.* (1968) Washington Square Press

MAmP Major American Poets to 1914. *Francis Murphy, ed.* (c.1967) D. C. Heath and Company

MAP Modern American Poetry. *Louis Untermeyer, ed.* (5th rev. ed., c.1936) Harcourt, Brace and Company. For the sixth and seventh revised editions, *see* MoAmPo

MAPA Modern American Poets. *Conrad Aiken, ed.* (1927) The Modern Library. Enlarged edition of 1963 has title Twentieth-Century American Poetry. *See* TwAmPo

MaPo Major Poets, The; English and American. *Charles M. Coffin and Gerrit Hubbard Roelofs, eds.* (c.1954; 2d ed., c.1969) Harcourt, Brace & World

MaRV Masterpieces of Religious Verse. *James Dalton Morrison, ed.* (c.1948) Harper & Brothers

MasP Master Poems of the English Language. *Oscar Williams, ed.* (1966) Trident Press

MaVP Major Victorian Poets, The. *William H. Marshall, ed.* (1966) Washington Square Press

MBW 1–2 Major British Writers, Vols. I–II. *G. B. Harrison, ed.* (c.1959) Harcourt, Brace & World

MC My Country. *Burton Egbert Stevenson, ed.* (1932) Houghton Mifflin Company

MCCG Magic Casements. *George S. Carhart and Paul A. McGhee, comps.* (1926, reissue, 1948) The Macmillan Company

MeEL Medieval English Lyrics; a Critical Anthology. *R. T. Davies, ed.* (1964) Northwestern University Press

MeEV Medieval English Verse and Prose, in Modernized Versions. *Roger Sherman Loomis and Rudolph Willard, eds.* (c.1948) Appleton-Century-Crofts.

MeLP Metaphysical Lyrics & Poems of the Seventeenth Century. *Herbert J. C. Grierson, ed.* (1921, reissue, 1947) Oxford University Press

MemP Memorable Poetry. *Sir Francis Meynell, ed.* (c.1965) Franklin Watts

MePo Metaphysical Poets, The. *Helen Gardner, ed.* (c.1957) Penguin Books

MERP Major English Romantic Poets, The. *William H. Marshall, ed.* (1966) Washington Square Press

MeWo Men and Women; the Poetry of Love. *Louis Untermeyer, ed.* (c.1970) American Heritage Press

MiAP Mid-Century American Poets. *John Ciardi, ed.* (c.1950) Twayne Publishers

ML Marvelous Light, The; Poets and Poetry. *Helen Plotz, ed.* (c.1970) Thomas Y. Crowell Company

MMA Men Who March Away; Poems of the First World War. *I. M. Parsons, ed.* (c.1965) The Viking Press

MoAB Modern American & Modern British Poetry. *Louis Untermeyer, ed.,* in consultation with *Karl Shapiro and Richard Wilbur*. (Rev., shorter ed., c.1955) Harcourt, Brace and Company

MoAmPo Modern American Poetry. *Louis Untermeyer, ed.* (6th rev. ed., c.1942; mid-century ed. [7th rev. ed.], c.1950; 8th rev. ed., c.1962) Harcourt, Brace and Company. For the fifth revised edition, *see* MAP

MoAuPo Modern Australian Poetry. *H. M. Green, comp.* (2d ed., rev., 1952) Melbourne University Press

MoBrPo Modern British Poetry. *Louis Untermeyer, ed.* (5th rev. ed., c.1942; mid-century ed. [6th rev. ed.], c.1950; 7th rev. ed., c.1962) Harcourt, Brace and Company

MoBS Modern Ballads and Story Poems. *Charles Causley, ed.* (1965) Franklin Watts, Inc. English edition, published in 1964 by Brockhampton Press Ltd., had title Rising Early

MoCV Modern Canadian Verse. *A. J. M. Smith, ed.* (1967) Oxford University Press

MoLP Modern Love Poems. *D. J. Klemer, ed.* (c.1961) Doubleday & Company

MoPo Modern Poetry; American and British. *Kimon Friar and John Malcolm Brinnin, eds.* (c.1951) Appleton-Century-Crofts

MoPW Modern Poets' World, The (The Poetry Bookshelf). *James Reeves, ed.* (1957) William Heinemann

MoRP Modern Religious Poems; a Contemporary Anthology. *Jacob Trapp, ed.* (c.1964) Harper & Row

MoShBr Moon Is Shining Bright as Day, The; an Anthology of Good-humored Verse. *Ogden Nash, ed.* (c.1953) J. B. Lippincott Company

MoSiPe More Silver Pennies. *Blanche Jennings Thompson, comp.* (c.1938) The Macmillan Company

MoVE Modern Verse in English, 1900-1950. *David Cecil and Allen Tate, eds.* (c.1958) The Macmillan Company

MP Modern Poets, The; an American-British Anthology. *John Malcolm Brinnin and Bill Read, eds.* (c.1963) McGraw-Hill Book Company. Revised edition of 1970 has title Twentieth Century Poetry; American and British (1900-1970). *See* TwCP

MPB My Poetry Book. *Grace Thompson Huffard, Laura Mae Carlisle, and Helen Ferris, comps.* (1934, rev. ed., c.1956) John C. Winston Company

MuSP Music & Sweet Poetry. *John Bishop, comp.* (c.1968) John Baker

MWA 1–2 Major Writers of America, Vols. I-II. *Perry Miller and others, eds.* (c.1962) Harcourt, Brace & World

MyFE My Favourite English Poems. *John Masefield, ed.* (1950) The Macmillan Company

NA Nonsense Anthology, A. *Carolyn Wells, ed.* (c.1930) Charles

Scribner's Sons. Paperback edition of 1958 published by Dover Publications

NAMP New Anthology of Modern Poetry, A. *Selden Rodman, ed.* (1938) Random House, *later pub. by* The Modern Library

NaP Naked Poetry; Recent American Poetry in Open Forms. *Stephen Berg and Robert Mezey, eds.* (c.1969) Bobbs-Merrill

NBM 19th Century British Minor Poets. *W. H. Auden, ed.* (c.1966) Delacorte Press

NBP New Black Poetry, The. *Clarence Major, ed.* (1970) International Publishers Company

NCEP New Canon of English Poetry, A. *James Reeves and Martin Seymour-Smith, eds.* (c.1967) Barnes & Noble

NeAP New American Poetry, The, 1945–1960. *Donald M. Allen, ed.* (c.1960) Grove Press

NeBP New British Poets, The. *Kenneth Rexroth, ed.* (1949) New Directions

NeHB New Home Book of Best Loved Poems, The. *Richard Charlton MacKenzie, ed.* (c.1946) The Blakiston Company

NeIP New Irish Poets. *Devin A. Garrity, ed.* (1948) The Devin-Adair Company

NeLNL New Land, New Language; an Anthology of Australian Verse. *Judith Wright, comp.* (1957) Oxford University Press

NeMA New Modern American & British Poetry, The. *Louis Untermeyer, ed.* (Mid-century ed. [4th ed.], c.1950) Harcourt, Brace and Company

NePA New Pocket Anthology of American Verse from Colonial Days to the Present, The. *Oscar Williams, ed.* (c.1955) World Publishing Company

NePoAm New Poems by American Poets. *Rolfe Humphries, ed.* (1953) Ballantine Books

NePoAm-2 New Poems by American Poets #2. *Rolfe Humphries, ed.* (1957) Ballantine Books

NePoEA New Poets of England and America. *Donald Hall, Robert Pack, and Louis Simpson, eds.* (c.1957) Meridian Books

NePoEA-2 New Poets of England and America; Second Selection. *Donald Hall and Robert Pack, eds.* (c.1962) The World Publishing Company

NMP New Modern Poetry, The. *M. L. Rosenthal, ed.* (c.1967) The Macmillan Company

NNP New Negro Poets: U.S.A. *Langston Hughes, ed.* (c.1964) Indiana University Press

NoP Norton Anthology of Poetry, The. *Arthur M. Eastman and others, eds.* (c.1970) W. W. Norton and Company

NP New Poetry, The. *Harriet Monroe and Alice Corbin Henderson, eds.*

	(New ed., rev. and enl., 1932, reissue 1947) The Macmillan Company
NYBP	New Yorker Book of Poems, The. (c.1969) The Viking Press
NYTB	New York Times Book of Verse, The. *Thomas Lask, ed.* (c.1970) The Macmillan Company
OA	Out of the Ark; an Anthology of Animal Verse. *Gwendolyn Reed, comp.* (1970) Atheneum
OAEP	Oxford Anthology of English Poetry, An. *Howard Foster Lowry and Willard Thorp, eds.* (c.1935, 2d ed., 1956) Oxford University Press
OBB	Oxford Book of Ballads, The. *Arthur Quiller-Couch, ed.* (1910, reissue, 1927, 1946) Oxford University Press
OBCV	Oxford Book of Canadian Verse in English and French, The. *A. J. M. Smith, ed.* (1960) Oxford University Press
OBEC	Oxford Book of Eighteenth Century Verse, The. *David Nichol Smith, ed.* (1926) Oxford University Press
OBEV	Oxford Book of English Verse, The. *Sir Arthur Quiller-Couch, ed.* (1st ed., 1900, new ed., rev. and enl., 1939) Oxford University Press
OBMV	Oxford Book of Modern Verse, The, 1892-1935. *William Butler Yeats, ed.* (1936) Oxford University Press
OBNC	Oxford Book of Nineteenth-Century English Verse, The. *John Hayward, ed.* (c.1964) Oxford University Press
OBRV	Oxford Book of Regency Verse, The, 1798–1837. *H. S. Milford, ed.* (1928) Oxford University Press. Edition of 1935 has title Oxford Book of English Verse of the Romantic Period, 1798–1837
OBS	Oxford Book of Seventeenth Century Verse, The. *H. J. C. Grierson and G. Bullough, eds.* (1934) Oxford University Press
OBSC	Oxford Book of Sixteenth Century Verse, The. *E. K. Chambers, comp.* (1932) Oxford University Press
OBVV	Oxford Book of Victorian Verse, The. *Arthur Quiller-Couch, comp.* (1912, reissue, 1925) Oxford University Press
OCS	On City Streets. *Nancy Larrick, comp.* (c.1968) M. Evans & Company
OHFP	One Hundred and One Famous Poems. *Roy J. Cook, comp.* (1929, rev. ed., c.1958) Reilly & Lee Company
OHIP	Our Holidays in Poetry. *Mildred P. Harrington and Josephine H. Thomas, comps.* (1929, reissue, 1935, 1950) The H. W. Wilson Company
OnHM	100 Modern Poems. *Selden Rodman, comp.* (1949) Pellegrini & Cudahy
OnMSP	100 More Story Poems. *Elinor Parker, comp.* (c.1960) Thomas Y. Crowell Company
OnPM	One Thousand and One Poems of Mankind; Memorable Short Poems

from the World's Chief Literatures. *Henry W. Wells, comp.* (c.1953) Tupper and Love

OnPP 100 Poems about People. *Elinor Parker, comp.* (c.1955) Thomas Y. Crowell Company

OnSP 100 Story Poems. *Elinor Parker, comp.* (c.1951) Thomas Y. Crowell Company

OnYI 1000 Years of Irish Poetry. *Kathleen Hoagland, ed.* (c.1947) The Devin-Adair Company

OPoP 100 Postwar Poems. *M. L. Rosenthal, ed.* (c.1968) The Macmillan Company

OQP 1000 Quotable Poems. *Thomas Curtis Clark, ed.* (1937) Willett, Clark and Company, *later pub. by* Harper & Brothers

OTD On This Day; an Anthology of Poetry and Prose for Every Day of the Year. *Phyllis Detz and Kermit M. Stover, eds.* (c.1970) J. G. Ferguson Publishing Company

OtMeF Other Men's Flowers. *A. P. Wavell, Earl Wavell, comp.* (1944) Jonathan Cape

OTPC One Thousand Poems for Children. *Roger Ingpen, ed.* (Rev. and enl. ed., 1923) *Elizabeth Hough Sechrist, ed.* (1946) Macrae-Smith-Company

OuHeWo Our Heritage of World Literature. *Stith Thompson and John Gassner, eds.* (Rev. ed., c.1942, 2 books in 1) The Dryden Press. Book One, Literature in Translation; Book Two, Literature in Our Own Tongue. Also published separately

OuSiCo Our Singing Country; a Second Volume of American Ballads and Folk Songs. *John A. Lomax and Alan Lomax, comps.* (1941, reissue, 1949) The Macmillan Company

OxBA Oxford Book of American Verse, The. *F. O. Matthiessen, ed.* (1950) Oxford University Press

OxBB Oxford Book of Ballads, The. *James Kinsley, ed.* (1969) Oxford University Press

OxBI Oxford Book of Irish Verse, The; XVIIth Century–XXth Century. *Donagh MacDonagh and Lennox Robinson, comps.* (1958) Oxford University Press

OxBoCh Oxford Book of Christian Verse, The. *Lord David Cecil, ed.* (1940) Oxford University Press

OxBoLi Oxford Book of Light Verse, The. *W. H. Auden, ed.* (1938, repr., with corr., 1939) Oxford University Press

OxBS Oxford Book of Scottish Verse, The. *John MacQueen and Tom Scott, comps.* (1966) Oxford University Press

OxNR Oxford Nursery Rhyme Book, The. *Iona Opie and Peter Opie, comps.* (1955) Oxford University Press

PaA Patriotic Anthology, The. *Introduced by Carl Van Doren.* (c.1941) Doubleday, Doran & Company

PAH Poems of American History. *Burton Egbert Stevenson, ed.* (Rev. ed., 1922) Houghton Mifflin Company

PAL Patriotic Poems America Loves. *Jean Anne Vincent, comp.* (1968) Doubleday & Company

PAn Poetry Anthology, A. *Marlies K. Danziger and Wendell Stacy Johnson, eds.* (c.1968) Random House

PAP Poems of American Patriotism. *Brander Matthews, ed.* (Rev. and enl. ed., 1922) Charles Scribner's Sons

PaPo Parlour Poetry; a Casquet of Gems. *Michael R. Turner, ed.* (c.1969) The Viking Press

Par Parodies; an Anthology from Chaucer to Beerbohm—and After. *Dwight Macdonald, ed.* (c.1960) The Modern Library

PBA Poems from Black Africa. Langston Hughes, *ed.* (c.1963) Indiana University Press

PCD Poet's Craft, The. *Helen Fern Daringer and Anne Thaxter Eaton, comps.* (1935) World Book Company

PCH Poems for the Children's Hour. *Josephine Bouton, comp.* (c.1927, 1945). The Platt & Munk Company

PDV Piping down the Valleys Wild; Poetry for the Young of All Ages. *Nancy Larrick, ed.* (c.1968) Delacorte Press

PeCV Penguin Book of Canadian Verse, The. *Ralph Gustafson, ed.* (c.1958; rev. ed., c.1967) Penguin Books

PEDC Pieces for Every Day the Schools Celebrate. *Norman H. Deming and Katharine I. Bemis, comps.* (Enl. ed. 1931, rev. and enl. ed., 1949) Noble & Noble, Publishers

PeER Penguin Book of English Romantic Verse, The. *David Wright, ed.* (c.1968) Penguin Books

PeRV Penguin Book of Restoration Verse, The. *Harold Love, ed.* (c.1968) Penguin Books

PeSA Penguin Book of South African Verse, The. *Jack Cope and Uys Krige, eds.* (c.1968) Penguin Books

PeVV Penguin Book of Victorian Verse, The. *George MacBeth, ed.* (c.1969) Penguin Books

PFY Poems for Youth. *William Rose Benét, comp.* (1925) E. P. Dutton & Company

PG Poet's Gold. *David Ross, ed.* (c.1933, rev. and enl. ed., 1945) The Macaulay Company, *later pub. by* Dial Press. (2d rev. ed., 1956) The Devin-Adair Company

PGD Poems for the Great Days. *Thomas Curtis Clark and Robert Earle Clark, comps.* (c.1948) Abingdon-Cokesbury Press

PIA Poetry; an Introductory Anthology. *Hazard Adams, ed.* (c.1968) Little, Brown and Company

Po Poem, The; a Critical Anthology. *Josephine Miles, ed.* (1959) Prentice-Hall

PoAn Poem, The; an Anthology. *Stanley B. Greenfield and A. Kingsley Weatherhead, eds.* (c.1968) Appleton-Century-Crofts

PoAu 1–2 Poetry in Australia. Vols. I–II. Vol. I: From the Ballads to Brennan. *T. Inglis Moore, comp.* Vol. II: Modern Australian Verse. *Douglas Stewart, comp.* (1965) University of California Press

PoCH Poet's Choice. *Paul Engle and Joseph Langland, eds.* (1962) The Dial Press

PoDB Poems of Doubt and Belief; an Anthology of Modern Religious Poetry. *Tom F. Driver and Robert Pack, eds.* (c.1964) The Macmillan Company

PoE Poems in English, 1530-1940. *David Daiches and William Charvat, eds.* (c.1950) The Ronald Press Company

PoEL 1–5 Poets of the English Language, Vols. I–V. *W. H. Auden and Norman Holmes Pearson, eds.* (1950) The Viking Press. Vol. I: Langland to Spenser; Vol. II: Marlowe to Marvell; Vol. III: Milton to Goldsmith; Vol. IV: Blake to Poe; Vol. V: Tennyson to Yeats

PoeP Poets & Poems. *Herbert Goldstone and Irving Cummings, eds.* (c.1967) Wadsworth Publishing Company

PoFr Poetry of Freedom, The. *William Rose Benét and Norman Cousins, eds.* (c.1945) Random House, *later pub. by* The Modern Library

PoFS Poems for Study; a Critical and Historical Introduction. *Leonard Unger and William Van O'Connor, eds.* (c.1953) Rinehart & Company

PoG Poet's Garden, The. *Stevie Smith, ed.* (c.1970) The Viking Press

PoIE Poetry in English. *Warren Taylor and Donald Hall, eds.* (c.1963; 2d ed., 1970) The Macmillan Company

PoLF Poems That Live Forever. *Hazel Felleman, ed.* (1965) Doubleday & Company

PoLi Poetry and Life; an Anthology of English Catholic Poetry. *F. J. Sheed, comp.* (1942) Sheed and Ward

PoMa Poems for a Machine Age. *Horace J. McNeil, ed.* (c.1941) McGraw-Hill Book Company. Edition of 1949, published by the Globe Book Company, has title Living Poetry

PoMS Poems of Magic and Spells. *William Cole, ed.* (c.1960) World Publishing Company

PoNe Poetry of the Negro, The, 1746–1970. *Langston Hughes and Arna Bontemps, eds.* (1949; rev. ed., c.1970) Doubleday & Company

PoOW Poems of the Old West; a Rocky Mountain Anthology. *Levette J. Davidson, ed.* (c.1951) The University of Denver Press

PoPl Poetry for Pleasure; the Hallmark Book of Poetry. (c.1960) Doubleday & Company

PoPo Poems and Poets. *David Aloian, ed.* (c.1965) Webster Division, McGraw-Hill Book Company

PoRA Poems to Read Aloud. *Edward Hodnett, ed.* (c.1957; rev. ed., c.1967) W. W. Norton & Company

PoRh Pocketful of Rhymes, A. *Katherine Love, ed.* (c.1946) Thomas Y. Crowell Company

PoRL Poems for Red Letter Days. *Elizabeth Hough Sechrist, comp.* (c.1951) Macrae Smith Company

PoSa Poetry Sampler, A. *Donald Hall, ed.* (c.1962) Franklin Watts

PoSC Poems for Seasons and Celebrations. *William Cole, ed.* (c.1961) The World Publishing Company

PoToHe Poems That Touch the Heart. *A. L. Alexander, comp.* (c.1941, new, enl. ed., c.1956) Garden City Publishing Company

POTE Poems of Our Time, 1900–1942 (Everyman's Library). *Richard Church and M. M. Bozman, eds.* (1945) J. M. Dent & Sons
Poems of Our Time, 1900–1960 (Everyman's Library). *Richard Church, Mildred Bozman, and Edith Sitwell, eds.* (1959) J. M. Dent & Sons

POTi Poets of Our Time. *F. E. S. Finn, comp.* (c.1965) John Murray

PoVP Poetry of the Victorian Period. *George Benjamin Woods and Jerome Hamilton Buckley, eds.* (Rev. ed., c.1955) Scott, Foresman and Company

PP Poems on Poetry; the Mirror's Garland. *Robert Wallace and James G. Taaffe, eds.* (1965) E. P. Dutton & Co.

PPL Pinafore Palace. *Kate Douglas Wiggin and Nora Archibald Smith, eds.* (1907) Doubleday, Doran & Company

PPON Poems of Protest Old and New. *Arnold Kenseth, ed.* (c.1968) The Macmillan Company

PrWP Presenting Welsh Poetry. *Gwyn Williams, ed.* (c.1959) Faber and Faber

PRWS Posy Ring, The. *Kate Douglas Wiggin and Nora Archibald Smith, eds.* (1903, reissue, 1935) Doubleday, Doran & Company

PTK Poetry to Know. *Editors of the Book of Knowledge.* (c.1966) Franklin Watts

PV Pith and Vinegar. *William Cole, ed.* (c.1969) Simon and Schuster

QAH Quickly Aging Here; Some Poets of the 1970's. *Geof Hewitt, ed.* (c.1969) Doubleday Anchor Books

QFR Quest for Reality. *Yvor Winters and Kenneth Fields, eds.* (c.1969) The Swallow Press

ReEn Renaissance England; Poetry and Prose from the Reformation to the Restoration. *Roy Lamson and Hallett Smith, eds.* (c.1956) W. W. Norton & Company. Edition of 1942 had title The Golden Hind

ReIE Renaissance in England, The; Non-dramatic Prose and Verse of the Sixteenth Century. *Hyder E. Rollins and Herschel Baker, comps.* (c.1954) D. C. Heath and Company

ReMP Reading Modern Poetry (Key Editions). *Paul Engle and Warren Carrier, eds.* (c.1955) Scott, Foresman and Company

RePo Reading of Poetry, The. *William D. Sheldon, Nellie Lyons, and Polly Rouault, eds.* (c.1963) Allyn and Bacon

RG Rainbow Gold. *Sara Teasdale, comp.* (1922) The Macmillan Company

RIS Rainbow in the Sky. *Louis Untermeyer, ed.* (c.1935) Harcourt, Brace and Company

RoGo Roofs of Gold; Poems to Read Aloud. *Padraic Colum, ed.* (c.1964) The Macmillan Company

SAS Sugar and Spice. *Mary Wilder Tileston, comp.* (1928, reissue, 1942) Little, Brown & Company

SaSa Saucy Sailor and Other Dramatized Ballads, The. *Alice M. G. White and Janet E. Tobitt, comps.* (1940) E. P. Dutton & Company

SCAP Seventeenth-Century American Poetry. *Harrison T. Meserole, ed.* (c.1968) Doubleday Anchor Books

Second Treasury of the Familiar, A. *See* TreFS

SCC Songs of the Cattle Trail and Cow Camp. *John A. Lomax, comp.* (c.1919, new ed., 1950) The Macmillan Company, *later pub. by* Duell, Sloan and Pearce

SCEP 1–2 17th Century English Poetry, Vols. I–II. *Miriam K. Starkman, ed.* (1967) Alfred A. Knopf

SD Sprints and Distances; Sports in Poetry and the Poetry in Sport. *Lillian Morrison, comp.* (c.1965) Thomas Y. Crowell Company

SeCePo Seven Centuries of Poetry; Chaucer to Dylan Thomas. *A. N. Jeffares, ed.* (1955) Longmans, Green & Company

SeCeV Seven Centuries of Verse, English & American. *A. J. M. Smith, ed.* (2d ed., rev. and enl., c.1957; rev. and enl. ed., c.1967) Charles Scribner's Sons

SeCL Seventeenth Century Lyrics. *Norman Ault, ed.* (2d ed., c.1950) William Sloane Associates

SeCP Seventeenth Century Poetry; the Schools of Donne and Jonson. *Hugh Kenner, ed.* (c.1964) Holt, Rinehart and Winston

SeCSL Seventeenth Century Songs and Lyrics. *John P. Cutts, ed.* (1959) University of Missouri Press

SeCV 1–2 Seventeenth-Century Verse and Prose, Vols. I–II. *Helen C. White, Ruth C. Wallerstein, and Ricardo Quintana, eds.* (c.1951, 1952) The Macmillan Company. Vol. I: 1600–1660; Vol. II: 1660–1700

SeEP Seventeenth-Century English Poetry (The Harper English Literature Series). *R. C. Bald, ed.* (c.1959) Harper & Brothers

SGR Songs of the Gold Rush, The. *Richard A. Dwyer and Richard E. Lingenfelter, eds.* (1964) University of California Press

ShBV 1–4 Sheldon Book of Verse, The. Books I–IV. *P. G. Smith and J. F. Wilkins, comps.* (1959) Oxford University Press

ShM Shrieks at Midnight; Macabre Poems, Eerie and Humorous. *Sara Brewton and John E. Brewton, eds.* (c.1969) Thomas Y. Crowell Company

ShS Shantymen and Shantyboys; Songs of the Sailor and Lumberman. *William Main Doerflinger, comp.* (1951) The Macmillan Company

SiCE Sixteenth-Century English Poetry (The Harper English Literature Series). *Norman E. McClure, ed.* (c.1954) Harper & Brothers

SiPS Silver Poets of the Sixteenth Century (Everyman's Library). *Gerald Bullett, ed.* (1947) J. M. Dent and Sons

SiSoSe Sing a Song of Seasons. *Sara Brewton and John E. Brewton, eds.* (c.1955) The Macmillan Company

SiSw Silver Swan, The. *Horace Gregory and Marya Zaturenska, eds.* (c.1968) The Macmillan Company, Collier Books

SiTL Silver Treasury of Light Verse, The (A Mentor Book). *Oscar Williams, ed.* (c.1957) The New American Library

SoAmSa Songs of American Sailormen. *Joanna C. Colcord, ed.* (Enl. and rev. ed., c.1938) W. W. Norton & Company. Edition of 1924, published by the Bobbs-Merrill Company, had title Roll and Go, Songs of American Sailormen

Sonn Sonnet, The. *Robert M. Bender and Charles L. Squier. eds.* (1965) Washington Square Press

SoP Sourcebook of Poetry. *Al Bryant, comp.* (c.1968) Zondervan Publishing House

SoPo Sound of Poetry, The. *Mary C. Austin and Queenie B. Mills, eds.* (c.1963) Allyn and Bacon

SP Silver Pennies. *Blanche Jennings Thompson, comp.* (1925) The Macmillan Company

StaSt Stars to Steer By. *Louis Untermeyer. ed.* (c.1941) Harcourt, Brace and Company

STF Speaker's Treasury of 400 Quotable Poems, The. *Croft M. Pentz, comp.* (c.1963) Zondervan Publishing House

StJW Story of Jesus in the World's Literature, The. *Edward Wagenknecht, ed.* (c.1946) Creative Age Press

StP Studying Poetry; a Critical Anthology of English and American Poems. *Karl Kroeber and John O. Lyons, eds.* (c.1965) Harper & Row

StPo Story Poems, New and Old. *William Cole, ed.* (c.1957) World Publishing Company

StVeCh Story and Verse for Children. *Miriam Blanton Huber, ed.* (c.1940, reissue, 1947; rev. ed., c.1955) The Macmillan Company

SUS Sung Under the Silver Umbrella. *Association for Childhood Education.* (1935) The Macmillan Company

SyP Symbolist Poem, The. *Edward Engelberg, ed.* (1967) E. P. Dutton & Company

Third Treasury of the Familiar, A. *See* TreFT

TDP Three Dimensions of Poetry. *Vincent Stewart, ed.* (c.1969) Charles Scribner's Sons

ThGo Thread of Gold, A; an Anthology of Poetry. *Eleanor Graham, comp.* (c.1964) The Bodley Head

ThLM This Land Is Mine; an Anthology of American Verse. *Al Hine, ed.* (c.1965) J. B. Lippincott Company

ThO 31 New American Poets. *Ron Schreiber, ed.* (c.1969) Hill & Wang

ThWaDe This Way, Delight; a Book of Poetry for the Young. *Herbert Read, ed.* (c.1956) Pantheon Books

TIHL These I Have Loved. *Gilbert Hay, comp.* (c.1969) Simon and Schuster

TiPo Time for Poetry. *May Hill Arbuthnot, comp.* (General ed., c.1952, rev. ed., c.1959) Scott, Foresman and Company

TNV Today's Negro Voices. *Beatrice M. Murphy, ed.* (c.1970) Julian Messner

TOP Types of Poetry. *Jacob Zeitlin and Clarissa Rinaker, comps.* (1926, reissue, 1946) The Macmillan Company

ToPo Today's Poets; American and British Poetry since the 1930's. *Chad Walsh, ed.* (c.1964) Charles Scribner's Sons

TPM To Play Man Number One. *Sara Hannum and John Terry Chase, comps.* (1969) Atheneum

TrAS Treasury of American Song, A. *Olin Downes and Elie Siegmeister, comps.* (2d ed., rev. and enl., 1943) Alfred A. Knopf

TreF Treasury of the Familiar, A. *Ralph L. Woods, ed.* (c.1942, reissue, 1945) The Macmillan Company

TreFS Treasury of the Familiar, A Second. *Ralph L. Woods, ed.* (1950) The Macmillan Company

TreFT Treasury of the Familiar, A Third. *Ralph L. Woods, ed.* (c.1970) The Macmillan Company

TrGrPo Treasury of Great Poems, English and American, A. *Louis Untermeyer, ed.* (1942, rev. and enl. ed., 1955) Simon and Schuster

TrJP Treasury of Jewish Poetry, A. *Nathan Ausubel and Marynn Ausubel, eds.* (c.1957) Crown Publishers

TrPWD Treasury of Poems for Worship and Devotion, A. *Charles L. Wallis, ed.* (c.1959) Harper & Brothers

TRV Treasury of Religious Verse, The. *Donald T. Kauffman, comp.* (c.1962) Fleming H. Revell Company

TSW This Singing World. *Louis Untermeyer, ed.* (1923) Harcourt, Brace and Company

TTY 3000 Years of Black Poetry. *Alan Lomax and Raoul Abdul, eds.* (c.1970) Dodd, Mead & Company

TuPP Tudor Poetry and Prose. *J. William Hebel, Hoyt H. Hudson, Francis R. Johnson, A. Wigfall Green, and Robert Hoopes, eds.* (c.1953) Appleton-Century-Crofts. Copyright (in part) 1929 by F. S. Crofts & Company under title Poetry of the English Renaissance

TVC Treasury of Verse for Little Children, A. *M. G. Edgar, ed.* (Rev. and enl. ed., 1927, new ed., 1946) Thomas Y. Crowell Company

TwAmPo Twentieth-Century American Poetry. *Conrad Aiken, ed.* (rev. ed., c.1963) The Modern Library. Edition of 1927 had title Modern American Poets. *See* MAPA

TwCaPo Twentieth Century Canadian Poetry. *Earle Birney, ed.* (c.1953) The Ryerson Press

TwCP Twentieth Century Poetry; American and British (1900–1970). *John Malcolm Brinnin and Bill Read, eds.* (c.1963, rev. ed., c.1970) McGraw-Hill Book Company. Text edition entitled The Modern Poets; for the 1963 edition, *see* MP

UnPo Understanding Poetry. *Cleanth Brooks and Robert Penn Warren, eds.* (c.1938, 3d ed., c.1960) Henry Holt and Company, *later pub. by* Holt, Rinehart and Winston

UnS Untune the Sky; Poems of Music and the Dance. *Helen Plotz, comp.* (c.1957) Thomas Y. Crowell Company

UnTE Uninhibited Treasury of Erotic Poetry, An. *Louis Untermeyer, ed.* (1963) The Dial Press

UTS Under the Tent of the Sky. *John E. Brewton, comp.* (1937) The Macmillan Company

VA Victorian Anthology, A, 1837–1895. *Edmund Clarence Stedman, ed.* (c.1895) Houghton Mifflin Company

VaPo Variety of Poetry, The; an Anthology. *Edward A. Bloom, Charles H. Philbrick, Elmer M. Blistein, eds.* (c.1964) The Odyssey Press

ViBoFo Viking Book of Folk Ballads of the English-speaking World, The. *Albert B. Friedman, ed.* (1956) The Viking Press

ViBoPo Viking Book of Poetry of the English-speaking World, The. *Richard Aldington, ed.* (c.1941; rev., mid-century ed., 1959, in 2 vols). The Viking Press

ViPo Victorian Poetry. *E. K. Brown and J. O. Bailey, eds.* (1942; 2d ed., c. 1962) Thomas Nelson and Sons, *later pub. by* The Ronald Press Company

ViPP Victorian Poetry and Poetics. *Walter E. Houghton and G. Robert Stange, eds.* (c.1959) Houghton Mifflin Company

VP Victorian Poetry; Ten Major Poets. *Robert Bernard Martin, ed.* (c.1964) Random House

WaaP War and the Poet . . . from Ancient Times to the Present. *Richard Eberhart and Selden Rodman, eds.* (1945) The Devin-Adair Company

WaKn Way of Knowing, A; a Collection of Poems for Boys. *Gerald D. McDonald, comp.* (c.1959) Thomas Y. Crowell Company

WaP War Poets; The; an Anthology of the War Poetry of the 20th Century. *Oscar Williams, ed.* (c.1945) The John Day Company

WaPE Wayside Poems of the Early Eighteenth Century. *Edmund Blunden and Bernard Mellor, eds.* (1964) Hong Kong University Press (U.S. agent: Oxford University Press)

WBLP World's Best-loved Poems, The. *James Gilchrist Lawson, comp.* (1927) Harper & Brothers

WBP World's Best Poems, The. *Mark Van Doren and Garibaldi M. Lapolla, eds.* (ċ.1929, 1946) Albert & Charles Boni, *later pub. by* The World Publishing Company. *Same as* JAWP

WePo Wealth of Poetry, A; Selected for the Young in Heart. *Winifred Hindley, ed., with the assistance of John Betjeman.* (c.1963) Basil Blackwell

WGRP World's Great Religious Poetry, The. *Caroline Miles Hill, ed.* (1934) The Macmillan Company

WHA Winged Horse Anthology, The. *Joseph Auslander and Frank Ernest Hill, eds.* (1929) Doubleday, Doran & Company

WhC What Cheer; an Anthology of American and British Humorous and Witty Verse. *David McCord, ed.* (c.1945) Coward-McCann

WHL With Harp and Lute. *Blanche Jennings Thompson, comp.* (1935) The Macmillan Company

WHW Wind Has Wings, The; Poems from Canada. *Mary Alice Downie and Barbara Robertson, eds.* (c.1968) Henry Z. Walck, Oxford University Press

WiR Wind and the Rain, The; an Anthology of Poems for Young People. *John Hollander and Harold Bloom, eds.* (c.1961) Doubleday & Company

WIRo Wind Is Round, The. *Sara Hannum and John Terry Chase, comps.* (1970) Atheneum

WoL World Literature. *Arthur E. Christy and Henry W. Wells, eds.* (c.1947) American Book Company

WOW Writing on the Wall, The. *Walter Lowenfels, ed.* (c.1969) Doubleday & Company

WSL We Speak as Liberators; Young Black Poets. *Orde Coombs, ed.* (c.1970) Dodd, Mead & Company

YaCaBo Yale Carol Book, The. *H. Frank Bozyan and Sidney Lovett, eds.* (1944) Yale University Press

YaD Yankee Doodles. *Ted Malone, ed.* (c.1943) McGraw-Hill Book Company. Edition of 1948, published by the Garden City Publishing Company, has title The All-American Book of Verse

YAP Young American Poets, The. *Paul Carroll, ed.* (c.1968) Big Table Publishing Company (Follett)

YAT Young American's Treasury of English Poetry, A. *Shirley E. Marshall, ed.* (1967) Washington Square Press

YeAr Year Around, The; Poems for Children. *Alice I. Hazeltine and Elva S. Smith, comps.* (c.1956) Abingdon Press

YT Yesterday and Today. *Louis Untermeyer, ed.* (c.1926) Harcourt, Brace and Company

TITLE AND FIRST LINE INDEX

A, a, a, a!/ Nunc gaudet ecclesia. *Unknown.* EnPo
A. A violent order is disorder. Connoisseur of Chaos. Wallace Stevens. CABA; LiTM (rev. ed.); MoPo; Po
A. Apple Pie. Edward Lear. *See* Nonsense Alphabet, A ("A was once an apple-pie").
A, B & C of It, The. William Carlos Williams. PoeP
A, B, C. Charles Stuart Calverley. *See* Alphabet, The.
A. B. C., An [*or* The]. Chaucer. CoBE
(La Prière de Nostre Dame, *mod. vers. by* Anselm M. Townsend.) ISi
Well of Pity, The, *sel.* PoLi
A B C. Eliza Cook. OTPC (1923 ed.)
A B C. *Unknown, tr. fr. German.* SAS
A B C Bunny, The. Wanda Gág. TiPo
A B C D. *Unknown.* OxNR
A, B, C, D, E, F, G,/ Little Robin Redbreast sitting on a tree. *Unknown.* OxNR
A, B, C, D, E, F, G. The Alphabet. *Unknown.* PCH
A. B. C. of Devotion, An. *Unknown.* MeEL
A B C you know. A B C. *Unknown, tr. fr. German.* SAS
A B C s ("The word forms"). Charles Olson. PoAn
A B C s ("What we do not know of ourselves"). Charles Olson. PoAn
A B C's in Green. Leonora Speyer. DD; HBMV; HBVY; OHIP; OQP
A celuy que pluys eyme en mounde. Lines from Love Letters [*or* To the One I Love Most]. *Unknown.* MeEL; OBEV (new ed.)
A Clymène. Paul Verlaine, *tr. fr. French by* Arthur Symons. AWP; JAWP; WBP
A' day aboot the hoose I work. Nocht o' Mortal Sicht. Bessie J. B. Macarthur. OxBS
A Deux. William Wood. BoLP; ELU
A Dieu! and Au Revoir. John Oxenham. MaRV
A dis, a dis, a green grass. Green Grass. *Unknown.* BoTP; CH; LO; OxBoLi; OxNR
A. E. Emily Brontë. *See* Two Children, The.
A.E.F. Carl Sandburg. CMoP; CoBA; HBMV; MAP; MoAB; MoAmPo; WaaP
A. E. Housman and a Few Friends. Humbert Wolfe. FiBHP; WhC
("What lads have done with labor.") Par
A E I O U. Swift. BoTP
A 11. Louis Zukofsky. CoPo
A Fauxbourg. George Croly. *Fr.* Paris in 1815. OBRV
A for Apple, big and red. The A B C Bunny. Wanda Gág. TiPo
A for the animals out in the stable. An Alphabet of Christmas. *Unknown.* ChBR
A! [*or* Ah!] fredome [*or* freedom] is a noble thing! Freedom. John Barbour. *Fr.* The Bruce. FaBoCh; GoTS; LoGBV; OBEV; OxBS; PoFr; TrGrPo; ViBoPo
A Ha Ha Ha! This World Doth Passe. *Unknown.* AtBAP; PoEL-2
(Idle Fyno.) ChTr
A ho! A ho!/ Love's horn doth blow. Song [*or* Love Goes a-Hawking]. Thomas Lovell Beddoes. *Fr.* The Bride's Tragedy. BiS; ChER; VA
A. "I was a Have." B. "I was a 'Have-not.'" "Equality of Sacrifice." Kipling. *Fr.* Epitaphs of War. BrPo; FaBoTw; NoP; OAEP (2d ed.)
A is an angel of blushing eighteen. The Alphabet [*or* A, B, C]. Charles Stuart Calverley. HBV; SiTL
A is an apple, sour and green. *Unknown.* WhC
A is for Acting, the shantyboys' life. The Shantyboys' Song. Kenneth Zwicker. ShS
A is for Alex. Line-up for Yesterday. Ogden Nash. SD
A Is for Alpha: Alpha Is for A. Conrad Aiken. NePA
A is for ax, and that we all know. The Lumberman's Alphabet. *Unknown.* ShS
A is our army so true and so brave. The Alphabet. *Unknown.* BFSS
A is to begin with, and A began with Adam. Genesis of Vowels. James Broughton. CrMA
A la Carte. Kenneth Fearing. CMoP
A la promenade. Paul Verlaine, *tr. fr. French by* Arthur Symons. AWP
À l'Ange Avantgardien. F. R. Scott. MoCV
A! Mercy, Fortune. *Unknown.* MeEL
A Mhic, ná Meabhraigh Eigse. *Unknown, tr. fr. Irish by* Máire MacEntee. OxBI
"A, my dere, a, my dere Son." Mary Weeps for Her Child. *Unknown.* OxBoLi
A! My Herte, A! What Aileth The. Sir Thomas Wyatt. AtBAP
A peels an apple, while B kneels to God. A Primer of the Daily Round. Howard Nemerov. NYBP
A Perigord pres del muralh. Bertrand de Born, *tr. fr. Provençal by* Ezra Pound. CTC
A putta putta putt. Riding in a Motor Boat. Dorothy W. Baruch. FaPON; MPB
A Quoi Bon Dire. Charlotte Mew. HBMV
A. R. U., *with music. Unknown.* AS
A sè stesso. Giacomo Leopardi, *tr. fr. Italian by* Lorna de' Lucchi. AWP; JAWP; WBP
A Solis Ortus Cardine. Ford Madox Ford. ViBoPo
A soun tres chere et special. Lines from Love Letters. *Unknown.* OBEV (new ed.)
A Terre. Wilfred Owen. LiTM (rev. ed.); MMA; WaP
A' the boys of merry Lincoln. Hugh of Lincoln. *Unknown.* OBB
A was an ape. Nonsense Alphabet. Edward Lear. SAS
A was an apple pie;/ B bit it. Mother Goose. BoChLi; OTPC; OxNR; PCH
A was an apple pie. The Alphabet. Kate Greenaway. HBVY
A was an archer, who shot at a frog. Tom Thumb's Alphabet. *Unknown.* HBV; HBVY; OTPC; OxNR; SiTL
A was once an apple-pie. Nonsense Alphabet [*or* A. Apple Pie]. Edward Lear. PPL; SoPo; SUS; TiPo
A ye wha are sae guid yoursel. *See* O ye wha are sae guid yoursel.
Aa the skippers of bonny Lothen. Young Allan. *Unknown.* ESPB
Aa went te Blaydon Races, 'twas on the ninth o' June. Blaydon Races. *Unknown.* ELP
Aardvark. Julia Fields. BOLo
Aaron. Edwin Denby. ANYP
Aaron. George Herbert. MaMe; MeLP; MePo; OAEP; OBS; PoFS; SCEP-1
Aaron Burr. Stephen Vincent Benét. InMe
Aaron Burr's Wooing. Edmund Clarence Stedman. PAH
Aaron had a passion for the lost chord. Aaron. Edwin Denby. ANYP
Aaron Hatfield. Edgar Lee Masters. *Fr.* Spoon River Anthology. LiTA; NP
Aaron Stark. E. A. Robinson. MoAB; MoAmPo (1950 ed.); Sonn
Abalone, *with music. Unknown.* AS
Abandonado, El, *with music. Unknown, tr. fr. Spanish by* Frank Dobie. ABF; AS
Abandoned. Madison Cawein. YT
Abandoned, The. Arthur Symons. SyP
Abandoned. *Unknown.* SoP
Abandoned Copper Refinery. Dan Gillespie. QAH
Abandoned is the house. Murder House. Elizabeth J. Coatsworth. FiSC
Abandoned on the beach. Akiko Yosano, *tr. fr. Japanese by* Kenneth Rexroth. LiTW
Abasis. Christopher Middleton. *Fr.* Herman Moon's Hourbook. NePoEA-2
Abbé Liszt, The/ Hit the piano with his fist. Liszt. E. C. Bent-

Abbé (continued)
ley. *Fr.* Biography for Beginners. UnS
Abbess, The ("The Abbess was of noble blood"). Sir Walter Scott. *Fr.* Marmion, II. GoBC
Abbey, The. José M. Eguren, *tr. fr. Spanish by* Thomas Walsh. CAW
Abbey Asaroe. William Allingham. OnYI; OxBI
Abbie Ben Adams, *parody*. Carolyn Wells. CIV
Abbot of Derry, The. John Bennett. HBMV
Abbot of Inisfalen, The. William Allingham. GN; HBV; OnMSP
Abbreviated Interviews with a Few Disgruntled Literary Celebrities. Reed Whittemore. FiBHP
Abdelazer, *sel.* Aphra Behn.
Song: "Love in fantastic [*or* fantastique] triumph sate." AtBAP; HBV; OBEV; TrGrPo; ViBoPo
(Love Armed.) SeCL
(Love in Fantastic Triumph [Sate].) CBEP; OAEP; OnPM
(Song: Love Arm'd.) CavP; OBS
Abdication of Fergus Mac Roy, The. Sir Samuel Ferguson. AnIL
Abdication Street Song. *Unknown.* PV
Abdolonymus the Sidonian. Jones Very. AP
Abdul A-Bul-Bul A-Mir. *Unknown.* TreF
(Abdul, the Bulbul Ameer, *with music.*) AS
(Abdullah Bulbul Amir.) BLPA; StPo
(Ballade of Ivan Petrofsky Skevar, Ye, *with music.*) ABF
(Ivan Skavinsky Skavar.) GSP
Abe Lincoln stood at the White House gate. Lord Lovel (B *vers., parody*). *Unknown.* ViBoFo
Abel. Demetrios Capetanakis. AtBAP; GTBS-P; WaaP
Abélard Tells His Love to Héloïse. Herbert E. Palmer. POTE
Abelard was: God is. Sic et Non. Herbert Read. FaBoTw
Abenamar, Abenamar. *Unknown*, *tr. fr. Spanish by* Robert Southey. AWP; OuHeWo
Abide in Me, *sel.* Harriet Beecher Stowe.
"Soul alone, like a neglected harp, The." ChIP
Abide with Me. Henry F. Lyte. BLRP; FaBoBe; FaFP; FaPL; HBV; MaRV; NeHB; SoP; TreF; VA; WBLP; WGRP
(Hymn: "Abide with me; fast falls the eventide.") NBM
Abide with me, O Christ; Thou must not go. It Is toward Evening. *Unknown.* BePJ
Abide with Us. Horatius Bonar. BePJ; VA
Abiding. A. B. Simpson. SoP; STF
Abiding Love, The. John White Chadwick. BLPA; FaBoBe; NeHB
(Auld Lang Syne.) MaRV; WGRP
Abiding Snake. Prologue: Moments in a Glade. Alan Stephens. QFR
Abiku. Wole Soyinka. PBA
Abishag. Jacob Fichman, *tr. fr. Hebrew by* Sholom J. Kahn. TrJP
Abishag. Rainer Maria Rilke, *tr. fr. German by* Jethro Bithell. AWP
Abishag. André Spire, *tr. fr. French by* Emanuel Eisenberg. TrJP
Abla. Antara, *tr. fr. Arabic by* E. Powys Mathers. *Fr.* The Mu'allaqát. AWP; JAWP; LiTW; WBP
Abnegation. Martial, *tr. fr. Latin by* Thomas Moore. UnTE
Abnegation. Christina Rossetti. Monna Innominata, XII. VA
("If there be any one can take my place.") ViPo; VP
Abnormal Is Not Courage, The. Jack Gilbert. CoAP
Aboard a train three thousand miles. The Hand. Irving Feldman. AmPC
Aboard at a Ship's Helm. Walt Whitman. NePA; OxBA
Abode of the nightingale is bare, The. Alone. Walter de la Mare. ChTr; EnLoPo
Abolitionist Hymn, *with music.* *Unknown.* TrAS
Aboriginal Mother's Lament, An. Charles Harpur. ACV; VA
Aboriginal Sin. John Hay. NePoAm-2
Abortive tears! Thaw. Jean Starr Untermeyer. AtBAP
Abou Ben Adhem. Leigh Hunt. BeLS; BLPA; DD; EnLi-2; EnRP; EPN; FaBoBe; FaBV; FaFP; GBV (1952 ed.); GN; GoTP; HBV; HBVY; MaRV; MCCG; MemP; NeHB; OBEV (new ed.); OBVV; OHFP; OnSP; OQP; OTD; OTPC; PoPo; RIS; StVeCh (1940 ed.); TIHL; TreF; TRV; WBLP; WGRP; YAT
(Abou Ben Adhem and the Angel.) EnLit; FaPON
(Abu Ben Adhem.) BoC
Abou Ben Adhem's name led all the rest. Holy Order. J. B. Boothroyd. FiBHP
About a fierce highwayman my story I will tell. Brennan on the Moor. *Unknown.* OuSiCo
About a well-spring, in a little mead. Of Three Damsels in a Meadow. John Payne. OBVV
About an Allegory. Walter Conrad Arensberg. AnAmPo
About ane bank, where birdis on bewis. Alexander Montgomerie. *Fr.* The Cherry and the Slae. GoTS
About Animals. Hilda Conkling. UTS
About Buttons. Dorothy Aldis. MoSiPe
About Face. Anne Waldman. YAP
About fifty years since, in the days of our daddies. Paddy's Metamorphosis. Thomas Moore. OnYI
About Glenkindie and his man. Glenkindie. William Bell Scott. HBV; VA
About her head or floating feet. My Father's Child. "Stuart Sterne." AA
About his brow the laurel and the bay. A Man. Clinton Scollard. OHIP; PEDC
About me the night, moonless, wimples the mountains. Vancouver Lights. Earle Birney. CaP
About my temples go triumphant bays. Ovid. *Fr.* Elegies. RelE
About Savannah. *Unknown.* PAH
About suffering they were never wrong. Musée des Beaux Arts. W. H. Auden. BWP; CABA; CaFP; CBV; ChMP; CMoP; CoBMV; DiPo; EnL; ExPo; FaFP; ForPo; FosPo; GTBS; LiTB; LiTG; LiTM; MaPo; MoAB; MoPo; NePA; NoP; OAEP (2d ed.); PG (1955 ed.); PIA; PoAn; PoFS; PoIE; PoRA; PoSa; SeCePo; SeCeV; StP; TreFT; TrGrPo (rev. ed.); TwCP
About the august and ancient Square. Oxford Nights. Lionel Johnson. BrPo; EnLit
About the chambers of my heart. *See* About the little chambers of my heart.
About the chilly, ragged lawns they lie. Autumn Leaves. Minnie Case Hopkins. OQP
About the Cool Water. Kenneth Rexroth. ErPo
About the dog days folks complain. A Dog Day. Rachel Field. SiSoSe
About the Fairies. Jean Ingelow. BoTP
About the fashions of the day. Hug Me Tight. John Kendall. WhC
About the Grass. James L. Weil. NYTB
About the heights, soft clouds, a few. Alfred Domett. *Fr.* Ranolf and Amohia. AnNZ
About the hilltop how the clouds are cool. Summer Days. Roy Daniells. CaP
About the little chambers of my heart. Gone. Mary Elizabeth Coleridge. HBV; OBEV (new ed.); OBNC; OBVV; OQP; TOP
About the mountains it is useless to argue. Alpine. R. S. Thomas. BoNaP
About the Shark, phlegmatical one. The Maldive Shark. Herman Melville. AmP; AmPP (4th ed.); AP; CBEP; CBV; LoGBV; MAmP; MWA-1; NePA; NoP; OxBA; PoEL-5; PoFS; PoG; TDP
About the Shelleys. *Unknown, quoted by* Wordsworth. WhC
About the sweet bag of a bee. The Bag of the Bee. Robert Herrick. OAEP
About the year of one B.C. Jonah and the Whale. *Unknown.* BLPA
About their prince each took his wonted seat. Pluto's Council. Tasso. *Fr.* Godfrey of Bulloigne. OBSC
About these column faces. The Crosses. Besmilr Brigham. ThO
About this lady many fruitful trees. The Lady with the Unicorn. Vernon Watkins. LiTB; TwCP
About this time when dusk falls like a shutter. Adolescents in the Dusk. Iain Fletcher. FaBoMo
About to marry and invest. The Dorking Thigh. William Plomer. WePo
About twenty years ago. Wild Oats. Philip Larkin. PoeP
About with this brimmer my bullyes. *Unknown.* SeCSL
About Women. H. Phelps Putnam. AnFE; CoAnAm; MAP; MoAmPo (1942 ed.); TwAmPo
About Yule, when [*or* quhen] the wind blew cule. Young Waters. *Unknown.* EnLit; ESPB; OBB; OxBB; TOP
Above a rough altar, coarse cement all. La Mambo dans le Hounfort. Charles F. Pressoir. PoNe

Above a stretch of still unravaged weald. The Garden Party. Donald Davie. NePoEA
Above a world entrapped by fear. The Forgotten Star. Thomas Curtis Clark. PGD
Above and below the ship, this blue. Becalmed. John Blight. BoAV; PoAu-2
Above, below, in sky and sod. The Over-Heart. Whittier. OQP; WGRP
Above dark cities build. To Young Dreamers. Lucia Trent. OQP
Above earth's bloody battlefields. "With Whom Is No Shadow of Turning." Martha Snell Nicholson. SoP
Above finespun, unruffled sheets. Lovebirds. William Jay Smith. ErPo
Above me the abbey, grey arches on the cliff. Cædmon. Norman Nicholson. FaBoTw
Above my face is a map. The Cloud-Mobile. May Swenson. GoTP
Above my head the shields are stained with rust. The Lamp of Poor Souls. Marjorie Pickthall. HBV
Above Myself. Carlton Buck. SoP
Above on the bare mountain. Little Town. Federico García Lorca. OnPM
Above Pate Valley. Gary Snyder. CoAP; NaP
Above St. Irénée. Duncan Campbell Scott. VA
Above Salerno. Ada Foster Murray. HBV
Above the Arno. May Swenson. NYBP
Above the Battle's Front. Vachel Lindsay. StJW
Above the beach, the vineyard. The Flower. Robert Penn Warren. PoPl
Above the cannon's roar we hear His voice. Look Up. Martha Snell Nicholson. BePJ
Above the city, where I dwell, guarding it close, runs an embattled wall. The City Wall. Eunice Tietjens. NP
Above the cloistral valley. The Sleeper. Clinton Scollard. HBV
Above the clouds. The Moon. Azumamaro. OnPM
Above the Dock. T. E. Hulme. FaBoMo; GTBS-P; WePo
Above the forest of the parakeets. The Bird with the Coppery, Keen Claws. Wallace Stevens. AnFE; APA; CoAnAm; NoP; PoeP
Above the fresh ruffles of the surf. Voyages, I. Hart Crane. AmPP (5th ed.); AP; CABA; CABL; CMoP; ForPo; NoP; OxBA; Po; PoIE; TDP
(The Sea.) CrMA
Above the graves of countless millions slain. In the Name of Our Sons. Dorothy Gould. PGD
Above the height of Mikasa in Kasuga. Wine and the Moon. *Unknown. Fr.* Manyo Shu. OnPM
Above the hemispheres there floats. The Elements. Oscar Williams. NAMP
Above the High. Geoffrey Grigson. EnLoPo
Above the Hills of Time. Thomas Tiplady. MaRV; SoP; TRV
Above the Lake of Galilee. Immortal Words. Aline Badger Carter. ChIP
Above the last squeak-squeal of wheels. Climbers. Earle Birney. TwCaPo
Above the laughter, O sea. The Signal. Eugenio Florit. OnPM
Above the Nile. Horace E. Hamilton. NYTB
Above the pine trees. Cazador (Hunter). Federico García Lorca. Po
Above the pines the moon was slowly drifting. Dickens in Camp. Bret Harte. HBV; OTD; PoRL
Above the place where children play. A Sussex Legend. Charles Dalmon. BoTP
Above the pools, above the valley of fears. Elevation. Baudelaire. AWP
Above the quiet dock in midnight. Above the Dock. T. E. Hulme. FaBoMo; GTBS-P; WePo
Above the quiet valley and unrippled lake. Spring Oak. Galway Kinnell. BoNaP; ELU; NePoAm
Above the River that is East. Look, Hart, That Horse You Ride Is Wood. Peter Viereck. ML
Above the road to Bethlehem. The Road to Bethlehem. Watson Kirkconnell. MaRV
Above the Stable. Nona Keen Duffy. BrR; ChBR
Above the unfathomed deep. The Precipice. John Banister Tabb. AmP
Above the violent park. A Star. George MacBeth. NYBP
Above the voiceful windings of a river. At the Grave of Henry Vaughan. Siegfried Sassoon. ChMP; CMoP; EaLo; GTBS-P; POTE
Above the water, in her rocky niche. The Strawberry Plant. Ruth Pitter. POTE
Above the weary waiting world. Christmas Song. Bliss Carman. PeCV; PoSC; StJW
Above the whispering sea. Air Raid Across the Bay of Plymouth. Stephen Spender. TPM
Above them spread a stranger sky. The Indian's Welcome to the Pilgrim Fathers. Lydia Huntley Sigourney. AA; DD
Above these bleak Wyoming plains. Winter Juniper. Joseph Langland. NePoEA
Above this bramble-overarched long lane. The Clearing. Robert Graves. NYBP
Above, through lunar woods a goddess flees. The Lovers. William Jay Smith. MoAmPo (1962 ed.)
Above us hangs the jewelled night. Waking. John Le Gay Brereton. BoAu
Above yon sombre [*or* somber] swell of land. The Plough [*or* Plow]. Richard Henry Horne. HBV; OBEV; OBVV; VA
Abracadabra. Dorothy Livesay. WHW
Abraham. Edwin Muir. MoRP
Abraham and Isaac. Genesis, XXII: 1-13, Bible, *O.T.* EnLi-1 (1949 ed.); OuHeWo
Abraham and Isaac. *Unknown. Fr.* Chester Miracle Play. FlW
Abraham Davenport. Whittier. AmePo; AmPP; AnNE; CoBA; NoP
Abraham Lincoln. A. S. Ames. OHIP
Abraham Lincoln. Joseph Auslander. YaD
Abraham Lincoln. Rosemary Benét *and* Stephen Vincent Benét. LiPo; NAMP; PoSC; TiPo; YeAr
Abraham Lincoln. Joel Benton. DD
Abraham Lincoln. Henry Howard Brownell. GN, *abr.*
Abraham Lincoln. Bryant. DD; MC; PaA; PAH; PoPo
(Death of Lincoln, The.) AmePo; AmP; AP; CoBA; ForPo; InP; LiPo
(To the Memory of Abraham Lincoln.) OHIP
Abraham Lincoln. Samuel Valentine Cole. OHIP; PEDC
Abraham Lincoln. James Russell Lowell. *Fr.* Ode Recited at the Harvard Commemoration, July 21, 1865. PAP
(Lincoln.) AnNE
(Our Martyr-Chief.) OHIP; PEDC
("Such was he, our Martyr-Chief.") InP
Abraham Lincoln. Mildred Plew Meigs. PAL; TiPo
Abraham Lincoln. Francesca Falk Miller. PEDC
Abraham Lincoln. Edmund Clarence Stedman. LiPo; PAH
Abraham Lincoln ("Not as when some great captain falls"). Richard Henry Stoddard. AA; FaBoBe; LiPo; PAH
Abraham Lincoln ("This man whose homely face"). Richard Henry Stoddard. DD; GN; HH; OHIP; OTPC (1946 ed.); PEDC; PGD
(Lincoln's Birthday.) PoRL
Abraham Lincoln. Tom Taylor, *sometimes wr. at. to* Mark Lemon *and to* Shirley Brooks. HBV; MCCG; PaA; PAH; VA
Abraham Lincoln. Robert Whitaker. HH
Abraham Lincoln. Whittier. *Fr.* The Emancipation Group. SoP
Abraham Lincoln, the dear president. The Dear President. John James Piatt. DD; MC; PAH
Abraham Lincoln, the Master. Thomas Curtis Clark. OHIP; PEDC
(Master, The.) OQP
Abraham Lincoln Walks at Midnight. Vachel Lindsay. AmFN; AmLP; AmPP; AnFE; ATP (1935 ed.); CMoP; CoAnAm; CoBA; FaBV; FaFP; FaPON; HBV; InP; LaNeLa; LiPo; LiTA; MAP; MaRV; MC; MCCG; MoRP; MoAmPo; MoVE; MPB; NAMP; NP; OHFP; OHIP; OnPP; OQP; OTD; OxBA; PaA; PAH; PAL; PEDC, *abr.*; PG (1945 ed.); PoPl; PoPo; PoRL, 6 *sts.*; PPON; RePo; ThLM; TIHL; TreF
Abraham Lincoln was ten feet tall. Abraham Lincoln. Joseph Auslander. YaD
Abraham, my servant, Abraham. Abraham and Isaac. *Unknown. Fr.* Chester Miracle Play. FlW
Abraham to kill him. Emily Dickinson. MWA-2
Abraham's Daughter, *with music.* Septimus Winner. TrAS
Abraham's Knife. George Garrett. PoPl
Abraham's Madness. Bink Noll. ToPo
Abram Brown, *with music. Unknown.* SoAmSa
Abroad. Alfred Starr Hamilton. QAH

Abroad and at Home. Swift. WhC
(Epigram: "As Thomas was cudglled one day by his wife.") WePo
Abroad on a winter's night there ran. A Christmas Legend. Frank Sidgwick. OHIP
Abroad the royal banners fly. Vexilla Regis. Fortunatus. CAW; WHL
Abroad Thoughts from Home. Donald Hall. NePoEA
Absalom and Achitophel, Pt. I. Dryden. CABL; CEP; EiCL; EiPP; EnLi-1; MBW-1; NoP; OAEP; SeCV-2; SeEP; TOP
Sels.
Achitophel. AWP, *br. sel.*; JAWP; SeCePo; WBP; WHA, *br. sel.*
(Characters from the Satires: Achitophel.) InPo
(Earl of Shaftesbury, The.) FaBoEn
(Enemies of David, The.) PeRV
(False Achitophel, The.) FiP
(Lord Shaftesbury.) LoBV
("Of these the false Achitophel was first.") AtBAP; PoEL-3; ViBoPo
(Shaftesbury.) OBS
Duke of Buckingham, The. FaBoEn
"From hence began that plot; the nation's curse." PeRV
"In pious times, e'r priestcraft did begin." MaPo (1969 ed.)
Popish Plot, The. ACP
"This Plot, which failed for want of common sense." CoBE
Zimri. AnFE; AWP; JAWP; SeCePo; ShBV-4; WBP
(Characters from the Satires: Zimri.) InPo
(George Villiers, Duke of Buckingham.) PoSa
("In the first rank of these did Zimri stand.") PoFS; ViBoPo
(Malcontents, The.) OBS
Absalom and Achitophel, Pt. II, *sels.* Nahum Tate *and* John Dryden.
"Levi, thou art a load, I'll lay thee down." Dryden. AtBAP; SeEP
"Next these, a troop of buisy spirits press." Dryden. CEP; SeCV-2
"Now stop your noses readers, all and some." Dryden. PeRV
Og and Doeg. Dryden. AWP; FiP, *shorter sel.*; JAWP; WBP
("And hasten Og and Doeg to rehearse.") MBW-1
(Characters from the Satires: Og and Doeg.) InPo
("Doeg though without knowing.") PoEL-3
"Some in my speedy pace I must outrun." Dryden. PIA
Thomas Shadwell the Poet, 2 *ll.* Dryden. ChTr
Absence. Matthew Arnold. Switzerland, VI. CBEP; MBW-2; PoVP; ViPP; VP
("In this fair stranger's eyes of grey.") OAEP
Absence. John Arthur Blaikie. VA
Absence. Robert Bridges. BoPe; OBEV (1st ed.)
("When my love was away.") BrPo; EG; LO
Absence. Jean Burden. NYTB
Absence. John Hoskins, *sometimes at. to* John Donne. FosPo; LiTL; MeLP; UnPo (1st ed.)
("Absence, heare my protestation.") EG
(Ode: "Absence, hear thou.") EIL; ReEn; TuPP
(Present in Absence.) GTBS; GTBS-D; GTBS-P; GTBS-W; GTSE; GTSL
(That Time and Absence Proves Rather Helps than Hurts to Loves.) OBEV (1st ed.)
Absence. Richard Jago. HBV; OBEV
Absence. Frances Anne Kemble. NeHB
What Shall I Do? *sel.* PoToHe (new ed.)
Absence ("Here, ever since you went abroad"). Walter Savage Landor. OBEV (1st ed.); TOP
Absence ("Ianthe! you resolve to cross the sea"). Walter Savage Landor. EnRP
("Ianthe, you resolve to cross the sea.") OBNC; OBVV
Absence, The. Denise Levertov. NaP
Absence. Pierre Louys, *tr. fr. French by* Horace M. Brown. *Fr.* The Songs of Bilitis. UnTE
Absence. James Russell Lowell. CBV
Absence. Claude McKay. CDC
Absence. Charlotte Mew. ChMP; MoAB; MoBrPo
Absence. Shakespeare. *See* Sonnets, LVII.
Absence. William Shenstone. Pastoral Ballad, Pt. I. OBEC
Absence. Sir Philip Sidney. SiPS
("Finding those beams, which I must ever love.") FCP
Absence ("Western wind"). *Unknown.* *See* Western Wind, When Wilt Thou Blow?
Absence ("When I think on the happy days"). *Unknown.* GTSL
Absence, The. Sylvia Townsend Warner. MoBrPo
Absence absenting causeth me to complain. Sir Thomas Wyatt. FCP; SiPS
Absence and Presence. Fulke Greville. Caelica, XLV [XLIV]. OBSC
("Absence, the noble truce.") EnRePo; NCEP; PoEL-1
Absence from thee is something worse than death. George Henry Boker. Sonn
Absence, hear thou my [*or* hear my *or* hear thou this] protestation. Absence [*or* Ode *or* Present in Absence *or* That Time and Absence Proves. . .]. John Hoskins, *sometimes at. to* John Donne. EG; EIL; FosPo; GTBS; GTBS-D; GTBS-P; GTBS-W; GTSE; GTSL; LiTL; MeLP; OBEV (1st ed.); ReEn; TuPP; UnPo (1st ed.)
Absence of Occupation ("Lucrative offices are seldom lost"). William Cowper. *Fr.* Retirement. OBEC
Absence, the noble truce. Absence and Presence. Fulke Greville. Caelica, XLV [XLIV]. EnRePo; NCEP; OBSC; PoEL-1
Absences. Philip Larkin. PoCH
Absent, The. Edwin Muir. MoRP
Absent Creation. D. S. Savage. NeBP
Absent Daughter. Barend Toerien, *tr. fr. Afrikaans by* Barend Toerien. PeSA
Absent face, remote and sharp, as far, An. The Beaches, III. "Robin Hyde." AnNZ
Absent from thee I languish still. A Song [*or* Return]. Earl of Rochester. CavP; ELP; EnLoPo; FaBoEn; LO; LoBV; MePo; OBEV; OBS; PeRV; PoFS; SeCePo; SeCL; SeCV-2; SeEP; ViBoPo
Absent Lover. *Unknown, tr. fr. Xhosa by* A. C. Jordan. PBA
Absent Minded Birch Tree, The. Kathleen Millay. PEDC
Absent-Minded Professor. Howard Nemerov. ELU
Absent Yet Present. Sir Edward Bulwer-Lytton. OBVV; UnPo
Absinthe-Drinker, The. Arthur Symons. BrPo; FaBoTw
Absolute, An/ patience. The Breathing. Denise Levertov. NaP; WIRo
Absolute and Abitofhell. Ronald Arbuthnott Knox. CenHV
Absolute knowledge I have none. Source of News. *Unknown.* TreF
Absolute, pity the visionless. Address to an Absolute. Roy McFadden. NeIP
Absolution. Siegfried Sassoon. MMA
Absolution. Edward Willard Watson. AA
Absolvers, The. Robert Southey. *Fr.* A Vision of Judgement. EnRP
Abstemia. Gelett Burgess. NA
Abstinence and Desire. Blake. OnPM
("Abstinence sows sand all over.") EiCL; ERoP-1; ExPo; TrGrPo
(Poems from MSS.) ViBoPo
Abstract Painter. Gerta Kennedy. NYTB
Abstract Painter in Spring. Rosamond Haas. NYTB
Abstrosophy. Gelett Burgess. CenHV; NA
Abt Vogler. Robert Browning. BEL; CoBE; DiPo; EPN; GoTL; HBV; MBW-2; NoP; OAEP; PoVP; TOP; VA; ViPo; ViPP; VP; WGRP
Sels.
"Builder and maker Thou." OQP
"Therefore to whom turn I but to thee, the ineffable Name?" MaRV
Abu Ben Adhem. Leigh Hunt. *See* Abou Ben Adhem.
Abu Nowas for the Barmacides. *Unknown, tr. fr. Arabic by* E. Powys Mathers. *Fr.* The Thousand and One Nights. AWP
Abundant Life. Henry W. Frost. SoP
Abused Lover Seeth His Folly and Entendeth to Trust No More, The. Sir Thomas Wyatt. ReIE
Abyss, The. Baudelaire, *tr. fr. French by* Robert Lowell. SyP
Acacia Leaves, The. Allen Upward. *Fr.* Scented Leaves from a Chinese Jar. NP
Academic. Theodore Roethke. CrMA; ELU; MiAP; PoeP; StP
Academic Discourse at Havana. Wallace Stevens. MoPo
Academic Visit to the Continent, An. Richard Porson. *See* Epigram on an Academic Visit to the Continent.
Academy. Sister Mary Jeremy. JKCP (1955 ed.)
Academy of the future is opening its doors, The. Sonnet. Ted Berrigan. ANYP; FRC

Acadia, *sel.* Joseph Howe.
"In ev'ry thought, in ev'ry wish I own." CaP
Accents in Alsace, *sels.* Gertrude Stein. AtBAP
Alsace or Alsatians.
Watch on the Rhine, The.
Accept each gift, though it be small. Lines for a Wedding Gift. Wesley Trimpi. NePoEA
Accept My Full Heart's Thanks. Ella Wheeler Wilcox. PoToHe
Accept Our Tribute. Isaac Watts. BePJ
Accept this garland and this girl together. Double Gift. *Unknown.* UnTE
Accept thou shrine of my dead saint. The Exequy [*or* Exequy on His Wife]. Henry King. AnAnS-2; AtBAP; ATP; BWP; CABA; CaFP; CLwM; EP; FaBoEn; ForPo; InvP; LiTL; LoBV; MeLP; MePo; NoP; OBEV; OBS; PoEL-2; QFR; ReEn; SeCePo; SeCL; SeCP; SeEP; ViBoPo; WHA
Acceptance. Robert Frost. CMoP; MoRP; OxBA
Acceptance. Langston Hughes. NePoAm-2
Acceptance. Willard Wattles. OQP
(Comrades of the Cross.) HBMV
Acceptation. Margaret Junkin Preston. MC; PAH
"Accepted." *Unknown.* SoP
Accepted and Will Appear. "Parmenas Mix." BOHV
Accident, The. Raymond Richard Patterson. CAD
Accident in Art. Richard Hovey. HBV
Accidents will happen—still, in time. A Bedtime Story [*or* If I Should Die Before I Wake]. Robert Mezey. NePoEA; NYBP
Accidian. Henry Charles Beeching. OBVV
Acclamation, An. Sir John Davies. *Fr.* Nosce Teipsum. OxBoCh; TuPP
Accompanied by clamor and by noise. Power. Grace Noll Crowell. PoMa
Accomplished Facts. Carl Sandburg. WHA
According to Brueghel. Landscape with the Fall of Icarus. William Carlos Williams. TDP
According to eternal laws. Walter Savage Landor. EiCP
"According to the Mighty Working." Thomas Hardy. CMoP; OnPM; ReMP
According to The Gracious Word. James Montgomery. MaRV
(This Do in Remembrance of Me.) SoP
According to [*or* to the] tradition. The Tryst. Christopher Morley. ALV; BOHV; HBMV
Account Me Not. Henry Longan Stuart. JKCP (1955 ed.)
Account of the Cruelty of the Papists, An. Benjamin Harris. SCAP
Accountability. Paul Laurence Dunbar. AnAmPo; PoLF; YaD
Accountant in His Bath, The ("The accountant dried his imperfect back"). Adrian Mitchell. NYBP
Accountants hover over the earth like helicopters. A Dream of Suffocation. Robert Bly. NaP
Accounte of W. Canynge's Feast, The. Thomas Chatterton. EnLi-2
Accursed, The. Baudelaire, *tr. fr. French by* F. P. Sturm. LiTW
Accursed be love . . . *See* Accurst Be Love.
Accursèd power which stands on Privilege, The. On a Great [*or* General] Election. Hilaire Belloc. MoVE; OxBoLi; WhC
Accursed the man, whom fate ordains, in spite. The Pains of Education. Charles Churchill. SiTL
Accurst Be Love! Thomas Lodge. PoIE (1970 ed.); SiCE
Accusation, The. James Wright. AmPC
Accusation of the Inward Man, The. Edward Taylor. *Fr.* God's Determinations. LiTA
Accusèd though I be without desert. Sir Thomas Wyatt. FCP; SiPS
Ace—Pride of parents. The Airman's Alphabet. W. H. Auden. *Fr.* Journal of an Airman. NAMP
Aceldama. Longfellow. StJW
Achaians Have Got Troy, upon This Very Day, The. Aeschylus, *tr. fr. Greek by* Richmond Lattimore. *Fr.* Agamemnon. WaaP
Ache, The. Lewis Mac Adams. YAP
Ache of wide millions, The. Return of a Reaper. Alan Creighton. CaP
Achievement. Morris Abel Beer. PoMa
Achievement. Berta Hart Nance. MaRV
Achilles, *sel.* John Gay.
Song: "Think of dress in ev'ry light," *fr.* III. OBEC
(Think of Dress in Every Light.) InvP
Achilles. Ernest Myers. OBVV
Achilles and the King. John Logan. AmPC
Achilles' baneful wrath resound, O goddess that impos'd. Homer. *Fr.* The Iliad, I. ReIE
Achilles Deatheridge. Edgar Lee Masters. AmFN; MaC; PoMa
Achilles' Shield. Homer, *tr. fr. Greek by* George Chapman. *Fr.* The Iliad, XVIII. ReEn
("This said, he left her there, and forth did to his bellows go.") TuPP
Achilles Shows Himself in the Battle by the Ships. Homer, *tr. fr. Greek by* George Chapman. *Fr.* The Iliad, XVIII. OBS
Achilles to Lycaon. Homer, *tr. fr. Greek by* Richmond Lattimore. *Fr.* The Iliad, XXI. LiTW; WaaP
Achitophel. Dryden. *Fr.* Absalom and Achitophel, Pt. I. AWP, *br. sel.*; JAWP; SeCePo; WBP; WHA, *br. sel.*
(Characters from the Satires: Achitophel.) InPo
(Earl of Shaftesbury, The.) FaBoEn
(Enemies of David.) PeRV
(False Achitophel, The.) FiP
(Lord Shaftesbury.) LoBV
("Of these the false Achitophel was first.") AtBAP; PoEL-3; ViBoPo
(Shaftesbury.) OBS
Achtung. Sappho, *tr. fr. Greek by* Thomas Hardy. CTC
Acis and Galatea, *sels.* John Gay.
Love in Her Eyes Sits Playing. ELP; EnLi-1 (1949 ed.); OBEC; OnPM; ViBoPo
(Song: "Love in her eyes sits playing.") FaBoEn
O Ruddier than the Cherry. ELP; LiTL; ViBoPo
(Air: "O ruddier than the cherry.") EiCL
(Song: "O ruddier than the cherry.") EiPP; HBV; OBEC; OBEV (1st ed.)
Recitativo: "I rage, I melt, I burn." EiCL
Acme and Septimius. Catullus, *tr. fr. Latin by* Abraham Cowley. AWP; UnTE
Aconite, The. A. M. Graham. BoTP
Acorn, The. *Unknown.* BoTP
Acorn and the Pumpkin, The. La Fontaine, *tr. fr. French by* Elizur Wright. BoChLi
Acorns. Edith King. GFA
Acquaintance. David Morton. MCCG
Acquainted with the Night. Robert Frost. AmP; AP; BWP; ChTr; CMoP; CoBMV; DiPo; ForPo; InP; LiTM; MaPo; MemP; MoAmPo (1962 ed.); MWA-2; NePA; NP; OCS; PDV; PIA; PoeP; PoFS; PoG; PoIE; PoLF; PoSa; Sonn; TDP; TPM; TwCP
Acre of Grass, An. W. B. Yeats. CMoP; GTBS-D; MBW-2; POTE
Acrobat. Rachel Field. *Fr.* A Circus Garland. SoPo; StVeCh
Acrobat from Xanadu Disdained All Nets, The. Dan Georgakas. ThO
Acrobat on the border of the sea, An. The Woman That Had More Babies than That. Wallace Stevens. LiTA
Across a sage-grown upland. The Path of the Padres. Edith D. Osborne. AmFN
Across clear drops of dew. Bunya no Asayasu, *tr. fr. Japanese by* I. W. Furukami. LiTW
Across Illinois. John Stoltze. PoMa
Across its wastes a universe I trod. Search. T. Moore Atkinson. ChIP
Across my loom of years there fell a shadow, gaunt and gray. The Shadow on the Loom. Nellie Burget Miller. OQP
Across North Wales. Dafydd ap Gwilym Resents the Winter. Rolfe Humphries. NYBP
Across Roblin Lake, two shores away. Wilderness Gothic. Alfred Purdy. MoCV; PeCV (1967 ed.)
Across the ages they come thundering. Say This of Horses. Minnie Hite Moody. PoLF
Across the azure spaces. The Winds of God. Clinton Scollard. PoRL
Across the barrage, the cities of Europe remember. Homage of War. Bruce Williamson. NeIP
Across the bitter centuries I hear the wail of men. Thy Kingdom Come. Willard Wattles. OQP
Across the boughs of a swinging, sunlit tree. Service. Sybil Leonard Armes. FaChP
Across the bristled and sallow fields. The Hawk. Raymond Knister. OBCV
Across the brook of time man leaping goes. Laus Mariae. Sidney Lanier. Sonn

Across the courtyard. The Wedding. Boris Pasternak. HW
Across the craggy indigo. Business as Usual 1946. A. J. M. Smith. NMP
Across the crests of the naked hills. Laramie Trail. Joseph Mills Hanson. PoOW
Across the dark linked loveliness of lakes. Dawn. "Æ." BEL
Across the Delaware. Will Carleton. MC; PAH
Across the desert dry as bone. The Upas Tree. Pushkin. LiTW
Across the dewy lawn she treads. Paean. Jonathan Henderson Brooks. CDC
Across the dim frozen fields of night. Night Train. Robert Francis. LOW
Across the Door. Padraic Colum. HBV
Across the drifted square from street and lane. Independence Square, Christmas, 1783. Arthur Guiterman. PEDC
Across the eastern sky has glowed. The Crowing of the Red Cock. Emma Lazarus. AA; HBV
Across the edges of the world there blows a wind. The Spring of God. William Alexander Percy. *Fr.* In April Once. OQP
Across the empty garden-beds. The Sailing of the *Sword.* William Morris. CoBE; ILP; OAEP; OBVV; PoVP
Across the Fens. Gilbert Thomas. HaMV
Across the Fields. Walter Crane. VA
Across the fields of yesterday. Sometimes. Thomas S. Jones, Jr. HBV; InP; MaRV; OQP; PoMa; TreFT; TRV
Across the Fields to Anne. Richard Burton. HBV
Across the floor flits the mechanical toy. Cirque d'Hiver. Elizabeth Bishop. FiMAP; LiTA; MiAP
Across the foaming river. The Bridge. Frederick Peterson. HBV
Across the gardens of Life they go. Love and Time. Beatrix Demarest Lloyd. AA
Across the German Ocean. Little Gottlieb. Phoebe Cary. OTPC (1946 ed.); TVC
Across the grass I see her pass. The Milkmaid. Austin Dobson. HBV
Across the Great Divide. Phyllis C. Michael. SoP
Across the greening lawn. A Northern Spring. Gene Baro. NePoEA-2
Across the heavy sands running they came. Pan and Syrinx. W. R. Rodgers. NMP
Across the hills of Arcady. To Arcady. Charles Buxton Going. HBV
Across the lonely beach we flit. *See* Across the narrow beach we flit.
Across the moorlands of the Not. Moorlands of the Not. *Unknown.* NA
Across the mud the line drags on and on. Ration Party. John Manifold. WaP
Across the narrow [*or* lonely] beach we flit. The Sandpiper. Celia Thaxter. AA; BBV (1923 ed.); BoChLi; DD; FaBoBe; FaPON; GN; HBV; HBVY; PTK; UTS; WBLP
Across the open countryside. Unsettled Motorcyclist's Vision of His Death. Thom Gunn. ForPo; NePoEA-2
Across the page of history. Lincoln Leads. Minna Irving. HH; OHIP
Across the pearly distance. Autumn Haze. Richard Kendall Munkittrick. PoRL
Across the places deep and dim. The Road to Anywhere. Bert Leston Taylor. HBMV; MPB; TSW
Across the plain the wind whines through the sage. The Snowstorm. Pearl Riggs Crouch. PoOW
Across the round field, under the dark male tower. The Lovers. Alex Comfort. NeBP
Across the sands of Syria. The Legend of the First Cam-u-el. Arthur Guiterman. ALV; BOHV; CenHV
Across the sea a land there is. A Land across the Sea. William Morris. *Fr.* The Earthly Paradise. VA
Across the sea, along the shore. "What Went Ye Out for to See?" Arthur Hugh Clough. PoVP; StJW
Across the seas of Wonderland to Mogadore we plodded. Forty Singing Seamen. Alfred Noyes. AnFE; BBV; BEL; BoChLi; GBV; OnMSP; ShBV-1; StPo; TOP
Across the shaken bastions of the year. Sonnets of a Portrait Painter, XLVII. Arthur Davison Ficke. AnAmPo
Across the shimmering meadows. The Hawthorn Tree. Willa Cather. HBMV
Across the silent stream. From the Hills of Dream. "Fiona Macleod." MoSiPe
Across the sky run streaks of white light, aching. Before Olympus. John Gould Fletcher. MAP; MoAmPo
Across the snow the silver bells. Silver Bells. Hamish Hendry. BoTP
Across the sombre prairie sea. Prairie. Herbert Bates. AA
Across the Stony Mountains, o'er the desert's drouth and sand. The Crisis. Whittier. PAH
Across the stony ridges. Ballad of the Drover. Henry Lawson. PoAu-1
Across the storm-swept plain. A Traveler Caught in a Storm. Kiokusui. GaP
Across the Straits. Rosemary Dobson. PoAu-2
Across the swamps and marshlands of the hours. A Sea-Change: For Harold. Joseph Langland. LiTM (1970 ed.)
Across the swiffling waves they went. The Cruise of the *P. C.* *Unknown.* NA
Across the tapestry-lands of the Middle Ages. The Witches. Leah Bodine Drake. FiSC
Across the way my neighbor's windows shine. Intolerance. Molly Anderson Haley. MaRV
Across the Western Ocean, *with music. Unknown.* AmSS; AS; SoAmSa
Across the wrack besprinkled bay. The Glaucous-Gull's Death. Daniel James O'Sullivan. NeIP
Across the years he could recall. The Secret Heart. Robert P. Tristram Coffin. OTD; PoRL; PoSC
Across this dream of seas blue mountains fall. Between Seasons. Anne Welsh. PeSA
Across thousands of mountains no birds fly. Ice in a Stream. Liu Tsung-yuan. OnPM
Acrostick on Mrs. Elizabeth Hull, An. John Saffin. SCAP
Acrostick on Mrs. Winifret Griffin, An. John Saffin. SCAP
A-Cruising We Will Go. *Unknown.* AmSS
Act, The. William Carlos Williams. CBV; ELU
Act V (Midnight). Thomas Bailey Aldrich. PFY
Act of Love. Nicholas Moore. NeBP
Act of Love. Vernon Scannell. ErPo
Act II. Katherine Davis. PoPl
Actaeon. Rayner Heppenstall. FaBoTw
Actaeon. *Unknown. See* I Would I Were Actaeon.
Actea. Sir Rennell Rodd. VA
Acteon. Ovid, *tr. fr. Latin by* Arthur Golding. *Fr.* Metamorphoses, III. CTC
Action. James Oppenheim. TrJP
Action is transitory—a step, a blow. Wordsworth. *Fr.* The Borderers. PeER
Action Rhyme. E. M. Adams. BoTP
Action runs left to right, The. Movies, Left to Right. Robert Sward. NYBP
Actions. Marcel Schwob, *tr. fr. French by* William Brown Meloney. TrJP
Actor, An. "Peter Pindar." BOHV
Actor, The. Thomas Snapp. NYBP
Actor's dead, and memory alone, The. J. B. Henry Cuyler Bunner. AA
Actress, The. Dorothy Parker. PoPo
Actress of emotional roles, An. The Tattooed Man. Harry B. Smith. *Fr.* The Idol's Eye. InMe
Acts, The, *sels.* Bible, *N.T.*
"Chief captain commanded him to be brought into the castle, The," XXII: 24-30. PoFr
Paul on the Road to Damascus, IX: 3-6. TreF
Acts of Youth, The. John Wieners. CoPo
Actual evidence I have none. Rumors [*or* When the War Will End]. Reginald Arkell. InMe; TreFT
Actual Willow. Winifred Welles. MAP
Actuality. Sir John Suckling. *See* Doubt of Martyrdom, A.
Ad. Kenneth Fearing. CMoP
Ad Amicam. Francis Thompson. Sonn
Ad Castitatem. Francis Thompson. PoLi
Ad Chloen, M. A. Mortimer Collins. BOHV; HBV
Ad Coelum. Harry Romaine. BLPA; FaBoBe; NeHB
Ad Collegium Wintoniensem. John Heath. TuPP
Ad Curiosum Lectorem. Thomas Bastard. SiCE
Ad Deum. George Chapman. ReIE
Ad Domnulam Suam. Ernest Dowson. HBV; PG
Ad Eandem. Thomas Bastard. SiCE
Ad Finem. Heine, *tr. fr. German by* Elizabeth Barrett Browning. AWP; JAWP; WBP
Ad Finem. Ella Wheeler Wilcox. BLPA
Ad Gulielmum Shakespeare. John Weever. ReIE; SiCE; TuPP

Ad Gulielmum Warner. John Weever. ReIE
Ad Henricum Wottonem ("Wotton my little Bere dwells on a hill"). Thomas Bastard. SiCE
Ad Henricum Wottonum ("Wotton, the country and the country swain"). Thomas Bastard. SiCE
Ad Jo. [*or* Io.] Marston & [*or* et] Ben. Jonson [*or* Johnson *or* Ionson]. John Weever. ReIE; SiCE; TuPP
Ad Lectorem ("How quickly doth the reader pass away"). Thomas Bastard. SiCE; TuPP
Ad Lectorem ("If my books easy of digestion be"). Thomas Bastard. SiCE
Ad Lectorem ("Reader, my book flies low, and comes not near"). Thomas Bastard. SiCE
Ad Lectorem ("Reader, there is no biting in my verse"). Thomas Bastard. SiCE
Ad Lectorem. John Weever. ReIE
Ad Lesbiam. Catullus, *tr. fr. Latin by* Niall Sheridan. OxBI
Ad Leuconoen. Franklin P. Adams, *after the Latin of* Horace. AWP; JAWP; WBP
Ad Leuconoen. Francis Sylvester Mahony. IrPN
Ad Librum. Samuel Danforth, Jr. SCAP
Ad Majorem Dei Gloriam. Frederick George Scott. MaRV; VA
Ad Majorem Hominis Gloriam. John Gould Fletcher. MAP; MoAmPo
Ad Mariam. Sister Mary Edwardine. WHL
Ad Matrem. Julian Fane. HBV
Ad Matrem, in Caelis. Charles L. O'Donnell. WHL
Ad Matrem in Coelis. Linda Lyon Van Voorhis. GoBC
Ad Michaelem Drayton. John Weever. ReIE
Ad Ministram. Thackeray, *after the Latin of* Horace. HBV
(Persicos Odi.) OBEV (new ed.)
Ad Modernos Epigrammatistas. John Heath. SiCE; TuPP
Ad Musam. Sir John Davies. ReIE; SiCE
Ad Patriam, *sel.* William Dudley Foulke.
Land of My Heart. PAL; PGD
Ad Patriam. Clinton Scollard. PaA; PAH; PEDC
(Land of Our Fathers.) MC
Ad Persephonen. Franklin P. Adams. InMe
Ad Reginam Elizabetham ("Live long Elisa, that the wolf of Spain"). Thomas Bastard. SiCE
Ad Reginam Elizabetham ("Mother of England, and sweet nurse of all"). Thomas Bastard. SiCE
Ad Samuelem Daniel. John Weever. ReIE
Ad Samuelem Danielem. Thomas Bastard. SiCE
Ad Tho. Bastardum Epigrammatistam. John Heath. TuPP
Ad Xanthium Phoceum. Franklin P. Adams, *after the Latin of* Horace. AWP; JAWP; WBP
Ad Zoilum. John Heath. TuPP
Adakrue Nemontai Aiona. Emerson. MWA-1
Adam. Philip Booth. MoLP
Adam. Anthony Hecht. CoPo
Adam. Rainer Maria Rilke, *tr. fr. German by* M. D. Herter Norton. MoRP
Adam. *Unknown. See* Adam Lay Ibounden.
Adam/ Had 'em. On [*or* Lines on] the Antiquity of Microbes. Strickland Gillilan. InP; TreFT; WhC
Adam and Eve. Genesis, II: 7—III: 23, Bible, *O.T.* TreFT
Adam and Eve. Itzig Manger, *tr. fr. Yiddish by* Jacob Sonntag. TrJP
Adam and Eve ("Birds their choir apply; airs, vernal airs, The"). Milton. *Fr.* Paradise Lost, IV. CLwM
(Eternal Spring, The.) GN
Adam and Eve ("So passed they naked on, nor shunned the sight"). Milton. *Fr.* Paradise Lost, IV. SeCePo
Adam and Eve. Karl Shapiro. AmP; FiMAP; ReMP
Sels.
Recognition of Eve, The. MoAB; ToPo
Sickness of Adam, The. AP; CoBMV; MoAB
Adam and Eve, like us. A Circle. Theodore Spencer. NYBP
Adam and God. Anne Wilkinson. MoCV
Adam Bell [*or* Bel], Clym of the Clough, and William of Cloudesley. *Unknown.* BuBa; ESPB; OBB; OxBB
Adam Birkett took his gun. Birkett's Eagle. Dorothy S. Howard. MoBS
Adam, First Man of Men. Milton. *Fr.* Paradise Lost, VIII. MaPo
Adam in the Garden Pinnin' Leaves, *with music. Unknown.* OuSiCo
Adam is a pupil of mine. Athlete. Don Maynard. PoAu-2
Adam Lay Ibounden [*or* I-bowndyn *or* Ybounden]. *Unknown.* AtBAP; BoW; CBEP; ChTr; CTC; EG; EnPo; FosPo; GoBC; ILP; LO; NoP; OAEP; OnPM; OxBoCh; OxBoLi; PoEL-1; PoIE; PoLi; SeCeV; ThGo; YAT
(Adam.) CH
(Adam Lay in Bondage.) MeEL
("O Felix Culpa.") ACP; CAW
Adam, Lilith, and Eve. Robert Browning. HBV; MeWo; PoVP; ViPP
"Adam, my child, my son." Adam. Anthony Hecht. CoPo
Adam on His Way Home. Robert Pack. ErPo; PoDB
Adam Pos'd. Countess of Winchilsea. EiCL; Po
Adam scriveyn, if ever it thee bifalle. Chaucers Wordes unto Adam, His Owne Scriveyn. Chaucer. BEL
Adam stood by the sleeping lion. Eden. F. R. Scott. TwCaPo
Adam—the First Kiss. Hal Porter. ACV
Adam the goodliest man of men since born. A Scene in Paradise. Milton. *Fr.* Paradise Lost, IV. GN
Adam to Lilith. Christopher Brennan. *Fr.* Lilith. PoAu-1
Adam, walking in the summer garden. Lord of Eden. Marie de L. Welch. AnAmPo
Adam was my grandfather. For All Blasphemers. Stephen Vincent Benét. AtBAP; OxBA
Adam, who thought himself immortal still. The Discovery. Monk Gibbon. OnYI
Adamant, The. Theodore Roethke. NYTB
Adamastor, whom Camoens and the sea. David Wright. *Fr.* A Voyage to Africa. BoSA
Adams and Liberty. Robert Treat Paine. MC; PAH
Adam's Complaint. Theophanes, *tr. fr. Greek by* John Mason Neale. SoP
Adam's Curse. W. B. Yeats. CMoP; CoBMV; DiPo; Po; PP; ViPo (1962 ed.)
Adam's first wife had soft lips but no soul. Lilith. X. J. Kennedy. UnTE
Adam's Footprint. Vassar Miller. NePoEA; ToPo
Adam's Hymn in Paradise. Joost van den Vondel, *tr. fr. Dutch by* Sir John Bowring. WGRP
(Hymn of Adam.) CAW
Adam's Morning Hymn. Milton. *Fr.* Paradise Lost, V. WGRP
(Morning Hymn of Adam, *abr.*) TrPWD
(Morning Hymn of Adam and Eve.) OxBoCh
(These Are Thy Glorious Works.) MaRV
Adam's Race. Sadi, *tr. fr. Persian by* Edward B. Eastwick. LiTW
Adam's Song of the Visible World, *much abr.* Ridgely Torrence. TrPWD
Adam's Song to Heaven. Edgar Bowers. QFR
Adam's Wonder. George O'Neil. NP
Adapt Thyself. Shem-Tob ben Joseph Palquera, *tr. fr. Hebrew by* Rabbi Ettelson. TrJP
Adare, *sel.* John Francis O'Donnell. IrPN
"Morn comes freshly from the east, The."
Add but a handle. The Fan. Sokan. GFA
Addict. Mabel MacDonald Carver. FiSC
Addict, The. Larry Rubin. GoYe
Addict, The. Anne Sexton. TPM
Additional Verses to "Hail Columbia." Oliver Wendell Holmes. PAH
Address, The. *Unknown.* PCH
Address Not Known. John Heath-Stubbs. ChMP
Address of Richard III to His Army, The. Shakespeare. King Richard III, *fr.* V, iii. UnPo (1st ed.)
Address of Ruth to Naomi. Ruth, Bible, *O.T. See* Intreat Me Not to Leave Thee.
Address to a Child during a Boisterous Winter Evening. Dorothy Wordsworth. OTPC (1923 ed.)
Wind, The, *sel.* BoTP
Address to a Haggis. Burns. ViBoPo
Address to a Lady. Burns. *See* Oh Wert Thou in the Cauld Blast.
Address to a Lark, *sel.* John Clare.
Address to a Lark Singing in Winter. BiS
Address to a Mummy. Horace Smith. HBV; RoGo, *sl. abr.*
Address to an Absolute. Roy McFadden. NeIP
Address to His Elbow-Chair, New Cloath'd, An. William Somervile. CEP; OBEC
Address to Miss Phillis Wheatley, An, *sel.* Jupiter Hammon.
"O come you pious youth! adore." AmPP (5th ed.)

Address to My Infant Daughter. Wordsworth. EvOK; Par
Address to My Soul. Elinor Wylie. AmLP; AnFE; APA; AWP; CoAnAm; LiTM; MoRP; OxBA; PoFr
Address to Plenty, *sel.* John Clare.
"'Tis not great, what I solicit." OBRV
Address to the Body. Francis Maguire. JKCP (1955 ed.)
Address to the Crown. Charles L. O'Donnell. GoBC
Address to the Deil. Burns. CEP; EiCP; EiPP; EnPE; EnRP; GoTS; OAEP; OxBS; PoE; PoEL-4; UnPo (1st ed.)
Address to the Doomed, *sel.* George Dillon.
"Say it is life that matters. Say the bone," I. NP
Address to the New Year. Dinah Maria Mulock Craik. PEDC
Address to the Ocean. Byron. *See* Ocean, The.
Address to the Parents, The. Marvin Bell. YAP
Address to the Scholars of New England. John Crowe Ransom. AmPP; LiTM (rev. ed.); NePA
Address to the Soul Occasioned by a Rain, An. Edward Taylor. AP; OxBA; Po; PoEL-3
(When Let by Rain.) MAmP
Address to the Toothache. Burns. BOHV
Address to the Unco Guid, or the Rigidly Righteous. Burns. AnFE; BEL; BoLiVe; CEP; CoBE; EiCL; EiPP; EnLit; EnPE; EnRP; FosPo; HBV; LoBV; OAEP; OBEC; OxBS; PoFr; SeCeV; TOP; TreFS; TrGrPo; ViBoPo
"Then gently scan your brother man," 2 *sts.* MaRV
Address to the Vacationers at Cape Lookout, An. William Stafford. NYBP
Address to Venus. Lucretius, *tr. fr. Latin by* Spenser. *Fr.* De Rerum Natura *and fr.* The Faerie Queene, IV, 10. AnEnPo; AWP
(Prayer to Venus.) EIL
Addressed to a Gentleman at Table, Who Kept Boasting of the Company He Kept. Burns. PV
Addressed to a Young Lady. William Cowper. *See* To a Young Lady.
Addressed to Haydon ("Great spirits now on earth are sojourning"). Keats. EnRP; OBNC
(Addressed to the Same.) MERP
("Great spirits now on earth. . .") Sonn
(Sonnet Addressed to Haydon.) PeER
(To Haydon.) MBW-2
Addressed to Haydon ("Highmindedness, a jealousy for good"). Keats. CBEP; MERP
Ad-dressing of Cats, The. T. S. Eliot. GoTP
Adela Cathcart, *sel.* George Macdonald.
Sir Lark and King Sun, *fr. ch.* 16. HBV; HBVY; OTPC
Adelaide Crapsey. Carl Sandburg. HBMV
Adelaide Neilson. William Winter. AA
Adelita, *with music.* *Unknown.* *tr. fr. Spanish by* F. S. Curtis, Jr. AS
Adepts, The. Lawrence Durrell. *Fr.* Eight Aspects of Melissa. ErPo; NeBP
Adequacy. Elizabeth Barrett Browning. SoP
Adeste Fideles. *Unknown.* *See* O Come, All Ye Faithful.
Adew, my King, court, cuntrey, and my kin. To Henry Constable and Henry Keir. Alexander Montgomerie. OxBS
Adhesive: for Earlene. Robert Hass. YAP
Adieu. Thomas Carlyle. HBV; OBRV; VA
"Adieu." John Clare. FIW
Adieu. Eleanor Elizabeth Montgomery. VA
Adieu, adieu, fair Annie, he did say. Fair Annie (B *vers.*). *Unknown.* BaBo
Adieu, adieu! my native shore. Childe Harold's Farewell to England [*or* Childe Harold's Good Night]. Byron. *Fr.* Childe Harold's Pilgrimage. MBW-2; OHFP; PoPl
Adieu, dear object of my love's excess. Orinda to Lucasia Parting, October, 1661, at London. Katherine Philips. OBS
Adieu, fair isle! I love thy bowers. Farewell to Cuba. Maria Gowen Brooks. AA
Adieu, Farewell, Earth's Bliss [*or* Blisse]! Thomas Nashe. *Fr.* Summer's Last Will and Testament. AtBAP; CaFP; CBV; CH; EIL; ELP; InvP; LoBV; OAEP; PoE; PoG, 3 *sts.*; PoIE; PoSa; QFR; SiCE; TuPP; ViBoPo
(Death's Summons.) HBV; SoP
(Dust Hath Closed Helen's Eye.) SeCePo
(In a Time of Pestilence.) HoPM; PoFS; TrGrPo
(In Plague Time.) FaBoCH; LoGBV; OBSC
(In Time of Pestilence 1593.) CBEP; DTC; LiTG; MemP; OBEV; OtMeF
(In Time of Plague.) EnRePo; EP
(Litany in Time of Plague, A.) BEL; BWP; CABA; EnLi-1 (1949 ed.); ForPo; FosPo; NoP; PoRA; ReEn
(Lord, Have Mercy On Us.) ChTr
(Song.) DiPo; FaBoEn; MyFE; PoEL-2; StP
(Song in Plague-Time.) FOL
"Adieu, for now I've made an end." John Gower. *Fr.* Confessio Amantis: Conclusion. MeEV
Adieu, kind Life, though thou hast often been. Departure. May Riley Smith. AA
Adieu Love, Untrue Love. *Unknown.* *See* Faithless Shepherdess, The.
"Adieu [*or* Adiew], madame [*or* madam], my mother dear." Lord Maxwell's [Last] Good-Night. *Unknown.* ESPB, (B *vers.*); OBB
Adieu, O Daisy of Delight! Alexander Montgomerie. LO
Adieu, sweet Angus, Maeve, and Fand. The Passing of the Shee. J. M. Synge. OnYI
Adieu the woods and waters' side. Lines on Leaving a Scene in Bavaria. Thomas Campbell. OBNC
Adieu to Belashanny [*or* Ballyshannon]! where I was bred and born. The Winding Banks of Erne [*or* Adieu to Belashanny]. William Allingham. AnIV; IrPN; NBM; OxBI
Adieu to Bon County, *with music.* *Unknown.* ABF
Adieu to France. John Hunter-Duvar. *Fr.* De Roberval. VA
Adieu to the Stone Walls, *with music.* *Unknown.* OuSiCo
Adieu? why so? deare Castaminda stay. *Unknown.* SeCSL
Adieux à Marie Stuart. Swinburne. PoVP
Adina. Harold Telemaque. PoNe; TTY
Adios. Donald C. Babcock. NePoAm-2
Adios. Joaquin Miller. OQP
Adjectives. Moishe Nadir, *tr. fr. Yiddish by* Joseph Leftwich. TrJP
Adjuration. Frank Belknap Long. FiSC
Adjuration. Charles Enoch Wheeler. AmNP; PoNe
Adjust, Adjust. Christopher Bursk. WOW
Adjustment. Whittier. WGRP
Adlatts parke is wyde and broad. Will Stewart and John. *Unknown.* ESPB
Adlestrop. Edward Thomas. BrPo; CH; CLwM; FIW; GoJo; GTBS; GTBS-W; HT; LiTB; LiTM; NP; OBEV (new ed.); PoG; ShBV-2
Admiral. John Alexander Allen. NYBP
Admiral, Admiral, sailing home. The Homing. John Jerome Rooney. AA
Admiral Benbow. *Unknown.* CBEP; EnSB
Admiral Byrd. Ogden Nash. InMe; YaD
Admiral Hosier's Ghost. Richard Glover. HBV; ViBoPo
Admiral's Caravan, The, *sel.* Charles Edward Carryl.
Plaint of the Camel, The. AnAmPo; BoTP; FaPON; HBV; HBVY; OTPC (1946 ed.); PoRh; SP; StVeCh; UTS
(Camel's Complaint, The.) AmePo
(Camel's Lament, The.) GoTP
Admiral, the prisoner of your giant's. Admiral. John Alexander Allen NYBP
Admiral's Ghost, The. Alfred Noyes. BBV; PoMS; TiPo (1952 ed.)
Admire the face of plastered stone. Quebec Farmhouse. John Glassco. PeCV (1967 ed.)
Admire thy wreath? And wherefore should I not. To a Plagiarist. Moses ibn Ezra. TrJP
Admire, when you come here, the glimmering hair. Vuillard: "The Mother and Sister of the Artist." W. D. Snodgrass. CoAP
Admission. Henry Vaughan. AnAnS-1; MeP
Admit the ruse to fix and name her chaste. The Romantic. Louise Bogan. NP
Admit thou darlinge of myne eyes. *Unknown.* SeCSL
Admonition. John Peale Bishop. TwAmPo
Admonition. John L. Bonn. JKCP (1955 ed.)
Admonition. Philip Stack. BLPA
Admonition before Grief. Hazel Hall. NP
Admonition for Spring. L. A. MacKay. CaP; OBCV; PeCV
Admonition to a Traveller. Wordsworth. GTBS; GTBS-D; GTBS-P; GTBS-W; GTSE; GTSL
Admonition to Montgomerie. James I, King of England. OxBS
Admonitions. Margaret Bell Houston. MoSiPe
Adolescence. P. K. Page. CaP; OBCV; TwCaPo
Adolescents in the Dusk. Iain Fletcher. FaBoMo

Adolicus; that's a creeper rug, its small. The Houses, III. "Robin Hyde." AnNZ
Adolphus Elfinstone. Gelett Burgess. BBGG; GaP; PoRL
Adon 'Olam. *Unknown, tr. fr. Hebrew by* F. De Sola Mendes. EaLo
Adonais. Will Wallace Harney. AA; HBV
Adonais; an Elegy on the Death of John Keats. Shelley. AtBAP; ATP; BEL; BoLiVe; CABA; ChER; EnL; EnLi-2; EnLit; EnRP; EPN; ERoP-2; FaPL; FiP, *much abr.*; FosPo, *abr.*; GoTL; HBV; HoPM; LoBV; MaPo; MasP; MBW-2, *abr.*; MCCG; MERP; NoP; OAEP; OBRV; PAn; PoE; PoEL-4; PoIE, *much abr.*; StP; TOP; TrGrPo; UnPo (1st ed.); ViBoPo, *abr.*; WHA; WoL, *abr.*
Sels.
"Alas ! that all we love." OHIP
Go Thou to Rome. ChTr
"He has outsoared the shadow of our night." BoC; PeER; PoSa
"He is a portion of the loveliness." MemP
"He is made one with Nature." WGRP
"Here pause: these graves are all too young as yet." MyFE
"One remains, the many change and pass, The." InP
(Lumen de Lumine.) GoBC
One with Nature ("He lives, he wakes"). MaRV
"Peace, peace! he is not dead, he doth not sleep." FaBoEn; LO
(Against Oblivion.) TreFS
(Elegy on the Death of John Keats, An.) OBNC
(He Is Not Dead.) MaRV
Adonis. Hilda Doolittle ("H. D."). AP; AWP; InPo; JAWP; LiTA; PoPl; WBP
Adorable images. To the Mannequins. Howard Nemerov. CBV
Adoration. Henry W. Frost. SoP
Adoration. Mme Guyon, *tr. fr. French.* SoP; STF; WGRP
(By Thy Life I Live.) MaRV; TRV
Adoration. David Morton. MaRV
Adoration. Christopher Smart. *Fr.* A Song to David. FaBoEn
Adoration. Henry van Dyke. *See* Hymn of Joy.
Adoration—A Carol. E. Margaret Clarkson. SoP
Adoration of the Disk by King Akhnaten and Princess Nefer Neferi-u Aten. *Unknown, tr. fr. Egyptian by* Robert Hillyer. *Fr.* The Book of the Dead. AWP; JAWP; WBP
"Cattle roam again across the field, The," *sel.* FaPON
Adoration of the Shepherds, The. St. Luke, Bible, *N.T.* ChrBoLe (II: 1-16)
(Angels of Bethlehem, The, II: 8-16.) BoC
(Christmas Eve, II: 8-14.) BiCB; ChBR; GaP; PCH; SiSoSe
(Christmas Story, The, II: 8-14.) MaRV
(First Christmas, The.) OTPC (1946 ed.) (II: 8-16); PoRL (II: 8-16); SoPo (II: 8-16); TreFS (II: 1-19)
(Tidings of Great Joy, II: 8-14.) FaPON
Adoration of the Wise Men, The. Cecil Frances Alexander. HBVY; PRWS
Adoro Te Devote. St. Thomas Aquinas, *tr. fr. Latin.* CAW, *tr. by* Dom F. Cabrol; WHL, *abr.,* tr. unknown
A-down the road and gun in hand. Whiskey Bill; a Fragment. *Unknown.* SCC
Adrasta, *sel.* John Jones.
Come, Lovers, Bring Your Cares. SeCL; TuPP
Adrian Block's Song. Edward Everett Hale. PAH
Adriani Morientis ad Animam Suam. Emperor Hadrian. *See* To His Soul.
Adriatic. Robert Conquest. PP
Adrift. Elizabeth Dickinson Dowden. WGRP
Adrift! A little boat adrift! Emily Dickinson. MWA-2
Adrift in space. Autumn Grove after Rain, by Wen Tien. James Kirkup. *Fr.* Seven Pictures from China. POTi
Adsum. Richard Henry Stoddard. AA
Adulescentia, *sel.* Robert Fitzgerald.
"Miraculously, through prayer to Saint Anthony." SD
Adult Lullaby, An. *Unknown.* MeEL
Adulterers and customers of whores. Womanisers. John Press. ErPo
Adulteries, murthers, robberies, thefts. Roger Williams. SCAP
Adults Only. William Stafford. CBV
Advance your choral motions now. Song: To the Masquers Representing Stars [*or* The Stars Dance]. Thomas Campion. *Fr.* The Lords' Mask. LoBV; OBSC
Advantage of the Outside, The. Richard Eberhart. NePA
Advantages of Learning, The. Martial, *tr. fr. Latin by* Kenneth Rexroth. ErPo
Advantages of living with two cultures, The. Bonne Entente. F. R. Scott. FiBHP; OBCV; PeCV; SiTL
Advent. Brother Antoninus. NeAP
Advent. W. H. Auden. *Fr.* For the Time Being. OAEP (2d ed.)
Advent. John Gould Fletcher. MAP; MaRV; MoAmPo
Advent. F. W. H. Myers. *Fr.* Saint Paul. MaRV
Advent. Christina Rossetti. PoVP
Advent Lyrics, *sels.* *Unknown, tr. fr. Anglo-Saxon by* Charles W. Kennedy. *Fr.* Christ 1. AnOE
"Bless earth with Thine Advent, O Savior Christ!" VIII.
"Hail, O most worthy in all the world!" IX.
"O holy Jerusalem, Vision of peace," III.
". . . .to the King./ Thou art the wall-stone the workers rejected," I.
Advent Meditation. Alice Meynell. *See* No Sudden Thing of Glory.
Adventure. Harry Behn. TiPo (1959 ed.)
Adventure. Laura Benét. GaP; HBMV; TSW
Adventure. Adelaide Crapsey. NP
Adventure. Thomas Wade Earp. PoMa
Adventure. Mary Fullerton. BoAV
Adventure. Guy Mason. CaP
Adventure. Grace Fallow Norton. HBMV
Adventure. Nancy Byrd Turner. StVeCh (1955 ed.)
Adventure with a Lady, An. Donald Hall. TPM
Adventurer, The. Odell Shepard. HBMV
Adventurers, The. May Byron. HBV
Adventurers, The. John Thompson. PoAu-2
Adventures. Arthur Kramer. BiCB
Adventures of Huckleberry Finn, The, *sel.* "Mark Twain."
Ode to Stephen Dowling Bots, Dec'd. FiBHP
Adventures of Isabel. Ogden Nash. CenHV; MoAmPo; MoShBr; NeMA; OnMSP; PDV; TiPo (1959 ed.)
"Isabel met an enormous bear." ShM
Adventures of Master F. I. [*or* F. J.], The, *sels.* George Gascoigne.
And If I Did, What Then? EIL; FaBoEn; NCEP; PoEL-1; ReIE
(Farewell, A.) LoBV; OBSC
"As some men say there is a kind of seed." ReIE
"Fair Bersabe the bright, once bathing in a well." ReIE
Adventures of my separate bark, The. Charles Madge. *Fr.* Poem by Stages. BoSA
Adventures of Oberon, King of the Fairies, While Searching for Queen Mab, The. Michael Drayton. *Fr.* Nymphidia; or, The Court of Fairy. OA
Adventures of Simon Swaugum, a Village Merchant, The. Philip Freneau. PoEL-4
Adventures of Tom Sawyer, The, *sel.* "Mark Twain."
Missouri Maiden's Farwell to Alabama, A, *fr. ch.* 21. InMe
Adventurous bird walking upon the air. The Bird. Edwin Muir. POTE
Adversaries. Louis Johnson. ACV
Advertisement of a Lost Day. Lydia Huntley Sigourney. WBLP
Advertising Agency Song, The. *Unknown.* PV
Advice. Gwendolyn B. Bennett. CDC
Advice, The. Thomas Flatman. CavP
Advice. Walter Savage Landor. HBV; VA
Advice, The. Sir Walter Ralegh. FCP; NCEP; SiPS
Advice. Hugh Rhodes. GoTP
Advice, The ("Phyllis, for shame, let us improve"). Charles Sackville. *See* Song: "Phyllis, for shame. . ."
Advice, The ("Wou'd you in love succeed, be brisk, be gay"). Charles Sackville. PeRV
Advice. *Unknown.* CBV
Advice against Travel. James Clarence Mangan. OBVV
Advice from a Nightwatchman. Ian Healy. Poems from the Coalfields, II. PoAu-2
Advice from an Expert. John Kieran. InMe
Advice to a Blue-Bird. Maxwell Bodenheim. HBMV; MAP; MoAmPo (1942 ed.)
Advice to a Fair Wanton. Ovid, *tr. fr. Latin by* Christopher Marlowe. *Fr.* Amores. UnTE
Advice to a Forest. Maxwell Bodenheim. TrJP
Advice to a Girl. Thomas Campion. *See* Never Love Unless You Can.
Advice to a Knight. T. H. Jones. FIW

Advice to a Lady in Autumn. Earl of Chesterfield. CEP; OBEC
Advice to a Lover. S. Charles Jellicoe. HBV
Advice to a Lover. *Unknown. See* Sea Hath Many Thousand Sands, The.
Advice to a Prophet. Richard Wilbur. AmPP (5th ed.); CoPo; MoAmPo (1962 ed.); MoRP; NMP; NYBP; OPoP; TDP; ToPo; TwCP
Advice to a Raven in Russia, December, 1812. Joel Barlow. AmePo; AmLP; AmPP (4th ed.); NePA; OxBA
Advice to a Young Friend on the Choice of His Library. William Wycherley. PeRV
Advice to a Young Man (of Letters) Who Doesn't Know How to Take Care of Himself. Irwin Edman. InMe
Advice to a Young Prophet. Thomas Merton. WOW
Advice to Bachelors. *Unknown, tr. fr. German by* Louis Untermeyer. UnTE
Advice to Bores. Abraham ibn Chasdai, *tr. fr. Hebrew by* Joseph Chotzner. TrJP
Advice to Colonel Valentine. Robert Graves. NYBP
Advice to Country Girls. *Unknown, tr. fr. German by* Louis Untermeyer. UnTE
Advice to Hotheads. Samuel ben Elhanan Isaac Archevolti of Padua, *tr. fr. Hebrew by* A. B. Rhine. TrJP
Advice to Julia, *sels.* Henry Luttrell.
  After the Wedding. IrPN
  Dress. OBRV
  Honeymoon, The. OBRV
  Lovers and Friends. OBRV
  Peace, The. OBRV
Advice to Kyrnos. Theognis, *tr. fr. Greek by* T. F. Higham. LiTW
Advice to Small Children. Edward Anthony. GoTP
Advice to the Grub-Street Verse-Writers. Swift. EiCL
Advice to the Ladies of London in the Choice of Their Husbands. *Unknown.* CoMu
Advice to the Old Beaux. Sir Charles Sedley. CEP; PeRV; SeCV-2
Advice to the Same ("Who doth desire that chaste his wife should be"). Sir Philip Sidney. *See* Truth Doth Truth Deserve.
Advice to Travelers. Walker Gibson. NePoAm-2
Advice to Worriers. George S. Kaufman. ALV
Advice to Writers for the Daily Press. Joel Chandler Harris. OTD
Advice to Young Children. Stevie Smith. ELU
Advices from Rexroth's Bestiary. Kenneth Rexroth. *See* Bestiary, A.
Advocate with the Father, An. Edward Taylor. *See* Preparatory Meditations: "Oh! What a thing is man. . ."
Ae boat anerlie nou. Largo. Sidney Goodsir Smith. NeBP
Ae Fond Kiss. Burns. AnFe; BEL; CABA; CEP; EiCL; EiPP; ELP; EnLi-2; EnLit; EnRP; ForPo; HBV; MeWo; OAEP; OBEC; OBEV; OuHeWo; PoEL-4; SeCeV; TreFT; WePo; WHA
  (Ae Fond Kiss, and Then We Sever.) LO; ViBoPo
  (Farewell to Nancy.) FaFP; TreF; WoL
Ae weet forenicht i' the yow-trummle. The Watergaw. "Hugh MacDiarmid." GoTS; NeBP; PoIE
Aedh Tells of the Rose in His Heart. W. B. Yeats. *See* Lover Tells of the Rose in His Heart, The.
Aedh Wishes for the Cloths of Heaven. W. B. Yeats. MoBrPo; NeMA; OBEV (new ed.); OBVV
  (He Wishes for the Cloths of Heaven.) BoPe; CMoP; OTD; SP
Aegean. Louis Simpson. NYBP
Aegean Islands 1940-41. Bernard Spencer. NeBP
Aeglamour's Lament. Ben Jonson. *See* Here She Was Wont to Go.
Aelf-scin, the Shining Scimmer the Gleam, the Shining, The. Michael McClure. CoPo
Aeliana's Ditty. Henry Chettle. *See* Wily Cupid.
Aella; a Tragycal Enterlude, *sels.* Thomas Chatterton.
  Minstrel's Song. HBV; LoBV; PeER; TrGrPo, *sl. abr.*; WHA
    (My Love Is Dead.) WiR
    (Mynstrelles Songe.) AnFE; BEL; CEP; EiCL; EiPP; EnLi-2; EnLoPo; EnRP; OBEC
    (O, Sing unto My Roundelay, *abr.*) CH
    (Song: "O sing unto my roundelay.") ATP (1935 ed.), *sl. abr.*; LiTL; LO,*abr.*
    (Song from "Aella.") LiTG; OBEV; TOP
  Mynstrelles Songe: "Angelles bee wrogte to bee of neidher kynde." EnLoPo
  Song of the Three Minstrels. PeER; TrGrPo
    ("Budding floweret blushes at the light, The.") ViBoPo
    (Mynstrelles Songe.) EiCL; EnRP
Aeneas at Washington. Allen Tate. AP; LiTA; MoPo; MoVE; NePA; OxBA
Aeneas dead, Ascanius reign'd; Ascanius dead, his brother. William Warner. *Fr.* Albion's England. ReIE
Aeneid. Claire McAllister. NePA
Aeneid, The, *sels.* Vergil, *tr. fr. Latin.*
  "Aurora now from Titan's purple bed," *fr.* IV, *tr. by* the Earl of Surrey. EnPo
  Batalis and the Man, *fr.* I, *tr. by* Gawin Douglas. CTC
  Battle of Actium, *fr.* VIII, *tr. by* Dryden. OBS
  Boat Race, The, *fr.* V, *tr. by* Rolfe Humphries. SD
  Boxing Match, The, *fr.* V, *tr. by* Rolfe Humphries. SD
  "But now the wounded queen, with heavy care," *fr.* IV, *tr. by* the Earl of Surrey. FCP; ReIE
  Death of Turnus, The, *abr., fr.* XII, *tr. by* Dryden. WoL
  Destiny of Rome, The, *fr.* VI, *tr. by* Dryden. PeRV
  Destruction of Troy, The, *fr.* II, *tr. by* Sir John Denham. SeCV-1
  Dido among the Shades, *fr.* VI, *tr. by* Dryden. OBS
  Dido to Aeneas, *fr.* IV, *tr. by* Richard Stanyhurst. AnIV
  Dido's Hunting, *fr.* IV, *tr. by* the Earl of Surrey. OBSC
    (Fourth Book of Virgil, The.) ReEn
  Entrance to Hell, The, *fr.* VI, *tr. into Middle English by* Gawin Douglas. GoTS
  "Full soon the Queen this crafty sleight 'gan smell," *fr.* IV, *tr. by* the Earl of Surrey. EnLit
  Golden Bough, The, *fr.* VI, *tr. by* Dryden. PeRV
  "I that my slender oaten pipe in verse was wont to sound," *fr.* I, *tr. by* Thomas Phaer. ReIE
  "It was then night; the sounde and quiet slepe," *fr.* IV, *tr. by* the Earl of Surrey. PoEL-1; YAT
  Marcellus, *fr.* VI, *tr. by* Dryden. OBS
  Prologue to Book VII, The, *tr. by* Gawin Douglas. OxBS
  Rang'd on the Line Opposed, Antonius Brings, *fr.* VIII, *tr. by* Dryden. WaaP
  Sixth Book of the Aeneis, The, *tr by* Dryden. SeCV-2
    (Destiny of Rome, The.) PeRV
  "Then from the seas the dawning gan arise," *fr.* IV, *tr. by* the Earl of Surrey. ReEn
  "Then Mercury 'gan bend him to obey," *fr.* IV, *tr. by* the Earl of Surrey. ViBoPo
  "They whisted all, with fixed face attent," *fr.* II, *tr. by* the Earl of Surrey. EnLi-1; FCP; TuPP
    (Second Book of Virgil's Aeneid, The.) SiCE; SiPS
    (Translation from Virgil's Aeneid.) LiTB
  Welcome to the Sun, *fr.* XII, *tr. by* Gawin Douglas. ACP
  "With tentive list'ning each wight was settled in hark'ning," *fr.* II, *tr. by* Richard Stanyhurst. ReIE
Aeolian Harp. William Allingham. OnYI
Aeolian Harp, An. "Michael Field." VA
Aeolian Harp, The. Herman Melville. AmePo; AmPP (5th ed.); AP; MAmP; MWA-1
Aeolian Harp, The. Samuel Taylor Coleridge. *See* Eolian Harp, The.
Aeolus. Rolfe Humphries. RePo
Aeons of history float. Prisoner. Marguerite George. GoYe
Aeronaut to His Lady, The. Frank Sidgwick. WhC
Aeroplane. Mary McBride Green. SoPo; TiPo
Aeroplane, The. Jeannie Kirby. BoTP
Aeschylus. Aeschylus, *wr. at. to* Simonides, *tr. fr. Greek by* Lord Neaves. OnPM
Aesop. Andrew Lang. VA
Aesop, *sel.* Sir John Vanbrugh.
  In the Sprightly Month of May. UnTE
  Nightingale, The. SeCL
Aesop at Play. Phaedrus, *tr. fr. Latin by* Christopher Smart. AWP; JAWP; WBP
Aesthete, The. W. S. Gilbert. *See* Bunthorne's Song.
Aestivation. Oliver Wendell Holmes. *Fr.* The Autocrat of the Breakfast Table, *ch.* 11. AmPP; AnNE; BOHV; InMe; NA; WhC
  (Intramural Aestivation, or Summer in Town, by a Teacher of Latin.) ChTr
Aestuary, An. George Croly. IrPN
Aetate XIX. Herman Charles Merivale. OBVV; VA

Aetatis suae fifty-two. The Progress of Marriage. Swift. EiCP
Aeterna Poetae Memoria. Archibald MacLeish. Sonn
Aeternall love! what 'tis to love thee well. In Amorem Divinum (Hermannus Hugo). Richard Crashaw. MaMe
Æthelstan [or Athelston] King,/Lord among Earls. The Battle of Brunanburh. *Unknown, tr. by* Tennyson. BEL; CoBE; EnLit; ExPo; FOL; PeVV; TrGrPo; WaaP
Æthelston King, lord of earls. The Battle of Brunanburh. *Unknown, tr. by* Charles W. Kennedy. AnOE
Aether. Allen Ginsberg. CoPo
Afar in the Desert. Thomas Pringle. BoSA; HBV; OA, 2 *sts.*
Afar on the Floodways. *Unknown. Fr.* The Seafarer. PoLi
Afar the hunt in vales below has sped. Meeting of Orion and Artemis. Richard Henry Horne. *Fr.* Orion. VA
Affable Irregular, An. The Road at My Door. W. B. Yeats. Meditations in Time of Civil War, V. CABL; LiTB; PIA
Affair of Honour. George Whalley. MoCV
Affaire d'Amour. Margaret Deland. HBV
Affection and Desire. Sir Walter Ralegh. *See* Conceit Begotten by the Eyes.
Affectionate Shepherd, The, *sel.* Richard Barnfield.
Daphnis to Ganymede. ElL; ThWaDe
Affection's charm no longer gilds. The Personified Sentimental. Bret Harte. NA
Affections, instincts, principles, and powers. Written in Butler's Sermons. Matthew Arnold. MBW-2
Affections of My Soul, The. Richard Langhorn.
"O, Father of Mercy." PeRV
Affidavit in Platitudes. E. B. White. InMe
Affinity. "Ricketty Kate." MoAuPo
Affinity. R. S. Thomas. HaMV; POTi
Affinity, The. Anna Wickham. HBMV; MoBrPo
Affirmation, An. Minot Judson Savage. MaRV
Affirmations (I-III). Peter Viereck. MiAP
Affliction. Lamentations, III: 1-15, Bible, *O.T.* TrJP
Affliction. Sir John Davies. *Fr.* Nosce Teipsum. OBSC
Affliction ("Broken in pieces all asunder"). George Herbert. AnAnS-1; LoBV; MaMe; MeP
Affliction ("Kill me not ev'ry day"). George Herbert. MaMe
Affliction ("My God, I read this day"). George Herbert. MaMe
Affliction ("My heart did heave"). George Herbert. MaMe
Affliction ("When first thou didst entice to thee my heart"). George Herbert. AnAnS-1; BWP; CABA; EP; LiTB; MaMe; MaPo; MeLP; MeP; MePo; NoP; OBS; OxBoCh; SCEP-1; SeCP
Affliction is a stormy deep. Submission in Affliction. *Unknown.* STF
Affliction of Margaret, The. Wordsworth. EnRP; GTBS; GTBS-D; GTBS-P; GTBS-W; GTSE; GTSL; OBRV; PeER; PoEL-4
Affliction of Richard, The. Robert Bridges. QFR
Afforestation. E. A. Wodehouse. FiBHP; SD
Afield, afield, out in the open field! How the Grain Grows. *Unknown.* OnPM
Afloat; We Move. Delicious! Arthur Hugh Clough. *Fr.* Dipsychus. PoVP; ViPP
Afoot. Sir Charles G. D. Roberts. CaP; HBV; VA
Afoot and light-hearted I take to the open road. Song of the Open Road [*or* The Open Road]. Walt Whitman. AtBAP; FaFP; GTSE; HBVY; MAP; MoAmPo; NeMA; NePA; OQP; PoMa; StaSt; TiPo; TreFT; ViBoPo; WHA
Aforetime, by the waters wan. Roast Swan Song. *Unknown.* FlW; LiTW
Aforetime, fruitfulness and tilth were here. Deserted Farms. Richard Burton. AnAmPo
Afraid. Walter de la Mare. ThGo
Afraid. Emily Dickinson. *See* Afraid? Of whom am I afraid?
Afraid? Esther P. Moore. SoP
Afraid? Of What? E. H. Hamilton. SoP
Afraid? Of whom am I afraid? Emily Dickinson. OHIP
Africa. Lewis Alexander. CDC
Africa. David Diop, *tr. fr. French by* Ulli Beier. PBA; TTY
Africa. Claude McKay. BALP
Africa. Adèle Naudé. PeSA
Africa. *Unknown.* MaRV; SoP; StJW
Africa, my Africa. Africa. David Diop. PBA; TTY
Africa Speaks. Michael Dei-Anang. ACV
Africa, you were once just a name to me. The Meaning of Africa [*or* The Continent That Lies Within Us]. Abioseh Nicol. ACV; PBA
African Affair, The. Bruce McM. Wright. AmNP; PoNe
African blues. Notes for a Speech. LeRoi Jones. CoPo
African Chief, The. Bryant. AnNE; BLPA; PaPo; TreFS
African China. Melvin B. Tolson. Kal
African Dance. Langston Hughes. FaPON; MoSiPe; RePo; TiPo (1952 ed.)
African Easter. Abioseh Nicol. PBA
African Heaven. Frank Parkes. ACV
African in Louisiana. Kojo Gyinaye Kyei. PBA
African Moonrise. Roy Campbell. CoBE
African Song, An. Thomas Chatterton. LoBV
African Trader's Complaint, The. Dennis C. Osadebay. PBA
African Tramp, The. Geoffrey Haresnape. PeSA
Africa's Plea. Roland Tombekai Dempster. PBA; TTY
Afrikaans Homestead. Peter Jackson. BoSA
Afro-American Fragment. Langston Hughes. NoP; PoNe
After. Robert Browning. BoLiVe; TrGrPo
(Avenger Speaks, The.) EG
After. Caroline Grayson. BLRP
After. Robert Hershon. ThO
After. Ralph Hodgson. MoBrPo
After. Philip Bourke Marston. HBV
After. Lizette Woodworth Reese. HBV
Daily Round, *sel.* ThGo
After. Oswald J. Smith. SoP
After a banquet. The Cynneddf. Rolfe Humphries. CrMA
After a Dolmetsch Concert. Arthur Upson. PFY
After a fearful maze where doubt. Chimera. Barbara Howes. TwCP
After a Game of Squash. Samuel L. Albert. GoYe; NePoAm-2
After a hundred years. Emily Dickinson. AWP; FaBoEn; InPo; MoPo; OxBA; PoeP
After a Journey. Thomas Hardy. AtBAP; BWP; ChMP; CMoP; DTC; ELP; EnLopo; FaBoEn; GTBS-D; GTBS-P; MoPW; MoVE; OBNC; PoEL-5
After a Lecture on Keats. Oliver Wendell Holmes. AA; ViBoPo
After a Line by John Peale Bishop. Donald Justice. PoCh
After a little I could not have told. The Song of the Tortured Girl. John Berryman. CoAP
After a Little While. James Ryder Randall. CAW
After a Lobster Dinner and Playing like Kids on a King-Sized Bed. Roger Aplon. YAP
After a Parting. Alice Meynell. PoVP
After a Passage in Baudelaire. Robert Duncan. OPoP
After a Retreat. Robert Hugh Benson. JKCP
After a soiree, with his dark head bent. Hazlitt Sups. Katharine Day Little. GoYe
After a sunrise heavy with unease. The Blizzard. Lenore A. Pratt. TwCaPo
After a thousand mazes overgone. A Sleeping Youth. Keats. *Fr.* Endymion, II. SeCePo
After a Time. Catherine Davis. NePoEA; TDP
After Alcman. Dick Gallup. ANYP
After All. Donald Jeffrey Hayes. CDC
After All. William Winter. PAP
After all,/ One country, brethren! One Country. Frank Lebby Stanton. AA; PaA; PAL
After All and After All. Mary Carolyn Davies. GaP; MPB; SP; TiPo (1952 ed.)
After all and after all. After All. Donald Jeffrey Hayes. CDC
After an Accident. Donald Davie. OPoP
After an Interval. Walt Whitman. AA
After Anacreon. Lew Welch. NeAP
After Annunciation. Anna Wickham. MoBrPo
After Apple-picking. Robert Frost. AmP; AmPP (5th ed.); AnAmPo; AnNE; AP; BWP; CaFP; CMoP; CoBMV; DiPo; ForPo; LiTA; MAP; MaPo (1969 ed.); MoAB; MoAmPo; MoPo; MoVE; MWA-2; NP; OxBA; PoAn; ReMP; RoGo; StP; TDP; UnPo; ViBoPo; WoL
After, at sea a tall ship did appeare. The Visions of Petrarch, II. *Tr. by* Spenser. EnLi-1
After Aughrim. Arthur Gerald Geoghegan. OnYI
After Aughrim. Emily Lawless. OBEV (new ed.); OxBI
After Battle ("Better to live on beggar's bread"). *Unknown, tr. fr. Sanskrit by* Sir Edwin Arnold. *Fr.* Bhagavad-Gita. MaRV
After Battle ("When after many battles past"). *Unknown.* MaRV

After being beaten. Satirical Poems on Daimyos, V. Issa. PoFr
After Blenheim. Robert Southey. *See* Battle of Blenheim, The.
After Bombardment. John Pudney. WaP
After careful meditation. Thomas Love Peacock. *Fr.* Crotchet Castle. ALV
After casting the first act, checking sections. God and Man. Samuel Hazo. ELU
After Catullus: Song, to Celia. Ben Jonson. *See* Come, My Celia, Let Us Prove.
After Christmas. W. H. Auden. *Fr.* For the Time Being. MoAB; MoBrPo (1950 ed.)
(Well, So That Is That.) LiTA
After Christmas. Consuelo Valencia. MaRV
After Christmas a Landlord Remembers. Elizabeth J. Coatsworth. StJW
(Reminiscences of a Landlord.) ChrBoLe
After-Christmas Poem. Elizabeth-Ellen Long. ChBR
After-Comers, The. Robert Traill Spence Lowell. AA
After completing a book for one now dead. Indian Summer. William Ellery Leonard. *Fr.* Two Lives, Pt. III. PG (1945 ed.)
After Construing. A. C. Benson. VA
After Dark. Adrienne Rich. LiTM (1970 ed.)
After dark,/ Near the South Dakota border. Having Lost My Sons, I Confront the Wreckage of the Moon. James Wright. CoAP; FRC
After Dark Vapours [*or* Vapors]. Keats. BWP; CBEP; EnRP; ERoP-2
(Sonnet: "After dark vapours have oppressed our plains.") AtBAP; OBNC
After Dead Souls. Allen Ginsberg. CBV
After Death. R. A. K. Mason. AnNZ
After Death. Fanny Parnell. AnIV; OBVV; OnYI; OxBI; VA
(Post-Mortem.) PoFr
After Death. Charles Francis Richardson. AA
After Death. Christina Rossetti. EnLi-2; PoVP; VA; VP
After Death. Swinburne. PeVV
After Death in Arabia, *abr.* Sir Edwin Arnold. *Fr.* Pearls of the Faith. HBV; VA; WGRP
"Farewell, friends! yet not farewell," *sel.* MaRV
After death, nothing is. Chorus. Seneca. *Fr.* Troas, II. PeRV
After Depression Came Soul. Tommy Whitaker. TNV
After Dilettante Concetti. Henry Duff Traill. BOHV; CenHV; HBV; Par
After dinner Erasmus. E. C. Bentley. *Fr.* Clerihews. CenHV
After Dinner We Take a Drive into the Night. Tony Towle. ANYP
After Drinking All Night with a Friend, We Go Out in a Boat at Dawn to See Who Can Write the Best Poem. Robert Bly. NaP
After, each, word, he, places, a, comma. "Poet." William Jay Smith. RePo
After eleven years and a couple of children. Adversaries. Louis Johnson. ACV
After Ever Happily; or, The Princess and the Woodcutter. Ian Serraillier. BoLP; FIW
After experience taught me that all the ordinary. W. D. Snodgrass. CoAP
After G. de Nerval. Lewis Mac Adams. YAP
After Galen. Oliver St. John Gogarty. OBMV; PoRA
After Goliath. Kingsley Amis. NePoEA-2; PoCh
After Gray Vigils, Sunshine in the Heart. George Santayana. Sonnets, XLIX. MAP; MoAmPo; WHA
After great pain, a formal feeling comes. Emily Dickinson. AmePo; AmPP (5th ed.); AP; CABA; CBV; CoBA; ForPo; InPo; LiTA; LiTG; MAmP; MAP; MaPo; MoAB; MoAmPo; MoPo; MoVE; MWA-2; NePA; NoP; PAn; Po; PoAn; PoE; PoeP; PoIE; ReMP; UnPo
After great storms the calm returns. Sir Thomas Wyatt. FCP; SiPS
After Greece. James Merrill. NYBP
After he concluded that. The Vanishing Act. Alan Stephens. TDP
After He Had Gone. Sylvia Townsend Warner. MoBrPo
After Horace. A. D. Godley. BOHV
After Horace ("Not marble, nor the gilded"). Shakespeare. *See* Sonnets, LV.
After hot loveless nights, when cold winds stream. The Sisters. Roy Campbell. ChMP; ErPo; FaBoTw; MoVE; OBMV
After Hours. Robert Mezey. AmPC; NaP; ToPo
After I forgot about the horses. Marching. Charles Simic. YAP
After I got religion and settled down. "Butch" Weldy. Edgar Lee Masters. *Fr.* Spoon River Anthology. NePA; PoPo
After it became obvious that the strange rain would never stop. Tentative Description of a Dinner [Given] to Promote the Impeachment of President Eisenhower. Lawrence Ferlinghetti. CoPo
After Jena. Thomas Hardy. *Fr.* The Dynasts, Pt. II, Act I, sc. vii. WaaP
After Johnson's Dance. Charles H. Souter. PoAu-1
After Laughter. Grace Buchanan Sherwood. GoYe
After Les Fleurs (Paul Eluard). Anne Waldman. YAP
After Light and the shaping of Land he came. The Elder Brother (Poem for All Good and Loyal Dogs). Elma Dean. NeMA
After lilacs come out. Lilacs. Hilda Conkling. NP
After London. John Dynham Cornish Pellow. GTBS
After long journey in sun. Ear Is Not Deaf. Irene Dayton. GoYe
After Long Silence. W. B. Yeats. BWP; CBV; CMoP; DiPo; ELU; EnLoPo; GTBS-W; HoPM; LiTL; LiTM; MBW-2; OBMV; PoAn; PoeP; PoPl; POTE; UnPo
After long storms' [*or* stormes] and tempests' sad assay. Amoretti, LXIII. Spenser. BEL; EnLit; FaBoEn; NoP; OAEP; OBSC; SiCE
After Looking into Carlyle's Reminiscences. Swinburne. ViPo
After Lorca. Robert Creeley. NaP
After Love. Arthur Symons. NeHB
After many scornes like these. What Hee Suffered. Ben Jonson. *Fr.* A Celebration of Charis. AnAnS-2; SeCP
After many strange thoughts. After Working. Robert Bly. NaP; WIRo
After Mardi Gras. Sister Mary Honora. NePoAm-2
After Margrave died, nothing. History of a Literary Movement. Howard Nemerov. NePoEA; PP
After Midnight. Charles Vildrac, *tr. fr. French by* Jethro Bithell. AWP; JAWP; WBP
After much dissension and strife. Peter's Tears. Thomas Hood. TreFT
After Music. Josephine Preston Peabody. AA
After night, the waking knowledge. Awaking. Stephen Spender. NYBP
After night's thunder far away had rolled. Haymaking. Edward Thomas. AnFE; BrPo; MoAB; MoBrPo; SeCePo
After one moment when I bowed my head. The Convert. G. K. Chesterton. GoBC; InP; JKCP (1926 ed.)
After one more grandiloquent effort he slips back. The Beetle in the Country Bathtub. John Hall Wheelock. WIRo
After our fierce loving. The Profile on the Pillow. Dudley Randall. BP
After Pain. Marjorie Meeker. NP
After Parting. Sara Teasdale. TOP
After Passing the Examination. Po Chü-i, *tr. fr. Chinese by* Arthur Waley. Po
After Rain. Eleanor Farjeon. BoChLi
After Rain. Tu Fu, *tr. fr. Chinese by* Chi Hwang Chu *and* Edna Worthley Underwood. OnPM
After rain, through afterglow, the unfolding fan. Train Ride. John Wheelwright. AnFE; CoAnAm; MoPo; TwAmPo
After Reading a Book on Abnormal Psychology. Ernest. G. Moll. ELU
After Reading a Child's Guide to Modern Physics. W. H. Auden. NYBP
After Reading Certain Books. Mary Elizabeth Coleridge. EaLo
After Reading in a Letter Proposals for Building a Cottage. John Clare. OBRV
After Reading Milne. Ruth Powell. PCD
After Reading St. John the Divine. Gene Derwood. LiTM; NePA; Sonn
After Reading Saint Teresa, Luis de Leon and Ramon Lull. Muna Lee. CAW
After Reading the Reviews of "Finnegans Wake." Melville Cane. WhC
After Reading Translations of Ancient Texts on Stone and Clay. Charles Reznikoff. SiSw
After Reading Twenty Years of Grantland Rice. Don Skene. InMe

After Ronsard. Charles Williams. GTBS
After St. Augustine. Mary Elizabeth Coleridge. MaRV; SoP; TrPWD; TRV
After scanning its face again and again. John Muir on Mt. Ritter. Gary Snyder. *Fr.* Myths & Texts: Burning. FlW
After School: Room Three. William Stafford. NYTB
After Seeing "Lear." Marie Syrkin. NYTB
After Shakespeare. Alex Comfort. ErPo
"After sharp showers," said Peace, "how shining the sun!" The Harrowing of Hell. William Langland. *Fr.* The Vision of Piers Plowman. BoPe
After she/ had complained about. The Proposition. Paul Blackburn. ErPo
After Six Thousand Years. Victor Hugo, *tr. fr. French by* Selden Rodman. WaaP
After so long a race as I have run. Amoretti, LXXX. Spenser. ReEn; ReIE; SiCE
After so many concurring petitions. To the Five Members of the Honourable House of Commons. Sir John Denham. NCEP
After so many deaths to breathe again. Variations on a Theme by George Herbert. Marya Zaturenska. TrPWD
After Some Day of Decision. Reed Whittemore. NePoEA
After Speaking of One Dead a Long Time. Padraic Colum. GoYe
After Storm. David Morton. HBMV
After such years of dissension and strife. Epigram [*or* Natural Tears *or* Dust to Dust]. Thomas Hood. FiBHP; GoTP; HBV; ShM
After Summer. Philip Bourke Marston. HBV; VA
After Sunday Dinner We Uncles Snooze. John Ciardi. ToPo
After Sunset. William Allingham. IrPN
After Sunset. Grace Hazard Conkling. AnAmPo; EPN; HBMV; MaRV; MoRP; YT
After Sunset, *sel.* Swinburne.
"If light of life outlive the set of sun," III. BEL; EPN; OQP
After Sunset. Arthur Symons. *Fr.* At Dieppe. BrPo; SyP
After supper stand a while. Rhymes to Remember. *Unknown.* StaSt
After that moment when at last you let. The Confidence. Elizabeth Jennings. BoPe
After the Agony in the Garden. Daryl Hine. PeCV
After the Annunciation. Eileen Duggan. ISi
After the Armistice I was at Tours. First World War. Kenneth Slade Alling. NePoAm
After the Ball. Charles Kassell Harris. TreF
After the Battle. Richard Chenevix Trench. VA
After the Battle. George Sylvester Viereck. GoYe
After the blast of lightning from the East. The End. Wilfred Owen. CH; HBMV; MMA; MoVE
After the brief bivouac of Sunday. The Stenographers. P. K. Page. CaP; LiTM (1970 ed.); OBCV; PeCV; TwCaPo
After the Broken Arm. Ron Padgett. ANYP
After the bronzed, heroic traveller. The Mapmaker on His Art. Howard Nemerov. NYBP
After the Burial. James Russell Lowell. AA; CoBA; MWA-1; TOP; UnPo
After the Centennial. Christopher Pearse Cranch. PAH
After the centres' naked files, the basic line. The Lines. Randall Jarrell. CrMA
After the cloud embankments. Reconnaissance. Arna Bontemps. AmNP; Kal
After the Club-Dance. Thomas Hardy. At Casterbridge Fair, III. BEL; EnLi-2 (1949 ed.); EnLit; PoVP
After the Comanches. *Unknown.* PAH
After the comfortable words come these. Sursum Corda. Annie Lake Townsend. OQP
After the Concert. David Stapleton. MuSP
After the Dark. Enola Chamberlain. STF
After the darkness and storm. After. Caroline Grayson. BLRP
After the day is over. The Tales the Barbers Tell. Morris Bishop. ALV
After the Dazzle of Day. Walt Whitman. NePA
After the door shuts and the footsteps die. A Hunt in the Black Forest. Randall Jarrell. CoAP
After the emotion of rain. This Morning. Hildegarde Flanner. NP
After the experience of waves. Ground Swell. G. Stanley Koehler. NePoAm-2
After the eyes that looked, the lips that spake. Lincoln at Gettysburg. Bayard Taylor. *Fr.* The Gettysburg Ode. OHIP; PAH
After the Fair. Thomas Hardy. At Casterbridge Fair, VII. BEL; CMoP; EnLi-2 (1949 ed.); EnLit; PoVP
After the fall drive, the last. Montana Eclogue. William Stafford. NYBP
After the Festival. Stefan George, *tr. fr. German by* Carol North Valhope *and* Ernst Morwitz. LiTw
After the fierce midsummer all ablaze. Friendship after Love. Ella Wheeler Wilcox. CBV
After the Fire. Oliver Wendell Holmes. MC; PAH
After the first powerful plain manifesto. The Express. Stephen Spender. AnFe; BBV (1951 ed.); CMoP; EnL; EnLi-2 (1949 ed.); EnLit; ExPo; GoJo; LiTM; MoAB; MoBrPo; MoVE; NAMP; NeMA; PoPl; RoGo; SeCeV; ShBV-3; TwCP; VaPo
After the five hour flight the confusion. Arrival: the Capital. Desmond O'Grady. NMP
After the Flood. Sir David Lindsay. *Fr.* The Monarche. OxBS
After the Flood Went Down, God Said. Genesis, VIII: 22, IX: 12, Bible, *O.T.*. ThGo
After the Fourth of July. M. Phelps Dawson. DD
After the Funeral. Dylan Thomas. CMoP; CoBMV; DiPo; FaBoMo; GTBS-W; MaPo; MoVE; OAEP (2d ed.); PoIE; ReMP; ToPo
(In Memory of Ann Jones.) LiTB; MoAB; MoBrPo (1950 ed.); MoPo; NeBP; PoE
After the Gale. Robert Bridges. *See* Upon the Shore.
After the good fairy. The Birth of the Poet. Quandra Prettyman. BOLo
After the heaped piles and the cornsheaves waiting. Harvest and Consecration. Elizabeth Jennings. NePoEA-2
After the honey drops of pearly showers. The Rose. William Hammond. OBS
After the Hunt. Detlev von Liliencron, *tr. fr. German by* Ludwig Lewisohn. AWP
After the Industrial Revolution. Robert Bly. CoAP
After the Japanese. Lynn Strongin. ThO
After the joys of earth. What Then? *Unknown.* SoP
After the Last Bulletins. Richard Wilbur. CoAP; MoAB; MoAmPo (1962 ed.); NePoAm; NYBP; TrGrPo (rev. ed.); ViBoPo (1958 ed.)
After the Last Dynasty. Stanley Kunitz. NMP
After the leaves have fallen, we return. The Plain Sense of Things. Wallace Stevens. PIA
After the light has set. The Return. George MacBeth. NYBP; OPoP
After the lights and after the rumba and after the bourbon. A Charm for Cantinflas. Muriel Rukeyser. FiMAP
After the long wake, when many were drunk. Attitudes. Richard Eberhart. ToPo
After the Martyrdom. Scharmel Iris. MaRV
After the May time and after the June time. Midsummer. Ella Wilcox Wheeler. HBV
After the murder, like parades of fools. Murder Mystery. David Wagoner. TwAmPo
After the noise and spasm of battle, a lull. Sky Full of Dead. Robert Mezey. TDP
After the Opera. D. H. Lawrence. MuSP
After the Order of Melchisedec. Robert Norwood. MaRV
After the Pangs of a Desperate Lover. Dryden. *Fr.* An Evening's Love, II, i. ELP; OAEP; StP; UnTE; ViBoPo
(Love's Fancy.) ErPo
(Song: "After the pangs of a desperate lover.") FaBoEn
After the Party. Frances Cornford. ELU
After the Party. William Wise. FaPON
After the Persian. Louise Bogan. NePoAm; NYBP
After the Plague. *Unknown, tr. fr. Arabic by* Sir Charles Lyall. LiTW
After the planes unloaded, we fell down. The Dead in Europe. Robert Lowell. CMoP; DTC; LiTM (1970 ed.); NePA; NePoEA; OxBA; ToPo
After the Pleasure Party. Herman Melville. AP; MAmP; MWA-1; PoEL-5
After the Quarrel. Paul Laurence Dunbar. CDC
After the Quarrel. Adam Lindsay Gordon. OBVV
After the Rain. Edward A. Collier. BLRP
After the Rain. Stanley Crouch. WSL
After the rain comes on the lawn. Mister Angleworm. —— Manchester. GFA

After the rain the mossy house-steps are green. Descriptive Poem. Han Wu. OnPM
After the rare arch-poet Jonson died [*or* dy'd]. Upon M. Ben. Jonson, Epigram. Robert Herrick. HoPM; OAEP
After the Record Is Broken. James A. Emanuel. NYTB
After the red leaf and the gold have gone. A Spell before Winter. Howard Nemerov. LiTM (1970 ed.); ToPo; WIRo
After the Release of Ezra Pound. Dannie Abse. NMP; OPoP
After the Round-up. *At. to* D. J. White. *See* When The Work's All Done This Fall.
After the satyr's twilight in the park. Homecoming—Massachusetts. John Ciardi. NYBP
After the Sea-Ship. Walt Whitman. CBEP; NePA
After the sea, the harbor. Sequence. Edgar Daniel Kramer. BLRP
After the shameful trial in the hall. The Ninth Hour. Caroline Hazard. ChIP; OQP
After the shot the driven feathers rock. Rainbow. Robert Huff. NePoEA-2
After the Show. Sam Harrison. NeIP
After the Shower. Archibald Lampman. CaP
After the siege and the assault of Troy. Sir Gawain and the Green Knight. *Unknown.* BEL; EnLit
After the squealing brass. Saint's Parade. Robert Layzer. NePoEA
After the stars were all hung separately out. The Book of How. Merrill Moore. BoLiVe (1939 ed.); MAP; MoAmPo; NeMA
After the Storm. Elizabeth Bartlett. GoYe
After the Storm. Thackeray. *Fr.* The White Squall. PRWS
After the Storm. Annie Howe Thomson. SoP
After the Storm. Henry Vaughan. *See* Bird, The.
After the Supper and Talk. Walt Whitman. MAP; MoAmPo
After the Surprising Conversions. Robert Lowell. AmPP (5th ed.); AP; CABA; CoBMV; FiMAP; NePoEA; NoP; PIA; PoAn; PoeP; SeCeV
After the thorns I came to the first page. The Sleeping Beauty; Variation of the Prince. Randall Jarrell. FiMAP
After the tiff there was silence, till. The Lovers. W. R. Rodgers. WePo
After the Visit. Thomas Hardy. FaBoEn; GTBS-D; OBNC
After the War. Richard Le Gallienne. MC; PAH
After the Wedding. Henry Luttrell. *Fr.* Advice to Julia. IrPN
After the whipping, he crawled into bed. Portrait of a Boy. Stephen Vincent Benét. HBMV; MCCG; NeMA; PoMa
After the whistle's roar has bellowed and shuddered. Night Landing. John Gould Fletcher. Down the Mississippi, VI. HT; LiTA; NP
After the wind. The Blizzard Ape. Kenneth Pitchford. CoPo
After the Winter. Claude McKay. BANP; GoSl; IDB; PoNe
After the winter, so cold and so drear. After. Oswald J. Smith. SoP
After the winter thawed away, I rose. The Assignation. James Wright. NePoEA
After the Wise Men went, and the strange star. The Vigil of Joseph. Elsa Barker. StJW
After these weeks at sea, my native land. Durban Revisited. R. N. Currey. BoSA
After these years of lectures heard. To a Friend, on Her Examination for the Doctorate in English. J. V. Cunningham. EiCP; TwAmPo
After They Have Tired [of the Brilliance of Cities]. Stephen Spender. AtBAP; FaBoMo; LiTM
After They Put Down Their Overalls. Lenrie Peters. TTY
After thinking this fortnight of Whig and of Tory. My Opinion. Charles Sackville. PeRV
After those reverend papers, whose soule is. To Sir H. W. [*or* Wotton] at His Going Ambassador to Venice. John Donne. MaMe; MeLP; OBS; SeEP
After-Thought. *See* Afterthought.
After Tschaikowsky. Wallace Gould. AnAmPo
After twenty years of expensive foods. Song for Mother's Day. T. S. Matthews. ELU
After two sittings, now our Lady State. The Last Instructions to a Painter. Andrew Marvell. MaMe
After Two Years. Richard Aldington. GTSL; HBV; MoBrPo; PG; PoPl; WHA
After volcanoes husht [*or* Over dead craters, hushed] with snows. The Christ of the Andes. Edwin Markham. PEDC; PoRL
After we, dear friends, have drunk together. Friends Drinking Together. Lady Otomo of Sakanoye. OnPM
After we fled away from the shuddering dock. On the Way to the Island. David Ferry. NePoAm-2
After we'd left off loving, long after that. The People, I. "Robin Hyde". AnNZ
After Wings. Sarah M. B. Piatt. AA; HBV
After Winter. Carolyn Sherwin Bailey. PCH
After Winter. Sterling Brown. GoSl; PoNe
After Woman, The. Francis Thompson. ISi
After Work. John Oxenham. MaRV; TRV
After Working. Robert Bly. NaP; WIRo
After You, Madam. Alex Comfort. ErPo; UnTE
After your death. Poem. William Knott. YAP
Afterglow, The. Basho, *tr. fr. Japanese by* Harold Gould Henderson. WoL
After-Glow, The. Mathilde Blind. OBNC
Afterglow. Jorge Luis Borges, *tr. fr. Spanish by* Norman Thomas di Giovanni. NYBP
Aftermath, An. Thomas Blackburn. NMP
Aftermath, The. Euripides, *tr. fr. Greek by* Richmond Lattimore. *Fr.* Iphigenia in Aulis. WaaP
Aftermath. Longfellow. AP; MAmP
Aftermath. Margaret McCulloch. PGD
Aftermath. Siegfried Sassoon. AnFE; BrPo; GTSL; MaRV; MCCG; MoBrPo; NeMA; TrJP; ViBoPo; WaP
Afternoon. Wendell Phillips Garrison. *Fr.* Post-Meridian. AA
Afternoon./ Teacher and nun, bleak refugee, a stone. Street Scene. Robert Mezey. LiTM (1970 ed.); ToPo
Afternoon: Amagansett Beach. John Hall Wheelock. BoNaP; MoVE; NePA; PoRA (rev. ed.); WIRo
Afternoon dark increases with the clock, The. Late Tutorial. Vincent Buckley. PoAu-2
Afternoon for a Small Boy. Bink Noll. ToPo
Afternoon foreclosing, see, The. The Swimmer. Irving Layton. PeCV
Afternoon in a Church. Raymond Kresensky. ChIP
Afternoon in a Tree. Sister Maris Stella. GoBC
Afternoon in Anglo-Ireland. Bruce Williamson. NeIP
Afternoon in Artillery Walk, An; Mary Milton Loquitur. Leonard Bacon. AnAmPo; ATP
Afternoon in the Tropics. Rubén Darío, *tr. fr. Spanish by* Pauline Cook. LiTW
Afternoon is dark and not with rain, The. The Breaking of the Day. Peter Davison. CoPo
Afternoon late summer, in a room, An. At My Grandmother's. David Malouf. PoAu-2
Afternoon lies glazed upon the wall, The. Glass Poem. Karl Shapiro. PoIE
Afternoon of a Faun, The. Stéphane Mallarmé. *See* Après-Midi d'un faune, L'.
Afternoon on a Hill. Edna St. Vincent Millay. BoTP; FaPON; MPB; OxBA; PDV; SoPo; StVeCh (1955 ed.); TiPo (1952 ed.); TSW
Afternoon Sleep. Robert Bly. NaP
Afternoon Tea. Arthur Guiterman. TOP
Afternoon turned dark early, The. During December's Death. Delmore Schwartz. NYBP
Afternoon wears on, The. Pastoral. David Wright. NYBP
Afternoon with Grandmother. Barbara A. Huff. FaPON
Afternoon with heavy hours, The. The Traveler. Allen Tate. LiTM
Afternoons. Philip Larkin. TDP
After-Song. Richard Watson Gilder. *Fr.* The New Day. AA; TrPWD
Afterthought. Justin Richardson. PV
After-Thought. Wordsworth. The River Duddon, XXXIV. EnL; EnRP; EPN; FaBoEn; MBW-2; OBNC; PeER; SeCePo
(After-Thought to "The River Duddon.") OAEP; OBRV
("I thought of thee, my partner and my guide.") EnLi-2
(Valedictory Sonnet to the River Duddon.) OBEV
Afterthoughts of Donna Elvira. Carolyn Kizer. NePoAm-2
Afterward. Mary Matheson. CaP
Afterward. Elizabeth Stuart Phelps Ward. HBV
Afterward he may take thought. The Airman. W. R. Rodgers. WaP
Afterwards. "Violet Fane." HBV; OBVV; VA
Afterwards. Thomas Hardy. AnFE; BEL; BoNaP; CBEP; CBV; CH; ChMP; ChTr; CMoP; EnLi-2 (1949 ed.); FaBoEn; ForPo; GTBS-P; LiTB; LiTG; LiTM (rev. ed.);

MoAB; MoBrPo; MoVE; NAMP; NoP; OBNC; PoAn; PoEL-5; PoeP; PoIE; POTE; QFR; SeCeV; ShBV-3; TreFT; TrGrPo; ViBoPo; ViPP; YT
("When the present has latched its postern behind my tremulous stay.") EG
Afterwards. Frances Ridley Havergal. *See* Light after Darkness.
Afterwards. Edward Lucie-Smith. HYE
Afterwards, *sel.* Gertrude Stein.
"I like to have a home life in the house." LOW
Afterwards. Mary Dixon Thayer. GFA
Afterwards, let us make riddles. Riddles. Patrick F. Kirby. GoBC
Afterwards, They Shall Dance. Bob Kaufman. PoNe (1970 ed.); TwCP
Afterword to My Father, An. Marvin Bell. YAP
Afton Water. Burns. *See* Flow Gently, Sweet Afton.
Again. Frantisek Halas, *tr. fr. Czech by* Karl W. Deutsch. WaaP
Again. Charlotte Mew. MoAB; MoBrPo; NeMA
Again, again, I sinful see. In Dream. J. M. Synge. SyP
Again and again. For "Poems of Two." Lynn Strongin. ThO
Again and again I kiss thy gates at departing. Roma. Rutilius. CTC
Again and again I make the intolerable journey. The Repeated Journey. Thomas McGrath. NePoEA
Again and then again. . .the year is born. New Year's Day. Robert Lowell. AmPP (5th ed.); CABA; LiTM (1970 ed.); NePoEA
Again at Christmas did we weave. In Memoriam, LXXVIII. Tennyson. EnL; EnLi-2; EnLit; EPN; OAEP; ViPo; VP
Again Beginning. Sophia Castro-Leon. QAH
Again Columbia's stripes, unfurl'd. *Enterprise* and *Boxer*. *Unknown.* PAH
Again December shadowed and gray. An Anniversary; a Country Burial. Ann Stanford. TPM
Again for You. Sister Mary Catherine. JKCP (1955 ed.)
Again God plants the tree of doom. Mutans Nomen Evae. Eric Gill. CAW
Again I hear that creaking step. My Familiar. John Godfrey Saxe. AnNE; HBV; TreFS
Again I reply to the triple winds. January. William Carlos Williams. MAP; MoAB; MoAmPo; NP
Again I see my bliss at hand. Meeting [*or* The Lake]. Matthew Arnold. Switzerland, I. CBEP; ELP; MaVP; MBW-2; OAEP; ViPP; VP
Again, I see you, ah my queen. Juana. Alfred de Musset. AWP; JAWP; WBP
Again last night I dreamed the dream called laundry. The Mad Scene. James Merrill. CoAP
Again maternal Autumn grieves. Mater Dolorosa. John Banister Tabb. AnAmPo; StJW
Again? New tumults in my breast? Horace, *tr. by* Pope. Odes, IV, i. SiSw
Again next spring when the heath blows white and pink. Sun Orchids. Douglas Stewart. NeLNL
Again on the morrow morning doth Sigurd the Volsung ride. Sigurd Rideth to the Glittering Heath. William Morris. *Fr.* The Story of Sigurd the Volsung. PoEL-5
Again rejoicing Nature sees. Song [*or* Composed in Spring]. Burns. BoNaP; CBEP; HBV
Again the ancient, meaningless. Logging, V. Gary Snyder. *Fr.* Myths & Texts. NaP
Again the day. If the Stars Should Fall. Samuel Allen. IDB; NNP
Again the native hour lets down the locks. More Sonnets at Christmas, I. Allen Tate. LiTA; LiTM; NePA; WaP
Again the Story Is Told. Ada Jackson. MaRV
Again the Summoning. Lawrence S. Cumberbatch. WSL
Again the veld revives. Namaqualand after Rain. William Plomer. ACV; BoSA
Again, the year's decline, midst storms and floods. Robert Bloomfield. *Fr.* The Farmer's Boy. OBRV
Again they peal, the wistful Yuletide chimes. Another Christmas. J. Sidlow Baxter. SoP
Again this morning trembles on the swift stream the image of the sun. Images. Kathleen Raine. NYBP
Again tonight I read "Before Disaster." A Letter to Yvor Winters. Kenneth Rexroth. ML
Again we climb the little hill—again. Pilgrimage. Catherine Parmenter. PEDC
Again we smelled for days on end. Again. Frantisek Halas. WaaP
Again your kindly, smiling face I see. Mother. Max Ehrmann. PoToHe
Againe. Robert Herrick. SeCP
Against a Second Coming, *sel.* Sidney Keyes.
Walking Woman, The. AtBAP; POTE
Against a Thorn. *Unknown.* SoP
Against an Atheist. Sir John Harington, *after the Latin of* Martial. SiCE
Against an elm a sheep was tied. The Wild Boar and the Ram. John Gay. *Fr.* Fables. EiCP; PPON
Against an Extreme Flatterer That Preached at Bath on the Queen's Day the Fortieth Year of Her Reign. Sir John Harington. SiCE
Against Art. David Mus. YAP
Against Blame of Women. Gerald, Earl of Desmond, *tr. fr. Late Middle Irish by* the Earl of Longford. AnIL
Against Borders. Yevgeny Yevtushenko, *tr. fr. Russian by* Anselm Hollo. CAD
Against Consummation. Petronius Arbiter. *See* Doing a Filthy Pleasure Is.
Against Death. Peter Redgrove. NMP; OPoP
Against Despair. Sister Mary Ada. JKCP (1955 ed.)
Against Feasting. Sir John Harington. SiCE
Against Fruition. Sir John Suckling. ErPo; SCEP-2
Against Fulfillment of Desire. *Unknown.* TrGrPo
Against Garnesche, *sel.* John Skelton.
"What, have ye kithèd you a knight." ViBoPo
Against Gaudy, Bragging, Undoughty Daccus. John Davies of Hereford. SiCE
Against God I daily offend by frailty. Of Rebellion. John Heywood. ReIE
Against Hope. Abraham Cowley. *Fr.* The Mistress. GTBS-W; LiTB; LiTG; LoBV; MeLP; OBS; SeCV-1
(Hope.) MaMe; SCEP-1
(On Hope.) MaMe; MePo
Against Idleness and Mischief. Isaac Watts. *See* How Doth the Little Busy Bee.
Against Indifference. Charles Webbe. HBV; OBEV
(More Love or More Disdain.) SeCL
Against Irresolution. Richard Crashaw. *See* To the Noblest and Best of Ladies.
Against Jealousy. Clive Matson. ThO
Against Love. Sir John Denham. CBEP
Against Modesty in Love. Matthew Prior. ErPo
Against Mosquitoes. Meleager, *tr. fr. Greek by* Dudley Fitts. LiTW
Against Mustolphus His Lying. John Davies of Hereford. SiCE
Against my love shall be, as I am now. Sonnets, LXIII. Shakespeare. OBSC; ReEn; SiCE
Against my will was I married. "Ho There, Death!" *Unknown.* OnPM
Against Oblivion. Shelley. *See* He Is Not Dead.
Against Paulus. Sir John Harington. SiCE
Against Platonick Love. *Unknown.* OBS
Against Publishing Satires. Colin Ellis. MemP
Against Quarrelling and Fighting. Isaac Watts. *See* Let Dogs Delight to Bark and Bite.
Against Romanticism. Kingsley Amis. NePoEA
Against Seasons. Robert Mezey. AmPC; NYBP
Against Still Life. Margaret Atwood. MoCV
Against summer, the leaf-lovely wide and lively trees. B-52's. Arnold Kenseth. PPON
Against Suspicion, *sel.* Mark Akenside.
Benevolence. OBEC
Against that time, if ever that time come. Sonnets, XLIX. Shakespeare. BWP; Sonn
Against the Age. Louis Simpson. NePoEA-2
Against the Barons' Enemies. *Unknown.* *See* Song of Lewes, The.
Against the broad sky. Takahama Kyoshi, *tr. fr. Japanese by* Geoffrey Bownas *and* Anthony Thwaite. FIW
Against the burly air I strode. Genesis. Geoffrey Hill. ACV; NePoEA
Against the clear intensity of dawn. Budding Spring. Jack Lindsay. PoAu-1
Against the Cold. Witter Bynner. MAP; MoAmPo (1942 ed.)

Against the Court of Rome. Petrarch, *tr. fr. Italian by* Sir Thomas Wyatt. Sonnets to Laura: To Laura in Life, CVII. LiTW
Against the day of sorrow. Trifle. Georgia Douglas Johnson. AmNP
Against the Dispraisers of Poetry. Richard Barnfield. SiCE; Sonn; TuPP
Against the evening sky the trees are black. The Winter Trees. Clifford Dyment. POTi
Against the False Magicians. Thomas McGrath. NePoEA; PP
Against the Fantastical Attire That Many Ladies Wear Nowadays. John Davies of Hereford. SiCE
Against the Fear of Death. Lucretius, *tr. fr. Latin by* Dryden. *Fr.* De Rerum Natura, III. BWP; MBW-1
"What has this bugbear death to frighten man." AWP; CTC; JAWP; WBP
Against the flare and descant of the gas. Warning to a Guest. John Holloway. NePoEA
Against the Grain. Michael Brownstein. ANYP; YAP
Against the green flame of the hawthorn-tree. On Hampstead Heath. W. W. Gibson. EPN; HBV; NP
Against the guide of Truth. Epigram V. *Unknown. Fr.* Duel with Verses over a Great Man. TrJP
Against the heavy yellow skies. Impression de Paris. Oscar Wilde. SyP
Against the Hope of Reconstruction. F. T. Marinetti, *tr. fr. Italian by* Selden Rodman. OnHM
Against the Love of Great Ones. Richard Lovelace. AnAnS-2
Against the moon now eldritch-thin. Sorceress. Gertrude Claytor. FiSC
Against the pure, reflective tiles. My Six Toothbrushes. Phyllis McGinley. GoYe
Against the rigors of an austere season. The Bird. Sister Mary Thérèse. JKCP (1955 ed.)
Against the swart magnolia's sheen. Carolina Spring Song. Hervey Allen. HBMV
Against the wall of this sky. Elegy on an Empty Skyscraper. John Gould Fletcher. AmP
Against the window pane. Summer Rain. Sir Herbert Read. LiTM; POTE
Against Them Who Lay Unchastity to the Sex of Women. William Habington. *Fr.* Castara, II. AnAnS-2; CLwM; MePo; OBS; SeCP; SeEP
Against these turbid turquoise skies. Les Ballons. Oscar Wilde. SyP
Against this wrong of the Teutonic might. The Arsenal of the Lord. William Stanley Braithwaite. PoNE
Against Time. Louis Untermeyer. MoAmPo (1942 ed.)
Against Unworthy Praise. W. B. Yeats. AnFE
Against Women. Juvenal, *tr. fr. Latin by* Dryden. *Fr.* The Satires, VI. LiTW; UnTE
Against Women. *Unknown.* MeEL
Against Women either Good or Bad. Thomas Norton. EIL; ViBoPo
(Man May Live Thrice Nestor's Life, A.) InvP
Against Women Unconstant. Chaucer. NoP
(Ballade against Woman Inconstant, A.) CABA
Against Women's Fashions. John Lydgate. ACP
Against Writers That Carp at Other Men's Books. Sir John Harington. *See* Critics and Cooks.
Agamemnon, *sels.* Aeschylus, *tr. fr. Greek.*
Achaians Have Got Troy, upon This Very Day, The, *tr. by* Richmond Lattimore. WaaP
Cassandra's Lament, *tr. by* Richmond Lattimore. LiTW
Chorus: "Great Fortune is an hungry thing," *tr. by* Gilbert Murray. AWP; JAWP; WBP
Chorus: "O Zeus our king and Night our friend," *tr. by* Louis MacNeice. LiTW
"Dead are not to rise, The," *tr. by* J. S. Blackie. PoFr
God of War, The. PPON
God of War, Money Changer of Dead Bodies, The, *tr. by* Richmond Lattimore. WaaP
Hymn to Zeus, *tr. by* Gilbert Murray. WGRP
If I Were to Tell of Our Labours, Our Hard Lodging, *tr. by* Louis MacNeice. WaaP
Signal Fire, The, *tr. by* Dallam Simpson. CTC
Agamemnon before Troy. John Frederick Nims. Sonn
Agamemnon's Tomb. Sacheverell Sitwell. LiTB; OBMV
"One by one, as harvesters," *sel.* MoBrPo
Aganis the Thievis of Liddisdale. Sir Richard Maitland. GoTS
Agatha. Alfred Austin HBV VA
Agatha Christie to. Said. George Starbuck. PV
Agatha Morley. Dust. Sydney King Russell. ShM
Agathon, *sel.* George Edward Woodberry.
Song of Eros. AA; HBV
Agbor Dancer. John Pepper Clark. PBA
Age, The. Herbert Edwin Clarke. VA
Age. Abraham Cowley, *after the Greek of* Anacreon. AWP; CavP; JAWP; OnPM; WBP
Age. *At. to* H. S. Fritsch *and to* Edward Tuck. *See* How Old Are You?
Age. Richard Garnett. VA
(Sonnet: Age.) OBVV
Age. Walter Savage Landor. ELU; NBM; PoEL-4
Age. Philip Larkin. CMoP
Age. Sir Thomas More. EnRePo; TuPP
Age. R. S. Thomas. ToPo
Age. *At. to* Edward Tuck *and to* H. S. Fritsch. *See* How Old Are You?
Age. William Winter. HBV
Age after age and all alone. The Wandering Moon. James Reeves. RePo
Age after age our bird through incense flies. Bird, Bird. Gene Derwood. LiTA; Sonn
Age and Youth. Shakespeare. *See* Crabbed Age and Youth.
Age and Youth. *Unknown, tr. fr. German by* Louis Untermeyer. UnTE
Age being mathematical, these flowers, An. Tulips. Padraic Colum. ImOP
Age came not my conifer, O. From the Beaumont Series. Dick Gallup. ANYP
Age cannot reach me where the veils of God have shut me in. Immortality. Susan L. Mitchell. OnYI
Age cannot wither her, nor custom stale. Her Infinite Variety [*or* A Shakespeare Gallery: Cleopatra]. Shakespeare. *Fr.* Antony and Cleopatra, II, ii. MaC
Age cannot wither her whom not gray hairs. Evening. Wendell Phillips Garrison. *Fr.* Post-Meridian. AA
Age Demanded, The ("For this agility chance found"). Mauberley, III. Ezra Pound. *Fr.* Hugh Selwyn Mauberley. CoBMV; LiTA; LiTM (rev. ed.); MoPo; NoP
Age demanded an image, The. Hugh Selwyn Mauberley, II. Ezra Pound. AmPP (5th ed.); CMoP; CoBMV; InPo; LiTA; LiTM (rev. ed.); MoAmPo (1962 ed.); MoPo; PoIE
Age grips the body but the heart stays young. Love Is Bitter. *Unknown.* PeSA
Age in her embraces past, An. The Mistress; a Song [*or* His Mistress]. Earl of Rochester. AtBAP; CavP; MePo; OBS; OnPM; PeRV; ViBoPo
Age in Prospect. Robinson Jeffers. BoLiVe; MAP; MoAB; MoAmPo; NeMA
Age in Youth. Trumbull Stickney. MAP; MoAmPo (1942 ed.); NCEP
Age is a quality of mind. How Old Are You? [*or* Age]. *At. to* Edward Tuck *and to* H. S. Fritsch. BiCB; PoLF; PoRL; PoToHe; SoP
Age is dull and mean, The. Men creep. For Righteousness' Sake. Whittier. AmePo; PoEL-4
Age Is Great and Strong, The. Victor Hugo, *tr. fr. French by* W. J. Robertson. WGRP
Age Not to Be Rejected. Robert Herrick. *See* To a Gentlewoman Objecting to Him His Gray Hairs.
Age of a Dream, The. Lionel Johnson. OBMV; ViPP
Age of Gold. Pietro Metastasio, *tr. fr. Italian by* Ezra Pound. CTC
Age of Gold, The. Sotère Torregian. YAP
Age of Innocence. Graham Hough. PoRA (rev. ed.)
Age of Sheen, The. Dorothy Hughes. NYBP
Age of Wisdom, The. Thackeray. *Fr.* Rebecca and Rowena. ALV; HBV; VA; WhC
(Love at Two Score.) PoVP
"Age takes in pitiless hands." All Gone. Walter de la Mare. BoPe
Age with devouring fingers spareth naught. Rome. Marcelino Menéndez y Pelayo. CAW
Ageanax. Edward Cracroft Lefroy. *Fr.* Echoes from Theocritus. OBVV
Aged Aged Man, The. "Lewis Carroll." *See* White Knight's Song, The.
Aged Carle, The. Sir Walter Scott. *See* Why Sit'st Thou by That Ruined Hall.

Aged catch their breath, The. Preface. W. H. Auden. *Fr.* The Sea and the Mirror. LiTA; SeCeV
Aged Fisherman. Witter Bynner. GoYe
Aged Lover Renounceth Love, The. Thomas, Lord Vaux. ElL; EnPo; EnRePo; EP; OAEP; PoEL-1; ReEn; SiCE; TuPP
(Image of Death, The.) GoTL; OBSC; PoLi
Aged man, that mowes [*or* mows] these fields. A Dialogue betwixt Time and a Pilgrime. Aurelian Townshend. AnAnS-2; MePo; OBS; PoEL-2; SeCP; SeEP
Aged man, when he beheld winter approaching, The. The Acacia Leaves. Allen Upward. NP
Aged Mother, Mary, even though—when that thing. Complaint. Ted Hughes. PoDB
Aged Ninety Years. Wilbert Snow. AnAmPo
Aged Stranger, The. Bret Harte. AA; AmFN; LHV; MaC; MAP; MoAmPo (1942 ed.); NeMA; TreFS
Aged twenty-six. Birthdays. C. J. Driver. PeSA
Aged Writer, An. Roy McFadden. NeIP
Ageing Athlete, The. Neil Weiss. SD
Ageless. *Unknown*, *tr. fr. Greek by* Louis Untermeyer. UnTE
Ageless Christ, The. B. L. Byer. BePJ
Ageless, the Mantinean woman speaks. ". . .Discourse Heard One Day. . ." Donald C. Babcock. NePoAm-2
Agent of obscure. The Unbroken Code. Robert Dana. NYTB
Ages. Friedrich Hölderlin, *tr. fr. German by* Iwan Goll. OnPM
Ages and Ages Returning at Intervals. Walt Whitman. AP
Ages of Man, The. *At. to* Abraham ibn Ezra, *tr. fr. Hebrew by* Nina Davis Salaman. TrJP
Aghadoe. John Todhunter. AnIL; AnIV; BoLP; OBEV (1st ed.); OBVV; OxBI; PoVP
Agile noisy jungle flower he files, An. Pretty Polly. E. Merrill Root. MAP
Agincourt. Michael Drayton. BEL; BeLS; CBEP; ElL; FaBoBe; FaBoCh; FOL; GoTL; HBV; LoGBV; MCCG; MemP; OBEV; OnSP; PTK; ShBV-1; WHA
(Ballad of Agincourt, The.) EnRePo; PoRA
(Battle of Agincourt, The.) GN
(His Ballad of Agincourt.) NoP
(Ode to the Cambro-Britains and Their Harp, His Ballad of Agincourt.) EnLi-1
(To the Cambro-Britons [*or* -Britains] and Their Harp, His Ballad of Agincourt.) AnFE; EnL; OAEP; OBS; ReEn; RelE; SeEP; TOP; TuPP
Agincourt ("Agincourt, Agincourt!"). *Unknown.* OTPC (1923 ed.)
Aging Coquette, The. John Trumbull. *Fr.* The Progress of Dulness. AnNE
Agitation of the air, An. End of Summer. Stanley Kunitz. AmLP; CrMA; MoAmPo (1962 ed.); PoAn
Agitato Ma Non Troppo. John Crowe Ransom. OxBA
Aglaia. Nicholas Breton. *Fr.* The Passionate Shepherd. OBSC
Aglaura, *sels.* Sir John Suckling.
Song: "No, no, fair heretic, it needs must be," *fr.* IV, i. AnAnS-2; AtBAP; CABA; LiTL; LoBV; OBS; PoIE; ReEN; SeEP
(No, No, Fair Heretic.) CBEP
Why So Pale and Wan Fond Lover? *fr.* IV, ii. ALV; AnFE; AWP; BBV (1923 ed.); BEL; BoLP; CaFP; CBEP; CBV; CoBE; DiPo; EG; ELP; EnL; EnLi-1; EnLit; EvOK; FaBV; HoPM; InPo; JAWP; LiTG; LiTL; MCCG; MemP; MeWo; OBEV; OBS; OnPM; OtMeF; OuHeWo; PoFS; PoMA; PoRA; SeCePo; SeCL; ShBV-4; TOP; TreFS; TrGrPo; ViBoPo; WBP; WHA
(Constant Lover, The.) NeHB; PG
(Encouragements to a Lover.) FaFP; GTBS; GTBS-D; GTBS-P; GTBS-W; GTSE; GTSL
(Orsames' Song.) AnEnPo
(Song: "Why so pale and wan, fond lover.") AnAnS-1; CABA; EnLoPo; EP; ForPo; HBV; InP; LoBV; MePo; NoP; PoE; PoEL-3; PoIE; PoPl; ReEn; SCEP-2; SeCP; SeCV-1; SeEP; YAT
Agnes. Henry Francis Lyte. ATP (1935 ed.); GTSL
Agnes and the Hill-Man. *Unknown*, *tr. fr. Danish by* William Morris. PoVP
Agnes lived with geraniums on the window-sills. Short Short Story. Josephine Jacobsen. NePoAm-2
Agnes, thou child of harmony, now fled. Whither. Philip Becker Goetz. AA
Agnes went through the meadows a-weeping. Agnes and the Hill-Man. *Unknown*, *tr. by* William Morris. PoVP
Agnosco Veteris Vestigia Flammae. J. V. Cunningham. QFR; TwAmPo
Agnostic's Creed, The. Walter Malone. HBV
ΑΓΝΩΣΤΩι ΘΕΩι Agnosto Theo (To an Unknown God). Thomas Hardy. MoPo;WGRP
Agnus Dei. Victor Kinon, *tr. fr. French by* Richard C. Savage. CAW
Agog, in rain house-deep. Apologia. Jean Garrigue. LiTA
Agonie [*or* Agony], The. George Herbert. AnAnS-1; EP; MaMe; MeP; MePo; SCEP-1
(Philosophers Have Measured Mountains.) TRV
Agony, An. As Now. LeRoi Jones. AmPP (5th ed.); BALP; LiTM (1970 ed.); OPoP
Agony of God, The. Georgia Harkness. MaRV
Agreed that all these birds. All These Birds. Richard Wilbur. FiMAP; Po
Agricultural Irish Girl, The. *Unknown.* OnYI
Agrigento. Alan Ross. POTi
Aguinaldo. Bertrand Shadwell. PAH
Ah, a bud! all blue and white. Blossoms. Mary Fenollosa. PCH
Ah, ah the falce fatall tale I read. *Unknown.* SeCSL
Ah, all the sands of the earth lead unto heaven. Persian Miniature. William Jay Smith. CoAP; MoVE
Ah, Are You Digging on My Grave? Thomas Hardy. BrPo; EnLi-2; EnLit; ILP; MoAB; MoBrPo; PoAn; PoPo; PoVP; VP
Ah, Be Not False. Richard Watson Gilder. AA; HBV; HBVY
Ah, be not vain! In yon flower-bell. Dewdrop, Wind and Sun [*or* The Dewdrop]. Joseph Skipsey. OBVV; VA
Ah, bed! the field where joy's peace some do see. Astrophel and Stella, XCVIII. Sir Philip Sidney. EnLoPo; FCP; ReEn; SiPS
Ah Ben!/ Say how, or when. An Ode for Ben Jonson [*or* An Ode for Him]. Robert Herrick. AnAnS-2; AWP; BEL; CoBE; DiPo; EG; EnLi-1; EnLit; InPo; InvP; JAWP; LoBV; MaPo; NoP; OAEP; OBS; PoE; PoFS; PoSa; SCEP-2; SeCP; SeCV-1; SeEP; TOP; TrGrPo; UnPo; WBP
Ah, blackbird, thou art satisfied. The Blackbird. *Unknown.* AnIL; OnYI
Ah, blessedness at work! the aimless mind. Work. Louis James Block. AA
Ah, Bring It Not. Dollie Radford. VA
Ah, broken is the golden bowl! the spirit flown forever! Lenore. Poe. AA; AmP; AmPP; AnFE; AP; APA; CoAnAm; CoBA; LiTA; MWA-1; TreFS; WHA
Ah! but the third one, ah! but the third. The Judgment of Paris. *Unknown.* OtMeF
Ah! cease this kind persuasive strain. Ode to a Friend. William Mason. OBEC
Ah Chloris [*or* Cloris]! that [*or* could] I now could [*or* but] sit. Child and Maiden [*or* Song *or* To Chloris]. Sir Charles Sedley. *Fr.* The Mulberry Garden, III, ii. CavP; GTBS; GTBS-D; GTBS-P; GTBS-W; GTSE; GTSL; HBV; LiTL; OAEP; OBEV; OBS; SeCL; SeCV-2; TOP; ViBoPo
Ah, Christ, I love you rings to the wild sky. Sonnets at Christmas, II. Allen Tate. AmP; AP; GTBS-W; LiTA; LiTM; NePA; PoDB; PoNe (1970 ed.); ReMP; Sonn
Ah, Clemence! when I saw thee last. La Grisette. Oliver Wendell Holmes. AA; HBV
Ah Cloris! that I now could sit. Sir Charles Sedley. *See* Ah Chloris . . .
Ah, comic officer and gentleman. Elegy: E. W. L. E. Sissman. NYBP
Ah, could I grow in some remote degree. Sonnet. George Henry Boker. *Fr.* Sonnets: Sequence on Profane Love. AmePo
Ah could we wake in mercy's name. Song for an Allegorical Play. John Ciardi. PoCh
Ah! County Guy, the hour is nigh. County Guy [*or* Serenade *or* Song]. Sir Walter Scott. *Fr.* Quentin Durward. BEL; CH; EPN; GTBS; GTBS-D; GTBS-P; GTBS-W; GTSE; GTSL; OAEP; OBRV; TOP
Ah Cupid, I mistook thee. Francis Davison. EG
Ah, Dear Heart. *Unknown.* TuPP
Ah! dear one, we were young so long. Alas, So Long! Dante Gabriel Rossetti. PoVP
Ah, dearest Jesus, holy child. A Bed in My Heart. Martin Luther. SoP
Ah! dearest love, sweet home of all my fears. Keats. *Fr.* Ode to Fanny. ChER

Ah, did he climb, that man, nigher to heaven than I. Dark Rapture. "Æ." SeCePo

Ah, did you once see Shelley plain. Memorabilia. Robert Browning. ACV; BEL; BoLiVe; CABA; CLwM; EnLi-2; EnLit; EPN; FaBoEn; FiP; GTBS-W; HBV; ILP; LoBV; OAEP; MBW-2; ML; NoP; OBNC; PoVP; PP; SeCePo; TOP; TreFT; VA; ViPo; ViPP; WHA

Ah, drink again. Lethe. Edna St. Vincent Millay. PG

Ah, drops of gold in whitening flame. To Daisies. Francis Thompson. HBV

Ah, Fading Joy. Dryden *Fr.* The Indian Emperor, IV, iii. ChTr; FiP;LoBV; OAEP; TreFT;ViBoPo
("Ah, fading joy, how quickly art thou past!" MaPo
(Song: "Ah fading joy, how quickly art thou past!") FaBoEn; NoP

Ah! fair and lovely bloom the flowers of youth. Youth and Age. Mimnermus. AWP; OnPm

Ah! fair face gone from sight. Lionel Johnson. *Fr.* In Memory. FaBoEn; OBNC; PoEL-5

Ah faire [*or* fair] Zenocrate, divine Zenocrate. Fair Is Too Foul an Epithet. Christopher Marlowe. *Fr.* Tamburlaine, Pt. I, Act V, sc.ii. AtBAP; LiTB; PoEL-2; ViBoPo

Ah Faustus,/ Now hast thou but one bare hour [*or* hower] to live. Christopher Marlowe. *Fr.* Dr. Faustus. AtBAP; BoLiVe; ChTr; FIW; MyFE; PoEL-2; ShBV-4; TrGrPo; ViBoPo; WHA; YAT

Ah! First snow! Transient Beauty. Basho. OnPM

Ah, Flood of Life on which I am a wave. Watson Kirkconnell. *Fr.* The Tide of Life. CaP

Ah, flow on, flow on. Sail Peacefully Home. Simeon Frug. TrJP

Ah for one hour of youthful joy! The Old Man Dreams. Oliver Wendell Holmes. PoLF

Ah for the throes of a heart sorely wounded! The Damsel. Omar b. Abi Rabi'a. AWP; LiTW

Ah! fredome [*or* freedom] is a noble thing! See A! fredome is a noble thing!

Ah! from mine eyes the tears unbidden start. Sonnet: On a Distant View of England. William Lisle Bowles. CEP

Ah! gentle, fleeting, wavering sprite. On the Soul. Emperor Hadrian, *tr. by* Byron. WoL

Ah gentle shepherd, thine the lot to tend. John Dyer. *Fr.* The Fleece. PoEL-3

Ah, gentle, tender lady mine. The Chronicle of the Drum. Thackeray. ViBoPo

Ah! Give Me, Lord, the Single Eye. Augustus Montague Toplady. OxBoCh

Ah, give us back our dear dead Land of Dreams. The Land of Dreams. Henry Martyn Hoyt. HBMV

Ah, God! to see the branches stir. Rupert Brooke. *Fr.* The Old Vicarage. Grantchester. HT

Ah, great it is to believe the dream. The Dream. Edwin Markham. OQP

Ah, had you seen the Coolun. *See* O had you seen the Coolun.

Ah, Happiness: Who called you "Earandell." A Song of Happiness. Ernest Rhys. NP

Ah, happy blindness! Enion sees not the terrors of the uncertain. It is Not So with Me. Blake. *Fr.* Vala; or, The Four Zoas. SeCePo

Ah, happy who have seen Him, whom the world. Francis W. Bourdillon. *Fr.* A Lost God. WGRP

Ah, happy youths, ah, happy maid. On a Picture by Poussin Representing Shepherds in Arcadia. John Addington Symonds. FaBoBe; HBV

Ah hate to see de evenin' sun go down. St. Louis Blues. W. C. Handy. NAMP

Ah! he is fled! The Brittish Church. Henry Vaughan. AnAnS-1; MeP

Ah, here it is! the sliding rail. The Crooked Footpath. Oliver Wendell Holmes. *Fr.* The Professor at the Breakfast Table. HBV; TreF

Ah, how poets sing and die! Dunbar. Anne Spencer. BANP; CDC; Kal

Ah How Sweet It Is to Love. Dryden. *Fr.* Tyrannic Love, IV, i. EiCL; EnLi-1; HBV; HoPM; LiTL; MaPo; OBEV (1st ed.); PoIE; ViBoPo
(Song: "Ah how sweet it is to love.") CavP; EiPP; FaBoEn; PeRV

Ah How the Throat of a Girl. Archibald MacLeish. *Fr.* Conquistador. AtBAP

Ah, I know what happiness is! Poem. Blanche Taylor Dickinson. CDC

Ah! I remember Stillwater, as it were yesterday. Arnold at Stillwater. Thomas Dunn English. PAH

Ah, I remember well—and how can I. Early Love [*or* First Flame]. Samuel Daniel. *Fr.* Hymen's Triumph. BoLP; ErPo

Ah! if we only dreamed how close they stand. Comfort. May Doney. HBMV

Ah! I'm feared thou's come to sooin. To a Daisy. John Hartley. VA

Ah in the thunder air. Trees in the Garden. D. H. Lawrence. CMoP; MoAB; MoBrPo; Po

Ah, Jack it was, and with him little Jill. Jack and Jill. Harriet S. Morgridge. *Fr.* Mother Goose Sonnets. AA

Ah Jean Dubuffet. Naphtha. Frank O'Hara. ANYP

Ah, June is here, but where is May? Unfulfilment. Frances Louisa Bushnell. AA

Ah! lay by your lute. Wit Predominant. Thomas Rymer. *Fr.* Edgar. SeCL

Ah! leave the smoke, the wealth, the roar. Ballade to Theocritus, in Winter [*or* To Theocritus. . .]. Andrew Lang. InP; VA

Ah, let us go, whom nature gave firm minds and courage fast. The Draught of Life. Abu-l-Ala al-Maarri. LiTW

Ah! liberal-handed lady, though. The Good Tradition. *Unknown.* AnIL

Ah, life is good! and good thus to behold. Summons. Arthur Davison Ficke. Sonnets of a Portait Painter, XIV. HBMV

Ah! light lovely lady with delicate lips aglow. At Mass. *Unknown, tr. by* Robin Flower. OxBI

Ah! little flower, upspringing, azure-eyed. Fruitionless. Ina Donna Coolbrith. AA

Ah! little fly, alighting fitfully. Calvus to a Fly. Charles Tennyson Turner. Sonn

Ah, little mill, you're rumbling still. An Oxford Idyll. Thomas Edward Brown. PoVP

Ah, little road, all whirry in the breeze. The Road. Helene Johnson. AmNP; BANP; CDC; GoSl; PoNe

Ah! little they know of true happiness, they whom satiety fills. Labor Song. Denis Florence MacCarthy. *Fr.* The Bell-Founder. DD

Ah, London, London! our delight. A Ballad of London. Richard Le Gallienne. HBMV

Ah! long ago since I or thou. Before and After. Oliver Madox Brown. VA

Ah, look./ How sucking their last sweetness from the air. The Divers. Peter Quennell. MoBrPo; MoVE

Ah, Love, but a day. James Lee's Wife. Robert Browning. EPN, *sel.*; ViPP

Ah Love! could you and I with Him conspire. A Wish. Omar Khayyám, *tr. by* Edward Fitzgerald. *Fr.* The Rubáiyát. OnPM; PoPl

Ah, Love, I cannot die, I cannot go. Rispetto. Agnes Mary Frances Robinson. Tuscan Cypress, XV. HBMV

Ah, Love, Let Us Be True. Matthew Arnold. *Fr.* Dover Beach. OQP

Ah! Love, my master, hear me swear. Of His Death. Meleager. AWP

Ah, love, the teacher we decried. A Pure Hypothesis. May Kendall. VA

Ah love! where is thy abydinge? *Unknown.* SeCSL

Ah, lovely Devon. Oh, to Be in England Now the Weather's There! *Unknown.* SiTL

Ah Lucasta, why so bright! To Lucasta. Richard Lovelace. AnAnS-2

Ah, Marian mine, the face you look on now. To Mrs. L. H. Leigh Hunt. Sonn

Ah! marvel not if when I come to die. For He Had Great Possessions. Richard Middleton. HBV

Ah! Matt.: old age has brought to me. Senex to Matt. Prior. James Kenneth Stephen. *Fr.* Two Epigrams. BOHV; CenHV; FiBHP; WhC

Ah me./ Was there a time. For Lucas Cranach's Eve. Adelaide Crapsey. QFR

Ah Me! Am I the Swaine. George Wither. OBS

Ah me, but it might have been! On a Nankin Plate. Austin Dobson. PoVP

Ah Me, Do You Remember Still. Agnes Mary Frances Robinson. WHA

Ah me, dread friends of mine—Love, Time, and Death. Love,

Time, and Death. Frederick Locker-Lampson. HBV
Ah me! full sorely is my heart forlorn. The Schoolmistress. William Shenstone. CEP; EiPP; EnPE; GoTL; LaA
Ah, me! I know how like a golden flower. The Grand Ronde Valley. Ella Higginson. AA
Ah me, if I grew sweet to man. The Tragic Mary Queen of Scots. "Michael Field." EnLoPo; OBMV
Ah me, my friend! it will not, will not last! Elegy: He Complains How Soon the Pleasing Novelty of Life Is Over [*or* Elegy XI]. William Shenstone. CEP; OBEC
Ah me the hand upon the body. Legerdemain. Kenneth Mackenzie. BoAV; PoAu-2
Ah Me! The Mighty Love. George Frederick Cameron. CaP
Ah me! those old familiar bounds. Ode on a Distant Prospect of Clapham Academy. Thomas Hood. CBEP
Ah me! to many deaths decreed. To Many Deaths Decreed. John Crowne. *Fr.* Regulus. SeCL
Ah me! Why may not love and life be one? Love and Life. Henry Timrod. *Fr.* Most Men Know Love but as a Part of Life. OQP
Ah! might I in some humble Kentish dale. Lines Written at Cambridge, to W. R., Esquire. Phineas Fletcher. EIL
Ah, moment not to be purchased. Bayard Taylor. *Fr.* The Sunshine of the Gods. AA
Ah, more than any priest, O soul, we too believe in God. Walt Whitman. *Fr.* Passage to India. WGRP
Ah mother of a mighty race. Bryant. *See* O Mother of a Mighty Race.
Ah Music, thou sweet sprite. To Music. William Kean Seymour. HBMV
Ah my Anthea! Must my heart still break? To Anthea [*or* What Shame Forbids to Speak]. Robert Herrick. SCEP-2; UnTE
Ah, my Clio! every day. To Clio. John Dyer. WaPE
Ah my dear angry [*or* deare angrie] Lord. Bitter-Sweet. George Herbert. MaMe; NoP; OxBoCh; TrPWD
Ah, my dear father and my parent sweet. His Apology of His Good Father. Gabriel Harvey. *Fr.* Greene's Memorial. ReIE
Ah My Dere ("Ah my dere, ah my dere Son"). *Unknown.* AtBAP; BoW
Ah, my God,/ What might I not have made of thy fair world. We Needs Must Love the Highest. Tennyson. *Fr.* Idylls of the King: Guinevere. MaRV
Ah! my heart, ah! what aileth thee. To His Heart. Sir Thomas Wyatt. FCP; OBSC; SiPS
Ah! my heart is weary waiting. Summer Longings. Denis Florence MacCarthy. HBV
Ah, my heart, the storm and sadness! Liebesweh. Dora Wilcox. BoAu
Ah my Perilla! do'st thou grieve to see. To Perilla. Robert Herrick. AnAnS-2; AtBAP; NoP; OBS; SCEP-2; SeCP; SeCV-1; SeEP; UnPo (1st ed.)
Ah, my sweet sweeting. My Sweet Sweeting. *Unknown.* CH; LO
Ah Night! blind germ of days to be. A Ballad of High Endeavor. *Unknown.* BOHV; NA
Ah, no; he is not dead; he only sleeps. In Memoriam. Henry W. Frost. SoP
Ah! no, no, it is nothing, surely nothing at all. The Wind. William Morris. NBM; PoVP
Ah, no, not these! Parentage. Alice Meynell. PeVV
Ah! not because our Soldier died before his field was won. Raglan. Sir Edwin Arnold. VA
Ah nothing is too late till the tired heart shall cease to palpitate. Old Age. Longfellow. *Fr.* Morituri Salutamus. SoP
Ah, Now I Know What Day This Is. Statius, *tr. fr. Latin by* D. A. Slater *and* Virginia Tufte. *Fr.* Epithalamium for Stella and Violentilla. HW
Ah! on Thanksgiving Day, when from East and from West. The Pumpkin. Whittier. DD; OHIP; PoRL; PoSC
Ah, pity love where e'r it grows! The old Man's Complaint: by Mr. Wells. *Unknown.* PeRV
Ah! poor intoxicated little knave. To a Fly. "Peter Pindar." BOHV
Ah Posthumus! Our yeares hence flye. His Age. Robert Herrick. SeCP
Ah, Poverties, Wincings, and Sulky Retreats. Walt Whitman. CBEP
Ah, ra, chickera. *Unknown.* OxNR
"Ah Robin,/ Jolly Robin." Sir Thomas Wyatt. FCP; SiPS
Ah! sad wer we as we did peace. The Turnstile. William Barnes. CH; OBVV
Ah! say you so, bold sailor. The Herald Crane. Hamlin Garland. HBV
Ah, see the fair chivalry come, the companions of Christ! Te Martyrum Candidatus. Lionel Johnson. ACP; BoC; CAW; HBV; JKCP; OBMV; OxBoCh; PoLi
Ah, Spain, already your tragic landscapes. The Spanish War. "Hugh MacDiarmid." NMP
Ah stay! ah turn! ah whither would you fly. Song. Congreve. *Fr.* The Fair Penitent (*by* Nicholas Rowe). AtBAP; LoBV; OBEC
Ah, stay thy treacherous hand, forbear to trace. Verses on Sir Joshua Reynolds's Painted Window at New-College Oxford. Thomas Warton, the Younger. CEP; EiCL; OBEC; PoEL-3
Ah, stern cold man. A Woman and Her Dead Husband. D. H. Lawrence. NP
Ah! Sunflower [Weary of Time]. Blake. *Fr.* Songs of Experience. AtBAP; AWP; CABA; CBEP; CBV; DiPo; EG; EiCL; EiPP; ELP; ELU; EnLi-2; EnLit; EnRP; ERoP-1; ExPo; ForPo; GTBS-D; GTBS-W; InPo; JAWP; MaPo; NoP; OAEP; OBEC; OBNC; OuHeWo; PAn; PoE; PoEL-4; SeCeV; ShBV-4; TOP; UnPo; ViBoPo; WBP
(Sunflower, The.) BEL; BoLiVe; ChTr; PoFS; TrGrPo
Ah, sweet Content, where is thy mild abode? Sonnet [*or* Content]. Barnabe Barnes. Parthenophil and Parthenophe, LXVI. EIL; OBSC; ReEn; Sonn; TuPP
Ah, Sweet Is Tipperary. Denis A. McCarthy. HBV
"Ah, sweet Kitty Neil, rise up from that wheel." Kitty Neil. John Francis Waller. HBV; VA
Ah, sweet, thou little knowest how. Serenade. Thomas Hood. HBV
Ah! take those lips away; no more. Deadly Kisses. Pierre de Ronsard. AWP
Ah, That I Were Far Away. Arthur Hugh Clough. *Fr.* Amours de Voyage. OBNC
Ah! the May was grand this mornin'! The Song of the Thrush. T. A. Daly. MAP; NeMA
Ah! the morning is grey. Chimney-Tops. *Unknown.* BoTP
Ah the Poetry of Miss Parrot's Feet Demonstrating the Tango. Tom Raworth. HYE
Ah! the Sighs. William Cornish. TuPP
Ah! then the grassy-meäded May. Zummer Stream. William Barnes. BoNaP
Ah, there is no abiding! Change. Mary Elizabeth Coleridge. MoVE
Ah! there's the lily, marble pale. The Rose of May. Mary Howitt. HBV
Ah, those hours when by-gone sages. Half Hours with the Classics. H. J. DeBurgh. BOHV; InMe
Ah! thou, too. Dante, Shakespeare, Milton. Sydney Dobell. *Fr.* Balder. VA
Ah, through the open door. Spring Morning. D. H. Lawrence. BoLP; BrPo; CMoP; MoAB; MoBrPo
Ah! To be all alone in a little cell. The Desire for Hermitage. *Unknown.* AnIL
Ah, to be by Mooni now. Mooni. Henry C. Kendall. BoAu
Ah, vale of woe, of gloom and darkness moulded. Song. Rachel Morpurgo. TrJP
Ah, wasteful woman, she that may. Unthrift [*or* Preludes, I]. Coventry Patmore. *Fr.* The Angel in the House. FaPL; GoBC; HBV
Ah, we are neither heaven nor earth, but men. John Masefield. *Fr.* Sonnets ("Long long ago"). EPN
Ah! weak and wide astray! Blake. *Fr.* Jerusalem. OBRV
Ah, well, Friend Death, good friend thou art. Helen Hunt Jackson. *Fr.* Habeas Corpus. OHIP
Ah, well, I abandon you, cherrywood smokestack. The Artist. Kenneth Koch. AmPC; HYE
Ah, well it is—since she is gone. Reply. Hartley Coleridge. OBRV
Ah! were she pitiful as she is fair. Fawnia [*or* In Praise of His Loving and Best-beloved Fawnia]. Robert Greene. *Fr.* Pandosto. AtBAP; EG; HBV; OBEV; OBSC; PoEL-2; TrGrPo; ViBoPo
Ah! what a weary race my feet have run. Sonnet: To the River Lodon [*or* Loddon]. Thomas Warton, the Younger. CEP; CoBE; OBEC; Sonn; ViBoPo
Ah, what are strength and beauty? Hymn. Synesius. CAW
Ah! What Avails the Sceptred Race! Walter Savage Landor. *See* Rose Aylmer.

Ah, what can ail thee, wretched wight [*or* knight-at-arms]. *See* O what can ail thee, knight-at-arms.

Ah, what can ever be more stately and admirable to me than mast-hemmed Manhattan? Walt Whitman. *Fr.* Crossing Brooklyn Ferry. AA

Ah, what if Time forgot to light the stars. World-Ruin. Hugh Wilgus Ramsaur. MaRV

Ah! what is love? It is a pretty thing. The Shepherd's Wife's Song [*or* The Shepherd and the King]. Robert Greene. *Fr.* Greene's Mourning Garment. EG; EIL; HBV; LoBV; OBSC; PG; PTK; ReEn; SiCE; TOP; TuPP; ViBoPo

Ah! what joy, the bagpipe and the flute. Paul Fort. *Fr.* Ballad of the Bells. WoL

Ah! what pleasant visions haunt me. The Secret of the Sea [*or* The Galley of Count Arnaldos]. Longfellow. AnNE; EtS; GoTP; OBEV (new ed.); OBVV; RIS

Ah! what time wilt thou come? when shall that cry. The Dawning. Henry Vaughan. CAW; MemP; MePo; OxBoCh; ReEn; SoP; TrPWD

Ah! What Woes Are Mine. Edmond O'Ryan, *tr. fr. Modern Irish by* Charlotte Brooke. OnYI

Ah, when the means are gone that buy this praise. Shakespeare. *Fr.* Timon of Athens, II, ii. MyFE

Ah! when will this long weary day have end. Spenser. *Fr.* Epithalamion. LO

Ah, where, Kincora! is Brian the Great? *See* Oh, where, Kincora! is Brian the Great?

Ah! where must needy poet seek for aid. Swift. *Fr.* A Description of a City Shower. ViBoPo

Ah wherefore with infection should he live. Sonnets, LXVII. Shakespeare. SiCE

Ah! whither doost thou now, thou greater Muse. Two Cantos of Mutabilitie. Spenser. *Fr.* The Faerie Queene. ReEn

Ah whither, Love, wilt thou now carrie me? An Hymne in Honour of Beautie. Spenser. ReEn; SiCE

Ah! who can tell how hard it is to climb. The Minstrel, I. James Beattie. CEP; EiPP; EnPE

Ah! who has seen the mailèd lobster rise. Wonders of Nature. *Unknown.* BOHV

Ah! why those piteous sounds of woe. The Forlorn One. "Thomas Ingoldsby." BOHV

Ah! why will my dear little girl be so cross. Washing and Dressing. Ann Taylor. SAS

Ah, with the Grape my fading Life provide. Omar and Death [*or* Ritual of the Grape]. Omar Khayyám, *tr. by* Edward Fitzgerald. *Fr.* The Rubáiyát. GTBS-P; GTBS-W; GTSE; OBEV; OBVV; OnPM

Ah! with what freedom [*or* freedome] could I once have pray'd. The Sigh. Nathaniel Wanley. OBS; OxBoCh

Ah! without the moon, what white nights. Without the Moon. Jules Laforgue. LiTW

Ah Woe Is Me. Propertius, *tr. fr. Latin by* F. A. Wright. Elegies, I, 1. AWP

Ah! woe is me, condemned to bear. For One in Doubt. Charles Wesley. Three Hymns, 3. WaPE

Ah woe is me, of passion naught I knew. Ah Woe Is Me. Propertius. AWP

Ah yah, tair um bam, boo wah. Jungle Mammy Song. *Unknown.* AS

Ah, Yes, I Wrote It. Gelett Burgess. *See* Cinq Ans Après.

Ah, Yes, I Wrote the "Purple Cow." Gelett Burgess. *See* Cinq Ans Après.

"Ah, yes, the works are busy on the Hook." A Hook for Leviathan. Norman Cameron. ChMP

Ah! yesterday was dark and drear. Dare Quam Accipere. Mathilde Blind. OBVV

Ah! Yet Consider It Again! Arthur Hugh Clough. EPN; PoVP; TOP; VA
(Old Things Need Not Be Therefore True.) ViPP

Ah, you are cruel. Neighbors. Anne Spencer. CDC

Ah, you mistake me, comrades, to think that my heart is steel! Arnold at Stillwater. Thomas Dunn English. PAH

Ah (You Say), This Is Holy Wisdom. Hilda Doolittle ("H. D."). *Fr.* Tribute to the Angels. CrMA

Ah, you should see Cynddylan on a tractor. Cynddylan on a Tractor in Spring. R. S. Thomas. BoC

Ahab Mohammed. James Matthew Legaré. AA

Ahead. *Unknown.* SoP

Ahkoond of Swat, The. George Thomas Lanigan. *See* Threnody, A: "What, what, what. . ."

Ahkoond [*or* Ahkond] of Swat, The. Edward Lear. *See* Akond of Swat, The.

Ah'm Broke an' Hungry, *with music.* Lawrence Gellert. TrAS

Ah'm goin' whah nobody knows my name, Lawd, Lawd. Levee Moan (A *and* B *vers.*). *Unknown.* AS

Ah'm gonna build mahself a raft. De [*or* The] Blues Ain' Nothin'. *Unknown.* AS; TrAS

Ah'm sick, doctor-man, Ah'm sick! Calling the Doctor. John wesley Holloway. BANP; IHA

Ahmed. James Berry Bensel. AA

Ahoy and ahoy, birds. Wings and Wheels. Nancy Byrd Turner. SoPo; StVeCh (1955 ed.); SUS; TiPo

"Ahoy! and O-ho! and it's who's for the ferry?" Twickenham Ferry. Théophile Marzials. HBV; VA

A-Hunting. Jennie Dunbar. BoTP

A-Hunting We Will Go. Henry Fielding. *Fr.* Don Quixote in England, II. HBV; OTPC (1923 ed.); ViBoPo
(Hunting Song.) CEP; OBEC; OxBoLi; StP

Ai, ai, my small red man. Song of Welcome. Hermia Harris Fraser. CaP

Aid me Bellona, while the dreadful fight. The Battle [*or* Battel] of the Summer-Islands. Edmund Waller. AnAnS-2; CEP; ReEn; SCEP-2; SeCV-1

Aidenn. Katrina Trask. AA

Aids to Composition. Robert Conquest. PP

Aiken Drum. *Unknown.* FaBoCh; LoGBV; OxNR

Aileen Aroon. Gerald Griffin. *See* Eileen Aroon.

Ailill the king is vanished. The Downfall of Heathendom. *Unknown.* KiLC

Ailing Parent, The. Lora Dunetz. NePoAm-2

Aim, The. Sir Charles G. D. Roberts. MaRV; PeCV

Aim of Life, The. Philip James Bailey. *Fr.* Festus. OQP
(Country Town, A, 4 *ll.*) PoToHe (new ed.)
(We Live in Deeds.) MaRV

Aim Was Song, The. Robert Frost. HH; NoP; NP; PP

Aimirgin's Invocation. *At. to* Amergin. *See* Invocation to Ireland.

Aimless. Louis Palagyi, *tr. fr. Hungarian by* Watson Kirkconnell. TrJP

Aimless business of your feet, The. Cecidit, Cecidit Babylon Magna! Theodore Maynard. JKCP

Ain' but de one thing I done wrong. Rosie. *Unknown.* ABF

Ain' Go'n to Study War No Mo', *with music. Unknown.* AS

Ain' No Mo' Cane on de Brazis, *with music. Unknown.* ABF

Ain't Gonna Rain, *with music. Unknown.* AS

Ain't It Awful, Mabel? John Edward Hazzard. BOHV

Ain't it fierce to be so beautiful. Beautiful. *Unknown.* ABF

"Ain't It Fine Today!" Douglas Malloch. SoP; WBLP
(It's Fine Today.) BLPA

Ain't It Hard to Be a Right Black Nigger, *with music. Unknown.* OuSiCo

Ain't Nature Commonplace! Arthur Guiterman. FiBHP; InMe

Ain't too much happening around town anymore. A Short Poem for Frustrated Poets. Johnie Scott. WSL

Ain't Workin' Song, *with music. Unknown.* OuSiCo

Air. Edwin Denby. CrMA
("Thin air I breathe and birds use for flying.") ANYP

Air. Kathleen Raine. MoAB; MoBrPo (1962 ed.)

Air: "I ne'er could any luster see." Sheridan. *Fr.* The Duenna. HBV

Air: "Naturally it is night." W. S. Merwin. AmPC; CoPo; NaP

Air: "O ruddier than the cherry." John Gay. *See* O Ruddier than the Cherry.

Air: Sentir avec Ardeur. Marie-Françoise-Catherine de Beauveau, Marquise de Boufflers, *tr. fr. French by* Ezra Pound. CTC

Air [or Aire] and Angels. John Donne. AnAnS-1; AtBAP; BoW; BWP; CBEP; EnRePo; MaMe; MBW-1; MeLP; MePo; NoP; OBS; PIA; PoFS; SCEP-1; SeCP; SeCV-1; TuPP
("Twice or thrice had I loved thee.") EG

Air as the fuel of owls. Snow. Iowa. Michael Dennis Browne. NYBP

Air bears little creatures, The. Riddle: Gnats. *Unknown.* YAT

Air breathes frost, The. A thin wind beats. City Autumn. Joseph Moncure March. OCS

Air by Sammartini, An. Louis Dudek. OBCV

Air comes in tickly. Sneezing. Marie Louise Allen. SoPo

Air cool and soft, The. Chaka. F. T. Prince. BoSA
Air in Spring, The. Basil Dowling. AnNZ
Air is a mill of hooks, The. Mystic. Sylvia Plath. NYBP
Air is full of a farewell, The. On Leaving Ullswater. Kathleen Raine. NeBP
Air is full of diamond dust tonight, The. Frozen Fire. Floris Clarke McLaren. CaP
Air is interesting, The. Sunglasses. Tom Clark. ANYP
Air is like a butterfly, The. Easter. Joyce Kilmer. MPB; NP; PDV; SoPo; TiPo
Air is mild, not quite. A Sleep. Larry Eigner. CoPo
Air is soft and balmy, The. In April. Emily Gail Arnold. PEDC
Air is sweetest that a thistle guards, The. Variations: The Air Is Sweetest That a Thistle Guards. James Merrill. NePoEA
Air is thick with nerves and smoke, The: pens tremble in sweating hands. University Examinations in Egypt. D. J. Enright. MoPW; TwCP
Air is white and winds are crying, The. Snow Storm. Sister Mary Madeleva. GoBC
Air Mail, Special. Sister Mary Philip. JKCP (1955 ed.)
Air of June Sings, The. Edward Dorn. NeAP
Air of the museum, The. The Frozen Hero. Thomas H. Vance. NYBP
Air Plant, The (Grand Cayman, W.I). Hart Crane. MAP; MoAB; MoAmPo; NoP; PoIE
Air Raid across the Bay of Plymouth. Stephen Spender. TPM
Air Sentry, The. Patrick Barrington. CenHV
Air Shaft. Ian Healy. Poems from the Coalfields, I. PoAu-2
Air sings of marble by the soothing sea, The. The Temple by the Sea. Geoffrey Dutton. ACV
Air Tunnel, Monticello. Bink Noll. ToPo
Air was calm, the sun was low, The. On the Victory of Poland and Her Allies over the Sultan Osman, 1621. Casimir Sarbiewski. CAW
Air, which is not anything. Elements. Carolyn Wilson Link. GoYe
Airborn. Louis Grudin. PG (1955 ed.)
Airborne dragonfly, An. Hunter's Moon. Stephen Sandy. NYBP
Aircraft, Landing. Colin Thiele. ACV
Aircrews have had it and the war goes on. "For Whom the Bell Tolls." Gavin Ewart. WaP
Aire and Angels. John Donne. *See* Air and Angels.
Airedale, erect beside the chauffeur of a Rolls-Royce, An. Fashions in Dogs. E. B. White. FiBHP
Airly Beacon. Charles Kingsley. GTBS; GTSL; HBV; OBEV; PoVP
Airmail. *See* Air Mail.
Airman, The. W. R. Rodgers. WaP
Airman Who Flew over Shakespeare's England, The. Hyam Plutzik. PoPl
Airman's Alphabet, The. W. H. Auden. *Fr.* Journal of an Airman. NAMP
Airman's Prayer, An. Hugh R. Brodie. MaRV
(Sergeant's Prayer, A.) PGD
Airmen's Hymn, The. Harry Webb Farrington. MaRV
Airplane, The. Rowena Bastin Bennett. FaPON; GFA; OTPC (1946 ed.)
Airplane, The. Annette Wynne. GFA
Airplane has gigantic wings, An. The Airplane. Rowena Bastin Bennett. FaPON; GFA; OTPC (1946 ed.)
Airplane taxied to the station's gate, The. First Flight. Robert P. Tristram Coffin. PoMa
Airplane taxis down the field, The. Taking Off. Mary McB. Green. SoPo; TiPo
Air's advice is all, The. Prelude to Commencement. Marie de L. Welch. NYBP
Airs from the sea blown back. Ovid on the Dacian Coast. Dunstan Thompson. NYBP
Airs of Pei, *sel.* Confucius, *tr. fr. Chinese by* Ezra Pound.
Efficient Wife's Complaint, The. CTC
Airs! that wander and murmur round. The Siesta. *Unknown.* AWP; JAWP; WBP
Airship. Hy Sobiloff. NePA
Airstrip in Essex, 1960, An. Donald Hall. LiTM (1970 ed.); PoCh
Airy, fairy Lilian. Lilian. Tennyson. HBV; PoVP
Airy Tomb, The. R. S. Thomas. ToPo
Aishah Schechinah. Robert Stephen Hawker. ACP (1926 ed.); GoBC; ISi; OBNC; OxBoCh
Aisling. Austin Clarke. AnIV
Aix-la-Chappelle, 1945. Edgar Bowers. NePoEA
Ai-yee! My yellow-bird-woman. Beat against Me No Longer. Lew Sarett. NP
Ajanta. Muriel Rukeyser. FiMAP; LiTA; LiTM; MiAP; MoAB; MoAmPo (1950 ed.); TwAmPo
Aja's Lament over His Dead Wife, *abr.* Kalidasa, *tr. fr. Sanskrit by* Arthur W. Ryder. LiTW
Ajax *sels.* Sophocles, *tr. fr. Greek.*
Ajax, before His Suicide, *tr. by* F. Storr. LiTW
Chorus: "Fair Salamis, the billow's roar," *tr. by* Winthrop Mackworth Praed. AWP; JAWP; WBP
Universal Change, *tr. by* Charles Stuart Calverley. LiTW
Ajax and Ulysses. James Shirley. *See* Contention of Ajax and Ulysses, The.
Ajax, before His Suicide. Sophocles, *tr. fr. Greek by* F. Storr. *Fr.* Ajax. LiTW
Akathistos Hymn, The. *Unknown, tr. fr. Greek by* Vincent McNabb. ISi
Akbar's Dream, *sel.* Tennyson.
Hymn: "Once again thou flamest heavenward, once again we see thee rise." PoVP
Akhnaton. Thomas S. Jones, Jr. AnAmPo
Akinetos. Richard Henry Horne. *Fr.* Orion. VA
Akond of Swat, The. Edward Lear. ALV; CenHV; FaBoCh; FiBHP; GoTP; OnPP; SiTL
(Ahkoond [*or* Ahkond] of Swat, The.) BOHV; NA; RIS
Al Aaraaf. Poe. AmP; AP
Sels.
Song: "Neath blue-bell or streamer." APA
('Neath Blue-Bell or Streamer.) AmPP (3d ed.)
(Song from "Al Aaraaf.") AmPP (4th ed.); AnFE; CoAnAm; NePA; OxBA
Song: "Spirit! that dwellest where. CoBA
Sonnet to Science. Prologue. AmePo; AmP; AmPP; AnAmPo; AnFE; AP; APA; CBV; CoAnAm; CoBA; ILP; MAmP; MWA-1; NePA; NoP; OxBA; PPON
(To Science.) CBEP; Sonn
Al Fitnah Muhajir. Nazzam Al Sudan. NBP
Al Nist by the Rose. *Unknown.* AtBAP
Al the Meryere. *Unknown.* AtBAP; BoW
Ala, mala, mink, monk. *Unknown.* OxNR
Alabado, *with music.* *Unknown, tr. fr. Spanish.* TrAS
Alabama, The. Maurice Bell. PAH
Alabama. Julia Fields. PoNe (1970 ed.)
Alabama. Julia S. Tutwiler. PoRL
Alabama, The. *Unknown.* ShS, 2 *vers. with music;* SoAmSa, *with music.*
Alabama Bound, *with music.* *Unknown.* ABF
Alabama Centennial. Naomi Long Madgett. BALP
Alabama Earth. Langston Hughes. AmFN; GoSl
Alabama, good-bye! I love thee well! A Missouri Maiden's Farewell to Alabama. "Mark Twain." InMe
Alack-a-day,/ Who is he? I say. Behind the Looking Glass. Daniel Carter Beard. OTD
Alack! what poverty my Muse brings forth. Sonnets, CIII. Shakespeare. CLwM
Aladdin. James Russell Lowell. AnNE; BBV (1951 ed.); HBV; NeHB; OTD; PoMS; RoGo; StVeCh (1940 ed.); TreFT; WaKn
Aladdin and the Jinn. Vachel Lindsay. AnAmPo; AnFE; APA; CoAnAm; GTBS-W; LiTM; NP; OnPP
(Poems about the Moon [VI].) MAPA; TwAmPo
Aladdin Throws Away His Lamp. Elias Lieberman. PoMa
Alafia. Odaro (Barbara Jones). BF
Alamance. Seymour W. Whiting. PAH
Alan. Raymond Roseliep. FiSC
Alarm and time clock still intrude too early. And on This Shore. M. Carl Holman. AmNP; PoNe
Alarm Clock, The. Mari Evans. BOLo
Alarm clocks tick in a thousand furnished rooms, The. North Infinity Street. Conrad Aiken. AP
Alarm in 1645, An, *sel.* Thomas Jordan.
Cavalier's Lullaby for His Mistress, A. SeCL
Alarmed Skipper, The. James Thomas Fields. BOHV; EtS; GoTP; HBV; LHV; YaD
(Nantucket Skipper, The.) AmSS
Alarum, The. Sylvia Townsend Warner. MoBrPo
Alas. Walter de la Mare. CLwM

Alas! Sadi, *tr. fr. Persian by* L. Cranmer-Byng. *Fr.* The Gulistan. AWP; WoL
Alas! *Unknown.* IHA
Alas, Alack. Walter de la Mare. EvOK; FaPON; GFA; MPB; PoRh; TiPo
Alas! alas! The while. A Night with a Holy-Water Clerk. *Unknown.* MeEL
Alas! alas! thou turn'st in vain. Claim to Love. Giovanni Battista Guarini. AWP
Alas! and am I born for this. On Liberty and Slavery. George Moses Horton. Kal; PoNe
Alas, and well-a-day! they are talking of me still. A Maori Girl's Song. Alfred Domett. OBVV
Alas, dear duchess. Toast to a Departing Duchess. Clément Marot. HW
Alas, dear heart! what hope had I. Love Me Again. *Unknown.* EIL
Alas! deceite that in truste is nowe. Trust Only Yourself. *Unknown.* MeEL
Alas! fond child. Emblems, I, 3. Francis Quarles. EP
Alas! for all the pretty women who marry dull men. Meditation at Kew. Anna Wickham. AnEnPo; FaBoTw; MeWo; MoBrPo
Alas for him that for any of the vile rude world's estates. He Who Forsakes the Clerkly Life. *Unknown.* *Fr.* The Life of St. Cellach of Killala. OnYI
Alas for him who never sees. Whittier. *Fr.* Snow-bound. InP
Alas for me, who loved a falcon well. Sonnet: A Lady Laments for Her Lost Lover. *Unknown.* AWP
Alas! for Peter not a helping hand. George Crabbe. *Fr.* The Borough, Letter XXII. OBRV
Alas! for the going of swiftness, for the feet of the running of thee. Johnny, I Hardly Knew Ye: In Swinburnese, *parody.* Robert Yelverton Tyrrell. OnYI
Alas for the voyage, O High King of Heaven. Farewell [*or* Colum-Cille's Farewell] to Ireland. *At. to* St. Columcille, *tr. by* Douglas Hyde. AnIV; AWP; JAWP; LiTW; WBP
Alas! for them, their day is o'er. Indians. Charles Sprague. *Fr.* Centennial Ode. GN
Alas for Youth. Firdausi, *tr. fr. Persian by* R. A. Nicholson. AWP; JAWP; LiTW; WBP
Alas, have I not pain enough, my friend. Astrophel and Stella, XIV. Sir Philip Sidney. FCP; MaPo (1969 ed.); NoP; ReEn; SiPS; TuPP
Alas! how can I sleep? who truly loves. Thomas Middleton. *Fr.* Blurt, Master Constable. LO
Alas! how dismal is my tale. The Curse of Doneraile. Patrick O'Kelly. OnYI
Alas, how easily things go wrong! Sweet Peril. George Macdonald. BLPA; FaBoBe; NeHB; TreFS
Alas! how frail and weak a little boat. A Summer Storm. Lord Alfred Douglas. JKCP (1926 ed.)
Alas! how full of fear. The Fate of the Prophets. Longfellow. *Fr.* Christus; a Mystery. WGRP
Alas How Long ("Alas how long shall I and my maidenhead lie"). *Unknown.* ErPo
Alas, how pleasant are their dayes. The Unfortunate Lover. Andrew Marvell. MaMe
Alas, How Soon the Hours Are Over. Walter Savage Landor. *See* Plays.
Alas, I am a heavy child. Stout. Rue Carpenter. RIS
Alas, I am so faint I may not stand. The Desertion of Beauty and Strength. *Unknown.* *Fr.* Everyman. ACP
Alas! I have lost my God. Rejected. Lord Alfred Douglas. PeVV
Alas, Kind Element. Léonie Adams. MoVE
Alas, Madam, for Stealing of a Kiss. Sir Thomas Wyatt. FCP; OAEP
Alas! my child, where is the pen. The Hen. Oliver Herford. LBN; NA
Alas! my dear friend, what a state of affairs! Epistle of Condolence. Thomas Moore. OnYI
Alas, My God. Thomas Shepherd. *Fr.* For Communion with God. OxBoCh
("Alas, my God, that we should be," *shorter sel.*) TrPWD
Alas, my hart will brek in three. Fearful Death. *Unknown.* MeEL
Alas, my heart is black. The New Heart. *Unknown.* WGRP
Alas, my heart! mine eye hath wrongèd thee. Corydon to His Phyllis. Sir Edward Dyer. EIL; SiCE
Alas! my Lord is going. Comfort in Extremity. Christopher Harvey. OxBoCh
Alas, my love, ye [*or* you] do me wrong. Greensleeves [*or* Lady Greensleeves]. *Unknown.* *See also* Greensleeves was all my joy. AtBAP; LoGBV; MeWo; PoEL-2; UnTE.
Alas, my Postumus, our years. To Postumus. Horace. Odes, II, 14. LiTW; OuHeWo
Alas! my son, you little know. Wedlock. Jenny Grahame. LiTL
Alas, my worthy master honourable. *See* Allas! my worthy maister honorable.
Alas! noble Prince Leopold, he is dead. The Death of Prince Leopold. William McGonagall. EvOK
Alas, O King of Kings. The Song of the Heads. *Unknown.* KiLC
Alas! our young affections run to waste. Desire and Disillusion. Byron. *Fr.* Childe Harold's Pilgrimage. EPN
Alas poor Death, where does thy great strength lye? Meditations for July 25, 1666. Philip Pain. SCAP
Alas, poor Death, where is thy glory? A Dialogue Anthem. George Herbert. MaMe; StJW
Alas, poor heart, I pity thee. Medieval Norman Songs, IX. *Unknown, tr. by* John Addington Symonds. AWP
Alas, poor man, what hap have I. Sir Thomas Wyatt. FCP; SiPS
Alas! Poor Queen. Marion Angus. ACV; GoTS; OxBS; SiSW
Alas so all things now do hold their peace. A Complaint by Night of the Lover Not Beloved [*or* Night]. Earl of Surrey, *after* Petrarch. AWP; EIL; EnRePo; FaBoEn; FCP; LoBV; OBSC; OuHeWo; ReEn; SiCE; SiPS; Sonn; TuPP
Alas, So Long! Dante Gabriel Rossetti. PoVP
Alas! that all we loved of him should be. Shelley. *Fr.* Adonais. OHIP
Alas! that ever [*or* evyr] that speche was spoken [*or* spokyn]. *Unknown.* *Fr.* Eva's Lament. AtBAP; EnLoPo
Alas! that men must see. Love and Death. Margaret Deland. AA; HBV
Alas, that my heart is a lute. My Heart Is a Lute. *At. to* Lady Ann Lindsay *and to* Lady Blanche Lindsay. HBV; VA
Alas the grief and deadly woeful smart! Sir Thomas Wyatt. FCP; SiPS
Alas! the love of women! it is known. Byron. *Fr.* Don Juan, II. CoBE
Alas, the moon should ever beam. The Water Lady. Thomas Hood. CH; HBV; VA; ViBoPo
Alas! they had been friends in youth. Broken Friendship [*or* The Scars Remaining.] Samuel Taylor Coleridge. *Fr.* Christabel. LO; MCCG; OBNC; OBRV; TreFT
Alas 'tis true I have gone here and there. Sonnets, CX. Shakespeare. CBEP; EnLi-1 (1949 ed.); EP; MaPo; OAEP; OBSC; PoE; ReEn; ReIE; SiCE; ViBoPo
Alas! 'tis very sad to hear. Walter Savage Landor. GTBS-P
Alas! too well we know our loss. Concerning Them That Are Asleep. R. W. Raymond. STF
Alas, unhappy land; ill-fated spot. Dirge of the Moolla of Kotal. George Thomas Lanigan. BOHV; NA
Alas, what pleasure, now the pleasant spring. A Canzon Pastoral in Honor of Her Majesty. Edmund Bolton. TuPP
Alas! What Shall I Do for Love? Henry VIII, King of England. PrWP
Alas! what shul we freres do. A Friar Complains. *Unknown.* MeEL
Alas, whence came this change of looks? Astrophel and Stella, LXXXVI. Sir Philip Sidney. FCP; SiPS
Alas! who knows or cares, my love. Laura's Song. Oliver Madox Brown. OBVV; VA
Alas, with what tormenting fire. Chorus [*or* Of Death]. Robert Garnier, *tr. by* the Countess of Pembroke. *Fr.* Antonius. EIL; TuPP
Alas! you son of her who is short-eared. Lion. *Unknown.* PeSA
Alaska. Joaquin Miller. OTD; PAH; ThLM
Alaska. *Unknown.* PoRL
Alastor; or, The Spirit of Solitude. Shelley. BEL; CABL; EnLi-2 (1949 ed.); EnRP; MERP; OAEP
Sels.
"As an eagle grasped." ChER
"Earth, ocean, air, belovèd brotherhood!" FiP
(Invocation.) WHA
(Invocation to Nature.) EPN

Alba ("Creeper grows over thorn"). Confucius, *tr. fr. Chinese by* Ezra Pound. *Fr.* Songs of T'ang. CTC
Alba ("When the nightingale to his mate"). Ezra Pound. *Fr.* Langue d'Oc. PoIE
Alba, *sel.* Robert Tofte.
Love's Labour Lost. EIL
Alba. Derek Walcott. GoJo
Alba after Six Years. Christopher Middleton. NePoEA-2
Alba Innominata. *Unknown, tr. fr. Provençal by* Ezra Pound. AWP; LiTW
Albany schmalbany/ Governor W. George Starbuck. PV
Albatross, The. Baudelaire, *tr. fr. French.* EnLi-2, *tr. by* Frances Winwar; OnPM, *tr. by* Lilian Spencer Walker; ReMP, *tr. by* Warren Carrier; SyP, *tr. by* Richard Wilbur; WoL, *tr. by* George Dillon
Albatross, The. John Biram. NYTB
Albatross. Charles Burgess. NePoAm-2
Albatross, The. William Pember Reeves. AnNZ
Albatross. Charles Warren Stoddard. AA; EtS
Albeit the Venice girls get praise. Ballad of the Women of Paris. Villon, *tr. by* Swinburne. AWP; JAWP; MeWo; OuHeWo; UnTE; WBP
"Albemarle" Cushing. James Jeffrey Roche. PAH
Albert Dürer. W. Leslie Nicholls. PV
Albert Sidney Johnston. Kate Brownlee Sherwood. MC; PAH
Albert Sidney Johnston. Francis Orrery Ticknor. PAH
Albi, Ne Doreas, *wr.* [Doleas]. Horace, *tr. fr. Latin by* Austin Dobson. Odes, I, 33. AWP
Albion and Albanius, *sel.* Dryden.
Song of the River Thames, A. FaBoEn
Albion's England, *sels.* William Warner.
"Aeneas dead, Ascanius reign'd; Ascanius dead, his brother," *fr. Bk.* II, *ch.* 13. ReIE
"Eight Henry, heir indubitate of York and Lancaster," *fr. Bk.* VIII, *ch.* 38. TuPP
Fate of Narcissus, The, *fr. Bk.* IX, *ch.* 46. OBSC
"Now of the conqueror this isle had Brutain unto name," *fr. Bk.* III, *ch.* 14. ReIE
Albuera. Thomas Hardy. *Fr.* The Dynasts, Pt. II, Act VI, sc. iv. WaaP
Album, The. C. Day Lewis. ChMP; EnLoPo; FaBoEn; OxBI
Album Verses. Oliver Wendell Holmes. *Fr.* The Autocrat of the Breakfast Table, *ch.* 1. AmPP
Alcaics; to H. F. B. Robert Louis Stevenson. NBM; OBEV (new ed.); OBVV; ShBV-3
("Brave lads in olden musical centuries.") EG
Alcestis, *sels.* Euripides, *tr. fr. Greek.*
It Is a Gracious House and Ever Was, *tr. by* Dudley Fitts *and* Robert Fitzgerald. LiTW
Strength of Fate, The. *tr. by* A. E. Housman. AWP; JAWP; WBP
Alcestis. Isabel Williams Verry. GoYe
Alcestis in Ely. Nicholas Moore. NeBP
Alchemist, The. Louise Bogan. AWP; MAP; MoAmPo
Alchemist, The, *sels.* Ben Jonson.
"Come on, sir. Now, you set your foot on shore," *fr.* II, i-ii. AtBAP; PoEL-2
"I have blown, sir,/ Hard for your worship," *fr.* II, ii. LO
"No. I'll have no bawds," *fr.* II, ii. ViBoPo
Alchemist, The. Robert Kelly. CoPo
Alchemist, The. Ezra Pound. CMoP; LiTA; NePA; TwAmPo
Alchemist in the City, The. Gerard Manley Hopkins. NoP
Alchemy. Francis Carlin. JKCP
Alchemy. Adelaide Love. PGD
Alcibiades to a Jealous Girl. Arthur Davison Ficke. HBMV
Alcilia, *sel.* "J. C."
Frailty of Beauty, The. EIL
Alciphron and Leucippe. Walter Savage Landor. OBEV
Alcohol. Louis MacNeice. LiTM
Alcohol. Peter Schjeldahl. YAP
Alcoholic. F. D. Reeve. NYBP
Alcyone. Frances Laughton Mace. AA
Aldebaran at Dusk. George Sterling. PFY
Alder by the river, The. Spring. Celia Thaxter. BoChLi; DD; HH; OTPC (1946 ed.); PRWS
Aldfrid's Itinerary through Ireland. *Unknown, tr. fr. Middle Irish by* James Clarence Mangan. OnYI
Aldhelm. Edgar Lee Masters. CMoP
Alec Yeaton's Son. Thomas Bailey Aldrich. EtS
Alex, perhaps a colour of which neither of us had dreamt. Letter to Alex Comfort. Dannie Abse. FaBoTw; TwCP
Alexander and Campaspe, *sels.* John Lyly.
Apelles' Song: "Cupid and my Campaspe played," *fr.* III, v. ATP; EnLi-1; EnLit; NeHB; OuHeWo; TOP; TrGrPo
(Cards and Kisses.) HoPM; LiTL; OBEV
(Cards for Kisses.) MeWo
(Cupid and Campaspe.) AtBAP; BEL; EIL; GTBS; GTBS-D; GTBS-P; GTBS-W; GTSE; GTSL; HBV; ILP; LiTG; SeCeV; UnPo (1st ed.); WHA
(Cupid and My Campaspe Played [*or* Play'd].) CABA; ExPo; NoP; OAEP; PoRA; ReEn; SiCE; TuPP; ViBoPo
(Song: "Cupid and my Campaspe playd.") YAT
(Song by Apelles.) ALV
(Song of Apelles.) OBSC
Serving Men's Song, A: "O! for a bowl of fat Canary," *fr.* I, iii. *Also in* A Mad World, My Masters (*by* Thomas Middleton). ALV; OBSC
(Oh, for a Bowl of Fat Canary.) NoP
Trico's Song: "What bird so sings", *fr.* V, i. OBSC; TrGrPo
(Spring, The.) CH; MemP
(Spring's Welcome.) AnEnPo; BEL; OBEV; TOP
(What Bird So Sings.) EG; EIL; SiCE; ThWaDe; TuPP; ViBoPo
(Who Is't Now We Hear?) BiS
Alexander Campbell, *sel.* Vachel Lindsay.
My Fathers Came from Kentucky. AmFN; HBMV
Alexander Graham Bell Did Not Invent the Telephone. Robert P. Tristram Coffin. OTD; TiPo (1959 ed.)
Alexander Jannai. C. P. Cavafy, *tr. fr. Modern Greek by* Simon Chasen. TrJP
Alexander Pope at Stanton Harcourt. Sidney Keyes. *Fr.* Sour Land. FaBoTw
Alexander Selkirk during His Solitary Abode in the Island of Juan Fernandez. William Cowper. *See* Verses Supposed to Be Written by Alexander Selkirk. . .
Alexander the Great. *Unknown.* CH
Alexander's Feast; or, The Power of Music [*or* Musique]. Dryden. ACP; AnFE; ATP; BEL; BoLiVe; CEP; CoBE; EiCL; EiPP; EnL; EnLi-1; EnLit; FiP; GN, *sts.* 1-2; GoBC; GTBS; GTBS-D; GTBS-P; GTBS-W; GTSE; GTSL; HBV; LiTB; LoBV; MBW-1; NoP; OAEP; OBS; OtMeF, *st.* 1; OuHeWo; PoE; SeCeV; SeCV-2; SeEP; StP; TOP; TrGrPo; WHA; WiR; YAT, 3 *sts.*
War, *br. sel.* TreFS
Alexandria. Lawrence Durrell. MoVE; ToPo
Alexias, the Complaint of the Forsaken Wife of Sainte Alexis. Richard Crashaw. MaMe
Alexis, here she stayed; among these pines. Sonnet [*or* Spring Bereaved]. William Drummond of Hawthornden. EIL; HBV; LO; OBEV; OBS
Alfonso was his name; his sad cantina. Skin Diving in the Virgins. John Malcolm Brinnin. NYBP
Alfred, a Masque, *sel.* James Thomson *and* David Mallet.
Rule, Britannia, *fr.* II, v. Thomson. BEL; CEP; EiCP; EiPP; EnLi-2 (1949 ed.); EnLit; GTBS; GTBS-D; GTBS-P; GTBS-W; GTSE; GTSL; HBV; NoP; OAEP; OBEC; PoFr; TreF; WBLP; YAT
Alfred Corning Clark. Robert Lowell. PoeP
Alfred de Musset. Byway in Biography. Maurice Hare. MemP; RIS
Alfred Lord Tennyson. Reed Whittemore. PP; SiTL
Alfred-Seeable Philadelphia Sky. Eli Siegel. CAD
Alfred the Harper. John Sterling. BeLS
Alfred was a ninny. Alfred, Lord Tennyson. Reed Whittemore. PP; SiTL
Algerian Refugee Camp, Aïn-Khemouda. Alan Ross. POTi
Algernon Sidney fills this tomb. On Algernon Sidney. *Unknown.* PeRV
Algonkian Burial. Alfred Goldsworthy Bailey. OBCV
Algy Met [*or* Saw] a Bear. *Unknown.* FaPON; MoShBr; ShM
Ali. Lloyd M. Corbin, Jr. BOLo
Alibi. Hughes Mearns. *Fr.* Later Antigonishes. InMe
Alice. Herbert Bashford. HBV
Alice. Charles Cotton. *See* Resolution in Four Sonnets. . . Concerning Four Rural Sisters.
Alice B, *with music. Unknown.* AS
Alice Brand. Sir Walter Scott. *Fr.* The Lady of the Lake, IV. BeLS; HBV; HBVY; OnMSP; OTPC (1946 ed.)
Alice, dear, what ails you. A Frosty Night. Robert Graves. CH; MoAB; MoBrPo; MoBS

Alice Fell. Wordsworth. BEL; BeLS; OTPC
Alice for Annie, An. R. H. W. Dillard. TDP
Alice, for whom my love is deep. Proof Positive. Deems Taylor. UnTE
Alice grown lazy, mammoth but not fat. Last Days of Alice. Allen Tate. AmP; AtBAP; OxBA; TwAmPo; UnPo
Alice is tall and upright as a pine. Alice [*or* Two Rural Sisters]. Charles Cotton. *Fr.* Resolution in Four Sonnets . . . Concerning Four Rural Sisters. CLwM; EG; EnLoPo; PeRV; PoEL-3; Sonn; TrGrPo; UnTE
Alice Lee stood awaiting her lover one night. The Lips That Touch Liquor Shall Never Touch Mine. Harriet A. Glazebrook. PaPo
Alice 1963. G. Bishop-Dubjinsky. ThO
Alice Ray. Sarah Josepha Hale. AA
Alice's Adventures in Wonderland, *sels.* "Lewis Carroll."
Evidence Read at the Trial of the Knave of Hearts, *fr. ch.* 12. FaFP; GTBS-P; LiTG; NBM; OxBoLi; SiTL
Father William, *fr. ch.* 5. BiCB; BOHV; FaPL; FaPON; FiBHP; GoJo; GoTP; HBV; HoPM; InMe; LBN; LiTB; LiTG; OnPP; OTPC (1946 ed.); PCD; PDV; PoLF; PoRA; PoVP; RePo; RIS; SiTL; StaSt; TOP; TreF; TrGrPo; TSW; WaKn
(You Are Old, Father William.) ALV; BoChLi; Par; ShBV-2; TiPo; WhC; YAT
How Doth the Little Crocodile, *fr. ch.* 2. BoChLi; CBV; FaBoCh; FaFP; FaPON; LoGBV; MoShBr; MPB; OTPC (1946 ed.); Par; ShM; SoPo; TiPo; TreFS; WaKn; WhC; YAT; YT
(Crocodile, The.) EnLi-2 (1949 ed.); GFA; GoTP; HoPM; PoFS; TrGrPo
Lobster Quadrille, The [*or* A], *fr. ch.* 10. BoChLi; BoTP; FaPON; MoShBr; OTPC (1946 ed.); Par; PCD; PCH; PRWS; RIS; SAS; StVeCh; UTS
(Mock Turtle's Song, The.) ChTr; MPB (1956 ed.); PoVP
(Quadrille, A.) EnLi-2
(Whiting and the Snail, The.) HBV; HBVY
("'Will you walk a little faster?' said a whiting to a snail.") TiPo (1952 ed.)
Of Alice in Wonderland, *introd.* VA
Speak Roughly to Your Little Boy, *fr. ch.* 6. FaBoCh; LoGBV; Par
(Dutchess' Lullaby, The.) BBGG
Turtle Soup. InMe
("Beautiful soup, so rich and green.") Par
Twinkle, twinkle, Little Bat! *fr. ch.* 7. Par; WhC
Voice of the Lobster, The, *fr. ch.* 10. EvOK; SAS; SiTL
("'T is the voice of the Lobster; I heard him declare.") Par
Alice's Supper. Laura E. Richards. MPB
Alicia's Bonnet. Elisabeth Cavazza. AA
Alien. Helen Frazee-Bower. HBMV
Alien. Donald Jeffrey Hayes. AmNP
Alien. Archibald MacLeish. EtS
Alien. William Price Turner. OxBS
Alienation. Harry Kemp. HBMV
Alike. Dorothy Aldis. RePo
Alike from love and marriage hurry. Advice to Bachelors. *Unknown.* UnTE
Alimentary. Clifton Fadiman. PV
Aliscamp, The. Frédéric Mistral, *tr. fr. Provençal by* Harriet Waters Preston. CAW
Alison. *Unknown. See* Alisoun.
Alison and Willie. *Unknown.* BaBo; ESPB
Alison Gross. *Unknown.* BuBa; FaBoCh; OBB; OxBB
(Allison Gross.) BaBo; CH; ESPB
Alisoun. *Unknown.* AtBAP; CTC; MeEV, *mod. by* Mabel Van Duzee; PoEL-1
(Alison.) MeEL; NoP; OBEV
(Alysoun.) BEL; CoBE; EnL; EnLi-1; EnLit; GoBC
(Bytuenë Mersh and Averil.) ViBoPo
Aliter. Confucius, *tr. fr. Chinese by* Ezra Pound. *Fr.* Songs of Ch'en. CTC
Aliud. Thomas Freeman. TuPP
Alive. Nellie Goode. SoP
Alive for Evermore. Amos Niven Wilder. MaRV
Alive where I lie and hide. The Veteran. Louis O. Coxe. MoVE
All. Antoni Slonimski, *tr. fr. Polish.* PoFr, *tr. by* Marion Moore Coleman; TrJP, *tr. by* Wanda Dynowska
All, The. *Unknown, tr. fr. Sanskrit by* Joseph Nadin Rawson. *Fr.* The Upanishads. OnPM
All a green willow, willow, willow. A Green Willow Is My Garland. John Heywood. CoBE; EIL
"All aboard! All aboard!" is the cry. Shearing. David McKee Wright. AnNZ
All Aboard for Bombay. Leroy F. Jackson. BrR
All Adam's race are members of one frame. Adam's Race. Sadi. LiTW
All after pleasures as I rid one day. Christmas. George Herbert. MaMe; OxBoCh; SCEP-1; SeCV-1
All, All. Baudelaire, *tr. fr. French by* George Dillon. WoL
All, All a-Lonely. *Unknown.* ChTr; OxBoLi
("Three little children sitting on the sand.") ExPo
All, all for immortality. Walt Whitman. *Fr.* Song of the Universal. MaRV
All, all my trust, Lord, I have put in Thee. Psalm XXXI. *Paraphrased by* Sir Philip Sidney. FCP
All, All of a Piece [Throughout]. Dryden. *Fr.* The Secular Masque. CBEP; ChTr; ELP; ELU; GTBS-W
(Chorus: "All, all of a piece throughout.") OnPM; ViBoPo
All alone—alone,/ Calm, as on a kingly throne. Solitude. Edward Rowland Sill. AnNE
All alone as I strayed by the banks of the river. The Lost Jimmie Whalen. *Unknown.* ABF
All alone on the hillside. The "Grey Horse Troop." Robert W. Chambers. HBV; PAH
All Alone Tree, The. F. O'Neil Gallagher. PCH
All along the backwater. Duck's [*or* Ducks'] Ditty. Kenneth Grahame. *Fr.* The Wind in the Willows. BoTP; FaPON; GoJo; MoShBr; MPB; OTPC (1946 ed.); PCH; PDV; PoRh; SoPo; SUS; TiPo; UTS; WaKn
All along the rail. The Wait. Quincy Troupe. WSL
All along the valley, stream that flashest white. In the Valley of Cauteretz. Tennyson. EPN; MaPo (1969 ed.); MBW-2; OBVV; PoVP; TOP; ViPo
All Animals Like Me. Raymond Souster. WHW
All are architects of Fate. The Builders. Longfellow. FaFP; MaRV; OHFP; TreFS
All are but parts of one stupendous whole. Pope. *Fr.* An Essay on Man, Epistle I. WGRP
All are keen. Aideen. *Unknown.* KiLC
All are not moralists, like Southey, when. The Lake Poets. Byron. *Fr.* Don Juan, III. UnPo (1st ed.)
All are not taken; there are left behind. Consolation. Elizabeth Barrett Browning. OBEV (1st ed.); PoVP
All around him Patmos lies. Patmos. Edith M. Thomas. HBV
All around the kitchen, cocky doodle doodle doo. Cocky Doodle Doodle Doo. *Unknown.* OuSiCo
All around the mulberry bush. Mother Goose. OTPC (1946 ed.)
All Around the Town, *sels.* Phyllis McGinley.
"B's the Bus." FaPON; SoPo; TiPo
"C is for the Circus." SoPo; TiPo
"E is the Escalator." TiPo
"F is the fighting Firetruck." FaPON
"J's the jumping Jay-walker." FaPON; TiPo (1952 ed.)
"P's the proud Policeman." SoPo; TiPo
"R is for the Restaurant." TiPo (1959 ed.)
"U is for Umbrellas." TiPo
"W's for Windows." TiPo
All as a Sea, the World No Other Is. *Unknown.* RelE
All at Sea. Frederick Moxon. BOHV
All Awry. Justin Richardson. SiTL
All beaded with dew. Hunting, VII. Gary Snyder. *Fr.* Myths & Texts. NaP
All Beautiful the March of Days. Frances Whitmarsh Wile. MaRV
All beautiful things bring sadness, nor alone. Sonnet. Richard Chenevix Trench. VA
All beauty calls you to me and you seem. From the Sea. Sara Teasdale. MoLP
All beauty, resonance, integrity. Le Livre Est sur la Table. John Ashbery. ANYP
All beginnings start right here. The Move Continuing. Al Young. WSL
All beneath the white-rose tree. The Three Captains. *Unknown.* AWP
All blisse/ Consists in this. Blisse. Thomas Traherne. PeRV
All bones but yours will rattle when I say. The Sea-Serpent. James Robinson Planché. NA

All buildings are but monuments of death. Epigram: Fatum Supremum [*or* Fatum Supremum]. *Unknown.* OBS; SeCL
All busy punching tickets. Crickets. David McCord. PDV
All but Blind. Walter de la Mare. FaPON; HBMV; MoAB; MoBrPo; PDV; ShBV-2; UnPo (1st ed.); WaKn; WePo
All but unutterable Name! The Divine Presence. Aubrey Thomas De Vere. *Fr.* May Carols. GoBC; MaRV
"All calligraphy transferred onto cubes." Some Feathers. Dick Gallup. ANYP
All children sound the same. The Core. John Holmes. MiAP
All Christians and lay-elders too. The Four-legg'd Elder; or, A Horrible Relation of a Dog and an Elder's Maid. Sir John Birkenhead. CoMu
All Christmas night upon the shelf. The Mouse. Hugh McCrae. PoAu-1
All Clowns Are Masked. Delmore Schwartz. The Repetitive Heart, III. LiTA; OxBA; ViBoPo
All day a steady snow had drifted down. The Slide at the Empire Mine. Harriet L. Wason. PoOW
All day a strong wind blew. A Strong Wind. Austin Clarke. BoNaP
All day across the sagebrush flat. The Sheep-Herder. Badger Clark. IHA; SCC
All day, all night, we hear, we feel. Standard Forgings Plant. William Stephens. NAMP
All day along potato hills, this woman. Potato Digger. Frances Frost. NYTB
All day and all day, as I sit at my measureless turning. The Mother's Song. Virginia Woodward Cloud. AA
All Day and All October. Laurence Lerner. PeSA
All day and every day the sea shone, steeped in its blueness. When I Was Young. Alun Llywelyn Williams. PrWP
All day and many days I rode. A Wish. Hamlin Garland. AA
All day and night, save winter, every weather. Aspens. Edward Thomas. ChMP
All day beneath the bleak, indifferent skies. Prometheus. W. W. Gibson. EPN
All day beneath the hurtling shells. The Dancers. W. W. Gibson. MMA
All day beside the shattered tank he'd lain. Reconciliation. C. Day Lewis. TwCP
All day cars mooed and shrieked. Klaxon. James Reaney. TwCaPo
All day from that deep well of life within. Alone into the Mountain. Katharine Lee Bates. ChIP; MaRV; StJW
All day has the battle raged. King Olaf's Death-Drink. Longfellow. *Fr.* The Saga of King Olaf. AmPP (4th ed.)
All day he stood at Weeping Cross. Karl. Charles Spear. AnNZ
All day I bar you from my slightest thought. Compensation. Lizette Woodworth Reese. HBMV
All day I did the little things. The Blue Bowl. Blanche Bane Kuder. BLPA; FaBoBe; NeHB
All day I follow. The Plowman. Raymond Knister. OBCV; PeCV; TwCaPo
All day I have been completely alone, and now the night. Separation. D. S. Savage. NeBP
All day I have been tossed and whirled in a preposterous happiness. The Day with a White Mark. C. S. Lewis. BoPe
All Day I Hear [the Noise of Waters]. James Joyce. Chamber Music, XXXV. CBV; FaBoCh; FlW; LoGBV; MoBrPo; NP; OnYI; PoRA
(Noise of Waters, The.) FaPON; TiPo (1959 ed.); TSW
All day I heard a humming in my ears. The Awaking of the Poetic Faculty. George Henry Boker. Sonn
All day I tell my rosary. Love's Rosary. Alfred Noyes. HBV
All day I watch the stretch of burning sand. Le Repos en Egypte; the Sphinx. Agnes Repplier. CAW; ISi; JKCP; StJW
All day in exquisite air. Larks. Katharine Tynan. OnYI
All day in Mother's garden here. Bedtime. Helen Coale Crew. GFA
All day it had been raining; now, the leaves. Hunt. Melvin Walker La Follette. NePoEA
All Day It Has Rained. Alun Lewis. GTBS-P; WePo
All day, knowing you dead. The Hours. John Peale Bishop. MoVE; OxBA
All day long/ The sun shines bright. The Night Sky. *Unknown.* BoTP
All day long/ The gray rain beating. Rain. "Seumas O'Sullivan." OnYI
All day long and every day. The Chapel in Lyoness. William Morris. PoVP; ViPo
All day long, day after day. The Nile. Elizabeth Coatsworth. HT
All day long I glance against. The Old Lecher. Louis O. Coxe. TwAmPo
All day long I have been working. Madonna of the Evening Flowers. Amy Lowell. AmLP; MAP; MoAmPo; NeMA; TOP; TreFT
All day long I played in an orchard. And of Laughter That Was a Changeling. Elizabeth Rendall. HBMV
All day long o'er the ocean I fly. Gaelic Folk Song. *Unknown.* GFA
All day long on the highway. The Highway. Louise Driscoll. HBV
All day long on the prairie I ride. The Cowboy. *Unknown.* CoSo (B *vers.*)
All day long the clouds go by. Flight. George Johnston. WHW
All day long the guns at the forts. The Surrender of New Orleans. Marion Manville. PAH
All day long till the west was red. Making Port. J. T. McKay. EtS
All day my sheep have mingled with yours. Shepherdess. Norman Cameron. Three Love Poems, III. FaBoTw; GTBS-P; OxBS
All day my wife, the maid[s], the men. After Christmas a Landlord Remembers [*or* Reminiscences of a Landlord]. Elizabeth J. Coatsworth. ChrBoLe; StJW
All day on the prairie in the saddle I ride. The Cowboy. *Unknown.* CoSo (A *vers.*)
All day rain fell. Ode on Contemplating Clapham Junction. Christopher Middleton. *Fr.* Herman Moon's Hourbook. NePoEA-2
All day red hatpins fall out. The Destination. James Tate. YAP
All day she hurried to get through. Mis' Smith. Albert Bigelow Paine. BOHV; PoLF
All day she sits behind a bright brass rail. The Travel Bureau. Ruth Comfort Mitchell. HBMV
All day that metronome, thrice gallant heart. Dirge for Two Clavichords and Bowler Hat. Kendrick Smithyman. AnNZ
All day the bird-song here has seemed. Random Reflections on a Summer Evening. John Hall Wheelock. NYBP
All day, the burning furnace of the plain. The Road to Granada. Arthur Ketchum. HT
All day the coast of Africa was seen. To Naples. H. B. Mallalieu. WaP
All day the gopher-killing boys. David. Eli Mandel. PeCV (1967 ed.)
All day the great guns barked and roared. Molly Pitcher. Laura E. Richards. MC; PAH; ThLM; YaD
All day the light wind blew on the house. Day on Kind Continent. Robert David Cohen. NYBP
All day the rain on this long voyage into wreckage plunges. Dreams of the Accuser. Randy Blasing. YAP
All day the sand, like golden chains. Scot in the Desert. Laurie Lee. POTi; ToPo
All day the stormy wind has blown. Take Heart. Edna Dean Proctor. HBV
All day the unnatural barking of dogs. The Dog. Valentin Iremonger. NeIP
All day the waves assailed the rock. Nahant [*or* Waves]. Emerson. AA; AmPP (5th ed.); MWA-1
All day the wind has made love. On Lake Pend Oreille. Richard Shelton. NYBP
All day Theseus marched, and all th' ensuing night. The Knight's Tale. Chaucer. *Fr.* The Canterbury Tales. BEL; TOP
All day they loitered by the resting ships. The *Wanderer.* John Masefield. BrPo; CABL; MCCG
All day this spring—the first he's known. The Rabbit. Camilla Doyle. StaST
All day to the loose tile behind the parapet. The Wasps' Nest. George MacBeth. FlW
All day today the sea gulls cried. Out in the Cold. George Starbuck. NYBP
All day under acrobat. Ruins under the Stars. Galway Kinnell. NaP

All day we had ridden through scarred, tawny hills. Spain, 1809. F. L. Lucas. HaMV
All day we have sat and watched the shadows' feet. Cerne Abbas. Hal Summers. HaMV
All day we watched the gulls. Torn Down from Glory Daily. Anne Sexton. WIRo
All do not seek the exalted fire. Earth and Fire. Vernon Watkins. NYBP
All down the years thy tale has rolled. To Homer. John Malcolm Bulloch. ATP (1935 ed.)
All Dressed Up for Easter. Aileen Fisher. RePo
All dripping in tangles green. The Tuft of Kelp. Herman Melville. CBV; ChTr; MAmP; MWA-1
All dull, my Lord, my spirits flat, and dead. Meditation Seven [*or* He Sent a Man before Them, Even Joseph, Who Was Sold.] Edward Taylor. *Fr.* Preparatory Meditations, Second Series. MAmP; MWA-1
All earthly beauty hath one cause and proof. Robert Bridges. The Growth of Love, XXXV. PoVP
All else for use, one only for desire. Deo Optimo Maximo. Louise Imogen Guiney. TrPWD
All-Embracing, The. Frederick William Faber. *See* There's a Wideness in God's Mercy.
All endeavor to be beautiful. Primer of Plato. Jean Garrigue. MoVE
All evening, while the summer trees were crying. Evening in Summer [*or* While the Summer Trees Were Crying *or* Time, the Faithless]. Valentin Iremonger. AnIV; NeIP; OxBI
All eyes were on Enceladus's face. Hyperion's Arrival [*or* Hyperion and Saturn]. Keats. *Fr.* Hyperion. OBRV; SeCePo
All feeling hearts must feel for him. "The Coming Storm." Herman Melville. MWA-1
All Fellows, *sel.* Laurence Housman.
"Dear love, when with a two-fold mind." WGRP
All fixed: early arrival at the flat. Nothing to Fear. Kingsley Amis. ErPo
All Flesh. Francis Thompson. BrPo
All Flesh Is Grass. Isaiah, XL: 6-8, Bible, *O.T.* TrJP
All flesh is grass and so are feathers too. Epitaph on Lady Ossory's Bullfinch. Horace Walpole. ChTr; OA
All Fools' Day. *Unknown.* PoRL; SiSoSe; SoPo
(April Fool's Day.) PCH
("First of April, some do say, The.") BoTP
All for Love. Byron. *See* Stanzas Written on the Road between Florence and Pisa.
All For Love, *sels.* Dryden.
Cleopatra and Antony, *fr.* II. FiP
Epilogue: "Poets, like disputants, when reasons fail." DiPo
"How I loved/ Witness, ye days and nights," *fr.* II. LO
Prologue: "What flocks of critics hover here to-day." DiPo
"Portents and prodigies are grown so frequent," *fr.* I. AtBAP
(Wild Weather.) BoW
"She comes. She's here," *fr.* III. MyFE
All for Love. *Unknown, tr. fr. German by* Louis Untermeyer. UnTE
All French folk, whereso'er ye be. If I Were King. Justin Huntly M'Carthy, *par. fr. the French of* Villon. *Fr.* If I Were King. HBV
All gather from the village here. Where Is Dominga? Francisco de Sá de Miranda. OnPM
All generous hearts lament. John Fitzgerald Kennedy. John Masefield. PAL
All gentlemen and yeomen good. Robin Hood and the Shepherd. *Unknown.* ESPB
All Girls Drill Team, The. Marvin Bell. TDP
All glass may yet be whole. The Scarred Girl. James Dickey. ToPo
All glorious as the Rainbow's birth. Young Love. Gerald Massey. OBVV
All glory cannot vanish from the hills. The Passing of the Forest. William Pember Reeves. AnNZ
All Goats. Elizabeth J. Coatsworth. PoMa
All God's Chillun Got Wings. *Unknown.* BoAN-1, *with music*; TreFS
(I Got a Robe.) SiTL
All Gold. *Unknown, tr. fr. Irish by* Frank O'Connor. KiLC
All Gone. C. Day Lewis. FaBoMo
All Gone. Walter de la Mare. BoPe
All good things have not kept aloof. To——. Tennyson. OBRV
All Greece hates. Helen. Hilda Doolittle ("H. D."). FaBoTw; LiTM (1970 ed.); MAP; MoAmPo; MoVE
"All green things on the earth, bless ye the Lord!" Benedicite. Anna Callender Brackett. AA
All hail, inexorable lord! To Ruin. Burns. CoBE
All hail, once pleasing, once inspiring shade. Lines Written in Windsor Forest. Pope. SiSw
All Hail, the Pageant of the Years. John Haynes Holmes. MaRV
All hail the power of Jesus' name! Coronation. Edward Perronet. HBV; MaRV; TreFS; WGRP
All hail, thou glorious morn. Washington's Birthday. Charles S. Davis. HH
All Hail, Thou Noble Guest. Martin Luther, *tr. fr. German by* Arthur Tozer Russell *and* Catherine Winkworth. TrPWD
All hail! thou noble land. America to Great Britain. Washington Allston. AA; HBV; PaA
All hail to Pennsylvania. Pennsylvania. Helen Hall Bucher. PoRL
All Hail to the Days That Merit More Praise, *with music.* Thomas D'Urfey, *and others.* YaCaBo
All hail to the State that we honor. The State We Honor. Fanny J. Crosby. PoRL
All hail! Unfurl the Stripes and Stars! God Save Our President. Francis de Haes Janvier. PaA; PAH; PAL
All hail, ye tender martyr-flowers. The Holy Innocents. Prudentius. CAW
All haile sweet poet, more full of more strong fire. To Mr. T. W. John Donne. MaMe
All hallelujahs, Oh ye heav'nly quires. A Poem upon the Triumphant Translation of . . . Mrs. Anne Eliot. John Danforth. SCAP
All Hallow Eve. Carolyn Wells. DD
"All hands alive! We're goin' about!" Hen Overboard. Robert P. Tristram Coffin. RePo
All Hands Unmoor! William Falconer. *Fr.* The Shipwreck. EtS
All heavy minds. Sir Thomas Wyatt. EG; FCP; SiPS
All hollow vaults and dungeons sealed from sight. Sacred Night. Michelangelo. OnPM
All holy influences dwell within. The Children Band. Sir Aubrey De Vere. OBEV
All honest folk throughout the land. *Unknown.* *Fr.* La Carmagnole. PoFr
"All honor to him who shall win the prize [*or* fight]." For Those Who Fail. Joaquin Miller. MaRV; OQP; PoToHe; TSW
All honor to that day which long ago. Washington's Birthday. Arthur J. Burdick. OHIP
All houses wherein men have lived and died. Haunted Houses. Longfellow. AnNE
All how silent and how still. Noon. John Clare. OBRV; SeCePo
All human progress up to God. The Martyr's Hymn. Francis H. Rose. MaRV
All human race wou'd fain be wits. Swift. *Fr.* On Poetry; a Rapsody. EiCL; PoEL-3
All human things are subject to decay. Life's Brevity. Simonides. OnPM
All human [*or* humane] things are subject to decay. MacFlecknoe. Dryden. AnFE; AtBAP; ATP (1953 ed.); BEL; BWP; CABA; CABL; CEP; CoBE; DiPo; EiCL; EiPP; EnLi-1; EnLit; ExPo; FiP; ForPo; FosPo; MaPo; MBW-1; NoP; OAEP; OBS; OxBoLi; PAn; PeRV; Po; PoAn; PoE; PoFS; PoIE; PP; QFR; SeCV-2; SeEP; SiTL; StP; TrGrPo; ViBoPo
All Hushed and Still within the House. Emily Brontë. FaBoCh
All hushed the trees are waiting. Tree Shadows. *Unknown.* GFA
All Hybla's honey, all that sweetnesse can. Upon Our Lords Last Comfortable Discourse with His Disciples. Richard Crashaw. MaMe
All I can give you is broken-face gargoyles. Broken-Face Gargoyles. Carl Sandburg. AmPP (5th ed.); ILP; MAP; MoAmPo; OxBA
All I can offer now is a cracked china jug. Winter Offering. D. S. Savage. LiTB; LiTM; NeBP
All I can say is—I saw it! Natural Magic. Robert Browning. PoVP
All I could see from where I stood. Renascence. Edna St. Vincent Millay. AmPP; FaFP; HBV; MAP; MoAB;

MoAmPo; NeMA; NePA; OHFP; PDV; PFY; TIHL; TwAmPo
All I Do, de Church Keep a-Grumblin', *with music.* *Unknown.* BoAN-2
"All I do is dole out minutes." Gallop, Gallop to a Rhyme. Monica Shannon. SiSoSe
All I have got of wealth and wisdom, I. Confession. Kenneth Mackenzie. BoAV
All I need to make me happy. *Unknown.* GoTP
All I shall ask, at last, when I put forth to sea. The Voyage. Henry W. Frost. SoP
All I want in this creation. Black-eyed Susie. *Unknown.* ABF
All Ignorance Toboggans into Know. E. E. Cummings. AmPP; OxBA; WaP
All impulses of soul and sense. Samuel Taylor Coleridge. *Fr.* Love. LO
All in a Garden Green. W. E. Henley. OBMV
All in a garden green. *Unknown.* LO
All in All. Edith Nesbit. PoFr
All in All. John Banister Tabb. OQP
All in All. Tennyson. *See* In Love, If Love Be Love.
All in Green Went My Love Riding. E. E. Cummings. AmLP; CLwM; CMoP; CoBA; FaBV; FlW; GoJo; InPo; LiTA; LiTM; NePA; NoP; OxBA; PoRA; SD; ThWaDe; VaPo
(Song: "All in green went my love riding.") ViBoPo
All in our marriage garden. Our Wee White Rose. Gerald Massey. *Fr.* The Mother's Idol Broken. HBV
All in Red. Eileen Mathias. BoTP
All in the April evening [morning, *wr.*]. Sheep and Lambs. Katharine Tynan. AnIV; BoPe; BoTP; HBV; JKCP; OBEV; OBVV; OnYI; OTPC (1946 ed.); OxBI; PoRL; PRWS; StJW; ThGo; VA; WHL
All in the Downs. Tom Hood. ALV; CenHV
All in the Downs the fleet was moored [*or* moor'd]. Blacked-eyed Susan [*or* Sweet William's Farewell to Black-eyed Susan]. John Gay. BeLS; CEP; EiPP; EtS; GTBS; GTBS-D; GTBS-P; GTBS-W; GTSE; GTSL; HBV; NoP; OBEC; RoGo; TreFS
All in the golden weather, forth let us ride today. The King's Highway. John S. McGroarty. HBV; HT
All in the groves of dragon-fungus. The Chickamungus. James Reeves. GoTP
All in the land of Essex. News from Colchester. Sir John Denham. PeRV
All in the leafy darkness, when sleep had passed. Care. Virginia Woodward Cloud. AA; HBV
All in the lilac-rain. In the Lilac-Rain. Edith M. Thomas. HBV
All in the merry month of May. Barbara Allen [*or* Barbara Allen's Cruelty]. *Unknown.* FaBoBe; MaC; MeWo
All in the Morning. *Unknown.* BiCB
All in the morning early. The Blue Boy in London. William Brighty Rands. OTPC
All in the pleasant afternoon. The Lost Playmate. Abbie Farwell Brown. HBVY
All in the pleasant evening, together comers we. *See* All in this pleasant evening . . .
All in the town were still asleep. The Little Dog's Day. Rupert Brooke. ShBV-1
All in their lofty bower so still. Medelwold and Sidselille. *Unknown.* BaBo
All in this pleasant evening, together come are we. Old May Song. *Unknown.* AtBAP; BoTP; CH; HH
All-intellectual eye, our solar round. James Thomson. *Fr.* To the Memory of Sir Isaac Newton. ImOP
All Is Best. Milton. *Fr.* Samson Agonistes. SeCePo
("All is best, though we oft doubt.") BoC; MyFE; OBEV; OBS
(Choruses from "Samson Agonistes.") SeCeV
(Epilogue.) FaBoEn
(Final Chorus.) ExPo
(Last Chorus.) ShBV-4
All is changing now—it seems as though all must be parted. Goethe. *Fr.* Hermann and Dorothea. PoFr
All is divine/ which the Highest has made. The Queen of Seasons. Cardinal Newman. GoBC
All is dying; hearts are breaking. Unchanging Jesus. Karl Johann Philipp Spitta. BLRP
All is over! fleet career. The Last Leap. Adam Lindsay Gordon. BoAu
All is phantom that we mid fare. Phantasy. *Unknown.* ACP
All is quiet and the desert moon. Guard. Michael C. Martin. WaP
All is secure. The Hapsburg on his throne. Mozart's "Linz" Symphony. Margaret Stanley-Wrench. MuSP
All Is Sold ("All is sold, all is lost, all is plundered"). "Anna Akhmatova," *tr. fr. Russian by* Babette Deutsch. OnPM
All is still/ Under the Pines. Under the Pines. Arthur S. Bourinot. OBCV
All is the same still. Earth and heaven locked in. Emily Brontë. C. Day Lewis. ChMP; GTBS-P
All Is Vanity. Ecclesiastes, I: 14-15, III: 19, Bible, *O.T.* TRV
All Is Vanity. *Unknown, at. to* Philip Rosseter. HBV
("Whether men do laugh or weep.") OBSC
All Is Well. Arthur Hugh Clough. BEL; EnLi-2; EPN; PoVP
(Whate'er You Dream with Doubt Possest.) OAEP
All June I bound the rose in sheaves. One Way of Love. Robert Browning. HBV; OtMeF; PoVP; TOP; VA
All kings, and all their favourites [*or* favorites]. The Anniversary [*or* The Anniversarie]. John Donne. AnAnS-1; AnFE; CBEP; DiPo; EP; ExPo; HoPM; LiTB; LiTG; MaMe; MBW-1; MeLP; MePo; NoP; OAEP; OBS; PoeP; ReIE; SCEP-1; SeCeV; SeCP; SeCV-1; SeEP; TuPP; UnPo (1st ed.)
All kings are hollow. The Cool, Cool Country. John Shaw Neilson. PoAu-1
All-knowing Lamp. *Unknown, tr. fr. Greek by* Louis Untermeyer. UnTE
All landscapes are his land. A Wealthy Man. William Allingham. IrPN
All Last Night. Lascelles Abercrombie. FaBoTw; HBV
All Legendary Obstacles. John Montague. OPoP
All lesser reasons for loving die away. Come to Birth. Abbie Huston Evans. NePoAm
All Life. Paul Eluard, *tr. fr. French by* Glauco Cambon. OnPM
All life, tumbled together in a storm. For Posterity. Kathleen Raine. NeBP
All look and likeness caught from earth. Phantom. S. T. Coleridge. ERoP-1; LO; PoEL-4; SiSw
All looks be pale, hearts cold as stone. A Lamentation. Thomas Campion. CH; OHIP
All love at first, like generous wine. Love. Samuel Butler. CBEP; SeCL
All loved and lovely women dear to rhyme. Immortals. David Morton. HBV
All Lovely Things. Conrad Aiken. CBV; PoRA
All Lovely Things. Richard Aldington. NeMA
All lovely things: a bell across the snow. A Joy as Old as Breathing. Etta May Van Tassel. JKCP (1955 ed.)
All-loving, The. Robert Browning. *Fr.* An Epistle Containing the Strange Medical Experience of Karshish, the Arab Physician. MaRV; OQP
("So, the All-great were the All-loving too.") ChIP; TRV
All matronly in her stoop, her wings canted. The Black Angel. Henri Coulette. NYBP
All meet here with us, finally. Ostriches & Grandmothers! LeRoi Jones. NeAP
All men are brothers and each people is my own. My Song to the Jewish People. Leib Olitski. TrJP
All Men Are Free! Elliott Napier. BoAu; InP
All men are wormes: but this no man. In silke. On Court-Worme. Ben Jonson. SeCP
All men know it, the young when the enemy in them. The Fear of Dying. John Holmes. MiAP
All men,—the preacher saith,—whate'er or whence. Frederick Goddard Tuckerman. *Fr.* Sonnets. PoIE
All Morning. Theodore Roethke. NaP; NoP
All mortal men, this day rejoice. Easter Day. Jasper Heywood. ReIE
All moveless stand the ancient cedar-trees. In the Dark. George Arnold. HBV
All moves within the visual frame. A Monument. Charles Madge. FaBoMo
All music, sauces, feasts, delights and pleasures. Measure. Thomas Traherne. *Fr.* Christian Ethics. UnS
All must be used. Barracks Apt. 14. Theodore Weiss. CoAP; NePoAm-2; TwAmPo
All my emprises have been fill'd with Thee. Walt Whitman. *Fr.* Prayer of Columbus. TRV

All my favourite characters have been. Mythology. Lawrence Durrell. DTC
All My Heart This Night Rejoices. Paul Gerhardt, *tr. fr. German by* Catherine Winkworth. MaRV; SoP
All my life they have told me. More Letters Found near a Suicide. Frank Horne. BANP
All my love for my sweet. Song. John Hall Wheelock. NP
All My Luve, Leave Me Not. *Unknown.* GoTS
All my past life is mine no more. Love of Life. Earl of Rochester. BWP; CavP; CBV; CEP; CLwM; EG; EiCL; ELP; EnLoPo; FaBoEn; HBV; LiTL; LoBV; MePo; OBEV; OBS; PeRV; PoEL-3; SeCL; SeCV-2; SeEP; TrGrPo; ViBoPo
All my pleasure is in catching of birds. The English Schoolboy. John Heywood. *Fr.* The Play of the Weather. ACP
All My Pretty Ones. Anne Sexton. CoPo
"All My Pretty Ones? Did You Say All?" Bink Noll. ToPo
All my sense thy sweetness gained. Sir Philip Sidney. FCP
All my senses, like beacon's flame. Caelica, LVI. Fulke Greville. EnRePo; InvP; PoEL-1; QFR
All my sheep/ Gather in a heap. Last Words before Winter. Louis Untermeyer. GoTP; MAP; MoAmPo; NeMA
All my stars forsake me. Song of the Night at Daybreak. Alice Meynell. CH; PoVP; VA
All my thoughts always speak to me of love. Divided Thoughts. Dante. *Fr.* La Vita Nuova. AWP; OnPM
All names I will not mention, as you may understand. Lumberjacks and Teamsters. *Unknown.* OuSiCo
All nature has a feeling: woods, fields, brooks. Eternity of Nature. John Clare. StP
All Nature Has a Voice to Tell. J. Gilchrist Lawson. BLRP
All nature is a temple where the alive. Correspondences. Baudelaire. AWP; LiTW
All Nature seems at work. Slugs leave their lair. Work without Hope. Samuel Taylor Coleridge. BEL; BoNaP; BoTP, 4 *ll.*; CABA; EnLi-2; EnRP; EPN; ERoP-1; FiP; HBV; ILP; LoBV; MaPo (1969 ed.); MBW-2; NoP; OBEV; OBRV; OQP; PG; Sonn; YAT, 6 *ll.*
All Nature Sings. Phyllis C. Michael. SoP
All Needs Met. J. H. Sammis. BLRP
All night a noise of leaping fish. The Fisher. Roderic Quinn. BoAV; PoAu-1
All night and all day the wind roared in the trees. Mid-Country Blow. Theodore Roethke. BoNaP
All night around the Thorn Tree. The Fairy Tree. Temple Lane. StJW
All night between my dreams the thought of you. Flight. Helen Frazee-Bower. *Fr.* Two Married. HBMV
All Night by the Rose. *Unknown.* CBEP; NoP
(Rose's Scent, The.) WiR
All night fell hammers, shock on shock. A London Fete. Coventry Patmore. NBM; PeVV
All night had shout of men and cry. Easter Night. Alice Meynell. ChIP; OHIP; StJW
All night he sits and plays at solitaire. Expatriate. Mary Brown Onstott. PoMa
All night I could not sleep. A "Tzu-yeh" Song. *Unknown.* OnPM
All night I hear the hammers. The Students of Justice. W. S. Merwin. NaP
All Night I Heard. Gertrude MacGregor Moffat. CaP
All night I lie awake and hear. Remembering. "Michael Lewis." *Fr.* Cherry Blossoms. UnTE
All night I muse, all day I cry. Sighs. *Unknown.* LO; SeCL
All night I raced the moon. Laurence Dakin. *Fr.* Tancred, II, i. CaP
All night I thought on those wise men who took. Twelfth Night. John Peale Bishop. UnPo (3d ed.)
All night I watched awake for morning. Dawn-Angels. Agnes Mary Frances Robinson. HBV; VA
All night I wearied utterly of the pillow of darkness. In a Wood Clearing. Wilson MacDonald. CaP
All night, in May, dogs barked in the hollow woods. Eidolon. Robert Penn Warren. FiMAP; TDP
All Night Long, *with music. Unknown.* AS
All night long and every night. Young Night Thought. Robert Louis Stevenson. GaP; NeHB; RIS
All night long into my sleeping bag's head pad the blood. The Far Side of Introspection. Al Lee. CoAP
All night long the window. Night, Window, Wind. Jack Anderson. ThO
All night long through the starlit air and the stillness. The Cattle of His Hand. Wilbur Underwood. AA; WGRP
All night rain fell. The Old Adam. William Rose Benét. YaD
All night the crickets chirp. Crickets at Dawn. Leonora Speyer. PFY
All night the men whipped the dead horse and then. Parable. Peggy Bennett. ELU
All night the small feet of the rain. April. Dora Sigerson Shorter. HBMV; HBVY
All night the sound had. The Rain. Robert Creeley. CoAP
All night the water has worked without pause. The Cocks. Boris Pasternak. LiTW
All night the wind swept over the house. Winter Morning. William Jay Smith. BoNaP
All night there had sought in vain. The Reminder. Léonie Adams. MoVE
All night they marched, the infantrymen under pack. 1935. Stephen Vincent Benét. MAP; MoAmPo; NeMA
All night they toiled, those men of Galilee. Launch Out into the Deep. Ida Norton Munson. ChIP
All night they whine upon their ropes and boom. Nocturne of the Wharves. Arna Bontemps. BANP; PoNe (1970 ed.)
All night under the moon. For G. W. W. Gibson. LO
All night upon the guarded hill. The Defence of Lawrence. Richard Realf. MC; PAH
All night, without the gates of slumber lying. On a Steamship. Upton Sinclair. MaRV
All of a sudden bicycles are toys. A Certain Age. Phyllis McGinley. NePoAm-2
All of a sudden the big nasturtiums. The Big Nasturtiums. Robert Beverly Hale. BoNaP; NYBP; PoMS; SiTL
All of Her. Samuel L. Albert. NePoAm-2
All of the Fruits Had Fallen. Delmore Schwartz. OPoP
All of them the wind took, all of them the light lured. Alone. Hayyim Nahman Bialik. TrJP
All of Us Always Turning Away for Solace. Delmore Schwartz. The Repetitive Heart, I. OxBA
All One in Christ. John Oxenham. *See* No East or West.
All One People. Carl Sandburg. AmFN
All or Nothing. Congreve. MeWo
All other joys of life he strove to warm. Modern Love, IV. George Meredith. GTBS-D; OAEP; VA; ViPo; VP
All Our Griefs to Tell. John Newton. BePJ
All Our Joy Is Enough. Geoffrey Scott. OBMV
All our stones like as much sun as possible. Forecast. Josephine Miles. CrMA
All out of doors looked darkly in at him. An Old Man's Winter Night. Robert Frost. AmPP; AnAmPo; AnEnPo; AnNE; AWP; BoLiVe; CoBA; HBMV; JAWP; MAP; MoAB; MoAmPo; MoVE; MWA-2; NP; OnPP; OxBA; PoMa; WBP
All over America railroads ride through roses. Landscape as Metal and Flowers. Winfield Townley Scott. AmFN; GoJo; HoPM; MiAP
All-over Love. Abraham Cowley. *Fr.* The Mistress. LiTL; SeCL
All over the earth are roads. Alone. Hermann Hesse. TwGP
All Over the World. Geoffrey Johnson. HaMV
All over the world. Waiting Mothers. Ann Zucker. PEDC
All over the world, I wonder, in lands that I never have trod. Meditations of a Hindu Prince. Sir Alfred Comyn Lyall. VA; WGRP
All over this unsettled country, bands/ Of wild and unowned horses roam. Wild Horse Jerry's Story. Sarah Elizabeth Howard. PoOW
All overgrown by cunning moss. For Charlotte Brontë. Emily Dickinson. CoBA
All own the young Silvia is fatally fair. Young Silvia. ——De la Sale. SeCL
All passes. Art alone. Austin Dobson, *after* Théophile Gautier. *Fr.* Ars Victrix. CTC
All Paths Lead to You. Blanche Shoemaker Wagstaff. BLPA; FaBoBe; NeHB
All peacefully gliding. The Rapid. Charles Sangster. CaP; WHW
All people that on earth do dwell. The Hundredth Psalm [*or* Old Hundredth *or* Scotch Te Deum]. William Kethe. MaRV; OtMeF; SoP; WGRP
All perished—brides and infants. Song of a Jewish Boy. "M. J." TrJP

All-powerful Ruler of angels, The. Fall of Angels and of Man. Cædmon(?). *Fr.* Genesis. PoLi
All Praise. Stanley Crouch. WSL
All praise to him of Nazareth. Communion Hymn. Bryant. SoP
All praise to Jesus' hallowed name. Praise to Jesus. Martin Luther. SoP
All praise to Thee, my God, this night. An Evening Hymn. Thomas Ken. OBS
All Quiet along [*or* on] the Potomac. Ethel Lynn Beers. *See* Picket-Guard, The.
All Revelation. Robert Frost. BWP; CABA; MoPo; NePA
All right: and with that wry acceptance you follow the cow-track. The Dogwood. Robert Penn Warren. *Fr.* Dark Woods. PoDB
All right. I may have lied to you and about you. Love 20 cents the First Quarter Mile. Kenneth Fearing. MeWo
All right, I was Welsh. Does it matter? A Welsh Testament. R. S. Thomas. POTi; ToPo
All right now, boys. Sis Joe. *Unknown*. OuSiCo
All roads that lead to God are good. The Goal. Ella Wheeler Wilcox. MaRV; OQP
All rose before the aged apparition. The Apparition. Blake. *Fr.* America. BoW
All round the horizon black clouds appear. On a Sea-Storm nigh the Coast. Richard Steere. SCAP
All Ruin Is the Same. Emanuel Litvinoff. WaP
All Saints'. Edmund Yates. BOHV; HBV; SiTL
All saints revile her, and all sober men. The White Goddess. Robert Graves. MoBrPo (1962 ed.); PoIE
All Scottish legends did his fancy fashion. Robert Burns. William Alexander. HBV
All Seasons in One. *Unknown*. MeWo; TrGrPo
(“April is in my mistress' face.”) CBV; EG; OBSC; ReEn; SiCE
All Seasons Shall Be Sweet. Samuel Taylor Coleridge. *Fr.* Frost at Midnight. BoTP
All-seeing Gods, The. Longfellow. *Fr.* The Masque of Pandora. OQP
All Service Ranks the Same with God. Robert Browning. *Fr.* Pippa Passes, Introd. BEL; MaRV; OQP; TreFT
(God's View of Service.) SoP
(Service.) TrGrPo; TSW
(Song: “All service ranks the same with God.”) LoBV
All silence says music will follow. Onion Bucket. Lorenzo Thomas. BF
All singers have shadows. The Green Singer. Shaw Neilson. BoAu
All smatterers are more brisk and pert. Smatterers. Samuel Butler. BOHV
All sorts of grain which our land doth yield. The Plymouth Harvest. William Bradford. PCH
All Souls. Liboria E. Romano. FiSC
All-Souls' Day. Siegfried Sassoon. MoRP
All souls enact an image of their dream. Chartres Cathedral. Donald C. Babcock. NYTB
All Souls' Eve. Mary E. Mannix. GoBC
All Souls' Night. Frances Cornford. Two Poems, II. EnLoPo
All Souls' Night. Dora Sigerson Shorter. VA
All Souls' Night. W. B. Yeats. *Fr.* A Vision. MoVE; ReMP
All souls that struggle and aspire. Whittier. *Fr.* The Shadow and the Light. TrPWD
All strangest things the multitudinous years. Universal Change. Sophocles. *Fr.* Ajax. LiTW
All such proclivities are tabulated. The Quiet Glades of Eden. Robert Graves. ErPo
All suddenly a stormy whirlwind blew. The Mask of Cupid. Spenser. *Fr.* The Faerie Queene, III. OBSC
All-sufficient Christ, The. Bernice W. Lubke. BLRP
All summer long the people knelt. At the President's Grave. Richard Watson Gilder. PAH
All summer watch the children in the public garden. A Prospect of Children. Lawrence Durrell. *Fr.* Eight Aspects of Melissa. NeBP
All Sung. Richard Le Gallienne. OBVV
All that a man might ask, thou hast given me, England. A Petition. Robert Ernest Vernède. InP
All that blesses the step of the antelope. “Else a Great Prince in Prison Lies.” Denise Levertov. NaP
All That Glisters Is Not Gold. Shakespeare. *Fr.* The Merchant of Venice, II, vii. CTC
All That Glitters Is Not Gold. *Unknown*. TreFT
All that have two or but one ear. The Four-legg'd Quaker. *Unknown*. CoMu
All, that he came to give. A Friend. Lionel Johnson. HBV; JKCP
All that I am to Earth belongs. Life's Testament, XI. William Baylebridge. BoAV; PoAu-1
All that I ask. My Desk. Humbert Wolfe. YT
All that I do is clumsy and ill timed. The Double-Goer [or Doppelganger]. Daryl Hine. MoCV; OBCV
All that I dream. Sunset on the Spire. Elinor Wylie. CoBA
All that I got from love. A Poem about Love. G. S. Fraser. NeBP
All that I had I brought. Exchanges. Ernest Dowson. OBMV
All that I know / Of a certain star. My Star. Robert Browning. BEL; BoLiVe; EPN; EvOK; FaPON; HBV; MBW-2; OAEP; OTPC (1946 ed.); PoVP; StaSt; TOP; TrGrPo; UnPo (1st ed.); ViPo; ViPP
All that I know of you is that you wore. The True Romance. Herbert Jones. HBMV
All that I may swynk of swet. Care Away. *Unknown*. OxBoLi
All that in this wide world we see. “I Will Send Them Prophets and Apostles.” Bryant. SoP
All That Is, and Can Delight. Robert Farren. OxBI
All That Is Left. Basho, *tr. fr. Japanese by* Curtis Hidden Page. WaaP
(“Old battle field, fresh with spring flowers again.”) AWP; LiTW; PoPo
All That Is Lovely in Men. Robert Creeley. NaP
All that is moulded of iron. Woodworkers' Ballad. Herbert Edward Palmer. HaMV; OBEV (new ed.)
All That Matters. Edgar A. Guest. ATP
All That Matters. Walter Sorell. GoYe
All that matters is to be at one with the living God. Pax. D. H. Lawrence. MaRV
All that night I walked alone and wept. Gethsemane. Arna Bontemps. CDC
All that remains for me. Envoi. Arthur Symons. UnTE
All That Summer. Lora Dunetz. NePoAm-2
All that was beautiful and just. In the Streets of Catania. Roger Casement. AnIV
All That Was Mortal. Sara Teasdale. MoRP
All that we know of April is her way. Acquaintance. David Morton. MCCG
All that we say returns. Recompense. John Richard Moreland. OQP
All that we see, about, abroad. On the Universality and Other Attributes of the God of Nature. Philip Freneau. AmePo; AmP; AP; ForPo
All that which Egypt whilom did devise. Ruins of Rome, VIII. Joachim du Bellay. OnPM
All that which lies outside our sort of why. Objects. W. H. Auden. NePoAm-2
All That's Bright Must Fade. Thomas Moore. OxBI
All That's Past. Walter de la Mare. AnFE; CoBE; GoJo; InP; MoAB; NP; OAEP (2d ed.); OBMV; PG (1945 ed.); POTE; SeCeV; ShBV-4; StP; ThWaDe; TreFT; TrGrPo; ViBoPo; WHA
All the afternoon there has been a chirping of birds. Free Fantasia on Japanese Themes. Amy Lowell. MAP; MoAmPo
All the animals in my poems go into the ark. Prologue. Jon Silkin. PoDB
All the apostles of freedom, I've hated them all my life. Goethe. *Fr.* Venetian Epigrams. PoFr
All the beauty and the grandeur. I Thank Thee, Lord. Myra Brooks Welch. SoP
All the bells of heaven may ring. A Child's Laughter. Swinburne. EPN; HBV; PoLF; PoVP; PRWS; TOP
All the bells were ringing. The Broken Doll. Christina Rossetti. *Fr.* Sing-Song. MPB; TiPo
All the birds have come again. Spring's Arrival. *Unknown*. FaPON
All the boys of merry Lincoln. Hugh of Lincoln. *Unknown*. ACP
All the breath and the bloom of the year in the bag of one bee. Summum Bonum. Robert Browning. BoLP; CBV;

All (continued)
ELU; EnLi-2 (1949 ed.); EPN; GTSL; HBV; LiTL; NeHB; OHFP; PG (1955 ed.); PoVP; TIHL; YAT
All the Cats. Kate Greenaway. *See* Cats Have Come to Tea, The.
All the complicated details. Winter Trees. William Carlos Williams. NP
All the earth a hush of white. Nocturne. Amelia Josephine Burr. HBV
All the Farewells. Byron Vazakas. MoPo
All the flowers are sleeping. Blue Jay. Hilda Conkling. BiS
All the Flowers of the Spring. John Webster. *Fr.* The Devil's Law Case. AtBAP; CBEP; EG; ElL; ELP; ExPo; GTBS-W; LiTB; LiTG; OBS; PoEL-2; PoFS; PoRA; SiCE; ViBoPo
(Burial, The.) CH; LoBV
(Nets to Catch the Wind.) TrGrPo
(Song: "All the flowers of the spring.") HBV
(Speech by Romelio.) PoIE
(Vanitas Vanitatum.) BEL; OBEV; PoFR, 4 *ll.*
All the forms are fugitive. Emerson. *Fr.* Woodnotes, II. WGRP
All the foul fiends and demons of the air. Static. Rolfe Humphries. UnS
All the full-moon night in the coomb. In the Night of the Full Moon. Carl Busse. AWP
All the glorious Spring makes me color blind. Sorrow. Marie Tello Phillips. GoYe
All the grass/ dies. A Night Sky. Robert Creeley. FRC
All the Heaven. Petronius, *tr. fr. Latin by* Walter K. Kelly. OnPM
All the Hills and Vales Along. Charles Hamilton Sorley. EnLit; FaBoCh; HBMV; MMA; MoBrPo
(Route March.) POTE
All the Hosts of Heaven. Simeon ben Isaac ben Abun of Mainz, *tr. fr. Hebrew by* Nina Davis Salaman. TrJP
All the inventions that the world contains. Inventions. Samuel Butler. CBV; PV
All the islands have run away. Islands. Rachel Field. GFA
All the Little Hoofprints. Robinson Jeffers. Po
All the long August afternoon. In August. William Dean Howells. AmePo; GN; PoRL
All the long forenoon, the loitering of insects. The Forenoon. Christopher Middleton. *Fr.* Herman Moon's Hourbook. NePoEA-2
All the long night. The Happy Farmer. Tse Nan. OnPM
All the long school-hours, round the irregular hum. A Snowy Day in School. D. H. Lawrence. FIW
All the maidens are in the street! Apart. *Unknown.* OnPM
All the materials of a poem. Lumber of Spring. Anne Ridler. NYBP
All the names I know from nurse. The Flowers. Robert Louis Stevenson. FaPON; MPB
All the night/ And all day long. Blacksmith. B. K. Pyke. BoTP
All the night in woe. The Little Girl Found. Blake. *Fr.* Songs of Experience. CBEP; DiPo
All the night sleep came not upon my eyelids. Sapphics. Swinburne. AnEnPo; Po; PoEL-5; PoVP; TOP; ViPo
All the night they heard birds passing. The Night before America. Norma Farber. FOL
All the others translate: the painter sketches. The Composer. W. H. Auden. MuSP; PoPo; UnS
All the paths of the Lord are lovingkindness and truth. *Fr.* Psalm XXV, Bible, *O.T.* BoC
All the people in my poems walk into the dark. Epilogue. Jon Silkin. PoDB
All the Pretty Little Horses. *Unknown.* ABF, *with music*; OxBoLi
All the promises of the world are lies. The Promises of the World. Moses ibn Ezra. *Fr.* The World's Illusion. TrJP
All the Road to Egypt. Katharine Lee Bates. ChrBoLe
All the Roary Night. Kenneth Patchen. LiTM (1970 ed.)
All the Robin Redbreasts. Valentines to My Mother (1885). Christina Rossetti. BoChLi; DD
All the roses are but one rose. The Only Rose. Juan Ramón Jiménez. OnPM
All the Saturdays met one day. The Saturdays' Party in Fairyland. Mary Carolyn Davies. TVC
All the Scenes of Nature Quicken. Christopher Smart. ELP
All the selves that have been slain. Fugue. R. A. K. Mason. OnPM
All the skippers o Scarsburgh. Young Allan. *Unknown.* BaBo
All the Smoke. Eli Siegel. CAD; ELU; FiBHP
All the soldiers marching along. Remembering Day. Mary Wright Saunders. DD; HH; OTPC (1946 ed.); PEDC; YeAr
All the starlings in the world. In the Lane. L. A. G. Strong. HaMV
All the storm has rolled away. On the Bridge. Arthur Reed Ropes. VA
All the streets are a-shine with rain. Rain in the City. Rachel Field. GFA
All the time they were praying. The Death Bed. Waring Cuney. CDC; PoNe
All the Tree's Hands. Jeannette Nichols. MeWo
All the trees they are so high. The Trees So High. *Unknown.* OBB; OxBoLi; SiTL
All the voices of the wood called "Muriel!" Then I Saw What the Calling Was. Muriel Rukeyser. FiMAP
All the way back, the moon. The Moon. Kotomichi. OnPM
All the Way My Saviour Leads Me. Fanny J. Crosby. SoP; STF
All the way to Tir na n'Og are many roads that run. The King of Ireland's Son. Nora Hopper. AnIL
All the whole world is living without war. Canzone: He Speaks of His Condition through Love. Forcachiero de' Folcachieri. AWP
All the wide air was trawled for cloud. L'Ile du Levant; the Nudist Colony. Barbara Howes. NePoAm-2; PoCh
All the wise men that ever were, by aught that I can witness. Poverty Not All Loss. William Langland. *Fr.* The Vision of Piers Plowman. PoLi
All the woods are now in flower. The Wooing. *Unknown.* UnTE
All the words that I utter. Where My Books Go. W. B. Yeats. OBEV; OBVV
All the World. *Unknown, tr. fr. Hebrew by* Israel Zangwill. TrJP
All the World Moved. June Meyer. NBP
All the world over, I wonder, in lands that I never have trod. Meditations of a Hindu Prince. Sir Alfred Comyn Lyall. VA; WGRP
All the world over, nursing their scars. Kipling. BoPe
All the world shall come to serve Thee. All the World. *Unknown.* TrJP
All the World's a Stage. Sir Walter Ralegh. *See* On the Life of Man.
All the World's a Stage. Shakespeare. *Fr.* As You Like It, II, vii. DiPo; FiP; GoTP; LiTB; LiTG; MasP; PoLF; PoSa; TIHL; TrGrPo; YAT
(Seven Ages of Man, The.) FaFP; GTBS-W; OQP; PoPo; PTK; TreF
All the year we travel. The Crossroads. Catherine Parmenter. PEDC
All the young men. Mediocracy. Caryll Houselander. JKCP (1955 ed.)
All their lives in a box! What generations. The Silkworms. Douglas Stewart. AnMoPo; FIW; PoAu-2
All these and more came flocking; but with looks/ Down-cast. Mustering the Hosts of Hell. Milton. *Fr.* Paradise Lost, I. MyFE
All these are your essence, you are their flesh and their force. Dick Diespecker. *Fr.* Between Two Furious Oceans. CaP
All These Birds. Richard Wilbur. FiMAP; Po
All these borders—/ they/ bug me! Against Borders. Yevgeny Yevtushenko. CAD
All these maneuverings to avoid. Love's Stratagems. Donald Justice. NYBP
All these numbers, several are possibly aghast. James Brodey. *Fr.* Identikit. ANYP
All these on whom the sacred seal was set. An Unbeliever. Anna Hempstead Branch. MaRV; PFY; WGRP
All these things are in my mind also, lady; but I fear still. Hektor to Andromache. Homer. *Fr.* The Iliad, VI. WaaP
All these years behind windows. The Animals. W. S. Merwin. FRC
All these years I have remembered a night. Grievance. Amy Lowell. ViBoPo (1941 ed.)
All things announce her coming and her praise. Celebration of

Love. James McAuley. MoAuPo
All Things Are a Flowing. R. P. Blackmur. TwAmPo
All things are best when first begun. I Love the Beginning of All Rain. Geoffrey Scott. POTE
All things are changed save thee—thou art the same. To the Spirit of Poetry. Philip Bourke Marston. VA
All Things Are Current Found. Henry David Thoreau. *Fr.* A Week on the Concord and Merrimack Rivers. AnNE; OnPM; ViBoPo; WoL
All things are doubly fair. Art. Théophile Gautier, *tr. by* George Santayana. AWP; JAWP; LiTW; WBP; WoL
All things are hushed, as Nature's self lay dead. Midnight. Dryden. ACP
All Things Are Thine. Whittier. SoP, *abr.*
All things are wonderful to him. The Eyes of Wonder. Jessie Corrigan Pegis. JKCP (1955 ed.)
All Things Be Dear but Poor Mens Labour; or The Sad Complaint of Poor People. "L. W." CoMu
All Things Bright and Beautiful. Cecil Frances Alexander. BoChLi (1950 ed.); MaRV; NeHB; OHIP; PRWS; SoP; StVeCh; ThGo; TVC, *abr.*
(All Things Beautiful, *abr.*) PEDC
(Creation, The.) FaPON; OTPC
All things burn with the fire of God. Revelation. Verne Bright. BLRP; OQP; WBLP
All Things Can Tempt Me. W. B. Yeats. CMoP
All things change, we are told, in this world of change and sorrow. Four Folk-Songs in Hokku Form, 3. *Unknown.* LiTW
All Things Drink. Thomas Stanley, *after the Greek of* Anacreon. *See* Fruitful Earth Drinks Up the Rain.
All Things except Myself I Know. Villon, *tr. fr. French by* Henry Carrington. BOHV
All things find their road. The bee its hive. Puzzle. Sidney Cooksley. NYTB
All things God can do, but this thing He will not. Judgment and Mercy. Dorothy L. Sayers. *Fr.* The Devil to Pay. MaRV
All Things Have Savour [*or* Savor]. *Unknown.* LiTG; SiTL
All things he saw, even to the ends of the earth. Gilgamesh. *Tr. by* William Ellery Leonard. WoL
All Things in Jesus. J. Danson Smith. SoP
All things journey: sun and moon. Song of the Zincali. "George Eliot." *Fr.* The Spanish Gypsy. VA
All Things Must Have an End: The World Itself. Longfellow. AmePo
All things return, Nietzsche said. The Recurrence. Edwin Muir. MoPo
All things shall die and decay, but the kingdom of Allah endureth. His Face is Forever. *Unknown.* OnPM
All things that are on earth shall wholly pass away. The Love of God. Bernard Rascas, *tr. by* Bryant. CAW; WGRP
All things that go deep enough. The Ice Skin. James Dickey. NYBP
All things that pass. Passing and Glassing. Christina Rossetti. FaBoEn; OBNC; VA
All things turned to Orpheus' hand. The Greater Music. Theodore Weiss. NePoAm-2
All things uncomely and broken, all things worn out and old. The Lover [*or* Aedh] Tells of the Rose in His Heart. W. B. Yeats. BrPo; CMoP; CoBE; EnLi-2 (1949 ed.); MoBrPo; ViBoPo; ViPo (1962 ed.)
All Things Wait upon Thee. Christina Rossetti. GN
All things whate'er they be. Being Underived. Dante, *tr. by* Longfellow. *Fr.* Divina Commedia: Paradiso. CAW
All things within this fading world hath end. Before the Birth of One of Her Children. Anne Bradstreet. MAmP
All this indigo, nonviolent light will triumph. Sunday Evenings. John Hollander. NYBP
All this is one. My Faith. Ananda Acharya. WGRP
All this is vanity. Peace. Brian Vrepont. BoAu
All this night shrill chanticleer. Chanticleer [*or* Carol]. William Austin. OxBoCh; SeCL
All this (said she) we know. Achilles Shows Himself in the Battle by the Ships. Homer. *Fr.* The Iliad, XVIII. OBS
All this smacking. Just a Smack at Smacking. *Unknown.* SiTL
All This Sunday Long. B. S. Johnson. ELU
All This World's Riches. Spenser. *See* Amoretti, XV.
All those dark days in spring when we would sew. Compensation. Ruth Comfort Mitchell. PEDC
All those Germans. Some Europeans. *Unknown.* SiTL
All Those Hymnings up to God. Abbie Huston Evans. MoRP
All those that do but rob and steal enough. The Law. Samuel Butler. CBV
All those treasures that lie in the little bolted box whose tiny space is. Slow Movement. William Carlos Williams. NP
All those who journey, soon or late. Gethsemane. Ella Wheeler Wilcox. MaRV; OQP
All those who knew you are dispersed or dead. Sestina for Khasan Israelov. John Wain. *Fr.* Wildtrack. ToPo
All those who seek Thee tempt Thee. I Would Comprehend Thee. Rainer Maria Rilke. OnPM
All those years that you ate and changed. Peasant. W. S. Merwin. NYBP
All thoughts, all passions, all delights. Love. Samuel Taylor Coleridge. BEL; BeLS; ChER; EnRP; EPN; ERoP-1; GTBS; GTBS-D; GTBS-P; GTBS-W; GTSE; GTSL; HBV; LiTL; LoBV; OAEP; OBEV; TOP; TreFT
All thro' the breathing night there seemed to flow. A Venetian Night. Hugo von Hofmannsthal. AWP; JAWP; WBP
All thro' the Year. *Unknown.* BLRP
All through an empty place I go. The Loss of Love. Countee Cullen. PoNe
All through life I see a cross. The Christian Paradox. Walter Chalmers Smith. MaRV
All through that summer at ease we lay. The Castle. Edwin Muir. LiTB
All through the garden I went and went. The Butterbean Tent. Elizabeth Madox Roberts. GoJo; StVeCh; SUS
All through the golden weather. A Song of Autumn. Sir Rennall Rodd. HBV
All through the Night ("Sleep, my love, and peace attend thee"). Harold Boulton. TreFS
All through the Night ("Sleep, my babe, lie still and slumber"). *Unknown.* FaPON
(Welsh Lullaby.) GoTP
All through the night in silence they come and go. Charing Cross. Cecil Roberts. HBMV
All through the night the happy sheep. The Happy Sheep. Wilfrid Thorley. GFA; PCH; SoPo
All through the Stranger's Wood. Isaac Leibush Peretz, *tr. fr. Yiddish by* Joseph Leftwich. TrJP
All through the sultry hours of June. My Thrush. Mortimer Collins. HBV; OTPC (1923 ed.)
All through the windless night the clipper rolled. John Masefield. *Fr.* Dauber, VI. AnFE; CMoP
All told the gray world. The Tall Toms. Edwin Honig. NePA
All Too Slowly. Lucia Trent. ChIP
All travail of high thought. The Beginnings of Faith. Sir Lewis Morris. WGRP
All travellers at first incline. Stella's Birthday, 1720. Swift. ILP; OxBI; PoEL-3
All trees, all leavy groves confesse the spring. Out of Virgil, In the Praise of the Spring. Richard Crashaw. MaMe
All truths wait in all things. Walt Whitman. Song of Myself, XXX. PFY
All Turns into Yesterday. *Unknown.* MeEL
All uncompelled, weightless as the notes. Cædmon. George Garrett. NePoAm-2
All under the leaves, and the leaves of life. Seven Virgins, The. *Unknown.* CH; ChTr; OBB; OBEV; OxBoCh
All unseen the Master walketh. My Grace is Sufficient for Thee. *Unknown.* BePJ
All up and down in shadow-town. The Shadows. Frank Dempster Sherman. AA
All Virgil's idylls end in sunsets; pale. The Voice. Edmund Wilson. NYBP
All visible, visibly. Runner. W. H. Auden. SD
All wars are planned by old men. Two Sides of War. Grantland Rice. TreFT
All was as it was when I went in. Apopemptic Hymn. Dorothy Auchterlonie. PoAu-2
All was for you: and you are dead. Beyond. Lionel Johnson. BrPo
All was play, all was sport. *Unknown.* *Fr.* The Combat of Ferdiad and Cuchulain. OnYI
All we have achieved, the machine threatens to rule. Sonnets to

All (continued)
Orpheus, Pt. II, X. Rainer Maria Rilke, *tr. by* Jessie Lemont. OnPM
All we have gained the machine threatens. Sonnets to Orpheus, Pt. II, X. Rainer Maria Rilke, *tr. by* M. D. Herter Norton. PoFr
All we have is God's, and yet. Give to Caesar. Richard Crashaw. MaMe
All we make is enough. All Our Joy Is Enough. Geoffrey Scott. OBMV
All week, the maid tells me, bowing. A Walk in Kyoto. Earle Birney. GoYe
All were too little for the merchant's hand. Seven Sonnets in Sequence, V. George Gascoigne. Sonn
All who have and have all can cry: "Peace!" Editorial Poem On An Incident Of Effects Far-Reaching. Russell Atkins. NBP
All who have loved, be sure of this from me. Richard Watson Dixon. *Fr.* Love's Consolation. OBNC
All will go right—will go right—will go right. *Unknown. Fr.* Ça ira! PoFr
All windows open, moths. Three Part Invention. Paul Blackburn. CoPo
All winter long you listened for the boom. The Stoic: for Laura von Courten. Edgar Bowers. CoAP; NePoEa; QFR
All winter through I bow my head. The Scarecrow. Walter de la Mare. MoBrPo; ShBV-1
All wisdom and renown are worth. Summer Interlude. Lionel Stevenson. CaP
All women born are so perverse. Triolet. Robert Bridges. HBV; PoVP; PV; SeCePo
All women loved dance in a dying light. They Sing. Theodore Roethke. *Fr.* The Dying Man. NYBP; PoDB
All Wool. Abbie Farwell Brown. TiPo (1952 ed.)
All work and no play makes Jack a dull boy. *Unknown.* OxNR
All worldly shapes shall melt in gloom. The Last Man. Thomas Campbell. EnRP; OBRV
All ye poets of the age. Namby-Pamby. Henry Carey. Par
All Ye That Go Astray. Moses ibn Ezra, *tr. fr. Hebrew by* Solomon Solis-Cohen. *Fr.* The World's Illusion. TrJP
All ye that handle harp and viol and pipe. Chorus. Moses Hayyim Luzzatto of Padua. *Fr.* Unto the Upright Praise. TrJP
All ye that lovely lovers be. Harvester's Song. George Peele. *Fr.* The Old Wives' Tale. TrGrPo
All Ye That Pass. Dante, *tr. fr. Italian by* Dante Gabriel Rossetti. La Vita Nuova, II. LiTW
("All ye that pass along Love's trodden way.") AWP; JAWP; WBP
"All Ye That Pass By." John Masefield. CMoP
All ye that passe by this holy place. A Second Epitaph. *Unknown.* MeEL
All ye who love the springtime. The Dawning o' the Year. Mary Elizabeth McGrath Blake. AA
All ye woods, and trees, and bowers. The God of Sheep [*or* To Pan]. John Fletcher. *Fr.* The Faithful Shepherdess, V, v. EIL; FaBoCh; LoGBV; TrGrPo
All yee forsaken lovers come & pitty my distress. *Unknown.* SeCSL
All you lords of Scottland ffaire. Tom Potts. *Unknown.* ESPB
All you on emigration bent. The Settler's Lament. *Unknown.* PoAu-1
All you possessed with indepressed spirits. Hymnus in Noctem. George Chapman. *Fr.* The Shadow of Night. TuPP
All you that are enamored of my name. Demos. E. A. Robinson. AP; NP
All you that are to mirth inclin'd, come tarry here a little while. The Country Girl's Policy; or, The Cockney Outwitted. *Unknown.* CoMu
All you that delight to spend some time. Little John a Begging. *Unknown.* BaBo; ESPB (B *vers.*); ESPB
All you that desire to here of a jest. The Unfortunate Miller; or, The Country Lasses Witty Invention. *Unknown.* CoMu; OxBB
All you that pass along. The Dumb Maid. *Unknown.* CoBE
All you that to feasting and mirth are inclined. Old Christmas Returned. *Unknown.* GN; OHIP
All you that weep, all you that mourn. Resurrexit. Henry Longan Stuart. CAW
All you violated ones with gentle hearts. For Malcolm X. Margaret Walker. BP
All young men should take note of the case. Limerick. M. B. Thornton. LiBL
All Your Fortunes We Can Tell Ye. Ben Jonson. *Fr.* The Gypsies Metamorphosed. ChTr
All yow that crye O hone! O hone! A Lementable New Ballad upon the Earle of Essex Death. *Unknown.* CoMu
Allá en El Rancho Grande, *with music. Unknown, tr. fr. Spanish.* ABF
Allace depairting, grund of wo. *Unknown.* OxBS
Allace! So Sobir Is the Micht. Mersar. OxBS
Allah. Siegfried August Mahlmann, *tr. fr. German by* Longfellow. AWP
Allah. *Unknown, tr. fr. Arabic by* Sir Edwin Arnold. OnPM
Allah Akbar!/ All things vanish after brief careering. Night Is Nearing. James Clarence Mangan, *after the Persian.* IrPN
"Allah!" Bi-'smi-'llah! Say that God is one. Allah. *Unknown.* OnPM
Allah gives light in darkness. Allah. Siegried August Mahlmann. AWP
Allah, the Artificer. *Unknown, tr. fr. Arabic by* Sir Edwin Arnold. OnPM
Allah's Tent. Arthur Colton. HBV
Allalu Mo Wauleen. *Unknown.* AnIV
Allan Water. Matthew Gregory Lewis. HBV; OTPC (1923 ed.)
Allas! my worthy maister honorable. Lament for Chaucer. Thomas Hoccleve. *Fr.* De Regimine Principum. OBEV
Allas the Wo! Allas, the peynes stronge. Chaucer. *Fr.* The Canterbury Tales: The Knight's Tale. LO
Allatoona. *Unknown.* PAH
Alle that beth of herte trewe. The Death of King Edward I. *Unknown.* MeEL
Alle Vögel Sind Schon Da. Frances Chesterton. UnS
Allegorical Figure of Brooklyn, The. Tony Towle. ANYP
Allegory of the Adolescent and the Adult. George Barker. LiTB; MasP
Allegra Agonistes. Grace Fallow Norton. NP
Allegro. "McM." InMe
Alleluia! Alleluia! Let the Holy Anthem Rise. *Unknown.* PoSC
Alleluya. Rubén Darío, *tr. fr. Spanish by* Lysander Kemp. TTY
Allen-a-Dale. Sir Walter Scott. *Fr.* Rokeby, III. EnRP; OTPC (1946 ed.); StPo; TOP
Allenby Enters Jerusalem. Stephen Chalmers. PoMa
Allergy. Walker Gibson. NePoAm
Alley Cat. Frank Stevens. CIV
Alley Cat, An. Nancy Byrd Turner. CIV
Alleyway. Salvatore Quasimodo, *tr. fr. Italian by* Jack Bevan. FIW
Alli Veri Figlioli Delle Muse. *Unknown. Fr.* Zepheria. ReIE; TuPP
Alliance of Education and Government, The, *abr.* Thomas Gray. CEP
Alliances. Nathalia Crane. MAP
Allie ("Allie, call the birds in"). Robert Graves. FaPON; GoJo; LOW
Alligator on the Escalator. Eve Merriam. OCS
Allison Gross. *Unknown. See* Alison Gross.
Alliteration; or, The Siege of Belgrade. *Unknown, at. to* Alaric A. Watts. *See* Siege of Belgrade, The.
Allotted a four-by-four square. Sapling. Yvette Johnson. TNV
All's but naught. Shakespeare. *Fr.* Antony and Cleopatra, IV, xv. MemP
All's ill and will be so. The Wind Is Ill. John Malcolm Brinnin. LiTA
All's over, then: does truth sound bitter. The Lost Mistress. Robert Browning. CBEP; FaBoEn; FiP; GTSE; HBV; MeWo; OBEV; OBNC; OBVV; PoVP
All's peace to-day at Beecher Isle. Beecher Island. Arthur Chapman. PoOW
All's Vast. Francis Thompson. *See* Heart, The.
"All's Well!" William Allen Butler. HBV
All's Well. Harriet McEwen Kimball. AA
All's Well. William A. Quayle. MaRV
All's Well. Whittier. CBEP; FaChP; OBVV; SoP
All's Well That Ends Well, *sel.* Shakespeare.

For I the Ballad Will Repeat, *fr.* I, iii. ViBoPo
All's Well That Ends Well ("A friend of mine"). *Unknown.* BOHV; FaFP; SiTL
Allusion to Horace, An. The 10th Satire of the 1st Book. Earl of Rochester. OBS; PeRV; SeEP
Alma Mater. Mary Elizabeth Osborn. NePoAm
Alma Mater. Sir Arthur Quiller-Couch. OBVV
Alma Mater, Forget Me. William Cole. FiBHP
Alma Mater's Roll. Edward Everett Hale. AA
Alma; or, The Progress of the Mind, *sel.* Matthew Prior.
"Matthew met Richard; when or where." EiCP
Alma Redemptoris. *Unknown.* WHL
Alma Redemptoris Mater. *At. to* Hermanus Contractus, *tr. fr. Latin by* Winfred Douglas. ISi
Alma Venus, *sel.* Bernard O'Dowd.
"Door of existence, beacon of our haze." PoAu-1
Almae Matres. Andrew Lang. OBVV; TOP
Almanac, An. James Schuyler. ANYP
Almanac. May Swenson. NYBP
Almanac Verse. Samuel Danforth. SCAP
Almanac Verse. *Unknown.* SCAP
Almanack for the Year of Our Lord, 1657, An. Samuel Bradstreet. SCAP
Almería. "Pablo Neruda," *tr. fr. Spanish by* Angel Flores. LiTW; WaaP
Almightie Judge, how shall poore wretches brook. Judgement. George Herbert. AnAnS-1; MaMe; MeP; SeCP
Almightie Lord, who from thy glorious throne. The Church Militant. George Herbert. MaMe
Almighty, The. Edward Taylor. *See* Preparatory Meditations: "O! What a thing is might. . ."
Almighty and all [*or* al] merciable queen [*or* quene]. An A. B. C. [*or* La Prière de Nostre Dame *or* The Well of Pity.] Chaucer. CoBE; ISi; PoLi
Almighty and all present Power. An Airman's [*or* A Sergeant's] Prayer. Hugh R. Brodie. MaRV; PGD
Almighty and everlasting God, we thank Thee. Prayer for Every Day. *Unknown.* PBA
Almighty Builder, bless, we pray. The Cornerstone. Edward A. Church. MaRV
Almighty crowd, thou shorten'st all dispute. Vox Populi. Dryden. *Fr.* The Medal. OBS; PeRV
Almighty Father, Son, and Holy Ghost. With Thee, O God! Saint Columcille. SoP
Almighty Framer of the skies! A Hymn for Christmas Day. Thomas Chatterton. MaRV; OTPC (1923 ed.)
Almighty God, Fader of Hevene. A Prayer to the Trinity. *Unknown.* MeEL
Almighty God, the Wonderful. That's Jesus! Grace B. Renfrow. BePJ
Almighty God, unchangeable. Prayer to the Crucifix. Mossén Juan Tallante. CAW
Almighty God, Whose Justice Like a Sun. Hilaire Belloc. Sonnets, XXI. TrPWD
Almighty Lord, with One Accord. M. Woolsey Stryker. MaRV
Almighty Maker God! Sincere Praise. Isaac Watts. CEP; TrPWD
Almighty Vigour strove through all the void. Description of Chaos. Sir Richard Blackmore. *Fr.* Prince Arthur. PeRV
Almighty! What Is Man? Solomon ibn Gabirol, *tr. fr. Hebrew by* Emma Lazarus. TrJP
Almighty Wisdom made the land. The Sea Is His. Edward Sandford Martin. EtS
Almond Blossom. Sir Edwin Arnold. GN; HBV; OTPC
Almond Blossom in Wartime. Stephen Spender. ACV
Almond Blossoms. Charles Dalmon. *Fr.* Three Pictures. TSW
Almond groves of Samarkand, The. The East a-Callin'. Oscar Wilde. *Fr.* Ave Imperatrix! OtMeF
Almost. Rachel Field. SUS
Almost a girl it was and issued forth. Four Sonnets to Orpheus. Rainer Maria Rilke, *tr. by* M. D. Herter Norton. *Fr.* Sonnets to Orpheus. LiTW
Almost a girl it was, then, issuing. Rainer Maria Rilke, *tr. by* W. D. Snodgrass. *Fr.* Sonnets to Orpheus. ReMP
Almost afraid they led her in. Transfigured. Sarah Morgan Bryan Piatt. AA
Almost emptied of sound and light. Great Silence. Sister Mary St. Virginia. JKCP (1955 ed.)
Almost happy now, he looked at his estate. Voltaire at Ferney. W. H. Auden. LiTA
Almost Human. C. Day Lewis. CMoP
Almost I, yes, I hear. W. S. Graham. *Fr.* The Dark Dialogues. OxBS
Almost Ninety. Ruth Whitman. NYTB
Almost Revolutionist, The. Tena L. Lockett. WSL
Almost the body leads the laggard soul. Grieve Not for Beauty. Witter Bynner. *Fr.* The New World. NP
Almost-tropic night crept through my door, The. Vampire. Walter H. Kerr. FiSC
Almost tuneless treble, The. That is Tad. Sister Mary Norbert Körte. ThO
Almost two thousand years ago today. Easter Message. John Van Brakle. ChIP
Almost yesterday, those gentle ladies stole. The Lost Ingredient. Anne Sexton. CoPo
Alms, *sel.* Robert Herrick.
"Give, if thou canst, an alms," 2 *ll.* MyFE
Alms in Autumn. Rose Fyleman. PCH
Almswomen. Edmund Blunden. BoPe; GTBS; OBMV; POTE; ShBV-3
Alnwick Castle. Fitz-Greene Halleck. AA
Aloe Plant, The. Henry Harbaugh. BLPA
Aloft he guards the starry folds. The Eagle of the Blue. Herman Melville. AA
Aloft in Heavenly Mansions, Doubleyou One. The Playboy of the Demi-World; 1938. William Plomer. FaBoTw
Aloft, in secret veins of air. Waldeinsamkeit. Emerson. HBV; WGRP
Aloft upon an old basaltic crag. Kane. Fitz-James O'Brien. PAH
Aloft we all must go oh. John Dameray. *Unknown.* ShS
Aloha. William Griffith. HBMV
Aloha Oe. Don Blanding. PoToHe (new ed.)
Alone? William Alexander. SoP
Alone. Hayyim Nahman Bialik, *tr. fr. Hebrew by* Jessie Sampter. TrJP
Alone. Walter de la Mare. ChTr; EnLoPo
Alone. John Farrar. BoChLi; GaP; GFA; MPB; YeAr
Alone. Robert Finch. CaP; PeCV
Alone. Francis Jammes, *tr. fr. French by* J. F. Mullen. CAW
Alone. James Joyce. InvP; NP
Alone. Elsie Laurence. CaP
Alone. Joseph Paget-Fredericks. StVeCh
Alone. Poe. CBV; CLwM; LaNeLa; MAmP; MWA-1; PoSa (From Childhood's Hour.) NePA; PoEL-4
Alone. Sappho, *tr. fr. Greek by* William Ellery Leonard. AWP
(Lonely Night, *tr. by* H. De Vere Stacpoole.) LiTW
(Moon Has Set, The, *tr. unknown.*) ChTr
Alone. Siegfried Sassoon. BoLiVe; MoBrPo; TrGrPo (1942 ed.); WePo; YT
(When I'm Alone.) OBMV; POTE; ShBV-3
Alone. Richard Shelton. NYBP
Alone. *Unknown.* NA
Alone. Carolyn Wells. PoToHe
Alone. Hubert Witheford. AnNZ
Alone?/ In wilderness of lofty, virgin trees. Abraham Lincoln. Francesca Falk Miller. PEDC
Alone, alone, about a dreadful wood. Advent. W. H. Auden. *Fr.* For the Time Being. OAEP (2d ed.)
Alone! Alone! I sit in the solitudes of the moonshades. Alone. *Unknown.* NA
Alone amid the forest of his soul. Alone. Francis Jammes. CAW
Alone by the Hearth. George Arnold. HBV
Alone, dear Lord, in solitude serene. Alone with Him. Alice E. Sherwood. SoP
Alone far in the wilds and mountains I hunt. Song of Myself, X. Walt Whitman. CoBA; SeCeV
Alone God Sufficeth. St. Teresa of Avila, *tr. by* Longfellow. *See* Lines Written in Her Breviary.
Alone I sit at eventide. Our Native Birds. Nathan Haskell Dole. BOHV
Alone I stay; for I am lame. A Board School Pastoral. May Kendall. VA
Alone I walked the ocean strand. A Name in the Sand. Hannah Flagg Gould. AA; SoP
Alone in a cold autumn I stood. Midstream. Mao Tse-Tung. MoCV
Alone, in an Inn (at Southampton). Aaron Hill. EiCL

Alone in April. James Branch Cabell. HBMV
Alone, in silence, at a certain time of night. A Local Train of Thought. Siegfried Sassoon. AtBAP
Alone in the atoning belfry how I grieve. Giotto's Campanile. Guy Butler. PeSA
Alone in the dreary, pitiless street. Nobody's Child. Phila H. Case. TreF
Alone in the hot sun. The Song-Maker. Kingsley Fairbridge. ACV; BoSA
Alone in the night. Stars. Sara Teasdale. BoChLi; FaPON; HBMV; MoRP; NP; PoPo; SP; TiPo; YT
Alone in these woods. The Cloisters. William M. Hoffman. ThO
Alone in this desert under the cold moon. If I Forget Thee. Emanuel Litvinoff. TrJP
Alone into the Mountain. Katharine Lee Bates. ChIP; MaRV; StJW
Alone Lord God, in Whom our trust and peace. Out of the Deep Have I Called unto Thee, O Lord. Christina Rossetti. VP
Alone on Lykaion since man hath been. Mt. Lykaion [*or* Alone on Lykaion]. Trumbull Stickney. AmLP; AnAmPo; AnFE; APA; CoAnAm; MAP; MoAmPo (1942 ed.); MoVE; NePA; OxBA; Sonn; TrGrPo
Alone on the hill where the sun goes down. Box-Car Letters. Karle Wilson Baker. InP
Alone on the lawn. The Dancing Cabman. J. B. Morton. MoShBr; ShBV-4
Alone on the shore in the pause of the nighttime. The Full Heart. Robert Nichols. BoNaP; HBMV
Alone one noon on a sheet of igneous rock. Myths. Guy Butler. BoSA; PeSA
Alone, remote, nor witting where I went. The Altar. E. A. Robinson. PoDB
Alone she feeds the white swans. Swans of Vadstena. Ralph Gustafson. MoCV
Alone the pallid cuckoo now. Pallid Cuckoo. David Campbell. PoAu-2
Alone to sacrifice Thou goest, Lord. Good Friday; the Third Nocturn. Peter Abelard. LiTW
Alone, upon a summer's eve. Swansong on the Moorlands. Steingrímur Thorsteinsson. LiTW
Alone, upon the broad, low bench, he sits. To Borglum's Seated Statue of Abraham Lincoln. B. Jordan. OHIP
Alone upon the housetops to the North. The Love Song of Har Dyal. Kipling. BoPe; GBV; OtMeF
Alone Walking. *Unknown.* CBEP
(Wishing My Death.) MeEL
Alone walking/ And oft musing. The Bailey Beareth the Bell Away. *Unknown.* SeCePo
Alone was I born,/ a comfort to my folk. Christ Tells of His Passion. Cynewulf. *Fr.* Christ. PoLi
Alone we are born/ And die alone. High Country Weather. James K. Baxter. AnNZ
Alone with God. Elizabeth Payson Prentiss. SoP
Alone with God. *Unknown.* SoP
Alone with God for one sweet solemn hour. The Quiet Hour. Louise Hollingsworth Bowman. BLRP
Alone with Him. Alice E. Sherwood. SoP
Alone, yet never lonely. Lindbergh. Aline Michaelis. DD
Along a dustless clay road in wet weather. Leaf Mirrors. James Applewhite. YAP
Along a river-side, I know not where. The Washers of the Shroud. James Russell Lowell. AP; CoBA; HBV; PAH; PAP
Along Ancona's hills the shimmering heat. Poppies in the Wheat. Helen Hunt Jackson. AA; PFY
Along came the F. F. V., the fastest on the line. The Wreck on the C. & O.; or, The Death of Jack Hinton. *Unknown.* ABF
Along Highway 40, blare. The Shape of Autumn. Virginia Russ. GoYe
Along how many Main Streets have I walked. The Eternal Return. Robert Hillyer. NYBP
Along in September comes Toe River Fair. An Episode. Muriel Earley Sheppard. IHA
Along my ways of life you never came. Sonnets, XII. Muna Lee. HBMV; NP
Along Shore. Herbert Bashford. AA
Along the avenue of cypresses. Giorno dei Morti. D. H. Lawrence. BrPo; POTE; SeCePo; ShBV-4
Along the beach the great Achilles went. The Wrath of Achilles. Homer. *Fr.* The Iliad, XIX. BBV (1923 ed.)
Along the black. Night Ride. Sir Herbert Read. BoLP; WePo
Along the blushing borders, bright with dew. Spring Flowers. James Thomson. *Fr.* The Seasons: Spring. AtBAP; OBEC
Along the Brittle Treacherous Bright Streets. E. E. Cummings. NoP
Along the country roadside, stone on stone. Stone Walls. Julie Mathilde Lippmann. AA
Along the dark aisles. The Way of the Cross. Leonard Feeney. WHL
Along the dark and silent night. The Bell-Man. Robert Herrick. CH; OBS; PCD; PoeP
Along the dark wet lanes of golden light. A Drunken Man on Highgate Hill. Paul Hasluck. MoAuPo
Along the earth and up the sky. Pandora's Songs. William Vaughn Moody. *Fr.* The Fire-Bringer. GBV
Along the Field as We Came By. A. E. Housman. A Shropshire Lad, XXVI. CLwM; HBV; LiTL; MasP; MoAB; MoBrPo; OAEP; PoVP; UnTE; ViPo
Along the garden terrace, under which. Modern Love, XXXVII. George Meredith. ViPo; VP
Along the garden ways just now. A Love Symphony. Arthur O'Shaughnessy. HBV
Along the graceless grass of town. A Dead Harvest. Alice Meynell. MoVE
Along the grass sweet airs are blown. A New Year's Burden. Dante Gabriel Rossetti. AtBAP
Along the grave green downs, this idle afternoon. On Scratchbury Camp. Siegfried Sassoon. HaMV
Along the just-returning green. Wonder and a Thousand Springs. William Alexander Percy. HBMV
Along the lane beside the mead. A Pastoral. Norman Gale. HBV
Along the line of smoky hills. Indian Summer. Wilfred Campbell. CaP; OBCV; PoPl; WHW
Along the pastoral ways I go. A Holiday. Lizette Woodworth Reese. AA
Along the path that skirts the wood. The Three Musicians. Aubrey Beardsley. ACP (1926 ed.); JKCP (1926 ed.); MuSP; PeVV
Along the Potomac. Emily Dickinson. *See* When I was small, a woman died.
Along the Rand in eighty-five. Johannesburg. William Plomer. BoSA
Along the rims of outer space. Lord of All. Phyllis C. Michael. SoP
Along the Road. Robert Browning Hamilton. BLPA; NeHB; TreFS
(Pleasure and Sorrow.) MaRV
Along the road. Summer Night. Victor Contoski. ThO
Along the road all shapes must travel by. Prolonged Sonnet. Simone dall' Antella. AWP
Along the roadside, like the flowers of gold. Prelude. Whittier. *Fr.* Among the Hills. AmePo; AP; CoBA; OxBA; PoEL-4; TOP
Along the roof-line, sharp and red. My Jack. John Francis O'Donnell. IrPN
Along the Sacred Road I strolled one day. The Bore. Horace. *Fr.* Satires. ATP
Along the sea-edge, like a gnome. The Sandpiper. Witter Bynner. HBMV
Along the serried coast the Southerly raves. Sea-Grief. Dowell O'Reilly. BoAu; PoAu-1
Along the shore of the Great Bitter Lake. Commandos Embarking. George Whalley. TwCaPo
Along the shore the slimy brine-pits yawn. The Witch's Whelp. Richard Henry Stoddard. AA; AnAmPo
Along the Strand. Alfred Mombert, *tr. fr. German by* Jethro Bithell. TrJP
Along the thousand roads of France. The Good Joan. Lizette Woodworth Reese. FaPON; MoShBr; MPB; SP; TiPo (1952 ed.); WHL
Along the wind-swept platform, pinched and white. Morning Express. Siegfried Sassoon. HaMV; ShBV-3; WePo
Along the woodland path we took. Where You Passed. Amelia Josephine Burr. HBMV
Along these low pleached lanes, on such a day. On a Country Road. Swinburne. *Fr.* A Midsummer Holiday. PoVP; TOP
Along this path he walked, great Washington. At Mount Ver-

non. Thomas Curtis Clark. PAL; PGD
Alons au bois le may cueillir. Charles d'Orléans, *tr. fr. French by* W. E. Henley. AWP; JAWP; WBP
Alonso to Ferdinand. W. H. Auden. *Fr.* The Sea and the Mirror. MoPo
Aloof. Christina Rossetti. The Thread of Life, I. BoLiVe; OBEV; OBVV; TrGrPo; YT
(Thread of Life, The.) FaBoEn; OBNC; VA
Aloof upon the day's immeasured dome. The Black Vulture. George Sterling. AmLP; AnAmPo; HBV; MAP; MoAmPo (1942 ed.); NP; PFY; PoMa
Aloofe, aloofe, and come no neare. The Sea Marke. John Smith. SCAP
Alow and aloof. The Windy Night. Thomas Buchanan Read. GN
Alpha and Omega. Frederic William Henry Myers. *Fr* Saint Paul. OQP
Alphabet, The. Charles Stuart Calverley. HBV
(A, B, C.) SiTL
Alphabet, An. Charles Edward Carryl. LBN
Alphabet, The. Kate Greenaway. HBVY
Alphabet, The. James Reaney. ACV
Alphabet, The. Karl Shapiro. MoRP
Alphabet, The ("A, B, C, D, E, F, G"). *Unknown.* PCH
Alphabet, The ("A is our army so true"), *with music. Unknown.* BFSS
Alphabet noodles. Baby Toodles. Joseph S. Newman. BBGG
Alphabet of, The/ the trees. The Botticellian Trees. William Carlos Williams. AmP; AmPP (5th ed.); LiTA; NoP; NP; PoeP
Alphabet of Christmas, An. *Unknown.* ChBR
Alphabet of Famous Goops, An, *sel.* Gelett Burgess.
"Bohunkus would take off his hat, and bow and smile, and things like that." BBGG
Alphabet rejoiced to hear, The. A Literary Squabble. James Robinson Planché. CenHV
Alphabetical Song on the Corn Law Bill. *Unknown.* OxBoLi
Alpheus and Arethusa. Eugene Howell Daly. AA
Alphonso of Castile. Emerson. AP
Alpine. R. S. Thomas. BoNaP
Alpine Descent. Wordsworth. *See* Simplon Pass, The.
Alpine Flowers, The. Lydia Huntley Sigourney. AnAmPo
Alpine Spirit's Song. Thomas Lovell Beddoes. OBNC
Alpine View. Melville Cane. PoPl
Alps on Alps. Pope. *See* Little Learning Is a Dangerous Thing, A.
Already. Stephen Spender. FaBoMo
Already batter'd, by his lee they lay. The Sea Battle. Dryden. *Fr.* Annus Mirabilis. FiP
Already blushes in thy cheek. Nemesis. Emerson. AtBAP; PoIE
Already fallen plum-bloom stars the green. The Poor Man's Pig. Edmund Blunden. MoBrPo
Already in the dew-wrapped vineyards dry. Among the Orchards. Archibald Lampman. PeCV
Already it's late summer. Sun-bathers go. The Divine Insect. John Hall Wheelock. GoYe; NYBP
Already Late. Lou Lipsitz. YAP
Already our kingdoms are beginning to totter. Charles Rann Kennedy. *Fr.* The Terrible Meek. ChIP
Already the slim crocus stirs the snow. Joy. Oscar Wilde. *Fr.* Humanitad. PCH
Already, through the splendour ere the morn. Virgil's Farewell to Dante. Dante. *Fr.* Divina Commedia: Purgatorio. FaBoTw
Already was Tithonus' mistress fair. Dante. *Fr.* Divina Commedia: Purgatorio, IX. EnLi-1
Already you are beginning to become. Already. Stephen Spender. FaBoMo
Alright if I have to be famous let it be for this great. Poem. William Knott. YAP
Als I me rode this endre day. The Singing Maid. *Unknown.* MeEL
Alsace or Alsatians. Gertrude Stein. *Fr.* Accents in Alsace. AtBAP
Also Ulysses once—that other war. Kilroy. Peter Viereck. MoAmPo (1950 ed.); NeMA; PoRA; ThLM
Alta Quies. A. E. Housman. SeCEV
Altar, The. George Herbert. AnAnS-1; ATP; MaMe; MeP; PAn; PoFS; PoSa; ReEn; SCEP-1; SeCP; SeCV-1; TrGrPo; VaPo
Altar, The. E. A. Robinson. PoDB
Altar, The. Jean Starr Untermeyer. HBMV
Altar and Sacrifice to Disdain for Freeing Him from Love, An. *Unknown.* ReIE; SiCE
Altar Boy, The. Leonard Feeney. WHL
Altar Smoke. Rosalie Grayer. GoTP
Altars. Sybil Leonard Armes. FaChP
Altars. Bernard Freeman Trotter. MaRV
Altars Raised to God. Martha Snell Nicholson. FaChP
Altarwise by Owl-Light (I-X). Dylan Thomas. CoBMV; LiTM; MasP
Sels.
"Altarwise by owl-light in the half-way house," I. CMoP; Sonn; ToPo
(Sonnet; "Altarwise by owl-light in the half-way house.") LiTM
(Two Sonnets.) MoAB; MoBrPo (1950 ed.)
"Death is all metaphors, shape in one history," II. CMoP; Sonn
"First there was the lamb on knocking knees," III. CMoP
"From the oracular archives and the parchment," IX. CMoP; Sonn
"Let the tale's sailor from a Christian voyage," X. CMoP
"Now stamp the Lord's Prayer on a grain of rice," VII. GTBS-W; Sonn
"This was the crucifixion on the mountain," VIII. CMoP
"What is the metre of the dictionary?" IV. CMoP
Alter! When the hills do. Emily Dickinson. AA; AmPP (5th ed.); AnNE; FaBoBe
Altered look about the hills, An. Emily Dickinson. OxBA
Alternative Endings to an Unwritten Ballad. Paul Dehn. FiBHP
Although a gem be cast away. On True Worth. Sadi. LiTW
Although a lumberman 'tis clear. Paddy the Beaver. Thornton Burgess. RePo
Although accustomed to picking them, it always. The Woman and the Aloe. Perseus Adams. PeSA
Although as yet my cure be incomplete. Retractions, I. James Branch Cabell. HBMV
Although beneath this grave-mound thy white bones now are lying. A Hound. Simonides, *tr. fr. Greek by* F. L. Lucas. WoL
Although confused with details and a dunce. To a History Professor. *Unknown.* UnTE
Although crowds gathered once if she but showed her face. Fallen Majesty. W. B. Yeats. InP
Although he has not seen Pepita, Loam. Loam Norton. Gwendolyn Brooks. BP
Although his actions won him wide renown. Anonymous Gravestone. Erich Kästner. ELU
Although I can see him still. The Fisherman. W. B. Yeats. BWP; CMoP; CoBMV; MaPo (1969 ed.); MBW-2; NoP; NP; SD; ShBV-4
Although I do not hope to turn again. T. S. Eliot. Ash Wednesday, VI. FaBoEn
Although I do not know. Saigyo Hoshi, *tr. fr. Japanese by* Arthur Waley. AWP
Although I enter not. At the Church Gate. Thackeray. *Fr.* Pendennis. EPN; HBV; VA
Although I Had a Check. Earl of Surrey. NoP; SiPS
Although I put away his life. Emily Dickinson. CoBA; MAP; MoAmPo
Although I shelter from the rain. The Lamentation of the Old Pensioner. W. B. Yeats. MaPo; NoP; PeVV; PoPo; PPON
"Although I'd lie lapped in linen." Under the Round Tower. W. B. Yeats. SiSw
Although it is a cold evening. At the Fishouses. Elizabeth Bishop. CoAP; FiMAP; LiTM (1970 ed.); MoVE; NYBP; PoRA (rev. ed.)
Although it is not plainly visible to the eye. Fujiwara no Toshiyuki, *tr. fr. Japanese by* Arthur Waley. *Fr.* Kokin Shu. AWP; JAWP; WBP
Although it may appear archaic. Eppur Si Muove? Robert Hillyer. GoYe
Although my clothes are fine and gay. Clothes. Abbie Farwell Brown. PPL
Although my eyes may never see. My Galilees. Belle Chapman Morrill. MaRV

Although my father's only child. Cecilia. *Unknown.* WHW
Although she feeds me bread of bitterness. America. Claude McKay. AnAmPo; BALP; CDC; NoP; PoFr; PoNe; TTY
Although the aepyornis. He "Digesteth Harde Yron." Marianne Moore. CMoP
Although the bed, by hollow shadowing. A Simpler Thing, a Chair. Robert Mezey. NePoEA
Although the Borgias/ Were rather gorgeous. Important People. Louis Untermeyer, *and others.* StaSt
Although the lattice had dropped loose. The Bride's Prelude. Dante Gabriel Rossetti. SeCePo
Although the night is damp. The Firefly Lights His Lamp. *Unknown.* MPB; SoPo
Although the ship's bell marks the time, it is. Concert at Sea. Hubert Creekmore. WaP
Although the snow still lingers. Last Snow. Andrew Young. MoBrPo (1942 ed.); POTE; StaST
Although thy hand and faith and good works too. Change. John Donne. Elegies, III. LiTG; MaMe; ViBoPo
Although Tormented. Kalonymos ben Judah, *tr. fr. Hebrew.* TrJP
Although we do not all the good we love. John Davies of Hereford. Sonn
Although with lives, submerged and brief. Coral Islands. Louis Ginsberg. OQP
Although you died in a distant land. Vigil. Marjorie Freeman Campbell. CaP
Although your charms are many. To Natalie. Morrie Ryskind. HBMV
Altitude. Lola Ridge. NP
Altitudes. Richard Wilbur. CMoP
Alton Locke, *sels.* Charles Kingsley.
  Alton Locke's Song, 1848. PoFr
  Sands of [*or* o'] Dee, The. BBV (1923 ed.); BeLS; BoChLi; CH; FaPON; GBV (1952 ed.); GN; GTBS; GTBS-D; GTSE; GTSL; HBV; MCCG; MPB; NeHB; OBEV (1st ed.); OnSP; OTPC; PoMS; PoVP; PTK; RG; ShBV-2; TreF; TSW; VA; WBLP
Altruism. David Starr Jordan. OQP
Alulvan. Walter de la Mare. GBV (1952 ed.); MoVE
Alum. Richard Burns. NYTB
Alumnus Football. Grantland Rice. PoLF
  Sels.
  "For when the One Great Scorer comes." MaRV
  "You'll find the road is long and rough, with soft spots far apart." TreFS
Alun Mabon's Song. John Ceiriog Hughes. WePo
Always a "little boy" to her. Her Little Boy. *Unknown.* PEDC
Always alone, star-told? Man. Samuel Greenberg. CrMA
Always Another Viewpoint. Kenneth Patchen. TPM
Always at dusk, the same tearless experience. The Eyes of My Regret. Angelina Weld Grimké. CDC
Always Battling. Thomas O'Brien. NeIP
Always before, We sped in the same Direction. The Queen. Kenneth Pitchford. NYBP
Always before Your Voice [My Soul]. E. E. Cummings. AnFE; CoAnAm; CoBA; LiTA; MAP; MoAmPo; NePA; TwAmPo (Song: "Always before your voice. . .") APA
Always driven, always in the bite of the blast. And Yet We Are Here! Karl Wolfskehl. TrJP
Always Finish. *Unknown.* BLPA; FaBoBe; NeHB; WBLP (Perseverance.) TreFT
Always have these clear sounds been in your ear. Poem for You. Robert Pack. NePoEA
Always He feared you. The Crowd. Irene McKeighan. ChIP; MaRV
Always he sits in his accustomed place. Habitué. Helen Frith Stickney. GoYe
Always, here where I sleep, I hear the sound of the sea. The Sound of the Sea. John Hall Wheelock. EtS
Always I lay upon the brink of love. Judas. Vassar Miller. MoAmPo (1962 ed.)
Always—I tell you this they learned. House Fear. Robert Frost. *Fr.* The Hill Wife. NP
Always in the Parting Year. Else Lasker-Schüler, *tr. fr. German by* Ralph Manheim. TrJP
Always on Monday, God's in the morning papers. The Day after Sunday. Phyllis McGinley. MoAmPo (1962 ed.)
Always, or nearly always, on old apple trees. Somewhere around Christmas. John Smith. FIW
Always place in God thy trust. Trust. Thomas á Kempis. SoP
Always prudent but unprepared. Poem. Alan Dugan. CBV
Always remembering always remembering. Be Still. William Closson Emory. NP
Always she goes like a captured wild bird. Sappho. Jack Cope. PeSA
Always she loved the sound of bells. Joan of Arc. Hugh McCrae. PoAu-1
Always the Following Wind. W. H. Auden. MoBrPo
Always the ghost of these will wake again. Oxford Bells. Sister Maris Stella. GoBC
Always the heavy air. The Lion House. John Hall Wheelock. HBMV
Always the Melting Moon Comes. Margot Osborn. CaP
Always the month of April fills. April. Isobel McFadden. MaRV
Always the path leads back. Finale. Douglas Le Pan. TwCaPo
Always the same, when on a fated night. The Onset. Robert Frost. AmP; AnNE; AP; CMoP; CoBMV; MoAB; MoAmPo; NeMA; OxBA
Always there is someone who has turned away. The Hermit. Howard Moss. NePoAm
Always too eager for the future, we. Next, Please. Philip Larkin. EiCP; MoBrPo (1962 ed.); NePoEA; PoIE
Always waiting at the back of my mind. Landscape with Children. Sister Maris Stella. JKCP (1955 ed.)
Always we are following a light. The Lamp of Life. Amy Lowell. MaRV
Always we have believed. Disguises. Elizabeth Jennings. NePoEA-2
Always well behaved am I. Grisette Dines. Antoinette Deshoulières. CIV
Always with us, always with us. I Am with You Alway. Edwin Henry Nevin. BePJ
Always with Us!—The Black Preacher. Herman Melville. BiS
Always within me lies. Homage to Ghosts. Jean Garrigue. TwAmPo
Alysoun ("Bytuene Mersh and Averil"). *Unknown. See* Alisoun.
Alysoun ("Lenten ys come with love to towne"). *Unknown. See* Lenten Is Come.
Am Driven Mad. Allen Polite. NNP
Am I a black man or a goat? Who I Am. Luis Gonzaga Pinto da Gama. TTY
Am I a king, that I should call my own. From My Arm-Chair. Longfellow. BLPA
Am I a soldier of the cross? Holy Fortitude. Isaac Watts. SoP
Am I a stone, and not a sheep. Good Friday. Christina Rossetti. ChIP; MaRV; PoEL-5; SoP; StJW; TRV; VP
Am I Alone. Recitation and Song [*or* Bunthorne's Recitative and Song]. W. S. Gilbert. *Fr.* Patience. CoBE; PoVP; WoL
Am I alone—or is it you, my friend? Toussaint L'Ouverture. E. A. Robinson. PoNe
Am I despised [*or* despis'd] because, you say. To a Gentlewoman Objecting to Him His Gray Hairs [*or* Age Not to Be Rejected]. Robert Herrick. MyFE; OBS
Am I emptied, Lord, of self? Heartsearch. Evelyn K. Gibson. STF
Am I failing? For no longer can I cast. Modern Love, XXIX. George Meredith. CABA; FaPL; ViPo; VP
Am I mad, O noble Festus. The Distracted Puritan. Richard Corbet. OxBoLi
Am I My Neighbor's Keeper? Richard Eberhart. PoAn; ToPo
Am I Nearer Heaven To-night? Henry Dobbs Holt. SoP
Am I Running from You, Jesus? Warren Risch. SoP
Am I sincere? I say I dote. To Anthea, Who May Command Him Anything. Alfred Cochrane. HBV
Am I the bullet? Cause and Effect. May Swenson. TPM
Am I the slave they say. Soggarth Aroon. John Banim. GoBC; VA
Am I thy gold? Or purse, Lord, for thy wealth. Meditation Six [*or* Another Meditation at the Same Time]. Edward Taylor. *Fr.* Preparatory Meditations, First Series. AmLP; AmPP (4th ed.); AP; AtBAP; LiTA; MeP; NePA; NoP; OxBA
Am I to tell you next of the storms and stars of autumn? Virgil, *tr. by* C. Day Lewis. *Fr.* The Georgics, I. FIW
Am I with you, or you with me. Songs in Absence, XI. Arthur Hugh Clough. EPN
Am not I in blessed case. My Dear Lady. *Unknown. Fr.*

The Trial of Treasure. EIL; TuPP
Amagansett Beach Revisited. John Hall Wheelock. NYBP
Amanda, *with music.* *Unknown.* BFSS
Amanda's Complaint. Philip Freneau. AP
Amantium Irae. Ernest Dowson. HBV; NoP
Amantium Irae [Amoris Redintegratio Est]. Richard Edwards. EIL; HBV; LoBV; OBEV; OBSC; PoE; ReEn; ReIE; SiCE; TuPP
(In Going to My Naked Bed.) CBEP
Amaranth, The. Coventry Patmore. The Angel in the House, II, xii, 2. LoBV (1949 ed.)
Amarantha sweet and faire. To Amarantha, That She Would Dishevel Her Haire. Richard Lovelace. AnAnS-2; EG; EP; HBV; HoPM; LiTL; LO; MePo; MeWo; NoP; OBEV; PoFS; SCEP-2; SeCP; SeCV-1; TrGrPo; UnTE; ViBoPo
Amarillis [*or* Amaryllis]. Thomas Campion. *See* I Care Not for These Ladies.
Amarillis teare thy haire. *Unknown.* SeCSL
Amaryllis I did woo. George Wither. EG
Amasis. Laurence Binyon. OBVV
Amateur, driving too fast, An. Aristophanes, *tr. by* F. A. Wright. *Fr.* The Wasps. LiBL
Amateur Flute, The. *Unknown.* Par
Amaturus. William Johnson Cory. GTBS; HBV
A-Maying, a-Playing. Thomas Nashe. *Fr.* Summer's Last Will and Testament. EIL
(Clownish Song, A.) OBSC
Amaze. Adelaide Crapsey. AnAmPo; QFR
Amazement fills my heart to-night. Thanksgiving. Robert Nichols. MMA
Amazing, Beauteous Change! Philip Doddridge. SoP
Amazing Facts about Food. *Unknown.* BOHV
Amazing Grace, *with music.* *Unknown.* ABF
Amazing monster! that, for aught I know. A Fish Answers [*or* Fish to Man]. Leigh Hunt. *Fr.* The Fish, the Man, and the Spirit. FiBHP; MoShBr; OA
Amazing sight, the Savior stands. Henry Alline. *Fr.* Christ Inviting Sinners to His Grace. CaP
Ambassador Puser the ambassador. Memorial Rain. Archibald MacLeish. AmPP (5th ed.); AnFE; BoLiVe; CMoP; CoAnAm; CoBA; LiTA; MAP; MoAB; MoAmPo; TwAmPo
Amber. Holger Drachmann, *tr. fr. Danish by* Charles Wharton Stork. LiTW
Amber Bead, The. Robert Herrick. *See* Trapped Fly, A.
Amber Beads. Audrey Alexandra Brown. CaP
Amber eyed girls continue to stand naked. Quellisma. G. Bishop-Dubjinsky. ThO
Amber morning floats a tree, The. Adam's Wonder. George O'Neil. NP
Amber the wine. At the Party. Freda Laughton. NeIP
Ambience of Love, The. Isidor Schneider. PG (1933 ed.)
Ambiguous Dog, The. Arthur Guiterman. PoMa
Ambiguous Lines. *Unknown.* *See* I Saw a Peacock.
Ambiguous Time, I heard you sighing. Montgomery. J. C. Hall. ChMP
Ambition. Edith Agnew. GaP; TiPo
Ambition. Morris Bishop. AmFN
Ambition. W. H. Davies. MoBrPo; TrGrPo
Ambition. Aline Kilmer. HBMV; LHV; WHL
Ambition. Anne Blackwell Payne. GFA
Ambition. Shakespeare, *and probably* John Fletcher. *See* Higher Loyalty, The.
Ambitious Gorgons, wide-mouthed Lamians. John Marston. *Fr.* Satire V. ViBoPo
Ambitious Mouse, The. John Farrar. PCH; TSW
Ambitious Nile, thy banks deplore. De Rosis Hibernis. Sir Edmund Gosse. VA
Ambitious Statesman, The, *sel.* John Crowne.
"Whilst th'iron hand." PeRV
Amboyna, *sel.* Dryden.
Song: "Day is come, I see it rise, The." HW
Ambrosia of Dionysus and Semele, The. Robert Graves. NYBP
Ambulance flies at a furious gait, The. Hell's Bells. Margaret Fishback. ShM
Ambuscade. Hugh McCrae. BoAV; PoAu-1
Ambushed by Angels. Gustav Davidson. •FiSC; GoYe
Ameinias. John Simon. ELU
Amelia Mixed the Mustard. A. E. Housman. WhC
Amen. A. C. Benson. OBVV
Amen. Frederick G. Browning. BLRP
Amen. Richard W. Thomas. BF
Amendment. Thomas Traherne. SCEP-1; SeCV-2
Amends for Ladies, *sel.* Nathaniel Field.
Rise, Lady Mistress, Rise! EIL; TuPP
(Matin Song.) HBV
(Song: "Rise Lady Mistresse, rise.") OBS
Amends to Nature. Arthur Symons. GTSL; HBMV; PoVP; YT
Amends to the Tailors and Soutars. William Dunbar. CBEP
America. Donald C. Babcock. NePoAm
America. Arlo Bates. *Fr.* The Torch-Bearers. AA; PaA; PAL
"America, last hope of man and truth," *sel.* PGD
America, *sels.* Blake.
Apparition, The. BoW
Empire Is No More. EnRP
America ("O mother of a mighty race"). Bryant. *See* O, Mother of a Mighty Race.
America. Florence Earle Coates. PEDC
America. Arthur Cleveland Coxe. *Fr.* England and America. MC; PAH
America. Sydney Dobell. EPN; OBVV
"Nor force nor fraud shall sunder us!" *sel.* HBV; PaA; PAL
America. Henry Dumas. BOLo
America. Allen Ginsberg. CoAP; NaP; NMP; PoIE (1970 ed.)
America. Bobb Hamilton. BOLo
America. Alfred Kreymborg. NP
America. Claude McKay. AnAmPo; BALP; CDC; NoP; PoFr; PoNe; TTY
America. Bernadette Mayer. ANYP
America. Herman Melville. MAmP
America. Samuel Francis Smith. AA; DD; FaBoBe; FaFP; FaPON; GFA; HBV; HBVY; HH; MaRV, *with add. st. by* Longfellow; MC; OTPC; PaA; PAL; PEDC; PoFr; PoLF; PoRL; TreF; WBLP; YaD
(National Hymn.) SoP
America. Bayard Taylor. *Fr.* National Ode, Read at the Celebration in Independence Hall, Philadelphia, July 4, 1876. AA; PAL; PoFr
America/ I/ carry/ you. The Pinta, the Nina and the Santa Maria. John Tagliabue. AmFN
America; a Prophecy. Blake. *See* America.
America always! American Feuillage. Whitman. Po
America! dear brother land! Greeting from England. *Unknown.* PAH
America First. G. Ashton Oldham. MaRV; PGD
America for Me. Henry van Dyke. BLPA; FaFP; HBVY; MC; MPB; OHFP; OTPC (1946 ed.); PaA; PAL; PCD; PTK; RePo; SP; TreFS; WBLP
"I know that Europe's wonderful, yet something seems to lack," *sel.* MaRV
America Greets an Alien. *Unknown.* PAL; PGD
(Welcome over the Door of an Old Inn.) PoToHe (new ed.)
America has nourished wiser sons. The Prophet. Thomas Curtis Clark. HH; PEDC
"America, I Love You." Bert Kalmar *and* Harry Ruby. FiBHP; InMe
America Is Corn. Robert P. Tristram Coffin. WaKn
America Is Great Because. *At. to* Alexis de Tocqueville. TreFT
America is West and the wind blowing. Archibald MacLeish. *Fr.* American Letter. AmFN
America I've given you all and now I'm nothing. America. Allen Ginsberg. CoAP; NaP; NMP; PoIE (1970 ed.)
America, last hope of man and truth. Arlo Bates. *Fr.* The Torch-Bearers. PGD
America, My Country. Emerson. AmePo; AmPP
America, my own! National Song. William Henry Venable. DD; MC; PAH
America, O Power benign, great hearts revere your name. Land of the Free. Arthur Nicholas Hosking. BLPA; PaA; PAL
America Prays. Arthur Gordon Field. PGD
America Remembers, *sel.* Paul Engle.
"Here by this midland lake," *much abr.* NAMP
America Resurgent. Wendell Phillips Stafford. MC
America the Beautiful. Katharine Lee Bates. BLPA; DD; EaLo; FaBoBe; FaBV; FaFP; FaPL; FaPON; HBMV; HBVY; MARV; MC; MCCG; MPB; NeHB; OQP; OTD; OTPC (1946 ed.); PaA; PAL; PCH; PEDC; PoRL; PTK; TIHL; TreF; WBLP; WGRP; YaD

America, the land beloved. The Name of Washington. Arthur Gordon Field. PAL; PGD
America! thou fractious nation. A Proclamation. *Unknown.* PAH
America to England. George Edward Woodberry. AA
America to Great Britain. Washington Allston. AA; HBV; PaA
America, unbend that troubled brow! To Thee, My Country. Louise Burton Laidlaw. PAH
America was always promises. Archibald MacLeish. *Fr.* America Was Promises. AmFN
America was forests. America Was Schoolmasters. Robert P. Tristram Coffin. PAL; WaKn
America Was Promises, *sels.* Archibald MacLeish. CABL; LiTB;
"America was always promises." AmFN
"America was promises—to whom?/ Jefferson knew." PAL; PoFr
America Was Schoolmasters. Robert P. Tristram Coffin. PAL; WaKn
American Book of the Dead, The, *sels.* John Giorno. ANYP
"Astronaut Jim Lovell."
"Father, A/ accused of shooting."
"Stray deer, A/ pursued by four Newark policemen."
"Swallows, The/ returned at dawn today."
"Vivian Beaumont, The/ Theatre."
"With a brilliant sun causing his tears."
American Boy, The *Unknown.* PEDC
American Change. Allen Ginsberg. CABL; NoP
American Dream, The *sel.* Johnie Scott.
"'Speech, or dark cities screaming.'" NBP
American eagle is not aware he is, The. Eagle Plain. Robert Francis. AmFN
American Feuillage. Whitman. Po
American Flag, The. Joseph Rodman Drake. AA; AmePo; AmLP; DD, *much abr.*; FaBoBe; FaFP; GN; HBV; HBVY; HH; MaRV; MC; OTPC, *abr.*; PaA; PAH; PAL; PAP; PaPo; PGD, *abr.*; PoFr; PTK; TreF; WBLP
American Flag, The. Lena E. Faulds. HH
American Flag, The. Charles Constantine Pise. CAW
American Freedom, The. Matthew Biller. PoRL
American frigate, a frigate of fame, An. Paul Jones' Victory. *Unknown.* TrAS
American frigate from Balitmore came, An. Paul Jones. *Unknown.* OTD; PAH; PAL
American Girl, An. Brander Matthews. AA
American Heartbreak. Langston Hughes. AmPP (5th ed.); LiTM (1970 ed.)
American Gothic. Samuel Allen. *See* To Satch.
American Hero, The. Nathaniel Niles. PoFr; WaaP
(Bunker Hill, *with music.*) TrAS
American hero must triumph over, The. Eisenhower's Visit to Franco, 1959. James Wright. NaP; NMP
American History. Marguerite Janvrin Adams. PoRL
American History. W. R. Moses. LiTA
American in England, An. Elinor Wylie. HT
American Independence. Francis Hopkinson. PAH
American Independence. Alfred Billings Street. PEDC
American Indian, The. *Unknown.* FiBHP; SiTL
(Indian, The.) LiTG
American jump, American jump. *Unknown.* OxNR
American land is a land of freedom, The. The American Freedom. Matthew Biller. PoRL
American Laughter. Kenneth Allan Robinson. AmFN; PaA; TreFS
American Letter. Archibald MacLeish. AmPP; ILP; NoP; OxBA
Sel.
"America is West and the wind blowing." AmFN
American Love-Ode, An. Thomas Warton, the Elder. CEP
American muse, whose strong and diverse heart. Invocation. Stephen Vincent Benét. *Fr.* John Brown's Body. AmFN; CrMA; MPB; NP; PaA; PAL
American Names. Stephen Vincent Benét. AmFN; AmP; BoLiVe (1945 ed.); HT; InP; LaNeLa; LoGBV; NP; OxBA; PG; TreFT; WaKn; YaD
American Nights. Richmond Lattimore. TPM
American now mind my song. John Chinaman's Appeal. Mart Taylor. SGR
American Patriot's Prayer, The. *Unknown.* PAH
American Patrol. William Brown. QAH
American Poetry. Stuart Peterfreund. QAH
American Poetry. Louis Simpson. ELU; PP
American Primitive. William Jay Smith. MoAmPo (1962 ed.); NePoAm; NePoEA; PoPl; PPON; TwCP
American Rhapsody. Kenneth Fearing. MoAmPo; TrGrPo (1942 ed.)
American Soldier's Hymn, The. *Unknown.* PAH
American Spring Song. Sherwood Anderson. NP
American Takes a Walk, An. Reed Whittemore. MoVE
American to France, An. Alice Duer Miller. HBMV
American Traveller, The. "Orpheus C. Kerr." BOHV; WhC
American Twilights, 1957. James Wright. CoAP
American Vineyard. Mildred Cousens. GoYe
American Yarns. Carl Sandburg. *See* They Have Yarns.
Americans! Philip Freneau. *Fr.* Reflections. PPON
Americans All. Minna Irving. PEDC
Americans Are Afraid of Lizards. Karl Shapiro. AmFN
Americans are always moving on. Stephen Vincent Benét. *Fr.* Western Star. AmFN
Americans, rejoice. Old Song Written during Washington's Life. *Unknown.* OHIP
Americans, Who Whistle As You Go! Stephen Vincent Benét. PTK
America's Answer. R. W. Lillard. BLPA; HH; PAL; PEDC
America's Gospel. James Russell Lowell. MaRV; PGD
America's Prosperity. Henry van Dyke. PGD
America's Welcome Home. Henry van Dyke. MC
Americus, as he did wend. The Noble Tuck-Man. Jean Ingelow. NA
Ametas and Thestylis Making Hay-Ropes. Andrew Marvell. ALV; CavP; InvP; MaMe; SeCL; SeCP
Amherst Train, The. Emily Dickinson. *See* I like to see it lap the miles.
Amico Suo. Herbert P. Horne. VA
Amid a rabble cry. For Me. *Unknown.* SoP
Amid a wilderness of rock-piled towers. From Sappho's Death: Three Pictures by Gustave Moreau. T. Sturge Moore. SyP
Amid all Triads let it be confest. Epigram. Richard Garnett. OBVV
Amid curled leaves and green. Peach Tree with Fruit. Padraic Colum. BoNaP
Amid my bale I bathe in bliss. A Strange Passion of a Lover. George Gascoigne. EnLit; EnRePo; EP; ReEn; RelE; SiCE; TuPP
Amid the cares of married strife. Tell Her So. *Unknown.* PoToHe (new ed.)
Amid the chapel's chequered gloom. Heliotrope. Harry Thurston Peck. AA; HBV
Amid the cloistered gloom of Aachen's aisle. The Opening of the Tomb of Charlemagne. Sir Aubrey De Vere. HBV
Amid the deafening traffic of the town. To a Passer-by. Baudelaire. SyP
Amid the Din of Earthly Strife. Henry Warburton Hawkes. SoP; TRV
Amid the fairest things that grow. Her Dwelling Place. Ada Foster Murray. HBV
Amid the garden's fragrance laid. Ode: Allusion to Horace. Mark Akenside. CEP
Amid the Myrtles. Judah Halevi, *tr. fr. Hebrew by* Ephraim Sando *and* William Cutter. HW
Amid the non-committed compounds of the mind. Metagnomy. N. H. Pritchard. NBP
Amid the nut grove, still and brown. The Faerie's Child. Thomas Caulfield Irwin. OnYI
Amid the stony slapping of the waves. Barnacle Geese. Charles Higham. PoAU-2
Amid the thunders of the falling Dark. The Coat of Fire. Edith Sitwell. FaBoTw; OAEP (2d ed.)
Amid Tibetan snows the ancient lama. What Hath Man Wrought Exclamation Point. Morris Bishop. NYBP
Amid this hot green glowing gloom. Interlude. Edith Sitwell. MoAB; MoBrPo; NeMA
Amidst the fairest mountain tops. Cynthia. Sir Edward Dyer. OBEC
Amidst thy sacred effigies. The Emancipation Group. Whittier. LiPo
Aminta, *sel.* Tasso, *tr. fr. Italian.*
Pastoral, A: "Oh happy golden age," *tr. by* Samuel Daniel. PoEL-2; ReEn; RelE
(Golden Age, The.) AWP, *tr. by* Leigh Hunt; WoL
(O Bella Età de l'Oro, *tr. by* Henry Reynolds.) FosPo

(Pastoral of Tasso, A, *tr. by* Samuel Daniel.) OBSC
Amintas and Claudia; or The Merry Shepherdess. *Unknown.* CoMu
Amintor oh thou faithless swane. *Unknown.* SeCSL
Amitabha's Vow, X. Gary Snyder. *Fr.* Myths & Texts: Burning. NaP
Amitié Amoureuse. Luc Grimard, *tr. fr. French by* Edna Worthley Underwood PoNe
Amnesiac. Sylvia Plath. NYBP
Amo Amas. John O'Keeffe. BoLP;ChTr
("Amo, amas,/ I love a lass.") LO
(Jingle.) IrPN
Among/ of/ green. The Locust Tree in Flower. William Carlos Williams. PIA
Among a people who doubted. Zechariah. Earl Marlatt. MoRP
Among All Lovely Things My Love Had Been. Wordsworth. *See* Glow-Worm, The.
Among all the myths and masks and make-believes. Charles Madge. *Fr.* Poem by Stages. BoSA
Among Foes. Nietzsche, *tr. fr. German by* Paul Victor Cohn. PoFr
Among green shades and flowering ghosts, the remembrances of love. The Two Fires. Judith Wright. MoBrPo (1962 ed.)
Among his books he sits all day. A Tragedy. Edith Nesbit. HBV
Among left trucks, mailbags, chums. Homing Pigeons. Ted Walker. NYBP
Among other things profiting in our tongue. John Heywood. *Fr.* A Dialogue Containing the Number of the Effectual Proverbs in the English Tongue. ReIE
Among our young lass[i]es is [or there's] Muirland Meg. Muirland Meg [or She'll Do It]. Burns. ErPo; UnTE
Among poppies in a field of maize. Death in the Corn. Detlev von Liliencron. WaaP
Among School Children. W. B. Yeats. AnIL; ATP (1953 ed.); CABA; CaFP; ChMP; CMoP; CoBMV; DiPo; FaBoEn; ForPo; FosPo; GTBS-P; ILP; LiTB; LiTG; LiTM (rev. ed.); MaPo; MBW-2; MoAB; MoBrPo; MoVE; NoP; OAEP (2d ed.); PAn; PIA; PoAn; PoeP; PoIE; PoVP; ReMP; SeCeV; TDP; TrGrPo; UnPo
Among Shadows. Arthur Davison Ficke. NP
Among that band of Officers was one. Wordsworth. *Fr.* The Prelude. ChER
Among the anthropophagi. Funebrial Reflections. Ogden Nash. CenHV; ImOP
Among the Beautiful Pictures. Alice Cary. BLPA
Among the bumble-bees in red-top hay. Adelaide Crapsey. Carl Sandburg. HBMV
Among the cigarettes and the peppermint creams. Far West. A. J. M. Smith. PeCV
Among the contemporaries of Shakespeare. Clerihews. E. C. Bentley. OnPP
Among the Daffadillies. Giles Farnaby. OAEP
Among the Ferns. Edward Carpenter. WGRP, *abr.*
"I lay among the ferns," *sel.* OQP
"Among the few things/ I brought with me." A Cross on a Hill [*or* Symbol of Hope]. Carl S. Weist. BePJ; ChIP
Among the first and farthest! Elk and deer. John Day, Frontiersman. Yvor Winters. PoSa
Among the first to go are always a few. Only the Beards Are Different. Bruce Dawe. PoAu-2
Among the greatest plagues, one is the third day ague. Of Scolding Wives and the Third Day Ague. Henricus Selyns. SCAP
Among the guests who often stayed. Shelley. *Fr.* Peter Bell the Third. ChER
Among the Heather. William Allingham. IrPN
Among the high-branching, leafless boughs. The View from an Attic Window. Howard Nemerov. CoAP
Among the Hills, *sel.* Whittier
Prelude: "Along the roadside, like the flowers of gold." AmePo; AP; CoBA; OxBA; PoEL-4; TOP
Among the hills of Athol he was born. The Wanderer. Wordsworth. *Fr.* The Excursion, I. EnRP
Among the hills of St. Jerome. At St. Jerome. Frances Harrison. WHW
Among the iodoform, in twilight-sleep. The Leg. Karl Shapiro. MoAB; MoAmPo (1950 ed.); NeMA; TPM; TrGrPo (rev. ed.); UnPo (3d ed.)
Among the Lions Night Is Still. Sister Mary Norbert Körte. ThO
Among the meadows of the countryside. The Old-fashioned Garden. John Russell Hayes. AA
Among the Millet. Archibald Lampman. CaP; WHW
Among the mountains I wandered and saw blue haze and red crag and was amazed. The Poor. Carl Sandburg. NP
Among the Nuts. *Unknown.* BoTP; TVC
Among the orchard weeds, from every search. Hen's Nest. John Clare. OA; Sonn
Among the Orchards. Archibald Lampman. PeCV
Among the people who work at small trades. In the Land of Magic. Henri Michaux. LiTW
Among the pickled foetuses and bottled bones. "Siena Mi Fe'; Disfecemi Maremma." Ezra Pound. *Fr.* Hugh Selwyn Mauberley, VII. AmPP (5th ed.); CMoP; CoBMV; LiTA; LiTM (rev. ed.); MoAmPo (1962 ed.); MoPo
Among the plastic flowers one honest one. The Woolworth Philodendron. Stephen Sandy. CoPo
Among the priceless gems and treasures rare. Pastel. Francis Saltus Saltus. AA
Among the rain. The Great Figure. William Carlos Williams. QFR
Among the rest by Fortune overthrown. How Shore's Wife. Was by King Richard Despoiled of All Her Goods and Forced to Do Open Penance. Thomas Churchyard. *Fr.* A Mirror for Magistrates. ReIE
Among the Rocks. Robert Browning. James Lee's Wife, VII. BoLiVe
(Ancient Doctrine, The.) OBVV
"O good gigantic smile," *sel.* EPN; YT
Among the signs of autumn I perceive. Tall Ambrosia. Henry David Thoreau. PoEL-4
Among the silver cornstalks. Eve. Robert L. Wolf. HBMV
Among the smoke and fog of a December afternoon. Portrait of a Lady. T. S. Eliot. AnAmPo; CoAnAm; ForPo; HBMV; LiTG; MAP; MAPA; MoAmPo (1942 ed.); NP; TwAmPo; TwCP
Among the Stars. Wordsworth. *See* Crescent Boat, The.
Among the Stuart heads. Watson and the Shark. Paul Petrie. NYTB
Among the sullen peaks she stood at bay. The Mountain Woman. DuBose Heyward. AnAmPo; NP; OnPP
Among the thistles on the hill. Little Sorrow. "Marian Douglas." SAS; TVC
Among the thousand, thousand spheres that roll. Alcyone. Frances Laughton Mace. AA
Among the Violets, Fair Lillies and Roses. *Unknown.* SeCL
(Dying Damsel's Doleful Destiny, The.) SeEP
Among the woods and tillage. Yattendon. Sir Henry Newbolt. HBMV
Among the Worst of Men That Ever Lived. Henry David Thoreau. PoEL-4
Among these latter busts we count by scores. Protus. Robert Browning. FOL
Among These Troopes of Christs Souldiers, Came . . . Mr. Roger Harlackenden. Edward Johnson. SCAP
Among These Turf-Stacks. Louis MacNeice. LiTB; LiTM; SeCePo; ShBV-4; WaP
(Turf-Stacks.) OBMV
Among those joys, 'tis one at eve to sail. Sailing upon the River. George Crabbe. *Fr.* The Borough. OBNC
Among Those Killed in the Dawn Raid Was a Man Aged One [*or* a] Hundred. Dylan Thomas. InPo; MoPo; Sonn
Among those mountain-skirts a league away. The Lough. William Allingham. IrPN
Among those things that make our love complete. Consummation. Elsa Barker. *Fr.* The Spirit and the Bride. HBMV
Among those who promised us our honors. Palermo, Mother's Day, 1943. William Belvin. PoPl
Among thy fancies, tell me this. The Kisse. Robert Herrick. CavP
Among twenty snowy mountains. Thirteen Ways of Looking at a Blackbird. Wallace Stevens. AP; CABA; CMoP; CoBMV; DiPo; LiTM; MAPA; MaPo (1969 ed.); PoeP; PoFS; PoSa; TDP; TwAmPo
Amongst the mourners that attend his hearse. Charles Cotton. ReEn
Amongst the princely paragons. A Princely Ditty in Praise of the English Rose. Thomas Deloney. BoTP

Amongst the pure ones all. The Quaker's Song. *Unknown.* CoMu
Amor Aeternalis. Clark Ashton Smith. FiSC
Amor Dei. *Unknown.* BoC
Amor Mundi. Christina Rossetti. NBM; PoEL-5; PoVP; ViPo
Amor Mysticus. Sister Marcela de Carpio de San Félix, *tr. fr. Spanish by* John Hay. AWP; CAW; JAWP; LiTW; WBP
Amor Profanus. Ernest Dowson. PoVP
Amor que te tenía, El, *with music. Unknown, tr. fr. Spanish.* ABF
Amor Triumphans, *sel.* Arthur Symons.
V. Return, The. BrPo
Amores, *sels.* Ovid, *tr. fr. Latin.*
Advice to a Fair Wanton, III, 14, *tr. by* Christopher Marlowe. UnTE
Apology for Loose Behavior, II, 4, *tr. by* Christopher Marlowe. UnTE
"If for thy self thou wilt not watch thy whore," *fr.* II, 19, *tr. by* Dryden. PeRV
In Love with two, *fr.* II, 10, *tr. by* Christopher Marlowe. MeWo
"In summer's heat and mid-time of the day," I, 5, *tr. by* Christopher Marlowe. CLwM
(In Summer's Heat.) UnTE
(Ovid's Fifth Elegy.) NCEP
Long Have I Borne Much, *fr.* III, 10, *tr. by* Christopher Marlowe. MeWo
Possessive Lover, The, I, 4, *tr. by* Christopher Marlowe. UnTE
Shameful Impotence, III, 8, *tr. by* Christopher Marlowe. ErPo
(Impotent Lover, The.) UnTE
To Corinna's Chamber-maid, *fr.* I, 8, *tr. by* Thomas Creed. PeRV
Amoret. Mark Akenside. HBV; OBEV
Amoret. Congreve. *See* A Hue and Cry after Fair Amoret.
Amoretti, *sels.* Spenser.
I. "Happy ye leaves! when as those lily [*or* lilly] hands." ATP; BEL; CoBE; EnLi-1; EnLit; LoBV; MaPo (1969 ed.); Po; PoAn; ReEn; ReIE; SiCE; Sonn
III. "The sovereign beauty which I do admire." ATP; HBV; OAEP; PAn;
("Soverayne beauty which I doo admyre, The.") PoEL-1; SiCE
IV. "New yeare forth looking out of Ianus gate." ReEn
V. "Rudely thou wrongest my dear heart's desire." EIL; ReIE; SiCE; Sonn
VIII. "More than most fair[e], full of the living fire." BoLiVe; CABA; HBV; MeWo; NoP; OAEP; Sonn; TrGrPo
IX. "Long-while I sought to what I might compare." PoE; Sonn
X. "Unrighteous Lord of love, what law is this." NoP; PIA
XIII. "In that proud port, which her so goodly graceth." BWP; ReIE; Sonn
XV. "Ye tradeful merchants, that with weary toil [*or* toyle]." BoLiVe; LiTB; LiTG; ReEn; ReIE; SiCE; Sonn; TrGrPo
(All This World's Riches.) LiTL
XVI. "One day as I unwarily did gaze." ReEn
XIX. "The merry cuckow [*or* cuckoo], messenger of spring." ILP; MaPo (1969 ed.); OBSC; ReEn; ReIE; Sonn
XXI. "Was it the work of Nature or of Art."
(Art of Eyes, The.) LiTL
XXII. "This holy season, fit to fast and pray." ReEn; SiCE
XXIII. "Penelope for her Ulysses' [*or* Ulisses] sake." BWP; CoBE; ReEn; ReIE
XXIV. "When I behold that beauty's [*or* beauties] wonderment." BEL; HBV
XXV. "How long shall this like dying life endure." EnRePo; Sonn
XXVI. "Sweet is the rose, but grows [*or* growes] upon a brere [*or* brier]." EIL; EP; ILP; ReEn
(Sweet and Sour.) HBV
XXVII. "Fair proud, now tell me, why should fair be proud." Sonn
XXVIII. "The laurel leaf, which you this day do wear." CABA; ReIE
XXX. "My love is like to ice, and I to fire." ATP; BoLiVe; CBV; ErPo; LiTB; LiTG; LiTL; PG (1955 ed.); TrGrPo
XXXIII. "Great wrong I do[e], I can it not deny." ReEn; ReIE
XXXIV. Like [*or* Lyke] as a ship, that through the ocean wide [*or* wyde]." AnFE; BEL; CoBE; DiPo; EnLi-1; EnLit; EtS; HBV; ILP; MaPo (1969 ed.); OBSC; PAn; PoAn; PoFS; PoIE; ReEn; ReIE; SiCE; YAT
XXXV. "My hungry eyes through greedy covetize." BWP
XXXVII. "What guile [*or* guyle] is this, that those her golden tresses." ForPo; InP; LiTL; NoP; OBSC; ReEn; SiCE; Sonn; StP; TrGrPo
XL. "Mark when she smiles with amiable cheer." OBSC
XLI. "Is it her nature or is it her will." OAEP
XLIV. "When those renoumed noble peers of Greece." CABA; ReIE
XLV. "Leave, lady, in your glass of crystal clean." CBV; PoAn
XLVI. "When my abodes prefixed time is spent." PoFS
XLVII. "Trust not the treason of those smiling looks." BoLiVe; CBV; LO; TrGrPo
LIII. "The panther knowing that his spotted hide." EnRePo
LIV. "Of this worlds theatre in which we stay." NoP; ReEn; ReIE
LV. "So oft as I her beauty do[e] behold." BoLiVe; HBV; PoIE; SiCE; Sonn; TrGrPo
LVI. "Fair [*or* Fayre] ye be sure, but cruell and unkind." EnLit; NoP; Sonn
LVII. "Sweet warrior when shall I have peace with you?" StP
LVIII. "Weak is the assurance that weak flesh reposeth."
(By Her That Is Most Assured to Her Self.) EnRePo
LX. "They, that in course of heavenly spheres are skilled." Sonn
LXI. "The Glorious image of the Maker's beauty." SiCE; Sonn
LXII. "The weary year[e] his race now having run." OBSC; ReIE; SiCE
LXIII. "After long storm[e]s and tempests sad assay." BEL; EnLit; FaBoEn; NoP; OAEP; OBSC; SiCE
LXIV. "Com[m]ing to kisse her lyps (such grace I found)." LoBV; Sonn
LXV. "The doubt which ye misdeem, fair love, is vain." SiCE; Sonn
LXVII. "Like [*or* Lyke] as a huntsman after weary chase [*or* chace]." BoLiVe; EnRePo; ForPo; ILP; NoP; OAEP; PoEL-1; PoIE; PoSa; ReEn; SeCePo; SiCE; Sonn; TrGrPo
LXVIII. "Most glorious Lord of life [*or* lyfe]! that on this day." ATP; BoC; CABA; EIL; EnRePo; HBV; LiTB; MaPo (1969 ed.); NoP; OBEV; OxBoCh; PoE; ReEn; ReIE; SeCeV; SiCE; Sonn; TrPWD
(Easter.) CAW; FaChP; StJW
(Easter Morning.) DD; MaRV; OHIP; TRV
LXIX. "The famous warriors of the antique [*or* anticke] world." CoBE; ReEn; SiCE
LXX. "Fresh spring, the herald of love's mighty king." AWP; BEL; BWP; CABA; ChTr; EIL; EnLit; FaBoEn; HBV; JAWP; LiTB; NoP; OBEV; OBSC; OnPM; PoFS; ReEn; ReIE; SeCeV; SiCE; Sonn; StP; TOP; ViBoPo; WBP
(Make Haste, Sweet Love.) LiTL
LXXI. "I joy to see how in your drawen work." MaPo (1969 ed.); SiCE
LXXII. "Oft when my spirit doth spre[a]d her bolder wing [e]s." EG; EnLi-1; OAEP; OBSC; SiCE; Sonn
LXXIII. "Being my[e]self [*or* my selfe] captived [*or* captyved] here in care." CoBE; LoBV
LXXV. "One day I wrote her name upon the strand." AnFE; ATP; AWP; BEL; BoLiVe; BWP; CABA; CBEP; CoBE; EIL; EnLi-1; EnLit; EP; FiP; ForPo; HBV; ILP; JAWP; LiTB; LiTG; LiTL; MaPo (1969 ed.); NoP; OAEP; PAn; PG (1955 ed.); PIA; PoE; PoFS; ReEn; ReIE; SeCeV; SiCE; Sonn; StP; TOP; ViBoPo; WBP
(Her Name Upon the Strand.) SeCePo
LXXVII. "Was it a dream, or did I see it plain?" ReIE
LXXVIII. "Lacking my love, I go from place to place." EIL; ViBoPo
LXXIX. "Men call you fair [*or* fayre], and you do[e] credit it." ATP; AWP; BEL; EnLi-1; FaBoBe; HBV; JAWP; LiTL; NoP; PoAn; PoFS; ReIE; SiCE; Sonn; TOP; WBP
LXXX. "After so long a race as I have run." ReEn; ReIE; SiCE
LXXXI. "Fair is my love, when her fair golden hairs [*or* heares]." EIL; LiTL; NoP; PoE; Sonn
LXXXII. "Joy of my life! full oft for loving you." BEL; ReIE
LXXXV. "The world that cannot deeme of worthy things." ReEn

LXXXVI. "Venemous toung, tipt with vile adders sting." ReEn
LXXXVII. "Since I did leave the presence of my love." EG; ReEn
LXXXVIII. "Since I have lacked the comfort of that light." EnRePo
LXXIX. "Like [*or* Lyke] as the culver on the bared bough." EG; MaPo (1969 ed.); Sonn
Amoris Exsul, *sel.* Arthur Symons.
In the Bay, III. OBNC; PoVP
Amoris Victima, *sel.* Arthur Symons.
"And yet, there was a hunger in your eyes." PeVV
Amorist, The. Nahum Tate. SeCL
Amorist, The. *Unknown,* *tr. fr. Greek by* Louis Untermeyer. UnTE
Amorous Bigot, The, *sel.* Thomas Shadwell.
Fire of Love, The, *at. to* Shadwell *and to* Charles Sackville, Earl of Dorset. SeCL
Amorous Dialogue between John and his Mistress, An. *Unknown.* CoMu; PeRV
(Amorous Dialogue between the Mistris and Her Aprentice, An.) UnTE
Amorous M. A., An. Limerick. *Unknown.* LiBL
Amorous Silvy, The. *Unknown.* *See* On a Time the Amorous Silvy.
Amorous Temper, An. John Trumbull. *See* Tom Brainless Seeks a Wife.
Amorous War, The, *sel.* Jasper Mayne.
Time. OBEV; SeCL
(First Song, Sung by Two Amazons, The.) SeEP
(Time Is the Feather'd Thing.) CLwM; EG
Amorous Worms' Meat, The. Petrarch, *tr. fr. Italian by* Anna Marie Armi. Sonnets to Laura: To Laura in Death, XXXVI. LiTW
Amos, *sel.* Bible, *O.T.*
O Ye That Would Swallow the Needy, VIII: 4-10. TrJP
Amour, *sels.* Paul Verlaine, *tr. fr. French by* John Gray. SyP
Crucifix, A.
Parsifal.
Amours de Marie, *sels.* Pierre de Ronsard, *tr. fr. French by* Andrew Lang.
His Lady's Death. AWP
His Lady's Tomb. AWP; JAWP; WBP
To His Young Mistress. AWP; OuHeWo
To the Moon. AWP
Amours de Voyage. Arthur Hugh Clough. ViPP
Sels.
Ah, That I Were Far Away, Canto III, *introd.* OBNC
"*Dulce* it is, and *decorum,* no doubt, for the country to fall," Canto II, ii. OAEP
"Is it illusion? or does there a spirit from perfecter ages," Canto II, *introd.* EPN
(Spirit from Perfecter Ages, A.) OBNC
Juxtaposition, Canto III, vi. OBNC; VA
Letter from Rome, A, Canto I, v. LoBV
"Over the great windy waters, and over the clear-crested summits," Canto I, *introd.* EPN
"Rome disappoints me still; but I shrink and adapt myself to it," Canto I, ii. EPN
Rome Is Fallen, I Hear, Canto V, vi. BEL
"So, I have seen a man killed," Canto II, vii. PeVV
"There are two different kinds, I believe, of human attraction," Canto II, xi. GTBS-P
"Tibur is beautiful, too, and the orchard slopes, and the Anio," Canto III, xi. GTBS-P
(So Not Seeing I Sung.) OBNC
"Whither depart the souls of the brave that die in the battle," Canto V, vi. OAEP
Ye Ancient Divine Ones, Canto I, x. OBNC
"Yes, as I walk, I behold, in a luminous, large intuition," Canto III, vii. GTBS-D
"Yes, we are fighting at last, it appears," Canto II, v. PeVV
Amphibious Crocodile. John Crowe Ransom. AnAmPo
Amphimachos the Dandy. Vincent McHugh. NePoAm-2
Amphitryon, *sels.* Dryden.
Fair Iris and Her Swain, *fr.* IV, i. ViBoPo
Song, A: "Celia, that I once was blest," *fr.* III, i. CavP
Song: "Fair Iris I love, and hourly I die," *fr.* IV, i. AWP; JAWP; LiTL; WBP; WOL
(Fair Iris I Love.) InPo; OnPM
(False and Fickle.) MeWo
(Hourly I Die.) UnTE
(Mercury's Song to Phaedra.) CEP; MBW-1; PoEL-3; SeCV-2
Amphora, The. "Feodor Sologub," *tr. fr. Russian* by Babette Deutsch *and* Avrahm Yarmolinsky. AWP; JAWP; WBP
(In a Gay Jar.) OnPM
"Ample heaven of fabrik sure, The." A Summer's Day. Alexander Hume. *Fr.* Summer Day. CH
Ample make this bed. Emily Dickinson. AP; AtBAP; MAP; MoAB; MoAmPo; NoP; OxBA; PoEL-5
Ampler Circumscription, The. William Baylebridge. BoAV
Amsterdam. Francis Jammes, *tr. fr. French by* Jethro Bithell. AWP; JAWP; WBP
Robinson Crusoe Returns to Amsterdam, *sel.* FaPON
Amsterdam Letter. Jean Garrigue. NYBP
Amulet of Love, The. Michelangelo, *tr. fr. Italian by* John Addington Symonds. OnPM
Amusements. George Crabbe. *Fr.* The Borough, Letter IX. OBRV
Amy. James Matthew Legaré. AA
Amy Elizabeth Ermyntrude Annie. Queenie Scott-Hopper. BoTP; TiPo (1952 ed.)
Amy Margaret. William Allingham. BiCB
Amy Wentworth. Whittier. BeLS
Amynta. Sir Gilbert Elliot. HBV
Amyntas. Tasso. *See* Aminta.
Amyntas Led Me to a Grove. Aphra Behn. *Fr.* The Dutch Lover. ErPo
(Willing Mistress, The.) UnTE; ViBoPo
Amyntas; or, The Impossible Dowry, *sel.* Thomas Randolph, *tr. fr. Latin by* Leigh Hunt.
Fairies' Song. ALV; PoMS
(Fairy Song.) HBV
(Song of Fairies Robbing an Orchard.) OBRV
An' Charlie he's my darling. Charlie He's My Darling. Burns. *See also* 'Twas on a Monday morning. ALV; CH.
An der Beach, an der Beach. An Unserer Beach. Kurt M. Stein. InMe
An' I couldn't hear nobody pray, O, Lord. I Couldn't Hear Nobody Pray. *Unknown.* BoAN-1
An Thou Were My Ain Thing. Allan Ramsay. EiPP; ViBoPo, 5 *sts.*
An Unserer Beach. Kurt M. Stein. InMe
An' zoo o' Monday we got drough. Easter Monday. William Barnes. PoVP
Anabasis, *sels.* "St.-J. Perse," *tr. fr. French by* T. S. Eliot.
"For my soul engaged in far matters," Pt. V.
(Three Sections from "Anabasis.") LiTW
I Have Built Myself, with Honour and Dignity, Pt. I. AtBAP
Song: "I have halted my horse by the tree of the doves."
(Three Sections from "Anabasis.") LiTW
Song: Under the Bronze Leaves. AtBAP; PoPl
(Three Sections from "Anabasis.") LiTW
Such Is the Way of the World, Pt. IV. AtBAP
(Thus Was the City Founded.) OnHM
We Shall Not Dwell Forever in These Yellow Lands, Pt. VII. AtBAP
Anabasis. Eithne Wilkins. NeBP
Anacreon to the Sophist. "B. H." InMe
Anacreon's Dove. Samuel Johnson, *after the Greek of* Anacreon. AWP; JAWP; WBP
Anacreontic. Robert Herrick. OAEP; OnPM; OxBoLi; SCEP-2; WoL
Anacreontic on Drinking. Abraham Cowley. *See* Drinking.
Anacreontick. Charles Cotton. PeRV
Anacreontick, An. William Oldys. *See* On a Fly Drinking out of His Cup.
Anactoria, *sels.* Swinburne.
"For who shall change with prayers or thanksgivings." AtBAP
"Thee too the years shall cover; thou shalt be." ViBoPo
Anagram, The, II. John Donne. *Fr.* Elegies. MaMe
Analogous to floral pageantry. Land of the Free. Sister Mary Honora. NePoAm-2
Analysis of Love, The. Sir Herbert Read. FaBoMo; LiTG
"Nature has perpetual tears," *sel.* MoBrPo (1942 ed.)
Ana(Mary Army)gram. George Herbert. CABA; MaMe; SCEP-1
Anansi son name Stan'-up-stick. Sweet Riley. *Unknown.* BaBo
Anastasis. Albert E. S. Smythe. CaP

Anathemata, The, *sels.* David Jones.
Rite and Fore-Time. AtBAP
"Stands a lady/ on a mountain." PrWP
Anatole France at Eighty. Gladys Oaks. AnAmPo
Anatomie [*or* Anatomy] of the World, An; the First Anniversary. John Donne. AnAnS-1; MaMe; MasP; MBW-1; MeP; SCEP-1
Sels.
Doth Not a Tenarif, or Higher Hill. ChTr
"How witty's ruin! how importunate." ReEn
New Philsophy, The. ExPo
"She, she is dead." MyFE
"So did the world from the first hour decay." TuPP
"When that rich Soule which to her heaven is gone." SeCV-1; SeEP
Anatomy Lesson. Ilo Orleans. RIS
Anatomy of a Lover, The. George Gascoigne. ReIE
Anatomy of Angels, The. Alden Nowlan. PeCV (1967 ed.)
Anatomy of Baseness, The, *sel.* John Andrews.
To the Detracted. EIL, 8 *ll.*; LO, 16 *ll.*; SeEP
Anatomy of Happiness, The. Ogden Nash. LiTA; LiTM; SiTL
Anatomy of Humor, The. Morris Bishop. InMe; WhC
Anatomy of Melancholy, The, *sels.* Robert Burton.
Authors Abstract of Melancholy, The. OBS; SeCL
"Dost ask (my dear) what service I will have?" *after the Latin of* Terence. LO
Anatomy of the World, An. John Donne. *See* Anatomie of the World, An.
"Ancestor remote of Man, The." Man and the Ascidian. Andrew Lang. HBV
Ancestors, The. Christopher Middleton. NMP; OPoP
Ancestors, The. Judith Wright. BoAV
Ancestral Dwellings, The. Henry van Dyke. PoMa
Ancestral Faces. Kwesi Brew. PBA
Ancestral Houses. W. B. Yeats. Meditations in Time of Civil War, I. CABL; ChMP; LiTB; MoVE; PIA
Ancestry. Stephen Crane. The Black Riders, XXII. AA
Ancestry. William A. Donaghy. JKCP (1955 ed.)
Anchises. Blanaid Salkeld. OxBI
Anchor: "Oft I must strive with wind and wave." *Unknown, tr. fr. Anglo-Saxon by* Charles W. Kennedy. *Fr.* Riddles. AnOE
Anchor is weighed, and the sails they are set, The. Away, Rio! *Unknown.* AmSS; LoGBV
Anchorage, The. Pat Wilson. AnNZ
Anchored to the Infinite. Edwin Markham. MaRV; OQP
Anchor's Aweigh, The, *with music.* *Unknown.* ShS
Ancient. "Æ." SeCePo
Ancient and leaden-lidded he treads. Chameleon. Anthony Delius. BoSA
Ancient and Modern Muses, The. Francis Turner Palgrave. VA
Ancient Ballad of Chevy-Chase, The. *Unknown.* *See* Chevy Chase.
Ancient Barbarossa, the Kaiser Frederick old, The. Barbarossa. Friedrich Rückert. AWP
Ancient bridge, and a more ancient tower, An. My House. W. B. Yeats. Meditations in Time of Civil War, II. CABL; LiTB; PIA
Ancient Carol, An. *Unknown.* *See* I Sing of a Maiden.
Ancient Castle, An. William Morris. *Fr.* Golden Wings. SeCePo
Ancient cavern, huge and wide, An. The Cavern and the Hut. John Hookham Frere. OTPC (1923 ed.)
Ancient chestnut's blossoms threw, An. Alciphron and Leucippe. Walter Savage Landor. OBEV
Ancient Christmas Carol, An. *Unknown.* *See* I Sing of a Maiden.
Ancient Degree, An. Bernadette Mayer. ANYP
Ancient Doctrine, The. Robert Browning. *See* Among the Rocks.
Ancient Historian. Chris Wallace-Crabbe. PoAu-2
Ancient Lights. Austin Clarke. NMP; OPoP; OxBI
Ancient long-horned bovine, An. The Last Longhorn. *At. to* R. W. Hall. CoSo
Ancient Lullaby. Gerald Griffin. IrPN
Ancient Mansion, The, *sel.* George Crabbe. *Fr.* Posthumous Tales.
Spring to Winter. ChTr
Ancient Mariner, The. Samuel Taylor Coleridge. *See* Rime of the Ancient Mariner, The.
Ancient Music. Ezra Pound. FIW; LiTM; NePA; OxBA; Par; PIA; PoE; PPON; SiTL
Ancient of Days. William Croswell Doane. AA
Ancient pages of the Talmud. The Talmud. Simeon Frug. TrJP
Ancient person, for whom I. A Song of a Young Lady to Her Ancient Lover. Earl of Rochester. CavP; CBV; EP; ErPo; MePo; PeRV
Ancient Phyllis. Congreve. *Fr.* The Double-Dealer. SeCL
Ancient poets and their learned rhymes, The. An Answer to Some Verses Made in His Praise. Sir John Suckling. PP
Ancient pond, The. Haiku. Basho. CaFP
Ancient Prayer, An. T. H. B. Webb. *See* Prayer, A: "Give me a good digestion, Lord."
Ancient Prophecy, An. Philip Freneau. OTD; PAH
Ancient Proverb, An. Blake. ERoP-1
Ancient Quatrain. *Unknown, tr. fr. Chinese by* David Rafael Wang. HW
Ancient Race, The Michael Tormey. JKCP (1926 ed.)
Ancient readers of heaven's book, Th'. Ode: Of Cynthia. *Unknown.* OBSC; SiCE
Ancient Sacrifice, The. Mahlon Leonard Fisher. AnAmPo
Ancient saga tells us how, An. Dead Cow Farm. Robert Graves. BrPo
Ancient Sage, The. Tennyson. EPN; ViPP
Sels.
Cling to Faith. OQP
Faith ("Thou canst not prove the Nameless"). MaRV
"Thou canst not prove that thou art body alone." WGRP
Ancient songs pass deathward mournfully, The. Choricos. Richard Aldington. HBMV; NP
Ancient Sorrow. Giosuè Carducci, *tr. fr. Italian by* Glauco Cambon. OnPM
Ancient sowed an acorn from His mind, The. Oak. Philip Child. CaP
Ancient story I'll tell you anon, An. King John and the Abbott of Canterbury. *Unknown.* BoChLi; BoHV; BoTP; EnSB; GN; GoTP; HBV; OBB; OnSP; OTPC; RG; StaSt; TrGrPo
Ancient Thought, The. Watson Kerr. SoP; TRV; WGRP
Ancient to Ancients, An. Thomas Hardy. ChMo; ChMP; CMoP; CoBMV; GTBS-P; LiTM (rev. ed.); MoPo; MoVE; PoVP; TOP
Ancient Virgin, An. George Crabbe. *Fr.* The Parish Register. OBNC
Ancient Winter. Salvatore Quasimodo, *tr. fr. Italian by* Glauco Cambon. OnPM
Ancient wood, fit for the work designed, An. The Golden Bough. Vergil, *tr.* by Dryden. *Fr.* The Aeneid, VI. PeRV
Anciently in this village. Ivy and Holly. E. H. W. Meyerstein. ELU
And a ah-la-dee. Little Mathey Grove. *Unknown.* BFSS
And a Certain Priest Comming That Way Looked on Him and Passed By. Richard Crashaw. MaMe
And a clam caught my little finger. The Little Girl That Lost a Finger. "Gabriela Mistral." FaPON
And a dog, lying there, lifted its head and pricked its ears. Homer. *Fr.* The Odyssey, XVII. LO
And a great sign appeared in heaven. A Woman Clothed with the Sun. Apocalypse (Revelation), Bible, *N.T.* (*Douay vers.*). ISi
And after all, it's there for the listening. The Oracle of Delphi. Adèle Naudé. BoSA
And after Calvary, a garden, green. They Saw and Believed. Esther Lloyd Hagg. ChIP
And after he has come to hide. Compensation. Phoebe Cary. OQP
"And all her silken flanks with garlands drest." Vlamertinghe: Passing the Chateau, July 1917. Edmund Blunden. MMA; Sonn
And all is well, tho' faith and form. In Memoriam A. H. H., CXXVII. Tennyson. BEL; CoBE; EnLi-2; EPN; HBV; OAEP; ViPo; VP
And all the sails hang limp. Comes Fog and Mist. William Hart-Smith. *Fr.* Christopher Columbus. PoAu-2
"And All the While the Sky Is Falling. . ." Lora Dunetz. NePoAm
And all the while they mocked him and reviled. The Martyr. Natalie Flohr. ChIP; PGD
And all these years I have hidden it. Spel IV. Robert Kelly. *Fr.* Thor's Thrush. YAP

And all things are of God. God Was in Christ. Second Corinthians, Bible, *N.T.* TRV
And Already the Minutes. Conrad Aiken. Priapus and the Pool, V [VI]. InPo
And always through my window pane. Girl's Song. Marya Zaturenska. TPM
And Angling, Too. Byron. *Fr.* Don Juan. SD
And are ye one of Hermitage. The Inquiry. Thomas Hardy. At Casterbridge Fair, V. BEL; EnLi-2 (1949 ed.); EnLit; PoVP
And [*or* But] are ye [*or* you] sure the news is true. The Sailor's Wife [*or* The Mariner's Wife *or* There's Nae Luck about the House]. William Julius Mickle, *also at. to* Jean Adam. BeLS; GN; GTBS; GTBS-D; GTBS-P; GTBS-W; GTSE; GTSL; HBV; LO; OBEC; ViBoPo
And Art Thou Come, Blest Babe? *Unknown.* OxBoCh
And art thou come to this at last. Alexander McLachlan. *Fr.* To an Indian Skull. CaP
And art thou fallen and lowly laid. Lament for Tabby. *Unknown.* CIV
And art thou grieved, sweet and sacred dove? Grieve Not the Holy Spirit. George Herbert. AnAnS-1; MaMe; MeP
And art thou he, now "Fallen on evil days." Milton: On the Busts of Milton, in Youth and Age. William Lisle Bowles. Sonn
And art Thou mine, my dearest Lord? On the Sacrament. Elizabeth Rowe. Three Hymns, 2. WaPE
And as Dame Fame was in laudation. Stephen Hawes. *Fr.* The Pastime of Pleasure. ReIE
And as for me, though that my wit be lite [*or* thogh that I can but lyte]. Chaucer. *Fr.* The Legend of Good Women. CH; ViBoPo
And as he journeyed, he came near Damascus. Paul on the Road to Damascus. The Acts, Bible, *N.T.* TreF
And as I have said before and elsewhere: If I. Ogden Nash Gets All the Cash. David McCord. ML
And as, my friend, you ask me what makes me sad and still. Utah Carroll. *Unknown.* CoSo
And as she backward cast her busy eye. Be Bold. Spenser. *Fr.* The Faerie Queene, III. MyFE
And, as the path of duty is made plain. His Strength. Whittier. *Fr.* First Day Thoughts. FaChP; SoP
And as we spoke the Nicene Creed we were called out. Barnfire during Church. Robert Bly. NePoEA
And as we walked the grass was faintly stirred. Hawks. James Stephens. HBMV; NP
And at Lake Geneva, Which is in Wisconsin. At Lake Geneva. Richard Eberhart. LiTA
And at last when I go. Daily Prayer. Marion Strobel. NP
And at the last from inner Egypt came. Nyarlathotep. H. P. Lovecraft. HYE
And before hell mouth; dry plain. Ezra Pound. *Fr.* Canto XVI. ExPo; MoPo
And, behold, a certain lawyer stood up, and tempted him. The Good Samaritan. St. Luke, Bible, *N.T.* TreF
. . . And behold thrones were kingless, and men walked. The Day of Liberty. Shelley. *Fr.* Prometheus Unbound, III, iv. EPN
And, behold, two of them went that same day to a village called Emmaus. On the Road to Emmaus. St. Luke, Bible, *N.T.* TreFS
And boys, be in nothing so moderate as in love of man. Robinson Jeffers. *Fr.* Shine, Perishing Republic. TRV
And by "his kind" this scoundrel means no less. Lawyer in Search of Six Poets. *Unknown.* SiTL
And call it the maiden ladies day. April Thirty first. Barbara L. Greenberg. QAH
And call the vales, and bid them hither cast. Milton. *Fr.* Lycidas. WePo
And call ye this to utter what is just. Psalm LVIII. Countess of Pembroke. EP
And Can the Physician Make Sick Men Well. *Unknown.* *Fr.* Robin Goodfellow, Pt. II. AtBAP
(And Can the Physician?) ELP
(Lily, Germander, and Sops-in-Wine.) AnFE
(Song: "And can the physician make sick men well?"). EIL; LoBV; ThWaDe
And canst thou find God in the crystal sphere. Immanence. F. Barrie Flint. OQP
And cells in breaking. The Solitary. Jason Miller. ThO
And change with hurried hand has swept these scenes. Elegy in Six Sonnets. Frederick Goddard Tuckerman. *Fr.* Sonnets. NoP; QFR
And chiefly shone. Variations and Elegy: White Stag, Black Bear. James Merrill. NoP
And children still grow up with longing eyes. Twilight of the Outward Life. Hugo von Hofmannsthal, *tr. by* Peter Viereck. OnHM
And cruell maid, because I see. The Cruell Maid. Robert Herrick. CavP
And Dancing. Ivy O. Eastwick. MPB (1956 ed.)
And David lamented with this lamentation over Saul and over Jonathan his son. David's Lament. *Fr.* Second Samuel, Bible, *O.T.*. ChTr
And Death Shall Have No Dominion. Dylan Thomas. ACV; ChMP; CMoP; CoBE; EaLo; ExPo; LiTM; MaPo; MemP; MoAB; MoBrPo (1950 ed.); MoRP; MoVE; NeBP; OAEP (2d ed.); OnHM; PoDB; PoIE; POTE; SeCePo; ShBV-4; ToPo; WePo
And deep-eyed children cannot long be children. Ballad of the Outer Life. Hugo von Hofmannsthal. AWP; JAWP; LiTW; TrJP; WBP
And deisel oil/ having the wrong/ chemistry. The Wind Was Out of the North. James Koller. FRC
And Dick said, "Look what I have found!" Crescent Moon. Elizabeth Madox Roberts. SUS; TiPo (1952 ed.)
And did ever a man go black with sun in a Belgian swamp. Nigger. Karl Shapiro. OxBA
And Did Those Feet in Ancient Time. Blake. *Fr.* Milton. AtBAP; ATP; AWP; BEL; CABA; CaFP; CBEP; EG; EiPP; EnRP; ERoP-1; FaBoCh; FaBV; FOL; InPo; JAWP; LoBV; LoGBV; MaRV; NoP; OAEP; OBRV; PAn; PG (1945 ed.); PoAn; PoE; PoEL-4; PoFS; PoRA; PoSa; SeCeV; StJW; TOP; UnPo (1st ed.); ViBoPo; WBP; WGRP
(Chariot of Fire.) OnPM
(Jerusalem.) BBV (1951 ed.); BoTP; EaLo; EvOK; GTBS-W; MemP; OBEV (new ed.); OtMeF; PPON; ShBV-2; WaaP
(New Jerusalem, A [*or* The].) BoLiVe; FaBoEn; LiTB; LiTG; PTK; TrGrPo
(Preface.) EiCL; ILP; PoIE
(Preface to "Milton".) AnFE; CEP; NeHB; PoeP
(Prelude.) OBNC
(Song: "And did those feet in ancient time.") WoL
(Stanzas from "Milton.") EnLi-2; EnLit
(Till We Have Built Jerusalem.) OQP
And did thy sapphire shallop slip. To a New-born Baby Girl. Grace Hazard Conkling. HBV
And did you not hear of a mirth that befell. Away to Twiver, Away, Away! *Unknown.* EIL
"And did you once see Shelley plain?" A Travelogue; Clovelly. Carolyn Wells. InMe
And did young Stephen sicken. Ode to Stephen Dowling Bots, Dec'd. "Mark Twain." *Fr.* The Adventures of Huckleberry Finn. FiBHP
And didst thou die, dear Mother of our Life? Our Lady's Death. Benjamin Dionysius Hill. JKCP
And didst Thou love the race that loved not Thee? Kinsman. Jean Ingelow. MaRV
And do I see some cause a hope to feed. Astrophel and Stella, LXVI. Sir Philip Sidney. FCP; ReEn; SiPS
And do our loves all perish with our frames? Immortality. Richard Henry Dana. AA; WGRP
And do they so? have they a sense? Rom. Cap. 8. Ver. 19. Henry Vaughan. AnAnS-1; MeLP; MeP; OBS; ReEn; SCEP-1; SeEP
And dost thou faithlessly abandon me? The Unrealities. Schiller. AWP; WoL
And doun on knes anoon-ryght I me sette. This Fresshe Flour. Chaucer. *Fr.* The Legend of Good Women. SeCePo
And dragging their shining skins. Deeply Gone. Jon Silkin. FiSC
And Dust to Dust. Charles David Webb. NePoAm-2
And Each Man's Leave. Roland Robinson. NeLNL
And early in the morning he came again into the temple. The Woman Taken in Adultery. St. John, Bible, *N.T.* TreFT
And Ellen, when the graybeard years. To Ellen. Emerson. TOP
"And Enoch walked with God." The Secret. Joan Suisted. SoP
"And even our women," lastly grumbles Ben. The Girl of All Periods. Coventry Patmore. VA

And even silence found a tongue. John Clare. *Fr.* Secret Love. LO
And ever must I fan this fire? Camoens. Herman Melville. ViBoPo
And every beast of beating heart grew bold. Shelley. *Fr.* The Witch of Atlas. MyFE
And every prodigal greatness. The Flowering Urn. Laura Riding. FaBoMo; LiTA
And Every Sky Was Blue and Rain. Ralph Hodgson. *Fr.* To Deck a Woman, II. LOW
And every year a world my will did deem. Seven Sonnets in Sequence, III. George Gascoigne. Sonn
And faces, forms and phantoms, numbered not. Elegy in Six Sonnets. Frederick Goddard Tuckerman. *Fr.* Sonnets. QFR
And Fall Shall Sit in Judgment. Audre Lorde. NNP
And finally, ladies and gentlemen, perhaps in his quiet way. Tithonus. D. M. Thomas. HYE
And first behold the merriest man alive. The Characters of the Wits. John Sheffield, Duke of Buckingham and Normanby. *Fr.* An Essay on Satyr. PeRV
And first Morency, far famed water, you. Standish O'Grady. *Fr.* The Emigrant. CaP
And first, the lamp-posts whose burning match-heads. Jewish Main Street. Irving Layton. CaP
And for the soul,/ if it is to know itself. Argonautica. George Seferis. OnHM
"And forasmuch that he made Nature." Stephen Hawes. *Fr.* The Pastime of Pleasure. RelE
"And Forgive Us Our Trespasses." Aphra Behn. MeWo; PeRV
And forth h' is brought unto th' accomplishment. Samuel Daniel. *Fr.* The Civil Wars, II. RelE
. . . & Forty-second Street. Archibald MacLeish. CoBA
And Freedom rear'd in that august sunrise. Tennyson. *Fr.* The Poet. PoFr
And from a northern coast the Lovers watch'd. Three Fragments, I. William Allingham. IrPN
And from Sardes her/ thoughts. Arignota Remembers. Sappho. LiTW
And from the windy West came two-gunned Gabriel. Altarwise by Owl-Light, V. Dylan Thomas. CoBMV; LiTM; MaSP
And glad to find, on again looking at it. Quayside. Robert Graves. FaBoMo
And God Created the Great Whales. Milton. *Fr.* Paradise Lost, VII. EtS
And God said, How do you know? Job. R. S. Thomas. NYTB
And God said . . . I do set my bow in the cloud. The Rainbow. Genesis, Bible, *O.T.* BoC
And God saw that the wickedness of man was great in the earth. Noah and the Flood. Genesis, Bible, *O.T.* OuHeWo
And God spake all these words, saying. The Ten Commandments. Exodus, Bible, *O.T.* TreF
And God stepped out on space. The Creation. James Weldon Johnson. BALP; BANP; CDC; FaBV; GoSl; MAP; MaRV; MoAmPo; NP; PoNe; PoPl; PoRA (rev. ed.); TiPo (1952 ed.); WePo; YaD
And Grow. John Hay. WaP
And Gwydion said to Math, when it was spring. The Wife of Llew. Francis Ledwidge. CLwM; PoMS
And haply, bason'd in some unsunn'd cleft. Samuel Taylor Coleridge. *Fr.* To a Young Friend. ChER
And hark! how blithe the throstle sings! Let Nature Be Your Teacher. Wordsworth. *Fr.* The Tables Turned. MaRV
And hasten Og and Doeg to rehearse. Og and Doeg [*or* Characters from the Satires]. Dryden. *Fr.* Absalom and Achitophel, Pt. II. AWP; InPo; JAWP; MBW-1; WBP
And have I heard her say, "O cruel pain!" Sir Philip Sidney. FCP
And have the bright immensities. Via Lucis. Howard Chandler Robbins. MaRV; OQP
And have we done with war at last? Two Fusiliers. Robert Graves. MMA
"And having taken bread, he broke it." Holy Week. Phoebe Smith Bachelder. ChIP
And He Answered Them Nothing. Richard Crashaw. EP; MaMe; MePo
And he cast it down, down, on the green grass. The New Ghost. Fredegond Shove. BoPe; ChMP; HBMV; MoVE; OxBoCh
And he is risen? Well, be it so. A Drizzling Easter Morning. Thomas Hardy. CMoP
And he looked up, and he saw the rich men casting their gifts. The Widow's Mite. St. Luke, Bible, *N.T.* TreFT
And he said, A certain man had two sons. The Prodigal Son. St. Luke, Bible, *N.T.* BoC; TreF
And he said to himself. Between Worlds. Carl Sandburg. MoAmPo (1950 ed.)
And he said to them all, If any man will come after me. On Taking up One's Cross. St. Luke, Bible, *N.T.* TreFT
And he shall charm and soothe, and breathe and bless. Christ's Reign of Peace. Stephen Phillips. ChIP
And he showed me a pure river of water of life. There Shall Be No Night. Revelation, Bible, *N.T.* TrGrPo
And he spake this parable unto certain which trusted. The Pharisee and the Publican. St. Luke, Bible, *N.T.* TreFT
And he went unto Ramah. There he met. The Dance of Saul with the Prophets. Saul Tchernichowsky. TrJP
And heed not them that warn or chide thee. The Rosy Days Are Numbered. Moses ibn Ezra. *Fr.* Wine-Songs. TrJP
And here face down beneath the sun. You, Andrew Marvell. Archibald MacLeish. AmLP; AmP; AmPP; AnAmPo; AnEnPo; AnFE; AP; APA; AWP; BoLiVe; CaFP; CBV; CMoP; CoAnAm; CoBA; CoBMV; FaBV; FosPo; GTBS-W; HoPM; InP; InPo; LiTA; LiTM; MAP; MoAB; MoAmPo; MoVE; NeMA; NoP; NP; OxBA; PoAn; PoIE; PoMa; PoRA; StP; TDP; TreFT; TrGrPo; TwAmPo; TwCP; VaPo; ViBoPo; WoL
And here is dear old Boston. The New Order. Phyllis McGinley. AmFN
And here, sweet friend, I go my way. Adios. Joaquin Miller. OQP
And [*or* Loe] here the precious dust is laid [*or* layd]. Maria Wentworth [*or* The Inscription on the Tomb[e] of the Lady Mary Wentworth *or* Epitaph on Maria, Lady Wentworth]. Thomas Carew. AnAnS-2; ATP; EP; MeLP; MePo; OBS; SeCV-1; SeEP
And here where all is waste and wild. Syracuse. Elizabeth Coatsworth. HT
And here's good luck to the shanty boys. Lumberjacks and Teamsters. *Unknown.* OuSiCo
And here's the happy, bounding flea. The Flea [*or* The Happy Bounding Flea]. Roland Young. PoPl; SiTL; WaKn; WhC
And Herod said: "Supposing you had been in my shoes?" Innocents' Day. Norman Nicholson. POTi
And him beside rides fierce revenging Wrath. Spenser. *Fr.* The Faerie Queene, I. MyFE
And Him evermore I beheld. Follow Me. Longfellow. PGD
And His Name Shall Be Called Wonderful. Martha Snell Nicholson. BePJ; SoP
And his son Judas, who was called Maccabeus. Judas Maccabeus. First Maccabees, Bible, Apocrypha. TrJP
And how much of this. The Death of Nick Charles. LeRoi Jones. CoPo
And I am only a little man. A Little Man. *Unknown.* SiTL
And I behold once more. The River. Emerson. MAmP
And I bowed my body and beheld all about. William Langland. *Fr.* The Vision of Piers Plowman. CTC
And I can remember still your first lies America. Q. R. Hand. BF
"And I fare you well, Lady Ouncebell." Lord Lovel (A *vers.*). *Unknown.* BaBo; ESPB; NoP
And I have come upon this place. L'An Trentiesme de Mon Eage (*or* Age) [*or* In My Thirtieth Year]. Archibald MacLeish. AmLP; AnFE; APA; CoAnAm; LiTM; MAP; MoAmPo; MoVE; SiSw; NePA; NP; TwAmPo
And I have learned how diving's done. Fantasia. Dorothy Livesay. MoCV; OBCV
And I have seen again the marvellous child. Sonnet. Paul Verlaine. LiTW
"And I, if I Be Lifted Up, Shall Draw All Men." E. P. Dickie. MaRV
("If I Be Lifted Up.") ChIP
And I said to the man who stood at the gate of the year. God Knows. Minnie Louise Haskins. *Fr.* The Gate of the Year. FaChP; MaRV; SoP; TreFS; TRV; WePo
And, I said, you can take your rich aunts and uncles. The Day

I Kicked a Bankroll out the Window. Charles Bukowski. WOW
And I saw a great white throne. The Last Judgment. Revelation, Bible, *N.T.* TreF
And I saw a new heaven and a new earth. The New Jerusalem. Revelation, Bible, *N.T.* TrGrPo
And I say nothing—no, not a word. My Sister Jane. Ted Hughes. FIW
And I say unto you, Ask, and it shall be given you. Effective Prayer. St. Luke, Bible, *N.T.* TreFT
And I thought of how impossibly alone we were. After a Game of Squash. Samuel L. Albert. GoYe; NePoAm-2
And I took her down by the river. The Faithless Wife. Federico García Lorca. ErPo
And I Turned from the Inner Heart. Jon Silkin. PoDB
And ich bowede my body and bihelde al aboute. A Vision of Nature. William Langland. *Fr.* The Vision of Piers Plowman. PoEL-1
And if. Tangere. Theodore Enslin. CoPo
And If an Eye May Save or Slay. Sir Thomas Wyatt. FCP; MaPo (1969 ed.); SiPS
And If at Last. Louise Labé, *tr. fr. French by* Frederic Prokosch. LiTW
And if by such bright tokens. To Our Lady, the Ark of the Covenants. Raymond E. F. Larsson. ISi
And if Fate remember later, and come to claim her due. Carpe Diem. "Laurence Hope." OtMeF
And if he ever should come back. The Last Words. Maeterlinck. AWP; JAWP; PoPl; WBP
And if he should come again. Ylen's Song. Richard Hovey. *Fr.* The Birth of Galahad. AA
"And if he's gone away," said she. Story. Dorothy Parker. InMe; MaC
And If I Did, What Then? George Gascoigne. *Fr.* The Adventures of Master F. I. EIL; FaBoEn; NCEP; PoEL-1; ReIE (Farewell, A.) LoBV; OBSC
And If I Die before I Wake. Clay Goss. WSL
And if I love you, we'll fight. Mulata—to Skinny. Frank Lima. ANYP
And if I loved you Wednesday. Thursday. Edna St. Vincent Millay. InMe
And if I say I love you, what of that? Another Song. Marion Strobel. MoLP
And if, my friend, you'd have it end. They Part. Dorothy Parker. ALV
And if some day. Thomas Hardy. EG
And if the dead, and the dead/ Of spirit now join. The Conspirators. Frederic Prokosch. LiTM; NAMP; NePA; WaP
"And if the name of 'Mage' offends these gentlemen." A Brief Introduction to the History of Culture. Weldon Kees. TwAmPo
And if tomorrow shall be sad. Today. *Unknown.* OQP
And if tonight my soul may find her peace. Shadows. D. H. Lawrence. OAEP (2d ed.)
And if ye stand in doubt. John Skelton. *Fr.* Colin Clout. EnPo; ReEn
And, if you asked of him to say. Charles Stuart Calverley. *Fr.* Gemini and Virgo. FiBHP
And if you meet the Canon of Chimay. Concerning Geffray Teste Noire. William Morris. PoVP; ViPo
And in a moment will create. Milton. *Fr.* Paradise Lost, VII. YAT
And in Her Morning. Jessica Powers. ISi
And in meanewhyle the gentyll porteres. Stephen Hawes. *Fr.* The Passetyme of Pleasure. EnPo
And in September, O what keen delight! September. Folgore da San Geminiano. *Fr.* Sonnets of the Months. AWP; SD
And in strange lands. I Shall Remember. H. D. Carberry. PoNe
And in that land dwells a king. Sir Cawline. *Unknown.* ESPB
And in the frosty season, when the sun. On the Frozen Lake [*or* Skating]. Wordsworth. *Fr.* The Prelude. FaBoCh; GN; GoTP; InP; LoGBV; MyFE; PoMa; ShBV-3
And in the Hanging Gardens. Conrad Aiken. MAP; MAPA; MoAB; MoAmPo
And in the midst of all a fountaine stood. The Bower of Bliss. Spenser. *Fr.* The Faerie Queene, II. CH
And in the morning the king loved you most. Arcanum One. Gwendolyn MacEwen. MoCV
And, in the night, the Spirit came. The Messenger. Alfred Noyes. GoBC
And in the sixth month, the angel Gabriel was sent from God. Mary and Gabriel. St. Luke, Bible, *N.T.* (*Douay vers.*). ISi
And in the world, as in the school. Sportsmanship. Thackeray. OTD
And is he gone, whom these arms held but now. Quaerit Jesum Suum Maria. Richard Crashaw. ACP; CAW; MaMe
And Is It Night? *Unknown.* EIL
And is our life, a life wherein we borrow. Matthew X. 28. Roger Wolcott. SCAP
And is the great cause lost beyond recall? Faith. Ada Cambridge. PoAu-1
And is the swallow gone? The Departure of the Swallow. William Howitt. VA
And is there care in heaven? and is there love. Guardian Angels [*or* The Bright Squadrons *or* Guardian Angels of Men *or* Heavenly Aid]. Spenser. *Fr.* The Faerie Queene, II, 8. BoC; GoBC; MaRV; OBSC; OxBoCh
And is this—Yarrow!—This the stream. Yarrow Visited [1814]. Wordsworth. BEL; EnLi-2; EnRP; GTBS; GTBS-D; GTBS-P; GTBS-W; GTSL; HBV; MERP
And Ishmael crouch'd beside a crackling briar. Ishmael. Herbert Edward Palmer. OBEV (new ed.); POTE
And it came to pass after these things, that God did tempt Abraham. Abraham and Isaac. Genesis, Bible, *O.T.* EnLi-1 (1949 ed.); OuHeWo
And It Came to Pass at Midnight. Yannai, *tr. fr. Hebrew.* TrJP
And it came to pass in an eveningtide. David and Bathsheba. Second Samuel, Bible, *O.T.* OuHeWo
And it came to pass in those days. The Adoration of the Shepherds [*or* The First Christmas]. St. Luke, Bible, *N.T.* ChrBoLe; TreFS
And it came to pass, that, as Jesus sat at meat in his house. Jesus Eats With Sinners. St. Mark, Bible, *N.T.* TreFT
And it shall come to pass in the day that the Lord shall give thee rest. Isaiah, Bible, *O.T.* PoFr
And it shall come to pass in the end of days. In the End of Days. Isaiah, Bible, *O.T.* TrJP
And it shall come to pass when the days shall grow long. When the Days Shall Grow Long. Hayyim Nahman Bialik. TrJP
And it was in the winter. Contrast. Charles Granville Hamilton. ChIP
And it's fare you well, fare you well. Runagate Runagate. Robert E. Hayden. PoNe
And it's ladies to the center. Shoot the Buffalo. *Unknown.* ABF
And Jephthah vowed a vow unto the Lord. Jephthah's Daughter. Judges, Bible, *O.T.* OuHeWo
And Jesus answered them, saying, The hour is come. Children of the Light. St. John, Bible, *N.T.* WoL
And Jesus said, A certain man had two sons. St. Luke, Bible, *N.T.* LO
And Jesus said unto them, I am the bread of life. I Am the Bread of Life. St. John, Bible, *N.T.* TreFS
And Jesus Wept. Matthew Bridges. BePJ; SoP
And just by crossing the short sea. Channel Crossing. George Barker. ACV; ChMP; GTBS-P; ToPo
And King Olaf heard the cry. King Olaf's Return. Longfellow. *Fr.* The Saga of King Olaf. AmPP (4th ed.)
And ladders leaning against damson trees. The Looker-on. Frank Kendon. POTE
And learn O voyager to walk. Seafarer. Archibald MacLeish. NoP
And Left Me Stranded on a Hush. Doyle Hennessy. JKCP (1955 ed.)
And let the canakin clink, [clink]. Shakespeare. *Fr.* Othello, II, iii. LiBL
And Lightly, like the Flowers. Pierre de Ronsard, *tr. fr. French by* W. E. Henley. AWP
And like a dying lady, lean and pale. The Moon [*or* The Waning Moon]. Shelley. AnFE; BoLiVe; CH; ChER; FaBoCh; LoGBV; OBEV; PoG; TDP; TrGrPo
And like the riptide riven reef-swirls. Reef Wrack. Clement B. Christesen. BoAu
And like thy father sing in tunefulness. A Barren Soul. Joseph Ezobi. *Fr.* The Silver Bowl. TrJP

And, lo! leading a blessed host comes one. Lincoln. Harriet Monroe. *Fr.* Commemoration Ode. AA; LiPo
And lo! the sea that fleets about the land. *See* For lo! the sea that fleets about the land.
And Lo, the Star! Molly Anderson Haley. PGD
And long ere dinner-time I have. On a Day's Stint. Sir Walter Scott. NBM
And Los beheld the mild Emanation, Jerusalem, eastward bending. In Deadly Fear. Blake. *Fr.* Jerusalem. SeCePo
And Love Hung Still. Louis MacNeice. Trilogy for X, II. LiTL; MoBrPo
("And love hung still as crystal over the bed.") ErPo
And man is a spirit. Louis MacNeice. *Fr.* Holes in the Sky. TRV
"And Man is left alone with Man." 'Tis well! At the Worst. Israel Zangwill. WGRP
And many an endless, endless lake. Wordsworth. *Fr.* Ruth. MyFE
And Mary rising up in those days. Mary and Elizabeth. St. Luke, Bible, *N.T.* (*Douay vers.*). ISi
And Mary said, "Before the void was filled." Ex Maria Virgine. Norbert Engels. ISi
And Mary said: My soul doth magnify the Lord. The Magnificat. St. Luke, Bible, *N.T.* (*Douay vers.*). ISi
And Mary stood beside the cross! Her soul. Mary at the Cross. Clyde McGee. MaRV; PGD
And mathematics, fresh as May. Edmund Blunden. *Fr.* Reliques. ImOP
And may my humble dwelling stand. Matthew Green. *Fr.* The Spleen. LoBV
And me happiest when I compose poems. The Birth of Tragedy. Irving Layton. MoCV; OBCV; PeCV
And me my winter's task is drawing over. Frederick Goddard Tuckerman. *Fr.* Sonnets. QFR
And mightier grew the joy to meet full-faced. Swimming. Swinburne. *Fr.* Tristram of Lyonesse. GN
And Mr. Ferritt. Judith Wright. MoBrPo (1962 ed.)
And Monelle said: I will speak to you of actions. Actions. Marcel Schwob. TrJP
And Monelle said: I will speak to you of moments. Moments. Marcel Schwob. TrJP
And Monelle said: I will speak to you of things dead. Things Dead. Marcel Schwob. TrJP
And mony ane sings o' grass, o' grass. *Unknown.* *Fr.* The Birth of Robin Hood. ViBoPo
And much fruit, the swan. See in the Midst of Fair Leaves. Marianne Moore. MoAB
And must I say that God is Christ. Faith. Edwin McNeill Poteat. ChIP; MaRV
And must we part, because some say. The Suspition upon His Over-much Familiarity with a Gentlewoman. Robert Herrick. CavP
And my dear one sat in the shadows; very softly she wept. Ford Madox Ford. *Fr.* On Heaven. ViBoPo
And my poor fool is hang'd! No, no, no life! Death of Lear. Shakespeare. *Fr.* King Lear, V, iii. FiP
And my young sweetheart sat at board with me. Idyl. Alfred Mombert. AWP; JAWP; WBP
And Naomi said/ Unto her two daughters-in-law. Naomi and Ruth. Ruth, Bible, *O.T.* TrJP
And natheless there is no man. *Unknown.* LO
And nature, the old nurse, took. The Manuscripts of God. Longfellow. *Fr.* The Fiftieth Birthday of Agassiz. MaRV; SoP; TRV
And near me on the grass lies Glanvil's book. Matthew Arnold. *Fr.* The Scholar Gipsy. ACV
And near some river-mouth—shoal—marshy-wide. Alfred Domett. *Fr.* Ranolf and Amohia. AnNZ
And new Philosophy calls all in doubt. The New Philosophy. John Donne. *Fr.* An Anatomy of the World. ExPo
And Nicodemus came by night. Nicodemus. Harry Kemp. OQP
And nigh thereto a little Chappell stoode. Spenser. *Fr.* The Faerie Queene, V, 6. MBW-1
And nigh this toppling reed, still as the dead. Edmund Blunden. *Fr.* The Pike. OA
And none but Love their woeful hap did rue. *Unknown.* *Fr.* Love Winged My Hopes. LO
And nor will these tears be the last. Nor Will These Tears Be the Last. Goethe. LiTW
And nothing was missing. Master Canterel at Locus Solus. David Shapiro. ANYP
"And Now. . ." J. B. Boothroyd. FiBHP
And now all nature seemed in love. On a [*or* the] Bank as I Sat a-Fishing [*or* A Description of the Spring *or* A May Day]. Sir Henry Wotton. AnAnS-2; CH; LoBV; MyFE; OBS; SeCL; SeCP
And now. An attempt. Behold the Lilies of the Field. Anthony Hecht. CoPo; NePoEA-2; PoIE (1970 ed.)
And now at last. Robert E. Lee. Stephen Vincent Benét. *Fr.* John Brown's Body. AmFN
And now at last I come to it: spring. Spring,/ etc. Reed Whitemore. WaKn
And now at length the joyful time drew on. Endymion's Convoy. Michael Drayton. *Fr.* Endimion and Phoebe. OBSC
And now, behold! as at the approach of the morning. The Celestial Pilot. Dante. *Fr.* Divina Commedia: Purgatorio. WGRP
And now beware the tearful rogue. The Peace. Ralph Hodgson. CBV
And now both bands in close embraces met. Heaps on Heaps. Matthew Concanen. *Fr.* A Match at Football. SD
And now four days the sun had seen our woes. The Great Fire. Dryden. *Fr.* Annus Mirabilis. FiP
And now gentlemen. The Base of All Metaphysics. Walt Whitman. AmePo; NePA
And, now gives Time, her states description. George Chapman. *Fr.* Euthymiae Raptus. PoEL-2
And now I have another lad! The Danger of Writing Defiant Verse. Dorothy Parker. InMe
And Now in Age I Bud Again. George Herbert. *Fr.* The Flower. CBEP
And now, kind friends, what I have wrote. What I Have Wrote. Julia A. Moore. FiBHP; SiTL
And now Love sang: but his was such a song. Willowwood, 2. Dante Gabriel Rossetti. The House of Life, L. MaVP; OAEP; PoVP; ViPo; VP
And now, man-slaughtering Pallas tooke in hand. The End of the Suitors. Homer. *Fr.* The Odyssey, XXII. OBS
And now methinks I could e'en chide myself. Cyril Tourneur. *Fr.* The Revenger's Tragedy. ViBoPo
And now only I still remain to gather the strands. The Final Soliloquy. Colin Thiele. *Fr.* Burke and Wills. NeLNL
"And now," said the Governor, gazing abroad on the piled-up store. The First Thanksgiving Day. Margaret Junkin Preston. MC; PAH; ThLM
And now she cleans her teeth into the lake. Camping Out. William Empson. CMoP; FaBoMo; MoVE; ToPo
And now spring. Tanka, VI. Lewis Alexander. CDC
And now take thought, my sonnet, who is he. Sonnets of the Months: Conclusion. Folgore da San Gemignano. AWP
And now th'art set wide ope, the speare's sad art. I Am the Doore. Richard Crashaw. MaMe; OAEP
And now the dark comes on, all full of chitter noise. The Sound of Night. Maxine W. Kumin. BoNaP
And now the earth they had spurned rose up against them in anger. The Flight. C. Day Lewis. *Fr.* A Time to Dance. FaBoMo
And now the final toast. The Final Toast. Tom Veitch. ANYP
And now the green household is dark. In the Tree House at Night. James Dickey. NoP; PIA; ToPo
And now the long, long lines of the Nation's graves. For Decoration Day, II. Rupert Hughes. AA
And now the Queen, to glad her sons, proclaims. Pope. *Fr.* The Dunciad, II. NoP
And now the rain again. The Rain and the Rainbow. Leo Fredericks. ACV
And now the sea-scoured temptress, having failed. The Re-Birth of Venus. Geoffrey Hill. NePoEA
And now the trembling light. Shoreham: Twilight Time. Samuel Palmer. ERoP-2; NBM
And Now There Is Nothing Left. George Barker. *Fr.* Pacific Sonnets. LiTM (rev. ed.)
("And now there is nothing left to celebrate.") NeBP; Sonn
And now they nigh approachèd to the stead. The Mermaids. Spenser. *Fr.* The Faerie Queene, II, 12. ChTr; MBW-1
And now they were diverted by their suite. Byron. *Fr.* Don Juan, III. FosPo; MBW-2

And now 'tis time; for their officious haste. Heroic [*or* Heroique] Stanzas. Dryden. CEP; SeCV-2
And now, to all the other memories. Threnody for a Pet Cat. Mazie V. Caruthers. CIV
"And now to God the Father," he ends. In Church. Thomas Hardy. *Fr.* Satires of Circumstance. DiPo; DTC; FosPo; MoAB; MoBrPo; PoDB; VaPo; VP
And now to the abbyss I pass. Andrew Marvell. *Fr.* Appleton House. AtBAP
And now to what remains!—Since I've resolved. Origins of Vegetable and Animal Life. Lucretius, *tr. by* William Ellery Leonard. *Fr.* De Rerum Natura. OuHeWo
And now, unveil'd, the toilet stands display'd. The Toilet [*or* Belinda's Morning]. Pope. *Fr.* The Rape of the Lock. ExPo; OBEC
And now we climb this bare eroded hill. Dombashawa. Peter Jackson. BoSA
And now we will write the praises of our Lady. Weddase Maryam. *Unknown.* ISi
And now what are we? unbelievers both. In Doubt of Doubt. Robert Browning. *Fr.* Bishop Blougram's Apology. MaRV
And now what monarch would not gardener be. To Amanda Walking in the Garden. Nicholas Hookes. SeCL
And now where're he strays. Richard Crashaw. *Fr.* Saint Mary Magdalene. LiTG; Par
And now, with gleams of half-extinguished thought. Wordsworth. *Fr.* Tintern Abbey. ViBoPo
And now you live dispersed on ribbon roads. T. S. Eliot. *Fr.* The Rock. TiPo
And now you're ready who while she was here. Epigram. J. V. Cunningham. ErPo
And O and O,/ The daisies blow. Song of Spring. Keats. BoTP
And, oh! there lives within my heart. A Hope. Anne Brontë. MaRV
And oh, to think the sun can shine. Adelaide Neilson. William Winter. AA
And o'er the first bumbarrel's nest. Birds' Nests. John Clare. *Fr.* Childhood. BiS
And of Columbus. Horace Gregory. CMoP
And of Laughter That Was a Changeling. Elizabeth Rendall. HBMV
And oft, while wonder thrill'd my breast, mine eyes. Waterspout. Luis de Camoes. EtS
And on My Eyes Dark Sleep by Night. "Michael Field." OBMV
And on that day, upon the heavenly scarp. Psalm VI. A. M. Klein. *Fr.* The Psalter of Avram Haktani. PeCV
And on the porch, across the upturned chair. The Poet at Seven. Donald Justice. TwAmPo
And on the wall was limned a mouldering corse. On the Wall. Immanuel di Roma. TrJP
And on This Shore. M. Carl Holman. AmNP; PoNe
And once again I was within that house. The Dream. John Peale Bishop. LiTA; LiTM (rev. ed.)
And once, in some swamp-forest, these. Coal Fire. Louis Untermeyer. GoTP
And once more the necromancer. The White Kite. *Unknown.* *Fr.* Song of Quetzalcoatl. LiTW
And one morning while in the woods. Between the World and Me. Richard Wright. AmNP; IDB; LiTM (1970 ed.); PoNe
And one of the malefactors which were hanged railed on him. St. Luke, Bible, *N.T.* BoC
And One Shall Live in Two. Jonathan Henderson Brooks. PoNe
"And one that dips with me the sop." — "Not I!" Judas. Howard McKinley Corning. ChIP
And Only Our Shadow Walks with Us. Eithne Wilkins. NeBP
And/Or. Clarence Day. WhC
And Other Poems. R. S. Morgan. FIW
And our/ namby-nimby-pamby-pimby shuffles. If Beer Cans Were Bullets. Arthur Pfister. WSL
And out in the black chart. Beyond Astronaut. John Fairfax. HYE
And Paris be it or Helen dying. Fragment on [*or* of] Death. Villon, *tr. by* Swinburne. AWP; CTC; OuHeWo; PeVV
And Pergamos,/ City of the Phrygians. Chorus. Euripides. *Fr.* Iphigenia in Aulis. AWP; LiTW
And perhaps on another planet, on one. Perhaps Where He Is Only Loving Rockets Can Land. Brian Patten. HYE
And Phoebus stooped under the craggy roof. Hymn to Mercury. *Unknown.* *Fr.* Homeric Hymns. LiTW
And Pilate wrote a title, and put it on the cross. Inscription on the Cross. St. John, Bible, *N.T.* TreFT
"And pray, who are you?" The Tax-Gatherer. John Banister Tabb. GN; UTS
And preparing a net. Wave. Barbara Guest. AmPC
And Rest in a Flame. Francis Maguire JKCP (1955 ed.)
And ride in triumph through Persepolis! Christopher Marlowe. *Fr.* Tamburlaine, Pt. I, Act II, sc. v. FOL; MyFE; TrGrPo; WHA
And rise, O moon, from yonder down. Tennyson. *Fr.* In Memoriam A. H. H.: Epilogue. OAEP
And round these men spread the sub-tropic latitudes. Anthony Delius. *Fr.* The Great Divide. BoSA
And rustling flowers for some third party waited. Their Lonely Betters. W. H. Auden. LOW
And Ruth said, "Intreat [*or* Entreat] me not to leave thee." Intreat Me Not to Leave Thee [*or* Address of Ruth to Naomi]. Ruth, Bible, *O.T.* GBV (1952 ed.); LO; PoPl; TreF
And saxophones were oboes become bassoon. Mock Pop Forsooth: A Tale of Life and Death. James W. Thompson. WSL
And "Science" said. The Dunce. Walter de la Mare. ImOP
And sedge-warblers, clinging so light. Edward Thomas. *Fr.* Sedge-Warblers. BiS
And see th' expected hour is on the wing. Prospect of the Future Glory of America. John Trumbull. AmPP (5th ed.)
And seeing the multitudes, he went up into a mountain. The Sermon on the Mount. St. Matthew, Bible, *N.T.* OuHeWo; PoPl; ReIE
And several strengths from drowsiness campaigned. The Sermon on the Warpland. Gwendolyn Brooks. LiTM (1970 ed.)
And shall I then the fact deny? Sir Eustace Grey. George Crabbe. MyFE
And shall I weep that Love's no more. Le Roi Est Mort. Agnes Mary Frances Robinson. OBVV
And she aloof to laughter—till I don't know. Big, Fat Summer —and the Lean and Hard. Frederick Bock. NYBP
And she, being old, fed from a mashed plate. Old Woman. Iain Crichton Smith. NePoEA-2
And she, her beauty never made her cold. Frederick Goddard Tuckerman. *Fr.* Sonnets. AmePo
And she is with me—years roll, I shall change. Andromeda. Robert Browning. *Fr.* Pauline. OBRV
And she said. Ritratto. Ezra Pound. PP
And she was there. The little boat. Orpheus' Dream. Edwin Muir. SiSw
And She Washed His Feet with Her Tears, and Wiped Them with the Hairs of Her Head. Sir Edward Sherburne, *after the Italian of* Giambattista Marini. CBEP; ChTr; MeLP; OBS; OxBoCh; SeCL; SeEP
(Magdalen, The.) ACP; GoBC
(Proud Egyptian Queen, The.) MemP
And should my soul be torn with grief. My Bible. Edgar A. Guest. *Fr.* My Books and I. MaRV
And silence. The End of Man Is His Beauty. LeRoi Jones. AmNP; BALP
And Simeon blessed them, and said to Mary his mother. Mary and Simeon. St. Luke, Bible, *N.T.* (*Douay vers.*). ISi
"And sitting down they watched Him there." They Watched Him There. Shirley Elizabeth Reitz. SoP
And sitting down they watched him there. Gambler. G. A. Studdert-Kennedy. ChIP; MaRV
And sleeps thy heart when flower and tree. Summer. Johannes Carl Andersen. BoAu
And slowly answered Arthur from the barge. Prayer. Tennyson. *Fr.* Morte D'Arthur (*also in* Idylls of the King: The Passing of Arthur). BoPe; FaBoEn; GTSL
And so an easier life our Cyclops drew. The Cyclops. Theocritus, *tr. by* Elizabeth Barrett Browning. Idylls, XI. AWP; EnLi-1; JAWP; OuHeWo; WBP
And so, Anne Everard, in those leafy Junes. Anne's Book. Mary Webb. OnPP
And So at Last. David Starr Jordan. MaRV
And so depart into dark. Homage to Ezra Pound. Gilbert Highet. Par
And so, farewell for ever. George Chapman. *Fr.* The Tragedy of Charles, Duke of Byron. MyFE

And so he called her Pigeon. Husband Betrayed. John Crowe Ransom. TwAmPo
And so I cross into another world. New Heaven and Earth. D. H. Lawrence. CMoP
And so I find it well to come. Whittier. *Fr.* The Meeting. FaChP
And so I must lose her whose mind. Prothalamium. Donagh MacDonagh. NeIP
And so I somehow-nohow played. Robert Browning. *Fr.* Fifine at the Fair. Par
And so it came to that last day. The Wanderer: St. James' Grove. William Carlos Williams. TwAmPo
And so, like most young poets, in a flush. The Ferment of New Wine. Elizabeth Barrett Browning. *Fr.* Aurora Leigh, I. VA
And So Men Say, I Love Thee! Derwent Coleridge. CBEP
And so, night after night. Saint Cecilia. John Heath-Stubbs. MuSP
And so, one day when the tide was away out. The Farewell. Pat Wilson. AnNZ
And so our royal relative is dead! A Dirge Concerning the Late Lamented King of the Cannibal Islands. William Augustus Croffut. BOHV; InMe
And So Should You. Anna Temple Whitney. *See* Kneeling Camel, The.
And so that all these ages, these years. From the Domain of Arnheim. Edwin Morgan. HYE
And so the day drops by; the horizon draws. Frederick Goddard Tuckerman. *Fr.* Sonnets. AmePo; AnNE; PoIE
And so the Mother, shutting up the duty-book. Seven-year-old Poet. Arthur Rimbaud. OnHM
And so the river moves. The Lost Children. Richard Eberhart. NePoAm-2
And so thou hast burst forth from place of death. Resurrection. Henry W. Frost. SoP
And so to a chambre full solacious. Dame Music [*or* Musike]. Stephen Hawes. *Fr.* The Pastime of Pleasure. MuSP; PoEL-1
And so we labored all the good night long. At the Last. Vincent David Engels. CAW
And so we two [*or* too] came where the rest have come. The Question. F. T. Prince. ChMP; GTBS-P; PeSA
And so, when the time came. In Memoriam. Frank A. Collymore. PoNe
And so you find them somewhat thin. The Old Songs. Sir Owen Seaman. InMe
And so you found that poor room dull. Appearances. Robert Browning. CBEP; PoVP
And softe he cougheth with a semysoun. Young Woman. Chaucer. *Fr.* The Canterbury Tales: The Miller's Tale. BoW
"And something that. . .that is theirs—no longer ours." The Dispossessed. John Berryman. AP; PoCh
And sometimes in the cool night I see you are an animal. Ode for Soft Voice. Michael McClure. NeAP
And sometimes the speech. Invisible Trumpets Blowing. E. J. Pratt. *Fr.* Brébeuf and His Brethren. CaP
And, star and system rolling past. Tennyson. *Fr.* In Memoriam A. H. H.: Epilogue. ImOP
And still he climbed, and through the grey leaves thrust. The Olive Garden. Rainer Maria Rilke. BoPe
And still the picnickers come on. Sunday in the Park. William Carlos Williams. *Fr.* Paterson. CrMA
And still they come and go: and this is all I know. Picture-Show. Siegfried Sassoon. CMoP
And still we stood and stared far down. "Therefore Is the Name of It Called Babel." Sir Osbert Sitwell. MMA
And still you paint, and still I stand. The Painter's Mistress. James Elroy Flecker. BrPo
And Suddenly It's Evening. Salvatore Quasimodo. *tr. fr. Italian by* Glauco Cambon. OnPM
And suddenly the flowing night stands still. Burning Bush. Louis Untermeyer. MAP; MoLP
And summer mornings the mute child, rebellious. Eleven. Archibald MacLeish. CMoP
And Tangi and his tribe thus much had gained. Alfred Domett. *Fr.* Ranolf and Amohia. AnNZ
And tell how Oberon doth fare. The Adventures of Oberon, King of the Fairies, While Searching for Queen Mab. Michael Drayton. *Fr.* Nymphidia; or, The Court of Fairy. OA
And that is all I really have to say. The Epilogue of the Wandering Jew. Colin Newbury. AnNZ
And that was the hottest summer. Miller. Stuart Peterfreund. QAH
And that's what sits upon its torse. A Tail for the Horse. *Unknown.* SiTL
And the age ended, and the last deliverer died. W. H. Auden. *Fr.* In Time of War. CMoP; ExPo; Sonn
And the angel spoke and made an effort. Joseph's Suspicion. Rainer Maria Rilke. MoRP
And the betrayers of language. Ezra Pound. *Fr.* Canto XIV. MoPo
And the bitter storm augments; the wild winds wage. John Josselyn. SCAP
And the child grew, and waxed strong in spirit. The Child of Nazareth. St. Luke, Bible, *N.T.* ChrBoLe
And the children of Israel were fruitful. The Child Moses. Exodus, Bible, *O.T.* OuHeWo
And the corn singing Millennium! Background with Revolutionaries. Archibald MacLeish. Frescoes for Mr. Rockefeller's City, VI. UnPo
And the curtains, the lamp. True to a Dream. Donald Petersen. NePoEA-2
And the day arrives at last, my friends. Nightmare of a Cook. Chester Kallman. CrMA
And the Days Are Not Full Enough. Ezra Pound. FIW
And the Dead. Sean Jennett. NeBP
And the Earth Rebelled. Yuri Suhl, *tr. fr. Yiddish by* Max Rosenfeld. TrJP
And the first grey [*or* gray] of morning fill'd the east. Sohrab and Rustum. Matthew Arnold. BEL; CABL; DTo; EPN; MaVP; PoVP; ShBV-2; TOP; ViPo; ViPP; VP
And the Greatness of These. J. R. Perkins. OQP
And the Green Grass Grew All Around, *with music. Unknown.* BFSS
And the hunger. The Hunger. Shirley Kaufman. QAH
And the ladies dress in silk. On the High Cost of Dairy Products. James McIntyre. FiBHP
"And the Life Everlasting." Percy Clough Ainsworth. MaRV
And the light, a wakened heyday of air. November Sunday Morning. Alvin Feinman. CoAP; FosPo
And the Lord God formed man of the dust of the ground. Adam and Eve. Genesis, Bible, *O.T.* TreFT
And the Lord God whispered and said to me. Angela Morgan. *Fr.* God Prays. OQP
And the Lord said to Moses. *Unknown.* SiTL
And the Lord said unto Samuel, How long wilt thou mourn for Saul. David and Goliath. First Samuel, Bible, *O.T.* TreFS
And the Lord Was Not in the Whirlwind. Louis MacNeice. *Fr.* Visitations, VII. EaLo
And the many days and the many nights that I lay as one barren. A Canticle to the Christ in the Holy Eucharist. Brother Antoninus. ToPo
And the mist: and the rain in the west: and the wind steady. The Omelet of A. MacLeish. Edmund Wilson. NYBP; Par
And the next who came in was a sailor. When Johnson's Ale Was New. *Unknown.* ShS
And the Old Women Gathered. Mari Evans. Kal; NNP
And the Pear Trees Shiver. Jocelyn Macy Sloan. FiSC
And the raying sun from behind breaks out east. Heraclitus in the West. Charles G. Bell. NePoAm
And the sea parted before and closed again behind. The Discovery. Charles Brasch. *Fr.* Genesis. AnNZ
And the soil was not refused. The Constancy. Jason Miller. ThO
And the subway gives such refinement. The Subway. Conrad Kent Rivers. Kal
And the trunk: "So sweet those words to me that I." Pier delle Vigne. Dante. *Fr.* Divina Commedia: Inferno. HoPM
And the voice said: Walk. Little Falls. Robert Hogg. MoCV
And the voice that was calmer [*or* softer] than silence said. James Russell Lowell. *Fr.* The Vision of Sir Launfal, Pt. II. ChIP; MaRV
And the whole multitude of them arose. The Death of Jesus. St. Luke, Bible, *N.T.* TreF
And the word of the Lord came unto me, saying. Unfaithful Shepherds. Ezekiel, Bible, *O.T.* WoL
"And the Word Was Made Flesh." Laurence Housman. MaRV

And the World's Face. Julian Symons. WaP
And their faces were pale. Departure. Guillaume Apollinaire. OnPM
And then/ He made the stars also. Stars. Florence S. Edsall. MoSiPe
And Then Her Burial. Merrill Moore. MAP; MoAmPo (1942 ed.)
And then I pressed the shell. The Shell. James Stephens. BoNaP; BoTP; CH; CMoP; FIW; MoAB; MoBrPo; MoShBr; MoVE; NeMA; POTE; YT
And then I sat me down, and gave the rein. Sonnets, II. Gustave Rosenhane. AWP; JAWP; WBP
And then I wakened up in such a fright. Midnight. James Stephens. DTC
And Then It Rained. Mark Van Doren. BoNaP
And Then No More. Friedrich Rückert, *tr. fr. German by* James Clarence Mangan. AnIV; BLPA; IrPN
And then one day Hershey played by the door. You Are a Jew! Delmore Schwartz. *Fr.* Genesis. TrJP
And then she saw me creeping. Fossils. James Stephens. OnYI
And then the old inhabitants, so kind. Fishing Village. Louis Dudek. *Fr.* Provincetown. MoCV
And Then the Sun. Pradip Sen. ACV
And Then There. Frantisek Halas, *tr. fr. Czech by* Michael Flach. LiTW
And then went down to the ship. Canto I. Ezra Pound. AmPP; AP; AtBAP; CMoP; CoBMV; LiTA; MAP; MoAB; MoAmPo; MoVE; PoIE; SeCeV; TrGrPo (rev. ed.)
And there a lovely cloistered court he found. The Lady of the Land. William Morris. *Fr.* The Earthly Paradise. TOP
And there appeared a great wonder in heaven. Revelation, Bible, *N.T.* CAW
And there followed him a great company of people. St. Luke, Bible, *N.T.* LO
And there I found a gray and ancient ass. Pegasus Lost. Elinor Wylie. MAP; MoAmPo; NeMA
And there I saw the seed upon the mountain. Preludes to Definition, I. Conrad Aiken. TwAmPo
And there is no answer. This our liberty. The Usurpers. Edwin Muir. CMoP
And There Shall Be No More Death, *sel.* Ruth Gilbert.
"That which the long scythe whispered to the grass." AnNZ
And There Shall Come Forth. Isaiah, Bible, *O.T.* *See* Rod of Jesse, The.
And there she's leand her back to a thorn. The Cruel Mother. *Unknown.* ESPB
And there the knight stands, wringing his hands. St. Cuthbert Intervenes. "Thomas Ingoldsby." *Fr.* The Lay of St. Cuthbert. NBM
And there they were: with fire everywhere. A New Dance. S. E. Anderson. NBP
And there two runners did the sign abide. Atalanta's Race. William Morris. *Fr.* The Earthly Paradise. BEL
"And There Was a Great Calm." Thomas Hardy. ChTr; CMoP; LiTM; MoRP; TDP
And there was grass on the floor of the temple. Ezra Pound. *Fr.* Canto XXI. MoPo
And there was great mourning in Israel in every place. Great Mourning. First Maccabees, Bible, Apocrypha. TrJP
And There Was Mary Magdalene and the Other Mary, Sitting Over against the Sepulchre. W. R. Rodgers. WePo
And there we were together again. The Return of Morgan and Fingal. E. A. Robinson. TOP
And there were in the same country shepherds [*or* shepherds in the same country] abiding in the field. The Adoration of the Shepherds [*or* The First Christmas *or* Christmas Eve *or* Tidings of Great Joy *or* The Angels of Bethlehem]. St. Luke, Bible, *N.T.* BiCB; BoC; ChBR; FaPON; GaP; MaRV; OTPC (1946 ed.); PCH; PoRL; SiSoSe; SoPo
And there were spring-faced cherubs that did sleep. The Sea of Death. *Unknown.* CH
And there will be just as rich fruits to cull. After Death. R. A. K. Mason. AnNZ
And therefore praise I even the most high. James Branch Cabell. *Fr.* Retractions. HBMV
And therewith cast I doun mine eye again. Walking under the Tour. James I, King of Scotland. *Fr.* The Kingis Quair. SeCePo
And these few precepts in thy memory. Polonius' Advice to Laertes [*or* This above All]. Shakespeare. *Fr.* Hamlet, I, iii. GN; MasP; TrGrPo
And these mountains which my eyes have seen. The Seven Metal Mountains. Enoch, Bible, Pseudepigrapha. TrJP
And they, and all, in one loud symphony. Shelley. *Fr.* The Revolt of Islam, V. PoFr
And they both lived happily ever after. After Ever Happily; or, The Princess and the Woodcutter. Ian Serraillier. BoLP; FIW
And they brought young children to him. Jesus and the Children. St. Mark, Bible, *N.T.* TreFT
And they had fixed the wedding day. Wordsworth. *Fr.* The Thorn. EvOK
And they have thrust our shattered dead away in foreign graves. The Martyrs of the Maine. Rupert Hughes. PAH
And They Shall Beat Their Swords into Plowshares. Micah, IV: 1-15, Bible, *O.T.* TreF
(Neither Shall They Learn War Any More.) TRV
And this comely dame. John Skelton. *Fr.* Elinor Rumming. ViBoPo
And this digester, this digester of food. Poem. Conrad Aiken. *Fr.* Time in the Rock. VaPo
And this freedom will be the freedom of all. A Free Nation. Edwin Markham. MaRV; TRV
And this I hate—not men, nor flag, nor race. The Hymn of Hate. Joseph Dana Miller. PGD
And this is England! June's undarkened green. This Is England. Laurence Binyon. BoTP
"And this is freedom!" cried the serf; "At last." Bondage. Owen Innsley. AA
And this is [*or* this is to *or* Here's to] good old Boston. A Boston Toast [*or* Boston]. John Collins Bossidy. AmFN; BLPA; CenHV; GoTP; HBV; NeHB; TreFS; WhC; YaD
And this is now their home. H. H. Dugmore. *Fr.* A Reminiscence of 1820. ACV
And this is the song that the white woman sings. Goosey Goosey Gander—by Various Authors (Kipling's Version). William Percy French. CenHV
And this is the way the baby woke. The Way the Baby Woke. James Whitcomb Riley. AA
And this is the way they ring. Ringing the Bells. Anne Sexton. NMP
And this is to good old Boston. *See* And this is good old Boston.
And this July—its nakedness burned out. Tansy for August. Theodore Enslin. CoPo
And this our life exempt from public haunt. Good in Everything. Shakespeare. *Fr.* As You Like It, II, i. PoToHe
And this place our forefathers made for man! The Dungeon. Samuel Taylor Coleridge. *Fr.* Remorse (Osorio), V. MCCG
And this reft house is that the which he built. On a Ruined House in a Romantic Country [*or* The House That Jack Built]. Samuel Taylor Coleridge. BOHV; Par; Sonn
And this of all my hopes. Emily Dickinson. ForPo
And those dear loved of ours we miss so sorely. We'll Meet Them. Mrs. Donald A. Day. FaChP
And those two young ladies of Birmingham. Limerick. *Unknown.* LiBL
And those who husbanded the golden grain. Omar Khayyám, *tr. by* Edward Fitzgerald. *Fr.* The Rubáiyát. PoFr
And thou, America,/ For the scheme's culmination. Walt Whitman. *Fr.* Song of the Universal, IV. PGD
And Thou Art Dead, as Young and Fair. Byron. AtBAP; ERoP-2; PoEL-4; TOP
(Elegy on Thyrza.) GTBS; GTBS-D; GTBS-P; GTBS-W; GTSE; GTSL
And thou art gone, most loved, most honored friend! On the Late S. T. Coleridge. Washington Allston. AA
And thou art now no longer near! To the Parted One. Goethe. AWP; JAWP; WBP
And thou hast walked about (how strange a story!). Address to a Mummy. Horace Smith. HBV; RoGo
And thou, O Life, the lady of all bliss. Newborn Death, 2. Dante Gabriel Rossetti. The House of Life, C. MaVP; PoVP; ViPo
And Thou, O Lord! by whom are seen. Whittier. *Fr.* The Eternal Goodness. TrPWD
And thou, O Virgin, Daughter, Mother, Bride. Appeal for Illumination. Luigi Pulci, *tr. by* Byron. *Fr.* Il Morgante maggiore. ISi

And thou that art the flower of virgins all. Invocatio ad Mariam. Chaucer. *Fr.* The Canterbury Tales: The Prologue to the Second Nun's Tale. ISi
And Thou! whom earth still holds, and will not yield. Wordsworth. William Wilberforce Lord. *Fr.* Ode to England. AA
And Thou Would'st Not! Winifred Stoddard LeBar. ChIP
And Three Hundred and Sixty-six in Leap Year. Ogden Nash. NePA
And thus a moon roll'd on, and fair Haidée. Juan and Haidée. Byron. *Fr.* Don Juan, II. MaPo
And thus all-expectant abiding I waited not long, for soon. He Heard Her Sing. James Thomson. VA
And thus as we were talking to and fro. Complaint [*or* Compleynt] of the Common [*or* Comoun] Weill of Scotland. Sir David Lindsay. *Fr.* The Dreme. GoTS; OxBS
And thus continuing, she said. The Sailor's Mother. Wordsworth. Par
And Thus He Spoke. John A. Stone. SGR
And Thus in Nineveh. Ezra Pound. PP
And thus she spoke to the bright Marygold of Leutha's vale. The Marigold. Blake. *Fr.* Visions of the Daughters of Albion. AtBAP
And thus went out this lamp of light. An Account of the Cruelty of the Papists. Benjamin Harris. SCAP
And timid, funny, brisk little bunny. Christina Rossetti. *Fr.* Sing-Song. TiPo
And to the Young Men. Merrill Moore. BoLiVe (1939 ed.); MAP; MoAmPo
And, truly, I would rather be struck dumb. Keats. *Fr.* Endymion. ViBoPo
And truth, you say, is all divine. Realism. A. C. Benson. VA
And two bird-children. Poem for Thel—the Very Tops of Trees. Joseph Major. NBP
And walked across Potomac into Thebes. Effigy. Georgia Lee McElhaney. CoPo
And was it good for you this time? The Love-making: His and Hers. Eve Merriam. UnTE
And was it true,/ The stranger standing so. The Annunciation. John Duffy. ISi
And was not death a lusty struggler. Of a Cozener. John Hoskins. TuPP
And was the day of my delight. In Memoriam A. H. H., XXIV. Tennyson. EnLi-2; EPN; ViPo; VP
And wasna he a roguey. The Piper o' Dundee. *Unknown.* OxBS
And we love Art for Art's sake. Art for Art's Sake. Marc Blitzstein. *Fr.* The Cradle Will Rock. TrJP
And we marched against them there in the next spring. Archibald MacLeish. *Fr.* Conquistador. ThLM
And we might trust these youths and maidens fair. Youth, Love, and Death. Philip James Bailey. *Fr.* Festus. VA
And welcom now (Great Monarch) to your own. Dryden. *Fr.* Astraea Redux. OBS
And what are you that, missing you. The Philosopher. Edna St. Vincent Millay. CMoP; TOP
And what is a kiss, when all is done? Edmond Rostand. *Fr.* Cyrano de Bergerac. OTD
And what is death? Death. James Oppenheim. WGRP
And what is faith? The anchored trust that at the core of things. Sam Walter Foss. *Fr.* The Higher Catechism. OQP
And what is love? It is a doll dress'd [*or* dressed] up. Modern Love. Keats. CBEP; OBNC
And what is love? Misunderstanding, pain. Epigram. J. V. Cunningham. NePoAm
And what is so rare as a day in June? June [*or* A Day in June]. James Russell Lowell. *Fr.* The Vision of Sir Launfal. AmLP; BBV; FaBoBe; FaBV; FaFP; FaPL; FaPON; GoTP; NePA; PoRL; PTK; StaSt; StVeCh (1955 ed.)
And what, my thoughtless Sons, should fire you more. Britannia's Empire. James Thomson. *Fr.* Britannia. OBEC
And what of Hodge, and where stood he. Hodge in the Strife. Maurice Hewlett. *Fr.* The Song of the Plow. PoFr
And what of you? You also shall not say. Insights. Catherine Davis. QFR
And What Shall You Say? Joseph Seamon Cotter, Jr. BANP; CDC; PoNe
And What Sordello Would See There. Robert Browning. *Fr.* Sordello. MyFE
And What though Winter Will Pinch Severe. Sir Walter Scott. *Fr.* Old Mortality. EnRP
And what were roses. Perfume? for I do. Sonnet. E. E. Cummings. NP
And What with the Blunders. Kenneth Patchen. NaP
"And When He Had Scourged Jesus, He Delivered Him to Be Crucified." W. R. Rodgers. WePo
And when he saw the multitude he went up into a mountain. St. Matthew, Bible, *N.T.* RelE
And when he was himself again, she questioned him withal. *Unknown.* *Fr.* Tsar Lazar and Tsaritsa Militsa. PoFr
And when he was twelve years old, they went up after the custom of the feast. St. Luke, Bible, *N.T.* BoC
And when her broken thoughts went following after. Seven Sad Sonnets, V. Mary Aldis. HBMV
And When I Am Entombèd. Emerson. ViBoPo
And when I heard their voices on the stair. The Betrayal. Josephine W. Johnson. MoRP
And When I Lamented. Heine, *tr. fr. German by* Emma Lazarus. *Fr.* Homeward Bound. TrJP
And when I pay death's duty. Poem. Robin Blaser. NeAP
And when, immortal mortal, droops your head. To My Godchild M. W. M. Francis Thompson. JKCP
"And when it comis to the ficht." Bruce Addresses His Army. John Barbour. *Fr.* The Bruce, XIII. GoTS
And, when it was darkest, I came to a strong City. The Strong City. Alfred Noyes. *Fr.* The Last Voyage. GoBC
And when—its force expended. After the Storm. Thackeray. *Fr.* The White Squall. PRWS
And when Joseph came home. Genesis, Bible, *O.T.* LO
And when my work is over, to Cheyenne then I'll head. Dodge City, the End of the Trail. *Unknown.* CoSo
And when new regions prompt their feet to roam. Timothy Dwight. *Fr.* Greenfield Hill. Po
And when night comes they will sing serenades. Evening. Walter James Turner. HT
And when religious sects ran mad. Intolerance. Winthrop Mackworth Praed. MaRV
And when Saul saw David go forth against the Philistine. First Samuel, Bible, *O.T.* LO
And when the rain had gone away. The Cricket. Marjorie Barrows. BoChLi (1950 ed.)
And when the sun puts out his lamp. To the Mountains. Henry David Thoreau. PoEL-4
And When They Fall. James J. Montague. HBMV
And when they see me coming. Beware of Larry Gorman. Larry Gorman. ShS
And when this work all brought was to an end. Now Welcome Summer. Chaucer. *Fr.* The Parlement of Foules. PoLi
And when thou hast on foot the purblind hare. Poor Wat. Shakespeare. *Fr.* Venus and Adonis. OBSC; UnPo (1st ed.)
And when thy heart is resting. Emily Brontë. LO
And when you walk the world lifts up its head. To a Very Beautiful Lady. Ruthven Todd. NeBP
"And where have you been, my Mary." The Fairies of the Caldon Low. Mary Howitt. BeLS; HBV; HBVY; OTPC; PRWS; TVC
"And where now, Bayard, will thy footsteps tend?" Bayard Taylor. Whittier. DD; HBV
And while my visitor prattled. Secret Thoughts. Christopher Morley. *Fr.* Translations from the Chinese. EvOK
And Who Has Seen a Fair Alluring Face. George Peele. ErPo
And who has seen the moon, who has not seen. Moonrise. D. H. Lawrence. GTBS-W; LiTM; NP
And who shall say. Magic. Thomas Wolfe. PoPl
And who shall separate the dust. Common Dust. Georgia Douglas Johnson. AmNP; TTY
And who will lead the way? Love Comes. Ernest Crosby. OQP
And why, in God's name, is that elegant bureau? Ballad of a Sweet Dream of Peace. Robert Penn Warren. TwAmPo
And why not, as hee. To Himselfe and the Harpe. Michael Drayton. OBS
And why so coy? what is your rose. *Unknown.* SeCSL
And why to me this, thou lame Lord of fire. An Execration upon Vulcan. Ben Jonson. AnAnS-2; ReEn; SeCP
And Will He [*or* A'] Not Come Again? Shakespeare. *Fr.* Hamlet, IV, v. EG; InPo; PoEL-2; ViBoPo
(Ophelia's Songs, 1.) AnFE; TrGrPo

And will she never hold her tongue. The Power of Silence. W. H. Davies. BrPo
And will they cast the altars down. In Portugal, 1912. Alice Meynell. OxBoCh
And will tomorrow come? And if it comes. The Humming Stair. Joseph Payne Brennan. FiSC
"And will you cut a stone for him." The Stone. W. W. Gibson. MoBrPo; NeMA; PoPo
And wilt thou leave [*or* wylt thow leve] me thus? An Earnest Suit to His Unkind Mistress Not to Forsake Him [*or* The Appeal *or* The Lover's Appeal]. Sir Thomas Wyatt. AtBAP; BEL; CBEP; EG; ElL; EnLit; EnLoPo; EnRePo; FCP; GoBC; GTBS; GTBS-D; GTBS-P; GTBS-W; GTSE; GTSL; LiTL; LoBV; NoP; OAEP; OBEV; OBSC; PoIE; ReEn; ReIE; SiCE; SiPS; TOP; TuPP; YAT
And with great fear I inhabit the middle of the night. The Acts of Youth. John Wieners. CoPo
And with No Language but a Cry. Amos Niven Wilder. MaRV
And worth the blossoms that acacias. Poplar Tree. Padraic Colum. NePoAm
And Would You See My Mistress' Face. *At. to* Thomas Campion. OAEP; OBSC
"And would you sign my copy sir?" "A Scotch?" The Poet at Fifty. Laurence Lerner. PeSA
And wouldst Thou, Holy Shepherd, leave. At the Ascension. Luis de León, *tr. by* Thomas Walsh. CAW
And wylt thow leve me thus. *See* And wilt thou leave me thus.
And ye sall walk in silk attire. The Siller Croun. Susanna Blamire. HBV
And Yet. Arthur B. Rhinow. BLRP
And Yet. Errol B. Sloan. BLRP
And yet, because thou overcomest so. Sonnets from the Portuguese, XVI. Elizabeth Barrett Browning. OAEP; ViPo
And yet but lately have I seen, e'en here. A Winter-Piece. Ambrose Philips. SeCePo
And yet, dear heart! remembering thee. Whittier. *Fr.* Snow-bound. MaRV
And Yet Fools Say. George S. Holmes. OTD
And yet how lovely in thine age of woe. Greece. Byron. *Fr.* Childe Harold's Pilgrimage, II. OBRV
And yet I cannot reprehend the flight. To Delia, XXXII. Samuel Daniel. HBV; OAEP; OBEV
And yet I really must complain. The Modern Traveller. Hilaire Belloc. OtMeF
And yet one arrives somehow. Arrival. William Carlos Williams. PoAn
And yet the southern whale does sometime come. The Whales. Marguerite Young. ReMP
And yet, there was a hunger in your eyes. Arthur Symons. *Fr.* Amoris Victima. PeVV
And yet this great wink [wing, *wr.*] of eternity. Voyages, II. Hart Crane. AmLP; AmPP (5th ed.); AnFE; BoLiVe (1939 ed.); CoAnAm; CoBMV; DTC; ExPo; FaBoEn; ForPo; GTBS-W; LiTM; MAP; MoAB; MoAmPo; MoPo; MoVE; NAMP; NePA; NP; Po; PoDB; PoFS; PoIE; TwAmPo; UnPo (3d ed.); VaPo; ViBoPo (1958 ed.)
And Yet We Are Here! Karl Wolfskehl, *tr. fr. German by* Carol North Valhope *and* Ernst Morwitz. TrJP
And you as well must die, belovèd dust. Sonnet. Edna St. Vincent Millay. GTBS-W; MasP; NP; PoLF; PoRA
And you begin to grow, but no one notices. Grow in Hope and Grace. Barbara Anne Baker. TNV
And you believed that I would do it so? Broken Monologue. "Michael Lewis." UnTE
"And you, Sir Poet, shall you make, I pray." The Poet and the Child. Winifred Howells. AA
And you who love, you who attach yourselves. Conrad Aiken. *Fr.* Time in the Rock. ViBoPo
"And you will cut a stone for him." The Stone. W. W. Gibson. GSP
And you, ye stars. Matthew Arnold. *Fr.* Empedocles on Etna, II. VA
And your eyes look on me. Epistle for Spring. R. Ellsworth Larsson. CAW
Andalusian Lute, The: Another Baedeker. Raymond Dipalma *and* Stephen Shrader. QAH
Andalusian merchant, that returns, The. *Unknown. Fr.* Wonders. FaBoCh
Andalusian Sereno, The. Francis Saltus Saltus. AA
Andante, ma Non Assai. Rufinus Domesticus, *tr. fr. Greek by* Dudley Fitts. ErPo; LiTW
André. Charlotte Fiske Bates. MC; PAH
Andre. Gwendolyn Brooks. RePo; TiPo (1959 ed.)
Andrea del Sarto. Robert Browning. ATP; BEL; CABA; CoBE; CTC; DiPo; EnL; EnLi-2; EnLit; EPN; FosPo; HBV; MaPo; MaVP; MBW-2; NoP; OAEP; PAn; PoE; PoEL-5; PoVP; StP; TOP; ViPo; ViPP; VP; WHA
Andreas, *sels. Unknown, tr. fr. Anglo-Saxon.*
Christ to the Sufferer. PoLi
St. Andrew's Voyage to Mermedonia, *tr. by* Charles W. Kennedy. AnOE
André's Request to Washington. Nathaniel Parker Willis. MC; PAH
André's Ride. Augustus Henry Beesly. HBV
Andrew. Thomas William Parsons. AA
Andrew and Maudlin, Rebecca and Will. A Ballad of Andrew and Maudlin. Thomas Durfey. CoMu; PeRV
Andrew Bardeen, *with music. Unknown.* BFSS
Andrew Jackson. Stephen Vincent Benét. InMe
Andrew Jackson. Martha Keller. AmFN; GoTP; MaC
Andrew Jackson/ Was an Anglo-Saxon. *Unknown.* RIS
Andrew Jackson/ Was Anglo-Saxon. Important People. Louis Untermeyer, *and others.* StaSt
Andrew Lammie. *Unknown.* ESPB
(Trumpeter of Fyvie, The.) OXBB
Andrew M'Crie. Robert Fuller Murray. CenHV
Andrew Magrath's Reply to John O'Tuomy. Andrew Magrath. *tr. fr. Modern Irish by* John O'Daly, *vers. by* James Clarence Mangan. OnYI
Andrew Rose, *with music. Unknown.* SoAmSa
Andrew Rykman's Prayer, *sels.* Whittier.
"If there be some weaker one." FaChP; MaRV; TRV
"Make my mortal dreams come true." TrPWD
"Pardon, Lord, the lips that dare." TrPWD
Andromache, *sel.* Euripides, *tr. fr. Greek by* George Allen.
Chorus: Kings of Troy, The. WaaP
Andromache, I think of you! The stream. The Swan. Baudelaire. SyP
Andromeda. Thomas Bailey Aldrich. AA; AmePo
Andromeda. Robert Browning. *Fr.* Pauline. OBRV
Andromeda. Gerard Manley Hopkins. FaBoMo; LiTB
Andromeda, *sels.* Charles Kingsley.
Andromeda and the Sea-Nymphs. VA
Nereids, The. NBM
"Whelming the dwellings of men, and the toils of the slow-footed oxen." PeVV
Andromeda. James Jeffrey Roche. AA; HBV; JKCP
Andromeda and the Sea Nymphs. Charles Kingsley. *Fr.* Andromeda. VA
Andromeda, by Perseus saved and wed. Aspecta Medusa. Dante Gabriel Rossetti. PoVP
Andy Warhol,/ there are empty cans of Campbell soup. First Essay on the Art of the U.S. Ron Welburn. BF
Andy's Gone with Cattle. Henry Lawson. PoAu-1
Ane Ballat of Our Lady. William Dunbar. *See* Ballad of Our Lady.
Ane doolie sessoun to ane cairfull dyte. The Testament of Cresseid. Robert Henryson. CABL; GoTS; OxBS
Ane Sang of the Birth of Christ, with the Tune of Baw Lula Low. John Wedderburn, *after the German of* Martin Luther.
"My saul and life stand up and see," *sel.* ChTr
Ane Satyre [*or* Satire] of the Threi [*or* Three] Estaitis. Sir David Lindsay. *See* Satire of the Three Estates, The.
Ane Supplication in Contemptioum of Syde Taillis, *abr.* Sir David Lindsay. GoTS
Anear the centre of that northern crest. Melancholia [*or* Melencolia]. James Thomson. The City of Dreadful Night, XXI. AnEnPo; FaBoEn; GTBS-P; OAEP; VA
Anecdote for Fathers. Wordsworth. EnRP
Anecdote in Verse. Rolfe Humphries. CBV
Anecdote of Men by the Thousand. Wallace Stevens. Po
Anecdote of the Jar. Wallace Stevens. AmPP (5th ed.); AP; CaFP; CBV; CMoP; CoBMV; ExPo; FosPo; GTBS-W; LiTA; MaPo (1969 ed.); MoAB; MoAmPo; MoVE; NePA; OxBA; PAn; PoAn; PoeP; PoIE; VaPo
Anecdote of the Sparrow. Robert Pack. NePA
Anecdote of 2 A.M. John Wain. NMP
Anecdotes of the Late War, *sel.* Charles Olson.
"That (like the man sd) Booth." LiPo

Anemone. Dawn Finlay. SoP
Anemones for Miss Austen. Bernard Bergonzi. HaMV
Anemones of Collioure, The. John Unterecker. ThO
Angel, The ("I asked a thief..."). Blake. *See* I Asked a Thief.
Angel, The ("I dreamt a dream!"). Blake. *Fr.* Songs of Experience. CH; EiPP; EnRP
Angel, The. Alfred Hayes. TrJP
Angel ("My work is done"). Cardinal Newman. *Fr.* The Dream of Gerontius. GoBC
Angel ("Softly and gently, dearly-ransom'd soul"). Cardinal Newman. *Fr.* The Dream of Gerontius. OxBoCh
"Angel." Robin Skelton. NMP
Angel and Stone. Howard Nemerov. NoP; NYBP
Angel and the girl are met, The. The Annunciation. Edwin Muir. CMoP
Angel and the Shepherds, The. *Unknown, tr. fr. Flemish by* Alfred R. Bellinger. ChrBoLe
Angel at the Ford, The. William James Dawson. VA
Angel came by night, The. Adsum. Richard Henry Stoddard. AA
Angel came with lilies three, The. Annunciation to All Women. Agnes C. Foote. ChIP
Angel choirs on high are singing. The Joys of Heaven. Thomas à Kempis. CAW
Angel Describes Truth, An. Ben Jonson. *Fr.* Hymenaei. OBS
Angel Gabriel, The. *Unknown.* OBB
Angel Hair sleeps with a boy in my head. What Is Going on inside His Head. Jonathan Cott. YAP
Angel, hast thou betrayed me? Long ago. Vers la Vie. Arthur Upson. HBV
Angel in the Apple Tree, The. Winifred Welles. StVeCh
Angel in the House, The, *sels.* Coventry Patmore.
  Abdication, The, *fr.* I, xii.
    (Honoria's Surrender.) VA
  Amaranth, The, II, xii, 2. LoBV (1949 ed.)
  Attainment, The, I, iii, 4. OBVV
    (Preludes, II.) GoBC
  Constancy [Rewarded], II, xi, 4. OBVV
  Courtesy, *fr.* I, xi, 2. OBVV
  Dance, The, *fr.* I, xi,.
    ("My memory of Heaven awakes!") EG
  Dean, The, *fr.* I, vi.
    (Dean's Consent, The.) VA
  Foreign Land, The, II, ix, 2. HBV
    (Woman.) OBVV
  Going to Church, *fr.* I, x. LoBV; PeVV
  Honor and Desert, II, iv, 1. FaPL; HBV
  Impossibility, The, *fr.* I, i, 1. PoVP
  Joyful Wisdom, The, I, x, 1. HBV
  Kiss, The, II, viii, 3. ALV; EnLoPo; FiBHP; LiTL; MemP; MeWo; OBVV
  Love at Large, I, ii, 2. HoPM; PoVP; StP
  Love in Action, *fr.* II, x. EG
  Love Serviceable, I, vi, 3. EnLoPo; MaRV
  Lover, The, I, iii, 1. PoVP
  Love's Reality, *fr.* I, i, 1. PoVP
  Married Lover, The, II, xii, 1. EPN; FaPL; GoBC; GTBS; HBV; LiTL; MeWo; OBEV; PoVP; TreFT; TrGrPo; VA
    ("Why having won her, do I woo?") EG
  Nearest the Dearest, II, i, 4. HBV
  Rainbow, The, II, iii, 2. GTBS-P
  Revelation, The, I, viii, 2. EnLoPo; GTBS-P; NBM; OBNC; PoG
    ("Idle poet, here and there, An.") EG; ViBoPo
    "Love wakes men, once a life-time each," *sel.* LO
  Rose of the World, The, I, iv, 1. HBV
  Sensuality, *fr.* I, ix, 2. OBVV
  Shame, *fr.* I, ix, 2. OBVV
  Spirit's Epochs, The, I, viii, 3. GoBC
    ("Not in the crises of events.") EG
  Tribute, The, I, iv, 2. FaPL; HBV; OBNC
  Unthrift, I, iii, 3. FaPL; HBV
    (Preludes, I.) GoBC
  Wedding Sermon, The, II, xi, 3. PoVP
Angel, king of streaming morn. Sun. Henry Rowe. OBEV
Angel living near the moon, An. To Dick, on His Sixth Birthday. Sara Teasdale. BiCB
Angel of cinnamon, An. Two Spanish Gypsy Lullabies. *Unknown.* FIW
Angel of God, my guardian dear. To the Guardian Angel. *Unknown.* WHL
Angel of Life, The. Richard Rowe. BoAu
Angel of Patience, The. Whittier, *after the German.* WGRP
Angel of poets,/ Tell us how. Prayer for All Poets at This Time. Irwin Edman. TrPWD
Angel of the Agony. Cardinal Newman. *Fr.* The Dream of Gerontius. OxBoCh
Angel of the Lord declared unto Mary, The. Angelus Domini. *Unknown.* WHL
Angel of words, in vain I have striven with thee. A Child Asleep. Walter de la Mare. POTE
Angel, robed in spotless white, An. Dawn. Paul Laurence Dunbar. AmNP; GoSl; PoLF; PoNe
Angel Roll de Stone Away, De, *with music.* *Unknown.* BoAN-2
Angel Singing, An. Blake. RIS
Angel song still trembles, The. After Christmas. Consuelo Valencia. MaRV
Angel Spirits of Sleep. Robert Bridges. CH
  (Spirits.) OBEV; OBVV
Angel spoke and tried to hold, The. Joseph's Suspicion. Rainer Maria Rilke. ReMP
Angel stepping through her window said, An. L'Annunciazione. Ned O'Gorman. TwAmPo
Angel that presided o'er my birth, The. Injunction. Blake. BoLiVe; ERoP-1; OBRV; TrGrPo
Angel thus til him can sai, An. The Flight into Egypt. *Unknown.* *Fr.* Cursor Mundi. CoBE
Angel told Mary, An. A Christmas Carol. Harry Behn. BiCB
Angel Unawares, An. *Unknown.* BLRP; MaRV; TRV
Angel Voices. Mary B. Stevenson. ChIP
Angelic Chorus, The. D. J. Donahoe. JKCP
Angelic Guidance. Cardinal Newman. GoBC
Angelic Vilancete, The. Gil Vicente. *Fr.* The Auto of the Four Seasons. CAW
Angelica and the Ork. Ariosto, *tr. fr. Italian by* Sir John Harington. *Fr.* Orlando Furioso, X. OBSC
Angelina. Paul Laurence Dunbar. HBV
Angelles bee wrogte to bee of neidher kynde. Mynstrelles Songe. Thomas Chatterton. *Fr.* Aella. EnLoPo
Angells sung a carole at thy birth, The. When They Had Sung an Hymn. Edward Taylor. *Fr.* Preparatory Meditations, Second Series. MWA-1
Angelo Orders His Dinner. Bayard Taylor. BOHV; Par
Angels, The. William Drummond of Hawthornden. GN; HBV
  (Angels for the Nativity of Our Lord, The.) OxBoCh
  (Nativitie, The.) OBS
Angels. Gertrude Hall. AA
Angels/ might fall that way. Snowfall: Four Variations. George Amabile. NYBP
Angels Adoring. Jonathan Cott. YAP
Angels are bright still, though the brightest fell. Lucifer. D. H. Lawrence. OAEP (2d ed.)
Angels are stooping, The. A Cradle Song. W. B. Yeats. PoPl; POTE; TSW
Angels, as well as birds, on silent wing. On Angels. W. W. E. Ross. MoCV
Angels at Hamburg, The. Randall Jarrell. AmP
Angels at the foot. Watching Angels. Christina Rossetti. *Fr.* Sing-Song. PPL
Angels bending, The. The Empty Cradle. José Selgas y Carrasco. CAW
Angels Came a-Mustering, The. *Unknown, tr. fr. Hebrew by* Israel Zangwill. EaLo; TrJP
Angels' eyes, whom veils cannot deceive, The. Of the Blessed Sacrament of the Altar. Robert Southwell. OBEV (new ed.)
Angels for the Nativity of Our Lord, The. William Drummond of Hawthornden. *See* Angels, The.
Angels from the long ago. The Light Now Shineth. *Unknown.* STF
Angels, from the Realms of Glory. James Montgomery. YaCaBo, *with music*
  (Good Tidings of Great Joy to All People.) HBV
  (Nativity.) MaRV; OBRV
Angels guide him now, The. In Memory of a Child. Vachel Lindsay. InP

Angels have talked with him, and showed him thrones. The Mystic. Tennyson. OAEP
Angels in Heab'n Gwineter Write My Name, De, *with music.* *Unknown.* BoAN-2
Angels in Heav'n as we may say. A Poem upon the Caelestial Embassy. Richard Steere. SCAP
Angels in high places, The. Azrael. Robert Gilbert Welsh. HBV; MaRV; OQP
Angels, in the early morning. Emily Dickinson. MWA-2
Angels inhabit love songs. But they're sprites. The Anatomy of Angels. Alden Nowlan. PeCV (1967 ed.)
Angels of Bethlehem, The. St. Luke, Bible, *N.T.* *See* Adoration of the Shepherds, The.
Angels of Buena Vista, The. Whittier. BeLS; PAH
Angels Prayer, An. Lefty Sims. BF
Angels received his dying breath. On the Death of a Journalist. Roy Campbell. CoBE
Angels, Roll the Rock Away! Thomas Scott. BePJ; SoP
Angels' Song, The. Edmund Hamilton Sears. *See* It Came upon the Midnight Clear.
Angel's Story, The. Adelaide Anne Procter. DD
Angels to the shepherds sang, The. A Carol. Fred E. Weatherly. YeAr
Angels We Have Heard on High. *Unknown.* TreFS; YaCaBo, *with music*
Angels, where you soar. A Prayer. Alfred Noyes. PoPl
Angel's Whisper, The. Samuel Lover. OnYI; PRWS
Angelus, The. Florence Earle Coates. HBV
Angelus, The, *sel.* Edwin Markham.
  True Work Is Worship. MaRV
Angelus. "Yehoash," *tr. fr. Yiddish by* Elbert Aidline. LiTW
Angelus Domini. *Unknown.* WHL
Angelus inquit pastoribus. Now the Most High Is Born. James Ryman. MeEL
Angelus-Time near Dublin. William Bedell Stanford. NeIP
Anger. Robert Creeley. CoPo; NaP
Anger ("Anger in its time and place"). Charles *and* Mary Lamb. FaBoBe; HBV; HBVY; OTPC (1923 ed.); ThGo
Anger of Christ, The. Richard Watson Gilder. StJW
Angina Pectoris. W. R. Moses. LiTA
Anglais Mort à Florence. Wallace Stevens. AP
Angle of Geese. N. Scott Momaday. QFR
Angler, The. Bhartrihari, *tr. fr. Sanskrit by* Paul Elmer More. LiTW
Angler, The (*in* Izaak Walton's The Compleat Angler). John Chalkhill. HBV
Angler named Ezekiel Hutt, An. Haulage. E. E. Nott-Bower. WhC
Angler's Ballad, The. Charles Cotton. CavP; CEP
Angler's Invitation, The. Thomas Tod Stoddart. GN; HBV
Angler's Reveille, The. Henry van Dyke. *Fr.* The Toiling of Felix. BBV (1923 ed.); GN; StVeCh
Angler's Song, The (*in* Izaak Walton's The Compleat Angler). William Basse. OBS
  "As inward love breeds outward talk," *sel.* SD
Angler's Song, The. John Dennys. *Fr.* The Secrets of Angling. ElL
  ("Let me live harmlessly, and near the brink.") MyFE
Angler's Song, The ("Man's life is but vain") (*in* Izaak Walton's The Compleat Angler). *Unknown.* SeCL
Angler's Wish, An. Henry van Dyke. AA
Angler's Wish, The. Izaak Walton. *Fr.* The Compleat Angler. HBV; SeCL
Angleworm. Herbert Cahoon. SiTL
Anglo-Eire Vignette. Patric Stevenson. NeIP
Anglo-Irishman's Complaint, An. *Unknown.* AnIL
Anglo-Saxon. E. L. Mayo. MiAP
Angola Question Mark. Langston Hughes. TTY
Angora anger who art in heaven. Lyric. Gil Orlovitz. ToPo
Angry future like a winter builds, The. Poem on Hampstead Heath. Louis Adeane. NeBP
Angry Lover, The. Matthew Prior. *See* A Lover's Anger.
Angry threat of silence, ever present, The. Woman Telephoning. Joseph Joel Keith. FiSC
Angry Word, An. Margaret E. Bruner. PoToHe
Angry young husband called Bicket, An. Limerick. John Galsworthy. CenHV
Anguish. Stéphane Mallarmé, *tr. fr. French by* Arthur Symons. AWP; SyP
Anguish, The. Edna St. Vincent Millay. NeMA
Anguish. Henry Vaughan. MemP; SoP
Anguish of the earth absolves our eyes, The. Absolution. Siegfried Sassoon. MMA
Anguish'd Doubt Broods over Eden, The. Christopher Brennan. *Fr.* Lilith. PoAu-1
Anguishes of poets are, The. Poets Easily Consoled. Christopher Morley. LHV
Angus McGregor. Lew Sarett. PoMa
Anima Christi. St. Ignatius Loyola, *tr. fr. Latin.* WHL
Animal Crackers. Christopher Morley. BoChLi; FaPON; GFA; MPB; OTPC (1946 ed.); PCD; SoPo; SP; SUS; TiPo; UTS
Animal Fair. Philip Booth. NePoAm-2
Animal Fair. *Unknown.* AS, *with music*; BLPA; FaBoBe; GoTP; MoShBr; SiTL; SoPo; YaD
Animal Howl, The. M. J., *tr. fr. Polish by* A. Glanz-Leyeless. TrJP
Animal Kingdom. Sydney Clouts. PeSA
Animal runs, it passes, it dies, The. And it is the great cold. Death Rites II. *Unknown.* TTY
Animal Store, The. Rachel Field. OTPC (1946 ed.); PDV; SoPo; TiPo; UTS
Animal that I am, I come to call. The Man in the Dress Suit. Robert L. Wolf. HBMV
Animal Tranquillity and Decay. Wordsworth. *See* Old Man, An.
Animal willows of November. The Willows of Massachusetts. Denise Levertov. WIRo
Animals, The. Stephen Berg. NaP
Animals, The. Josephine Jacobsen. GoYe
Animals, The. Lewis Mac Adams. ANYP; YAP
Animals, The. W. S. Merwin. FRC
Animals, The. Edwin Muir. CMoP; MoBrPo (1962 ed.); MoPW; PoDB
Animals. Walt Whitman. *Fr.* Song of Myself, XXXII. FaFP; GTBS-W; LiTG; MCCG; NePA; PoPL; PPON; SiTL
  (Beasts, The.) CBEP; HBV; OBVV
  ("I think I could turn and live with animals.") AnEnPo; BoC; LoBV; PDV; PG (1955 ed.); PoG; PoMa; TrGrPo; WGRP
Animals are my friends and my kin and my playfellows. About Animals. Hilda Conkling. UTS
Animals Are Passing from Our Lives. Philip Levine. CoAP
Animals are silent in the hold, The. Noah's Song. Evan Jones. PoAu-2
Animals came in two by two, The. One More River. *Unknown.* SiTL
Animals in the Ark, The. *Unknown.* *Fr.* The Deluge. ChTr
Animals Mourn with Eve, The. Christina Rossetti. *Fr.* Eve. OA
Animals of the forest and plants of the field are friends. William Harmon. *Fr.* Treasury Holiday. QAH
Animals own a fur world. Adults Only. William Stafford. CBV
Animals we have seen, all marvelous creatures, The. The Park in Milan. William Jay Smith. CAD; CoAP
Animals will never know, The. If They Spoke. Mark Van Doren. ImOP
Animula. T. S. Eliot. AmPP; LiTB; MAP; MoAmPo (1942 ed.); MoPW; MoVE; TwAmPo
Animula Blandula Vagula. Emperor Hadrian. *See* To His Soul.
Animula Vagula. A. Y. Campbell. HBMV
Anke von Tharau. *Unknown,* *tr. fr. German by* Christa Wolf *and* Virginia Tufte. HW
Ankle's chief end is exposiery, The. The Limeratomy: The Ankle. Anthony Euwer. HBMV
Ann and the Fairy Song. Walter de la Mare. *Fr.* A Child's Day. FaBV
Ann, Ann!/ Come! quick as you can! Alas, Alack. Walter de la Mare. EvOK; FaPON; GFA; MPB; PoRh; TiPo
Ann Rutledge. Edgar Lee Masters. *See* Anne Rutledge.
Ann stood and watched the combers race to shore. Andrew Merkel. *Fr.* Tallahassee. CaP
Anna. Burns. TrGrPo; UnTE
  (Gowden Locks of Anna, The.) CBEP
Anna Elise, she jumped with surprise. *Unknown.* OxNR
Anna-Marie, Love, Up Is the Sun. Sir Walter Scott. *Fr.* Ivanhoe, *ch.* 40. ViBoPo
Anna Susanna. *Unknown.* SAS

Annabel Lee, *parody.* Stanley Huntley. BOHV
Annabel Lee. Poe. AA; AmePo; AmP; AmPP; AnFE; AP; APA; AWP; BBV; BeLS; BLPA; BoLiVe; BoLP; CH; CLwM; CoAnAm; CoBA; DiPo; EtS; FaFP; FaPL; FaPON; GoTP; GTBS-W; GTSE; HBV; HBVY; HoPM; InPo; JAWP; LiTA; LiTG; LiTL; LoEn; LoGBV; MaC; MAmP; MCCG; MemP; MPB; MWA-1; NeHB; NePA; NoP; OBEV (1st ed.); OBVV; OnMSP; OTD; OtMeF; OTPC, *abr.*; OuHeWo; OxBA; PCD; PG; PoFS; PoG; PoPl; PoPo; PTK; RoGo; SeCeV; StaSt; StPo; StVeCh; TOP; TreF; TrGrPo; ViBoPo; WBP; WBLP; YT
Annales, *sel.* Ennius, *tr. fr. Latin by* John Wight.
Like a Shower of Rain. WaaP
Annals. Maxine Cassin. TDP
Annan Water. *Unknown.* BaBo; BuBa; CH; HBV; OBB
Annar-Mariar's Christmas Shopping. Eleanor Farjeon. ChBR
Anne. Lizette Woodworth Reese. AA
Anne Grenville, Countess Temple, Appointed Poet Laureate to the King of the Fairies. Horace Walpole. *See* Countess Temple, Appointed Poet Laureate.
Anne Hutchinson's Exile. Edward Everett Hale. PAH
Anne [*or* Ann] Rutledge. Edgar Lee Masters. *Fr.* Spoon River Anthology. AmFN; AmLP; AmP; CMoP; FaFP; ILP; InPo; LiPo; LiTA; LiTM (rev. ed.); MAP; MoAmPo; MoVE; NeHB; NeMA; NePA; NP; OHFP; OxBA; PaA; PG (1945 ed.); PoPl; PoSa; PoSC; PTK; ThLM; TrGrPo
Anne, who are dead. Wonderful Things. Ron Padgett. YAP
Anne's Book. Mary Webb. OnPP
Annette Myers; or, A Murder in St. James's Park. *Unknown.* OxBoLi
Annie and Rhoda, sisters twain. The Sisters. Whittier. AWP; InPo
Annie and Willie's Prayer. Sophia P. Snow. BeLS; BLPA
Annie Bolanny. *Unknown.* ChTr
Annie Breen, *with music. Unknown.* CoSo
Annie Died the Other Day. E. E. Cummings. ErPo
Annie Laurie. William Douglas, *revised by* Lady John Scott. FaBoBe; FaBV; FaFP; GN; GTBS-W; HBV; InP; LiTG; LiTL; MCCG; OTPC; PTK; SiTL; TreF; WBLP
Annie McConkus. Amy Belle Adams. StaSt
Annie of Lochroyan. *Unknown. See* Lass of Lochroyan, The.
Annie Shore and Johnnie Doon. Patrick Orr. BANP; HBV
Annie's Garden. Eliza Lee Follen. PPL
Annihilation. Conrad Aiken. CrMA; LO; MAP; MoAB; MoAmPo
Annihilation of Nothing, The. Thom Gunn. NePoEA-2
Anniversaries. Donald Justice. TDP
Anniversary [*or* Anniversarie], The. John Donne. AnAnS-1; AnFE; CBEP; DiPo; EP; ExPo; HoPM; LiTB; LiTG; MaMe; MBW-1; MeLP; MeP; MePo; NoP; OAEP; OBS; PoeP; RelE; SCEP-1; SeCeV; SeCP; SeCV-1; SeEP; TuPP; UnPo (1st ed.)
"Only our love hath no decay," *sel.* LO
Anniversary. Richmond Lattimore. NYBP; PoCh
Anniversary, An. Richard Lovelace. LoBV
Anniversary. R. S. Thomas. ToPo
Anniversary. John Wain. NePoEA-2; ToPo
Anniversary, An; a Country Burial. Ann Stanford. TPM
Anniversary in September. Beatrice Curtis Brown. BiCB
Anniversary of Antonia Pozzi's Death by Suicide. Vittorio Serini. *tr. fr. Italian by* Glauco Cambon. OnPM
Anno Domini. John Bellenden. ACP (1926 ed.)
Anno 1829. Heine, *tr. fr. German by* Charles Stuart Calverley. AWP; JAWP; WBP; WOL; LiTW, *tr. by* Louis Untermeyer
Anno Santo. Stephen Spender. FaBoMo
Annot Lyle's Song: "Birds of Omen." Sir Walter Scott. *Fr.* The Legend of Montrose, VI. EnRP
Annotation for an Epitaph. Adrienne Rich. TwAmPo
Annotations of Auschwitz. Peter Porter. FOL; NMP
Annotators agree Composer X. A St. Cecilia's Day Epigram. Peter Porter. ELU
Announce it here with triple leading. Rarae Aves. Franklin P. Adams. WhC
Announced by all the trumpets of the sky. The Snow-Storm. Emerson. AA; AmePo; AMP; AmPP; AnNE; AP; BoLiVe; BoNaP; CoBA; DiPo; FaBoBe; GTBS-D; GTBS-W; InP; LaNeLa; LiTA; LiTG; MAmP; MWA-1; NePA; NoP; OHFP; OTPC; OuHeWo; OxBA; PCH; PG (1945 ed.); PoE; PoEL-4; PoFS; PoLF; PoPo; PTK; StP; TDP; TiPo; TreFT; TrGrPo; VaPo; WiR; YT
Announcement. Elizabeth J. Coatsworth. *See* Conquistador.
Announcement. James T. Stewart. BF
Ann's House. Dick Lourie. ThO
Annual Gaiety. Wallace Stevens. MAP; MoAB; MoAmPo
Annual Legend. Winfield Townley Scott. CoAP; GTBS-W; LiTA; LiTM; WaP
Annual Solution, The. Edwin Meade Robinson. InMe
Annuity, The. George Outram. BOHV; HBV; PeVV
Annul Wars. Nahman of Bratzlav, *tr. fr. Hebrew by* Jacob Sloan. TrJP
Annunciation, The. Margaret Devereaux Conway. ISi; JKCP (1955 ed.)
Annunciation, The. Abraham Cowley. *Fr.* Davideis. OxBoCh
Annunciation. John Donne. AnAnS-1; ISi; MaMe; MeP; OBS; Sonn
Annunciation, The. John Duffy. ISi
Annunciation. Ruth Gilbert. *Fr.* The Blossom of the Branches. ACV
Annunciation. D. G. Jones. PeCV (1967 ed.)
Annunciation, The. W. S. Merwin. AP
Annunciation, The. Edwin Muir. CMoP
Annunciation, The. St. Nerses, *tr. fr. Armenian by* W. H. Kent. ISi
Annunciation, The. Adelaide Anne Procter. JKCP
Annunciation, The. John Banister Tabb. ISi
Annunciation, The ("Gabriel, fram Hevene King"). *Unknown.* MeEL
Annunciation, The ("Our Lady went forth pondering"). *Unknown, tr. fr. German.* ISi
Annunciation Night. Katherine E. Conway. CAW; ChIP
Annunciation Night. Abby Maria Hemenway. *Fr.* Mary of Nazareth. ISi
Annunciation to All Women. Agnes C. Foote. ChIP
Annunciations. Geoffrey Hill. NePoEA-2
Annuntiation and Passion, The. John Donne. MaMe
Annus Mirabilis, *sels.* Dryden.
"But ah! how unsincere are all our joys!" SeEP
Fire of London, The. ChTr; FaBoEn, *shorter sel.*
Fourth Day's Battle, The. OBS
Great Fire, The. FiP
New London, The. FaBoCh; OBS
(London.) SeCePo
(Rebirth of London, The.) PeRV
Sea Battle, The. FiP
"Warlike prince had sever'd from the rest, The." PeRV
"Yet London, empress of the northern clime." ViBoPo
Anodyne, The. Sarah N. Cleghorn. OQP
Anodyne, An. Thomas Ken. OxBoCh
Anon out of the earth a fabric huge. Pandemonium and Its Architect. Milton. *Fr.* Paradise Lost, I. PoFS; TreFS
Anonymous. John Banister Tabb. AA
Anonymous Alba. *Unknown, tr. fr. French by* Stanley Burnshaw. OuHeWo
Anonymous as cherubs. Two Voices in a Meadow. Richard Wilbur. CaFP; CBV; NePoAm-2; UnPo (3d ed.)
Anonymous Drawing. Donald Justice. CoAP; NePoEA-2
Anonymous Gravestone. Erich Kästner, *tr. fr. German by* Patrick Bridgewater. ELU
Anonymous—nor needs a name. Anonymous. John Banister Tabb. AA
Another. Abraham Cowley, *after the Greek of* Anacreon. SeCP
Another [Fantastic Simile]. Thomas Lovell Beddoes. Sonn
Another [Upon the Death of Mr. Herrys]. Richard Crashaw. MaMe
Another [To His Booke]. Robert Herrick. AnAnS-2
Another [Beggar Poem] ("For one copper"). Issa, *tr. fr. Japanese by* Max Bickerton. PoFr
Another ("As I beheld a winters evening air"). Richard Lovelace. SeCP
Another ("The Centaur, Syren, I forego"). Richard Lovelace. AtBAP; PoEL-3
Another age ground down by civil strife! The Horrors of Civil War. Horace. WoL
Another Altar. Edmund Blunden. MoPW
Another and the Same. Samuel Rogers. *Fr.* Human Life. OBNC
Another armored animal—scale. The Pangolin. Marianne Moore. AP; CoBMV; CrMA

Another Beggar Poem ("A bleak day!"). Issa, *tr. fr. Japanese by* Max Bickerton. PoFr
Another Birthday. Ben Jonson. WiR
Another Charm. Robert Herrick. OTPC (1923 ed.)
Another Christmas. J. Sidlow Baxter. SoP
Another cove of shale. On the Marginal Way. Richard Wilbur. CoAP
Another Cross. John Masefield. *Fr.* The Everlasting Mercy. MaRV
Another Cynical Variation. "Helen." InMe
Another Dark Lady. Edwin Arlington Robinson. CLwM
Another Day. Isabella Maria Brown. PoNe (1970 ed.)
Another Day. Alice Hansche Mortenson. SoP
Another day when being. Being and Wind. Gregory Orr. QAH
Another dreadful tale of woe as I will here unfold. Annette Myers; or, A Murder in St. James's Park. *Unknown.* OxBoLi
Another epic! Who inflicts again. Byron. *Fr.* English Bards and Scotch Reviewers. EiCP
Another Fan Belonging to Mademoiselle Mallarmé. Stéphane Mallarmé, *tr. fr. French by* Roger Fry. SyP
Another four I've left yet to bring on. The Four Seasons of the Year. Anne Bradstreet. SCAP
Another Generation. J. C. Squire. HBMV
Another good cow-puncher has gone to meet his fate. Charlie Rutledge. *Unknown, at. to.* D. J. White (D. J. O'Malley). CoSo
Another Grace for a Child ("Here a little child I stand"). Robert Herrick. *See* Grace for a Child.
Another guest that winter night. Prophetess. Whittier. *Fr.* Snow-bound. AA
Another hill town. Hotel Paradiso e Commerciale. John Malcolm Brinnin. NYBP; PoCh; TwCP
Another If. *Unknown.* SoP
Another. In Defence of Their Inconstancie. Ben Jonson. *See* In Defense of Their Inconstancy.
Another irresistible force. Today. Clive Matson. ThO
Another Island Groupage. Kenward Elmslie. ANYP
Another Kind of Burning. Ruth Fox. NYBP
Another knight smote Saint Thomas in that self wound. Becket's Diadem. *Unknown.* ACP
Another Ladyes Exception Present at the Hearing. Ben Jonson. *Fr.* A Celebration of Charis. AnAnS-2; SeCP
Another Late Edition, *sel.* Olga Cabral.
This Morning the Sun. PPON
Another Letter to Her Husband, Absent upon Publick Employment. Anne Bradstreet. *See* Letter to Her Husband, Absent upon Publick Employment.
Another Little Drink, *with music.* *Unknown.* TrAS, *with* Old Zip Coon
Another Meditation at the Same Time. Edward Taylor. *See* Preparatory Meditations: "Am I thy gold. . ."
Another might have spared your pride. What I Have. Robert Farren. JKCP (1955 ed.)
Another New Year. Phyllis C. Michael. SoP
Another New-Yeeres Gift, or Song for the Circumcision. Robert Herrick. SCEP-2
Another nickel in the slot. A Hero in the Land of Dough. Robert Clairmont. WaKn; WhC
Another night, and yet no tidings come. The Parting of King Philip and Marie. John Westland Marston. *Fr.* Marie de Meranie. VA
Another Night in the Ruins. Galway Kinnell. CoAP
Another Night with Telescope. Leonard Cohen. PeCV (1967 ed.)
Another Ode to the North-East Wind. *Unknown.* Par
Another, of Another Mind ("A king, oh boon for my aspiring mind!"). "F. M." TuPP
Another, of Another Mind ("The greatest kings do least command content"). *Unknown.* TuPP
Another, of His Cynthia. Fulke Greville. *See* Of His Cynthia.
Another of the Same ("The praise of meaner wits"). Sir Walter Ralegh. FCP; SiPS
Another of the Same. Excellently Written by a Most Woorthy Gentleman. *At. to* Sir Edward Dyer. *See* Epitaph on Sir Philip Sidney.
Another of the Same Nature, Made Since ("Come live with me and be my dear"). *Unknown.* CLwM
Another on the University Carrier. Milton. *See* On the Oxford Carrier.
Another Plum-Cake. Ann Taylor. *See* Plum-Cake, The.
Another Reply to "In Flanders Fields." C. B. Galbreath, *sometimes at. to* J. A. Armstrong. BLPA; PAL
(In Flanders Fields; an Answer.) HH
Another Return. Winfield Townley Scott. ELU
Another sate near him, whose harp of gold. Fenton Johnson. *Fr.* The Vision of Lazarus. BANP
Another scorns the homespun thread of rhymes. Satire VI. Joseph Hall. *Fr.* Virgidemiarum. SiCE; TuPP
Another September. Thomas Kinsella. PoCh
Another side, umbrageous grots and caves. Paradise. Milton. *Fr.* Paradise Lost, IV. OBS
Another Song. Donald Justice. *See* Tune for a Lonesome Fife.
Another Song. William Ross, *tr. fr. Gaelic.* GoTS
Another Song. Marion Strobel. MoLP
Another Song of a Fool. W. B. Yeats. OA
Another Sonnet to Black Itself. Lord Herbert of Cherbury. EP; SeEP
Another Spirit Advances. Jules Romains, *tr. fr. French by* Joseph T. Shipley. AWP; JAWP; WBP
Another Spring. Christina Rossetti. VP
Another Time. W. H. Auden. MemP; OxBA
Another to the Same. Horace, *tr. fr. Latin by* William Browne. Odes, I, 5. WiR
Another to Urania. Benjamin Colman. SCAP
Another Tribute to Wyatt ("In the rude age, when knowledge was not rife"). Earl of Surrey. SiPS
(In the Rude Age.) NCEP
("In the rude age when science was not so rife.") FCP
Another Version. George Herbert. *See* To My Successor.
Another Villon-ous Variation. Don Marquis. HBMV
Another Way. Ambrose Bierce. AA; LHV
Another Way of Love. Robert Browning. PoVP
Another Weeping Woman. Wallace Stevens. MoVE; NP
Another While. Morris Rosenfeld, *tr. fr. Yiddish.* TrJP
Another writes because his father writ. Edward Young. SiTL
Another Year. Frances Ridley Havergal. *See* Another Year Is Dawning.
Another Year. Thomas O'Hagan. PEDC
Another Year ("Another year has now been born"). Oswald J. Smith. STF
Another year! another deadly blow! November, 1806. Wordsworth. OBRV; PoFr
Another Year Come. W. S. Merwin. NYBP
Another year has struck the vibrant chime. Washington. Mae Winkler Goodman. PGD
Another year I enter. A New Year's Promise. *Unknown.* BLRP
Another Year Is Dawning. Frances Ridley Havergal. BLRP; SoP; STF; WBLP
Another year passed over—gone. Another Year. Thomas O'-Hagan. PEDC
Anster Fair, *sel.* William Tennant.
On the Road to Anster Fair. OBRV
Answer, The. George Herbert. MaMe
Answer. Harriet Hoock. WHL
Answer, The. Robinson Jeffers. CMoP; GoYe; MoRP
Answer, The. Orrick Johns. NP
Answer, An. Henry S. Leigh. YT
Answer, An. Sir Tobie Matthew. SeCL
("Say, but did you love so long?") SeCV-1
Answer. Merrill Moore. NeMA
Answer. Thomas Osbert Mordaunt. *See* Sound, Sound the Clarion.
Answer. Leonora Speyer. PG (1945 ed.)
Answer, The. Sara Teasdale. NP
Answer, The. John Hall Wheelock. WIRo
Answer for Hope. Richard Crashaw. *See* For Hope.
Answer that ye made to me, my dear, The. Sir Thomas Wyatt. FCP; SiPS
Answer to a Child's Question. Samuel Taylor Coleridge. BiS; DD; EnRP; FaBoBe; HBV; HBVY; NeHB; OTPC; PEDC; PRWS; ThGo; ThWaDe; TVC; UTS
(Birds, The.) BoTP
Answer to a Worldly One. Li Po, *tr. fr. Chinese by* C. W. Luh. OnPM
Answer to Another Persuading a Lady to Marriage, An. Katherine Philips. *See* To One Persuading a Lady to Marriage.

Answer (continued)
Answer to Chloe [*or* Cloe] Jealous. Matthew Prior. ALV; OBEC; SeCePo; SeCL
(Answer to Jealousy.) MeWo
(Better Answer [to Cloe Jealous], A.) AWP; CEP; EiCL; EiPP; ELP; ExPo; FaBoEn; InPo; JAWP; PIA; PoE; PoEL-3; SeCeV; TOP; WBP
(To Chloe [*or* Cloe] Jealous [a Better Answer].) HBV; LiTL LO; ViBoPo
Answer to Jealousy. Matthew Prior. *See* Answer to Chloe Jealous.
Answer to Marlowe. Sir Walter Ralegh. *See* Nymph's Reply to the Shepherd, The.
Answer to Master Wither's Song. Ben Jonson. BOHV; InMe
Answer to Pauper. Thomas Hood. NBM
Answer to Some Verses Made in His Praise, An. Sir John Suckling. PP
Answer to the Cuckold's Complaint, An. *Unknown.* *See* Scolding Wives Vindication, The.
Answer to the Parson, An. Blake. OxBoLi
(Epigram: An Answer to the Parson.) SiTL
Answer to Twenty-one Years, An. *Unknown.* *See* Little Willie's My Darlin'.
Answer you, Sirs? Do I understand aright? Giuseppe Caponsacchi. Robert Browning. The Ring and the Book, VI. PoVP; VP
Answered Prayer, The. Annie Johnson Flint. STF
Answered Thus by Sir P. S. Sir Philip Sidney. TuPP
Answering a Letter from a Younger Poet. Brewster Ghiselin. PoCh
Answering Vice-Prefect Chang. Wang Wei, *tr. fr. Chinese by* Witter Bynner *and* Kiang Kang-hu. OuHeWo
Answers, The. Robert Clairmont. GoTP; SiTL; SoPo; WhC
(When Did the World Begin.) WaKn
Answers. Elizabeth Jennings. NePoEA; PoDB
Ant, The. Richard Armour. PoPo
Ant, The. Oliver Herford. LBN
Ant, The. Samuel Johnson. CBV; EiCL
Ant, The. Ogden Nash. FaBV
Ant, a prodigy of strength, The. The Ant. Richard Armour. PoPo
Ant and the Cricket, The. *Unknown.* GoTP; HBV; HBVY; OTPC (1923 ed.); PRWS
Ant Explorer, The. C. J. Dennis. NeLNL
Ant has made himself illustrious, The. The Ant. Ogden Nash. FaBV
Ant on the tablecloth, An. Departmental. Robert Frost. AmP; AmPP; AnNE; DiPo; GoYe; HoPM; MoAB; MoAmPo
Ant Sun, The. Christopher Middleton. *Fr.* Herman Moon's Hourbook. NePoEA-2
Ant Village, The. Marion Edey. FaPON; TiPo
Antagonist, The. David Ferry. NePoAm-2
Antagonists, The. Muriel Rukeyser. *Fr.* Ninth Elegy. FiMAP
Ante-Bellum Sermon, An. Paul Laurence Dunbar. BALP; YT
Ante Mortem. Robinson Jeffers. MAP; MoAmPo; MoVE
Antecedents. Charles Tomlinson. CMoP
Antelope. William Jay Smith. TiPo (1959 ed.)
Antelopes, The. James K. Baxter. AnNZ
Antenora. Hugh MacDiarmid. SeCePo
Anteroom, The. Denise Levertov. NeBP
Anteros. William Johnson Cory. OBVV
(Dirge, A.) OBNC
Anthem for Doomed Youth. Wilfred Owen. AnFE; BoLiVe; BrPo; ChTr; CMoP; CoBMV; EnLi-2 (1949 ed.); EvOK; FaBoMo; FaFP; FIW; FosPo; GTBS-D; GTBS-P; GTBS-W; GTSL; HBMV; LiTM; MaRV; MoAB; MoBrPo; MoPW; MoVE; NeMA; NoP; NP; OAEP (2d ed.); OBEV (new ed.); PoE; PoPo; POTE; SeCePo; ShBV-4; Sonn; TreFT; TrGrPo; ViBoPo; WaP; WHA
Anthem for St. Cecilia's Day. W. H. Auden. *See* Song for St. Celilia's Day.
Anthill, The ("The anthill lay unsheltered in the sun"). Donald C. Babcock. NePoAm
Anthologistics. Arthur Guiterman. InMe; WhC
Anthony Munday unto All Young Gentlemen in Commendation of this Gallery and Workmen Thereof. Anthony Munday. RelE
Anthony Wayne. Arthur Guiterman. TiPo (1959 ed.)
Anthropos apteros for days. The Labyrinth. W. H. Auden. GTBS-W; LiTA; LiTM (rev. ed.); NePA; SiTL
Anti-Platonicke. George Daniel. CavP
Anti-Politician, The. Alexander Brome. CavP
Anti-Symbolist, The. Sidney Keyes. MoPo
Anti-aircraft seen from a certain distance. Dam Neck, Virginia. Richard Eberhart. LiTA; MoAB; WaP
Antichrist. Edwin Muir. EaLo
Antichrist, or the Reunion of Christendom; an Ode. G. K. Chesterton. SeCePo
Antichrist, playing his lissome flute and merry. Armageddon. John Crowe Ransom. LiTA
Anticipation. Emily Brontë. OBNC
Anticipation. Lord De Tabley. ELP; GTBS-D
Anticipation. Sarah Carter Lewis. SoP
Anticipation. Joseph Tusiani. GoYe
Antigone, *sels.* Sophocles, *tr. fr. Greek.*
Choral Ode: "Numberless are the world's wonders," *tr. by* Dudley Fitts *and* Robert Fitzgerald. LiTW
Higher Command, The, *tr. unknown.* MaRV
Thebes of the Seven Gates, *tr. by* Dudley Fitts *and* Robert Fitzgerald. WaaP
Antigone and Helen—would they laugh. Two Sonnets. David P. Berenberg. HBMV
Antigonish. Hughes Mearns. InMe; PoLF; WhC
(Case, A.) LiTM; SiTL
(Little Man, The.) StaSt
(Little Man Who Wasn't There, The.) FaFP; FaPON; SoPo
Antinous. Quentin Stevenson. POTE (1959 ed.)
Antipater of Thessalonica. Kenneth Rexroth. CrMA
Antiphon: "Let all the world in ev'ry corner sing." George Herbert. MaMe
("Let all the world in every corner sing.") ThGo
Antiphon: "Praised be the God of love." George Herbert. MaMe
Antiphony. William Morris. *See* Song from "Ogier the Dane."
Antiplatonick, The. John Cleveland. AnAnS-2; MePo; SeCP
Antiquary. John Donne. CLwM; MaMe; TuPP
Antiquary, The. Martial, *tr. fr. Latin by* Paul Nixon. LiTW
Antiquary, The, *sels.* Sir Walter Scott.
Harlaw, *fr. ch.* 40. EnLi-2
(Red Harlaw.) OxBB
Why Sit'st [*or* Sitt'st] Thou by That Ruin'd Hall. EnRP; EPN
(Aged Carle, The.) OAEP
Antique. John Stevens Wade. NYTB
Antique Carved Figures. Raymond E. F. Larsson. JKCP (1955 ed.)
Antique Glimpses, *sel.* Thomas Caulfield Irwin.
"Grey-faced Spirit! let us sit." IrPN
Antique Harvesters. John Crowe Ransom. AnFE; AP; APA; CoAnAm; CoBMV; CrMA; FaBoEn; InPo; MAP; MoAB; MoAmPo; NoP; OxBA; WoL
Antique Shop. Carl Carmer. FaPON; MoSiPe; RePo
Antiques of old Auctus will bore me to death, The. The Antiquary. Martial. LiTW
Antiquity of Freedom, The. Bryant. AA; AnNE; AP; CoBA; TOP
"Oh Freedom! thou art not, as poets dream," *sel.* PoFr
Antiseptic Baby and the Prophylactic Pup, The. Strictly Germproof. Arthur Guiterman. BLPA; BOHV; HBV; TreF; TrJP; YaD
Antlers of a buried intelligence. A Change of Heart. Peter Fellowes. QAH
Antonio. Laura E. Richards. MoShBr; PDV; PoRh; SoPo; TiPo (1959 ed.)
Antonio and Mellida, *sel.* John Marston.
"My thoughts are fixed." ViBoPo
Antonio, Antonio,/ Was tired of living alonio. Antonio. Laura E. Richards. MoShBr; PDV; PoRh; SoPo; TiPo (1959 ed.)
Antonio Sarto ees buildin' a wall. The Blossomy Barrow. T. A. Daly. LHV
Antonio Torres Heredia. The Arrest of Antoñito el Camborio in the Streets of Seville. Federico García Lorca. PoFr
Antonio's Revenge, *sel.* John Marston.
Prologue: "Rawish dank of clumsy winter ramps, The." LoBV; ViBoPo
Antonius, *sel.* Robert Garnier, *tr. fr. French by* the Countess of Pembroke.
Chorus: "Alas, with what tormenting fire." TuPP

(Of Death.) ElL
Antony and Cleopatra (3 *sonnets*). José Maria de Heredia, *tr. fr. French by* Henri Coulette. NePoEA
Antony and Cleopatra. William Haines Lytle. *See* Antony to Cleopatra.
Antony and Cleopatra, *sels.* Shakespeare.
"All's but naught," *fr.* IV, xv. MemP
"Antony's dead," *fr.* II, v. MemP
Cleopatra, *fr.* II, ii. CLwM; DiPo; FOL; LiTB; LiTG; LiTL
"Barge she sat in, like a burnish'd throne, The." MemP
(Cleopatra and Her Barge.) TreF
(Cleopatra's Barge.) PoFS; TrGrPo
Cleopatra's Lament, *fr.* V, ii. UnPo
"His legs bestrid the ocean: his rear'd arm." MemP
Come, Thou Monarch of the Vine, *fr.* II, vii. BEL; OAEP; OnPM; ViBoPo
(Drinking Song, A.) OBSC
"Crown o' the earth doth melt, The," *fr.* IV, xv. MemP
Death of Cleopatra, *fr.* V, ii. FiP; TreFS
(Cleopatra's Death.) TrGrPo
("Give me my robe, put on my crown.") AtBAP; MemP
"Her gentlewomen, like the Nereids," *fr.* II, ii. MemP
"I am dying, Egypt, dying," *fr.* IV, xv. MemP
(Death of Antony.) FiP
"I will o'ertake thee, Cleopatra, and, *fr.* IV, xiv. MemP
"Now boast thee, death, in thy possession lies," *fr.* V, ii. MemP
"O Charmian,/ Where think'st thou he is now," *fr.* I, v. MemP
"Oh Sunne,/ Burne the great sphere thou mov'st in," *fr.* IV, xv. AtBAP
(Shakespeare Gallery, A: Cleopatra. MaC
Antony to Cleopatra. William Haines Lytle. AA; BeLS; HBV; OnPP
(Antony and Cleopatra.) BLPA; NeHB; TreF
Antony's Oration. Shakespeare. *Fr.* Julius Caesar, III, ii. LiTB; PoPl; TreF; TrGrPo
("Friends, Romans, countrymen, lend me your ears.") FOL
(I Come to Bury Caesar.) WHA
(Mark Antony's Lament.) TreFS
(Mark Antony's Speech.) PTK
Ants. Alfred Kreymborg. MAPA
Ant's a Centaur, The. Ezra Pound. *Fr.* Canto LXXXI. PoSa
(Pull Down Thy Vanity.) FaBoEn
Ants and Others. Adrien Stoutenburg. NYBP
Ants are walking under the ground, The. The People. Elizabeth Madox Roberts. GoJo; SoPo; TiPo
Antwerp and Bruges. Dante Gabriel Rossetti. PIA
Antwerp: Musée Des Beaux-Arts. Alan Ross. NYBP
Antwerp to Ghent. Dante Gabriel Rossetti. *Fr.* A Trip to Paris and Belgium. PeVV
Anvil, The—God's Word. John Clifford. BLPA; NeHB; OQP; PoToHe (new ed.)
(Anvil of God's Word, The.) BLRP; STF
(God's Word.) FaChP; MaRV; SoP; TRV
(Hammers and Anvil.) WBLP
Anvil of God's Mercy, The. Anna Hamilton Wood. OQP
Anvil of God's Word, The. John Clifford. *See* Anvil, The—God's.
Anxiety, *sel.* Emerson.
"Some of your hurts you have cured." MaRV
(Borrowing.) WhC
(Needless Worry.) TreFT
Anxiety of a Young Lady to Get Married. *Unknown, tr. fr. Chinese by* James Legge. OuHeWo
Anxious Dead, The. John McCrae. OHIP
Anxious Farmer, The. Burges Johnson. BoNaP
Any Author to Any Friend. Martial, *tr. fr. Latin by* Dudley Fitts. ML
Any Bird. Ilo Orleans. RIS
Any Day Now. David McCord. ShM
Any Father to Any Son. Francis Burdett Money-Coutts. OBVV
"Any floozie." Overheard at a Sculpture Show at a Museum. *Unknown.* SiTL
Any honest housewife would sort them out. The Poets. Robert Graves. MoPW
Any hound a porcupine nudges. The Porcupine. Ogden Nash. MemP
Any Human to Another. Countee Cullen. MoRP
Any Husband or Wife. Carol Haynes. *See* Any Wife or Husband.
Any Lover, Any Lass. Richard Middleton. HBV; OBVV
Any Man to His Secretary. Hilary Corke. ErPo
Any Man's Advice to His Son. Kenneth Fearing. CMoP
Any of the several names. Eulogy for Populations. Ron Welburn. BF
Any Saint, *abr.* Francis Thompson. MoBrPo
Any Sunset. Louis Untermeyer. GoTP
Any time you hears da cheers and tables crack. Signs of Rain. Edward Jenner. *ad. by* Alex Rogers. StaSt
Any way the old world goes. The Song on the Way. *Unknown.* MPB
Any Wife or Husband. Carol Haynes. BLPA; NeHB
(Any Husband or Wife.) PoToHe
Any Wife to Any Husband. Robert Browning. FaBoEn; OBNC; OtMeF; PoVP
Any Woman. Hazel Hall. MAP; MoAmPo (1942 ed.)
Anybody/ Better than/ Nobody. Desert. Langston Hughes. Kal
Anyhow, anyhow, anyhow my Lord! I'm Gwine Up to Heab'n Anyhow. *Unknown.* BoAN-2
Anyone Lived in a Pretty How Town. E. E. Cummings. AP; CABA; CaFP; CBV; CMoP; CoBMV; DiPo; EvOK; ILP; LiTA; LiTM; MoAB; MoAmPo (1962 ed.); MoPo; NoP; Po; PoSa; ShBV-3; TwAmPo; TwCP
Any One Will Do. *Unknown.* BOHV
Anything, God, but Hate. *Unknown.* TreFT
Anything Remembered. Alfred Starr Hamilton. QAH
Anything this/ recognizable. Downy Hair in the Shape of a Flame. Coleman Barks. PV
Anyway, the old man said, and winked at the barmaid. Yes Please Gentlemen. A. R. D. Fairburn. ACV
Anzac Cove. Leon Gellert. PoAu-1
Aodh Ruadh O'Domhnaill. Thomas McGreevy. AnIV; OBMV; OxBI
(Red Hugh.) OnYI
Aoibhinn, a leabhráin, do thriall. *Unknown, tr. fr. Irish.* AnIV, *tr. by* Flann O'Brien; OxBI, *tr. by* Brian O Nolan
Apart. *Unknown, tr. fr. Russian by* W. R. S. Ralston. OnPM
Apartment House. Gerald Raftery. AmFN; OCS; PoMa
Ape, The. La Fontaine, *tr. fr. French by* Elizur Wright. OnPM
Ape, The. Roland Young. PoPl; WhC
Ape, the Monkey and Baboon Did Meet, The. *Unknown.* NCEP
Apelles' Song. John Lyly. *Fr.* Alexander and Campaspe, III, v. ATP; EnLi-1; EnLit; NeHB; OuHeWo; TOP; TrGrPo
(Cards and Kisses.) HoPM; LiTL; OBEV
(Cards for Kisses.) MeWo
(Cupid and Campaspe.) AtBAP; BEL; ElL; GTBS; GTBS-D; GTBS-P; GTBS-W; GTSE; GTSL; HBV; ILP; LiTG; SeCeV; UnPo (1st ed.); WHA
(Cupid and My Campaspe Played [or Play'd].) CABA; ExPo; NOP; OAEP; PoRA; ReEN; SiCE; TuPP; ViBoPo
(Song: "Cupid and my Campaspe playd.") YAT
(Song by Apelles.) ALV
(Song of Apelles.) OBSC
Apelles the Painter. Leonidas of Tarentum, *tr. fr. Greek by* Lord Neaves. OnPM
Apeneck Sweeney spreads his knees. Sweeney among the Nightingales. T. S. Eliot. AmPP (5th ed.); AnEnPo; AnFE; AP; APA; BoLiVe; BWP; CABA; CaFP; ChMP; CMoP; CoAnAm; CoBMV; DiPo; EnL; EnLit; FaBoMo; ILP; InPo; InvP; LiTA; LiTM; MAP; MAPA; MaPo; MBW-2; MoAmPo (1942 ed.); MoVE; NePA; NoP; NP; OAEP (2d ed.); OBMV; OxBA; PoAN; ReMP; SeCeV; TwAmPo
Apes and Ivory. Alfred Noyes. TSW
Apes yawn and adore their fleas in the sun, The. The Jaguar. Ted Hughes. LiTM (1970 ed.); NoP; PoPl; POTE (1959 ed.); POTi; ToPo
Apex. Nate Salsbury. InMe; WhC
Aphrodite. Floyce Alexander. QAH
Aphrodite Metropolis. Kenneth Fearing. CAD
Aphrodite Pandemos. *Unknown, tr. fr. Greek by* Louis Untermeyer. UnTE
Apis! the men you boxed with, grateful that you. The World's Worst Boxer. Lucilius. SD
Apocalypse. Bible, *N.T. See* Revelation.
Apocalypse. D. J. Enright. NMP; OPoP
Apocalypse. Theodore Maynard. JKCP
Apocalypse. John Frederick Nims. MiAP
Apocalypse. Francis Ernest Kobina Parkes. PBA
Apocalypse. Edith Lovejoy Pierce. MoRP

Apocalypse. Richard Realf. PaA; PAP

Apocrypha. Bible, *O.T. See* Baruch; Ecclesiasticus; First Maccabees; Judith; Tobit; Wisdom of Solomon, The.

Apocrypha. Babette Deutsch. HBMV

Apocrypha. X. J. Kennedy. PV

Apocryphal Apocalypse. John Wheelwright. MoVE

Apoem I. Henri Pichette, *tr. fr. French by* Richard Wilbur. LiTW

Apollo. Matthew Arnold. *See* Song of Callicles'.

Apollo Alone Approves. Mark Turbyfill. NP

Apollo and Daphne. W. R. Rodgers. ErPo; LiTB

Apollo and Daphne, *sel.* Paul Whitehead.
Hunting Song, A. EiCL; OBEC; OxBoLi

Apollo and Daphne. Yvor Winters. Sonn

Apollo kept my father's sheep. A Daughter of Admetus. T. Sturge Moore. FaBoTw

Apollo once a yeare may merry be. *Unknown.* SeCSL

Apollo sings, his harpe resounds; give roome. Upon Master Fletchers Incomparable Playes. Robert Herrick. OBS

Apollo then, with sudden scrutiny and gloomless eyes. Keats. *Fr.* Hyperion. OBRV

Apollo's Song. Ben Jonson. *Fr.* The Masque of Augurs. LoBV

Apollo's Song. John Lyly. *See* Daphne.

Apollyonists, The. Phineas Fletcher. *See* Locusts, or Apollyonists, The.

Apologia. Herbert Farjeon. PV

Apologia. Jean Garrigue. LiTA

Apologia. David Gascoyne. ChMP

Apologia. Oscar Wilde. PoVP

Apologia Addressed to Ireland in the Coming Days. W. B. Yeats. *See* To Ireland in the Coming Times.

Apologia pro Poemate Meo. Wilfred Owen. ChMP; CoBE; CoBMV; LiTM (rev. ed.); MoAB; MoBrPo; NeMA; NP; PoFr

Apologia pro Vita Sua. Samuel Taylor Coleridge. EnRP; ERop-1; PP

Apologie for Having Loved Before, An. Edmund Waller. *See* Apology for Having Loved Before, An.

Apologie for the Precedent [*or* Fore-going] Hymne [*or* Hymnes]. Richard Crashaw. AnAnS-1; MaMe; MeP; SCEP-1

Apologies. Marge Piercy. ThO

Apology, The. Emerson. AmePo; AmPP (3d ed.); AP; CLwM; CoBA; PG (1945 ed.)

Apology. Edith Henrich. NYTB

Apology. Amy Lowell. BoLiVe; NP

Apology. Vassar Miller. NePoEA

Apology, An: "Of Heaven or Hell I have no power to sing." William Morris. *Fr.* The Earthly Paradise. AWP; BEL; BLPA; CoBE; EnLi-2; EnLit; EPN; GTBS; GTBS-W; GTSL; InP; OAEP; OBNC; PolE; PoVP; TOP; ViPP
(Earthly Paradise, The: Prologue.) OtMeF
("Of Heaven or Hell I have no power to sing.") LiTB; LoBV; NoP; ViBoPo, *abr.*; ViPo
(Prologue: "Of Heaven or Hell . . .") FaBoEn
(Singer's Prelude, The.) HBV; Va

Apology. Richard Wilbur. NePoAm

Apology for Actors, An, *sel.* Thomas Heywood.
Author to His Booke, The. PoVP

Apology for Bad Dreams. Robinson Jeffers. AmP; AmPP; AnFE; AP; CoAnAm; CoBMV; ILP; LiTA; MAP; MoAB; MoAmPo; NoP; OxBA; SeCeV; TwAmPo

Apology [*or* Apologie] for Having Loved Before, An. Edmund Waller. MePo; OAEP

Apology for Loose Behavior. Ovid, *tr. fr. Latin by* Christopher Marlowe. *Fr.* Amores. UnTE

Apology for Love. Boccaccio, *tr. fr. Italian by* Dryden. LiTW

Apology for Understatement. John Wain. NePoEA-2; ToPo

Apology for Vagrants. John Langhorne. *Fr.* The Country Justice. OBEC

Apology for Youth. Sister Mary Madeleva. PoPl

Apology of Genius. Mina Loy. QFR

Apology of the Young Scientists. Celia Dimmette. GoYe

Apology: Why Do I Write Today? William Carlos Williams. OxBA; PoeP

Apon the Midsummer evin, mirriest of nichtis. The Tretis of the Tua Mariit Wemen and the Wedo. William Dunbar. GoTS; OxBS

Apopemptic Hymn. Dorothy Auchterlonie. PoAu-2

Apostasy. Aus of Kuraiza, *tr. fr. Arabic by* Hartwig Hirschfeld. TrJP

Apostasy. Mary Mills. NePoAm

Apostasy, The *sel.* Thomas Traherne.
"One star / Is better far." CoBE

Apostate, The. A. E. Coppard. OBMV

Apostle, citizen, and artisan! Love's Cosmopolitan. Annie Matheson. OBVV

Apostles of the hidden sun. The Last Supper. Oscar Williams. FaFP; GTBS-W; LiTA; LiTM; MoRP; NePA; TwAmPo

Apostles of the risen Christ, go forth! His Glory Tell. Horatius Bonar. BePJ

Apostrophe to a Pram Rider. E. B. White. InMe

Apostrophe to Death. Caelius Sedulius, *tr. fr. Latin by* George Sigerson. *Fr.* Carmen Paschale. OnYl

Apostrophe to the Island of Cuba. James Gates Percival. PAH

Apostrophe to the Ocean. Byron. *See* Ocean, The.

Apostrophic Notes from the New-World Physics. E. B. White. ImOP

Apotheosis, *abr.* Joseph Bajza, *tr. fr. Hungarian by* William N. Loew. PoFr

Appalachian Front. Robert Lewis Weeks. AmFN; NYBP

Apparel of green woods and meadows gay. On Revisiting Cintra, after the Death of Catarina. Luís de Camoes. AWP

Apparelled as a Payhim in pilgrim's wise. The Palmer. William Langland. *Fr.* The Vision of Piers Plowman. ACP; CAW

Apparent Failure. Robert Browning. PoVP

"It's wiser being good than bad," *sel.* MaRV

Apparently the Nibelungs. Operatic Note. Melville Cane. UnS

Apparently with no surprise. Emily Dickinson. AmePo; AmPP; AnFE; AnNE; AP; APA; CABA; CaFP; CBV; CoAnAm; CoBA; ILP; OmPM; TrGrPo

Apparition. John Peale Bishop. MoVE

Apparition, The. Blake. *Fr.* America. BoW

Apparition, The. John Donne. AnAns-1; AtBAP; BWP; CABA; CBEP; EnLoPo; EnRePo; EP; ExPo; LoBV; MaMe; MePo; OBEV (new ed.); OBS; PoeP; ReEn; SCEP-1; SeCP; SeCV-1; SeEP; ViBoPo

Apparition. John Erskine. HBMV

Apparition. W. E. Henley. *Fr.* In Hospital. BEL; EnLi-2 (1949 ed.); PoVP; TrGrPo

Apparition, The. Herman Melville. MAmP; MWA-1; NoP

Apparition, The. Stephen Phillips. OBEV (new ed.); OBVV (Dream, A.) MaRV

Apparition of His Mistresse Calling Him to Elizium, The. Robert Herrick. AnAnS-2; ExPo; SCEP-2; SeCP; SeCV-1

Apparition of Splendor. Marianne Moore. NePoAm

Apparition of these faces in the crowd, The. In a Station of the Metro. Ezra Pound. AmP; AmPP (5th ed.); CABA; CAD; CaFP; CBV; ExPo; ForPo; InP; MAP; MoAB; MoAmPo; NeMA; NoP; OxBA; PoAn; PolE; UnPo; VaPo

Apparitions. Robert Browning. *See* Such a Starved Bank of Moss.

Apparitions. Thomas Curtis Clark. MaRV; OQP; PGD; TRV (It Shall Not Be Again!) PEDC; PoRL

Apparitions. Alice Corbin. NP

Apparitions. The. W. B. Yeats. CMoP; LiTM (rev. ed.); PoFS; PolE (1970 ed.)

Apparitions Are Not Singular Occurrences. Diane Wakoski. CoPo; YAP

Apparuit. Ezra Pound. APA; CoAnAm; TwAmPo

Appeal, The. Emily Brontë. BoPe; LoBV
("If grief for grief can touch thee.") EnLoPo

Appeal, The. Walter Savage Landor. VA
(Remain.) OBEV (1st ed.)
(Remain, Ah Not in Youth Alone.) OAEP; OBNC

Appeal. Noemia de Sousa, *tr. fr. Portuguese by* Dorothy Guedes *and* Philippa Rumsey. TTY

Appeal, The. Sir Thomas Wyatt. *See* Earnest Suit to His Unkind Mistress Not to Forsake Him, An.

Appeal for Are to the Sextant of the Old Brick Meetinouse, A. Arabella M. Willson. BOHV

Appeal for Illumination. Luigi Pulci, *tr. fr. Italian by* Byron. *Fr.* Il Morgante maggiore. ISi

Appeal to Cats in the Business of Love, An. Thomas Flatman. EnLoPo

Appeal to Harold, The. H. C. Bunner. AA

Appeal to the Phoenix. Louis Untermeyer. UnTE

Appear, O mother, was the perpetual cry. Invocation. Wilfred Watson. MoCV
Appearances. Robert Browning. CBEP; PoVP
Appeasement of Demeter, The. George Meredith. EnLi-2
Appendix. Coleman Barks. *Fr.* Body Poems. QAH
Appian Way, The. Geoffrey Johnson. JKCP (1955 ed.)
Appile Tree, De. Joel Chandler Harris. IHA; TSW
Applauding youths laughed with young prostitutes. The Harlem Dancer. Claude McKay. BALP; BANP; MAP
Applause flutters onto the open air. A Snapshot for Miss Bricka Who Lost in the Semi-final Round of the Pennsylvania Lawn Tennis Tournament at Haverford, July, 1960. Robert Wallace. SD
Apple, The. Lady Margaret Sackville. OBVV
Apple and Mole. Donald Davidson. MAP; MoAmPo (1942 ed.)
Apple-Barrel, The. Edwin L. Sabin. DD
Apple-Barrel of Johnny Appleseed, The. Vachel Lindsay. AmFN; CMoP; MAP; MoAmPo; NeMA; OxBA
Apple Blossom. Kate Louise Brown. GFA; OTPC (1946 ed.)
Apple blossom is crystal white. Brown Bear's Honey Song. Kathryn Jackson. RePo
Apple Blossoms. Ralph Bergengren. GFA
Apple Blossoms. Lucy Larcom. YeAr
Apple Blossoms. Helen Adams Parker. BoTP
Apple Blossoms. Helen Wing. GFA
Apple blossoms, budding, blowing. Apple Blossoms. Lucy Larcom. YeAr
Apple blossoms grow so high, The. Apple Blossoms. Helen Wing. GFA
Apple blossoms look like snow. A Comparison. John Farrar. BrR; FaPON; MPB; TSW
Apple Dumplings and a King. "Peter Pindar." OBEC
Apple-Elf, The. Sheila E. Braine. GFA
Apple Gathering, An. Christina Rossetti. BoLP; OBNC; PoVP
Apple-green west and an orange bar. "Frost To-Night." Edith M. Thomas. MCCG; PCD
Apple Harvest. Helen Leuty. BoTP
Apple Howling Songs ("Here stands a good apple tree"). *Unknown.* OTPC (1923 ed.)
(Two Apple-howling Songs, 1.) PCH
Apple Howling Songs ("Here's to thee, old apple tree"). *Unknown.* OTPC (1923 ed.)
("Here's to thee, old apple tree.") OxNR
(Two Apple-howling Songs, 2.) PCH
Apple Offering. *Unknown, tr. fr. Greek by* Louis Untermeyer. UnTE
Apple Orchard in the Spring, The. William Wesley Martin. GN; OTPC
Apple orchard smells like wine, An. Wise. Lizette Woodworth Reese. HBV
Apple Peeler. Robert Francis. CrMA; NePoAm
Apple-Pie and Cheese. Eugene Field. LHV
Apple-pie, apple-pie. *Unknown.* OxNR
Apple Rhyme, The. Madeleine Nightingale. BoTP
Apple Season. Frances Frost. BrR; SiSoSe
Apple-Seed John. Lydia Maria Child. DD, *abr.*; OHIP; OTPC
Apple Song. Frances Frost. FaPON; TiPo (1959 ed.)
Apple Tree, The. Beatrice Curtis Brown. SiSoSe
Apple-Tree, The. Nancy Campbell. AnIV; NP
Apple Tree, The. Brian Vrepont. BoAu; PoAu-2
Apple trees are hung with gold, The. Endymion. Oscar Wilde. HBV
Apple trees are made to sing in. The Comfortable Apple Trees. Grace Taber Hallock. RePo
Apple-trees, with burdens of white bloom, The. Messengers. Charles Hanson Towne. CAW
Apples. Laurie Lee. POTi; WePo
(Autumn Apples.) BoC
Apples. Lisel Mueller. NePoAm-2
Apples. Lizette Woodworth Reese. YT
Apples. Swift. *Fr.* Verses for Fruitwomen. AnIV; OnYI
(Verses Made for Women Who Cry Apples.) NCEP
Apples and Water. Robert Graves. PoIE
Apples are ripe in the orchard, The. After All. William Winter. PAP
Apples are seasoned, The. Apple Song. Frances Frost. FaPON; TiPo (1959 ed.)
Apples falling from the tree, The. Night Magic. Amelia Josephine Burr. MPB; SP
Apples in New Hampshire. Marie Gilchrist. BoNaP; PoMa
Apples of gold the Hero dropt. Good Luck. Oliver St. John Gogarty. JKCP (1926 ed.)
Apples ripen under yellowing leaves, The. Sonnet. Thomas Caulfield Irwin. IrPN
Appleton House. Andrew Marvell. *See* Upon Appleton House.
Applicant, The. Sylvia Plath. NaP; TwCP
Apply for the position (I've forgotten now for what). In Order To. Kenneth Patchen. NaP; Po
Appoggiatura. Donald Jeffrey Hayes. AmNP; PoNe
Appointed in the newe moon. Jason and Medea. John Gower. *Fr.* Confessio Amantis. ACP
Appointed lot has come upon me, mother, The. Farewell to My Mother. "Plácido," *tr. by* Bryant. BANP
Appointed winners in a long-stretch'd game, The. To-Day and Thee. Walt Whitman. NePA
Appointment, The. Sully-Prudhomme, *tr. fr. French by* Arthur O'Shaughnessy. OxBI
Appointment, An. W. B. Yeats. AnEnPo; PoFr
Appointment in Doctor's Office. Josephine Miles. FiMAP
Appomattox. MacKinlay Kantor. AnAmPo
Appraisal. Sara Teasdale. MAP; MoAmPo
Appreciation. Thomas Bailey Aldrich. AA
Appreciation. Clarence Edwin Flynn. SoP
Appreciation. George Meredith. ViBoPo
Apprehension. James Anderson Fraser. MaRV; OQP
Apprehension. *Unknown, tr. fr. Sanskrit by* Douglas Ainslie. OBVV
Apprenticed. Jean Ingelow. *Fr.* Songs of the Night Watches. LiTL; OBVV
Approach, The. Thomas Traherne. *Fr.* The Third Century. OxBoCh
("That childish thoughts such joys inspire.") AnAnS-1; MeP
"O Lord, I wonder at thy Lov," *sel.* TrPWD
Approach, my soul, the mercy-seat. The Effort. John Newton. SoP
Approach of Evening. George Croly. IrPN
Approach of Pharaoh, The. Cædmon, *tr. fr. Anglo-Saxon by* C. W. Kennedy. *Fr.* Genesis. ACP; WaaP
(Coming of Pharaoh, The.) CAW
Approach of Winter. James Thomson. *Fr.* The Seasons: Winter. OBEC
Approach this court with deference. On Entering a Forest. Elinor Lennen. PGD
Approach to a City. William Carlos Williams. CAD; PoRA (rev. ed.)
Approaches. George Macdonald. MaRV; OQP; TRV
Approaching America. J. C. Squire. HBMV
Approaching by the gate (Class of '79). Views of the Favorite Colleges. John Malcolm Brinnin. LiTA; MoAB; OnHM
Approximations. Robert Hayden. PoIE (1970 ed.)
Aprèes-Midi d'un faune, L'. Stéphane Mallarmé, *tr. fr. French by* Aldous Huxley. AWP; LiTW
(Afternoon of a Faun, The.) PIA, *tr. by* C. F. MacIntyre; ReMP, *tr. by* Roger Fry; SyP, *tr. by* Roger Fry
"Proud of my music, let me often make," *sel., tr. by* Aldous Huxley. ErPo
April. Obadiah Cyrus Auringer. AA
April. Remy Belleau, *tr. fr. French by* Andrew Lang. AWP
April. Godfrey Fox Bradby. ShBV-1
April. Vidame de Chartres, *tr. fr. French by* Swinburne. AWP
April. Emerson. ViBoPo
April. Theodosia Garrison. DD; HBMV; MPB
April. Robert Loveman. AA
April. Isobel McFadden. MaRV
April. John Francis O'Donnell. IrPN
April. Ezra Pound. CMoP
April. Ted Robinson. GoTP
April. Dora Sigerson Shorter. HBMV; HBVY
April [*or* Aprill]. Spenser. *Fr.* The Shepheardes Calender. EnLi-1; PoEL-1; ReEn; ReIE; SiCE
Sels.
Ditty, A: "See where she sits upon the grassie greene," 6 *sts.* OBEV
("See where she sits upon the grassy green," 2 *sts.*) ViBoPo
Elisa. OBSC
("Ye dayntye nymphs, that in this blessed brooke.") AtBAP

April. Francis Sweeney. JKCP (1955 ed.)
April. Sara Teasdale. FaPON; GFA; OTPC (1946 ed.); PCH; PDV; PoSC; SoPo; StVeCh; TiPo; TSW; YeAr
April. Eunice Tietjens. SoPo; YeAr
April. Sir William Watson. *See* Song: "April, April."
April. Yvor Winters. ELU
April Adoration, An. Sir Charles G. D. Roberts. HBV
April again and it is a year again. Elegy. Sidney Keyes. FaBoMo; WaP
April again, and its message unvaried, the same old impromptu. The Burden of Junk. John Classco. OBCV
April—and Dying. Anne Reeve Aldrich. AA
April and May. Emerson. *Fr.* May-Day. GN; OHIP
April and May. Anne Robinson. SUS
April, April,/ Laugh thy girlish laughter. Song [*or* April]. Sir William Watson. BoTP; DD; FaBV; GN; GoTP; HBV; HBVY; MoBrPo (1942 ed.); OBVV; PoRL; PoSC; TreF; TrGrPo; TSW; YT
April cold with dropping rain. April and May. Emerson. *Fr.* May-Day. GN; OHIP
April Day, An. Joseph Seamon Cotter, Jr. CDC
April Earth, The. Max Eastman. AnEnPo
April, 1885. Robert Bridges. NBM
April Fantasie. Ellen Mackay Hutchinson Cortissoz. AA
April Fool. Elizabeth J. Coatsworth. RePo; YeAr
April Fool. Eleanor Hammond. GFA; SoPo
April Fools. Katherine Brégy. JKCP (1955 ed.)
April Fool's Day. Marnie Pomeroy. OTD; PoSC
April Fool's Day. *Unknown. See* All Fools' Day.
April Fool's Day, or, St. Mary of Egypt. John Berryman. The Dream Songs, XLVII. NaP
April Fourth. Robert Mezey. NaP
April in England. Robert Browning. *See* Home Thoughts from Abroad.
April Inventory. W. D. Snodgrass. AP; CABA; CoAP; LiTM (1970 ed.); NePoEA; PoPl; TwCP
April is a laundress. April and May. Anne Robinson. SUS
April is in my mistress' face. All Seasons in One. *Unknown.* CBV; EG; MeWo; OBSC; ReEn; SiCE; TrGrPo
April is no month for burials. Rite of Spring. Leo Kennedy. CaP
April is the cruellest [*or* cruelest] month, breeding. The Burial of the Dead. T. S. Eliot. The Waste Land, I. AmPP; AP; AtBAP; ATP (1953 ed.); CABA; CMoP; CoBMV; EnLit; FaBoMo; LiTA; LiTM; MasP; MBW-2; MoAB; MoAmPo (1950 ed.); MoPo; MoVE; MWA-2; NePA; NoP; OAEP (2d ed.); OxBA; ReMP; UnPo (3d ed.)
April Lights. Alfred Starr Hamilton. QAH
April Love. Ernest Dowson. PG
April Midnight. Arthur Symons. SyP
April Moment. Arthur Davison Ficke. HBMV
April Morning, An. Bliss Carman. DD; GBV; HBMV; HBVY
April Mortality. Léonie Adams. AnAmPo; MAP; MoAB; MoAmPo; TrGrPo, 2 *sts;*
April, 1940. Patrick Maybin. NeIP
April, 1942. Mark Van Doren. WaP
April 1962. Paul Goodman. NMP
April of Our Desire. Lola Ridge. MAP; MoAmPo (1942 ed.)
April of the Ages, The. Digby Mackworth Dolben. GoBC
April, pride of woodland ways. April. Remy Belleau. AWP
April Puddle. Rowena Bennett. TiPo (1959 ed.)
April Rain. Mathilde Blind. HBV
April Rain. Robert Loveman. BoTP; DD; HBV; HBVY; MaRV; RIS; SUS; TrJP
 (Rain Song, The.) MPB; OQP; TreFT; WBLP
April Rain Song. Langston Hughes. FaPON; OTD; PDV; PoRh; SUS; TiPo
April rain, the April rain, The. April Rain. Mathilde Blind. HBV
April Rise. Laurie Lee. BoC; FIW; GTBS-D; OnHM; POTi
April Showers. James Stephens. TiPo (1959 ed.)
April Snow, The. Jones Very. AP
April Thirty-first. Barbara L. Greenberg. QAH
April this year, not otherwise. Song of a Second April. Edna St. Vincent Millay. CMoP; OxBA
April 29th. Alexander Bergman. WOW
April, up on a twig a leaftuft stands. First Warm Days. Edwin Denby. GTBS-W; LiTM
April walks beside me still in budded cloak of brown. Hurdy-Gurdy Days. Martha Haskell Clark. MPB
April Weather. Jessie McDermott. OTPC (1946 ed.); PCH
April Weather. Lizette Woodworth Reese. DD; HBMV
April whispered this to me. The Secret. John Richard Moreland. OQP
April Winds. Michael Lewis. TSW
 (In Spring.) StaSt
April winds are magical, The. April. Emerson. ViBoPo
April world is misted with emerald and gold, The. Gypsy-Heart [*or* Gipsy-Heart]. Katharine Lee Bates. HBMV; PoTo
Aprill. Spenser. *See* April.
April's Amazing Meaning. George Dillon. AmLP; BoLP; MAP; MoAmPo (1942 ed.)
April's sweet hand in the margins betrayed. Fifth Sunday after Easter. Thomas Kinsella. NMP
Apron of Flowers, The. Robert Herrick. SeCV-1
Apt Prayer, An. A. F. Thomas. SoP
Aquarium, An. Amy Lowell. PFY
Aquarium. George T. Wright. NYBP
Aquarium Dream, The. Florence Trefethen. NYTB
Ar, these is 'appy days! An' 'ow they've flown. The Stoush o' Day. C. J. Dennis. NeLNL
Arab Love-Song, An. Francis Thompson. AWP; MemP; MeWo; MoAB; MoBrPo; OtMeF; POTE; YT
 ("Hunchèd camels of the night, The.") EG
Arab Music. D. J. Enright. MuSP
Arab Song. Richard Henry Stoddard. AA
Arab to His Favorite Steed, The. Caroline E. S. Norton. BeLS; TreFS
 (Arab's Farewell to His Horse.) BLPA
 (Arab's Farewell to His Steed, The.) PaPo; PTK
Arabia. Walter de la Mare. GTBS; HBMV; POTE; WHA
Arabian Nights. *Unknown. See* Thousand and One Nights, The.
Arabian Nights Entertainments. *Unknown. See* Thousand and One Nights The.
Arabian Proverb ("He who knows. . .") *Unknown, tr. fr. Arabic.* TreF
 (He Who Knows.) BLPA; GoTP; NeHB
Arabian Shawl, The. Katherine Mansfield. *Fr.* Two Nocturnes. HBMV
Arabs. Alfred Kreymborg. MAPA; TwAmPo
Arabs complain—or so I have been told. For the Rain It Raineth Every Day. Robert Graves. NYBP
Arab's Farewell to His Horse [*or* Steed]. Caroline E. S. Norton. *See* Arab to His Favorite Steed, The.
Arachne. Rose Terry Cooke. AA; AnAmPo
Arachne. William Empson. InvP; MoVE; OBMV
Arachnida, Female. Aletha Humphreys. FiSC
Arac's Song. W. S. Gilbert. *Fr.* Princess Ida. FiBHP; WhC
Araucana, La, *much abr.* Alonso de Ercilla y Zúñiga, *tr. fr. Spanish by* Paul Thomas Manchester *and* Charles Maxwell Lancaster. OuHeWo
Arawata Bill. Denis Glover. ACV
Arbasto, *sels.* Robert Greene.
 In Time We See That Silver Drops. ReIE; SiCE
 (Doralicia's Song.) LoBV; OBSC
 Whereat Erewhile I Wept, I Laugh. EIL
Arbor Amoris. Villon, *tr. fr. French by* Andrew Lang. AWP
Arbor Day. Dorothy Brown Thompson. SiSoSe
Arbor Day Song. Mary A. Heermans. HH
Arbor Day Tree, An. *Unknown.* DD; HH; OHIP; RePo
Arbor Una Nobilis. Sister Thomas Aquinas. JKCP (1955 ed.)
Arbor Vitae. Coventry Patmore. The Unknown Eros, II, iii. GoBC; LoBV; NBM; OBNC; PeVV; SeCePo
Arbutus. Adelaide Crapsey. MoAmPo (1942 ed.)
Arcades. Milton. MaPo (1969 ed.)
 Sels.
 Song: "Nymphs and shepherds, dance no more." AtBAP; CBEP; ELP; FiP; SeCL; ViBoPo
 Song: "O'er [*or* O're] the smooth enamel[l]ed green." AtBAP; BoLiVe; InPo; LoBV; OBEV; SeCL; ThWaDe; TrGrPo; ViBoPo
Arcadia, *sels.* Sir Philip Sidney.
 Country Song, A: "Lad Philisides, The." OBSC; SiPS
 ("Lad Philisides, The.") FCP
 Cupid. SiPS
 Double Sestine. AtBAP LiTB; PoEL-1
 (Sestina.) LiTG; StP

("Ye goatherd gods, that love the grassy mountains.") BWP; FCP; SiCE
Echo. SiPS
("Fair rocks, goodly rivers, sweet woods.") FCP
Epithalamium: "Let mother earth now deck herself in flowers." SiPS
(O Hymen, Long Their Coupled Joys Maintain!) HW
Excellent Sonnet of a Nymph, An. RelE
("Virtue, beauty, and speech did strike, wound, charm.") FCP
"Farewell, O sun, Arcadia's clearest light." FCP
"Feed on my sheep, my charge, my comfort feed." FCP
Geron and Histor. SiPS
Get Hence Foule Griefe. AtBAP; PoEL-1
(Contentment.) SiPS
Gifts of the Animals to Man, The. OA
Graven Thoughts. SiPS
In Vain, Mine Eyes. SiPS
"Leave off my sheep, it is no time to feed." FCP
"Lock up, fair lids, the treasure of my heart." SiCE
(Sleep.) OBSC; SiPS
(Sonnet: "Lock up, fair lids, the treasure of my heart.") EG; EIL
Love and Jealousy. SiPS
Love and Reason. SiPS
Loved I Am, and Yet Complaine of Love. PoEL-1
(Complaint of Love.) SiPS
Madrigal: "Why dost thou haste away." EG; OBSC; SiPS
"My sheep are thoughts, which I both guide and serve." SiCE; SiPS
(Dorus His Comparisons.) RelE
My True Love Hath My Heart [and I Have His]. AtBAP; BoLiVe; CBEP; CH; CoBE; DiPo; EG; EP; FaBoBe; FCP; HBV; ILP; LiTG; LiTL; MaPo; MeWo; OAEP; OnPM; PoE; PoEL-1; PTK; ReEn; SeCeV; SiCE; TrGrPo; ViBoPo
(Arcadian Duologue.) SiPS
(Bargain, The.) OBEV; OtMeF; PG; TreFS
(Ditty, A: "My true-love hath my heart and I have his.") AWP; GTBS; GTBS-D; GTBS-P; GTBS-W; GTSE; GTSL; InPo; JAWP; PoRL; TOP
(Ditty: Heart Exchange.) EnLit
(Heart Exchange.) LiTB; LoBV
(Just Exchange.) FaBoEn
(My True Love.) WePo
(Song: "My true love hath my heart.") EnLi-1
(Sonnet: "My true love hath my heart.") EIL; WHA
(True Love.) ALV; BoPe; ChTr; MemP; OBSC
Night. SiPS
O Sweet Woods (*three sonnets*). AtBAP; CoBE, *first sonnet*; PoEL-1; TuPP
(Delight of Solitariness, The.) LiTB
(Dorus's Song.) LoBV
("O sweet woods the delight of solitariness!") FCP; SiCE
(Solitariness.) OBSC; SiPS
O Words Which Fall Like Summer Dew on Me. MaPo
(Rural Poesy.) EIL
Old Age. SiPS
Sapphics. SiPS
("If mine eyes can speak to do hearty errand.") FCP
Shepherd Song: "As I my little flock on Ister bank." SiPS
Shepherd's Tale, A. SiPS
Since So Mine Eyes. SiPS
"Sweet glove, the witness of my secret bliss." FCP
Sweeter Saint I Serve, A. SiPS
Tale for Husbands, A. SiPS
Truth Doth Truth Deserve. HBV; LiTL
(Advice to the Same.) SiPS
"What length of verse can serve brave Mopsa's good to show." RelE
What Tongue Can Her Perfections Tell? EnRePo; SiPS
(Her Perfections.) CLwM
When Two Suns Do Appear. EnRePo; SiPS
Why Fear to Die? SiPS
Wronged Lover, The. SiPS
Arcadia was of old (said he) a state. Rhotus on Arcadia. John Chalkhill. *Fr.* Thealma and Clearchus. OBS
Arcadian Duologue. Sir Philip Sidney. *See* My True Love Hath My Heart.
Arcana Sylvarum. Charles De Kay. AA
Arcanum One. Gwendolyn MacEwen. MoCV
Arch Armadillo, The. Carolyn Wells. PCH
Archaeological Picnic, The. John Betjeman. EnLoPo
Archaeologist of the Future, The. Leonard Bacon. WhC
Archaeology of Love, The. Richard Murphy. EnLoPo
Archaic Apollo. William Plomer. ChMP
Archaic Torso of Apollo. Rainer Maria Rilke, *tr. fr. German by* Vernon Watkins. LiTW; PIA
Archangel, The. Byron. *See* At the Gate of Heaven.
Archbishop Tait. *Unknown.* ChTr
Archer, The. Clinton Scollard. FaPON; GaP
Archer, The. A. J. M. Smith. OBCV; PeCV
Archer. Lynn Strongin. ThO
Archer, The. *Unknown, tr. fr. Sanskrit by* Douglas Ainslie. OBVV
Archer is wake [*or* awake], The! Peace on Earth. William Carlos Williams. LiTA; LOW; MAP; NP; PFY; ViBoPo
Archer, the Archer, The. The Archer. *Tr. by* Douglas Ainslie. OBVV
Archers of the King. Sister Mary Genoveva. GoBC
Arches. Helen Hoyt. NP
Arches on arches! as it were that Rome. The Coliseum. Byron. *Fr.* Childe Harold's Pilgrimage, IV. BEL; CoBE; EPN
Archibald Higbie. Edgar Lee Masters. *Fr.* Spoon River Anthology. InP; NP
Archibald MacLeish Suspends the Five Little Pigs, *parody.* Louis Untermeyer. MoAmPo
Archie o' [*or* of] Cawfield [*or* Cafield] (*diff. vers.*). *Unknown.* BaBo; BuBa; ESPB; OBB; OxBS
Archilochus's seaside tomb you see. A Slanderer. *Unknown.* OnPM
Archin' here and arrachin' there. Water Music. "Hugh MacDiarmid." GoTS
Architect, The. Molly Anderson Haley. ChIP
Architect told us our house had original features, The. The Treasure of the Haunted Rambler. John Sladek. HYE
Architects of Dream. Lucia Trent. PGD
Architects plant their imagination, weld their poems on rock. Earthfast. A. S. J. Tessimond. POTE
Archy a Low Brow. Don Marquis. *Fr.* Archys Life of Mehitabel. WhC
Archy and Mehitabel, *sels.* Don Marquis.
Archy Confesses. EvOK; FiBHP
Ballade: "Outcast bones from a thousand biers." WhC
Cheerio My Deario. ShBV-4
Flattered Lightning Bug, The. StPo
Freddy the Rat Perishes. OCS
Hen and the Oriole, The. EvOK; FiBHP
Mehitabel Sings a Song. InME
Song of Mehitabel, The. FiBHP; TreFS
Trouble. TreFT
Wail of Archy, The, *sel.*
"Gods I am pent in a cockroach." FiBHP
Warty Bliggens, the Toad. FiBHP
Archy Confesses. Don Marquis. *Fr.* Archy and Mehitabel. EvOK; FiBHP
Archy Does His Part, *sel.* Don Marquis.
Fate Is Unfair. EvOK
Archy Experiences a Seizure. Don Marquis. *Fr.* Archys Life of Mehitabel. WhC
(Hero Cockroach, The.) TSW
Archy, the Cockroach, Speaks. Don Marquis. *Fr.* Certain Maxims of Archy. FaPON
Archygrams. Don Marquis. *Fr.* Archys Life of Mehitabel. WhC
Archys Autobiography. Don Marquis. *Fr.* Archys Life of Mehitabel. CrMA
Archys Last Name. Don Marquis. *Fr.* Archys Life of Mehitabel. CrMA
Archys Life of Mehitabel, *sels.* Don Marquis.
Archy a Low Brow. WhC
Archy Experiences a Seizure. WhC
(Hero Cockroach, The.) TSW
Archygrams. WhC
Archys Autobiography. CrMA
Artists Shouldn't Have Offspring. CrMA
Ballade of the Under Side. InvP
Mehitabel Tries Marriage. WePo
Arcite's Farewell. Chaucer, *mod. vers. by* John Hall Wheelock. *Fr.* The Canterbury Tales: The Knight's Tale. LiTL
Arctic Convoy. J. K. Annand. OxBS
Arctic honey blabbed over the report causing darkness, The. Leaving the Atocha Station. John Ashbery. ANYP

Arctic Moon, The. Joaquin Miller. *Fr.* The Yukon. MAP; MoAmPo (1942 ed.)
Arctic moon hangs overhead, The. The Wolf Cry. Lew Sarett. FaPON; PoMa
Arctic Ox, The. Marianne Moore. NYBP
Arctic raven tracks the caribou, The. Epigram. Raymond Wilson. PV
Arctic Tern in a Museum. Mary Effie Lee Newsome. PoNe
Arctic Vision, An. Bret Harte. MC; PAH
Arcturus in Autumn. Sara Teasdale. NP
Arcturus is his other name. Emily Dickinson. FaBV; StaSt
Ardan Mór. Francis Ledwidge. AnIV; AWP; JAWP; WBP
(Herons, The.) ACP; OnYI; OxBI
Arden of Feversham, *sel.* *Unknown.*
"Ungentle Alice, thy sorrow is my sore." LO
Ardent lover cannot find, The. The Disappointed Wife. Hetty Wright. WaPE
Ardent owl flew, An. Flight. William Walden. NYTB
Ardor. Gamaliel Bradford. HBMV
Ardor [*or* Ardour] and Memory. Dante Gabriel Rossetti. The House of Life, LXIV. MaVP; PoVP; ViPo
Ardour of red flame is thine, The. Lionel Johnson. *Fr.* The Dark Angel. LO
Are all the birds imprisoned there. Alle Vögel Sind Schon Da. Frances Chesterton. UnS
Are All the Children In? *Unknown.* SoP; STF
Are God and Nature then at strife. Tennyson. *Fr.* In Memoriam A. H. H., LV. TRV
Are lovers full of fire? Upon His Timorous Silence in Her Presence. Francis Davidson. EG; TuPP
". . . Are not molesters of women" the book says. Pocket Guide for Servicemen. Hubert Creekmore. WaP
Are not the joys of morning sweeter? Blake. EiCL
Are the Children at Home? Margaret E. Sangster. HBV
Are the desolate, dark weeks. These. William Carlos Williams. AP; CoBMV; MoAB; MoAmPo; NoP; OxBA; PIA
". . . Are the horns of the hall on fire?" The Battle of Finnsburg. *Unknown.* AnOE
Are the living so much use. At the Cenotaph. "Hugh MacDiarmid." NAMP
"Are the reindeer in the rain, dear?" Conversation between Mr. and Mrs. Santa Claus. Rowena Bennett. ChBR; SiSoSe; TiPo (1959 ed.)
Are there favoring ladies above thee? Valse Jeune. Louise Imogen Guiney. AA
Are there no roses in your garden. Jardin des Fleurs. Charles David Webb. NePoAm-2
Are these the honors they reserve for me. Columbus in Chains. Philip Freneau. MC; PAH
Are these the strings that poets feign. On Lutestrings Cat-eaten. Thomas Master. CLwM; MuSP
Are these the tracks of some unearthly friend. Angelic Guidance. Cardinal Newman. GoBC
Are they clinging to their crosses. Antichrist, or the Reunion of Christendom; an Ode. G. K. Chesterton. SeCePo
Are They Dancing. Edward Dorn. NeAP
Are they exiles here from the rest of the world? What Do the Birds Think? Alfred Purdy. MoCV
Are They Not All Ministering Spirits? Robert Stephen Hawker. CoBE; EPN; GoBC; HBV; OBEV (1st ed.)
Are They Shadow[e]s [That We See]? Samuel Daniel. *Fr.* Tethys' Festival. AtBAP; ATP; EIL; ExPo; InvP; LoBV; NoP; PoIE; SeCeV; TuPP
("Are they shadows that we see?") CH; SiCE
(Eidola.) LO
(Shadows.) OBSC
(Song: "Are they shadowes that we see?") PoEL-2
Are thine eyes weary? is thy heart too sick. November. William Morris. *Fr.* The Earthly Paradise. EPN; GTSL; ViPo; ViPP
Are those two stars, her eyes, my life's light gone. Licia, XLIII. Giles Fletcher. Sonn
Are we mere pieces in the hand. Fate. James Fenimore Cooper. HBMV
Are we not all of race divine. Patriots of Mankind. Christopher Smart. PoFr
Are We Not the People, *sel.* Al Samau'al ibn Adiya, *tr. fr. Arabic by* Hartwig Hirschfeld.
"Now listen to boasting which leaves the heart dazed." TrJP
Are We Thankful? ("Are we being fair, I wonder"). *Unknown.* STF
Are we, then, wholly fallen? Can it be. Freedom. James Russell Lowell. PaA
Are Women Fair? *At. to* Francis Davison. BOHV; HBV
Are ye so strong, O kings, O strong men? Nay. Swinburne. *Fr.* A Year's Burden, 1870. PoFr
Are you a giant, great big man, or is your real name Smith? Big Smith. Juliana Horatia Ewing. TVC
Are You a Marsupial? John Becker. RePo
Are you alive? The Pool. Hilda Doolittle ("H. D."). CMoP; ExPo; NP
Are you almost disgusted with life, little man? How to Be Happy. *Unknown.* BLPA
Are you an active member. Do You Just Belong? *Unknown.* STF
"Are you an eland?" Yes! Yes! A Story from the Bushmen. Joseph Ceravolo. ANYP
Are you asleep, Mother? Mary's Vision. *Unknown.* ISi
"Are you awake." Haunting Fingers. Thomas Hardy. MaPo
Are you awake? Do you hear the rain? Rain at Night. Helen Hoyt. LiTM; NP
"Are you awake, Gemelli." Star-Talk. Robert Graves. BoNaP; GoJo; HBMV; MoBrPo; RG
Are You Born? Muriel Rukeyser. MoRP
Are you busy in the corner? Your Corner. Mary Harrington. SoP
Are you coming or going? The opening. Surabaja. Bill Berkson. ANYP; YAP
Are you dreaming of Christmas? Christmas 1942. Robert Nathan. PoFr
"Are you flying through the night." The Fire-Fly. John Banister Tabb. UTS
Are you groping for a blessing. Get Somewhere. A. B. Simpson. FaChP
"Are you looking for someone, you who come pattering." Thoughts of Thomas Hardy. Edmund Blunden. PoCh
Are You looking for us? We are here. The 151st Psalm. Karl Shapiro. EaLo
"Are you ready for your steeple-chase, Lorraine, Lorraine, Lorèe?" Lorraine [*or* Lorraine Lorèe]. Charles Kingsley. BBV; PoVP; VA
"Are you ready, O Virginia." The Call to the Colors. Arthur Guiterman. PaA; PAH
Are you sheltered, curled up and content by your world's warm fire? For the New Year. Edwin Markham. OQP
Are you so weary? Come to the window. Wind in the Grass. Mark Van Doren. FaBV
Are you standing at "Wit's End Corner?" Wit's End Corner. Antoinette Wilson. BLRP; SoP; STF
Are You New Person Drawn toward Me? Walt Whitman. NePA
Are You There? Strickland Gillilan. PoToHe (new ed.)
Are you tir'd? Rosamond at Woodstock. Swinburne. *Fr.* Rosamond. VA
Are you very weary? Rest a little bit. Rest. *Unknown.* PoToHe
"Are you waking?" shout the breezes. Christmas Bells. George Cooper. HH
Are you washed in the blood. For His Sake. Annie Denman. BePJ
Are you whistling. Moreso. Alfred Starr Hamilton. QAH
Are you worsted in a fight? Laugh It Off. Henry Rutherford Elliot. WBLP
Are your rocks shelter for ships. The Shrine. Hilda Doolittle ("H. D."). AnAmPo; MaPa; NP
Are zebras black with broad white stripes. Zebra. William Jay Smith. TiPo (1959 ed.)
Areopagitica, *sel.* Milton.
"This is true liberty," *tr. fr. the Greek of* Euripides. PoFr
Ares. Albert Ehrenstein, *tr. fr. German by* Babette Deutsch *and* Avrahm Yarmolinsky. TrJP
Ares at last has quit the field. Under Which Lyre. W. H. Auden. MoAB; MoBrPo (1950 ed.)
Arethusa. Shelley. DTo; EnRP; EPN; GN; HBV; MBW-2; OBRV; WiR
Aretina's Song. Sir Henry Taylor. VA
Argalus and Parthenia, *sels.* Francis Quarles.
Authour's Dreame, The. OBS
Hos Ego Versiculos. OBS; SeEP. *See also* Man's Mortality, *sl. diff. vers. at. to* Simon Wastell, *fr.* Microbiblion.
Argenteuil County. Peter Dale Scott. MoCV

Argentina in one swing of the bell skirt. The Beautiful Train. William Empson. MoVE
Arglwydd Arwain. William Williams. *See* Christian Pilgrim's Hymn, The.
Argonautica. George Seferis, *tr. fr. Modern Greek by* Rex Warner. OnHM
Argument, The, *sel.* Conrad Aiken.
Do Not Believe Your Shakespeare's Grief. OA
Argument, The. Archibald MacLeish. *Fr.* Conquistador. AtBAP
Argument, An. Thomas Moore. EnLoPo
Argument. Mildred Weston. PoMa; WhC
Argument of His Book, The. Robert Herrick. AnAnS-2; AtBAP; AWP; BEL; BoLiVe; CoBE; EnL; EnLi-1; EnLit; ForPo; HBV; InP; InPo; InvP; NoP; OAEP; OBS; PoE; PoEL-3; PoeP; PoIE; PoRA; ReEn; SCEP-2; SeCePo; SeCeV; SeCP; SeCV-1; SeEP; TrGrPo; ViBoPo; WHA
(Argument of This Book, *abr.*) HBVY
(Hesperides.) ForPo; MyFE
Argument of the Book, The. James I, King of England. Sonn
Argument, An—Of the Passion of Christ. Thomas Merton. CrMA
Argument of This Book. Robert Herrick. *See* Argument of His Book.
Argument with a Millionaire, An. "David Grayson." OTD
(Happy Farmer, The.) GoTP
Argumentum ad Hominem. Hyam Plutzik. FiMAP
Argus ("Argus was a puppy"). Eleanor Farjeon. GBV (1952 ed.)
Aria. Rolfe Humphries. NYBP
Aria. Delmore Schwartz. ErPo
Aria for Flute and Oboe. Joseph Langland. NePoEA
Aria Senza da Capo. Robert Finch. MoCV
Ariake, Japanese friend, I regard. To Ariake Kambara. Norman Rosten. NYBP
Ariana. Franklin Benjamin Sanborn. AA
Arid Lands, The. Herbert Bashford. AA
Aridity. "Michael Field." BoC; FaChP; OBMV; OxBoCh; TRV
Aridity. C. S. Lewis. BoC
Ariel. David Campbell. NeLNL; PoAu-2
Ariel. Sylvia Plath. NMP; OPoP
Ariel in the Cloven Pine. Bayard Taylor. AA
Ariel to Miranda:—Take. With a Guitar, to Jane [*or* To a Lady with a Guitar]. Shelley. BEL; EnRP; EPN; ERoP-2; GTBS; GTBS-D; GTBS-P; GTBS-W; GTSE; GTSL; HBV; MERP
Ariel was glad he had written his poems. The Planet on the Table. Wallace Stevens. ML; PoeP
Ariel's Dirge. Shakespeare. *See* Ariel's Song: "Full fathom five . . ."
Ariel's Song: "Come unto these yellow sands." Shakespeare. *Fr.* The Tempest, I, ii. CTC; EG; FaBoCh; GN; GoJo; LoBV; LoGBV; MaPo (1969 ed.); MCCG; MPB (1956 ed.); PCH; PTK; ThWaDe
("Come unto these yellow sands.") AnFE; AtBAP; BEL; BoTP; CBEP; CH; ElL; InPo; NoP; OBSC; OTPC (1923 ed.); PoEL-2; PoIE; SiCE; TOP; ViBoPo
(Fairy Land.) OBEV
(Fairy Life, The, 2.) GTSL
(Fairy Songs.) HBV
(Remote Bermudas, The.) CLwM
Ariel's Song: "Full fathom five thy father lies." Shakespeare. *Fr.* The Tempest, I, ii. BoLiVe; EG; FaBoEn; FlW; GN; LoBV; PTK; SeCePo; TreFT
(Ariel's Dirge.) EvOK; GoJo; ThWaDe
(Fairy Land.) OBEV
("Full fathom five thy father lies.") AnFE; AtBAP; ATP; BEL; CABA; CaFP; CBEP; ChTr; DiPo; ElL; ELP; EnLi-1; ExPo; FaBoCh; GTSL; HoPM; ILP; InPo; LiTB; LiTG; LoGBV; MaPo; NoP; OAEP; OBSC; OTPC; OuHeWo; PAn; PIA; PoEL-2; PoeP; PoIE; PoRA; SeCeV; ShBV-1; SiCE; TOP; ViBoPo; WHA
(Sea Dirge, A.) AnEnPo; EtS; GTBS; GTBS-D; GTBS-P; GTBS-W; GTSE; HBV; MCCG; TrGrPo
(Song: "Full fathom five thy father lies.") CBV; ForPo; FosPo; NeHB; YAT
(Songs from the Plays.) AWP; JAWP; WBP
Ariel's Song: "Where the bee sucks, there suck I." Shakespeare. *Fr.* The Tempest, V, i. AnEnPo; EG; GN; MaPo (1969 ed.); MCCG; NoP; PCD; PDV; PTK
(Fairy Land.) OBEV
(Fairy Life, The, 1.) GTSL
(Fairy Songs.) HBV; HBVY; RIS
(Fairy's Life, A.) PCH; PoPL
(Song: "Where the bee sucks, there suck I.") YAT
(Songs from the Plays.) AWP; JAWP; WBP
("Where the bee sucks, there suck I.") AnFE; BEL; BoTP; CABA; CBEP; CTC; CH; DiPo; ElL; EnLi-1; EnLit; EnRePo; FaBV; FoBA; ILP; InPo; MPB; OBSC; OTPC; PoRh; SeCeV; SiCE; ThWaDe; TiPo; TOP; UTS; ViBoPo; WHA
Arise and go now to the city of slaughter. The City of Slaughter. Hayyim Nahman Bialik. TrJP
Arise! Arise! Louis Untermeyer. StaSt
Arise arise, faire Sun restore the daye. *Unknown.* SeCSL
Arise faint Muse bring one heart-melting verse. An Elegie on the Deploreable Departure of the . . . Chieftain John Hull. John Saffin. SCAP
Arise, Get Up, My Dear Love. *Unknown.* TuPP
("Arise, get up, my dear love, rise, make haste, begone thee!") ReEn
Arise, My Love, My Fair One. The Song of Solomon, II: 8-14, Bible, *O.T.* LoPo
Arise, my slumbering soul! arise. Soul and Country. James Clarence Mangan. VA
Arise, O soul, and gird thee up anew. A Challenge. James Benjamin Kenyon. AA
Arise, Saint Aodh, and find, on rising. The Scribe. F. R. Higgins. JKCP (1926 ed.)
Arise—'Tis the day of our Washington's glory. Crown Our Washington. Hezekiah Butterworth. DD; HH; PEDC; PoRL
Arise up on thy feet, O Quiet Heart. He Biddeth Osiris to Arise from the Dead. *Unknown.* *Fr.* Book of the Dead. AWP
Arise, ye kings of Macha. *Unknown.* *Fr.* The Combat of Ferdiad and Cuchulain. OnYI
Arise, you who will not be bondslaves. Ch'i Lai'. Shih Ee. PoFr
Aristeides. Antipater of Sidon, *tr. fr. Greek by* Charles Whibley. AWP
Aristippus, *sel.* Thomas Randolph.
Drinking Song. SeCL
Aristocratic Trio, An. Judson France. PV
Aristocrats. Keith Douglas. NePoEA
Aristocrats of Labor. W. Stewart. *Fr.* The True Aristocrat. OQP; PGD
Aristotelian Elegy, An. Donald E. Bogle. TNV
Aristotle to Phyllis. John Hollander. PoCh
Arithmetic. Carl Sandburg. FlW; ImOP; RePo; WaKn
"Arithmetic is where numbers fly like pigeons in and out of your head," *sel.* FaPON
Arithmetique nine digits, and no more. Upon the Losse of His Little Finger. Thomas Randolph. AnAnS-2
Arizona. Margaret Rowe Clifford. PoRL
Arizona. Sharlot Mabridth Hall. PAH
Arizona. *Unknown.* ABF
Arizona Boys and Girls, *with music.* *Unknown.* BFSS; CoSo
Arizona Poems, *sels.* John Gould Fletcher.
Mexican Quarter, II. NP
Rain in the Desert, VI.
(Rain in the Street.) NP
Windmills, The, IV. CrMA; PoMa
Arizona Village. Robert Stiles Davieau. AmFN
Ark, The. Irving Feldman. AmPC
Ark, The. Milton. *Fr.* Paradise Lost, XI. EtS
Ark and the *Dove*, The. Daniel Sargent. EtS
Ark of the Covenant. Louise Townsend Nicholl. ImOP
Arkansas Traveler, The. *At. to* Sanford C. Faulkner. PoRL
Arkansaw Traveler, The. *Unknown.* *See* State of Arkansas, The.
Arlington. David McKee Wright. AnNZ
Arlington Cemetery Looking toward the Capitol. Winthrop Palmer. GoYe
Arlo Will. Edgar Lee Masters. *Fr.* Spoon River Anthology. LiTA; NP
Arm, Arm, Arm, Arm. John Fletcher. *Fr.* The Mad Lover. ElL
Armada, The. Macaulay. BeLS; FaBoCh; LoGBV; OBRV; OTPC (1923 ed.); ShBV-2; WBLP
(Armada, The; a Fragment.) GN; HBV

Sels.
England's Standard. OtMeF
"Night sank upon the dusky beach, and on the purple sea." OBNC; PeVV
Armada of Thirty Whales, An. Daniel G. Hoffman. NePA
Armadillo, The. Lesley Gordon. GFA
Armadillo, The—Brazil. Elizabeth Bishop. NYBP
Armageddon. John Crowe Ransom. LiTA
Armand Dussault. Wilson MacDonald. WhC
Arme, arme, arme, arme, great Neptune rowze, awake. John Smith of His Friend Master John Taylor. John Smith. SCAP
Armed Vision. N. P. van Wyk Louw, *tr. fr. Afrikaans by* Jack Cope *and* Uys Krige. PeSA
Armful, The. Robert Frost. CMoP
Armida, the Sorceress. Tasso, *tr. fr. Italian by* Edward Fairfax. *Fr.* Jerusalem Delivered, IV. EnLi-1
Armies joined, The; I saw the Prince of Peace. The Retreat from Heaven. J. A. R. McKellar. MoAuPo
Arming of Pigwiggen, The Michael Drayton. *Fr.* Nymphidia; or, The Court of Fairy. GN; OTPC
(Pigwiggen.) BoTP
(Pigwiggen Arms Himself.) MoShBr
Armistice. Charles Buxton Going. DD; HBMV; PEDC
Armistice. Sophie Jewett. AA
Armistice. Eunice Mitchell Lehmer. PGD
Armistice. Thomas Lodge. *See* For Pity, Pretty Eyes, Surcease.
Armistice. Margaret E. Sangster. PEDC
Armistice Day. John Freeman. MMA
Armistice Day. Roselle Mercier Montgomery. MC; PoRL
Armistice Day. Lucia Trent. PGD
Armistice Day Vow. Dorothy Gould. PGD
Armistice Night. Curtis Wheeler. HH
Armor. James Dickey. CoAP
Armor of Mars, The. Pause. Rosa Zagnoni Marinoni. FiSC
Armor the Bud. Frances Frieseke. JKCP (1955 ed.)
Armorer's Song, The. Harry Bache Smith. AA; OHIP
Armorial. Ralph Gustafson. ACV; MoCV; PeCV (1967 ed.)
Armour's Undermining Modesty. Marianne Moore. AP; CoBMV
Armoury, An. Alcaeus, *tr. fr. Greek by* Gilbert Highet. WaaP
Arms & Exit. James W. Thompson. WSL
Arms and the Boy. Winfred Owen. AnEnPo; BrPo; CMoP; FaFP; FosPo; GTBS-W; LiTB; LiTM; MoAB; MoBrPo; NAMP; NP; OAEP (2d ed.); PoPo; WaP
Arms and the heroes signalised in fame. Passage to India. Luís de Camoes. *Fr.* The Lusiads. WoL
Arms and the man I sing, and sing for joy. Epigram. J. V. Cunningham. NePoAm
Arms of the sea are extended, The. A Delusion of Reference. R. A. D. Ford. PeCV
Arms reversed and banners craped. A Dirge for McPherson. Herman Melville. AP; PAH; PoEL-5
Armstrong at Fayal, The. Wallace Rice. PAH
Army Corps on the March, An. Walt Whitman. AmPo; CoBA; NoP; PAL; PoLF
Army Correspondent's Last Ride. George Alfred Townsend. AA
Army Hymn. Oliver Wendell Holmes. SoP
Army, Navy. *Unknown.* OxNR
Army of the Red Cross, The. Katrina Trask. PEDC
Army of the Sidhe, The. Lady Gregory. SP
Army was ours that spring, The. Landing in England. North Pickenham. Coman Leavenworth. *Fr.* Norfolk Memorials. LiTA
Arnold at Stillwater. Thomas Dunn English. PAH
Arnold, Master of the *Scud.* Bliss Carman. EtS
Arnold, the Vile Traitor. *Unknown.* PAH
Arnold von Winkelried. James Montgomery. BeLS
(Make Way for Liberty.) PoFr, *abr.*; TreFS
(Patriot's Pass-Word, The.) HBV
Arnold, warm with God. The Last Warmth of Arnold. Gregory Corso. CoPo
Arno's Vale. Charles Sackville. WaPE
Around, above my bed, the pitch-dark fly. Truth. Howard Nemerov. LiTM (1970 ed.); MoVE
Around, above the world of snow. February. James Berry Bensel. GoTP
Around and around a dusty little room. Margaret Johnson. SAS
Around Assisi's convent gate. St. Francis' Sermon to the Birds. Longfellow. OTPC
Around Cape Horn, *with music. Unknown.* AmSS
Around me the images of thirty years. The Municipal Gallery Revisited. W. B. Yeats. GTBS-P; LiTB
Around my garden the little wall is low. Losing a Slave-Girl. Po Chü-i. AWP
Around the battlements go by. War on the Periphery. George Johnston. PeCV (1967 ed.)
Around the bend we streaked it with the leaders swingin' wide. The Oro Stage. H. H. Knibbs. IHA
Around the Child. Walter Savage Landor. HBV
Around the Corner. Charles Hanson Towne. PoLF; PoToHe
Around the fireplace, pointing at the fire. On Falling Asleep by Firelight. William Meredith. NYBP
Around the Fish; after Paul Klee. Howard Moss. MoPo
Around the headland, at the end. The Lives of Gulls and Children. Howard Nemerov. FiMAP; NePoEA
Around the house the flakes fly faster. Birds at Winter Nightfall. Thomas Hardy. BiS; ELU; MoBrPo
Around the magnet, Faraday. Induced Current. Herbert Mayo. PoMa
Around the quays, kicked off in twos. Fishing Boats in Martigues. *Unknown.* PeSA
Around the rick, around the rick. *Unknown.* OxNR
Around the rocky headlands, far and near. The Sea's Voice. William Prescott Foster. EtS
Around the vase of Life at your slow pace. The Vase of Life. Dante Gabriel Rossetti. The House of Life, XCV. MaVP; PoVP; SyP; ViPo
Around the weedy grass-grown fields. I Planted Little Trees To-Day. James B. Carrington. PEDC
Around the World. Kate Greenaway. OTPC; PPL
(In Go-Cart So Tiny.) FaPON; SAS; TiPo
Around their legs girl athletes twist. Girl Athletes. Haniel Long. HBMV
Around this lovely valley rise. Midsummer. John Townsend Trowbridge. AA; DD; HBV; HBVY
Around us lies a world invisible. Lone-Land. John Banister Tabb. OQP
Around us summer wrote its last farewell. September Afternoon. Margaret Haley Carpenter. GoYe
Around were all the roses red. Spleen. Paul Verlaine, *tr. by* Ernest Dowson. AWP; EnLi-2; JAWP; OnPM; SyP; WBP
Arouse, arouse, ye friends of right. The World Hymn. J. Gilchrist Lawson. WBLP
A-Roving. Victor Daley. BoAu
A-Roving ("In Amsterdam. . ."). *Unknown. See* Fair Maid of Amsterdam, The.
A-Roving ("In Plymouth Town. . ."). *Unknown.* UnTE
Arques—Afternoon. Arthur Symons. PoVP
Arraigned before his worldly gods. The Execution of Cornelius Vane. Sir Herbert Read. BrPo
Arraigned, poor captive at the bar I stand. Fidessa, More Chaste than Kind, V. Bartholomew Griffin. ReIE; SiCE; Sonn; TuPP
Arraignment, *sel.* William Rose Benét.
"What did you do with the world that you bade us to bow to anew?" MaRV
Arraignment. Helen Gray Cone. AA
Arraignment of a Lover, The. George Gascoigne. ReIE; SiCE
(Gascoigne's Arraignment.) ReEN; TuPP
Arraignment of Paris, The, *sels.* George Peele.
Dirge: "Welladay, welladay, poor Colin." EIL
(Shepherd's Dirge, The.) OBSC
Fair and Fair. EIL; OBEV; ViBoPo
("Fair and fair, and twice so fair.") ReEn; SiCE; TuPP
(Cupid's Curse.) BEL; TOP
(Song of Oenone and Paris.) OBSC
Not Iris in Her Pride. ViBoPo
O Gentle Love. EIL
(Colin, the Enamored Shepherd, Singeth This Passion of Love.) ReIE
(Colin's Passion of Love.) OBSC
Oenone's Complaint. EIL; OBSC
Arran. *Unknown, tr. fr. Irish by* Kuno Meyer. FaBoCh; LoGBV; ChTr, *tr. by* Kenneth Jackson.

Arrange the scene with only a shade of difference. An Incident. Douglas Le Pan. ACV; MoCV; PeCV
Arranged by two's as peaches are. Nine Nectarines and Other Porcelaine. Marianne Moore. OxBA
Arrangements of molecules held together by. Meditation on Indentity. David Wright. OPoP
Arras. P. K. Page. MoCV; OBCV
Arrest of Antoñito el Camborio in the Streets of Seville, The. Federico García Lorca, *tr. fr. Spanish by* A. L. Lloyd. PoFr
Arrest of Oscar Wilde at the Cadogan Hotel, The. John Betjeman. CMoP; DTC; InvP; LiTM (rev. ed.); MoBrPo (1962 ed.); SiTL
Arrested like marble horses. A Frieze. John Peale Bishop. MoPo
Arrival. William Carlos Williams. PoAn
Arrival and Departure. Charles Eglington. BoSA; PeSA
Arrival at Santos. Elizabeth Bishop. FiMAP; OPoP
Arrival at the Waldorf. Wallace Stevens. PP
Arrival of a Guest, The. Tu Fu, *tr. fr. Chinese by* Soame Jenyns. WoL
Arrival of the Bee Box, The. Sylvia Plath. NaP; TPM
Arrival of the Greenhorn, The. John A. Stone. IHA; RePo; SGR, *with music*
Arrival of the San Francisco, *with music.* Isaac W. Baker. SGR
Arrival: The Capital. Desmond O'Grady. NMP
Arrivals and Departures. Melvin Walker La Follette. CoPo
Arrivals, Departures. Philip Larkin. MoBrPo (1962 ed.)
Arriv'd now at our ship, we launch'd, and set. Ulysses Hears the Prophecies of Tiresias. Homer. *Fr.* The Odyssey, XI. LoBV
Arrived from scattered cities, several lands. Shipment to Maidenek. Ephim G. Fogel. TrJP
Arrived in heaven, when his sands were run. The Crusader. Dorothy Parker. ShM
Arrived upon the downs of asphodel. Classic Encounter. "Christopher Caudwell." POTE
Arrogance Repressed. John Betjeman. FiBHP
Arrogant Frog and the Superior Bull, The. Guy Wetmore Carryl. StPo
Arrogant kings, with envious lust [*or* with hate and lust]. The Coins of Love. John Richard Moreland. *Fr.* What of the Night? ChIP; MaRV
Arrow, The. Richard Henry Stoddard. *See* Flight of the Arrow, The.
Arrow, The. Clarence Urmy. HBMV
Arrow, The. W. B. Yeats. EG
Arrow and the Song, The. Longfellow. AA; AnAmPo; AnNE; BBV (1951 ed.); DD; FaFP; HBV; HBVY; MaRV; NeHB; OQP; OTPC; PG; PoPl; PoToHe (new ed.); TreF
Arrow rides upon the sky, An. Love Song. Samuel Allen. NNP
Arrowhead Field. Lawrence Hetrick. TPM
Arrows of Love. Bhartrihari, *tr. fr. Sanskrit by* Arthur W. Ryder. OnPM
Arrowtown. Denis Glover. AnNZ
Ars Amoris. J. V. Cunningham. QFR
Ars Poetica. X. J. Kennedy. ErPo; PP; PV
Ars Poetica. Archibald MacLeish. AmP; AmPP; AP; AWP; CaFP; CBV; CMoP; CoBMV; DiPo; ExPo; HoPM; InP; InPo; LiTA; LiTM; MAP; MoAB; MoAmPo; NeMA; NP; OxBA; PoAn; PoPl; PoPo; PoRA (rev. ed.); PP; ReMP; SeCeV; TwAmPo; VaPo
("Poem should be palpable and mute, A.") NAMP
Ars Poetica. Victor van Vriesland, *tr. fr. Dutch by* Adriaan J. Barnouw. TrJP
Ars Poetica about Ultimates. Tram Combs. TwCP
Ars Victrix. Austin Dobson, *after the French of* Théophile Gautier. HBV; HBVY; MoBrPo (1942 ed.); PoVP; SyP; VA
Sels.
"All passes. Art alone." CTC
"O Poet, then, forbear" InP
Arsenal at Springfield, The. Longfellow. AmPP; AnNE; AP; CoBA; DD, *abr.*; GTBS; HBV; MCCG; MWA-1; WaaP
Sels.
"Were half the power, that fills the world with terror." PGD
When War Shall Be No More. MaRV
Arsenal of the Lord, The. William Stanley Braithwaite. PoNe
Arsenic. Howard Moss. CoAP; NYBP
Arsinoë's Cats. Rosamund Marriott Watson. CIV
Arson and Cold Lace. Worth Long. NBP
Art. Emerson. AmePo; MAmP
Art. Théophile Gautier, *tr. fr. French by* George Santayana. AWP; JAWP; LiTW; WBP; WoL
Art. Herman Melville. AmPP (5th ed.); AP; CBV; MAmP; MWA-1; PoFS; PoIE; ViBoPo
Art. Alfred Noyes. OBEV (new ed.)
Art. Sir Gilbert Parker. *Fr.* A Lover's Diary. VA
Art. Lilla Cabot Perry. AA
Art. José Asunción Silva, *tr. fr. Spanish by* Thomas Walsh. CAW
Art, *sels.* James Thomson.
"Singing is sweet; but be sure of this," III. EnLi-2
"What precious thing are you making fast," I. EnLi-2; OBVV; PoVP
Art. *Unknown.* BLPA
Art above Nature; to Julia. Robert Herrick. AnAnS-2
Art and Life. Lola Ridge. HBMV
Art and Nature. Francisco de Medrano, *tr. fr. Spanish by* Longfellow. OnPM
Art for Art's Sake. Marc Blitzstein. *Fr.* The Cradle Will Rock. TrJP
Art has taught this man to writhe in marble. Carrara. Philip Murray. NePoAm
Art is unmade/ To nature and the wild again. An Open Air Performance of "As You Like It." E. J. Scovell. ChMP
Art Master, An. John Boyle O'Reilly. AA
Art of Biography, The. E. C. Bentley. *Fr.* Clerihews. CenHV; FiBHP; PV
Art of Book-keeping, The. Laman Blanchard. BOHV
Art of Eyes, The. Spenser. *See* Amoretti, XXI.
Art of Love, The. Samuel Butler. *Fr.* Hudibras. FaBoEn
Art of Love, The, *sels.* Ovid, *tr. fr. Latin by* Dryden.
"In Cupid's school whoe'er would take degree." UnTE
"Kiss if you can: Resistance if she make." ErPo
Art of Love, The. Sir John Suckling. LO
Art of lying is you cannot stand, The. Just a Fishing Smack at Empson. George Barker. SiTL
"Art of Our Necessities Is Strange, The." Forrest Izard. WhC
Art of Poetry, The. Nicholas Boileau-Despréaux. *See* Art poétique, L'.
Art of Poetry, The. Horace, *tr. fr. Latin by* the Earl of Roscommon. EnLi-1
Art of Poetry, An. James McAuley. ACV
Art of Poetry, The. Dennis Trudell. QAH
Art of Poetry, The. Paul Verlaine. *See* Art poétique.
Art of Politicks, The, *sel.* James Bramston.
Time's Changes, *abr.* OBEC
Art of Preserving Health, The, *sels.* John Armstrong. OBEC
Blest Winter Nights, *fr.* III.
Home of the Naiads, The, *fr.* II.
Art of the Sonnet, *sels.* Gil Orlovitz. ToPo
"Bowed negress, who aghast but the light."
"If I could rise and see my father young."
"Such folly of margins that may retaliate."
Art poétique, L', *sels.* Nicholas Boileau-Despréaux, *tr. fr. French by* Sir William Soames *and* John Dryden.
"Lucilius was the man, who, bravely bold," II. EnLi-1
"Rash author, 'tis a vain presumptuous crime," I. EnLi-1; PP
Art Poétique. Paul Verlaine, *tr. fr. French by* Arthur Symons. AWP
(Art of Poetry, The.) SyP
Art thou a Statist in the van. A Poet's Epitaph. Wordsworth. EnRP; MBW-2; OBRV; PeER; UnPo (1st ed.)
Art thou alive? It cannot be. On a Lady with Foul Breath. Thomas Parnell. PoE
Art Thou Gone in Haste? *Unknown.* *Fr.* The Thracian Wonder. ElL; ELP; LO; OxBoLi; ThWaDe
("Art thou gon in haste Ile not forsake thee," *longer vers.*) SeCSL
(Chase, The.) CH
(Pursuit of Love.) ChTr
Art thou gone so far. Ode: The Spirit Wooed. Richard Watson Dixon. OBNC
Art thou Heywood with the mad mery wit? Of [*or* Art Thou] Heywood. John Heywood. NCEP; ReIE; SiCE; TuPP
Art thou in love? it cannot be? *Unknown.* SeCSL
Art Thou Lonely? John Oxenham. PoToHe
Art thou not hungry for thy children, Zion? To Zion. Judah Halevi. AWP; JAWP; WBP
Art thou not lovely? Abélard Tells His Love to Héloïse. Herbert E. Palmer. POTE

Art thou pale for weariness. The Moon [*or* To the Moon]. Shelley. AnFE; BoLiVe; BoNaP; ChER; EnRP; EPN; ERoP-2; GTBS; GTBS-D; GTBS-P; GTBS-W; GTSE; GTSL; LoBV; MBW-2; MCCG; OBEV; OnPM; RePo; TrGrPo; ViBoPo
Art thou poor, yet hast thou golden slumbers? The Happy Heart [*or* Content *or* O Sweet Content *or* The Basket-Maker's Song]. Thomas Dekker. *Fr.* The Pleasant Comedy of Patient Grissell, I, i. AtBAP; BBV (1923 ed.); BEL; CBEP; CH; EG; EIL; EnLi-1; EnLit; GTBS; GTBS-D; GTBS-P; GTBS-W; GTSE; GTSL; HBV; LoBV; MemP; OAEP; OBEV; OBSC; OtMeF; PG; PTK; ShBV-2; SiCE; ThWaDe; TOP; TreFT; TrGrPo; TuPP; ViBoPo; WHA; WoL
Art thou some wingèd Sprite, that, fluttering round. To a Maple Seed. Lloyd Mifflin. AA
Art Thou That She. *Unknown.* OnPM; SeCL; SeCSL; ViBoPo
Art thou the bird whom man loves best. The Redbreast Chasing a Butterfly. Wordsworth. OTPC
Art Thou the Same. Frances Dorr Tatnall. AA
Art Thou Weary? John Mason Neale, *after the Greek of* St. Stephen the Sabaite. CAW; SoP
(Art Thou Weary, Art Thou Troubled.) MaRV
Artegall and Radigund. Spenser. *Fr.* The Faerie Queene, V, 5. OBSC
"Artemidora! Gods invisible." The Death of Artemidora. Walter Savage Landor. *Fr.* Pericles and Aspasia. BEL; EnRP; EPN; InP; OBNC; SeCeV; VA; ViBoPo
Artemis. Peter Davison. ErPo
Artemis. Dulcie Deamer. PoAu-1
Artemis. Gérard de Nerval, *tr. fr. French by* Hubert Creekmore. LiTW
Artemis Prologizes. Robert Browning. AnEnPo; LoBV (2d ed.)
Arthur. Ogden Nash. FiBHP
Arthur. William Winter. AA
Arthur Allen, when he lived. Bolyai, the Geometer. Donald Davie. OPoP
Arthur, king most wroth, heard that Modred. Arthur's Last Battle. Layamon. *Fr.* The Brut. BEL
Arthur Mitchell. Marianne Moore. PoNe (1970 ed.)
Arthur o'Bower has broken his band[s]. The Wind [*or* The High Wind]. *Unknown.* ChTr; FaBoCh; LoGBV; OxNR
Arthur Ridgewood, M.D. Frank Marshall Davis. Kal
Arthur, to Robert, made a sign. The Nest. Mary Elliott. OTPC (1923 ed.)
Arthur turns into Tuscany when the time is favorable. *Unknown, tr. fr. Middle English. Fr.* Morte Arthure. MeEV
Arthur with a lighted taper. Wallace Irwin. *Fr.* Science for the Young. ShM
Arthur's Disillusionment. Tennyson. *Fr.* Idylls of the King. TreFS
Arthur's Dream. Layamon, *tr. fr. Middle English. Fr.* The Brut. MeEV
Arthur's Last Fight. Layamon, *tr. fr. Middle English. Fr.* The Brut. MeEV
(Arthur's Last Battle, *pr. tr.*) BEL
Arthur's Seat, *sel.* Thomas Mercer.
("Where is the gallant race that rose.") OxBS
Articles of War. Dunstan Thompson. WaP
Artificer. X. J. Kennedy. TwCP
Artificial Beauty. Lucian, *tr. fr. Greek by* William Cowper. AWP; JAWP; OnPM; WBP
Artillerie [*or* Artillery]. George Herbert. MaMe; MaPo; NoP; PoEL-2; SeCV-1
Artillery Shoot. James Forsyth. WaP
Artisan, The. Alice Brown. TrPWD
Artist, The. Arthur Grissom. AA
Artist, The. Kenneth Koch. AmPC; HYE
Artist. Ernestine Mercer. InMe
Artist, The. Sir Walter Raleigh. WhC
Artist, The. William Carlos Williams. HoPM; NYBP; PIA
Artist and Ape. Gordden Link. GoYe
Artist and his luckless wife, The. The Artist. Sir Walter Raleigh. WhC
Artist and His Work, The. Michelangelo, *tr. fr. Italian by* John Addington Symonds. RBL
Artist as Cuckold, The. *Unknown, tr. fr. Greek by* Louis Untermeyer. UnTE
Artist on Penmaenmawr, The. Charles Tennyson-Turner. OBNC
Artist Paints Dawn, An. Rochelle Ratner. QAH
Artist, who underneath the table. On a Spider. Edward Littleton. WaPE
Artistically weather-proof. On Moving into a Skylight Room. Sister Rita Agnes. JKCP (1926 ed.)
Artists Shouldn't Have Offspring. Don Marquis. *Fr.* Archys Life of Mehitabel. CrMA
Art's use; what is it but to touch the springs. Art. Sir Gilbert Parker. *Fr.* A Lover's Diary. VA
Arundel Tomb, An. Philip Larkin. NePoEA-2
Arvia, east of the morning. Invitation. Ridgely Torrence. NP
As a bath tub lined with white porcelain. The Bath Tub. Ezra Pound. CBV
As a [*or* For] beauty I'm not a great star [*or* I am not a star]. Limerick [*or* My Face *or* The Face]. Anthony Euwer. *Fr.* The Limeratomy. BOHV; FaFP; GoTP; HBMV; HBV; HBVY; InvP; LiBL; LiTM; NePA; PoLF; SiTL; TreF; WhC
As a Bell in a Chime. Robert Underwood Johnson. AA
As a Black Child I was a dreamer. Four Sheets to the Wind and a One-Way Ticket to France. Conrad Kent Rivers. AmNP
As a Boy with a Richness of Needs I Wandered. Clifford Dyment. HaMV
As a child/ I bought a red scarf. Four Sheets to the Wind and a One-Way Ticket to France. Conrad Kent Rivers. IDB; NNP; PoNe (1970 ed.)
As a child holds a pet. Port Bou. Stephen Spender. MoPo; TwCP
As a corpse face in shadow of a shrub. Sagittarius or the Archer. Joseph Gordon Macleod. NP
As a dancer dancing in a shower of roses before her King. The Joys of Art. Rachel Annand Taylor. OBVV
As a dare-gale skylark scanted in a dull cage. The Caged Skylark. Gerard Manley Hopkins. CMoP; LiTM; MoAB; MoBrPo; MoPo; OBMV; PoeP; Sonn; TDP; ViPP; VP
As a drenched, drowned bee. A Baby Asleep after Pain. D. H. Lawrence. BoPe; NP
As a fond mother, when the day is o'er. Nature. Longfellow. AA; AmePo; AmPP (3d ed.); AnNE; AP; BoNaP; CoBA; FaBoBe; HBV; InP; MaRV; PoLF; PoMa; SoP; TOP; TreFT; TrGrPo; TRV; WHA
As a fond mother, when the daylight fades. Comforted. Henry W. Frost. SoP
As a friend to the children, commend me the Yak. The Yak. Hilaire Belloc. ALV; BOHV; FaBV; FaPON; HBVY; InMe; MoBrPo; MPB; NA; PCH; PoRh; StaSt; TDP; TreFS; TSW; UTS
As a guest who may not stay. In Memory of James T. Fields. Whittier. OBVV
As a Man Soweth. Goethe, *tr. fr. German.* FaChP; MaRV
As a Masai warrior. Black Music Man. Lethonia Gee. BF
As a mote in at a minster door, so mighty were its jaws. Jonah. *Unknown. Fr.* Patience. ACP
As a naked man I go. In Waste Places [*or* The Waste Places]. James Stephens. CaFP; CBV; GTSL; HBV; MoAB; MoBrPo; MoVE; NP; PoFr
As a Plane Tree by the Water. Robert Lowell. AP; CMoP; CoAP; CoBMV; CrMA; DTC; ForPo; GTBS-W; LiTM (rev. ed.); MoAB; MoAmPo (1950 ed.); NePA; NePoEA; OxBA; PoDB; SiSw; TrGrPo (rev. ed.); UnPo (3d ed.); VaPo
As a Possible Lover. LeRoi Jones. AmNP
As a queen sits down, knowing that a chair will be there. Walking to Sleep. Richard Wilbur. NYBP
As a rule, man is [*or* man's] a fool. Man Is a Fool [*or* Generalization]. Joseph Capp. FaFP; SiTL; TreFT, *diff. vers.*
As a Seal upon Thy Heart. The Song of Solomon, Bible, *O.T.* *See* Love.
As a shy deer that hurtles into sunlight. For Simone Weil. Sister M. Thérèse. MoRP
As a signet of carbuncle in a setting of gold. Music. Ecclesiasticus, Bible, Apocrypha. TrJP
As a sloop with a sweep of immaculate wing on her delicate spine. Buick. Karl Shapiro. CaFP; CMoP; CoBA; HoPM; MiAP; MoAB; PoIE; TrGrPo (rev. ed.); ViBoPo (1958 ed.)
As a stream that runs to sea. Bonds. Laurence Housman. MaRV
As a torn paper might seal up its side. The Pruned Tree. Howard Moss. NYBP
As a twig trembles, which a bird. She Came and Went. James Russell Lowell. AA; CoBA; FaPL; HBV; ViBoPo
As a water lily only blooms. Hope's Forecast. Ethel Romig Fuller. RePo

As a white candle. The Old Woman. Joseph Campbell. ACV; AWP; GoBC; HBMV; JAWP; MCCG; MoBrPo; NeHB; NeMA; NP; OnYI; OxBI; POTE; PoToHe (new ed.); TreFT; ViBoPo; WBP; YT
As a young child the wisest could adore him. W. H. Auden. *Fr.* In Time of War. CMoP
As a young Child, whose Mother, for a jest. The Child's Purchase. Coventry Patmore. CoBE; ISi
As a young lobster roamed about. The Lobster. *Unknown.* GoTP
As a young stag the thicket passed [*or* past]. The Tame Stag. John Gay. *Fr.* Fables. CBEP; EiCP
As a youth. Yesterday's Child. Robert Reedburg. TNV
As Adam Early in the Morning. Walt Whitman. AP; MAmP; OxBA
As after noon, one summer's day. Cupid Mistaken. Matthew Prior. ALV; EiCL; EiCP; InMe; ViBoPo
As Ah walked oot, yah Sunday morn. Bleeberrying. Jonathan Denwood. MoBS
As Always. James F. Gallagher. JKCP (1955 ed.)
As Amoret with Phyllis Sat. Sir Carr Scrope. *Fr.* The Man of Mode (*by* Sir George Etherege). SeCL
As an eagle grasped/ In folds of the green serpent. Shelley. *Fr.* Alastor. ChER
As an intruder I trudged with careful innocence. Old Mansion. John Crowe Ransom. OxBA
As an Old Mercer. Mahlon Leonard Fisher. HBV
As an unperfect actor on the stage. Sonnets, XXIII. Shakespeare. BEL; EnL; HBV; InvP; OAEP; ReEN; SiCE; Sonn
As And to Aus, and Aus to Bis. The Passionate Encyclopedia Britannica Reader to His Love. "Maggie." InMe
As Ann came in one summer's day. The Sleeper. Walter de la Mare. MoAB; MoBrPo; SeCeV; YT
As, at a railway junction, men. Sic Itur. Arthur Hugh Clough. NCEP
As at noon[e] Dulcina rested. Dulcina [*or* The Shepherd's Wooing Dulcina *or* Come to Me Soon *or* On Dulcina]. *At. to* Sir Walter Ralegh. ALV; CoMu; TuPP; UnTE
As Bad as a Mile. Philip Larkin. ELU
As beautiful as the hands. For Miriam. Kenneth Patchen. ToPo
As beautiful Kitty one morning was tripping. Kitty of Coleraine. *At. to* Charles Dawson Shanly, *also to* Edward Lysaght. BOHV; HBV; MCCG; OnYI; StPo
As Bees, that when the skies are calm and fair. Bees and Monks. John Hookham Frere. *Fr.* King Arthur and His Round Table. OBRV
As beneath the moon I walked. The Whisperers. W. W. Gibson. HBV
As billows upon billows roll. The Surrender at Appomattox. Herman Melville. MC; PAH
As Birds Are Fitted to the Boughs. Louis Simpson. BoLP; CBV; NePoEA
As birds their infant brood protect. Jehovah-Shammah. William Cowper. NoP
As biting Winter flies, lo, Spring with sunny skies. To Lucius Sestius. Horace. Odes, I, 4. OuHeWo
As black as ink and isn't ink. *Unknown.* OxNR
As boring as the fact of a marvelous friend. The Rainy Season. William Meredith. NePoEA
As bronze may be much beautified. Fragment: The Abyss of War. Wilfred Owen. POTE
As Brothers Live Together. Longfellow. *Fr.* The Song of Hiawatha, I. TreFT
As bryght Phebus, scheyn soverane hevynnys e. Prologue to Book VII, The. Vergil, *tr. by* Gawin Douglas. Aeneid: Prologue to Book VII. OxBS
As burnish'd gold, such are my sovereign's hears. Robert Tofte. *Fr.* Laura. ReIE
As butterflies are but winged flowers. Butterflies. W. H. Davies. BoPe
As by occasion late, towards Brutus' city old. A Winter's Morning Muse. Thomas Howell. SiCE
As by the dead we love to sit. Emily Dickinson. NePA
As by the instrument she took her place. Virtuosa. Mary Ashley Townsend. AA
As cages, think of department stores and certain zoos. Cages. Marvin Solomon. NYBP
As Catholics make of the Redeemer. Brand Speaks. Ibsen. *Fr.* Brand, I. WGRP
As cedars beaten with continual storms. George Chapman. *Fr.* Bussy d'Ambois, I, i. ViBoPo
As Celia rested in the shade. A Pastorall Dialogue. Thomas Carew. AnAnS-2; CavP
As children bring their broken toys. Reproof. *Unknown.* STF
As chimes that flow o'er shining seas. Far-away. George Sigerson. JKCP (1926 ed.)
As Chloe [*or* Cloe] came into the room t'other day. A [*or* The] Lover's Anger [*or* The Angry Lover]. Matthew Prior. ErPo; LO; MeWo; SeCL; UnTE
As cities that to the fierce conquerors yield. The Statue in Stocks-Market. Andrew Marvell. MaMe
As clever Tom Clinch, while the Rabble was bawling. Clever Tom Clinch going to Be Hanged. Swift. CEP; CoMu; SeCeV
As Cloe on flowers reclin'd o'er the stream. Chloe Resolved. John Hoadly. EiCL
As Cloris [*or* Chloris] full of harmless thoughts. A Song. Earl of Rochester. ErPo; UnTE
As concerning Man. Alexander Radcliffe. PeRV
As Consequent from Store of Summer Rains. Walt Whitman. MAmP
As convicts go, when it is time, to cells. The Convict. Anthony Frisch. CaP
As cruel as a Turk: whence came. On Mammon. Herman Melville. *Fr.* Clarel. OxBA
As Cupid in a garden strayed. The Bee. *Unknown.* TrAS
As custome was, the pepill far and neir. The Assembly of the Gods. Robert Henryson. *Fr.* The Testament of Cresseid. PoEL-1
As Day Begins to Wane. Helena Coleman. CaP
As day dawns bright by heaven's grace. Of the Night, Let the Bridegroom Sing. Statius. *Fr.* Epithalamium for Stella and Violentilla. HW
As day did darken on the dewless grass. The Wind at the Door. William Barnes. AtBAP; CBEP; ELP; GTBS-P; LO; NBM; PoEL-4
As Dew in Aprille. *Unknown. See* I Sing of a Maiden.
As doctors give physic by way of prevention. For My Own Monument. Matthew Prior. CEP; EiCP; HBV; LoBV; OBEC; OBEV
As does his heart who travels far from home. To a Young Child. Eliza Scudder. AA
As Dolly and her favorite swain. The Unfortunate Reminder. William Pattison. UnTE
As down by Banna's banks I strayed. Mailligh Mo Stor. George Ogle. IrPN
As down the road she wambled slow. Bessie Bobtail. James Stephens. NP
As Down the Woodland Ways. Sir Charles G. D. Roberts. TwCaPo
As due by many titles I resign[e]. Holy Sonnets, II. John Donne. AnAnS-1; MaMe; MasP; MeP; MePo; OBS; PIA; SCEP-1; SeEP; Sonn
As dyed in blood the streaming vines appear. Woodbines in October. Charlotte Fiske Bates. AA
As Eponina brought, to move the king. Frederick Goddard Tuckerman. *Fr.* Sonnets. AmePo
As, even today, the airman, feeling the plane sweat. Icarus. Valentin Iremonger. NeIP; OnYI; OxBI
As evening slowly spreads his mantle hoar. Ode Written at Vale-Royal Abbey in Cheshire. Thomas Warton, the Younger. CoBE
As far as human need exists. Love. Charles Russell Wakeley. OQP
As far as I can see this autumn haze. The Cocoon. Robert Frost. MWA-2
As far as most of what you call people, my darling, are. Suburban Homecoming. John Ciardi. ToPo
As fast as thou shalt wane, so fast thou grow'st. Sonnets, IX. Shakespeare. Sonn
As fire, unfound ere pole approaches pole. William Baylebridge. *Fr.* Love Redeemed. PoAu-1
As flame streams upward, so my longing thought. He Made Us Free. Maurice Francis Egan. AA; JKCP
As flames are drawn from the scuttle of turbines' roar. Homeward Bound. James Brodey. ANYP
As flow the rivers to the sea. Inheritance. "Æ." EPN; PoVP
As fly the shadows o'er the grass. The Irish Wolf-Hound. Denis Florence MacCarthy. *Fr.* The Foray of Con O'Donnell. VA

As for my life, I've led it. A Placid Man's Epitaph. Thomas Hardy. MoBrPo
As Fowlers Lie in Wait. Jeremiah, V: 26-31, Bible, *O.T.* TrJP
As Freedom Is a Breakfastfood. E. E. Cummings. AnFE; CMoP; CoAnAm; LiTA; LiTM; OxBA; TwAmPo
As for God, His way is perfect! God's Way Is Perfect. Avis B. Christiansen. SoP
As for me, when I saw you. America. Bernadette Mayer. ANYP
As from a darkn'd roome some optick glass. The Epilogue Spoken to the King at the Opening the Play-House at Oxford. Dryden. EiCL
As from an ancestral oak. Similes for Two Political Characters. Shelley. CBEP; PeER
As from my window at first glimpse of dawn. At the Dawn. Alice Macdonald Kipling. MaRV
As from our dream we died away. Parting. "Æ." PoVP
As from the Dorset shore I travell'd home. The White Horse of Westbury. Charles Tennyson Turner. PeVV
As from the moist and gelid sleep. George Darley. *Fr.* Nepenthe. OnYI
As gay for you to take your father's ax. To a Young Wretch. Robert Frost. NeMA; PoDB
As gillyflowers do but stay. A Lady Dying in Childbed. Robert Herrick. EG
As Glycera was perfect, so. The Grammar of Love. Martial. ALV
As God claps hands of time and space. Chant. Oscar Williams. MoRP
As good enough as a feast: yea, God save it. Of Enough and a Feast. John Heywood. SiCE; TuPP
As good to write, as for to lie and groan. Astrophel and Stella, XL. Sir Philip Sidney. FCP; SiPS; TuPP
As great as earth with child or sun with fire. The Phoenix. Richard Selig. MemP
As growth of form or momentary glance. Transfigured Life. Dante Gabriel Rossetti. The House of Life, LX. MaVP; PoVP; ViPo
As hags hold sabbaths, not for joy but spite. Pope. *Fr.* Moral Essays. ExPo
As hang two mighty thunderclouds. The Guns in the Grass. Thomas Frost. MC; PAH
As Happy Dwellers by the Seaside Hear. Celia Thaxter. EtS
As hath been, lo, these many generations. First Travels of Max. John Crowe Ransom. MAP; MoAmPo
As he climbs down our hill, my kestrel rises. Esyllt. Glyn Jones. DTC
As He Is. W. H. Auden. MoPo
As He Lay Dying. Randolph Stow. FIW
As he said vanity, so vain say I. The Vanity of All Worldly Things. Anne Bradstreet. SCAP
As he taught and healed the multitudes. God Must Be Like That. Kenneth W. Sollitt. SoP
As he that loves oft looks on the dear form. On the "Vita Nuova" of Dante. Dante Gabriel Rossetti. MaVP; PoVP
As he that sees a dark and shadie grove. H. Baptisme. George Herbert. MaMe; SCEP-1
As he that sees a starre fall, runs apace. The Bridegroomes Coming. John Donne. MaMe
As he trudged along to school. The Story of Johnny Head-in-Air. Heinrich Hoffmann. BBGG; TiPo
As He Walked with Us. Harry Webb Farrington. ChIP; SoP
As hearts have broken, let young hearts break. Little Dirge. Jean Starr Untermeyer. HBMV
As Helen Once. Muna Lee. HBMV
As Hermes once took to his feathers light. On a Dream [*or* A Dream, after Reading Dante's Episode of Paolo and Francesca]. Keats. CBEP; DiPo; EnRP; ERoP-2; MBW-2
As his great wings the albatross. Albatross. Charles Burgess. NePoAm-2
As Holy Kirke makes mind. The Nativity. *Unknown.* MeEL
As home again I travelled regretfully through London. Town Maid. Clifford Bax. POTE
As honest Jacob on a night. The Patriarch. Burns. CoMu
As I am a rhymer. On My Joyful Departure from the City of Cologne. Samuel Taylor Coleridge. InvP; WhC
As I am now so you will [*or* must] be. A Curt Addendum. *Unknown.* ShM; WhC
As I beheld a winters evening air. Another. Richard Lovelace. SeCP
As I cam in by Dunidier. The Battle of Harlaw. *Unknown.* ESPB
"As I cam in by Glasgow [*or* boney Glassgow] town." Glasgow Peggie. *Unknown.* BaBo; ESPB
As I cam thro the Garrioch land. The Battle of Harlaw (B *vers.*). *Unknown.* ESPB
As I Came Down from Lebanon. Clinton Scollard. AA; AnAmPo; HBV; HT
As I Came Down Mount Tamalpais. Clarence Urmy. AA; HBMV
As I came down Talbingo Hill. Bullocky Bill. *Unknown.* PoAu-1
As I came down the Bowery. Can't You Dance the Polka? *Unknown.* SoAmSa
As I came down the hillside. Despair. Edward Bliss Reed. HBMV
As I came down to the long street by the water. South Street. Francis E. Falkenbury. EtS; PFY
As I came home the other night. The Drunken Fool. *Unknown.* BFSS
As I came in by Fiddich-side. Willie Macintosh. *Unknown.* ESPB (B *vers.*)
As I came O'er Cairney Mount. Burns. CoMu (My Bonnie Highland Laddie.) UnTE
As I came out of the New York Public Library. Nuns in the Wind. Muriel Rukeyser. FiMAP
As I Came Over the Grey, Grey Hills. Joseph Campbell. AnIL
As I came over the humpbacked hill. The Green Fiddler. Rachel Field. BoChLi; StPo
As I came over the rise by Stewart's ash. Country Miracle. Abbie Huston Evans. LiTM
As I came over Windy Gap. Running to Paradise. W. B. Yeats. BoLiVe; LOW; OxBoLi
As I came past the Brimham Rocks. The Song of Nidderdale. Dorothy Una Ratcliffe. HBMV
As I came round the harbor buoy. The Long White Seam. Jean Ingelow. GN; HBV; OTPC; VA
As I Came through the Desert. James Thomson. *Fr.* The City of Dreadful Night, IV. LiTB; NBM ("As I came through the desert thus it was.") LiTG; PoEL-5
As I came to the edge of the woods. Come In. Robert Frost. AmPP; AnNE; BoNaP; BWP; DiPo; FaBV; ForPo; GTBS-W; LiTA; LiTM; MaPo; MemP; MoAB; MoAmPo; NeMA; PoAn; PoeP; PoIE; ReMP; TrGrPo; UnPo (3d ed.); WePo
As I came to the sea wall that August day. On the Sea Wall. C. Day Lewis. SeCePo
As I came up the sandy road that lifts above the sea. The Spell. Henry Martin Hoyt. HBMV
As I came wandering down Glen Spean. The Emigrant Lassie. John Stuart Blackie. VA
As I descended black, impassive rivers. The Drunken Boat. Arthur Rimbaud. PIA; SyP
As I did roam the other day. Thomas of Erceldoune. *Unknown.* MeEV
As I did walk abroad one time. The Mourning Conquest. *Unknown.* CoMu
As I did walke my selfe alone. King James and Brown. *Unknown.* ESPB
As I drive to the junction of lane and highway. At Castle Boterel. Thomas Hardy. DTC; FaBoEn; GTBS-D; GTBS-P; MoVE; OBNC; PeVV; PoSa
As I Ebb'd with the Ocean of Life. Walt Whitman. AmPP (5th ed.); LoBV; MAmP; MWA-1
As I fell—from mind-perch precarious. This Here Is Hell. Samuel M. Bradley. FiSC
As I gaed down to Collistown. The Cunning Clerk. *Unknown.* OxBB
As I gaed in by the Duke o' Athole's gates. The Duke o' Athole's Nurse. *Unknown.* OxBB
As I gaed in yon greenwood-side. The Duke of Athole's Nurse. *Unknown.* BaBo
As I Gird on for Fighting. A. E. Housman. CMoP
As I Go down the Sunset Hill. Alice Hansche Mortenson. SoP
As I Go on My Way. Strickland Gillilan. MaRV
As I Grew Older. Langston Hughes. AmPP (5th ed.); BANP; TPM
As I Grow Old. *Unknown.* FaChP; MaRV; OQP
As I have seene when on the breast of Thames. Praise of

Poets. William Browne. *Fr.* Britannia's Pastorals, II, Song 2. OBS
As I hear it, now when there is company. Grandmother and Grandson. W. S. Merwin. NePoEA-2
As I in hoary [*or* hoarie] winter's night stood shivering in the snow. The Burning Babe. Robert Southwell. ACP; AnAnS-1; AnFE; AtBAP; BEL; BoW; CABA; CAW; CBEP; CBV; CH; CoBE; EG; ElL; EnLit; FaBoCh; FaBoEn; FlW; GoBC; HBV; HoPM; ILP; LiTB; LiTG; LoBV; LoGBV; MaRV; MeP; MePo; NoP; OBEV; OBSC; OxBoCh; PoEL-2; PoG; PoIE; PoLi; PTK; ReEn; ReIE; SeCePo; SiCE; StJW; StP; TOP; TrGrPo; TuPP; UnPo (1st ed.); ViBoPo
As I lay asleep in Italy. The Mask of Anarchy. Shelley. CABL; EnRP; FOL; PeER
As I lay awake in the white moonlight. Sleepyhead. Walter de la Mare. TiPo
As I lay in a winter's night. The Debate of the Body and the Soul. *Unknown.* CoBE
As I Lay Musing ("As I lay musing all alone"). *Unknown.* CoMu
(Friar and the Fair Maid, The, *shorter vers.*) UnTE
(Friar in the Well, The, A *and* B *vers.*) ESPB
As I lay musing all alone/ upon my resting bed. The Poore Man Payes for All. *Unknown.* CoMu
As I Lay Quiet. Margaret Widdemer. GoYe
As I lay sleeping. *Unknown.* EG; LO; TrGrPo
As I lay upon a night. Jesus Reassures His Mother. *Unknown.* MeEL
As I lay upon a night. My Thought Was on a Maid So Bright. *Unknown.* ISi
As I Lay with My Head in Your Lap Camerado. Walt Whitman. OxBA
As I Laye a-Thynkynge. "Thomas Ingoldsby." HBV
(Last Lines.) OBVV
As I lie here in the sun. Jonah. Randall Jarrell. MoRP
As I lie in bed. A Prayer. Joseph Seamon Cotter, Jr. BANP
As I lie roofed in, screened in. On the Porch. Harriet Monroe. NP
As I listened from a beach-chair in the shade. Their Lonely Betters. W. H. Auden. GoJo
As I look back upon your first embrace. Surrender. Amelia Josephine Burr. HBV
As I look into each different face. Through the Varied Patterned Lace. Margaret Danner. Kal
As I looked out of my window. Run Along, You Little Dogies. *Unknown.* OuSiCo
As I looked out one May morning. The Princess and the Gypsies. Frances Cornford. StPo
As I looked, the poplar rose in the shining air. The Deceptive Present, the Phoenix Year. Delmore Schwartz. BoNaP
As I mused by the hearthside. At Home, Alone with the Cat. Walter de la Mare. BoC
As I my little flock on Ister bank. Shepherd Song. Sir Philip Sidney. *Fr.* Arcadia. SiPS
As I one ev'ning [*or* evening] sat before my cell. Artillerie [*or* Artillery]. George Herbert. MaMe; MaPo; NoP; PoEL-2; SeCV-1
As I once came from Tottingham. Tottingham Frolic. *Unknown.* UnTE
As I passed [*or* pass'd] by a river side. The Carnal [*or* Crow] and the Crane. *Unknown.* BuBa, *abr.*; ESPB; OBB; StJW
As I passed by Tom Sherman's bar-room. The Cowboy's Lament (A *vers.*). *Unknown.* ViBoFo
As I Pondered in Silence. Walt Whitman. WHA
As I proceeded down along impassive rivers. The Drunken Boat. Arthur Rimbaud. LiTW
As I returned from London. Johnny German. *Unknown.* BFSS
As I ride, as I ride. Through the Metidja to Abd-el-Kadr. Robert Browning. PoVP
As I rode down the arroyo through yuccas [*or* yucas] belled with bloom. In the Mohave. Patrick Orr. BANP; LiTM
As I rode out one evening down by a river side. Two Lovers Discoursing. *Unknown.* ShS
As I rose in the early dawn. Wanderers. James Hebblethwaite. BoAu; NeLNL
As I rose like a lover from the ravished sea. To a Poet Who Has Never Travelled. Charles Causley. POTE (1959 ed.)
As I roved out impatiently. In the Ringwood. Thomas Kinsella. NMP; OxBI
As I roved out on a May morning. Johnny's the Lad I Love [*or* As I Roved Out]. *Unknown.* AnIV; DTC; OxBoLi
As I roved out on a summer's morning. Castle Hyde [*or* Castlehyde]. Edward Kenealy. IrPN; OnYI
As I roved out one summer's morning, speculating most curiously. Colleen Rue. *Unknown.* OnYI
As I rowed out to the light-house. The Light-House-Keeper's White-Mouse. John Ciardi. PDV
As I rummaged thro' [*or* through] the attic. My Trundle Bed. J. G. Baker. BLPA; FaBoBe
As I sail home to Galveston. A Sailor's Song. Hazel Harper Harris. EtS
As I sail o'er life's wide ocean. The Pilot. *Unknown.* STF
As I Sat at My Spinning-Wheel. *Unknown.* CoMu
As I sat at the café I said to myself. Spectator ab Extra [*or* As I Sat at the Café]. Arthur Hugh Clough. *Also in* Dipsychus. ALV; ELP; FiBHP; GTBS-P; LiTG; NBM; OxBoLi; PeVV; SeCePo; SiTL; ViPP; WePo
As I sat by my window last evening. Miss Foggerty's Cake. *Unknown.* BLPA
As I sat down t' play a game o' coon can. Po' Boy. *Unknown.* TrAS
As I sat down to breakfast in state. The Country Clergyman's Trip to Cambridge. Macaulay. NBM; OxBoLi
As I Sat on a Sunny Bank. *Unknown.* *See* I Saw Three Ships.
As I Sat under a Sycamore Tree. *Unknown.* *See* I Saw Three Ships.
As I sd to my/ friend. I Know a Man. Robert Creeley. AmPC; CoPo
As I Set Down to Play Tin-Can. *Unknown.* *See* Po' Boy.
As I sit looking out of a window of the building. The Instruction Manual. John Ashbery. NeAP
As I sit on a log here in the woods among the clean-faced beeches. Choir Practice. Ernest Crosby. AA
As I sit with others, at a great feast, suddenly, while the music is playing. Thought. Walt Whitman. MaRV
As I stand by the cross on the lone mountain's crest. The Two Ships. Bret Harte. MaRV
As I start for a saunter, I turn and say. When He Goes to Play with the Boys. Strickland Gillilan. PEDC
As I Step Over a Puddle at the End of Winter. James Wright. FRC; NaP
As I stood at the door. The [*or* In the] College of Surgeons. James Stephens. AnIL; LOW
As I stood by yon roofless tower. The Vision. Burns. PoFr
As I stray'd o'er the common on Cork's rugged border. Mary Le More. George Nugent Reynolds. OnYI
As I strolled out one evening, out for a night's career. The Fire Ship. *Unknown.* AmSS
As I strole the city, oft I. A Character, Panegyric, and Description of the Legion Club. Swift. EiCL
As I sunk the lobster-pots. Fisherman's Luck. W. W. Gibson. EtS
As I suppose, and as I suppose. *Unknown.* SiTL
As I walk down NYC I wonder into the ground. Big City. Michael Brownstein. ANYP
As I walk through the streets. Prayer. F. S. Flint. TrPWD
As I Walk'd by Myself. *Unknown.* *See* As I Walked by Myself.
As I walk'd out one evening just as the sun went down. *See* As I walked out one evening just as the sun went down.
As I walk'd thinking through a little grove. Catch: On a Wet Day. Franco Sacchetti, *tr. by* Dante Gabriel Rossetti. AWP; BoNaP; JAWP; WBP
As I Walked [*or* Walk'd] by Myself. *Unknown.* ChTr; OTPC (1923 ed.); OxNR; SiTL
(As I Walked, 1 *st.*) MPB (1956 ed.)
(On K. W. 3d.) PeRV
(Song on King William III, A.) NA
As I walked down by the river. A Ballad for Katharine of Aragon. Charles Causley. FaBoTw; NePoEA
As I walked down the waterside. The Sleepers. W. H. Davies. AnFE; WoL
As I walked fforth one morninge. Christopher White. *Unknown.* ESPB
As I Walked in the Woods. *Unknown.* UnTE
As I walked me this endurs day. Here I Sit Alone. *Unknown.* OxBoCh

As I Walked Out in the Streets of Laredo. *Unknown.* *See* Cowboy's Lament, The.
As I walked out in yonder dell. The Elfin Knight (B *vers.*). *Unknown.* ViBoFo
As I walked out of St. James's Hospital. The Bad Girl's Lament. *Unknown.* ViBoFo
As I walked out of Tom Sherman's barroom. The Cowboy's Lament (A *vers.*). *Unknown.* BFSS
As I walked out one cold winter night. The Lass of Roch Royal (C *vers.*). *Unknown.* ViBoFo
As I Walked Out One Evening. W. H. Auden. AtBAP; ChMP; DiPo; LiTM; MaPo (1969 ed.); NoP; OAEP (2d ed.); PIA; PoFS; PoSa; POTE; SeCeV; TDP; TwCP; UnPo (3d ed.); PoAn (Song: As I Walked Out One Evening.) MoAB; MoBrPo (1950 ed.)
As I walked [*or* walk'd] out one evening just as the sun went down. The Shanty-Boy and the Farmer's Son. *Unknown.* ABF; IHA
As I walked out one evening late, a-drinking of sweet wine. My Old True Love. *Unknown.* OuSiCo
As I walked out one May morning,/ One May morning so early. I'm Seventeen Come Sunday. *Unknown.* UnTE
As I walked out one May morning/ To see if the leaves had come. John of Hazelgreen (B *vers.*). *Unknown.* BFSS
As I walked out one May morning,/ When May was all in bloom. The Bold Fisherman. *Unknown.* BaBo
As I walked out one midsummer's morning. The Banks of Sweet Primroses. *Unknown.* ELP
As I walked out one morning down by the Sligo dock. Yellow Meal. *Unknown.* ShS
As I walked out [*or* was a-walking] one morning for pleasure. Whoopee Ti Yi Yo, Git Along, Little Dogies [*or* Git Along, Little Dogies *or* Whoopee High Ogie]. *Unknown.* ABF; AmPP; AS; BFSS; CoSo; FaPON; IHA; InP; MoShBr; MPB; OTPC (1946 ed.); StVeCh; TiPo; TreF; TSW; WaKn
As I walked out one morning in May,/ For my recreation. The Lass of Mohea. *Unknown.* SoAmSa
As I walked out one morning in May,/ Just before the break of day. Archie o Cawfield (B *vers.*). *Unknown.* BaBo
As I walked out one morning in May/ To hear the birds sing sweet. Who Will Shoe Your Feet? *Unknown.* BFSS
As I walked out one night, it being dark all over. The Sailor's Return. *Unknown.* LO; OxBoLi
As I walked out one summer's evening. John Riley. *Unknown.* OuSiCo
As I walked out that sultry night. Full Moon. Robert Graves. FaBoEn; POTE
As I walked out upon the road one day. Poor Old Man. *Unknown.* ShS
As I walked over London bridge. Georgie. *Unknown.* BFSS
As I walked over the hill [*or* hills] one day. A Nursery Song. Ann A. G. Carter. OTPC (1923 ed.); PPL; SAS
As I walked the heights of Meelin on a tranquil autumn day. The Fairy Harpers. James B. Dollard. CaP
As I walked thinking through a little grove. *See* As I walk'd thinking . . .
As I walked through my garden. Butterfly. Hilda Conkling. NP; TiPo
As I walked through the rumorous streets. Vistas. Odell Shepard. HBMV
As I wandered in the forest. Wild Flower's Song. Blake. BoTP
As I wandered on the beach. The Great Blue Heron. Carolyn Kizer. CoAP; FRC; NePoEA-2; PIA
As I wandered round the homestead. My Mother's Prayer. T. C. O'Kane. BLPA; FaBoBe
As I wandered the forest. The Wild Flower's Song. Blake. CBEP
As I was a-gwine [*or* goin'] down the road. Turkey in the Straw. *Unknown.* AS; FaFP; TrAS; TreFS; YaD
As I was a-hoeing, a-hoeing my lands. The Six Badgers. Robert Graves. GoJo
As I was a-roaming for pleasure one day. The Little Mohee. *Unknown.* BaBo
As I was a-walkin' /All by the seashore. Little Mohee. *Unknown.* AmSS
As I was a-walkin' [*or* a-walking *or* walking] down Paradise Street. Blow the Man Down. *Unknown.* ABF; AmSS (*vers.* II); AS; IHA; SoAmSa (B *vers.*).
As I Was a-Walking. *Unknown.* BiS
(The Lark in the Morning.) ChTr
As I was a walking, I cannot tell where. Narcissus, Come Kiss Us! *Unknown.* ErPo
As I was a-walking [*or* walking] mine alane [*or* alone]. Archie of [*or* o'] Cawfield [*or* Cafield]. *Unknown.* BuBa; ESPB (B *vers.*); OBB; OxBS
As I was a-walking on Westminster Bridge. *Unknown.* OxNR
As I was a-walking one morning down by the Clarence Dock. Heave Away, *vers.* I. *Unknown.* ShS
As I was a-walking one morning for pleasure. *See* As I walked out one morning for pleasure.
As I was a-walking the other day. The Shoemaker. *Unknown.* FaPON; GFA; SoPo
As I was a-walking the streets of Laredo. Cowboy's Lament. *Unknown.* ThLM
As I was carving images from clouds. Opifex. Thomas Edward Brown. OBVV; PoVP
As I was cast in my first [*or* ffirst] sleepe. Younge Andrew. *Unknown.* ESPB; OBB; OxBB
As I was climbing Ardan Mór. Ardan Mór [*or* The Herons]. Francis Ledwidge. ACP; AnIV; AWP; JAWP; OnYI; OxBI; WBP
As I was coming down the stair. *Unknown.* CenHV
As I was driving my waggon one day. Gee Ho, Dobin. *Unknown.* CoMu
As I was falling down the stair. Later Antigonishes. Hughes Mearns. InMe
As I was fishing off Pondy Point. Jim Desterland. Hyam Plutzik. FiSC
As I was goin' down the road. *See* As I was a-gwine down the road.
As I was going along, long, long [*or* along, along]. Mother Goose. OxNR; TiPo (1952 ed.)
As I was going by candlelight. Copper Song. Ethel Talbot Scheffauer. PoMS
As I was going by Charing Cross. *Unknown.* CH; FaBoCh; LoGBV; OxNR; RIS
As I was going down Treak Street. Micky Thumps. *Unknown.* WePo
As I was going o'er London Bridge. *Unknown.* OxNR; SiTL
As I was going o'er Tipple Tine. *Unknown.* OxNR
As I was going o'er Westminster bridge. *Unknown.* OTPC (1946 ed.); PPL
As I was going to Banbury. *Unknown.* OxNR
As I was going to Bethlehem-town. Bethlehem-Town. Eugene Field. WBLP
As I was going to Derby,/ Upon a market day. The Derby Ram [*or* The Ram]. *Unknown.* OxNR; SiTL; ViBoFo
As I was going to Derby, all on a market day. The Wonderful Derby Ram. *Unknown.* BoTP
As I was going to Derby, 'twas on a market day. Derby Ram. *Unknown.* SoAmSa
As I was going to my father's house. The Cruel Mother [*or* Two Little Babes]. *Unknown.* BFSS
As I Was Going to Saint Ives. Daniel G. Hoffman. NYBP
As I was going to St. Ives. Mother Goose. BoChLi; HBV; HBVY; OTPC; OxNR; PPL; RIS; SiTL; SoPo; StVeCh
As I was going to sell my eggs. *Unknown.* OxNR
As I was going to town. Me Alone. Lula Lowe Weeden. CDC
As I was going up Pippen Hill. *Unknown.* OxNR
As I was going up the hill. Jack the Piper. *Unknown.* ChTr; OxNR
As I was going [*or* walking] up the stair. Antigonish [*or* A Case *or* The Little Man Who Wasn't There]. Hughes Mearns. FaFP; FaPON; InMe; LiTM; PoLF; SiTL; SoPo; StaSt; WhC
As I was hiking past the woods, the cool and sleepy summer woods. Out There Somewhere. H. H. Knibbs. BLPA
As I Was Laying on the Green. *Unknown.* FiBHP; SiTL; WhC
As I was letting down my hair. The Lady with Technique. Hughes Mearns. *Fr.* Later Antigonishes. FiBHP; InMe; SiTL; WhC
As I was lumberin' down the street. Louisiana Girls. *Unknown.* ABF
As I was lumb'ring down de street. Lubly Fan. Cool White. TrAS
As I was marching in Flanders. Comrades. W. W. Gibson. BEL
As I was old sometime and sometime young. Time's Mutability. Bertholt Brecht. ELU
As I was on the high-road. Wet or Fine. Amory Hare. HBMV

As I was out upon the road one day. Sacramento, *vers.* II. *Unknown.* ShS
As I was out walking for pleasure one day. The Indian Mohee. *Unknown.* BFSS
As I was playing on the green. *Unknown.* WhC
As I was reading the book of nature. The Book of Nature. Richard Eberhart. PoDB
As I was robbing Chelsea Bank. Later Antigonishes. Hughes Mearns. InMe
As I was rumbling through the mountain rift. Reward of Virtue. Arthur Guiterman. InMe
As I was sailing down the coast. The High Barbaree. Laura E. Richards. SoPo
As I was sitting in my chair. The Perfect Reactionary. Hughes Mearns. SiTL; WhC
As I was, so be ye. Epitaph. *Unknown.* TreFS
As I Was Standing in the Street. *Unknown.* SiTL
As I was strolling down a woodland way. Down a Woodland Way. Mildred Howells. AA
As I was travelling one morning in May. The Bachelor's Lay. *Unknown.* OuSiCo
As I was traveling toward the city of satisfactions. The City of Satisfactions. Daniel Hoffman. CoPo
As I was waiting for the bus. Sight Unseen. Kingsley Amis. ErPo; NePoEA-2
As I was wa'kin' all alone. The Wee Wee Man. *Unknown.* *See* As I was walking mine alane.
As I Was Walkin' down Wexford Street, *with music.* *Unknown.* AS
As I was walkin' the jungle round, a-killin' of tigers an' time. A Ballad. Guy Wetmore Carryl. BOHV; InMe; Par
As I was walking. Kore. Robert Creeley. CoPo; NMP; OPoP
As I was walking all alane [*or* alone]. The Twa [*or* Two] Corbies. *Unknown.* AnFE; BaBo (B *vers.*); BoLiVe; BuBa; CBEP; CH; ELP; EnL; EnLi-1; EnLit; EnSB; ESPB; ExPo; FaBoCh; FIW; FosPo; GoTS; GTBS; GTBS-D; GTBS-P; GTBS-W; GTSE; GTSL; HBV; ILP; InP; InPo; LO; LoGBV; NoP; OBB; OBEV; OxBS; PIA; Po; PoAn; SeCePo; SeCeV; ShBV-2; StP; StPo; TOP; ViBoFo (B *vers.*)
As I was walking all alone. The Wee Wee Man. *Unknown.* *See* As I was walking mine alane.
As I was walking down Paradise Street. *See* As I was a-walkin' down Paradise Street.
As I was walking home just now, from seeing. The Departure from Hydra. Kenneth Koch. AmPC; ANYP
As I was walking I met a woman. An Old Air. F. R. Higgins. AnIL
As I was walking in a field of wheat. *Unknown.* OxNR
As I was walking mine alane. Archie o' Cawfield. *Unknown.* *See* As I was a-walking mine alane.
As I was walking [*or* wa'kin' *or* wa'king] mine [*or* all] alane [*or* alone]. The Wee Wee Man. *Unknown.* BaBo; BuBa; CH; ELP; ESPB; FaBoCh; OBB; OTPC (1946 ed.); OxBB
As I was walking one midsummer morning. O Dear O. *Unknown.* ErPo
As I was walking one morning in spring. I Shall Be Married on Monday Morning. *Unknown.* ErPo
As I was walking out one morning, I met a buxom lass. Buxom Lass. *Unknown.* ErPo
As I was walking out upon the road one day. Sacramento, *vers.* III. *Unknown.* ShS
As I was walking up the stair. *See* As I was going up the stair.
As I walking up the street. O Mally's Meek, Mally's Sweet. Burns. GN; HBV; OTPC
As I watched, the animals. An Adventure with a Lady. Donald Hall. TPM
As I watched the unlikely ones at the bar. Dramas of the Rose. James Schevill. FiMAP
As I went a-walking all by the seashore. The Little Mohee. *Unknown.* ABF
As I Went a-Walking down Ratcliffe Highway, 2 *vers.*, *with music.* *Unknown.* ShS
As I Went a-Walking One Fine Summer's Evening, *with music.* *Unknown.* OuSiCo
As I went by a dyer's door. The Dyer. *Unknown.* ChTr; OxNR
As I went down by Hastings Mill I lingered in my going. Hastings Mill. Cicely Fox Smith. HBV; WaKn
As I Went Down by Havre de Grace. Elinor Wylie. HT
As I went down the hill along the wall. Meeting and Passing. Robert Frost. MaPo; OxBA
As I went down the hill I heard. The Voice. Norman Gale. HBV; OHIP
As I went down the village green. Ducks. Norman Ault. BoTP
As I went down the village street. Village Christmas. Margaret Widdemer. RePo
As I went down through Dublin City. Dublin; the Old Squares. Padraic Colum. NePoAm
As I went down to Darby town. The Ram of Darby. *Unknown.* OuSiCo
As I went down to Dymchurch Wall. In Romney Marsh. John Davidson. GoTS; GTBS; GTBS-D; HT; OBVV; POTE; ShBV-3; ViBoPo
As I went down to Rotten Lake I remembered. Rotten Lake Elegy. Muriel Rukeyser. MoPo; NePA
As I went down to the old depot. The Maid Freed from the Gallows (D *vers.*). *Unknown.* ViBoFo
As I went on Yol Day. Jankin, the Clerical Seducer. *Unknown.* MeEL
As I went out a Crow. The Last Word of a Bluebird. Robert Frost. FaPON; GoJo; StVeCh (1955 ed.); ThGo; TiPo
As I Went Out for a Ramble, *with music.* *Unknown.* OuSiCo
As I Went Out on Christmas Day. *Unknown.* CBEP
As I went out one evening. The Mermaid. *Unknown.* OuSiCo
As I went out one morning to breathe the morning air. Lolly Too-Dum. *Unknown.* OuSiCo
As I went out to walk. Country Tune. Elizabeth Riddell. BoAV; NeLNL
As I went over London Bridge. Riddle. *Unknown.* ChTr
As I went over the Far Hill. Beyond Rathkelly. Francis Carlin. HBMV
As I went over the water. *Unknown.* OxNR; SiTL
As I went over Tipple Tyne. Riddle. *Unknown.* ChTr
As I Went Singing over the Earth. Mary Elizabeth Coleridge. UnS
As I went through the [*or* a] garden gap. Mother Goose. BoChLi; HBV; HBVY; OTPC; PPL; RIS
As I went through the marshes. A Doe at Evening. D. H. Lawrence. BrPo
As I went through the tangled wood. The Haughty Aspen. Nora Archibald Smith. ChrBoLe
As I went to Bonner. *Unknown.* OxBoLi; OxNR; SiTL
As I went to Totnam. The Maid of Tottenham. *Unknown.* CoMu
As I went to Walsingham. Francis' New Jig. George Attowell. ReIE
As I went up and he came down, my little six-year boy. The Meeting. Katharine Tynan. BoPe
As I went up by Heartbreak Road. Heartbreak Road. Helen Gray Cone. HBMV
As I went up the Brandy Hill. Brandy Hill. *Unknown.* CBEP; OxNR
As I went up the garden. *Unknown.* BoTP
As I went up to Craigbilly Fair. Craigbilly Fair. *Unknown.* ChTr
"As I went up to London." Going Up to London. Nancy Byrd Turner. GaP; HBMV
As I went walking. Song in Spring. Louis Ginsberg. YeAr
As I went walking one March day. One March Day. *Unknown.* PCH
As I wer readen ov a stwone. The Readen ov a Head-Stwone [*or* The Head-Stone]. William Barnes. CH; HBV; OBVV
As I were a-walking upon a fine day. Because I Were Shy. *Unknown.* StPo
As I'd Nothing Else to Do. Herbert Fry. TreFS
As if a cast of grain leapt back to the hand. An Event. Richard Wilbur. TwAmPo
As if a left-handed god had placed my village. Emigrant's Iconoclasm. Taner Baybars. NyTB
As If Awakened, Summoned. Wordsworth. *Fr.* The Prelude. AtBAP
As If from Her Nest. *Unknown.* *tr. fr. Russian by* Michael Daly. HW
As it it were. Merritt Parkway. Denise Levertov. AmPP (5th ed.); NeAP; ToPo
As if it were a scene made up by the mind. Often I Am Permitted to Return to a Meadow. Robert Duncan. NMP
As if stone Caesar shook. Fragment. Hugh McCrae. BoAV
As if the storme meant him. Why Are Yee Afraid, O Yee of Little

As (continued)
Faith? Richard Crashaw. MaMe
As if the sun had trodden down the sky. Heat. John Gould Fletcher. Down the Mississippi, II. HT; LiTA; NP
As if you could not leave the jug alone! The Broken Jug. William Barnes. PoVP
As I'm sitting all alone in the gloaming. Bantry Bay. James Lyman Molloy. OnYI
As imperceptibly as grief. Emily Dickinson. AP; CMoP; DiPo; ExPo; FaBoEn; ForPo; FosPo; LiTA; LiTM (rev. ed.); NoP; PAn; PIA; PoEL-5; PoFS; QFR
As in a dream of flood from which we rose intact but alone. The Break. E. N. Sargent. NYBP
As in a Dusky and Tempestuous Night. William Drummond of Hawthornden. LO, 4 *ll.*
(Sonnet: "As in a duskie and tempestuous night.") FaBoEn; OBS
As in a porch of stars we stand; the night. The Porch of Stars. Laurence Binyon. LHV
As in a Rose-Jar. Thomas S. Jones, Jr. PoLF
As in a royal army, led by a king. Christ's Coming to Judgment. Thomas Dekker. AnEnPo
As in a Watteau fete of rose and silver blue. The Tempest. Marya Zaturenska. MoAmPo; TrGrPo (1942 ed.)
As in Silks My Julia Goes. Robert Herrick. *See* Upon Julia's Clothes.
As in smooth oil the razor best is whet. Epigram. *Unknown.* HBV
As in some countries, far remote from hence. Idea, L. Michael Drayton. ReIE
As in the age of shepherd king and queen. Dans l'Allée [or The Avenue]. Paul Verlaine. AWP; SyP
As in the cool air'd road I come by. My Love's Guardian Angel. William Barnes. AtBAP; NBM; PoEL-4
As in the gardens, all through May, the rose. His Lady's Tomb. Pierre de Ronsard. *Fr.* Amours de Marie. AWP; JAWP; WBP
As in the greatest of societies. Proemium I. Everard Guilpin. *Fr.* Skialetheia. ReIE; SiCE
As in the house I sate. Poverty. Thomas Traherne. OxBoCh
As in the Midst of Battle There Is Room. George Santayana. Sonnets, XXV. AnFE; APA; AWP; CoAnAm; JAWP; LiTM (1946 ed.); MAP; MoAmPo; NePA; WBP
As in the night I restless lie. An Anodyne. Thomas Ken. OxBoCh
As in the Night We See the Sparks Revived. *Unknown.* ReIE
As in your innocent eyes last night. Birthday Poem, November 4th. John Thompson, Jr. WaP
As inward love breeds outward talk. The Angler's Song. William Basse. OBS; SD
As it befel[l] [*or* itt beffell] in midsummertime. Sir Andrew Barton. *Unknown.* BaBo; EnSB; ESPB; OBB; OxBB; ViBoFo
As it befell on a bright holiday. The Bitter Withy. *Unknown.* ChTr
As it befell upon one time. Hughie Grame. *Unknown.* ESPB
As It Began to Dawn. George Edward Hoffman. ChIP
As it fell. The Camellia. Basho. RePo
As it fell [out] on a holy-day. John Dory. *Unknown.* Buba; ESPB
As it fell one [*or* on one *or* out on a high *or* on a light] holy-day. Little Musgrave and Lady Barnard [*or* Little Mousgrove and the Lady Barnet]. *Unknown.* BaBo (A *vers.*); CABL; ErPo; ESPB; InvP; NoP; OBB; OxBB; ViBoFo
As it fell out on a high holy day. *See* As it fell one holy day.
As it fell out on a holy day. The Bitter Withy. *Unknown.* BaBo; NoP; OAEP; PoIE; ViBoFo
As it fell out on a holy-day. John Dory. *Unknown.* *See* As it fell on a holy-day.
As it fell out on [*or* in] a long summer's day. Fair Margaret and Sweet William. *Unknown.* ESPB; OBB; OxBB; TOP
As it fell out one May morning. The Holy Well. *Unknown.* FaBoCh; LoGBV; OBB; OxBoCh
As it fell out upon a day. Dives [*or* Diverus] and Lazarus [*or* Lazarus]. *Unknown.* ATP; BaBo; ELP; ESPB; FlW; NoP; OBB; OxBB; SaSa
As It Fell upon a Day. Richard Barnfield. *See* Nightingale, The.
As it is true that I, like all, must die. Scene-Shifter Death. Mary Devenport O'Neill. NeIP
As It Looked Then. E. A. Robinson. CMoP; MaPo; NePA
As It Was. Lilla Cabot Perry. Meeting after Long Absence, II. AA
As it/ Were tissue of silver. Fate Defied. Adelaide Crapsey. NP; YT
As it were upon the sea. Under the wind's hand. The Desert Travellers. L. D. Lerner. BoSA
As itt beffell in midsummer-time. *See* As it befel . . .
As Jack walked out of London city, no one on Jack to take pity. Jack the Jolly Tar. *Unknown.* BaBo
As Jock the Leg and the merry merchant. Jock the Leg and the Merry Merchant. *Unknown.* ESPB
As Joe Gould says. E. E. Cummings. FiBHP
As Joseph knocked upon his door. No Room. Dorothy Conant Stroud. STF
As Joseph Was a-Walking [*or* a-Waukin']. *Unknown.* BoTP; DD; OHIP; PCH; PTK; StVeCh; ViBoPo
(Cherry-Tree Carol, The.) ChrBoLe; ThGo
(Christmas Carol.) GN; HBV; HBVY; HH; OTPC
As junco is with winter. Different Winter. Louise Townsend Nicholl. NePoAm-2
As Jupiter's all-seeing eye. The Eagle, and the Assembly of Animals. John Gay. *Fr.* Fables. EiCP
As Kaethe Kollwitz knew. Death Swoops. Kenneth Pitchford. CoPo
As Kingfishers Catch Fire, Dragonflies Draw Flame. Gerard Manley Hopkins. CMoP; DiPo; EaLo; ExPo; FaBoMo; LiTM; MoRP; NoP; PoeP; VP
(What I Do Is Me.) MoAB; MoBrPo
As Lambs into the Pen. Dorothy Wellesley. FaBoTw
As landscapes richen after rain, the eye. Foliage of Vision. James Merrill. MoPo
As late I journey'd o'er the extensive plain. Life. Samuel Taylor Coleridge. EnRP
As late I sought the spangled bowers. Odes of Anacreon, *tr. by* Thomas Moore. OuHeWo
As laurel leaves that cease not to be green. The Promise of a Constant Lover. *Unknown.* ElL; ReIE
As life runs on, the road grows strange. Sixty-eighth Birthday. James Russell Lowell. PoEL-5; StP
As Life What Is So Sweet. *Unknown.* SeCL
As Like the Woman as You Can. W. E. Henley. HBV
As Lise however my mother was white. The Black Man's Son. Oswald Durand. PoNe
As little Jenny Wren/ Was sitting by the shed. *Unknown.* OxNR
As lonely I strayed by the banks of the river. Lost Jimmie Whalen. *Unknown.* BaBo
As long ago we carried to your knees. Mother. Kathleen Norris. PoToHe
As long as I go forth on ships that sail. A Seaman's Confession of Faith. Harry Kemp. TrPWD
As long as I live. Me. Walter de la Mare. BiCB; FaPON; ThGo; TiPo (1959 ed.)
As long as people. On Wearing Ears. William J. Harris. BOLo
As long as the blade has never. Shame. Arthur Rimbaud. SyP
As long as you allowed her complete liberty. The Incentive. Martial. UnTE
As Love is cause of joy. Love. Anthony Munday. *Fr.* Zelanto, the Fountain of Fame. OBSC
As lovers, banished from their lady's face. Before Her Portrait in Youth. Francis Thompson. EPN
As loving hind that (hartless) wants her deer. A [*or* Another] Letter to Her Husband, Absent upon Publick Employment. Anne Bradstreet. CBEP; OxBA; SCAP
As Lucy Went a-Walking. Walter de la Mare. RIS
As mad sexton's bell, tolling. Song on the Water. Thomas Lovell Beddoes. EG; FaBoCh; LoGBV; PoE
As man and his motor have brought it about. Streamlined Stream-Knowledge. Arthur W. Bell. WhC
As many as the leaves fall from the tree. The Golden Apples. William Morris. *Fr.* The Earthly Paradise. EPN
As many, Mother, are your moods and forms. Bernard O'-Dowd. *Fr.* The Bush. PoAu-1
As men, for fear the starres should sleep and nod. Divinitie. George Herbert. MaMe
"As men from men." Despondency Corrected. Wordsworth. *Fr.* The Excursion, IV. EnRP
As men who fight for home and child and wife. Battle of Oriskany. Charles D. Helmer. PAH

As men who see a city fitly planned. Proofs of Buddha's Existence. *Unknown.* WGRP
As my hand dropt a seed. Sowing Seed. Laurence Binyon. POTE
As my lady was in her daisy garden. The Spanish Man. F. R. Higgins. JKCP (1926 ed.)
As near beauteous Boston lying. A New Song. *Unknown.* PAH
As near Porto-Bello lying. Admiral Hosier's Ghost. Richard Glover. HBV; ViBoPo
As newer comers crowd the fore. The Superseded. Thomas Hardy. TOP
As Night Comes On. Cecil Cobb Wesley. GoYe
As night drew on, and, from the crest. The Winter Night. Whittier. *Fr.* Snow-Bound. PTK; TrGrPo; YT
As Ocean's Stream. Feodor Ivanovich Tyutchev, *tr. fr. Russian by* Babette Deutsch *and* Avrahm Yarmolinsky. AWP
As o'er my latest book I pored. Printer's Error. P. G. Wodehouse. FiBHP
As o'er the cold sepulchral stone. Lines Written in an Album at Malta. Byron. InP
As o'er the hill we roam'd at will. Wanderers. Charles Stuart Calverley. CenHV
As Oft as I Behold and See. Earl of Surrey. EP; SiPS
As oft I doe record. *Unknown.* SeCSL
As often as some where before my feet. Francis Daniel Pastorius. SCAP
As on a daye Clorinda fayre was bathinge. *Unknown.* SeCSL
As on a window late I cast mine eye. Love-Joy. George Herbert. MaMe
As on Euphrates shady banks we lay. Paraphrase on the Psalms of David: Psalm CXXXVII. George Sandys. OBS
As on my bed at dawn I mused and prayed. The Lattice at Sunrise. Charles Tennyson Turner. OBVV; Sonn; VA
As on Serena's Panting Breast. *Unknown.* UnTE
As on the bank the poor fish lies. The Restless Heart. *Unknown.* WGRP
As on the gauzy wings of fancy flying. Oliver Wendell Holmes. *Fr.* The Iron Gate. AA
As on the Heather. Reinmar von Hagenau, *tr. fr. German by* Jethro Bithell. AWP
As on the hedge they danced one night. Wild Marjorie. "Jean Lorrain." CAW
As once grave Pluto drove his royal wheels. Proserpine's Ragout. Mary Leapor. WaPE
"As once Hippolytus from Athens fled." Paradise. Dante. *Fr.* Divina Commedia. EnLi-1
As once I played beside the sea. The Tides. Thomas Tapper. GFA
As once, if not with light regard. Ode on the Poetical Character. William Collins. CEP; EiCL; EiCP; EiPP; EnPE; EnRP; ERoP-1; OAEP; PeER; PoEL-3; PoFS; StP
As once in black I disrespected walked. On a Maid of Honour Seen by a Scholar in Somerset Garden. Thomas Randolph. EP
As one advances up the slow ascent. Solitude. Philip Henry Savage. AA
As one, at midnight, wakened by the call. Prelude. W. W. Gibson. MoBrPo
As one by one the singers of our land. The Succession. Frances Laughton Mace. AA
As one dark morn I trod a forest glade. The Forest Glade. Charles Tennyson Turner. VA
As One Finding Peace. Sister Mary Madeleva. JKCP
As One Finding Peace. Sister Mary of the Visitation. JKCP (1926 ed.)
As one of the curious gatherers. Party Line. Joseph Joel Keith. FiSC
As one put drunk into the packet-boat. Tom May's Death. Andrew Marvell. MaMe
As one sees on the branch in the month of May the rose. Roses. Pierre de Ronsard. LiTW
As one that for a a weary space has lain. The Odyssey. Andrew Lang. GTBS-D; HBV; InP; LoBV; OBEV; OBNC; OBVV; OtMeF; PoLF; PoRA; PoVP; TOP; VA; ViBoPo; WHA; YT
As one that strives, being sick, and sick to death. To Celia, upon Love's Ubiquity. Thomas Carew. AnAnS-2
As one who after long and far-spent years. Sonnet to Hampstead. Leigh Hunt. Sonn
As One Who Bears beneath His Neighbor's Roof. Robert Hillyer. MAP; MoAmPo
As one who came with ointments sweet. Spikenard. Laurence Housman. TrPWD
As one who cleaves the circumambient air. Timon of Archimedes. Charles Battell Loomis. NA
As one who cons at evening o'er an album all alone. An Old Sweetheart of Mine. James Whitcomb Riley. BLPA; TreFS
As one who follows a departing friend. Last Days. Elizabeth Stoddard. AA; AnAmPo
As one who hangs down-bending from the side. A Dedicated Spirit. Wordsworth. *Fr.* The Prelude. SeCePo
As one who has sailed across an unknown sea. The Solitary. Rainer Maria Rilke. TrJP
As one held herself apart. Sister. Whittier. *Fr.* Snow-bound. AA
As one who, long by wasting sickness worn. Hope. William Lisle Bowles. EnRP
As one who long hath fled with panting breath. Victor and Vanquished. Longfellow. CoBA
As one who, long in populous city pent. Satan Beholds Eve. Milton. *Fr.* Paradise Lost, IX. PoFS
As one who, long in thickets and in brakes. The Garden. William Cowper. The Task, III. CEP; EiCL; EiPP; EnPE
As one who strives from some fast steamer's side. O. M. B. Ford Madox Brown. VA
As one who, walking in the twilight gloom. Dedication. Longfellow. *Fr.* The Seaside and the Fireside. MAmP; MWA-1
As one who walks and weeps by alien brine. Frederick Goddard Tuckerman. *Fr.* Sonnets. AmePo
As one who walks in sleep, up a familiar lane. The Road. John Gould Fletcher. HBMV; TSW
As One Who Wanders into Old Workings. C. Day Lewis. FaBoMo; LiTM (rev. ed.)
As one whose country is distraught with war. Conflict. Caroline Clive. OBVV
As one would stand who saw a sudden light. Love's Outset. Sir Gilbert Parker. *Fr.* A Lover's Diary. VA
As other men, so I myself do muse. Idea, IX. Michael Drayton. EnLi-1 (1949 ed.); ReEn; SiCE; Sonn; TuPP
As Others See Us. Burns. *Fr.* To a Louse. MaRV
As our king lay musing on his bed. King Henry Fifth's Conquest of France. *Unknown.* BaBo (A *vers.*); ESPB
As over muddy shores a dragon flock. The Fear. Lascelles Abercrombie. OBMV
As over the swelling ocean's tide. On the Banishment of Cicero. Philip Wharton. WaPE
As Oyster Nan Stood by Her Tub. *Unknown.* CoMu
As patience paints the flower red, so grass. And Grow. John Hay. WaP
As pilot well expert in perilous wave. The Cave of Mammon. Spenser. *Fr.* The Faerie Queene, II. PoEL-1
As pools beneath stone arches take. Invocation. John Drinkwater. HBMV; NP
As power and wit will me assist. Sir Thomas Wyatt. FCP; SiPS
As proude Bayard ginneth for to skip. Chaucer. *Fr.* Troilus and Criseyde, I. MyFE
As Pure Water. *Unknown, tr. fr. Sanskrit by* Joseph Nadin Rawson. *Fr.* The Upanishads. OnPM
As rays around the source of light. St. Stephen's Day. John Keble. CoBE
As rising from the vegetable World. James Thomson. *Fr.* The Seasons: Spring. PoEL-3
As Rivers of Water in a Dry Place. Anna Bunston de Bary. HBMV
As Rochefoucault [*or* Rochefaucauld] his maxims drew. Verses on [*or* On] the Death of Dr. Swift. Swift. CABL; CEP; CoBE; EiCL; EiCP; EiPP; LoBV; MasP; MBW-1; PoEL-3; PoFS
As rock to sun or storm. Poem. Niall Sheridan. OnYI
As round as an apple, as deep as a cup. Mother Goose. OxNR; PPL; StVeCh (1940 ed.); TiPo
As round the pine-clad top of Morna's hill. A Distant Prospect of the City of Armagh. James Stuart. *Fr.* Morna's Hill. IrPN
As sea-foam blown of the winds, as blossom of brine that is drifted. Home, Sweet Home, with Variations, II. H. C. Bunner. BOHV; CenHV; InMe

As Severn Lately in her ebbs that sank. The Severn. Michael Drayton. *Fr.* The Baron's War, I. ChTr
As shadows cast by cloud and sun. Christmas [*or* The Holy Star]. Bryant. BePJ; ChIP; MaRV; SoP
As Shakespeare couldn't write his plays. By Deputy. Arthur St. John Adcock. CenHV
As She Feared It Would Be. Lilla Cabot Perry. Meeting after Long Absence, I. AA
As shepherd and shepherdess, how many summers had we. Out of That Sea. David Ferry. NePoAm-2
As shining sand-drift. An Epitaph. Lady Margaret Sackville. HBMV
As ships, becalmed at eve, that lay. Qua Cursum Ventus. Arthur Hugh Clough. BEL; EnLi-2; EnLit; EPN; ETS; GTBS; HBV; OAEP; OBEV (new ed.); OBVV; PoIE; PoVP; TOP; TreFT; VA; ViPo; ViPP
As sickly plants betray a niggard earth. The Alliance of Education and Government. Thomas Gray. CEP
As silent as a mirror is believed. Legend. Hart Crane. CABA; InPo; MoVE; OxBA; SyP; TwAmPo
As simple an act. Way Out West. LeRoi Jones. NeAP; NMP
As sinewy as biltong, as narrow. My Grandmother. Perseus Adams. PeSA
As Sir Launfal made morn through the darksome gate. Sir Launfal and the Leper. James Russell Lowell. *Fr.* The Vision of Sir Launfal, Pt. I. GN; OTPC
As slow I climb the cliff's ascending side. At Tynemouth Priory, after a Tempestuous Voyage. William Lisle Bowles. Sonn
As slow our ship her foamy track. The Journey Onwards. Thomas Moore. GTBS; GTBS-D; GTBS-P; GTBS-W; GTSE; GTSL; HBV; SeCePo
As soft as silk, as white as milk. Mother Goose. HBV; HBVY; OTPC (1946 ed.); OxNR; PPL
As solid as it is, yet gold may fail. God's Gift. Enola Chamberlin. SoP
As some brave admiral, in former war. The Maimed [*or* Maim'd] Debauchee [*or* Satire]. Earl of Rochester. CABA; CBEP; EiCL; EP; NCEP; PeRV; PoEL-3; UnPo (3d ed.)
As some day it may happen that a victim must be found. Ko-Ko's Song [*or* They'll None of 'em Be Missed]. W. S. Gilbert. *Fr.* The Mikado. EnLi-2 (1949 ed.); LiTB; PoVP; SiTL
As some fond virgin, whom her mother's care. Epistle to Miss Blount [*or* To a Young Lady], on Her Leaving the Town, after the Coronation. Pope. BWP; CaFP; CBV; CEP; DiPo; ExPo; MBW-1; OBEC; PoEL-3; SeCeV; WePo
As some lone miser visiting his store. Real Happiness. Goldsmith. *Fr.* The Traveller. OBEC
As some men say there is a kind of seed. George Gascoigne. *Fr.* The Adventures of Master F. I. ReIE
As Some Mysterious Wanderer of the Skies. Henry Jerome Stockard. AA
As some true chief of men, bowed down with stress. The Sun's Shame, 2. Dante Gabriel Rossetti. The House of Life, XCIII. MaVP; PoVP; ViPo
As sometimes in a dead man's face. In Memoriam A. H. H., LXXIV. Tennyson. EPN; LiTB; LiTG; ViPo; VP
As sometimes with a sable cloud. The First Meeting. Lord Herbert of Cherbury. AnAnS-2
As soon/ As a squirrel. Song for Thrift Week. Mildred Weston. WhC
As soon as/ I speak, I. The Pattern. Robert Creeley. FRC
As Soon as Ever Twilight Comes. Walter de la Mare. SiSoSe
As Soon As He Learned. Dan Georgakas. ThO
As soon as I saw before me the sons of Huyayy. Bragging Song. *Unknown.* LiTW
As soon as I'm in bed at night. Mrs. Brown. Rose Fyleman. BoTP; GaP; TiPo
As soon as night comes my demon springs up out of the ground. Magdalene. Boris Pasternak. MoRP
As soon as the fire burns red and low. The Sleepy Song. Josephine Daskam Bacon. OTPC (1946 ed.); PCH; PPL; StVeCh; SUS; UTS
As soon as the idea of the Flood had abated. After the Flood. Arthur Rimbaud, *tr. by* Helen Rootham. BoW
As supple as a tiger's skin. The Prayer Rug. Sara Beaumont Kennedy. HBMV
As sure as we have a fatherland. Fellow-Citizens. Verner von Heidenstam. PoPl
As Sylvia in her garden strayed. Sylvia and the Bee. Mary Leapor. WaPE
As tapering pines, still stately watchers. Suspense. William J. Grace. JKCP (1955 ed.)
As Tate grows old some child will fondle him. From Gestures to the Dead. John Wheelwright. MoVE
As the bee through the garden ranges. God. Emerson. *Fr.* Woodnotes, II. OQP
As the black storm upon the mountain top. Residence in London [*or* The Blind Beggar]. Wordsworth. *Fr.* The Prelude, VII. ERoP-1; PoEL-4
As the bow unto the cord is. Longfellow. *Fr.* The Song of Hiawatha. TRV
As the brown mowers strode across the field. The Swathe Uncut. John Hewitt. NeIP
As the cat/ climbed over. Poem. William Carlos Williams. CABA; FaPON; InvP; LOW; NoP; PDV; PoAn; ThWaDe
As the chafed hart which brayeth. Psalm XLII. *Paraphrased by* Sir Philip Sidney. FCP
As the child knows not if his mother's face. From Dawn to Noon. Dante Gabriel Rossetti. The House of Life, LXXX. MaVP; PoVP; ViPo
As the clouds that are so light. The Clouds That Are So Light. Edward Thomas. FaBoTw
As the coin of her ear-ring. June Song of a Man Who Looks Two Ways. Leslie Daiken. NeIP
As the Crow Flies, *sel.* Samuel Hoffenstein.
"How much we pay to say, *Je suis.*" WhC
As the Day Breaks. Ernest McGaffey. AA
As the days grow longer. Mother Goose. PPL
As the Dead Prey upon Us. Charles Olson. NeAP
As the deep blue of heaven brightens into stars. God's Promises. *Unknown.* BLRP
As the flight of a river. Absent yet Present. Sir Edward Bulwer-Lytton. OBVV; UnPo
As the gods began one world, and man another. Snakecharmer. Sylvia Plath. NePoEA-2; PP
As the golden grass burns out. September Evening, 1938. William Plomer. SeCePo
As the hand moves over the harp, and the strings speak. Inspiration. *Unknown.* *Fr.* Solomon. WGRP
As the hart panteth after the water brooks. Psalm XLII, Bible, *O.T.* AWP; BoC; JAWP; TrGrPo; TrJP; TRV; WGRP; WoL
As the Holly Groweth Green. Henry VIII, King of England. *See* Green Groweth the Holly.
As the image of the sun. Estuary. Ted Walker. NYBP
As the immense dew of Florida. Nomad Exquisite. Wallace Stevens. AtBAP
As the inhastening tide doth roll. The Visiting Sea. Alice Meynell. BoPe
As the insect from the rock. The Making of Man. John White Chadwick. AA
As the kindling glances. The Voice. Matthew Arnold. ViPP
As the leading agronomist. Plant Poems. Edward Field. FRC
As the Liberty lads o'er the sea. Song for the Luddites. Byron. PoFr
As the marsh-hen secretly builds on the watery sod. Sidney Lanier. *Fr.* The Marshes of Glynn. FaChP; MaRV; OQP
As the moon sinks on the mountain-edge. Far beyond Us. *Unknown.* OnPM
As the mute nightingale in closest groves. The Nightingale [*or* To the Blessed Virgin Mary]. Gerald Griffin. CAW; JKCP; OnYI
As the Old Year seeks the shadows. New Year Prayer. Edgar Daniel Kramer. PEDC
As the poem drifts under the cry of the sea. Adriatic. Robert Conquest. PP
As the proud horse with costly trappings gay. Shortening Sail. William Falconer. *Fr.* The Shipwreck, II. EtS
As the rain falls. Rain. William Carlos Williams. AP; CoBMV
As the Sculptor. Toyohiko Kagawa, *tr. fr. Japanese.* OQP
As the sin that was sweet in the sinning. The Poets at Tea, 3. Barry Pain. Par
As the skull of man grows broader. Don Marquis. *Fr.* The God-Maker, Man. OQP
As the slanting sun drowsed lazily. Cape Coloured Batman. Guy Butler. BoSA; PeSA
As the soft yield of water cleaves obstinate stone. Lesson of Wa-

ter. *Unknown, at. to* Lao-tzu. *Fr.* Tao Teh King. OnPM
As the stars go out so let me go. Wilson MacDonald. *Fr.* The Last Portage. MaRV
As the stars hide in the light before daybreak. Avoiding News by the River. W. S. Merwin. NaP
As the starved maelstrom laps the navies. Emily Dickinson. MWA-2
As the sun rose. Pigeons Just Awake. Hilda Conkling. YT
As the sunbeams stream through liberal space. Emerson. *Fr.* Woodnotes, II. OHIP
As the sweet sweat of roses in a still. The Comparison. John Donne. Elegies, VIII. ErPo; MaMe
As the Team's Head-Brass. Edward Thomas. ExPo; GTBS-P; MMA
As the through-train of words with white-hot whistle. Express. W. R. Rodgers. MoVE
As the transatlantic tourists. The Doves of Venice. Laurence Hutton. AA
As the trees shake off their leaves and lift their branches to heaven. A Thanksgiving Psalm. *Unknown.* SoP
As the Twig Is Bent. Pope. *Fr.* Moral Essays, Epistle I. TreF
As the used anger drips from his hands like blood. The Murderer. Paul Petrie. NYBP
As the war-trumpet drowns the rustic flute. Pindar. Antipater of Sidon. AWP
As the weeders went trimming the corn young and green. The Legend of Babe Jesus and the Weeders. *Unknown.* ChrBoLe
As the wind at play with a spark. Louisa May Alcott. Louise Chandler Moulton. AA
As the wise men of old brought gifts. The Gift. William Carlos Williams. MoRP; NePoAm-2; PoPl
As the words dissolve from the fading page. The Moths. William H. Matchett. WIRo
As the World Turns. Swift. OTPC (1946 ed.); RIS
As the years go by, give me but peace. Answering Vice-Prefect Chang. Wang Wei. OuHeWo
As the young phoenix, duteous to his sire. Renewal. "Michael Field." OBVV
As there, along the elmy hedge, I go. Troubles of the Day. William Barnes. GTBS-P
As there I left the road in May. The Surprise. William Barnes. PoVP
As there is music uninform'd by art. To My Honor'd Friend Sir Robert Howard, on His Excellent Poems. Dryden. EiPP
As they came in by the Eden side. The Slaughter of the Laird of Mellerstain. *Unknown.* ESPB
As they join their various voices. The Birds. Blossius Aemilius Dracontius. CAW
As they sat sipping their glasses in the courtyard. Dinner at the Hotel de la Tigresse Verte. Donald Evans. AnAmPo
As things be/come. Word Poem (Perhaps Worth Considering). Nikki Giovanni. BOLo
As this comes in/ Call you. The Lute in the Attic. Kenneth Patchen. OnHM
As Thomas was cudgelled one day by his wife. Abroad and at Home [*or* Epigram]. Swift. WePo; WhC
As those of old drank mummia. Mummia. Rupert Brooke. BrPo
As those we love decay, we die in part. Verses Occasioned by the Death of Dr. Aikman [*or* On the Death of a Particular Friend]. James Thomson. OBEC; OBEV
As those who are not athletic at breakfast day by day. Nature Morte. Louis MacNeice. CMoP
As though an aged person were to wear. Elegy for the Monastery Barn. Thomas Merton. CoPo
As though he could hold all in consciousness. Elegy against a Latter Day. Kendrick Smithyman. AnNZ
As though the streets were all downhill. Evangel. Jean Burden. NYTB
As threads spilling dew-drops. The Dolphins. Hamish Maclaren. EtS
As thro' [*or* through] the Land at Eve We Went. Tennyson. *Fr.* The Princess, Pt. I. AnFE; AtBAP; GTBS; GTBS-W; LiTB; LiTG; LiTL; MaRV; OBVV; PoVP; TreFS; VA
(Reconciliation, The.) HBV
(Songs from "The Princess.") OAEP; ViPo
(We Kiss'd Again with Tears.) PoToHe
As through the palms ye wander. The Lullaby. Lope de Vega. CAW
As through the void we went I heard his plumes. The Doors. Lloyd Mufflin. AA
As through the wild green hills of Wyre. A. E. Housman. A Shropshire Lad, XXXVII. PoVP
As thus I stand beside the murmuring stream. Corston. Robert Southey. Sonn
As thus the snows arise, and foul and fierce. The Lost Shepherd. James Thomson. *Fr.* The Seasons: Winter. CoBE; SeCePo
"As thy day thy strength shall be!" Daily Strength. Frances Ridley Havergal. SoP
As Thy Days. Grant Colfax Tullar. BLRP
As Thy Days So Shall Thy Strength Be. "George Klingle." BLRP; TRV
As thy friend's face, with shadow of soul o'erspread. Life the Beloved. Dante Gabriel Rossetti. The House of Life, XCVI. MaVP; PoVP; ViPo
As Time One Day by Me Did Pass. Henry Vaughan. AnAnS-1; MeLP; MeP; SCEP-1; SeCV-1
As to a bird's song she were listening. Deaf. H. C. Bunner. AA
As to a sacrament/ Quiet I go. Love's Language. Donagh MacDonagh. NeIP
As to Being Alone. James Oppenheim. PoMa; TrJP
As to democracy, fellow-citizens. John Hancock Otis. Edgar Lee Masters. *Fr.* Spoon River Anthology. PoFr; TOP
As to His Choice of Her. Wilfrid Scawen Blunt. *See* To Manon, as to His Choice of Her.
As to kidnap the Congress has long been my aim. General Howe's Letter. *Unknown.* PAH
As to marshals and statesmen, and all their whole lineage. French Cookery. Thomas Moore. *Fr.* The Fudge Family in Paris. OBRV
As to naps. Perambulator Poems, VI. David McCord. WhC
As to that poet (if so great a one as he). A Letter from the Country to a Friend in Town. John Oldham. PP
As to the blooming prime. To Favonius. Edmund Bolton. OBSC
As to the lanes I took my way. Summer Morning. Jean Ingelow. ThGo
As to the seer in ancient time. A Prayer for Teachers. Marguerite Emilio. OQP
As to the Weather. *Unknown.* BOHV
As Toilsome I Wander'd [*or* Wandered] Virginia's Woods. Walt Whitman. AmePo; AmPP (3d ed.); HBV; InP; LO; MaPo (1969 ed.); PCD; SeCeV; ViBoPo
As Tom and his wife were discoursing one day. Too Candid by Half. John Godfrey Saxe. HBV
As Tom the Porter went up Ludgate-Hill. Tom the Porter. John Byrom. CEP
As Tommy Snooks and Bessy [*or* Bessie] Brooks. Mother Goose. BoChLi; HBV; HBVY; OTPC; OxNR; PCH; PPL, *sl. diff.*; RIS, *sl. diff.*
As trails a sadly wounded deer the hound. The Quarry. Juan Boscán. LiTW
As travellours when the twilight's come. The Pilgrimage. Henry Vaughan. AnAnS-1; MeP; NCEP
As treading some long corridor. My Soul and I. Charles Buxton Going. MaRV
As Troylus did rejoice. To His Friend Riding to Londonward. George Turberville. ReIE
As true as I was born into. Halfway. Maxine W. Kumin. GoYe
As True as Thy Faith, This Riddle Thus Saith. Thomas Tusser. *See* Praise of Husbandry, The.
As tuned harp-strings sad noates take. *Unknown.* SeCSL
As Turpin was riding across the moor. Dick Turpin and the Lawyer. *Unknown.* ViBoFo
As twilight fell. I Saw a Ghost. Joan Boilleau. TiPo
As two men were a-walking, down by the sea-side. The Duke of Grafton. *Unknown.* ChTr
As two whose love, first foolish, widening scope. Known in Vain. Dante Gabriel Rossetti. The House of Life, LXV. EnLi-2; MaVP; PoVP; ViPo
As unto Francis poverty. Brother Juniper. Blanche Mary Kelly. GoBC; JKCP
As unto heaven thou'rt soaring. At the Assumption. Luis de León. CAW
"As unto the bow the cord is." Hiawatha's Wooing. Longfel-

As (continued)
low. *Fr.* The Song of Hiawatha. BeLS; TreFS
As up by Kennetside I rode. An Old Thought. Maurice Hewlett. *Fr.* The Song of the Plow. PoFr
As usual, Election Day/ approaches us. A Way of Judging Politics. Lou Lipsitz. YAP
As Venus from her mother's bosom rose. Apelles the Painter. Leonidas of Tarentum. OnPM
As Vesta was from Latmos Hill descending. *Unknown.* OAEP
As virtuous men pass [*or* passe] mildly away. A Valediction Forbidding Mourning. John Donne. AnAnS-1; BWP; CABA; CaFP; CBV; CoBE; DiPo; EnL; EnLi-1; EnLit; EnRePo; ExPo; FaBoEn; FaPL; ForPo; HoPM; ILP; LiTB; MaMe; MaPo; MasP; MBW-1; MeLP; MeP; MePo; NoP; OAEP; OBS; PAn; PIA; Po; PoAn; PoEL-2; PoeP; PoFS; PoIE; ReEn; ReIE; SCEP-1; SeCeV; SeCP; SeCV-1; SeEP; TDP; TreFT; TuPP; UnPo; VaPo
As vonce I valked by a dismal swamp. The Old Cove. Henry Howard Brownell. PAH
As warm north rain breaks over suburb houses. Rocket Show. James K. Baxter. AnNZ
As water rained upon a height. As Pure Water. *Unknown. Fr.* The Upanishads. OnPM
As We Are So Wonderfully Done with Each Other. Kenneth Patchen. ErPo
As we come marching, marching, in the beauty of the day. Bread and Roses. James Oppenheim. OQP
As We Dance Round. *Unknown.* CH; HH
As we entered by that door. Dirge of the Lone Woman. Mary M. Colum. AnIV
As we get older we do not get any younger. Chard Whitlow. Henry Reed. DTC; FiBHP; LiTM (rev. ed.); ML; MoBrPo (1962 ed.); OnHM; Par; SiTL
As We Grow Older. Rollin J. Wells. PoToHe
(Growing Old.) TreFT; WBLP
(Growing Older.) BLPA
As we hammer out iron we shall hammer out new days. Tomorrow. Regino Pedroso. PoFr
As we lay musing in our beds. The Mermaid. *Unknown.* BaBo; ESPB
As we passed northward along the oiled ribbon leading out of Gallup. The Lightning. Myron H. Broomell. CBV
As We Pray. John Keble. *Fr.* Oh, Timely Happy, Timely Wise. MaRV; SoP
(Help Us to Live.) TRV
As we rowed from our ships and set foot on the shore. The Savages. Josephine Miles. FiMAP; LiTM (1970 ed.)
As We Rush, as We Rush in the Train. James Thomson. Sunday at Hampstead, X. GTBS; GTBS-W; LiTG; PoVP; ViBoPo
(In the Train.) BoTP; OBEV; PCD
As we sailed down the Chyannel of old Engeland. Let Go the Reef Tackle. *Unknown.* ShS
As we sailed on the water blue. Whisky Johnny. *Unknown.* ABF; AS
As we the withered ferns. Ballade of Dead Friends. E. A. Robinson. AA
As we wax older on this earth. "The Things That Are More Excellent." Sir William Watson. OHFP
As Weary Pilgrim, Now at Rest. Anne Bradstreet. AnNE; PoEL-3; SCAP
(Longing for Heaven.) AnFE; APA; CoAnAm; LiTA
As Well As Can Be Expected. W. H. Auden. *See* Taller Today, We Remember.
As wet as a fish—as dry as a bone. Similies [*or* Comparisons]. *Unknown.* BOHV; GoTP; HBVY
As, when a beauteous nymph decays. Stella's Birthday. Swift. PP
As when a child on some long winter's night. Charles Lamb. Sonn
As, when a lofty pile is raised. To Stella. Swift. EiCP
As when a maide, taught from her mother's wing. Practising the Virginals. William Browne. MuSP
As when a man, that sails in a balloon. Tennyson. *Fr.* A Dream of Fair Women. ChER; OBRV; RoGo
As when a scout. New Worlds. Milton. *Fr.* Paradise Lost, III. OBS
As when a stone is dropped in water, the harmonies of the universe. Buddha. Theodore Holmes. CoPo
As when a tree's cut down, the secret root. Prologue to "The Tempest." Dryden. EiPP; EnL; MBW-1; NoP; PoE
As when a vulture on Imaus bred. Milton. *Fr.* Paradise Lost, III. HoPM
As when a wretch (who conscious of his crime). Priam and Achilles. Homer, *tr. by.* Pope. *Fr.* The Iliad, XXIV. OBEC
As when desire, long darkling, dawns, and first. Bridal Birth. Dante Gabriel Rossetti. The House of Life, II. MaVP; OAEP; PoVP; Sonn; ViPo; VP
". . . As When Emotion Too Far Exceeds Its Cause." G. C. Oden. AmNP; Kal
As when far off the warbled strains are heard. La Fayette. Samuel Taylor Coleridge. EnRP; Sonn
As when, of amorous night uncertain birth. A Summer Storm. Charles Whitehead. OBRV
As when one layeth/ His worn-out robes away. Death. *Unknown. Fr.* Bhagavad-Gita. MaRV
As when some dire usurper Heav'n provides. The Fire of London. Dryden. *Fr.* Annus Mirabilis. ChTr
As when some skilful cook, to please each guest. On a Miscellany of Poems to Bernard Lintott. John Gay. CEP; EiCL; EiPP
As when the bright cerulean firmament. Gulling Sonnets, II. Sir John Davies. Sonn
As when the moon hath comforted the night. George Chapman. *Fr.* The Conspiracy of Charles, Duke of Byron. ViBoPo
As when the scepter dangles from the hand. George Santayana. Sonnets, XLII. ATP
As when the sun new-risen. Lucifer. Milton. *Fr.* Paradise Lost, I. UnPo (1st ed.)
As when two men have loved a woman well. Lost on Both Sides. Dante Gabriel Rossetti. The House of Life, XCI. GTSL; MaVP; NoP; PoVP; SeCePo; ViPo; ViPP
As when, upon a trancèd summer-night. Keats. *Fr.* Hyperion, I. ViBoPo
As wildly ranged the tea-imbibing throng. Afternoon Tea. Arthur Guiterman. TOP
As William walking with his wife was seen. A Fair Exchange. La Fontaine. UnTE
As, with enforced yet unreluctant pace. The Social Future. John Kells Ingram. OnYI
As with Gladness Men of Old. William Chatterton Dix. MaRV; SoP
As with My Hat. Samuel Johnson. LBN
As with varnish red and glistening. Casualty. W. E. Henley. *Fr.* In Hospital. PoVP
As withereth the primrose by the river. A Palinode. Edmund Bolton. EIL; InvP; OBSC; PoEL-2; SiCE; TuPP
As Wulfstan said on another occasion. Speech for the Repeal of the McCarran Act. Richard Wilbur. CMoP; NePoAm
As Ye Came from the Holy Land. *Unknown, sometimes at. to* Sir Walter Ralegh. *See* As You Came from the Holy Land.
As Ye Do It unto These. *Unknown.* ChIP; SoP
As ye go through those palm-trees. A Song of the Virgin Mother. Lope de Vega, *tr. by* Ezra Pound. AWP; JAWP; LiTW; WBP
As ye see, a mountaine lion fare. Sarpedon's Speech. Homer, *tr. by* Chapman. *Fr.* The Iliad, XII. OBS
As years do grow, so cares increase. To Mistress Anne Cecil, upon Making Her a New Year's Gift. William Cecil, Lord Burghley. *See* Lamp, The. EIL; OBSC; PrWP
As You [*or* Ye] Came from the Holy Land. *Unknown, sometimes at. to* Sir Walter Ralegh. AtBAP; ChTr; EG; EIL; EnLoPo; FCP; LiTL; LoBV; NoP; OBEV; PG; PoEL-2; PoSa; ReEn; ReIE; SiCE; TrGrPo; TuPP; ViBoPo
(Holy Land of Walsinghame, The.) EnSB
(Lover's Complaint, A.) FaBoEn
(Walsinghame.) CBEP; FaBoCh; FosPo; LiTB; LoGBV; OBSC; SeCeV; UnPo (1st ed.)
As you drank deep as Thor, did you think of milk or wine? Fish Food. John Wheelwright. AnFE; CoAnAm; LiTA; TwAmPo
"As you go down to yondos town." Rosemary and Thyme. *Unknown.* BFSS
"As you go into yonders town." The Cambric Shirt (A *vers.*). *Unknown.* BFSS
As you know, the kangaroo. Advices from Rexroth's Bestiary. Kenneth Rexroth. *Fr.* A Bestiary. SiTL
As you lay in sleep. Cartography. Louise Bogan. PoPl
As You Leave Me. Etheridge Knight. BP
As You Leave the Room. Wallace Stevens. AP

As You Like It, *sels.* Shakespeare.
All the World's a Stage, *fr.* II, vii. DiPo; FiP; GoTP; LiTB; LiTG; MasP; PoLF; PoSa; TIHL; TrGrPo; YAT
(Seven Ages of Man, The.) FaFP; GTBS-W; OQP; PoPo; PTK; TreF
Blow, Blow, Thou Winter Wind, *fr.* II, vii. AnFE; ATP (1935 ed.); BEL; BoLiVe; CBEP; CH; ChTr; CoBE; DiPo; EG; ElL; ELP; EnLi-1 (1949 ed.); EnLit; EnRePo; FaFP; GTBS; GTBS-D; GTBS-P; GTBS-W; GTSE; GTSL; HBV; ILP; InPo; LiTB; LiTG; LO; MaPo; MCCG; NoP; OAEP; OBEV; OBSC; OQP; OTPC; OuHeWo; PG (1945 ed.); PIA; PoEL-2; PoIE; PoPo; PTK; RG; SeCeV; ShBV-1; SiCE; TOP; UnPo (1st ed.); ViBoPo; WaKn; WePo; WHA; WiR
(Blow, Thou Winter Wind.) TreF
(Ingratitude.) BBV
(Song: "Blow, Blow, Thou Winter Wind.") CBV; CTC; FiP
(Songs from the Plays.) AWP; JAWP; WBP
(Songs of the Greenwood.) TrGrPo
(Two Songs by Amiens, 1.) BoLiVe
"Come apace, good Audrey. I will fetch up your goats, Audrey," *fr.* III, iii. PP
"Good shepherd, tell this youth what 'tis to love," *abr., fr.* V, ii. LO
High Wedlock Then Be Honoured, *fr.* V, iv. HW
If It Do Come to Pass, *fr.* II, v. ViBoPo
It Was a Lover and His Lass, *fr.* V, iii. BEL; CBEP; CH; CLwM; EG; ElL; ELP; EnL; EnLi-1; EnLit; ExPo; GTBS; GTBS-D; GTBS-P; GTBS-W; GTSE; GTSL; HBV; InPo; LiTB; LiTG; LiTL; LO; LoBV; NoP; OBEV; PIA; PoRA; ShBV-1; SiCE; SiTL; TOP; UnTE; ViBoPo
(Country Song.) TrGrPo
(In the Spring-Time.) MeWo
(Lover in Spring-Time.) MCCG
(Pages' Song, The.) OBSC; SeCePo
(Song: "It was a lover and his lass.") CTC; FiP; YAT
(Song of the Two Pages.) BoLiVe
(Songs from the Plays.) AWP; JAWP; WBP
Motley's the Only Wear, II, vii. TrGrPo
(Worthy Fool, A.) TreFT
Orlando's Rhymes, *fr.* III, ii. OBSC
Song: "If the scorn of your bright eyne," *fr.* IV, iii. CTC
Under the Greenwood Tree, *fr.* II, v. AnFE; BBV (1923 ed.); BEL; BoNaP; BoTP; CBEP; CH; EG; ElL; ELP; EnLi-1; EnLit; EnRePo; ExPo; FaBoBe; FaFP; FaPON; GBV; GN; GTBS; GTBS-D; GTBS-P; GTBS-W; GTSE; GTSL; HoPM; InPo; LiTB; LiTG; MCCG; MPB; NoP; OAEP; OBEV; OBSC; OHIP; OTPC; OuHeWo; PCH; PoeP; PTK; RG; SeCeV; ShBV-2; SiCE; TiPo; TOP; TreFS; ViBoPo; WHA; WiR; WoL
(Greenwood Tree, The.) RIS
(In the Greenwood.) AnEnPo
(Song: "Under the greenwood tree.") CTC; FiP MemP
(Songs from the Plays.) AWP; JAWP; WBP
(Songs of the Greenwood.) TrGrPo
(Two Songs by Amiens, 2.) BoLiVe
Uses of Adversity, The, *fr.* II, i. LiTB; TreFS; TrGrPo
(Banished Duke [Living in the Forest] Speaks to His Retainers, The.) LiTG
(Good in Everything, *much abr.*) PoToHe
(Sweet Are the Uses of Adversity, 6 *ll.*) MaRV
Wedding Is Great Juno's Crown, *fr.* V, iv. ViBoPo
What Shall He Have That Kill'd the Deer? *fr.* IV, ii. OBSC; ViBoPo
(Song: "What shall he have that kill'd the deer?") CTC
Why Should This a Desert Be, *fr.* III, ii. CTC
Worthy Fool, A, *fr.* II, vii. TreFT
(Motley's the Only Wear.) TrGrPo
As you love me, let there be. A Dieu! and Au Revoir. John Oxenham. MaRV
As you read, a white bear leisurely. To the Reader. Denise Levertov. AmPP (5th ed.); CoPo
As You Say; an Anti-Poem. Karl Shapiro. *Fr.* The Bourgeois Poet. CaFP
"As you say (not without sadness), poets don't see, they feel." PP
As you were out a-riding. The Balloon Man. ——Morton. GFA
Ascendancy. Herbert A. Simmons. NBP
Ascension, The. Joseph Beaumont. OxBoCh
Ascension. John Donne. *See* Ascention.
Ascension, The. Edwin Markham. StJW
Ascension and the Assumption, The. Ramón López Velarde, *tr. fr. Spanish by* H. R. Hays. HW
Ascension Day. Sheila Kaye-Smith. CAW
Ascension-Day. Henry Vaughan. AnAnS-1; MeP; OxBoCh
Ascension Hymn. The Venerable Bede. *See* Hymn of Glory Let Us Sing, A.
Ascension Hymn. Jean Baptiste de Santeuil, *tr. fr. French by* Allan G. McDougall. CAW
Ascension-Hymn ("Dust and clay"). Henry Vaughan. AnAnS-1; MeP; SCEP-1; SeCV-1
Ascension-Hymn ("They are all gone into the World of Light"). Henry Vaughan. *See* They Are All Gone into the World of Light.
Ascent. Wendell Berry. AP
Ascent. Charles G. Blanden. OQP
Ascent, The. John Stevens Wade. ThO
Ascent of F 6, The, *sel.* W. H. Auden *and* Christopher Isherwood.
"At last the secret is out, as it always must come in the end." NAMP; SeCePo
Ascent of Mount Snowdon. Wordsworth. *See* In One of Those Excursions.
Ascent to the Sierras. Robinson Jeffers. AmPP (3d ed.); HT; LoGBV; OxBA
Ascention. John Donne. AnAnS-1; MaMe; MeP; OBS; Sonn
Ascetic, The. Victor J. Daley. PoAu-1
Ascot Waistcoat. David McCord. *See* Sportif.
Ascribe unto the Lord of Light. Psalm XXIX. *Paraphrased by* Sir Philip Sidney. FCP
Ase I me rod this ender day. The Five Joys of Mary. *Unknown.* MeEL
A-settin' on the ice till my feet got cold. Sweet Thing: The Crawdad Song. *Unknown.* OuSiCo
Ash. George MacBeth. NMP
Ash and the Oak, The. Louis Simpson. NePoAm
Ash-Boughs. Gerard Manley Hopkins. BoPe
Ash-heap of four cultures. Conon in Alexandria. Lawrence Durrell. MoPo
Ash on an Old Man's Sleeve. T. S. Eliot. *Fr.* Four Quartets: Little Gidding. FaBoTw; GTBS-W; PoFS
Ash tree is the only one, The. The Timid Ash Tree. Kathleen Millay. PEDC
Ash Wednesday. T. S. Eliot. ACV; AmPP; AnFE; AP; CoAnAm; CoBMV; LiTA; LiTG; MoAB; MoAmPo; MoPo; OxBA; Po; SeCeV; TwAmPo
Sels.
"Although I do not hope to turn again," VI. FaBoEn
"Because I do not hope to turn again," I. ATP (1953 ed.); OxBoCh
"If the lost word is lost, if the spent word is spent," V. OxBoCh
"Lady, three white leopards sat under a juniper-tree," II. LO; LoBV; SiSw
(Salutation.) AnAmPo
Ash Wednesday. Rosa Zagnoni Marinoni. PoRL; WHL
Ashamed at times that I am silent. The Praises of Laura Transcend His Poetic Power. Petrarch. *Fr.* Sonnets to Laura: To Laura in Life. EnLi-1; OuHeWo
Ashamed of Jesus. Joseph Grigg. BePJ
(Not Ashamed of Christ.) SoP
Ashamed of tears? This world of ours. Tears. *Unknown.* SoP
Ashby. John Reuben Thompson. AA
Ashcake. Thomas Nelson Page. AA
Ashen feelers of the frigid morrow, The. The Specter. Ernst Hardt. AWP
Ashes. Heine. *See* Sag', wo ist dein schönes Liebchen.
Ashes in the fire stir, The. The Fireside Kitten. Elizabeth J. Coatsworth. CIV
Ashes of Life. Edna St. Vincent Millay. FaBoBe; HBV; LiTL; NP
Ashes of Roses. Elaine Goodale Eastman. AA; HBV
Ashes of the Christmas Tree. Yetza Gillespie. ChBR
Ashes on the Slide. Eugene Field. BBV (1923 ed.)
Ashokan. Dachine Rainer. NePoAm
Ashore. "Laurence Hope." HBV
Ashtabula Disaster, The. Julia Moore. EvOK
Asia. Shelley. *Fr.* Prometheus Unbound, II, v. PoFS; ViBoPo
(Asia's Song.) ATP (1935 ed.); UnPo (1st ed.)
Asian Birds. Robert Bridges. VA
Asian Desert. Dorothy Wellesley. OBMV
Asian Peace Offers Rejected without Publication. Robert Bly. NaP

Asians Dying, The. W. S. Merwin. CoAP; NaP; NYBP
Asia's Song. Shelley. *See* Asia.
Asides from the Clowns, *sel.* Jules Laforgue, *tr. fr. French by* William Jay Smith.
"My clear-cut heart, my tender soul." PoPl
Asides on the Oboe. Wallace Stevens. AP; MoAB; MoAmPo
A-Sitting on a Gate. "Lewis Carroll." *See* White Knight's Song, The.
Ask and Have. Samuel Lover. HBV; TreFS
(How to Ask and Have.) BOHV
Ask and it shall be given. Choice. Ellen Coit Elliott. OQP
Ask, and it shall be given you; seek, and ye shall find. St. Matthew, VII: 7, 8, Bible, *N.T.* BoC
Ask, and Ye Shall Receive. Mrs. Havens. BLRP
Ask any question in this town. "Round Cape Horn." *Unknown.* EtS
Ask God to give thee skill. Sympathy. Anna E. Hamilton. OQP
Ask if I love thee? Oh, smiles cannot tell. Margaret to Dolcino. Charles Kingsley. HBV
Ask, is it well, O thou consumed of fire. The Burning of the Law. Mëir of Rothenburg. TrJP
Ask Me No More. Thomas Carew. *See* Ask Me No More Where Jove Bestows.
Ask me no more: I've enough Chablis. To an Importunate Host. *Unknown.* BOHV
Ask me no more: the moon may draw the sea. Tennyson. *Fr.* The Princess, Pt. VI. AnFE; AtBAP; BoLiVe; EnLi-2; EnLit; EPN; GTBS-W; HBV; LiTB; MaPo; MeWo; OAEP; OBNC; PoEL-5; PoVP; TreFT; TrGrPo; UnTE; VA; ViPo; ViPP
Ask Me No More Where Jove Bestows. Thomas Carew. AWP; BEL; CoBE; EG; ELP; EnLit; JAWP; LiTL; MeWo; OAEP; PoRA; SeCePo; SeCL; TOP; TrGrPo; ViBoPo; WBP; WHA
(Song, A: "Ask [*or* Aske] me no more where Jove bestowes.") AnAnS-2; AtBAP; ATP (1953 ed.); CABA; CavP; CBV; CH; EnLoPo; FaBoEn; FaFP; ForPo; FosPo; GTBS-W; HBV; HoPM; InPo; LiTB; LiTG; LO; LoBV; MasP; MeLP; MePo; NeHB; NoP; OBEV; OBS; PG; PoE; PoEL-3; PoFS; PoIE; SCEP-2; SeCP; SeCV-1; SeEP; TreFT; TrGrPo
Ask me no more, why there appears. Pyms Anarchy. *At. to* Thomas Jordan. OBS
Ask me why I live among the greens mountains? Answer to a Worldly One. Li Po. OnPM
Ask me why I send you here. The Primrose. Robert Herrick. HBV; OBEV; ViBoPo
Ask night how it feels to be dark. To Be Black, to Be Lost. Hannah Kahn. GoYe
Ask No Return. Horace Gregory. Chorus for Survival. CMoP; MAP; MoAmPo; TrGrPo (1942 ed.); TwAmPo
Ask not for whom the bells toll. Donne Redone. Joseph Paul Tierney. ShM
Ask not overmuch for fair. He That Loves a Rosy Cheek. Heinrich von Rugge. AWP; JAWP; WBP
Ask not the cause, why sullen spring. Song to a Fair Young Lady Going Out of the Town in the Spring [*or* To a Fair Young Lady . . .]. Dryden. BWP; CABA; HBV; LiTL; MaPo; MBW-1; OBEV; OBS; PoIE; SeCL; SeEP
Ask Not to Know This Man. Ben Jonson. CABA
(Little Shrub Growing By, A.) CBEP; EnRePo
Ask Not Ungainly. Horace, *tr. fr. Latin by* Ezra Pound. Odes, I, 2. CTC
Ask not why hearts turn magazines of passions. A Funeral Elogy upon . . . Mrs. Anne Bradstreet. John Norton. SCAP
Ask not why sorrow shades my brow. Montross. Charles Cotton. SeCL
Ask nothing more of me, sweet. The Oblation. Swinburne. BoLP; EnLit; HBV; PoVP
Ask of your soul this question, What is strength? Strength. Jessie Wilmore Murton. ChIP; MaRV; OQP
Ask the dead. They Know. Ryah Tumarkin Goodman. FiSC
Ask the Empresse of the night. The Magnet. Thomas Stanley. MePo
Ask what love is? It is a passion. A True Description of Love. *Unknown.* TuPP
Ask you what provocation I have had? Satire [*or* In Defence of Satire]. Pope. *Fr.* Epilogue to the Satires Dialogue II. CoBE; OBEC
Asked of Echo, t'other day. Echo. John Godfrey Saxe. BoHV
Askest thou of these graves? They'll tell thee. Gheluvelt. Robert Bridges. BrPo
Asking for It. Siegfried Sassoon. MoRP
Aslant the shoulder of each prisoner. Sara Bard Field. *Fr.* Barabbas. PoFr
Asleep. Alcman, *tr. fr. Greek by* Olga Marx *and* Ernst Morwitz. LiTW
Asleep. Witter Bynner. *Fr.* Chapala Poems. NP
Asleep. Wilfred Owen. MMA; POTE; WePo
Asleep. William Winter. AA
Asleep at last! For fourscore years. Oliver Wendell Holmes. William Hamilton Hayne. DD
Asleep at the Switch. George Hoey. BeLS; PaPo
Asleep in Jesus. Margaret Mackay. BePJ
Asleep in the Bosom of Youth. Judah Halevi, *tr. fr. Hebrew by* Nina Salaman. LiTW
Asleep in the Deep. Arthur J. Lamb. TreFT
Asleep, My Love? Shakespeare. *Fr.* A Midsummer Night's Dream, V, i. CTC; LBN
Asleep or waking is it? for her neck. Laus Veneris. Swinburne. MaVP; PoVP; ViPP
Asleep within the deadest hour of night. To ——. Robert Nichols. HBMV
A-sleepin' at length on the sand. The Sea Serpant. Wallace Irwin. FiBHP
Asmodai. Geoffrey Hill. NePoEA
Asolando, *sels.* Robert Browning.
Dubiety. MaPo (1969 ed.)
Epilogue: "At the midnight in the silence of the sleep-time." BEL; BoLiVe; CoBE; EnL; EnLi-2; EnLit; EPN; FaBoEn; FaBV; FiP; GTSL; HBV; HBVY; InP; MaRV; MBW-2; OAEP; OBNC; OBVV; OHFP; OQP; OuHeWo; PoIE; PoVP; TOP; TreFT; TrGrPo; VA; ViBoPo; ViPo; ViPP
Prologue: "Poet's age is sad, The." PoVP; ViPo; ViPP
Aspatia's Song. Beaumont *and* Fletcher. *Fr.* The Maid's Tragedy, II, i. AWP; HBV; InPo; JAWP; OBEV; OBS; TOP; TrGrPo; WBP
(I Died True.) CH
(Lay a Garland on My Hearse.) AtBAP; ElL; ILP; InP; OAEP; SiCE; TuPP; ViBoPo; WHA
Aspecta Medusa. Dante Gabriel Rossetti. PoVP
Aspects. Norman MacCaig. NYTB; OxBS
Aspects of Robinson. Weldon Kees. CoAP; NaP; NYBP; TwAmPo
Aspects of Some Forsythia Branches. Ralph Gustafson. PeCV (1967 ed.)
Aspects of Spring in Greater Boston. George Starbuck. NYBP
Aspects of the Pines. Paul Hamilton Hayne. AA; AmPP (3d ed.); AnAmPo; HBV
Aspen and the Stream, The. Richard Wilbur. NYBP
Aspens. Edward Thomas. ChMP
Aspens and the maple now, The. Valentine's Day. Aileen Fisher. YeAr
Asperius Nihil Est Humili cum Surgat in Altum. Henry Parrot. SiCE
Asphalt morning found him; he was dead, The. Raccoon on the Road. Joseph Payne Brennan. GoYe
Asphodel, That Greeny Flower, *sel.* William Carlos Williams.
"Of asphodel, that greeny flower." PP
Aspiration. Mário de Andrade, *tr. fr. Portuguese by* John Nist. TTY
Aspiration. William Drennan. IrPN
Aspiration. Eileen Duggan. JKCP (1955 ed.)
Aspiration. Mary Lamb. *See* Maternal Lady with the Virgin Grace.
Aspiration, The. John Norris. LoBV; OxBoCh
Aspiration. John Banister Tabb. LO
Aspiration. Edward William Thomson. OBVV
Aspiration. George Wither. MaRV
Aspirations. Adam G. Oehlenschlaeger. SoP
Ass, The. Edwin Allan. PoPl; WhC
Ass, The. Moses Mendes. *Fr.* The Chaplet. TrJP
Ass-Face. Edith Sitwell. OBMV
Ass in the Lion's Skin, The. ("An ass put on a lion's skin and went). Aesop, *rhymed tr. fr. Greek by* William Ellery Leonard. AWP; JAWP; LiTW; OA; WBP
Ass Speaks, The. Katherine Tynan. MaRV
Assassin, The. Donald Hall. TPM
Assassination, The. Robert Hillyer. AnNE; MoAmPo; TrGrPo (1942 ed.)

Assassination. Don L. Lee. BOLo; BP
Assault, The. Robert Nichols. MCCG
Assault on the Fortess, The. Timothy Dwight. PAH
Assemble, all ye maidens, at the door. Elegy on a Lady, Whom Grief for the Death of Her Betrothed Killed. Robert Bridges. CoBMV; OBEV (new ed.); OBVV
Assembling of the Fays, The. Joseph Rodman Drake. *Fr.* The Culprit Fay. GN
Assembly; Harlem School. Eugene T. Maleska. GoYe
Assembly of the Gods, The. Robert Henryson. *Fr.* The Testament of Cresseid. PoEL-1
Assert ten barren love day made. A Play on Words. Eugene Field. WhC
Asses, *sel.* Padraic Colum.
"I know where I'd get." LOW
Asses milk, half a pint, take at seven, or before. Advice to a Lady in Autumn. Earl of Chesterfield. CEP; OBEC
Assignation, The, *sel.* Dryden.
Long betwixt Love and Fear. LiTL; SeCL; ViBoPo
(Song: "Long betwixt love and fear Phillis tormented.") SeEP
Assignation, The. Imr el Kais, *tr. fr. Arabic by* Howard Mumford Jones. LiTW
Assignation, The. James Wright. NePoEA
Assimilation. Irving Feldman. AmPC
Assisi. Alfred Noyes. GoBC
Assistance, The. Paul Blackburn. NeAP
Association Copy. Paula Kurth. JKCP (1955 ed.)
Assorted Relishes. Richard Armour. WhC
Assuagement. Sister Claude of Jesus. JKCP (1955 ed.)
Assumes it is true to put down roots. The Poem That Tries to Be a Tree. Phillip Hey. YAP
Assumpta Est Maria. Liam Brophy. ISi
Assumpta Maria. Francis Thompson. ISi
Assumption, The. Sir John Beaumont. ACP (1952 ed.); CAW; GoBC
Assumption, The. John Gilland Brunini. ISi
Assumption, The. St. Nerses, *tr. fr. Armenian by* W. H. Kent. CAW
Assumption, The. John Banister Tabb. ISi
Assunpink and Princeton. Thomas Dunn English. MC; PAH
Assurance, An. Nicholas Breton. OBSC
Assurance. Grace Noll Crowell. PoRL
Assurance. George Herbert. MaMe; OxBoCh
Assurance. Ida Norton Munson. PGD
Assured of worthiness we do not dread. Internal Harmony. George Meredith. EPN
Assyrian came down like the [*or* a] wolf on the fold, The. The Destruction of Sennacherib. Byron. ATP; BEL; BeLS; BLPA; BoLiVe; CoBE; DiPo; EnLi-2; EnLit; EnRP; ERoP-2; EvOK; FaBoBe; FaBoCh; FaFP; FaPON; FOL; GN; GoTP; HBV; InP; LiTG; LoGBV; MaRV; MCCG; MPB (1956 ed.); MemP; NeHB; NoP; OAEP; OnMSP; OTPC; OuHeWo; PAn; PaPo; PCD; Po; PoE; PoIE; PoLF; PTK; RG; ShBV-1; SoP; TIHL; TOP; TreF; WBLP; WGRP
Assyrian[s'] king in peace, with foul desire, The. Sardanapalus [*or* The Portrait of Henry VIII]. Earl of Surrey. ACP (1952 ed.); EnPo; EP; FCP; FOL; SiPS
Astarte Syriaca. Dante Gabriel Rossetti. PoVP
Aster. Plato. *See* Morning and Evening Star.
Astonished Listener Hears the Radio Announcer Bat Out the Long Balls of Verbs, Nouns and Adjectives, An. James Schevill. FiMAP
Astonished poplars hide. Paysage Moralisé. John Hollander. ErPo; NePoEA
Astonished stood Lucrece and Nara. Lucrece and Nara. Laura Riding. FaBoMo
Astounding the bucolic grass. Park Concert. James Michie. MuSP
Astraea. Emerson. AnNE
Astraea. Whittier. AA
Astraea at the Capitol. Whittier. PAH
Astraea Redux. Dryden. CEP
Sels.
"And welcom now (Great Monarch)." OBS
"Now with a general peace the world was blest." OBS
Astride on steel. Motorcycle. Benjamin Sturgis Pray. GoYe
Astride the pivot of the world. Seesaw. Gerardo Diego. LiTW
Astrologers own eyes are set, The. Two Songs at the Marriage of the Lord Fauconberg and the Lady Mary Cromwell. Andrew Marvell. MaMe
Astrologer's Song, An. Kipling. MoBrPo; NeMA
Astrology. Tom Marshall. PeCV (1967 ed.)
Astronaut Jim Lovell. John Giorno. *Fr.* The American Book of the Dead. ANYP
Astronomer, The. Kevin F. Doherty. JKCP (1955 ed.)
Astronomers of Mont Blanc, The. Edgar Bowers. QFR
Astronomers predict his sun is dying. Protagonist. Edith Henrich. MoRP
Astrophel. Spenser. StP
Astrophel and Stella. Sir Philip Sidney. FCP; SiPS
Sonnets:
I. "Loving in truth, and fain in verse my love to show." AnFE; AWP; BEL; BWP; CABA; CBEP; CBV; CoBE; EG; EnL; EnLi-1; EnLit; FaBoEn; FCP; ForPo; GTBS-W; HBV; ILP; InPo; JAWP; LiTB; LiTG; MaPo; MasP; NoP; OAEP; OBSC; PAn; Po; PoFS; PoIE; PP; ReEn; ReIE; SeCePo; SeCeV; SiCE; SiPS; Sonn; TOP; TreFT; TrGrPo; TuPP; ViBoPo; WBP; YAT
(Look into Thy Heart.) LiTL
II. "Not at the first sight, nor with a dribbed shot." FCP; MaPo; PIA; ReEn; ReIE; SiCE; SiPS; TuPP
III. "Let dainty wits cry on the Sisters nine." FCP; OBSC; ReEn; ReIE; SiCE; SiPS; Sonn; TuPP
IV. "Virtue, alas, now let me take some rest." FCP; MaPo; ReEn; SiPS
V. "It is most true, that eyes are formed to serve." FCP; MaPo; NoP; OBSC; ReEn; SiCE; SiPS; Sonn; TuPP
VI. "Some lovers speak, when they their muses entertain." FCP; PIA; ReEn; ReIE; SiPS; Sonn; TuPP
VII. "When Nature made her chief work, Stella's eyes." CABA; FCP; ReEn; ReIE; SiCE; SiPS; Sonn; TuPP
VIII. "Love born in Greece, of late fled from his native place." FCP; SiPS; Sonn
X. "Reason, in faith thou art well serv'd that still." FCP; MaPo; ReEn; SiCE; SiPS
XI. "In truth, O Love, with what a boyish kind." ElL; FCP; InvP; ReEn; SiCE; SiPS
XII. "Cupid, because thou shin'st in Stella's eyes." FCP; ReEn; SiPS
XIV. "Alas have I not pain enough my friend." FCP; MaPo (1969 ed.); NoP; ReEn; SiPS; TuPP
XV. "You that do search for every purling spring." CoBE; FCP; ILP; MaPo (1969 ed.); OBSC; ReEn; ReIE; SiCE; SiPS; Sonn; TuPP
XVIII. "With what sharp checks I in myself am shent." FCP; ReEn; SiPS; Sonn
XX. "Fly, fly, my friends, I have my death wound; fly." FCP; MaPo; PAn; ReIE; SiPS; TuPP
XXI. "Your words, my friend, right healthful caustics, blame." CABA; FCP; ReEn; ReIE; SiCE; SiPS; TuPP
XXII. "In highest way of heaven the sun did ride." FCP; OBSC; SiPS; Sonn
XXIII. "The curious wits, seeing dull pensiveness." FCP; ReEn; SiPS
XXIV. "Rich fools there be, whose base and filthy heart." MaPo (1969 ed.); OAEP; ReEn; ReIE; SiCE; SiPS; TuPP
XXV. "The wisest scholar of the wight most wise." FCP; NoP; ReEn; SiPS
XXVI. "Though dusty wits dare scorn astrology." FCP; ReEn; SiPS; Sonn
XXVII. "Because I oft in dark abstracted guise." FCP; ReEn; SiCE; SiPS
XXVIII. "You that with allegory's curious frame." FCP; ILP; ReEn; ReIE; SiCE; SiPS; TuPP
XXX. "Whether the Turkish new moon minded be." CLwM; FCP; ReEn; ReIE; SiPS; Sonn; TuPP
XXXI. "With how sad steps, O Moon, thou climb'st at the skies!" AnEnPo; AnFE; AtBAP; AWP; BEL; BoLiVe; BWP; CaFP; CH; ChTr; CoBE; DiPo; EG; ElL; EnL; EnLi-1; EnLit; EnLoPo; EnRePo; EP; FaBoEn; FCP; ForPo; GTSL; HBV; ILP; InvP; JAWP; LiTL; MaPo; MeWo; NoP; OAEP; OBSC; PoAn; PoE; PoEL-1; PoIE; PoRA; ReEn; ReIE; SeCeV; SiCE; SiPS; Sonn; StP; TOP; TrGrPo; TuPP; ViBoPo; WBP; WHA
(His Lady's Cruelty.) OBEV
(Languishing Moon, The.) BoNaP
(Moon, The.) LoBV
(To the Moon.) LiTG
XXXII. "Morpheus, the lively son of deadly sleep." ReEn; SiPS
XXXIII. "I might—unhappy word—O me, I might." FCP; OBSC; ReEn; SiPS; Sonn; TuPP

Astrophel (continued)
XXXIV. "Come, let me write. And to what end? To ease." FCP; ReIE; SiPS; TuPP
XXXV. "What may words say, or what may words not say." CABA; FCP; ReIE; SiCE; SiPS; TuPP
XXXVII. "My mouth doth water, and my breast doth swell." FCP; ReEn; ReIE; SiPS; Sonn; TuPP
XXXVIII. "This night while sleep begins with heavy wings." BWP; FCP; NoP; SiPS
XXXIX. "Come, sleep, O sleep, the certain knot of peace." AnFE; BEL; BoLiVe; CABA; CBEP; CBV; CoBE; EIL; EnL; EnLi-1; EnLit; EnRePo; EP; FCP; ForPo; HBV; InP; LiTG; MaPo (1969 ed.); MyFE; NoP; OAEP; OBSC; PoE; PoFS; PoIE; PoRA; ReEn; ReIE; SiCE; SiPS; Sonn; StP; TreFS; TrGrPo; TuPP; ViBoPo; WHA
(Sleep.) FaPL; GTSL; LoBV; OBEV
(To Sleep.) ShBV-4
XL. "As good to write as for to lie and groan." FCP; SiPS; TuPP
XLI. "Having this day my horse, my hand, my lance." AnFE; ATP; BEL; CLwM; CoBE; EG; EnL; EnLit; EnRePo; FCP; ILP; MaPo (1969 ed.); NoP; OAEP; OBSC; PoFS; ReEn; ReIE; SiCE; SiPS; Sonn; TOP; TuPP; YAT
XLII. "O eyes, which do the spheres of beauty move." FCP; SiPS; Sonn
XLV. "Stella oft sees the very face of woe." FCP; PoE; ReEn; SiCE; SiPS; TuPP
XLVII. "What, have I thus betrayed my liberty [*or* libertie]?" AtBAP; FCP; PoEL-1; ReEn; SiPS
(Yoke of Tyranny, The.) TrGrPo
XLVIII. "Soul's joy, bend not those morning stars from me." FCP; MaPo; NoP; SiPS
XLIX. "I on my horse, and Love on me, doth try." FCP; NoP; ReEn; SiPS
L. "Stella, the fullness of my thoughts of thee." FCP; ReEn; SiPS
LII. "A strife is grown between Virtue and Love." FCP; ReEn; SiPS
LIII. "In martial sports I had my cunning tried." FCP; ReEn; ReIE; SiPS
LIV. "Because I breathe not love to every one." BoLiVe; FCP; OAEP; OBSC; PoAn; ReEn; SiCE; SiPS; TOP; TrGrPo; TuPP
LV. "Muses, I oft invoked your holy aid." FCP; SiPS; TuPP
LVI. "Fie, school of patience, fie! Your lesson is." FCP; ReEn; SiPS
LVII. "Woe having made, with many fights, his own." FCP; ReEn; SiPS
FCP; ReEn; SiPS
LIX. "Dear, why make you more of a dog than me?" FCP; MaPo (1969 ed.); OAEP; SiPS
LXII. "Late tired with woe, even ready for to pine." EnLit; FCP; HBV; ReEn; SiPS
LXIII. "O grammar rules, O now your virtues show." FCP; SiPS; TuPP
XIV. "No more, my dear, no more these counsels try." BEL; CoBE; FaPL; FCP; HBV; OBSC; ReEn; SiCE; SiPS; Sonn; TOP; TuPP
LXV. "Love, by sure proof I may call thee unkind." FCP; SiPS; Sonn
LXVI. "And do I see some cause a hope to feed." FCP; ReEn; SiPS
LXVII. "Hope, art thou true, or dost thou flatter me?" FCP; ReEn; SiPS
LXVIII. "Stella, the only planet of my light." FCP; OBSC; ReEn; SiPS
LXIX. "O joy too high for my low style to show!" BoLiVe; FCP; MaPo; PoFS; ReEn; SiCE; SiPS; TrGrPo; TuPP
LXX. "My Muse may well grudge at my heavenly joy." FCP; ReEn; SiPS
LXXI. "Who will in fairest book of Nature know." BWP; CABA; FCP; MaPo; NoP; PAn; ReEn; ReIE; SiCE; SiPS
LXXII. "Desire, though thou my old companion art." FCP; ReEn; SiPS
LXXIII. "Love still a boy and oft a wanton is." EG; FCP; HBV; MyFE; OAEP; ReEn; SiPS; Sonn
LXXIV. "I never drank of Aganippe well." CABA; EnRePo; FCP; OBSC; ReEn; ReIE; SiCE; SiPS; Sonn; TuPP
LXXVI. "She comes, and straight therewith her shining orbs [*or* twins] do move." CABA; FCP; ReIE; SiPS
LXXIX. "Sweet kiss, thy sweets I fain would sweetly indite." FCP; ReEn; SiPS
LXXXI. "O kiss, which dost those ruddy gems impart." FCP; SiPS; Sonn
LXXXII. "Nymph of the garden where all beauties be." FCP; InvP; SiPS
LXXXIV. "Highway, since you my chief Parnassus be." EIL; EnRePo; FCP; ILP; OAEP; OBSC; ReEn; SiPS
(Highway, The.) GTBS-W; LiTB; LiTG; OBEV
(Via Amoris.) GTSL
XC. "Stella, think not that I by verse seek fame." EnLit; FCP; OBSC; ReEn; SiCE; SiPS; TuPP
XCII. "Be your words made, good sir, of Indian ware." FCP; ReEn; SiPS
XCIV. "Grief, find the words; for thou hast made my brain." FCP; ReEn; SiPS
XCVI. "Thought, with good cause thou likest so well the night." FCP; ReEn; SiPS
XCVII. "Dian, that fain would cheer her friend the Night." FCP; ReEn; SiPS
XCVIII. "Ah, bed! the field where joy's peace some do see." EnLoPo; FCP; ReEn; SiPS
XCIX. "When far-spent night persuades each mortal eye." CABA; FCP; FosPo; MaPo; OBSC; ReEn; SiPS; Sonn
C. "O tears, no tears, but rain from Beauty's skies." FCP; ReIE; SiPS; Sonn
CIII. "O happy Thames that didst my Stella bear!" FCP; HBV; ReEn; SiPS
CIV. "Envious wits, what hath been mine offence." FCP; SiPS; Sonn; TuPP
CVII. "Stella since thou so right a princess[e] art." FCP; HBV; MaPo; NoP; ReEn; SiPS
CVIII. "When sorrow (using mine own fire's might)." FCP; MaPo (1969 ed.); SiPS; Sonn
CIX. "Thou blind man's mark, thou fool's self-chosen snare." *Sometimes considered part of* Astrophel and Stella; *also in* Certain Sonnets. BWP; CABA; EnRePo; ErPo; FCP; FosPo; NoP; PoSa; ReEn; ReIE; SiCE; Sonn; TuPP; VaPo; ViBoPo
(Desire.) LiTB; LiTG; MaSP; SiPS; TrGrPo
CX. "Leave me, O love, which reachest but to dust." *Sometimes considered part of* Astrophel and Stella; *also in* Certain Sonnets. BWP; CABA; DiPo; EG; EIL; EnLit; EnRePo; EP; ExPo; FCP; ForPo; LiTB; LiTG; MaPo; OAEP; OxBoCh; PAn; PIA; PoAn; PoE; PoIE (1970 ed.); PoRA; PoSa; ReEn; ReIE; SeCePo; SeCeV; SiCE; Sonn; TOP; TreFT; TrPWD; TuPP; ViBoPo; WHA
(Farewell, A.) UnPo (1st ed.)
(Farewell World.) FaBoEn
(Splendidis Longum Valedico Nugis.) LO; OBEV; OBSC; SiPS
Songs.
First Song: "Doubt you to whom my Muse these notes intended [*or* entendeth]." AtBAP; FCP; HBV; OBSC; PoFS; ReIE; SiCE; SiPS; Sonn; TuPP
(To Stella.) EIL; WHA
(To You! To You!) LiTL
Second Song: "Have I caught my heavenly jewel." FCP
(Stella Sleeping.) SiPS
Third Song: "If Orpheus' voice [*or* voyce] had force." FCP; PoEL-1; ReIE; SiPS
Fourth Song: "Only [*or* Onely] joy, now here you are." AtBAP; EIL; EnRePo; FaPL; FCP; InvP; OBSC; ReEn; ReIE; SiCE; SiPS; TuPP; UnTE
Sixth Song: "O you that hear[e] this voice." FCP; OBSC; SiPS
Eighth Song: "In a grove most rich of shade." FCP; OBSC; SiPS
(Eighth Sonnet, The.) OAEP
Ninth Song: "Go, my flock, go get you hence." FCP; SiPS
Tenth Song: "O dear life, when shall it be?" EnRePo; FCP; SiPS
Eleventh Song: "Who is it that this dark[e] night." AtBAP; EIL; EnLi-1; EnRePo; FCP; FosPo; NoP; OBSC; PoEL-1; ReEn; ReIE; SiCE; TuPP; ViBoPo; WoL
(Dialogue, A.) CLwM; EG
(Lovers' Dialogue.) SiPS
(Underneath My Window.) SeCePo
(Voices at the Window.) OBEV
Astrophel's Love Is Dead. Sir Philip Sidney. *See* Ring Out Your Bells.
Asunder shall the clouds be rolled. The Day of Judgment. Dugald Buchanan. GoTS
A-swell within her billowed skirts. The Mad Woman of Punnet's Town. L. A. G. Strong. MoBrPo
Asylum. David R. Clark. PPON
Asylum. John Freeman. OBMV
At a Bach Concert. Adrienne Cecile Rich. NePoEA

At a Bible House. Robert Lowell. PoeP
At a Burial. Sir William Watson. MaRV
At a bygone Western country fair. At a Country Fair. Thomas Hardy. VP
At a Calvary near the Ancre. Wilfred Owen. MoRP
At a certain time in life it becomes essential. Cartier at St. Malo. Francis Webb. *Fr.* A View of Montreal. BoAV
At a Child's Baptism. Vassar Miller. GoJo; NYTB
At a Concert of Music. Conrad Aiken. CMoP; MAP; MoAB; MoAmPo; UnS
At a Country Dance in Provence. Harold Monro. OBVV
At a Country Fair. Thomas Hardy. VP
At a Country Fair. John Holmes. MoShBr
At a Country Hotel. Howard Nemerov. PoRA (rev. ed.)
At a Cowboy Dance. James Barton Adams. HBV; IHA; PoOW; RePo; SCC
(Idaho Cowboy Dance, An.) ABF
At a dinner so various, at such a repast. The Retaliation. Goldsmith. CEP; OAEP; TOP
At a distance, young voices are whooping. On Returning to Teach. Marvin Bell. YAP
At a gay reception given in a mansion grand and old. The Moth and the Flame. George Taggert. TreF
At a Loss. James L. Weil. GoYe
At a Lunar Eclipse. Thomas Hardy. MoPW; POTE; TOP
At a Parade. F. T. Prince. NeBP; WaP
At a pleasant evening party I had taken down to supper. Ferdinando and Elvira. W. S. Gilbert. BOHV; FiBHP; LBN; NA
At a pot-house bar as I chanced to pass. What the Trumpeter Said. Sebastian Evans. VA
At a round-up on the Gila. The Legend of Boastful Bill. Badger Clark. SCC
At a Solemn Music [*or* Musick]. Milton. EG; ExPo; GTBS; GTBS-D; GTBS-P; GTBS-W; GTSE; GTSL; HBV; LoBV; MaPo (1969 ed.); MeP; OAEP; OBEV; OBS; PoE; PoEL-3; SeCeV; SeCL; SeEP; TOP
(Blest Pair of Sirens.) OxBoCh
"Blest pair of sirens, pledges of heaven's joy," *sel.* UnS
At a Solemn Musick. Delmore Schwartz. MoRP; TwAmPo
At a spring-well [*or* springe wel] under a thorn. The Spring under a Thorn. *Unknown.* MeEL; NoP
At a Time. Ray Mathew. PoAu-2
At a university women's sort of charity fair. The Fortune Teller. John Holmes. NePoAm-2
At a Vacation Exercise [in the College, Part Latin, Part English]. Milton. OBS
"Hail native Language, that by sinews weak," *sel.* PP
At a Watering-Place. Thomas Hardy. CMoP
At a Window. Carl Sandburg. FaBoBe; HBMV; MoLP; NP; PCD; PoToHe; TrPWD
At Aberdeen. *Unknown.* *See* Epitaph: "Here lie I, Martin Elginbrodde."
At Algeciras—Meditation upon Death. W. B. Yeats. NoP
At Amberley Wild Brooks. Andrew Young. OA
At an Inn. Thomas Hardy. VP
At an Old Battlefield. Umaki, *tr. fr. Japanese by* Asataro Miyamori. OnPM
At anchor in Hampton Roads we lay. The *Cumberland.* Longfellow. AA; AnNE; EtS; MC; PaA; PAH; PAP
At Baia. Hilda Doolittle ("H. D."). AnFE; APA; CoAnAm; LiTA; MAPA; NP; TwAmPo
At Bannockburn the English lay. Bannockburn. Burns. PoPo
At Barstow. Charles Tomlinson. TwCP
At beauty's bar as I did stand. The Arraignment of a Lover [*or* Gascoigne's Arraignment]. George Gascoigne. ReEn; ReIE; SiCE; TuPP
At Bedtime. Mariana Griswold Van Rensselaer. HBMV
At Beltane, when ilk body bownis. Peblis to the Play. *Unknown.* GoTS
At Benediction. Eleanor Rogers Cox. JKCP
At Best. John Boyle O'Reilly. AA
At Best, Poets. Robert Graves. MemP
At Bethlehem. John Banister Tabb. The Child, I. AA
(Child at Bethlehem, The.) PRWS
At Beverly Farms, a portly, uncomfortable boulder. Terminal Days at Beverly Farms. Robert Lowell. FRC
At Birth. Anthony Thwaite. NePoEA-2
At Boot Hill in Tombstone, Arizona. *Unknown.* ShM
At break of day I chanced to stray. The Oul' Grey Mare. *Unknown.* AnIV
At Breakfast. I. M. Mills. BoTP
At breakfast a husband is cheery or blue. Sentimental Journey. "Elspeth." WhC
At Brill on the hill. *Unknown.* OxNR
At Bungendore. James McAuley. PoAu-2
At Cambridge. Audrey McGaffin. NePoAm
At Candle-lightin' Time. Paul Laurence Dunbar. IHA
At Carbis Bay. Arthur Symons. PoVP
At Carcassonne. Winfred Ernest Garrison. OQP
At Carmel. Mary Austin. AmFN
At Casterbridge Fair. Thomas Hardy. BEL; EnLit; PoVP
Sels.
Ballad-Singer, The, I. LO; MeWo; NoP
Former Beauties, II. FaBoEn; OBMV; OBNC
At Castle Boterel. Thomas Hardy. DTC; FaBoEn; GTBS-D; GTBS-P; MoVE; OBNC; PeVV; PoSa
At Castle Wood. Emily Brontë. ViBoPo
At Chappaqua. Joel Benton. AA
At Christmastide. Laura Simmons. PGD
At Christmas Time. Mary Brennan Clapp. GFA
At Christmas time so long ago. The Little Fir Tree. Margaret Rose. BoTP
At Church Next Sunday. *Unknown.* BLRP
At Cockcrow. Lizette Woodworth Reese. TrPWD
At Common Dawn. Vivian Locke Ellis. CH
At cool of day, with God I walk. Eventide. Caroline Atherton Briggs Mason. MaRV; TreFS
At Cooloolah. Judith Wright. MoBrPo (1962 ed.)
At counters where I eat my lunch. Marble-Top. E. B. White. FiBHP; WhC
At Court. Spenser. *Fr.* Mother Hubberds Tale. PoFr
At court I met it, in clothes brave enough. On Something That Walks [*or* Walkes] Somewhere. Ben Jonson. CoBE; SeCP; SeCV-1; TuPP
At Cove on the Crooked River. William Stafford. LiTM (1970 ed.); NaP
At Creçy by Somme in Ponthieu. Creçy. Francis Turner Palgrave. BeLS; HBV
At Darien Bridge. James Dickey. NoP
At Dawn. Rose Fyleman. BoChLi
At Dawn. Victor Hugo, *tr. fr. French by* Alan Conder. OnPM
At Dawn. Arthur Symons. OBNC
At Dawn. J. M. Synge. SyP
At Dawn. Charles Williams. FaBoTw
"At dawn," he said, "I bid them all farewell." The Volunteer. Elbridge Jefferson Cutler. AA
At dawn of day I saw a man. The Drunkard's Doom. *Unknown.* AS
At Dawn of the Year. "George Klingle." PGD
At dawn she lay with her profile at that angle. Daybreak. Stephen Spender. LiTL; MoLP; POTE
At dawn she sought the Saviour slain. Mary Magdalene. Richard Burton. ChIP
At dawn the dark birds flew. The Ninth of April. Otto Gelsted. PoFr
At dawn, the joyful choir of bells. Ave Maria Bells. Charles Warren Stoddard. ISi; JKCP
At Dawn the Light Will Come. N. P. Van Wyk Louw, *tr. fr. Afrikaans by* Uys Krige *and* Jack Cope. PeSA
At dawn the ridge emerges massed and dun. Attack. Siegfried Sassoon. MCCG; MoBrPo; PoMa
At dawn, when England's childish tongue. Dandelion. Annie Rankin Annan. HBV
At Daybreak. Helen Hoyt. BiCB
At daybreak, dawn of desire. A Garland of Peacock Feathers. Dafydd ap Gwilym. BoPe
At daybreak, when the falcon claps his wings. Ballade for a Bridegroom. Villon, *tr. by* Swinburne. AWP; MeWo
At Day's End. *Unknown.* TreFT
At de feet o' Jesus. Feet o' Jesus. Langston Hughes. NP
At Dead Low Water. Allen Curnow. AnNZ
At dead of night, the sailors sprawled on deck. Nearing La Guaira. Derek Walcott. TTY
At Delft. Charles Tomlinson. NYBP
At Delos. Duncan Campbell Scott. PeCV
At Dieppe, *sels.* Arthur Symons.
After Sunset. BrPo; SyP
Grey and Green. PeVV; SyP
On the Beach. PoVP; SyP

At (continued)
Rain on the Down. BrPo; OBNC; SyP
At Dingle Bank. Edward Lear. WhC
At dinner, she is hostess, I am host. Modern Love, XVII. George Meredith. EnLit; ILP; OAEP; Sonn; VA; ViPo; VP
At Dirty Dick's and Sloppy Joe's. Song of the Master and Boatswain. W. H. Auden. *Fr.* The Sea and the Mirror. DTC; FaBoTw
At Dover Cliffs. William Lisle Bowles. *See* Dover Cliffs.
At Dunwich. Anthony Thwaite. MoBS
At dusk/ from the island in the river. If the Owl Calls Again. John Haines. BoNaP; CoAP
At dusk it is. Mrs. Southern's Enemy. Sir Osbert Sitwell. AtBAP
At each moment we rise vainly from the dead. Vain Cry; Lydian Campaign, 1941. Glauco Cambon. OnPM
At early dawn I once had been. The Dawning of the Day. *Unknown.* OnYI
At Early Morn. Binga Dismond, *fr. the French of* Catulle Mendes. PoNe
At Ease. Walter de la Mare. ChMP; GTBS-P
At Easter Time. Laura E. Richards. BoChLi; DD; HH; MPB; OHIP; OTPC (1946 ed.)
At Ecelin. Robert Browning. *Fr.* Sordello. MyFE
At 8:00 he rises, bathes, and dresses. Mr. Eliot's Day. Robert Francis. NYBP
At Eighty-seven. Dachine Rainer. NePoAm
At Eighty-three, *sel.* Thomas Durley Landels.
"Thank God for life, with all its endless store." MaRV
At Epidaurus. Lawrence Durrell. LiTB; MoPo
At Eutaw Springs the valiant died. To the Memory of the Brave Americans [*or* Eutaw Springs]. Philip Freneau. AA; AmP; AmPP; AP; BeLS; CoBA; NeHB; PaA; PAH; PAL; PAP; PoLF
"At eve should be the time," they said. Datur Hora Quieti. Robert Stephen Hawker. GoBC
At eve the horse is freed of plough and wain. An Evening Falls. James Stephens. SUS
At Even. Frederic Manning. NP
At even o' Hallowmas no sleep I sought. The Spell. John Gay. DD
At Even, when the Sun Was Set. Henry Twells. MaRV
At Evening. Dora Wilcox. BoAu
At evening, sitting on this terrace. Bat. D. H. Lawrence. BrPo; GTBS-P
At evening when I go to bed. Daisies. Frank Dempster Sherman. TSW; TVC
At evening when the lamp is lit. The Land of Story-Books. Robert Louis Stevenson. FaBoBe; FaPL; FaPON; GoTP; HBV; HBVY; MPB; NeHB; OTD; OTPC; PoVP; PRWS; TiPo; TreFS; TSW
At Eventide. *Unknown, tr. fr. German by* Robert Bridges. MaRV
At every proper christening. To Patricia on Her Christening Day. Edith Ballinger Price. BiCB
At every step he heard the devil's moan. Borderline. R. H. Grenville. FiSC
At every stroke his brazen fins do take. The Whale. John Donne. *Fr.* The Progress of the Soul. ChTr; PoSa
At Ferns Castle. Padraic Colum. NePoAm
At fifteen I went with the army. Return. *Unknown.* LiTW
At first cock-crow. The Neighbors. Theodosia Garrison. HBMV
At first he stirs uneasily in sleep. Dog at Night. Louis Untermeyer. GoTP; StaSt
At first, he wondered why he should be spared. The Madman. Constance Urdang. PoPl
At first I feared the color of the dark. The Pulse of Darkness. John Fandel. JKCP (1955 ed.)
At first I hoped she would accept a dime. Femme Fatale. Vincent Starrett. FiSC
At first I prayed for Light. The Larger Prayer [*or* Prayer—Answer]. Ednah Dow Cheney. BLRP; MaRV; OQP; SoP; STF; WGRP
At first I said: "I will not have, I think." Birthday. Elaine V. Emans. BiCB
At first I thought a pest. Armour's Undermining Modesty. Marianne Moore. AP; CoBMV
At first I thought some animal, wounded. Near Barbizon. Galway Kinnell. NePoAm-2
At first I went apart. And now I see. Tammuz. Rayner Heppenstall. WaP
At first I would not reply, and my shame showed upon my cheeks. Remorse. Pierre Louys. *Fr.* The Songs of Bilitis. UnTE
At first, in that place, at all times, above the earth. The Walam Olum. *Unknown.* WoL
At first it will seem tame. Money. Victor Contoski. ThO
At first nothing is. Nothing Is. Sun-Ra. BF
At first she thought it a fantastic dream. Ballade of Charon and the River Girl. J. B. Morton. WhC
At first the river's very small. The Growing River. Rodney Bennett. BoTP
At first there all sea-water on the top land. On the Creation and Ontogony. *Unknown. Fr.* Wallam Olum. LiTA
At first we sat imprisoned in this place. Conversation in Black and White. May Sarton. GoYe
At first when I heard the old song. I Heard the Old Song. B. W. Vilakazi. PeSA
At first when we saw a girl. Sunday Afternoon. Philip Levine. NaP
At five in the afternoon. Lament for the Death of a Bullfighter [*or* Lament for Ignacio Sanchez Mejias]. Federico García Lorca. LiTW; ReMP
At five o'clock he milks the cow. The Breakfast Song. Emilie Poulsson. HBVY
At Flores in the Azores Sir Richard Grenville lay. The *Revenge* [*or* A Ballad of the Fleet]. Tennyson. BBV; BEL; BeLS; DTo; EnLi-2; EnLit; EPN; FaBoCh; FOL; HBV; HoPM; MaC; MCCG; OAEP; OnMSP; OTPC; PCD; PoRA; PoVP; ShBV-1; TOP; UnPo (1st ed.); ViPo
At Fontainebleau. Arthur Symons. VA
At Fotheringay. Robert Southwell. PoEL-2
(Decease, Release: Dum Morior Orior.) NCEP; SiCE
Martyrdom of Mary, Queen of Scots, The, *sel.* ACP
At four in the morning the smoke of the forded river. While We Slept. David Wolff. AnAmPo; TrJP
At four o'clock. Roosters. Elizabeth Bishop. AmLP; CrMA; FiMAP LiTM; NePA; OnHM
At four o'clock in the morning. Waking Time. Ivy O. Eastwick. SiSoSe; TiPo (1959 ed.)
At 14th Street and First Avenue. Strawberries in Mexico. Ron Padgett. ANYP
At Francis Allen's on the Christmas-eve. The Epic (Introduction to "Morte d'Arthur"). Tennyson. MBW-2; PoVP; ViPP
At Fredericksburg (December 13, 1862). John Boyle O'Reilly. MC; PAH
At Fyvie's yetts there grows a flower. Andrew Lammie [*or* The Trumpeter of Fyvie]. *Unknown.* ESPB; OxBB
At Galway Races. W. B. Yeats. SD
At Gibraltar (*Sonnets* I *and* II). George Edward Woodberry. AA; AnAmPo; GN
"England, I stand on thy imperial ground," *sel.* HBV
At Glastonbury. Henry Kingsley. *See* Magdalen.
At Glenalough lived a young saint. St. Kevin. Samuel Lover. OnYI
At Golgotha I stood alone. Edwin John Ellis. *Fr.* Himself. OBMV
At Graduating Time. *Unknown.* DD; PEDC; PoRL
At Grantchester. Charles Causley. POTi
At Grass. Philip Larkin. HaMV; NePoEA; PoeP; SD; WIRo
At Great Torrington, Devon. *Unknown.* ShM; SiTL
At Gull Lake: August, 1810. Duncan Campbell Scott. OBCV
At half-past six A.M. the sun. Beside the Sea. George Johnston. ACV
At half-past three a single bird. Emily Dickinson. AmLP; AP; MAmP; MoAmPo (1950 ed.); MWA-2; OxBA; TDP
At Hallowmas, whan nights grow lang. Hallow-Fair. Robert Fergusson. OxBS
At Haroun's court it chanced, upon a time. The World's Way. Thomas Bailey Aldrich. HBV; LHV
At Harvest. Joseph Campbell. NP
At hawthorn-time in Wiltshire travelling. Lob. Edward Thomas. MoVE
At her doorway Mrs. Mayle. The Lavender Bush. Elizabeth Fleming. BoTP
At Her Fair Hands. Walter Davison. *See* How Can the Heart Forget Her.
At Her Grave. Arthur O'Shaughnessy. PoVP; VA
At Her Window. Frederick Locker-Lampson. HBV; OBEV (1st ed.); OBVV

At High Mass. Robert Hugh Benson. CAW
At His Feet. Lois R. Carpenter. BePJ
At His Grave. Alfred Austin. VA
At his heart stood/ the poisoned point. Death in Battle. *Unknown. Fr.* The Battle of Maldon. PoLi
At Home. Christina Rossetti. PoVP; VA
At home alone, O Nomades. Home, Sweet Home, with Variations, IV. H. C. Bunner. BOHV; CenHV; InMe
At Home, Alone with the Cat. Walter de la Mare. BoC
At Home, Alone with the Dog. Harold Monro. *See* Hearthstone.
At home, as in no other city, here. Oxford. Keith Douglas. NePoEA
At Home in Heaven. James Montgomery. HBV; VA
At Home in Heaven. Robert Southwell. AnAnS-1; MeP
At home, in my flannel gown, like a bear to its floe. 90 North. Randall Jarrell. AP; CoAP; CoBMV; FiMAP; ILP; MoAB; MoPo; MoVE
At home it seems to be the rule. Ma's Tools. *Unknown.* PEDC
At home the hearth lies in sorrow such as this. The God of War. Aeschylus. *Fr.* Agamemnon. PPON
At home the sea is in the town. The Sea Eats the Land at Home. Kofi Awoonor. CAD
At Husking Time. E. Pauline Johnson. VA
At insular café tables under awnings. Green Coconuts. Lawrence Durrell. FaBoMo
At Ithaca. Hilda Doolittle ("H. D."). AnAmPo
At its far limits, the universe is daft. Quasistellar Radio Sources. Howard McCord. NYTB
At its margin. Ode to Arnold Schoenberg. Charles Tomlinson. NePoEA-2
At its own distance. Siciliana; the Landings at Gela. G. Stanley Koehler. NePoAm-2
At Knaresborough. Donald Davie. NePoEA
At Lagos you knew sad faced girls. Langston Hughes. Jacques Roumain. PoNe
At Lake Geneva. Richard Eberhart. LiTA
At Lanier's Grave. John Banister Tabb. AmP
At Last. Philip Bourke Marston. VA
At Last. Sir Lewis Morris. VA
At Last. Richard Henry Stoddard. HBV
At Last. Katrina Trask. AA
At Last. Whittier. AP; NeHB, *abr*; OQP, *abr.*; SoP; TreFS; TrPWD; WGRP
(To Paths Unknown.) MaRV; TRV
At last he came unto a gloomy glade. Spenser. *Fr.* The Faerie Queene, II, 7. MBW-1
At last her face was turned to him who knew. Seven Sad Sonnets, II. Mary Aldis. HBMV
At last I have a Sabine farm. My Sabine Farm. Eugene Field. InMe
At last I have ceased repining, at last I accept my fate. The Agnositc's Creed. Walter Malone. HBV
At last I put off love. He Abjures Love. Thomas Hardy. OBNC
At last Jeane come down stairs, a-drest. Jeane's Wedden Day in Mornen. William Barnes. PoVP
At last like a divining rod. Symphony. Christopher Hassall. MuSP
At last, O thou serene retreat. To Retirement. Luis de León. TrJP
At last our dull Earth listens. Earth Listens. Katharine Lee Bates. PGD
At last she calls to mind where hangs a piece. Troy Depicted. Shakespeare. *Fr.* The Rape of Lucrece. OBSC
At last she chauncèd by good hap to meet. Spenser. *Fr.* The Faerie Queene, I, 7. MBW-1
At last, so faire a ladie did I spie. The Visions of Petrarch. *Tr. by* Spenser. EnLi-1
At last the beautiful Palm Sunday comes. Palm Sunday. Francis Jammes. CAW
At last the bird that sang [*or* sung] so long. Good Friday Night. William Vaughn Moody. APA; StJW
At last the dawn throws the forest in relief. After the Agony in the Garden. Daryl Hine. PeCV
At Last the Secret Is Out. W. H. Auden *and* Christopher Isherwood. *Fr.* The Ascent of F 6. NAMP; SeCePo
At last to be identified! Emily Dickinson. WGRP
At last we are met—but I hope with no other. The Pacific Engagement. *Unknown. Fr.* Bungiana. WhC
At last we parley: we so strangely dumb. Modern Love, XLVI. George Meredith. EnLit; VA; ViPo
At last withdraw your cruelty. Sir Thomas Wyatt. FCP; SiPS
At last you are tired of being single. Poem Read at Joan Mitchell's. Frank O'Hara. ANYP
At last you do not find—you have—the dark. In Time of Darkness. Raymond Roseliep. FiSC
At last you yielded up the album, which. Lines on a Young Lady's Photograph Album. Philip Larkin. EnLoPo; NoP; ToPo
At least, it was a life of swords. Comrades. Lionel Johnson. HBV
At least—to pray—is left—is left. Emily Dickinson. AmePo; AP
At Leeds. *Unknown.* PV; WhC
At length a reverend sire among them came. The Ark. Milton. *Fr.* Paradise Lost, XI. EtS
At length arrived, your book I take. On Receiving a Copy of Mr. Austin Dobson's "Old World Idylls." James Russell Lowell. AP
At length, by so much importunity pressed [*or* press'd]. The Lover; a Ballad. Lady Mary Wortley Montagu. CEP; LO; OBEC
At length I saw a lady within call. Tennyson. *Fr.* A Dream of Fair Women. PoG
At length my chariot wheel about the mark hath found the way. Arthur Golding. ReIE
At length, my friends, the feast of life is o'er. On the Death of an Epicure. Richard Graves. CBEP
At length the finished garden to the view. James Thomson. *Fr.* The Seasons: Spring. ViBoPo
At length the term's ending. A Letter. Sir Arthur Quiller-Couch. CenHV
At length their long kiss severed, with sweet smart. Nuptial Sleep. Dante Gabriel Rossetti. The House of Life, VI. LoBV; MaVP; ViPo; ViPP; VP
At length there dawns the glorious day. Brotherhood. Ozora Stearns Davis. MaRV
At length came into a larger space. The Cave of Mammon. Spenser. *Fr.* The Faerie Queene, II, 7. FiP
At length 'tis done, the glorious conflict's done. On the Late Successful Expedition against Louisbourg. Francis Hopkinson. PAH
At length we have settled a pastor. Wanted, a Minister's Wife. *Unknown.* BLPA; TreFS
At length with jostling, elbowing and the aid. At the Gate of Heaven. Byron. *Fr.* The Vision of Judgment. OBRV
At Les Eboulements. Duncan Campbell Scott. VA
At liberty I sit and see. The Lover in Liberty Smileth at Them in Thraldom, That Sometime Scorned His Bondage. *Unknown.* EIL
At Lincoln. Oscar Fay Adams. AA
At Little Virgil's Window. Edwin Markham. TRV
At London in England, not a very long time. Saint Erkenwald. *Unknown.* MeEV
At Lord's. Francis Thompson. MemP
At Loschwitz above the city. The Birch-Tree at Loschwitz. Amy Levy. TrJP
At low tide like this how sheer the water is. The Bight. Elizabeth Bishop. NYBP; PoSa
At lucky moments we seem on the brink. W. H. Auden. PV
At Madame Tussaud's in Victorian Years. Thomas Hardy. MuSP
At Magnolia Cemetery. Henry Timrod. *See* Ode: "Sleep sweetly in your humble graves."
At Majority. Adrienne Rich. NePoEA-2
At Manhood End the older dead lie thick. Manhood End. Anthony Thwaite. NMP
At Manly. Leonard Mann. MoAuPo
At Marshfield. William Cleaver Wilkinson. *Fr.* Webster, an Ode. AA
At matyne houre in midis of the nicht. Honour with Age. Walter Kennedy. OxBS
At Melville's Tomb. Hart Crane. AmLP; AP; ATP (1953 ed.); CBV; CoBMV; FosPo; InPo; MoAmPo (1962 ed.); NePA; NoP; Po; PoIE; ReMP; SeCeV (1967 ed.); UnPo
At Memphis Station. Johannes V. Jensen, *tr. fr. Danish by* S. Foster Damon. WoL
At midday they looked up and saw their death. Three Memorial Sonnets, III. George Barker. WaP
At Midnight. Frank Dempster Sherman. AA; MAP

At Midnight. Joel Sloman. ThO
At midnight by the stream I roved. Lewti: or, The Circassian Love-Chaunt. Samuel Taylor Coleridge. EnRP; MERP
At midnight Death dismissed the chancellor. Lines on the Death of Bismarck. John Jay Chapman. PoEL-5
At midnight, death's and truth's unlocking-time. The Crystal. Sidney Lanier. AmP
At midnight, flaking down like chromium. Closing Time. David Wagoner. NYBP
At midnight from the zenith burst a light. The Angelic Chorus. D. J. Donahoe. JKCP
At midnight, in his guarded tent. Marco Bozzaris. Fitz-Greene Halleck. AA; BELS; FOL; GN; HBV; HoPM; PFY; TreF; WBLP
At midnight in the alley. The Tomcat. Don Marquis. CIV; PoMa; PoRA
At midnight, in the garden never planted. They Also Stand . . . Merrill Moore. CrMA
At midnight, in the month of June. The Sleeper. Poe. AA; AmePo; AmPP; AnFE; AP; APA; CBEP; CoAnAm; CoBA; InP; LiTA; MWA-1; NePA; OBVV; OxBA; PoEL-4; PoFS; TDP; TrGrPo; UnPo (1st ed.)
At midnight in the silence of the sleep-time. *See* At the midnight . . .
At midnight, sudden, dim-lit isolation. The Crow-Marble Whores of Paris. James Schevill. NMP
At midnight when cattle are sleeping. The Cowboy's Meditation. *Unknown.* CoSo
At Midnight's Hour I Raised My Head. Henry David Thoreau. PoEL-4
At Mrs. Appleby's. Elizabeth Upham McWebb. SiSoSe; StVeCh (1955 ed.); TiPo
At Monday dawn, I climbed into my skin. Diary. David Wagoner. CoAP
At moost mischief. My Lute and I. Sir Thomas Wyatt. MeEL
At morn, at noon, at eve, and middle night. The Poet. Keats. ERoP-2
At morn, at noon, at twilight dim. Hymn [*or* Hymn of the Angelus]. Poe. CAW; ISi
At morn I prayed, "I fain would see." Trinitas. Whittier. AmePo; SoP
At Morning an Iris. Patrick Evans. NeBP
At morning from the coldness of Mount Brandon. Aisling. Austin Clarke. AnIV
At morning's call. Our Hymn. Oliver Wendell Holmes. BOHV
At most mischief. Sir Thomas Wyatt. FCP; SiPS
At Mount Vernon. Thomas Curtis Clark. PAL; PGD
At Mürren let the morning lead thee out. Morgenlied. John Addington Symonds. Sonn
At my casement I sat by night, while the wind remote in dark valleys. Epilogue. Aubrey Thomas De Vere. IrPN
At My Father's Grave. Matthias Claudius, *tr. fr. German by* Ralph Marcus. WoL
At My Father's Grave. "Hugh MacDiarmid." ELU; GTBS-P; PoIE
At My Grandmother's. David Malouf. PoAu-2
At My Mother's Knee. John H. Styles, Jr. *See* My Altar.
At My Whisper. Lyle Donaghy. AnIV
At my windowpane a bird. That Is All I Heard. "Yehoash." TrJP
At Nazareth. Katharine Lee Bates. StJW
At Nebra, by the Unstrut. The Inn of Care. Samuel Waddington. OBVV; VA
At Newmarket. Samuel Bishop. PV
At Night ("My brain is like the ravaged shores"). Frances Cornford. MoBrPo
At Night ("On moony nights the dogs bark shrill"). Frances Cornford. StaSt; TSW
At Night. Alice Meynell. BoPe; Ch; HBV; LiTL; OBVV
(To W. M.) GoBC
At Night. George Edgar Montgomery. AA
At Night. Anne Blackwell Payne. GFA; UTS
At night, alone, the animals came and shone. The Animals. Josephine Jacobsen. GoYe
At night, as drough the mead I took my way. To Me. William Barnes. NBM; PoEL-4
At night, by the fire. Domination of Black. Wallace Stevens. AmPP; AnFE; AP; CoAnAm; CoBMV; ILP; MAP; MAPA; MoAB; MoAmPo; OxBA; PIA; PoeP; TDP; TPM; TwAmPo
At night here in the park it is different. The Man Among the Seals. Denis Johnson. QAH
At night in each other's arms. Love's Vision. Edward Carpenter. WGRP
At Night in the Wood. Nancy M. Hayes. BoTP
(Night in the Wood, A.) TVC
At night the Front like coloured barley-sugar; but now. Cricket at Brighton. Alan Ross. POTi
At night the ticking of the clock. The Clock. Jean Jaszi. SoPo
At night through the city in a song. For Them All. John Hall Wheelock. HBMV; TSW
At night what things will stalk abroad. Lux in Tenebris. Katharine Tynan. OxBI; TrPWD
At night when ale is in. Of Drunkenness. George Turberville. TuPP
At night when dying proceeds to sever all seams. Landscape of Screams. Nelly Sachs. NYBP
At night when I am tired of play. Bed Time. Ella Young. BoChLi (1950 ed.)
At night when sick folk wakeful lie. The Dead Coach. Katharine Tynan. HBV; VA
At night, when the black water-hen. The Heron. John Lyle Donaghy. NeIP
At night when there are no lights my city is a man who arises. The Lame One. Sherwood Anderson. AnAmPo
At night while/ whitey sleeps. Black Warrior. Norman Jordan. BF
At Nightfall. Charles Hanson Towne. BLPA; FaBoBe; NeHB
(Nightfall.) PoToHe (new ed.)
At nightfall, as the sea darkens. Ghost Crabs. Ted Hughes. HYE
At nine in the morning there passed a church. Faintheart in a Railway Train. Thomas Hardy. CTC; EnLoPo
At nine o'clock the bus snouts cityward. Nine o'Clock. Louis Simpson. PoNe
At noon in the desert a panting lizard. At the Bomb Testing Site. William Stafford. CoAP; LiTM (1970 ed.)
At noon she left her cavern cell. Imogen—in Wales. Thomas Caulfield Irwin. IrPN
At noon the sun puffed up, outsize. Idyll. Francis Webb. PoAu-2
At noon they buried her. The day was fair. Death on the Rancherie. Emily Leavens. TwCaPo
At noon, Tithonus, withered by his singing. The Wedding. Conrad Aiken. AnAmPo; CMoP; NoP
At once, from hence, my lines and I depart. To Mr. T. W. John Donne. MaMe; PP
At once in blacke I desrespected walkt. On a Maide of Honour Seene by a Schollar in Sommerset Garden. Thomas Randolph. MePo
At once whatever happened starts receding. Whatever Happened? Philip Larkin. Sonn
At once with him they rose. Hell. Milton. *Fr* Paradise Lost, II. OBS
At once with resolution fatal. John Trumbull. *Fr.* M'Fingal. AmPP (5th ed.)
At one o'clock the wind with sudden shift. The Shipwreck. Byron. *Fr.* Don Juan, II. MCCG
At one point of the journey, a memorable one. A Valentine. Hal Summers. ChMP
At one the Apocalypse had Spoken. Recapitulations, II. Karl Shapiro. FiMAP
At one time. An Aristotelian Elegy. Donald E. Bogle. TNV
At Only That Moment. Alan Ross. ErPo
At Ostend. William Lisle Bowles. *See* Sonnet: At Ostend.
At Palomar. Sister Mary Edwardine. JKCP (1955 ed.)
At Paris, hard by the Maine barriers. Thackeray. *Fr.* The Chronicle of the Drum. OtMeF
At Paris it was, at the opera there. Aux Italiens. "Owen Meredith." BeLS; BLPA; FaBoBe; HBV; TreFS; VA
At Parting. Swinburne. HBV; ViBoPo
At Parting. *Unknown.* SeCL
At Penshurst ("Had Sacharissa liv'd when mortals made"). Edmund Waller. AnAnS-2; NoP; PoFS; ReEn; SCEP-2
(At Penshurst Another.) SeCV-1
At Penshurst ("While in the park I sing, the listning deer."). Edmund Waller. AnAnS-2; OAEP
At Perigord near to the wall. A Periogord pres del muralh. Bertrans de Born. CTC

At Piccadilly Circus. Vivian de Sola Pinto. OBMV
At Polwart on the Green. Polwart on the Green. Allan Ramsay. CEP; EiCL
At Port Royal. Whittier. PAH, *abr.*; PAP
Song of the Negro Boatman, *sel.* GN
At Prayer Meeting. Margaret E. Sangster. SoP
At Prime Jesus was y-led. William of Shoreham. *Fr.* Hours of the Passion. ACP; CAW
At Quebec. Jean Blewett. CaP
At Quincey's moat the squandering [*or* straggling] village ends. Almswomen. Edmund Blunden. BoPe; GTBS; OBMV; POTE; ShBV-3
At Rest. Henry W. Frost. SoP
At Rest in the Blast. Marianne Moore. MoAB; MoAmPo (1950 ed.)
At Richmond the people walked along by the river. Mr. Symons at Richmond, Mr. Pope at Twickenham. Julian Symons. WaP
At Robert Fergusson's Grave, October 1962. Robert Garioch. OxBS
At Roblin Lake. Alfred Purdy. PeCV (1967 ed.)
At Rochecoart,/ Where the hills part. Provincia Deserta. Ezra Pound. CrMA; OxBA
At Runnymede, at Runnymede. The Reeds of Runnymede. Kipling. FOL
At Sagamore the Chief lies low. Sagamore. Corinne Roosevelt Robinson. HBMV; PoRL
At St. Jerome. Frances Harrison. WHW
At Saint Patrick's Purgatory. *At. to* Donnchadh mor O'Dala, *tr. fr. Middle Irish by* Seán O'Faoláin. AnIL; LiTW; OnYI
At Sainte-Marguerite. Trumbull Stickney. LiTA; MoVE; NCEP; OxBA; TwAmPo
At School-Close. Whittier. PoRL
At school I sometimes read a book. My Education. James Kenneth Stephen. WhC
At Sea. Allan Cunningham. *See* Wet Sheet and a Flowing Sea, A.
At Sea. Vera E. Guerard. TNV
At Sea. D. H. Rogers. AnNZ
At Sea. Jean Toomer. BALP
At Sea. John T. Trowbridge. AmePo; EtS
At Seeing Archbishop Williams's Monument at Carnarvonshire. Sneyd Davies. EiCL
At Sestos, Hero dwelt; Hero the fair[e]. Hero the Fair[e]. Christopher Marlowe. *Fr.* Hero and Leander. FaBoEn; WHA
At Set of Sun. "George Eliot." *See* Count That Day Lost.
At Set of Sun. Mary Ashley Townsend. AA
At setting day and rising morn. Song. Allan Ramsay. HBV
At seven, when I go to bed. A Child's Thought. Robert Louis Stevenson. BoTP
At seventeen I spent cold cash. Hearthside Story. X. J. Kennedy. CoPo
At Shakespeare's Grave. Irving Browne. AA
At Shelley's birth. To Shelley. John Banister Tabb. AA
At six o'clock. The Sound of Morning in New Mexico. Reeve Spencer Kelley. AmFN
At six o'clock we were waiting for coffee. A Miracle for Breakfast. Elizabeth Bishop. AmP; FiMAP; LiTA; MiAP; StP
At sixteen I came West, riding. A Living Pearl. Kenneth Rexroth. LiTM (1970 ed.)
At sixteen she was a potential celebrity. Clara. Ezra Pound. DTC
At sixteen years she knew no care. Butterflies. John Davidson. HBV
At steeplecock height. Quebec. Eldon Grier. PeCV
At Stratford-on-Avon. Mackenzie Bell. VA
At such an hour on such a day. I Broke My Trust with God. *Unknown.* SoP
At summer eve, when Heaven's ethereal bow. Thomas Campbell. *Fr.* The Pleasures of Hope. EnRP
At Sunrise. Rosa Zagnoni Marinoni. PoToHe
At Sunset. Ivy O. Eastwick. BoTP
At Sunset. Louis V. Ledoux. HBV
At sunset my brown nightingales. Nightingales. Grace Hazard Conkling. HBMV
At sunset only swamp. The Slough of Despond. Robert Lowell. SyP
At sunset, only to his true love. Bird of Paradise. Robert Graves. BoPE
At sunset, when the night-dews fall. The Snail. James Reeves. RePo
At table yonder sit the man we seek. At the Mermaid Inn. Charles Lotin Hildreth. AA
At Tara [*or* Tarah] today, in this awful hour. St. Patrick's Hymn before Tara [*or* Tarah]. James Clarence Mangan. EnRP; GoBC
At Tea. Thomas Hardy. Satires of Circumstance, I. PoVP; VaPo
At Teignmouth, *sel.* Keats.
Song of Spring. BoTP
At ten a clock, when I the fire rake. Epigrams. Francis Daniel Pastorius. SCAP
At ten A.M. the young housewife. The Young Housewife. William Carlos Williams. BWP; NoP
At Ten o'Clock in the Morning. Joseph Cardarelli. QAH
At Thames faire port. Praise of Poets. William Browne. *Fr.* Britannia's Pastorals, II, Song 1. OBS
At Thanksgiving. Jo Ann Leichliter. NYTB
At that hour when all things have repose. James Joyce. Chamber Music, III. HW
At that instant there came a crash. The Farmer's Head. Ron Padgett. ANYP
At That Moment. Raymond Patterson. WOW
At that so pleasant season of the year. On Fleet. Shepheard's Takeing away a Child's Bread and Butter. Matthew Prior. PeRV
At that time, saith the Lord, they shall bring out the bones. Peace! and There Is No Peace. Jeremiah, Bible, *O.T.* WoL
At the Abbey Theatre. W. B. Yeats. Sonn
At the Airport. John Malcolm Brinnin. MoAB
At the Alter-Rail. Thomas Hardy. Satires of Circumstance, IX. MoAB; MoBrPo; PoVP
At the Aquarium. Max Eastman. AnAmPo; FaPON; HBMV; OTPC (1946 ed.); PoMa; PoPo; StaSt; WGRP
At the Ascension. Luis de León, *tr. fr. Spanish by* Thomas Walsh. CAW
At the Assumption. Luis de León, *tr. fr. Spanish by* Thomas Walsh. CAW
At the Back of the North Wind, *sels.* George Macdonald.
Baby, The, *fr. ch.* 23. BiCB; FaPON; HBV; HBVY; MPB; OTPC; SoP; TreF; TRV; TVC; VA
(Song: "Where did you come from, baby dear?") PaPo
(Where Did You Come From?) BLPA; FaFP
At the Ball Game. Roswell Martin Field. InMe
At the Ball Game. William Carlos Williams. *See* Crowd at the Ball Game, The.
At the Battery Sea-Wall. Clifford James Laube. GoYe
At the big trumpet, we must all put on. Rise and Shine. Richmond Lattimore. NYBP
At the black wood's corner, not one green bud. Pluviose. Julian Bell. ChMP
At the boarding house where I live. Folk Song. *Unknown.* ShM
At the Bomb Testing Site. William Stafford. CoAP; LiTM (1970 ed.)
At the bonfire. Bonner's Ferry. Peter Schjeldahl. ANYP
At the Bottom of the Well. Louis Untermeyer. GoJo; MAP
At the break of Christmas Day. The Waits. Margaret Deland. DD; HH
At the British Museum. Richard Aldington. MoBrPo
At the British War Cemetery, Bayeux. Charles Causley. BoPE; POTE (1959 ed.); POTi
At the Cannon's Mouth. Herman Melville. PAH
At the Carnival. Anne Spencer. BANP; CDC; Kal; PoNe
At the Cedars. Duncan Campbell Scott. CaP; VA
At the Cenotaph. "Hugh MacDiarmid." NAMP
At the Cenotaph. Siegfried Sassoon. CMoP
(Make Them Forget.) MaRV
At the Church Gate. Thackeray. *Fr.* Pendennis, *ch.* 32. EPN; HBV; VA
At the Circus. Dorothy Aldis. TiPo (1952 ed.); UTS
Bare-Back Rider.
Elephants, The.
Seals, The.
At the close of a winter day. The Rhyme of the Three Captains. Kipling. BeLS
At the Closed Gate of Justice. James David Corrothers. BANP
At the Comedy. Arthur Stringer. HBV
At the corner of Wood Street, when daylight appears. The Reverie of Poor Susan. Wordsworth. CBEP; CH; EnRP;

At (continued)
ERoP-1; GTBS; GTBS-D; GTBS-P; GTBS-W; GTSE; GTSL; HBV; MBW-2; MCCG; MERP; OTPC (1923 ed.); OxBoLi; ShBV-1; WiR
At the Cross. *Unknown.* STF
At the cross her station keeping. Stabat Mater [Dolorosa]. *At. to* Jacopone da Todi, *tr. fr. Latin by* Richard Mant *and* Edward Caswall. TreFS; WGRP; WHL
At the Crossroads. Richard Hovey. BBV (1951 ed.); HBV; MAP; MoAmPo (1942 ed.); NeMA; PFY; PoMa
At the cross-roads I came upon the delinquent moon. Templeogue. Blanaid Salkeld. NeIP
At the cry of the first bird. The Crucifixion. *Unknown.* OnYI; OxBI
At the dance in the village. Mairgread ni Chealleadh. Edward Walsh. IrPN
At the Dark Hour. Paul Dehn. WaP
At the Dawn. Alice Macdonald Kipling. MaRV
At the dawn I seek Thee. Morning Song. Solomon ibn Gabirol. TrJP
At the day's end we have visions, sometimes, and. Phases of the Moon. John Dos Passos. OTD
At the dead centre of the boundless plain. The Riders. Edwin Muir. *Fr* Variations on a Time Theme. MoVE; PIA
At the Discharge of Cannon Rise the Drowned. Hubert Witheford. AnNZ
At the Dog Show. Christopher Morley. MoShBr; MPB
At the Door. Lillie Fuller Merriam. PoToHe
At the door of his hut sat Massasoit. The Peace Message. Burton Egbert Stevenson. PAH
At the door on summer evenings. Hiawatha's Childhood [*or* Firefly Song]. Longfellow. *Fr.* The Song of Hiawatha. BoTP; PCD
At the Doors. "Der Nistor," *tr. fr. Yiddish by* Joseph Leftwich. TrJP
At the Draper's. Thomas Hardy. Satires of Circumstance, XII. EnLi-2 (1949 ed.); MoAB; MoBrPo; PoeP; VaPo
At the earliest ending of winter. Not Ideas about the Thing but the Thing Itself. Wallace Stevens. ViBoPo (1958 ed.)
At the Ebony Circle. Helen G. Quigless. TNV
At the Edge. Sister Mary Norbert Körte. ThO
At the edge of all the ages. The Song of Finis. Walter de la Mare. MoBrPo
At the Edge of the Bay. Thomas Caldecot Chubb. EtS
At the Edge of the Day. Clarence Urmy. HBMV
At the end I will bellow my challenge. Phantoms. Harry McGuire. CAW
At the end of a full day of walking we found. Passion. Galway Kinnell. NePoAm
At the end of a long-walled garden. The Cottage Hospital. John Betjeman. GTBS-P; MoBrPo (1962 ed.); MoVE; UnPo (3d ed.)
At the end of my yard there is a vat. Riddle. *Unknown.* ChTr
At the end of the bough! Sweet Apple. James Stephens. CMoP
At the End of the Day. Richard Hovey. HBVY; StaSt; YT
At the end of the garden. Pumpkins. John Cotton. BoNaP
At the end of the garden walk. The Cold Green Element. Irving Layton. OBCV
At the end of the third act, poetry gutters down. After Shakespeare. Alex Comfort. ErPo
At the End of Things. Arthur Edward Waite. WGRP
"Cast away fear," *sel.* TRV
At the end will be but rust. The Empty Soul. Walter R. Bowie. MaRV
At the equinox when the earth was veiled in a late rain. Continent's End. Robinson Jeffers. AnFE; AWP; CoAnAm; FaBV; ImOP; InPo; JAWP; ReMP; TwAmPo; WBP
At the Executed Murderer's Grave. James Wright. AmPC
At the far end of a trip north. Nooksack Valley. Gary Snyder. NaP
At the feast of Belshazzar and a thousand of his lords. The Handwriting on the Wall. Knowles Shaw. BLPA
At the first hour from dawn. Journey through the Night. John Holloway. NePoEA
At the first hour, it was as if one said, "Arise." Spring. John Gould Fletcher. PFY
At the first peep of dawn she roused me! The Wanderer: Paterson—the Strike. William Carlos Williams. MAPA; TwAmPo
At the first sound the golden sun arises from the deep. Enitharmon Revives with Los. Blake. *Fr.* Vala; or, The Four Zoas. OBNC
At the first stepping-stone, the past of water. The Stepping Stones. Conrad Aiken. CrMA
At the Fishhouses. Elizabeth Bishop. CoAP; FiMAP; LiTM (1970 ed.); MoVE; NYBP; PoRA (rev. ed.)
At the Fishing Settlement. Alistair Campbell. AnNZ
At the Florists' Feast in Norwich. Matthew Stevenson. SeCL
At the focus of thought there is no face. The Crystal Skull. Kathleen Raine. CMoP; FaBoMo; NeBP
At the foot of a great pine, in the wild country. Reconciliation. John Hall Wheelock. CrMA
At the foot of yon mountain, where the fountain doth flow. Red River Shore. *Unknown.* ABF; CoSo
At the foot of your dry well. Reunion. W. S. Merwin. AmPC
At the Fountain. Marcabrun, *tr. fr. French by* Harriet Waters Preston. AWP; JAWP; WBP
At the Front. John Erskine. HBMV
At the game which is my life. The Game. Conrado Nalé Roxlo. OnPM
At the Garden Gate. David McCord. FaPON; RIS; StaSt
At the Garden Rail. A. M. Buckton. BoSA
At the Gate. Chaucer. *Fr.* Troilus and Criseyde. SeCePo
At the Gate of Heaven. Byron. *Fr.* The Vision of Judgment. OBRV
(Archangel, The.) LoBV
At the gate of old Granada, when all its bolts are barred. The Lamentation for Celin. *Unknown, tr. by* John Gibson Lockhart. AWP; JAWP; OuHeWo; PoFr; WBP
At the gate of the West I stand. "Scum o' the Earth." Robert Haven Schauffler. HBV; PaA; PoFr; TIHL
At the Goal. Christina Rossetti. OQP
At the Grave of a Land-Shark. Ernest G. Moll. WhC
At the Grave of Burns [1803]. Wordsworth. Memorials of a Tour in Scotland, 1803, II. BEL; EnLi-2; EnRP; MERP
At the Grave of Cecil Rhodes. Peter Jackson. BoSA
At the Grave of Champernowne. John Albee. HBV
At the Grave of Dante Gabriel Rossetti. Mackenzie Bell. VA
At the Grave of Henry James. W. H. Auden. LiTA; MoPo
At the Grave of Henry Vaughan. Siegfried Sassoon. ChMP; CMoP; EaLo; GTBS-P; POTE
At the Grave of John Clare, *sel.* Charles Causley.
"Walking in the scythed churchyard." FIW
At the Grave of Selvaggia. Cino da Pistoia. *See* Sonnet: Of the Grave of Selvaggia.
At the Grave of Walker. Joaquin Miller. AA; AnAmPo; AnFE; APA; CoAnAm
At the Great Wall of China. Edmund Blunden. GTBS-P; HaMV
At the great water's edge/ Golden Narcissus lies. Narcissus. Alistair Campbell. AnNZ
At the grey dawn, amongst the falling leaves. A Bird from the West. Dora Sigerson Shorter. OBVV
At the Hacienda. Bret Harte. AA
At the heart of the cyclone tearing the sky. The Place of Peace. Edwin Markham. FaChP; MaRV; OQP; SoP; TreFT; TRV
At the high ridge. The Wooden Christ. Martha Foote Crow. ChIP; StJW
At the inn there was no room. The Loan of a Stall. James L. Duff. ISi
At th' ivory tribunall of your hand. Two Dedicatory Poems. Richard Crashaw. MaMe
At the Keyhole. Walter de la Mare. DTC; MoAB; MoBrPo
At the king's gate the subtle noon. Coronation. Helen Hunt Jackson. AA; BeLS; GN; HBV; PFY; PTK
At the kitchen table with Mrs. Hartman. The Young Man. Lewis Mac Adams. ANYP
At the large foot of a fair hollow tree. The Country Mouse. Abraham Cowley. SeCP
At the Last. Vincent David Engels. CAW
At the Last. Philip Bourke Marston. HBV; VA
At the last, tenderly. The Last Invocation [*or* The Imprisoned Soul]. Walt Whitman. AmP; AnFE; APA; BoLiVe; CoAnAm; GTBS-D; HBV; MAP; MaRV; MoAmPo; NeMA; OBEV; OQP; OxBA; PoEL-5; SoP; TOP; TreFT; TrGrPo; TrPWD; TRV; WGRP
At the last tumult of the railroad. Anniversary of Antonia Pozzi's Death by Suicide. Vittorio Serini. OnPM
At the Lavendar Lantern. Charles Divine. HBMV

At the Leap of the Waters. Edward F. Garesché. JKCP
At the Lincoln Memorial. William E. Brooks. OQP
At the Lincoln Tomb. John H. Bryant. PGD
At the little window is the tiny hand. Clean and Clear. Michael Brownstein. ANYP
At the long meadow's end, where the road runs. The Pond. Howard Nemerov. FiMAP
At the Lord's table waiting, robed and stoled. An Incident. Frederick Tennyson. GoBC
At the Mermaid, *sel.* Robert Browning.
My Sun Sets to Rise Again. MaRV
At the Mermaid Cafeteria. Christopher Morley. PFY
At the Mermaid Inn. Charles Lotin Hildreth. AA
At the Mid Hour of Night. Thomas Moore. AnIV; FaBoEn; GoBC; GTBS; GTSE; GTSL; HBV; NBM; OAEP; OBEV; OBNC; OBRV; OxBI; PeER; PoEL-4; TreFS; ViBoPo
("At the mid hour of night, when stars are weeping, I fly.") GTBS-D; GTBS-P; GTBS-W
At the Mid Hour of Night. *Unknown, tr. fr. Greek by* Thomas Stanley. WoL
At the midnight in the silence of the sleep-time. Epilogue. Robert Browning. *Fr.* Asolando. BEL; BoLiVe; CoBE; EnL; EnLi-2; EnLit; EPN; FaBoEn; FaBV; FiP; GTSL; HBV; HBVY; InP; MaRV; MBW-2; OAEP; OBNC; OBVV; OHFP; OQP; OuHeWo; PoIE; PoVP; TOP; TreFT; TrGrPo; VA; ViBoPo; ViPo; ViPP
At the midsummer, when the hay was down. Four Years. Dinah Maria Mulock Craik. HBV
At the muezzin's call for prayer. Ad Coelum. Harry Romaine. BLPA; FaBoBe; NeHB
At the Nadir. Gerta Kennedy. PoPl
At the New Year. Kenneth Patchen. AnFE; CoAnAm; LiTM (1970 ed.); ToPo
(Before the Bells of this New Year Ring.) WOW
At the next vacancy for God, if I am elected. In Place of a Curse. John Ciardi. CaFP; ToPo
At the Ninth Hour. John Lancaster Spalding. *Fr.* God and the Soul. AA
At the Ocean's Verge. Ralph Gustafson. OBCV
At the old concert hall on the Bowery. She Is More to Be Pitied than Censured. William B. Gray. BeLS; BLPA; TreF
At the Pantomime. Oliver Wendell Holmes. AnNE
At the Party. W. H. Auden. PoIE (1970 ed.)
At the Party. Freda Laughton. NeIP
At the Place of the Roman Baths. "Richard Scrace." CaP
At the Place of the Sea. Annie Johnson Flint. BLPA; FaChP; OQP; STF
(Red Sea Place in Your Life, The.) BLRP; SoP
At the Poem Society a black-haired man stands up to say. Fresh Air. Kenneth Koch. NeAP; PP
At the Portal. Frances Ridley Havergal. BLRP
At the President's Grave. Richard Watson Gilder. PAH
At the Railway Station, Upway. Thomas Hardy. FIW
At the road's end glimmer the station lights. Fetching the Wounded. Laurence Binyon. MMA
At the Roman Baths, Bath. Edward Lucie-Smith. NePoEA-2
At the round earth's imagin'd [*or* imagined] corners, blow. Holy Sonnets, VII. John Donne. AnAnS-1; AnEnPo; AtBAP; ATP (1953 ed.); BWP; CABA; CBEP; CBV; ChTr; CoBE; DiPo; EaLo; EnRePo; EP; ExPo; FaBoEn; FIW; ForPo; FosPo; ILP; InPo; LiTB; LiTG; LoBV; MaMe; MaPo; MasP; MBW-1; MeLP; MeP; MePo; MyFE; NoP; OAEP; OBS; OxBoCh; PAn; PIA; Po; PoAn; PoEL-2; PoFS; PoIE; QFR; ReEn; SCEP-1; SeCeV; SeCP; SeCV-1; SeEP; ShBV-4; Sonn; StP; TDP; TreFT; TuPP; VaPo; ViBoPo; YAT
At the rude goodness. Vernal Showers. David O'Neil. AnAmPo
At the safari's end a porter. H. C. Bosman. *Fr.* The Luck in the Square Stone. BoSA
At the Salon. Florence Wilkinson Evans. HBV
At the San Francisco Airport. Yvor Winters. ForPo; QFR
At the Saturday Club. Oliver Wendell Holmes. AmePo; AmPP (3d ed.); CoBA
At the Savoy Chapel. Robert Graves. HW
At the Seaside. Robert Louis Stevenson. FaPON; GFA; MPB (1956 ed.); OTPC; StVeCh (1940 ed.); SUS; TiPo
At the Seed and Feed. J. Edgar Simmons. NYTB
At the segregated party. Evening in the Suburbs. Stella Barnett. PV
At the Setting of the Sun. *Unknown.* CBEP
At the Ship. R. P. Lister. FiBHP
At the Shrine. Richard Kendall Munkittrick. AA
At the side of my husband. Eliza Spaulding. Donald Burnie. PaA
At the siege of Belle Isle. *Unknown.* OxNR
At the Sign of the Cock. Sir Owen Seaman. BOHV
At the Slackening of the Tide. James Wright. AmPC; CABA; UnPo (3d ed.)
At the source of my forces my memory. All Life. Paul Eluard. OnPM
At the station exit, my bundle in hand. No More Hiroshimas. James Kirkup. POTi
At the stern sat Hiawatha. Hiawatha's Fishing. Longfellow. *Fr.* The Song of Hiawatha. PoG
At the summit of perception. Prince Henry the Navigator. Sydney Clouts. PeSA
At the Sunrise in 1848. Dante Gabriel Rossetti. PoVP
At the Symphony. Robert Nathan. HBMV; MAP; PoRL; TSW
At the table beyond us. Black Slippers: Bellotti. Ezra Pound. NoP
At the Telephone Club. Henri Coulette. CoAP
At the Tennis Clinic. I. L. Martin. SD
At the Theater. Rachel Field. FaPON; GFA; MPB
At the Theater. A. P. Herbert. FiBHP
At the time it seemed unimportant: he was lying. The Day. Roy Fuller. ToPo
At the time of Matines, Lord thu were itake. The Hours of the Passion. *Unknown.* MeEL
At the Tomb of Rachel. "Yehoash," *tr. fr. Yiddish by* Isidore Goldstick. TrJP
At the Tomb of Washington. Clinton Scollard. DD; MC; OHIP; PEDC
At the Tombs of the House of Savoy. William Jay Smith. NePoAm-2
At the Top of My Voice. Vladimir Mayakovsky, *tr. fr. Russian by* Herbert Marshall. OnHM
"My verse will reach you," *sel., tr. by* Babette Deutsch. LiTW
At the top of the house the apples are laid in rows. Moonlit Apples. John Drinkwater. BoNaP; BoPe; BoTP; OBMV; PoRA
At the Top of the Road. Charles Buxton Going. HBV
At the top of the world, where fields of snow. Mrs. Santa Claus' Christmas Present. Alice S. Morris. PoSC
At the training depot that first morning. The Misfit—1939-1945. C. Day Lewis. BoC
At the village emporium in Woodstock. Limerick. Frederick Winsor. WhC
At the Wedding March. Gerard Manley Hopkins. HW; PoLi
At the White Mass. Lilies. Padraic Colum. NePoAm
At the window holding. Saint. Stéphane Mallarmé. SyP
At the Winter Solstice. Daniel G. Hoffman. StP
At the Worst. Israel Zangwill. WGRP
"Evil is here? That's work for us to do," *sel.* TRV
At the "Ye That Do Truly." Charles Williams. OxBoCh
At the Zoo. A. A. Milne. FaPON; TiPo (1959 ed.)
At the Zoo. Anne May Smith. PCH
At the Zoo. Israel Zangwill. TrJP
At thee the Mocker sneers in cold derision. The Maid of Orleans. Schiller. AWP; JAWP; WBP
At Thermopylae. Simonides. *See* Thermopylae.
At these high words great heaven began to shake. A Prayer Brings Rain. Tasso, *tr. by* Edward Fairfax. *Fr.* Godfrey of Bulloigne. OBSC
At these two men well may we churchmen scoff. Simon and Judas. Kenneth W. Porter. ChIP
At thieves I bark'd, at lovers wagg'd my tail. Epitaph on the Lap-Dog of Lady Frail. John Wilkes. ALV
At Thirty Years. Byron. *Fr.* Don Juan, I. FiP
At This Farewell. Wordsworth. *See* Dear Native Regions.
At This Moment of Time. Delmore Schwartz. TwAmPo
At this our solstice of history. Prayer to St. Lucy. John Heath-Stubbs. BoPe
At this the last yet second meeting. The Encounter. Lawrence Durrell. *Fr.* Eight Aspects of Melissa. NeBP
At three in the morning. Pointed Boots. Christopher Middleton. *Fr.* Herman Moon's Hourbook. NePoEA-2
At Tide Water. Sir Charles G. D. Roberts. PeCV
At Timber Line. Frank H. Mayer. PoOW
At times I am fast confined by my Master. A Storm. *Unknown. Fr.* Riddles. EnLi-1; OuHeWo

At times I resort, beyond man's discerning. Wind. *Unknown.* *Fr.* Riddles. AnOE
At times I see it, present. A Bright Day. John Montague. NYTB
At times I travel in tracks undreamed of. A Storm, II. *Unknown.* *Fr.* Riddles. OuHeWo
At times when we're walking. Underground Rumbling. James S. Tippett. GFA
At Timon's Villa. Pope. *See* Timon's Villa.
At Toledo. Arthur Symons. BrPo
At Trumpyngtoun nat fer from Cantebrigge. The Reeve's Tale. Chaucer. *Fr.* The Canterbury Tales. ViBoPo
At Twelfth Night twilight now. Twelfth Night. Philip Booth. NePoEA
At twelve bell answers bell. Angelus-Time near Dublin. William Bedell Stanford. NeIP
At twelve, the disintegration of afternoon. What We See Is What We Think. Wallace Stevens. SyP
At twenty-one Jupe ran away. Slave Story. Hodding Carter. PoNe (1970 ed.)
At Twilight. Peyton Van Rensselaer. AA
At two A.M. a thing, jumping out of a manhole. News Report. David Ignatow. ErPo; TwCP
At Tynemouth Priory, after a Tempestuous Voyage. William Lisle Bowles. Sonn
At Vallauris and Vence, Picasso and Matisse. Picasso and Matisse. Robert Francis. NePoAm
At Venice. Arthur Hugh Clough. ViPo
In the Piazza at Night.
On the Lido.
At Viscount Nelson's lavish funeral. 1805. Robert Graves. ChMP; EvOK; FaBoCh; HaMV; LoGBV
At War. Russell Atkins. AmNP
At War. Charles Madge. FaBoMo
At Warm Springs. William Rose Benét. PoRL
At Wednesbury there was a cocking. Wednesbury Cocking. *Unknown.* EnSB
At Welbedacht. A. M. Buckton. BoSA
At what a great cost God gave to the world. He's Come! The Savior Has Come! Alice Mortenson. BePJ
At whiles (yea oftentimes) I muse over. Dante. *Fr.* La Vita Nuova. AWP; JAWP; WBP
At Whose Sheltering Shall the Day Sea. W. S. Graham. FaBoMo
At Winchester was a wedding. The Winchester Wedding. Thomas D'Urfey. CavP
At Winter's End. Sister Mary Madeleva. JKCP
At Woodlawn I heard the dead cry. The Lost Son. Theodore Roethke. AP; CoBMV; FiMAP; LiTM (1970 ed.); MiAP; MoPo; NePA; PIA; PoeP; ReMP; TrGrPo (rev. ed.); TwAmPo
At Woodward's Gardens. Robert Frost. ImOP
At Wu Shan, of an autumn night. The Fireflies. Tu Fu. OnPM
At Year's-End. Richard Wilbur. LiTM (rev. ed.); MiAP; NePA; NYBP
(Year's-End.) CoAP; FiMAP; NePoEA; PoAn; PoIE
At Your Service; the Panama Gang. Berton Braley. BLPA
At your voice,/ Panic, despair, flee away. Contagion of Courage. Matthew Arnold. *Fr.* Rugby Chapel. MaRV
Atalanta in Calydon. Swinburne. ViPo
Sels.
Before the Beginning of Years. ACV; BEL; EnL; EPN; FaFP; HBV; LiTB; LiTG; MasP; NoP; OAEP; PoFS; PoVP; ViPP; VP; WHA
(Chorus: "Before the beginning of years.") EnLit; GTBS-D; GTBS-W; LoBV; OBVV; TRV
(Chorus from "Atalanta.") CBEP; OBEV (new ed.)
(Choruses from "Atalanta in Calydon.") EnLi-2; GTSE; ViBoPo
(Life of Man, The.) TOP
(Man.) BoLiVe; TrGrPo
Chorus: "Who hath given man speech?" MaVP
(Choruses from "Atalanta in Calydon.") ViBoPo
Death of Meleager, The. OBVV; PoVP
"Maiden, and mistress of the months and stars." PoEL-5
(Invocation.) PoVP
Not as with Sundering of the Earth. PoVP
We Have Seen Thee, O Love. BEL; PoVP
(Chorus: "We have seen thee, O Love.") MaVP; VA
(Choruses from "Atalanta in Calydon.") EnLi-2
When the Hounds of Spring [Are on Winter's Traces]. BoLiVe; CoBE; EnL; EvOK; FaBoBe; HBV; LiTB; MasP; NoP; PoFS; PoVP; TreF; TrGrPo; ViPP; VP
(Chorus: "When the hounds of spring are on winter's traces.") AnFE; AWP; CTC; EnLit; EPN; ExPo; FaBoEn; GTBS-P; ILP; InPo; JAWP; OBEV; OuHeWo; Po; PoIE; PoSa; RG, *abr.*; SeCeV; ShBV-4; TOP; VA; WBP; YAT
(Chorus from "Atalanta.") GTSL
(Choruses from "Atalanta in Calydon.") EnLi-2; ViBoPo
(Hounds of Spring, The.) BEL; FaBV; YT
Atalanta in Camden-Town. "Lewis Carroll." ALV; CenHV
Atalanta's Defeat. William Morris. *Fr.* The Earthly Paradise. VA
Atalanta's Race. William Morris. *Fr.* The Earthly Paradise. BEL; DTo; ViPo
Atalanta's Victory. William Morris. *Fr.* The Earthly Paradise. VA
Ataraxia. Bert Leston Taylor. HBMV; InMe
Atavism. Elinor Wylie. AnEnPo; FiSC; HBMV; NP
Athalie, *sel.* Racine, *tr. fr. French by* Charles Randolph.
Chorus: "God whose goodness filleth every clime, The." CAW; WGRP
Athanasia. Oscar Wilde. BrPo
Atheist. E. Y. Harburg. PV
Atheist and the Acorn, The. Countess of Winchilsea. EiCL
Atheist Buries His Son, The. Abu'l Atahija, *tr. fr. Arabic by* Henry Baerlein. LiTW
Atheist's Tragedy, The, *sels.* Cyril Tourneur.
"Cease that harsh musick; we are not pleas'd with it," *fr.* V, i. AtBAP
"His body lies interred within this mold," *fr.* III, i. SiCE
(Epitaph on a Soldier.) ElL
Walking Next Day upon the Fatal Shore, *fr.* II, i. ViBoPo; WaaP
Soldier's Death, A, *shorter sel.* SeCePo
Athelstan King. Battle of Brunanburh. *Unknown, See* Æthelstan King. *tr. fr. Anglo-Saxon by* Tennyson.
Athenian Aeschylus, Euphorion's son,/ This tomb at Gela holds. Aeschylus. Aeschylus (Simonides, *wr.*), *tr. by* Lord Neaves. OnPM
Athenian Dead, The. Simonides, *tr. fr. Greek by* T. F. Higham. WoL
Athenian Garden, An. Trumbull Stickney. NCEP
Athens. Milton. *Fr.* Paradise Regained, IV. OBS
("Look once more ere we leave this specular Mount," *shorter sel.*) SeEP; ViBoPo
(Vision of Athens, *shorter sel.*) TOP
Athens, a fragile kingdom by the foam. Triumph. John Crowe Ransom. HBMV
Athirst in spirit, through the gloom. The Prophet. Pushkin. AWP; EaLo; JAWP; LiTW; WBP; WGRP
Athlete. Don Maynard. PoAu-2
Athlete, virtuoso. For One Who Would Not Take His Life in His Hands. Delmore Schwartz. NAMP
Athletes. Walker Gibson. SD
Athletic Code. George Santayana. AmePo
Athletic Employment. *Unknown.* SD
Athulf's Death Song. Thomas Lovell Beddoes. *Fr.* Death's Jest Book, IV, iii. VA
Athwart the island here, from sea to sea. Inscriptions for the Caledonian Canal. Robert Southey. NBM
Athwart the jangling of our creeds is heard. Come, Follow Me! Thomas Curtis Clark. ChIP
Athwart the sky a lowly sigh. London. John Davidson. OBNC; StP; VA
Athwart the sod which is treading for God. Francis Thompson. *Fr.* A Judgment in Heaven. CoBE
Athwart the sunrise of our western day. Achilles. Ernest Myers. OBVV
Atisket, Atasket. *Unknown.* *See* Itiskit, Itaskit.
"Atkins." George Meredith. PoVP
Atlantic Charter; 1942. Francis Brett Young. *Fr.* The Island. BBV (1951 ed.); PAL
(Atlantic Charter, A.D. 1620-1942.) AmFN; TiPo (1952 ed.)
Atlantic is a stormy moat, and the Mediterranean, The. The Eye. Robinson Jeffers. AmLP; AP; CoBMV; CrMA; FaBoEn; GTBS-W; LiTA; LiTM; OxBA; PoPo; WaP
Atlantic Moonrise. Vivian L. Virtue. PoNe
Atlandid islands, phantom-fair. Frederick William Henry Myers. *Fr.* Teneriffe. OBVV
Atlantides, The. Henry David Thoreau. *Fr.* A Week on the

Concord and Merrimack Rivers. BWP; ViBoPo
Atlantis. Conrad Aiken. *Fr.* Priapus and the Pool. SiSw
("There was an island in the sea.") CMoP
Atlantis. W. H. Auden. FaBoTw; PoPl
Atlantis. Gordon Bottomley. POTE
Atlantis. Stanton A. Coblentz. FiSC
Atlantis. Hart Crane. *Fr.* The Bridge. AmLP; AnFE; AtBAP; CoAnAm; LiTA; LiTM; MoPo; NePA; TwAmPo
Atlantis, *sel.* Louis Dudek.
Marine Aquarium, The. MoCV
Atlas, The, *sels.* Kenneth Slessor. PoAu-2
Dutch Seacoast.
King of Cuckooz, The.
Mermaids. NeLNL
Post-Roads.
Atoll in the Mind, The. Alex Comfort. FaBoMo; GTBS-W; LiTB; LiTM; POTE; SeCePo
Atom from Atom. Emerson. *Fr.* Fragments on Nature and Life. ImOP
("Atom from atom yawns as far.") TiPo (1959 ed.)
Atomic Courtesy. Ethel Jacobson. FaFP; LiTM (rev. ed.); ShM; SiTL
Atonement. Margaret E. Bruner. MaRV
Atonement, The. Gerald Gould. POTE
Atonement. Marie LeNart. ChIP; OQP
Atonement, The. Milton. *Fr.* Paradise Lost, III. OBS
Atonement? Lord, who doth atone today? Atonement. Marie LeNart. ChIP; OQP
A-traipsin' from a shindig, I unsaddles. Agamemnon Before Troy. John Frederick Nims. Sonn
Atropos. John Myers O'Hara. AnAmPo
Attack, The. Thomas Buchanan Read. PAH
Attack. Siegfried Sassoon. MCCG; MoBrPo; PoMa
Attack me, Father, now. Prayer for Peace. Johnstone G. Patrick. TrPWD
Attack on Finnsburg, The. *Unknown, tr. fr. Anglo-Saxon by* Francis B. Gummere. BEL
Attainment. Madison Cawein. WGRP
Attainment, The. Coventry Patmore. The Angel in the House, I, iii, 4. OBVV
(Preludes, II.) GoBC
Attainment. Algernon Tassin. AA
Attainment. Ella Wheeler Wilcox. OQP; WGRP
Attend [*or* Come], all ye who list to hear our noble England's praise. The Armada. Macaulay. BeLS; BHV; FaBoCh; GN; HBV; LoGBV; OBRV; OTPC (1923 ed.); ShBV-2; WBLP
Attend Church? Of course we do. Attending Church. *Unknown.* STF
Attend my fable if your ears be clean. Roy Campbell. *Fr.* The Wayzgoose. BoSA
Attend, my Muse, and, if you can, approve. In Praise of Young Girls. Raymond Asquith. OtMeF
Attend my words, my gentle knave. Stans Puer ad Mensam. Sir Walter Raleigh. WhC
Attend, ye mournful parents, while. Another to Urania. Benjamin Colman. SCAP
Attendant angel, mark this one. Mill Girl. James K. Baxter. AnNZ
Attenders to this day. This and More. Glenn Siebert. HW
Attending Church. *Unknown.* STF
Attentive eyes, fantastic heed. A Poet. Thomas Hardy. VP
Attic, The. Charles Bruce. *Fr.* The Flowing Summer. CaP
Attic, The. Henri Coulette. NePoEA-2; PoPl; PoRA (rev. ed.)
Attic, The. Richard Eberhart. *Fr.* Burr Oaks. MoAB
Attic, The. Rose Fyleman. PCH
Attic. William Hathaway. QAH
Attic and the cedar chest—nostalgia! The Attic. Richard Eberhart. *Fr.* Burr Oaks. MoAB
Attic Landscape, The. Herman Melville. MWA-1
Attic maid! with honey fed. A Swallow. Euenus, *tr. by* William Cowper. WoL
Attic window's in the ceiling, The. The Attic. Rose Fyleman. PCH
Atticus. Pope. *Fr.* Epistle to Dr. Arbuthnot. AWP; JAWP; MaPo; OBEC; PoSa; SeCePo; ShBV-4; WBP; WHA
(Characters from the Satires: Atticus.) InPo
("Peace to all such! but were there One whose fires.") PoFS; ViBoPo
(Portrait of Atticus.) UnPo (1st ed.)
Attila's spirit rides again the red roads of the East. Ave, Vita Nostra! Clifford James Laube. ISi
Attired in black, spangled with flames of fire. The Spirit of Night. Thomas Rogers. ElL
Attitudes. Richard Eberhart. ToPo
Attitudes for a New Zealand Poet, III. Allen Curnow. AnNZ
Attorney was taking a turn, An. The Briefless Barrister. John G. Saxe. ShM
Attraction. *Unknown.* STF
Attractions of a Fashionable Irish Watering Place, The. Francis Sylvester Mahony. IrPN; NBM
Atween the world o' licht. Scotland. William Soutar. OxBS
Au Jardin des Plantes. John Wain. FlW; NePoEA-2
Au Tombeau de Mon Père. Ronald McCuaig. PoAu-2
Aubade. Sir William Davenant. *See* Lark Now Leaves His Wat'ry Nest, The.
Aubade. William Empson. FaBoTw; LiTB; ToPo
Aubade. Dilys Laing. NMP
Aubade. Louis MacNeice. ViBoPo
Aubade. Shakespeare. *See* Hark! Hark! the Lark.
Aubade. Edith Sitwell. CMoP; ExPo; InP; MoAB; MoBrPo; NeMa; NP; PoRA; TrGrPo, *abr.*; WePo
Aubade. Eric Torgersen. QAH
Aubade: Dick, the Donkey-Boy. Sir Osbert Sitwell. HaMV
Aubade for Hope. Robert Penn Warren. MAP; MoAmPo
Aubade: Lake Erie. Thomas James Merton. NYBP
Auburn. Goldsmith. *See* Village, The ("Sweet Auburn. . .").
Auburn. Paul Verlaine. *tr. fr. French by* Lawrence M. Bensky. ErPo
Aucassin and Nicolete. Francis William Bourdillon. HBV
Aucassin and Nicolete. *Unknown, tr. fr. French by* Andrew Lang. OuHeWo; WoL
Who Would List, *sel.* CTC
Aucassin and Nicolette. Edmund Clarence Stedman. *See* Provençal Lovers.
"Auchanachie Gordon is bonny and braw." Lord Saltoun and Auchanachie. *Unknown.* BaBo; ESPB
Auction. John Holmes. WaKn
Auction Sale, The. Henry Reed. MoBrPo (1962 ed.)
Auction Sale—Household Furnishings. Adele de Leeuw. PoToHe (new ed.)
Auctioneer. Carl Sandburg. PDV
Auctioneer of parting, The. Emily Dickinson. AP; PoEL-5
Audacious painters have nine worthies made. In Decium. Sir John Davies. TuPP
Auden, MacNeice, Day Lewis, I have read them all. British Leftish Poetry, 1930-40. "Hugh MacDiarmid." NMP; OPoP
Audience pricks an intellectual ear, The. Concert-Interpretation. Siegfried Sassoon. CBEP; MuSP
Auditions. Ruby C. Saunders. WSL
Auditors In. Patrick Kavanagh. OxBI
Audley Court. Tennyson. PeVV
Audubon, Drafted. LeRoi Jones. Kal; TTY
Auf dem Wasser zu Singen. Stephen Spender. EnLoPo
Auf meiner Herzliebsten Augelein. Heine, *tr. fr. German by* Richard Garnett. AWP
Auf Wiedersehen. Donald Jeffrey Hayes. CDC
Auf Wiedersehen, *sel.* Longfellow.
"It were a double grief." OQP
Auf Wiedersehen. James Russell Lowell. AA; CoBA; HBV
Augsburg Adoration, The. Randall Jarrell. NYBP
Auguries of Innocence. Blake. AnFE; AtBAP; BoLiVe, *abr.* CABA; CABL; CoBE, 4 *ll.*; DiPo; EiCL; EiPP; EnLi-2, 4 8ll.; EnLit, 4 *ll.*; EnRP; ERoP-1; FaBoCh, *abr.*; FaBoEn; FaBV; FaFP; GTBS-W; ILP; IMOP, 4 *ll.*; InP, 4 *ll.*; LiTB; LiTG; LoBV; LoGBV, *abr.*; MaRV, *abr*; MasP; NoP; OAEP; OBNC; OBRV, *abr.*; OtMeF; PeER; Po; PoEL-4; PoFr, *abr.*; PoFS; RePo, 4*ll.*; SeCeV; TOP, *sl. abr.*; TreFS, 4 *ll.*; TrGrPo, *abr.*; ViBoPo, 4 *ll.*; WoL
(Augury of Innocence, An, 4 *ll.*) OnPM
(To See a World.) GoTP
("To see a world in a grain of sand.") BEL, 4 *ll.*; EG, *much abr.*; LO, *much abr.*; TRV, 4 *ll.*; WGRP, *much abr.*; WHA, 4 *ll.*; YAT, 4 *ll.*
"Every night and every morn." PoG
"God appears, and God is Light." TRV
Robin Redbreast, A, *much. abr.* SiSoSe; UTS
(Many Birds.) ThGo
("Robin redbreast in a cage, A," *sl. abr.*) OxBoLi; TreFT
(Things to Remember, *br. sel.*) RIS

Auguries (continued)
(Three Things to Remember, *br. sel.*) FaPON; MoShBr; OTD; OTPC (1946 ed.); PCD
Augury. Stefan George, *tr. fr. German by* Carol Hope Valhope *and* Ernst Morwitz. SiSw
August. Brother Antoninus. ToPo
August. Laurence Binyon. SyP
August. Eunice Fallon. BoTP
August. Folgore da San Geminiano, *tr. fr. Italian by* Dante Gabriel Rossetti. *Fr.* Sonnets of the Months. CTC
August. Francis Ledwidge. OxBI; SiSw
August. Michael Lewis. GoTP; OTD
August. Louis MacNeice. CMoP; FaBoEn; LiTM
August. Norman Nicholson. POTi
August ("The sixth was August"). Spenser. *Fr.* The Faerie Queene, VII, 7. GN
August ("Tell me, Perigot"). Spenser. *Fr.* The Shepheardes Calender. OAEP; ReEn
Perigot and Willye, *sel.* LoBV
(It Fell upon a Holy Eve.) PoE
(Roundelay, A: "It fell upon a holy eve.") EIL
August. Swinburne. AtBAP; WiR
August. Celia Thaxter. FaPON; YeAr
August. Helen Maria Winslow. YeAr
August. Elinor Wylie. AnEnPo; FosPo; MAP; MoAB; MoAmPo; NeMA
August Afternoon. Marion Edey. YeAr
August and on the vine eight melons sleeping. Eight Melons. Malcolm Cowley. TwAmPo
August for the People. W. H. Auden. WaP
August from My Desk. Roland Flint. AmFN
August Hail. J. V. Cunningham. PoIE; PoSa
August is a lazy girl. August Smiles. Elizabeth J. Coatsworth. SiSoSe
August is nearly over, the people. Louis MacNeice. *Fr.* Autumn Journal. CMoP
August Midnight, An. Thomas Hardy. BrPo; PoMa
August Night. Elizabeth Madox Roberts. YeAr
August Night. May Swenson. MoLP
August Night. Sara Teasdale. MAP; MoAmPo
August Night, 1953. Elizabeth B. Harrod. NePoEA
August, 1914. John Masefield. HBV
August, revered,/ Our nation's sire. His Task—and Ours. Dorothy Gould. PGD
August Saturday Night on the Negro Street. Karl Shapiro. ToPo
August Smiles. Elizabeth J. Coatsworth. SiSoSe
August 'twas the twenty fifth. Bars Fight. Lucy Terry. PoNe
Augustus was a chubby lad. The Story of Augustus, Who Would Not Have Any Soup. Heinrich Hoffman. BBGG; GoJo; HBV; HBVY; MoShBr; OTPC; ShM; TiPo
Auld Daddy Darkness. James Ferguson. HBV; HBVY; PCH; PRWS; RG
Auld Deil cam to the man at the pleugh, The. The Farmer's Curst Wife (B *vers.*). *Unknown.* ESPB
Auld House, The. Lady Nairne. HBV; OTPC (1923 ed.)
Auld House, The. William Soutar. OxBS
Auld Lang Syne. Burns. AWP; BEL; CEP; CoBE; EiCP; EiPP; EnLi-2; EnLit; EnPE; EnRP; FaFP; GoTS; GTBS-W; HBV; InP; InPo; JAWP; LiTB; LiTG; LiTL; MCCG; NeHB; OAEP; OBEC; OBEV; OuHeWo; OxBS; PAn; PoE; PoLF; PTK; SiTL; TOP; TreF; WBP; YAT
Auld Lang Syne. John White Chadwick. *See* Abiding Love, The.
Auld Man's Mear's Dead, The. Patrick Birnie. GoTS
Auld Matrons. *Unknown.* BaBo; ESPB
Auld mune on her back, The. Leander Stormbound. Sydney Goodsir Smith. OxBS
Auld Noah was at hame wi' them a'. Parley of Beasts. "Hugh MacDiarmid." LO; MoBrPo; OA; OBMV
Auld Reikie. Robert Fergusson. CABL
Auld Robin Gray. Lady Anne Lindsay. BeLS; CH; GoTS; GTBS; GTBS-D; GTBS-P; GTBS-W; GTSE; GTSL; HBV; OBEC; OBEV; OnPP; ViBoPo
Auld Sang. William Soutar. OxBS
Auld Seceder Cat, The. *Unknown.* SiTL
Auld Wife [Sat at Her Ivied Door], The. Charles Stuart Calverley. *See* Ballad: "Auld wife sat at her ivied door, The."
Auld wumman cam' in, a mere rickle o' banes, An. Old Wife in High Spirits. "Hugh MacDiarmid." NMP; OPoP
Auncient Acquaintance, Madam. John Skelton. EnPo; PoEL-1
Aunt, The. Daniel Berrigan. TwAmPo
Aunt Alice has a birthday. Shops. John Farrar. PCH
Aunt Alice in April. William H. Matchett. TPM
Aunt Cora. Kenneth Pitchford. CoPo
Aunt Eliza. Harry Graham. ALV; ChTr; FaFP; NA; SiTL; WhC
(Four Ruthless Rhymes.) MaC
Aunt Eliza. *Unknown.* ShM
Aunt Eliza's Slow Ear. Winifred Welles. GaP
Aunt Helen. T. S. Eliot. PoSa
Aunt Jane. Herbert Asquith. GaP
Aunt Jane ("Aunt Jane, of whom I dreamed"). Alden A. Nowlan. FiSC
Aunt Jane Allen. Fenton Johnston. GoSl; IDB; PoNe
Aunt Jane's in such a hurry. Aunt Jane. Herbert Asquith. GaP
Aunt Jennifer's Tigers. Adrienne Rich. TPM
Aunt Liza./ Yes? Me, Colored. Peter Abrahams. *Fr.* Tell Freedom. PBA
Aunt Mary ("Aunt Mary died of eating twelve red peppers"). John Ciardi. PoDB
Aunt Mary; a Christmas Chant. Robert Stephen Hawker. JKCP; OHIP
Aunt Matilda. Barbara Euphan Todd. BoC
Aunt Maud. Harry Graham. *See* Waste.
Aunt Nerissa's Muffin. Wallace Irwin. FiBHP
Aunt Rose—now—might I see you. To Aunt Rose. Allen Ginsberg. LiTM (1970 ed.); NoP
Aunt Selina. Carol Haynes. HBMV; HBVY; MPB
Aunt Tabitha. Oliver Wendell Holmes. CenHV
Aunt was on the garden seat. The Fox Rhyme. Ian Serraillier. ELU
Aunt Zillah Speaks. Herbert Palmer. FaBoTw
Auntie, did you feel no pain. Some Ruthless Rhymes, III. Harry Graham. CenHV; SiTL
Aunties know all about fairies. Grown-ups. Rose Fyleman. HH
Auntie's Skirts. Robert Louis Stevenson. MPB (1956 ed.); PoVP
Aura amara, L'. Arnaut Daniel, *tr. fr. Provençal by* Ezra Pound. CTC
Auras of Delight. Coventry Patmore. The Unknown Eros, II, xi. ACP; CAW; LoBV; OBVV
Aurelia. Robert Nichols. OBMV; POTE
Aureng-Zebe, *sels.* Dryden.
Epilogue: "Pretty task, A; and so I told the fool." SeEP
Prologue to "Aureng-Zebe" ATP; BWP; CEP; EiPP; FiP; OBS; OxBoLi; SeCeV; SiTL
(Prologue: "Our author, by experience, finds it true.") CBEP; EiCL; MBW-1; PP; SeCV-2; SeEP
Plant That Will Not Grow, A. *fr.* Prologue.
When I Consider Life, *fr.* IV, i. FiP
Aurora. Emily Dickinson. *See* Of bronze and blaze.
Aurora, *sels.* Earl of Stirling.
"Clear moving cristall, pure as the sunne beames." Sonnet XXV. OxBS
"I envy not Endymion now no more," Sonnet XXIX. EIL; Sonn
"I hope, I fear, resolved, and yet I doubt," Sonnet LXVIII. Sonn
"Ile give thee leave my love, in beauties field," Sonnet XXVI. OxBS
"Let others of the world's decaying tell," Sonnet XCVIII. EIL; Sonn
"O happy Tithon!" Song IX, *sts.* 1-2. OBEV
"Oh, if thou knew'st how thou thyself dost harm," Sonnet XXXIII. EIL; Sonn
(To Aurora.) GTBS; GTBS-D; GTBS-P; GTBS-W; GTSE; GTSL
"Then whilst that Latmos did contain her bliss, Sonnet XXVIII. ViBoPo
"When in her face mine eyes I fix," Madrigal I. EIL
Aurora Leigh, *sels.* Elizabeth Barrett Browning.
Books ("Or else I sat on in my chamber green"), *fr.* I. VA
By Solitary Fires, *fr.* V. VA
"Critics say that epics have died out, The," *fr.* V. PeVV
"Earth's crammed with heaven," *fr.* VII. TRV
England, *fr.* I. VA
Ferment of New Wine, The, *fr.* I. VA
Glory in the Commonplace, *fr.* VII. MaRV
"I dared to rest, or wander," *fr.* I.

"I just knew it when we swept," *fr.* VII. PeVV
Motherless, *fr.* I. VA
Paris, *fr.* VI. ViP
Poets, The, *fr.* I. VA
Reading, *fr.* I. GN; HH
("Good from a Book.") PoRL
Romney and Aurora, *fr.* IX. VA
"Truth, so far, in my book; the truth which draws," *fr.* VII. WGRP
"Where There Is No Vision," *fr.* II. *abr.* MaRV
Aurora now from Titan's purple bed. Vergil. *Fr.* The Aeneid, IV. EnPo
Auroras of Autumn, The, *sels.* Wallace Stevens. CMoP
"Farewell to an idea...A cabin stands."
"This is where the serpent lives, the bodiless."
"Unhappy people in a happy world, An."
Aurore Pradère, *with music.* *Unknown,* *tr. fr. French.* ABF
Aus einer Kindheit. Kenneth Koch. AmPC
Auspex. James Russell Lowell. AmLP; AmPP (3d ed.); AnFE; AnNE; AP; APA; CoAnAm; GTBS-W; HBV; NePA; OBVV; PoEL-5
Auspice of Jewels. Laura Riding. FaBoMo; LiTA
Austere the Music of My Songs. "Feodor Sologub," *tr. fr. Russian by* Babette Deutsch *and* Avrahm Yarmolinsky. AWP
Austerity is not asperity. At the Winter Solstice. Daniel G. Hoffman. StP
Austerity of Poetry. Matthew Arnold. BEL; CLwM; EnLi-2; EPN; OAEP; OBVV; PoFS; PoVP; TOP; VP
(Jacopone da Todi.) CAW; GoBC
Australasia, *sels.* William Charles Wentworth.
"Celestial poesy! whose genial sway." BoAu
"Land of my birth! though now, alas! no more." PoAu-1
Australia. A. D. Hope. ACV; BoAV; MoAuPo; OnHM
Australia. Eve Langley. BoAV
Australia. Bernard O'Dowd. BoAu; NeLNL; PoAu-1
Australia. Dowell O'Reilly. BoAu
Australia, *abr.* John Laurence Rentoul. PoFr
Australia and the Amazon. John A. Stone. SGR
Australia Day, 1942; in Memoriam W. J. Miles. Ian Mudie. BoAu
Australia, 1894. William Gay. BoAu
Australia is a part of us. Soldier Overseas. Leonard Mann. BoAu
Australia, 1905. Archibald T. Strong. *Fr.* Sonnets of the Empire. BoAu
Australia, 1914. Archibald T. Strong. *Fr.* Sonnets of the Empire. BoAu
Australia to England. Archibald T. Strong. *Fr.* Sonnets of the Empire. BoAu; PoFr
Australian, The. Arthur H. Adams. BoAu; PoAu-1
Australian Federation. William Gay. BoAu; PoFr
Australian Girl, An. Ethel Castilla. VA
Australian Spring. Hugh McCrae. BoAu
Australian Symphony, An. G. Essex Evans. ACV; BoAu
Australia's on the Wallaby. *Unknown.* PoAu-1
Austrian Archduke, assaulted and assailed, An. The War: A-Z. John R. Edwards. BOHV
Austrian Army, An. *Unknown,* *at. to* Alaric A. Watts. *See* Siege of Belgrade, The.
Aut Caesar aut Nullus. Lilian White Spencer. CAW
Autet e bas. Arnaut Daniel. *See* Canzo of Bird-Songs and Love.
Authentic, The! Shadows of it. Matins. Denise Levertov. AmPP (5th ed.); CoPo; PIA; ToPo
Author and God of freedom, Thou dost plant. The Spirit of Freedom. *Unknown.* PoFr
Author Loving These Homely Meats [Specially], The. John Davies of Hereford. ElL; Sonn
(Buttered Pippin-Pies.) ChTr
(Homely Meats.) FaBoCh; LoGBV
Author of *Christine,* The. Richard Howard. CoAP
Author of Light. Thomas Campion. AtBAP
("Author of light, revive my dying spright.") SiCE
Author of the "Pobble," The. Edward Lear. *See* How Pleasant to Know Mr. Lear.
Author to a Daughter of Nine Years Old, The. Sir John Harington, *after the Latin of* Martial. SiCE
Author to Her Book, The. Anne Bradstreet. AmPP; AP; MAmP; NePA; OxBA; SCAP
(Author and Her Book, The.) StP
Author to His Book, The. George Alsop. SCAP
Author to His Booke, The. Thomas Heywood. *Fr.* An Apology for Actors. OBS
Author to His Wife, of a Woman's Eloquence, The. Sir John Harington. ErPo
Author to Queen Elizabeth, in Praise of Her Reading, The. Sir John Harington. SiCE
Author Unknown. William Montgomerie. OxBS
Authority. William Reed Huntington. AA
Author's Abstract of Melancholy, The. Robert Burton. *Fr.* The Anatomy of Melancholy. OBS; SeCL
Authors and actors and artists and such. Bohemia. Dorothy Parker. CrMA; NAMP
Author's Entreaty for His Lay. Eysteinn Asgrímsson, *tr. fr. Icelandic by* Eirik Magnusson. *Fr.* Lilya. ISi
Author's Epitaph, The. *Unknown.* FiBHP
Author's Epitaph, Made by Himself the Night before His Death, The. Sir Walter Ralegh. *See* Conclusion, The.
Author's favourite pipe am I, An. The Pipe. Sir John Squire. PoPl
Author's Life, The. Thomas Tusser. ReIE
Author's Mock-Song to Mark Anthony, The. John Cleveland. AnAnS-2
Authors Motto, The. Richard Crashaw. MaMe
Author's Purpose, The. Byron. *Fr.* Don Juan, IV. EPN
("Nothing so difficult as a beginning.") BEL; CoBE; EnRP; PoFS
(Romantic to Burlesque, *shorter sel.*) FiP
Author's Resolution [in a Sonnet], The. George Wither. *See* Shall I, Wasting in Despair.
Authour's Dreame, The. Francis Quarles. *Fr.* Argalus and Parthenia. OBS
Auto of the Bark of Purgatory, The, *sel.* Gil Vicente, *tr. fr. Spanish by* Aubrey F. G. Bell.
Song of the Three Angels. CAW
Auto of the Four Seasons, The, *sel.* Gil Vicente, *tr. fr. Spanish by* Aubrey F. G. Bell.
Angelic Vilancete, The. CAW
Auto Wreck. Karl Shapiro. AmLP; CMoP; FlW; ILP; LiTM; MiAP; MoVE; NePA; PoAn; PoPl; PoPo; ReMP
Autobiographical. A. M. Klein. MoCV
Autobiographical Fragment. Kingsley Amis. NePoEA-2
Autobiography, An. Bairam at Tunisie, *tr. fr. Turkish by* Herbert Howarth *and* Ibrahim Shukrallah. LiTW
Autobiography. Charles Causley. LiTM (1970 ed.); Sonn
Autobiography. Mbella Sonne Dipoko. TTY
Autobiography. Louis MacNeice. FaBoTw; FlW
Autobiography. Dorothy Parker. WhC
Autobiography, An. Ernest Rhys. ACV; OBEV (new ed.); OBVV; POTE; PrWP; VA
Autochthon. Sir Charles G. D. Roberts. CaP; VA
Autocrat of the Breakfast Table, The, *sels.* Oliver Wendell Holmes.
Aestivation, *fr. ch.* 11. AmPP; AnNE; BOHV; InMe; NA; WhC
Album Verses, *fr. ch.* 1. AmPP
Chambered Nautilus, The, *fr. ch.* 4. AA; AmePo; AmLP; AmP; AmPP; AnAmPo; AnNE; AP; DD; DiPo; EtS; FaBoBe; FaFP; GN; GTBS; GTBS-W; HBV; HBVY; HoPM; IHA; LiTA; MaRV; MCCG; NeHB; NePa; NoP; OBVV; OHFP; OQP; OTPC; OuHeWo; PCD; PG (1955 ed.); PoEL-5; PoLF; PTK; TiHL; TreF; UnPo (1st ed.); WGRP; YT
("Build thee more stately mansions, O my soul," *last st.*) TRV
Contentment, *fr. ch.* 11. AmPP (4th ed.); AnNE; AP; BOHV; HBV; InMe; OnPP; OxBA; TOP; TreF
Deacon's Masterpiece, The; or, The Wonderful "One-Hoss Shay", *fr. ch.* 11. AmePo; AmP; AmPP; AnNE; AP; BBV (1923 ed.); BOHV; CoBA; FaFP; HBV; HBVY; InMe; LHV; LiTA; LoGBV; MoShBr; NePA; OHFP; OnSP; OTPC; OxBA; PaPo; Po; PoIE; PoLF; PoRA; PTK; RIS; SiTL; StPo; StVeCh; WBLP; YT
(One-Hoss Shay, The; or, The Deacon's Masterpiece.) TreF
(Wonderful "One-Hoss Shay," The.) BeLS; FaBoBe; YaD
Latter-Day Warnings, *fr. ch.* 1. PCD
Living Temple, The, *fr. ch.* 7. AA; AmePo; AmPP (3d ed.); AP
Voiceless, The, *fr. ch.* 12. AA; CoBA; ViBoPo
Autograph, An. James Russell Lowell. AA

Autograph, An. Whittier. AA
Autolycus [*or* Autolycus' Songs]. Shakespeare. *See* Jog On, Jog On *and* Lawn as White as Driven Snow *and* When Daffodils Begin to Peer.
Autolycus' Song (in Basic English). Richard L. Greene. WhC
Automaton whose stiffened gesture writes. Record Perpetual Loss. Mary Stanley. AnNZ
Automobile, The. Percy MacKaye. AnAmPo
Automobile Mechanics. Dorothy W. Baruch. FaPON; SoPo; TiPo
Automobiles/ In a row. Stop—Go. Dorothy W. Baruch. FaPON; SUS; TiPo
Autonomous. Mark Van Doren. LiTA; PG (1955 ed.)
Autosonic Door. Dorothy Brown Thompson. GoYe
Autostrada, The. Geoffrey Johnson. NYTB
Autres Bêtes, Autres Moeurs. Ogden Nash. *See* Turtle, The.
Autumn. D. R. Beeton. PeSA
Autumn. Roy Campbell. GTBS-P; JKCP (1955 ed.); MoBrPo; OBMV; POTE; TrGrPo (1942 ed.)
Autumn. Amy Carmichael. FaChP
Autumn. William Herbert Carruth. MPB
Autumn ("I love the fitful gust.") John Clare. BoTP, 3 *sts.*; GTBS-D; PCH, 2 *sts.*
("I love the fitful gust that shakes.") EG
Autumn ("The thistledown's flying"). John Clare. BoNaP; NBM; PoEL-4
Autumn. Victor Contoski. ThO
Autumn. Edwin Curran. HBMV; TSW
Autumn. Walter de la Mare. GTBS-D; POTE
(Lost Playmate, The.) OTPC (1923 ed.)
Autumn. Emily Dickinson. *See* Morns are meeker than they were, The.
Autumn. Florence Hoatson. BoTP
Autumn ("I saw old Autumn in the misty morn"). Thomas Hood. LiTB; NoP; OBEV; PCD; PeER; ViBoPo
(Ode: Autumn.) ERoP-2; ILP; OBNC; OBRV; PoEL-4; VA
(Ode to Autumn.) HBV
Autumn. Patricia Hubbell. PDV
Autumn. T. E. Hulme. CBV; FaBoMo; LoBV; LOW; MoBrPo (1942 ed.); SeCePo; ViBoPo
Autumn. Thomas Caulfield Irwin. IrPN
Autumn. Kalidasa, *tr. fr. Sanskrit by* Arthur W. Ryder. *Fr.* The Seasons. AWP; JAWP; WBP
Autumn. Arthur A. Knipe. GFA
Autumn. Walter Savage Landor. *See* Mild Is the Parting Year.
Autumn. Detlev von Liliencron, *tr. fr. German by* Ludwig Lewisohn. AWP; JAWP; WBP
Autumn ("Thou comest, Autumn, heralded by the rain"). Longfellow. OBVV
Autumn. Itzig Manger, *tr. fr. Yiddish by* Joseph Leftwich. TrJP
Autumn. Thomas Nashe. *Fr.* Summer's Last Will and Testament. ElL; EnRePo; LoBV; OBSC; QFR; TrGrPo; TuPP
Autumn. Pushkin, *tr. fr. Russian by* Max Eastman. AnEnPo; AWP
Autumn. Stan Rice. QAH
Autumn. Rainer Maria Rilke, *tr. fr. German.* MoAuPo, *tr. by* James McAuley; OnPM, *tr. by* Jessie Lemont; PoPo, *tr. by* M. D. Herter Norton; TrJP, *tr. by* C. F. MacIntyre
Autumn. Elizabeth Madox Roberts. AnAmPo; YaD
(Dick and Will.) BiCB
Autumn. W. R. Rodgers. NeBP
Autumn. Siegfried Sassoon. NP
Autumn, *sel.* Vernon Scannell.
"It is the football season once more." FIW
Autumn. Shelley. CH; OTPC
(Autumn; a Dirge.) HBV
Autumn. Alexander Smith. *See* Sea-Marge.
Autumn. Stevie Smith. ELU
Autumn. William Jay Smith. NePoAm; RePo
Autumn. Spenser. *Fr.* The Faerie Queene, VII, 7. GN
Autumn. Rabindranath Tagore. BoPe; WGRP
Autumn. Allen Tate. Seasons of the Soul, II. MoVE
Autumn. James Thomson. *Fr.* The Seasons. CEP
"But see the fading many-colour'd woods." EnRP; LoBV
"Fled in the blasted verdure." OAEP
Lavinia. OBEC
Love of Nature. OBEC
Moonlight in Autumn, *abr.* OBEC
Autumn! Nancy Byrd Turner. YeAr
Autumn ("Autumn's good, a cosy season"). *Unknown, tr. fr. Irish by* Frank O'Connor. KiLC; PoSC
Autumn ("Woman full of wile"). *Unknown, See* Growing Old. *tr. fr. Irish by* Frank O'Connor.
Autumn. Jean Starr Untermeyer. HBMV; MAP; MCCG; MoAmPo; NeMA; PFY
Autumn. Sir William Watson. OBVV
Autumn. Frances Winwar. GoYe
Autumn. Humbert Wolfe. PoLF
Autumn; a Dirge. Shelley. *See* Autumn.
Autumn again, the leopardlike and burning. Howard Sergeant. *Fr.* The Leaves of Europe. ToPo
Autumn along the Beaches. John Hall Wheelock. AnAmPo
Autumn; an Ode. Charles Gullans. NePoEA
Autumn and the elms unleaving. Autumn Is a Season. James F. Cotter. JKCP (1955 ed.)
Autumn Apples. Laurie Lee. *See* Apples.
Autumn Begins in Martins Ferry, Ohio. James Wright. NaP
Autumn Bird. Howard McKinley Corning. MAP; MoAmPo (1942 ed.)
Autumn Birds. John Clare. OA
Autumn Breeze, An. William Hamilton Hayne. AA
Autumn Burial: a Meditation. Charles Gullans. QFR
Autumn, cloud blades on the horizon. Clear after Rain. Tu Fu. PoPl
Autumn Color. Tom Robinson. YeAr
Autumn comes, a maiden fair, The. Autumn. Kalidasa. *Fr.* The Seasons. AWP; JAWP; WBP
Autumn comes on slippered feet. Autumn's Fete. Alice Sutton McGeorge. YeAr
Autumn constellations, The. Moon Festival. Tu Fu. NaP
Autumn, Crystal Eye. Margot Ruddock. OBMV
Autumn, Dark Wanderer. Elizabeth Daryush. QGR
Autumn Dawn. Antonio Machado, *tr. fr. Spanish by* Jean Rogers Longland. PoPl
Autumn Day. Rainer Maria Rilke, *tr. fr. German by* C. F. MacIntyre. TrJP
Autumn Daybreak. Edna St. Vincent Millay. LaNeLa
Autumn Days. Margaret Knowled Speidel. SoP
Autumn Eve. Amelia Andriello. SiSoSe
Autumn Evening. John Clare. ThWaDe
Autumn Fancies. *Unknown.* FaPON; MPB; StVeCh
Autumn Fashions. Edith M. Thomas. DD; YeAr
Autumn Fields. Elizabeth Madox Roberts. BrR
Autumn Fires. Robert Louis Stevenson. BrR; GFA; SUS; TiPo; YeAr
Autumn Flitting, An. George Cotterell. VA
Autumn Flowers. Jones Very. MAmP
Autumn, Forsake These Hills. Frank Ernest Hill. PoMa
Autumn frosts will lie upon the grass, The. Wild Peaches, II. Elinor Wylie. LiTA; NAMP; OxBA
Autumn Garden, An. Bliss Carman. HBV
Autumn Gloves. Mildred D. Shacklett. GFA
Autumn Grove after Rain, by Wen Tien. James Kirkup. *Fr.* Seven Pictures from China. POTi
Autumn hath all the summer's fruitful treasure. Autumn. Thomas Nashe. *Fr.* Summer's Last Will and Testament. ElL; EnRePo; LoBV; OBSC; QFR; TrGrPo; TuPP
Autumn Haze. Richard Kendall Munkittrick. PoRL
Autumn Healing. Jean Ward. LaNeLa
Autumn Hour. George Chapman. JKCP (1955 ed.)
Autumn House, The. George M. Brady. OnYI
Autumn Idleness. Dante Gabriel Rossetti. The House of Life, LXIX. ILP; MaVP; PoVP; ViPo; ViPP
Autumn in Carmel. George Sterling. HT
Autumn in King's Hintock Park. Thomas Hardy. PoVP
Autumn in the Highlands. Arthur Hugh Clough. *See* Engagement, The.
Autumn in the Plains. William Hunt. YAP
Autumn in the West. William Davis Gallagher. AA; AnAmPo
Autumn Is a Season. James F. Cotter. JKCP (1955 ed.)
Autumn is a train that travels. Autumn Train. Mildred D. Shacklett. GFA
Autumn is for older men. Adios. Donald C. Babcock. NePoAm-2
Autumn is in the air. London Interior. Harold Monro. BrPo

Autumn is only winter in disguise. Against the Cold. Witter
Bynner. MAP; MoAmPo (1942 ed.)
Autumn is over the long leaves that love us. The Falling of the
Leaves. W. B. Yeats. PoPo
Autumn is very wild though. In My Crib. Joseph Ceravolo.
ANYP
Autumn is weary, halt, and old. The October Redbreast.
Alice Meynell. MoBrPo
Autumn Journal, *sels.* Louis MacNeice.
"August is nearly over, the people." CMoP
"Conferences, adjournments, ultimatums." WaP
Good-bye Now, Plato and Hegel. OnHM
"Nightmare leaves fatigue." AnIL
"Now we are back to normal, now the mind is." CMoP
"Sleep serene, avoid the backward." CMoP
"These days are misty, insulated, mute." CMoP
Autumn Journey. Denise Levertov. NeBP
Autumn Leaves. W. Hodgson Burnet. PoMa
Autumn Leaves. Janie Screven Heyward. HBMV; MPB
Autumn Leaves. Minnie Case Hopkins. OQP
Autumn Leaves. Margaret P. Sutphen. PCH
Autumn Leaves. Toshiyuki, *tr. fr. Japanese by* Basil Hall Chamberlain. OnPM
Autumn Leaves, The. *Unknown.* NA
Autumn Love. Ibycus, *tr. fr. Greek by* Olga Marx *and* Ernst
Morwitz. LiTW
Autumn Memories. George Francis Savage-Armstrong. VA
Autumn Moon. Chisato, *tr. fr. Japanese by* Basil Hall Chamberlain. OnPM
Autumn Morning. Frances Frost. RePo
Autumn Morning, An. *Unknown.* BoTP
Autumn Morning. Adeline White. BoTP
Autumn Morning at Cambridge. Frances Cornford. HBMV;
MoVE; OBVV; PoRA (rev. ed.)
Autumn Movement. Carl Sandburg. NP
Autumn, my Alan, is a spectre. Alan. Raymond Roseliep.
FiSC
Autumn Night. Evelyn Scott. AnAmPo
Autumn 1940. W. H. Auden. LiTA
Autumn on the Land. R. S. Thomas. POTi
Autumn Park, An. David Gascoyne. MoPo
Autumn Races. Emilie Blackmore Stapp. GFA
Autumn Rain. Aileen Fisher. RePo
Autumn Rain. D. H. Lawrence. BrPo
Autumn Refrain. Wallace Stevens. LiTA; Sonn; TDP
Autumn Riddle, An. *Unknown.* OTPC (1946 ed.)
Autumn Road, An. Glenn Ward Dresbach. HBMV
Autumn Robin, The. John Clare. BoTP
Autumn Rose-Tree, An. Michael Earls. JKCP
Autumn Scene. Basil Dowling. BoNaP
Autumn seems to cry for thee, The. Helen. "Susan Coolidge." AA
Autumn Sequence. Adrienne Rich. NoP
Autumn Song. Noel Harry Brettell. ACV
Autumn Song, An. Edward Dowden. ACV; OnYI
Autumn Song. Elizabeth-Ellen Long. SiSoSe
Autumn Song. Margaret Rose. BoTP
Autumn Song. Dante Gabriel Rossetti. ViBoPo; YAT
Autumn Song. Edmund Clarence Stedman. DD
(Going a-Nutting.) BBV (1923 ed.); GN
Autumn Song. Johann Ludwig Tieck, *tr. fr. German by* James
Clarence Mangan. AWP
Autumn Song. Paul Verlaine, *tr. fr. French by* Gerard Previn Meyer. LiTW
Autumn Squall—Lake Erie. Lola Ingres Russo. AmFN
Autumn Storm, The. Basho, *tr. fr. Japanese by* Harold G.
Henderson. RePo
Autumn Testament. Dennis Schmitz. YAP
Autumn: the ninth year of Yüan Ho. The Temple. Po Chü-i. OBMV
Autumn-time has come, The. My Triumph. Whittier. AnNE
Autumn time is with us, The. Autumn in the West. William
Davis Gallagher. AA; AnAmPo
Autumn Train. Mildred D. Shacklett. GFA
Autumn Twilight. Henri de Régnier, *tr. fr. French by* L. R.
Lind. LiTW
Autumn upon us was rushing, The. Ravings. Thomas Hood, the
Younger. Par
Autumn Valentine. Dorothy Parker. NeMA
Autumn Walk, An. Witter Bynner. GoYe
Autumn was cold in Plymouth town. Her Picture. Ellen
Mackay Hutchinson Cortissoz. AA
Autumn Wind, The. John Clare. BoNaP
Autumn Wind, The. Wu Ti, *tr. fr. Chinese by* Arthur Waley. FaBoCh; LoGBV
Autumn wind blows mournfully, The. At an Old Battlefield.
Umaki. OnPM
Autumn wind came stealing. The Thief. Irene F. Pawsey.
BoTP
Autumn wind, The—oh, hear it howl! Hallowe'en. Arthur
Cleveland Coxe. DD
Autumn wind rises; white clouds fly. The Autumn Wind.
Wu Ti, *tr. by* Arthur Waley. FaBoCh; LoGBV
Autumn wind's a pirate, The. Pirate Wind. Mary Jane Carr.
BrR; SiSoSe
Autumn wins you best by this its mute. Scene in a Garden.
Robert Browning. *Fr.* Paracelsus, I. PCH
Autumn Woods. Bryant. AnNE
Autumn Woods. James S. Tippett. BoChLi; SUS; TiPo
Autumnal. Horatio Colony. TwAmPo
Autumnal. Louis O. Coxe. TwAmPo
Autumnal, The. John Donne. Elegies, IX. MaMe; NoP;
PoEL-2; ReEn; SCEP-1; SeCV-1; TuPP; ViBoPo
(Elegy IX: Autumnal, The.) AtBAP; DiPo; OAEP; SeEP
(Elegy: "No spring nor summer beauty hath such grace.")
EnL
Autumnal. Ernest Dowson. OBNC
Autumnal. Rolfe Humphries. MoRP
Autumnal. James Wright. TPM
Autumnal Clouds. John Gould Fletcher. MAPA
Autumnal Consummation. Patric Stevenson. NeIP
Autumnal Equinox on Mediterranean Beach. Robert Penn Warren. VaPo
Autumnal Evening, An. "Fiona Macleod." GBV; PoSC; SyP
Autumnal Ode. Aubrey Thomas De Vere. OBNC
Autumnal Song. Walter Savage Landor. *See* Very True, the
Linnets Sing.
Autumnal Spring Song. Vassar Miller. NePoEA; PoSa
Autumnall. Joseph Bennett. NePA
Autumnall, The. John Donne. *See* Autumnal, The.
Autumn's Fete. Alice Sutton McGeorge. YeAr
Autumn's good, a cosy season. Autumn. *Unknown.* KiLC;
PoSC
Autumn's Mirth. Samuel Minturn Peck. GN
Autumn's Processional. Dinah Maria Mulock Craik. GN
Autumn's wind on suthering wings, The. The Autumn Wind.
John Clare. BoNaP
Autumnus. Joshua Sylvester. EIL; LO; OBS; SeEP; StP; UnPo
(1st ed.)
Auvergnat. Hilaire Belloc. MemP
Aux Carmélites. Katharine Tynan. OnYI
Aux Italiens. "Owen Meredith." BeLS; BLPA; FaBoBe;
HBV; TreFS; VA
Aux taureaux Dieu cornes donne. Peter Parasol. Wallace Stevens. NP
'Av 'ee met a Cornish miner. The Cornish Miner. Walter F.
Gries. IHA
Avalanche. Adrien Stoutenburg. NYBP
Avalon. Thomas Holley Chivers. AnFE; APA; CoAnAm
Avalon. Audrey McGaffin. NePoAm
Avant Garde. Louis Dudek. *Fr.* Provincetown. MoCV
Avarice. George Herbert. MaMe; LiTB
("Money, thou bane of bliss and source of woe.") GTBS-W
Avarice. William Langland, *mod. by* Henry W. Wells. *Fr.*
The Vision of Piers Plowman, Passus V. PoLi
Avarice. Luis de León, *tr. fr. Spanish by* Audrey F. G. Bell.
WoL
Avaro ("Avaro sick is seen to shiver"). John Swanwick Drennan. IrPN
Avast, honest Jack! now, before you get mellow. The Battle of
Erie. *Unknown.* PAH
Ave. Dante Gabriel Rossetti. GoBC; ISi; OxBoCh; ViPo
Ave atque Vale. Dryden. *Fr.* Sigismonda and Guiscardo.
OBS
Ave atque Vale. Swinburne. EnLi-2; MaVP; OAEP; OBEV;
OBNC; PoVP; StP; SyP; ViBoPo; ViPP; VP
Ave atque Vale. Rosamund Marriott Watson. HBV; VA
Ave Caesar. Robinson Jeffers. MoVE; OxBA
Ave Crux, Spes Unica! Edward Shillito. ChIP; MaRV; OQP
Ave Eva. John Wheelwright. MoPo
Ave Imperatrix. Oscar Wilde. HBV; PeVV; VA
East a-Callin', The, *sel.* OtMeF

Ave Maria. Byron. *Fr.* Don Juan, III. ISi, 2 *sts.*; MCCG, 6 *sts.*
Ave Maria. Henriette Charasson, *tr. fr. French by* Frederic Thompson. CAW; ISi
Ave Maria. Hart Crane. *Fr.* The Bridge. AtBAP; LiTA; MoPo; NePA; PoDB
Ave Maria. Frank O'Hara. ANYP
Ave Maria. John Jerome Rooney. JKCP
Ave Maria. Sir Walter Scott. *See* Hymn to the Virgin.
Ave Maria Bells. Charles Warren Stoddard. ISi; JKCP
Ave Maria! blessèd be the hour! Ave Maria. Byron. *Fr.* Don Juan, III. ISi; MCCG
Ave Maria Gratia Plena. Oscar Wilde. ACP (1926 ed.); CAW; ChIP; ISi; JKCP (1926 ed.); StJW
Ave Maria! Maiden mild! Hymn to the Virgin [*or* Ave Maria]. Sir Walter Scott. *Fr.* The Lady of the Lake, III. EnRP; GoBC; ISi
Ave Maris Stella ("Ave maris stella, the star of the sea"). *Unknown.* CTC
Ave, Maris Stella ("Hail, Thou star of ocean"). *Unknown, tr. fr. Latin.* WHL
Ave Maris Stella ("Star of ocean fairest"). *Unknown, tr. fr. Latin.* ISi
Ave! Nero Imperator. Duffield Osborne. AA
Ave Regina ("Hail, O Queen of heaven enthroned"). *Unknown, tr. fr. Latin.* WHL
Ave Regina Coelorum ("Queen of the heavens, we hail thee"). *Unknown, tr. fr. Latin by* Winfred Douglas. ISi
Ave Sanctissima! *Unknown.* WHL
Ave Verum Corpus Natum, *abr.* *Unknown, tr. fr. Latin.* WHL
Ave, Vita Nostra! Clifford James Laube. ISi
'Ave you 'eard o' the Widow at Windsor. The Widow at Windsor. Kipling. BrPo; FOL; OAEP (2d ed.)
Avenge O Lord thy slaughtered saints, whose bones. On the Late Massacre in Piedmont [*or* Piemont]. Milton. ATP; AWP; BEL; BWP; CABA; CBEP; CBV; DiPo; EnL; EnLi-1; EnLit; ExPo; FOL; GTBS; GTBS-D; GTBS-P; GTBS-W; GTSE; GTSL; HBV; ILP; InP; InPo; JAWP; LiTB; LoBV; MaPo; MBW-1; NoP; OAEP; OBS; OnPM; OuHeWo; PAn; PIA; Po; PoAn; PoEL-3; PoFS; PoIE; SeCeV; SeCL; SeEP; ShBV-3; Sonn; StP; TOP; OnPo; ViBoPo; WaaP; WBP; WHA; WoL
Avenger, The. James Wright. TwAmPo
Avenger Speaks, The. Robert Browning. *See* After.
Avengers, The. Robert Graves. HBMV
Avengers, The. Edwin Markham. MAP; MoAmPo; NeMA
Avenging Daughters, The. *Unknown, tr. fr. Danish by* E. M. Smith-Dampier. LiTW
Avenue, The. Paul Verlaine. *See* Dans l'Allée.
Avenue Bearing the Initial of Christ into the New World, The. Galway Kinnell. CoPo; LiTM (1970 ed.); NePoEA-2, *abr.*; PoDB
Sels.
"Behind the Power Station on 14th, the held breath." NaP
"Children set fires in ashbarrels." NaP
"First Sun Day of the Year. Tonight." NaP
"Fishmarket closed, the fishes gone into flesh, The." NaP
"From the Station House." NMP
"In the pushcart market, on Sunday." NaP; NMP
"In sunlight on the avenue." NMP
"Pcheek pcheek pcheek pcheek pcheek." CAD
"Promise was broken too freely, The." NaP
Avenue of the Allies, The. Alfred Noyes. PoFr
Avenue of Trees, The. Tsurayuki, *tr. fr. Japanese by* Basil Hall Chamberlain. OnPM
Average. P. K. Page. TwCaPo
Average Man, The. William Langland, *mod. by* Henry W. Wells. *Fr.* The Vision of Piers Plowman. PoLi
Average Man, The. Margaret E. Sangster. WBLP
Avert, High Wisdom, never vainly wooed. On the Danger of War. George Meredith. CoBE; EPN; PPON
Avery Anameer. Joseph Payne Brennan. FiSC
Avesta. *See* Gathas.
Aviator, The. Aleksandr Blok, *tr. fr. Russian by* Payson Loomis. OnHM
Aviators. Jon Anderson. YAP
Avoid the reeking herd. The Eagle and the Mole. Elinor Wylie. AnFE; APA; AWP; BoLiVe; CoAnAm; CoBA; GTBS-W; HBMV; LiTA; LiTM; MAP; MoAB; MoAmPo; NeMA; NP; OA; PG; PoE; PoPo; TreFT; TSW; ViBoPo; WHA
Avoiding News by the River. W. S. Merwin. NaP
Avon, The. Henry Jacobs. AnNZ
Avondale Mine Disaster, The. *Unknown.* BaBo; ThLM; ViBoFo
Avowal. A. M. Sullivan. JKCP (1926 ed.)
Aw, quit yer cryin', kid—I know it's tough. Cell-Mates. Louis Untermeyer. HBMV
Aw, Sally Brown, I been a long while a-courtin' ya. Sally Brown, *vers.* II. *Unknown.* ShS
Awaits no solar quadriga. The Welcome. Freda Laughton. NeIP
Awake! Song of Solomon, IV: 16, Bible, *O.T.* FaPON ("Awake! oh, north wind.") SUS
Awake. Mary Elizabeth Coleridge. OBNC
Awake! W. R. Rodgers. LiTM (rev. ed.); WaP
Awake! Walther von der Volgelweide, *tr. fr. German by* Jethro Bithell. AWP; JAWP; OnPM; WBP (Awake! The Day Is Coming Now.) WoL
Awake, Aeolian lyre, awake. The Progress of Poesy. Thomas Gray. ATP; AWP; BEL; CBEP; CEP; CoBE; EiCL; EiCP; EiPP; EnLi-2 (1949 ed.); EnLit; EnPE; EnRP; GTBS; GTBS-D; GTBS-P; GTBS-W; GTSE; GTSL; HBV; NoP; OAEP; OBEC; OBEV; PoFS; PP; ViBoPo
Awake, alone, aware. Insomniac Poem. Ron Loewinsohn. NeAP
Awake and praise, O dwellers in the dust! The Resurrection. John Gilland Brunini. MaRV
Awake, arise,/ Pull out your eyes. *Unknown.* OxNR
Awake! arise! shake off thy dreams! To My Native Land. James Clarence Mangan. AnIL; IrPN
Awake! arise, ye men of might! To Arms. Park Benjamin. PAH
Awake, Awake! Thomas Campion. ELP; SiCE
Awake! Awake! Sir William Davenant. *See* Lark Now Leaves His Wat'ry Nest, The.
Awake! Awake! Ruskin. *Fr.* Song of the Dawn. HBV ("Awake! awake! the stars are pale.") PoFr
Awake! Awake! The Bells. William Young. *Fr.* Wishmakers' Town. AA
Awake, awake, Deborah. Judges, Bible, *O.T.* PoFr
Awake! awake! my gallant friends. The Battle of Tippecanoe. *Unknown.* PAH
"Awake, awake, my little boy!" The Land of Dreams. Blake. BeLS; CH; OBRV
Awake, Awake, My Lyre! Abraham Cowley. *See* Supplication, A.
Awake, awake, O Church of God! The Clarion-Call. *Unknown.* BLRP
Awake! awake! the stars are pale, the east is russet gray. Awake! Awake! Ruskin. *Fr.* Song of the Dawn. HBV; PoFr
Awake, awake! thou heavy sprite. Awake, Awake! Thomas Campion. ELP; SiCE
Awake, Awake to Love and Work. G. A. Studdert-Kennedy. TRV
Awake, awake, you weary sleepers. Rules of the Road. *Unknown.* SoAmSa
Awake but not yet up, too early morning. Out of Sleep. Allen Curnow. AnNZ
Awake, fair[e] Muse; for I intend. An Ode. William Browne. OBS; SeEP
Awake! for Morning in the bowl of Night. Omar Khayyám, *tr. by* Edward Fitzgerald. *Fr.* The Rubáiyát. GTBS-D; ILP; LoBV; MemP; OxBI; PeVV; PoFS; ShBV-4. *See also* Wake! for the Sun who scattered into flight.
Awake from slumbering lethargy! To His Muse. Edward Benlowes. *Fr.* Theophila; or, Love's Sacrifice. SeCL
Awake! Glad Heart! Henry Vaughan. *See* Christ's Nativity.
Awake, great sir, the sun shines here. On New-Year's Day, 1640. To the King. Sir John Suckling. SCEP-2; SeCV-1
Awake, like a hippopotamus with eyes bulged. Monday. William Stafford. NYBP
Awake, Mine Eyes! *Unknown.* ElL
Awake, My Fair. Judah Halevi, *tr. fr. Hebrew by* Alice Lucas. TrJP
Awake, My Heart to Be Loved. Robert Bridges. GTBS-P; HBV; MoAB; MoBrPo; OBEV (new ed.); OBVV; VA
Awake, My Lute! C. S. Lewis. CenHV
Awake, my St. John! leave all meaner things. An Essay on

Man. Pope. BEL; CEP; EiCL; EiPP; EnL; EnLi-1; MBW-1; NoP; OAEP; PAn; PoEL-3; TOP
Awake, My Soul. Philip Doddridge. SoP; WGRP
Awake, My Soul. Moses ibn Ezra, *tr. fr. Hebrew by* Solomon Solis-Cohen. *Fr* Wine-Songs. TrJP
Awake, My Soul. Thomas Ken. *See* Morning Hymn.
Awake, O, north wind. Song of Solomon, Bible, *O.T.* FaPON; SUS
Awake sad heart, whom sorrow ever drowns. The Dawning. George Herbert. AnAnS-1; MaMe; MeP
Awake sound sleeper! hark, what dismal knells. Upon the Death of His Much Esteemed Friend Mr. Jno Saffin Junr. Grindall Rawson. SCAP
Awake!—the crimson dawn is glowing. Thirty-first of May. Frederick Tennyson. VA
Awake! the dawn is on the hills. Morning Serenade. Madison Cawein. HBV
Awake! The Day Is Coming Now. Walther von der Vogelweide. *See* Awake!
Awake thee, my Bessy, the morning is fair. Song. Jeremiah Joseph Callanan. IrPN; OnYI
Awake thee, my lady-love! Morning-Song [*or* Serenade]. George Darley. *Fr* Sylvia; or, The May Queen. HBV; VA
Awake, thou wintry earth. Easter Hymn. Thomas Blackburn. HH
Awake to the cold light. March. Hart Crane. BoNaP
Awake, ye forms of verse divine! The National Paintings. Fitz-Green Halleck *and* Joseph Rodman Drake. *Fr.* The Croaker Papers. AA
Awake, ye nations, slumbering supine. Sonnets Written in the Fall of 1914. George Edward Woodberry. HBV; MC; PAH
Awake yee westerne nymphs, arise and sing. Samuel Danforth. SCAP
Awakened, I behold through dewy leaves. Sonnet. Thomas Caulfield Irwin. IrPN
Awakened War God, The. Margaret Widdemer. WGRP
Awakening, The. Conrad Aiken. The Kid, VII MoVE
Awakening. Robert Bly. NaP
Awakening, The. Robert Creeley. NeAP
Awakening, The. K. William Kgositsile. BF
Awakening, The. Don Marquis. HBMV
Awakening, The. Angela Morgan. OHIP
Awakening. Margaret E. Sangster. AA
Awakening, The. *Unknown.* *See* On a time the Amorous Silvy.
Awakening of Dermuid, The. Austin Clarke. *Fr.* The Vengeance of Finn. AnIV
Awakening of Epimenides, The, *sel.* Goethe, *tr. fr. German by* F. Melian Stawell *and* Nora Purtscher-Wydenbruck.
"Up my brothers! Set all men free!" PoFr
Awakening of Man, The. Robert Browning. *See* Man's Destiny.
Awakening swan grows tired at last, The. The Swan. Edmund Gosse. SyP
Awaking. Stephen Spender. NYBP
Awaking of the Poetic Faculty, The. George Henry Boker. Sonn
Award. Gertrude Callaghan. JKCP (1955 ed.)
Award. Ray Durem. IDB; PPON
"Well, old spy," *sel.* BP; NNP; TTY; WOW
Aware. D. H. Lawrence. BoNaP; MoBrPo
Aware Aware. Tram Combs. TwCP
Awareness. Don L. Lee. BOLo
Awareness. Miriam Teichner. FaChP; MaRV; OQP
Awareness is on us, now, of the several heavens. Chorus for Easter. David Morton. MaRV
Away. Walter de la Mare. CMoP; NoP
Away. Max Ehrmann. PoToHe
Away. James Whitcomb Riley. BLRP, *abr.*; MaRV; TreFT; TRV; WGRP, *abr.*
(He Is Not Dead.) BLPA; NeHB
Away above a Harborful. Lawrence Ferlinghetti. *Fr.* Pictures of the Gone World. ErPo; NMP; OPoP
Away, Away! Shelley. *Fr.* To Jane: The Invitation. GoTP
Away! away! The Complaint. Mark Akenside. OBEV
Away, away, from men and towns. Away, Away! Shelley. *Fr.* To Jane: The Invitation. GoTP
Away, away in the Northland. A Legend of the Northland. Phoebe Cary. GoTP; HBV; HBVY; OnMSP; OTPC; RIS
Away, away, my steed and I. Byron. *Fr* Mazeppa. FOL
Away, Away, Vex Me No More. *Unknown.* SeCL
Away beyond the Jarboe house. Strange Tree. Elizabeth Madox Roberts. BoChLi; BoNaP; FaPON; MPB; NP; SP
Away by the haunts of the Yang-tse-boo. The Rhyme of the Kipperling. Sir Owen Seaman. CenHV
Away, Delights! Beaumont *and* Fletcher. *Fr.* The Captain, III, iv. ElL; OBEV; ViBoPo
("Away, delights! go seek some other dwelling.") LO
(Sad Song, The.) FaBoEn
Away despair; my gracious Lord doth heare. The Bag. George Herbert. AnAnS-1; MaMe; MeP; SCEP-1; SeCP
Away down South in old Tennessee. A Long Time Ago, *vers.* I. *Unknown.* ShS
Away down South where I was born. A Long Time Ago. *Unknown.* ShS, *vers.* II; SoAmSa
Away feare with thy projectes, noe false fyre. William Alabaster. AnAnS-1
Away, fond thing! tempt me no more. To Plautia. Sir Aston Cokayne. CavP
Away, for we are ready to a man! The Golden Journey to Samarkand: Epilogue (*also in* Hassan). James Elroy Flecker. ShBV-3
Away from friends, away from home. The Wanderer's Grave. Rufus B. Sage. PoOW
Away, haul away, Rock and roll me over. Haul Away, Joe, *vers.* I. *Unknown.* ShS
Away, haul away, Oh, haul and sing together. Haul Away Joe. *Unknown.* SoAmSa
Away, haul away, Oh, haul away together. Haul Away, Joe. *Unknown.* AmSS
Away, haunt thou not me. In a Lecture-Room. Arthur Hugh Clough. EPN; PoVP; VA; ViPo
Away in a Manger. Martin Luther. *See* Cradle Hymn.
Away in foreign lands they wondered how. Missionaries. *Unknown.* SoP
Away; let nought to love displeasing. Winifreda. *Unknown.* HBV; OBEC; OBEV (new ed.)
Away, my friends, with god of war and strife. Preparing for the Wedding. Claudian. *Fr.* Epithalamium for Honorius and Maria. HW
Away my verse! and never fear. To His Verse. Walter Savage Landor. OBVV
Away out in old Texas, that great Lone Star State. Only a Cowboy. *Unknown.* CoSo
Away out yonder in Arizony. Whoppers. John A. Lomax. OuSiCo
Away, Rio! *Unknown.* AmSS, *with music*; LoGBV
Away! the moor is dark beneath the moon. Stanzas—April, 1814 [*or* Remorse]. Shelley. ChER; EnRP; ERoP-2; FiP; LoBV; MBW-2; MyFE; OAEP; OBEV; OBNC
Away thou fondling motley humorist. Satires, I. John Donne. MaMe; OAEP
Away to the brook. The Angler's Ballad. Charles Cotton. CavP; CEP
Away to Twiver, Away, Away! *Unknown.* ElL
Away Up on the Yuba, *with music.* John A. Stone. SGR
Away, useless trifles! Of the Sad Lot of the Humanists in Paris. George Buchanan. GoTS
Away, 'way off 'cross the seas and such. The Little Toy Land of the Dutch. *Unknown.* GFA; MPB; OTPC (1946 ed.)
Away We Go. Aileen Fisher. TiPo (1959 ed.)
Away with Bloodshed. A. E. Housman. ShM; WhC
Away with Funeral Music. Robert Louis Stevenson. TreFT; WePo
Away with recipes in books. Old German Mottos. *Unknown.* StaSt
Away with silks, away with lawn. Clothes Do but Cheat and Cozen Us [*or* Away with Silks]. Robert Herrick. ALV; ErPo; MeWo
Away with that tradition of wretched glory. The Technique of Love. Jascha Kessler. AmPC
Away with these self-loving lads. Of [*or* Song to] His Cynthia [*or* Cynthia]. Fulke Greville. Caelica, LII. AtBAP; ElL; ELP; EnRePo; NoP; OBSC; ReIE; SiCE; TuPP; ViBoPo
Away with this cash. *Unknown.* SeCSL
"Away with you, away with you, James de Grant!" James Grant. *Unknown.* ESPB
Away with your fictions of flimsy romance. The First Kiss of Love. Byron. HBV
Away, ye gay landscapes, ye gardens of roses! Lachin y Gair. Byron. OxBS
Away yee barb'rous woods; how ever yee be plac't. Michael

Away (continued)
Drayton. *Fr.* Polyolbion: Third Song. OBS
Aw'd by her own rash words she was still: and her eyes to the seaward. Andromeda and the Sea-Nymphs. Charles Kingsley. *Fr.* Andromeda. VA
Aweary Am I. Abu-l-Ala al-Maarri, *tr. fr. Arabic by* R. A. Nicholson. AWP; LiTW
Awesome are the works of God. The Works of God. Moses ibn Ezra. TrJP
Awful Responsibility, An. Keith Preston. PoPl; WhC
Awful shadow of some unseen Power, The. Hymn to Intellectual Beauty. Shelley. AnEnPo; AnFE; BEL; BoLiVe; CoBE; EnL; EnLi-2; EnLit; EnRP; EPN; ERoP-2; ILP; MBW-2; MERP; NoP; OAEP; OBNC; OBRV; OuHeWo; PIA; Po; PoAn; PoE; PoFS; TOP; UnPo (1st ed.)
Awful tempest mashed the air, An. Emily Dickinson. MCCG
Awhile she lay all passive to the touch. An Indian Mother About to Destroy Her Child. James Montgomery. PaPo
Awkward was she yesterday. The Maiden. Peter Hille. AWP
Awltho I no how 2 and fro. My Own Simplified Spelling. E. V. Knox. SiTL
A-Working on the Railway. Arthur H. Clark. IHA
Awright, awright, ev'rybody get ready. Steel Laying Holler. *Unknown.* ABF
Axe, The. Isabella Valancy Crawford. VA
(Axe of the Pioneer, The.) CaP
Axe angles, An/ From my neighbor's ashcan. Junk. Richard Wilbur. CaFP; NoP; TDP
Axe has cut the forest down, The. Conquest. Elizabeth J. Coatsworth. AmFN; BrR; MPB (1956 ed.)
(Wilderness is Tamed, The.) FaPON; StVeCh
Axe-Helve, The. Robert Frost. CABL; OxBA
Axe in the Wood, The. Clifford Dyment. ACV; POTE; POTi
Axe of the Pioneer, The. Isabella Valancy Crawford. *See* Axe, The.
Axle Song. Mark Van Doren. MoPo
Axolotl, The. David McCord. FiBHP; WhC
Ay, an old story, yet it might. A Legend. May Kendall. VA
Ay ant lak pie-plant pie so wery vell. Sonnet on Stewed Prunes. William F. Kirk. WhC
Ay, ay, and away she goes. Highland Laddie. *Unknown.* ShS
Ay, ay; good man, kind father, best of friends. "Bona de Mortuis." Thomas Lovell Beddoes. ELU
Ay, beshrew you! by my fay. Mannerly Margery Milk and Ale. John Skelton. NoP; ReEn
Ay, but to die, and go we know not where. Fear of Death, The. Shakespeare. *Fr.* Measure for Measure, III, i. TreFT
Ay, buzz and buzz away. Dost thou suppose. Luther to a Bluebottle Fly (1540). Eugene Lee-Hamilton. Sonn
Ay! drop the treacherous mask! throw by. Butler's Proclamation. Paul Hamilton Hayne. PAH
Ay, Dwainie!—My Dwainie! Dwainie. James Whitcomb Riley. *Fr.* Flying Islands of the Night. AA
Ay, it is fitting on this holiday. Ode in Memory of the American Volunteers Fallen for France. Alan Seeger. PAH
Ay, let it rest! And give us peace. The Gospel of Peace. James Jeffrey Roche. PAH
Ay, little larky! what's the reason. Address to a Lark Singing in Winter. John Clare. *Fr.* Address to a Lark. BiS
Ay, man is manly. Here you see. On the Photograph of a Corps Commander. Herman Melville. MWA-1
Ay, Me, Alas. *Unknown.* FaBoCh; LoGBV
(Ay Me, Alas, Heigh Ho!) CH
(Madrigals, 3.) OxBoLi; SiTL
Ay me alas! the beautiful bright hair. Canzone: His Lament for Selvaggia. Cino da Pistoia. AWP; JAWP; WBP
Ay me, ay me! I sigh to see the scythe afield. A Proper Sonnet, How Time Consumeth All Earthly Things [*or* Sic Transit]. *Unknown, at. to* Thomas Proctor. ChTr; EIL; OBSC; SiCE; TrGrPo; TuPP
Ay me! for aught that ever I could [*or* I could ever] read. The Course of True Love. Shakespeare. *Fr.* A Midsummer Night's Dream, I, i. TreFS; WHA
"Ay, not at home, then, didst thou say?" A Call on Sir Walter Raleigh. Sarah M. B. Piatt. AA
Ay or Nay? Ralph Schomberg. *Fr.* The Judgment of Paris. TrJP
Ay, shout and rave, thou cruel sea. Herndon. S. Weir Mitchell. PAH
Ay, since beyond these walls no heavens there be. Herbert Trench. *Fr.* To Arolilia. LO
Ay [*or* Aye], tear her tattered ensign down! Old Ironsides. Oliver Wendell Holmes. AA; AmePo; AmLP; AmPP (3d ed.); AnNE; AP; BBV; BLPA; CoBA; DD; EtS; FaBoBe; FaFP; FaPL; FaPON; GN; HBV; HBVY; MaC; MC; MCCG; NeHB; OTD; OuHeWo; PaA; PAH; PAL; PoPl; PoRL; PTK; ThLM; TreF; YaD
Ay—There It Is. Emily Brontë. ChER
Ay, this is freedom!—these pure skies. The Hunter of the Prairies. Bryant. AA
Ay, thou art for the grave; thy glances shine. To——: Bryant. Sonn
Ay! thou look'st cold on me, pomp-loving Moon. To the Moon. George Darley. Sonn
Ay, 'Tis Thus. *Unknown, tr. fr. Hebrew by* Israel Zangwill. TrJP
Ay, 'twas here, on this spot. Atalanta in Camden-Town. "Lewis Carroll." ALV; CenHV
Ay! Unto thee belong. Theocritus. Annie Fields. AA
Aye, at times on summer evenings. Mirth and Music. William Barnes. MuSP
"Aye! I am a poet and upon my tomb." And Thus in Nineveh. Ezra Pound. PP
Aye, lads, aye, we fought 'em. Off Manilly. Edmund Vance Cooke. PAH
Aye me can love and bewtie soe conspire. *Unknown.* SeCSL
"Aye, squire," said Stevens, "they back him at evens." How We Beat the Favo[u]rite. Adam Lindsay Gordon. OtMeF; PeVV; VA
Aye, tear her tattered ensign down! *See* Ay, tear her tattered ensign down!
Aye, up at the feast, by Melhill's brow. Melhill Feast. William Barnes. CBEP; OBNC
Aye Waukin' O! *Unknown.* GoTS
Ayee! Ai! This is [*or* This] heavy earth on our shoulders. Burying Ground by the Ties. Archibald MacLeish. Frescoes for Mr. Rockefeller's City, III. AmPP (4th ed.); MAP; MoAmPo; NAMP; UnPo; WoL; WOW
Aylmer's Field, *sel.* Tennyson.
Leolin and Edith. GN
Azalea, The. Coventry Patmore. The Unknown Eros, I, vii. ELP; GoBC; PoVP
Azaleas—whitest of white. White Azaleas. Harriet McEwen Kimball. AA; HBV
Aziola, The. Shelley. CBEP; PeER; SiSw
Azra, The. Heine, *tr. fr. German by* John Hay. AWP; JAWP; WBP
Azrael. Longfellow. Tales of a Wayside Inn: The Spanish Jew's Tale, Pt. III. AnAmPo; MWA-1
Azrael. Robert Gilbert Welsh. HBV; MaRV; OQP
Aztec City, The. Eugene Fitch Ware. AA; HBV; HT; PTK
Aztec sacrifice, An. Le Musée Imaginaire. Charles Tomlinson. NePoEA-2
Azur'd vault, the crystal circles bright, The. *See* Azured vault, the crystal. . .
Azure sky, An/ All star bestrewn. Christmas. *Unknown.* BoTP
Azure, 'tis I, come from Elysian shores. Hélène (Helen, the Sad Queen). Paul Valéry, *tr. by* Janet Lewis. Po
Azure, 'tis I; from the caves of death withdrawn. Helen, the Sad Queen. Paul Valéry. *tr. by* Joseph T. Shipley. AWP;CAW;JAWP;WBP
Azured [*or* Azur'd] vault, the crystal circles bright, The. Heaven and Earth [*or* Sonnet]. James I, King of England. ChTr; EIL;SeCePo
Azzoomm, azzoomm loud and strong. Riding in an Airplane. Dorothy W. Baruch. FaPON

B

B. Larry Eigner. NeAP
B-52's. Arnold Kenseth. PPON
B Negative. X. J. Kennedy. NePoEA-2

B Stands for Bear. Hilaire Belloc. *Fr.* A Moral Alphabet. ShM
Baa, baa, black sheep, have you any wool? Mother Goose. BoChLi; FaBoBe; FaFP; HBV; HBVY; OTPC; OxNR; PCH; PPL; RIS; SAS; SiTL; SoPo; StVeCh; TiPo
Baal Shem Tov. A. M. Klein. CaP; TrJP
Bab-Lock-Hythe. Laurence Binyon. MoVE; SD; WePo
Babbitt and the Bromide. Ira Gershwin. *Fr.* Funny Face. ALV
Babbitt, your tribe is passing away. The Virginians Are Coming Again. Vachel Lindsay. NP
Babe, The. Monk Gibbon. OxBI
Babe is born all of a May, A. Three Christmas Carols, I. *Unknown.* ACP
Babe is cold, The. Candle and Star. Elizabeth J. Coatsworth. BiCB
Babe Jesu lying/ On my little pallet lonely. Saint Ita's Fosterling. *At. to* St. Ita. OnYI
Babe Jesus is here. The Little Lord Jesus. *Unknown.* ChrBoLe
Babe of Bethlehem, The. Henry Beer. BePJ
Babe of Bethlehem, The. Condé Benoist Pallen. JKCP
Babes in the Wood [*or* Woods], The ("My dear, do you know/ How, a long time ago"). *Unknown.* OTPC (1946 ed.); RIS
("My dear, do you know how a long time ago.") PPL
Babes in the Wood [*or* Woods], The ("Now ponder well, you parents dear"). *Unknown.* HBV; HBVY; OTPC (1923 ed.)
(Children in the Wood, The.) EnSB; OBB; OnSP
Babiaantje, The. F. T. Prince. ACV; BoSA; ChMP; MoBrPo (1962 ed.)
Babie, The. Jeremiah Eames Rankin, *wr. at. to* Hugh Miller. AA; HBV
Babies, The. Mark Strand. NYBP
Babies haven't any hair. More Hair. Samuel Hoffenstein. SiTL
Baboon ("Heretse!/ Heretse!"). *Unknown, tr. fr. Hottentot.* PeSA
Baboon 2 ("You hollow-cheeked son"). *Unknown, tr. fr. Hottentot.* PeSA
Babushka; a Russian Legend. Edith M. Thomas. ChrBoLe; OnMSP; OTPC (1946 ed.)
(Babouscka.) MPB
Baby. Elaine Goodale Eastman. AA
Baby. Florence Kiper Frank. HBMV
Baby, The. Sir William Jones, *after the Sanskrit of* Kalidasa. TreFS
(Epigram: "On parent knees, a naked new-born child.") CBV; OBEV; PoPl
(Moral Tetrastich, A.) OBEC; PrWP
(On Parent Knees.) HBV
Baby, The. George Macdonald. *Fr.* At the Back of the North Wind, *ch.* 23. BiCB; FaPON; HBV; HBVY; MPB; OTPC; SoP; TreF; TRV; TVC; VA
(Song: "Where did you come from, baby dear?") PaPo
(Where Did You Come From?) BLPA; FaFP
Baby, The. Ann Taylor. DD, *abr.*; OHIP
Baby,/ You shall be free. Kadia the Young Mother Speaks. Jessie Sampter. TrJP
Baby and I/ Were baked in a pie. *Unknown.* OxNR
Baby and Mary. *Unknown.* NA
Baby Asleep after Pain, A. D. H. Lawrence. BoPe; NP
Baby at Play. *Unknown.* HBV; HBVY; OTPC
("Brow bender.") PPL
Baby, baby, lay your head. Good Night. Jane Taylor. BoChLi; HBV; HBVY; OTPC; PPL; SAS, *st.* 1
Baby, baby, naughty baby. *Unknown.* OxNR
Baby, baby, ope your eye. Good-Morning. *Unknown.* SAS
Baby Beds. *Unknown.* BoTP
Baby Bell. Thomas Bailey Aldrich. HBV
Baby born in Bethlehem. Little Child of Mary. H. T. Burleigh. StJW
Baby bye. The Fly. Theodore Tilton. RIS
Baby cat is soft and sweet, A. Cats. Marchette Chute. SoPo
Baby Christ, when He was born, The. The Birthday of the Lord. Mary Jane Carr. BiCB; ChBR
Baby Cobina. Gladys May Casely Hayford. CDC
Baby Corn. Lydia Avery Coonley Ward. GFA; PRWS
Baby Dear. Samuel Lover. OTPC (1946 ed.)
Baby dear, good-night, good-night. *Unknown.* SAS
Baby Goes Out to Tea. *Unknown.* SAS
Baby Goes to Boston, The. Laura E. Richards. SAS; TiPo
Baby in the Basket, The. Emily Carter. SAS
Baby is born [*or* borne], us bliss [*or* blis] to bring, A. Dear Son, Leave Thy Weeping [*or* Jesus Comforts His Mother *or* A Baby Is Born]. *Unknown.* CTC; MeEL; NoP
Baby King Jesus came down to His own, The. Christmas Legend. Edna Randolph Worrell. ChBR
Baby-Land. George Cooper. *See* Babyland.
Baby Lapp's Ride. *Unknown.* SAS
Baby Livingston. *Unknown.* OBB
Baby Lon. *Unknown.* *See* Babylon; or, The Bonnie Banks o' Fordie.
Baby loves to play with me. Hide and Seek. Phyllis Drayson. BoTP
Baby lying on his mother's breast, A. Man's Pillow. Irving Browne. AA
Baby Making Cakes. *Unknown.* SAS
Baby May. William Cox Bennett. HBV; OTPC (1923 ed.); VA
Baby moon, a canoe, a silver papoose canoe, The. Early Moon. Carl Sandburg. LaNeLa; PG
Baby mustn't frown. The Gravel Path. Laurence Alma-Tadema. PPL
Baby new to earth and sky, The. In Memoriam A. H. H., XLV. Tennyson. EnLi-2; EPN; ViPo; VP
Baby, O baby, fain you are for bed. Cradle Song. Louis Esson. BoAu
Baby on Her Travels. *Unknown.* SAS
Baby Running Barefoot. D. H. Lawrence. MoPW; NoP
Baby sat on the window-seat. Baby and Mary. *Unknown.* NA
Baby, see the flowers! In a Garden. Swinburne. PRWS
Baby Seed Song. Edith Nesbit. BoChLi; DD; FaPON; HBV; HBVY; MPB; OTPC; PCH; PRWS; SP; TVC
Baby Seeds. *Unknown.* OTPC (1946 ed.); PCH
Baby Show, De. Wilson MacDonald. WhC
Baby, Sleep. Christina Rossetti. *Fr.* Sing-Song. OTPC (1946 ed.)
Baby Sleeps. Samuel Hinds. HBV
Baby takes to her bed at night, The. Household Gods. J. H. Macnair. PoMa
Baby Ten Months Old Looks at the Public Domain, A. William Stafford. NYBP
Baby Toes. Carl Sandburg. FaPON; LaNeLa; SUS; TSW
Baby Toodles. Joseph S. Newman. BBGG
Baby Tortoise. D. H. Lawrence. BoPe; CMoP
Baby Verse, A ("Tit-tat-toe,/ My first go"). *Unknown.* BoTP
("Tit, tat, toe.") OxNR
Baby Villon. Philip Levine. CoAP; NaP
Baby wades alone across the lawn, The. Errantry. Robert Fitzgerald. NYBP
Baby wants a lullaby. Lullaby. William Brighty Rands. PPL
Baby wants his breakfast. Baby's Breakfast. Emilie Poulsson. HBV; HBVY; PPL
Baby was sleeping, A. The Angel's Whisper. Samuel Lover. OnYI; PRWS
Baby watched a ford, whereto, A. Wagtail and Baby. Thomas Hardy. HBMV
Baby wept, The. Baby Sleeps. Samuel Hinds. HBV
Babyhood. Josiah Gilbert Holland. *See* Cradle Song: "What is the little one thinking about?"
Babyland [*or* Baby-Land]. George Cooper. BoTP; HBV; HBVY; OTPC; PPL
Babylon. "Æ." HBMV
Babylon. Laura Benét. FiSC
Babylon. Robert Graves. HBMV
Babylon. Ralph Hodgson. BrPo; HBMV
Babylon. Robert Eyres Landor. *Fr.* The Impious Feast, I. OBRV
Babylon ("Babylon that was beautiful is Nothing now"). Siegfried Sassoon. MoRP
Babylon. A. G. Stephens. BoAu
Babylon. Viola Taylor. HBV
Babylon ("How many miles to Babylon"). *Unknown.* CBEP
Babylon ("King and Queen of Cantelon"). *Unknown.* ChTr
Babylon ("There were three ladies lived in a bower"). *Unknown.* *See* Babylon; or, The Bonnie Banks o' Fordie.
Babylon and Sion (Goa and Lisbon). Luís de Camoes, *tr. fr. Portuguese by* Richard Garnett. AWP; WoL
Babylon, Babylon, Babylon the Great. Vachel Lindsay. LiPo

Babylon has fallen! Aye; but Babylon endures. Babylon. A. G. Stephens. BoAu
Babylon; or, The Bonnie Banks o' Fordie. *Unknown.* BaBo (A *and* B *vers.*); EnLi-1; ESPB; TOP
(Baby Lon.) SeCePo
(Babylon: "There were three ladies. . .") OBB; OxBB
(Bonnie Banks of Fordie, The.) BuBa
Babylonia, *sel.* "Owen Meredith."
Tempora Acta. VA
Baby's been in Sleepyland. Sleepyland. Laura E. Richards. SAS
Baby's Birthday, The. Eliza Lee Follen. PPL
Baby's brain is tired of thinking. A Boston Lullaby. James Jeffrey Roche. BOHV
Baby's Breakfast. Emilie Poulsson. HBV; HBVY; PPL
Baby's Debut, The. Horace Smith *and* James Smith. ALV; BOHV; OBRV; Par
Baby's Eyes, A. Swinburne. Etude Réaliste, III. TSW
Baby's Feet, A. Swinburne. Etude Réaliste, I. FaPON; InP; PoVP; TSW; VA
Baby's Hands. Gomei, *tr. fr. Japanese.* MPB
Baby's hands in Bethlehem, A. The Hands of Christ. Leslie Savage Clark. ChIP; MaRV
Baby's in Jail; the Animal Day Plays Alone. Charles Henri Ford. MoVE
Baby's Name, The. Tudor Jenks. BiCB
Baby's World. Rabindranath Tagore. FIW
Baccalaureate. David McCord. WhC
Bacchae, *sels.* Euripides, *tr. fr. Greek by* Gilbert Murray.
Home of Aphrodite, The. AWP
Where Shall Be Wisdom Be Found? UnS, 6 *ll.*
Bacchanal. Irving Layton. OBCV
Bacchanalia; or, A Description of a Drunken Club, *sel.* Charles Darby.
"But by this time tongues 'gan to rest." PeRV
Bacchanalia; or, The New Age. Matthew Arnold. PoVP
Bacchanalian Verse, A. Robert Herrick. BEL
Bacchante to Her Babe, The. Eunice Tietjens. HBMV; NP
Bacchus. Emerson. AmePo; AmP; AmPP; AnAmPo; AnFE; AnNE; AP; APA; AWP; CoAnAm; HBV; LiTA; MAmP; OBEV; OxBA; PoEL-4; ViBoPo
Bacchus. William Empson. PoCh
Bacchus. Thomas Love Peacock. *Fr.* Rhododaphne. OBRV
Bacchus. Frank Dempster Sherman. MAP
Bacchus by the lonely ocean. Bacchus. Thomas Love Peacock. *Fr.* Rhododaphne. OBRV
Bacchus in Tuscany, *sels.* Francesco Redi, *tr. fr. Italian.*
Bacchus's Opinion of Wine, and Other Beverages, *tr. by* Leigh Hunt. AWP
Bacchus on Beverages, *tr. by* Leigh Hunt, *shorter sel.* LiTW
Bacchus must now his power resign. A Drinking-Song. Henry Carey. OBEV
Bacchus, the father of drunken Nowls. The Man in the Moon Drinks Clarret. *Unknown.* CoMu
Bacchus's Opinion of Wine, and Other Beverages. Francesco Redi, *tr. fr. Italian by* Leigh Hunt. *Fr.* Bacchus in Tuscany. AWP
Bacchus on Beverages, *shorter sel.* LiTW
Bacchylides. George Meason Whicher. AA
Bach Cantata, A. Margaret Stanley-Wrench. MuSP
Bachelor, The. William Barnes. PeVV
Bachelor Hall. Eugene Field. BLPA
Bachelor's Ballade, The. David Fisher Parry. InMe
Bachelors' Buttons. Maud Morin. BoTP
Bachelor's Dream, The. Thomas Hood. BOHV
Bachelor's Hall. John Finley. HBV
Bachelor's Lay, The, *with music.* *Unknown.* OuSiCo
Bachelor's Mono-Rhyme, A. Charles Mackay. BOHV
Bachelor's Song, The. Thomas Flatman. *See* On Marriage.
Back. W. W. Gibson. GTSL; MaRV; TreFT
Back. Weldon Kees. NaP; TwAmPo
Back Again from Yucca Flats. Reeve Spencer Kelley. AmFN
Back Again, Home. Don L. Lee. BALP
Back and Forth. Lucy Sprague Mitchell. FaPON
Back and forth, back and forth. Fall 1961. Robert Lowell. OPoP; TPM
Back and Side Go Bare, Go Bare. *At. to* William Stevenson. *Fr.* Gammer Gurton's Needle. BEL; EG; EnLi-1; FosPo; InvP; LiTB; OAEP; PoRA; ReEn; SiCE; TOP; TuPP; ViBoPo
(Drinking Song.) WiR, *at. to* John Still.
(I Cannot Eat but Little Meat.) ExPo
(In Praise of Ale.) TrGrPo
(Jolly Good Ale [and Old].) HBV; NoP; OBEV; SeCeV; SiTL; TDP
(Of Jolly Good Ale and Old.) ElL
(Song of Ale, A.) AnFE; OBSC; UnPo (1st ed.)
Back at San Francisco Greyhound, leaning. Poem. James Brodey. ANYP
Back behind the mirror is another pussy-cat. The Looking-Glass Pussy. Margaret Widdemer. UTS
Back from the cordial grave I drag thee. Emily Dickinson. MWA-2
Back from the kill. Contest. Florence Victor. SD
Back from the line one night in June. Corporal Stare. Robert Graves. BrPo
Back from the Paved Way. Robert D. Fitzgerald. PoAu-2
Back from the trebly crimsoned field. Wanted—a Man. Edmund Clarence Stedman. LiPo; PAH
Back home the black women are all beautiful. W. W. LeRoi Jones. NBP
Back in the dear old thirties' days. The Poet of Bray. John Heath-Stubbs. ML
Back in the years when Phlagstaff, the Dane, was monarch. The Rejected "National Hymns," I. "Orpheus C. Kerr." BOHV; InMe
Back Lane. R. D. Murphy. PoAu-2
Back of Chicago the open fields—were you ever there? Evening Song. Sherwood Anderson. NP
Back of God, The. J. R. Perkins. MaRV; OQP
Back of the beating hammer. The Thinker. Berton Braley. BLPA; NeHB; OQP; PEDC; PoMa; StVeCh (1940 ed.); WBLP
Back of the Bus, *sel.* *Unknown.*
"If you miss me on the picket line." WOW
Back of the door the child is playing that. Resolution. W. S. Merwin. NYBP
Back of the loaf is the snowy flour. Our Daily Bread [*or* "Give Us This Day Our Daily Bread"]. Maltbie D. Babcock. MaRV; OQP; SoP; TRV
Back out of all this now too much for us. Directive. Robert Frost. AmPP (5th ed.); AP; BWP; CABA; CBV; CMoP; CoBMV; CrMA; DiPo; ForPo; FosPo; LiTA; LiTM (rev. ed.); MaPo; MasP; MoAB; MoAmPo (1962 ed.); MWA-2; NePA; PIA; PoDB; PoeP; SeCeV
Back Road Farm. Charles Bruce. CaP
Back Room Joys. Justin Richardson. FiBHP
Back she came through the trembling dusk. Folk-Song. Louis Untermeyer. HBV; MeWo
Back side of Albany stands Lake Champlain. Siege of Plattsburg. *Unknown.* ABF
Back through clouds. Train Tune. Louise Bogan. NePoAm
Back to Dublin. R. A. D. Ford. CaP; MoCV
Back to Griggsby's Station. James Whitcomb Riley. BLPA
Back to the bewildering vision. Kinship. Sir Charles G. D. Roberts. CaP
Back to the flower-town, side by side. In Memory of Walter Savage Landor. Swinburne. HBV; PoEL-5; PoFS; PoVP; VA
Back to the Ghetto. Jacob Glatstein, *tr. fr. Yiddish by* Joseph Leftwich. TrJP
Back to the green deeps of the outer bay. The Herring Weir. Sir Charles G. D. Roberts. PeCV
Back Yard, July Night. William Cole. BoNaP
Backyard on Fulton Street, The. Gail Dusenbery. ThO
Backstair Ballad. David McCord. BOHV
Backward—Forward. *Unknown.* BLRP
Backward, turn backward, film guy in your flight. Two Parodies. *Unknown.* CoSo
Backward, turn backward, O Time, in your flight. Rock Me to Sleep [Mother]. Elizabeth Akers Allen. AA; AmePo; BLPA; DD; FaBoBe; FaFP; NeHB; PaPo; TreF; WBLP
Backward, turn backward, O Time with your wheels. Two Parodies. *Unknown.* CoSo
Backward we look regretful, forward we glance with dread. Resurgam. W. Nelson Bitton. BLRP
Backwater Pond: The Canoeists. W. S. Merwin. PoPl
Backwoods Hero, A, *sel.* Alexander McLachlan.
"Where yonder ancient willow weeps." CaP

Bacon and Eggs. A. P. Herbert. WhC
Bacon's Epitaph, Made by His Man. *Unknown, at. to* John Cotton. AnAmPo; PAH; SCAP
Bad Boy, The, *with music.* *Unknown.* CoSo
Bad breed of the natives with their hates, The. D. C. Karl Shapiro. NYBP
Bad Children, The. Carl Bode. ToPo
Bad Dreams. Robert Browning. OAEP; PoVP
Bad Girl's Lament, The. *Unknown.* ViBoFo
Bad I am, but yet thy child. Gerard Manley Hopkins. BoC
Bad Joke, A. Martial, *tr. fr. Latin by* Louis Untermeyer. UnTE
Bad Kittens, The. Elizabeth J. Coatsworth. FaPON; MoSiPe; MPB; PoRL; RePo; YT
Bad Luck to This Marching. Charles James Lever. OnYI
Bad Man Ballad, *with music.* *Unknown.* ABF
Bad Man from the Brazos, The. *Unknown.* CoSo
Bad Season Makes the Poet Sad, The. Robert Herrick. AnAnS-2; CABA; LiTB; OAEP; SeCeV; UnPo (1st ed.)
Bad Times. Joseph Beaumont. MaRV
Badger, The. P. R. Chalmers. BoPe
Badger. John Clare. CBEP; EnRP; ERoP-2; ExPo; LiTB; NBM; NCEP; NoP; PoE; PoEL-4; UnPo (3d ed.); WiR
Badger, The. Eden Phillpotts. BoTP
Badminton. Sir Alfred Comyn Lyall. *Fr.* Studies at Delhi, 1876. OBVV; PeVV
Bad-tempered Wife, The. *Unknown.* *See* Farmer's Curst Wife, The.
Baffled Knight, The. *Unknown.* BaBo; ESPB; NoP; ViBoFo
(Courteous Night, The *with music.*) OxBB
(There Was a Knight.) UnTE
(There was a Knight and He Was Young.) CoMu
Bag, The. George Herbert. AnAnS-1; MaMe; MeP; SCEP-1; SeCP
Bag of the Bee, The. Robert Herrick. OAEP
Bag of Tools, A. R. L. Sharpe. BLPA; FaChP; MaRV; NeHB; PoToHe (new ed.); TreFT; YaD
Bagel, The. David Ignatow. TwCP
Baggot Street Deserta. Thomas Kinsella. NMP
Bagheera's Song. Kipling. *Fr.* The Second Jungle Book. PoFr
Bagley Wood. Lionel Johnson. AnFE
Bagpipe Man, The. Nancy Byrd Turner. BoChLi; GaP; TiPo
Bagpipe Music. Louis MacNeice. ExPo; GTBS-P; ILP; LiTB; LiTM; NoP; OAEP (2d ed.); OnYI; PoE; PoSa; SeCePo; SeCeV; SiTL; ViBoPo (1958 ed.)
Bags Under the Eyes. Coleman Barks. *Fr.* Body Poems. QAH
Bah! spite of Fate, that says us nay. The Indolent. Paul Verlaine. SyP
Bahamas. George Oppen. NYBP
Baharistan, *sel.* Jami, *tr. fr. Persian.*
Fragment: "Though decked the tray." CIV
Bahnhofstrasse. Clifford Dyment. POTi
Baiamai's Never-failing Stream. William Hart-Smith. BoAV
Bailey Beareth the Bell Away, The. *Unknown.* *See* Maidens Came, The.
Bailiff, The. Ebenezer Elliott. *Fr.* The Splendid Village. NBM
Bailiff's Daughter of Islington, The. *Unknown.* BaBo (A *vers.*); BFSS, *with music*; ESPB; GN; GoTP; HBV; LoEn; NoP; OAEP; OBB; OnSP; OTPC; OxBB; OxBoLi; PoPo; RePo; SaSa, *with music*; ViBoFo, *with music*
(Love Token, The, B *vers.*) BaBo
Bairnies cuddle doon at nicht, The. Cuddle Doon. Alexander Anderson. GN; HBV; OHFP; VA
Bait [*or* Baite], The. John Donne. AnEnPo; CABA; CBV; CLwM; DiPo; ErPo; HoPM; ILP; LiTL; MaMe; OAEP; PoRA; SCEP-1; SD; StP; TuPP; WhC
Baith Gud[e] and Fair and Womanly [*or* Womanlie]. *Unknown.* GoTS; OxBS
Baker's Boy, The. Mary Effie Lee Newsome. CDC; GoSl
Baker's Duzzen Uv Wize Sawz, A. Edward Rowland Sill. FaBoBe; FaFP; HBV; HBVY; InMe; SiTL; TreFS
Bakers have perfumed the dawn, The. Sun. Iwan Goll. OnPM
Baker's Reply to the Needle Peddler, The. *Unknown.* SiTL
("I need not your needles.") OxNR
Baker's Tale, The. "Lewis Carroll." *Fr.* The Hunting of the Snark, III. BoChLi; PoVP
Balaam. John Keble. OBNC; OBVV
Balaam's Blessing. Numbers, XXIV: 5-9, Bible, *O.T.* TrGrPo
Balade: "Hyd[e], Absolon [*or* Absalon], thy gilte tresses clere." Chaucer. *Fr.* The Legend of Good Women. AtBAP; AWP; ChTr; FiP; InPo; JAWP; LiTG; LoBV; OBEV; PIA; SeCeV; WBP
(Hyd, Absolon, Thy Gilte Tresses Clere.) ExPo
(Of His Lady, *sl. diff.*) EG
Balade de [*or* of] Bon Conseyl [*or* Conseil *or* Conseill]. Chaucer. BEL; LiTG; TrGrPo; ViBoPo
(Ballad of Good Counsel.) ACP; CAW; GoBC, *sl. mod. vers. by* Wordsworth
(Ballade of Good Counsel, *mod. by* Henry van Dyke.) TrGrPo
(Truth.) AWP; CBEP; MaPo; MyFE; NoP; PAn; PoG, 1*st.*; PoLi
(Truth Shall Set You Free.) MeEL
Balance of Europe, The. Pope. CBV; SeCeV; TOP
Balancing of gaudy broad pavilions, The. Irradiations, IV [VI]. John Gould Fletcher. AnFE; APA; MAPA; TwAmPo
Balancing spaces are not disturbed, The. The Known Soldier. Kenneth Patchen. WaaP
Balankin was as gude a mason. Lamkin (B *vers.*). *Unknown.* ESPB
Balboa. Nora Perry. PAH
Balcon, Le. Baudelaire, *tr. fr. French by* Lord Alfred Douglas. AWP
(Balcony, The, *tr. by* F. P. Sturm.) PIA
Balcony Scene, The. Shakespeare. *See* He Jests at Scars . . .
Balcony with Birds, A. Howard Moss. NePoEA
Bald-bare, bone-bare, and ivory yellow: skull. The U.S. Sailor with the Japanese Skull. Winfield Townley Scott. FiMAP; LiTM (1970 ed.); MiAP; NMP; WaP
Bald-headed Tyrant, The. Mary E. Vandyne. BOHV
Bald heads forgetful of their sins. The Scholars. W. B. Yeats. CaFP; CMoP; ML; NoP; TDP
Bald Old Woman, The. *Tr. fr. Chinese by* I. T. Headland. GaP
Balder, *sels.* Sydney Dobell.
Chanted Calendar, A. BoC; BoTP; DD; GBV; GTSE; HBV; HBVY; OBEV; RG
(Procession of the Flowers.) GN; OTPC
Dante, Shakespeare, Milton. VA
Sea Ballad. VA
Balder Dead, *sels.* Matthew Arnold.
"But when the Gods and Heroes heard, they brought." PeVV
"Forth from the east, up the ascent of Heaven." PeVV
Incremation, The. VA
Second Asgard, The. FiP
Balder's Wife. Alice Cary. AA; AnAmPo
Baldness and the Swan. Winfield Townley Scott. FiMAP
Baldpate Pond. E. F. Weisslitz. NYBP
Baldy Bane. W. S. Graham. NePoEA
Baldy Green. *Unknown.* PoOW
Balearic Idyll. Frederick Packard. FiBHP
Balefire kindled in the night, A. Carlyle and Emerson. Montgomery Schuyler. AA; PoMa
Balin and Balan. Tennyson. *See* Idylls of the King.
Balkis. Lascelles Abercrombie. *Fr.* Emblems of Love: Judith. HBV
(Song: "Balkis was in her marble town.") MoBrPo
Ball. Kate Greenaway. PCH
Ball, The ("The ball no question makes of ayes and noes"). Omar Khayyám, *tr. fr. Persian by* Edward Fitzgerald. *Fr.* The Rubáiyát. OnPM
Ball and the Club, The. Forbes Lindsay. SD
Ball of fire shoots through the tamarack, A. The Scarlet Tanager. Joel Benton. AA; AmLP
Ball Poem, The. John Berryman. CoAP; MoAmPo (1950 ed.)
"What is the boy now, who lost his ball," *sel.* OCS
Ball will bounce, but less and less, A. Juggler. Richard Wilbur. AmP; CMoP; FiMAP; LiTM (rev. ed.) MoAB; NePA; NePoEA; NYBP; PoIE
Ballad: A.D. 1400. Charles Kingsley. *See* Ballad of Earl Haldan's Daughter, The.
Ballad, A: "As I was walkin' the jungle round, a-killin' of tigers an' time." Guy Wetmore Carryl. BOHV; Par
Ballad: "Auld wife sat at her ivied door," The. Charles Stuart Calverley. BOHV; CenHV; FiBHP; HBV; InMe; OnSP; Par; PCD; PoVP; SiTL; TSW; WiR; WhC

Ballad (continued)
(Auld Wife [Sat at Her Ivied Door], The.) EnLi-2 (1949 ed.); NA
Ballad: "Father, through the dark that parts us." Roy Fuller. ELU
Ballad: "Follow, follow me into the South." Marjorie Allen Seiffert. HBMV
Ballad: "He pulled a flower." Leonard Cohen. PeCV
Ballad: "He said: 'The shadows darken down.'" May Kendall. HBV
Ballad: "In the summer even." Harriet Prescott Spofford. HBV
Ballad: "It was not in the winter." Thomas Hood. *See* Time of Roses.
Ballad: La Belle Dame sans Merci. Keats. *See* La Belle Dame sans Merci.
Ballad: "Mother mine, Mother mine, what do you see?" Annemarie Ewing. NePoAm
Ballad: "My lady was found mutilated." Leonard Cohen. OBCV
Ballad: "Noble Ritter Hugo, Der." Charles Godfrey Leland. *See* Ballad of the Mermaid.
Ballad: "Oh, come my joy, my soldier boy." Henry Treece. WaP
Ballad: "O! shairly ye hae seen my love." William Soutar. NeBP; WePo
Ballad: O What Is That Sound? W. H. Auden. *See* O What Is That Sound Which So Thrills the Ear?
Ballad: "Of all the girls that e'er were seen." John Gay. CoMu; ErPo
Ballad: "Roses in my garden, The." Maurice Baring. HBV
Ballad: "Spring it is cheery." Thomas Hood. VA
Ballad: "'Twas when the seas were roaring." John Gay. *Fr.* The What D'Ye Call It. CEP; HBV; StP; ViBoPo
Ballad: White Rose. Sacheverell Sitwell. POTE (1959 ed.)
(White Rose.) SiSw
Ballad against the Enemies of France. Villon, *tr. fr. French by* Swinburne. AWP; PoFr
Ballad by Hans Breitmann. Charles Godfrey Leland. *See* Ballad of the Mermaid.
Ballad Call'd the Hay-Markett Hectors, A. *At. to* Andrew Marvell. PeRV
Ballad for Gloom. Ezra Pound. LiTM (rev. ed.); MAP; MoAmPo; NeMA; NePA; OBVV
Ballad for Katharine of Aragon, A. Charles Causley. FaBoTw; NePoEA
Ballad for the Dead Ladies. Robert Lowell. TDP
Ballad from the Seven Dials Press, A. *Unknown.* CoMu
Ballad in Blonde Hair Foretold. Robert Bagg. NePoAm-2
Ballad in "G," A. Eugene Fitch Ware. PoLF
Ballad, A, in the Manner of R-dy-rd K-pl-ng, *parody.* Guy Wetmore Carryl. InMe
Ballad of a Barber, The. Aubrey Beardsley. SyP
Ballad of a Bridal. Edith Nesbit. VA
Ballad of a Bun, A. Sir Owen Seaman. CenHV
Ballad of a Mine, A. Robin Skelton. MoBS
Ballad of a Nun, A. John Davidson. BeLS; EnLit; HBMV; MoBrPo; OnMSP; PoVP
Ballad of a Strange Thing. H. Phelps Putnam. MAP; MoAmPo (1942 ed.); MoVE; OxBA
Ballad of a Sweet Dream of Peace. Robert Penn Warren. TwAmPo
Ballad of Adam's First, The. Leland Davis. HBMV
Ballad of Agincourt, The. Michael Drayton. *See* Agincourt.
Ballad of All [the] Trades, A. *Unknown.* CoMu; ErPo; UnTE
Ballad of Andrew and Maudlin, A. Thomas Durfey. CoMu; PeRV
Ballad of Another Ophelia. D. H. Lawrence. ChTr; CoBMV; MoVE
Ballad of Banners (1944), The. John Lehmann. MoBS
Ballad of Bedlam. *Unknown.* NA
Ballad of Billie Potts, The. Robert Penn Warren. AmPP (3d ed.); MoAmPo (1950 ed.); OxBA
Ballad of Billy Rose, The. Leslie Norris. MoBS
Ballad of Bouillabaisse, The. Thackeray. ALV; BOHV; HBV; InMe; OBEV (new ed.); OBVV; PoVP; VA; ViBoPo
Ballad of Bunker Hill, The. Edward Everett Hale. MC; PAH
Ballad of Burdens, A. Swinburne. EnLi-2; PoVP
Ballad of Camden Town, The. James Elroy Flecker. EnLit; HBV
Ballad of Captain Kidd, The. *Unknown.* *See* Captain Kidd.
Ballad of Cassandra Brown, The. Helen Gray Cone. BOHV; InMe
Ballad of Charity, The. Charles Godfrey Leland. BOHV; GSP; InMe
Ballad of Charlotte Dymond, The. Charles Causley. POTi
Ballad of Chickamauga, The. Maurice Thompson. MC; PAH
Ballad of Chicken Bill, The. F. E. Vaughn. PoOW
Ballad of China, A. Laura E. Richards. RePo
Ballad of Christmas, A. Walter de la Mare. StJW
Ballad of Culinary Frustration. Phyllis McGinley. FiBHP
Ballad of Davy Crockett, The, *with music.* *Unknown.* ABF
Ballad of Dead Ladies, A ("I wonder in what Isle of Bliss"). Justin Huntly M'Carthy, *par. fr. the French of* Villon. *Fr.* If I Were King. HBV
Ballad of Dead Ladies, The. Villon, *tr. fr. French by* Dante Gabriel Rossetti. ALV; ATP (1935 ed.); AWP; BEL; CTC; EnLi-2; ExPo; FaFP; GoBC; HBV; InP; JAWP; LO; OuHeWo; PoFS; PoRA; PoVP; TOP; VA; ViBoPo; ViPP; WBP
(Ballade of Dead Ladies, *tr. by* Andrew Lang.) HBV
(Snows of Yester-Year, The, *tr. by* Dante Gabriel Rossetti.) WiR
Ballad of Death, A. Swinburne. MaVP; PoVP
Ballad of Despair, A. Wade Wellman. FiSC
Ballad of Don Juan Tenorio and the Statue of the Comendador. Roy Campbell. PeSA
Ballad of Douglas Bridge. Francis Carlin. AnIV; HBMV; OxBI
Ballad of Downal Baun. Padraic Colum. SUS
Ballad of Dowsabell, The. Michael Drayton. *See* Cassamen and Dowsabel.
Ballad of Dreamland, A. Swinburne. EPN; HBV; ILP; PoVP
Ballad of Earl Haldan's Daughter, The. Charles Kingsley. OTPC
(Ballad: A.D. 1400.) GN
Ballad of East and West, The. Kipling. AnFE; BBV (1951 ed.); BEL; BeLS; BrPo; FaBoBe; FaBV; HBV; MaC; PoPo; PoVP; TSW; VA
"Oh, East is East, and West is West," *sel.* MaRV, 4 *ll.*; TRV
Ballad of Father Gilligan, The. W. B. Yeats. AnIV; EaLo; EnLit; HBV; InP; InPo; MoBrPo; NeMA; OnYI; PoPo; PoRA; WaKn; WePo
(Father Gilligan.) TSW
Ballad of Fisher's Boardinghouse, The. Kipling. PoRA
Ballad of François Villon, A. Swinburne. BEL; EnLi-2; PoEL-5; PoRA; PoVP; ViPP
Ballad of Good Counsel. Chaucer. *See* Balade de Bon Conseyl.
Ballad of Halfmoon Bay, The, *sel.* Keith Sinclair.
"Edward Edwards was a castaway sealer." AnNZ
Ballad of Hampstead Heath, The. James Elroy Flecker. MoBrPo
Ballad of Heaven, A. John Davidson. BeLS; EnLit; HBMV; PoVP; VA
Ballad of Hell, A. John Davidson. ACV; AnEnPo; AnFE; HoPM; MoBrPo; PoVP; StP; WHA
Ballad of Heroes, A. Austin Dobson. HBV; HBVY; InP; OHIP; PoRL
Ballad of High Endeavor, A. *Unknown.* BOHV; NA
Ballad of Hope and Fear. Charles Madge. FaBoMo
Ballad of Human Life. Thomas Lovell Beddoes. BeLS; VA
Ballad of Imitation, The. Austin Dobson. HBV
Ballad of Ishmael Day, The. *Unknown.* PAH
Ballad of Jack and Jill, The. Anthony C. Deane. *See* Here Is the Tale.
Ballad of John Cable and Three Gentlemen. W. S. Merwin. CoAP; NePoEA
Ballad of John Silver, A. John Masefield. BoChLi (1939 ed.); EvOK; MPB; TSW
Ballad of Johnny Appleseed, A. Helmer O. Oleson. SiSoSe; TiPo (1959 ed.)
Ballad of Judas Iscariot, The. Robert Buchanan. HBV; VA
Ballad of Keith of Ravelston, The. Sydney Dobell. *Fr.* A Nuptial Eve. OBEV; OBVV; TOP
(Keith of Ravelston.) CH; GTBS
"Ravelston, Ravelston," *sel.* LO
Ballad of Kynd Kittok, The. William Dunbar. GoTS; OxBoLi
Ballad of Ladies' Love, Number Two. Villon. *See* Ballade of Ladies' Love.
Ballad of Late Annie, The. Gwendolyn Brooks. CBV

Ballad of Lieutenant Miles. Clinton Scollard. MC
(Deed of Lieutenant Miles, The.) PAH
Ballad of Life, A. Swinburne. HBV; MaVP; PoVP
Ballad of London, A. Richard Le Gallienne. HBMV
Ballad of Longwood Glen, The. Vladimir Nabokov. NYBP
Ballad of Low-lie-down. Madison Cawein. HBV
Ballad of Manila Bay, A. Sir Charles G. D. Roberts. PAH
Ballad of Mistress Death. Denis Devlin. NMP
Ballad of Nat Turner, The. Robert E. Hayden. BALP
Ballad of New Orleans, The. George Henry Boker. PAH
Ballad of O'Bruadir, The. F. R. Higgins. EtS; OBMV
Ballad of Oriskany, The. Obadiah Cyrus Auringer. AA
Ballad of Orleans, A. Agnes Mary Frances Robinson. HBV; VA
Ballad of Our Lady. William Dunbar. ACP; CAW; ISi, *mod. vers. by* E. M. Clerke
(Ane Ballat of Our Lady.) OxBS
(Hymn to Mary, A.) MeEL
Ballad of Paco Town, The. Clinton Scollard. PAH
Ballad of Past Meridian, A. George Meredith. PeVV; PoVP
Ballad of Persse O'Reilly, The. James Joyce. *Fr.* Finnegans Wake. LiTB; SiTL
Ballad of Poor Chimney Sweeps. Villon, *tr. fr. French by* John Payne. WoL
Ballad of Private Chadd, The. A. A. Milne. CenHV
Ballad of Queensland (Sam Holt), A. G. H. Gibson. PoAu-1
Ballad of Reading Gaol, The. Oscar Wilde. AnFE; BeLS; BrPo; DTo; EnLi-2; EnLit; FaPL; HBV; LiTG, *much abr.*; OBMV, *abr.*; OnYI; OtMeF, *abr.*; PoVP; TreF
Sels.
"He did not wear his scarlet coat," *fr.* I *and* II. MoBrPo; OBNC
Hope ("We did not dare to breathe a prayer"), *br. sel. fr.* III. MaRV
"I know not whether Laws be right," V. ACP (1926 ed.); MaRV, 7 *sts.*; SoP
(In Prison, 3 *sts.*) OQP
"I never saw a man who looked / With such a wistful eye," *fr.* II. PoFr
"In Debtor's Yard the stones are hard," *fr.* III, *abr.* ViBoPo
In Reading Gaol by Reading Town, VI. FaFP; LiTB; PoPl
"There is no chapel on the day," *fr.* IV. OxBI
(Capital Punishment.) WePo
Yet Each Man Kills the Thing He Loves, *fr.* I. LO, 3 *sts.*; TrGrPo, 14 *sts. fr.* I *and* II; WHA, *br. sel.*
Ballad of Red Fox, The. Melvin Walker La Follette. LOW; NePoEA
Ballad of Redhead's Day, A. Richard Butler Glaenzer. MC; PAH
Ballad of Remembrance, A. Robert E. Hayden. AmNP; IDB; PoNe
Ballad of Riding, A. Marjorie Allen Seiffert. NP
Ballad of St. Thomas, A. Charles A. Brady. JKCP (1955 ed.)
Ballad of Sally in Our Alley, The. Henry Carey. *See* Sally in Our Alley.
Ballad of Sarsfield, A. Aubrey Thomas De Vere. GoBC; HBV
Ballad of Semmerwater, The. Sir William Watson. PoVP
Ballad of Sir Brian and the Three Wishes, The. Newman Levy. FiBHP
Ballad of Sir John Franklin, A. George Henry Boker. AA; HBV; OnMSP
Ballad of Sir Patrick Spens. *Unknown.* *See* Sir Patrick Spens.
Ballad of Sister Anne, The. Sir Osbert Sitwell. AtBAP
Ballad of Sue Ellen Westerfield, The. Robert Hayden. AmPP (5th ed.); Kal
Ballad of Sweet P, The. Virginia Woodward Cloud. PAH
Ballad of the Angel, The. Theodosia Garrison. HBV
Ballad of the Battle of Gibeon, The. G. K. Chesterton. YT
Ballad of the Bells, *sel.* Paul Fort, *tr. fr. French by* Joseph T. Shipley.
"Ah! what joy, the bagpipe and the flute." WoL
Ballad of [*or* to] the *Billycock,* The. Anthony C. Deane. ALV; NeMA; TSW
Ballad of the Boat, The. Richard Garnett. HBV; VA
Ballad of the Boll Weevil, The. *Unknown.* *See* Ballet of de Boll Weevil, De.
Ballad of the Boston Tea-Party, A. Oliver Wendell Holmes. MC; PaA; PAH; PAL; PoFr, *abr.*; ThLM
Ballad of the Bushman. Eileen Duggan. CoBE
Ballad of the Canal. Phoebe Cary. BOHV
Ballad of the Captains, A. E. J. Brady. EtS
Ballad of the Children of the Czar, The. Delmore Schwartz. MiAP; OnHM
Ballad of the Common Man (for the Jefferson Memorial). Alfred Kreymborg. PAL; PoFr
Ballad of the Conemaugh Flood, A. Hardwicke Drummond Rawnsley. PAH
Ballad of the Courtier and the Country Clown, A. *Unknown.* CoMu
Ballad of the Cross, The. Theodosia Garrison. HBMV; HBVY
Ballad of the Dark Ladie, The. Samuel Taylor Coleridge. EnRP
Ballad of the Days of the Messiah. A. M. Klein. TrJP
Ballad of the Despairing Husband. Robert Creeley. AmPC; NeAP; ToPo
Ballad of the Double Bed. Eve Merriam. UnTE
Ballad of the Drinker in His Pub. N. P. van Wyk Louw, *tr. fr. Afrikaans by* Uys Krige, Jack Cope, *and* Ruth Miller. PeSA
Ballad of the Drover. Henry Lawson. PoAu-1
Ballad of the Emeu, The. Bret Harte. BOHV
Ballad of the Epiphany. Charles Dalmon. HBMV; OnMSP; TSW
Ballad of the Equinox. Vernon Watkins. PrWP
Ballad of the Erie Canal. *Unknown.* ABF; IHA
Ballad of the Faded Field. Robert Burns Wilson. AA
Ballad of the Faithful Clerk. Albert Stillman. InMe
Ballad of the Fiddler, The. "Seumas O'Sullivan." MPB
Ballad of the Flood. Edwin Muir. MoBS
Ballad of the Fox. *Unknown.* *See* Fox, The.
Ballad of the Foxhunter, The. W. B. Yeats. EnLit
Ballad of the French Fleet, A. Longfellow. HBV; MC; PAH
Ballad of the Gibbet. Villon. *See* Epitaph in Form of a Ballad, The.
Ballad of the Golden Bowl. Sara Henderson Hay. OnMSP
Ballad of the Good Lord Nelson, A. Lawrence Durrell. ErPo; LiTM; OnHM; SiTL
Ballad of the Goodly Fere. Ezra Pound. CAW; CMoP; FOL; FosPo; HBV; LiTA; LiTM; MAP; MoAB; MoAmPo; MoBS; NePA; NP; PoRA; PoSa; TrGrPo
Ballad of the Happy Christmas Wind. Sister Mary Madeleva. ChrBoLe
Ballad of the Harp-Weaver, The. Edna St. Vincent Millay. MaC; StPo; YT
Ballad of the *Ivanhoe,* The. Bill Adams. BBV
Ballad of the King's Jest, The. Kipling. GBV
Ballad of the Landlord. Langston Hughes. TPM
Ballad of the Lincoln Penny. Alfred Kreymborg. YaD
Ballad of the Little Black Hound. Dora Sigerson Shorter. OnYI; StPo
Ballad of the Londoner. James Elroy Flecker. EnLoPo
Ballad of the Long-legged Bait. Dylan Thomas. CoBMV; SeCeV
Ballad of the Lords of Old Time. Villon, *tr. fr. French by* Swinburne. AWP; JAWP; PeVV; WBP
Ballad of the Mermaid. Charles Godfrey Leland. FiBHP
(Ballad by Hans Breitmann.) BOHV; CenHV
(Ballad; "Der noble Ritter Hugo.") PaPo
Ballad of the Merry Ferry, The. Emma Rounds. MPB; RIS
Ballad of the Mouse. Robert Wallace. NYBP
Ballad of the Mulberry Road, A. Ezra Pound. LOW
Ballad of the Outer Life. Hugo von Hofmannsthal, *tr. fr. German by* Jethro Bithell. AWP; JAWP; LiTW; TrJP; WBP
(Twilight of the Outward Life, *tr. by* Peter Viereck.) OnHM
Ballad of the Oysterman, The. Oliver Wendell Holmes. AmePo; AmPP; AnAmPo; AnNE; AP; BOHV; EtS; FaFP; HBV; HBVY; MCCG; MoShBr; OnSP; PCD; PTK; TreFS; YT
Ballad of the Primitive Jest. Andrew Lang. BOHV
(Ballade of the Primitive Jest.) HBV
Ballad of the Rising in the North, A. *Unknown.* ACP
Ballad of the Sailor Ben. Jack Mitchell.
(Hints on Writing Verse.) PCD
Ballad of the Spanish Civil Guard. Federico García Lorca, *tr. fr. Spanish by* Lysander Kemp. LiTW
Ballad of the Strange and Wonderful Storm of Hail, A. *Unknown.* CoMu
Ballad of the Tempest. James Thomas Fields. BeLS; EtS; FaBoBe; HBV (8th ed.); PoLF; YaD
(Captain's Daughter, The.) FaFP; HBV (6th ed.); HBVY
(Tempest, The.) TreF
Ballad of the Trial of Sodom. Vernon Watkins. MoRP

Ballad of the Two Tapsters. Vernon Watkins. MoBS
Ballad of the Unmiraculous Miracle. Vassar Miller. ToPo
Ballad of the Western Island in the North Country. *Unknown, tr. fr. Chinese by* Arthur Waley. SiSw
Ballad of the White Horse, The, *sels.* G. K. Chesterton.
"Before the gods that made the gods." ACP (1952 ed.)
Harp of Alfred, The. MoVE
Songs of Guthrum and Alfred, The. HBV
King Alfred Answers the Danes. OxBoCh
"To sweat a slave to a race of slaves." PoFr
Ballad of the Women of Paris. Villon, *tr. fr. French by* Swinburne. AWP; JAWP; OuHeWo; WBP
(Ballade of the Women of Paris.) MeWo; UnTE
Ballad of Trees and the Master, A. Sidney Lanier. AA; AmePo; AmP; AnAmPo; AP; CAW; ChIP; CoBA; GoBC; GTBS-W; HBV; LaNeLa; LiTA; MAmP; MAP; MaRV; MoAmPo (1942 ed.); OQP; OxBA; PFY; PoEL-5; PoLF; PoRL; PTK; SoP; StJW; TOP; TreFT; TRV; WGRP; WHL
(Cross, The.) BePJ
Ballad of Two Kings. Grant Code. FiSC
Ballad of William Sycamore, The. Stephen Vincent Benét. AnAmPo; BoLiVe; HBMV; MAP; MoAmPo; MPB; OnSP; PFY; PoRA; TreFT
Ballad of Wise Men, A. George M. P. Baird. ChrBoLe
Ballad of Wonder, A. Eleanor Slater. MaRV
Ballad of Yukon Jake, The. Edward E. Paramore, Jr. BeLS; BLPA; NeHB
Ballad on the Taxes, A. Edward Ward. OxBoLi; PPON; SiTL
Ballad Riding in the North, A. *Unknown.* ACP
Ballad Singer, The. Thomas Hardy. At Casterbridge Fair, I. BEL; EnLi-2 (1949 ed.); EnLit; LO; NoP; PoVP
(Sing, Ballad-Singer.) MeWo
Ballad Singers. John Gay. *See* Of Ballad-Singers.
Ballad to a Traditional Refrain. Maurice James Craig. SeCePo
Ballad to Queen Elizabeth, A. Austin Dobson. ALV; GTBS; OBVV; ShBV-2
Ballad to the *Billycock,* The. Anthony C. Deane. *See* Ballad of the *Billycock,* The.
Ballad to the Tune of Bateman, A. Sir Charles Sedley. CoMu; PeRV
Ballad to the Tune of "The Cut-Purse," A. Swift. PP
Ballad to William of Nassau. *Unknown, tr. fr. Dutch by* A. J. Barnouw. PoFr, 7 *sts.*
Ballad upon a Wedding, A. Sir John Suckling. AtBAP; CABA; CABL; CavP; CBEP; HBV, *sl. abr.*; InvP; LoBV; NoP; OBS; Par; ReEn; SeCeV; SCEP-2; SeCL; UnTE; ViBoPo
(Ballade upon a Wedding, A.) AnAnS-2; CoMu; SeCP; SeCV-1; SeEP
(Wedding, A.) BOHV
Sels.
Bride, The ("Her feet beneath her petticoat"). MeWo; TrGrPo
"Maid, The (and therby hangs a tale)." LO
Ballad upon the Popish Plot, A. John Gadbury. CoMu
Ballad Warning Men to Beware of Deceitful Women, A, *sel.* John Lydgate.
"Women, of kinde, have conditions three." LO
Ballad with an Ancient Refrain. *Unknown.* NA
Ballad Written for a Bridegroom. Villon, *tr. fr. French by* Swinburne. AWP
(Ballade for a Bridegroom.) MeWo
Ballade: "Here ends this cycle of my poems for you." Karl Shapiro. MeWo
Ballade: "Looking one day toward the coast of France." Charles d'Orléans, *tr. fr. French by* William Stirling. LiTW
Ballade: "O sely ankir, that in thi selle." Charles d'Orléans. EnPo
(Go Sad Complaint.) MeEL
Ballade: "Outcast bones from a thousand biers." Don Marquis. *Fr.* Archy and Mehitabel. WhC
Ballade: "Pretty maid she died, she died, in love-bed as she lay, The." Paul Fort, *tr. fr. French by* Frederick York Powell. AWP; JAWP; WBP
(Pretty Maid, The.) OBMV
Ballade: To a Fish of the Brooke. John Wolcot. CBEP
Ballade: "When fresshe Phebus, day of Seynt Valentyne." Charles d'Orléans. EnPo
Ballade against Woman Inconstant, A. Chaucer. *See* Against Women Inconstant.
Ballade by the Fire. E. A. Robinson. InP
Ballade Catalogue of Lovely Things, A. Richard Le Gallienne. HBMV
Ballade de Marguerite. *Unknown, tr. fr. French by* Oscar Wilde. AWP; JAWP; WBP
Ballade d'une Grande Dame. G. K. Chesterton. OxBoLi
Ballade for a Bridegroom. *See* Ballad Written for a Bridegroom.
Ballade for the Duke of Orléans. Richard Wilbur. TDP
Ballade in a Bad Temper. Louis MacNeice. PoFr
Ballade Made in the Hot Weather. W. E. Henley. AnFE; MoBrPo
(Made in the Hot Weather.) GN
Ballade of a Conspicuous Omission from "The Book of Humorous Verse." Carolyn Wells. BOHV
Ballade of a Friar. Clément Marot. *See* Friar Lubin.
Ballade of a Ship. E. A. Robinson. TSW
Ballade of a Summer Hotel. "Junia." WhC
Ballade of a Toyokuni Color-Print. W. E. Henley. PoVP
Ballade of an Anti-Puritan, A. G. K. Chesterton. BOHV
Ballade of Andrew Lang. Dugald Sutherland MacColl. CenHV
Ballade of Any Father to Any Son, A. J. C. Squire. WhC
Ballade of Ballade-Mongers, A. Augustus M. Moore. BOHV
Ballade of Big Plans. Dorothy Parker. InMe
Ballade of Blue China. Andrew Lang. PoVP; TSW
(Of Blue China.) VA
Ballade of Charon and the River Girl. J. B. Morton. WhC
Ballade of Dead Actors. W. E. Henley. ALV; InP; OBMV; PoVP
Ballade of Dead Friends. E. A. Robinson. AA
Ballade of Dead Ladies. Villon. *See* Ballad of Dead Ladies, The.
Ballade of Diminishing Control, A. J. C. Squire. WhC
Ballade of England. Louis MacNeice. NYBP
Ballade of Evolution, A. Grant Allen. ATP (1935 ed.)
Ballade of Expansion. Hilda Johnson. PAH
Ballade of Faith. Tom MacInnes. CaP
Ballade of Forgotten Loves. Arthur Grissom. BOHV
Ballade of Good Counsel. Chaucer. *See* Balade de Bon Conseyl.
Ballade of Hell and of Mrs. Roebeck. Hilaire Belloc. MoVE
Ballade of His Choice of a Sepulcher. Andrew Lang. PoVP
(Of His Choice of a Sepulchre.) VA
Ballade of Illegal Ornaments. Hilaire Belloc. ACP (1952 ed.)
Ballade of Islands, A. Lucy Catlin Robinson. AA
Ballade of Ivan Petrofsky Skevar, Ye. *Unknown. See* Abdul A-Bul-Bul A-Mir.
Ballade of Ladies' Love. Villon, *tr. fr. French by* John Payne. UnTE
(Ballad of Ladies' Love, Number Two.) ErPo
Ballade of Ladies' Names. W. E. Henley. HBV
Ballade of Lawn Tennis, A. Franklin P. Adams. SD
Ballade of Lost Objects. Phyllis McGinley. PoCh; PoRA (rev. ed.)
Ballade of Middle Age. Andrew Lang. HBV
Ballade of Muhammad Din Tilai. *Unknown, tr. fr. Pushtu by* E. Powys Mathers. PG (1945 ed.)
Ballade of My Lady's Beauty. Joyce Kilmer. HBV
Ballade of Playing Cards, A. Gleeson White. VA
Ballade of Primitive Man. Andrew Lang. *See* Double Ballade of Primitive Man.
Ballade of Prose and Rhyme, The. Austin Dobson. MoBrPo (1942 ed.)
Ballade of Schopenhauer's Philosophy. Franklin P. Adams. HBMV
Ballade of Soporific Absorption. J. C. Squire. InMe
Ballade of Spring. W. E. Henley. TSW
Ballade of Spring's Unrest, A. Bert Leston Taylor. PoMa; YT
Ballade of Suicide, A. G. K. Chesterton. BOHV; FiBHP; HBV; InMe; JKCP (1955 ed.)
Ballade of the Ancient Wheeze. Nate Salsbury *and* Newman Levy. InMe
Ballade of the Dreamland Rose. Brian Hooker. HBMV
Ballade of the Fair Helm-Maker. Villon, *tr. fr. French by* John Payne. UnTE
Ballade of the Gibbet. Villon. *See* Epitaph in Form of a Ballad, The.
Ballade of the Golfer in Love. Clinton Scollard. BOHV
Ballade of the Goth. Sir Walter Raleigh. WhC
Ballade of the Hanged Men. Villon. *See* Epitaph in Form of a Ballad.

Ballade of the Harrowing of Hell. D. B. Wyndham Lewis. CoBE; JKCP (1955 ed.)
Ballade of the Heresiarchs. Hilaire Belloc. MoVE
Ballade of the Nurserie, A. John Twig. NA
Ballade of the Poetic Life. J. C. Squire. OBMV; WhC
Ballade of the Primitive Jest. Andrew Lang. *See* Ballad of the Primitive Jest.
Ballade of the Scottyshe Kynge, A. John Skelton. CoMu
Ballade of the Session after Camarillo. David Galler. NMP
Ballade of the Southern Cross. Andrew Lang. InP
Ballade of the Unchanging Beauty. Richard Le Gallienne. InP
Ballade of the Under Side. Don Marquis. *Fr.* Archys Life of Mehitabel. InvP
Ballade of the Women of Paris. Villon. *See* Ballad of the Women. . .
Ballade of Unfortunate Mammals. Dorothy Parker. ALV; BOHV; InMe
Ballade of Villon and Fat Margot. Villon, *tr. fr. French by* John Payne. UnTE
Ballade of Youth and Age. W. E. Henley. PoVP
Ballade on Eschatology. Sister Mary Madeleva. GoYe
Ballade to My Psychoanalyst. Kenneth Lillington. FiBHP
Ballade to Our Lady. Sebastian Brant, *tr. fr. German by* Alexander Barclay. *Fr.* The Ship of Fools. ISi
Ballade to Our Lady of Czestochowa. Hilaire Belloc. ACP (1952 ed.); ISi
Ballade to Rosamund. Chaucer. *See* To Rosamond.
Ballade to Theocritus, in Winter. Andrew Lang. InP
(To Theocritus, in Winter.) VA
Ballade un Peu Banale. A. J. M. Smith. MoCV; SiTL
Ballads of the Last Prince, The, *sel.* Ernest Rhys.
Mountain Liberty. PoFr
Ballads on Napoleon, *sels.* *Unknown.*
Hop-o-My-Thumb. CoBE
Island, The. CoBE
Ballade upon a Wedding, A. Sir John Suckling. *See* Ballad upon a Wedding, A.
Ballata: Concerning a Shepherd-Maid. Guido Cavalcanti, *tr. fr. Italian by* Dante Gabriel Rossetti. AWP
Ballata: He Reveals His Increasing Love for Mandetta. Guido Cavalcanti, *tr. fr. Italian by* Dante Gabriel Rossetti. AWP
Ballata: He Will Gaze upon Beatrice. Dante, *tr. fr. Italian by* Dante Gabriel Rossetti. AWP; JAWP; WBP
(Sonnet: "Because mine eyes can never have their fill.") GoBC
Ballata: His Talk with Certain Peasant-Girls. Franco Sacchetti, *tr. fr. Italian by* Dante Gabriel Rossetti. AWP
Ballata: In Exile at Sarzana. Guido Cavalcanti, *tr. fr. Italian by* Dante Gabriel Rossetti. AWP JAWP; WBP
Ballata V: "Light do I see within my Lady's eyes." Guido Cavalcanti, *tr. fr. Italian by* Ezra Pound. CTC
Ballata: Of a Continual Death in Love. Guido Cavalcanti, *tr. fr. Italian by* Dante Gabriel Rossetti. AWP
Ballata: Of His Lady among Other Ladies. Guido Cavalcanti. *See* Ballata: "With other women I beheld my love."
Ballata: Of True and False Singing. *Unknown, tr. fr. Italian by* Dante Gabriel Rossetti. AWP
(Ballata of True and False Spring.) UnS
(True and False Singing.) OnPM
Ballata: One Speaks of the Beginning of His Love. *Unknown, tr. fr. Italian by* Dante Gabriel Rossetti. AWP
Ballata: "With other women I beheld my love." Guido Cavalcanti, *tr. fr. Italian by* Dante Gabriel Rossetti. OnPM
(Ballata: Of His Lady among Other Ladies.) AWP
Ballata of Love's Power. Guido Cavalcanti, *tr. fr. Italian by* Hubert Creekmore. LiTW
Ballata of Myrrha's Eyes. Angelo Poliziano, *tr. fr. Italian by* John Addington Symonds. LiTW
(Three Ballate, II.) AWP
Ballata of True and False Spring. *Unknown.* *See* Ballata: Of True and False Singing.
Ballatetta. Ezra Pound. NoP
Ballet [*or* Ballad] of de [*or* the] Boll Weevil, De (diff. versions). *Unknown.* ABF, *with music*; AS, *with music*; IHA; ViBoFo, *with music*
(Ballad of the Boll Weevil, The.) ThLM; TrAS
(Boll Weevil Song, The.) AS
Ballet of the Fifth Year, The. Delmore Schwartz. MoAB; OxBA; TwCP
Ballet Song of Mary, A. Elizabeth Madox Roberts. MAP; MoAmPo; NP
Balloon, The. Karla Kuskin. PDV
Balloon, The. Tennyson. *See* Dream of Fair Women, A.
Balloon Faces. Carl Sandburg. CMoP
Balloon Man, The. Dorothy Aldis. TiPo
Balloon Man. Hazel I. Dannecker. PoMa
Balloon Man, The. Rose Fyleman. BoTP; SoPo; SUS
Balloon Man, The. E. Herbert. BoTP
Ballon Man, The. ——Morton. GFA
Balloon Man. Jessica N. North. GaP; SoPo
Balloon Seller, The. Elizabeth Fleming. BoTP
Balloons. Sylvia Plath. TPM
Balloons hang on wires in the Marigold Gardens, The. Balloon Faces. Carl Sandburg. CMoP
Ballot, The. John Pierpont. AA; AmePo; InP; PoRL
Ballroom Dancing Class. Phyllis McGinley. MoShBr
Ball-room was filled with fashion's throng, The. A Bird in a Gilded Cage. Arthur J. Lamb. TreFT
Ball's lost, lost, gone. The Lost Ball. Lucy Sprague Mitchell. TiPo (1959 ed.)
Ballyhoo for a Mendicant. Carlton Talbott. AnAmPo
Ballykinlar, May, 1940. Patrick Maybin. NeIP
Ballyshannon foundered off the coast of Cariboo, The. Etiquette. W. S. Gilbert. BOHV; CenHV; EnLi-2; FaBoCh; FiBHP; MaC
Ballytullagh. William Allingham. *Fr.* Laurence Bloomfield in Ireland. IrPN
Balme. Spenser. *Fr.* The Faerie Queene, I, 11. CH
Balmy warmth comes wafted o'er the seas, A. Farewell to Bithynia. Catullus. OuHeWo
Baloo, loo, lammy, now baloo, my dear. Lullaby. Lady Nairne. HBV
Balow. *Unknown.* LO; OBEV
(By-low, My Babe, *abr.*) TrGrPo
(Lady Anne Bothwell's Lament.) HBV
Balow, my babe, weep not for me. The New Balow. *Unknown.* CoMu
Balthasar's Song. Shakespeare. *See* Sigh No More, Ladies.
Balulalow. James, John, *and* Robert Wedderburn. LoBV; OxBoCh
(Cradle Song: "O my deir hert, young Jesu sweit.") EaLo; OBEV
Balzac. Darcy Gottlieb. NYTB
Bam, Bam, Bam. Eve Merriam. PDV
Bambini picking daisies in the new spring grass. Daisies of Florence. Kathleen Raine. NYBP
Bamboo. William Plomer. PeSA
Ban of Time there is no disobeying, The. Lament. Gelett Burgess. InMe
Bañalbufar, a Brazier, Relativity, Cloud Formations & the Kindness & Relentlessness of Time. Paul Blackburn. CoPo
Banana. Charles G. Bell. ErPo; NePoAm-2
Banana. Adrian Mitchell. PV
Banana-stuffed, the ape behind the brain. After Sunday Dinner We Uncles Snooze. John Ciardi. ToPo
Bananas ripe and green, and ginger-root. The Tropics in New York. Claude McKay. AmNP; GoSl; Kal; PoNe; TTY
Banbury Fair. Edith G. Millard. BoTP
Band, The. —— John. GFA
Band blares, The. Circus. Eleanor Farjeon. MPB; SUS; UTS
Band in the Pines, The. John Esten Cooke. AA
Band makes a tunnel of the open street. The Bands and the Beautiful Children. P. K. Page. PeCV
Band Music. John Fuller. NePoEA-2
Band o' Gideon, De. *Unknown.* BoAN-1, *with music*
Band of Gideon, The. Joseph S. Cotter, Jr. BANP; CDC
Band of Military Officers, A. Wordsworth. *Fr.* The Prelude, IX. EnLi-2
Band of the bold were gathered together, The. The Parting of the Red Sea. *Unknown.* *Fr.* Exodus. AnOE
Band Played On, The. John F. Palmer. TreF
Banded Cobra, The. C. Louis Leipoldt, *tr. fr. Afrikaans by* Uys Krige, Jack Cope, *and* Ruth Miller. PeSA
Bandit. A. M. Klein. WHW
Bandit Peter Mancino's Death, The. *Unknown, tr. fr. Italian by* Maria Graham. CAW
Bandit's Grave, The. Charles Pitt. SCC
Bandog, The. Walter de la Mare. BrPo; EvOK; TiPo
Bands and the Beautiful Children, The. P. K. Page. PeCV

Bandusia, Stainless Mirror ("O fons Bandusiae"). Horace, *tr. fr. Latin by* Charles Stuart Calverley. Odes, III, 13. OnPM
Bang Bang Bang/ Said the nails in the Ark. The History of the Flood. John Heath-Stubbs. FlW; MoBS
Bangidero, *with music. Unknown.* SoAmSa
Bangkok. F. R. Scott. MoCV; OBCV
Bangkolidye. Barry Pain. BOHV
Bangum Rode the Riverside, *with music. Unknown.* BFSS
Banish the scent of sherry and cigars. After the Party. Frances Cornford. ELU
Banished, The. Arturo Serrano Plaja, *tr. fr. Spanish by* Rolfe Humphries. PoFr
Banished, dispossessed dead, The. Litany of the Rooms of the Dead. Franz Werfel. TrJP
Banished Duke [Living in the Forest] Speaks to His Retainers, The. Shakespeare. *See* Uses of Adversity, The.
Banished Duke of Grantham, The. *Unknown.* EnSB
Banishment, The. Milton. *Fr.* Paradise Lost. XII. OBS
Banishment from Paradise. Milton. *Fr.* Paradise Lost,XII. TreFS
Banisht!/ It greev'd me much to heare the sentence. John Webster. *Fr.* The White Devil, I, i. AtBAP
Banjo Boomer. Wallace Stevens. WaKn
Banjo of the Past, The. Howard Weeden. AA
Banjo Player, The. Fenton Johnson. AnAmPo; BANP; GoSl; Kal; PoNe
Bank had closed, The; my earthly store had vanished from my hand. God's Bank Ain't Busted Yet. Alice P. Moss. SoP
Bank holiday. A sky of guns. The river. At Grantchester. Charles Causley. POTi
Bank of the Arkansaw, The, *with music. Unknown.* OuSiCo
Bank Thief, The. J. R. Farrell. BeLS; BLPA
Bankers Are Just like Anybody Else, except Richer. Ogden Nash. ATP (1953 ed.); LiTA
Banking Coal. Jean Toomer. PoNe (1970 ed.)
Bankis of Helicon, The, *sel. Unknown.*
"Declair, ye bankis of Helicon." OxBS
Bankrupt. Cortlandt W. Sayres. PoLF; PoToHe (new ed.)
Banks o' Doon, The. Burns. BoLiVe; BoLP; CEP; EiCL; EnLi-2; InP; LoBV; MCCG; MeWo; NeHB; OBEC; OBEV; OtMeF; OuHeWo; PoMa; TreFS; TrGrPo; ViBoPo; WBLP; WHA
(Bonie Doon.) BEL; NoP
(Bonnie Doon.) EnLit; HBV
(False Love.) LiTL
(Ye Banks and Braes [o' Bonnie Doon].) AtBAP; CBEP; CH; EiPP; ELP; GTBS-P; GTSE; GTSL; StP; WePo
(Ye Flowery Banks [o' Bonnie Doon].) AWP; CABA; CEP; EG; EnRP; ForPo; GTBS; GTBS-D; GTBS-W; InPo; JAWP; OAEP; OBEC; PeER; PoEL-4; TOP; WBP
Banks of Banna, The. George Ogle. IrPN
Banks of Dundee, The. *Unknown.* BaBo
Banks of Gaspereaux, The. *Unknown.* BaBo
(Banks of the Gaspereaux, The.) ShS
Banks of Newfoundland, The, *with music. Unknown.* ShS; SoAmSa
Banks of Sacramento, The, *with music. Unknown.* AmSS; AS
Banks of Sweet Primroses, The. *Unknown.* ELP
Banks of the Condamine, The. *Unknown.* PoAu-1
Banks of the Gaspereaux, The. *Unknown. See* Banks of Gaspereaux, The.
Banks of the Pamanaw, The. *Unknown.* ABF
Banks of the Roses, The, *with music. Unknown.* ShS
Banks of Wye, The, *sels.* Robert Bloomfield. OBNC
Coracle Fishers, The.
Meandering Wye.
Banner of England, not for a season, O banner of Britain, hast thou. The Defence of Lucknow. Tennyson. BeLS
Banner of Freedom high floated unfurled, The. The *United States* and *Macedonian. Unknown.* PAH
Banner of the Cross, The. George Washington Doane. BePJ
Banner of the Jew, The. Emma Lazarus. AA; TrJP
Bannockburn. Burns. PoPo. *See also* Scots Wha Hae.
Banquet, The. Louise Driscoll. MaRV
Banquet, The. George Herbert. AnAnS-1; MaMe; MeP
Banquet, The. Keats. *Fr.* Lamia. SeCePo
Banquet-cups, of many a hue and shape, The. The Respite. Maria Gowen Brooks. *Fr.* Zophiel; or, The Bride of Seven. AA
Bansha Peeler wint won night, A. The Peeler and the Goat. *Unknown.* AnIL
Banshee, The. John Todhunter. OnYI; VA
Bantam Husband, The. *Unknown. See* Petit Mari, Le.
Bantams in Pine-Woods. Wallace Stevens. AtBAP; CBV; CMoP; InPo; MoVE; OxBA; PoAn; PoeP; SeCeV
Bantry Bay. James Lyman Molloy. OnYI
Bantu on a Bicycle. Alan Ross. POTi
Banty Tim. John Hay. MAP; MoAmPo (1942 ed.)
Baptism, The. Leonard Aaronson. FaBoTw
Baptism. Charles G. Bell. AmFN
Baptism. Claude McKay. AnEnPo; PoNe
Baptist, The. William Drummond of Hawthornden. *See* For the Baptist.
Bar, The. *Unknown.* PoToHe (new ed.); STF
Bar at Night, A. Sakutaro Hagiwara, *tr. fr. Japanese by* Katue Kitasono. LiTW
Bar is closed and I come, The. Night on Clinton. Robert Mezey. NaP
Bar is crossed, The: but Death—the pilot—stands. Becalmed. John Banister Tabb. AA
Bar Kochba. Emma Lazarus. TrJP
Bar Not the Door. Thomas Campion. UnTE
Bar to heaven, a door to hell, A. The Bar. *Unknown.* STF
Bar was black with blistered age, The. Ghost-Town Saloon: Winter. Joseph Payne Brennan. FiSC
Bar-Z on a Sunday Night. Percival Combes. SCC
Barabbas, *sels.* Sara Bard Field. PoFr
"Aslant the shoulder of each prisoner," *fr.* III.
"In secret mountain fastnesses we stored," *fr.* I.
Barabbas, Judas Isçariot. The Morning After. Dorothy Wellesley. OBMV
Barabbas Speaks. Edwin McNeill Poteat. MaRV
Barbara. Alexander Smith. GoTS; GTBS; HBV; OBEV (1st ed.); OBVV
Barbara/ Van Gogh Poem. Lew Welch. FRC
Barbara Allen [*or* Allan]. *Unknown.* BeLS; BFSS, *with music*; CABA; CBEP; DiPo; EnSB; FaFP; ForPo; MaC; MeWo; TrAS *with music*; TreF; ViBoFo (A *and* C *vers.*; B *vers., with music*)
(Barbara Allen's Cruelty.) FaBoBe; HBV; OBB; OBEV; OnSP; OTPC (1923 ed.); ViBoPo
(Barbara Ellen.) IHA
(Barbra Allen, *with music.*) AS
(Bonny Barbara Allan.) AWP; BaBo (A, B, *and* C *vers.*); BEL; BoLiVe; CH, *abr.*; CoBE; EnLi-1 (1949 ed.); EnLit; ESPB (A *and* B *vers.*); InPo; JAWP; LiTB; LiTL; LoEn; NoP; OuHeWo; OxBB; TOP; TrGrPo; WBP
(Bonny Barbara Ellen.) Po
("In Scarlet Town where I was born.") LO
(Sir John Graeme and Barbara Allan.) OxBoLi
Barbara Frietchie. Whittier. AmePo; AmPP (3d ed.); AnNE; AP; BBV; BeLS; BoTP; CTC; DD; FaBoBe; FaBV; FaFP; FaPL; FaPON; GN; GoTP; GSP; HBV; HBVY; MaC; MC; NeHB; OnSP; OTD; OTPC; PaA; PAH; PAL; PAP; PaPo; PoLF; PoSC; PTK; RIS; StVeCh (1940 ed.); ThLM; TreF; TrGrPo; WBLP; YaD; YT
Barbara, think what'd happen if Van Gogh'd ever seen. Barbara/ Van Gogh Poem. Lew Welch. FRC
Barbarian. Arthur Rimbaud, *tr. fr. French by* Hubert Creekmore. LiTW
Barbarians in the hills, The. Morning Moon. Victor Contoski. ThO
Barbarossa, *sel.* Giovanni Battista Niccolini, *tr. fr. Italian by* William Dean Howells.
"When will you dream,/ You Germans." PoFr
Barbarossa. Friedrich Rückert, *tr. fr. German.* AWP
Barb'd blossom of the guarded gorse. A Song of Winter. Emily Davis Pfeiffer. ACV; PrWP; VA
Barbed Wire. Eithne Wilkins. NeBP
Barber, The. Moses Browne. WaPE
Barber, The. John Gray. SyP
Barber, barber, shave a pig. Mother Goose. BoChLi; EvOK; GaP; HBV; HBVY; OTPC; OxNR; RIS
Barber Shaved the Mason, The. *Unknown.* OTPC (1923 ed.); OxNR
Barber shop is blank, The. Through the Barber Shop Window. Violet Anderson. CaP
Barber snips and snips, The. Barber's Clippers. Dorothy Baruch. SoPo
Barber, Spare Those Hairs. John Love, Jr. YaD

Barbered woman's man, A. Contemporaries. Richard Hovey. MAP; MoAmPo (1942 ed.)
Barberries. Mary Aldis. HBMV
Barberries ripe. Chant for Skippers. Katharine Gallagher. SiSoSe
Barberry-Bush, The. Jones Very. AP
Barber's, The. Walter de la Mare. GaP; GoJo; MPB; PCH; SoPo; SUS
Barber's art, no trivial whim, The. The Barber. Moses Browne. WePE
Barber's Clippers. Dorothy Baruch. SoPo
Barber's Cry, *with music*. *Unknown*. TrAS
Barbra Allen. *Unknown*. *See* Barbara Allen.
Barcarole of James Smith, The. Herbert S. Gorman. HBMV
Barcarolle. Arthur O'Shaughnessy. NBM
Bard, The. Blake. *See* Hear the Voice of the Bard.
Bard, The. Thomas Gray. BEL; CEP; EnL; EnLi-2; EiCP; EiPP; EnPE; EnRP; GTBS; GTBS-D; GTBS-P; GTBS-W; GTSE; GTSL; OAEP; OBEC; PAn; Po; PoFr, *abr.*; ShBV-4; StP; TOP
Sels.
Curse upon Edward. OBEV
"On a rock, whose haughty brow." SeCePo
Bard, The. James Shirley. ErPo
Bard is buried here, not strong, but sweet, A. The Epitaph of Eusthenes. Edward Cracroft Lefroy. *Fr.* Echoes from Theocritus. AWP; OBVV
Bard of Love, The. *Unknown, tr. fr. Greek by* Byron. OuHeWo
Bard who is singing of Wollombi Jim, The. Jim the Splitter. Henry Kendall. PoAu-1
Bards, The. Walter de la Mare. DTC; PV
Bards, The. Robert Graves. DTC; FaBoMo; GTBS-W; LiTM (rev. ed.); SeCePo; ViBoPo (1958 ed.)
(Lust in Song.) OxBI; ViBoPo (1941 ed.)
Bard's Chant. James Shirley. *Fr.* Saint Patrick for Ireland. ACP
Bard's Epitaph, A. Burns. EiPP; InP
Bards falter in shame, their running verse, The. The Bards, [*or* Lust in Song]. Robert Graves. ViBoPo. *See also* Their cheeks are blotched for shame, their running verse.
Bards of brow funereal. Mystical Poets. Amado Nervo. CAW
Bards of Passion and of Mirth. Keats. *See* Ode: "Bards of Passion and of Mirth."
Bards of the Future! you that come. On the Future of Poetry. Austin Dobson. PoVP
Bard's Song, The. Sir Robert Stapylton. SeCePo
Bards We Quote, The. Bert Leston Taylor. HBMV; WhC
Bare Almond-Trees. D. H. Lawrence. FlW
Bare and bow your Christian. Elegy for a Lady. Walt Delegall. BF
Bare-handed, I hand the combs. Stings. Sylvia Plath. NaP
Bare mud, slippery, wet and brown. Highway to Nowhere. Grant Code. FiSC
Bare skin is my wrinkled sack. The Shrouded Stranger. Allen Ginsberg. NeAP
Bare uncovered bulb, A. Reality. Yvette Johnson. TNV
Bare Winter owns the earth at last. Winter Life and Scenery. Thomas Caulfield Irwin. IrPN
Bareback. William Haskell Simpson. *Fr.* In Arizona. NP
Bare-Back Rider. Dorothy Aldis. *Fr.* At the Circus. UTS
Barefoot and ragged, with neglected hair. On a Fair Beggar. Philip Ayres. EnLoPo; LO; OBS; SeCL; SeEP
Barefoot Boy, A. James Whitcomb Riley. FaFP
Barefoot Boy, The. Whittier. AA; AmePo; AmPP (3d ed.); AnNE; CoBA; FaBoBe; GN; GTBS-W; HBV; HBVY; LaNeLa; LiTA; NeHB; OBVV; OHFP; OnPP; OTPC; PoLF; PTK; TreF; WBLP, *abr.*
"Blessings on thee, little man," *sel.* FaPON; PoPl
Barefoot boy, A! I mark him at his play. A Barefoot Boy. James Whitcomb Riley. FaFP
Barefoot Days. Rachel Field. FaPON; YeAr
Barefoot friar all in brown, A. The Irish Franciscan. Rosa Mulholland. CAW
Barefoot I went and made no sound. The Viper. Ruth Pitter. FaBoTw
Barefoot without a stitch she walks. Dance with Banderillas. Richard Duerden. NeAP
Barefooted boys scud up the street. A Sudden Shower. James Whitcomb Riley. PRWS
Barefooted, in his hood and cloak of brown. The Friar. Julián del Casal. CAW; WHL
Barely a twelvemonth after. The Horses. Edwin Muir. ACV; BoPe; CMoP; HaMV; MoBrPo (1962 ed.); NMP; PoIE; PoSa
Bargain, The. Anna Bunston de Bary. MaRV
Bargain. Louise Driscoll. HBMV
Bargain, The. Neidhart von Reuental, *tr. fr. German by* Jethro Bithell. LiTW
Bargain, The. Sir Philip Sidney. *See* My True Love Hath My Heart.
Bargain Basement. F. T. Macartney. MoAuPo
Bargain Sale, A. S. E. Kiser. PoToHe (new ed.)
Barge, The. Rose Fyleman. BrR
Barge glided, The. Vision. Israel Zangwill. TrJP
Barge she sat in, like a burnish'd throne, The. Cleopatra. Shakespeare. *Fr.* Antony and Cleopatra, II, ii. CLwM; DiPo; FOL; LiTB; LiTG; LiTL; MemP; PoFS; TreF; TrGrPo
Barine, the Incorrigible. Horace, *tr. fr. Latin by* Louis Untermeyer. Odes, II, 8. UnTE
Bark and boom of guns and shrieking flight, The. The Silent Stars. Eric H. Daniell. MaRV
Bark leaps love-fraught from the land, The; the sea. The Thousand Islands. Charles Sangster. *Fr.* The St. Lawrence and the Saguenay. OBCV
Bark smells like pineapple: Jeffries. Foxtail Pine. Gary Snyder. CoPo; NaP
Bark that bare me through foam and squall. Boatman's Hymn. *At. to* Andrew Magrath. OnYI
Bark that held the prince went down, The. He Never Smiled Again. Felicia Dorothea Hemans. HBV
Barking sound the shepherd hears, A. Fidelity. Wordsworth. PeER
Barks the melancholy dog. Wakeful in the Township. Elizabeth Riddell. PoAu-2
Barley-break. Sir John Suckling. *See* Love, Reason, Hate.
Barley-Mowers' Song, The. Mary Howitt. OTPC (1923 ed.)
Barn, The. Edmund Blunden. MoBrPo; SeCePo
Barn, The. Elizabeth J. Coatsworth. AnNE; BiCB; ChBR; GoTP; SoPo; UTS
Barn, The. Stephen Spender. HaMV
Barn in Winter, The. Claire Harris MacIntosh. CaP
Barn Swallow. Charles G. Bell. NYTB
Barn-Swallow, The. William Sargent. RIS
Barnabe Rich, Gentleman Soldier, in Praise of the Author. Barnabe Rich. ReIE
Barnacle, The. A. P. Herbert. RIS
Barnacle Bill the Sailor. *Unknown*. *See* Abram Brown.
Barnacle Geese. Charles Higham. PoAu-2
Barnacles. Sidney Lanier. OQP
(Sailing.) SoP
Barney Bodkin broke his nose. *Unknown*. OxNR; SiTL
Barney McGee. Richard Hovey. BOHV; HBV; InMe; TreFS
Barney O'Hea. Samuel Lover. OnYI
Barney's Invitation. Philip Freneau. PAH
Barnfire during Church. Robert Bly. NePoEA
Barnfloor and Winepress. Gerard Manley Hopkins. ACP; CAW
Barnyard, The. Maud Burnham. PCH; PPL; TiPo
Barnyard Song, *with music*. *Unknown*. TrAS
(Farmyard, The, *with music.*.) BFSS
(Farmyard Song, *arr. by* Maria Hastings.) SoPo
("I had a cat and the cat pleased me.") OxNR
Baron has decided to mate the monster, The. The Bride of Frankenstein. Edward Field. CoAP; FRC
Baron hath the landward park, the fisher hath the sea, The. The Sea Fowler. Mary Howitt. VA
Baron o' [*or* of] Brackley [*or* Braikley], The. *Unknown*. BaBo; ESPB (A *and* B *vers.*); OBB; OxBB
Baron of [*or* o] Leys, The. *Unknown*. ESPB; OxBB
Baron of Smaylho'me rose with day, The. The Eve of Saint John. Sir Walter Scott. EnRP; EPN; PoEL-4
Baron Renfrew's Ball. Charles Graham Halpine. PAH
Baroness and the Black Musician, The. Larry Neal. BF
Baroness Mu Impeded in Her Wish to Help Famine Victims in Wei. Confucius, *tr. fr. Chinese by* Ezra Pound. *Fr.* Yung Wind. CTC
Barons Bold, The. William Johnson Fox. PoFr; VA
Baron's Last Banquet, The. Albert Gorton Greene. AA; BeLS
Baron's War, The, *sel.* Michael Drayton.

Baron's (continued)
Severn, The, *fr.* I. ChTr
Baroque Comment. Louise Bogan. CrMA
Baroque Gravure, A. Thomas Merton. CoPo
Baroque-handled and sharp. The Compasses. George MacBeth. NePoEA-2
Baroque Wall-Fountain in the Villa Sciarra, A. Richard Wilbur. AmPP (5th ed.); NePoEA; NoP; NYBP; PoCh; ToPo; TwCP
Barque of phosphor. Fabliau of Florida. Wallace Stevens. NP
Barrack-Room Ballads, *sel.* Kipling.
Dedication: "Beyond the path of the outmost sun through utter darkness hurled." ViPP
Barrack-square, washed clean with rain, The. In Barracks. Siegfried Sassoon. FaBoTw
Barrack Yard, The. Nettie Palmer. NeLNL
Barracks Apt. 14. Theodore Weiss. CoAP; NePoAm-2; TwAmPo
Barrage. Richard Aldington. BrPo
Barred Islands. Philip Booth. NePoEA
Barrel-Organ, The. Alfred Noyes. EnLit; FaBV; HBV; MCCG; MoBrPo; NeMA, *sl. abr.*; PoRA; TreF, *sl. abr.*
"Go Down to Kew in Lilac-Time, *sel.* BoTP
Barrels of blue potato spray, The. Spraying the Potatoes. Patrick Kavanagh. OxBI
Barren. "Rachel," *tr. fr. Hebrew by* L. V. Snowman. TrJP
Barren Fig Tree, The. Elizabeth Bartlett. WOW
Barren Moors, The. William Ellery Channing. AA
Barren Soul, A. Joseph Ezobi, *tr. fr. Hebrew by* D. I. Friedmann. *Fr.* The Silver Bowl. TrJP
Barren Spring. Dante Gabriel Rossetti. The House of Life, LXXXIII. FaBoEn; MaVP; NoP; OBNC; PoEL-5; PoVP; Sonn; VaPo; ViPo
Barren Stone. Nicolás Guillén, *tr. fr. Spanish by* Langston Hughes. PoNe
Barricade—a wall—a stronghold, A. The Breech. Michael McClure. NeAP
Barricades, The. Denise Levertov. NeBP
Barrier, The. Louis Lavater. MoAuPo
Barrier, The. Claude McKay. BANP
Barrier. John Frederick Nims. JKCP (1955 ed.)
Barrier stone has rolled away, The. Easter. Edwin L. Sabin. DD; HH; OHIP; PoRL; PoSC
Bar-Room Matins. Louis MacNeice. EaLo; NYBP
Bars Fight. Lucy Terry. PoNe
Bars go by, and watching them his sight, The. The Panther. Rainer Maria Rilke. PIA
Barter. Marie Blake. PoPl; PoToHe (new ed.)
Barter. Earle V. Eastwood. OQP
Barter. Sara Teasdale. FaBV; FaPON; MCCG; MPB; OQP; OTPC (1946 ed.); SP; TIHL; TreFS
Barter. Margaret Widdemer. HBMV; WGRP
Barthélemon at Vauxhall. Thomas Hardy. UnS
Bartholdi Statue, The. Whittier. PaA; PAH; ThLM
Bartholomew. Norman Gale. BiCB; HBV; HBVY; OTPC; SP
Bartholomew Benjamin Bunting. The Singular Sangfroid of Baby Bunting. Guy Wetmore Carryl. NA
Bartholomew is very sweet. Norman Gale. BiCB; HBV; HBVY; OTPC; SP
Bartimeus. Laura Simmons. ChIP
Bartleme Fair. George Alexander Stevens. ELP
Bartol. Amos Bronson Alcott. AA
Baruch, *sel.* Bible, Apocrypha.
Path of Wisdom, The, III: 9-IV: 4. TrJP
Bas Bleu, *sel.* Hannah More.
Conversation. OBEC
Bas-Relief. Carl Sandburg. CrMA
Base Details. Siegfried Sassoon. CBV; MemP; MMA; MoBrPo; NeMA
Base mettell hanger by your master's thigh! One Writeing against His Prick. *Unknown.* PeRV
Base of All Metaphysics, The. Walt Whitman. AmePo; NePA
Base Stealer, The. Robert Francis. GoJo; SD
Base words are uttered only by the base. W. H. Auden. PV
Baseball. Tom Clark. ANYP
Baseball Note. Franklin P. Adams. SD
Baseball's Sad Lexicon. Franklin P. Adams. FaFP; InMe; SD; TreFS
Bashful Earthquake, The, *sel.* Oliver Herford.
If This Little World To-night. ShM
(Poem: "If this little world tonight.") AA
Basia. Thomas Campion. *See* Turn Back, You Wanton Flyer.
Basia, *sels.* Johannes Secundus, *tr. fr. Latin by* John Nott. UnTE
Insatiate, The.
Neaera's Kisses.
Basic. Ray Durem. PoNe (1970 ed.)
Basic Communication. Thomas Hornsby Ferril. NePoAm-2
Basie Band, The. Julian Cooper. MuSP
Basilisk, The. D. M. Black. HYE
Basilisk, The. Philip Child. CaP
Basket Maker's Song. Thomas Dekker. *See* Happy Heart, The.
Basket of roses for the Royal House of David, A. A Gift of Flowers. Leonard Feeney. WHL
Basket over his head, A. Monk Begging, Kyoto. Edith Shiffert. NYTB
Baskets of ripe fruit in air. Gardener Janus Catches a Naiad. Edith Sitwell. MoAB; MoBrPo
Basking in peace in the warm spring sun. The Romance of the Carpet. Robert J. Burdette. BOHV
Bast. William Rose Benét. HBMV
Bastard, The, *sel.* Richard Savage.
(Bastard's Lot, The.) CBEP; OBEC
Bat. John Clare. *Fr.* Childhood. OA
Bat. D. H. Lawrence. BrPo; GTBS-P
Bat, The. Ogden Nash. PV
Bat, The. Ruth Pitter. WePo
Bat, The. Theodore Roethke. FIW; GoJo; GoTP; NYTB; PDV
Bat, bat, come under my hat. Mother Goose. OTPC; OxNR
Bat in the Monastery, A. John L'Heureux. YAP
Bat is born, A. Bats. Randall Jarrell. OA
Batalis and the Man, The. Vergil, *tr. fr. Latin by* Gawin Douglas. *Fr.* The Aeneid, I. CTC
Batchelor leads an easy life, A. Good & Bad Wives. *Unknown.* CoMu
Batchelor's Song, The. Thomas Flatman. CEP; PeRV
Batchin'. S. Omar Barker. IHA
Bath, The. Harry Graham. CenHV; ShM
Bath, The. Joel Oppenheimer. NeAP
Bath, The; or, The Western Lass, *sel.* Thomas Durfey.
Second Dialogue between Crab and Gillian. PeRV
Bath Tub. *See* Bathtub.
Bathe me O God in thee, mounting to thee. Walt Whitman. *Fr.* Passage to India. TrPWD
Bathed Is My Blood. Oliver La Grone. NNP
Bather in a Painting, A. Ashton Greene. NePoAm
Bathers, The. Arthur Hugh Clough. *Fr.* The Bothie of Tober-na-Vuolich. VA
"There is a stream, I name not its name, lest inquisitive tourist," *sel.* BoNaP
Bathers, The. Hart Crane. SyP
Bathers. Terence Tiller. ChMP; FaBoMo; NeBP
Bathing. John Keble. OTPC (1923 ed.)
Bathing Girl, A. Johannes V. Jensen, *tr. fr. Danish by* Charles W. Stork. PoPl
Bathing herself, a girl with silver feet. The Young Bather. *Unknown.* UnTE
Bathing of Oisin's Head, The. *Unknown, tr. fr. Early Modern Irish by* Eoin MacNeill. AnIL
Bathing Song. Anne Ridler. NYBP
Baths of Rome and Babylon. A City Song. John Hanlon Mitchell. CaP
Bathsheba: to whom none ever said scat. Epitaph. Whittier. CIV
Bathsheba came out to the sun. Telling the Bees. Lizette Woodworth Reese. AA
Bathsheba's Song. George Peele. *See* Bethsabe's Song.
Bath Tub, The. Ezra Pound. CBV
Bathtub Bay. Lenore Riggs. GFA
Bathtub Gin. Philip H. Rhinelander. WhC
Bathtubs. Richmond Lattimore. NYBP
Bathymeter. William Hart-Smith. BoAV
Bats. Philip Dow. QAH
Bats, The. Robert Hillyer. GoYe
Bats. Randall Jarrell. OA
Bats. Mary Effie Lee Newsome. GoSl
Batson, *with music. Unknown.* OuSiCo
Batt he gets children, not for love to reare 'em. Upon Batt. Robert Herrick. AnAnS-2

Battel of the Summer-Islands, The. Edmund Waller. *See* Battle of the Summer Islands, The.
Batter my heart, three person'd God; for, you. John Donne. *Fr.* Holy Sonnets, XIV. AnAnS-1; AnEnPo; AnFE; BoLiVe; BWP; CABA; CaFP; CBEP; CBV; DiPo; EaLo; EnL; EnRePo; EP; ExPo; FaFP; ForPo; FosPo; GoBC; GTBS-W; ILP; LiTB; LiTG; MaMe; MaPo; MaRV; MasP; MBW-1; MeLP; MeP; MePo; NoP; OAEP; OBS; OxBoCh; PAn; PIA; Po; PoAn; PoE; PoEL-2; PoeP; PoFS; PoIE; ReEn; SCEP-1; SeCePo; SeCeV; SeCP; SeCV-1; SeEP; Sonn; StP; TDP; TreFT; TrGrPo; TrPWD; TuPP; VaPo
Batter'd wreck'd old man, A. Prayer of Columbus. Walt Whitman. AmPP (4th ed.); ATP; WGRP
Battered roof where stars went tripping, A. The Sleepers. F. W. Harvey. MMA
Batteries Out of Ammunition. Kipling. *Fr.* Epitaphs of the War. MMA; PoVP
Battery grides and jingles, The. The Day's March. Robert Nichols. MMA
Battery Moving Up to a New Position from Rest Camp: Dawn. Robert Nichols. MMA
Batte's Song: "What is love but the desire." Michael Drayton. *Fr.* The Shepherd's Garland, Eclogue, VII. LoBV
Battle, The. Chu Yuan, *tr. fr. Chinese by* Arthur Waley. WaaP
Battle, The. W. H. Davies. BrPo
Battle. Robinson Jeffers. *See* May-June, 1940.
Battle, The ("By this, though deep the evening fell"). Sir Walter Scott. *See* Flodden.
Battle, The ("Not far advanc'd was morning day"). Sir Walter Scott. *See* Marmion: Marmion and Douglas.
Battle, The. Louis Simpson. TPM
Battle Autumn of 1862, The. Whittier. MC; PAH
Battle Ballad, A. Francis Orrery Ticknor. PAH
Battle between a Cock and a Capon, The. Thomas Heyrick. PeRV
Battle Cry. John G. Neihardt. HBMV
Battle Cry, A. Lee Shippey. MaRV
Battle Cry. William Henry Venable. PAH
Battle Cry of Freedom, The. George Frederick Root. FaBoBe; PaA; PAH; PoFr; TreFS; YaD
Battle Eve of the [Irish] Brigade, The. Thomas Osborne Davis. AnIV; OnYI
Battle-fear mounted. Cynewulf. *Fr.* Elene. YAT
Battle-Flag of Sigurd, The. Dora Greenwell. OBVV
Battle grows more hard and harder yet, The. The Last Battle. *Unknown.* *Fr.* The Song of Roland. LiTW
Battle: Hit. W. W. Gibson. *See* Hit.
Battle Hymn. Michael Altenburg, *tr. fr. German by* Catherine Winkworth. WGRP
Battle Hymn of the American Republic. Julia Ward Howe. *See* Battle Hymn of the Republic.
Battle Hymn of the Chinese Revolution (1912). *Unknown, tr. fr. Chinese.* PoFr
Battle Hymn of the Republic. Julia Ward Howe. AA; AmLP; AnAmPo; AnFE; APA; BBV (1923 ed.); BLPA; CH; CoAnAm; CoBA; DD; EaLo; FaBoBe; FaFP; FaPL; FaPON; GN; GoTP; HBV; HBVY; InP; LiTG; MaRV; MC; NeHB; NePA; OHIP; PAL; OQP; OTPC; PaA; PAH; PAP; PoFr; PTK; RG; SoP; ThLM; TIHL; TOP; TrAS, *with music*; TreF; WBLP; WGRP; YaD
(Battle Hymn of the American Republic.) OBVV; OtMeF
(Mine Eyes Have Seen the Glory.) TRV
Battle Hymn of the Spanish Rebellion. L. A. MacKay. OBCV
(Battle Hymn of the Spanish Republic.) OnPM
Battle in the Clouds, The. William Dean Howells. PAH
Battle is fought and won, The. Scanderbeg. Longfellow. *Fr.* Tales of a Wayside Inn. PFY
Battle of Actium. Vergil, *tr. fr. Latin by* Dryden. *Fr.* The Aeneid, VIII. OBS
Battle of Agincourt. Michael Drayton. *See* Agincourt.
Battle of Argoed Llwyfain, The. Taliesin, *tr. fr. Welsh by* Gwyn Williams. PrWP
Battle of Aughrim, The, *sels.* Richard Murphy. OPoP
Country Woman and a Country Man, A.
Rapparees.
Story I Have to Tell, The.
Battle of Baltimore, The. *Unknown.* PAH
Battle of Bath, The. Layamon, *tr. fr. Middle English.* *Fr.* The Brut. MeEV
Battle of Bennington, The. Thomas P. Rodman. MC; PAH
Battle of Blenheim, The. Robert Southey. BeLS; BoChLi; BOHV; EnLit; EnRP; EPN; FaBV; FOL; GN; GoTP; HBV; HBVY; InMe; MCCG; NeHB; OBNC; OBRV; OnSP; OTPC; PaPo; PoLF; PoPo; PoSa; PTK; StP; StVeCh (1940 ed.); TIHL; TOP; TreF; TrGrPo; WBLP
(After Blenheim.) BBV; GTBS; GTBS-D; GTBS-P; GTBS-W; GTSE; GTSL; MemP; TRV
"Now tell us what 'twas all about," *sel.* OQP
Battle of Bothwell Bridge, The. *Unknown.* *See* Bothwell Bridge.
Battle of Bridgewater, The. *Unknown.* PAH
Battle of Brunanburh. *Unknown, tr. fr. Anglo-Saxon by* Tennyson. BEL; CoBE; EnLit; ExPo; FOL; PeVV; TrGrPo; WaaP
—— *Tr. by* Charles W. Kennedy. AnOE
—— *Tr. by* Stith Thompson. EnLi-1 (1949 ed.)
Battle of Bunker Hill, The. *Unknown.* PAH
Battle of Charlestown, The. Henry Howard Brownell. PAH
Battle of Charleston Harbor, The. Paul Hamilton Hayne. PAH
Battle of Erie, The. *Unknown.* PAH
Battle of Eutaw, The. William Gilmore Simms. PAH
Battle of Finnsburg, The. *Unknown, tr. fr. Anglo-Saxon by* Charles W. Kennedy. AnOE
Battle of Gettysburg, The. Stephen Vincent Benét. *Fr.* John Brown's Body. BeLS
Battle of Harlaw, The. *Unknown.* ESPB (A *and* B *vers.*)
Battle of Hohenlinden, The. Thomas Campbell. *See* Hohenlinden.
Battle of Ivry, The. Macaulay. *See* Ivry.
Battle of Killiekrankie, The. William E. Aytoun. FOL
Battle of King's Mountain, The. *Unknown.* PAH
Battle of La Prairie, The. William Douw Schuyler-Lighthall. MC; PAH; VA
Battle of Lake Champlain, The. Philip Freneau. PAH
Battle of [the] Lake Regillus, The, *sels.* Macaulay.
Death of Herminius, The. OtMeF
Fight in the Centre, The. OtMeF
"From every warlike city." PoG
Herminius's Horse. PoG
Battle of Lexington, The. Sidney Lanier. *Fr.* The Psalm of the West. PAP
Battle of Lookout Mountain, The. George Henry Boker. MC; PAH
Battle of Lovell's Pond, The. Longfellow. PAH
Battle of Maldon, The. *Unknown, tr. fr. Anglo-Saxon.* AnOE, *tr. by* Charles W. Kennedy
Sels.
Death in Battle. PoLi
"Wilt thou hear, O sailor, what this people say?" PoFr
Battle of Manila, The. Richard Hovey. PAH
Battle of Monmouth, The. Thomas Dunn English. PAH
Battle of Monmouth, The. "R. H." PAH
Battle of Morris' Island, The. *Unknown.* PAH
Battle of Murfreesboro, The. Kinahan Cornwallis. PAH
Battle of Muskingum, The. William Harrison Safford. PAH
Battle of Naseby, The. Macaulay. FOL; GTBS; HBV; OBRV; ShBV-3; VA
Battle of Navarino, The. *Unknown.* CoMu
Battle of New Orleans, The. Thomas Dunn English. PAH; PAP; ThLM
Battle of Oriskany. Charles D. Helmer. PAH
Battle of Otterbourne [*or* Otterburn], The. *Unknown.* BaBo (A *and* B *vers.*); ESPB (A, B, *and* C *vers.*); FaBoCh; GoTS; HBV; OBB, *mod. Eng.*; OnMSP; OxBB
Fey, *sel.* OtMeF
Battle of Peace, The. Wilson MacDonald. MaRV
Battle of Philiphaugh, The. *Unknown.* ESPB
Battle of Plattsburg, The. *Unknown.* PAH
Battle of Plattsburg Bay, The. Clinton Scollard. MC; PAH
Battle of Queenstown, The. William Banker, Jr. PAH
Battle of Salamis, The. Aeschylus. *See* Salamis.
Battle of Somerset. Cornelius C. Cullen. PAH
Battle of Stonington on the Seaboard of Connecticut, The. Philip Freneau. PAH
Battle of the Baltic, The. Thomas Campbell. CBEP; CoBE; FOL; GN; GTBS; GTBS-D; GTBS-P; GTBS-W; GTSE; GTSL; HBV; NBM; OBEV; OTPC (1923 ed.); RoGo
Battle of the *Bonhomme Richard* and the *Serapis.* Walt Whitman. *See* Old-Time Sea-Fight, A.

Battle of the Cowpens, The. Thomas Dunn English. PAH; PAP
Battle of the Jarama, The. "Pablo Neruda," *tr. fr. Spanish by* Angel Flores. WaaP
Battle of the Kegs, The. Francis Hopkinson. PaA
(British Valor Displayed.) PAH
Battle of the King's Mill. Thomas Dunn English. MC; PAH
Battle of the Lake Regillus, The. Macaulay. *See* Battle of Lake Regillus, The.
Battle [*or* Battel] of the Summer Islands, The. Edmund Waller. AnAnS-2; CEP
"Aid me, Bellona! while the dreadful fight," I. ReEn; SCEP-2; SeCV-1
Battle of Tippecanoe, The. *Unknown.* PAH
Battle of Trenton, The. *Unknown.* MC; PAH; PAP
Battle of Valparaiso, The. *Unknown.* PAH
Battle of Waterloo. Byron. *See* Waterloo ("There was a sound...").
Battle-Plane in France, A. O. C. A. Child. PaA
Battle Problem. William Meredith. NYBP
Battle rent a cobweb diamond-strung. Range-finding. Robert Frost. AmLP; CABA; MaPo; TPM
Battle Report. Bob Kaufman. CAD; TTY
Battle-smoke still fouled the day, The. The Red Cross Nurse. Edith M. Thomas. PEDC
Battle Song. Ebenezer Elliott. OBEV (1st ed.); OBRV
Battle Song. Robert Burns Wilson. MC; PAH
Battle-Song of Failure. Amelia Josephine Burr. HBMV
Battle-Song of the *Oregon.* Wallace Rice. PaA; PAH
Battle Songs of the King Tshaka. *Unknown, tr. fr. Zulu.* PeSA
Battle Within, The. Christina Rossetti. MaRV; TRV
(Who Shall Deliver Me?) OxBoCh
Battlefield. Richard Aldington. MMA
Battlefield, The. Bryant. AA; AmePo; CoBA; PAL; PoLF
Truth, Crushed to Earth. NeHB; OQP
("Truth crushed to earth shall rise again.") MaRV; SoP; TRV
(Truth, the Invincible.) TreF
Battle-Field, The. Emily Dickinson. *See* They dropped like flakes, they dropped like stars.
Battlefield, The. Lloyd Mifflin. PAH
Battles? No! Agonies! And before the agonies. César Vallejo. *Fr.* Hymn to the Volunteers of the Republic. PoFr
Battles nor songs can from oblivion save. Immortality. Lizette Woodworth Reese. AA; HBMV; HBVY
Battles of the Centaurs, *sel.* Sacheverell Sitwell.
Centaurs and Lapithae. AtBAP
Battus, though bound from drinking wine of late. Ebrius Dissimulans. Henry Parrot. TuPP
Baucis. Erinna. *See* Erinna to Her Friend.
Baucis and Philemon. Ovid, *tr. fr. Latin by* Dryden. *Fr.* Metamorphoses, VIII. AWP; JAWP; MBW-1; WBP; WoL
(Philemon and Baucis, *tr. by* Arthur Golding.) CTC; OBSC
Baucis and Philemon. Swift. CEP; EiCP; EiPP; GN, *abr.*; GoTL; GSP, *abr.*; NoP; OBEC; OTPC (1946 ed.); PAn; StPo
Baudelaire. Delmore Schwartz. ML; TwCP
Bavarian Gentians. D. H. Lawrence. AtBAP; CMoP; DiPo; FaBoCh; FaBoMo; GoJo; GTBS-P; LiTB; LoGBV; NoP; OAEP (2d ed.); PoE; PoIE; PoSa; SeCeV; UnPo (3d ed.); ViBoPo
Baviad, The, *sel.* William Gifford.
Della Cruscans, The. OBEC
Bawl of a steer, The. The Cowboy's Life. *At. to* James Barton Adams. AmFN; CoSo; MPB; SoPo; TiPo
Bay Fight, The. Henry Howard Brownell. PaA; PAH; PAP, abr.
"Three days through sapphire seas we sailed," *sel.* PFY
Bay is gouged by the wind, The. Green Lions. Douglas Stewart. AnNZ
Bay is not blue but somber yellow, The. Self-Criticism in February. Robinson Jeffers. AmPP
Bay is set with ashy sails, The. At Les Eboulements. Duncan Campbell Scott. VA
Bay today breaks, The. Today. James Schuyler. ANYP
Bay Violets. Sister Maris Stella. GoBC
Bay was anchor, sky, The. Offshore. Philip Booth. SD
Bay was bronze with sunset, and so light, The. Wings. William Rose Benét. PoMa
Bayadere, The. Francis Saltus Saltus. AA
Bayard Taylor. Longfellow. DD
Bayard Taylor. Whittier. DD; HBV
Baying Hounds, The. Mary Gilmore. BoAV; PoAu-1
Bayonet, The. Shawn O'Leary. MoAuPo
Bayonet Charge. Ted Hughes. POTi
Be a god, your spirit cried. To William Blake. Olive Tilford Dargan. HBMV
Be aisy an' list to a chune. Tim the Dragoon. Sir Arthur Quiller-Couch. WhC
Be always in time. *Unknown.* OxNR
Be anxious if Christ presses on your life. If Any Man Would Come after Me. Edwin McNeill Poteat. ChIP
Be assured, the Dragon is not dead. Vanity. Robert Graves. GTBS-P
Be aware. Squanderings. Witter Bynner. MoLP
Be Beautiful, Noble, like the Antique Ant. José Garcia Villa. AnFE; CoAnAm; TwAmPo
(Be Beautiful.) CrMA
Be Bold. Spenser. *Fr.* The Faerie Queene, III, 11. MyFE
Be brave, faint heart. Optimism. Newton Mackintosh. BOHV
Be Careful. *Unknown.* SoP
Be careful what/ You say or do. Zoo Manners. Eileen Mathias. BoTP
Be Careful What You Say. Joseph Kronthal. STF
Be Comforted. Tennyson. *Fr.* The Death of the Duke of Clarence and Avondale. MaRV
Be composed—be at ease with me—I am Walt Whitman. To a Common Prostitute. Whitman. AnAmPo; MAP; MoAmPo; ViBoPo
Be Daedalus. Nanina Alba. PoNe (1970 ed.)
Be dark, be deep, wait there for me between. The Upper Lake. Francis Stuart. NeIP
Be Different to Trees. Mary Carolyn Davies. DD; FaPON; HBMV; HBVY; MPB
(Be Deferent to Trees.) OHIP
Be dumb ye infant chimes, thump not the metal. Great Tom. Richard Corbet. OxBoLi
Be dumb you beggars of the rhythming trade. The Hecatomb to His Mistress. John Cleveland. AnAnS-2
Be ever meek and humble, nor essay. The Meek and the Proud. Abraham ibn Chasdai. TrJP
Be extra careful by this door. The Whisperer. Mark Van Doren. AnFE; CoAnAm; MAP; MoAmPo; UnTE
Be for a little while eternal. O Mors Aeterna. Horace Gregory. CMoP
Be Friendly. Walter E. Isenhour. STF
Be gay, be merry, and don't be wary of milking the modest minute. Samuel Hoffenstein. *Fr.* Song, on Reading that the Cyclotron Has Produced Cosmic Rays. ShM
Be gentle/ When you touch bread. Bread. *Unknown.* MaRV
Be glad in heart, grow great before the Lord. A Brave-hearted Maid. *Unknown.* ISi; PoLi
Be glad, O youth, in your young manhood. To the Bridegroom. Judah Halevi. HW
Be glaid, al ye that luvaris bene. May Poem. *Unknown.* OxBS
Be governour baith guid and gratious. To the Queen. Lord Darnley. OxBS
Be his memory forever green and rich. Baal Shem Tov. A. M. Klein. CaP; TrJP
Be Hopeful. Strickland Gillilan. PoToHe
Be Hopeful. Celia Thaxter. SoP
Be hushed, all voices and untimely laughter. A Dead March. Mary C. Gillington. PeVV
Be in me as the eternal moods. Δώρια (Doria). Ezra Pound. FIW; MAP; MoAB; MoAmPo; MoVE; NP; PoIE; ViBoPo
Be it not mine to steal the cultured flower. Simple Nature. George John Romanes. HBV
Be it right or wrong, these men among. The Nut-brown Maid. *Unknown.* LiTL; MeEV; OBB; OBEV; OBSC
Be joyfull in the Lorde. Psalm C, Bible, *O.T.* (*The Great Bible*). YAT
Be just, and fear not. For a Patriot. Shakespeare. King Henry VIII, *fr.* III, ii. PGD
Be just (domestick monarchs) unto them. George Alsop. SCAP
Be Kind. Margaret Courtney. PoToHe
Be kind and tender to the Frog. The Frog. Hilaire Belloc. BoChLi; BOHV; FaBoBe; FaBV; FaPON; FiBHP; GoJo; HBV; InMe; MoShBr; MPB; NA; RePo; TSW

Be kind, good sir, and I'll lift my sark. Confucius. *Fr.* Songs of Cheng. CTC
Be Kind Now. *Unknown.* SoP
Be Kind Promptly. *Unknown, tr. fr. Greek by* Lord Neaves. OnPM
Be kind to all dumb animals. Humane Thought. Rebecca McCann. YaD
Be kind to her O Time. To End Her Fear. John Freeman. OBMV
Be kind to the panther! for when thou wert young. Kindly Advice [*or* The Panther]. *Unknown.* BoHV; NA
Be kind to thy father: for when thou wert young. Be Kind. Margaret Courtney. PoToHe
Be life what it has been, and let us hold. To His Wife. Decimus Magnus Ausonius. AWP; JAWP; WBP
Be like the Bird. Victor Hugo, *tr. fr. French.* FaPON; OTPC (1946 ed.); SoPo; SUS; TiPo; UTS
(Wings.) MaRV
"Be like the hummingbird," they said. Hummingbird. Violet Alleyn Storey. PoMa
Be Merciful. John T. McFarland. OQP
Be Mine, and I Will Give Thy Name. William Cox Bennett. VA
Be mute, this autumn; gather in the world. In March. Philip Martin. PoAu-2
Be natural. The Name. Robert Creeley. CoPo; ToPo
Be Natural, Baby. Ruby C. Saunders. WSL
Be nèar me when my light is low. In Memoriam A. H. H., L. Tennyson. AnFE; AtBAP; BEL; CoBE; ELP; EnL; EnLi-2; EPN; LiTB; LiTG; MemP; OAEP; PoE; PoEL-5; PoFS; TOP; UnPo; ViPo; VP
Be near to me, O white shadowless Light of my soul's swift venture. Psalm to the Holy Spirit. A. M. Sullivan. TrPWD
Be neither song, nor game, nor feast. Ring Out, Wild Bells. Tennyson. *Fr.* In Memoriam A. H. H., CV-CVI. WiR
Be not afeard [*or* afeared *or* affeard]; the isle is full of noises [*or* noyses]. Caliban [*or* To Dream Again]. Shakespeare. *Fr.* The Tempest, III, ii. AtBAP; FiP; FIW; TrGrPo; UnS
Be Not Afraid. Robert Nathan. GBV (1952 ed.)
Be Not Afraid. Walt Whitman. *Fr.* The Song of the Open Road. MaRV
Be not afraid, O Dead, be not afraid. Struthers Burt. *Fr.* The Land. DD; HBMV
Be not afraid of every stranger. A Spell. George Peele. *Fr.* The Old Wives' Tale. ChTr
Be not afraid to pray—to pray is right. Prayer. Hartley Coleridge. MaRV; OQP; Sonn; TreFT; VA
Be not angry with me that I bear. Apology. Amy Lowell. BoLiVe; NP
Be not dismayed, whate'er betide. God's Goodness. C. D. Martin. WBLP
Be not frighted with our fashion. All Your Fortunes We Can Tell Ye. Ben Jonson. *Fr.* The Gypsies Metamorphosed. ChTr
Be not proud, nor coye nor cruell. *Unknown.* SeCSL
Be not proud pritty one. *Unknown.* SeCSL
Be Not Silent. David ben Meshullam, *tr. fr. Hebrew.* TrJP
Be not so desolate. Promise. "Æ." BoC; POTE
Be not sparing. Herrings. Swift. *Fr.* Verses for Fruitwomen. AnIV; OnYI
Be not too certain, life! The Hill. Horace Holley. WGRP
Be not too forward, painter; 'tis. To the Painter Preparing to Draw M. M. H. James Shirley. CavP
Be not too proud, imperious Dame. The Defiance. Thomas Flatman. CEP; OBS
Be not too wise, nor too foolish. Instruction of King Cormac. Cormac, King of Cashel. PoToHe (new ed.)
Be of Good Cheer. St. John, XVI: 1-33, Bible, *N.T.* WoL
Be of Good Cheer; I Have Overcome the World, 19-33. TreFS
Be our daily bread withheld, be it given. Thanksgiving. Amos Niven Wilder. MaRV
Be Patient. "George Klingle." PoToHe
Be patient, O be patient! Put your ear against the earth. Patience. William James Linton. VA
Be pitiful, my God! Mea Culpa. "Ethna Carbery." CAW; JKCP; TrPWD
Be Present at Our Table, Lord. *Unknown, at. to* John Cennick. BLRP; TreFT
(John Wesley's Grace before Meals, *at. to* John Wesley.) TreFT
Be proud New-York of your prize domes. . . . & Forty-second Street. Archibald MacLeish. CoBA
Be proud you people of these graves. City of Monuments. Muriel Rukeyser. NAMP
Be quick, be quick, my eyes, my ears. Harvesting. Selma Robinson. InMe
Be Quiet; Fear Not. Frances Ridley Havergal. *See* Thy Presence.
"Be quiet, good Trusty." Trusty Learning A, B, C. Eliza Lee Follen. SAS
Be Quiet, Sir! *Unknown.* ErPo
(Cautious Struggle, The.) UnTE
Be real, show organs, show blood, Oh let me. Oh Ease Oh Body-Strain Oh Love Oh Ease Me Not! Wound-Bore. Michael McClure. CoPo
Be rootfast. Never yield. Last Rally. Clifford J. Laube. JKCP (1955 ed.)
Be sad, be cool, be kind. The Long Shadow of Lincoln. Carl Sandburg. LiPo; MoAmPo (1950 ed.); TPM
Be seated, pray. "A grave appeal"? A Virtuoso. Austin Dobson. PeVV
Be secret, heart, and if your dreams have come. Sonnet. Anna Virginia Mitchell. OQP
Be She Fair as Lilies Be. *Unknown.* SeCL
Be silent, secret [*or* hidden], and conceal. Silentium. Feodor Ivanovich Tyutchev. LiTW; OnPM; PoPl; WoL
Be slow. Fold the daily news. A Nickle Bet. Etheridge Knight. CAD
Be staid; be careful; and be not too free. Week-end. Harold Monro. SeCePo
Be Still. William Ward Ayer. BLRP
Be Still. William Closson Emory. NP
Be Still. Betsy W. Kline. STF
Be Still. Edith Willis Linn. FaChP
Be Still. "G. W. S." SoP
Be Still. Katharina von Schlegel. *See* Be Still, My Soul.
Be Still! ("Be still! Just now be still!). *Unknown.* SoP
Be Still ("'Stand still,' my soul, for so thy Lord commands"). *Unknown.* SoP
Be still and know that I am God! Be Still. William Ward Ayer. BLRP
"Be still and know that I am God." Quietness. ——Doran. FaChP; SoP
Be Still and Sleep. Edward Rowland Sill. Sop
Be Still as You Are Beautiful. Patrick MacDonogh. AnIV; NeIP; OxBI
Be still: be still: nor dare. Holy Hill. "Æ." AWP; JAWP; WBP
Be still! Just now be still! Be Still! *Unknown.* SoP
Be still, Mr. Wind, be still! Take Care. Rose Waldo. GFA
Be Still My Heart. Rosco Gilmore Scott. SoP
Be Still My Heart ("I will commit my way, O Lord, to Thee"). *Unknown.* SoP
Be Still, My Heart ("Not so in haste, my heart"). *Unknown. See* Not So in Haste, My Heart.
Be still, my heart, and listen. Khristna and His Flute. "Laurence Hope." HBV
Be still my heart! We murmur, you and I. Be Still, My Heart. Rosco Gilmore Scott. SoP
Be still, my little, dancing feet. A Song of Diligence. Helen Frazee-Bower. HBMV
Be Still, My Soul. Katharina von Schlegel, *tr. fr. German by* Jane L. Borthwick. SoP; TRV
(Be Still.) MaRV
Be still, my soul and listen. Be Still. "G. W. S." SoP
Be Still, My Soul, Be Still. A. E. Housman. A Shropshire Lad, XLVIII. AnFE; MoAB; MoBrPo; OAEP; OBNC; PoVP; TrGrPo
Be still, my soul: the Lord is on thy side. Be Still, My Soul. Katharina von Schlegel. MaRV; SoP; TRV
Be still, sad soul, be still. Resignation. Seumas MacManus. JKCP
Be Still. The Hanging Gardens Were a Dream. Trumbull Stickney. AmePo; AmLP; AnAmPo; AnFE; APA; CoAnAm; LiTA; NCEP; NePA; TwAmPo
Be still, while the music rises about us. At a Concert of Music. Conrad Aiken. CMoP; MAP; MoAB; MoAmPo; UnS
Be Strong! Maltbie Davenport Babcock. BLPA; FaBoBe; FaFP; MaRV; NeHB; OHFP; OQP; SoP; WBLP
Be Strong. Adelaide Anne Procter. MaRV
Be strong! We are not here to play. Be Strong! Maltbie Davenport Babcock. BLPA; MaRV; NeHB; OHFP; OQP; WBLP

Be Such a Man. Phillips Brooks. SoP
Be swift, dear heart, in saying. Kindness. *Unknown.* SoP; STF
Be Swift O Sun. R. A. K. Mason. AnNZ
Be Thankful. Mark Bullock. STF
Be Thankful unto Him. Psalms, C, Bible, *O.T.* *See* Thanksgiving.
Be the Best. Douglas Malloch. SoP
Be the Best of Whatever You Are. Douglas Malloch. BLPA; YaD
Be the mistress of my choice. What Kind of Mistress He Would Have. Robert Herrick. TrGrPo; UnTE
Be the New Year sweet and short. Prosit Neujahr. George Santayana. InMe
Be then your counsels, as your subject, great. To the Federal Convention. Thomas Dwight. PAH
Be this the fate/ Of the man who would shut his gate. A Curse on a Closed Gate. James H. Cousins. AnIV
Be thou at peace this night. Nocturne. Edward Davison. CH
Be thou guardian of the weak. Joseph B. Gilder, *wr. at. to* Jeannette L. Gilder. *Fr.* The Parting of the Ways. AA; HBV; MaRV; OQP; PAH
Be Thou My Guide. Florence Earle Coates. TrPWD
Be thou my priestess, who hast ever stood. To Nature. Mahlon Leonard Fisher. AnAmPo
Be Thou my vision, O Lord of my heart. A Prayer. *Unknown.* OnYI
Be thou our country's Chief. A National Hymn. John William DeForest. *Fr.* Miss Ravenel's Conversion. PAL
Be thou praised, my Lord, with all Thy creatures. Praise of Created Things. St. Francis of Assisi. FaPON; GBV (1952 ed.)
Be thoughtful when you touch the bread. The Bread of the Sacrament. *Unknown.* SoP
Be thy duty high as angels flight. Duty Our Ladder. Robert Leighton. OQP
Be to her Persephone. Prayer to Persephone. Edna St. Vincent Millay. *Fr.* Memorial to D. C. NP
Be True. Horatius Bonar. FaBoBe; GN; HBV; MaRV; TRV
(Be True Thyself.) SoP
(Honesty.) HBVY
(Thou Must Be True.) OQP
Be True. Shakespeare. *See* Polonius' Advice to Laertes.
Be True Thyself. Horatius Bonar. *See* Be True.
Be True to Your Condition in Life. John Audelay. MeEL
Be True to Yourself. *Unknown.* SoP
Be uncovered! Wild Provoke of the Endurance Sky. Joseph Ceravolo. ANYP
Be Useful, *abr.* George Herbert. GN
Be vengeance wholly left to powers divine. Conversion [*or* The World Well Lost *or* Worldly Vanity]. Dryden. *Fr.* The Hind and the Panther, III. ACP; CAW FiP; PoLi
Be ware, squire, yeoman and page. Service Is No Heritage. *Unknown.* CBEP
Be wary, lad; the road up which you go. To a Negro Boy Graduating. Eugene T. Maleska. PoNe (1970 ed.)
"Be well assured, wife, all these things in my kind cares are weighed." Hector to Andromache. Homer. *Fr.* The Iliad. ReEn
Be Wise, and Fly Not. Thomas Campion. UnTE
Be wise, and ne'er to publick view produce. To Sir George Etheridge. William Wycherley. PeRV
Be wise to-day; 'tis madness to defer. Procrastination. Edward Young. *Fr.* Night Thoughts, I. AnEnPo; OBEC
Be with me, Beauty, for the fire is dying. On Growing Old. John Masefield. BEL; CMoP; CoBE; FaFP; HBMV; InP; LiTB; LiTM; MoAB; MoBrPo; MoRP; PG; PoLF; PoRA; TreFS; ViBoPo; WHA
Be with Me, Lord! John Oxenham. *See* Prayer, A: "Through every minute of this day."
Be with me, Luis de San Angel, now. Ave Maria. Hart Crane. *Fr.* The Bridge. AtBAP; LiTA; MoPo; NePA; PoDB
Be with us, Lord, at eventide. Grace at Evening. Edwin McNeill Poteat. ChIP; TrPWD; TRV
Be with us, Lord, today. Soul-feeding Hyacinths. Corinne Farley. ChIP
Be Ye Also Ready. Bryant. *Fr.* Thanatopsis. MaRV
Be Ye Also Ready. Annie Johnson Flint. FaChP
Be Ye in Love with April-Tide. Clinton Scollard. AA; HBV
Be you still, trembling heart. To His Heart Bidding It Have No Fear. W. B. Yeats. BoPe
Be your words made, good Sir, of Indian ware. Astrophel and Stella, XCII. Sir Philip Sidney. FCP; ReEn; SiPS
Beach Burial. Kenneth Slessor. BoAV; MoAuPo; PoAu-2
Beach Encounter. Charles A. Wagner. NYTB
Beach Fire. Frances M. Frost. TiPo
Beach Head, The. Thom Gunn. ToPo
Beach holds and sifts us through her dreaming fingers, The. Poem. William Knott. YAP
Beach House. Mary Rita Hurley. PoPl
Beach Queen. David Campbell. BoAV
Beach you've never seen is where I've been, A. For You. Anne Waldman. YAP
Beachcomber, The. W. H. Oliver. AnNZ
Beached on the meadow, close by the sea's/ Accustomed lap. The Old Boat. Lenore Pratt. CaP
Beaches, The, *sels.* "Robin Hyde." AnNZ
"Absent face, remote and sharp, as far, An," III.
"Close under here, I watched two lovers once," VI.
"This is my secret, this is the chord most perfectly strung," V.
Beacon Light. Leslie Savage Clark. ChIP; PGD
Beacons, The. Henry Hart Milman. *Fr.* Samor. OBRV
Bead Mat, The. Walter de la Mare. CBEP; MoPW
Beads from Blackpool. Anne Ridler. NMP
Beagles. W. R. Rodgers. FaBoTw; OnYI; SD
Beagle's Cry, The. *Unknown, tr. fr. Late Middle Irish by* Eoin MacNeill. OnYI
Beale Street, Memphis. Thurmond Snyder. NNP
Beam of Light, A. John Jerome Rooney. AA
Bean Eaters, The. Gwendolyn Brooks. Kal; NoP; TTY
Bean Spasms. Ted Berrigan. ANYP
Beanfield, The. John Clare. BoTP
Bear, The. John Randell Carpenter. NYTB
Bear, The. Robert Frost. AmP; MAP; MoAB; MoAmPo; PoeP
Bear, The. Galway Kinnell. CoAP; PoIE (1970 ed.)
Bear, The/ from the mountain. Poem for the Disappearing Bear. Dan Gillespie. QAH
Bear cub, chained and tethered to a stake, A. Squaring the Circle. Louis O. Coxe. NYBP
Bear down lightly. To Destiny. *Unknown.* EaLo
Bear down under the cliff, A. This Poem Is for Bear. Gary Snyder. *Fr.* Myths & Texts: Hunting. NaP
Bear him, comrades, to his grave. The Burial of Barber. Whittier. PAH
Bear Hunt, The. Margaret Widdemer. FaPON; MPB; UTS
Bear in mind/ That death is a drum. Drum. Langston Hughes. MAP; MoAmPo
Bear in Mind, O Ye Recording Angels. Norman Cameron. ELU
Bear in the Hill, The, *with music.* *Unknown.* ABF
Bear on, proud billows; Boreas blow. Mr. Le Strange His Verses in the Prison at Linn. Sir Roger L'Estrange. SeCL
Bear on the Delhi Road, The. Earle Birney. MoCV; NYBP; PoAn; PoCh
Bear puts both arms around the tree above her, The. The Bear. Robert Frost. AmP; MAP; MoAB; MoAmPo; PoeP
Bear sleeps in the cellar hole, A, where pine needles. New Hampshire. Donald Hall. NePoEA-2
Bear that breath[e]s [*or* breaks] the northern blast, The. Upon a Wasp Chilled with Cold. Edward Taylor. AmPP (4th ed.); AtBAP; CBEP; FaBoEn; GTBS-W; PoEL-3
Bear the News, Mary, *with music.* *Unknown.* ABF
Bear untamable and wild, A. Infant Innocence. A. E. Housman. PoPo
Bear Up Awhile. James Thomson. MaRV
Bear went over the mountain, A. Mother Goose. StVeCh (1955 ed.)
Bear with me, Master, when I turn from Thee. Prayer. Edith Lovejoy Pierce. ChIP; TrPWD
Bearded goldfish move about the bowl, The. Goldfish. Howard Nemerov. NYTB
Bearded grass waves in the summer breeze, The. Death and Night. James Benjamin Kenyon. AA
Bearded Oaks. Robert Penn Warren. AmP; AnFE; CoAnAm; FiMAP; LiTM; MoAmPo (1950 ed.); MoVE; OnHM; ReMP; TDP; TwCP; VaPo

Bearded one sees the joy, The. Wayward Child. David Llorens. TNV
Bearded outlaw, A. Outlaw. John Giorno. ANYP
Bearded relatives I never knew. Montana Visit. Craig Sterry. QAH
Bearded "teach": walking. pissing thots. on church-coated stools. Pome. For Weird. Hearts. & All You Mothers. Ahmed Legraham Alhamisi. BF
Bearer of finches and clouds, pale atmosphere. Oxygen. Joan Swift. NYBP
Bearer of Freedom's holy light. Democracy. Whittier. PoFr; StaSt
Bearing their birds and gardens on their hats. L'Après Midi d'une Fille aux Cheveux de Lin. Ronald McCuaig. PoAu-2
Bearings. Jack Marshall. YAP
Bears. Arthur Guiterman. PoRA
Bears. Adrienne Cecile Rich. NePoEA; NYBP; TPM
Bears are in the cabbage again. The Wrath of Lester Lame Bull. James Welch. YAP
Bear's Song, The. *Tr. fr. Haida Indian song by* Constance Lindsay Skinner. AWP; JAWP; WBP
Beast, The. Theodore Roethke. AmLP
Beast and bird must bow aside. Epilogue for a Masque of Purcell. Adrienne Cecile Rich. NePoEA; NYBP
Beast in View. Muriel Rukeyser. FiMAP
Beast Section, The. Welton Smith. BF
Beast with Chrome Teeth, The. Thurmond Snyder. NNP
Beasts. Paul Engle. PoCh
"That was a shocking day, *sel.*" ReMP
Beasts, The. Walt Whitman. *See* Animals.
Beasts. Richard Wilbur. AmPP (5th ed.); CrMA; FiMAP; NePoAm; ToPo; TwAmPo; TwCP
Beast's backing up, The. His ass. The Beautiful Day #9. A. B. Spellman. BF
Beasts, Birds, and Fishes. Adelaide O'Keeffe. OTPC (1923 ed.)
Beasts' Confession, The. Swift. ATP (1935 ed.); CEP; EiCL; EiPP; TOP
Beasts in the Tower, The. Charles *and* Mary Lamb. OTPC (1923 ed.)
Beasts in their major freedom. Beasts. Richard Wilbur. AmPP (5th ed.); CrMA; FiMAP; NePoAm; TwAmPo; TwCP
Beasts onely capable of sense, enjoy. John Ford. *Fr.* The Broken Heart. PoEL-2
Beat, The. James R. Lucas. WSL
Beat against Me No Longer. Lew Sarett. NP
Beat and beat and growl of the Basie band, The. The Basie Band. Julian Cooper. MuSP
Beat—beat—beat—drums—beat. Drums of Haiti. Marcus B. Christian. GoSl
Beat! Beat! Drums! Walt Whitman. AP; ATP (1935 ed.); CoBA; FaBV; LaNeLa; NoP; PoLF
Beat hell out of it. Paterson; Episode 17. William Carlos Williams. OxBA
Beat on, proud billows [*or* billowes]; Boreas blow. Loyalty Confin'd [*or* In Prison *or* Liberty and Requiem of an Imprisoned Royalist]. Sir Roger L'Estrange. OBS; SeCL
Beat on the Tom-toms, and scatter the flowers. The Bride. "Laurence Hope." HBV
Beat the drums of skins. War Comes. Zalman Schneour. TrJP
Beat the drums of tragedy for me. Fantasy in Purple. Langston Hughes. BANP; CDC
Beat the knife on the plate and the fork on the can. Going In to Dinner. Edward Shanks. OBMV
Beata l'Alma. Sir Herbert Read. LiTG
Beata Solitudo. Ernest Dowson. PoVP
Beaten and a baffled man, A. The Black Knight. John Todhunter. OBVV; PoVP
Beaten, beaten, beaten, beaten. The Copper Song. Hermia Harris Fraser. CaP
Beaten like an old hound. Mad Day in March. Philip Levine. NYBP
Beaten Path, The. Anne Goodwin Winslow. HBMV
Beati Omnes. Psalms, CXXVIII, Bible, *O.T.*, *tr. by* Thomas Sternhold. ReIE; SiCE
Beatific Sea, The. Thomas Campbell. EtS
Beatific Vision, The. G. K. Chesterton. MoRP
Beating Heart, The. Heine, *tr. fr. German by* Louis Untermeyer. UnTE
Beating heart! we come again. At Her Window. Frederick Locker-Lampson. HBV; OBEV (1st ed.); OBVV
Beating hearts. Untitle. Kuwasi Balagon. BF
Beating of the guns grows louder, The. The Assault. Robert Nichols. MCCG
Beatitudes, The. St. Matthew, V, Bible, *N.T.* *Fr.* The Sermon on the Mount. TrGrPo (3-10)
(Beatitudes of Jesus, The.) MaRV (3-12)
Beatitudes for a Housewife. Mary Mae Oesch. PoToHe (new ed.)
Beatrice, *sel.* Joseph Sheridan Le Fanu.
Hymn: "Hush! oh ye billows." OnYI
Beatrice is gone up into high Heaven. Sonnet. Dante, *tr. by* Dante Gabriel Rossetti. *Fr.* La Vita Nuova. GoBC
Beatrice's Last Words. Shelley. *Fr.* The Cenci, V, iv. FiP
Beatus Vir. Psalms, I, Bible, *O.T.*, *tr. by* Thomas Sternhold. ReIE; SiCE
Beatus Vir. Richard Le Gallienne. HBMV; OHIP
Beau, The. *Unknown.* WaPE
Beaucourt Revisited. A. P. Herbert. MMA
Beauing, belling [*or* belle-ing], dancing, drinking. The Rakes of Mallow. *Unknown.* IrPN; OnYI
Beaumont and Fletcher. Swinburne. *Fr.* Sonnets on English Dramatic Poets. PoVP
Beauregard. Catherine Anne Warfield. MC; PaA; PAH
Beau's Receipt for a Lady's Dress, The. *Unknown.* CoMu
Beau's Reply. William Cowper. EiCL; FaBoCh; OA; OTPC (1923 ed.); PRWS
Beauté, La. Baudelaire. *See* Beauty.
Beauteous Ethel's father has, The. A Piazza Tragedy. Eugene Field. FiBHP
Beauteous, Yea Beauteous More than These. Christopher Smart. *Fr.* A Song to David. EaLo
Beautie, and the life, The. *See* Beauty, and the life, The.
Beautie, I know, is good, and bloud is more. Ben Jonson. *Fr.* Epistle to Elizabeth, Countess of Rutland. FaBoEn
Beautie, sweet love, is like the morning dewe. *See* Beauty, sweet love, is like the morning dew.
Beauties, Have Ye Seen This Toy. Ben Jonson. *Fr.* The Hue and Cry after Cupid. OAEP
(Beauties, Have Ye Seen.) TuPP
(Cupid.) BOHV, *abr.*; InMe
(Venus' Runaway.) HBV; ReEn
Beauties of Santa Cruz, The. Philip Freneau. MAmP
Sels.
"From the vast caverns of old ocean's bed." AmPP (4th ed.)
"Sick of thy northern glooms, come shepherd, seek." CoBA
Beautiful. W. A. Bixler. WBLP
Beautiful, The. W. H. Davies. ELU; POTE
Beautiful, The. John Aylmer Dorgan. AA
Beautiful, *with music.* *Unknown.* ABF
Beautiful always the littoral line. The Innocent. Gene Derwood. NePA; WaP
Beautiful American Word, Sure, The. Delmore Schwartz. CrMA; LiTA
Beautiful and blond they come, the Californians. The Californians. Theodore Spencer. NYBP
Beautiful and happy girl, A. Memories. Whittier. AP; CoBA; OBVV
Beautiful and rich is an old friendship. Old Friendship. Eunice Tietjens. NP
Beautiful are the fingers of the loved one. When She Plays upon the Harp or Lute. Moses ibn Ezra. TrJP
Beautiful as the flying legend of some leopard. Judith of Bethulia. John Crowe Ransom. CrMA; DTC; FaBoMo; LiTA; LiTM (rev. ed.); MoPo; NePA
Bearer of Evil Things, The. Robert Frost. CBEP
Beautiful as the pomegranate is the white face of Ophrah. The Hot Flame of My Grief. Moses ibn Ezra. TrJP
Beautiful, Beautiful Mother, give. Immaculate Palm. Joseph Joel Keith. ISi
Beautiful bird, in as your wings as vivid. To the Rosella in the Poinsettia Tree. James Picot. BoAV
Beautiful, black womanhood. Death of Days and Nights of Life. Clarence Franklin. BF
"Beautiful body made of ivory." Conrad Aiken. *Fr.* Variations, XIV. PG (1945 ed.)
Beautiful Boy, The. *Unknown, tr. fr. Arabic by* E. Powys Mathers. *Fr.* The Thousand and One Nights. LiTW
Beautiful cashier's white face has risen once more, The. Before the Cashier's Window in a Department Store. James Wright. CoAP; NYBP

Beautiful Changes, The. Richard Wilbur. CMoP; CoAP; FiMAP; ILP; SeCeV (1967 ed.)
Beautiful Creatures Brief as These. D. G. Jones. MoCV
Beautiful Day #9, The. A. B. Spellman. BF
Beautiful, delicate bright gazelle, The. A Love-Song. W. J. Turner. OBMV
Beautiful Evelyn Hope is dead! Evelyn Hope. Browning. BoLiVe; HBV; MaPo; MBW-2; OuHeWo; PoVP; TrGrPo; VA; ViPo
Beautiful face of a child. Three Portraits of Prince Charles. Andrew Lang. PoVP; VA
Beautiful faces are those that wear. Beautiful Things. Ellen Palmer Allerton. BLPA; NeHB; WBLP
Beautiful Gift, The. Grace Noll Crowell. PEDC
Beautiful girl said something in your praise, A. To a Friend on His Marriage. F. T. Prince. LiTM
Beautiful glooms, soft dusks in the noonday fire. Sidney Lanier. *Fr.* The Marshes of Glynn. PFY
Beautiful habitations, auras of delight! Auras of Delight. Coventry Patmore. *Fr.* The Unknown Eros. ACP; CAW; LoBV; OBVV
Beautiful Hands. Ellen M. H. Gates. TreF
Beautiful Horses, The. Donald Hall. NePoAm-2
Beautiful Hsi-shih, The. Wang Wei, *tr. fr. Chinese by* Witter Bynner *and* Kiang Kang-hu. OuHeWo
Beautiful is she, this woman. Love Song. *Unknown.* AWP; JAWP; WBP
Beautiful is the large church. Churches. *Unknown.* MaRV; SoP
Beautiful Is the Loved One. Moses ibn Ezra, *tr. fr. Hebrew by* Solomon Solis-Cohen. TrJP
Beautiful Isle of Somewhere. Jessie B. Pounds. TreFT
Beautiful ladies through the orchard pass. Les Demoiselles De Sauve. John Gray. PeVV
Beautiful lady named Psyche, A. Limerick. *Unknown.* LiBL; LiTG; SiTL; WhC
Beautiful landscape! I could look on thee. On a Beautiful Landscape. William Bowles. PoPo
Beautiful Lie the Dead. Stephen Phillips. POTE
Beautiful lily!/ So gently unfolding. Beautiful Lily. Alice Mortenson. BePJ
Beautiful Meals. T. Sturge Moore. BoTP
Beautiful Mistress, A. Thomas Carew. OBS
("If when the sun at noon displays.") EG
(Song: Beautiful Mistress, A.) SeEP
Beautiful mother is bending, The. Nativity Song. Jacopone da Todi. OHIP
Beautiful must be the mountains whence ye come. Nightingales. Robert Bridges. AtBAP; BrPo; BWP; CMoP; CoBMV; EnLi-2 (1949 ed.); ExPo; FaBoEn; ForPo; GTBS; HBMV; LiTB; LiTM; MoAB; MoBrPo; MoPo; OA; OBEV; OBMV; OBNC; OBVV; Po; PoPl; PoVP; SeCeV; SiSW; TrGrPo; UnPo
Beautiful, my delight. To Be Sung on the Water. Louise Bogan. MoVE
Beautiful Necessity, The, *sel.* Claude Bragdon.
Point, the Line, the Surface and Sphere, The, 2 *ll.* ImOP
Beautiful Negress, The. Ruth Pitter. MoVE
Beautiful Night, A. Thomas Lovell Beddoes. *Fr.* Fragments Intended for the Dramas. ChER; LoBV
(Lines: "How lovely is the heaven of this night.") NBM
Beautiful Night, A. Naoyoshi, *tr. fr. Japanese by* Asataro Miyamori. OnPM
Beautiful, O beautiful—/ In all the mountain passes. The April of the Ages. Digby Mackworth Dolben. GoBC
Beautiful place is the town of Lo-yang, A. Lo-yang. Emperor Ch'ien Wen-ti. AtBAP; AWP; JAWP; WBP
Beautiful Proud Sea. Sara Teasdale. NP
Beautiful Railway Bridge of the Silv'ry Tay. The Tay Bridge Disaster. William McGonagall. EvOK
Beautiful rain falls, the unheeded angel, The. In Time. Kathleen Raine. CMoP; NeBP
Beautiful Saviour. Charlotte M. Kruger. BePJ
Beautiful? Sir, you may say so. Thar isn't her match in the country. Chiquita. Bret Harte. AA; IHA; PFY
Beautiful Snow, The. John Whittaker Watson. BLPA; TreF; WBLP
Beautiful soup, so rich and green. Turtle Soup. "Lewis Carroll." *Fr.* Alice's Adventures in Wonderland. InMe; Par
Beautiful spoils! borne off from vanquisht death! Rose Aylmer's Hair, Given by Her Sister. Walter Savage Landor. VA
Beautiful star in heav'n so bright. Star of the Evening. James M. Sayles. Par
Beautiful sun that giveth us light. Beautiful. W. A. Bixler. WBLP
Beautiful Sunday. "Jake Falstaff." *See* Day in Spring, A.
Beautiful, tender, wasting away for sorrow. Luscious and Sorrowful. Christina Rossetti. PoEL-5; SeCePo
Beautiful Things. Ellen Palmer Allerton. BLPA; NeHB; WBLP
Beautiful, through clear skies newly blue. Spring Landscape. Melvin Walker La Follette. NePoEA-2
Beautiful Train, The. William Empson. MoVE
Beautiful Virgin! clothèd with the sun. To the Virgin Mary. Petrarch. Sonnets to Laura, Canzone VIII. CAW
Beautiful vision! how bright it rose. The Reign of Peace. Eliza Thornton. PEDC
Beautiful, which mocked his fond pursuing, The. The Beautiful. John Aylmer Dorgan. AA
Beautiful Woman, The. Tu Fu, *tr. fr. Chinese by* Soame Jenyns. WoL
Beautiful woman, a cup of wine, and a garden, A. Joy of Life. Moses ibn Ezra. *Fr.* The Book of Tarshish. TrJP
Beautiful World, The. W. L. Childress. OHIP
Beautiful world of new, superber birth, that rises to my eyes. Walt Whitman. *Fr.* Thou Mother with Thy Equal Brood. PoFr
Beautiful you rise upon the horizon of heaven. The Hymn to the Sun. Ikhnaton. TTY
Beautiful young men and women, The. Earth's Winter Song. Robert Duncan. FRC
Beautiful Young Nymph Going to Bed, A. Swift. EiCP; UnTE
Corinna, Pride of Drury-Lane, *sel.* PPON
Beautifully Janet slept. Janet Waking. John Crowe Ransom. AmLP; AmP; AnAmPo; CMoP; ExPo; ForPo; MAP; MoAB; MoAmPo; PoIE; PoPo; ThWaDe
Beauty. Kenneth Slade Alling. HBMV
Beauty. Basho. *See* They Also.
Beauty. Baudelaire, *tr. fr. French.* LO, *tr. by* Alan Conder; OnPM, *tr. by* Arthur Symons
(Beauté, La, *tr. by* Lord Alfred Douglas.) AWP; JAWP; WBP
Beauty. Laurence Binyon. MoBrPo
Beauty. Abraham Cowley. AnFE; LiTB; PoEL-2; SiTL; TrGrPo
Beauty. Emerson. MWA-1
Beauty. E Yeh Shure'. FaPON; TiPo
Beauty, The, *sel.* Thomas Hardy.
"I hate my beauty in the glass." LO
Beauty. Peter Hille, *tr. fr. German by* Jethro Bithell. AWP
Beauty. Christopher Marlowe. *See* If All the Pens That Poets Ever Held.
Beauty. John Masefield. BEL
Beauty. Isaac Rosenberg. TrJP
Beauty. Sappho. *See* One Girl.
Beauty. Mary Craig Sinclair. OQP
Beauty. Alexander Smith. VA
Beauty. Spenser. *Fr.* An Hymne in Honour of Beautie. OBSC
(Soul Is Form, *abr.*) GoBC
Beauty. Joel Elias Spingarn. HBMV
Beauty. Thomas Stanley, *after the Greek of* Anacreon. AWP; JAWP; PG (1945 ed.); WBP
(Horns to Bulls Wise Nature Lends.) OnPM
Beauty. Edward Thomas. NP
Beauty ("Beauty is but a vain and doubtful good"). *Unknown.* The Passionate Pilgrim, XIII. OBSC
Beauty. Elinor Wylie. NP; OxBA
Beauty—a beam, nay, flame. Fading Beauty. Giambattista Marini. AWP
Beauty, a Silver Dew. *Unknown.* CBEP
(Epigram: "Beauty, a silver dew that falls in May.") OBSC
Beauty, Alas, Where Wast Thou Born. *At. to* Thomas Lodge *and to* Robert Greene. ElL
Beauty all stainless, a pearl of a maiden, A. The Geraldine's Daughter. Egan O'Rahilly. AnIL; IrPN; OnYI
Beauty and Duty. Ellen S. Hooper. *See* Duty.
Beauty and Terror. Lesbia Harford. MoAuPo; PoAu-1
Beauty and the Artist. Michelangelo, *tr. fr. Italian by* John Addington Symonds. PoFr
Beauty [*or* Beautie], and the life, The. Madrigal [*or* Her Pass-

ing]. William Drummond of Hawthornden. AtBAP; EIL; OBEV; PoEL-2
Beauty and Truth. Emily Dickinson. *See* I died for beauty.
Beauty and youth, with manners sweet, and friends. On the Grave of a Young Cavalry Officer Killed in the Valley of Virginia. Herman Melville. AP
Beauty, arise, show forth thy glorious shining! A Bridal Song [*or* Beauty, Arise!]. Thomas Dekker, *and others. Fr.* The Pleasant Comedy of Patient Grissell. EIL; OBSC; TrGrPo; TuPP
Beauty as a Shield. Elsie Robinson. BLPA; PoToHe (new ed.)
Beauty at the Plough. Arthur Joseph Munby. *Fr.* Dorothy; a Country Story. VA
Beauty Bathing. Anthony Munday. *See* Beauty Sat Bathing by a Spring.
Beauty blue and beauty white. Shopping Day. Orrick Johns. InMe
Beauty calls and gives no warning. Evensong. Ridgely Torrence. HBV
Beauty Clear and Fair. John Fletcher. *Fr.* The Elder Brother, III, v. BEL; CBEP; HoPM; LO; OAEP; OBEV; SeCL; SeEP; ViBoPo
(Beauty Cleere and Fair.) AtBAP
(Song: "Beauty clear and fair.") OBS
Beauty depends on simplicity. The Inner Man. Plato. PoPl
Beauty does not walk through lovely days. Beauty and Terror. Lesbia Harford. MoAuPo; PoAu-1
Beauty Extolled [*or* Extoll'd]. *Unknown, at. to* Henry Noel *and to* William Strode. ChTr; OBS
(Gaze Not on Swans.) ELP
("Gaze not on swans in whose soft breast.") LO
(On His Mistress.) PoEL-2
Beauty for Ashes. Martha Snell Nicholson. SoP
Beauty goes out to meet a greater beauty. Dying. Jessie Holt. ChIP; PGD
Beauty growing on a thorn. Chiaroscuro. John B. Thompson. OQP
Beauty had first my pride. The Star. Willoughby Weaving. HBMV; HBVY
Beauty Imposes. John Shaw Neilson. PoAu-1
Beauty in Trouble. Robert Graves. NYBP
Beauty in woman; the high will's decree. Sonnet: He Compares All Things with His Lady. Guido Cavalcanti, *tr. by* Dante Gabriel Rossetti. AWP
Beauty in Worship. *Unknown. Fr.* A Poem, in Defence of the Decent Ornaments of Christ-Church. . . OBS
Beauty is a lily. Reflection. Lew Sarett. MoSiPe
Beauty Is a Lovely Sweet. *Unknown.* SiCE; TuPP
Beauty Is a Witch. Shakespeare. *Fr.* Much Ado about Nothing, II, i. TrGrPo
Beauty is but a flower. Thomas Nashe. *Fr.* Summer's Last Will and Testament. LO
Beauty Is but a Painted Hell. Thomas Campion. AtBAP
Beauty is but a passenger; she will not. Vale. Patrick Mary Plunkett. JKCP (1955 ed.)
Beauty is but a vain and doubtful good. Beauty. *Unknown.* The Passionate Pilgrim, XIII. OBSC
Beauty Is Ever to the Lonely Mind. Robert Nathan. HBMV
Beauty is gone from the hills, the high brooks are forsaken. Vespers. Ian Maxwell. MoAuPo
Beauty is gull. The Bull. Francis Maguire. JKCP (1955 ed.)
Beauty Is Most at Twilight's Close. Pär Lagerkvist, *tr. fr. Swedish by* G. Kenneth Laycock. LiTW; PoPl
Beauty is never satisfied. Mythmaking. Kathleen Spivack. YAP
Beauty Is Not Bound. Thomas Campion. *See* Give Beauty All Her Right.
Beauty is not caused—it is. Emily Dickinson. LiTA; PoPo
Beauty is seen. Beauty. E Yeh Shure'. FaPON; TiPo
Beauty is still immortal in our eyes. The Immortal. Marjorie Pickthall. CaP
Beauty like hers is genius. Not the call. Genius in Beauty. Dante Gabriel Rossetti. The House of Life, XVIII. EnLit; InP; MaVP; OAEP; PoVP; TOP; ViPo; VP
Beauty may be the path to highest good. The Straight Road. Ellen Hooper. HBV
Beauty no more the subject be. Song. Thomas Nabbes. *Fr.* Hannibal and Scipio. SeCL; TuPP
Beauty, no other thing is, then a beam[e]. The Definition of Beauty. Robert Herrick. Po
Beauty of, The/ the terrible faces. Apology: Why Do I Write Today? William Carlos Williams. OxBA
Beauty of Israel is slain, The. David's Lament [*or* How Are the Mighty Fallen]. Second Samuel, Bible, *O.T.* AWP; LiTW; LO; ShBV-3; TrGrPo; WaaP
Beauty of Jesus in Me, The. Alice Hansche Mortenson. SoP
Beauty of Job's Daughters, The. Jay Macpherson. ACV; MoCV; PoCh
Beauty of manhole covers, The—what of that? Manhole Covers. Karl Shapiro. AmFN; GoJo
Beauty of the northern dawns, The. Christine. John Hay. AA
Beauty of the Stars, The. Moses ibn Ezra, *tr. fr. Hebrew by* Solomon Solis-Cohen. TrJP
Beauty of the World. Frank Wilmot. MoAuPo
Beauty of the world hath made me sad, The. The Wayfarer. Padraic Pearse. OxBI
Beauty of This Earth. Martin Opitz, *tr. fr. German by* Werner Heider. LiTW
Beauty Paramount. Sir William Killigrew. *Fr.* Selindra. SeCL
Beauty Rohtraut. Eduard Mörike, *tr. fr. German by* George Meredith. AWP; JAWP; WBP; WoL
Beauty Sat Bathing [by a Spring]. Anthony Munday. *Fr.* Primaleon of Greece. CBEP; EIL; UnTE
(Beauty Bathing.) OBEV; PG (1955 ed.)
(Colin.) GTBS; GTBS-D; GTBS-P; GTBS-W; GTSE; GTSL
(To Colin Clout.) OAEP; OBSC; TuPP; ViBoPo
Beauty, Since You So Much Desire. Thomas Campion. ErPo
(Place of Cupid's Fire, The.) UnTE
Beauty-sleep for the writer, and the beauty. Harvard. Robert Lowell. NoP
Beauty still walketh on the earth and air. Beauty. Alexander Smith. VA
Beauty [*or* Beautie], sweet love, is like the morning dew. Sonnet [*or* Beauty, Time, and Love, 5]. Samuel Daniel. To Delia, XLII [XLVII]. BWP; EIL; EnRePo; FaBoEn; HBV; OBEV; OBSC; TuPP; ViBoPo
Beauty That All Night Long, A. Jalal ed-Din Rumi, *tr. fr. Persian by* R. A. Nicholson. AWP; LiTW
Beauty Then Is Being. James W. Thompson. WSL
Beauty! thou art a wanderer on the earth. Behold, O Aspasia! I Send You Verses. Walter Savage Landor. *Fr.* Pericles and Aspasia. LoBV; OBNC; ViBoPo
Beauty, thou wild fantastic ape. Beauty. Abraham Cowley. AnFE; LiTB; PoEL-2; SiTL; TrGrPo
Beauty, Time, and Love (7 *sonnets*). Samuel Daniel. *Fr.* To Delia. OBEV
Beauty, Too, Seeks Surrender. Jessica Powers. JKCP (1955 ed.)
Beauty—what is it? A perfume without name. Epitaph for the Poet V., III. Arthur Davison Ficke. HBMV
Beauty which all men admire. *Unknown.* SeCSL
Beauty with the flame shawl, do not repulse me. Ghazal of Isa Akhun Zada. *Unknown, tr. fr. Pushtu by* E. Powys Mathers. PG (1945 ed.)
Beauty's Glass. Samuel Daniel, *after the French of* Philippe Desportes. OnPM
(To Delia, XXXIV, *sl. diff.*) ReIE
Beauty's Hands Are Cool. Karle Wilson Baker. GoYe
Beauty's Pageant. Dante Gabriel Rossetti. The House of Life, XVII. MaVP; PoVP; ViPo; VP
Beauty's Queen. Kisa'i of Merv, *tr. fr. Persian by* R. A. Nicholson. LiTW
Beauty's Self. *Unknown. See* My Love in Her Attire.
Beauty's Soliloquy during Her Honeymoon, A. Thomas Hardy. PoVP
Beaver Brook, *sel.* James Russell Lowell.
"Hushed with broad sunlight lies the hill." CoBA
Beaver Island Boys, The, *with music. At. to* Daniel Malloy. OuSiCo
Beaver Pond. Anne Marriott. ACV
Beaver roars hoarse with meltin' snows. Mr. Hosea Biglow to the Editor of the Atlantic Monthly. James Russell Lowell. *Fr.* The Biglow Papers, 2d series, No. X. PoEL-5
Beaver Sign. Kenneth Porter. NePoAm
Beaver's Story, The. Vernon Watkins. NYBP
Becalmed. John Blight. BoAV; PoAu-2
Becalmed. John Banister Tabb. AA
Becalmed in old Back Bay's dead water sulk. George Starbuck. Poems from a First Year in Boston, IV. PoDB

Because. Edward Fitzgerald. HBV
Because. Edward Teschemacher. TreFT
Because. B. W. Vilakzi, *tr. fr. Zulu.* PeSA
Because a woman's lips were red. History. "Paul Tanaquil." HBMV
"Because, because," the sound of the hard road said. Proud, Unhoped-for Light. Raymond Holden. MAP; MoAmPo (1942 ed.)
Because, dear Christ, your tender, wounded arm. Brier. E. Pauline Johnson. MaRV
Because, dear Lord, their way is rough and steep. Prayer for Shut-Ins. Ruth Winant Wheeler. PoToHe (new ed.)
Because, forsooth, you're young and fair. To His Young Mistress. Anacreon. UnTE
Because Going Nowhere Takes a Long Time. Kenneth Patchen. NaP
Because he had spoken harshly to his mother. Revelation. Robert Penn Warren. AnFE; CoAnAm; FiMAP; LiTA; MoPo; NePA; TwAmPo
Because he is young. Okura, *tr. fr. Japanese by* Arthur Waley. *Fr.* Manyo Shu. AWP; JAWP; LiTW; WBP
Because He Liked to Be at Home. Kenneth Patchen. NaP; ToPo
Because He Lives. Adele Lathrop. BLRP
Because he puts the compromising chart. Zola. E. A. Robinson. AmePo; FOL; MoVE; NePA; OxBA
Because he seemed to walk with an intent. James Thomson. *Fr.* The City of Dreadful Night. EnLit
Because he was a butcher and thereby. Reuben Bright. E. A. Robinson. AmP; AnNE; MAP; MaPo; MoAB; MoAmPo; NePA; NoP; PAn; PoPo; Sonn; StP; TrGrPo
Because he was gone, without a goodbye. Song. Lysander Kemp. NYTB
Because He Was Tempted. *Unknown.* STF
Because Heaven's cost is Hell, and perfect joy. Cost. Richard Watson Gilder. StJW
Because his soup was cold, he needs must sulk. House-Mates. Leon Gellert. MoAuPo
Because I am bewildered, because I must decide. Herod. W. H. Auden. *Fr.* For the Time Being. OnHM
Because I am idolatrous and have besought. Epigram. Ernest Dowson. ACP
"Because I am mad about women." The Wild Old Wicked Man. W. B. Yeats. AnIL; AtBAP; CMoP; MBW-2
Because I believe in the community of little children. The Massacre of the Innocents. William Jay Smith. EaLo
Because I bid her clean the pots for supper. The Land of Heart's Desire. W. B. Yeats. PoVP
Because I breathe not love to every one. Sir Philip Sidney. Astrophel and Stella, LIV. BoLiVe; FCP; OAEP; OBSC; PoAn; ReEn; SiCE; SiPS; TOP; TrGrPo; TuPP
Because I could not stop for Death. Emily Dickinson. AmePo; AmLP; AmP; AmPP (4th ed.); AnAmPo; AnFe; AnNE; AP; APA; AWP; CABA; CaFP; CBEP; CBV; CMoP; CoAnAm; DiPo; ExPo; FlW; ForPo; GTBS-W; ILP; InPo; LiTA; LiTM; MAmP; MAPA; MaPo; MaRV,*st.* 1; MasP; MoAB; MoAmPo; MoPo; MoRP; MoVE; MWA-2; NePA; NoP; OQP; OxBA; PAn; PIA; PoAn; PoE; PoEL-5; PoeP; PoFS; PoIE; PoPo; ReMP; SeCeV; TDP; TreFS; TRV; TwAmPo; UnPo (3d ed.); WGRP
Because I do not always know. A Prayer for Charity. Edwin O. Kennedy. TrPWD
Because I do not hope to turn again. Ash Wednesday. T. S. Eliot. ACV; AmPP; AnFE; AP; ATP (1953 ed.); CoAnAm; CoBMV; LiTA; LiTG; MoAB; MoAmPo; MoPo; OxBA; OxBoCh; Po; SeCeV; TwAmPo
Because I feel that, in the Heavens above. To My Mother. Poe. AnAmPo; AP; DD; LaNeLa; MAmP; MaRV; MCCG; NePA; OxBA; PoPo
Because I had loved so deeply. Compensation. Paul Laurence Dunbar. AmNP; HBV; PoNe; PTK
Because I have been given much. Because of Thy Great Bounty. Grace Noll Crowell. OQP; SoP; TrPWD
Because I have called to you. Calls. Carl Sandburg. NP
Because I have loved life, I shall have no sorrow to die. A Song of Living. Amelia Josephine Burr. HBV
Because I Liked You Better. A. E. Housman. EnLit; PeVV; VP; WePo
Because I Live. Evelyn Ames. GoYe
Because I love and serve a whore *sans glose.* Ballade of Villon and Fat Margot. Villon. UnTE
Because I love her. Gerald Bullett. LO
Because I oft in dark abstracted guise. Astrophel and Stella, XXVII. Sir Philip Sidney. FCP; ReEn; SiCE; SiPS
Because I once beat you up. For a Far-out Friend. Gary Snyder. NeAP
Because I set no snare. Michael's Song. W. W. Gibson. BoTP
Because I think not ever to return. Ballata: In Exile at Sarzana. Guido Cavalcanti. AWP; JAWP; WBP
Because I used to shun. The Spark. Joseph Mary Plunkett. AnIV; AWP; JAWP; WBP
Because I waddle when I walk. The Dachshund. Edward Anthony. GoTP
Because I was content with these poor fields. Musketaquid. Emerson. AP; CoBA
Because I Were Shy. *Unknown.* StPo
Because in these so malcontented times. Against Paulus. Sir John Harington. SiCE
Because in This Sorrowing Statue of Flesh. Kenneth Patchen. NaP
Because it is the day of Palms. Palm Sunday: Naples. Arthur Symons. BrPo; PeVV
Because, just then, I'd nothing else to do. World's End. G. K. Chettur. ACV
Because mine eyes can never have their fill. Ballata: He Will Gaze upon Beatrice [*or* Sonnet]. Dante, *tr. by* Dante Gabriel Rossetti. AWP; GoBC; JAWP; WBP
Because my brook is fluent. Emily Dickinson. MWA-2
Because My Faltering Feet. Hilaire Belloc. Sonnets, XVII. OxBoCh
(Her Faith.) GoBC
(Sonnet.) POTE
Because My Grief Seems Quiet and Apart. Robert Nathan. MAP
(Sonnet: "Because my grief seems quiet and apart.") TrJP
Because My Hands Hear the Flowers Thinking. Kenneth Patchen. ToPo
Because my joy is less than joy. Courage. Helen Frazee-Bower. HBMV
Because my will is simple as a window. The Blessed Virgin Mary Compared to a Window. Thomas Merton. ISi
Because of body's hunger are we born. Sehnsucht. Anna Wickham. MoBrPo
Because of Clothes. Laura Riding. LiTA
Because of endless pride. Posturing. C. S. Lewis. BoPe
Because of Her Who Flowered So Fair. Leonard Feeney. *Fr.* Song for a Listener. ISi
Because of little children soiled. Come, Lord Jesus. Amy Carmichael. FaChP
Because of one small low-laid head all crowned. Through Sorrow to Service. *Unknown.* MaRV
Because of the light of the moon. Alchemy. Francis Carlin. JKCP
Because of the memory of one we held dear. In a Province. F. T. Prince. BoSA; MoVE
Because of Thy Great Bounty. Grace Noll Crowell. OQP; SoP; TrPWD
Because of You. W. Cestrian. OQP
Because of You. Sophia Almon Hensley. HBV
Because of you I bear aloft the standard. Because of You. W. Cestrian. OQP
Because of you we will be glad and gay. Julian Grenfell. Maurice Baring. HBMV; POTE
Because of your firm faith, I kept the track. The Stimulus of Friendship. *Unknown.* OQP
Because on the branch that is tapping my pane. In the Hospital. Arthur Guiterman. MaRV; WGRP
Because our lives are cowardly and sly. The Road. James Stephens. HBMV
Because our talk was of the cloud-control. Secret Parting. Dante Gabriel Rossetti. The House of Life, XLV. MaVP; PoVP; ViPo; VP
Because river-fog. River-Fog. Kiyowara Fukayabu. *Fr.* Shui Shu. AWP; FaPON; JAWP; LiTW; WBP
Because Sometimes You Can't Always Be So. Kenneth Patchen. NaP
Because somewhere there was a man in a candystripe silk shirt. Homage to the Empress of the Blues. Robert E Hayden. PoNe
Because that you are going. Emily Dickinson. MoAmPo
Because the day that stretches out for me. A Nurse's Pray-

er. Ruth Winant Wheeler. FaChP
Because the ground-creature looked so sad. The Little Green Blackbird. Kenneth Patchen. PoCh
Because the Old French *chatepelose* meant hairy cat. D-9. James Schevill. FiMAP
Because the paint is not the shadow of branches. Camouflage. John Manifold. WaP
Because the rose must fade. Song. Richard Watson Gilder. HBV
Because the shadows deepen'd verily. At the Last. Philip Bourke Marston. HBV; VA
Because, the singer of an age, he sang. Shakespeare. Agnes Lee. NP
Because the snow is deep. The Fox. Kenneth Patchen. AnAmPo
Because the spirit of delight has laid. As One Finding Peace. Sister Mary of the Visitation. JKCP (1926 ed.)
Because the upper and the nether stones. To a Baffled Idealist. J. G. E. Hopkins. JKCP (1926 ed.); MaRV
Because the warm honey. Sanctuary. Bruce Boyd. NeAP
Because the years are few, I must be glad. The Debt. Katharine Lee Bates. OQP
Because there is safety in derision. The Apparitions. W. B. Yeats. CMoP; LiTM (rev. ed.); PoFS; PoIE (1970 ed.)
Because there was no other place. Flee on Your Donkey. Anne Sexton. NYBP
Because they are not. The Deceptrices. William Carlos Williams. NYBP
Because they could not give it too much ground. In a Bird Sanctuary. Richard Wilbur. FiMAP
Because They Were Very Poor That Winter. Kenneth Patchen. NaP
Because thou canst not see. The Philosopher to His Mistress. Robert Bridges. CMoP; LiTM (rev. ed.); OAEP; PoEL-5
Because thou hast the power and own'st the grace. Elizabeth Barrett Browning. Sonnets from the Portuguese, XXXIX. VA
Because thou wast the daughter of a king. To Saint Catherine. Henry Constable. GoBC
Because time kept. Pre Domina. Jean Lipkin. PeSA
Because time subdues sharp angles and closes wounds. Burial. Paulin Joachim. TTY
Because to-day is some religious festival. She Turns the Dolls' Faces to the Wall. W. B. Yeats. Upon a Dying Lady, III. LiTB
Because upon the first glad Easter day. Easter Light. Ida Norton Munson. ChIP
Because We Do Not See. *Unknown.* BLRP
Because we felt there could not be. God's Acre. Witter Bynner. AnEnPo
Because we love bare hills and stunted trees. Hound Voice. W. B. Yeats. POTE; SyP
Because we were baffled. The White Bird. Wilfred Watson. MoCV
Because ye have broken your own chain. The Curse. Elizabeth Barrett Browning. *Fr.* A Curse for a Nation. PoVP
Because ye made your backs your shields, it came. To the Guelf Faction. Folgore da San Geminiano. FOL
Because you are simple people, kindly and romantic. Fourth Act. Robinson Jeffers. LiTA; WaP
Because You Care. Frank Crane. PoToHe (new ed.)
Because you come to me with naught save love. Because. Edward Teschemacher. TreFT
Because you have increased my hurt. The Storm. Robert David Cohen. NYBP
Because you have no fear to mingle. To a Sparrow. Francis Ledwidge. HBMV; TSW
Because you have thrown off your prelate lord. On the New Forcers of Conscience under the Long Parliament. Milton. CABA; PoFr; Sonn; StP
Because you left her name unnamed. Joseph Mary Plunkett. Wilfrid Meynell. ISi
Because you love me I have much achieved. Encouraged. Paul Laurence Dunbar. TRV
Because you made me glad, I was the net. Affirmations. Peter Viereck. MiAP
Because you passed, and now are not. A Ballad of Heroes. Austin Dobson. HBV; HBVY; InP; OHIP; PoRL
Because You Passed My Way. Eleanor Taylor Rhodes. SoP
Because You Prayed. "C. B. B." STF
Because You Prayed. Ruth Margaret Gibbs. SoP
Because You Take Life in Your Stride. E. E. Cummings. TDP
Because your voice was at my side. Chamber Music, XVII. James Joyce. WePo
Becket, *sel.* Tennyson.
Duet: "Is it the wind of the dawn that I hear in the pine overhead?" SiSw
Becket's Diadem. *Unknown.* ACP
Beckie, my luve!—What is't, ye twa-faced tod. Sonnet. George Campbell Hay. OxBS
Beclouded. Emily Dickinson. *See* The sky is low, the clouds are mean.
Becoming a Dad. Edgar A. Guest. PoLF
Bed, The. Robert Creeley. StP
Bed, The. Giambattista Marino, *Tr. fr. Italian by* Virginia Tufte. HW
Bed, The. James Merrill. NePoEA
Bed, The. John Owen, *tr. fr. Latin by* Thomas Harvey. *Fr.* Four Epigrams. PrWP
Bed, The. Karl Shapiro. NYBP
Bed Charm. *Unknown. See* Matthew, Mark, Luke, and John.
Bed in My Heart, A. Martin Luther, *tr. fr. German.* SoP
Bed in Summer. Robert Louis Stevenson. GFA; GoJo; OTD; OTPC; PCH; PoPl; PoVP; PTK; RIS; StVeCh; TreFT
Bed is the boon for me! Old Lizette on Sleep. Agnes Lee. HBMV
Bed of ashes and a half-burned brand, A. Morning in Camp. Herbert Bashford. AA
Bed of Campanula, A. "John Crichton." CaP
Bed Time. *See* Bedtime.
Bed was made, the room was fit, The. Camper's Night Song. Robert Louis Stevenson. *Fr.* Travels with a Donkey. BBV
Bed without a Woman, A. Raymond Souster. ELU; ErPo
Bedbug, The. Tony Harrison. PV
Bedbug. *Unknown.* GoSl
Bedlam Hills. Vivian Smith. PoAu-2
Bedouin Song. Bayard Taylor. AA; AmePo; AmP; AnAmPo; BoLP; FaBoBe; GBV; HBV; MCCG; NeHB; PaPo; PFY; TreFT
(Bedouin Love-Song.) BBV
Bedouins of the Skies, The. James Benjamin Kenyon. AA
Bed-ridden, laid by an age's malady. Final Poem. Robert Bhain Campbell. MoPo; NePA
Beds are made close to a wall flat. Saturday Morning. Richard Howard. ErPo
Beds of Fleur-de-Lys, The. Charlotte Perkins Gilman. AA
Bed-Time. Laurence Alma-Tadema. BoTP
Bedtime. Elizabeth J. Coatsworth. ThGo
Bedtime. Helen Coale Crew. GFA
Bedtime. Francis Erskine, Earl of Rosslyn. HBV; HBVY; PRWS; VA
Bedtime. Eleanor Farjeon. SoPo; TiPo
Bed-Time. *At. to* Thomas Hood. BoTP; OTPC (1946 ed.)
Bed-Time. Ralph M. Jones. HBMV
Bedtime. Denise Levertov. FRC; NaP; TwCP
Bed Time. Ella Young. BoChLi (1950 ed.)
Bed-Time Song. Emilie Poulsson. HBV; HBVY
Bed-Time Story. Melville Cane. GoTP
Bedtime Story. George MacBeth. HYE; NePoEA-2
Bedtime Story, A. Robert Mezey. NePoEA
(If I Should Die Before I Wake.) NYBP
Bedtime Story for My Son. Peter Redgrove. BoPe; NePoEA-2
Bedtime Tales. Joseph Joel Keith. FiSC
Bedtime's come fu' little boys. Lullaby. Paul Laurence Dunbar. BoChLi; GoSl; MPB; StVeCh (1940 ed.); TSW
Bee, The. Emily Dickinson. *See* Like trains of cars.
Bee, The. John Fandel. GoYe
Bee, The. Charles Fitzgeffrey. *Fr.* Sir Francis Drake. ElL
Bee, The. Henry Hawkins. ACP
Bee, The ("As Cupid in a garden strayed"), *with music.* *Unknown.* TrAS
Bee, The ("Summer's nectar gathering bee"). *Unknown.* SeCL
Bee, The ("There is a little gentleman"). *Unknown.* PCH
Bee, The. Isaac Watts. *See* How Doth the Little Busy Bee.
Bee and the Cuckoo, The. Tomás de Iriarte, *tr. fr. Spanish by* George H. Devereux. BoChLi
Bee and the Lily, The. Thomas Westwood. TVC
Bee and the Petunia, The. Katherine Hoskins. ErPo
Bee-balm for humming-birds. Garden Song. Arthur Guiterman. MoSiPe

Bee, he has white honey, The. Dulce Ridentem. Stephen Vincent Benét. LOW
Bee his burnished carriage, A. Emily Dickinson. MWA-2; TDP
Bee is a rover, The. The Happy World [*or* Brown Bee]. William Brighty Rands. OTPC (1946 ed.); PCH; PPL; StVeCh (1940 ed.)
Bee is not afraid of me, The. Emily Dickinson. LaNeLa
Bee Is Such a Busy Soul, The. *Unknown.* SiTL
Bee-Master. V. Sackville-West. HaMV
Bee-Orchis, The. Andrew Young. ChTr
Bee quick my boyes drinke off your wine. *Unknown.* SeCSL
Bee Sets Sail, A. Katharine Morse. UTS
Bee Song. Carl Sandburg. PDV
Bee, the Ant, and the Sparrow, The. Charles Cotton. RIS
Bee to the heather, The. Song. Sir Henry Taylor. OBVV
Beech, The. Theodore Daeubler, *tr. fr. German by* Glauco Cambon. OnPM
Beech, The. Andrew Young. BoNaP
Beech and Oak. Thomas Love Peacock. CBEP
Beech Leaves. James Reeves. RePo
Beech says, The: my power is the foliage. The Beech. Theodore Daeubler. OnPM
Beech Trees. Sister Mary Madeleva. BBV (1951 ed.)
Beech Tree's Petition, The. Thomas Campbell. GTSL; HBV
Beecher Island. Arthur Chapman. PoOW
Beeg Irish cop dat walk hees beat. Two 'Mericana Men. T. A. Daly. MPB
Beehive. Jean Toomer. IDB; PoNe; TTY
Beehould a cluster to itt selfe a vine. Sonnet. William Alabaster. AnAnS-1; MeP
Beekeeper, The. Jack Matthews. NYTB
Beëlzebub Rises to Speak. Milton. *Fr.* Paradise Lost, II. UnPo (1st ed.)
Been in dat jailhouse, expectin' a fine. Sun Gonna Shine in My Door Some Day. *Unknown.* OuSiCo
Been in the Pen So Long, *with music.* *Unknown.* AS
Been on the hummer since ninety-four. A. R. U. *Unknown.* AS
Been out in the lifeboat often? The Lifeboat. George R. Sims. PaPo
Been to Pike's Peak, lost all my dimes. Soliloquy of the Returned Gold Adventurer. *Unknown.* PoOW
Beeny Cliff. Thomas Hardy. OBNC; PoVP
Beer. George Arnold. AA; TreFT
Beer. Charles Stuart Calverley. CenHV
"But hark! a sound is stealing on my ear," *sel.* FiBHP
Beer. *Unknown.* *See* Limerick: "Man to whom illness was chronic, A."
Beer and Skittles. Diana Barrett. StaSt
Beerbottle armada bobs in the rainbow, A. Marina. Gregory Orr. QAH
Bees. Marchette Chute. BoChLi (1950 ed.)
Bees, The. Monk Gibbon. OnYI
Bees, The. Lola Ridge. FaPON; MPB
Bees. Frank Dempster Sherman. PPL
Bees and Monks. John Hookham Frere. *Fr.* King Arthur and His Round Table. OBRV
Bees are black, with gilt surcingles. Emily Dickinson. MWA-2
Bees before Winter. Merrill Moore. RIS
Bees build in the crevices, The. The Stare's Nest by my Window. W. B. Yeats. Meditations in Time of Civil War, VI. CABL; GTBS-P; LiTB; PIA
Bees don't care about the snow. Bees. Frank Dempster Sherman. PPL
Bees in the clover are making honey, and I am making my hay, The. The Mower in Ohio. John James Piatt. AA
Bees in the late summer sun. Bee Song. Carl Sandburg. PDV
Bees of Christ, The. Clifford J. Laube. JKCP (1955 ed.)
Bees of Middleton [*or* Myddleton] Manor, The. May Probyn. GoBC; JKCP; VA
Bees over the gooseberry bushes. The Bees. Lola Ridge. FaPON; MPB
Bees' Song, The. Walter de la Mare. OTPC (1946 ed.); WhC; YT
Beethoven. Edward Carpenter. PoMa
Beethoven Andante, A. Grace Hazard Conkling. PFY
Beethoven's Death Mask. Stephen Spender. MuSP; UnS
Beetle, The. Edith King. GFA
Beetle, The. James Whitcomb Riley. PCD
"Shrilling locust slowly sheathes, The," *sel.* FaPON
Beetle Bemused. R. P. Lister. PV
Beetle in the Country Bathtub, The. John Hall Wheelock. WIRo
Beetle loves his unpretending track, The. Wordsworth. *Fr.* Liberty. FiBHP; Par
Beetle on the Shasta Daylight. Shirley Kaufman. NYBP
Beetles,/ noisy bumble bees. Come Visit My Garden. Tom Dent. NNP
Beets. Alden Nowlan. PeCV (1967 ed.)
Before, *sel.* Robert Browning.
"Our wars are wars of life, and wounds of love." ChIP; StJW
Before. W. E. Henley. In Hospital, IV. BEL; EnLi-2; MoBrPo; OuHeWo; PoVP
Before. Mary Sinton Leitch. OQP
Before a Statue of Achilles. George Santayana. HBV
Before a Statue of Apollo. Saul Tchernichowsky, *tr. fr. Hebrew by* Sholom J. Kahn. LiTW
(Before the Statue of Apollo, *tr. by* L. V. Snowman.) TrJP
Before Action. Leon Gellert. BoAV
Before Action. W. W. Gibson. BEL; TOP
Before Action. William Noel Hodgson. MaRV; WGRP
Before Agincourt. Shakespeare. *Fr.* King Henry V, *prologue to* IV. ChTr
Before all Time, before all worlds. Namdev. *Fr.* Everlasting to Everlasting. MaRV
Before an Old Painting of the Crucifixion. N. Scott Momaday. QFR
Before and After. Oliver Madox Brown. VA
Before and after Marriage. Anne Campbell. PoToHe (new ed.)
Before Bannockburn. Burns. *See* Scots Wha Hae.
Before Bannockburn. John Barbour. *Fr.* The Bruce. OxBS
Before Christ left the Citadel of Light. His Laureate. Joyce Kilmer. StJW
Before Communion. Self-Examination. *Unknown.* SoP
Before Dawn. Elinor Chipp. HBMV
Before Dawn. Walter de la Mare. ChrBoLe
Before Dawn. Horace Hamilton. NYBP
Before Dawn in the Woods. Marguerite Wilkinson. HBMV
Before Day. Siegfried Sassoon. WGRP
Before daybreak, before dew breaks. Youth. Barend Toerien. PeSA
Before Disaster. Yvor Winters. HoPM; QFR
Before Exile. Louise Mack. BoAu
Before fruit, the flower. In Cycle Repeated. Katherine Garrison Chapin. NYTB
Before God's footstool to confess. Success [*or* Judgment]. *Unknown.* PoToHe; TreFT
Before Harvest. Robert Fitzgerald. PoPl
Before he embarks on shipboard. Three Dangers. *Unknown.* OnPM
Before He formed a star. His Plan. *Unknown.* STF
Before he pass'd from mortal view. Solemn Rondeau. Charles Dent Bell. OBVV
Before Her Portrait in Youth. Francis Thompson. EPN
Before her supper where she sits. The Daughter at Evening. Robert Nathan. HBMV; TSW
Before Him weltered like a shoreless sea. Judgment Day. William Dean Howells. AA; AmePo; PFY
Before His Throne. *Unknown.* SoP
Before I began to burn. Interval with Fire. Dorothy Livesay. CaP
Before I brand a brother. Before. Mary Sinton Leitch. OQP
Before I came across the sea. The Native Irishman. *Unknown.* OnYI
Before I got my eye put out. Emily Dickinson. LiTA; LiTM (rev. ed.)
Before I joined the army. Death and the Fairies. Patrick MacGill. HBMV
Before I knew how cruel. Gossip. Lexie Dean Robertson. MoSiPe
Before I knew, the dawn was on the road. The Road to Dieppe. John Finley. MCCG
Before I Knocked and Flesh Let Enter. Dylan Thomas. FaBoTw
Before I saw the spring. Spring in Hiding. Frances Frost. YeAr
Before I sigh my last gasp[e], let me breath[e]. The Will.

John Donne. ATP (1935 ed.); LiTB; LiTG; MaMe; MePo; SCEP-1; SeEP; TOP; TuPP
Before I Stumbled. Francis Carlin. HBMV
Before I trust my fate to thee. A Woman's Question[s]. Adelaide Anne Procter. HBV; LiTL; LO; VA
Before I was a travelled bird. Regarding (1) the U. S. and (2) New York. Franklin P. Adams. HBMV
Before I woke I knew her gone. The Flower of Flame. Robert Nichols. OBMV
Before I woke, the customed thews. Male Torso. Christoper Middleton. NePoEA-2
Before Invasion, 1940. John Betjeman. MoVE
Before It Is Too Late. Frank Herbert Sweet. PoToHe (new ed.)
Before man came to blow it right. The Aim Was Song. Robert Frost. HH; NoP; NP; PP
Before man parted for this earthly strand. Revolutions. Matthew Arnold. EPN; PoVP
Before Man's labouring wisdom gave me birth. The Ship and Her Makers. John Masefield. CoBE
Before me you bowed as before an altar. Homage. Helen Hoyt. AnAmPo
Before mine eye, to feed my greedy will. Seven Sonnets in Sequence, II. George Gascoigne. Sonn
Before My Face the Picture Hangs. Robert Southwell. *See* Upon the Image of Death.
Before my lady's window gay. Medieval Norman Songs, IV. *Unknown, tr. by* John Addington Symonds. AWP
Before my light goes out for ever if God should give me a choice of graces. Impenitentia Ultima. Ernest Dowson. BrPo; HBV
Before Olympus. John Gould Fletcher. MAP; MoAmPo
Before our eyes a pageant rolled. After the Centennial. Christopher Pearse Cranch. PAH
Before our lady came on earth. Song from "The Hill of Venus." William Morris. *Fr.* The Earthly Paradise. PoVP
Before our lives divide for ever. The Triumph of Time. Swinburne. MaVP; PoVP; ViPo; ViPP; VP
Before Pilate. Leslie Savage Clark. ChIP
Before remembrance we moved here, withheld. The Font in the Forest. Léonie Adams. CrMA
Before Rereading Shakespeare's Sonnets. T. Sturge Moore. BrPo
Before Saint Anne. The Good Bishop. *Unknown.* CAW; WGRP
Before Salamis. William Bedell Stanford. NeIP
Before Sedan. Austin Dobson. MoBrPo (1942 ed.); NeMA; PeVV; TreFS
Before Sentence Is Passed. R. P. Blackmur. LiTA
Before she first had smiled or looked with calm. E. J. Scovell. *Fr.* The First Year. FaBoMo
Before she has her floor swept. Portrait by a Neighbor. Edna St. Vincent Millay. FaPON; GaP; LOW; MoShBr; MPB; PDV; SP; TiPo; TSW
Before she saw him in the wood. The Quickening. Stella Weston Tuttle. GoYe
Before she went from grieving. Apples. Lizette Woodworth Reese. YT
Before sheep came, before my fathers drove. Frances Frost. *Fr.* Woman of This Earth. AnAmPo
Before Sleep. Prudentius, *tr. fr. Latin by* Helen Waddell. LiTW
Before Sleep. Anne Ridler. NeBP
Before Sleeping. *Unknown. See* Matthew, Mark, Luke and John.
Before Spring. P. A. Ropes. BoTP
Before sunrise. Looking for Jonathan. Jon Anderson. YAP
Before Sunrise in Winter. Edward Rowland Sill. AA
Before Sunset. Swinburne. StP
("In the lower lands of day.") EG
Before that my loved one. Apprehension. *Tr. by* Douglas Ainslie. OBVV
Before the altar in his heart he knelt. The Dissenter. Lillian M. Swenson. ChIP
Before the Anaesthetic; or, A Real Fright. John Betjeman. SeCePo
Before the Barn-Door Crowing. John Gay. *Fr.* The Beggar's Opera. CBEP; ELU
(Song.) ErPo; PoEL-3
Before the Beginning. Christina Rossetti. OxBoCh
(Last Prayer.) OBVV
Before the Beginning of Years. Swinburne. *Fr.* Atalanta in Calydon. ACV; BEL; CBV; EnL; EPN; FaFP; HBV; LiTB; LiTG; MasP; NoP; OAEP; PoFS; PoVP; ViPP; VP; WHA
(Chorus: "Before the beginning of years.") EnLit; GTBS-D; GTBS-W; LoBV; OBVV; TRV
(Chorus from "Atalanta.") CBEP; OBEV (new ed.)
(Choruses from "Atalanta in Calydon.") EnLi-2; GTSE; ViBoPo
(Life of Man, The.) TOP
(Man.) BoLiVe; TrGrPo
Before the beginning Thou hast foreknown the end. Before the Beginning [*or* Last Prayer]. Christina Rossetti. OBVV; OxBoCh
Before the Bells of This New Year Ring. Kenneth Patchen. *See* At the New Year.
Before the Big Storm. William Stafford. NaP
Before the Birth of One of Her Children. Anne Bradstreet. MAmP
Before the blond horseman rode into our village. An Event. Edward Field. CoAP
Before the Carnival. Thom Gunn. NePoEA
Before the Cashier's Window in a Department Store. James Wright. CoAP; NYBP
Before the cathedral in grandeur rose. How the Great Guest Came [*or* The Great Guest Comes.]. Edwin Markham. BeLS; BLPA; WBLP
Before the Coming of Winter. Dennis Schmitz. YAP
Before the Crucifix. Princess Gabrielle Wrede, *tr. fr. German by* Robert Huntington. StJW
Before the dawn-wind swept the troubled sky. A Vision. Geoffrey Dearmer. HBMV
Before the ending of the day. Evening Prayer. *Unknown.* FaChP
Before the falling summer sun. Musings. William Barnes. OBNC
Before the Feast of Shushan. Anne Spencer. BANP
Before the glare o' dawn I rise. The Shearer's Wife. Louis Esson. BoAu; PoAu-1
Before the gods that made the gods. G. K. Chesterton. *Fr.* The Ballad of the White Horse. ACP (1952 ed.)
Before the grass is out the people are out. William Carlos Williams. *Fr.* Paterson. ReMP
Before the Great Void, we burn the fragrant incense. To Purity and Truth. *Unknown.* TrJP
Before the Ikon of the Mother of God. Constantine of Rhodes, *tr. fr. Greek by* G. R. Woodward. ISi
Before the listening world behold him stand. The Violin. Richard Watson Gilder. PoRL
Before the living bronze Saint-Gaudens made. *See* Before the solemn bronze. . .
Before the Mirror. Swinburne. OBVV
"Glad, but not flush'd with gladness," *sel.* OBEV (new ed.)
Before the mountains were brought forth, before. Later Life, I. Christina Rossetti. Sonn
Before the Paling of the Stars. Christina Rossetti. CBEP; ChIP; DD; HBVY; MaRV; OTPC (1946 ed.)
(Christmas Carol, A: "Before the paling of the stars.") BiCB
(Christmas Daybreak.) GoTP
Before the prim old mirror. Hair-dressing. Louis Untermeyer. UnTE
Before the Rain. Thomas Bailey Aldrich. GN
Before the Rain. Amélie Rives. AA
Before the Roman Came to Rye. G. K. Chesterton. *See* Rolling English Road, The.
Before the sixth day of the next new year. On the Cards and Dice. Sir Walter Ralegh. EnRePo; FCP; SiPS
Before the solemn [*or* living] bronze Saint Gaudens made. An Ode in Time of Hesitation. William Vaughn Moody. AmePo; AmPP; AnFE; AP; APA; ATP; CoAnAm; HBV; OxBA; PaA; PAH; TOP
Before the sonne had guilde the morne of silver daij. *Unknown.* SeCSL
Before the Squall. Arthur Symons. PoVP
Before the Statue of Apollo. Saul Tchernichowsky. *See* Before a Statue of Apollo.
Before the stirring of the notes at the lecture. Madonna of the Dons. Arthur MacGillivray. ISi; JKCP (1955 ed.)
Before the Storm. Richard Dehmel, *tr. fr. German by* Ludwig Lewisohn. AWP; JAWP; WBP

Before the Storm. Kenneth O. Hanson. CoAP
Before the sun rose at yester-dawn. Kitty Bhan. Edward Walsh. ACP
Before the urchin well could go. The Fair Thief. Charles Wyndham. HBV
Before the work and toil of day. The Solitary Place. Carlton Buck. SoP
Before the World Was Made. W. B. Yeats. GTBS-P
Before the world was made. Words in the Wilderness. Sister Claude of Jesus. JKCP (1955 ed.)
Before there was in Egypt any sound. Monadnock through the Trees. E. A. Robinson. InP; TOP
Before they come I hear their talk. People Going By. Elizabeth Madox Roberts. GaP
Before thir eyes in sudden view appear. Description of Chaos. Milton. *Fr.* Paradise Lost. PeRV
Before this coiling planet shall be cold. Edna St. Vincent Millay. Epitaph for the Race of Man, I. AmP
Before this time another year, I may be gone. Oh, Lawd, How Long? *Unknown.* ABF
Before those golden altar-lights we stood. Victory. Alfred Noyes. BEL
Before Thy cross I'm kneeling. Before the Crucifix. Princess Gabrielle Wrede. StJW
Before Thy cross, O Saviour, we confess. Hymn to the Perfect. Edith Lovejoy Pierce. ChIP
Before thy door too long of late. Extremum Tanain. Horace. Odes, III, 10. AWP; JAWP; WBP
Before thy grisly front no man may stand. Christus Triumphans. Condé B. Pallen. CAW
Before Thy Throne. William Boyd Carpenter. SoP; TRV
Before us in the sultry dawn arose. The Slave. Richard Henry Horne. VA
Before Vespasian's regal throne. Death of Gaudentis. "Harriet Annie." WBLP
Before Vicksburg. George Henry Boker. PAH
Before Waterloo. Thomas Hardy. *Fr.* The Dynasts, Pt. III, Act VI, sc. viii. MoAB; PoVP; WaaP
(Chorus: "Yea, the coneys are scared by the thud of hoofs.") LoBV
(Chorus of the Years.) CMoP
(Field of Waterloo, The.) FaBoCh; LoGBV
Before we came the moon-soaked dews were here. Prelude to Cricket. Thomas Moult. *Fr.* Summer Days. MemP; POTE
Before we light the tribal fires again. Since We Are Property. Lilith Lorraine. FiSC
Before we shall again behold. Song. Sir William Davenant. MeLP; MePo; OBS; SeEP
Before Winter. Frederick R. McCreary. MAP
Before you bid, for Christmas' sake. For Them. Eleanor Farjeon. ChBR; ThGo
Before you kissed me only winds of heaven. The Kiss. Sara Teasdale. HBV
Before you love. A Proverb. *Unknown.* BoLP
Before you touch the bolt that locks this gate. Spoken at a Castle Gate. Donald Davidson. MAP; MoAmPo (1942 ed.)
Before your tiger roar was heard. Chang Liang. Li Po. PoFr
Beforehand. Witter Bynner. HBMV
Beg Parding. *Unknown.* ChTr
Bega. Marjorie Pickthall. CaP
Begetting. Dorothea Spears. PeSA
Begetting of Cain, The. Hyam Plutzik. FiMAP
Beggar, The. Margaret E. Bruner. PoToHe
Beggar, The. H. L. Doak. HBMV
Beggar. F. S. Flint. MoBrPo (1942 ed.)
Beggar. Nicanor Parra, *tr. fr. Spanish by* Miller Williams. CAD
Beggar and Poet, The. Samuel Wesley. PeRV
"Beggar," he sayes. Little John a Begging. *Unknown.* ESPB
Beggar in dirt. Dervish. Georgia Lee McElhaney. CoPo
Beggar Laddie, The. *Unknown.* ESPB
Beggar Maid, The. Tennyson. BeLS; BoTP; HBV; OnMSP; OTPC; PoVP
Beggar man came over the lea, A. The Jolly Beggar. *Unknown.* BFSS
Beggar on the Beach, The. Horace Gregory. NMP
Beggar to Beggar Cried. W. B. Yeats. CMoP
Beggar to Burgher. A. R. D. Fairburn. AnNZ
Beggar, to Mab the Fairy Queen, The. Robert Herrick. OTPC (1923 ed.)
Beggar to the graveyard hied, A. Poverty. *Unknown.* *Fr.* The Panchatantra. AWP; PoFr
Beggar Wind, The. Mary Austin. BoNaP
Beggars. Rhys Carpenter. HBMV
Beggars. Francis Davidson. CH
Beggars. Ella Higginson. AA
Beggars, The. Margaret Widdemer. NP
Beggars' Bush, *sel.* John Fletcher.
Cast Our Caps and Cares Away *fr.* II. SiCE; TuPP; ViBoPo
Beggar's Opera, The, *sels.* John Gay.
Before the Barn-Door Crowing, *fr.* II, i. CBEP; ELU
(Song: "Before the barn-door crowing.") ErPo; PoEL-3
"Fox may steal your hens, sir, A," *fr.* I, i. CEP
Highwaymen, The. WiR
"How happy could I be with either," *fr.* II, ii. ViBoPo
"If the heart of a man is deprest with cares," *fr.* II, i. CEP; NoP
(If the Heart of a Man.) ATP (1935 ed.); CBEP; ELP
"Let us take the road," *fr.* II, i. ATP (1935 ed.); CEP
(Highwaymen, The.) WiR
"Man may escape from rope and gun," *fr.* II, ii. CEP
"Modes of the court so common are grown, The," *fr.* III, iv. NoP
"O Polly, you might have toy'd and kist," *fr.* I, i. EnLoPo
Song: "Can love be controll'd by advice?" *fr.* I, viii. LoBV
Song: "If any wench Venus's girdle wear," *fr.* I, i. PoEL-3
Song: "Thus when the swallow, seeking prey," *fr.* II, ii. PoEL-3
"Through all the employments of life," *fr.* I, i. CEP; StP
(Employments of Life, The.) PV
Were I Laid on Greenland's Coast, *fr.* I, i. AtBAP; CBEP; CEP; NoP
(Macheath and Polly.) LoBV
(Over the Hills and Far Away.) ATP (1935 ed.); EnLi-1 (1949 ed.)
(Song: "Were I laid on Greenland's coast.") OBEC; OxBoLi; PoEL-3; SeCeV
"Youth's the season made for joys," *fr.* II, i. CEP
(Song.) OBEC
(Youth's the Season.) WiR
Beggar's Rhyme. *Unknown.* ChBR; GaP; PCH
("Christmas is coming, the geese are getting fat.") OxNR; SoPo; TiPo (1952 ed.)
Beggar's Serenade. John Heath-Stubbs. ErPo; NeBP
Begging. Henry Vaughan. AnAnS-1; MeP
Begging Another, on Colour of Mending the Former. Ben Jonson. *Fr.* A Celebration of Charis. AnAnS-2; LO; OAEP; PoEL-2; SCEP-2; SeCP; TuPP
(Begging Another Kiss.) StP
(For Love's Sake.) UnTE
(Kiss, The.) AtBAP
Begin Again. "Susan Coolidge." MaRV; SoP
Begin again. There is no law which says. Five Epigrams, 1. Donald Hall. NePoAm-2
Begin before birth with swept-back fins. The Matin Pandemoniums. Richard Eberhart. NYBP
Begin Summer. Ingrid Jonker, *tr. fr. Afrikaans by* Jack Cope *and* Uys Krige. PeSA
Begin the Day With God. Horatius Bonar. FaChP
(Begin with God.) SoP
Begin the Day with God ("Every morning lean thine arms awhile"). *Unknown.* MaRV; SoP; TRV
Begin the day with God. Rules for Daily Life. *Unknown.* SoP; STF
Begin to charme, and as thou stroak'st mine eares. To Musick. Robert Herrick. MuSP
Begin unto my God with timbrels. "... With Timbrels." Judith, Bible, Apocrypha. TrJP
Begin with God. Horatius Bonar. *See* Begin the Day with God.
Beginner, The. Kipling. *Fr.* Epitaphs of the War. FaBoTw
Beginner,/ Perpetual beginner. What Can I Tell My Bones? Theodore Roethke. AmPP (5th ed.)
Beginners. Walt Whitman. AA
Beginning, The. Wallace Stevens. TPM
Beginning. James Wright. FRC
Beginning and the End, The. *Unknown,* *tr. fr. Icelandic by* Henry Adams Bellows. *Fr.* The Elder Edda. LiTW, *abr.*
(Voluspo.) AWP

Beginning in half darkness. The Morning Track. Edward Parone. NYBP
Beginning My Studies. Walt Whitman. CBEP; OxBA
Beginning of a Long Poem on Why I Burned the City, The. Lawrence Benford. NBP; TTY
Beginning of an Undergraduate Poem. *Unknown.* SiTL
Beginning of eternity, the end of time and space, The. Rhyming Riddle. *Unknown.* TreFT
Beginning of fall, The. The End of Summer. Basho. RePo
Beginning of Heliodorus, The. Richard Crashaw. MaMe
Beginning of Love, The. Keats. *Fr.* Isabella; or, The Pot of Basil. UnPo (1st ed.)
Beginning to dangle beneath. In the Marble Quarry. James Dickey. AmFN; NoP
Beginning to Squall. May Swenson. NYTB
Beginnings of Civilization. Lucretius, *tr. fr. Latin by* William Ellery Leonard. *Fr.* De Rerum Natura (Of the Nature of Things). OuHeWo
Beginnings of Faith, The. Sir Lewis Morris. WGRP
Beg-Innish. J. M. Synge. MoBrPo; NeMA; OnYI; OxBI
Begon thou fatall fyery feaver. *Unknown.* SeCSL
"Begone, thou fond presumptuous Elf." The Waterfall and the Eglantine. Wordsworth. OTPC
Begone, you, sir. Here, shepherd, call your dog. The Shepherd Dog of the Pyrenees. Ellen Murray. PoRL
Begotten by the meeting of rock with rock. Sea Holly. Conrad Aiken. AP; LiTM; MAPA; NePA
Begracde with glory, gloried with grace. Meditation. Edward Taylor. *Fr.* Preparatory Meditations, First Series. MeP
Behave Yoursel' before Folk. Alexander Rodger. BOHV; HBV
Behaviour of Money. Bernard Spencer. LiTB
Behind Devaney's barn I saw. A Little Pig Asleep. Leroy F. Jackson. BrR
Behind him lay the gray [*or* great] Azores. Columbus [*or* Sail On!]. Joaquin Miller. AA; AmePo; AmPP (3d ed.); BBV; BeLS; DD; FaBoBe; FaFP; FaPON; GN; HBV; HBVY; MC; MCCG; MPB; NeHB; NeMA; OHFP; OnSP; OQP; OTPC (1946 ed.); PaA; PAH; PAL; PaPo; PCD; PEDC; PFY; PGD; PoPo; PoRL; PTK; SoP; StaSt; StVeCh; ThLM; TIHL; TiPo (1952 ed.); TreF; TSW; WaKn; YaD; YeAr; YT
Behind him the hotdogs split and drizzled. Suicide off Egg Rock. Sylvia Plath. NMP
Behind me dips eternity. Emily Dickinson. AP; WoL
Behind me lies the mistress of the East. The Pilgrim. Eleanor Downing. JKCP
Behind me the house was asleep. Happening. Edwin Honig. NePA
Behind our house there is a mere. The White Drake. *Unknown.* WHW
Behind shut doors, in shadowy quarantine. The First Time. Karl Shapiro. ErPo
Behind that white brow. To a Dead Journalist. William Carlos Williams. QFR
Behind the black watertower. Christmas Eve. Bill Berkson. ANYP
Behind the board fence at the banker's house. The Last Antelope. Edwin Ford Piper. PoMa
Behind the Closed Eye. Francis Ledwidge. MCCG
Behind the Door. Bert Leston Taylor. LHV
Behind the granite church. Fugue. Constance Carrier. GoYe
Behind the hilltop drops the sun. Evening Songs, IV. John Vance Cheney. AA
Behind the house is the millet plot. Melilot. Muna Lee. NP
Behind the house the upland falls. After the Pleasure Party. Herman Melville. AP
Behind the Line. Edmund Blunden. ChMP
Behind the Log, *sel.* E. J. Pratt.
"There is a language in a naval log." MoCV
"Whatever doubt the eye might have imposed." TwCaPo
Behind the Looking Glass. Daniel Carter Beard. OTD
Behind the mountain ledge. Looking at the Moon on Putting out from the Shore at Nagato. *Unknown.* FlW
Behind the Plough. James H. Cousins. OxBI
Behind the Power Station on 14th, the held breath. Galway Kinnell. *Fr.* The Avenue Bearing the Initial of Christ into the New World. NaP
Behind the tree, behind the house, behind the stars. Seen in a Glass. Kathleen Raine. ChMP
Behind the wall of St. John's in the city. The Garden at St. John's. May Swenson. NePoEA; PoPl
Behind the Waterfall. Winifred Welles. PoMS; StVeCh; TiPo
Behind the Wheel. Michael Brownstein. ANYP
Behind the wild-bird's throat. Wood-Thrush. John Hall Wheelock. NePoAm; PoDB
Behind thee leave thy merchandise. God Hide the Whole World in Thy Heart. Emerson. *Fr.* Woodnotes, I. OQP
Behind thy pasteboard, on thy battered hack. Don Quixote. Austin Dobson. HBV; HBVY
Behind yon hills where Lugar flows. My Nanie, O [*or* Song: Nanie, O]. Burns. EnLi-2
Behold a critic, pitched like the *castrati.* Pipling. Theodore Roethke. NePA; SiTL
Behold! a giant am I! The Windmill. Longfellow. MoShBr
Behold a hag whom life denies a kiss. Opportunity. Madison Cawein. AA
Behold! a new white world! A New Year. Dora Sigerson Shorter. YeAr
Behold a silly [*or* helpless *or* little] tender babe. New Prince, New Pomp [*or* Humble Pomp *or* In Freezing Winter Night]. Robert Southwell. AnAnS-1; EG; ELP; EP; FlW; GN; GoTP; MaRV; MeP; OBSC; OHIP; ReIE; SiCE; StJW; ThWaDe; TuPP
Behold, a stranger's at the door! Christ at the Door. Joseph Grigg. BePJ; SoP
Behold a virgin shall conceive, and bear a son. The Messiah. Isaiah, Bible, *O.T.* AWP
Behold a woman! The Justified Mother of Men. Walt Whitman. *Fr.* Faces. OHIP
Behold a Wonder Here! *Unknown.* ALV; OBSC; TrGrPo
"Behold another singer!" Criton said. "Song, to the Gods, Is Sweetest Sacrifice." Annie Fields. AA
Behold, bless ye the Lord. Psalm CXXXIV, Bible, *O.T.* TRV
Behold, four Kings in majesty rever'd. The Playing Cards. Pope. *Fr.* The Rape of the Lock. ChTr
Behold from sluggish winter's arm. Primo Vere. Giosuè Carducci. AWP; JAWP; WBP
Behold, from the land of the farther suns. The Black Riders, XXIX. Stephen Crane. AP
Behold, God is great, and we know him not. Job, Bible, *O.T.* ImOP
Behold great Neptunes risen from the deep. *At. to* Henry Hughes. SeCSL
Behold her Seven Hills loom white. Resurge San Francisco. Joaquin Miller. PAH
Behold her, single in the field. The Solitary Reaper [*or* The Reaper]. Wordsworth. AnEnPo; AnFE; AtBAP; ATP; AWP; BEL; BoLiVe; BoPe; BWP; CABA; CaFP; CBEP; CBV; CH; ChER; CoBE; DiPo; EG; EnL; EnLi-2; EnLit; EnRP; EPN; ERoP-1; ExPo; FaBoCh; FaBoEn; FiP; ForPo; GBV; GN; GTBS; GTBS-D; GTBS-P; GTBS-W; GTSE; GTSL; HBV; HoPM; ILP; InP; InPo; JAWP; LiTB; LiTG; LiTL; LoBV; MaPo; MBW-2; MCCG; MERP; NoP; OAEP; OBEV; OBNC; OBRV; OnPP; OTPC; OuHeWo; PAn; PCD; PoAn; PoE; PoEL-4; PoeP; PoFS; PoIE; PoRA; PoSa; PTK; RG; RoGo; SeCeV; ShBV-3; StP; TDP; ThWaDe; TOP; TreF;
Behold Him now as He comes! The Real Christ. Richard Watson Gilder. *Fr.* The Passing of Christ. ChIP; MaRV; OQP
Behold him, priests, and though he stink of sweat. George Gascoigne. *Fr.* The Steel Glass. ReEn
Behold, how good and how pleasant it is for brethren to dwell in unity! To Dwell Together in Unity. Psalm CXXXIII, Bible, *O.T.* AWP; JAWP; OnPM; TreFT; TrJP; TRV
Behold, I Come! Annie Johnson Flint. SoP
Behold, I gathered mine offenses. The Caravan. Hovhannes Blouz. CAW
Behold I see the haven nigh at hand. Spenser. *Fr.* The Faerie Queene, I. FosPo
Behold in swaddling clothes a Child. A Christmas Hymn. Harry Baker. SoP
Behold! in various throngs the scribbling crew. Byron. *Fr.* English Bards and Scotch Reviewers. EnRP; ERoP-2
Behold, love, thy power how she despiseth! Sir Thomas Wyatt. FCP
Behold me waiting—waiting for the knife. Before. W. E. Henley. In Hospital, IV. BEL; EnLi-2; MoBrPo; OuHeWo; PoVP
Behold, My Cross Was Gone! Alice Mortenson. BePJ

Behold, my fair, where'er we rove. The Winter's Walk. Samuel Johnson. CBEP; EiCP
Behold, My Servant. Isaiah, LII: 13-LIII: 9, Bible, *O.T.* OuHeWo
Behold, O Aspasia! I Send You Verses. Walter Savage Landor. *Fr.* Pericles and Aspasia. LoBV; OBNC
Behold, O Man. Spenser. *Fr.* The Faerie Queene, II, 6. EIL
Behold, O noble Lady, O Mother piteous. Prayer to Santa Maria del Vade. Juan Ruiz, Archpriest of Hita. CAW
Behold, O world, the toiling man. Edwin Markham. *Fr.* The Toiler. PGD
Behold, of dreams the best will I tell. The Dream of the Rood. *Unknown.* CAW
Behold once more with serious labor here. To the Reader. Samuel Daniel. OBSC; PP; SiCE
Behold, One of Several Little Christs. Kenneth Patchen. NaP
Behold our first great warrior of the sea. John Paul Jones. Richard Watson Gilder. PoRL
Behold Pelides with his yellow hair. Before a Statue of Achilles. George Santayana. HBV
Behold, slow-settling o'er the lurid grove. The Storm. James Thomson. *Fr.* The Seasons: Summer. LoBV
Behold that which I have seen. Enjoy the Good. Ecclesiastes, Bible, *O.T.* TreFT
Behold the apples' rounded worlds. Apples [*or* Autumn Apples]. Laurie Lee. BoC; POTi; WePo
Behold the birds. God Provides. St. Matthew, Bible, *N.T.* BLRP
Behold the blind their sight receive. The Divine. Isaac Watts. SoP
Behold the brand of beauty tossed! The Dancer. Edmund Waller. PoFS; TrGrPo
Behold the cot! where thrives th' industrious swain. George Crabbe. *Fr.* The Parish Register, I. OBRV
Behold the Deeds! H. C. Bunner. ALV; BOHV; HBV; InMe; LHV
Behold the duck. The Duck. Ogden Nash. MoShBr; WhC
Behold the fatal day arrive! Swift. *Fr.* Verses on the Death of Dr. Swift. ViBoPo
Behold, the Fields Are White, *sel.* Samuel Longfellow.
"Where prophets' word, and martyrs' blood." FaChP
Behold, the grave of a wicked man. Why? Stephen Crane. The Black Riders XXV. AA
Behold the hippopotamus! The Hippopotamus. Ogden Nash. FaBV
Behold the Lilies of the Field. Anthony Hecht. CoPo; NePoEA-2; PoIE (1970 ed.)
Behold the Man! *Unknown.* STF
Behold the man alive in me. Ecce Homo. Witter Bynner. WGRP
Behold the mansion reared by Daedal Jack! The Domicile of John. *Unknown. Sometimes at. to* Pope. InMe
Behold the Meads. Guillaume de Poitiers, *tr. fr. French by* Harriet Waters Preston. AWP; OuHeWo
Behold the mighty dinosaur. The Dinosaur. Bert Leston Taylor. ImOP; LHV; PoMa
Behold! the mother bird. The Assumption. John Banister Tabb. ISi
Behold the portal: open wide it stands. The Garden Where There Is No Winter. Louis James Block. AA
Behold the ravens on the trees. Contentment. Benjamin Schlipf. BLRP
Behold the reed of scorn. Two Easter Lilies. John Banister Tabb. StJW
Behold the rocky wall. The Two Streams. Oliver Wendell Holmes. AP
Behold, the rosy dawn. The Nymphs' Song. Michael Drayton. *Fr.* The Muses' Elysium. SeCL
Behold the Saviour of mankind. The Saviour. Samuel Wesley. BePJ
Behold the Sea, *sel.* Aaron Kurtz.
They Got You Last Night. PPON
Behold the wicked little barb. The Question Mark. Persis Greely Anderson. PoMa; WhC
Behold the wonders of the mighty deep. The Sea. *Unknown.* NA
Behold the works of William Morris. Rondel. *Unknown.* Par
Behold these woods, and mark, my sweet. A Pastoral Courtship. Earl of Rochester. UnTE
Behold This Dreamer. Elizabeth Bartlett. NePoAm-2
Behold this fleeting world, how all things fade. An Epitaph of the Death of Nicholas Grimald. Barnabe Googe. EnRePo; ReIE; SiCE; TuPP
Behold this little bane. Emily Dickinson. AmePo
Behold this needle: when the Arctic stone. On the Needle of a Sundial [*or* A Compass Needle.]. Francis Quarles. CBEP; OBS; TrGrPo
Behold this ruin! 'Twas a skull. To a Skeleton. *Unknown.* BLPA
Behold, Thou Art Fair. The Song of Solomon, Bible, *O.T.* MeWo; TrJP; WoL
Behold through the veil of distance a pleasing image. Jonathan. "Rachel." TrJP
Behold thy darling, which thy lustfull care. Francis Quarles. *Fr.* Emblems. AnAnS-1; MeP
Behold upon the swelling seas. A-Cruising We Will Go. *Unknown.* AmSS
Behold, we go up to Jerusalem again. Lent. Miriam LeFevre Crouse. ChIP
Behold, we have gathered together our battleships, near and afar. "Mene, Mene, Tekel, Upharsin." Madison Cawein. PAH
Behold, we stand at many doors and knock. The Untried Door. Edward Shillito. ChIP
Behold what furies still. Chorus. Samuel Daniel. *Fr.* Cleopatra. LoBV
Behold what homage to his idol paid. With Petrarch's Sonnets. Walter Savage Landor. InP
Behold where on the Aegean shore a city stands. Vision of Athens. Milton. *Fr.* Paradise Regained, IV. TOP
Behold within our Hayden Planetarium. Ode to the Hayden Planetarium. Arthur Guiterman. ImPO
Behold, within the leafy shade. The Sparrow's Nest. Wordsworth. EnRP
Behold yon hill, how it is swell'd with pride. Describes the Place where Cynthia Is Sporting Herself. Girolamo Petri. EnLoPo
Behold yon mountain's hoary height. To Thaliarchus [*or* Ode to Thaliarchus]. Horace. Odes, I, 9. AWP; CavP; JAWP; LiTW; MBW-1; PeRV; WBP
Behold yon new-born infant, griev'd. The Ignorance of Man. James Merrick. OxBoCh
Behold you not this globe, this golden bowl. Thomas Dekker. *Fr.* Old Fortunatus. ViBoPo
Behold Your King! Frances Ridley Havergal. BePJ; SoP
Beholde me, I pray thee, with all thine whole reson. Wofully Araide. *Unknown.* MeEL
Beholde the father, is his daughters sonne. The Nativitie of Christ. Robert Southwell. MeP
Beholders, The. James Dickey. AP
Beholding element, in whose pure eye. The Aspen and the Stream. Richard Wilbur. NYBP
Beholding youth and hope in mockery caught. The Sun's Shame, 1. Dante Gabriel Rossetti. The House of Life, XCII. MaVP; PoVP; ViPo
Bei Hennef. D. H. Lawrence. BrPo
Being, The. James Dickey. NMP
Being. Jacob Glatstein, *tr. fr. Yiddish by Jacob Sloan. Fr.* The Bratzlav Rabbi to His Scribe. LiTW
Being a Christian. *Unknown.* STF
Being a Gypsy. Barbara Young. *See* Being Gypsy.
Being a woman, I am/ not more than man nor less. The Wife Speaks. Mary Stanley. AnNZ
Being and Wind. Gregory Orr. QAH
Being at last on our way. Departure. William Hart-Smith. *Fr.* Christopher Columbus. PoAu-2
Being born the lowest of the low. Satirical Poems on Daimyos, IV. Issa. PoFr
Being cleaves the moonlit air, A. Hans Christian Andersen. Sir Edmund Gosse. VA
Being Forsaken of His friend He Complaineth. "E. S." EIL ("Why should I longer long to live."). SiCE
Being Gypsy. Barbara Young. SoPo; TiPo (Being a Gypsy.) BrR
Being Her Friend. John Masefield. GTSL
Being his resting place. A Dog Sleeping on my Feet. James Dickey. PP
Being homeward bound on the mighty deep. Lady Franklin's Lament, *vers.* I. *Unknown.* ShS
Being Importunate, at the Length He Obtaineth. Richard Edwards. TuPP
Being in thought of love, I chanced to see. Ballata: He Reveals

His Increasing Love for Mandetta. Guido Cavalcanti, *tr. by* Dante Gabriel Rossetti. AWP
Being myself captived [*or* captyved] here in care. Amoretti, LXXIII. Spenser. CoBE; LoBV
Being newly-married before all the world. *Unknown.* HW
Being now completely wet through to the skin. Wet Through. Hal Summers. HaMV
Being now three or four years more than sixty. The World's Wonders. Robinson Jeffers. NePA; PoDB
Being one day at my window all alone. The Visions. Petrarch, *tr. by* Spenser. *Fr.* Sonnets to Laura: Songs. AWP; EnLi-1; JAWP; WBP
Being out of heart with government. An Appointment. W. B. Yeats. AnEnPo; PoFr
Being Scorned, and Disdained, He Inveighs against His Lady. *Unknown. See* Since Just Disdain.
Being set, let's sport a while, my fair. Thomas Randolph. *Fr.* A Pastoral Courtship. ViBoPo
Being set on the idea. Atlantis. W. H. Auden. FaBoTw; PoPl
Being Sick. Jimmy Garthwaite. BrR
Being slowly lifted up, thou long black arm. On Seeing a Piece of Our Artillery Brought into Action. Wilfred Owen. LiTM (1946 ed.)
Being so tired, it is hard to hide from you. A Man Walks in the Wind. Maurice Lesemann. AnAmPo; LiTL
Being suspicious of great happiness. Being Unused to Joyous Consciousness. Delmore Schwartz. FiMAP
Being to Timelessness as It's to Time. E. E. Cummings. NePA
Being Twins. Kathryn Jackson. BiCB
Being Underived. Dante, *tr. by* Longfellow. *Fr.* Divina Commedia: Paradiso. CAW
Being Unused to Joyous Consciousness. Delmore Schwartz. FiMAP
Being with you. Margaret Atwood. *Fr.* The Circle Game. MoCV
Being without quality. Vox Humana. Thom Gunn. NePoEA-2
Being your slave, what should I do but tend. Sonnets, LVII. Shakespeare. BoLP; CLwM; EG; GTBS; GTBS-D; GTBS-P; GTBS-W; GTSE; GTSL; LiTL; OBEV; PoEL-2; ViBoPo; WoL
Beinn Naomh, *sel.* Kathleen Raine.
Summit, The, IV. OxBS
Bel m'es quan lo vens m'alena. Arnaut Daniel, *tr. fr. Provençal by* Harriet Waters Preston. AWP; JAWP; LiTW; WBP
Belagcholly Days. *Unknown.* BOHV; StaSt
Belated Violet, A. Oliver Herford. AA
Belden Hollow. Leslie Nelson Jennings. GoYe
Beleaguered Cities. F. L. Lucas. HaMV; POTE
Beleaguered City, The. Longfellow. MWA-1
Belfast; High Street. Padraic Colum. NePoAm
Belfry, The. Laurence Binyon. CH
Belfry, The. R. S. Thomas. BoPe
Belfry of Bruges, The. Longfellow. HBV; HT
Sel.
Carillon. CoBA
Belgravia. Barbara Guest. AmPC
Belief. Ruth Fitch Bartlett. InMe
Belief. Josephine Miles. CBV; FiMAP
Belief and Unbelief. Robert Browning. *Fr.* Bishop Blougram's Apology. FaBV
Belief and Unbelief. Philip Freneau. AmePo
Belief in Plan of Thee. Walt Whitman. TRV
Believe! And if, while standing under a shower. To My Children. Marion Strobel. NP
Believe and Take Heart. John Lancaster Spalding. AA; JKCP
Believe as I believe, no more, no less. The Over-Confident Man. *Unknown.* SoP
"Believe in me," the Prophet cried. Infallibility. Thomas Stephens Collier. AA
Believe Me, Dearest Susan, *with music. Unknown.* SoAmSa
Believe me, I say to the gentleman with the pince-nez. In the Library. Elizabeth Brewster. OBCV
Believe me, I understand your refusal. Letter to Pasternak. Ralph Pomeroy. CoPo
Believe Me, if All Those Endearing Young Charms. Thomas Moore. AnFE; BEL; BLPA; CBEP; ELP; EnLi-2 (1949 ed.); EnLit; EnRP; FaBoBe; FaBV; FaFP; GTBS-W; HBV; InP; LiTB; LiTG; LiTL; MCCG; NeHB; OBNC; OBRV; OnYI; PoEL-4; PoPl; PTK; SiTL; TreF; WBLP; YAT
Believe me, knot of gristle, I bleed like a tree. Give Way, Ye Gates. Theodore Roethke. FiMAP; NMP; OPoP
Believe me, Love, this vagrant life. To Cordelia. Joseph Stansbury. CaP
Believe Not. Isaac Leibush Peretz, *tr. fr. Yiddish by* Solomon Liptzin. TrJP
Believe Not Him. *Unknown.* SeCL
Believe not that the world is for naught, made. Believe Not. Isaac Leibush Peretz. TrJP
Believe the Bible. A. B. Simpson. *See* It Means Just What It Says.
"Believe Ye That I Am Able to Do This?" Dawn Finlay. SoP
Believer he and unbeliever both. Epitaph. Robert Francis. PoIE
Belinda has such wond'rous charms. Belinda the Charitable. *Unknown.* MeWo
Belinda lived in a little white house. The Tale of Custard the Dragon. Ogden Nash. FaPON; GoTP; PoPl; PoRA; ShBV-1; TiPo (1959 ed.); WePo
Belinda the Charitable. *Unknown.* MeWo
Belinda's Morning. Pope. *See* Toilet, The.
Belinda's Recovery from Sickness. William Broome. OBEV (1st ed.)
Belinda's Window. Margaret Widdemer. PEDC
Belisarius. Longfellow. PoEL-5; WiR
Beliza shade your shining eyes. *Unknown.* SeCSL
Bell, A. Clinton Scollard. AA
Bell-Birds. Henry C. Kendall. BoAu; PoAu-1
Bell-Bottom [*or* Bottomed] Trousers. *Unknown.* AmSS; UnTE
Bellbuoy. Sol Funaroff. WOW
Bell Buoy. W. S. Merwin. OPoP
Bell doth tolle, The. The Knell. George Herbert. MaMe
Bell-Founder, The, *sel.* Denis Florence MacCarthy.
Labor Song. DD
Bell horses, bell horses,/ What time of day? A London Clock [*or* What Time of Day?]. Mother Goose. BoTP; OxNR; PCH; SiSoSe; TiPo
Bell in the convent tower hung, The. The Book of Hours of Sister Clotilde. Amy Lowell. APA
Bell-Man. *See* Bellman.
Bell, my silver tonguéd bell. Theme. Carl Spitteler. PoPl
Bell of the Hermitage, The. *Unknown, tr. fr. Old Irish.* CAW
Bell-rope that gathers God at dawn, The. The Broken Tower. Hart Crane. AmP; AmPP (5th ed.); AP; CMoP; CoBMV; GTBS-W; LiTM (1970 ed.); MoAB; MoAmPo (1962 ed.); MoPo; MoVE; NoP; OxBA; Po; PoIE; SyP; TrGrPo (rev. ed.); VaPo
Bell Speech. Richard Wilbur. AP; CABA; MoAB; MoAmPo (1962 ed.); MoVE
Bell that tolls my syllables can tell, The. S.S. *City of Benares.* G. S. Fraser. NeBP; OnHM
Bell Tower. Léonie Adams. AmLP; AnAmPo; MAP; MoAB; MoAmPo; PoPl
Bella was young and Bella was fair. Unhappy Bella. *Unknown.* ErPo
Belle, *with music. Unknown.* OuSiCo
Belle-de-nuit. Ignace Nau, *tr. fr. French by* Edna Worthley Underwood. PoNe
Belle Isis; Ballad of a Rose. Sacheverell Sitwell. Rosario d'Arabeschi; Poems and Rose Portraits, I. POTE (1959 ed.)
Belle of the Balkans, The. Newman Levy. ALV; FiBHP
Belle of the Ball-Room, The. Winthrop Mackworth Praed. Every-Day Characters, III. ALV; EnRP; HBV; InMe; ViBoPo, 2 *sts.*
(Belle of the Ball, The.) BOHV
Belle Saison, La. Jacques Prévert, *tr. fr. French by* Lawrence Ferlinghetti. CAD
Bellerophon, *sel.* Euripides, *tr. fr. Greek by* John Addington Symonds.
There Are No Gods. EaLo
Belles of the eighties were soft, The. Reflections Outside of a Gymnasium. Phyllis McGinley. SD
Bellies bitter with drinking. Final Chorus. Archibald MacLeish. *Fr.* Panic. MAP; MoAmPo
Bellman, The. Robert Herrick. CBEP; CH; OBS; PCD; PoeP
Bellman of Night, if I about shall go. Cock-Crow. Robert Herrick. MyFE
Bellman's Good-Morrow, The. *Unknown.* PoLi

Bellman's Song, The. *Unknown.* DiPo; EIL; SeCePo
Bellow of good Master Bull, The. Ballade un Peu Banale. A. J. M. Smith. MoCV; SiTL
Bells, The. Antonio Fogazzaro, *tr. fr. Italian.* CAW
Bells, The. Poe. AA; AmePo; AmPP (3d ed.); BBV; CoBA; FaFP; FaPL; GN; HBV; LiTA; NeHB; NePA; OHFP; OTPC; PCD; PCH, *st.* 1; PG (1945 ed.); PoLF; PoPo; PTK; ShBV-1; TreF; WBLP
Sels.
"Hear the mellow wedding bells." PoPl
"Hear the sledges with the bells." FaPON
Bells. Duncan Campbell Scott. CaP
Bells, The. *Unknown.* BOHV; FiBHP
Bells, The. William Young. *Fr.* Wishmakers' Town. AA
Bells across the Snow. Frances Ridley Havergal. SoP
Bells are booming down the bohreens. Ireland with Emily. John Betjeman. GTBS-P
Bells are tolling, The. Tolling Bells. Lady Kasa. OnPM
Bells assault the maiden air, The. Ou Phrontis. Charles Causley. AtBAP; NePoEA
Bells at Midnight, The. Thomas Bailey Aldrich. PAH
Bells chime clear, The. The Christening. Walter de la Mare. BiCB
Bell's Dream, *abr.* Frederic Edward Weatherly. OTPC
Bells for John Whiteside's [Whitesides, *wr.*] Daughter. John Crowe Ransom. AmLP; AmP; AmPP; AnFE; AP; CaFP; CBV; CMoP; CoAnAm; CoBMV; CrMA; DTC; FosPo; GTBS-D; ILP; InP; InPo; LiTA; LiTM (rev. ed.); MAP; MoAB; MoAmPo; MoVE; NePA; NoP; NP; OxBA; PIA; PoAn; PoIE; PoPo; PPON; ReMP; StP; TDP; TreFT; TwAmPo; UnPo (3d ed.); VaPo
Bells for William Wordsworth. Dom Moraes. BoPe; ML
Bells have wide mouths and tongues, but are too weak. Upon a Ring of Bells. Bunyan. CH
Bells in the Country. Robert Nathan. HBMV; OTPC (1946 ed.); PCH; TSW
Bells in the Rain. Elinor Wylie. YT
Bells of Heaven, The. Ralph Hodgson. BoTP; BrPo; EaLo; GoJo; GTBS-W; LiTM; MemP; MoAB; MoBrPo; OBEV (new ed.); OtMeF; PoIE; PoSa; PPON; ShBV-1; SiSoSe; SP; TreFT; UTS
Bells of London, The. *Unknown.* BoTP; EvOK; HBV; HBVY; PCH; PoRA; SiTL
("Gay go up and gay go down.") OTPC; OxNR; PPL
(London Bells.) ChTr; LiTB; LiTG; OxBoLi
Bells of Lynn, The. Longfellow. AA
Bells of New Year. Arthur Gordon Field. PGD
Bells of Oria, The. The Bells. Antonio Fogazzaro. CAW
Bells of Osenèy, The. Chanson of the Bells of Osenèy. Cale Young Rice. AnFE; APA; CoAnAm; HBV
Bells of Ostend, The. William Lisle Bowles. *See* Sonnet: At Ostend, July 22, 1787.
Bells of Peace, The. Aileen Fisher. SiSoSe
Bells of Ste. Anne des Monts, The. Leo Cox. CaP
Bells of San Blas, The. Longfellow. AmP; AmPP (3d ed.); OxBA
Bells of San Gabriel, The. Charles Warren Stoddard. CAW; JKCP
Bells of Shandon, The. Francis Sylvester Mahony. ACP; AnIV; CAW; CH; ChTr; GoBC; HBV; HT; IrPN; OBEV; OBRV; OBVV; RoGo; TreFS; UnPo
(Shandon Bells, The.) GTBS; OnYI; ShBV-2; VA
Bells of Sunday rang us down, The. Song. John Ciardi. WaP
Bells of the Cherokee Ponies, The. D. A. Levy. WOW
Bells of waiting Advent ring, The. Christmas. John Betjeman. BoC; POTi; WePo
Bells of Youth, The. "Fiona Macleod." BoTP
Bells, Ostend, The. William Lisle Bowles. *See* Sonnet: At Ostend, July 22, 1787.
Bells ring clear as bugle note, The. Christmas Morning. Joaquin Miller. MaRV
Bells their Christmas message send o'er earth, The. Perpetual Christmas. Arthur Gordon Field. PGD
Belly Dancer. Diane Wakoski. YAP
Belonging to Summer. Mildred D. Shacklett. GFA
Belongings, The. Theodore Enslin. CoPo
Belovèd. Elizabeth Barrett Browning. *See* Belovèd, my Belovèd . . .
Beloved, The. May Probyn. GoBC
Beloved, The. Katharine Tynan. HBV
Beloved, do you pity not my doleful case. Lament of the Mangaire Sugach. Andrew Magrath. OnYI
Belovèd friends! More glorious times than ours. To My Friends. Schiller. AWP; LiTW
Belovèd, from the Hour That You Were Born. Corinne Roosevelt Robinson. HBMV
Beloved, gaze in thine own heart. The Two Trees. W. B. Yeats. BrPo; MaPo; POTE
Beloved Head, A. Michael Benedikt. HYE; YAP
Beloved, in the noisy city here. James Russell Lowell. Sonn
Belovèd, It Is Morn. Emily Henrietta Hickey. CAW; GoBC; JKCP; OnYI; VA
(Song: "Belovèd, it is morn.") OBVV
Beloved land is yon land in the east, A. Deirdre's Farewell to Scotland. *Unknown.* OnYI
Beloved, let us love: love is of God. Love Is of God. Horatius Bonar. MaRV; SoP; TRV
Beloved, Let Us Once More Praise the Rain. Conrad Aiken. Preludes for Memnon, VII. LiTA; TwAmPo
Beloved, may your sleep be sound. Lullaby. W. B. Yeats. FaBoTw; OBMV; POTE
Belovèd, my Belovèd, when I think. Sonnets from the Portuguese, XX. Elizabeth Barrett Browning. CoBE; MaRV; OAEP; Sonn TOP; VA; ViPo
Beloved person must I think, The. Ki no Akimine. *Fr.* Kokin Shu. AWP
Beloved, the black swans of my eyes. Birds. Hildegarde Flanner. NP
Beloved, thou hast brought me many flowers. Sonnets from the Portuguese, XLIV. Elizabeth Barrett Browning. ILP; OAEP; OBNC; ViPo
Beloved to the Spouse, The. William Baldwin. *See* Christ. to His Spouse.
Beloved Vagabond, The. W. G. Tinckom-Fernandez. BFP
Below lies one whose name was traced in sand. My Epitaph. David Gray. MaRV; OBVV; VA
Below me trees unnumber'd rise. John Dyer. *Fr.* Grongar Hill. FaBoEn
Below my watchtower window, over the scarecrow-sticked. The Coastguardsman in the Fog. James Schevill. FiMAP
Below the dancing larches freckled. "Adam Drinan." *Fr.* Men of the Rocks. OxBS
Below the down the stranded town. A Cinque Port. John Davidson. BrPo
Below the Heights. Walter Herries Pollock. VA
Below, the river scrambled like a goat. God's Little Mountain. Geoffrey Hill. BoPe; NePoEA
Below the thunders of the upper deep. The Kraken. Tennyson. CABA; CaFP; GTBS-D; MBW-2; OBNC; OBRV; PeER; Po; PoEL-5; PoG; PoVP; SyP; VaPo; ViPP; WiR
Below this music, grave and slow. Receive, Beloved. Virginia Earle. JKCP (1955 ed.)
Belphegor; or, The Marriage of the Devil, *sel.* John Wilson.
Were I to Take Wife. SeCL
Belshazzar had a letter. Emily Dickinson. AmePo; CBEP; MoRP
Belshazzar. Heine, *tr. fr. German..* SoP
Belshazzar's Feast. Daniel, V: 1-31, Bible, *O.T.* TreF
Belsnickel. Arthur Guiterman. BBGG
Ben-Arabie was the Camel. Exile. Virna Sheard. PeCV
Ben Backstay. *Unknown.* AmSS
Ben Battle was a soldier bold. Faithless Nelly [*or* Nellie] Gray. Thomas Hood. BOHV; EnRP; HBV; InMe; InP; NA; ShBV-2; ShM; SiTL; TOP; TreF; TSW; WePo
Ben Bluff. Thomas Hood. BOHV
Ben Bolt. Thomas Dunn English. AA; AmePo; FaBoBe; FaFP; HBV; TreF
Ben Dorain. Duncan Ban MacIntyre. *See* Praise of Ben Dorain, The.
Ben Franklin munched a loaf of bread while walking down the street. Benjamin Franklin. Rosemary Benét *and* Stephen Vincent Benét. FaPON; TiPo
Ben Franklin's Head (1728). Mark Antony DeWolfe Howe. WaKn
Ben Hall was out on the Lachlan side. The Death of Ben Hall. Will H. Ogilvie. PoAu-1
Ben-Hur, *sel.* Lew Wallace.
"Wake not, but hear me, love!" AA
Ben Jonson. Swinburne. Sonnets on English Dramatic Poets (1590-1650), III. BEL; PoVP; Sonn

Ben Jonson Entertains a Man from Stratford. E. A. Robinson. AmPP; APA; ATP; CoAnAm; MAP; MAPA; MoAB; MoAmPo; MoPo; TwAmPo
"You are a friend then, as I make it out," *sel.* InP
Ben Jonson's [*or* Johnsons] Sociable Rules for the Apollo. Ben Jonson, *tr. fr. Latin by* Alexander Brome. SeCV-1; TuPP
Ben Karshook's Wisdom. Robert Browning. PoVP
Ben Milam. William H. Wharton. PAH
Bench, the sewermouth, the hydrant placed, The. Northern Boulevard. Edwin Denby. CrMA
Benches are broken, the grassplots brown and bare, The. South End. Conrad Aiken. CMoP; MoVE; OxBA
Bend as the Bow Bends. Conrad Aiken. CMoP
("Bend as the bow bends, and let fly the shaft.") Sonn
Bend back thy bow, O Archer, till the string. The Archer. A. J. M. Smith. OBCV; PeCV
Bend low again, night of summer stars. Summer Stars. Carl Sandburg. LOW; RePo; YeAr
Bend low, O dusky night. To-Night. Louise Chandler Moulton. AA
Bend now thy body to the common weight. The Breaking. Margaret Steele Anderson. HBV
Bend willow, willow bend down deep. Willow Bend and Weep. Herbert Clark Johnson. PoNe
Bendemeer. Thomas Moore. *See* By Bendemeer's Stream.
Bending back with the horror of it. Soft-Man 3. Ed Sanders. ANYP
Bending sails shall whiten on the sea, The. The Ships. Theodore Maynard. EtS
Bendix. John Updike. NYBP
Beneath a churchyard yew. O Sweet Anne Page [*or* Slender's Ghost]. William Shenstone. EiPP; SeCePo
Beneath a Cool Shade. Aphra Behn. UnTE
Beneath a goblin yew-tree's shade. Immortals in Exile. Arthur Davison Ficke. PFY
Beneath a holm repaired two jolly swains. Corydon and Thyrsis. Vergil. Eclogues, VII. AWP
Beneath a myrtle shade. Song of the Zambra Dance [*or* The Zambra Dance]. Dryden. *Fr.* The Conquest of Granada. AtBAP; CEP; ErPo; MBW-1; OAEP; PoEL-3; SeCV-2; UnTE
Beneath a palm-tree by a clear cool spring. A Lesson of Mercy. George Murray. VA
Beneath a withered bush the serpent waits. The Serpent Waits. Joseph Payne Brennan. FiSC
Beneath an Indian palm a girl. The Palm-Tree and the Pine. Richard Monckton Milnes. HBV
Beneath him with new wonder now he views. The Garden. Milton. *Fr.* Paradise Lost, IV. MaPo (1969 ed.)
Beneath its morning caul, this ravaged land. Dakota Badlands. Elizabeth Landeweer. AmFN
Beneath my palm trees, by the river side. Keats. *Fr.* Endymion, IV. ViBoPo
Beneath my window in a city street. The Steam Shovel. Eunice Tietjens. NP
Beneath our consecrated elm. New-come Chief. James Russell Lowell. *Fr.* Under the Old Elm, III. MC
Beneath our feet and o'er our head. The Holy Field. Henry Hart Milman. OxBoCh
Beneath our feet, the shuddering bogs. On Yes Tor. Sir Edmund Gosse. CH
Beneath Such Rains. James E. Warren, Jr. ChIP
Beneath the barren artifice of red. City Girl. Maxwell Bodenheim. HBMV
Beneath the blistering tropical sun. Wheeler's Brigade at Santiago. Wallace Rice. MC
Beneath the branch of the green may. Medieval Norman Songs, XIII. *Unknown, tr. by* John Addington Symonds. AWP; JAWP; WBP
Beneath the branches of the olive yard. Etruscan Tombs. Agnes Mary Frances Robinson. WHA
Beneath the brown, lustrous haze. Reflection. Margaret Allonby. BoSA
Beneath the burning brazen sky. The Ute Lover. Hamlin Garland. AA; PFY
Beneath the Cross. Elizabeth Cecilia Clephane. MaRV
Beneath the curious gaze of all the dead. The Gown. Mary Carolyn Davies. HBMV
Beneath the Cypress Shade. Thomas Love Peacock. *See* Grave of Love, The.
Beneath the deep my broken timbers lie. The Spirit of the *Bluenose.* Claire Harris MacIntosh. CaP
Beneath the Flag. *Unknown.* HH
Beneath the flat and paper sky. Clowns' Houses. Edith Sitwell. SyP
Beneath the Forms of Outward Rite. James A. Blaisdell. MaRV
Beneath the fourteen pointed arches. Cataclysm. N. H. Brettell. BoSA
Beneath the golden cope of dawn. The Shepherd of Meriador. Wilfred Rowland Childe. HBMV
Beneath the loveliest dream there coils a fear. A Dream. Theodore Watts-Dunton. Sonn
Beneath the low-hung night cloud. The *Three Bells.* Whittier. EtS
Beneath the Malebolge lies Hastings Street. Christ Walks in This Infernal District Too. Malcolm Lowry. MoCV
Beneath the Memnonian shadows of Memphis, it rose from the slime. The Reed. Henry Bernard Carpenter. AA
Beneath the midnight moon of May. The Night Watch. William Winter. AA
Beneath the ocean's sapphire lid. The Gardens of the Sea. George Sterling. EtS
Beneath the sagging roof. Ezra Pound. *Fr.* Hugh Selwyn Mauberley. MoAmPo (1962 ed.); PoIE
Beneath the sand-storm John the Pilgrim prays. John the Pilgrim. Theodore Watts-Dunton. MaRV
Beneath the shaded calm of his cottage now. Evening Fantasy. Friedrich Hölderlin. LiTW
Beneath the shadow of dawn's aerial cope. Hope and Fear. Swinburne. FaBoBe; HBV; PoVP; VA
Beneath the silent chambers of the earth. Hell. Abraham Cowley. *Fr.* Davideis, I. OxBoCh; SeEP
Beneath the thorn tree's spikey shade. Conceit with Aunties, Urn and Puss. Michael T. Leech. NYTB
Beneath the warrior's helm, behold. On an Intaglio Head of Minerva. Thomas Bailey Aldrich. HBV; InMe
Beneath the Wattle Boughs. Frances Gill. VA
Beneath these alien stars. Pioneer Woman. Vesta Pierce Crawford. PoOW
Beneath these fruit-tree boughs that shed. The Green Linnet. Wordsworth. AtBAP; CBEP; EnRP; EPN; ERoP-1; GTBS; GTBS-D; GTBS-P; GTBS-W; GTSE; GTSL; HBV; OTPC; PeER
Beneath these poppies buried deep. Epitaph on Robert Southey [*or* a Well-known Poet]. Thomas Moore. InMe; PP; SiTL
Beneath these shades, beside yon winding stream. On Visiting the Graves of Hawthorne and Thoreau. Jones Very. AP
Beneath these stones repose the bones. On an Old Toper Buried in Durham Churchyard, England. *Unknown.* ShM
Beneath these sun-warm'd pines among the heather. A South Coast Idyll. Rosamund Marriott Watson. OBVV
Beneath this narrow jostling street. Fleet Street. Arthur Adams. BoAu
Beneath this plain pine board is lying. Joshua Hight. *Unknown.* ShM
Beneath this silent stone is laid. Epitaph on a Talkative Old Maid. Benjamin Franklin. WhC
Beneath this slab. Lather as You Go. Ogden Nash. WePo
Beneath this starry arch. On, On, Forever. Harriet Martineau. VA
Beneath this stone, a lump of clay. Epitaphs. *Unknown.* SiTL
Beneath this stone lies one good man; and when. An Epitaph. W. H. Davies. ChMP
Beneath this stone lies the body of Hengist. Hengest Cyning. Jorge Luis Borges. NYBP
Beneath this stone our baby lies. *Unknown.* WhC
Beneath this stone, reader, there lieth flat. Epitaph on Mr. John Sprat, Late Steward of Grayes-Inn. Alexander Radcliffe. PeRV
Beneath this stony roof reclined. Inscription in a Hermitage. Thomas Warton, the Younger. HBV
Beneath this tent, clutching this glass of beer. Blues for an Old Blue. Walker Gibson. NYBP
Beneath thy spell, O radiant summer sea. The Sea's Spell. Susan Marr Spalding. AA; EtS
Beneath Thy Wing. Hayyim Nahman Bialik, *tr. fr. Hebrew by* Helena Frank. TrJP
Beneath Time's roaring cannon. When the Mississippi Flowed in Indiana. Vachel Lindsay. Three Poems about Mark Twain, II. CMoP
Beneath yon birch with silver bark. The Ballad of the Dark La-

Beneath (continued)
die. Samuel Taylor Coleridge. EnRP
Beneath yon larkspur's azure bells. The Blue-Bird. Herman Melville. MWA-1
Beneath yon ruined abbey's moss-grown piles. The Solemn Noon of Night. Thomas Warton, the Younger. *Fr.* The Pleasures of Melancholy. OBEC; SeCePo
Beneathe an ancient oake one daye. A Christmas Legend. Oliver Herford. PoMS
Benedetta Barzini. Gerard Malanga. YAP
Benedicite. Anna Callender Brackett. AA
Benedicite, What Dreamed I This Night!. *Unknown.* EnPo; LO; NCEP; PoEL-1
(Dream, A.) OBSC
(What Dreamed I?) CBEP
Benedictine Garden, A. Alice Brown. HBV
Benedictine Ultima, The. *Unknown, tr. fr. Latin.* CAW
Benedictio Domini. Ernest Dowson. CAW; JKCP
Benediction. Numbers, VI: 24-26, Bible, *O.T.*. TrGrPo
(Blessing, A.) ThGo
(Blessing of the Priests.) TrJP
Benediction, The. John Donne. MaMe
Benediction. Frederick Ebright. NYTB
Benediction. Donald Jeffrey Hayes. AmNP; PoNe
Benediction. Georgia Douglas Johnson. GoSl
Benediction. Bob Kaufman. PoNe (1970 ed.); WOW
Benediction. Stanley Kunitz. MoRP
Benediction. Stephen Phillips. *Fr* Herod. MaRV
Benediction. Mark Turbyfill. NP
Benedictus. St. Luke, I: 68-79, Bible, *N.T.* MaRV
Benefit Night at the Opera, A. Martin Bell. MuSP
Benevolence. Mark Akenside. *Fr.* Against Suspicion. OBEC
Benighted on a lone and dreary wild. I Will Guide Thee. W. L. Alexander. SoP
Benjamin. Ogden Nash. NePA; SiTL
Benjamin Franklin [1706-1790]. Rosemary Benét *and* Stephen Vincent Benét. FaPON; TiPo
Bennie's kisses left me cold. Georgie Porgie. Franklin P. Adams. HBMV
Bennington. W. H. Babcock. PAH
Benny Havens, Oh! ——O'Brien. ABF
Bent and heavy with rain. Roadside near Moscow. R. A. D. Ford. PeCV; TwCaPo
Bent double, like old beggars under sacks. Dulce et Decorum Est. Wilfred Owen. AnFE; CBEP; CBV; CMoP; CoBMV; FaBoTw; FaBV; InP; InvP; LiTB; LiTM (rev. ed.); MMA; MoAB; MoBrPo; MoPW; OAEP (2d ed.); PoIE; PPON; ShBV-3; WaP
Bent Sae Brown, The *Unknown.* ESPB
Bents and Broom, The. *Unknown.* OxBB
Beowulf. *Unknown, tr. fr. Anglo-Saxon.* BEL (*sl. abr., tr. by* Francis B. Gummere); EnL (*pr. tr. by* Chauncey B. Tinker); EnLi-1 (*mod. vers., sl. abr., tr. by* J. Duncan Spaeth); EnLit (*pr. tr. by* Albert C. Baugh); OuHeWo (Prologue *and* I-XXXI, *pr. tr. by* Chauncey B. Tinker); TOP (*pr. tr. by* Chauncey B. Tinker); ViBoPo (Prologue, *tr. by* C. K. Scott-Moncrieff)
Sels.
Beowulf and Wiglaf Slay the Dragon, *tr. by* Charles W. Kennedy. AnOE
Beowulf's Death, *tr. by* Charles W. Kennedy. AnOE
Beowulf's Fight with Grendel, *tr. by* Richard L. Hoffman. YAT
Beowulf's Voyage to Denmark, *tr. by* Michael Alexander. FIW
Defeat of Grendel, The, *tr. by* Richard L. Hoffman. YAT
Feasting and Giving of Treasure in the Hall, The, *tr. by* Richard L. Hoffman. YAT
Fire-Dragon and the Treasure, The, *tr. by* Charles W. Kennedy. AnOE
Funeral Pyre, The, *tr. by* Charles W. Kennedy. AnOE
Lay of Finn, The, *tr. by* Charles W. Kennedy. AnOE
Slaughter of Grendel by Beowulf, The, *tr. by* Charles W. Kennedy. LiTW
Tale of Sigemund, The, *tr. by* Charles W. Kennedy. AnOE
Beowulf. Richard Wilbur. CrMA
Beowulf and Wiglaf Slay the Dragon. *Unknown, tr. fr. Anglo-Saxon by Charles W. Kennedy.* *Fr.* Beowulf. AnOE
Beowulf's Death. *Unknown, tr. fr. Anglo-Saxon by* Charles W. Kennedy. *Fr.* Beowulf. AnOE
Beowulf's Fight with Grendel. *Unknown, tr. fr. Anglo-Saxon by* Richard L. Hoffman. *Fr.* Beowulf. YAT
Beowulf's Voyage to Denmark. *Unknown, tr. fr. Anglo-Saxon by* Michael Alexander. *Fr.* Beowulf. FIW
Beppo. Byron. BEL; CABL; ERoP-2
Italy, *sel.* OBRV SeCePo
Bequest of His Heart, A. Alexander Scott. OBEV
Berceuse Ariettes, *sel.* Alfred Kreymborg.
"Our window is stained." PG (1955 ed.)
Bereaved. Emily Dickinson. *See* If he were living—dare I ask.
Bereaved. James Whitcomb Riley. AA; MaRV
Bereaved Maid, The. *Unknown. See* Falcon, The.
Bereaved of all, I went abroad. Emily Dickinson. MAPA; TwAmPo
Bereaved Swan, The. Stevie Smith. FaBoTw
Bereavement of the Fields. Wilfred Campbell. CaP
Bereft. Robert Frost. AnFE; AtBAP; CoAnAm; FaPL; LiTM; MAP; MoAB; MoAmPo; OxBA; PoDB; TwAmPo
Berg, The. Herman Melville. AmP; AmPP (5th ed.); AP; AtBAP; CBEP; LiTA; MAmP; MWA-1; NoP; PoEL-5; PoFS
Bermuda Suite. Winfield Townley Scott. MiAP
"Flared down from broken cloud the calipered light," V. FiMAP
Bermudas. Andrew Marvell. AnAnS-1; AtBAP; AWP; CABA; CBEP; CEP; CH; ChTr; CoBE; EnL; ExPo; FaBoCh; FaBoEn; GN; HBV; ILP; InPo; LoBV; LoGBV; MaMe; MeP; MePo; NoP; OAEP; OBEV; OBS; PAH; PoE; PoFS; ReEn; SCEP-2; SeCeV; SeCL; SeCP; SeCV-1; SeEP; ThLM; ViBoPo
(Song of the Emigrants in Bermuda.) GTBS; GTBS-D; GTBS-P; GTBS-W; GTSE; GTSL; OTPC (1923 ed.); OxBoCh; ShBV-3
Bernál Díaz's Preface to His Book. Archibald MacLeish. *Fr.* Conquistador. AmPP (3d ed.)
"We saw that city on the inland sea," *sel.* AtBAP
Bernard reads late, alone; and twilight falls. The Vision of St. Bernard. M. Whitcomb Hess. ISi
Berries. Walter de la Mare. AtBAP; BoChLi; MoBrPo; OnSP; RG; StaSt; TiPo
Berries on the outwash plain. Unaware that Avessek. Colette Inez. QAH
Berry Picking. Irving Layton. MoCV
Berrying. Emerson. AtBAP
Bert Kessler. Edgar Lee Masters. *Fr.* Spoon River Anthology. AnFE; APA; CoAnAm
Bert Schultz. Colin Thiele. PoAu-2
Bertrand and Raton—a monkey and a cat. The Monkey and the Cat. La Fontaine. CIV
Beset Wife, The. Robert Farren. OxBI
Beshrew that heart that makes my heart to groan. Sonnets, CXXXIII. Shakespeare. CBEP; InvP; ReIE
Beside a Baby's Bed. Walter E. Isenhour. SoP
Beside a Balance Wheel. MacKnight Black. NP
Beside a chapel I'd a room looked down. Dread. J. M. Synge. MoBrPo
Beside a dune high as a tree. The Desert. Clifford Dyment. POTi
Beside a green meadow a stream used to flow. The Cow and the Ass. Jane Taylor. BoTP; OTPC (1923 ed.)
Beside a hill there is a still. Good Ol' Mountain Dew. *Unknown.* ABF
Beside a lofty waterfall I've stood. A Waterfall. Hugh McMillan. SoP
Beside a primrose 'broider'd rill. Phyllis Lee. Oliver Herford. BOHV
Beside a runnel build my shed. After Reading in a Letter Proposals for Building a Cottage. John Clare. OBRV
Beside dim wharves, the battered ships are dreaming. Old Ships. Louis Ginsberg. HBMV
Beside he was a shrewd philosopher. Hudibras the Sectarian. Samuel Butler. *Fr.* Hudibras. SeCePo
Beside her ashen heath she sate her down. The Fortunate One. Harriet Monroe. AA
Beside his heavy-shouldered team. Bullocky. Judith Wright. BoAV; MoAuPo; NeLNL; PoAu-2; SeCePo
Beside his wife at Passover in spring. Passover Eve. Fania Kruger. GoYe
Beside Lilia Dead. Sister Mary Catherine. JKCP (1955 ed.)
Beside me she sat, hand hooked and hovering. An Egyptian Passage. Theodore Weiss. CoPo
Beside me there is resting. The Dead Bee. Nathalia Crane. MAP; MoAmPo (1942 ed.)
Beside still waters. Twenty-Third Psalm. Dawn Finlay. SoP

Beside that tent and under guard. Geronimo. Ernest McGaffey. AA; PAH; ThLM
Beside the Bed. Charlotte Mew. AnEnPo; MoAB; MoBrPo; NeMA; NP; TrGrPo
Beside the bed where parting life was laid. The Village Preacher. Goldsmith. *Fr.* The Deserted Village. TrGrPo
Beside the Blackwater. Norreys Jephson O'Conor. HBMV
Beside the crater and the tattered palm. The Dead in Melanesia. Randall Jarrell. MiAP
Beside the dark sand and the winged foam. Poem by the Clock Tower, Sumner. James K. Baxter. ACV
Beside the dead I knelt for prayer. Christus Consolator. Rossiter W. Raymond. HBV; MaRV; OQP
Beside the empty sepulcher she lingered. Mary. "W. B." ChIP
Beside the haunted lake where nereids seem. Mademoiselle Richarde. Edith Sitwell. MoVE
Beside the idle summer sea. Rondel. W. E. Henley. OBNC
Beside the landsman knelt a dame. The Manor Lord. George Houghton. AA
Beside the lone river. Little Big Horn. Ernest McGaffey. PAH
Beside the Mead of Memories. The Dead Quire. Thomas Hardy. OAEP
Beside the mountain roads, the men. Blue Smoke. Frances Frost. RePo; SiSoSe
Beside the old hall-fire—upon my nurse's knee. Fairy Days. Thackeray. GoTP; OTPC (1946 ed.)
Beside the pale water. The Pool. Fritz S. Burnel. BoAu
Beside the pleasant Mill of Trompington. Wordsworth. *Fr.* The Prelude. OBRV
Beside the pool where shadows flit. The Fool of Love. *Unknown.* UnTE
Beside the pounding cataracts. The City of the End of Things. Archibald Lampman. OBCV; VA
Beside the rail, despite the gale. The Missing Link. Oliver Herford. CenHV
Beside the rivers of the midnight town. Madrigal. John Frederick Nims. MiAP
Beside the Sea. Ella Higginson. OTPC (1946 ed.)
Beside the Sea. George Johnston. ACV
Beside the slew the poplars play. A Prairie Water Colour. Duncan Campbell Scott. OBCV
Beside the stolid opaque flow. The Gravel-Pit Field. David Gascoyne. NeBP
Beside the ungathered rice he lay. The Slave's Dream. Longfellow. AnNE; CoBA; GTBS; MemP; OBVV; PoNe; TSW; WePo
Beside yon church, that beams a modest ray. Church and School. Timothy Dwight. *Fr.* Greenfield Hill. AmPP (3d ed.)
Beside yon straggling fence that skirts the way. The Village Schoolmaster [*or* The Schoolmaster]. Goldsmith. *Fr.* The Deserted Village. OBEC; OTPC (1946 ed.); PoSa; ShBV-2; TrGrPo
Beside you. Nightsong. Philip Booth. MoLP
Besides the autumn poets sing. Emily Dickinson. MAmP; OxBA
Besieged. Zalman Schneour, *tr. fr. Yiddish by* Joseph Leftwich. TrJP
Besieged Heart, The. Sir John Suckling. *See* Siege, The.
Besom-Man, The. Joseph Campbell. OnYI
Besse Bunting. *Unknown.* MeEL
("In Aprell and in May.") EnPo
Bessie Bell and Mary Gray. Mother Goose. *See* Bessy Bell and Mary Gray.
Bessie Bell and Mary Gray (*ballad*). *Unknown.* BFSS; OBB
(Bessy Bell and Mary Gray.) ESPB; OxBB; ViBoFo
Bessie Bobtail. James Stephens. NP
Bessie Brown, M.D. Samuel Minturn Peck. BOHV
Bessy [*or* Bessie] Bell and Mary Gray. Mother Goose. OTPC (1923 ed.); OxNR; PCH; PPL; RIS
Bessy Bell and Mary Gray (*ballad*). *Unknown.* *See* Bessie Bell and Mary Gray.
Best, The. Elizabeth Barrett Browning. OBVV
Best, The. Carl Sandburg. *Fr.* The People, Yes. MaRV
Best and brightest, come away! To Jane: The Invitation [*or* The Invitation *or* The Invitation to Jane]. Shelley. CH; EPN; ERoP-2; GTBS; GTBS-D; GTBS-P; GTBS-W; GTSE; GTSL; HBV; MBW-2; OBEV; OBRV; OTPC; SeCeV
Best and the Worst, The. *Unknown.* *See* World, The.
Best Choice, The. *Unknown.* SoP; STF
Best Firm, The. Walter G. Doty. HBV; HBVY; RIS
Best for Me, The. E. Margaret Clarkson. *See* This I Know.
Best for Us, The. Olive H. Burnett. STF
Best Friend, The. W. H. Davies. OBMV
Bestfriend, The. Dick Lourie. *Fr.* Calls on the Dream Telephone. ThO
Best Game the Fairies Play, The. Rose Fyleman. GFA; SoPo; TiPo (1952 ed.); YT
Best Man in the Vield, The. William Barnes. PeVV
Best Memory Course, The. *Unknown.* STF
Best Not to Be Born. Archias, *tr. fr. Greek by* William Hay. OnPM
Best of All, The. Fanny Crosby. BLRP
Best of All, The. Margaret G. Rhodes. BoTP
Best of All. *Unknown.* WBLP
Best of All. J. M. Westrup. BoTP
Best Old Feller in the World, The (A *vers., with music*). *Unknown.* BFSS
Best preacher is the heart, The. The Best. Carl Sandburg. *Fr.* The People, Yes. MaRV
Best Religion, The. Heine, *tr. fr. German by* Emma Lazarus. *Fr.* Tannhäuser. TrJP
Best Road of All, The. Charles Hanson Towne. HBMV; OQP
Best Song as It Seems to Me, The. *Unknown.* CoBE
Best thing in the world, but I better be quick about it, The. Biotherm. Frank O'Hara. CoPo
Best Time of All, The. Nancy Byrd Turner. GFA
Best Treasure, The. John J. Moment. MaRV; TRV
Bestiary, The *sel.* William Rose Benét.
"Comtemplate Pliny's crocodile." OA
Bestiary. A. M. Klein. OBCV
Bestiary, A, *sels.* Kenneth Rexroth.
Deer. HoPM
Herring. HoPM
Kangaroo.
(Advices from Rexroth's Bestiary.) SiTL
Lion. HoPM
Racoon. FiBHP
(Advices from Rexroth's Bestiary.) SiTL
Trout.
(Advices from Rexroth's Bestiary.) SiTL
Wolf.
(Advices from Rexroth's Bestiary.) SiTL
You. HoPM
Bête Humaine. Francis Brett Young. CH; HBMV
Beth Gêlert. William Robert Spencer. BeLS; GoTP; GSP; OnSP; OTPC; TreFS
(Beth Gêlert or the Grave of the Grayhound.) BLPA
Beth has some mittens. Richer. Aileen Fisher. BiCB
Bethel. A. J. H. Duganne. PAH
Bethesda. Arthur Hugh Clough. PoVP
Bethinking Himself of His End, Writeth Thus. Thomas, Lord Vaux. *See* Latter Day, The.
Bethlehem. William Canton. BoTP; YeAr
Bethlehem. Harry Webb Farrington. OQP
Bethlehem. Arthur Ketchum. ChrBoLe
Bethlehem. Clinton Scollard. MaRV
Bethlehem of Judea. *Unknown.* BiCB; ChBR
Bethlehem Road, The. Ida Norton Munson. ChIP
Bethlehem Star, The, Shines On! Alice Mortenson. BePJ
Bethlehem-Town ("As I was going to Bethlehem-town"). Eugene Field. WBLP
"Unto a Child in Bethlehem-town," *sel.* PGD
Bethlehem's Babe. Henry W. Frost. SoP
Bethou Me, Said Sparrow. Wallace Stevens. Notes toward a Supreme Fiction, XVI. CrMA; LiTM (rev. ed.); NePA
("Bethou me, said sparrow, to the crackled blade.") MoPo
Bethsabe's Song. George Peele. *Fr.* David and Bethsabe, I, i. ATBAP; ATP; CBEP; EnRePo; OBSC; OxBoLi; SeCeV
(Bathsheba's Song.) InPo
(Bethsabe Bathing.) EIL; ExPo; LoBV; TrGrPo
("Hot sun, cool fire, tempered with sweet air.") LO; NoP; PoEL-2; SiCE; TuPP
Betimes a wise guest. Always with Us!—The Black Preacher. Herman Melville. BiS
Betrayal. Hester H. Cholmondeley. MaRV; OQP; TRV
(Still as of Old.) PGD
Betrayal, The. Alice Furlong. AnIV

Betrayal, The. Josephine W. Johnson. MoRP
Betrayal, The. Sidney Lanier. *Fr.* The Jacquerie. AA
Betrayal. John Banister Tabb. ACP
Betrayal. *Unknown.* OQP
Betrayal. Sir Thomas Wyatt. *See* How Should I Be So Pleasant.
Betrayal of the Rose, The. Edith M. Thomas. AA
Betrayed by friend dragged from the garden hailed. Ecce Homunculus. R. A. K. Mason. AnNZ
Betrothal, The. Edna St. Vincent Millay. NP; PG
Betrothed, The. Kipling. HBV
Betrothed, The, *sel.* Sir Walter Scott.
Woman's Faith, *fr. ch.* 20. CBV; ViBoPo
Betsey and I Are Out. Will Carleton. PaPo
Betsey Trotwood's Cat. Louella C. Poole. CIV
Betsy from Pike. *Unknown, See* Sweet Betsy from Pike. *at. to* John A. Stone.
Betsy Jane's Sixth Birthday. Alfred Noyes. BiCB; SiSoSe
Betsy's Battle-Flag. Minna Irving. DD; MC; PAH; PEDC; PoRL
Better a Day of Faith. Henry Burke Robins. MaRV
Better Answer (to Cloe Jealous), A. Matthew Prior. *See* Answer to Chloe Jealous.
Better Bargain, The. Congreve. *See* Song: "Tell me no more I am deceived."
Better be early and have to wait. Rhymes to Remember. *Unknown.* StaSt
Better disguised than the leaf insect. The Lake. Ted Hughes. NYBP
Better Eros, The. Asclepiades, *tr. fr. Greek by* Robert Guthrie MacGregor. OnPM
Better go outdoors now, shut the door on trouble. First Concerns. Abbie Huston Evans. NP
Better in the Wild. Bhartrihari, *tr. fr. Sanskrit by* Arthur W. Ryder. OnPM
Better it were, my brother. Man to Man. John McClure. HBMV
Better late than never: yea, mate. Of Late and Never. John Heywood. TuPP
Better love than mine, A. The Bible. Nathaniel Frothingham. SoP
Better music ne'er was known. Beaumont *and* Fletcher. *Fr.* The Knight of the Burning Pestle. SiCE; TuPP
Better never trouble Trouble. Trouble. David Keppel. FaFP; PoLF; TreF; WBLP
Better one bird in hand, than ten in the wood. Of Birds and Birders. John Heywood. SiCE
Better Part, The. Matthew Arnold. ChIP; EPN; MaRV; PoVP; StJW; TOP; ViPP
Better Part, The. Bhartrihari, *tr. fr. Sanskrit by* Arthur W. Ryder. OnPm
Better Path, The. Ecclesiastes, VII: 1-5 Bible, *O.T.* TreFS (It Is Better. . ., 1-9.) TrJP
Better Resurrection, A. Christina Rossetti. FaChP; HBV; OxBoCh; PoVP; StJW; TrPWD; ViPo; VP
Better than flowers. William Carlos Williams. *Fr.* Paterson. MoLP
Better than Gold ("Better than grandeur. . ."). Abram J. Ryan, *at. also to* Alexander Smart. FaFP; MaRV; PoToHe
Better than granite, Spoon River. Aaron Hatfield. Edgar Lee Masters. *Fr.* Spoon River Anthology. LiTA; NP
Better the empty sorrow in the dark. Night of Rain. Bernice Kenyon. HBMV
Better to Be Brave. Lucillius, *tr. fr. Greek by* Lord Neaves. OnPM
Better to be the rock above the river. La Crosse at Ninety Miles an Hour. Richard Eberhart. AmFN
Better to dwell in mountains wild. Better in the Wild. Bhartrihari. OnPM
Better to live on beggar's bread. After Battle. *Unknown. Fr.* Bhagavad-Gita. MaRV
Better to see your cheek grown hollow. Madman's Song. Elinor Wylie. LOW; MAP; MoAB; MoAmPo; MoSiPe; PoRA
Better trust all and be deceived. Faith [*or* Trust]. Frances Anne Kemble. FaBoBe; HBV; MaRV; NeHB; OBVV; VA
Better Way, The. "Susan Coolidge." PaA
Better Way, The. *Unknown.* SoP
Better, Wiser and Happier. Ella Wheeler Wilcox. WBLP (Kindness.) SoP
Betty at the Party. Mary E. Bradley. BiCB; BoTP
Betty Botter bought some butter. *Unknown.* OxNR; SiTL
Betty by the Sea. Ronald McCuaig. BoAV
Betty Perrin. A. E. Coppard. MoBrPo (1942 ed.)
Betty Pringle [Had a Little Pig]. *Unknown.* OTPC (1923 ed.); PPL
Betty told Dupree, "Daddy, I want a diamond ring." *Unknown.* OuSiCo
Betty Zane. Thomas Dunn English. PAH; PAL
Between a sunny bank and the sun. Two Houses. Edward Thomas. ChMP; FaBoCh; LoGBV
Between Adam and me the great difference is. Upon Being Obliged to Leave a Pleasant Party. Thomas Moore. BOHV
Between Botallack and the light. A Ballad of a Mine. Robin Skelton. MoBS
Between Brielle and Manasquan. Oliver St. John Gogarty. OnYI
Between Cellini's Perseus and the Sabine Rape. More Nudes for Florence. Harold Witt. ErPo
Between decision and ensuing act. Birdwatcher. Henry Treece. WaP
Between extremities. Vacillation. W. B. Yeats. MoVE; PoDB
Between fields of popcorn. "America, I Love You." Bert Kalmar *and* Harry Ruby. FiBHP; InMe
Between God's Eyelashes. José Garcia Villa. CrMA
Between me and the moving world's. Presence. John Moffit. MoRP
Between me and the rising sun. Cobwebs. E. L. M. King. BoTP
Between me and the sunset, like a dome. The Man against the Sky. E. A. Robinson. AmPP; AP; APA; CMoP; CoAnAm; CoBMV; LiTA; MAPA; MoVE; NAMP; OxBA; TwAmPo
Between Midnight and Morning. Sir Owen Seaman. *See* Victory.
Between Motions. Jerome Mazzaro. NYTB
Between my eyes and her so thin the screen. Ideal Passion, XXXVII. George Edward Woodberry. HBMV
Between my finger and my thumb. Digging. Seamus Heaney. TwCP
Between my love and me there runs a thread. Sonnets. Irene Rutherford McLeod. HBMV
Between my suppertime and bed. A Busy Person. Alfarata Hilton. PCH
Between Namur and Liège. William Wordsworth. EPN; MCCG
Between Nose and Eyes a strange contest arose. The Nose and the Eyes [*or* Dispute between Nose and Eyes *or* Report of an Adjudged Case]. William Cowper. BOHV; MPB; OTPC
Between Seasons. Anne Welsh. PeSA
Between such animal and human heat. The Partner. Theodore Roethke. *Fr.* Four for Sir John Davies. NePA; NePoAm
Between the Acts. Stanley Kunitz. ELU
Between the amber portals of the sea. The Peach Tree. Edith Sitwell. NP
Between the avenue of cypresses. Service of All the Dead. D. H. Lawrence. NP
Between the dark and the daylight. The Children's Hour. Longfellow. AA; AmePo; AmP; AnNE; CoBA; FaBoBe; FaBV; FaFP; FaPL; FaPON; GoTP; HBV; HBVY; MPB; NeHB; OHFP; OTPC; PCH; PoEL-5; PoLF; PoPl; PTK; TreF; TSW; WBLP
Between the earth and the drowned platinum. The Battle of the Jarama. "Pablo Neruda." WaaP
Between the erect and solemn trees. The Temple of the Trees. J. D. C. Pellow. PGD
Between the exhilaration of Beginning. The Middle-Time. Lona M. Fowler. FaChP; TRV
Between the falling leaf and rose-bud's breath. The Term of Death. Sarah Morgan Bryan Piatt. AA
Between the first pangs and the last of love. This Little Vigil. Charles G. Bell. MoLP; NePoAm
Between the fosse and inner wall. The Defender. Arthur M. Sampley. GoYe
Between the gardening and the cookery. A Bookshop Idyll. Kingsley Amis. NePoEA
Between the gray pastures and the dark wood. *See* Between the grey. . .
Between the green bud and the red. Prelude to "Songs before

Sunrise." Swinburne. MaVP; PoVP; ViPo
Between the grey [*or* gray] pastures and the dark wood. The Valley of White Poppies. "Fiona Macleod." MoSiPe; PoVP
Between the gutter and sidewalk. A Blade of Grass. Oscar Williams. NYTB
Between the hands, between the brows. Love-Lily. Dante Gabriel Rossetti. AtBAP; PoVP
Between the hill and the brook, ook, ook. The Rabbits. *Unknown, tr. fr. German.* PCH; PPL; SAS
Between the Karim Shahir. Rochelle Owens. CoPo
Between the legs. The Mother. Raymond Souster. PeCV
Between the Lines. W. W. Gibson. MCCG
Between the midnight and the morn. The Secret Muse. Roy Campbell. BoC; PeSA
Between the mountains and the sea. Santa Barbara. Francis Fisher Browne. AA
Between the perfect. Somewhere the Equation Breaks Down. Daniel Berrigan. NYBP
Between the pleasant lands, the sunlit places. Program Note on Sibelius. Donald Babcock. UnS
Between the Porch and the Altar. Robert Lowell. FiMAP; MiAP; NePoEA
Between the railway and the mine. The Blackberry. Norman Nicholson. MoBrPo (1950 ed.); NeMA
Between the Rapids. Archibald Lampman. VA
Between the rice swamps and the fields of tea. The Quarry. William Vaughn Moody. AnAmPo
Between the roadside and the wood. A Windflower. Bliss Carman. VA
Between the roses. Five Roses. Jacinto Verdaguer, *tr. by* Thomas Walsh. CAW
Between the rough hills of gabbro and the cold sea. In Our Time. Michael Roberts. WaP
Between the Showers. Amy Levy. VA
Between the spaces. The Dark-red Shadow-Spots. Yumei Kanbara. LiTW
Between the Sunken Sun and the New Moon. Paul Hamilton Hayne. AA
Between the Sunset and the Sea. Swinburne. *See* Mary Beaton's Song.
Between the swung rope and the sound of the bell. Interval. Rolfe Humphries. ML
Between the Traveller and the Setting Sun. Henry David Thoreau. PoEL-4
Between the Walls of the Valley. Elisabeth Peck. AmFN
Between the wheeze of her torpor and the wind of her falling. Faintly and from Far Away. Vassar Miller. CoPo
Between the World and Me. Richard Wright. AmNP; IDB; LiTM (1970 ed.); PoNe
Between their sandspit ends. Barred Islands. Philip Booth. NePoEA
Between thirty and forty, one is distracted by the Five Lusts. On Being Sixty. Po Chü-i. AWP
Between town and the. The Quarry Pool. Denise Levertov. ToPo
Between trains, on this day of snow. At the Roman Baths, Bath. Edward Lucie-Smith. NePoEA-2
Between Two Furious Oceans, *sels.* Dick Diespecker.
"All these are your essence, you are their flesh and their force." CaP
"You have asked me, 'What am I?' " TwCaPo
Between Two Loves. T. A. Daly. BOHV; MAP; MoAmPo (1942 ed.); PoMa; StVeCh (1940 ed.)
Between Two Prisoners. James Dickey. AP; NoP
Between two russet [*or* golden] tufts of summer grass. Lying in the Grass. Sir Edmund Gosse. OBVV; TOP; VA
Between Two Worlds. Rosemary Thomas. NYBP
Between Us. Stephen Berg. NaP
Between us lie/ The mountains and the plain. With One Swift Thought. Sister Maryanna. JKCP (1955 ed.)
Between wise men and fools, among things many. Of Difference between Wise Men and Fools. John Heywood. ReIE
Between Worlds. Carl Sandburg. MoAmPo (1950 ed.)
Betwene Mersh and Averil. *Unknown. See* Alisoun.
Betwixt and Between. Hugh Lofting. BiCB; GaP
Betwixt the actual and unseen, alone. Beethoven. Edward Carpenter. PoMa
Betwixt the quarters, flows a golden sea. Battle of Actium. Vergil, *tr. by* Dryden. *Fr.* The Aeneid, VIII. OBS
Betwixt the stirrop and the ground. Grave-stones, III. *Unknown.* OtMeF
Betwixt twelve hours and eleven. Amends to the Tailors and Soutars. William Dunbar. CBEP
Betwixt two billows of the downs. The Winnowers. Robert Bridges. OAEP
Beverley Maid and the Tinker, The. *Unknown.* CoMu
Bewail with me, all ye that have professed. On the Death of Phillips. *Unknown.* OBSC
Bewailing in my chamber thus allone. He Sees His Beloved [*or* The Coming of Love]. James I, King of Scotland. *Fr.* The Kingis Quair. GoTS; PoEL-1
Bewar, squier, yeman, and page. A Warning to Those Who Serve Lords. *Unknown.* MeEL
Beware. Dora Sigerson Shorter. GTSL
Beware, beware the snare of "victory." Victory. Roger Axford. PGD
Beware: Do Not Read This Poem. Ishmael Reed. NoP
Beware Fair Maid. Joshua Sylvester. OBS
Beware, My Child. Shel Silverstein. PDV
Beware, my friend, of fiends and their grimaces. Sonnet to a Cat. Heine. CIV
Beware of a pirate who will scuttle your ship. Convention. Alfred Kreymborg. MAPA
Beware of Doubleness. John Lydgate. EnPo
(Duplicity of Women, The, *shorter vers.*) MeEL
Beware of Larry Gorman, *with music.* Larry Gorman. ShS
Beware of Sirens. ——Bewe. ReIE
("When sage Ulysses sailed by.") SiCE
Beware, take heede, take heede, beware, beware. How Collingbourne was Cruelly Executed for Making a Foolish Rhyme. William Baldwin. NCEP
Beware the Cuckoo. E. G. Moll. BoAV
Beware the deadly Sitting habit. Cave Sedem! Theodore F. McManus. HBV
Beware! The Israelite of old, who tore. The Warning. Longfellow. AmePo; CoBA
Bewhiskered raticide, whose velvet paw. The Eternal Question. D. B. Van Buren. CIV
Bewick and Graham. *Unknown.* BaBo; ESPB
(Bewick and the Graeme, The.) OxBB
(Graeme and Bewick.) CBEP; EnSB
Bewick Finzer. E. A. Robinson. AnNE; AP; BoLiVe (1945 ed.); CMoP; CoBMV; ForPo; MAP; MoAB; MoAmPo; NeMA
Bewildered Arab, The. Jami, *tr. fr. Persian by* Edward Fitzgerald. *Fr.* Salámán and Absál. WoL
Bewildered Guest, The. William Dean Howells. AmePo
Bewildered in the morning down dry roads. The Bullocks. Alex Comfort. FaBoTw
Bewildered with the broken tongue. Words in Time. Archibald MacLeish. CrMA; PoCH; NePA; PoRA
Bewilderment at the Entrance of the Fat Boy into Eden, A. Daryl Hine. OBCV
Bewitched. Walter de la Mare. PoMS
Bewteis of the Fute-Ball, The. *Unknown.* GoTS; OxBS
Bewty of hir amorus ene, The. Off Womanheid Ane Flour Delice. *Unknown.* OxBS
Beyond. Lionel Johnson. BrPo
Beyond. Hannah Parker Kimball. AA
Beyond. John Gibson Lockhart. MaRV
Beyond, The. Ella Wheeler Wilcox. MaRV
Beyond a hundred years and more. Pope at Twickenham. Charles Kent. VA
Beyond all this, the wish to be alone. Wants. Philip Larkin. GTBS-P
Beyond antiseptic white. Semi-Private. Mabel MacDonald Carver. FiSC
Beyond Arcturus and the Pleiades. White Splendor. Leslie Savage Clark. ChIP
Beyond Astronaut. John Fairfax. HYE
Beyond, beyond the mountain line. Dreams. Cecil Frances Alexander. OnYI
Beyond Biology. Robert Francis. NePoAm
Beyond earshot of others, furtively. The Conspirators. Kenneth Burke. TwAmPo
Beyond Electrons. Adelaide P. Love. OQP
Beyond Kerguelen. Henry C. Kendall. BoAu; PoAu-1
Beyond my window in the night. A Town Window. John Drinkwater. BoTP; GTBS; NeMA
Beyond Nagel's Funeral Parlor. The Elizabethans Called It Dying. James Schuyler. NeAP

Beyond Possession. Elizabeth Jennings. BoC; NePoEA
Beyond Rathkelly. Francis Carlin. HBMV
Beyond Recall. Mary E. Bradley. AA
Beyond Religion. Lucretius, *tr. fr. Latin by* William Ellery Leonard. *Fr.* De Rerum Natura. AWP
"Whilst human kind/Throughout the lands lay miserably crushed," *sel.* PoFr
Beyond surprise, my ribs start up from the ground. The Defeated. W. S. Merwin. AmPC
Beyond the Atlas roams a glutton. The Glutton. Robert Graves. CMoP
Beyond the blue, the purple seas. The Hunter. Walter James Turner. HBMV
Beyond the bourn of mortal death and birth. At Last. Katrina Trask. AA
Beyond the Chagres. James Stanley Gilbert. PoLF
Beyond the Chiltern coast, this church. Edlesborough. Anne Ridler. NeBP
Beyond the corn-rows from our Barracks stood. The Quaker Meeting-House. William Ellery Leonard. PFY
Beyond the cypress unexpected drifts. Samarian Nights. Yaakov Fichman. LiTW
Beyond the desolate expanse of plain. Then and Now. George Sterling. PoMa
Beyond the doorway of the tiny room. Blue Homespun. Frank Oliver Call. *Fr.* A Sonnet Series of French Canada. CaP
Beyond the East the sunrise, beyond the West the sea. Wander-Thirst [*or* Wanderlust]. Gerald Gould. HT; PoMa; StaSt; TiPo; TSW
Beyond the edge of the world, past crater terrain. The Antelopes. James K. Baxter. AnNZ
Beyond the End. Denise Levertov. NeAP
Beyond the famous river Utva. Field of Tears. *Unknown.* OnPM
Beyond the fence she hesitates. Midwife Cat. Mark Van Doren. OA
Beyond the ferry water. Ferry Hinksey. Laurence Binyon. HBV
Beyond the field where crows cawed at a hawk. Two Lives and Others. Winfield Townley Scott. PoPl
Beyond the Grave. Margaret E. Bruner. PoToHe
Beyond the great valley an odd instinctive rising. Ascent to the Sierras. Robinson Jeffers. AmPP (3d ed.); HT; LoGBV; OxBA
Beyond the Horizon. Robert Freeman. MaRV; OQP
Beyond the hour we counted rain that fell. Old Countryside. Louise Bogan. AmLP; LiTA; NePA; NP; TwAmPo
Beyond the Hunting Woods. Donald Justice. NePoEA; NYBP; PoPl
Beyond the image of the willow. The Importance of Poetry, or the Coming Forth from Eternity into Time. Hyam Plutzik. PP
Beyond the last gate, where I made my first halt. On Scafell Pike. Ted Walker. NYBP
Beyond the last horizon's rim. The Hills of Rest. Albert Bigelow Paine. HBV; MaRV; OQP; WGRP
Beyond the Last Lamp. Thomas Hardy. MoVE; OBNC; PoVP
Beyond the little [*or* narrow] window. The Tree-Top Road. May Riley Smith. HBV; MaRV
Beyond the low marsh-meadows and the beach. The Pines and the Sea. Christopher Pearse Cranch. AA; AmLP; AnAmPo; HBV; ILP
Beyond the mountains there are other mountains. Songs of the Blue-Light Dakini. Lenore Kandel. FRC
Beyond the murk that swallows me. Irene Rutherford McLeod. *Fr.* The Rebel. WGRP
Beyond the narrow window. *See* Beyond the little window.
Beyond the pale of memory. Amor Profanus. Ernest Dowson. PoVP
Beyond the Panther. John Stevens Wade. ThO
Beyond the path of the outmost sun through utter darkness hurled. Dedication. Kipling. *Fr.* Barrack-Room Ballads. ViPP
Beyond the Potomac. Paul Hamilton Hayne. PAH
Beyond the Profit of Today. *Unknown.* PoToHe (new ed.)
Beyond the sea, I know not where. Vivérols. David Starr Jordan. AA
Beyond the shadow of the ship. Samuel Taylor Coleridge. *Fr.* The Rime of the Ancient Mariner. BoC
Beyond the Smiling and the Weeping. Horatius Bonar. HBV
(Little While, A.) VA
Beyond the sphere which spreads to widest space. La Vita Nuova, XXIX [*or* Sonnet]. Dante, *tr. by* Dante Gabriel Rossetti. AWP; CTC; JAWP; OnPM; OuHeWo; WBP
Beyond the square of the old church tower. Vespers. Henry W. Frost. SoP
Beyond the Tapestries. Norma Farber. GoYe
Beyond the thickets of my self. Nightmare. Joseph Payne Brennan. FiSC
Beyond the turning sea's far foam. At War. Russell Atkins. AmNP
Beyond the vague Atlantic deep. Our Mother Tongue [*or* An Envoy to an American Lady]. Richard Monckton Milnes. GN; OTPC; VA
Beyond The Veil. Henry Vaughan. *See* They Are All Gone.
Beyond the war-clouds and the reddened ways. The Morning Breaks [*or* The Coming Day]. John Oxenham. MaRV; OQP
Beyond the white dust flushed by the carriers. Patrol; Buonamary. Bernard Gutteridge. WaP
Beyond the window, the tyre-coloured road deflates. North London. Alan Ross. POTi
Beyond the window's tracery. The Woman at the Window. Donald Wandrei. FiSC
Beyond th'old pillers many have travailed. Sir John Wingefield. John Donne. MaMe
Beyond Today. *Unknown.* SoP
Bhagavad [*or* Bhagavat]-Gita, *sels.* *Unknown, tr. fr. Sanskrit.*
After Battle, *tr. by* Sir Edwin Arnold. MaRV
Considerations of Murder, *tr. by* Swami Prabhavananda *and* Christopher Isherwood. LiTW
Death ("As when one layeth/ His worn-out robes away"), *tr. by* Sir Edwin Arnold. MaRV
Debate between Arjuna and Sri Krishna, *tr. by* Swami Prabhavananda *and* Christopher Isherwood. Waap
Eternal Self, The, *tr. by* Charles Johnston. WoL
Give Me Your Whole Heart, *tr. by* Swami Prabhavananda *and* Christopher Isherwood. MaRV
"Never the spirit was born," *tr. by* Sir Edwin Arnold. MaRV; TreFT
Transfiguration, The, *tr. by* Sir Edwin Arnold. OuHeWo
Wise, The, *tr. by* Sir Edwin Arnold. OQP
Bi a forrest as I gan fare. By a Forest. *Unknown.* NCEP
Bianca. Arthur Symons. PeVV; UnTE
Bianca among the Nightingales. Elizabeth Barrett Browning. GTBS-P; ViPo
Bible, The. Bishop Anderson. SoP
Bible, The. Bernard Barton. SoP
Bible, The. Henry W. Frost. SoP
Bible, The. Nathaniel Frothingham. SoP
Bible, The. H. H. Halley. SoP
Bible, The, *sel.* David Levi, *tr. fr. Italian by* Mary A. Craig.
"Thou, Zion, old and suffering." TrJP
Bible, The. Sir Walter Scott. *See* Book of Books, The.
Bible, The. Dorothy Conant Stroud. STF
Bible, The. Thomas Traherne. LoBV (1949 ed.)
Bible, A ("A stern destroyer"). *Unknown, tr. fr. Anglo-Saxon by* Stith Thompson. *Fr.* Riddles. EnLi-1; OuHeWo
Bible, The ("Study it carefully"). *Unknown.* SoP
Bible, The ("When I am tired, the Bible is my bed"). *Unknown.* OQP; SoP
Bible, The. Whittier. *Fr.* Miriam. MaRV; NeHB; OQP; SoP; TreFT
(Book Our Mothers Read, The.) BLRP; TRV
(Knowledge.) PoToHe (new ed.)
("We search the world for truth. We cull.") FaChP
Bible is an antique volume, The. Emily Dickinson. AmePo; MAmP; NoP
Bible of the Race, The. James Russell Lowell. OQP
Bible Stories. Lizette Woodworth Reese. BrR; MoSiPe; MPB; StJW; TSW
Bible Stories. *Unknown.* LiTG
Bible Study. Martha Snell Nicholson. FaChP
Bibliolatres. James Russell Lowell.
God Is Not Dumb, *sel.* MaRV; OQP; WGRP
Bibliomaniac's Prayer, The. Eugene Field. AA
"Biby's" Epitaph. *Unknown.* FiBHP
Bicycalamity. Edmund W. Peters. SD
Bicycle Rider, The. David Shapiro. ANYP
Bicycling Song. Henry Charles Beeching. *See* Going down Hill on a Bicycle.

Bid Adieu to Maidenhood. James Joyce. Chamber Music, XI. LiTG; LiTL; OBEV (new ed.)
(Bid Adieu, Adieu, Adieu.) HW; OnYI
(Bid Adieu to Girlish Days.) HBV
Bid me go asleep: I scorn it with my heels. Samuel Rowlands. SiCE
Bid me live, and I will live. *See* Bid me to live. . .
Bid me not go where neither suns nor showers. A Valediction. William Cartwright. EG; OBS; SeCL; SeEP
Bid me remember, O my gracious Lord. Mary Elizabeth Coleridge. *Fr.* Death. TrPWD
Bid Me Sin No More. Charles Wesley. BePJ
Bid me to live, and I will live. To Anthea, Who May Command Him Any Thing. Robert Herrick. AnAnS-2; BoC; BoLiVe; CavP; CBEP; CoBE; EnLit; GTBS; GTBS-D; GTBS-P; GTBS-W; GTSE; GTSL; HBV; LoBV; MeWo; NeHB; OAEP; OBEV; OBS; PoeP; ReEn; SCEP-2; SeCL; SeCP; SeCV-1; SeEP; TOP; TrGrPo; ViBoPo
Bid not farewell for fate can ne're divorce. *Unknown.* SeCSL
Bid the din of battle cease! The Message of Peace. Julia Ward Howe. PGD
Biddy, Biddy, *with music.* *Unknown.* OuSiCo
Bide a Wee! John Oxenham. TRV
Bide thou thy time! The Patient Church. Cardinal Newman. GoBC
Bi-focal. Hal Porter. BoAV
Bi-focal. William Stafford. NoP
Biftek aux Champignons. Henry Augustin Beers. AA; AmLP; HBV
Big and Little Things. Alfred H. Miles. OTPC (1923 ed.)
Big Arm-Chair, The. "E. H. R." GFA
Big Baboon, The. Hilaire Belloc. InP; MoBrPo; MoShBr; RIS
Big Bell in Zion, The. Theodore Henry Shackleford. BANP
Big Billie Potts was big and stout. The Ballad of Billie Potts. Robert Penn Warren. AmPP (3d ed.); MoAmPo (1950 ed.); OxBA
Big black nigger, lying on the log. When de Good Lord Sets You Free. *Unknown.* ABF
Big blue-jean, the summer-bored boy next door, The. Carry Me Back. John Holmes. AmFN; NePoAm-2
Big box/ Little box. *Unknown.* OxNR
Big Brother. Elizabeth Madox Roberts. FaPON; GaP; MPB
Big Chief Wotapotami. David McCord. WhC
Big City. Michael Brownstein. ANYP
Big Clock, The. *Unknown.* SoPo; TiPo
Big Crash Out West. Peter Viereck. PoPl
Big Daddy Lipscomb, who used to help them up. Say Good-Bye to Big Daddy. Randall Jarrell. PoNe (1970 ed.)
Big Dam. W. R. Moses. AmFN
Big Engines, The. Chorus. Jack Kerouac. *Fr.* Mexico City Blues. NeAP
Big, Fat Summer—and the Lean and Hard. Frederick Bock. NYBP
Big Fat Woman, *with music.* *Unknown.* OuSiCo
Big feet,/ Black Feet. Feet. Irene Thompson. BoTP
Big Five-Gallon Jar, The, *with music.* *Unknown.* ShS
Big grey elephant, A. Just Jumbo. Eileen Mathias. BoTP
Big guns again. Imperator Victus. Hart Crane. OxBA
Big house,/ Little house. *Unknown.* OxNR
Big iron horse with lifted head. The Little Boy to the Locomotive. Benjamin R. C. Low. HBMV
Big Jim. *Unknown.* ABF
Big mountains sit still in the afternoon light, The. Sinners. D. H. Lawrence. CBV; ViBoPo
Big Nasturtiums. Robert Beverly Hale. BoNaP; NYBP; PoMS; SiTL
Big Rock Candy Mountain[s], The. *Unknown.* ChTr; MaC; TreFT; WePo
Big Smith. Juliana Horatia Ewing. TVC
Big Steamers. Kipling. Par
Big stones of the cistern behind the barn, The. Twilights. James Wright. NaP
Big strong work horses working every day. Work Horses. Edith Newlin Chase. SoPo
Big Swing-Tree Is Green Again, The. Mary Jane Carr. BrR; SiSoSe
Big Tent under the Roof, The. Ogden Nash. RePo
Big Thompson Canon. Jean Milne Gower. PoOW
Big trucks for steel beams. Trucks. James S. Tippett. FaPON; GFA; OTD
Big trucks with apples. Country Trucks. Monica Shannon. BrR; FaPON; TiPo (1950 ed.)
Big Turtle, A. *Unknown.* SoPo
Big-uddered piebald cattle low. Christmas Holiday. Alun Lewis. PrWP
Big Wind. Theodore Roethke. AmPP (5th ed.); GoJo; InvP; NoP; ViBoPo (1958 ed.)
Big yam taters in de sandy lan'. Sandy Lan'. *Unknown.* ABF
Big yellow trolley lumbers [*or* limbers] along. There Are So Many Ways of Going Places. Leslie Thompson. FaPON; SoPo
Big young bareheaded woman, A. Proletarian Portrait. William Carlos Williams. OCS
Bigamist born in Zambezi, A. Lessons in Limericks, I. David McCord. InMe
Bigerlow, *with music.* *Unknown.* AS
Bigger Day, The. G. E. Bishop. WBLP
Bigger the box the more it holds, The. Boxes and Bags. Carl Sandburg. RePo
Biggest Killing, The. Edward Dorn. CoPo
Bight, The. Elizabeth Bishop. NYBP; PoSa
Bigler, The (*diff. versions*), *with music.* *Unknown.* AmSS; OuSiCo
(Bigler's Crew, The.) IHA
(Cruise of the *Bigler*, The, *with music.*) SoAmSa
Biglow Papers, The, *sels.* James Russell Lowell.
1st Series, No. I.
Letter from Mr. Ezekiel Biglow of Jaalam to the Hon. Joseph T. Buckingham, A ("Thrash away, you'll hev to rattle"). AmPP; OxBA
(Mr. Hosea Biglow Speaks.) PAH
("Thrash away, you'll hev to rattle.") AmePo; CoBA
(To a Recruiting Sergeant.) AnNE
Ez fer War, 4 *sts.* PPON
War, 1 *st.* MaRV
1st Series, No. II.
Letter, from Mr. Hosea Biglow to the Hon. J. T. Buckingham, A ("This kind of sogerin"). OxBA
1st Series, No. III.
What Mr. Robinson Thinks. AA; AmPP; AnNE; BOHV; HBV; IHA; InMe; LHV; PAH; TOP; YaD
("Guvener B. is a sensible man.") AmePo
1st Series, No. V.
Debate in the Sennit, The. HBV; PAH
1st Series, No. VI.
Pious Editor's Creed, The. AmePo; AnNE; TOP
(Candidate's Creed, The, *abr.*) BOHV; YaD
1st Series, No. VII.
Letter from Candidate for the Presidency, A ("Dear Sir,—You wish to know my notions").
(Candidate's Letter, The.) AA
2d Series, Introduction.
Courtin', The. AA; AmePo; AmPP; AnNE; BeLS; BOHV; CoBA; HBV; IHA; InMe; LHV; MCCG; OBVV; StVeCh; TreFS; YT
2d Series, No. II.
Mason and Slidell; a Yankee Idyll, *sel.*
Jonathan to John. CoBA; PaA; PAH; PAP
2d Series, No. VI.
Sunthin' in the Pastoral Line. AmPP (3d ed.); AP; CoBA; MWA-1; PFY, *abr.*
(Spring.) FaBV; MCCG, *abr.*
2d Series, No. X.
Mr. Hosea Biglow to the Editor of the *Atlantic Monthly.* AA, *abr.*; PoEL-5
(Hosea Biglow's Lament, *abr.*) PFY
Bigness of cannon, The. La Guerre. E. E. Cummings. MAP; MoAB; MoAmPo
Bigot. Eleanor Slater. MaRV
Bilitis. Pierre Louys, *tr. fr. French by* Horace M. Brown. *Fr.* The Songs of Bilitis. UnTE
Bill. J. L. Salzburg. BiCB
Bill/ Was ill. Careless Talk. Mark Hollis. FiBHP
Bill and Joe. Oliver Wendell Holmes. AA; HBV; PCD
Bill dug a well. A Narrative. Theodore Spencer. NeMA; WaKn; WhC
Bill Haller's Dance. Robert V. Carr. PoOW
Bill Jones had been the shining star upon his college team. Alumnus Football. Grantland Rice. PoLF
Bill Jones was cynical and sad. Jim and Bill. Franklin P. Adams. LHV

Bill Jupp lies 'ere, aged sixty year. From the Greek Anthology. L. A. G. Strong. WhC
Bill Manning. Joseph I. C. Clarke. JKCP (1926 ed.)
Bill Martin and Ella Speed, *with music*. *Unknown*. ABF
Bill Peters, the Stage Driver. *Unknown*. CoSo; IHA
(Bill Peters.) TSW
Bill the Bachelor lived by himself. Bachelors' Buttons. Maud Morin. BoTP
Bill the Whaler. Will Lawson. PoAu-1
Bill Venero. *Unknown*. CoSo, *with music*
Billiards. Walker Gibson. NePoAm
Billows swell, the winds are high, The. Temptation. William Cowper. EiCP
Billowy headlands swiftly fly, The. Battle-Song of the *Oregon*. Wallace Rice. PaA; PAH
Billy. Harry Graham. *See* Tenderheartedness.
Billy Barlow, *with music*. *Unknown*. OuSiCo
Billy Boy. Dorothy King. BoTP
Billy Boy. *Unknown*. ABF, *with music*; BLPA; IHA; SiTL
("Where have ye [*or* you] been all the day,/ Billy Boy?") LO; OxNR
Billy Boy, Billy Boy, where are you riding to? Billy Boy. Dorothy King. BoTP
Billy Budd, Foretopman, *sel*. Herman Melville.
Billy in the Darbies. AmePo; AmPP (4th ed.); AtBAP; CBEP; ExPo; LoBV; MAmP; NCEP; OxBoLi; PoEL-5
Billy goat's a handsome gent, The. The Goat. Roland Young. WhC
Billy, He's in Trouble. James Barton Adams. YaD
Billy, in one of his nice new sashes. Tenderheartedness [*or* Billy]. Harry Graham. Some Ruthless Rhymes, II. CenHV; FaFP; LiTM; MaC; SiTL; TreFT; WhC; WePo
Billy in the Darbies. Herman Melville. *Fr.* Billy Budd, Foretopman. AmePo; AmPP (4th ed.); AtBAP; CBEP; ExPo; LoBV; MAmP; NCEP; OxBoLi; PoEL-5
Billy the Kid. Jack Spicer. CoPo
Billy the Kid ("Billy was a bad man"). *Unknown*. ABF; CoSo
Billy the Kid ("I'll sing you a true song of Billy the Kid"). *Unknown*. ABF, *with music*; CoSo, *with music*; FaBoBe; ThLM
Billy Venero heard them say. Bill Venero. *Unknown*. CoSo
Billy was a bad man. Billy the Kid. *Unknown*. ABF; CoSo
Billy's Rose ("Billy's dead, and gone to glory"). George R. Sims. PaPo
Bim Bam. Dorothy Rosenberg. PoNe (1970 ed.)
Bimbo's Pome. Paul Klee, *tr. fr. German by* Anselm Hollo. FIW
Bind us the Morning, mother of the stars. Thefts of the Morning. Edith M. Thomas. AA
Bindlestiff. Edwin Ford Piper. HBMV; MAP
Bind-Weed. "Susan Coolidge." GN; OTPC (1923 ed.)
Bindweed, The. Walter de la Mare. BrPo
Bingen on the Rhine. Caroline Elizabeth Sarah Norton. BeLS; BLPA; HBV; NeHB; TreF; WBLP
Bingo. *Unknown*. CH; OTPC (1946 ed.)
(Bobby Bingo.) RIS
Bingo Has an Enemy ("Bingo is kind and friendly"). Rose Fyleman. TiPo; UTS
Binker ("Binker—what I call him—is a secret of my own"). A. A. Milne. PoPl
Binnorie. *Unknown*. *See* Two Sisters, The.
Binsey Poplars (Felled 1879). Gerard Manley Hopkins. BoNaP; BrPo; CoBMV; EG; ELP; FIW; MoVE; NoP; PIA; PoPo; UnPo (3d ed.); VP
Biography. Charles Bruce. CaP; PeCV
Biography. A. M. Klein. TrJP
Biography. Mavor Moore. TwCaPo
Biography. "Jan Struther." InMe
Biography for Beginners. E. C. Bentley. *See* Clerihews.
Biography for Traman, *sel*. Winfield Townley Scott.
"Let us record/ The evenings when we were innocents of twenty." ErPo
Biography of an Agnostic. Louis Ginsberg. TrJP
Bion's Lament for Adonis. Bion. *See* Lament for Adonis.
Biotherm. Frank O'Hara. CoPo
Birch. Louis Simpson. ELU; PoIE (1970 ed.)
Birch begins to crack its outer sheath, The. A Young Birch. Robert Frost. BoNAP; LiTA
Birch-Tree at Loschwitz, The. Amy Levy. TrJP
Birch tree, you remind me. Birch. Louis Simpson. ELU; PoIE (1970 ed.)
Birch Trees. John Richard Moreland. DD; HBMV; HBVY; OHIP
Birches, The. Walter Prichard Eaton. StVeCh
Birches. Robert Frost. AmPP; AnNE; CMoP; CoBA; DiPo; FaBV; HaMV; HBMV; ILP; LiTA; LiTM; LoGBV; MAP; MAPA; MaPo (1969 ed.); MCCG; MoAB; MoAmPo; MoVE; NeMA; NoP; OxBA; PAn; PFY; PoFS; PoIE; PoLF; PoPl; PoRA; StP; TOP; TreF; TrGrPo; TwAmPo; UnPo (3d ed.)
Birches that dance on the top of the hill, The. Parenthood. John Farrar. MPB; OHIP
Bird, The. William Allingham. OTPC
Bird, A. Emily Dickinson. *See* Bird came down the walk, A.
Bird, The. Robert Greacen. NeIP
Bird, The. Samuel Hoffenstein. FiBHP; PV
Bird, The. Jorge de Lima, *tr. fr. Portuguese by* Dudley Poore. LiTW
Bird, The. Max Michelson. NP; TrJP
Bird, The. Edwin Muir. POTE
Bird, The. Louis Simpson. NePoEA-2
Bird, The. Rabindranath Tagore, *tr. fr. Bengali by* Rabindranath Tagore. The Gardener, LXVII. LiTW; PoPl
Bird, The. Sister Mary Thérèse. JKCP (1955 ed.)
Bird, The. Henry Vaughan. AnAnS-1; AtBAP; LoBV; MeP; OBEV (new ed.); PoEL-2; SCEP-1; SeCL; SeCV-1
(After the Storm.) BoC
(To a Bird after a Storm.) TRV
Bird, The. Countess of Winchilsea. EiPP
Bird, The. Andrew Young. POTE
Bird, a man, a loaded gun, A. *Unknown*. WhC
Bird and Brook, *sel*. Sir Samuel Ferguson.
"Bird that pipest on the bough." IrPN
Bird and the Tree, The. Ridgely Torrence. HBMV; MAP; MoAmPo (1942 ed.); NP; PoFr; PoNe
Bird appears a thoughtless thing, A. Crumbs to the Birds. Charles *and* Mary Lamb. OTPC
Bird at Dawn, The. Harold Monro. BoTP; GoTP; MoBrPo (1950 ed.)
Bird at Night. Marion Ethel Hamilton. GoYe
Bird Bath, The. Florence Hoatson. BoTP
Bird, Bird. Gene Derwood. LiTA; Sonn
Bird, bird don't edge me in. The Reply. Theodore Roethke. NoP; NYBP
Birdcage, The. Conrad Aiken. BiS
Bird Cage, *sel*. David Campbell.
Magpie Singing His Delight, The. BiS
Bird came down the walk, A. Emily Dickinson. AmePo; AmLP; AmPP (5th ed.); AnAmPo; AnFE; AP; APA; CABA; CMoP; CoAnAm; CoBA; DiPo; FaPON, 8 *ll*.; GoJo; InvP; LiTA; LiTM (rev. ed.); MAmP; MAPA; MaPo; MoAmPo; MoShBr; MoVE; MPB; NoP; PAn; PDV; OxBA; PG; PoLF; PoPo; PoRA; PoRh; SeCeV; SoPo; StVeCh, 8 *ll*.; TDP; TiPo; TreFT; TwAmPo; UTS
Bird Catcher. *See* Birdcatcher.
Bird Fancier, The. James Kirkup. PoPo
Bird flew tangent-wise to the open window, A. The Bird. Robert Greacen. NeIP
Bird flies and I gum it to a concept, A. Letter to Anne Ridler. G. S. Fraser. OxBS
Bird from the West, A. Dora Sigerson Shorter. OBVV
Bird in a Cage, The. William Lisle Bowles. TVC
Bird in a Cage, The, *with music*. *Unknown*. AS
Bird in a Gilded Cage, A. Arthur J. Lamb. TreFT
Bird in my bower, A. Song. Francis Howard Williams. AA
Bird in my heart is calling through a far-fled, tear-grey sea, The. Blanid's Song. Gordon Bottomley. *Fr.* The Crier by Night. BrPo
Bird in Search of a Cage, A. Robert Pack. NePoEA
Bird in the Bush, A. Lord Kennet. PV
Bird in the Hand, A. Frederic E. Weatherly. BOHV; VA
Bird in the Room, The. Rudolph Chambers Lehmann. HBMV; HBVY
Bird is lost, The. Yardbird's Skull. Owen Dodson. AmNP; IDB
Bird is my neighbour, a whimsical fellow and dim, The. The Crane Is My Neighbour. John Shaw Neilson. PoAu-1
Bird is out-to-lunch. Expansion to Aveline's. James Brodey. ANYP
Bird kept saying that birds had once been men, The. On an Old Horn. Wallace Stevens. LiTA

Bird, Let Loose in Eastern Skies, The. Thomas Moore. HBV; OTPC (1923 ed.)
Bird may curve across the sky, A. Flight. Hazel Hall. AnAmPo; MAP; MoAmPo (1942 ed.)
Bird of Night, The. Randall Jarrell. BiS
Bird of Paradise, The. Laura Benét. PFY
Bird of Paradise, The. W. H. Davies. AtBAP; BrPo; MoVE
Bird of Paradise. Robert Graves. BoPe
Bird of the bitter bright gray golden morn. A Ballad of François Villon. Swinburne. BEL; EnLi-2; PoEL-5; PoRA; PoVP; ViPP
Bird of the fierce delight. To a Sea-Gull. Arthur Symons. PoVP
Bird of the spray, the tree of bones. Loss. Randall Jarrell. FiMAP
Bird of the wilderness. The Skylark. James Hogg. ATP; DD; GN; HBV; HBVY; OTPC; PTK
Bird of Time, The. Omar Khayyám, *tr. fr. Persian by* Edward Fitzgerald. *Fr.* The Rubáiyát. OnPM
("Come, fill the cup, and in the fire of spring.") FaBV; InP; TreF; WGRP
(Fifteen Rubáiyát.) LiTW
Bird ran up the onyx steps of night, A. Fantasy. Louis Untermeyer. TSW
Bird Raptures. Christina Rossetti. ViPo
Bird shadows mounting. Larry Eigner. CoPo
Bird-shaped island, with secretive bird-voices. New Guinea. James McAuley. PoAu-2
Bird sings on a matin tree, A. Lyric. Kathleen Raine. CMoP
Bird sings the selfsame song, A. The Selfsame Song. Thomas Hardy. CMoP; TOP
Birdsong. Blake. *See* Nightingale and Flowers.
Bird Song. John Hay. NePoAm-2
Bird Song. Laura E. Richards. HBV
Bird-Song. Mary Dixon Thayer. CAW
Bird that discoursest from yon poplar bough. Sonnet. James Clarence Mangan. IrPN
Bird that flies to climates crisper, The. Spring. Oscar Williams. LiTA
Bird that I don't know, A. A Country Life. Randall Jarrell. MiAP; MoAmPo (1950 ed.)
Bird that pipest on the bough. Sir Samuel Ferguson. *Fr.* Bird and Brook. IrPN
Bird, that's fetch't from Phasis floud, The. Out of Petronius. Richard Crashaw. MaMe
Bird Trades. *Unknown.* DD; HH
Bird walks by the shore, The. Northern Water Thrush. D. G. Jones. PeCV (1967 ed.)
Bird Was Singing, A. Dietmar von Aist, *tr. fr. German by* Jethro Bithell. AWP; LiTW
Birdwatcher. Henry Treece. WaP
Birdwatchers of America. Anthony Hecht. CoPo
Bird watchers top my honors list. Up from the Egg; the Confessions of a Nuthatch Avoider. Ogden Nash. FiBHP; PoRA (rev. ed.)
Bird with a Broken Wing, The. Hezekiah Butterworth. FaChP; WBLP
(Broken Pinion, The.) MaRV
Bird with the Coppery, Keen Claws, The. Wallace Stevens. AnFE; APA; CoAnAm; NoP; PoeP
Bird-witted. Marianne Moore. CMoP
Bird Wounded by an Arrow, The. La Fontaine, *tr. fr. French by* Elizur Wright. OnPM
Bird you caught me, with blue feathers, The. Letter: The Japanese, to Her Husband at War. William Walsh. PoPl
Birdcatcher, The. Ralph Hodgson. AtBAP; MoBrPo; NeMA; PoIE
Bird-Catcher, The. Elizabeth Turner. OTPC (1923 ed.)
Bird Catcher, The. *Unknown, tr. fr. Egyptian by* Ulli Beier. TTY
Birdcatcher's Song. William John Courthope. *Fr.* The Paradise of Birds. VA
Birdie. Eliza Lee Follen. OTPC; SAS
"Birdie, Birdie, will you pet?" The Bird. William Allingham. OTPC
Birdie with a yellow bill, A. Time to Rise [*or* Time to Get Up]. Robert Louis Stevenson. BoChLi; InP; OTPC (1946 ed.); PCH; PoVP; RIS; SiSoSe; StVeCh; ThGo; UTS
Birdies' Breakfast, The. *Unknown.* BoTP
Birdies, can there be any doubt. November. James Reaney. *Fr.* A Suit of Nettles. OBCV; PIA
Birdies with Broken Wings. Mary Mapes Dodge. *See* Mother.
Birdless heaven, seadusk, one lone star, A. Tutto è Sciolto. James Joyce. OBMV; OxBI
Bird-like, my heart was glad to soar and vault. Voyage to Cythera. Baudelaire. SyP
Birds, *sels.* Aristophanes, *tr. fr. Greek.*
Chorus of Birds, *tr. by* Swinburne. AWP; JAWP; WBP; WoL, *tr. by* Benjamin Bickely Rogers
(Grand Chorus of Birds, *tr. by* Swinburne.) PoEL-5
Take My Wings and Dance with Me, *tr. by* Ann Stanford. HW
Birds, The. Hilaire Belloc. JKCP
Birds, The. Blake. CH; OBRV
Birds, The. Samuel Taylor Coleridge. *See* Answer to a Child's Question.
Birds, The. Blossius Aemilius Dracontius, *tr. fr. Latin by* Thomas Walsh. CAW
Birds. Hildegarde Flanner. NP
Birds. Robinson Jeffers. AP; CoBMV; TwAmPo
Birds. "Llywelyn." PoAu-2
Birds. Ruth Miller. PeSA
Birds, The. Ogden Nash. *Fr.* The Carnival of Animals. UnS
Birds. "Moira O'Neill." HBV
Birds. "Seumas O'Sullivan." OxBI
Birds, The. David Posner. NYBP
Birds, The. J. C. Squire. HBMV
Birds. Richard Henry Stoddard. AA; HBV
Birds, The ("From out of a wood did a cuckoo fly"). *Unknown, tr. fr. Czech.* ChrBoLe
Birds ("Wild pigeon of the leaves"). *Unknown, tr. fr. Arabic by* E. Powys Mathers. *Fr.* The Thousand and One Nights. AWP; LiTW
Birds All Singing. Norman MacCaig. ChMP
Birds and Bees. *Unknown, tr. fr. German by* Louis Untermeyer. UnTE
Birds and bees and butterflies. Out of Doors. E. North. BoTP
Birds and butterflies. Brownstone. Rod McKuen. TPM
Birds are coming home soon, The. The Coming of Spring. *Unknown.* PEDC
Birds are gone to bed, the cows are still, The. Hares at Play. John Clare. CBEP; OA
Birds are of passage now. Words for the Raker of Leaves. Léonie Adams. PoCh
Birds are our angels—out of heaven. Birds. "Llywelyn." PoAu-2
Birds are singing round my window. Birds. Richard Henry Stoddard. AA; HBV
Birds at Winter Nightfall. Thomas Hardy. BiS; ELU; MoBrPo
Birds, Bags, Bears, and Buns. *Unknown.* *See* Common Cormorant, The.
Birds' Ball, The. Charles William Bardeen. BLPA
Birds' Courting Song, The, *with music.* *Unknown.* TrAS
Birds Do Thus, The. Robert Frost. AmePo
Bird's egg, a green branch, A. That's June. Mary F. Butts. YeAr
Bird's Epitaph, A. Martin Armstrong. BiS; POTE
(On a Little Bird.) CH
Birds far-off and open in the evening. The Gentle Hill. Salvatore Quasimodo. PoPl
Birds feed on birds, beasts on each other prey. Wretched Man. Earl of Rochester. *Fr.* A Satire against Mankind. SeCePo
Birds Go By, The. Shaw Neilson. MoAuPo
Birds go fluttering in the air, The. The Silent Snake. *Unknown.* BoTP; FaPON; TiPo (1959 ed.)
Birds have been singing today, The. In Februrary. John Addington Symonds. DD; PRWS; YeAr
"Birds have hid, the winds are low, The." John Vance Cheney. Evening Songs, I. AA
Birds in a whirl, drift to the rooftops. This Poem Is for Birds. Gary Snyder. Myths & Texts: Hunting. NaP
Birds in April. W. E. Henley. *See* World Still Young, A.
Birds in Spring. Thomas Nashe. *See* Spring, the Sweet Spring.
Birds in Spring. James Thomson. *Fr.* The Seasons: Spring. OBEC
("Blackbird whistles from the thorny brake, The.) PeER
Birds in Summer. Mary Howitt. HH; MPB; OTPC; PRWS
Birds in the air. Mary's Song. Eleanor Farjeon. ThGo

Birds in the Fens. Michael Drayton. Polyolbion, Song 25. ChTr
Birds in the first light twitter and whistle, The. A Little Morning Music. Delmore Schwartz. BoNaP; NYBP
Birds in the Flax. Stanley Snaith. HaMV
Birds in the Garden. *Unknown.* ThGo
Birds in the high Hall-garden. Tennyson. *Fr.* Maude. OTPC (1923 ed.); PeVV
Birds in their oratory of leaves. Per Diem et per Noctem. Mary Stanley. AnNZ
Birds, joyous birds of the wandering wing! The Birds of Passage. Felicia Dorothea Hemans. OTPC
Birds' Lament. John Clare. PoEL-4
Bird's Nest, The. John Drinkwater. EvOK; PDV; SoPo; StVeCh
Bird's Nest, The. Elizabeth Turner. OHIP; OTPC (1923 ed.)
Birdsnest, A, built on the palm of the high-/ Most bough. Lightness. Richard Wilbur. FiMAP
Birds' Nests. John Clare. *Fr.* Childhood. BiS; ERoP-2
Birds' Nests. Millicent Seager. BoTP
Birds' Nests. *Unknown.* BoTP; MPB
Birds of a feather will flock together. *Unknown.* GoTP
Birds of America, The. James Broughton. AmFN
Birds of Bethlehem, The. Richard Watson Gilder. AA
Birds of Killingworth, The. Longfellow. *Fr.* Tales of a Wayside Inn: The Poet's Tale. OnMSP; OxBA
"Do you ne'er think that wondrous beings these?" *sel.* WBLP
Birds of omen dark and foul. Annot Lyle's Song. Sir Walter Scott. *Fr.* The Legend of Montrose. EnRP
Birds of Paradise, The. John Peale Bishop. GoJo
Birds of Paradise. Christina Rossetti. VP
Birds of Passage. Felicia Dorothea Hemans. OTPC
Birds of Passage, *sel.* Walt Whitman.
In This Earth Perfection. OQP
Birds of Rhiannon, The. Euros Bowen, *tr. fr. Welsh by* Gwyn Williams. PrWP
Birds of the Air, The. Hollis Freeman. STF
Birds of Tin, The. Charles Madge. NeBP
Birds on the School Windowsill, The. Evelyn Dainty. BoTP
Birds' Rondel, The. Chaucer. *See* Roundel, A: "Now welcom, somer, with thy sonne softe."
Bird's Song at Morning. William James Dawson. VA
Bird's Song in Spring. Edith Nesbit. *See* Child's Song in Spring.
Bird's Song, the Sun, and the Wind, The. Sir Charles G. D. Roberts. VA
Birds stayed not their singing. Armistice Day. John Freeman. MMA
Birds that were gray in the green are black in the yellow. September. "Seranus". VA
Birds their choir [*or* quire] apply, The; airs, vernal airs. Adam and Eve [*or* The Eternal Spring]. Milton. *Fr.* Paradise Lost, IV. CLwM; GN
Birds their love-notes warble, The. Alice Ray. Sarah Joseph Hale. AA
Bird's wing lies under your swing, A. Look, See the Cat. Nancy Price. NYTB
Birdsong. *See* Bird Song.
Birdwatcher. *See* Bird Watcher.
Birkenhead, The, *sel.* Sir Henry Yule.
"Not with the cheer of battle." OtMeF
Birkett's Eagle. Dorothy S. Howard. MoBS
Birks of Aberfeldy, The. Burns. CTC; ViBoPo
Birks of Endermay, The. David Mallet. OBEC
Birlinn Chlann-Raghnaill. Alexander MacDonald, *tr. fr. Gaelic by* "Hugh MacDiarmid." GoTS
Birmingham. Julia Fields. PoNe (1970 ed.)
Birmingham. Louis MacNeice. CMoP; ILP; MoAB; MoBrPo
Birmingham Sunday. Langston Hughes. PoNe (1970 ed.)
Birth, A. James Dickey. FRC
Birth, The. Rosemary Dobson. PoAu-2
Birth. Grace Raymond. AA
Birth, A. Muriel Rukeyser. FiMAP
Birth and Death. Swinburne. MaVP
Birth and Death. Thomas Wade. VA
Birth and death, twin-sister and twin-brother. Birth and Death. Swinburne. MaVP
Birth-Bond, The. Dante Gabriel Rossetti. The House of Life, XV. HBV; MaVP; OAEP; PoVP; Sonn; ViPo; VP
Birth by Anesthesia. George Scarbrough. GoYe
Birth-Dues. Robinson Jeffers. MAP; MoAB; MoAmPo
Birth in a Narrow Room, The. Gwendolyn Brooks. PoNe; TPM
Birth of a Great Man. Robert Graves. NYBP
Birth of a Shark, The. David Wevill. TwCP
Birth of Arachne, the Spider, The. James Schevill. FiMAP
Birth of Arthur, The. Layamon, *tr. fr. Middle English. Fr.* The Brut. MeEV
Birth of Australia, The. Percy Russell. VA
Birth of Christ. Rainer Maria Rilke, *tr. fr. German by* M. D. Herter Norton. MoRP
Birth of Galahad, The, *sel.* Richard Hovey.
Ylen's Song. AA
Birth of Lucifer, The. John Gould Fletcher. MAP; MoAmPo
Birth of Mary. Rainer Maria Rilke, *tr. fr. German by* M. D. Herter Norton. MoRP
Birth of Moshesh, The. D. G. T. Bereng, *tr. fr. Sotho by* Dan Kunene *and* Jack Cope. PeSA; TTY
Birth of Robin Hood, The. *Unknown.* BuBa; OBB; OxBB; ViBoPo, *last 2 sts.*
(Willie and Earl Richard's Daughter, A, B, *and* C *vers.*) ESPB
Birth of Saint Patrick, The. Samuel Lover. BOHV; DD; HBV; OTD; PoRL; PoSC
Birth of Speech, The. Hartley Coleridge. VA
Birth of the Flowers, The. Mary NcNeil Fenollosa. OQP
Birth of the Poet, The. Quandra Prettyman. BOLo
Birth of the Squire, The; an Eclogue. John Gay. EiCL; EiCP; PoEL-3
Birth of Tragedy, The. Irving Layton. MoCV; OBCV; PeCV
Birth of Venus, The. *Unknown.* EtS
Birth seems like chance, and life appears uncertain. Lincoln. Rembrandt William B. Ditmars. HBMV
Birth Song of Christ, The. Edmund H. Sears. BePJ
(Christmas Hymn, A.) SoP
Birthday. Elaine V. Emans. BiCB
Birthday, A. Rachel Field. BiCB; SiSoSe; TiPo (1959 ed.)
Birthday, A. Christina Rossetti. AWP; BoLiVe; BoLP; CH; CoBE; EnLi-2; FaFP; FaPL; GTBS; GTSE; GTSL; InvP; JAWP; LiTB; LiTG; LiTL; LoBV; MeWo; OAEP; OBEV; OBVV; OuHeWo; PCD; PeVV; PoE; PoVP; ShBV-4; ThWaDe; TOP; TreFS; TrGrPo; TSW; ViBoPo; ViPo; VP; WBP; WHA; WiR; YT
("My heart is like a singing bird.") EG
Birthday. Jean Starr Untermeyer. MAP; MoAmPo (1942 ed.)
Birthday, birthday; little boy has a birthday. Birthday Gifts. Louise Binder Scott *and* J. J. Thompson. BiCB
Birthday Bus, The. Mary Ann Hoberman. BiCB
Birthday Cake, The. Victoria Chase. BiCB
Birthday Cake. Ivy O. Eastwick. BiCB
Birthday Cake. Aileen Fisher. BiCB; PDV
Birthday-Cake Glockenspiel, The. Elizabeth Henley. BiCB
Birthday Candle, A. Donald Justice. NYBP
Birthday Candles. Louise Binder Scott *and* J. J. Thompson. BiCB
Birthday candles, shine your brightest. Six Birthday Candles Shining. Mary Jane Carr. BiCB
Birthday Child, The. Rose Fyleman. BiCB; FaPON; SiSoSe
Birthday Crown, The. William Alexander. OBVV
Birthday Garden. Ivy O. Eastwick. BiCB
Birthday Gift. Ethel Barnett de Vito. BiCB
Birthday Gift, A. Christina Rossetti. *See* Christmas Carol, A: "In the bleak mid-winter."
Birthday Gifts. Herbert Asquith. BiCB; SiSoSe
Birthday Gifts. Louise Binder Scott *and* J. J. Thompson. BiCB
Birthday Morning. Jean Ingelow. *See* Seven Times One.
Birthday of Catharine Tufton, The, *sel.* Countess of Winchilsea.
Portrait, The. OBEC
Birthday of Daniel Webster. Oliver Wendell Holmes. DD
Birthday of the Lord, The. Mary Jane Carr. BiCB; ChBR
Birthday Poem for Thomas Hardy. C. Day Lewis. CoBMV
Birthday Poem, November 4th. John Thompson, Jr. WaP
Birthday Prayer, A. John Finley. TrPWD
Birthday Rhyme. *Unknown.* BiCB
Birthday Song, A. Richard Watson Gilder. PoRL
Birthday Sonnet. Elinor Wylie. BoLiVe; MAP; MoAB; MoAmPo; OnPM
Birthday Wish, A. Dorothy Nell McDonald. PoToHe (new ed.)
Birthday, with Leaves. James Applewhite. YAP

Birthdays. Marchette Chute. BiCB; SiSoSe; StVeCh
Birthdays. C. J. Driver. PeSA
Birthdays from the ocean one desert april noon. That "Craning of the Neck." Isabella Gardner. NePA
Birthdays? yes, in a general way. Imitation of Robert Browning [*or* Sincere Flattery of R. B.]. James Kenneth Stephen. InMe; Par
Birthplace, The. Robert Frost. LoGBV
Birthplace of Mr. William Shakespeare author, The. Verses for a Centennial. Archibald MacLeish. NoP
Birthplace Revisited. Gregory Corso. CAD; NeAP; OCS
Birthright. John Drinkwater. CH; HBV; POTE; WHA
Bishop and a bold dragoon, A. A Recent Dialogue. Thomas Moore. NBM
Bishop and His Portmanteau, The. *Unknown.* ALV
Bishop Blougram's Apology. Robert Browning. OBNC; OtMeF, *abr.*; PoEL-5; ViPo; ViPP
Sels.
Belief and Unbelief. FaBV
Common Problem, The. OQP
In Doubt of Doubt. MaRV
"When the fight begins within himself." MaRV;TRV
Bishop Boundary-rides His Diocese, The. Allen Curnow. *Fr.* Not in Narrow Seas. AnNZ
Bishop Butler of Kilcash. *Unknown.* OnYI
Bishop Doane on His Dog ["Cluny"]. William Croswell Doane, *wr. at. to* George Washington Doane. BBV (1951 ed.); BLPA; FaBoBe; NeHB
Bishop Hatto [and the Rats]. Robert Southey. *See* God's Judgment on a Wicked Bishop.
Bishop Loreless. *Unknown.* NoP
Bishop of Atlanta, The: Ray Charles. Horace Julian Bond. AmNP
Bishop of Rum-ti-Foo, The. W. S. Gilbert. CenHV; PoVP
Bishop Orders His Tomb at Saint Praxed's Church, The. Robert Browning. ATP; AWP; BEL; BoLiVe; BWP; CABA; CaFP; CBV; DiPo; EnLi-2; EnLit; EPN; ExPo; FiP; ForPo; GTSE; HBV; ILP; MaPo; MaVP; MBW-2; MyFE; NoP; OAEP; OtMeF; PAn; PIA; Po; PoAn; PoE; PoIE; PoVP; SeCeV; ShBV-4; VA; VaPo; ViBoPo; ViPo; ViPP; VP
Bishop sat in lordly state and purple cap sublime, The. Tangmalangaloo. P. J. Hartigan. PoAu-1
Bishop seduces the world with his voice, The. The Bishop of Atlanta: Ray Charles. Horace Julian Bond. AmNP
Bishop Spaniel's Sermons. Colin Ellis. *See* Spaniel's Sermon.
Bishop tells us, The: "When the boys come back." "They." Siegfried Sassoon. CMoP; HBMV; MaRV
Bishop's Harp, The. Robert Mannyng. ACP
Bishop's See, The. *Unknown.* CoMu
Bison, The. Hilaire Belloc. NA
Bit of color against the blue, A. A Song for Our Flag. Margaret E. Sangster. FaFP
Bit of Colour, A. Horace Smith. BoTP
Bit of the Book, A. Margaret E. Sangster. FaChP; SoP; TRV
"Bite deep and wide, O Axe, the tree." Isabella Valancy Crawford. *Fr.* Malcolm's Katie. OBCV
Biter Bit, The. William Edmonstoune Aytoun. BOHV; InMe
Bits and Pieces. Gregory J. Ford. TNV
Bits of song—what else? Hokku. Yone Noguchi. NP
Bits of Straw. John Clare. *See* I Peeled Bits Of Straw.
Bitten. Mark Van Doren. AnAmPo
Bitter air, The. L'aura amara. Arnaut Daniel. CTC
Bitter, bitter/ Is my fate. Misery. Shao Ch'ang Heng. OnPM
Bitter black bitterness. Poem (No Name No. 2). Nikki Giovanni. BOLo
Bitter in sooth is the wind to-night. The Viking. Whitley Stokes. OnYI
Bitter king in anger to be gone, A. Like an Old Proud King in a Parable. A. J. M. Smith. OBCV
Bitter Purple Willows, The. Allen Upward. *Fr.* Scented Leaves from a Chinese Jar. NP
Bitter Question. Arthur R. Macdougall, Jr. PGD
Bitter Sanctuary. Harodl Monro. FaBoMo; LiTB; OBMV
Bitter-Sweet. George Herbert. MaMe; NoP; OxBoCh; TrPWD
Bitter-sweet, *sels.* Josiah Gilbert Holland.
Cradle Song: "What is the little one thinking about?" HBV; PCD
(Babyhood.) AA
Hymn: "For summer's bloom and autumn's blight." TrPWD
Song of Faith. WGRP
Bitter the storm to-night. The Vikings. *Unknown.* ChTr
Bitter was it, Oh to view. *Unknown.* *Fr.* A Lament for the Priory of Walsingham. ChTr
Bitter Withy, The. *Unknown.* BaBo; ChTr; NoP; OAEP; PoIE; ViBoFo, *with music.*
Bitter World of Spring, The. William Carlos Williams. PoeP
Bitterness of days like these we know, The. Salutamus. Sterling A. Brown. CDC
Bitterness of death and bitterer scorn, The. John Marston. Swinburne. *Fr.* Sonnets on English Dramatic Poets. Sonn
Bitwene Mersh and Averil. *Unknown.* *See* Alisoun.
Bivouac. Alun Lewis. ChMP
Bivouac of the Dead, The. Theodore O'Hara. AA; AnAmPo; BLPA; DD, *much abr.*; FaPL; GA, *much abr.*; HBV; HH; MC; NeHB; PaA; PAH; PAL; PAP; TreF
"Muffled drum's sad roll has beat, The," *sel.* PoRL
Bivouac on a Mountain Side. Walt Whitman. AA; AmP; AP; ChTr; CoBA; MWA-1; NoP; OxBA; PAL; PO; PoLF
Bizarre Deity, dark as infernal nights. Sed Non Satiata. Baudelaire. OnPM
Black absence hides upon the past. Stanzas. John Clare. EnLoPo
Black All Day. Raymond Richard Patterson. BOLo
Black and Gold. Nancy Byrd Turner. MPB; SoPo; TiPo; YeAr
Black and White. Esther Lillian Duff. HBMV
Black and white. Things to Learn About. John Becker. RePo
Black and White Shuffle. Harry Elmore Hurd. WhC
Black and White Spring. Christopher Hampton. NYTB
Black and yellow. Bumble Bee. Margaret Wise Brown. PDV
Black Angel, The. Henri Coulette. CoAP; NYBP
Black Angel. Lewis Thompson. AtBAP
Black Are the Stars. Raymond Roseliep. FiSC
Black Army, The. S. E. K. Mqhayi, *tr. fr. Xhosa by* C. M. Mcanyangwa *and* Jack Cope. PeSA
Black Art. LeRoi Jones. BF; BP
Black as a battering-ram the massive head. Buffalo. Roy Daniells. CaP
Black as a chimney is his face. "Sooeep!" Walter de la Mare. BoTP
Black Ball Line, The, *with music.* *Unknown.* ABF; AmSS; SoAmSa, *diff. vers.*
(Blow, Boys, Blow, *vers. IV, diff. vers.*) ShS
Black beamy hairs, which so seem to arise. To Her Hair. Lord Herbert of Cherbury. NoP; SeEP
Black beauty, which above that common light. Sonnet of Black Beauty. Lord Herbert of Cherbury. AnAnS-2; AtBAP; BoW; EP; MePo; SeCL; SeEP
Black Betty, *with music.* *Unknown.* ABF
Black Bird. *See* Blackbird.
Black, black, black is the color of my true love's hair. Black Is the Color of My True Love's Hair. *Unknown.* TreFT
Black, black, the sheen of his back and shoulders. Toro. W. S. Merwin. NePA
Black Blues. Bloke Modisane. PBA
Black Book of Carmarthen, The, *sels.* *Unknown,* *tr. fr. Welsh.*
Englyn, *tr. by* Gwyn Williams. PrWP
On Christians, Mercy Will Fall, *tr. by* D. M. Lloyd. PrWP
Song of the Graves, The, *tr. by* Ernest Rhys. OBMV
Winter, *tr. by* Kenneth Jackson. PrWP
Wisdom in Winter, *tr. by* Gwyn Williams. PrWP
Black Boundary, The. Lewis Warsh. YAP
Black Boy. Carl Carmer. AnAmPo
Black Boy. Norman Rosten. TrJP
Black boy rose from his bed, The. Samuel. Alan Paton. BoSA
Black boy, the night hides you. Black Boy. Norman Rosten. TrJP
Black brother, think you life so sweet. Time to Die. Ray Garfield Dandridge. BANP
Black-burnin' shame is your garb, quo' they. The Scarlet Woman. "Hugh MacDiarmid." ACV
Black Cat. Lora Dunetz. NePoAm-2
Black cat among roses, A. The Garden by Moonlight. Amy Lowell. NP; PFY; TOP; YT
Black cat, black cat, with the lucky white spot at your neck. Black Cat. Lora Dunetz. NePoAm-2
Black Cat Crossed His Luck, De. James D. Corrothers. CIV
Black cat yawns, The. The Cat. Mary Britton Miller.

Black (continued)
BoChLi; SoPo; StVeCh; SUS; TiPo; UTS
Black cats, grey cats, green cats miau. The Conscientious Deacon. Vachel Lindsay. MemP
Black Christ, The. Arthur Shearly Cripps. BoSA
Black Church on Sunday. Joseph M. Mosley, Jr. NBP
Black Cop's Communion, A. Arnold Kemp. WSL
Black Cottage, The. Robert Frost. AmPP; CoBA; MWA-2
"Black" Country, The. D. J. Enright. HaMV
Black Crispus Attucks taught. Dark Symphony. Melvin B. Tolson. AmNP; BALP; PoNe
Black crosses on the skyline, like a squad heedless of levies. Erris Coast, 1943. Hugh Connell. NeIP
Black ear crawls on the window, A. It is. New World of Will. David Shapiro. ANYP
Black enormous cat, A. Cloud Fantasies, I. Christian Morgenstern. OnPM
Black-eyed Susan. John Gay. EtS; GTBS; GTBS-D; GTBS-P; GTBS-W; GTSE; GTSL; HBV; RoGo; TreFS
(Sweet William's Farewell to Black-eyed Susan.) BeLS; CEP; EiPP; NoP; OBEC
Black-eyed Susie, *with music*. *Unknown*. ABF
Black eyes if you seem dark. To Her Eyes. Lord Herbert of Cherbury. OBS
Black eyes, in your dark orbs doth lie. Upon Black Eyes, and Becoming Frowns. James Howell. SeCL
Black faces lifted to the heavens...searching. Evolution. Thelma Parker Cox. TNV
Black Finger, The. Angelina W. Grimké. AmNP; PoNe
Black fool, why winter here? These frozen skies. Advice to a Raven in Russia, December, 1812. Joel Barlow. AmePo; AmLP; AmPP (4th ed.); NePA; OxBA
Black Friday. Louella C. Poole. CIV
Black gain a whit(e;) (jetty): (a color again). Kay Price and Stella Pajunas. Vito Hannibal Acconci. YAP
Black Gal, De, *with music*. *Unknown*. ABF
Black girl black girl. Blackberry Sweet. Dudley Randall. BOLo; NBP
Black Girl Goes By, A. Emile Roumer, *tr. fr. French by* Edna Worthley Underwood. TTY
Black grows the southern sky, betokening rain. Sudden Shower. John Clare. CBEP; OBRV; PoSC
Black Hair. Muhammadji, *tr. fr. Persian by* E. Powys Mathers. LiTW
Black-haired girl, The. The Yawn. Paul Blackburn. ELU
Black horse came to visit us, A. Snow on the East Wind. Lord Dunsany. MoBrPo (1942 ed.)
Black I am and much admired. *Unknown*. OxNR
Black in the fog and in the snow. Waifs and Strays. Arthur Rimbaud. WoL
Black Is a Soul. Joseph White. IDB
Black Is Beautiful. Townsend T. Brewster. TNV
Black Is Best. Larry Thompson. BOLo
Black is no color; white is all of sense. Five Epigrams, 4. Donald Hall. NePoAm-2
Black is not. A Poem Looking for a Reader. Don L. Lee. BP
Black [*or* Blacke] is the beauty of the brightest day. Divine Zenocrate [*or* To Entertain Divine Zenocrate]. Christopher Marlowe. *Fr.* Tamburlaine the Great, Pt. II. AtBAP; BoW; ChTr; ViBoPo; WHA
Black Is the Color of My True Love's Hair. *Unknown*. TreFT
Black is the night they are marching through. What Though the Dark! Archie Edwards. BePJ
Black is what the prisons are. The African Affair. Bruce McM. Wright. AmNP; PoNe
Black Jack David come ridin' through the woods. The Gypsy Laddie (B *vers*.). *Unknown*. ViBoFo
Black Jack Davy [*or* Davie]. *Unknown*. *See* Wraggle Taggle Gipsies, The.
Black Jackets. Thom Gunn. CBV; TwCP
Black Jess. Peter Kane Dufault. NYBP
Black Judgement. Nikki Giovanni. TNV
Black Knight, The. John Todhunter. OBVV; PoVP
Black Lady in an Afro Hairdo Cheers for Cassius. R. Ernest Holmes. WSL
Black, long-tailed, The/ one then. The Yellow Season. William Carlos Williams. MoAB; MoAmPo (1950 ed.)
Black Lotus. Alicia Ley Johnson. NBP
Black Madonna, The. Albert Rice. CDC
Black Magdalens. Countee Cullen. BANP
Black magnet of hate has sucked up our flight, The. The Man without a Road, X. Erik Lindegren. LiTW
Black Mammies. John Wesley Holloway. BANP
Black Man Speaks, The. Langston Hughes. TreFT
Black man straddling the unbalanced scale. Split Standard. Hart Leroi Bibbs. BF
Black Man Talks of Reaping, A. Arna Bontemps. AmNP; BANP; CDC; IDB; Kal; PoNe
Black Man's Feast. Sarah Webster Fabio. PoNe (1970 ed.)
Black Man's Son, The. Oswald Durand, *tr. fr. French by* Edna Worthley Underwood. PoNe; TTY
Black Marble. Arthur O'Shaughnessy. SyP
Black Marigolds. Bilhana, *formerly at. to* Chauras. *tr. fr. Sanskrit by* E. Powys Mathers. AWP; ErPo, *abr.*; LiTW, *abr.*
Sels.
Death Sends Me the Flickering of Powdery Lids. OnPM
Her Mouth Carelessly Scented. OnPM
I Have a Need. OnPM
I Have No Surety. OnPM
I Know My Princess. OnPM
I Know That I Have Savoured. OnPM
I Love Long Black Eyes. OnPM; SiGo
I Mind That I Went Round with Men and Women. OnPM
I Mind the Coming. OnPM
I Mind the Time of the Falling of Blossoms. OnPM
I See Her. OnPM
I See the Heavy Startled Hair. OnPM
I Seem to See My Prison Walls. OnPM
If I See in My Soul. OnPM
If My Girl with Lotus Eyes. OnPM
Love Is a God. OnPM
My Eyes That Hurry to See. OnPM
Pleased Intimacy, The. OnPM
She Swims Back in the Crowning Hour. OnPM
She with Young Limbs. OnPM
Spread We Our Nets. OnPM
Stainless Fair Appearance, The. OnPM
When All My Heavy Heart. OnPM
Woodcutter and the Fisherman Turn Home, The. OnPM
Black milk of the dawn we drink it evenings. Death Fugue. Paul Celan. TrJP
Black Mountain, Los Altos. Robert Hass. YAP
Black mountains pricked with pointed pine. The Watershed. Alice Meynell. POTE
Black Music Man. Lethonia Gee. BF
Black Narcissus. Gerald William Barrax. Kal
Black Narrator, The. Ahmed Alhamisi. BP
Black night./ White snow. The Twelve. Aleksandr Aleksandrovich Blok. AWP; LiTW; PoFr
Black night bends down upon the tangled woods. In the Forest. Alexander Petofi. LiTW
Black night came down in rain and wrath and storm, The. Sing Thou, My Soul. Theodosia Garrison. CAW
Black night without, and blacker night within. Rachel. Ruth Gilbert. AnNZ
Black-nosed kitten will slumber all the day, A. Choosing a Kitten. *Unknown*. StVeCh
Black November Turkey, A. Richard Wilbur. AmLP; FiMAP; MoAB
Black on flat water past the jonquil lawns. The Black Swan. James Merrill. MoPo
Black one, last as usual, swings her head, The. Fetching Cows. Norman MacCaig. FIW
Black Orpheus. Frederick J. Bryant, Jr. BF
Black Panther, The. John Hall Wheelock. HBMV; LiTG; LiTM; PFY; TPM
Black Patch on Lucasta's Face, A. Richard Lovelace. AnAnS-2; SCEP-2; SeCP
Black Pebble, The. James Reeves. PDV
Black people/ have got to be black. Doughtry Long, Jr. ("Doc Long"). TNV
Black people, arise. There Are Seeds to Sow. Bernette Golden. TNV
Black people think. Awareness. Don L. Lee. BOLo
Black pitchy night, companion of my woe. Sonnet. Michael Drayton. Idea's Mirrour, LXX [XLV]. LoBV; OBSC; ReIE; SiCE; TuPP
Black Poetry Day, A. Alicia Loy Johnson. BOLo
Black poets should live—not leap. For Black Poets Who Think of Suicide. Etheridge Knight. BP
Black ponds and boughs of clay and sulky sedge. Muffled. Edmund Blunden. Sonn

Black Poplar-Boughs. John Freeman. HBMV
Black reapers with the sound of steel on stones. Reapers. Jean Toomer. CDC; Kal
Black, Red, and Gold, *sel.* Ferdinand Freiligrath, *tr. fr. German by* J. L. Joynes.
"True Freedom breaks the yokes that gall." PoFr
Black Regiment, The. George Henry Boker. GN; HBV; PAH; PAP
Black Revolution is passing you bye, The. Poem. Nikki Giovanni. WSL
Black Riders, The, *sels.* Stephen Crane.
Ancestry ("Once I saw mountains angry"), XXII. AA
"Behold, from the land of the farther suns," XXIX. AP
"Black riders came from the sea," I. AP
(Black Riders, The.) AA; AmP
Blades [*or* Blade] of Grass, The ("In heaven/ Some little blades of grass"), XVIII. AmP; AP; MAP; MaRV; MoAmPo; NeMA; PoPl; PoPo; TreFT
Book of Wisdom, The ("I met a seer"), XXXVI. CoBA; HoPM; MAP; MoAmPo
"God fashioned the ship of the world carefully," VI. AP
God in Wrath, A, XIX. AP; NoP
"God lay dead in heaven," LXVII. AmPP (5th ed.); AP
"I looked here," VIII. AP
I Saw a Man [Pursuing the Horizon], XXIV. AmePo; AmPP (5th ed.); AP; CoBA; HoPM; LiTA; LiTM (1970 ed.); LoGBV; MAP; MoAmPo; NeMA; NePA; OTD
"I stood musing in a black world," XLIX. AP
I Stood upon a High Place, IX. AmePo; AmP; AP; LiTA; NePA; PoPo
"I stood upon a highway," XXXIV. AP
If I Should Cast Off This Tattered Coat, LXVI. AmePo; AP
In the Desert, III. AmePo; AP; CrMA; LiTM (1970 ed.)
(Heart, The.) HoPM; MAP; MoAmPo; NeMA
It Was Wrong to Do This, Said the Angel, LIV. AmP; AP; LiTA; NePA
Learned Man, A ("A learned man came to me once"), XX. LiTA; MoAmPo (1950 ed.); NePA
Livid Lightnings Flashed in the Clouds, XXXIX. AmePo; AP
"Love walked alone," XLI. AP
"Man feared that he might find an assassin, A," LVI. MWA-2
Man Saw a Ball of Gold in the Sky, A, XXXV. AmP; EvOK; LiTA; NePA; OTD; PoPl; PoPo
"Man went before a strange God, A," LI. AP
"Many red devils ran from my heart," XLVI. AP
Many Workmen, XXXI. LiTA; NePA; PoPo
"Ocean said to me once, The," XXXVIII. MWA-2
"Places among the stars," XXIII. AP
"Sage lectured brilliantly, The," LVIII. AnAmPo; YaD
'Scaped ("Once I knew a fine song"), LXV. AA
"Should the wide world roll away," X. AmPP (5th ed.); AP
"There was, before me," XXI. AP
There Was Crimson Clash of War, XIV. AP; NoP
" 'Truth,' said a traveller," XXVIII. AP
"Two or three angels," XXXII. AnAmPo
"Upon the road of my life," LX. AP
"Well then, I hate Thee, unrighteous picture," XII. AP
Why? ("Behold the grave of a wicked man"), XXV. AA
Youth in Apparel That Glittered, A, XXVII. AmePo; AnAmPo; LiTA; NePA
(Content.) AA
(Youth, A.) MoAmPo (1950 ed.)
Black riders came from the sea. The Black Riders, I. Stephen Crane. AA; AmP; AP
Black Rock of Kiltearn, The. Andrew Young. FaBoTw
Black Rook in Rainy Weather. Sylvia Plath. LiTM (1970 ed.); NePoEA-2; NoP; PoDB; PP
Black Sailor's Chanty. Charles Keeler. EtS
Black Sheep. Richard Burton. AA
Black Slippers: Bellotti. Ezra Pound. NoP
Black-smocked smiths, smattered with smoke. *See* Swarty, sweaty smiths, smutched with smoke.
Black Snake, The. Patricia Hubbell. PDV
Black Soul of the Land. Lance Jeffers. BF
Black Spirit. Tom Poots. FiSC
Black Spring. Robert Lowell, *ad. fr. the Russian of* Innokentii Annensky. NaP
Black spruce and Norway pine. Pare Lorentz. *Fr.* The River. AmFN; NAMP
Black Stick with a Ball of Cotton for a Head and a Running Machine for a Mouth, A. Calvin C. Hernton. BF
Black Students. Julia Fields. NBP
Black Sunrise. Art Wilson. WSL
Black swallows swooping or gliding. The Skaters. John Gould Fletcher. MAP; MoAmPo; NeMA; PFY; PoMa; SD
Black Swan, The. Randall Jarrell. CMoP; FiMAP; NMP
Black Swan, The. James Merrill. MoPo
Black Tail Range, The, *with music.* *Unknown.* CoSo
Black Tambourine. Hart Crane. AP; CBEP; CoBMV; NAMP; OxBA; PoNe
Black texture of the leafy trees, engraved. Three Fragments, III. William Allingham. IrPN
Black, the sun floats melting. The Inhuman Rain Rejoiced. Don Shea. QAH
Black Thing. *Unknown.* CoMu
Black Tower, The. W. B. Yeats. CMoP; NoP
Black Tragedy lets slip her grim disguise. Masks. Thomas Bailey Aldrich. AA
Black Virgin, The. G. K. Chesterton. ISi
Black Vulture, The. George Sterling. AmLP; AnAmPo; HBV; MAP; NP; PFY; PoMa
Black Wall-Flower, The. Frances Anne Kemble. VA
Black Warrior. Norman Jordan. BF
Black Water and Bright Air. Constance Carrier. SD
Black wave the trees in the forest. Adventure. Laura Benét. GaP; HBMV; TSW
Black we are but [*or* though] much admired. *Unknown.* OTPC (1946 ed.); RIS
Black wings and white in the hollow. Behind the Plough. James H. Cousins. OxBI
Black within and red without. Mother Goose. BoChLi; OxNR; PPL; RIS
Black Woman. R. Ernest Holmes. WSL
Black Woman. Georgia Douglas Johnson. BALP
Black Woman. Léopold Sédar Senghor, *tr. fr. French by* Anne Atik. TTY
Black Your Shoes, Your Honour? *Unknown.* PCH
("Here's Finiky Hawkes.") OxNR
Blackberry, The. Norman Nicholson. MoBrPo (1950 ed.); NeMA
Blackberry Fold. *Unknown.* *See* Squire and Milkmaid.
Blackberry Girl, The. Nancy Dennis Sproat. BLPA
Blackberry-Picking. Seamus Heaney. BoNaP
Blackberry Sweet. Dudley Randall. BOLo; NBP
Blackberry Thicket, The. Ann Stanford. WIRo
Blackberry Winter. John Crowe Ransom. OnHM; OxBA; PoRA
Blackberrying. Sylvia Plath. NYBP
Blackbird, A. Marcus Argentarius, *tr. fr. Greek by* Sir William Marris. LiTW
Blackbird, The. William Barnes. GTSE; HBV
Blackbird, The. Henry Charles Beeching. OBVV
Blackbird, The. Dinah Maria Mulock Craik. BoTP; GoTP
Blackbird, The. Phyllis Drayson. BoTP
Black Bird, The. John Hall-Stevenson. Makarony Fables, IV. EiCL
Blackbird, The. W. E. Henley. *See* To A. D.
Blackbird, The. A. E. Housman. *See* When Smoke Stood Up from Ludlow.
Blackbird, The. Tennyson. OTPC
Blackbird, The. Frederick Tennyson. HBV; VA
Blackbird, The ("Ah, blackbird, thou art satisfied"). *Unknown, tr. fr. Middle Irish by* Kuno Meyer. AnIL; OnYI
Blackbird, The ("In midst of woods or pleasant grove"). *Unknown.* *See* In Midst of Woods.
Blackbird, The ("On a fair summer's morning of soft recreation"). *Unknown.* OnYI
Blackbird, The. Humbert Wolfe. BoTP; FaPON; GoJo; HBMV; HBVY; MPB; PCH; RePo; StVeCh; SUS; TiPo; TSW; UTS
Blackbird, blackbird in the cage. The Bird and the Tree. Ridgely Torrence. HBMV; MAP; MoAmPo (1942 ed.); NP; PoFr; PoNe
Blackbird by Belfast Lough, The. *Unknown, tr. fr. Irish by* Frank O'Connor. BiS; KiLC
Blackbird darted through the boughs, The. The Bird. Andrew Young. POTE
Blackbird flew down to the almond tree, A. Opposites. José Moreno Villa. OnPM

Blackbird of Derrycairn, The. Austin Clarke, *after the Irish.* NeIP
Blackbird of Litir Lone, The. On Not Hearing the Birds Sing in Ireland. Padraic Colum. NePoAm
Black bird of my heart, whose breasts are oranges. Three Haitian Creole Moods. Emile Roumer. OnHM
Blackbird Singing, A. R. S. Thomas. BoC; FlW; POTi; WePo
Blackbird startles from the homestead hedge, The. John Clare. *Fr.* Child Harold. PeER
Blackbird Suddenly, A. Joseph Auslander. MaRV; MPB; PoRL; RePo; TiPo
Blackbird whistles from the thorny brake, The. Birds in Spring. James Thomson. *Fr.* The Seasons: Spring. OBEC; PeER
Blackcaps pipe among the reeds, The. Before the Rain. Amélie Rives. AA
Blacke is the beauty of the brightest day. *See* Black is the beauty of the brightest day.
Blacken thy heavens, Jove. Prometheus. Goethe. AWP; JAWP; WBP; WoL
Blackened and bleeding, helpless, panting, prone. Chicago. Bret Harte. PAH; ThLM
Blacker than night. Two from the Country. R. Ernest Holmes. WSL
Blackfeet, Blood and Piegan Hunters. James Welch. YAP
Blackfriars. John Betjeman. NoP
Blackie Speaks on Campus: a Valentine for Vachel Lindsay. Stanley Crouch. BF
Blackie, the Electric Rembrandt. Thom Gunn. FlW
Blackie Thinks of His Brothers. Stanley Crouch. BF
Blackjack Davy, The. *Unknown.* *See* Wraggle Taggle Gipsies, The.
Blackmwore Maidens. William Barnes. EPN; GTBS; HBV; PoVP; ShBV-3; VA
Black'on frowns east on Maidon. After the Club-Dance. Thomas Hardy. At Casterbridge Fair, III. BEL; EnLi-2 (1949 ed.); EnLit; PoVP
Blackout. Arthur Gregor. SiSw
Black-out. Robinson Jeffers. LiTA; LiTM (rev. ed.); NePA; WaP
Blackpool Breezes. *Unknown.* CoMu
Blacksmith. B. K. Pyke. BoTP
Blacksmith, The. *Unknown, tr. fr. German.* SAS
Blacksmith did not hobble here, The. Old Hundred. Mark Van Doren. UnS
Blacksmith Pain. Otto Julius Bierbaum, *tr. fr. German by* Jethro Bithell. AWP; JAWP; WBP
Blacksmiths, The. *Unknown.* CABA; EnL; WiR (Smoke-blackened Smiths.) MeEL
Blacksmith's boy went out with a rifle, The. Legend. Judith Wright. BoAV; FlW
Blacksmith's Serenade, The. Vachel Lindsay. StPo
Blackstone Rangers, The. Gwendolyn Brooks. BALP
"There they are," *sel.* CAD
Blacktail Deer. Lew Sarett. NP
Blade is sharp, the reaper stout, The. Theology. Joyce Kilmer. TSW
Blade of Grass, A. Oscar Williams. NYTB
Blade of Grass Sings to the River, The. Leah Goldberg, *tr. fr. Hebrew by* Robert Friend. TrJP
Blades, [*or* Blade] of Grass, The. Stephen Crane. The Black Riders, XVIII. AmP; AP; MAP; MaRV; MoAmPo; NeMA; PoPl; PoPo; TreFT
Blades of Harden, The. Will H. Ogilvie. *Fr.* Whaup o' the Rede. GoTS
Bladud had one son, Leir was he called. Leir and His Daughters. Layamon. *Fr.* The Brut. MeEV
Bladyn's Song of Cloten. Charles M Doughty. *Fr.* The Dawn in Britain. PoEL-5
Blake. John Gould Fletcher. InP
Blake saw a treeful of angels at Peckham Rye. Mad Blake. William Rose Benét. HBMV
Blame Not My Cheeks. Thomas Campion. EG; UnPo
Blame Not My Lute. Sir Thomas Wyatt. EIL; EnRePo; FCP; FosPo; MaPo (1969 ed.); ReEn; ReIE; SiCE; SiPS; TuPP (Lute Obeys, The.) OBSC; QFR
Blanaid's Song ("Blanaid loves roses"). Joseph Campbell. OxBI
Blanche comme la neige, *with music.* *Unknown, tr. fr. French.* OuSiCo
Blanche is/ And navy the tree full of holes. Song in a Winter Night. Bink Noll. ToPo
Blancheflour and Jellyflorice. *Unknown.* ESPB
Bland many-eyed walls, The. Prevailing Winds. Lee Anderson. TwAmPo
Blanid's Song. Gordon Bottomley. *Fr.* The Crier by Night. BrPo
Blank Book Letter, The. Samuel Greenberg. LiTA
"Blank Misgivings of a Creature Moving About in Worlds Not Realized," *sel.* Arthur Hugh Clough.
"How often sit I, poring o'er," V. EPN; GTBS-D
Blanket Street. Inez Hogan. BiCB
Blare of trumpet and roll of drum! The Victor. William Young. HBMV
Blast from Freedom's Northern hills, upon its Southern way, The. Massachusetts to Virginia. Whittier. AmPP; AnNE; CoBA; WoL
Blast of War, The. Shakespeare. *See* Once More unto the Breach.
Blast of Wind, A, a Momentary Breath. Barnabe Barnes. *See* Life of Man, The.
Blasted and bored and undermined. The Chalk-Cliff. Andrew Young. POTE
Blasted Herb, The. Meshech Weare. PAH
Blasted with sighs, and surrounded with teares [*or* tears]. Twicknam [*or* Twickenham] Garden[s]. John Donne. AnAnS-1; CBEP; DiPo; EnLoPo; LoBV; MaMe; MBW-1; MeLP; MePo; OBS; PIA; PoEL-2; PoFS; ReIE; SeCP; SeEP; TuPP
Blasting from Heaven. Philip Levine. CoAP
Blauen Veilchen der Äugelein, Die. Heine. *See* Withered Heart, The.
Blaydon Races. *Unknown.* ELP
Blazing Heart, The. Alice Williams Brotherton. AA
Blazon Columbia's emblem. Columbia's Emblem. Edna Dean Proctor. GN
Bleak and barren mountains keep, The. Loch Coruisk (Skye). "Fiona Macleod." SyP
Bleak day, A! Another Beggar Poem. Issa. PoFr
Bleak-faced Winter, with his braggart winds, The. Australian Spring. Hugh McCrae. BoAu
Bleak season was it, turbulent and wild. Wordsworth. *Fr.* The Recluse. ERoP-1
Bleak the February light. Kingdom of Heaven. Léonie Adams. MAP; MoAB; MoAmPo
Bleat of Protest. Mildred Weston. FiBHP
Bleeberrying. Jonathan Denwood. MoBS
Blend of mirth and sadness, smiles and tears, A. Lincoln [*or* The Masterpiece]. Walter Malone. InP; PGD
Blenheim. Addison. *Fr.* The Campaign. OBEC
Blennerhassett's Island. Thomas Buchanan Read. *Fr.* The New Pastoral. PAH; ThLM
Bless, Dear Saviour, This Child. Thomas Beck. BePJ
Bless earth with Thine Advent, O Saviour Christ! Advent Lyrics, VIII. *Unknown.* *Fr.* Christ 1. AnOE
Bless Him ("Bless Him, O constant companions"). *Unknown, tr. fr. Hebrew by* Israel Abrahams. TrJP
Bless love and hope. Full many a withered year. Love and Hope. Dante Gabriel Rossetti. The House of Life, XLIII. MaVP; PoVP; ViPo; VP
Bless me, 'tis cold! how chill the air. An Ode in Imitation of Horace. Congreve. PeRV
Bless the Blessed Morn. Horatius Bonar. BePJ; SoP
Bless the Dear Old Verdant Land. Denis Florence MacCarthy. VA
Bless the four corners of this house. House Blessing. Arthur Guiterman. BrR; MaRV; TiPo; TrPWD
Bless the Lord, O my soul; and all that is within me. Psalm CIII, Bible, *O.T.* AWP; JAWP; TiPo (1952 ed.); WGRP
Bless the Lord, O my soul; O Lord my God, Thou art very great. Psalm CIV, Bible, *O.T.* OHIP; TrJP; WGRP
Bless This House. Helen Taylor. SoP, 2 *sts.*; TreFT, 4 *sts.*; TRV, 1 *st.*
Bless Thou the gifts our hands have brought. In Thy Hand. Samuel Longfellow. FaChP
Bless Thou this year, O Lord! Prayer [*or* A Prayer for a Happy New Year]. A. S. C. Clarke. BLRP; PGD
Bless you, bless you, bonnie [*or* burnie] bee. *Unknown.* BoTP; OxNR; SAS
Bless you, Mother. On the Appeal from the Race of Sheba: II. Léopold Sédar Senghor. TTY

Bless'd art Thou, O Lord of all. Prayer before Sleep. Alice Lucas. TrJP
Blessed. Freda Hanbury Allen. SoP
Blessed. Soné, *tr. fr. Hebrew by* David Kuselewitz. TrJP
Blessed. *Unknown.* OQP; SoP
(How God Answers.) MaRV
Blessed Agitator, The. Lucia Trent. ChIP
Blessed Are the Eyes That See. *See* My Peace I Give unto You.
Blessed are the poor in spirit. The Beatitudes. St. Matthew, Bible, *N.T.* ExPo; GoTP; MaRV; TrGrPo
Blessed Are They. Wilhelmina Stitch. PoToHe
Blessed are they of the Easter faith. Easter Beatitudes. Clarence M. Burkholder. BLRP
Blessed are they that have eyes to see. Some Blesseds. John Oxenham. WGRP
Blessed Are They That Mourn. Bryant. SoP
Blessed are they who are pleasant to live with. Blessed Are They. Wilhelmina Stitch. PoToHe
Blessed are they who sow but do not reap. Blessed. Soné. TrJP
Blessed are those who have not seen. In Stratis Viarum. Arthur Hugh Clough. PoVP
Blessed art Thou, O God our Lord. Blessings for Chanukah. Jessie E. Sampter. TiPo (1952 ed.)
Blessed Art Thou, O Lord. *Unknown, tr. fr. Hebrew by* Theodor H. Gaster. *Fr.* The Dead Sea Scrolls. TrJP
Blessed art thou that fearest God. Beati Omnes. Psalm CXXVIII, Bible, *O.T.*, *tr. by* Thomas Sternhold. ReIE; SiCE
Blessed be that lady bright. A Cause for Wonder. *Unknown.* MeEL
Blessed be the day which bids my grief subside. To Mr. William Long, on His Recovery from a Dangerous Illness. William Hayley. Sonn
Blessed be the English and all their ways and works. Jobson's Amen. Kipling. AnFE
Blessed be the God of love. *See* Blest be the God of love.
Blessed Be the Holy Will of God. *Unknown, tr. fr. Modern Irish by* Douglas Hyde. OnYI
Blessed be the Lord God of Israel; for he hath visited and redeemed his people. Benedictus. St. Luke, Bible, *N.T.* MaRV
Blessed be the Maker's name. The Stars. Dafydd ap Gwilym. BoPe
Blessed Be the Paps Which Thou Hast Sucked. Richard Crashaw. MaMe
(Luke 11.) CABA
Blessed be this place. Blood and the Moon. W. B. Yeats. MBW-2
Blessed be your name, my God. Paul Claudel. *Fr.* Five Grand Odes. OnHM
Blessed Bible, sacred treasure. The Best of All. Fanny Crosby. BLRP
Blessed Damozel, The. Dante Gabriel Rossetti. AnFE; AWP; BEL; BoLiVe; CoBE; DiPo; EnL; EnLi-2; EnLit; EPN; GBV; GoTL; GTBS; GTSL; HBV; ILP; LiTB; LiTG; LoBV; MasP; MaVP; NoP; OAEP; OBEV; OBNC; OBVV; OHFP; OuHeWo; PAn; PoE; PoEL-5; PoIE; PoVP; SeCeV; ShBV-4; TOP; TrGrPo; TSW; VA; ViPo; ViPP; VP; WHA
Blessed Face, The. Ray Palmer. *See* Jesus, These Eyes Have Never Seen.
Blessed is every one that feareth the Lord. Psalm CXXVIII, Bible, *O.T.* TRV
Blessed Is God ("Blessed is God that liveth forever"). Tobit, XIII, Bible, Apocrypha. *Tr. fr. Greek by* D. C. Simpson. TrJP
Blessed is he whose faith is not offended. Blessed. Freda Hanbury Allen. SoP
Blessed is she whose daily tasks are a labor of love. Beatitudes for a Housewife. Mary Mae Oesch. PoToHe (new ed.)
Blessed is the man, O Virgin Mary. St. Bonaventure. *Fr.* Psalter of the Blessed Virgin Mary. ISi
Blessed is the man that beholdeth the face of a friend in a far country. The Face of a Friend. Henry van Dyke. OQP
Blessed is the man that walketh not in the counsel of the ungodly. The Godly and the Ungodly. Psalm I, Bible, *O.T.* AWP; EnLi-1; JAWP; TreF; WGRP; WoL
Blessed is the man whose filthy stain. Psalm XXXII. *Paraphrased by* Sir Philip Sidney. FCP
Blessed Journey, The. Gerhard Tersteegen. FaChP
Blessed land of Judea! thrice hallowed of song. Palestine. Whittier. WBLP
Blessed Little Jesus of the Cradle. A Christmas Prayer. Lucy Embury. ChrBoLe
Blessed Mary, moder virginal. A Short Prayer to Mary. *Unknown.* MeEL
Blessed Match, The. Hannah Senesh, *tr. fr. Yiddish.* TrJP
Blessed Name, The. George W. Bethune. BLRP
Blessed Nearness. Mary Bullock. STF
Blessed of the Lord Be His Land. Deuteronomy, XXXIII: 13-16, Bible, *O.T.* BrR
(Give Ear, O Ye Heavens.) PCH
Blessed Offendo[u]r: who thyself hast tried [*or* haist try'd]. To Saint Mary Magdalen. Henry Constable. LoBV (2d ed.); PoEL-2
Blessed poster girl leaned out, The. The Poster Girl. Carolyn Wells. HBV; InMe
Blessed Received in Paradise, The. James Kirkup. BoPe
Blessed Road, The. Charles Buxton Going. ChIP
Blessed Saviour, Thou Art Mine. Oswald J. Smith. SoP
Blessed Secret, The. Albert Simpson Reitz. SoP
Blessed Spot, A. Abulfadhel Ahmed, *tr. fr. Arabic by* Leigh Hunt. OnPM
Blessed story of the Christ, The. The Babe of Bethlehem. Henry Beer. BePJ
Blessed Task, The. Harriet McEwen Kimball. BePJ
Blessed the match that was burned. The Blessed Match. Hannah Senesh. TrJP
Blessed thou, Simon. Poems by the Roadside. St. Matthew, Bible, *N.T.* CAW
Blessed Trinity have pity! Childless. Giollabhrighde Mac Conmidhe. KiLC
Blessed Virgin Compared to the Air We Breathe, The. Gerard Manley Hopkins. BrPo; ISi; MoPo; OxBoCh; PeVV; PoLi
Blessed Virgin Mary Compared to a Window, The. Thomas Merton. ISi
Blessed Virgin's Expostulation, The Nahum Tate. ISi
Blessed with a joy that only she. The Gift of God. E. A. Robinson. AnAmPo; AP; CoBMV; MAP; MAPA; MaPo (1969 ed.); MoAB; MoAmPo; OxBA; TwAmPo
Blessèd, yet sinful one, and broken-hearted! To Mary Magdalen. Bartholome Leonardo de Argensola. CAW
Blessing, A. Numbers, VI: 24-26, Bible, *O.T.* *See* Benediction.
Blessing, The. Mary Colborne-Veel. BoAu
Blessing. John Frederick Nims. CBV
Blessing, A [*or* The]. James Wright. AmPC; FIW; NaP; OPoP; StP; TwCP
Blessing and Honor. Horatius Bonar. SoP; TRV
Blessing for the Blessed, A. Laurence Alma-Tadema. BoTP; PRWS
(Sunset.) GFA
Blessing his handiwork, his drawbridge closed. Artificer. X. J. Kennedy. TwCP
Blessing in Disguise, A. John Ashbery. ANYP
Blessing Mrs. Larkin. Margery Mansfield. GoYe
Blessing of St. Francis, The. Sister Maura. CaP
Blessing of the Priests. Numbers, Bible, *O.T.* *See* Benediction.
Blessing of Toil. Samuel Ellsworth Kiser. PEDC
Blessing on Little Boys. Arthur Guiterman. TrPWD
Blessing on the hand of women! *See* Blessings on the hand. . .
Blessing on you, Mrs. Larkin, for planting my trees, A! Blessing Mrs. Larkin. Margery Mansfield. GoYe
Blessing over Food. Hayyim Nahman Bialik. YeAr
Blessing the Dance. Irwin Russell. *Fr.* Christmas-Night in the Quarters. AnAmPo
Blessing the Hounds. Mary Winter. GoYe
Blessings as rich and fragrant crown your heads. To the Best and Most Accomplished Couple. Henry Vaughan. HW
Blessings for Chanukah. Jessie E. Sampter. TiPo (1952 ed.)
Blessings, in abundance come. The Good-Night or Blessing. Robert Herrick. ALV
Blessings of God, The. Mary D. Hughes. SoP
Blessings of Surrender, The. Mary J. Helphingtine. STF
Blessings on all the kids who improve the signs in the subways. Graffiti. Edward Field. CoPo
Blessings on Doneraile. Patrick O'Kelly. OnYI
Blessings on the Bride-Bed. Shakespeare. *See* Oberon and Titania to the Fairy Train.
Blessings [*or* Blessing] on the hand of women! The Hand That Rocks the Cradle Is the Hand That Rules the World. William

Blessings (continued)
Ross Wallace. FaFP; PoLF; TreF; WBLP
Blessings on thee, little man. The Barefoot Boy. Whittier. AA; AmePo; AmPP (3d ed.); AnNE; CoBA; FaBoBe; FaPON; GN; GTBS-W; HBV; HBVY; LaNeLa; LiTA; NeHB; OBVV; OHFP; OnPP; OTPC; PoLF; PoPl; PTK; TreF; WBLP
Blessings That Remain, The. Annie Johnson Flint. BLRP
Blest are the pure in heart. Purity of Heart. John Keble. *Fr.* The Purification. BLRP
Blest are your North parts, for all this long time. To Mr. I. L. John Donne. MaMe; SeCP
Blest be God/ Who did create. Blessing over Food. Hayyim Nahman Bialik. YeAr
Blest be the bric-a-brac that still survives. In the Shadowy What-not Corner. Robert Hillyer. NePoAm
Blest [*or* Blessed] be the God of love. Even-Song [*or* Even-song]. George Herbert. AnAnS-1; EP; FaBoEn; MaMe; MeP
Blest Be the Tie That Binds. John Fawcett. HBV; SoP
Blest beyond earth's bliss, with heaven I deem him. To a Bride. Sappho. WoL
Blest, Blest and Happy He. *Unknown.* GoTS
Blest he who thinks on human destiny. At Dawn. Victor Hugo. OnPM
Blest infant bud, whose blossom-life. The Burial of an Infant. Henry Vaughan. OAEP
Blest is he that seeketh rest. The Tree of the Cross. "Angelus Silesius." CAW
Blest is the man who never lent. The Patriot. Thomas Godfrey. PoFr
Blest Leaf! whose aromatic gales dispense. In Imitation of Pope. Isaac Hawkins Browne. *Fr.* A Pipe of Tobacco. OBEC; Par
Blest Order, which in power dost so excell. The Priesthood. George Herbert. AnAnS-1; MaMe; MeP
Blest pair of sirens, pledges of heav'ns [*or* heaven's] joy. At a Solemn Music [*or* Musick]. Milton. EG; ExPo; GTBS; GTBS-D; GTBS-P; GTBS-W; GTSE; GTSL; HBV; LoBV; MaPo (1969 ed.); MeP; OAEP; OBEV; OBS; OxBoCh; PoE; PoEL-3; SeCeV; SeCL; SeEP; TOP; UnS
Blest payre of swans, Oh may you interbring. The Benediction. John Donne. MaMe
Blest Retirement. Goldsmith. *Fr.* The Deserted Village. OBEC
Blest Spirit of Calm that dwellest in these woods! Charles Sangster. *Fr.* Sonnets Written in the Orillia Woods. PeCV
Blest Statesman He, Whose Mind's Unselfish Will. Wordsworth. EPN
Blest the Infant Babe. Wordsworth. *Fr.* The Prelude. AtBAP
Blest Winter Nights. John Armstrong. *Fr.* The Art of Preserving Health, III. OBEC
Bleue Maison. Edmund Blunden. BrPo
Blight. Arna Bontemps. BANP
Blight. Emerson. AmePo; AP; CDC; NoP
Blight rests in your face, The. To a Publisher. . . Cut-out. LeRoi Jones. NeAP
"Blighters." Siegfried Sassoon. FaBoTw; MMA; MoVE
Blin' Man Stood on de Road [*or* Way] an' Cried, De. *Unknown.* ABF; BoAN-1, *with music*
(Blind Man, *with music.*) TrAS
Blind. John Kendrick Bangs. MaRV; OQP; PoToHe; SoP
Blind, The. Baudelaire, *tr. fr. French by* T. Sturge Moore. SyP
Blind. Fanny Crosby. MaRV
Blind. Harry Kemp. HBMV; PFY; PoMa
Blind. Norman V. Pearce. MaRV; PoToHe
Blind as the song of birds. Lines to a Blind Girl. Thomas Buchanan Read. AA
Blind Bartimeus [*or* Bartimaeus]. Longfellow. ChIP; SoP
(Jericho's Blind Beggar.) WBLP
Blind Beggar, The. Wordsworth. *See* Residence in London.
Blind Beggar's Daughter of Bednall-Green, The. *Unknown.* LoEn; OBB; OTPC (1923 ed.), *sl. abr.*
(Blind Beggar of Bednall Green, The, *diff. vers.*) BaBo
Blind Boy, The. Colley Cibber. CEP; GTBS; GTBS-D; GTBS-P; GTBS-W; GTSE; GTSL; HBV; NeHB; OBEC; PRWS; RoGo; TreFS
Blind Boy's Pranks, The. William Thom. OBEV
Blind but Happy. Fanny J. Crosby. FaChP; MaRV; OTD; TRV
Blind Child, The. *Unknown.* MaRV; SoP
Blind Cured by the Word of Our Saviour, The. Richard Crashaw. MaMe
Blind Date. Conrad Aiken. MoVE; ViBoPo (1958 ed.)
Blind Eateth Many a Fly, The. *Unknown.* NoP
Blind for the lamp she's smashed and the riving tears. Nuit Blanche. Katherine Hoskins. NMP
Blind Geronimo. Bill Berkson. ANYP
Blind Girl, The. Nathalia Crane. MAP; MCCG; MoAmPo (1942 ed.)
Blind Girl. W. S. Merwin. NePoEA-2
Blind girl singing on the radio, A. Singing in the Dark. Irma Wassall. PoNe
Blind Highland Boy, The. Wordsworth. OTPC
Blind, I Speak to the Cigarette. Joanne de Longchamps. GoYe
Blind Louise. George Washington Dewey. AA
Blind Love. Shakespeare. *See* Sonnets, CXLVIII.
Blind Man. Michael Hamburger. NePoEA-2
Blind Man. Jason Miller. ThO
Blind Man, The. Margaret E. Sangster. PoToHe
Blind Man. *Unknown.* *See* Blin' Man Stood on de Road an' Cried, De.
Blind Man, The. Andrew Young. BiS
Blind Man at the Fair, The. Joseph Campbell. AnIV; AWP; JAWP; WBP
Blind man, blind man. *Unknown.* OxNR
Blindman by the name of La Fontaine, A. Haec Fabula Docet. Robert Frost. PoeP
Blind man, A. I can stare at him. A Solitude. Denise Levertov. NePoEA-2
Blind Man Lay beside the Way, *with music.* *Unknown.* AS
Blind Man Prays, A. Catherine Baird. SoP
Blind Man's Morning, The. Viola Meynell. MemP; MoBrPo (1942 ed.)
Blind Man's Regret, The, *with music.* *Unknown.* BFSS
Blind men add the figures, draw the maps, The. Great Powers Conference. Edith Lovejoy Pierce. PGD
Blind Men and the Elephant, The. John Godfrey Saxe. AmePo; AnNE; BBV (1951 ed.); BLPA; BoTP; FaBoBe; GoTP; GSP; HBV; HBVY; MaC; MaRV; NeHB; OnMSP; OTPC; PCD; PoToHe (new ed.); StPo; StVeCh (1940 ed.); TreF; TSW; WBLP
Blind Peddler, The. Sir Osbert Sitwell. MoBrPo (1942 ed.)
Blind Psalmist, The. Elizabeth Clementine Kinney. AA
Blind Samson. William Plomer. PeSA
Blind Sheep, The. Randall Jarrell. NYBP
Blind Singer, The. Friedrich Hölderlin, *tr. fr. German by* J. B. Leishman. LiTW
Blind Steersmen. Francis Ernest Kobina Parkes. PBA
Blind Thamyris, and blind Maeonides. Ode to the Human Heart. Laman Blanchard. BOHV; InMe; NA
Blind to all reasoned aim, this furtive folk. The Termites. Robert Hillyer. OA
Blind Youth, The. Clive Sansom. MemP
Blinded and deafened by the seas. Meditation. Blanaid Salkeld. OnYI
Blinded Bird, The. Thomas Hardy. AnFE; CMoP; EaLo; LiTM (rev. ed.); PAn; VP
Blinded parson gingering down the neo-Gothic steps, A. The Four. Geoffrey Grigson. WaP
Blinded Soldier to His Love, The. Alfred Noyes. PoPl
Blindest buzzard that I know, The. A Sketch. Christina Rossetti. GTBS-P
Blindfolded and alone I stand. Not As I Will. Helen Hunt Jackson. OQP
Blinding spot burned on the snow, A. Mistress of the Matchless Mine. Clyde Robertson. PoOW
Blinding sun at ten o'clock, The. The Church. Edwin Ford Piper. WGRP
Blind-Man's Buff. Blake. WiR
Blindman's Buff. Peter Viereck. LiTM (1970 ed.); MiAP; MoAmPo (1950 ed.)
Blindness of Samson, The. Milton. *Fr.* Samson Agonistes. LiTB; UnPo
Bliss for which our spirits pine, The. The True Heaven. Paul Hamilton Hayne. WGRP
Bliss is the plaything of the child. Emily Dickinson. MWA-2
Blisse. Thomas Traherne. PeRV
"Blissful," quoth [*or* said] I, "can [*or* may] this be true?" The

Queen of Courtesy. *Unknown.* *Fr.* The Pearl. ACP; CAW; ISi
Blissit mot be the heye goddis all. James I, King of Scotland. *Fr.* The Kingis Quair. AtBAP
Blistered and dry was the desert I trod. The Palm. Roy Campbell. MoBrPo
Blithe [*or* Blith] and Bonny Country Lass, A. Thomas Lodge. *Fr.* Rosalynde. ALV
(Corydon's [*or* Coridon's] Song.) ReIE; UnTE
"Blithe-fronted, lofty, young too, wilt thou, Day." The Swan. Stéphane Mallarmé. SyP
Blithe Mask, The. Dollett Fuguet. MaRV; TRV
Blithe playmate of the summer time. To a Humming Bird in a Garden. George Murray. VA
Blithe the bright dawn found me. John O'Dwyer of the Glen. Thomas Furlong. AnIV
Blizzard, The. Lenore A. Pratt. TwCaPo
Blizzard Ape, The. Kenneth Pitchford. CoPo
Bloated Biggaboon, The. Henry Cholmondeley-Pennell. NA
Block City. Robert Louis Stevenson. FaPON; MPB; PCH; SoPo; TiPo
Block of marble caught the glance, A. Discipline. *Unknown.* SoP
Block the cannon; let no trumpets sound. Sunset Horn. Myron O'Higgins. AmNP; PoNe
"Block time, baby, let's walk." On the Block: Another Night Search. Jay Wright. ThO
Blockhouse. Olga Kirsch, *tr. fr. Afrikaans by* Jack Cope. PeSA
Blocks. Frank O'Hara. ANYP
Blond Alice who looms large. An Alice for Annie. R. H. W. Dillard. TDP
Blond cowl terse as a blunt threat to injure, The. Love among the Manichees. William Dickey. PoCh
Blonde mouths are awake on the tree, The. Poem Written During Sleep. Sotère Torregian. YAP
Blondel. Clarence Urmy. AA; HBMV; PFY
Blondie Goes to Heaven. *Unknown.* MemP; OtMeF
Blood. Ray Bremser. NeAP
Blood and the Moon. W. B. Yeats. MBW-2
Blood falling in drops to the earth. Where Are the Men Seized in This Wind of Madness? Aldo do Espirito Santo. TTY
Blood flows in me, but what does it have to do. Living by the Red River. James Wright. FRC
Blood hath been shed ere now, i' the olden time. Shakespeare. *Fr.* Macbeth, III, iv. MyFE
Blood Horse, The. "Barry Cornwall." GN; HBV; OTPC; VA
Blood Is Thicker than Water. Wallace Rice. PaA; PAH
Blood locked as I am, sun bound, and hot as a pistol. Life Must Burn. John Hay. NePoAm
Blood-Red Ring Hung round the Moon, A. John E. Logan. VA
Blood-red the aloes flank. Farm Gate. Uys Kirge. PeSA
Blood thirsty care goe packe. *Unknown.* SeCSL
Blood thudded in my ears. I scuffed. First Confession. X. J. Kennedy. NePoEA-2
Blood, wine, and glee. The Dance of the Sword. *Unknown.* WaaP
Bloodhound, The. Edward Anthony. GoTP
Bloodhounds look like sad old judges, The. Nice Day for a Lynching. Kenneth Patchen. PoNe
Blood-strained Banders, The, *with music.* *Unknown.* OuSiCo
Bloodtotem. Keith Wilson. ThO
Bloody and a sudden end, A. John Kinsella's Lament for Mrs. Mary Moore. W. B. Yeats. AtBAP; CMoP; DTC; LiTM; MoAB; OAEP (2d ed.); SiTL
Bloody, and stained, and with mothers' cries. The Innocents. Jay Macpherson. OBCV
Bloody Bill. D. M. Ross. AnNZ
Bloody Brother, The, *sels.* John Fletcher, *and others.*
Drink To-Day [and Drown All Sorrow], *fr.* II, ii. EnLit; HBV; OAEP; ViBoPo
(Drinking Song.) ElL; TuPP
(Song, The: "Drink to-day and drown all sorrow.") SeEP
Take, O Take, Those Lips Away, *fr.* V, ii; *st.* 1 *also in* Shakespeare's Measure for Measure. AtBAP; FaBoEn; HBV; NoP; PoEL-2; TuPP
(Hide, Oh, Hide Those Hills, *st.* 2.) ViBoPo
Bloody Conquests of Mighty Tamburlaine, The. Christopher Marlowe. *See* Tamburlaine the Great.
Bloody Cranesbill on the Dunes. E. J. Scovell. ChMP
Bloody day subsided, A; the volcano's lips. Postlude: for Goya. Ramon Guthrie. NMP
Bloody Injians, The. *Unknown.* CoSo
Bloody Mary's venomous flames can curl. The Martyrdom of Bishop Farrar. Ted Hughes. PoDB
Bloody Sire, The. Robinson Jeffers. CMoP; LiTM; NePA; VaPo
Bloody trunk [*or* Bloudy trunck] of him who did possess[e], The. The Fall. Sir Richard Fanshawe. *Fr.* Il Pastor Fido. MePo; OBS
Bloom. Alfred Kreymborg. HBMV; TSW
Bloom is result. To meet a flower. Emily Dickinson. PoEL-5
Bloom of beauty! early flower. Ode to the Hon. Miss Carteret. Ambrose Philips. WaPE
Bloom of tenderer flowers is past, The. Winter. Kalidasa. *Fr.* The Seasons. AWP
Blooming Nelly. Burns. UnTE
Blooming of the White Thorn, The. Edith M. Thomas. ChrBoLe
Blossom, The. Blake. *Fr.* Songs of Innocence. CBEP; EiCL; FosPo; GoJo; OTPC (1923 ed.); ThWaDe
Blossom, The. John Donne. AWP; InPo; LiTB; MBW-1; SeEP; UnPo (1st ed.)
(Blossome, The.) AnAnS-1; MaMe; MeLP; OBS; SCEP-1; SeCP
"But thou which lov'st to be," *sel.* LO
Blossom. Jason Miller. ThO
Blossom, The. Shakespeare. *See* On a Day—Alack the Day!
Blossom of the almond trees. Almond Blossom. Sir Edwin Arnold. GN; HBV; OTPC
Blossom of the Branches, The, *sels.* Ruth Gilbert. ACV
Annunciation.
Nativity.
Quickening, The.
Blossom of the Soul, The. Robert Underwood Johnson. AA
Blossom on the plum. March. Nora Hopper. HBV
Blossom Themes. Carl Sandburg. FIW
Blossom Time. Wilbur Larremore. AA
Blossome, The. John Donne. *See* Blossom, The.
Blossoms. Mary Fenollosa. PCH
Blossoms. Otomo Yakamochi, *tr. fr. Japanese by* Ishii *and* Obata. OnPM
Blossoms and Storm. Sadaiye, *tr. fr. Japanese by* H. G. Henderson. OnPM
Blossoms dropped before we really saw them, The. The Quick. Sean Jennett. NeBP
Blossoms fall like snowflakes, The. Butterflies. Chu Miao Tuan. FIW
Blossoms of babies. Handfuls. Carl Sandburg. AP; NP
Blossoms of the plum. Tanka. *Unknown.* InP
Blossomy Barrow, The. T. A. Daly. LHV
Blot in the 'Scutcheon, A, *sel.* Robert Browning.
Earl Mertoun's Song. HBV; OBEV; PTK
("There's a woman like a dew-drop.") UnTE
Blou Northerne Wynd. *Unknown.* *See* Blow, Northern Wind.
Bloudy trunck of him who did possesse, The. *See* Bloody trunk of him who did possess, The.
Blouzelinda's Funeral. John Gay. *Fr.* The Shepherd's Week: Friday. OBEC
Blow, blow over me, sweet-scented breath. Wind of the Prairie. Grace Clementine Howes. GoYe
Blow! blow! The winds are so hoarse they cannot blow! The Winter Storms [*or* Storm at Sea]. Sir William Davenant. RoGo; SeCL
Blow, Blow, Thou Winter Wind. Shakespeare. *Fr.* As You Like It, II, vii. AnFe; ATP (1935 ed.); BEL; BoLiVe; CBEP; CH; ChTr; CoBE; DiPo; EG; ElL; ELP; EnLi-1 (1949 ed.); EnLit; EnRePo; GTBS; GTBS-D; GTBS-P; GTBS-W; GTSE; GTSL; HBV; ILP; InPo; LiTB; LiTG; LO; MaPo; MCCG; NoP; OAEP; OBEV; OBSC; OQP; OTPC; OuHeWo; PG (1945 ed.); PIA; PoEL-2; PoIE; PoPo; PTK; RG; SeCeV; ShBV-1; SiCE; TOP; UnPo (1st ed.); ViBoPo; WaKn; WePo; WHA; WiR
(Blow, Thou Winter Wind.) FaFP; TreF
(Ingratitude.) BBV
(Song: Blow, blow, thou winter wind!") CBV; CTC; FiP
(Songs from the Plays.) AWP; JAWP; WBP
(Songs of the Greenwood.) TrGrPo
(Two Songs by Amiens, 1.) BoLiVe
Blow, Boys, Blow ("Blow, my bullies, I long to hear you"). *Unknown.* IHA; ShS (*vers.* I)

Blow, Boys, Blow ("I served my time in the Black Ball Line"). *Unknown. See* Black Ball Line, The.
Blow, Boys, Blow ("Now, it's blow, you winds"). *Unknown.* ShS (*vers.* III)
Blow, Boys, Blow ("A Yankee ship came down the river"), *with music. Unknown.* ShS (*vers.* II); SoAmSa; TrAS
(Blow, Bullies, Blow, *diff. vers.*) AmSS, *with music*
Blow, Bugle! Thomas Curtis Clark. PGD
Blow, bugle, blow! Bugle Song of Peace. Thomas Curtis Clark. PEDC; WBLP; WGRP
Blow, Bugle, Blow. Tennyson. *See* Bugle Song, The.
Blow, Bugles, Blow. John Steven McGroarty. DD; HBV; PaA
Blow, Bullies, Blow. *Unknown. See* Blow, Boys Blow.
Blow cold against the flame. Incarnation. Edith Lovejoy Pierce. MaRV
Blow Fish. A. Kirby Congdon. NYTB
Blow gently over my garden. The Beloved. Katharine Tynan. HBV
Blow gently passion in my faire ones breast. *Unknown.* SeCSL
Blow, golden trumpets, sweet and clear. Easter Music. Margaret Wade Deland. ChIP; HH; OQP; PoRL
Blow High, Blow Low. Charles Dibdin. HBV
Blow Me Eyes! Wallace Irwin. BOHV; BoLP; GSP; HBMV; InMe; StPo
Blow, my bullies, I long to hear you. Blow, Boys, Blow. *Unknown.* IHA
Blow, Northern Wind. *Unknown.* OBEV
(Blou Northerne Wynd.) AtBAP
(Love for a Beautiful Lady.) MeEL
Blow on the embers, an' sigh at the sparkles! A Bud in the Frost. "Moira O'Neill." POTE
Blow out the candles of your cake. For K. R. on Her Sixtieth Birthday. Richard Wilbur. ML
Blow out, you bugles, over the rich dead! The Dead. Rupert Brooke. 1914, III. BEL; FaPL; MCCG; OQP; PoFr; TreF; WGRP
Blow, shepherds, blow your pipes, with gladsome glee resounding. *Unknown.* ReEn; SiCE
Blow Softly, Thrush. Joseph Russell Taylor. HBV
Blow, summer wind, from yonder ocean blow. Spring. Thomas Caulfield Irwin. IrPN
Blow the fife and clarinet. Jonathan Bing Dances for Spring. Beatrice Curtis Brown. SiSoSe
Blow the fire, blacksmith. *Unknown.* OxNR
Blow the Man Down. *Unknown.* ABF, *with music*; AmSS, 2 *vers., with music*; AS, *diff. vers., with music*; IHA, *sl. diff. vers.*; ShS, 5 *vers., with music*; SoAmSa (A, B, *and* C *vers.*), *with music*; TrAS, *with music*
Blow the Stars Home. Eleanor Farjeon. PDV
Blow the Winds, I-ho! *Unknown.* OxBoLi
Blow [*or* Blowe] there, sweet Zephyrus [*or* Zephirus]! where thou shalt find[e]. Song. *Unknown.* SeCL; SeCSL
Blow, Thou Winter Wind. Shakespeare. *See* Blow, Blow, Thou Winter Wind.
Blow, wind, blow! Winter Night. Mary Frances Butts. OTPC; PRWS; TiPo (1952 ed.)
Blow, wind, blow! And go, mill, go! Mother Goose. BrR; HBV; OTPC; OxNR; PCH; PPL; SoPo; StVeCh; TiPo
Blow, wind, blow, sing through yard and shroud. A Christmas Song. William Cox Bennett. VA
Blow, Winds. Shakespeare. *Fr.* King Lear, III, ii. TrGrPo; WHA
("Blow winds [*or* windes], and crack your cheeks; rage, blow.") AtBAP; FlW; TreFT
Blow, Ye Winds. *Unknown.* AmSS, *with music*; IHA; SoAmSa, *with music*
Blow Your Trumpets, Angels. John Donne. *See* Sonnet: "At the round earth's imagin'd corners, blow."
Blowe there sweet Zephirus where thou shalt finde. *See* Blow there, sweet Zephyrus . . .
Blowing around this barren-seeming prairie. Note from Thoreau, N.M. John Morgan. YAP
Blowing Bubbles. William Allingham. GN
(Bubble, The.) OnYI
Blown [*or* Blowne] in the morning, thou shalt fade ere noon. A Rose [*or* The Rose of Life]. Sir Richard Fanshawe. *Fr.* Il Pastor Fido. AWP; CavP; HBV; OBEV; OBS; PoEL-2; SeCePo; SeCL; SeEP
Blows the Wind To-Day. Robert Louis Stevenson. *See* To S. R. Crockett.
Bludoo Baby, Want Money, and Alligator Got It to Give. LeRoi Jones. BF
Bludy Serk, The. Robert Henryson. OBEV (1st ed.); OxBoCh
Blue and the Gray, The. Francis Miles Finch. AA; AmePo; BLPA; CoBA; DD, *abr.*; FaBoBe; HBV; HH; MC; NeHB; PaA; PAH; PAL; PAP; PaPo; PCD; PEDC; PTK; ThLM, *abr.*; TreF; WBLP
Blue and White. Mary Elizabeth Coleridge. OBEV (new ed.); OBVV
Blue and white are the heavens. Two Folk Songs, 1. *Unknown.* LiTW
Blue are the beautiful skies! Sweeping the Skies. Elizabeth Anna Hart. CenHV
Blue as the blowpipe's petal of flame. Blue Flag. Dorothy Donnelly. NYBP
Blue Battalions, The. Stephen Crane. AP
(When a People Reach the Top of a Hill.) AmePo
Blue Black. Bloke Modisane. PBA
Blue-black Nubian plucking oranges, A. Color. W. W. Gibson. InP; NP
Blue Blood. James Stephens, *after* O'Bruaidar. MoAB; MoBrPo; OBMV; OxBI
Blue Bonnets over the Border. Sir Walter Scott. *See* Border Ballad.
Blue Bottle, *with music. Unknown.* OuSiCo
Blue Bowl, The. Blanche Bane Kuder. BLPA; FaBoBe; NeHB
Blue Boy in London, The. William Brighty Rands. OTPC
Blue-Butterfly Day. Robert Frost. NeMA
Blue Closet, The. William Morris. NBM; PoVP; VA; ViPo; ViPP
Blue Cockerel. W. S. Merwin. TwAmPo
Blue crane fishing in Cooloolah's twilight, The. At Cooloolah. Judith Wright. MoBrPo (1962 ed.)
Blue day, A, a blue jay. March. Elizabeth Coatsworth. PDV
Blue drifted the sea; the waters of the sun. The Sea. Herman Gorter. LiTW
Blue Duck, The. Lew Sarett. NP
Blue dusk, The, ran between the streets: my love was winged within my mind. Babylon. "Æ." HBMV
Blue Ey'd Mary. *Unknown.* CoMu
Blue-eyed and bright of face but waning fast. Staff-Nurse: New Style. W. E. Henley. *Fr.* In Hospital. NBM; PoVP
Blue-eyed phantom far before, A. Christina Rossetti. EG
Blue-eyed was Elf the minstrel. The Harp of Alfred. G. K. Chesterton. *Fr.* The Ballad of the White Horse. MoVE
Blue eyes, against the whiteness pressed. Songs for Fragoletta, IV. Richard Le Gallienne. HBV
Blue eyes looking up at me. Songs for Fragoletta, II. Richard Le Gallienne. HBV
Blue, faded purple, horizon mount, The. Peace. Samuel Greenberg. CrMA
Blue Funk. Joel Oppenheimer. NeAP
Blue Ghosts. Stanley Snaith. ChMP
Blue giant is passing, The. Larkspur. John Haines. ThO
Blue Girls. John Crowe Ransom. AmP; AnFE; APA; CBV; ChTr; CMoP; CoAnAm; HoPM; LiTA; LiTL; MAP; MoAB; MoAmPo; MoPW; MoVE; NP; PoPo; PoSa; ReMP; TreFT; TwAmPo
Blue gulf all around us. Burial of the Dane. Henry Howard Brownell. AA; HBV
Blue Hen's Chickens, The. Arthur Guiterman. PaA
Blue Heron, The. Theodore Goodridge Roberts. CaP; OBCV; PeCV; TDP; TwCaPo
Blue Hills beneath the Haze. Charles Goodrich Whiting. AA
Blue Homespun. Frank Oliver Call. *Fr.* A Sonnet Series of French Canada. CaP
Blue Horse, The. Melvin Walker La Follette. NePoEA
Blue Horses, The. J. P. McAuley. BoAV
Blue in a lupin-leaf. Dewdrop. Ted Walker. NYTB
Blue in the west the mountain stands. Vickery's Mountain. E. A. Robinson. MAP; MoAmPo
Blue is Our Lady's colour. Blue and White. Mary Elizabeth Coleridge. OBEV (new ed.); OBVV
"Blue Is the Hero." Bill Berkson. ANYP
Blue is true. *Unknown.* GoTP
Blue Island Intersection. Carl Sandburg. MAP; MoAmPo
Blue Jay. Hilda Conkling. BiS
Blue Jay. Robert Francis. ELU
Blue-Jay, The. Susan Hartley Swett. PRWS
Blue jay, fly to my windowsill! Invitation. Harry Behn. FaPON; SoPo

Blue jay scuffling in the bushes follows, The. On the Move. Thom Gunn. ForPo; LiTM (1970 ed.); NePoEA-2; NMP; NoP; OPoP; ShBV-4; ToPo; TwCP; UnPo (3d ed.)
Blue Juniata, *sels.* Malcolm Cowley.
Blue Juniata. MAP; MoAmPo (1942 ed.)
Farm Died, The. MAP; MoAmPo (1942 ed.)
Mine No. 6. InP; MAP; MoAmPo (1942 ed.)
Urn, The. AnAmPo; MoVE; NP
William Wilson. AnAmPo; MoVE
Winter; Two Sonnets. MAP; MoAmPo (1942 ed.)
Blue Kinds. Clark Coolidge. YAP
Blue laguna rocks and quivers, The. Port of Holy Peter. John Masefield. AtBAP; OBMV; POTE; ShBV-2
Blue Larkspur. Sister Mariella. JKCP (1955 ed.)
Blue Meridian, The. Jean Toomer. *See* Brown River, Smile.
Blue Moles. Sylvia Plath. NePoEA-2; PoAn
Blue Moonshine. Francis G. Stokes. NA
Blue mountains to the north of the walls. Taking Leave of a Friend. Li Po, *tr. by* Ezra Pound. CoAnAm; PoFS; TwAmPo
Blue on White. Elizabeth J. Coatsworth. RePo
Blue Persian. Isabel Fiske Conant. CIV
Blue Peter. Stanislaus Lynch. OnYI
Blue, pink and yellow houses, and, afar. Tropical Town. Salomón de la Selva. HBV
Blue Ribbon at Amesbury, A. Robert Frost. NePA
Blue Ribbon Cats. Lalia Mitchell Thornton. CIV
Blue Ridge, The. Harriet Monroe. HBMV
Blue robe on their shoulders, A. The Seven Fiddlers. Sebastian Evans. OnMSP; PoMS; RIS
Blue sea, blue sky, blue eggs. Reflection in Blue. David McCord. MoAmPo (1942 ed.)
Blue Shoes. Kate Greenaway. MPB
Blue skies and bluer sea with its white teeth showing. Sand Dunes and Sea. John Richard Moreland. HBMV
Blue skies bend and are about her furled, The. Roma Mater Sempaeterna. Shaemas O'Sheel. JKCP
Blue sky, blue noon, and the secret line is flung. The Sounding. Conrad Aiken. CrMA
Blue sky, green fields, and lazy yellow sun! Spring Passion. Joel Elias Spingarn. HBV
Blue Sleigh. Winfield Townley Scott. NePoAm; PG (1955 ed.)
Blue Smoke. Frances Frost. RePo; SiSoSe
Blue smoke eclipsed, The. Eclipse. Amir Rashidd. NBP
Blue Squills. Sara Teasdale. HBMV; NP
Blue Symphony, The. John Gould Fletcher. AnAmPo; MAPA; NP; TwAmPo
Blue-Tail Fly, The [*or* De]. *Unknown.* FaFP; SiTL; TreFT; ViBoFo
Blue Tanganyika. Lebert Bethune. BF
Blue Texarkana. Glenn Stokes. WSL
Blue Valentine, A. Joyce Kilmer. ISi; JKCP; LHV
Blue water. . . a clear moon. Nocturne. Li Po. OnPM
Blue waves are sleeping, The. Serenade. Jeremiah Joseph Callanan. IrPN; OnYI
Blue wave's slumber and the rocky brow, The. Olive Grove. James Merrill. NePoAm
Blue waves within the stone. The Immobile Wind. Yvor Winters. NP
Bluebeard's Closet. Rose Terry Cooke. AA
Bluebeard's Wife. Daryl Hine. ACV
Bluebell, The. Emily Brontë. OTPC (1923 ed.)
Bluebell. Geoffrey Taylor. NeIP
Bluebell is the sweetest flower, The. The Bluebell. Emily Brontë. OTPC (1923 ed.)
Bluebells. Walter de la Mare. MPB
Bluebells. Patric Dickinson. BoPe; POTi
Bluebells. Olive Enoch. BoTP
Bluebells. Juliana Horatia Ewing. BoTP
Bluebells. Lucia Clark Markham. HBMV
Bluebells. P. A. Ropes. BoTP
Bluebells [*or* Blue Bells] of Scotland, The. *Unknown, sometimes at. to* Mrs. Grant of Laggan. HBV; OTPC; TreFS
Blue Bird, The. Mary Elizabeth Coleridge. *See* L'Oiseau Bleu.
Bluebird. Hilda Conkling. GFA
Blue-Bird, The. Herman Melville. MWA-1
Bluebird, The. Emily Huntington Miller. GFA; MPB; OTPC (1946 ed.); PRWS
Bluebird, The. Eben Eugene Rexford. *See* Sign of Spring, A.
Bluebird, The. *Unknown.* SoP
Blue-Bird, The. Alexander Wilson. AA
Bluebird lives in yonder tree, A. To Miguel de Cervantes Saavedra. Richard Kendall Munkittrick. AA
Blue Flag. Dorothy Donnelly. NYBP
Blue-Flag in the Bog, The. Edna St. Vincent Millay. AnAmPo
Blue-Fly, The. Robert Graves. CMoP; ILP; MoVE; NYBP
Blue Fly. Joaquim Maria Machado de Assis, *tr. fr. Portuguese by* Frances Ellen Buckland. TTY
Blueprint. Joel Sloman. ThO
Blueprint. D. B. Steinman. GoYe
Blues. Bob Maxey. WSL
Blues. Horace Mungin. BOLo
Blues. Quandra Prettyman. BOLo
Blues. Sonia Sanchez. BF
Blues/ Never climb a hill. Get Up, Blues. James A. Emanuel. AmNP; BOLo
Blues Ain' Nothin', The [*or* De], *with music. Unknown.* AS; TrAS
Blues and Bitterness. Lerone Bennett. NNP
Blues Ballad. Kenneth Pitchford. *Fr.* Good for Nothing Man. CoPo
Blues #8. *Unknown, tr. fr. Chinese by* David Rafael Wang. HW
Blues for an Old Blue. Walker Gibson. NYBP
Blues for Bessie. Myron O'Higgins. PoNe
Blues, for Sallie. Stanley Crouch. WSL
Blues guitar-blues people. Twang. T. L. Robinson. WSL
Blues is a fine/ sister. Blues. Horace Mungin. BOLo
Blues is the black o' the face, The. Black Blues. Bloke Modisane. PBA
Blues meant Swiss-Up, The. Riding Across John Lee's Finger. Stanley Crouch. WSL
Blues Today, The. Mae Jackson. BOLo
Bluff King Hal was full of beans. Henry VIII. Eleanor *and* Herbert Farjeon. OnPP; StPo
Bluish, pale, The. Moontan. Mark Strand. NYBP
Blum. Dorothy Aldis. MoShBr
Blurb, The. Richard Armour. SiTL
Blurt, Master Constable, *sels.* Thomas Middleton.
"Alas! how can I sleep? who truly loves." LO
"Love for such a cherry lip." EG; ViBoPo
(Lips and Eyes.) HBV
(Song: "Love for such a cherry lip.") EIL
"Love is like a lamb, and love is like a lion." BoLP
(Song: Love Is like a Lamb.) AtBAP
Midnight. EIL; SeCePo
True Love Ditty, A. EIL
Blush as of roses, A. Le Marais du Cygne. Whittier. PAH
Blush is on the flower, and the bloom is on the tree, The. My Own Cáilin Donn. George Sigerson. FaBoBe; HBV
Blush Not Redder than the Morning. Nathaniel Lee. *Fr.* Caesar Borgia. SeCL
Blushing rose and purple flower, The. Song [*or* A Song of Pleasure]. Philip Massinger. *Fr.* The Picture, III, v. LiTL; SeCL; UnTE; ViBoPo
Blythe bell, that calls to bridal halls. A Thought. Walter Savage Landor. VA
Blythe was your comin. For My Newborn Son. Sydney Goodsir Smith. ACV
Boadicea. William Cowper. BeLS; FOL; HBV; OTPC
Boar, The. Robert Kelly. CoPo
Boar and the Dromedar, The. Henry Beissel. WHW
Boar Hunt, The. Homer, *tr. fr. Greek by* Robert Fitzgerald. *Fr.* The Odyssey, XIX. FIW
Board Meets, The. John Gloag. FiBHP
Board School Pastoral A. May Kendall. VA
Boarder, The. Louis Simpson. PoPl
Boarding nettings are triced for fight, The. Jack Creamer. James Jeffrey Roche. MC; PAH
"Boarding of Pan American Flight 207 Will Be Delayed Ten Minutes." Barbara L. Greenberg. QAH
Boar's Head, The [That We Bryng Here]. *Unknown. See* Borys Hede. . .
Boar's Head Carol, The ("The boar's head in hands I bring"). *Unknown.* MeEL; MeEV
(Carol Bringing in the Boar's Head, A.) TuPP
Boast no more fond love, thy power. A Song. Thomas D'Urfey. CavP

Boast Not, Proud English. Roger Williams. *Fr.* A Key into the Language of America. AmPP (4th ed.); SCAP
Boast not your fresh unmingled sweets. On Her Absence. Thomas Rymer. SeCL
Boast of heraldry, the pomp of power, The. Thomas Gray. *Fr.* Elegy Written in a Country Churchyard. LO
Boast of Masopha. Z. D. Mangoaela, *tr. fr. Sotho.* PeSA
Boastful Husbandman. *Unknown, tr. fr. German by* Louis Untermeyer. UnTE
Boasting Drunk in Dodge, The. *Unknown.* CoSo
Boasting of Sir Peter Parker, The. Clinton Scollard. PAH
Boat, The. Rose Fyleman. BrR
Boat, The. Robert Kelly. CoPo
Boat, The. Robert Pack. CoAP; NePoEA-2; TPM
Boat, The. Joseph Addison Richards. *See* Master of My Boat, The.
Boat, a Boat, A. *Unknown.* CBEP
("Boat a boat haste to the ferry, A.") SeCSL
Boat, beneath a sunny sky, A. Of Alice in Wonderland. "Lewis Carroll." *Fr.* Alice's Adventures. . ., introd. VA
Boat-Haven, Co. Mayo. Geoffrey Taylor. NeIP
Boat is chafing at our long delay, The. Song. John Davidson. OBEV; OBVV
Boat is ready in which I must embark, The. On Setting Out. William Dickey. CBV
Boat Lost, A. *Unknown, tr. fr. Japanese by* Ishii *and* Obata. OnPM
Boat on the Sea, A. Ethel Turner. BoAu
Boat on the Serchio, The, *sel.* Shelley. MyFE
"Stars burnt out in the pale blue air, The."
Boat ploughed on, The. Going Back to School. Stephen Vincent Benét. LaNeLa
Boat Race, The. Vergil, *tr. fr. Latin by* Rolfe Humphries. *Fr.* The Aeneid, V. SD
Boat Sails Away, The. Kate Greenaway. MoShBr
Boat Song. Sir Walter Scott. *Fr.* The Lady of the Lake, II. BEL; EnLi-2 (1949 ed.); OAEP; PeER; PoEL-4
(Hail to the Chief Who in Triumph Advances!) EnRP
Boatman, The. Jay Macpherson. MoCV; OBCV; PIA
Boatman, The. Christina Rossetti. *See* Ferry Me across the Water.
Boatman he can dance and sing, The. Dance the Boatman. *Unknown.* ThLM
Boatman of Kinsale, The. Thomas Osborne Davis. VA
Boatman's Hymn. *At. to* Andrew Magrath, *tr. fr. Modern Irish by* Sir Samuel Ferguson. OnYI
Boatman's Song, The. Thomas Hardy. *See* Night of Trafalgar, The.
Boats. Rowena Bastin Bennett. GFA; SoPo; TiPo
Boats Are Afloat, The. Chu Hsi, *tr. fr. Chinese by* Kenneth Rexroth. NaP
Boats at Night. Edward Shanks. CH; FIW; MCCG; POTE
Boats go out and the boats come in, The. The Fisher's Widow. Arthur Symons. HBV; PoMa
Boats in a Fog. Robinson Jeffers. AmPP; NoP; OxBA
Boats Sail on the Rivers [*or* River]. Christina Rossetti. *Fr.* Sing-Song. BoChLi; BoTP; BrR; CoBE; OTPC (1946 ed.); PCH; PoRh; PoVP; RIS; StVeCh; TiPo; TSW
(Rainbow, The.) GFA; SoPo
Boats that carry sugar. Freight Boats. James S. Tippett. BrR; FaPON; GFA; MPB; StVeCh (1955 ed.)
Boats that sail in Nancy's fleet, The. Bathtub Bay. Lenore Riggs. GFA
Bob Anderson, My Beau. *Unknown.* PAH
Bob Friede/ was 25 years old. She Tasted Death. John Giorno. ANYP
Bob has blown a hundred eggs. Eggs. Herbert Asquith. BrR
Bob Southey! You're a poet—Poet laureate. Dedication [*or* Southey and Wordsworth]. Byron. *Fr.* Don Juan. BEL; BoLiVe; CTC; EnLi-2 (1949 ed.); EnLit; EnRP; FiP; ILP; InP; LoBV; OAEP; PoFS; TrGrPo
Bob Stanford. *Unknown.* CoSo
Bob was bathing in the Bay. Some Ruthless Rhymes, V. Harry Graham. CenHV
Bob White. George Cooper. DD; GoTP; HBVY; OTPC (1946 ed.); StVeCh (1940 ed.)
(Bobwhite.) MPB
Bobby Bingo. *Unknown. See* Bingo.
Bobby Blue. John Drinkwater. FaPON; GaP; SoPo
Bobby Shaftoe's [*or* Shafto's *or* Shafto has] gone to sea. Mother Goose. AtBAP; BoChLi; BrR; HBV; MPB (1956 ed.); OTPC; OxNR; PPL; RIS
Bobby's First Poem. Norman Gale. FiBHP; MoShBr; PV
Bobolink, The. Thomas Hill. HBV
Bobolink! Max Schling, Max Schling, Lend Me Your Green Thumb. Ogden Nash. PV
Bobolink! that in the meadow. The Bobolink. Thomas Hill. HBV
Bobolinks, The. Christopher Pearse Cranch. AA; GN, *abr.*; OTPC, *abr.*
Bobwhite. *See* Bob White.
Boddynge flourettes bloshes atte the lyghte, The. *See* Budding floweret blushes. . .
Bodhisattva Undoes Hell, A. Jerome Rothenberg. CoPo
Bodies of Men and Women Engirth Me, The. Walt Whitman. AmePo
Bodies that gleam like rare bronze in the fire. The War Dance. Robert V. Carr. PoOW
Bodiless amid bodies, The. Omnipresent Self. *Unknown. Fr.* The Upanishads. OnPM
Bodiless, nameless God. Prayer of the Young Stoic. Stephen P. Dunn. TrPWD
Bodily Beauty. George Rostrevor Hamilton. HBMV
Body and Spirit. W. H. Davies. AtBAP
Body and Spirit I surrendered whole. The Wonder. Kipling. *Fr.* Epitaphs of the War. PoVP
Body English. Ron Padgett. YAP
Body grows without, The. Emily Dickinson. MWA-2; PoeP
Body, if age or uppish soul. Address to the Body. Francis Maguire. JKCP (1955 ed).
Body is a threshold not a waterfall, The. Frances. John Gill. ThO
Body is not fallen like the soul, The. Piero della Francesca. Anne Ridler. FaBoMo
Body Job. John Stevens Wade. ThO
Body, long oppressed, The. This Corruptible. Elinor Wylie. AnFE; CoAnAm; MAP; MoAB; MoAmPo; MoRP
Body my house. Question. May Swenson. LiTM (1970 ed.); NePoEA
Body of, The. Epitaph. Benjamin Franklin. TRV
Body of a Rook. David Wevill. MoCV
Body of Jesus. Arthur Cleveland Coxe. BePJ
Body of John. R. A. K. Mason. AnNZ
Body of Summer, The. "Odysseus Elytis," *tr. fr. Modern Greek by* Kimon Friar. LiTW
Body of the Queen. Donald Evans. AnAmPo
Body Poems, *sels.* Coleman Barks. QAH
Appendix.
Bags under the Eyes.
Brain.
Ear Lobe.
Elbow.
Forehead.
Heart.
Inner Ear.
Navel.
Scar.
Skull.
Stomach.
Body Politic, The. Donald Hall. NePoEA; TwCP
Body slumbers, humble as the dead, The. Lines in Order to Be Slandered. Paul Verlaine. SyP
Body's Beauty. Dante Gabriel Rossetti. The House of Life, LXXVIII. ATP (1953 ed.); EnL; HBV; ILP; MaVP; PAn; PoVP; Sonn; TrGrPo; ViPo; ViPP
(Lilith.) PoEL-5
Body's Eye, The. Anne Welsh. BoSA
Body's Freedom. Helen Neville. NePA
Body's Speech, The. Donal MacCarthy, first Earl Clancarty, *tr. fr. Irish by* Frank O'Connor. KiLC
Boer War, The. William Plomer. BoSA
Bofors A.A. Gun, The. Gavin Ewart. WaP
Bog Lands, The. William A. Byrne. AnIV; JKCP (1926 ed.)
Bogac Bán. Darrell Figgis. AnIV
Boggy Creek. *Unknown. See* Buffalo Skinners, The.
Bohemia. Dorothy Parker. CrMA; NAMP
Bohemian Girl, The, *sels.* Alfred Bunn.
I Dreamt I Dwelt in Marble Halls. TreFS
When Other Lips and Other Hearts. TreF
Bohemian Hymn, The. Emerson. OQP; PFY; WGRP
Bohemians, The. Ivor Gurney. MMA

Bohemond and Tancred and Raymond St. Giles. God Wills It. Richard F. Grady. JKCP (1955 ed.)
Bohernabreena. Leslie Daiken. OnYI
Bohunkus. *Unknown.* YaD
Bohunkus would take off his hat, and bow and smile, and things like that. Gelett Burgess. *Fr.* An Alphabet of Famous Goops. BBGG
Boisterous Poem about Poetry, A, *sel.* John Wain.
"I have a notion that the world is round." PP
Boke of Phyllyp Sparowe. John Skelton. *See* Phyllyp Sparowe.
Boke of Two Ladies, *sel.* David Morton.
Petition for a Miracle. ISi
Bold, amiable, ebon outlaw, grave and wise! To a Crow. Robert Burns Wilson. AA
Bold Captain of the Body-Guard. Zagonyi. George Henry Boker. PAH
Bold Daniels [*or* Bold Manan]. *Unknown.* SoAmSa
Bold Fisherman, The. *Unknown.* BaBo
Bold Lanty was in love, you see, with lively Rosie Carey. Lanty Leary. Samuel Lover. BOHV; BoLP; ChTr
Bold Manan. *Unknown.* *See* Bold Daniels.
Bold Manning, *with music.* *Unknown.* ShS
Bold Peddler [*or* Pedlar] and Robin Hood, The. *Unknown.* BaBo; ESPB
Bold Phelim Brady, the Bard of Armagh. *Unknown.* OnYI
Bold *Princess Royal,* The, *with music.* *Unknown.* ShS (2 *vers.*)
(Fair *Princess Royal,* The, *with music.*) SoAmSa
Bold Rangers, *with music.* *Unknown.* BFSS
Bold Robert Emmet. Tom Maguire. OnYI
Bold Satirist, The, *abr.* Horace, *tr. fr. Latin by* Philip Francis. WoL
Boldness[e] in Love. Thomas Carew. AnAnS-2; ErPo; MePo; SCEP-2; SeCL; SeCV-1; SeEP; UnTE
(Mark How the Bashful Morn [in Vain]). EG; LiTL
Boll Weevil Song, The. *Unknown.* *See* Ballet of de Boll Weevil, De.
Boll-weevil's coming, and the winter's cold. November Cotton Flower. Jean Toomer. CDC
Bologna, and Byron. Samuel Rogers. *See* Byron Recollected at Bologna.
Bolschevik who never gave heed to queen or to king, A. Dain do Eimhir, XXX. Sorley Maclean. NeBP
Bolsum Brown, *with music.* *Unknown.* AS
Bolt and bar the front door. Hallowe'en. Molly Capes. MoSiPe
Bolt and bar the shutter. Mad as the Mist and Snow. W. B. Yeats. AtBAP; ChTr; MBW-2
Bolyai, the Geometer. Donald Davie. OPoP
Bombardment. Richard Aldington. MMA
Bombardment. D. H. Lawrence. MMA
Bombardment, The. Amy Lowell. YT
Bombardment of Bristol, The. *Unknown.* PAH
Bombay. Josephine Miles. FiMAP
Bombay Arrival. Laurie Lee. POTi; ToPo
Bombed Happiness, The. Stephen Spender. CMoP
Bombed in London. Kipling. *Fr.* Epitaphs of the War. PoVP
Bomber, The. Robert Lowell. WaaP
Bomber, The. Brian Vrepont. BoAV
Bomber climb out on the roof. The Bomber. Robert Lowell. WaaP
Bombers. C. Day Lewis. CMoP; MoAB
Bombing Casualties: [in] Spain. Sir Herbert Read. FaBoTw; PPON
"Bon jour, Madame Sans Souci." Madame Sans Souci. *Unknown.* BOHV
Bon Mot, A. *Unknown.* ErPo
"Bon soir, ma chérie." Comrades in Arms: Conversation Piece. *Unknown.* ErPo
"Bona de Mortuis". Thomas Lovell Beddoes. ELU
Bonac. John Hall Wheelock. HT; MoVE
Bond Street. Norman Nicholson. POTi
Bondage. "Owen Innsley." AA
Bondmen of Mizraim/ Were our fathers. Flowering without End. Stefan Zweig. *Fr.* Jeremiah. TrJP
Bonds. Laurence Housman. MaRV
Bond-slave to Christ, and in my bonds rejoicing. Paul. John Oxenham. TRV
Bonduca, *sel.* John Fletcher.
"Had we a difference with some petty isle." PoFr
Bone-aged is my white horse. Song [*or* Song—Talysarn]. Brenda Chamberlain. NeBP; NeIP
Bone China. R. P. Lister. NYBP
Bone that has no marrow, The. Emily Dickinson. AmePo
Bone Thoughts on a Dry Day. George Starbuck. GoYe; NYBP; TDP; TwCP
Bone to bone. Tomb. Besmilr Brigham. ThO
"Boneless tongue, so small and weak, The." The Tongue. Phillips Burrows Strong. PoToHe (new ed.); SoP; TreFT; WBLP
Bones. Walter de la Mare. FiBHP; ShM
Bones, The. W. S. Merwin. LiTM (1970 ed.); NePoEA-2
Bones Go to Church, The. Florence Dolby Wolfe. SoP
Bones of a French Lady in a Museum. Richard Gillman. NePoAm
Bones of Chuang Tzu, The. Chang Heng, *tr. fr. Chinese by* Arthur Waley. AtBAP; AWP
Bones of Incontention, The. Robert David Cohen. NYBP
Bones of the children cried out upon the mountain, The. On the Mountain. M. K. Joseph. AnNZ
Boney ("Boney was a warrior"), *with music.* *Unknown.* AmSS; ShS (2 *vers.*); SoAmSa, *sl. diff. vers.*
Bonfire, The. Robert Frost. InvP
Bonfire of Kings. Donald Evans. AnAmPo
Bonhomme Richard and *Serapis,* The. Philip Freneau. PAH
Bonie Doon. Burns. *See* Banks o'Doon, The.
Bonie lassie, will ye go. *See* Bonnie lassie. . .
Bonnard: A Novel. Richard Howard. CoAP; NYBP
Bonne Entente. F. R. Scott. FiBHP; OBCV; PeCV; SiTL
Bonner's Ferry. Peter Schjeldahl. ANYP
Bonnie Annie. *Unknown.* ESPB (A *and* B *vers.*); OBB (*combined vers.* A *and* B, *sl. diff.*)
Bonnie Annie Livieston. *Unknown.* OxBB
Bonnie Banks o'Fordie, The. *Unknown.* *See* Babylon; or, The Bonnie Banks o'Fordie.
Bonnie Blue Flag, The ("Come, brothers! rally for the right"). Annie Chambers Ketchum. PaA; PAH; ThLM
Bonnie Bessie Lee. Robert Nicoll. VA
Bonnie Black Bess. *Unknown.* *See* My Bonny Black Bess.
Bonnie, bonnie bairn who sits poking in the ase, The. Castles in the Air. James Ballantine. HBV
Bonnie Bower. *Unknown.* *See* Lament of the Border Widow, The.
Bonnie Broukit Bairn, The. "Hugh MacDiarmid." FaBoCh; GoTS
Bonnie Charlie's now awa'. Will Ye No Come Back Again? Lady Nairne. ShBV-1
Bonnie Doon. Burns. *See* Banks o'Doon, The.
Bonnie Dundee. Sir Walter Scott. *See* Bonny Dundee.
Bonnie Earl of Murray [*or* Moray], The. *Unknown.* *See* Bonny Earl of Murray, The.
Bonnie George Campbell. *Unknown.* AWP; BEL; BoLiVe; CH; ELP; EnLit; EnRP; HBV; InPo; NoP; OxBB; PoPo
(Bonny George Campbell.) GoTS; OBB; OxBoLi; PCD, *shorter vers*; ViBoPo
(Bonnie [*or* Bonny] James Campbell.) BaBo (A *and* B *vers.*); BFS, *with music*; CBEP; ESPB (A, B, C, *and* D *vers.*)
Bonnie [*or* Bonny] House o' [*or* of] Airlie, The. *Unknown.* BaBo (A *and* B *vers.*); BuBa; ESPB; OBB; OBEV; OxBB; OxBS
(Lady Ogalbie, *with music.*) BFSS
Bonnie James Campbell. *Unknown.* *See* Bonnie George Campbell.
Bonnie Jeanie. J. B. Morton. ShBV-4
Bonnie [*or* Bonny] Kilmeny gaed up the glen. Kilmeny. James Hogg. *Fr.* The Queen's Wake. CABL; GBV; GoTS; HBV; OBEV; OnSP
Bonnie Laddie's Lang a-Grouwin', The. *Unknown.* OxBS
Bonnie [*or* Bonie] lassie, will ye go. The Birks of Aberfeldy. Burns. CTC; ViBoPo
Bonnie Lesley [*or* Leslie]. Burns. AtBAP; CTC; GTBS; GTBS-D; GTBS-P; GTBS-W; GTSE; GTSL; OBEC; OBEV; PoIE
(O, Saw Ye Bonnie Lesley?) HBV
(Saw ye Bonny [*or* Bonie] Lesley?) CBEP; OxBS
Bonnie Wee Thing. Burns. HBV
Bonniest Bairn in A' the Warl', The. Robert Ford. GN
Bonniest lass that ye meet neist, The. For A' That an' A' That. *At. to* Robert Burns. CoMu: UnTE
Bonny Baby Livingston. *Unknown.* BaBo; ESPB (A and C vers.)
Bonny Barbara Allen. *Unknown.* *See* Barbara Allen.

Bonny Bee Hom. *Unknown.* BaBo; ESPB; OBB, *sl. diff. vers.*
Bonny Birdy, The. *Unknown.* ESPB
Bonny Black Bess. Charles Sackville. *See* Song: "Methinks the poor town has been troubled too long."
Bonny Black Bess. *Unknown.* *See* My Bonny Black Bess.
Bonny, bonny bird I had, A. Richard Brome. *Fr.* The Northern Lass. TuPP
Bonny, Bonny Owl, The. Sir Walter Scott. *Fr.* Kenilworth, *ch.* 2. BiS
Bonny Broom, The, *with music.* *Unknown.* BFSS
Bonny Brown Girl, The. *Unknown.* *See* Brown Girl, The.
Bonny Bunch of Roses, O, The. *Unknown.* OxBoLi
Bonny burgh is Edinbro', the city brave and bright, A. Edinburgh. Arthur Guiterman. WhC
Bonny Dundee. Sir Walter Scott. *Fr.* The Doom of Devorgoil, II, ii. BEL; EnRP; FaBoCh; HBV; LoGBV; OBRV; OxBoLi; OxBS; SeCeV; ToP
(Bonnie Dundee.) OTPC (1923 ed.); Par, *abr.*
Bonny Earl of Livingston, The. *Unknown.* *See* Fair Mary of Wallington.
Bonny [*or* Bonnie] Earl of Murray [*or* o'Moray], The. *Unknown.* AnFE; BaBo (A *and* B *vers.*); BEL; BuBa; CBEP; ELP; EnLit; ESPB (A *and* B *vers.*); FaBoCh; GoTS; HBV; LoGBV; OBB; OBEV; OBS; OxBB; OxBS; ViBoFo
Bonny fine maid of a noble degree, A. Robin Hood and Maid Marian. *Unknown.* BaBo; ESPB
Bonny George Campbell. *Unknown.* *See* Bonnie George Campbell.
Bonny Harvest Moon, The. John Barr of Craigielee. AnNZ
Bonny heir, and the well-faird [*or* faur'd *or* favoured] heir, The. The Heir of Linne. *Unknown.* BaBo; BuBa; ESPB (B *vers.*); OBB
Bonny Hind [*or* Heyn], The. *Unknown.* ESPB; OxBB; ViBoFo
Bonny James Campbell. *Unknown.* *See* Bonnie George Campbell.
Bonny John Seton. *Unknown.* BaBo; ESPB
Bonny Kilmeny gaed up the glen. *See* Bonnie Kilmeny. . .
Bonny Lass of Anglesey, The *Unknown.* ESPB (A *and* B *vers.*)
Bonny Lassie O. John Clare. CH
Bonny Lizie Baillie. *Unknown.* BaBo; ESPB
Bonum Est Mihi Quod Humiliasti Me, *abr.* Earl of Surrey. SiPS
("Storms are past, these clouds are overblown, The.") FCP
Boogie-woogie Ballads. St. Clair McKelway. PoNe
Book, A ("He ate and drank the precious words"). Emily Dickinson. *See* He ate and drank the precious words.
Book, A [*or* The] ("There is no frigate like a book"). Emily Dickinson. *See* There is no frigate like a book.
Book, The. William Drummond of Hawthornden. *See* Book of the World, The.
Book, The. Helen Frazee-Bower. SoP
Book, The. Winfred Ernest Garrison. OQP; TRV
Book, A. Hannah More. HH; OTPC; PoRL; PoSC
(Riddle, A: Book, A.) GN
Book, A. Lizette Woodworth Reese. YeAr
Book, The. Henry Vaughan. EnL; SCEP-1; SeCV-1
Book, a friend, a song, a glass, A. William Thompson. *Fr* The Happy Life. ViBoPo
Book and a jug and a dame, A. Limerick. *Unknown.* LiBL
Book & Bookplate. John Masefield. WhC
Book, Book. Annette Wynne. HH
Book Buying in the Tenderloin. Robert Hass. YAP
Book for Christmas, A. Margaret Allonby. BoSA
Book I Held Grew Cold, The. Ernst Toller, *tr. fr. German by* Ashley Dukes. TrJP
Book Is an Enchanted Gate, A. Morris Abel Beer. HH
Book may be a flower, A. A Book. Lizette Woodworth Reese. YeAr
Book-Moth. *Unknown.* *See* Book-Worm, A.
Book of a Thousand Nights and a Night, The. *Unknown.* *See* Thousand and One Nights, The.
Book of Books, The. Sir Walter Scott. *Fr.* The Monastery, *ch.* 12. MaRV; NeHB; OQP; SoP; TreFT
(Bible, The.) BLRP; TRV
(Divine Volume, The.) FaChP
(Sir Walter Scott's Tribute.) WBLP
Book of books, holy, sublime and true, The. The Bible. Henry W. Frost. SoP
Book of God, The. Horatius Bonar. SoP
Book of Good Love, The, *sel.* Juan Ruiz, Archpriest of Hita, *tr. fr. Spanish.*
Praise of Little Women, *tr. by* Longfellow. AWP
Book of Hours, The, *sel.* Rainer Maria Rilke, *tr. fr. German by* Jessie Lemont.
"Many have painted her." CAW
Book of Hours of Sister Clotilde, The. Amy Lowell. APA
Book of How, The. Merrill Moore. BoLiVe (1939 ed.); MAP; MoAmPo; NeMA
Book of Kells, The. Howard Nemerov. EaLo
Book of Leinster, *sel.* Cormac, *tr. fr. Old Irish by* George Sigerson.
Heavenly Pilot, The. OnYI
Book of Los, The, *sel.* Blake.
Immortal, The, *fr. ch.* 2. LiTB; LoBV
Book of Merlin, The. Jack Spicer. CoPo
Book of Nature, The. Richard Eberhart. PoDB
Book of Odes, The. *Unknown.* *See* Shi King.
Book of Orm, The, *sel.* Robert Buchanan.
Dream of the World without Death, The. VA
Book of Percival, The. Jack Spicer. CoPo
Book of Philip Sparrow, The. John Skelton. *See* Phyllyp Sparowe.
Book of Rights, *sel.* *Unknown,* *tr. fr. Middle Irish by* James Clarence Mangan.
Testament of Cathaeir Mor, The. OnYI
Book of Shells, A. Randy Blasing. YAP
Book of Songs. *Unknown.* *See* Shi King.
Book of Tarshish, The, *sel.* Moses ibn Ezra, *tr. fr. Hebrew by* Solomon Solis-Cohen.
Joy of Life. TrJP
Book of the Dead, *sels.* *Unknown,* *tr. fr. Egyptian by* Robert Hillyer.
Adoration of the Disk by King Akhnaten and Princess Nefer Neferiu Aten. AWP; JAWP; WBP
"Cattle roam again across the field, The." FaPON
Dead Man Ariseth and Singeth a Hymn to the Sun, The. AWP; JAWP; WBP
He Approacheth the Hall of Judgment. AWP; JAWP; WBP
He Asketh Absolution of God. AWP
He Biddeth Osiris to Arise from the Dead. AWP
He Cometh Forth into the Day. AWP; JAWP; WBP
He Commandeth a Fair Wind. AWP
He Defendeth His Heart against the Destroyer. AWP
He Embarketh in the Boat of Ra. AWP
He Entereth the House of the Goddess Hathor. AWP
He Establisheth His Triumph. AWP; JAWP; WBP
He Holdeth Fast to the Memory of His Identity. AWP; JAWP; WBP
He Is Declared True of Word. AWP; JAWP; WBP
He Is like the Lotus. AWP; EaLo; JAWP; WBP
He Is like the Serpent Saka. AWP
He Kindleth a Fire. AWP
He Knoweth the Souls of the East. AWP
He Knoweth the Souls of the West. AWP; JAWP; WBP
He Maketh Himself One with Osiris. AWP
He Maketh Himself One with the God Ra. AWP
He Maketh Himself One with the Only God, Whose Limbs Are the Many Gods. AWP; JAWP; WBP
He Overcometh the Serpent of Evil in the Name of Ra. AWP
He Prayeth for Ink and Palette That He May Write. AWP
He Singeth a Hymn to Osiris the Lord of Eternity. AWP
He Singeth in the Underworld. AWP; JAWP; WBP
He Walketh by Day. AWP; JAWP; WBP
Hymn to Ra, *pr. tr. by* E. A. Wallis Budge. OuHeWo
"I am the past and the present, and I bear," *tr. by* Lindley W. Hubbell. LiTW
Other World, The. AWP; JAWP; WBP
Book of the Duchesse, The, *sels.* Chaucer.
Dream, The. FiP
May Morning. WHA
Book of the Native, The, *sel.* Sir Charles G. D. Roberts.
When the Sleepy Man Comes. HBV; HBVY; MPB
Book of the Two Married Women and the Widow, The. William Dunbar. *See* Tua Mariit Wemen and the Wedo, The.
Book of the World, The. William Drummond of Hawthornden. HBV; TOP
(Book, The.) CH; MCCG; PCD
(Lessons of Nature, The.) GTBS; GTBS-D; GTBS-P; GTBS-W; GTSE; GTSL

(On the Margin Wrought.) SeCePo
(Sonnet; "Of this fair volume which we world do name.") SeCL
Book of Thel, The. Blake. BEL; CEP; ChER; EiPP; EnRP; ERoP-1; NoP; OBNC; Po; PoEL-4
Sels.
"Clod of Clay heard the Worm's voice and raised her pitying head, The." LO
Thel's Motto ("Does the eagle know what is in the pit?"). ChTr; DiPo; LO
"Why cannot the ear be closed to its own destruction?" FaBoEn
Worm, The. FlW
Book of True Love, The, *sel.* Juan Ruiz, Archpriest of Hita, *tr. fr. Spanish by* Hubert Creekmore.
"When you're together with her, and you have a good excuse." ErPo
Book of Urizen, The. Blake. ERoP-1
Book of verses underneath the bough, A. Omar Khayyám, *tr. by* Edward Fitzgerald. *Fr.* The Rubáiyát. AnFE; DiPo; EG; FosPo; GTBS-W; HoPM; LiTL; MeWo; OBEV; OBVV; OnPM; OQP; SeCePo; SeCeV; SiTL; YT
Book of Wild Flowers, The Joseph Ceravolo. ANYP
Book of Wisdom, The. Stephen Crane. The Black Riders, XXXVI. HoPM; MAP; MoAmPo
("I met a seer.") CoBA
Book Our Mothers Read, The. Whittier. *See* Bible, The.
Book Review. David Ross. PG (1945 ed.)
Book was dull, its pictures, The. The Bride. Ralph Hodgson. HBMV; InP
Book was writ of late called *Tetrachordon*, A. On the Detraction Which Followed upon My Writing Certain Treatises. Milton. SeCeV; Sonn
Book which thou dost read, it is, The. To Fidentinus. Martial, *tr. by* Timothe Kendall. TuPP
Book you may buy for a shilling, A. Barter. Earle V. Eastwood. OQP
Booker T. and W. E. B. Dudley Randall. BP; Kal
Booker Washington Trilogy, The, *sels.* Vachel Lindsay.
John Brown, II. AnAmPo; MAP; MoAmPo; NP
Simon Legree—a Negro Sermon, I. CoBa; HBMV; InMe; LiTA; LoGBV; MoVE; NAMP; NePA; ShBV-2
(Negro Sermon, A: Simon Legree.) AnAmPo; ATP (1935 ed); MAP; MoAmPo; PFY
Bookmark. St. Teresa of Avila. *See* Lines Written in Her Breviary.
Bookra. Charles Dudley Warner. AA; HBV
Books. Elizabeth Barrett Browning. *Fr.* Aurora Leigh, I. VA
Books. Hilda Conkling. HH
Books. George Crabbe. *Fr.* The Library. OBEC
Books. Eleanor Farjeon. YeAr
Books. Joseph Joel Keith. StVeCh (1955 ed.)
Books. Florence Van Cleve. HH
Books. Wordsworth. *Fr.* The Prelude, V. MBW-2; PoEL-4
Books and the Man I sing, the first who brings. Pope. *Fr.* The Dunciad CEP; EiCL
Books are bridges. Golden Spurs. Virginia Scott Miner. PoRL; SiSoSe; StaSt
Books Are Keys. Emilie Poulsson. HH; SiSoSe
Books are more than words. Books. Joseph Joel Keith. StVeCh (1955 ed.)
Books Are Soldiers. Annette Wynne. HH
Books, books, that I love so. Books. Hilda Conkling. HH
Books collide—/ Or books in a library do. To W. H. Auden on His Fiftieth Birthday. Barbara Howes. ML
Books composed before our day, The. Prolog. John Gower. *Fr.* Confessio Amantis. MeEV
Books grow clear upon the shelf, The. Her Second Song. James K. Baxter. Cressida, IX. AnNZ
Books I have are made of lead, The. Convalescence, VIII. David McCord. WhC
Books men write are but a fragrance blown, The. The Book. Helen Frazee-Bower. SoP
Books say well, my Brothers, The!, each man's life. Nirvana. Sir Edwin Arnold. *Fr.* Light of Asia. VA
Bookshop Idyll, A. Kingsley Amis. NePoEA
Bookworm, The. Walter de la Mare. TiPo (1959 ed.)
Book-Worm, A [*or* The]. *Unknown, tr. fr. Anglo-Saxon. Fr.* Riddles. CoBE; EnLi-1, *tr. by* Stith Thompson
(Book-Moth: "Moth ate a word, A. To me it seemed," *tr. by* Charles W. Kennedy.) AnOE; OA
("Moth ate words, A. To me that seemed," *tr. by* Harold S. Stine.) EnLit
Book-Worms, The. Burns. ChTr; ELU; FiBHP
Boolee, the Bringer of Life. Mary Gilmore. BoAV
Boom! Howard Nemerov. LiTM (1970 ed.); PoDB
Boom above my knees lifts, and the boat, The. Sailing to an Island. Richard Murphy. NMP
Boomerang, The. Carrie May Nichols. PoToHe
Boomerang. John Perreault. ANYP
Boon, A. William Meredith. NePoEA
Boon Companion, The. Oliver St. John Gogarty. *See* To a Boon Companion.
Boon Nature to the woman bows. The Tribute. Coventry Patmore. *Fr.* The Angel in the House. FaPL; HBV; OBNC
Boosting the Booster ("Boost your city, boost your friend"). *Unknown.* WBLP
Boot and a Shoe and a Slipper, A. High and Low. John Banister Tabb. BrR
Boot and Saddle ("Boot, saddle, to horse, and away!"). Robert Browning. Cavalier Tunes, III. EnLi-2; EnLit; PoPo; PoVP; ShBV-1; ViPo
Boot-soles and overalled haunches to the street. Janitor Working on Threshold. Margaret Avison. PeCV (1967 ed.)
Booth led boldly with his big bass drum. General William Booth Enters into Heaven. Vachel Lindsay. AmLP; AmPP; ATP; BoC; CMoP; CoBA; FaBoMo; HBV; ILP; InPo; LiTA; LiTM; MAP; MaRV; MoAB; MoAmPo; MoPo; NP; OxBA; ReMP; SeCeV; TOP; TreFS; TrGrPo; WGRP
Boots. Kipling. BLPA; MoBrPo; PoVP; ShBV-2; WHA
Boots,/ Shoes. *Unknown.* OxNR
Boots and Saddles. Nicolas Saboly, *tr. fr. Provençal.* OHIP
Boots and Shoes. Lilian McCrea. BoTP
Bo-peep,/ Little Bo-peep. *Unknown.* OxNR
Bo-peeper. *Unknown.* OxNR
Bora Ring. Judith Wright. NeLNL
Border Affair, A. Badger Clark. SCC
Border Ballad. Sir Walter Scott. *Fr.* The Monastery, *ch.* 25. EnLit; EPN; GN; HBV; PCD
(Blue Bonnets over the Border.) OxBS
(Border March.) EnRP
(March, March [Ettrick and Teviotdale].) ViBoPo
Border River. Alfred Goldsworthy Bailey. CaP
Borderers, The, *sel.* Wordsworth.
"Action is transitory—a step, a blow." PeER
Borderline. R. H. Grenville. FiSC
Border Line. Langston Hughes. PoCh
Borderline Ballad. Richard Weber. PPON
Bore, The. Horace, *tr. fr. Latin.* Satires, I, 9. ATP, *tr. by* John Conington; EnLi-1, *tr. by* Sir Theodore Martin; OuHeWo; *tr. by* Sir Theodore Martin
Boreas blows on his high wood whistle. In Winter. C. H. Bretherton. InMe
Bored Mirror, The. Syuichi Nagayasu, *tr. fr. Japanese by* Katue Kitasono. LiTW
Boredom. Ramón de Campoamor, *tr. fr. Spanish by* Beatrice Gilman Proske. *Fr.* Doloras. OnPM
Bores hed in hondes I bring, The. The Boar's Head Carol. *Unknown.* MeEL
Borgia, thou once wert [*or* were] almost too august. On Lucretia Borgia's Hair [*or* On Seeing a Hair of Lucretia Borgia]. Walter Savage Landor. AnFE; CABA; EnRP; OAEP; TOP; UnPo [1st ed.]; VA
Born are we of fire. Mothers and Children. Orrick Johns. AnAmPo; HBMV
Born by a whim. Signature. Dorothy Livesay. OBCV
Born I was to be old. Anacreontic. Robert Herrick. OAEP; OnPM; OxBoLi; WoL
Born[e] I was to meet with age. On Himself[e]. Robert Herrick. ChTr; SeCV-1
Born in a borrowed cattle shed. Evaluation. Elinor Lennen. OQP
Born in a fence-corner. Tumbling Mustard. Malcolm Cowley. AmFN
Born in a hovel, trained in Hardship's school. Abraham Lincoln. A. S. Ames. OHIP
Born in a trance, we wake, observe, inquire. Another and the Same. Samuel Rogers. OBNC
Born in my mouth, the naked beast leaned out. A Warning to

Born (continued)
My Love. David Wagoner. NePoEA-2
Born in the comet tail of a war. Orphans. Randy Rhody. WOW
Born in the garret, in the kitchen bred. A Sketch [from Private Life]. Byron. ERoP-2; OBNC; OBRV
Born in these metal tubes beneath. A Winter's Tale. Ruth Lechlitner. HYE
Born, nurtured, wedded, prized, within the pale. La Fayette. Dolly Madison. PaA; PAH; PAL; ThLM
Born of my voiceless time, your steps. The Footsteps. Paul Valéry. LiTW
Born of Tears. W. H. Davies. GTBS-D
Born of the sorrowful of heart. For Paul Laurence Dunbar. Countee Cullen. Four Epitaphs, 3. AmNP; BALP; CDC; GoSl; Kal
Born of the union of Chaos and Time. Erda. Vera Bishop Konrick. FiSC
Born of the Colorado. Cowboy to Pitching Bronco [*or* Cowboy Talks to a Pitching Horse]. *Unknown.* ABF; CoSo
Born with a monocle he stares at life. En Monocle. Donald Evans. AnAmPo; NP
Born with all arms, he sought a separate peace. The Deserter. John Manifold. WaP
Born with the Vices. Thomas D'Urfey. *See* To Cynthia: a Song.
Born without a Chance. Edmund Vance Cooke. BLPA
Born Yesterday. Philip Larkin. HaMV
Borne ("Borne across a river of grey, life forces"). Daniel J. Owens. TNV
Borne-heid demoniac. Defeat o' the Hert. Sidney Goodsir Smith. AtBAP
Borne on a whispered sigh. Fallen Leaves. Kathryn Munro. CaP
Borough, The, *sels.* George Crabbe.
Amusements, *fr.* Letter IX. OBRV
"Can scenes like these,"*fr.* Letter I. OBRV
Caroline, The, *fr.* Letter XI. SeCePo
"'Decribe the Borough'—though our idle Tribe," Letter I. CABL
Peter Grimes, Letter XXII. EiCL; EnPE; EnRP; MemP; NoP; PoEL-4
"Alas! for Peter not a helping hand," *sel.* OBRV
"Thus by himself compell'd to live each day," *sel.* FaBoEn; OBNC; SeCePo
"Now lived the youth in freedom, but debarred," *sel.* WePo
Players, *fr.* Letter XII. EiCL
Poor of the Borough, The; the Parish Clerk, *fr.* Letter XIX. EiCL
Sailing upon the River, *fr.* Letter IX. OBNC
Schools, *fr.* Letter XXIV. CTC
Slum Dwelling, A, *fr.* Letter XVIII. OBNC
Thoughts by the Shore. PoG
Vicar, The, *fr.* Letter III. OBNC
Winter Storm at Sea, The, *fr.* Letter I. EtS
Winter Views Serene, *fr.* Letter IX. OBNC
"Your plan I love not; with a number you," *fr.* Letter XVIII. LO
Borrow and borrow. Rhymes to Remember. *Unknown.* StaSt
"Borrowed." *Unknown.* *See* Cross Was His Own, The.
Borrowed Child, The. Howard Weeden. AA
Borrowed wings on his ankles. Perseus. Louis MacNeice. CoBMV; GTBS-W; LiTM; ReMP; StP
Borrower of Salt, The. Oscar Williams. *Fr.* Variations on a Theme. LiTA; NePA
Borrowing. Emerson. *Fr.* Anxiety. WhC
(Needless Worry.) TreFT
("Some of your hurts you have cured.") MaRV
Borys Hede That We Bryng Here, The. *Unknown.* YAT
(Christmas Carol, A.) EnLit
Bos'n Hill. John Albee. AA
Bosnia. November. And the mountain roads. Sarajevo. Lawrence Durrell. GTBS-P
Bosom, A, of/ green buds. Mare Nostrum. Joel Oppenheimer. NeAP
Boss I have seen Mehitabel the cat. Mehitabel Tries Marriage. Don Marquis. *Fr.* Archys Life of Mehitabel. WePo
Boss I just discovered what. Archys Last Name. Don Marquis. *Fr.* Archys Life of Mehitabel. CrMA
Boss, I saw a picture. Archy a Low Brow. Don Marquis. *Fr.* Archys Life of Mehitabel. WhC
Boss knows what shape I'm in, The. He tells me. Drunk Last Night with Poets, I Go to Work Anyway. Philip Dow. QAH
Bossy and the Daisy. Margaret Deland. PPL
Boston ("And this is good old Boston"). John Collins Bossidy. *See* Boston Toast, A.
Boston ("I come from the city of Boston"). *At. to* Samuel C. Bushnell. LiTM; OxBoLi; SiTL.
See also Boston Toast, A.
Boston. Emerson. MC; PAP
Boston. John Boyle O'Reilly. PAH
Boston ("From Boston harbor we set sail"), *with music.* *Unknown.* SoAmSa
Boston Boy Went out to Yuma, A. "D. D." ShM
Boston Burglar, The *Unknown.* ViBoFo
Boston Cats, The. Arthur Macy. CIV
Boston Charlie. Walt Kelly. FiBHP; GoJo
Boston Come All Ye, The, *with music.* *Unknown.* ABF; SoAmSa
(Fishes, The.) TrAS
Boston Evening Transcript, The. T. S. Eliot. BWP; MWA-2; NePA
Boston has a festival. In the Public Garden. Marianne Moore. NoP
Boston Hymn. Emerson. AnNE; LaNeLa; MC; MWA-1; PaA; PAH; PAL; TOP; TRV; WGRP
"Word of the Lord, The," *sel.* DD, *diff. and abr.*
Boston. Lord God, the ocean never to windward. Poems from a First Year in Boston. George Starbuck. NePoEA-2; TwAmPo
Boston Lullaby, A. James Jeffrey Roche. BOHV
Boston Nursery Rhymes. Joseph Cook. BOHV; InMe
Boston Road Blues ("Boston Road is as wide as a boulevard"). David Henderson. BF
Boston Tea Party, The. *Unknown.* *See* New Song, A.
Boston Toast, A ("And this is [*or* is to *or* Here's to] good old Boston"). John Collins Bossidy. BLPA; NeHB; YaD
("And this is good old Boston.") CenHV
(Boston.) AmFN; GoTP
(Boston, *sl. diff. vers.*: "I come from the city of Boston.") LiTM (*Unknown*); OxBoLi (*At. to* Samuel C. Bushnell); SiTL (*Unknown*)
(On the Aristocracy of Harvard.) HBV; WhC
(On the Aristocracy of Harvard, *sl. diff. vers.*: "I come from good olde Boston,"*at. to* Samuel C. Bushnell.) BOHV
(To Boston.) TreFS
Boswell by my bed. Reading in War Time. Edwin Muir. WaP
Botanic Garden, The, *sels.* Erasmus Darwin.
Pt. I. The Economy of Vegetation.
Immortal Nature, *fr.* Canto IV. OBEC
Steam Power, *fr.* Canto I. OBEC
Pt. II. The Loves of the Plants.
Stay thy Soft Murmuring, *fr.* Canto I. OA
Vegetable Loves, *fr.* Canto I. OBEC; SeCePo
Botany Bay. *Unknown.* PoAu-1; ViBoFo
Both gentlemen, or yoemen bould. A True Tale of Robin Hood. *Unknown.* ESPB
Both Less and More. Richard Watson Dixon. LoBV
Both old and young, I pray lend an ear. The *Nightingale.* *Unknown.* ShS
Both power and being are denied to us. The Life within Our Forms. Jami. OnPM
Both robb'd of air [*or* rob'd of aire], we both lie [*or* lye] in one ground. Hero and Leander. John Donne. MaMe; ReIE
Both roof, and floor, and walls were all of gold. Mammon's House. Spenser. *Fr.* The Faerie Queene, II. MyFE
Both Sides. Mary Abigail Dodge. CIV
Both thou and I alike, my Bacchic urn. On an Urn. Richard Garnett. VA
Both you two have. To the Yew and Cypress to Grace His Funeral. Robert Herrick. QFR
Bothering Me at Last. David Ignatow. WOW
Bothie of Tober-na-Vuolich, The, *sels.* Arthur Hugh Clough.
Bathers. VA
("There is a stream, I name not its name, lest inquisitive tourist.") BoNaP
Engagement, The. NBM
(Autumn in the Highlands.) GTSE

Bothwell, *sel.* Swinburne.
John Knox's Indictment of the Queen. VA
Bothwell Bridge. *Unknown.* BaBo; ESPB
(Battle of Bothwell Bridge, The.) OxBB
Botticellian Trees, The. William Carlos Williams. AmP; AmPP (5th ed.); LiTA; NoP; NP; PoeP
Bottle, The. Walter de la Mare. MoPo; POTE
Bottle O! *with music.* *Unknown.* SoAmSa
Bottle of Chianti, The. Raymond Souster. ELU
Bottle of perfume that Willie sent, The. Limerick. *Unknown.* GoTP; WhC
"Bottle Should Be Plainly Labeled 'Poison'." Sara Henderson Hay. GoYe
Bottled, New York. Helene Johnson. GoSl
(Bottled.) CDC
Bottles are empty, the breakfast was good, The. The Morning After. Heine. ErPo; UnTE
Bottomed by tugging combs of water. The Swan. W. R. Rodgers. NeBP; NMP
Bottom's Song. Shakespeare. *Fr.* A Midsummer Night's Dream, III, 1. CTC
(Ousel Cock, The.) ViBoPo
Bough of the plane tree, where is the clear-beaked bird. Woodcock of the Ivory Beak. Elizabeth Madox Roberts. MAP; MoAmPo
Bough will bend, the leaf will sometime fall, The. Fable. Mary Mills. NePoAm
Boughs do shake and the bells do ring, The. Harvest Song. *Unknown.* BOTP; OxNR
Boughs, the boughs are bare enough, The. Winter the Gulf Stream. Gerard Manley Hopkins. CMoP; ExPo; SyP
Bought. Francis Douglas Davison. NeBP
Bought Embrace, A. G. S. Fraser. WaP
Bought Locks. Martial, *tr. fr. Latin by* Sir John Harington. AWP; JAWP; LiTW; OuHeWo; WBP; WoL
Boule's Hop. *Unknown.* IHA
Boulogne to Amiens and Paris. Dante Gabriel Rossetti. *Fr.* A Trip to Paris and Belgium. PeVV
Bounce ball! Bounce ball! Song for a Ball-Game. Wilfrid Thorley. BoTP
Bounce, buckram, velvet's dear. *Unknown.* OxNR
Bouncing Ball. Sara Ruth Watson. SoPo
Bound Down to Newfoundland, *with music.* *Unknown.* ShS
Bound for holy Palestine. The Crusade. Thomas Warton, The Younger. EiPP
Bound for Sourabaya! Charles Henry Souter. BoAu
Bound lion, almost blind from meeting their gaze and popcorn. Riverdale Lion. John Robert Colombo. PeCV (1967 ed.)
Bound No'th Blues. Langston Hughes. AmNP
Bound to a boy's swift feet, hard blades of steel. River Skater. Winifred Welles. SD
Bound to his torment on the wheel that turns. The Dream. "Michael Field." SyP
Bound to my heart as Ixion to the wheel. Dirge for the New Sunrise. Edith Sitwell. *Fr.* Three Poems of the Atomic Age. ACV; AtBAP; CMoP; EaLo; MoAB; MoBrPo (1950 ed.); MoRP; SeCePo
Bound Together. Ruth Lisa Schechter. WOW
Bound upon the accursed tree. The Crucifixion. Henry Hart Milman. BePJ
Boundaries. Catherine Cate Coblentz. OQP
Boundaries. Jessica Powers. JKCP (1955 ed.)
Boundary Rider, The. Thomas Heney. BoAu
Bounded unbrokenly by summer weather. The Made Lake. Louise Townsend Nicholl. NePoAm-2
Bountiful in charity. Praise of Mary. *Unknown.* ISi
Bounty of Our Age, The. Henry Farley. *See* To See a Quaint Outlandish Fowl.
Bouquet of Belle Scavior. Wallace Stevens. MoAB; MoAmPo
Bouquet of zephyr-flowers hitched to a hitching post in far off Roanoke, A. You at the Pump (History of North and South). Frank O'Hara. ANYP
Bourgeois Poet, The, *sels.* Karl Shapiro.
"As you say (not without sadness), poets don't see, they feel." PP
(As You Say; an Anti-Poem.) CaFP
"Bourgeois poet closes the door of his study and lights his pipe, The." PP
Bourne, The. Christina Rossetti. CBV; ELP; FaBoEn; HBV; LoBV; OBNC
Bourtree, bourtree, crookit rung. The Elder Tree. *Unknown.* ChTr
'Bout th'husband oke, the vine. To Castara, upon an Embrace. William Habington. AnAnS-2
Bout with Burning. Vassar Miller. LiTM (1970 ed.); MoAmPo (1962 ed.); NePoEA; PIA; TDP; ToPo
Bow all desires—even unknown ones—I had. After Reading a Book on Abnormal Psychology. Ernest G. Moll. ELU
Bow Down, Dear Land. James Russell Lowell. Ode Recited at the Harvard Commemoration, July 21, 1865, XI, *abr. and* XII. DD
Bow down, my song, before her presence high. Morton Luce. *Fr.* Thysia. HBV
Bow down my soul in worship very low. Russian Cathedral [*or* St. Isaac's Church, Petrograd]. Claude McKay AmNP; CDC; Kal; PoNe
Bow Down Your Head and Cry. *Unknown.* CoSo
Bow Lamkin, *with music.* *Unknown.* BFSS
Bow-wow, says the dog. *Unknown.* OxNR
Bow, wow, wow,/ Whose dog art thou? Greeting. Mother Goose. OxNR; PCH; PPL; RIS; SAS; StVeCh; TiPo
Bowed by the weight of centuries he leans. The Man With the Hoe. Edwin Markham. AA; AmePo; AmLP; AnAmPo; AnFE; APA; BLPA; CoAnAm; DD; EaLo; FaFP; FaPL; GTBS-W; HBV; LiTA; LiTM; MAP; MaRV; MCCG; MoAmPo; NAMP; NeHB; NeMA; OHFP; OQP; OTD; PEDC; PFY; PoFr; PoMa; PoPo; PPON; SoP; TreF; TrGrPo; TRV; WBLP; WGRP; WoL; WOW
Bowed negress, who aghast but the light. Gil Orlovitz. *Fr.* Art of the Sonnet. ToPo
Bower of Bliss, The. Spenser. *Fr.* The Faerie Queene, II, 12. CH; FaBoEn; FiP; LoBV; OBSC; PoEL-1
("Eftsoons they heard a most melodious sound.") UnS, 2 *sts.*; ViBoPo
(Gather the Rose.) ElL; WHA
("Thence passing forth, they shortly doe arrive." ATP
Bower of Peace, The. Robert Southey. *Fr.* Ode Written during the War with America, 1814. MC; PAH
Bowery, The. Charles Hale Hoyt. TreF; YaD
Bowery bum, The. Empire City. Dan Georgakas. ThO
Bowge of Court, The. John Skelton. ReIE
Bowl. Wallace Stevens. NP
Bowl full of ambrosia, A. To the Bridegroom. Sappho. HW
Bowl of Goldfish, The; a Fable. James Kirkup. POTi
Bowl of October, A. Helen Bevington. RePo
Bowl of Roses, A. W. E. Henley. EnLi-2; MeWo; MoBrPo; OuHeWo
Bowline, The. A. P. Herbert. WhC
Bows glided down, and the coast, The. Ballad of the Long-legged Bait. Dylan Thomas. CoBMV; SeCeV
Box-Car Letters. Karle Wilson Baker. InP
Box cars run by a mile long. Work Gangs. Carl Sandburg. CoBA
Boxer. Joseph P. Clancy. SD
Boxer's Face, The. Lucilius, *tr. fr. Latin by* Humbert Wolfe. SD
Boxes and Bags. Carl Sandburg. RePo
Boxing. Kipling. *Fr.* Verses on Games. OtMeF
Boxing Match, The. Vergil, *tr. fr. Latin by* Rolfe Humphries. *Fr.* The Aeneid. SD
Boy. William Allingham. PRWS
Boy, A. John Ashbery. NeAP
Boy, The. Eugene Field. NA
Boy. Winifred Welles. NP
Boy, A/ Blew west. In Praise of Johnny Appleseed. Vachel Lindsay. StVeCh
Boy among the reeds on Severn shore, A. Edward Elgar. C. Day Lewis. MuSP
Boy and a Pup, A. Arthur Guiterman. MPB; UTS
Boy and His Top, The. John Hookham Frere. OTPC (1923 ed.)
Boy and Tadpoles. Louis Untermeyer. YT
Boy and the Angel, The. Robert Browning. OTPC; PoVP
Boy and the Flute, The. Björnstjerne Björnson, *tr. fr. Norwegian by* Sir Edmund Gosse. AWP; JAWP; PoPl; WBP
Boy and the Geese, The. Padraic Fiacc. NeIP
Boy and the Mantle, The. *Unknown.* BaBo; ESPB; OBB; OxBB; UnTE
Boy and the Parrot, The. John Hookham Frere. OTPC (1923 ed.)

Boy and the Schoolmaster, The. La Fontaine, *tr. fr. French by* Elizur Wright. WoL
Boy and the Sheep, The. Ann Taylor. *See* Sheep, The.
Boy and the Squirrel, The. F. Hey. SAS
Boy and the Wolf, The. Aesop, *ad. fr. Greek by* Louis Untermeyer. MaC; OTD
Boy and the Wolf, The. John Hookham Frere. HBV; HBVY; OTPC (1923 ed.)
Boy at the Door. Louis J. Sanker. JKCP (1955 ed.)
Boy at Target Practice; a Contemplation. W. R. Moses. NYBP
Boy, Bare Your Head. Nancy Byrd Turner. PCD; PCH
Boy! bring an ounce of Freeman's best. Isaac Hawkins Brown. *Fr.* A Pipe of Tobacco. Par
Boy, bristle thy courage up; for Falstaff he is dead. Shakespeare. King Henry V, *fr.* II, iii. LO
Boy Brittan. Forceythe Willson. MC; PAH
Boy called to his team, The. Late Autumn. Andrew Young. HaMV; MoVE
Boy Christ, The. Helene Mullins. StJW
Boy Columbus, The. *Unknown.* HH; PEDC (1923 ed.)
Boy drove into the city, his wagon loaded down, A. The Little Black-eyed Rebel. Will Carleton. FaPON; GoTP; PAH; PAP
Boy employed to guard the sheep, A. The Boy and the Wolf. Aesop, *ad. fr. Greek by* Louis Untermeyer. MaC; OTD
Boy Fishing, The. E. J. Scovell. HaMV; ThWaDe
Boy from his bedroom window, The. The Boy. William Allingham. PRWS
Boy from Rome, Da. T. A. Daly. FaPON; MPB
Boy He Had an Auger, A, *with music.* *Unknown.* AS
Boy, I detest these modern innovations. Persicos Odi. Charles Edmund Merrill, Jr. AA
Boy, I hate their empty shows. Persian Fopperies [*or* Persian Pomp]. Horace, *tr. by* William Cowper. *Fr.* Odes. AWP; EnLi-1; JAWP; OnPM; WBP; WoL
Boy, I hate this Persian frippery. Frippery. Horace, *tr. by* L. R. Lind. *Fr.* Odes. LiTW
Boy in a Pond. James Whaler. *Fr.* Runaway. OA
Boy in Ice. Laurie Lee. NYBP
Boy in the Lamont Poetry Room, Harvard. D. G. Jones. PeCV (1967 ed.)
Boy in the Wilderness. Samuel Taylor Coleridge. *See* Fruit Plucker, The.
Boy in the Wind. George Dillon. MAP; MoAmPo (1942 ed.)
Boy Is a Boy, A. Phyllis C. Michael. SoP
Boy Jesus, The. John Banister Tabb. StJW
Boy looked out of eyes like Euclid's eyes, The. Form Was the World. Maurice English. NYBP
Boy-Man. Karl Shapiro. NYBP
Boy named Simon sojourned in a dale, A. Simple Simon. Harriet S. Morgridge. *Fr.* Mother Goose Sonnets. AA
Boy of eighteen years 'mid myrtle-boughs, A. Le Jeune Homme Caressant Sa Chimère. John Addington Symonds. OBVV; PoVP
Boy of five years old, serene and gay, A. Dead Child. Lucian. OnPM
Boy of Old Manhattan, A. Morris Abel Beer. HH
Boy of Winander, The. Wordsworth. *See* There Was a Boy.
Boy Playing an Organ. Francis Sweeney. GoBC
Boy, presuming on his intellect, A. At Woodward's Gardens. Robert Frost. ImOP
Boy Reciter, The. David Everett. *See* Tall Oaks from Little Acorns Grow.
Boy Remembers in the Field. Raymond Knister. CaP
Boy Riding Forward Backward. Robert Francis. NePoAm-2
Boy should have an open fireplace, A. A Boy's Need. Herbert Clark Johnson. PoNe
Boy stood in the supper-room, The. *Unknown.* CenHV
Boy stood on the burning deck, The/ Whence all but him [*or* he] had fled. Casabianca. Felicia Dorothea Hemans. BeLS; BLPA; EtS; FaBoBe; FaFP; FaPON; FOL; GoTP; HBV; HBVY; NeHB; OnSP; PaPo; OTPC; TreF; WBLP
Boy stood on the burning deck, The/ Eating peanuts by the peck. Peanuts. *Unknown.* FaFP; GoTP; SiTL
Boy stood on the burning deck, The,/ His fleece was white as snow. Familiar Lines. *Unknown.* FiBHP
Boy that is good, A. *Unknown.* OxNR
Boy that is truthful and honest, A. The Boy We Want. *Unknown.* WBLP
Boy, the giant beauty. Instruction in the Art. Philip Booth. SD
Boy Was Born at Bethlehem, A. Edward Hilton Young. *See* Christmas.
Boy was born 'mid little things, A. Two Gods. Sam Walter Foss. MaRV
Boy Washington, The. Dorothy Brown Thompson. SiSoSe
Boy We Want, The. *Unknown.* WBLP
Boy wears a grin, The. A Boy and a Pup. Arthur Guiterman. MPB; UTS
Boy, who in my festive home. To His Cup Bearer. Catullus. OnPM
Boy Who Laughed at Santa Claus, The. Ogden Nash. BBGG; CenHV; MaC; StPo
Boy, whose little, confiding hand. Locomotive to the Little Boy. Benjamin R. C. Low. HBMV
Boy with a Cart, The, *sel.* Christopher Fry.
"In our fields, fallow and burdened, in grass and furrow." LiTB
Rain. BoC
Boy with a Mouth Organ. James Kirkup. MuSP
Boy with His Hair Cut Short. Muriel Rukeyser. ExPo; FiMAP; LiTM (1970 ed.); MoAB; NAMP; PoPl; RoGo; TwAmPo; TwCP
Boyhood. Wordsworth. *See* Influence of Natural Objects.
Boyhood Etchings. Walter Adolphe Roberts. PoNe
Boyne Walk, The. F. R. Higgins. OxBI
Boyne Water, The. *Unknown.* AnIV; OnYI
Boys, The. Oliver Wendell Holmes. CoBA HBV; WBLP
Boys. Winifred M. Letts. HBMV
Boys and girls come out to play. *Unknown.* OxNR; RIS
Boys and girls who live in books, The. Adventures. Arthur Kramer. BiCB
Boys, by Girls Held in Their Thighs. John Peale Bishop. ErPo
Boy's Day. Ruth Evelyn Henderson. BiCB
Boys flying kites haul in their white-winged birds. Words. *Unknown.* OQP; PoLF
Boy's Head, A. Miroslav Holub, *tr. fr. Czech by* Ian Milner. FIW
Boys in October. Irving Layton. OBCV
Boys in sporadic but tenacious droves. The Horse Chestnut Tree. Richard Eberhart. AtBAP; CaFP; CMoP; CrMA; FiMAP; LiTM (1970 ed.); MoAB; MoAmPo (1962 ed.); NePA; NePoAm; Po; PoDB; PoPl; PoPo; ToPo
Boys like puppets dangling. Spring Is a Looping-free Time. Martin Robbins. SD
Boy's Mother, A. James Whitcomb Riley. DD; HBVY; HH; OHIP; OTPC; PoRL; PPL
Boys' Names. Eleanor Farjeon. BiCB; SUS; TiPo
Boy's Need, A. Herbert Clark Johnson. PoNe
Boys of the Island, The, *with music.* "Larry Gorman." ShS
Boys of the Island, The. *Unknown.* IHA
Boys of Wexford, The. *Unknown.* ELP
Boys out in the trenches, The. Destroyer Life. *Unknown.* ABF
Boys's Place, A. Rose Burgunder. PDV
Boy's Playthings. Leonidas, *tr. fr. Greek by* Lord Neaves. OnPM
Boy's Poem, A., *sel.* Alexander Smith.
"Steamer left the black and oozy wharves, The." PeVV
Boy's Prayer, A. Henry Charles Beeching. *See* Prayers.
Boy's Prayer. A. B. Ponsonby. MaRV
Boy's Song, A. James Hogg. BoChLi; BoTP; CH; FaPON; GaP; HBV; HBVY; LiTG; MoShBr; OBEV; OTPC (1946 ed.); PCH; PoRh; PRWS; RIS; StVeCh (1940 ed.); TVC; WaKn; WiR
Boy's Song to Mariana. Shakespeare. *See* Take, O Take Those Lips Away.
Boy's Summer Song, A. Paul Laurence Dunbar. OTD; RePo; SiSoSe
Boys Will Be Princes. William Heyen. NYTB
Bozzy and Piozzi, *sel.* "Peter Pindar."
Introduction and Anecdotes. PoEL-3
Brace of sinners, for no good, A. The Pilgrims and the Peas. "Peter Pindar." BOHV
Braced against the rise and fall of ocean. Korea Bound, 1952. William Childress. AmFN
Bracelet, The. John Donne. Elegies, XI. MaMe
Bracelet, The. Thomas Stanley. AnAnS-2
Bracelet of Grass, The. William Vaughn Moody. AP
Bracelet, The: To Julia. Robert Herrick. HBV; MeWo; OBEV; TrGrPo

("Why I tie about thy wrist.") EG
Bracken on the hillside. November. Aileen Fisher. SiSoSe; TiPo (1959 ed.)
Brackish reach of shoal off Madaket, A. The Quaker Graveyard in Nantucket. Robert Lowell. AmLP; AP; CABL; CMoP; CoBMV; FiMAP; HT; LiTM (1970 ed.); MiAP; MoAB; MoPo; MoVE; NePA; NMP; NoP; OxBA; PoeP; PoIE; ReMP; SeCeV (1967 ed.); ToPo; TwAmPo; UnPo (3d ed.); ViBoPo (1958 ed.)
Braddock's Defeat. *Unknown.* ABF
Braddock's Fate, with an Incitement to Revenge. Stephen Tilden. PAH; ThLM
Brady (A *and* B *vers.*), *with music. Unknown.* AS
(Duncan and Brady, *sl. diff., with music.*) OuSiCo
Brady's Bend. Martha Keller. StPo
Braes o' Gleniffer, The. Robert Tannahill. OBRV
Braes o' Yarrow, The. *Unknown. See* Dowie Houms o' Yarrow, The.
Braes of Yarrow, The. William Hamilton. CEP; EiCL; EiPP; OBEC
Braes of Yarrow, The. John Logan. GTBS; GTBS-D; GTBS-P; GTBS-W; GTSE; GTSL; HBV; OBEC
Braggart! Denis Wrafter. OnYI
Braggart March stood in the season's door, The. The Passing of March. Robert Burns Wilson. HBV
Bragging Song. *Unknown, tr. fr. Arabic by* Sir Charles Lyall. LiTW
Brahma. Emerson. AA; AmePo; AmLP; AmP; AmPP; AnAmPo; AnFE; AnNE; AP; APA; AWP; BoLiVe; BWP; CBEP; CBV; CoAnAm; CoBA; DiPo; EaLo; GTBS; GTBS-D; GTBS-W; HBV; InPo; JAWP; LiTA; LiTG; MAmP; MemP; MWA-1; NePA; NoP; OBEV; OBVV; OxBA; PFY; Po; PoAn; PoIE; PoPo; PoRA; SeCeV; ShBV-4; TreF; TrGrPo; UnPo; ViBoPo; WBP; WGRP; WHA; WoL
Brahma. Andrew Lang. CenHV
Brahma, the World Idea. *Unknown. Fr.* Rigveda. WGRP
Brahmin, fat and debonair, A. The Irreverent Brahmin. Arthur Guiterman. LHV
Brahms, The. Herbert Morris. NePoAm-2
Brahms Peruses the Score of "Siegfried." Roy Fuller. MuSP
Braid Claith. Robert Fergusson. CEP; GoTS; OBEC; OxBS
Braille. *Unknown.* OTD
Brain. Coleman Barks. *Fr.* Body Poems. QAH
Brain, The. Emily Dickinson. *See* Brain within its groove, The, *and* Brain is wider than the sky, The.
Brain, be ice. Mens Creatrix. Stanley J. Kunitz. NP
Brain forgets but the blood will remember, The. The Dark Chamber. Louis Untermeyer. MAP; MeWo; MoAmPo; MoLP; TOP; WHA
Brain is wider than the sky, The. Emily Dickinson. AmP; AmPP (4th ed.); AnNE; CaFP; MAmP; MAP; MoAB; MoAmPo; NoP; OxBA; PoFS
Brain, the blood, the busy thews, The. Life's Testament, II. William Baylebridge. BoAV; PoAu-1
Brain within it's groove, The. Emily Dickinson. AP; CoBA; DiPo; OnPM
Brainstorm. Howard Nemerov. NoP; ToPo
Brainwashing Dramatized. Don Johnson. PoNe (1970 ed.)
Bramble Briar, The, *with music. Unknown.* BFSS
Bramble Jam. Irene F. Pawsey. BoTP
Bran. George H. Moorse. NYTB
Branch of the apple-tree from Emain, The. *Unknown. Fr.* The Voyage of Bran. AnIL
Branch of the Sweet and Early Rose. William Drennan. IrPN
Branching head of, The. The Lily. William Carlos Williams. TDP
Brand, *sel.* Ibsen, *tr. fr. Norwegian by* C. H. Herford.
Brand Speaks, *br. sel.* WGRP
Brand Fire New Whaling Song Right from the Pacific Ocean. *Unknown.* EtS
Brand Speaks. Ibsen. *Fr.* Brand. WGRP
Branding Iron Herd, The. Ralph Rigby. PoOW
Brandish't sword of God before them blaz'd, The. Expulsion from Paradise. Milton. *Fr.* Paradise Lost, XII. ChTr
Brandy Hill. *Unknown.* CBEP
Branwell's Sestina. James Reaney. *Fr.* A Suit of Nettles. MoCV
Braque. M. K. Joseph. AnNZ
Brash and bare and whistling cold. Song of January. Gerta Kennedy. PoPl
Brass band blares, The. Circus. Eleanor Farjeon. BoChLi; MPB; SUS; UTS
Brass Horse, The. Drummond Allison. FaBoTw
Brass Spittoons. Langston Hughes. BANP; MAP; MoAmPo; NeMA
Bratzlav Rabbi to His Scribe, The. Jacob Glatstein, *tr. fr. Yiddish by* Jacob Sloan. TrJP
Being, *sel.* LiTW
Brave and high-souled Pilgrims, you who knew no fears. Thanksgiving Day. Annette Wynne. OHIP
Brave as a falcon and as merciless. To Manon, Comparing Her to a Falcon [*or* The Falcon]. Wilfrid Scawen Blunt. The Love Sonnets of Proteus, II. ACP; OBVV; VA
Brave as the firstborn flame upsprings the statue. At the Salon. Florence Wilkinson Evans. HBV
Brave at Home, The. Thomas Buchanan Read. *Fr.* The Waggoner of the Alleghanies. HBV; PAP
Brave Donahue. *At. to* Jack Donahue. PoAu-1
Brave English language, you are strong as trees. Rhyme for a Phonetician. Frances Cornford. YT
Brave flowers, that I could gallant it like you. A Contemplation upon Flowers. Henry King. ATP (1935 ed.); BoNaP; BWP; CBEP; EG; ELP; HBV; LoBV; MeLP; MePo; NoP; OBEV; OBS; PG; SeCL; SeCP; SeEP; StP; TrGrPo
Brave infant of Saguntum, clear[e]. To the Immortal Memory and Friendship of That Noble Pair, Sir Lucius Cary, and Sir Henry Morison [*or* Pindaric Ode]. Ben Jonson. AnAnS-2; MaPo (1969 ed.); NoP; OBS; PoEL-2; PoFS; SCEP-2; SeCP; SeCV-1; SeEP; StP; TuPP
Brave iron, brave hammer, from your sound. The Song of the Cyclops. Thomas Dekker. *Fr.* London's Tempe. ShBV-1; TuPP
Brave lads in olden musical centuries. Alcaics; to H. F. B. Robert Louis Stevenson. EG; NBM; OBEV (new ed.); OBVV; ShBV-3
Brave little bird that fears not God, A. The Meadow Lark. Hamlin Garland. AA
Brave men have followed. The Flag Speaks. Emily Greene Balch. PGD
Brave New World. Archibald MacLeish. AmP; OxBA
Brave New World. Shakespeare. *Fr.* The Tempest, V, i. TrGrPo
Brave News Is Come. *Unknown.* OTPC (1923 ed.)
("Brave news is come to town.") OxNR; PPL
Brave Old Oak, The. Henry Fothergill Chorley. FaBoBe; HBV
Brave Old Ship, the *Orient*, The. Robert Traill Spence Lowell. AA; FaBoBe
Brave Old World. Elisabeth Lambert. FaFP; SiTL
Brave Paulding and the Spy. *Unknown.* MC; PAH
(Major André, *with music.*) BFSS
Brave rose, (alas!) where art thou? Church-Rents and Schismes. George Herbert. MaMe
Brave Rover. Max Beerbohm. OA
Brave Wolfe. *Unknown.* BaBo (A *and* B *vers.*); PAH; ThLM; TrAS, *with music, sl. diff.*; ViBoFo
(Quebec, *sl. diff.*) BSNS
Brave young city by the Balboa seas, The. Twilight at the Heights. Joaquin Miller. AA
Brave young Prince a young Princess adores, A. The Essence of Opera. *Unknown.* OnPM
Brave-Hearted Maid, A. *Unknown, tr. fr. Anglo-Saxon by* Mother Margaret Williams. ISi; PoLi
Braver than sea-going ships with the dawn in their sails. To My Wife. William Rose Benét. PoMa
Bravest Battle, The. Joaquin Miller. *See* Mothers of Men, The.
Bravest names for fire and flames, The. General John. W. S. Gilbert. GoTP; NA
Brawling of a sparrow in the eaves, The. The Sorrow of Love. W. B. Yeats. PeVV; PoeP
Brawn of England's Lay. John Hunter-Duvar. VA
Brazen Tongue. William Rose Benét. MAP; MoAmPo
Brazier Coals, The. Miguel de Unamuno, *tr. fr. Spanish by* Thomas Walsh. OnPM
(Domestic Scenes.) LiTW; WoL
Brazil. Ronald de Carvalho, *tr. fr. Portuguese by* Dudley Poore. WoL
Bread. Stanley Burnshaw. TrJP
Bread. Leslie Savage Clark. ChIP
Bread. James Dickey. NoP

Bread. Nancy Keesing. PoAu-2
Bread. A. M. Klein. PeCV
Bread. R. S. Thomas. BoC
Bread. *Unknown.* MaRV
Bread. H. E. Wilkinson. BoTP
Bread and Milk. Christina Rossetti. *Fr.* Sing-Song. CBEP
("Bread and milk for breakfast.") SAS
(Winter.) PCH
Bread and Music. Conrad Aiken. *See* Music I Heard.
Bread and Roses. James Oppenheim. OQP
Bread is a lovely thing to eat. Lovely Things. H. M. Sarson. BoTP
Bread of Brotherhood. Lucia Trent. PGD
Bread of Life, The. Mary A. Lathbury. *See* Break Thou the Bread of Life.
Bread of the Sacrament, The. *Unknown.* SoP
Bread of the World. Reginald Heber. MaRV; SoP
Bread that bringeth [*or* giveth] strength I want to give, The. I Shall Not Pass Again This Way. Ellen H. Underwood. BLRP; FaChP; MaRV; OQP; SoP; TreF; WBLP
Bread the Holy. Elizabeth J. Coatsworth. MoRP
Break, The. E. N. Sargent. NYBP
Break, Break, Break. Tennyson. ATP; AWP; BEL; BoLiVe; CABA; CBV; DiPo; EnL; EnLi-2; EnLit; EPN; EtS; FaBoBe; FaBoEn; FaBV; FiP; GoJo; GTBS; GTBS-P; GTBS-W; GTSE; GTSL; HBV; ILP; InP; InPo; JAWP; LiTB; LiTG; MaPo (1969 ed.); MaRV; MaVP; MBW-2; MCCG; NeHB; NoP; OAEP; OBNC; OTPC; OuHeWo; PAn; PG (1945 ed.); Po; PoAn; PoE; PoEL-5; PoFS; PoG; PoPl; PoRA; PoSa; PoVP; PTK; ShBV-2; TOP; TreF; TrGrPo; ViPo; ViPP; WBP; WHA; YAT; YT
Break—break it open; let the knocker rust. Dedication to the Generation Knocking at the Door. John Davidson. BrPo
Break Down the Walls. John Oxenham. OQP
Break forth, break forth, O Sudbury town. Lydia. Lizette Woodworth Reese. AA
Break forth in song, ye trees. Centennial Hymn. John Pierpont. AnNE; PAL
Break My Heart of Stone. Charles Wesley. BePJ
(Prayer for Forgiveness, A.) SoP
Break not his sweet repose. A Soldier's Grave. John Albee. AA
Break not my loneliness, O Wanderer! The Dove's Loneliness. George Darley. OBNC
Break of Day. John Clare. CBEP
Break [*or* Breake] of Day. John Donne. CABA; ElL; EnRePo; ErPo; LiTB; LiTG; LiTL; MaMe; MeWo; PoeP; TrGrPo; TuPP
(Daybreak.) OBEV; TOP
("Stay, O sweet, and do not rise!") EG
Break of Day, The. John Shaw Neilson. BoAU; BoAV; PoAu-1
Break of Day in the Trenches. Isaac Rosenberg. BrPo; FaBoMo; FOL; GTBS-P; MMA; MoBrPo; SeCePo; ViBoPo; WaaP; WaP
"Break off your argument." The Shape of a Bird. Laurence Whistler. MoVE
Break the Heart's Anger, *sel.* Paul Engle.
"I will make a new song of the word," *abr., fr.* Prologue. PoFr
Break the News to Mother. Charles Kassell Harris. TreFS
Break the patterns! Shatter the images! Down icons! Would You Believe? Tuli Kupferberg. WOW
Break thou my heart, ah, break it. Arab Song. Richard Henry Stoddard. AA
Break Thou the Bread of Life. Mary A. Lathbury. MaRV; TRV
(Bread of Life, The.) STF OQP
Breake hart in twayne, fayre Ronile may se. *Unknown.* SeCSL
Breakfast. W. W. Gibson. OBMV
Breakfast. Mary Lamb. OTPC (1923 ed.)
Breakfast in a Bowling Alley in Utica, New York. Adrienne Rich. CoPo
Breakfast Song, The. Emilie Poulsson. HBVY
Breakfast Time. James Stephens. SUS
Breakfast with Gerard Manley Hopkins. Anthony Brode. FiBHP; Par
Breaking. J. Alexander Allan. PoAu-2
Breaking, The. Margaret Steele Anderson. HBV
Breaking a line of pines, a wide white gate. Alan Mulgan. *Fr.* Golden Wedding. ACV
Breaking from under that thy cloudy Veil [*or* Vail]. Upon Combing Her Hair. Lord Herbert of Cherbury. SeEP; StP
Breaking In a Tenderfoot. *Unknown.* IHA
Breaking of the Day, The. Peter Davison. CoPo
Breaking out, trying to find. Out. Howard McCord. YAP
Breaking Point. Sylvia Auxier. GoYe
Breaking through the sandy soil. Personal Letter to the Ephesians. Carl Bode. ToPo
Breaking waves dashed high, The. The Landing of the Pilgrim Fathers in New England [*or* Pilgrim Fathers]. Felicia Dorothea Hemans. BeLS; BLPA; BoTP; DD; FaBoBe; FaBV; FaFP; FaPL; FaPON; GN; GoTP; HBV; HBVY; HH; MaRV; MC; NeHB; OHIP; OnSP; OTPC; PaA; PAH; PAL; PaPo; PCH; PGD; PoFr; PoRL; PTK; SoP; ThLM; TreF; WBLP
Breakthrough. John Sinclair. NBP
Breakwaters. Ted Walker. NYBP
Breast to breast in the whirling. Boolee, the Bringer of Life. Mary Gilmore. BoAV
Breastplate of Saint Patrick, The. *At. to* St. Patrick. *See* Deer's Cry, The.
Breath, A ("A breath can fan love's flame to burning"). "Madeline Bridges." AA
Breath o' the grass. Susurro. "Fiona Macleod." *Fr.* Sospiri di Roma. VA
Breath of Air, A. James Wright. PoPl
Breath of Avon, The. Theodore Watts-Dunton. VA
Breath of dew, and twilight's grace, The. A Friend's Song for Simoisius. Louise Imogen Guiney. PFY
Breath of Hampstead Heath. Edith M. Thomas AA
Breath of life imbued those few dim days, The. Fragment. Jessie Redmond Fauset. CDC
Breath of Night, The. Randall Jarrell. CrMA
Breath of Prayer, A. Frances McKinnon Morton. SoP
(The Meaning of Prayer.) FaChP
Breath on the Oat. Joseph Russell Taylor. HBV; PAH
Breathe balmy airs, ye fragrant flowers. Flower-strewn Graves. Samuel Francis Smith. MaRV
Breathe Julia, breathe and I'll protest. Of Her Breath. Robert Herrick. EG
Breathe not, hid Heart: cease silently. To an Unborn Pauper Child. Thomas Hardy. CoBMV; GTBS-P; LiTB; MaPo (1969 ed.); ReMP; ViBoPo
Breathe on Me, Breath of God. Edwin Hatch. MaRV; SoP
Breathe, trumpets, breathe. Requiem. George Lunt. AA; PaA
Breathes there a bard who isn't moved? On Being Chosen Poet of Vermont. Robert Frost. ML
Breathes There a Man. Samuel Hoffenstein. PoPl; WhC
("Breathes there a man with hide so tough.") FiBHP
Breathes there a man who claimeth not. Gethsemane. Edmund Leamy. JKCP; OQP
Breathes there a man with hide so tough. Breathes There a Man. Samuel Hoffenstein. FiBHP; PoPl; WhC
Breathes There the [*or* a] Man [with Soul So Dead]. Sir Walter Scott. *Fr.* The Lay of The Last Minstrel, VI. BBV; BLPA; EnRP; FaFP; InP; MaRV; NeHB; OAEP; OBRV; OxBS; PGD; TreF
(Innominatus.) OBEV; PAL; TOP
(Love of Country.) OHFP; OQP; OTD; PaPo; WBLP
(My Native Land.) GN; MPB (1956 ed.); OTPC (1923 ed.); PTK; StaSt
(My Own, My Native Land.) StVeCh (1940 ed.)
(Native Land.) TrGrPo
(Patriot, The.) OBNC
(Patriotism.) PCD; PG (1945 ed.); SoP; TRV
Breathing, The. Denise Levertov. NaP; WIRo
Breathing do I draw that air to me. Song of Breath. Peire Vidal. AWP; JAWP; WBP
Breathing something German at the end. The Gift to Be Simple. Howard Moss. ImOP; MoRP; TwCP
Breathless Awe. Edwin Markham. *See* Third Wonder, The.
Breathless, we flung us on the windy hill. The Hill. Rupert Brooke. BoLP; EnLit; GTSL; HBV; LiTL; MeWo; MoBrPo; MoLP; OTD; POTE; Sonn; ViBoPo; WePo
Breaths. Birago Diop, *tr. fr. French by* Anne Atik. TTY
Breaths of kissing night and day, The. Dream-Tryst. Francis Thompson. AnFE; EnLit; VA
Brébeuf and His Brethren, *sels.* E. J. Pratt.
"Fury of taunt was followed by fury of blow, The." *fr.* XII. PeCV; TwCaPo
Invisible Trumpets Blowing, *shorter sel.* CaP

Martydom of Brébeuf and Lalemant, 16 March 1649, The. OBCV
"Three miles from town to town over the snow." ACV
Brechva's Harp Song. Ernest Rhys. VA
Bred in a low place, lord of little deeds. A Man of Men. Leonard Charles Van Noppen. PGD
Bred in distant woods, the clown. The Country Clown. John Trumbull. AnAmPo
Bredon Hill. A. E. Housman. A Shropshire Lad, XXI. BEL; BrPo; CLwM; EnLi-2; FosPo; LiTL; MeWo; MoAB; MoBrPo; NeMA; PAn; PoVP; TreF; ViPo; VP; WHA
(Summer Time on Bredon.) GBV (1952 ed.)
Breech, The. Michael McClure. NeAP
Breed of Athletes, The. Euripides, *tr. fr. Greek by* Moses Hadas. SD
Breeze, The. *Unknown. See* Summer Breeze.
Breeze and Billow. Albert Durrant Watson. CaP
Breeze blows o'er the lake, A. Herons. *Unknown.* SUS
Breeze has swelled the whitening sale, The. Song of the Pilgrims. Thomas Cogswell Upham. MC; PAH
Breeze is on the bluebells, The. Bluebells. Juliana Horatia Ewing. BoTP
Breeze is sharp, the sky is hard and blue, The. Frederick Goddard Tuckerman. *Fr.* Sonnets. AP
Breeze was crisp and the sea lay blue, The. The Pirates' Fight. Joseph Schull. *Fr.* The Legend of Ghost Lagoon. CaP
Breezes went steadily through the tall pines, The. Nathan Hale. *Unknown.* PAH
Breeze wipes creases off my forehead, A. Poem in June. Milton Acorn. WHW
Breezeways in the tropics winnow the air. A Letter from the Caribbean. Barbara Howes. CoAP
Brendan, holy Brendan of the blessed beard. Saint Brendan's Prophecy. *Unknown.* OnYI
Brennan on the Moor. *Unknown.* BaBo; OnYI; OuSiCo, *with music*; ViBoFo, *with music*
Brennbaum. Ezra Pound. Hugh Selwyn Mauberley. MoAmPo (1962 ed.).
Brer Tarrypin tired er prom'nadin' roun'. How Brer Tarrypin Learned to Fly. Joel Chandler Harris. TSW
Brererton Omen, The, *sel.* Felicia Dorothea Hemans.
"Yes! I have seen the ancient oak." CTC
Brest Left Behind. John Chipman Farrar. PAH
Bretagne had not her peer. In the province far or near. Lady of Castlenoire. Thomas Bailey Aldrich. BeLS; LoEn
Breton Afternoon. Ernest Dowson. OBNC
Breughel's Winter. Walter de la Mare. SeCePo
Breviary on the Subway. Leonard McCarthy. JKCP (1955 Ed.)
Brevities. Siegfried Sassoon. PoLF
Brew your potion, mix your spell. Comrade in Arms. T. Inglis Moore. PoAu-2
Brewer, A. *Unknown.* WhC
Brewer's Coachman, The. William Taylor. WaPE
Brewer's Man, The. L. A. G. Strong. DTC; ELU; FiBHP; WhC
Brewing of Soma, The. Whittier. AmePo; PoEL-4
Dear Lord and Father of Mankind, *sel.* MaRV; SoP; TrPWD; TRV
(Prayer: "Dear Lord and Father of mankind.") TreFT
Brian O'Linn. *Unknown.* OnYI
Briar, a blunder, a/ bungalow. Index. Bernadette Mayer. ANYP
Briar-Rose. *Unknown, tr. fr. German by* Louis Untermeyer. RIS
Brick, The. Paul Roche. NYBP
Brick distinguishes this country. Amsterdam Letter. Jean Garrigue. NYBP
Bricklayer Love. Carl Sandburg. AmP
Bricklayer tells the busdriver, The. The Continuity. Paul Blackburn. CAD; NeAP
Bricklayer's Lunch Hour, The. Allen Ginsberg. CBV
Bridal Birth. Dante Gabriel Rossetti. The House of Life, II. MaVP; OAEP; PoVP; Sonn; ViPo; VP
Bridal deer stand amid the myrtles, The. Amid the Myrtles. Judah Halevi. HW
Bridal Hymn. Catullus, *tr. fr. Latin by* W. H. Mallock. WoL
Bridal Morning. *Unknown. See* Maidens Came, The.
Bridal Pair, The. William Young. *Fr.* Wishmakers' Town. AA
Bridal Song ("Cynthia, to thy power"). Beaumont *and* Fletcher. *Fr.* The Maid's Tragedy, I, ii. OBEV; TuPP
Bridal Song ("Hold back thy hours"). Beaumont *and* Fletcher. *Fr.* The Maid's Tragedy, I, ii. ElL; ErPo; TrGrPo
("Hold back thy hours, dark Night, till we have done.") EG; ILP; UnTE; ViBoPo
Bridal Song. Clemens Brentano, *tr. fr. German by* Christa Wolf *and* Virginia Tufte. HW
Bridal Song ("Now, sleep, bind fast the flood of air"). George Chapman. *See* Now, Sleep, Bind Fast. *Fr.* The Masque of the Middle Temple and Lincoln's Inn.
Bridal Song ("O come, soft rest of cares! come, Night!"). George Chapman. *Fr.* Hero and Leander, Fifth Sestiad. OBEV
(Come, Night.) OnPM
("O come, soft rest of cares! come, Night!") EG
(Song.) ViBoPo
Bridal Song. Thomas Dekker, *and others. Fr.* The Pleasant Comedy of Patient Grissell, V, ii. OBSC; TrGrPo
(Beauty, Arise!). ElL; TuPP
Bridal Song. Fletcher *and* Shakespeare. *Fr.* The Two Noble Kinsmen I, i. CBEP; ElL; OBEV; OBSC
("Roses, their sharp spines being gone."). EG; HW; MyFE; NoP; SiCE; ViBoPo
Bridal Song, A. Hugh McCrae. BoAu
Bridal Song, A. Shelley. HW; OBRV
Bridal Song to Amala. Thomas Lovell Beddoes. *Fr.* Death's Jest Book, IV, iii.
(Epithalamia.) PoEL-4
(Song: "We have bathed, where none have seen us.") ChER; FaBoEn; OBNC
(Song[s] at Amala's Wedding.) LoBV; PoE
Briddes that han left their song, The. Guillaume de Lorris. *Fr.* The Romaunt of the Rose. EG
Bride, The. Henry Alford. OBEV (1st ed.)
(Master's Call, The.) SoP
Bride, The. Ambrose Bierce. AA
Bride, The. Ralph Hodgson. HBMV; InP
Bride, The. "Laurence Hope." HBV
Bride, The. D. H. Lawrence. BoPe
Bride, A. Meleager, *tr. fr. Greek by* H. C. Beeching. WoL
Bride, The. Ruth Comfort Mitchell. HBMV
Bride, The. L. A. G. Strong. POTE
Bride, The. Sir John Suckling. *Fr.* A Ballad upon a Wedding. MeWo; TrGrPo
Bride, The/ Sips about a dewdrop. *Unknown.* HW
Bride cam' out o' the byre, The. Wooed and Married and A'. *Unknown.* HBV
Bride in the '30's, A. W. H. Auden. FaBoMo
Bride loved old words, and found her pleasure marred. Five Epigrams. J. V. Cunningham. UnTE
Bride of Abydos, The. Byron. OAEP
Sels.
Know Ye the Land, *fr.* I. BEL; MCCG
"Winds are high on Helle's wave, The," *fr.* II. OBRV
Bride of Frankenstein, The. Edward Field. CoAP; FRC
Bride of Lammermoor, The, *sel.* Sir Walter Scott.
Lucy Ashton's Song, *fr. ch.* 3. EnRP; GoTS; OBEV; OtMeF; OxBS
(Look Not Thou.) CBEP; OBRV
Bride puts them away, The. *Unknown.* HW
Bride she bound her golden hair, The. Sir Turlough; or, The Churchyard Bride. William Carleton. IrPN
Bride, so filled with rosy longings. To the Bride. Sappho. HW
Bride Song. Christina Rossetti. *Fr.* The Prince's Progress. OBEV; OBVV; TOP
(Too Late for Love.) PoVP
Bridegroom, The. Kipling. *Fr.* Epitaphs of the War. CLwM
Bridegroom Dick, *sel.* Herman Melville.
"Where's Commander All-a-Tanto?" PoEL-5
Bridegroom Is So Tall, The. Sappho, *tr. fr. Greek by* Virginia Tufte. HW
Bridegroom none but death alone. A Bride. Meleager, *tr. fr. Greek by* H. C. Beeching. WoL
Bridegroom of Cana, The. Marjorie Pickthall. CaP
Bridegroomes Comming, The. John Donne. MaMe
Brides Going to Bed, The. John Donne. MaMe
Bride's Lament. Sappho, *tr. fr. Greek by* Virginia Tufte. HW
Bride's Marriage-Cake, The, *sel. Unknown.*
Fairy Chorus. HW

Bride's Prelude, The. Dante Gabriel Rossetti. SeCePo
Bride's Toilette, The. Ellen M. Hutchinson Cortissoz. AA
Bride's Tragedy, The, *sels.* Thomas Lovell Beddoes.
"Dear, I could weep, but that my brain is dry." LO
Hesperus Sings. VA
("Poor old pilgrim Misery."). EnRP
Love Goes a-Hawking. VA
(Song: "A ho! A ho!") BiS; ChER
Bridge. A R. Ammons. CoAP
Bridge, The. Hart Crane. LiTA
Sels.
Atlantis. AmLP; AnFE; AtBAP; CoAnAm; LiTM; MoPo; NePA; TwAmPo
Ave Maria. AtBAP; MoPo; NePA; PoDB
Cape Hatteras. WoL
"Nasal whine of power whips a new universe, The." MoAB
Power: Cape Hatteras. MAP; MoAmPo
Cutty Sark. AmPP; FaBoMo; NP
Powhatan's Daughter.
Dance, The. AnAmPo; AnFE; CoAnAm; LiTM; MoAB; MoAmPo; OxBA; SeCeV; TwAmPo
Harbor Dawn, The. AmP; MoPo; NePA; OxBA
Indiana. AnFE; CoAnAm; TwAmPo
River, The. AmP; AmPP; AnFE; AP; CMoP; CoAnAm; CoBA; CoBMV; MoAB; MoAmPo; NAMP; OxBA; TwAmPo; ViBoPo (1958 ed.)
"Down, down—born pioneers in time's despite." TrGrPo
"You will not hear it as the sea." ViBoPo (1941 ed.)
Van Winkle. AmP; AmPP; CrMA; FaBV; MAP; MoAB; MoAmPo; ReMP
Quaker Hill. LiTM (rev. ed.)
Three Songs
National Winter Garden. AmP; ErPo; LiTM (rev. ed.); OxBA; TDP
To Brooklyn Bridge. AmPP; AP; CABA; CoBMV; CrMA; DiPo; ExPo; FaBoEn; GTBS-W; HT; ILP; LiTA; LiTM; MoAB; MoAmPo (1950 ed.); MoPo; NePA; OxBA; PIA; PoDB; PoE; PoIE; PoPl; ReMP; SeCeV; TDP; ThLM
(Proem: To Brooklyn Bridge.) AmP; CMoP; NoP
Tunnel, The. AmP; AP; CMoP; LiTA; LiTG; MAP; MoAB; MoAmPo; MoVE; NePA; OxBA; PoFS
Bridge. S. Foster Damon. AnAmPo
Bridge, The. Willibald Köhler, *tr. fr. German by* George N. Shuster. CAW
Bridge, The. Longfellow. CoBA; FaPL; HBV; TreF
Bridge, The. Frederick Peterson. HBV
Bridge, The. James Thomson. Sunday Up the River, II. OBVV; TOP
("Oh, what are you waiting for here, young man?") PoVP
Bridge, The. Albert Verwey, *tr. fr. Dutch by* A. J. Barnouw. LiTW
Bridge Builder, The. Will Allen Dromgoole. FaChP; MaRV; NeHB; OQP; PoToHe; TreFS; TRV
(Building the Bridge for Him.) SoP; STF
Bridge-Guard in the Karroo. Kipling. BoSA
Bridge Instead of a Wall, A. *Unknown.* PoToHe (new ed.)
Bridge of Death, The. *Unknown, tr. fr. French by* Andrew Lang. AWP
Bridge of Sighs, The. Thomas Hood. BEL; BeLS; EnLi-2; EnLit; EnRP; GTBS; GTBS-D; GTBS-P; GTBS-W; GTSE; GTSL; HBV; HoPM; LiTG; OBEV; OBVV; PG; TreF; VA; WBLP; WHA
Bridge says, The: Come across, try me; see how good I am. Potomac Town in February. Carl Sandburg. EvOK; WaKn
Bridge weaves its arch with pearls, A. The Rainbow—a Riddle. Schiller. OTPC (1946 ed.)
Bridge You'll Never Cross, The. Grenville Kleiser. MaRV
Bridges. Rhoda W. Bacmeister. SoPo
Bridges, The. Arthur Rimbaud, *tr. fr. French by* Oliver Bernard. FlW
Bridges are essential in a place. Covered Bridge. Robert P. Tristram Coffin. AmFN
Bridges are for going over water. Over and Under. William Jay Smith. TiPo (1959 ed.)
Bridges that, a little because of absence. For the Princess Hello. David Shapiro. ANYP
Bridle-reins hang loose in the hold of his lean left hand, The. The Boundary Rider. Thomas Heney. BoAu
Brief Autumnal. *Unknown. tr. fr. Greek by* Dudley Fitts. LiTW
Brief Biography. Marguerite George. FiSC
Brief, den du geschrieben, Der. Heine, *tr. fr. German by* Louis Untermeyer. ALV
Brief Elegie on My Dear Son John, A. John Saffin. SCAP
Brief Farewell. Anthony Delius. PeSA
Brief History. Olga Hampel Briggs. GoYe
Brief Introduction to the History of Culture, A. Weldon Kees. TwAmPo
Brief is Erinna's song, her lowly lay. Erinna. Antipater of Sidon. AWP
Brief Lines in Not So Brief. Ogden Nash. ML
Brief, on a flying night. Chimes. Alice Meynell. AnFE; BoTP; CH; MoBrPo; NP; TSW; WHA
Brief Sermon, A. *Unknown.* TreFS
Briefless Barrister, The. John G. Saxe. ShM
Brier. E. Pauline Johnson. MaRV
"Brigade Must Not Know, Sir, The." *Unknown.* MC; OTD; PAH; ThLM
Brigadier. *Unknown, tr. fr. French-Canadian by* A. J. M. Smith. MoCV; NMP
Brigg, The. Robin Skelton. NMP
Brigham Young (A *and* B *vers.*). *Unknown.* CoSo
Bright Abandon. Tessa Sweazy Webb. GoYe
Bright and Morning Star, The. Edward Taylor. *See* Preparatory Meditations: "Star, bright morning star. . ."
Bright are the heavens, the narrow bay serene. The Indian's Grave. George J. Mountain. CaP
Bright as the Day, and like the Morning fair. Cloe. George Granville. SeEP
Bright as Venus' golden star. The Insatiate. Johannes Secundus. *Fr.* Basia. UnTE
Bright axe breaks the silence in the wood, The. Tree Felling. George Woodcock. NeBP
Bright Babe! whose awfull beautyes [*or* beauties] make. In the Glorious Epiphanie of Our Lord God [*or* A Hymne for the Epiphanie]. Richard Crashaw. AnAnS-1; MaMe; MeP; PoEL-2; SCEP-1
Bright Be the Place of Thy Soul! Byron. HoPM
Bright be the skies that cover thee. To Laura W——, Two Years Old. Nathaniel Parker Willis. HBV
Bright beach glittering in the morning sun, A. On the Edge of the Pacific. Theodore Maynard. CAW
Bright berries on the roadside. On the March. Richard Aldington. BrPo
Bright books! the perspectives to our weak sights. To His Books. Henry Vaughan. EP; QFR
Bright breaks the warrior o'er the ocean wave. The Ocean Wanderer. *Unknown.* BOHV; NA
Bright Cap and Streamers. James Joyce. Chamber Music, X. CBV; HW
Bright captures, wing-shimmers, facts. Spider. Richmond Lattimore. PP
Bright cards above the fire bring no friends near. Christmas 1944. Denise Levertov. NeBP
Bright clasp of her whole hand around my finger. To My Daughter. Stephen Spender. BoC
Bright Clouds. Edward Thomas. BrPo; POTE
Bright Day, A. John Montague. NYTB
Bright drips [*or* drops] the morning from its trophied nets. Sonnet of Fishes. George Barker. FaBoMo; FlW; Sonn
Bright earth moves in destined grooves, The. Final Thoughts on the Weather in England during 1953. David Daiches. SiTL
Bright eyes and laughing lips. Rain. Patrick F. Kirby. GoBC
Bright Eyes, Light Eyes! Daughter of a Fay! The Faery Foster-Mother. Robert Buchanan. VA
Bright Flower! whose home is everywhere. To the Daisy. Wordsworth. CoBE; EnRP; EPN; MERP
Bright glows the east with blushing red. The Farm. Jane Taylor. OTPC (1923 ed.)
Bright goddesse (Whether Jove thy father be). Out of Barclay's Euphormion. Richard Crashaw. MaMe
Bright-haired Spirit! Golden Brow! Onward to Far Ida. George Darley. *Fr.* Nepenthe. OBNC
Bright Hillside, The. Rhoda Coghill. NeIP; OxBI
Bright Is the Ring of Words. Robert Louis Stevenson. BrPo; OBNC; PoVP; TrGrPo
(Words.) GoTP
Bright light of the stars is dimmed, The. Standing at the Foot of the Steps at Night. Yüan Mei. FlW
Bright little maid of St. Thomas, A. Limerick. *Unknown.* HBV

Bright moon lifts from the Mountain of Heaven, The. The Moon at the Fortified Pass. Li Po. LiTW; WaaP
Bright Night, A. *Unknown, tr. fr. Japanese by* Arthur Waley. *Fr.* Manyo Shu. WoL
("Shall we make love.") AWP; LiTW
Bright on the banners of lily and rose. Welcome to the Nations. Oliver Wendell Holmes. PAH
Bright portals [*or* portalles] of the sky. An Hymne [*or* Song] of the Ascension. William Drummond of Hawthornden. OBS; SeCL
Bright Queen of Heaven, God's Virgin Spouse. The Knot. Henry Vaughan. ISi
Bright ran thy line, O Galloway. Lord Galloway. Burns. OxBoLi
Bright sea washed beneath her feet, The. The Return. Annie Fields. AA
Bright shadows of true rest! some shoots of blisse. Son [*or* Sun]-Dayes. Henry Vaughan. AtBAP; MemP; SeCP
Bright shine the golden summits in the light. A Calm Sea. Robert Southey. EtS
Bright shines the sun on Clinch's Hill. The Vance Song. Abner Vance. OuSiCo
Bright shines the sun; play, beggars, play! In Praise of a Beggar's Life [*or* A Song in Praise of a Beggar's Life *or* Play, Beggars, Play!]. "A. W." ElL; OBSC; PTK; SiCE; TrGrPo; WHA
Bright Sirius! that when Orion pales. The Star Sirius. George Meredith. VP
Bright soule, instruct poore mortalls how to mourne. *Unknown.* SeCSL
Bright spark, shot from a brighter place. The Starre. George Herbert. AnAnS-1; AtBAP; MaMe; MeP
Bright Sparkles in the Churchyard. *Unknown.* AA
Bright Squadrons, The. Spenser. *See* Guardian Angels.
Bright Star. Keats. *See* Bright Star! Would I Were Steadfast as Thou Art.
Bright star of beauty, fairest fair alive. To His Mistress. Richard Barnfield. *Fr.* Cynthia. SiCE; TuPP
Bright star of beauty, on whose eyelids sit. Idea, IV. Michael Drayton. HBV; SiCE
Bright Star! Would I Were Steadfast [*or* Stedfast] as Thou Art. Keats. ATP; BEL; BoLiVe; BoPe; CABA; CBV; CoBE; EnL; EnLi-2; EnLit; EnLoPo; EPN; ExPo; GTBS; GTBS-D; GTBS-P; GTBS-W; GTSE; ILP; LiTB; LiTG; LO; MaPo; MERP; OuHeWo; PoAn; PoE; PoeP; PoFS; PoIE; PoPo; SeCeV; ShBV-4; Sonn; TOP; TreFS; TrGrPo; ViBoPo
(Bright Star.) BWP; DiPo; EnRP; ERoP-2; FaPL; ForPo; LiTL; MBW-2; MeWo; NoP; PAn; PG (1955 ed.); WHA
(His Last Sonnet.) LoBV
(Last Sonnet.) AnFE; ChER; GTSL; HBV; NeHB; OBEV
(Sonnet: "Bright star.") AnEnPo; FaBV; FiP; OAEP; OBNC; PoEL-4; ShBV-4
(Written on a Blank Page in Shakespeare's Poems [Facing "A Lover's Complaint"].) FaBoEn; OBRV
Bright stars, light stars. Stars. Rhoda W. Bacmeister. BrR
Bright swords. Bright spears. They blur, blot, the world. Farewell to Han So. Tu Fu. OnPM
Bright thro' the valley gallops the brooklet. Eros. Coventry Patmore. GTSE
Bright vocabularies are transient as rainbows. Precious Moments. Carl Sandburg. MAP; MoAmPo
Bright was the morn—the waveless bay. Perry's Victory on Lake Erie. James Gates Percival. PaA; PAP
Bright Was the Morning. Thomas D'Urfey. OBS
Bright was the summer's noon when quickening steps. Summer Vacation. Wordsworth. *Fr.* The Prelude, IV. MBW-2
Bright water: like the salty tears of infancy. Memory. Arthur Rimbaud. LiTW
Bright waves scour the wound of Carthage, The. Rome Remember. Sidney Keyes. MoAB
Bright were the mornings first impearl'd. And Jesus Wept. Matthew Bridges. BePJ; SoP
Brightest and Best of the Sons of the Morning. Reginald Heber. GN; HBVY; MaRV; OTPC; SoP; WGRP; YaCaBo, *with music*
(Epiphany.) PoRL
(Hymn.) NBM
Brightly colored for a new season. Merry-go-round. Oliver Jenkins. GoYe
Brightly shone the sun in my hut. Those Who Lost Everything. David Diop. PBA
Brightness of Brightness. Egan O'Rahilly, *tr. fr. Irish by* Frank O'Connor. KiLC
Brigid, the daughter of Duffy, she wasn't like other young things. Saint Brigid. Denis A. McCarthy. JKCP
Brignall Banks. Sir Walter Scott. *Fr.* Rokeby, III. BEL; EnRP; EPN; OBEV; TOP
(Edmund's Song.) EnLi-2; PoRA
(Outlaw, The.) GTBS; GTBS-D; GTBS-P; GTBS-W; GTSE; GTSL; OtMeF
(Song: "O Brignall banks are wild and fair.") HBV; OAEP; OBRV
Brigs of Ayr, The, *sel.* Burns.
"When heavy, dark, continued, a'-day rains." MCCG
Brilliancies of Winter, The. Thomas Love Peacock. PeER
Brilliant seaside glitters its farewell, The. A Summer Gone. Howard Moss. NePoEA
Brindabella. Douglas Stewart. PoAu-2
Bring a Torch, Jeannette, Isabella. *At. to* Nicolas Saboly, *tr. fr. Provencal.* ChrBoLe; OHIP; YaCaBo *with music*
Bring Back. Anne Ridler. ACV
Bring cypress, rosemary and rue. Grover Cleveland. Joel Benton. DD; PAH
Bring Daddy home. *Unknown.* OxNR
Bring down the moon for genteel Janet. Goodbye Now; or, Pardon My Gauntlet. Ogden Nash. FiBHP
Bring every child. Christmas Songs. Gerta Kennedy. PoPl
Bring flowers, to strew again. Ode for Decoration Day. Henry Peterson. OHIP
Bring flowers to strew His way. Easter. Katharine Tynan. YT
Bring forth the flowers. Song for Decoration Day. Helen C. Bacon. HH
Bring from the craggy haunts of birch and pine. Song [*or* O Mighty, Melancholy Wind]. John Todhunter. OBVV; OnYI; PoVP
Bring Good Ale. *Unknown. See* Bring Us in Good Ale.
Bring hemlock, black as Cretan cheese. Epigram. Robert Hillyer. WhC
Bring Home the Poet. Patrick MacDonough. OnYI
Bring, in this timeless grave to throw. A. E. Housman. A Shropshire Lad, XLVI. PoVP
Bring Kateen-beug and Maurya Jude. Beg-Innish. J. M. Synge. MoBrPo; NeMA; OnYI; OxBI
Bring me a cherry without a stone. Captain Wedderburn's Courtship (C *vers.*). *Unknown.* BaBo
Bring me a cup of good red wine. Rinaldo. Henry Peterson. AA
Bring me a letter, postman! The Postman. Alice Todd. BoTP
"Bring me a long sharp knife for we are in danger." The Sunflowers. Douglas Stewart. BoAV
Bring me a rose. Grief-in-Idleness. Thomas Lovell Beddoes. *Fr.* Early Fragments. AtBAP
Bring Me Men. Sam Walter Foss. *Fr* The Coming American. OQP
("Bring me men to match my mountains.") AmFN; BBV (1951 ed.); BLPA; FaBoBe; MaRV: NeHB; OTD; PaA; WaKn
Bring me my dead! Tennyson. Thomas Henry Huxley. HBV; VA
"Bring me soft song," said Aladdin. Aladdin and the Jinn. Vachel Lindsay. AnAmPo; AnFE; APA; CoAnAm; GTBS-W; LiTM; MAPA; NP; OnPP; TwAmPo
Bring Me the Cup. Moses ibn Ezra, *tr. fr. Hebrew by* Solomon Solis-Cohen. *Fr* Wine-Songs. TrJP
Bring me the sunflower to transplant. The Sunflower. Eugenio Montale. OnPM
Bring me the sunset in a cup. Emily Dickinson. AP; MAP; MoAmPo; MWA-2
Bring me those needles, Martha. Owen Dodson. *Fr.* The Confession Stone. Kal
Bring me to the blasted oak. Crazy Jane and the Bishop. W. B. Yeats. AtBAP; CMoP; LiTM (1970 ed.)
Bring me wine, but wine which never grew. Bacchus. Emerson. AmePo; AmP; AmPP; AnAmPo; AnFE; AnNE; AP; APA; AWP; CoAnAm; HBV; LiTA; MAmP; OBEV; OxBA; PoEL-4; ViBoPo
Bring no jarring lute this way. A Woodland Grave. Lord De Tabley. VA
Bring not bright candles, for her eyes. The Dreamer. Walter de la Mare. OTPC (1923 ed.)
Bring, O Morn, thy music! Bring, O night, thy hushes! "Who

Bring (continued)
Wert and Art and Evermore Shalt Be." William Channing Gannett. TrPWD
Bring on the pomp and pride of old Castile. Alfred Noyes. *Fr.* Drake, XI. CAW
Bring out all the set ideas. Borderline Ballad. Richard Weber. PPON
Bring out the hemlock! bring the funeral yew! Dirge of the Munster Forest. Emily Lawless. OBVV; OnYI
Bring snow-white lilies, pallid heart-flushed roses. The Pantheist's Song of Immortality. Constance C. W. Naden. VA
Bring that red mouth of yours. Madrigal de Verano. Federico García Lorca. ErPo
Bring the biggest bath you've seen. The Song of the Bath. Margaret Gibbs. BoTP
Bring the bowl which you boast. Glee for King Charles. Sir Walter Scott. *Fr.* Woodstock, *ch.* 20. CoBE; EPN
Bring the comb and play upon it! Marching Song. Robert Louis Stevenson. BoTP; FaPON; OTPC; TiPo
Bring the good old bugle, boys, we'll sing another song. Marching through Georgia. Henry Clay Work. OTPC; PaA; PAH
Bring the Soul Blocks. Victor Hernandez Cruz. CAD
Bring Them Not Back. James Benjamin Kenyon. AA
Bring to me then all passionate, crimson flowers. She Plans Her Funeral. Louise Morey Bowman. CaP
Bring to me white roses, roses, pinks, and lavender. The Patchwork Quilt. Dora Sigerson Shorter. HBMV
Bring Torches. A. M. Stephen. CaP
Bring Us In Good Ale. *Unknown.* CH; EG; MeEL; ViBoPo
(Bring Good Ale.) SeCePo
Bring where our Beauty lies. Certain Artists Bring Her Dolls and Drawings. W. B. Yeats. Upon a Dying Lady, II. LiTB
Bringer of sun, arrower of evening, star-begetter and moon-riser. Hymnal. Harold Vinal. TrPWD
Bringers. Carl Sandburg. NP
Bringers of the Hemlock. Stanton A. Coblentz. ChIP
Bringing Him Up. Lord Dunsany. BBGG; PV
Bringing in the Wine. Li Po, *tr. fr. Chinese by* Witter Bynner *and* Kiang Kang-hu. OuHeWo
Bringing Our Sheaves. Elizabeth Akers Allen. HBV
Brisk encounter between a Youngman and His Love, A. *Unknown.* *See* Wil the Merry Weaver, and Charity the Chamber-Maid.
Brisk Girl, The. *Unknown.* *See* There Was a Brisk Girle.
Brisk methinks I am, and fine. Five Wines. Robert Herrick. BOHV
Brisk wielder of the birch and rule. The Schoolmaster. Whittier. *Fr.* Snow-bound. GoTP
Brisk Wind, A. William Barnes. UnPo (3d ed.)
Brisk young lover came a-courting me, A. Died of Love. *Unknown.* CBEP
Brissit brawnis and broken banis. The Bewteis of the Fute-Ball. *Unknown.* GoTS; OxBS
Bristling beard was his peculiarity, A. His Hirsute Suit. Frank Sidgwick. WhC
Bristol and Clifton. John Betjeman. CMoP; POTi
Bristowe Tragedie; or the Dethe of Syr Charles Bawdin. Thomas Chatterton. CEP; EiCL; EiPP; EnRP; OBEC; OxBB
Britain's Ida. Phineas Fletcher. *See* Brittain's Ida.
Britannia, *sel.* James Thomson.
Britannia's Empire. OBEC
Britannia Rules of Orthography. "Firth." InMe; WhC
Britannia rules the waves. England and America; On a Parisian Boulevard. James Kenneth Stephen. InMe
Britannia to Columbia. Alfred Austin. *See* To America.
Britannia's Empire. James Thomson. *Fr.* Britannia. OBEC
Britannia's gallant streamers. Yankee Thunders. *Unknown.* PAH
Britannia's Pastorals, *sels.* William Browne.
Frolic Mariners of Devon, The, *fr.* II, Song 3. ChTr
Gentle Nymphs, Be Not Refusing, *fr.* I, Song 3. EIL; ViBoPo
Glide Soft, Ye Silver Floods, *fr.* II, Song 1. EIL
Memory ("Marina's gone, and now sit I"), 7 *sts. fr.* III, Song 1. HBV
(Celadyne's Song.) OBS
(So Shuts the Marigold Her Leaves, *shorter sel.*) ChTr
Memory ("So shuts the marigold her leaves"), 3 *sts. fr.* III, Song 1. OBEV
(Since She Is Gone.) LiTL
("So shuts the marigold her leaves.") EG; ViBoPo
Praise of Poets ("At Thames faire port"), *fr.* II, Songs 1 *and* 2. OBS
Shall I Tell You Whom I Love? *fr.* II, Song 2. EIL; SeEP
(Song: "Shall I tell you whom I love?") HBV
Venus and Adonis, *fr.* II, Song 2. CLwM; EIL
("Venus, by Adonis' side.") SeEP
Britannia's sons, though slaves ye be. Hymn. John Bramwich. PoFr
British, The. A. S. J. Tessimond. ChMP
British Church, The. George Herbert. AnAnS-1; MaMe; MeP; PoE
British Commerce. John Dyer. *Fr.* The Fleece, IV. OBEC
British Commerce. James Thomson. *Fr.* Liberty, IV. OBEC
British Grenadiers, The ("Some talk of Alexander, and some of Hercules"). *Unknown.* CBEP; EiCL; HBV; OBEC; OxBoLi
British Grenadier, The ("Come, come fill up your glasses"). *Unknown.* PAH
British in branding their betters, The. Lessons in Limericks, II. David McCord. InMe
British Journalist, The. Humbert Wolfe. FiBHP; PV
("You cannot hope.") BoC
British Leftish Poetry, 1930-1940. "Hugh MacDiarmid." NMP; OPoP
British Lyon Roused, The. Stephen Tilden. PAH
British Museum Reading Room, The. Louis MacNeice. LiTM; MoAB; MoBrPo; SeCePo; WaP
British Prison Ship, The, *sel.* Philip Freneau.
Hospital Prison Ship, The, III. AmPP (5th ed.)
British puss demurely mews, The. Philological. John Updike. ELU
British Tar, The. W. S. Gilbert. *Fr.* H. M. S. Pinafore. ALV
British Valor Displayed. Francis Hopkinson. *See* Battle of the Kegs, The.
Britomart in the House of Busirane. Spenser. *Fr.* The Faerie Queene, III, 11-12. FiP
("There they dismounting drew their weapons bold.") MBW-1
Britons and Guests. Edith M. Thomas. PaA
Briton Who Shot at His King. David Ross. ShM
Britons grown big with pride. A Poem Containing Some Remarks on the Present War. *Unknown.* PAH
Brittaine, the mighty oceans lovely bride. To the Queen: Upon the Duke of Yorke His Birth a Panegyricke. Richard Crashaw. MaMe
Brittain's Ida, *sel.* Phineas Fletcher.
Song: "Fond men! whose wretched care the life soon ending." EIL
Brittan's Remembrancer, *sel.* George Wither.
"I know that if thou please thou canst provide." SeCV-1
Brittish Church, The. Henry Vaughan. AnAnS-1; MeP
Brittle Beauty. Earl of Surrey. AnFE; PoFS; TrGrPo
("Brittle beauty, that Nature made so frail.") EnLoPo; FCP; SiPS
(Frailty and Hurtfulness of Beauty, The.) HoPM; ReIE; SiCE; TuPP; VaPo
Brittle World. Lew Sarett. MoSiPe
"Broad acres, sir." You hear them in my talk. At Knaresborough. Donald Davie. NePoEA
Broad-Axe [*or*-Ax], The. Walt Whitman. *Fr.* Song of the Broad-Axe. MAP; MoAmPo
Broad-backed hippopotamus, The. The Hippopotamus. T. S. Eliot. AmPP; AnAmPo; AWP; HoPM; LiTB; LiTM (1946 ed.); NAMP; OBMV; PoDB; PoPl; PoSa
Broad bars of sunset-slanted gold. Ballad of the Faded Field. Robert Burns Wilson. AA
Broad-based, broad-fronted, bounteous, multiform. Ben Jonson. Swinburne. *Fr.* Sonnets on English Dramatic Poets. BEL; PoVP; Sonn
Broad beach, The / Sea wind and the sea's irregular rhythm. Afternoon; Amagansett Beach. John Hall Wheelock. BoNaP; MoVE; NePA; PoRA (rev. ed.); WIRo
Broad, but not deep, along his rock-chafed bed. Castleconnell. Air Aubrey De Vere. IrPN
Broad Gold. "Anna Akhmatova," *tr. fr. Russian by* Babette Deutsch. LiTW
Broad is the gate and wide the path. The Bath. Harry Graham. CenHV; ShM
Broad shadows fall. On all the mountain side. A Sunset at Les

Eboulements. Archibald Lampman. OBCV
Broad sun, The/ The bright day. The Far-Farers. Robert Louis Stevenson. BoTP
Broadcast, The. John W. Simons. JKCP (1955 ed.)
Broadcast to the Scholars in the Eyrie. David Ross. PG (1945 ed.)
Broadcasting. Mildred D. Shacklett. GFA
Broadway: Twilight. Tom Prideaux. OCS
Broadway's Canyon. John Gould Fletcher. InP
Brobdingnag. Adrien Stoutenburg. NYBP
Brobinyak has dragon eyes, The. What You Will Learn about the Brobinyak. John Ciardi. EvOK
Brocadós and Damasks, and Tabbies, and Gawzes. An Excellent New Song on a Seditious Pamphlet. Swift. CoMu
Brocks snuffle from their holt within. The Badgers. Eden Phillpotts. BoTP
Brogan's Lane. Louis Esson. BoAu
Broke an' hungry, ragged an' dirty too. The "Cholly" Blues. *Unknown.* ABF
Broken altar, Lord, thy servant rears, A. The Altar. George Herbert. AnAnS-1; ATP; MaMe; MeP; PAn; PoFS; PoSa; ReEn; SCEP-1; SeCP; SeCV-1; TrGrPo; VaPo
Broken Appointment, A. Thomas Hardy. BWP; CBEP; DTC; MoPW; NoP; OAEP (2d ed.); ViPo; ViPP
Broken Bodies. Louis Golding. HBMV; MaRV
Broken bones were left to brokenness. Richard Eberhart. *Fr.* Brotherhood of Men. OnHM
Broken Bowl, The. Jones Very. AP
Broken dike, the levee washed away, The. Edna St. Vincent Millay. *Fr.* Epitaph for the Race of Man, X. CMoP
Broken Doll, The. Christina Rossetti. *Fr.* Sing-Song. MPB
("All the bells were ringing.") TiPo
Broken-down Digger, The. *Unknown.* PoAu-1
Broken-down Squatter, The. *Unknown.* PoAu-1
Broken-Face Gargoyles. Carl Sandburg. AmPP (5th ed.); ILP; MAP; MoAmPo; OxBA
Broken Friendship. Samuel Taylor Coleridge. *Fr.* Christabel, Pt. II. TreFT
("Alas! they had been friends in youth.") LO; OBRV
(Friendship, *abr.*) MCCG
(Scars Remaining, The.) OBNC
Broken Heart, The. Thomas Beedome. OBS
Broken Heart, The. John Donne. AtBAP; DiPo; ILP; LiTL; MaMe; PoFS; ReEn; SCEP-1; TuPP
Broken Heart, The, *sels.* John Ford.
"Beasts onely capable of sense, enjoy," *fr.* IV, ii. PoEL-2
Can You Paint a Thought? *fr.* III, ii. AtBAP; CBEP; InvP; LO; OAEP; PoEL-2; TuPP; ViBoPo
"Glories, pleasures, pomps, delights, and ease,," *fr.* V, iil. TuPP; ViBoPo
(Broken Heart, A.) OnPM
(Dirge.) LoBV
(Song, A.) OBS
"Oh, no more, no more, too late," *fr.* IV, iii. AtBAP; ELP; LO; PoEL-2; TuPP; ViBoPo
(Now Love Dies.) SeCL
(Song.) LoBV; OBS; SeCePo; SeEP
Broken-hearted Gardener, The. *Unknown.* ChTr
Broken Hearts. M. P. Ferguson. SoP
Broken Home, The. James Merrill. NYBP
Broken in pieces all asunder. Affliction. George Herbert. AnAnS-1; LoBV; MaMe; MeP
Broken Jug, The. William Barnes. PoVP
Broken Kaleidoscope, The Walter de la Mare. NYTB
Broken Monologue. "Michael Lewis," *fr. the German.* UnTE
Broken moon lay in the autumn sky, The. To——. Alexander Smith. VA
Broken Music. Dante Gabriel Rossetti. The House of Life, XLVII. MaVP; PoVP; VA; ViPo; VP
Broken Oar, The. Longfellow. AmePo
Broken One, The. John Holmes. MiAP
Broken pillar of the wing jags from the clotted shoulder, The. Hurt Hawks. Robinson Jeffers. AmP; AmPP; AP; AtBAP; BoLiVe; CMoP; CoBA; CoBMV; DiPo; LiTA; LiTM (1970 ed.); MAP; MoAB; MoAmPo; MoVE; NeMA; NoP; NP; OxBA; PoPo
Broken Pinion, The. Hezekiah Butterworth. *See* Bird with a Broken Wing, The.
Broken Pitcher, The. William Edmondstoune Aytoun. BOHV; InMe; PoVP
Broken Ring, The. *Unknown.* *See* Dark-eyed Canaller.
Broken Shell. Winfield Townley Scott. NYTB
Broken snow should leave the traces, The. The Snow. Robert Creeley. AP
Broken Song, A. "Moira O'Neill." OBVV; PG (1945 ed.)
Broken String, The. *Unknown,* *fr. fr. Bushman by* W. H. I. Bleek. PeSA
Broken Sword, The. Edward Rowland Sill. *See* Opportunity.
Broken Things. Bob Jones, Jr. SoP
Broken Tower, The. Hart Crane. AmP; AmPP (5th ed.); AP; CMoP; CoBMV; GTBS-W; LiTM (1970 ed.); MoAB; MoAmPo (1962 ed.); MoPo; MoVE; NoP; OxBA; Po; PoIE; SyP; TrGrPo (rev. ed.); VaPo
Broken wagon wheel that rots away beside the river, A. Pioneers. Badger Clark. FaBoBe
Brome, Brome on Hill. *Unknown.* *Fr.* The Broomfield Hill. AtBAP
Bronc Peeler's Song. *Unknown.* CoSo
Bronc That Wouldn't Bust, The. *Unknown.* SCC
Broncho Dan halts midway of the stream. A Health at the Ford. Robert Cameron Rogers. AA; FaBoBe
Broncho That Would Not Be Broken, The. Vachel Lindsay. ATP (1935 ed.); BBV (1951 ed.); LaNeLa; LiTM (rev. ed.); NePA; PFY; PTK; RoGo; YT
Broncho versus Bicycle. *Unknown.* SCC
Bronx. Joseph Rodman Drake. AmePo; AnAmPo
Bronze. Alfred Starr Hamilton. QAH
Bronze. Derek Walcott. ToPo
Bronze daggers pierced the darkened night. Stormy Night. Barbara Drake Johnston. SoP
Bronze Frog, The. *Unknown,* *tr. fr. Greek by* Lord Neaves. OnPM
Bronze Head, A. W. B. Yeats. LiTB; MBW-2
Bronze Statuette of Kwan-yin, A. Charles Wharton Stork. GoYe
Bronzeville Man with a Belt in the Back. Gwendolyn Brooks. IDB
Brooding/ their faces seem to shrink. Yellow Apples. Rochelle Ratner. QAH
Brooding Grief. D. H. Lawrence. CMoP; LoBV
Brooding of Sigurd, The. William Morris. *Fr.* The Story of Sigurd the Volsung. SeCePo
Brook, The. William Wilberforce Lord. AA
Brook, The. Tennyson. *See* Brook, The; an Idyl.
Brook, The. Edward Thomas. MoVE; SeCeV
Brook, The, *sel.* William Bull Wright.
"Through his million veins are poured." AA
Brook, The; an Idyl, *sels.* Tennyson.
Brook, The. BoNaP; BoTP; EPN; FaBV; FaPON; GN; GoJo; GTBS; MCCG; MPB; OTPC; PCH; RIS; ShBV-2
(Brook's Song, The.) FaBoBe; FaFP; HBV; HBVY; PTK; TreF
(Song: "I come from haunts of coot and hern.") MemP
(Song of the Brook, The.) BoChLi; PoVP
"I chatter over stony ways," *abr.* GFA
Brook and road, The. The Simplon Pass. Wordsworth. *Fr.* The Prelude, VI. InPo; OBRV; PoeP; PoFs; SyP
Brook and the Willow Tree, The. *Unknown,* *tr. fr. Japanese.* GFA
Brook in February, The. Sir Charles G. D. Roberts. BoNaP; OBCV; WHW
Brook in the City, A. Robert Frost. OxBA; TSW
Brook in Winter, The. James Russell Lowell. *Fr.* The Vision of Sir Launfal: Prelude to Pt. II. GN; OTPC
(December.) GoTP
("Down swept the chill wind.") TreF
Brook of the Heart, The. Emily Dickinson. *See* Have you got a brook in your little heart?
Brook Song. James Herbert Morse. AA
Brook That Runs to France, The. John Clair Minot. DD
Brook, would thou couldst flow. Brook Song. James Herbert Morse. AA
Brook wound through the woods behind, The. The Crayfish. Robert Wallace. WaKn
Brooke whose streame so great, so good, A. An Epitaph upon Doctor Brooke. Richard Crashaw. MaMe
Brookfield. William E. Marshall.
"But see this happy village festival," *sel.* CaP
Brooklyn at Santiago, The. Wallace Rice. PAH
Brooklyn Bridge, The. Edna Dean Proctor. MC; PAH
Brooklyn Bridge. Sir Charles G. D. Roberts. PAH

Brooklyn Bridge at Dawn. Richard Le Gallienne. HBMV
Brooklyn Heights. John Wain. LiTM (1970 ed.); ToPo
Brooklynese Champion. Margaret Fishback. WhC
Brook's Song, The. Tennyson. *See* Brook, The; an Idyl.
Brooks that flush, The. The Thrush. John Duffy. JKCP (1955 ed.)
Brookside, The. Richard Monckton Milnes. HBV; TreFS; VA
Broom. John Farrar. GFA
Broom, The. Giacomo Leopardi, *tr. fr. Italian.* LiTW, *tr. by* John Heath-Stubbs; WoL, *tr. by* R. C. Trevelyan
Broom Flower, The. Mary Howitt. HBV
Broom, Green Broom. *Unknown. See* Green Broom.
Broom of Cowdenknows, The. *Unknown.* ESPB
Broom out the floor now, lay the fender by. June. Francis Ledwidge. OnYI; HBMV
Broomfield Hill, The. *Unknown.* BaBo; ESPB (A *and* B *vers.*); OBB; OxBB; ViBoFo
("O where were ye, my milk-white steed.") CH
Brome, Brome on Hill, *sel.* AtBAP
Brooms. Dorothy Aldis. GFA; SoPo
Broomstick Train, The. Oliver Wendell Holmes. MCCG
"Look out! Look out, boys! Clear the track!" *sel.* FaPON; PoMS
Brother, The. Semyon Yakovlevich Nadson, *tr. fr. Russian by* H. Badanes. TrJP
Brother and Sister. "Lewis Carroll." BBGG; ChTr; ShM
Brother and Sister, *abr.* "George Eliot." GN
Brother, are the cakes all done? Baby Making Cakes. *Unknown.* SAS
Brother Ass. Eric Irvin. BoAV
Brother Ass and St. Francis. John Banister Tabb. AnAmPo
Brother, come!/ And let us go unto our God. And What Shall You Say? Joseph Seamon Cotter, Jr. BANP; CDC; PoNE
Brother Dog. Luis Aníbal Sánchez, *tr. fr. Spanish by* Muna Lee. CAW
Brother Fire. Louis MacNeice. AtBAP; FaBoMo; FOL; MoAB; MoPW; OAEP (2d ed.); TPM; WaaP
Brother Green, *with music. Unknown.* BFSS
Brother Harlem Bedford Watts Tells Mr. Charlie Where Its At. Bobb Hamilton. BF
Brother, I am fire. Kin. Carl Sandburg. NP
Brother, I come from many seas and lands. Rite at a Brother's Grave. Catullus. OnPM
Brother Jonathan's Lament for Sister Caroline. Oliver Wendell Holmes. CoBA; HBV; PaA; PAH; ThLM
Brother Juniper. Blanche Mary Kelly. GoBC; JKCP
Brother, Lift Your Flag with Mine. Josephine Daskam Bacon. PoSC
Brother Malcolm: Waste Limit. Clarence Major. BP
Brother Noah, *with music. Unknown.* AmSS
Brother of mine, good monk with cowlëd head. Thomas à Kempis. Lizette Woodworth Reese. AA
Brother, sing your country's anthem. Brother, Lift Your Flag with Mine. Josephine Daskam Bacon. PoSC
Brother Solon's Hunting Song. Thomas D'Urfey. *See* Hunting Song.
Brother, thou art gone before us. Burial Hymn. Henry Hart Milman. VA
Brother to the firefly. Morning Light the Dew-Drier. Mary Effie Lee Newsome. AmNP; CDC; PoNe
Brother Tree. Idealists. Alfred Kreymborg. PoMa; TSW
Brotherhood. First John, II: 9-11, IV: 20-21, Bible, *N.T.* TreFT
Brotherhood. Ozora Stearns Davis. MaRV
Brotherhood. Edwin Markham. BBV (1951 ed.); MaRV; NeMA; OQP; PEDC; PGD; PoRL
Brotherhood, *sel.* Sir Lewis Morris.
"There shall come from out this noise of strife and groaning." PGD
Brotherhood is not by the blood certainly, The. Speech to Those Who Say Comrade. Archibald MacLeish. AmPP; OxBA
Brother of Men, *sel.* Richard Eberhart.
"Broken bones were left to brokenness." OnHM
Brotherly Love. John Fawcett. SoP
Brothers. George E. Day. MaRV
Brothers. Solomon Edwards. NNP
Brothers, The. Amy Groesbeck. FiSC
Brothers, The. John Holloway. NMP
Brothers. Gerard Manley Hopkins. OAEP
Brothers. James Weldon Johnson. BANP
Brothers. Elias Lieberman. PoMa
Brothers, The. Edwin Muir. GTBS-P
Brothers, The. Charles Sprague. AA
Brothers/ brothers/ everywhere. Utopia. Jewel C. Latimore. WSL
Brothers/ Who/ Will/ Lead/ Us? We Must Lead. Herbert Lee Pitts. WSL
Brothers and men that shall after us be. Ballad [*or* Ballade] of the Gibbet. Villon. AWP; JAWP; WBP; WoL
Brothers and sisters I have many. Which is the Favourite? Charles *and* Mary Lamb. OTPC (1923 ed.)
Brothers in blood! They who this wrong began. To the United States of America. Robert Bridges. HBV; PaA; PAH; PoFr
Brothers, let us discover our hearts again. Open Letter. Owen Dodson. BALP
Brothers of the Faith. John Oxenham. *See* No East or West.
Brothers, the day declines. Evening Hymn of the Alpine Shepherds. William Beattie. SoP
Brought here in slave ships and pitched over board. Love Your Enemy. Yusef Iman. BF; TTY
Broughty Wa's. *Unknown.* ESPB
Brow austere, a circumspective eye, A. How to Make a Man of Consequence. Mark Lemon. BOHV
Brow bender. Baby at Play. *Unknown.* HBV; HBVY; OTPC; PPL
Brow, brow, brenty. *Unknown.* OxNR
Brow of Nephin, The. *Unknown, tr. fr. Modern Irish by* Douglas Hyde. AnIL
Brown Adam. *Unknown.* BuBa; ESPB (A *and* B *vers.*); OBB; OxBB
Brown and Furry. Christina Rossetti. *See* Caterpillar, The.
Brown arms of the mothering plateau, The. The Lowveld. Charles Eglington. PeSA
Brown Baby Cobina, with his large black velvet eyes. Baby Cobina. Gladys May Casely Hayford. CDC
Brown Bear, The. Mary Austin. FaPON; MPB; OTPC (1946 ed.); PoSC; UTS; WaKn
Brown Bear's Honey Song. Kathryn Jackson. RePo
Brown Beauty, The. Lord Herbert of Cherbury. AnAnS-2
Brown bed of earth, still fresh and warm with love. Irradiations, VIII [XIV]. John Gould Fletcher. MAPA; TwAmPo
Brown Bee. William Brighty Rands. *See* Happy World, The.
Brown Bird, The. Walt Whitman. *See* Out of the Cradle Endlessly Rocking.
"Brown, black-spotted butterfly, A." Aphrodite. Floyce Alexander. QAH
Brown bunny sits inside his burrow. The Rabbit. Edith King. BoTP; GFA; HBMV; SoPo; StVeCh
Brown-dappled fawn, The. The Fawn in the Snow. William Rose Benét. AnAmPo; MAP; MoAmPo; OA
Brown Dwarf of Rügen, The. Whittier. PoMS
Brown earth-line meets gray heaven. In November. Anne Reeve Aldrich. AA
Brown enormous odor he lived by, The. The Prodigal. Elizabeth Bishop. CoAP; FiMAP; InvP; LiTM (1970 ed.); MoAB; NYBP; TwCP
Brown-eyed Lee, *with music. Unknown. See* Sherman Cyclone, The.
Brown eyes,/ Straight nose. Polly. William Brighty Rands. GoTP; OTPC (1923 ed.); PRWS; VA
Brown Fingers/ the salt. Flowers: Calabria. George Amabile. YAP
Brown Frog, The. Mary K. Robinson. BoTP
Brown from the sun's mid-afternoon caress. Spectrum. William Dickey. ELU
Brown Girl, The ("I am as brown as brown can be"). *Unknown.* BaBo (A *and* B *vers.*); ELP; ESPB (A *and* B *vers.*); OBB
(Bonny Brown Girl, The.) OxBB
Brown Girl Dead, A. Countee Cullen. BP; Kal
Brown Girl, or Fair Eleanor, The. *Unknown. See* Lord Thomas and Fair Annet.
Brown Is My Love. *Unknown.* CBEP; ElL
(Brown Is My Love, but Graceful[l].) AtBAP; EG; OBSC
(Song Set by Nicholas Yonge.) CTC
Brown Jug, The. Francis Fawkes, *after* Amaltheus. CBEP; ViBoPo
Brown lived at such a lofty farm. Brown's Descent. Robert Frost. EvOK; MAP; MoAmPo; PoRA; StP; StPo; WhC
Brown o' San Juan. Home, Sweet Home with Variations, III. Henry Cuyler Bunner. BoHV; InMe

Brown of Ossawatomie. Whittier. AmePo; DD; HBV; MC; OTPC; PAH; ThLM
Brown on brown stretches the pastureland. At Thanksgiving. Jo Ann Leichliter. NYTB
Brown owl sits in the ivy bush, The. The Great Brown Owl. Ann Hawkshaw. OTPC (1923 ed.)
Brown Penny. W. B. Yeats. BoLP; CLwM; CMoP; ELP; ExPo; FaBoCh; LoGBV
Brown River, Smile. Jean Toomer. AmNP
(Blue Meridian, The.) PoNe (1970 ed.)
"Each new American," *sel.* BALP
Brown Robin. *Unknown.* ESPB (A *and* B *vers.*); OxBB
Brown Robin's Confession. *Unknown.* ACP; WHL
(Brown Robyn.) CH
(Brown Robyn's Confession.) ESPB; OBB
Brown round of the continent tonight, The. Australia. Eve Langley. BoAV
Brown, sad-coloured hillside, where the soil, A. The Sower. Sir Charles G. D. Roberts. CaP; OBCV
Brown sails of fishing boats. The Fishing Fleet. Lincoln Colcord. HBMV
Brown, this is a short letter. Weather Report. Charles Wright. PIA
Brown Thrush, The. Lucy Larcom. BoChLi; BoTP; DD; FaPON; HBV; HBVY; MPB; OTPC; PEDC; PPL; RIS; TVC; UTS
Brownie, Brownie, Let Down Your Milk. Christina Rossetti. *Fr.* Sing-Song. RIS
Browning at Asolo. Robert Underwood Johnson. AA
Browning, old fellow, your leaves grow yellow. In a Copy of Browning. Bliss Carman. HBMV
Brown's Descent. Robert Frost. EvOK; MAP; MoAmPo; PoRA; StP; StPo; WhC
Brown's for Lalage, Jones for Lelia. Ballade of Ladies' Names. W. E. Henley. HBV
Brown's wife, herself a normal type. Family Life. Allan M. Laing. FiBHP
Brownstone. Rod McKuen. TPM
Browny Bee. Irene F. Pawsey. BoTP
Browny Hen, The. Irene F. Pawsey. BoTP
Bruadar and Smith and Glinn. *Tr. fr. Irish by* Douglas Hyde. AnIV
Bruce, The, *sels.* John Barbour.
Before Bannockburn. OxBS
Bruce Addresses His Army. GoTS
Bruce Consults His Men. GoTS
Freedom. FaBoCh; GoTS; LoGBV; OBEV; TrGrPo
("A! fredome is a noble thing!") PoFr; ViBoPo
(Fredome.) OxBS
"Storys to rede ar delitabill." OxBS
Bruce and the Spider. Bernard Barton. BeLS
Bruce Consults His Men. John Barbour. *Fr.* The Bruce. GoTS
Bruce [*or* Bruce's Address] to His Army [*or* Men] at Bannockburn. Burns. *See* Scots Wha Hae.
Bruce's March to Bannockburn. Burns. *See* Scots Wha Hae.
Bruised and battered. Tenement Room; Chicago. Frank Marshall Davis. GoSl
Bruised by a heel he strove to die. The Death of a Snake. William Plomer. ELU
Bruised Titans, The. Keats. *Fr.* Hyperion; a Fragment. OBNC
("Just as the self-same beat of Time's wide wings.") OBRV
Bruisers of England, the men of tremendous renown, The. The Fancy. William Rose Benét. SD
Brumana. James Elroy Flecker. BrPo; HT
Brummell at Calais. John Glassco. MoCV; PeCV (1967 ed.)
Brushes and paints are all I have. Quatrains. Gwendolyn B. Bennett. CDC
Brussels Cross Inscription. *Unknown, tr. fr. Anglo-Saxon by* Chauncey B. Tinker. InP
Brut, The, *sels.* Layamon, *tr. fr.* Middle English.
Arthur's Dream. MeEV
Arthur's Last Battle, *orig. and mod. English pr.* BEL
Arthur's Last Fight. MeEV
Battle of Bath, The. MeEV
Birth of Arthur, The. MeEV
Building of London, The. MeEV
Leir and His Daughters. MeEV
Prolog, The: "There was a priest in the land." MeEV
Prophecy of Diana, The. MeEV
Round Table, The. EnLi-1, *tr. by* Stith Thompson; MeEV
Bruton Town. *Unknown. See* In Brunton Town.
Brutus. Shakespeare. *See* Portrait of Brutus.
Brutus Explains Why He Murdered Caesar. Shakespeare. *Fr.* Julius Caesar, III, ii. TreFT
Brutus held Britain, and Corineus, Cornwall. The Building of London. Layamon. *Fr.* The Brut. MeEV
Brutus, that brave and complete cavalier. Henry Parrot. SiCE
Brutus took Ignogen and upon the ship led her. The Prophecy of Diana. Layamon. *Fr.* The Brut. MeEV
Bryan, Bryan, Bryan, Bryan. Vachel Lindsay. CMoP; CrMA; LiTA; OxBA; OxBoLi
Bryan O'Lin had no breeches to wear. Mother Goose. BrR
Bryant. James Russell Lowell. *Fr.* A Fable for Critics. AnNE; AP
("There is Bryant, as quiet, as cool, and as dignified.") CoBA
Bryant Dead. Paul Hamilton Hayne. DD
Bryant on His Seventieth Birthday. Whittier. DD
Bryng us in good ale, and bryng us in good ale. *See* Bring Us in Good Ale.
B's the Bus. Phyllis McGinley. *Fr.* All Around the Town. FaPON; SoPo; TiPo
Bubble, The. William Allingham. *See* Blowing Bubbles.
Bubble, The. John Banister Tabb. AA
Bubble-breasted swells the dome. Frascati's. Aldous Huxley. InPo; ViBoPo
Bubble, bubble, light and airy. Bubbles. George H. Shorey. PCH
Bubble of the silver-springing waves, The. The Poetic Land. William Caldwell Roscoe. OBVV
Bubbles. L. Nicholson. BoTP
Bubbles. George H. Shorey. PCH; PoPl
Bubbles soar and die in the sterile bottle, The. Notes for the Chart in 306. Ogden Nash. NYBP
Bubbling brook doth leap when I come by, The. Nature. Jones Very. AnAmPo; AP; HBV
Bubbling Wine. Abu Zakariya, *tr. fr. Arabic by* A. J. Arberry. TTY
Bubbs Creek Haircut. Gary Snyder. FRC
Buccaneer, The, *sel.* Richard Henry Dana.
Island, The. AnNE
Buccaneer, The. Nancy Byrd Turner. TiPo
Buccaneers, The. Young E. Allison. *See* Derelict.
Buck in the Snow, The. Edna St. Vincent Millay. AmLP; CrMA; NP; OTD
Buckdancer's Choice. James Dickey. NoP; NYBP; PoAn; PoNe (1970 ed.)
Buckee, Bene. *Unknown.* CH
Bucket, The. Samuel Woodworth. *See* Old Oaken Bucket, The.
Bucket of Bees, A. David McCord. MAP; MoAmPo (1942 ed.)
Bucket of Sea-Serpents. Howard Ant. GoYe
Bucking Bronco. *Unknown. At. to* Belle Star. ABF; CoSo
Buckingham Palace. A. A. Milne. PDV
Buckle, The. Walter de la Mare. BrR; PoRh; PTK
Buckle the spur and belt again. Lofty Lane. Edwin Gerard. PoAu-1
Buckles glitter, billies lean, The. American Twilights, 1957. James Wright. CoAP
Bucko-Mate. Samuel Schierloh. GoYe
Buckskin Joe. *Unknown.* CoSo
Bucolic. W. S. Merwin. NMP
Bucolic Eclogues, *sel.* Ethel Anderson.
Waking, Child, While You Slept. PoAu-2
Bucyrus. John Holmes. CrMA; NePoAm
Bud in the Frost, A. "Moira O'Neill." POTE
Buddha. Theodore Holmes. CoPo
Buddha. Arno Holz, *tr. fr. German by* William Ellery Leonard. AWP
Buddha at Kamakura, The. Kipling. LoBV
Buddha in Glory. Rainer Maria Rilke, *tr. fr. German by* Jessie Lemont. OnPM
Budding [*or* Boddynge] floweret[s] blushes at the light, The. Song of the Three Minstrels [*or* Mynstrelles Songe]. Thomas Chatterton. *Fr.* Aella. EiCL; EnRP; PeER; TrGrPo; ViBoPo
Budding Spring. Jack Lindsay. PoAu-1
Budding-Time Too Brief. Evaleen Stein. AA
Budging the sluggard ripples of the Somme. Hospital Barge at

Budging (continued)
Cérisy. Wilfred Owen. CBEP
Budmouth Dears. Thomas Hardy. *Fr.* The Dynasts, Pt. III, Act II, sc.i. CH; MoVE; PoVP
("When we lay where Budmouth Beach is.") LO
Buds are backward and winter lingers. At Winter's End. Sister Mary Madeleva. JKCP
Buds awake at touch of Spring, The. Spring's Immortality. Mackenzie Bell. VA
Buds of April dare not yet unfold, The. Like an April Day. Johan Sebastian Cammermeyer Welhaven. LiTW
Buen Matina. Sir John Salusbury. EIL
Buena Vista. Albert Pike. PAH
Buffalo. Florence Earle Coates. PAH
Buffalo. Roy Daniells. CaP
Buffalo. Charles Eglington. PeSA
Buffalo, The. Herbert Price. ACV
Buffalo Bill's. E. E. Cummings. AmPP; CABA; CoBA; FosPo; LiTA; NePA
(Buffalo Bill's Defunct.) AmFN
(Portrait.) AnNE; MAP; MoAB; MoAmPo; UnPo
Buffalo Creek. John Le Gay Brereton. BoAu; PoAu-1
Buffalo Dusk. Carl Sandburg. OA; PDV; TiPo
Buffalo Herds, The. Charles Mair. *Fr.* Tecumseh. VA
Buffalo Hunters, The. *Unknown.* CoSo; IHA
Buffalo loomed at the far loop of the field, The. The Difference. Winfield Townley Scott. NePoAm
Buffalo Moon and Sun-Go-Under. Reservation. David McCord. WhC
Buffalo Skinners, The. *Unknown.* ABF, *with music*; AS, *with music*; BaBo; BFSS, *with music*; CoSo, *with music*; ThLM; ViBoFo
(Boggy Creek, *cowboy vers.*) CoSo
(Jolly Lumbermen, The, *diff. vers., with music.*) TrAS
Buffaloes are gone, The. Buffalo Dusk. Carl Sandburg. OA; PDV; TiPo
Buffel's Kop. Roy Campbell. ChMP; PeSA
Bufo. Pope. *Fr.* Epistle to Dr. Arbuthnot. OBEC
Bugger Burns, *with music.* *Unknown.* OuSiCo
Bugle, The. Tennyson. *See* Bugle Song, The.
Bugle and battle-cry are still. Happy Death. John Freeman. HBMV
Bugle calls coiling through the rocky valley. A Northern Legion. Sir Herbert Read. FaBoMo; SeCePo
Bugle echoes shrill and sweet, The. Memorial Day. Joyce Kilmer. MaRV
Bugle Song. Tennyson. *Fr.* The Princess, III. ATP; BEL; BoChLi; EnLit; FaPON; GN; HBV; MCCG; MPB; PCD; PG (1945 ed.); StVeCh; TreF; VA
(Blow, Bugle, Blow.) ChTr; FaFP; GTBS-W; LiTB; LiTG; OBEV; TSW; UnS; WePo; WiR
(Bugle, The.) ShBV-2
(Horns of Elfland, The.) GBV
(Lyrics from "The Princess.") OuHeWo
(Our Echoes Roll from Soul to Soul.) MaRV
(Song: "Splendor [*or* Splendour] falls on castle walls, The.") ExPo; LoBV; MemP; NeHB; PoPl; ThWaDe; TOP
(Songs from "The Princess.") AWP; InPo; JAWP; OAEP; ViPo; WBP
(Splendor [*or* Splendour] Falls [on Castle Walls], The.) AnFE; AtBAP; BoLiVe; CBEP; CBV; CH; CoBE; ELP; EnL; EnLi-2; EPN; FaBoCh; FaBV; FiP; GoJo; GTBS; GTBS-D; GTBS-P; GTSL; ILP; InP; LoGBV; MaPo (1969 ed.); MBV-2; NoP; OBNC; OBVV; OQP; OTPC; PeVV; PoE; PoEL-5; PoIE; PoVP; RoGo; TrGrPo; ViBoPo; ViPP; VP
Bugle Song of Peace. Thomas Curtis Clark. PEDC; WBLP; WGRP
Bugle sounds the measured call to prayers, The. Sunday: New Guinea. Karl Shapiro. AmFN; PoPl
Bugler boy from barrack, A (it is over the hill). The Bugler's First Communion. Gerard Manley Hopkins. OAEP (2d ed.); VP
Bugler named Dougal MacDougal, A. Edouard. Ogden Nash. NePA; SiTL
Bugler sent a call of high romance, The. The Last Post. Robert Graves. MMA
Bugler's First Communion, The. Gerard Manley Hopkins. OAEP (2d ed.); VP
Bugles! And the Great Nation thrills and leaps to arms! The Call of the Bugles. Richard Hovey. AA
Bugle's call, The. . .the drum's low beat. "Disabled"—Armistice Day. Catherine Parmenter. PEDC
Bugles of Dreamland, The. "Fiona Macleod." OTPC (1946 ed.)
Bugles of England were blowing o'er the sea, The. For England. J. D. Burns. BoAu
Bugs. Will Stokes. BBV (1923 ed.); MoShBr
Bugville team was surely up against a rocky game, The. Casey—Twenty Years Later. S. P. McDonald. BLPA
Buick. Karl Shapiro. CaFP; CMoP; CoBA; HoPM; MiAP; MoAB; PoIE; TrGrPo (rev. ed.); ViBoPo (1958 ed.)
Buik of Alexander, The, *sel.* John Barbour.
Prologue to the Avowis of Alexander. OxBS
Build a Fence of Trust. Mary Frances Butts. *See* Today.
Build a house of gold for Punch. Conrad Aiken. *Fr.* Punch, The Immortal Liar. NP
Build a little fence of trust. Today. Mary Frances Butts. MaRV; SoP; TreFT; TRV
"Build at Kallundborg by the sea." Kallundborg Church. Whittier. BeLS; GBV
Build for yourself a strong box. Then Laugh. Bertha Adams Backus. BLPA; NeHB; PoToHe (new ed.); TreFT; WBLP; YaD
Build high your white and dazzling palaces. To February. Ethelwyn Wetherald. VA
Build me a castle of sand. Sand Castles. W. Graham Robertson. MPB
"Build me straight, O worthy Master!" The Building of the Ship. Longfellow. AmePo; AnNE; CoBA; EtS
Build on, and make thy castles high and fair. Challenge to Youth. Longfellow. *Fr.* The Castle Builder. MaRV
Build thee more stately mansions, O my soul. Oliver Wendell Holmes. *Fr.* The Chambered Nautilus. TRV
Build your houses, build your houses, build your towns. Beleaguered Cities. F. L. Lucas. HaMV; POTE
Builder, The. Caroline Giltinan. HBMV
Builder, The. Francis Sherman. CaP
Builder, The. *Unknown.* BLPA; MaRV
(Builders.) SoP
(Building a Temple.) OQP
Builder, The. Willard Wattles. AnAmPo; HBMV; OQP
Builder and maker Thou, of houses not made with hands! Robert Browning. *Fr.* Abt Vogler. OQP
Builder builded a temple, A. The Builder [*or* Builders *or* Building a Temple]. *Unknown.* BLPA; MaRV; OQP; SoP
Builder of Houses, The. Jane Cooper. AmPC
Builder who first bridged Niagara's gorge, The. Anchored to the Infinite. Edwin Markham. MaRV; OQP
Builders. Purd E. Deitz. MaRV; SoP; TRV
Builders, The. Ebenezer Elliott. VA
Builders. Hortense Flexner. HBMV
Builders, The. Longfellow. FaFP; MaRV; OHFP; TreFS
Builders. *Unknown.* *See* Builder, The.
Builders, The. Henry van Dyke. OQP
"Grant us the knowledge that we need," *sel.* TrPWD
Builders, The. Judith Wright. SeCePo
Builder's Lesson, A. John Boyle O'Reilly. PoLF
"How shall I a habit break?" *sel.* PoToHe (new ed.)
Builders of the State. Richard Watson Gilder. PoRL
Building. G. K. Chesterton. SoP
Building. Ella Wheeler Wilcox. OQP
Building a House. Dick Gallup. ANYP
Building a Skyscraper. James S. Tippett. MPB
Building a Temple. *Unknown.* *See* Builder, The.
Building for Eternity. N. B. Sargent. BLPA
Building in Stone. Sylvia Townsend Warner. MoBrPo
Building of London, The. Layamon, *tr. fr. Middle English.* *Fr.* The Brut. MeEV
Building of Sand. Grant Code. FiSC
Building of the *Long Serpent*, The. Longfellow. *Fr.* Tales of a Wayside Inn: The Musician's Tale, Pt. I. EtS
Building of the Nest, The. Margaret Sangster. DD; HBV; HBVY
Building of the Ship, The. Longfellow. AmePo; AnNE; CoBA; EtS
Sels.
Ship of State, The. FaBoBe; HBVY; MaRV; NeHB; OHIP; OQP; PAL; PAP
(Republic, The.) AA; DD; HH; MC; PAH; WGRP
(Sail On, O Ship of State!) FaPON; PoFr; TreF
("Thou, too, sail on, O Ship of State!") PaA; PGD; YaD
"Then the Master with a gesture." OHFP

Building the Bridge for Him. Will Allen Dromgoole. *See* Bridge Builder, The.
Buildings are fountains jetting stone. Waterfalls of Stone. Louis Ginsberg. PoMa
Buke of the Howlat, The, *sel.* Sir Richard Holland.
"Roye Robert the Bruss the rayke he avowit, The." OxBS
Bulb, A. Richard Kendall Munkittrick. AA
Bulbul, The ("Bulbul hummeth like a book, The"). Sir Owen Seaman. NA
Bulbul Wail'd, The. "Oh Rose. all night I sing." Song without a Sound. Sir Edwin Arnold. *Fr.* With Sa'di in the Garden. VA
Bulge, The. George Johnston. MoCV; PV
Bulging rampart streaked with pink and jade, The. The Watchers. Charles Spear. AnNZ
Bulkeley, Hunt, Willard. Hosmer, Meriam, Flint. Hamatreya. Emerson. AmePo; AmP; AmPP; AP; CoBA; MAmP; MWA-1; NoP; OxBA; PAn; PoE; PoEL-4; SeCeV; WoL. *See also* Minott Lee, Willard, Hosmer...
Bull, The. Ralph Hodgson. AnFE; BrPo; EnLi-2 (1949 ed.); EnLit; LiTG; LiTM (rev. ed.); MoAB; MoBrPo; MoVE; OBMV; ShBV-2; TOP; YT
"See an old unhappy bull," *sel.* OA
Bull, The. Freda Laughton. NeIP
Bull, The. Francis Maguire. JKCP (1955 ed.)
Bull, The. William Carlos Williams. LiTM (1970 ed.); MoVE; NoP; TDP; TwCP
Bull, The. Judith Wright. PoAu-2
Bull be took bad, says old Sam—wunnot fancy 'is fodder, Th'. From My Rural Pen. T. S. Watt. FiBHP
Bull Calf, The. Irving Layton. OBCV; PeCV
Bull Fight, The. L. Worthington Green. SCC
Bull Shit. Jayne Cortez. WSL
"Bull, the Fleece are cramm'd, and not a room, The." Audley Court. Tennyson. PeVV
Bull with the fierce eyes that none dares look at. Praises of King George VI. A. Z. Ngani. PeSA
Bulldozer, The. Donald A. Stauffer. WaP
Bulletin of the boarding school, The. Under All This Slate. James Hayford. NePoAm-2
Bullfrog. Ted Hughes. NYBP
Bullocks, The. Alex Comfort. FaBoTw
Bullocky. Judith Wright. BoAV; MoAuPo; NeLNL; PoAu-2; SeCePo
Bullocky Bill. *Unknown.* PoAu-1
Bull's eyes and targets. *Unknown.* OxNR
Bullwhacker, The. *Unknown.* ABF; CoSo
Bully, The. *At. to the* Earl of Rochester *and to* Thomas D'Urfey. CBEP; InvP; SeCL
(Song: Noble Name of Spark, The.) SeCePo
Bully ship and a bully crew, A. Sacramento. *Unknown.* SoAmSa
Bully ship and bully crew, A. Lowlands, *vers.* III. *Unknown.* ShS
Bulrush stood on the river's brim, A. The Vainglorious Oak and the Modest Bulrush. Guy Wetmore Carryl. TSW
Bum. W. Dayton Wedgefarth. BLPA
Bumblebeaver, The. Kenyon Cox. *Fr.* Mixed Beasts. RIS; TiPo
Bumble Bee. Margaret Wise Brown. PDV
Bumblebee. Edna D. Wood. PCH
Bumble-Bee and Clover. *Unknown.* GFA
Bumblebee, I'm sure I like you. Bumblebee. Edna D. Wood. PCH
Bumblebee went flying, A. The Easter Airplane. Carolyn R. Freeman. GFA
Bumble-Bug and Bumble-Bee. Famous Battle of Bumble-Bug and Bumble-Bee. *Unknown.* FTB
Bumper of good liquor, A. Sheridan. *Fr.* The Duenna, II, iii. WhC
Bumpety, bumpety, bump. Fan, the Filly. Wilfrid Thorley. BoTP
Bums, on Waking. James Dickey. CBV; NYBP
Bunch of Grapes, The. George Herbert. AnAnS-1; MaMe; MeP; SCEP-1
Bunch of grass, a wild rose, A. That's July. Mary F. Butts. YeAr
Bunch of Roses, A. John Banister Tabb. HBVY; PRWS; SP
Bunch of the boys were whooping it up in the Dixie-Belle, on Lex, A. The Tale of the Dixie-Belle. Frank Chase. InME
Bunch of the boys were whooping it up in the Malamute saloon, A. The Shooting of Dan McGrew. Robert W. Service. BeLS; FaBoBe; FaFP; MaC; NeHB; PoLF; PoRA; TreF; WHW
Bunch of Wild Flowers. Luke Zilles. RePo
Bunches of Grapes. Walter de la Mare. BOHV; GoJo; HBV; HBVY; MoShBr; OTPC; PoRH; SUS; TiPo
Bundle is a funny thing, A. Bundles. John Farrar. BrR; ChBR; GFA; PCH; TiPo
Bundles. John Farrar. BrR; ChBR; GFA; PCH; TiPo
Bundles. Carl Sandburg. MAP; MoAmPo
Bung Yer Eye. Stewart Edward White. ABF; IHA; RePo
Bungalows, The. John Ashbery. CoAP
Bungiana, *sel.* *Unknown.*
Pacific Engagement, The. WhC
Bunhill's Fields. Anne Ridler. NeBP
Bunk-House Orchestra, The. Badger Clark. SCC
Bunker Hill. George Henry Calvert. BeLS; DD, *abr.*; FaBoBe, *abr.*; MC
Bunker Hill. Nathaniel Niles. *See* American Hero, The.
Bunks in the bogus square, The. Another Island Groupage. Kenward Elmslie. ANYP
Bunny Rabbit ("Bunny creeps out and caresses his nose"). *Unknown.* BoTP
Buns for Tea. Dorothy M. Richardson YT
Bunthorne's Recitative and Song ("Am I alone"). W. S. Gilbert. *See* Recitation and Song.
Bunthorne's Song ("If you're anxious for to shine"). W. S. Gilbert. *Fr.* Patience. FiBHP; LiTB; NBM; SiTL; VaPo
(Aesthete, The.) ALV; EnLi-2
(Song: Bunthorne.) PoVP
Bunyip, The. Douglas Stewart. MoAuPo; OA
Bunyip and the Whistling Kettle, The. John Manifold. LiTB; LiTM; NeLNL; PoAu-2; PoMS; SiTL; WaP
Buonaparte. Tennyson. PoVP; Sonn
Buoy-Bell, The. Charles Tennyson Turner. EtS; PeVV; Sonn; VA
Buoy like a man in a red sou'wester, A. Beginning to Squall. May Swenson. NYTB
Burbank with a Baedeker; Bleistein with a Cigar ("Burbank crossed a little bridge"). T. S. Eliot. HBMV; MAP; MoAmPo (1942 ed.)
Burd Ellen and Young Tamlane ("Burd Ellen sits in her bower windowe"). *Unknown.* ESPB
Burd Helen was her mother's dear. Broughty Wa's. *Unknown.* ESPB
Burd Isabel and Earl Patrick. *Unknown.* BaBo; ESPB
Burden, The. "Marianne Farningham." OQP
Burden, The. Toyohiko Kagawa. MaRV
Burden, The. Francesca Yetunde Pereira. PBA
Burden of an ancient rhyme, The. Poems, CXL. Walter Savage Landor. PG
Burden of Everyday, The. Buddhadeva Bose, *tr. fr Bengali by* Buddhadeva Bose. LiTW
Burden of fair women, The. Vain delight. A Ballad of Burdens. Swinburne. EnLi-2; PoVP
Burden of Junk, The. John Glassco. OBCV
Burden of Love, The. "Owen Innsley." AA
Burden of Nineveh, The. Dante Gabriel Rossetti. MaVP; OAEP; PoVP
Burden of Strength The. George Meredith. EPN
Burden of Tyre, The, *sel.* Christopher Brennan.
"Let them devour and be devour'd!" NeLNL
Burdened with years and full of sinfulness. A Prayer for Strength. Michaelangelo. OnPM
Burdens. William Haskell Simpson. *Fr.* In Arizona. NP
Burdens of Water Jars. Burdens. William Haskell Simpson. *Fr.* In Arizona. NP
Burdock leaves beside the hedge, The. A Brisk Wind. William Barnes. UnPo (3d ed.)
Burgeis, thou haste so blowen atte the cole. Too Much Sex. *Unknown.* MeEL
Burges, *with music.* *Unknown.* ABF
Burges, B. R. Lieut. Second Bttn. The Royal Ulster. In Memoriam. Lewis MacAdams. ANYP
Burgesses of Calais, The. Laurence Minot. ACP
Burghers' Battle, The. William Morris. PoVP; VA
Burglar Bill. "F. Anstey." CenHV; FiBHP
Burglar of Babylon, The. Elizabeth Bishop. NYBP
Burgundian Carol. Bernard de la Monnoye, *tr. fr. French by* Percy Dearmer. UnS
(Patapan.) ChBR

Burial. Paulin Joachim, *tr. fr. French by* Oliver Bernard. TTY
Burial, The. Kipling. BoSA
Burial. Richard C. Raymond. NYTB
Burial. Mark Van Doren. MoBS
Burial, The. John Webster. *See* All the Flowers of the Spring.
Burial at Sea. E. J. Pratt. *Fr.* The *Roosevelt* and the *Antinoe.* CaP
Burial Hymn. Henry Hart Milman. VA
Burial of an Infant, The. Henry Vaughan. OAEP
Burial of Barber. Whittier. PAH
Burial of King Cormac, The. Sir Samuel Ferguson. AnIL; IrPN; OnYI
Burial of Latané, The. John Reuben Thompson. PAH
Burial of Moses. Cecil Frances Alexander. BeLS; BLPA; BLRP; GN; HBV; NeHB; OTPC; WBLP
Burial of Robert Browning, The. "Michael Field." VA
Burial of Saint Brendan, The. Padraic Colum. OxBI
Burial of Sir John McKenzie, The. Jessie Mackay. AnNZ
Burial of Sir John Moore after [*or* at] Corunna, The. Charles Wolfe. AnIV; BBV; BEL; CBEP; ChTR; EnRP; EPN; FaFP; FaPL; FOL; GN; GTBS; GTBS-D; GTBS-P; GTBS-W; GTSE; GTSL; HBV; HBVY; InP; LiTG; MaC; MCCG; MemP; NeHB; OBEV; OBRV; OnSP; OnYI; OTPC (1923 ed.); PaPo; PCD; OxBI; PoRA; RoGo; TOP; TreF; WaaP; WBLP; WHA
Burial of Terror, The. Carl Bode. ToPo
Burial of the Dane, The. Henry Howard Brownell. AA; HBV
Burial of the Dead. John Keble. OBEV (1st ed.)
Burial of the Dead, The. Prudentius, *tr. fr. Latin by* Helen Waddell. LiTW
Burial of the Linnet. Juliana Horatia Ewing. PRWS
Burial of the Minnisink. Longfellow. LaNeLa
Burial of the Spirit. Richard Hughes. MoBrPo
Burial of the Young Love. Waring Cuney. BANP; PoNe
Burial Song. *Unknown, tr. fr. Chinese by* Arthur Waley. WoL
Buriall. Henry Vaughan. SeCV-1
Burials. George Crabbe. *Fr.* The Parish Register Pt. III. EiCL
Sels.
"My record ends." OBRV
"There was, 'tis said, and I believe, a time." EiPP
Buriel at Springs. James Schuyler. ANYP; CoAP
Buried Child, The. Dorothy Wellesley. Deserted House: Epilogue. DTC; GTBS-D; OBMV
Buried Fire. Emperor Meiji, *tr. fr. Japanese by* Asataro Miyamori., OnPM
Buried in the shades of horrid night. On His Late Espoused Saint. Sir Kenelm Digby. ACP
Buried Lake, The. Allen Tate. CrMA
Buried Life, The. Matthew Arnold. BEL; BoLiVe; BoPe; BWP; EnL; EnLi-2; EnLit; EPN; ForPo; MaVP; MBW-2; OAEP; OuHeWo; PoFS; PoVP; SeCeV; VA; ViPo; ViPP; VP
Buried statue through the marble gleams, The. Form. Eva Gore-Booth. MaRV
Buried Thy Sins. *Unknown.* SoP
Burke and Wills. Ken Barratt. BoAV; PoAu-2
Burke and Wills, *sels.* Colin Thiele. NeLNL
Final Soliloquy, The.
Wills Dies in Solitude.
Burlesque of Lope de Vega. Samuel Johnson. *See* If the Man Who Turnips Cries.
Burly and big, his books among. Hodge, the Cat. "Susan Coolidge." CIV
Burly, dozing humble-bee. The Humble-Bee. Emerson. AA; AmePo; AmPP; AnNE; FaPON; GN; HBV; HBVY; LaNeLa; LHV; OTPC; OxBA
Burma Hills. Bernard Gutteridge. WaP
Burman Lover, The. Calder Campbell. *See* Ossian's Serenade.
Burn, Baby, Burn. Marvin E. Jackmon. BF
Burn me, Tongue of Fire! Paraclete. Jorge de Lima. PoFr
Burn on, sweet fire, for I live by that fuel. Parthenophil and Parthenope, LXXXVII. Barnabe Barnes. TuPP
Burn Out Burn Quick ("Burn out, my life, burn quick"). Abraham Reisen, *tr. fr. Yiddish by* Joseph Leftwich. TrJP
Burn Ovid with the rest. Lovers will find. Penal Law. Austin Clarke. ELU; GTBS-P
Burn stilly, thou; and come with me. To a Candle. Walter de la Mare. ChMP; ELP; GTBS-D
Burncombe Hollow. William Barnes. OBNC
Burned and dusty garden said, The. An Athenian Garden. Trumbull Stickney. NCEP
Burned in this element. Letter II. W. S. Graham. NePoEA
Burning. Galway Kinnell. CoAP
Burning, *abr.* Gary Snyder. *Fr.* Myths & Texts. NeAP
Sels.
Amitabha's Vow, X. NaP
John Muir on Mt. Ritter, VIII. FlW
Maitreya the Future Buddha, IV. NaP
"Night here, a covert," IX. NaP
"Spikes of new smell driven up nostrils," XIII. NaP
"Stone-flake and salmon," XV. NaP
Text, The, XVII. NaP
Burning—at first—would be probably worst, The. Heaven and Hell. James Kenneth Stephen. CenHV
Burning Babe, The. Robert Southwell. ACP; AnAnS-1; AnFE; AtBAP; BEL; BoW; CABA; CAW; CBEP; CBV; CH; CoBE; EIL; EnLit; FaBoCh; FaBoEn; FlW; GoBC; HBV; HoPM; ILP; LiTB; LiTG; LoBV; LoGBV; MaRV; MeP; MePo; NoP; OBEV; OBSC; OxBoCh; PoEL-2; PoG; PoIE; PoLi; PTK; ReEn; ReIE; SeCePo; SiCE; StJW; StP; TOP; TrGrPo; TuPP; UnPo (1st ed.); ViBoPo
("As I in hoary winter's night stood shivering in the snow.") EG
Burning Bush. Karle Wilson Baker. HBMV
Burning Bush. Martin Feinstein. TrJP
Burning Bush, The. Norman Nicholson. EaLo; NeBP; SeCePo
Burning Bush. Louis Untermeyer. MAP; MoLP
Burning Bush, The. Henry van Dyke. TRV
Burning eye, The. The Skeptic. Loring Williams. FiSC
Burning-Glass, The. Walter de la Mare. StJW
Burning in the Night. Thomas Clayton Wolfe. *arr. in verse by* John S. Barnes. AmFN
Burning Love Letters. Howard Moss. HoPM
Burning Mountain. W. S. Merwin. NYBP
Burning of Auchindown. *Unknown. See* Willie Macintosh.
Burning of Books, The. Bertolt Brecht, *tr. fr. German by* H. R. Hays. PoPl
Burning of Jamestown, The. Thomas Dunn English. PAH
Burning of the Law, The. Mëir of Rothenburg, *tr. fr. Hebrew by* Nina Davis Salaman. TrJP
Burning of the Leaves, The. Laurence Binyon. ChMP; DTC; GTBS-P; MoVE; POTE
"Now is the time for the burning of the leaves," *sel.* GTBS-D
Burning of the Temple, The. Isaac Rosenberg. FaBoMo; TrJP
Burning the Bee-Tree. Ruth Pitter. POTE
Burning the Christmas Greens. William Carlos Williams. AP; CABL; CoBMV; LiTM (1970 ed.); MoPo; NePA; TwAmPo
Burning the Letters. Randall Jarrell. MiAP; MoAB; MoAmPo (1950 ed.)
Burning upon some hidden shore. The Lighthouse. Marjorie Wilson. BoTP
Burnished, burned-out, still burning as the year. The Public Garden. Robert Lowell. AP; NoP; PoeP; PoRA (rev. ed.)
Burnished with copper light, burnished. Mending the Bridge. Douglas Stewart. AnNZ
Burns. Fitz-Greene Halleck. AA
Burns. Whittier. CoBA
Burns and His Highland Mary, *with music. Unknown.* ShS
Burn's Log Camp, *with music. Unknown.* ShS
Burnt Bridge, The. Louis MacNeice. SiSw
Burnt Lands. Sir Charles G. D. Roberts. VA
Burnt lawns and iron-bound pastures. Midsummer. Sybil Horatia Calverley. BiS
Burnt Norton. T. S. Eliot. *Fr.* Four Quartets. AnFE; AtBAP; CABL; CMoP; CoAnAm; LiTG; LiTM (rev. ed.); MoAB; MoAmPo (1950 ed.); MoPo; PAn; PoE; TwAmPo
Sels.
"Garlic and sapphires in the mud," *fr.* II. GTBS-W
"Words move, music moves," *fr.* V. UnS; ViBoPo (1958 ed.)
Burnt Ship, A. John Donne. MaMe; WaaP
Burr Oaks, *sel.* Richard Eberhart.
Attic, The. MoAB
Burro, The. J. J. Gibbons. PoOW
Burro once, sent by express, A. Advice to Travelers. Walker Gibson. NePoAm-2
Burro with the Long Ears. *Tr. fr. Navajo Indian by* Hilda Faunce Wetherill. FaPON

Burrowing mole lives under the ground, The. The Mole. Edith King. GFA
Bursting with pride, the loath'd impostume swells. My Lord All-Pride. Earl of Rochester. PeRV
Bursts from a rending East in flaws. Hard Weather. George Meredith. EPN; Po; ViPP
Bury Her at Even. "Michael Field." CAW; OBMV
Bury him deep. So damned a work should lie. Fragment. Thomas Lovell Beddoes. ELU
Bury me deep when I am dead. Requiescat. Rosamund Marriott Watson. HBV
Bury Me Not on the Chickamauga, *with music. Unknown.* BFSS
Bury Me Not on the Lone Prairie. *Unknown. See* Dying Cowboy, The ("Oh, bury me not. . .").
Bury Me Out on the Prairie, *with music. Unknown.* CoSo
"Bury me," the bishop said. St. Swithin. Daniel Henderson. HBMV; ShM
Bury the Dragon's Teeth! Bury Them. Henry Howard Brownell. PAH
Bury the Great Duke. Ode on the Death of the Duke of Wellington. Tennyson. BEL; EmBrPo; HBV; OBVV; PCD; PoVP; TOP; UnPo (1st ed.); VA; ViPo; ViPP
Bury Them. Henry Howard Brownell. PAH
Bury your heart in some deep green hollow. Saturday Market. Charlotte Mew. HBMV
Burying Ground by the Ties. Archibald MacLeish. Frescoes for Mr. Rockefeller's City, III. AmPP (4th ed.); MAP; MoAmPo; NAMP; UnPo; WoL; WOW
Bus, The. Leonard Cohen. CAD
Bus, The. "Peter." BoTP
Bus driver,/ Tram driver. We Thank You! L. E. Cox. BoTP
Bus Ride. Selma Robinson. *Fr.* Ferry Ride. FaPON
Bus rides like a room across the night, The. The Sea Dike. M. Vasalis. LiTW
Bus Trip, The. Joel Oppenheimer. NeAP
Bush, The. James Lister Cuthbertson. BoAu
Bush, The, *sels.* Bernard O'Dowd.
"As many, Mother, are your moods and forms."
Last Stanzas of "The Bush." BoAu
"Where is Australia, singer, do you know?" PoFr
Bush aboon Traquair, The. John Campbell Shairp. OBVV
Bush Christening, A. Andrew Barton Paterson. PoAu-1
Bush-Fiddle, The. Judith Green. PoAu-2
Bush Goblins. H. M. Green. BoAu
Bush on Mount Venus, The. Donald Finkel. CoPo
Bush that has most briers and bitter fruit, The. The Barberry-Bush. Jones Very. AP
Bushed. Earle Birney. MoCV; OBCV; PeCV
Bushes lean in the wind, The. Need of an Angel. Raymond Souster. CaP
Bushfeller, The. Eileen Duggan. AnNZ; JKCP (1955 ed.)
Bushman's Song, A. Andrew Barton Paterson. BoAu; PoAu-1
Bushman's stature is not great, The. The Fat-buttocked Bushmen. Earnest A. Hooton. WhC
Bushrangers, The. Edward Harrington. PoAu-1
Busie enquiring heart, what wouldst thou know? The Discharge. George Herbert. MaMe
Busie old foole, unruly Sunne. *See* Busy old fool, unruly Sun.
Business and bluebirds waken first in spring. Spring's on the Curb. Hildegarde Flanner. AnAmPo
Business as Usual 1946. A. J. M. Smith. NMP
Business Girls. John Betjeman. WePo
Business Is Business. Berton Braley. WBLP
Businessman of Alicante, The. Philip Levine. NaP
Business Man's Prayer, A. William Ludlum. BLRP
Business Men. Ch'en Tzu-ang, *tr. fr. Chinese by* Arthur Waley. MoPW; OnPM; WoL
Business of the Day, The. Patience Strong. SoP
Business of the lambing ewes would make me, The. Eagles over the Lambing Paddock. Ernest G. Moll. BoAu; PoAu-2
Businesse. George Herbert. MaMe
Busk ye, busk ye, my bonny bonny bride. The Braes of Yarrow. William Hamilton of Bangour. CEP; EiCL; EiPP; OBEC
Bussy d'Ambois, *sels.* George Chapman.
"As cedars beaten with continual storms," *fr.* I, i. ViBoPo
"Ile sooth his plots: and strow my hate with smiles," *fr.* IV, ii. PoEL-2
Invocation, An: "I long to know," *fr.* V, iii. ViBoPo
Now all ye peaceful regents of the night," *fr.* II, ii. LO; PoEL-2
"Now shall we see, that nature hath no end," *fr.* V, ii. PoEL-2
"Since I am free,/ Offending no just law, let no law make," *fr.* II, i. MyFE
Bust, The. W. H. Davies. MoPW
Bustan, The, *sels.* Sadi, *tr. fr. Persian by* Sir Edwin Arnold.
Dancer, The. AWP; JAWP; OuHeWo; WBP
Great Physician, The. AWP; OuHeWo
Busted Lute, The: a Baedeker. Raymond Dipalma *and* Stephen Shrader. QAH
Buster's got a popper gun. To China. Leroy F. Jackson. StVeCh (1940 ed.)
Bustle in a house, The. Emily Dickinson. AmePo; AmLP; AmPP; AnFE; AP; APA; CBEP; CoAnAm; CoBA; DiPo; ELU; FaBV; MaPo; MoRP; NePA; NoP; OnPM; OxBA; PoEL-5; PoLF; StP; WGRP
Busts and Bosoms Have I Known. *Unknown.* ErPo; PV
Busy Bee, The. Isaac Watts. *See* How Doth the Little Busy Bee.
Busy Body, The. Rachel Field. InMe
Busy Carpenters. James S. Tippett. SoPo; StVeCh
Busy, curious, thirsty fly! On a Fly Drinking Out of [*or* from] His Cup [*or* The Fly *or* To a Fly *or* An Anacreontick]. William Oldys. CBEP; EG; EiCL; FaFP; GoTP; GTBS-W; LiTG; OBEC; OBEV; OTPC (1923 ed.); TDP; TrGrPo; ViBoPo
Busy Day. James Laughlin. OnHM
Busy Day, A. *Unknown.* PCH
(Cock's on the Housetop, The.) OTPC (1946 ed.)
(Summer.) RIS
Busy day is over, The. The Happy Hour. Mary Frances Butts. DD
Busy Heart, The. Rupert Brooke. HBV; MemP; MoBrPo
Busy Man, The. *Unknown.* SoP
Busy [*or* Busie] old fool, unruly Sun. The Sun [*or* Sunne] Rising. John Donne. AnAnS-1; AnFE; AtBAP; BoLiVe; BWP; CABA; CBEP; CBV; DiPo; EG; EnRePo; EP; ExPo; GTSE; ILP; InvP; LiTB; LiTG; LiTL; LoBV; MaMe; MaPo (1969 ed.); MBW-1; MeLP; MePo; MeWo; NoP; OAEP; PoAn; PoE; PoEL-2; PoeP; PoFr; PoFS; PoIE; ReEn; ReIE; SCEP-1; SeCePo; SeCeV; SeCP; SeCV-1; SeEP; TrGrPo; TuPP; UnTE; VaPo
Busy Person, A. Alfarata Hilton. PCH
Busy wind is out today, The. My Kite. Beatrice Brown. GFA
Busy? Yes, Lord, in the midst of the conflict. Inventory. Ellen McKay Trimmer. SoP
But/ if it/ isn't. Abroad. Alfred Starr Hamilton. QAH
But a little while ago. Winter and Spring. *Unknown.* BoTP
But afar on the headland exalted. By the North Sea, VII. Swinburne. PoVP
But Agamemnon, as the rites demand. Preparation of the Pyre for Patroclus. Homer. *Fr.* The Iliad, XXIII. UnPo (1st ed.)
But ah! how unsincere are all our joys! The Fire of London. Dryden. *Fr.* Annus Mirabilis. SeEP
But ah! let me under some Kentish hill. Phineas Fletcher. *Fr.* The Purple Island. ViBoPo
But, ah! Maecenas is yclad in clay. Spenser. *Fr.* The Sheepheardes Calender: October. MyFE
But all my night has been sleepless! And now, at dawn. The Swallows. Agathias Scholasticus. LiTW
But All the Roses. Claire Goll, *tr. fr. French by* Claire Goll. OnPM
But all too soon, the much-loved father died. His Youth. John Oxenham. StJW
But are ye [*or* you] sure the news is true? *See* And are ye sure the news is true?
But Art Thou Come, Dear Saviour? *Unknown.* OxBoCh
But as they left the dark'ning heath. Flodden. Sir Walter Scott. *Fr.* Marmion, VI. ELP; FOL
But Bacchus was not so content: he quyght forsooke their land. King Midas. Ovid. *Fr* Metamorphoses. CTC
But he contented: when that fell arrest. Sonnets, LXXIV. Shakespeare. CBEP; OBSC; PoeP; Sonn
But beggars about midsummer go breadless to supper. Prayer for the Poor. William Langland. *Fr.* The Vision of Piers Plowman. PoFr; PoLi
But, breaking day, their several flutes. The Moment. Kendrick Smithyman. AnNZ
But bringing up the rear of this bright host. At the Gate of

But (continued)
Heaven [*or* The Archangel]. Byron. *Fr.* The Vision of Judgment. LoBV; OBRV
But by this time tongues 'gan to rest. Charles Darby. *Fr.* Bacchanalia; or, A Description of a Drunken Club. PeRV
But Can See Better There, and Laughing There. Gwendolyn Brooks. *See* "Pygmies Are Pygmies Still, Though Percht on Alps."
But chief by numbers of industrious hands. A Nation's Wealth. John Dyer. *Fr.* The Fleece. OBEC
But Choose. John Holmes. MiAP
But Christ can give thee heart who loveth thee. Christ Can Give Thee Heart. Christina Rossetti. ChIP
But did no paradise itself contain. Age of Innocence. Graham Hough. PoRA (rev. ed.)
But do not let us quarrel any more. Andrea del Sarto. Robert Browning. ATP; BEL; CABA; CoBE; CTC; DiPo; EnL; EnLi-2; EnLit; EPN; FosPo; HBV; MaPo; MaVP; MBW-2; NoP; OAEP; PAn; PoE; PoEL-5; PoVP; StP; TOP; ViPo; ViPP; VP; WHA
But do we truly mourn our soldier dead. For Decoration Day, I. Rupert Hughes. AA
But does every man feel like this at forty. The Second Life. Edwin Morgan. OxBS
But dwell in darkness, for your god is blind. A Coronet for His Mistress Philosophy, II. George Chapman. Sonn
But evening now. Alfred Domett. *Fr.* Ranolf and Amohia. AnNZ
But Fear Thou Not, O Jacob. Jeremiah, XLVI: 27-28, Bible, *O.T.* TrJP
But for a brief. A Grasshopper. Richard Wilbur. CBV; NoP
But for an hour's sleep in a filthy bed. Recall. Reed Whittemore. NYBP
But for Lust. Ruth Pitter. FaBoTw
But for the steady wash of rain. No Country You Remember. Robert Mezey. AmPC; PIA; ToPo
But for your Terror. To Death. Oliver St. John Gogarty. MaRV; OBMV; OtMeF
But Gebir when he heard of her approach. Walter Savage Landor. *Fr* Gebir. OBRV
But give me for my soul, those beauteous maids. Those Beauteous Maids. Moses ibn Ezra. TrJP
But Give Me Holly, Bold and Jolly. Christina Rossetti. *Fr.* Sing-Song. BrR; ChBR; TiPo
But give them me, the mouth, the eyes, the brow! Eurydice to Orpheus [*or* Orpheus and Eurydice]. Robert Browning. CTC; EPN
But God. Annie Johnson Flint. SoP
But God has no machine. Eclogue: Queen Elizabeth's Day. John Davidson. BrPo
But God is never so far off. God's Presence. Frederick William Faber. SoP
But God's Own Descent. Robert Frost. *Fr.* Kitty Hawk. EaLo; MoRP
But, gracious [*or* gratious] God, how well dost Thou provide. The Church's Testimony [*or* Confession of Faith *or* Conversion]. Dryden. *Fr.* The Hind and the Panther, I. ACP; CAW; PoLi; TrPWD; UnPo (1st ed.)
But grant, in public, men sometimes are shown. Woman's Ruling Passions. Pope. *Fr.* Moral Essays. OBEC
But grant, the virtues of temp'rate prime. Life's Last Scene. Samuel Johnson. *Fr.* The Vanity of Human Wishes. OBEC; SeCePo
But, grant thy poetry should find success. A Dissuasive against Poetry. John Oldham. *Fr.* A Satire. PeRV; ViBoPo
But, gratious God, how well dost Thou provide. *See* But, gracious God. . .
But half of me is woman grown. To a Vagabond. Constance Davies Woodrow. CaP
But hark! a sound is stealing on my ear. Charles Stuart Calverley. *Fr.* Beer. FiBHP
But, hark, 'tis late; the Whistlers knock from Plough. Evening Prayer. Edward Benlowes. *Fr.* Theophila. FaBoEn
But hark! What hubbub now is this that comes. Charles Harpur. *Fr.* The Temple of Infamy. PoAu-1
But harken, my American, my own. The Errand Imperious. Edwin Markham. PAL; PGD
But haste we!—'Tis that merry time of year. Spring. William Allingham. IrPN
But he comes! the Messiah of royalty comes! George the Fourth in Ireland. Byron. OBRV
But he [*or* He *or* Pa] followed the pair to Pawtucket. Limerick. *Unknown.* *Fr.* That Nantucket Limerick. HBV (8th ed.); LiBL; LiTG; TreF
But he his wonted pride. Satan and His Host. Milton. *Fr.* Paradise Lost, I. OBS
But He Was Cool. Don L. Lee BP
"But hear. If you stay, and the child be born." In the Restaurant. Thomas Hardy. Satires of Circumstance, XI. MoAB; MoBrPo
But here, at starting, I must just premise. John Moultrie. *Fr.* Sir Launfal. OBRV
But His lone cross and crown of thorns. Easter. John Oxenham. OQP
"But hold y. . .hold y. . .," says Robin. The Jolly Pinder of Wakefield. *Unknown.* ESPB
But how can I describe the doleful sight. Vision of Sorrow. Thomas Sackville. *Fr.* Induction to "The Mirror for Magistrates." LoBV
But How It Came from Earth. Conrad Aiken. MAP; MoAB; MoAmPo
But how many months [*or* monthes] be in the year [*or* yeere]. Robin Hood and the Curtal Friar. *Unknown.* ESPB; OBB
But how many moons be in the year? Robin Hood and the Curtal Friar. *Unknown.* BuBa
But how shall I, unblamed, express. Dress. Henry Luttrell. *Fr.* Advice to Julia. OBRV
But how shall we this union well express? The Soul and the Body [*or* In What Manner the Soul Is United to the Body]. Sir John Davies. *Fr.* Nosce Teipsum. CTC; LiTB; OBSC; PoEL-2
But I Am Growing Old and Indolent. Robinson Jeffers. AP
But "I" being less than soul, of dustier plume. Some Lines in Three Parts, II. Peter Viereck. MoAmPo (1950 ed.)
But I came from the dancing place. Ashore. "Laurence Hope." HBV
But I Do Not Need Kindness. Gregory Corso. CoPo; NeAP
But I don't know. Psyche. Alfred Starr Hamilton. QAH
But I hae dream'd a dreary dream. Fey. *Unknown.* OtMeF
But I remember when the fight was done. The Staff Officer. Shakespeare. King Henry IV, Pt. I, *fr.* I, iii. OtMeF
But I Shall Weep. Beatrice Redpath. CaP
But I think the king of that country comes out from his tireless host. Henry van Dyke. *Fr.* The Gospel of Labor. WGRP
But I want you to understand. The Gardener at Thirty. Jascha Kessler. AmPC
But I *was* dead, an hour or more. Escape. Robert Graves. BrPo; ILP; MoBrPo
But I was first of all the kings who drew. Tennyson. *Fr.* Idylls of the King: Guinevere. GTSL; YAT
But if that I may have truly. Back and Side Go Bare [*or* A Song of Ale]. *At. to.* William Stevenson. *Fr.* Gammer Gurton's Needle. AnFE; OBSC; PoRA; UnPo
But if the darkness and corruption leave. Christina Rossetti. *Fr.* Remember. LO
But if thou needs will hunt, be ruled by me. Shakespeare. *Fr.* Venus and Adonis. SiCE
But in the crowding darkness not a word did they say. The Old Marrieds. Gwendolyn Brooks. AmNP; PoNe
But in the darkest hour of night. Only a Beauty, Only a Power. John Masefield. MoRP
But in the evening the oppression lifted. W. H. Auden. *Fr.* In Time of War. EnLit
But in the last days it shall come to pass. And They Shall Beat Their Swords into Plowshares [*or* Neither Shall They Learn War Any More]. Micah, Bible, *O.T.* TreF; TRV
But it could never be true. Devil's Dream. Kenneth Fearing. CMoP
"But it is not Black," they will tell you, "any longer." The "Black" Country. D. J. Enright. HaMV
But it seems that something has happened that has never happened before. When the Church Is No Longer Regarded. T. S. Eliot. *Fr.* The Rock. MaRV
"But it was even thou. . ." Roundel of Passion-Tide. *Unknown.* CAW
But, knowing now that they would have her speak. The Defence [*or* Defense] of Guenevere. William Morris. EnL; EnLi-2; EnLit; PoVP; StP; ViPo; ViPP
But, leaving these vain trifles of men's souls. Christopher Marlowe. *Fr.* Dr. Faustus. MyFE

But let applause be dealt in all we may. The Vicar. George Crabbe. *Fr.* The Borough. OBNC
But letting go. . .hands, eyes, teeth, body, all ways. The People, IV. "Robin Hyde." AnNZ
But, like a graven image. Herminius's Horse. Macaulay. *Fr.* Lays of Ancient Rome: The Battle of Lake Regillus. PoG
But lo! at length the day is lingered out. Francis Thompson. *Fr.* Sister Songs. OBMV
But, lo! from forth a copse that neighbours by. The Courser and the Jennet. Shakespeare. *Fr.* Venus and Adonis. LoBV; OBSC
But lo we see, we touch, sayeth John. Of the Holy Eucharist. *Unknown.* ACP (1952 ed.)
But lo, what think you; suddenly. A Moon Rainbow. Robert Browning. BoC
But looke where sadly the poore wretch comes reading. Shakespeare. *Fr.* Hamlet, II, ii. AtBAP
"But Lord," she said, "my shoulders still are strong." At the Top of the Road. Charles Buxton Going. HBV
But love, first learnèd in a lady's eyes. Shakespeare. *Fr.* Love's Labour's Lost. PP
But love whilst that thou may'st [*or* maist] be loved again[e]. Samuel Daniel. To Delia, IX [XXXVII]. AtBAP; NoP; OBSC; SiCE; TuPP
But love's true passion is of immortal happiness. Robert Bridges. *Fr.* The Testament of Beauty. LO
But Man, Proud Man. Shakespeare. *Fr.* Measure for Measure, II, ii. WHA
But meanwhile in the centre. The Fight in the Centre. Macaulay. *Fr.* The Battle of Lake Regillus. OtMeF
But Men Loved Darknesse Rather Then Light. Richard Crashaw. MaMe
But mind, but thought—/ If these have been the master part of us. Life and Thought. Matthew Arnold. *Fr.* Empedocles on Etna. FiP
But Minerva fetch'd/ The winds from sea. Homer. *Fr.* The Odyssey, V. EnLi-1
But mortal man/ Was then far hardier in the old champaign. Of Human Progress. Lucretius, *tr. by* William Ellery Leonard. *Fr.* De Rerum Natura (Of the Nature of Things). WoL
But most by numbers judge a poet's song. Poetical Numbers. Pope. *Fr.* An Essay on Criticism. AnFE; InP; OBEC; PP; SeCePo
But my good little man, you have made a mistake. To a Boy-Poet of the Decadence. Sir Owen Seaman. CenHV; FiBHP
But My Neighbor Is My Treasure. Ruth Pitter. BoPe
But "nameless somethings" and "unbounded spaces." Roy Campbell. *Fr.* A Veld Eclogue: The Pioneers. BoSA
But nevertheless there are some other kinds of blue skies. April Lights. Alfred Starr Hamilton. QAH
But no, the familiar symbol, as that the/ curtain. Conrad Aiken. *Fr.* Time in the Rock. FaBoMo
But not on a shell, she starts. The Paltry Nude Starts on a Spring Voyage. Wallace Stevens. NP
But not so odd. A Reply. Cecil Browne. SiTL
But now Athenian mountains they descry. William Falconer. *Fr.* The Shipwreck, III. GoTL
But now Mr. Ferritt. And Mr. Ferritt. Judith Wright. MoBrPo (1962 ed.)
But now more serious let me grow. Matthew Green. *Fr.* The Spleen. PoEL-3
But now my muse, toil'd with continual care. Sonnet. Richard Barnfield. ReIE
But now the dentist cannot die. Andrew Lang. CenHV
But now the salmon-fishers moist. Carrying Their Coracles. Andrew Marvell. *Fr.* Upon Appleton House. ChTr
But now the sun had pass'd the height of Heaven. The Incremation. Matthew Arnold. *Fr.* Balder Dead. VA
But now the wholesome music of the wood. The Fire of Heaven. Tennyson. *Fr.* Idylls of the King. EPN
But now the wounded queen with heavy care. Certain Books of Virgil's Aeneid. Vergil, r. by the Earl of Surrey. *Fr.* The Aeneid, IV. FCP; ReIE
But Now They Have Seen, and Hated. Richard Crashaw. MaMe
But now to chase these phantoms out of sight. The Cause of Thunder. Lucretius. *Fr.* De Rerum Natura. PeRV
But now, to thee, faire bride, it is some wrong. Raising of the Bride. John Donne. MaMe
But O my God! though grovelling I appear. Aspiration. George Wither. MaRV
But, O my Lord, I thank Thee. Christ and the Common Day. Marguerite Wilkinson. BePJ
But O, my Muse, what numbers wilt thou find. Blenheim. Addison. *Fr.* The Campaign. OBEC
But oh! o'er all, forget not Kilda's race. St. Kilda. William Collins. *Fr.* Ode on the Popular Superstitions of the Highlands. FaBoEn
But oh, the night! oh, bitter-sweet! oh, sweet! Romney and Aurora. Elizabeth Barrett Browning. *Fr.* Aurora Leigh, IX.
But Once. Theodore Winthrop. AA
But once I pass this way. The Pilgrim Way. John Oxenham. OQP
But once upon a time. Cranach. Sir Herbert Read. BrPo; FaBoMo
But one apocalyptic lion's whelp (in flesh). There Is No Opera Like "Lohengrin." John Wheelwright. NYBP; OnHM; WhC
But one of the whole mammoth-brood still kept. Keats. *Fr.* Hyperion; a Fragment, I. OBRV
But only to be memories of spiritual gate. Immortality. Samuel Greenberg. LiTA
But, our Winter come, in vain. Sir Richard Fanshawe. LO
But peaceful was the night. The Peaceful Night. Milton. *Fr.* On the Morning of Christ's Nativity. ChrBoLe; FaBoCh; LoGBV
But piteous things we are—when I am gone. Sonnets to Aurelia, III. Robert Nichols. OBMV
"But plett a wand o bonnie birk." Sweet William's Ghost (G vers.). *Unknown.* ESPB
But poets are name-proud craftsmen; Greeks and Jews. Karl Shapiro. *Fr.* Essay on Rime. PP
But quiet to quick bosoms is a hell. Byron. *Fr.* Childe Harold's Pilgrimage, III. PoFr
But quit thy meaner game, indignant Muse. Bryant. *Fr.* The Embargo. CoBA
But Robin he walkes in the g[reene] fforest. Robin Hood and the Butcher. *Unknown.* ESPB
But say thou very woman, why to me. To His Unconstant Friend. Henry King. AnAnS-2
But see the fading many-coloured woods. Autumn. James Thomson. *Fr.* The Seasons: Autumn. EnRP; LoBV
But see this happy village festival. William E. Marshall. *Fr.* Brookfield. CaP
But since I know thy falsehood and thy pride. Abraham Cowley. LO
But so long as/ This prison-planet. Peter Preradovic. *Fr.* Ode to Slavdom. PoFr
But sometimes let me leave the noisy roads. The Pleasure of Walking through an Alley. John Gay. *Fr.* Trivia; or, The Art of Walking the Streets of London, II. EnLi-1 (1949 ed.)
But souls that of His own good life partake. In Him We Live. Henry More. MaRV
But stay, here comes Tityrus Griswold, and leads on. James Russell Lowell. *Fr.* A Fable for Critics. AmePo
But stay, my thoughts, make end, give fortune way. Sir Walter Ralegh. *Fr.* The Ocean to Cynthia, XI. TuPP
But still the thunder of Los peals loud, and thus the thunders cry. Blake. *Fr.* Jerusalem. PoIE
But stricken with the high cafard, the town. Anthony Delius. *Fr.* The Great Divide. BoSA
But That from Slow Dissolving Pomps of Dawn. Arthur Hugh Clough. ViPP
But That Is Another Story. Donald Justice. CoAP; NePoEA-2
But that my lord may plainly understand. George Gascoigne. *Fr.* The Steel Glass. ReEn
But that thou art my wisdome, Lord. Submission. George Herbert. MaMe
"But that was nothing to what things came out." Welsh Incident. Robert Graves. BoC; CMoP; ShBV-3; WePo
But That Was Yesterday. Aileen Fisher. SoPo
But that which most I wonder at, which most. Innocence. Thomas Traherne. AnAnS-1; MeP
But, the Africans Walked at Night. Stan Steiner. WOW
But the broad light glares and beats. Tennyson. Maud, Pt. II, xiii. SyP
But the chaste blackbird, to its partner true. Goldsmith, *tr. fr. the Latin of* Addison. LO

But the chief/ Are poets. Poets. Mark Akenside. *Fr.* The Pleasures of Imagination, IV. OBEC
But the copperbelt night is a snake. The Leader. Dorothy Livesay. MoCV; PeCV (1967 ed.)
But the majestic river floated on. Oxus. Matthew Arnold. *Fr.* Sohrab and Rustum. VA
But the men who are now dying. Breakthrough. John Sinclair. NBP
But the morn to the noon hath fallen, and the afternoon to the eve. The Brooding of Sigurd. William Morris. *Fr.* The Story of Sigurd the Volsung. SeCePo
But the vast pile th' amazed vulgar views. The Destruction of Troy. Vergil, *tr. by* Sir John Denham. *Fr.* The Aeneid. SeCV-1
But the wyld man, contrarie to her feare. Spenser. *Fr.* The Faerie Queene, VI. MBW-1
But Thee, but Thee, O sovereign Seer of Time. The Crystal Christ. Sidney Lanier. *Fr.* The Crystal. BePJ; ChIP; MaRV; TrPWD
But then there comes that moment rare. Voices of the Air. Katherine Mansfield. HBMV
But there are richer entanglements. Love and Friendship. Keats. *Fr.* Endymion, I. OBRV
But there is no black jaw which cannot be broken by our word. Kenneth Patchen. *Fr.* The Journal of Albion Moonlight. NaP
But there is one, they say. He Walks at Peace. *Unknown. Fr.* Tao Teh King. TRV
But these were only a few, there were others, too, many others. Trippers. Sir Osbert Sitwell. HaMV
But they that wait upon the Lord shall renew their strength. Isaiah, Bible, *O.T.* TiPo (1952 ed.)
But this also/ is part of my charm. There Must Be a Lone Ranger!!! Leroi Jones. WOW
But, this I found. Robert Norwood. *Fr.* The Man of Kerioth. CaP
But this is learning; to have skill to throw. Learning. George Chapman. *Fr.* Euthymaie Raptus; or, The Tears of Peace. SeCePo
But this: to know Thy life, without a stain. The True Need. Thomas Curtis Clark. OQP
But thou, Beth-lehem Ephratah. The Prince of Peace. Micah, Bible, *O.T.* ChrBoLe
But thou, Israel, My servant. Israel, My Servant. Isaiah, Bible, *O.T.* TrJP
But thou which lov'st to be. John Donne. *Fr.* The Blossom. LO
But to His Mother Mary. Milton. *Fr.* Paradise Regained, II. ISi
But to reach the archimedean point. "Mysticism Has Not the Patience to Wait for God's Revelation." Richard Eberhart. MoPo
But Troy, alas, methought above them all. Troy. Thomas Sackville. *Fr.* Induction to "The Mirror for Magistrates." SeCePo
But twelve short years you lived, my son. His Son. Callimachus. AWP; JAWP; WBP
But Two There Are. . . C. Day Lewis. OxBI
But undiscerning Muse, which heart, which eyes. Equality of Persons. John Donne. MaMe
But unto him came swift calamity. Frederick Goddard Tuckerman. *Fr.* Sonnets. AP
But usually, words fill our heads, which we bring. Gerald Butler. *Fr.* This Side of Orion. QAH
But, venture on the darkness; and within. A Fauxbourg. George Croly. *Fr.* Paris in 1815. OBRV
But Venus first. Sister Juana Inés de la Cruz, *tr. fr. Spanish by* Samuel Beckett. *Fr.* First Dream. AnMP
But we by a love, so much refined. John Donne. LO
But We Shall Bloom. Haim Guri, *tr. fr. Hebrew by* David Kuselewitz. TrJP
But well away, so is mine heart woe. To Chaucer. Thomas Hoccleve. *Fr.* De Regimine Principum. ACP
But Whan the Cok. Chaucer. *Fr.* Troilus and Criseide, III. AtBAP
But what, by the fur on your satin sleeves. The Retort Discourteous. Stephen Vincent Benét. HBMV
But what dark flag. Shark's Fin. Eithne Wilkins. NeBP
But What's in the Larder? Tennyson. ThGo
But what's that? a mass meeting? No, there come in lots. James Russell Lowell. *Fr.* A Fable for Critics. AmePo
But when grandpa, the miner, came back from the States. Une Vie. Pentti Saarikoski. ELU
But when that comely he covered his wits. The Temptation of Sir Gawain. *Unknown. Fr.* Sir Gawain and the Green Knight. ACP
But when the Gods and Heroes heard, they brought. Matthew Arnold. *Fr.* Balder Dead. PeVV
But when the Pharisees had heard that he had put the Sadducees. The Great Commandment. St. Matthew, Bible, *N.T.* TreFT
But when the water roars around us. The Ocean. Louis Dudek. *Fr.* Provincetown. MoCV
But when with her white horses day shone fair. Salamis. Aeschylus. *Fr.* Persians. WaaP
But When Ye Pray. Frances Crosby Hamlet. OQP
But where began the change; and what's my crime? Modern Love, X. George Meredith. EnLit; NBM; PoEL-5; ViPo; VP
But where shall wisdom be found? Where Shall Wisdom Be Found? Job Bible, *O.T.* TreFT
But where to find the happiest spot below. The First, Best Country. Goldsmith. *Fr.* The Traveller. GN
But wherefore do not you a mightier way [*or* waie]. Sonnets, XVI. Shakespeare. FaBoEn
But whether in the uncoloured light of truth. Seven Sonnets, IV. Arthur Hugh Clough. ViPP
"But who art thou, with curious beauty graced." Opportunity. Machiavelli. AWP; JAWP; WBP
But who considers well will find indeed. Andrew Marvell. *Fr.* The Loyal Scot. ViBoPo
But who is this, what thing of sea or land? Delilah. Milton. *Fr.* Samson Agonistes. SeCePo
But Who the Melodies of Morn Can Tell? James Beattie. *Fr.* The Minstrel, I. ViBoPo
(Nature and the Poets, *longer sel.*) OBEC; SeCePo
But whoso may, thrice happy man him hold. Spenser. *Fr.* An Hymne of Heavenly Beauty. WGRP
"But why do you go?" said the lady, while both sate under the yew. Lord Walter's Wife. Elizabeth Barrett Browning. BeLS
But will you woo this wild-cat? Petruchio Is Undaunted by Katharina. Shakespeare. *Fr.* The Taming of the Shrew, I, ii. TreFT
But wine was cheap in old Judea. And bread. Passover. John Beauchamp Thompson. ChIP
But word is come to Warrington. Sir John Butler. *Unknown.* ESPB
But yesterday she played with childish things. The Dead Child. George Barlow. OBVV; VA
But yesterday the earth drank like a child. A Letter to His Friend Isaac. Judah Halevi. TrJP
But yesterday these few and hoary sheaves. The Two Harvests. Francisco de Medrano. OnPM
But yet one thought has often stayed by me. Harriet Eleanor Hamilton King. *Fr.* The Sermon in the Hospital. BoC
But you are over-blest. Plenty this day. Feasts and Revells. John Donne. MaMe
But you are tir'd—I'll tell a tale.—"Agreed." Sir Balaam. Pope. *Fr.* Moral Essays. MaPo
But you can Life upon the Poor bestow. To a Good Physician. William Wycherley. ACP
But you, Thomas Jefferson. Brave New World. Archibald MacLeish. AmP; OxBA
But you were wrong that desolate dusk. For Thomas Hardy. Jane Cooper. AmPC
But you who seek to give and merit fame. Pope. *Fr.* An Essay on Criticism, Pt. I. EnL
"Butch" Weldy. Edgar Lee Masters. *Fr.* Spoon River Anthology. NePA; PoPo
Butcher Boy, The. *Unknown.* BaBo; ViBoFo
(Butcher's Boy, The, B *vers., with music.*) BSO
Butcher Shop. Jorge Luis Borges, *tr. fr. Spanish by* H. R. Hays. OnPM
Butchers. Redmond Phillips. NeLNL
Butcher's Boy, The. *Unknown. See* Butcher Boy, The.
Buthaina ("Buthaina, if the flower of youth could raise its head anew"). Jamil, *tr. fr. Arabic by* Howard Mumford Jones. LiTW
Butler's Proclamation. Paul Hamilton Hayne. PAH
Butterbean Tent, The. Elizabeth Madox Roberts. GoJo; StVeCh; SUS

Buttercup, A. *Unknown.* BoTP
Buttercup Cow. Elizabeth Rendall. TiPo
Buttercup Farm. *Unknown.* SAS
Buttercup nodded and said good-by. August. Celia Thaxter. FaPON; YeAr
Buttercup, the cow, had a new baby calf. The New Baby Calf. Edith Newlin Chase. SoPo; TiPo
Buttercups. Louis Ginsberg. HBVY; YT
Buttercups. Dolly Radford. RIS
Buttercups. Wilfrid Thorley. DD; FaPON; GaP; HBV; HBVY; OBVV
Buttercups. *Unknown.* BoTP
Buttercups and Daisies. Mary Howitt. BoTP; DD; HBV; HBVY, *abr.*; OHIP; OTPC; TVC
Buttercups, buttercups, stretching for miles. Buttercups. Dolly Radford. RIS
Buttercups, buttercups, what do you hold? Buttercups. Louis Ginsberg. HBVY; YT
Buttercups golden and gay. Buttercups. *Unknown.* BoTP
Buttercups in the sunshine look. A Fairy Song. Elizabeth T. Dillingham. OTPC (1946 ed.); PCH
Butterflies. Chu Miao Tuan, *tr. fr. Chinese* by Henry H. Hart. FlW
Butterflies. John Davidson, *sometimes at. to* François Coppée. HBV
Butterflies. W. H. Davies. BoPo
Butterflies. Kageki, *tr. fr. Japanese by* Asataro. Miyamori. OnPM
Butterflies. Haniel Long. HBMV
Butterflies. Alfred Noyes. BoC
Butterflies, butterflies. Corn-grinding Song. *Unknown, tr. fr. Laguna Indian by* Natalie Curtis. AWP; JAWP; SUS; WBP
Butterfly, The. Margaret Avison. ExPo; OBCV
Butterfly, The. Gray Burr. CoPo
Butterfly ("As I walked through my garden"). Hilda Conkling. NP; TiPo
Butterfly ("Butterfly,/ I like the way you wear your wings"). Hilda Conkling. PoRh; TVC
Butterfly, The. Alice Archer James. AA
Butterfly, The. Kikaku, *tr. fr. Japanese by* Harold G. Henderson. SoPo
Butterfly. Kwaso, *tr. fr. Japanese by* Harold G. Henderson. OnPM
Butterfly, The. Adelaide O'Keeffe. HBV; HBVY
Butterfly, The. Alice Freeman Palmer. HBV; MaRV
Butterfly, The. Margaret Rose. BoTP
Butterfly, The. Clinton Scollard. GFA
Butterfly, The. Joseph Skipsey. VA
Butterfly. William Jay Smith. GoJo; RePo; TiPo (1959 ed.)
Butterfly, The. Spenser. *Fr.* Muiopotmos. BoC
Butterfly. John Banister Tabb. OTPC (1946 ed.); UTS
Butterfly,/ I like the way you wear your wings. Butterfly. Hilda Conkling. PoRh; TVC
Butterfly, a [or the] cabbage-white, The. Flying Crooked. Robert Graves. FaBoMo; FlW; LiTM (rev. ed.); OA; TwCP
Butterfly, an idle thing, The. The Butterfly. Adelaide O'Keeffe. HBV; HBVY
Butterfly and the Bee, The. William Lisle Bowles. HBV; HBVY
Butterfly and the Caterpillar, The. Joseph Lauren. OnMSP; RIS; StaSt
Butterfly and wasp, The. Encounter. John L'Heureux. YAP
Butterfly Bones; or Sonnet against Sonnets. Margaret Avison. LiTM (1970 ed.)
Butterfly, butterfly, brilliant and bright. To a Butterfly. Lady Flora Hastings. OTPC (1923 ed.)
Butterfly, butterfly, sipping the sand. Butterfly. John Banister Tabb. OTPC (1946 ed.); UTS
Butterfly from flower to flower, The. The Butterfly. Joseph Skipsey. VA
Butterfly in Church, A. George Marion McClellan. BANP
Butterfly, one summer morn, A. The Butterfly and the Caterpillar. Joseph Lauren. OnMSP; RIS; StaSt
Butterfly the ancient Grecians made, The. Psyche. S. T. Coleridge. ERoP-1
Butterfly, the cabbage-white, The. *See* Butterfly, a Cabbage-white, The.
Butterfly's Ball, The. William Roscoe. BoChLi; GoTP; OTPC, *diff. vers.*; TVC
Butterfly's First Flight, The. *Unknown.* OTPC
Butterfly's Funeral, The. *Unknown.* OTPC (1923 ed.)
Butternut and walnut. Hillside Pause. Catharine Morris Wright. GoYe
Buttery, sugary, syrupy waffle, A. The Groaning Board. "Pink." InMe
Buttocks of the ruffed grouse, The. Painting by Chimes. Bernadette Mayer. ANYP
Button to chin. *Unknown.* OxNR
Buttons. Walter de la Mare. DTC
Buttons. Raymond Turner. WSL
Buttons, a farthing a pair. *Unknown.* OxNR
Buttons: brilliant, beautiful buttons. Buttons. Raymond Turner. WSL
Buxom Joan. Congreve. *See* Soldier and a Sailor, A.
Buxom Lass. *Unknown.* ErPo
Buy Me an Ounce and I'll Sell You a Pound. E. E. Cummings. OxBA
Buy my English posies! The Flowers. Kipling. OBVV
Buying a Pig. John Heywood. SiCE
Buz, Quoth the Blue Fly. Ben Jonson. *Fr.* Oberon, the Fairy Prince. NA; TuPP
("Buzz, quoth the blue fly," *sl. diff.*) OXNR
(Catch, A.) ElL
Buzz-saw snarled and rattled in the yard, The. Out, Out. Robert Frost. AmPP (4th ed.); CABA; CBV; ILP; InP; OxBA; PoeP; PoIE; PoPo; PreP; TDP; UnPo
"Buzz!" went the Bee, with a merry din. The Bee and the Lily. Thomas Westwood. TVC
Buzzards, The. Martin Armstrong. HBMV; POTE
Buzzards over Pondy Woods, The. Pondy Woods. Robert Penn Warren. MAP; MoAmPo
Buzzing, buzzing, buzzing, my golden-belted bees. The Bees of Middleton Manor. May Probyn. GoBC; JKCP; VA
Buzzy Brown. Leroy F. Jackson. GaP
Bwagamoyo. Lebert Bethune. BF
By a bank as I lay. Dawn. *Unknown.* OBSC
By a Bank of Pinks and Lilies. *Unknown.* ErPo
By a broken-down old dwellin', lookin' somethin' like a shoe. Mandy's Lay. Louis Untermeyer. StaSt
By a Chapel as I Came. *Unknown.* ChTr
By a clear well, within a little field. Of Three Girls and [of] Their Talk. Boccaccio. *Fr.* Sonnets. AWP; JAWP OnPM; WBP
By a dim road, o'ergrown with dry thin grass. Cut It Down. Mary Elizabeth Coleridge. MoVE
By a dim shore where water darkening. The Reed-Player. Duncan Campbell Scott. VA
By a dismal cypress lying. A Song from the Italian. Dryden. *Fr.* Limberham; or, The Kind Keeper. CEP; SeCV-2
By a flat rock on the shore of the sea. The Rock. *Unknown.* ChTr
By a Forest. *Unknown.* NCEP
By a gentle river laid. Love's Arithmetic. Sir Edward Sherburne. CaVP
By a Lake in Minnesota. James Wright. AmFN; FRC
By a peninsula the painter sat and/ Sketched. Conduct. Samuel Greenberg. CrMA; LiTA
By a peninsula the wanderer sat and sketched. Emblems of Conduct. Hart Crane, *after* Samuel Greenberg. LiTA; LiTM (rev. ed.); NAMP; NePA
By a quiet little stream on an old mossy log. The Frog and the Bird. Vera Hessey. BoTP
By a Rich Fast Moving Stream. John Tagliabue. ELU
By a route obscure and lonely. Dream-Land. Poe. AmePo; AmP; AmLP; AmPP; AnFE; AP; APA; CBEP; CoAnAm; CoBA; LiTA; MWA-1; NePA; OxBA; PoFS
By a sliver fountain. Fairy Frolic. Annie Isabel Rentoul. GFA
By Achmelvich Bridge. Norman MacCaig. OxBS
By all means sing of love, but if you do. The Truest Poetry Is the Most Feigning; or, Ars Poetica for Hard Times. W. H. Auden. NYBP
By all the deeds to thy dear glory done. Australia to England. Archibald T. Strong. *Fr.* Sonnets of the Empire. BoAu; PoFr
By all the Dodos! These are thoughts of weight. Dodoism. W. J. Courthope. *Fr.* The Paradise of Birds. OtMeF
By all the glories of the day. Before Action. William Noel Hodgson. MaRV; WGRP
By all thy gloryes willingly I goe. *Unknown.* SeCSL
By Allah! while the days endure. The Mock Caliph. *Unknown.* EnLi-1
By an alley lined with tumble-down shacks. Mexican Quarter.

By (continued)
John Gould Fletcher. Arizona Poems, II. NP
By an Ancient Sea. Thomas Curtis Clark. ChIP
By an Ant-Heap. Terence Heywood. BoSA
By an' By, *with music*. *Unknown*. BoAN-1
By an Evolutionist. Tennyson. BEL; EnLi-2; EPN; PoVP
"If my body come from brutes," 2 *sts*. MaRV
By and by. Epitaph on a Waiter [*or* On a Waiter]. David McCord. PoPo; WhC
By April mist. Spring Song. Katharine O'Brien. GoYe
By apt comparisons I thought to praise thee. Missed Again. John T. Durward. JKCP (1926 ed.)
By archy/ the roach that scurries. Ballade of the Under Side. Don Marquis. *Fr.* Archys Life of Mehitabel. InvP
By Arthur's Dale as late I went. Bonny Bee Hom. *Unknown*. BaBo; ESPB; OBB, *sl. diff. vers.*
By ashing sods where shadows mope. The Finding of the Táin. Robert Farren. CoBE
By, baby bunting. *See* Bye, baby bunting.
By banks where burned awhile the rose. Renascence. Muredach J. Dooher. OnYI
By Bendemeer's Stream. Thomas Moore. *Fr.* Lalla Rookh. OTPC (1946 ed.); RG
(Bendemeer.) OBRV
By Blue Ontario's Shore, *sels.* Walt Whitman.
"I swear I begin to see the meaning of these things." PoIE
Poet, The, IX XVII. MoAmPo (1950 ed.)
By bluster, graft, and doing people down. A Tribute to the Founder. Kingsley Amis. NePoEA-2
By brake unleaved and hedgerow. In Terra Nostra. Alan C. Tarbat. BoPe
By Broad Potomac's Shore. Walt Whitman. PoIE (1970 ed.)
By Candlelight. Lorie C. Gooding. SoP
By Canoe through the Fir Forest. James Dickey. NYBP
By Cavité on the bay. The Battle of Manila. Richard Hovey. PAH
By Chance I Walk. Yüan Mei, *tr. fr. Chinese by* David Mackay. FIW
By channels of coolness the echoes are calling. Bell-Birds. Henry C. Kendall. BoAu; PoAu-1
By Chickamauga's crooked stream the martial trumpets blew. The Ballad of Chickamauga. Maurice Thompson. MC; PAH
By childrens births, and death, I am become. Niobe. John Donne. MaMe
By chivalries as tiny. Emily Dickinson. MWA-2
By Cobequid Bay. Alexander Louis Fraser. CaP
By Coelia's Arbor. Sheridan. OnYI
By Cool Siloam's Shady Rill. Reginald Heber. ELP; MaRV; OxBoCh; PRWS
By copse and hedgerow, waste and wall. Knapweed. A. C. Benson. HBV; VA
By dark severance the apparition head. Painted Head [*or* Painting: a Head]. John Crowe Ransom. AP; CoBMV; CrMA; LiTA; LiTG; LiTM (rev. ed.); MAP; MoAB; MoAmPo; MoPo; MoVE; OxBA; PoIE; ReMP
By David's mouth, God spoke, "Be still and see that I am God." Canticle of Quietness. Sister Mary Paulinus. JKCP (1955 ed.)
By day. The Jefferson Highway. Sister Mariella. JKCP (1955 ed.)
By Day and by Night. W. S. Merwin. AmPC
By day Golgotha sleeps, but when night comes. Night at Gettysburg. Don C. Seitz. OHIP
By day my timid passions stand. Serenade. Richard Middleton. HBV; LoP
By day she woos me, soft, exceeding fair. The World. Christina Rossetti. Sonn; VP
By day the bat is cousin to the mouse. The Bat. Theodore Roethke. FIW; GoJo; GoTP; NYTB; PDV
By day the fields and meadows cry. The Poet's Call. Thomas Curtis Clark. WGRP
By day, the returning terror of swifts, the scream. Flight. Laurence Whistler. POTE
By day the skyscraper looms in the smoke and sun and has a soul. Skyscraper. Carl Sandburg. PoMa; PoPl
By day . . . tireless smokestacks. Five Towns on the B. and O. Carl Sandburg. OnPM; WoL
By Deputy. Arthur St. John Adcock. CenHV
By dint of dart, by push of sharpened spear. A Merry Ballad of Vintners. John Payne. ALV
By divination came the Dorians. In Arcadia. Lawrence Durrell. FaBoMo; MoBrPo (1962 ed.)
By dusk on shore he's waiting. Song of the Withy Greatcoat. Norma Farber. NYTB
By ear, he sd. I, Maximus of Gloucester, to You. Charles Olson. FRC; NeAP
By easy slope to west as if it had. Cheyenne Mountain. Helen Hunt Jackson. PoOW
By every ebb of the river-side. Pisgah. Willard Wattles. WGRP
By every light, in every pose. In God's Eternal Studios. Paul Shivell. *Fr.* The Studios Photographic. HBV
By Faith ("By faith and not by sight"). E. Margaret Clarkson. SoP
By far/ The naughtiest. Extremely Naughty Children. Elizabeth Godley. BBGG
By fate, not option, frugal Nature gave. Xenophanes. Emerson. AnNE; MWA-1
By favorable breezes fanned. Cythère. Paul Verlaine. AWP; SyP
By feathers green, across Casbeen. The Phoenix. A. C. Benson. OBEV; OBVV; ShBV-4
By Ferry to the Island. Iain Crichton Smith. BoPe
By Fiat of Adoration. Oscar Williams. GTBS-W; LiTL; LiTM; NePA
By flowers of china-pink and lily pads. Die Pelzaffen. Charles Spear. AnNZ
By force I live, in will I wish to die. Life Is but Loss. Robert Southwell. SiCE
By Gentle Love. *Unknown*. TRV
By Glistening, Dancing Seas. Lethonia Gee. BF
By God I hate to grow old. Covent Garden Market. Carl Bode. *Fr.* London Sonnets. ToPo
By granting charters of peace. An Anglo-Irishman's Complaint. *Unknown*. AnIL
By hard journeys in a dead land. Omphalos; the Well. Seán Jennett. NeIP
By Heaven 'tis false, I am not vain. The Defiance. Aphra Behn. EnLoPo
By heaven's high gift, in case revived were. Concerning Virgil's Aeneids. Nicholas Grimald. ReIE
By Heaven's! 'twas bravely done! Spoken Extempore. Earl of Rochester. SeCePo
By hell 'twas bravely done! what less than this? Satire I: Garnet's Ghost Addressing to the Jesuits. John Oldham. *Fr.* Satires upon the Jesuits. SeEP
By Her Aunt's Grave. Thomas Hardy. Satires of Circumstance, III. MoAB; MoBrPo; PoPo; PoVP; VaPo
By her that is most assured to her self. Amoretti, LVIII. Spenser. EnRePo
By Herndyke Mill there haunts, folks tell. The Silver Bird of Herndyke Mill. Edmund Blunden. GoTL (1949 ed.)
By Him. Ben Jonson. TRV
By him lay heavy Sleep, the cousin of Death. Sleep. Thomas Sackville. *Fr.* Induction to "The Mirror for Magistrates." WHA
By his commandment he maketh the snow to fall apace. Snow. Ecclesiasticus, Bible, Apocrypha. BoC
By his evening fire the artist. Gaspar Becerra. Longfellow. AnNE
By itself and from a distance. The Brick. Paul Roche. NYBP
By June our brook's run out of song and speed. Hyla Brook. Robert Frost. AnFE; AnNE; APA; BoNaP; CoAnAm; MAPA; TwAmPo
By Killarney's lakes and fells, em'rald isles and winding bays. Killarney. Edmund Falconer. TreFS
By Langley Bush I roam, but the bush hath left its hill. Enclosure. John Clare. *Fr.* Remembrance. NBM
By Lea's dear banks, where joined in play. Musing by a River. Moses Browne. WaPE
By Life, or by Death. Will H. Houghton. SoP
By Logan's streams that rin sae deep. Logan Braes. John Mayne. OxBS
By loss in play men oft forget. The Gambler's Repentance. Gerald, Baron of Offaly. AnIV
By lost Clonard the river meads still hold. Clonard. Thomas S. Jones, Jr. HBMV
By-low, My Babe. *Unknown*. *See* Balow.
By man I am forsaken and the world. A Flute. Nobutsuna. OnPM

By many a saint and many a scholar led. Memorial Sonnet. Marjorie Meeker. AnAmPo
By Master Saville who, conceivably, from the accuracy of the drawing. *The River Map* and We're Done. Charles Olson. CoPo
By Memory Inspired. *Unknown.* AnIV
By mid-day it was warm enough; she climbed. Aunt Alice in April. William H. Matchett. TPM
By miracles exceeding power of man. Crucifying. John Donne. AnAnS-1; MaMe; MeP; OBS; Sonn
By Momba Tracks. Roderic Quinn. NeLNL
By Moonlight. May Sarton. MoLP
By Moonlight. *Unknown, tr. fr. French by* Louis Untermeyer. UnTE
By Moscow Self-devoted to a Blaze. Wordsworth. PoFr
By my life I vow. The Vow. Sir Edward Sherburne. SeCL
By Myself. Robert Frost. RIS
By Nebo's lonely mountain. Burial of Moses. Cecil Frances Alexander. BeLS; BLPA; BLRP; GN; HBV; NeHB; OTPC; WBLP
By Night. Philip Jerome Cleveland. MaRV; TRV
By night around my temple grove. Buddha. Arno Holz. AWP
By night on my bed I sought him whom my soul loveth. On My Bed I Sought Him. The Song of Solomon, Bible, *O.T.* TrJP
By night we linger'd on the lawn. In Memoriam A. H. H., XCV. Tennyson. AnFE; EnL; EPN; FosPo; LoBV; OAEP; OBNC; PoEL-5; ViPo; VP
By night within my bed I roamed here and there. The Most Excellent Song Which Was Salomon's. Michael Drayton. *Fr.* The Harmony of the Church. ReIE
By none but me can the tale be told. The White Ship. Dante Gabriel Rossetti. OnSP; PoVP
By numbers here from shame of censure free. Poverty in London. Samuel Johnson. *Fr.* London. ChTr; EnLi-1 (1949 ed.); OBEC; ViBoPo
By One Great Heart. Margaret Deland. OQP
(Life.) MaRV; WGRP
By One, Unsure. Melville Cane. NYTB
By orange grove and palm-tree, we walked the southern shore. Hemlock Mountain. Sarah N. Cleghorn. HBV
By our first strange and fatal interview. On His Mistress [*or* Elegy on His Mistress]. John Donne. Elegies, XVI. AnAnS-1; CABL; CBV; CLwM; LiTB; LiTG; LoBV; MaMe; MeLP; MePo; MyFE; PoEL-2; ReEn; SCEP-1; SeCeV; SeCP; SeCV-1; SeEP; TuPP; ViBoPo
By Parcels Post. George R. Sims. BOHV
By proud New York and its man-piled Matterhorns. Proud New York. John Reed. HBMV; NP
By reason of despair we set forth behind you. The Murder of Moses. Karl Shapiro. EaLo
By Return Mail. Richard Aldridge. NePoAm-2
By right of fires that smelted ore. The Man and the Machine. E. J. Pratt. WoL
By rocks and twigs and garter snakes. Elsie's House. Stanley McNail. FiSC
By rose and verdant valley. Earth-born. Robert E. Howard. FiSC
By Saint [*or* Saynt] Mary, my lady. To Mistress [*or* Maystres] Isabel[l] Pennell. John Skelton. *Fr.* The Garlande of Laurell. AtBAP; CBEP; CH; EG; EnPo; FlW; LiTG; LiTL; LO; OAEP; OBEV (new ed.); OBSC; OxBoLi; PoEL-1; PoFS; PoIE; SeCeV; StP; TrGrPo; TuPP; ViBoPo; YAT
By Sandy Waters. Jesse Stuart. AmFN
By Saturday I said you would be better on Sunday. The Operation. Robert Creeley. NaP; ToPo
By scattered rocks and turbid waters shifting. The Mountain Heart's-Ease. Bret Harte. HBV
By seven vineyards on one hill. The Mystic. Witter Bynner. HBV
By Shaded Wells. Bhartrihari, *tr. fr. Sanskrit by* Paul Elmer More. OnPM
By sloth on sorrow fathered. Lollocks. Robert Graves. ChTr; DTC; EvOK; FlW; MoPW
By Solitary Fires. Elizabeth Barrett Browning. *Fr.* Aurora Leigh, V. VA
By some peculiar force centrifugal. To a Book. Elinor Wylie. LiTA
By some sad means, when Reason holds no sway. Philip Freneau. *Fr.* The House of Night. AmPP; PoEL-4
By something formed, I nothing am. In a Glass. Swift. RIS
By special lens, photo-electric cells. A Different Speech. Louise Townsend Nicholl. ImOP
By Stubborn Stars, *sels.* Kenneth Leslie.
Sonnet: "Silver herring throbbed thick in my seine, The," I. PeCV; TwCaPo
Sonnet: "Warm rain whispers, but the earth knows best, A." PeCV; TwCaPo
By such an all-embalming summer day. Near Helikon. Trumbull Stickney. AnFE; CoAnAm; LiTA; NCEP; TwAmPo
By that evening window where. Verses for the 60th Birthday of T. S. Eliot. George Barker. ChMP
"By the Babylonish waters." By the Waters of Babylon. Heine. *Fr.* Hebrew Melodies. TrJP
By the beard of the Prophet the Bashaw swore. How We Burned the *Philadelphia.* Barrett Eastman. PaA; PAH
By the Beautiful Sea. Thomas Cole. NePoAm-2
By the Bivouac's Fitful Flame. Walt Whitman. AP; MaPo (1969 ed.); NoP; OxBA; Po; TDP
By the blue taper's trembling light. A Night-Piece on Death. Thomas Parnell. CEP; EiPP; OBEC
By the Bridge. Ted Walker. NYBP
By the city dead-house by the gate. The City Dead-House. Walt Whitman. AmePo
By the Conemaugh. Florence Earle Coates. PAH
By the cool water the breeze murmurs, rustling. Orchard Song. Sappho. LiTW
By the Cradle. George Macdonald. OTPC (1946 ed.)
By the cross of expiation/ The Mother stood, and kept her station. Stabat Mater [Dolorosa.] *At. to.* Jacopone da Todi. ISi
By the Deep Sea. Byron. *See* Ocean, The.
By the Earth's Corpse. Thomas Hardy. PoDB; ViPo
By the edge of the divan. A Song of Self-Pity. Geoffrey Vivien. TwCaPo
By the Exeter River. Donald Hall. MoBS
By the Fire. Elizabeth J. Coatsworth. RePo
By the Fireside. Robert Browning. MBW-2; NoP
By the Flat Cup. Horace, *tr. fr. Latin by* Ezra Pound. *Fr.* Odes. CTC
By the flow of the inland river. The Blue and the Gray. Francis Miles Finch. AA; AmePo; BLPA; BoPo; CoBA; DD; FaBoBe; HBV; HH; MC; PaA; PAH; PAL; PAP; PaPo; PCD; PEDC; PTK; ThLM; TreF; WBLP
By the Fountain. Anyte, *tr. fr. Greek by* Lord Neaves. OnPM
(Shepherd's Gift, A, *tr. by* John William Burgon.) AWP
By the gate with star and moon. Medallion. Sylvia Plath. NoP
By the glim of a midwinterish early morning. Son and Father. C. Day Lewis. EaLo
By the grim grace of the Puritans she had been brought. Sarah Threeneedles. Katharine Lee Bates. HBMV
By the Hoof of the Wild Goat. Kipling. *Fr.* Plain Tales from the Hills. OBNC
(Predestination.) LoBV
By the Isar, in the twilight. River Roses. D. H. Lawrence. BrPo; CMoP; SiSw; ViBoPo
By the Lake. Lawrence Durrell. *Fr.* Eight Aspects of Melissa. NeBP
By the lake the orchards lie. Intermezzo. Robert Hillyer. NePoAm
By the lamplit stall I loitered, feasting my eyes. Sight. W. W. Gibson. MoBrPo; NeMA; PoMa
By the light of the Moon God. Dialogue. Prince Yuhara. OnPM
By the little river, still and deep and brown. The Willows. Walter Prichard Eaton. DD; FaPON; HBMV; MPB; OHIP
By the long flow of green and silver water. Water and Shadow. Marya Zaturenska. SiSw
By the Margin of the Great Deep. "Æ." HBMV; OBEV; OBVV; PoVP
By the margin of the ocean, one morning in the month of June. The Bonny Bunch of Roses O. *Unknown.* OxBoLi
By the merest chance, in the twilight gloom. What My Lover Said. Homer Greene. AA; HBV; TreFS
By the Moon We Sport and Play. *Unknown. at. to* John Lyly *and to* Thomas Ravenscroft. *Fr.* The Mayde's Metamorphosis. OTPC; TuPP
(By the Moon.) CH
(Fairy Dances, 1.) EIL

By (continued)
(Fairy Frolic, The.) PCH, *longer sel.*
(Urchins' Dance, The.) BoTP
By the morning hours. The Morning Hours. *Unknown.* PoPl
By the North Gate, the wind blows full of sand. Lament of the Frontier Guard. Li Po, *tr.* by Ezra Pound. AP; CoAnAm; CoBMV; TwAmPo; WaaP
By the North Sea. Swinburne.
Sels.
"But afar on the headland exalted," VII. PoVP
"Land that is lonelier than ruin, A," I. PoEL-5; PoVP
By the old Moulmein Pagoda, lookin' eastward to [*or* lazy at] the sea. Mandalay. Kipling. ATP; BEL; BoLiVe; BrPo; EnLi-2; EnLit; FaBV; HBV; LiTB; LiTM (rev. ed.); MoBrPo; PoVP; ShBV-2; SiTL; StaSt; TOP; TreF; TrGrPo; YT
By the Pacific. Herbert Bashford. AA
By the Pacific Ocean. Joaquin Miller. AA; AnAmPo; MAP; MoAmPo (1942 ed.)
By the pool. Tanka, VII. Lewis Alexander. CDC
By the Potomac. Thomas Bailey Aldrich. PAH; Sonn
By the public hook for the private eye. River Song. Weldon Kees. TwAmPo
By the purple haze that lies. Indian Summer. Susanna Moodie. CaP
By the Rio Grande. The Rio Grande. Sacheverell Stiwell. SeCePo
By the River. Harold Lenoir Davis. NP
By the River. Judith Gautier, *tr. fr. French by* Stuart Merrill. SiSw
By the River Eden. Kathleen Raine. NYBP
By the rivers gently flowing, Illinois, Illinois. Illinois. C. H. Chamberlain. PoRL
By the rivers [*or* waters] of Babylon, there we sat down. Psalm CXXXVII, Bible, *O.T.* AWP; CaFP; ExPo; JAWP; LiTW; OBS; OnPM; PG (1955 ed.); StaSt; TrGrPo; TrJP
By the Road to the Air-Base. Yvor Winters. CrMa; Po
By the road to the contagious hospital. Spring and All [*or* Poem]. William Carlos Williams. AP; CABA; CMoP; CoBMV; ExPo; ForPo; LiTM (1970 ed.); MAP; MoAB; MoAmPo; MoVE; NeMA; OxBA; PoeP; PoIE; PoSa; QFR; UnPo (3d ed.); VaPo
By the roadside, rain or shine. Ragged Robin and Bouncing Bet. Alice Reid. DD
By the roots of my hair some god got hold of me. The Hanging Man. Sylvia Plath. CBV
By the rosy cliffs of Devon, on a green hill's crest. Where Love Is. Amelia Josephine Burr. HBV; LoP
By the rude bridge that arched the flood. Concord Hymn [*or* Hymn]. Emerson. AA; AmePo; AmFN; AmP; AmPP; AnAmPo; AnNE; AP; AWP; BBV; BLPA; BoPo; CoBA; DD; ExPo; FaBoBe; FaBoEn; FaFP; FaPL; FaPON; GN; GTBS-W; HBV; HBVY; HH; HT; InP; InPo; JAWP; LiTA; LiTG; MaRV; MC; MCCG; MPB; MWA-1; NeHB; NePA; NoP; OHFP; OnPM; OQP; OTD; OTPC; OuHeWo; OxBA; PaA; PAH; PAL; PAP; PEDC; PG (1945 ed.); Po; PoFr; PoFS; PoIE; PoPl; PoRL; PTK; SeCeV; StVeCh; ThLM; ToP; TreF; TrGrPo; ViBoPo; WaaP; WBP; WoL; YaD; YT
By the ruined arch, where the bougainvillea bled. The World Comes Galloping; A True Story. Robert Penn Warren. Mexico Is a Foreign Country, III. FiMAP
By the rushy-fringèd bank. Milton. *Fr.* Comus. TOP
By the sad waters of separation. Exile. Ernest Dowson. BrPo
By the Salpêtrière. Thomas Ashe. VA
By the Salt Margin. Abbie Huston Evans. NePoAm
By the Saltings. Ted Walker. NYBP; WIRo
By the Sea. Marchette Chute. StVeCh (1955 ed.)
By the Sea. Emily Dickinson. *See* I started early, took my dog.
By the Sea. Richard Watson Dixon. OBNC
By the Sea. John Hollander. AmPC
By the Sea. Christina Rossetti. BoNaP
By the Sea. Wordsworth. *See* It Is a Beauteous Evening, Calm and Free.
By the Sea of Galilee. Katharine Lee Bates. ChIP
By the seven stars of her halo. Lady of O. James J. Galvin. ISi
By the shore, a plot of ground. The Ruined Chapel. William Allingham. IrPN
By the shores [*or* shore] of Gitche [*or* Gitchee] Gumee. Hiawatha's Childhood. Longfellow. *Fr.* The Song of Hiawatha. BoChLi; FaPON; GFA; MPB; OHFP; PoRh; RePo; ShBV-1; StVeCh; TiPo; WBLP
By the shot tower. Blackfriars. John Betjeman. NoP
By the shrouded gleam of the western skies. Keenan's Charge. George Parsons Lathrop. AA; BBV; HBV; MC; PAH; PAP; PFY
By the side of a green stagnate pool. A Pastoral. G. A. Stevens. CoMu; ErPo
By the side of a murmuring stream an elderly gentleman sat. The Elderly Gentleman. George Canning. BoHV; NA
By the side of the railway track. The Telephone Pole. Karel van den Oever. OnPM
By the Statue of King Charles at Charing Cross. Lionel Johnson. BoC; BrPo; CoBE; HBV; JKCP; MoBrPo; NBM; OBEV (new ed.); OBMV; OBNC; OBVV; PeVV; PIA; PoEL-5; PoVP; RoGo; ShBV-4; ViPP
By the time he's suited. Cold Fact. Dick Emmons. PoPl
By the time you swear you're his. Unfortunate Coincidence. Dorothy Parker. ALV; PoPl; PoPo; TreF; WhC
By the Turnstile. John Francis O'Donnell. IrPN; NBM
By the Waterfall. Friedrich Adler, *tr. fr. German by* Jethro Bithell. TrJP
By the Waters of Babylon. Heine, *tr. fr. German by* Charles Godfrey Leland. *Fr.* Hebrew Melodies. TrJP
By the waters of Babylon, there we sat down. *See* By the rivers of Babylon. . .
By the waters of Babylon we sat down and wept. Super Flumina Babylonis. Swinburne. AnFE; MaVP; OBVV; PoEL-5; PoFr; PoVP; ViPo
By the waters of Life we sat together. An Old Man's Idyl. Richard Realf. AA; HBV
By the wave rising, by the wave breaking. The Crow. P. K. Page. WHW
By the Way, *sel.* William Allingham.
"You see/ Nestled into a hollow of the downs." IrPN
By the wayside, on a mossy stone. Old. Ralph Hoyt. AA
By the wayside, three crows sat on a cross. Adam on His Way Home. Robert Pack. ErPo; PoDB
By the Weir. W. W. Gibson. MoVE; POTE
By the wide lake's margin I marked her lie. Shelter. Charles Stuart Calverley. PCD
By the wild sea-wall I wandered. Keats at Teignmouth: 1818. Charles Causley. MemP; ML; POTi
By the wireless I can hear. Wireless. Rodney Bennett. BoTP
By the Wood. Robert Nichols. ChMP; HBMV; MMA; NP
By these presents be it known. Countess Temple [*or* Anne Grenville, Countess Temple], Appointed Poet Laureate to the King of the Fairies. Horace Walpole. CEP; OBEC
By these slow shadows and the frosted air. Calvinist Autumnal. Elizabeth B. Harrod. NePoEA
By thine own tears thy song must tears beget. The Song-Throe. Dante Gabriel Rossetti. The House of Life, LXI. MaVP; PoVP; ViPo
By this body's lonely ark. To Fear. Clifford J. Laube. JKCP (1926 ed.)
By this bright bank the easy noon. The River Glideth in a Secret Tongue. Anthony Ostroff. NePoAm-2
By this cold shuddering fit of fear. The Glen of Silence. "Hugh MacDiarmid." NeBP
By this he knew she wept with waking eyes. Modern Love, I. George Meredith. AnEnPo; BEL; EnLi-2; EnLit; EnLoPo; HBV; HoPM; ILP; NBM; OAEP; Po; PoAn; PoEL-5; PoVP; Sonn; StP; ViPo; ViPP; VP
By this, Leander, being near the land. Christopher Marlowe. *Fr.* Hero and Leander. ErPo
By this low fire I often sit to woo. Frederick Goddard Tuckerman. *Fr.* Sonnets. AP; Sonn
By this, the dreadfull beast drew nigh to hand. The Death of the Dragon. Spenser. *Fr.* The Faerie Queene, I. WHA; YAT
By this the northerne wagoner had set. Spenser. *Fr.* The Faerie Queene, I. FosPo
By this the sun was all one glitter. Lines. John Masefield. *Fr.* The Everlasting Mercy. GBV
By this, though deep the evening fell. Flodden [*or* The Battle]. Sir Walter Scott. *Fr.* Marmion, VI. PoEL-4; PoFr
By those soft tods of wooll. A Conjuration, to Electra. Robert Herrick. AtBAP; PoEL-3; SiSw
By Thy Life I Live. Mme Guyon. *See* Adoration.
By thys fyre I warme my handys. The Months. *Unknown.* ChTr

By Way of Preface. Edward Lear. *See* How Pleasant to Know Mr. Lear.
By way of pretext. Pretext. Yakamochi. *Fr.* Manyo Shu. AWP; JAWP; LiTW; WBP; WoL
By ways remote and distant waters sped. On the Burial of His Brother. Catullus. AWP; EnLi-1; JAWP; OuHeWo; WBP
By Wellesbourne and Charlcote ford. Women Singing. Sir Henry Taylor. OBVV
By what astrology of fear or hope. Longfellow. *Fr.* To a Child. FaBoEn
By what bold passion am I rudely led. Sir William Davenant. *Fr.* Gondibert, I. FaBoEn; OBS
By what sends. Children's Rhymes. Langston Hughes. BOLo
By what strange prescience he plucks the green. The Well-Finder. Harold Vinal. FiSC
By What Sweet Name. Gotthold Lessing. *See* I Asked My Fair, One Happy Day.
By what word's power, the key of paths untrod. Heart's Hope. Dante Gabriel Rossetti. The House of Life, V. EnLit; EPN; HBV; MaVP; PoVP; ViPo; VP
By Wood and Wold. Adam Lindsay Gordon. BoAu
By World Laid Low. *Unknown, tr. fr. Irish.* ChTr
By yon bonnie banks and by yon bonnie braes. Loch Lomond. Lady John Scott. TreFS
By Yon Burn Side. Robert Tannahill. HBV
By yon castle wa', at the close of the day. There'll Never Be Peace. Burns. CBEP
By your unnumbered charities. Hospital for Defectives. Thomas Blackburn. GTBS-P
Bye Baby Bunting. Boston Nursery Rhymes. Joseph Cook. BOHV
Bye [*or* By], baby bunting. Mother Goose. BoChLi; HBV; HBVY; OTPC; OxNR; PPL; RIS; SAS; SoPo; StVeCh; TiPo; TrAS, *with music*
Bye, baby, your path diagonal. To C., Crossing the Park. Pamela Millward. FRC
Bye Bye. *Unknown. See* When Little Birdie Bye-bye Goes.
Bye, bye, baby bunting/ Your Daddy's gone a-hunting. *Unknown.* OxNR
By-Election Idyll. Peter Dickinson. FiBHP
Bye-o, baby, bye. Mamma's Gone to the Mail Boat. *Unknown.* OuSiCo
Bygones. Bert Leston Taylor. BOHV; HBMV
By'm By, *with music. Unknown.* AS
B'york! but it's lovely under the leaf. Spring Song. Donald Finkel. NYBP
Byrnies, The. Thom Gunn. NePoEA-2
Byron, *sel.* Joaquin Miller.
In Men Whom Men Condemn [as Ill]. HBV; MaRV; MoAmPo; NeMA; OQP; OTD; PoLF; TreFT
(Byron.) MAP
(Lines: "In men whom men condemn as ill.") BBV (1951 ed.)
Byron! how sweetly sad thy melody! Sonnet to Byron. Keats. ERoP-2; MBW-2
Byron Recollected at Bologna. Samuel Rogers. *Fr.* Italy. OBNC
(Byron and Bologna.) OBRV
Byron the Voluptuary. Sir William Watson. VA
Byron's Conspiracy. George Chapman. *See* Conspiracy of Charles, Duke of Byron, The.
Byron's Tragedy. George Chapman. *See* Tragedy of Charles, Duke of Byron, The.
Byrontown, *with music.* Larry Gorman. ShS
Bytuene Mersh and Averil. *Unknown. See* Alisoun.
Byway in Biography. Maurice Hare. MemP
By ways, The/ of my oaten straw? Hayseed. Theodore Weiss. TwAmPo
Byzantium. W. B. Yeats. CABA; CBV; CMoP; CoBMV; DiPo; FaBoEn; FaBoMo; GTBS-W; ILP; LiTM; LoBV; MaPo; MoAB; MoBrPo (1962 ed.); MoPo; NoP; OAEP (2d ed.); OnYI; PAn; PoE; PoeP; PoIE; SeCePo; SeCeV; StP; VaPo

C

CCC, The. Thomas Whitbread. NYBP
C. C. Rider (A *and* B *vers.*), *with music. Unknown.* AS
C Is for the Circus. Phyllis McGinley. *Fr.* All around the Town. SoPo; TiPo
C. L. M. John Masefield. BoLiVe; HBV; LiTM; MoBrPo
(To His Mother, C. L. M.) OBVV
C. S. A. Commissioners, The. *Unknown.* PAH
C Stands for Civilization. Kenneth Fearing. TrJP
Ça ira! *sel. Unknown, tr. fr. French by* John Oxenford.
"All will go right—will go right—will go right," 3 *sts.* PoFr
Ca' the Yowes to the Knowes. Burns. EnRP; PoE
(Hark! the Mavis.) OBEV
Ca' the Yowes to the Knowes. Isobel Pagan. OBEV
Ca' the Yowes to the Knowes. *Unknown.* OxBS
Cabin in the Clearing, A. Robert Frost. TDP
Cable Hymn, The. Whittier. PAH; ThLM
Cablegram. Aaron Kramer. NYTB
Cables entangling her. She Is Far from the Land. Thomas Hood. DTC; WiR
Caboose Thoughts. Carl Sandburg. AnAmPo; CMoP
Cachalot, The, *sels.* E. J. Pratt.
"Thousand years now had his breed, A." MoCV; OBCV
"Where Cape Delgado strikes the sea." CaP; MoCV
Cackle, cackle, Mother Goose. *Unknown.* OxNR; SiTL
Cacoëthes Scribendi. Oliver Wendell Holmes. AA; BoHV
Cactus. Terence Heywood. BoSA
Cactus towers, straight and tall, The. In Mexico. Evaleen Stein. AA
Cacus, if any chance on him to call. In Cacum. Thomas Bastard. SiCE
Cadences. John Payne. VA
Cadenus and Vanessa. Swift. EiCL
"Cupid tho' all his Darts were lost," *sel.* OxBI
Cadenza. Ted Hughes. NYBP; OPoP
Cadenza. Miriam Waddington. CaP
Cadgwith. Lionel Johnson. CoBE; GTBS; JKCP; OBVV; PoVP
"Mary Star of the sea," III. ISi
Cadmus and Harmonia. Matthew Arnold. *Fr.* Empedocles on Etna. OBVV; ViPo
("Far, far from here.") GTBS-P
(Song of Callicles, The.) FiP
Caecus awaked, was told the Sun appeared. Nullum Stimulum Ignavis. Henry Parrot. SiCE
Cædmon. George Garrett. NePoAm-2
Cædmon. Thomas S. Jones, Jr. InP
Cædmon. Norman Nicholson. FaBoTw
Caelia, *sels.* William Browne.
"Lo, I the man that whilom loved and lost," I. Sonn
"So sat the Muses on the banks of Thames," IV. Sonn
Caelia. Richard Duke. PeRV
Caelia, *sel.* Sir David Murray.
Sonnet: "Ponder thy cares, and sum them all in one." ElL
Caelia's fair, the charming toast. On a Painted Lady. William Pattison. WaPE
Caelica. Fulke Greville. FCP
Sels.
"Absence, the noble truce," XLV [XLIV]. EnRePo; NCEP; PoEL-1
(Absence and Presence.) OBSC
"All my senses, like beacon's flame," LVI. EnRePo; PoEL-1; QFR
"Away with these self-loving lads," LII. AtBAP; EnRePo; ReIE; SiCE
(Another, of His Cynthia.) TuPP
(Cynthia.) OBSC
(Of His Cynthia.) ElL; ELP; NoP
(Song to His Cynthia.) ViBoPo
"Caelica, I overnight was finely used," XXXVIII. EnRePo; EP; Sonn; TuPP
"Caelica, while you doe sweare you love me best," LXI. NCEP
"Cupid, my little boy, come home againe," XXXV. AtBAP
"Cupid, my pretty boy, leave off thy crying," XXV. AtBAP
"Cupid, thou naughty boy, when thou wert loathed," XII. EnRePo; NCEP; Sonn; TuPP
"Cynthia, because your horns look diverse ways," LIV. SiCE
"Down [*or* Downe] in the depth of mine iniquity," XCIX [C]. EnRePo; EP; ForPo; OBS; PoIE; QFR; SiCE
(Down in the Depth.) LiTG
(Saving God, The.) LoBV (2d ed.)
"Earth, The, with thunder torn, with fire blasted," LXXXVI [LXXXVII]. EnRePo; QFR; SiCE; Sonn; TuPP
"Eternal [*or* Eternall] Truth, almighty, infinite," XCVII [XCVIII]. EnRePo; OBS; OxBoCh; SiCE

Caelica (continued)
"Faction, that ever dwells," XXIX. EnRePo
(Love and Fortune.) OBSC
"Farewell, sweet boy; complain not of my truth," LXXXIV [LXXXV]. EnRePo; EP; NCEP; QFR; Sonn
(Farewell to Cupid.) OBSC
"Fie [or Fye], foolish Earth, think you the heaven wants glory,"XVI. EnRePo; LO; PoEL-1; ReIE; SiCE; Sonn; TuPP
(Love's Glory.) OBSC
"I offer wrong to my beloved Saint," XVIII. NCEP
"I, with whose colors [or colours] Myra dressed [or drest] her head," XXII. AtBAP; EG; EnRePo; PoE; QFR
(Myra.) CBEP; EIL; GTBS-W; LoBV; OBEV; OBSC
(To Myra.) LiTB; LiTG; LiTL; ViBoPo
"In night, when colors all to black are cast," C. EnRePo; EP; QFR; Sonn
"In the time when herbs and flowers," LXXVI.
(Caelica and Philocell.) OBSC
"In the window of a grange," LXXIV.
(Love and Honour.) OBSC
"Juno, that on her head Love's livery carried," XI. EP; NCEP
"Love, the delight of all well-thinking minds," I. OBSC; PoE; SiCE
"Malice and love in their ways opposite," XVC. SiCE
"Man, dream [or dreame] no more of curious mysteries," LXXXVIII [LXXXIX]. EnRePo; MePo; OBS; QFR
"Men that delight to multiply desire," XCIV [XCV]. OBS; SiCE
"Merlin, they say an English prophet borne," XXIII. NCEP
"More than most fair, full of that heavenly fire," III. EIL; SiCE
(To His Lady.) OBSC
"Nurse-life wheat, within his green husk growing, The," XL. EnRePo; EP; NCEP
(Youth and Maturity.) OBSC
"O false and treacherous Probability," CIII [CIV]. OBS; OxBoCh
"Sathan, no woman, yet a wandering spirit," XXI. NCEP
"Selfe-pitties teares, wherein my hope lyes drown'd," VIII. AtBAP
"Sion lies [or Syon lyes] waste, and thy Jerusalem," CIX [CX]. EnRePo; NoP; OxBoCh; PoEL-1; QFR; ReIE; SiCE; TuPP
"Three things there be in man's opinion deare," CV [CVI]. LiTB; LiTG; OBS; PoEL-1; SiCE
"Under a throne I saw a virgin sit," LXXXI [LXXXII]. ReIE; SiCE; TuPP
"When all this All doth pass from age to age," LXIX. EnRePo; EP
"Whenas [or When as] man's life, the light of human lust," LXXXVII [LXXXVIII]. EP; GTBS-W; LiTB; MePo; OBS; OxBoCh; PoEL-1; PoIE
"Who ever sailes neere to Bermuda coast," LXI. NCEP
"Who grace, for zenith had, from which no shadowes grow," LXXXIII [LXXXIV]. PoEL-1
(Despair.) OBSC
"World, that all contains, The, is ever moving," VII. EnRePo; ReIE; SiCE; TuPP
(Change.) OBSC
"Wrapped [or Wrapt] up, O Lord, in man's degeneration," XCVIII [XCIX]. EnRePo; EP; ForPo; OxBoCh; QFR; SiCE
"You little stars [or starres] that live in skies [or skyes]," IV. CBEP; EIL; NCEP; ReIE; SiCE; TuPP
(His Lady's Eyes.) OBSC
"You that seek what life is in death," LXXXII [LXXXIII]. EnRePo
(Time and Eternity.) OBSC
Caelica and Philocell. Fulke Greville, Caelica, LXXVI. OBSC
Caelica, I overnight was finely used. Caelica, XXXVIII. Fulke Greville. EP; Sonn; TuPP
Caelica, while you doe sweare you love me best. Caelica, LXI. Fulke Greville. NCEP
Caelius, my Lesbia, that one, that only Lesbia. Whom Lesbia Loved. Catullus. LiTW
Caesar. W. S. Merwin. FRC; NaP
Caesar. Paul Valéry, *tr. fr. French by* C. F. MacIntyre. WaaP
Caesar, afloat with his fortunes! The Turtle. *Unknown.* PAH
Caesar and Pompey. George Chapman. *See* Tragedy of Caesar and Pompey, The.
Caesar Borgia, *sel.* Nathaniel Lee.
Blush Not Redder than the Morning. SeCL
Caesar Remembers. William Kean Seymour. HBMV; OnPP
Caesar, serene Caesar, your foot on all. Caesar. Paul Valéry. WaaP
Caesar, that proud man. Caesar Remembers. William Kean Seymour. HBMV; OnPP
Caesar, when that the traitor of Egypt. Sir Thomas Wyatt. FCP
Caesar's Lost Transport Ships. Robert Frost. AmePo
Caesura. Kenneth Mackenzie. BoAV
Café Scene. Saunders Lewis, *tr. fr. Welsh by* Gwyn Williams. PrWP
Café Tableau. May Swenson. ErPo
Caffer Commando, The, *sel.* Thomas Pringle.
"Hark! heard ye the signals of triumph afar?" ACV
Cage, The. Martin Armstrong. PoFr; POTE
Cage, The. Elizabeth Bartlett. NePoAm-2
Cage, The. Eric Torgersen. QAH
Caged Bird, The. Arthur Symons. BrPo
Caged in old woods, whose reverend echoes wake. Captivity. Samuel Rogers. FaBoEn; OBNC
Caged Mongoose, The. Constance Hollar. PoNe
Caged Skylark, The. Gerard Manley Hopkins. CMoP; LiTM; MoAB; MoBrPo; MoPo; OBMV; PoeP; Sonn; TDP; ViPP; VP
Cages. Marvin Solomon. NYBP
Caiaphas, Pilate and Herod. Fellowship. Elinor Lennen. ChIP
Caileach Bein-y-Vreich. John Campbell Shairp. VA
Cain. Irving Layton. MoCV; PeCV (1967 ed.)
Cain Shall Not Slay Abel Today on Our Good Ground. Malcolm Lowry. OBCV; PeCV
Cainsmorning. Dom Moraes. MemP
Cairo Jag. Keith Douglas. NePoEA
Caisson Song, The. Edmund L. Gruber. PAL; TreF
Cake. Miriam Clark Potter. BiCB
Cakes and Ale. *Unknown. See* I Gave Her Cakes; I Gave Her Ale.
Calabash wherein she served my food, The. The Serving Girl. Gladys May Casely Hayford. CDC; GoSl; PoNe
Calais, August, 1802. Wordsworth. MERP; Sonn
Calais Sands. Matthew Arnold. OAEP
Calamity. F. R. Scott. PeCV (1967 ed.)
Calculation, The. David Wagoner. NYBP
Caldwell of Springfield. Bret Harte. PAH
Caledonian Market, The. William Plomer. ChMP; HaMV
Calendar. Witter Bynner. *Fr.* Chapala Poems. NP
Calendar, A. Sara Coleridge. *See.* Garden Year, The.
Calendar Rhyme. Flora Willis Watson. BoTP
Calenture. Alastair Reid. NYBP
Cales and Guyana. John Donne. MaMe
Calf-Path, The. Sam Walter Foss. HBV; HBVY; PoLF
Caliban ("Be not afeard; the isle is full of noises"). Shakespeare. *Fr.* The Tempest, III, ii. FiP
("Be not afeard [or affeard or afeared], the isle is full of noises [or noyses].") AtBAP; FlW; UnS
(To Dream Again.) TrGrPo
Caliban in the Coal Mines. Louis Untermeyer. HBV; MAP; MaRV; MoAmPo; NeMA; PDV; PoMa; PoPl; PoPo; TreFS; TrJP; TRV; WePo
Caliban upon Setebos. Robert Browning. AWP; EPN; MaVP; NoP; OAEP; PeVV; PoVP; ViPo; VP; WGRP
Calico Pie. Edward Lear. CBEP; FaBoCh; FaPON; GoTP; LoGBV; MPB; SAS; SoPo; TrGrPo; WhC
California. Thomas Lake Harris. AA
California. Lydia Huntley Sigourney. MC; PAH
California, *with music. Unknown.* AS
California as It Is and Was, *with music.* John A. Stone. SGR
California Ball, *with music.* John A. Stone. SGR
California Bank Robbers, *with music.* John A. Stone. SGR
California Bloomer, *with music.* John A. Stone. SGR
California Humbugs, *with music.* Mart Taylor. SGR
California Joe. "Captain Jack" Crawford. CoSo
California Legislature. John A. Stone. SGR
California over the Left. "Jack the Grumbler." SGR
California people are determined if they find, The. California Bank Robbers. John A. Stone. SGR
California song, A. Song of the Redwood-Tree. Walt Whitman. AmPP (5th ed.)
California Stage Company, The. John A. Stone. CoSo; SGR, *with music*
California Winter, *sel.* Karl Shapiro.

"This land grows the oldest living things," 6 *ll.* AmFN
Californians, The. Theodore Spencer. NYBP
Caligula. Robert Lowell. CoPo
Caligula, envying the bright fames. Of the Small Respect Had of Learned Men in General. John Davies of Hereford. SiCE
Caliph shot a gazelle, The. Humorous Verse. Abu Dolama. TTY
Caliph's Draught, The. Sir Edwin Arnold. VA
Calisto, *sel.* John Crowne.
Kind Lovers, Love On. InvP
(Song: "Kind lovers, love on.") ALV; SeCL
Call, The. Thomas Curtis Clark. PGD
Call, The. Daniel Corkery. OnYI
Call, The. James Dickey. *See* Owl King, The.
Call, The. John Hall. FaBoEn; LO; MeLP; MePo; OBS; SeCL; ViBoPo
Call, The. George Herbert. MaMe
Call, The. Reginald Wright Kauffman. HBV
Call, The. Charlotte Mew. ChMP
Call, The. Thomas Osbert Mordaunt. *See* Sound, Sound the Clarion.
Call, The. Jones Very. MAmP
Call, The. *Unknown.* OBEV
"Call All." *Unknown.* PAH
Call all hands to man the capstan. Rolling Home, *vers.* I. *Unknown.* ShS
Call Back. *Unknown.* SoP
Call—call—and bruise the air. Expression. Isaac Rosenberg. MoBrPo
"Call down the hawk from the air." The Hawk. W. B. Yeats. AtBAP; FIW
Call for the Robin Redbreast [and the Wren]. John Webster. *Fr.* The White Devil, V, iv. AtBAP; CaFP; CBEP; ChTr; ExPo; FaBoCh; LoGBV; NoP; OAEP; PoE; PoEL-2; PoRA; ReEn; SeCePo; SeCeV; SiCE; StP; TuPP; ViBoPo
(Cornelia's Song.) OBS; PoIE; TrGrPo
(Dirge, A: "Call for the robin redbreast and the wren.") BEL; EIL; EnLi-1; FaBoEn; GTBS; GTSE; GTSL; HBV; LiTB; OBEV; ThWaDe; UnPo; WHA
(Funeral Dirge for Marcello.) AnFE
(Land Dirge, A.) CH; GTBS-D; GTBS-P; GTBS-W; LoBV
(Song: "Call for the robin redbreast and the wren.") CBV; ShBV-3
Call for True Repentance, A. Jeremiah, VII: 1-20, Bible, *O.T.* WoL
Call Him the Lover and call me the Bride. The Song the Body Dreamed in the Spirit's Mad Behest. Brother Antoninus. ErPo
Call into Death. D. H. Lawrence. BoPe
Call is for belief, The. The Fundament Is Shifted. Abbie Huston Evans. MoRP; NYBP
Call it a crescent. Kalymniad, II. Robert Lax. ThO
Call It Goofus. Bill Berkson. ANYP
Call it neither love nor spring madness. Without Name. Pauli Murray. AmNP; PoNe
Call it not vain—they do not err. The Minstrel Responds to Flattery. Sir Walter Scott. *Fr.* The Lay of the Last Minstrel, V. OBNC; OBRV
Call John the Boatman, *with music.* *Unknown.* ShS
"Call Junius!" From the crowd a shadow stalked. At the Gate of Heaven. Byron. *Fr.* The Vision of Judgment. OBRV
Call Martha Corey. The Trial. Longfellow. *Fr.* Giles Corey of the Salem Farms. PAH
Call me friend or foe. The Comrade. Lee Wilson Dodd. HBMV
Call me no more. His Lachrimae or Mirth, Turn'd to Mourning. Robert Herrick. SCEP-2; SeCV-1; SeEP
Call me no more, O gentle stream. To a River in the South. Sir Henry Newbolt. CH
Call me no more the cursed tree. I Saw Death Slain. William Capell. ChIP
Call Me Not Back from the Echoless Shore. *Unknown.* BLPA
Call Me Not Dead. Richard Watson Gilder. HBV; WGRP
Call me not false, beloved. The Bridegroom. Kipling. *Fr.* Epitaphs of the War. CLwM
Call no faith false which e'er has brought. Tolerance. Sir Lewis Morris. OBVV
Call not on comfort lest she come. Passivity. Mary Fullerton. BoAV
Call not thy wanderer home as yet. Germinal. "Æ." MoBrPo; OBEV (new ed.); OBMV
Call of the Bugles, The. Richard Hovey. AA
Call of the Christian, The. Whittier. SoP
Call of the East, The. Henry W. Frost. SoP
Call of the Morning, The. George Darley. OnYI
Call of the Plains, The. Ethel MacDiarmid. SCC
Call of the River Nun, The. Gabriel Okara. PBA
Call of the Spring, The. Alfred Noyes. SUS
Call of the Wild, The. Robert W. Service. CaP
Call off your eyes from care. A Young Man's Exhortation. Thomas Hardy. ViPP
Call on Sir Walter Raleigh, A. Sarah M. Bryan Piatt. AA
Call on thy children of the hill. Carolina. Henry Timrod. PoRL
Call out, celebrate the beam. The Tears of a Muse in America. F. T. Prince. FaBoMo
"Call Rose Costara!" The Night Court. Ruth Comfort Mitchell. HBV
Call the cows home! Thunder. Walter de la Mare. BoNaP
Call the roller of big cigars. The Emperor of Ice-Cream. Wallace Stevens. AmLP; AmP; AmPP(4th ed.); AP; CABA; CaFP; CMoP; CoBMV; FaBoMo; FosPo; LiTA; MoPo; MoVE; NePA; OxBA; PoAn; PoeP; PoFS; PoIE; PoSa; TDP; ViBoPo (1958 ed.)
Call to a Scot, The. Ruth Guthrie Harding. HBV
Call to Action, A. Callinus, *tr. fr. Greek by* T. F. Higham. WaaP
(Rallying Song, *tr. by* H. N. Coleridge.) PoFr
Call to Arms, A. Mary Raymond Shipman Andrews. MC; PAH
Call to Conflict. *Unknown.* STF
Call to Pentecost, A. Inez M. Tyler. BLRP
Call to the Colors, The. Arthur Guiterman. PaA; PAH
Call to the Guard by a Drum, A. Alexander Radcliffe. PeRV
Call to the Strong, The. William Pierson Merrill. BLRP
Call to the swan and bid him bring. Childless. L. A. G. Strong. POTE
Call to the Wild, A. Lord Dunsany. OnYI
Callahan. *Unknown.* OuSiCo
Called Aside. *Unknown.* SoP
Called Away. Richard Le Gallienne. *See* I Meant to Do My Work Today.
Called Back. Emily Dickinson. *See* Just lost when I was saved!
Called out by fife and drum. Memorial Day. Alma Adams Wiley. PEDC
Called son by many lands. St. Patrick's Treasure. Patrick J. Carroll. JKCP
Caller Herrin'. Lady Nairne. HBV; MCCG; OBRV; OxBS
Callicles' Song. Matthew Arnold. *See* Song of Callicles.
Callimachus to Heraclitus. Callimachus, *tr. fr. Greek by* Ralph Marcus. OnPM
Calling, The. Luis Felipe Contardo, *tr. fr. Spanish by* Thomas Walsh. CAW
Calling, The. George Sigerson. JKCP (1926 ed.)
Calling all butterflies of every race. Pod of the Milkweed. Robert Frost. LiTM (1970 ed.)
Calling and the melody all night long, The. Chapultepec Park. Muriel Rukeyser. FiMAP
Calling Eagles. Leo Kennedy. TwCaPo
Calling in the Cat. Elizabeth J. Coatsworth. AnAmPo; NeMA; OA
Calling the Cows Home. Jean Ingelow. *Fr.* The High Tide on the Coast of Lincolnshire (1571). ThGo
Calling the Doctor. John Wesley Holloway. BANP; IHA
Calling, the heron flies athwart the blue. The Creek-Road. Madison Cawein. AA
Calling the Violet. Lucy Larcom. MPB
Calling to mind, my eyes went long [*or* mine eye long went] about. The Excuse. Sir Walter Ralegh. FCP; SiPS
Calling to mind [*or* minde], since first my love begun. Idea, LI. Michael Drayton. EnRePo; OBSC; PoEL-2; SiCE
Calliope *with music.* *Unknown.* AS
Calloused grass lies hard, The. By the Road to the Air-Base. Yvor Winters. CrMA; Po
Callow young were huddling in the nests, The. Scorned. Alexander Smith. OBVV
Calls, The. Wilfred Owen. BoPe
Calls. Carl Sandburg. NP
Calls on the Dream Telephone, *sels.* Dick Lourie. ThO
Bestfriend, The.

Calls (continued)
WhenIwas, The.
Callst thou me friend? What rhetorick is this? Meditation. Edward Taylor. *Fr.* Preparatory Meditations, Second Series. MeP
Calm. Stanton A. Coblentz. EtS
Calm, The. John Donne. CABL; LoBV; ReEn; ReIE; SeEP; StP; TuPP
(Calme, The.) MaMe; MePo
Calm. Whittier. SoP
Calm after Storm. Frank Yerby. AmNP
Calm and Full the Ocean. Robinson Jeffers. WaP
Calm and implacable. Imitation. Anthony C. Deane. BOHV
Calm as that second summer which precedes. Charleston. Henry Timrod. AA; AmePo; AmLP; AmP; AmPP; AP; CoBA; MAmP; OxBA; PAH
Calm as the Cloudless Heaven. "Christopher North." EtS
Calm, cool face, The. Suicide's Note. Langston Hughes. CDC
Calm Death, God of crossed hands and passionless eyes. Death. George Pellew. AA
Calm is all nature as a resting wheel. Written in Very Early Youth. Wordsworth. EnRP
Calm is the landcape when the storm has passed. Peace in the Welsh Hills. Vernon Watkins. ChMP; GTBS-P
Calm is the morn without a sound. In Memoriam A.H.H., XI. Tennyson. BoLiVe; ChTr; CoBE; ELP; EnLi-2; EPN; ExPo; FaBoEn; FiP; ForPo; FosPo; GTBS-D; GTSL; LiTB; MaPo (1969 ed.); OAEP; OBEV (1st ed.); OBNC; PIA; PoE; PoEL-5; PoFS; SeCeV; ShBV-4; TrGrPo; ViPo; VP
Calm martyr of a noble cause. Jefferson Davis. Walker Meriwether Bell. PAH
Calm Me, My God. Horatius Bonar. SoP
Calm Morning at Sea. Sara Teasdale. EtS
Calm Nature's idle spy, I follow. Swallows. Afanasi Afanasievich Fet. OnPM
Calm of heaven rests upon my heart, The. Blessed Nearness. Mary Bullock. STF
Calm on the bosom of thy God. Dirge [*or* A Death-Hymn]. Felicia Dorothea Hemans. *Fr.* The Siege of Valencia. HBV; OBEV; OBRV
Calm on the listening ear of night. The Birth Song of Christ [*or* A Christmas Hymn]. Edmund H. Sears. BePJ; SoP
Calm, sad, secure; behind high convent walls. Nuns of the Perpetual Adoration. Ernest Dowson. PoVP; TOP; ViPP
Calm Sea, A. Robert Southey. EtS
Calm Soul of All Things. Matthew Arnold. *Fr.* Lines Written in Kensington Gardens. TrPWD; TRV; WGRP
(Inward Peace.) MaRV
Calm, strong and gentle Man of Galilee. As He Walked with Us. Harry Webb Farrington. ChIP; SoP
Calm the boy sleeps, though death is in the clouds. Infant Noah. Vernon Watkins. NeBP
Calm, the surrounding mountains look upon. The Submerged Village. James Kirkup. POTi
Calm (*or* Calme] was the day, and through the trembling air [*or* ayre]. Prothalamion. Spenser. AnFE; AtBAP; ATP; AWP; BEL; CABA; CaFP; ChTr; CoBE; ElL; EnL; EnLi-1; EnLit; EnRePo; FaBoEn; FosPo; GoTL; GTBS; GTBS-D; GTBS-P; GTBS-W; GTSE; GTSL; HBV; HW; InPo; LiTB; LiTG; LiTL; LoBV; MaPo; MCCG; NoP; OBEV; OBSC; OuHeWo; PAn; PIA; PoE; PoIE; ReEn; ReIE; SeCePo; ShBV-4; SiCE; StP; TOP; UnPo (1st ed.); VaPo; ViBoPo; WHA
Calm Was the Even [and Clear Was the Sky]. Dryden. *Fr.* An Evening's Love; or, The Mock-Astrologer, IV, i. DiPo; MaPo; OAEP
(Song: "Calm was the even, and clear was the sky.") CavP; CBV; CEP; MBW-1; SeCV-2
Calm was the evening and clear was the sky (*longer vers.*). Amintas and Claudia; or, The Merry Shepherdess. *Unknown.* CoMu
Calm Winter Sleep. Hilary Corke. NYBP
Calme, The. John Donne. *See* Calm, The.
Calmly as the morning's soft tears shed. On a Lady Sleeping. *Unknown.* SeCL
Calmly beside her tropic strand. Charleston. Paul Hamilton Hayne. PAH
Calmly, breathe calmly all your music, maids! The Last Music. Lionel Johnson. PoVP
Calmly we walk through this April's day. Time Is the Fire [*or* For Rhoda]. Delmore Schwartz. The Repetitive Heart, IV. LiTA; LiTM; MoAB; MoAmPo; MoVE; OxBA
Calumny. Frances Sargent Osgood. AA; HBV
Calvaries, The. Peter Williamson. NYTB
Calvary. Henry W. Frost. SoP
Calvary. Mary Hallet. ChIP; PGD
Calvary. William Dean Howells. AmePo; ChIP; OQP
Calvary. Hugh Robert Orr. ChIP
Calvary. E. A. Robinson. AmePo; AnNE; ChIP; CoBA; MAP; MaRV; MoAmPo; NeMA; OQP; PoDB; PoPo; Sonn; StJW; TreFS; WGRP
Calvary. Libby Stopple. GoYe
Calvary ("Ev'ry time I think about Jesus"), *with music.* *Unknown.* BoAN-1
Calvary ("I walked alone to my Calvary"). *Unknown.* OQP
Calvary and Easter. "Susan Coolidge." OQP; PGD; WBLP
(Easter Song, An.) BLRP; SoP; TRV
Calvary is a continent. Still the Cross. E. Merrill Root. MaRV; StJW
Calvary was just one more. Daily Cross. Earl Bigelow Brown. ChIP
Calvary's Cry. John William Cunningham. BePJ
Calved from a glacier near Godhaven coast. The Iceberg. E. J. Pratt. *Fr.* The *Titanic.* TwCaPo
Calvinist Autumnal. Elizabeth B. Harrod. NePoEA
Calvinist in Love, A. Jack R. Clemo. ChMP
Calvinist Sang. Alexander Scott. OxBS
Calvus, if any joy from mortal tears. Quintilia Dead. Catullus. OnPM
Calvus to a Fly. Charles Tennyson Turner. Sonn
Calypso. William Carlos Williams. NePoAm-2
Calypsomania. Anthony Brode. FiBHP
Calypso's Island. Archibald MacLeish. MoAB; NoP
Calyx of the Oboe Breaks, The. Conrad Aiken. NYBP
(Music.) AP
Cam' Ye By ("Cam' ye by the salmon fishers?"). *Unknown.* AtBAP; CH
Cambric Shirt, The. *Unknown.* *See* Elfin Knight, The.
Cambridge, an outdoor library stack of bricks. Vale. John Ciardi. MiAP
Cambridge and the Alps. Wordsworth. The Prelude, VI. ERoP-1
Sels.
"Melancholy slackening that ensued, The." PoEL-4
"When the third summer freed us from restraint." MBW-2
Cambridge Ladies [Who Live in Furnished Souls], The. E. E. Cummings. *Fr.* Sonnets—Realities. AmPP (5th ed.); AnAmPo; CBEP; CoBA; MoPW; MoVE; NoP; OxBA; PoSa; PPON; Sonn; ViBoPo (1958 ed.)
Cambyses, *sel.* Elkanah Settle.
She That with Love Is Not Possessed. SeCL
Camden Magpie. Hugh McCrae. PoAu-1
Camden, most reverend head, to whom I owe. To William Camden. Ben Jonson. AnAnS-2; AWP; InPo; OBS; PoFS; ReEn; ReIE; SCEP-2; SeCV-1; SeEP; TuPP
Came a merchantman of yore. The Pearl of Great Price. William Chatterton Dix. SoP
Came a roaring bumble-bee. Bumble-Bee and Clover. *Unknown.* GFA
Came first, five hundred miles from port. Approaching America. J. C. Squire. HBMV
Came in my full youth to the midnight cave. Ajanta. Muriel Rukeyser. FiMAP; LiTA; LiTM; MiAP; MoAB; MoAmPo (1950 ed.); TwAmPo
Came, on a Sabbath morn [*or* noon], my sweet. Meet We No Angels, Pansie? Thomas Ashe. HBV; OBEV (1st ed.); OBVV
Came the morning of that day. Sumter. Edmund Clarence Stedman. MC; PAH
Came the relief. "What, sentry, ho!" Relieving Guard. Bret Harte. RoGo
Came to lakes; came to dead water. A Field of Light. Theodore Roethke. LiTM (1970 ed.); PoeP; ToPo; TwCP
Camel. Gene Derwood. NePA
Camel, The. Carmen Bernos de Gasztold, *tr. fr. French by* Rumer Godden. OA
Camel. W. S. Merwin. NePA
Camel. Mary Britton Miller. TiPo (1959 ed.); UTS
Camel, The. Ogden Nash. CenHV; SoPo
Camel. Jon Stallworthy. NYTB
Camel, at the close of day, The. The Kneeling Camel [*or*

Submission and Rest *or* Rest and Work]. Anna Temple Whitney. BLPA; BLRP; FaChP; MaRV; SoP; STF
Camel bells are sounding, The. The Little King. Irene Gass. ChrBoLe
Camel has a funny hump, The. Primer. Samuel Hoffenstein. BOHV
Camel has a single hump, The. The Camel. Ogden Nash. CenHV; SoPo
Camel Rider, The. *Unknown, tr. fr. Arabic by* Wilfrid Scawen Blunt. AWP; FaBoTw
Camellia, The. Basho, *tr. fr. Japanese by* Harold G. Henderson. RePo
"Camels are coming, The." huzza, huzza! The Camels Have Come. *Unknown.* PoOW
Camel's Complaint, The. Charles Edward Carryl. *See* Plaint of the Camel, The.
Camels Have Come, The. *Unknown.* PoOW
Camel's Hump, The. Kipling. *Fr.* Just-so Stories. BoChLi; EvOK
Camel's Lament, The. Charles Edward Carryl. *See* Plaint of the Camel, The.
Camel's Nose, The. Lydia Huntly Sigourney. OTPC (1923 ed.); PRWS
Cameo, The. Edna St. Vincent Millay. LiTA; MAP; MoAmPo
Cameos. Jeannette Bliss Gillespy. AA
Forgiven?
Valentine, A.
Camerados. Bayard Taylor. BOHV; Par
Cameronian Cat, The. *Unknown.* BOHV; CIV
Camilla. Charles Augustus Keeler. AA
Camille St. Saëns was racked with pains. Introduction. Ogden Nash. *Fr.* The Carnival of Animals. UnS
Camoens. Herman Melville. ViBoPo
Camoens in the Hospital. Herman Melville. ViBoPo
Camoes, alone, of all the lyric race. Luis de Camoes. Roy Campbell. BoSA; FaBoTw; PeSA
Camouflage. John Manifold. WaP
Camp. Patrick Anderson. OBCV
Camp Chums. Rose Waldo. MPB
Camp Fire. Beatrice Marion Bromley. ACV
Camp Hymn, The. Mary S. Edgar. *See* God, Who Touchest Earth. . .
Camp in the Prussian Forest, A. Randall Jarrell. AP; CMoP; MiAP; MoAmPo (1950 ed.); NeMA; NMP
Camp within the West, The. Roderic Quinn. BoAu; PoAu-1
Campaign, The. Addison. CEP
Blenheim, *sel.* OBEC
Campaign, The: Letters from the Front. Stephen Shrader. QAH
Campaigners, The; or, The Pleasant Adventures at Brussels, *sel.* Thomas D'Urfey.
Scotch Song, *fr.* III, i. CEP
Campañero, The, *with music.* *Unknown.* ShS
Campers. Robert Finch. TwCaPo
Camper's Night Song. Robert Louis Stevenson. *Fr.* Travels with a Donkey. BBV
Campi Flegrei. Barend Toerien, *tr. fr. Afrikaans by* Barend Toerien. PeSA
Camping Out. William Empson. CMoP; FaBoMo; MoVE; ToPo
Campion white, The/ Above the grass. The Lamp Flower. Margaret Cecilia Furse. BoTP
Camp's asleep and thro' the gloom, The. Silhouette in Sepia. Robert V. Carr. PoOW
Camps of Green. Walt Whitman. PoE
Camptown. John Ciardi. ThLM; WaP
Camptown Races, De, *with music.* Stephen Collins Foster. TrAS
Campus, The. David Posner. NYBP
Campus on the Hill, The. W. D. Snodgrass. AP; LiTM (1970 ed.); ToPo; TwCP
Can a bell ring in the heart. When Death Came April Twelve 1945. Carl Sandburg. AP
Can a Maid That Is Well Bred. *Unknown.* TuPP
Can anyone lend me two twelve-pound rats? Wanted. Shel Silverstein. PV
Can death be faithful or the grave be just. The Resurrection. Nathaniel Wanley. LoBV
Can death be sleep, when life is but a dream. On Death. Keats. SyP
Can Doleful Notes to Mesur'd Accents Set. John Danyel. UnS
(Chromatic Tunes.) MuSP
Can freckled August—drowsing warm and blonde. The Rain-Crow. Madison Cawein. AA
"Can God?" "J. A. R." SoP
Can he that loves be man. *Unknown.* SeCSL
Can I Believe. Ariosto, *tr. fr. Italian by* "Moira O'Neill." CAW
Can I Forget? Sidney Goodsir Smith. NeBP; SeCePo
Can I forget. Childhood. Henri Percikow. OCS
Can I forget that winter night. A Leap-Year Episode. *At. to* Eugene Field. BoLP
Can I forget the sickle mune. Can I Forget? Sidney Goodsir Smith. NeBP; SeCePo
Can I forget the sweet days that have been. Days That Have Been. W. H. Davies. PrWP
Can I not come to Thee, my God, for these. To His Ever-loving God. Robert Herrick. AnAnS-2; TrPWD
Can I not sin, but thou wilt be. To His Conscience. Robert Herrick. AnAnS-2; MaPo; OxBoCh; PoEL-3
Can I Not Sing [but Hoy!]. *Unknown.* ViBoPo
(Jolly Wat.) BuBa; OBB
(Joly Joly Wat.) MemP, 5 *sts.*
(Joly Wat.) AnEnPo
(Shepherd upon a [*or* the] Hill, The.) CBEP; GoBC; OxBoCh
Can—I—poet. For Some Poets. Mae Jackson. BOLo
Can I see another's woe. On Another's Sorrow. Blake. *Fr.* Songs of Innocence. AWP; CBEP; CEP; EiCL; EnRP; FaBV; LiTG; MaRV; OTPC (1923 ed.); PeER; PoEL-4; SoP; ViBoPo
Can I, who have for others oft compiled. Of My Dear Son [*or* Sonne], Gervase Beaumont. Sir John Beaumont. OBS; SeCL; SeEP; ViBoPo
Can it be possible no words shall welcome. Comforting Line. *Unknown.* STF
Can it be right to give what I can give? Sonnets from the Portuguese, IX. Elizabeth Barrett Browning. CTC; HBV; Sonn; VA
Can it roast a duck? American Poetry. Stuart Peterfreund. QAH
Can Life Be a Blessing. Dryden. *Fr.* Troilus and Cressida. ATP (1935 ed.); EiCL; SeCePo; SeCL; ViBoPo
(Song: "Can life be a blessing.") CEP; NoP; SeCV-2; SeEP
Can love be controll'd by advice? Song. John Gay. *Fr.* The Beggar's Opera. LoBV
Can man be free if woman be a slave? Shelley. *Fr.* Revolt of Islam, II. PoFr
Can rules or tutors educate. Culture. Emerson. AmePo
Can scenes like these withdraw thee from thy wood. George Crabbe. *Fr.* The Borough, Letter I. OBRV
Can She Excuse My Wrongs with Virtue's Cloak. *Unknown.* ReIE
Can that hackneyed jade be sane? On an Unpleasant Woman. Catullus. OnPM
Can the lover share his soul. Epithalamium. W. J. Turner. OBMV
Can the Mole Take. C. Day Lewis. OBMV
Can the sun forget its rising? He Will Never Fail. H. H. Savage. SoP
Can there be a moon in heaven to-night. Isabelle. James Hogg. Par
Can these movements which move themselves. Belly Dancer. Diane Wakoski. YAP
Can they still live. Ghosts. J. R. Ackerley. POTE
Can This Be Death? Martin Wedge. SoP
Can this be he. Milton. *Fr.* Samson Agonistes. InP
Can this be love men yield me in return. Renewal. Gladys Cromwell. AnAmPo; NP
Can this be the bird to man so good. The Redbreast Chasing a Butterfly. Wordsworth. OTPC
Can tyrants but by tyrants conquer'd be. Byron. *Fr.* Childe Harold's Pilgrimage, IV. PoFr
Can we believe — by an effort. Cities. Hilda Doolittle ("H. D."). ViBoPo (1941 ed.)
Can we fail to be touched by the thought. Sanctuary. J. B. Boothroyd. FiBHP
Can we not consecrate. Love and Sacrifice. Bernard O'Dowd. BoAu; BoAV
Can we not force from widowed [*or* widdowed] poetry. An

Can (continued)
Elegie [*or* Elegy] upon the Death of the Deane of Pauls, Dr. John Donne. Thomas Carew. AnAnS-2; CABA; MeLP; MePo; NoP; OBS; PP; SCEP-2; SeCP; SeCV-1; SeEP; StP
Can ye [*or* you] play me Duncan Gray. Duncan Gray[*or* The Thrusting of It]. Burns. CoMu; ErPo; UnTE
Can Ye Sew Cushions? *unknown.* FaBoCh; LoGBV
Can you dance? Music. Eleanor Farjeon. TiPo (1959 ed.)
Can you make me a cambric shirt. The Cambric Shirt [*or* Lovers' Tasks]. *Unknown.* BaBo; CBEP; OxNR
Can You Paint a Thought? John Ford. *Fr.* The Broken Heart, III, ii. AtBAP; CBEP; InvP; LO; OAEP; PoEL-2; TuPP; ViBoPo
Can you play me Duncan Gray. *See* Can ye play me . . .
Can you recall an ode to June. A Drawing-Room Ballad. Henry Duff Traill. CenHV
Can you see our way home? Millea Kenin. WOW
Can you see the bird coming through bushes. Nowhere. Floyce Alexander. QAH
"Can you spare a threepenny bit." War Relief. Oliver Herford. BOHV
Can you the author of our joy. Thomas Campion. *Fr.* A Relation of the Late Royal Entertainment Given by the Lord Knowles. SiCE
Canaan. Muriel Spark. NYBP
Canada. Sir Charles G. D. Roberts. PeCV; PoFr; VA
Canada; Case History. Earle Birney. TwCaPo
Canada to England. Marjorie Pickthall. PoFr
Canaday I. O. Ephraim Braley. BaBo; ViBoFo, *with music*
Canadian Authors Meet, The. F. R. Scott. ACV; OBCV; WhC
Canadian Boat Song, A. Thomas Moore. GoBC; HBV; OBRV; PTK
Canadian Boat Song. *Unknown, at. to* John Galt. BLPA; CaP; CBEP; FaBoCh; GoTS; LoGBV; OBEV (new ed.); OBNC; OBRV; OxBS
Scotland Yet, 4 *ll.* OtMeF
Canadian Exile, The. Antoine Gerin-Lajoie, *tr. fr. French-Canadian by* John Boyd. CaP
Canadian Farmer. Genevieve Bartole. CaP
Canadian Folk Song. Wilfred Campbell. PCH; VA
Canadian Herd-Boy, The. Susanna Moodie. OBCV
Canadian Hunter's Song. Susanna Moodie. VA
Canadian Rossignol, The. Edward William Thomson. CaP
Canal, The. Aldous Huxley. HBMV
Canal Bank Walk. Patrick Kavanagh. MoBrPo (1962 ed.)
Canaries in the morning, orchestras/ In the afternoon. Academic Discourse at Havana. Wallace Stevens. MoPo
Canaries were his hobby. The Glass Blower. James Scully. NYBP; TwCP
Canary, The. Ogden Nash. FiBHP
Canary, The. Elizabeth Turner. OTPC (1923 ed.)
Canary-birds feed on sugar and seed. The Plaint of the Camel [*or* The Camel's Complaint]. Charles Edward Carryl. *Fr.* The Admiral's Caravan. AmePo; AnAmPo; BoTP; EvOK; FaPON; GoTP; HBV; HBVY; OTPC (1946 ed.); PoRh; SoPo; SP; StVeCh; UTS
Canberra in April. J. R. Rowland. PoAu-2
Cancelled First Stanza. Keats. *Fr.* The Ode on Melancholy. ERoP-2; SyP
Cancelled Itinerary. Frederick Mortimer Clapp. LiTM (rev. ed.)
Cancer Cells, The. Richard Eberhart. HoPM; LiTM (1970 ed.); MiAP; ToPo
Cancion: "O love, I never, never thought." John II of Castile, *tr. fr. Spanish by* George Ticknor. AWP; JAWP; WBP
Candid Friend, The. George Canning. TreFT
Candid Man, The. Stephen Crane. War Is Kind, IX. MAP; MoAmPo
Candid Physician, The. *Unknown, See* On Dr. Isaac Letsome. *at. to* John C. Lettsom.
Candidate; Now, Mr. Echo, will you vote for me? By-Election Idyll. Peter Dickinson. FiBHP
Candidate's Creed, The. James Russell Lowell. *See* Pious Editor's Creed, The.
Candidate's Letter, The ("Dear Sir,—You wish to know my notions"). James Russell Lowell. The Biglow Papers, 1st Series, No.VII. AA
Candle, A. Leroy F. Jackson. PCH
Candle, A. Sir John Suckling. ErPo
Candle, The, a Saint. Wallace Stevens. PoRA; Sonn
Candle and Book. Nina Willis Walter. TRV
Candle and Star. Elizabeth J. Coatsworth. BiCB
Candle-blossoms of horse-chestnut left, The. What Trinkets? Thomas Hornsby Ferril. NePoAm-2
Candle Burning in the Night, A. Susan B. Warner. ThGo
Candle, candle. Christmas Chant. Isabel Shaw. ChBR; SiSoSe
Candle Flame, The. Janet Lewis. CrMA
Candle Indoors, The. Gerard Manley Hopkins. BWP; DiPo; FaBoMo; FlW; GTBS-W; LiTB; LiTM; OxBoCh; PoEL-5; ReMP; ViPP
Candle is out, The. The Lady. Elizabeth J. Coatsworth. InP; MaC
Candle lit in darkness of black waters, A. On the Lake. V. Sackville-West. ChMP; MoVE; OBMV
Candle Song. Anna Elizabeth Bennett. GoYe
Candle-lighting Song. Arthur Ketchum. HBMV
Candlemas. Hugh Francis Blunt. JKCP(1955 ed.)
Candlemas. Alice Brown. AA; PoRL
Candlemas. *Unknown.* PoRL
Candles. Sister Mary Eleanore. JKCP(1955 ed.)
Candles. *Unknown.* GoBC
Candles are lighted, the fire blazes bright, The. The Shadows. Mary Lundie Duncan. OTPC (1923 ed.)
Candles gutter and burn out, The. Winter Night. A. R. D. Fairburn. AnNZ
Candles. Red Tulips, ninety cents the bunch. Recipe for an Evening Musicale [*or* Evening Musicale]. Phyllis McGinley. Sonn; UnS; WHC
Candles splutter, The; and the kettle hums. The Still Small Voice. A. M. Klein. OBCV; PeCV
Candles toppling sideways in tomato-cans. Flash-Lights. Mary Aldis. NP
Candor. H.C. Bunner. HBV
Candy Bar. Tom Veitch. ANYP
Candy/ Is dandy. Reflections on Ice-breaking. Ogden Nash. FaFP; LiTM; NePA; ShBV-4; SiTL
Cane. Nicolás Guillén, *tr. fr. Spanish by* Langston Hughes. PoNe
Cane-bottomed Chair, The. Thackeray. HBV; OTPC; PaPo; PoVP
Canis Major. Robert Frost. *Fr.* A Sky Pair. MAP; MoAB; MoAmPo
Canner, exceedingly [*or* remarkably] canny, A. Limerick. Carolyn Wells. FaPON; HBV; HBVY; LiBL; TWS; YaD
Cannery, The. Lucien Stryk. NYTB
Cannibal bold of Penzance, A. Limerick. *Unknown.* LiBL
Cannibal Hymn, The. *Unknown, tr. fr. Egyptian by* Samuel A. B. Mercer. TTY
Cannon's voice is dumb, The. Peace. Harold Trowbridge Pulsifer. MC; PEDC
Canny moment, lucky fit. The Nativity Chant. Sir Walter Scott. *Fr.* Guy Mannering. ChTr; FaBoCh; LoGBV
Canny old codger at Yalta, A. Limerick. *Unknown.* LiBL
Canoe. Patrick Anderson. SD
Canoe, The. Isabella Valancy Crawford. OBCV; OnYI; VA
"O love, art thou a silver fish?" *sel.* ACV
Canoe. Keith Douglas. NeBP
Canoe Song at Twilight. Laura E. McCully. CaP
Canoe Speaks, The, *sel.* Robert Louis Stevenson.
"On the great streams the ships may go." SD
Canoe-Trip. Douglas Le Pan. CaP; OBCV; PeCV; TwCaPo
Canogait kirkyaird in the failing year. At Robert Fergusson's Grave, October 1962. Robert Garioch. OxBS
Canon for Apocreos, The. St. Theodore of Studium, *tr. fr. Greek by* John Mason Neale. CAW
Canonical Hours. William Dickey. CoAP
Canonicus and Roger Williams. *Unknown.* PAH
Canonization, The. John Donne. AnAnS-1; ATP; BEL; BoLiVe; BWP; CABA; CaFP; CBEP; CBV; CoBE; DiPo; ElL; EnL; EnLi-1 (1949 ed.); EnLoPo; EnRePo; EP; ForPo; FosPo; GTBS-W; GTSE; LiTB; LiTG; LiTL; MaMe; MaPo; MasP; MBW-1; MePo; NoP; OBS; PAn; Po; PoAn; PoE; PoEL-2; PoeP; PoFS; PoIE; ReEn; ReIE; SCEP-1; SeCeV; SeCP; SeCV-1; SeEP; StP; TDP; TOP; TrGrPo; TuPP; UnTE; VaPo; ViBoPo
(Canonisation, The.) LoBV; SeCePo
Canopus. Bert Leston Taylor. ALV; FiBHP; HBMV; InMe; WhC
Canso Strait, *with music. Unknown.* ShS
Canst be idle? canst thou play. Businesse. George Herbert. MaMe

Canst thinke the cargoe wherewith ship is fraught. Upon the Decease of Mrs. Anne Griffin. John Fiske. SCAP
Canst thou by searching find out God? The Eternal Quest [*or* Job's Comforters]. Job, Bible, *O.T.* MaRV; WGRP
Canst thou draw out leviathan with an hook? Leviathan [*or* Of God's Great Power in the Leviathan]. Job, Bible, *O.T.* PoG; TrGrPo
"Canst thou indeed be he that still would sing." Dante. *Fr.* La Vita Nuova. AWP
Canst thou love and lie alone? The Courtier's Good-Morrow to His Mistress. *Unknown.* ElL
Canst thou love me, lady? Love. Charles Stuart Calverley. ALV; FiBHP
Canst thou not minister to a mind diseased? Remorse. Shakespeare. *Fr.* Macbeth, V, iii. MaRV; TRV
Canst thou take the barren soil? He Can. *Unknown.* SoP
Cant. W. H. Davies. MoRP
Can't. Harriet Prescott Spofford. DD; MC; PAH
Can't They Dance the Polka! *with music.* *Unknown.* ShS
Can't You Dance the Polka? *with music.* *Unknown.* SoAmSa
Can't You Live Humble? *with music.* *Unknown.* BoAN-2
Cante Hondo. Ellen de Young Kay. NePoEA
Cantelope, The. Bayard Taylor. BOHV
Cantemus Cuncti Melodum. Notker Balbulus, *tr. fr. Latin by* John Mason Neale. CAW
Canterbury. Basil Dowling. AnNZ
Canterbury Tales, The, *sels.* Chaucer.
Prologue. BEL; BoLiVe, *abr.*; CaFP, *much abr.*; CoBE, *abr.*; CTC, *much abr.*; EnL, *sl. abr.*; EnLi-1; EnLit; FiP, *much abr.*; FlW, *abr., orig., with mod. vers. by* Nevill Coghill; ILP; MaPo, *much abr.*; MBW-1; NoP; OAEP; OuHeWo, *mod. by* J. U. Nicolson; PoIE, *abr.*; SeCeV; TOP, *much abr.*; ViBoPo, *much abr.*; WoL, *abr., mod.*; YAT, *abr.*
Clerk of Oxenford, The, *mod. by* Frank Ernest Hill. OnPP
Good Parson, The, *mod vers. by* H. C. Leonard. BoPe; MaRV; WGRP
(Parish Priest, The.) PoLi
("Parson of a country town was he, The," *mod. vers. by* H. C. Leonard.) TRV
(Poor Parson, The, *mod. vers. by* H. C. Leonard.) ACP; CAW
(Poure Persoun, The.) GoBC
Knight, A. GoTP, *mod. vers. by* Louis Untermeyer
(Seven Pilgrims, *orig., with mod. vers. by* Louis Untermeyer.) TrGrPo
(Ten of Chaucer's People, *mod. vers. by* Nevill Coghill.) PoSa
(Three Canterbury Pilgrims, *mod. vers. by* Louis Untermeyer.) MaC
Miller, A. GoTP, *mod. vers. by* Louis Untermeyer; WePo, *mod. vers. by* Nevill Coghill
Portrait of the Prioress, The. MaPo (1969 ed.)
Shipman, The. ACP, *mod.*; EtS
Squire, A. GoTP, *mod. vers. by* Louis Untermeyer; WePo, *mod. vers. by* Nevill Coghill
"Whan that Aprille with his shoures so[o]te," *br. sels.* ChTr; DiPo; GoBC; InP; TrGrPo, *orig., with mod. vers. by* Louis Untermeyer
(Than Longen Folk to Goon on Pilgrimages.) ATP
Wife of Bath, The ATP; WePo *mod. vers. by* Nevill Coghill
Clerk's Tale, The. MBW-1
(Patient Griselda, *mod. by* Edward Hodnett.) PoRA
Chaucer's Envoy to the Story of Patient Griselda, *mod. by* W. W. Skeat. AnEnPo
"That thee is sent, receyve in buxumnesse." PoG
Franklin's Tale. CABL; MBW-1; OAEP
Friar's Tale, The. EnLi-1 (1949 ed.), *mod. vers by* Edwin M. Everett; PoAn, *orig. and mod. vers.*
Knight's [*or* Knightes] Tale, The. BEL; GoTL; TOP
Arcite's Farewell, *mod. by* John Hall Wheelock. LiTL
("Allas the Wo! Allas, the peynes stronge.") LO
Emily's Prayer to Diana. MyFE
"I am, thow woost, yet of thy compaignye." PoG
Prayer to Venus, *mod. by* John Hall Wheelock. LiTL
Introduction to the Man of Law's Prologue. FiP
Maunciple's [*or* Manciple's] Tale, The.
Lat Take a Cat. ChTr
Take Any Bird. OA
Merchant's Tale, The, *abr., mod. vers. by* Frank Ernest Hill. UnTE
Miller's [*or* Milleres] Tale, The. MBW-1; OxBoLi
Carpenter's Young Wife, The. ExPo
Young Woman, 3 *ll.* BoW
Monk's Tale, The.
Croesus. MyFE
Tale of Hugelin, Count of Pisa, The. MyFE
Nun's Priest's [*or* Nonne Preestes] Tale, The. AnFE; AtBAP; BEL; CABL; CoBE; EnL, *mod. by* Theodore Morrison; EnLi-1; MaPo; MBW-1; NoP; OAEP; OuHeWo, *mod. by* J. U. Nicolson; PoEL-1; SeCeV; StP; TOP, *abr.*; TrGrPo, *orig., with mod. vers. by* Frank Ernest Hill
Murder Will Out. MyFE
Poor Widow's Cock, The, 6 *ll.* MyFE
"There lived, as authors tell, in days of yore," 36 *ll.* MBW-1, *mod. by* Dryden.
"This Chauntecleer stood hye up-on his toos." FiP
Pardoner's Tale, The. BEL; CABL; CoBE, *sl. abr.*; EnL, *mod. by* Theodore Morrison; EnLi-1; EnLit; FiP, *abr.*; FosPo; MBW-1; NoP; OAEP; PoEL-1; PoIE
Introduction: "'Thou beel amy, thou Pardoner,' he sayde," 11 *ll.* FosPo
"Thise ryotoures three, of which I tell." MyFE
"These rioters, of whom I make my rime," *mod. vers.* WHA
Prioress' Tale, The. ACP, *mod.*; BEL; GoBC, *mod. by* Wordsworth; ISi, *mod. by* Frank Ernest Hill; LoBV; MBW-1; OAEP; OxBoCh
Invocation: "O mother maid! O maiden-mother free," *mod. by* Frank Ernest Hill. ISi
(O Mooder Mayde.) BoW
(Prayer to the Blessed Virgin, *shorter sel., mod.*) CAW
(Two Invocations of the Virgin, 2, *mod.*) ACP
Prologue of [*or* to] the Pardoner's Tale. BEL; CABL; CoBE; EnL, *mod. by* Theodore Morrison; FosPo; MBW-1; NoP; OAEP
Prologue of the Prioresses Tale. AtBAP; MBW-1; OAEP
Prologue to Sir Thopas. Par
Prologue to the Man of Law's Tale. FiP
Reeve's Tale, The, *mod. vers. by* Frank Ernest Hill. UnTE
"At Trumpyngtoun Nat Fer From Cantebrigge." ViBoPo
Second Nun's Tale, The.
Invocatio ad Mariam, *fr. prologue, mod. by* Frank Ernest Hill. ISi
("Thou maid and mother, daughter of thy Son," *mod.*) GoBC
(Two Invocations of The Virgin, 1, *mod.*) ACP
Sir Thopas. BEL; Par
Wife of Bath's Prologue, The. EnL, *mod. by* Theodore Morrison; EnLi-1 (1949 ed.); MBW-1; OxBoLi, *abr.*; PoEL-1; WePo, *mod vers. by* Nevill Coghill
"My fifthe housbonde, god his soule blesse!" FiP
Wife of Bath's Tale, The. EnL, *mod. by* Theodore Morrison; EnLit; MBW-1
"In days of old, when Arthur filled the throne," *mod. by* Dryden, 45 *ll.* MBW-1
"In th'olde dayes of the Kyng Arthour," 25 *ll.* ViBoPo
Cantica: Our Lord Christ. St. Francis of Assisi, *tr. fr. Italian by* Dante Gabriel Rossetti. AWP; JAWP; WBP
(Of Order in Our Lord Christ.) CAW; GoBC
(Order.) OnPM
Canticle. Wendell Berry. AP
Canticle. William Griffith. DD; HBMV; HBVY
Canticle. James McAuley. PoAu-2
Canticle. Michael McClure. NeAP
Canticle. John Norris. SeCL
(Second Chap. of the Cant. from the 10. Verse to the 13.) SeEP
Canticle. Francis Quarles. *See* My Beloved Is Mine, and I Am His.
Canticle of Bernadette, The, *abr.* *Unknown.* WHL
Canticle of Canticles. Bible *O.T.* *See* Song of Solomon, The.
Canticle of Darkness. Wilfred Watson. ACV; MoCV
Canticle of Quietness. Sister Mary Paulinus. JKCP (1955 ed.)
Canticle of the Sun. St. Francis of Assisi, *tr. fr. Italian by* Matthew Arnold. BoC; OuHeWo; TreFS; WGRP, *tr. by* Maurice Egan; WHL, *tr. unknown; WoL, tr. by* Eleanor L. Turnbull
(Canticle [*or* Song] of the Creatures, *tr. by* Matthew Arnold.) CAW; GoBC; LiTW; MaRV

Canticle (continued)
(Cantico del Sole, *tr.* *by* Ezra Pound.) CTC
Canticle of the Sun Dancing on Easter Morning. John Heath-Stubbs. BoPe
Canticle to the Christ in the Holy Eucharist,A. Brother Antoninus. ToPo
Canticle to the Waterbirds, A. Brother Antoninus. NeAP; StP
Cantico del Sole. St. Francis of Assisi. *See* Canticle of the Sun.
Canticus Troili. Chaucer. *See* Song of Troilus.
Cantiga: "White and crimson, cheek and breast." Gil Vicente, *tr. fr. Portuguese and Spanish by* Thomas Walsh. CAW; ISi
Canto I: "Of Men, nay Beasts; worse, Monsters; worst of all." Phineas Fletcher. *Fr.* The Locusts, or Apollyonists. SeCV-1; SeEP
Canto I: "And then went down to the ship." Ezra Pound. AmPP; AP; AtBAP; CMoP, *abr.*; CoBMV; LiTA; MAP; MoAB; MoAmPo; MoVE; PoIE; SeCeV; TrGrPo (rev. ed.)
Canto II: "Hang it all, Robert Browning." Ezra Pound. AmPP (4th ed.); AP; AtBAP; CoBMV; MoAB; MoAmPo (1962 ed.); NePA; OxBA; TwAmPo
Canto XIII: "Kung walked/ by the dynastic temple." Ezra Pound. CMoP; FaBoMo; NP
Canto XIV, *sel.* Ezra Pound.
"And the betrayers of language." MoPo
Canto XV, *sel.* Ezra Pound.
"Skin-flakes, repetitions, erosions." MoPo
Canto XVI, *sel.* Ezra Pound.
"And before hell mouth; dry plain/and two mountains." ExPo; MoPo
Canto XVII: "So that the vines burst from my fingers." Ezra Pound. ExPo; LoBV; NAMP; OBMV; Po; ReMP
Canto XX, *sel.* Ezra Pound.
"Jungle:/ Glaze green and red feathers, jungle." MoPo
"And there was grass on the floor of the temple," *sel.* MoPo
Canto XXIX, *sel.* Ezra Pound.
"She is submarine, she is an octopus, she is/ A biological process." MoPo
Canto XLV: "With Usura/ With usura hath no man a house of good stone." Ezra Pound. CMoP; LiTM (rev. ed.); MoPo; NePA; PoIE; ReMP
Canto XLVII: "Who even dead, yet hath his mind entire!" Ezra Pound. CrMA; MoPo
Canto LXXIX, *sel.* Ezra Pound.
"O Lynx, wake Silenus and Casey." AtBAP; POTE (1959 ed.)
Canto LXXX, *sel.* Ezra Pound.
"Tudor indeed is gone and every rose."
(From "The Pisan Cantos.") FaBoTw
Canto LXXXI, *sels.* Ezra Pound.
"Ant's a centaur in his dragon world, The." PoSa
(From "The Pisan Cantos.") FaBoEn
"What thou lovest well remains." GTBS-D; MoAB; NePA; OxBA; SeCeV; UnPo (3d ed.); ViBoPo (1958 ed.)
(From "The Pisan Cantos.") FaBoTw
"Yet/ Ere the season died a-cold." MoVE
Canto CXIII, *sel.* Ezra Pound.
'Then a partridge-shaped cloud over dust storm." NYBP
Canto Amor. John Berryman. CoAP; MoAmPo (1950 ed.); MoPo; MoVE; NePA
Canto Espiritual. Juan Maragall, *tr. fr. Spanish by* Thomas Walsh. CAW
Canto First. George Canning. *Fr.* The Progress of Man, *sel.* EiCL
Canto the Third. Byron. *Fr.* Childe Harold's Pilgrimage. ERoP-2
Canute the Great, *sel.* "Michael Field."
"She dared not wait." VA
Canvas leaves, the painted trees, The. Midsummer Night's Dream. Byron Vazakas. NePA
Canzo: "When fresh grass-blades and leaves appear." Bernard de Ventadour, *tr. fr. Provençal by* Hubert Creekmore. LiTW
Canzo of Bird-Songs and Love. Arnaut Daniel, *tr. fr. Provençal by* Ezra Pound. LiTW
(Autet e bas.) CTC
Canzon Pastoral in Honor of Her Majesty, A. Edmund Bolton. TuPP
Canzone: "Clear, fresh, sweet waters." Petrarch, *tr. fr. Italian by* William D. Foulke. Sonnets to Laura: To Laura in Life, Canzone XIV. LiTW
Canzone: Donna Mi Priegha. Guido Cavalcanti, *tr. fr. Italian by* Ezra Pound. CTC
Canzone: He Beseeches Death for the Life of Beatrice. Dante, *tr. fr. Italian by* Dante Gabriel Rossetti. AWP
Canzone: He Perceives His Rashness in Love. Guido Guinicelli, *tr. fr. Italian by* Dante Gabriel Rossetti. AWP; JAWP; WBP
Canzone: He Rebukes the Evil of That Time, *sel.* Siciliano Inghilfredi, *tr. fr. Italian by* Dante Gabriel Rossetti.
"Let none who have not wisdom govern you." PoFr
Canzone: He Speaks of His Condition through Love. Folcachiero de' Folcachieri, *tr. fr. Italian by* Dante Gabriel Rossetti. AWP
Canzone: His Lament for Selvaggia. Cino da Pistoia, *tr. fr. Italian by* Dante Gabriel Rossetti. AWP; JAWP; WBP
Canzone: His Portrait of His Lady. Fazio degli Uberti. *tr. fr. Italian by* Dante Gabriel Rossetti. AWP
Canzone: "Lady asks me, A/ I speak in season." Guido Cavalcanti, *tr. fr. Italian by* Ezra Pound. LiTW
Canzone: Of His Dead Lady. Giacomino Pugliesi. *tr. fr. Italian by* Dante Gabriel Rossetti. AWP; JAWP; WBP
Canzone: Of His Love. Prinzivalle Doria, *tr. fr. Italian by* Dante Gabriel Rossetti. AWP
Canzone: Of the Gentle Heart. Guido Guinicelli, *tr. fr. Italian by* Dante Gabriel Rossetti. AWP; CTC; LiTW
(Of the Gentle Heart.) GoBC; Wol
Canzone: To Love and to His Lady. Guido delle Colonne, *tr. fr. Italian by* Dante Gabriel Rossetti. AWP
Canzone: To the Lady Pietra, of Sienna. Dante, *tr. fr. Italian by* John Heath-Stubbs. LiTW
Canzone: "When shall we learn, what should be clear as day." W. H. Auden. LiTA; LiTM; MoVE
Canzonet. *Unknown.* ElL
("See, see, mine own sweet jewel.") EG, LO
Canzonetta: Bitter Song to His Lady, A. Pier Moronelli di Fiorenza, *tr. fr. Italian by* Dante Gabriel Rossetti. AWP JAWP; WBP
Canzonetta: He Will Neither Boast Nor Lament to His Lady. Jacopo da Lentino, *tr. fr. Italian by* Dante Gabriel Rossetti. AWP
Canzonetta: Of His Lady and of His Making Her Likeness. Jacopo da Lentino, *tr. fr. Italian by* Dante Gabriel Rossetti. AWP
Canzonetta: Of His Lady in Absence. Giacomino Pugliesi, *tr. fr. Italian by* Dante Gabriel Rossetti. AWP
Canzoniere. Petrarch. *See* Sonnets to Laura.
Caoilte. *Unknown, tr. fr. Irish by* Frank O'Connor. KiLC
Caow-hand with a gun or two, A. Western Formula. *Unknown.* PoOW
Cap and Bells, The. W. B. Yeats. BrPo; ChTr; FlW; GTSL; MoAB; MoBrPo; OBVV; OnMSP
Cap That Fits. Austin Dobson. TSW
Cape Ann. T. S. Eliot. Landscapes, V. EvOK; GoJo; LoGBV; ThWaDe
Cape Ann: a View. John Malcolm Brinnin. NYBP
Cape Cod. George Santayana. AmePo
Cape Cod Girls. *Unknown.* AmSS; TrAS, *with music*
Cape Coloured Batman. Guy Butler. BoSA; PeSA
Cape Hatteras. Hart Crane. *Fr.* The Bridge. LiTA
"Nasal whine of power whips a new universe, The," *sel.* MoAB
(Cape Hatteras: "The nasal whine of power.") WoL
(Power.) MAP; MoAmPo
Cape Horn Gospel—I ("'I was in a hooker once,' said Karlssen"). John Masefield. StPo
Cape Horn Gospel—II ("Jake was a dirty Dago lad"). John Masefield. ShBV-3
Cape of Tempests, The. Luís de Camoes, *Tr. fr. Portuguese by* Sir Richard Fanshawe. *Fr.* The Lusiads. LiTW
Capilano ("Capilano, in the canyon"). A. M. Stephen. CaP
Capital, The. W. H. Auden. CMoP; MoPW
Capital Punishment. Oscar Wilde. *Fr.* The Ballad of Reading Gaol. WePo
("There is no chapel on the day.") OxBI
Capital ship for an ocean trip, A. A Nautical Ballad [*or* The Walloping Window-Blind]. Charles Edward Carryl. *See also* O, a capital ship for an ocean trip. *Fr.* Davy and the Goblin. FaPON; GFA; GoTP; HBV; InMe; LBN; MPB; NA; OTPC (1946 ed.); RePo; StVeCh; TreFS; WhC.
Capital Square. Patrick Anderson. OBCV
Capitals Are Rocked, The. Nikolai Alekseyevich Nekrasov, *tr.*

fr. Russian by Babette Deutsch. AWP; OnPM
"Cap'n". Arthur Wallace Peach. EtS
Cap'n, I Believe, *with music.* *Unknown.* AS
Cap'n was drunk and he went below, The. Bottle O! *Unknown.* SoAmSa
Capped arbiter of beauty in this street. For the Marriage of Faustus and Helen (III). Hart Crane. FaBoMo; LiTM
Capriccio. Babette Deutsch. HBMV; TSW
Capriccio Dramatico, Il, *sel.* Lorenzo da Ponte, *tr. fr. Italian by* John Mazzinghi.
To an Artful Theatre Manager. TrJP
Caprice. William Dean Howells. ALV
Capstan Chantey, A. Edwin James Brady. HBMV
Capsule Conclusions. *Unknown,* *ad. fr. German by* Louis Untermeyer. MeWo
Captain, The, *abr.* John G. C. Brainard. EtS
Captain, The. Dorothea Day. *See* My Captain.
Captain, The, *sels.* Beaumont *and* Fletcher.
Away, Delights! *fr.* III, iv. ElL; OBEV; ViBoPo
("Away, delights! go seek some other dwelling.") LO
(Sad Song, The.) FaBoEn
Tell me, Dearest, What Is Love? *fr.* II, ii. *Diff. vers.,* 2 *sts., given in* The Knight of the Burning Pestle. ElL; SeEP; ViBoPo
(What Is Love?) HBV
Captain, The. Jon Manchip White. NePoEA
Captain and the Mermaids, The. W. S. Gilbert. YT
Captain Arthur Phillip and the Birds. Lex Banning. PoAu-2
Captain bold, in [*or* from] Halifax, who [*or* that] dwelt in country quarters, A. Unfortunate Miss Bailey [*or* Miss Bailey's Ghost]. George Colman, the Younger. BOHV; DTC; FiBHP; OxBoLi; ViBoFo
Captain Busby put his beard in his mouth and sucked it. Poems. Philip O'Connor. LiTM
Captain Car; or, Edom o Gordon. *Unknown.* *See* Edom o'Gordon.
Captain Carpenter. John Crowe Ransom. AnFE; AP; APA; AtBAP; CBV; CoAnAm; CoBMV; FaBoMo; FosPo; GTBS-W; LiTA; LiTG; LiTM; LoBV (2d ed.); MAP; MasP; MoAB; MoAmPo; MoVE; NePA; OxBA; PIA; PoIE; PoSa; SeCeV; StP; TwAmPo; TwCP
Captain Cook. Alfred Domett. *Fr.* Ranolf and Amohia. FOL
Captain Craig, *sel.* E. A. Robinson.
"I doubt if ten men in all Tilbury Town." PoEL-5
Captain Death. *Unknown.* CoMu
Captain, I have seen. A Warning for Abraham Lincoln. Jacinto Fombona Pachano. PoFr; WoL
Captain Jinks. *Unknown,* *at. to* T. Maclagan. BLPA; FaFP; OnPP; TreF
Captain Kelly Lets His Daughter Go to Be a Nun. Thomas Butler Feeney. PoPl
Captain Kidd. Stephen Vincent Benét. ThLM
Captain Kidd. *Unknown.* BBV (1923 ed.); IHA; MoShBr, *shorter vers.;* SoAmSa, *longer vers., with music;* TrAS, *with music;* ViBoFo
(Ballad of Captain Kidd, The.) AmSS
(Captain Robert Kidd, *longer vers.*) ABF
Captain Loredan. Edward King. PFY
Captain Molly. William Collins. PAL
"Captain, oh, captain, what will you give me." The Low-down, Lonesome Low. *Unknown.* OuSiCo
Captain of St. Kitts, The. Beulah May. EtS
Captain of the *Oberon,* The. Francis Webb. *Fr.* A Drum for Ben Boyd. ACV; NeLNL
Captain of the *Shannon* came sailing up the bay, The. The *Shannon* and the *Chesapeake.* Thomas Tracy Bouvé. MC; PAH
Captain of the Western wood. Madroño. Bret Harte. AA
Captain of the Years. Arthur R. Macdougall, Jr. TRV
Captain or Colonel, or Knight in Arms. When the Assault Was Intended to the City. Milton. GTBS; GTBS-D; GTBS-P; GTSE; GTSL; MBW-1; NoP; OuHeWo; RoGo; SeEP; Sonn
Captain Quiros and Mr. William Lane. Terra Australis. Douglas Stewart. BoAV; MoAuPo
Captain Reece. W. S. Gilbert. CenHV; EvOK; FiBHP; GN; HBV; MaC; OTPC
Captain Robert Kidd. *Unknown.* *See* Captain Kidd.
Captain Rodgers' Cruelty. *Unknown.* *See* Andrew Rose.
Captain Stood on the Carronade, The. Frederick Marryat. *Fr.* Snarleyyow; or, The Dog Fiend. BBV (1923 ed.); EtS; HBV; OTPC; RePo
(Old Navy, The.) PaPo; StPo
Captain Stratton's Fancy. John Masefield. MoBrPo; OBEV (new ed.); OnPP
Captain Sword. Leigh Hunt. GN
Captain Ward and the *Rainbow.* *Unknown.* BaBo; ESPB; ViBoFo
Captain Wattle and Miss Roe. Charles Dibdin. OxBoLi
Captain! we often heretofore. To Our House-Dog Captain. Walter Savage Landor. NBM; PoEL-4
Captain Wedderburn's Courtship. *Unknown.* BaBo (A *and* C *vers.*); ESPB (A *and* B *vers.*); ViBoFo (A *and* B *vers.*)
(Old Man's Courtship.) BFSS
(Six Questions, B *vers.*) BaBo; BFSS
Captain Went Below, The, *frag.* *Unknown.* AmSS
Captain went to sea at seventeen, The. Clipper Captain. Shirley Barker. WaKn
Captains, The. Walter Adolphe Roberts. PoNe
Captain's Daughter, The. James Thomas Fields. *See* Ballad of the Tempest.
Captain's Feather, The. Samuel Minturn Peck. AA
Captains of Small Farms, The. Robert P. Tristram Coffin. RePo
Captains of the Years, The. Arthur R. Macdougall, Jr. ChIP; MaRV; OQP
Captain's Table. Witter Bynner. AnFE; CoAnAm
Captain's Walk; Salem. Oliver Jenkins. PoMa
Captive. Peretz Hirshbein, *tr. fr. Yiddish by* Joseph Leftwich. TrJP
Captive, The. Kipling. BoPe
Captive. John Richard Moreland. PoMa
Captive. Marion Strobel. ErPo
Captive Bird of Paradise, The. Ruth Pitter. SiSw
Captive Escaped in the Wilds of America, The. Charlotte Smith. Sonn
Captive flourished like, The. Portrait. Alan Dugan. TPM
Captive of Love, A. Ovid, *tr. fr. Latin by* Christopher Marlowe. Elegies, 1, 2. AWP
Captive Ships at Manila, The. Dorothy Paul. PAH
Captive snake half dead with fright, A. The Snake and the Mouse. Bhartrihari. OnPM
Captives, The. *Unknown,* *tr. fr. Ukrainian by* Florence Randal Livesay. PoFr
Captive's Hymn, The. Edna Dean Proctor. PAH
Captivity. Samuel Rogers. FaBoEn; OBNC
Captivity, The; an Oratorio, *sels.* Goldsmith.
Hope, *fr.* II. OBEC; TreFT
"Hope, like a gleaming taper's light." MaRV
Memory, *fr.* I. OBEC, *sl. diff. vers.;* OBEV
(Song: "O memory, thou fond deceiver.") ViBoPo
Capture of Edwin Alonzo Boyd, The. Peter Miller. MoCV
Capture of Little York. *Unknown.* PAH
Captured. Archibald MacLeish. HBMV
Captured. *Unknown.* SoP
Capturing a Spring. Rosemary Joseph. NYTB
Caput apri refero [*or* differo]. The Boar's Head Carol [*or* A Carol Bringing in the Boar's Head]. *Unknown.* MeEL; MeEV; TuPP
Caput Mortuum. E. A. Robinson. NP
Car is heavy with children, The. The Road Back. Anne Sexton. NYBP
Car swerves,/ injures 11. Aram Saroyan. ANYP
Caravan, The. Hovhannes Blouz, *tr. fr. Armenian by* Thomas Walsh. CAW
Caravan, The. Gwendolyn MacEwen. MoCV
Caravan, The. Madeleine Nightingale. BoTP; GaP; MPB
Caravan from China Comes, A. Richard Le Gallienne. BrR; MoSiPe
Caravans. Hal Borland. MoSiPe
Caravans. Emily Patterson. ChIP
Caravans. Josephine Preston Peabody. AA
Caravans. Irene Thompson. BoTP
Caravels of Columbus, The. Elias Lieberman. PEDC (1949 ed.)
Carcassonne. Gustave Nadaud, *tr. fr. French by* John R. Thompson. BLPA; FaBoBe; HBV; HT; NeHB; PTK
Carcosa. Lin Carter. FiSC
Card Burning in Central Park. William Hathaway. QAH
Card-Dealer, The. Dante Gabriel Rossetti. MaVP; NBM; PoVP; ViPo
Card of Invitation to Mr. Gibbon, at Brighthelmstone, A. William Hayley. OBEC
Cardinal. Jim Harrison. WIRo
Cardinal, A. W. D. Snodgrass. PP

Cardinal, The. Robert Penn Warren. Kentucky Mountain Farm, IV. BiS; MoVE
Cardinal Bird, The. William Davis Gallagher. AA
Cardinal Fisher. John Heywood. ACP
Cardinal, lover of shade. The Cardinal. Robert Penn Warren. Kentucky Mountain Farm, IV. BiS; MoVE
Cardinal Manning. Aubrey Thomas De Vere. JKCP; VA
Cardinal Wolsey's Farewell. Shakespeare, *and probably* John Fletcher. *See* Wolsey's Farewell to his Greatness.
Cardinal's Dog, The. John Glassco. MoCV
Cardinal's Soliloquy, The. Sir Edward Bulwer-Lytton. *Fr.* Richelieu; or, The Conspiracy, III, i. VA
Cards and Kisses. John Lyly. *See* Apelles' Song.
Care. Virginia Woodward Cloud. AA; HBV
Care. Josephine Miles. NYBP
Care and heavy thought weigh me down. Estat ai en greu cossirier. Beatriz de Dia. ErPo
Care Away. *Unknown.* OxBoLi
Care away goe thow from me. *Unknown.* SeCSL
Care-Charmer Sleep [Son of the Sable Night.]. Samuel Daniel. To Delia. AtBAP; ATP; CaFP; CBEP; CBV; CoBE; EG; EnLi-1; EnLit; EnRePo; FaBoEn; ForPo; GTBS; GTBS-D; GTBS-P; GTBS-W; GTSE; GTSL; HBV; LiTB; LiTG; LoBV; NoP; OAEP; PoIE; ReEn; ReIE; SiCE; Sonn; TOP; TreFS; TrGrPo; TuPP; VaPo; ViBoPo
(Sonnet.) EIL; PoEL-2 (XLIV)
(Sonnets to Delia.) BEL; OBSC
Care-charmer sleep, sweet ease in restless misery. Sleep. Barthlomew Griffin. Fidessa, More Chaste than Kind, XV. OBSC; ReEn; ReIE; SiCE; Sonn; TuPP
Care-charming Sleep, [Thou Easer of All Woes]. John Fletcher. *Fr.* The Tragedy of Valentinian, V, ii. AtBAP; BEL; ELP; OAEP; OnPM; SeEP; TrGrPo; TuPP; ViBoPo
(Into Slumbers.) SeCePo
(Invocation to Sleep.) AnEnPo; WHA
(Song: "Care-charming Sleep. . .") LoBV; PoEL-2
(Song for the Sick Emperor.) FaBoEn
(Song to Sleep.) OxBoLi
(Thou Easer of All Woes.) TreFT
(To Sleep.) EnLi-1; PoRA
Care in Heaven. John Heath-Stubbs. BoPe
Care Is Heavy. Conal O'Riordan. CAW
Careful Angler, The. Robert Louis Stevenson. SD
Careful for Nothing. Avis B. Christiansen. SoP
Careful Husband, The. *Unknown, tr. fr. Late Middle Irish by* the Earl of Longford. OnYI; OxBI
Careful man I ought to be, A. A Little Fellow Follows Me [*or* The Little Chap Who Follows Me *or* Service Supreme]. *Unknown.* PoToHe (new ed.); SoP; STF
Careful observers may foretel[l] the hour. A Description of a City Shower. Swift. BWP; CABL; CBEP; CEP; CIV; EiCL; EiCP; EiPP; EnLi-1 (1949 ed.); ExPo; LoBV; NoP; OnYI; PoE; PoFS; PoIE; SeCePo; SeCeV; UnPo (3d ed.); VaPo
Careful Penman, The. *Unknown.* BOHV
Carefully on tiptoe stealing. It Was the Cat. W. S. Gilbert. *Fr.* H. M. S. Pinafore. CIV
Carefully the birch tree. The Absent Minded Birch Tree Kathleen Millay. PEDC
Careles of love & free from feares. *At. to* Thomas Carew. SeCSL
Careless Content. John Byrom. CEP; HBV; OBEC
"I am content, I do not care, *sel.*" LO
Careless Delight. Omar Khayyám, *tr. fr. Persian by* Edward Fitzgerald. *Fr.* The Rubáiyát. OnPM
Careless Fairy, The. Nancy Byrd Turner. BoChLi
Careless for an instant I closed my child's fingers in the jamb. Fingers in the Door. David Holbrook. NePoEA-2
Careless forever, beautiful proud sea. Beautiful Proud Sea. Sara Teasdale. NP
Careless Gallant, The. Thomas Jordan. CoMu; OxBoLi; SeCL; SiTL
(Coronemus Nos Rosis Antequam Marcescant.) HBV; OBEV
(Epicure, The, Sung by One in the Habit of a Town Gallant.) SeEP
Careless Good Fellow, The. John Oldham. CEP; PeRV; SeCV-2
Careless I lived, accepting day by day. Epitaph on a Vagabond. Alexander Gray. HBMV
Careless Kittens, The. *Unknown.* *See* Three Little Kittens.
Careless Love. Stanley Kunitz. WaP
Careless Love, *with music.* *Unknown.* AS; BFSS, *with music*; TrAS; UnTE
Careless Lover, The. Sir John Suckling. CavP
Careless Niece, The. Carolyn Wells. ShM
Careless rhymer, it is true. Chloe, M. A. Mortimer Collins. BOHV
Careless Seems the Great Avenger. James Russell Lowell. *Fr.* The Present Crisis. TreFT; TRV
Careless she lies along the Southern Main. Australia, 1905. Archibald T. Strong. *Fr.* Sonnets of the Empire. BoAu
Careless Talk. Mark Hollis. FiBHP
Careless Willie. *Unknown.* BBGG
Careless Willie. *Unknown.* FaPON
Carentan O Carentan. Louis Simpson. CoAP; MoBS; NMP; OPoP
Cares and anxieties. For Sleep When Overtired. Sarah N. Cleghorn. OQP
Cares of Majesty, The. Shakespeare. King Henry IV, Pt. II, *fr.* III, i. LiTB; TreF
(Soliloquy on Sleep.) FiP
Caresses. Elsa Barker. *Fr.* The Spirit and the Bridge. HBMV
"Carest Thou not"—how may times the cry. Peace, Be Still. Maude Steenburg. SoP
Cargoes. John Masefield. AnEnPo; ATP; BEL; CMoP; DiPo; EnLi-2 (1949 ed.); EnLit; ExPo; FaBV; FaPON; FosPo; GTBS-D; GTSL; ILP; LiTM; MCCG; MoAB; MoBrPo; NP; OBEV (new ed.); OBMV; OBVV; OtMeF; PCH; PoPo; PoRA; PTK; RoGo; SeCeV; ShBV-1; SP; TiPo (1952 ed.); TOP; TreF; WePo; YT
Cargoes of the Radanites. Harry Alan Potamkin. TrJP
Caria and Philistia considered. Cry Faugh! Robert Graves. CoBMV; MoBrPo (1962 ed.)
Caribbean, The. Stephanie Ormsby. PoNe
Carillon, The. Rosalia Castro de Murguía, *tr. fr. Spanish by* Garrett Strange. CAW
Carillon. Longfellow. *Fr.* The Belfry of Bruges. CoBA
Caring. F. R. Scott. PeCV
Caring is loving, motionless. Caring. F. R. Scott. PeCV
Carl Hamblin. Edgar Lee Masters. *Fr.* Spoon River Anthology. AmP; CMoP; ILP; LiTA; LiTM (rev. ed.)
Carle He Came o'er the Croft, The. Allan Ramsay. OxBS
Carlino! what are thou about, my boy? To My Child Carlino. Walter Savage Landor. NoP; OBRV
Carlyle and Emerson. Montgomery Schuyler. AA; PoMa
Carlyle combined the lit'ry life. Thomas Carlyle. *Unknown.* FiBHP
Carlyle on Burns. William Jeffrey. *Fr.* On Glaister's Hill. OxBS
Carma, *sel.* Jean Toomer.
"Wind is in the cane. Come along." Kal
Carmagnole, La, *sel.* *Unknown, tr. fr. French by* John Oxenford.
"All honest folk throughout the land," 6 *sts.* PoFr
Carman's Account of a Law-Suit, A. Sir David Lindsay. BOHV
Carmen. Victor Hernandez Cruz. CAD
Carmen. Newman Levy. ALV; FiBHP
Carmen Bellicosum. Guy Humphreys McMaster. AA; ALV; DD; GN; HBV; MC; PaA; PAH; PAL
(Old Continentals, The.) PAP
Carmen Elegiacum. Thomas Morton. SCAP
Carmen Genesis. Francis Thompson. CoBE; PoLi
Carmen Paschale [*or* Easter Song], *sels.* Caelius Sedulius, *tr. fr. Latin.*
Apostrophe to Death, *tr. by* George Sigerson. OnYI
Christ Quiets the Tempest, *tr. by* George Sigerson. OnYI
Hail, Maiden Root, *tr. by* Raymond F. Roseliep. ISi
Invocation: "Eternal God omnipotent! The One," *tr. by* George Sigerson. OnYI
Magi Visit Herod, The, *tr. by* H. T. Henry. CAW
Miracle, The, *tr. by* H. T. Henry. CAW
Slaughter of the Innocents by Order of King Herod, The, *tr. by* George Sigerson. OnYI
Carmen Possum. *Unknown.* BLPA
Carmina. Robert Mezey. ToPo
Carmina Burana, *sels.* *Unknown, tr. fr. Latin.*
Winter Love Song, *tr. by* Helen Waddell. LiTW
Gaudeamus Igitur, *tr. by* John Addington Symonds. HBV; WoL

Carnal and Spiritual Love. Michelangelo, *tr. fr. Italian by* John Addington Symonds. OnPM
Carnal and the Crane, The. *Unknown.* ESPB; OBB; StJW
(Crow and the Crane, The.) BuBa, *abr.*
Carnival. J. R. Hervey. AnNZ
Carnival of Animals, The, *sels.* Ogden Nash. UnS
Birds, The.
Introduction: "Camille St. Saëns was racked with pains."
Carnival Songs, *sel.* Lorenzo de' Medici, *tr. fr. Italian by* Richard Aldington.
Triumph of Bacchus and Ariadne. CTC
Carol: "All this night shrill chanticler." William Austin. *See* Chanticleer.
Carol, A: "Angels to the shepherds sang, The." Fred E. Weatherly. YeAR
Carol: "Deep in the fading leaves of night." W. R. Rodgers. ChMP; DTC; FaBoTw; FlW
Carol: "Fire is what's precious now." Alison Boodson. NeBP
Carol: Five Joys of the Virgin, The. *Unknown.* ACP; ISi
Carol: "He came all so still." *Unknown. See* I Sing of a Maiden.
Carol: "I sing of a maiden." *Unknown. See* I Sing of a Maiden.
Carol: "I was a lover of turkey and holly." Anne Wilkinson. OBCV
Carol, A: "Joseph was an old man." Lizette Woodworth Reese. StJW
Carol: "Mary laid her Child among." Norman Nicholson. NeBP; StJW
Carol, A: "Mary the Mother sang to her Son." Lizette Woodworth Reese. HBMV
Carol: "Mary, the mother, sits on the hill." Langdon Elwyn Mitchell. OHIP
(Song: "Mary, the mother. . .") ChrBoLe
Carol: "Month can never forget the year, The." John McClure. HBMV
Carol, A: "Sweet Music, sweeter far." Edmund Bolton. OxBoCh
Carol: "There was a Boy bedded in bracken." John Short. DTC; FaBoCh; FaBoTw; LoGBV
Carol: "Villagers all, this frosty tide." Kenneth Grahame. *Fr.* The Wind in the Willows. OHIP
(Christmas Carol.) FaPON; MPB
Carol, A: "Vines branching stilly." Louise Imogen Guiney. CAW; OBVV
(Five Carols for Christmastide, II.) ISi
Carol: "We saw Him sleeping in His manger bed." Gerald Bullett. DD; HBVY
Carol: "When the herds were watching." William Canton. DD; HBVY; OHIP
Carol Bringing in the Boar's Head, A. *Unknown. See* Boar's Head Carol, The.
Carol, Brothers, Carol. William Muhlenberg. TiPo (1952 ed.)
Carol, Christians! Christ is here! Christ Is Here. Robert Lowell. BePJ
Carol, every violet has. Epilogue. Alfred Noyes. *Fr.* The Flower of Old Japan. MoBrPo
Carol for Candlemas Day. *Unknown.* SeCL
Carol for Children, A. Ogden Nash. EaLo
Carol for Christmas Day, A. *Unknown.* TuPP
Carol for Christmas Eve, A. Eleanor Farjeon. BoChLi
Carol for His Darling on Christmas Day. Derek Stanford. NeBP
Carol for Saint Stephen's Day, A. *Unknown. See* St. Stephen and Herod.
Carol for Twelfth Day, A. *Unknown.* OHIP
Carol in Praise of the Holly and Ivy. *Unknown. See* Holly and Ivy.
Carol Naive. John McClure. HBMV
Carol of Agincourt, A. *Unknown.* MeEL
Carol of St. George, A. *Unknown.* MeEL
Carol of the angels, The. Adoration—A Carol. E. Margaret Clarkson. SoP
Carol of the Birds. *Unknown, tr. fr. French.* OHIP
(Whence Comes This Rush of Wings?) ChrBoLe
Carol of the Russian Children. *Unknown.* OHIP
Carol of Three Kings, The. Nora Hopper Chesson. ChrBoLe
Carol on Corfu. Lawrence Durrell. MemP
Carol round the ruddy hearth, A. For Christmas Day. Eleanor Farjeon. ChBR; TiPo (1952 ed.)
Carol Singers, The. Eleanor Farjeon. MemP
Carol Singers, The. Margaret G. Rhodes. BoTP
Carol to Our Lady: "I sing of a Maiden." *Unknown. See* I Sing of a Maiden.
Carol with Variations. Phyllis McGinley. PoPo
Carolina. Henry Timrod. MC; PAH; PoRL
Carolina! Carolina! heaven's blessings attend her. The Old North State. William Gaston. PoRL
Carolina Spring Song. Hervey Allen. HBMV
Caroline, The. George Crabbe. *Fr.* The Borough. SeCePo
Caroline Cricket. C. Lindsay McCoy. GFA
Caroline of Edinborough Town. *Unknown.* BFSS, *with music*
Caroline, II: To the Evening Star. Thomas Campbell. *See* To the Evening Star.
Caron oh Caron come away. *Unknown.* SeCSL
Carousel, The. G. C. Oden. AmNP; Kal
Carpe Diem. "Laurence Hope." *Fr.* In the Early, Pearly Morning. OtMeF
Carpe Diem. Thomas Lodge. *See* Pluck the Fruit and Taste the Pleasure.
Carpe Diem. Theóphile Marzials. VA
Carpe Diem. Shakespeare. *See* O Mistress Mine.
Carpe Diem. Ridgely Torrence. *Fr.* The House of a Hundred Lights. AA
Carpe Diem. *Unknown. See* Hey Nonny No!
Carpenter, The. Amy Bruner Almy. ChIP
Carpenter. Leslie Savage Clark. ChIP
Carpenter. Isabel Fiske Conant. StJW
Carpenter, The. Clifford Dyment. POTi
Carpenter, The. Phyllis Hartnoll. ChIP
Carpenter. E. V. Lucas. StVeCh
Carpenter, The. George Macdonald. TrPWD; TRV
Carpenter, The. G. A. Studdert-Kennedy. ChIP; OQP; StJW
Carpenter Christ. Mildred Fowler Field. PGD
Carpenter, he worked with wood, A. Carpenter of Eternity. E. Merrill Root. ChIP; PGD
Carpenter is intent on the pressure of his hand, The. El Greco: Espolio. Earle Birney. MoCV; PeCV (1967 ed.)
Carpenter of Eternity. E. Merrill Root. ChIP; PGD
Carpenter of Galilee, The. Hilda W. Smith. ChIP; MaRV; TRV
Carpenter of Nazareth, The. George Blair. StJW
Carpenter of Nazareth, The. Walter Smith. ChIP
Carpenter was not afraid to die, The. The Divine Rebel. George Scheftel. ChIP
Carpenter, what are you building now? Not Made with Hands. Lilith Lorraine. ChIP
Carpenter's Plane, The. Vasili Kazin, *tr. fr. Russian by* Babette Deutsch. OnPM
Carpenter's Son. Annie Johnson Flint. BePJ
Carpenter's Son, The. A. E. Housman. A Shropshire Lad, XLVIII. BoLiVe; CoBMV; MoAB; MoBrPo; NeMA; PoAn; PoVP; VaPo
Carpenter's Son, The. Kathryn Blackburn Peck. BePJ
Carpenter's Wife. *Unknown.* OxBB
Carpenter's Young Wife, The. Chaucer. *Fr.* The Canterbury Tales: The Miller's Tale. ExPo
Carrara. Philip Murray. NePoAm
Carrefour. Amy Lowell. MoLP
Carriage brushes through the bright, The. Solo for Ear-Trumpet. Edith Sitwell. MoAB; MoBrPo; NeMA
Carriage from Sweden, A. Marianne Moore. LiTA; LiTM (rev. ed.); MoAB; NePA; TwCP
Carrickfergus. Louis MacNeice. AnIL; OnYI
Carrier's Address. *Unknown.* PoOW
Carrion, A. Baudelaire, *tr. fr. French by* Allen Tate. AWP; LiTW
Carrion. Clifford Dyment. POTi
Carrion. Harold Monro. Youth in Arms, IV. MMA
Carrion Comfort. Gerard Manley Hopkins. AnFE; AtBAP; BoC; BWP; CABA; CoBE; EnLi-2; LiTB; LiTG; MaPo; MoVE; NoP; OAEP; OxBoCh; PoDB; PoEL-5; PoeP; PoIE; PoLi; PoVP; Sonn; VaPo; ViPo; ViPP; VP
(Not, I'll Not, Carrion Comfort.) CMoP
(Sonnet: "Not, I'll not, carrion comfort, Despair, not feast on thee.") FaBoEn; OBNC
(Terrible Sonnets, The, I.) MoPo
Carrion Crow, The. Thomas Lovell Beddoes. *See* Song: "Old Adam, the carrion crow."
Carrion crow sat on an oak, A. Mother Goose. OTPC (1923 ed.); OxNR
Carrion-eater's nobility calls back from God, The. A Dreamed Realization. Gregory Corso. NeAP

Carroll's Sword. *At. to* Dallan MacMore. *See* Song of Carroll's Sword, The.
Carrot has a green fringed top, A. Vegetables. Rachel Field. GFA; SoPo
Carrouse to the Emperor, the Royal Pole, and the Much-wronged Duke of Lorrain, A. *Unknown.* CoMu
Carrowmore. "Æ." BEL; HBMV
(Gates of Dreamland, The.) HBV
Carry Her over the Water. W. H. Auden. FaBoTw
Carry Me Back. John Holmes. AmFN; NePoAm-2
Carry Me Back to Old Virginny. James A. Bland. FaBoBe; FaBV; FaFP; GoSl; PoRL; TreF
Carry me out. Discharged. W. E. Henley. *Fr.* In Hospital. PoVP
Carry me over the long last mile. The Long Last Mile. Lauchlan MacLean Watt. MaRV; SoP
Carry On! Thomas Curtis Clark. OQP
Carry On! Robert W. Service. HBV; MaRV
Carry your grief alone. Alone. Robert Finch. CaP; PeCV
Carrying a bunch of marigolds. A Negro Woman. William Carlos Williams. BWP; PoIE
Carrying his mandolin in the curve of afternoon. At the Seed and Feed. J. Edgar Simmons. NYTB
Carrying Their Coracles. Andrew Marvell. *Fr.* Upon Appleton House. ChTr
Carrying their packages of groceries in particular. Old Men and Old Women Going Home on the Street Car. Merrill Moore. MAP; MoAmPo
Cars/ In the Park. Central Park Tourney. Mildred Weston. AmFN; OCS
Cars Go Fast. Annette Wynne. GFA
Cars in the mirror come swiftly forward, The. Rear Vision. William Jay Smith. NYBP
Cars speed up and down, The. Under the surface lie. The Roman Wall. Patric Dickinson. POTi
Cart that carries hay, The. Farm Cart. Eleanor Farjeon. BrR
Carta Canadensis. Ralph Gustafson. PeCV (1967 ed.)
Cartagena de Indias. Earle Birney. MoCV
Carthon, a Poem. James Macpherson. EiPP; EnRP
Sels.
"King of Morven," Carthon said, "I fall in the midst of my course." EnPE
Ossian's Address to the Sun. BEL
Carthusians. Ernest Dowson. JKCP; PoVP
Cartier at St. Malo. Francis Webb. *Fr.* A View of Montreal. BoAV
Cartography. Louise Bogan. PoPl
Cartography. Joel Oppenheimer. CoPo
Cartoons of slashes on the tide-traced crater. Altarwise by Owl-Light, VI. Dylan Thomas. CoBMV; LiTM; MaSP
Carts of the Wee Blind Lass, The. Kenneth Patchen. ToPo
Caruso: a voice. Sleeping with Women. Kenneth Koch. ANYP
Carve your name upon a tree. Poem of Circumstance. Jean Cocteau. CAW
Carved by a mighty race whose vanished hands. The Sphinx Speaks. Francis Saltus Saltus. AA; HT
Carved Stone, A. *Unknown, tr. fr. Greek by* Lord Neaves. OnPM
Carver, The. Conrad Aiken. *See* See, as the Carver Carves a Rose.
Carver and the Rock Are One, The. Besmilr Brigham. ThO
Caryatid. Léonie Adams. LiTM (1970 ed.); MoVE
Casa d'Amunt. Alastair Reid. NePoEA
Casa Guidi Windows, *sels.* Elizabeth Barrett Browning.
"Cry is up in England, which doth ring, A," *fr.* II. PoVP
Juliet of Nations. VA
Sursum Corda. VA
Casabianca. Elizabeth Bishop. SiSw
Casabianca. Felicia Dorothea Hemans. BeLS; BLPA; EtS; FaBoBe; FaFP; FaPON; FOL; GoTP; HBV; HBVY; NeHB; OnSP; OTPC; PaPo; TreF; WBLP
Casa's Dirge. David Macbeth Moir. VA
Cascade, The. Edgell Rickword. ChMP; FaBoTw
Cascade, The. Tadamine, *tr. fr. Japanese by* Basil Hall Chamberlain. OnPM
Cascading streamers down of palest green. Weeping Willow. Richard Aldridge. NePoAm-2
Case, A. Hughes Mearns. *See* Antigonish.
Case for the Miners, The. Siegfried Sassoon. PoFr
Case History. Arthur W. Bell. WhC
Case History. Lilith Lorraine. FiSC
Case is Altered, The, *sel.* Ben Jonson.
"'Tis not to be told/ What servile villainies men will do for gold." LO
Case of Thomas More, The. Sister Mary St. Virginia. GoBC
Casey at the Bat. Ernest L. Thayer. AmePo; BBV (1951 ed.); BeLS; BLPA; BOHV; FaBoBe; FaFP; FaPON; GSP; HBV; IHA; InMe; LHV; MaC; NeHB; OnSP; OTD; PaPo; PoPl; PoRA; PTK; SD; StPo; TIHL; TreF; YaD
Casey Jones. Edward Vincent Swart. LiTM; PeSA
Casey Jones. *Unknown.* ABF, *with music*; AmPP; APW, *diff. vers.*; AS, *with music*; ATP; BeLS; FaBV, *arr. by* T. Lawrence Seibert; IHA, *sl. abr.*; MaC, *arr. by* T. Lawrence Seibert; OxBoLi; PoPo; ThLM; TreF; TrGrPo; ViBoFo (A, B, C, D, E, F, *and* G *vers.*)
(Mama, Have You Heard the News, *diff vers., with music.*) AS
(Natchul-born Easman, *diff. vers.*) ABF
Casey Jones, befo' he died. Natchul-born Easman. *Unknown.* ABF
Casey Jones has left today. Casey Jones. Edward Vincent Swart. LiTM; PeSA
Casey Jones was a brave engineer. Casey Jones (D *vers.*). *Unknown.* ViBoFo
Casey Jones was engineer. Casey Jones (F *vers.*). *Unknown.* ViBoFo
Casey Jones was long and tall. Casey Jones (E *vers.*). *Unknown.* ViBoFo
Casey—Twenty Years After. *Unknown, at. to* S. P. McDonald. BLPA; GSP
Casey would waltz with a strawberry blonde (*refrain*). The Band Played On. John F. Palmer. TreF
Casey's Daughter at the Bat, *parody.* Al Graham. InMe
Casey's Revenge. James Wilson. BLPA; OnMSP; TreFS
Casey's Table d'Hote. Eugene Field. PoOW
Cashed in his chips. Epitaph for a Man from Virginia City. Kenneth Porter. NePoAm-2
Cashel of Munster. *Unknown, At. to.* William English, *tr. fr. Modern Irish by* Sir Samuel Ferguson. AnIV; IrPN; OBEV; OBVV; OnYI; OxBI
Casino. W. H. Auden. MoPo
Casket, The. Nathaniel Wanley. SeCL
Casket Song, A. Shakespeare. *See* Tell Me Where Is Fancy Bred.
Caspar, Melchior, Balthazar. The Gift. Laura Spencer Portor. StJW
Cassamen and Dowsabell. Michael Drayton. *Fr.* The Shepherd's Garland. OBSC
(Ballad of Dowsabell, The.) LoBV
(Dowsabel.) UnTE
(Eighth Eclogue.) ReEn; TuPP
Cassandra. Louise Bogan. AnAmPo; MAP; MoAmPo; MoVE; NP
Cassandra. Robinson Jeffers. LiTA; LiTM; NePA; VaPo; WaP
Cassandra. E. A. Robinson. AmPP; CMoP; ExPo; LiTA; LiTM (rev. ed.); MaPo; NePA; NP; OxBA; PoFr; PPON; SeCeV
Cassandra Southwick. Whittier. PAH; PoIE
Cassandra, treading the Titanic deck. Captain's Table. Witter Bynner. AnFE; CoAnAm
Cassandra's Epithalamium. Euripides, *tr fr. Greek by* Ann Stanford. *Fr.* The Trojan Women. HW
Cassandra's Lament. Aeschylus, *tr. fr. Greek by* Richmond Lattimore. *Fr.* Agamemnon. LiTW
Cassie O'Lang. *Unknown.* ShM
Cassius Hueffer. Edgar Lee Masters. *Fr.* Spoon River Anthology. OxBA
Cassius Poisons Brutus' Mind. Shakespeare. *Fr.* Julius Caesar, I, ii. TreFS
Cast all your cares on God; that anchor holds. Cast Your Cares on God. Tennyson. *Fr.* Enoch Arden. MaRV; TRV
Cast aside dull books and thought. Invitation to the Dance. *Unknown.* UnTE
Cast away care, he that loves sorrow. Thomas Dekker *and* John Ford. *Fr.* The Sun's Darling. ReEn; TuPP
Cast away fear. Arthur Edward Waite. *Fr.* At the End of Things. TRV
Cast away those silkne clouds. *Unknown.* SeCSL
Cast Down, but Not Destroyed. *Unknown.* PAH
Cast on the water by a careless hand. The Cocoa-Tree.

Charles Warren Stoddard. AA; AmePo; CAW
Cast our caps and cares away. John Fletcher. *Fr.* Beggars' Bush. SiCE; TuPP; ViBoPo
Cast Thy Bread Upon the Waters. Ecclesiastes, XI: 1-6, Bible. *O.T.* AWP; JAWP; TiPo (1952 ed.), 2 *ll.*; WBP
(Life's Uncertainty, XI: 1-10.) TreFS
(Youth and Age, XI:I-XII:7.) OuHeWo
Cast wide the folding doorways of the East. From the Night of Forebeing. Francis Thompson. OBVV; OtMeF
Cast Your Cares on God. Tennyson. *Fr.* Enoch Arden. MaRV; TRV
Castara, *sels.* William Habington.
Against Them Who Lay Unchastity to the Sex of Women, *fr.* II. AnAnS-2; CLwM; MePo; OBS; SeCP; SeEP
Castara ("Like the violet, which alone"), *fr.* I. HBV; LiTL
(Description of Castara.) AnAnS-2; CaVP
Melancholy, *fr.* II. LoBV
Nox Nocti Indicat Scientiam, *fr.* III. ACP; AnAnS-2; CAW; GoBC; GTSL; HBV; LoBV; MeLP; MePo; OBEV; OBS; PoFr; PoLi; SeCL
(When I Survey the Bright.) OxBoCh
To Castara: The Reward of Innocent Love, *fr.* II. ACP; CaVP; LoBV
To Castara, upon Beauty, *fr.* II. AnAnS-2; CoBE; SeCP
To Roses in the Bosom of Castara, *fr.* I. AnAnS-2; CaVP; CLwM; EnLoPo; GoBC; HBV; LoBV; MeLP; OBEV; PoAn; SeCL; SeCP; SeEP; UnTE; ViBoPo
Upon Castara's Absence. AnAnS-2
Upon Castara's Departure, *fr.* I. SeCL
Upon Thought Castara May Die, *fr.* I. ACP
Castara, see that dust, the sportive wind. To Castara, upon Beauty. William Habington. *Fr.* Castara, II. AnAnS-2; CoBE; SeCP
Castaway, The. William Cowper. AtBAP; BEL; BWP; CABA; CBEP; CBV; CEP; CoBE; EiCL; EiCP; EiPP; ELP; EnLi-2; EnLit; EnPE; EnRP; FaBoEn; FiP; GTSL; InPo; NoP; OAEP; OBEC; PeER; PoE; PoEL-3; PoFS; PoSa; TDP; TOP
Castaways, The. Marya Zaturenska. TrGrPo (1942 ed.)
Castiglione has many a frontier. The Road to Bologna. Roy Macnab. PeSA
Castile. Miguel de Unamuno, *tr. fr. Spanish by* Eleanor L. Turnbull. PoPl
Castilian. Elinor Wylie. AnAmPo; HBMV; NAMP
Casting All Your Care upon God, for He Careth for You. Thomas Washbourne. OxBoCh
Casting All Your Care upon Him. *Unknown.* STF
Casting the times with their strong signes. Richard Crashaw. *Fr.* Sospetto d'Herode, I. MaMe; SCEP-1
Castle, The. Sidney Alexander. PoNe
Castle, The. Robert Graves. NoP
Castle, The. Edwin Muir. LiTB
Castle Builder, The. La Fontaine, *tr. fr. French.* OTPC
Castle Builder, The, *sel.* Longfellow.
Challenge to Youth ("Build on, and make thy castles high and fair"). MaRV
Castle by the Sea, The. Ludwig Uhland, *tr. fr. German by* Longfellow. AWP; JAWP; WBP
Castle Hyde. Edward Kenealy. IrPN
(Castlehyde, *sl. diff.*) OnYI
Castle in the Fire, The. Mary Jane Carr. BrR
Castle of Indolence, The, *sels.* James Thomson.
Canto I. BEL; CEP; EiCP; EiPP
"Doors that knew no shrill alarming bell, The," *fr.* I. ViBoPo
"In lowly dale, fast by a river's side," *fr.* I. EnRP; ViBoPo
(Land of Indolence.) OBEC; SeCePo
Indifference to Fortune, *fr.* II. OBEC
"O mortal man, who livest here by toil," *fr.* I. EnLi-2 (1949 ed.)
Praise of Industry, The, *fr.* II. OBEC
"Sometimes the pencil, in cool airy halls," *fr.* I. PoEL-3
Sons of Indolence, *fr.* I. OBEC
Witching Song, A, *fr.* I. OBEC
Wondrous Show, A, *fr*, I. OBEC
Castle Ruins The. William Barnes. VA
Castleconnell. Sir Aubrey De Vere. IrPN
Castled crag of Drachenfels, The. Byron. *Fr.* Childe Harold's Pilgrimage. ViBoPo
Castlehyde. Edward Kenealy. *See* Castle Hyde.
Castles. A. Glanz-Leyeless, *tr. fr. Yiddish by* Joseph Leftwich. TrJP
Castles and Distances. Richard Wilbur. FiMAP
Castles in the Air. James Ballantine. HBV
Castles in the Air. Thomas Love Peacock. HBV
Castles in the Sand. Dorothy Baker. BoTP
Castles with lofty. Soldier's Song. Goethe. *Fr.* Faust. AWP
Casual/ turning to a window. Blind Man. Jason Miller. ThO
Casual glance on me, The. Old Essex Door. Agnes MacCarthy Hickey. GoYe
Casual Gold. Maud E. Uschold. SoPo; YeAr
Casual Lines. Su Shih, *tr. fr. Chinese by* Theresa Li. FlW
Casual Man, The. Denis Glover. AnNZ
Casual Meeting. Margaret E. Bruner. PoToHe
Casual Song, A. Roden Noel. HBV
Casualty. W. E. Henley. *Fr.* In Hospital. PoVP
Casualty. Robert Nichols. MMA
Casualty. Edwin McNeill Poteat. MaRV
Casualty. Diana Witherby. ChMP
Casuarina. Roland Robinson. BoAV
Cat. Dorothy Baruch. SoPo; SUS; TiPo; UTS
Cat, The. Baudelaire, *tr. fr. French by* Roy Campbell. PoPl
Cat, The. Joseph Payne Brennan. ShM
Cat, The. Charles Stuart Calverley. *Fr.* Sad Memories. ChTr
Cat, The. Oliver Herford. FaBV
Cat, A. Jules Lemaître, *tr. fr. French.* CIV
Cat. Sinclair Lewis. GoTP
Cat, The. Mary Britton Miller. BoChLi; SoPo; StVeCh; SUS; TiPo; UTS
Cat, The. Walter Adolphe Roberts. CIV
Cat, The. Christopher Smart. *See* My Cat Jeoffry.
Cat. "Jan Struther." GoTP
Cat, A. Edward Thomas. BrPo
Cat, The. Helen Hay Whitney. GFA
Cat and I. Fight. Jean Jaszi. RePo
Cat and Mouse. Ted Hughes. EaLo
Cat and Northern Lights. The. Elizabeth J. Coatsworth. CIV
Cat and the Bird, The. George Canning. BiS; ChTr
Cat and the Bird, The. Marvin Solomon. NePoAm-2
Cat and the Fish, The. Thomas Gray. *See* Ode on the Death of a Favorite Cat.
Cat and the Miser, The. Mark Van Doren. TPM
Cat and the Moon, The. W. B. Yeats. CMoP; ExPo; FaBoCh; FlW; GoJo; InPo; LoGBV; LOW; NoP; Po; PoMS; RoGo; ShBV-1; ThWaDe; WePo
Cat and the Weather. May Swenson. WIRo
Cat Ballerina Assoluta. Emilie Glen. GoYe
Cat came fiddling out of a barn, A. Mother Goose. BoChLi; BoTP; OTPC; PCH; PPL; SAS; StVeCh
Cat Changed into a Woman, The. La Fontaine, *tr. fr. French.* CIV
Cat-eyed owl, although so fierce, The. Owl. Edward Brathwaite. NYTB
Cat-Goddesses. Robert Graves. MoVE; NYBP
Cat I live with is an animal, The. A Domestic Cat. Edwin Denby. ANYP
Cat I sing, of famous memory, A. A Catalectic Monody. *Unknown.* BOHV; CIV
Cat, if cat there be, merely harmonizes, The. Supposition at 2 A.M. Phillip Hey. YAP
Cat, if you go outdoors you must walk in the snow. On a Night of Snow. Elizabeth J. Coatesworth. CIV; GoTP; MAP; MoAmPo; MoShBr
Cat in distress, A. Verses on a Cat. Shelley. CIV
Cat in the Long Grass. Alan Dixon. FlW
Cat in the Snow, The. F. Hey. SAS
Cat is in the parlour, The. Indifference. *Unknown.* BOHV
Cat May Look at a King, A. *Unknown.* OxBoLi
Cat may look on a king, and what of that A. Of a Cat's Look. John Heywood. SiCE; TuPP
Cat-o'-Nine-Tails, The. John Blight. BoAV; NeLNL
Cat of Cats, The. William Brighty Rands. *Fr.* The White Princess. CIV
(Kitten Speaks, The.) RIS
(Kitty: What She Thinks of Herself.) MoShBr
Cat on Couch. Barbara Howes. PoSa
Cat on the Porch at Dusk. Dorothy Harriman. GoYe
Cat runs races with her tail, The. Signs of Winter. John Clare. BoNaP; ERoP-2; PoE; PoSC; WaKn; WiR
Cat said, A, on the corner. Vietnam #4. Clarence Major. BOLo; WOW
Cat sat asleep by the side of the fire, The. *Unknown.* OxNR
Cat sat quaintly by the fire, A. Hearth. Peggy Bacon. FaPON

Cat takes a look at the weather. Cat and the Weather. May Swenson. WIRo
Cat that comes to my window sill, The. That Cat. Ben King. FiBHP
Cat That Followed His Nose, The. John Kaye Kendall. CenHV
Cat to Her Kittens, A. Eliza Grove. OTPC (1923 ed.)
Cat was once a weaver, The. What the Gray Cat Sings. Arthur Guiterman. MoShBr; MPB; PoMS; PoRL
Cat went here and there, The. The Cat and the Moon. W. B. Yeats. CMoP; ExPo; FaBoCh; FlW; GoJo; InPo; LoGBV; LOW; NoP; Po; PoMS; RoGo; ShBV-1; ThWaDe; WePo
Cat! who has[t] pass'd thy grand climacteric. To a Cat [*or* To Mrs. Reynolds's Cat]. Keats. BoC; CIV; DiPo; FaBoCh
Cataclysm. N. H. Brettell. BoSA
Cataclysm. Catullus, *tr. fr. Latin by* Horace Gregory. LiTW
Cataclysm. Louis Johnson. AnNZ
Cataclysmic if it were so. "What You See Is Me". Barbara Gibbs. NYBP
Catalectic Monody, A. *Unknown.* BOHV; CIV
Cataline, Cato,/ Pericles and Plato. Food for Thought. Michael Lewis. RIS
Catalog. Rosalie Moore. GoTP; StaSt
Catalogue. Louis Untermeyer. HBMV
Catalpa Tree. Miriam Waddington. MoCV; OBCV
Catalpa Trees. Padraic Colum. NePoAm; NYTB
"Catamount Tavern" is lively to-night, The. Parson Allen's Ride. Wallace Bruce. MC; PAH
Cataract. Margoret Smith. NYBP
Cataract of Lodore, The. Robert Southey. BOHV; GN; HBV; OTPC; PTK; TreFS; WBLP
(How the Waters Come Down at Lodore.) PoPo
Cataract, whirling to the precipice, The. Fragment. John Clare. BoNaP
Catarina to Camoens, *sel.* Elizabeth Barrett Browning.
"Keep my riband, take and keep it." GTSE
Catastrophe. Edwin Brock. NMP
Catawba Wine. Longfellow. LHV
Catch, A: "Buz, quoth the blue fly." Ben Jonson. *See* Buz, Quoth the Blue Fly.
Catch, A: "If all be true that I do think." Henry Aldrich. *See* Reasons for Drinking.
Catch, A: "If you were queen of bloaters." Tom Hood. CenHV
Catch, A: "Ne'er trouble thyself at the times or their turnings." *Unknown.* SeCL
Catch: On a Wet Day. Franco Sacchetti, *tr. fr. Italian by* Dante Gabriel Rossetti. AWP; JAWP; WBP
(On a Wet Day.) BoNaP
Catch, A: "Once the head is gray." Richard Henry Stoddard. AA
Catch, A: "Seamen three!" Thomas Love Peacock. *See* Three Men of Gotham.
Catch: "Two boys uncoached are tossing a poem together." Robert Francis. PP
Catch, A: "Wisemen were but seven, The." *Unknown.* SeCL; SeEP
Catch a Little Rhyme. Eve Merriam. PDV
Catch by the Hearth, A. *Unknown.* ChBR; OHIP
(Christmas Hearth Rhyme.) PCH
Catch for Singing, A. W. W. Gibson. AnFE
Catch for Spring, A. Robert Nichols. GBV
Catch her and hold her if you can. Defiance. Walter Savage Landor. HBV
Catch him coming off the thing after a state of the union. Strategies. Welton Smith. NBP
Catch him, crow! Carry him, kite! *Unknown.* OxNR
Catching yourself, hands lathery. In the Round. Theodore Weiss. NMP
Catechism, The. Walter de la Mare. CMoP
Categorical Courtship. *Unknown.* BOHV; CIV
Caterpillar, The. Robert Graves. TSW
Caterpillar, The. Alfred Noyes. BoPe
Caterpillar. R. E. Rashley. CaP
Caterpillar. Christina Rossetti. *Fr.* Sing-Song. BoChLi (1950 ed.); BoTP; FaPON; GFA; GoJo; GoTP; MPB; OTPC (1946 ed.); RIS; SoPo; StVeCh
(Brown and Furry.) SUS; UTS
Caterpillar and the Ant, The. Allan Ramsay. SeCePo
Caterpillar and the Butterfly, The. José Rosas Moreno, *tr. fr. Spanish by* Bryant. OnPM
Caterpillars. John Freeman. ChMP
Caterpillar's Apology for Eating a Favorite Gladiolus, A. Charles Dalmon. TSW
Catfish. John Farrar. GFA
Catfish. Oliver Herford. BOHV
Catfish, The. Jack Mathews. TPM
Catfish with whiskers that lives in the brook, The. Catfish. John Farrar. GFA
Cathedral, The. Thomas S. Jones, Jr. MaRV
Cathedral, The. James Russell Lowell. AmePo; MAmP; MWA-1
Life's Purpose ("This life were brutish did we not sometimes"). MaRV
"Whatsoe'er/ The form of building or the creed professed." ChIP
(Sovereign Emblem, The.) MaRV
Witness of God. OQP
Cathedral by Sea. Norman Levine. PeCV
Cathedral of Rheims, The. Emile Verhaeren, *tr. fr. French by* Joyce Kilmer. CAW
Cathedral of St. Louis, The. Carl Carmer. MoSiPe
Cathemerinon, *sel.* Prudentius, *tr. fr. Latin by* Raymond F. Roseliep.
O Noble Virgin, *Hymn* XI, *verses* 53-60. ISi
Catherine. Karla Kuskin. PDV
Catherine Kinrade. Thomas Edward Brown. OBVV
Catherine Takes a Stroll. John Cournos. CLwM
Cath-Loda, *sel.* James Macpherson.
"Tale of the times of old, A!" BEL
Catholic Amen, The. Christopher Smart. *Fr.* A Song to David. GoBC
("He sang of God—the mighty source.") GBV; GTSL; LiTG; TRV
(Song of David, The.) GTBS-W
Catholic Bells, The. William Carlos Williams. CMoP; OxBA
Catholic Church, The. Dryden. *Fr.* The Hind And the Panther, II. OBS
("One in herself not rent by schism, but sound.") SeEP
Catholic Faith, The. Kenelm H. Digby. CAW
Catkin. *Unknown.* GFA; MPB; OTPC (1946 ed.); TiPo
(Little Gray Pussy.) SoPo
Cato, *sels.* Addison.
Cato's Soliloquy, *fr.* V, i. MaRV; TreFs; WBLP
(Immortality, *br. sel.*) OQP
"My voice is still for war," *fr.* II, i. PoFr
"Sempronius, why, why wilt thou urge the fate," *fr.* III, v. PoFr
Cato, *sel.* Jonathan Mitchell Sewall.
War and Washington. PAH
Cato's Address to His Troops in Lybia. Lucan, *tr. fr. Latin by* Nicholas Rowe. *Fr.* Pharsalia. OBEC
Cato's Soliloquy. Addison. *See* Cato.
Cats, The. Baudelaire, *tr. fr. French by* Arthur Symons. OnPM
Cats. Edith Richmond Blanchard. CIV
Cats. Marchette Chute. SoPo
Cats. Eleanor Farjeon. PDV; ThGo
Cats, The. Weldon Kees. NaP
Cats. Francis Scarfe. NeBP
Cats. John Banister Tabb. CIV
Cats. A. S. J. Tessimond. HaMV; POTE; ShBV-4
Cats. William Wallace Whitelock. CIV
Cats and Humans. All the Same. Anthony Euwer. CIV
Cats and Kings. Alfred Noyes. MemP
Cat's at the window, and Shock's at the door, The. The Bird-Catcher. Elizabeth Turner. OTPC (1923 ed.)
Cats caught a yellow-vented bulbul, The. Parliament of Cats. D. J. Enright. NMP
Cats Climb Trees. Tom Veitch. ANYP
Cat's Conscience, The. E.V. Lucas. The Nature of the Cat, IV. CIV; PoLF
Cat's Eye. Paul Engle. PoMa
Cats Have Come to Tea, The. Kate Greenaway. OTPC (1946 ed.); PCH
(All the Cats.) SAS
Cat's Meat. Harold Monro. OBMV; TSW
Cats no less liquid than their shadows. Cats. A. S. J. Tessimond. HaMV; POTE; ShBV-4
Cats of Baddeck, The. Phoebe Hoffman. CIV
Cats of Kilkenny, The. *Unknown.* *See* Kilkenny Cats, The.
Cats sleep/ Anywhere. Cats. Eleanor Farjeon. PDV; ThGo

Cats sleep fat and walk thin. Catalog. Rosalie Moore. GoTP; StaSt
Cats' Tea-Party, The. Frederic Edward Weatherly. OTPC (1923 ed.); SAS; TiPo
Cat's World. Bernice Kenyon. CIV
Cattail fluff. Porous. William Carlos Williams. NYBP
Cattle. Banko, *tr. fr. Japanese.* MPB
Cattle. Frederick Mortimer Clapp. LiTM (1946 ed.)
Cattle. *Unknown.* SoPo
Cattle of His Hand, The. Wilbur Underwood. AA; WGRP
Cattle roam again across the field, The. Adoration of the Disk. *Unknown. Fr.* The Book of the Dead. FaPON
Cattle-Round-up, The. H. D. C. McLachlan. SCC
Cattle Show. "Hugh MacDiarmid." GoTS; MoBrPo; OBMV
Cattle-trains edge along the river, The. Ceiling Unlimited. Muriel Rukeyser. MoAmPo
Catts as other creatures doe, The. *Unknown.* SeCSL
Catullan Hendecasyllables. Samuel Taylor Coleridge. PoG
Catullus de Lesbia. Swift. *See* Lesbia Railing.
Catullus to Lesbia. James Reeves. ErPo
Catullus Talks to Himself (Catullus, you're a fool. I said). Catullus, *tr. fr. Latin by* Louis Untermeyer. UnTE
Catwise. Philip Booth. NePoAm-2
Caucasus, The ("The Caucasus lay vast in light"). Boris Pasternak, *tr. fr. Russian by* Eugene M. Kayden. PoPl
"Caudal" Lecture, A. William Sawyer. BOHV
Caughnawaga Beadwork Seller, The. William Douw Lighthall. CaP
Caught by Chance. T. W. Ramsey. HaMV
Caught in the centre of a soundless field. Myxomatosis. Philip Larkin. CMoP; ELU
Caught in the exhaustion of an endless loneliness. Creation. V. N. Bhushan. ACV
Caught in the glib catcher's net. Sockeye Salmon. Ronald Hambleton. CaP; OBCV; PeCV
Caught still as Absalom. Chagrin. Isaac Rosenberg. ChMP; MoBrPo
Caught upon a thousand thorns, I sing. 1934. Richard Eberhart. TwAmPo
Caught without wife and mother, child. Getting Drunk with Daughter. Robert Huff. NePoEA-2
Cauld are the ghaisties in yon kirk yaird. Ghaisties. Robert Garioch. NeBP
Cauld blaws the wind frae east to west. Up in the Morning Early. Burns. PoSC
Cauld blows the wind frae north to south. Cold Blows the Wind. John Hamilton. CH
Cauld Lad of Hilton, The. *Unknown.* OxBoLi
(Cauld Lad's Song, The.) ChTr
(Ghost's Song, The.) FaBoCh; LoGBV
(Wandering Spectre, The.) AtBAP; CBEP; CH
Cauliflower, The. John Haines. ThO
Caulker, The. M. A. Lewis. StPo
Cause and Effect. May Swenson. TPM
Cause for Wonder, A. *Unknown.* MeEL
"Cause of loving God is God alone, The." The One Thing Needful. Vassar Miller. PoCh
Cause of Our Joy. Sister Maris Stella. ISi
Causc of This I Know Not, The. Haniel Long. HBMV; NP
Cause of Thunder, The. Lucretius, *tr. fr. Latin by* Thomas Creech. *Fr* De Rerum Natura, VI. PeRV
Caution. *Unknown, tr. fr. German by* Louis Untermeyer. UnTE
Caution to Everybody, A. Ogden Nash. NePA
Caution to Poets, A. Matthew Arnold. CBEP; PoVP; PV
Cautionary Tale, A. Anne Wilkinson. OBCV; PeCV (1967 ed.)
Cautionary Verses [to Youth of Both Sexes]. Theodore Hook. BOHV; HBV
Cautious collapsible cow, The. Limerick. *Unknown.* LiBL
Cautious Lovers, The, *sel.* Countess of Winchilsea.
To Silvia. HBV
Cautious Struggle, The. *Unknown. See* Be Quiet, Sir!.
Cavalier, The. Alexander Brome. PeRV
Cavalier. Richard Bruce. CDC
Cavalier Tunes. Robert Browning. BEL; EnLit; EPN; HBV; MCCG; OAEP; PoVP; ShBV-1; TOP; VA
Sels.
Boot and Saddle, III. EnLi-2; ViPo
Give a Rouse, II. EnLi-2; ViPo
(Cavalier Tune, A.) BoLiVe
Marching Along, I. ATP (1935 ed.); EnLi-2; ViPo; YT
Cavalier's Escape, The. George Walter Thornbury. FaBoBe; GN; HBV; OTPC
Cavalier's Lullaby for His Mistress, A. Thomas Jordan. *Fr.* An Alarm in 1645. SeCL
Cavalier's Song. Robert Graham. *See* If Doughty Deeds.
Cavalier's Song, The. William Motherwell. GN; HBV; OTPC
Cavalry Crossing A Ford. Walt Whitman. AA; AmePo; AmP; AmPP; AP; BWP; CABA; CBEP; CBV; ChTr; CoBA; MaPo (1969 ed.); MWA-1; NoP; Po; PoPl; PoPo; OxBA; RePo; StP; TDP; UnPo (3d ed.)
Cave, A. James Kirkup. BoPe
Cave-Boy, The. Laura E. Richards. FaPON
Cave-Drawing, The. Vernon Watkins. LiTB
Cave of Despair, The. Spenser. *Fr.* The Faerie Queene, I, 9. LoBV
Cave of Mammon, The. Spenser. The Faerie Queene, II, 7. FiP, 12 *sts.*; PoEL-1
(House of Richesse, The, 3 *sts.*) CH
Cave Rock is made of toffee. For a Child. Denis Glover. AnNZ
Cave Sedem. Theodore F. MacManus. HBV
Cavern, The. Charles Tomlinson. NMP
Cavern and the Hut, The. John Hookham Frere. OTPC (1923 ed.)
Caverns of my mind are wrinkled, The. Trapped. Vernoy E. Hite. TNV
Caverns of the Grave I've Seen, The. Blake. NCEP
Caves, The. Michael Roberts. ChMP
Caw, Caw. F. Hey. SAS
"Caw," said the rook. Birds' Nests. Millicent Seager. BoTP
Cazador (Hunter). Federico García Lorca, *tr. fr. Spanish by* Stephen Spender *and* J. L. Gili. Po
Cean Dubh Deelish. *Unknown. See* Dear Dark Head.
Cean-Salla. James Clarence Mangan. OnYI
Cease not thou heavnly voiced glorious creature. *Unknown.* SeCSL
Cease, sorrow cease, & doe noe more torment. *Unknown.* SeCSL
Cease that harsh musick; we are not pleas'd with it. Cyril Tourneur. *Fr.* The Atheist's Tragedy, V, i. AtBAP
Cease then nor Order Imperfection name. Whatever Is, Is Right. Pope. *Fr.* An Essay on Man, Epistles I-II. OBEC
Cease thy wishes gentle boy. *Unknown.* SeCSL
Cease, warring thoughts, and let his brain. James Shirley. *Fr.* The Triumph of Beauty. TuPP
Cease ye this farness; 'bate this pride of you. The Mock Caliph. *Unknown, tr. by* Richard F. Burton. EnLi-1
Ceaselessly the weaver, Time. The Weaver. William H. Burleigh. BLPA
Cecidit, Cecidit Babylon Magna! Theodore Maynard. JKCP
Cecilia. *Unknown, tr. fr. French-Canadian by* William McLennan. WHW
Cedar and jagged fir. The Lonely Land. A. J. M. Smith. CaP
Cedar Mountain. Annie Fields. MC; PAH
Cedar Waxwing. William H. Matchett. ELU; WIRo
Cedars of Lebanon, The. Alphonse Marie Louis de Lamartine, *tr. fr. French by* Toru Dutt. AWP; JAWP; WBP
Ceiling of his bedroom, The. Cartography. Joel Oppenheimer. CoPo
Ceiling Unlimited. Muriel Rukeyser. MoAmPo
Ceilings of knobbled gold. Paganini. Christopher Middleton. MuSP
Ceix and Alceone, *sel.* John Gower. *Fr.* Confessio Amantis.
House of Sleep, The. AtBAP
Celadyne's Song. William Browne. *See* Memory ("Marina's gone. . .").
Celanta at the Well of Life. George Peele. *See* Song at the Well, The.
Celebrate the season of the death. The Kimono. Don Gordon. WOW
Celebrated Return. Clarence Major. AmNP
Celebration. Leonard Cohen. ErPo
Celebration. John L'Heureux. YAP
Celebration, A. May Sarton. NePoAm-2
Celebration in the Plaza, The. Adrienne Cecile Rich. NePoEA; TwAmPo
Celebration of Charis, A. Ben Jonson. AnAnS-2; SCEP-2; SeCP

Celebration (continued)
Begging Another, on Colo[u]r of Mending the Former. LO; OAEP; PoEL-2; TuPP
(Begging Another Kiss.) StP
(For Love's Sake). UnTE
(Kiss, The.) AtBAP
Claiming a Second Kiss by Desert. LiTL
"Do but look on her eyes, they do light." LO
Have You Seen But a Bright Lily Grow. MemP; OTPC (1923 ed.)
("Have you seen but a bright lily grow.") EG; FaBoCh; LoGBV; ReEn
(So Sweet Is She.) GN
(So White, So Soft, So Sweet.) MeWo; TrGrPo; UnTE
(Triumph, The.) PG, 8 *ll.*
Her Man Described by Her Own Dictamen. AtBAP
His Excuse for Loving. EnRePo; PoEL-2; QFR; SeCV-1; SeEP; TuPP
How He Saw Her. AtBAP, 4 *ll.*; EnRePo; OAEP; QFR; SeCV-1
Triumph of Charis, The. BEL; CABA; CBEP; ELP; ExPo; GoBC; LiTB; LoBV; NoP; SeCeV; TOP; WHA
(Her Triumph.) AtBAP; CaFP; CTC; ElL; FaBoEn; HBV; InPo; LiTL; MaPo; OAEP; PAn; Po; PoEL-2; SeCV-1; SeEP; TuPP; ViBoPo
(See the Chariot at Hand Here of Love.) InvP; SiCE
(Triumph, The.) AnFE; OBEV
Celebration of Love. James McAuley. MoAuPo
Celebrations. Austin Clarke. OxBI
Celery. Ogden Nash. FaPON; RePo; WePo
Celestial Bird. Jessica Powers. JKCP (1955 ed.)
Celestial Body. Louise Townsend Nicholl. NePoAm.
Celestial choir, enthron'd in realms of light. His Excellency, General Washington. Phillis Wheatley. Kal
Celestial City, The. Giles Fletcher. Christ's Victory and Triumph, IV. OBS
Celestial Country, The. Bernard of Cluny. *See* Jerusalem, the Golden.
Celestial Love, *sel.* Emerson.
Love's Nobility. TreF
Celestial Love. Michelangelo, *tr. fr. Italian by* John Addington Symonds. AWP; JAWP; WBP
Celestial Passion, The. Richard Watson Gilder. AA; AnAmPo
Celestial Pilot, The. Dante, *tr. fr. Italian by* Longfellow. *Fr.* Divina Commedia: Purgatorio. WGRP
Celestial poesy! whose genial sway. William Charles Wentworth. *Fr.* Australasia. BoAu
Celestial Queen. Jacopo Sannazaro, *tr. fr. Latin by* John C. Eustace. *Fr.* De Partu Virginis. ISi
Celestial Surgeon, The. Robert Louis Stevenson. BBV; BoC; BrPo; EPN; GBV (1922 ed.); GoTP; HBV; HBVY; MaRV; MemP; MoBrPo; OQP; PoToHe (new ed.); PoVP; TreFS; TrGrPo; TrPWD; TRV; ViBoPo; WGRP
Celestial Wisdom. Juvenal, *tr. fr. Latin by* Samuel Johnson. The Satires, X. AWP; JAWP; WBP
Celestina, *sel.* Fernando de Rojas, *tr. fr. Spanish by* James Mabbe.
Now Sleep, and Take Thy Rest. SeCL
Celestine. Robert Fitzgerald. MoVE
Celestine Silvousplait Justine de Mouton Rosalie. Propinquity Needed. Charles Battell Loomis. BOHV; InMe
Celia. Thomas Duffett. SeCL
Celia and Belinda. Colley Cibber. *Fr.* Woman's Wit. SeCL
Celia Bleeding, to the Surgeon. Thomas Carew. AnAnS-2; SeCP
Celia Is Gone. William Browne. SeCL
Celia, my fairest Celia, fell. Charles Cotton. LO
Celia sat beside the seaside. *Unknown.* SiTL
Celia Singing ("Hark, how my Celia"). Thomas Carew. OAEP
Celia Singing ("You that think Love can convey"). Thomas Carew. CLwM; EnLit; LO; SeCL
(Her Sweet Voice.) LiTL
(Song: Celia Singing.) SeEP
("You that think Love can convey.") EG
Celia Singing. Thomas Stanley. AnAnS-2
Celia, that I once was blest. A Song. Dryden. *Fr.* Amphitrion. CavP
Celia, thy sweet angels face. *At. to* the Countess of Winchilsea. SeCSL
Celia, too late you would repent. Upon a Favour Offered. William Walsh. SeCL
Celia turnes awaye her eyes. *Unknown.* SeCSL
Celia, when you bid me. Night. Witter Bynner. NP
Celia's Home-coming. Agnes Mary Frances Robinson. OBEV (new ed.); OBVV; VA
Celibacy. Austin Clarke. JKCP (1926 ed.)
Celimena, of my heart. Song [*or* Damon and Celimena.]. Dryden. *Fr.* An Evening's Love. CavP; InvP; PeRV; SeCL
Celinda, by what potent art. Song. Thomas Stanley. CavP
Cell, The. George Rostrevor Hamilton. SoP; TrPWD
Cell-Mates. Louis Untermeyer. HBMV
Cell of Himself, The. Arthur Freeman. TwCP
Cellar, The. Hilda Conkling. PCH
Cello, The. Richard Watson Gilder. AA
Cello sobs, the symphony begins, The. The Festival. Frederic Prokosch. LiTA; LiTM (1946 ed.); WaP
'Cellos, setting forth apart, The. At the Symphony. Robert Nathan. HBMV; MAP; PoRL; TSW
Cells Breathe in the Emptiness. Galway Kinnell. NaP
Celluloid of a photograph holds them well, The. Six Young Men. Ted Hughes. POTi
Celt Speaks, The. Arthur Stringer. PoFr
Celtic Cross. Norman MacCaig. OxBS
Celtic Cross, The. Thomas D'Arcy McGee. OnYI; VA
Celts, The. Thomas D'Arcy McGee. OnYI; OxBI
Cemeteries are places for departed souls. Lines Written at the Grave of Alexandre [*or* Alexander] Dumas. Gwendolyn B. Bennett. CDC; PoNe
Cemetery, A. Emily Dickinson. *See* This quiet dust was gentlemen and ladies.
Cemetery at Academy, California, The. Philip Levine. NaP; NYBP
Cemetery by the Sea, The. Paul Valéry, *tr. fr. French by* Barbara Gibbs. LiTW; OnHM, *tr. by* Selden Rodman; PIA
(Marine Cemetery, The, *tr. by* Sidney Alexander.) ReMP
Cemetery Is, The. Audrey McGaffin. NePoAm-2
Cemetery Plot of Ed Sanders Shall Consist of, The. Ed Sanders. ANYP
Cemetery stone New England autumn, The. Voices of Heroes. Horace Gregory. PoFr; TrGrPo (1942 ed.)
Cenci, The. Shelley. EnRP
Beatrice's Last Words, *sel fr.* V, iv. FiP
Cenotaph. Brian Fitzpatrick. MoAuPo
Cenotaph, The. Charlotte Mew. MMA
Cenotaph of Lincoln, The. James T. McKay. OHIP
Censorship. Arthur Waley. WaP
Centaur, The. Theodore Roethke. NePoAm-2
Centaur, The. May Swenson. NePoAm-2; TwAmPo; TwCP
Centaur does not need a horse, The. The Centaur. Theodore Roethke. NePoAm-2
Centaur in the Groundlevel Apartment. Eric Pfeiffer. NYTB
Centaur Overheard, The. Edgar Bowers. NYTB
Centaur, Syren, I foregoe, The. Another. Richard Lovelace. AtBAP; PoEL-3
Centaurs, The. James Stephens. AnEnPo
Centaurs and Lapithae. Sacheverell Sitwell. *Fr.* Battles of the Centaurs. AtBAP
Centenarian's Story, The. Walt Whitman. CTC
Centennial Hymn. Bryant. PAH
Centennial Hymn. John Pierpont. AnNE; PAL
Centennial Hymn. Whittier. AA; MC; PaA; PAH; PAL; TOP
Centennial Meditation of Columbia, The. Sidney Lanier. PAH
Dear Land of All My Love, *sel.* DD; GN; HBVY; MPB; StVeCh
("Long as thine Art shall love true love.") PGD
Centennial Ode, *sel.* Charles Sprague.
Indians. GN
Centennial of Melville's birth this morning. Japanese City. Kenward Elmslie. YAP
Center of all centers, germ of germs. Buddha in Glory. Rainer Maria Rilke. OnPM
Center well upon his promise. Eyes Up! Mary Gustafson. SoP
Centipede, The. Samuel Hopkins Adams. InMe
Centipede, A [*or* The]. Mrs. Edward Craster. *See* Centipede Was Happy Quite, A.
Centipede, The. A. P. Herbert. CenHV
Centipede, The. Ogden Nash. FaPON

Centipede along the threshold crept, The. Thomas Hood. *Fr.* The Haunted House. ERoP-2; WiR
Centipede is not quite nice, The. The Centipede. A. P. Herbert. CenHV
Centipede Was Happy Quite, A. Mrs. Edward Craster. ALV; SoPo
(Centipede, A [*or* The].) GoTP; PCH; PoMa; TiPo (1959 ed.)
(Puzzled Centipede, The.) FaPON; RePo; UTS
(Quandary.) TreFS
Central, *sel.* John Curtis Underwood.
"Though men may build their bridges high." PoMa
Central America, painted so fine, The. Loss of the *Central America.* John A. Stone. SGR
Central Europe. Norman Cameron. MoPW
Central Park. Robert Lowell. LiTM (1970 ed.)
Central Park: It's About This Eden Thing. John Morgan. YAP
Central Park Tourney. Mildred Weston. AmFN; OCS
Centuries Are His, The. Georgia Moore Eberling. SoP; TRV
Centuries shall not deflect. To E. A. R. Lola Ridge. NP
Centuries, since Christ to earthland came, The. His Is the Way. Thomas Curtis Clark. ChIP
Centurion, The. Helen Purcell Roads. ChIP
Century of Couplets, A, *sel.* Richard Chenevix Trench.
"Who praises God the most." OBRV
Century since, out in the West, A. Betty Zane. Thomas Dunn English. PAL
Cerelle. Margaret Bell Houston. PoMa
Ceremonial Ode Intended for a University. Lascelles Abercrombie. OBVV
Ceremonies. Ann Stanford. HW
Ceremonies for Candlemas Day, The ("Kindle the Christmas brand"). Robert Herrick. EnLit; OAEP
Ceremonies for Candlemas Day, The. Ben Jonson. OAEP
Ceremonies for Candlemas[s] Eve ("Down with the rosemary and bays"). Robert Herrick. ILP; OAEP; OBS; OTPC (1923 ed.); SeEP
Ceremonies for Christmas[se] ("Come bring with a noise"). Robert Herrick. AnAnS-2; GN; HBV; OHIP; OTPC (1923 ed.); TiPo (1952 ed.)
Ceremony. Joanne De Longchamps. NYTB
Ceremony. Vassar Miller. NePoEA
Ceremony. Richard Wilbur. CoAP; FiMAP; MiAP; Po; PP; ReMP
Ceremony after a Fire Raid. Dylan Thomas. CMoP; CoBMV; ExPo; MoPo; PoDB; WaP
Ceremony for Birth and Naming. Ridgely Torrence. MoRP
Ceremony for Candlemas Day, A ("Down with the rosemary and so"). Robert Herrick. OTPC; PoRL
Ceremony must be found, The. Speaking of Poetry. John Peale Bishop. LiTA; LiTM (rev. ed.); OxBA; PP; TwAmPo
Ceres, most bounteous lady, thy rich leas. Shakespeare. *Fr.* The Tempest, IV, i. AtBAP
Cerne Abbas. Hal Summers. HaMV
Certain Age, A. Phyllis McGinley. NePoAm-2
Certain American Poets. Odell Shepard. InP
Certain Artists Bring Her Dolls and Drawings. W. B. Yeats. Upon a Dying Lady, II. LiTB
Certain Books of Vergil's Aeneis, *sels.* Vergil, *tr. fr. Latin by* the Earl of Surrey. *Fr.* The Aeneid.
"Aurora now from Titan's purple bed," *fr.* IV. EnPo
"But now the wounded queen with heavy care," *fr.* IV. FCP; ReIE, *abr.*
"They whisted all, with fixed face attent," *fr.* II. EnLi-1; EPP; FCP; SiPS; TuPP
(Second Boke of Virgiles Aenaeis, The.) SiCE
(Translation from Virgil's Aeneid.) LiTB
Certain branches cut. October. Denise Levertov. NoP
Certain Eclogues [*or* Egloges], *sels.* Alexander Barclay.
Prologue, The: "Famous poets with the muses nine, The." ReIE
""Winter snowes, all covered is the ground, The," *fr.* V. EnPo
Certain man in physic skilled, A. Of Fuscus, a Drunkard. Sir Thomas More, *tr. by* Timothe Kendall. TuPP
Certain Maxims of Archy. Don Marquis. InMe
Archy, the Cockroach, Speaks, *sel.* FaPON
Certain Maxims of Hafiz. Kipling. HBV
Maxim: "If he play," 2 *ll.* OtMeF
Certain Mercies. Robert Graves. CoBMV; GTBS-P
Certain pasha, dead five thousand years, A. A Turkish Legend. Thomas Bailey Aldrich. GN; HBV; HBVY; OTPC (1946 ed.); YT
Certain people would not clean their buttons. The Bohemians. Ivor Gurney. MMA
Certain poets/ have written good poems. On the Poet's Leer. David Ray. NePoEA-2
Certain Presbyterian pair, A. The Presbyterian Wedding. *Unknown.* CoMu; ErPo
Certain Rich Man, A. Theodore Maynard. OQP
Certain Saturday, A. Edith Lovejoy Pierce. ChIP
Certain Slant of Light, A. Emily Dickinson. *See* There's a certain slant of light.
Certain True Woords Spoken Concerning One Benet Corbett after Her Death. Richard Corbett. AnAnS-2; SeCP
Certain young fellow, named Bobbie, A. Limerick. *Unknown.* LiBL
Certain young gourmet of Crediton, A. Limerick. *Unknown, sometimes at. to* Charles Inge. CenHV; LiBL; WhC
Certain Young Lady, A. Washington Irving. FaBoBe; HBV; OnPP
Certain Young Man of Great Gumption, A. *Unknown.* ShM
Certain youthful lady in Thoulouse, A. Sonnet: Of the Eyes of a Certain Mandetta. Guido Cavalcanti. AWP
Certainties. Kenneth W. Porter. ChIP
Certainties. Margaret Widdemer. HBMV
Certainty. Emily Dickinson. *See* I never saw a moor.
Certainty. Evelyn Hardy. HBMV
Certainty Enough. Amelia Josephine Burr. HBMV
Certainty We Two Shall Meet, The. Gwendolyn Brooks. CBV
Cervantes. E. C. Bentley. EvOK
("People of Spain think Cervantes, The.) CenHV; FiBHP
Cervantes, Dostoievsky, Poe. A Poem Intended to Incite the Utmost Depression. Samuel Hoffenstein. BOHV; SiTL
Cervera. Bertrand Shadwell. PAH
Cerylas, jesting, called his pretty jade. Hors d'Oeuvre. Deems Taylor. UnTE
César Franck. Joseph Auslander. HBMV
Cetewayo, chief of the Zulus. Anthony Delius. PeSA
Ceylon. A. Hugh Fisher. HBV
Cézanne. Alfred Kreymborg. NP
Chace, The, *sel.* William Somervile.
Hare-hunting, *fr.* II. OBEC
Chaeronean Plutarch, to thy deathless praise. Plutarch [*or* Epigram on Plutarch]. Agathias Scholasticus. AWP; JAWP; MBW-1; WBP
Chaffinch flies fast, The. Cherry Tree. Ivy O. Eastwick. BoTP
Chaffinch's Nest at Sea, The. William Cowper. OTPC (1923 ed.)
Chagrin. Isaac Rosenberg. ChMP; MoBrPo
Chahcoal Man, *with music. Unknown.* AS
Chain I gave was fair to view, The. From the Turkish. Byron. HBV
Chain of Princes Street, The. Elizabeth Fleming. PCH
Chained by stern duty to the rock of state. Lincoln. S. Weir Mitchell. PAH
Chained in the market-place he stood. The African Chief. Bryant. AnNE; BLPA; PaPo; TreFS
Chains. Patrick Carey. SeCL
Chair, Dog, and Clock. Hilary Corke. NYBP
Chairman of many committees. Clubwoman. Mary Carter Smith. PoNe (1970 ed.)
Chairoplane Chant. Nancy Byrd Turner. RIS
Chairs. Annette Wynne. GFA
Chaka. F. T. Prince. BoSA
Chalk-Cliff, The. Andrew Young. POTE
Chalk from Eden. Howard Moss. NePA
Chalk-Pit, The. Edward Thomas. BrPo
Challenge. Sterling A. Brown. CDC
Challenge. Thomas Curtis Clark. MaRV; PGD
Challenge. John Drinkwater. PoMa
Challenge. Harry W. Falconer. PoToHe (1941 ed.)
Challenge. Samuel Hazo. SD
Challenge, A. James Benjamin Kenyon. AA
Challenge, The. Grenville Kleiser. BLRP
Challenge, The. Longfellow. AP
Challenge. Kenton Foster Murray. HBV
Challenge, The. Pope. PIA; PoEL-3
Challenge. Sir Walter Scott. *Fr.* Marmion, V. OtMeF

Challenge, The. *Unknown, tr. fr. Spanish by* Louis Untermeyer. UnTE
Challenge comes, The. The Challenge. Grenville Kleiser. BLRP
Challenge for Beauty, A, *sel.* Thomas Heywood.
"I remember,/ There lived a Spanish Princess of our name." LO
Challenge of Life, The. Tennyson. *Fr.* Ulysses. MaRV
(Experience.) OQP
Challenge of Thor, The. Longfellow. The Saga of King Olaf, 1. AmPP (4th ed.)
Challenge to Youth. Longfellow. *Fr.* The Castle Builder. MaRV
Challenger, The. Donald Wandrei. FiSC
Challengers. Alfred Dorn. GoYe
Chalse a Killey. Thomas Edward Brown. PoVP
Chamber Music. James Joyce. *Poems indexed separately by titles and first lines.*
Chamber over the Gate, The. Longfellow. AP; MAmP
Chamber Scene. Nathaniel Parker Willis. HBV
Chambered Nautilus, The. Oliver Wendell Holmes. *Fr.* The Autocrat of the Breakfast-Table, *ch.* 4. AA; AmePo; AmLP; AmP; AmPP; AnAmPo; AnNE; AP; DD; DiPo; EtS; FaBoBe; FaFP; GN; GTBS; GTBS-W; HBV; HBVY; HoPM; LiTA; MaRV; MCCG; NeHB; NePA; NoP; OBVV; OHFP; OQP; OTPC; OuHeWo; PCD; PG (1955 ed.); PoEL-5; PoLF; PTK; TIHL; TreF; UnPo (1st ed.); WGRP; YT
"Build thee more stately mansions, O my soul," *sel.* TRV
Chambermaid's Second Song, The. W. B. Yeats. ErPo
Chameleon. Susan Axelrod. QAH
Chameleon. Anthony Delius. BoSA
Chameleon. Paul Engle. CrMA
Chameleon, The. A. P. Herbert. FaPON; PCD
Chameleon. Gordon LeClaire. EtS
Chameleon, The. James Merrick, *after* De la Motte. HBV
Chameleon changes his color, The. The Chameleon. A. P. Herbert. FaPON; PCD
Chameleon, knowing I am near. Chameleon. Paul Engle. CrMA
Chamonix. George Hookham. OBVV
Champ de Manoeuvres. Sir Herbert Read. BrPo
Champagne Rosée [*or* Rosé]. John Kenyon. OBEV; OBRV; OBVV; VA
Champion of those who groan beneath. To William Lloyd Garrison. Whittier. CoBA; PAH
Chance, The. Robert Creeley. FRC
Chance, The. John Holmes. NePoAm-2
Chance and Change. Thomas Campion. *See* What if a Day . . .
Chance Met. Rosemary Dobson. NeLNL
Chancellor mused as he nibbled his pen, The. Love and War. Arthur Patchett Martin. VA
Chances, The. Wilfred Owen. MMA
Chancing upon the Devil in the doorway. The Devil and the Angel, 1. Rosemary Dobson. ACV; BoAV
Chandler Nicholas. Edgar Lee Masters. *Fr.* The New Spoon River. NAMP
Chang Liang. Li Po, *tr. fr. Chinese by* W. J. B. Fletcher. PoFr
Chang-an in utter confusion. War in Chang-An City. Wang Tsan. PPON
Chang'd, Yet Constant. Thomas Stanley. AnAnS-2
Change. Mary Elizabeth Coleridge. MoVE
Change, The. Abraham Cowley. *Fr.* The Mistress. AnAnS-2; BEL; CoBE; FaBoEn; LO; MeLP; MePo; OBS; ReEn; SCEP-2; SeCP; SeCV-1
Change. John Donne. Elegies, III. LiTG; MaMe; ViBoPo
Change. Earl of Essex. *See* Change Thy Mind.
Change. Fulke Greville. Caelica, VII. OBSC
(Sonnet.) RelE
("World, that all contains, is ever moving, The.") EnRePo; SiCE; TuPP
Change. William Dean Howells. AA
Change. Raymond Knister. CaP; OBCV; PeCV
Change. Stanley J. Kunitz. NP
Change. Lalia Mitchell Thornton. CIV
Change/ compels me more. Icons. Edgar Paiewonsky. QAH
Change in the Year, A. Wordsworth. *Fr.* To My Sister. BoTP
Change is the circumstance of our delight. The Prism. H. A. Pinkerton. NePoAm
"Change me, some God, into that breathing rose!" The River Duddon, VII. Wordsworth. Sonn
Change of Address. Kathleen Fraser. NYBP; YAP
Change of Heart, A. Peter Fellowes. QAH
Change of Heart, A. Valine Hobbs. SiSoSe
Change of Raiment. Gerhardt Tersteegen, *tr. fr. German.* SoP
Change of Subject, A. Daniel Sargent. JKCP (1955 ed.)
Change of World, A. Adrienne Rich. TPM
Change Should Breed Change. William Drummond of Hawthornden. *Fr.* Flowers of Sion. OBEV; OxBoCh
Change Thy Mind [since She Doth Change]. Earl of Essex. ElL; TuPP
(Change.) OBSC
Changed. Charles Stuart Calverley. ALV; FiBHP
Changed Woman, The. Louise Bogan. HBMV
Changeful Beauty. *Unknown, tr. fr. Greek by* Andrew Lang. EnLoPo
Changeless. Edith Hickman Divall. OQP
(In Whom Is No Variableness.) MaRV
Changeless. Alice Meynell. VA
Changeless Shore. Sarah Leeds Ash. GoYe
Changeling. Leah Bodine Drake. PoMS
Changeling, The. Charlotte Mew. CH; MPB
Changeling, The, *sels.* Thomas Middleton.
"Here we are, if you have any more," *fr.* V, iii. AtBAP; PoEL-2
"What makes your lip so strange?" *fr.* III, iv. AtBAP; PoEL-2
Changeling. Barbara Young. MoSiPe
Changeling Grateful, A. Josephine Preston Peabody. AA
Changelings. Mary Potter Thacher Higginson. AA
Changes. Charles Barter. *Fr.* Stray Memories of Natal and Zululand. BoSA
Changes. "Owen Meredith." PoLF
Changes; or, Love in a Maze, *sel.* James Shirley.
"Melancholy, hence! go get." TuPP
Changing guests, each in a different mood, The. Inclusiveness. Dante Gabriel Rossetti. The House of Life, LXIII. EnLi-2; MaVP; NBM; NCEP; PoVP; SyP; VA; ViPo
Changing Road, The. Katharine Lee Bates. HBV
Changing Wind, The. Julian Orde. NeBP
Changing World, The. Jami, *tr. fr. Persian by* F. Hadland Davis. OnPM
Changing Year, The. Lloyd Roberts. DD
Channel Crossing. George Barker. ACV; ChMP; GTBS-P; ToPo
Channel Firing. Thomas Hardy. BrPo; CABA; CBV; CMoP; CoBMV; EnL; ExPo; ForPo; ILP; LiTB; MaPo; MoPo; NoP; OAEP (2d ed.); PAn; PoAn; PoEL-5; PoeP; PoFS; PoIE; PoRA; PPON; SeCeV; StP; TDP; UnPo; ViPP; VP; WaaP
Channel moon went down, as ignorance, The. The Outlanders. Andrew Glaze. NYBP
Channel Passage, A. Rupert Brooke. FaBoTw
Channel U.S.A.—Live. Adrien Stoutenburg. AmFN; ThLM
Channing. Amos Bronson Alcott. AA
Chanson de Chateaulaire. Herbert Gorman. AnAmPo
Chanson de Roland. *Unknown. See* Song of Roland, The.
Chanson de Rosemonde. Richard Hovey. HBV
Chanson d'Or. Ann Hamilton. HBMV
Chanson mystique. *Unknown, tr. fr. French by* Percy Allen. CAW
(Mystic Song, A.) WGRP
Chanson Naïve. John McClure. HBMV
Chanson of the Bells of Osenèy. Cale Young Rice. AnFE; APA; CoAnAm; HBV
Chanson sans Paroles. Ernest Dowson. PoVP
Chanson un Peu Naïve. Louise Bogan. HBMV
Chansons d'Automne. Paul Verlaine, *tr. fr. French by* Arthur Symons. AWP; JAWP; WBP
(Song of Autumn.) OnPM; WoL
Chansons Innocentes, *sels.* E. E. Cummings.
I. In Just-/Spring When the World Is Mud. AmLP; AmPP; CAD; FaBV; FaPON; GoTP; MAP; MoAB; MoAmPo; MoShBr; NoP; NP; PoAn; ReMP; RePo; ThWaDe
II. Little Tree. FIW; LOW; PDV; PoSC; RoGo
Chant, A. W. H. Davies. BoPe
Chant. Oscar Williams. MoRP
Chant for Reapers. Wilfrid Thorley. OBEV (new ed.); OBVV

Chant for Skippers. Katharine Gallagher. SiSoSe
Chant of Departure; a Missionary's Prayer. Alfred J. Barrett. GoBC; ISi
Chant of Hate against England, A. Ernst Lissauer, *tr. fr. German by* Barbara Henderson. HBV
Hymn of Hate against England, A, *sel.* OtMeF
Chant of the Box Cars. Harry Kemp. PoMa
Chant of the Ninth Order of Seraphim. Inigo de Mendoza, *tr. fr. Spanish by* Roderick Gill. CAW
Chant Out of Doors, A. Marguerite Wilkinson. SP; TrPWD
Chant-Pagan. Kipling. OAEP (2d ed.)
Chant Royal from a Copydesk. Rufus Terral. InMe
Chant Royal of High Virtue. Sir Arthur Quiller-Couch. HBV
Chant Royal of the Dejected Dipsomaniac. Don Marquis. HBMV
Chant you loud of punishments. Three Poems, 2. Stephen Crane. AP
Chanted Calendar, A. Sydney Dobell. *Fr.* Balder. BoC; BoTP; DD; GBV; GTSE; HBV; HBVY; OBEV; RG
(Procession of the Flowers, The.) GN; OTPC
Chantey of Notorious Bibbers. Henry Morton Robinson. InMe
Chanticleer. William Austin. OxBoCh
(Carol: "All this night shrill chanticler.") SeCL
Chanticleer. John Farrar. GFA; PCH; SoPo; TiPo; UTS
Chanticleer. Margaret Irvin. PoAu-2
Chanticleer. Celia Thaxter. PRWS; TVC
Chanticleer. Katharine Tynan. HBV; HBVY; MPB; OTPC; TiPo; TSW
Chanting Cherubs, The—A Group by Greenough. Richard Henry Dana. AA
Chanting the Square Deific. Walt Whitman. AmePo; NoP; PoE; PoIE
Chants Communal, *sel.* Horace Traubel.
What Can I Do? TrJP
Chants, incense, and the glory pass and die. December 26. George Edward Hoffman. PGD
Chanty: "When rain falls, I say." Ronald McCuaig. MoAuPo
Chao-Mong-Mu freely laid his hands over the sky. Sermon. Emanuel Carnevali. NP
Chaos. Pope. *See* Conclusion: "In vain, in vain . . ."
Chaos—and the Way Out, *sel.* John Oxenham.
Law of Love, The. OQP
Chaos of night eternal; realm opposed. Epithalamium for Murder. Seneca. *Fr.* Medea. HW
Chapala Poems, *sels.* Witter Bynner. NP
Asleep.
Calendar.
Montezuma.
Web, The.
Chapel Deacon. R. S. Thomas. ACV; ToPo
Chapel in Lyoness, The. William Morris. PoVP; ViPo
Chaperon, The. H. C. Bunner. AA; HBV
Chaplet, The. Witter Bynner. PFY
Chaplet, The, *sels.* Moses Mendes. TrJP
Ass, The.
Philanderer, The.
Chaplinesque. Hart Crane. AP; CMoP; CrMA; LiTG; LiTM (rev. ed.); OxBA; ReMP
Chaplin's Sad Speech. Rafael Alberti, *tr. fr. Spanish by* Lloyd Mallan. LiTW
Chapultepec Park. Muriel Rukeyser. FiMAP
Character, A. Charlotte Fiske Bates. AA
Character, A. Blake. *See* Epigram: Character, A.
Character. Emerson. AA; AnFE; AnNE; APA; CoAnAm; LiTA
Character, A. Tennyson. PeER
Character and Talent. Jules Laforgue, *tr. fr. French by* Patricia Terry. OnPM
Character Building. Edward Anthony. GoTP
Character of a Happy Life, A. Sir Henry Wotton. AnAnS-2; DD; EIL; FaPL; GTBS; GTBS-D; GTBS-P; GTBS-W; GTSE; GTSL; HBV; HBVY; LiTB; LiTG; MaRV; MCCG; OBEV; OBS; OTPC (1923 ed.); PCD; PoFr; PoIE; PoPo; SeEP; ShBV-2; SoP; StaSt; TOP; TreF; TrGrPo; ViBoPo
(Happy Life, The.) MyFE, *abr.*
Character of Holland, The. Andrew Marvell. CABL; MaMe
"Holland, that scarce deserves the name of land." ChTr
Character of Love Seen as a Search for the Lost, The. Kenneth Patchen. NaP
Character of Sydrophel, The. Samuel Butler. *See* Portrait of Sidrophel.
Character of the Dutch, A. *At. to* Henry Nevile Payne. *Fr.* A Description of Holland by Mr. Nevell. PeRV
Character of the Happy Warrior. Wordsworth. BEL; BoLiVe, *abr.*; EnLit; EnRP; EPN; FaBoBe; FaFP; HBV; HBVY; LiTB; LiTG; LoBV; MaRV, *abr.*; MBW-2; MERP; OBRV; TOP; TreF
(Happy Warrior, The.) OHFP; OQP, *abr.*; TIHL
Character, Panegyric, and Description of the Legion Club, A. Swift. EiCL
Character "Treasure" written on the sail, The. Treasure Boat. Seiki Fujino. HW
Characteristics of a Child Three Years Old. Wordsworth. ERoP-1; OBRV
Characterization, A. Sir Henry Taylor. VA
Characters from the Satires: Achitophel. Dryden. *See* Achitophel.
Characters from the Satires: Atticus. Pope. *See* Atticus.
Characters from the Satires: Chloe. Pope. *See* Chloe.
Characters from the Satires: Og and Doeg. Dryden. *See* Og and Doeg.
Characters from the Satires: Sporus. Pope. *See* Sporus.
Characters from the Satires: Wharton. Pope. *See* Wharton.
Characters from the Satires: Zimri. Dryden. *See* Zimri.
Characters of great and small, The. The Skeleton in the Cupboard. Frederick Locker-Lampson. HBV; VA
Characters of the Wits, The. John Sheffield, Duke of Buckingham and Normanby. *Fr.* An Essay on Satyr. PeRV
Characters of Women: Flavia, Atossa, and Cloe. Pope. *Fr.* Moral Essays, Epistle II. OBEC
Chloe, *sel.* AWP; JAWP; WBP
Characters of Women. Edward Young. *Fr.* Love of Fame, the Universal Passion, V. OBEC
Charade. Winthrop Mackworth Praed. GN
Charcoal-Burner, The. Sir Edmund Gosse. OBVV
Charcoal-Burner's Son, The. Erik Gustaf Geijer, *tr. fr. Swedish by* Charles W. Stork. WoL
Charcoal Man, *with music.* *Unknown.* TrAS
Charcoal-Seller, The. Po Chü-i, *tr. fr. Chinese by* Arthur Waley. WoL
Chard Whitlow. Henry Reed. DTC; FiBHP; LiTM (rev. ed.); ML; MoBrPo (1962 ed.); OnHM; Par; SiTL
Charge, The. Denise Levertov. NePoEA-2
Charge, A. Herbert Trench. HBV; OBEV (new ed.); OBVV
Charge at Santiago, The. William Hamilton Hayne. MC; PAH
Charge by the Ford, The. Thomas Dunn English. PAH
Charge not thyself with the weight of a year. Day by Day. *Unknown.* SoP
Charge of the Light Brigade, The. Tennyson. BBV; BEL; BeLS; BLPA; EPN; FaBoBe; FaBV; FaFP; FaPON; FOL; GN; HBV; HBVY; HoPM; MaC; MaVP; MCCG; NeHB; OHFP; OnSP; OTD; OTPC; PaPo; PCD; PeVV; PoPl; PoVP; PTK; ShBV-1; TOP; TreF; VA; WBLP; YAT
Charge the Can Cheerily, *with music.* *Unknown.* AmSS
Charge to Keep I Have, A. Charles Wesley. SoP
(The Lord's Charge.) HBV
Charing Cross. Cecil Roberts. HBMV
Charing Cross. *Unknown.* CBEP
Chariot, The. Emily Dickinson. *See* Because I could not stop for Death.
Chariot of Fire. Blake. *See* And Did Those Feet in Ancient Time.
Chariot Race, The. Vergil, *tr. fr. Latin by* Smith Palmer Bovie. *Fr.* Georgics. SD
Charioteer. Witter Bynner. AnFE; CoAnAm
Charioteer, The. Shelley. *Fr.* Prometheus Unbound, II, iv. ShBV-3
("My coursers are fed with the lightning.") OBRV
Chariots. Witter Bynner. HBMV
Charis guess[e], and do[e] not miss[e]. Claiming [*or* Clayming] a Second Kiss[e] by Desert. Ben Jonson. *Fr.* A Celebration of Charis. AnAnS-2; LiTL; SeCP
Charis one day in discourse. Urging Her of a Promise. Ben Jonson. *Fr.* A Celebration of Charis. AnAnS-2; SeCP
Charitas Nimia; or, The Dear[e] Bargain. Richard Crashaw. AnAnS-1; MaMe; MeP; MePo; OxBoCh; PoFS; PoLi; ReEn; SeEP
"Lord, what is man?" *sel.* MaRV
Charity. First Corinthians, XIII, Bible, *N.T.* ShBV-4; StVeCh
(Gospel of Love, The.) OuHeWo

Charity (continued)
(Greatest of These, The.) TrGrPo, *abr.*
(Greatness of Love, The.) MaRV
(Love.) TRV
(Love Is Patient.) TIHL
(Love the Indispensable and Crowning Grace.) PG (1955 ed.)
(St. Paul on Charity.) TreF
("Though I speak with the tongues of men . . .") LO
Charity. George Parsons Lathrop. CAW; JKCP
Charity. Pope *Fr.* An Essay on Man, III. OBEC
("For forms of government let fools contest.") ViBoPo
Charity. *Unknown, at. to* Edward Wallis Hoch. BLPA; NeHB
(Good and Bad.) TreFS
Charity in Thought. Samuel Taylor Coleridge. WhC
Charity Overcoming Envy. Marianne Moore. NYBP
Charity, Thou Art a Lie. Stephen Crane. AmePo
Charlemagne. Longfellow. Tales of a Wayside Inn: The Poet's Tale, Pt. III. AnAmPo; FaFP; MWA-1
Charlemagne carried it far. The Cross. Ruby Weyburn Tobias. ChIP
Charles. Leonard Clark. FIW
Charles at the Siege. George Hetherington. AnIV
Charles Augustus Fortescue. Hilaire Belloc. OnPP
Charles Carville's Eyes. E. A. Robinson. MaPo; NePA; OxBA
Charles—for it seems you wish to know. A Gage d'Amour. Austin Dobson. VA
Charles Guiteau. *Unknown.* BFSS, *with music;* ViBoFo
(Garfield's Murder.) ThLM
Charles Gustavus Anderson, 2 *vers., with music. Unknown, at. to* Joseph Keating, Sr. ShS
Charles Lamb. Pakenham Beatty. VA
Charles! my slow heart was only sad. Sonnet to a Friend Who Asked How I Felt When the Nurse First Presented My Infant to Me. Samuel Taylor Coleridge. EnRP
Charles O'Malley, the Irish Dragoon, *sels.* Charles Lever.
It's Little for Glory I Care. OnYI
(Mickey Free's Song.) ALV
Larry M'Hale. OnYI
Widow Malone, The. BOHV; HBV; TreFS
Charles II. Andrew Marvell. *Fr.* Last Instructions to a Painter. OBS
Charles II, *sel.* Douglas Brooke Wheelton Sladen.
Refrain. VA
Charles II of Spain to Approaching Death. Eugene Lee-Hamilton. VA
Charles the Fifth and the Peasant. Robert Lowell, *after the French of* Paul Valéry. MiAP
Charles the First, *sel.* Shelley.
"Widow bird sate mourning for her love, A," *fr.* sc. v. AtBAP; BoTP; CBEP; CH; ELP; EPN; FaPON; GTBS; GTBS-D; GTBS-P; GTBS-W; GTSE; LO; MemP; MPB; OBRV; OTPC (1946 ed.); PoG; SeCeV; WePo
(Song, A.) FaBoEn; LoBV; OBNC; PoEL-4; ShBV-1; ThWaDe
(Winter.) StaSt
Charles the First, *sel.* William Gorman Wills.
Cromwell and Henrietta Maria. VA
Charles the Second. Earl of Rochester. *Fr.* The History of the Insipids. FOL
Charles XII. Samuel Johnson. *Fr.* The Vanity of Human Wishes. FOL; OBEC, *abr.*
("On what foundation stands the warrior's pride.") ViBoPo
Charles used to watch Naomi, taking heart. Laboratory Poem. James Merrill. NePoEA-2; TwCP
Charleston. Richard Watson Gilder. PAH
Charleston (February, 1865). Paul Hamilton Hayne. PAH
Charleston. Henry Timrod. AA; AmePo; AmLP; AmP; AmPP; AP; CoBA; MAmP; OxBA; PAH
Charleston Garden, A. Henry Bellamann. PoLF
Charleston in the 1860s. Adrienne Rich. CoAP
Charleville. Arthur Rimbaud, *tr. fr. French by* John Gray. SyP
Charley Barley, butter and eggs. *Unknown.* OxNR
Charley, Charley. *Unknown.* OxNR
Charley Lee. Henry Herbert Knibbs. WaKn
Charley Snyder. *Unknown.* ABF
Charley III. Stephen Sandy. NYTB
Charley Warlie had a cow. *Unknown.* OxNR
Charlie Chaplin Went to France. *Unknown, at. to* Carl Withers. FaFP; MoShBr; SiTL
Charlie, he's a young man. *Unknown.* LaNeLa
Charlie, He's My Darling. Burns. ALV; CH; ViBoPo
(Charlie Is My Darling.) HBV
Charlie Is My Darling. James Hogg. OTPC (1946 ed.)
Charlie MacPherson. *Unknown.* ESPB
Charlie Piecan. F. Murray *and* F. Leigh. OxBoLi
Charlie Rutledge. *Unknown, at. to* D. J. White (D. J. O'-Malley. CoSo
Charlie Wag. *Unknown.* OxNR
Charlotte [*or* Charlottie] liv'd on a mountaintop in a bleak and lonely spot. The Frozen Girl. *Unknown.* AS; IHA
Charm, A. Dryden. ChTr
Charm, A ("If ye fear to be affrighted"). Robert Herrick. ChTr
Charm, A ("In the morning when you rise"). Robert Herrick. OTPC (1923 ed.)
Charm, A. Kipling. OtMeF
Charm, A. Thomas Randolph. *Fr.* The Jealous Lovers. SeCL
Charm, The. Shakespeare. *See* Witches' Spell, The.
Charm against a Magpie, A. *Unknown.* ChTr
Charm: Against a Swarm of Bees. *Unknown, tr. fr. Anglo-Saxon by* Richard L. Hoffman. YAT
Charm against Enemies. *Unknown, tr. fr. Irish by* Lady Wilde. JKCP (1926 ed.)
Charm against the Stitch, A. *Unknown, tr. fr. Anglo-Saxon by* Gavin Bone. FIW
Charm against the Toothache, A. John Heath-Stubbs. BoPe; FIW; NePoEA; TwCP
Charm for a Sudden Stitch. *Unknown, tr. fr. Anglo-Saxon by* Charles W. Kennedy. AnOE
Charm for Bees, A. *Unknown, tr. fr. Old High German.* CAW
Charm for Cantinflas, A. Muriel Rukeyser. FiMAP
Charm for Going a-Hunting. Mary Austin. RePo
Charm for Spring Flowers, A. Rachel Field. TiPo (1959 ed.)
Charm for the Ear-Ache, A. James Kirkup. BoPe; POTi
Charm for Unfruitful Land. *Unknown, tr. fr. Anglo-Saxon by* Charles W. Kennedy. AnOE
Charm is a woman's strongest arm. If They Meant All They Said. Alice Duer Miller. BOHV
Charm is the measure of attraction's power. What Is Charm? Louisa Carroll Thomas. BLPA; NeHB
Charm me asleep, and melt me so. To Music [*or* Musique], to Becalm [*or* Becalme] His Fever. Robert Herrick. ATP; EG; GoJo; HBV; MuSP; OBEV; OBS; QFR; ReEn; SeCL; SeCV-1; UnS
Charm, or an Allay for Love, A. Robert Herrick. FaBoCh; LoGBV
Charm to Call Sleep, A. Henry Johnstone. PRWS
Charm to Quell a Rival. *Unknown, tr. fr. Sanskrit by* R. J. H. Griffith. *Fr.* The Rigveda. LiTW
Charm to Save Cattle. *Unknown, tr. fr. Russian by* W. R. S. Ralston. OnPM
Charming Oysters I cry. Oysters. Swift. ErPo
Charming Woman, The. Helen Selina Sheridan. ALV; OBRV
Charms, The. Emma A. Opper. DD
Charms and Knots. George Herbert. MaMe
Charms of Nature, The. Joseph Warton. *Fr.* The Enthusiast; or, The Lover of Nature. OBEC; SeCePo
Charon, O Charon, draw thy boat to th' shore. The New Charon. Robert Herrick. ReEn
Chart, The. Walter de la Mare. CoBMV
Chart, The. Michael Lewis. StaSt
Charter of all true liberty, The. The Bible. Bishop Anderson. SoP
Charter of Salvation, The. George Arthur Clarke. MaRV
Chartist Song. Thomas Cooper. VA
Chartivel, *sel.* Marie de France, *tr. fr. French by* Arthur O'Shaughnessy.
Song from "Chartivel." AWP; JAWP; LiTW; WBP
("Hath any loved you well, down there.") EnLoPo; PoVP
(Sarrazine's Song to Her Dead Lover.) HBV
Chartless. Emily Dickinson. *See* I never saw a moor.
Chartres Cathedral. Donald C. Babcock. NYTB
Chase, The. W. H. Davies. BrPo
Chase, The ("Harp of the North!"). Sir Walter Scott. *See* Harp of the North.

Chase, The ("Art thou gone in haste?"). *Unknown.* *See* Art Thou Gone in Haste?
Chase, The ("Here's a moccasin track in the drifts"). *Unknown.* SCC
Chase and the Race, The. Adam Lindsay Gordon. *Br. sel. fr.* Ye Wearie Wayfarer, Fytte VII. OtMeF
Chasm, A. Michael Silverton. PV
Chast, pious, prudent, Charles the Second. Charles the Second. Earl of Rochester. *Fr.* The History of the Insipids. FOL
Chaste and Lost Lovers, The, *sel.* William Bosworth.
See'st Not, My Love. SeCL
Chaste Arabian Bird, The. Earl of Rochester. ErPo; SiTL
Chaste Cloris doth disclose the shames. Cloris and Mertilla. Michael Drayton. *Fr.* The Muses' Elysium. LoBV
Chaste Cynthia bids me love, but hope no more. Platonic Love. Philip Ayres. Sonn
Chaste Florimel. Matthew Prior. ErPo
Chaste Goddesse, wel wostow that I. Emily's Prayer to Diana. Chaucer. *Fr.* The Canterbury Tales: The Knight's Tale. MyFE
Chaste Maid in Cheapside, A, *sel.* Thomas Middleton.
"Weep eyes, break heart!" TuPP
(Parting.) ElL
Chaste maids which haunt fair Aganippe's well. Lament. William Drummond of Hawthornden. *Fr.* Tears on the Death of Meliades. LoBV
Chastelard, *sels.* Swinburne.
Between the Sunset and the Sea. PoVP
(Mary Beaton's Song.) HBV
Chastelard and Mary Stuart. VA
Chasten your fears, I have not been destroyed. Sonnet VI. Mark Van Doren. MoLP
Chastity. Milton. *Fr.* Comus. OBS
Château Papineau. S. Frances Harrison. CaP; VA
Chatter of a death demon from a tree-top, The. War Is Kind, XIX. Stephen Crane. AP
Chatter thins, lights dip, and dusty crimson, The. A Benefit Night at the Opera. Martin Bell. MuSP
Chattering finch and water-fly. The Skeleton. G. K. Chesterton. FaBoTw
Chattering swallow! what shall we. The Swallow. Thomas Stanley. AWP
Chaucer. Benjamin Brawley. BANP
Chaucer. Longfellow. AA; AmePo; AmLP; AmP; AmPP; AP; ATP (1935 ed.); AWP; CBEP; CBV; CLwM; DiPo; InPo; InvP; JAWP; MAmP; ML; MWA-1; NePA; NoP; OBEV (new ed.); OBVV; OnPP; OxBA; PoIE (1970 ed.); PoRA; PP; PTK; Sonn; TOP; TrGrPo; WBP
Chaucer is dead; and Gower lies in grave. Against the Dispraisers of Poetry. Richard Barnfield. SiCE; Sonn; TuPP
Chaucer's Complaint to His Empty Purse. Chaucer. *See* Compleint of Chaucer to His Empty Purse, The.
Chaucer's Envoy to the Story of Patient Griselda. Chaucer, *mod. by* W. W. Skeat. *Fr.* The Canterbury Tales: The Clerk's Tale. AnEnPo
Chaucers Word[e]s unto Adam, His Owne Scriveyn. Chaucer. BEL
Chavez. Mildred I. McNeal Sweeney. HBV
Che Guevara Is Dead. Peter Schjeldahl. ANYP
Che Sara Sara. Victor Plarr. HBV
Cheat of Cupid, The; or, The Ungentle Guest. Robert Herrick, *after the Greek of* Anacreon. AWP; PG (1945 ed.); SeCeV
Check. James Stephens. AnIL; GTSL; HBMV; LOW; PoRh; SiSoSe; SP; SUS; TiPo
(Night, The.) BoTP
(Night Was Creeping.) StVeCh
Checking the Traps. Denis Johnson. QAH
Cheddar Pinks. Robert Bridges. ChMP; MoVE; POTE; SeCePo
Cheeks as soft as July peaches. Baby May. William Cox Bennett. HBV; OTPC (1923 ed.); VA
Cheer and salute for the Admiral, and here's to the Captain bold, A. The Men behind the Guns. John Jerome Rooney. AA; BLPA; EtS; FaBoBe; HBV; JKCP; MC; PaA; PAH; YaD
Cheer of the *Trenton,* The. Walter Mitchell. EtS
Cheer the New Year. Carlton Buck. SoP
Cheer up, all you young men. Brave Wolfe (B *vers.*). *Unknown.* BaBo
Cheer up, my [*or* ye] young men all [*or* your hearts, young men], let nothing fright you. Brave Wolfe. *Unknown.* BaBo (A *vers.*); PAH; ThLM; TrAS; ViBoFo
Cheered with this hope, to Paris I returned. Residence in France. Wordsworth. *Fr.* The Prelude. PoEL-4
Cheerfu' supper done, wi' serious face, The. Burns. *Fr.* The Cotter's Saturday Night. WGRP
Cheerful and industrious beast, A. The Bumblebeaver. Kenyon Cox. *Fr.* Mixed Beasts. RIS; TiPo
Cheerful Horn, The. *Unknown.* CH
Cheerful old bear at the Zoo, A. *Unknown.* GoTP
Cheerful Welcome, A. *Unknown.* MeEL
Cheerfulness. *Unknown.* *See* I'm Glad.
Cheerfulness Taught by Reason. Elizabeth Barrett Browning. *See* Complaints.
Cheerily carols the lark. Mad Margaret's Song. W. S. Gilbert. *Fr.* Ruddigore. RIS
Cheerio My Deario. Don Marquis. *Fr.* Archy and Mehitabel. ShBV-4
Cheer'ly, Man. *Unknown.* AmSS; SoAmSa, *with music* (Cheer'ly, O! *diff. vers.*) AmSS
Cheese-Mites Asked, The. *Unknown.* WhC
Cheetah. Charles Eglington. BoSA
Cheetie-Poussie-Cattie, O. *Unknown.* *See* There Was a Wee Bit Mousikie.
Chef whose hat is celluloid and green, A. Owed to Dickens, 1956. Jan Burroway. NePoAm-2
Chelmsfords Fate. Benjamin Tompson. SCAP
Chemist to His Love, The. *Unknown.* BOHV; InMe
Chemistry of Character, The. Elizabeth Dorney. BLPA
Cheops. James Schevill. FiMAP
Chequer-Board of mingled Light and Shade, A? Life's Chequer-Board. John Oxenham. TRV
Cher Maître:/ Neither my explication. A Letter to Wilbur Frohock. Daniel Hoffman. CoPo
Chercheuses de Poux, Les. Arthur Rimbaud, *tr. fr. French by* T. Sturge Moore. AWP
(Lice-Finders, The, *tr. by* T. Sturge Moore.) SyP
(Lice-Hunters, The, *tr. by* Robert Lowell.) SyP
(Louse-Catchers, The, *tr. by* Roy Campbell.) LiTW
Cherrie-ripe. Robert Herrick. *See* Cherry-ripe.
Cherries. Zalman Schneour, *tr. fr. Yiddish by* Joseph Leftwich. TrJP
Cherries. Frederic E. Weatherly. SAS
Cherries at the Eta Temple. On the Eta, the Untouchables. Issa. PoFr
Cherry. Gene Baro. ErPo
Cherry and Pear are white, The. The Crowns. John Freeman. CH
Cherry and the Slae, The, *sel.* Alexander Montgomerie.
"About ane bank, where birdis on bewis." GoTS
Cherry-Blossom Wand, The. Anna Wickham. MeWo; MoBrPo; TSW
Cherry Blossoms, *sels.* "Michael Lewis," *after the Chinese.* UnTE
Cursing and Blessing.
Leaving.
Living and Dying.
Longing.
Remembering.
Cherry-blossoms, more. Onitsura, *tr. fr. Japanese by* Harold Gould Henderson. LiTW
Cherry Creek store shoulders up to the bridge, The. The Snake Charmer. Muriel Earley Shepperd. IHA
Cherry Fair, A. *Unknown.* ChTr
Cherry-lipped Adonis in his snowy shape. Richard Barnfield. *Fr.* Cynthia. Sonn
Cherry-Pit. Robert Herrick. OAEP
Cherry-ripe. Thomas Campion. *See* There Is a Garden in Her Face.
Cherry-ripe. Robert Herrick. CH; CoBE; ELP; EnL; LiTL; OBEV; OTPC (1923 ed.); PoE; PoeP; PoFS; ShBV-1
(Cherrie-ripe.) CavP; SCEP-2; SeCP; SeCV-1
("Cherry-ripe, ripe, ripe, I cry.") EG
Cherry Robbers. D. H. Lawrence. MoAB; MoBrPo; PoIE
Cherry Tree. Ivy O. Eastwick. BoTP
Cherry Tree. Christina Rossetti. YeAr
Cherry Tree. Sacheverell Sitwell. AtBAP
Cherry-Tree Carol, The (*diff. versions*). *Unknown.* AnEnPo; BaBo (A *and* B *vers.*); BoLiVe; CBEP; ChTr; DiPo; ELP; EnSB; ESPB (A *and* B *vers.*); LoBV; NoP; OAEP; OBB; OnMSP; OxBB; OxBoCh; OxBoLi; PoAn; SeCeV; StJW;

Cherry-Tree (continued)
ThGo; TrGrPo; VaPo; ViBoFo, *with music*
(Joseph and Mary.) BFSS
(Joseph Was an Old Man.) BFSS, *with music*; ViBoPo
(Old Christmas Carol, An.) RG
Cherry-Tree Carol, The: As Joseph Was a-Walking. *Unknown.* *See* As Joseph . . .
Cherry tree's shedding, The. May Morning. Marjorie Barrows. GFA
Cherry year, A. *Unknown.* OxNR
Cherrylog Road. James Dickey. CoAP; NYBP; TPM; TwCP
Cherub-Folk, The. Enid Dinnis. CAW
Cherub in armor. Love to Stephen. Elinor Wylie. ML
Cherubic Pilgrim, The. "Angelus Silesius," *tr. fr. German.* "I have wandered." WGRP
Cherubim, The, *sel.* Thomas Heywood. WGRP
Cherwell! how pleased along thy willowed edge. The River Cherwell. William Lisle Bowles. Sonn
Cherwell Water Lily [*or* Waterlily], The. Frederick W. Faber. CAW:GoBC
Chesapeake. Gerta Kennedy. NYBP
Chesapeake and the *Shannon,* The. ("The *Chesapeake* so bold.") *Unknown.* PAH; ViBoFo, *with music*
Cheshire Cat. Kenneth Allott. NeBP
Chess. John Thompson. BoAu
Chess-Board, The. "Owen Meredith." HBV; OBVV; VA
Chesspieces. Joseph Campbell. OxBI
Chester, *with music.* William Billings. TrAS
Chester Miracle Play, *sel.* *Unknown.*
Abraham and Isaac. FlW
Chestnut Buds. Evelyn M. Williams. BoTP
Chestnut Casts His Flambeaux [and the Flowers], The. A. E. Housman. AtBAP; BrPo; CBV; CLwM; CMoP; EG; EnLit; LiTB; MoAB; MoBrPo; OBMV; POTE; ReMP; TDP; ViPo; VP
Chestnut Roasters, The. Joseph Payne Brennan. FiSC
Chestnut Stands. Rachel Field. SiSoSe
Chestnut's a fine tree, The. A Christmas-Tree Song. Rodney Bennett. BoTP
Chevalier de maison rouge, Le, *sel.* Alexandre Dumas, *tr. fr. French by* John Oxenford.
Girondins, The. PoFr
Chevalier Malheur, Le. Paul Verlaine, *tr. fr. French by* John Gray. *Fr.* Sagesse. SyP
Chevy Chase [*or* Chace]. *Unknown.* BFSS; BuBa; EnLi-1 (1949 ed.); EnSB; GN; HBV; OBB, *older vers.*; OxBB; TOP, *abr.*; ViBoFo, *with music*; ViBoPo, *older vers.*; WHA, *older vers.*
(Ancient Ballad of Chevy-Chase, The, *older vers.*) EnRP
(Hunting of the Cheviot, The.) BaBo (A, B, *and* C *vers.*); BEL, *older vers.*; ESPB (A *and* B *vers.*); OAEP
Cheyenne, *with music.* *Unknown.* CoSo
Cheyenne Mountain. Helen Hunt Jackson. PoOW
Chez Brébant. Francis Alexander Durivage. AA
Chez Jane. Frank O'Hara. CoAP; NeAP
Chez Madame. Sam Harrison. NeIP
Chez-Nous. A. G. Austin. PoAu-2
Chi ama, crede: mother. Study No. X. Pierre Coupey. PeCV (1967 ed.)
Chi è questa. Guido Cavalcanti. *See* Sonetto VII: "Who is she that comes, makyng turn every man's eye."
Ch'i Lai' (March of the Volunteers). Shih Ee, *tr. fr. Chinese by* Li Pao-sheng *and* Liu Liang-mo. PoFr
Chiaroscuro. Carole Bergé. ErPo
Chiaroscuro. John B. Thompson. OQP
Chiaroscuro: Rose. Conrad Aiken. MAPA
Chicago. Sherwood Anderson. NP
Chicago, *sel.* John Gill.
"Chicago/ the backyard." ThO
Chicago. Bret Harte. PAH; ThLM
Chicago. Galway Kinnell. NePoAm
Chicago. John Boyle O'Reilly. PAH
Chicago. Carl Sandburg. AmPP; AP; CMoP; CoBA; FaBV; HBMV; HT; InP; LiTM (rev. ed.); LoGBV; MAP; MoAmPo; MoVE; NePA; NoP; NP; OxBA; PoIE; PoPl; TOP; TreF; ViBoPo (1958 ed.); YaD
Chicago. Whittier. MC; PAH; PoRL
Chicago/ the backyard. John Gill. *Fr.* Chicago. ThO
Chicago *Defender* Sends a Man to Little Rock, Fall, 1957, The. Gwendolyn Brooks. AmNP
Chicago Idyll. E. Merrill Root. AnAmPo
Chicago Kid Winters. Douglas Blazek. WOW
Chicago Picasso, The. Gwendolyn Brooks. *Fr.* Two Dedications. LiTM (1970 ed.)
Chicago Poem. Lew Welch. FRC; NeAP
Chicago ran a fever of a hundred and one. The Shooting of John Dillinger outside the Biograph Theater, July 22, 1934. David Wagoner. CoAP
Chicago was a small boy once. Chicago Kid Winters. Douglas Blazek. WOW
Chick! my naggie. *Unknown.* OxNR
Chickadee, The. Hilda Conkling. BoChLi; TiPo; TSW
Chickadee, The. Emerson. *Fr.* The Titmouse. FaPON; GFA; OTPC (1946 ed.); PCH
Chickadee. Marion Mitchell Walker. GFA
Chickadee in the apple tree, The. The Chickadee. Hilda Conkling. BoChLi; TiPo; TSW
Chickadee-dee-dee is not a bird, The. Scarabs for the Living, VII. R. P. Blackmur. CoAnAm; TwAmPo
Chickadees, The. John Hay. NePoAm-2
Chickamungus, The. James Reeves. GoTP
Chicken. Walter de la Mare. NeMA; TiPo
Chicken-skin, delicate, white. On a Fan That Belonged to the Marquise de Pompadour. Austin Dobson. ALV; HBV; OBVV; PoVP; VA; ViBoPo
Chicken wants, The. *Unknown, tr. fr. Japanese by* Geoffrey Bownas *and* Anthony Thwaite. FlW
Chickens, The. Rose Fyleman. TiPo (1952 ed.)
Chickens, The. *Unknown.* *See* Five Little Chickens.
Chickens a-crowin' [*or* crowin'] on Sourwood Mountain. Sourwood Mountain. *Unknown.* ABF; AS; TrAS
Chickens Are a-Crowing, The, *with music.* *Unknown.* TrAS
Chickens in Trouble. *Unknown, tr. fr. Norwegian by* Emilie Poulsson. PPL
Chickens the Weasel Killed. William Stafford. NaP
Chickens they are crowing, a-crowing, a-crowing, The. The Chickens Are a-Crowing. *Unknown.* TrAS
Chickory. Zerubavel Gal'ed, *tr. fr. Hebrew.* TrJP
Chide, chide no more away. Expectation [*or* Destiny]. Thomas Stanley. AnAnS-2; LoBV; OBS; SeCL; SeEP
Chief captain commanded him to be brought into the castle, The. The Acts, Bible, *N.T.* PoFr
Chief Centurions, The. John Masefield. *Fr.* The Tragedy of Pompey the Great. POTE
("Man is a sacred city, built of marvellous earth.") WGRP
Chief defect of Henry King, The. Henry King. Hilaire Belloc. BBGG; CenHV; DTC; HBMV; ShM; TSW
Chief in thy generation born of men. Dickens. Swinburne. PoVP
Chief of organic numbers! On Seeing a Lock of Milton's Hair. Keats. PP
Chief of the West, Darkling, The. David Knight. MoCV
Chief Petty Officer. Charles Causley. POTi
Chief reply'd, The: This time forbids to rest. Homer, *tr.* by Pope. *Fr.* The Iliad, VI. ATP; CEP
Chief [*or* Chiefe] use then in man of that he knows [*or* knowes], The. Man's Service. Fulke Greville. *Fr.* Of Humane Learning. OBS; PoFr; SiCE
Chiefly, it is blue. People use. A Vacation on Earth. Thomas M. Disch. HYE
Chiefly to Mind Appears. C. Day Lewis. MoAB; MoBrPo
Chiefs of State marched up the hill, The. Alpine View. Melville Cane. PoPl
Chief's Prayer after the Salmon Catch, The. Constance Lindsay Skinner. *Fr.* Songs of the Coast Dwellers. NP
Chiefs that bow to Capet's reign, The. On the Anniversary of the Storming of the Bastille. Philip Freneau. AmPP (3d ed.); CoBA
Chieftain Iffucan of Azcan in caftan. Bantams in Pine-Woods. Wallace Stevens. AtBAP; CBV; CMoP; InPo; MoVE; OxBA; PoAn; PoeP; SeCeV
Chieftain, to the Highlands bound, A. Lord Ullin's Daughter. Thomas Campbell. BBV (1923 ed.); BeLS; BoTP; EnRP; FaPON; GN; GTBS; GTBS-D; GTBS-P; GTBS-W; GTSE; GTSL; HBV; HBVY; LoEn; OnSP; OTPC; RoGo; TreF; WBLP
Chiffons! William Samuel Johnson. HBV
Child, The. Sara Coleridge. OBEV (1st ed.)
Child, A. Richard Watson Gilder. AA
Child, The. Donald Hall. NePoEA-2
Child, A. Mary Lamb. *See* Parental Recollections.

Child, The. Reginald Massey. ACV
Child. Sylvia Plath. FlW
Child, The. Ivor Popham. EaLo
Child. Carl Sandburg. SoP; OQP; StJW; TRV
Child. E. N. Sargent. NYBP
Child, The. John Banister Tabb. AA
(Child at Bethlehem, The, *sel.*) PRWS
Child, The. George Edward Woodberry. Wild Eden, XXX. AA
Child, A/ Curious and innocent. To Robert Louis Stevenson. W. E. Henley. MoBrPo
Child,/ You are my brother. The Mists Are Rising Now. Hasye Cooperman. GoYe
Child, a Wasp, and an Apricot Tree, A. Diane Wakoski. YAP
Child Accepts, A. Michael Hamburger. NMP
Child alone a poet is, The. Babylon. Robert Graves. HBMV
Child and Maiden. Sir Charles Sedley. *Fr.* The Mulberry Garden, III, ii. GTBS; GTBS-D; GTBS-P; GTBS-W; GTSE; GTSL; LiTL; TOP
("Ah Cloris! that I now could sit.") OAEP; OBS
(Song: "Ah Chloris [*or* Cloris]! that I now could sit.") SeCV-2; ViBoPo
(To Chloris.) HBV; OBEV; SeCL
Child and Mother. Eugene Field. HH; MPB
Child and Poet. Swinburne. EnLit; EPN; PoVP
Child and the Fairies, The. *Unknown.* OTPC (1946 ed.); PCH; PRWS; StVeCh (1940 ed.)
Child and the Mariner, The. W. H. Davies. CH
Child and the Shadow, The. Elizabeth Jennings. NePoEA-2
Child and the Sparrow, The. Thomas Westwood. BiS
Child and the World, The. Kate Douglas Wiggin. PPL
Child and the Year, The. Celia Thaxter. DD; HH
Child Asleep, A. Walter de la Mare. POTE
Child Asleep, A. Elizabeth Madox Roberts. AnAmPo
Child at a Crèche, A. Alice Isabel Hazeltine. ChrBoLe
Child at Bethlehem, The. John Banister Tabb. *See* At Bethlehem.
Child at Sand. Robert Hershon. ThO
Child at school who fails to pass, A. The Untutored Giraffe. Oliver Herford. PoMa
Child awaits the angel, The. He stares. The Angel. Alfred Hayes. TrJP
Child, behold the lovely pattern. Mathematics. Lionel Wiggam. PoMa
Child came to a pool in the heart of a thicket, The. The Pool. Leah Bodine Drake. FiSC
Child, Child. Sara Teasdale. HBV
Child Compassion. The. Margot Ruddock. OBMV
Child Crying. Anthony Thwaite. NePoEA-2
Child! do not throw this book about! Dedication on the Gift of a Book to a Child [*or* A Foreword]. Hilaire Belloc. HBVY; ThGo; TSW
Child Drowns in the Sea of Its Own Imagining, A. Kathleen Fraser. YAP
Child Dying, The. Edwin Muir. ChMP; FaBoTw; GTBS-D; GTBS-P
Child Eros, The. Meleager, *tr. fr. Greek by* John Herman Merivale. OnPM
(Love, the Vagrant) WoL
Child fell, turning slowly with arms outstretched like a doll, The. For Brian Priestman. F. R. Scott. TwCaPo
Child, feverish, frowning, only saw red, The. Les Chercheuses de Poux. Arthur Rimbaud. SyP
"Child, follow me," the Master said. Follow Me! *Unknown.* SoP
Child grabbed my hand and made me run with him, The. Into the Wind. Winfield Townley Scott. NMP
Child Harold, *sels.* John Clare.
"Blackbird startles from the homestead hedge, The." PeER
Stanzas: "How beautiful this hill of fern swells on!" OBNC
Child He was, and had not learned to speak, A. The Incarnation. Giles Fletcher. StJW
Child, I will give you rings to wear. Declaration. Arthur Symons. *Fr.* Violet. BrPo; ViBoPo
Child Ill, A. John Betjeman. DTC
Child — in all the flying sky. Poem. Josephine Strongin. AnAmPo
Child in Our Soul, The. Björnstjerne Björnson, *tr. fr. Norwegian by* Arthur Hubbell Palmer. WoL
Child in the Garden, The. Henry van Dyke. HBV; MaRV
Child in the Sabbath peace, there, A. A Sunday. Walter de la Mare. NYTB; POTE
Child in the Street, The. John James Piatt. AA
Child Is Born, A. *Unknown.* STF
Child is holy and most wise, The. The Child. Ivor Popham. EaLo
Child is not dead, The. The Child Who Was Shot Dead by Soldiers at Nyanga. Ingrid Jonker. PeSA
Child Jesus, The. Francis Quarles. *See* On the Infancy of Our Saviour.
Child Jesus in the Garden, The. *Unknown.* ChrBoLe
Child Jesus to Mary the Rose, The. John Lydgate. CAW; GoBC; ISi
Child-King, The. Morris Wintchevsky, *tr. fr. Yiddish by* Alter Brody. TrJP
Child Looks Out, The. Dorothy Livesay. TwCaPo
Child Margaret. Carl Sandburg. FlW
Child Maurice. *Unknown. See* Childe Maurice.
Child Moses, The. Exodus, I: 7-II: 15, Bible, *O.T.* OuHeWo
Child most infantine, A. A Child of Twelve. Shelley. *Fr.* The Revolt of Islam. GN
Child Musician, The. Austin Dobson. GN; MuSP
Child My Choice, A. Robert Southwell. CAW; GoBC; HBV; OxBoCh; PoLi; SiCE
Child need not be very clever, A. Grandpa Is Ashamed. Ogden Nash. PV
Child Next Door, The. Rose Fyleman. FaPON; GaP; MPB; SP
Child Noryce is a clever young man. Child Maurice (B *vers*). *Unknown.* ESPB
Child of a Day. Walter Savage Landor. VA
(On a Child.) OBVV
Child of Loneliness. Norman Gale. WGRP
Child of My Love. Frank J. Exeley. SoP
Child of My love, lean hard. Lean Hard. *Unknown.* FaChP; SoP
Child of my love! though thou be bright as day. Shadow. Mary Elizabeth Coleridge. PoVP
Child of my winter, born. Heart's Needle. W. D. Snodgrass. AmPC; CoPo; MoAmPo (1962 ed.); PIA
Child of Nazareth, The. St. Luke, II: 40-52, Bible, *N.T.* ChrBoLe
Child of Peace, The. Selma Lagerlöf, *tr. fr. Swedish by* Charles W. Stork. PoPl
Child of sin and sorrow. Exhortation. Thomas Hastings. AA
Child of the frightened face. Frightened Face. Marion Strobel. HBMV
Child of the gorgeous East, whose ardent suns. To an Egyptian Boy. H. W. Berry. WhC
Child of the Long Grass. Roy Macnab. BoSA
Child of the Romans. Carl Sandburg. LaNeLa
Child of the season of adventure, child of the heart. Child. E. N. Sargent. NYBP
Child of the Sun, in whom his rays appear. La Gialletta Gallante; or, The Sun-burn'd Exotique Beauty. Lord Herbert of Cherbury. AtBAP
Child of the World. Edna L. S. Barker. GoYe
Child of To-Day, A. James Buckham. AA
Child of Twelve, A. Shelley. *Fr.* The Revolt of Islam. GN
Child on the Curbstone, The. Elinor Wylie. OCS
Child on the Judgment Seat, The. Elizabeth Rundle Charles. BLPA
Child on Top of a Greenhouse. Theodore Roethke. AtBAP; ELU; LOW; MiAP; PoPl; StP; WePo
Child Owlet. *Unknown.* ESPB
Child Reads an Almanac, The. Francis Jammes, *tr. fr. French by* Ludwig Lewisohn. AWP; FaPON; JAWP; WBP
Child riding the stormy mane of noon, A. Are You Born? Muriel Rukeyser. MoRP
Child Said *What Is the Grass?* A. Walt Whitman. *See* Grass, The.
Child should always say what's true, A. Whole Duty of Children. Robert Louis Stevenson EvOK; HBV; HBVY; NeHB; OTPC; PoVP; SAS; ThGo; TreFS
Child should have a pocket, A. Pockets. Susan Adger Williams. BrR
Child skipping jump on the quay at the Mill, A. Poor Old Horse. David Holbrook. NePoEA-2

Child That Has a Cold, A. Thomas Dibdin. ChTr; PV
Child, the current of your breath is six days long. Unknown Girl in the Maternity Ward. Anne Sexton. CoPo
Child-Thought, A. Wilfrid Thorley. PCH
Child upon the Stair, The. Carolyn Hall. TSW
Child was gone, The: the Mother stood alone. Madonna of the Empty Arms. Maurice Francis Egan. ISi
Child [*or* Childe] Waters. *Unknown.* BaBo; ESPB (A *and* B *vers.*); OAEP; OBB, *longer vers.*; OxBB; ViBoFo
Child, weary of thy baubles of to-day. The Human Plan. Charles Henry Crandall. AA
Child Who Was Shot Dead by Soldiers at Nyanga, The. Ingrid Jonker, *tr. fr. Afrikaans by* Jack Cope *and* Uys Krige. PeSA
Child, who went gathering the flowers of death. Haroun Al-Rachid for Hearts-Life. *Unknown. Fr.* The Thousand and One Nights. AWP
Child Wife. Joseph Joel Keith. FiSC
Child with Shell. R. G. Everson. PeCV (1967 ed.)
Child with the hungry eyes. Beggars. Ella Higginson. AA
Child, your white face is chanting memories. Elegy. Karel van de Woestijne. LiTW
Childbirth. Ted Hughes. ToPo
Childe Harold to the dark tower, L-two. The Letter. John Holmes. NePoAm
Childe Harold to the Round Tower Came. William Carlos Williams. PoeP
Childe Harold's Farewell to England. Byron. *Fr.* Childe Harold's Pilgrimage, I. OHFP; PoPl
Childe Harold's Good Night. Byron. *Fr.* Childe Harold's Pilgrimage, I. MBW-2
Childe Harold's Pilgrimage. Byron. *See individual selections and first lines.*
Childe [*or* Child] Maurice. *Unknown.* BaBo; ESPB (A, B, *and* D *vers.*); OBB; TrGrPo, *abr.*; ViBoFo
"Childe Maurice hunted the Silver Wood," *sel.* HoPM
"Childe Roland to the Dark Tower Came." Robert Browning. AnFE; ATP; BEL; DTo; EnL; FosPo; MaVP; MBW-2; OAEP; OtMeF; PeVV; Po; PoVP; SeCeV; TOP; VA; ViPo; ViPP; VP
Childe Waters. *Unknown. See* Child Waters.
Childe-hood. Henry Vaughan. *See* Childhood.
Childheart, time alone is not enough. A Late Spring. James Scully. NYBP
Childhood. Jens Baggesen, *tr. fr. Danish by* Longfellow. AWP; JAWP; WBP
Childhood, *sel.* John Clare.
Bat OA
Birds' Nests. BiS
Childhood. John Erskine. MaRV
Childhood. Louis Ginsberg. RIS
Childhood. Donagh MacDonagh. NeIP
Childhood. Sir Thomas More. EnRePo; TuPP
(I Am Called Childhood.) NCEP
Childhood. Edwin Muir. CMoP; SeCePo
Childhood. Ned O'Gorman. PoPl
Childhood. Henri Percikow. OCS
Childhood. Sir Herbert Read. BrPo
Childhood, *sels.* Arthur Rimbaud, *tr. fr. French.*
"I am the saint at prayer on the terrace," IV, *tr. by.* Louise Varèse. PoPl
"This idol with black eyes and yellow hair," I, *tr. by* T. Sturge Moore. SyP
Childhood, A. Stephen Spender. NeBP
Childhood. John Banister Tabb. HBV
Childhood. Thomas Traherne. TrGrPo
(Review, The.) CBEP
Childhood. *Unknown, tr. fr. Scottish by* G. R. D. McLean. FlW
Childhood [*or* Childe-hood]. Henry Vaughan. OxBoCh; SCEP-1; SeEP
Childhood. Margaret Walker. BOLo; Kal; TDP
Childhood ("When he had left the mountains and received"). Wordsworth. *Fr.* The Prelude, I. CoBE
Childhood Ambition. David Hilton. QAH
Childhood and School-Time. Wordsworth. *See* Fair Seed-Time Had My Soul. *Fr.* The Prelude, I.
Childhood Church, The. Pat Wilson. AnNZ
Childhood Fled. Charles Lamb. EnRP
("We were two pretty babes, the youngest she.") Sonn
Childhood is when the mouth tastes earth. Childhood. Ned O'Gorman. PoPl
Childhood of James V, The. Sir David Lindsay. *Fr.* The Complaynt of Schir David Lindesay. AtBAP
Childhood remembrances are always a drag. Nikki-Roasa. Nikki Giovanni. BP; CAD; NBP
Childhood's Trials. Mrs. C. F. Alexander. ThGo
Childish Game, A. Reinmar von Hagenau, *tr. fr. German.* AWP; JAWP; WBP
Childless. Giollabhrighde MacConmidhe, *tr. fr. Irish by* Frank O'Connor. KiLC
Childless. L. A. G. Strong. POTE
Childless Father, The. Wordsworth. CH
Childless Woman in Heaven, The. Katharine Tynan. BoC
Childlike Heart. Ellen Weston Catlin. PGD
Children, The. Charles Monroe Dickinson, *wr. at. to* Charles Dickens. AA; HBV
Children, The. Clifford Dyment. ChMP
Children. Euripides, *tr. fr. Greek by* T. F. Higham. WoL
Children. Walter Savage Landor. DD
Children. Longfellow. GTBS
Children, The. William Soutar. POTE
Children, The. Jane Stembridge. WOW
Children. Swinburne. PoVP
Children, The. Constance Urdang. CoAP
Children, The. William Carlos Williams. NePoAm-2
Children and pets, please note. In a Closed Universe. James Hayford. NePoAm-2
Children and Sir Nameless, The. Thomas Hardy. NoP
Children are at the door. At the Door. Lillie Fuller Merriam. PoToHe
Children are dumb to say how hot the day is. The Cool Web. Robert Graves. AWP; ChMP; GTBS-D; GTBS-P; NoP
Children are frightening. The Journey to Golgotha. K. Raghavendra Rao. ACV
Children are not visas, sure to enter, The. The Address to the Parents. Marvin Bell. YAP
Children are off somewhere, The. Lights I Have Seen Before. Philip Levine. TDP
Children are what the mothers are. Children. Walter Savage Landor. DD
Children (as such forgive them) have I known. Religious Isolation. Matthew Arnold. EPN; MBW-2
Children at Night. Samuel French Morse. NYTB
Children Band, The. Sir Aubrey De Vere. OBEV
Children, behold the chimpanzee. The Chimpanzee. Oliver Herford. CenHV; FaBV; FiBHP; InP; LBN; NA
Children born of fairy stock. I'd Love to Be a Fairy's Child. Robert Graves. BiCB; BoTP; FaPON; HBVY; PDV; SoPo; TSW
Children builded in the sand, The. The Master Builder. Myra Brooks Welch. SoP
Children, Children, Don't Forget. Dora Owen. MPB
Children conceived when two nightgowns. The Submarine Bed. John Peale Bishop. LiTA
Children dear, was it yesterday. Matthew Arnold. *Fr.* The Forsaken Merman. BoTP
Children, do you ever. My Other Me. Grace Denio Litchfield. AA; HBV
Children go. Follow Me! Eliza Lee Follen. PPL
Children, if you dare to think. Warning to Children. Robert Graves. FaBoCh; FaFP; FlW; GTBS-W; LoGBV; NoP; PoIE; SiTL
Children in a Christian home, The. Poor and Wealthy Children. Edward L. Crane. SoP
Children in the Market-Place. Henry van Dyke. SoP; TRV
Children in the Wood, The. *Unknown. See* Babes in the Wood; The ("Now ponder well").
Children indeed are we—children that wait. We Are Children. Robert Buchanan. VA
Children, It's Time. Michael Brownstein. ANYP
Children Look at the Parents, The. A. S. J. Tessimond. ChMP
Children look down upon the morning-grey. C. Day Lewis. BoC
Children March, The. Elizabeth Riddell. MoAuPo
Children model the dust. In a City Square. Eleanor Glenn Wallis. NePoAm-2
Children now awake to birds. Lines for the Margin of an Old Gospel. Sheila Wingfield. ChMP
Children of a Future Age. Blake. *See* A Little Girl Lost.
Children of Greenock, The. W. S. Graham. FaBoTw
Children of Israel prayed for [*or* wanted] bread, The. Old Sam's

Wife [*or* On The Wife of a Parish Clerk]. *Unknown.* ChTr; ShM
Children of Light. Robert Lowell. AP; CBV; CMoP; FiMAP; MoAB; OxBA; PoAn; PoPl; ToPo
Children of light, The—mongoloid. The Bad Children. Carl Bode. ToPo
Children of Love. Harold Monro. MoBrPo
Children of Martha. Gilean Douglas. TwCaPo
Children of my happier prime. Immolated. Herman Melville. ViBoPo
Children of Stare, The. Walter de la Mare. BrPo
Children of the cold sun and the broken horizon. The City. Ben Maddow. LiTM (1946 ed.); WaP
Children of the Cosmos. Kuwasi Balagon. BF
Children of the Czar, The. The Ballad of the Children of the Czar. Delmore Schwartz. MiAP; OnHM
Children of the future age. A Little Girl Lost [*or* Children of a Future Age]. Blake. *Fr.* Songs of Experience. CBEP; ERoP-1
Children of the Heavenly King. John Cennick. WGRP
Children of the Light. St. John, XII: 23-36, Bible, *N.T.* WoL
Children of the Night, The. E. A. Robinson. AmPP (4th ed.); NePA; OxBA
Children of the Poor, The, *sel.* Gwendolyn Brooks.
"What shall I give my children? who are poor." PoCh
Children of the Poor, The. Victor Hugo. *See* Poor Children, The.
Children of the Sun. Fenton Johnson. BANP
Children of the Wind. Carl Sandburg. *See* These Children of the Wind.
Children of the world are on the march, The. The Children March. Elizabeth Riddell. MoAuPo
Children of the world who're wanting, The. The Children. Jane Stembridge. WOW
Children of Tomorrow. Zona Gale. OQP
Children of yesterday, heirs of tomorrow. Song of Hope [*or* Room for Him! Room!]. Mary A. Lathbury. BLPA; ChIP; MaRV; SoP
Children picking up our bones. A Postcard from the Volcano. Wallace Stevens. AmPP; AP; LiTA; PoeP
Children played with horrors and utopias, The. The Golden Age. Robert Conquest. HYE
Children romp within the graveyard's pale, The. Four Epigrams. Sir William Watson. MoBrPo (1942 ed.)
Children set fires in ashbarrels. Galway Kinnell. *Fr.* The Avenue Bearing The Initial of Christ into the New World. NaP
Children she had missed, The. The Childless Woman in Heaven. Katharine Tynan. BoC
Children sing in far Japan, The. Singing. Robert Louis Stevenson. ThGo
Children, the Sandbar, That Summer. Muriel Rukeyser. FiMAP
Children today—tomorrow—men! Tomorrow's Men. Georgia Douglas Johnson. GoSL
Children Waking: Indian Hill Station. R. N. Currey. PeSA
Children were frightened by crescendoes, The. A Fete. Larry Eigner. NeAP
Children were shouting together, The. Frolic. "Æ." BoTP; FaPON; GTSL; MoBrPo; OTPC (1946 ed.)
Children When They're Very Sweet. John Ciardi. BBGG
Children, who extend their smile of crystal. The Bombed Happiness. Stephen Spender. CMoP
"Children who paddle where the ocean bed shelves steeply." Advice to Young Children. Stevie Smith. ELU
Children, you are very little. Good and Bad Children. Robert Louis Stevenson. BBGG; FaBoCh; FaFP; HBV; HBVY; LoGBV; NBM; OTPC (1923 ed.); PoVP; ThGo; TreF
Children's Bells, The. Eleanor Farjeon. BoTP; CH
Children's Crusade, The. Philip Levine. NaP
Children's Crusade 1939. Bertolt Brecht, *tr. fr. German by* Michael Hamburger. MoBS
Children's Don't, A, *sel.* Harry Graham.
"Don't tell Papa his nose is red." BBGG
Children's Elegy. Muriel Rukeyser. *Fr.* Eighth Elegy. FiMAP
Children's Ghosts, The. Winifred M. Letts. HBMV
Children's Hour, The. Longfellow. AA; AmePo; AmP; AnNE; CoBA; FaBoBe; FaBV; FaFP; FaPL; FaPON; GoTP; HBV; HBVY; LaNeLa; MPB; NeHB; OHFP; OTPC; PCH; PoEL-5; PoLF; PoPl; PTK; TreF; TSW; WBLP
Children's Playground, The. Oscar Williams. SiTL
Children's Rhymes. Langston Hughes. BOLo
Children's Song. Ford Madox Ford. HBV
Children's Song, The. Kipling. *See* Land of our Birth.
Children's Song. R. S. Thomas. BoC
Children's Song, The. *Unknown, tr. fr. Greek by* John Addington Symonds. FaPON
(Greek Children's Song.) OTPC (1946 ed.)
Children's voices in the orchard. New Hampshire. T. S. Eliot. Landscapes, I. FaBoCh; GTBS-P; LoBV; LoGBV; LOW; NoP; PoSa; ThWaDe
Child's a plaything for an hour, A. Parental Recollections [*or* A Child *or* In Memoriam]. Mary Lamb. GTSL; OBEV; OBRV
Child's Appeal, The. Mamie Gene Cole. MaRV; OQP
Child's Carol. Eleanor Farjeon. RePo
Child's castle crumbles, The; hot air shimmers. M. K. Joseph. *Fr.* Mercury Bay Eclogue. AnNZ
Child's Christmas Carol, A. Christine Chaundler. BoTP
Child's Christmas Song, A. T. A. Daly. BiCB
Child's cough scratches at my heart—my head, The. New York—December, 1931. Babette Deutsch. ImOP
Child's Day, A, *sels.* Walter de la Mare.
Ann and the Fairy Song. FaBV
"Softly, drowsily." SoPo; SUS; TiPo (1952 ed.)
(Child's Day Begins, A.) StVeCh
Child's Dream, The. *Unknown, tr. fr. Russian by* W. R. S. Ralston. OnPM
Child's Evening Hymn. Sabine Baring-Gould. *See* Now the Day Is Over.
Child's Evening Prayer, A. Samuel Taylor Coleridge. *See* Pains of Sleep, The.
Child's Evening Prayer, A. Mary Lundie Duncan. MaRV; OTPC
(Jesus, Tender Shepherd [Hear Me].) BLRP; PCH
("Jesus, tender shepherd, hear me.") ThGo
Child's Evensong. Ethel Robb. GFA
Child's eyes to see. The Vision Clear. J. M. Westrup. BoTP
Child's Fancy, A. "A." PRWS
Child's First Grief, The. Felicia D. Hemans. BLPA; NeHB
(First Grief, The.) CH
Child's Future, A. Swinburne. EnLi-2
Child's Game, A. Karle Wilson Baker. PCD
Child's Grace, A. Burns. BrR; FaPON; MoShBr; MPB; PCH; PRWS; StVeCh
(Two Graces.) FaBoCh; LoGBV
Child's Grace, A ("Here a little child I stand"). Robert Herrick. *See* Grace for a Child.
Child's Heritage, The. John G. Neihardt. HBV
Child's Hymn, A. Matilda Betham-Edwards. *See* Child's Prayer, A.
Child's Hymn, The. Mary Howitt. GoTP
Child's Hymn of Praise, A. Jane Taylor. OTPC (1923 ed.)
Child's Laughter, A. Swinburne. BiCB; EPN; HBV; PoLF; PoVP; PRWS; TOP
Child's Morning Prayer, A. Mary Lundie Duncan. OTPC
Child's Morning Prayer, A. Jeannie Kirby. BoTP
Child's Natural History, *sels.* Oliver Herford.
Geese. HBV
(Some Geese.) FiBHP; NA
Mon-Goos, The. AA; AmePo; HBV
Seal, A. HBV; HBVY
Yak, The. HBV; HBVY
Child's Offering, A. *Unknown.* MaRV
Child's Pet, A. W. H. Davies. CH
Child's Poem. Kay Smith. TwCaPo
Child's Portrait, A. William James Dawson. VA
Child's Power of Wonder, The. P. K. Saha. ACV
Child's Prayer, A. Matilda Betham-Edwards. OTPC; PRWS
(Child's Hymn, A.) TVC
Child's Prayer, A. William Canton. BoTP
Child's Prayer, The. Comte Robert de Montesquiou-Fezensac, *tr. fr. French by* Joseph T. Shipley. CAW
Child's Prayer, A, Siegfried Sassoon. BoTP
Child's Prayer, A. John Banister Tabb. FaPON; TreF; YaD
(Little Child's Prayer, A.) GaP
Child's Prayer, A. Francis Thompson. DD; FaChP; HBVY; OHIP; PoRL; TreFS; TSW
(Ex Ore Infantium.) BoTP; ChrBoLe; FaBV; GTSE; HBV; OBVV; PoRH; SUS
(Little Jesus.) MaRV; PoVP; SoP; StJW; TRV

Child's Prayer, A ("Father, lead me, day by day"). *Unknown.* BLRP
Child's Prayer, A. Charles Wesley. FaChP
Child's Prayer, A. *At. to* R. J. Weston. *See* Prayer: 'Father, we thank thee for the night."
Child's Present to His Child-Saviour, A. Robert Herrick. *See* To His Saviour, a Child; a Present by a Child.
Child's Purchase, The. Coventry Patmore. The Unknown Eros, II, xvii. CoBE; ISi
Child's Quest, The. Frances Shaw. NP
Child's Question, The. Emily Dickinson. *See* Will there really be a morning?
Child's Question, A. Emma Huntington Nason. AA
Child's Song, A. William Allingham. *See* Robin Redbreast.
Child's Song. Gerald Gould. BoTP
Child's Song. Kate Greenaway. OTPC (1946 ed.); PCH
(Naughty Blackbird, The.) HBVY
Child's Song. Robert Lowell. NMP
Child's Song. Thomas Moore. GoBC; OxBI; SUS; ViBoPo
(Garden Song, A.) BoNaP
Child's Song. Swinburne. GTSL; OBVV; PoVP
Child's Song in Spring. Edith Nesbit. BoTP; DD; HBV; HH; OHIP; OTPC
(Bird's Song in Spring.) PRWS
Child's Song of Christmas, A. Marjorie Pickthall. BoTP; HBV; HBVY; YeAr
Child's Song to Her Mother, A. Winifred Welles. HBMV
Child's Star, The. John Banister Tabb. PPL
Child's Talk in April. Christina Rossetti. GN; OTPC (1923 ed.)
Child's Thought, A. Bertha Moore. PaPo
Child's Thought, A. Robert Louis Stevenson. BoTP
Child's Thought of God, A. Elizabeth Barrett Browning. FaPON; MPB; OTPC; PCH; PRWS; SoP; TRV
Child's Thought of Harvest, A. "Susan Coolidge." BoChLi (1939 ed.); DD; OHIP; OTPC (1946 ed.); PoSC
Child's Winter Evening, A. Gwen John. CH
Child's Wish, A. Abram J. Ryan. AA; CAW; JKCP
Child's Wish Granted, The. George Parsons Lathrop. AA; HBV; JKCP
Child's World, The. William Brighty Rands. *See* Wonderful World, The.
Chiliasm. Richard Eberhart. EaLo
Chill, A. Christina Rossetti. BoTP; PRWS
Chill, chill! Winter. *Unknown.* KiLC
Chill New England sunshine, The. The Death of Goody Nurse. Rose Terry Cooke. PAH
Chill November day was done, The. A Little Goose. Eliza Sproat Turner. BOHV
Chill of the Eve. James Stephens. CMoP; OnYI
Chilled into a serenity. To an Icicle. Blanche Taylor Dickinson. CDC
Chilled with salt dew, tossed on dark waters deep. A Mermaiden. Thomas Hennell. FaBoTw
Chillingham. Mary Elizabeth Coleridge. BoTP
Chilly Dovebber with his boadigg blast. Belagcholly Days. *Unknown.* BOHV; StaSt
Chilly Water, *with music.* *Unknown.* BoAN-2
Chilly Winds, *with music.* *Unknown.* OuSiCo; TrAS
Chilterns, The. Rupert Brooke. MoBrPo
Chime of a bell of gold, The. Songs' End. John Payne. VA
Chime of the Sea, The. Dante Gabriel Rossetti. *See* Sea Limits, The.
Chimera. Barbara Howes. TwCP
Chimes. Alice Meynell. AnFE; BoTP; CH; MoBrPo; NP; TSW; WHA
Chimes. Dante Gabriel Rossetti. OBNC
Chimes, The. *Unknown.* SoP
Chiming a dream by the way. To My Mother. W. E. Henley. PoVP
Chimney, breathing a little smoke, A. February. James Schuyler. ANYP; NeAP
Chimney of my neighbor's house, The. Soliloquy to Absent Friends. D. G. Jones. MoCV
Chimney Swallows. Horatio Nelson Powers. HBV; OTPC (1923 ed.)
Chimney Sweeper, The ("A little black thing among the snow"). Blake. *Fr.* Songs of Experience. AtBAP; BoW; BWP; CABA; CBEP; EiCL; EiPP; EnL; EnLi-2 (1949 ed.); EnLit; EnPE; ERoP-1; ForPo; PAn; PoeP; PoIE; TDP; YAT
Chimney Sweeper, The ("When my mother died I was very young"). Blake. *Fr.* Songs of Innocence. AtBAP; BoW; BWP; CaFP; CBEP; CEP; CH; DiPo; EiCL; EiPP; EnPE; EnRP; ERoP-1; FosPo; ILP; PAn; PoeP; PoIE
Chimney-Tops. *Unknown.* BoTP
Chimneys, rank on rank, The. Evening. Richard Aldington. MoBrPo; SeCePo
Chimpanzee, The. Oliver Herford. FaBV; FiBHP; InP; LBN; NA
("Children, behold the chimpanzee.") CenHV
Chimpanzee, The/ Is a most embarrassing animal to see. Muriel Sly. FiBHP
Chin in, I doubt the praying mantis prays. The Chance. John Holmes. NePoAm-2
Chinatown Chant. Tom MacInnes. CaP
Chinese Ballad. William Empson. ToPo
Chinese Ballad. Li Chi, *ad. fr. Chinese by* William Empson. NoP
Chinese Banyan, The. William Meredith. NePoEA
Chinese Lullaby. Dorothy Henderson. GaP; GFA; OTPC (1946 ed.)
Chinese Nightingale, The. Vachel Lindsay. AmPP (3d ed.); HBMV; LiTM (rev. ed.); MAP; MAPA; MoAmPo; NePA; NP; OnSP
Chinese Nursery Rhyme, A. *Unknown, tr. fr. Chinese by* I. T. Headland. TVC
Chinese Poem Written in B.C. 718, A ("The K'e still ripples to its banks"). *Unknown, tr. fr. Chinese.* WePo
Chinese Poem Written B.C. 1121, A ("White clouds are in the sky"). *Unknown, tr. fr. Chinese.* WePo
Chinese Poems: Arthur Waley. "C. A. Fair." PeSA
Chinese sandmen,/ Wise and creepy. Chinese Lullaby. Dorothy Henderson. GaP; GFA; OTPC (1946 ed.)
Chinoiseries. Amy Lowell. AnAmPo; NP; PoRA (rev. ed.)
Chip on His Shoulder, A. *Unknown.* BLPA; WBLP
Chipeta. Eugene Field. PoOW
Chipeta's Ride. John W. Taylor. PoOW
Chipmunk, The. Millen Brand. NYTB
Chipmunk ("The chipmunk thinks I am a tree") Leigh Hanes. StaSt
Chipmunk. Marie de L. Welch. RePo
Chipmunk chewing the Chippendale. Exit, Pursued by a Bear. Ogden Nash. NYBP
Chipmunks jump, and. Valentine. Donald Hall. BoLP
Chipmunk's Song, The. Randall Jarrell. PDV
Chippewa Legend, A. James Russell Lowell. MPB
Chiquita. Bret Harte. AA; IHA; PFY
Chirrupy Cricket, The. Martha Banning Thomas. GFA; PCH
Chisel in hand stood a sculptor boy. Life-Sculpture [*or* Sculptors of Life]. George Washington Doane. BPLA; MaRV; OHFP; OQP; WBLP
Chiseler, The. Francis X. Maynard. JKCP (1955 ed.)
Chisholm Trail, The. *Unknown.* *See* Old Chisholm Trail, The.
Chivalry. "Æ." MoRP; ViBoPo
Chivalry at a Discount. Edward Fitzgerald. HBV
"Chkk! chkk!" hopper-grass. Confucius. *Fr.* Shao and the South. CTC
Chloe. Burns. GN; HBV; OTPC
Chloe. Charles Mordaunt, Earl of Peterborough. CEP; OBEC
Chloe. Pope. *Fr.* Moral Essays. AWP; JAWP; WBP
(Characters from the Satires: Chloe.) InPo
("Yet Cloe sure was form'd without a spot.") ErPo
Chloe. *Unknown.* UnTE
Chloe Divine. Thomas D'Urfey. HBV; LO; OBEV
Chloe found Amyntas lying. Rondelay [*or* Kiss Me, Dear]. Dryden. ALV; CavP; DiPo; MaPo; PAn; PeRV; SeCL; SeEP; UnTE; ViBoPo
Chloe, M.A. Mortimer Collins. BOHV
Chloe Resolved. John Hoadly. EiCL
Chloe, the contours of your bust. To Chloe. Earnest Albert Hooton. UnTE
Chloe, thou fliest me like a fawn. To Chloe. Horace, *tr. by* Goldwin Smith. OuHeWo
Chloe, why wish you that your years. To Chloe Who [for His Sake] Wished Herself Young Enough for Me. William Cartwright. EP; HBV; LiTB; LiTL; MePo; OBS; SeCL; SeEP; ViBoPo
Chloe, you shun me like a hind. To Chloe ("Vitas hinnuleo"). Horace, *tr. by* Austin Dobson. AWP; JAWP; WBP
Chloe's a Nymph in flowery groves. Chloe Divine. Thomas D'Urfey. HBV; LO; OBEV; UnTE
Chlora, come view my soul, and tell. *See* Clora, come view. . .

Chloride of Lime and Charcoal. Louis Zukofsky. CoPo
Chloris, *sels.* William Smith.
"Colin, my dear and most entire beloved," *dedication.* ReEn
(To the Most Excellent and Learned Shepherd, Colin Clout.) TuPP
"Feed, silly sheep, although your keeper pineth," III. Sonn; TuPP
"My love, I cannot thy rare beauties place," XVIII. InvP
(Sonnet.) EIL
"When I more large thy praises forth shall show," XLIV. Sonn; TuPP
"Whole showers of tears to Chloris I will pour," IV. Sonn; TuPP
Chloris a Constant Comfort. Henry Hughes. SeCL
Chloris and Hylas. Edmund Waller. SeCL
(Chloris and Hilas. Made to a Saraban.) SeCV-1
Chloris Farewell. Edmund Waller. *See* Song: "Chloris! farewell. I now must go."
Chloris, Forbear Awhile. Henry Bold. LO; SeCL
Chloris [*or* Cloris], I cannot say your eyes. To Cloris. Sir Charles Sedley. CEP; LO; PeRV
Chloris, I swear by all I ever swore. Lover's Play of Words. Martial. OnPM
Chloris in the Snow. William Strode. *See* On Chloris Walking in the Snow.
Chloris, it is not thy disdain. *See* Cloris, it is not thy disdaine.
Chloris made my heart to stop. A Winter Madrigal. Morris Bishop. InMe
Chloris, 'Tis Not in Your Power. Sir George Etherege. OBS
Chloris [*or* Cloris], when I to thee present. A Song. *Unknown.* OBS; SeCSL
Chloris, whilst thou and I were free. Sonnet. Charles Cotton. PeRV; ViBoPo
Chloris! yourself you so excel. To a Lady Singing a Song of His Own Composing. Edmund Waller. ReEn; SeCL; SeEP
Chocolate-Cream. E. V. Lucas. *Fr.* Counsel to Those That Eat. BOHV
Chocolate, pained, vaned, hysterical, box. The Hammer. Clark Coolidge. ANYP
Choice, The. Thomas Beedome. CavP; SeCL
Choice, The. Avis B. Christiansen. SoP
Choice, The. Hilary Corke. NYBP
Choice. Emily Dickinson. *See* Of all the souls that stand create.
Choice. Ellen Coit Elliott. OQP
Choice. John Farrar. BrR; SiSoSe
Choice, The. John Masefield. Lollingdon Downs, VIII. MoAB; MoBrPo
Choice. Angela Morgan. PoLF
Choice, The. John Norris. CavP
Choice, The. Dorothy Parker. BoLP
Choice, The. John Pomfret. CEP; EiCL; EiPP; OBEC; PoE; TOP
Sels.
"If Heaven the grateful liberty would give." PoFS; YAT
"Would bounteous Heaven one more indulge, I'd choose." LO
Choice, The. Dante Gabriel Rossetti. The House of Life, LXXI-LXXIII. ATP; BEL; EnL; EnLi-2; GTBS-P; MaVP; MyFE; OBVV; PoVP; TOP; ViBoPo; ViPo
"Eat thou and drink," LXXI. WHA
"Think thou and act," LXXIII. OBEV (new ed.); OHIP; WHA
Choice, The. Nahum Tate. MemP
Choice, A. Edward de Vere, Earl of Oxford. *See* Were I a King.
Choice, The. George Wither. OBEV
Choice, The. W. B. Yeats. CMoP; PoeP
Choice of Love, The. Marion Wilmshurst. SoP
Choice of the Cross, The. Dorothy L. Sayers. *Fr.* The Devil to Pay. MaRV
Choice of Weapons, A. Stanley Kunitz. LiTM (1970 ed.)
Choice soul, in whom, as in a glass, we see. The Doom of Beauty. Michelangelo. AWP; JAWP; LiTW; WBP
Choicest gifts at christenings, The. Gifts. Hazel Harper Harris. BiCB
Choir Boys, The. Heine, *tr. fr. German by* Ezra Pound. *Fr.* Die Heimkehr. LiTW
("Mutilated choir boys, The.") AWP
Choir Invisible, The. "George Eliot." *See* O May I Join the Choir Invisible.
Choir of bright beauties in spring did appear, A. The Lady's Song. Dryden. MBW-1; SeCeV
Choir of Day, The. Blake. *See* Nightingale and Flowers.
Choir of spirits on a cloud, A. William Baylebridge. *Fr.* Life's Testament. PoAu-1
Choir Practice. Ernest Crosby. AA
Choir-Boys on Christmas Eve. Louise Townsend Nicholl. TSW
Choirmaster's Burial, The. Thomas Hardy. DTC; MuSP
Choirs. George Rostrevor Hamilton. MuSP
Choirs of Heaven are tokened in a harp-string, The. The Counsels of O'Riordan, the Rann Maker. T. D. O'Bolger. AnIV
"Cholly" Blues, The, *with music.* *Unknown.* ABF
Chook, chook, chook, chook, chook. *Unknown.* OxNR
Choose. Verna Bishop. STF
Choose. Carl Sandburg. NP
Choose Life. Deuteronomy, XXX, Bible, *O.T.* TreFT
Choose me your Valentine. To His Mistress. Robert Herrick. ViBoPo
Choose Something like a Star. Robert Frost. AnNE; MoAB; MoAmPo (1950 ed.); NeMA; PoCh
Choose the darkest part o' the grove. Incantation to Oedipus [*or* A Spell]. Dryden. *Fr.* Oedipus. SiSw; WiR
Choose Thou for Me. Horatius Bonar. SoP
Choose You a Seat 'n Set Down, *with music.* *Unknown.* OuSiCo
Choose you this day whom you will serve. Choose. Verna Bishop. STF
Choosing. Coleman Barks. QAH
Choosing. Eleanor Farjeon. TiPo
Choosing a Homesite. Philip Booth. TPM
Choosing a Kitten. *Unknown.* StVeCh
Choosing a Mast. Roy Campbell. BoC; FaBoTw; GTBS-D; PeSA
Choosing a Name. Mary Lamb. HBV; OTPC (1923 ed.)
Choosing Coffins. Raymond Souster. MoCV
Choosing Shoes. ffrida Wolfe. BrR; SoPo; SUS; TiPo
Chop-Cherry. Robert Herrick. ALV; CBEP; EnLoPo; MyFE; SeEP; UnTE
Chopin in London. Philip Hobsbaum. *Fr.* Study in a Minor Key. MuSP
Chopin Prelude. Eleanour Norton. HBMV
Chopping Fire-Wood. Robert Pack. NePoEA-2
Chops Are Flyin. Stanley Crouch. NBP
Chopsticks. Yüan Mei, *tr. fr. Chinese by* Robert Kotewall and Norman L. Smith. FlW
Choral Ode: "Numberless are the world's wonders." Sophocles, *tr. fr. Greek by* Dudley Fitts *and* Robert Fitzgerald. *Fr.* Antigone. LiTW
Choral Poem "Land beloved of horsemen, fair, The." Sophocles, *tr. fr. Greek by* Robert Fitzgerald. *Fr.* Oedipus at Colonus. LiTW
Choral Symphony Conductor. Carol Coates. CaP
Chorale: "Often had I found her fair." A. D. Hope. ErPo; UnTE
Chorale for Autumn. Marya Zaturenska. NP
Chords knotted together like insane nouns, The. You (IV). Tom Clark. ANYP
Choric Song: "There is sweet music here that softer falls." Tennyson. *Fr.* The Lotos-Eaters. GTSL; LiTG; OuHeWo; WHA
(Choric Song of the Lotos-Eaters.) FaFP; GTBS-W; ViBoPo
(Song: "There is sweet music here.") OBNC
(Song of the Lotos-Eaters., OBEV
(There Is Sweet Music Here.) FaBV; HT
Choricos. Richard Aldington. HBMV; NP
Chorister in Avalon, A. Humbert Wolfe. BoPe
Choristers, The. Bliss Carman. ACV
Choros: "Give me your poppies." Hilda Doolittle ("H. D."). *Fr.* Morpheus. FaBoMo
Chorus: "After death, nothing is." Seneca, *tr. fr. Latin by* the Earl of Rochester. *Fr.* Troas, II. PeRV
Chorus: "Alas, with what tormenting fire." Robert Garnier, *tr. fr. French by* the Countess of Pembroke. *Fr.* Antonius. TuPP
(Of Death.) EIL
Chorus: "All, all of a piece throughout." Dryden. *See* All, All of a Piece Throughout.
Chorus: "All ye that handle harp and viol and pipe." Moses Hayyim Luzzatto of Padua, *tr. fr. Hebrew by* Nina Davis Salaman. *Fr.* Unto the Upright Praise. TrJP
Chorus: "And Pergamos." Euripides, *tr. fr. Greek by* Hilda Doolittle ("H. D."). *Fr.* Iphigenia in Aulis. AWP; LiTW

Chorus (continued)
Chorus: "Before the Beginning of years." Swinburne. *See* Before the Beginning of Years.
Chorus: "Behold what furies still." Samuel Daniel. *Fr.* Cleopatra. LoBV
Chorus: "Big Engines, The." Jack Kerouac. *Fr.* Mexico City Blues. NeAP
Chorus: "Climb at Court for me that will." Seneca, *tr. fr. Latin by* Andrew Marvell. *Fr.* Thyestes. OnPM
(Quiet Life, The.) LiTW
(Senec. Traged. ex Thyeste Chor. 2.) SeCV-1
Chorus: "Could I take me to some cavern for mine hiding." Euripides. *See* O for the Wings of a Dove.
Chorus: "Darkness has dawned in the East." Shelley. *Fr.* Hellas. EnRP
Chorus: "Doom is dark and deeper than any sea-dingle." W. H. Auden. *See* Doom is Dark.
Chorus: "Doth not our chiefest bliss then lie." Sidney Godolphin. LO
Chorus: "Essence of Existence, The." Jack Kerouac. *Fr.* Mexico City Blues. NeAP
Chorus: "Fair Salamis, the billow's roar." Sophocles. *Fr.* Ajax. AWP; JAWP; WBP
Chorus: "For this one thing above all I would be praised as a man." Sophocles, *tr. fr. Greek by* W. B. Yeats. *Fr.* Oedipus Rex. LiTW
Chorus: "Give away her gowns." Edna St. Vincent Millay. *Fr.* Memorial to D. C. NP
Chorus: "Glenn Miller and I were heroes." Jack Kerouac. *Fr.* Mexico City Blues. NeAP
Chorus: "God whose goodness filleth every clime, The." Racine. *Fr.* Athalie. CAW; WGRP
Chorus: "Got up and dressed up." Jack Kerouac. *Fr.* Mexico City Blues. NeAP
Chorus: "Great fortune is an hungry thing." Aeschylus, *tr. fr. Greek by* Sir Gilbert Murray. *Fr.* Agamemnon. AWP; JAWP; WBP
Chorus: "He is the Way." W. H. Auden. *Fr.* For the Time Being. AnFE
(He Is the Way.) EaLo; MaRV
Chorus: "Hail to the Headlong! the Headlong Ap-Headlong!" Thomas Love Peacock. *Fr.* Headlong Hall, *ch.* 13. OBRV; PeER
Chorus: "How dost thou wear and weary out thy days." Samuel Daniel. *Fr.* The Tragedie of Philotas. OBSC
Chorus: "If I drink water while this doth last." Thomas Love Peacock. *Fr.* Crotchet Castle, *ch.* 6. ViBoPo
Chorus: "In an old house there is always listening." T. S. Eliot. *Fr.* The Family Reunion. MWA-2
Chorus: "In wonder and time-mists." Lord De Tabley. *Fr.* Philoctetes. PoVP
Chorus: "It is hard for those who have never known persecution." T. S. Eliot. *Fr.* The Rock, Chorus VI. LiTM
Chorus: Kings of Troy, The. Euripides, *tr. fr. Greek by* George Allen. *Fr.* Andromache. WaaP
Chorus: "Land of running horses, fair, The." Sophocles, *tr. fr. Greek by* Robert Fitzgerald. *Fr.* Oedipus at Colonus. SiSw
Chorus: "Life may change, but it may fly not." Shelley. *Fr.* Hellas. EnRP; EPN
Chorus: "Life of Life! thy lips enkindle." Shelley. *See* Life of Life.
Chorus: Love Song. Euripides, *tr. fr. Greek by* Shelley. AWP; JAWP; WBP
Chorus: "Love's multitudinous boneyard." Jack Kerouac. *Fr.* Mexico City Blues. NeAP
Chorus: "Nobody knows the other side." Jack Kerouac. *Fr.* Mexico City Blues. NeAP
Chorus: "Oh, may my constant feet not fail." Sophocles, *tr. fr. Greek by* Robert Whitelaw. *Fr.* Oedipus Rex. WGRP
Chorus: "O Slavery! thou frost of the world's prime." Shelley. *Fr.* Hellas. PoFr
Chorus: "On wearisome condition of humanity!" Fulke Greville. *See* Chorus Sacerdotum. *Fr.* Mustapha.
Chorus: "O Zeus our king and Night our friend." Aeschylus, *tr. fr. Greek by* Louis MacNeice. *Fr.* Agamemnon. LiTW
Chorus: "Old Man Mose." Jack Kerouac. *Fr.* Mexico City Blues. NeAP
Chorus: "Only awake to Universal Mind." Jack Kerouac. *Fr.* Mexico City Blues. NeAP
Chorus: "Praised be man, he is existing in milk." Jack Kerouac. *Fr.* Mexico City Blues. NeAP
Chorus: "Saints, I give myself up to thee." Jack Kerouac. *Fr.* Mexico City Blues. NeAP
Chorus: "Since you have come thus far." C. Day Lewis. *Fr.* Noah and the Waters. OAEP (2d ed.)
Chorus: "Son of Man, behold with thine eyes, and hear with thine ears." T. S. Eliot. *Fr.* The Rock. PoDB
Chorus: "Spring all the Graces of the age." Ben Jonson. *Fr.* Neptune's Triumph. OBS; SeCL
Chorus: "Sweet are the ways of death to weary feet. Lord De Tabley. *Fr.* Medea. NBM; OBEV (new ed.); OBVV
Chorus: "Then thus we have beheld." Samuel Daniel. *Fr.* Cleopatra. OBSC
Chorus: "Throned are the gods and in. Lord De Tabley. *Fr.* Philoctetes. NBM
Chorus: "Tis not enough for one that is a wife." Lady Elizabeth Carew. *Fr.* Mariam. LiTL
Chorus: "To throw away the key and walk away." W. H. Auden. *Fr.* Paid on Both Sides. MoBrPo
(Walking Tour, The.) CMoP
Chorus: "Upward and back to their fountains the sacred rivers are stealing." Euripides, *tr. fr. Greek by* Arthur S. Way. PoFr
Chorus: "Vain man, born to no happiness." Sidney Godolphin. LoBV
Chorus: "Void that's highly embraceable, The. Jack Kerouac. *Fr.* Mexico City Blues. NeAP
Chorus: "We do not like to look out of the same window." T. S. Eliot. *Fr.* The Family Reunion. MWA-2
Chorus: "We have seen thee, O love." Swinburne. *See* We Have Seen Thee, O Love.
Chorus: "What man is he that yearneth." Sophocles. *See* Old Age.
Chorus: "Wheel of the quivering meat, The." Jack Kerouac. *Fr.* Mexico City Blues. NeAP
Chorus: "When love has passed its limits." Euripides, *tr. fr. Greek by* Frederic Prokosch. *Fr.* Medea. LiTW
Chorus: "When the hounds of spring are on winter's traces." Swinburne. *See* When the Hounds of Spring.
Chorus. "Who hath given man speech?" Swinburne. *Fr.* Atalanta in Calydon. MaVP
(Choruses from "Atalanta in Calydon.") ViBoPo
Chorus: "Word of the Lord came unto me, The." T. S. Eliot. *Fr.* The Rock. LiTB
Chorus: "World's great age begins anew, The." Shelley. *Fr.* Hellas. AtBAP; ERoP-2; ExPo; FaBoEn; HBV; InPo; LoBV; MyFE; OAEP; PoE; PoEL-4; SeCeV; TOP; WoL
(Choruses from "Hellas."). EnRP
(Final Chorus.) BEL; BoLiVe; EnLiT; OBRV; PoFS; SeCePo
(Hellas.) ChTr; EPN; OBEV; ShBV-4
(New World, A.) TrGrPo
(World's Great Age Begins Anew, The.) AWP; FiP; JAWP; NoP; PoIE; TreFS; WBP
Chorus: "Worlds on worlds are rolling ever." Shelley. *Fr.* Hellas. EnRP; OAEP
(Worlds on Worlds Are Rolling Ever.) NoP; PoFS
"Power from the unknown God, A," *sel.* StJW
Chorus: "Yea, the coneys are scared by the thud of hoofs." Thomas Hardy. *See* Before Waterloo.
Chorus: "You have seen the house built, you have seen it adorned." T. S. Eliot. *Fr.* The Rock. PoDB
Chorus for Easter. David Morton. MaRV
Chorus for Refusal. Margaret Marks. MAP
Chorus for Survival, *sel.* Horace Gregory.
"Ask no return for love that's given." CMoP; TwAmPo
(Ask No Return.) MoAmPo; TrGrPo
"Tell us that love/ returns." CMoP
"Waking from sleep we heard the Greats Lakes' tide." AtBAP
Chorus from a Tragedy. Leonard Bacon. ViBoPo
Chorus from "Atalanta in Calydon." Swinburne. *See* Atalanta in Calydon.
Chorus from "Hellas." Shelley. *See* Chorus: "World's great age begins anew, The."
Chorus of Angels. Cardinal Newman. *See* Praise to the Holiest in the Height.
Chorus of Batavian Women. Joost van den Vondel, *tr fr. Dutch by* Sir John Bowring. WoL
Chorus of Birds. Aristophanes, *tr. fr Greek by* Swinburne.

Fr. The Birds. AWP; JAWP; WBP; WoL, *tr. by* Benjamin Bickley Rogers
(Grand Chorus of Birds.) PoEL-5
Chorus of Frogs, The. Ann Hawkshaw. OTPC
Chorus of Satyrs, Driving Their Goats. Euripides, *tr. fr. Greek by* Shelley. *Fr.* The Cyclops. AWP; JAWP; WBP
Chorus of Sirens. George Darley. *See* Mermaiden's Vesper Hymn, The.
Chorus of Spirits. George Darley. *Fr.* Sylvia; or, The May Queen. OnYI; VA
Chorus of Spirits: "From unremembered ages we." Shelley. *Fr.* Prometheus Unbound. LoBV
Chorus of the Clouds. Aristophanes. *See* Song of the Clouds.
Chorus of the Elements. Cardinal Newman. *See* Elements, The.
Chorus of the Furies ("Look, sisters, look!"). Aeschylus, *tr. fr. Greek by* John Stuart Blackie. *Fr.* Eumenides. WoL
Chorus of the Unborn. Nelly Sachs, *tr. fr. German by* Ruth Mead *and* Matthew Mead. NYBP
Chorus of the Years. Thomas Hardy. *See* Before Waterloo.
Chorus of Women. Aristophanes. *See* Women Speak Out in Defense of Themselves, The.
Chorus Primus: Wise Counsellors. Fulke Greville. *Fr.* Mustapha. OBS
Chorus Quintus: Tartarorum. Fulke Greville. *Fr.* Mustapha. OBS
Chorus Sacerdotum. Fulke Greville. *Fr.* Mustapha. ATP (1935 ed.); FaBoEn; InvP; MePo; OBS; PoEL-1; SeCePo; SiCE; TuPP
(Chorus: "O wearisome condition of humanity!") ViBoPo
(O Wearisome Condition.) CBEP; CBV
(O Wearisome Condition of Humanity.) EG; LiTB; PoIE (1970 ed.); SeCeV
Chorus Tertius: Of Time: Eternitie. Fulke Greville. *Fr.* Mustapha. OBS
Choruses from "Atalanta in Calydon." Swinburne. *See* Atalanta in Calydon.
Chosen. Catherine Baird. SoP
Chosen. W. B. Yeats. CMoP
Chosen Lessons. Frances Ridley Havergal. SoP
Chosen of God. Stefan Zweig, *tr. fr. German by* Eden *and* Cedar Paul. *Fr.* Jeremiah. TrJP
Chosen People, The. W. N. Ewer. ALV; SiTL
(Epigram: "How odd/ Of God.") OtMeF
Chou and the South, *sel.* Confucius, *tr. fr. Chinese by* Ezra Pound.
"In the South be drooping trees." CTC
Choucoune. Oswald Durand, *tr. fr. French by* Edna Worthley Underwood. PoNe
Chough, The. James Reaney. OBCV; PeCV
Chough. Rex Warner. PoRA (rev. ed.)
Chough and crow to roost are gone, The. The Outlaw's Song [*or* Song of the Outlaws]. Joanna Baillie. *Fr.* Orra OBEV; OBRV; OTPC; PoFr
Chough, said a dictionary, The. The Chough. James Reaney. OBCV; PeCV
Choyce, The. Thomas Beedome. *See* Choice, The.
Chrismus on the Plantation. Paul Laurence Dunbar. IHA
Christ. Robert Jones Burdette. *Fr.* My Guide. BePJ
Christ, *sels.* Cynewulf, *tr. fr. Anglo-Saxon.*
Christ Tells of His Passion. PoLi
Heaven. PoLi
Last Judgment, The, *tr. by* Charles W. Kennedy. AnOE
(Human Race Comes to Be Judged, The, *diff. tr.*) PoLi
Maiden Ring-adorned, A, *tr. by* Mother Margaret Williams. ISi; PoLi, *shorter sel.*
Voyage of Life, The, *tr. by* Charles W. Kennedy. AnOE
("Our Life is likest a long sea-voyage," *tr. by* J. Duncan Spaeth.) EnLi-1, *br. sel.*
Christ. Giles Fletcher. *See* Excellency of Christ.
Christ. Theodore Holmes. CoPo
Christ, The. John Oxenham. TRV
Christ 1, *sels.* *Unknown*, *tr. fr. Anglo-Saxon by* Charles W. Kennedy. AnOE
Advent Lyrics.
"Bless earth with Thine Advent, O Saviour Christ!" VIII.
"Hail, O most worthy in all the world!" IX.
"O holy Jerusalem, Vision of peace," III.
". . . to the King./ Thou art the-wall stone the workers rejected," I.
Christ ("Christ for sickness"). *Unknown.* BePJ
Christ, The. Edgar William Whan. ChIP
Christ,/ Grant us this boon. A Prayer for Brotherhood. John S. Hoyland. MaRV
Christ All-sufficient. Frederic W. H. Myers. *Fr.* Saint Paul. MaRV
("Christ, I am Christ's, and let the name suffice you.") ChIP; TRV
Christ Alone. Shel Helsley. STF
Christ Alone. Theodore Monod. *See* None of Self and All of Thee.
Christ and His Mother at the Cross. Jacopone da Todi, *tr. fr. Italian by* Thomas Walsh. CAW
Christ and his Mother, heavenly maid. Founder's Day. Robert Bridges. OBVV
Christ and Satan, *sels.* Cædmon (?), *tr. fr. Anglo-Saxon.*
Lamentations of the Fallen Angels, *tr. by* Charles W. Kennedy. AnOE
Christ and the Common Day. Marguerite Wilkinson. BePJ
Christ and the Little Ones. Julia Gill. BLPA
Christ and the Mourners. Katherine E. Conway. ChIP; OQP
Christ and the Pagan. John Banister Tabb. CAW; JKCP
Christ and the Winds. John Banister Tabb. StJW
Christ—and We. Annie Johnson Flint. *See* World's Bible, The.
Christ and We. Robert Herrick. ChIP
(Christ's Incarnation.) StJW
Christ at the Door. Joseph Grigg. BePJ; SoP
Christ bears a thousand crosses now. Quatrain. Charles G. Blanden. ChIP; PGD
Christ before Pilate. George Herbert Clarke. StJW
Christ bids the dumbe tongue speake, it speakes, the sound. The Dumbe Healed, and the People Enjoyned Silence. Richard Crashaw. MaMe
Christ Brought Home. *Unknown.* PoLi
Christ, by dark clouds of worldliness concealed. Prayer before Meat. Una W. Harsen. ChIP; TrPWD
Christ, by Thine own darkened hour. Christ the Comrade. Padraic Colum. CAW; JKCP
Christ Calls Man Home. *Unknown.* MeEL
Christ came to earth again, and made his plea. The Second Coming. Stanton A. Coblentz. ChIP
Christ Can Give Thee Heart. Christina Rossetti. ChIP
Christ Candle, The. Kate Louise Brown. *See* Christmas Candle, The.
Christ-Child, The. G. K. Chesterton. *See* Christmas Carol, A: "Christ-Child lay on Mary's lap, The."
Christ-Child, The. Gregory of Narek, *tr. fr. Armenian by* Alice Stone Blackwell. CAW
Christ-Child, The. Laura Spencer Portor. StJW
(Christ Child's Christmas, The.) PEDC
Christ Child. Henry Treece. MaRV
Christ-Child Day in Australia, A. Ethel Turner. BoAu
Christ-child lay in the ox's stall, The. Ox and Donkey's Carol. Sister Maris Stella. PoRL
Christ child lay on Mary's lap, The. A Christmas Carol [*or* The Christ-Child]. G. K. Chesterton. BoTP; ChBR; ChrBoLe; FaFP; GaP; GoBC; HBV; HBVY; MaRV; OHIP; PoRL; StJW; SUS; TiPo (1952 ed.); WHL
Christ Child's Christmas, The. Laura Spencer Portor. *See* Christ-Child, The.
Christ! Christ! Christ! That the World. Kenneth Patchen. ToPo
Christ Church Bells. *At. to* Henry Aldrich. CBEP; SeCL
Christ Church Meadows, Oxford. Donald Hall. NYBP
Christ claims our help in many a strange disguise. The Man of Sorrows. *Unknown.* ChIP; MaRV; OQP; PGD
Christ Climbed Down. Lawrence Ferlinghetti. MoRP
Christ comes to mind and comes across the mind. Burns Singer. *Fr.* Sonnets for a Dying Man. NePoEA-2
Christ Complains to Sinners. *Unknown.* MeEL
Christ-Cross Rhyme, A. Robert Stephen Hawker. ACP (1926 ed.); CAW; GoBC; StJW
Christ Crucified. Richard Crashaw. GoBC; OBEV; PoRL
Christ for a dream was given from the dead. A Christmas Night. John Drinkwater. StJW
Christ for Everything ("Christ for life, and Christ for living"). R. A. Belsham. STF
Christ for sickness, Christ for health. Christ. *Unknown.* BePJ

Christ, forgive us! Except Ye Repent. J. Franklin Pineo. ChIP
Christ gave a yoke, a sword, a cross. Gifts. Chauncey R. Piety. PGD
Christ God who savest man, save most. Count Gismond. Robert Browning. BEL; MBW-2; PoVP; ViPP
Christ God's red shadow hangs upon the wall. Christmas in Black Rock. Robert Lowell. ToPo
Christ has no hands but our hands. The World's Bible [*or* Jesus Christ—and We]. Annie Johnson Flint. FaChP; MaRV; OQP; SoP; STF; TRV
Christ Has Risen. "Susan Coolidge." ChIP
Christ hath a garden walled around. Isaac Watts. FaBoCh; LoGBV
Christ His Cross shall be my speed! A Christ-Cross Rhyme. Robert Stephen Hawker. ACP (1926 ed.); CAW; GoBC; StJW
Christ Honored, Loved, Exalted. *Unknown. See* Not I.
Christ, I am Christ's and let the name suffice you. Christ All-sufficient. Frederic W. H. Myers. *Fr.* Saint Paul. ChIP; MaRV; TRV
Christ, I have walked around your erection. Reality! Reality! What Is It? Richard Eberhart. FiMAP
Christ, I was twelve. Jon Anderson. *Fr.* The Summer Deaths. YAP
Christ in Introspect. Charlotte Brontë. MaRV
Christ in the Andes. Carl John Bostelmann. ChIP
Christ in the City. Frank Mason North. MaRV
(City, The.) WGRP
("Where cross the crowded ways of life.") SoP
Christ in the Clay-Pit. Jack Clemo. GTBS-P
Christ in the Hospital. Roy Campbell. BoC
Christ in the Street. Jay G. Sigmund. ChIP; SoP
Christ in the Tempest. Anatolius. *See* Fierce Was the Wild Billow.
Christ in the Universe. Alice Meynell. ACP; CAW; GoBC; HBMV; JKCP; MemP, *abr.*; MoBrPo; StJW
(Or His Bestowals There.) BoC
Christ in Woolworth's. Teresa Hooley. ChIP; StJW
Christ in You. *Unknown.* STF
Christ Inviting Sinners to His Grace, *sel.* Henry Alline.
"Amazing sight, the Saviour Stands," *fr.* Bk. II, Hymn XXXVII. CaP
Christ Is All. Horatius Bonar. BePJ
Christ is born! Tell forth His fame! Tell Forth His Fame. *Unknown.* BePJ
Christ Is Coming. W. Macomber. STF
Christ Is Coming. Heyman Wreford. BePJ
Christ Is Crucified Anew. John Richard Moreland. ChIP; MaRV; PGD
Christ Is Here. Robert Lowell. BePJ
Christ is on the throne. Fears. Henry W. Frost. SoP
Christ Is Risen! Mrs. D. H. Dugan. BLRP
Christ Is Risen! Christoph Christian Sturm. BePJ
"Christ is risen, Christ is risen!" the glad voices glibly say. The Stone. Kenneth W. Porter. ChIP
Christ is the Fact of facts, the Bible's Theme. The Greatest Person in the Universe. Daniel L. Marsh. BLRP
Christ Jesus was born in a stable. A Christmas Thought. Mrs. Frank A. Breck. BePJ
Christ keep the Hollow Land. Song. William Morris. *Fr.* The Hollow Land. AtBAP; ChTr; NBM; PoEL-5; ThWaDe
Christ leads me through no darker rooms. Death. Richard Baxter. FaChP
Christ made a trance on Friday view. Good Friday. *Unknown.* ChTr
Christ maketh to man a fair present. Christ's Gift to Man. *Unknown.* ACP
Christ maketh to man a fair present. Love Unlike Love. *Unknown.* MeEL
Christ Militant, The. Thomas Curtis Clark. ChIP
Christ, My Beloved. William Baldwin. ElL; ELP; OxBoCh
(Spouse to the Beloved, The.) OBSC
Christ, My Life. Margaret J. Lucas. SoP
Christ, My Salvation ("Christ, my Lord is my salvation"). Eva Gray. STF
Christ never asks of us such busy labor. Dwell in Stillness. *Unknown.* SoP
Christ of Common Folks, The. George T. Liddell. OQP
Christ of Everywhere. Henry van Dyke. MaRV
Christ of God, The. Russell E. Kauffman. BePJ
Christ of His gentleness. In the Wilderness. Robert Graves. BoC; CBV; CH; GTBS-D; MoAB; MoBrPo; SeCePo; ShBV-3
Christ of Judea, look thou in my heart! Richard Watson Gilder. *Fr.* Credo. TrPWD
Christ of the Andes, The. Florence Earle Coates. StJW
Christ of the Andes, The. Edwin Markham. PEDC; PoRL
"O Christ of Olivet, you hushed the wars," *sel.* TrPWD
"Christ of the Andes," Christ of Everywhere. Christ of Everywhere. Henry van Dyke. MaRV
Christ of the council chamber. The Ageless Christ. B. L. Byer. BePJ
Christ of the glowing heart and golden speech. The Final Armistice. Frank B. Cowgill. OQP
Christ of the World's Highway, The. Dorothy Clarke Wilson. MaRV
Christ of Today, The. Thomas Curtis Clark. SoP
Christ on Madison Street. Raymond Kresensky. ChIP
Christ Our All in All, *sel.* Christina Rossetti.
Lord Carry Me. SoP
Christ Our Contemporary. William Charles Braithwaite. MaRV
Christ Our Example in Suffering. James Montgomery. *See* Go to Dark Gethsemane.
Christ Our Lord. George Herbert. *See* Love ("Love bade me welcome, yet my soul drew back").
Christ placed all rest, and had no resting place. Wondrous Love. Countess of Pembroke. BePJ
Christ Quiets the Tempest. Caelius Sedulius, *tr. fr. Latin by* George Sigerson. *Fr.* Carmen Paschale. OnYI
Christ Speaks. Gerard Manley Hopkins. *See* To Him Who Ever Thought with Love of Me.
Christ Speaks. Wade Oliver. MaRV
Christ Supreme. Carlton Buck. SoP
Christ Tells of His Passion. Cynewulf. *Fr.* Christ. PoLi
Christ the Answer. Richard Watson Gilder, *also at. to* George Macdonald. *See* Doubter, The.
Christ the Carpenter. Leslie L. Haskin. BePJ
Christ the Comrade. Padraic Colum. CAW; JKCP
Christ, the Conqueror, *abr.* Aaron Crossley Hobart Seymour, *wr. at. to* Henry Foster Burder. BePJ
Christ the Consoler. Henry W. Baker. BePJ
Christ the Corner Stone. *Unknown, tr. by* John Chandler. SoP
Christ the dew in the clod. Johnny Appleseed's Hymn to the Sun. Vachel Lindsay. MoRP
Christ, the Good Physician. Charles Wesley. BePJ
Christ the Lord is risen again. Resurrection Hymn. Michael Weiss. BePJ
Christ the Lord Is Risen To-Day. Charles Wesley. *See* Easter Hymn.
Christ the Lord is risen today. Victimae Paschali [Laudes]. Wipo, *tr. fr. Latin.* CAW; WHL
"Christ the Lord is risen today," sons of men and angels say. Easter Hymn [*or* For Easter-Day]. Charles Wesley. BePJ; CEP; DD; HH; MaRV; OHIP; SoP; TRV
Christ the Man. W. H. Davies. MaRV; WGRP
Christ, the Way. George Washington Doane. BePJ
(Way, the Truth, the Life, The.) MaRV
Christ, there is a swarm of bees outside. A Charm for Bees. *Unknown.* CAW
Christ! These are her angels. The Unicorn and The Lady. Jean Garrigue. NYBP
Christ to His Spouse. William Baldwin. ElL; OxBoCh
[Beloved to the Spouse, The.) OBSC
Christ to the Sufferer. *Unknown. Fr.* Andreas. PoLi
Christ to the young man said: "Yet one thing more." Hymn—for My Brother's Ordination. Longfellow. SoP
Christ to Thomas. Richard Crashaw. StJW
Christ took our nature on Him, not that He. Christ and We [*or* Christ's Incarnation]. Robert Herrick. ChIP; StJW
Christ Unconquered, *sel.* Arthur J. Little.
Invocation: "Mother of God, mother of man reborn," *fr.* Bk. IX. ISi
Christ Walking on the Water. W. R. Rodgers. AnIL; MoAB; OxBI
Christ Walks in This Infernal District Too. Malcolm Lowry. MoCV
Christ was born on Christmas Day. Christmas Carol. *At. to* Thomas Helmore. OHIP

Christ was no prisoner of time. No Prisoner of Time. William H. Hudnut, Jr. ChIP
Christ washed the feet of Judas! The Feet of Judas. George Marion McClellan. BANP; PoNe
Christ, when a Child, a garden made. A Legend. Peter Ilich Tchaikovsky, *tr. fr. Russian by* Nathan Haskell Dole. ChIP; MaRV; OHIP
Christ when He Died. Christ's Victory. Richard Crashaw. MaRV; StJW
Christ Whose Glory Fills the Skies. Charles Wesley. *See* Morning Hymn, A.
Christ will prove the true attraction. Attraction. *Unknown.* STF
Christ with me, Christ before me, Christ behind me. Phyllis Garlick. *Fr.* St. Patrick. TRV
Christ wow/ now I get. Insight. Lionel Kearns. PeCV (1967 ed.)
Christabel. Samuel Taylor Coleridge. BEL; CoBE; EnL; EnLi-2; EnLit; EnRP; EPN; ERoP-1; GoTL; MBW-2; MERP; OAEP; TOP; WHA
Sels.
"Alas! they had been friends in youth", *fr.* Pt. II. LO; OBRV
(Broken Friendship.) TreFT
(Friendship, *abr.*) MCCG
(Scars Remaning, The.). OBNC
Christabel, Pt. I. CH, *ll.* 1-65; FiP; OBRV; ShBV-3
("'Tis the middle of night by the castle clock.") SeCePo
Little Child, a Limber Elf, A, *fr.* Pt. II. LoBV; ViBoPo
"Lovely lady, Christabel, The," *fr.* Pt. I. LO
Christendom. Thomas Traherne. PoEL-2
"Things native sweetly grew," *sel.* FaBoEn
Christening, The. Walter de la Mare. BiCB
Christening, The. A. A. Milne. BiCB
Christening-Day Wishes for My God-Child, Grace Lane Berkley II. Robert P. Tristram Coffin. BiCB
Christening Remembered, A. Vernon Watkins. FaBoMo
Christian, A. Thomas Russell Ybarra. *See* Christian Is a Man Who Feels, A.
Christian, be up before the end of day. Epistle. Robert Nathan. MaRV
Christian Camp, The. Artemisia E. Strout. SoP
Christian, Dost Thou See Them? St. Andrew of Crete, *tr. fr. Greek by* John Mason Neale. MaRV
Christian Ethics, *sels.* Thomas Traherne.
"All music, sauces, feasts, delights and pleasures." UnS
Contentment Is a Sleepy Thing. OxBoCh
For Man to Act. OxBoCh
Mankind Is Sick. OxBoCh
Christian Freedom. George Matheson. *See* Christ's Bondservant.
Christian Herald, The. Bourne H. Draper. SoP
Christian Home, The. Gail Brooks Burket. SoP
Christian Is a Man Who Feels, A. Thomas Russell Ybarra. WhC
(Christian, A.) SiTL
Christian Life, The. Samuel Longfellow. SoP; WGRP
Christian Life, The. *Unknown.* SoP
Christian, like his Lord of old, The. My Friend. *Unknown.* SoP
Christian Militant, The. Robert Herrick. HoPM
Christian Mother, A. Phyllis E. Parlett. SoP
Christian Mother's Love, A. Raymond H. Crawford. SoP
Christian Paradox, The. Walter Chalmers Smith. MaRV
Christian Paradox. *Unknown.* MaRV; SoP
Christian Pilgrim's Hymn, The. William Williams, *tr. fr. Welsh by* Peter Williams, *ad. by* John Keble. SoP; WGRP
(Arglwydd Arwain.) PrWP
(Divine Hand, The, *much abr.*) BLRP
Christian, rise, and act thy creed. Rise [*or* Laborare Est Orare]. Francis Albert Rollo Russell. MaRV; SoP
Christian, seek not yet repose. Watch and Pray. Charlotte Elliott. SoP; STF
Christian Soldier, The. G. A. Studdert-Kennedy. *See* Suffering God, The.
Christian Soul. Louise Betts Edwards. SoP
Christian Year, The, *sel.* John Keble.
Who Runs May Read. SoP; VA
"There is a book, who runs may read," 1 *st.* FaChP
Christian's "Good-Night," The. Sarah Doudney. BLPA
Christian's New-Year Prayer, The, *sel.* Ella Wheeler Wilcox.
"If my vain soul needs blows and bitter losses." TrPWD
Christians Reply to the Phylosopher, The. Sir William Davenant. MeLP
Life and Death, *sel.* BOC; OBS
Christian's Testimony, A. *Unknown.* SoP
Christian's Victory—Triumph. J. Haskell. SoP
Christians were on the earth ere Christ was born. An Early Christian. Robert Barnabas Brough. OBVV
Christie's Portrait. Gerald Massey. VA
Christina. Louis MacNeice. OxBI
Christine. John Hay. AA
Christmas. Margaret Avison. TwCaPo
Christmas. John Betjeman. BoC; POTi; WePo
Christmas. Bryant. ChIP; MaRV
(Holy Star, The.) BePJ; SoP
Christmas. Marchette Chute. BrR; ChBR; SiSoSe
Christmas. Mary Mapes Dodge. BiCB
Christmas. George Herbert. MaMe; OxBoCh; SCEP-1; SeCV-1
Shall I Be Silent? *sel.* SoP; TRV
Christmas. Gertrude von Le Fort, *tr. fr. German by* Margaret Chanler. ISi
Christmas. Catherine Parmenter. DD
Christmas. Elizabeth Stanton Rice. StJW
Christmas. Sir Walter Scott. *See* Christmas in the Olden Time.
Christmas. Shakespeare. *See* Gracious Time, The.
Christmas. Betty Scott Stam. BePJ
Christmas. Nahum Tate. *See* While Shepherds Watched Their Flocks by Night.
Christmas. Henry Timrod. MAmP
Christmas ("An azure sky,/ All star bestrewn"). *Unknown.* BoTP
Christmas. Edward Hilton Young. StJW; TSW
(Boy Was Born at Bethlehem, A.) MaRV
Christmas Amnesty. Edith Lovejoy Pierce. PGD
Christmas and Common Birth. Anne Ridler. FaBoTw
Christmas and Ireland. Lionel Johnson. JKCP
Christmas Antiphon[e], A. Swinburne. ChIP, 2 *sts.*; PGD, 2 *sts.*; TrPWD, *abr.*; TRV, *abr.*
(Peace-Giver, The.) MaRV; OTPC (1946 ed.)
Christmas at Babbitt's. Henry Hallam Tweedy. MaRV; TRV
Christmas at Freelands. James Stephens. ILP
Christmas at Indian Point. Edgar Lee Masters. NP
Christmas at Melrose. Leslie Pinckney Hill. BANP
Christmas at Sea. Robert Louis Stevenson. BBV (1951 ed.); BrPo; CH; EtS; FaBoBe; FaBV; HBV; MCCG; OBVV; OTPC (1946 ed.); PeVV; PoVP; ShBV-2; StaSt; StPo; YAT
Christmas Bells. George Cooper. HH; PEDC
Christmas Bells. Longfellow. AmePo; BLRP; ChIP, *abr.*; DD; FaFP; FaPON; GoTP; HBV; HBVY; HH; MaRV; OQP; PGD, *abr.*; PoRL; RePo; SoP; TreFT; WBLP
(I Heard the Bells on Christmas Day.) NeHB; PoSC
Christmas Bells. Alice Mortenson. BePJ
Christmas Bells. Tennyson. *See* in Memoriam A. H. H.: "Time draws near the birth of Christ, The."
Christmas bells are ringing sweetly. Christmas Bells. Alice Mortenson. BePJ
Christmas Birthday. Grace Ellen Glaubitz. BiCB; SiSoSe
Christmas Blessing. Franklin D. Elmer, Jr. ChIP
Christmas Brownie. Rowena Bennett. ChBR
Christmas cakes. Birthday Cake. Ivy O. Eastwick. BiCB
Christmas Candle, The. Kate Louise Brown. PoRL; SoPo
(Christ Candle.) OTPC (1946 ed.)
Christmas Carol, A: "Angel told Mary, An." Harry Behn. BiCB
Christmas Carol: "As Joseph was a-walking." *Unknown. See* As Joseph Was a-Walking.
Christmas Carol, A: "Before the paling of the stars." Christina Rossetti. *See* Before the Paling of the Stars.
Christmas Carol, A: "Borys hede that we bryng here, The." *Unknown. See* Borys Hede That We Bryng. . .
Christmas Carol, A: "Christ-child lay on Mary's lap, The." G. K. Chesterton. BoTP; ChBR; ChrBoLe; FaFP; GaP; GoBC; HBV; HBVY; MaRV; OHIP; PoRL; StJW; SUS; TiPo (1952 ed.)
(Christ-Child, The, *abr.*) WHL
Christmas Carol: "Christ was born on Christmas day." *At. to* Thomas Helmore. OHIP
Christmas Carol: "Earth has grown old with its burden of care, The." Phillips Brooks. HH; MaRV; PEDC
Christmas Carol, A: "Everywhere, everywhere Christmas tonight." Phillips Brooks. OHIP; PCH, *st.* 1; SoPo

Christmas (continued)
(Christmas Everywhere.) FaFP; GoTP; MaRV
(Everywhere, Everywhere Christmas Tonight.) HH; OTPC; PoRL; SoP
Christmas Everywhere, *sel.* BLRP; NeHB; OHFP; WBLP
Christmas Carol: "From the starry heav'ns descending." J. R. Newell. BLRP
Christmas Carol: "God bless the master of this house." *Unknown.* BoTP; BrR; ChBR; OHIP; OxNR; RePo; SiSoSe; StVeCh; TiPo
(Good-Bye, *with music.*) YaCaBo
(Grace, A.) MoShBr
Christmas Carol, A: "Holly wreath that now, The." Fred Cogswell. ACV
Christmas Carol, A: "In the bleak mid-winter." Christina Rossetti. ChTr; OHIP; RG
(In the Bleak Mid-winter.) BoC; OxBoCh; SoP, *abr*; StJW; SUS; TRV, *abr.*
(What Can I Give Him? *abr.*) ThGO
My Gift, *st.* 5. BrR; ChBR; FaPON; MaRV; OTPC (1946 ed.); SiSoSe
(Birthday Gift, A.) PRWS
("What can I give Him?") BiCB; FaChP
Christmas Carol: "It came upon the midnight clear." Edmund Hamilton Sears. *See* It Came upon the Midnight Clear.
Christmas Carol: "Kings they came from out the south, The." Sara Teasdale. ChrBoLe; StJW
Christmas Carol, A: "Lacking samite and sable." May Probyn. ACP; CAW; GoBC; HBMV; ISi; OBVV
Christmas Carol: "Land grew bright in a single flower, The." Sister Francisca Josefa del Castillo, *tr. fr. Spanish by* Thomas Walsh. CAW
Christmas Carol, A: "Night in the far Judean land." Mary A. O'Reilly. JKCP
Christmas Carol, A: "Shepherds had an Angel, The." Christina Rossetti. *See* Shepherds Had an Angel, The.
Christmas Carol, A: "Shepherds went their hasty way, The." Samuel Taylor Coleridge. ISi; OxBoCh; SoP
(Shepherds, The.) StJW
Christmas Carol, A: "So, now is [*or* has] come our joyfullest [*or* joyful] feast." George Wither. OBS; SeEP; UnPo (1st ed.); ViBoPo
(Our Joyful Feast.) ChBR; OHIP; SiSoSe
Christmas Carol, A: "Star that shone on Bethlehem, shine on London city." Gilbert Thomas. MoRP
Christmas Carol, A: "There's a song in the air!" Josiah Gilbert Holland. AA; AmePo; DD; HBVY; RG
(There's a Song in the Air!) ChIP; FaChP; MaRV; SoP; TRV
Christmas Carol, A: "Three damsels in the queen's chamber." Swinburne. StJW
Christmas Carol: "Three outas from the bleak Karoo." D. J. Opperman, *tr. fr. Afrikaans by* Anthony Delius. PeSA
Christmas Carol, A: "Thys ender nyght." *Unknown.* TrGrPo, *abr.*
("This endris nyght.") OAEP
Christmas Carol: "Villagers all, this frosty tide." Kenneth Grahame. *See* Carol: "Villagers all. . ."
Christmas Carol, A: "What means this glory 'round our feet." James Russell Lowell. ChIP; DD; PGD; StJW
Christmas Carol, A: "What sweeter music can we bring." Robert Herrick. MPB
(Christmas Caroll, A, Sung to the King in the Presence at White-Hall.) GoJo
"We see Him come, and know Him ours," 3 *ll.* MyFE
Christmas Carol: "When Christ was born in Bethlehem." *Unknown, tr. fr. Italian by* Longfellow. ChrBoLe; OHIP
Christmas Carol, Sung to the King in the Presence at Whitehall, A. Robert Herrick. *See* Christmas Carol, A: "What sweeter music can we bring."
Christmas Carols. Gui Barozai, *par. by* Longfellow. BoTP
Christmas Chant. Isabel Shaw. ChBR; SiSoSe
Christmas Child, The. *Unknown, tr. fr. Spanish by* Katharine B. Clay. PCH
Christmas Childhood, A. Patrick Kavanagh. AnIL; OxBI
"My father played the melodion," *sel.* DTC
Christmas Chimes ("Little Penelope Socrates"). *Unknown.* BOHV
Christmas Comes. Earle Birney. ACV
Christmas comes. School after Christmas. Wymond Garthwaite. ChBR
Christmas comes but once a year. *Unknown.* OxNR; SoPo
Christmas Comes to Moccasin Flat. James Welch. YAP
Christmas Cradlesong, A. Lope de Vega. *See* Madonna, to Her Sleeping Child, The.
Christmas Dawn. Fleur Adcock. ACV
Christmas Dawn at Sea, A. Evan Morgan. EtS
Christmas Day. Margaret E. Sangster. PEDC
Christmas Day. Christopher Smart. Hymns and Spiritual Songs, Hymn XXXII. ChTr
Christmas Day in the Workhouse. George R. Sims. BeLS; BLPA; TreF
(In the Workhouse: Christmas Day.) PaPo
Christmas Day Is Come. Luke Wadding. OxBI
Christmas Day was coming, the Christmas Eve drew near, The. The Little Christmas Tree. "Susan Coolidge." DD; PEDC
Christmas Daybreak. Christina Rossetti. *See* Christmas Carol, A: "Before the paling of the stars."
Christmas declares the glory of the flesh. Christmas and Common Birth. Anne Ridler. FaBoTw
Christmas Dusk. Wilbur D. Nesbit. PEDC
Christmas, 1898. Edward Sandford Martin. DD
Christmas 1898, *sel.* Sir Lewis Morris. TrPWD
"'Tis nigh two thousand years."
Christmas Eve. Bill Berkson. ANYP
Christmas Eve. St. Luke, Bible, *N.T.* *See* Adoration of the Shepherds, The.
Christmas-Eve. Robert Browning. *See* Christmas-Eve and Easter-Day.
Christmas Eve. Liam P. Clancy. ISi
Christmas Eve. Charlotte Druitt Cole. BoTP
Christmas Eve. John Davidson. MPB; OHIP
Christmas Eve. C. Day Lewis. EaLo
Christmas Eve. John Drinkwater. HBMV
Christmas Eve. Marion Edey. YeAr
Christmas Eve. Eugene Field. OHIP
Christmas Eve. Florence Hoatson. GFA
Christmas Eve. Catherine Parmenter. PEDC; PGD
Christmas Eve. Edna Kingsley Wallace. BoTP
Christmas Eve. Kate Douglas Wiggin. *See* Romance of a Christmas Card, The.
Christmas-Eve and Easter-Day, *sels.* Robert Browning.
"Earth breaks up, time drops away." ChIP
Life. OQP
Rest Remaineth. OQP; PoRL
Christmas Eve, and twelve of the clock. The Oxen. Thomas Hardy. BoLiVe; BoPe; BoTP; BWP; CaFP; ChrBoLe; CLwM; CMoP; CoBMV; EnL; FosPo; GTBS-W; GTSL; HBMV; LiTM; MaPo; MaRV; MoAB; MoBrPo; MoRP; NoP; OAEP; PAn; PIA; OTPC (1946 ed.); Po; PoAn; PoDB; PoeP; PoIE; PoSa; PoVP; ShBV-2; SoP; StJW; TSW; ViPP; VP
Christmas Eve—Another Ceremony. Robert Herrick. OHIP
Christmas Eve—Another to the Maids. Robert Herrick. OHIP
Christmas Eve: Australia. Karl Shapiro. NYBP; PoAn; ReMP
Christmas Eve Choral, A. Bliss Carman. ISi
Christmas Eve in France. Jessie Redmond Fauset. BANP
Christmas Eve in Ireland. Katharine Tynan. ChrBoLe
Christmas Eve in Whitneyville, 1955. Donald Hall. UnPo (3d ed.)
Christmas Eve Legend. Frances Frost. BiCB
Christmas Eve; Market Square. P. K. Page. TwCaPo
Christmas Eve Meditation. Margaret E. Bruner. MaRV
Christmas Eve under Hooker's Statue. Robert Lowell. AP; NePA; OxBA; PoDB; ThLM
Christmas Everywhere. Phillips Brooks. *See* Christmas Carol, A: "Everywhere, everywhere, Christmas tonight."
Christmas Exchange, The. Arthur Guiterman. BrR; ChBR
Christmas Folk-Song, A. Lizette Woodworth Reese. ChBR; ChrBoLe; DD; FaPON; GFA; HBMV; HBVY; MPB; OHIP; OnMSP; OTPC (1946 ed.); PoRh; PoRL; SP; StJW; SUS; ThGo; TiPo (1952 ed.); TSW; UTS
Christmas Ghost Story, A. Thomas Hardy. EnLi-2
Christmas "Good Night." Ethel Robb. GFA
Christmas Greeting ("Sing hey! Sing hey!"). *Unknown.* BrR; ChBR; SiSoSe
(Old Christmas Greeting, An.) FaPON; MPB; TiPo
Christmas Greeting ("When Bill gives me a book, I know"). *Unknown.* BrR
Christmas hath made an end. Carol for Candlemas Day. *Unknown.* SeCL

Christmas Hearth Rhyme. *Unknown.* *See* Catch by the Hearth, A.
Christmas Holiday. Alun Lewis. PrWP
Christmas Holly, The. Eliza Cook. OTPC (1946 ed.); PRWS
Christmas Husbandly Fare. Thomas Tusser. SiCE; TuPP
Christmas Hymn, A. Cecil Frances Alexander. *See* Once in Royal David's City.
Christmas Hymn, A. Harry Baker. SoP
Christmas Hymn, A. Alfred Domett. DD; GN; GTBS; HBV; OTPC; WGRP
(Christmas Hymn, 1837.) OBVV
(Christmas Hymn, A: Old Style, 1837.) VA
"It is the calm and solemn night," *sel.* PGD
Christmas Hymn, *sel.* St. Ephrem, *tr. fr. Syriac by* W. H. Kent.
Virgin Truly Full of Wonder. ISi
(Christmas Hymn, The.) CAW
Christmas Hymn, A. Richard Watson Gilder. MaRV; StJW
Christmas Hymn, A. Edmund H. Sears. *See* Birth Song of Christ, The.
Christmas Hymn, A. Richard Wilbur. CoPo; MoRP
Christmas Hymn, 1837. Alfred Domett. *See* Christmas Hymn.
Christmas, Ibiza, 1966. Thomas Hanna. QAH
Christmas in Black Rock. Robert Lowell. ToPo
Christmas in the Heart. *Unknown.* RePo
Christmas Hymn, A: New Style, *sel.* Alfred Domett.
"To murder one so young!" VA
Christmas Hymn, A: Old Style, 1837. Alfred Domett. *See* Christmas Hymn, A.
Christmas in England. Sir Walter Scott. *See* Christmas in the Olden Time.
Christmas in lands of the fir tree and pine. Everywhere, Everywhere Christmas Tonight. Phillips Brooks. HH; OTPC; PoRL
Christmas in Olden Time. Sir Walter Scott. *See* Christmas in the Olden Time.
Christmas in Provence. Sister Mary Madeleva. WHL
Midnight Mass, II.
Serenade, The, I.
Christmas in the Heart. *Unknown.* ChBR; MaRV; OHIP; SiSoSe
Christmas in the North. Margaret E. Sangster. PEDC
Christmas in the Olden Time. Sir Walter Scott. *Fr.* Marmion, *Introd. to* VI. GoBC; OTPC; PCH, 3 *ll.*
(Christmas: "The damsel donned her kirtle sheen," *abr.*) PCH
(Christmas in England, *abr.*) GN
(Christmas in Olden Time.) PoRL
("Heap on more wood!—the wind is chill," 3 *ll.*) TiPo
(Old Christmas-Tide.) ChBR, 3 *ll.*; DD; MBP; SiSoSe, 3 *ll.*
Christmas in the Woods. Frances Frost. BrR; ChBR; TiPo (1952 ed.)
Christmas is a bitter day. David, Aged Four. Mildred Focht. MaRV
Christmas is coming, the geese are getting fat. Beggar's Rhyme. *Unknown.* ChBR; GaP; OxNR; PCH; SoPo; TiPo (1952 ed.)
Christmas is here. The Mahogany Tree. Thackeray. HBV; VA
Christmas is in the air. Five Days Old. Francis Webb. PoAu-2
Christmas Is Remembering. Elsie Binns. BiCB; ChBR; SiSoSe
Christmas Island. Katharine Lee Bates. HBMV; HBVY; TSW
Christmas knows a merry, merry place. Wassail Chorus at the Mermaid Tavern. Theodore Watts-Dunton. OBEV (1st ed.)
Christmas Landscape. Laurie Lee. BoPe; FIW; POTi
Christmas Legend, A. Oliver Herford. PoMS
Christmas Legend, A. Frank Sidgwick. OHIP
Christmas Legend. Edna Randolph Worrell. ChBR
Christmas Legends. Denis A. McCarthy. ChBR; ChrBoLe
Christmas Letter from Australia, A. Douglas Brooke Wheelton Sladen. VA
Christmas Lullaby, A. John Addington Symonds. PRWS
Christmas Lullaby. Ulrich Troubetzkoy. YeAr
Christmas Lullaby for a New-born Child. Yvonne Gregory. AmNP
Christmas morn, the legends say. Christmas Legends. Denis A. McCarthy. ChBR; ChrBoLe
Christmas Morning. Elsie Melchert Fowler. ChBR
Christmas Morning. Joaquin Miller. MaRV
Christmas Morning. Elizabeth Madox Roberts. ChBR; ChrBoLe; GoTP; MAP; MaRV; MoAmPo; MPB; PCH; PoRh; PoSC; RePo; StJW; StVeCh; SUS; TSW; WHL
Christmas Morning, I. Carol Freeman. BF; PoNe (1970 ed.); TTY
Christmas Mourning. Vassar Miller. CoPo; MoAmPo (1962 ed.)
Christmas Mystery we now present, A. The Star. Bertha Palmer Lane. ChrBoLe
Christmas Night, A. John Drinkwater. StJW
Christmas Night. Alice Isabel Hazeltine. ChrBoLe
Christmas Night. Marion Lochhead. MaRV
Christmas Night. Hugh MacCawell, *tr. fr. Irish by* Frank O'-Connor. KiLC
Christmas Night. Alice Meynell. StJW
Christmas Night. B. E. Milner. BoTP
Christmas-Night in the Quarters, *sels.* Irwin Russell.
Blessing the Dance. AnAmPo
Fust Banjo, De. AA; BLPA; HBV; IHA; PFY
(First Banjo, The.) BOHV; LHV
Christmas Night of '62. William Gordon McCabe. AA
Christmas 1959 et Cetera. Gerald William Barrax. Kal
Christmas 1945. Al Hine. ThLM
Christmas 1944. Denise Levertov. NeBP
Christmas 1942. Eric Irvin. BoAV; PoAu-2
Christmas 1942. Robert Nathan. PoFr
Christmas, 1930. Anderson M. Scruggs. CAW
(Christmas Today.) MaRV; OQP
(How Can They Honor Him.) StJW
Christmas: 1924. Thomas Hardy. PV
Christmas on Three Continents. John Peter. BoSA
Christmas Pageant. Margaret Fishback. PoSC
Christmas Party, A. Carolyn Sherwin Bailey. PCH
Christmas Party, The. Adeline White. BoTP
Christmas Pastoral. Robert Hillyer. MaRV
Christmas Prayer. Ralph Spaulding Cushman. MaRV
Christmas Prayer, A. Lucy Embury. ChrBoLe
Christmas Prayer, A. Molly Anderson Haley. PGD
Christmas Prayer, A. Herbert H. Hines. ChIP; MaRV; OQP; PGD
Christmas Prayer, A. George Macdonald. SUS
Christmas Prayer. Madeline Morse. PGD
Christmas Present, The. Patricia Hubbell. PDV
Christmas Pudding, The. *Unknown.* TiPo (1952 ed.)
Christmas Rede. Jane Barlow. OBVV
Christmas Rose. Margaret Evelyn Singleton. ChIP
Christmas Sermon, A, *sel.* Robert Louis Stevenson.
To Be Honest, to Be Kind. PoLF
Christmas Shoppers. Aileen Fisher. ChBR
Christmas Silence, The. Margaret Deland. ChrBoLe; OHIP; PRWS
Christmas Singing. Elsie Williams Chandler. ChBR; SiSoSe
Christmas Snow. John Moore. StaSt
Christmas Song, A. William Cox Bennett. VA
Christmas Song, A. Teresa Brayton. JKCP
Christmas Song. Bliss Carman. PeCV; PoSC; StJW
Christmas Song, A. Florence Evelyn Dratt. MaRV
Christmas Song. Eugene Field, *wr. at. to* Lydia Avery Coonley Ward. DD; HH; OHIP; PRWS; YeAr
(Song: "Why do the bells of [*or* do bells for] Christmas ring?") BoTP; GaP; GFA; PCH; TiPo (1952 ed.)
(Why Do the Bells of Christmas Ring.) SoPo
Christmas Song. Elizabeth-Ellen Long. ChBR; SiSoSe
Christmas Song, A: "Winds through the olive trees softly did blow." *Unknown.* *See* Long, Long Ago.
Christmas Songs. Gerta Kennedy. PoPl
Christmas Sonnet, A. E. A. Robinson. EaLo; MaRV; PoDB
Christmas Star. Boris Pasternak, *See* Star of the Nativity.
Christmas Star, The. Nancy Byrd Turner. MaRV
Christmas star burns overhead, The. Childlike Heart. Ellen Weston Catlin. PGD
Christmas Still Lives. William Hawkes. BePJ
Christmas Story, The. St. Luke, Bible, *N.T.* *See* Adoration of the Shepherds, The.
Christmas Symbol, The. *Unknown.* OQP
Christmas, the Year One, A.D. Sara Henderson Hay. PoRA
Christmas Thought, A. Mrs. Frank A. Breck. BePJ
Christmas Today. Anderson M. Scruggs. *See* Christmas, 1930.

Christmas Tree, A. William Burford. NePA
Christmas Tree, The. C. Day Lewis. GTBS-D
Christmas Tree, The. Isabel de Savitzsky. BoTP
Christmas Tree. Aileen Fisher. ChBR; PDV
Christmas Tree, The. Mary E. Wilkins Freeman. PEDC
Christmas Tree, The. Edward Shillito. ChIP; OQP
Christmas Tree in the Nursery, The. Richard Watson Gilder. DD; HBVY; OHIP
Christmas-Tree Song, A. Rodney Bennett. BoTP
Christmas tree stood by the parlor door, The. Golden Cobwebs. Rowena Bennett. ChBR
Christmas Trees, The. Mary Frances Butts. OHIP; PRWS
Christmas Trees. Violet Alleyn Storey. StJW
Christmas twigs crispen and needles rattle, The. New Year's Poem. Margaret Avison. LiTM (1970 ed.); OBCV
Christmas Verse, A. "Kay." BoTP
Christmas was in the air and all was well. Karma. E. A. Robinson. AmPP; AnNE; AP; CMoP; CoBMV; ILP; MoAB; MoAmPo (1950 ed.)
Christmas Wish, A. Eugene Field. ChBR
Christmas Wish, A. Rose Fyleman. BoTP
Christmas-Time. Rose Fyleman. ChBR
"Christo et Ecclesiae" 1700. Oliver Wendell Holmes. *Fr.* Two Sonnets: Harvard. AP
Christofero had a mind. The Great Discovery. Eleanor Farjeon. PoSC
Christofo Columbo, *with music. Unknown.* AmSS
Christofo Colombo was a hungry man. Mysterious Biography. Carl Sandburg. SiSoSe
Christoph. Charles Spear. AnNZ
Christophe. Russell Atkins. *See* Poem: "Upstood upstaffed passing sinuously away."
Christopher Columbus. Franklin P. Adams. InMe
Christopher Columbus. Rosemary Benét *and* Stephen Vincent Benét. PoRh; RePo
Christopher Columbus, *sels.* William Hart-Smith.
 Cipangu. PoAu-2
 Comes Fog and Mist. PoAu-2
 Departure. PoAu-2
 Space. PoAu-2
 (Columbus Goes West.) BoAV; NeLNL
 Waterspout, The. PoAu-2
Christopher Columbus. Annette Wynne. HH
Christopher Marlowe. Michael Drayton. *Fr.* To Henry Reynolds, of Poets and Poesy. ChTr
Christopher Marlowe. Swinburne. *Fr.* Sonnets on English Dramatic Poets. BEL; PoVP; Sonn; TOP; TrGrPo
Christopher of the Shenandoah, A. Edith M. Thomas. PAH
Christopher Robin goes. Hoppity. A. A. Milne. FaBV; TiPo
Christopher White. *Unknown.* ESPB
Christ's Bloody Sweat. Robert Southwell. ReIE
Christ's Bondservant. George Matheson. MaRV; SoP; STF; TRV
 (Christian Freedom.) TrPWD
Christ's Call. *Unknown.* SoP
Christ's Coming in Triumph. Jeremy Taylor. BePJ
 (Christ's Coming O Jerusalem in Triumph.) StJW
 (Lord, Come Away!) MaRV
Christ's Coming to Judgment. Thomas Dekker. AnEnPo
Christ's Gift to Man. *Unknown.* ACP
Christ's Giving. Anna E. Hamilton. ChIP; OQP
Christ's Incarnation. Robert Herrick. *See* Christ and We.
Christ's Invitation. *Unknown.* SoP
Christ's Kirk on the Green. *At. to* James V King of Scotland. OxBS
Christ's Nativity. Henry Vaughan. AnAnS-1; AtBAP; MeP; StJW
 (Awake! Glad Heart!) GoTP
Christ's Prayer in Gethsemane. *Unknown.* SeCePo
Christ's Reign of Peace. Stephen Phillips. ChIP
Christ's Reply. Edward Taylor. *Fr.* God's Determinations. MAmP; MWA-1; PoEL-3
Christs Returne out of Egypt. Robert Southwell. MeP
Christs Sleeping Friends. Robert Southwell. AnAnS-1; MeP
Christ's Spirit taketh breath again. Christ Our Contemporary. William Charles Braithwaite. MaRV
Christ's Sympathy. Sir Edward Bulwer-Lytton. BePJ
Christ's Tear Breaks My Heart. *Unknown.* MeEL
Christ's Triumph after Death. Giles Fletcher. *See* Christ's Victory and Triumph.
Christ's Triumph over Death. Giles Fletcher. *See* Christ's Victory and Triumph.
Christ's Victory. Richard Crashaw. MaRV; StJW
Christ's Victory and Triumph, *sels.* Giles Fletcher.
 Christ's Triumph after Death, IV.
  Celestial City, The. OBS
  Easter Morn. EIL
  "Had I a voice of steel to tune my song." LoBV
  Heavenly Jerusalem, The. OxBoCh
 Christ's Triumph over Death, III.
  On the Crucifixion. OxBoCh
  "So down the silver streams of Eridan." LoBV
 Christ's Victory in Heaven, I.
  Excellency of Christ. BePJ; MaRV; SoP; StJW; WGRP
  (Christ.) FaChP
  (He Is a Path.) ChIP; TRV
  "She was a Virgin of austere regard." ViBoPo
 Christ's Victory on Earth, II.
  "His haire was blacke, and in small curls did twine." SeCV-1
  "Love is the blossom where there blows." LO; ViBoPo
  (Wooing Song.) EIL; HBV; OBEV
  "Twice had Diana bent her golden bowe." SeEP
Christ's Victory in Heaven. Giles Fletcher. *See* Christ's Victory and Triumph.
Christ's Victory on Earth. Giles Fletcher. *See* Christ's Victory and Triumph.
Christus; a Mystery, *sels.* Longfellow.
 Fate of the Prophets, The, *fr.* I, Introitus. WGRP
 Flight into Egypt, The, *fr.* II, 3. OBVV
 Love and Hate, *fr.* I, 1st Interlude. MaRV
 "My work is finished; I am strong." ChIP
Christus Consolator. Rossiter W. Raymond. HBV; MaRV; OQP
Christus Matthaeum et Discipulos Alloquitur. Sir Edward Sherburne. ACP
Christus Triumphans. Condé Benoist Pallen. CAW
Chromatic Tunes. John Danyel. *See* Can Doleful Notes to Mesur'd Accents Set.
Chromis. Phineas Fletcher. Piscatorie Eclogues, IV. LoBV
Chromium-plated Hat, A; Inlaid with Scenes from Siegfried. Howard Nemerov. FiMAP
Chronicle, The. Abraham Cowley. *See* Chronicle, The; a Ballad.
Chronicle, *sel. At. to* Robert of Gloucester.
 "Thus com, lo! Engelond in-to Normandies hond." YAT
Chronicle, A. *Unknown.* NA; SiTL
Chronicle, The; a Ballad. Abraham Cowley. BOHV; CEP; GoTL; SeCV-1; ViBoPo
Chronicle of Meola Creek, The. Keith Sinclair. AnNZ
Chronicle of the Drum, The, *sels.* Thackeray.
 "Ah, gentle, tender lady mine!" ViBoPo
 "At Paris, hard by the Maine barriers." OTMeF
Chronicler, The. Alexander Bergman. TrJP
Chronometer, The. A. M. Sullivan. WaKn
Chronos, Chronos, mend thy pace. The Secular Masque. Dryden. DiPo; EiCL; ExPo; MaPo; MBW-1; PoEL-3; SeCeV; SeCV-2; SeEP
Chrysalis, A. Mary Emily Bradley. AA; HBV
Chrysalis, The. John James Piatt. InP
Chrysanthemum Legend, The. Arthur Davison Ficke. PoMa
Chrysanthemum Show, The. C. Day Lewis. MoVE
Chrysanthemums. F. S. Flint. MoBrPo (1942 ed.)
Chryseis. Walter Conrad Arensberg. AnAmPo
Chrysolites and Rubies, The. Walter Savage Landor. EPN
Chrysothemis. Henry Reed. MoVE
"Chuff! chuff! chuff!" An' a mountain bluff. A Song of Panama. Damon Runyon. PAH; ThLM
Chug! Puff! Chug! Tugs. James S. Tippett. FaPON; GFA
Chugachimute I Love the Name. Rochelle Owens. CoPo
Chums. Buson, *tr. fr. Japanese.* GaP
Chums. Arthur Guiterman. GaP; MPB
Chunky together, the marchers blacken their way. May Day Demonstrators. Maurice Lindsay. ACV
Church, The. Edwin Muir. MoRP
Church, The. Edwin Ford Piper. WGRP
Church, The. Jules Romains, *tr. fr. French by* Jethro Bithell. WGRP
Church, The. Nancy Willard. ThO
Church,/ Chapel. *Unknown.* OxNR
Church and Church-yard at Night. Robert Blair. *Fr.* The Grave. OBEC

("See yonder hallow'd fane! the pious work.") ViBoPo
Church and Clouds. James Applewhite. *Fr.* Steps from the Stream. YAP
Church and School. Timothy Dwight. *Fr.* Greenfield Hill. AmPP (3d ed.)
Church and State. W. B. Yeats. CMoP
Church and the World walked far apart, The. The Church Walking with the World. Mathilda C. Edwards. BLPA
Church Bell in the Night, The. *Unknown, tr. fr. Old Irish by* Kuno Meyer. AnIL
(Church Bell at Night, The, *tr. by* Howard Mumford Jones.) OnYI
Church bells are ringing, The. Sunday up the River, IV. James Thomson. OAEP
Church bells at Christmas-time, The. Christmas-Time. Rose Fyleman. ChBR
Church bells thunder out their roundest tone, The. The Unbidden Wedding Guest. Kurt Marti. HW
Church bells toll a melancholy round, The. Sonnet Written in Disgust of Vulgar Superstition. Keats. ERoP-2
Church bells were ringing, the Devil sat singing, The. A Parable from Liebig. Charles Kingsley. SoP
Church-Builder, The. Thomas Hardy. BEL
Church do zeem a touchèn zight [*or* seem a touching sight], The. Vo'k a-Comen into Church [*or* In Church]. William Barnes. OxBoCh; WePo
Church flings forth a battled shade, The. The Church-Builder. Thomas Hardy. BEL
Church-Floor[e], The. George Herbert. AnAnS-1; ATP; ExPo; MaMe; MeLP; MeP; OBS; PoE; SeCePo; SeCeV
Church Going. Philip Larkin. CMoP; ForPo; GTBS-P; HaMV; ILP; LiTM (1970 ed.); MoBrPo (1962 ed.); NePoEA; NoP; PIA; PoDB; PoeP; PoIE; ToPo; TwCP; UnPo (3d ed.)
Church has pieces jutting out, The. The Pilaster. Elizabeth Madox Roberts. NP
Church in the Heart, The. Morris Abel Beer. MaRV; TRV
("Who builds a church within his heart.") PoToHe
Church is a business, and the rich, The. After Lorca. Robert Creeley. NaP
"Church is dead, The," said brother Brown. The Pastor's Friend. *Unknown.* STF
Church is man when his awed soul goes out, The. What Is the Church? Sam Walter Foss. OQP
Church-Lock and Key. George Herbert. AnAnS-1; MaMe; MeP
Church Militant, The, *sel.* George Herbert. MaMe
L'Envoy: "King of Glorie, King of Peace," *sel.* AnAnS-1; MaMe; MeP; SCEP-1
Church-Monuments. George Herbert. AnAnS-1; CABA; EP; ForPo; MaMe; MaPo; MeP; NoP; PIA; PoIE; QFR
Church-Music [*or* Musick]. George Herbert. AnAnS-1; EP; MaMe; MeP; MuSP; SCEP-1; SeCV-1; UnS
Church of a Dream, The. Lionel Johnson. OBMV; PoVP
Church of Brou, The, *sel.* Matthew Arnold.
Tomb, The. PoVP
Church of England, The. Dryden. *Fr.* The Hind and the Panther, I. OBS
Church of San Antonio de la Florida, The. Paul Petrie. NYBP
Church of the Holy Innocents, Dunedin. "Robin Hyde." ACV
Church of the Revolution. Hezekiah Butterworth. PAH
Church of the Sacred Heart, The. Ashton Greene. NePoAm
Church out, I walked over town. Church and Clouds. James Applewhite. *Fr.* Steps from the Stream. YAP
Church-Porch, The. George Herbert. AnAnS-1; MaMe; SCEP-1, *much abr.*; YAT, *much abr.*
Courage. PCD; PCH
Dare to be True. GoTP
"Let vain or busy thoughts have there no part." TRV
On Worship. MaRV
"Thou, whose sweet youth and early hopes inhance." MeP
Church-Rents and Schismes. George Herbert. MaMe
Church Romance, A. Thomas Hardy. FaBoTw
Church Scene, The. Longfellow. *Fr.* Evangeline. TreF
Church Street wears ever a smile, from having watched bright belles. Streets. Douglas Goldring. HBMV
Church Today, The. Sir William Watson. MaRV; WGRP
Church tower crowned the town, A. The Glass Town. Alastair Reid. NYBP
Church Triumphant. S. Ralph Harlow. MaRV
Church Triumphant, The. John Addington Symonds. *See* Loftier Race, A.
Church Universal, The. Samuel Longfellow. MaRV; SoP; WGRP
Church Walking with the World. Mathilda C. Edwards. BLPA
Church Windows, The. George Herbert. *See* Windows, The.
Church-Windows, The, *abr. Unknown. Fr.* A Poem, in Defence of the Decent Ornaments of Christ-Church, Oxon. OBS
Church Within, The. A. L. Alexander. SoP
Churches. *Unknown.* MaRV; SoP
Churches, lord, all the dark churches, The. Crag Jack's Apostasy. Ted Hughes. EaLo
Churches of Rome and of England, The. Dryden. *Fr.* The Hind and the Panther, I. ACP
Church's One Foundation, The. Samuel J. Stone. MaRV; SoP; TreFT; WGRP
Church's one foundation, The. Battle Hymn of the Spanish Rebellion [*or* Republic]. Louis Alexander Mackay. OBCV; OnPM
Church's Testimony, The. Dryden. *Fr.* The Hind and the Panther, I. ACP; CAW
("But, gratious God, how well dost thou provide.") TrPWD
(Confession of Faith.) UnPo (1st ed.)
(Conversion.) PoLi
Churchyard, The. Robert Buchanan. HBV; VA
Churchyard in Wales, A. *Unknown.* SiTL
("Our Life is but a summer's day.") WhC
Churchyard leans to the sea with its dead, The. The Old Churchyard of Bonchurch. Philip Bourke Marston. HBV; NBM; OBNC; OBVV; VA
Churchyard of St. Mary Magdalene, Old Milton. John Heath-Stubbs. NePoEA
Churchyard on the Sands, The. Lord De Tabley. CH, *abr.*; GTBS-D, *abr.*; HBV; LoBV; OBNC
Churl in spirit, up or down, The. In Memoriam A. H. H.., CXI. Tennyson. EPN; ViPo; VP
Churl that wants another's fare, The. The Dog in the River. Phaedrus. AWP; JAWP; OnPM; WBP
Chus doth so often to the doctor go. In Chus. *Unknown.* TuPP
Ciampino. Edwin Denby. ANYP
Ciaran, the Master of Horses and Lands. Joseph Campbell. JKCP (1926 ed.)
Cicada. Libero de Libero, *tr. fr. Italian by* Frederick Mortimer Clapp. LiTW
Cicada, The. H. M. Green. PoAu-1
Cicada, A. Li Shang-yin, *tr. fr. Chinese by* Witter Bynner *and* Kiang Kang-hu. OuHeWo
Cicada, The. Ou-yang Hsiu, *tr. fr. Chinese by* Arthur Waley. AWP
Cicada. Adrien Stoutenburg. NYBP
Cicada (*fr.* Anacreontics). *Unknown, tr. fr. Greek by* Addison. OuHeWo
Cicada cries out, The. Peasant and Geisha Songs. *Unknown.* LiTW
Cicada-Shell. Basho, *tr. fr. Japanese.* SoPo
Cicadas, The. Aldous Huxley. POTE
Cicadas. Richard Wilbur. FiMAP
(Cigales.) NePoEA
Cicadas, The. Judith Wright. FIW
Ciceronis Amor. Robert Greene. *See* Tullie's Love.
Cid, The, *sel.* Corneille, *tr. fr. French by* Paul Landis.
Two Lovers in the Toils of Honor. LiTW
Cid, The, *sel. Unknown, tr. fr. Spanish by* R. Selden Rose *and* Leonard Bacon.
Pawning the Coffers of Sand. LiTW
Cid of the West. Edna Dean Proctor. DD
Cider. Philip Booth. WIRo
Cider Song. Mildred Weston. BoNaP
Cid's Rising, The. Felicia Hemans. FOL; OBRV
Cigales. Richard Wilbur. *See* Cicadas.
Cigar Smoke, Sunday, after Dinner. Louise Townsend Nicholl. NePoAm
Cigarette, The. Jules Laforgue, *tr. fr. French by* William Jay Smith. LiTW
Cigarette for the Bambino. Gavin Ewart. WaP
Cigarettes in my mouth. The End of Ethnic Dream. Jay Wright. BF; ThO
Cigarettes Will Spoil Yer Life *with music. Unknown.* AS

Cincinnatus of the West, The. Byron. *See* Washington.
Cincirinella Had a Mule. *Unknown, tr. fr. Italian by* Maria Cimino. FaPON
Cincophrenicpoet. Bob Kaufman. PoNe (1970 ed.)
Cinderella. Cynthia Pickard. PoPl
Cinderella's Song. Elizabeth Madox Roberts. PoRh
Cindy, *with music. Unknown.* TrAS, *with music*; TreFS
Cinema, at the Lighthouse. Henri Coulette. *Fr.* The War of the Secret Agents. NePoEA-2
Cinq Ans Après. Gelett Burgess. HBV; TreFS
(Ah, Yes, I Wrote It.) SiTL
(Ah, Yes, I Wrote the "Purple Cow.") FiBHP; PoPl
(Nonsense Quatrains.) CenHV
Cinque Port, A. John Davidson. BrPo
Cipangu. William Hart-Smith. *Fr.* Christopher Columbus. PoAu-2
Circe. Lord De Tabley. VA
Circe. Hilda Doolittle ("H. D."). PoRA (rev ed.)
Circe. Alfred Kreymborg. MAPA
Circe. Louis MacNeice. LO; OBMV
Circe, *sel.* Augusta Webster.
"Sun drops luridly into the west, The." PeVV
Circe Undersea. George MacBeth. HYE
Circle, The. Carol Coates. CaP
Circle, The. Jean Garrigue. LiTA; MoPo
Circle, A. Theodore Spencer. NYBP
Circle and wheel of. Who cares what I'll. Song. Robert Kelly. YAP
Circle Game, The, *sels.* Margaret Atwood. MoCV
"Being with you," II.
"Returning to the room," IV.
"Summer again," VII.
Circle of Struggle. William Pitt Root. NYBP
Circle One. Owen Dodson. Kal
Circle to the left, the old Brass Wagon. Old Brass Wagon. *Unknown.* AS
Circle will remain, of mountain, hill, The. The World's Centre. Ruth Dallas. AnNZ
Circled by a Horsefly. Helen G. Quigless. TNV
Circles. Carl Sandburg. AmFN; FIW
Circles. Miriam Waddington. PeCV
Circles never fully round, but change, The. Perspective of Coordination. Arthur Davison Ficke. NP
Circlet, The. The Numbers. Joel Oppenheimer. CoPo
Circling Hearths, The. Roderic Quinn. BoAu
Circling months begin this day, The. The New Year's Gift to Phyllis. Matthew Prior. CBEP
Circling on high, in cloudless sky. On the Plains. Francis Brooks. *Fr.* Intaglios. AA
Circling upon his star. The Sleepwalker. Nelly Sachs. NYBP
Circuit closes, The. House and heart. Winter Night. Louis O. Coxe. NYBP
Circular star, glowing. Death of the Moonshine Supermen. Reginald Lockett. BF
Circumstance. Thomas Bailey Aldrich. AA
Circumstance. Frederick Locker-Lampson. BOHV
Circumstance. Shelley. CBEP; MBW-2
Circumstance without Pomp. John Kendall. WhC
Circumstances. Albert Simpson Reitz. SoP
Circus, The. Fannie Stearns Davis. PCH
Circus. Eleanor Farjeon. BoChLi; MPB; SUS; UTS
Circus, The. Milton Kaplan. GoYe
Circus, The. Kenneth Koch. ANYP; FRC
Circus, The. Elizabeth Madox Roberts. FaPON; GFA; MPB; SoPo; UTS
Circus, The. E. B. White. InMe
Circus Animals' Desertion, The. W. B. Yeats. CMoP; DiPo; FaBoTw; LiTB; MaPo (1969 ed.); OAEP (2d ed.); PoeP; PoIE; PP
"Circus comes this week, The!" The Circus. Fannie Stearns Davis. PCH
Circus Elephant. Kathryn Worth. BrR
Circus Garland, A, *sels.* Rachel Field.
Acrobat. SoPo; StVeCh
Elephant, The. SoPo; StVeCh
Epilogue. UTS
Equestrienne. UTS
Girl on the Milk-white Horse, The. SoPo; StVeCh
Next Day. SoPo; StVeCh
Parade. SoPo; StVeCh; UTS
Performing Seal, The. SoPo; StVeCh; TiPo (1959 ed.); UTS
Circus Maximus. George Bowering. PeCV (1967 ed.)
Circus Nerves and Worries. Kenward Elmslie. ANYP
Circus of battleships carrying heavy laughter, A. Celebrated Return. Clarence Major. AmNP
Circus Parade, The. Olive Beaupré Miller. GFA; SoPo; TiPo
Circus Parade. James S. Tippett. UTS
Circus-postered Barn, The. Elizabeth J. Coatsworth. MAP; MoAmPo
Circus Ship *Euzkera*, The. Walker Gibson. *See* In Memory of the Circus Ship *Euzkera*. . .
Circus was never meant for children, The. The Circus. Milton Kaplan. GoYe
Cirque d'Hiver. Elizabeth Bishop. FiMAP; LiTA; MiAP
Cirrus bow of surf is blown, The. A Fantasy of Little Waters. James Scully. NYBP
Cistern Dry & the Well, The. James Koller. FRC
Cit, a Common-Council-Man by place, The. What Is't to Us? Charles Churchill. *Fr.* Night. SeCePo
Citation and Examination of William Shakespeare, The, *sel.* Walter Savage Landor.
Maid's Lament, The. GTBS; HBV; OBEV; OBNC; OBRV; OBVV; VA
Citation for Horace Gregory. Muriel Rukeyser. NAMP
Cities, The. "Æ." OBMV
Cities. Hilda Doolittle ("H. D.") ViBoPo (1941 ed.)
Cities and Science. David McCord. AmFN
Cities and Seas. Norman Jordan. PoNe (1970 ed.)
Cities and Thrones and Powers. Kipling. *Fr.* Puck of Pook's Hill. CBV; FaBoEn; GoJo; GTBS-D; MemP; MoVE; OBNC; PoEL-5; POTE; PoVP; SeCeV; ShBV-4; ViPP
Cities, The, are mine! The Devil's Meditation. Michael Sweany. MaRV
Cities #8, *sel.* Victor Hernandez Cruz.
"Little cousins/ play on your." BOLo
Cities, The, send to one another saying: "My sons are mad." Vala, or, The Four Zoas. Blake. ViBoPo
Citizen. Louis Grudin. NePA
Citizen, The. Vilma Howard. NNP
Citizen. Peter Schjeldahl. ANYP
Citizen and the Red Lion of Brentford, The. Christopher Smart. NCEP
Citizen Bacillus. John Brunner. HYE
Citizen, myself, or personal friend. More Sonnets at Christmas, IV. Allen Tate. LiTM; WaP
Citizen of the World. Joyce Kilmer. OQP; StJW
Citizen Turned Gentleman, The, *sel.* Edward Ravenscroft.
I Sigh All the Night. SeCL
Citizens in the Round. Robert P. Tristram Coffin. RePo
Citizenship; Form 8889512, Sub-section Q. G. K. Chesterton. OxBoLi
City, The. "Æ." WGRP
City, The. W. H. Auden. Sonn
City. Langston Hughes. FaPON; PDV
(City; San Francisco.) AmFN; GoSL
City, The ("In Homer's time"). Emmett Jarrett. *Fr.* Design for the City of Man. ThO
City, The ("Set over against lust"). Emmett Jarrett. *Fr.* Design for the City of Man. ThO
City, The. Ben Maddow. LiTM (1946 ed.); WaP
City, The. Edwin Muir. PIA
City, The. Frank Mason North. *See* Christ in the City.
City about whose brow the north winds blow. Ottawa. Duncan Campbell Scott. VA
City Afternoon. Barbara Howes. AmFN; TPM
City Afternoon, A. Edith Wyatt. LiTM (1946 ed.); NP
City and Country Life. William Cowper. *Fr.* The Task. CoBE
City and the Trucks, The. Dorothy Brown Thompson. BrR
City Asleep. Maurice Lesemann. NP
City Autumn. Joseph Moncure March. OCS
City Beautiful, The. *Unknown.* SoP
City Bird. Theda Kenyon. PoMa
City Birds. Spud Johnson. PoMa
City by Night. Vittorio Sereni, *tr. fr. Italian by* Glauco Cambon. OnPM
City Child, The. Tennyson. BoTP; OTPC; PRWS
City child, A, rooms are to him no mere places to live in. Ten Years Old. Louis Untermeyer. TSW
City Church, The. "E. H. K." WGRP
City Clerk, The. Thomas Ashe. OBVV

City clocks point out the hours, The. Belfast; High Street. Padraic Colum. NePoAm
City considered as a Tulip Tree, The. Carl Bode. *Fr.* London Sonnets. ToPo
City Council, *with music.* David G. Robinson. SGR
City Dead-House, The. Walt Whitman. AmePo
City dwellers all complain, The. August. Michael Lewis. GoTP; OTD
City Enscriber, The. Bob Maxey. WSL
City Financier, The/ walks in the gardens. Thrushes. Humbert Wolfe. MoBrPo
City Flower, A. Austin Dobson. BoPe
City Girl. Maxwell Bodenheim. HBMV
City God Hath Made, The. Sabine Baring-Gould. SoP
City has streets, The. City Streets and Country Roads. Eleanor Farjeon. BrR; SoPo; TiPo
City, I never told you yet. To Sydney. Louise Mack. BoAu
City in the Sea, The. Poe. AA; AmePo; AmLP; AmP; AmPP; AnAmPo; AnEnPo; AnFE; AP; APA; BoLiVe; CBEP; CoAnAm; CoBA; FaBoEn; ForPo; GTBS-D; HBV; ILP; LiTA; MAmP; MWA-1; NePA; NoP; OxBA; PeER; PoE; PoEL-4; PoFS; PoIE; SiSw; TDP; TrGrPo; ViBoPo; WHA
(Doomed City, The.) OBRV
City in the Throes of Despair, The. Tony Towle. ANYP
City is cutting a way, The. New York. Arthur Guiterman. PaA
City is in imminent danger of being destroyed. Overture. Emmett Jarrett. *Fr.* Design for the City of Man. ThO
City is of Night, The; perchance of death. James Thomson. *Fr.* The City of Dreadful Night, I. AnFE; EnLit; LiTB; OAEP; PoEL-5; ViBoPo
City Life. D. H. Lawrence. CAD; OAEP (2d ed.); PoIE (1970 ed.)
City Lights. Karle Wilson Baker. PCD
City Lights. Rachel Field. FaPON; GFA; PDV
City, The: Midnight. Bruce Dawe. PoAu-2
City misted in rain, dim wet flashes of light, The. Ombres Chinoises. Babette Deutsch. TPM
City Mouse and the Garden Mouse, The. Christina Rossetti. *Fr.* Sing-Song. BoChLi; BoTP; FaBoBe; FaPON; GoTP; HBV; HBVY; MPB; OTPC; PPL; StVeCh; UTS
(City Mouse and the Country Mouse, The.) PCH
("City mouse lives in a house, The.") SUS; TiPo
City Nature. Esther Pinch. PoMa
City Nights: In Bohemia. Arthur Symons. SyP
(In Bohemia.) BrPo
City Nights: In the Train. Arthur Symons. SyP
City Number. Carl Sandburg. OCS
City of Baltimore, The, *with music.* *Unknown.* ShS
City of Beggars, The. Alfred Hayes. WaP
City of Dreadful Night, The. James Thomson. OBNC, *abr.*; PoVP
Sels.
"Anear the centre of that northern crest," XXI. FaBoEn; GTBS-P; OAEP
(Melancholia.) AnEnPo; VA
"As I came through the desert thus it was," *fr.* IV. LiTB; LiTG; NBM; PoEL-5
"Because he seemed to walk with an intent," II. EnLit
"City is of Night, The; perchance of Death," I. AnFE; EnLit; LiTB; OAEP; PoEL-5; ViBoPo
"He stood alone within the spacious square," IV. AnFE; EnLi-2; WiR
"How the moon triumphs through the endless nights!" XVII. GTSL
"I sat me weary on a pillar's base," XX. NBM; OAEP
(Sphinx, The.) EPN
"Large glooms were gathered in the mighty fane," XIV. OAEP
"Of all things human which are strange and wild," XIII. LoBV (XIII-XIV); ViBoPo
Proem: "Lo, thus, as prostrate, 'In the dust I write.'" EnLit; GoTS; OAEP; OxBS; ViBoPo
City of Christmas, here, I love your season. Christmas Eve; Market Square. P. K. Page. TwCaPo
City of Falling Leaves, The. Amy Lowell. 1777, II. MAPA; SUS; TiPo; TwAmPo
City of God. Samuel Johnson. AA; MaRV; TRV; WGRP
City of God. R. H. Long. BoAu
City of God, The. Francis Turner Palgrave. MaRV; WGRP
City of God, The. Henry B. Robins. MaRV
City of God, The. Anna Louise Strong. MaRV
City of God, how broad and far. City of God. Samuel Johnson. AA; MaRV; TRV; WGRP
City of Golf, The. Robert Fuller Murray. SD
City of mist and rain and blown grey spaces. Edinburgh. Alfred Noyes. HBV; HT
City of Monuments. Muriel Rukeyser. NAMP
City of Orgies. Walt Whitman. MWA-1
City of Our Hopes, The. Felix Adler. *See* Hail! the Glorious Golden City.
City of Prague, The. William Jeffery Prowse. CenHV
City of Satisfactions, The. Daniel Hoffman. CoPo
City of Slaughter, The. Hayyim Nahman Bialik, *tr. fr. Hebrew by* A. M. Klein. TrJP
City of the Dead, The. Richard Burton. HBV
City of the dead is zoned, The. Part-Time Tenant. Edna Meudt. FiSC
City of the End of Things, The. Archibald Lampman. OBCV; VA
City of the North, A. James Kirkup. POTi
City of the Soul, The. Lord Alfred Douglas. HBMV
"Each new hour's passage is the acolyte," *sel.* MoBrPo (1942 ed.); WHA
City Park, A. Alter Brody. OCS
City Priest. Anne Higginson Spicer. OQP
City Rain. Rachel Field. SoPo; TiPo
City rolls, The. On the Expressway. Robert Dana. OCS
City Roofs. Charles Hanson Towne. BLPA
(Roof-Tops.) PoToHe
City; San Francisco. Langston Hughes. *See* City.
City Show, The. Eleanor Farjeon. GaP
City Shower, A. Swift. *See* Description of a City Shower.
City shuffles through the snow, the whirling snow, The. Dead of Winter. Anthony Towne. NYBP; StP
City sleeps in its unconcern, but the highways are awake, The. The City and the Trucks. Dorothy Brown Thompson. BrR
City Song, A. John Hanlon Mitchell. CaP
City Songs. Mark Van Doren. NYBP
City Sparrow. Alfred Kreymborg. OCS
City stirred about me softly as air, The. The Hours of the Day. George Dillon. NP
City-Storm. Harold Monro. MoBrPo
City Streets and Country Roads. Eleanor Farjeon. BrR; SoPo; TiPo
City Summer. Lou Lipsitz. YAP
City to which its prince turns not in compassion, sighs itself away into silence, The. Lamentation of Nippur. *Unknown.* LiTW
City Traffic. Eve Merriam. OCS; PDV
City Tree, The. Isabella Valancy Crawford. CaP
City Trees. Vere Dargan. OQP; PGD
City Trees. Edna St. Vincent Millay. FaPON; LaNeLa; OCS; PoMa; RePo
City Trees. Anderson M. Scruggs. PoMa
City Wall, The. Eunice Tietjens. NP
City which thou seest no other deem, The. Rome. Milton. *Fr.* Paradise Regained, IV. OBS
City without Walls. W. H. Auden. NYBP
City's Crown, The. William Dudley Foulke. HBMV; MaRV; OQP; WGRP
City's steeple-towers remove away, The. On Leaving Bruges. Dante Gabriel Rossetti. CBEP
City's taken off her winter things, The. Spring. Vladimir Mayakovsky. CAD
Civil Irish and Wild Irish. Laoiseach Mac an Bhaird, *tr. fr. Late Middle Irish by* Kenneth Jackson. AnIL
Civil War. Charles Dawson Shanly. HBV; PAH
Civil War. Mark Van Doren. MoVE
Civil Wars, The, *sels.* Samuel Daniel.
"And forth h' is brought unto th' accomplishment," *fr.* II. ReIE
"I sing the civil wars, tumultuous broils," *fr.* I. ReIE
Richard II as Captive, *fr.* II. SiCE
Civile, res ago [*or* si ergo]. See, Will, 'Ere's a Go. *Unknown.* ChTr; WhC
Civilian for a pause of hours. Goodmorning with Light. John Ciardi. WaP
Civilities. Thomas Whitbread. SD
Civilization. Stanton A. Coblentz. OQP
Civilization. Yüan Chieh, *tr. fr. Chinese by* Arthur Waley. LiTW

Civilization and Its Discontents. John Ashbery. TwCP
Civilized, crying how to be human again: this will tell you how. Signpost. Robinson Jeffers. GoYe; PoPo; ViBoPo
Civilizing the Child. Lisel Mueller. TPM
Civitas Dei. Edith Lovejoy Pierce. MaRV
Clack your beaks you cormorants and kittiwakes. A Canticle to the Waterbirds. Brother Antoninus. NeAP; StP
Clad All in White. Abraham Cowley. *Fr.* The Mistress. SeCV-1
Claes Oldenburg Story, The. Lewis Mac Adams. YAP
Claim That Has the Canker on the Rose, The. Joseph Plunkett. OxBI
Claim to Love. Giovanni Battista Guarini, *tr. fr. Italian by* Thomas Stanley. AWP
Claiming [*or* Clayming] a Second Kiss by Desert. Ben Jonson. *Fr.* A Celebration of Charis. AnAnS-2; LiTL; SCEP-2; SeCP
Claiming the Promise. Charles Wesley. BePJ
Clair de Lune. Anthony Hecht. NYBP
Clair de Lune. Arthur Symons. SyP
Clair de lune. Paul Verlaine, *tr. fr. French by* Arthur Symons. AWP
(Moonlight.) SyP, *tr. by* John Gray.
(Pastel, A.) SyP, *tr. by* Arthur O'Shaughnessy.
Clam, A. *Unknown. See* Nirvana.
Clamming. Reed Whittemore. NoP; NYBP
Clamor of cannon dies down, the furnace mouth of the battle is silent, The. Lincoln. John Gould Fletcher. HBMV; MAP; SP
Clancy of The Overflow. Andrew Barton Paterson. BoAu; PoAu-1
"Clang!" goes the high-framed, feather-tufted gong. "Tan Ta Ra, Cries Mars. . ." David Wagoner. NePoAm-2
Clap, clap handies. Mother Goose. PPL
Clap, clap the double nightcap on! William Gifford. Walter Savage Landor. GTBS-P
Clap Hands. Doug Palmer. ThO
Clap hands, clap hands. *Unknown.* OxNR
Clap hands, Daddy comes. *Unknown.* OxNR
Clap hands, Daddy's coming. *Unknown.* OxNR
Clap hands with festal joy, O holy people. Hymn for Laudes; Feast of Our Lady of Good Counsel. *Unknown.* ISi
Clapping her platter stood plump Bess. Chicken. Walter de la Mare. NeMA; TiPo
Clara. Ezra Pound. DTC
Clarastella Distrusting. Robert Heath. SeCL
Clare Coast. Emily Lawless. OxBI
Clare de Kitchen. *Unknown.* BLPA
Clarel, *sels.* Herman Melville.
Epilogue: "If Luther's day expand to Darwin's year." AmePo; AnAmPo; AP; ImOP; MAmP
Nathan. MAmP
Of Rome. OxBA
On Mammon. OxBA
Prelusive. AmPP (5th ed.)
Seedsmen of Old Saturn's Land. AmPP (3d ed.)
Sodom. AmPP (5th ed.)
Ungar and Rolfe. OxBA
Vine and Clarel. MAmP
Clare's Dragoons. Thomas Osborne Davis. OnYI
Clari, the Maid of Milan, *sel.* John Howard Payne.
Home, Sweet Home. AA; BLPA; FaBoBe; FaFP; HBV; MaRV; NeHB; OTPC; TreF; WBLP
Claribel. Tennyson. AtBAP; PeER; PoVP; ViPo
Clarified into present. The Exchanges II. Robert Kelly. CoPo
Clarimonde. Théophile Gautier, *tr. fr. French by* Lafcadio Hearn. AWP; JAWP; WBP
Clarindon's House-Warming. Andrew Marvell. MaMe
Clarion. Thomas O. Mordaunt. *See* Sound, Sound the Clarion.
Clarion-Call, The. *Unknown.* BLRP
Clark Colven and his gay ladie. Clerk Colvill (A *vers.*) *Unknown.* ESPB
Clark Sanders. *Unknown. See* Clerk Saunders.
Clash of arms which shook the Persian state, The. Abdolonymus the Sidonian. Jones Very. AP
Clasp her and hold her and love her. At Sunset. Louis V. Ledoux. HBV
Clasp you the God within yourself. The Last Round. Anna Wickham. MoBrPo
Clasped, dear girl, in your embrace. Vanity of Kissing. Bonefonius. OnPM
Clasping of Hands. George Herbert. MaMe; PoEL-2
Class Dismissed. *Unknown, tr. fr. Greek by* Louis Untermeyer. UnTE
("Lifting my eyes from Hesiod's great book.") MeWo
Classic Case, A. Gilbert Sorrentino. NeAP
Classic Encounter. "Christopher Caudwell." POTE
Classic landscapes of dreams are not, The. The Snowfall. Donald Justice. NePoEA-2
Classic Ode, A. Charles Battell Loomis. NA
Classic Scene. William Carlos Williams. AmP; OxBA; WoL
Classic Waits for Me, A. E. B. White. NYBP; Par; WhC
Classical Criticism. George Lynde Richardson. AA
Classroom in October. Elias Lieberman. GoYe
Claud Halcro's Invocation. Sir Walter Scott. *Fr.* The Pirate, *ch.* 23. NBM
Claudia Peregrina is marrying Pudens my son. For a Son's Marriage. Martial. HW
Claudius Gilbert. John Wilson. SCAP
Clavering. E. A. Robinson. CrMA; HBMV; OxBA
Clavichord, The. May Sarton. UnS
Claw-free love, when I was. Roc's Brood. Samuel M. Bradley. FiSC
Clay. E. V. Lucas. HBV
Clay Hills. Jean Starr Untermeyer. HBMV; MAP; MoAmPo (1942 ed.); NeMA; NP
Clay Pipe. Joel Sloman. ThO
Clayming a Second Kisse by Desert. Ben Jonson. *See* Claiming a Second Kiss by Desert.
Clean and Clear. Michael Brownstein. ANYP
Clean as a lady. Tulip. Humbert Wolfe. MoBrPo; NP; TSW
Clean as the ivoried hoofs of antelopes. Mountain Dawn. Gene Boardman Hoover. StaSt
Clean birds by sevens. A Charm against a Magpie. *Unknown.* ChTr
Clean Clara. William Brighty Rands. BOHV; HBV; HBVY
Clean Curtains. Carl Sandburg. WoL
Clean de ba'n and sweep de flo'. Uncle Eph's Banjo Song. James Edwin Campbell. BANP
Clean Gentleman, The. George Abbe. FiSC
Clean Hands. Austin Dobson. TrPWD
Clean in the light, with nothing to remember. Aspects. Norman MacCaig. NYTB; OxBS
Clean Platter, The. Ogden Nash. BOHV
Clean the spittoons, boy. Brass Spittoons. Langston Hughes. BANP; MAP; MoAmPo; NeMA
Clean Wind Blowing, A. *Unknown.* FaChP
Cleaning Ship. Charles Keeler. EtS
Cleaning the Candelabrum. Siegfried Sassoon. HaMV
Cleaning Up. Edward Dyson. PoAu-1
Cleaning woman opened the rusty door, A. The Church of San Antonio de la Florida. Paul Petrie. NYBP
Cleanliness. Charles *and* Mary Lamb. OTPC (1923 ed.); PRWS
Cleanly rush of the mountain air, The. The Dead Knight. John Masefield. CH; GTBS-P
Cleanly, sir, you went to the core of the matter. A Correct Compassion. James Kirkup. ChMP; FaBoTw; FlW; ImOP; SeCePo
Cleanse with the burning log of oak. *See* Light with the burning log of oak.
Cleansing. Heinrich Suso Waldeck, *tr. fr. German by* George N. Schuster. CAW
Cleansing Fires. Adelaide Anne Procter. WGRP
Cleanthes of Andros, The. To a Greek Ship in the Port of Dublin. William Bedell Stanford. NeIP
Clear after Rain. Tu Fu, *tr. fr. Chinese by* Kenneth Rexroth. PoPl
Clear air and grassy lea. Early Morning at Bargis. Hermann Hagedorn. HBV
Clear Air of October, The. Robert Bly. NaP
Clear and cool, clear and cool. The Tide River. Charles Kingsley. *Fr.* The Water Babies. BoNaP; GN; HBV; PoVP; PTK
Clear and gentle stream. Elegy. Robert Bridges. BrPo; OAEP
Clear and high, a mountain. The Hike. Neil Weiss. SD

Clear and sweet in the crystal weather. Off Banks Peninsula. Denis Glover. AnNZ
Clear Anker, on whose silver-sanded shore. Michael Drayton. Idea, LIII, *also in* Idea's Mirrour. TuPP
Clear as air, the western waters. The Grave of Rury. Thomas W. Rolleston. AnIL; AnIV; IrPN; OnYI
Clear brown eyes, kindly and alert, The. Portrait. Kenneth Fearing. MoAmPo
Clear cool note of the cuckoo which has ousted the legitimate nest-holder, The. Sincere Flattery [*or* Of W. W. (Americanus)]. James Kenneth Stephen. FiBHP; HBV; InMe; Par; WhC
Clear Eyes ("Clear eyes do dim at last"). Walter de la Mare. MoVE; ViBoPo
Clear, fresh, sweet waters. Canzone. Petrarch, *tr. by* William D. Foulke. Sonnets to Laura: To Laura in Life, Canzone XIV. LiTW
Clear frost succeeds, and thro' the blew serene. James Thomson. *Fr.* The Seasons: Winter. FaBoEn
Clear [*or* Cleere] had the day been from the dawn. A Fine Day [*or* The Sixth Nymphal]. Michael Drayton. *Fr.* The Muses' Elysium. BoTP; GN; LoBV; OBS; OTPC; PCH; TuPP
Clear Midnight, A. Walt Whitman. NeMA
Clear on the air, their pulsing cadence pealing. Convent Echoes. Helen Louise Moriarty. JKCP
Clear or Cloudy, Sweet as April Showering. *Unknown.* ElL; OBSC
Clear, placid Leman! thy contrasted lake. Lake Leman [*or* Night and Storm in the Alps]. Byron. *Fr.* Childe Harold's Pilgrimage, III. MaPo; MCCG; OBNC
Clear ringing of a bell. New Years and Old. Maud Frazer Jackson. PGD
Clear Rock's Chisholm Trail, *with music. Unknown.* CoSo
Clear the field for the grand tournament of the nations! The Tournament of Man. Ernest Crosby. PGD
Clear—the senses bright—sitting in the black chair—Rocker. Peyote Poem, I. Michael McClure. NeAP
Clear the Track, *with music. Unknown.* SoAmSa
Clear the way and build the road! The Road. Zalman Schneour. TrJP
Clear water in a brilliant bowl. The Poems of Our Climate. Wallace Stevens. AmP; MoPo; OxBA; PP; TrGrPo (rev. ed.); TwCP
Clear water; like the salt of childhood tears. Memory. Arthur Rimbaud, *tr. by* Wallace Fowlie. ReMP
Cleare moving cristall, pure as the sunne beames. Sonnet. Earl of Stirling. Aurora, XXV. OxBS
"Cleared." Kipling. PeVV
Clearing, The. Robert Graves. NYBP
Clearing, The. LeRoi Jones. CoPo
Clearing at Dawn. Li Po, *tr. fr. Chinese by* Arthur Waley. AWP; JAWP; WBP
Clearing for the Plough. E. G. Moll. MoAuPo
Clearing in the forest. The Lincoln Child. James Oppenheim. HBMV; MAP; MoAmPo (1942 ed.)
Cleary Pioneer, A. Fred Crewe. PaA
Cleator Moor. Norman Nicholson. FaBoTw; NeBP; POTi
Cleavage. Louise Townsend Nicholl. NePoAm
Cleave ever to the sunnier side of doubt. Cling to Faith. Tennyson. *Fr.* The Ancient Sage. OQP
Cleere had the day bin from the dawne. *See* Clear had the day been from the dawn.
Clefs de la prison, Les, *with music. Unknown.* OuSiCo
Cleitagoras. Leonidas of Tarentum, *tr. fr. Greek by* William M. Hardinge. AWP
Cleo on the Section Gang. The Park. Robin Blaser. CoPo
Cleobulus' Epitaph. Simonides, *tr. fr. Greek by* Richmond Lattimore. PoPl
Cleomenes, *sel.* Dryden.
No, No, Poor Suffering [*or* Suff'ring] Heart, *fr.* II, ii. AtBAP; GTBS-W; LiTB; LiTG; LiTL; LoBV; QFR; ViBoPo
(One Happy Moment.) OBEV (new ed.)
(Song: "No, no, poor suffering heart.") CEP; NoP; SeCV-2
Cleon. Robert Browning. MaVP; MBW-2; OAEP; PoVP; StP; ViPo; ViPP; VP
Greece, *br. sel.* OtMeF
Cleon and I. Charles Mackay. MaRV
Cleon the poet (from the sprinkled isles). Cleon. Robert Browning. MaVP; MBW-2; OAEP; OtMeF; PoVP; StP; ViPo; ViPP; VP
Cleonicos. Edward Cracroft Lefroy. Echoes from Theocritus, XXVII. AWP; JAWP; WBP
Cleopatra, *sels.* Samuel Daniel.
Chorus: "Behold what furies still." LoBV
Chorus: "Then thus we have beheld." OBSC
O Fearful, Frowning Nemesis. PoEL-2
Cleopatra. Shakespeare. *Fr.* Antony and Cleopatra, II ii. CLwM; DiPo; FOL; LiTB; LiTG; LiTL
("Barge she sat in, like a burnish'd throne, The.") MemP
(Cleopatra and Her Barge.) TreF
(Cleopatra's Barge.) PoFS; TrGrPo
Cleopatra. William Wetmore Story. AA
Cleopatra. Swinburne. BeLS
Cleopatra and Antony. Dryden. *Fr.* All For Love. FiP
Cleopatra and Her Barge. Shakespeare. *See* Cleopatra.
Cleopatra Dying. Thomas Stephens Collier. BLPA; FaBoBe; NeHB; OTD; TreFT
Cleopatra, who thought they maligned her. Limerick. Newton Mackintosh. LiBL; NA
Cleopatra's Barge. Shakespeare. *See* Cleopatra.
Cleopatra's Death. Shakespeare. *See* Death of Cleopatra.
Cleopatra's Lament. Shakespeare. *Fr.* Antony and Cleopatra, V, ii. UnPo
Clepsydra. Charles Cotton. CavP; PeRV
Clergyman, in want, A. Limerick [*or* Rhymes]. Ronald Arbuthnott Knox. OxBoLi; WhC
Clergyman out in Dumont, A. Limerick. Morris Bishop. LiBL; WhC
Cleric Courts His Lady, A. *Unknown.* MeEL
Clerical Oppressors. Whittier. PAH; PPON
Clerihews, *sels.* E. C. Bentley.
"After dinner Erasmus." CenHV
"Among the contemporaries of Shakespeare." OnPP
"Art of Biography, The. CenHV; FiBHP; PV
"Digestion of Milton, The. PV
"Dr. Clifford." CenHV
"Geoffrey Chaucer." PV
"George the Third." PV
"Great Duke of Wellington, The." CenHV
"Great Emperor Otto, The," PV
"'I quite realized,' said Columbus." FiBHP; OnPP
"If only Mr. Roosevelt." CenHV
"Intrepid Ricardo, The." CenHV
"It was a rule of Leonardo da Vinci's." OnPP
"It was a weakness of Voltaire's." OnPP
"John Stuart Mill." FiBHP
(J. S. Mill.) BOHV; OxBoLi; WhC
Liszt. UnS
"Mr. Bernard Shaw." CenHV
"Mr. Hilaire Belloc." CenHV
"People of Spain think Cervantes, The." CenHV; FiBHP
Sir Christopher Wren. BOHV; CenHV; FiBHP; InMe; LiTG; MoShBr; PV; ShBV-3; SiTL; WhC
(Important People, 8.) StaSt
Sir Humphry Davy. CenHV; ImOP; ShBV-3
"Sir Walter Raleigh." CenHV
"'Susaddah!' exclaimed Ibsen." PV
"What I like about Clive." CenHV
(Clive.) ShBV-3
(Lord Clive.) BOHV; MoShBr; OxBoLi; WhC
"Younger Van Eyck, The." FiBHP
Clerimont's Song. Ben Jonson. *See* Simplex Munditiis.
Clerk Colvill[e]. *Unknown.* BaBo; EnSB; ESPB (A *and* B *vers.*); OxBB; ViBoFo
(Clerk Colven.) BuBa; OBB
Clerk in the Hospital Record Room in Summer. Merrill Moore. Sonn
Clerk of Oxenford, The. Chaucer, *mod. by* Frank Ernest Hill. *Fr.* The Canterbury Tales: Prologue. OnPP
Clerk Saunders (*diff. versions*). *Unknown.* AnFE; BaBo; CBEP; ESPB (A, B, *and* F *vers.*); LO; OAEP; OBB; OBEV; OxBS; SeCeV; ViBoFo
(Clark Sanders.) OxBB
(Clerk Sanders.) NoP
Clerk Ther Was of Cauntebrigge Also, A. W. W. Skeat. Par
Clerk ther was of Oxenford also, A. Seven Pilgrims. Chaucer. *Fr.* The Canterbury Tales: Prologue. TrGrPo
Clerkes Tale. *See* Clerk's Tale.
Clerks, The. E. A. Robinson. AA; AnNE; CABA; MAmP; MAP; MaPo (1969 ed.); MoAB; MoAmPo; MoVE; NeMA; PIA; PoEL-5

Clerk's [*or* Clerkes] Tale, The. Chaucer. *Fr.* The Canterbury Tales. MBW-1
Sels.
Chaucer's Envoy to the Story of Patient Griselda, *mod. by* W. W. Skeat. AnEnPo
(Patient Griselda, *mod. by* Edward Hodnett.) PoRA
"That thee is sent, receyve in buxumnesse." PoG
Clerk's Twa Sons o Owsenford, The. *Unknown.* BaBo; ESPB
Clevedon Church. Andrew Lang. GoTS, *abr.*
Cleveland. William Goldsmith Brown. DD
Clever man builds a city, A. Woman. *Unknown. Fr.* Shi King. AWP; LiTW
Clever Tom Clinch Going to Be Hanged. Swift. CEP; CoMu; SeCeV
Click, click! like an elfin musket. Photograph. James J. Galvin. JKCP (1955 ed.)
Click Go the Shears, Boys. *Unknown.* PoAu-1
Click o' the Latch. Nancy Byrd Turner. HBMV
Clickety-clack. Song of the Train. David McCord. FaPON; SoPo
Cliff Dwelling, The. Arthur W. Monroe. PoOW
Cliff Klingenhagen. E. A. Robinson. AmePo; AmP; AmPP; AP; CaFP; CoBMV; MAP; MoAB; MoAmPo; NeMA; Sonn; TreFS
Cliff-locked port and a bluff sea wall, A. Reid at Fayal. John Williamson Palmer. PAH
Cliff Rose, The. Ernest Fewster. CaP
Cliff-Top, The. Robert Bridges. BoNaP; BoTP; GFA, *st.* 1
Cliffs of scarlet cloud gleam in the west. The Return. Tu Fu. LiTW
Cliffs that rise a thousand feet. Sailing Homeward. Chan Fang-sheng, *tr. by* Arthur Waley. AWP FaBoCh; JAWP; LoGBV; WBP
Clifton Chapel. Sir Henry Newbolt. OBEV (new ed.); OBVV
Clifton Grove, *sel.* Henry Kirke White.
"Lo! in the West, fast fades the ling'ring light." OBNC
Climacteric. Emerson. MWA-1
Climate, The. Edwin Denby. ANYP
Climate of Thought, The. Robert Graves BoPe; MoAB; ViBoPo (1958 ed.)
Climax of passion, the dancers are trembling, The. Rumba. José Zacarías Tallet. TTY
Climb. Winifred Welles. BiCB; TSW
Climb at Court for me that will. Chorus [*or* The Quiet Life]. Seneca, *tr. by* Andrew Marvell. *Fr.* Thyestes. LiTW; MaMe; OnPM; SeCV-1
Climb then by spiral stairways of cold thought. The Ghost in the Cellarage. John Heath-Stubbs. NeBP
Climbers. Earle Birney. TwCaPo
Climbers, The. Elizabeth Jennings. NePoEA
Climbing from the Lethal dead. Orpheus. Yvor Winters. MoVE
Climbing in Glencoe. Andrew Young. SD
Climbing northward. The Herds. W. S. Merwin. FRC; NaP; NYBP
Climbing sun had drunk the shade, The. Blue Ghosts. Stanley Snaith. ChMP
Climbing the beanstalk of your mind, I reach. High Kingdom. Howard Sergeant. ToPo
Climbing through the January snow, into the Lobo canyon. Mountain Lion. D. H. Lawrence. AtBAP; HaMV; ShBV-2
Climbing to the Light. Charles Mackay. RIS
Climbing up the hillside beneath the summer stars. Man in Nature. William Roscoe Thayer. AA
Clime of the brave! the high heart's home. New England. George Denison Prentice. AA
Clime of the unforgotten brave! Byron. *Fr.* The Giaour. PoFr
Clinch Mountain. *Unknown. See* Rye Whiskey.
Cling to Faith. Tennyson. *Fr.* The Ancient Sage. OQP
Cling together in your dust: the frost. Earthly Love. Joseph Bennett. NePA
Clink, clink, clinkety-clink. The Milkman. *Unknown.* BoTP
Clink of the Ice, The. Eugene Field. InMe
Clinker, The. *Unknown.* PEDC; StVeCh (1940 ed.)
Clinton South of Polk. Carl Sandburg. AmFN
Clio. Ernest Rhys. POTE
Clip-clop go water-drops and bridles ring. Nude in a Fountain. Norman MacCaig. OxBS
Clipped Wings. Lew Sarett. PoMa
Clipper, The. Thomas Fleming Day. EtS
Clipper Captain. Shirley Barker. WaKn
Clipper Loitered South, The. John Masefield. *Fr.* Dauber. EtS
Clipper Ship *Dreadnaught*, The. *Unknown.* IHA
Clipper Ships. John Anderson. EtS
Clipper Ships and Captains. Rosemary Benét *and* Stephen Vincent Benét. RePo; StVeCh (1955 ed.)
Clippety cloppity. George Starbuck. PV
Clipping. Tom Veitch. ANYP
Clippity clop, clippity clop. The Milkman. Jane W. Krows. SoPo
Cliques and Critics. Sa'ib of Isfahan, *tr. fr. Persian by* Edward G. Browne. LiTW
Clive. E. C. Bentley. *See* Lord Clive.
Cloak, The. Violet Anderson. CaP
Cloak of Laughter. Abigail Cresson. PoToHe
Clock, The. Baudelaire, *tr. fr. French by* Alan Conder. LO
Clock, The. Jovan Ducic, *tr. fr. Serbo-Croatian by* Oliver Elton. LiTW
Clock, The. Jean Jaszi. SoPo
Clock. Harold Monro. BrPo
Clock, The. Francis Scarfe. NeBP
Clock, The ("Tick, tock, tick, tock"). *Unknown.* OTPC (1946 ed.); PCH
Clock, A ("Twelve little figures around me"). *Unknown.* OTPC (1946 ed.)
Clock-a-Clay. John Clare. CBEP; ERoP-2; FaPON; LiTB; LoBV; NBM; OBNC; PoEL-4; SeCeV; ThWaDe; WHA
(Clock-o'-Clay.) PoFS; TrGrPo
Clock is on the stroke of six, The. Father Is Coming. Mary Howitt. OTPC
Clock is striking autumn at the apple vendor's fair, The. Autumn. Patricia Hubbell. PDV
Clock-o'-Clay. John Clare. *See* Clock-a-Clay.
Clock of God, The. Clarence Edwin Flynn. SoP
Clock Shop, The. Jeannette C. Shirk. GFA
Clock shows nearly five, The. To a Salesgirl, Weary of Artificial Holiday Trees. James Wright. NYBP
Clock stopped, A. Emily Dickinson. AmPP (5th ed.); AnFE; AP; APA; CABA; CoAnAm; MAmP; MAPA; MaPo; MWA-2; NCEP; NoP; PoEL-5; TwAmPo
Clock Symphony. John Frederick Nims. MiAP
Clock ticks slowly, slowly in the hall, The. The Twenty-fourth of December. *Unknown.* PCH
Clock Time by the Geyser. John White. ShM
Clock Tower, The. Colleen Thibaudeau. WHW
Clock within us, speaking time, The. Making Love, Killing Time. Anne Ridler. NMP
Clock Works, The. Lewis Mac Adams. ANYP; YAP
Clocked with the sun and by his journey paced. Homestead—Winter Morning. Mary Ballard Duryee. GoYe
Clocking Hen, The. Ann Hawkshaw. *See* Clucking Hen, The.
Clocks. Louis Ginsberg. TrJP
Clocks. Carl Sandburg. CrMA
Clocks are chiming in my heart, The. Past. John Galsworthy. HBV
Clocks begin, civicly simultaneous, The. At Delft. Charles Tomlinson. NYBP
Clock's Song, The. Rose Hawthorne Lathrop. AA; JKCP
Clock's untiring fingers wind the wool of darkness, The. Cradle Song. Louis MacNeice. MoAB; MoBrPo
Clock-Winder, The. Thomas Hardy. PoVP
Clockwork beings, winding out their lives. Insects. Isidor Schneider. AnAmPo; TrJP
Clod, The. Edwin Curran. HBMV
Clod and the Pebble, The. Blake. *Fr.* Songs of Experience. AWP; BEL; BoLiVe; CABA; CBEP; EiPP; EnL; EnLi-2; EnLit; EnLoPo; EnRP; FaBoEn; FaBV; ForPo; JAWP; LoBV; MaPo (1969 ed.); OAEP; OBEC; OBNC; OnPM; OtMeF; PeER; PoAn; PoeP; TOP; TrGrPO; ViBoPo; WBP
("Love seeketh not itself to please.") LO
Clod of Clay heard the Worm's voice and raised her pitying head, The. Blake. *Fr.* The Book of Thel. LO
Clods of battlefields are red, The. Stanzas from "Elegy for Edward Thomas." Charles Dalmon. POTE
Cloe. George Granville. SeEP
Cloe, by your command, in verse i write. A Letter from Ar-

temisa in the Town, to Cloe, in the the Country. Earl of Rochester. SeCV-2
Cloe Jealous. Matthew Prior. CEP; EiPP
Cloe's the wonder of her sex. To Cloe. George Granville. PV
Clogged and soft and sloppy eyes. The Parents; People Like Our Marriage. Gwendolyn Brooks. TPM
Cloister. Conrad Aiken. Preludes for Memnon, XX. MAP; MoAmPo; MoAB
(So in the Evening, to the Simple Cloister.) LiTA
Cloister. Charles L. O'Donnell. CAW
Cloistered. Alice Brown. AA; MaRV
Cloisters, The. William M. Hoffman. ThO
Cloisters, The. Samuel Yellen. NePoAm
Clonard. Thomas S. Jones, Jr. HBMV
Clonmacnoise. Angus O'Gillan. *See* Dead at Clonmacnois, The.
Clootie. *Unknown.* BuBa
Clora! Conde Bernardino de Rebolledo, *tr. fr. Spanish by* Sir John Bowring. OnPM
Clora [*or* Chlora] come view my soul, and tell. The Gallery. Andrew Marvell. AnAnS-1; MaMe; MeLP; OBS; ReEn; SeEP; SiSw
Clora! to church—your sad complaint. Clora! Conde Bernardino de Rebolledo. OnPM
Clorinda and Damon. Andrew Marvell. AnAnS-1; MaMe; SeCP
Cloris and Mertilla. Michael Drayton. *Fr.* The Muses' Elysium. LoBV
Cloris, I cannot say your eyes. *See* Chloris, I cannot say your eyes.
Cloris I faine would try to love againe. *Unknown.* SeCSL
Cloris, I justly am betray'd. To Cloris. Sir Charles Sedley. PeRV
Cloris I wish that envye were. *Unknown.* SeCSL
Cloris, [*or* Chloris], it is not thy disdaine. Song [*or* To Chloris *or* To the Tune of, In Fayth I Cannot Keepe My Fathers Sheepe]. Sidney Godolphin. EG; MeLP; OBS; SeCL
Cloris, since my death doth com from you. *Unknown.* SeCSL
Cloris when I to thee present. *See* Chloris, when I to thee present.
Close, The. Richard Crashaw. MaMe
Close all open things, O God! Prayer for Sophistication. Mark Turbyfill. NP
Close as the stars along the sky. Reine d'Amour. Francis Turner Palgrave. GBV (1952 ed.)
Close by a fringed banke I found. *Unknown.* SeCSL
Close by the margin of the brook. Dame Duck's First Lecture on Education [*or* Dame Duck's Lecture to Her Ducklings]. Ann Hawkshaw. OTPC (1923 ed.); SAS
Close by the threshold of a door nailed [*or* nail'd] fast. The Colubraid. William Cowper. BOHV; CIV; OTPC (1923 ed.)
Close by those meads, for ever crown'd [*or* crowned] with flowers. Pope. *Fr.* The Rape of the Lock. FiP; OxBoLi; WHA
Close Clan, The. Mark Van Doren. GoYe
Close eyes, bow head. *Unknown.* ThGo
Close gray sky, A. The Lark. Lizette Woodworth Reese. GFA; HBMV; OTPC (1946 ed.)
Close her eyes; she must not peep! By the Cradle. George Macdonald. OTPC (1946 ed.)
Close his eyes; his work is done! Dirge for a Soldier. George Henry Boker. AA; AnFE; APA; CoAnAm; DD; HBV; MC; OBVV; PaA; PAH; PAP; WaaP
Close in a cage a bird I'll keep. Riddles, 2. *Unknown.* CoBE
Close in the hollow bank she lies. The Stockdove. Ruth Pitter. HaMV; SeCePo
Close, Mortal Eyes. Ruth Pitter. BoC
Close not thy hand upon the innocent joy. Forbearance. "Owen Meredith." PCD
Close now thine eyes, and rest secure. A Good-Night. Francis Quarles. OBS; SeCL; SeEP; TrGrPo
Close of Day, The. Wesley Curtwright. CDC
Close on the edge of a midsummer dawn. A Shadow of the Night. Thomas Bailey Aldrich. AA
Close ranks and ride on! The Riderless Horse. Harold Trowbridge Pulsifer. MaRV
Close softly thine arms about me like a girdle. Endearments. Pierre Louys. *Fr.* The Songs of Bilitis. UnTE
Close thine [*or* thy] eyes, and sleep secure. On a Quiet Conscience. Charles I, King of England. CH; PCD
Close to Me. "Gabriela Mistral," *tr. fr. Spanish by* Langston Hughes. PoPl
Close to the breast of night. Life of Life. Johannes Edfelt. LiTW
Close to the frontier of Eternity is my patrimony. The Migrant. Donald C. Babcock. NePoAm
Close to the road's impurity. A Primrose by the Wayside. Anna Bunston de Bary. MaRV
Close to the Sacred Heart, it nestles fair. Ladye Chapel at Eden Hall. Eleanor C. Donnelly. JKCP
Close to the sod. The Snowdrop. Anna Bunston de Bary. BoTP; HBMV; MaRV
Close under here, I watched two lovers once. The Beaches, VI. "Robin Hyde." AnNZ
Close up the casement, draw the blind. Shut Out That Moon. Thomas Hardy. BrPo; CMoP; MoVE; ViBoPo
Close up the Ranks. Edward S. Van Zile. PEDC
Close-wrapped in living thought I stand. All-Souls' Day. Siegfried Sassoon. MoRP
Close Your Eyes! Arna Bontemps. AmNP; CDC; Kal; PoNe
Closed Door, The. Theodosia Garrison. BLPA; PoToHe
Closed eyes can't see the white roses. Give Them the Flowers Now. Leigh M. Hodges. WBLP
Closed for Good. Robert Frost. MoAmPo (1950 ed.)
Closer to Christ. Lucy Larcom. SoP
Closer Walk with God, A. William Cowper. *See* Walking with God.
Closes and courts and lanes. Song. John Davidson. BrPo; HBV; PoVP
Closest to men, thou pitying Son of Man. To Jesus of Nazareth. Frederic Lawrence Knowles. TrPWD
Closing Cadence. John Moffit. MoRP
Closing Doxology, The. Psalms, CL, Bible, *O.T.* (Smith-Goodspeed *tr.*). MaRV
Closing Music, A. Laurence Whistler. MuSP
Closing of the Rodeo, The. William Jay Smith. NePoEA; RePo; SD; TwCP
Closing Prayer. Johnstone G. Patrick. TrPWD
Closing Scene, The. Thomas Read. AA; HBV
Closing the Doors. Irene Pettit McKeehan. MaRV; OQP
Closing Time. James Michie. NePoEA-2
Closing Time. David Wagoner. NYBP
Clote, The (Water-Lily). William Barnes. ELP; GTBS-D; PoEL-4
Cloth of Gold. F. R. Scott. MoCV
Clothed in yellow, red, and green. *Unknown.* OxNR
Clother of the lily, Feeder of the sparrow. A Prayer [*or* They Toil Not neither Do They Spin.] Christina Rossetti. OBVV; TrPWD
Clothes. Abbie Farwell Brown. PPL
Clothes. Frances Frost. RePo
Clothes Do but Cheat and Cozen Us. Robert Herrick. ALV; ErPo
(Away with Silks.) MeWo
Clothes-Line, The. Charlotte Druitt Cole. BoTP
Clothes make no sound when I tread ground. A Riddle. *Unknown.* ChTr
Clothing's New Emperor, The. Donald Finkel. NePoEA
Cloud, The. Salvador Diaz Mirón, *tr. fr. Spanish by* Alice Stone Blackwell. PoFr
Cloud, The. Oliver Herford. BOHV
Cloud. Samuel Hoffenstein. AnAmPo
Cloud, The. Sidney Lanier. AmePo
Cloud, The. Shelley. ATP; BEL; BoLiVe; CBEP; ChER; EnL; EnLi-2; EnLit; EnRP; EPN; ERoP-2; FaPON; GN; GTBS-W; HBV; ImOP, *abr.*; InP; LiTB; LiTG; MBW-2; MCCG; MERP; MPB; NoP; OAEP; OBRV; OHFP; OTPC; OuHeWo; PCH, *much abr.*; PoE; PoEL-4; PoIE; RePo; RG; RIS, *sts.* 1-2; SeCeV; StaSt, *br. sel.*; TOP; TreF; TrGrPo; ViBoPo
Cloud and Flame. John Berryman. AP
Cloud and Wind. Dante Gabriel Rossetti. The House of Life, XLIV. MaVP; PoVP; ViPo VP
Cloud assumes fantastic shapes, The. Cloud. Samuel Hoffenstein. AnAmPo
Cloud-backed heron will not move, The. The Heron. Vernon Watkins. ChMP; GTBS-P; TwCP; UnPo (3d ed.)
Cloud-bank lies in a red-gold ring, The. Judith Remembers. Maxwell Anderson. *Fr.* Judith of Minnewaulken. WHA
Cloud-capp'd towers, the gorgeous palaces, The. Our Revels Now

Cloud-capp'd (continued)
Are Ended. Shakespeare. *Fr.* The Tempest, IV, i. MaRV; PoPl
Cloud Confines, The. Dante Gabriel Rossetti. BEL; EnLi-2; TOP
Cloud Country. James Merrill. NePoEA
Cloud doth gather, the green wood roar, The. Thekla's Song. Schiller. *Fr.* The Piccolomini. AWP; JAWP; WBP
Cloud Fantasies, I. Christian Morgenstern, *tr. fr. German by* Babette Deutsch *and* Avrahm Yarmolinsky. OnPM
Cloud House, The. Adrian Mott. GaP
Cloud is the post office between continents, The. To Modigliani to Prove to Him That I Am a Poet. Max Jacob. TrJP
Cloud lay cradled near the setting sun, A. The Evening Cloud. "Christopher North." HBV
Cloud-maidens that float on forever. Song of the Clouds. Aristophanes. *Fr.* The Clouds. AWP
Cloud-Messenger, The, *sel.* Kalidasa, *tr. fr. Sanskrit by* Arthur W. Ryder.
"O cloud, the parching spirit stirs thy pity." LiTW
Cloud-Mobile, The. May Swenson. GoTP
Cloud moved close, A. The bulk of the wind shifted. The Visitant. Theodore Roethke. NMP; PoIE; UnPo (3d ed.)
Cloud of Carmel, The. Jessica Powers. ISi
Cloud of dust on the long, white road, A. The Teams. Henry Lawson. BoAu; NeLNL; PoAu-1
Cloud of grasshoppers, A. Credo. Leonard Cohen. PeCV (1967 ed.)
Cloud of Unknowing, The. Philip Murray. NePoAm-2
Cloud only goes, A. Clouds. Jean Jaszi. RePo
Cloud-piercing mountains! Chance and Change. Fest. Puritatis. Aubrey Thomas De Vere. *Fr.* May Carols. PoVP
Cloud possessed the hollow field, A. The High Tide at Gettysburg. Will Henry Thompson. AA; BeLS; BLPA; FaBoBe; HBV; MC; OTD; PaA; PAH; PAL; PaPo; PFY; PoFr; TreFS
Cloud-puffball, torn tufts, tossed pillows. That Nature Is a Heraclitean Fire and of the Comfort of the Resurrection. Gerard Manley Hopkins. AtBAP; BrPo; CABA; CoBMV; DiPo; FaBoMo; GTBS-P; LiTB; MaPo; MoAB; MoPo; MoVE; NoP; OAEP (2d ed.); PAn; PoEL-5; ViPo (1962 ed.); ViPP
Cloud-riders leap for Normandy. On the Cliff. Hal Summers. ChMP
Clouded Morning, The. Jones Very. AP
Clouded vision, light obscure. Such Is Love. Rodrigo Cota de Maguaque. OnPM
Clouded with snow. Winter. Walter de la Mare. OBMV
Cloudless night like this, A. A Walk after Dark. W. H. Auden. MaPo
Clouds. Dorothy Aldis. SoPo
Clouds, The, *sel.* Aristophanes, *tr. fr. Greek.*
Song of the Clouds, *tr. by* Oscar Wilde. AWP
(Chorus of the Clouds, *tr. by* T. F. Higham.) LiTW
Clouds. Norman Ault. HBVY
Clouds. Rupert Brooke. BoC; BrPo; GTSL; MoVE; OBEV (new ed.); OBMV; POTE
Clouds. John Jay Chapman. EtS
Clouds, The. William Croswell. AA
Clouds. Frank Ernest Hill. AnAmPo
Clouds. Jean Jaszi. RePo
Clouds. James Reaney. WHW
Clouds. Shakespeare. *See* Our Revels Now Are Ended.
Clouds. Frank Dempster Sherman. PRWS
Clouds. *Unknown, wr. at. to* Christina Rossetti. BrR; OTPC (1946 ed.); PCH; SoPo; StVeCh
(White Sheep, *wr. at. to* W. H. Davies.) BoTP
("White sheep, white sheep.") TiPo
Clouds, The. William Carlos Williams. MoPo
Clouds. Helen Wing. GFA
Clouds across the Canyon. John Gould Fletcher. Grand Canyon of the Colorado, IV. HT
Clouds are scudding across the moon, The. Storm Song. Bayard Taylor. BBV (1923 ed.); EtS; HBV; OTD
Clouds, clouds, clouds in the sky. Washerwoman's Song. L. A. G. Strong. YT
Clouds, ever drifting in air. Chorus of the Clouds. Aristophanes. *Fr.* The Clouds. LiTW
Clouds go rolling over, The. Ron Padgett. *Fr.* Tone Arm. YAP
Clouds grow clear, the pine-wood glooms and stills, The. A Summer Evening. Archibald Lampman. PeCV
Clouds had made a crimson crown, The. A Moment. Mary Elizabeth Coleridge. PoVP
Clouds hang heavy around my way, The. Trust. *Unknown.* SoP
Clouds Have Left the Sky, The. Robert Bridges. CH; EG; PoVP
Clouds in the sky at twilight. The Violin Calls. Florence Randal Livesay. CaP
Clouds, lingering yet, extend in solid bars. Composed by the Side of Grasmere Lake. Wordsworth. BWP; ChER; MERP; Sonn
Clouds of Evening. Robinson Jeffers. MAP; MoAB; MoAmPo
Clouds or waves? Waves or Clouds? A View of the Sea. Mabuchi. OnPM
Clouds spout upon her. Rain on a Grave. Thomas Hardy. CoBMV; HBV; OAEP
Clouds That Are So Light, The. Edward Thomas. FaBoTw
Clouds, the source of rain, one stormy night. Lost in Heaven. Robert Frost. MAP; MoAmPo
Clouds, then the glory of sunset. Contrasts. Henry Meade Bland. SoP
Clouds weave a shawl, The. Garment. Langston Hughes. GoSl
Clouds were all brushed up and back, The. Snow Advent. Joseph Auslander. MoSiPe
Clouds were fishbone, The. Walden in July. Donald Junkins. NYBP
Clouds, which rise with thunder, slake, The. All's Well. Whittier. CBEP; FaChP; OBVV; SoP
Clover, The. Margaret Deland. AA
Clover. Lope de Vega, *tr. fr. Spanish by* Jessie Read Wendell. LiTW
Clover. John Banister Tabb. AA; AnAmPo; AnFE; APA; CoAnAm
Clover-burr was two feet high, and the billabongs were full, The. Irish Lords. Charles H. Souter. PoAu-1
Clover, dear Christ, what fragrance! Clover. Lope de Vega. LiTW
Clover for Breakfast. Frances Frost. RePo; StVeCh (1955 ed.)
Clovers, The. Jean Garrigue. MoPo
Clover's simple fame, The. Emily Dickinson. MWA-2; NoP
Clown, The. Dorothy Aldis. PDV
Clown, The. Margaret E. Bruner. PoToHe
Clown, The. D. L. Graham. BF
Clown, The. Donald Hall. NYBP
Clown, The. Mary Catherine Rose. SoPo
Clown, The: He Dances in the Clearing by Night. Ramon Guthrie. NMP; OPoP
Clownish Song, A. Thomas Nashe. *See* A-Maying, a-Playing.
Clown's Baby, The. "Margaret Vandegrift." PaPo; SCC
Clown's Courtship, The. *Unknown. See* Quoth John to Joan.
Clowns' Houses. Edith Sitwell. SyP
Clowns in a garish air. On panicky pedals. The Necromancers. John Frederick Nims. PoCh
Clown's Song, The ("Come away, come away, death"). Shakespeare. *See* Come Away, Come Away, Death. *Fr.* Twelfth Night.
Clown's Song ("O mistris mine where are you roming?"). Shakespeare. *See* O Mistress Mine.
Cloying sea envelopes man at birth, A. Adventure. Guy Mason. CaP
Clubby! thou surely art, I ween. Verses on a Cat. Charles Daubeny. CIV; HBV
Clubwoman. Mary Carter Smith. PoNe (1970 ed.)
Cluck, Cluck, *with music. Unknown.* FTB
Clucking Hen, The. Ann Hawkshaw. BoTP; PPL
(Clocking Hen, The.) HBVY; OTPC; SAS
Clue, The. Charlotte Fiske Bates. AA
Clumps of ghostly buckeye. Black Mountain, Los Altos. Robert Hass. YAP
Clunton and Clunbury. A. E. Housman. A Shropshire Lad, L. PoVP; ViPo
Clustering rainbow-grapes. Balloon Man. Jessica Nelson North. GaP; SoPo
Clusters in Thy vineyard turn to gold, The, O God. Grape-gathering. Abraham Shlonsky. TrJP
Clusters of electric bulbs. The Excavation. Max Endicoff. PoMa

Cluttered Temples. George Herbert. SoP
Clyde [*or* Clyde's] Water[s]. *Unknown.* *See* Mother's Malison, The; or, Clyde's Waters.
Coach. Eleanor Farjeon. PoRh
Coach,/ Carriage. *Unknown.* OxNR
Coach is at the door at last, The. Farewell to the Farm. Robert Louis Stevenson. BoChLi (1939 ed.); BoTP; FaPON; GaP; MPB; OTPC; TiPo
Coach of Time, The. Pushkin, *tr. fr. Russian by* C. M. Bowra. LiTW
Coachman's Yarn, The. E. J. Brady. PoAu-1
Coal Fire. Louis Untermeyer. GoTP
Coal for Mike. Bertolt Brecht, *tr. fr. German by* H. R. Hays. PoPl
Coal Man, The. Hugh Chesterman. GFA
Coal Miner's Child, The. *Unknown.* *See* Orphan Girl, The.
Coal-Owner and the Pitman's Wife, The. *Unknown.* CoMu
Coal-white bird appeares this spring, A. Almanac Verse. Samuel Danforth. SCAP
Coals of Fire. A. P. Herbert. ALV
Coame, Malkyn, Hurle Thine Oyz at Hodge Trillindle. *Unknown.* NCEP
Coarse/ jocosity/ catches the crowd. Archy Confesses. Don Marquis. *Fr.* Archy and Mehitabel. EvOK; FiBHP
Coast, The—I think it was the coast that I. Juan and Haidee; Ways of Love. Byron. *Fr.* Don Juan, II. EPN
Coast of Peru, The. *Unknown.* EtS; ShS; SoAmSa, *with music, diff. vers.*
Coasters, The. Thomas Fleming Day. AA; PFY
Coastguard House, The. Robert Lowell, *ad. fr. the Italian of* Eugenio Montale. NaP
Coastguardsman in the Fog, The. James Schevill. FiMAP
Coasts of High Barbary, The. *Unknown.* OnSP
Coastwise Lights, The. Kipling. EtS
Coat, A. W. B. Yeats. CMoP; GTBS-W; LiTG; LiTM (rev. ed.); ML; PoEL-5
Coat of Fire, The. Edith Sitwell. FaBoTw; OAEP (2d ed.)
Coaxing a Fairy Fiddler. Monica Shannon. BoChLi
Cobb Would Have Caught It. Robert Fitzgerald. InvP; SD; TwCP
Cobbe's Prophecies. *Unknown.* NA
Cobbled with stars. Lament for a Man Who Loved God. James Schevill. FiMAP
Cobbler. Peggy Bacon. OCS; PoMa
Cobbler, The. Eleanor Alletta Chaffee. GaP; SoPo; TiPo
Cobbler, The. *Unknown.* BoTP
Cobbler and the Rich Man, The. La Fontaine, *tr. fr. French by* Elizur Wright. OuHeWo
Cobbler bent at his wooden foot, The. John Masefield. *Fr.* Reynard the Fox. ViBoPo
Cobbler, cobbler, mend my shoe. Mother Goose. OxNR; RIS; StVeCh (1940 ed.)
Cobbler in Willow Street, The. George O'Neil. HBMV
Cobbler sang from morn till night, A. The Cobbler and the Rich Man. La Fontaine. OuHeWo
Cobbler's Song, The. *At. to* George Peele, *also at. to* Charles Tilney. *Fr.* Locrine, II, iii. OBSC
(Strumbo, Dorothy, Trumpart, Cobbling Shoes.) TuPP
Coble o Cargill, The. *Unknown.* ESPB
Coblerone I'm told, A. Mutton and Leather. *Unknown.* CoMu
Cobweb. Winifred Welles. AnAmPo
Cobwebs. E. L. M. King. BoTP
Cobwebs. Christina Rossetti. NoP
Cobwebs. *Unknown.* GFA
Cobwebs and dust have long. Hut near Desolated Pines. Alistair Campbell. AnNZ
Cocaine Lil. *Unknown.* AS, *with music*; TrAS, *with music*
(Cocaine Lil and Morphine Sue.) OxBoLi; SiTL
Cock, The. Eleanor Farjeon. RIS
(For a Cock.) PoRh
Cock, The. Rose Fyleman. UTS
Cock. Anthony Ostroff. NYTB
Cock-a-doodle-doo!/ My dame has lost her shoe. Mother Goose. BoTP; HBVY; OTPC; OxNR; RIS; StVeCh (1940 ed.)
Cock-a-doodle-doo the brass-lined rooster says. Dog. John Crowe Ransom. LiTA
Cock a doodle do! 'tis the bravest game. Cock-throwing. Martin Lluellyn. SeCL
Cock Again, The. Kikaku, *tr. fr. Japanese by* Harold G. Henderson. SoPo
Cock and Hens. Eliza Lee Follen. SAS
Cock and his hen perching in the night, A. The Cock and the Hen. John Heywood. ReIE
Cock and the Bull, The. Charles Stuart Calverley. ALV; BOHV; InMe; NA; Par
Cock and the Hen, The. John Heywood. ReIE
Cock and the Pearl, The. La Fontaine, *tr. fr. French by* Elizur Wright. OnPM
Cock, cock, cock, cock. Cock and Hens. Eliza Lee Follen. SAS
Cock, cock, cock, cock. *Unknown.* OxNR
Cock-Crow. R. N. Currey. PeSA
Cock-Crow, *sl. abr.* Robert Herrick. MyFE
Cock Crow. Edward Thomas. GTBS-P; MoAB; MoBrPo; NeMA
Cockcrow. Eithne Wilkins. NeBP
Cock-Crow Song. *Unknown,* *tr. fr. Chinese by* Arthur Waley. LiTW
Cock-Crow; Woodstock. Henry Morton Robinson. CAW
Cock-Crowing. Henry Vaughan. AnAnS-1; AtBAP; MaPo; MeP; MePo; SCEP-1; SeCV-1
Cock crows, The/ But no queen rises. Depression before Spring. Wallace Stevens. WIRo
Cock crows in the morn. The Cocks [*or* Rules of Behavior]. Mother Goose. HBVY; PPL; RIS
Cock doth crow, The. Mother Goose. OxNR; PCH; TiPo
Cock had first performed and roused the dogs, The. Morning Overture; Chorus of Dogs. Pearl Strachan. GoTP
Cock has crow'd an hour ago, The. The Morning Quatrains. Charles Cotton. PeRV
Cock is crowing, The. The Farm Yard. Eliza Lee Follen. OTPC (1946 ed.)
Cock is crowing, The. Written in March [*or* In March *or* The Merry Month of March]. Wordsworth. BoChLi; BoNaP; BoTP; DD; EnRP; EvOK; FaPON; GoJo; GoTP; HBV; HBVY; LiTG; MoShBr; MPB; OTD; OTPC; PCH; PoG; PoRL; PRWS; PTK; RG; RIS; ShBV-1; SoPo; StaSt; SUS; ThWaDe; TiPo; UnPo (3d ed.); WaKn; YeAr
Cock-Pheasant. Laurie Lee. POTi
Cock Robin got up early. *Unknown.* BoTP; OxNR; RIS
Cock Robin, he got a new tippet in spring. The Red Robin. John Clare. BiS
Cock scratch'd up, one day, A. The Cock and the Pearl. La Fontaine. OnPM
Cock Shall Crow, The. Ditty. Robert Louis Stevenson. TrGrPo
Cock stubble-searching pheasant, delicate. Pheasant. Sidney Keyes. HaMV
Cock that crew when Peter lied, The. Cock-Crow; Woodstock. Henry Morton Robinson. CAW
Cock that crowed this dawn up, heard, The. Robert D. Fitzgerald. *Fr.* Copernicus. BoAV
Cock-throwing. Martin Lluellyn. SeCL
Cockayne Country. Agnes Mary F. Robinson. OBVV; VA
Cockcrow. *See* Cock-Crow.
Cockerel Sun. Rosemary Dobson. MoAuPo
Cockerel, the Cat, and the Young Mouse, The. La Fontaine, *tr. fr. French by* Elizur Wright. WoL
Cockies of Bungaree. *Unknown.* PoAu-1
Cockles and Mussels. *Unknown.* ELP; OnYI
("In Dublin's fair city, where the girls are so pretty.") LO
(Molly Malone.) MaC
Cockle-Shell and Sandal-Shoon. Herbert T. J. Coleman. CaP
Cockley Moor, Dockray, Penrith. Norman Nicholson. NeBP
Cockney of the North, The. Harry Graham. CenHV
Cockney Outwitted, The, *Unknown.* *See* Country Girl's Policy, The.
Cockpit in the Clouds. Dick Dorrance. FaPON; PoMa; TiPo
Cockroach Song. *Unknown.* *See* Cucaracha, La.
Cockroach stood by the mickle, The. Archy Experiences a Seizure [*or* The Hero Cockroach]. Don Marquis. *Fr.* Archys Life of Mehitabel. TSW; WhC
Cocks, The. Boris Pasternak, *tr. fr. Russian by* J. M. Cohen. LiTW
Cocks are crowing, The. Eerily Sweet. Elizabeth J. Coatsworth. ChBR
Cocks crow. What They Do. Eleanor Farjeon. ThGo
Cocks crow in the morn. Mother Goose. GoTP; TiPo
Cock's on the housetop blowing his horn, The. A Busy Day [*or*

Cock's (continued)
Summer]. *Unknown.* OTPC (1946 ed.); PCH; RIS
Cock's on the wood pile, The. *Unknown.* OxNR
Cocktail is a pleasant drink, The. R-e-m-o-r-s-e. George Ade. ALV; FiBHP; TreFT
Cocktail Party, The. Harriet Zinnes. NYTB
Cocky Doodle Doodle Doo, *with music.* *Unknown.* OuSiCo
Cocky Walkers, The. Mervyn Peake. POTE; ShBV-4
Cocoa-Tree, The. Charles Warren Stoddard. AA; AmePo; CAW
Coconut, The. "Ande." FiBHP
Cocoon, The. Robert Frost. MWA-2
Cocoon. David McCord. PoPo
Cocooning, The. Frédéric Mistral, *tr. fr. French by* Harriet Waters Preston. *Fr.* The Mirèio. AWP; JAWP; PoPl; WBP; WoL
Cocteau's *Opium*: 1. Donald Finkel. CoPo
Cocteau's *Opium*: 2. Donald Finkel. CoPo
Cod Liver Ile, *with music.* *Unknown.* OuSiCo
Coda. Louis MacNeice. TDP
Coda. Dorothy Parker. BOHV; InMe; TreFS
Coda. James Tate. NYBP
Code, The. Robert Frost. MaC; NP; YT
Code, The. Christopher Morley. LHV
Code arrives, A; language; lingo; slang. Carl Sandburg. *Fr.* Good Morning, America. ReMP
Code of Morals, A. Kipling. OnSP
Code of the Cow Country. S. Omar Barker. PoOW
Codes. Lois Seyster Montross. HBMV
Codfish lays ten thousand eggs, The. It Pays to Advertise. *Unknown.* TreFT
Codfish Shanty, The, *with music.* *Unknown.* SoAmSa
Cod-Fisher, The. Joseph C. Lincoln. EtS
Codicil. Mabel MacDonald Carver. GoYe
Codicil for Pvt. John Hogg's Will. Winfield Townley Scott. FiMAP
Cod-Piece That Will House, The. Shakespeare. *Fr.* King Lear, III, ii. ViBoPo
Codrus, a shepherd lusty, gay, and stout. The Fourth Egloge of Alexander Barclay. Alexander Barclay. ReIE
Coelia, *sels.* William Percy.
"If it be sin so dearly for to love thee," VII. ReIE
"It shall be said I died for Coelia," XIX. ReEn; ReIE; Sonn; TuPP
(Sonnet.) EIL
"Judged by my goddess' doom to endless pain," I. ReIE; Sonn; TuPP
"Receive these writs, my sweet and dearest friend," XX. ReIE
"Relent, my dear yet unkind Coelia," XVII. Sonn; TuPP
"What is the fair to whom so long I plead?" XV. ReIE
Coelo et in Terra. Thomas Walsh. JKCP
Coeur de Lion to Berengaria. Theodore Tilton. AA
Coexistence. Marie Syrkin. NYTB
Coffee. J. V. Cunningham. MoAmPo (1962 ed.)
Coffee cups cool on the Vicar's harmonium. A Game of Consequences. Paul Dehn. ErPo; FiBHP
Coffeepot Face, A. Aileen Fisher. MPB
Coffee-House Lecture, A. Robert Mezey. CABA
Coffin, The. Heine, *tr. fr. German by* Louis Untermeyer. AWP; JAWP; WBP
Coffin-Worm, The. Ruth Pitter. MoBrPo; TrGrPo (1942 ed.)
Cogitabo pro Peccato Meo. William Habington. CoBE
Coil upon coil, the grave serpent holds. An Equation. Hyam Plutzik. FiMAP
Coilyear, The, gudlie in feir, tuke him be the hand. *Unknown.* *Fr.* Rauf Coilyear. OxBS
Coin, The. Sara Teasdale. HBMV; RePo; SP; TiPo (1952 ed.)
Coin in the Fist. Florence Kerr Brownell. GoYe
Coin of Pity, The. George Meredith. Modern Love, XLIV. VA
Coins and Coffins under My Bed. Diane Wakoski. CoPo
Coins of Love, The. John Richard Moreland. *Fr.* What of the Night? MaRV
("Arrogant kings, with envious lust.") ChIP
Cois na Teineadh. T. W. Rolleston. AnIV
Cokaygne. *Unknown.* *See* Land of Cokaigne, The.
Cokkils. Sydney Goodsir Smith. OxBS
Cold. Robert Francis. NePoAm-2
Cold. Margaret Parton. PCD
Cold, The/ with steely clutch. Winter. Adelaide Crapsey. MPB
Cold against the sky. Tanka, IV. Lewis Alexander. CDC
Cold and brilliant streams the sunlight on the wintry banks of Seine. Funeral of Napoleon I. Sir John H. Hagarty. CaP
Cold and chill is de winter wind. Big Jim. *Unknown.* ABF
Cold and clear-cut face, why come you so cruelly meek. Tennyson. *Fr.* Maud, I. SyP
Cold and holy oak. Rumba of the Three Lost Souls. Charles Madge. NeBP
Cold and the colors of cold: mineral, shell. Cold. Robert Francis. NePoAm-2
Cold Are the Crabs. Edward Lear. GoJo
(Sonnet, A.) CenHV
Cold as a mountain in its star-pitched tent. Kinship with the Stars. George Meredith. *Fr.* Modern Love, IV. GTBS-W
Cold as the breath of winds that blow. Lucasta's World. Richard Lovelace. SCEP-2; SeCP
Cold as the thin Marquis who bit when kissing. The Lucifer. Guy Glover. CaP
Cold August. Jim Harrison. NYTB
Cold blast at the casement beats, The. The Heart's Summer. Epes Sargent. AA
Cold Blast of Debt. Catullus, *tr. fr. Latin by* George Lamb. OnPM
Cold-blooded Creatures. Elinor Wylie. ImOP
Cold Blows the Wind. John Hamilton. CH
Cold blows the wind to my true love. The Unquiet Grave. *Unknown.* ViBoFo
Cold blows the winter wind: 'tis Love. Love at the Door. Meleager. AWP
Cold, clear, and blue, the morning heaven. The Morning Star. Emily Brontë. ChTr
Cold coiled line of mottled lead, A. The Massasauga. Hamlin Garland. AA
Cold, cold!/ Cold to-night is broad Moylurg. A Song of Winter. *Unknown.* AnIL; CH; OnYI
Cold. Cold. Cold winds and colder heart. A Knight of Ghosts and Shadows. Dunstan Thompson. NePA
Cold, cold is the north wind and rude is the blast. The Battle of Lovell's Pond. Longfellow. PAH
Cold, cold the year draws to its end. Old Poem. *Unknown.* AWP
Cold Colloquy. Patrick Anderson. Poem on Canada, V. CaP; PeCV
("What are you...? they ask.") TwCaPo
"Cold coming we had of it, A." Journey of the Magi. T. S. Eliot. AmP; BoC; BWP; CABA; CaFP; CoBA; DiPo; DTC; EaLo; FaBoCh; FaBoMo; FaFP; GTBS-D; GTBS-W; ILP; InPo; LiTA; LiTM; LoGBV; MAP; MaPo; MoAB; MoAmPo; MoRP; MWA-2; NePA; NoP; OAEP (2d ed.); OBMV; PAn; PIA; PoAn; PoE; PoIE; PoPo; PoSa; ShBV-3; StJW; TIHL; TrGrPo; TwCP; UnPo (3d ed.); WePo
Cold, deserted and silent. *Unknown.* *Fr.* Winter on Black Mingo. FiBHP
Cold Divinities, The. James Wright. AmPC
Cold Earth Slept Below, The. Shelley. *See* Lines: "Cold earth slept below, The."
Cold eyelids that hide like a jewel. Dolores. Swinburne. MaVP; PoVP; ViPo; VP
Cold Fact. Dick Emmons. PoPl
Cold Fall. Richard Eberhart. FiMAP
Cold Fire. George Starbuck. NYBP
Cold, gray light of the dawning, The. Ticonderoga. V. B. Wilson. OTPC; PaA; PAL; PAP
Cold Green Element, The. Irving Layton. OBCV
Cold grey hills they bind me around, The. The King on the Tower. Ludwig Uhland. OBVV
Cold Heaven, The. W. B. Yeats. AWP; CTC; GTBS-P; InPo; JAWP; MoVE; NAMP; NP; OAEP (2d ed.); WBP
Cold heritique. *Unknown.* SeCSL
Cold hours pass, The. Night Piece. Edith Sitwell. NP
Cold in the earth—and the deep snow piled above thee. Remembrance [*or* R. Alcona to J. Brenzaida]. Emily Brontë. BoPe; BWP; CH; EnLi-2; EnLit; EnLoPo; FaBoEn; FaFP; ForPo; GTBS-D; GTBS-W; GTSL; HBV; LiTB; LiTG; LiTL; LO; MasP; OAEP; OBEV

(1st ed.); OBNC; OxBI; PeER; PoEL-5; PoIE; PoVP; TreFT; TrGrPo
Cold Iron. Kipling. OnMSP
Cold is the wind to-night, and rough the sea. In the Monastery. Norreys Jephson O'Conor. CAW
Cold limbs of the air, The. A Mountain Wind. "Æ." AWP; JAWP; WBP
Cold Logic. Barney Hutchinson. SD
Cold moon hangs to the sky by its horn, The. The Night of the Dance. Thomas Hardy. BrPo
Cold Night, A. Bernard Spencer. WaP
Cold Oxford unfamiliar now, around. Above the High. Geoffrey Grigson. EnLoPo
Cold, Sharp Lamentation. Douglas Hyde, *tr. fr. Irish by* Lady Gregory. OBMV
Cold shuttered loveless star, skulker in clouds. News of the World I. George Barker. FaBoMo; LiTB
Cold, smoldering, The. A Love Dirge to the Whitehouse. Bob Fletcher. NBP
Cold Spring, A. Elizabeth Bishop. FiMAP; Po; StP; TwCP
Cold steel may penetrate the flesh. Heart Wounds. Claire Richcreek Thomas. PoToHe (new ed.)
Cold, strange, withdrawn our friendly court and still. November 2 A.M. Conspiracy. Sara Bard Field. AnEnPo
Cold, the dull cold! What ails the sun. A Seamark. Bliss Carman. PeCV
Cold transparent ham is on my fork, The. Sonnet to Vauxhall. Thomas Hood. PoEL-4
Cold, uncompassionate, bare. Across the Fens. Gilbert Thomas. HaMV
Cold Waltzes. Colette Inez. QAH
Cold was the day, when in a garden bare. The Child Jesus in the Garden. *Unknown.* ChrBoLe
Cold was the night wind, drifting fast the snows fell. The Widow. Robert Southey. OBEC
Cold Water Flat. Philip Booth. NePoAm
Cold-Weather Love. Ronald Everson. MoCV
Cold Weather Proverb. Robert Graves. CBV
Cold wind of autumn, blowing loud. Autumn Daybreak. Edna St. Vincent Millay. LaNeLa
Cold winds swept the mountain's height, The. The Mother in the Snow-Storm. Seba Smith. PaPo
Cold winter now is in the wood. Elizabeth J. Coatsworth. TiPo
Cold winter's in the wood. In the Wood. Eileen Mathias. BoTP
Colder Fire. Robert Penn Warren. *Fr.* To a Little Girl, One Year Old, in a Ruined Fortress. LiTM (1970 ed.)
("It rained toward day. The morning came sad and white.") MoVE
Colder the Air, The. Elizabeth Bishop. MiAP
Coldest day in all the year, The. The Smithfield Market Fire. Fred Dallas. WePo
Coldly, sadly descends. Rugby Chapel [November, 1857]. Matthew Arnold. ATP (1935 ed.); BEL; CBEP; EnL; EnLi-2; EnLit; EPN; GTBS; MaVP; MBW-2; OAEP; OxBoCh; PoE; PoEL-5; PoVP; TOP; ViPo; ViPP; VP; WGRP
Coldness that falls upon the hours, The. Cold Fall. Richard Eberhart. FiMAP
Cold's the Wind. Thomas Dekker. *Fr.* The Shoemaker's Holiday, V, iv. ViBoPo
("Cold's the wind, and wet's the rain.") ReEn; TuPP
(Drinking Song.) TrGrPo
(Hey Derry Derry.) SeCePo
(Saint Hugh.) OBSC
(Troll the Bowl!) EIL
Cole, that unwearied prince of Colchester. Variations on [*or* of] an Air: After Lord Tennyson. G. K. Chesterton. InP; Par
Cole Younger. *Unknown.* BeLS; BFSS, *with music.*
Coleridge. Aubrey Thomas De Vere. GoBC
Coleridge. George Sidney Hellman. AA
Coleridge. Theodore Watts-Dunton. HBV; OBVV; Sonn; VA
Coleridge caused his wife unrest. Theme and Variation. Peter De Vries. NYBP
Coleridge, they say, lived in fantasy. A Plea for Alias. James Schevill. FiMAP
Colin. Anthony Munday. *See* Beauty Sat Bathing by a Spring.
Colin and Lucy. Thomas Tickell. CEP; EiPP; OBEC
(Lucy and Colin.) OTPC (1923 ed.)
Colin Clout. John Skelton. *See* Colyn Cloute.
Colin Clout's Come Home Again. Spenser. CABL
Sels.
Colin Clout at Court. OBSC
Her Heards Be Thousand Fishes. ChTr
"Shepheards boy, The (best knowen by that name)." ReIE
Colin, my dear and most entire beloved. To the Most Excellent and Learned Shepherd, Colin Clout. William Smith. *Fr.* Chloris. ReEn; Sonn; TuPP
Colin, my deare, when shall it please thee sing. November. Spenser. *Fr.* The Shepheardes Calender. MaPo; PoEL-1
Colin, the Enamored Shepherd, Singeth This Passion of Love. George Peele. *See* O Gentle Love.
Colin's Complaint. Nicholas Rowe. OBEC
Colin's gone home, the glory of his clime. In Obitum Ed. Spenser Poetae Prestaniss. John Weever. ReIE
Colin's Passion of Love. George Peele. *See* O Gentle Love.
Coliseum, The ("Arches on arches"). Byron. *Fr.* Childe Harold's Pilgrimage, IV. BEL; EPN
("Arches on arches! as it were that Rome," *abr.*) CoBE
Coliseum, The ("The stars are forth"). Byron. *Fr.* Manfred, III, iv. MCCG
Coliseum, The. Poe. AmPP (5th ed.); AP; MWA-1
Colkelbie Sow, *sel.* *Unknown.*
"Penny lost in the lak, The." OxBS
Collaboration. Tony Towle. ANYP
Collages and Compositions. Richmond Lattimore. PP
Collar, The. George Herbert. AnAnS-1; AtBAP; ATP; AWP; BEL; BWP; CABA; CaFP; CBEP; CBV; CoBE; EaLo; EnL; EnLi-1; EnLit; ExPo; FaBoEn; FaPL; ForPo; FosPo; GTBS-W; HBV; ILP; InPo; JAWP; LiTB; LiTG; LoBV; MaMe; MaPo; MaRV; MasP; MeLP; MemP; MeP; MePo; NoP; OAEP; OBS; OuHeWo; OxBoCh; PAn; PoAn; PoE; PoEL-2; PoFS; PoIE; PoRA; ReEn; SCEP-1; SeCePo; SeCeV; SeCL; SeCP; SeCV-1; SeEP; StP; TOP; TrGrPo; UnPo (1st ed.); ViBoPo; WBP; WHA
Collar-Bone of a Hare, The. W. B. Yeats. AtBAP; EnL; NP
Collect the silver on a Sunday. The Lucky Coin. Austin Clarke. NeIP
Collection of Emblemes, Ancient and Moderne, A, *sel.* George Wither.
"Why, silly Man! so much admirest thou." SeCV-1
Collective Portrait, The. Robert Finch. MoCV
Collector, The. Raymond Souster. ErPo; OBCV
Colleen Oge Asthore. *Unknown.* OnYI
Colleen Rue. *Unknown.* OnYI
College Cat, The. Alfred Denis Godley. CenHV
College Colonel, The. Herman Melville. AA; AmePo; MWA-1
College Formal: Renaissance Casino. Langston Hughes. BALP
College of Surgeons, The. James Stephens. AnIL
(In the College of Surgeons.) LOW
College Song. Ed Anthony. InMe
Collegiate Angels, The. Rafael Alberti, *tr. fr. Spanish by* Mark Strand. FIW
Collegiate damsel named Breeze, A. *Unknown.* GoTP
Collen say why sittst thou soe. *Unknown.* SeCSL
Colley fell ill, and is no more! On an Insignificant Fellow. Lord Curzon. PV
Collier, The. Vernon Watkins. DTC; FaBoTw; FIW; MoVE
Collier's Wife, The. D. H. Lawrence. HaMV
Collies, The. Edward Anthony. GoTP
Collige Rosas. W. E. Henley. *See* O Gather Me the Rose.
Colloque sentimental. Paul Verlaine, *tr. fr. French by* Ernest Dowson. BrPo; EnLi-2
(Sentimental Colloquy, *tr. by* Alan Conder.) LO
(Sentimental Conversation.) SyP
Colloquial. Rupert Brooke. BrPo
Colloquy. Weldon Kees. NaP; NYBP
Colloquy at Peniel. W. S. Merwin. NePoEA
Colloquy in Black Rock. Robert Lowell. AnNE; AP; CoBMV; FiMAP; MiAP; MoAB; MoAmPo (1950 ed.); Po; PoDB; ReMP
Colloquy of the Ancients, The, *sel.* *Unknown, tr. fr. Late Middle Irish by* Standish Hayes O'Grady *and* Kuno Meyer, *arr. by* Kathleen Hoagland.
"MacLugach! says Finn." OnYI
Colloquy with a King-Crab. John Peale Bishop. LiTA; MoPo
Colloquy with Cockroach. Robert Penn Warren. CBV
Colloquy with God, A. Sir Thomas Browne. *See* Evening Hymn.

Collusion between a Alegaiter and a Water-Snaik. J. W. Morris. NA
Colly, My Cow. *Unknown.* EvOK
Colm had a cat. The Pets. Robert Farren. CoBE; OA; OxBI
Cologne. John Bate. NeBP
Cologne. Samuel Taylor Coleridge. BOHV; HBV; InMe; PV; WhC
(Epigram: "In Köln, a town of monks and bones.") ALV
Cologne Cathedral. Frances Shaw. NP
Colombine. Hugh McCrae. BoAV; NeLNL; PoAu-1
Colomen. Mary Webb. LoEn
Colonel B. Constance Carrier. NePoAm-2
Colonel B/ Drove from the tee. Afforestation. E. A. Wodehouse. FiBHP; SD
Colonel Ellsworth. Richard Henry Stoddard. PAH
Colonel Fantock. Edith Sitwell. AnFE; MoAB; MoBrPo; MoVE; OBMV
Colonel rode by his picket-line, The. The Two Wives. William Dean Howells. AA
Colonel Sharp. *Unknown.* BaBo
Colonial Set. Alfred Goldsworthy Bailey. OBCV
Colonist in His Garden, A. William Pember Reeves. ACV; AnNZ
Colonized Mind. Barbara Marshall. TNV
Colonos. Henry Alford. VA
Colophon. Oliver St. John Gogarty. OBMV
Color. Rowena Bennett. MPB (1956 ed.)
Color. Melville Cane. RePo
Color. W. W. Gibson. InP; NP
Color, The. John Haines. ThO
Color. Langston Hughes. BOLo
Color. Christina Rossetti. *See* What Is Pink?
Color Alone Can Speak. Louise Townsend Nicholl. NePoAm
Color Blind. Carol Paine. PV
Color—caste—denomination. Emily Dickinson. EaLo; MWA-2
Color gladdens all your heart, The. Sympathy. Althea Gyles. HBV
Color of silence is the oyster's color, The. Earliness at the Cape. Babette Deutsch. NePoAm-2; NYBP
Color of stone when leaves are yellow, The. Autumn. William Jay Smith. NePoAm; RePo
Color of the ground was in him, the red earth, The. Edwin Markham. *Fr.* Lincoln, the Man of the People. MaRV; PGD
Color of walls of scratches of cracks of brightness. The Aelf-scin, the Shining Scimmer the Gleam, the Shining. Michael McClure. CoPo
Colorado. John D. Dillenback. PoOW
Colorado. Robert Fitzgerald. MoPo
Colorado Sand Storm, A. Eugene Field. PoOW
Colorado Trail, The, *with music.* *Unknown.* AS; CoSo
Colored Band, The. Paul Laurence Dunbar. MPB
Colored like fallen needles, the red squirrel goes. Squirrel. Frances Frost. BoChLi
Colored pictures. The Songs of Maximus. Charles Olson. NeAP
Colors, The. Nathalia Crane. MAP; NeMA; StaSt
(Standards.) GoTP
Colors in the sun, colors at night, the Army, Navy and Marines. The Lagoon. Ashton Greene. NePoAm
"Colors," she said, "are never so fine." The Green and the Black. Anthony Bailey. NYBP
Colors we depend on are, The. The Love Bit. Joel Oppenheimer. CoPo
Colosseum. Harold Norse. TrJP
Colossus, The. Sylvia Plath. LiTM (1970 ed.); NePoEA-2
Colour. *Unknown.* BoTP
Colour. Adeline White. BoTP
Colour is a lovely thing. Colour. *Unknown.* BoTP
Colour of God's Face, The, *sels.* Dorothy Livesay. PeCV (1967 ed.)
Land, The.
People, The.
Coloured lanterns lit the trees, the grass, The. Episode of a Night of May. Arthur Symons. Scènes de la Vie de Bohème, I. BrPo; PeVV
Coloured long-shore fishermen unfurl, The. The Gamblers. Anthony Delius. BoSA; PeSA
Colours of Love, The. Denis Devlin. OxBI
Colours of the setting sun, The. The Sliprails and the Spur. Henry Lawson. BoAu; PoAu-1
Colt, The. Raymond Knister. TwCaPo
Colt is tethered at the appointed gate, The. The Ride to Jerusalem. Norman Nicholson. StJW
Coltrane must understand how. Soul. D. L. Graham. Kal
Colubriad, The. William Cowper. BOHV; CIV; OTPC (1923 ed.)
Columbia. Timothy Dwight. HBV; MC; PaA; PAH
(Star of Columbia, *with music.*) TrAS
Columbia,/ If aught but loss of honor. Roosevelt. Peter Fandel. PEDC
Columbia appear! To thy mountains ascend. Perry's Victory. *Unknown.* PAH
Columbia, Columbia, to glory arise. Columbia [*or* Star of Columbia]. Timothy Dwight. HBV; MC; PaA; PAH; TrAS
Columbia, the Gem of the Ocean. David T. Shaw. FaBoBe; PAL
(Red, White, and Blue.) WBLP
Columbiad, The, *sel.* Joel Barlow.
"Eager he look'd. Another train of years," *fr.* X. AmPP (5th ed.)
(League of Nations, A.) CoBA
(One Centred System.) AP
Columbian Ode. Paul Laurence Dunbar. PoRL
Columbia's Emblem. Edna Dean Proctor. GN
Columbine, The. Jones Very. AP
Columbus. Arthur Hugh Clough. AmFN; DD; MC; PoSC
Columbus. Florence Earle Coates. DD; MC
Columbus. Charles Buxton Going. HH
(Great Master Dreamer.) PEDC (1931 ed.)
Columbus. Edward Everett Hale. DD; HH; MC; PAH
Columbus. Percy Hutchison. EtS
Columbus. Leroy F. Jackson. SiSoSe
Columbus, *sel.* James Russell Lowell.
"One day more/ These muttering shoalbrains leave the helm to me." PGD
Columbus. Joaquin Miller. AA; AmePo; AmPP (3d ed.); BBV; BeLS; DD; EtS; FaBoBe; FaFP; FaPON; GN; HBV; HBVY; MC; MCCG; MPB; NeHB; NeMA; OHFP; OnSP; OQP; OTPC (1946 ed.); PaA; PAH; PAL; PaPo; PCD; PEDC; PFY; PGD; PoPo; PoRL; PTK; StaSt; StVeCh; ThLM; TIHL; TiPo (1952 ed.); TreF; TSW; WaKn; YaD; YeAr; YT
(Sail On!) SoP
Columbus. James Montgomery. *Fr.* The West Indies. PEDC
(Inspiration, The.) PAH
Columbus. Lydia Huntley Sigourney. AA; DD; HBV; HH; MC; OTPC; PAH
Columbus. Annette Wynne. HH; MPB; TiPo
Columbus and the *Mayflower.* Richard Monckton Milnes. MC; PAH
Columbus at the Convent. John Townsend Trowbridge. DD; MC; PAH
Columbus Day. Tennyson. HH; PEDC
Columbus Dying. Edna Dean Proctor. MC; PAH
Columbus Goes West. William Hart-Smith. *See* Space.
Columbus in Chains. Philip Freneau. MC; PAH
Columbus is remembered by young men. And of Columbus. Horace Gregory. CMoP
Columbus looked; and still around them spread. The First American Congress. Joel Barlow. PAH
Columbus looks towards the New World. Space [*or* Columbus Goes West]. William Hart-Smith. *Fr.* Christopher Columbus. BoAV; MoAuPo; NeLNL; PoAu-2
Columbus Never Knew. Gail Brook Burket. PGD
Columbus sailed over the ocean blue. Columbus. Leroy F. Jackson. SiSoSe
Columbus stands in the night alone, and passing grave. The Triumph. Sidney Lanier. *Fr.* The Psalm of the West. PAH
Columbus the World-Giver. Maurice Francis Egan. OQP; PGD
Columbus to Ferdinand. Philip Freneau, *wr. at. to* Jonathan Mason. PAH
Columcille the Scribe. *At. to* St. Columcille. *See* St. Columcille the Scribe.
Colum-Cille's Farewell to Ireland. *At. to* St. Columcille. *See* Farewell to Ireland.
Columcille's Greeting to Ireland, *abr.* *At. to* St. Columcille, *but*

probably 12th cent., tr. fr. Middle Irish by William Reeves *and* Kuno Meyer. OnYI
Column A. Michael Silverton. PV
Colyn Cloute [*or* Colin Clout], *sels.* John Skelton.
"And if ye stand in doubt/ Who brought this rhyme about." EnPo; ReEn
Prelates, The. TrGrPo
"What can it avail/ To drive forth a snail." SiCE; TuPP
Com, com sad turtle mateles moaninge. *Unknown.* SeCSL
Com home againe! Christ Calls Man Home. *Unknown.* MeEL
Comanche. Tom Clark. ANYP
Comarnad it is a very bonny place. Richie Story (B *vers.*). *Unknown.* ESPB
Comatas. Harry Mathews. ANYP
Comb out your golden hair and whisper, monkeys, monkeys. Flying Foxes and Others. Kay Boyle. AnAmPo
Combat, The. Matthew Arnold. *Fr.* Sohrab and Rustum. VA
Combat, The. Edwin Muir. ChMP; CMoP; GTBS-D; LiTB; MoBrPo (1962 ed.)
Combat, The. Thomas Stanley, *after the Greek of* Anacreon. AWP
Combat of Ferdiad and Cuchulain, The, *sels. Unknown, tr. fr. Middle Irish.*
"All was play, all was sport," *tr. by* Joseph Dunn. OnYI
(Cuchulain's Lament for Ferdiad, *tr. by* George Sigerson.) AnIL
(Cuchullain's Lament over Ferdiad, *tr by* George Sigerson.) AnIV
"Arise ye kings of Macha," *tr by* Joseph Dunn. OnYI
"Ravens shall pick," *tr. by* Joseph Dunn. OnYI
"Roll of a chariot, The," *tr. by* Joseph Dunn. OnYI
Combat raged not long, The; but ours the day. The Burial of Latané. John Reuben Thompson. PAH
Combe, The ("The combe was ever dark"). Edward Thomas. GTBS-P; PoIE; PrWP
Combed by the cold seas, Bering and Pacific. Love Letter from an Impossible Land. William Meredith. WaP
Combination of Wagner and burlesque. Job. E. W. Mandel. PeCV
Come! William Barnes. CH
Come. *Unknown.* SoP
Come,/ Let us roam the night together. Harlem Night Song. Langston Hughes. OCS
"Come a little nearer, doctor—thank you—let me take the cup." Forceythe Willson. *Fr.* The Old Sergeant. AA; BeLS; PaA
Come about the meadow. What May Happen to a Thimble. "B." PRWS
Come again to the place. After the Visit. Thomas Hardy. FaBoEn; GTBS-D; OBNC
Come, all brother sailors, I hope you'll draw nigh. The Beaver Island Boys. *At. to* Daniel Malloy. OuSiCo
Come all fair maids both far and near and listen unto me. Tragic Verses. *Unknown.* CoMu
Come all gallant (*or* you gallant] seamen that unite a meeting. The Death of Nelson [*or* A New Song Composed on the Death of Lord Nelson]. *Unknown.* CoMu; OxBoLi
Come all good people, I'd have you draw near. Naomi Wise. *Unknown.* ViBoFo
Come, all my boys and listen, a song I'll sing to you. The *Bigler* [*or* The *Bigler's* Crew]. *Unknown.* IHA; OuSiCo
Come all my fair ones. Jack Tar. *Unknown.* ShS
Come, all of you bold rangers. Bold Rangers. *Unknown.* BFSS
Come all of you bold shanty boys, and list while I relate. The Jam on Gerry's Rock. *Unknown.* BaBo
Come all of you, my brother scouts. The Old Scout's Lament. William F. Drannan. CoSo; PoOW
Come all of you people, I pray you draw near. The Arizona Boys and Girls. *Unknown.* CoSo
Come all old maids that are squeamish. Eurynome. Jay Macpherson. NMP; OBCV; PV
Come all that loves good company. The Merry Hoastess. *Unknown.* CoMu
Come all who desire to hear of a jest. The Foolish Miller. *Unknown.* UnTE
Come, all ye bold Americans, to you the truth I tell. The Surrender of Cornwallis. *Unknown.* PAH
Come all ye bold sailors/ Who sail round Cape Horn. The Coast of Peru. *Unknown.* EtS
Come all ye [*or* you] bold sailors that follow the Lakes. Red Iron Ore. *Unknown.* ABF; AS; IHA; TiPo (1952 ed.)
Come all ye boys of Liverpool I'd have you to beware. Van Dieman's Land. *Unknown.* BaBo
Come all ye brave Americans. *See* Come all you brave Americans.
Come All Ye Fair and Tender Maidens. *Unknown. See* Come, All You Fair Maidens.
Come all ye fine young fellows. Hunt the Buffalo. *Unknown.* TrAS, *with* Shoot the Buffalo
Come all ye good people, wherever you be. Polly Williams. *Unknown.* ABF
Come all ye Irish gentlemen, a story I would tell. How We Built a Church at Ashcroft. Jack Leahy. PoOW
Come all ye [*or* you] jolly fellows, wherever you may be. Gerry's Rocks. *Unknown.* ABF
Come all ye jolly good shanty boys, come listen to my song. Jim Porter's Shanty Song. *Unknown.* IHA
Come all ye jolly lumbermen, and listen to my song. Canaday I. O. Ephraim Braley. BaBo; ViBoFo, *with music*
Come all ye jolly lumbermen who lumbered on Gaspereaux. The Banks of the Gaspereaux. *Unknown.* ShS
Come all ye jolly sailors bold. Captain Ward and the Rainbow. *Unknown.* ViBoFo
Come all ye jolly shepherds. When the Kye Comes Hame. James Hogg. HBV; OxBS
Come all ye lads and lassies and listen to me a while. The Maid of the Sweet Brown Knowe. *Unknown.* AnIV; OnYI
Come all ye lads who know no fear. Barney's Invitation. Philip Freneau. PAH
Come all ye maids of Simcoe, give ear to what I write. The Maids of Simcoe. *Unknown.* ShS
Come all ye pretty fair maids, O if ye did but know. Sailors' Come -All-Ye. *Unknown.* SoAmSa
Come all ye railroad section men an' listen to my song. Jerry, Go an' Ile That Car. *Unknown.* AS; IHA
Come all ye river-drivers, if a tale you wish to hear. How We Logged Katahdin Stream. Daniel G. Hoffman. MaC
Come all ye rounders if you want to hear. *See* Come all you rounders. . .
Come, all ye seamen bold. Admiral Benbow. *Unknown.* CBEP; EnSB
Come all ye sons of Brittany. Braddock's Fate, with an Incitement to Revenge. Stephen Tilden. PAH; ThLM
Come, all ye sons of Canada, wherever you may dwell. The Hanging Limb. *Unknown.* IHA
Come all ye tender-hearted people. Garfield's Murder. *Unknown.* ThLM
Come all ye [*or* you] true-born shanty-boys, wherever you may be [*or* whoever that ye be]. The Jam on Gerry's Rock [*or* Young Monroe at Gerry's Rock]. *Unknown.* AmSS; AS; IHA; ViBoFo
Come all ye true-bred Irishmen. The *City of Baltimore. Unknown.* ShS
Come all ye who list to hear our noble England's praise. *See* Attend, all ye. . .
Come all ye wits, that with immortal rhymes. Invites Poets and Historians to Write in Cynthia's Praise. Philip Ayres. Sonn
Come all ye Yankee sailors, with swords and pikes advance. The *Constellation* and the *Insurgente. Unknown.* PAH
Come all ye young fellows of Prince Edward Island. The Boys of the Island. Larry Gorman. ShS
Come all ye [*or* you] young fellows that [*or* who] follow the sea. Blow the Man Down [*or* The Black Ball Line]. *Unknown.* AmSS; ShS *vers.* II; SoAmSa
Come all ye young females, I pray you'll attend. Sally Monroe. *Unknown.* ShS
Come all ye young people, come fathers and mothers, too. The Rowan County Crew. *Unknown.* OuSiCo
Come, all ye young sailormen, listen to me. The Boston Come-All-Ye [*or* The Fishes]. *Unknown.* ABF; SoAmSa; TrAS
Come all ye young tars who are cruising for sperm. Coast of Peru. *Unknown.* SoAmSa
Come, All Ye Youths. Thomas Otway. *Fr.* The Orphan. OAEP
Come all you blessed Christians dear. A Ballad from the Seven Dials Press. *Unknown.* CoMu
Come All You Bold Canadians, *with music. Unknown.* ShS

Come all you bold fishermen, listen to me. Song of the Fishes. *Unknown.* AmSS
Come all you bold ox teamsters. Teamster's Song. *Unknown.* TrAS
Come all you bold robbers and open your ears. Quantrell. *Unknown.* ABF; CoSo
Come all you bold sailors that follow the Lakes. *See* Come all ye bold sailors . . .
Come, all you bold shanty boys. The Jam at Gerry's Rock. *Unknown.* BFSS
Come, all you bold undaunted men. Jack Donahoo [*or* Donahoe]. *Unknown.* ABF; CoSo
Come all you bold, undaunted ones. Fifteen Ships on George's Banks. *Unknown.* BaBo
Come all you [*or* ye] brave Americans. Brave Paulding and the Spy [*or* Major André]. *Unknown.* BFSS; MC; PAH
Come all you brave Annapolis boys. Corbitt's Barkentine. *At. to* Tom Reynolds. ShS
Come, all you brave gallants, and listen awhile. Robin Hood and the Butcher. *Unknown.* BuBa; ESPB (B *vers.*); OBB; RG
Come all you brave Sailors, that sails on the Main. The Famous Fight at Malago; or The Englishmen's Victory over the Spaniards. *Unknown.* CoMu
Come all you brave soldiers, both valiant and free. On Independence. Jonathan Mitchell Sewall. PAH
Come all you brave young shanty boys, I pray you. James Whaland. *Unknown.* AS; IHA
Come all you British hearts of oak, and listen unto me. The Glorious Victory of Navarino! *Unknown.* CoMu; FOL
Come all you Californians, I pray open [*or* ope] wide your ears. Crossing the Plains. John A. Stone. ABF; SGR
Come, All You Fair Maidens ("Come, all you fair and tender ladies"). *Unknown.* BFSS, *with music*
(Come All Ye Fair and Tender Maidens.) TreFT
Come all you fine young fellows with hearts so warm and true. Flat River Girl. *Unknown.* AS
Come all you gallant poachers, that ramble void of [*or* free from] care. Van Diemans Land. *Unknown.* CoMu; PeVV
Come all you gallant seamen that unite a meeting. *See* Come all gallant seamen. . .
Come all you good old boys and listen to my rhymes. Lackey Bill. *Unknown.* CoSo
Come all you hardy sons of toil, pray lend an ear to me. The History of Prince Edward Island. Larry Gorman. ShS
Come all you hearty roving blades, and listen to my song. The Frolicsome Parson Outwitted. *Unknown.* CoMu
Come all you humane countrymen, with pity lend an ear. Charles Gustavus Anderson, *vers.* II. *At. to* Joseph Keating, Sr. ShS
Come all you joky boys. Katy Dorey. *Unknown.* OuSiCo
Come all you jolly buffalo skinners and listen to my song. *See* Come all you jolly fellows. . .
Come all you jolly cowboys that follow the bronco steer. The Crooked Trail to Holbrook. *Unknown.* CoSo
Come all you jolly dogs, in the Grapes, and King's Head, and Green Man, and Bell Taps. Tom Tatter's Birthday Ode. Thomas Hood. LoBV
Come all you jolly fellows [*or* buffalo skinners *or* skinners] and listen to my song. The Buffalo Skinners. *Unknown.* ABF; AS; BFSS; CoSo; ThLM; ViBoFo
Come, all you jolly fellows, wherever you may be. *See* Come, all ye jolly. . .
Come all you jolly freighters that has freighted on the road. Freighting from Wilcox to Globe. *Unknown.* CoSo
Come all you jolly lumbermen and listen to my song. The Jolly Lumbermen. *Unknown.* TrAS
Come all you jolly lumbermen, I'd have you for to know. The Banks of Gaspereaux. *Unknown.* BaBo
Come all you jolly railroad men, and I'll sing you if I can. Way Out in Idaho. *Unknown.* OuSiCo
Come all you jolly river boys, I'll have you all draw near. The Jam on Gerry's Rock, *vers.* I. *Unknown.* ShS
Come all you jolly sailormen that follow the salt sea. The Schooner *Blizzard.* Henry Burke. ShS
Come all you jolly skinners and listen to my song. *See* Come all you jolly fellows. . .
Come all you jolly soldiers, I will sing to you a song. War Song. *Unknown.* ABF
Come all you jolly travellers that's out of work, just mind. Cockies of Bungaree. *Unknown.* PoAu-1
Come, all you little runabouts. A Tract for Autos. Arthur Guiterman. MPB; RePo
Come all you Louisiana girls and listen to my noise. The Texian Boys. *Unknown.* CoSo
Come all you melancholy folks and listen unto me. The Melancholy Cowboy. *Unknown.* CoSo
Come all you men and maidens dear, to you I will relate. The Lexington Miller. *Unknown.* BaBo
Come all you men of Arkansas. Annie Breen. *Unknown.* CoSo
Come all you men of learning. Botany Bay. *Unknown.* ViBoFo
Come all you Milltown rowdies that drink and have no fear. Tomah Stream. Larry Gorman. ShS
Come, all you Mississippi girls, and listen to my noise. Mississippi Girls. *Unknown.* BFSS
Come all you old cow-punchers, a story I will tell. A Man Named Hods. *Unknown.* CoSo
Come all you old-time cowboys and listen to my song. Boggy Creek. *Unknown.* CoSo
Come all you old-timers and listen to my song. John Garner's Trail Herd. *Unknown.* CoSo
Come all you pretty girls, to you these lines I'll write. The Buffalo Hunters. *Unknown.* CoSo; IHA
Come all you rambling sailor lads and listen unto me. The *Flying Cloud, vers.* I. *Unknown.* ShS
Come all you range riders and listen to me. The Range Riders. *Unknown.* CoSo
Come all you [*or* ye] rounders if you want [*or* for I want you] to hear. Casey Jones. *Unknown.* ABF; AmPP; AS; ATP; BeLS; FaBV, *arr. by* T. Lawrence Seibert; IHA; OxBoLi; PoPo; ThLM; TreF; TrGrPo; ViBoFo (A *and* B *vers.*)
Come all you sailors bold. The Death of Admiral Benbow. *Unknown.* CoMu
Come, all you sailors of the southern waters. Phantoms All. Harriet Prescott Spofford. AA; PFY
Come all you sons of Erin, attention now I crave. Morrissey and the Russian Sailor. *Unknown.* AS
Come, all you sons of Liberty, that to the seas belong. The *General Armstrong. Unknown.* PAH
Come all you swaggering farmers, whoever you may be. The Times Have Altered. *unknown.* CoMu
Come, all you tender Christians. Charles Guiteau; or The Murder of James A. Garfield. *Unknown.* BFSS; ViBoFo
Come, all you Texas Rangers, wherever you may be. The Texas Rangers. *Unknown.* BFSS; CoSo; OuSiCo
Come all you thoughtless young men, a warning take by me. The Murder of Maria Marten. W. Corder. CoMu
Come all you true-born shanty-boys, wherever you may be. *See* Come all ye true-born. . .
Come, all you true boys from the river. Johnny Stiles, or the Wild Mustard River. *Unknown.* OuSiCo
Come all you true lovers and the truth I'll unfold. The Jolly Young Sailor and the Beautiful Queen. *Unknown.* ShS
Come, all you wild young people, and listen to my song. Young Edwin in the Lowlands Low (A *vers.*) *Unknown.* BaBo
Come all you woolly waddies. The Harrington Barn Dance. *Unknown.* CoSo
Come all you young Canadian boys, wherever that you be. The Jam on Jerry's Rock, *vers.* II. *Unknown.* ShS
Come, all you young companions. Young Companions. *Unknown.* CoSo
Come all you young fellows that carry a gun. At the Setting of the Sun. *Unknown.* CBEP
Come all you young fellows that [*or* who] follow the sea. *See* Come all ye young. . .
Come, all you young gallants that follow the gun. Young Molly Bawn. *Unknown.* OnYI
Come all you young ladies and make no delay. *Unknown.* OxNR
Come all you young men from the Nashwaak. Young Forbest. *Unknown.* ShS
Come all you young men [*or* people] who handle a [*or* the] gun. Molly Bawn [*or* Shooting of His Dear]. *Unknown.* BaBo; OxBoLi
Come all you young people and listen to my song. The Young Man Who Wouldn't Plow Corn. *Unknown.* BFSS
Come, all you young people, I pray you draw near. Arizona Boys and Girls. *Unknown.* BFSS
Come all you young people, I pray you draw near. Naomi (Omie) Wise (A *vers.*). *Unknown.* BaBo

Come all you young people who handle the gun. *See* Come all you young men who handle a gun.
Come all you young sailors who cruise round Cape Horn. The Coast of Peru. *Unknown.* ShS
Come, all young girls, pay attention to my noise. Kansas Boys. *Unknown.* AS; IHA
Come, all young men and maidens, attend unto my rhyme. Caroline of Edinborough Town. *Unknown.* BFSS
Come along boys, and listen to my tale. The Old Chisholm [*or* Chizzum] Trail. *Unknown.* ABF; BeLS; BFSS; CoSo; FaBoBe; TreFT
Come along, children, come along. Raise a Rukus Tonight. *Unknown.* ABF
Come along, get you ready. A Hot Time in the Old Town. Joe Hayden. YaD
Come along, 'tis time, ten or more minutes past. Spectator ab Extra: Le Diner. Arthur Hugh Clough. OxBoLi; PeVV
Come and buy—/Have a try. Lemonade Stand. Dorothy Brown Thompson. SiSoSe
Come and get your quinine, and come and get your pills. Words for Army Bugle Calls: Sick Call. *Unknown.* TreF
Come and kiss me, mistress Beauty. Refrain. Douglas Brooke Wheelton Sladen. *Fr.* Charles II. VA
Come and let me make thee glad. The Builder. Francis Sherman. CaP
Come, and let us drink of that new river. Easter Hymn. St. John of Damascus. BePJ
Come and let us live my deare. Counting Kisses [*or* Out of Catullus]. Catullus. CavP; LiTW; MaMe
Come, and pass, and go. Quiet. Yaha. WoL
"Come and see! Come and see!" What the Thrush Says. Queenie Scott-Hopper. BoTP
Come and see her as she stands. Fanny. Anne Reeve Aldrich. HBV
Come and see the chimney-pots, etched against the light! Paris; the Seine at Night. Charles Divine. HBMV
Come and smile into my eyes. Dawn. Kenton Kilmer. JKCP (1955 ed.)
Come and Welcome. Thomas Haweis. BePJ
"Come and you shall see." Shadow. Ann Mars. GoYe
Come apace, good Audrey. I will fetch up your goats, Audrey. Shakespeare. *Fr.* As You Like It, III, iii. PP
Come, arm ye! Come, arm ye! The Garibaldi Hymn. Luigi Mercantini. WBLP
Come away,/ Make no delay. Dooms-Day. George Herbert. MaMe; SCEP-1; SeCP; SeCV-1
Come away, away, away, James Shirley. *Fr.* The Triumph of Peace. TuPP
Come Away, Come Away, Death. Shakespeare. *Fr.* Twelfth Night, II, iv. AnFE; AtBAP; CBEP; CenL; EG; EIL; EnLi-1 (1949 ed.); ExPo; ILP; InPo; MaPo; NoP; OAEP; OBSC; SiCE; TOP; ViBoPo; WHA
(Clown's Song, The.) CTC
(Come Away, Death.) DiPo; ELP; PAn; PoRA; SeCeV
(Dirge.) OBEV
(Dirge of Love.) GTBS; GTBS-D; GTBS-P; GTBS-W; GTSE; GTSL
(Feste's Song.) VaPo
(Love's Despair.) TrGrPo
(Song.) FiP; PoEL-2
(Two of Feste's Songs.) BoLiVe
Come away, come away from the straightness of the road. Song of the Foot-Track. Elsie Cole. BoAu
Come Away, Come, Sweet Love. *Unknown.* EnRePo; OAEP; OBSC; PoEL-2; ReEn; ReIE
(Come Away, Sweet Love.) LoBV
(To His Love.) EIL; ELP
Come Away, Death. E. J. Pratt. PeCV
Come Away, Death. Shakespeare. *See* Come Away, Come Away, Death.
Come away, elves, while the dew is sweet. Water-Lilies. Felicia Dorothea Hemans. OTPC
Come away from them. Truth. Donald Green. WSL
Come Away, Sweet Love. *Unknown.* *See* Come Away, Come, Sweet Love.
Come, Baby, come quick, for I want you to see. Baby Goes Out to Tea. *Unknown.* SAS
Come Back. Arthur Hugh Clough. NCEP
Come Back. Henry William Herbert. AA
Come Back. W. S. Merwin. NaP
Come back again, my olden heart! Come Back. Arthur Hugh Clough. NCEP
Come back and bring my life again. Come Back. Henry William Herbert. AA
"Come back at dead of night and speak to me." The Two Societies. John Hall Wheelock. PoCh
Come back before the birds are flown. The Recall. James Russell Lowell. AP
Come Back, Lincoln. Chauncey R. Piety. PGD
Come Back to Erin. Charlotte Alington Barnard. TreFS
Come back to me. Another Night with Telescope. Leonard Cohen. PeCV (1967 ed.)
Come back to me, who wait and watch for you. Monna Innominata, I. Christina Rossetti. ViPo; VP
Come back, ye wandering Muses, come back home. On [*or* Proem to] the Hellenics. Walter Savage Landor. *Fr.* The Hellenics. BEL; EnRP; EPN; ViBoPo
Come, bairns, come all to the frolic play. The Last Day of the Year. Alexander Smart. PCH
Come balmy sleep! tired nature's soft resort! To Sleep. Charlotte Smith. Sonn
Come, be my valentine! Phyllis Inamorata. Francis Andrewes. SeCL
Come buy my fine wares. Apples [*or* Verses Made for Women Who Cry Apples]. Swift. *Fr.* Verses for Fruitwomen. AnIV; NCEP; OnYI
"Come, before the summer passes." Travel Song. Anne Glenny Wilson. BoAu
Come, Blessed Bird. *Unknown.* NCEP
Come, blessed sleep, most full, most perfect, come. Invitation to Sleep. Christina Rossetti. GTSE
Come boyes, fill us a bumper, we'l make the Nation roare. The Courtier's Health; or, Merry Boys of the Times. *Unknown.* CoMu
Come, brave soldiers, come, and see. In Cicatrices Domini Jesu. Richard Crashaw. MaMe
Come, Break with Time. Louise Bogan. ATP (1953 ed.); MAP; MoAmPo; NP
Come, break your heart, then, with the world's beauty. Sic Transit Gloria Mundi. James Wreford Watson. CaP
Come, bring thy gift. If blessings were as slow. An Offering. George Herbert. MaMe
Come bring with a noise. Ceremonies for Christmas[se]. Robert Herrick. AnAnS-2; GN; HBV; OHIP; OTPC (1923 ed.); TiPo (1952 ed.)
Come, brother, come. Let's lift it. Cotton Song. Jean Toomer. CDC
Come, brothers! rally for the right! The Bonnie Blue Flag. Annie Chambers Ketchum. PaA; PAH; ThLM
"Come, Buck, come, Bouncer, my three bloodhounds." Johnie Cock (D *vers*). *Unknown.* BaBo
Come, butter, come. Mother Goose. OxNR; PCH; StVeCh
Come Buy! Come Buy!. Shakespeare. *See* Lawn as White as Driven Snow.
Come Buy My Nice Muffins. *Unknown.* PCH
Come, Captain Age. Sarah N. Cleghorn. HBMV
Come Carol, Make Carol. C. C. Gould. MemP
Come, Celia, let's agree at last. Song. John Sheffield. HBV
Come, Charles, blow the trumpet. The Baby's Birthday. Eliza Lee Follen. PPL
Come, cheer up, my lads, like a true British band. A Song. *Unknown.* PAH
Come, cheer up, my lads! 'tis to glory we steer. Heart of Oak. David Garrick. HBV; OBEC; OxBoLi
Come, Cheerful Day! Thomas Campion. BEL; EIL
("Come cheerful day, part of my life to me.") EG; SiCE
(Sic Transit.) GTSL; TOP
Come, children, hear the joyful sound. The Big Bell in Zion. Theodore Henry Shackleford. BANP
Come, Children of Tomorrow, come! Children of Tomorrow. Zona Gale. OQP
Come, Chloe, and Give Me Sweet Kisses. Sir Charles Hanbury Williams, *after the Latin of* Martial. HBV; UnTE
(Epigram of Martial Imitated, An.) OBEC
Come, choose your road and away, my lad. The Call of the Spring. Alfred Noyes. SUS
Come close to me, dear Annie, while I bind a lover's knot. Pot and Kettle. Robert Graves. HBMV
Come, Come Away! Richard Brome. *Fr.* The Merry Beggars. BiS
Come, come away. To His Tutor. John Hall. EG

Come, come away! the spring. Come, Come Away. Richard Brome. *Fr.* The Merry Beggars. BiS
"Come, come away, to the Tavern I say." *Unknown.* OBS
Come, come dear[e] night, Love's mart of kisses. Epithalamion Teratos [*or* Teratus]. George Chapman. *Fr.* Hero and Leander. AtBAP; ElL; LoBV
Come, come fill up your glasses. The British Grenadier. *Unknown.* PAH
Come, come, lie down, and thou shalt see. *Unknown.* *Fr.* The Marriage of Wit and Science. TuPP
Come, come my hearts, a-hunting let us wend. The Hunting Song. *Unknown.* TuPP
Come, come, no time for lamentation now. Death of Samson. Milton. *Fr.* Samson Agonistes. ChTr; FiP
"Come, come," said Tom's father, "at your time of life." On Taking a Wife [*or* Epigram *or* A Joke Versified]. Thomas Moore. ALV; BOHV; HBV; LiTG; SiTL; TreF; WhC
Come come sweet Love why dost thou stay. *Unknown.* SeCSL
Come, come, thou glorious object of my sight. Beauty Paramount. Sir William Killigrew. *Fr.* Selindra. SeCL
Come, Come, What Doe I Here? Henry Vaughan. AnAnS-1; MeP; MePo; SCEP-1; SeCV-1
Come, comrades, come, your glasses clink. Down among the Dead Men. William Morris. PoVP
"Come!" cried Helen, eager Helen. Sisters. Eleanor Farjeon. FaPON
"Come!" cried my mind and by her might. The Wanderer: Clarity. William Carlos Williams. TwAmPo
Come cuddle close in daddy's coat. The Fairy Folk. Robert N. Bird. GFA; HBV; HBVY; OTPC; PRWS; TVC
Come dally me, darling, dally me with kisses. Psyche to Cupid: Her Ditty. James Broughton. ErPo
Come dance a jig. *Unknown.* OxNR
Come, dark-eyed Sleep, thou child of Night. And on My Eyes Dark Sleep by Night. "Michael Field." OBMV
Come, day, glad day, day running out of the night. Glad Day. Louis Untermeyer. TrJP
Come day, go day. Traveller's Ditty. Miriam Allen deFord. HBMV
Come, dear children, let us away. The Forsaken Merman. Matthew Arnold. ATP (1935 ed.); BBV (1923 ed.); BEL; BeLS; BoLiVe; CBEP; EnL; EnLi-2; EnLit; EPN; EtS; FaBoCh; FiP; ForPo; GBV (1922 ed.); GN; GTBS; GTBS-D; GTSL; HBV; LoEn; LoGBV; MaVP; MBW-2; MCCG; MPB; NoP; OAEP; OBEV (1st ed.); OBVV; OnSP; OTPC; OuHeWo; PAn; PoVP; RG; ShBV-1; TOP; VA; ViBoPo; ViPo; ViPP; VP; WHA; YAT; YT
Come, dear Heart! Corpus Christi. Evelyn Underhill. StJW
Come, dear old comrade, you and I. Bill and Joe. Oliver Wendell Holmes. AA; HBV; PCD
Come, Death, but free from pain. Song to Death. Juan Escrivá. LiTW
Come death, come bands, nor do you shrink, my eares. I Am Ready Not Onely to Be Bound But to Dye. Richard Crashaw. MaMe
Come, Death, I'd have a word with thee. Motley. Walter de la Mare. MMA
Come, Death—My Lady Is Dead. Charles d'Orleans(?). MeEL
Come Down. George Macdonald. TrPWD
Come down at dawn from windless hills. Sunrise on Rydal Water. John Drinkwater. GBV; HBV; LiTM; NP
Come down, come down, my Lord, come down. My Lord's a-Writin' All de Time. *Unknown.* BoAN-1
"Come down, come down," said the farmer to his son. The Yorkshire Bite. *Unknown.* BaBo
Come down, come down to the Square. The Cat That Followed His Nose. John Kaye Kendall. CenHV
Come down, dear love, be quick. A Lover's Words. Vernon Watkins. DTC
Come down from heaven to meet me when my breath. Invocation. Siegfried Sassoon. MoBrPo
Come down, O Christ, and help me! reach thy hand. E Tenebris. Oscar Wilde. BrPo; CABA; CAW; ChIP; JKCP (1926 ed.); MaRV; MoBrPo; PoLi; Sonn; StJW; TreFT; TrPWD
Come Down, O Maid [from Yonder Mountain Height]. Tennyson. *Fr.* The Princess, Pt. VII. AnEnPo; AnFE; AtBAP; BoPe; CABA; CaFP; CBEP; DiPo; EG; EnL; FosPo; GTBS; GTBS-P; MaPo; OBEV; OBNC; OBVV; PoE; PoVP; ShBV-3; TOP; TreFT; ViBoPo; ViPo; ViPP; WHA
(Idyl, An.) TrGrPo
(Shepherd's Song.) LoBV
(Song.) FaBoEn
(Songs from "The Princess.") EnLi-2; OAEP; SeCeV
Come down, ye graybeard mariners. A Cry from the Shore. Ellen Mackay Hutchinson Cortissoz. AA
Come Down, You Bunch of Roses, Come Down, *with music.* *Unknown.* ShS
Come drawer some wine or wele pull downe your signe. *Unknown.* SeCSL
Come, drop your branches, strow the way. Palm-Sunday [*or* The Triumphant Entry]. Henry Vaughan. AtBAP; MaRV; StJW
Come, drunks and drug-takers: come, perverts unnerved! Several Voices Out of a Cloud. Louise Bogan. ExPo; MoVE
Come, each death-doing dog who dares venture his neck. Hot Stuff. Edward Botwood. PAH
Come, earth, wreathed now with nuptial spring. Sing, Woods and Rivers All. Claudian. *Fr.* Fescennine Verses in Honor of the Marriage of the Emperor Honorius. HW
Come, Evening, once again, season of peace. Winter Evening [*or* Evening]. William Cowper. *Fr.* The Task, IV. CoBE; OBEC
Come exorcise the illness of this lovely girl. No Harm to Lovers. Albius Tibullus. LiTW
Come! fill a fresh bumper—for why should we go. Ode for a Social Meeting. Oliver Wendell Holmes. BOHV
Come, fill the beaker, while we chaunt a pean of old days. Fort Duquesne. Florus B. Plimpton. PaA; PAH
Come, fill the cup, and in the fire of spring. The Bird of Time [*or* Fifteen Rubáiyát]. Omar Khayyám, *tr. by* Edward Fitzgerald. *Fr.* The Rubáiyát. FaBV; InP; LiTW; OnPM; TreF; WGRP
Come fleetly, come fleetly, my hookabadar. Cossimbazar. Henry S. Leigh. BOHV; NA
Come follow, follow me. The Fairy Queen [*or* The Queen of Fairies]. *Unknown.* BoTP; OTPC; PCD; PCH; PoRh; RG; ViBoPo
Come follow, heart upon your sleeve. A Maine Trail. Gertrude Huntington McGiffert. HBV
Come, Follow Me. Thomas Campion. EnRePo
Come, Follow Me! Thomas Curtis Clark. ChIP
Come, follow me by the smell. Onions. Swift. *Fr.* Verses for Fruitwomen. AnIV; OnYI
Come Follow Me, You Country Lasses. John Fletcher *or* William Rowley. *Fr.* The Maid in the Mill. SeCL
Come, forsake your city street! October. T. A. Daly. JKCP
Come forth, and let us through our hearts receive. Foliage. Felicia Dorothea Hemans. OBRV
Come Forth, Come Forth. "Christopher North." OBRV
Come forth; for Night is falling. The Invitation to the Gondola. John Addington Symonds. *Fr.* In Venice. PoVP
Come forth! for Spring is singing in the boughs. April Moment. Arthur Davison Ficke. Sonnets of a Portrait Painter, XI. HBMV
Come forth, you workers! Reveille. Lola Ridge. AnAmPo; HBMV; PoFr
Come forthe, sire sergeaunt, with your stately mace. The Dance. John Lydgate. *Fr.* The Dance of Death. PoEL-1
Come, Freemen of the land. Put It Through. Edward Everett Hale. MC; PAH
Come, freighted heart, within this port. Lovemusic. Carolyn Kizer. ErPo
Come, friendly bombs, and fall on Slough. Slough. John Betjeman. MoBrPo (1962 ed.)
Come from a distant country. At Birth. Anthony Thwaite. NePoEA-2
Come from my first, ay, come! Charade. Winthrop Mackworth Praed. GN
Come Gather round Me, Parnellites. W. B. Yeats. PoFr
Come, Gaze with Me upon This Dome. E. E. Cummings. CBV; OxBA
Come, Gentle Death! Thomas Watson. *Fr.* Hecatompathia. ElL
("Come gentle Death. Who calls? One that's oppressed.") SiCE
Come, gentle death! come silently. Welcome Death. Juan Escrivá. OnPM

Come, Gentle Night. Shakespeare. *Fr.* Romeo and Juliet, III, ii. HW
Come gentle sleep, I woo thee: come and take. The Growth of Love, XLVIII. Robert Bridges. Sonn
Come, gentle Spring, ethereal mildness, come. The Seasons: Spring. James Thomson. EiCP; PeER
Come, gentle tripe, the hungry carter's joy. Tripe. J. B. Morton. InMe
Come, gentle Zephyr, tricked with those perfumes. George Peele. *Fr.* David and Bethsabe. ViBoPo
Come, gentlemen all, and listen a while. Robin Hood and the Bishop of Hereford. *Unknown.* BaBo; BuBa; ESPB; OBB
Come, gentlemen Tories, firm, loyal and true. Sir Henry Clinton's Invitation to the Refugees. Philip Freneau. PAH
Come, Georgia boy, come listen to my song. Georgia Boy. *Unknown.* OuSiCo
Come, gie's a sang, Montgomery cried [*or* cry'd]. Tullochgorum. John Skinner. GoTS; OBEC; OxBS
Come Green Again. Winfield Townley Scott. PoPl
Come, guard this night the Christmas pie. Christmas Eve—Another Ceremony. Robert Herrick. OHIP
Come. . .have do with dillying. Shrine to What Should Be. Mari Evans. NNP
Come, Heavenly Child, and on this place. Two Inscriptions for the Christmas Candle. Anna Hempstead Branch. MaRV
Come heavy hart, whose sighs thy sorrowes shew. *Unknown.* SeCSL
Come, Heavy Sleep. *Unknown.* ReIE
Come, heavy souls, oppressed that are. Casting All Your Care upon God, for He Careth for You. Thomas Washbourne. OxBoCh
Come, here are a slate, and a pencil, and string. Learning to Draw. Ann *or* Jane Taylor. SAS
"Come here, come here, you freely feed." Kemp Owyne [*or* Kempion], B *vers.* *Unknown.* ESPB; OxBB
Come here, good people great and small, that wander far abroad. My Bath. John Stuart Blackie. VA
Come Here, Little Robin. *Unknown.* BoTP; OTPC (1923 ed.)
Come Here Lord! *with music.* *Unknown.* BoAn-2
Come here, my boy; hould up your head. The Irish Schoolmaster. James A. Sidney. BOHV; FiBHP
Come Here, My Friends. Tim Hall. WOW
"Come here, my sweet Landlady, pray, how d'ye do?" Matthew Prior. *Fr.* Down Hall. MyFE
Come here, said my hostess, her face making room. Literary Dinner. Vladimir Nabokov. FiBHP
Come here to papa, and I'll tell my dear boy. Of What Are Your Clothes Made? Ann *and* Jane Taylor. OTPC (1923 ed.)
Come Hither. John Clare. NoP
Come Hither. *Unknown.* *See* Come Hither, Little Puppy-Dog.
Come hither all sweet maidens soberly. On a Picture [*or* an Engraved Gem] of Leander [*or* Sonnet]. Keats. CBEP; EnRP; TOP
Come hither and behold this lady's face. Laura Sleeping. Louise Chandler Moulton. AA
Come hither Apollo's bouncing girl. Square-Cap. John Cleveland. AnAnS-2
Come hither, boy: if ever thou shalt love. Shakespeare. *Fr.* Twelfth Night, II, iv. LO
Come hither, child! and rest. Villanelle of Sunset. Ernest Dowson. BrPo
Come hither, Evan Cameron! Come, stand beside my knee. The Execution of Montrose. William Edmondstoune Aytoun. GTBS; HBV; OnMSP; VA
Come hither, gallers of renown. To Some Reviewers Who Have Wilfully Abused Certain True Poets. Herbert Palmer. FaBoTw
Come hither, lads, and harken [*or* hearken], for a tale there is to tell. The Day Is Coming. William Morris. EnLi-2; OAEP; PoVP; ViPo; WGRP
Come hither, lads, and hearken, for a tale there is to tell. The Day Is Coming, *parody.* Sir Walter Besant. CenHV
Come Hither, Little Puppy Dog. *Unknown.* OTPC (1923 ed.); PPL
(Come Hither.) FTB
(Robin Knows Great A.) SAS
"Come hither, my boy, tell me what thou seest there." Lacedemonian Instruction. Blake. ERoP-1
Come Hither, My Dear One. John Clare. BoLP; ELP
Come hither, my heart's darling. The Husband's Petition. William Edmondstoune Aytoun. BOHV
Come hither my sparrows. The Marriage Ring. Blake. HW
Come hither, Sir John, my picture is here. On a Lady Who Beat Her Husband. *Unknown.* FiBHP
Come Hither, Sweet Robin, *abr.* *Unknown.* PPL
(Feeding the Robin.) SAS
Come hither, womankind and all their worth. Kissing. Lord Herbert of Cherbury. EnLoPo; LiTL; ViBoPo
Come hither, ye who thirst. Come Hither. John Clare. NoP
Come Hither, You That Love. John Fletcher. ELP
Come, Holy Babe! Mary Dickerson Bangham. ChIP; PGD
Come, Holy Dove,/ Descend on silent pinion. Hymn to the Holy Spirit. Richard Wilton. OxBoCh
Come Holy Ghost, Creator blest. Veni, Creator Spiritus. *Unknown.* WHL
Come Holy Ghost eternal God, and ease the woeful grief. For Whitsunday. Francis Kinwelmarsh. SiCE
Come, Holy Ghost, our souls inspire. John Cosins, *ad. fr. Latin.* BoC
Come, Holy Ghost! thou fire divine! Veni, Sancte Spiritus. Robert II of France. HBV
Come, Holy Spirit, Heavenly Dove. Isaac Watts. SoP
Come Home. *Unknown, tr. fr. Zulu by* Jack Cope. PeSA
Come Home, Father. Henry Clay Work. *See* Father, Dear Father, Come Home with Me Now.
Come home with me a little space. Christmas at Melrose. Leslie Pinckney Hill. BANP
Come home with white gulls waving across gray. Winter Landscape. Stephen Spender. MoAB; MoBrPo
Come, honest sexton, take thy spade. The Passing Bell. *Unknown.* SeCL; SeEP
Come, Hooker, come forth of thy native soile. Yee Shall Not Misse of a Few Lines in Remembrance of Thomas Hooker. Edward Johnson. SCAP
Come, I will make the continent indissoluble. For You O Democracy. Walt Whitman. AmePo; CoBA; PaA; PoFr; StaSt; TrGrPo
Come I'll sing you a song, just for want of some other. Hop-o-My-Thumb. *Unknown.* *Fr.* Ballads on Napoleon. CoBE
Come In. Robert Frost. AmPP; AnNE; BoNaP; BWP; DiPo; FaBV; ForPo; GTBS-W; LiTA; LiTM; MaPo; MemP; MoAB; MoAmPo; NeMA; PoAn; PoeP; PoIE; ReMP; TrGrPo; UnPo (3d ed.); WePo
"Come in an' sit ye down," old Gruda said. Second Sight. H. S. Neill. FiSC
Come in from the veranda and the blaze. Michael. Val Vallis. NeLNL
Come in, she said, but. Invitation. Victor Contoski. PV
Come in sweet grief. Tricked Again. Ridhiana. NBP
Come in the evening, or come in the morning. The Welcome. Thomas Osborne Davis. HBV; IrPN, 8 *ll.*; TreFT, 4 *ll.*; VA
Come in the garden. The Snowman. E. M. Adams. BoTP
Come! in this cool retreat. A New Zealand Regret. Eleanor Elizabeth Montgomery. VA
Come in this hour to set my spirit free. Before Day. Siegfried Sassoon. WGRP
Come into Animal Presence. Denise Levertov. AP; NaP
Come into my black hands. Invitation. Raymond R. Patterson. WSL
Come into the garden, Kate. The Tryst. E. V. Knox. CenHV
Come into the Garden, Maud. Tennyson Maud, Pt. I, xxii. BEL; BoLP; CBEP; EnLit; EPN; ExPo; FaBV; FiP; GTBS; GTSE; GTSL; HBV; LiTG; LiTL; MaVP; MCCG; OBVV; PaPo; PoIE; TreF; UnPo (1st ed.); VA
(Lyric from "Maud.") EnLi-2
(Maud.) GTBS-W; OBEV
(Song [from "Maud"].) AWP; InPo; JAWP; TOP; WBP
Come into the Whenceness Which. Whenceness of the Which. *Unknown.* BOHV
Come, John, sit thee down I have somewhat to say. An Amorous Dialogue between John and His Mistress [*or* between the Mistris and Her Aprentice]. *Unknown.* CoMu; PeRV; UnTE
Come join hand in hand, brave Americans all. The Liberty Song [*or* A Song of American Freedom]. John Dickinson. AmPP; PoFr; TrAS
Come join us, come join us, beautiful bride. Bridal Song. Clemens Brentano. HW
Come, keen iambics, with your badger's feet. John Cleveland. *Fr.* The Rebel Scot. OBS; ViBoPo
Come, ladies and gentlemen, listen to my song. Down on

Come (continued)
Roberts' Farm. Claude Reeves. ThLM

Come, Landlord, Fill the Flowing Bowl. *Unknown.* OxBoLi

Come lasses and lads. The Rural Dance about the Maypole [*or* May Pole Dance]. *Unknown.* OxBoLi; SeCL; WePo

Come learn with me the fatal song. The Mighty Heart. Emerson. Fr. Woodnotes, II. AA

Come leave the loathed stage. Ode to Himself[e]. Ben Jonson. AnAns-2; OBS; ReEn; SeCP; SeEP

Come, leave this loathed country-life. Upon Himself. Robert Herrick. SeEP

Come! leave this sullen state, and let not wine. To His Retired Friend. Henry Vaughan. ViBoPo

Come leave thy care, and love thy friend. The Anti-Politician. Alexander Brome. CavP

Come, let me sing into your ear. Those Dancing Days Are Gone. W. B. Yeats. AtBAP

Come, let me write. And to what end? To ease. Astrophel and Stella, XXXIV. Sir Philip Sidney. FCP; ReIE; SiPS; TuPP

Come let us be going my brothers. Come Home. *Unknown.* PeSA

Come! let us draw the curtains. Autumn. Humbert Wolfe. PoLF

Come, let us drink away the time. Ode. Charles Cotton. CavP

Come let us drink away the time. A Song of Sack. *Unknown.* OBS

Come, Let Us Eat and Drink Today. Juan del Encina, *tr. fr. Spanish by* Sir John Bowring. OnPM

Come, Let Us Find. W. H. Davies. HBMV

Come, let us go a-roaming! Travellers. Arthur St. John Adcock. BoTP

Come, let us join our friends above. The Ever-living Church. Charles Wesley. STF

Come, Let Us Kiss and Part. Michael Drayton. *See* Idea: "Since there's no help, come let us kiss and part."

Come, Let Us Make Love Deathless. Herbert Trench. EG; HBMV; OBVV

(Love, *br. sel.*) MaRV

Come, let us mount the breezy down. Harvest Home. Frederick Tennyson. OBVV

Come, let us now resolve at last. The Reconcilement. John Sheffield, Duke of Buckingham and Normanby. CEP; LiTL; LO; OBEV

Come, let us pity those who are better off than we are. The Garret. Ezra Pound. NP; PoPI

Come, let us plant the apple tree. The Planting of the Apple Tree. Bryant. AA; AnNE; DD; GN; HBV; HBVY; LaNeLa; MPB (1956 ed.) OHIP; PoSC; StVeCh

Come let us rejoice. About Savannah. *Unknown.* PAH

"Come let us sigh a requiem over love." Robert Nichols. Sonnets to Aurelia, IV. OBMV

Come, Let Us Sing, *with music.* *Unknown.* BFSS

Come, let us sing! it is the time for summer. For an Eskimo. Annie Charlotte Dalton. CaP

Come, Let Us Sound with Melody [the Praises]. Thomas Campion. PoAn; ReIE; SiCE; UnS

Come let us take another's word's and change the meaning. Preludes for Memnon, XXXVII. Conrad Aiken. NoP

Come, let us tune our loftiest song. Worship and Thanks to Him Belong. Robert A. West. SoP

Come let's begin to revel 't out. Madrigal. *Unknown.* BoTP

Come, let's to bed. Mother Goose. OnPM; OTPC; OxBoLi; OxNR; RIS; SiTL

("To bed, to bed, says sleepy-head.") SAS

Come light and listen, you gentlemen all. Robin Hood and the Beggar, I. *Unknown.* BaBo; ESPB

Come, list and hark! the bell doth toll. The Passing Bell. Thomas Heywood. *Fr.* The Rape of Lucrece. SeCL

Come list to me, ye heroes, ye nobles, and ye braves. The Raging Can-all. *Unknown.* ABF

Come list ye landsmen, all to me. The Wonderful Crocodile. *Unknown.* ABF

Come listen a while and I'll sing you a song. Hard Times. *Unknown.* ABF

Come listen a while, you gentlemen all. Robin Hood Newly Revived. *Unknown.* BaBo; ESPB

Come, listen all unto [*or* listen to] my song. How Cyrus Laid the Cable. John Godfrey Saxe. MC; PaA; PAH

Come listen, and hear me tell/ the end of a tale so true. The

Lass of Lynn's New Joy, for Finding a Father for Her Child. *Unknown.* CoMu

Come listen and I'll tell you. The Yankee Privateer. Arthur Hale. PaA; PAH

Come listen awhile, and I'll sing you a song. The Silly Old Man. *Unknown.* CoMu

Come, listen, good neighbors of every degree. The Liberty Pole. *Unknown.* *Fr.* The Procession with the Standard of a Faction; a Cantata. PAH

Come listen, good people, to accommodate. The Silk Merchant's Daughter. *Unknown.* BFSS

"Come, listen, my men, while I tell you again." How to Recognize a Snark [*or* The Snark]. "Lewis Carroll." *Fr.* The Hunting of the Snark. BOHV; MPB; TSW

Come listen, O Love, to the voice of the dove. The Voice of the Dove. Joaquin Miller. AA

Come, listen to a ranger, you kindhearted stranger. The Disheartened Ranger. *Unknown.* BFSS; CoSo

Come listen to another song. The Old Scottish Cavalier. William Edmondstoune Aytoun. GN; HBV; PoVP

Come listen to me, you [*or* ye] gallants so free. Robin Hood and Allen [*or* Allan *or* Alan *or* Allin]-a-Dale. *Unknown.* BaBo; BoChLi; BuBa; EnLit; ESPB; FaBoBe; GoTP; HBV; LoEn; MCCG; MoShBr; OBB; OnSP; StVeCh (1940 ed.)

Come listen to my ditty/ 'Twill not detain you long. Baldy Green. *Unknown.* PoOW

Come, listen to my song. *See* Come, listen all unto my song.

Come listen to my story, Molly Bawn. Molly Bawn and Brian Oge. *Unknown.* OnYI

Come, listen to my story, ye landsmen, one and all. Raging Canawl. *Unknown.* AS

Come, listen to my tragedy, good people, young and old. Henry Green. *Unknown.* BaBo

Come listen to the story of brave Lathrop and his Men. The Lamentable Ballad of the Bloody Brook. Edward Everett Hale. HBV; PAH

Come listen unto me a while. Old Sailor's Song. *Unknown.* SoAmSa

Come, little babe, come, silly soul. A Sweet Lullaby [*or* Cradle Song]. Nicholas Breton. EIL; GTSL; HBV; OBEV; OBSC; PoIE; SiCE; TOP; TuPP; ViBoPo

Come, little boy, to mother's knee. Christmas Dusk. Wilbur D. Nesbit. PEDC

Come, little children, gather round. The Shepherd's Madrigal. Geraldine Farrar. StJW

"Come, little cottage girl, you seem." The Poets at Tea, 6. Barry Pain. Par

Come, little Drummer Boy, lay down your knapsack here. The Soldier's Friend. George Canning *and* John Hookham Frere. OBEC; Par

Come little infant, love me now. Young Love. Andrew Marvell. EP; MaMe

Come, Little Leaves. George Cooper. FaPON; MPB; OTPC; PCH; PPL; RIS

(Wind and the Leaves, The.) BoTP

Come live and be merry. Laughing Song. Blake. *Fr.* Songs of Innocence. SoPo

Come live with me, and be my dear. Another of the Same Nature, Made Since. *Unknown.* CLwM

Come, Live with Me and Be My Love. C. Day Lewis. AtBAP; CLwM; CoBMV; ILP; MaRV; OBMV; StP

Come live with me and be my love. An Invitation to Phyllis. Charles Cotton. CLwM

Come live with me, and be my love. The Bait[e]. John Donne. AnEnPo; CABA; CBV; CLwM; DiPo; ErPo; HoPM; ILP; LiTL; MaMe; OAEP; PoRA; SCEP-1; SD; StP; TuPP; WhC

Come live with me and be my love. That Strain Again. Ronald Hambleton. CaP

Come live with me and be my Love. The Passionate Shepherd to His Love [*or* The Shephard to His Love *or* The Shepherd's Plea]. Christopher Marlowe. AnEnPo; ATP; AWP; BEL; BoLiVe; BoLP; BWP; CABA; CaFP; CBEP; CBV; CLwM; CoBE; CTC; DiPo; EG; EIL; ELP; EnL; EnLi-1; EnLit; EP; ExPo; FaBoBe; FaBoEn; FaFP; FCP; FosPo; GBV (1952 ed.); GN; GTBS; GTBS-D; GTBS-P; GTBS-W; GTSE; GTSL; HBV; HoPM; ILP; InPo; JAWP; LiTB; LiTG; LiTL; LoBV; MemP; MeWo; NeHB; NoP; OAEP; OBEV; OBSC; OnP; OTD; OTPC (1923 ed.); OuHeWo; PAn;

PG (1945 ed.); Po; PoE; PoFS; PoIE; PoLF; PoPo; PoRA; PoSa; ReEn; ReIE; RG; SeCePo; SeCeV; SiCE; SiPS; SiTL; StP; ThWaDe; TOP; TreF; TrGrPo; TuPP; UnPo (1st ed.); UnTE; ViBoPo; WBP; WePo; WHA; YAT
Come live with me and be my whofe. The Wooing Rogue. *Unnknown.* CoMu
Come live with me and be my wife. A Modern Romance. Paul Engle. PoPl
Come, Lord Jesus. Amy Carmichael. FaChP
Come, Lord Jesus. Charles Wesley. BePJ
Come Lord, my head doth burn, my heart is sick. Home. George Herbert. MaMe
Come, Love, Let's Walk. *Unknown.* ElL
Come Love or Death. Will Henry Thompson. AA
Come, lovely and soothing Death. Death Carol. Walt Whitman. *Fr.* When Lilacs last the Door-yard Bloom'd. AnFE; APA; CoAnAm; MaRV; MoRP
Come, Lovers, Bring Your Cares. John Jones. *Fr.* Adrasta. SeCL; TuPP
Come lusty ladyes come come with pensive thoughte ye pyne. *Unknown.* SeCSL
Come, madam, come, all rest my powers defie. Going to Bed [*or* To His Mistress Going to Bed]. John Donne. Elegies, XIX. AnAnS-1; EnRePo; EP; ErPo; LiTB; LiTG; MaMe; MePo; NoP; ReEn; SeCP; SiTL; UnTE
Come, men, stack arms! Pile on the rails. Stonewall Jackson's Way. John Williamson Palmer. AA; DD; HBV; MC; PAH
Come Michaelmas. A. Newberry Choyce. HBMV
Come Micky and Molly and dainty Dolly. The Flitch of Dunmow. James Carnegie. HBV; VA
Come mighty Must! The Mighty Must. W. S. Gilbert. *Fr.* Princess Ida. BOHV
Come, mint me up the golden gorse. The Casual Man. Denis Glover. AnNZ
Come, Muse, migrate from Greece and Ionia. The Muse in the New World. Walt Whitman. *Fr.* Song of the Exposition, II, III, *abr.* MAP; MoAmPo; PP
Come, Muses, come, and help me to lament. Deep Desire Sung This Song. George Gascoigne. TuPP
Come muster, my lads, your mechanical tools. The New Roof. Francis Hopkinson. PAH
Come, my brothers. The Only Tourist in Havana Turns His Thoughts, Homeward. Leonard Cohen. MoCV
Come, My Celia, Let Us Prove. Ben Jonson. *Fr.* Volpone, III, vii. AtBAP; ElL; EnLi-1 (1949 ed.); FosPo; MaPo; SiCE; WHA
(After Catullus: Song, to Celia.) CLwM
(Come, My Celia.) CABA; FaBV; MeWo; NoP; PAn; TrGrPo
("Come, my Celia, let us prove.") EnRePo
(Song to Celia.) EnL; ErPo; OBS; SCEP-2; SeCeV; SeCP; SeCV-1; SiTL; TuPP
(To Celia.) AnAnS-2; FaBoEn; LoBV; ReEN; ReIE; UnTE
(Vivamus Mea Lesbia atque Amemus.) EG
Come, my dainty doxies. Thomas Middleton. *Fr.* More Dissemblers besides Women, IV, i. TuPP
Come, my dearest, come, my fairest. The Saucy Sailor. *Unknown.* SaSa
Come, my fine cat, against my loving heart. The Cat. Baudelaire. PoPl
Come, my friends. Tennyson. *Fr.* Ulysses. TRV
Come my friends and listen unto me. The Parson Grocer. *Unknown.* CoMu
Come, my lad, and sit beside me: we have often talked before. The Story of a Stowaway. Clement Scott. PaPo
Come, my little Robert, near. Cleanliness. Charles *and* Mary Lamb. OTPC (1923 ed.); PRWS
Come, my Lucasia, since we see. Friendship's Mystery. Katherine Philips. ViBoPo
Come, my *moo sarge,* let us go up that shining mountain. Wabanaki Song. *Unknown.* PeCV
Come my Oenone lett us doe. *Unknown.* SeCSL
Come, My Sheep. Dorothy B. Polsue. SoP
Come, my songs, let us express our baser passions. Further Instructions. Ezra Pound. AnAmPo; NP; TwCP
Come, my sweet, whiles every strain. William Cartwright. EG
Come my tan-faced children. Pioneers! O Pioneers! Walt Whitman. AmePo; AmPP; ATP; CoBA; FaBoBe; MPB; PaA; TOP; UnPo (1st ed.); WHA
Come, my way, my truth, my life. The Call. George Herbert. MaMe
Come, mysterious night. A Hymn to Night. Max Michelson. NP; TrJP
Come near me, for the night. Microcosmos, XL. Nigel Heseltine. NeBP
Come, Night. George Chapman. *See* Bridal Song ("O come . . .").
Come night,/ the ugly weather's fire-cracker simmer. News from Mount Amiata. Robert Lowell, *ad. fr. Italian of* Eugenio Montale. NaP
Come Night, Come Romeo. Shakespeare. *Fr.* Romeo and Juliet, III, ii. BoLP; LiTL; MemP
Come not again! I dwell with you. The Flown Soul. George Parsons Lathrop. AA
Come not in terrors clad, to claim. To Death. Caroline Anne Bowles. OBEV (1st ed.)
Come Not Near. Mary Elizabeth Osborn. NePoAm-2
Come Not near My Songs. *Unknown, tr. fr. Shoshone Indian by* Mary Austin. AWP; JAWP; PG; WBP
Come not the earliest petal here, but only. Quiet. Marjorie Pickthall. OBCV; PeCV; TwCaPo
Come Not the Seasons Here. E. J. Pratt. PeCV
Come Not to Me for Scarfs. Aurelian Townshend. AnAnS-2
Come Not, When I Am Dead. Tennyson. PeVV; PoVP; ViPo
(Go By.) OBNC
Come, Now! Archibald Rutledge. SoP
Come now, and let us wake them: time. Serenade. *Unknown.* AWP; JAWP; WBP
Come now behold. The Glory of and Grace in the Church Set Out. Edward Taylor. *Fr.* God's Determinations. AmPP (5th ed.); AnNe; AP; NoP
Come now each gen'rous feeling heart. The Framework-Knitters Lamentation. *Unknown.* CoMu
Come, now, you most careful layers of T-squares. Come, Now! Archibald Rutledge. SoP
Come now, you who carry. A Coffee-House Lecture. Robert Mezey. CABA
Come, O Come. Thomas Campion. *See* Come, Oh, Come, My Life's Delight.
Come, oh come in pious Laies. Hymne I: A Generall Invitation to Praise God. George Wither. *Fr.* Hallelujah; or, Britain's Second Remembrancer. SeCV-1
Come, Oh, Come, My Life's Delight. Thomas Campion. EG; ElL; InvP; LO; OBSC; SiCE
(Come, O Come.) AtBAP
(My Life's Delight.) MeWo; TrGrPo
Come, O Creator Spirit blest! Hymn to the Holy Spirit. *Unknown.* SoP
Come, O Friend, to Greet the Bride. Heine. *after the Hebrew of* Solomon Halevi Alkabez, *tr. fr. German by* Louis Untermeyer. *Fr.* Hebrew Melodies. TrJP
Come, O Lord, like Morning Sunlight. Milton S. Littlefield. TrPWD
Come, oh, songs! Come, oh, dreams! The Wild Rose. Hermann Hagedorn, Jr. PFY
Come, O thou traveller unknown. Wrestling Jacob. Charles Wesley. CEP; EiCL; EiPP; OBEC; OBEV (new ed.); OxBoCh; PeER; PoEL-3; SeCePo; SoP
Come o'er the hills, and pass unto the wold. A Winter Hymn —to the Snow. Ebenezer Jones. OBNC
Come o'er the stream, Charlie. McLean's Welcome. James Hogg. OxBS
Come off to the stable, all you who are able. Words for Army Bugle Calls: Stable Call. *Unknown.* TreF
Come on! Come on! This hillock hides the spire. Sunday Afternoon Service in St. Enodoc Church, Cornwall. John Betjeman. MoVE
Come on, don't be afraid you'll spoil me. Serenade. Emanuel Carnevali. AnAmPo
Come On In. *Unknown.* SD
Come on, sir. Now, you set your foot on shore. Ben Jonson. *Fr.* The Alchemist, II, i-ii. AtBAP; PoEL-2
Come on then, ye dwellers by nature in darkness. Chorus of Birds [*or* Grand Chorus of Birds]. Aristophanes, *tr. by* Swinburne. *Fr.* The Birds. AWP; JAWP; PoEL-5; WBP
Come, on thy swaying feet. The Spirit of the Fall. Danske Dandridge. AA
Come on ye critticks! find one fault who dare. On Mr. Edward

Come (continued)
Howard upon His British Princes. Charles Sackville. PeRV
Come, Ophrah, fill my cup—but not with wine. The Splendor of Thine Eyes. Moses ibn Ezra. TrJP
"Come out and hear the waters shoot, the owlet hoot, the owlet hoot." Apprenticed. Jean Ingelow. *Fr.* Songs of the Night Watches. LiTL; OBVV
Come out and join the revels! A Song for May Day. Frederick Herbert Adler. DD
Come out and walk. The last few drops of light. A Night Piece. Edward Shanks. HBMV
Come out, come out, this sunny day. Hay-Time. C. M. Lowe. BoTP
Come Out, Come Out, Ye Souls That Serve. Christopher Brennan. *Fr.* The Wanderer. PoAu-1
Come out for a while and look from the outside in. Christmas Eve. C. Day Lewis. EaLo
Come out in the night when darkness has fallen. Stars. Martha Hird. SoP
Come Out into the Sun. Robert Francis. NYBP
Come out o' door, 'tis Spring! 'tis May. May. William Barnes. GTBS-D; PoSC
Come out of the classroom, Katya. Invitation. Emmett Jarrett. ThO
Come out, 'tis now September. The Ripe and Bearded Barley. *Unknown.* BoNaP; ChTr
"Come out with me!" cried the little red sled. The Little Red Sled. Jocelyn Bush. PCH; SoPo; TiPo
Come over the bourn [*or* born], Bessy. A Song[e] between the Queen's Majesty and England. William Birche. CoMu; TuPP
Come, pass about the bowl to me. The Royalist. Alexander Brome. CavP
Come, Phyllis, I've a cask of wine. To Phyllis. Eugene Field, *after* Horace. InMe
Come play with me. To a Squirrel at Kyle-na-no. W. B. Yeats. FaPON; PDV; ThWaDe
Come, pretty lamb, do stay with me. The Lamb. *Unknown.* OTPC (1923 ed.)
Come, put off your gown of smooth lilac. Winter and Red Berries. Nicholas Moore. NeBP
Come, read to me some poem. Longfellow. *Fr.* The Day Is Done. YT
Come rede me, dame, come tell me, dame. Nine Inch Will Please a Lady. Burns. ErPo
Come, rejoice, 'tis Easter Day. Christ Is Risen. Mrs. D. H. Dugan. BLRP
Come, rest beneath my pine-tree, murmuring sweet. Spoken by the God Pan. *Unknown.* OnPM
Come, Rest in This Bosom. Thomas Moore. EnRP
(Song: "Come, rest in this bosom, my own stricken deer.") PG
(Stricken Deer, The.) GoBC
Come ride and ride to the garden. Lady Gregory. SUS
Come, Ride with Me to Toyland. Rowena Bennett. ChBR; SiSoSe
Come, rouse up, ye bold-hearted Whigs of Kentucky. Old Tippecanoe. *Unknown.* PAH; ThLM
Come, Sable Night. *Unknown.* EnRePo
Come, Says Jesus' Voice. Anna Letitia Barbauld. BePJ
"Come!" said Old Shellover. Old Shellover. Walter de la Mare. AtBAP; BoTP; UTS
Come sail with me o'er the golden sea. The Lord of the World. G. A. Studdert-Kennedy. PGD
Come, sail-i-ors, landsmen, one and all. Erie Canal. *Unknown.* ABF
Come sapless blossom, creep not stil on earth. The Sap. Henry Vaughan. AnAnS-1; MeP
Come, Saviour! Antoinette Bourignon. SoP
Come, Says Jesus' Voice. Anna Letitia Barbauld. BePJ
(Home.) SoP
Come, see the *Dolphin's* anchor forged—'tis at a white heat now. The Forging of the Anchor. Sir Samuel Ferguson. HBV; IrPN; PoVP
Come See the Place Where the Lord Lay. Richard Crashaw. MaMe
Come, see thy friend, retir'd without regret. Nil Admirari. Congreve. *Fr.* Of Improving the Present Time. OBEC
Come sell your pony, cowboy. Sweetgrass Range. Edwin Ford Piper. MAP; PFY
Come, set thee down by these cool streams. Then Lose in Time Thy Maidenhead. *Unknown.* ErPo
Come, shall we come out of the listening season into the city. Entry. Josephine Miles. AnAmPo
Come sheathe your swords! my gallant boys. Sergeant Champe. *Unknown.* PAH
Come, Shepherds, Come! John Fletcher. *Fr.* The Faithful Shepherdess, I, iii. EG; ElL; ErPo
Come shepherds, come! Your silent sheep. The Angel and the Shepherds. *Unknown.* ChrBoLe
Come, Silence, thou sweet reasoner. Silence. James Herbert Morse. AA
Come, Sirrah Jack, Ho! *Unknown.* NCEP; OAEP
Come sit aneath this pinetree, whose lofty tressed crown. Country Music. Plato. LiTW
Come, Sleep. Beaumont *and* Fletcher. *Fr.* The Woman-Hater, III, i. ElL; ELP
("Come, sleep, and with thy sweet deceiving.") EG; SiCE
(Lullaby: "Come sleep, and with the sweet deceiving.") FaBoEn
(Sleep.) HBV; OBEV (1st ed.)
Come, Sleep! but mind ye! if ye come without. To Sleep. Walter Savage Landor. VA
Come, sleep, O sleep, the certain knot of peace. Astrophel and Stella, XXXIX. Sir Philip Sidney. AnFE; BEL; BoLiVe; CABA; CBEP; CBV; CoBE; ElL; EnL; EnLi-1; EnLit; EnRePo; EP; FaPL; FCP; ForPo; GTSL; HBV; InP; LiTG; LoBV; MaPo (1969 ed.); MyFE; NoP; OAEP; OBEV; OBSC; PoE; PoFS; PoIE; PoRA; ReEn; ReIE; ShBV-4; SiCE; SiPS; Sonn; StP; TreFS; TrGrPo; TuPP; ViBoPo; WHA
Come slowly, Eden! Emily Dickinson. CMoP; MeWo; UnTE
Come Slowly, Paradise. James Benjamin Kenyon. AA
Come solemn Muse and help me sing. A Sonet to the Tune of A Hone a Hone. Nicholas Breton. SiCE
Come, Sons of Mars, who thirst for Blood. A Drinking-Song, against All Sorts of Disputes in Drinking. William Wycherley. SeCV-2
Come sons of summer, by whose toile. The Hock-Cart, or Harvest Home. Robert Herrick. AnAnS-2; NoP; OAEP; OBS; OTPC (1923 ed.); PoE; PoeP; ReEn; SCEP-2; SeCP; SeCV-1; SeEP; StP; ViBoPo
Come Sorrow wrap me in thy sable cloake. *Unknown.* SeCSL
Come, sound up your trumpets and beat up your drums. The Young Earl of Essex's Victory over the Emperor of Germany. *Unknown.* ESPB
Come, Spirit of Thy Holy Love. My Heart's Desire. *Unknown.* STF
Come, spread foam rubber on the floor. I Can't Have a Martini, Dear, but You Take One. Ogden Nash. PoRA (rev. ed.)
Come, sprite, and dance! The sun is up. The Bacchante to Her Babe. Eunice Tietjens. HBMV; NP
Come, spur [*or* spurre] away. An Ode to Mr. [*or* Master] Anthony Stafford to Hasten Him into the Country [*or* Ode on Leaving the Great Town]. Thomas Randolph. AnAnS-2; EG; FaBoEn; GoTL; HBV; OBEV; OBS; SeCL; SeEP; ViBoPo
Come, stack arms, men; pile on the rails. Stonewall Jackson's Way. John Williamson Palmer. AA; DD; HBV; MC; OTPC (1946 ed.); PaA; PAH
Come, stand we here within this cactus-brake. A Sicilian Night. Edward Cracroft Lefroy. Echoes from Theocritus, IV. VA
Come, Stumpy, old man, we must shift while we can. The Broken-down Squatter. *Unknown.* PoAu-1
Come suddenly, O Lord, or slowly come. The Coming of the Lord. Jones Very. BePJ; MAmP
"Come; sun and laughter wait us at the end!" Aut Caesar aut Nullus. Lilian White Spencer. CAW
Come! supper is ready. The Good Moolly Cow. Eliza Lee Follen. PPL
"Come, surly fellow, come! A song!" The Haunted House. Robert Graves. OxBI
Come, swallow your bumpers, ye Tories, and roar. Massachusetts Song of Liberty. Mercy Warren. PAH
Come, Sweet Lass. *Unknown.* SeCL
Come take a carouse. *Unknown.* SeCSL
Come take up your hats and away let us haste. The Butterfly's Ball. William Roscoe. BoChLi; GoTP; OTPC, *diff. vers.*; TVC
Come the little clouds out of the Ice-Caves. Indian Songs.

Louis Mertins. StVeCh (1955 ed.)
Come, the wind may never again. Emily Brontë. EnLoPo
Come then, a song; a winding gentle song. In a Garden by Moonlight. Thomas Lovell Beddoes. *Fr.* Torrismond. VA
Come then, and like two doves with silv'ry [*or* silv'rie] wings. The Apparition of His Mistress Calling Him to Elysium [*or* Elizium]. Robert Herrick. AnAnS-2; ExPo; SCEP-2; SeCP; SeCV-1
Come then, as ever, like the wind at morning! Invocation to Youth. Laurence Binyon. OBEV; OBVV
Come then, my friend, my genius! Come along! Henry St. John, Viscount Bolingbroke. Pope. *Fr.* An Essay on Man. OBEC
Come then, tell me, sage divine. Ode on a Sermon against Glory. Mark Akenside. CEP; EiCL
Come, thou almighty King. *Unknown, wr. at. to* Charles Wesley. WGRP
Come, thou Fount of every blessing. Hymn of Praise. Robert Robinson. SoP
Come, Thou Holy Spirit, come. The Golden Sequence. Pope Innocent III. CAW
Come, Thou Monarch of the Vine. Shakespeare. *Fr.* Antony and Cleopatra, II, vii. BEL; OAEP; OnPM; ViBoPo (Drinking Song, A.) OBSC
Come Thou My Light. Hugh Thomson Kerr. MaRV
Come thou, who art the wine and wit. His Winding Sheet. Robert Herrick. AnFE; HBV; OBEV
Come through the quiet fields; April again. April, 1940. Patrick Maybin. NeIP
Come to Birth. Abbie Huston Evans. NePoAm
Come to Britain; a Humble Contribution to the Movement. A. P. Herbert. WhC
Come to Calvary's Holy Mountain. James Montgomery. BePJ
Come to conquer. Cold Water Flat. Philip Booth. NePoAm
Come to Me. *Unknown. tr. fr. Japanese by* Ishii *and* Obata. *Fr.* Manyo Shu. OnPM
Come to me, angel of the weary-hearted! To Sleep. Frances Sargent Osgood. AA
Come to Me, Beloved. Digby Mackworth Dolben. OxBoCh (Homo Factus Est.) TrPWD
Come to me broken dreams and all. The Still Voice of Harlem. Conrad Kent Rivers. IDB; Kal; NNP
Come to Me, Dearest. Joseph Brenan. HBV
Come to me, Eros, if you needs must come. To the God of Love. Edmund G. V. Knox. ALV; HBMV
Come to me God; but do not come. To God. Robert Herrick. AnAnS-2
Come to me, grief for ever. A Funerall Song. *Unknown.* CH
Come to me in my dreams, and then. Longing. Matthew Arnold. BoPe; CBEP; HBV; LO, *st.* 1; MBW-2; OAEP; PoLF; VP
Come to me in the silence of the night. Echo. Christina Rossetti. CH; ELP; GTBS-D; LiTL; LO; LoBV; MeWo; NoP; OBNC; PoEL-5; SeCeV; ViBoPo; ViPo; VP
Come to me, my dearest. Come to Me. *Unknown. Fr.* Manyo Shu. OnPM
Come to me, O ye children! Children. Longfellow. GTBS
Come to me, O ye sorrowful and hungry. My Clarion Call. Alberto Ghiraldo. PoFr
Come to Me Soon. Sir Walter Ralegh. *See* Dulcina.
Come to me when the swelling wind assails the wood with a sea-like roar. Late Light. Edmund Blunden. EnLoPo
Come to me, you with the laughing face, in the night as I lie. Pirates. Alfred Noyes. MCCG
Come to my window in the evening twilight. Sunset. Hayyim Nahman Bialik. TrJP
Come to our well-run desert. W. H. Auden. *Fr.* For The Time Being. TRV
Come to sunny Prestatyn. Sunny Prestatyn. Philip Larkin. PoeP
Come to the festal board to-night. The Festal Board. *Unknown.* BLPA; TreFS
Come to the judgment, golden threads. The Judgment of the May. Richard Watson Dixon. OBNC
Come to the terrace, May—the sun is low. A Sonnet in Dialogue. Austin Dobson. YT
"Come to the window, Mamma, and look out." Flying Flowers. Mrs. Motherly. SAS
Come to this land of sunshine. Arizona. Margaret Rowe Clifford. PoRL
Come to Your Heaven, You Heavenly Choirs! Robert Southwell. *See* New Heaven, New War.
Come tomorrow night. Young Man's Fancy. Ray Mathew. BoAV
Come, triumphe, enter Church, courte, citty, towne. A Gratulatory Elegy of the Peaceable Entry of King James. Sir John Harington. SiCE
Come trotting up. Foal. Mary Britton Miller. PDV
"Come, try your skill, kind gentlemen." The Gipsy Girl. Ralph Hodgson. EnLit; MCCG; MoBrPo; POTE
Come Turn to Mee, Thou Pretty Little One. *Unknown.* CoMu
Come unto Me. Katharine Lee Bates. ChIP
Come unto Me. St Matthew, XI: 28-30, Bible, *N.T.* MaRV (My Yoke Is Easy.) TreFS
Come unto Me. Flora Osgood. STF
Come unto Me. John Stuart. STF
Come unto me, ye heroes. Saratoga Song. *Unknown.* PAH
Come Unto Me, Ye Weary. William C. Dix. SoP
Come unto these yellow sands. Ariel's Song. Shakespeare. *Fr.* The Tempest, I, ii. AnFE; AtBAP; BEL; BoTP; CBEP; CH; CLwM; CTC; EG; EIL; FaBoCh; GN; GoJo; GTSL; HBV; InPo; LoBV; LoGBV; MaPo (1969 ed.); MCCG; MPB (1956 ed.); NoP; OBEV; OBSC; OTPC (1923 ed.); PCH; PoEL-2; PoIE; PTK; SiCE; ThWaDe; TOP; ViBoPo
Come Up From the Fields, Father. Walt Whitman. AmePo; AmPP; ATP (1935 ed.); CoBA; MAP; MCCG; MoAmPo (1950 ed.); NeMA; OuHeWo; OxBA; PoPo
Come up here, O dusty feet! Fairy Bread. Robert Louis Stevenson. GBV (1922 ed.); OTPC (1946 ed.)
Come up in the orchard with grass to your knee. Apple Season. Frances Frost. BrR; SiSoSe
Come Up, Methuselah. C. Day Lewis. OBMV
Come up, my horse, to Budleigh Fair. *Unknown.* OxNR
Come up to me at early dawn. Invitation. Solomon ibn Gabirol. TrJP
Come, virgin tapers of pure wax. Epithalamium. Richard Crashaw. HW; ReEn; ViBoPo
Come Visit My Garden. Tom Dent. NNP
Come Visit Us. James Freeman Clarke. FaChP
Come Vyolle come lett me thy necke embrace. *Unknown.* SeCSL
Come walk with me. Walk on a Winter Day. Sara Van Alstyne Allen. YeAr
Come walk with me along this willowed lane. May. Henry Sylvester Cornwell. HBV
Come, Walter Savage Landor, come this way. Landor. John Albee. AA
Come, Wandering Sheep. Edward Caswall. BePJ
Come Wary One. Ruth Manning Sanders. CH
Come, we shepherds, whose blest sight [*or* who have seen]. In the Holy Nativity of Our Lord God [*or* Holly Nativity of Our Lord God *or* Hymn of the Nativity *or* The Nativity]. Richard Crashaw. AnAnS-1; AtBAP; BEL; CABA; CoBE; EIL; MaMe; MeLP; MeP; MePo; OBS, *sl. abr.*; OxBoCh; PoEL-2; PoLi; SCEP-1; SeCeV; SeCV-1; SeEP; UnPo (1st ed.); WGRP, *sl. abr.*
Come, we who love the Lord. Emmanuel's Land. Isaac Watts. SoP
Come wench, are we almost at the well? The Song at the Well [*or* Fair Maiden]. George Peele. *Fr.* The Old Wives' Tale. AtBAP; PoEL-2
Come, when no graver cares employ. To the Rev. F. D. Maurice. Tennyson. GTBS-P
Come when you're called. Rules of Behavior. Mother Goose. HBV; HBVY; OxNR; SAS
Come Where My Love Lies Dreaming. Stephen Collins Foster. TreFS
Come while the afternoon of May. Expectation. Theodore Wratislaw. VA
"Come, wife," said good old Farmer Gray. The Little Dog under the Wagon. *Unknown.* PoLF
Come with bird's voices when the light grows dim. The Holy Spirit. Evelyn Underhill. BoC
Come with me/ on a safari. Safari. Worth Long. WOW
Come with me, under my coat. The Coolin. James Stephens. POTE
Come, with our voyces, let us warre. The Musicall Strife; in a Pastorall Dialogue. Ben Jonson. SCEP-2
Come with rain, O loud Southwester! To the Thawing

Come (continued)
Wind. Robert Frost. LOW; OxBA; RIS
Come with the Spring-time, forth Fair Maid, and be. The Meddow Verse; or, Aniversary to Mistris Bridget Lowman. Robert Herrick. SeCV-1
Come, Woeful Orpheus. *Unknown.* EnRePo
Come, workers! Poets, artists, dreamers, more and more. Angela Morgan. *Fr.* Let Us Declare! PGD
Come, worthy Greek, Ulysses, come. Ulysses and the Siren [*or* Syren]. Samuel Daniel. BWP; CABA; ElL; EnRePo; LoBV; NoP; OBEV; OBSC; PoEL-2; ReEn; ReIE; SiCE; StP; TuPP; ViBoPo
Come, Ye Disconsolate. Thomas Moore. CAW; MaRV; WGRP
Come, ye fair, ambrosial flowers. A Nosegay for Laura. Francis Fawkes. WaPE
Come, ye heavy states of night. *Unknown.* OBSC
Come ye hither all, whose taste. The Invitation. George Herbert. AnAnS-1; MaMe; MeP
Come, Ye Lads, Who Wish To Shine. *Unknown.* PAH
Come Ye Sons of Art. Henry Purcell. UnS
Come, ye thankful people, come. Harvest Home. Henry Alford. MaRV; SoP; WGRP
Come, ye that love the Saviour's name. Before His Throne. *Unknown.* SoP
Come ye yourselves apart and rest awhile. Come. *Unknown.* SoP
Come you gallants all, to you I do call. Robin Hood's Chase. *Unknown.* BaBo; ESPB
Come you ladies and you gentlemen and listen to my song. Hard Times in the Country. *Unknown.* OuSiCo
Come, You Pretty False-eyed Wanton. Thomas Campion. ELP; NoP; OBSC; StP
Come, You Whose Loves Are Dead. Beaumont *and* Fletcher. *Fr.* The Knight of the Burning Pestle, IV, iv. AtBAP; ElL; SiCE; TuPP
Comedian. Louis Johnson. AnNZ
Comedian as the Letter C, The. Wallace Stevens. NePA; OxBA; TwAmPo
Comedy. Mark Van Doren. NePoAm-2
Comedy of Patient and Meek Grissell, *sel.* John Phillip.
"Lulla by baby, lulla by baby." ReEn; TuPP
(Lullaby: "Lullaby baby, lullaby baby.") ElL
Comely and capable one of our race. On the Portrait of a Woman about to Be Hanged. Thomas Hardy. CMoP
Come a cry from Cuban water. Cuba Libre. Joaquin Miller. MC; PAH; ThLM
Comes a dun in the morning and raps at my door. The Poet and the Dun. William Shenstone. PP
Comes any good from Nazareth? From Nazareth. Margaret E. Sangster. ChIP
Comes Fall. Robert Nathan. HBMV
Comes Fog and Mist. William Hart-Smith. *Fr.* Christopher Columbus. PoAu-2
Comes not the springtime here. Come Not the Seasons Here. E. J. Pratt. PeCV
Comes something down with eventide. Eventide. Thomas Burbidge. VA
Comes the deer to my singing. Hunting Song [*or* Navajo Hunting-Song]. *Unknown, tr. by* Natalie Curtis. AWP; JAWP; WBP
Comes the lure of green things growning. Afoot. Sir Charles G. D. Roberts. CaP; HBV; VA
Comes the New Year; wailing the north winds blow. Thysia XVI. Morton Luce. HBV
Comes the time. Algonkian Burial. Alfred Goldsworthy Bailey. OBCV
Comes the time when it's later. A Wicker Basket. Robert Creeley. AmPC; ToPo
Comes to knock and knock again. Galileo Galilei. William Jay Smith. PoCh
Comes with autumn the spent moment. Three Trees at Solstice. Mary Finnin. BoAV
Comet. Mary Fullerton. NeLNL
Comet at Yell'ham, The. Thomas Hardy. CMoP; ExPo
Comet of Going-to-the-Sun, The. Vachel Lindsay. CMoP
Comet that my father saw, The. Comet. Mary Fullerton. NeLNL
Comfort. Elizabeth Barrett Browning. HBV; SoP; TRV
Comfort. May Doney. HBMV
Comfort. J. J. Lynch. SoP
Comfort. Margaret Widdemer. GoYe
Comfort but a queer companion, A. Woman. *Unknown.* UnTE
Comfort for Poor Poets, A. Sir John Harington. SiCE
Comfort for the Sleepless. H. C. Bradby. BoC
Comfort in Affliction. William E. Aytoun. BOHV; InMe
Comfort in Extremity. Christopher Harvey. OxBoCh
Comfort in Puirtith. Helen B. Cruickshank. OxBS
Comfort me with stars, not apples. Star Drill. T. Inglis Moore. PoAu-2
Comfort of the Fields. Archibald Lampman. CaP
Comfort of the Stars, The. Richard Burton. AnAmPo
Comfort of the Trees, The. Richard Watson Gilder. OTD; PAH
Comfort thee, O thou mourner, yet awhile. To the Sister of Elia [*or* To Mary Lamb]. Waller Savage Landor. HBV; TOP
Comfort thyself, my woeful heart. Sir Thomas Wyatt. Songs and Lyrics, XXXV. FCP; SiPS
Comfort to a Youth That Had Lost His Love. Robert Herrick. OBEV
Comfort When Work Seems Difficult. Isaiah, XLI: 6-7, 9-10, Bible, *O.T.* BoC
Comfort Ye, Comfort Ye My People. Isaiah, XL, Bible, *O.T.* EaLo; TreFS; TrJP; WoL
Comfort ye, my people. Listening to Handel's "Messiah". A. L. Rowse. MuSP
Comfortable Apple Trees, The. Grace Taber Hallock. RePo
Comforted. Amy Carmichael. SoP; TRV
Comforted. Henry W. Frost. SoP
Comforter of sorrow and care, The. Work. Edwin L. Sabin. DD
Comforters, The. Dora Sigerson Shorter. CH; HBMV
Comforting Lines. *Unknown.* STF
Comforts were few in eighteen-fifty-five. The Early Days. Basil Dowling. AnNZ
Comic Miseries. John Godfrey Saxe. BOHV
Comica Man, Da. T. A. Daly. StaSt
Comical Girl, The. M. Pelham. BOHV
Comical Revenge, The; or, Love in a Tub, *sels.* Sir George Etherege.
If She Be Not as Kind as Fair, *fr.* II, iii. SeCL
(Song: "If she be not as kind as fair.") CEP
Song: "Ladies, though to your conquering eyes," *fr.* V, iii. HBV; LO; OBEV (1st ed.); OBS
Comin' thro' [*or* through] the Rye (*diff. versions*). Burns. EiCL; ExPo; FaFP; HBV; LiTB; LiTG; LiTL; OxBS; TreF; UnTE
Comin' through the craigs o' Kyle. Owre the Muir amang the Heather. Jean Glover. HBV
Comin' through the Rye. *Unknown.* WBLP
Comin' through [*or* thro'] the Rye, poor body. Comin' Thro' the Rye. Burns. EiCL; HBV; OxBS; UnTE.
See also Gin a body meet a body.
Coming, The. Anthony Delius. ACV; BoSA
Coming. Philip Larkin. MoBrPo (1962 ed.)
Coming American, The, *sel.* Sam Walter Foss.
Bring Me Men. OQP
("Bring me men to match my mountains.") AmFN; BBV (1951 ed.); BLPA; FaBoBe; MaRV; NeHB; OTD; PaA; WaKn
Coming and the Appearing, The. *Unknown.* STF
Coming around a corner of the dark trail. . .what was wrong with the valley? The Inquisitors. Robinson Jeffers. MoAmPo (1950 ed.)
Coming around the Horn. John A. Stone. ABF; SGR, *with music*
Coming Awake. D. H. Lawrence. BrPo
Coming back and. Thinking of Our Visits. Craig Sterry. QAH
Coming Back to America. James Dickey. NYBP
Coming back to school again. Getting Back. Dorothy Brown Thompson. SiSoSe
Coming by evening through the wintry city. At a Bach Concert. Adrienne Cecile Rich. NePoEA
Coming Child, The. Richard Crashaw. *See* Welcome!
Coming Day, The. John Oxenham. *See* Morning Breaks, The.
Coming down/ I on. Old Love. Keith Wilson. ThO
Coming down Cleveland Avenue. James Tate. YAP
Coming down the mountain in the twilight. Where the Hayfields Were. Archibald MacLeish. LOW

Coming down the mountain road. The Mountain Road. Enid Derham. BoAu
Coming down the sluice of morning, Billy the Kid. The Return of Philista. Dick Gallup. ANYP
Coming for to carry me home (*refrain*). Swing Low, Sweet Chariot. *Unknown.* GoSl
Coming Forth by Day of Osiris Jones, The, *sel.* Conrad Aiken.
Nursery, The. LOW
Coming Home. Rolfe Humphries. MoRP
Coming Homeward Out of Spain. Barnabe Googe. EIL; EnRePo; ReIE; SiCE; TuPP
(Commynge Homewarde Out of Spayne.) EnPo
Coming in splendor through the golden gate. This Is the Last. Gilbert Waterhouse. PGD
Coming into a circle. Fire Song. Jason Miller. ThO
Coming into the store at first angry. The Man Who Finds That His Son Has Become a Thief. Raymond Souster. OBCV
Coming late, as always. The Poem. W. S. Merwin. PP
Coming of Christ, The. *Unknown.* ACP
Coming of Dusk upon a Village in Haiti, The. Henry Rago. HoPM
Coming [*or* Comming] of Good Luck, The. Robert Herrick. AtBAP; CBEP; ELU
Coming of His Feet, The. Lyman W. Allen. BLPA; MaRV; NeHB; SoP
Coming of Love, The. James I, King of Scotland. *See* He Sees His Beloved.
Coming of Love, The, *sel.* Theodore Watts-Dunton.
First Kiss, The. HBV; VA
Coming of Mary Louise, The. Gertrude Boughton Urquhart. PCH
Coming of Night, The. Thomas Wade. ERoP-2
Coming of Pharaoh, The. Cædmon(?). *See* Approach of Pharaoh, The.
Coming of Spring, The. Nora Perry. DD; HBVY; HH; PRWS; SoPo
(Coming of the Spring, The.) YeAr
Coming of Spring, The. *Unknown.* PEDC
Coming of the Fog. Clifford Dyment. POTi
Coming of the King, The. *Unknown.* *See* Yet if His Majesty, Our Sovereign Lord.
Coming of the Lord, The. Jones Very. BePJ; MAmP
Coming of the Plague, The. Weldon Kees. NaP
Coming of the Spring, The. Nora Perry. *See* Coming of Spring, The.
Coming of the Trees, The. Arthur Guiterman. PEDC
Coming of the White Man, The. Patrick Anderson. *Fr.* Poem on Canada. CaP; MoCV
Coming of War, The: Actaeon. Ezra Pound. CMoP; NP
Coming of Wisdom with Time, The. W. B. Yeats. DiPo
Coming out from a movie. Catwise. Philip Booth. NePoAm-2
Coming out of the bathroom. When I Think More of My Own Future Than of Myself. Ron Padgett. YAP
Coming out of the house on a fresh March morning. March 1st. Kathleen Spivak. NYBP
Coming out of the mountains of a summer evening. St. Gervais. Michael Roberts. FaBoCh; LoGBV
"Coming Storm, The." Herman Melville. MWA-1
Coming through the rye, poor body. *See* Comin' through the rye, poor body.
Coming [*or* Comming] to kiss[e] her lips [*or* lyps] (such grace I found). Amoretti, LXIV. Spenser. AtBAP; LoBV; Sonn
Coming up England by a different line. I Remember, I Remember. Philip Larkin. PoeP
Coming upon it unawares. Pittsburgh. Witter Bynner. AmFN
Comings and Goings, *sels.* Jean Follain, *tr. fr. French by* Dori Katz. CoFP
"Should the stroller absentmindedly kick."
"Sound of the wind revives former days, The."
Commanders of the Faithful. Thackeray. ALV
Commanding Elephants. Philip Levine. NaP
Commandos Embarking. George Whalley. TwCaPo
Commemoration. Claude McKay. BANP
Commemoration. Sir Henry Newbolt. FaBoTw; OBVV
Commemoration for the Physicist X, A. Paul Oppenheimer. NYTB
Commemoration Ode, The. James Russell Lowell. *See* Ode Recited at the Harvard Commemoration, July 21, 1865.
Commemoration Ode (World's Columbian Exposition, Chicago, 1892), *sels.* Harriet Monroe.
Democracy. AA
Lincoln. AA
Two Heroes. OHIP
Washington. AA; FaBoBe; MaRV; OQP; PoRL
Commemorative of a Naval Victory. Herman Melville. AP
Commencement. Margaret Elizabeth Sangster. PEDC
Commendation of Her Beauty, Stature, Behavior, and Wit. Francis Davison. *See* Her Commendation.
Commendation of Music, The. William Strode. *See* In Commendation of Music.
Commendations of Mistress Jane Scrope, The. John Skelton. *Fr.* Phyllyp Sparowe. OBSC
("Howe [*or* How] shall I report," *abr.*) EG; ViBoPo
Comment. Dorothy Parker. ALV
(Some Beautiful Letters: Comment.) InMe
Commentary, *sel.* W. H. Auden.
"Some of our dead are famous, but they would not care." MoPo
Commercial Candour. G. K. Chesterton. ALV; WhC
Commination. Walter Savage Landor. ALV
Comming of Good Luck, The. Robert Herrick. *See* Coming of Good Luck, The.
Comming to kisse her lyps (such grace I found). *See* Coming to kiss her lips . . .
Commingling sky, A. Freely Espousing. James Schuyler. ANYP; NeAP
Commissary Report. Stoddard King. ALV; ShM
Commission. Ezra Pound. CBV; TwCP
Commissioned. Henry W. Frost. SoP
Commissioner bet me a pony, The—I won. Songs [*or* Song] of the Squatter[s]. Robert Lowe. PoAu-1; VA
Commit thou all thy griefs. Commitment. Paul Gerhardt. SoP
Commit Thy Way. Paul Gerhardt, *tr. fr. German by* Elizabeth Rundle Charles. SoP
Commitment. Paul Gerhardt, *tr. fr. German by* John Wesley. SoP
Commitment. James Russell Lowell. *See* Slaves.
Committee, The. C. Day Lewis. CMoP
Committee—now a permanent body, The. Dream. Marianne Moore. NYBP
Common Bill, *with music.* *Unknown.* AS
Common Blessings. Thomas Curtis Clark. TrPWD
Common Conditions, *sel.* *Unknown.*
"Lustily, lustily, lustily let us sail forth." ReEn; SiCE; TuPP
Common Cormorant, The. *Unknown.* FaBoCh; FiBHP; GoTP; LoGBV; SiTL; WhC
(Birds, Bags, Bears, and Buns.) OtMeF
(Common Cormorant or Shag, The.) ChTr
Common Dawn. Guy Butler. PeSA
Common Dust. Georgia Douglas Johnson. AmNP; TTY
Common Form. Kipling. *Fr.* Epitaphs of the War. FaBoTw; PoVP; PV
Common Grave, The. James Dickey. CoAP
Common Ground, A, *sel.* Denise Levertov.
"Not 'common speech.'" PP
Common Inference, A. Charlotte Perkins Gilman. AA; AmePo; AnAmPo; WGRP
Common Lot, The. Adelbert Sumpter Coats. TrPWD
Common Lot, The. Lizette Woodworth Reese. NP
Common Man, The. Goldsmith. *Fr.* The Deserted Village. MaRV
("Ill fares the land.") TreFT; TRV
Common practice is the reverse of Tessie's. Report. Robert Finch. TwCaPo
Common Problem, The. Robert Browning. *Fr.* Bishop Blougram's Apology. OQP
Common rain had come again, The. The First Night of Fall and Falling Rain. Delmore Schwartz. NYTB
Common Road, The. Silas H. Perkins. BLPA; FaBoBe; NeHB
Common Sense. James Thomas Fields. AA
Common Sense. Harry Graham. *See* Mr. Jones.
Common Sense and Genius. Thomas Moore. NBM
Common speech is, spend and God will send, The. Gascoigne's Memories, III [*or* Magnum Vectigal Parcimonia]. George Gascoigne. EnPo; EnRePo; EP
Common Street, The. Helen Gray Cone. AnAmPo; HBV

Common Tasks, The. Grace Noll Crowell. PoToHe (new ed.)
Common Terns. Patric Dickinson. POTi
Common Things. Ann Hawkshaw. OTPC (1923 ed.)
Common Things, The. Barbara Young. OQP
Commonplace. "Susan Coolidge." *See* Commonplaces.
Commonplace, The. Walt Whitman. MAP; MoAmPo; TrGrPo; TSW
("Commonplace I sing, The.") YT
"Commonplace life, A," we say, and we sigh. Commonplaces [*or* Commonplace]. "Susan Coolidge." OQP; TreFT
Commonplaces. "Susan Coolidge." OQP
(Commonplace.) TreFT
God's Plan, *sel.* MaRV
Commonplaces. Kipling. BOHV; HBV
Commonwealth of Birds, The. James Shirley. GoBC
Commonwealth of the Bees, The. Shakespeare. King Henry V, *fr.* I, ii. GN
Commotion of these waves, however strong, cannot disturb. Louis Dudek. *Fr.* Europe. OBCV
Communal. Mary Fullerton. PoAu-1
Communication. Elizabeth Jennings. NePoEA
Communication on His Thirtieth Birthday. Marvin Bell. CoAP
Communication to Nancy Cunard, A. Kay Boyle. PoNe
Communication to the City Fathers of Boston. George Starbuck. NYBP
Communion. Phoebe Smith Bachelder. ChIP
Communion. Loren W. Burch. ChIP
Communion. Edward Dowden. MaRV; TrPWD
Communion. Hildegarde Flanner. NP
Communion. Caroline Giltinan. CAW; JKCP
Communion. Wallace Gould. AnAmPo
Communion. P. M. Snider. PoToHe (new ed.)
Communion. J. L. Spicer. BLRP
Communion. John Banister Tabb. MaRV; WGRP
Communion. T. Turner. LO
Communion. Wordsworth. *Fr.* The Excursion, I. MaRV
("Such was the Boy—but for the growing Youth.") OBRV
Communion Hymn. Bryant. SoP
Communion Hymn. Henry W. Frost. SoP
Communion Hymn. William Gay. ChIP
Communion Hymn. Alice Freeman Palmer. MaRV; TrPWD
Communion Hymn of the Ancient Irish Church. *Unknown.* *See* May the Sweet Name of Jesus.
Communion of Saints. Benjamin Beddome. SoP
Communion with Nature ("For I would walk alone"). Wordsworth. *Fr.* The Prelude, II. TOP
Communion with Nature ("Think you 'mid all this mighty sum"). Wordsworth. *Fr.* Expostulation and Reply. MaRV
Community. John Donne. Po
(Communitie.) MaMe
Commuter. E. B. White. OCS; PV; TreFT; WhC
(Commuters.) BOHV
Commynge Homewarde Out of Spayne. Barnaby Googe. *See* Coming Homeward Out of Spain.
Companion, The. Yevgeny Yevtushenko, *tr. fr. Russian by* Robin Milner Gulland *and* Peter Levi. FIW
Companion Fear is at my side. The News. "Sec." TRV
Companion me. Closing Cadence. John Moffit. MoRP
Companion of Her Lord till Death. *Unknown, tr. fr. Chinese by* Arthur Waley. *Fr.* The Book of Songs. HW
Companioned by long loneliness. En Route. George Dillon. NP
Companions. Charles Stuart Calverley. BOHV; HBV; NA; PoVP; TOP; TSW; VA
Companions, The. Howard Nemerov. NYBP
Companions. Adrien Stoutenburg. WIRo
Companions. Margaret Widdemer. FiSC
Companions were we in the grove and glen! Frederick Goddard Tuckerman. *Fr.* Sonnets. AP
Companionship. Maltbie D. Babcock. *See* No Distant Lord.
Companionship. Mary Elizabeth Coleridge. NBM
Company. William Dean Howells. AmePo
Company Cook, The. *Unknown.* ABF
Company of boatmen I'll have you to know, A. Jacket So Blue; or, A Company of Boatmen. *Unknown.* BFSS
Company of Lovers, The. Judith Wright. BoAV; MoAuPo
Company of vessels on the sea, A. Battle Problem. William Meredith. NYBP
Company One Keeps, The. Aimor R. Dickson. *See* Judged by the Company One Keeps.
Compare a stick with the wood. Family Screams. Hy Sobiloff. TwAmPo
Compare me to the child that plays with fire. Fidessa, More Chaste than Kind, XIII. Bartholomew Griffin. SiCE; Sonn; TuPP
Compare needles to the shrewd injectors of the State. Poem for a Painter. Floyce Alexander. QAH
Compared with Christ. Augustus Montague Toplady. BePJ
Comparison, The. Thomas Carew. AnAnS-2; CavP
Comparison, The. Catullus, *tr. fr. Latin by* George Lamb. OnPM
Comparison, The. John Donne. Elegies, VIII. ErPo; MaMe
Comparison, A. John Farrar. BrR; FaPON; MPB; TSW
Comparison. Mary Ann Hoberman. BiCB
Comparison, A. *Unknown.* STF
Comparison and Complaint, The. Isaac Watts. TrPWD
Comparison of His Love with the Faithful and Painful Love of Troilus to Cressid, A. *Unknown.* ReIE
Comparison of Life and Death. John Harington. *See* Elegy Wrote in the Tower, 1554.
Comparison of Love to a Streame Falling from the Alpes. Sir Thomas Wyatt. FaBoEn
("From these high hills as when a spring doth fall.") FCP
Comparison of the Life of Man, A. Richard Barnfield. OBSC; SiCE
Comparison of the Sonnet and the Epigram. Sir John Harington. SiCE; TuPP
Comparisons. *Unknown.* *See* Similes.
Compass Needle, A. Francis Quarles. *See* On the Needle of a Sundial.
Compasses, The. George MacBeth. NePoEA-2
Compassion. James A. Sanaker. SoP
Compassion for the Lost. *Unknown.* SoP
Compassion in the world againe is bred. Ralphius. John Donne. MaMe
Compassion is love, plus desire to share. Compassion. James A. Sanaker. SoP
Compassion So Divine. Anne Steele. BePJ
Compassionate eyes had our brave John Brown. John Brown; a Paradox. Louise Imogen Guiney. DD
Compassionate Fool, The. Norman Cameron. CBEP; GTBS-P
Compatience perses, reuth and marcy stoundes. The Passion of Jesus. *Unknown.* MeEL
Compel Them to Come In. Leonard Dodd. BLRP
Compelled to Love. Walter Stone. ErPo
Compensate. Patrick D. Moreland. InP
Compensation. E. M. Brainard. PoToHe
Compensation. James Edwin Campbell. BANP
Compensation, *sl. abr.* Phoebe Cary. OQP
Compensation. Elizabeth Rundle Charles. SoP
Compensation. Thomas Stephens Collier. AA
Compensation. Paul Laurence Dunbar. AmNP; HBV; PoNe; PTK
Compensation ("The wings of Time"). Emerson. AmPP (5th ed.); AP; ForPo; MWA-1
Compensation ("Why should I keep holiday"). Emerson. AnFE; AnNE; APA; CoAnAm; LiTA
Compensation. Henry W. Frost. SoP
Compensation. Gerald Gould. HBMV
Compensation. Robinson Jeffers. MAP; MoAB; MoAmPo; NeMA
Compensation. Ruth Comfort Mitchell. PEDC
Compensation. Lizette Woodworth Reese. HBMV
Compensation. Celia Thaxter. HBV
Compensation. Ridgely Torrence. *Fr.* The House of a Hundred Lights. AA
Complacencies of the peignoir, and late. Sunday Morning. Wallace Stevens. AmLP; AmP; AmPP (4th ed.); AnFE; AnNE; AP; APA; BWP; CABA; CABL; CaFP; CBV; CMoP; CoAnAm; CoBA; CoBMV; CrMA; FaBoEn; ForPo; FosPo; InPo; LiTA; LiTG; LiTM; MAP; MAPA; MaPo (1969 ed.); MasP; MoAB; MoAmPo; MoVE; NePA; NoP; OxBA; PAn; PoAn; PoDB; PoeP; PoIE; QFR; ReMP; SeCeV; StP; TDP; TwAmPo
Complacent Cliff-Dweller, The. Margaret Fishback. PoLF
Complain we may, much is amiss. Totus Mundus in Maligno Positus. *Unknown.* SiCE; TuPP
"Complaine my lute, complaine on him." A Pleasant New Ballad

of Two Lovers. *Unknown.* CoMu
Complaining. George Herbert. MaMe
Complains, Being Hindered the Sight of His Nymph. Philip Ayres. SeCL
Complaint, The. Mark Akenside. OBEV
Complaint. Joseph Bennett. LiTA; StP
Complaint, The. Catullus, *tr. fr. Latin by* Leigh Hunt. OnPM
Complaint, A. Lady Chwang Këang, *tr. fr. Chinese by* James Legge; *revised by* Helen Waddell. OuHeWo
Complaint. Samuel Taylor Coleridge. *See* Good, Great Man, The.
Complaint. Ted Hughes. PoDB
Complaint. William Carlos Williams. QFR
Complaint, A. Wordsworth. ATP; CBEP; OBRV; PoEL-4
Complaint, The; or, Night Thoughts. Edward Young. *See* Night Thoughts.
Complaint by Night of the Lover Not Beloved, A. Earl of Surrey *after* Petrarch. AWP; ElL; FaBoEn; OuHeWo; SiCE; Sonn; TuPP
("Alas, so all things now do hold their peace!") ReEn; SiPS
(Complaint by Night, A.) LoBV
(Night.) OBSC
Complaint for True Love Unrequited. Sir Thomas Wyatt. ReIE
("What vaileth truth? or, by it, to take pain?") FCP
Complaint of a Lover Forsaken of His Love, The. *Unknown.* CoMu OBSC
(Green Willow, The.) OBSC
Complaint of a Lover Rebuked. Petrarch, *tr. fr. Italian by* the Earl of Surrey. *Fr.* Sonnets to Laura: To Laura in Life. AWP; BEL; CABA; CBV; CoBE; EnLi-1 (1949 ed.); EnLit; LiTW; OAEP; OnPM; ReIE; SiCE; Sonn; TrGrPo; TuPP
(Love That Doth Reign.) ILP
("Love that doth reign and live within my thought.") ReEn; SiPS
Complaint of a Lover That Defied Love and Was by Love After the More Tormented. Earl of Surrey. *See* Love's Rebel.
Complaint of Chaucer to His Empty Purse, The. Chaucer. *See* Compleint of Chaucer to His Empty Purse, The.
Complaint of Henrie Duke of Buckinghame, The. Thomas Sackville. *See* Mirror for Magistrates, A.
Complaint of Love. Sir Philip Sidney. *See* Loved I Am, and Yet Complaine of Love.
Complaint of New Amsterdam, The. Jacob Steendam. PAH
Complaint of Rosamund, The, *abr.* Samuel Daniel. OAEP; ReEn; ReIE; SiCE; TuPP
Sels.
Henry's Lament. OBSC
Lonely Beauty. CTC; OBSC
Rosamond's Appeal. OBSC
Complaint of Tarpeia's Door, The. Propertius, *tr. fr. Latin by* Frances Fletcher. LiTW
Complaint of the Absence of Her Lover Being upon the Sea. Earl of Surrey. ElL; OBEV; SiCE
(Lady Complains of Her Lover's Absence, A.) SiPS
("O happy dames, that may embrace.") ReEn
(Seafarer, The.) OBSC
Complaint of the Black Knight, The. John Lydgate.
"In May, when Flora, the fresshe lusty quene,"*sel.* EnPo
Complaint of the Common Weill of Scotland. Sir David Lindsay. *Fr.* The Dreme. GoTS
(Compleynt of the Comoun Weill of Scotland, The.) OxBS
Complaint of the Fair Armouress, The. Villon, *tr. fr. French by* Swinburne. AWP;CTC;UnTE; Wol
(Lament of "La Belle Heaulmière," The, *tr. by* Lewis Wharton.) LiTW
(Lament of the Lovely Helmet-Dealer, *tr. by* Hubert Creekmore.) ErPo
(Old Woman's Lamentations, An, *pr. tr. by* J. M. Synge.) OBMV
(Two Translations from Villon, *pr. tr. by* J. M. Synge.) MoBrPo
Complaint of the Lover Disdained. Earl of Surrey. BEL; Sonn
("In Cypress Springs—whereas dame Venus dwelt.") FCP
Complaint of the Morepethshire Farmer, The. Basil Bunting. CTC
Complaint of Troilus, The. Chaucer. *Fr.* Troilus and Criseyde, V. DiPo; OBEV (new ed.)
Complaint on the Oblivion of the Dead. Jules Laforgue, *tr. fr. French by* William Jay Smith. LiTW
Complaint That His Ladie after She Knew of His Love Kept Her Face Alway Hidden from Him. Earl of Surrey. *See* Cornet, The.
Complaint to His Purse. Chaucer. *See* Compleint of Chaucer to His Empty Purse.
Complaints. Elizabeth Barrett Browning. FaChP
(Cheerfulness Taught by Reason.) PoVP
Complaisant Swain, The. Ovid, *tr. fr. Latin by* F. A. Wright. AWP
Complaynt of Schir David Lindesay, The, *sel.* Sir David Lindsay.
Childhood of James V, The. AtBAP
Compleat Angler, The, *sel.* Izaak Walton.
Angler's Wish, The. HBV; SeCL
Compleint [*or* Compleinte *or* Compleynt] of Chaucer to His Empty Purse [*or* Purs], The. Chaucer. CoBE; EnLi-1; EnLit
(Chaucer's Complaint to His Empty Purse, *mod. vers. by* Louis Untermeyer.) TrGrPo
(Complaint of Chaucer to His Empty Purse, The.) BEL; EnL; GoBC *mod. vers. by* Belle Cooper; WHA
(Complaint of Chaucer to His Purse, The.) CLwM; PAn; SiTL; ViBoPo; YAT
(Complaint to His Purse.) CABA; NoP
(Compleynt of Chaucer to His Purse, The) PoIE
(Song to His Purse for the King, A.) MeEL
(To My Empty Purse.) BOHV
Complement, The. Thomas Carew. CavP
Complete Destruction. William Carlos Williams. PoeP
Complete Hen, The. Elizabeth J. Coatsworth. GoTP
Complete Lover, The. William Browne. HBV; LiTL
(Song: "For her gait, if she be walking.") CLwM; OBEV
Complete Misanthropist, The. Morris Bishop. FiBHP; SiTL
Completion. Eunice Tietjens. HBMV; NP
Complex Autumnal. Carolyn Kizer. FRC
Compleynt of Chaucer to His Purse, The. Chaucer. *See* Compleint of Chaucer to His Empty Purse.
Compleynt of the Comoun Weill of Scotland. Sir David Lindsay. *See* Complaint of the Common Weill of Scotland.
Complicated gentleman allow me to present, A. Sir Bailey Barre. W. S. Gilbert. *Fr.* Utopia, Limited. PCD
Compliment, The. William Habington. ACP
Compline. Patrick F. Kirby. GoBC
Compline. Duncan Campbell Scott. GoBC
Composed among the Ruins of a Castle in North Wales. Wordsworth. BWP
Composed at Neidpath Castle, the Property of Lord Queensberry, 1803. Wordsworth. GTBS; GTBS-D; GTBS-P; GTBS-W; GTSE; GTSL
Composed at Rydal on May Morning, 1838. Wordsworth. PeER
Composed by the Sea-Side, near Calais, August, 1802. Wordsworth. ATP; CoBE; EnLi-2; EnRP; MBW-2; MERP; OAEP; OuHeWo; PoE; Sonn; TOP; UnPo (1st ed.)
Composed by the Side of Grasmere Lake. Wordsworth. BWP; MERP; Sonn
(Sonnet: Composed by the Side of Grasmere Lake.) ChER
Composed, generally defined. The Map. Mark Strand. NYBP
Composed in Spring. Burns. *See* Song: "Again rejoicing Nature sees."
Composed in the Tower before his execution. "More Light! More Light!" Anthony Hecht. CoAP; NePoEA-2; TwCP
Composed in the Valley near Dover. Wordsworth. MERP
Composed near Calais, on the Road Leading to Ardes. Wordsworth. MERP
Composed on a Journey Homeward. Samuel Taylor Coleridge. *See* Sonnet: Oft o'er My Brain.
Composed on the Eve of the Marriage of a Friend in the Vale of Grasmere. Wordsworth. HW
Composed upon an Evening of Extraordinary Splendor and Beauty. Wordsworth. EnRP; MBW-2; PoE
Composed upon Westminster Bridge, Sept. 3, 1802. Wordsworth. AnEnPo; AnFE; ATP; AWP; BEL; BoLiVe; BWP; CABA; CaFP; CBEP; CBV; ChTr; CoBE; DiPo; EnL; EnLit; EnRP; EPN; ERoP-1; ExPo; FaBoCh; FaBV; FaFP; ForPo; HT; ILP; InP; InPo; InvP; JAWP; LoGBV; MaPo; MBW-2;

Composed (continued)
MERP; NoP; OAEP; OBNC; OBRV; OuHeWo; PAn; PoAn; PoE; PoEL-4; PoeP; PoFS; PoG; PoIE; PoLF; PoMa; PoPl; PoPo; Sonn; TOP; TrGrPo; UnPo (1st ed.); VaPo; WBP; WePo; YAT
(Earth Has Not Anything to Show More Fair.) EG; WHA
(Sonnet: Composed upon Westminster Bridge, September 3, 1802.) FiP; HBV; OTPC
(Upon Westminster Bridge.) BoPe; GTBS; GTBS-D; GTBS-P; GTBS-W; GTSE; GTSL; LiTB; LiTG; MCCG; MemP; OBEV; PoSa; SeCeV; ShBV-3; StP; TreF
(Westminster Bridge.) LoBV; PoRA; ViBoPo
Composed While under Arrest. Mikhail Yurevich Lermontov, *tr. fr. Russian by* Max Eastman. AWP
Composer, The. W. H. Auden. MuSP; PoPo; UnS
Composer Liszt, The/ Banged the piano with his fist. Important People. Louis Untermeyer, *and others.* StaSt
Composing scales beside the rails. The Harmonious Heedlessness of Little Boy Blue [*or* Little Boy Blue]. Guy Wetmore Carryl. ALV; MPB; YT
Composite whose body is of light, A. Wine. Dakiki. LiTW
Composition for a Nativity. John Ciardi. MiAP
Composition in Late Spring. Irving Layton. PeCV
Composition of Distances, The. Pien Chih-lin, *tr. fr. Chinese by* Pien Chih-lin. LiTW
Composition of Pat Young, The. Pat Young. Kenneth Mackenzie. PoAu-2
Compost Heap, The. Vernon Watkins. NYBP
Compounded out of nothingness and all. This Sharpening Tension. Sister Mary St. Virginia. JKCP (1955 ed.)
Compromise. Laurence McKinney. InMe
Computation, The. John Donne. ATP (1935 ed.); DiPo; MaMe; OAEP; TuPP
Comrade, The. Lee Wilson Dodd. HBMV
Comrade Christ. Verne Bright. ChIP; OQP
Comrade, Do Not Forget! Vasili Lebedev-Kumach, *tr. fr. Russian by* Dan Levin. PoFr
Comrade in Arms. T. Inglis Moore. PoAu-2
Comrade Jesus. Ralph Cheyney. ChIP; PGD
Comrade Jesus. Sarah N. Cleghorn. AnAmPo; HBMV; MaRV; NAMP; OQP; PoFr; StJW; WGRP
Comrade, Remember. Raymond Kresensky. PGD
Comrade Rides Ahead, A. Douglas Malloch. HBMV
Comrade, with your finger on the playback switch. The Bedbug. Tony Harrison. PV
Comrade, within your tent of clay. Comrade, Remember. Raymond Kresensky. PGD
Comradery. Madison Cawein. AA
Comrades. Henry Ames Blood. AA
Comrades. Henry R. Dorr. MC; PAH
Comrades. W. W. Gibson. BEL
Comrades. Laurence Housman. HBV
Comrades. Richard Hovey. MAP; MoAmPo (1942 ed.); PC
Comrades. Lionel Johnson. HBV
Comrades. George Edward Woodberry. HBV; PFY
Comrades as We Rest Within. Ronald Hambleton. CaP
Comrades in Arms: Conversation Piece. *Unknown.* ErPo
Comrades, leave me here a little, while as yet 'tis early morn. Locksley Hall. Tennyson. ATP (1935 ed.); BEL; CABA; CABL; DiPo; EnL; EnLi-2; EnLit; EPN; FaFP; HBV; LiTG; MaVP; MBW-2; OAEP; PoVP; TOP; ViPo; ViPP; WHA
Comrades of risk and rigour long ago. Prisoners. F. W. Harvey. MMA
Comrades of the Cross. Willard Wattles. *See* Acceptance.
Comrades, pour the wine tonight. Comrades. Richard Hovey. MAP; MoAmPo (1942 ed.)
Comrades, the Morning Breaks. Hafiz, *tr. fr. Persian by* Richard Le Gallienne. *Fr.* Odes. AWP
Comrades, when the air is sweet. At a Country Dance in Provence. Harold Monro. OBVV
Comrades, you may pass the rosy. The Lay of the Love-lorn [*or* The Cry of the Lovelorn]. William E. Aytoun *and* Sir Theodore Martin. BOHV; CenHV
Comus; a Masque Presented at Ludlow Castle. Milton. OAEP
Sels.
"By the rushy-fringèd bank." TOP
Chastity ("A hidden strength"). OBS
He That Has Light Within, 5 *ll.* MaRV
"O foolishness of men! that lend their ears." AtBAP; ViBoPo
(Comus's Praise of Nature.) PoEL-3
Sabrina Fair. AtBAP; ATP (1935 ed.); CBEP; EG; ELP; FaBoCh; InPo; LoGBV; OBEV; PoEL-3; SeCeV; SeCL; TOP; ViBoPo
(Sabrina.) CH; UnPo (1st ed.)
(Song: "Sabrina fair.") LoBV
"She that has that is clad in cómplete steel." InP
"Some say no evil thing that walks by night." LO
"Star that bids the shepherd fold, The." EG; FaBoCh; LoGBV; OBEV, *abr.*; SeCeV; TOP; ViBoPo; WHA
(Comus' Invocation to His Revelers.) BoLiVe; TrGrPo
(Invocation of Comus, The.) OBS
(Mask, A.) FiP
"Sweet Echo, sweetest nymph, that liv'st unseen." AtBAP; EG; ELP; ExPo; SeCeV; SeCL; TOP; ViBoPo
(Echo.) CBEP; OBEV; OBS
(Lady's Song.) BoLiVe; TrGrPo
(Song: "Sweet Echo, sweetest nymph that liv'st unseen.") LoBV
Temperance and Virginity. OBS
"There is a gentle nymph not far from hence." MyFE; SeEP
(Sabrina.) OBS
"To the ocean now I fly." AtBAP; OBEV; OBS; SeCeV; ViBoPo
(Farewell of the Attendant Spirit.) BoLiVe; TrGrPo
Concealment, The: Ishi, the Last Wild Indian. William Stafford. NaP
Conceit Begotten by the Eyes. Sir Walter Ralegh. EnRePo; SiPS
(Affection and Desire.) CBEP; OBSC
(Poesy to Prove Affection Is Not Love, A. FCP
Conceit with Aunties, Urn and Puss. Michael T. Leech. NYTB
Conceits. Arlo Bates. AA
Concentred here th' united wisdom shines. The Federal Convention. *Unknown.* PAH
Conception. Waring Cuney. BANP; PoNe
Concerning brave Captains. Great-Heart. Kipling. HBV
Concerning Geffray Teste Noire. William Morris. PoVP; ViPo
Concerning Love. Josephine Preston Peabody. CIV;WhC
Concerning Mme. Robert. Deems Taylor. *tr. fr. French.* UnTE
Concerning the Nature of Love. Lucretius. *tr. fr. Latin by* Dryden. *Fr.* De Rerum Natura, IV. ErPo; PeRV
Concerning the Nature of Things. Lucretius. *See* De Rerum Natura.
Concerning Them That Are Asleep. R. W. Raymond. STF
Concerning Unnatural Nature: An Inverted Form. Hollis Summers. ErPo
Concerning Virgil's Aeneids. Nicholas Grimald. ReIE
Concert, The. Phyllis McGinley. YeAr
Concert. Helen Quigless. NBP
Concert at Sea. Hubert Creekmore. WaP
Concert-hall creaked like a full-dress shirt, The. Unfamiliar Quartet. Stephen Vincent Benét. WhC
Concert-Interpretation. Siegfried Sassoon. CBEP; MuSP
Concert, The: Oratorio for a Season of Wrath. John L'Heureux. YAP
Concert Party, A. Siegfried Sassoon. EnLit; MMA; MuSP
Concert Scene. John Logan. NePoEA-2
Concierge at the front gate where relatives, The. Aeterna Poetae Memoria. Archibald MacLeish. Sonn
Conclusion. Lord De Tabley. PoVP
Conclusion, The. Sir Walter Ralegh. BEL; EvOK; FaPL; HBV; OBEV; OtMeF; PCD; PTK; SoP; TOP; WGRP
(Author's Epitaph, [Made by Himselfe], The.) BoC; EnLi-1 (1949 ed.); EnLit; FaBoEn; FaChP; OAEP; OxBoCh; SiCE
(Epitaph: "Even such is Time, which takes in trust.") CTC; OBSC; TRV
(Even Such Is Time.) ChTr; EG; ElL; EnRePo; EP; ExPo; FCP; ForPo; GTBS-W; LiTB; OnPM; PG (1955 ed.); PoE; PoRA; SeCeV; SiPS; WHA; WoL
(His Epitaph.) TrGrPo
(Last Lines.) ShBV-3
(Lines Written the Night before His Execution.) SoP
(Sir Walter Ralegh the Night before His Death.) PoFS; PoPo
(Sir Walter Raleigh's Verses, Found in His Bible in the Gatehouse at Westminster.) MaRV
(Verses: "Even such is time.") PoIE

(Verses Found in His Bible in the Gate-House at Westminster.) EnL
(Verses Written in His Bible.) ViBoPo
(Written on the Night before His Execution.) WePo
Conclusion. Siegfried Sassoon. MoBrPo
Conclusion, The. Delmore Schwartz. TwAmPo
Conclusion, The. *Unknown.* SoP
Conclusion. Wordsworth. *See* In One of Those Excursions.
Conclusion: "In vain, in vain—the all-composing hour." Pope. *Fr.* The Dunciad, IV. EnLi-1; ViBoPo
(Chaos.) LoBV
(Reign of Chaos, The.) FiP
(Triumph of Ignorance, The.) CoBE
Conclusion: "It was a close, warm, breezeless summer night." Wordsworth. *Fr.* The Prelude, XIV. MBW-2; PoEL-4
(Conclusion: "It was a summer's night, a close warm night," *sl. diff.*) FaBoEn; OBNC
Conclusion: "Now have I brought a woork too end which neither Joves fierce wrath." Ovid, *tr. fr. Latin by* Arthur Golding. *Fr.* Metamorphoses, XV. CTC
Conclusion of the Whole Matter, The. Ridgely Torrence. *Fr.* The House of a Hundred Lights. AA; HBV
Conclusion to the May Queen and New Year's Eve. Tennyson. *Fr.* The May Queen. OTPC (1923 ed.)
Conclusive Voyage, The. Juan Ramón Jiménez, *tr. fr. Spanish by* H. R. Hays. PoPl
Concord. Robert Lowell. MaPo (1969 ed.); TDP
Concord Hymn. Emerson. AA; AmePo; AmFN; AmP; AmPP; AnAmPo; AP; AWP; BBV; BLPA; CoBA; DD; ExPo; FaBoBe; FaBoEn; FaFP; FaPL; FaPON; GN; GTBS-W; HBV; HBVY; HH; HT; InP; InPo; JAWP; LiTA; LiTG; MaRV; MC; MCCG; MPB; MWA-1; NeHB; NePA; NoP; OHFP; OnPM; OQP; OTD; OTPC; OuHeWo; OxBA; PaA; PAH; PAL; PEDC; Po; PoFr; PoFS; PoIE; PoRL; PTK; SeCeV; StVeCh; ThLM; TOP; TreF; TrGrPo; ViBoPo, *sts.* 1-2; WaaP; WBP; WoL; YaD; YT
(Hymn: "By the rude bridge that arched the flood.") AnNE; PG (1945 ed.)
(Hymn Sung at the Completion of the Concord Monument.) PAP; PoPl
Concrete Mixers. Patricia Hubbell. PDV
Concrete Poem, A. Anthony Mundy. PV
Concubine, The (Sir Martyn), *sels.* William Julius Mickle. OBEC
Sunset, *fr.* II.
Wild Romantic Dell, A, *fr.* II.
Condemnation. Thich Nhat Hanh. PPON
Condemned, The. Edward Howland. AA
Condemned [*or* Condemn'd] to hope's delusive mine. On the Death of Mr. [*or* Dr.] Robert Levet. Samuel Johnson. BWP; CBEP; CEP; EiCL; EiCP; EiPP; FaBoEn; HBV; NoP; OBEC; OBEV; PoE; PoEL-3; PoFS; VaPo
Condemned Women. John Gray, *after* Baudelaire. SyP
Condors. Padraic Colum. GoJo
Conduct. Samuel Greenberg. CrMA; LiTA
Conducted Tour. Emma Swan. NYTB
Conductor Bradley. Whittier. PaPo
Conductor when he receives a fare, The. The Passenjare. Isaac H. Bromley. FiBHP
Conemaugh. Elizabeth Stuart Phelps Ward. PAH
Coney Island Life, A. James L. Weil. AmFN
Coney Island of the Mind, A, *sels.* Lawrence Ferlinghetti.
"Constantly risking absurdity." LiTM (1970 ed.); NeAP; ToPo
"Dove sta amore." ToPo
Funny Fantasies Are Never so Real as Oldstyle. ErPo
In a Surrealist Year. PPON
"In Golden Gate Park that day." ToPo
"In Goya's greatest scenes we seem to see." LiTM (1970 ed.); NeAP
(In Goya's Greatest Scenes.) NMP
"Poet's eye obscenely seeing, The." LiTM (1970 ed.)
"Wounded wilderness of Morris Graves, The." NeAP
Confederates in this white field. Meeting. Charles Eglington. BoSA
Conference, The, *sel.* Charles Churchill. OBEC
Conscience.
Conference-meeting through at last, The. The Doorstep. Edmund Clarence Stedman. HBV; LHV
Conferences, adjournments, ultimatums. Autumn Journal, VII. Louis MacNeice. WaP
Confess Jehovah, *with music.* *Unknown.* TrAS
Confess'd from yonder slow-extinguish'd clouds. Summer Evening and Night. James Thomson. *Fr.* The Seasons: Summer. OBEC
Confessed. Josephine Miles. FiMAP
Confessio Amantis, *sels.* John Gower.
"Adieu, for now I've made an end," Conclusion, *fr.* VIII, *cond., mod. by* Muriel Bowden. MeEV
"Flees he tok and goth to Bote, The," *fr.* V. AtBAP
Florent and the Loathly Hag, *fr.* I, *mod. by* Muriel Bowden. MeEV
House of Sleep, The, *fr.* IV. AtBAP
Jason and Medea, *fr.* V. ACP
Parting of Venus and Old Age, The, *fr.* VIII. PoEL-1
Poet Meets Venus and Her Priest, The, *fr.* I, *cond., mod. by* Muriel Bowden. MeEV
Prolog: "Books composed before our day, The," *cond., mod. by* Muriel Bowden. MeEV
Confession. Elsa Barker. *Fr.* The Spirit and the Bride. HBMV
Confession. Pearl Cleage. WSL
Confession, A. Henry W. Frost. SoP
Confession. George Herbert. AnAnS-1; MaMe; MeP; ReEN
Confession, The. "Thomas Ingoldsby." BOHV; FiBHP
Confession. Kenneth Mackenzie. BoAV
Confession, A. Robert Mezey. NaP
Confession. Charles d'Orléans, *tr. fr. French.* *See* My Ghostly Father.
Confession. Ralph Pomeroy. CoPo
Confession. D. S. Savage. NeBP
Confession, A. Paul Verlaine, *tr. fr. French by* Arthur Symons. CAW; WGRP
Confession, The. Wen Yi-tuo, *tr. fr. Chinese by* Ho Yung. ChTr; LiTW
Confession in Holy Week. Christopher Morley. HBMV
Confession of a Stolen Kiss. Charles d'Orléans. *See* My Ghostly Father.
Confession of Faith. Dryden. *See* Church's Testimony, The.
Confession of Faith. Elinor Wylie. AnAmPo; AnFE; APA; CoAnAm; MAP; MoAmPo
Confession of Golias, The. "The Archpoet of Cologne," *tr. fr. Latin by* George F. Whicher. LiTW, *abr.*
Confession of the Deadly Sins, The. William Langland, *tr. fr. Middle English.* *Fr.* The Vision of Piers Plowman. MeEV
(Confessions of the Seven Deadly Sins, The, *shorter sel., tr. by* W. A. Neilson *and* K. G. T. Webster.) EnLi-1 (1949 ed.)
("King and his knights went to church, The.") BEL
Confession Overheard in a Subway. Kenneth Fearing. LiTA; LiTM (rev. ed.); WaP
Confession Stone, The. Owen Dodson. TTY
"Bring me those needles, Martha," *sel.* Kal
Confessional, The. Robert Browning. OtMeF; PoVP; ViBoPo
Confessional, The. Helen Parry Eden. JKCP
Confessional, The. *Unknown, tr. fr. Latin by* Louis Untermeyer. UnTE
Confessions ("Face to face in my chamber"). Elizabeth Barrett Browning. OBVV
Confessions ("What is he buzzing in my ears?"). Robert Browning. ELP; EPN; GTBS-D; GTBS-P; MBW-2; PoVP; ViBoPo; ViPo
Confessions of the Seven Deadly Sins, The. William Langland. *See* Confession of the Deadly Sins, The.
Confessor, The. G. G. Belli, *tr. fr. Italian by* Harold Norse. ErPo
Confide in a Friend. *Unknown.* PoToHe (new ed.)
Confide ye aye in Providence. Its Ain Drap o' Dew. James Ballantine. HBV
Confidence. Avis B. Christiansen. SoP
Confidence. Marsden Hartley. AnFE; CoAnAm
Confidence. Frances Ridley Havergal. *See* Thy Presence.
Confidence, The. Elizabeth Jennings. BoPe
Confidence. *Unknown.* BLRP
Confidential. Winfield Townley Scott. ELU
Confidential Data on the Loyalty Investigation of Herbert Ashenfoot. James Schevill. FiMAP
Configurations of time and singing. Beast in View. Muriel Rukeyser. FiMAP
Confined Love. John Donne. AnEnPo; MaMe; TuPP
Confirmation, The. Edwin Muir. OxBS; POTE; WePo
Confirmation, The. Karl Shapiro. ErPo

Confiteor. *Unknown.* CoBE
Conflict. Caroline Clive. OBVV
Conflict, The. C. Day Lewis. AnEnPo; EnLit; FaBoMo; LiTB; LiTM; MoAB; MoBrPo
Conflict. Lincoln Fitzell. AnAmPo
Conflict. F. R. Scott. CaP; PeCV
Conflict and Victory. Henry W. Frost. SoP
Conflict of Convictions, The. Herman Melville. AP; MAmP; MWA-1
Conformers, The. Thomas Hardy. EnLi-2 (1949 ed.); ViBoPo
Confuse me not with impious things. A Caterpillar's Apology for Eating a Favorite Gladiolus. Charles Dalmon. TSW
Confused Dawn, The. William Douw Lighthall. VA
Confusion. Christopher Hervey. Par
Congal, *sels.* Sir Samuel Ferguson. IrPN
"Land Is Ours, The."
Simile.
Conger Eel, The. Patrick MacGill. OnYI
Congo, The. Vachel Lindsay. AmP; AmPP; CMoP; CoBA; FaFP; FaPL; GTBS-W; HoPM; LiTA; LiTG; MAP; MCCG; MoAB; MoAmPo; NeMA; NP; OxBA; PFY; PoMa; PoNe; PoRA; ShBV-3; TreF (I *and* III); WHA
In the Congo, *sel.* WePo
Congratulations ("Fortunate bridegroom"). Sappho, *tr. fr. Greek by* Virginia Tufte. HW
Congratulations ("You lucky man, you"). Sappho, *tr. fr. Greek by* Virginia Tufte. HW
Congratulatory Poem to the Honoured Edmund Morris, Esq., on His Happy Marriage, A, *abr.* Elkanah Settle. HW
Congress, 1878. Victor Alexis de la Montagne, *tr. fr. Flemish by* Jethro Bithell. WoL
Conjecture, A. Charles Francis Richardson. AA
Conjectured to Be upon the Death of Sir Walter Raleigh. Henry King. *See* Elegy, An: "I will not weep, for 'twere as great a sin."
Conjergal Rights. T. E. Brown. *Fr.* In the Coach. PeVV
Conjugal Conjugations. A. W. Bellaw. BOHV
Conjugal Conundrum, A. *Unknown.* BOHV
Conjuh Man, De. James Edwin Campbell. BANP
Conjunction of Jupiter and Venus, The, *sel.* Bryant.
I Would Not Always Reason. OQP
Conjuration, to Electra, A. Robert Herrick. AtBAP; PoEL-3; SiSw
Conjured. John Gill. ThO
Conjuror, The. E. V. Lucas. BiCB; BoChLi; PoMS
Connacht Caoine, A. *Unknown, tr. fr. Irish.* AnIV
Connais-tu le Pays? Richard Shelton. NYBP
Connaught Rangers, The. Winifred M. Letts. HBMV
Connecticut Elm, The. Emma Swan. PoPl
Connecticut Peddler, The, *with music. Unknown.* ABF
Connecticut River, The. Reuel Denney. TwAmPo
Connecticut Road Song. Anna Hempstead Branch. HT
Connoisseur of Chaos. Wallace Stevens. CABA; LiTM (rev. ed.); MoPo; Po; PoeP
Connoisseur of pearl, A. African China. Melvin B. Tolson. Kal
Connolly. Liam MacGowan. OnYI
Connubii Flores; or, The Well-Wishes at Weddings. Robert Herrick. HW
Conon in Alexandria. Lawrence Durrell. MoPo
Conon in Exile. Lawrence Durrell. ToPo
Conor the king. The King of Ulster. *Unknown.* KiLC
"Conquer the gloomy night of thy sorrow." Defiance. Solomon ibn Gabirol. TrJP
Conquered. Zoë Akins. HBMV
Conquered Banner, The. Abram Joseph Ryan. AA; DD, *abr.*; FaPL; HBV; JKCP; PaA; PAH; PEDC; TreF
Conquered King, The, *sel.* George Wither.
"Kings who without control the sceptre sway'd," 4 *ll.* PoFr
Conquered the flower-maidens, and the wide embrace. Parsifal. Paul Verlaine. *Fr.* Amour. SyP
Conquering Love of Jesus, The. Charles Wesley. BePJ
Conqueror, The. Ruth M. Williams. BePJ
Conqueror Renowned, The. Bernard of Clairvaux, *tr. fr. Latin.* BePJ
Conqueror Worm, The. Poe. *Fr.* Ligeia, *pr. tale.* AA; AmePo; AmP; AnAmPo; AnFE; AP; APA; AWP; CoAnAm; CoBA; HBV; InPo; LiTA; MAmP; MWA-1; TDP
Conquerors, The. Paul Laurence Dunbar. AmePo
Conquerors, The. Harry Kemp. AnAmPo; ChIP; HBV; MaRV
Conqueror's Grave, The. Bryant. AA
Conquest. Leslie Savage Clark. ChIP
Conquest. Elizabeth J. Coatsworth. AmFN
Conquest. Philippe Desportes. *See* Those Eyes Which Set My Fancy on Afire.
Conquest, The. Oliver St. John Gogarty. OBMV
Conquest. Georgia Douglas Johnson. AmNP
Conquest, A. Walter Herries Pollock. OBVV; VA
Conquest of Granada, The, *sels.* Dryden.
Epilogue: "They who have best succeeded on the stage," *fr.* Pt. II. CEP; EiCL; EiPP; FiP; MBW-1; SeCV-2; SeEP
How Unhappy a Lover Am I, *fr.* Pt. II, Act IV, sc. iii. SeCL
Love ("Love is that madness"), *fr.* Pt. II, Act III, sc. iii. FiP
Song of the Zambra Dance, *fr.* Pt. I, Act III, sc. i. AtBAP; ErPo; OAEP; PoEL-3
(Beneath a Myrtle Shade.) UnTE
(Zambra Dance, The.) CEP; MBW-1; SeCV-2
Wherever I Am, *fr.* Pt. I, Act IV, sc, ii. DiPo; MaPo
(Phyllis.) SeCL
(Song: "Wherever I am, and whatever I doe.") YAT
Conquest of Love, The. Racine, *tr. fr. French by* Lacy Lockert. *Fr.* Phedre. LiTW
Conquests of Tamburlaine, The. Christopher Marlowe. *See* Tamburlaine the Great.
Conquistador. Elizabeth J. Coatsworth. GoTP
(Announcement.) MAP
Conquistador. A. D. Hope. MoAuPo
Conquistador. Georgia Lee McElhaney. CoPo
Conquistador, *sels.* Archibald MacLeish.
Ah How the Throat of a Girl, *fr.* Bk. 10. AtBAP
"And we marched against them there in the next spring." ThLM
Agrument, The. AtBAP
Bernál Díaz's Preface to His Book. AmPP (3d ed.)
Bernal Diaz' Preface: "We saw that city on the inland sea," *sel.* AtBAP
Dawn on the Wall-Head There, *fr.* Bk. 13. AtBAP
Conrad in Twilight. John Crowe Ransom. OxBA
Conscience. Byron. MaRV
Conscience. Charles Churchill. *Fr.* The Conference. OBSC
Conscience. George Herbert. AnAnS-1; EP; MaMe; MeP
Conscience. Shakespeare. *See* Sleep.
Conscience. Sir Edward Sherburne. ACP
Conscience. Charles William Stubbs. *See* Conscience and Future Judgment.
Conscience. Henry David Thoreau. *Fr.* A Week on the Concord and Merrimack Rivers. AnNE; BWP; HBV
Conscience and Future Judgment. Charles William Stubbs. MaRV
(Conscience.) BLPA
Conscience and Remorse. Paul Laurence Dunbar. MaRV
Conscience-Curst, The. "F. Anstey." CenHV
Conscience is instinct bred in the house. Conscience. Henry David Thoreau. *Fr.* A Week on the Concord and Merrimack Rivers. AnNE; BWP; HBV
Conscience is you and God. For the Existentialists. Winthrop Palmer. NYTB
Conscience-Keeper, The. William Young. *Fr.* Wishmakers' Town. AA
Conscience's Song. Robert Wilson. *See* New Brooms.
Conscientious Deacon, The. Vachel Lindsay. MemP
Conscientious Objector, The. Karl Shapiro. AmPP (4th ed.); OxBA
Conscious. Wilfred Owen. MMA
Conscript, The. W. W. Gibson. MaRV
Conscripts of the Dream, *sel.* Edwin Markham.
"Give thanks, O heart, for the high souls." PGD
Consecration. "Marianne Farningham." FaChP; MaRV
Consecration. Ann Hoppe. BePJ
Consecration. Patrick F. Kirby. GoBC
Consecration. Loma Ried Lauden. SoP
Consecration, A. John Masefield. BEL; EnLit; HBMV; InP; MCCG; MoAB; MoBrPo; NeMA; OtMeF; PoFr; WHA
Consecration. Murdoch O'Daly, *tr. fr. Irish by* Eleanor Hull. JKCP (1926 ed.)
Consecration. Benjamin Schmolck. *See* My Jesus, as Thou Wilt.
Consecration. Edgar Tramp. SoP
Consecration. *Unknown.* TRV
Consecration of the Common Way, The. Edwin Markham. StJW

Consecration of the House. W. S. Fairbridge. NeLNL; PoAu-2
Conservative, A. Charlotte Perkins Gilman. AA; AmePo; HBV
Conservative Shepherd to His Love, The, *parody.* Jack D'Arcy. InMe
"Conservatrix of Milesien." Ezra Pound. *Fr.* Hugh Selwyn Mauberley. CMoP
Consider. Giovanni Pico della Mirandola, *tr. fr. Italian by* Sir Thomas More. CAW
Consider. Christina Rossetti. GN; SoP; TRV
Consider a new habit—classical. Arras. P. K. Page. MoCV; OBCV
Consider for a moment how the body of a dancer. Female Dancer. James Camp. Sonn
Consider, if you can, the heads. On Viewing a Florist's Whimsy at Fifty-ninth and Madison. Margaret Fishback. WhC
Consider me a memory, a dream that passed away. Recessional. Georgia Douglas Johnson. CDC; PoNe
Consider, O my soul, what morn is this! A Meditation for Christmas. Selwyn Image. OBEV (new ed.)
Consider, please, the jacket blurb. The Blurb. Richard Armour. SiTL
Consider, reader, what fatigues I've known. John Gay. *Fr.* Trivia; or, The Art of Walking the Streets of London, III. EnLi-1 (1949 ed.)
Consider the auk. A Caution to Everybody. Ogden Nash. NePA
Consider the Lilies. William Channing Gannett. MaRV; WGRP
Consider the lilies of the field, whose bloom is brief. Consider. Christina Rossetti. GN; SoP; TRV
Consider the lowering Lynx. Limerick. Langford Reed. CenHV
Consider the mysterious salt. In Time like Air. May Sarton. MoLP; NYBP
Consider the ravens; for they neither sow nor reap. To His Disciples. St. Luke, Bible, *N.T.* CAW
Consider the sages who pulverize boulders. P Is for Paleontology. Milton Bracker. FiBHP; InMe; WhC
Consider the sea's listless chime. The Sea Limits [*or* The Chime of the Sea]. Dante Gabriel Rossetti. AnEnPo; BoC; EPN; EtS; NBM; PoVP; TOP; VA
Consider them, my soul, how horrible! The Blind. Baudelaire. SyP
Consider These, for We Have Comdemned [Them]. C. Day Lewis. LiTB; LiTM; NAMP; SeCePo
Consider These Greek Widows of America. Dan Georgakas. ThO
Consider This and in Our Time. W. H. Auden. LiTB; LiTG
Consider this man in the field beneath. Affinity. R. S. Thomas. HaMV; POTi
Consider [*or* do but consider] this small dust. The Hour-Glass [*or* Houre-Glasse]. Ben Jonson. CBEP; EnLoPo; EnRePo; GTBS-W; LiTB; LiTG; PIA; SeCP; SiTL
Consider Well. Sir Thomas More. ACP; CAW; GoBC; SoP
Consider when thou art movèd to be wroth. Consider. Giovanni Pico della Mirandola. CAW
Considerable Speck, A. Robert Frost. AmP; AmPP; MoAB; MoAmPo; WhC
Considerations of Murder. *Unknown, tr. fr. Sanskrit by* Swami Prabhavananda *and* Christopher Isherwood. *Fr.* Bhagavad-Gita. LiTW
(Debate between Arjuna and Sri Krishna.) WaaP
Considerations of Norfolk Island, *sel.* Kendrick Smithyman.
"High in the afternoon the dove." AnNZ
Considerations on Certain Music of J. S. Bach, *sel.* J. C. Beaglehole.
"Meditating in silence after the last note." AnNZ
Consideratus Considerandus. John Saffin. SCAP
Considering the Snail. Thom Gunn. FIW; LiTM (1970 ed.); NePoEA-2; TDP; TwCP; WIRo
Consigned for lading, marked for repairs. Chant of the Box Cars. Harry Kemp. PoMa
Consignee of silent storms and unseen lightning. Lynx. R. A. D. Ford. CaP
Consolation. Matthew Arnold. ViPo
Consolation. Elizabeth Barrett Browning. OBEV (1st ed.); PoVP
Consolation. George Darley. ERoP-2
Consolation. Rose Fyleman. GaP
Consolation. Longfellow. SoP
Consolation, A. Shakespeare. *See* Sonnets, XXIX.
Consolation. Earl of Surrey. OBSC
Consolation. *Unknown, See* There Is Never A Day So Dreary. *at. to* Lilla M. Alexander.
Consolation in July. Rayner Heppenstall. NeBP
Consolation in War. Lewis Mumford. NYBP
Consolation of Philosophy, *sel.* Boethius, *tr. fr. Latin by* Elizabeth I, Queen of England.
Happy Too Much. CTC
Consolatory! St. John Emile Clavering Hankin. CenHV
Consolatory Poem Dedicated unto Mr. Cotton Mather, A. Nicholas Noyes. SCAP
Conspiracy in Iowa. William Hathaway. QAH
Conspiracy of Charles, Duke of Byron, The, *sels.* George Chapman.
"As when the moon hath comforted the night," *fr.* III, i. ViBoPo
"Give me a spirit that on this life's rough sea," *fr.* III, i. MyFE; ViBoPo
(Master Spirit, The.) EtS
"Ile weare those golden spurres upon my heeles," *fr.*. III, i. PoFr
"To fear a violent good, abuseth goodness," *fr.* I, i. MyFE
Conspirators, The. Kenneth Burke. TwAmPo
Conspirators, The. Frederic Prokosch. LiTM; NAMP; NePA; WaP
Constancie. George Herbert. MaMe
Constancies. *Unknown, tr. fr. German by* Louis Untermeyer. UnTE
Constancy. Samuel Daniel. *Fr.* Hymen's Triumph. OBSC
Constancy, The. Jason Miller. ThO
Constancy. John Boyle O'Reilly. BOHV; OnYI
Constancy. Coventry Patmore. The Angel in the House, II, xi, 4. OBVV
Constancy. Earl of Rochester. CaVP; GTSL; HBV; OBEV; OBS; SeCL; TOP
(I Cannot Change as Others Do.) EnLi-1 (1949 ed.)
(Song; "I cannot change...") SeEP
Constancy. Sir Charles Sedley. PeRV
Constancy. Sir John Suckling. *See* Constant Lover, The.
Constancy. *At. to* Joshua Sylvester. *See* Were I as Base as Is the Lowly Plain.
Constancy. Minor Watson. HBV
Constancy. Sir Thomas Wyatt. *See* Perdye I Saide Yt Not.
Constancy of a Lover, The. George Gascoigne. EnRePo; QFR
Constancy to an Ideal Object. Samuel Taylor Coleridge. ERoP-1
Constancye. Sidney Godolphin. MePo
Constant. Emily Dickinson. *See* Alter? When the hills do.
Constant. Frederic Thompson. JKCP (1926 ed.)
Constant Affection. *Unknown.* SeCL
Constant Bridegrooms, The. Kenneth Patchen. CrMA; LiTM (1970 ed.); NaP
Constant Cannibal Maiden, The. Wallace Irwin. BOHV
Constant keeping-past of shaken trees, A. London to Folkestone. Dante Gabriel Rossetti. *Fr.* A Trip to Paris and Belgium. PeVV
Constant Lover, The. Louis Simpson. NYBP
Constant Lover, The ("Out upon it"). Sir John Suckling. AWP; CLwM; EnLi-1; FaBV; FaFP; GTBS-W; HBV; InPo; JAWP; LiTB; LiTG; LiTL; MCCG; MeWo; OBEV; OuHeWo; PoMa; ReEn; SeCePo; TOP; TreFS; TrGrPo; WBP
(Constancy.) AnEnPo; BEL; CoBE; LoBV
(Out upon It [I Have Loved].) AnFE; BOHV; BoLP; CABA; EG; EnL; EnLit; ErPo; ForPo; ILP; LO; NoP; OBS; PoE; PoEL-3; PoIE; PoRA; PoSa; SeCeV; SeEP; SiTL
(Poem, A: "Out upon it! I have loved.") ViBoPo
(Poem with the Answer, A.) CavP; SCEP-2; YAT
(Sir J.S.) AnAnS-2; SeCV-1
(Song: "Out upon it, I have loved.") EP; FosPo; MeLP; MePo; SeCL; SeCP; WHA
Constant Lover, The ("Why so pale and wan"). Sir John Suckling. *See* Why So Pale and Wan?
Constant Lover, The. Aurelian Townsend. *See* Though Regions Far Divided.
Constant North, The. J. F. Hendry. NeBP; OxBS
Constant One, The. George Dillon. AmLP
Constant Penelope sends to thee, careless Ulysses! *Unknown.* EnLoPo; SiCE

Constant running up the path. Constant. Frederic Thompson. JKCP (1926 ed.)
Constant Swain and Virtuous Maid, The. *Unknown.* HBV
Constantine's Vision of the Cross. Cynewulf, *tr. fr. Anglo-Saxon by* Charles W. Kennedy. *Fr.* Elene. AnOE
Constantly near you, I never in my entire. The Horse Show. William Carlos Williams. CMoP
Constantly risking absurdity. Lawrence Ferlinghetti. *Fr.* A Coney Island of the Mind. LiTM (1970 ed.); NeAP; ToPo
Constellation. Merrill Moore. TrGrPo (1942 ed.)
Constellation, The. Henry Vaughan. SCEP-1; SeCV-1
Constellation and the *Insurgente,* The. *Unknown.* PAH
Constitution and *Guerrière,* The, *with music. Unknown.* ABF, *abr.*; SoAmSa
(*Constitution* and the *Guerrière,* The.) AmSS, *with music;* PAH; ViBoFo
Constitution for a League of Nations. Arthur Guiterman. InMe
Constitution of Athens, The. Solon, *tr. fr. Greek by* John Herman Merivale. PoFr
Constitution's Last Fight, The. James Jeffrey Roche. MC; PAH
Constricted by my tortured thought. Prayer before Study. Theodore Roethke. TrPWD
Construction. Patricia Hubbell. OCS
Consuelo at the Country Club. Selden Rodman. NAMP
Consummate Happiness. Wordsworth. *Fr.* The Prelude. OBNC
Consummation. Elsa Barker. *Fr.* The Spirit and the Bride. HBMV
Consummation. Witter Bynner. *Fr.* To Celia. NP
Consummation. Thomas Traherne. SCEP-1; SeCV-2
Consummation. *Unknown, tr. fr. Greek by* Louis Untermeyer. UnTE
Consummation. James Terry White. OQP
Contact. Dorothy Livesay. CaP
Contagion of Courage. Matthew Arnold. *Fr.* Rugby Chapel. MaRV
Contagious Hospital, The. William Carlos Williams. *See* Spring and All.
Contains:/ Best Loved Words. The Bible. H. H. Halley. SoP.
Contemplate all this work of Time. In Memoriam A. H. H., CXVIII. Tennyson. BEL; CoBE; EnL; EnLi-2; EPN; MaPo; OAEP; PoFS; SeCeV; TOP; UnPo; ViPo; VP
Contemplate Pliny's crocodile. William Rose Benét. *Fr.* The Bestiary. OA
Contemplation. John Alden Carpenter. RIS
Contemplation. Francis Thompson. BrPo; LoBV
Sels.
"Nature one hour appears a thing unsexed." OBNC
"River has not any care, The." FaBoEn
Contemplation of Our State in Our Deathbed. John Donne. *Fr.* Of the Progresse of the Soule. OBS
Contemplation on Night, A. John Gay. CEP
Contemplation upon Flowers, A. Henry King. ATP (1935 ed.); BoNaP; BWP; CBEP; ELP; HBV; LoBV; MeLP; MePo; NoP; OBEV; OBS; PG; SeCL; SeCP; SeEP; StP; TrGrPo
("Brave flowers, that I could gallant it like you.") EG
Contemplations. Anne Bradstreet. AmPP; AnFE; AnNE; AP; APA; CoAnAm; MAmP; PoEL-3, *abr.*; SCAP
Sels.
Stanzas from "Contemplations" ("Some time now past in the autumnal tide"). Po
When I behold the heavens as in their prime." AmLP; MaRV
Contemplative, The. Sister Mary Thérèse. MoRP
Contemplative Quarry, The. Anna Wickham. HBMV; NP
Contemplative Sentry, The. W. S. Gilbert. *Fr.* Iolanthe. ALV; EnLi-2; FiBHP; PoVP
Contemporaries. Richard Hovey. MAP; MoAmPo (1942 ed.)
Contemporary. Sara Bard Field. ChIP
Contemporary Nursery Rhyme. *Unknown.* PV
Contemporary Poets. Byron. *Fr.* Don Juan, XI. OBRV
Contemporary Song. Theodore Spencer. LiTA
Contempt for Dylan Thomas, A. Wilfred Watson. PeCV
Contempt of Poetry, The. Spenser. *See* October.
Contempt of the World. *Unknown. See* Ubi Sunt Qui ante Fuerunt?
Contemptuous of kings, Empedocles. Empedocles. Thomas S. Jones, Jr. AnAmPo
Contend in a sea which the land partly encloses. The Yachts. William Carlos Williams. AmPP; AP; CMoP; CoBMV; ExPo; FIW; ILP; InPo; LiTA; LiTM; MasP; MoAB; MoAmPo (1950 ed.); MoPo; MoVE; NAMP; NePA; NoP; OxBA; Po; PoeP; PoFS; ReMP; SeCeV; TwAmPo; VaPo; ViBoPo (1958 ed.)
Contending with her streams, renascent stars. Aria for Flute and Oboe. Joseph Langland. NePoEA
Content. Barnabe Barnes. *See* Sonnet: "Ah, sweet Content."
Content. Elizabeth Barrett Browning. MaRV
Content. Thomas Campion. OBSC
Content. Stephen Crane. *See* Youth in Apparel That Glittered, A.
Content. Thomas Dekker. *See* Happy Heart, The.
Content. Earl of Essex. *See* Happy Were He.
Content. Norman Gale. HBV; VA
Content. Robert Greene. *See* Sweet Are the Thoughts That Savor of Content.
Content. Dora Greenwell. PoToHe
Content. George Herbert. MaMe
Content ("My crown is in my heart"). Shakespeare. King Henry VI, Pt. III, *fr.* III, i. MaRV
("My crown is in my heart, not on my head.") PoToHe (new ed.)
Content. Henry Vaughan. SCEP-1
Content. Thomas, Lord Vaux. *See* Of a Contented Mind.
Content. Geffrey Whitney. EIL
("In crystal towers, and turrets richly set.") SiCE
(Song: "In crystal towers [towns, *wr.*] and turrets richly set.") ACP
Content and Rich. Robert Southwell. OBSC; SiCE
Content, content! within a quiet room. Content. Dora Greenwell. PoToHe
Content in you. New Legends. Robert Graves. AtBAP
Content thee, greedie heart. The Size. George Herbert. MaMe
Content Thyself with Thy Estate. *Unknown.* EIL
Content with Thee. Amy Carmichael. SoP
Content within his wigwam warm. Canonicus and Roger Williams. *Unknown.* PAH
Contented at Forty. Sarah N. Cleghorn. HBMV
Contented Bachelor, The. John Kendall. InMe
Contented evening; comfortable joys. Week-End Sonnets, III. Harold Monro. YT
Contented John. Jane Taylor. HBV; HBVY
Contented Lover, The. *Unknown.* SeCL
Contented Man, The. Pope. *See* Ode on Solitude.
Contented Mind, A. Joshua Sylvester. HBV; PoToHe (1941 ed.)
Contented wi' Little and Cantie wi' Mair. Burns. BEL
Contention between Four Maids Concerning That which Addeth Most Perfection to That Sex. Sir John Davies. SiPS
Contention betwixt a Wife, a Widow, and a Maid, A. Sir John Davies. OBSC; SiPS
Contention of Ajax and Ulysses, The, *sel.* James Shirley.
Glories of Our Blood and State, The *fr.* sc. iii. BWP; CavP; CBEP; ChTr; EG; ExPo; ILP; InvP; LiTG; NoP; OBS; PG; PoRA; ReEn; SeEP; TrGrPo; TuPP; ViBoPo; WaaP; YT
(Death the Leveller.) FosPo; GTBS; GTBS-D; GTBS-P; GTBS-W; GTSE; GTSL; LiTB; LoBV; MaRV; MemP; OBEV; OtMeF; PoLi; PPON; SeCeV; ShBV-4
(Death's Final Conquest.) HBV
(Dirge, A.) ACP; AnFE; AWP; BEL; EnLit; InPo; JAWP; PoEL-2; TOP; TreFT; WBP
(Equality.) AnEnPo
(Of Death.) SeCL; WHA
(Our Blood and State.) GoBC
(Song.) CBV; FaBoEn
Contentions. *Unknown. See* It Was a Lording's Daughter.
Contentment. Charles Stuart Calverley. ALV
Contentment. William Cowper.
(Olney Hymns.) CEP
Contentment. Fanny J. Crosby. SoP
Contentment. Sir Edward Dyer. *See* My Mind to Me a Kingdom Is.
Contentment. Oliver Wendell Holmes. *Fr.* The Autocrat of the Breakfast Table, *ch.* 11. AmPP (4th ed.); AnNE; AP; BOHV; HBV; InMe; OnPP; OxBA; TOP; TreF
Contentment. Martial, *tr. fr. Latin by* Owen Felltham. CavP
Contentment. Sadi, *tr. fr. Persian by* L. S. Costello. LiTW

Contentment. Benjamin Schlipf. BLRP
Contentment. Sir Philip Sidney. *See* Get Hence Foule Griefe.
Contentment in Poverty. Issa, *tr. fr. Japanese by* Harold G. Henderson. RePo
Contentment Is a Sleepy Thing. Thomas Traherne. *Fr.* Christian Ethics. OxBoCh
Contentment of Willoughby, The. Frances Alexander. GoYe
Contentment; or, The Happy Workman's Song. John Byrom. CEP; OBEC
Contentment, parent of delight. A Cure for the Spleen. Matthew Green. *Fr.* The Spleen. OBEC
Contents of the Scedule Which Sir John of Bordeaux Gave to His Sons, The. Thomas Lodge. *Fr.* Rosalynde. ReIE; SiCE
Contest. Florence Victor. SD
Contest between Court and Country, A. *Unknown.* SeCL
(Court and Country Love.) UnTe
Continent That Lies within Us, The. Abioseh Nicol. *See* The Meaning of Africa.
Continental Crossing. Dorothy Brown Thompson. AmFN
Continent's End. Robinson Jeffers. AnFE; AWP; CoAnAm; FaBV; ImOP; InPo; JAWP; ReMP; TwAmPo; WBP
Continual Conversation with a Silent Man. Wallace Stevens. LiTM (rev. ed.); NePA
Continual deprivation, now. Deprivation. H. A. Pinkerton. NePoAm
Continuation of Lucan, *br. sel.* Thomas May.
Death ("The wisest men are glad to die"). MaRV
Continuannce/ Of remembraunce. A Lover Left Alone. *Unknown.* MeEL
Continued. Matthew Arnold. *See* To a Republican Friend, 1848, Continued.
Continuing Christ, The. W. Russell Bowie. ChIP; MaRV
Continuing City, The. Laurence Housman. WGRP
Continuity. "Æ." MoBrPo; NBM; NeMA; PoVP
Continuity, The. Paul Blackburn. CAD; NeAP
Continuous, a medley of old pop numbers. The Songs. Martin Bell. MuSP
Contours of Fixation, The. Weldon Kees. NaP
Contract. Frederick Nicklaus. NYTB
Contraption, The. May Swenson. TPM
Contraption,—that's the bizarre, proper slang. The Crystal Palace. John Davidson. PeVV
Contrapuntalist, A—/ composer of chorales. Melchior Vulpius. Marianne Moore. AP
Contrarious Passions in a Lover, The. Petrarch, *See* Description of the Contrarious Passions . . . *tr. by* Sir Thomas Wyatt.
Contrary, The. Alexander Brome. CavP
Contrary Boy, The. Gaston V. Drake. BBGG
Contrary Experience, The. Sir Herbert Read. FaBoMo
Contrary Joe. L. A. G. Strong. PoMa
Contrary Mary. Nancy Byrd Turner. HBMV; HBVY; TSW
Contrary Theses, I. Wallace Stevens. OxBA
Contrast. Aubert Edgar Bruce. ChIP
Contrast, The. Helen Gray Cone. AA
Contrast. Eileen Duggan. ACV; AnNZ
Contrast. Charles Granville Hamilton. ChIP
Contrast. Issa, *tr. fr. Japanese by* Max Bickerton. PoFr
Contrast, The. C. Morris. BOHV
Contrast Rooster's white feathers. Guardian. Alfred Starr Hamilton. QAH
Contrasts. Henry Meade Bland. SoP
Contravention. René Char, *tr. fr. French by* David Lunde. CoFP
Contretemps, The. Thomas Hardy. CMoP; LiTM (rev. ed.)
Contribution, The. David Shapiro. ANYP
Contrite Heart, The. William Cowper. EiCP; PoEL-3; TrPWD
(Lord Will Happiness Divine, The.) OxBoCh
"Thy Saints are comforted, I know," *sel.* MyFE
Contrition across the Waves. Caroline Giltinan. WHL
Contrition twines me like a snake. Fulani Cattle. John Pepper Clark. PBA
Contrivances, The, *sel.* Henry Carey. Maiden's Ideal of a Husband, A. HBV
(Maid's Husband, The.) WaPE
Conundrum of the Workshops, The. Kipling. HBV; MoBrPo; PoVP; VA
Convalescence, I-VIII. David McCord. WhC
Conveniently near to where. The Gastronomic Guile of Simple Simon. Guy Wetmore Carryl. GoTP; YT
Convent, The. Jeanne D'Orge. AnAmPo
Convent Cemetery, Mount Carmel. Sister Mary St. Virginia. GoBC
Convent Echoes. Helen Louise Moriarty. JKCP
Convent of Pleasure, The, *sel.* Margaret Cavendish, Duchess of Newcastle.
Sea-Goddess, The. SeCL
(My Cabinets Are Oyster Shells.) ELP
(Song by Lady Happy, as a Sea-Goodess.) SiSw
Convent Threshold, The. Christina Rossetti. MasP; PoEL-5; PoVP
Sels.
"For what is knowledge duly weighed?" LO
"I tell you what I dreamed last night." PeVV
Conventicle. Gerrit Lansing. CoPo
Convention. Alfred Kreymborg. MAPA
Convention. Agnes Lee. HBMV; PoMa
Convention Song. *Unknown.* PAH
Conventionality. Eloise Hackett. MaRV
Convergence of the Twain, The; Lines on the Loss of the *Titanic.* Thomas Hardy. BrPo; BWP; CBV; CoBMV; EnL; FaBoTw; ILP; InPo; LiTB; LiTM (1970 ed.); MaPo; MoAB; MoBrPo; MoPo; MoVE; NoP; OAEP (2d ed.); PAn; PeVV; PoAn; PoeP; SeCeV; ShBV-3; ViPP; VP
Conversation. John Berryman. LiTA; LiTM; NePA; WaP
Conversation. William Cowper. BCEP, *much abr.*
Walk to Emmaus, The, *sel.* SoP; StJW
Conversation. Berenice C. Dewey. InMe
Conversation. Rose Fyleman. BoTP
Conversation. Louis MacNeice. FaBoMo
Conversation. Hannah More. *Fr.* Bas Bleu. OBEC
Conversation, The. Alex Raybin. ThO
Conversation. Anne Robinson. SUS
Conversation. Sir Walter Scott. OTD
Conversation, A. Shelley. *Fr.* Julian and Maddalo. ERoP-2
Conversation. William F. Walsh. JKCP (1955 ed.)
Conversation between Mr. and Mrs. Santa Claus. Rowena Bennett. ChBR; SiSoSe; TiPo (1959 ed.)
Conversation Galante. T. S. Eliot. HBMV; MAP; MoAmPo (1942 ed.)
Conversation in Avila. Phyllis McGinley. EaLo; PoPo
Conversation in Black and White. May Sarton. GoYe
Conversation in Clichés. James Edward Tobin. JKCP (1955 ed.)
Conversation in the Drawing Room, The. Weldon Kees. TwAmPo
Conversation is but carving. Conversation. Sir Walter Scott. OTD
Conversation of Prayer, The. Dylan Thomas. GTBS-P; NoP
Conversation on V. Owen Dodson. Kal
Conversation Piece. Arthur Freeman. ErPo
Conversation Piece. Philip Hobsbaum. NYTB
Conversation with a Friend. George Abbe. NYTB
Conversation with an April Fool. Rowena Bennett. SiSoSe
Conversation with Rain. Louise D. Gunn. GoYe
Conversation with Three Women of New England. Wallace Stevens. NePA
Conversational. *Unknown.* ALV; BoLP; FiBHP
Conversational Neighbor, A. Richard Kirk. PoMa
Conversational Reformer, The. Harry Graham. InMe; YaD
Conversations are simple, The: about food. Under the Window: Ouro Preto. Elizabeth Bishop. NYBP
Conversations in Courtship, *sel.* *Unknown,* *tr. fr. Egyptian into Italian by* Boris de Rachewiltz, *tr. into English by* Ezra Pound.
"Darling, you only, there is no duplicate." CTC
Conversion. Frances Angermayer. PoLF; TreFS
(Last Thoughts of a Fighting Man.) PGD
Conversion ("Be vengeance wholly left to powers divine"). Dryden. *Fr.* The Hind and the Panther, III. ACP; CAW
(World Well Lost, The.) PoLi
(Worldly Vanity.) FiP
Conversion ("But, gracious God, how well dost Thou provide"). Dryden. *See* Church's Testimony, The.
Conversion. T. E. Hulme. FaBoMo; LoBV; MoBrPo (1942 ed.); ViBoPo
Conversion. Andrew Young. *Fr.* Nicodemus. MaRV
Conversion of the Magdalene, The, *sel.* Pedro Malon de Chaide, *tr. fr. Spanish by* Thomas Walsh.
"Encircling Thee Thy holy brides." CAW

Convert, The. G. K. Chesterton. GoBC; InP; JKCP (1926 ed.)
Converted Cannibals, The. G. E. Farrow. BOHV
Convict, The. Anthony Frisch. CaP
Convict, The. *Unknown.* CoSo
Convict of Clonmel [*or* Clonmala], The. *Unknown, tr. fr. Modern Irish by* Jeremiah Joseph Callanan. AnIL; AnIV; IrPN; NBM; OxBI; OnYI; SD
Conviction, The. J. M. Synge. SyP
Convict's Lament on the Death of Captain Logan, A. *Unknown.* PoAu-1
Convicts working on the frontier forts, The. On the Danube. Robert Conquest. NMP
Convinced by Sorrow. Elizabeth Barrett Browning. *Fr.* The Cry of the Human. BLRP; OQP; WBLP
("'There is no God,' the foolish saith.") MaRV; PoVP
Convoy. Charles Causley. POTi
Convoy. William Jay Smith. WaP
Convulsions came; and, where the field. The Apparition. Herman Melville. MAmP; MWA-1; NoP
Coo-Coo, *with music. Unknown.* AS
Coo, coo, coo! The Dove and the Wren [*or* Country Rhyme]. *Unknown.* RIS; ThGo
Coogan's Wood. Francis Stuart. NeIP
Coogee. Henry Clarence Kendall. VA
Cook County. Archibald MacLeish. CrMA
(Weather.) MAP; MoAmPo
Cook was a captain of the Admiralty. Five Visions of Captain Cook. Kenneth Slessor. BoAV
Cook we had upon the deck, The. The Erie Canal Ballad. *Unknown.* ABF
Cool, and palm-shaded from the torrid heat. The Pipe-Player. Sir Edmund Gosse. VA
Cool as a cucumber. Lily McQueen. Sara Jackson. BoLP
Cool, Cool Country, The. John Shaw Neilson. PoAu-1
Cool Gold Wines of Paradise, The. Robert Farren. AnIV; SeCePo
Cool it is, and still. Crescent Moon. Basho. OnPM
Cool shades, air-fanning groves. M. Antonio Flaminio: To His Farm. John Ashmore. CLwM
Cool sky opens like a hand, The. William Blake Sees God. Roy McFadden. NeIP
Cool-slick-fly. Impressions. Kirk Hall. BF
Cool small evening shrunk to a dog bark and the clank of a bucket, A. Encounter. Ted Hughes. ToPo
Cool Tombs. Carl Sandburg. AmP; AmPP; AnFE; AP; AtBAP; BoLiVe; CMoP; CoAnAm; CoBA; HBMV; MAP; MoAB; MoAmPo; MoVE; NeMA; PAL; PoLF; PoPo; TrGrPo; TwAmPo; ViBoPo; WHA; WOW
Cool Web, The. Robert Graves. AWP; ChMP; GTBS-D; GTBS-P; NoP
Cool with the touch of autumn, waters break. Lament for My Brother on a Hayrake. James Wright. TwAmPo
Coole Park and Ballylee, 1931. W. B. Yeats. CMoP; GTBS-P; MaPo (1969 ed.); NoP; OBMV; TDP
Coole Park, 1929. W. B. Yeats. MBW-2; OBMV; OxBI; PoeP
Cooleen, The. Douglas Hyde. OBVV
Coolin, The. James Stephens. POTE
Coolness in Summer. Ryusui, *tr. fr. Japanese by* Harold G. Henderson. RePo
Coolun, The. Maurice O'Dugan, *fr. Late Middle Irish by* Sir Samuel Ferguson. AnIV; OnYI; OxBI
Coomb-Firtrees say that life is a moan. Yell'ham-Wood's Story. Thomas Hardy. TOP
Coon Can (Poor Boy), *with music. Unknown.* AS
Coon explains it. Evolution. Rochelle Owens. CoPo
Cooper. James Russell Lowell. *Fr.* A Fable for Critics. AnNE; AP; OxBA
("Here's Cooper, who's written.") CoBA; MWA-1
Cooper O'Dundee, The. *Unknown.* CoMu
Cooper, whose name is with his country's woven. Red Jacket. Fitz-Greene Halleck. AA
Co-operation. J. Mason Knox. BLPA; YaD
Cooper's Hill. Sir John Denham. AnAnS-2; CEP; EiCL; SeCP; SeCV-1; SeEP
Sels.
"My eye, descending from the hill, surveys." ReEn; ViBoPo
(Thames from Cooper's Hill, The.) OBS; SeCePo
Thames, The. FaBoEn
Cop slumps alertly on his motorcycle, The. Corner. Ralph Pomeroy. CAD; CoPo
Copernicus, *sel.* Robert D. Fitzgerald.
"Cock that crowed this dawn up, heard, The." BoAV
Cophetua. "Hugh MacDiarmid." OxBS
Cophetua was a merry King. King Cophetua and the Beggar Maid. Don Marquis. HBMV; InMe
Coplas de Manrique, *sel.* Longfellow.
"To One alone my thoughts arise." ChIP
Coplas on the Death of His Father. Jorge Manrique. *See* Ode on the Death of His Father.
Copper bowl I keep, The. Objet d'Art. Lucien Stryk. NYTB
Copper cobra comes out of his slit, The. The Banded Cobra. C. Louis Leipoldt. PeSA
Copper concave of a sky, A. A Christ-Child Day in Australia. Ethel Turner. BoAu
Copper-green Phillip. Captain Arthur Phillip and the Birds. Lex Banning. PoAu-2
Copper Song, The. Hermia Harris Fraser, *ad. fr. Haida Indian song.* CaP
Copper Song. Ethel Talbot Scheffauer. PoMS
Copperfaces, The ("The copperfaces, the red men, handed us tobacco"). Carl Sandburg. *Fr.* The People, Yes. RePo
Copse, The. Thomas Wade. ERoP-2
Coptic Poem ("A Coptic deputation, going to Ethiopia"). Lawrence Durrell. FaBoMo
Copy of an Intercepted Despatch. Thomas Moore. NBM
Copy of Verses, A. John Wilson. SCAP
Copy of Verses sent by Cleone to Aspasia, A. Walter Savage Landor. *Fr.* Pericles and Aspasia. LoBV
Coquette, The. Aphra Behn. TrGrPo
(Coquet, The.) ViBoPo
Coquette, The. Muriel Earley Sheppard. IHA
Coquette Conquered, A. Paul Laurence Dunbar. MAP; MoAmPo (1942 ed.); NeMA
Cor Cordium. Swinburne. ATP (1935 ed.); EPN; MaVP; PoVP; TOP; ViPo; VP
Cora Punctuated with Strawberries. George Starbuck. NMP
Coracle, The. Lucan, *tr. fr. Latin by* Sir Walter Ralegh. ChTr
Coracle Fishers, The. Robert Bloomfield. *Fr.* The Banks of Wye. OBNC
Coral. Christina Rossetti. *See* O Sailor, Come Ashore.
Coral Grove, The. James Gates Percival. AA; AmLP; AnAmPo; AnNE; EtS; GN; GoTP
Coral Islands. Louis Ginsberg. OQP
Coral Reef, The. Laurence Lieberman. CoAP
Corbitt's Barkentine, *with music. At. to* Tom Reynolds. ShS
Corda Concordia, *sel.* Edmund Clarence Stedman.
Quest. AA
Cordova. Ibn Zaydun, *tr. fr. Arabic by* H. A. R. Gibb. AWP; LiTW
Core, The. John Holmes. MiAP
Coridon and Melampus' Song. George Peele. *See* Song of Coridon and Melampus.
Coridon and Phillis. Robert Greene. *Fr.* Perimedes. OBSC
(Phillis and Corydon.) HBV
Coridon's Song. John Chalkhill. HBV; ViBoPo
Coridon's Song. Thomas Lodge. *See* Blithe and Bonny Country Lass, A.
Coridon's Supplication to Phillis. Nicholas Breton. SiCE
(Supplication.) OBSC
Corinna. Thomas Campion. *See* When to Her Lute Corinna Sings.
Corinna Bathes. George Chapman. *Fr.* Ovid's Banquet of Sense. OBSC
(Natures Naked Jem.) FaBoEn
Corinna, from Athens, to Tanagra. Walter Savage Landor. *Fr.* Pericles and Aspasia. OBEV (new ed.); OBVV
(Corinna to Tanagra.) OBNC; OBRV; ViBoPo, *abr.*
(Corinna to Tanagra from Athens.) TOP
Corinna Goes a-Singing. Frank Sidgwick. WhC
Corinna in Vendome. Pierre de Ronsard, *tr. fr. French by* Robert Mezey. ErPo
Corinna Is Divinely Fair. *Unknown.* SeCL
Corinna, pride of Drury-Lane. A Beautiful Young Nymph Going to Bed. Swift. EiCP; PPON; UnTE
Corinna to Tanagra from Athens. Walter Savage Landor. *See* Corinna, from Athens, to Tanagra.
Corinna with a graceful air. Upon a Sickly Lady. *At to* Charles Burnaby *and to* William Burnaby. *Fr.* The Reformed Wife. SeCL
Corinna's Going a-Maying. Robert Herrick. AnAnS-2; AtBAP; ATP; BEL; BoLiVe; BoNaP; CABA; CBEP; CBV; CLwM;

CoBE; DD, *abr.*; DiPo; EnL; EnLi-1; EnLit; ExPo; FosPo; HBV; MaPo; NoP; OAEP; OBEV; OBS; OuHeWo; PAn; PIA; Po; PoAn; PoEL-3; PoeP; PoFS; PoIE; ReEn; SCEP-2; SeCeV; SeCP; SeCV-1; SeEP; TOP; TreFT, *abr.*; TrGrPo; UnPo (1st ed.); WHA
(Corinna's Maying.) GTSL; PoRL, *sts.* 1-3
(Going a-Maying.) GN; OTPC (1923 ed.)
Corinthian of dogs, how word the grace. To an English Setter. Thomas Walsh. PFY
Corinthians I. *See* First Corinthians.
Coriolan, *sel.* T. S. Eliot.
Triumphal March. BWP; ShBV-4; WaaP
Corliss Engine-Wheel. MacKnight Black. AnAmPo
Cormorants. John Blight. FIW
Corn. Esther Antin. *Fr.* On Our Farm. RIS
Corn. Sidney Lanier. AP; CoBA; LaNeLa; MAmP
Corn. Bernadette Mayer. ANYP
Corn and the Lilies, The. Emily A. Braddock. SoP
Corn Cañon. Patric Stevenson. NeIP
Corn comes flowing down the hills, The. Tamazunchali. Witter Bynner. NYTB
Corn Crake, The. James H. Cousins. OnYI
Corn Dance, The. Fanny Howe. QAH
Corn does not hurry, and the black grape swells. Second Wisdom. Henry Morton Robinson. GoYe
Corn-grinding Song. *Unknown, tr. fr. Laguna Indian by* Natalie Curtis. AWP; JAWP; SUS; WBP
Corn-grinding Song. *Unknown, tr. fr. Zuni Indian by* Natalie Curtis. RePo; SUS
Corn grows up, The. Incantation for Rain. *Unknown.* ExPo
Corn Husker, The. Emily Pauline Johnson. CaP
Corn is a small hard seed. Corn. Bernadette Mayer. ANYP
Corn Must Be Sown. Thomas Carlyle. ThGo
Corn Rigs Are Bonny. Burns. *See* Rigs o' Barley.
Corn-Song, A. Paul Laurence Dunbar. AA
Corn Song, The. John Wesley Holloway. BANP
Corn Song, The. Whittier. *Fr.* The Huskers. GN; OHIP; OTPC
Cornelia, *sel.* Thomas Kyd.
Of Fortune, *abr.* EiL
Cornelia's Song. John Webster. *See* Call for the Robin Redbreast.
Corner, The. Walter de la Mare. BiCB
Corner. Ralph Pomeroy. CAD; CoPo
Corner bank has lost a great window, The. High Wind at the Battery. Ralph Pomeroy. NYBP
Corner Boys. Bryan MacMahon. OnYI
Corner Knot, The. Robert Graves. NYBP
Corner Meeting. Langston Hughes. CAD
Corner of the Field, The. Frances Cornford. BoLP; ELU
Corner Seat. Louis MacNeice. MoVE
Cornerstone, The. Edward A. Church. MaRV
Corner Stone, The. Walter de la Mare. BrPo
Cornet, The. Earl of Surrey. OBSC
(Complaint That His Ladie after She Knew of His Love Kept Her Face Alway Hidden from Him, *sl. diff.*) PoEL-1; PoIE
("I never saw you, madam, lay apart.") SiPS
Cornet Solo. C. Day Lewis. MuSP
Cornfield. Leo Cox. CaP
Cornfield, The. Elizabeth Madox Roberts. GoJo; SUS
Cornfield, The, *sel.* Muriel Rukeyser.
"For those given to voyages: these roads." FiMAP
Cornfield Holler, *with music.* *Unknown.* ABF
Cornfields, *abr.* Mary Howitt. OTPC (1923 ed.)
"When on the breath of autumn breeze," *sel.* PRWS; VA
Cornish Magic. Ann Durell. FaPON
Cornish Miner, The. Walter F. Gries. IHA
Cornwallis led a country dance. The Dance [*or* Cornwallis's Country Dance]. *Unknown.* PAH; TrAS, *with* Yankee Doodle
Cornwallis's Surrender. *Unknown.* PAH
Coromandel Fishers. Sarojini Naidu. BBV; EtS; MCCG; RePo
Corona Inutilis. James Lister Cuthbertson. BoAu
Coronach. Alexander Scott. OxBS
Coronach ("He is gone on the mountain"). Sir Walter Scott. *Fr.* The Lady of the Lake, III. AnFE; BEL; CH; EnLi-2 (1949 ed.); EnLit; EnRP; GTBS; GTBS-D; GTBS-P; GTBS-W; GTSL; HBV; InP; OAEP; OBRV; OHIP; PCD; PoRA; ShBV-1; TOP; TreFS; TrGrPo; ViBoPo; WHA; WiR; YAT
("He is gone on the mountain.") EPN
Coronary Thrombosis. William Price Turner. OxBS
Coronation. Helen Hunt Jackson. AA; BeLS; GN; HBV; PFY; PTK
Coronation. Edward Perronet. HBV; MaRV; TreFS; WGRP
Coronation Day at Melrose. Peter Bladen. PoAu-2
Coronemus Nos Rosis Antequam Marcescant. Thomas Jordan. *See* Careless Gallant, The.
Coronet, The. Andrew Marvell. AnAnS-1; FosPo; LoBV; MaMe; MaPo (1969 ed.); MeLP; MeP; MePo; NCEP; OBS; OxBoCh; PIA; PP; SCEP-2; SeCV-1; StJW
Coronet for His Mistress Philosophy, A, *sels.* George Chapman.
"But dwell in darkness, for your god is blind," II. Sonn
"Love flows not from my liver but her living," III. Sonn
"Muses that Fame's loose feathers beautify," X. RelE; Sonn
"Muses that sing love's sensual empery," I. CoBE; EIL; LoBV; PoE; Sonn; TuPP
(Love and Philosophy.) OBSC; SeCePo
"Corporal Green!" the orderly cried. Roll-Call. Nathaniel Graham Shepherd. AA; BBV (1923 ed.); DD; HBV; OHIP; PaA
Corporal Stare. Robert Graves. BrPo
Corporeal and Mental Vision. Thomas Wade. ERoP-2
Corposant. Peter Redgrove. NePoEA-2
Corpse, clad with carefulness. Of Misery. Thomas Howell. EIL; TuPP
Corpse-Plant, The. Adrienne Rich. CoPo
Corpses in the Wood. Ernst Toller, *tr. fr. German by* E. Ellis Roberts. TrJP
Corpus Christi. Evelyn Underhill. StJW
Corpus Christi Carol. *Unknown.* *See* Falcon, The.
Correct Compassion, A. James Kirkup. ChMP; FaBoTw; FIW; ImOP; SeCePo
Correction, A. Robert Frost. WhC
Correggio's Cupolas at Parma. Aubrey Thomas De Vere. Sonn
Correlated Greatness. Francis Thompson. *See* Heart, The.
Correspondence School Instructor Says Goodbye to His Poetry Students, The. Galway Kinnell. CBV
Correspondences. Baudelaire, *tr. fr. French.* AWP, *tr. by* Allen Tate; LiTW, *tr. by* Allen Tate; SyP, *tr. by* Arthur Symons; ReMP, *tr. by* R. G. Stern
Correspondent. Witter Bynner. AnFE; CoAnAm
Corrib: An Emblem. Donald Davie. PoCh
Corridor, The. Thom Gunn. NePoEA; ToPo
Corroded flat as hills allow. Bedlam Hills. Vivian Smith. PoAu-2
Corruption. Henry Vaughan. AnAnS-1; CAW; FaBoEn; MeP; OBS; OxBoCh; SCEP-1; SeCP; SeCV-1
Corrymeela. "Moira O'Neill." AnIV; AWP; HBV; JAWP; WBP
Corsage Bouquet, A. Charles Henry Luders. HBV
Corsair, The, *sels.* Byron.
Song of the Corsairs, *fr.* I. EtS
Summer, *fr.* III. OBRV
Sunset over the Aegean, *fr.* III. OBNC
Corsons Inlet. A. R. Ammons. CoAP
Corston. Robert Southey. Sonn
Cortège. Jerome G. Rothenberg. OPP
Cortège. Paul Verlaine, *tr. fr. French by* Arthur Symons. AWP; OnPM; WoL
Cortege for Colette. Jean Garrigue. NYBP
Cortège for Rosenbloom. Wallace Stevens. TwAmPo
Corydon and Thyrsis. Vergil, *tr. fr. Latin by* Dryden. Eclogues, VII. AWP
Corydon and Tityrus. *Unknown, tr. fr. Dutch by* Montgomery Carmichael. CAW
Corydon to His Phyllis. Sir Edward Dyer. EIL
("Alas, my heart! my eye hath wrongèd thee.") SiCE
Corydon, Arise, My Corydon! *Unknown.* *See* Phyllida's Love-Call.
Corydon's Complaint. Samuel Pordage. CavP
Corydon's Song. Thomas Lodge. *See* Blithe and Bonny Country Lass, A.
Corythos, *sel.* Walter Savage Landor.
Helen and Corythos. LoBV
Cosmic Age, The. Sun-Ra. BF
Cosmic Egg, The. *Unknown.* BOHV
Cosmic Fabric, The. Yakov Polonsky, *tr. fr. Russian by* Av-

Cosmic (continued)
rahm Yarmolinsky *and* Cecil Cowdery. EaLo
Cosmic Leviathan, that monstrous fish. Cosmogony. Edgell Rickword. FaBoTw
Cosmogony. David Daiches. LiTM
Cosmogony. Edgell Rickword. FaBoTw
Cosmopolitan Woman, A. Sam Walter Foss. BOHV
Cospatrick. *Unknown.* OBB
Cossimbazar. Henry S. Leigh. BOHV; NA
Cost. Richard Watson Gilder. StJW
Cost, The. Flora L. Osgood. STF
Cosy fire is bright and gay, The. The Poets at Tea, 4. Barry Pain. Par
Cot, The. Grover Amen. NYBP
Côte d'Azur. Katherine Hoskins. NYBP
Cottage, The. Jones Very. OxBA
Cottage Hospital, The. John Betjeman. GTBS-P; MoBrPo (1962 ed.); MoVE; UnPo (3d ed.)
Cottage was a thatch'd one, The. Little Jim. Edward Farmer. PaPo
Cottager, The, *sel.* John Clare.
"True as the church clock." OBRV
Cottager and His Landlord, The. Milton, *tr. fr. Latin by* William Cowper. OTPC (1923 ed.)
Cottager to Her Infant, The. Dorothy Wordsworth. CH; HBV; OTPC (1923 ed.); PRWS
Cottager's Hymn, The. Patrick Brontë. MaRV
Cottager's Lullaby, The. Dorothy Wordsworth. *See* Cottager to Her Infant, The.
Cotter's Saturday Night, The. Burns. BEL; BeLS; CEP; EiCL; EiCP; EiPP; EnL; EnLi-2; EnLit; EnRP; FaBoBe; HBV; MCCG; OAEP; OBEC, *abr.*; TOP
Sels.
"Cheerfu' supper done, The," *br. sel.* WGRP
November Evening. UnPo (1st ed.)
Prayer for My Native Land. MaRV
Cotton blouse you wear, your mother said, The. McDonogh Day in New Orleans. Marcus B. Christian. AmNP; PoNe
Cotton Boll, The. Henry Timrod. AA; AmPP; MAmP
Cotton Cat, The. Mary Effie Lee Newsome. GoSl
Cotton Eye Joe ("Where did you come from"), *with music. Unknown.* OuSiCo
Cotton-eyed Joe ("If it had not 'a' been for Cotton-eyed Joe"), *with music. Unknown.* ABF
Cotton Field Song, *with music. Unknown.* ABF
Cotton Mather. Stephen Vincent Benét. ThLM
Cotton-Mill Colic, *with music. Unknown.* OuSiCo
Cotton Song. Jean Toomer. CDC
Cottonmouth Country. Louise Glück. CoAP; YAP
Cottonwood Leaves. Badger Clark. TiPo
Cou'd our first father, at his toilsome plough. Adam Pos'd. Countess of Winchilsea. EiCL
Cough dyed heavy, The. Among the Lions Night Is Still. Sister Mary Norbert Körte. ThO
Coughing in a shady grove. Ipecacuanha. George Canning. ChTr
Could all this be forgotten? Yes, a schism. Keats. *Fr.* Sleep and Poetry. ChER
Could Be ("Could be Hastings Street"). Langston Hughes. OCS
Could but this be brought. Technique. Langdon Elwyn Mitchell. *Fr.* To a Writer of the Day. AA
Could every time-worn heart but see Thee once again. The Nativity. Henry van Dyke. *Fr.* To the Child Jesus. MaRV; TrPWD
Could he have made Priscilla share. Llewellyn and the Tree. E. A. Robinson. BeLS; HBMV
Could he return to us, how would we greet him? Woodrow Wilson. Robert Underwood Johnson. DD
Could I Believe. Ewart Milne. OxBI
Could I but hear. Tanka, VIII. Lewis Alexander. CDC
Could I but retrace. Tanka, I. Lewis Alexander. CDC
Could I but teach a man to believe. Adios. Joaquin Miller. OQP
Could I have said while he was here. In Memoriam A. H. H., LXXXI. Tennyson. EnLi-2; EPN; ViPo; VP
Could I pluck down Aldebaran. The Unloved to His Beloved. William Alexander Percy. HBMV
Could I remount the river of my years. A Fragment. Byron. ERoP-2
Could I take me to some cavern for mine hiding. O for the Wings of a Dove [*or* Longing *or* Chorus]. Euripides. *Fr.* Hippolytus. AWP; BoPe; JAWP; PCD; ShBV-4; WBP
Could It Have Been a Shadow? Monica Shannon. FaPON; GaP; SoPo; StVeCh (1955 ed.); TiPo
Could Juno's self more sovereign presence wear. Venus Victrix. Dante Gabriel Rossetti. The House of Life, XXXIII. MaVP; PoVP; ViPo; VP
Could Love for ever. Stanzas. Byron. HBV; NoP; ViBoPo
Could Man Be Drunk Forever. A. E. Housman. Last Poems, X. EG; EnLi-2 (1949 ed.); EnLit; InPo; LiTM; OBMV; OtMeF; PoE
Could mortal lip divine. Emily Dickinson. DiPo
Could my heart but see Creation as God sees it—from within. Immanence. Edmond G. A. Holmes. MaRV
Could not once blinding me, cruel, suffice? Sampson to His Dalilah. Richard Crashaw. MaMe; TrGrPo
Could our first father, at his toilsome plough. Adam Posed. Countess of Winchilsea. Po
Could she come back who has been dead so long. Separation. Alice Learned Bunner. *Fr.* Vingtaine. AA
Could then the babes from yon unshelter'd cot. Sonnet. Thomas Russell. OBEC
Could these faint numbers glow with equal fire. To the Fair Unknown. William Taylor. WaPE
Could Time, his night reversed, restore the hours. William Cowper. *Fr.* On the Receipt of My Mother's Picture. WHA
Could We. *Unknown.* STF
Could we but draw back the curtains. If Only We Understood. *Unknown.* STF
Could we forget the widow'd hour. In Memoriam A. H. H., XL. Tennyson. EPN; ViPo; VP
Could we only see the goodness. Could We. *Unknown.* STF
Could ye come back to me, Douglas, Douglas. Douglas, Douglas, Tender and True [*or* Too Late]. Dinah Maria Mulock Craik. BLPA; HBV; NeHB; OBVV; TreF; VA
"Could Ye Not Watch One Hour?" Godfrey Fox Bradby. MaRV
Could you bid an acorn. Lover's Reply to Good Advice. Richard Hughes. MoBrPo
Could you care for me, as I care for my cat? Plea for a Cat. Jewell Bothwell Tull. CIV
Could You Do That? Burns. UnTE
Could you indeed come lightly. Song for a Departure. Elizabeth Jennings. NMP
Could you not drink her gaze like wine? The Card-Dealer. Dante Gabriel Rossetti. MaVP; NBM; PoVP; ViPo
Could You Once Regain. Kendrick Smithyman. AnNZ
Could You Spare Some Time for Jesus? Lester Knickman. STF
Could you tell me the way to Somewhere. Somewhere. Walter de la Mare. FaPON
Couldn't Stand the Press. Mart Taylor. SGR
Couldst thou, Great Fairy, give to me. The Pines. Harriet Prescott Spofford. AA
Could'st thou (O Earth) live thus obscure. George Alsop. SCAP
Couldst thou portray that face whose holy spell. Our Madonna at Home. Rafael Pombo. CAW
Council Held by the Rats, The. La Fontaine. *tr. fr. French by* Elizur Wright. OuHeWo
("Old Rodilard, a certain cat.") CIV
("Tyrant Cat, by surname Nibbelard, A," *diff. tr.*) CIV
Council of Horses, The. John Gay. *Fr.* Fables. BoChLi; GN
Council of Satan, The. Milton. *Fr.* Paradise Lost, I. PoEL-3
Councillor, The. Cullen Gouldsbury. BoSA
Counsel, The. Alexander Brome. CavP
Counsel. Roselle Mercier Montgomery. HBMV
Counsel. Mollie E. Moore. HBV
Counsel of Moderation, A. Francis Thompson. MoBrPo
Counsel to Girls. Robert Herrick. *See* To the Virgins, to Make Much of Time.
Counsel to Girls. Archibald Stodart-Walker. *Fr.* The Moxford Book of English Verse. CenHV
Counsel to Those That Eat, *sels.* E. V. Lucas.
Chocolate-Cream. BOHV
Potatoes. GaP
Counsel upon Marriage. Chaucer. PoLi
Counselor, The. Dorothy Parker. InMe

Counsels of O'Riordan, the Rann Maker, The. T. D. O'Bolger. AnIV
Counsels of Sigrdrifa. *Unknown, tr. fr. Icelandic by* William Morris *and* Eiríkur Magnusson. *Fr.* The Elder Edda. AWP
Count Basie's. Ted Wilson. BF
Count each affliction, whether light or grave. Sorrow. Aubrey Thomas De Vere. BLPA; EPN; GoBC; HBV; JKCP; MaRV; NeHB; OBEV (1st ed.); OQP; VA; WGRP
Count Filippo, *sels.* Charles Heavysege. PeCV
"Now let the drums roll muffled; let the bells'."
Song: "Who is lord of lordly fate."
Count Gismond. Robert Browning. BEL; MBW-2; PoVP; ViPP
Count me o'er earth's chosen heroes—they were souls that stood alone. James Russell Lowell. *Fr.* The Present Crisis. WGRP
Count not thyself a starveling soul. The Kingdom Within. Percy Clough Ainsworth. MaRV
Count of Senlis at His Toilet, The. Lord De Tabley. PeVV
Count Orlo in England. Jon Manchip White. NePoEA
Count Ten. Bonaro Overstreet. PoToHe (new ed.)
Count That Day Lost. "George Eliot." MaRV; NeHB; OQP; TreFT
(At Set of Sun.) OTD; PoToHe (new ed.); PoPl; TRV
Count the flashes in the surf. Song for Music. Sir Edmund Gosse. VA
Count the sighs, and count the teares. The Broken Heart. Thomas Beedome. OBS
Count the white horses you meet on the way. White Horses. Eleanor Farjeon. PDV; PoRh
Count up those books whose pages you have read. Indolence. Vernon Watkins. FaBoTw
Count William's Escapade. Guillaume de Poitiers, *tr. fr. Provençal by* Hubert Creekmore. ErPo
Count your blessings. *Unknown.* ThGo
Countee Cullen. Eugene T. Maleska. PoNe (1970 ed.)
Countenance like lightning, why do you stand. Colloquy at Peniel. W. S. Merwin. NePoEA
Counter-Attack. Siegfried Sassoon. BrPo; EnLit; MoBrPo; WaP
Counterpart, The. Elizabeth Jennings. LiTM (1970 ed.)
Counterpoint, A. Robert Creeley. NeAP
Counters. Elizabeth J. Coatsworth. GaP; PoRh; SoPo; SUS
(To Think.) MPB
Counter-Serenade; She Invokes the Autumn Instant. Peter Viereck. CrMA
Countershadow, The. Philip Booth. NYBP
Countersign. Arthur Ketchum. *Fr.* Legends for Trees. HBMV
Countersign, The. Charles J. Quirk. *Fr.* Quatrains. CAW
Countersigns, The, *with music. Unknown.* SoAmSa
Countess, I see the flying year. To My Mistress. Frederick Locker-Lampson. VA
Countess Laura. George Henry Boker. BeLS
Countess of Montgomery's Urania, The, *sel.* Lady Mary Wroth.
Love, What Art Thou? SeCL
Countess of Pembroke's Arcadia, The. Sir Philip Sidney. *See* Arcadia.
Countess Temple, Appointed Poet Laureate to the King of the Fairies. Horace Walpole. CEP
(Anne Grenville, Countess Temple, Appointed Poet Laureate to the King of the Fairies.) OBEC
Countesse of Douglas out of her boure she came, The. The Knight of Liddesdale. *Unknown.* ESPB
Counting. Fenton Johnson. AmNP
Counting. Carl Sandburg. MoLP
Counting Kisses. Catullus, *tr. fr. Latin by* Richard Crashaw. LiTW
(Out of Catullus.) CavP; MaMe
Counting Man, The. William Vaughn Moody. PoMS
Counting on Flowers. John Ciardi. PP
Counting-out Rhyme. Edna St. Vincent Millay. GoJo; MoShBr
Counting-out Rhyme. *Unknown.* ChTr
Counting-out Rhyme for March. Frances Frost. YeAr
Counting Sheep. Aileen Fisher. SoPo
Counting Small-Boned Bodies. Robert Bly. NaP
Counting the Beats. Robert Graves. CBV; DTC; ELP; GTBS-P; Po; PoIE; ViBoPo (1958 ed.)
Counting the Days. James S. Tippett. ChBR
Counting the Mad. Donald Justice. NePoEA; PPON; UnPo (3d ed.); WOW
Countless gold of a merry heart, The. Riches. Blake. *Fr.* Gnomic Verses. BoLiVe; PoG; StaSt; TrGrPo
Countless stars, which to our human eye, The. The Starry Host. John Lancaster Spalding. *Fr.* God and the Soul. AA; HBV
Countrie men of England, who live at home with ease. *See* Countrymen of England . . .
Countries tears, be ye my spring, The; my hill. To the Memory of the Learned and Reverend, Mr. Jonathan Mitchell. Francis Drake. SCAP
Country Bedroom, The. Frances Cornford. MemP; MoBrPo
Country Burying (1919). Robert Penn Warren. LiTM (1970 ed.)
Country Cat. Elizabeth J. Coatsworth. GoTP
Country Child, The. Irene Thompson. BoTP
Country Church. Robert P. Tristram Coffin. MaRV
Country Church, A. Violet Alleyn Storey. OQP
Country Clergy, The. R. S. Thomas. BoPe; GTBS-P; PoIE
Country Clergyman's Trip to Cambridge, The. Macaulay. NBM; OxBoLi
Country Clown, The. John Trumbull. AnAmPo
Country Club Sunday. Phyllis McGinley. CrMA; PoPo
Country curate, visiting his flock, A. The Lost Spectacles. *Unknown.* BOHV
Country Dance. Judith Wright. MoAuPo
Country Doctor, The. Will M. Carleton. BLPA
Country Faith, The. Norman Gale. BoTP; HBV; OBEV (new ed.); OBVV; OQP; OTPC; VA; WGRP
Country farmer had a friend at court, A. Henry Parrot. SiCE
Country folk who pass have said to me, The. The Grave. John Lyle Donaghy. NeIP
Country Girl, Don't Stay Away. Luis Carlos López, *tr. fr. Spanish by* Donald Devenish Walsh. WoL
Country Girl's Policy, The; or, The Cockney Outwitted. *Unknown.* CoMu
Country Glee. Thomas Dekker *and* John Ford. *Fr.* The Sun's Darling. OBSC
("Haymakers, rakers, reapers, and mowers.") ELP; ViBoPo
Country God, A. Edmund Blunden. MoBrPo
Country Gods. Cometas, *tr. fr. Greek by* T. F. Higham. FaBoCh; LoGBV
Country Graveyard. Dave Etter. ThO
Country Graveyard. Charles F. Pressoir, *tr. fr. French by* Edna Worthley Underwood. PoNe
Country Gulliver, A. The Reports Come In. J. D. Reed. NYBP
Country Inn, The, *sel.* Joanna Baillie.
Song: "Though richer swains thy love pursue." OBRV
Country Innocence. *Unknown. See* Happy Husbandman, The.
Country is no country I have seen, The. Civil War. Mark Van Doren. MoVE
Country Justice, The. John Langhorne. LaA
Apology for Vagrants, I. OBEC
Country Kisses. Arthur Joseph Munby. *Fr.* Dorothy; a Country Story. VA
Country Lad, The. Nicholas Breton. *See* Merry Country Lad, The.
Country lad and bonny lass, A. Have-at a Venture. *Unknown.* CoMu; ErPo
Country Lane. Margaret Stanion Darling. FiSC
Country Lasses Witty Invention, The, *Unknown. See* Unfortunate Miller, The.
Country Letter. John Clare. CBEP; NCEP
Country Life. Horace, *tr. fr. Latin by* Dryden. Epodes II. AWP
(Revery of a Business Man.) WoL
Country Life, A. Randall Jarrell. MiAP; MoAmPo (1950 ed.)
Country Life. Frank Kendon. POTE
Country life is sweet, A! The Useful Plough. *Unknown.* DD; HBV; OTPC (1923 ed.); RIS
Country Life, A; to His Brother, M. Tho: Herrick. Robert Herrick. SeCP; SeCV-1
Country Lovers, The. *Unknown.* UnTE
Country Lover's Complaint, The. *Unknown. See* Phillada Flouts Me.
Country men of England. *See* Countrymen of England . . .
Country Miracle. Abbie Huston Evans. LiTM
Country Mouse, The. Abraham Cowley, *after* Horace. SeCP

Country Music. Plato, *tr. fr. Greek by* Robert Bridges. LiTW
Country of a Thousand Years of Peace, The. James Merrill. PoCh
Country of hunchbacks!—where the strong, straight spine. Sonnet to Gath. Edna St. Vincent Millay. CMoP; CoBA; MAP; MoAB; MoAmPo
Country of No Lack. Jean Starr Untermeyer. MAP; MoAmPo
Country Parson, The. Goldsmith. *See* Village Preacher, The.
Country Pastor. Mitsuko Inoue, *tr. fr. Japanese by* Katue Kitasono. LiTW
Country Pleasures. Martial, *tr. fr. Latin by* F. A. Wright. AWP; OnPM
Country Proverbs. *Unknown.* StaSt
Country Reverie. Carol Coates. CaP
Country Rhyme. *Unknown. See* Dove and the Wren, The.
Country roads are yellow and brown. Street Lanterns. Mary Elizabeth Coleridge. BoTP; PoRA (rev. ed.)
Country Saying. *Unknown. See* He That Would Thrive.
Country School. Allen Curnow. AnNZ
Country Song. Nicholas Breton. *See* Report Song, A.
Country Song. Shakespeare. *See* It Was a Lover and His Lass.
Country Song, A. Sir Philip Sidney. *Fr.* Arcadia. OBSC; SiPS
Country Store, The. *Unknown.* BLPA
Country Summer. Léonie Adams. AnEnPo; ATP (1953 ed.); BoLiVe (1939 ed.); GoJo; LiTM; MAP; MoAB; MoAmPo; MoPo; MoVE; TrGrPo; TwAmPo; ViBoPo (1958 ed.)
Country Summer Pastoral, A, *sl. abr.* Sam Walter Foss. BOHV
Country Thought. Sylvia Townsend Warner. MoBrPo; NeMA
Country Town, A. Philip James Bailey. *See* Aim of Life, The.
Country Towns. Kenneth Slessor. MoAuPo; NeLNL; PoAu-2
Country Trucks. Monica Shannon. BrR; FaPON; TiPo (1950 ed.)
Country Tune. Elizabeth Riddell. BoAV; NeLNL
Country Vegetables. Eleanor Farjeon. *See* Vegetables.
Country Walk, The. John Dyer. PrWP
Country Walk, A. Thomas Kinsella. NMP; OPoP
Country Walk. Geoffrey Taylor. OxBI
Country Ways. Marcia Masters. Impressions of My Father, I. GoYe
Country Wedding, The. *Unknown.* HBV
Country Witch, A. William Barnes. *See* Witch, A.
Country without a Mythology, A. Douglas Le Pan. MoCV
Country Words. Wallace Stevens. NYTB
Countryman's God. Roger Winship Stuart. MaRV
Countryman's Wooing, A. Theocritus, *tr. fr. Latin by* Charles Stuart Calverley. Idylls, XXVII. ErPo
Countrymen, The. John Masefield. *Fr.* Reynard the Fox, I. CMoP
Countrymen [*or* Countrie men] of England, who live at home with ease. Sailors [*or* Saylors] for My Money. Martin Parker. CoMu; SeCL; TuPP
Country Woman and a Country Man, A. Richard Murphy. *Fr.* The Battle of Aughrim. OPoP
Countrywoman of Mine, A. Elaine Goodale Eastman. AA
County Ball, The, *sel.* Winthrop Mackworth Praed.
County Member, The. OBNC
County Guy. Sir Walter Scott. *Fr.* Quentin Durward, *ch.* 4. BEL; EPN; OAEP; OBRV; TOP
(Serenade, A: "Ah! County Guy.") GTBS; GTBS-D; GTBS-P; GTBS-W; GTSE; GTSL
(Song: "Ah! County Guy.") CH
County Mayo, The. Anthony Raftery, *tr. fr. Modern Irish.* AnIL, *tr. by* James Stephens; KiLC, *tr. by* Frank O'Connor
County of Mayo, The. *At. to* Thomas Flavell [*or* Lavelle], *tr. fr. Modern Irish by* George Fox. AnIV; IrPN; OBEV; OnYI; OxBI
County Sligo. Louis MacNeice. OnYI
Coup d'Etat. Ruth Herschberger. LiTA
Coup de Grace, The. Edward Rowland Sill. AA
Couple, The. Sandra Hochman. NYBP
Couple, The. Joel Oppenheimer. CoPo
Couple, A. Carl Sandburg. ReMP
Couple. Walter Stone. NYBP
Couplet on Newton. Pope. *See* Epitaph Intended for Sir Isaac Newton.
Courage. Arthur Adams. BoAu
Courage. Matthew Arnold. MBW-2
Courage. Maltbie D. Babcock. SoP
Courage. Karle Wilson Baker. MaRV
Courage. Stopford Brooke. WGRP
Courage. Ozora Stearns Davis. OQP
Courage. Amelia Earhart. MaRV; MoSiPe
Courage. Helen Frazee-Bower. HBMV; OTD
Courage. John Galsworthy. OtMeF
Courage. Paul Gerhardt. *See* Give to the Winds Thy Fears.
Courage. George Herbert. *See* Dare to Be True.
Courage. Lowell Mason. OTD
Courage. Sadi, *tr. fr. Persian by* Sir Edwin Arnold. *Fr.* The Gulistan. AWP; JAWP; OnPM; WBP
Courage, All. Edwin Markham. HBMV
Courage, brother! do not stumble. Trust in God and Do the Right. Norman Macleod. BLRP; PaPo; TreFT
Courage for the Pusillanimous. Paul Roche. GoYe
Courage Has a Crimson Coat. Nancy Byrd Turner. MoSiPe; PCD; PCH
"Courage!" he said, and pointed toward the land. The Lotos Eaters. Tennyson. AtBAP; BEL; BoLiVe; ChTr; CoBE; DiPo; EnL; EnLi-2; EnLit; EPN; ExPo; FiP; ForPo; GoTL; HBV; LiTB; MaPo; MaVP; MBW-2; MCCG; NoP; OAEP; OBRV; OnMSP; OTPC; PAn; PIA; PoAn; PoE; PoEL-5; PoFS; PoIE; PoVP; PTK; SeCeV; ShBV-4; TOP; TreFT; VA; ViPo; ViPP; VP
Courage is a fabric. To Archbishop Stepinac. Sister Mary Eulalia. JKCP (1955 ed.)
Courage is armor. Courage. Karle Wilson Baker. MaRV
Courage is the price that life exacts for granting peace. Courage. Amelia Earhart. MaRV; MoSiPe
Courage Means Running. William Empson. LiTB
Courage my Soul, now learn to wield. A Dialogue, between the Resolved Soul, and Created Pleasure. Andrew Marvell. AnAnS-1; EP; FosPo; MaMe; MeLP; MeP; MePo; OBS; SCEP-2; SeCP; SeCV-1
Courage, my Soul! now to the silent wood. Peace. Bhartrihari. AWP
Courage to Live. Grace Noll Crowell. PoToHe
Courage: your tongue has left. Stutterer. Alan Dugan. NYBP
Courageous Turk, The, *sel.* Thomas Goffe.
"Drop golden showers, gentle sleep." SeCL; SeEP
Coureurs de Boise. Douglas Le Pan. CaP; MoCV
Couriers from Chihuahua go, The. The Bull Fight. L. Worthington Green. SCC
Course, The. Robert Huff. CoAP
Course bread and water's most their fare. Roger Williams. SCAP
Course of a Particular, The. Wallace Stevens. ForPo; PoIE; QFR
Course of each life must vary, The. Bread of Brotherhood. Lucia Trent. PGD
Course of my long life hath reached at last, The. On the Crucifix. Michelangelo. CAW
Course of Time, The, *sel.* Robert Pollok. Ocean, *fr.* I. EtS
Course of True Love, The. Shakespeare. *Fr.* A Midsummer Night's Dream, I, i. TreFS; WHA
Courser and the Jennet, The. Shakespeare. *Fr.* Venus and Adonis. LoBV
(Courser, The.) OBSC
Court and Country Love. *Unknown. See* Contest between Court and Country, A.
Court Historian, The. Walter Thornbury. HBV; OBVV; PeVV
Court is kept att leeue London, The. Hugh Spencer's Feats in France. *Unknown.* ESPB
Court Lady, A. Elizabeth Barrett Browning. BeLS; HBV; VA
Court of Charles II, The. Pope. *Fr.* To Augustus. OBEC
Court of Neptune, The. John Hughes. EtS
Court of Sapience, *sel.* John Lydgate.
Lament: "Farewell Mercy, farewell thy piteous grace." PoEL-1
Courteous kind gallants all. Sir Walter Rauleigh His Lamentation. *Unknown.* CoMu
Courteous Knight, The. *Unknown. See* Baffled Knight, The.
Courteous Pagan Shall Condemn, The. Roger Williams. *Fr.* A Key into the Language of America. AmPP (4th ed.); SCAP
Courtesies of good-morning and good-evening. On Dwelling.

Robert Graves. CBEP; CMoP; MoPW; MoVE
Courtesy. Hilaire Belloc. ACP (1952 ed.); BoC; HBMV; JKCP; OtMeF
Courtesy. Mary Mapes Dodge. BrR
Courtesy. Coventry Patmore. *Fr.* Angel in the House, I, xi, 2. OBVV
Courthouse Square. Herbert Merrill. AmFN
Courtier, whose heart with pride so mighty grows. Up-start Courtier. Samuel Rowlands. SiCE
Courtier's a Riddle, A. Ralph Schomberg. *Fr.* The Judgment of Paris. TrJP
Courtier's Good-Morrow to His Mistress, The. *Unknown.* ElL
Courtier's Health, The, or, Merry Boys of the Times. *Unknown.* CoMu
Courtier's Life, The. Sir Thomas Wyatt. CBV; ReIE
Courtin', The. James Russell Lowell. *Fr.* The Biglow Papers, 2d series, Introduction. AA; AmePo; AmPP; AnNE; BeLS; BOHV; CoBA; HBV; IHA; InMe; LHV; MCCG; OBVV; StVeCh (1940 ed.); TreFS; YT
Courting in Kentucky. Florence E. Pratt. BOHV
Courting of Olga Karg, The. Watson Kirkconnell. TwCaPo
Courtling, I rather thou should'st utterly. To Censorious Courtling. Ben Jonson. ReIE
Courts, The. Alice Meynell. BoPe; MemP
Courtship. Alexander Brome, *after the Latin of* Catullus. CavP
Courtship, Merry Marriage, and Picnic Dinner of Cock Robin and Jenny Wren, The. *Unknown.* HBV; OTPC
("It was a merry time.") PPL
("It was on a merry time." Mother Goose *vers.*) BoChLi (1939 ed.)
Courtship of Miles Standish, The, *parody.* William F. Kirk. PoMa
Courtship of Miles Standish, The. Longfellow. BeLS; TreFS, *abr.*
Sels.
Expedition to Wessagusset, *fr.* V *and* VII. PAH
War-Token, The, *fr.* IV. PAH
Courtship of the Yonghy-Bonghy-Bo, The. Edward Lear. EnLoPo; EvOK; GoTP; HBV; OnMSP; OTPC; WiR
(Yonghy-Bonghy-Bo, The.) BOHV; LBN; NA
Courtyard Thaw, A. Richard Wilbur. FosPo
Cousin Emily and the Night Visitor. Kendrick Smithyman. ACV
Cousin Florence. Richard Eberhart. ToPo
Cousin Nancy. T. S. Eliot. MWA-2; PoSa
Covenant of His Grace, The. Charles Wesley. BePJ
Covenanter's Lament for Bothwell Brigg, The. Winthrop Mackworth Praed. OBRV
Covent Garden Market. Carl Bode. *Fr.* London Sonnets. ToPo
Coventry Carol. *Unknown.* ELP; MeEL; YaCaBo, *with music*
Cover. Frances Frost. SUS
Cover Me Over. Richard Eberhart. FiMAP
Cover me over. Bringers. Carl Sandburg. NP
Cover my eyes with your palm. Ruth Miller. *Fr.* Cycle. PeSA
Cover the embers. Longfellow. *Fr.* Curfew. WaKn
Cover your eyes with your hands. The Cripple. Robert P. Tristram Coffin. StVeCh (1955 ed.)
Covered Bridge, The. Madison Cawein. YT
Covered Bridge. Robert P. Tristram Coffin. AmFN
Covered with snow, the herd, with none to guide. Without the Herdsman. Diotimus. AWP
Covering the Subject. Richard Armour. RePo; WaKn
Covertly under the line tree aspen. Epithalamium for Cavorting Ghosts. Dachine Rainer. NePoAm-2
Coves of Crail, The. "Fiona Macleod." VA
Covey of cotton-dressed, apple-breasted girls, A. Wax. Winfield Townley Scott. ErPo
Cow, The. Oliver Herford. *Fr.* More Animals. NA
Cow. Harold Massingham. FlW
Cow, The. Mrs. Motherly. PPL; SAS
Cow, The. Ogden Nash. CenHV
Cow, The. Bernard O'Dowd. BoAu; PoAu-1
Cow, The. Theodore Roethke. FiBHP
Cow, The. Robert Louis Stevenson. BoChLi; BrPo; FaPON; GFA; MPB; OTPC (1946 ed.); PoVP; PPL; RIS; SAS; SoPo; StVeCh; SUS; TiPo; UTS
Cow, The. Ann *or* Jane Taylor. BoChLi; HBV; HBVY; MPB; OTPC; UTS
(Pretty Cow.) PoRh; StVeCh; TVC
(Thank You, Pretty Cow.) BoTP; PCH, *st.* 1; PRWS; SAS
Cow, The. Bert Leston Taylor. RIS
Cow and a calf, A. *Unknown.* OxNR
Cow and the Ass, The. Jane Taylor. BoTP; OTPC (1923 ed.)
Cow at Sullington, A. Charles Dalmon. TSW
Cow-bosses are good-hearted chunks, The. Dogie Song. *Unknown.* CoSo
Cow Camp on the Range, A. *Unknown.* CoSo
Cow-Chace, The. John André. PAH
Cow Dance. Bruce Beaver. PoAu-2
Cow eats green grass, The. Response to Rimbaud's Later Manner. T. Sturge Moore. HBMV; SyP
Cow has a cud, The. David McCord. TiPo (1959 ed.)
Cow in Apple Time, The. Robert Frost. CABA; MAP; MoAB; MoAmPo; OA; PoeP; PoLF
Cow is of the bovine ilk, The. The Cow. Ogden Nash. CenHV
Cow is too well known, I fear, The. The Cow. Oliver Herford. *Fr.* More Animals. NA
Cow Time. Monica Shannon. SiSoSe
Cow walks away from him, The. Thomas in the Fields. Lois Moyles. NYBP
Cow Wandering in the Bare Field, The. Randall Jarrell. MoVE
Coward. Harold Lewis Cook. NP
Coward, The. Roland R. Greenwood. YT
Coward, The. Kipling. *Fr.* Epitaphs of the War. FaBoTw; GTBS; OAEP (2d ed.); PoVP
Coward, The. Eve Merriam. TrJP
Coward,—of heroic size. Grizzly. Bret Harte. AA; AnAmPo; OA
Cowards ("Cowards die many times before their deaths"). Shakespeare. *Fr.* Julius Caesar, II, ii. MaRV
(Death of Cowards, The.) TreFS
(That Men Should Fear.) TrGrPo
Cowards fear to die, but courage stout. On the Snuff of a Candle. Sir Walter Ralegh. FCP; SiPS
Cowboy, The. John Antrobus. AA; FaBoBe; FaPON; OTPC (1946 ed.); PoRL
Cowboy ("I'm wild and wooly"). Baird Boyd. *See* Drunken Desperado, The.
Cowboy, The ("All day on the prairie"), *with music.* *Unknown.* CoSo (A *and* B *vers.*)
Cowboy, The ("He wears a big hat"). *Unknown.* MaC; SCC
Cowboy, The ("It was only a few short years ago"). *Unknown.* CoSo
Cowboy, The ("Oh, a man there lives"). *Unknown.* CoSo
Cowboy Alone with His Conscience, A. James Barton Adams. SCC
Cowboy and His Love, The, *with music.* John Milton Hagen. CoSo
(Song of the Cattle Trail.) SCC
Cowboy and the Maid, The. *Unknown.* SCC
Cowboy at Church, The. *Unknown.* CoSo, *with music*
Cowboy at the Carnival, A. *Unknown.* SCC
Cowboy at Work, The. *Unknown.* CoSo
Cowboy Boasting Chants. *Unknown.* ABF
Cowboy Dance Song, A. *Unknown.* CoSo
Cow-Boy Fun. Wallace D. Coburn. PoOW
Cowboy Grace: "Eat your meat and save the skin." *Unknown.* CoSo
Cowboy Grace: "Thar's the bread, thar's the meat." *Unknown.* CoSo
Cowboy Grace: "Yes, we'll come to the table." *Unknown.* CoSo
Cowboy he lay on the prairie, A. Dry-Landers. *Unknown.* CoSo
Cowboy Jack, *with music.* *Unknown.* CoSo
Cowboy Race, A. J. C. Davis. SCC
Cowboy Song ("I come from Salem County"). Charles Causley. NePoEA; PoRA (rev. ed.); PoSa; POTi
Cowboy Song, A ("I could not be so well content"). *Unknown.* SCC
Cowboy Song. Tom Veitch. ANYP
Cowboy Songs ("Oh, slow up, dogies, quit your roving round"). *At. to* Harry Stephens. *See* Night-herding Song.
Cowboy stands beneath, The. Vaquero. Edward Dorn. NeAP
Cowboy Talks to a Pitching Horse. *Unknown.* *See* Cowboy to Pitching Bronco.
Cowboy to His Friends in Need. Burke Jenkins. SCC

Cowboy to Pitching Bronco, *with music*. *Unknown*. ABF
(Cowboy Talks to a Pitching Horse, *st.* 1.) CoSo
Cowboy Toast, A. James Barton Adams. SCC
Cowboy up to Date, The. Charles F. Thomas, Jr. CoSo
Cowboy versus Broncho. James Barton Adams. SCC
Cowboys' Ball, The. Henry Herbert Knibbs. SCC
(Cowboy's Ball, The.) PoOW
Cowboy's Christmas Ball, *with music*. Larry Chittenden. CoSo, *with music*; SCC
Cowboys, come and hear a story of Roy Bean in all his glory. Roy Bean. *Unknown, at. to* Charles J. Finger. ABF; BeLS; CoSo
Cowboy's Dance Song, The, *with music*. James Barton Adams. CoSo; SCC
Cowboy's Dream, The ("Last night as I lay on the prairie"). Charles J. Finger. BFSS, *with music*; CoSo, *with music*; IHA; MaC; YT
Cowboy's Dream, The ("When I think of the last great round-up"). *Unknown*. ABF
(Great Round-up, The.) CoSo
Cowboy's Fate, The. Wallace D. Coburn. PoOW
Cowboy's Gettin'-up Holler, *with music*. *Unknown*. ABF; CoSo; TrAS
Cowboy's Hopeless Love, A. James Barton Adams. SCC
Cowboy's Lament, The. *Unknown*. BFSS, *with music*; ChTr; CoSo, *with music*; FaFP; MaC; ThLM; TreFS; ViBoFo (A *and* B *vers*.); WaKn
(As I walked Out in the Streets of Laredo, *with music*.) AS
Cowboy's Life, The. *At. to* James Barton Adams, *ad. by* John A. *and* Alan Lomax. AmFN; CoSo; MPB; SoPo; TiPo
Cowboy's life is a dreary, dreary life, A. The Kansas Line. *Unknown*. CoSo
Cowboy's Love Song, The. *Unknown*. SCC
Cowboy's Meditation, The. *Unknown*. CoSo
Cowboy's Prayer, A. Badger Clark. SoP
Cowboy's Return, The, *with music*. *Unknown*. BFSS
Cowboy's Salvation Song. Robert V. Carr. PoOW
Cowboy's Son, A. *Unknown*. SCC
Cow-Boy's Song, The. Anna Maria Wells. PRWS
Cowboy's Valentine, The. Charles Fletcher Lummis. SCC
Cowboy's Worrying Love, A. James Barton Adams. SCC
Cowdung-colored mud, The. Five Poems from Mexico. Denise Levertov. PoAn
Cowhorn-crowned, shockheaded, cornshuck-bearded. The Knight, Death, and the Devil. Randall Jarrell. CrMA
Cowman's Prayer, The, *with music*. *Unknown*. CoSo
Cowper. John Clare. PeER
Cowper. Norman Nicholson. ML
Cowper at Olney. Sylvia Lynd. POTE
Cowper, the poet of the fields. Cowper. John Clare. PeER
Cowper's Grave. Elizabeth Barrett Browning. HBV; OBVV; PoVP; ViPo
Cows. James Reeves. PoSC
Cows! Cows! With ears like mouths of telephones. Band Music. John Fuller. NePoEA-2
Cows low in the pasture on the hill, The. The Song of the Robin. Beatrice Bergquist. SUS
Cows with eyes of buttered moons. Country Graveyard. Dave Etter. ThO
Cowslips. Walter Savage Landor. *See* With Rosy Hand.
Coxcomb Bird, The. Pope. *Fr.* Moral Essays. LiTB; SiTL
Coxswain's Line, The. H. E. Cressman. RePo
Coy Clelia, veil those charming eyes. To Clelia. Matthew Coppinger. CavP; SeCL
Coy in a covert of the glossy bracken. Illusion. Edmund Gosse. SyP
Coy Lass Dress'd Up in Her Best, The. *Unknown*. ErPo
Coy nature (which remain'd though [*or* tho] aged grown). Abraham Cowley. *Fr.* Ode upon Dr. Harvey. Par; PoEL-2
Coy Shepherdess, The; or, Phillis and Amintas. *Unknown*. CoMu
Coyote and the Locust, The. *Tr. fr. Zuni Indian by* Frank Cushing. AWP; JAWP; WBP
(Locust, The.) FaPON; RePo; SUS
Cozy. T'ao Ch'ien, *tr. fr. Chinese by* C. W. Luh. OnPM
Cozzo Grillo. H. B. Mallalieu. WaP
Crab. John Blight. BoAV
Crab-Apple. Ethel Talbot. BiCB; PCH; TiPo
Crab-Apple Crisis, The. George MacBeth. HYE
Crab, the bullace, and the sloe, The. Grave-Digger's Song. Alfred Austin. *Fr.* Prince Lucifer. VA
Crab Tree, The. Oliver St. John Gogarty. AnIL; OxBI
Crabbed Age and Youth. Shakespeare. The Passionate Pilgrim, XII. CBV; HBV; LiTB; OBEV; ReEn; TreFS; UnTE; ViBoPo
(Age and Youth.) ElL; FaBoEn
("Crabbed age and youth cannot live together.") SiCE; YAT
(Madrigal, A: "Crabbed age and youth.") GBV (1952 ed.); GTBS; GTBS-D; GTBS-P; GTBS-W; GTSE; GTSL
(Youth and Age.) OBSC
Crabbing. Norman Levine. CaP; OBCV
Crabe dans Calalou, *with music*. *Unknown*. OuSiCo
Crabfish, The, *with music*. *Unknown*. SaSa
Crack, The. Michael Goldman. NYBP
Crack, The. J. C. Hall. HaMV
Cracked Bell, The. Baudelaire, *tr. fr. French by* Arthur Symons. OnPM
Crackle and blaze. A Winter Song. William Cox Bennett. PCH
Crackling embers on the hearth are dead, The. Night. Hartley Coleridge. NCEP
Crackling Twig, The. James Stephens. *See* Satyr, The.
Cradle, The. Austin Dobson. VA
Cradle and the Cross, The. A. S. Reitz. STF
Cradle and Throne. *Unknown*. STF
Cradle Carol. Eleanor Slater. MaRV
Cradle Hymn. Martin Luther, *tr. fr. German*. BiCB; BoChLi; BoTP; ChBR; DD; FaPON; GaP; GFA; GoTP; HH; MPB; OHIP; OTPC (1946 ed.); PCH; PRWS; StVeCh; SUS; TiPo (1952 ed.)
(Away in a Manger.) ChrBoLe; MaRV; ThGo; TreFS; YaCaBo, *with music*
Cradle Hymn, A. Isaac Watts. CEP; EiPP; HBV; LoBV; NoP; OBEC; OBEV; PoEL-3; PRWS; SoPo; SUS; TreFS
(Cradle Song, A.) BoChLi; OTPC; OxBoCh; ThGo
Cradle of the Deep. Emma Hart Willard. *See* Rocked in the Cradle of the Deep.
Cradle Song, A: "Angels are stooping, The." W. B. Yeats. PoPl; POTE; TSW
Cradle Song: "Baby, O baby, fain you are for bed." Louis Esson. BoAu
Cradle Song: "Christ by Thine own darkened hour." Padraic Colum. CAW
Cradle Song: "Clock's untiring fingers wind the wool of darkness, The." Louis MacNeice. MoAB; MoBrPo
Cradle Song, A: "Come little babe, come silly soul." Nicholas Breton. *See* Sweet Lullaby, A.
Cradle Song: "From groves of spice." Sarojini Naidu. BrR; FaPON; MoSiPe; MPB
(Hindu Cradle Song.) BoTP
Cradle Song: "Golden slumbers kiss your eyes." Thomas Dekker, *and others*. *See* Golden Slumbers.
Cradle Song, A: "Hush, my dear, lie still and slumber." Isaac Watts. *See* Cradle Hymn.
Cradle Song: "Lord Gabriel, wilt thou not rejoice." Josephine Preston Peabody. HBV; NP
Cradle Song: "Lullaby, my little one." Karl Mikael Bellman, *tr. fr. Swedish*. FaPON
Cradle-Song: "Madonna, Madonna [*or* Madonnina]." Adelaide Crapsey. HBMV; ISi
Cradle Song, A: "O men from the fields." Padraic Colum. AS; GoBC; ISi; MP; OnYI; OxBI; StJW; WHL
Cradle Song: "O my deir hert, young Jesus sweit." James, John, *and* Robert Wedderburn. *See* Balulalow.
Cradle Song: "Out in the dark something complains." F. R. Higgins. POTE
Cradle Song, A: "Sleep, baby, sleep,/ Thy father watches the sheep." *Unknown*. *See* Sleep, Baby, Sleep.
Cradle Song: "Sleep enfold thee,/ Jesukin." James L. Duff. ISi
Cradle Song: "Sleep, my child, my little daughter." *Unknown, tr. fr. Yiddish by* Joseph Leftwich. TrJP
Cradle Song: "Sleep, my darling, sleep." Louis MacNeice. OxBI; PoPl
Cradle Song, A: "Sleep! sleep! beauty bright." Blake. EnLi-2; EnRP; GTSL; HBV; HBVY; OBEC; OBEV; PoFS; PoLF; PoPl
(Sleep! Sleep! Beauty Bright.) CBEP; OTPC
Cradle Song, A: "Sweet dreams, form a shade." Blake. *Fr.* Songs of Innocence. AnFE; BEL; CBEP; EiPP; EnLi-2; EnLit; EnRP; OAEP; RIS; ViBoPo
(Sweet Dreams Form a Shade.) OTPC

Cradle Song: "What does little birdie say." Tennyson. *See* What Does Little Birdie Say?
Cradle Song: "What is the little one thinking about?" Josiah Gilbert Holland. *Fr.* Bitter-sweet. HBV; PCD
(Babyhood.) AA
Cradle Song at Bethlehem. E. J. Falconer. BoTP
Cradle Song of a Celtic Queen. James Edward Tobin. JKCP (1955 ed.)
Cradle Song of the Elephants. Adriano del Valle, *tr. fr. Spanish by* Alida Malkus. FaPON; RePo
Cradle Song of the Virgin ("Jesu, my sweet Son dear"). *Unknown.* ISi
Cradle Will Rock, The, *sel.* Marc Blitzstein.
Art for Art's Sake. TrJP
Cradling my funnybone. Elbow. Coleman Barks. *Fr.* Body Poems. QAH
Craft of a Keeper of Sheep, The. Moschus, *tr. fr. Greek by* Ernest Meyers. AWP
Craft of Verse, The. Pope. *See* Sound and Sense.
Craftsman, The. Marcus B. Christian. PoNe
Crafty Farmer, The. *Unknown.* BaBo; ESPB; TiPo (1952 ed.)
Crafty Miss of London, The; or, The Fryar Well Fitted. *Unknown.* CoMu; OxBB
Crag Jack's Apostasy. Ted Hughes. EaLo
Crags lay dark in strange eclipse, The. The Sea-Watcher. Aubrey Thomas De Vere. IrPN
Craigbilly Fair. *Unknown.* ChTr
Cramped like sardines on the Queens, and sedated. Tourists. Howard Moss. FiBHP; NYBP
Cranach. Sir Herbert Read. BrPo; FaBoMo
Cranberry Road. Rachel Field. MoSiPe
Crane. Joseph Langland. NYBP
Crane, The. Charles Tomlinson. MoBrPo (1962 ed.)
Crane Is My Neighbour, The. John Shaw Neilson. PoAu-1
Cranes, The. Po Chü-i, *tr. fr. Chinese by* Arthur Waley. MoBrPo (1942 ed.)
Cranes of Ibycus, The. Emma Lazarus. AA; PFY
Crankadox leaned o'er the edge of the moon, The. Spirk Troll-Derisive. James Whitcomb Riley. BOHV; LBN; NA
Cranmer's Prophecy of Queen Elizabeth. Shakespeare *and probably* John Fletcher. King Henry VIII, *fr.* V, v. WGRP
Crash at Leithfield. Allen Curnow. AnNZ
Crashed through the woods that lumbering coach. The East Coachload. Walter de la Mare. SeCePo
Crashing sky has swept old paths aside, The. Make Way! Florence Crocker Comfort. PGD
Crass Times Redeemed by Dignity of Souls. Peter Viereck. MiAP
"Tenderness of dignity of souls, The," *sel.* HoPM
Craven. Sir Henry Newbolt. BBV (1923 ed.); HBV; HBVY; PAH
Craven rook, and pert jackdaw, The. On the Gentlemen in *The Dunciad. Unknown.* EiCL
Craving of Samuel Rouse for clearance to create, The. The Slave and the Iron Lace. Margaret Danner. AmNP
Crawdad Song, The. *Unknown.* *See* Sweet Thing.
Crawford Long and William Morton. Rosemary Benét *and* Stephen Vincent Benét. OTD; PoMa
Crawl Blues. Vincent McHugh. ErPo
Crawl, crawl, clock on the wall. Pendulum Rhyme. Selma Robinson. InMe
Crawl into Bed. Quandra Prettyman. BOLo
Crawlin' aboot like a snail in the mud. The Image o' God. Joe Corrie. OxBS
Crayfish, The. Robert Wallace. WaKn
Crazed Girl, A. W. B. Yeats. Sonn
Crazy. Lawrence Ferlinghetti. CBV
Crazy bookcase, placed before, A. Epilogue to the Breakfast Table Series. Oliver Wendell Holmes. *Fr.* The Poet at the Breakfast Table. AA
Crazy Jane and Jack the Journeyman. W. B. Yeats. AtBAP; CMoP
Crazy Jane and the Bishop. W. B. Yeats. AtBAP; CMoP; LiTM (1970 ed.)
Crazy Jane Grown Old Looks at the Dancers. W. B. Yeats. AtBAP; CMoP; PoeP
Crazy Jane on God. W. B. Yeats. AtBAP; CMoP; MoAB; PoDB
Crazy Jane on the Day of Judgment. W. B. Yeats. AtBAP; CMoP
Crazy Jane on the Mountain. W. B. Yeats. AtBAP; CMoP
Crazy Jane Reproved. W. B. Yeats. AtBAP; CMoP
Crazy Jane Talks with the Bishop. W. B. Yeats. AtBAP; CABA; CBV; CMoP; CoBMV; DiPo; ErPo; ExPo; ILP; LiTG; LiTM (rev. ed.); OAEP (2d ed.); PAn; PoeP
Crazy Lady, The. William Hathaway. QAH
Crazy old vinegar man is dead, The. The Vinegar Man. Ruth Comfort Mitchell. MPB
Crazy Song to the Air of "Dixie." "Andy Lee." AS
Crazy tugs, The. East River. Rosemary Thomas. AmFN
Crazy World, The. William Gay. BoAu; BoAV; PoAu-1
Creak out of the marsh in the dark hollow, A. Facing Up. James Scully. WIRo
Creamcheese babies square and downy as bolsters. The Peaceable Kingdom. Marge Piercy. TwCP; WOW
Cream-cups, butter-cups. A Little Song of Spring. Mary Austin. YeAr
Cream of phosphorescent light, A. Jonah. Aldous Huxley. ChTr
Create Great Peace. James Oppenheim. *Fr.* 1914—and After. MaRV
Created, The. Jones Very. AmP; MAmP; PoIE; QFR
Created by the poet to sing my song. The Reaper. Robert Duncan. CrMA
Created for whose sake? The praying. Don't Sit under the Apple Tree with Anyone Else but Me. Robert Pack. CoPo
Created purely from glass the saint stands. In Piam Memoriam. Geoffrey Hill. NePoEA-2
Created Universe, The. Mark Akenside. *See* Nature's Influence on Man.
Creation, The. Cecil Frances Alexander. *See* All Things Bright and Beautiful.
Creation. V. N. Bhushan. ACV
Creation, The. Genesis, Bible, *O.T.* TreF (I: 1-II: 3); WoL (I: 1-III: 24)
("In the beginning God created the heaven and the earth," I: 1-31.) ImOP
Creation. Ambrose Bierce. AA; LHV; PFY
Creation, The. Cædmon. *See* Hymn of the World's Creator, The.
Creation, The. Abraham Cowley. *Fr.* The Davideis, I. OBS
Creation, The. James Weldon Johnson. BALP; BANP; CDC; FaBV; GoSl; MAP; MaRV; MoAmPo; NP; PoNe; PoPl; PoRA (rev. ed.); TiPo (1952 ed.); WePo; YaD
Up from the Bed of the River, *sel.* EaLo
Creation. Louise Townsend Nicholl. GoYe
Creation. Alfred Noyes. GoBC; OBVV
Creation Hymn, The. *Unknown, tr. fr. Vedic by* R. T. H. Griffith. *Fr.* The Rig-Veda. OuHeWo
Creation of Man, The. Milton. *Fr.* Paradise Lost, VII. PeRV
Creation of My Lady, The. Francesco Redi, *tr. fr. Italian by* Sir Edmund Gosse. AWP
Creation of the World, The. Milton. *Fr.* Paradise Lost, VII. MaPo
Creation of Woman, The. Milton. *Fr.* Paradise Lost, VIII. PeRV
Creation's and Creator's crowning good. To the Body. Coventry Patmore. *Fr.* The Unknown Eros. GoBC; OxBoCh; PoEL-5; PoLi
Creation's crust and crumb, breaking of bread. Bread. A. M. Klein. PeCV
Creation's Lord, We Give Thee Thanks. William De Witt Hyde. MaRV
Creative Force. Maude Miner Hadden. GoYe
Creativity. *Unknown, tr. fr. Chinese by* Y. S. Han. OQP
Creator, The ("Creator of all men"). *Unknown, tr. fr. Egyptian.* PCH
Creator of night and of birth, The. Special Starlight. Carl Sandburg. MoRP
Creator Spirit, by whose aid. Veni Creator Spiritus. *Unknown, paraphrased by* Dryden. AWP; CEP; CoBE; GoBC; HBV; MaRV; OuHeWo; SeCV-2; WBP; WGRP
Creatrix. Anna Wickham. MoBrPo; TrGrPo (1942 ed.)
Creature of God, thy coat. Hymn to the Seal. Stevie Smith. PoG
Creature was a changeling child, The. Stranger Bride. Jocelyn Macy Sloan. FiSC
Creatures all eyes and brows, and tresses streaming. Correggio's Cupolas at Parma. Aubrey Thomas De Vere. Sonn
Crèche, The. Carol Ryrie Brink. ChrBoLe
Creçy. Francis Turner Palgrave. BeLS; HBV

Credences of Summer. Wallace Stevens. AP; CoBMV
Credibility. John Ciardi. ToPo
Credit. *Unknown.* STF
Creditor, The. Louis MacNeice. EaLo; ShBV-3
Credo. Leonard Cohen. PeCV (1967 ed.)
Credo. Zona Gale. TrPWD
Credo, *sel.* Richard Watson Gilder.
"Christ of Judea, look thou in my heart!" TrPWD
Credo. Robinson Jeffers. AnEnPo; MAP; MoAB; MoAmPo; PoPl
Credo. Georgia Douglas Johnson. BALP
Credo. Alfred Kreymborg. AnAmPo
Credo. "Seumas O'Sullivan." OnYI
Credo. John Oxenham. BLRP; ChIP; MaRV; OQP; StJW
Credo. E. A. Robinson. AmePo; AmPP; AnNE; AP; CMoP; CoBA; GTBS-W; ILP; LiTM (rev. ed.); MaRV; MoAmPo; NeMA; NePA; OQP; OxBA; TreFT; WGRP
Credo. Arthur Symons. OBVV; OQP
Credo. Saul Tchernichowsky. *See* I Believe.
Credo, A. Thackeray. HBV
Creed, A. Ellen Glasgow. OQP
Creed, A. Edgar A. Guest. HH; PEDC
Creed. Walter Lowenfels. PoNe (1970 ed.)
Creed, A. Norman Macleod. WGRP
Creed, A ("Here is the truth in a little creed"). Edwin Markham. *See* Quatrain: "Here is the truth. . ."
Creed, A ("There is a destiny that makes us brothers"). Edwin Markham. BLPA; FaBoBe; FaFP; MaRV; NeHB; PoPl; PoRL; TreFS
Creed, A. John Masefield. HBMV; MoRP; WGRP
Creed. Anne Spencer. CDC
Creed. Mary Ashley Townsend. BLPA; FaBoBe; NeHB
Creed, A. *Unknown.* *See* My Daily Creed.
Creed and Deed. Robert Loveman. MaRV; OQP
Creed in a Garden, A. Newman Flower. MaRV
Creed thy father built, wherein his soul, The. Creeds. William O. Partridge. OQP
Creede. Cy Warman. PoOW
Creedless Love, The. Sam Walter Foss. OQP
Creeds. Karle Wilson Baker. HBMV; WGRP
Creeds. William O. Partridge. OQP
Creeds. Willard Wattles. HBMV; InP; MaRV; OQP
Creek, The. W. W. E. Ross. MoCV; OBCV
Creek of the Four Graves, The, *sel.* Charles Harpur.
"Settler in the olden times went forth, A." PoAu-1
Creek-Road, The. Madison Cawein. AA
Creek, shining, The. The Creek. W. W. E. Ross. MoCV; OBCV
Creep afore Ye Gang. James Ballantine. HBV
Creep into thy narrow bed. The Last Word. Matthew Arnold. BEL; BoLiVe; CABA; CBV; EnLi-2; FaBoEn; FiP; GTBS-D; HBV; MaRV; MBW-2; MCCG; MemP; OBNC; OBVV; PG; PoEL-5; PoFS; PoRA; PoSa; PoVP; TOP; TreFT; TrGrPo; ViPo
Creeper grows over thorn. Alba. Confucius. *Fr.* Songs of T'ang. CTC
Creeps in half wanton, half asleep. Wagner. Rupert Brooke. MuSP; NAMP
Cremation. Robinson Jeffers. ELU
Cremation. William Sawyer. BOHV
Cremation of Sam McGee, The. Robert W. Service. FaFP; GSP; MaC; PoLF; ShM; StPo; TreF; TwCaPo; YT
Cremona. Sir Arthur Conan Doyle. HBV
Creole Girl. Leslie M. Collins. PoNe
Creole Slave-Song, A. Maurice Thompson. AA
Creon. Sophocles, *tr. fr. Greek by* F. Storr. *Fr.* Oedipus Rex. PoFr
Crepe de Chine. Tennessee Williams. NYBP
Crept side by side beyond the thresh. Epithalamium. Vassar Miller. NePoEA
Crepuscular. Richard Howard. TwCP
Crescent Boat, The. Wordsworth. *Fr.* Peter Bell. ThWaDe
(Among the Stars.) GoTP
Crescent Moon. Basho, *tr. fr. Japanese by* H. G. Henderson. OnPM
Crescent Moon. Elizabeth Madox Roberts. SUS; TiPo (1952 ed.)
Cresophontes, *sel.* Euripides, *tr. fr. Greek by* Moses Hadas.
Prayer to Peace. PoPl
Cresseid's Complaint against Fortune. Robert Henryson. *Fr.* The Testament of Cresseid. MeEL
Cressid. Nora Perry. AA
Cressida, *sels.* James K. Baxter. AnNZ
Her Decision, XI.
Her First Song, V.
Her Second Song, IX.
In the Lecture Room, I.
Lounge Bar, XII.
Parting, The, VI.
Sestina: "Swept clean of leaves, with stripped boughs, the garden," XV.
Cressida's Leprosy. Robert Henryson. *Fr.* The Testament of Cresseid. SeCePo
Cressid's Complaint. George Whetstone. ReIE
Crest and crowning of all good, The. Brotherhood. Edwin Markham. BBV (1951 ed.); MaRV; NeMA; OQP; PEDC; PGD; PoRL
Crest Jewel, The. James Stephens. AnIL; MoAB; MoBrPo
Crested heron flies over the lake, The. The Heron. Brian Vrepont. MoAuPo
Crethis. Callimachus, *tr. fr. Greek by* Richard Garnett. AWP
Creüsa cried for, through the tomb of Troy. Aeneid. Claire McAllister. NePA
Crew Cut. David McCord. SD
Crew Poem, A. Edward Augustus Blount, Jr. AA
Crew Practice on Lake Bled, in Jugoslavia. James Scully. NYBP
Crewel. Nancy Willard. ThO
Crib, The. Christopher Morley. BiCB
Cricket, The. Marjorie Barrows. BoChLi (1950 ed.)
Cricket, The. Vincent Bourne, *tr. fr. Latin by* William Cowper. HBV; HBVY; OTPC; PoLF
Cricket. Eleanor Alletta Chaffee. StaSt
Cricket. Emily Dickinson. *See* 'Twas later when the summer went.
Cricket. Clinton Scollard. HBV
Cricket, The. Tu Fu, *tr. fr. Chinese by* Chi Hwang Chu *and* Edna Worthley Underwood. OnPM
Cricket, The. Frederick Goddard Tuckerman. MAmP; NoP; QFR
Cricket and the Star, The. Mary Effie Lee Newsome. GoSl
Cricket at Brighton. Alan Ross. POTi
Cricket Bowler, A. Edward Cracroft Lefroy. OBVV
Cricket, chirring in the autumn twilight. Cricket. Clinton Scollard. HBV
Cricket does not sing, The. Pauses, II. José Gorostiza. OnPM
Cricket in the garden is awake, The. A Little Night Music. Felix Stefanile. FiSC
Cricket is a slight creature, The. The Cricket. Tu Fu. OnPM
Cricket on his cymbal sounds, The. Cricket. Eleanor Alletta Chaffee. StaSt
Cricket sang, The. Emily Dickinson. GBV (1952 ed.); MAPA; TwAmPo
Cricket Triolet, A. Coulson Kernahan. CenHV; WePo
Crickets. David McCord. PDV
Crickets. Aram Saroyan. ANYP; YAP
Crickets. Helen Wing. GFA
Crickets and Mice. Joseph Joel Keith. StVeCh (1955 ed.)
Crickets are making the merriest din. September [Is Here]. Edward Bliss Reed. DD; HBMV; HBVY; MPB; YeAr
Crickets at Dawn. Leonora Speyer. PFY
Crickets sing, and mans ore-labor'd sense, The. Shakespeare. *Fr.* Cymbeline, II, ii. AtBAP
Cricket's Story The. Emma Huntington Nason. HBV; HBVY
Crier, The. Michael Drayton. EIL; InvP; OAEP; TuPP; WhC
(Cryer, The.) PoEL-2; SeEP
Crier by Night, The, *sel.* Gordon Bottomley.
Blanid's Song. BrPo
Cries, The. *Unknown.* SoP
Cries of Evening, The. Stephen Spender. NoP
Cries Out of Blindness. Tristan Corbière, *tr. fr. French by* Harold Rosenberg. LiTW
Cries Sue to Will, in matrimonial strife. Epigram. *Unknown.* ALV
Cries Sylvia to a reverend Dean. Epigram. Robert Dodsley. ALV
Crime. Robert Penn Warren. AmP

Crime and Punishment. Kahlil Gibran. *Fr.* The Prophet. PoToHe (new ed.)
Crime Club. Weldon Kees. NaP
Crime Note. Hughes Mearns. *Fr.* Later Antigonishes. InMe
Crime Story. Charles Higham. NYTB
Crime Took Place at Granada, The. Antonio Machado, *tr. fr. Spanish by* Rolfe Humphries. PoFr
Crimean Heroes, The. Walter Savage Landor. ALV
Crimes of Lizzie Borden, The. *Unknown.* *See* Lizzie Borden.
Criminality of War, The. Edward Young. PGD
Crimp and whorl of conch, The. A Mantelpiece of Shells. Ruthven Todd. NYBP
Crimson Cherry Tree, The. Henry Treece. LiTM (1946 ed.); WaP
Crimson leafage fires the lawn, The. A Letter from Newport. Frederic William Henry Myers. VA
Crimson roses burn and glow, The. Vigil. Richard Dehmel. AWP; JAWP; LiTW; WBP
Crinog, melodious is your song. To Crinog. *Unknown.* AnIL; OnYI
Crinolines and Bloomers. *Unknown.* ThLM
Criole Candjo, *with music.* *Unknown, tr. fr. French.* ABF
Cripple, The. Robert P. Tristram Coffin. StVeCh (1955 ed.)
Cripple Dick upon a stick. *Unknown.* OxNR
Cripple in the wheelchair, The. Busy Day. James Laughlin. OnHM
Cripples. Kathleen Spivack. YAP
Crisis. W. H. Auden. AtBAP; ReMP
Crisis. G. S. Fraser. NeBP
Crisis, The. Whittier. PAH
Crisis is a hair. Emily Dickinson. MWA-2
Crispus Attucks. John Boyle O'Reilly. PAH
Cristina. Robert Browning. EPN; MaVP; MBW-2; OAEP; PoVP; ViPo
Critic, The. John Farrar. GaP; SoPo
Critic, A. Walter Savage Landor. ChTr
Critic, The. *Unknown.* SoP
Critic of the days of yore, The. Narcissus and Some Tadpoles. Victor J. Daley. PoAu-1
Critical Fribble, A. Charles Churchill. *Fr.* The Rosciad. OBEC
(Criticaster, A.) FaBoEn
Critics. George Crabbe. PP
Critics, The. Lawrence Durrell. ToPo
Critics. Sir John Harington. *See* Critics and Cooks. *after* Martial.
Critics, The. Theodore Spencer. NYBP
Critics. Swift. *Fr.* On Poetry; a Rhapsody. OBEC; SeCePo
Critics all were jealous, The. Why My Poems Died. Bhartrihari. OnPM
Critics and Connoisseurs. Marianne Moore. AmPP (5th ed.); AnAmPo; AnEnPo; CMoP; NePA; OxBA; PIA
Critics and Cooks. Sir John Harington, *after the Latin of* Martial. OnPM
(Against Writers That Carp at Other Men's Books.) TuPP
(Critics.) AWP
(Epigram: "Readers and the hearers like my books, The.") ALV
Critics avaunt! Tobacco is my theme. In Imitation of Young. Isaac Hawkins Browne. *Fr.* A Pipe of Tobacco. OBEC
Critics cry unfair, The. In Defense of Black Poets. Conrad Kent Rivers. BOLo
Critic's heel is on ye, sure, Th'. To th' Minstrel Girl. T. A. Daly. BOHV
Critic's Rules, The. Robert Lloyd. *Fr.* Shakespeare; an Epistle to Mr. Garrick. OBEC
Critics say that epics have died out, The. Elizabeth Barrett Browning. *Fr.* Aurora Leigh, V. PeVV
Critics sipping cups of tea. Obituary. Anthony Brode. FiBHP
Croak of a raven hoar, The. Mammon Marriage. George Macdonald. CBEP; NBM; OBVV
"Croak!" Said the Toad. *Unknown.* *See* Toad and the Frog, The.
Croaker Papers, The, *sels.* Fitz-Greene Halleck *and* Joseph Rodman Drake. AA
Man Who Frets at Worldly Strife, The.
National Paintings, The.
Ode to Fortune.
Crocodile, A. Thomas Lovell Beddoes. *Fr.* The Last Man. AnFE; CBV
Crocodile, The. "Lewis Carroll." *See* How Doth the Little Crocodile.
Crocodile, The. Laura E. Richards. UTS
Crocodile The. *Unknown.* CBEP
Crocus, The. Walter Crane. OTPC (1946 ed.); PCH; SoPo
Crocus. Sarah J. Day. MPB
Crocus, The. Mary Elliott. OTPC (1923 ed.)
Crocus, The. Harriet Eleanor Hamilton King. VA
Crocus. Alfred Kreymborg. HBMV; MAP
Crocus, The. Norman Nicholson. BoPe; POTi
Crocus ("Warm sunshine came down"). *Unknown.* GFA
Crocus. Marion Mitchell Walker. GFA
Crocus grows in any spot, The. To the Crocus—with My Love. Marion Sturges-Jones. BOHV
Crocus had slept in his little round house, The. Crocus. Sarah J. Day. MPB
Crocus, while the days are dark, The. The Year [*or* The Year's Round *or* Round the Year]. Coventry Patmore. BoTP; GTSE; OTPC (1946 ed.); PoRL; ThWaDe
Crocuses. Josa, *tr. fr. Japanese by* William N. Porter. MPB; TiPo
Crocuses. Anna M. Platt. BoTP
Crocuses in the Grass. John Gray. CAW
Crocuses in the Square, The. Extras. Richard Burton. AA
Croesus. Chaucer. *Fr.* The Canterbury Tales: The Monk's Tale. MyFE
Croesus in Autumn. Robert Penn Warren. AnAmPo
Crofters few but crafty. Shore Tullye. Robert Rendall. OxBS
"Crom Cruach and his sub-gods twelve." The Burial of King Cormac. Sir Samuel Ferguson. AnIL; IrPN; OnYI
Cromek ("A pretty sneaking knave"). Blake. FiBHP; PV
Cromwell and Henrietta Maria. William Gorman Wills. *Fr.* Charles the First. VA
Cromwell Dead. Andrew Marvell. *Fr.* A Poem upon the Death of Oliver Cromwell. ChTr
("I saw him dead.") OBS;PeRV;ViBoPo
Cromwell, I charge thee, fling away ambition. The Higher Loyalty [*or* Ambition]. Shakespeare, *and probably* John Fletcher. King Henry VIII, *fr.* III, ii. MaRV; TrGrPo
Cromwell, I did not think to shed a tear. Wolsey's Farewell to Cromwell [*or* Wolsey's Regrets]. Shakespeare, *and probably* John Fletcher. King Henry VIII, *fr.* III, ii. InP; OTPC (1923 ed.); TreFS
Cromwell, our chief of men, who through a cloud. To the Lord General Cromwell [*or* To Oliver Cromwell]. Milton. AnEnPo; BEL; CABA; EnLit; MaPo; MBW-1; NoP; OBS; OuHeWo; PAn; SeCeV; Sonn; TrGrPo; ViBoPo
Cronie Is Dead, *with music.* *Unknown.* BFSS
Crooked Footpath, The. Oliver Wendell Holmes. *Fr.* The Professor at the Breakfast Table. HBV; TreF
Crooked Gun, The, *with music.* *Unknown.* OuSiCo
Crooked heels/ And scuffy toes. The Cobbler. Eleanor Alletta Chaffee. GaP; SoPo; TiPo
Crooked paths go every way, The. The Goat Paths. James Stephens. AnIV; AWP; BoPe; CH; GoJo; JAWP; LiTB; OA; OxBI; PG; PoDB; UnPo (3d ed.); WBP; WHA
Crooked Sixpence, The. Mother Goose. *See* There was a crooked man . . .
Crooked Trail to Holbrook, The. *Unknown.* CoSo
Croppy Boy., The. William B. McBurney. OnYI
Croppy Boy, The. *Unknown.* AnIL; AnIV; CBEP; OxBoLi; PoFr
Cross, The. Thomas Bancroft. StJW
Cross, The. John Bowring. *See* In the Cross of Christ I Glory.
Cross, The. Charles S. Braden. ChIP
Cross, The. Pedro Calderón de la Barca, *tr. fr. Spanish by* Richard Chenevix Trench. *Fr.* La Devocion de la Cruz. CAW
(Dying Eusebio's Address to the Cross, The, *longer sel., tr. by* D. F. MacCarthy.) OuHeWo
Cross, The. William Cowper. SoP
Cross, The. Donald Earl Edwards. ChIP
Cross, The. Leon Gellert. BoAu
Cross, The. Eva Gore-Booth. ChIP; MaRV
Cross. Langston Hughes. AmNP; AnAmPo; BANP; IDB; LiTM (1970 ed.); PoLF; PoNe

Cross, The. Sidney Lanier. *See* Ballad of Trees and the Master, A.
Cross, The. Charles N. Pace. BePJ; BLRP; SoP
Cross, The. Shelley. BoC
Cross, The. Allen Tate. AP; AWP; MAP; MoAmPo; MoVE; OxBA; PoDB
Cross, The. Ruby Weyburn Tobias. ChIP
Cross, The. Shirley Dillon Waite. ChIP; OQP
Cross a Crown, The. Amos R. Wells. SoP
Cross and the Crown, The. Thomas Kelly. MaRV
(Victor, The.) FaChP
Cross and the Tomb, The. Annie Johnson Flint. STF
Cross and the Tree, The. William L. Stidger. ChIP; PGD
Cross and Throne. Horatius Bonar. BePJ
Cross at the Crossways, The. John Oxenham. MaRV
Cross at the morning. Once and Upon. Madeline Gleason. NeAP
Cross I bore seemed heavy, and, The. Behold, My Cross Was Gone! Alice Mortenson. BePJ
Cross in God's own service I have ta'en, The. The Pilgrimage. Albrecht von Johannsdorf. LiTW
Cross is such a simple thing, The. The Cross. Charles N. Pace. BePJ; BLRP; SoP
Cross it standeth fast, The. Cross and Throne. Horatius Bonar. BePJ
Cross leaves marks the tree we fancy, A. An Owl Is an Only Bird of Poetry. Robert Duncan. NeAP
Cross Makers. Clyde McGee. MaRV
(Free Enterprise.) ChIP
Cross of Calvary, The. The Key. John Oxenham. BePJ
Cross of Gold, The. David Gray. AA
Cross of Snow, The. Longfellow. AmePo; AmP; AmPP; AnAmPo; AP; CoBA; FaPL; MAmP; MaRV; MWA-1; OxBA
Cross of the angels, The. Prayer before Going to Sleep. *Unknown.* JKCP (1926 ed.)
Cross of the Dumb, The. "Fiona Macleod." ChrBoLe
Cross on a Hill, A. Carl S. Weist. BePJ
(Symbol of Hope.) ChIP
Cross, A—One staggering beneath the weight. There Was a Garden. Marie Barton. OQP
Cross-patch,/ Draw the latch. Mother Goose. BrR; ChTr; EvOK; OTPC; OxNR; PPL; SAS; SiTL
Cross Section of a Landscape. Donald Davidson. MAP; MoAmPo (1942 ed.)
Cross Speaks, The. *Unknown.* *Fr.* The Dream of the Rood. PoLi
Cross stands firm, The; no blast of time. The Same Forever. Horatius Bonar. BePJ
Cross Talk. Cyril Cusack. NYTB
Cross, A? That? The Cross. Charles S. Braden. ChIP
Cross that bears my Master slain, The. Interpretation. Sheldon Shepard. ChIP
Cross, the Cross, The. Tortoise Shell. D. H. Lawrence. BoPe; CMoP; ExPo
Cross, the Cross is tainted, The! O most Just. The Temptation of Saint Anthony. Arthur Symons. BrPo
Cross, the icon, The. The Paradox. Francesca Yetunde Pereira. PBA
Cross they raised against the rain, The. The Suffering God. Raymond Kresensky. ChIP
Cross Ties. X. J. Kennedy. CoPo
Cross Was His Own, The. *Unknown.* BePJ; BLPA, *abr.*; MaRV
("Borrowed.") BLRP
Cross was such an ugly thing, The. Transformation. Lon Woodrum. SoP
Cross-bars and posts, the echo of distant bells. Football Field; Evening. J. A. R. McKellar. NeLNL
Crossbow wanted a child. The Children's Crusade. Philip Levine. NaP
Crosse, The. John Donne. MaMe
Crosse, The. George Herbert. AnAnS-1; MaMe; MeP
Crosse of Jesu Christ be ever oure spede. An A. B. C. of Devotion. *Unknown.* MeEL
Crossed Apple, The. Louise Bogan. NP
Crossed bridges before I got to them. I, a Justified Sinner. Arnold Price. NYTB
Crossed Legs. Charles Johnson. WSL
Crossed Swords, The. Nathaniel Langdon Frothingham. AA
Crossed the River. James Koller. FRC
Crosses, The. Besmilr Brigham. ThO
Crosses. Mabel Hicks. PEDC
Crossing, The. Paul Blackburn. NYBP
Crossing. Philip Booth. AmFN
Crossing a Creek. Herbert Clark Johnson. PoNe
Crossing Alone the Nighted Ferry. A. E. Housman. ChMP; GTBS-P; MaPo (1969 ed.)
Crossing at Fredericksburg, The. George Henry Boker. PAH
Crossing Boston Common. Louise Dyer Harris. WhC, *st.* 1
Crossing Brooklyn Ferry. Walt Whitman. AmePo; AmPP; AP; ATP; CABA; CABL; CoBA; DiPo; LiTA; MAmP; MWA-1; PoIE
Sels.
"Ah, what can be more stately." AA
"It avails not, time nor place—distance avails not." NeMA
Crossing Kansas by Train. Donald Justice. NYBP
Crossing the Alps ("The only track now visible was one"). Wordsworth. *Fr.* The Prelude, VI. CoBE
Crossing the Bar. Gavin Ewart. CBV
Crossing the Bar. Tennyson. BEL; BLRP; BoLiVe; CABA; CBV; DD; DiPo; EnL; EnLi-2; EnLit; EPN; EtS; FaBoEn; FaBV; FaFP; FaPL; FiP; GTBS-W; GTSL; HBV; HBVY; ILP; InP; LiTB; LiTG; MaRV; MaVP; MBW-2; MCCG; NeHB; NoP; OAEP; OBEV (new ed.); OBNC; OBVV; OHFP; OQP; OTD; OTPC (1946 ed.); OuHeWo; PG (1945 ed.); PoAn; PoE; PoLF; PoPo; PoRA; PoVP; ShBV-3; SoP; StJW; TIHL; TOP; TreF; TrGrPo; TRV; TSW; UnPo (1st ed.); VA; ViBoPo; ViPo; ViPP; VP; WBLP; WGRP; WHA; YAT
"Sunset and evening star," *sel., st.* 1 YT
Crossing the Blackwater. Robert Dwyer Joyce. VA
Crossing the border, the first city I came to. Three Cities. George Rostrevor Hamilton. POTE
Crossing the County Line. Elizabeth Randall-Mills. GoYe
Crossing the Mountain Alone. Princess Daihaku, *tr. fr. Japanese by* Arthur Waley. *Fr.* Manyo Shu. WoL
("How will you manage.") AWP; JAWP; WBP
Crossing the Park. Howard Moss. NYBP
Crossing the Plains. Joaquin Miller. AA; AmePo; AmLP; AmPP (3d ed.); AnAmPo; GN; MAP; MoAmPo (1942 ed.); PaA
Crossing the Plains. John A. Stone. ABF; SGR, *with music.*
Crossing the shallow holdings high above sea. The Hungry Grass. Donagh MacDonagh. NeIP; OxBI
Crossing the Straits. Charles Brasch. AnNZ
Crossing the street. The Broken Home. James Merrill. NYBP
Crossing the Tropics. Herman Melville. AA
Crossing the uplands of time. The Quest. Grace Goodhue Coolidge. OTD
Crossing there under the trees with leaden pace. False Enchantment. Jean Starr Untermeyer. MoAmPo (1950 ed.)
Crossroads. Miguel Otero Silva, *tr. fr. Spanish by* Donald Devenish Walsh. WoL
Crossroads, The. Catherine Parmenter. PEDC
Crossroads, The. E. Randall. SoP
Crotalus. Bret Harte. AA; PFY
Crotalus Rex. Brewster Ghiselin. MoVE
Crotchet Castle, *sels.* Thomas Love Peacock.
"After careful meditation," *fr. ch.* 6. ALV
Chorus: "If I drink water while this doth last," *fr. ch.* 6. ViBoPo
In the Days of Old, *fr. ch.* 18. HBV
Greatness ("He took castle and towns"). OtMeF
Priest and the Mulberry Tree, The, *fr. ch.* 18. BoTP; GN; OnMSP; OTPC; RIS; StPo
Crouched down by a roadside windbreak. Listening to the Mourners. James Wright. FRC
Crouched [*or* Crouch'd] on the pavement, close by Belgrave Square. West London. Matthew Arnold. EPN; MCCG; OAEP; PoFr; PoPo; PoVP; Sonn
Crow, The. Mrs. Alexander. BoTP; OTPC (1946 ed.); PCH
Crow, A. Basho, *tr. fr. Japanese by* H. G. Henderson. OnPM
Crow, The. William Canton. GoTP; HBV
Crow, The. John Clare. WePo
Crow, The. P. K. Page. WHW
Crow, The. Henry David Thoreau. BiS
Crow. Mark Van Doren. OA
Crow and Pie. *Unknown.* ESPB
Crow and the Crane, The. *Unknown.* *See* Carnal and the Crane, The.
Crow and the Fox, The. La Fontaine, *tr. fr. French by* Sir Edward Marsh. AWP; JAWP; MaC; WBP

Crow and the Nighthawk, The. Watson Kirkconnell. CaP
Crow Country. Kenneth Slessor. BoAV
Crow, in pulpit lone and tall. In the Pauper's Turnip-Field. Herman Melville. PoEL-5
Crow lies over the cornfield, The. Ballad in Blonde Hair Foretold. Robert Bagg. NePoAm-2
Crow-Marble Whores of Paris, The. James Schevill. NMP
Crow sat perched upon an oak, A. The Crow and the Fox. La Fontaine. AWP; JAWP; MaC; WBP
Crow, The—the crow! the great black crow! The Great Black Crow. Philip James Bailey. BOHV
Crow will tumble up and down, The. Crows in Spring. John Clare. EnRP
Crowd, The. Irene McKeighan. ChIP; MaRV
Crowd advances like a sounding sea, The. Song of the General Strike. Mario Bravo. PoFr
Crowd at the Ball Game, The. William Carlos Williams. OxBA
(At the Ball Game.) CMoP; ExPo
Crowd back the hills and give me room. Soul Lifted. Albert Durrant Watson. CaP
Crowd is thrilled to see a fighter downed, The. He Falls. William A. Donaghy. *Fr.* The Stations of the Cross. JKCP (1955 ed.)
Crowd of beauteous Quinta prate, The. The Comparison. Catullus. OnPM
Crowd was gathering beneath the tent, A. The Clown. Margaret E. Bruner. PoToHe
Crowd was thronging my doorstep, A. Christ the Carpenter. Leslie L. Haskin. BePJ
Crowded Out. Florence White Willett. STF
Crowded Ways of Life. Walter J. Gresham. BLPA
Crowdieknow. "Hugh MacDiarmid." OxBS
Crowdpleasers/ coming down the aisles. Goosepimples. Coleman Barks. PV
Crowing of the Red Cock, The. Emma Lazarus. AA; HBV
Crown Him with Many Crowns. Matthew Bridges. MaRV
(Seraphs' Song, The.) SoP
Crown o' the earth doth melt, The. Shakespeare. *Fr.* Antony and Cleopatra, IV, xv. MemP
Crown of Age. "M. H." SoP
Crown of Days. *Unknown, tr. fr. Hebrew by* Herbert Loewe. TrJP
Crown of empire, The—must thou yield it now? I Have Overcome the World [*or* World Conqueror]. Laura Simmons. ChIP; MaRV
Crown of ivy, A! I submit my head. On Receiving a Crown of Ivy from the Same (Keats). Leigh Hunt. Sonn
Crown of thorns, A. Lord, Is It I? John Philo Trowbridge. SoP
Crown of thorns men gave to Christ, A. The Earth Worshiped! Catherine Cate Coblentz. ChIP
Crown Our Washington. Hezekiah Butterworth. DD; HH; PEDC; PoRL
Crown the Year. Frances Ridley Havergal. SoP
Crown we our heroes with a holier wreath. Lincoln. George Henry Boker. *Fr.* Our Heroic Times. DD; MC; OHIP
Crown'd with the sickle, and the wheaten sheaf. Autumn. James Thomson. *Fr.* The Seasons. CEP
Crowned. Amy Lowell. HBV
Crowned, girdled, garbed and shod with light and fire. Christopher Marlowe. Swinburne. *Fr.* Sonnets on English Dramatic Poets. BEL; PoVP; Sonn; TOP; TrGrPo
Crowned or Crucified. *Unknown.* SoP
Crowned Poet, A. Anne Reeve Aldrich. AA
Crowned with flowers, I saw fair Amarillis. *Unknown.* EnLoPo; SiCE
Crowning a bluff where gleams the lake below. Pontoosuce. Herman Melville. MAmP
Crowning Gift, The. Gladys Cromwell. HBMV; MAP; NP
Crowning of Arthur, The. Charles Williams. FaBoMo
Crowning of Dreaming John, The. John Drinkwater. HBMV
Crowning Wonder, The. John Oxenham. StJW
Crowns. Louise Upham Brooks. ChIP
Crowns, The. John Freeman. CH
Crows, The. Louise Bogan. YT
Crows, The. David McCord. MAP; MoAmPo; PDV; TiPo (1959 ed.)
Crows. Lizette Woodworth Reese. MAP; MoAmPo (1942 ed.)
Crows, The. *Unknown.* RIS
("On the first of March.") OxNR
Crows are come again to pick my eyes, The. Soliloquy on Death. F. K. Fiawoo. PBA
Crows are flying above the foyer of summer, The. The Novel. Wallace Stevens. ReMP
Crows crowd croaking overhead. Summer Evening. John Clare. BoTP
Crow's harsh dissyllables, A. A Valediction. Melvin Walker La Follette. CoPo
Crows in Spring. John Clare. EnRP
Crows in the Garden, *with music. Unknown.* ABF
Crow's Nest. Richard F. Armknecht. GoYe
Crucified. Patrick Dacus Moreland. StJW
Crucified to the World. *Unknown.* MeEL
Crucifix, The. Alphonse de Lamartine, *tr. fr. French by* Henry Logan Stuart. CAW
Crucifix, The. Robert Lowell. NoP
Crucifix. Elder Olson. MoRP
Crucifix. Edith Lovejoy Pierce. ChIP
Crucifix, The. Pushkin, *tr. fr. Russian by* Frances Cornford *and* E. P. Salaman. LiTW
Crucifix, The. Sir Herbert Read. BrPo
Crucifix, A. Paul Verlaine, *tr. fr. French by* John Gray. *Fr.* Amour. SyP
Crucifixion. Waring Cuney. BANP; GoSl
Crucifixion. Eva Gore-Booth. MaRV; WGRP
Crucifixion. Hugh O. Isbell. ChIP; PGD
Crucifixion, The. John W. Lynch. JKCP (1955 ed.)
Crucifixion. Earl Marlatt. ChIP
Crucifixion, The. Alice Meynell. OxBoCh; PoLi
Crucifixion, The. Henry Hart Milman. BePJ
Crucifixion. Mrs. Roy L. Peifer. STF
Crucifixion. Frederick George Scott. ChIP MaRV; OQP
Crucifixion, The. G. A. Studdert-Kennedy. *See* Indifference.
Crucifixion, The ("At the cry of the first bird"). *Unknown, tr. fr. Middle Irish by* Kuno Meyer. OxBI; OnYI, *tr. by* Howard Mumford Jones
Crucifixion, The ("I sike when I singe"). *Unknown.* MeEL
Crucifixion ("They [*or* Dey] crucified my Lord"). *Unknown.* BoAN-1, *with music*; MaRV; TrGrPo
Crucifixion. Carl S. Weist. ChIP
Crucifixion and the Harrowing of Hell, The. William Langland, *tr. fr. Middle English. Fr.* The Vision of Piers Plowman. MeEV
Crucifixion of Noel, The. Marsden Hartley. AnAmPo
Crucifixion to the World, by the Cross of Christ. Isaac Watts. *See* When I Survey the Wond'rous Cross.
Crucifixus pro Nobis. Patrick Carey. SeCL
(Hymn: Crucifixus pro Nobis.) OxBoCh
Cruciform. Winifred Welles. LO; NYBP; POTE
Crucifying. John Donne. AnAnS-1; MaMe; MeP; OBS; Sonn
Crude Foyer. Wallace Stevens. LiTM (rev. ed.); NePA
Cruel, and fair! when this soft down. To Ligurinus. Horace. Odes, IV, 10. CavP
Cruel Brother, The, *sel.* Sir William Davenant.
What Is Past, *fr.* V, i. TrGrPo
Cruel Brother, The. *Unknown.* BaBo (A *and* B *vers.*); EnLit; ESPB (A *and* B *vers.*); LoEn; OBB; OxBB; TOP; ViBoFo; YAT
Cruel Clever Cat. Geoffrey Taylor. ChTr; LiTM; SiTL
Cruel flames have entirely devoured the house in which I was born, The. Prose Poem: House in the Heart. Judith Gautier. OnPM
Cruel Mistress, The. William Hammond. *See* Tell Me, O Love.
Cruel Moon, The. Robert Graves. TSW
Cruel Mother, The (*diff. versions*). *Unknown.* BaBo; BFSS, *with music*; CBEP; ESPB; NoP; OBB; OxBB; ViBoFo
(Fine Flowers in the Valley.) FosPo
(Two Little Babes, *diff. vers. with music.*) BFSS
Cruel Naughty Boy, The. *Unknown.* BBGG
(Naughty Darkey Boy, The.) BOHV
Cruel Sister, The. *Unknown. See* Two Sisters, The.
Cruel Solstice, The. Sidney Keyes. POTE
Cruel You Be. George Puttenham. ElL
Cruell Clarinda tell me why. *Unknown.* SeCSL
Cruell Maid, The. Robert Herrick. CavP
Cruell Mistris, A. Thomas Carew. AnAnS-2
Cruelly, Love. E. E. Cummings. CLwM
Cruelty. Margaret E. Bruner. CIV

Cruelty has a human heart. A Divine Image. Blake. AtBAP; ChTr; NoP; OBNC; PoeP; PoIE
Cruise of the *Fair American,* The. *Unknown.* PAH
Cruise of the *Monitor,* The. George Henry Boker. MC; PAH; ThLM
Cruise of the P. C., The. *Unknown.* NA
Cruisers, destroyers, carriers align. Victory Parade. George Edward Hoffman. PGD
Cruiskeen Lawn, The. *Unknown.* HBV; OnYI
Crumb for Robin. Emily Dickinson. *See* If I shouldn't be alive.
Crumbling [*or* Crumpling] a pyramid, humbling a rose. The Dust. Nathalia Crane. MAP; NeMA
Crumbling centuries are thrust, The. The Jewels. Austin Clarke. MoAB
Crumblin is not an instant's act. Emily Dickinson. AmPP (5th ed.); AP; DiPo
Crumbs. Walter de la Mare. SoPo
Crumbs or the Loaf. Robinson Jeffers. CMoP
Crumbs to the Birds. Charles *and* Mary Lamb. OTPC
Crumpling a pyramid, humbling a rose. *See* Crumbling a pyramid . . .
Crusade. Hilaire Belloc. GoBC
Crusade, The. Rinaldo d'Aquino, *tr. fr. Italian by* "Moira O'Neill." CAW
Crusade, The. Thomas Warton, the Younger. EiPP
Crusader, The. Dorothy Parker. ShM
Crusader Chorus. Charles Kingsley. *Fr.* The Saint's Tragedy. FOL, *abr.*; VA
Crusaders. Elizabeth Waddell. ChIP; OQP
Crusaders Behold Jerusalem, The. Tasso. *See* Crusaders Reach Jerusalem, The.
Crusader's Hymn. *Unknown.* *See* Fairest Lord Jesus.
Crusaders Reach Jerusalem, The. Tasso, *tr. fr. Italian by* Edward Fairfax. *Fr.* Jerusalem Delivered, III. EnLi-1
(Crusaders Behold Jerusalem, The, *tr. by* J. H. Wiffen.) CAW
Crusaders' Song. *Unknown,* *tr. fr. French by* Walter Clifford Meller. CAW
Cruse, The. Louise Townsend Nicholl. NYBP
Crushed by the waves upon the crag was I. Sea Dirge. Archias of Byzantium. AWP
Crushed Fender. Rosa Zagnoni Marinoni. MaRV; PoToHe (1941 ed.)
Crushing of a thousand petals, Lord, The. The Poet Prays. Grace Noll Crowell. TrPWD
Crusoe. Floris Clark McLaren. PeCV; TwCaPo
Crust of Bread, The. *Unknown.* HBV; HBVY; OTPC (1923 ed.)
Crust of bread and a corner to sleep in, A. Life. Paul Laurence Dunbar. AmNP; CDC
Crustaceans. Roy Fuller. NeBP; ToPo
Crusts. Walter Shea. ChIP
Crusty Critics. George Crabbe. *Fr.* The Library. OBEC
Cry, A. Francesco Bianco. CLwM
Cry, A. Herbert Edwin Clarke. VA
Cry, The. Federico García Lorca, *tr. fr. Spanish by* Eleanor L. Turnbull. OnPM
Cry, a greenish hollow undulation, A. High Dive. William Empson. AtBAP
Cry-baby, cry. *Unknown.* GoTP
Cry Faugh! Robert Graves. CoBMV; MoBrPo (1962 ed.)
Cry for a Dead Soldier. Mary L. Inman. NYTB
Cry for Light, A. *Unknown.* BLRP
Cry from the Battlefield. Robert Menth. ISi
Cry from the Canadian Hills, A. Lilian Leveridge. BLPA
Cry from the Ghetto, A. Morris Rosenfeld, *tr. fr. Yiddish by* Charles Weber Linn. TrJP
Cry from the green-grained sticks of the fire, A. Surview. Thomas Hardy. ChMP; LO
Cry from the Shore, A. Ellen Mackay Hutchinson Cortissoz. AA
Cry in Distress, A ("My God, my God, why hast thou forsaken me?"). Psalms, XXII, Bible, *O.T.* TrGrPo
Cry The, is: "Back to God!" Without respite. The Homeward Journey. L. Aaronson. FaBoTw; TrJP
Cry is up in England, which doth ring, A. Elizabeth Barrett Browning. *Fr.* Casa Guidi Windows, II. PoVP
Cry Kismet! and take heart. Eros is gone. Retractions, XII. James Branch Cabell. HBMV
Cry of a Dreamer, The. John Boyle O'Reilly. *See* Cry of the Dreamer, The.
Cry of Faith, A. M. Allen Gibson. SoP
Cry of man's anguish went up to God, The. Lord, Take Away Pain [*or* Pain]. *Unknown.* MaRV; OQP
Cry of ruin strides the sky, A. The Traitors. Morton Dauwen Zabel. NP
Cry of the Age, The. Hamlin Garland. OQP; WGRP
Cry of the Children, The. Elizabeth Barrett Browning. BEL; EnLi-2; HBV; MaRV, *much abr.*; OAEP; PoFr, *sl. abr.*; PoVP; VA; ViBoPo; ViPo
"They look up with their pale and sunken faces," *sel.* NBM
Cry of the cicada, The. Hokku. Basho. InP
Cry of the Dreamer, The. John Boyle O'Reilly. OnYI
(Cry of a Dreamer, The.) BLPA; NeHB; TreFS
Cry of the Daughter of My People, The. Jeremiah, VIII: 18-23, Bible, *O.T.* TrJP
Cry of the Human, The. Elizabeth Barrett Browning. PoVP
Convinced by Sorrow, *sel.* BLRP; OQP; WBLP
("'There is no God,' the foolish saith.") MaRV
Cry of the Lovelorn, The. William E. Aytoun *and* Sir Theodore Martin. *See* Lay of the Love-lorn, The.
Cry of the People. John G. Neihardt. MAP; PoFr
Cry of the Peoples, The. Alter Brody. TrJP
Cry of the Stag. Emperor Jomei, *tr. fr. Japanese by* Ishii *and* Obata. OnPM
Cry of those being eaten by America, The. Those Being Eaten by America. Robert Bly. CoAP; FRC; NaP
Cry to Arms, A. Henry Timrod. PAH
Cry to Mary, A. St. Godric. MeEL
Cry to Music, A. John Masefield. MuSP
Cryderville Jail, The, *with music.* *Unknown,* *add. sts. by* C. E. Scoggins. ABF
(Po' Boy, *frag.*) ABF
Cryer, The. Michael Drayton. *See* Crier, The.
"Crying crane and wheeling crows." The Answer. Orrick Johns. NP
Crying of Water, The. Arthur Symons. AnEnPo; MoBrPo
Cryptic Streets, The. Abu-l-Ala al-Maarri, *tr. fr. Arabic by* Ameen Rihani. LiTW
Crystal, The. George Barker. LiTM; OBMV; POTE
Crystal, The. Titus Munson Coan. AA
Crystal, The. Sidney Lanier. AmePo; AmP
Sels.
Crystal Christ, The. MaRV
("But Thee, but Thee, O sovereign Seer of Time.") BePJ; ChIP; TrPWD
"Oh, what amiss may I forgive in Thee." TRV
Crystal and silver. The Islands of the Ever Living. *Unknown,* *tr. fr. Irish by* Padraic Colum. AnIV
Crystal Anniversary. Philip Appleman. MeWo
Crystal Cabinet, The. Blake. CH; DiPo; ERoP-1; FaBoCh; FosPo; LoGBV; NCEP; OBNC; OBRV; PIA; PoEL-4
Crystal Christ, The. Sidney Lanier. *Fr.* The Crystal. MaRV
("But Thee, but Thee, O sovereign Seer of Time.") BePJ; ChIP; TrPWD
Crystal Gazer, The. Sara Teasdale. MAP; MoAmPo; NeMA
Crystal mirror, I, A. Submission. Jessie E. Williams. OQP
Crystal Night. Denise Levertov. *Fr.* During the Eichmann Trial. NMP
Crystal Palace, The. John Davidson. PeVV
Crystal Palace, The. Thackeray. BoHV; InMe
(Mr. Molony's Account of the Crystal Palace.) PeVV
Crystal parting the meads. The River in the Meadows. Léonie Adams. AnAmPo; MAP; MoAB; MoAmPo; NP
Crystal Skull, The. Kathleen Raine. CMoP; FaBoMo; NeBP
Cuatro Palomitas Blancas, *with music.* *Unknown,* *tr. fr. Spanish.* ABF
Cuba. Harvey Rice. PAH
Cuba. Edmund Clarence Stedman. PAH
Cuba, disheveled, naked to the waist. On a Monument to Marti. Walter Adolphe Roberts. PoNe; TTY
Cuba Libre. Joaquin Miller. MC; PAH; ThLM
Cuba to Columbia. Will Carleton. MC; PAH
Cuban Voyage. Paul Engle. ReMP
Cubbyhole I live in is a box, The. Out of Superstition. Boris Pasternak. LiTW
Cubes. Mary Fullerton. PoAu-1
Cubic Triolet, A. *Unknown.* PV
Cubism. Hy Sobiloff. SiTL
Cubs of bears a living lump appear, The. The Phoenix Selfborn. Ovid, *tr. by* Dryden. *Fr.* Metamorphoses, XV. ChTr

Cucaracha, La (The Cockroach), *with music.* *Unknown,* *tr. fr. Spanish.* AS; TrAS
Cuccu Song. *Unknown.* *See* Sumer Is Icumen In.
Cuchulain Comforted. W. B. Yeats. CMoP; LiTG; LiTM (rev. ed.)
Cuchulain's Fight with the Sea. W. B. Yeats. AnIL; PoVP
(Death of Cuchulain, The.) ChTr; GoTL; ViPo (1926 ed.)
Cuchullain's Lament over Fardiad. *Unknown,* *tr. fr. Middle Irish by* George Sigerson. *Fr.* The Combat of Ferdiad and Cuchulain. AnIV
(Cuchulain's Lament for Ferdiad.) AnIL
Cuckoo! Hilaire Belloc. MoVE
Cuckoo, The. Patrick Reginald Chalmers. CenHV
Cuckoo, The. Rose Fyleman. UTS
Cuckoo, The. Gerard Manley Hopkins. MoAB; MoBrPo
(Fragment: "Repeat that, repeat.") ELU
(Repeat That, Repeat.) FlW
Cuckoo, The. Kodo, *tr. fr. Japanese by* Kenneth Yasuda. FlW
Cuckoo, The. Frederick Locker-Lampson. HBV
Cuckoo, The. Edward Thomas. BrPo
Cuckoo, The ("The cuckoo's a bonny [*or* fine] Bird"). *Unknown.* ChTr; RIS
(Cuckoo Is a Fine Bird, The.) OTPC (1923 ed.)
Cuckoo, The ("In April/ Come he will"). *Unknown.* BoTP
("Cuckoo, cuckoo,/ What do you do?" *sl. diff.*) RIS
Cuckoo ("In former days my father and mother"). *Unknown,* *tr. fr. Anglo-Saxon by* Charles W. Kennedy. *Fr.* Riddles. AnOE
Cuckoo, The ("O meeting is a pleasure, but parting is grief"). *Unknown.* CBEP
Cuckoo. *Unknown.* *See* Sumer Is Icumen In.
Cuckoo. Andrew Young. ChTr
Cuckoo and the Nightingale, The. Thomas Clanvowe, *tr. fr. Middle English by* Wordsworth. MeEV
Cuckoo! calls the cuckoo. The Captives. *Unknown.* PoFr
Cuckoo Clock, The. John Farrar. GFA
Cuckoo clock on the nursery wall, The. Ticking Clocks. Rachel Field. TiPo (1959 ed.)
Cuckoo comes in April, The. *Unknown.* OxNR
"Cuckoo! The," cried my child, the while I slept. The Oo-cuck. Justin Richardson. FiBHP
Cuckoo, cuckoo!/ In April skies were blue. Cuckoo Song. Katharine Tynan. OnYI
Cuckoo, cuckoo!/ Is it thy double note I hear. Cuckoo. Andrew Young. ChTr
Cuckoo, cuckoo,/ What do you do? *Unknown.* OxNR; RIS
Cuckoo, cuckoo, cherry tree. *Unknown.* OnNR
Cuckoo in the clock by day, The. The Cuckoo Clock. John Farrar. GFA
Cuckoo in the Pear-Tree. William Brighty Rands. BiS
Cuckoo Is a Fine Bird, The. *Unknown.* *See* Cuckoo, The.
Cuckoo is a merry bird, The. *Unknown.* OxNR
Cuckoo is a tell-tale, The. The Cuckoo. Rose Fyleman. UTS
Cuckoo sat in the old pear-tree, The. Cuckoo in the Pear-Tree. William Brighty Rands. BiS
Cuckoo Song. Katharine Tynan. OnYI
Cuckoo Song. *Unknown.* *See* Sumer Is Icumen In.
Cuckoo-throb, the heartbeat of the Spring, The. Ardour and Memory. Dante Gabriel Rossetti. The House of Life, LXIV. MaVP; PoVP; ViPo
Cuckoo Waltz, *with music.* *Unknown.* AS
Cuckoo, when the lambkins bleat, The. The Cuckoo. Patrick Reginald Chalmers. CenHV
Cuckoos. Andrew Young. ChTr; MoPW
Cuckoo's [*or* cuckoo is] a bonny [*or* fine] bird, The. The Cuckoo. *Unknown.* ChTr; OTPC (1923 ed.); RIS
Cuckoo's double note, The. Wiltshire Downs. Andrew Young. ChMP; GTBS-D; GTBS-P
Cuckoo's Palace. William Brighty Rands. BiS
Cuckoo's Song, The. Josui, *tr. fr. Japanese by* William N. Porter. MPB
Cuddle Doon. Alexander Anderson. GN; HBV; OHFP; VA
Cuddle Down, Dolly. Kate Douglas Wiggin. PPL
Cuddy [*or* Cuddie], for shame hold up thy heavy head. October [*or* The Contempt of Poetry]. Spenser. *Fr.* The Shepheardes Calender. EnPo; OBSC; PP; ReEn; ReIE; SiCE
Cudgelled but Contented Cuckold, The. La Fontaine. UnTE
Cui Bono? Thomas Carlyle. HBV; OBRV; WGRP
Cuisine Bourgeoise. Wallace Stevens. LiTA
Cul-de-Sac, The. "Jan Struther." LO
Culbin Sands. Andrew Young. GTBS-P; OxBS
Cullen ("Cullen renounced his cradle at fifteen"). P. K. Page. CaP
Culloden and After. Iain Crichton Smith. OxBS
Culprit, The. A. E. Housman. PG (1955 ed.); VP
Culprit Fay, The, *sels.* Joseph Rodman Drake.
Assembling of the Fays, The. GN
Elfin Song. AA; PoMS
Fairy Dawn. GN
Fairy in Armor, A. FaPON; GaP; GFA; OTPC; PRWS
(Elfin Knight, An.) BoTP
Fay's Crime, The. GN
Fay's Sentence, The. GN
First Quest, The. AA
(Fay's Departure, The, *shorter sel.*) GN
Second Quest, The. AA
"Soft and pale is the moony beam. PFY
Throne of the Lily-King, The. GN
Cultural Exchange. Langston Hughes. PoNe (1970 ed.)
Cultural Notes. Kenneth Fearing. CMoP
Cultural Presupposition, The. W. H. Auden. CABA; MaPo
(Culture.) MoPW
Culture. Emerson. AmePo
Culture in the Slums. W. E. Henley. BOHV; CenHV; HBV; InMe
Cultured gentleman, mature, congenial, refined. Personal. Samuel Yellen. NYBP
Cultured Girl Again, The. Ben King. FiBHP
Cum Invocarem. Psalms, IV, Bible, *O.T.,* *tr. by* Thomas Sternhold. SiCE
Cum, listen w'ile yore Unkel sings. 'Ittle Touzle Head. Ray Garfield Dandridge. BANP
Cumberbunee, The. Paul West. BOHV; NA
Cumberland, The. Longfellow. AA; AnNE; EtS; MC; PaA; PAH; PAP
Cumberland, The. Herman Melville. PAH
Cumberland Gap. *Unknown.* ABF; AmFN
Cumberland's Crew, The, *with music.* *Unknown.* ShS
Cummerbund, The. Edward Lear. CenHV
Cumnor Hall. William Julius Mickle. BeLS; CEP; OBEC; OxBB
"Dews of summer night did fall, The," *sel.* ViBoPo
Cun-ne-wa-bum—"one who looks on stars." Portrait of a Cree. "Katherine Hale." CaP
Cunning arts man, The/ Faltered not in a line. John Ford. *Fr.* The Lover's Melancholy. MyFE
Cunning Clerk, The. *Unknown.* OxBB
Cunning Cobbler Done Over, The. *Unknown.* CoMu
Cunning hand that carved this face, The. On an Intaglio Head of Minerva. Thomas Bailey Aldrich. HBV
Cunning, wise, cautious, folly is, by which. Upon the Most Useful Knowledge, Craft or Cunning, Which Is More Wisdom, as 'Tis Less Wit. William Wycherley. SeCV-2
Cup, The. Martha Snell Nicholson. SoP
Cup, The. John Oldham, *after the Greek of* Anacreon. AWP; PeRV
Cup, The. Frederick T. Roberts. ChIP
Cup, The. John Townsend Trowbridge. HBV
"Cup for hope! A," she said. Three Seasons. Christina Rossetti. CBV; HBV
Cup I sing is a cup of gold, The. The Cup. John Townsend Trowbridge. HBV
Cup in hand, I can enjoy, A. Snow. Munetake. OnPM
Cup of Blessing, The. Charles Wesley. BePJ
Cup of Happiness, The. Gilbert Thomas. MaRV; TrPWD
Cup of life is not so shallow, The. Good Hope. Emerson. OnPM
Cup of O'Hara, The. Turlough Carolan, *tr. fr. Modern Irish by* Sir Samuel Ferguson. OnYI
(When Kian O'Hara's Cup Was Passed to Turlough O'Carolan.) AnIV
Cupboard, The. Walter de la Mare. BrR; FaPON; PCH; PoRh; SoPo; TiPo
Cupid. Blake. BOHV
Cupid. Ben Jonson. *See* Beauties, Have Ye Seen This Toy.
Cupid. Sir Philip Sidney. *Fr.* Arcadia. SiPS
Cupid. *Unknown.* ElL
Cupid Abroad Was Lated. Robert Greene. *Fr.* Greene's Orpharion. TuPP
Cupid and Campaspe. John Lyly. *See* Apelles' Song.
Cupid and Death, *sels.* James Shirley.

Cupid (continued)
Love's Victories. GoBC
Victorious Men of Earth. CBEP; OBS; TrGrPo
(Death, the Conqueror.) GoBC
(Death's Emissaries.) LoBV
(Death's Subtle Ways.) HBV
(Last Conqueror, The.) GTBS; GTBS-D; GTBS-P; GTBS-W; GTSE; GTSL
(Song: "Victorious men of Earth, no more.") FaBoEn; SeCL
("Victorious men of earth, no more.") TuPP
Cupid and My Campaspe. John Lyly. *See* Apelles' Song.
Cupid and Venus. Mark Alexander Boyd. *See* Sonnet: "Fra bank to bank, fra wood to wood, I rin.
Cupid, as he lay among. The Wounded Cupid. Robert Herrick. AWP
Cupid, because thou shin'st in Stella's eyes. Astrophel and Stella, XII. Sir Philip Sidney. FCP; ReEn; SiPS
Cupid, beware, there'll come a day. Warning to Cupid. *Unknown.* UnTE
Cupid blushes to behold. *Unknown.* SeCSL
Cupid did cry, his mother chid him so. The Compliment. William Habington. ACP
Cupid Drowned. Leigh Hunt, *after the Greek of* Anacreon. HBV
Cupid, dumb idol, peevish saint of love. Idea, XXVI. Michael Drayton. EnRePo
Cupid, I hate thee, which I'd have thee know. Idea, XLVIII. Michael Drayton. LO
Cupid, I Scorn to Beg the Art. Sir Francis Fane. *Fr.* Love in the Dark. SeCL; SeEP
Cupid if thou tell-tale prove. *Unknown.* SeCSL
Cupid in a Bed of Roses. *Unknown.* ElL
Cupid laid by his brand and fell asleep. Sonnets, CLIII. Shakespeare. Sonn
Cupid Mistaken. Matthew Prior. ALV; EiCL; EiCP; InMe
(Cupid's Mistaken.) ViBoPo
Cupid, My Little Boy, Come Home Again. Fulke Greville. Caelica, XXXV. AtBAP
Cupid my mistriss hart assaild. *Unknown.* SeCSL
Cupid, my pretty boy, leave off thy crying. Fulke Greville. Caelica, XXV. AtBAP
Cupid Stung ("Cupid once upon a bed.") Thomas Moore. HBV
Cupid tho' all his darts were lost. Swift. Fr. Cadenus and Vanessa. OxBI
Cupid thou art a sluggish boye. *Unknown.* SeCSL
Cupid, thou naughty boy, when thou wert loathed. Caelica, XII. Fulke Greville. EnRePo; NCEP; Sonn; TuPP
Cupid Turned Plowman. Moschus, *tr. fr. Greek by* Matthew Prior. AWP; OnPM
Cupid Ungodded. James Shirley. GoBC
Cupidon. William Jay Smith. NePoEA
Cupids Call. James Shirley. ErPo
Cupid's Curse. George Peele. *See* Fair and Fair.
Cupid's Darts. A. P. Herbert. BOHV; CenHV
Cupids in vain around them hover. After the Wedding. Henry Luttrell. *Fr.* Advice to Julia. IrPN
Cupid's Indictment. John Lyly. *Fr.* Galathea. ElL
(Song of Diana's Nymph, A: "Oyes, Oyes! if any maid.") OBSC
Cupid's Mistaken. Matthew Prior. *See* Cupid Mistaken.
Cupid's Pastime. *At. to* Francis Davison *and to* "A. W." *See* Fiction, A.
Cupid's Revenge, *sel.* Beaumont *and* Fletcher.
Lovers, Rejoice! ElL; FaBoEn
Cupids wearie of the Court. *Unknown.* SeCSL
Cupping her chin and lying there, the Bren. Defensive Position. John Manifold. MoBrPo (1950 ed.)
Cups of Illusion. Henry Bellamann. HBMV
Curate and the spinster sit, The. The Curate's Christmas Eve. Harold Monro. FaBoTw
Curate Thinks You Have No Soul, The. St. John Lucas. BLPA
Curate's Christmas Eve, The. Harold Monro. FaBoTw
Curate's Kindness, The. Thomas Hardy. CoBMV; ILP; PoVP; VP
Curb for stubborn steed. Hymn to Christ the Savior [*or* Earliest Christian Hymn]. Clement of Alexandria. CAW; WGRP
Curbstones are to balance on. What They Are For. Dorothy Aldis. SoPo
Cure, The. William Carlos Williams. ML
Cure All, The. Don L. Lee. CAD
Cure for Exhaustion, The. Piet Hein. TIHL
Cure for Fault-finding, A. Strickland W. Gillilan. *See* Watch Yourself Go By.
Cure for Poetry, A. *Unknown.* *See* Seven Wealthy Towns.
Cure for the Spleen, A. Matthew Green. *Fr.* The Spleen. OBEC
Curé in his windy gown, The. Saint Francis. John Peale Bishop. EaLo
Cure me with quietness. For Sleep, or Death. Ruth Pitter. TrPWD; WePo
Curé's Progress, The. Austin Dobson. HBV; PoVP; VA
Curfew. Longfellow. AA; MCCG; OxBA; PCD; TDP
"Cover the embers," *sel.* WaKn
Curfew bells are softly pealing. An Evening Prayer. Henry W. Frost. SoP
Curfew Must Not Ring Tonight. Rose Hartwick Thorpe. BeLS; BLPA; FaBoBe; FaPON; GSP; HBV; NeHB; PaPo; TreF; WBLP
Curfew tolls the knell of parting day, The. Elegy Written in a Country Churchyard. Thomas Gray. AnEnPo; AnFE; AtBAP; ATP; AWP; BEL; BoLiVe; CABA; CABL; CaFP; CBEP; CEP; CoBE; DiPo; EiCL; EiCP; EiPP; EnL; EnLi-2; EnLit; EnPE; EnRP; ExPo; FaBoBe; FaBoEn; FaFP; FaPL; FosPo; GN; GoTL; GTBS; GTBS-D; GTBS-P; GTBS-W; GTSE; GTSL; HBV; HBVY; HoPM; ILP; InP; InPo; JAWP; LaA; LiTB; LiTG; LoBV; MaRV; MasP; MCCG; MemP; MyFE; NeHB; NoP; OAEP; OBEC; OBEV; OHFP; OQP; OTD; OTPC; OuHeWo; PAn; PG (1945 ed.); PIA; Po; PoAn; PoE; PoEL-3; PoFS; PoIE; PoLF; PoPo; PoSa; SeCeV; ShBV-3; StP; TDP; TIHL; TOP; TreF; TrGrPo; UnPo; ViBoPo; WBLP; WBP; WHA; WoL; YAT
Curfew tolls the knell of parting day, The. If Gray Had Had to Write His Elegy in the Cemetery of Spoon River Instead of in That of Stoke Poges, *parody.* J. C. Squire. WhC
Curio, aye [*or* ay] me! Thy mistress' monkey's dead. Satire VIII. John Marston. *Fr.* The Scourge of Villainy. ReEn; ReIE
Curiosity. Harry Behn. SoPo
Curiosity, *sels.* Charles Sprague. AA
Fiction.
News, The.
Curious child, who dwelt upon a tract, A. Shells. Wordsworth. *Fr.* The Excursion, IV. BoPe; WGRP
Curious, curious Tiggady Rue. Tiggady Rue. David McCord. RIS; TiPo (1959 ed.)
Curious knot God made in Paradise, A. Upon Wedlock and Death of Children. Edward Taylor. AmPP (5th ed.); AP; NoP
Curious reticence afflicts my generation, A. The Event Itself. Hayden Carruth. WOW
Curious Something. Winifred Welles. TiPo
Curious, the ways of these folk of humble and hardy condition. Country Kisses. Arthur Joseph Munby. *Fr.* Dorothy; a Country Story. VA
Curious twists, The. Energy for a New Thang. Ernie Mkalimoto. NBP
Curious wits, seeing dull pensiveness, The. Astrophel and Stella, XXIII. Sir Philip Sidney. FCP; ReEn; SiPS
Curled in his fist, though nothing's there. Flogged Child. Joseph Joel Keith. FiSC
Curled up and sitting on her feet. L' Eau Dormante. Thomas Bailey Aldrich. HBV
Curlew's Call, A. Jane Barlow. VA
Curliest Thing, The. *Unknown.* BoTP
Curls powdered with chalk like a black roman bust. Native Working on the Aerodrome. Roy Fuller. NeBP
Curly locks! Curly locks! wilt thou be mine? Mother Goose. HBV; HBVY; OTPC; OxNR; PCH; PPL; RIS; SAS; SoPo
Current, The. James Merrill. NYBP
Currente Calamo. Arthur Hugh Clough. *Fr.* Mari Magno. LoBV
Curry odors, mustard in the kitchen. Saturday Night. Gail Dusenbery. ThO
Curse, The. Elizabeth Barrett Browning. *Fr.* A Curse for a Nation. PoVP
Curse, The. John Donne. CBEP; MaMe; OAEP; SCEP-1
Curse, The. Edna St. Vincent Millay. NP
Curse, A. Rabi'a, Daughter of Ka'b, *tr. fr. Persian by* R. A. Nicholson. LiTW

Curse, The. Shelley. *Fr.* Prometheus Unbound, I. PoFr
Curse, The. J. M. Synge. ChTr; PV; SiTL; TreFT
Curse for the Saxophone, A. Vachel Lindsay. ATP (1935 ed.)
Curse for a Nation, A., *sels.* Elizabeth Barrett Browning. PoVP
Curse, The.
Prologue.
"Curse God, and die," Job's wife advised. Hast Thou Considered Job's Wife. Esther Archibald. SoP
Curse God and Die, You Said to Me. Archibald MacLeish. *Fr.* J. B. EaLo
Curse of Cain was on the earth, The. The First Thanksgiving. Arthur Guiterman. DD
Curse of Cromwell, The. W. B. Yeats. SeCePo
Curse of Doneraile, The. Patrick O'Kelly. OnYI
Curse of Faint Praise, The. Irwin Edman. InMe
Curse of Kehama, The, *sels.* Robert Southey.
Kehama's Curse. OBNC
("I charm thy life.") LoBV; OBRV
Love Indestructible. OBNC
("They sin who tell us.") OBRV
"Stream descends on Meru Mountain, A." OBRV
"Two forms inseparable in unity." OBRV
Curse on a Closed Gate, A. James H. Cousins, *fr. the Irish.* AnIV
Curse on the Cat, A. John Skelton. *See* Cursing of the Cat, The. *Fr.* Phyllyp Sparowe.
Curse the tongue in my head. Good Night! Good Night! John Holmes. PoToHe
Curse upon Edward, The. Thomas Gray. *Fr.* The Bard. OBEV
Cursed Be the Day. Jeremiah, XX: 14-18, Bible, *O.T.* TrJP
Cursed by the gods and crowned by shame. The Wife of Loki. Lady Charlotte Elliot. VA
Curses upon this land; till plague devours. Edmond Rostand. *Fr.* The Woman of Samaria. StJW
Cursing and Blessing. "Michael Lewis," *after the Chinese. Fr.* Cherry Blossoms. UnTE
Cursing of the Cat, The. John Skelton. *Fr.* Phyllyp Sparowe. OA
(Curse on the Cat, A, *shorter sel.*) EvOK
(O Cat of Carlish Kind.) ChTr
(Vengence on Cats.) PoSa
Cursive crawl, the squared-off characters, The. Writing. Howard Nemerov. NYBP
Cursor Mundi, *sel.* *Unknown.*
Flight into Egypt, The. CoBE
Curt Addendum, A. *Unknown.* ShM
("As I am now, so you must be.") WhC
Curtain! Paul Laurence Dunbar. CenHV
Curtain, The (Old Tabor Grand Opera House). Jean Milne Gower. PoOW
Curtain. Helen Spalding. POTE
Curtain on the grouping dancers falls, The. The Music-Hall. Theodore Wratislaw. VA
Curtain Poem, The. Edwin Brock. NMP
Curtain rises on Act II, The. Act II. Katherine Davis. PoPl
Curtains are of lace, softening darkness, The. Curtains for a Spinster. Walter H. Kerr. NePoAm-2
Curtains drawn back, the door ajar. Robinson at Home. Weldon Kees. CoAP; NYBP; TwAmPo
Curtains for a Spinster. Walter H. Kerr. NePoAm-2
Curtains Now Are Drawn, The. Thomas Hardy. CMoP
Curtains of rock. Orpheus in the Underworld. David Gascoyne. FaBoTw
Curtains were half drawn, the floor was swept, The. After Death. Christina Rossetti. EnLi-2; PoVP; VA; VP
"Cusha! Cusha! Cusha!" calling. Calling the Cows Home. Jean Ingelow. *Fr.* The High Tide on the Coast of Lincolnshire (1571). ThGo
Cusha-Ma-Chree. John Philpot Curran. DD; HBV
Cushy Cow. Laura Benét. MPB; TSW
Cushy cow bonny, let down thy milk. Mother Goose. BoChLi; OxNR; PPL; SAS; StVeCh
Cushy Cow has curly horns. Cushy Cow. Laura Benét. MPB; TSW
Custer. Edmund Clarence Stedman. PAH
Custer's Last Charge. Frederick Whittaker. DD; HBV; MC; OnMSP; PaA; PAH; PoLF; ThLM
Custer's Last Fierce Charge, *with music.* *Unknown.* BFSS
Cut down that timber! Bells, too many and strong. The Planster's Vision. John Betjeman. PoPl
Cut Flower, A. Karl Shapiro. BoNaP
Cut from the joints of this immense. The Night. Lawrence Durrell. *Fr.* Eight Aspects of Melissa. NeBP
Cut is the branch that might have grown full straight. Epilogue. Christopher Marlowe. *Fr.* Dr. Faustus. ViBoPo
Cut It Down. Mary Elizabeth Coleridge. MoVE
Cut mats are even. Laura Cashdollars. Bernadette Mayer. ANYP
Cut out/ the insides. Hegel. LeRoi Jones. CoPo
Cut out as if in porphyry against the sky. Cattle. Frederick Mortimer Clapp. LiTM (1946 ed.)
Cut out the deep design of life. Plan for a Novel. Frederic Thompson. JKCP (1955 ed.)
Cut the Cables. Robert Burns Wilson. PAH
Cut thistles in May. *Unknown.* OxNR
Cut your nails [*or* them] on Monday, cut them for news [*or* health]. Old Superstitions [*or* Old Wives' Sayings]. *Unknown.* HBV; OxNR; StaSt
Cutbert our cobbler can no more forbear. Henry Parrot. SiCE
Cuthullin sat by Tura's wall. James MacPherson. *Fr.* Fingal; an Ancient Epic Poem. EnLi-2
Cuttin Down to Size. Henry Dumas. BF
Cutting Edge, The. Philip Levine. NYBP
Cutting that jungle road from Lugardville. Surveyor. Guy Butler. PeSA
Cutting the Jewish Bride's Hair. Ruth Whitman. HW
Cuttings, Later. Theodore Roethke. AP; PoIE
Cutty Sark, The. George Barker. *Fr.* Dreams of a Summer Night, VI. FIW
Cutty Sark. Hart Crane. *Fr.* The Bridge. AmPP; FaBoMo; LiTA; NP
Cutty Wren, The. *Unknown.* CBEP; GTBS-W; LiTG; NCEP; OxBoLi; SiTL; WiR
Cuvier Light. Pat Wilson. AnNZ
Cwa een like milk-wort and bog-cotton hair! Milk-Wort and Bog Cotton. "Hugh MacDiarmid." NeBP
Cyanide jar seals life, as sonnets move, The. Butterfly Bones; or Sonnet against Sonnets. Margaret Avison. LiTM (1970 ed.)
Cyclamen, The. Arlo Bates. AA; HBV
Cycle. Langston Hughes. FaPON; GoSl
Cycle, *sel.* Ruth Miller.
"Cover my eyes with your palm." PeSA
Cycle, The. Theodore Roethke. ToPo
Cycle; Seven War Poems. Seán Jennett. WaP
I Was a Labourer, *sel.* OnYI
Cycle sings, A. Nature. Walter Stone. NYBP
Cycle was closed and rounded, A. Bennington. W. H. Babcock. PAH
Cycling to Dublin. Robert Greacen. OnYI
Cyclone at Sea, A. William Hamilton Hayne. AA
Cyclone Blues. *Unknown.* CoSo
Cyclops, *sels.* Euripides, *tr. fr. Greek by* Shelley.
Chorus: Love Song. AWP; JAWP; WBP
Chorus of Satyrs, Driving Their Goats. AWP; JAWP; WBP
Cyclops. Ovid, *tr. fr. Latin by* Arthur Golding. *Fr.* Metamorphoses, XIII. CTC
Cyclops, The. Theocritus, *tr. fr. Greek by* Elizabeth Barrett Browning. Idylls, XI. AWP; EnLi-1; JAWP; OuHeWo; WBP
Cydonian Spring with her attendant train. The Spring. Ezra Pound. Po
Cygnet crested on the purple water, The. Similes. Edward Noxon. OBRV
Cymbals crash, The. A Victory Ball [*or* Dance]. Alfred Noyes. EnLit; PoLF
Cymbeline, *sels.* Shakespeare.
"Crickets sing, and mans ore-labor'd sense, The," *fr.* II, ii. AtBAP
Fear No More the Heat O' the Sun, *fr.* IV, ii. AnFE; ATP; BEL; CABA; CBEP; ChTr; CoBE; EG; EnL; EnLi-1; ExPo; GTSL; ILP; LoBV; MaPo; NoP; OAEP; OuHeWo; PAn; PoAn; PoE; PoRA; QFR; SeCeV; TOP; WHA
(Dirge: "Fear no more the heat o' the sun.") CAW; EnLit; HBV
(Fear No More.) CH; DiPo; ElL; ELP; EnRePo; FaFP; InPo; LiTB; LiTG; PoeP; PoFS; PoG; PoIE; PoSa; PTK; RoGo; TrGrPo; ViBoPo

Cymbeline (continued)
("Feare no more the heate o' the sun.") AtBAP; PoEL-2; SiCE
(Fidele.) BoC; GTBS; GTBS-D; GTSB-P; GTBS-W; GTSE; MCCG; OBEV; OQP; PoPo; ShBV-4
(Fidele's Dirge.) FaBoCh; LoGBV; OBSC; WePo
(Lament for Imogen.) TreF
(Lament of Guiderius and Arviragus.) FaBoEn
(Song: "Fear no more the heat o' the sun.") AWP; CBV; CTC; FiP; ForPo; FosPo; JAWP; MemP; VaPo; WBP
(Song of the Two Brothers.) BoLiVe
Hark! Hark! The Lark, *fr.* II, iii. AnFE; AtBAP; ATP; BEL; BoTP; CBEP; CH; ChTr; CoBE; DiPo; EnL; EnLi-1 (1949 ed.); EnLit; EnRePo; ExPo; FaBoCh; FaBV; FaFP; FaPON; HBV; ILP; InP; InPo; LiTB; LiTG; LoBV; LoGBV; NoP; OTPC; OuHeWo; PoIE; PTK; SeCeV; SiCE; TOP; TreF; TrGrPo; ViBoPo; WHA
(Aubade.) OBEV; ShBV-3
(Morning Song, A.) GN; PCH
(Morning Song for Imogen, A.) AnEnPo
(Song: "Hark! hark! the lark at heaven's gate sings.") AWP; CLwM; ElL; FiP; JAWP; WBP
(Song of the Musicians.) BoLiVe
(Song to Imogen.) EG; OBSC
(Three Songs.) UnPo (1st ed.)
Cymochles and Phaedria. Spenser. *Fr.* The Faerie Queene, II, 6. OBSC
Cymon and Iphigenia, *sel.* Dryden.
Power of Love, The. OBS
Cynara. Ernest Dowson. *See* Non Sum Qualis Eram Bonae sub Regno Cynarae.
Cynddylan on a Tractor [in Spring]. R. S. Thomas. BoC
Cynddylan's Hall. *Unknown, tr. fr. Welsh by* William Barnes. PrWP
Cynic, The. Theodosia Garrison. HBMV
Cynic breaks stained window, The. Destroyer. A. M. Sullivan. ALV
Cynic of the Woods, The. Arthur Patchett Martin. VA
Cynical Ode to an Ultra-Cynical Public. Charles Mackay. BOHV
Cynical Portraits. Louis Paul. InMe
Cynics say that every rose, The. The Wisdom of Folly. Ellen Thorneycroft Fowler. HBV
Cynicus to W. Shakespeare [*or* Shakspere]. James Kenneth Stephen. *Fr.* Two Epigrams. BOHV; CenHV; WhC
Cynneddf, The. Rolfe Humphries. CrMA
Cynotaph, The, *sel.* "Thomas Ingoldsby."
Not a Sou Had He Got. HBV
Cynthia, *sels.* Richard Barnfield.
"Cherry-lipped Adonis in his snowy shape." Sonn
"Now was the welkin all inveloped." ReIE
"Sighing, and sadly sitting by my love." Sonn
To His Mistress. SiCE; TuPP
Cynthia. Sir Edward Dyer. OBEC
Cynthia ("Away with these self-loving lads"). Fulke Greville. *See* Of His Cynthia.
Cynthia, because your horns look diverse ways. Caelica, LIV. Fulke Greville. SiCE
Cynthia, Cynthia. Propertius, *tr. fr. Latin by* James Cranstoun. LiTW
Cynthia in the Snow. Gwendolyn Brooks. TiPo (1959 ed.)
Cynthia on Horseback. Philip Ayres. EnLoPo; Sonn
Cynthia, Queen of seas and lands. The Mariner's Song. Sir John Davies. OBSC
Cynthia, to thy power and thee. Bridal Song. Beaumont *and* Fletcher. *Fr.* The Maid's Tragedy. OBEV; TuPP
Cynthia's Revels, *sels.* Ben Jonson.
Glove, The, *fr.* IV. ElL
"Queen[e] and huntress[e], chaste, and fair[e]." CH; EG; ILP; OBEV; OBS; PoE; ReEn; SiCE
(Hesperus' Hymn to Cynthia.) LoBV; SeCV-1
(Hesperus' Song.) GN
(Hymn[e], The: "Queen[e] and huntress, chaste and fair [e].") AnAnS-2; AtBAP; PoEL-2; SCEP-2; ViBoPo; YAT
(Hymn to Cynthia.) MaPo (1969 ed.); SeCePo
(Hymn to Diana.) AnFE; AWP; BEL; BoLiVe; ChTr; ElL; EnLi-1 (1949 ed.); EnLit; EnRePo; GTBS; GTBS-D; GTBS-P; GTBS-W; GTSE; GTSL; InPo; JAWP; MemP; PoRA; RG; QFR; SeCP; ShBV-4; TOP; TrGrPo; WBP; WHA; WiR
(Queen and Huntress.) CABA; CBEP; EnL; NoP; OAEP; PAn; TuPP
(Song: To Cynthia.) HBV
(To Diana.) OTPC
"Slow, slow, fresh fount, keep time with my salt tears," *fr.* I, ii. CH; EG; ExPo; ILP; OAEP; OBS; ReEn; SiCE
(Echo's Lament of Narcissus.) AnEnPo
(Echo's [*or* Eccho's] Song.) BoLiVe; LoBV; PoIE; SeCV-1; TrGrPo
(Slow, Slow, Fresh Fount.) ChTr; ElL; ELP; EnLi-1 (1949 ed.); MaPo (1969 ed.); NoP; SeCeV; TuPP; UnPo; WHA
(Song: "Slow, slow, fresh fount, keepe time with my salt teares.") AnAnS-2; AtBAP; CBV; EnRePo; EP; FaBoEn; PoEL-2; SeCP; ViBoPo
(Song of Echo.) GoBC
Song: "O, that joy so soon should waste," *fr.* IV, iii. LiTL; TuPP; ViBoPo
(Kiss, The.) HBV; UnTE
Cypress, The. Thomas Love Peacock. CLwM
Cypress. John Peter. BoSA
Cypress-bough, and a rose-wreath sweet, A. Athulf's Death Song. Thomas Lovell Beddoes. *Fr.* Death's Jest Book, IV. VA
Cypress Curtain of the Night [Is Spread], The. Thomas Campion. LoBV; ReIE
Cypress stood up like a church, The. Bianca among the Nightingales. Elizabeth Barrett Browning. GTBS-P; ViPo
Cypress swamp around me wraps its spell, The. Down the Bayou. Mary Ashley Townsend. AA; AnAmPo
Cyprian Woman, A; Greek Folk Song. Margaret Widdemer. AnAmPo; HBV; NP
Cyrano de Bergerac, *sels.* Edmond Rostand, *tr. fr. French by* Brian Hooker.
"And what is a kiss, when all is done?" *fr.* III. OTD
Cyrano de Bergerac Discusses His Nose, *fr.* I. TreFS
Cyriack, this three years' day these eyes, though clear. To [Mr.] Cyriack Skinner Upon His Blindness. Milton. AnEnPo; ATP (1935 ed.); BEL; BWP; DiPo; EnLi-1; MBW-1; PoIE; Sonn; TOP; TrGrPo
Cyriack, whose grandsire on the royal bench. To Cyriack Skinner [*or* Sonnet]. Milton. GTBS; GTBS-D; GTBS-P; GTBS-W; GTSE; GTSL; LoBV; NoP; OBEV; OBS; SeEP; Sonn
Cyrus Brown's Prayer. Sam Walter Foss. *See* Prayer of Cyrus Brown.
Cythère. Paul Verlaine, *tr. fr. French by* Arthur Symons. AWP
(Cythera.) SyP

D

D. C. Karl Shapiro. NYBP
D-Dawn. Margaret McGarvey. GoYe
D. L. and W.'s Phoebe Snow, The. *Unknown.* TreF
D Minor, The. E. L. Mayo. MiAP
D-9. James Schevill. FiMAP
"D. O. M." Sir Henry Wotton. *See* Eternall Mover.
D-Y Bar. James Welch. YAP
Da Capo. H. C. Bunner. HBV
Da Silva Gives the Cue. Walter Hart Blumenthal. TrJP
Dabbling in the Dew. *Unknown.* CH; UnTE
Daccus is all bedaubed with golden lace. Against Gaudy, Bragging, Undoughty Daccus. John Davies of Hereford. SiCE
Dachshund, The. Edward Anthony. GoTP
Dachshunds. William Jay Smith. TDP
Dacus, with some good color and pretense. In Dacum. Sir John Davies. TuPP
Dad, a Home Guard, when in liquor. *Unknown.* WhC
Dada would have liked a day like this. Pictures of the Gone World, Sec. 23. Lawrence Ferlinghetti. NeAP
Daddy. Rose Fyleman. SiSoSe
Daddy. Sylvia Plath. CoAP; LiTM (1970 ed.); NaP; NMP; OPoP; TwCP
Daddy drinks/ lots of/ beer. Idle Chatter. Charles Cooper. BOLo
Daddy Fell into the Pond. Alfred Noyes. FaPON; PDV; RePo
Daddy fixed breakfast. Mummy Slept Late and Daddy Fixed Breakfast. John Ciardi. PDV

Daddy goes a-riding in a motor painted grey. Differences. Rose Fyleman. GFA
Daddy had a little boy. Does Daddy Go? *Unknown.* STF
Daddy Shot a Bear, *with music. Unknown.* OuSiCo
Dad's Greatest Job. *Unknown.* STF
Daedalus. Ovid, *tr. fr. Latin by* Ezra Pound. *Fr.* Metamorphoses, VIII. CTC
Daedalus. Alastair Reid. NYBP
Daedalus to Icarus. Louis Coxe. NYTB
Daemon, The. Louise Bogan. NYBP
Daemon, The. Mikhail Lermontov. *See* Demon, The.
Daemon Lover, The. *Unknown.* *See* Demon Lover, The.
Daemon of the World, The, *sel.* Shelley.
"How wonderful is Death," *fr.* Pt. I. PeER
Trackless Deeps, The, *fr.* Pt. II. EtS
Daffadowndilly/ Has come up to town. Mother Goose. *See* Daffy-down-dilly is new come to town.
Daffodils. Gina Ballantyne. BoAu
Daffodils. Ruth Guthrie Harding. HBMV
Daffodils. Robert Herrick. *See* To Daffodils.
Daffodils. Kikurio, *tr. fr. Japanese.* SoPo; SUS; TiPo
Daffodils. Lizette Woodworth Reese. AA
Daffodils. P. A. Ropes. BoTP
Daffodils. Wordsworth. *See* I Wandered Lonely as a Cloud.
. . . daffodils/ That come before the swallow dares. Shakespeare. *Fr.* The Winter's Tale, IV, iii. TiPo (1959 ed.)
Daffodils over Night. David Morton. PCH
Daffodil's Return. Bliss Carman. CaP
Daffy-down-dilly. Anna B. Warner. MPB; OTPC; PRWS; TVC
Daffy-down-dilly is new come [*or* Daffadowndilly/ Has come up] to town. Mother Goose. BoChLi; BrR; OxNR; RIS; SoPo; TiPo
Daft Days, The. Robert Ferguson. CEP
Dafydd ap Gwilym Resents the Winter. Rolfe Humphries. NYBP
Dagger, The Jorge Luis Borges, *tr. fr. Spanish by* Norman Thomas di Giovanni. NYBP
Dagger. Mikhail Yurevich Lermontov, *tr. fr. Russian by* Max Eastman. AWP; JAWP; WBP
Dagger rests in a drawer, A. The Dagger. Jorge Luis Borges. NYBP
Dago shovelman sits by the railroad track, The. Child of the Romans. Carl Sandburg. LaNeLa
Dagonet, the fool, whom Gawain in his mood. The Last Tournament. Tennyson. *Fr.* Idylls of the King. ViPo
Dagonet's Canzonet. Ernest Rhys. HBV; SiSw
Daguerreotype, The. William Vaughn Moody. AnAmPo
Dahlias. Edith Agnew. GaP
Dahlias. Padraic Colum. GoJo; NePoAm
Dai horse neighs against the bleak wind of Etsu, The. South-Folk in Cold Country. Ezra Pound. CrMA
Daily Bread. *Unknown.* BePJ
Daily Cross. Earl Bigelow Brown. ChIP
Daily Globe, The. Howard Nemerov. TPM
Daily Grind, The. Fenton Johnson. AmNP
Daily Manna, The. Sara Henderson Hay. GoYe
Daily News. Tom Clark. ANYP
Daily Paradox. Sara Henderson Hay. InMe
Daily Prayer. Marion Strobel. NP
Daily Round, The. Ronald McCuaig. BoAV
Daily Round. Lizette Woodworth Reese. *Fr.* After. ThGo
Daily Strength. Frances Ridley Havergal. SoP
Daily the bending skies solicit man. Fragments on Nature and Life. Emerson. TOP
Daily the fishers' sails drift out. Beside the Sea. Ella Higginson. OTPC (1946 ed.)
Daily the rooms in which. Minding Our Own Business. William Brown. QAH
Daily Trials. Oliver Wendell Holmes. PoEL-5
Daily walked the fair and lovely. The Azra. Heine. AWP; JAWP; WBP
Daily with You. Annie Johnson Flint. BLRP
Daily Work. *Unknown.* SoP
Daily work in narrow space is bound, The. Escape. *Unknown.* MaRV
Dain do Eimhir, *sels.* Sorley Maclean. NeBP
"Bolshevik who never gave heed to queen or to king, A," XXX.
"I do not see the sense of my toil putting thoughts in a dying tongue," LV.
"I gave you immortality and what did you give me?" XIX.
"I walked with my reason out beside the sea," XXII.
(I Walked with My Reason.) LiTW
"Multitude of the skies, gold riddle of millions of stars," XVII.
"You were dawn on the Cuillin," LIV.
Dain Eile, *sel.* Sorley Maclean.
"My eye is not on Calvary, nor on Bethlehem the Blessed." NeBP
Daintiest draught thy pensill ever drew, The. He Is a New Creature. Edward Taylor. *Fr.* Preparatory Meditations, First Series. MWA-1
Dainty fairy lace-work, O so finely spun. Cobwebs. *Unknown.* GFA
Dainty Fine Bird. *Unknown.* TuPP
(Prisoners). ElL
Dainty little cups of color. Crocus. Marion Mitchell Walker. GFA
Dainty little maiden, whither would you wander? The City Child. Tennyson. BoTP; OTPC; PRWS
Dainty Sang, A. Allan Ramsay. *Fr.* Gentle Shepherd, The. OBEC
Dainty Sweet Bird. *Unknown.* EnRePo; NCEP
Dainty thing's the villanelle, A. Villanelle W. E. Henley. InP; TOP
Daisies, The. Bliss Carman. BoNaP; HBV MaRV; MoAmPo (1942 ed.); NeMA; PFY; TSW
Daisies, The. Kate Greenaway. MPB
Daisies. Frank Dempster Sherman. TSW; TVC
Daisies, The. James Stephens. AnIV; AWP; JAWP; WBP
Daisies. Andrew Young. GoJo
Daisies and Grasses. *Unknown.* BoTP
Daisies are broken. Love Song. William Carlos Williams. NP
Daisies of Florence. Kathleen Raine. NYBP
Daisies so bright,/ Grasses so green. Daisies and Grasses. *Unknown.* BoTP
Daisy, The. Burns. *See* To a Mountain Daisy.
Daisy, The. Chaucer. *Fr.* The Legend of Good Women: Prologue.
("And as for me, thogh that I can but lyte.") CH
("And as for me, though that my wite be lite.") ViBoPo
("Of all the floures in the mede," *shorter sel.*) LO
Daisy, The. James Montgomery. OTPC (1923 ed.)
(Field Flower, A.) HBV
"There is a flower, a little flower," *sel.* BoTP
Daisy, The. Sir Rennell Rodd. VA
Daisy, The. Jane Taylor. *See* Field Daisy, The.
Daisy, The. Tennyson. EnLoPo; OBNC; OBVV; PoEL-5; VA
Daisy. Francis Thompson. AnEnPo; AWP; BeLS; BrPo; EnLit; GoBC; FaBV; GTBS-D; HBV; MoAB; MoBrPo; NeMA; OBEV (new ed.); OBNC; OBVV; VA; WHA
Tokens, The, *br. sel.* OtMeF
Daisy. William Carlos Williams. MAP; MoAB; MoAmPo
Daisy, The. Marya Zaturenska. MoAmPo
"Daisy and Lily." Waltz. Edith Sitwell. OAEP (2d ed.)
Daisy Bell. Harry Dacre. TreF
Daisy Fraser. Edgar Lee Masters. *Fr.* Spoon River Anthology. CMoP; MoVE; NP
Daisy's Song, A. Keats. BoNaP; OTPC; PRWS
Dakota Badlands. Elizabeth Landeweer. AmFN
Dakota: Five Times Six. Joseph Hansen. NYBP
Dakota Land, *with music. Unknown.* AS; CoSo
Daley's Dorg Wattle. W. T. Goodge. PoAu-1
Dalliance of Leopards, The. *Unknown, tr. fr. Sanskrit by* E. Powys Mathers. OnPM
Dalliance of the Eagles, The. Walt Whitman. AA; AmPP (5th ed.); BWP; CABA; FaBoEn; MWA-1; NoP; TDP
Dalmatian Nocturne. Aleksa Santic, *tr. fr. Serbo-Croatian by* Paul Selver. LiTW
Dalyaunce. *Unknown.* CH
"Welcome, fayre chylde, what is thy name?" *sel.* AtBAP
Dam, The. Patric Dickinson. POTi
Dam Bellona, The. Der Blinde Junge. Mina Loy. QFR
Dam Neck, Virginia. Richard Eberhart. LiTA; MoAB; WaP
Damage You Have Done, The. Ellis Ayitey Komey. PBA
Damascus. Edna Holroyd Yelland. CIV
Damascus Road, The. Daniel Hughes. ChIP
Dame, dame! the watch is set. The Witches' Charms. Ben Jonson. *Fr.* The Masque of Queens. ElL; PoMS; ThWaDe

Dame Duck's First Lecture on Education. Ann Hawkshaw. OTPC (1923 ed.)
(Dame Duck's Lecture to Her Ducklings.) SAS
(Mother Duck.) BoTP
Dame, get up and bake your pies. *Unknown.* BoTP; OxNR
Dame Goose, the sun shines cheerfully. Fox and Goose. F. Hey. SAS
Dame Gunild, she dwells in Spire, The. Ravngard and Memering. *Unknown.* BaBo
"Dame, how the moments go." The Bride's Toilette. Ellen Mackay Hutchinson Cortissoz. AA
Dame Jane a sprightly nun and gay. The Penitent Nun. John Lockman. ErPo; UnTE
Dame Liberty Reports from Travel. Dorothy Cowles Pinkney. GoYe
Dame Music. Stephen Hawes. *Fr.* The Pastime of Pleasure. PoEL-1
(Dame Musike.) MuSP
Dame Nature. Spenser. *Fr.* The Faerie Queene, VII, 7. PoEL-1
Dame, said the Panther, times are mended well. Dryden. The Hind and the Panther, II. PoEL-3
Dame Trot and Her Cat. *Unknown.* BoTP; OxNR
(Dame Trot and Her Comical Cat.) FTB
Dame Wiggins of Lee and Her [Seven] Wonderful Cats. *Unknown, at. to* Richard Scrafton Sharpe. CIV; FaBoBe
Damelus' Song to His Diaphenia. *At. to* Henry Constable *and to* Henry Chettle. *See* Diaphenia.
Dames of France are fond and free, The. The Girl I Left behind Me. Thomas Osborne Davis. AmSS; FaBoBe; FaFP; HBV; OnYI; TreF
Damien lived with lepers. Contrition across the Waves. Caroline Giltinan. WHL
Damis, an author cold and weak. Epigram. *Unknown.* HBV
Dam it all! all this our South stinks peace. Sestina: Altaforte. Ezra Pound. AmP; CaFP; CMoP; CoBMV; FaBoTw; LiTA; LiTG; LiTM (1946 ed.); MoAB; MoAmPo (1950 ed.); PoIE; StP
Damn the Filipinos, *with music.* *Unknown.* ABF
Damnation of Byron, The. A. D. Hope. MoAuPo
Damnation of Vancouver, *sel.* Earle Birney.
Speech of the Salish Chief. OBCV
Damned Minoan crevices, that I clog them up! Paranoia in Crete. Gregory Corso. NeAP
Damned ship lurched and slithered, The. Quiet and quick. A Channel Passage. Rupert Brooke. FaBoTw
Damocles. Robert Graves. NYBP
Damon and Celimena. Dryden. *See* Song: "Celimena of my heart."
Damon and Cupid. John Gay. EnLoPo; SeCeV
Damon come drive thy flocks this way. Clorinda and Damon. Andrew Marvell. AnAnS-1; MaMe; SeCP
Damon died young; no bell was tolled for him. Toll the Bell for Damon. Maxwell Anderson. InMe
Damon the Mower. Andrew Marvell. AnAnS-1; BWP; MaMe; SCEP-2
Damp clods with corn may thank the showers. The Snake. Roy Campbell. AtBAP
Dampe, The. John Donne. MaMe; SCEP-1; SeCP
Damsel, The. Omar b. Abi Rabi'a, *tr. fr. Arabic by* W. G. Palgrave. AWP; LiTW
Damsel donned her kirtle sheen, The. Christmas. Sir Walter Scott. *Fr.* Marmion. PCH
Dan Bartholmew's Dolorous Discourses. George Gascoigne. EnRePo
Dan Dunder. John Ciardi. BBGG
Dan Pope first in vogue. The Lass of Isleworth Mill. Richard Wooddeson. WaPE
Dan Taylor, *with music.* *Unknown.* CoSo
Danaë. Simonides, *tr. fr. Greek by* T. F. Higham. LiTW
Dance, The. Hart Crane. *Fr.* The Bridge: Powhatan's Daughter. AnAmPo; AnFE; CoAnAm; LiTA; LiTM; MoAB; MoAmPo; OxBA; SeCeV; TwAmPo
Dance, The. Robert Duncan. NeAP
Dance, The. John Haines. ThO
Dance, The. LeRoi Jones. CoPo
Dance, The. Rudolph Chambers Lehmann. HBMV
Dance, The. John Lydgate. *Fr.* The Dance of Death. PoEL-1
Dance, The. Theodore Roethke. Four for Sir John Davies, I. CoBMV; CrMA; FiMAP; NePoAm; ReMP; UnS
Dance, The Spenser. *See* Dance of the Graces, The.
Dance, The. R. S. Thomas. BoPe
Dance, The ("Cornwallis led a country dance"). *Unknown.* PAH
(Cornwallis's Country Dance, *abr., with* Yankee Doodle.) TrAS
Dance, The. *Unknown, at. to* Thomas Campion. ElL; FaBoCh; LoBV; LiTL; LoGBV
Dance. Lula Lowe Weeden. CDC
Dance, The. William Carlos Williams. AmP; AmPP (5th ed.); CMoP; ExPo; GoJo; LiTM (1970 ed.); LoGBV; NoP; OxBA; PoeP; TDP
Dance a baby diddy. *Unknown.* OxNR
Dance at Silver Valley, The. William Maxwell. SCC
Dance at the Ranch, A. *Unknown.* SCC
Dance Band. A. S. J. Tessimond. MuSP
Dance begins with the sun descending, The. Marrakech. Richard Eberhart. LiTM (1970 ed.)
Dance by the Roadside, The. Gustaf Fröding, *tr. fr. Swedish by* Charles W. Stork. WoL
Dance Called David, The. Theodore Weiss. CoPo
Dance Chant, A. *Tr. fr. Iroquois Indian by* E. S. Parker. WGRP
Dance Chant, A. *Tr. fr. Osage Indian by* D. G. Brinton. WGRP
Dance, dance in this museum case. Love Song to Eohippus. Peter Viereck. MoAmPo (1950 ed.)
Dance Figure (for the Marriage in Cana of Galilee). Ezra Pound. AnAmPo; CoAnAm; HW; MAP; MoAB; MoAmPo; NP; ReMP; TwAmPo
Dance for Ma Rainey, A. Al Young. NBP
Dance for Militant Dilettantes, A. Al Young. WSL
Dance for Rain, A. Witter Bynner. HT
Dance from its dancers circulates among the other, The. The Dance. Robert Duncan. NeAP
Dance in the township hall is nearly over, The. Country Dance. Judith Wright. MoAuPo
Dance is on the Bridge of Death, The. The Bridge of Death. *Unknown.* AWP
Dance, little baby, dance up high. The Baby's Dance. Mother Goose. GFA; OTPC; OxNR; PPL
Dance, little children, it is holy twilight. Snow-Dance for the Dead. Lola Ridge. AnAmPo
Dance My Baby Diddy. *Unknown.* OTPC (1923 ed.)
Dance of blue-bells in the shady places, A. Sweet Surprises. S. Doudney. BoTP
Dance of Death, The. Austin Dobson. HBV; TOP
Dance of Death. Kimball Flaccus. AnAmPo
Dance of Death, The, *sel.* John Lydgate.
Dance, The. PoEL-1
"Ye that amonge lordis and barouns." EnPo
Dance of Despair, The. Hayyim Nahman Bialik, *tr. fr. Hebrew by* A. M. Klein. TrJP
Dance of Love, The. Sir John Davies. *Fr.* Orchestra. ElL; SeCePo
Dance of Saul with the Prophets, The. Saul Tchernichowsky, *tr. fr. Hebrew by* I. M. Lask. TrJP
Dance of the Abakweta. Margaret Danner. Far from Africa, 2. AmNP; NNP; PoNe (1970 ed.)
Dance of the Daughters of Herodias, The. Arthur Symons. BrPo
Dance of the Graces, The. Spenser. *Fr.* The Faerie Queene, VI, 10. OBSC
(Dance, The, *shorter sel.*) TrGrPo
Dance of the Macabre Mice. Wallace Stevens. CMoP; NePA; OxBA; SeCeV
Dance of the Rain, The. Eugene Marais. *tr. fr. Afrikaans by* Jack Cope *and* Uys Krige. PeSA
Dance of the Sevin Deidly Synnis, The. William Dunbar. GoTS; OxBS
Dance of the Sword, The. *Unknown, tr. fr. Breton by* Tom Taylor. WaaP
Dance Song, A. Burkhard von Hohenfels, *tr. fr. German by* Jethro Bithell. LiTW
Dance Song. *Unknown, tr. fr. Chinese by* Arthur Waley. FaBoCh; LoGBV
(Unicorn's Hoofs, The.) OA
Dance-Song of the Lightning. *Unknown, tr. fr. Hottentot.* PeSA
Dance the Boatman. *Unknown.* ThLM
Dance, Thumbkin, dance. *Unknown.* OxNR

Dance to the beat of the rain, little fern. Fern Song. John Banister Tabb. PRWS
Dance to your daddy. [*or* daddie]. Mother Goose. OxNR; PPL; RIS; SAS; TiPo
Dance with Banderillas. Richard Duerden. NeAP
Dancer, The. Joseph Campbell. OBMV; OxBI; POTE
Dancer, The. Ednah Proctor Clarke. AA
Dancer, The. Sadi, *tr. fr. Persian by* Sir Edwin Arnold. *Fr.* The Bustan. AWP; JAWP; OuHeWo; WBP
Dancer, The. W. J. Turner. OBMV; POTE
Dancer, The. Edmund Waller. PoFS; TrGrPo
Dancer at Cruachan and Cro-Patrick, The. W. B. Yeats. UnS
Dancer: O you translation. Rainer Maria Rilke. Sonnets to Orpheus, Pt. II, XVIII. OnPM
Dancers, The. Babette Deutsch. HBMV
Dancers, The. "Michael Field." VA
Dancers, The. W. W. Gibson. MMA
Dancers, The. Roland E. Robinson. ACV
Dancers with a Hop, The. James Schevill. FiMAP
Dances Inspired by Love. Ben Jonson. *Fr.* Love Restored. UnS
Dancing. Eleanor Farjeon. StVeCh (1955 ed.)
Dancing. Yang Kuei-fei, *tr. fr. Chinese by* Florence Ayscough *and* Amy Lowell. FaPON
Dancing All Alone. Al Young. WSL
Dancing Cabman, The. J. B. Morton. MoShBr; ShBV-4
Dancing dancing down the street. Rain. Ella Young. TiPo (1952 ed.)
Dancing, drinking, gambling, fighting. Off Guard. *Unknown.* CoSo
Dancing Faun, The. Robert Cameron Rogers. AA
Dancing firefly, A! The Firefly. Taigi. OnPM
Dancing Girl, A. Frances Sargent Osgood. AA
Dancing lamely on a lacquered plain. The Tillaquils. Laura Riding. FaBoMo
Dancing Lesson, The. Eliza Grove. OTPC (1923 ed.)
Dancing on the Shore. M. M. Hutchinson. BoTP
Dancing on the Shore. Al Young. WSL
Dancing Partners. Philip Child. CaP
Dancing Ploughmen, The. M. K. Joseph. ACV
Dancing Sea, The. Sir John Davies. *Fr.* Orchestra. ChTr
(Sea Danceth, The.) EtS
Dancing Seal, The. W. W. Gibson. HBMV; OnMSP; PoMS
Dancing through the air. Butterflies. Kageki. OnPM
Dancing with such salacious gestures. Familiarity Breeds Indifference. Martial. UnTE
Dandelion. Annie Rankin Annan. HBV
Dandelion. Kate L. Brown. TVC
Dandelion. Hilda Conkling. BoChLi; FaPON; GFA; MPB; PDV; PoRh; TiPo; TSW; TVC
Dandelion. Nellie M. Garabrant. GFA
Dandelion, The. Vachel Lindsay. BrR
Dandelion, The. Katharine Pyle. DD
Dandelion, The ("O dandelion, yellow as gold"). *Unknown.* PCH
(O Dandelion.) BoTP
Dandelion ("There was a pretty dandelion"). *Unknown.* GFA
Dandelion Puff, The. Mary K. Robinson. BoTP
Dandelion stares, The. The Little Dandelion. Lula Lowe Weeden. CDC
Dandelions. John Albee. AA
Dandelions. Marchette Chute. BiCB
Dandelions, The. Helen Gray Cone. DD; GFA; HBV; PRWS
Dandelions. Frances M. Frost. TiPo
Dandelions. Howard Nemerov. NePA; TwAmPo
Dandelions. Sacheverell Sitwell. RIS
Dandelions, The. *Unknown.* BoTP
Dandelions, wrecked on their stems, The. Late Dandelions. Ben Belitt. NYBP
Dandoo ("Little old Man came in from plow."), *with music. Unknown.* BFSS
Dandoo ("There was a man lived in the west.") *Unknown. See* Wife Wrapt in Wether's Skin, The.
Dandy Cat, The. Laura E. Richards. CIV
Dandy Dandelion. Christopher Morley. GFA
Dandy O, The. *Unknown.* CoMu
Danger. Helen Hunt Jackson. AnFE; APA; CoAnAm
Danger. Theodora L. Paine. PGD
Danger at Funny Junction, The. Marvin Bell. YAP
Danger is not in action, but in sloth. Tyrannicide. Walter Savage Landor. PoFr
Danger is silent in the bloodless square. Capital Square. Patrick Anderson. OBCV
Danger of Writing Defiant Verse, The. Dorothy Parker. InMe
Dangers of Football, The. John Gay. *Fr.* Trivia; or, The Art of Walking the Streets of London, II: Of Walking the Streets by Day. EnLi-1 (1949 ed.); SD
Dangers of the Journey to the Happy Land. Joseph Ceravolo. ANYP
Daniel, *sel.* Bible, *O.T.*
Belshazzar's Feast, V. TreF
Daniel. Vachel Lindsay. ChTr; PoE; ShBV-1; WePo
(Daniel Jazz, The.) CBEP; PTK; TrGrPo
Daniel and Abigail. Epitaph. Miguel de Barrios. TrJP
Daniel, beside the subject of thy verse. Ad Samuelem Danielem. Thomas Bastard. SiCE
Daniel Boone. Stephen Vincent Benét. AmFN; NAMP; PoPl
Daniel Boone. Arthur Guiterman. FaPON; MaC; MoShBr; MPB; OnSP; PaA; PoFr
Daniel Defoe. Walter Savage Landor. NCEP
Daniel Gray. Josiah Gilbert Holland. AA; HBV
Daniel Jazz, The. Vachel Lindsay. *See* Daniel.
Daniel Saw de Stone, *with music. Unknown.* BoAN-2
Daniel, thou in tragic note excels. Ad Samuelem Daniel. John Weever. ReIE
Daniel Webster. Oliver Wendell Holmes. PAH
Daniel Webster's Horses. Elizabeth J. Coatsworth. AmFN; AnNE; FiSC; MAP; MoAmPo; PoMS
Danish Barrow, A. Francis Turner Palgrave. VA
Danish conqueror, on his royal chair, The. A Fact, and an Imagination. Wordsworth. FOL
Danish Cradle Song, A. *Unknwon.* BoTP
Danish Wit. John Hollander. PV
Dank, limber verses, stuft with lakeside sedges. Some of Wordsworth. Walter Savage Landor. ChTr
Dankwerts, scholarship boy from the slums. Our Supervisors Will Do That for Us! David Holbrook. NePoEA-2
Danny. J. M. Synge. AnEnPo; PeVV
Danny Deever. Kipling. AnFE; BBV (1923 ed.); BEL; BrPo; CaFP; DiPo; EnLi-2 (1949 ed.); ExPo; GTBS-P; HBV; InP; LiTB; LiTM (rev. ed.); MaC; MCCG; MoBrPo; NeMA; NoP; OAEP (2d ed.); OxBoLi; PeVV; PoE; PoFS; PoLF; PoPo; PoVP; SeCePo; ShBV-3; TOP; TreFS; TrGrPo; TSW; UnPo (3d ed.); VA; VaPo; WaaP
Danny Murphy. James Stephens. BoTP; RoGo
Danny Was a rascal. The Buccaneer. Nancy Byrd Turner. TiPo
Danny's Wooing. David McKee Wright. PoAu-1
Dans l'Allée. Paul Verlaine, *tr. fr. French by* Arthur Symons. AWP
(Avenue, The.) SyP
Danse Macabre. Antonia Y. Schwab. FiSC
Danse Russe. William Carlos Williams. CMoP; ForPo; NoP
Dante. Bryant. ViBoPo
Dante ("Oft have I seen"). Longfellow. *See* Oft Have I Seen . . .
Dante ("Tuscan, that wanderest"). Longfellow. AA; AnNE; CoBA; MAmP
Dante. Michelangelo, *tr. fr. Italian by* Longfellow. AWP; JAWP; WBP
Dante, a sigh that rose from the heart's core. Sonnet: To Dante Alighieri (He Reports the Successful Issue of Lapo Gianni's Love). Guido Cavalcanti. AWP
Dante Alighieri, a dark oracle. Inscription for a Portrait of Dante [*or* A Tribute to Dante]. Boccaccio. AWP; GoBC; JAWP; OnPM; WBP
Dante Alighieri, Cecco, your good friend. Sonnet: To Dante Alighieri (On the Last Sonnet of the "Vita Nuova"). Cecco Angiolieri da Siena. AWP
Dante Alighieri, if I jest and die. Sonnet: To Dante Alighieri (He Writes to Dante). Cecco Angiolieri da Siena. AWP
Dante Alighieri in Becchina's praise. Sonnet: He Rails against Dante. Cecco Angiolieri da Siena. AWP; JAWP; WBP
Dante and Beatrice in the Earthly Paradise. Dante, *tr. fr. Italian by* Dorothy Sayers. *Fr.* Divina Commedia: Purgatorio. BoC
Dante at Verona. Dante Gabriel Rossetti. MaVP
Dante attained the purgatorial hill. The Vigil. Theodore Roethke. *Fr.* Four for Sir John Davies. PoDB

Dante, if thou within the sphere of Love. Sonnets: To Dante in Paradise [*or* Fiammetta]. Boccaccio. AWP; GoBC
Dante, Shakespeare, Milton. Sydney Dobell. *Fr.* Balder. VA
Dante, whenever this thing happeneth. Sonnet: To Dante Alighieri (He Conceives of Some Compensation in Death). Cino da Pistoia. AWP
Dante's Angels. Dante, *tr. fr. Italian by* Dorothy Sayers. *Fr.* Divina Commedia: Purgatorio. BoC
Dante's Heaven. Dante, *tr. fr. Italian by* Dorothy Sayers. *Fr.* Divina Commedia: Paradiso. BoC
Danube River, The. Hamilton Aïdé. VA
Danube to the Severn gave, The. In Memoriam A. H. H., XIX. Tennyson. EnL; EnLi-2; EPN; GTBS-P; LoBV; OAEP; TOP; ViPo; VP
Daphnaida, *sel.* Spenser.
"She fell away in her first ages spring." OBEV
Daphne. Bliss Carman. OBCV
Daphne. Hildegarde Flanner. HBMV
Daphne. David Galler. NYTB
Daphne. Thomas S. Jones, Jr. OHIP
Daphne. John Lyly. *Fr.* Midas. ElL
(Apollo's Song.) HBV
("My Daphne's hair is twisted gold.") SiCE
(Song of Daphne to the Lute, A.) OBSC
Daphne. Claire McAllister. TwAmPo
Daphne. Selden Rodman. PoNe
Daphne. Edith Sitwell. HBMV
Daphne and Apollo. George Macy. InMe
"Daphne with her thighs in bark." Ezra Pound. *Fr.* Hugh Selwyn Mauberley. CMoP
Daphnis and Chloe. Andrew Marvell. MaMe
Daphnis Came on a Summer's [*or* Sommers] Day. *Unknown.* SeCSL; ViBoPo
Daphnis must from Chloe part. Daphnis and Chloe. Andrew Marvell. MaMe
Daphnis to Ganymede. Richard Barnfield. *Fr.* The Affectionate Shepherd. ElL; ThWaDe
Dappled sky, a world of meadows, A. Jean Ingelow. *Fr.* Divided. OBNC
Darby and Joan. St. John Honeywood. AA; LHV
Darby and Joan. Frederic Edward Weatherly. VA
Darby and Joan were dressed in black. *Unknwon.* OxNR
Dare not too farre Castara, for the shade. To Castara, Ventring to Walke Too Farre in the Neighbouring Wood. William Habington. AnAnS-2
Dare Quam Accipere. Mathilde Blind. OBVV
Dare to Be Free. Georg Herwegh, *tr. fr. German by* J. L. Joynes. PoFr
Dare to Be True. George Herbert. *Fr.* The Church Porch. GoTP
(Courage.) PCD; PCH
Dare we despair? Through all the nights and days. He Leads Us Still. Arthur Guiterman. OHIP; OQP
Dare You? Edward Rowland Sill. AnNE
Dare you haunt our hallow'd green? The Fairies' Dance. *Unknown.* MPB
Dare you see a soul at the white heat? Emily Dickinson. MAmP
Darest Thou Now O Soul. Walt Whitman. AmLP; ATP (1935 ed.); CoBA; HBV; InP; MaRV; NePA; PoFS; TOP; TrGrPo; TRV; ViBoPo; WGRP
Darien. Sir Edwin Arnold. MC; PAH
Daring young lady of Guam, A. *Unknown.* GoTP
Darius Green and His Flying-Machine. John Townsend Trowbridge. BeLS; BoChLi; BOHV; FaBoBe; HBV; HBVY; IHA; InMe; MoShBr; PoLF; StVeCh (1940 ed.); YaD
Darius the Mede was a king and a wonder. Daniel [*or* The Daniel Jazz]. Vachel Lindsay. CBEP; ChTr; PoE; PTK; ShBV-1; TrGrPo; WePo
Dark, The. "George Eliot." *Fr.* The Spanish Gypsy. VA
Dark accurate plunger down the successive knell. The Subway. Allen Tate. AP; TDP
Dark and Falling Summer, The. Delmore Schwartz. NYBP
Dark and more dark the shades of evening fell. Sonnet: Composed after a Journey across the Hamilton Hills, Yorkshire. Wordsworth. ChER
Dark and the Fair, The. Stanley Kunitz. PoCh
Dark Angel. Elizabeth Bartlett. NePoAm-2
Dark Angel, The. Lionel Johnson. ACP; CAW; CoBE; GTBS-P; GTBS-W; JKCP; LiTB; LiTG; LiTM (rev. ed.); MoBrPo; OBMV; PoLi; PoVP; ViPP; WHA
"Ardour of red flame is thine, The," *sel.* LO
Dark Angel and I met as the long hand was vertical, The. Night Attack. Donald M. Woodruff. TwCaPo
Dark angel of the night, you come on folded wings. Dark Angel. Elizabeth Bartlett. NePoAm-2
Dark Angel, with thine aching lust. The Dark Angel. Lionel Johnson. ACP; CAW; CoBE; GTBS-P; GTBS-W; JKCP; LiTB; LiTG; LiTM (rev. ed.); MoBrPo; OBMV; PoLi; PoVP; ViPP; WHA
Dark as the clouds of even. The Black Regiment. George Henry Boker. GN; HBV; PAH; PAP
Dark blue of early autumn, The. Sleep Impression. Carl Sandburg. RePo
Dark brain. Poem to the Man on My Fire Escape. Diane Wakoski. CoPo
Dark Brother, The. Lewis Alexander. CDC
Dark brown is the river. Where Go the Boats? Robert Louis Stevenson. BoChLi; FaBoBe; FaBoCh; GoJo; LoGBV; MPB; PRWS; PTK; SoPo; StVeCh (1940 ed.); SUS; TreFT; TiPo
Dark brown mould's upturned, The. Pain. Maltbie D. Babcock. FaChP
Dark bull quartered in my eye, The. Jerome Rothenberg. *Fr.* Three Landscapes. CoPo
Dark Cat, The. Audrey Alexandra Brown. CaP
Dark Cavalier, The. Margaret Widdemer. HBMV; PFY
Dark Chamber, The. Louis Untermeyer. MAP; MeWo; MoAmPo; MoLP; TOP; WHA
Dark Château, The. Walter de la Mare. BrPo
Dark City, The. Clifford Dyment. POTi
Dark cloud raged, The. Thunder Shower. Hilda Conkling. NP
Dark Corner. Graham Hough. NMP
Dark creeping Ivy, with thy berries brown. To the Ivy. John Clare. CBEP
Dark Cup, The, *sel.* Sara Teasdale.
May Day. MemP
Dark Danny. Ivy O. Eastwick. BrR; FaPON; TiPo
Dark, dark lay the drifters against the red West. Kilmeny. Alfred Noyes. EnLit
Dark Day, A. Dante Gabriel Rossetti. The House of Life, LXVIII. MaVP; PoVP; ViPo
Dark, deep and cold the current flows. Plaint [*or* The Land Which No One Knows]. Ebenezer Elliott. HBV; OBEV; OBVV
Dark Dialogues, The, *sels.* W. S. Graham. OxBS
"Almost I, yes, I hear," II.
"Now in the third voice," III.
Dark Earth and Summer. Edgar Bowers. QFR
Dark Eleanor and Henry sat at meat. The Rose of the World. John Masefield. PoRA
Dark, elusive shadow, A. Shadows. Arthur J. Peel. MoSiPe
Dark eyed/ O woman of my dreams. Dance Figure. Ezra Pound. AnAmPo; CoAnAm; HW; MAP; MoAB; MoAmPo; NP; ReMP; TwAmPo
Dark-eyed Canaller. *Unknown.* *See* Dark-eyed Sailor, The.
Dark-eyed Gentleman, The. Thomas Hardy. MoAB; MoBrPo; PoIE; PoeP
Dark-eyed Lad Columbus. Nancy Byrd Turner. SiSoSe
Dark-eyed Sailor, The, *with music.* *Unknown.* ShS
(Dark-eyed Canaller, *with music.*) OuSiCo
Dark Eyes at Forest Hills. I. L. Martin. SD
Dark eyes, wonderful, strange and dear they shone. The Half Door. "Seumas O'Sullivan." AnIV
Dark fell the night, the watch was set. Alfred the Harper. John Sterling. BeLS
Dark Flows the River. Arthur S. Bourinot. CaP
Dark Forest, The. Edward Thomas. NoP
Dark-fringed eyelids slowly close, The. Tucking the Baby In. Curtis May. HBV
Dark frost was in the air without. Winter Dusk. Walter de la Mare. AnEnPo
Dark Girl. Arna Bontemps. GoSl
Dark Girl Dressed in Blue, The. *Unknown.* BeLS
Dark Girl's Rhyme, The. Dorothy Parker. InMe
Dark Glass, The. Dante Gabriel Rossetti. The House of Life, XXXIV. EPN; HBV; MaVP; PoVP; TOP; VA; ViPo; VP
Dark gray clouds, The. Natalia M. Belting. PDV
Dark, gray receding tide uncovers, The. By the Sea. John Hollander. AmPC
Dark green and seaweed-cold, the snake-bright hair. The Mer-

maid. A. J. M. Smith. TwCaPo
Dark green truck on the cement platform, The. Train Window. Robert Finch. OBCV; PeCV
Dark Hills, The. E. A. Robinson. AP; CBV; CoBMV; FaFP; GoJo; GTBS-W; ILP; InP; LiTA; LiTM; MAP; MaPo (1969 ed.); MoAB; MoAmPo; NeMa; NePA; OnPM; PoIE; PoSa; TOP
Dark Hotel. Alfred Dorn. FiSC
Dark house, by which once more I stand. In Memoriam A. H. H., VII. Tennyson. BEL; BWP; CoBE; DiPo; EnL; EnLi-2; EnLit; EPN; FaBoEn; FosPo; GTBS-P; LiTB; MaPo; OAEP; OBNC; PoE; PoEL-5; PoIE; PoSa; SeCeV; UnPo; ViPo; VP
Dark house, dark lonely grave. The Grave. T. Gwynn Jones. LiTW
Dark House in Autumn. Conrad Pendleton. FiSC
Dark is kind and cozy, The. God's Dark. John Martin. MaRV; PoLF
Dark is shattered, The. New Things and Old. Sister Mary Madeleva. GoBC
Dark is the face of Harriet. Harriet Tubman. Margaret Walker. PoNe
Dark is the forest and deep, and overhead. The Dark Forest. Edward Thomas. NoP
Dark is the house, the hall, the mirror silent. Garden Party. Mary Mills. NePoAm
Dark is the sapphire night. Half-Light. Jean Percival Waddell. CaP
Dark is the sky! and veiled the unknown morrow! He Goes Before. J. Danson Smith. SoP
Dark is the stair, and humid the old walls. The Belfry. Laurence Binyon. CH
Dark Lily without blame. A Scot to Jeanne d'Arc. Andrew Lang. VA
Dark Man, The. Nora Hopper. HBV
Dark Memory, The. John Hall Wheelock. LiTL
Dark mountain has grown black, The. The Three Pipes. *Unknown.* OnPM
Dark night! Black image of my foul despair. Parthenophil and Parthenophe, LXXXIII. Barnabe Barnes. Sonn
Dark Night of the Soul, The. St. John of the Cross. *See* Obscure Night of the Soul, The.
Dark Palace, The. Alice Milligan. AnIV
Dark People. Kattie M. Cumbo. BOLo
Dark Rapture. "Æ." SeCePo
Dark red roses in a honeyed wind swinging. June. Nora Hopper. YeAr
Dark-red Shadow-Spots, The. Yumei Kanbara, *tr. fr. Japanese by* Yone Noguchi. LiTW
Dark Road, The. Ethel Clifford. HBV
Dark Rosaleon. *Unknown, at. to* Hugh O'Donnell, *tr. fr. Late Middle Irish by* James Clarence Mangan. ACP; AnFE; AnIL; AnIV; AWP; CH; CoBE; EnRP; GTSL; HBV; IrPN; JAWP; JKCP; LiTW; LO, *abr.*; OBEV; OBVV; OnYI; OxBI; PoFr, *abr.*; PTK, *abr.*; VA; ViBoPo; WBP
(Little Dark Rose, The, *tr. by* Padraic Pearse.) OnYI
(Roisin Dubh, *tr. by* Eleanor Hull.) OnYI
Dark Rosaleen, *sels.* David McKee Wright. PoAu-1
"My Love is the voice of a song," IX.
"On a shining silver morning long ago," I.
Dark Shadows. John Hall. NBP
Dark Song. Edith Sitwell. *Fr.* Façade. CMoP; FaBoTw
Dark Stag, The. Isabella Valancy Crawford. PeCV (1967 ed.)
Dark suffocates the world; but such. An Autumn Park. David Gascoyne. MoPo
Dark Symphony. Melvin B. Tolson. AmNP; BALP; PoNe
Dark Testament. Pauli Murray. AmNP
Dark theme keeps me here, A. In Evening Air. Theodore Roethke. NYBP
Dark, thinned, beside the wall of stone. In Time of Grief. Lizette Woodworth Reese. AA; ATP (1935 ed.); PFY
Dark thoughts are my companions. I have wined. J. V. Cunningham. QFR
Dark-time. The little ones like bees. Little Lullaby. Irving Feldman. NYBP
Dark to me is the earth. Dark to me are the heavens. The Desolate City. *Unknown, tr. by* Wilfrid Scawen Blunt. AWP; JKCP; MoBrPo (1942 ed.); OBEV; OBVV
Dark was de night an' col' was de groun'. A Group of Negro Songs. *Unknown.* NAMP
Dark was the forest, dark was the mind. The Awakening. Conrad Aiken. The Kid, VII. MoVE
Dark was the night when Jesus suffered. Light After Darkness. Carlton Buck. SoP
Dark was the sky, and not one friendly star. Death. Philip Freneau. *Fr.* The House of Night. AP
Dark water, underground. The Cycle. Theodore Roethke. ToPo
Dark! Well what of that? What of That? *Unknown.* SoP
Dark Wings. James Stephens. NP
Dark Women. Ted Hughes. ToPo
Dark Wood, The. John Hall Wheelock. PG (1955 ed.)
Dark Woods, *sel.* Robert Penn Warren.
Dogwood, The, II. PoDB
Dark World, A. E. J. Scovell. MoVE
Dark Yuggoth. Lin Carter. FISC
Darkened hut outlined against the sky, A. The Sunrise of the Poor. Robert Burns Wilson. AA
Darkened Mind, The. James Russell Lowell. MAmP; MWA-1
Darkening Garden, The. *Unknown.* BoTP
Darkening the azure roof of Nero's world. Domine, Quo Vadis? Sir William Watson. WGRP
Darkling Summer, Ominous Dusk, Rumerous Rain. Delmore Schwartz. WIRo
Darkling Thrush, The. Thomas Hardy. AnFE; ATP (1953 ed.); BoLiVe; BrPo; BWP; CaFP; CBV; CMoP; CoBE; CoBMV; DiPo; EnL; EnLi-2 (1949 ed.); EPN; EvOK; ExPo; FaFP; ForPo; GTBS-W; GTSL; HBMV; ILP; InP; LiTB; LiTG; LiTM; MaPo (1969 ed.); MasP; MoAB; MoBrPo; MoPo; NeMA; NoP; OAEP; OBEV (new ed.); OBNC; OBVV; PAn; PG (1955 ed.); PoAn; PoDB; PoeP; PoFS; PoIE; PoSa; POTE; PoVP; ReMP; RoGo; SeCeV; ShBV-4; StP; TreFT; TrGrPo; ViPo; ViPP; VP; WaP
Darkly their glibs o'erhang. The Fate of King Dathi. Thomas Osborne Davis. OnYI
Darkness. Peggy Bacon. BrR
Darkness. Byron. EnRP; EPN; ERoP-2; ILP; LiTB; MBW-2; OAEP; PoEL-4
Darkness, The. Lionel Johnson. BrPo
Darkness. James Naumburg Rosenberg. AA
Darkness and death? Nay, Pioneer, for thee. Walt Whitman. Francis Howard Williams. AA; DD
Darkness and stars i' the midday! They invite. A Rhapsody. Henry Vaughan. ReEn
Darkness comes out of the earth. Twilight. D. H. Lawrence. OBMV
Darkness crumbles away, The. Break of Day in the Trenches. Isaac Rosenberg. BrPo; FaBoMo; FOL; GTBS-P; MMA; MoBrPo; SeCePo; ViBoPo; WaaP; WaP
Darkness encloses the concert hall. Choral Symphony Conductor. Carol Coates. CaP
Darkness Gathers, The. Hjalmar Söderberg, *tr. fr. Swedish by* Charles W. Stork. OnPM
Darkness has called to darkness, and disgrace. As a Plane Tree by the Water. Robert Lowell. AP; CMoP; CoAP; CoBMV; CrMA; DTC; ForPo; GTBS-W; LiTM (rev. ed.); MoAB; MoAmPo (1950 ed.); NePA; NePoEA; OxBA; PoDB; SiSw; TrGrPo (rev. ed.); UnPo (3d ed.); VaPo
Darkness has dawned in the East. Chorus. Shelley. *Fr.* Hellas. EnRP
Darkness is not dark, nor sunlight the light of the sun. Foal. Vernon Watkins. FaBoMo
Darkness o'er the world is creeping. Ancient Lullaby. Gerald Griffin. IrPN
Darkness passes, The; storms shall not abide, The Day Shall Yet Be Fair. Celia Thaxter. MaRV
Darkness rools upward, The. The Blue Symphony. John Gould Fletcher. AnAmPo; MAPA; NP; TwAmPo
Darkness steals the forms of all the queens, The. Grief. D. H. Lawrence. NP
Darkness still is deep'ning, The. Praise at Midnight. Carrie Judd Montgomery. SoP
Darkness succeeds to twilight. Lines Suggested by the Fourteenth of February. Charles Stuart Calverley. ALV
Darkness: the rain sluiced down; the mire was deep. The Redeemer. Siegfried Sassoon. MMA; WGRP
Darkness was a richness in the room, The. From a Childhood. Rainer Maria Rilke. SiSw; TrJP
Darkness wears off, and, dawning into light. The Figures on the Frieze. Alastair Reid. ErPo; NYBP
Darky Sunday School. *Unknown.* ABF, *with music*; OxBoLi; SiTL

Darling, at last my tiny lute. Ad Persephonen. Franklin P. Adams. InMe
Darlin', *with music. Unknown.* ABF
Darling, at the Beautician's you buy. A Valentine for a Lady. Lucillius. LiTW
Darling! Because My Blood Can Sing. E. E. Cummings. InvP; OxBA
Darling Birds, The. *Unknown.* PPL
Darling Cora, *with music. Unknown.* TrAS
(Darling Corey, *diff. vers., with music.*) OuSiCo
Darling, each morning a blooded rose. Corinna in Vendome. Pierre de Ronsard. ErPo
Darling, I am growing old. Silver Threads among the Gold. Eben E. Rexford. FaFP; TreF
Darling, If You Only Knew. Edward Newman Horn. ErPo
Darling, my darling!—It was mother singing low. At Bedtime. Mariana Griswold Van Rensselaer. HBMV
Darling Nelly Gray. Benjamin R. Hanby. TrAS, *with music*; TreFS
Darling of God and Men, beneath the gliding stars. Lucretius. *Fr.* De Rerum Natura. PoPl
Darling, Tell Me Yes. John Godfrey Saxe. HBV
Darling, this is good-bye. The words are ordinary. Parting. Kathleen Raine. LiTL
Darling, you only, there is no duplicate. *Unknown. Fr.* Conversations in Courtship. CTC
Darned Mounseer, The. W. S. Gilbert. *Fr.* Ruddigore. TSW
Dar's a lazy, sortah hazy. Sprin' Fevah. Ray Garfield Dandridge. BANP
Dar's a poe-ful rassle 'twixt de good and de bad. Time Goes by Turns. Joel Chandler Harris. *Fr.* Uncle Remus, His Songs and His Sayings. IHA
Dar's a shakin' an' er achin' amongst dese old bones. I Kilt er Cat. Virginia Frazer Boyle. CIV
Dart of Izdabel prevails! 'twas dipt, The. The Dying Indian. Joseph Warton. EiCL
D'Artagnan's Ride. Gouverneur Morris. AA
Dartmoor. Coventry Patmore. NBM
Dartmouth Winter-Song. Richard Hovey. AA
Darwin and Mendel laid on man the chains. Progress. David McCord. ImOP
Darwinian Ballad, A. *Unknown.* BOHV
Darwinism. Agnes Mary Frances Robinson. VA
Darwinism in the Kitchen. *Unknown.* FiBHP
Darwinity. Herman C. Merivale. BOHV; InMe; NA
Da's All Right, Baby, *with music. Unknown.* ABF
Das Liebesleben. Thom Gunn. ErPo
Dash Back. Tennyson. LiTG; SiTL
Dash for the Colors, The. Frederick G. Webb. BeLS
Dashing through [*or* thro'] the snow in a one-horse open sleigh. Jingle Bells. James S. Pierpont. FaFP; TreF; YaD
Dat Lonesome Stream, *with music. Unknown.* ABF
Dat nigger fum Shiloh. Pick a Bale o' Cotton. *Unknown.* ABF
Dat prodjeckin' son wuz de beatenest chap. De Prodjeckin' Son. Booth Lowrey. IHA
Dat Sunshine Special comin' around de bend. C. C. Rider. *Unknown.* AS
Data, data, data. Transfigured Night. Ralph Gustafson. MoCV
Data for Accreditation. Sister Mary Maura. JKCP (1955 ed.)
Dates. *Unknown, tr. fr. Arabic by* E. Powys Mathers. *Fr.* The Thousand and One Nights. AWP; FaPON; JAWP; LiTW; WBP
Dat's a mighty quare tale 'bout de appile tree. De Appile Tree. Joel Chandler Harris. IHA; TSW
Dat's very cole an' stormy night on Village St. Mathieu. De Stove Pipe Hole. William Henry Drummond. IHA
Datur Hora Quieti. Robert Stephen Hawker. GoBC
Datur Hora Quieti. Sir Walter Scott. *Fr.* The Doom of Devorgoil, I. GTBS; GTBS-D; GTBS-P; GTBS-W; GTSE; GTSL
Dauber, *sels.* John Masefield.
"All through the windless night the clipper rolled," VI. AnFE; CMoP
Clipper Loitered South, The, *fr.* IV. EtS
Rounding the Horn, *fr.* VI. EtS; MoAB; MoBrPo; NeMA; WHA
(Dauber Rounds Cape Horn, The,) BBV
"Si talked with Dauber, standing by the side," *fr.* I. InP
Daughter at Evening, The. Robert Nathan. HBMV; TSW
Daughter, how the door is creaking. Evening Prayer. Arthur Fitger. AWP
Daughter of Admetus, A. T. Sturge Moore. FaBoTw
Daughter of Debate, The. Elizabeth, Queen of England. *See* Doubt of Future Foes, The.
Daughter of Egypt, veil thine eyes! Song. Bayard Taylor. AA
Daughter of her whose face, and lofty name. Sonnets to Miranda, I. Sir William Watson. HBV
Daughter of Jove, relentless power. Hymn to [*or* of] Adversity. Thomas Gray. CEP; EiPP; EnRP; GTBS; GTBS-D; GTBS-P; GTBS-W; GTSE; GTSL; OBEC; StP
Daughter of Mendoza, The. Mirabeau B. Lamar. AA; HBV
Daughter of the ancient Eve. The After Woman. Francis Thompson. ISi
Daughter of the Farrier, The. *Unknown.* GoTP
Daughter of the Regiment, The. Clinton Scollard. PAH
Daughter of the Slava, The, *sel.* Jan Kollar, *tr. fr. Czech by* Edna Worthley Underwood.
"He only is worthy of freedom." PoFr
Daughter of the warrior Gileadite, The. Jepthah's Daughter. Tennyson. FOL
Daughter of Venice, fairer than the moon! To an Old Venetian Wine-Glass. Lloyd Mifflin. AA
"Daughter, thou art come to die." Very Old Song. "William Laird." HBV
Daughter to that good Earl, once President. To the Lady Margaret Ley [*or* Two Sonnets]. Milton. GTBS; GTBS-D; GTBS-P; GTBS-W; GTSE; GTSL; OBEV; OBS; Sonn
Daughters, daughters, do ye grieve? Thammuz. William Vaughn Moody. AP
Daughters, in the winds boisterous roughing. Vernal Equinox. Ruth Stone. MoAmPo (1962 ed.)
Daughters of Blum, The. Charles Wright. CoAP
Daughters of Jove, whose voice is melody. Hymn to the Moon [*or* Hymn to Selene]. *Unknown. Fr.* Homeric Hymns. AWP; LiTW
Daughters of Philistia. Walter C. Smith. *Fr.* Olrig Grange. VA
Daughters of the Horseleech, The. Stanley Kunitz. CrMA
Daughters of the Seraphim led round their sunny flocks, The. The Book of Thel [*or* The Lament of Thel]. Blake. BEL; CEP; ChER; EiPP; EnRP; ERoP-1; NoP; OBNC; Po; PoEL-4
Daughters of Time, the hypocritic Days. Days. Emerson. AA; AmePo; AmPP; AnAmPo; AnFE; AnNE; AP; APA; ATP; BoLiVe; BWP; CaFP; CBEP; CBV; CoAnAm; CoBA; ForPo; GTBS-W; ILP; LiTA; MAmP; MWA-1; NoP; OBVV; OnPM; OQP; OuHeWo; OxBA; PAn; PFY; Po; PoAn; PoE; PoEL-4; PoFS; PoIE; PoPo; SeCeV; TreFT; TrGrPo; UnPo (1st ed.); ViBoPo; WHA
Daughters of Troy, The. Euripides. *See* Trojan Women.
Daughters of War. Isaac Rosenberg. BrPo
Daughter's Rebellion, The. Francis Hopkinson. PAH
Dauncing (bright Lady) then began to be[e]. Sir John Davies. *Fr.* Orchestra; or, A Poem of Dancing. AtBAP; FaBoEn; PoEL-2
D'Avalo's Prayer. John Masefield. *See* Prayer: "When the last sea is sailed."
Dave Lilly. Joyce Kilmer. JKCP (1926 ed.)
David. Earle Birney. CaP; TwCaPo
David. Guy Butler. BoSA
David. Mary Carolyn Davies. HBMV
David. Walker Gibson. CrMA; NePoAm
David. Eli Mandel. PeCV (1967 ed.)
David, Aged Four. Mildred Focht. MaRV
David and Bathsheba. Second Samuel, XI: 2-XII: 18, Bible, *O.T.* OuHeWo
David and Bethsabe, *sels.* George Peele.
"Come, gentle Zephyr, tricked with those perfumes," *fr.* sc. i. ViBoPo
"Hot sun, cool fire, tempered with sweet air," *fr.* sc. i. LO; NoP; PoEL-2; SiCE; TuPP
(Bathsheba's Song.) InPo
(Bethsabe Bathing.) EIL; ExPo; LoBV; TrGrPo
(Bethsabe's Song.) AtBAP; ATP; CBEP; EnRePo; OBSC; OxBoLi; SeCeV
"Now comes my lover tripping like the roe," *fr.* sc. i. ViBoPo
"Now for the crown and throne of Israel," *fr.* sc. xii. ViBoPo

David and Goliath. First Samuel, XVI, XVII: 1-51, Bible, *O.T.* TreFS
David and Goliath. John Banister Tabb. PoMa
David and I that summer cut trails on the Survey. David. Earle Birney. CaP; TwCaPo
David ap Gwillam's Mass of the Birds. Padraic Colum. CAW
David Drummond's destinie. The Coble o Cargill. *Unknown.* ESPB
David Exorcising Malzah, the Evil Spirit from the Lord. Charles Heavysege. *Fr.* Saul, a Drama. VA
David Garrick. Goldsmith. *Fr.* Retaliation. CBEP; OBEC; SeCeV
David Garrick, the Actor, to Sir John Hill, a Physician Who Wrote Plays. David Garrick. TreFT
David Jazz, The. Edwin Meade Robinson. HBMV
David Livingstone. *Unknown.* MaRV
David sang to his hooknosed harp. King David. Stephen Vincent Benét. HBMV
David, the king, was grieved and moved. David's Lamentation. William Billings. TrAS
David was a shepherd lad, beautiful as you. David. Mary Carolyn Davies. HBMV
David was a Young Blood, David was a striplin'. The David Jazz. Edwin Meade Robinson. HBMV
Davideis, *sels.* Abraham Cowley.
  Annunciation, The, *fr.* II. OxBoCh
  "Beneath the silent chambers of the earth," *fr.* I. SeEP
  Creation, The, *fr.* I. OBS
  Hell, *fr.* I. OxBoCh
  "I sing the Man who Judah's Scepter bore," *fr.* I. SCEP-2; SeEP
  Power of Numbers, The, *fr.* I. OBS
  Supplication, A, *fr.* III. GTBS; GTBS-D; GTBS-P; GTBS-W; GTSE; GTSL
    (Awake, Awake, My Lyre.) SCEP-2; SeCL
  "Whilst thus his wrath with threats the tyrant fed," *fr.* I. SeEP
  "With sober pace an heav'enly maid walks in," *fr.* II *and* III. SeCV-1
David's Lament. Second Samuel, I: 19-27, Bible, *O.T.* ChTr (I: 17, 19-27); TrGrPo; TrJP
  ("Beauty of Israel is slain, The," I: 19-26.) LO
  (David's Lament for Saul and Jonathan.) AWP
  (David's Lament over Saul and Jonathan.) ShBV-3
  (How Are the Mighty Fallen.) LiTW; WaaP
David's Lament for Jonathan. Peter Abelard, *tr. fr. Latin by* Helen Waddell. LiTW
David's Lamentation, *with music.* William Billings. TrAS
David's Peccavi. Robert Southwell. EP
David's Song. Robert Browning. *Fr.* Saul, IX. BoLiVe; FaBV
  (Joy of Living, The.) ShBV-2
  (Oh, The Wild Joy of Living.) TreFT
  (Saul: "Oh, our manhood's prime vigor!") OtMeF
  (Youth.) BoTP
Davis Matlock. Edgar Lee Masters. *Fr.* Spoon River Anthology. LiTA; LiTM (rev. ed.)
Davy and the Goblin, *sels.* Charles Edward Carryl.
  My Recollectest Thoughts, *fr. ch.* 7. HBV; HBVY; NA
  Nautical Ballad, A, *fr. ch.* 8. FaPON; GFA; HBV; MPB; OTPC (1946 ed.); StVeCh
    (Walloping Window-Blind, The.) GoTP; InMe; LBN; MoShBr; NA; TreFS; WhC
  Robinson Crusoe's Story, *fr. ch.* 11. BeLS; BoChLi; BOHV; FiBHP; InMe; MCCG; OnPP; OTPC (1946 ed.); PCD; PoRA; PoRh; TSW
    (Robinson Crusoe.) AA; HBV; HBVY; LHV; MPB; TreFT
Davy came trippling o'er the hills. The Blackjack Davy. *Unknown.* BFSS
Davy Crockett in his woodman dress. Lament for the Alamo. Arthur Guiterman. AmFN; RePo
Davy Davy Dumpling. *Unknown.* OxNR
Davy Dicar's Dream. Thomas Churchyard. ReIE
Davy, the Dicer. Sir Thomas More. *Fr.* Two Short Ballettes . . . Made for His Pastime While He Was Prisoner in the Tower of London. DiPo; TuPP
Dawlish Fair. Keats. PeER
Dawn. "Æ." BEL
Dawn. Baudelaire, *tr. fr. French by* Edna St. Vincent Millay. WoL
Dawn. Gordon Bottomley. *Fr.* Night and Morning Songs. BiS; BoTP; MoBrPo; NP
Dawn, The. Robert Buchanan. GTSE
Dawn. Isabel Butchart. PoMA
Dawn. Miriam LeFevre Crouse. ChIP
Dawn. Louis Dudek. PeCV
Dawn. Paul Laurence Dunbar. AmNP; GoSl; PoLF; PoNe
Dawn. John Ford. *See* Fly Hence Shadows.
Dawn. Kenton Kilmer. JKCP (1955 ed.)
Dawn. George B. Logan, Jr. HBV
Dawn. "P. S. M." MCCG
Dawn. John Masefield. BrPo
Dawn, *sel.* Harold Monro.
  God. WGRP
Dawn. "Rachel," *tr. fr. Hebrew by* Abraham M. Klein. TrJP
Dawn. Frederick George Scott. CaP; MaRV; PoPl
Dawn. Frank Dempster Sherman. MAP; TRV
Dawn ("By a bank as I lay"). *Unknown.* OBSC
Dawn, The ("One morning I rose and looked upon the world"). *Unknown.* PoToHe (new ed.)
Dawn ("Thou enemy of love"). *Unknown. tr. fr. Greek by* Louis Untermeyer. UnTE
Dawn. William Carlos Williams. MAP; MoAB; MoAmPo; PoPl
Dawn, The. W. B. Yeats. MaPo; MoVE; NP
Dawn amid Scotch Firs. "Fiona Macleod." SyP
Dawn an unsympathetic yellow. Electrical Storm. Elizabeth Bishop. WIRo
Dawn—and a magical stillness; on earth, quiescence profound. Dawn on the Headland. Sir William Watson. HBV
Dawn and Dark. Norman Gale. HBV; TSW; VA
Dawn: and foot on the cold stair treading. Aubade for Hope. Robert Penn Warren. MAP; MoAmPo
Dawn; and the jew's-harp's sawing seesaw song. Pilots, Man Your Planes. Randall Jarrell. MoAB; MoAmPo (1950 ed.)
Dawn—and the mist across the silent lane. A Hillside Farmer. John Farrar. HBMV
Dawn-Angels. Agnes Mary Frances Robinson. HBV; VA
Dawn at Flying-Fish Point. Clement B. Christesen. BoAu
Dawn at Liverpool. Archibald T. Strong. *Fr.* Sonnets of the Empire. BoAu
Dawn at the Rain's Edge. Joseph Auslander. MAP; MoAmPo (1942 ed.)
Dawn Boy's Song. *Unknown, tr. fr. Navaho Indian by* Washington Matthews. FaBV
Dawn breaking as I woke. Alba. Derek Walcott. GoJo
Dawn breeze, The. Sand Paintings. Alice Corbin. AnAmPo; NP
Dawn came wild with rain, and all day long, The. Moonlight on Lake Sydenham. Wilson MacDonald. CaP
Dawn comes cold: the haystack smokes, The. Dawn. John Masefield. BrPo
Dawn cried out: the brutual voice of a bird. In All These Acts. Brother Antoninus. OPoP; ToPo
Dawn drives the dreams away, yet some abide. Omnia Somnia. Rosamund Marriott Watson. HBV
Dawn, enemy of love, how slow you creep. *Unknown, ad. fr. Greek by* Louis Untermeyer. MeWo
Dawn from the foretop! Dawn from the barrel! The Ice-Floes. E. J. Pratt. CaP
Dawn Has Yet to Ripple In. Melville Cane. MAP; MoAmPo
Dawn Hippo. Sydney Clouts. PeSA
Dawn in Britain, The, *sels.* Charles M. Doughty.
  Bladyn's Song of Cloten. PoEL-5
  Druids' Hymn to the Sun. FaBoTw
  Gauls Sacrifice Their Prisoners, The. FaBoTw
  Roman Officer Writes Home, A. FaBoTw
Dawn in Inishtrahull. D. J. O'Sullivan. OnYI
Dawn in the Heart of Africa. Patrice Lumumba. PBA; TTY
Dawn is a/ slugger. Improvisation III. Harold Silverman. TwCaPo
Dawn is comin', callin', The. Forest Boat Song. Richard Clyde Ford. IHA
Dawn is dense with twitter. Wings at Dawn. Joseph Auslander. HBMV
Dawn is here. Now I must go. Leaving. "Michael Lewis." *Fr.* Cherry Blossoms. UnTE
Dawn is lonely for the sun, The. Chanson de Rosemonde. Richard Hovey. HBV
Dawn is not distant, The. Longfellow. *Fr.* Tales of a Wayside Inn: The Saga of King Olaf. TRV
Dawn is smiling on the dew that covers, The. The Genesis of

Dawn (continued)
Butterflies. Victor Hugo. AWP; JAWP; WBP
Dawn of a bright June morning. Mass of Love. *Unknown.* LiTW; PoPl
Dawn of a pleasant morning in May. Lee to the Rear. John Reuben Thompson. MC; PaA; PAH
Dawn of Day. William Browne. *Fr.* The Shepherd's Pipe. ElL
Dawn of Peace, The. Alfred Noyes. *Fr.* The Wine Press: Epilogue. MaRV
Dawn of Womanhood. Harold Monro. HBV
Dawn off the Foreland—the young flood making. Mine Sweepers. Kipling. ShBV-4
Dawn on Mid-Ocean. John Hall Wheelock. EtS
Dawn on the East Coast. Alun Lewis. FaBoMo
Dawn on the Headland. Sir William Watson. HBV
Dawn on the Lievre, The. Archibald Lampman. CaP
Dawn on the Night-Journey. Dante Gabriel Rossetti. NCEP
Dawn on the Somme. Robert Nichols. POTE
Dawn on the Wall-Head There. Archibald MacLeish. *Fr.* Conquistador, Bk. 13. AtBAP
Dawn Patrol; Chicago. Richard V. Durham. GoSl
Dawn peered through the pines as we dashed at the ford. Riding with Kilpatrick. Clinton Scollard. PAH
Dawn shakes the candle, shoots a flame. May It Be. Boris Pasternak. TrJP
Dawn Song. Linwood D. Smith. TNV
Dawn Song—St. Patrick's Day. Violet Alleyn Storey. YeAr
Dawn-Song to Waken the Lovers. *Unknown, tr. fr. Latin by* Helen Waddell. LiTW
Dawn songs in the dews of young orange trees. In England's Green & (a Garland and a Clyster). Jonathan Williams. CoPo
Dawn talks to-day. William Morris. *Fr.* Love Is Enough. AtBAP
Dawn turned on her purple pillow. A December Day [*or* Winter Solstice]. Sara Teasdale. BoChLi; PoRL; YeAr; YT
Dawn was apple-green, The. Green. D. H. Lawrence. ELU; MoBrPo; NeMA; NP
Dawne to darke. Lines for a Sundial. Thomas Herbert Warren. OBVV
Dawning, The. George Herbert. AnAnS-1; MaMe; MeP
Dawning, The. Henry Vaughan. CAW; MemP; MePo; OxBoCh; ReEn; SoP; TrPWD, *abr.*
Dawning o' the Year, The. Mary Elizabeth McGrath Blake. AA
Dawning of morn, the day-light's sinking, The. Thee, Thee, Only Thee. Thomas Moore. OBNC
Dawning of the Day, The. James Clarence Mangan. GoBC
Dawning of the Day, The. *Unknown, tr. fr. Modern Irish by* Edward Walsh. OnYI
Dawns. Alfred Kreymborg. MAP
Dawn's Awake, The. Otto Leland Bohanan. BANP
Dawns leaden day: a grey. In Jerusalem. *Unknown.* StJW
Dawn's precise pronouncement waits, The. The Edge of Day. Laurie Lee. NYBP; ToPo
Daw's Dinner. Joyce Kilmer. CAW
Dawson City mining man lay dying in the ice, A. Just from Dawson. *Unknown.* ABF
Day, The. Horatius Bonar. FaChP
Day, The. George M. Brady. NeIP
Day, The. Witter Bynner. PGD; PoFr
Day, A. Emily Dickinson. *See* I'll tell you how the sun rose.
Day, The. Roy Fuller. ToPo
Day, The. John Glassco. MoCV
Day, The. Edwin Muir. PoDB
Day, The. Theodore Spencer. PoPo
Day. Sir Cecil Spring-Rice. BoTP
Day, A. William L. Stidger. PoToHe
Day. Jones Very. AnNE
Day!/ Faster and more fast. Pippa Passes. Robert Browning. GTSL, *sel.*; OQP, *sel.*; PoVP; ViPP
"Day a Dancer Learned to Sing of Dreamless Escapades, The." L. Goodwin. BF
Day, a night, an hour of sweet content, A. Content. Thomas Campion. OBSC
Day; a Pastoral. John Cunningham. OBEC
Day after Day. Rabindranath Tagore. Gitanjali, LXXV. OBMV
Day after day/ The muffled shuttling of Her blood. Our Lady's Labor. John Duffy. ISi
Day after day her nest she moulded. The Swallow's Nest. Sir Edwin Arnold. OTPC (1946 ed.); PRWS
Day after day, O Lord of my life, shall I stand. Day after Day. Rabindranath Tagore. Gitanjali, LXXV. OBMV
Day after day, thro' following night on night. The Ship and the Sea. B. E. Baughan. AnNZ
Day after day we kept the dusty road. The City. Edwin Muir. PIA
Day after Sunday, The. Phyllis McGinley. MoAmPo (1962 ed.)
Day agone, as I rode sullenly, A. Dante. *Fr.* La Vita Nuova. AWP
Day and Dark. George Cabot Lodge. AnAmPo; AnFE; APA; CoAnAm
Day and Night. Lewis Alexander. CDC
Day and Night. Victor Daley. BoAu
Day and Night. Baldoon Dhingra. ACV
Day and Night. Lady Anne Lindsay. ThGo
Day and Night. James Stephens. BoTP
Day and night are never weary. Greek Epigram. Ezra Pound. MAP; MoAB; MoAmPo; NeMA
Day and Night Are Thine. *Unknown.* SoP
Day and night I wander widely through the wilderness of thought. God. Gamaliel Bradford. MaRV; TRV; WGRP
Day and Night My Thoughts Incline. Richard Henry Stoddard. *See* Jar, The.
Day and Night Songs. William Allingham. VA
Day and the Work, The. Edwin Markham. OQP; PEDC
Day and then a week passed by, A. The Cardinal Bird. William Davis Gallagher. AA
Day at the Farm, A. "L. J." BoTP
Day Aviva Came to Paris, The. Irving Layton. MoCV
Day-Bed, The. Richard Eberhart. FiMAP
Day Before, The. *Unknown.* SoP
Day before April, The. Mary Carolyn Davies. BoTP; FaPON; GaP; SP; SUS; TiPo (1952 ed.)
Day before Christmas. Marchette Chute. ChBR
Day before Christmas, The. Raymond Souster. PeCV (1967 ed.)
Day before he died, a burnet moth, The. In Memory of Boris Pasternak. Denise Levertov. NoP
Day began with dismal doubt, The. *Unknown.* PoToHe (new ed.)
Day Begins, A. Denise Levertov. FRC; NaP
Day begins to droop, The. Winter Nightfall. Robert Bridges. GTBS-D; MoAB; MoBrPo; NeMA; OBEV; PoVP
Day Breaks, The. Thomas Curtis Clark. ChIP
Day breaks on England down the Kentish hills. The Dying Patriot. James Elroy Flecker. HBMV; ViBoPo
Day by Day. Josiah Conder. SoP
Day by Day. A. G. Fisher. STF
Day by Day. Julia Harris May. BLRP; MaRV
Day by Day. *Unknown.* SoP
Day by Day. Stephen F. Winward. TRV
Day by day I float my paper boats. Paper Boats. Rabindranath Tagore. FaPON; FIW; MCCG; PCH; SP
Day by day [the] manna fell. Day by Day [*or* Daily Bread]. Josiah Conder. BePJ; SoP
Day by day the organ-builder in his lonely chamber wrought. The Legend of the Organ-Builder. Julia C. R. Dorr. BeLS; BLPA; FaBoBe
Day by day the years are fleeting. The Passing Years. James McGinlay. SoP
Day came slow, till five o'clock, The. Emily Dickinson. AmPP
Day Closes, The. Carlton Talbott. ALV
Day comes. Perturbation at Dawn. Ibn Maatuk. LiTW
Day Comes. Tu Fu, *tr. fr. Chinese by* Chi Hwang Chu *and* Edna Worthley Underwood. OnPM
Day comes slowly up north. Northern View. Harriet Plimpton. NYTB
Day Dawn of the Heart. Mary T. Lathrop. ChIP; PGD
Day dawns with scent of must and rain, The. Mirror in February. Thomas Kinsella. GTBS-P; PIA
Day does not come with violence. Deer in Aspens. Kay DeBard Hall. GoYe
Day Dream. *See* Daydream.
Day ends:/ Breasting the North. Day's End. Toyohiko Kagawa. MaRV
Day Euterpe Died, The. Thomas M. Disch. HYE

Day goeth bold in cloth of gold. Day and Night. Victor Daley. BoAu
Day grows hot, and darts his rays, The. Noon Quatrains. Charles Cotton. LoBV
Day had awakened all the things that be. Daybreak. Shelley. GN
Day had fled, the moon arose, The. George Gordon McCrae. *Fr.* Mamba the Bright-eyed. PoAu-1
Day had gone; alone and weak, The. The Night Had Gone [*or* My Hand in His]. Annie Porter Johnson. SoP
Day has barred her windows close, and gangs wi' quiet feet. East Coast Lullaby. Lady Anne Lindsay. ETS
Day has her star, as well as Night. The Two Stars. W. H. Davies. MoBrPo
Day he first spoke to me of love, The. When He Spoke to Me of Love. M. A. Mokhomo. PeSA
Day I Kicked a Bankroll Out the Window, The. Charles Bukowski. WOW
Day! I lament that none can hymn thy praise. Day. Jones Very. AnNE
Day I rode through Devonshire, The. Beneath Such Rains. James E. Warren, Jr. ChIP
Day I was born, The. Children, It's Time. Michael Brownstein. ANYP
Day in Autumn, A. R. S. Thomas. BoNaP; WePo
Day in, day out. Corner Boys. Bryan MacMahon. OnYI
Day in Ireland, A. *Unknown, tr. fr. Irish by* Michael Cavanagh. AnIV
Day in June, A. James Russell Lowell. *See* June.
Day in Spring, A. "Jake Falstaff." BoC
(Beautiful Sunday.) BoNaP
Day in the City, A. L. E. Sissman. NYBP
Day in the Life of a Poet, A. Quincy Troupe. WSL
Day is a golden grain of corn. Day and Night. Baldoon Dhingra. ACV
Day is a Negro, The. Day and Night. Lewis Alexander. CDC
Day is again begun. Unrest. Richard Watson Dixon. OBNC
Day is cold, and dark, and dreary, The. The Rainy Day. Longfellow. AnNE; AWP; HBV; InPo; MaRV; NeHB; PoLF; PoPl; PTK; SoP; TreFT
Day is colorless like Swiss characters in a novel, The. For Guillaume Apollinaire. William Meredith. CoAP
Day is come, I see it rise, The. Song. Dryden. *Fr.* Amboyna. HW
Day Is Coming, The. Sir Walter Besant. CenHV
Day Is Coming, The. William Morris. EnLi-2; OAEP; PoVP; ViPo; WGRP
Day is curl'd about agen, The. An Anniversary. Richard Lovelace. LoBV
Day is dark, The. Sehnsucht; or, What You Will. "Corinna." FiBHP; InMe
Day is dark and the night, The. The Cloud Confines. Dante Gabriel Rossetti. BEL; EnLi-2; TOP
Day Is Dead. Augusta Davies Webster. VA
Day Is Done, The, *parody.* Phoebe Cary. ALV; BOHV
Day is Done, The. Longfellow. AmePo; AmPP (4th ed.); AnAmPo; BLPA; CoBA; FaBoBe; FaFP; HBV; MaRV, *abr.*; MCCG; NeHB; OHFP; OuHeWo; OxBA; PCD; PG; PoPl; PoRA; SoP, *abr.*; StaSt; TIHL; TreF; TrGrPo
"Come, read to me some poem," *sel.* YT
Day is done, The. Evening Hymn. Elizabeth Madox Roberts. TiPo
Day is done, gone the sun. God Is Nigh. *Unknown.* TRV
Day is done, night comes down, The. Run, Nigger Run! *Unknown.* ABF
Day is done, the winter sun, The. At Castle Wood. Emily Brontë. ViBoPo
Day is drawing to its fall, A. First Sight of Her and After. Thomas Hardy. PoEL-5
Day Is Dying in the West. Mary A. Lathbury, *also at. to* William F. Sherwin. SoP; TreFT; TRV; WGRP
Day is ended, The. Ere I sink to sleep. All's Well. Harriet McEwen Kimball. AA
Day Is Gone, The. Keats. EnRP
Day is here! Day is here, is here! Daylight. *Tr. by* Natalie Barnes. MPB
Day is ours together, The. Full Moon. Galway Kinnell. NePoAm-2
Day is over, Mother, see, The. Compline. Patrick F. Kirby. GoBC
Day is past and all the light has fled, The. At Rest. Henry W. Frost. SoP
Day is quenched, and the sun is fled, The. A Song of Doubt. Josiah Gilbert Holland. WGRP
Day is spent, & hath his will on mee, The. Even-Song. George Herbert. MaMe
Day is the children's friend. The Prejudice Against the Past. Wallace Stevens. LiTM (rev. ed.)
Day is Thine, The. Day and Night Are Thine. *Unknown.* SoP
Day is tired with idleness and awe, The. Solstice. Charles Weekes. OnYI
Day is warm, The. June. Aileen Fisher. PDV
Day Lady Died, The. Frank O'Hara. ANYP; NeAP
Day like a respectable woman went, The. Carnival. J. R. Hervey. AnNZ
Day, like our souls, is fiercely dark. Battle Song. Ebenezer Elliot. OBEV (1st ed.); OBRV
Day Lost, A. Gertrude Stein. AtBAP
Day most calm, most bright. Sunday. George Herbert. SCEP-1
Day of Atonement, The, *sel.* Joseph Leiser.
Kol Nidra. AA; TrJP
Day of Battle, The. A. E. Housman. A Shropshire Lad, LVI. OHIP; PoVP; WaaP
Day of Christ, the day of God, The. Thy Glorious Face Above. Charles Wesley. BePJ
Day of Days, The. William Morris. PoVP
Day of Doom, The. Michael Wigglesworth. SCAP
Sels.
Heathen and the Infants, The. AmPP (3d ed.)
Infants' Petition, The. AnNE
Men of Good Works. AmPP
Day of glory! Welcome day! The Fourth of July. John Pierpont. AnNE; DD; HH; MC; OTPC (1946 ed.); PAH; PAL; PoRL; YeAr
Day of hunting done. Twilight in California. Philip Dow. QAH
Day of Inverlochy, The. Iain Lom, *tr. fr. Gaelic.* GoTS
Day of Joy, The. Lucy Larcom. HH
Day of joy, A, a holiday! On Lincoln's Birthday. John Kendrick Bangs. HH
Day of Judgement [*or* Judgment], The. Swift. BWP; CEP; EiCL; EiPP; FaBoEn; NoP
(On the World.) AnIV
Day of Judgement [*or* Judgment], The. Isaac Watts. CEP; EiPP; LoBV; NoP; OBEV; SeCePo
Day of Judgement, The. Edward Young. OxBoCh
Day of Judgment, The. Dugald Buchanan, *tr. fr. Gaelic.* GoTS
Day of Liberty, The. Shelley. *Fr.* Prometheus Unbound, III, iv. EPN
Day of Love, A. Dante Gabriel Rossetti. The House of Life, XVI. MaVP; PoVP; ViPo; VP
Day of Love, The, *abr.* Shelley. *Fr.* Prometheus Unbound, IV. EPN
Day of my life! Where can she get? Good-Night, Babette! Austin Dobson. HBV; OBVV; PoVP; VA
Day of reappearing! The, how it speeds! The Day. Horatius Bonar. FaChP
Day of Resurrection, The. St. John of Damascus, *tr. fr. Greek by* John Mason Neale. MaRV
(Resurrection, The.) PGD, *st.* 1; SoP
Day of tender memory, A. Memorial Day. Emma A. Lent. OQP; WBLP
Day of the Circus Horse, The. T. A. Daly. RIS; UTS
Day of the Crucifixion, The. "Hugh MacDiarmid." PV
Day of the king most righteous. The Day of Wrath. St. Columcille. OxBI
Day of the Slaves, The. Leonard Bacon. PoFr
Day of the Wolf. Keith Wilson. WIRo
Day of These Days. Laurie Lee. AtBAP; BoNaP; FaBoMo; MoVE
Day of Wrath, The. St. Columcille, *tr. fr. Latin by* Helen Waddell. OxBI
Day of wrath, that day of burning. Dies Irae. Thomas of Celano, *tr. by* Abraham Coles. AA; CAW; HBV
Day of wrath, the years are keeping. Dies Irae. Thomas of Celano, *tr. by* Swinburne. LiTW
Day on Kind Continent. Robert David Cohen. NYBP

Day recedes in white, The. A Still Day. Joseph Cherwinski. RePo
Day Returns, The. Burns. HBV
Day Returns, The. Robert Louis Stevenson. SoP; TRV
Day Shall Yet Be Fair, The. Celia Thaxter. MaRV
Day she came, the trees and bushes slept, The. The Visit. Robert Mezey. AmPC
Day she visited the dissecting room, The. Two Views of a Cadaver Room. Sylvia Plath. GoYe; NMP
Day tell me Joe Turner's come and gone. Joe Turner Blues. *Unknown.* TrAS
Day that ends the world will be the one, The. Like a Whisper. Ethan Ayer. GoYe
Day That I Have Loved. Rupert Brooke. BEL; GTSL; PoLF
Day that I was christened, The. Godmother. Dorothy Parker. PoRA
Day that my dear came to us, The. Early Mornings. *Unknown.* AS
Day that Youth had died, The. The Funeral of Youth: Threnody. Rupert Brooke. FaBoTw; SeCeV
Day the big tree went, The. The Tree. Pat Wilson. AnNZ
Day the house and night the street. Through an Embrace. Paul Eluard. LiTW
Day, The—the Way. John Oxenham. FaChP; TRV
Day the Tide, The. Philip Booth. CoAP
Day the Weather Broke, The. Alastair Reid. TPM
Day the wind is white shall I be free, The. Apostasy. Mary Mills. NePoAm
Day the wind was hardly, A. Letter VI. W. S. Graham. ChMP
Day the Winds, The. Josephine Miles. FiMAP
Day unfolds like a lotus bloom, The. Sunrise in the Hills of Satsuma. Mary McNeil Fenollosa. AA
Day was a year at first, The. The Day. Theodore Spencer. PoPo
Day was breaking. The Leper. Nathaniel Parker Willis. WGRP
Day was here when it was his to know, The. The New Tenants. E. A. Robinson. NP
Day was hot, The. The forests were on fire. The Monkey. Vladislav Khodasevich. PoPo
Day was lingering in the pale northwest, The. Twilight. Charles Heavysege. VA
Day was one of weariness, The. The Beggar. Margaret E. Bruner. PoToHe
Day Well Spent, A. "George Eliot." *See* Count That Day Lost.
Day when Charmus ran with five, The. A Mighty Runner. E. A. Robinson. SD
Day when it will not matter, The. The Day. John Glassco. MoCV
Day Will Bring Some Lovely Thing, The. Grace Noll Crowell. TiPo (1952 ed.)
Day will dawn, when one of us shall harken, The. One of Us Two. Ella Wheeler Wilcox. PoToHe
Day will return with a fresher boon. Song of Faith. Josiah Gilbert Holland. *Fr.* Bitter-sweet. WGRP
Day will rise and the sun from eastward. Song. George Campbell Hay. OxBS
Day will soon be gone, The. Fujiwara no Michinobu. *Fr.* Hyaku-Nin-Isshu. AWP; JAWP; WBP
Day with a White Mark, The. C. S. Lewis. BoPe
Day with sky so wide, A. The Motion of the Earth. Norman Nicholson. ImOP
Day with the Foreign Legion, A. Reed Whittemore. CoAP; LiTM (1970 ed.); NePoEA
Day you came naked to Paris, The. The Day Aviva Came to Paris. Irving Layton. MoCV
Day you told me you had a bank account, The. A Poem of Love. Kay Boyle. WOW
Daybreak. John Donne. *See* Break of Day.
Daybreak. Longfellow. AmePo; AnNE; BoTP; HBV; PoLF; TreFT; WaKn
Daybreak. Carl Sandburg. PDV
Daybreak. Shelley. GN
Daybreak. Samuel F. Smith. *See* Morning Light Is Breaking, The.
Daybreak. Stephen Spender. LiTL; MoLP; POTE
Daybreak. Tony Towle. ANYP
Daybreak comes first. Daybreak. Carl Sandburg. PDV
Daybreak in a Garden. Siegfried Sassoon. BoTP
Daybreak in Alabama. Langston Hughes. AmFN
Daybreak upon the hills. Peace. Adeline D. T. Whitney. PAH
Day-Breakers, The. Arna Bontemps. AmNP; BP; CDC; GoSl; IDB; PoNe
Day Dream. Nancy Cardozo. MeWo
Day-Dream, The. Dante Gabriel Rossetti. SyP
Daydream. A. S. J. Tessimond. SeCePo
Day-Dreamer. *Unknown, ad. fr. German by* Louis Untermeyer. *Fr.* Proverbs. RIS; TiPo
Daydreamers. Norma L. Davis. PoAu-2
Day Dreams, or Ten Years Old. Margaret Johnson. BLPA
Dayley Island. Frederick Seidel. CoPo
Daylight. *Tr. fr. Pawnee Indian by* Natalie Barnes. MPB
Day-long bluster of the storm was o'er, The. The Drowned Spaniel. Charles Tennyson Turner. PeVV
Daylong this tomcat lies stretched flat. Esther's Tomcat. Ted Hughes. POTi
Days. Karle Wilson Baker. GFA; OQP; RePo; SP; TiPo
Days. Emerson. AA; AmePo; AmPP; AnAmPo; AnFE; AnNE; AP; APA; ATP; BoLiVe; BWP; CaFP; CBEP; CBV; CoAnAm; CoBA; ForPo; GTBS-W; ILP; LiTA; MAmP; MWA-1; NoP; OBVV; OnPM; OQP; OuHeWo; OxBA; PAn; PFY; Po; PoAn; PoE; PoEL-4; PoFS; PoIE; PoPo; SeCeV; TreFT; TrGrPo; UnPo (1st ed.); ViBoPo; WHA
Days, The. Theodosia Garrison. HBMV
Days. Edgar Paiewonsky. QAH
Days. Eliot Kays Stone. OQP
Day's Affirmation. Sir Herbert Read. FaBoTw
Days after daffodils were up. Easter Snowfall. Harry Behn. TiPo (1959 ed.)
Days and Nights. T. Sturge Moore. HBMV
Days are clear, The. Stay, June, Stay! Christina Rossetti. Fr. Sing-Song. RIS; TiPo; YeAr
Days are cold, the nights are long, The. The Cottager to Her Infant [*or* Cottager's Lullaby]. Dorothy Wordsworth. CH; HBV; OTPC (1923 ed.); PRWS
Days are filled with duties, The. Vesper Bells. Dwight Edwards Marvin. SoP
Days are gone, The. Older Grown. Kate Greenaway. BiCB
Days are sad, it is the Holy tide, The. The Holy Tide. Frederick Tennyson. OBEV; OBVV
Days are short, The. January. John Updike. PDV
Day's at end and there's nowhere to go, The. More Sonnets at Christmas, II. Allen Tate. LiTA; LiTM; NePA; WaP
Days dawn on us that make amends for many. The Interpreters. Swinburne. PoEL-5
Day's Demand, The. Josiah Gilbert Holland. *See* God Give Us Men.
Days drift by, The—as ships drift out to sea. In Summer. Charles Hanson Towne. HBMV
Day's End. Laurence Binyon. OBVV
Day's End. Lesbia Harford. PoAu-1
Day's End. Toyohiko Kagawa, *tr. fr. Japanese by* Lois J. Erickson. MaRV
Day's End. Sir Henry Newbolt. *See* Finis.
Days Gone By, The. James Whitcomb Riley. TreF
Days grow long, the mountains, The. South Wind. Tu Fu. FIW
Days grow short, The; but though the falling sun. The Pudding Prepared and Eaten. Joel Barlow. *Fr.* The Hasty Pudding, III. AnNE
Days grow shorter, the nights grow longer, The. Interlude [*or* Growing Old]. Ella Wheeler Wilcox. BLPA; HBV
Day's grown old, the fainting sun, The. Evening Quatrains [*or* Evening *or* Summer Evening]. Charles Cotton. ChTr; EG; ExPo; LoBV; PoEL-3; TrGrPo; WiR
Days like These. Ella Elizabeth Egbert. PoMa
Days like this, off Jake's, the August fog. Jake's Wharf. Philip Booth. NYBP
Day's March, The. Robert Nichols. MMA
Day's No Rounder than Its Angles Are, The. Peter Viereck. AmP
Days of Birth. *Unknown.* MoShBr
Days of Bute and Grafton's fame, The. The Eight-Day Clock. Alfred Cochrane. HBV
Days of Forty-nine, The. *Unknown, at. to* Charley Rhodes. CoSo, *with music*; IHA; MC; PAH; SGR, *with music*
Days of My Youth. St. George Tucker. AA; HBV

Days of 1964. James Merrill. CoAP; NoP
Days of Our Youth, The. *Unknown, tr. fr. Arabic by* Wilfrid Scawen Blunt. AWP; JAWP; WBP
Days of spring are here, The! The Eglantine. Hafiz. *Fr.* Odes. AWP; JAWP; WBP
Days of the Leaders, 1925, *sel.* L. Lamprey.
Deaf, The. BBV (1951 ed.)
Days of the Week, The. John Farrar. GFA
Days of the Week. *Unknown.* TreFT
Days pace by in weary seemliness, The. An Inhibited Persian. Richard Hart. CIV
Days pass like snaps of lightning. Earth. Brian Vrepont. NeLNL
Days Prior To. Jacques Wakefield. BF
Days shorten, the south blows wide for showers now, The. Salmon-fishing. Robinson Jeffers. AnEnPo; SD
Day's swim done, we found some grass and flung, The. Serendipity of Love. Richard Aldridge. NePoAm-2
Days That Have Been. W. H. Davies. PrWP
Days Too Short. W. H. Davies. MoBrPo; NeMA; POTE
Days will come when you will cease to know, The. Warning. Robert Frost. AmePo
Dayseye hugging the earth, The. Daisy. William Carlos Williams. MAP; MoAB; MoAmPo
Daysman, The. William J. Barnes. SoP
Dazel'd thus, with height of place. *See* Dazzled thus . . .
Dazzle on the sea, my darling, The. Leaving Barra. Louis MacNeice. CMoP; POTE
Dazzled, how the brown moth flutters. Where More Is Meant. Christopher Morley. RePo
Dazzled [*or* Dazel'd] thus with height of place. Upon the Sudden Restraint of the Earl[e] of Somerset, Then Falling from Favour. Sir Henry Wotton. AnAns-2; ELP; MePo; OBS; SeCP
Dazzling and Tremendous How Quick the Sun-Rise Would Kill Me. Walt Whitman. *Fr.* Song of Myself. AtBAP
Dazzling Day, The. Lewis Mac Adams. ANYP
De Amore. Ernest Dowson. OBNC
"Lord over life and all the ways of breath," *sel.* TrPWD
De Anima. Howard Nemerov. ToPo
De Bombycibus, *sel.* Marco Girolamo Vida, *tr. fr. Latin by* Francis Sylvester Mahony.
Silkworm, The. CAW
De Coenatione Micae. Martial, *tr. fr. Latin by* Robert Louis Stevenson. FaBoCh; LoGBV
De Consolatione Philosophiae. Boethius. *See* Consolation of Philosophy.
De Contemptu Mundi, *sels.* Bernard of Cluny, *tr. fr. Latin by* John Mason Neale.
Jerusalem, the Golden. CAW; MaRV; WGRP
(Celestial Country, The.) GoBC, *abr.*
(Jerusalem, *abr.*) HBV; OBVV
De Fesch. James Reeves. MuSP
De Gaulle Nods Once. Eugene Brooks. NYTB
De Gelu Diutino, Anno Dom. 1607. John Heath. SiCE
De Good Lawd Know My Name. Frank L. Stanton. WBLP
De Guiana, Carmen Epicum. George Chapman. OBSC
"De Gustibus." Robert Browning. EPN; HBV; MaVP; MBW-2; OAEP; PoVP; VA; ViPo; VP; YT
De Gustibus. St. John Emile Clavering Hankin. CenHV
De Ignoto. Everard Guilpin. *Fr.* Skialetheia. ReIE
De little black bull kem down de medder. Hoosen Johnny. *Unknown.* FaPON
De Lord he thought he'd make a man. Dese Bones Gwine to Rise Again. *Unknown.* SiTL
De Mense Ianuarii Quae Fuit An. Do. 1595. Thomas Bastard. SiCE
De Mexico ha venido, *with music. Unknown, tr. fr. Spanish.* TrAS
De Microcosmo. Thomas Bastard. SiCE
De Morte. *At. to* Sir Henry Wotton. OBS
"De Mortuis Nil Nisi Bonum." Richard Realf. HBV
De Naevo in Facie Faustinae. Thomas Bastard. LO
De Partu Virginis, *sel.* Jacopo Sannazaro, *tr. fr. Latin by* John C. Eustace.
Celestial Queen, *fr.* Bk. III. ISi
De Piscatione. Thomas Bastard. TuPP
De Poeta Martiali. Thomas Bastard. SiCE
De Profundis. Psalms, CXXX, Bible, *O.T.* BLRP; MaRV; TreF; WGRP; WHL
(Out of the Depths.) TrJP
(Psalm CXXX.) EnLi-1; LiTW (*Book of Common Prayer*); OnPM
(Song of Supplication, A.) TrGrPo
De Profundis, *sel.* Elizabeth Barrett Browning.
"Whatever's lost, it first was won." TrPWD
De Profundis. David Gascoyne. *Fr.* Miserere. NeBP
De Profundis. "Hugh MacDiarmid." SeCePo
De Profundis. George Macdonald. EPN
De Profundis. Dorothy Parker. ErPo
De Profundis. Christina Rossetti. CoBE; OuHeWo; PoVP; VP
De Profundis, *sel.* Tennyson.
"Out of the deep, my child, out of the deep," I. ILP
De Profundis. Georg Trakl, *tr. fr. German by* Glauco Cambon. OnPM
De Profundis. Katharine Tynan. VA
De Profundis. Amos N. Wilder. TrPWD
De Profundis Clamavi. Baudelaire, *tr. fr. French by* Arthur Symons. SyP
De railroad bridge's. Homesick Blues. Langston Hughes. WaKn
De Regimine Principum, *sels.* Thomas Hoccleve.
Hoccleve's Lament for Chaucer and Gower, *abr.* OAEP
Lament for Chaucer. OBEV
Prologue: "Musing upon the restles bisinesse." PoEL-1
To Chaucer. ACP
De Rerum Natura, *sels.* Lucretius, *tr. fr. Latin.*
Address to Venus, *fr.* I, *tr. by* Spenser, *fr.* The Faerie Queene, IV, 10. AnEnPo; AWP
("Darling of God and Men, beneath the gliding stars," *tr. by* Basil Bunting.) PoPl
(Prayer to Venus, *tr. by* Spenser.) ElL
Against the Fear of Death, *fr.* III, *tr. by* Dryden. BWP; MBW-1
Fear of Death, The, *fr.* III, LoBV
"What has this bugbear death to frighten man." AWP; CTC; JAWP; WBP
Cause of Thunder, The, *fr.* VI, *tr. by* Thomas Creech. PeRV
Concerning the Nature of Love, *fr.* IV, *tr. by* Dryden. ErPo; PeRV
(Nature of Love, The.) UnTE
No Single Thing Abides, *fr.* III, *tr. by* W. H. Mallock. AWP; ImOP, *abr.*; JAWP; PG (1945 ed); WBP
Of the Nature of Things, *tr. by* William Ellery Leonard.
Beginnings of Civilization, *fr.* V. OuHeWo
Beyond Religion. AWP; PoFr
Of Human Progress, *fr.* V. WoL
Origins and Savage Period of Mankind, *fr.* V. OuHeWo
Origins of Life, The. LiTW
Origins of Vegetable and Animal Life, *fr.* V. OuHeWo
Suave Mari Magno, *tr. by* W. H. Mallock. AWP
De Roberval; a Drama, *sels.* John Hunter-Duvar.
Adieu to France. VA
Gallant Fleet, The. VA
"Here, then, we stand on the Canadian shore." CaP
La Belle Sauvage. OBCV
Ohnáwa. VA
Twilight Song. VA; WHW
De Rosis Hibernia. Sir Edmund Gosse. VA
De Se. John Weever. ReIE; TuPP
De Senectute. Franklin P. Adams. HBMV
De Subiecto Operis Sui. Thomas Bastard. SiCE
De Tea Fabula. Sir Arthur Quiller-Couch. CenHV
Deacon's Masterpiece, The; or, The Wonderful "One-Hoss Shay." Oliver Wendell Holmes. *Fr.* The Autocrat of the Breakfast Table, *ch.* 11. AmePo; AmP; AmPP; AnNE; AP; BBV (1923 ed.); BOHV; CoBA; FaFP; HBV; HBVY; InMe; LHV; LiTA; LoGBV; MoShBr; NePA; OHFP; OnSP; OTPC; OxBA; PaPo; Po; PoIE; PoLF; PoRA; PTK; RIS; SiTL; StPo; StVeCh; WBLP; YT
(One-Hoss Shay, The; or, The Deacon's Masterpiece.) TreF
(Wonderful "One-Hoss Shay," The.) BeLS; FaBoBe; YaD
Dead, The. Mathilde Blind. EPN; OBVV; VA; WGRP
Dead, The. John Le Gay Brereton. BoAu
Dead, The ("Blow out, you bugles"). Rupert Brooke. 1914, III. BEL; FaPL; MCCG; OQP; PoFr; TreF; WGRP
Dead, The ("These hearts were woven"). Rupert Brooke. 1914, IV. AnFe; ATP; BrPo; CH; EnLit; GTSL; GTBS-W; LiTB; LiTG; MCCG; MMA; OtMeF; PoRL; POTE; SeCeV; ShBV-4; Sonn; TOP; YT
Dead. Rhoda Coghill. OnYI
Dead, The. Robert J. Crot. MaRV

Dead, The. C. Day Lewis. TwCP
Dead. Lionel Johnson. BrPo; FaBoEn; GTBS-D; OBNC; PoEL-5
Dead, The ("Think you the dead are lonely in that place"). David Morton. PAH
Dead, The. Jones Very. AA; AmePo; AnNE; AP; CBV; MAmP; OxBA
Dead, The. John Williams. NePoAm-2
Dead abide with us, The. Though stark and cold. The Dead. Mathilde Blind. EPN; OBVV; VA; WGRP
Dead and the Living One, The. Thomas Hardy. MMA
Dead are born from the dark again, The. Reversions. Alfred Dorn. FiSC
Dead, The, are not to rise; their roll our grief. Aeschylus. *Fr.* Agamemnon. PoFr
Dead are silent, The. Passionless and still. The Dead. Robert J. Crot. MaRV
Dead at Clonmacnois, The. Angus O'Gillan, *tr. fr. Middle Irish by* T. W. Rolleston. AnIL; HBV; HT; IrPN; OBEV; OBVV; OnYI; OxBI
(Clonmacnoise.) AnIV; OBMV
Dead Aviator, The. Francis Hackett. JKCP (1926 ed.)
Dead Bee, The. Nathalia Crane. MAP; MoAmPo (1942 ed.)
Dead Bird, A. Andrew Young. BiS
Dead Boy. Callimachus, *tr. fr. Greek by* Lord Neaves. OnPM
Dead Boy. John Crowe Ransom. CMoP; LiTA; MoPW; NoP; OxBA; TwCP
Dead Branch, The. Douglas Gibson. NYTB
Dead brood over Europe, the cloud and vision descends over cheerful France, The. Blake. The French Revolution, I. EiPP
Dead Brother, The. *Unknown.* EnSB
Dead Calm and Mist, A. "Fiona Macleod." SyP
Dead Center. Ruth Whitman. NYBP
Dead Child, The. George Barlow. OBVV; VA
Dead Child, The. Ernest Dowson. BrPo
Dead Child [*or* Childe], A. Lucian, *tr. fr. Greek.* LiTW, *tr. by* Timothe Kendall; OnPM, *tr. by* Lord Neaves
("Frowning fates have taken hence, The," *tr. by* Timothe Kendall.) EnLi-1
Dead Church, The. Charles Kingsley. VA
Dead City, The. Clinch Calkins. AnAmPo
Dead Cleopatra Lies in a Crystal Casket. Conrad Aiken. *Fr.* Discordants. CMoP
Dead Coach, The. Katharine Tynan. HBV; VA
Dead Cow Farm. Robert Graves. BrPo
Dead Crab, The. Andrew Young. FaBoTw; LoBV; OA
Dead dancer, how is this?—the laurel here. Vernon Castle. Harriet Monroe. HBMV
Dead do not specially depress me, The. At Morning an Iris. Patrick Evans. NeBP
Dead Eagle, The. Thomas Campbell. EnRP
Dead Faith, The. Fanny Heaslip Lea. HBV; WGRP
Dead Feast of the Kol-Folk, The. Whittier. PoEL-4
Dead Fiddle, The. Humbert Wolfe. TrJP
Dead Fires. Jessie Redmond Fauset. BANP; PoNe
Dead Friend, A. Norman Gale. VA
Dead hangs the fruit on that tall tree. Burial of the Spirit. Richard Hughes. MoBrPo
Dead Harvest, A. Alice Meynell. MoVE
Dead he lay among his books! Bayard Taylor. Longfellow. DD; HBV
Dead here look upon the light from caves, The. Girod Street Cemetery; New Orleans. Harry Morris. GoYe
Dead Heroes, The. Isaac Rosenberg. MoBrPo; TrGrPo (1942 ed.)
Dead Horse, The, *with music.* *Unknown.* AmSS; AS
Dead Host's Welcome, The. John Fletcher. *Fr.* The Lovers' Progress, III, i. SeCl; TrGrPo
('Tis Late and Cold.) ViBoPo
Dead in Europe, The. Robert Lowell. CMoP; DTC; LiTM (1970 ed.); NePA; NePoEA; OxBA; ToPo
Dead in Melanesia, The. Randall Jarrell. MiAP
Dead in Queens lean westward from their stones, The. A Day in the City. L. E. Sissman. NYBP
Dead in the battle,—dead in the field. The Soldier's Dirge. Elizabeth Herman. DD; HH
Dead in the Sierras. Joaquin Miller. AA; PFY
Dead in Wars and in Revolutions. Mary Devenport O'Neill. NeIP
Dead! Is it possible? He, the bold rider. Custer's Last Charge. Frederick Whittaker. DD; HBV; MC; OnMSP; PaA; PAH; PoLF; ThLM
Dead is the roll of the drums. Abraham Lincoln. Henry Howard Brownell. GN
Dead Knight, The. John Masefield. CH; GTBS-P
Dead Knock About, The. William Hunt. YAP
Dead Leaf, A. Howard Moss. NYBP
Dead leaves strew the forest walk, The. Stanzas. John G. C. Brainard. AnAmPo
Dead Letter, A. Austin Dobson. HBV; PoVP; VA
Dead Liar Speaks, A. Michael Lewis. GoTP
Dead lie drunk on heady rain, The. Lufoten. Quentin Stevenson. POTE (1959 ed.)
Dead, Long Dead. Tennyson. *Fr.* Maud. AtBAP; SyP, *shorter sel.*
Dead Love. Mary Mathews Adams. AA
Dead Make Rules, The. Mary Carolyn Davies. HBMV; PoFr
Dead Man, A. *Unknown,* *tr. fr. Japanese by* Ishii *and* Obata. OnPM
Dead Man Ariseth and Singeth a Hymn to the Sun, The. *Unknown,* *tr. fr. Egyptian by* Robert Hillyer. *Fr.* Book of the Dead. AWP; JAWP; WBP
Deadman's Dirge. George Darley. *See* Sea-Ritual, The.
Dead Man's Dump. Isaac Rosenberg. BrPo; CABL; FaBoMo; GTBS-P; LiTM; MMA; MoPo; TrJP; WaP
Dead March, A. Mary C. Gillington. PeVV
Dead March, A. Cosmo Monkhouse. HBV; VA
"play me a march," *sel.* OBVV
Dead Marine. Louis O. Coxe. WaP
Dead men are wisest, for they know. The Wise. Countee Cullen. PoNe
Dead men of 'ninety-two, also of 'ninety-three. Sonnet. Arthur Rimbaud. WaaP
Dead Men Tell No Tales. Haniel Long. HBMV; MCCG; NP
"Dead men tell no tales!" they chuckled. The Singing Saviors. Clement Wood. MaRV; OQP
Dead Men's Song, The. Young Ewing Allison. *See* Derelict.
Dead Metaphors. David Holbrook. NYTB
Dead Mole, A. Andrew Young. GTBS-P
Dead Moon, The. Danske Bedlinger Dandridge. AA
Dead Morning. Raymond Holden. MAP; MoAmPo (1942 ed.)
Dead Musician, The. Charles L. O'Donnell. CAW; JKCP
Dead Musicians. Siegfried Sassoon. BrPo
Dead of the Wilderness, The. Hayyim Nahman Bialik, *tr. fr. Hebrew by* Maurice Samuel. AWP
"Yonder great shadow," *sel.* JAWP; WBP
Dead of Winter. Anthony Towne. NYBP; StP
Dead! one of them shot by the sea in the east. Mother and Poet. Elizabeth Barrett Browning. HBV; VA
Dead Pan, The. Elizabeth Barrett Browning. PoVP; ViPo
Dead Past, A. *At. to* C. C. Munson. BLRP; WBLP
Dead Player, The. Robert Burns Wilson. AA
Dead Poet, The. Lord Alfred Douglas. CLwM; HBMV; MoBrPo (1942 ed.); PoVP; ViBoPo
Dead pomp sneering undergound. Stanzas on a Visit to Longleat House in Wiltshire, October 1953. George Barker. ToPo
Dead Ponies. Brenda Chamberlain. NeBP
Dead President, The. Edward Rowland Sill. LiPo; PAH
Dead Pussy Cat, The. *Unknown,* *at. to* John Bennett *and to* Marion Short. CIV
Dead Quire, The. Thomas Hardy. OAEP
Dead return to us continually, The. Ghosts. Brian Hooker. PFY
Dead Ride Fast, The. R. P. Blackmur. MoPo
Dead Sea Scrolls, The, *sels.* *Unknown,* *tr. fr. Hebrew.* TrJP
Blessed Art Thou, O Lord, *tr. by* Theodor H. Gaster.
Lo, I Am Stricken Dumb, *tr. by* Theodor H. Gaster.
My Soul in the Bundle of Life, *tr. by* E. Margaret Rowley.
Though Mine Eye Sleep Not, *tr. by* Theodor H. Gaster.
Dead Seal. Alfred Purdy. MoCV
Dead shalt thou lie; and nought. Achtung. Sappho. CTC
Dead Ship of Harpswell, The. Whittier. EtS
Dead Singer, A. John E. Logan. VA
Dead Singer, The. Mary Ashley Townsend. AA
Dead Snake. William Jay Smith. NePoAm-2
Dead Soldier. Nicolás Guillén, *tr. fr. Spanish by* Langston Hughes. PoNe; TTY
Dead Soldier, A. George Edgar Montgomery. AA
Dead Solomon, The. John Aylmer Dorgan. AA

Dead Song-Writer, A. Lucilius, *tr. fr. Greek by* Humbert Wolfe. WoL
Dead soul lay in the light of day, A. Judgment. Grace Ellery Channing. AA
Dead Sparrow, The. William Cartwright. CH
(Lesbia on Her Sparrow.) CavP
("Tell me not of joy: there's none.") LO
Dead Sparrow, The. Catullus, *tr. fr. Latin by* Byron. EnLi-1; OuHeWo
Dead Starling, The. Catullus. *See* Death of Lesbia's Bird, The.
Dead Statesman, A. Kipling. *Fr.* Epitaphs of the War, 1914-18. OAEP (2d ed.); PoVP
Dead. The dead year is lying at my feet. New Year's Eve—Midnight. Frederika Richardson Macdonald. VA
Dead, they'll burn you up with electricity. Marcus Argentarius. Kenneth Rexroth. CrMA
Dead Tribune, The. Denis Florence MacCarthy. ACP
Dead Wasp. Kenneth Slade Alling. NePoAm
Dead Wasp. Gregory Orr. QAH
Dead Water, The. Wen Yi-tuo, *tr. fr. Chinese by* Harold Acton *and* Ch'en Shih-hsiang. LiTW
Dead Warrior, A. Laurence Housman. HBMV
Dead Wingman, The. Randall Jarrell. MiAP
Dead, with their eyes to the foe. Melville and Coghill. Andrew Lang. VA
Dead woman lay in her first night's grave, The. The Dead and the Living One. Thomas Hardy. MMA
Dead wood with its load of stones. The Water-Wheel. Jack R. Clemo. ChMP
Dead Words, The. Vernon Watkins. LiTM (rev. ed.)
Dead young man stood up in his grave, The. Articles of War. Dunstan Thompson. WaP
Deader they die here, or at least. Fall Comes in Back-Country Vermont. Robert Penn Warren. NYBP
Deadfall. Martha Keller. GoYe
Deadly certain, death takes its time. Dirge for J. A. Rogers. Hart Leroi Bibbs. BF
Deadly Kisses. Pierre de Ronsard, *tr. fr. French by* Andrew Lang. AWP
Deadman's Dirge. George Darley. PoG
Deaf. H. C. Bunner. AA
Deaf. Barry O. Higgs. PeSA
Deaf, The. L. Lamprey. *Fr.* Days of the Leaders, 1925. BBV (1951 ed.)
Deaf and Dumb. "A." PRWS
Deaf and Dumb. Robert Browning. MaRV
Deaf-and-Dumb School. Anthony Delius. PeSA
Deaf is like. Deaf. Barry O. Higgs. PeSA
Deaf to God, who calls and walks. Doomsday Morning. Genevieve Taggard. MAP; MoAmPo
Deaf Woman's Courtship, The, *with music. Unknown.* BFSS; SaSa
Deafening/ The first solitary note of day. Trumpet and Flute. Gunnar Hernaes. LiTW
Deal out again the dog-eared poetry books. John Betjeman. *Fr.* Summoned by Bells. ML
Dean, The. Alan Porter. AnAmPo
Dean, if we believe Report, The. Swift. *Fr.* Verses on the Death of Dr. Swift. FaBoEn
Dean-bourn, a Rude River in Devon, by Which Sometimes He Lived ("Dean-bourn, farewell; I never look to see"). Robert Herrick. MaPo (1969 ed.); Po; PoeP; SeCV-1
(To Dean-bourn, a Rude River in Devon.) AnAnS-2; SCEP-2
Dean's Consent, The. Coventry Patmore. *Fr.* The Angel in the House, I, vi. VA
Dean's Lady, The. George Crabbe. LoBV
Dear. Howard McCord. YAP
Dear Agatha, I give you joy. The Doll's House. Anna Letitia Barbauld. OTPC (1923 ed.)
Dear Alice! you'll laugh when you know it. The Talented Man. Winthrop Mackworth Praed. ALV; CoBE; EnRP; FiBHP; HBV
Dear America. Robert Peterson. PPON
Dear and great Angel, wouldst thou only leave. The Guardian-Angel. Robert Browning. GoBC; HBV; PoVP
Dear Andrew, with the brindled hair. To Andrew Lang. Robert Louis Stevenson. PoVP
Dear Ann, wherever you are. For [*or* To] Ann Scott-Moncrieff. Edwin Muir. GTBS-P; SiSw
Dear architect of fine *chateaux en l'air.* To William Hayley, Esq. William Cowper. Sonn
"Dear as remembered kisses after death." Constancy. Minor Watson. HBV
Dear, back my wounded heart restore. The Divorce. Thomas Stanley. AnAnS-2; LO; MeLP
Dear Bargain, The. Richard Crashaw. *See* Charitas Nimia.
Dear, beauteous Death! the jewel of the just. Henry Vaughan. LO
Dear Bill,/ When I search the past for you. A Letter to William Carlos Williams. Kenneth Rexroth. OnHM; PP
Dear boy, of thy race thou'rt the blossom and pride. Quarrel with Juventius. Catullus. OnPM
Dear boy! whom, torn in early youth away. Memorial Trees. Juvenal. OnPM
Dear boy, you will not hear me speak. Pangloss's Song: A Comic-Opera Lyric. Richard Wilbur. AP; NePoAm-2
Dear Brook! Tomorrow's noon again. Wordsworth. *Fr.* An Evening Walk. CoBE; EnRP
Dear brother Robin, this comes from us all. Country Letter. John Clare. CBEP; NCEP
"Dear brother, when you go home to-night." Yonder School. *Unknown.* BFSS
Dear brother, would you know the life. A Letter. Emerson. OxBA
Dear charming nymph, neglected and decried. Farewell to Poetry. Goldsmith. *Fr.* The Deserted Village. OBEC
Dear Cherry Blossom. To a Japanese Girl Grieved over the War on China. Belle Chapman Morrill. MaRV
Dear child of Nature, let them rail! To a Young Lady. Wordsworth. EG; EnRP
Dear child! whom sleep can hardly tame. To a Child. John Sterling. VA
Dear child, you in your native land unfold. Yesterday. Ethel Anderson. NeLNL
"Dear children," they asked in every town. The Kings from the East. Heine. ChTr
Dear Chloe [or Cloe], how blubbered is that pretty face! Answer to Chloe Jealous [*or* A Better Answer (to Cloe Jealous]). Matthew Prior. ALV; AWP; CEP; EiCL; EiPP; ELP; ExPo; FaBoEn; HBV; InPo; JAWP; LiTL; LO; MeWo; OBEC; PIA; PoE; PoEL-3; SeCePo; SeCeV; SeCL; TOP; ViBoPo; WBP
Dear chorister, who from those shadows sends. *See* Dear quirister, who from those shadows sends.
Dear Citizens,/ I heard the newsboys shouting "Europe! Europe!" The True, the Good and the Beautiful. Delmore Schwartz. MiAP
Dear Cloe, how blubber'd is that pretty face. *See* Dear Chloe, how blubber'd is that pretty face.
Dear Colin, prevent my warm blushes. Restrained Passion. Lady Mary Wortley Montagu. MeWo
Dear common flower, that grow'st beside the way. To the Dandelion. James Russell Lowell. AP; CoBA; DD; FaPON; GN; HBV; HBVY; MPB; YT
Dear Cosmopolitan, I know. A Familiar Epistle. Austin Dobson. VA
Dear Craoibhin, look into our case. At the Abbey Theatre. W. B. Yeats. Sonn
Dear critic, who my lightness so deplores. To a Captious Critic. Paul Laurence Dunbar. Kal
Dear Cynthia, though thou bear'st the name. To Cynthia, on Her Changing. Sir Francis Kynaston. EG; MePo; SeCL
Dear, damned, distracted town, farewell! A Farewell to London in the Year 1715. Pope. CBEP; CEP
Dear Dark Head. *Unknown, tr. fr. Modern Irish by* Sir Samuel Ferguson. AnIV; BoLP; OnYI; OxBI; UnTE
(Cean Dubh Deelish.) ACV; IrPN; OBEV (1st ed.); SeCePo
Dear Dark Head. William Rooney. JKCP (1926 ed.)
Dear, dear, dear, is the rocky glen. The Thrush's Song. *Unknown, tr. by* William Macgillivray. CH; GoTP
Dear, dear! what can the matter be? Mother Goose. PPL
Dear, did you know how sweet to me. A Vain Desire. Theodore Wratislaw. VA
Dear, do not your fair beauty wrong. Love's Prime. Thomas May. *Fr.* The Old Couple, III, i. EG; SeCL; TuPP; ViBoPo
Dear Doctor, whose blandly invincible pen. To O. W. Holmes. Paul Hamilton Hayne. DD
Dear Doll, while the tails of our horses are plaiting. Miss

Dear (continued)
Biddy Fudge to Miss Dorothy. Thomas Moore. *Fr.* The Fudge Family in Paris. NBM
Dear Dove, that bear'st to my sole-laboring ark. Ad Amicam. Francis Thompson. Sonn
Dear dreamer, that I may plunge. Another Fan Belonging to Mademoiselle Mallarmé. Stéphane Mallarmé. SyP
Dear Emily, my tears would burn your page. To Emily Dickinson. Yvor Winters. Sonn
Dear Erin, how sweetly thy green bosom rises. Cushla-Ma-Chree. John Philpot Curran. DD; HBV
Dear eyes, set deep within the shade. The Protestation. Selwyn Image. VA
Dear Fanny. Thomas Moore. HBV; InMe
Dear father and dear mother: Let me crave. Erotion. Martial. AWP; JAWP; WBP
Dear Father/ hear and bless. Margaret Wise Brown. PDV
"Dear Father, tell me, Why are Worms?" Why? Walter de la Mare. FiBHP
Dear Father, whom we cannot see. A Prayer for Peace. John Oxenham. SoP
Dear fellow-artist, why so free. To a Young Beauty. W. B. Yeats. CMoP
Dear Fergusson—They've Ramsay's statue clean. Letter to Robert Fergusson. Alexander Scott. OxBS
Dear firstling of my little flock. To My Firstborn. Bernard Isaac Durward. JKCP (1926 ed.)
Dear friend, far off, my lost desire. In Memoriam A. H. H., CXXIX. Tennyson. EPN; MaPo; MaRV; TOP; ViPo; VP
Dear Friend, I fear my heart will break. Out of French. Sir Charles Sedley. PeRV
Dear friend, I pray thee, if thou wouldst be proving. Friendship. Ella Wheeler Wilcox. PoToHe
Dear friend, when those we love are in distress. To Julian. Robert Gould. PeRV
Dear friend! whose holy, ever-living lines. The Match. Henry Vaughan. AnAnS-1; MeP
Dear Friend, whose presence in the house. Come Visit Us. James Freeman Clarke. FaChP
Dear Friends. E. A. Robinson. AmePo
Dear Friends and Patrons of the *Denver News!* Carrier's Address. *Unknown.* PoOW
Dear friends, reproach me not for what I do. Dear Friends. E. A. Robinson. AmePo
Dear Fronto, famed alike in peace and war. Country Pleasures. Martial. AWP; OnPM
Dear George,/ At last the blowfly's buzz retreats. Letter to a Friend. John Thompson. BoAV; PoAu-2
Dear gentle hands have stroked my hair. Mother's Hands. W. Dayton Wedgefarth. PoToHe
Dear Gill I ne'er thought till last night. The New Married Couple; or A Friendly Debate between the Country Farmer and His Buxome Wife. *Unknown.* CoMu
Dear God,/ give us a flood of water. The Prayer of the Little Ducks. Carmen Bernos de Gasztold. PDV; ThGo
Dear God, another day is done. An Evening Prayer. *Unknown.* STF
Dear God, I humbly pray. Prayer of a Beginning Teacher. Ouida Smith Dunnam. TrPWD
Dear God, I stand with empty hands. Gifts. Mary Edgar Comstock. OQP
Dear God, I wish I could have been. Finding you. Mary Dixon Thayer. CAW
Dear God, my little boy of three. A Father's Prayer. *Unknown.* SoP; STF
Dear God our Father, at Thy knee confessing. For Deeper Life. Katharine Lee Bates. TrPWD
Dear God, the light is come, our outgrown creeds. A Prayer. *Unknown.* OQP
Dear God, Thou know'st how many tasks. A Prayer of Busy Hands. B. Y. Williams. MaRV
Dear God, though Thy all-powerful hand. Care Is Heavy. Conal O'Riordan. CAW
Dear God, Your roses bloom so very sweetly. Prayer in a June Garden. *Unknown.* FaChP
Dear Grandmamma, with what we give. Grandmamma's Birthday. Hilaire Belloc. ELU; FiBHP; PoPl
Dear, had the world in its caprice. Respectability. Robert Browning. EnLoPo; EpN; MBW-2; PoVP; VA; ViBoPo; ViPP
Dear Harp of My Country. Thomas Moore. AnIL; EnRP; OAEP
Dear head to one side, in summer dusk, Olga. Trastevere. Edwin Denby. ANYP
Dear heart, I think the young impassioned priest. "Quia Multum Amavi." Oscar Wilde. ACP (1926 ed.)
Dear, heaven-designing [*or* heavn-designed] soul! To a Young Gentle-Woman [*or* To the Same Party], Councel Concerning Her Choice. Richard Crashaw. AtBAP; MaMe; OBS
Dear, honored name, beloved for human ties. Name of Mary. John Boyle O'Reilly. JKCP
Dear hope! Earth's dowry and heaven's debt! For Hope [*or* Answer for Hope *or* Richard Crashaw's Answer; for Hope]. Richard Crashaw. GTBS-W; LiTB; LiTG; MaMe; MeLP; OBS; SCEP-1; SeCV-1; ViBoPo
Dear, I could weep, but that my brain is dry. Thomas Lovell Beddoes. *Fr.* The Bride's Tragedy. LO
Dear, I do not count it flighty. To a Lady across the Way. E. B. White. InMe
Dear, I have lit a candle for your birthday. Candles. Sister Mary Eleanor. JKCP (1955 ed.)
Dear, I must be gone. Parting. W. B. Yeats. FaBoTw
Dear If I with Guile. Thomas Campion. NCEP
Dear, If You Change. *Unknown.* CBEP; CBV; EIL; EnRePo; EP
("Dear, if you change, I'll never choose again.") EnLoPo; InvP; LO; OBSC; SiCE
(Deare, if You Change.) AtBAP; PoEL-2
Dear, if you love me, hold me most your friend. A Sonnet. Alice Duer Miller. AA
Dear Italy! The sound of thy soft name. Italian Rhapsody. Robert Underwood Johnson. HBV
Dear Jesus! ever at my side. The Nearest Friend. Frederick W. Faber. TreFS
Dear Lady of the Cherries, cool, serene. Sonnet for the Madonna of the Cherries. A. P. Wavell. OtMeF
Dear Lady, When Thou Frownest. Robert Bridges. LiTL
Dear Land of All My Love. Sidney Lanier. *Fr.* The Centennial Meditation of Columbia. DD; GN; HBVY; MPB; StVeCh
("Long as thine Art shall love true love.") PGD
Dear Land of Hope, thy hope is crowned. Land of Hope and Glory. A. C. Benson. PTK
Dear, let me dream of love. A Prayer. Selwyn Image. VA
Dear, let us two each other spy. Love's Vision. William Cavendish, Duke of Newcastle. LO; SeCL
Dear Lillian! (The "dear" one risks). To Lillian Russell. Bert Leston Taylor. WhC
Dear Little Arms, The. Walter E. Isenhour. SoP
Dear little child this little book. With a First Reader. Rupert Hughes. HBMV
Dear little Dorothy, she is no more! Dorothy. Rose Hawthorne Lathrop. AA
Dear little flag in the window there. The Service Flag. William Herschell. PEDC
Dear little house, dear shabby street. To the Little House. Christopher Morley. HBMV
Dear little, pretty, favourite ore. On a Half Penny which a Young Lady Gave a Beggar, and which the Author Redemmed for Half a Crown. Henry Fielding. CBEP
Dear little tree that we plant to-day. An Arbor Day Tree. *Unknown.* DD; HH; OHIP; RePo
Dear little Violet. Calling the Violet. Lucy Larcom. MPB
Dear Little Violets. John Moultrie. *See* Violets.
Dear Lizbie Browne. To Lizbie Browne. Thomas Hardy. DTC; ELP; EnLit; LO
Dear Lord and Father of Mankind. Whittier. *Fr.* The Brewing of Soma. MaRV; SoP; TreFT; TrPWD; TRV
Dear Lord—before I take my place. A Driver's Prayer. *Unknown.* STF
Dear Lord, for all in pain. A Prayer. Amy Carmichael. SoP; TRV
Dear Lord, I do not ask. Hand in Hand, a Child and I. *Unknown.* SoP
Dear Lord, I do not hesitate. A Business Man's Prayer. William Ludlum. BLRP
Dear Lord. I hold my hand to take. A Mother Understands. G. A. Studdert-Kennedy. OQP
Dear Lord, if ever I might hope for grace. Prayers of a Christian Bridegroom. Pierre Poupo. HW
Dear Lord, in the battle. *Unknown.* OTD
Dear Lord! Kind Lord! The Prayer Perfect [*or* Love's Pray-

er]. James Whitcomb Riley. AA; MaRV; OQP; TreFT
Dear Lord, let me recount to Thee. It is Finished. Christina Rossetti. VA
Dear Lord, receive my son, whose winning love. Of His Dear Son, Gervase. Sir John Beaumont. *Fr.* Of My Dear Son, Gervase Beaumont. GoBC; OBEV
Dear Lord, thy table is outspread. The Master's Invitation. Anson Davies Fitz Randolph. AA
Dear Lord, we bow our heads to pray. Grace for the Noonday Meal. William L. Stidger. SoP
Dear Lord, Who Sought at Dawn. Harry Webb Farrington. MaRV
Dear Lord, Whose serving-maiden. Hymn. Josephine Preston Peabody. TrPWD
Dear Lord's best interpreters, The. In Earthen Vessels. Whittier. *Fr.* The Friend's Burial. BLRP; SoP; TRV
Dear loss! since thy untimely fate. Henry King. *Fr.* The Exequy. ATP; LO; OBEV; OBS; WHA
Dear love, dost thou sleep fairly. Parting at Morning. Dietmar von Aist. AWP
Dear [*or* Deare] love, for nothing less [*or* lesse] than thee. The Dream [*or* Dreame]. John Donne. AnAnS-1; EG; EIL; GTBS-W; InvP; LiTB; LiTG; LiTL; LO; LoBV; MaMe; MBW-1; MeLP; MePo; OAEP; OBEV; OBS; SCEP-1; SeCP; SeEP; TOP
Dear Love, let me this evening die! The Dying Lover. Sir William Davenant. SeCL
Dear love, when with a two-fold mind. Laurence Housman. *Fr.* All Fellows. WGRP
"Dear love, why should you weep." A Lost World. Robert Graves. NYBP
Dear Lucy, you know what my wish is. Ad Ministram [*or* Persicos Odi]. Thackeray. HBV; OBEV (new ed.)
Dear madam, did you never gaze? On Mites. Stephen Duck. EiCL
Dear Madam, you have seen this play. At the Theater. A. P. Herbert. FiBHP
Dear maid, let me speak. Conjugal Conjugations. A. W. Bellaw. BOHV
Dear Maiden. Heine, *tr. fr. German by* John Todhunter. AWP
Dear March, come in! Emily Dickinson. YeAr
Dear Marge, hello. It is 5:15 a.m. Sonnet XVIII. Ted Berrigan. FRC
Dear marshes, by no hand of man. Flood-Time on the Marshes. Evaleen Stein. AA
Dear Master, for this coming year. New Year. *Unknown.* SoP
Dear Master, in Whose life I see. Dreams and Deeds. John Hunter. ChIP; MaRV; SoP; TRV
"Dear me!" exclaimed Homer. E. C. Bentley. FiBHP
Dear me! what signifies a pin. The Pin. Ann Taylor. HBV; HBVY
Dear Men and Women. John Hall Wheelock. NYBP
Dear Miss Dix, I am a young man of half-past thirty-seven. Two and One Are a Problem. Ogden Nash. FiBHP
Dear Mr. Editor: I wish to say. A Grievance. James Kenneth Stephen. HBV; Par
Dear Mr. Noman, does it ever strike you. On Noman, a Guest. Hilaire Belloc. PV
Dear Mistress, do not grieve for me. Leo to His Mistress. Henry Dwight Sedgwick. BLPA; CIV
Dear Mother, dear Mother, the Church is cold. The Little Vagabond. Blake. BOHV; CBEP; CEP; SeCeV; TDP
Dear mother, how pretty. The New Moon. Eliza Lee Follen. BoChLi; PPL; TVC
Dear Mother of the Savior, yet remaining. Last Antiphon; To Mary. James J. Donohue. ISi
"Dear mother," said a little fish. The Little Fish That Would Not Do as It Was Bid. Ann *or* Jane Taylor. OHIP
"Dear Mother," said a little maid. How Old Ought I to Be? *Unknown.* SoP
Dear murdered comrades, not in vain. Tulips from Their Blood. Edwin Brooks. NBP
Dear, my familiar hand in love's own gesture. Epigram. J. V. Cunningham. PV
Dear my friend and fellow-student. Lady Geraldine's Courtship. Elizabeth Barrett Browning. DTo
Dear native brook! wild streamlet of the West! Sonnet: To the River Otter. Samuel Taylor Coleridge. ChER; ERoP-1; Sonn
Dear native regions, I foretell. At This Farewell. Wordsworth. PoRL
Dear, near and true—no truer Time himself. A Dedication. Tennyson. EPN; PoVP
Dear Night, This World's Defeat. Henry Vaughan. EG; MaRV
(Night, The.) BoC; TrGrPo
Dear object of my love, whose manly charms. Pretty Maids Beware! *Unknown.* CoMu
Dear! of all happy in the hour, most blest. Safety. Rupert Brooke. *Fr.* 1914. BrPo; EnLoPo; PoFr
Dear old couple my grandparents were, A. The Child and the Mariner. W. H. Davies. CH
Dear Old Dad. Eva Gilbert Shaver. STF
Dear old ladies whose cheeks are pink, The. Autumn Leaves. Janie Screven Heyward. HBMV; MPB
Dear Old Mothers. Charles S. Ross. OQP; PGD
(Old Mothers.) PoToHe (new ed.); SoP
Dear Old Toiling One, The. David Gray. VA
Dear Old Village, The. John Betjeman. CMoP
Dear old woman in the lane, The. Neighboring. Christina Rossetti. *Fr.* Sing-Song. GaP; PCH
Dear, on a day of dumb rain. Rain. Howard Moss. ErPo
Dear Paulus it's a busy trade of late. Lines Descriptive of Thomson's Island. Benjamin Lynde. SCAP
Dear poet, your heart is not in question. To a Poet Who Has Had a Heart Attack. Richard Eberhart. ML
Dear Possible. Laura Riding. LiTA
Dear President, The. John James Piatt. DD, *sl. abr.*; MC; PAH
Dear quirister [*or* chorister], who from those shadows sends. Sonnet [*or* To the Nightingale]. William Drummond of Hawthornden. HBV; LO; ViBoPo
Dear Refuge of my weary soul. Prayer. Anne Steele. SoP
Dear reliques of a dislodg'd soul, whose lack. Death's Lecture at the Funeral of a Young Gentleman [*or* Upon Mr. Staninough's Death]. Richard Crashaw. MaMe; SeCP
Dear restless heart, be still; don't fret and worry so. Be Still. Edith Willis Linn. FaChP
Dear Reynolds! as last night I lay in bed. Epistle to John Hamilton Reynolds. Keats. OBNC
Dear Saint Thomas. Air Mail, Special. Sister Mary Philip. JKCP (1955 ed.)
Dear singer of our fathers' day. To John Greenleaf Whittier. William Hayes Ward. AA
Dear Sir, we in Row D are well aware. To the Gentleman in Row D. Virginia Graham. MuSP
Dear Sir,—You wish to know my notions. The Candidate's Letter. James Russell Lowell. *Fr.* The Biglow Papers, 1st Series, No. VII. AA
Dear Sir: Your astonishment's odd. Limerick. *Unknown.* LiBL
Dear Sirmio, that art the very eye. Home to Sirmiò. Catullus, *tr. by* Sir Theodore Martin. OuHeWo
Dear Sirs: Is it not time we formed a Boston. Communication to the City Fathers of Boston. George Starbuck. NYBP
Dear skilfull Betty, who dost far excell. To Corinna's Chambermaid. Ovid. *Fr.* Amores, I, 8. PeRV
Dear Smith, the sleest, paukie thief. Epistle to James Smith. Burns. CABL; HoPM; MCCG; OBEC
Dear Son, Leave Thy Weeping. *Unknown.* CTC
(Jesus Comforts His Mother.) MeEL
Dear Son, when the warm multitudes cry. Alonso to Ferdinand. W. H. Auden. *Fr.* The Sea and the Mirror. MoPo
Dear Sons of God,—of Him whom Sinai saw. Jesus. Ramón Pimentel Coronel. CAW
Dear soul be strong! Richard Crashaw. *Fr.* On a Prayer Book Sent to Mrs. M. R. ErPo
Dear steps may die away. Room. Robert Finch. MoCV
Dear stranger, reading this small, true book. Strength to War. Stephen Stepanchev. WaP
Dear, they are praising your beauty. Praise. "Seumas O'Sullivan." HBV
Dear, They Have Poached the Eyes You Loved So Well. Rupert Brooke. WhC
Dear Thomas, didst thou never pop. A Simile. Matthew Prior. BOHV; CEP; CoBE; EiPP; FaBoEn
Dear, though the Night Is Gone. W. H. Auden. InvP
Dear, though your mind stand so averse. Hear Me Yet. *Unknown.* EIL

Dear ties of mutual succor bind. Mutual Kindness. Bryant. SoP
Dear tiger lily, fanged and striped! you are the bravest. The Return. Conrad Aiken. NePA
Dear to me always was this lonely hill. The Infinite. Giacomo Leopardi. WoL
Dear to me were the three sides. The Wife of Aed mac Ainmirech, King of Ireland, Laments Her Husband. *Unknown.* AnIL
Dear to my heart are the ancestral dwellings of America. The Ancestral Dwellings. Henry van Dyke. PoMa
Dear to my soul! then leave me not forsaken! Sonnet. Henry Constable. *Fr.* Diana. ElL; OBSC; ReEn; ReIE; SiCE; Sonn; TuPP
Dear Tom, how melancholly I am grown. An Epistle from Mr. Duke to Mr. Otway. Richard Duke. PeRV
Dear Tom, this brown jug that now foams with mild ale. The Brown Jug. Francis Fawkes. CBEP; ViBoPo
Dear urge no more that killing cause. To One That Pleaded Her Own Want of Merit [*or* To Celia Pleading Want of Merit]. Thomas Stanley. MeLP; OBS
Dear victims, kindly bear with me a minute. Prologue for a Magician. Arthur Guiterman. PoMS
Dear Voyager, a lucky star be thine. Ageanax. Edward Cracroft Lefroy. Echoes from Theocritus, VI. OBVV
Dear, wakeful bird! I bid thine accents hail. The Landrail. Sir Aubrey De Vere. IrPN
Dear wanton, when the moon made light our bed. Mother of Men. Stephen Southwold. HBMV
Dear Was He. *Unknown, tr. fr. Late Middle Irish by* Standish Hayes O'Grady. *Fr.* The Life of St. Cellach of Killala. OnYI
Dear W——d, mark, in dirty hole. The Mole. *Unknown.* EiCL
Dear, when I did from you remove. Madrigal. Lord Herbert of Cherbury. ElL
Dear, when I went you. A Song of Two Wanderers. Marguerite Wilkinson. HBMV
Dear, when the sun is set. Give Me Not Tears: Joy. Rose Hawthorne Lathrop. AA
Dear, when we sit in that high, placid room. Touché. Jessie Fauset. CDC
Dear, when you see my grave. Give Me Not Tears: Despair. Rose Hawthorne Lathrop. AA
Dear Whizz, I remember you at St. Mark's in '39. To Auden on His Fiftieth. Richard Eberhart. ML
Dear [*or* Deare], why make you more of a dog then me? Sir Philip Sidney. Astrophel and Stella, LIX. FCP; MaPo (1969 ed.); OAEP; SiPS
Dear [*or* Deare], why should you command me to my rest. Idea, XXXVII [*or* Night and Day *or* Sonnets to "Idea," 11]. Michael Drayton. EG; ElL; FaBoEn; HBV; LiTB; LiTG; LiTL; LO; OAEP; OBSC; PoEL-2; ReEn; Sonn; TuPP; ViBoPo
Dear wife, last midnight, whilst I read. Dibdin's Ghost. Eugene Field. AA
Dear wife, let me have a fire made. Sir T. J.'s Speech to His Wife and Children. *Unknown.* CoMu
Dear youth, too early lost, who now art laid. On the Death of a Young and Favorite Slave. Martial. AWP; JAWP; LiTW; WBP
Deare friend sit down, and bear awhile this shade. The Palm-Tree. Henry Vaughan. AnAnS-1; MeP
Deare friend, sit down, the tale is long and sad. Love Unknown. George Herbert. MaMe; SCEP-1
Deare if I with guile would guild a true intent. Dear If I with Guile. Thomas Campion. NCEP
Deare, if You Change. *Unknown. See* Dear, if You Change.
Deare Lelipa, where hast thou bin so long. The Seventh Nimphall. Michael Drayton. *Fr.* The Muses Elizium. AnAnS-2
Deare love, for nothing lesse than thee. *See* Dear love, for nothing less than thee.
Deare reliques of a dislodg'd soule, whose lacke. Richard Crashaw. *See* Dear reliques . . .
Deare Venus, if thou wilt bee kinde. *Unknown.* SeCSL
Dearest all faire is in your browne. *Unknown.* SeCSL
Dearest and nearest brother. Stephen Spender. Elegy for Margaret, VI. FaBoEn
Dearest, Do Not You Delay Me. *At. to* John Fletcher. *Fr.* The Spanish Curate. SeCL; ViBoPo
Dearest Friend, Thou Art in Love. Heine, *tr. fr. German by* Emma Lazarus. *Fr.* Homeward Bound. TrJP
Dearest in friendship, if you'll know. My Happy Life. Mildmay Fane, Earl of Westmorland. CavP
Dearest love, do you remember. Weeping, Sad and Lonely. Charles Carroll Sawyer. TrAS
Dearest my wife who lies. Personal Poem. Kendrick Smithyman. AnNZ
Dearest of all the heroes! Peerless knight. Don Quixote. Arthur Davison Ficke. HBMV
"Dearest of men, for love of thee." Death in Bed. *Unknown. Fr.* The Life of Guthlac. PoLi
Dearest of thousands, now the time drawes neere. His Charge to Julia at His Death. Robert Herrick. SeCV-1
"Dearest papa," says my boy to me. The Legend of the Easter Eggs. Fitz-James O'Brien. BeLS
Dearest Poets, The. Leigh Hunt. HBV; OTPC (1923 ed.) (Poets, The.) Sonn
Dearest Spot on Earth, The. W. T. Wrighton. FaBoBe
Dearest, these household cares remit. The Blackbird. Henry Charles Beeching. OBVV
Dearest thy tresses are not threads of gold. The Comparison. Thomas Carew. AnAnS-2; CavP
Dearest, when your lovely head. But I Shall Weep. Beatrice Redpath. CaP
Death. Maltbie D. Babcock. MaRV; OQP; SoP; WGRP (Emancipation.) BLRP; FaChP; WBLP
Death. Richard Baxter. FaChP
Death. Maxwell Bodenheim. AnAmPo; LiTM; MAP; MAPA; MoAmPo (1942 ed.); NP; PFY; TrJP
Death ("O Death, rock me asleep"). *At. to* George Boleyn, *also to* Anne Boleyn. *See* O Death, Rock Me Asleep.
Death. Emily Brontë. OBNC
Death. Madison Cawein. AA
Death. John Clare. ERoP-2; GTBS-P; PeER
Death. Florence Earle Coates. HBV; OQP
Death, *sel.* Mary Elizabeth Coleridge.
"Bid me remember, O my gracious Lord." TrPWD
Death. Emily Dickinson. *See* Bustle in a house, the, *and* Death is a dialogue.
Death. John Donne. *See* Death, Be Not Proud.
Death. Philip Dow. QAH
Death. Thomas Flatman. *See* Sad Day, The.
Death. Philip Freneau. *Fr.* The House of Night. AP
Death. Henry W. Frost. SoP
Death. George Herbert. AnAnS-1; BWP; EP; MaMe; MeP; MePo; OBS; PoFS; PoIE; SCEP-1; SeCL; SeCP; SeCV-1
Death. Thomas Hood. ERoP-2; OBEV (It Is Not Death.) OBRV ("It is not death, that sometimes in a sigh." EG (Sonnet.) OBNC; ViBoPo
Death, A. Elizabeth Jennings. NMP; OPoP
Death. William Knott. YAP
Death. Walter Savage Landor. *See* Death Stands above Me.
Death. Arthur MacGillivray. JKCP (1955 ed.)
Death. Thomas May. *Fr.* Continuation of Lucan. MaRV
Death. Sir Thomas More. EnRePo
Death. James Oppenheim. WGRP
Death. George Pellew. AA
Death ("Death is here, and death is there"). Shelley. DiPo; UnPo (1st ed.)
Death ("What if some little paine the passage have"). Spenser. *See* What if Some Little Paine . . .
Death. Darwin T. Turner. BALP
Death ("As when one layeth/ His worn-out robes away"). *Unknown, tr. fr. Sanskrit by* Sir Edwin Arnold. *Fr.* Bhagavad-Gita. MaRV
Death ("I am stranger in the land"). *Unknown.* BLPA
Death ("Once he will miss, twice he will miss"). *Unknown. Fr.* The Thousand and One Nights. AWP; JAWP; WBP
Death. Henry Vaughan. NCEP
Death. William Walsh. *See* Sonnet on Death.
Death. William Carlos Williams. OxBA
Death. W. B. Yeats. ChMP; GTBS-D; MemP; POTE; ShBV-4
Death./ The death of a million. Pastoral. Ron Loewinsohn. NeAP
Death again has swooped and flown. Resurgence. John L. Bonn. JKCP (1955 ed.)
Death Alone. "Pablo Neruda," *tr. fr. Spanish by* Angel Flores. OnHM
Death, Always Cruel. Dante, *tr. fr. Italian by* Dante Gabriel

Rossetti. *Fr.* La Vita Nuova, III. LiTW
("Death, always cruel Pity's foe in chief.") AWP; JAWP; WBP
Death and Burial of Cock Robbin, The. *Unknown.* SiTL
Death & Co. Sylvia Plath. OPoP
Death, and darkness get you packing. Easter Hymn. Henry Vaughan. AnAnS-1; MemP; MeP; StJW
Death and Doctor Hornbook. Robert Burns. OxBS
Death and General Putnam. Arthur Guiterman. OnSP; PoMS; TIHL
Death and Last Confession of Wandering Peter, The. Hilaire Belloc. MemP; OtMeF; TIHL
Death and Life. Emily Dickinson. *See* Apparently with no surprise.
Death and Night. James Benjamin Kenyon. AA
Death and Resurrection. George Croly. WGRP
Death and the Fairies. Patrick MacGill. HBMV
Death and the kyng did, as it were, contende. Upon the Death of Sir Antony Denny. *Unknown.* EnPo
Death and the Lady. Léonie Adams. MAP; MoAmPo; MoAB;
Death and the Maiden. Dick Gallup. ANYP
Death and the Maiden, *sel.* W. H. Oliver.
"Mourn her in the valleys, you young lovers, and throughout your gloom." AnNZ
Death and the Maiden. *Unknown, tr. fr. Irish by* Frank O'Connor. KiLC
Death-angel smote Alexander McGlue, The. Out of the Hurly-Burly. "Max Adeler." CenHV
Death as a Lotus Flower. *Unknown.* *See* He Is Like the Lotus.
Death as History. Jay Wright. ThO
Death and Birth. Swinburne. MaVP
Death as the Fool. Frank T. Marzials. VA
Death as the Teacher of Love-Lore. Frank T. Marzials. VA
Death at Daybreak. Anne Reeve Aldrich. AA; OQP
Death at the headlands, Hesiod, long ago. Hesiod, 1908. Alexander Mair. GoTS; SiSw
Death, Be Not Proud. John Donne. Holy Sonnets, X. BoLiVe; CBEP; CBV; ChTr; CoBE; FaBV; FaFP; GoBC; GTBS-W; HBV; InvP; LiTB; LiTG; OnPM; PG (1955 ed.); PoE; PoFr; PoRA; PoSa; SoP; StP; TIHL; TreFS; TrGrPo; TRV; WHA
(Death.) ATP; BEL; BoC; EnLi-1; EnLit; FaChP; MaRV; OBEV; ShBV-4; TOP; UnPo (1st ed.)
("Death be not proud, though some have called thee.") AnAnS-1; AnEnPo; AnFE; AtBAP; BWP; CABA; CaFP; DiPo; ElL; EnL; EnRePo; ExPo; FaBoEn; ForPo; ILP; InPo; LoBV; MaMe; MaPo; MasP; MBW-1; MeLP; MeP; MePo; MyFE; NoP; OAEP; OBS; PAn; Po; PoAn; PoEL-2; PoeP; PoFS; PoIE; PoPo; PPON; ReEn; SCEP-1; SeCeV; SeCP; SeCV-1; SeEP; Sonn; TDP; TuPP; ViBoPo; YAT
Death Bed. *See* Deathbed.
Death before forty's no bar. Lo! Obit on Parnassus. F. Scott Fitzgerald. InMe; NYBP; WhC
Death-blow is a life-blow to some, A. Emily Dickinson. AmPP
Death by Rarity. Marguerite Young. LiTA
Death came to him so quickly. The Flies. Merrill Moore. AnAmPo; AnEnPo
Death cannot surprise us who are driven. The People Has No Obituary. Eunice Clark. NAMP
Death cannot yet extinguish that entyre. *Unknown.* SeCSL
Death Carol: "Come, lovely and soothing Death." Walt Whitman. *Fr.* When Lilacs Last in the Door-Yard Bloomed, XIV. AnFE; APA; CoAnAm; MaRV; MoRP
Death-cell, A? The shack of the coastguards. The Coastguard House. Robert Lowell, *ad. fr. Italian of* Eugenio Montale. NaP
Death-Child, The. "Fiona Macleod." VA
Death Come to My House He Didn't Stay Long, *with music. Unknown.* BoAN-2
Death comes like this, I know. Fog. John Reed. AnEnPo
Death could not come between us two. Deep Waters. Van Tassel Sutphen. AA
Death, death; O amiable lovely death! O Amiable Lovely Death. Shakespeare. *Fr.* King John, III, iv. TreFT
Death Deposed. William Allingham. OnYI
Death devours all lovely things. Passer Mortuus Est. Edna St. Vincent Millay. CMoP; MAP; MoAmPo; OxBA
Death done warn me right. Tokens. John Richard Moreland. IHA
Death-Doomed. Will Carleton. PaPo
Death from Cancer. Robert Lowell. *Fr.* In Memory of Arthur Winslow. FiMAP; PoSa; TDP; TwCP
Death Fugue. Paul Celan, *tr. fr. German by* Clement Greenberg. TrJP
Death Goes before Me. Yvor Winters. NP
Death-Grapple. Laura Bell Everett. OQP
Death Great Smoothener. May Swenson. TPM
Death has come to visit us today. On the Acequia Madre. Alice Corbin. NP
Death hunted me for life, wherefor. The Double Crucifixion. John Malcolm Brinnin. LiTM (rev. ed.)
Death-Hymn, A. Felicia Dorothea Hemans. *See* Dirge: "Calm on the bosom of thy God."
Death I recant, and say, unsaid by mee. Elegie on Mrs. Boulstred. John Donne. MaMe
Death, I repent. Invocation of Death. Kathleen Raine. MoAB
Death, I say, my heart is bowed. The Shroud. Edna St. Vincent Millay. NP
Death, if thou wilt, fain would I plead with thee. A Dialogue. Swinburne. PoEL-5
Death in Battle. *Unknown.* *Fr.* The Battle of Maldon. PoLi
Death in Bed. *Unknown.* *Fr.* The Life of Guthlac. PoLi
Death in Hospital, A. John Lehmann. AtBAP; ChMP
Death in Leamington. John Betjeman. ACV; NoP; PoPl
Death in Life. Thomas, Lord Vaux. *See* No Pleasure without Some Pain.
Death in Life. *Unknown.* OQP
Death-in-Love. Dante Gabriel Rossetti. The House of Life, XLVIII. MaVP; PoVP; ViPo; VP
Death in the Corn. Detlev von Liliencron, *tr. fr. German by* C. F. MacIntyre. WaaP
Death in the Desert, A. Robert Browning. GoTL; OxBoCh; PoVP; StJW
Sels.
"For life, with all it yields of joy and woe." OQP; TRV
(Truth.) MaRV
"I say, the acknowledgment of God in Christ," 3 *ll.* ChIP
Illimitable God, The. MaRV
Old Whom God Loves, The. BoC
Death in the Home. T. Sturge Moore. BrPo
Death in this tomb his weary limbs hath laid. Death's Epitaph. Philip Freneau. *Fr.* The House of Night. AA
Death Invoked. Philip Massinger. *See* Song: "Why art thou slow, thou rest of trouble, Death."
Death Is a Blessed Thing. "Angelus Silesius," *tr. fr. German by* Paul Carus. OnPM
Death is a clean bold word and has no second meaning. Rebecca Richmond. BoPe
Death is a dialogue between. Emily Dickinson. MaPo (1969 ed.); OQP; PoeP; WGRP
Death Is a Door. Nancy Byrd Turner. BLPA; NeHB
(Death Is Only a Door.) SoP
Death Is a Little Thing. George Abbe. FiSC
"Death is a voyage," I heard it lightly told. O Mariners! Archibald Rutledge. EtS
Death is all metaphors, shape in one history. Altarwise by Owl-Light, II. Dylan Thomas. CMoP; CoBMV; LiTM; MaSP; MoAB; MoBrPo (1950 ed.) Sonn
Death is another milestone on their way. The Funeral. Stephen Spender. CMoP; MoAB; MoBrPo; NAMP; PoAn
Death Is before Me To-Day. *Unknown, tr. fr. Egyptian.* MaRV
Death Is but Death. Will Dyson. BoAV; MoAuPo
Death is but life's escape: a rung. Youth and Death. E. Merrill Root. OQP
Death Is Dead. Paul Eluard, *tr. fr. French by* Patricia Terry. OnPM
Death is gwineter lay his cold icy hands on me. Death's Gwineter Lay His Cold Icy Hands on Me. *Unknown.* BoAN-2
Death is here and death is there. Death. Shelley. DiPo; UnPo (1st ed.)
Death is more than. One X. E. E. Cummings. FaBoMo
Death is no foeman, we were born together. Knights Errant. Sister M. Madeleva. CAW
Death is not a dream; death lives. Death. Darwin T. Turner. BALP
Death is only an old door. Death Is a Door. Nancy Byrd Turner. BLPA; NeHB; SoP
Death is stronger than all the governments because the govern-

Death (continued)
ments. Death Snips Proud Men. Carl Sandburg. CMoP; CoBA
Death is the strongest of all living things. Warning to One. Merrill Moore. MAP; MoAmPo; NP; TrGrPo; YaD
Death is the supple suitor. Emily Dickinson. StP
Death it can bring. Issa, *tr. fr. Japanese by* Harold Gould Henderson. LiTW
Death lay in ambush. Christopher Okigbo. *Fr.* Distances. TTY
Death Mask of a Fisherman. George Bruce. ACV
Death May Be . . . Oliver St. John Gogarty. POTE
(Death May Be Very Gentle.) PoRA
Death Motion. Paula Giddings. WSL
Death, my lifes mistress, and the soveraign queen. To His Mistress for Her True Picture. Lord Herbert of Cherbury. AnAnS-2; SeCP
Death never troubled Damocles. Damocles. Robert Graves. NYBP
Death of a Bird. Jon Silkin. NePoEA
Death of a Cat. James Schevill. NMP; OPoP
Death of a Dove, The. James Schevill. FiMAP
Death of a Hornet. D. G. Jones. PeCV
Death of a Jazz Musician. William Jay Smith. NePoAm-2
Death of a Peasant. R. S. Thomas. FIW; PoIE
Death of a Snake, The. William Plomer. ELU
Death of a Soldier, The. Wallace Stevens. BWP; ForPo; QFR
(Death of the Soldier.) AmPP
Death of a Son. Jon Silkin. GTBS-P; NePoEA; POTE (1959 ed.); TwCP
Death of a Squirrel in McKinley Park, The. Gerald William Barrax. Kal
Death of a Toad, The. Richard Wilbur. AmP; AP; CABA; CaFP; CMoP; ForPo; LiTM (1970 ed.); MiAP; MoVE; NMP; NoP; TwAmPo; VaPo
Death of a Vermont Farm Woman. Barbara Howes. MoAmPo (1962 ed.)
Death of a Whale. John Blight. PoAu-2
Death of a Zulu, The. William Plomer. BoSA
Death of Admiral Benbow, The. *Unknown.* CoMu
Death of Adonis, The. Shakespeare. *Fr.* Venus and Adonis. WHA
Death of Ailill, The. Francis Ledwidge. OnYI
Death of Alexander, The. *Unknown. See* When Alexander Our King Was Dead.
Death of an Aircraft. Charles Causley. MoBS; POTi
Death of an Elephant. Bertram J. Warr. TwCaPo
Death of an Old Man, The. Michael Hamburger. NePoEA
Death of Antony. Shakespeare. *Fr.* Antony and Cleopatra, IV, xv. FiP
("I am dying, Egypt, dying.") MemP
Death of Artemidora, The. Walter Savage Landor. *Fr.* Pericles and Aspasia, LXXXV. BEL; EnRP; EPN; InP; OBNC; SeCeV; VA
("Artemidora! Gods invisible.") ViBoPo
Death of Azron, The. Alice Wellington Rollins. AA
Death of Ben Hall, The. Will H. Ogilvie. PoAu-1
Death of Buckingham, The. Pope. *Fr.* Moral Essays, Epistle III: Of the Use of Riches. FiP
(Death of the Duke of Buckingham, The.) ExPo
(Duke of Buckingham.) OBEC
Death of Chiron, The. J. P. McAuley. BoAV
Death of Christ. Arthur R. Macdougall, Jr. ChIP
Death of Cleopatra, The ("Nunc est bibendum"). Horace, *tr. fr. Latin by* Sir Stephen E. De Vere. Odes, I, 37. EnLi-1; OuHeWo
Death of Cleopatra. Shakespeare. *Fr.* Antony and Cleopatra, V, ii. FiP; TreFS
(Cleopatra's Death.) TrGrPo
("Give me my robe, put on my crown.") AtBAP; MemP
Death of Colman, The. Thomas Frost. PAH
Death of Cowards, The. Shakespeare. *See* Cowards ("Cowards die many times before their deaths").
Death of Cuchulain. Eleanor Rogers Cox. JKCP
Death of Cuchulain [*or* Cuchullin], The. W. B. Yeats. *See* Cuchulain's Fight with the Sea.
Death of Custer, The. "Captain Jack" Crawford. PoOW
Death of Daphnis, The. Theocritus, *tr. fr. Greek by* Charles Stuart Calverley. Idylls, I. AWP; JAWP; WBP
(Song of the Death of Daphnis, The, *tr. by* J. H. Hallard.) EnLi-1
Death of David, The. Hayyim Nahman Bialik, *tr. fr. Hebrew by* Herbert Danby. TrJP
Death of Days and Nights of Life. Clarence Franklin. BF
Death of Death, The. Shakespeare. *See* Sonnets, CXLVI.
Death of Dermid, The. Sir Samuel Ferguson. IrPN
Death of Digenes Akritas, The. John Heath-Stubbs. NePoEA
Death of Dives, The. Richard Baxter. *Fr.* Madness. PeRV
Death of Don Pedro, The. *Unknown, tr. fr. Spanish by* John Gibson Lockhart. AWP
Death of Edward, The. Michael Drayton. *Fr.* Mortimeriados. ReIE
Death of Europe, The. Charles Olson. NeAP
Death of Eve, The, *sel.* William Vaughn Moody.
"Yea, Jubal?" Act I. WoL
Death of Friends, The. Adele Levi. GoYe
Death of Gaudentis. "Harriet Annie." WBLP
Death of General Pike, The. Laughton Osborn. PAH
Death of Goody Nurse, The. Rose Terry Cooke. PAH
Death of Grant, The. Ambrose Bierce. AA
Death of Haidée, The. Byron. *Fr.* Don Juan, IV. FiP; WHA, *longer sel.*
Death of Hamlet. Shakespeare. *Fr.* Hamlet, V, ii. FiP
Death of Hampden, The. Pakenham Beatty. VA
Death of Harrison, The. Nathaniel Parker Willis. PAH
Death of Hector, The. Homer, *tr. fr. Greek by* George Chapman. *Fr.* The Iliad, XXII. OBS
Death of Herminius, The. Macaulay. *Fr.* The Battle of the Lake Regillus. OtMeF
Death of Hoelderlin, The. Paul Oppenheimer. NYTB
Death of Jack Hinton, The. *Unknown. See* Wreck on the C. & O., The.
Death of Jefferson, The. Hezekiah Butterworth. PAH; ThLM
Death of Jesus, The. St. Luke, XXIII: 1-46, Bible, *N.T.* TreF
Death of Keats, The. Vernon Watkins. ML
Death of King Edward I, The. *Unknown.* MeEL
Death of King Edward VII, The. *Unknown.* OxBoLi
Death of Kings, The ("Let's talk of graves"). Shakespeare. King Richard II, fr. III, ii. TrGrPo
(Let's Talk of Graves.) DiPo
(Richard II's Dejection.) TreFS
Death of Leander, The. Thomas Hood. *Fr.* Hero and Leander. EnRP
Death of Lear. Shakespeare. *Fr.* King Lear, V, iii. FiP
Death of Leonidas, The. George Croly. BeLS
Death of Lesbia's Bird, The. Catullus, *tr. fr. Latin by* Samuel Taylor Coleridge. AWP
(Dead Starling, The.) OnPM
Death of Lincoln, The. Bryant. *See* Abraham Lincoln.
Death of Little Boys. Allen Tate. CBV; LiTA; MAP; MoAB; MoAmPo; TwCP
Death of Lord Warriston, The. *Unknown. See* Laird of Wariston, The.
Death of Lyon, The. Henry Peterson. PAH
Death of Marlborough, The. George Walter Thornbury. VA
Death of Master Tommy Rook, The. Eliza Cook. OTPC
Death of Meleager, The. Swinburne. *Fr.* Atalanta in Calydon. PoVP; OBVV
Death of Minnehaha, The. Longfellow. The Song of Hiawatha, Pt. XX. AA
Death of Moses, The. *Unknown, tr. fr. Hebrew by* Alice Lucas. TrJP
Death of My Aunt. *Unknown.* OxBoLi; SiTL
Death of Nelson, The. *Unknown.* OxBoLi
(New Song Composed on the Death of Lord Nelson, A.) CoMu
Death of Nick Charles, The. LeRoi Jones. CoPo
Death of Othello. Shakespeare. *See* Othello.
Death of Our Ladie, The. Robert Southwell. MeP
Death of Parcy Reed, The. *Unknown.* BaBo (A *and* B *vers.*); ESPB; OBB
Death of Peter Esson, The. George Mackay Brown. NePoEA-2
Death of Poetry, The, *sel.* Nathalia Crane.
Requiem. MoAmPo (1942 ed.)
Death of Polybius Jubb, The. Roy Campbell. *See* Limerick: "He died in attempting to swallow."
Death of Prince Leopold, The. William McGonagall. EvOK
Death of Puck, The. Eugene Lee-Hamilton. HBMV; OBVV
Death of Queen Jane, The. *Unknown.* BaBo (A, B *and* D

vers.); ESPB (A *and* B *vers.*); ViBoFo
(Jane Was a Neighbor, C *vers.*) BaBo
Death of Richard Wagner, The. Swinburne. LoBV
Death of Robert, Earl of Huntingdon, *sel.* Anthony Munday *and* Henry Chettle.
Dirge for Robin Hood. CBEP
(Dirge: "Weep, weep, ye woodmen, wail.") CTC; OBSC
(Robin Hood's Funeral.) WiR
(Song: "Weep, weep, ye woodmen, wail.") EIL; ThWaDe
(Weep, Weep, Ye Woodmen!) CH
Death of Robin Hood, The. William Rose Benét. OTPC (1946 ed.)
Death of Robin Hood, The. Eugene Field. StPo
Death of Robin Hood, The. *Unknown. See* Robin Hood's Death.
Death of Saint Guthlac. Cynewulf, *tr. fr. Anglo-Saxon. Fr.* Guthlac. ACP
Death of Samson. Milton. *Fr.* Samson Agonistes. ChTr
("Come, come, no time for lamentation now.") FiP
Death of Santa Claus, The. Vincent Starrett. FiSC
Death of Sir Nihil, book the *n* th. Tywater. Richard Wilbur. CMoP; GTBS-W; LiTA; LiTM (rev. ed.); MemP; MiAP; MoAB; NePA; PoSa; ReMP
Death of Slavery, The. Bryant. AA; DD, *much abr.*; PoFr, *abr.*
Death of Sohrab, The. Matthew Arnold. *Fr.* Sohrab and Rustum. FiP
(Sohrab's Death, *longer sel.*) WHA
Death of Tammuz, The. Saul Tchernichowsky, *tr. fr. Hebrew by* L. V. Snowman. TrJP
Death of the Ball Turret Gunner, The. Randall Jarrell. AP; CaFP; CBV; CMoP; CoBMV; ELU; ExPo; FiMAP; ILP; LiTM (1970 ed.); MiAP; MoAmPo (1950 ed.); NMP; NoP; OxBA; PoPl; PoPo; SeCeV (1967 ed.); ShBV-3; UnPo (3d ed.); WaaP; WaP
Death of the Bird, The. A. D. Hope. PoAu-2
Death of the Bull. Roy Campbell. FaBoTw
Death of the Craneman, The. Alfred Hayes. LiTA; NAMP; WaP
Death of the Day. Walter Savage Landor. NoP
Death of the Dragon, The. Spenser. *Fr.* The Faerie Queene, I, 11. WHA
Death of the Duke of Buckingham, The. Pope. *See* Death of Buckingham, The.
Death of the Duke of Clarence and Avondale, The, *sel.* Tennyson.
Be Comforted. MaRV
Death of the Flowers, The. Bryant. AA; AnAmPo; AnNE; BoNaP; CoBA; DD, *abr.*; GN; HBV; OTPC; PoLF; TreF; WBLP
Death of the Hired Man, The. Robert Frost. AmPP; AnNE; ATP; CMoP; CoBA; HoPM; MaC; MAP; MoAB; MoAmPo; NeMA; OxBA; SeCeV; TOP; TrGrPo; UnPo (1st ed.)
Home, *br. sel.* MaRV; TRV
(Home Defined.) TreF
Death of the innocent by the innocent. On Reading Gene Derwood's "The Innocent." Willard Maas. NePA
Death of the Kapowsin Tavern. Richard Hugo. PIA
Death of the Lincoln Despotism, The. *Unknown.* PAH
Death of the Moonshine Supermen. Reginald Lockett BF
Death of the Old Year. Tennyson. DD; HBV; HH; OTPC; PoSC, *abr.*
Death of the Sheriff, The. Robert Lowell. MoAB; MoAmPo (1950 ed.)
(Noli Me Tangere.) FiMAP
Death of the Soldier. Wallace Stevens. *See* Death of a Soldier, The.
Death, of thee do I make my moan. To Death, of His Lady. Villon, *tr. by* Dante Gabriel Rossetti. AWP; OuHeWo
Death of Turnus, The, *abr.* Vergil, *tr. fr. Latin by* Dryden. *Fr.* The Aeneid, XII. WoL
Death of Urgan, The. Swinburne. *Fr.* Tristram of Lyonesse. WHA
Death of Venus, The. Robert Creeley. AmPC; StP
Death of Vitellozzo Vitelli, The. Irving Feldman. TwCP
Death of Warren, The. Epes Sargent. MC; PAH
Death of Wolfe, The. *Unknown.* PAH
Death of Wyatt, The. Earl of Surrey. SiPS
(Divers Thy Death.) NCEP
("Divers thy death do diversely bemoan.") FCP
Death of Yeats, The. George Barker. LiTB
Death on a Live Wire. Michael Baldwin. MoBS
Death on Columbus Day. James Tate. YAP
Death on the Rancherie. Emily Leavens. TwCaPo
Death passing by and hearing Parsons play. Epitaph upon Master Parsons, Organist at Westminster. *Unknown.* MuSP
Death, poker-faced and wearing livery. Dark Hotel. Alfred Dorn. FiSC
Death, reaping the mad world, his crimson blade. The Foiled Reaper. William Kean Seymour. HBMV
Death Rites II. *Unknown, tr. by* C. M. Bowra. TTY
Death Room, The. Robert Graves. NYBP
Death Sends Me the Flickering of Powdery Lids. Bilhana, *formerly at. to Chauras, tr. fr. Sanskrit by* E. Powys Mathers. *Fr.* Black Marigolds. OnPM
Death shall be death forever unto thee. Forever Dead. Sappho, *tr. by* William Ellery Leonard. AWP; JAWP; LiTW; WBP
Death, since I find not one with whom to grieve. Canzone 17: He Beseeches Death for the Life of Beatrice. Dante. AWP
Death Snips Proud Men. Carl Sandburg. CMoP; CoBA
Death Song, A. Paul Laurence Dunbar. AA; BANP; CDC; PoLF; PoNe
Death Song. Robert Stephen Hawker. OBNC; OBRV; OBVY
Death Song. Alonzo Lewis. PAH
Death Song, A. William Morris. PoVP; VA
Death speaks: / When men my scythe and darts supply. Thomas Parnell. *Fr.* Night Piece on Death. OnYI
Death Stands above Me [Whispering Low]. Walter Savage Landor. AnFE; CBV; EnRP; EPN; LiTB; MaRV; MemP; NoP; OAEP; OBNC; PoEL-4; TOP; YAT
(Death.) FaBV; HBV
(Death Undreaded.) VA
(On Death.) BoLiVe; InP; TrGrPo
(On His Own Death.) OBVV
Death stately came to a young man. Death Deposed. William Allingham. OnYI
Death stood beside us on your night of birth. To Duncan. Jessica Nelson North. NP
Death stretched down two hands. Casualty. Diana Witherby. ChMP
Death Swoops. Kenneth Pitchford. CoPo
Death takes our loved ones. Selfishness. Margaret E. Bruner. MaRV; PoToHe
Death, that is small respecter of distinction. Trainwrecked Soldiers. John Frederick Nims. MiAP; ReMP
Death, that struck when I was most confiding. Death. Emily Brontë. OBNC
Death, the Conqueror ("Victorious men of earth! no more"). James Shirley. *See* Victorious Men of Earth.
Death the Great. Elis Wyn o Lasynys, *tr. fr. Welsh by* George Borrow. LiTW
Death the Leveller. James Shirley. *See* Glories of Our Blood and State.
Death, tho I see him not, is near. Age. Walter Savage Landor. ELU; NBM; PoEL-4
Death, Thou Hast Seized Me. Isaac Luzzatto, *tr. fr. Hebrew by* Nina Davis Salaman. TrJP
Death, thou wast once an uncouth hideous thing. Death. George Herbert. AnAnS-1; BWP; EP; MaMe; MeP; MePo; OBS; PoFS; PoIE; SCEP-1; SeCL; SeCP; SeCV-1
Death, though already in the world, as yet. The Legend of the Dead Lambs. "Owen Meredith." VA
Death, thou'rt a cordial old and rare. The Stirrup-Cup. Sidney Lanier. AA; AmePo; AmP; AmPP (5th ed.); CoBA; OQP; PFY; TOP
Death thresholded old man hold. Double Ritual. Dachine Rainer. CrMA
Death to the Lady said. Death and the Lady. Léonie Adams. MAP; MoAB; MoAmPo
Death to Us, A. Jon Silkin. NePoEA
Death to Van Gogh's Ear! Allen Ginsberg. NaP
Death Undreaded. Walter Savage Landor. *See* Death Stands above Me.
Death-Wake, The; or, Lunacy, *sel.* Thomas Stoddart.
Mirthful Lunacy. OBNC
Death walks through the mind's dark woods. Poem. Henry Treece. NeBP

Death Warnings. Francisco de Quevedo y Villegas. *See* Sonnet: Death Warnings.
Death Was a Woman. Sydney King Russell. GoYe
Death, what dost? O hold thy blow. Upon the Death of the Most Desired Mr. Herrys. Richard Crashaw. MaMe
Death, when I am ready, I. Pause en Route. Thomas Kinsella. OxBI
Death, when you come to me, tread with a footstep. So Might It Be. John Galsworthy. PoLF
Death, who one day taketh all. Epitaph for a Kitten. Miriam Vedder. CIV
Death, why hast thou made life so hard to bear. Canzone: Of His Dead Lady. Giacomino Pugliesi. AWP; JAWP; WBP
Death why so cruel [soe crewill]! What! no other way. Bacon's Epitaph, Made by His Man. John Cotton. AnAmPo; PAH; SCAP
Death-Wish, The. Louis MacNeice. AnFE
Death-Bed, A. James Aldrich. AA; HBV
Death Bed, The. Waring Cuney. CDC; PoNe
Death-Bed, The. Thomas Hood. BEL; CBV; EnRP; GTBS; GTBS-D; GTBS-P; GTBS-W; GTSE; GTSL; HBV; MaRV; MCCG; OBEV; OBNC; OBRV; OBVV; PG; TreFS; VA
(We Watch'd Her Breathing.) ELP
Death-Bed. A. L. Rowse. WePo
Death-Bed, The. Siegfried Sassoon. LiTM (1970 ed.); MMA; MoVE; POTE
Death-Bed Hymn of Saint Anthony of Padua. St. Anthony of Padua, *tr. fr. Latin by* Thomas Walsh. CAW
Deathless, The. Ednah Proctor Clarke. AA
Deathless Aphrodite, throned in flowers. Ode to Aphrodite. Sappho. AWP
Deathless Flower, A. Michelangelo. *See* Love's Justification.
Deathless Ones, The. Eleanor Glenn Wallis. NePoAm
Deathless Principle, Arise. Augustus Montague Toplady. OxBoCh
Deathless Tale, The. Charles Hanson Towne. ChIP; StJW
Deathless, though godheads be dying. In the Vastness, a God. *Unknown.* OQP
Deaths, The. Solveig von Schoultz, *tr. fr. Finnish by* Martin S. Allwood. LiTW
Death's a peculiar thing. The Coward. Roland R. Greenwood. YT
Death's Alchemy. William Sidney Walker. VA
Death's Apology. Francisco Manuel de Mello, *tr. fr. Spanish by* Edgar Prestage. CAW
Deaths at Paragon, Indiana, The. John Woods. CoPo
Death's but one more to-morrow. Thou art gray. Of One Who Seemed to Have Failed. S. Weir Mitchell. AA
Death's Conqueror. First Corinthians, XV: 20, 21, 53, 55, Bible, *N.T.* MaRV
Death's Emissaries. James Shirley. *See* Victorious Men of Earth.
Death's Epitaph. Philip Freneau. *Fr.* The House of Night. AA
Death's Final Conquest. James Shirley. *See* Glories of Our Blood and State.
Death's Gwineter Lay His Cold Icy Hands on Me, 2 *vers., with music. Unknown.* BoAN-2
Death's head on your hand you neede not weare, A. Thomas Dudley, Ah! Old Must Dye. *Unknown.* SCAP
Death's Jest Book, *sels.* Thomas Lovell Beddoes.
Athulf's Death Song ("Cypress bough, A, and a rose-wreath sweet"), *fr.* IV, iii. VA
Bridal Song to Amala ("We have bathed"), *fr.* IV, iii. OBVV
(Epithalamia.) PoEL-4
(Song.) ChER; FaBoEn; OBNC
(Song[s] at Amala's Wedding.) LoBV; PoE
Dirge: "If thou wilt ease thine heart," *fr.* II, ii. LiTB; LO; OBNC; OBRV; PoEL-4; VA
(Dirge for Wolfram.) PoE
(If Thou Wilt Ease Thine Heart.) EG; EnRP
(Wolfram's Dirge.) OBEV
Dirge: "Swallow leaves her nest, The," *fr.* I, iv. CBEP; LoBV; OBVV; PoEL-4
(Swallow Leaves Her Nest, The.) EPN
(Voice from the Waters, A.) OBNC; OBRV
Dirge: "We do lie beneath the grass, *fr.* V, iv. OBNC; WiR
(Second Dirge.) VA
(Sibylla's Dirge.) GTBS-D; NBM
(We Do Lie beneath the Grass.) ELP
"Durst thou again say life and soul has lifted," *fr.* III, iii. LO
"Fair and bright assembly, A: never strode," *fr.* II, iii. CTC
"I never knew before/ The meaning of this love," *fr.* II, iii. LO
Isbrand's Song, *fr.* III, iii. PoE
(Song by Isbrand.) OBNC
(Squats on a Toad-Stool under a Tree.) InvP
L'Envoi: "Who findeth comfort in the stars and flowers. LO; OBNC
(Dedicatory Stanzas.) ERoP-2
Mandrake's Song ("Folly hath now turned out of door"), *fr.* I, i. NBM; PeER
"My will lies there, my hope, and all my life," *fr.* II, ii. LO
Song: "Old Adam, the carrion crow," *fr.* V, iv. ChER; ERoP-2; LiTB; OBRV; PoEL-4; TOP
(Carrion Crow, The.) TrGrPo; WiR
(Old Adam.) *fr.* V, iv. ELP
(Old Adam the Carrion Crow.) EnRP; PoMS
(Song That Wolfram Heard in Hell, The.) PeER
(Wolfram's Song.) CBEP; GTBS-D; OBEV; OBVV; SiTL
"Then all the minutes of my life to come," *fr.* II, iv. LO
"Then listen, as I listened unto you," *fr.* III, iii. PoFr
To Sea, To Sea! *fr.* I, i. EtS; OTPC; PCD; VA
(Mariners' Song.) OBVV; YT
(Sailors' Song.) HBV
(Sea Song.) GoTP
(Song from the Ship.) GTBS-D; OBRV; PeER
(To Sea.) CH
Death's Lecture at the Funeral of a Young Gentleman. Richard Crashaw. MaMe; SeCP
(Upon Mr. Staningugh's Death.) MaMe
Death's nobility again. In Battle. Wallace Stevens. NP
Deaths of Myron and Klydone, The. Augusta Davies Webster. *Fr.* In a Day. VA
Death's Only Son. Jon Anderson. YAP
Death's pale cold orb has turned to an eclipse. Avalon. Thomas Holley Chivers. AnFE; CoAnAm
Death's Ramble. Thomas Hood. BOHV
Death's Songsters. Dante Gabriel Rossetti. The House of Life, LXXXVII. MaVP; PoVP; ViPo
Death's Subtle Ways. James Shirley. *See* Victorious Men of Earth.
Death's Summons. Thomas Nashe. *See* Adieu, Farewell, Earth's Bliss!
Death's Transfiguration. Israel Zangwill. TrJP
Death's Warning to Beauty. *Unknown, tr. fr. Early Modern Irish by* Robin Flower. AnIL
Debate between Arjuna and Sri Krishna. *Unknown. See* Considerations of Murder.
Debate in the Sennit, The. James Russell Lowell. The Biglow Papers, 1st Series, No. V. HBV; PAH
Debate of the Body and the Soul, The. *Unknown, ad. fr. Middle English.* CoBE, *abr., ad. by* Francis James Child; MeEV,*ad. by* Sir Theodore Martin
Debate on Marriage versus Virginity, A. Catullus, *tr. fr. Latin by* Virginia Tufte. HW
Debate with the Rabbi. Howard Nemerov. PoPl
Deborah danced, when she was two. Experience. Aline Kilmer. BiCB; HBMV
Debout, *sel.* Tchicaya U Tam'si, *tr. fr. French by* E. S. Yntema.
"Here is the stream again under the rainbow." PBA
Débris. Lola Ridge. NP
Debt, The. Katharine Lee Bates. OQP
Debt, The. Paul Laurence Dunbar. AmNP; BANP; CDC; Kal; MaRV; NoP; TRV
Debt, The. Theodosia Garrison. DD; PEDC
Debt. Sara Teasdale. NP
Debt is paid, The. The Past. Emerson. AmePo; AmP; FaBoCh; LiTA; LoGBV; PoEL-4
Debts. Jessie B. Rittenhouse. HBMV
Debutante was sitting in the parlor of her flat, A. Song: "Don't Tell Me What You Dreamt Last Night." Franklin P. Adams. FiBHP
Debutantrum. William Rose Benét. InMe; LHV
Decade, A. Amy Lowell. BoLP; MAP; MoAmPo; NeMA; PoPl
Decades behind me. A Right-of-Way, 1865. William Plomer. DTC
Decanter of Madeira, Aged 86, to George Bancroft, Aged 86. Silas Weir Mitchell. AA; ViBoPo
Decay. George Herbert. AnAnS-1; MaMe; MeP SeCP; SeCV-1

Decay of a People, The. William Gilmore Simms. AA
Decay of Cathedrals, The. William Carlos Williams. PoeP
Decay of Vanity, The. Ted Hughes. POTE (1959 ed.)
Decayed Monastery, A. Thomas Dermody. OnYI
Decease, Release: Dum Morior, Orior. Robert Southwell. *See* At Fotheringay.
Deceased, The. Keith Douglas. FaBoTw
Deceased authors thou admir'st alone. Reactionary Critic. Martial. OnPM
Deceitful snow, made of the gray sea. December Storm. John Hay. NePoAm
Deceiving world, that with alluring toys. A Palinode. Robert Greene. *Fr.* Greene's Groatsworth of Wit. OBSC; SiCE
December. Aileen Fisher. SiSoSe
December. Thomas Caulfield Irwin. IrPN; NBM
December. Keats. *See* "In a drear-nighted December."
December. James Russell Lowell. *See* Brook in Winter, The.
December. Ron Padgett. ANYP
December. Christina Rossetti. YeAr
December. James Schuyler. ANYP
December. Sanderson Vanderbilt. OCS
December among the Vanished. W. S. Merwin. NaP
December, and the closing of the year. Christmas Eve in Whitneyville, 1955. Donald Hall. UnPo (3d ed.)
December Day, Hoy Sound. George Mackay Brown. OxBS
December Day, A. Sara Teasdale. PoRL
(Winter Solstice.) BoChLi; YeAr; YT
December 18th. Anne Sexton. MeWo
December Fugitive. Henry Morton Robinson. AnEnPo
(November Fugitive.) GoYe
December is dying, her last minutes flying. The New Year. Donald E. Cooke. MPB (1956 ed.)
December, my dear, on the road to Nijmegen. The Road to Nijmegen. Earle Birney. OBCV
December: Of Aphrodite. W. S. Merwin. NePoEA
December Stillness. Siegfried Sassoon. CMoP; MoRP
December Storm. John Hay. NePoAm
December Twenty-fourth. Eleanor Slater. ChIP; MaRV; OQP
December 26. George Edward Hoffman. PGD
Decent Burial. Lois Seyster Montross. HBMV
Decent docent doesn't doze, The. History of Education. David McCord. WhC
Deceptions. Philip Larkin. CABA; CMoP; ErPo; GTBS-P; NePoEA; NMP
Deceptive Present, the Phoenix Year, The. Delmore Schwartz. BoNaP
Deceptrices, The. William Carlos Williams. NYBP
Decide on a sound. Pissarro's One Pure Note. G. Bishop-Dubjinsky. ThO
Deciduous Branch. Stanley Kunitz. HoPM; TwAmPo
Decision, The. Owen Dodson. PoNe
Decision. George Macdonald. *See* Obedience.
Decision, The. E. J. Pratt. CBV
Decision. *Unknown.* PoToHe (new ed.)
Deck thyself, maiden. Esthonian Bridal Song. Johann Gottfried von Herder. AWP; JAWP; WBP
Deck us all with Boston Charlie. Boston Charlie. Walt Kelly. FiBHP; GoJo
Declair, ye bankis of Helicon. *Unknown.* *Fr.* The Bankis of Helicon. OxBS
Declaration. Arthur Symons. *Fr.* Violet. BrPo; ViBoPo
Declaration, The. Nathaniel Parker Willis. BOHV
Declaration at Forty. Judson Crews. UnTE
Declare, my pretty maid. The Philanderer. Moses Mendes. *Fr.* The Chaplet. TrJP
Decline and Fall of a Roman Umpire. Ogden Nash. SD
Declining Days. Henry Francis Lyte. SoP
Decoration. Louise Bogan. MAP; MoAB; MoAmPo
Decoration. Thomas Wentworth Higginson. AA
Decoration Day. Julia Ward Howe. DD
Decoration Day. Longfellow. DD; HH; MC; MPB; OTD; PoSC
Decoration Day at Charleston. Henry Timrod. *See* Ode: "Sleep sweetly in your humble graves."
Decoration Day Prayer. Arthur Roszelle Bemis, Jr. OQP
Decoy. John Ashbery. ANYP
Decoys, The. W. H. Auden. CMoP; SyP
Decrees of God, The. Chao Ying-tou, *tr. fr. Chinese by* William C. White. TrJP
Decrepit old gasman, named Peter, A. Limerick. *Unknown.* FaFP; LiBL; SiTL
Dedicated Spirit, A. Wordsworth. *Fr.* The Prelude. SeCePo
Dedication: "As one who, walking in the twilight gloom." Longfellow. *Fr.* The Seaside and the Fireside. MAmP; MWA-1
Dedication: "Beyond the path of the outmost sun through utter darkness hurled." Kipling. *Fr.* Barrack-Room Ballads. ViPP
Dedication: "Bob Southey! You're a poet—Poet-laureate." Byron. *Fr.* Don Juan. BEL; BoLiVe; CTC; EnLi-2 (1949 ed.); EnLit; EnRP; ILP; InP, 4 *sts.*; OAEP, 5 *sts.*; PoFS
(Dedication to the Poet Laureate, *abr.* FiP
(Invocation.) LoBV
(Southey and Wordsworth.) TrGrPo
Dedication, A: "Dear, near and true—no truer Time himself." Tennyson. EPN; PoVP
Dedication: "Eugenius, thy son, who guards the Rock." Pope Eugenius III, *tr. fr. Latin by* Raymond F. Roseliep. ISi
Dedication: "From wounds and death they rest—this bow and quiver." *Unknown, tr. fr. Greek by* Robert Bland. OnPM
Dedication: "Had there been peace there never had been riven." Drummond Allison. FaBoTw
Dedication A: "He was, through boyhood's storm and shower." G. K. Chesterton. FiBHP
Dedication: "Holy Jesus, Thou art born." Victoria Saffelle Johnson. GoBC; TrPWD
Dedication: "I speak with a proud tongue of the people who were." Patrick MacGill. OnYI
Dedication: "I would the gift I offer here." Whittier. *Fr.* Songs of Labor. AmPP (4th ed.); AnNE; CoBA; OxBA
Dedication: "If the rose in meek duty." Francis Thompson. CoBE
Dedication, A: "Life of my learning, fire of all my Art." Mary Elizabeth Coleridge. TrPWD
Dedication: "Lord, in the strength of grace." Charles Wesley. MaRV
Dedication, The: "Lord, my first fruits present themselves to thee." George Herbert. AnAnS-1; MaMe; MeP; OAEP
Dedication, A: "Lucilla, saved from shipwreck on the seas." Claire McAllister. TwAmPo
Dedication, The: "My God, thou that didst dye for me." Henry Vaughan. AnAnS-1; MeP
Dedication, A: "My new-cut ashlar takes the light." Kipling. GTSL; HBV; MaRV; OBEV (1st ed.); OBVV
(My New-cut Ashlar.) PoEL-5
Dedication: "Nothing that is shall perish utterly." Longfellow. *Fr.* Michael Angelo: a Fragment. MAmP; MWA-1
Dedication, A: "Oh, Lord, I present myself to Thee." *Unknown.* SoP
Dedication: "O lyric Love, half angel and half bird." Robert Browning. *See* O Lyric Love.
Dedication: "O thou whose gracious presence blest," *abr.* Louis F. Benson. MaRV; SoP
(Dedication for a Home [John Oxenham, *wr.*], *abr.*) ChIP
(O Thou Whose Gracious Presence Blest.) TrPWD
Dedication: "Strongest and the noblest argument, The." Sir John Davies. *Fr.* Nosce Teipsum. SiPS
Dedication: "Tall unpopular men." Oliver St. John Gogarty. OBMV
Dedication: "These to his memory—since he held them dear." Tennyson. *Fr.* Idylls of the King. CABA; PoVP; ViPP
Dedication, A: "They are rhymes rudely strung with intent less." Adam Lindsay Gordon. BoAu; PoAu-1
Dedication: "They say my verse is sad: no wonder." A. E. Housman. *See* They Say My Verse Is Sad.
Dedication: "'They shall not die in vain,' we said." Ralph Gustafson. CaP; TwCaPo
Dedication: "This little book, my God and King." Sir James Chamberlayne. CavP
Dedication: "Thou, whose unmeasured temple stands." Bryant. BLRP; SoP; TRV
(How Amiable Are Thy Tabernacles!) TrPWD
(Thou, Whose Unmeasured Temple Stands.) MaRV
Dedication: To Leigh Hunt. Keats. *See* To Leigh Hunt, Esq.
Dedication: "To that clear majesty which in the north." Sir John Davies. *Fr.* Nosce Teipsum. SiPS
(To My Most Gracious Dread Sovereign.) ReIE; SiCE
(To Queen Elizabeth.) OBSC
Dedication: "We dedicate a church today." Ethel Arnold Tilden. MaRV; OQP; SoP

Dedication: "When I have ended, then I see." Laurence Housman. TrPWD
Dedication: "With favoring winds, o'er sunlit seas." Longfellow. *Fr.* Ultima Thule. ViBoPo
Dedication for a Building. Alan Dugan. CAD
Dedication for a Home. Louis F. Benson. [John Oxenham, *wr.*]. *See* Dedication: "O thou whose gracious presence blest."
Dedication for a Plot of Ground. William Carlos Williams. PoeP
Dedication of a Mirror. Plato, *tr. fr. Greek by* Dudley Fitts. LiTW
Dedication of a Ship. Macedonius, *tr. fr. Greek by* Lord Neaves. OnPM
Dedication of the Chronicles of England and France. Robert Fabyan. ISi
Dedication of the Cook. Anna Wickham. MoBrPo
Dedication of the Illustrations to Blair's "Grave," *sel.* Blake.
Door of Death, The. ChTr
(To the Queen.) EnRP
Dedication of the Ring and the Book. Robert Browning. *See* O Lyric Love.
Dedication on the Gift of a Book to a Child. Hilaire Belloc. HBVY; ThGo
(Foreward, A.: "Child! do not throw this book about!") TSW
Dedication to a Book of Stories Selected from the Irish Novelists, The. W. B. Yeats. NAMP
Dedication to Christina G. Rossetti. Swinburne. StP
Dedication to Poems and Ballads [First Series]. Swinburne. PoVP; ViPo
Dedication to the Generation Knocking at the Door. John Davidson. BrPo
Dedication to the Poet Laureate. Byron. *See* Dedication: "Bob Southey! You're a poet—Poet-laureate."
Dedication to the Sermons, The. Charles Churchill. QFR
Dedications [*of* Orchestra]. Sir John Davies. SiPS
I. To His Very Friend, Master Richard Martin.
II. To the Prince.
Dedicatory. Mary Gilmore. BoAV
Dedicatory Ode, *sel.* Hilaire Belloc.
They Say That in the Unchanging Place. PoLF
Dedicatory Sonnet to S. T. Coleridge. Hartley Coleridge. ERoP-2; Sonn
Dedicatory Stanzas. Thomas Lovell Beddoes. *See* L'Envoi: "Who findeth comfort in the stars and flowers."
Deean Tractorman, Clear, The. Edith Anne Robertson. OxBS
Deed of Lieutenant Miles, The. Clinton Scollard. *See* Ballad of Lieutenant Miles.
Deed you evra see Joy. Da Pup een da Snow. T. A. Daly. TSW
Deedle, deedle, dumpling, my son John. *See* Diddle, diddle, dumpling. . .
Deeds of Kindness. Epes Sargent, *sometimes at. to* Fanny Crosby. HBV; HBVY; OTPC; PPL
(Suppose.) TVC
Deeds of Valor at Santiago. Clinton Scollard. HBV; MC; PAH
Deeds That Might Have Been, The. Wilfried Scawen Blunt. TrGrPo
Deem as ye list, upon good cause. Songs and Lyrics, XCIX. Sir Thomas Wyatt. FCP; SiPS
Deem Not [because You See Me]. George Santayana. Sonnets, XI. AnEnPo; TrGrPo
Deem not devoid of elegance the sage. Sonnet: Written in a Blank Leaf of Dugdale's "Monasticon." Thomas Warton, the Younger. Sonnets, III. EiPP; OBEC; SeCePo; Sonn
Deep, The. John G. C. Brainard. AA; EtS
Deep affections of the breast, The. The Parrot. Thomas Campbell. OTPC
Deep and Dark Blue Ocean. Byron. *See* Ocean, The.
Deep and soft and far off over country. Before Harvest. Robert Fitzgerald. PoPl
Deep asleep, deep asleep. The Ballad of Semmerwater. Sir William Watson. PoVP
Deep black against the dying glow. An Autumnal Evening. "Fiona Macleod." GBV; PoSC; SyP
Deep cradled in the fringed mow to lie. Theophany. Evelyn Underhill. MaRV; WGRP
Deep Dark Night, The. Tennyson. *Fr.* The Devil and the Lady. SeCePo
Deep Dark River. Lloyd Roberts. CaP
Deep Desire Sung This Song. George Gascoigne. TuPP
Deep Discussion, A. Richard Moore. HoPM
Deep down in the Siberian mine. *See* Deep in the Siberian mine.
Deep down the Blackman's Mind. R. E. G. Armattoe. ACV
Deep flows the flood. Underground. Ian Mudie. BoAV; MoAuPo
Deep Honeysuckle! in the silent eve. To the Herald Honeysuckle. Emily Pfeiffer. VA
Deep in a distant bay, and deeply hidden. The Lonely Isle. Claudian. AWP; JAWP; WBP
Deep in a glassy ball, the future looks. Crystal Anniversary. Philip Appleman. MeWo
Deep in a Rose's glowing heart. Sent with a Rose to a Young Lady. Margaret Deland. AA
Deep in a vale where rocks on every side. Sonnets, I. Gustave Rosenhane, *tr. by* Sir Edmund Gosse. AWP; JAWP; WBP
Deep in Alabama earth. Alabama Earth. Langston Hughes. AmFN; GoSl
Deep in earth's opaque mirror. W. H. Auden. *Fr.* Symmetries and Asymmetries. FlW
Deep in grey dusk the mill turns faltering. The Mill. Emile Verhaeren. WoL
Deep in Love. *Unknown.* CBEP
Deep in my brain walks to and fro. My Cat. Baudelaire. CIV
Deep in my gathering garden. A Thrush Sings. W. E. Henley. YT
Deep in my heart I hear them, the gaunt hounds pacing. The Hounds of the Soul. Louis Ginsberg. TrJP
Deep in my soul there roared the crashing thunder. Calm after Storm. Frank Yerby. AmNP
Deep in the brown bosom. Bangkok. F. R. Scott. MoCV; OBCV
Deep in the cool, dark wood. Undertone. Dorothy Quick. FiSC
Deep in the fading leaves of night. Carol. W. R. Rodgers. ChMP; DTC; FaBoTw; FlW
Deep in the Georgia night when all. Georgia Towns. Daniel Whitehead Hicky. AmFN
Deep in the grass there lies a dead gazelle. Maytime. *Unknown. Fr.* Shi King. AWP
Deep in the heart of the forest the lily of Yorrow is growing. The Lily of Yorrow. Henry van Dyke. AA
Deep in the heart of the lake. Water Music. Alun Lewis. ChMP; GTBS-D; MemP
Deep in the leafy fierceness of the wood. Apollo and Daphne. Yvor Winters. Sonn
Deep in the man sits fast his fate. Fate. Emerson. ForPo
Deep in the shadow of slumber, one night I lay on my bed. The Harvest and the Tempest. Lon Woodrum. SoP
Deep in the shady sadness of a vale. Hyperion. Keats. AnEnPo; ATP; BEL; ChER; EnRP; EPN; ERoP-2; ExPo; FaBoEn; FiP; InP; LoBV; MBW-2; MyFE; OBNC; OBRV; PeER; PoEL-4; TrGrPo
Deep in the shelter of the cave. Neighbors of the Christ Night. Nora Archibald Smith. ChrBoLe; PRWS
Deep in [*or* down in] the Siberian mine. Message to Siberia. Pushkin. AWP; JAWP; PoFr; TTY; WBP; WoL
Deep in the study. The Phoenix. Ogden Nash. CenHV; NePA
Deep in the wave is a coral grove. The Coral Grove. James Gates Percival. AA; AmLP; AnAmPo; AnNE; EtS; GN; GoTP
Deep in the winter plain, two armies. Two Armies. Stephen Spender. ChMP; CoBMV; SeCeV; WaP
Deep in the Woods. Mildred D. Shacklett. GFA
Deep in [*or* into] the woods we'll go. Heart of the Woods. Wesley Curtright. GoSl; PoNe
Deep lines of honour all can hit. The Portrait. Countess of Winchilsea. *Fr.* The Birthday of Catharine Tufton. OBEC
Deep Living. *Unknown.* SoP
Deep loving, well knowing. Our Colonel. Arthur Guiterman. DD; HH; PoRL
Deep music of the ancient forest! Sancta Silvarum. Lionel Johnson. BrPo
Deep on the convent-roof the snows. St. Agnes' Eve. Tennyson. CAW; CoBE; EnL; EnLit; GoBC; GTBS-W; GTSL; HBV; ILP; LiTB; LiTG; MaVP; OAEP; OBEV; OBVV; OTPC; OxBoCh; PoVP; StJW; ViPo

Deep peace, pure white of the moon to you. "Fiona Macleod." *Fr.* Invocation of Peace. BoTP
Deep River ("Deep river, deep river, Lawd"), *with music.* *Unknown.* ABF
Deep River ("Deep river, my home is over Jordan"), with music. *Unknown.* BoAN-1; TrAS
Deep-Sea Fishing. "Hugh MacDiarmid." SeCePo
Deep Sea Soundings. Sarah Williams. EtS; WGRP
Deep seclusion of this forest path, The. Enchantment. Madison Caweii HBV
Deep Stuff. Keith Preston. WhC
Deep-Sworn Vow, A. W. B. Yeats. CMoP; ELU; PoPo; ReMP; UnPo
Deep was the first draught, deep the next, no stint was there. After the Plague. *Unknown.* LiTW
Deep Waters. Van Tassel Sutphen. AA
Deep well corporals ride alongside listen. Behind the Wheel. Michael Brownstein. ANYP
Deep well knows and knows it well, The. World Secret. Hugo von Hofmannsthal, *tr. by* Werner Heider. LiTW
Deep well knows it certainly, The. World-Secret. Hugo von Hofmannsthal, *tr. by* Charles Wharton Stork. TrJP
Deepe in the bottome of an huge great rocke. Spenser. *Fr.* The Faerie Queene, IV, 11-12. MBW-1
Deeper into the Forest. Roy Daniells. TwCaPo
Deeper Seas, The. Henry Bellamann. EtS
Deeper than sleep but not so deep as death. Night Feeding. Muriel Rukeyser. MiAP
Deeper than the narwhal sinketh. The Sea-Deeps. Thomas Miller. EtS
Deepest infamy man can attain, The. The Worst Treason. Victor Hugo. PoFr
Deepest thanksgiving I do give. A Thanksgiving. Carolyn Wells. PEDC
Deeply Gone. Jon Silkin. FiSC
Deer, The. Mary Austin. FaPON
Deer. John Drinkwater. CH
Deer. Kenneth Rexroth. *Fr.* A Bestiary. HoPM
Deer and Echo. Otomo Yakamochi, *tr. fr. Japanese by* Ishii *and* Obata. OnPM
Deer and the Snake, The. Kenneth Patchen. MoAmPo
Deer are gentle and graceful. Deer. Kenneth Rexroth. *Fr.* A Bestiary. HoPM
Deer are on the mountain, deer! Deer on the Mountain. Grace Fallow Norton. HBMV
Deer in Aspens. Kay DeBard Hall. GoYe
Deer is humble, The, lovely as God made her. The Deer and the Snake. Kenneth Patchen. MoAmPo
Deer of Ireland, The. Padraic Colum. PoFr
(Old Man Said, An.) OxBI
Deer on pine mountain, The. Onakatomi no Yoshinobu, *tr. fr. Japanese by* Kenneth Rexroth. *Fr.* Shui Shu. LiTW
Deer on the Mountain. Grace Fallow Norton. HBMV
Deer Sing, *sel.* Confucius, *tr. fr. Chinese by* Ezra Pound.
Fraternitas. CTC
Deer were bounding like blown leaves, The. Fire on the Hills. Robinson Jeffers. CMoP
Deer which lives, The. Onakatomi no Yoshinobu, *tr. fr.* Japanese. *Fr.* Shui Shu. AWP
Deere my deere why are you cruell. *Unknown.* SeCSL
Deere turne awaye thyne eyes soe bright. *Unknown.* SeCSL
Deere, why should you commaund me to my rest. *See* Dear, why should. . .
Deer's Cry, The. *At. to* St. Patrick, *tr. fr. Old Irish by* Whitley Stokes, John Strachan, *and* Kuno Meyer.
AnIL; CAW; OnYI; WGRP
(Breastplate of St. Patrick, The.) OxBI, *tr. by* Cecil Frances Alexander; WHL, *tr. by* Kuno Meyer; BBV, *sel.*
(St. Patrick's Breastplate, *tr. by* Cecil Frances Alexander.) FaBoCh; LoGBV; AnIV, *sel. tr. by* Kuno Meyer; MaRV, *sel.*; TRV, *sel.*
Deevil's Waltz, The. Sidney Goodsir Smith. FaBoTw
Defeat. Witter Bynner. PoNe
Defeat and Victory. Wallace Rice. MC; PAH
Defeat may serve as well as victory. Victory in Defeat. Edwin Markham. MaRV; OQP; PoLF; PoPl; StaSt; TreFT
Defeat o' the Hert. Sidney Goodsir Smith. AtBAP
Defeat of Grendel, The. *Unknown, tr. fr. Anglo-Saxon by* Richard L. Hoffman. *Fr.* Beowulf. YAT
Defeat of the Armada, The. *Unknown, at. to* William Warner. CoBE
("Some years of late, in eighty-eight.") FaBoCh; LoGBV
(Spanish Armado, The.) LiTG
Defeat of the Rebels. Robert Graves. WaP
Defeated, The. Alun Lewis. PrWP
Defeated, The. W. S. Merwin. AmPC
Defeated Farmer. Mark Van Doren. AnAmPo
Defence of Fort M'Henry. Francis Scott Key. *See* Star Spangled Banner.
Defence [*or* Defense] of Guenevere, The. William Morris. BEL; EnL; EnLi-2; EnLit; OAEP; PoVP; StP; ViPo; ViPP
Defence of Lawrence, The. Richard Realf. MC; PAH
Defence of Lucknow, The. Tennyson. BeLS
Defence of Night, The. Michelangelo, *tr. fr. Italian.* CAW, *tr. by* Longfellow; OnPM, *tr. by* John Addington Symonds.
Defence of the Alamo, The. Joaquin Miller. *See* Defense of the Alamo, The.
Defenceless Children, Your Great Enemy. Kendrick Smithyman. AnNZ
Defender, The. Arthur M. Sampley. GoYe
Defender of his country, The—the founder of liberty. Epitaph on Washington. *Unknown.* OHIP; PEDC
Defense of Guenevere, The. William Morris. *See* Defence of Guenevere, The.
Defense [*or* Defence] of the Alamo, The. Joaquin Miller. BeLS; DD; FaBoBe; HBV; MC; OnMSP; PaA; PAH
Defense Rests. Vassar Miller. MoAmPo (1962 ed.)
Defensive Position. John Manifold. MoBrPo (1950 ed.)
Defiance, The. Aphra Behn. EnLoPo
Defiance, The. Thomas Flatman. CEP; OBS
Defiance. Solomon ibn Gabirol, *tr. fr. Hebrew by* Emma Lazarus. TrJP
Defiance. Walter Savage Landor. HBV
Defiled Is My Name. Anne Boleyn. FOL
Definition. Grace Noll Crowell. PoToHe (new ed.)
Definition. Edwin Rolfe. NAMP
Definition. May Sarton. MoLP
Definition of Beauty, The. Robert Herrick. Po
Definition of Love, The. Andrew Marvell. AnAnS-1; AnFE; BoLiVe; BWP; CBEP; DiPo; EP; FaBoEn; ForPo; FosPo; GTBS-W; LiTB; LiTG; LiTL; LoBV; MaMe; MaPo; MeLP; MePo; NoP; OAEP; OBEV (new ed.); OBS; PIA; Po; PoE; PoEL-2; PoFS; PoIE; ReEn; SCEP-2; SeCePo; SeCeV; SeCL; SeCP; SeCV-1; SeEP; StP; TreFT; TrGrPo; VaPo; UnPo; WHA
Definition of My Brother. W. S. Graham. FaBoTw; NeBP
Definition of the Soul. Boris Pasternak, *tr. fr. Russian.* LiTW, *tr. by* J. M. Cohen; TrJP, *tr. by* Babette Deutsch
Definitions. Joseph Joel Keith. PoToHe (new ed.)
Deflective rhythm under seas. Einstein among the Coffee-Cups. Louis Untermeyer. WhC
Deflowered forever. Here the Stem Rises. Daniel Berrigan. TwAmPo
Deformed Mistress, The. Sir John Suckling. ErPo
Deftly, admiral, cast your fly. Song: "Deftly, Admiral, Cast Your Fly." W. H. Auden. GTBS-P
Degas called him "The Notary." Seurat. James Schevill. FiMAP
Degenerate Age, A. Solomon ibn Gabirol, *tr. fr. Hebrew by* Emma Lazarus. TrJP
Degenerate Douglas! O the unworthy lord! Composed at Neidpath Castle, the Property of Lord Queensberry, 1803. Wordsworth. GTBS; GTBS-D; GTBS-P; GTBS-W; GTSE; GTSL
Degrees of Gray in Philipsburg. Richard Hugo. CoAP
Degrees of Shade. H. A. Pinkerton. NePoAm
Deh was a princess propose to be married. The Maid Freed from the Gallows (C *vers.*). *Unknown.* BaBo; ViBoFo
Dei Genitrix. Aubrey Thomas De Vere. IrPN
Deid Folks' Ferry. Rosamund Marriott Watson. VA
Deid is now that divour and dollin in erd. The Widow Speaks. William Dunbar. *Fr.* The Tua Mariit Wemen and the Wedo. PoEL-1
Deidre's Lament for the Sons of Usnach. *Unknown.* *See* Deirdre's Lament for the Sons of Usnach.
Deigne [*or* Deign] at my hands this crown of prayer and praise. La Corona. John Donne. AnAnS-1; MaMe; MeP; OBS; Sonn
De'il's Awa wi' the Exciseman, The. Burns. OAEP; ViBoPo
(Exciseman, The.) GoTS
Deirdre, *sel.* Sir Samuel Ferguson.
Deirdre ("Give me my harp, and let me sing a song"). IrPN
Deirdre. James Stephens. AWP; CMoP; GTSL; HBMV;

Deirdre (continued)
JAWP; OBMV; OnPP; PG; PoRA; ViBoPo; WBP
Deirdre, *sel.* W. B. Yeats.
"'Why is it,' Queen Edain said." ViBoPo
Deirdre and the Poets. Ewart Milne. NeIP
Deirdre's Farewell to Alba. *Unknown, tr. fr. Middle Irish by* Sir Samuel Ferguson. IrPN; OnYI
(Deirdre's Farewell to Scotland, *tr. by* Whitley Stokes *and* Kuno Meyer.) OnYI
Deirdre's [*or* Deidre's] Lament for the Sons of Usnach. *Unknown, tr. fr. Middle Irish by* Sir Samuel Ferguson. IrPN; OnYI; SeCePo
(Deirdre's Lament, *tr. by* Whitley Stokes *and* Kuno Meyer.) LiTW; OnYI
Deirdre's Song at Sunrise. Sister Maura. CaP
Deities and Beasts. John Updike. ELU
Dejected Lover, The. George Crabbe. *Fr.* Tales of the Hall. FaBoEn
(Sad Lover, The.) OBNC
Dejection. Robert Bridges. QFR
Dejection; an Ode. Samuel Taylor Coleridge. AnEnPo; BEL; CABA; CBEP; EnL; EnLi-2; EnLit; EnRP; EPN; ERoP-1; FaBoEn; FiP; ForPo; HBV; LiTB; LoBV; MaPo; MasP; MBW-2; MERP; NoP; OAEP; OBNC; OBRV; PAn; PIA; PoE; PoEL-4; PoFS; PoIE; StP
Sels.
Dejection: A Letter (*Longer vers.*). PeER
"Well! If the Bard was weather-wise, who made." SeCePo
(Letter to Sara Hutchinson, A.) NCEP
Del Cascar. William Stanley Braithwaite. BANP; CDC
Delacroix pentit Chopin's head. Ye Mongers Aye Need Masks for Cheatrie. Sydney Goodsir Smith. OxBS
Delay. Saint Augustine, *tr. fr. Latin.* SoP
Delay. Charlotte Fiske Bates. AA
Delay. Elizabeth Jennings. NePoEA
Delay Has Danger, *sel.* George Crabbe. *Fr.* Tales of the Hall. Sad Lover, The. OBNC
Delayed till she had ceased to know. Emily Dickinson. AA
Delectable Dream, A, *sel.* Humphrey Gifford.
"Woman's face is full of wiles, A." ElL; SiCE; TuPP
Delia. Samuel Daniel. *See* To Delia.
Delicate Bird Who Is Flying Up Our Asses, The. Marvin Bell. YAP
Delicate corner shot, The. Civilities. Thomas Whitbread. SD
Delicate fabric of bird song, A. May Day. Sara Teasdale. *Fr.* The Dark Cup. BoNaP; MemP; OTD; PoSC
Delicate white body will be buried today, The. The Lament for Urien, II. *Unknown. Fr.* The Red Book of Hergest. OBMV
Delicate young Negro stands, A. Anonymous Drawing. Donald Justice. CoAP; NePoEA-2
Deliciae Sapientiae de Amore. Coventry Patmore. The Unknown Eros, II, ix. OxBoCh; PoVP
Delicious Beauty. *At. to* John Marston. UnTE
(Song: "Delicious beauty, that doth lie.") ElL
Delight in Books from Evening. Francis Daniel Pastorius. SCAP
Delight in Disorder. Robert Herrick. ALV; AnAnS-2; BoLiVe; CABA; CavP; CBEP; CBV; CoBE; EnLi-1 (1949 ed.); EnLit; EnLoPo; EP; ErPo; FaBoEn; FaBV; HBV; ILP; InMe; LiTB; LiTG; LiTL; LoBV; MaPo; MemP; MeWo; NoP; OAEP; OBEV; OBS; PAn; PG (1945 ed.); PIA; PoAn; PoE; PoeP; PoFS; PoIE; PoRA; PoSa; PP; ReEn; SCEP-2; SeCePo; SeCeV; SeCL; SeCP; SeCV-1; SeEP; StP; TDP; TreFS; TrGrPo; UnPo; VaPo; ViBoPo; WHA
(Poetry of Dress, I.) GTBS; GTBS-D; GTBS-W; GTSE; GTSL
(Sweet Disorder [in the Dress], A.) AnFE; AWP; EG; GTBS-P; InPo; JAWP; ShBV-4; TOP; WBP
Delight in God Only. Francis Quarles. *Fr.* Emblems, VI. MaRV
Delight in God's House. Henry Francis Lyte. SoP
Delight it is in youth and May. A. E. Housman. VP
Delight of Solitariness, The. Sir Philip Sidney. *See* O Sweet Woods.
Delightful, book, your trip. Aoibhinn, a leabhráin, do thriall. *Unknown, tr. fr. Irish.* AnIV, *tr. by* Flann O'Brien; OxBI, *tr. by* Brian O Nolan
Delightful I think it to be in the bosom of an isle. St. Columcille's Island Hermitage. *Unknown.* AnIL
Delightful to be on the Hill of Howth. Columcille's Greeting to Ireland. *At. to* St. Columcille. OnYI
Delights of the bottle and charms of old wine, The. Love and Wine. Thomas Shadwell. UnTE
Delilah. Kipling. BrPo
Delilah. Milton. *Fr.* Samson Agonistes. SeCePo
Delilah Aberyswith was a lady—not too young. Delilah. Kipling. BrPo
Delilie was a woman, fine an' fair. Samson. *Unknown.* OuSiCo
Delius in the Cathedral. Derek Parker. MuSP
Deliver Me. Amy Carmichael. SoP; STF
(Flame of God.) STF
(Make Me Thy Fuel.) FaChP
Deliver me, O beloved, from this evil. Lotuses. Witter Bynner. MoLP
Deliver Us From. . . . Amelia Josephine Burr. OQP
Deliverance. "M. E. B." SoP
Deliverance. William James Dawson. OBVV
Deliverance. Laurie Lee. BoPe
Deliverance of Jehovah, The. Psalms, XXVII, Bible, *O.T.* (*Moulton, Modern Reader's Bible*). WGRP
Deliverer, The. Milton. *Fr.* Samson Agonistes. OBS
(Choruses from Samson Agonistes.) SeCeV
("Oh, how comely it is and how reviving.") OBEV
Deliverer, Jove, The. *Unknown, tr. fr. Greek by* Lord Neaves. OnPM
Delivering Children. David Holbrook. NePoEA-2
Delivers papers to the doors of sleep. Herald. Josephine Miles. FiMAP
Della Cruscans, The. William Gifford. *Fr.* The Baviad. OBEC
Delmonico's is where he dines. A Splendid Fellow. H. C. Dodge. BOHV
Delos. Lawrence Durrell. NeBP
Delos. Bernard Spencer. FaBoMo
Delphic and Theban and Corinthian. Four Legs, Two Legs, Three Legs. William Empson. MoPo; ToPo
Delphy. Alice Corbin. *Fr.* Echoes of Childhood. PoNe
Delta, The. Michael Dennis Browne. NYBP
Deluded mortals, whom the great. A Libel on Doctor Delany and a Certain Great Lord. Swift. NCEP
Delug'd with tears, by what you heard before. To My Honoured Patron Humphery Davie. Benjamin Tompson. SCAP
Deluge. John Clare. BoNaP
Deluge, The, *sel. Unknown.*
Animals in the Ark, The. ChTr
Deluge, The. *Unknown, tr. fr. Lenape Indian by* C. S. Rafinesque. *Fr.* Wallam Olum. LiTA
Delusion of Reference, A. R. A. D. Ford. PeCV
Delusions VIII ("Placed in a country on a desert verging"). Charles Madge. BoSA
Delusions IV ("Sometimes at evening travellers have heard"). Charles Madge. FaBoMo
Delusions VI ("Without surprise, on that not distant shore"). Charles Madge. NeBP
Delusions of the days that once have been. Prologue. Longfellow. *Fr.* Giles Corey of the Salem Farms. PAH
Delve deep amongst the musty muniments. Nicolas Gatineau. Arthur S. Bourinot. CaP
Delve not so deep in the gloomy past. Ascent. Charles G. Blanden. OQP
Dem Bones, *with music. Unknown.* OuSiCo
Deme as Ye List upon Goode Cause. Sir Thomas Wyatt. PoEL-1
Demeter and Persephone. Tennyson. BWP; MBW-2; ViPP
Demeter devastated our good land. The Appeasement of Demeter. George Meredith. EnLi-2
Demiurge's Laugh, The. Robert Frost. OxBA
Democracy. Harriet Monroe. *Fr.* Commemoration Ode. AA
Democracy, *abr.* Whittier. PoFr; StaSt
Democritus Platonissans; or, An Essay upon the Infinity of Worlds out of Platonick Principles, *abr.* Henry More. SeCV-2
Demogorgon's Song. Shelley. *Fr.* Prometheus Unbound. MaPo (1969 ed.)
(Demogorgon's Speech.) LoBV
(Final Victory, The.) ShBV-3

("This is the day which down the void abysm.") EnLit; OQP; PoIE; SeCeV
Demon [*or* Daemon], The, *sel.* Mikhail Yurevich Lermontov, *tr. fr. Russian by* Babette Deutsch *and* Avrahm Yarmolinsky.
"On the sightless seas." AWP
("On the vast aerial ocean," *rev. tr. by* Babette Deutsch.) OnPM
Demon bydes in the breist in dern, A. Saagin. Sidney Goodsir Smith. AtBAP
Demon-Lover, The. James Abraham Hillhouse. AA
Demon Lover, The. *Unknown.* BuBa; CABA; EnL; EnSB; LiTB; PoAn; PoMS; PoPo; TOP; UnPo
(Carpenter's Wife, The.) OxBB
(Daemon Lover, The.) CBEP; EnLi-1; EnLit; FlW; OBB
(House Carpenter, The, *with music.*) AS; BFSS
(James Harris, *diff. vers.*) BaBo (A, B, C, *and* D *vers.*); ESPB (A, D, *and* F *vers.*); ViBoFo (A *vers.*; B *vers., with music*)
Demon of the Gibbet, The. Fitz-James O'Brien. PoMS
Demon of the Mirror, The. Bayard Taylor. BeLS
Demon Speaks, The. Pedro Calderon de la Barca, *tr. fr. Spanish by* Shelley. *Fr.* El Magico prodigioso. CAW
Demophilus. Henry Wellesley, *after the Greek of* Nicarchus. ALV
Demos. E. A. Robinson. AP; NP
Demosthenes to the Radio Announcer. David Ross. PG (1945 ed.)
Den of the Titans, The. Keats. *Fr.* Hyperion, II. WHA
Denial, A. Elizabeth Barrett Browning. OBNC
Denial. George Herbert. EnL; EP; InPo; LoBV (1949 ed.); NoP
(Deniall.) AnAnS-1; FaBoEn; MaMe; MeP; MePo; PoEL-2; SCEP-1
Denied, she screamed in rage, and ran away. You Can't Be Wise. Paul Engle. PoPl
Denise: A Letter Never Sent. Henri Coulette. *Fr.* The War of the Secret Agents. NePoEA-2
Dennis was hearty when Dennis was young. The Grand Match. "Moira O'Neill." HBMV
Denouement. Sister Mary Eulalia. JKCP (1955 ed.)
Denouement. Kenneth Fearing. OnHM
Dentist, The. Rose Fyleman. GaP; SoPo; TiPo
Dentist, A. *Unknown. See* Epitaph on a Dentist.
Dentists continue to water their lawns even in the rain. The Great Society. Robert Bly. CAD
Denunciation: or, Unfrock'd Again. Philip Whalen. NeAP
Denver Jim. Sherman D. Richardson. SCC
Deny and what will be given you? Song from the End of the Earth. William Hunt. YAP
Deny Yourself. Christopher Morley. LHV; YaD
Deo gracias, Anglia. A Carol of Agincourt. *Uknown.* MeEL
Deo Opt. Max. George Sandys. Paraphrase on the Psalms of David, Psalm CIV. OBS
Deo Optimo Maximo. Louise Imogen Guiney. TrPWD
Deor's Lament. *Unknown, tr. fr. Anglo-Saxon.*
—— *Tr. by* Francis B. Gummere. BEL
—— *Tr. by* Charles W. Kennedy. AnOE
—— *Tr. by* Harold S. Stine. EnLit
—— *Tr. by* Stith Thompson. EnLi-1; OuHeWo
(Deor, *tr. by* Burton Raffel.) CaFP
Depart, depart, depart! A Lament; 1547. Alexander Scott. CH; LO
Depart from Me. Mary Elizabeth Coleridge. TrPWD
Departed, The. John Bannister Tabb. AA
Departed Friend, A. Julia A. Moore. FiBHP
Departed Friend, The. Salvador Novo, *tr. fr. Spanish by* Muna Lee. WoL
Departed friend, I do not come. Exequy: To Peter Allt. Kildare Dobbs. OBCV
Departed Friends. Henry Vaughan. *See* They Are All Gone.
Departed out of parlement echone. The Despair of Troilus. Chaucer. *Fr.* Troilus and Criseyde, IV. LoBV
Departed—to the judgment. Emily Dickinson. CABA; MaPo; NoP; OnPM
Departmental. Robert Frost. AmP; AmPP; AnNE; DiPo; GoYe; HoPM; MoAB; MoAmPo
Departure. Kingsley Amis. NePoEA
Departure. Guillaume Apollinaire, *tr. fr. French by* Patricia Terry. OnPM
Departure. Thomas Hardy. Sonn
Departure. William Hart-Smith. *Fr.* Christopher Columbus. PoAu-2
Departure. Edna St. Vincent Millay. MAP; MoAmPo
Departure, The. Robert Pack. NePoEA
Departure. Coventry Patmore. The Unknown Eros, I, viii. ACP; CoBE; FaPL; GTBS-D; GTSL; HBV; JKCP; LO; OBEV; OBNC; OBVV; PG (1945 ed.); PoLi; PoVP; SeCePo; TreFT
Departure. May Riley Smith. AA
Departure. L. A. G. Strong. HaMV
Departure, The; an Elegy. Henry King. SeCP
Departure from Hydra, The. Kenneth Koch. AmPC; ANYP
Departure from Paradise, The. Milton. *Fr.* Paradise Lost, XII. OBS
Departure in the Dark. C. Day Lewis. ChMP; CoBMV; MoPo; TwCP
Departure of Martín Fierro, The, *abr.* José Hernández, *tr. fr. Spanish by* Walter Owen. PoFr
Departure of the Swallow, The. William Howitt. VA
Departure Platform. Kenneth Allott. NeBP
Dependence on God. Francis Quarles. MaRV
Deportation. "M. J.", *tr. fr. Polish by* A. Glanz-Leyeless. TrJP
Deposition by John Wilmot, A. Vincent McHugh. ErPo
Deposition from Beauty, A. Thomas Stanley. HBV
("Though when I lov'd thee thou wert fair.") EG
(When I Loved Thee.) LiTL
Deposition from Love, A. Thomas Carew. AnAnS-2; CavP; MeLP; OAEP; OBS
Deprecating Parrots. Beulah May. EtS
Depreciating Her Beauty. Wilfrid Scawen Blunt. The Love Sonnets of Proteus, VI. OBMV
Depressed by a Book of Bad Poetry, I Walk toward an Unused Pasture and Invite the Insects to Join Me. James Wright. PIA
Depression. Robert Bly. FRC; NaP
Depression. "Michael Field." SyP
Depression before Spring. Wallace Stevens. WIRo
Deprivation. H. A. Pinkerton. NePoAm
Deprived [*or* Depriv'd] of root, and branch and rind. A Maypole. Swift. CBEP; NCEP
Deprived of the green of that exclusive golf course, the scotch. Epistle to the Gentiles. Alfred Hayes. TrJP
Depths, The. Denise Levertov. NaP
Der Arme Poet. Michael Roberts. ML
Der Blinde Junge. Mina Loy. QFR
Der Heilige Mantel von Aachen. Benjamin Francis Musser. ISi
Der lived a king inta da aste. King Orfeo. *Unknown.* ESPB; OBB; OxBB; OxBoLi
Der Noble Ritter Hugo. *See* Noble Ritter Hugo, Der.
Deranged. Padraic Fiacc. NeIP
Derby Ram, The (*diff. vers.*). *Unknown.* SoAmSa, *with music*; ViBoFo, *with music*
("As I was going to Derby.") OxNR
(Ram, The.) SiTL
(Ram of Darby, The, *with music.*) OuSiCo
(Wonderful Derby Ram, The.) BoTP
Derbyshire Bluebells. Sacheverell Sitwell. ChMP
Derelict. Young E. Allison. BBV; BLPA; EtS; FaBoBe; FaFP; HBMV; MCCG; NeHB; OnMSP; TreFS
(Buccaneers, The.) ABF
(Dead Men's Song, The.) AnAmPo
Derelict, The. Lucius Harwood Foote. AA
Derelict, The. Henry W. Frost. SoP
Derelict, The. Kipling. BrPo
Derelict. Elisabeth Cavazza Pullen. AA
Dereliction. Edward Shillito. ChIP
Dere's a Han'writin' on de Wall, *with music. Unknown.* BoAN-2
Dere's a star in de Eas' on Christmas morn. Rise Up Shepherd an' Foller. *Unknown.* BoAN-2; ChrBoLe
Dere's No Hidin' Place down Dere, *with music. Unknown.* BoAN-1
Derricks and Rainbows. Joseph Auslander. PoMa
Dervish. Georgia Lee McElhaney. CoPo
Dervorgilla's supremely lovely daughter. Portrait with Background. Oliver St. John Gogarty. OBMV
Des a little cabin. A Little Cabin. Charles Bertram Johnson BANP
Descend, Fair Sun! George Chapman. *Fr.* The Masque of the Middle Temple and Lincoln's Inn. ElL; TuPP

Descend from heav'n Urania, by that name. Invocation to Urania. Milton. *Fr.* Paradise Lost, VII. FiP; MBW-1; OBS
Descend, Ye Nine. Pope. *Fr.* Ode for Music on St. Cecilia's Day. GN
Descended, Adam to the bower where Eve. Banishment from Paradise. Milton. *Fr.* Paradise Lost, XII TreFS
Descended of an ancient line. To Maecenas [*or* Horat. Ode 29. Book 3 *or* The Twenty Ninth Ode of the Third Book]. Horace. *paraphrased by* Dryden. *Fr.* Odes. AWP; CEP; JAWP; MBW-1; SeCV-2; WBP
Descending. Valentin Iremonger. *See* Going down the Mountain.
Descending. Robert Pack. NePoEA-2
Descending swans, The. Ritual. Gustav Davidson. NYTB
Descending towards Cairo, an arid. Egypt. Zulfikar Ghose. NYTB
Descent, The. James Tate. YAP
Descent, The. William Carlos Williams. MoAB; PoCh; ReMP
Descent for the Lost. Philip Child. CaP
Descent from the Cross, The, *sel.* Christina Rossetti.
Face of Jesus Christ, The. BePJ
("Is this the face that thrills with awe.") ChIP
Descent into Hell, The. William Langland. *Fr.* The Vision of Piers Plowman. PoEL-1
Descent of Odin, The; an Ode from the Norse Tongue. Thomas Gray. CEP; EiCP; EiPP
Descent of the Holy Ghost. John Gilland Brunini. JKCP (1955 ed.)
Descent on Middlesex, The. Peter St. John. PAH
"Describe the Borough"—though our idle tribe. George Crabbe. *Fr.* The Borough, Letter I. CABL
Describes the Place where Cynthia Is Sporting Herself. Girolamo Preti, *tr. by* Phillip Ayres. EnLoPo
Description, A. Lord Herbert of Cherbury. AnAnS-2; SeCP
Description and Praise of His Love Geraldine. Earl of Surrey. OAEP; ReIE; SiCE; TuPP
("From Tuscan[e] came my lady's worthy race.") FCP; ReEn; SiPS
Description of a City Shower, A. Swift. BWP; CABL; CBEP; CEP; EiCL; EiCP; EiPP; EnLi-1 (1949 ed.); ExPo; LoBV; NoP; OnYI; PoE; PoFS; PoIE; SeCePo; SeCeV; VaPo
(City Shower, A.) UnPo (3d ed.)
Sels.
"Ah! where must needy poet seek for aid." ViBoPo
"Careful observers may foretell." CIV
Description of a Gun. Pandolphus, *tr. fr. Latin by* Sir Thomas Wyatt. ReIE; TuPP
("Vulcan begat me; Minerva me taught.") FCP
Description of a Most Noble Lady, A. John Heywood. *See* Praise of His Lady, A.
Description of a New England Spring. John Josselyn. SCAP
Description of a Religious House and Condition of Life. Richard Crashaw. MaMe
Description of a Sea-Battle. John Banks. *Fr.* The Unhappy Favourite. PeRV
Description of a Strange (and Miraculous) Fish, A. Martin Parker. CoMu
Description of a Summer's Eve. Henry Kirke White. OBRV
Description of a View. William Empson. ACV
Description of an Envious and Naughty Neighbor, The. Thomas Tusser. SiCE
Description of an Irish Feast, The; or, O'Rourk's Frolic. Hugh MacGowran, *tr. fr. Modern Irish by* Swift. OnYI
(O'Rourk's Frolic.) LiTW
Description of Beauty, A. Samuel Daniel, *after the Italian of* Giambattista Marini. OBSC
(Fading Beauty.) AWP
Enjoy Thy April Now, *sel.* EIL; ELP; StP
Description of Castara, The. William Habington. *Fr.* Castara, I. AnAnS-2; CavP
("Like the violet, which alone.") HBV; LiTL
Description of Chaos. Sir Richard Blackmore. *Fr.* Prince Arthur. PeRV
Description of Chaos. Milton. *Fr.* Paradise Lost, II. PeRV
Description of Cozeners. George Whetstone. TuPP
Description of Elysium. James Agee. CrMA
Description of Elysium [*or* Elizium], The. Michael Drayton. *Fr.* The Muses Elysium. AnAnS-2; TuPP
(Poets' Paradise, The.) WiR
Description of His Ugly Lady, A. Thomas Hoccleve. *See* Hoccleve's Humerous Praise of His Lady.
Description of Holland by Mr. Nevell, A, *sel.* *At. to* Henry Nevile Payne.
Character of the Dutch, A. PeRV
Description of Life and Riches, A. Thomas Tusser. SiCE
Description of London, A. John Banks. WaPE
Description of Love, A. Sir Walter Ralegh. ALV; CBEP; EIL; ELP; LiTL; OBSC; PAn; PoFS; ReIE; TuPP; UnTE
(Now What Is Love.) HBV; PoLF
Description of Maidenhead, A. Earl of Rochester. UnTE
Description of Sir Geoffrey Chaucer, The. Robert Greene. *Fr.* Greene's Vision. AnFE; CTC; OBSC
(Sir Geoffrey Chaucer.) FaBoCh; LoGBV; WePo
Description of Spring [Wherein Each Thing Renews, Save Only the Lover]. Earl of Surrey, *after* Petrarch. AnEnPo; AtBAP; BEL; CoBE; EIL; EnLi-1; EnLit; ILP; LiTB; LoBV; OAEP; OBEV; PoE; ReIE; SeCePo; SeCeV; SiCE; Sonn; STP; TOP; TuPP
(Soote Season, The.) EnRePo; NoP
(Soote Season, That Bud and Blome Furth Bringes, The.) YAT
("Soote season that bud and bloom forth brings, The.") EG; FCP; ReEn; SiPS
(Spring.) FlW; OA; OBSC; PoIE
(Summer Comes.) OnPM
(Summer Is Come.) AWP; JAWP; OuHeWo; WBP
Description of Such a One as He Would Love, A. Sir Thomas Wyatt. TuPP
(Epigram: "Face that should content me wonders well, A.") CTC; OBSC
("Face that should content me wondrous well, A.") EnLoPo; FCP; ReEn; SiCE
Description of the Contrarious Passions in a Lover. Petrarch, *tr. fr. Italian by* Sir Thomas Wyatt. *Fr.* Sonnets to Laura: To Laura in Life. EnLi-1 (1949 ed.); OAEP; PoFS; ReIE; Sonn; TrGrPo; TuPP
(Contrarious Passions in a Lover, The.) LiTL
(I Find No Peace.) DiPo; LiTB; PoAn; PoIE
("I find no peace and all my war is done.") FCP; ReEn
(Love's Inconsistency.) AWP; JAWP; OuHeWo; WBP
(Sonnet: "I find no peace, and all my war is done.") SiPS
Description of the Lives of the Lasses of London, A. *Unknown.* *See* Innocent Country-Maid's Delight, The.
Description of the Morning, A. Swift. BWP; CABA; CaFP; CBV; CEP; EiCL; EiCP; EiPP; ExPo; FaBoEn; FosPo; ILP; PoFS; PoIE; SeCeV; StP; ViBoPo
Description of the Properties of Winds All the [*or* at All] Times of the Year, A. Thomas Tusser. ReIE; SiCE; TuPP
(Winds, The.) WiR
Description of the Spring, A. Sir Henry Wotton. *See* On a Bank as I Sat a-Fishing.
Description of the Spring; Wherein Each Thing Renews, Save Only the Lover. Earl of Surrey. *See* Description of Spring.
Description of Time and the Year, A. Thomas Tusser. SiCE
Description of Tyme, A. Alexander Montgomerie. OxBS
Description of Vertue. Theodore Beza, *tr. fr. Latin by* Nicholas Grimald. SiCE; TuPP
(Virtue.) OBSC
Description of Wallace, A. Henry the Minstrel. *Fr.* The Wallace, IX. GoTS
Descriptive Poem. Han Wu, *tr. fr. Chinese by* Arthur Christy. OnPM
Desdemona. Sister Mary Jeremy. JKCP (1955 ed.)
Desdemona's Song. Shakespeare. *Fr.* Othello, IV, iii. LoBV
Desdichado, El. Gerard de Nerval, *tr. fr. French by* Alan Conder. LO
Dese Bones Gwine to Rise Again. *Unknown.* ABF, *with music*; AS, *with music*; OxBoLi; SiTL
Desert, The. Clifford Dyment. POTi
Desert. Langston Hughes. Kal
Desert, The. Henry Herbert Knibbs. SCC
Desert, The ("Never have I found a place"). C. E. S. Wood. *Fr.* The Poet in the Desert. AnEnPo
Desert, The ("She is a nun"). C. E. S. Wood. *Fr.* The Poet in the Desert. AnAmPo; MAP
Desert Claypan. Frederick T. Macartney. PoAu-1
Desert does not have to be, A. Deserts. Anne Hamilton. MaRV; OQP
Desert Flowers. Keith Douglas. FaBoTw

Desert Fox. R. H. W. Dillard. TDP
Desert Gulls. Dan Gillespie. QAH
Desert Lark, The. Eugene Marais, *tr. fr. Afrikaans by* Jack Cope *and* Uys Krige. PeSA
Desert moves out on half the horizon, The. The Supper after the Last. Galway Kinnell. PoCh; TwAmPo
Desert murmurs to the sun a strange murmur, The. C. E. S. Wood. *Fr.* The Poet in the Desert. PoFr
Desert Music, The *sel.* William Carlos Williams.
"Music, The! the music! as when Casals struck. UnS
Desert of weed and water-darkened stone under my western windows, A. People and a Heron. Robinson Jeffers. ReMP
Desert Places. Robert Frost. AmPP (4th ed.); AnFE; AP; AtBAP; CABA; CBV; CMoP; CoAnAm; CoBMV; DiPo; ForPo; MAP; MaPo (1969 ed.); MoAB; MoAmPo; MoVE; MWA-2; OxBA; PAn; PoAn; PoIE; PoPo; ReMP; TwAmPo; UnPo
Desert River. Patricia Benton. GoYe
Desert Shipwreck. Barbara Leslie Jordan. GoYe
Desert Travellers, The. Laurence D. Lerner. BoSA
Desert Wanderings. Thomas Curtis Clark. ChIP
Deserted. Madison Cawein. MAP; MCCG
Deserted Buildings under Shefford Mountain. John Glassco. OBCV
Deserted City, The. Sir Charles G. D. Roberts. VA
Deserted City, The, *sel.* Francis Sherman.
House of Colour, The. CaP
Deserted Farms. Richard Burton. AnAmPo
Deserted Garden, The. Elizabeth Barrett Browning. HBV; OBEV (1st ed.)
Deserted Garden, The. Li Po, *tr. fr. Chinese by* C. W. Luh. OnPM
Deserted Home, A. Sidney Royse Lysaght. CH
Deserted Home, The. *Unknown, tr. fr. Irish by* Kuno Meyer. OxBI
(Ruined Nest, The.) OnYI
Deserted House, The. Mary Elizabeth Coleridge. BoTP; CH; MoVE; PCD; PoG; ThWaDe
Deserted House, The. Tennyson. PeER; VA
Deserted House, *sel* Dorothy Wellesley.
Buried Child, The: Epilogue. DTC; GTBS-D; OBMV
Deserted Kingdom, The. Lord Dunsany. AnIV
Deserted Pasture, The. Bliss Carman. HBV
Deserted Plantation, The. Paul Laurence Dunbar. IHA
Deserted Village, The. Goldsmith. BEL; BeLS; CEP; CoBE; EiCL; EiPP; EnL; EnLi-1; EnLit; EnPE; EnRP; FaFP; GoTL; HBV; ILP; LaA; LoBV, abr.; MasP; MCCG; NoP; OAEP; OnYI; OuHeWo; OxBI; Po, abr.; PoE; PoEL-3; TOP
Sels.
Blest Retirement. OBEC
Farewell to Poetry. OBEC
"Ill fares the land, to hastening ills a prey." TRV
(Common Man, The, 6 *ll.*) MaRV
(Ill Fares the Land, 6 *ll.*) TreFT
"Near yonder copse, where once the garden smiled." TRV
(Parson, The.) WePo
"Sweet Auburn! loveliest village of the plain." FOL; OTPC; TreFS; ViBoPo
(Auburn.) OBEC; SeCePo
(Sweet Auburn.) LiTB
(Village, The.) TrGrPo
"Sweet smiling village, loveliest of the lawn." AnFE; PoFr, *abr.*
(Sweet, Smiling Village.) PPON
"Sweet was the sound when oft at evening's close." FaBoEn
(Evening.) ShBV-2
Village Preacher, The. MaRV; TrGrPo, *shorter sel.*
(Country Parson, The.) OTPC (1923 ed.)
(Village Parson, The.) OBEC; WGRP
Village Schoolmaster, The. OBEC; PoSa; TrGrPo
(Schoolmaster, The.) OTPC (1946 ed.); ShBV-2
Still the Wonder Grew, 4 *ll.* TreF
Deserter, The. Joseph S. Cotter, Jr. CDC
Deserter, The. John Philpot Curran. ViBoPo
(Deserter's Lamentation, The.) IrPN; SeCePo
(Let Us Be Merry before We Go.) AnIV
Deserter, The. A. E. Housman. OBMV; SeCeV
Deserter, The. John Manifold. WaP
Deserter, The. Bayard Taylor. PaPo
Deserter from the Cause, The. Gerald Massey. VA; YT
"'Deserter!' Well, Captain, the word's about right." The Deserter. Bayard Taylor. PaPo
Deserter's Lamentation, The. John Philpot Curran. *See* Deserter, The.
Desertion of Beauty and Strength, The. *Unknown. Fr.* Everyman. ACP
Deserts. Anne Hamilton. MaRV; OQP
Deserts ("Deserts are more than shimmering heat and sand"). Leigh Hanes. GoYe
Deservings. *Unknown.* HBV
Desideravi. Theodore Maynard. HBMV
Desideria. Wordsworth. *See* Surprised by Joy—Impatient as the Wind.
Desiderium. Phineas Fletcher. *Fr.* The Purple Island, I. OBS
Desiderium Indesideratum. Francis Thompson. PoIE (1970 ed.); StJW
Design. Dryden. *See* What is the World?
Design. Robert Frost. AmLP; AP; BWP; CABA; CaFP; CBV; CMoP; CoBMV; CrMA; ForPo; ILP; MaPo (1969 ed.); NoP; Po; PoAn; PoDB; PoeP; PoIE; PoPo; SeCeV; Sonn
Design for a Bowl. Anacreon. *See* Odes.
Design for a List of Pictures. Arthur Symons. FaBoTw
Design for a Stream-lined Sunrise. Sister Mary Madeleva. GoBC; JKCP (1955 ed.)
Design for Mediaeval Tapestry. A. M. Klein. CaP
Design for Peace. Janet Norris Bangs. PGD
Design for the City of Man; a Vision, *sels.* Emmett Jarrett. ThO
City, The ("In Homer's time").
City, The ("Set over against lust").
Overture.
Sojourners, The.
Two Mad Songs.
Desire. "Æ." OBMV; TrPWD
Desire. Matthew Arnold. WGRP
Desire. William Cornish. OBSC; SeCeV
("Knight knock'd at the castle gate, The.") EG
Desire. Nathalia Crane. MAP; MoAmPo (1942 ed.)
Desire. Pierre Louys, *tr. fr. French by* Horace M. Brown. *Fr.* The Songs of Bilitis. UnTE
Desire. "Fiona Macleod." OQP
Desire. Kathleen Raine. MoPo
Desire. Sir Philip Sidney. *See* Thou Blind Man's Mark.
Desire. Thomas Traherne. OxBoCh
("For giving me desire.") LO
Desire, The. Katherine Tynan. HBV; TSW
Desire, alas, my master and my foe. Sir Thomas Wyatt. FCP
Desire and Disillusion. Byron. *Fr.* Childe Harold's Pilgrimage, IV. EPN
Desire for Hermitage, The. *Unknown, tr. fr. Old Irish by* Séan O'Faoláin. AnIL
Desire Is a Witch. C. Day Lewis. CMoP
Desire Knows. Asclepiades, *tr. fr. Greek by* Charles Glenn Wallis. LiTW
Desire of love, Joy, The. Desire. "Fiona Macleod." OQP
Desire of the Moth, The. Shelley. *See* One Word Is Too Often Profaned.
Desire of your light hands. Ancient Winter. Salvatore Quasimodo. OnPM
Desire that all men have is all my love. Love and Marriage. Ray Mathew. PoAu-2
Desire, though thou my old companion art. Astrophel and Stella, LXXII. Sir Philip Sidney. FCP; ReEn; SiPS
Desire We Past Illusions to Recall. Wordsworth. EPN
Desired Swan-Song, The. Samuel Taylor Coleridge. *See* On a Bad Singer.
Desiree,/ I find it most bitter that you. Denise: A Letter Never Sent. Henri Coulette. *Fr.* The War of the Secret Agents. NePoEA-2
Desire's Government. "A. W." EIL
Desires of Men and Women. John Berryman. LiTM
Desolate. Sydney Dobell. CBEP; NBM; OBNC
Desolate. Claude McKay. CDC
Desolate and lone. Lost. Carl Sandburg. AmPP (5th ed.); BrR; CMoP; NP; PDV; PoPl; PoPo; RePo; WHA
Desolate City, The. *Unknown, tr. fr. Arabic by* Wilfrid Scawen Blunt. AWP; JKCP; MoBrPo (1942 ed.); OBEV; OBVV
Desolate Lover, The. Eileen Shanahan. NeIP
Desolate Scythia. Edgar Lee Masters. NP
Desolate Shore, A. W. E. Henley. SyP

Desolate that cry as though world were unworthy. Chough. Rex Warner. PoRA (rev. ed.)
Desolate Valley, The, *sel.* Thomas Pringle.
"Then, couched at night in hunter's wattled shieling." BoSA
Desolate windmill, eyelid of the distance. The Windmill. Lord De Tabley. NBM
Desolation in Zion. Lamentations, I: 12-17, Bible, *O.T.* TrJP
Desolation Is a Delicate Thing. Elinor Wylie. MAP; MoAmPo
Despair. Fulke Greville. Caelica, LXXXIII [LXXXIV]. OBSC
("Who grace, for zenith had, from which no shadowes grow.") PoEL-1
Despair. Rose Hawthorne Lathrop. *Fr.* Give Me Not Tears. AA
Despair. W. S. Merwin. AmPC
Despair. Edward Bliss Reed. HBMV
Despair. Spenser. *Fr.* The Faerie Queene, I, 9. SeCePo, *shorter sel.*
(To Be or Not to Be.) FaBoEn
("Who Travels by the Weary Wandering Way.") PoG
Despair and Hope. Israel Zangwill. TrJP
Despair in Seascape. Richmond Lattimore. TwAmPo
Despair is given me. Where Fled. John Wieners. CoPo
Despair of the Old Woman, The. Baudelaire, *tr. fr. French by* Arthur Symons. OnPM
Despair of Troilus, The. Chaucer. *Fr.* Troilus and Criseyde, IV. LoBV
Despair, that seeking for the *Ding-an-sich.* Preludes for Memnon, V. Conrad Aiken. PoDB
Despairing beside a clear stream. Colin's Complaint. Nicholas Rowe. OBEC
Despairing Embrace, The. Pierre Louys, *tr. fr. French by* Horace M. Brown. *Fr.* The Songs of Bilitis. UnTE
Despairing Lover, The. William Walsh. ALV; BoLP; CEP; CLwM; EiCL; ELP; FaBoCh; LoGBV; OBEC; OxBoLi; WePo
Desperado, The. *Unknown.* CoSo; TreFS
Despise no spot. There's not a place. Appreciation. Clarence Edwin Flynn. SoP
Despise not any man that lives. Sam Walter Foss. *Fr.* Work For Small Men. PoToHe
Despise Not Thou the Chastening of the Almighty. Bernard Barton. SoP
Despise the World. *Unknown.* MeEL
Despised and Rejected. Katharine Lee Bates. OQP
Despised and Rejected. Christina Rossetti. MaRV; StJW
"Then I cried out upon him: Cease," *sel.* PeVV
Despite and Still. Robert Graves. CBEP
Despite its late exhibition at the. To Start a Controversy. Peter Porter. HYE
Despite the drums we were ready to go. The Mountaineers. Dannie Abse. PP
Despite their boastful Margraves and their flags. Central Europe. Norman Cameron. MoPW
Despondency. Matthew Arnold. PoVP
Despondency Corrected. Wordsworth. *Fr.* The Excursion, IV. EnRP
Desponding Phillis [*or* Phyllis] was endued. Phillis, or The Progress of Love. Swift. CLwM; EiCP; ExPo; PoEL-3
Desponding Soul's Wish, The. John Byrom. OBEC; TrPWD
(In Thy Love.) FaChP
(My Spirit Longeth for Thee.) BoC; OxBoCh
Despot treads thy sacred sands, The. Carolina. Henry Timrod. MC; PAH
Despot's heel is on thy shore, The. My Maryland [*or* Maryland, My Maryland]. James Ryder Randall. AA; AnAmPo; APA; CoBA; FaBoBe; FaFP; HBV; JKCP; MC; PaA; PAH; PoFr; PoRL; TreF
Dessert, The. Charles *and* Mary Lamb. OTPC (1923 ed.)
Destination, The. James Tate. YAP
Destined to war from very infancy. Epitaphs, VI. Gabriello Chiabrera. AWP; JAWP; WBP
Destined, while living, to sustain. An Epitaph on Herself. Hetty Wright. WaPE
Destiny. Sir Edwin Arnold. MaRV; PoLF
(Somewhere.) PoToHe (new ed.)
Destiny. Matthew Arnold. MBW-2; VP
Destiny. Nathalia Crane. GoTP; MAP; NeMA
Destiny. John Fletcher. *Fr.* Upon an Honest Man's Fortune. MaRV
Destiny. Harrison Smith Morris. AA
Destiny. Thomas Stanley. *See* Expectation.
Destiny. Whittier. MaRV
Destiny of Nations, The, *sels.* Samuel Taylor Coleridge.
"'Even so' (the exulting Maiden said)." ChER
"For what is Freedom, but the unfettered use." EnRP
Destiny of Rome, The. Vergil. *See* Sixth Book of the Aeneid, The.
Destroyer. A. M. Sullivan. ALV
Destroyer Life, *with music.* *Unknown.* ABF
Destroyer of Destroyers, The. Wallace Rice. PAH
Destroyers, The, *sel.* Archibald Fleming MacLiesh.
"Now all things melt and shift." NAMP
Destroyers in Collision. Kipling. *Fr.* Epitaphs of the War. PoVP
Destroying Angel. Hilary Corke. NYBP
Destruction of Bulfinch's House, The. Stephen Sandy. CoPo
Destruction of Jerusalem by the Babylonian Hordes, The. Isaac Rosenberg. SiSW
Destruction of Letters. Babette Deutsch. HoPM
Destruction of Sennacherib, The. Byron. ATP; BEL; BeLS; BLPA; BoLiVe; CoBE; DiPo; EnLi-2; EnLit; EnRP; ERoP-2; EvOK; FaBoBe; FaBoCh; FaFP; FaPON; GN; GoTP; HBV; InP; LiTG; LoGBV; MaRV; MCCG; MemP; MPB (1956 ed.); NeHB; NoP; OAEP; OnMSP; OTPC; OuHeWo; PAn; PCD; Po; PoE; PoIE; PoLF; PTK; RG; ShBV-1; SoP; TIHL; TOP; TreF; WBLP; WGRP
(Sennacherib.) FOL; PaPo
Destruction of Troy, The. Vergil, *tr. fr. Latin by* Sir John Denham. *Fr.* The Aeneid, II. SeCV-1
Desultory Poem, A, Written on the Christmas Eve of 1794, *sel.* Samuel Taylor Coleridge. *Fr.* Religious Musings.
"Lovely was the death." EnRP
Detach, Invading. Ron Padgett. ANYP
Detachment is a virtue, teachers say. Ballade on Eschatology. Sister Mary Madeleva. GoYe
Detail. Mary Ursula Bethell. AnNZ
Detail from an Annunciation by Crivelli. Rosemary Dobson. NeLNL; PoAu-2
Details. Luke Zilles. RePo
Determination. *Unknown.* TreFT
Determined to be peaceful, we played cards. A Game of Cards. Elizabeth Jennings. NYTB
Dethronement. Robert Graves. PIA
Detour—Gypsy Trail Closed. Sara Henderson Hay *and* Raymond Holden. StaSt
Detroit. Donald Hall. AmFN
Deus Absconditus. Anne Ridler. FaBoMo
Deus Immensa Trinitas. *Unknown,* *tr. fr. Latin by* Alan G. McDougall. CAW
Deus Meus. Mael-Isu, *tr. fr. Irish by* George Sigerson. CAW
Deus Noster Ignis Consumens. Laurence Housman. HBMV
Deuteronomy, *sels.* Bible, *O.T.*
Blessed of the Lord Be His Land, XXXIII: 13-16. BrR
(Give Ear, O Ye Heavens, XXXIII: 13-16, 27.) PCH
Choose Life, XXX: 15-19. TreFT
Give Ear, Ye Heavens, XXXII: 1-43. TrJP
Development. Robert Browning. MaVP; PoVP
Development of Idiotcy, A. Ebenezer Jones. OBNC; PeVV
Development of Man, The. Robert Browning. *Fr.* Paracelsus, V. EPN
Deviator, The. Bertram Warr. OBCV
Device. Sir Herbert Read. MoBrPo (1942 ed.)
Devil, The. *Unknown.* STF
Devil and the Angel, The, *sels.* Rosemary Dobson.
"Chancing upon the Devil in the doorway," I. ACV; BoAV
Methusalah, VI. PoAu-2
("The man was called Methusalah.") BoAV
Devil and the Farmer's Wife, The, *with music.* *Unknown.* TrAS
Devil and the Governor, The, *sel.* William Forster.
"In New South Wales, as I plainly see." PoAu-1
Devil and the Lady, The, *sel.* Tennyson.
Deep Dark Night, The. SeCePo
Devil daddied Cerberus, lamented of his progeny. Hybris, Nemesis, One, Two, Three. Alicia Ostriker. StP
Devil-Dancers, The. William Plomer. BoSA; PeSA
Devil Doll. Lisa Grenelle. FiSC
Devil, having nothing else to do, The. On Lady Poltagrue, a Public Peril. Hilaire Belloc. ALV; MoBrPo; PV; TreFT; WhC

Devil sprang from box. Jack-in-the-Box. Elder Olson. NePA
Devil to Pay, The, *sels.* Dorothy L. Sayers. MaRV
Choice of the Cross, The.
Judgment and Mercy.
Devil up my attic stair, The. All, All. Baudelaire. WoL
Devil was given permission one day, The. Arizona. *Unknown.* ABF
Devil, we're told, in hell was chained, The. Hell in Texas. *Unknown.* ABF; BLPA
Devilish Mary, *with music. Unknown.* OuSiCo
Devil's Advice to Story-Tellers, The. Robert Graves. CBEP; LiTM (rev. ed.)
Devil's Cauldron. Monk Gibbon. HaMV
Devil's Darning Needle. C. Lindsay McCoy. GFA
Devil's Dream. Kenneth Fearing. CMoP
Devil's Law Case, The, *sels.* John Webster.
All the Flowers of the Spring. AtBAP; CBEP; EG; ElL; ELP; ExPo; GTBS-W; LiTB; LiTG; OBS; PoEL-2; PoFS; PoRA; SiCE; ViBoPo
(Burial, The.) CH; LoBV
(Nets to Catch the Wind.) TrGrPo
(Song: "All the flowers of the spring.") HBV
(Speech by Romelio.) PoIE
(Vanitas Vanitatum.) BEL; OBEV
"Vain the ambition of kings," 4 *ll.* PoFr
"Oh heere's my mother: I ha strange newes for you." AtBAP
"O, I shall run mad!" LO
Devil's Meditation, The. Michael Sweany. MaRV
Devil's Nine Questions, The. *Unknown.* BFSS
Devil's Tribute to Moling, The, *sel. Unknown, tr. fr. Old Irish by* Whitley Stokes *and* John Strachan. OnYI
Holy Man, The.
Devil's Walk on Earth, The. Robert Southey *and* Samuel Taylor Coleridge. BoHV
(Devil's Thoughts, The, *much abr.*) OxBoLi
(Devil's Walk, The, 8 *ll.*) PV
"From his brimstone bed at break of day," *sel.* PoMS
Devocion de la Cruz, La, *sel.* Pedro Calderón de la Barca, *tr. fr. Spanish.*
Cross, The, *tr. by* Richard Chenevix Trench. CAW
(Dying Eusebio's Address to the Cross, The, *longer sel., tr. by* D. F. MacCarthy.) OuHeWo
Devoid of reason, thrall to foolish ire. Passion's Hounds. Thomas Lodge, *after* Pierre de Ronsard. Phyllis, XXXI. OnPM; ReEn; SiCE
Devon to Me. John Galsworthy. HBMV
Devonshire Lane, The. John Marriott. BOHV
Devonshire Rhyme, A ("Walk fast in snow"). *Unknown.* BrR; MPB; SiSoSe
Devonshire Song, A ("Thou ne're wilt riddle"). *Unknown, at. to* William Strode.. OBS; PoEL-2, *Sl. diff.*
Devotion ("Follow thy fair sun, unhappy shadow"). Thomas Campion. *See* Follow Thy Fair Sun.
Devotion ("Follow your saint, follow with accents sweet!"). Thomas Campion. *See* Follow Your Saint.
Devotion. Henry W. Frost. SoP
Devotion. *Unknown. See* Fain Would I Change That Note.
Devotion to Duty. Siegfried Sassoon. MoPW
Devotional Incitements. Wordsworth. OxBoCh
Devotions. Ellinor L. Norcross. OQP
Devouring Time, blunt thou the lion's [*or* lyons] paws. Sonnets, XIX. Shakespeare. AtBAP; AWP; BWP; CBEP; ChTr; DiPo; EG; EP; GTBS-W; InPo; MeWo; OBSC; PoEL-2; ReIE; SiCE; Sonn; TrGrPo; WHA
Devout Fits. John Donne. *See* Sonnet: "Oh, to vex me. . ."
Devout Lover, A. Thomas Randolph. HBV; HoPM; LiTL; OBEV
("I have a mistress, for perfections rare.") EG
Devout Man Prays to His Relations, The. William Herebert. MeEL
Devout Prayer of the Passion, A. *Unknown.* MeEL
Devoutly worshipping the oak. Canticle. William Griffith. DD; HBMV; HBVY
Dew. Franks S. Williamson. BoAu
Dew Each Trembling Leaf Inwreath'd, The. Mary Balfour. IrPN
Dew is gleaming in the grass, The. Among the Millet. Archibald Lampman. CaP; WHW
Dew is on the grasses, dear, The. Youth. Georgia Douglas Johnson. BANP; GoSl; PoNe
Dew is on the heather, The. The Captain's Feathers. Samuel Minturn Peck. AA
Dew it trembles on the thorn, The. Silent Love. John Clare. EnRP
Dew on a Dusty Heart. Jean Starr Untermeyer. MAP; MoAmPo
Dew-Plants. Ernest G. Moll. NeLNL
Dew Sat on Julia's Hair. Robert Herrick. *See* Upon Julia's Hair Filled with Dew.
Dew, the rain and moonlight, The. A Net to Snare the Moonlight. Vachel Lindsay. CMoP; PoLF
Dew upon the robin as he lilts there on the thorn. Dew. Frank S. Williamson. BoAu
Dew was falling fast, the stars began to blink, The. The Pet Lamb. Wordsworth. OTPC; PRWS; SAS
Dewdrop, A. Frank Dempster Sherman. PPL
Dewdrop, The. Joseph Skipsey. *See* Dewdrop, Wind and Sun.
Dewdrop. Ted Walker. NYTB
Dewdrop of the darkness born, A. The Immaculate Conception. John Banister Tabb. ISi
Dewdrop, Wind and Sun. Joseph Skipsey. OBVV
(Dewdrop, The.) VA
Dewdrops. John Clare. BoPe
Dewdrops, The. Lydia Miller Mackay. GFA
Dewdrops. Soin, *tr. fr. Japanese by* H. G. Henderson. OnPM
Dewdrops hang from leaf and stem. May Thirtieth. *Unknown.* PoSC
Dewdrops, limpid, small. Dewdrops. Soin. OnPM
Dewdrops on every blade of grass, The. Dewdrops. John Clare. BoPe
Dewey and His Men. Wallace Rice. PAH
Dewey at Manila. Robert Underwood Johnson. HBV; MC; PAH
Dewey in Manila Bay. Richard Voorhees Risley. DD; MC; PAH
Dews are all of one pale silvery white, The. Autumn Leaves. Toshiyuki. OnPM
Dews Disappear, The. Issa, *tr. fr. Japanese by* H. G. Henderson. OnPM
Dews drop slowly and dreams gather: unknown spears, The. The Valley of the Black Pig. W. B. Yeats. ChTr
Dews of summer night did fall, The. Cumnor Hall. William Julius Mickle. BeLS; CEP; OBEC; OxBB; ViBoPo
Dewy dawn from old Tihonus' bed, The. Jabberwocky. Junius Cooper. InMe
Dewy-eyed with shimmering hair. An Old Song by New Singers: Mr. Algernon C. Swinburne's Idea. A. C. Wilkie. BOHV
Dewy, roseate morn had with her hairs, The. Phyllis, IX. Thomas Lodge. SiCE
Dey crucified my Lord. Crucifixion. *Unknown.* MaRV
Dey had a gread big pahty down to Tom's de othah night. The Party. Paul Laurence Dunbar. AmNP
Dey is times in life when Nature. When de Co'n Pone's Hot. Paul Laurence Dunbar. BANP
Dey tell me Joe Turner he done come [*or* Joe Turner's come and gone]. Joe Turner [Blues]. *Unknown.* AS; TrAS
Dey was hard times jes fo' Christmas. An Indignation Dinner. James David Corrothers. BANP; PoNe
Deze eatin' folks may tell me ub de gloriz ub spring lam. Hog Meat. Daniel Webster Davis. BANP
Dharra and the Date-Stone, The. *Unknown, tr. fr. Arabic by* Sir Edwin Arnold. OnPM
Dhows, The. Francis Brett Young. EtS
Diaduminius. Pierre Benoit, *tr. fr. French by* Joseph T. Shipley. CAW
Diagnosis of our hist'ry [*or* history] proves, A. The Rejected "National Hymns," III. "Orpheus C. Kerr." BOHV; InMe
Dial faced the summer sun, The. The Song of the Dial. Peter Airey. OQP
Dial Tone, The. Howard Nemerov. NYBP; ToPo
Dialect Quatrain. Marcus B. Christian. AmNP
Dialectics of Flight. John Hall Wheelock. NePoAm-2
Dialogue, A. Austin Dobson. PoVP
Dialogue. John Erskine. HBMV
Dialogue. George Herbert. MaMe; MePo; OBEV; OBS; SeCV-1
Dialogue. Sister Mary Madeleva. CAW

Dialogue. Howard Nemerov. NYBP; PoPl
Dialogue, A. Sir Philip Sidney. *See* Astrophel and Stella: Eleventh Song.
Dialogue, A. Swinburne. PoEL-5
Dialogue. Prince Yuhara, *tr. fr. Japanese by* Ishii *and* Obata. OnPM
Dialogue-Antheme, A. George Herbert. MaMe; StJW
Dialogue at the Cross. Frederick Spee, *tr. fr. German by* Mary E. Mannix. CAW
Dialogue betweene Araphill and Castara, A. William Habington. AnAnS-2
Dialogue between Fleet Shepard and Will the Coffee Man, A. *Unknown.* PeRV
Dialogue between Mary and Gabriel. W. H. Auden. *Fr.* For the Time Being; a Christmas Oratorio. ISi
Dialogue between Strephon and Daphne, A. Earl of Rochester. CavP; SeCV-2
Dialogue between the Lovelorn Sir Hugh and Certain Ladies of Venice, A. Thomas Deloney. UnTE
Dialogue between the Resolved Soul, and Created Pleasure, A. Andrew Marvell. AnAnS-1; EP; FosPo; MaMe; MeLP; MeP; MePo; OBS; SCEP-2; SeCP; SeCV-1
Dialogue between the Soul and Body, A. Andrew Marvell. AnAnS-1; EP; MaMe; MeLP; MeP; MePo; OBS; OxBoCh; PAn; PIA; PoEL-2; PoFS; ReEn; SCEP-2; SeCP; SeCV-1; SeEP
Dialogue between the Two Horses, A. Andrew Marvell. MaMe
Dialogue between Thyrsis and Dorinda, A. Andrew Marvell. MaMe; SCEP-2; SeCP
Dialogue between Two Shepherds, Thenot and Piers, in Praise of Astrea, A. Countess of Pembroke. ReIE
Dialogue betwixt God and the Soul, A. *At. to* Sir Henry Wotton, *after* Horace. MeLP; OBS; OxBoCh
Dialogue betwixt Time and a Pilgrime, A. Aurelian Townshend. AnAnS-2; MePo; OBS; PoEL-2; SeCP; SeEP
Dialogue Containing the Number of the Effectual Proverbs in the English Tongue, A, *sels.* John Heywood. ReIE
"Among other things profiting in our tongue."
"Of mine acquaintance a certain young man."
Dialogue from Plato, A. Austin Dobson. BOHV; HBV
Dialogue from "The Dream Queen." Bhasa, *tr. fr. Sanskrit by* A. G. Shirreff *and* Panna Lall. *Fr.* The Dream Queen. LiTW
Dialogue I'll tell you as true as my life, A. The Coal-Owner and the Pitman's Wife. *Unknown.* CoMu
Dialogue in Praise of the Owl and the Cuckoo. Shakespeare. *See* When Daisies Pied .
Dialogue: Lover and Lady. Ciullo d'Alcamo, *tr. fr. Italian by* Dante Gabriel Rossetti. AWP
Dialogue of Self and Soul, A. W. B. Yeats. CABA; CMoP; ExPo; FaBoMo; LiTB; LiTM; MasP; MoBrPo (1962 ed.); OAEP (2d ed.); PIA; Po; PoDB; ReMP
"Living man is blind and drinks his drop, A," *sel.* DTC
Dialogue of the Way. Harold Stewart. BoAV
Dialogue on the Headland. Robert Graves. ACV
Dialogue—2 Dollmakers. Gregory Corso. NeAP
Dialogue with a Door. Catullus, *tr. fr. Latin by* John Nott. UnTE
Dialogue, without End. Isabel Harriss Barr. JKCP (1955 ed.)
Diamond. Michael Brownstein. YAP
Diamond. Robert Loveman. AA
Diamond Cut Diamond. Ewart Milne. FaBoCh; LoGBV; NeIP
Diamond Joe, *with music.* *Unknown.* CoSo; OuSiCo
Diamond you may draw, A. The Stubborn Fool. Bhartrihari. OnPM
Diamonds. Virginia Call. SoP
Dian, that fain would cheer her friend the Night. Astrophel and Stella, XCVII. Sir Philip Sidney. FCP; ReEn; SiPS
Diana, *sels.* Henry Constable.
"Dear to my soul, then leave me not forsaken!" OBSC; ReEn; ReIE; SiCE; Sonn; TuPP
(Sonnet.) EIL
"Fair grace of graces, muse of muses all." Sonn; TuPP
"Fair sun, if you would have me praise your light." OBSC; SiCE
"Grace full of grace, though in these verses here." OBSC
"Hope, like the hyena [*or* hyaena] coming to be old." EnLoPo; OBSC; SiCE; Sonn
"If ever sorrow spoke from soul that loves." SiCE
(Sonnet.) EIL
"Mine eye with all the deadly sins is fraught." SiCE; TuPP
"Miracle of the world! I never will deny." OBSC; ReEn
(To His Mistress.) TuPP
"My lady's presence makes the roses red." CoBE; HBV; OBSC; ReIE; SiCE
(Sonnet.) EIL
"My tears are true, though others be divine." OBSC
"Needs must I leave and yet needs must I love." InvP; OBSC; SiCE
"Not that thy hand is soft, is sweet, is white." OBSC
"Ready to seek out death in my disgrace." OBSC; SiCE
"Resolved to love, unworthy to obtain." Sonn
"Sun, his journey ending in the west, The." OBSC
"To live in hell, and heaven to behold." HBV; InvP; OBSC; ReEn; ReIE; SiCE; Sonn; TuPP
(If This Be Love.) LiTL
"Uncivil sickness, hast thou no regard." ReIE
"When your perfections to my thoughts appear." SiCE
"Whilst echo cries, 'What shall become of me?' " OBSC; ReEn; ReIE; SiCE; Sonn; TuPP
"You secret vales, you solitary fields." OBSC
Diana, *sels.* Jorge de Montemayor, *tr. fr. Spanish.*
Melisea, Her Song in Scorn of Her Shepherd Narcissus, *tr. by* Bartholomew Young. TuPP
Nymph Diana's Song, The, *tr. by* Bartholomew Young. ReIE
"Of this high grace with bliss conjoined," *tr. by* Sir Philip Sidney. FCP
"Shepherd, who can pass such wrong," *tr. by* Bartholomew Young. SiCE
(Nymph Selvagia, The, Her Song.) TuPP
(Song.) EIL
("What changes here, O hair.") FCP
Diana. Sir Walter Ralegh. *See* Praised Be Diana's Fair and Harmless Light.
Diana. Ernest Rhys. OBVV; VA
Diana Cecyll, that rare beauty thou dost show. To Mrs. Diana Cecyll. Lord Herbert of Cherbury. AnAnS-2
Diana Enamorada, *sel.* Gaspar Gil Polo, *tr. fr. Spanish by* Bartholomew Young.
Ring Forth, Nymphs, You Joyful Songs for Gladness. HW
Diana Fitzpatrick Mauleverer James. Miss James. A. A. Milne. MoShBr; MPB; TiPo
Diana guardeth our estate. Hymn to Diana. Catullus. AWP
Diana's Hunting-Song. Dryden. *Fr.* The Secular Masque. SeCePo; SeCL
(Songs from "The Secular Masque.") InPo
Diane de Poitiers, Josephine and Pompadour. Mother Goose Rhyme. Kenneth Rexroth. ErPo
Diaphenia. *At. to* Henry Constable *and to* Henry Chettle. CBEP; CH; EG; EIL; GoBC; GTBS; GTBS-D; GTBS-P; GTSB-W; GTSE
(Damelus' Song to His Diaphenia.) ELP; FaBoEn; HBV; OBSC; PoEL-2; TuPP; ViBoPo
("Diaphenia, like the daffadowndilly.") LO
Diaphenia, drunk with sleep. Male and Female Created He Them. Aldous Huxley. ALV
Diaphenia, like the daffadowndilly. *At. to* Henry Constable *and to* Henry Chettle. *See* Diaphenia.
Diary, *sel.* Ethel Romig Fuller.
"Old Year is a diary where is set, The." PGD
Diary. David Wagoner. CoAP
Diary of a Church Mouse. John Betjeman. BoC; POTi
Diary of a Nondescript. Garrett Oppenheim. NYTB
Diary of a Raccoon. Gertrude Ryder Bennett. GoYe
Diaspora, The. W. H. Auden. *See* Jew Wrecked in the German Cell, The.
Dibdin's Ghost. Eugene Field. AA
Dice Were Loaded, The. Mary Gilmore. BoAV; MoAuPo
Dick and Will [and Charles and I]. Elizabeth Madox Roberts. *See* Autumn.
Dick Daring, the Poacher. *Unknown.* *See* Shining Night, A.
Dick Hairbrain Learns the Social Graces. John Trumbull. *Fr.* The Progress of Dulness. AmPP (5th ed.)
"Dick, I marvel much why in every plat." The "Gloria Patri." John Heywood. ACP
Dick Johnson Reel, The. "Jake Falstaff." EvOK; WhC
Dick o' the Cow. *Unknown.* BaBo; ESPB; OBB; OxBB
Dick Said. Louis Untermeyer. TSW
Dick Straightup. Ted Hughes. POTi; ToPo
Dick Turpin and the Lawyer. *Unknown.* ViBoFo
Dick Turpin bold! Dick, hie away. My Bonny Black Bess. *Unknown.* CoMu

Dickens. Swinburne. PoVP
Dickens in Camp. Bret Harte. HBV; OTD, *abr.;* PoRL
Dickery, dickery, dare. Mother Goose. OxNR
Dickey-Bird, The. Mrs. Motherly. SAS
Dickie found a broken spade. The Worm. Elizabeth Madox Roberts. BoChLi; GFA; UTS; YT
Dicky-Birds. Natalie Joan. BoTP
Dicky of Ballyman. *Unknown.* OTPC (1946 ed.)
Dictum: For a Masque of Deluge. W. S. Merwin. AP
Dictum Sapienti. Charles Henry Webb. ALV
Did a blowing cherry blossom drift in? At Daybreak. Helen Hoyt. BiCB
Did a fairy's fancy spin you. To a Kitten. Rena M. Manning. CIV
Did Adam love his Eve from first to last? Christina Rossetti. *Fr.* Later Life, XV. LO
Did all the lets and bars appear. The March into Virginia. Herman Melville. AmP; AP; LiTA; LiTG; MWA-1; NoP; PoIE; TrGrPo; UnPo (3d ed.); ViBoPo; WaaP
Did any bird come flying. Christina Rossetti. EG
Did any one plan this? At Roblin Lake. Alfred Purdy. PeCV (1967 ed.)
Did any punishment attend. Horace. Odes, II, 8. PeRV
Did Bethlehem's stable loathe. Come, Holy Babe! Mary Dickerson Bangham. ChIP; PGD
Did Chaos form,—and water, air, and fire. Genesis. John Hall Ingham. AA
Did he say I said you said she said that? *Unknown.* SiTL
Did He smell the scents of the morning. In the Early Hours. Dawn Finley. SoP
Did he steal away from the great Omphale for a night. Drunken Heracles. Wallace Gould. AnAmPo
Did He who wrought the universe. This Little Earth. Lislie Savage Clark. ChIP
Did I ever think. Ono no Takamura. *Fr.* Kokin Shu. AWP
Did I follow Truth wherever she led. Herman Altman. Edgar Lee Masters. *Fr.* Spoon River Anthology. OxBA
Did I hear the news from Custer? The Death of Custer. "Captain Jack" Crawford. PoOW
Did I love thee? I only did desire. Rondo. George Moore. UnTE
Did I not know there is in heaven above. A Confession. Henry W. Frost. SoP
Did I see her? *Unknown.* HW
Did I stand on the bald top of Nefin. The Brow of Nephin. *Unknown.* AnIL
Did it yell. Cicada-Shell. Basho. SoPo
Did ivver ye see the like o' that? Pride. Violet Jacob. OxBS
Did life's penurious length? Emily Dickinson. MWA-2
Did love sojourn with you long. Black and White. Esther Lilian Duff. HBMV
Did Mary know when the Wise Men laid. Offering. Leslie Savage Clark. ChIP
Did my father curse his father for his lust I wonder. The Young Man Thinks of Sons. R. A. K. Mason. AnNZ
Did Not. Thomas Moore. ALV; ErPo; NBM
(Quantum Est Quod Desit.) EnLoPo
Did not each poet amorous of old. Troubadours. Arthur Davison Ficke. Sonnets of a Portrait Painter, X. HBMV
Did Not the Heavenly Rhetoric of Thine Eye. Shakespeare. *Fr.* Love's Labour's Lost, IV, iii. LiTB; LiTG; Sonn
(Heavenly Rhetoric, The.) GTBS-W
(Sonnet: "Did not the heavenly rhetoric. . .") ViBoPo
Did Sabine grace adorn my living line. Wordsworth. *Fr.* An Evening Walk. EiCP
Did she in summer write it, or in spring. Words on the Windowpane. Dante Gabriel Rossetti. SyP
Did Shriner die or make it to New York? A Disappearance in West Cedar Street. L. E. Sissman. TwCP
Did the harebell loose her girdle. Emily Dickinson. FaBV
Did the love of adventure, the promise of gold. Diego's Bold Shores. *Unknown.* SoAmSa
Did the people of Viet Nam/ use lanterns of stone? What Were They Like? Denise Levertov. PPON; WOW
Did the rose-bush or the oak. War. E. Merrill Root. OQP
Did they catch as it were in a vision at shut of day. Jezreel. Thomas Hardy. NoP
"Did they dare, did they dare, to slay Eoghan Ruadh [*or* Owen Roe] O'Neill?" Lament for the Death of Eohan Ruadh [*or* Owen Roe] O'Neill. Thomas Osborne Davis. AnIV; FOL; IrPN; OnYI; OxBI
Did times grow hard in Nazareth. Temple Offering. Leslie Savage Clark. ChIP
Did we abolish frost. Emily Dickinson. MWA-2
Did ye ever hear o guid Earl o Bran. Earl Brand. *Unknown.* BaBo (A *vers.*); ESPB
Did ye ever sleep at the foot o' the bed. Sleepin' at the Foot of the Bed. Luther Patrick. BLPA
Did you ask dulcet rimes from me? To a Certain Civilian. Walt Whitman. CoBA
Did you ask for the beaten brass of the moon? A House in Taos: Moon. Langston Hughes. CDC
Did you boys hear. Lord It's All, Almost Done. *Unknown.* OuSiCo
Did you deserve a quiet death? did you. Dream of a Decent Death. G. A. Borgese. NePoAm
Did you ever come to the place. Mother's Love. Ross B. Clapp. WBLP
Did You Ever, Ever, Ever? *with music.* *Unknown.* AS
Did you ever go to meetin', Uncle Joe. Hop Up, My Ladies. *Unknown.* OuSiCo
Did you ever hear a rustling. Ghosteries. Henry Cholmondeley Pennell. CIV
Did you ever hear about Cocaine Lil? Cocaine Lil and Morphine Sue. *Unknown.* AS; OxBoLi; SiTL; TrAS
Did You Ever Hear an English Sparrow Sing? Bertha Johnston. BLPA
Did you ever hear of Captain Wattle? Captain Wattle and Miss Roe. Charles Dibdin. OxBoLi
Did you ever hear of Editor Whedon. Daisy Fraser. Edgar Lee Masters. *Fr.* Spoon River Anthology. CMoP; MoVE; NP
Did you ever hear tell of sweet Betsy from Pike. Sweet Betsy from Pike. *Unknown.* ABF; CoSo
Did you ever hear the story 'bout Willy, the Weeper? Willy the Weeper. *Unknown.* AS
Did you ever hear the story of how one stormy night. The Stampede. Wallace D. Coburn. PoOW
Did you ever look. Raccoons. Aileen Fisher. PDV
Did you ever note the beauty of the soft New England grasses. A Painter in New England. Charles Wharton Stork. HBMV
Did you ever see an alligator. Arlo Will. Edgar Lee Masters. *Fr.* Spoon River Anthology. LiTA; NP
Did you ever see the nest. The Young Linnets. Ann Hawkshaw. OTPC
Did you ever sit and ponder, sit and wonder, sit and think. Life's a Funny Proposition after All. George M. Cohan. PoLF
Did you ever stand in a cavern's mouth? Emily Dickinson. MWA-2
Did you ever think as the hearse rolls by. The Hearse Song. *Unknown.* ABF; AS
Did you ever think how queer? A Birthday. Rachel Field. BiCB; SiSoSe; TiPo (1959 ed.)
Did you ever think you'd like to. Honest, Wouldn't You? *Unknown.* WBLP
Did you ever wait for daylight when the stars along the river. The Shallows of the Ford. Henry Herbert Knibbs. SCC
Did You Feed My Cow? *Unknown.* GoSl
Did you hear of the curate who mounted his mare. The Priest and the Mulberry Tree. Thomas Love Peacock. *Fr.* Crotchet Castle. BoTP; GN; OnMSP; OTPC; RIS; StPo
Did you hear of the fight at Corinth. The Eagle of Corinth. Henry Howard Brownell. PAH
Did you hear of the Widow Malone. The Widow Malone. Charles Lever. *Fr.* Charles O'Malley, the Irish Dragoon. BOHV; HBV; TreFS
Did you know, little child. The Welcome. Nettie Palmer. BoAu
Did you say. Didn't You Ever Search for Another Star? Alfred Starr Hamilton. QAH
Did you see my wife, did you see, did you see. *Unknown.* OxNR
Did you see Paidin. The Besom-Man. Joseph Campbell. OnYI
Did you tackle that trouble that came your way. How Did You Die? Edmund Vance Cooke. BLPA; MaRV; OHFP; OTD
Did you think of us this morning. Who Prayed? *Unknown.* STF
Didactic Poem, The. Richard Garnett. VA
Didactic Sonnet. Melvin Walker La Follette. NePoEA
Diddle, diddle [*or* Deedle, deedle], dumpling, my son John.

Diddle (continued)
Mother Goose. BoChLi; BoTP; BrR; OxNR; PCH; RIS; StVeCh
Diddledy, Diddledy, Dumpty. *Unknown.* OTPC (1923 ed.)
("Diddlety, diddlety, dumpty.") OxNR
Didn' [*or* Didn't] My Lord Deliver Daniel? *with music. Unknown.* BoAN-1; TrAS
Didn' Ol' John Cross the Water on His Knees, *with music. Unknown.* OuSiCo
Didn't it come like. Leyland King. WSL
Didn't know Flynn. Flynn of Virginia. Bret Harte. PTK
Didn't Old Pharaoh Get Los'? *with music. Unknown.* BoAN-1
Didn't You Ever Search for Another Sun? Alfred Starr Hamilton. QAH
Dido ("Dido was the Carthage Queen"). Thomas Campion. CBEP
Dido. Richard Porson. BOHV
Dido among the Shades. Vergil, *tr. fr. Latin by* Dryden. *Fr.* The Aeneid, VI. OBS
Dido My Dear, Alas, Is Dead. Spenser. *Fr.* The Shepheardes Calender: November. ChTr
("Up then Melpomene thou mournefulst Muse of nyne.") AtBAP
Dido to Aeneas. Vergil, *tr. fr. Latin by* Richard Stanyhurst. *Fr.* The Aeneid, IV. AnIV
Dido with the driven hair. The Beaten Path. Anne Goodwin Winslow. HBMV
Dido's Hunting. Vergil, *tr. fr. Latin by* the Earl of Surrey. *Fr.* The Aeneid, IV. OBSC
(Fourth Book of Vergil, The.) ReEn
Didst thou not find the place inspir'd. Upon My Lady Carlisle's [*or* Carliles] Walking in Hampton-Court Garden. Sir John Suckling. AnAnS-2; SCEP-2
Didyma. *Unknown, tr. fr. Greek by* Louis Untermeyer. UnTE
Didymus. Eileen Duggan. JKCP (1955 ed.)
Didymus. Louis MacNeice. EaLo
Die Black Pervert. Reginald Lockett. BF
Die, die my shriek, you will not be heard. Die My Shriek. Aaron Kushniroff. TrJP
Die in de Fiel', *with music. Unknown.* BoAN-1
Die My Shriek. Aaron Kushniroff, *tr. fr. Yiddish by* Joseph Leftwich. TrJP
Die Not, Fond Man. *Unknown.* EIL
Die Pelzaffen. Charles Spear. AnNZ
Die, pussy, die. *Unknown.* OxNR
Died of Love. *Unknown.* CBEP
Diego's Bold Shores, *with music. Unknown.* SoAmSa
Diella, *sel.* Richard Lynche.
"End this enchantment, love, of my desires," XXXV. Sonn; TuPP
"I *know*, within my mouth, for bashful fear," XIII.
(Love's Despair.) EIL
"Soon as the azure-colored gates of th' east," II. Sonn; TuPP
"Weary with serving where I nought could get," XXVIII. Sonn; TuPP
"What sugared terms, what all-persuading art," IV. ReEn; Sonn; TuPP
Dies Irae. James L. Duff. ChIP; JKCP; MaRV
Dies Irae. Inger Hagerup, *tr. fr. Norwegian by* Martin S. Allwood. LiTW
Dies Irae. Sir Walter Scott. *Fr.* The Lay of the Last Minstrel, VI. GoBC; MaRV, *shorter sel.*
("Nought of the bridal will I tell.") OBRV
Dies Irae. Thomas of Celano, *tr. fr. Latin by* Abraham Coles. AA; CAW, *abr., sl. diff.;* HBV
—— *Tr. by* Richard Crashaw. AWP; MaMe; OuHeWo
—— *Tr. by* the Earl of Roscommon. WGRP
—— *Par. by* Sir Walter Scott. *Fr.* The Lay of the Last Minstrel, VI. GoBC; MaRV
—— *Tr. by* Swinburne. LiTW
—— *Tr. by* Father Wingfield *and* Father Alward. WHL
(Hymn for the Dead: "That day of wrath.") OBRV, *longer sel.*
Dies Irae—Dies Pacis. John Oxenham. MaRV
Dietrich Bonhoeffer, Awaiting Execution in a Concentration Camp, Prays for His Fellow Prisoners. Dietrich Bonhoeffer, *tr. fr. German.* BoC
Dieu Qu'il la Fait. Charles d'Orléans, *tr. fr. French by* Ezra Pound. AWP
Difference. Thomas Bailey Aldrich. TOP
Difference, The. Eleanor A. Chaffee. BiCB
Difference, The. Benjamin Franklin. PoPo; WhC
Difference, The. Laura E. Richards. HBV; HBVY
("Eight fingers.") PPL
Difference, The. Winfield Townley Scott. NePoAm
Difference, The ("Drop an unkind word or careless"). *Unknown.* STF
Difference, The ("Twixt optimist and pessimist"). *Unknown, at. to* McLandburgh Wilson. GoTP
(Optimist and Pessimist.) TreFT
Difference between despair, The. Emily Dickinson. MWA-2; NoP; QFR
Differences. Paul Laurence Dunbar. TreFS
Differences. Rose Fyleman. GFA
Differences. Valerie Tarver. TNV
Different Bicycles. Dorothy W. Baruch. FaPON; SUS; TiPo
Different Speech, A. Louise Townsend Nicholl. ImOP
Different Way, A. Esther Lloyd Hagg. ChIP
Different Winter. Louise Townsend Nicholl. NePoAm-2
Difficult Land, The. Edwin Muir. BoPe
Difficult Times. Bertolt Brecht, *tr. fr. German by* Martin Esslin. ELU
Difficult to recall an emotion that is dead. The Patient is Rallying. Weldon Kees. NaP
Difficulties of Translation, The, *abr.* Gawin Douglas. *Fr.* Prologues to the Aeneid: Prologue to Bk. I. GoTS
Difficulty to think at the end of the day, The. A Rabbit as King of the Ghosts. Wallace Stevens. OA; ThWaDe
Difficulty with all, The. Knight, with Umbrella. Elder Olson. FiBHP
Diffugere Nives. Horace, *tr. fr. Latin by* A. E. Housman. Odes, IV, 7. MaPo (1969 ed.); NoP
Diffugere Nives, 1917. Maurice Baring. HBMV; POTE
Dig My Grave, *with music. Unknown.* OuSiCo
Digby, whence comes it that the world begins. To Master Everard Digby. Thomas Lodge. ReIE
Digdog. Ruth Pitter. AnFE
Digestion of Milton, The. Clerihews. E. C. Bentley. PV
Digger's Grave, The. Sarah Welch. VA
Diggers' Song, The, *abr.* Gerard Winstanley. PoFr
Digging. Seamus Heaney. TwCP
Digging. Edward Thomas. BrPo; MoAB; MoBrPo
Digging/ spade and sun will mock. Migrant Workers. Rochelle Ratner. QAH
Digging for China. Richard Wilbur. GoJo; LOW; TwCP
Digging It Out. John Hollander. AmPC
Dighton Is Engaged! Gelett Burgess. BOHV
Dignity. Bhartrihari, *tr. fr. Sanskrit by* Arthur W. Ryder. OnPM
Dignity of Labor, The. Robert Bersohn. PoPl; WhC
Dignity of Man—Lesson # 1, The. Walter H. Kerr. NePoAm-2
Digression from Husbandry to a Point or Two of Huswifery, A. Thomas Tusser. ReIE
Digression to Hospitality, A. Thomas Tusser. SiCE
Dilemma. Bhartrihari, *tr. fr. Sanskrit by* Paul Elmer More. LiTW
Dilemma. Orrick Johns. MAP
Dilemma. Dorothy Parker. InMe
Dilemma of the Elm. Genevieve Taggard. MAP; MoAmPo
Diligently I hope. Circles. Miriam Waddington. PeCV
Dillar, a dollar, A,/ A ten o'clock scholar. Mother Goose. BoChLi; FaBoBe; FaFP; GaP; HBV; HBVY; OTPC; OxNR; RIS; SAS; SiTL; TiPo
Dim, as the borrow'd beams of moon and stars. Religio Laici. John Dryden. AnAnS-2; CEP; EiCL; EiPP; FiP; LoBV; NoP; OBS; OxBoCh; PeRV; PoLi; SeCV-2; SeEP; ViBoPo
Dim-berried is the mistletoe. Before Dawn. Walter de la Mare. ChrBoLe
Dim Face of Beauty. "Fiona Macleod." PoVP
Dim, gradual thinning of the shapeless gloom. The Troops. Siegfried Sassoon. ChMP; CMoP; GTBS-D; GTSL; POTE
"Dim grows your face, and in my ears." A Colonist in His Garden. William Pember Reeves. ACV; AnNZ
Dim script on the yellow sheets of pioneer diaries, The. Missouri Rhapsody. James Daugherty. RePo
Dim sea glints chill, The. The Sign-Post. Edward Thomas. PoIE; ViBoPo
Dim stars wheeled above the frontier post, The. The Gold Seekers. Marion Muir Richardson. PoOW
Dim the light in your faces: be passionless in the room. The Image. Richard Hughes. OBMV

Dim vales—and shadowy floods. Fairy-Land. Poe. MWA-1; OTPC
Dim wind pillared the hills: stiller than mist it seemed. Sunrise Trumpets. Joseph Auslander. AnAmPo; TrJP
Dimidium Animae Meae. Charles A. Brady. GoYe
Diminutivus Ululans. Francis MacNamara. OxBI
Dimme eyes, deaf ears, cold stomach shew. Verses Found in Thomas Dudley's Pocket after His Death. Thomas Dudley. SCAP
Dimmest and brightest month am I. December. Christina Rossetti. YeAr
Dimple Diggers. "Robin Christopher." RIS
Dimpled and flushed and dewy pink he lies. Baby. Elaine Goodale Eastman. AA
Dimply damsel, sweetly smiling. To Miss Margaret Pulteney. Ambrose Philips. CEP; EiCL
Dinah. A. R. Ammons. PV
Dinah. Norman Gale. OTPC (1946 ed.)
Diner while dining at Crewe, A. Limerick [*or* New Limericks]. *Unknown.* RIS; StaSt
Ding dang, bell rang. *Unknown.* OxNR
Ding-Dong! Eliza Lee Follen. *See* Ding Dong! Ding Dong!
Ding Dong. A. C. Hilton. Par
Ding Dong. *Unknown.* *Fr.* Swetnam, the Woman Hater. ElL
Ding, dong, bell,/ Pussy's in the well! Mother Goose. BoChLi; OTPC; OxNR; PPL; RIS; SAS; SiTL; SoPo; StVeCh (1940 ed.); TiPo
Ding dong didero,/ Blow big bellows. Smith's Song. George Sigerson. OnYI
Ding Dong! Ding Dong! Eliza Lee Follen. SAS
(Ding-Dong!) BoTP
Ding dong, ding dong. Ding Dong. A. C. Hilton. Par
Ding-dong, ding-dong, ding-dong. A Dirge for a Righteous Kitten. Vachel Lindsay. CIV; SUS; UTS
Ding-dong! ding-dong! Merry, merry. Song from Fragment of an Eccentric Drama. Henry Kirke White. OBRV
Ding dong! The Castle Bell! *Unknown.* ExPo
Ding! Dong! The moon is gleaming. The Enchanted Garden. Marjorie Barrows. GFA
Dingaan and Retief. Charles Barter. *Fr.* Stray Memories of Natal and Zululand. BoSA
Dingle dingle doosey. *Unknown.* OxNR
Dingty diddlety. *Unknown.* OxNR
Dining-Room Tea. Rupert Brooke. BrPo; MoBrPo; POTE
Dinkey-Bird, The. Eugene Field. AA; BOHV; HBVY; LBN; NA; PFY; TreFS; TSW; UTS
Dink's Blues. *Unknown.* ABF
Dink's Song. *Unknown.* ABF, *with music*; ErPo; OxBoLi; SiTL
Dinky. Theodore Roethke. PoeP
Dinna Ask Me. John Dunlop. HBV
Dinner at Eight. Katie Louchheim. NYTB
Dinner at the Hotel de la Tigresse Verte. Donald Evans. AnAmPo
Dinner Guest. Oscar Williams. TwAmPo
Dinner Hour, The. "Owen Meredith." *Fr.* Lucille. VA
Dinner party, coffee, tea, A. Breakfast. Mary Lamb. OTPC (1923 ed.)
Dinner Party, 1940. Phillip M. Sherlock. PoNe
Dinner with Ligurinus. Martial, *tr. fr. Latin by* James Elphinston. OnPM
Dinnshenchas, *sels.* *Unknown, tr. fr. Middle Irish.* OnYI
Enchanted Fawn, The, *tr. by* Edward Gwynn.
Story of Macha, The, *tr. by* Sir Samuel Ferguson.
Tara, *tr. by* Edward Gwynn.
Dinogad's Petticoat. *Unknown, tr. fr. Welsh by* Gwyn Williams. PrWP
Dinosaur, The. Carl S. Junge. SoPo
Dinosaur, The. Bert Leston Taylor. ImOP; LHV; PoMa
Dinosaurs. Carolyn Stoloff. NYBP
Dinosaurs and violins played in the sky. Cubism. Hy Sobiloff. SiTL
Dinosaurs are not all dead, The. Steam Shovel. Charles Malam. PoMa; PoPo
Diodorus Siculus. *Unknown.* ErPo; PV
Diogenes. Max Eastman. HBV; OQP
Diogenes the Trainman. Pamela Millward. FRC
Dion of Tarsus. *Unknown, tr. fr. Greek by* Alma Strettell. AWP; JAWP; WBP
Dionysus. Irving Layton. ErPo
Dionysus. Winthrop Palmer. SiTL
Dip down upon the northern shore. In Memoriam A. H. H., LXXXIII [*or* Spring]. Tennyson. EnLi-2; EPN; HBV; MaPo; OAEP; ViBoPo; ViPo; VP
Diplomatic Platypus, The. Patrick Barrington. *See* I Had a Duck-billed Platypus.
Diplomats, The. Alfred Noyes. MaRV
Dipped in the instincts of heaven. Woman. Thomas O'Hagan. CAW
Dipsychus, *sels.* Arthur Hugh Clough.
"Afloat; we move. Delicious!" *fr.* Pt. II, sc. ii. PoVP; ViPP
As I Sat at the Café, I Said to Myself, *fr.* Pt. II, sc. ii, *also in* Spectator ab Extra. ELP; ViPP; WePo,*st.* 1
(From "Spectator ab Extra.") ALV; FiBHP; LiTG
(So Pleasant It Is to Have Money.) SeCePo
(Spectator ab Extra, 3 *sts.*) GTBS-P
"I dreamt a dream; till morning light," *abr., fr.* Pt. I, sc. v. OAEP
"I had a vision; was it in my sleep?" *fr.* Pt. II, sc. vii. PoVP
"O let me love my love unto myself alone," *fr.* Pt. II, sc. ii. OAEP; ViPP
"Our gaieties, our luxuries," *fr.* Pt. II, sc. ii. EPN
"Scene is different, and the place, The; the air," *fr.* Pt. I, sc. i. PeVV
"'There is no God!' the wicked saith," *fr.* Pt. I, sc. v. EPN; NBM; PoVP; ViPP
(Spirit's Song, The.) LoBV
(There Is No God.) FaPL; TreFS
"Where are the great, whom thou would'st wish to praise thee?" *fr.* Pt. II, sc. ii. EPN
(Isolation.) OBVV
"Yet I could think, indeed, the perfect call," *fr.* Pt. II, sc. v. OBNC
Dirce. Walter Savage Landor. *Fr.* Pericles and Aspasia. AnFE; AWP; BoLiVe; CBEP; CBV; CTC;1EnRP; ExPo; FaBoEn; InPo; JAWP; LiTB; LoBV; MemP; NoP; OAEP; OBEV; OBNC; OBRV; PoEL-4; PoRA; SeCeV; StP; TOP; TreFT; TrGrPo; VA; ViBoPo;1 WBP; WHA; WhC;
(Stand Close Around.) ChTr
("Stand close around, ye Stygian set.") EG; GTBS-D
Dire Dilemma, A. Pope. *Fr.* Epistle to Dr. Arbuthnot. WHA
Dire rebel though he was. Philip Van Artevelde. Sir Henry Taylor. VA
Direct retinal flood, The. Ed Sanders. ANYP
Direct Song. Eve Merriam. UnTE
Direct This Day. Thomas Ken. TRV
Direction to a Rebel. W. R. Rodgers. LiTM (rev. ed.)
Directions. Onitsura, *tr. fr. Japanese by* Harold G. Henderson. SoPo
Directions for a Birth-Day Song. Swift. EiCL
Directive. Robert Frost. AmPP (5th ed.); AP; BWP; CABA; CBV; CMoP; CoBMV; CrMA; DiPo; ForPo; FosPo; LiTA; LiTM (rev. ed.); MaPo; MasP; MoAB; MoAmPo (1962 ed.); MWA-2; NePA; PIA; PoDB; PoeP; SeCeV
Diretro al Sol. Charles G. Bell. NePoAm
Dirge: "Call for the robin redbreast and the wren." John Webster. *See* Call for the Robin Redbreast.
Dirge: "Calm on the bosom of thy God." Felicia Dorothea Hemans. *Fr.* The Siege of Valencia. HBV, *longer vers.*; OBEV
(Death Hymn, A.) OBRV
Dirge: "Come away, come away, death." Shakespeare. *See* Come Away, Come Away, Death.
Dirge: "Fear no more the heat o' the sun." Shakespeare. *See* Fear No More the Heat o' the Sun.
Dirge: For One Who Fell in Battle. Thomas William Parsons. AA; GN; HBV; PAH
Dirge, A: "Glories of our blood and state, The." James Shirley. *See* Glories of Our Blood and State.
Dirge: "Glories, pleasures, pomps, delights, and ease." John Ford. *See* Glories, Pleasures.
Dirge: "Hark, now everything is still." John Webster. *See* Hark! Now Everything . . .
Dirge: "Her house is become like a man dishonored." First Maccabees, II: 8-14, Bible, Apocrypha. TrJP
Dirge: "If thou wilt ease thine heart." Thomas Lovell Beddoes. *Fr.* Death's Jest Book, II, ii. LiTB; LO; OBNC; OBRV; PoEL-4; VA
(Dirge for Wolfram.) PoE
(If Thou Wilt Ease Thine Heart.) EG; EnRP
(Wolfram's Dirge.) OBEV
Dirge: "It is the endless dance." Quincy Troupe. WSL

Dirge: "Just at the blackest bit of my depression." Hazel Townson. PV
Dirge, A: "Looking on the peaceful face." Hisaki, *tr. fr. Japanese by* Asataro Miyamori. OnPM
Dirge, A: "Naiad, hid beneath the bank." William Johnson Cory. *See* Anteros.
Dirge: "Never the nightingale." Adelaide Crapsey. HBV; NP
Dirge: "O sad, sad world, O world that knows not Love." Edith Lovejoy Pierce. MaRV
Dirge: "1-2-3 was the number he played." Kenneth Fearing. AmP; CaFP; HoPM; LiTM; NAMP; PoIE; PoRA; PoSa; ThLM; TrJP
Dirge: "Peerless yet hapless maid of Q." *Unknown.* BOHV
Dirge: "Room for a soldier! lay him in the clover." Thomas William Parsons. PaA
Dirge, A: "Rough wind, that moanest loud." Shelley. BEL; BoLiVe; CABA; ChTr; DiPo; EnLi-2; EnLit; EnRP; EPN; GTSL; MCCG; OAEP; PoFS; PoRA; TOP; TrGrPo; WHA; WiR
Dirge: "She came—." Alfred Kreymborg. NP
Dirge: "Softly! She is lying with her lips apart." Charles Gamage Eastman. AA
Dirge: "Sorrow, lie still and wear." Thomas Lovell Beddoes. ERoP-2
Dirge: "Swallow leaves her nest, The" Thomas Lovell Beddoes. *Fr.* Death's Jest Book, I, iv. CBEP; LoBV; OBVV; PoEL-4
(Swallow Leaves Her Nest, The.) EPN
(Voice from the Waters, A.) OBNC; OBRV
Dirge: "Though you should whisper." Muna Lee. NP
Dirge: "Tuck the earth, fold the sod." William Alexander Percy. HBMV
Dirge: "Wail! wail ye o'er the dead!" George Darley. *Fr.* Sylvia; or, The May Queen. OBRV
Dirge: "We built our love up like a work of art." Louis Johnson. AnNZ
Dirge: "We do lie beneath the grass." Thomas Lovell Beddoes. *Fr.* Death's Jest Book, V, iv. OBNC; WiR
(Second Dirge.) VA
(Sibylla's Dirge.) GTBS-D; NBM
(We Do Lie beneath the Grass.) ELP
Dirge: "Weep, weep, ye woodmen, wail." Anthony Munday *and* Henry Chettle. *See* Dirge for Robin Hood.
Dirge: "Welladay, welladay, poor Colin." George Peele. *Fr.* The Arraignment of Paris. EIL
(Shepherd's Dirge, The.) OBSC
Dirge: "What longer need hath she of loveliness." Sarojini Naidu. ACV
Dirge: "What shall her silence keep." Madison Cawein. AA
Dirge: "Whose were they those voices? What footsteps came near me?" Aubrey Thomas De Vere. IrPN
Dirge, A: "Why were you born when the snow was falling?" Christina Rossetti. ChTr; LoBV; ViPo
Dirge, Concerning the Late Lamented King of the Cannibal Islands, A. William Augustus Croffut. BOHV; InMe
Dirge for a Bad Boy. E. V. Rieu. BBGG
Dirge for Ashby. Margaret Junkin Preston. PAH
Dirge for a Righteous Kitten, A. Vachel Lindsay. CIV; SUS; UTS
Dirge for a Soldier. George Henry Boker. AA; AnFE; APA; CoAnAm; DD; HBV; MC; OBVV; PaA; PAH; PAP; WaaP
Dirge for Ashby. Margaret Junkin Preston. PAH
Dirge for J. A. Rogers. Hart Leroi Bibbs. BF
Dirge for McPherson, A. Herman Melville. AP; PAH; PoEL-5
Dirge for Robin Hood. Anthony Munday *and* Henry Chettle. *Fr.* Death of Robert, Earl of Huntingdon. CBEP
(Dirge: "Weep, weep, ye woodmen, wail.") CTC; OBSC
(Robin Hood's Funeral.) WiR
(Song: "Weep, weep, ye woodmen, wail.") EIL; ThWaDe
(Weep, Weep, Ye Woodmen!) CH
Dirge for Summer, A. Sebastian Evans. VA
Dirge for the Barrel-Organ of the New Barbarism. Louis Aragon, *tr. fr. French by* Selden Rodman. OnHM; WaaP
Dirge for the New Sunrise. Edith Sitwell. *Fr.* Three Poems of the Atomic Age. ACV; AtBAP; CMoP; EaLo; MoAB; MoBrPo (1950 ed.); MoRP; SeCePo
Dirge for the Ninth of Ab. *Unknown, tr. fr. Hebrew by* Nina Davis Salaman. TrJP
Dirge for the Year. Shelley. DD; HBV; HBVY
"Orphan hours, the year is dead!" *sel.* GN
Dirge for Two Clavichords and Bowler Hat. Kendrick Smithyman. AnNZ
Dirge for Two Veterans. Walt Whitman. BoLiVe; MoAmPo (1950 ed.); NeMA; PoEL-5
(Two Veterans.) GN
Dirge for Wolfram. Thomas Lovell Beddoes. *See* Dirge: "If thou wilt ease thine heart."
Dirge in "Cymbeline." William Collins. *See* Song from Shakespeare's "Cymbeline," A.
Dirge in Woods. George Meredith. BoLiVe; EPN; OAEP; OBEV (new ed.); OBNC; OBVV; PoVP; TDP; TOP; VP; WHA; WiR
(Dirge in the Woods.) LoBV; SeCeV
("Wind sways the pines, A.") EG
Dirge is sung, the ritual said, The. I. H. B. William Winter. AA
Dirge of Alaric the Visigoth. Edward Everett. BeLS
Dirge of Kildare, The. Aubrey Thomas De Vere. IrPN
Dirge of Love. Shakespeare. *See* Come Away, Come Away, Death.
Dirge of O'Sullivan Bear. Jeremiah Joseph Callanan. *See* Lament for O'Sullivan, Beare, The.
Dirge of Rory O'More. Aubrey Thomas De Vere. IrPN
Dirge of the Lone Woman. Mary M. Colum. AnIV
Dirge of the Moolla of Kotal. George Thomas Lanigan. BOHV; NA
Dirge of the Munster Forest. Emily Lawless. OBVV; OnYI
Dirge of the Three Queens. Fletcher *and* Shakespeare. *See* Funeral Song ("Urns and odors, bring away").
Dirge on the Death of Art O'Leary. *Unknown, tr. fr. Irish by* Eleanor Hull. AnIV
Dirge upon the Death of the Right Valiant Lord, Bernard Stuart, A. Robert Herrick. SeCV-1
Dirge without Music. Edna St. Vincent Millay. AnNE; BoLiVe; CMoP; GTBS-W; LiTA; LiTG; LO; MoRP; NePA; NP; PG; PPON; TrGrPo
Dirge Written for a Drama. Thomas Lovell Beddoes. EnRP
Dirigible, The. Ralph W. Bergengren. FaPON; SoPo
Dirt and/ clean them clean them clean them. The Streetcleaner's Lament. Patricia Hubbell. OCS
Dirt and Deity. Louis Ginsberg. OQP
Dirty Floor, The. Edward Field. *See* Floor Is Dirty, The.
Dirty Hand, The. Mark Strand. YAP
Dirty Jim. Jane Taylor. HBV; HBVY
Dirty Little Accuser, The. Norman Cameron. OxBS
Dirty Man makes an obscene invitation, The. The Crazy Lady. William Hathaway. QAH
Dirty Mistreatin' Women, *with music. Unknown.* ABF
Dirty Old Man, The. William Allingham. PCD
Dirty river by religious explorers, The. Mystic River. John Ciardi. AmP; NYBP
Dirty Thoughts. Victor Contoski. ThO
Dirty Word, The. Karl Shapiro. CoAP; MiAP; PoCh
Dis Aliter Visum; or, Le Byron de Nos Jours. Robert Browning. ViPP
Dis is gospel weathah sho'. Song of Summer. Paul Laurence Dunbar. MCCG; OTPC (1946 ed.); TSW
Dis Mornin', Dis Evenin', So Soon. *Unknown. See* Old Bill .
Disabled. Wilfred Owen. BrPo; CMoP; LiTM (rev. ed.); MMA; NAMP; WaP
"Disabled"—Armistice Day. Catherine Parmenter. PEDC
Disagreeable Feature, A. Edwin Meade Robinson. HBMV
Disagreeable Man, The. W. S. Gilbert. *Fr.* Princess Ida. ALV; FiBHP; MPB; PoVP
Disagreeing with God. Beverly Haglund. SoP
Disappearance in West Cedar Street, A. L. E. Sissman. TwCP
Disappointed Shrimper, The. P. A. Ropes. BoTP
Disappointed Tenderfoot, The. Earl Alonzo Brininstool. SCC
Disappointed Wife, The. Hetty Wright. WaPE
Disappointment. Thomas Stephens Collier. AA
Disappointment, The. Earl of Rochester. UnTE
Disappointment. John Boyle O'Reilly. ACP; OnYI
Disappointment. *Unknown.* WBLP
Disappointment—His Appointment. Edith Lillian Young. BLRP; SoP
(Disappointment.) TRV
(His Appointment.) FaChP
Disarm the Hearts. Ethel Blair Jordan. PGD
Disarmament, *sel.* Whittier.
"'Put up the sword!' The voice of Christ once more." PGD
Disarmed. Laura Catherine Redden Searing. AA

Disaster. Charles Stuart Calverley. BOHV; CenHV; HBV
Disaster. James Clarence Mangan. IrPN
Disasters on disasters grow. Human Frailty. Philip Freneau. AnAmPo
Disastrous condition, The. Vietnam Turnpike. Thomas Hanna. QAH
Discarded Christmas Tree. Elizabeth-Ellen Long. ChBR
Discarding even the bag of chocolates and the novel. La Belle Dame sans Merci. A. R. D. Fairburn. AnNZ
Discardment, The. Alan Paton. BoSA
Discerning the Lord's Body. Carrie Judd Montgomery. STF
Discharge, The. George Herbert. MaMe
Discharged. W. E. Henley. In Hospital, XXVIII. PoVP
Disciple, The. Dwight Bradley. ChIP; OQP
Disciples, The, *sel.* Harriet Eleanor Hamilton King.
Palermo. VA
Discipleship. C. O. Bales. STF
Discipleship. Henry W. Frost. SoP
Discipline. George Herbert. BoLiVe; CoBE; ExPo; HBV; LiTB; LoBV; MaMe; MeLP; MemP; MePo; NoP; OBEV; OBS; OxBoCh; PAn; PG (1945 ed.); PoFS; PoLF; SeCePo; SeCeV; SeEP; TrGrPo; ViBoPo
"Throw away thy rod," *sel.* EG
Discipline. *Unknown.* SoP
Discipline in Education. William Cowper. *Fr.* The Task. CoBE
Discipline of Consequences, The. Eileen Duggan. JKCP (1955 ed.)
Discipline of Wisdom, The. George Meredith. EPN
Disclaimer of Prejudice. Eli Siegel. PV
Discobolus. David A. Locher. NYTB
Disconsolate and sad. Platonic[k] Love. Lord Herbert of Cherbury. AnAnS-2; OBS; SeEP
Discontent. Sarah Orne Jewett. PRWS; TVC
Discontented Colonel, The, *sel.* Sir John Suckling.
She's Pretty to Walk With. SeCL
Discontented Sugar Broker, A. W. S. Gilbert. PCD
Discontents in Devon. Robert Herrick. AnAnS-2; OAEP; PoeP; ReEn; SCEP-2; SeCV-1; SeEP
Discord and darkness—but the song and the star. Pilgrimage. Elinor Lennen. PGD
Discord in Childhood. D. H. Lawrence. CBEP; ELU; MoPW
Discordants. Conrad Aiken. BoLP
Sels.
Dead Cleopatra Lies in a Crystal Casket. CMoP
Music I Heard [with You], I. AWP; FaFP; GTBS-W; HBV; LiTA; LiTL; LiTM; OTD; OxBA; PG; PoMa; PoPo; PoRA; TreFT
(Bread and Music.) MAP; MoAB; MoAmPo; NeMA; YT
Discouraged. Lucille Stanaback. STF
Discouraged Cherry Tree, The. Kathleen Millay. PEDC
Discouragement's mold, the first cobweb of dispair. The Invaders. Jocelyn Macy Sloan. FiSC
". . . Discourse Heard One Day. . ." Donald C. Babcock. NePoAm-2
Discourse of the Adventures Passed by Master F. J., A. George Gascoigne. *See* Adventures of Master F. I., The.
Discourse of the Wanderer, and an Evening Visit to the Lake. Wordsworth. *Fr.* The Excursion, IX. EnRP
Discourse on the Real. Samuel Yellen. NePoAm
Discovered. Paul Laurence Dunbar. MAP; MoAmPo (1942 ed.)
Discovered in Mid-Ocean. Stephen Spender. MoBrPo
(He Will Watch the Hawk.) CBV; CMoP
Discoverer, The. Nathalia Crane. PoMa; YT
Discoverer, The. Arthur Gordon Field. PGD
Discoverer, The. Edmund Clarence Stedman. AA; HBV
Discoverer of the North Cape, The. Longfellow. AnNE; AtBAP; ShBV-1; StVeCh (1940 ed.)
Discoveries. Vernon Watkins. LiTM; PoIE; WaP
Discovering God Is Waking One Morning. John L'Heureux. BoNaP
Discovery. Hilaire Belloc. ViBoPo
Discovery, The. Charles Brasch. *Fr.* Genesis. AnNZ
Discovery. Carlton Buck. SoP
Discovery. Hildegarde Flanner. HBMV
Discovery. Philip Freneau. WoL
Discovery, The. Monk Gibbon. OnYI
Discovery. Benjamin Keech. PoToHe
Discovery, A. Arthur A. Knipe. GFA
Discovery. Raymond Kresensky. OQP
Discovery, The. Cardinal Newman. OBRV
Discovery. Catherine Parmenter. OQP
Discovery. E. A. Robinson. CMoP
Discovery, The. Stanley Snaith. LO; POTE
Discovery, The. J. C. Squire. *See* There Was an Indian.
Discovery of Pity. Shakespeare. *See* Take Physic, Pomp.
Discovery of San Francisco Bay, The. Richard Edward White. PAH
Discovery of This Time. Archibald MacLeish. LiTA; WaP
Discreet householder exclaims on the grandsire, A. Old Man Playing with Children. John Crow Ransom. MoPW
Discretion. *Unknown.* CBEP
Disdain ("If in the world"). Sir Thomas Wyatt. *See* If in the World There Be More Woe.
Disdain Me Not without Desert. Sir Thomas Wyatt. EnRePo; FCP; ReIE; SiPS
Disdain Me Still. William Herbert, Earl of Pembroke. ElL
Disdain [*or* Disdaine] Returned. Thomas Carew. AWP; CavP; EnLit; HBV; InPo; JAWP; OBS; OuHeWo; PoIE, 3 *sts.*; SCEP-2; SeCL; SeCV-1; SeEP; TOP; TrGrPo; ViBoPo, 2 *sts.*; WBP
(He That Loves a Rosy Cheek.) BEL; EG; FaBV, 2 *sts.*; LiTB; LiTG, 2 *sts.*
(Steadfast Mind, The.) OnPM
(True Beauty, The. GTBS; GTBS-D; GTBS-P, 2 *sts.*; GTBS-W; GTSE; GTSL; MCCG; PoPo, 2 8sts.
(Unfading Beauty, The.) AtBAP, 2 *sts.*; EnLi-1, 2 *sts.*; HoPM, 2 *sts.*; LiTL; OBEV
Disdaine me not sweet love though I be ould. *Unknown.* SeCSL
Disdainful Shepherdess, The. *Unknown.* *See* Phillada Flouts Me.
Disdaining butterflies. The Woman Who Loved Worms. Colette Inez. QAH
Disdains Zenocrate to live with me? Christopher Marlowe. *Fr.* Tamburlaine the Great, Pt. I. ViBoPo
Diseases, famine, enemies, in us no change have wrought. Marius Victor, *tr. fr. Latin by* Sir Walter Ralegh. FCP
Disembodied Spirit, The. Fernando de Herrera, *tr. fr. Spanish by* Longfellow. OnPM
Disenchanted. Louis Untermeyer. GoTP
Disenchantment. Charles Leonard Moore. AA
Disentangle lush water-lily cables. Summer's End. Ethel Kirk Grayson. TwCaPo
Disgrace he'd brought on an ancient name. "Rake" Windermere. Leonard Pounds. PaPo
Disguise upon disguise, and then disguise. Soul unto Soul Glooms Darkling. Charles Leonard Moore. AA
Disguised ("Disguised as my next door neighbor"). John Perreault. ANYP
Disguised He stands without in the street. Holy Communion. Speer Strahan. JKCP
Disguises. Thomas Edward Brown. WGRP
Disguises. Elizabeth Jennings. NePoEA-2
Dish for the bishop, a crushed and bitter dish, A. Almeria. "Pablo Neruda." LiTW; WaaP
Disheartened Ranger, The. *Unknown.* BFSS *with music*; CoSo
Dishonor. Edwin Denby. ErPo
Disillusion. Bessie B. Decker. PoToHe (new ed.)
Disillusion. Sister Mary Edwardine. JKCP (1955 ed.)
Disillusioned. "Lewis Carroll." CenHV
Disillusioned. Thomas Curtis Clark. ChIP
Disillusioned. Emily Dickinson. *See* It dropped so low in my regard.
Disillusionment of Ten o'Clock. Wallace Stevens. AmP; CMoP; CrMA; ForPo; FosPo; LOW; OxBA; PoIE; PoPo; PoSa
Disingenuous, The/ Charm of living. Limb and Mind. John Waller. NeBP
Disinherited. John Donne. MaMe
Disinherited, The, *sel.* Mary Gilmore.
"Sudden autumn winds, like hounds, The." PoAu-1
Dislike of a Governor. Issa. PoFr
Dismal and purposeless and gray. Pain. St. John Lucas. HBV
Dismal fog-hoarse siren howls at dawn, A. The Calls. Wilfred Owen. BoPe
Dismal Observations. John Hall Wheelock. ML
Dismantled Ship, The. Walt Whitman. AmPP (4th ed.); CABA; CBEP; NoP; OxBA

Dismiss the instruments that for your pleasure. Music in Venice. Louis Simpson. NYBP
Dismiss your apprehension, pseudo bard. At Shakespeare's Grave. Irving Browne. AA
Dismissal. Thomas Campion. *See* Hours of Sleepy Night, The.
Dismissal. Peter Redgrove. NMP; OPoP
Dismissing bees and bookmen from. Professor Nocturnal. Raymond Roseliep. FiSC
Dismounting from my horse I enter the ruins of the old city. Visiting the Ruins. Chang Ch'ien. OnPM
Dispensary, The, *sels.* Sir Samuel Garth.
"Not far from that most famous theatre." CEP
Portrait of a Physician. PeRV
Displeasure against Love, A. Nicholas Breton. SiCE
Dispossessed, The. John Berryman. AP; PoCh
Dispossessed Poet. Monk Gibbon. OnYI
Dispraise [*or* Disprayse] of a Courtly Life. Sir Philip Sidney. FCP; LoBV; OAEP; SiCE
Dispraise of Absalom, The. *Unknown, tr. fr. Irish by* Robin Flower. OxBI
Dispraise of Love, and Lovers' Follies. "A. W." EIL; HBV; OBSC
(Dispraise of Love.) TrGrPo
("If love be life, I long to die.") LO
Disprayse of a Courtly Life. Sir Philip Sidney. *See* Dispraise of a Courtly Life.
Dispute between Nose and Eyes. William Cowper. *See* Nose and the Eyes, The.
Dispute of the Heart and Body of François Villon, The. Villon, *tr. fr. French by* Swinburne. AWP
Dispute over Suicide, A. *Unknown, tr. fr. Egyptian by* T. Eric Peet. TTY
Disputes. Alonso Jerónimo de Salas Barbadillo, *tr. fr. Spanish by* Sir John Bowring. OnPM
Disquisition on Death, *sel.* A. R. D. Fairburn.
"I went through the market-place crying, There is no death." AnNZ
Dissatisfaction with Metaphysics. William Empson. CMoP
Dissembler, The. Abraham Cowley. AnAnS-2
Dissembler. Charles Shaw. GoYe
Dissenter, The. Lillian M. Swenson. ChIP
Dissolution, The. John Donne. ILP; MaMe; OAEP; SeCV-1
Dissolving in the chemic vat. Change. Stanley J. Kunitz. NP
Dissolving, the coals shift. Rain swaddles us. The Ruin. Charles Tomlinson. NePoEA-2
Dissuasive against Poetry, A. John Oldham. *Fr.* A Satire. PeRV
("But, grant thy poetry should find success.") ViBoPo
Distance. Robert Creeley. CoPo
Distance. Anthony Delius. PeSA
Distance. Babette Deutsch. PoMa
Distance nor death shall part us, dear. Love Song. Henry Treece. MaRV
Distance widens, The. Absence. Jean Burden. NYTB
Distances. Jeremy Kingston. NYBP
Distances, *sel.* Christopher Okigbo.
"Death lay in ambush." TTY
Distances, The. Charles Olson. NeAP
Distances to the Friend, The. Jonathan Williams. NeAP
Distant and long have I waited without going. To Mackinnon of Strath. Iain Lom. GoTS
Distant as the Duchess of Savoy. *Unknown.* MeEL
("O mestres, whye.") EnPo
Distant Drum, The. Calvin C. Hernton. BOLo; NNP; TTY
Distant Prospect of the City of Armagh, A. James Stuart. *Fr.* Morna's Hill. IrPN
Distant Runners, The. Mark Van Doren. LiTA; LiTM; LoGBV; MAP; MoAmPo; NePA
Distant View. Uys Krige, *tr. fr. Afrikaans by* Uys Krige *and* Jack Cope. PeSA
Distant View of England from the Sea. William Lisle Bowles. EnRP
Distich. Shuraikh, *tr. fr. Arabic.* TrJP
Distichs. John Hay. BOHV
Distinction. Mark Antony De Wolfe Howe. AA
Distinction is in fire and division, The. Poem. José Garcia Villa. POTE (1959 ed.)
Distinctions. Charles Tomlinson. CMoP
Distracted Puritan, The. Richard Corbet. OxBoLi
Distracted with care. The Despairing Lover. William Walsh. ALV; BoLP; CEP; CLwM; EiCL; ELP; FaBoCh; LoGBV; OBEC; OxBoLi; WePo
Distraction. Henry Vaughan. NCEP; SeCP
Distraction is the panacea, Sir! Modern Love, XXVII. George Meredith. ViPo; VP
Distraught for Meropé. Richard Henry Horne. *Fr.* Orion. VA
Distribution. Elsie B. Purcell. PoMa
District school not far away, A. The Smack in School. William P. Palmer. BOHV; HBV
District school-master was sitting behind his great bookladen desk, The. The School-Master's Guests. Will M. Carleton. IHA
Disturbed, the cat. *Unknown, tr. fr. Japanese by* Geoffrey Bownas *and* Anthony Thwaite. FIW
Disturbing it is/ To take your stick sedately talking. The River Walk. Padraic Fallon. OxBI
Disused Temple, The. Norman Cameron. ChMP; OxBS
Ditch is dear to the drunken man, The. Emily Dickinson. MWA-2
Dithyramb in Retrospect. Peter Hopegood. BoAV; PoAu-2
Ditty: "Cock shall crow, The." Robert Louis Stevenson. TrGrPo
Ditty: Heart Exchange. Sir Philip Sidney. *See* My True Love Hath My Heart.
Ditty: "Heavy of heart and light of purse." William Gibson. NYTB
Ditty, A: In Praise of Eliza, Queen of the Shepherds. Spenser. *See* Ditty, A: "See where she sits upon the grassie greene."
Ditty, A: "My true love hath my heart and I have his." Sir Philip Sidney. *See* My True Love Hath My Heart.
Ditty: "O holy Love, religious saint!" Sir Robert Chester. *Fr.* Love's Martyr. EIL
Ditty, A: "Peace, peace, peace, make no noise." John Day. *Fr.* Humour Out of Breath. EIL
Ditty, A: "See where she sits upon the grassy [*or* grassie] green [e]." Spenser. *Fr.* The Shepheardes Calender: April. FaBoCh; OBEV
("See where she sits upon the grassy green," 2 *sts.*) ViBoPo
Ditty: "Time was long and long ago, The." Ted Robinson. MaRV
Ditty, The: "Young Colin Clout." John Gay. *Fr.* The Shepherd's Week. LoBV
Ditty in Imitation of the Spanish ("Entre tanto que l'Avril"). Lord Herbert of Cherbury. AnAnS-2; EIL; OBS; SeEP
Ditty of the Pen Inveighing against Usury and False Dealing, A. John Hall. ReIE
Ditty of the Six Virgins, The. Thomas Watson. *See* With Fragrant Flowers We Strew the Way.
Ditty the City Sang, The. Alfred Kreymborg. NeMA
Divan, The. Richard Henry Stoddard. AA
Dive. Langston Hughes. CAD
Dive for Dreams. E. E. Cummings. TPM
Diver, The. Robert Hayden. AmPP (5th ed.); Kal
Diver, The. John Frederic Herbin. CaP
Diver, The. E. L. Mayo. CoAP
Diver, The. Leonard E. Nathan. ErPo
Diver, The. W. W. E. Ross. OBCV; PeCV; WHW
Diverging now (as if his quest had been). Wordsworth. *Fr.* The Excursion, II. OBRV
Divers, The. Peter Quennell. MoBrPo; MoVE
Divers [*or* Dyvers] Doth Use, as I Have Heard and Know. Sir Thomas Wyatt. EnL; EnPo; FCP; OAEP; ReEn; SiCE; Sonn; TuPP
(Sonnet: "Divers doth use . . .") SiPS
Divers thy death do diversely bemoan. The Death of Wyatt. Earl of Surrey. FCP; NCEP; SiPS
Diversely passioned is the lover's heart. The Eleveneth Property. Sir Thomas More. *Fr.* The Twelve Properties or Conditions of a Lover. EnRePo
Diversions of the Re-echo Club. Carolyn Wells. BOHV
Diversity. Everard V. Thompson. BePJ
Diverting History of John Gilpin, The. William Cowper. BeLS; BoChLi; BOHV; CEP; CoBE; EiCL; EiCP; EiPP; FaBoBe; FiP; GN; HBV; HBVY; InMe; OBEC; OnSP; OTPC; PTK; RIS; RoGo; TOP; TreFS; WePo
(John Gilpin.) CABL; InvP; ViBoPo

Dives and Lazarus. *Unknown.* BaBo; ELP; ESPB; FlW; NoP; OBB; OxBB
(Diverus and Lazarus.) ATP
(Dives and Laz'us.) ABF; TTY
(Lazarus, *with music.*) SaSa
Dives Asking a Drop. Richard Crashaw. MaMe
(On Dives.) ACP
Dives, when you and I go down to Hell. To Dives. Hilaire Belloc. CAW; HBMV
Divided. David Gray. AA
Divided. Jean Ingelow. HBV
"Dappled sky, a world of meadows, A," *sel.* OBNC
Divided Destinies. Kipling. BOHV
Divided Heart, The. George Wither. *See* I Wandered Out.
Divided Thought, A. *Unknown, tr. fr. Spanish by* Havelock Ellis. OnPM
Divided Thoughts. Dante, *tr. fr. Italian by* Dante Gabriel Rossetti. *Fr.* La Vita Nuova. OnPM
("All my thoughts always speak to me of Love.") AWP
Dividends. Hubert Creekmore. WaP
Divina Commedia, *sels.* Dante, *tr. fr. Italian.*
Inferno.
Francesca da Rimini, *fr.* V, *tr. by* Dante Gabriel Rossetti. EPN
Inferno. EnLi-1 (*fr.* V *and* XIII), *tr. by* Frances Winwar; OuHeWo, *abr., tr. by* Henry F. Cary
Midway the Journey, *fr.* I, *tr. by* Laurence Binyon. ExPo
Paolo and Francesca, *fr.* V. ExPo, *tr. by* Laurencė Binyon; TreFT, *tr. by* Byron
Pier delle Vigne, *fr.* XIII, *tr. by* John Ciardi. HoPM
"While I was all absorbed," *fr.* XXVIII, *tr. by* Longfellow. CAW
Paradiso.
Being Underived, *fr.* I, *tr. by* Longfellow. CAW
Dante's Heaven, *tr. by* Dorothy Sayers. BoC
"I raised my eyes aloft, and I beheld," 4 *ll.* TRV
"Into the Justice of eternity," *fr.* XIX, *tr. by* Jefferson Butler Fletcher, PoFr
"'Now say,' he said, 'were it not worse indeed,' " *fr.* VIII, *tr. by* Jefferson Butler Fletcher. PoFr
"O petty blood-nobility of ours!" *fr.* XVI, *tr. by* Jefferson Butler Fletcher. PoFr
One World, 4 *ll.* MaRV
Paradise, *abr., tr. by* Henry F. Cary. OuHeWo
Paradise: Cacciaquida's Prophecy to Dante, *fr.* XVII, *tr. by* Frances Winwar. EnLi-1
Primal Cause, The, *fr.* XXVIII, *tr. by* Longfellow. CAW
Saint Bernard's Prayer to Our Lady, *fr.* XXXIII, *tr. by* Louis How. ISi
("Thou Virgin Mother, daughter of thy Son," *tr. by* Longfellow.) CAW
Saints in Glory, The, *fr.* XXXI, *tr. by* Henry F. Cary. WGRP
Vision of God, The, *fr.* XXXIII, *tr. by* Laurence Binyon. ExPo
Vision of the Divine Mystery, *fr.* XXXIII, *tr. by* Laurence Binyon. LiTW
Purgatorio.
Celestial Pilot, The, *fr.* II, *tr. by* Longfellow. WGRP
Dante and Beatrice in the Earthly Paradise, *fr.* XXVIII, *tr. by* Dorothy Sayers. BoC
Dante's Angels, *fr.* VIII, *tr. by* Dorothy Sayers. BoC
"How haughty was thy mien," *fr.* VI, *tr. by* Jefferson Butler Fletcher. PoFr
Political Chaos in Italy, *fr.* VI, *tr. by* Longfellow. WoL
Purgatory, *abr., tr. by* Henry F. Cary. OuHeWo
Purgatory: Dante's Dream, *fr.* IX, *tr. by* Frances Winwar. EnLi-1
"'Twas now the hour that turneth," *fr.* VIII, *tr. by* Longfellow. CAW
"Veracious People, The," *fr.* XXX, *tr. by* Longfellow. CAW
Virgil's Farewell to Dante, *fr.* XXVII, *tr. by* Laurence Binyon. FaBoTw
Divina Commedia. (*poems introductory to* Longfellow's *tr. of the* Divine Comedy I-VI). Longfellow. AmePo; AmP; AmPP; AnAmPo; AnFE; AP; APA; CoAnAm; CoBA; NePA; NoP; OxBA
(Sonnets on the Divina Commedia.) ILP
Sels.
"How strange the sculptures that adorn these towers!" II. AnNE; DiPo; GoBC; MWA-1; PoE; PoFS; Sonn
"I enter, and I see thee in the gloom," III. AnNE; GoBC; MWA-1
"I lift mine eyes, and all the windows blaze," IV [V]. AnNE; GoBC; SeCeV; Sonn
"O star of morning and of liberty!" V [VI]. AnNE; GOBC
"Oft have I seen at some cathedral door," I. AnNE; ATP; GoBC; HBV; MWA-1; OQP; PoE; Sonn; TOP; TreF; ViBoPo
(Dante.) OBEV (new ed.)
(On Dante's "Divine Comedy.") AnEnPo
(Peace through Prayer.) MaRV
On Translating the "Divina Commedia," I, II, III, V. OuHeWo
"With snow-white veil and garments as of flame," IV. MWA-1; TreFT
Divination by a Cat. Anthony Hecht. StP
Divination by a Daffadil[l]. Robert Herrick. CavP; OBS; PoeP; SeCV-1; SeEP
Divine, The. Isaac Watts. SoP
Divine Abundance. *Unknown.* BLRP
Divine Awe. George Edward Woodberry. Wild Eden, XVI. AA
Divine Camenes, that with your sacred food. Of Edwards of the Chapel. Barnabe Googe. ReIE
Divine Care. Francis Quarles. MaRV
Divine Century of Spiritual Sonnets, A, *sels.* Barnabe Barnes.
"Fortress of hope, anchor of faithful zeal." TuPP
"Gracious, Divine, and most omnipotent." SiCE
Life of Man, The. OBSC
("Blast of wind, a momentary breath, A.") SiCE; Sonn; TuPP
"No more lewd lays of lighter loves I sing." Sonn; TuPP
World's Bright Comforter, The. OxBoCh
(God's Virtue.) OBSC
(Sonnet.) EIL
("World's bright comforter, whose beamsome light, The.") SiCE
Divine Comedy, The. Dante. *See* Divina Commedia.
Divine Compassion. Whittier. MAmP
Divine Hand, The. William Williams. *See* Christian Pilgrim's Hymn, The.
Divine Harmony, The. Shakespeare. *See* In Such a Night.
Divine Image, A ("Cruelty has a human heart"). Blake. AtBAP; ChTr; NoP; OBNC; PoeP; PoIE
Divine Image, The ("To Mercy, Pity, Peace, and Love"). Blake. *Fr.* Songs of Innocence. BoPe; BoTP; CBEP; CEP; EiPP; EnL; EnLit; EnPE; EnRP; ERoP-1; FaBoEn; LiTG; MaPo; MaRV; MemP; NoP; OAEP; OBEC; OBNC; OnPM; OxBoCh; PoEL-4; PoeP; PoIE; SoP; TRV; ViBoPo; WGRP
("To Mercy Pity Peace and Love.") LO
Divine Insect, The. John Hall Wheelock. GoYe; NYBP
Divine Love. Michael Benedikt. CoAP; YAP
Divine Love. Richard Crashaw. *See* Song, A: "Lord, when the sense of thy sweet grace."
Divine Love. Charles Wesley. *See* Love Divine.
Divine Lover, The. Charles Wesley. *See* Jesus, Lover of My Soul.
Divine Mistris, A. Thomas Carew. AnAnS-2
Divine Narcissus, The. Sister Juana Inés de la Cruz, *tr. fr. Spanish by* Roderick Gill. CAW
Divine Office of the Kitchen, The. Cecily Hallack. BLRP; PoLF; TreFT. *See also* Lord of All Pots and Pans and Things.
Divine Paradox, The. *Unknown.* *See* God and Yet a Man, A.
Divine Passion, The. Hortensio Félix Paravicino y Arteaga, *tr. fr. Spanish by* Thomas Walsh. CAW
Divine perfection, we have sinned, 'tis true. The Dean. Alan Porter. AnAmPo
Divine Poems, *sels.* José Garcia Villa.
"Much, beauty, is, less, than, the, face, of," 102. POTE (1959 ed.)
"My most. My most, O my lost!" 57. BoW; POTE (1959 ed.)
"Sir, I commend to you the spirit," 45. MoRP
"Within the city of my death," 74. MoRP
Divine Presence, The. Aubrey Thomas De Vere. *Fr.* May Carols. GoBC; MaRV
Divine Rapture, A. Francis Quarles. *See* My Beloved Is Mine, and I Am His.

Divine Rebel, The. George Scheftel. ChIP
Divine Ship Sails the Divine Sea for You, The. Walt Whitman. MoRP
Divine Songs to Ahura Mazda. Zoroaster, *tr. fr. Persian by* D. J. Irani. LiTW
Divine Volume, The. Sir Walter Scott. *See* Book of Books.
Divine Wooer, The, *sel.* Phineas Fletcher.
"Me Lord? can'st Thou mispend." TrPWD
Divine Zenocrate. Christopher Marlowe. *Fr.* Tamburlaine the Great, Pt. II, Act II, sc. iii. WHA
("Black [*or* Blacke] is the beauty of the brightest day.") AtBAP; BoW; ViBoPo
(To Entertain Divine Zenocrate.) ChTr
Divinely shapen cup, thy lip. On a Greek Vase. Frank Dempster Sherman. AA
Divinely Superfluous Beauty. Robinson Jeffers. LiTL; MAP; MoAmPo; MoLP; PoPl
Divinest Sense. Emily Dickinson. *See* Much madness is divinest sense.
Divinitie. George Herbert. MaMe
Divinity, The. Matthew Arnold. EPN
Divisibility. Hyam Plutzik. FiMAP
Division, The. Thomas Hardy. PG (1945 ed.); PoeP; VP
Division. John Ratti. NYBP
Division of Parts, The. Anne Sexton. NePoEA-2
Divorce, The. Thomas Stanley. AnAnS-2; LO, *sts.* 1-2; MeLP
Divorce. Anna Wickham. MoBrPo
Divorce. Charles Williams. POTE
Divorce me now, good Death, from Love and ling'ring Life. A Libel of Divorce. George Gascoigne. ReEn
Dixie ("I wish I was in de land ob cotton"). Daniel Decatur Emmett. ABF; FaFP; FaPON; HBV; PoFr; TrAS, *with music*; TreF; TrGrPo; YaD
Dixie ("Southrons, hear your country call you!"). Albert Pike. AA; HBV; MC; PaA; PAH
Dixie Lullaby, A. Strickland W. Gillilan. LHV
Dixie's Green Shore, *with music.* *Unknown.* BFSS
Dixon, a Choctaw, twenty years of age. A Savage. John Boyle O'Reilly. AA
Do. Melvin B. Tolson. *Fr.* Libretto for the Republic of Liberia. PoNe (1970 ed.)
Do all the good you can. John Wesley's Rule [*or* A Rule]. John Wesley. FaFP; HBVY; OTD; PCH; TreFT
Do' a-stan'in' on a jar, fiah a-shinin' thoo. Howdy, Honey, Howdy! Paul Laurence Dunbar. PoLF
Do but consider this small dust. *See* Consider this small dust.
Do but look on her eyes, they do light. Ben Jonson. *Fr.* A Celebration of Charis. LO
Do Come Back Again, *with music.* *Unknown.* OuSiCo
Do diddle di do. Jim Jay. Walter de la Mare. BrPo; CenHV; GaP; GoTP; HBMV; RG; RIS; SiSoSe
Do Don't Touch-a My Garment, Good Lord, I'm Gwine Home, *with music.* *Unknown.* BoAN-2
Do fishes gleam with hope or flowers feel. Credo. Alfred Kreymborg. AnAmPo
Do gold-tongued candles comfort Thee. Meditation in St. Mary's. Gertrude du Bois. ChIP
Do I give off in the wee. The Sickness of Friends. Henri Coulette. NYBP
Do I have to prove that I can sell anything? Horace Gregory. *Fr.* The Passion of M'Phail. CMoP
Do I Love Thee? John Godfrey Saxe. HBV
Do I love you? A Love Song. Raymond Richard Patterson. BOLo
Do I love you? The question might be well. In Consolation. Vassar Miller. CBV; ToPo
Do I not deal with angels. For Miriam. Kenneth Patchen. MeWo; ToPo
Do I not love thee, O my Lord? Lovest Thou Me? Feed My Lambs. Philip Doddridge. SoP
Do I Really Pray? John Burton. SoP; STF
Do I remember such and such an one? Pilate Remembers. Thomas Durley Landels. *Fr.* Pontius Pilate. MaRV
Do I sleep? Do I dream? De Tea Fabula. Sir Arthur Quiller-Couch. CenHV
Do I sleep? do I dream? Truthful James. Bret Harte. CenHV
Do I venture away too far. Song. Keith Douglas. NePoEA
Do It Now. Berton Braley. BLPA; FaFP; WBLP
Do It Now ("He was going to be all that a mortal should be"). *Unknown.* *See* Tomorrow.
Do It Now ("If you've got a job to do"). *Unknown.* BLPA; FaFP; WBLP
Do It Right. Samuel O. Buckner. WBLP
Do it, then. If you do. It. Richmond Lattimore. PP
Do It Yrself. Larry Eigner. NeAP
Do, my Johnny Boker. Johnny Boker. *Unknown.* ShS; SoAmSa
Do not ask me, charming Phillis. By the Bank of Pinks and Lilies. *Unknown.* ErPo
Do not ask of me. The Oracle. Coleman Barks. QAH
Do not ask: where? We Go. Karl Wolfskehl. TrJP
Do not beguile my heart. Complaining. George Herbert. MaMe
Do Not Believe Your Shakespeare's Grief. Conrad Aiken. *Fr.* The Argument. OA
Do not come when I am dead. My Hereafter. Juanita De Long. WGRP
Do not conceal[e] thy radiant eyes. To Cynthia, on Concealment of Her Beauty. Sir Francis Kynaston. CavP; EG; HBV; LiTL; LO; MeLP; MePo; OBS; SeCL; SeEP; ViBoPo
Do not conceive that I shall here recount. A Virgin Declares Her Beauties. Francesco da Barberino, *tr. by* Dante Gabriel Rossetti. AWP; ErPo
Do not crouch to-day and worship. The Present. Adelaide Anne Procter. WGRP
Do not despair. For Johnny. John Pudney. HaMV; WePo
Do not disdain, O straight up-raisèd pine. Graven Thoughts. Sir Philip Sidney. *Fr.* Arcadia. SiPS
Do Not Embrace Your Mind's New Negro Friend. William Meredith. WaP
Do not enforce the tired wolf. Prelude to an Evening. John Crowe Ransom. AP; CoBMV; ILP; MAP; MoAB; MoAmPo; MoPo; MoVE; NePA; OxBA; PoCh
Do not enquire from the centurion nodding. The Silver Age. Thom Gunn. ToPo
Do Not Expect Again a Phoenix Hour. C. Day Lewis. CMoP; LiTB; LiTM (rev. ed.); MoAB; MoBrPo; OxBI; PoRA
Do not fear. Release. Jean Grigsby Paxton. OQP
Do not fear, my love; no danger. Fürchte Nichts, geliebte Seele [*or* Precaution]. Heine, *tr. fr. German by* Louis Untermeyer. ALV; UnTE
Do not fear to claim His promise. A Sure Trust. *Unknown.* SoP
Do not fear to put thy feet. The River-God's Song. John Fletcher. *Fr.* The Faithful Shepherdess, III, i. CBEP; EIL; FaPON; MoShBr; OBS; PCH; ThWaDe; TuPP
Do not forget, Lord. The Prayer of the Cock. Carmen Bernos de Gasztold. TIHL
Do Not Go Gentle into That Good Night. Dylan Thomas. ACV; CABA; CBV; ChMP; CoBMV; DiPo; EnL; FaFP; FaPL; LiTM (1970 ed.); MaPo (1969 ed.); MoAB; MoBrPo (1962 ed.); MoVE; PAn; PG (1955 ed.) Po; PoSa; PPON; SeCeV; TDP; TIHL; ToPo; TreFT; TwCP; ViBoPo (1958 ed.); WePo
Do not hurry; have faith. Have Faith. Edward Carpenter. WGRP
Do not leave me, Lord, do not let the field lie fallow. Prayer for the Useless Days. Edith Lovejoy Pierce. TrPWD
Do not let any woman read this verse! Deirdre. James Stephens. AWP; CMoP; GTSL; HBMV; JAWP; OBMV; OnPP; PG; PoRA; ViBoPo; WBP
Do not look at my face. Sweet. *Unknown.* OnPM
Do not love me, my friend. Love Song. Flavien Ranaivo. PBA
Do Not Minute. Thomas Lovell Beddoes. LO
Do Not, Oh Do Not Prize. *Unknown.* CBEP; EIL
("Do [*or* Doe] not, O do not prize thy beauty at too high a rate.") EG; OBSC
(O Do Not Prize Thy Beauty.) LiTL
(Pride Is the Canker.) TrGrPo
Do Not Open until Christmas. James S. Tippett. ChBR
Do not pay too much attention to the stupid old body. The Stupid Old Body. Edward Carpenter. WGRP
Do not pay too much attention to the wandering lunatic mind. The Wandering Lunatic Mind. Edward Carpenter. WGRP
Do not profane the work of doing well. Musophilus. Samuel Daniel. ReEn

Do not rumple my top-knot. The Coy Lass Dress'd Up in Her Best. *Unknown.* ErPo

Do not speak to me of martyrdom. Malcolm. Sonia Sanchez. BP

Do not spend your time in fretting. When Things Go Wrong. *Unknown.* SoP; STF

Do not stifle me with the strange scent. Alien. Donald Jeffrey Hayes. AmNP

Do not suddenly break the branch. Usk. T. S. Eliot. Landscapes, III. CoBE; FaBoCh; LoGBV

"Do not take a bath in Jordan." Scotch Rhapsody. Edith Sitwell. TwCP

Do Not Torment Me, Woman ("Do not torment me, woman, for your honour's sake do not pursue me"). *Unknown, tr. fr. Late Middle Irish by* Kenneth Jackson. AnIL

Do not torment me, woman, let us set our minds at one. Reconciliation. *Unknown.* AnIL

Do not trust him gentle lady. The Gipsy's Warning. *Unknown.* BeLS

Do not try to adopt me. I'm on an Island. Tom Clark. ANYP

Do not unjustly blame. To His Mistress. Samuel Butler. SeCL

Do not waste your pity, friend. A Wasted Sympathy. Winifred Howells. AA

Do not waste your time. To a Boy. *Unknown.* KiLC

Do not weep, maiden, for war is kind. War Is Kind, I. Stephen Crane. AmePo; AmPP; AnAmPo; AnFE; AP; APA; CoAnAm; CoBA; DiPo; HBV; InPo; LiTA; LiTM (1970 ed.); MWA-2; PAL; PoLF; PoPo; StP; ThLM; ViBoPo; WaaP

Do not worry if I scurry from the grill-room in a hurry. Cupid's Darts. A. P. Herbert. BOHV; CenHV

Do skyscrapers ever grow tired. Skyscrapers. Rachel Field. FaPON; GFA; StVeCh

Do Something. *Unknown.* STF

Do the boys and girls still go to Siever's. Hare Drummer. Edgar Lee Masters. *Fr.* Spoon River Anthology. TOP

Do the Dead Know What Time It Is? Kenneth Patchen. MoAmPo

"Do the fish still glitter in the waterpool?" Fisherman. Sacheverell Sitwell. AtBAP

Do the wife and baby travelling to see. The Sick Nought. Randall Jarrell. OxBA

Do the Work That's Nearest. Charles Kingsley. MaRV

Do They Miss Me at Home? Caroline Atherton Briggs Mason. TreFS

Do They Miss Me at Home? A Parody, *with music.* Mart Taylor. SGR

Do They Think of Me at Home. Joseph Edward Carpenter. FaBoBe; TreFS

Do They Whisper. Delmore Schwartz. FiMAP

(Do They Whisper behind My Back?) LiTA

Do Thy Day's Work. *Unknown.* PEDC

Do we indeed desire the dead. In Memoriam A. H. H., LI. Tennyson. AtBAP; BEL; EnLi-2; EPN; OAEP; TOP; ViPo; VP

Do We Not Hear Thy Footfall? Amy Carmichael. TRV

(Footfall, The.) FaChP

Do What Thy Manhood Bids Thee Do. Sir Richard Francis Burton. TreFS

Do What You Will. Dorothy Hobson. GoBC

Do ye hear the children weeping, O my brothers. The Cry of the Children. Elizabeth Barrett Browning. BEL; EnLi-2; HBV; MaRV; OAEP; PoFr; PoVP; VA; ViBoPo; ViPo

Do ye ken hoo to fush for the salmon? Master and Man. Sir Henry Newbolt. WhC

Do ye know the little wood-mouse. The Wood-Mouse. Mary Howitt. TVC

Do you also hear the silence between us? A Resonant Silence. David Llorens. TNV

Do you ask me how I prove. The Heart's Proof. James Buckham. BLRP; OQP; WBLP

Do you ask me what I think of. What I Think of Hiawatha. J. W. Morris. Par

Do you ask [*or* know] what the birds say? Answer to a Child's Question [*or* The Birds]. Samuel Taylor Coleridge. BiS; BoTP; DD; EnRP; FaBoBe; HBV; HBVY; NeHB; OTPC; PEDC; PRWS; ThGo; ThWaDe; TVC; UTS

Do you carrot all for me? *Unknown.* SiTL

Do You Fear the Wind? Hamlin Garland. · AA; HBV;

HBVY; MPB; OQP; OTD; PoPl; TiPo (1952 ed.); TreFT; TSW; YaD

(Do you Fear the Force of the Wind?) MCCG; PoMA

Do you feel your heart discouraged as you pass along the way? When Thou Passest through the Waters. Henry Crowell. BLRP

Do you forget the shifting hole. To a Defeated Saviour. James Wright. NePoEA

Do you give yourself to me utterly. Sleep. Kenneth Slessor. BoAV; MoAuPo

Do You Guess It Is I? Eliza Lee Follen. OTPC (1946 ed.); PPL

Do you hear his whistle blowing. The Popcorn Man. Edith D. Osborne. GFA

Do you hear the angels singing? Praise. Henry W. Frost. SoP

Do you hear the cry as the pack goes by. Wind-Wolves. William D. Sargent. MPB; TiPo; UTS

Do you hear the East a-calling? The Call of the East. Henry W. Frost. SoP

"Do you herd sheep?" old gramma sighed. How Low Is Lowing Herd. Walt Kelly. FiBHP

Do You Just Belong? *Unknown.* STF

Do You Know? Christina Rossetti. *See* When the Cows Come Home.

Do You Know How Many Stars? *Unknown.* PPL

Do you know how the people of all the land. Potomac Side. Edward Everett Hale. From Potomac to Merrimac, I. PAH

Do you know how to begin? Preface to a Musician. Richard Church. MuSP

Do you know me now? From the Ballad of Evil. N. P. van Wyk Louw. PeSA

Do you know of the dreary land. The River Fight. Henry Howard Brownell. PaA; PAH; PAP

Do you know that your soul is of my soul such a part. Like Mother, Like Son [*or* To My Son]. Margaret Johnston Grafflin. BLPA; NeHB; PoToHe (new ed.)

Do you know the little wood-mouse. *See* Do ye Know . . .

Do you know the neighbor who lives in your block. Your Neighbor. H. Howard Biggar. PoToHe

Do you know the old man who. The Wild Flower Man. Lu Yu. NaP

Do you know there's lots of people. Get into the Boosting Business. *Unknown.* WBLP

Do you know what happened on that day. What Happened. Margaret D. Armstrong. FaChP

Do you know what I could wish? Song for a Hot Day. Elizabeth J. Coatsworth. StVeCh (1955 ed.)

Do you know what the birds say? *See* Do you ask what the birds say?

Do you know what's in my pottet? A Little Boy's Pocket. *Unknown.* PPL

Do you know why the rabbits are caught in the snare? Why. H. P. Stevens. BOHV

Do you know you have asked for the costliest thing. A Woman's Question. Lena Lathrop. BLPA; PoToHe; WBLP

Do you like marigolds? Marigolds. Louise Driscoll. BoTP

Do you love me?. *Unknown.* PoSC; SiTL

Do you 'member way last summer? You Kicked and Stomped and Beat Me. *Unknown.* OuSiCo

Do you mind the news while we eat? Dinner Party, 1940. Phillip M. Sherlock. PoNe

Do you ne'er think what wondrous beings these? Longfellow. *Fr.* The Birds of Killingworth. WBLP

Do You Not Father Me. Dylan Thomas. ToPo

"Do you not find something very strange about him?" The Assassination. Robert Hillyer. AnNE; MoAmPo; TrGrPo (1942 ed.)

Do You Not Hear? James Picot. BoAV

Do you not hear her song. Daphne. Thomas S. Jones, Jr. OHIP

Do you not hear me calling, white deer with no horns? He Mourns for the Change That Has Come upon Him and His Beloved, and Longs for the End of the World. W. B. Yeats. Po

"Do you not hear the Aziola cry." The Aziola. Shelley. CBEP; PeER; SiSW

Do you not see the Christmas star. Song of the Wise Men. Edith Lovejoy Pierce. PGD

"Do you not wish to renounce the Devil?" Epigram. Armand Lanusse. PoNe; TTY

Do you, now, as the news becomes known. Pay-Off. Kenneth Fearing. CMoP
Do You Plan to Speak Bantu? or Abbreviation Is the Thief of Sanity. Ogden Nash. FiBHP
Do you read. I Am Not the Constant Reader. Michael Brownstein. ANYP
Do you recall that night in June. The Danube River. Hamilton Aïdé. VA
"Do you realize how high kites are," he said. Kites. Michael Brownstein. ANYP
Do you recall what I recall? Rondeau. Louis Untermeyer. MeWo
Do You Remember. Thomas Haynes Bayly. HBV
Do you remember. Envoy. W. E. Henley. BrPo
Do you remember/ Honey-melon moon. New Orleans. Lola Ridge. MAP; MoAmPo (1942 ed.)
Do you remember/ How you won? To James. Frank Horne. *Fr.* Letters Found near a Suicide. BANP; BiCB; GoSl; Kal
Do you remember an inn. Tarantella. Hilaire Belloc. CH; FaBoCh; GoBC; HT; LoGBV; MoBrPo; MoShBr; MoSiPe; NeMA; OBMV; OtMeF; ShBV-2; WePo
Do you remember, Heart's Desire. A Hallowe'en Memory. Christopher Morley. LHV
Do you remember how the twilight stood. To Butterfly. William Alexander Percy. HBMV
Do you remember how we came that day. Two Married: The Heights. Helen Frazee-Bower. HBMV
Do you remember, Joan (O vain to wonder). The Saint. Humbert Wolfe. *Fr.* Requiem. CAW
Do you remember, long ago. After Aughrim. Arthur Gerald Geoghegan. OnYI
Do You Remember Me? Walter Savage Landor. *Fr.* Ianthe. EnRP; GTBS-D; OBNC; ViBoPo
(Ianthe's Question.) OBEV
Do you remember Mr. Goodbeare, the carpenter. Elegy for Mr. Goodbeare. Sir Osbert Sitwell. AnFE; MoBrPo
Do you remember, my sweet, absent son. The Child's Wish Granted. George Parsons Lathrop. AA; HBV; JKCP
Do you remember, O Delphic Apollo. Webster Ford. Edgar Lee Masters. *Fr.* Spoon River Anthology. NP
Do you remember one immortal. To F. C. in Memoriam Palestine. G. K. Chesterton. HBMV
Do you remember, passer-by, the path. James Garber. Edgar Lee Masters. *Fr.* Spoon River Antholoby. ILP
Do you remember that careless band. Fairyland. Anne Glenny Wilson. BoAu
Do You Remember That Night? *Unknown, tr. fr. Modern Irish by* Eugene O'Curry. AnIV; BoLP; OnYI; OxBI
—*Tr. by* George Petrie. IrPN; SiSW
Do you remember that still summer evening. The Golden Room. W. W. Gibson. POTE
Do you remember the dark months you held the sector at Mametz. Aftermath. Siegfried Sassoon. GTSL; MCCG
Do you remember the dark pool at Nîmes. The Pool. Alice Corbin. NP
Do you remember the meadow-field. The Meadow-Field. Charles Sangster. *Fr.* Pleasant Memories. OBCV
Do you remember, when we two were children. Over the Bridge. Li Kwang-t'ien. LiTW
Do you remember when you heard. Do You Remember. Thomas Haynes Bayly. HBV
Do you remember, when you were first a child. Message from Home. Kathleen Raine. ImOP
Do you see that bird in the sky? Bird-Song. Mary Dixon Thayer. CAW
Do you see that willow standing. The West Wind's Secret. Mary Jane Carr. BrR
Do you see them? I mean the Dead. Haunted Odysseus; the Last Testament. Horace Gregory. MoVE
Do you seek to bind me, ye gods. The Sword of Tethra. William Larminie. *Fr.* Moytura. OnYI
Do you suppose it's really really true. Run, Kitty, Run! Jimmy Garthwaite. BBGG
Do you think I'd marry a woman. A Bachelor's Mono-Rhyme. Charles Mackay. BOHV
Do you think, my boy, when I put my arms around you. The Lonely Child. James Oppenheim. NP
Do you think that because I sing. The Swan's Singing. *Unknown.* OnPM
Do you think that odes and sermons. Sexsmith the Dentist. Edgar Lee Masters. *Fr.* Spoon River Anthology. NePA
Do you think we skip. The Zobo Bird. Frank A. Collymore. GoJo
Do you wish the world were better? Better, Wiser and Happier [*or* Kindness]. Ella Wheeler Wilcox. Sop; WBLP
Do you wonder to see him in chains? Columbus Day. Tennyson. HH; PEDC
Do Your Best. *Unknown.* SoP
Do your days seem long, your pleasures few. He Cares. Owen C. Salway. STF
Doan't You Be What You Ain't. Edwin Milton Royle. BLPA
Dobe Bill, he came a-riding. The Killer. *Unknown.* ABF; CoSo
Doc Hill. Edgar Lee Masters. *Fr.* Spoon River Anthology. NP
Dock Rats. Marianne Moore. AnAmPo
Docks. Dorothy Wellesley. ShBV-3
Doctor and His Patients, The. Sir Charles Sedley. PeRV
Doctor Bill Williams. Ernest Walsh. InvP
Dr. Birch and His Young Friends, *sel.* Thackeray.
End of the Play, The. FaFP; GN; TreF; VA
Doctor Bottom was preparing to leave. Medical Aid. Walter Hard. WhC
Dr. Clifford. E. C. Bentley. *Fr.* Clerihews. CenHV
Dr. Coppelius. Wrey Gardiner. NeBP
Dr. Donne. Kenneth Slade Alling. NePoAm
Doctor Emmanuel. James Reeves. PV
Doctor Faustus. Geoffrey Hill. NePoEA-2; NMP
Dr. Faustus. Christopher Marlowe. CoBE; EnLi-1; EnLit
Sels.
"Ah Faustus,/ Now hast thou but one bare hour to live." AtBAP; BoLiVe; ChTr; FlW; MyFE; ViBoPo; YAT
(End of Dr. Faustus, The.) PoEL-2
(End of Faustus, The.) TrGrPo
(Faustus Faces His Doom.) TreFT
(Finale.) WHA
(Last Hour of Faustus, The.) ShBV-4
"But, leaving these vain trifles of men's souls." MyFE
"Cut is the branch that might have grown full straight," *fr.* Epilogue. ViBoPo, 8 *ll.*
"Was this the face that launch'd a thousand ships?" AtBAP; InP; LiTL; PTK; TreF, 3 *ll.*; TrGrPo; ViBoPo
(Face of Helen, The.) FaBV
(Faustus to Helen.) NeHB
(Helen.) FaFP; GTBS-W; LiTB; LiTG; WHA
"Tell me what is that Lucifer thy lord?" YAT
"That I might have unto my paramour." FaPL
Doctor Faustus was a good man. Mother Goose. GaP; OTPC (1946 ed.)
Doctor Fell. Thomas Brown. *See* I Do Not Love Thee, Doctor Fell.
Dr. Fell and Points West. Ogden Nash. RePo
Doctor Fell in a Deep Well, A. *Unknown.* GoTP; ShM
Doctor fingers my bruise, The. Passing Out. Philip Levine. AmPC
Doctor Foster is a good man. *Unknown.* OxNR
Doctor Foster went to Gloucester [*or* Glos'ter]. Mother Goose. BoChLi; OxBoLi; OxNR; PCH; RIS; SiTL
Dr. Hu/ speaks. Norman Mailer. ELU
Doctor Major. Lionel Johnson. BrPo
Dr. Newman with the crooked pince-nez. Robert Graves. *Fr.* Grotesques. DTC
Doctor punched my vein, The. Scyros. Karl Shapiro. HoPM; ILP; LiTA; LiTM; MoVE; NePA; SeCeV; WaP
Dr. Sigmund Freud Discovers the Sea Shell. Archibald MacLeish. PPON
Dr. Syntax in Search of the Picturesque, *sel.* William Combe.
In Search of the Picturesque. OBRV
Dr. Unlikely, we love you so. Horror Movie. Howard Moss. NePoEA-2; SiTL
Doctors' Row. Conrad Aiken. AP; PoPl
Doctor's Story, The. Will Carleton. BLPA
Doctrinal Point. William Empson. AtBAP; ToPo
Doctrine has wound of lovers' limbs. Chalk from Eden. Howard Moss. NePA
Dodder leans, against the rubus, The. The Newlyweds' Separation. Tu Fu. HW
Dodger, The, *with music.* *Unknown.* OuSiCo
Dodo, The. Hilaire Belloc. ChTr
Dodoism. W. J. Courthope. *Fr.* The Paradise of Birds. OtMeF

Dodona's Oaks Were Still. Patrick MacDonogh. NeIP
Doe at Evening, A. D. H. Lawrence. BrPo
Doe, doe!/ I shall dever see her bore! Lay of the Deserted Influenzaed. Henry Cholmondeley-Pennell. BOHV; InMe
Doe not their prophane orgies heare. To Castara. William Habington. AnAnS-2
Doe you not wonder at the strange rare sound. *Unknown.* SeCSL
Doeg, though without knowing how or why. Dryden. *Fr.* Absalom and Achitophel, Pt. II. PoEL-3
Does a tear fall from the eye. Tragedy. Howard Moss. NePoEA
Does Daddy Go? *Unknown.* STF
Does It Matter? Siegfried Sassoon. MoBrPo; NeMA; NP; PoPo; PPON; WaP; YT
Does man love Art? Man visits Art, but squirms. The Chicago Picasso. Gwendolyn Brooks. *Fr.* Two Dedications. LiTM (1970 ed.)
Does memory make you sad of heart? George Rostrevor Hamilton. MuSP
Does no one see that in your wood. Boy. Winifred Welles. NP
Does the eagle know what is in the pit? Thel's Motto. Blake. *Fr.* The Book of Thel. ChTr; DiPo; LO
Does the elephant remember. Circus Elephant. Kathryn Worth. BrR
Does the heart grieve on. The Heart Recalcitrant. Leonora Speyer. PG
Does the lily flower open? Star Song of the Bushman Women. *Unknown.* PeSA
Does the Pearl Know? Helen Hay Whitney. AA
Does the road wind up-hill all the way? Up-Hill. Christina Rossetti. BLP; BLPA; CH; CoBE; EG; EnLi-2; FaBoBe; FaChP; FaPL; GTBS; HBV; LoBV; MaRV; MCCG; MemP; NeHB; NoP; OAEP; OBEV; OBNC; OBVV; OQP; OtMeF; OTPC (1946 ed.); PCD; Po; PoFS; PoMa; PoRA; PoVP; ShBV-2; SoP; TOP; TreFS; TrGrPo; TSW; VA; ViBoPo; ViPo; VP; WGRP; WHA; WiR
Does your heart go back to Galway, to The Blazers and stone walls. Blue Peter. Stanislaus Lynch. OnYI
Doesn't thou 'ear my 'erse's legs, as they canters awaäy? *See* Dosn't thou 'ear . . .
Dog, The. W. H. Davies. MoBrPo
Dog. Lawrence Ferlinghetti. NoP
Dog, The (As Seen by the Cat). Oliver Herford. FaBV; RIS
Dog, The. Valentin Iremonger. NeIP
Dog, The. Sandford Lyne. QAH
Dog. Harold Monro. MoBrPo
(Dogs.) GoTP
Dog. John Crowe Ransom. LiTA
Dog. William Jay Smith. GoJo
Dog, The. *Unknown.* WBLP
Dog and a cat went out together, A. Mother Goose. PCH; SAS
Dog and the Cat, The. Grace Taber Hallock. RePo
Dog and the Cat, and the Duck and the Rat, The. Eliza Lee Follen. CIV
Dog and the Water-Lily, The. William Cowper. OAEP
Dog around the Block. E. B. White. OCS
Dog at Night. Louis Untermeyer. GoTP; StaSt
Dog barked, The; then the woman stood in the doorway. Roan Stallion. Robinson Jeffers. AmPP (4th ed.); BeLS; NAMP
Dog Barks, The. *Unknown.* RIS
Dog beneath the cherry-tree, The. The Ambiguous Dog. Arthur Guiterman. PoMa
Dog beneath the Skin, The, *sel.* W. H. Auden.
"You with shooting-sticks." NAMP
Dog called Sesamë slewed out, The. Stray Dog, near Ecully, Valley of the Rhône. Margaret Avison. OBCV
Dog Day, A. Rachel Field. SiSoSe
Dog Disappears, A. A Song of Autumn. Joseph Ceravolo. ANYP
Dog, Dog in My Manger. George Barker. LiTM
Dog emerges from the flies, A. Nino, the Wonder Dog. Roy Fuller. CBV
Dog Fiend, The. Frederick Marryat. *See* Snarleyyow, or, The Dog Fiend.
Dog fox rolls on his lolling tongue, The. The Hunt. Louis Kent. WaKn
Dog growing thinner, for want of a dinner, A. The Dog of Reflection. Jeffreys Taylor. OTPC
Dog in a Car. David McCord. RePo
Dog in the River, The. Phaedrus, *tr. fr. Latin by* Christopher Smart. AWP; JAWP; OnPM; WBP
Dog is black or white or brown, The. The Dog (As Seen by the Cat). Oliver Herford. RIS
Dog is man's best friend, The. An Introduction to Dogs. Ogden Nash. GoTP; MoShBr
Dog loved its churlish life, The. Lupercalia. Ted Hughes. NMP; ToPo
Dog means dog. Blum. Dorothy Aldis. MoShBr
Dog Named Ego [the Snowflakes as Kisses], A. Delmore Schwartz. The Repetitive Heart, X. AmP; LiTA; LiTM; MiAP
Dog of Art, The. Denise Levertov. FRC
Dog of Reflection, The. Jeffreys Taylor. OTPC
Dog over Snow. Marion Strobel. NP
Dog Sleeping on My Feet, A. James Dickey. PP
Dog stops barking after Robinson has gone, The. Robinson. Weldon Kees. NaP; NYBP; TwAmPo
Dog that is beat has a right to complain, The. On Sir Henry Clinton's Recall. *Unknown.* PAH
Dog that spoke, a monster born of sheep, A. Mongolian Idiot. Karl Shapiro. FiMAP
Dog trots freely in the street, The. Dog. Lawrence Ferlinghetti. *Fr.* Oral Messages. NoP; ToPo
Dog was there, outside her door, The. The Dog. W. H. Davies. MoBrPo
Dog Who Ate a Pond Lily. Winifred Wells. NP
Dog who knew the winter felt no spleen, The. The Watcher. Ruth Stone. NYBP
Dog will come when he is called, The. Beasts, Birds, and Fishes. Adelaide O'Keeffe. OTPC (1923 ed.)
Dog will often steal a bone, A. A Cat's Conscience. *Unknown.* The Nature of the Cat, IV. CIV. PoLF
Dog will roll, and wag his tail, and fawn, The. Dignity. Bhartrihari. OnPM
Dog yelped, skunk let fly, The. Larry Eigner. CoPo
Doggies went to the mill, The. *Unknown.* BoTP; OxNR
Dogie Song. *Unknown.* CoSo
Dogma. Babette Deutsch. MoLP
Dogrose. Patric Stevenson. NeIP
Dogs. Frances Cornford. *Fr.* Feri's Dream. ThGo
Dogs. Harold Monro. *See* Dog.
Dogs. Pope. *See* Epigram: "I am his Highness' dog at Kew."
Dogs and Weather. Winifred Welles. FaPON; StVeCh; TiPo
Dogs are quite a bit like people. Dog. William Jay Smith. GoJo
Dogs barking, dust awhirling. Hail and Farewell. Anne Higginson Spicer. HBMV
Dog's Cold Nose, The. Arthur Guiterman. StPo; TiPo (1959 ed.)
Dogs of Bethlehem, The. Katharine Lee Bates. ChrboLe
Dog's Vigil, A. Margaret E. Bruner. PoToHe
Dogwood, The. Robert Penn Warren. Dark Woods, II. PoDB
Dogwood Blossoms. George Marion McClellan. BANP
Dogwood flakes. Variations Done for Gerald van de Wiele. Charles Olson. NeAP
Dogwood tree was once as broad, The. The Legend of the Dogwood Tree. Geraldine Farrar. StJW
Doing a Filthy Pleasure Is [and Short]. Petronius Arbiter, *tr. fr. Latin by* Ben Jonson. CABA; CBV; ErPo
(Against Consummation.) UnTE
(Foeda Est in Coitu.) LiTW
(Fragmentum.) NoP
Doing Railroads for *The Rocky Mountain News.* Cy Warman. PoOW
Doing what the moon says, he shifts his chair. Orkney Interior. Ian Hamilton Finlay. NMP; OPoP
Dolcino to Margaret. Charles Kingsley. HBV; PoVP
(Hey Nonny!) OBVV
Dole of the King's Daughter, The. *Unknown, tr. fr. French by* Oscar Wilde. AWP
Doll, The. Robert Friend. NYTB
Doll, don't be too proud of those eyes. To Vanity. Darwin T. Turner. PoNe (1970 ed.)
Doll in the doll-maker's house, A. The Dolls. W. B. Yeats. BrPo; CMoP; MBW-2; StP
Doll Song. "Lewis Carroll." SoPo

Dolladine. William Brighty Rands. PRWS
Dollar a day is a sailor's pay, A. Leave Her Johnny (C *vers.*). *Unknown.* SoAmSa
Dollar and a Half a Day, A, *with music.* *Unknown.* TrAS
Dollar Bill. John Frederick Nims. MiAP
Dollar for Whitman, you are all stumbling, A. The Contribution. David Shapiro. ANYP
Dollar I Gave, A. *Unknown.* STF
Dollmaker, snug in your house. The Doll. Robert Friend. NYTB
Dolls, The. John Ciardi. ToPo
Dolls, The. Frederic Prokosch. LiTM (1946 ed.)
Dolls, The. W. B. Yeats. BrPo; CMoP; MBW-2; StP
Dolls' faces are rosier but these were children. Bombing Casualties in Spain. Sir Herbert Read. FaBoTw; PPON
Doll's hair concealing, A. Partial Resemblance. Denise Levertov. CoAP; NaP
Doll's House, The. Anna Letitia Barbauld. OTPC (1923 ed.)
Doll's Song. "Lewis Carroll." OTPC (1946 ed.)
Doll's Wooing, The. Eugene Field. RIS
Dolor. Theodore Roethke. AmP; AmPP (5th ed.); AP; CABA; CoBMV; FiMAP; ILP; LiTM (1970 ed.); MoVE; NMP; PoeP; PoIE; PoSa; PPON
Dolores. Swinburne. MaVP; PoVP; ViPo; VP
"We shift and bedeck and bedrape us," *sel.* UnTE
Dolphin. John Unterecker. ThO
Dolphins, The. Hamish Maclaren. EtS
Dolphins. Molly Michaels. RIS
Dolphins in Blue Water. Amy Lowell. LaNeLa; TSW
Dolphins rampant. An Exchange of Letters On Suicide Porpoises. William Brown. QAH
Dolphin's Tomb, The. Anyte, *tr. fr. Greek by* F. L. Lucas. OA
Dom Pedro, The, *with music.* *Unknown.* SoAmSa
Dombashawa. Peter Jackson. BoSA
Dome of Sunday, The. Karl Shapiro. AP; CMoP; CoAP; CoBMV; LiTM; MoAB; MoAmPo (1950 ed.); MoPo; NePA; OxBA; WaP
Dome of the capitol looks to the Potomac river, The. Smoke Rose Gold. Carl Sandburg. NeMA; YT
Domed with the azure of heaven. Vapour and Blue. Wilfred Campbell. CaP
Domenic Darragh walked the land. The Mountainy Childer. Elizabeth Shane. HBMV
Domestic Asides; or, Truth in Parentheses. Thomas Hood. EnRP
Domestic Cat, A. Edwin Denby. ANYP
Domestic: Climax. Merrill Moore. ErPo
Domestic Didactics by an Old Servant. Thomas Hood. OBRV
Domestic Economy. Anna Wickham. NeMA
Domestic Scenes. Miguel de Unamuno, *tr. fr. Spanish by* Thomas Walsh.
"Go, stir the brazier coals, my child." LiTW; WoL
(Brazier Coals, The.) OnPM
"Look not upon me with such eyes, my son." LiTW; WoL
"When Shades of night have come." WoL
Domestic Science. *Unknown.* WBLP
Domicile of John, The. *Unknown, sometimes at. to* Pope. InMe
Domination of Black. Wallace Stevens. AmPP; AnFE; AP; CoAnAm; CoBMV; ILP; MAP; MAPA; MoAB; MoAmPo; OxBA; PIA; PoeP; TDP; TPM; TwAmPo
Domine Cui Sunt Pleiades Curae. Sir Charles G. D. Roberts. VA
Domine Jesu! John Duffy. JKCP (1955 ed.)
Domine Quid Multiplicati Sunt. Psalms, III, Bible, *O.T., tr. by* Thomas Sternhold. SiCE
Domine, Quo Vadis? *Unknown.* ACP; CAW
Domine, Quo Vadis? Sir William Watson. WGRP
Dominic came riding down, sworded, straight and splendid. The Lovers of Marchaid. Marjorie Pickthall. HBV
Dominic Has a Doll. E. E. Cummings. PoPl
Dominion. Martha Snell Nicholson. FaChP
Dominion of Australia, The (a Forecast, 1877). Brunton Stephens. BoAu; PoAu-1; VA
Dominus Illuminatio Mea. Richard Doddridge Blackmore. MaRV; OBEV; OBVV; TreFS
(In the Hour of Death.) OQP
Don Giovanni, *sel.* Lorenzo da Ponte, *tr. fr. Italian by* Natalie MacFarren.
"Giovinette, che fate all' amore." TrJP
Don Giovanni on His Way to Hell (II). Jack Gilbert. NMP
Don Juan, *sels.* Byron.
"Alas! the love of women! it is known," *fr.* II. COBE
And Angling, Too, *fr.* XIII. SD
"And now they were diverted by their sulte," *fr.* III. FosPo; MBW-2
At Thirty Years, *fr.* I. FiP
Ave Maria, *fr.* III. ISi; MCCG
Canto I. NoP; OAEP, *sels.*
("I want a hero: an uncommon want.") EnL, *abr.*; EnLit, *sel.*; EnRP; MBW-2; Po, *sel.*
Canto III. EnLi-2, *sels.*; OAEP, *sels.*
Canto IV. BEL, *abr.*; CoBE, *abr.*; OAEP, *sel.*
Canto XI, *sels.* OAEP
Canto XII. MERP
Contemporary Poets, *fr.* XI. OBRV
Death of Haidee, The, *fr.* IV. FiP; WHA, *longer sel.*
Dedication: "Bob Southey! You're a poet—Poet laureate." BEL; BoLiVe; CTC; EnLi-2 (1949 ed.); EnLit; EnRP; ILP; InP, 4 *sts.*; OAEP, 5 *sts.*; PoFS
(Dedication to the Poet Laureate, *abr.*) FiP
(Invocation.) LoBV
(Southey and Wordsworth.) TrGrPo
Don Juan and Haidee, *fr.* II *and* IV. TOP
Don Juan's Education, *fr.* I. WHA
Donna Julia, *fr.* I. PoEL-4
Evening, *after* Sappho, *fr.* III. BoLiVe; OTPC; TrGrPo
(Hesperus.) OnPM, 1 *st.*
(Hesperus the Bringer.) AWP; JAWP; OuHeWo; WBP
(Hymn to Hesperus.) TOP
"For me, I know nought," *fr.* XIV. OBRV
"Fourth day came, but not a breath of air, The," *fr.* II. ChER
Fragment: "I would to heaven that I were so much clay," *on the back of poet's MS of* I. CTC; FiP; ILP; OAEP; PeER
Gulbeyaz, *fr.* V. PoEL-4
Haidee ("One of the two, according to your choice"), *fr.* IV. SeCePo
"In her first passion woman loves her lover," *fr.* I. ErPo; UnTE
"In the great world—which, being interpreted," *fr.* XI. OxBoLi
Isles of Greece, The, *fr.* III. AnFE; AWP; BEL, *longer sel.*; CBEP; ChTr; CoBE; EnLit; EPN, *longer sel.*; FaBoEn; FiP; HBV; HT, *abr.*; InPo; LiTB; MemP; OBEV; OBRV; OTPC, 3 *sts.*; PoFr; PoIE; PTK; RoGo; SeCeV, *longer sel.*; TOP; TreFS; ViBoPo; WHA
"It was the cooling hour," *fr.* II. ViBoPo
(Haidee [and Don Juan].) OBNC; OBRV
(Juan and Haidee.) EPN, *longer sel.*; MaPo
Juan in England, *fr.* XI. FiP
"Juan was taught from out the best edition," *fr.* I. PIA
Lady Adeline Amundeville, *fr.* XIII. PoEL-4
Lake Poets, The, *fr.* III. UnPo (1st ed.)
Lambro's Return, *fr.* III. OBRV
"Man's a strange animal, and makes strange use," *fr.* I. PeER
"Man's love is of man's life a thing apart," *fr.* I. TreF
My Days of Love Are Over, *fr.* I. FaBoEn; OBNC
("No more—no more—Oh! never more, my heart.") PeER
Norman Abbey, *fr.* XIII. OBRV
"Nothing so difficult as a beginning," *fr.* IV. BEL; CoBE; EnRP; PoFS
(Author's Purpose, The.) EPN
(Romantic to Burlesque, *shorter sel.*). FiP
"Oh ye! who teach the ingenuous youth of nations," *fr.* II. EnRP
"Old Lambro pass'd unseen a private gate," *fr.* III. EnRP
Poetical Commandments, *fr.* I. FiP; OBRV
("If ever I should condescend to prose.") OxBoLi
(Poet's Credo.) SeCePo
Shipwreck, The, *fr.* II. MCCG, *much abr.*; OBRV; WHA
Siege of Ismail, The, *fr.* VII *and* VIII, *abr.* WoL
"They tell me 'tis decided; you depart," *fr.* I. ViBoPo
"Tis pleasing to be schooled in a strange tongue," *fr.* II. ViBoPo
'Tis Sweet [to Hear], *fr.* I. MaPo; MCCG; ViBoPo
(First Love.) OBRV
(Pleasant Things, *shorter sel.*) OTPC (1923 ed.)

"'Twas midnight—Donna Julia was in bed," *fr.* I. UnTE
Wellington, *fr.* IX. OBRV
("Oh, Wellington! or 'Villainton'—for fame.") OxBoLi; PeER
(On Wellington.) FiP, *abr.*
"When Juan woke he found some good things ready," *fr.* II. EnLit
"'Whom the gods love die young' was said of yore," *fr.* IV. EnLit
Don Juan. Lucius Harwood Foote. AA
Don Juan and Haidee. Byron. *Fr.* Don Juan, II *and* IV. TOP
Don Juan Declaims. James Elroy Flecker. OnPP
Don Juan had got out on Shooter's Hill. Juan in England. Byron. *Fr.* Don Juan, XI. FiP; OAEP
Don Juan has ever the grand old air. Don Juan. Lucius Harwood Foote. AA
Don Juan in Hell. Baudelaire, *tr. fr. French by* James Elroy Flecker. AWP; SyP
Don Juan Muses. John Heath-Stubbs. MoPW
Don Juan's Address to the Sunset. Robert Nichols. OBMV; POTE
Don Juan's Education. Byron. *Fr.* Don Juan, I. WHA
Don' let Yo' Watch Run Down, *with music.* *Unknown.* AS
Don Quixote. Craven Langstroth Betts. AA
Don Quixote. Austin Dobson. HBV
Don Quixote. Arthur Davison Ficke. HBMV
Don Quixote in England, *sels.* Henry Fielding.
A Hunting We Will Go, *fr.* II. HBV; OTPC (1923 ed.); ViBoPo
(Hunting Song.) CEP; OBEC; OxBoLi; StP
Roast Beef of Old England, The, *fr.* I. CEP; OBEC
Donal o' Dreams has no bed for his sleeping. The Fiddler. Edna Valentine Trapnell. HBMV
Donal Ogue. *Unknown.* *See* Donall Oge.
Donald. Henry Abbey. AA
Donald, he's come to this town. Dugall Quin (B *vers.*). *Unknown.* ESPB
Donald Macdonald. James Hogg. PoFr
Donald of the Isles. *Unknown.* *See* Lizie Lindsay.
Donall [*or* Donal] Oge: Grief of a Girl's Heart. *Unknown, tr. fr. Modern Irish by* Lady Gregory. BoLP; OnYI; OxBI
(Donal Ogue, *tr. by* Frank O'Connor.) KiLC
(Grief of a Girl's Heart, The, *tr. by* Lady Gregory.) ChTr
Done For. Rose Terry Cooke. AA
Done Foun' My Los' Sheep, *with music.* *Unknown.* BoAN-1
Done is a battle [*or* battell] on the dragon black. Of [*or* On] the Resurrection of Christ. William Dunbar. MeEL; OxBoCh; OxBS; PoEL-1; PoLi
Done is the work that saves! The Work That Saves! Horatius Bonar. BePJ
Done to death by slanderous tongues. Epitaph. Shakespeare. *Fr.* Much Ado about Nothing, V, iii. CTC; OBSC
Donec Eris Felix Multos Numerabis Amicos. *Unknown.* EnPo
Doney Gal, *with music.* *Unknown.* CoSo; OuSiCo
Dong with a Luminous Nose, The. Edward Lear. CBEP; CenHV; ChTr; FaBV; LBN; NBM; PoEL-5; PoMS; SiTL; TOP; WiR
Donkey, The. G. K. Chesterton. ACP (1952 ed.); BoC; FaBV; GoBC; GTBS-D; MaRV; MemP; MoBrPo; NeHB; NeMA; OBEV (new ed.); PoLF; PoMa; PoPo; PoRL; POTE; ShBV-1; StaSt; StJW; TOP; TreFT; WGRP
Tattered outlaw, The," *sel.* HBVY
Donkey, The. Rose Fyleman. BoTP
Donkey, The. P. R. Kaikini. ACV
Donkey, The. *Unknown.* BiCB
Donkey. Mark Van Doren. EaLo
Donkey, Donkey, do not bray. *Unknown.* OxNR
Donkey Riding. *Unknown.* WHW
Donkey sat down on the roadside, The. Time Out. John Montague. NYTB
Donna Julia. Byron. *Fr.* Don Juan, I. PoEL-4
Donne Redone. Joseph Paul Tierney. ShM
Donne, the delight of Phoebus, and each muse. To John Donne. Ben Jonson. AnAnS-2; MaPo; OAEP; OBS; ReEn; SCEP-2; SeCV-1; SeEP; StP
Donnybrook Jig, The. Charles O'Flaherty. *See* Humours of Donnybrook Fair, The.
Don't. James Jeffrey Roche. HBV
Don't. *Unknown.* STF
Don't ask me how he managed. The Worm. Raymond Souster. WHW
Don't ask where is Wisdom to be sought as ecstatic music. The Undertaking. Gerrit Lansing. CoPo
Don't Be Foolish Pray. *Unknown.* CoMu
Don't Be Sorrowful, Darling. Rembrandt Peale. HBV
Don't blush, dear sir, your flame to own. To a Gentleman in Love with a Negro Woman. Sneyd Davies. WaPE
Don't boast your unbelief in woods! A Warning to Skeptics. Leah Bodine Drake. FiSC
Don't Break It. Joseph Ceravolo. ANYP
"Don't Care" and "Never Mind" ("'Don't care' is no friend of mine"). John Kendrick Bangs. FaFP
Don't Copy Cat. "Mark Twain." TreFT
Don't Ever Cross a Crocodile. Kaye Starbird. PDV
Don't fight Boy! How to Succeed. Arnold Kemp. WSL
Don't Find Fault. *Unknown.* SoP
Don't forget the crablike. The Hands. Denise Levertov. NeAP
Don't get discouraged when you hear. Don't. *Unknown.* STF
Don't get the wrong idea. Eyewitness. Rodney Hall. PoAu-2
Don't Give Up. Phoebe Cary. PCH
Don't Give Up. *Unknown.* FaFP; PoToHe (new ed.)
Don't give up hoping when the ship goes down. Hang to Your Grit! Louis E. Thayer. *Fr.* Keep Your Grit. WBLP
Don't Grow Weary, Boys. *Unknown.* CoSo
Don't Guess, Let Me Tell You. Ogden Nash. SiTL
Don't hurry spring/ the wind still trembles. Spring Song. Rod McKuen. CAD
Don't knock at my door, little child. Black Woman. Georgia Douglas Johnson. BALP
Don't know why I. Angola Question Mark. Langston Hughes. TTY
Don't leave/ wait. Turning. Sophia Castro-Leon. QAH
Don't let me lose you. How Tuesday Began. Kathleen Fraser. NYBP
Don't, like the cat, try to get more out. Don't Copy Cat. "Mark Twain." TreFT
Don't Look Now but Mary Is Everybody. Peter Viereck. LiTA; LiTM (rev ed.); ReMP
Don't love me, my sweet. Song of a Common Lover. Flavien Ranaivo. TTY
Don't neglect the quiet hour. Communion. J. L. Spicer. BLRP
Don't Pay. Ruby C. Saunders. WSL
"Don't pick all the flowers!" cried Daisy one day. Meadow Talk. Nora Archibald Smith. PPL
Don't pull off my boots and pull off my hat. The Dying Desperado. *Unknown.* CoSo
Don't Quit. *Unknown.* BLPA; SoP; STF
(You Mustn't Quit.) PoToHe
Don't Say You Like Tchaikowsky. Paul Rosner. FiBHP
Don't seek me where the myrtles bloom! My Camping Ground. Morris Rosenfeld. TrJP
"Don't send my boy to Harvard," the dying mother said. Old College Song with Variant Lines to Suit. *Unknown.* TreFT
Don't shirk. Proverbs: Good Advice [*or* Old German Mottos: Advice]. *Unknown, ad. by* Louis Untermeyer. RIS; StaSt; TiPo (1952 ed.)
Don't Sit under the Apple Tree With Anyone Else but Me. Robert Pack. CoPo
Don't stand at night by the gate, love. War Poem. Henry Treece. MaRV
Don't Talk about It, *with music.* *Unknown.* OuSiCo
Don't talk with food in your mouth. The Age of Gold. Sotère Torregian. YAP
Don't Tell All You Know. *Unknown.* PCH
Don't Tell Me. *Unknown.* STF
Don't tell me of buds and blossoms. Answer to Pauper. Thomas Hood. NBM
Don't tell Papa his nose is red. Harry Graham. *Fr.* A Children's Don't. BBGG
Don't tell your friends about your indigestion. Of Tact [*or* How Are You?]. Arthur Guiterman. MoShBr; WhC
Don't throw your arms around me in that way. Footnote to John II: 4. R. A. K. Mason. AnNZ
Don't Trouble Trouble. Mark Guy Pearse. MaRV; SoP; WBLP
Don't waste your time in longing. Shine Just Where You Are. *Unknown.* STF
Don't Worry. Elizabeth Porter Gould. FaChP

Don't worry about growing old. Prayerwheel 2. David Meltzer. NeAP
Don't you hear the big spurs jingle? The Dance at Silver Valley. William Maxwell. SCC
Don't You Hurry Worry with Me, *with music. Unknown.* OuSiCo
Don't You Like It? *with music. Unknown.* OuSiCo
Don't you remember sweet Alice, Ben Bolt. Ben Bolt. Thomas Dunn English. AA; AmePo; FaBoBe; FaFP; HBV; TreF
Don't you remember sweet Betsey from Pike. *See* Oh, don't you remember . . .
"Don't you take no sail off 'er," the Ol' Man said. What the Old Man Said. Cicely Fox Smith. EtS
Don't you think it's probable. Little Talk. Aileen Fisher. FaPON
Don't you think the trees remember. Ambition. Anne Blackwell Payne. GFA
Don't you trouble trouble till trouble troubles you. Don't Trouble Trouble. Mark Guy Pearse. MaRV; WBLP
Don'tcha worry, honey chile. On Limited Warfare. *Unknown.* SiTL
Don'ts. D. H. Lawrence. LiTB; LiTM; OxBoLi
Donzella and the *Ceylon,* The, *with music. At. to* Daniel Smith. ShS
Doodledy, doodledy, doodledy, dan. *Unknown.* OxNR
Dooley Is a Traitor. James Michie. NePoEA-2
Doom. Arthur O'Shaughnessy. MoBrPo (1942 ed.); OBVV
Doom-Bar, The. Alice E. Gillington. VA
Doom-devoted. Louis Golding. HBMV
Doom is Dark [and Deeper Than Any Sea-Dingle]. W. H. Auden. EnL; LiTB; UnPo
(Chorus.) GTBS-P; MoAB; MoBrPo
(Something Is Bound to Happen.) CMoP; CoBMV; EnLit; OAEP (2d ed.); PoRA
Doom of Beauty, The. Michelangelo, *tr. fr. Italian by* John Addington Symonds. AWP; JAWP; LiTW; WBP
Doom of Devorgoil, The, *sels.* Sir Walter Scott.
Bonny Dundee, *fr.* II, ii. BEL; EnRP; FaBoCh; HBV; LoGBV; OBRV; OxBoLi; OxBS; SeCeV; TOP
(Bonnie Dundee.) OTPC (1923 ed.); Par, *abr.*
Datur Hora Quieti, *fr.* I. GTBS; GTBS-D; GTBS-P; GTBS-W; GTSE; GTSL
Doomed. *Unknown.* CIV
Doomed City, The. Poe. *See* City in the Sea, The.
Doomed in the depths to dwell. Thanksgiving. David Abenatar Melo. TrJP
Doomed Man, The. Joseph Addison Alexander. *Fr.* The Hidden Line. MaRV; SoP; TRV
Doomed to death bodies opposed in defiance. To the Dead of the Revolution. Ernst Toller. PoFr
Dooms-Day. George Herbert. MaMe; SCEP-1; SeCP; SeCV-1
Doomsday. Elinor Wylie. CrMA
Doomsday Morning. Genevieve Taggard. MAP; MoAmPo
Doomsday Thought, A. Thomas Flatman. CEP
Doon Deeside cam Inverey. The Baron of Braikley. *Unknown.* OxBB
Door, The. W. H. Auden. Sonn
Door, The. Robert Creeley. NaP; NeAP; ToPo
Door, The. Mary Carolyn Davies. HBMV
Door, The. Robert Graves. LiTB
Door, The. Orrick Johns. NP
Door, The. Leonard A. G. Strong. MoBrPo
Door and the Window, The. Henry Reed. NeBP
Door and Window Bolted Fast. Mani Leib, *tr. fr. Yiddish by* Joseph Leftwich. TrJP
Door at the End of Our Garden, The. Frederic E. Weatherly. OTPC (1946 ed.)
Door behind me was you, The. You (I). Tom Clark. ANYP; YAP
Door closed against the splinters. Old Seawoman. Gordon LeClaire. CaP
Door creaks in the house, A. Outside the window. Scenario. D. S. Savage. NeBP
Door is on the latch to-night, The. The Romance of a Christmas Card [*or* Christmas Eve]. Kate Douglas Wiggin. MaRV; OQP; TRV
"Door is shut fast, The." Who's In? Elizabeth Fleming. BoTP; BrR; MoSiPe
Door-Mats. Mary Carolyn Davies. HBMV; YaD
Door of Death, The. Blake. *Fr.* Dedication of the Illustrations to Blair's "Grave." ChTr
(To the Queen.) EnRP
Door of existence, beacon of our haze. Bernard O'Dowd. *Fr.* Alma Venus. PoAu-1
Door still swinging to, and girls revive, The. A Dream of Fair Women. Kingsley Amis. NMP
Door to the Future, The. Dick Gallup. ANYP
Door was bolted and the windows of my porch, The. The Milkman. Isabella Gardner. NePA
Door was shut, as doors should be, The. Jack Frost. "Gabriel Setoun." BoTP; DD; GFA; HBV; HBVY; MPB; OTPC
Door was shut, The. I looked between. Shut Out. Christina Rossetti. NoP
Door-Bell, The. Charlotte Becker. PoToHe (new ed.)
Doorbells. Rachel Field. FaPON; GaP; StVeCh (1955 ed.); TiPo
Door-Keeper Has Big Feet, The. Sappho, *tr. fr. Greek by* Virginia Tufte. HW
Doors. Hermann Hagedorn. AnAmPo; PFY
Doors, The. Lloyd Mifflin. AA
Doors. Carl Sandburg. LOW
Doors are shut, the windows fast, The. Canadian Folk Song. Wilfred Campbell. PCH; VA
Doors close fly. Dry July. Arnold Adoff. CAD
Doors flapped open in Ulysses's house, The. The Return. Edwin Muir. CMoP; MoPW
Doors in the Temple, The, *abr.* William Watson, *sometimes at. to* George Mathesen. OQP
Doors of the Temple. Aldous Huxley. HBMV
Doors that knew no shrill alarming bell, The. James Thomson. *Fr.* The Castle of Indolence. ViBoPo
Doors were cedar, The. Four Preludes on Playthings of the Wind, II. Carl Sandburg. AmLP; AnAmPo; AnFE; CoBA; InP; MAP; MoAB; MoAmPo; NePA; NP; SeCeV
Doors, where my heart was used to beat. In Memoriam A. H. H., CXIX. Tennyson. DiPo; EPN; OBNC; PoEL-5; ViPo; VP
Doorstep, The. Edmund Clarence Stedman. HBV; LHV
Doppelganger, The. Daryl Hine. *See* Double-Goer, The.
Dora. Thomas Edward Brown. OBEV (1st ed.); PoVP
Dora. Howard McCord. YAP
Dora Markus. Eugenio Montale, *tr. fr. Italian by* Maurice English. OnHM
Dora versus Rose. Austin Dobson. ALV; BOHV
Doralicia's Song. Robert Greene. *See* In Time We See That Silver Drops.
Doran's Ass. *Unknown.* OnYI
Dorcas. George Macdonald. OBVV
Dorchester Giant, The. Oliver Wendell Holmes. FaPON; MPB; OnMSP
Doré knew this overhang. View from the Gorge. Ben Belitt. NYBP
Δώρια (Doria). Ezra Pound. FIW; MAP; MoAB; MoAmPo; MoVE; NP; PoIE; ViBoPo
Doric. Angelos Sikelianos, *tr. fr. Greek by* Edmund Kelley *and* Philip Sherrard. ErPo
Doricha. Poseidippus, *tr. fr. Greek by* E. A. Robinson. AWP; JAWP; WBP
Dorinda. Charles Sackville. *See* Song: "Dorinda's sparkling wit, and eyes."
Doris; a Pastoral. Arthur Joseph Munby. HBV; VA
Doris, I that could repell. The Snow-Ball. Thomas Stanley. CavP
Doris, see the amorous flame. *Unknown.* SeCSL
Dorking Thigh, The. William Plomer. WePo
Dormi, Jesu, mater ridet. Latin Lullaby. *Unknown.* CAW
Dormouse, The. Charlotte Druitt Cole. BoTP
Dormouse and the Doctor, The. A. A. Milne. WhC
Dormouse felt so sleepy, The. The Dormouse. Charlotte Druitt Cole. BoTP
Doron's Description of Samela. Robert Greene. *Fr.* Menaphon. AtBAP; LoBV; PoEL-2; ReIE; SiCE; TuPP
(Samela.) EIL; HBV; OBEV; OBSC; ViBoPo
Doron's Jig [*or* Jigge]. Robert Greene. *Fr.* Menaphon. AtBAP; PoEL-2; TuPP
(Jig, A.) EIL
Dorothea. Sarah N. Cleghorn. HBMV
Dorothy. Alfred Kreymborg. AnAmPo
Dorothy. Rose Hawthorne Lathrop. AA
Dorothy; a Country Story, *sels.* Arthur Joseph Munby. VA

Beauty at the Plough.
Country Kisses.
Dorothy.
Dorothy's Room.
Dorothy goes with her pails to the ancient well in the court-yard. Dorothy. Arthur Joseph Munby. *Fr.* Dorothy; a Country Story. VA
Dorothy Q. Oliver Wendell Holmes. AA; AmPP (3d ed.); AnNE; AP; CoBA; HBV; InMe; OnPP; TreFS
Dorothy's Room. Arthur Joseph Munby. *Fr.* Dorothy; a Country Story. VA
Dorus His Comparisons. Sir Philip Sidney. *See* My Sheep Are Thoughts.
Dorus's Song. Sir Philip Sidney. *See* O Sweet Woods.
Dosn't [*or* Doesn't] thou 'ear my 'erse's legs, as they canters awaäy? Northern Farmer: New Style. Tennyson. BOHV; BoLiVe; EPN; MBW-2; PeVV; PoVP; ShBV-4; ViPo
Dosser in Springtime, The. Douglas Stewart. ErPo; TDP
Dost ask (my dear) what service I will have? Robert Burton, *after the Latin of* Terence. *Fr.* The Anatomy of Melancholy. LO
Dost deem him weak that owns his strength is tried? The Strong. John Vance Cheney. AA
Dost not thou Castara read? A Dialogue betweene Araphill and Castara. William Habington. AnAnS-2
Dost see how unregarded now? Sonnet. Sir John Suckling. AnAnS-2; ELP; SCEP-2
Dost think he whom thy liberal table drew. Martial. Thomas Heyrick. CaVP
Dost thou deem that thyself. "Te Judice." Frederick George Scott. PeCV
Dost thou in conscience think—tell me, Emilia. Shakespeare. *Fr.* Othello, IV iii. MyFE
Dost thou look back on what hath been. In Memoriam A. H. H., LXIV. Tennyson. EPN; ViPo; VP
Dost thou not hear? Amid dun, lonely hills. An Aeolian Harp. "Michael Field." VA
Dost Thou not see about our feet. Edgar Lee Masters. *Fr.* Supplication. MaRV
Dost thou remember ever, for my sake. Mathilde Blind. *Fr.* Love in Exile. OBNC
Dost thou remember, friend of vanished days. In Tuscany. Eric Mackay. VA
Dost Thou Remember Me? Emily Dickinson. *See* Saviour, I've no one else to tell.
Dost thou still hope thou shalt be fair. The Fair Inconstant. Francis Thompson. GTSE
Dostoievsky to a Young Communist. Daniel J. Honan. JKCP (1955 ed.)
Dot is five and Jack is ten. A Puzzling Example. Virginia Sarah Benjamin. BiCB
Dotage. George Herbert. MaMe
Doth it not thrill thee, Poet. The Passionate Reader to His Poet. Richard Le Gallienne. HBV; VA
Doth love live in beauty's eyes? A Solemn Conceit. Nicholas Breton. SiCE
Doth most humbly show it. The Humble Petition of Poor Ben to the Best of Monarchs, Masters, Men, King Charles. Ben Jonson. PP
Doth Not a Tenarif, or Higher Hill. John Donne. *Fr.* An Anatomy of the World: The First Anniversary. ChTr
Doth not our chiefest bliss then lie. Chorus. Sidney Godolphin. LO
Doth not wisdom cry? and understanding put forth her voice? Proverbs, Bible, *O.T.* BoC
Doth some one say that there be gods above? There Are No Gods. Euripides. *Fr.* Bellerophon. EaLo
Doth Then the World Go Thus. William Drummond of Hawthornden. GTBS; GTSL
("Doth then the world go thus, doth all thus move?") GTBS-D; GTBS-P; GTBS-W; GTSE
Doting father once there was, A. Piano Practice. Ian Serraillier. BBGG
Double, The. Irving Feldman. NYBP
Double Ballad of Good Counsel, A. Villon, *tr. fr. French by* Swinburne. AWP
Double Ballade of Life and Fate. W. E. Henley. PoVP
Double Ballade of Primitive Man. Andrew Lang *and* Edward Burnett Tylor. BOHV; CenHV
(Ballade of Primitive Man, 3 *sts.*) ATP
Double Crucifixion, The. John Malcolm Brinnin. LiTM (rev. ed.)
Double-Dealer, The, *sel.* Congreve.
Ancient Phyllis. SeCL
Double Duty. W. E. Farbstein. PoPl; WhC
Double flower we are, A. A Waltz in the Afternoon. Beth Bentley. BoLP
Double Fortress, The. Alfred Noyes. GoBC
Double Gift. *Unknown, tr. fr. Greek by* Louis Untermeyer. UnTE
Double Goer, The. Daryl Hine. MoCV
(Doppelganger, The.) OBCV
Double-Headed Snake, The. John Newlove. MoCV
Double-Headed Snake of Newbury, The. Whittier. AmePo
Double Marriage, The, *sel.* John Fletcher *and* Philip Massinger.
" 'Tis a substantial thing, and not a word," *fr.* V, i. PoFr
Double Monologue. Adrienne Rich. NePoEA-2; NoP
Double moon, The. River Moons. Carl Sandburg. FIW
Double Play, The. Robert Wallace. PP; SD
Double Red Daisies. Robert Graves. PCH
Double Rock, The Henry King. AtBAP; CLwM
(Sonnet: Double Rock, The.) AnAnS-2; SeCP
Double Sestine. Sir Philip Sidney. *Fr.* Arcadia. AtBAP; LiTB; PoEL-1
(Sestina.) LiTG; StP
(Ye Goatherd Gods.) NoP
("Ye goat-herd gods that love the grassy mountains.") BWP; FCP; SiCE
Double Shame, The. Stephen Spender. GTBS-W; LiTB; LiTL; LiTM (rev. ed.)
Double Star, A. David McCord. MAP
Double Tree, The. Winfield Townley Scott. PoPl
Double Vision, The. C. Day Lewis. AtBAP
Doubled Mirrors. Kenneth Rexroth. OPoP
Doubt. Elinor Chipp. HBMV
Doubt. Margaret Deland. MaRV; TrPWD
Doubt. Fernand Gregh. WGRP
Doubt. Helen Hunt Jackson. WGRP
Doubt. Robert Cameron Rogers. AA
Doubt. Sara Teasdale. LO
Doubt. Tennyson. *See* In Memoriam A. H. H.: "You say, but with no touch of scorn."
Doubt and Prayer. Tennyson. EPN
Doubt me, my dim companion! Emily Dickinson. ViBoPo
Doubt no longer miracles. Miracles. Arna Bontemps. GoSl; PoNe
Doubt of Future Foes, The. Elizabeth I, Queen of England. CTC; TuPP
(Daughter of Debate, The.) LiBL, 1 *st.*; OBSC
("Doubt of future foes exiles my present joy, The.") ReEn; SiCE
Doubt of Martyrdom, A. Sir John Suckling. BEL; EnLi-1; HBV; OBEV
(Actuality.) LoBV
("O! for some honest lovers ghost.") CBEP; EnL; FosPo; Par
(Sonnet: "Oh! for some honest lovers ghost.") AnAnS-2; ATP; FaBoEn; MeLP; MePo; OBS; PoEL-3; ReEn; SCEP-2; SeCP; SeCV-1; SeEP
Doubt there hath been, when with his golden chain. Astrophel and Stella, LVIII. Sir Philip Sidney. FCP; ReEN; SiPS
Doubt which ye misdeem, fair love, is vain, The. Amoretti, LXV. Spenser. SiCE; Sonn
Doubt you to whom my Muse these notes entendeth. Astrophel and Stella: First Song. Sir Philip Sidney. AtBAP; ElL; FCP; HBV; LiTL; OBSC; PoFS; ReIE; SiCE; SiPS; Sonn; TuPP; WHA
Doubter, The. Richard Watson Gilder. TrPWD
(Christ the Answer, *with add. st., at. to* George Macdonald.) MaRV
Doubter's Prayer, The. Anne Brontë. MaRV; TrPWD; WGRP
Doubtful Choice, A. Edward de Vere, Earl of Oxford. *See* Were I a King.
Doubting Heart, A. Adelaide Anne Proctor. HBV; VA
Doubting Thomas and loving John. Dare You? Edward Rowland Sill. AnNE
Doubts. Rupert Brooke. CH; SiSw
Doubts ("Our doubts are traitors"). Shakespeare. *Fr.* Measure for Measure, I, iv. MaRV

Douglas, Douglas, Tender and True. Dinah Maria Mulock Craik. BLPA; NeHB; TreF
(Douglas.) OBVV
(Too Late.) HBV; VA
Douglas Gordon. Frederic Edward Weatherly. VA
Douglas Tragedy, The *diff. versions. Unknown.* BoLiVe; HBV; MaC; MeWo; NoP; OBB; OnSP; OxBB; PAn; PoPo; TrGrPo
(Earl Brand.) BaBo (A *and* B *vers.*); ESPB (A, B, *and* F *vers.*); OBB (A *vers., sl. abr.*); OxBB; ViBoFo (A *and* B *vers.*)
(Seven Sleepers, The, *with music.*) BFSS
(Sweet William, *with music.*) OuSiCo
Doun throu the sea. Cokkils. Sydney Goodsir Smith. OxBS
Dour thing in olive trees, The. Olive Trees. Bernard Spencer. FaBoMo
Dove, The. William Barnes. BiS
Dove, The. Walter de la Mare. CBV
Dove, The. T. S. Eliot. *Fr.* Four Quartets: Little Gidding. BoC
Dove, The. Judah Halevi, *tr. fr. Hebrew by* Amy Levy. TrJP
Dove, The. Keats. *See* I Had a Dove.
Dove and the Wren, The. *Unknown.* RIS
(Country Rhyme.) ThGo
Dove Apologizes to His God for Being Caught by a Cat, The. Anthony Eaton. PeSA
Dove colored, the shadows melt and mingle. Twilight. Feodor Tyutchev. OnPM
Dove descending breaks the air, The. The Dove. T. S. Eliot. *Fr.* Four Quartets. BoC
Dove of Dacca, The. Kipling. GN
Dove of New Snow, The. Vachel Lindsay. MAP; MoAmPo
Dove of rarest worth, A. The Dove. Judah Halevi. TrJP
Dove once pulled up a cyclamen. Three Paintings by Arthur Dove. Ronald Johnson. YAP
Dove returns; it found no resting place, The. Where We Must Look for Help. Robert Bly. NePoEA
Dove, The, says, "Coo, coo, what shall I do?" Mother Goose. BoTP; OxNR; PCH
Dove sta amore. Lawrence Ferlinghetti. *Fr.* A Coney Island of the Mind. ToPo
Dove walks with sticky feet, The. Pastoral. Kenneth Patchen. AtBAP; NaP
Dover Beach. Matthew Arnold. AnEnPo; ATP; AWP; BEL; BoLiVe; BoLP; BoPe; BWP; CABA; CaFP; CBEP; CBV; CoBE; DiPo; DTC; EaLo; EnL; EnLi-2; EnLit; EPN; EtS; ExPo; FaBoBe; FaBoEn; FaBV; FaFP; FaPL; FiP; ForPo; FosPo; GBV; GTBS-D; GTBS-P; GTBS-W; GTSL; HBV; HoPM; ILP; InP; InPo; InvP; JAWP; LiTB; LiTG; LiTL; LoBV; MaPo; MaRV; MasP; MaVP; MBW-2; MCCG; MeWo; NeHB; NoP; OAEP; OBNC; OBVV; OTPC (1946 ed.); OuHeWo; PAn; PeVV; PG; PIA; Po; PoAn; PoE; PoEL-5; PoFS; PoIE; PoPl; PoPo; PoRA; PoSa; PoVP; PPON; PTK; SeCePo; SeCeV; StP; TDP; TIHL; TOP; TreFS; TrGrPo; TRV; UnPo; VA; VaPo; ViBoPo; ViPo; ViPP; VP; WBP; WHA; YAT
Sels.
Ah, Love, Let Us Be True. OQP
"Sea is calm tonight, The." FlW; WePo
"Dover Beach"—A Note to That Poem. Archibald MacLeish. CBV; NoP
Dover Bitch, The. Anthony Hecht. CBV; NePoEA-2; PP
Dover Cliff. F. Wyville Home. VA
Dover Cliffs. William Lisle Bowles. HBV; Sonn
(At Dover Cliffs.) EnRP; ViBoPo
(Sonnet: At Dover Cliffs, July 20, 1787.) CEP; OBEC
Doves. E. J. Falconer. BoTP
Doves, The. Katharine Tynan. AnIV; AWP; JAWP; WBP
Dove's Loneliness, The. George Darley. OBNC
Dove's Nest. Joseph Russell Taylor. HBV
Doves of Venice, The. Laurence Hutton. AA
Doves that coo in Colomen, The. Colomen. Mary H. Webb. LoEn
Dowie Houms [*or* Dens] o' Yarrow, The. *Unknown.* GoTS; OBB; OBEV; OBS; OxBS
(Braes o' Yarrow, The.) BaBo; BFSS (A *and* B *vers., with music*); ESPB (A *and* E *vers.*); OXBB; ViBoFo
Down/ Down into the fathomless depths. Black Is a Soul. Joseph White. IDB
"Down a down!" Phoebe's Sonnet. Thomas Lodge. ViBoPo
Down a hill, then up a hill. An Autumn Road. Glenn Ward Dresbach. HBMV
Down a Sunny Easter Meadow. Nancy Byrd Turner. SiSoSe; SoPo
Down a Woodland Way. Mildred Howells. AA
Down Among the Dead Men. William Morris. PoVP
Down among the Wharves. Eleanore Myers Jewett. EtS
Down and Out. Clarence Leonard Hay. BeLS; BLPA
Down around the quay they lie, the ships that sail to sea. The Port o' Heart's Desire. John S. McGroarty. HBV
Down at the hall at midnight sometimes. Dance. Lula Lowe Weeden. CDC
Down below the combers drape. At Manly. Leonard Mann. MoAuPo
Down by the church-way walk, and where the brook. An Ancient Virgin. George Crabbe. *Fr.* The Parish Register. OBNC
Down by the bridge/ They sit and wait. Water-Front. Cecil ffrench Salkeld. OnYI
Down by the flash of the restless water. Ballade of a Ship. E. A. Robinson. TSW
Down by the Glenside. Peadar Kearney. AnIV
Down by the meadows, chasing butterflies. *Unknown.* BoTP
Down by the Old Mill Stream. John Read. TreFS
Down by the railroad in a green valley. Eye-Witness. Ridgely Torrence. HBMV
Down by the river. *Unknown.* OxNR
Down by the Salley Gardens. W. B. Yeats. BoLP; CMoP; CTC; EnLi-2 (1949 ed.); EnLoPo; GTBS-D; HBV; OBEV (new ed.); OBVV; OnYI; OxBI; PG; PoEL-5; POTE; ShBV-3; ViPo (1962 ed.)
(Old Song Resung, An.) BoLiVe; MoAB; MoBrPo; NeMA; VA
(Salley Gardens, The.) EG
Down by yon garden green. The Laird of Wariston [*or* Waristoun] (A *vers.*). *Unknown.* BaBo; ESPB
Down by yon weeping willow. The Jealous Lover [*or* Fair Florella]. *Unknown.* BaBo (A *vers.*); ViBoFo
"Down cellar," said the cricket. The Potatoes' Dance. Vachel Lindsay. BoChLi; FaPON; MPB; SP; SUS
Down, deeper down, thou sinful, sensual Self. Spiritual Conflict. Henry W. Frost. SoP
Down! Down! Eleanor Farjeon. SoPo; SUS; TiPo
Down, down—born pioneers in time's despite. Hart Crane. *Fr.* The Bridge: The River. TrGrPo
Down, Down Derry Down, *with music. Unknown.* AS
Down, Down, Down, *with music.* William Keating. OuSiCo
Down drop of the blackbird, The. Three Spring Notations on Bipeds. Carl Sandburg. AWP; InPo; JAWP; WBP
Down every passage of the cloister hung. Upon the Death of George Santayana. Anthony Hecht. AmLP; CoPo; NePA
Down from a drummed steel highway. Arrowhead Field. Lawrence Hetrick. TPM
Down from a sunken doorstep to the road. Romance. Mildred Howells. AA
Down from her dainty head. The Lily Princess. *Unknown.* MPB
Down from her head the earth has rolled. Nightfall. Feodor Tyutchev. LiTW
Down from his post in the tower. Across the Straits. Rosemary Dobson. PoAu-2
Down from the branches fall the leaves. Winter Love Song. *Unknown.* LiTW
Down from the neck unto that dainty breast. Robert Tofte. *Fr.* Laura. ReIE
Down from the rocky western steep. The Flock at Evening. Odell Shepard. HBMV
Down Hall. Matthew Prior. CEP
"Come here, my sweet Landlady, pray, how d'ye do?" *sel.* MyFE
Down hill I came, hungry, and yet not starved. *See* Downhill I came . . .
Down in a bed, and on a bed of down. An Elegy. Giles Fletcher. *Fr.* Licia. ReIE
Down in a Coal Mine. J. B. Geoghegan. TreFS
Down in a dark dungeon I saw a brave knight. *Unknown.* PPL
Down in a deep dark ditch sat an old cow munching a beanstalk. Hexameter and Pentameter. *Unknown.* ChTr
Down in a field, one day in June. Discontent. Sarah Orne Jewett. PRWS; TVC
Down in a Garden. *Unknown.* ALV; CBEP; SeCL; SeEP

(Riddle, The.) UnTE
Down in a garden golden. The Rose's Cup. Frank Dempster Sherman. AA
Down in a garden sat my dearest love. Down in a Garden. *Unknown.* ALV; CBEP; SeCL; SeEP; UnTE
Down in a green and shady bed. The Violet. Jane Taylor. BoChLi; HBV; HBVY; OTPC; PRWS; RIS; TreF; TVC
Down in a lonesome valley. Fair Florella; or, The Jealous Lover (B *vers.*). *Unknown.* BaBo
Down in a Wine Vault. Don Marquis. WhC
Down in adoration falling. Tantum Ergo Sacramentum. *Unknown.* WHL
Down in Alabama I was born. Roll the Cotton Down, *vers.* II. *Unknown.* ShS
Down in Carlisle there lived a lady. The Lady of Carlisle. *Unknown.* OuSiCo
Down in Dallas. X. J. Kennedy. CoPo
Down in Dumbarton there wonnd a rich merchant. Bonnie Annie (B *vers.*). *Unknown.* ESPB
Down in front of Casey's old brown wooden stoop. The Sidewalks of New York. James W. Blake. BLPA; FaBoBe; TreFS; YaD
Down in Lehigh Valley. *Unknown.* TreF
Down in New Mexico, where the plains are brown and sere. Old Buck's Ghost. Frank Benton. PoOW
Down in old Kentucky. Ballad of the Lincoln Penny. Alfred Kreymborg. YaD
Down in our cellar on a Monday and a Tuesday. Old Ellen Sullivan. Winifred Welles. FaPON; GaP; MPB; TiPo
Down in St. Louis at 12th and Carr. Brady (A *vers.*). *Unknown.* AS
Down in the bleak December bay. The *Mayflower.* Erastus Wolcott Ellsworth. AA; FaBoBe; HH; MC; PAH
Down [*or* Downe] in the depth of mine iniquity. Caelica, XCIX. Fulke Greville. EnRePo; EP; ForPo; LiTG; LoBV (2d ed.); OBS; PoIE; QFR; SiCE
Down in the grassy hollow. Merry Little Men. Kathleen M. Chaplin. BoTP
Down in the grassy lowland dells. Lilies of the Valley. Marion Mitchell Walker. GFA
Down in the Hollow. Aileen Fisher. SoPo; SUS
Down in the land of the center-fire saddle. *Unknown.* *Fr.* Up the Trail. CoSo
Down in the meadow, sprent with dew. Revelation. Alice Brown. *Fr.* The Road to Castaly. WGRP
Down in the Meadows. *Unknown.* CBEP
Down in the meadows fresh and gay. Deep in Love. *Unknown.* CBEP
Down in the meadows the other day. Down in the Meadows. *Unknown.* CBEP
Down in the park the children play. Song at Summer's End. A. R. D. Fairburn. AnNZ
Down in the rushes beside the pool. The Frogs' Singing-School. E. T. Carbell. SoPo
Down in the silent hallway. Unsatisfied Yearning. Richard Kendall Munkittrick. BOHV; InMe; PoMa
Down in the South, by the waste without sail on it. Beyond Kerguelen. Henry C. Kendall. BoAu; PoAu-1
Down in the Valley. *Unknown.* ABF, *with music*; AS, *with music*; FaFP; SiTL; TreFT
Down in the villages. The Murmuring of Pine Trees. Ryokwan. OnPM
Down in the west the shadows rest. Canoe Song at Twilight. Laura E. McCully. CaP
Down in yon garden sweet and gay. Willy Drowned in Yarrow. *Unknown.* GTBS-D; GTBS-P; GTBS-W
Down in Yonder Meadow. *Unknown.* CH
Down lay in a nook my lady's brach. Song. Sir Henry Taylor. *Fr.* Philip van Artevelde. VA
Down lay the shepherd swain. Pastoral Verses on Two Lovers. *Unknown.* CLwM
Down London Lanes, with swinging reins. Mosby at Hamilton. Madison Cawein. PAH
Down looked the moon, but looked no more. John Francis O'Donnell. *Fr.* Happy Christmases. IrPN
Down near the end of a wandering lane. A Rhyme of the Dream-Maker Man. William Allen White. PoLF
Down near "The river." Spring of Work Storm. Joseph Ceravolo. ANYP
Down Newport Street, last Sunday night. Newport Street, E. Douglas Goldring. HBMV
Down on My luck. A. R. D. Fairburn. AnNZ
Down on Roberts' Farm. Claude Reeves. ThLM
Down on the beach when the tide is out. Treasures. Mary Dixon Thayer. MPB; SoPo
Down on the big ranch, down where I lived. Allá en El Rancho Grande. *Unknown.* ABF
Down on the flat of the lake. Lake Harvest. Raymond Knister. AnCaPo; PeCV
Down on the shadowed stream of time and tears. Christ and the Mourners. Katherine E. Conway. ChIP; OQP
Down on the sunlit ebb with the wind in her sails and free. On the Embankment. W. W. Gibson. PoFr
Down on your knees, boys, holystone the decks. Cleaning Ship. Charles Keeler. EtS
Down South on the Rio Grande. *Unknown.* CoSo
Down stepped her old father dear. Lady Maisry (B *vers.*). *Unknown.* BaBo
Down, swelling thought, and do not press. His Despair. T. Beaumont. SeCL
Down swept the chill wind from the mountain peak. The Brook in Winter [*or* December]. James Russell Lowell. *Fr.* The Vision of Sir Launfal: Prelude to Pt. II. GN; GoTP; OTPC; TreF
Down the Bayou. Mary Ashley Townsend. AA; AnAmPo
Down the black highway where no whisper stirs. Sonnets from a Sequence, XXIV. Shirley Barker. AnAmPo
Down the blue night the unending columns press. Clouds. Rupert Brooke. BoC; BrPo; GTSL; MoVE; OBEV (new ed.); OBMV; POTE
Down the bright stream the Fairies float. The Last Voyage of the Fairies. William H. Davenport Adams. HBVY; PRWS
Down the carved hills the bison come. Gates of the Rockies. James Daugherty. RePo
Down the centuries, eternal. From a Venetian Sequence. Adèle Naudé. PeSA
Down the close, darkening lanes they sang their way. The Send-off. Wilfred Owen. BrPo; LiTB; MoAB; MoBrPo (1950 ed.); MoVE
Down the dawn-brown. The Current. James Merrill. NYBP
Down the deep steps of stone, through iron doors. Judgment. William Rose Benét. AnAmPo
Down the dimpled green-sward dancing. Song. George Darley. OnYI
Down the dripping pathway dancing through the rain. Rainy Song. Max Eastman. FaBoBe; HBMV
Down the Field. Rolfe Humphries. AnAmPo
Down the Glimmering Staircase. Siegfried Sassoon. *Fr.* Vigils. PoLF
Down the glutted river's throat. The Floating Island. Ruth Miller. BoSA
Down the goldenest of streams. Mater Amabilis. Emma Lazarus. OHIP
Down the green hillside fro' the castle window. Lady Jane. Sir Arthur Quiller-Couch. FiBHP; InMe; WhC
Down the lane by the Butts in the headlights. Delivering Children. David Holbrook. NePoEA-2
Down the Little Big Horn. Francis Brooks. PAH
Down the long hall she glistens like a star. Venus of the Louvre. Emma Lazarus. AA; AnAmPo
Down the long path beneath the garden wall. A Dream. V. Sackville-West. MoVE
Down the market. *Unknown.* RIS
Down the Mississippi. John Gould Fletcher. HT; LiTA; NP
Sels.
Embarkation, I. AmFN
Moon's Orchestra, The, IV. LaNeLa
Down the Ohio the flatboats go. Anthony Wayne. Arthur Guiterman. TiPo (1959 ed.)
Down the picket-guarded lane. "How Are You, Sanitary?" Bret Harte. PaA; PAP
Down the Rain Falls. Elizabeth J. Coatsworth. PoRh; SoPo
Down the rivers, o'er the prairies. As Brothers Live Together. Longfellow. *Fr.* The Song of Hiawatha, I. TreFT
Down the road someone is practicing [*or* practising] scales. Sunday Morning. Louis MacNeice. CoBMV; FaBoMo; LiTB; MoAB; MoBrPo; MoVE; NeMA; PoE; Sonn
Down the road to Llasa. The Pilgrims of Thibet. Cale Young Rice. PFY
Down the Simplon Pass. Wordsworth. *See* Simplon Pass, The.
Down the slide. Sliding. Marchette Chute. TiPo (1959 ed.)

Down (continued)
Down the stone stairs. After the Opera. D. H. Lawrence. MuSP
Down the street. The Sun-Shower. George Amabile. YAP
Down the street, down the street, flying down the street. Jonathan Bing's Tea. Beatrice Curtis Brown. WaKn
Down the sultry arc of day. Description of a Summer's Eve. Henry Kirke White. OBRV
Down the valleys of Languedoc. At Carcassonne. Winfred Ernest Garrison. OQP
Down the white steps of Heaven Christ came to meet him. Entrance into Heaven. Sara Henderson Hay. ChIP
Down the wintry mountain. Dinah Maria Mulock Craik. *Fr.* Highland Cattle. GN; OTPC
Down the Wolf river. Feasts of Death, Feasts of Love. Stuart Z. Perkoff. NeAP
Down the world with Marna! The Wander-Lovers. Richard Hovey. AA; HBV
Down the Yellowstone, the Milk, the White and Cheyenne. Pare Lorentz. *Fr.* The River. AmFN
Down there a poor woman. The Potter. *Unknown.* TTY
Down through the ancient Strand. Scherzando. W. E. Henley. London Voluntaries, III. BrPo
Down through the rocks where the dark roots dry. The Grave of Arthur. G. K. Chesterton. JKCP (1955 ed.)
Down through the snow-drifts in the street. The Boy. Eugene Field. NA
Down through the spheres that chant the Name of One. The Path of the Stars. Thomas S. Jones, Jr. ChIP; MoRP; WGRP
Down to a bank where it was always evening. The Island. Giuseppe Ungaretti. LiTW
Down to Sleep. Helen Hunt Jackson. GN
Down to the pond came a pretty fawn. Life. Alice Brown. AA
Down to the Puritan marrow of my bones. Puritan Sonnet [*or* Sonnet]. Elinor Wylie. Wild Peaches, IV. InP; LiTA; MAP; MoAB; MoAmPo; NAMP; NeMA; OxBA; TrGrPo
Down toward the deep-blue water, marching to throb of drum. Your Lad, and My Lad. Randall Parrish. MC; PAH
Down valley a smoke haze. Mid-August at Sourdough Mountain Lookout. Gary Snyder. NaP
Down, Wanton, Down! Robert Graves. CMoP; ErPo; FaBoTw; LiTM; SiTL
Down Went McGinty. Joseph Flynn. TreF; YaD
Down went the gunner, a bullet was his fate. Praise the Lord and Pass the Ammunition. Frank Loesser. YaD
Down Wind against the Highest Peaks. Clarence Major. NBP
Down with the lambs. *Unknown.* OxNR
Down with the rosemary and bayes [*or* bays]. Ceremonies for Candlemas Eve. Robert Herrick. ILP; OAEP; OBS; OTPC; SeEP
Down with the rosemary and so. A Ceremony for Candlemas Day [*or* Ceremony upon Candelmas Eve]. Robert Herrick. OTPC; PoRL
Down, you mongrel, Death! The Poet and His Book. Edna St. Vincent Millay. AmLP; MAP; MoAmPo; NePA
Downe downe afflicted soule and paie thy due. *Unknown.* SeCSL
Downe in a dale satt a nimph weeping. *Unknown.* SeCSL
Downe in a vale there satt a shepherdesse. *Unknown.* SeCSL
Downe in the depth of mine iniquity. *See* Down in the depth . . .
Downe to the King's most bright-kept baths they went. Homer. *Fr.* The Odyssey. CTC
Downe too farre usurping day. *Unknown.* SeCSL
Downfall of Heathendom, The. *Unknown, tr. fr. Irish by* Frank O'Connor. KiLC
Downfall of Piracy, The. *At. to* Benjamin Franklin. PAH
Downfall of the Gael, The. Fearflatha O'Gnive, *tr. fr. Late Middle Irish by* Sir Samuel Ferguson. AnIV; AWP; JAWP; OnYI; WBP
Downfall of the Tyrant. Isaiah, XIV: 4-19, Bible, *O.T.* TrGrPo
Downgoing. Gustav Davidson. FiSC
Downhill I came, hungry, and yet not starved. The Owl. Edward Thomas. BiS; ChTr; DTC; FaBoTw; GTBS-P; LiTB; MemP; NoP; PoIE; PoSa; UnPo (3d ed.)
Downhill through this upland meadow. Cider. Philip Booth. WIRo
Downing his drink to toasts of cut-rate jokes. 3 for 25. William Jay Smith. WaP
Down-Pullers, The. Walter E. Isenhour. STF
Downright Country-Man, The; or, The Faithful Dairy Maid. *Unknown.* CoMu
Downs will lose the sun, white alyssum, The. Head and Bottle. Edward Thomas. BrPo
Downstream they have killed the river and built a dam. The Fish Counter at Bonneville. William Stafford. AmFN
Downtown-Boy Uptown. David Henderson. NNP; PoNe (1970 ed.)
Downtown Swan Thing, The. Thomas Hanna. QAH
Downward through the evening twilight. Hiawatha's Childhood. Longfellow. *Fr.* The Song of Hiawatha. AnNE; FaBV
Downward was the wheeling Bear. At the Mid Hour of Night. *Unknown.* WoL
Downwards we hurried fast. Down the Simplon Pass [*or* Alpine Descent]. Wordsworth. *Fr.* The Prelude, VI. EPN; WHA
Downy Hair in the Shape of a Flame. Coleman Barks. PV
Dow's Flat—1856. Bret Harte. FaBoBe; HBV; IHA
Dowsabel. Michael Drayton. *See* Cassamen and Dowsabell.
Doxology. Jessica Powers. JKCP (1955 ed.)
Doxology for Peace. R. B. Y. Scott. MaRV
Doxy, oh! thy glaziers shine. The Maunder's Praise of His Strowling Mort. *Unknown.* OxBoLi
Doze, The. James Reeves. GoTP
Dozen machines, A. A Time for Building. Myra Cohn Livingston. PDV
Dozen sandaled saints I see, A. So Runs Our Song. Mary Eva Kitchel. ChIP; PGD
Dozens of girls would storm up. Embraceable You. Ira Gershwin. BoLP
Dozing on sand we make our fresh resolutions. Waiwera. Kendrick Smithyman. AnNZ
Dr. *See* Doctor.
Drab drugget paths protect these polished floors. Fantasia on a Wittelsbach Atmosphere. Siegried Sassoon. MoVE
Draft Horse, The. Robert Frost. CaFP
Draft Riot, The. Charles De Kay. PAH
Drag-Irons, The. E. J. Pratt. CBV
Drag of cans thrown around my mind, The. Crossed Legs. Charles Johnson. WSL
Dragged to her cell. Ed Sanders. *Fr.* Toe Queen Poems. ANYP
Dragging an iron rake. Tractor. William Hart-Smith. AnNZ
Dragon, The. Mary Mullineaux. BoTP
Dragon, The. Spenser. *Fr.* The Faerie Queene, I, 11. SeCePo
Dragon Flies. W. J. Turner. GTBS-D
Dragon of the Seas, The. Thomas Nelson Page. PAH
Dragon that our seas did raise his crest, The. Of the Great and Famous [Sir Francis Drake]. Robert Hayman. CH; FaBoCh; NoP
Dragonfly, The. Chisoku, *tr. fr. Japanese by* Harold G. Henderson. SoPo
Dragonfly, The. W. H. Davies. BoPe
Dragon-Fly, A. Eleanor Farjeon. FaPON; PDV
Dragon-Fly, The. Walter Savage Landor. OBEV (new ed.); OBVV
(Lines to a Dragon Fly.) OBNC; OBRV
Dragonfly, The. Theodore Harding Rand. CaP
Dragon-Fly, The. Tennyson. *Fr.* The Two Voices. OA
Dragon-fly and I together, The. Two of a Trade. Samuel Willoughby Duffield. AA
Dragonfly who hurries by, The. The Elfin Plane. Rowena Bennett. MPB (1956 ed.)
Draherin O Machree. *Unknown.* AnIV
Drake, *sels.* Alfred Noyes.
"Bring on the pomp and pride of old Castile," *fr.* XI. CAW
Drake, who the world hast conquered like a scroll. To the Noble Sir Francis Drake [*or* Epitaph on Drake]. Thomas Beedome. MemP; SeEP
Drake's Drum ("Drake he's in his hammock an' a thousand miles away"). Sir Henry Newbolt. AnFE; EtS; FaBoCh; FOL; GTBS; GTSL; HBV; HBVY; MCCG; MemP; OBMV; OBVV; OnSP; OtMeF; PaPo; PoRA; ShBV-2; TOP; TreF; TSW; WePo
Drama. William Hart-Smith. BoAV; NeLNL

Drama of Exile, A, *sel.* Elizabeth Barrett Browning.
Live and Love. OQP
Dramas of the Rose. James Schevill. FiMAP
Dramatic Fragment. Trumbull Stickney. CBEP; ELU; OxBA
Dramatic Idyls, *sel.* Robert Browning.
Epilogue: "Touch him ne'er so lightly, into song he broke." MBW-2; PoVP
Dramatis Personae, *sel.* Robert Browning.
"That one Face, far from vanish, rather grows," 3 *ll.* ChIP; MaRV
Drank lonesome water. Lonesome Water. Roy Helton. AmFN; MAP; MoAmPo; PoMS; WaKn
Draught of Life, The. Abu-l-Ala al-Maarri, *tr. fr. Arabic by* R. A. Nicholson. LiTW
Draught of Love, The. Meleager, *tr. fr. Greek by* Lord Neaves. OnPM
Draught-Ox, The. Addaeus, *tr. fr. Greek by* Lord Neaves. OnPM
Draw a circle round me thrice. In My End Is My Beginning. Rosemary Dobson. BoAV; NeLNL
Draw a Little Closer. *Unknown.* SoP
Draw a Pail of Water. *Unknown.* BoTP; MoShBr; OxNR
Draw back the cradle curtains, Kate. The King of the Cradle. Joseph Ashby-Sterry. HBV
Draw closer to me, God, than were I one. Prayer of an Unbeliever. Lizette Woodworth Reese. TrPWD
Draw me near [*or* nere], draw me near. The Jolly Juggler [*or* The Magician and the Baron's Daughter]. *Unknown.* EnPo; MeEL; NoP
Draw Me, Saviour, after Thee. Charles Wesley. BePJ
Draw near/ And list what with our council we have done. Richard II Banishes Bolingbroke. Shakespeare. King Richard II, *fr.* I, iii. PoFS
Draw near [*or* neer]/ You lovers that complain. The Exequies. Thomas Stanley. AnAnS-2; MeLP; OBS; SeCL; SeEP
Draw near, and see. Song. *Unknown.* SeCL
Draw near, brave sparks, whose spirits scorn to light. Francis Quarles. Emblems, I, 9. EP
Draw Near, O Son of God. Charles Wesley. BePJ
Draw near to the tables, ye that wear the cloaks. A Connacht Caoine. *Unknown.* AnIV
Draw On, Sweet Night. *Unknown.* TuPP
Draw the blanket of ocean. Convoy. Charles Causley. POTi
Draw thou my soul, O Christ. Closer to Christ. Lucy Larcom. SoP
Draw-to the curtains then, and let it rain. In Time of Suspense. Lawrence Whistler. POTE
Draw up the papers, lawyer. Betsey and I Are Out. Will Carleton. PaPo
Drawer, The. George MacBeth. NePoEA-2
Drawing-Room Ballad, A. Henry Duff Traill. CenHV
Drawn blinds and flaring gas within. City Nights: In Bohemia. Arthur Symons. BrPo; SyP
Drawn by the annual call, we now behold. Players. George Crabbe. *Fr.* The Borough. EiCL
Drawn upward from the glass-green element. From a Porthole in the Ice. William Vincent Sieller. NYTB
Drawn with th' attractive virtue of her eyes. To Delia, XLVIII. Samuel Daniel. ReIE
Dray, The. Laurence Binyon. SyP
Drayman, The. Giovanni Pascoli, *tr. fr. Italian by* Glauco Cambon. OnPM
Drayman, The. Walt Whitman. *Fr.* Song of Myself. PoNE
Dread. J. M. Synge. MoBrPo
Dreadful hour with leaden pace approached, The. Lisy's Parting with Her Cat. James Thomson. CIV
Dread are the death-pale kings. Still-Heart. Frank Pearce Sturm. OBMV
Dread of Height, The. Francis Thompson. JKCP
Dread Potter, in Thine hands we lay. A Pagan's Baptism. A. S. Cripps. BoSA
Dreaded Task, The. Margaret E. Bruner. PoToHe
Dreadful case of murder, A. Execution of Alice Holt. *Unknown.* OxBoLi
Dreadful Story of Pauline and the Matches, The. Heinrich Hoffmann, *tr. fr. German.* CIV
(Harriet and the Matches, *sl. diff.*) RIS
Dreadnought, The, *with music.* *Unknown.* AmSS; ShS (2 *vers.*); SoAmSa
Dream A. William Allingham. OxBI; VA
Dream, A. Matthew Arnold. GTBS-P; SeCePo
Dream, A. Thomas Lovell Beddoes. HoPM
Dream, The. John Peale Bishop. LiTA; LiTM (rev. ed.)
Dream, A. Blake. *Fr.* Songs of Innocence. CBEP; CH; EnRP; MPB; OA; PoRh; TVC
Dream, The. Louise Bogan. LiTA; LiTM; MoAB; MoAmPo (1950 ed.)
Dream, A. Emily Brontë. NBM
Dream. Witter Bynner. MoLP; NP
Dream, The. Byron. BeLS; CABL; ChER; ERoP-2
Dream, The. Chaucer. *Fr.* The Book of the Duchesse. FiP
Dream, A. Hugh Connell. NeIP
Dream. Richard Watson Dixon. LoBV; PeVV
Dream [*or* Dreame], The ("Deare love, for nothing lesse then thee"). John Donne. AnAnS-1; EIL; GTBS-W; InvP; LiTB; LiTG; LiTL; LO; LoBV; MaMe; MBW-1; MeLP; MePo; OAEP; OBEV; OBS; SCEP-1; SeCP; SeEP; TOP
("Deare love, for nothing lesse than thee.") EG
Dreame, The ("Image of her whom I love"). John Donne. Elegies, X. MaMe
Dream. Solomon Edwards. NNP; PoNe (1970 ed.)
Dream, The. "Michael Field." SyP
Dream, A. Mary Fullerton. BoAV
Dream, The. David Ignatow. CoAP
Dream, A. Helen Hunt Jackson. AnFE; APA; CoAnAm
Dream, The. Ben Jonson. *See* Dreame, The.
Dream, A. Keats. *Fr.* The Fall of Hyperion. OBNC
Dream, A. Elizabeth Clementine Kinney. AA
Dream, The. Edwin Markham. OQP
Dream, The. Francis Burdett Money-Coutts. OBVV
Dream. Marianne Moore. NYBP
Dream, A. Stephen Phillips. *See* Apparition, The.
Dream, A. Ruth Pitter. BoPe
Dream, A. Poe. MWA-1
Dream. Alex Raybin. ThO
Dream, The. Theodore Roethke. AmP; MoVE; NoP; NYBP
Dream, A. V. Sackville-West. MoVE
Dream. William Jay Smith. MoVE
Dream, The. Helen Spalding. ChMP
Dream, The. Arthur Symons. SyP
Dream, A ("Benedicite, what dreamed I this night?"). *Unknown.* *See* Benedicite, What Dreamed I . . .
Dream, The ("Last night I supped on lobster"). *Unknown.* OxBoLi
Dream, A. Theodore Watts-Dunton. Sonn
Dream, A. Charles Williams. OBEV (new ed.)
Dream across the Dark. Clifford J. Laube. JKCP (1955 ed.)
Dream after dream I see the wrecks that lie. Posted. John Masefield. Sonn
Dream, after Reading Dante's Episode of Paolo and Francesca, A. Keats. *See* On a Dream.
Dream Again, The. W. S. Merwin. FRC
Dream and Image. Heinrich von Morungen, *tr. fr. German by* Jethro Bithell. LiTW
Dream and the Blood, The. Louis Untermeyer. UnTE
Dream and the Song. James David Corrothers. BANP
Dream as Reported, A. Virginia Earle. GoYe
Dream Boogie. Langston Hughes. AmPP (5th ed.)
Dream Called Life, The. Pedro Calderón de la Barca, *tr. fr. Spanish by* Edward Fitzgerald. AWP; CAW; JAWP; OuHeWo; WBP
Dream-Daemon, The. Lin Carter. FiSC
Dream Data. Robert Duncan. NeAP
Dream Deferred. Langston Hughes. *See* Harlem.
Dream encounters. Otomo no Yakamochi, *tr. fr. Japanese by* I. W. Furukami. LiTW
Dream-fair, beside dream waters, it stands alone. The Shadow House of Lugh. "Ethna Carbery." AnIV
Dream Fairy, The. Thomas Hood. *Fr.* Queen Mab. BoTP
Dream Fantasy. "Fiona Macleod." WGRP
Dream Girl. Carl Sandburg. MoLP
Dream has spilled its genial plenitude, The. Eurydice. Margaret Allonby. BoSA
Dream House. Catherine Parmenter Newell. PoToHe
Dream House, The. Marjorie Allen Seiffert. HBMV
Dream in a dream the heavy soul somewhere. Canto Amor. John Berryman. CoAP; MoAmPo (1950 ed.); MoPo; MoVE; NePA
Dream in Early Spring, A. Fredegond Shove. MoVE

Dream is a cocktail at Sloppy Joe's, The. Havana Dreams. Langston Hughes. GoSl; PoNe
Dream Is a Cradle, The. Anca Vrbovska. WOW
Dream is the thought in the ghost, The. George Meredith. *Fr.* A Faith on Trial. WGRP
Dream it was in which I found myself, A. The Dream Called Life. Pedro Calderón de la Barca. AWP; CAW; JAWP; OuHeWo; WBP
Dream Land. Frances Anne Kemble. OBVV
Dreamland, *sel.* Charles Mair.
"We are not wholly blest who use the earth." CaP
Dream-Land. Poe. AmePo; AmLP; AmP; AmPP; AnFE; AP; APA; CBEP; CoAnAm; CoBA; LiTA; MWA-1; NePA; OxBA; PoFS
Dream Land. Christina Rossetti. EnLi-2; PoVP; ViPo; VP
Dream-Love. Christina Rossetti. CH; GTBS-D; GTSL; NBM; PoEL-5
Dream Motorcycle, The. Pete Winslow. PV
Dream not, O Soul, that easy is the task. Help. Whittier. Sonn
Dream not of noble service elsewhere wrought. Life's Common Duties. Minot J. Savage. WBLP
Dream Observed, A. Anne Ridler. NeBP
Dream of a Baseball Star. Gregory Corso. SD
Dream of a Boy Who Lived at Nine-Elms, The. William Brighty Rands. PPL; RIS
(Dream of a Little Boy Who Lived at Nine-Elms, The.) GaP
Dream of a Decent Death. G. A. Borgese. NePoAm
Dream of a Girl Who Lived at Seven-Oaks, The. William Brighty Rands. OTPC; PPL; RIS
(Dream of a Little Girl Who Lived at Seven-Oaks, The.) GaP
Dream of a Little Boy Who Lived at Nine-Elms, The. William Brighty Rands. *See* Dream of a Boy Who Lived at Nine-Elms, The.
Dream of a Little Girl Who Lived at Seven-Oaks, The. William Brighty Rands. *See* Dream of a Girl Who Lived at Seven-Oaks, The.
Dream of Ængus Og, The. Eleanor Rogers Cox. HBMV
Dream of Apricots, A. James Schevill. NYTB
Dream of Artemis, A, *sel.* Francis Ledwidge.
"God, whose kindly hand doth sow." TrPWD
Dream of Burial, A. James Wright. NaP
Dream of Chiangnan, A. Huang-fu Sung, *tr. fr. Chinese by* C. W. Luh. OnPM
Dream of Dakiki, The. Firdausi, *tr. fr. Persian by* A. V. Williams Jackson. WGRP
Dream of Death, A. "Owen Innsley." AA
Dream of Death, A. W. B. Yeats. POTE
Dream of dolorous women stole my sleep, A. Vampire Bride. Felix Stefanile. FiSC
Dream of Eugene Aram, The. Thomas Hood. BeLS; EnRP; HBV; StPo; VA
Dream of Fair Women, A. Kingsley Amis. NMP
Dream of Fair Women, A, *sels.* Tennyson. BEL; OBRV, *orig. vers.*; ViPo
Sels.
As When a Man, *first* 4 *sts. of orig. vers.* ChER
(Balloon, The.) RoGo
"At length I saw a lady within call." PoG
Dream of Flowers, A. Titus Munson Coan. AA
Dream of Gerontius, The. Cardinal Newman. PoVP
Sels.
Angel ("My work is done"). GoBC
Angel ("Softly and gently, dearly-ransom'd soul"). OxBoCh
Angel of the Agony ("Jesu! by that shuddering dread which fell on Thee"). OxBoCh
"Jesu, Maria—I am near to death." ACP; CoBE; EnLi-2
"Praise to the Holiest in the height." PoEL-5
(Chorus of Angels.) NBM
(Fifth Choir of Angelicals.) GoBC
Soul before God, The ("Take me away, and in the lowest deep"). OxBoCh
Dream of Governors, A. Louis Simpson. NYBP; PoSa
Dream of Horses, A. Ted Hughes. NePoEA-2
Dream of John Ball, A, *sel.* William Morris.
Sheriff, The. PoVP
Dream of Love. Bhai Vir Singh. *tr. fr. Punjabi by* Puran Singh. OnPM
Dream of Metals, A. Jack Anderson. ThO
Dream of November, A. Edmund Gosse. SyP
Dream of Suffocation, A. Robert Bly. NaP
Dream of Surreal Science, A. Sri Aurobindo Ghose. ACV
Dream of the Romaunt of the Rose, The. Guillaume de Lorris, *tr. fr. French by* Chaucer. *Fr.* The Romance of the Rose. LoBV
Dream of the Rood, A. *Unknown, at. to* Cynewulf, *tr. fr. Anglo-Saxon.* AnOE, *tr. by* Charles W. Kennedy; CAW, *tr. by* Sister Mary Madeleva; EnLi-1, *tr. by* Stith Thompson; OuHeWo, *tr. by* Stith Thompson; StJW, *tr. by* LaMotte Iddings
Sels.
Cross Speaks, The. PoLi
"I am remembering in the long ago." ACP
Poet Prays to the Cross, The. PoLi
Dream of the Unknown, A. Shelley. *See* Question, The ("I dreamed that, as I wandered by the way").
Dream of the walls of a cave. The Fossil. John Lyle Donaghy. NeIP
Dream of the World without Death, The. Robert Buchanan. *Fr.* The Book of Orm. VA
Dream of Venus, A. Bion. *See* I Dreamt I Saw Great Venus.
Dream of waking in some sleeper's eye, A. Hiroshima. Margaret Rockwell. PPON
Dream of Wrecks, A. Shakespeare. Richard III, *fr.* I, iv. ChTr
Dream-Pedlary. Thomas Lovell Beddoes. AnFE; AtBAP, *sts.* 1-2; BoTP; CBEP; CH; EnRP; EPN; FaBoBe; GTBS-W, *sts.* 1-2; LiTB; LoBV; NeHB; OBEV; OBNC; OBRV; OBVV; OQP; OtMeF; PCD; PG (1945 ed.), *sts.* 1-2; PoEL-4; TOP; TreFS; TrGrPo; VA; ViBoPo; WiR; YT
(Dreams to Sell.) OTPC (1946 ed.), *sts.* 1-2
("If there were dreams to sell.") EG
Dream Poem #1. Craig Sterry. QAH
Dream Poem #3. Craig Sterry. QAH
Dream Queen, The, *sel.* Bhasa, *tr. fr. Sanskrit by* A. G. Shirreff *and* Panna Lall.
Dialogue from "The Dream Queen" ("Look, look, my lord"). LiTW
Dream Sestina, A. Donald Justice. PIA; TDP
(Sestina.) NePoEA
Dream Ship, The. W. K. Holmes. BoTP
Dream Song. Lewis Alexander. PoNe
Dream-Song. Walter de la Mare. RePo
Dream Song. Richard Middleton. HBV
Dream Songs, The, *sels.* John Berryman.
April Fool's Day, or, St. Mary of Egypt, XLVII. NaP
"Full moon. Our Narragansett gales subside," LXI. CoAP
"Glories of the world struck me, made me aria, once, The," XXVI. NaP
"He lay in the middle of the world, and twitcht," LIII. OPoP
"Henry hates the world. What the world to Henry," LXXIV. NaP
Henry's Confession, LXXVI. NaP; TwCP
"I am, outside. Incredible panic rules," XLVI. NaP
"I don't operate often. When I do," LXVII. NaP
"I'm scared a lonely. Never see my son," XV. CoAP
"Let us suppose, valleys & such ago," XV. NaP
"Life, friends, is boring," XIV. LiTM (1970 ed.); NaP; TwCP
"Seedy Henry rose up shy in de world," LXXVII. NaP; TwCP
Snow Line, XXVIII. NaP
"Tell it to the forest fire, tell it to the moon," XLIV. NaP
"That dark brown rabbit," LXII. TwCP
"There sat down, once a thing on Henry's heart," XXIX. NMP; OPoP
"Turning it over, considering, like a madman," LXXV. NaP
Dream-Teller, The. Padraic Gregory. HBMV; OnYI
Dream the Great Dream. Florence Earle Coates. HBMV; PoMa
Dream Tryst. Richard Le Gallienne. HBMV
Dream-Tryst. Francis Thompson. AnFE; EnLit; VA
Dream Variation [*or* Variations]. Langston Hughes. AmNP; BALP; CDC; IDB; OTD; PoNe; PoPl
Dream within a Dream, A. Poe. AmP; AmPP; AnFE; AP; APA; BoLiVe; CBEP; ChTr; CoAnAm; CoBA; MAmP; MeWo; OxBA; SyP; TDP; TrGrPo
(To——: "Take this kiss upon thy brow!") LO
Dreame, The. John Donne. *See* Dream, The.
Dreame, The. Ben Jonson. PoEL-2
Dreamed Realization, A. Gregory Corso. NeAP
Dreamer, The. Walter de la Mare. CMoP; OTPC (1923 ed.)
Dreamer, The. Dorothy Gould. PGD
Dreamer, A. Arthur Guiterman. PoMa
Dreamer, The. Thomas Nunan. WBLP

Dreamer of Dreams. William Herbert Carruth. *See* Dreamers of Dreams.
Dreamer, waiting for darkness with sorrowful, drooping eyes. Forward. Edna Dean Proctor. HBV
Dreamers, The. Theodosia Garrison. GaP; HBMV
Dreamers, The. Sydney Jephcott. BoAu
Dreamers. Siegfried Sassoon. BrPo; CMoP; HBMV; MCCG; MoBrPo; NeMA; Sonn
Dreamers and the Sea, The. Eithne Wilkins. *Fr.* Parzival. NeBP
Dreamers Cry Their Dream, The. Lucia Trent. PGD
Dreamers of Dreams. William Herbert Carruth. MaRV; OQP
(Dreamer of Dreams.) PoLF
Dreamers of Dreams, The. Arthur O'Shaughnessy. *See* Ode: "We are the music-makers."
Dreamers turn, The. The Dreamers and the Sea. Eithne Wilkins. *Fr.* Parzival. NeBP
Dreamers upon the hilltops, The. The Dreamers Cry Their Dream. Lucia Trent. PGD
Dreamers, wake up! For you I beat the drum! I Beat the Drum. Jan Greshoff. PoFr
Dreaming along the haunted shore of time. Edgar Allan Poe. Clifford Lanier. PoRL
Dreaming in marble all the castle lay. Of Nicolette. E. E. Cummings. HBMV
Dreaming in the Trenches. William Gordon McCabe. AA
Dreaming of a prince. After All and after All. Mary Carolyn Davies. GaP; MPB; SP; TiPo (1952 ed.)
Dreaming of Cities Dead. Eleanor Rogers Cox. CAW; JKCP
Dreaming of honeycombs to share. Waiting. Harry Behn. SiSoSe; TiPo
Dreaming Spires. Roy Campbell. BoSA
Dreaming Trout, The. Charles Bruce. *Fr.* The Flowing Summer. CaP
Dreaming when dawn's left hand was in the sky. Omar Khayyám, *tr. by* Edward Fitzgerald. *Fr.* The Rubáiyát. PoSa
Dreaming with a Friend. Stephen Berg. NaP
Dreamland. *See* Dream Land.
Dreams. Cecil Frances Alexander. OnYI
Dreams. Victor J. Daley. PoAu-1
Dreams. Robert Herrick. SeEP
Dreams. Langston Hughes. BoChLi (1950 ed.); GoSl
Dreams. Poe. AmPP (4th ed.); CBEP; OxBA
Dreams. Philip M. Raskin. OQP
Dreams. Henry Timrod. AmePo
Dreams. Israel Zangwill. TrJP
Dreams Ahead, The. Edwin Carlile Litsey. PoToHe
Dreams and Deeds. John Hunter. ChIP; MaRV
Dreams and Realities, *sel.* Phoebe Cary.
"Sometimes, I think, the things we see." MaRV
Dreams are they—but they are God's dreams! God's Dreams. Thomas Curtis Clark. OQP
Dreams cross his sleep, The. The Valley of Sleep. Hendrik Marsman. *Fr.* The Zodiac. LiTW
Dreams fled away, this country bedroom, raw. Another September. Thomas Kinsella. PoCh
Dreams of a Summer Night, *sel.* George Barker.
Cutty Sark, The, VI. FIW
Dreams of the Accuser. Randy Blasing. YAP
Dreams of the Dreamer, The. Georgia Douglas Johnson. CDC
Dreams of the Sea. W. H. Davies. EtS
Dreams of Water. Donald Justice. NYBP
Dreams Old and Nascent. D. H. Lawrence. WGRP
Dreams that delude with flying shade men's minds. We Are Such Stuff as Dreams. Petronius Arbiter. AWP
Dreams to Sell. Thomas Lovell Beddoes. *See* Dream-Pedlary.
Dreams within Dreams. "Fiona Macleod." PoVP
Dreamscape in Kümmel. Harold Witt. NYBP
Dreamside Bestiary. Harold Bond. YAP
Dreamy crags with raucous voices croon, The. Hymn to the Sunrise. *Unknown.* NA
Dreamy rhymer's measur'd snore, The. Macaulay. Walter Savage Landor. VA
Dreary and brown the night comes down. Columbus at the Convent. John Townsend Trowbridge. DD; MC; PAH
Dreary Black Hills, The, *diff. versions.* *Unknown.* ABF, *with music*; AS, *with music*; CoSo, *with music*; IHA
Dreary Change, The. Sir Walter Scott. ERoP-1; OBNC; PeER ("Sun upon the Weirdlaw Hill, The.") EPN
Dreary lay the long road, dreary lay the town. The Toy Band. Sir Henry Newbolt. BoTP
Dreary season to a tragic tale, A. The Testament of Cresseid. Robert Henryson. MeEV
Dred of deth, sorow of sin. In His Utter Wretchedness. John Audelay. MeEL
Dredged in a net the slender god. Archaic Apollo. William Plomer. ChMP
Dree Night, The. *Unknown.* ChTr
Dregs. Ernest Dowson. HBV; NCEP; OBMV; SeCePo; ViPP
Dreidel Song. Efraim Rosenzweig. TiPo (1952 ed.)
Dreme, The, *sel.* Sir David Lindsay.
Complaint of the Common Weill of Scotland. GoTS
Compleynt of the Comoun Weill of Scotland, The. OxBS
Of the Realme of Scotland. OxBS
Drenched earth has a warm, sweet radiance all her own, The. The Robin's Egg. Annie Charlotte Dalton. CaP
Drenched saw Doris home, midnight gale. Edwin Denby. ANYP
Drenched with purple. Simaetha. Hilda Doolittle ("H. D."). MAPA
Dresden shepherdess was one day, A. In a China Shop. George Sidney Hellman. AA
Dress. Henry Luttrell. *Fr.* Advice to Julia. OBRV
Dress, The. Christopher Middleton. NMP
Dress of Spring, The. May Justus. YeAr
Dress that my brother has put on is thin, The. "The Lady of Sakanoye." *Fr.* Manyo Shu. AWP; JAWP; WBP
Dresscessional, A. Carolyn Wells. WBLP
Dressed in his clumsy, stiff, aquatic clothes. The Diver. E. L. Mayo. CoAP
Dressed Up. Langston Hughes. GoSl
Dressed up in my melancholy. Song. M. Carl Holman. AmNP; Kal; PoNe
Dressing. Henry Vaughan. AnAnS-1; MeP
Dressing the Doll. William Brighty Rands. PRWS; VA
Dried Apple Pies. *Unknown.* BLPA
Dried-up Fountain, The. Robert Leighton. VA
Drift ("Drift drift upon the beach"). Denis Glover. AnNZ
Drift descends like rattling dust, The. Avalanche. Adrien Stoutenburg. NYBP
Drifter, The. Dave Hughes. CoSo
Drifter off Tarentum, A. Kipling. *Fr.* Epitaphs of the War. MMA
Drifters are in Harlem, The. Neon Diaspora. David Henderson. BF
Drifting. James McConkey. SoP
Drifting. John Francis O'Donnell. IrPN
Drifting. Thomas Buchanan Read. AA; GN; HBV; HT
Drifting Away. Charles Kingsley. OxBoCh
Drifting mist beyond the bar, A. Dawn. Isabel Butchart. PoMa
Drifting night [*or* scent] in the Georgia pines. O Daedalus, Fly Away Home. Robert Hayden. IDB; NoP; PoNe
Drifting Petal, A. Mary McNeil Fenollosa. AA
Drifting Sands and a Caravan. Yolande Langworthy. BLPA; NeHB
Drifting smoke is gone, today, The. Fourth of July. S. S. Gardons. AmPC
Driftwood, *abr.* Trumbull Stickney. HBV
Driftwood. Richard Wilbur. FiMAP
Drill, The. Harry Brown. WaaP
Drilling in Russell Square. Edward Shanks. OBMV
Drilling Missed Holes. Don Cameron. PoOW
Drink. William Carlos Williams. OxBA
Drink about till the day find us. Song. Earl of Rochester. PeRV
Drink and Be Glad. *Unknown,* *tr. fr. Greek by* Bland *and* Wellesley. OnPM
Drink and be merry, merry, merry boys. *See* Drinke and be merry. . .
Drink, comrades, drink; give loose to mirth! The Death of Cleopatra. Horace. EnLi-1; OuHeWo
Drink! drink! to whom shall we drink? The Old Man's Carousal. James Kirke Paulding. AA
Drink, Friends. Moses ibn Ezra, *tr. fr. Hebrew by* Solomon Solis-Cohen. *Fr.* Wine-Songs. TrJP
Drink full ones, tinker, methinks the monks are dry. The Tink-

Drink (continued)
er and the Monks. Nathaniel Whiting. *Fr.* Le Hore di Recreatione. SeCL
Drink, gossips mine! we drink no wine. Medieval Norman Songs, XVIII. *Unknown, tr. by* John Addington Symonds. AWP
Drink in moods. Tanka, III. Lewis Alexander. CDC
Drink (ingurgitate, engulph, engorge, gulp). A Thesaurus Nightmare. J. Willard Ridings. WhC
Drink That Rot Gut. *Unknown.* ABF
(Drinking Song.) CoSo
Drink to Me Only with Thine Eyes. Ben Jonson. *See* To Celia ("Drink to me only. . .)
Drink To-Day [and Drown All Sorrow]. John Fletcher, *and others. Fr.* The Bloody Brother, II, ii. EnLit; HBV; OAEP; ViBoPo
(Drinking Song.) ElL; TuPP
(Song, The: "Drink to-day and drown all sorrow.") SeEP
Drink Wine in the Corner Store. Clive Matson. ThO
Drink with Something in It, A. Ogden Nash. PoPl
Drinke and be merry, merry, merry, boyes. The Songe. Thomas Morton. *Fr.* New English Canaan. AmPP; SCAP
Drinker. Patrick Anderson. PeCV
Drinking. Abraham Cowley, *after the Greek of* Anacreon. CABA; CEP; EnLi-1 (1949 ed.); HBV; LoBV; MePo; OBEV; OtMeF; PG; PoFS; PoSa; ReEn; SCEP-2; SeCP; SeCV-1; SeEP; ShBV-4; StP; TDP; TrGrPo; WhC
(Anacreontic on Drinking.) NoP; SeCePo
(Of Drinking.) ALV
(On Drinking.) WePo
(Thirsty Earth, The.) WiR
("Thirsty earth soaks up the rain, The.") EG
Drinking. Hsin Ch'i-chi, *tr. fr. Chinese by* Ching Ti. LiTW
Drinking Alone in the Moonlight: "If Heaven did not love wine." Li Po, *tr. fr. Chinese by* Amy Lowell *and* Florence Ayscough. AWP
Drinking Alone in the Moonlight: "Pot of wine among flowers, A." Li Po, *tr. fr. Chinese by* Amy Lowell *and* Florence Ayscough. AWP
(Drinking Alone with the Moon: "From a pot of wine among the flowers," *by* Witter Bynner.) LiTW
Drinking Bout, A. Liu Chia, *tr. fr. Chinese by* Henry H. Hart. OnPM
Drinking Fountain. Marchette Chute. TiPo (1959 ed.)
Drinking Song. Burns. *Fr.* The Jolly Beggars. PoFr; TrGrPo
Drinking-Song, A. Henry Carey. OBEV
Drinking Song. William Cartwright. *Fr.* The Royal Slave. SeCL
Drinking Song. Thomas Dekker. *See* Cold's the Wind.
Drinking Song. John Fletcher, *and others. See* Drink To-Day.
Drinking Song. Anthony Hecht. NMP
Drinking Song. Thomas Randolph. *Fr.* Aristippus. SeCL
Drinking Song, A. Shakespeare. *See* Come, Thou Monarch of the Vine.
Drinking Song. *At. to* William Stevenson *and to* John Still. *Fr.* Gammer Gurton's Needle. WiR
Drinking Song ("Drink that rot gut"). *Unknown. See* Drink That Rot Gut.
Drinking Song ("How happy's the prisoner that conquers his fate"). *Unknown.* SeCL
Drinking Song ("O night, O eyes of love!"). *Unknown, tr. fr. Arabic by* E. Powys Mathers. *Fr.* The Thousand and One Nights. LiTW
Drinking Song ("Tapster, fille another ale!"). *Unknown.* EnLit
Drinking Song, A. W. B. Yeats. CLwM
Drinking Song, A, against All Sorts of Disputes in Drinking; to One, Who Always Bawl'd to Have Reason Done Him, and Was Noisie, and Quarrelsom in His Cups. William Wycherley. SeCV-2
Drinking Song for Present-Day Gatherings. Morris Bishop. ALV
Drinking Time. D. J. O'Sullivan. OnYI
Drive It On, *with music. Unknown.* OuSiCo
Drive on, sharp wings, and cry above. The Redshanks. Julian Bell. LO; OBMV
Drive the pilings deep! Beach House. Mary Rita Hurley. PoPl
Drive-ins are out, to start with. One must always be. Movie-Going. John Hollander. CoAP
Driven by desire I did this deed. Sir Thomas Wyatt. FCP
Driven by Desire to Set Affection. *Unknown.* ReIE
Driven from the soil of France, a female came. Sonnet: September 1, 1802. Wordsworth. ChER
Driven to achievement by youth and love. Haute Politique. Granville Trace. AWP
Driver rubbed at his nettly chin, The. To the Four Courts, Please. James Stephens. HBMV; MoAB; MoBrPo; NemA
Driver Saying. Josephine Miles. FiMAP
"Driver, what stream is it?" I asked, well knowing. The Lordly Hudson. Paul Goodman. CoAP; NMP
Drivers are washing the concrete mixers, The. Concrete Mixers. Patricia Hubbell. PDV
Driver's Prayer, A. *Unknown.* STF
Drivin' Steel, *with music. Unknown.* AS
Drivin' steel, drivin' steel. Hammer Man. *Unknown.* AS
Driving Cattle to Casas Buenas. Roy Campbell. PeSA
Driving Cross-Country. X. J. Kennedy. TwCP
Driving down from the turf bog in the rain. Merchandise. Seán Jennett. NeIP
Driving Home the Cows. Kate Putnam Osgood. AA; AmePo; BeLS, HBV; PAH; TreFS
Driving in the Park. *Unknown.* OxBoLi
Driving Saw-Logs on the Plover. *Unknown.* AS, *with music*; IHA
Driving through Belgium. Michael Brownstein. ANYP
Driving to Town Late to Mail a Letter. Robert Bly. BoNaP; ELU; NaP
Driving toward the Lac Qui Parle River. Robert Bly. NaP
Drizzling Easter Morning, A. Thomas Hardy. CMoP
Drizzling murk of a March dawn, The. The Parting. James K. Baxter. Cressida, VI. AnNZ
Dromedary, The. Hilaire Belloc. WhC
Dromedary, The. Archibald Y. Campbell. HBMV; PoMa; StaSt
Dromedary is a cheerful bird, The. The Dromedary. Hilaire Belloc. WhC
Drone *v.* Worker. Ebenezer Elliott. NBM
Droning a drowsy syncopated tune. The Weary Blues. Langston Hughes. BALP; FaBV; NoP; PoNe; UnS
Droop, droop no more, or hang the head. Upon Julia's Recovery. Robert Herrick. AtBAP
Droop under doves' wings silent, breathing shapes. The Night Nurse Goes Her Round. John Gray. LoBV; OBNC
Drop a Pebble in the Water. James W. Foley. BLPA; PoToHe; SoP
Drop a pebble in the water. Influence. Joseph Norris. MaRV
Drop a stitch, drop a stitch. Forecast. Sydney King Russell. FiSC
Drop an unkind word or careless. The Difference. *Unknown.* STF
Drop down, drop down, white snowflakes! Winter [*or* Winter's Song.] *Unknown.* BoTP; PCH
Drop, drop, slow tears. A Hymn [*or* A Litany]. Phineas Fletcher. AtBAP; BoC; BoW; CBEP; ElL; LoBV; OBEV; OBS; OxBoCh; SeEP
Drop fell on the apple tree, A. Emily Dickinson. BoNaP
Drop Golden Showers, Gentle Sleep. Thomas Goffe. *Fr.* The Courageous Turk. SeCL; SeEP
Drop Me The Seed. John Masefield. MoRP
Drop of Dew, A. Schmuel Halkin, *tr. fr. Yiddish by* Jacob Sonntag. TrJP
Drop of Dew, A. Andrew Marvell. *See* On a Drop of Dew.
Drop of Ink, A. Joseph Ernest Whitney. AA
Drop of sepia in the fragrant vase, The. Dusk. Abraham Z. Lopez-Penha. TrJP
Drop, one drop, how sweetly one fair drop, A. Dives Asking a Drop [*or* On Dives]. Richard Crashaw. ACP; MaMe
Drop your offering in the box. Candles. *Unknown.* GoBC
Dropped feather from the wings of God. Poet Songs, III. Karle Wilson Baker. HBMV
Dropping back with the ball ripe in my palm. The Passer. George Abbe. SD
Dropping Down the River. Horatius Bonar. SoP
Dropping from bells a day draped in mourning. Return of Autumn. "Pablo Neruda." LiTW
Dropping Your Aitches. Joseph Warren Beach. NYBP
Drought. Betty Bruechert. SoP
Drought. Geoffrey Johnson. HaMV
Drought. Frederick E. Laight. OBCV
(Soliloquy.) CaP

Drought. Will H. Ogilvie. BoAu
Drought, *sel.* Francis Carey Slater.
"Sky is a blue, coiled serpent, The." ACV
Drouth. Mary Austin. NP
Drove-Road, The. W. W. Gibson. EnLit
Drover, A. Padraic Colum. AnIL; AnIV; AWP; HBV; HT; JAWP; MoBrPo; NP; OBMV; OxBI; ViBoPo; WBP
Droving Man. Thea Astley. PoAu-2
Drowned Lady, The. *Unknown.* ChTr
Drowned Mariner, The. Elizabeth Oakes Smith. AA
Drowned Sailor. Neufville Shaw. CaP
Drowned Seaman, The. Maude Goldring. HBMV
Drowned Spaniel, The. Charles Tennyson Turner. PeVV
Drowned Wife, The. Robert Horan. OnHM
Drowning is not so pitiful. Emily Dickinson. AnEnPo; CMoP; ExPo
Drowning of Conaing, The. *Unknown, tr. fr. Old Irish by* Frank O'Connor. AnIL
Drowning Poet, The. James Merrill. PP
Drowning with Others. James Dickey. CoPo
Drowsily come the sheep. Slumber Song. Louis V. Ledoux. FaPON; HBMV; MPB; UTS
Drowsing in my chair of disbelief. The Visitation. Robert Graves. BoPe
Drowsy, friendly, comfortable creak, The. Dawn at the Rain's Edge. Joseph Auslander. MAP; MoAmPo (1942 ed.)
Drowsy Herodotus holds him there, The. Ancient Historian. Chris Wallace Crabbe. PoAu-2
Drowsy Sleeper, The. *Unknown. See* Who's That at My Bedroom Window?
Drowsy sun went slowly to his rest, The. Evening. James Stephens. MoBrPo
Drowzy night hir wings has spred, The. *Unknown.* SeCSL
Drug Addict, The. Miriam Waddington. *Fr.* Three Prison Portraits. ACV
Drug Clerk, The. Eunice Tietjens. AmAmPo; HBMV
Drug Store. Karl Shapiro. AmPP (4th ed.); CMoP; FiMAP; ILP; MoVE; OxBA; TwCP
Drug Store. John V. A. Weaver. HBMV; NP; ThLM; YaD
Drugged. Walter de la Mare. BrPo
Druggist, The. Larry Rubin. FiSC
Druid, The. John Bannister Tabb. AA
Druidic Gums. T. I. Moore. MoAuPo
Druids' Hymn to the Sun. C. M. Doughty. *Fr.* The Dawn in Britain. FaBoTw
Drum, The. John Farrar. BrR; GFA
Drum. Langston Hughes. MAP; MoAmPo
Drum, The. John Scott of Amwell. CBEP; OBEC; ViBoPo
(Ode: "I hate that drum's discordant sound.") EiCL
(Retort on the Foregoing.) OBEV (new ed.); PPON
Drum for Ben Boyd, A, *sels.* Francis Webb.
Captain of the *Oberon*, The. ACV; NeLNL
Papuan Shepherd, A. PoAu-2
Drum Majah, De. Ray Garfield Dandridge. BANP
Drum on your drums, batter on your banjos. Jazz Fantasia. Carl Sandburg. AnFE; CoAnAm; MAP; MoAB; MoAmPo; NeMA; OCS; OTD; PoNe; TwAmPo; WePo
Drum, The; The Narrative of the Demon of Tedworth. Edith Sitwell. *Fr.* façade. BoW; FaBoTw
Drumlin Woodchuck. A. Robert Frost. GoYe; WaKn
Drummer, The. Anne Robinson. SUS
Drummer-Boy and the Shepherdess, The. William Brighty Rands. MoShBr
Drummer Boy of Waterloo. The ("When battle roused each warlike charm"). *with music. Unknown.* BFSS
Drummer Hodge. Thomas Hardy. AWP; BrPo; CoBMV; EnL; GTBS-P; ILP; InPo; JAWP; MaPo (1969 ed.;) NoP; PoE; PoeP; POTE; PoVP; SeCeV; ViPo; VP; WBP
Drum's a very quiet [*or* quiet little] fellow, The. The Drum. John Farrar. BrR; GFA
Drums of Haiti. Marcus B. Christian. GoSl
Drunk and senseless in his place. Ramon. Bret Harte. BeLS
Drunk in the Furnace, The. W. S. Merwin. CBV; LiTM (1970 ed.); NePoEA-2; TwCP
Drunk Last Night with Poets, I Go to Work Anyway. Philip Dow. QAH
Drunk: On Crutches. Raymond Souster. PeCV
Drunk on sour cherries, the harlequin of birds. Cedar Waxwing. William H. Matchett. ELU; WIRo
Drunk on the moon, a sage of dreams. A Hybrid Villanelle on a Line of Li Po. William Witherup. QAH
Drunk, Two Afternoons. Lou Lipsitz. YAP
Drunkard, The. Proverbs, XXIII: 29-35, Bible, *O.T.* TrJP
Drunkard, The. Fenton Johnson. AnAmPo
Drunkard, The. Philip Levine. NePoEA-2
Drunkard cannot meet a cork, A. Emily Dickinson. MWA-2
Drunkard to His Bottle, A. Joseph Sheridan Le Fanu. OnYI
Drunkards, The. Malcolm Lowry. NYBP
Drunkard's Doom, The. *Unknown.* ABF, *with music*; AS
Drunken Boat, The. Arthur Rimbaud, *tr. fr. French.* LiTW, *tr. by* Norman Cameron; PIA, *tr by* Stephen Stepanchev; ReMP, *tr. by* Ben Belitt; SyP, *tr. by* Stephen Stephanchev
Drunken Desperado, The. Baird Boyd. SCC
(Cowboy.) ChTr
(Cowboy Boasting Chants: "I'm wild and woolly," *st.* 1.) ABF
Drunken Fisherman, The. Robert Lowell. AmP; AmPP (5th ed.); AP; CBV; CMoP; CrMA; FiMAP; LiTA; LiTM (rev. ed.); MoPo; MoVE; OxBA; SeCeV; TwAmPo
Drunken Fool, The, *with music. Unknown.* BFSS
Drunken Gunners. M. K. Joseph. AnNZ
Drunken Heracles (Metropolitan Museum). Wallace Gould. AnAmPo
Drunken Lover. Owen Dodson. AmNP
Drunken Man on Highgate Hill, A. Paul Hasluck. MoAuPo
Drunken Preacher's Sermon, The. James Reaney. *Fr.* A Suit of Nettles. PeCV (1967 ed.)
Drunken Rose, The. Amarou, *tr. fr. Sanskrit by* E. Powys Mathers. AWP
Drunken Sailor, The; or, Early in the Morning, *with music. Unknown.* ShS; SoAmSa
Drunken Winter. Joseph Ceravolo. ANYP
Drunkenness of youth has passed like a fever, The. Inscription at the City of Brass. *Unknown. Fr.* The Thousand and One Nights. LiTW
Dry, and brown-withered and silent, they that remain. Winter Stalks. Bertram J. Warr. TwCaPo
Dry Be That Tear. Sheridan. OnYI
Dry Gap—a dingy general store. Western Town. David Wadsworth Cannon, Jr. PoNe
Dry July. Arnold Adoff. CAD
Dry-Landers, The, *with music. Unknown.* CoSo
Dry leaves fall, as if from far away, The. Autumn. Rainer Maria Rilke. PoPo
Dry leaves, soldier, dry leaves, dead leaves. The Wars. Conrad Aiken. *Fr.* The Soldier. WaaP
Dry lighted soul, the ray that shines in thee. To R. W. E. Ellen Hooper. AnAmPo
Dry Loaf. Wallace Stevens. AtBAP; CrMA; OxBA; PoRA
Dry-Point. Philip Larkin. CMoP; NMP
Dry Salvages, The. T. S. Eliot. *Fr.* Four Quartets. CABA; LiTB; MaPo; MBW-2; MWA-2; NoP; OxBA; SeCePo; SeCeV
Sels.
"Lady, whose shrine stands on the promontory," IV. ISi
"To communicate with Mars, converse with spirits," V. AmPP; ATP (1953 ed.)
"Where is there an end of it, the soundless wailing," *fr.* II. FaBoTw
Dry Time. Norma Davis. NeLNL
Dry vine leaves burn in an angle of the wall. The Thousand Things. Christopher Middleton. NePoEA-2; OPoP
Dry Wishing Well. Wally Ford. WSL
Dry Your Tears, Africa! Bernard Dadié, *tr. fr. French by* Donatus Ibe Nwoga. TTY
Dryad Song. Margaret Fuller. AA; WGRP
Dryad's home was once the tree, A. On Sivori's Violin. Frances Sargent Osgood. AA
Du Bartas His Divine Weeks, *sels.* Joshua Sylvester.
First Day of the First Week, The. Po
I Hear the Crane. OA
Du bist wie eine Blume. Heine, *tr. fr. German by* Kate Kroeker. *Fr.* Homeward Bound. AWP; JAWP; WBP; OuHeWo, *tr. by* Sir Theodore Martin
(Thou Seemest like a Flower, *tr. by* Emma Lazarus.) TrJP
(Translated Way, The, *tr. by* Franklin P. Adams.) BOHV
Du schönes Fischer-Mädchen. Heine. *See* Oh Lovely Fishermaiden.
Dual Site, The. Michael Hamburger. NePoEA-2

Duality. Kenneth Slade Alling. AnAmPo; CAW
Duality. Arthur Sherburne Hardy. AA
Duality. Katherine Thayer Hobson. GoYe
Dubiety. Robert Browning. *Fr.* Asolando. MaPo (1969); MBW-2; PoVP; ViPo
Dublin. Louis MacNeice. ACV; OxBI
Dublin Ballad, A; 1916. "Dermot O'Byrne." AnIV; OxBI
Dublin Bay. Ewart Milne. NeIP
Dublin Bay, *with music. Unknown.* BFSS
Dublin Limerick, A. Ray Bradbury. SiTL
Dublin Made Me. Donagh MacDonagh. AnIV; NeIP; OxBI
Dublin; the Old Squares. Padraic Colum. NePoAm
"Ducats take, The! I'll sign the bond to-day." Two Argosies. Wallace Bruce. AA
Duchess. Lilian Bowes Lyon. HaMV; POTE
Duchess of Malfi, The, *sels.* John Webster.
Dirge, A: "Hark, now everything is still," *fr.* IV, ii. CBEP
"Farewell Cariola!" *fr.* IV, ii. LO
Hark, Now Everything Is Still, *fr.* IV, ii. BEL; ElL; EnLi-1; HW; LoBV; NoP; OBS; QFR; SeCePo; SiCE; TuPP; ViBoPo
(General Mist of Error, A.) OnPM
(Hark.) CH
(Shrouding of the Duchess of Malfi, The.) OBEV
(Summons to Execution.) FaBoEn
"I am come to make thy tomb," *fr.* IV, ii. ChTr
"Is she dead?/ She is what you would have her," *fr.* IV, ii. AnFE
"It may be/ I'll join with thee in a most just revenge," 4 *ll. fr.* V, ii. PoFr
Oh, Let Us Howl Some Heavy Note, *fr.* IV, ii. InvP; SiCE
(Madman's Song, The.) ElL
"What hideous noyse was that?" *fr.* IV, ii. AtBAP; PoEL-2
"Yond's the Cardinall's window: This fortification," *fr.* V, iii. AtBAP; PoEL-2
Duck. John Lyle Donaghy. OxBI
Duck, The. Edith King. BoTP; GFA; HBVY; StVeCh
Duck, The. Ogden Nash. MoShBr; WhC
Duck and a drake, A. *Unknown.* OxNR
Duck, and Mallard first, the falconers' only sport, The. Birds in the Fens. Michael Drayton. *Fr.* Polyolbion. ChTr
Duck and the Kangaroo, The. Edward Lear. BoChLi; GFA; OTPC (1946 ed.); PoRh; TiPo (1952 ed.)
Duck-Chasing. Galway Kinnell. NMP; TwCP
Duck in Central Park. Frances Higginson Savage. GoYe
Duck is whiter than whey is, The. Quack! Walter de la Mare. TiPo
Duckle, Duckle, Daisy. Leroy F. Jackson. ChBR
Ducks. Norman Ault. BoTP
Ducks. Robert Bly. PV
Ducks. Roy Daniells. TwCaPo
Ducks. Frederick William Harvey. BoC; YT
"Yes, ducks are valiant things," *sel.* BoTP
Ducks, The. Alice Wilkins. GFA; TiPo
Duck's-assed and leather-jacketed. The Execrators. David Galler. NMP
Ducks at Dawn. James S. Tippett. SiSoSe; SoPo; TiPo; UTS
Duck's [*or* Ducks'] Ditty. Kenneth Grahame. *Fr.* The Wind in the Willows, *ch.* 2. BoTP; FaPON; GoJo; MoShBr; MPB; OTPC (1946 ed.); PCH; PDV; PoRh; SoPo; SUS; TiPo; UTS; WaKn
Ducks in the Millpond, *with music. Unknown.* OuSiCo
Ducks in the mill-pond eating up moss. Don't Grow Weary, Boys. *Unknown.* CoSo
Ducks require no ship and sail. What Ducks Require. John Crowe Ransom. FaBoMo
Dude, The. Martial, *tr. fr. Latin.* OnPM
Due Commendation of the Quipping Autor, A. Gabriel Harvey. *Fr.* Four Letters and Certain Sonnets. ReIE
Due North. Benjamin R. C. Low. EtS; HBMV
Duel, The. Abraham Cowley. AnAnS-2
Duel, The. Eugene Field. BeLS; BoChLi; CenHV; FaBoBe; FaFP; FaPON; GFA; HBV; HBVY; MoShBr; NeHB; OHFP; OnMSP; OnSP; OTPC (1946 ed.); PoLF; PoPl; PoRA; PTK; SoPo; StVeCh; TiPo; TreF; UTS; YT
Duel, The. Theodore Maynard. CAW
Duel, The. Harold Trowbridge Pulsifer. HBMV
Duel, The. *Unknown.* ShM
Duel in the Park. Lisa Grenelle. GoYe
Duel with Verses over a Great Man, *sels. Unknown, tr. fr. Hebrew.* TrJP
"Against the guide of Truth," Epigram V.
"Forgive us, son of Amram, be not wroth," Epigram III.
"Here lies a man, and still no man," Epitaph I.
"Thou fool profane, be silent!" Epigram II.
"Thou Guide to doubt, be silent evermore," Epigram I.
"What thought ye to burn, when ye kindled the pyre," Epigram IV.
Duellist, The, *sel.* Charles Churchill.
"Hail, Liberty! a glorious word." PoFr
Duenna, The, *sels.* Sheridan.
Air: "I ne're could any luster see," *fr.* I, ii. HBV
"Bumper of good liquor, A," *fr.* II, iii. WhC
Song: "Had I a heart for falsehood framed," *fr.* I, v. CEP; HBV; OBEC
Song: "If a daughter you have, she's the plague of your life," *fr.* I, iii. CEP; NeHB
Duet, A. T. Sturge Moore. OBEV; OBVV
Duet. Shakespeare. *See* In Such a Night.
Duet. Leonora Speyer. HBMV
Duet: "Is it the wind of the dawn that I hear in the pine overhead?" Tennyson. *Fr.* Becket. SiSw
Duff, The. David McKee Wright. AnNZ
Duffy's Hotel, *with music. Unknown.* ShS
Dugall Quin (A *and* B *vers.*). *Unknown.* ESPB
Dug-out, The. Siegfried Sassoon. AtBAP; CH; FlW; MCCG; MoBrPo; MoVE; NeMA; OHIP; POTE; WaaP; WaP
Duino Elegies, The, *sel.* Rainer Maria Rilke. *tr. fr. German.*
Third Duino Elegy, The, *tr. by* Stephen Spender *and* J. B. Leishman. LiTW
Duke di Broccoli and the Countess of Points, The. Pointillism. Joseph Bennett. SiTL
Duke Is the Lad, The. Thomas Moore. OnYI
Duke of Athol's [*or* Athole's] Nurse, The. *Unknown.* BaBo; ESPB (A *and* B *vers.*); OxBB
Duke of Benevento, The. Sir John Henry Moore. CEP; OBEC
Duke of Buckingham, The ("A numerous host"). Dryden. *Fr.* Absalom and Achitophel, Pt. I. FaBoEn
Duke of Buckingham, The. Pope. *See* Death of Buckingham, The.
Duke of Gordon's Daughter, The. *Unknown.* BuBa; ESPB; OBB, *sl. diff.*
Duke of Grafton, The. *Unknown.* ChTr
Duke of Merchant's daughter walked out one summer's day, The. Six Questions. *Unknown.* BaBo
Duke of Parma's Ear. Eli Siegel. ELU
Duke of Plaza-Toro, The. W. S. Gilbert. *Fr.* The Gondoliers. ALV; FaPON; FiBHP; OnPP; PCD
Duke of Rutland urged *The Times* to pray, The. You Can't Please Everybody. Edward Verrall Lucas. MemP
Dulce et Decorum. T. P. Cameron Wilson. HBMV
Dulce et Decorum Est. Wilfred Owen. AnFE; CBEP; CBV; CMoP; CoBMV; FaBoTw; FaBV; InP; InvP; LiTB; LiTM (rev. ed.); MMA; MoAB; MoBrPo; MoPW; OAEP (2d ed.); PoIE; PPON; ShBV-3; WaP
Dulce Ridentem. Stephen Vincent Benét. LOW
Dulcina. *St. to* Sir Walter Ralegh. ALV
(Come to Me Soon.) UnTE
(On Dulcina.) CoMu
(Shepherd's Wooing Dulcina, The.) TuPP
Dule's i' This Bonnet o' Mine, The. Edwin Waugh. HBV; VA
Dull and hard the low wind creaks. Suburb. Harold Monro. HBV
Dull as I was, to think that a court fly. A Black Patch on Lucasta's Face. Richard Lovelace. AnAnS-2; SCEP-2; SeCP
Dull day darkens to its close, The. "Fiona Macleod." Sonnet VII. SyP
Dull, dull, my Lord, my fancy dull I finde. Meditation CXXXI. Edward Taylor. *Fr.* Preparatory Meditations, Second Series. MAmP
Dull Is My Verse. Walter Savage Landor. PoEL-4
Dull masses of dense green. Embarkation. John Gould Fletcher. Down the Mississippi, I. AmFN; HT; LiTA; NP
Dull, sick day, A; the sky opaque—a cloudy screen. The Clock. Jovan Ducic. LiTW
Dull soul aspire. To the Soul. John Collop. TrGrPo
Dull to myself[e], and almost dead to these. The Bad Season Makes the Poet Sad. Robert Herrick. AnAnS-2; CABA; LiTB; OAEP; SeCeV; UnPo (1st ed.)
Dulled by the slow glare of the yellow bulb. A Wartime

Dawn. David Gascoyne. LiTM (1970 ed.); MoVE
Dulnesse. George Herbert. AnAnS-1; MaMe; MeP; SCEP-1
Dum Vivimus Vigilemus. Charles Henry Webb. AA
Dum Vivimus, Vivamus. Philip Doddridge. *See* Live While You Live.
Dumain's Rhymes. Shakespeare. *See* On a Day—Alack the Day!
Dumb are the heavens: sphere controlling sphere. Thomas Caulfield Irwin. *Fr.* To a Skull. IrPN
Dumb are the trumpets, cymbals. Solomon. Heine. TrJP
Dumb Dick. Leslie A. Fiedler. ErPo
Dumb, Dumb, Dumb. *Unknown.* OnYI
Dumb genius blows. From Another Room. Gregory Corso. NeAP
Dumb Maid, The, *with music.* *Unknown.* BFSS; CoBE
Dumb Mother of all maids, let me rest. Sonnet in a Garden. Josephine Preston Peabody. AA
Dumb Soldier, The. Robert Louis Stevenson. GoTP
Dumb Wife Cured, The. *Unknown.* MaC
Dumbe Healed, and the People Enjoyned Silence, The. Richard Crashaw. MaMe
Dumbo rescue report: the weather was dirty. Time Zones for Forty-four. Donald A. Stauffer. WaP
Dummer the shepherd sacrific'd. Epitaph. Cotton Mather. SCAP
Dun-Color. Ruth Pitter. MoVE; PoRA (rev. ed.)
Dun shades quiver down the lone long fallow. A Poem for Max Nordau. E. A. Robinson. AmePo
Duna. Marjorie Pickthall. HBV; MCCG; MLP
Dunbar. Anne Spencer. BANP; CDC; Kal
Dunbarton. Robert Lowell. NoP
Duncan and Brady. *Unknown.* *See* Brady.
Duncan and his brother was playing pool. Brady (B *vers.*). *Unknown.* AS
Duncan, Duncan was a-tendin' the bar. Duncan and Brady. *Unknown.* OuSiCo
Duncan Gray. Burns. BEL; CEP; CoMu; EiPP; EnLit; ErPo; GoTS; GTBS; GTBS-D; GTBS-P; GTBS-W; GTSE; GTSL; LiTL; MCCG; OBEC; PoMa; TOP
(Duncan Gray Cam' Here to Woo.) ALV
(Thrusting of It, The.) UnTE
Dunce, The. Walter de la Mare. ImOP
Dunce, The. Jacques Prévert, *tr. fr. French by* John Dixon Hunt. FlW
Dunces' Opera. Pope. *Fr.* The Dunciad, IV. MuSP
Dunciad, The, *sels.* Pope.
"And now the Queen, to glad her sons, proclaims," *fr.* II. NoP
"Books and the Man I sing," I (1729 ed.) CEP; EiCL
Conclusion: "In vain, in vain—the all-composing hour," *fr.* IV. EnLi-1; ViBoPo
(Chaos.) LoBV
(Reign of Chaos, The.) FiP
(Triumph of Ignorance, The.) CoBE
Dunces' Opera, *fr.* IV. MuSP
"High on a gorgeous seat, that far out-shone," *fr.* AtBAP
"In flowed at once a gay embroidered race," *fr.* IV. NoP
"Mighty mother, and her son, who brings, The," *fr.* I. AtBAP, *shorter sel.*; EiPP; FosPo
Triumph of Dulness, The. OBEC
"Yet, yet a moment, one dim ray of light, " *fr.* IV. AtBAP, *br. sel.*; EiPP; FosPo; MBW-1; PoEL-3
Duncton Hill. Hilaire Belloc. GoBC
Dunedin in the Gloaming. Jessie Mackay. BoAu
Dunedin Revisited. Denis Glover. AnNZ
Dungeon, The. Samuel Taylor Coleridge. *Fr.* Remorse (Osorio), V. MCCG
Dunkirk. Robert Nathan. MaC; OnSP
Dunkirk, *sel.* E. J. Pratt.
"From Dover to Dunkirk." PTK
Dunna thee tell me it's his'n, mother. Whether or Not. D. H. Lawrence. MoBrPo
Dunno a heap about the what an' why. Vagabond. John Masefield. OtMeF
Duns Scotus. Thomas Merton. CoPo
Duns Scotus's Oxford. Gerard Manley Hopkins. CoBE; GTBS-P; MaPo; NAMP; OBMV; PoE; PoEL-5; PoIE; VP
Duo. Olive Tilford Dargan. HBMV
Duo-tang. Kenward Elmslie. ANYP
Dupliciter Beatus. Henry Parrot. SiCE
Duplicity of Women, The. John Lydgate. *See* Beware of Doubleness.
Dupont's Round Fight. Herman Melville. MWA-1
Dupree. *Unknown.* OuSiCo, *with music*; ViBoFo (A *and* B *vers.*)
Durable Bon Mot, The. Keith Preston. HBMV
Duraluminum dove dives, The. Summary of the Distance between the Bomber and the Objective. Walter Benton. WaP
Durand of Blonden. Ludwig Uhland, *tr. fr. German by* James Clarence Mangan. AWP; JAWP; WBP
Durand Jail, The, *with music.* *Unknown.* CoSo
Durban Revisited. R. N. Currey. BoSA
Dürer would have seen a reason for living. The Steeple-Jack. Marianne Moore. *Fr.* Part of a Novel, Part of a Poem, Part of a Play. AmLP; AmPP; AP; CMoP; CoBMV; CrMA; ExPo; FaBoMo; ILP; MoPo; NoP; OnHM; OxBA; TwAmPo
Durham Field. *Unknown.* ESPB; OBB, *sl. diff.*
Durham Lock-out, The. *Unknown.* CoMu
Duriesdyke. Swinburne. OxBB
During a Bombardment by V-Weapons. Roy Fuller. ToPo
During a Chorale by César Franck. Witter Bynner. *Fr.* To Celia. AnAmPo; HBMV; NP
During December's Death. Delmore Schwartz. NYBP
During happy boyhood years. In Nazareth. Leslie Savage Clark. ChIP
During Music. Arthur Symons. MoBrPo; VA
During our encounters. For Sergeant Fetta. Ed Sanders. ANYP
During the Eichmann Trial, *sel.* Denise Levertov.
Crystal Night. NMP
During the past few months. Idaho. John Ashbery. ANYP
During the plague I came into my own. Tarantula or the Dance of Death. Anthony Hecht. CoAP
During the strike, the ponies were brought up. The Ponies. W. W. Gibson. WaKn
During the winter she began. Division. John Ratti. NYBP
During Wind and Rain. Thomas Hardy. CBV; CMoP; ELP; ExPo; ForPo; GTBS-P; PeVV; PIA; PoIE; PoSa; QFR; SeCeV; ViPP
Durst thou again say life and soul has lifted. Thomas Lovell Beddoes. *Fr.* Death's Jest Book. LO
Dusk. Basho, *tr. fr. Japanese by* H. G. Henderson. OnPM; WoL
Dusk. Angelina Weld Grimké. CDC
Dusk. DuBose Heyward. HBMV; HT
Dusk. Abraham Z. Lopez-Penha, *tr. fr. Spanish by* Thomas Walsh. TrJP
Dusk. Archibald MacLeish. HBMV
Dusk. Leonard E. Nathan. NYTB
Dusk. Helen Welshimer. PoToHe
Dusk for Me. Louis Paul Lehman, Jr. SoP
Dusk-haired and gold-robed o'er the golden wine. For the "Wine of Circe;" a Picture by Edward Burne-Jones. Dante Gabriel Rossetti. ATP (1953 ed.); MaVP; NoP; PoVP
Dusk in the Domain. Dorothea Mackellar. PoAu-1
Dusk in the Sugar Woods. Charles Malam. NYTB
Dusk in Winter. W. S. Merwin. NaP
Dusk made a thrust at my heart. The Star. Grace Hazard Conkling. HBMV
Dusk of day's decline was hard on dark, The. James Shirley. Swinburne. *Fr.* Sonnets on English Dramatic Poets. Sonn
Dusk of Horses, The. James Dickey. AP; LiTM (1970 ed.); NYBP; ToPo
Dusk of the Gods, *sel.* S. Funaroff.
"Of my deep hunger." NAMP
Dusk of this box wood, The. Hoof Dusk. Carl Sandburg. Po
Dusk Song. William H. A. Moore. BANP
Dusky night rides down the sky, The. A-Hunting We Will Go [*or* Hunting Song]. Henry Fielding. *Fr.* Don Quixote in England. CEP; HBV; OBEC; OTPC (1923 ed.); OxBoLi; StP; ViBoPo
Dust. "Æ." HBMV; OQP; WGRP
Dust. Sister Mary Angelita. JKCP (1926 ed.)
Dust. Rupert Brooke. ALV; HBV; MoBrPo; OBVV
Dust, The. Nathalia Crane. MAP; NeMA
Dust. Waring Cuney. CDC
Dust, The. Gertrude Hall. AA
Dust, The. Lizette Woodworth Reese. HBMV; PoMa
Dust. P. A. Ropes. BoTP
Dust. Sydney King Russell. ShM
Dust. Stanley Snaith. POTE
Dust. André Spire, *tr. fr. French by* Jethro Bithell. TrJP

Dust. Randolph Stow. PoAu-2
Dust always blowing about the town. A Peck of Gold. Robert Frost. LaNeLa; PDV; PoG
Dust and clay. Ascension-Hymn. Henry Vaughan. AnAnS-1; MeP; SCEP-1; SeCV-1
Dust blows up and down, The. The Dust. Lizette Woodworth Reese. HBMV; PoMa
Dust Bowl. Robert A. Davis. GoSl; IDB
Dust comes secretly day after day, The. Dusting. Viola Meynell. MoBrPo (1942 ed.)
Dust hangs thick upon the trail, The. The Cowboy and His Love [*or* Song of the Cattle Trail]. John Milton Hagen. CoSo; SCC
Dust Hath Closed Helen's Eye. Thomas Nashe. *See* Adieu, Farewell, Earth's Bliss!
Dust in a cloud, blinding weather. Apples and Water. Robert Graves. PoIE
Dust is such a pleasant thing. In Praise of Dust. Rachel Field. RePo
Dust is the end of all pursuit. Knell. George Chapman. MaRV
Dust of Love, The. Chad Walsh. NYTB
Dust of Snow. Robert Frost. AmPP; BiS; CMoP; InP; MaPo (1969 ed.); MoShBr; MoSiPe; OxBA; PDV; TiPo; UnPo; WePo
Dust of the Overland Trail, The. James Barton Adams. PoOW
Dust of Timas, the. E. A. Robinson, *after the Greek of* Sappho. AWP; JAWP; WBP
Dust through which. Dust. Waring Cuney. CDC
Dust to Dust. Walter de la Mare. TrPWD
Dust to Dust. Thomas Hood. *See* Epigram: "After such years of dissension and strife."
Dustbowl, The. Kenward Elmslie. ANYP
Duster, dust away, my friend. Dust. André Spire. TrJP
Dusting. Viola Meynell. MoBrPo (1942 ed.)
Dusting of the Books, The. Dorothy Hughes. GoYe
Dustman, The. Clive Sansom. BoTP
Dustman, The. *Unknown.* BoTP
Dustman, The. Frederic Edward Weatherly. HBV; OTPC
Dusty Answer, A. George Meredith. *See* Modern Love: "Thus piteously Love closed what he begot."
Dust road is mine to tread, A. Pedlar Jim. Florence Hoare. BoTP
Dutch, The. George Canning. OxBoLi
Dutch Courtesan, The, *sel.* John Marston.
  "O Love, How Strangely Sweet." AtBAP; TuPP
  (Song: "O Love, how strangely sweet.") ElL; LO
Dutch in the Thames [*or* the Medway], The. Andrew Marvell. *Fr.* The Last Instructions to a Painter. OBS; PeRV
Dutch Lover, The, *sel.* Aphra Behn.
  Amyntas Led Me to a Grove. ErPo
  (Willing Mistress, The.) UnTE; ViBoPo
Dutch Lullaby, A. Eugene Field. *See* Wynken, Blynken, and Nod.
Dutch Picture, A. Longfellow. AmPP (4th ed.); EtS; ExPo; HBVY; MoShBr; OnPP; PCD; PFY; YT
  (Simon Danz.) OBVV
Dutch Proverb, A. Matthew Prior. CEP
Dutch Seacoast. Kenneth Slessor. *Fr.* The Atlas. PoAu-2
Dutch Seamen and New Holland, The. William Pember Reeves. AnNZ
Dutchess' Lullaby, The. "Lewis Carroll." *See* Speak Roughly to Your Little Boy.
Dutchess of Monmouth's Lamentation for the Loss of Her Duke, The. *Unknown.* CoMu
Dutchesse of Malfy, The. John Webster. *See.* Duchess of Malfi, The.
Dutchman's Beeches. Arthur Guiterman. YT
Duties of Man, The. Romans, XII: 3-21, Bible, *N.T.* TreF
Duty ("In an age of fops and toys"). Emerson. Voluntaries, III. AnNE
  (In an Age of Fops and Toys.) LiTA
  (So Nigh Is Grandeur.) HBVY; TreFS; YT
  (Voluntaries, III.) MaRV
Duty ("So nigh is grandeur to our dust"), *last* 4 *ll.* FaFP; GN; HBV; TreF; YaD
  (Heroism.) OQP
  ("So nigh is grandeur to our dust.") TRV
Duty. Ellen S. Hooper. BLPA; NeHB; OQP; TreFS
  (Beauty and Duty.) HBV
Duty. Edwin Markham. HBMV; HBVY; OQP; TSW
Duty is a path of pain and peril. Motherhood. William L. Stidger. PGD
Duty of the Student. Edward Anthony. GoTP
Duty Our Ladder. Robert Leighton. OQP
Duty—That's to Say Complying. Arthur Hugh Clough. ViPP
Duty to Death, LD. Dick Roberts. WaP
Dwainie. James Whitcomb Riley. *Fr.* The Flying Islands of the Night. AA
Dwarf barefooted, chanting, The. The Peasants. Alun Lewis. FaBoMo; LiTM (1970 ed.)
Dwarf of Disintegration. Oscar Williams. LiTM (rev. ed.); MoPo; NePA; PoCh; TwAmPo
Dwarf pines; the wild plum on the wind-grassed shore. Colloquy with a King-Crab. John Peale Bishop. LiTA; MoPo
Dwell Deep, My Soul. *Unknown.* SoP
Dwell in Stillness. *Unknown.* SoP
Dwell in the Depths. J. E. Dean. SoP
Dwell with Me, Lovely Images. Theodore Maynard. GoBC
Dwelling Place, The. Henry Vaughan. MaRV; MeLP; OBS; OxBoCh; SeEP; TrPWD; WGRP
D'ye ken John Peel with his coat so gay [*or* gray]? John Peel [*or* Song]. John Woodcock Graves. CH; NBM; OxBoLi; PoG; SD
Dyer, The. *Unknown.* ChTr
  ("As I went by a dyer's door.") OxNR
Dying. Emily Dickinson. *See* I heard a fly buzz when I died.
Dying. Jessie Holt. ChIP; PGD
Dying. Martha Snell Nicholson. FaChP
Dying. Roden Noel. *See* Old, The.
Dying Airman, The. *Unknown.* FaFP; LiTM; OxBoLi; SiTL
  (Handsome Young Airman, The, *with music.*) AS
Dying: An Introduction. L. E. Sissman. NYBP
Dying Californian, The, *with music. Unknown.* BFSS; TrAS
Dying Child, The. John Clare. CBEP; EnRP; FIW; NCEP; TrGrPo
Dying Christian to His Soul, The. Pope, *par. fr. the Latin of* Emperor Hadrian. AWP; BoPe; CAW; GoBC; HBV; JAWP; MaRV; NeHB; OBEV; SoP; TreF; WBP
  (Ode: Dying Christian to His Soul, The.) CEP
  (Vital Spark of Heavenly Flame.) GTBS-W; LiTB; LiTG; PoPo
Dying Cowboy, The ("Oh, bury me not on the lone prairie"). *Unknown.* BFSS (A *vers., with music*); CoSo, *longer vers. with music*; FaBoBe
  (Bury Me Not on the Lone Prairie.) FaBV; FaFP; TrAS, *with music*; WOW
  (Lone Prairie, The.) ViBoFo
  (O, Bury Me Not on the Lone Prairie.) AS, *br. sel., with music*; ATP
Dying Cowboy of Rim Rock Ranch, The, *with music. Unknown.* CoSo
Dying Crane, The. Michael Drayton. OA
Dying Damsel's Doleful Destiny, The. *Unknown. See* Among the Violets, Fair Lilies and Roses.
Dying day pinches the tot. Daily News. Tom Clark. ANYP
Dying Desperado, The. *Unknown.* CoSo
Dying, dying. The Small Hours. Mary Ursula Bethell. OnPM
Dying Eagle, The. E. J. Pratt. ACV
Dying Enthusiast, The. James Clarence Mangan. IrPN
Dying Eusebio's Address to the Cross, The. Pedro Calderón de la Barca. *See* Cross, The.
Dying figure against the sky, A. Calvary. Mary Hallet. ChIP; PGD
Dying firelight slides along the quirt, A. The End of the Weekend. Anthony Hecht. LiTM (1970 ed.); NePoEA-2
Dying Fisherman's Song, The. *Unknown.* TreFT
Dying Girl, The. Richard D'Alton Williams. OnYI
Dying Hogger, The. *Unknown.* AS, *with music*; IHA
Dying Hymn, A. Alice Cary. HBV
Dying Indian, The. Joseph Warton. EiCL
Dying Lover, The. Sir William Davenant. SeCL
Dying Lover, The. Richard Henry Stoddard. HBV
Dying Man, The, *sels.* Theodore Roethke.
  Exulting, The. PoDB
  They Sing. NYBP
    They Sing, They Sing. PoDB
Dying Man in His Garden, The. George Sewell. GTBS; GTBS-D; GTBS-P; GTBS-W; GTSE

Dying man to the Whitefriar gave, The. Mountain Liberty. Ernest Rhys. *Fr.* The Ballads of the Last Prince. PoFr
Dying Men. Shakespeare. King Richard II, *fr.* II, i. MaRV
Dying Patriot, The. James Elroy Flecker. HBMV; ViBoPo
Dying Ranger, The, *with music. Unknown.* BFSS; CoSo
(Dying Soldier, The, *diff. vers., with music.*) ShS
Dying Reservist, The. Maurice Baring. HBV
Dying Soldier, The. *Unknown. See* Dying Ranger, The.
Dying Speech of an Old Philosopher. Walter Savage Landor. *See* On His Seventy-fifth Birthday.
Dying Stockman, The. *Unknown.* PoAu-1; ViBoFo
Dying sun, shine warm a little longer! Lament for Pasiphae. Robert Graves. FaBoTw
Dying Swan, The. T. Sturge Moore. GTBS-D; OBMV; SeCePo; SyP
Dying Swan, The. Tennyson. GTSE; OTPC; PeER; WiR
Dying Swan, The. *Unknown.* ChTr
Dying that I Might Live. Charles Wesley. BePJ
Dying Thief, The. J. S. Phillimore. OQP
Dying! To be afraid of thee. Emily Dickinson. MoPo
Dying Wife to Her Husband, A. Moses ibn Ezra, *tr. fr. Hebrew.* TrJP
Dying Words of Stonewall Jackson, The. Sidney Lanier. PAH
Dying Year, The. Clyde Walton Hill. PEDC
Dyke-Builder, The. Henry Treece. LiTB; LiTM; WaP
Dylan Thomas. Stephen Spender. ML
Dynastic Tiff. Geoffrey Hellman. ALV
Dynasties, the Sky Overhead, The. Randy Blasing. YAP
Dynasts, The, *sels.* Thomas Hardy.
After Jena, *fr.* Pt. II, Act I, sc. vii. WaaP
Albuera, *fr.* Pt. II, Act VI, sc. iv. WaaP
Chorus: "Yea, the coneys are scared by the thud of hoofs," *fr.* Pt. III, Act VI, sc. viii. LoBV
(Before Waterloo.) MoAB; PoVP; WaaP
(Chorus of the Years.) CMoP
(Field of Waterloo, The, *shorter sel.*) FaBoCh; LoGBV
Field of Talavera, The, *fr.* Pt. II, Act IV, sc. iv. CMoP
Men Who March Away, *fr.* Pt. I, Act I, sc. i. CH
Night of Trafalgar, The, *fr.* Pt. I, Act V, sc. vii. ChTr; FaBoCh; MoBrPo; OBMV; OTD; PoVP; ShBV-1
(Boatman's Song, The.) WaaP
(Trafalgar.) CH
Overworld, The, Pt. III, After Scene. WoL
"When we lay where Budmouth Beach is," *fr.* Pt. III, Act II, sc. i. LO
(Budmouth Dears.) CH; MoVE; PoVP
Dypsychus. Arthur Hugh Clough. *See* Dipsychus.
Dysynni Valley, The. Theodore Holmes. CoPo
Dyvers dothe use, as I have hard and kno. *See* Divers doth use. . .
Dyvers thy death doo dyverslye bemone. *See* Divers thy Death.

E

E. A. Poe/ disappeared. The Invaders. Ronald Johnson. HYE
E. B. B. James Thomson. HBV
$E=MC^2$ Morris Bishop. ImOP
E is the Escalator. Phyllis McGinley. *Fr.* All Around the Town. TiPo
E. P. Ode pour l'Election de Son Sepulchre. Ezra Pound. *Fr.* Hugh Selwyn Mauberley. AmPP (5th ed.); AP; CABA; CMoP; CoBMV; CrMA; FaBoEn; LiTA; LiTM (rev. ed.); MasP; MoAmPo (1962 ed.); MoPo; MoVE; NePA; OxBA; PoIE; PP; SeCeV; UnPo (3d ed.)
(Pour l'Election de Son Sepulchre.) FaBoMo; LiTG
E. Tenebris. Oscar Wilde. BrPo; CABA; CAW; ChIP; JKCP (1926 ed.); MaRV; MoBrPo; PoLi; Sonn; StJW; TrPWD
"Come down, O Christ, and help me! reach thy hand," *sel.* TreFT
E to the X dy! dx! Engineer's Yell (University of California). *Unknown.* WhC
'E was sittin' on a door-step. The Road to Vagabondia. Dana Burnet. PoLF
Each a Part of All. Augustus Wright Bamberger. *See* Out of the Vast.
Each and All. Emerson. AA; AmePo; AmP; AmPP; AnNE; AP; AWP; CoBA; HBV; ILP; MAmP; MCCG; MWA-1; NePA; OHFP; OQP; OxBA; PoIE; TOP; WGRP
Each beast can choose his fere according to his mind. Of a Lady That Refused to Dance with Him. Earl of Surrey. SiPS
Each blest drop, on each blest limn. On the Water of Our Lord's Baptism. Richard Crashaw. MaMe; SeEP
Each care-worn face is but a book. The Strangers. Jones Very. CBEP; OXBA
Each dawn is clear. Logging, VIII. Gary Snyder. *Fr.* Myths & Texts. NaP; NMP; OPoP
Each day another installment of the old. The Daily Globe. Howard Nemerov. TPM
Each day, dear love, my road leads far. The Homing Heart. Daniel Henderson. HBMV
Each day I live, each day the sea of light. Poem against the Rich. Robert Bly. NMP
Each day I open the cupboard. The Routine. Paul Blackburn. ELU
Each day I pray high God to give me strength anew. Give Me Strength. *Unknown.* FaChP
Each day I walk with wonder. A Prayer. Clinton Scollard. TrPWD
Each day into the upper air. Election Reflection. M. Keel Jones. PV
Each day sees die the lonely leaf, sees die. Threnos. J. R. Hervey. AnNZ
Each day she woke with sullen eyes. The Witch. Stanley McNail. FiSC
Each day the string that joined their natural selves. The Cat and the Bird. Marvin Solomon. NePoAm-2
Each day to her a miracle. Mother. *Unknown.* PGD
Each day, when the glow of sunset. "Are the Children at Home?" Margaret E. Sangster. HBV
Each day you live. Mother. Percy Waxman. PEDC
Each element to water yields. The First Olympionique to Hiero of Syracuse, Victorious in the Horse-Race. Pindar. *Fr.* Odes. ATP
Each eve earth falleth down the dark. The Day of Days. William Morris. PoVP
Each evening the sea casts starfish up on the beach. Prosepoem. William Knott. YAP
Each evening tulips close their eyes. The Sleepy Tulips. Marion Mitchell Walker. GFA
Each face its own phantom. Cartagena de Indias. Earl Birney. MoCV
Each fall I put down. About the Grass. James L. Weil. NYTB
Each for himself is still the rule. In the Great Metropolis. Arthur Hugh Clough. PoVP; ViPP
Each Found Himself at the End of. . . Ebbe Borregaard. NeAP
Each Friday morning, sharp at eight. Black Friday. Louella C. Poole. CIV
Each gesture. A Reason. Robert Creeley. NaP
Each golden note of music greets. Moonlight Song of the Mocking-Bird. William Hamilton Hayne. AA
Each has his saint, and one may dream. St. Peter. Eileen Duggan. WHL
Each hath his drug for sorrow. To Each His Own. Margaret Root Garvin. HBV
Each hour until we meet is as a bird. Winged Hours. Dante Gabriel Rossetti. The House of Life, XXV. EPN; MaVP; PoVP; ViPo; VP
Each, in himself, his hour to be and cease. Epilogue: Credo. Arthur Symons. OBVV; OQP; PoVP
Each in His Inmost Heart. John D. Sheridan. JKCP (1955 ed.)
Each in His Own Tongue. W. H. Carruth. AmePo; BBV; BLPA; HBV; MaRV; NeHB; OHFP; OQP; TRV; WBLP; WGRP
Each instant of his life a task, he never rests. The Poet. James Kirkup. PP
Each is beautiful. Tell Our Daughters. Besmilr Brigham. ThO
Each known mile comes late. The Train Runs Late to Harlem. Conrad Kent Rivers. IDB
Each life converges to some centre. Emily Dickinson. NoP
Each lonely haunt where vanished tribes have dwelt. The Cathedral. Thomas S. Jones, Jr. MaRV
Each lover's longing leads him naturally. Sonnet: To Dante Aligh-

Each (continued)
ieri (He Interprets Dante's Dream). Cino da Pistoia. AWP
Each man is captain of his soul. We Break New Seas Today. John Oxenham. OQP
Each man is limited by inborn traits. Love Is Kind. Benjamin Keech. PoToHe
Each man me telleth I change most my devise. Sir Thomas Wyatt. FCP; SiPS
Each man to his forced march; this is mine. Hitchhiker. Jack Marshall. NYBP
Each Morning. LeRoi Jones. *Fr.* Hymn for Lanie Poo. IDB; NNP
Each morning bees and butterflies. A Lovely Bed. Mattie Lee Hausgen. GFA
Each morning I lift my blind to stare. Urban Roses. Ted Isaac. PoPl
Each morning there were lambs with bloody mouth. Foxes among the Lambs. Ernest G. Moll. BoAu
Each new American. Jean Toomer. *Fr.* The Blue Meridian. BALP
Each New Hour's Passage Is the Acolyte. Lord Alfred Douglas. *Fr.* The City of the Soul. MoBrPo (1942 ed.); WHA
Each night has new meaning. On the Murder of Martin Luther King. Stan Rice. QAH
Each of us is like Balboa: once in all our lives do we. Rare Moments. Charles Henry Phelps. AA
Each of us like you. Adonis. Hilda Doolittle ("H.D."). AP; AWP; InPo; JAWP; PoPl; WBP
Each of us pursues his trade. The Scholar and the Cat. *Unknown.* KiLC
Each of us waking to the window's light. Exile. Donald Hall. NePA
Each on his own strict line we move. Too Late. Matthew Arnold. VP
Each one deserves great praise to have, but yet not like, I think. Fortitude; a Young Man of Egypt and Valerian. Richard Edwards. ReIE
Each one shall sit at table with his own cup and spoon. A Practical Program for Monks. Thomas Merton. CoPo
Each other we meet but live grief rises early. Definition of My Brother. W. S. Graham. FaBoTw; NeBP
Each pale Christ stirring underground. Words for a Resurrection. Leo Kennedy. OBCV; PeCV
Each soldier as he passes looks at their breasts. Namkwin Pul. Bernard Gutteridge. WaP
Each storm-soaked flower has a beautiful eye. Rain. Vachel Lindsay. CMoP
Each the herald is who wrote. Astraea. Emerson. AnNE
Each, the issue of a passioned kiss. On a Row of Nuns in a Cemetery. R. G. Howarth. ELU
Each time, greenbones, you pressed the neat trigger. Boy at Target Practice: a Contemplation. W. R. Moses. NYBP
Each time his will abdicated. Possession. Lynne Lawner. ErPo
Each time I return to Johannesburg it is summer. David Wright. *Fr.* Seven South African Poems. ACV; BoSA
Each to Each. Melville Cane. GoYe
Each to His Own Ground. John Stevens Wade. ThO
Each tree did boast the wished springtime's pride. Thomas Watson. *Fr.* The Tears of Fancy. Sonn; TuPP
Each tree stands alone in stillness. Sonnet XVII. Ted Berrigan. FRC
Each was honest after his way. The Diplomats. Alfred Noyes. MaRV
Each with each has borne in patience. To Edom. Heine. TrJP
Each year for a short season. Folk Wisdom. Thomas Kinsella. TwCP
Each year I have a birthday. A Giant's Cake. Evelina San Garde. BoTP
Eadem Mutato Resurgo. Selden Rodman. OnHM
Eadie, *with music.* *Unknown.* OuSiCo
Eager he look'd. Another train of years. A League of Nations [*or* One Centred System]. Joel Barlow. *Fr.* The Columbiad, X. AmPP (5th ed.); AP; CoBA
Eager he wandered the streets of Scythopolis. A Stranger in Scythopolis. Katharine Lee Bates. StJW
Eager Spring. Gordon Bottomley. MoBrPo; POTE
"Eager to search, in and throughout its ways." Dante and Beatrice in the Earthly Paradise. Dante. *Fr.* Divina Commedia: Purgatorio. BoC
Eagerly/ Like a woman hurrying to her lover. Four Glimpses of Night. Frank Marshall Davis. AmNP; PoNe
Eagle, The. James Daly. AnAmPo
Eagle, The. Tennyson. BEL; BoTP; BoLiVe; CaFP; CBEP; CBV; CH; DiPo; EG; EnL; ExPo; FaBoCh; FaPON; FiP; GN; GoJo; GoTP; GTBS-D; GTBS-P; GTSL; HBV; LoGBV; MaPo (1969 ed.); MBW-2; MemP; MyFE; NoP; OAEP; OTPC; PCD; PCH; PDV; PoIE; PoMa; PoPo; PoVP; PTK; RIS; SeCePo; SeCeV; ShBV-1; StaSt; StP; SUS; SyP; TDP; ThWaDe; TreFT; TrGrPo; UnPo (3d ed.); UTS; VaPo; ViPo; ViPP; WePo; WiR; YT
Eagle, The. Andrew Young. ELU; WePo
Eagle, and the Assembly of Animals, The. John Gay. *Fr.* Fables. EiCP
Eagle and the Mole, The. Elinor Wylie. AnFE; APA; AWP; BoLiVe; CoAnAm; CoBA; GTBS-W; HBMV; LiTA; LiTM; MAP; MoAB; MoAmPo; NeMA; NP; OA; PG; PoE; PoPo; TreFT; TSW; ViBoPo; WHA
Eagle and Vulture, The. Thomas Buchanan Read. PAH
Eagle, The, did ye see him fall? The Eagle's Fall. Charles Goodrich Whiting. AA
Eagle for an Emperor. Falconry. Anne Wilkinson. MoCV; OBCV
Eagle headed to the west, An. The Tall Axe-Man. Robert P. Tristram Coffin. PoFr
Eagle of Corinth, The. Henry Howard Brownell. PAH
Eagle of the armies of the West, The. The Flight of the War Eagle. Obadiah Cyrus Auringer. AA
Eagle of the Blue, The. Herman Melville. AA
Eagle on a Tombstone. Antipater of Sidon, *tr. fr. Greek by* John Leyden. OnPM
Eagle Plain. Robert Francis. AmFN
Eagle Soars in the Summit of Heaven, The. T. S. Eliot. *Fr.* The Rock. NAMP; OBMV; OnHM
(Knowledge without Wisdom.) MaRV
Eagle Song. Gordon Bottomley. *Fr.* Suilven and the Eagle. MoBrPo
Eagle Sonnets, *sels.* Clement Wood. HBMV
"Flower of the dust am I: for dust will flower," VII.
"I am a tongue for beauty," XIX.
"I have been sure of three things all my life," III.
"O bitter moon, O cold and bitter moon," IX.
"We are the singing shadows beauty casts," XX.
"When down the windy vistas of the years," XI.
Eagle Swift, The. Adam of St. Victor, *tr. fr. Latin.* BePJ
Eagle That Is Forgotten, The. Vachel Lindsay. AmP; AnFE; APA; ATP; AWP; CMoP; CoAnAm; HBV; InP; JAWP; LiTA; MAP; MoAB; MoAmPo; MoRP; NeMA; NePA; NP; OTD; OxBA; PFY; Po; PoFr; TOP; TwAmPo; ViBoPo (1958 ed.); WBP; WHA; WOW
Eagle Valor, Chicken Mind. Robinson Jeffers. ELU; LiTA; OxBA; WaP
Eagle! why soarest thou above that tomb? Spirit of Plato [*or* Plato's Tomb]. *Unknown, tr. by* Shelley. AWP; EnLi-1; FaBoCh; JAWP; LoGBV; WBP
Eagles and lions, kings of birds and beasts. Of Seals and Arms. John Taylor. CBEP
Eagles and Sparrows. José Santos Chocano, *tr. fr. Spanish by* Alice Stone Blackwell. PoFr
Eagle's Fall, The. Charles Goodrich Whiting. AA
Eagles, leave your sky. Broadcast to the Scholars in the Eyrie. David Ross. PG (1945 ed.)
Eagle's Nature, The. *Unknown, tr. fr. Middle English. Fr.* The Bestiary. MeEV
Eagles over the Lambing Paddock. Ernest G. Moll. BoAu; PoAu-2
Eagle's shadow runs across the plain. Zebra. "Isak Dinesen." GoJo
Eagle's Song, The. Mary Austin. NP
Eagle's Song, The. Richard Mansfield. DD; HBV; HBVY; MC; PaA; PAH
Eagles, that wheel above our crests. The Cedars of Lebanon. Lamartine. AWP; JAWP; WBP
Eaper Weaper. *Unknown.* OxBoLi
Ear Is Not Deaf. Irene Dayton. GoYe
Ear-Maker and the Mould-Mender, The. La Fontaine. UnTE
Ear the answer, The/ Hears the wrecked cry. The Hill of Intrusion. W. S. Graham. NePoEA
Earl Bothwell. *Unknown.* ESPB
Earl Brand. *Unknown. See* Douglas Tragedy, The.
Earl Crawford. *Unknown.* BaBo; ESPB

Earl March look'd on his dying child. The Maid of Neidpath [*or* Song]. Thomas Campbell. GoTS; GTBS; GTBS-D; GTBS-P; GTBS-W; GTSE; GTSL; HBV
Earl Mar's Daughter. *Unknown.* BuBa; GN; HBV; OBB; OnSP
(Earl of Mar's Daughter, The.) BaBo; CH,*abr.*; ESPB
Earl Mertoun's Song. Robert Browning. *Fr.* The Blot in the 'Scutcheon. HBV; OBEV; PTK
("There's a woman like a dewdrop.") UnTE
Earl Norman and John Truman. Charles Mackay. VA
Earl o' Quarterdeck, The. George Macdonald. BeLS; EtS; LoEn
Earl of Aboyne, The. *Unknown.* BaBo; ESPB
Earl of Errol, The. *Unknown.* ESPB
Earl of Mar's Daughter, The. *Unknown.* *See* Earl Mar's Daughter.
Earl of Shaftesbury, The. Dryden. *See* Achitophel.
Earl of Surrey to Geraldine, The. Michael Drayton. *See* Henry Howard, Earl of Surrey, to the Lady Geraldine.
Earl of Westmoreland, The. *Unknown.* ESPB
Earl of Wigton had three daughters, The. Richie Story. *Unknown.* BaBo; ESPB
Earl Percie of Northumberland. Chevy Chase. *Unknown.* EnSB
Earl Richard had but ae daughter. The Kitchie-Boy. *Unknown.* BaBo
Earl Rothes. *Unknown.* BaBo; ESPB
Earle Douglasse for this day doth with the Percies stand, The. Michael Drayton. *Fr.* Polyolbion. OBS
Earliest Christian Hymn ("Curb for stubborn steed"). Clement of Alexandria, *tr. fr. Greek by* Edward H. Plumptre. WGRP
(Hymn to Christ our Saviour.) CAW
Earliest Christian Hymn, The ("Shepherd of tender youth"). Clement of Alexandria. *See* Shepherd of Eager Youth.
Earliest Spring. William Dean Howells. OBEV; OBVV
Earliest spring, and clouds at dawn are few. Dialogue of the Way. Harold Stewart. BoAV
Earliness at the Cape. Babette Deutsch. NePoAm-2; NYBP
Ear Lobe. Coleman Barks. *Fr.* Body Poems. QAH
Early and late the backdrop is for joy. This World. Abbie Huston Evans. NePoAm
Early April. Robert Frost. YeAr
Early Bacon. Archibald Stodart-Walker. *Fr.* The Moxford Book of English Verse. CenHV
Early before the day doth spring. Of Astraea [*or* The Virgin Queen; an Anagram]. Sir John Davies. *Fr* Hymns of Astraea. SiCE; TrGrPo; TuPP
Early Bluebird, An. Maurice Thompson. AA
Early cheerful, mounting lark. To the Lark. Sir John Davies. *Fr.* Hymns of Astraea. SiCE
Early Christian, An. Robert Barnabas Brough. OBVV
Early Chronology. Siegfried Sassoon. FaBoTw
Early Dawn. Hilaire Belloc. *See* Early Morning, The.
Early Days, The. Basil Dowling. AnNZ
Early Death. Hartley Coleridge. HBV; MaRV; OBEV; TreFS
Early Death and Fame. Matthew Arnold. MBW-2
Early December in Croton-on-Hudson. Louise Glück. YAP
Early dew woos the half ripened flowers, An. Haroun's Favorite Song. *Unknown.* *Fr.* The Thousand and One Nights. AWP
Early Dutch. Jennie M. Palen. GoYe
Early, early, comes the dark. Witches' Song. Elizabeth J. Coatsworth. PoMS
Early, Early Easter Day. Aileen Fisher. SiSoSe
Early Evening Quarrel. Langston Hughes. HoPM
Early for God. Emily Dickinson. *See* It was too late for man.
Early Fragments, *sels.* Thomas Lovell Beddoes.
  Grief-in-Idleness. AtBAP
  Her Kisses. AtBAP
  ("Her Kisses are/ Soft as a snow-tuft. . .") LO
  I'll Be as True. AtBAP
Early have a miser's insinuating rub, The. Timers. Flora J. Arnstein. GoYe
Early I rose/ In the blue morning. Love Song. *Unknown, tr. by* Mary Austin. AWP; JAWP; LiTA
Early in One Spring,*with music.* *Unknown.* BFSS
Early in the Morning. Louis Simpson. PoIE; PoSa
Early in the Morning ("Way, hay, there she rises"). *Unknown.* AmSS
Early in the morning. A Watering Rhyme. P. A. Ropes. BoTP
Early in the morning, before the day began. The Angel in the Apple Tree. Winifred Welles. StVeCh
Early in the morning, when the dawn is on the roofs. The Milkman. Christopher Morley. GaP; MPB
Early in the spring when the snow is all gone. A Trip to the Grand Banks. *Unknown.* ShS
Early indians were our first poets, The. Lake Winnipesaukee. Olive Driver. RePo
Early Influences. Mark Akenside. *Fr.* The Pleasures of Imagination, IV. OBEC
Early light of the rising sun shines on the beams of my house, The. Getting up Early on a Spring Morning. Po Chü-i. FlW
Early Love. Samuel Daniel. *Fr.* Hymen's Triumph. ErPo
(First Flame.) BoLP
Early Lynching. Carl Sandburg. MAP; MoAmPo
Early Moon. Carl Sandburg. LaNeLa; PG
Early Morn with Jesus. *Unknown.* SoP
Early Morning, The. Hilaire Belloc. BoNaP; BoTP; GTBS-D; HBMV; HBVY; JKCP; POTE; RIS; WaKn
(Early Dawn.) ThGo
Early Morning. Morris Bishop. PV
Early Morning. Philip Dow. QAH
Early Morning at Bargis. Hermann Hagedorn. HBV
Early Morning Feed. Peter Redgrove. BoC
Early Morning in a Glade. Glenn Ward Dresbach. NP
Early Morning Meadow Song. Charles Dalmon. ALV; CH; HBMV
Early Mornings. *Unknown, tr. fr. Spanish by* Louis Untermeyer. AS
Early News. Anna Maria Pratt. AA
Early on a Monday morning. Kevin Barry. *Unknown.* AS
Early One Morning ("Early one morning in May I set out"). Edward Thomas. MoVE
Early One Morning ("Early one morning, just as the sun was rising"). *Unknown.* ChTr
Early one morning as I went out to plow. Farmer Jones's Wife. *Unknown.* BFSS
Early one morning the bay will be full of pelicans. The Pelicans My Father Sees. Sister Maris Stella. GoBC
Early rises the sun, summer draws nigh. His Delight. Meilir ap Gwalchmai. LiTW
Early Rising. Lady Flora Hastings. OTPC (1923 ed.)
Early Rising. John Godfrey Saxe. AnNE; BOHV; HBV; InMe; PoLF; WhC
Early Rising and Prayer. Henry Vaughan. *Fr.* Rules and Lessons. SoP
Early Spring. Kalidasa. *Fr.* The Seasons. AWP
Early Spring. Sidney Keyes. FaBoMo; MoBrPo (1962 ed.)
Early Spring. Tennyson. DD; HBV; HBVY
Early Summer Night. Wen Yi-tuo, *tr. fr. Chinese by* Ho Yung. LiTW
Early Summer Thought. Marie J. Post. SoP
Early sun on Beaulieu water. Youth and Age on Beaulieu River, Hants. John Betjeman. ChMP; FaBoTw; TwCP
Early Supper. Barbara Howes. GoJo; PoPl
Early that afternoon, as we keep. The "Portland" Going Out. W. S. Merwin. NYBP
Early this morning. The Strangers. Audrey Alexandra Brown. WHW
Early This Spring We'll Leave Nauvoo. Austin Fife *and* Alta Fife. OTD
Early thou goest forth, to put to rout. To a "Tenting" Boy. Charles Tennyson-Turner. OBNC
Early Thoughts. William Edward Hartpole Lecky. OnYI
Early to bed and early to rise. Early to Bed [*or* Rhymes to Remember *or* Some Proverbs in Verse]. *Unknown.* FaBoBe; PCH; StaSt
Early Unfinished Sketch. Austin Clarke. ErPo
Early Waking. Léonie Adams. LiTM (1970 ed.); MoVE
Earnest, earthless, equal, attuneable. Spelt from Sibyl's Leaves. Gerard Manley Hopkins. BrPo; CMoP; CoBMV; FaBoMo; LiTM; MaPo; MoPo; PoAn; PoDB; ViPo (1962 ed.); ViPP; VP
Early Winter. Weldon Kees. NaP
Earnest Suit to His Unkind Mistress Not to Forsake Him, An. Sir Thomas Wyatt. BEL; EnLit; GoBC; LiTL; TOP
("And wilt [*or* wylt] thou leave me thus?") AtBAP; EG; ElL; EnLoPo; OAEP; ReEn; ReIE; SiCE; SiPS; TuPP
(Appeal, The.) OBEV; OBSC

Earnest (continued)
(Lover's Appeal, The.) GTBS; GTBS-D; GTBS-W; GTSE; GTSL
(Say Nay.) LoBV
Ears in the Turrets Hear. Dylan Thomas. FaBoTw
Ears lack no food, for loaded time. Light Heart. T. Sturge Moore. POTE
Earth. Bryant. AmePo; AP
Earth, The. Emerson. AA
Earth. Oliver Herford. *Fr.* The Bashful Earthquake. (Proem: "If this little world tonight.") AA
Earth, The. Leonard Mann. BoAV; MoAuPo; NeLNL
Earth. William Caldwell Roscoe. VA
Earth. Rolland Snellings. BF
Earth, The. Jones Very. AmP; OxBA
Earth. Brian Vrepont. NeLNL
Earth ("Grasshopper, your fairy song"). John Hall Wheelock. AnFE; APA; CoAnAm; HBMV; InP; LiTA; MAP; MoAmPo; MoRP
Earth ("Planet, A, doesn't explode"). John Hall Wheelock. LiTM (1970 ed.); PV
Earth Abideth Forever, The. Ecclesiastes, I: 4-7, Bible, *O.T.* FaPON
Earth and Air. Frank Ernest Hill. MAP; MoAmPo (1942 ed.)
Earth and Fire. Vernon Watkins. NYBP
Earth and I Gave You Turquoise. N. Scott Momaday. PoPl
Earth and Man, The. Stopford Brooke. HBV; OnYI; OTPC
Earth and Man. George Meredith. EPN; ViPo
Earth and Sky. Euripides, *tr. fr. Greek by* C. M. Bowra. EaLo
Earth and Sky. Eleanor Farjeon. BoChLi; PoSC; SUS
Earth and water, air and stars. Immortality. "Nikolai Maksimovich Minski." TrJP
Earth Asks and Receives Rain, The. Phyllis Haring. PeSA
Earth-bound. Henry W. Frost. SoP
Earth Bows to the New Bomb. Aline Badger Carter. ChIP
Earth breaks up, time drops away. Robert Browning. *Fr.* Christmas-Eve and Easter-Day. ChIP
Earth Breath, The. "Æ." BEL
Earth-canonized. Henry Morton Robinson. CAW
Earth darkens and is beaded. Quod Tegit Omnia. Yvor Winters. MoVE; QFR
Earth dies to haze below, the cables sing. Clouds. Frank Ernest Hill. AnAmPo
Earth does not ever grow fat, The. Ngoni Burial Song. *Unknown.* PeSA
Earth does not lack. W. H. Davies Simplifies the Simplicities He Loves. Louis Untermeyer. WhC
Earth does not understand her child. The Return. Edna St. Vincent Millay. GTBS-W; InP; LiTA; MAP; MoAB; MoAmPo; MoPo; OxBA; FoPl
Earth draws her breath so gently, heaven bends. The Marriage of Earth and Heaven. Jay Macpherson. OBCV
Earth Felicities, Heavens Allowances. Richard Steere. SCAP
Earth from heavenly light conceived heat, The. George Chapman. *Fr.* Ovid's Banquet of Sense. ReIE
Earth from her winter slumber breaks. Decoration Day. Julia Ward Howe. DD; OHIP
Earth gave Thee a cradle, O Christ, and a cross. Cradle and Throne. *Unknown.* STF
Earth gets its price for what Earth gives us. James Russell Lowell. *Fr.* The Vision of Sir Launfal. TreF
Earth grows white with harvest; all day long, The. The Harvest of the Sea. John McCrae. EtS
Earth has borne a little son. The Aconite. A. M. Graham. BoTP
Earth has grown old with its burden of care, The. Christmas Carol. Phillips Brooks. HH; MaRV; PEDC
Earth has its rock: the body has its bone. Peasantry. Eileen Duggan. CoBE
Earth Has Not Anything to Show More Fair. Wordsworth. *See* Composed upon Westminster Bridge.
Earth has not anything to show more fair. On Mrs. W——. Nicolas Bentley. FiBHP
Earth Has Shrunk in the Wash. William Empson. CMoP
Earth in Spring, The. Judah Halevi, *tr. fr. Hebrew by* Edward G. King. TrJP
Earth is a jealous mother; from her breast. Coelo et in Terra. Thomas Walsh. JKCP
Earth is a place on which England is found, The. Geography. G. K. Chesterton. *Fr.* Songs of Education. HBMV
Earth is dark where you rest. Dark Earth and Summer. Edgar Bowers. QFR
Earth Is Enough. Edwin Markham. MaRV; OQP; SoP; TreFS; TRV
Earth Is Full of God's Goodness, The. James Montgomery. MaRV
Earth is God's, and what the globe of. Psalm XXIV. *Paraphrased by* Sir Philip Sidney. FCP
Earth is instinct with spirit everywhere. Immanence. Thomas Durley Landels. MaRV
Earth is like a spinning top, The. The Spinning Top. Sister Mary Angelita. WHL
Earth is raw with this one note. Crows. Lizette Woodworth Reese. MAP; MoAmPo (1942 ed.)
Earth is the Lord's and the fullness thereof, The. Psalm XXIV, Bible, *O.T.* AWP; EaLo; EnLi-1; FaPON; JAWP; OHIP; OnPM; OuHeWo; PCD; PCH; TiPo (1952 ed.); TreFT; TrGrPo; TrJP; WoL
"Earth is the Lord's and the fulness thereof, The." Spring Song. Helen Steiner Rice. FaChP
Earth is the tower of granite, the floor of loam. Earth and Air. Frank Ernest Hill. MAP; MoAmPo (1942 ed.)
Earth is weary of our foolish wars, The. Let Us Have Peace. Nancy Byrd Turner. MaRV; OQP; OTD; PoToHe
Earth keeps some vibration going, The. Fiddler Jones. Edgar Lee Masters. *Fr.* Spoon River Anthology. AmP; CMoP; LiTA; LoGBV; NP; OxBA; TDP; TrGrPo; UnS
Earth labored, and lo! Man lay in her lap. Afterthought. Justin Richardson. PV
Earth Late Choked with Showers, The. Thomas Lodge. *Fr.* Scillaes Metamorphosis. EIL; PoSa; SiCE; ViBoPo
(Melancholy.) OBSC
(Sonnet.) TuPP
Earth lay like one revealed. Thunder over Earth. Horatio Colony. TwAmPo
Earth, let thy softest mantle rest. Horace Greeley. Edmund Clarence Stedman. DD
Earth lies here in giant folds and creases, The. High Wheat Country. Elijah L. Jacobs. AmFN
Earth Listens. Katharine Lee Bates. PGD
Earth, Mother Earth, do you feel light flowing. Peace Triumphant. Cale Young Rice. PEDC
Earth, My Likeness. Walt Whitman. NePA; OxBA
Earth now is green, and heaven is blue. To the Spring. Sir John Davies. *Fr.* Hymns of Astraea. EIL; SiCE; TuPP
Earth, ocean, air, belovèd brotherhood! Alastor; or, The Spirit of Solitude. Shelley. BEL; CABL; EnLi-2 (1949 ed.); EnRP; EPN; FiP; MERP; OAEP; WHA
Earth out of Earth. *Unknown.* CBEP; ChTr; MeEL
Earth puts her colours by. Envoi. P. H. B. Lyon. BoTP
Earth raised up her head. Earth's Answer. Blake. *Fr.* Songs of Experience. CBEP; EiPP; EnPE; EnRP; ERoP-1
Earth rebelled, The. And the Earth Rebelled. Yuri Suhl. TrJP
Earth, receive an honoured guest. W. H. Auden. *Fr.* In Memory of W. B. Yeats ChMP; ChTr; FaBoTw; NeMA; PG (1955 ed.)
Earth rolls on through empty space, its journey's never done, The. The Ramble-eer. *Unknown.* PoAu-1
Earth, sea, and sky expand the air. The Chart. Michael Lewis. StaSt
Earth seems a desolate mother, The March. Charles Henry Webb. AA
Earth, Sky. Sydney Clouts. PeSA
Earth-Spirit, The. William Ellery Channing. AnNE; PFY
Earth, that let us in, was soft as fern, The. En Route. E. L. Mayo. MiAP
Earth, that nourished thee, shall claim. Bryant. *Fr.* Thanatopsis. YT
Earth to Earth. "Michael Field." VA
Earth to Earth. *Unknown.* OnPM; WoL
Earth to earth, and dust to dust! Death and Resurrection. George Croly. WGRP
Earth took from earth earth with woe. Earth to Earth. *Unknown.* OnPM; WoL
Earth travails. At Harvest. Joseph Campbell. NP
Earth Trembles Waiting. Blanche Shoemaker Wagstaff. PoLF
Earth Tremor in Lugano. James Kirkup. NYBP
Earth twitches its skin, The. Seismograph. A. M. Sullivan. JKCP (1955 ed.)
Earth upon Earth, *in mod. Eng.* *Unknown.* ChTr
Earth-Visitors. Kenneth Slessor. BoAV

Earth was green, the sky was blue, The. A Green Cornfield [*or* The Skylark]. Christina Rossetti. BoTP; GoTP; PoG
Earth was not Earth before her sons appeared. Appreciation. George Meredith. ViBoPo
Earth Will Stay the Same, The. Frank Ernest Hill. AnAmPo
Earth, with all its fullness, is the Lord's, The. Poor for Our Sakes. Mary Brainerd Smith. BLRP
Earth with its dark and dreadful ills. A Dying Hymn. Alice Cary. HBV
Earth, The, with thunder torn, with fire blasted. Fulke Greville. Caelica, LXXXVI. EnRePo; QFR; SiCE; Sonn; TuPP
Earth Worshiped, The! Catherine Cate Coblentz. ChIP
Earth yields nothing more divine, The. Life's Purpose. "George Eliot." *Fr.* A Minor Prophet. MaRV
Earth, you have had great lovers in your hour. Poets. Hortense Flexner. HBMV
Earth-Born. Robert E. Howard. FiSC
Earthborn. Peter McArthur. CaP
Earthen, An/ sound. Heart. Coleman Barks. *Fr.* Body Poems. QAH
Earthen Pot and the Iron Pot, The. La Fontaine, *tr. fr. French.* BoChLi
Earthfast. A.S.J. Tessimond. POTE
Earthly Illusion. Louise Leighton. GoYe
Earthly Love. Joseph Bennett. NePA
Earthly [*or* Eartly] nurse [*or* nourris] sits and sings, An. The [Great] Silkie of Sule Skerry [*or* Skerrie]. *Unknown.* BaBo (B *vers.*); BuBa; ChTr; ESPB; EtS; FaBoCh; OBB; ViBoFo (A *vers.*)
Earthly Paradise, The, *sels.* William Morris.
Apology, An. AWP; BEL; BLPA; CoBE; EnLi-2; EnLit; EPN; GTBS; GTBS-W; GTSL; InP; OAEP; OBNC; PoIE; PoVP; TOP; ViPP
("Of Heaven or Hell I have no power to sing.") LiTB; LoBV; NoP; ViBoPo,*abr.*; ViPo
(Prologue: "Of Heaven or Hell I have no power to sing.") FaBoEn; OtMeF
(Singer's Prelude, The.) HBV; VA
Atlanta's Race (*in* March). BEL; DTo; ViPo
Atlanta's Defeat. VA
Atlanta's Victory. VA
February, *abr.* ViPo
Golden Apples, The (*in* December). EPN
June. PoVP; ViPo, *abr.*
("O June, O June, that we desired so,"*abr.*) ViBoPo
King's Visit, The (*fr.* The Man Born to Be King, *in* March). VA
Lady of the Land, The (*in* June). PoVP; TOP
Land across the Sea, A (*fr.* The Watching of the Falcon, *in* July). VA
L'Envoi: "Here are we for the last time face to face." EnLi-2; PoVP; ViPo
March. HBV; OtMeF
November, *abr.* EPN; GTSL; ViPo; ViPP
"O love, this morn when the sweet nightingale" (*in* May). EG
October. EPN; OBNC; ViPP
("O love, turn from the unchanging sea, and gaze.") FaBoEn
Outlanders, Whence Come Ye Last? (Song from "The Land East of the Sun and West of the Moon," *in* September). OxBoCh; StJW
(Minstrels and Maids.) GN
Prologue: "Forget six countries overhung with smoke." BEL; EPN; ViPo
(Introduction.) ViPP
Road of Life, The. OBNC
Song: "Fair is the night and fair the day." HBV
Song from "Ogier the Dane" (*in* August). OAEP; PoVP
(Antiphony.) VA
("In the white-flowered hawthorn brake.") EG; ViBoPo
Song from "The Hill of Venus" ("Before our lady came on earth") (*in* February). PoVP
Song: To Psyche. VA
Earthly props are useless. Props. John Oxenham. FaChP; TRV
Earthly roses at God's call have made, The. On the Death of a Pious Lady. Olof Wexionius. AWP; JAWP; WBP
Earthly tree a heavenly fruit it bare, An. A Carol for Christmas Day. *Unknown.* TuPP
Earthquake. James Kirkup. POTi
Earth's Answer. Blake. *Fr.* Songs of Experience. CBEP; EiPP; EnPE; EnRP; ERoP-1
Earth's Bondman. Betty Page Dabney. GoYe
Earth's Burdens. Ernest Charles Jones. VA
Earth's Common Things. Minot J. Savage. MaRV; OQP
Earth's crammed with heaven. Glory in the Commonplace. Elizabeth Barrett Browning. *Fr.* Aurora Leigh, VII. MaRV; TRV
Earth's first Adam, he lay in the grass. Adam and Eve. Itzig Manger. TrJP
"Earth's Holocaust." James Schuler. ANYP
Earth's Immortalities. Robert Browning.
Fame. PoVP; PP
Love. EnLoPo; PoVP
Earth's Night. William Allingham. GTBS-W; IrPN; TRV
Earth's Secret. George Meredith. EPN; PoVP
Earth's Story. Thomas Curtis Clark. OQP
Earth's Winter Song. Robert Duncan. FRC
Earthy Anecdote. Wallace Stevens. CMoP; GoJo; ThWaDe
Eartly nourris sits and sings, An. *See* Earthly nurse sits and sings, An.
Easiest Way, The. *Unknown, tr. fr. Greek by* Louis Untermeyer. UnTE
Easily, my dear, you move, easily your head. A Bride in the '30's. W. H. Auden. FaBoMo
Easily to the old. Exit. Wilson MacDonald. CaP; ViBoPo
East, The. Matthew Arnold. *Fr.* Obermann Once More. OtMeF
East a-Callin', The. Oscar Wilde. *Fr.* Ave Imperatrix! OtMeF
East and the South have ruled us long, The. Andrew Jackson. Stephen Vincent Benét. InMe
East Anglian Bathe. John Betjeman. GTBS-D; SD
East bow'd low before the blast, The. The East. Matthew Arnold. *Fr.* Obermann Once More. OtMeF
East Coast—Canada. Elizabeth Brewster. CaP
East Coker. T. S. Eliot. *Fr.* Four Quartets. ChMP; FaBoMo; MoVE; NePA
East End. Bill Berkson. YAP
East is a clear violet mass, The. A Street Scene. Lizette Woodworth Reese. PCH; TSW
East is yellow as a daffodil, The. Sunrise. Lizette Woodworth Reese. TSW
East London. Matthew Arnold. EPN; MaRV; OAEP; OHIP; PoVP; StJW; WGRP
East-northeaster pounds the coast tonight, The. Euroclydon. Abbie Huston Evans. NePoAm
East of the long Duck Mountain range. The Courting of Olga Karg. Watson Kirkconnell. TwCaPo
East River. Rosemary Thomas. AmFN
East unrolled a sheet of gold, The. As Helen Once. Muna Lee. HBMV
East Virginia, *with music. Unknown.* OuSiCo
East was crowned with snow-cold bloom, The. Oversoul [*or* Krishna]. "Æ." MaRV; PoVP; VA
East Wind, The. George Cabot Lodge. AmePo
Easter. Thomas Curtis Clark. OQP
Easter. Elizabeth J. Coatsworth. YeAr
Easter. Hilda Conkling. HH; TiPo (1952 ed.)
Easter. Zula Evelyn Coon. SoP
Easter. Mary Carolyn Davies. OHIP
Easter. Henry W. Frost. SoP
Easter. Richard Watson Gilder. DD
Easter. George Herbert. AnAnS-1; MaMe; MeP; SCEP-1; SeCV-1; SeEP
"I got me flowers to straw [*or* strew] Thy way," *sel.* AtBAP, 3 *sts.*; BoC; BoTP; CH; EG; FaBoCh, 2 *sts., diff. vers.*; FaBoEn; LoGBV; OBEV, 2 *sts., diff. vers.*; OBS; OHIP; PCH, 1 *st.*; TrGrPo; TRV
Easter. Joyce Kilmer. MPB; NP; PDV; SoPo; TiPo
Easter. Martin Luther, *after the Latin of* John Huss. *tr. fr. German.* SoP
Easter. John G. Neihardt. *See* Easter, 1923.
Easter. John Oxenham. OQP
Easter. Edwin L. Sabin. DD; HH; OHIP; PoRL; PoSC
Easter. Spenser. *See* Amoretti LXVIII.
Easter. Charles Hanson Towne. *See* Easter Prayer, An.
Easter. Katharine Tynan. YT
Easter ("Sing, soul of mine"). *Unknown.* OQP
Easter. John Van Brakle. ChIP
Easter. Robert Whitaker. ChIP; PGD
Easter Airplane, The. Carolyn R. Freeman. GFA
Easter Beatitudes. Clarence M. Burkholder. BLRP
Easter Canticle, An: "In every trembling bud and bloom."

Easter (continued)
Charles Hanson Towne. ChIP; MaRV, *abr.*; OHIP; TrPWD
Easter Carol, An: "Flash forth, thou sun." Christina Rossetti. PCH; PoRL
Easter Carol: "O Earth! throughout thy borders." George Newell Lovejoy. ChIP; DD; OHIP; OQP; PGD
Easter Carol, An: "Spring bursts to-day." Christina Rossetti. DD; HH; MaRV; MPB; OHIip
Easter Chick, An. Thirza Wakley. BoTP
Easter Chorus: "Christ is arisen." Goethe, *tr. fr. German by* Arthur Cleveland Coxe. *Fr.* Faust. MaRV
(Easter Chorus from Faust, *abr., tr. by* Bayard Taylor.) WGRP
(Easter Hymn.) ChIP
Easter Communion. Gerard Manley Hopkins. BrPo
Easter dawn! Morning, Noon, and . . . Hawley Truax. NYBP
Easter Day. Arthur Hugh Clough. EPN; OAEP; PoVP; ViPP
"Weep not beside his tomb," *sel., fr.* II. PGD
Easter Day. Richard Crashaw. MaMe; PoLi
Easter Day. Henry W. Frost. SoP
Easter Day. Jasper Heywood. ReIE
Easter Day. Christina Rossetti. VP
Easter-Day. Henry Vaughan. AnAnS-1
Easter day breaks! Rest Remaineth. Robert Browning. *Fr.* Christmas-Eve and Easter-Day. PoRL
Easter, Day of Christ Eternal. Maurice Moore. STF
Easter Day was a holiday. Sir Hugh (C *vers.*). *Unknown.* ViBoFo
Easter Day we got up early. Early, Early Easter Day. Aileen Fisher. SiSoSe
Easter duck and Easter chick. Some Things That Easter Brings. Elsie Parrish. PCH; SoPo
Easter Eggs. *Unknown.* GFA
Easter Eucharist. *Unknown.* MaRV
Easter Eve. James Branch Cabell. HBMV; MaRV
Easter Eve, 1945. Muriel Rukeyser. MiAP; NePA
Easter Glory, The. A. J. Beattie. SoP
Easter Gloves. *Unknown.* PCH
("Rose is red, the violet blue, The.") SiTL
Easter has come around. W. D. Snodgrass. Heart's Needle, VI. NePoEA; NMP; OPoP; PIA
Easter Hymn. Thomas Blackburn. HH
Easter Hymn. A. E. Housman. CABA; CaFP; ChMP; EaLo; ILP; MaRV; MoAB; SeCeV
Easter Hymn. St. John of Damascus, *tr. fr. Greek by* John Mason Neale. BePJ; CAW
Easter Hymn. Michael Thwaites. MoRP
Easter Hymn. Henry Vaughan. AnAnS-1; MemP; StJW
Easter Hymn. Charles Wesley. DD; HD; MaRV; OHIP; TRV
(Christ the Lord Is Risen Today.) BePJ
(For Easter Day.) CEP; SoP
Easter in the Woods. Frances Frost. BrR; SiSoSe
Easter Island. Frederick George Scott. OBCV
Easter Joy. Daisy Conway Price. ChIP
Easter Joy. Nancy Byrd Turner. YeAr
Easter Light. Ida Norton Munson. ChIP
Easter lilies! Can you hear. On Easter Day. Celia Thaxter. FaPON; YeAr
Easter lilies freshly bloom. Mary's Easter. Marie Mason. DD
Easter Message. John Van Brakle. ChIP
Easter Monday. William Barnes. PoVP
Easter Morn. Giles Fletcher. *Fr.* Christ's Victory and Triumph. EIL
Easter Morning. St. Matthew, XXVIII: 1-10, Bible, *N.T.* TreF
Easter Morning. Phillips Brooks. MaRV; SoP
Easter Morning. Winfred Ernest Garrison. ChIP
Easter Morning. Spenser. *See* Amoretti, LXVIII.
Easter Music. Margaret Wade Deland. ChIP; HH; OQP; PoRL
Easter Must Be Reclaimed. George W. Wiseman. MaRV
Easter Night. Alice Meynell. ChIP; OHIP; StJW
Easter, 1916. W. B. Yeats. BrPo; BWP; CABA; ChMP; CMoP; CoBMV; DiPo; FaBoMo; LiTM; MaPo (1969 ed.); MBW-2; MoAB; NoP; OxBI; PIA; PoAn; PoeP; PoFS; PoIE; SeCeV; ShBV-4
"Too long a sacrifice,"*sel.* PoPo
Easter, 1923. John G. Neihardt. AmAmPo; HBMV
(Easter.) OHIP
Easter Parade. Marchette Chute. BrR; SiSoSe
Easter Poem. Kathleen Raine. LiTB
Easter Praise. Rodney Bennett. BoTP
Easter Prayer, An. Chester M. Davis. SoP
Easter Prayer. Frances Ridley Havergal. *See* For Easter.
Easter Prayer, An. Charles Hanson Towne. OQP; SoP
(Easter.) ChIP
Easter Prayer, An. *Unknown.* SoP
Easter Reveille, An. John R. Slater. MaRV
Easter Robin, The. Geraldine Farrar. StJW
Easter Sacraments. Henry Park Schauffler. OQP
Easter Snowfall. Harry Behn. TiPo (1959 ed.)
Easter Song. Leo Alishan, *tr. fr. Armenian by* Alice Stone Blackwell. CAW
Easter Song. "Susan Coolidge." *See* Calvary and Easter.
Easter Song. Mary A. Lathbury. OHIP
Easter Song. Kenneth Leslie. MoRP
Easter Song. Caelius Sedulius. *See* Carmen Paschale.
Easter stars are shining, The. Flight to the City. William Carlos Williams. AnAmPo
Easter Sunday, 1945. G. A. Borgese. NePoAm
Easter Surprise, An. Leona Covey. GFA
Easter Thought. Leo Cox. CaP
Easter Week. Charles Kingsley. DD; OHIP
Easter Week. *Unknown.* OnYI
Easter Wings. George Herbert. AnAnS-1; ATP; CABA; ExPo; LiTB; MaMe; MaPo (1969 ed.); MeLP; MePo; NoP; OAEP; OBS; PAn; PIA; PoEL-2; PoFS; PP; SCEP-1; SeCP; SeEP; StP; VaPo; YAT
"Lord, who createdst man in wealth and store," *sel.* PoSa
Easter Wish, An. *Unknown.* *See* My Easter Wish.
Easter Zunday. William Barnes. PoVP
Eastern Gate, The. *Unknown,* *tr. fr. Chinese by* Arthur Waley. FIW
Eastern Question, An. H. M. Paull. BOHV
Eastern Serenade. William E. Aytoun *and* Sir Theodore Martin. InMe
Eastern Shore. Charles Bruce. PeCV
Eastern Tempest. Edmund Blunden. MoBrPo
Eastertide. Carl Bode. *Fr.* The Sacred Seasons. ToPo
Eastmuir king, and Wastmuir king. Fause Foodrage (C *vers.*) *Unknown.* ESPB
Eastmure king, and the Westmure king, The. Fause Foodrage (B *vers.*). *Unknown.* ESPB
Eastward far anon. The Beacons. Henry Hart Milman. *Fr.* Samor. OBRV
Eastward I Stand, Mercies I Beg. *Unknown,* *tr. fr. Anglo-Saxon by* Sarah Plotz. EaLo
Easy as cove-water rustles its pebbles and shells. Part of a Letter. Richard Wilbur. CMoP
Easy Decision, An. Kenneth Patchen. LOW; ToPo
Easy is the triolet. Triolet. W. E. Henley. BOHV
Easy on your drums. Dark Girl. Arna Bontemps. GoSl
Easy roads are crowded, and, The. Upstream. *Unknown.* SoP
Easy the cry, while vengeance now is wrought. The Right of Asylum. Stephen Phillips. PoFr
Easy thing, O power divine, An. The Things I Miss [*or* Thank Thee]. Thomas Wentworth Higginson. SoP; TrPWD
Easy to Grow. John Giorno. ANYP
Eat and Walk. James Norman Hall. BLPA
Eat but simple food; go for early rising. Advice from an Expert. John Kieran. InMe
Eat-It-All Elaine. Kaye Starbird. PDV
"Eat my cake, eat," cried the young. To the Last Wedding Guest. Horace Gregory. NYBP
Eat no green apples or you'll droop. Advice to Small Children. Edward Anthony. GoTP
Eat thou and drink: to-morrow thou shalt die. The Choice, 1. Dante Gabriel Rossetti. The House of Life, LXXI. ATP; BEL; EnL; EnLi-2; HBV; MaVP; MyFE; OBVV; PoVP; TOP; ViBoPo; ViPo; WHA
Ear your meat and save the skin. Cowboy Grace. *Unknown.* CoSo
Eaten Heart, The. *Unknown,* *tr. fr. Middle English by* Pearl London. *Fr.* The Knight of Curtesy. TrGrPo
Eating Fish. George Johnston. WHW
Eating Poetry. Mark Strand. YAP
Eating Song. Sir Walter Raleigh. WhC

Eaves moan/ clapboards flap. In the Farmhouse. Galway Kinnell. WIRo
Ebb. John Lyle Donaghy. NeIP
Ebb and Flow. George William Curtis. AA; HBV
Ebb and Flow, The. Edward Taylor. AmP; AmPP; AnNE; AP; SCAP
Ebb slips from the rock, the sunken, The. Night. Robinson Jeffers. AmPP (3d ed.); AP; AWP; CoBMV; InPo; JAWP; LiTA; MAP; MoAmPo; MoPo; NoP; NP; OxBA; WBP; WHA
Ebb Tide. Marjorie Pickthall. CaP
Ebb Tide, The. Robert Southey. OBNC
Ebbtide at Sundown. "Michael Field." CAW
Ebb tide to me as of the sea! The Old Woman of Beare. *Unknown, tr. by* Kuno Meyer. OnYI
Ebbé Skammelson. *Unknown, tr. fr. Danish.* BaBo
Ebbed and flowed the muddy Pei-ho by the gulf of Pechili. Blood Is Thicker than Water. Wallace Rice. PaA; PAH
Ebbing, the wave of the sea. The Woman of Beare. *Tr. by* Stephen Gwynn. AnIV
Ebbs from soiled fields the last drab vestige of snow. February. D. S. Savage. NeBP
Ebenezer, The, *with music. Unknown.* ShS
Ebrius Dissimulans. Henry Parrot. TuPP
Ecce Homo. John Ackerson. MaRV
Ecce Homo. Witter Bynner. WGRP
Ecce Homo. David Gascoyne. *Fr.* Miserere. ChMP; FaBoTw; LiTM (rev. ed.); NeBP; OnHM
Ecce Homunculus. R. A. K. Mason. AnNZ
Ecce in Deserto. Henry Augustin Beers. AA; AnFE; APA; CoAnAm
Ecce Puer. James Joyce. PoIE; PoPl; StP
"Ecce Quomodo Mortiur Justus." Diogenes Laertius, *tr. fr. Greek by* Dudley Fitts. LiTW
Eccentric old person of Slough, An. Limerick. George Robey. CenHV
Eccho, The. Richard Leigh. MePo
Ecchoing Green, The. Blake. *See* Echoing Green, The.
Eccho's Song. Ben Jonson. *See* Slow, Slow, Fresh Fount.
Ecclesiast, The. John Ashbery. ANYP
Ecclesiastes. Bible, *O.T.* WoL, *abr.*
Sels.
All Is Vanity, I: 14-15, III: 19. TRV
Cast Thy Bread upon the Waters, XI: 1-6. AWP; JAWP; TiPo (1952 ed.); WBP
(Life's Uncertainty, XI: 1-10.) TreFS
Earth Abideth Forever, The, I: 4-7. FaPON
Enjoy the Good, V: 18-20. TreFT
"It Is Better. . .," VII: 1-9. TrJP
(Better Path, The, VII: 1-5.) TreFS
Light Is Sweet, The, XI: 7. FaPON
Live Joyfully, IX: 7-11. TreFS
("Live joyfully with the wife whom thou lovest," IX: 9-11.) PoG
Remember Now Thy Creator, XII: 1-7. AWP; ChTr (XII: 1-8); JAWP; LiTW; MaRV; ShBV-1; TreF (1-14); WBP
(Remember Also Thy Creator.) ExPo
("Remember now thy Creator in the days of thy youth," XII: 1-8.) EnLi-1 (1949 ed.)
(Remember Then Thy Creator, XII: 1-8.) TrJP
Time for Everything, A, III: 1-8. TrGrPo
"To every thing there is a season, and a time," III: 1-8. PoPl
Vanity, I: 12-II: 26. OuHeWo
Words of the Preacher, The, I: 2-11. TreFS
(Vanity of Vanities, I: 2-9.) TrJP
Youth and Age. OuHeWo (XI: 1-XII: 7); TrGrPo (XII:1-8)
Ecclesiastes. Morris Bishop. HBMV
Ecclesiastes. G. K. Chesterton. MoBrPo
Ecclesiastes. Joseph Langland. NePoEA; PoPl
Ecclesiastical Sonnets, *sels.* Wordsworth.
Conclusion ("Why sleeps the future"), Pt. III, Sonnet XLVII. MERP
Inside of King's College Chapel, Cambridge, Pt. III, Sonnet XLIII. EnLi-2; EnRP; EPN; GoBC; MaRV; OAEP; OBNC; OBRV; OxBoCh; PeER
(Within King's College Chapel, Cambridge.) GTBS; GTBS-D; GTBS-P; GTBS-W; GTSE; GTSL
Mutability, Pt. III, Sonnet XXXIV. BWP; EnLi-2; EnRP; EPN; ExPo; LiTB; NoP; OBRV; OQP; PeER; PoE; PoEL-4; SeCeV
("From low to high doth dissolution climb.") EG
Persuasion, Pt. I, Sonnet XVI. MaRV
Ecclesiasticus, *sels.* Bible, Apocrypha.
"He was as the morning star in the midst of a cloud, and as the moon at the full," L: 6-12. BoC
"I am the mother of fair love," XXIV: 24-28, *Douay vers.* ISi
Let Us Now Praise Famous Men, XLIV: 1-15, XXXVIII: 26-39. BoC; ChTr
(Our Fathers, XLIV: 1-15.) TrJP
(Praise of Famous Men, XLIV: 10-14.) MaRV
"Look upon the rainbow, and praise him that made it," XLIII: 12-13. BoC
Music, XXXII: 5-6. TrJP
"My son, if thou come to serve the Lord, prepare thy soul for temptation," II: 1-13. BoC
O Death, XLI: 1-4. TrJP
On Death—a Sonnet, XLI (*Moulton, Modern Reader's Bible*). MaRV
Snow, XLIII: 14-16, 18-24. BoC
Sun, Moon and Stars, XLIII: 1-11. BoC
Test of Men, The, XXVI: 5-8. TrJP
Ecclogue 1613. December 26. John Donne. MaMe
Ech, Sic a Pairish. *Unknown.* FiBHP
Echetlos. Robert Browning. ViPo
Echo. Walter de la Mare. MoVE; OBMV; SeCeV; ShBV-4
Echo. Viscountess Grey of Fallodon. CH; GBV (1922 ed.)
Echo. Elizabeth Stanton Hardy. GoYe
Echo. Milton. *See* Sweet Echo.
Echo. Thomas Moore. ELP; GoBC; OxBI
(Echoes.) CBEP; GTBS; GTBS-D; GTBS-P; GTBS-W; GTSE; GTSL
Echo. Christina Rossetti. CH; ELP; EPN; GTBS-D; LiTL; LoBV; MeWo; NoP; OBNC; PoEL-5; SeCeV; ViBoPo; ViPo; VP
("Come to me in the silence of the night.") LO
Echo. John Godfrey Saxe. AnNE; BOHV
Echo. Sir Philip Sidney. *Fr.* Arcadia. SiPS
Echo. *Unknown.* GFA
Echo. Mildred Weston. BoNaP; PoMa
Echo. Otomo Yakamochi, *tr. fr. Japanese by* Ishii *and* Obata. OnPM
Echo Club, The, *sel.* Bayard Taylor.
Palabras Grandiosas. BOHV
Echo from Willowwood, An. Christina Rossetti. VA
Echo [*or* Shepherd: Echo], I ween, will in the wood reply. A Gentle Echo on Woman. Swift. ALV; BOHV; FiBHP; LiTG; LiTL; OnYI; SiTL
Echo in a Church. Lord Herbert of Cherbury. AnAnS-2
("Where shall my troubled soule at large.") SeCSL
Echo of a Song, The. James W. Foley. PEDC
Echo of song I heard you sing, An. Lost Voice on This Hill. Burnham Eaton. FiSC
Echo of Victor Hugo, An, *sel.* Francis Thompson.
"Life's a veil the real has." MemP
Echo Poem. M. Allan. FiBHP
Echo, tell me, while I wander. Song. Addison. BOHV
Echo to a Rock. Lord Herbert of Cherbury. AtBAP; PoEL-2
Echoes. Walter de la Mare. RePo
Echoes. W. E. Henley. *Poems indexed separately by titles and first lines.*
Echoes. Thomas Moore. *See* Echo.
Echoes. Wordsworth. *See* There Was a Boy.
Echoes from Theocritus, *sels.* Edward Cracroft Lefroy, *after* Theocritus.
Ageanax, VI. OBVV
Cleonicos, XXVII. AWP; JAWP; WBP
Epitaph of Eusthenes, The, XXVIII. AWP; OBVV
Flute of Daphnis, The, XXIII. AWP; OBVV
Grave of Hipponax, The, XXX. AWP; JAWP; WBP
Monument of Cleita, The, XXIX. AWP; JAWP; WBP
Sacred Grove, A, XXIV. AWP
Shepherd Maiden, A, II. VA
Sicilian Night, A, IV. VA
Summer Day in Old Sicily, A, V. OBVV
Sylvan Revel, A, XXV. AWP; JAWP; WBP
Thyrsis, XXVI. AWP
Echoes of Childhood, *sels.* Alice Corbin. PoNe
Delphy.
Mandy's Religion.
Uncle Jim.
Echoes of Jesus. Lucile Coleman. ChIP
Echoes of Love's House. William Morris. GTSL
Echoing Cliff, The. Andrew Young. BiS

Echoing [*or* Ecchoing] Green, The. Blake. *Fr.* Songs of Innocence. BoTP; BWP; CaFP; CBEP; CBV; CEP; CH; DiPo; EiPP; ERoP-1; GBV (1952 ed.); OBEC; OTPC; PAn; PCH; PeER; PoeP; PoRH; PoSC; WiR
Echoing sounds of hammers, The. New Houses. Grace Noll Crowell. PEDC
Echo's Lament of Narcissus. Ben Jonson. *See* Slow, Slow, Fresh Fount.
Echo's Song. Ben Jonson. *See* Slow, Slow, Fresh Fount.
Eclipse. Albert E. Haynes, Jr. BF
Eclipse. Amir Rashidd. NBP
Eclipse. Ed Roberson. PoNe (1970 ed.)
Eclipse, The. Henry Vaughan. MemP; SoP
Eclipse of Faith, The. Theodore Dwight Woolsey. AA
Ecliptic, The: Cancer, or, The Crab, *sel.* Joseph Gordon Macleod.
"Moonpoison, mullock of sacrifice." NeBP
Eclog. III: "Fisher-lad, A (no higher dares he look)." Phineas Fletcher. *Fr.* Piscatorie Eclogues. SeCV-1
Eclogue: "Late 'twas in June, the fleece when fully grown." The Shepherd's Garland, Eclogue IX. Michael Drayton. OBSC
Eclogue: "Lycon begin—begin the mournful tale." William Diaper. *Fr.* Nereides; or, Sea-Eclogues. SeCePo
Eclogue: Merchantman, The. John Davidson. *See* Merchantman, The.
Eclogue: "No one dies cleanly now." Frederic Prokosch. ViBoPo
Eclogue: Queen Elizabeth's Day. John Davidson. BrPo
Eclogue: Two Farms in Woone. William Barnes. NBM
Eclogue: "When all the powers have fallen." Hal Summers. POTE
Eclogue: "Would'st thou know nature in her better part?" Thomas Chatterton. Eclogues, III. PeER
Eclogue for Christmas, An. Louis MacNeice. FaBoMo; MoPo; MoVE; OBMV
Eclogue the Second. William Collins. *Fr.* Persian Eclogues. CEP
Eclogue [*or* Eglogue] to Mr. Johnson, An. Thomas Randolph. SeEP
Poetry and Philosophy, *sel.* OBS
Eclogues, *sel.* Thomas Chatterton.
"Would'st thou know nature in her better part," III. PeER
Eclogues. Michael Drayton. *See* Shepherd's Garland, The.
Eclogues. Dennis Schmitz. YAP
Eclogues, *sels.* Vergil, *tr. fr. Latin.*
Corydon and Thyrsis, VII, *tr. by* Dryden. AWP
Lycidas and Moeris, IX, *tr. by* Dryden. AWP
(Ninth Eclogue, *tr. by* Dryden.) FosPo
Eighth Pastoral of Virgil, The, *tr. by* Dryden. EiCP
Messiah, The, IV, *tr. by* Dryden. AWP; JAWP; OuHeWo; WBP
(Fourth Eclogue, The, *tr. by* James Laughlin.) LiTW
"For thee little boy, will the earth pour forth gifts," *tr. by* James Laughlin. PoPl
Sibylline Prophecy, The, *tr. by* Roderick Gill. CAW
Shepherd's Gratitude, The, I. AWP, *tr. by* Charles Stuart Calverley
"What made thee then so keen to look on Rome?" *tr. by* Charles Stuart Calverley. PoFr
Economy of Vegetation, The. Erasmus Darwin. *See* Botanic Garden, The.
Ecstasie, rash production of the thoughts. George Darley. *Fr.* Errors of Ecstasie. OnYI
Ecstasies of Dialectic, The. Howard Nemerov. FiMAP; TwAmPo
Ecstasy, The. Abraham Cowley. Po
(Extasie, The.) AnAnS-2; SeCP
Ecstasy, The. John Donne. ATP; CABA; DiPo; EnRePo; ExPo; LiTB; LiTG; LO, *abr.,*; LoBV; MaPo; MBW-1; NoP; OBEV; PIA; PoFS; PoIE; ReEn; SeCePo; SeCeV; SeEP; StP; TDP; TrGrPo; TuPP; UnTE; ViBoPo
(Extasie, The.) AnAnS-1 AnFE; EnLoPo; FaBoEn; MaMe; MasP; MeLP; MeP; MePo; OBS; PoEL-2; SCEP-1; SeCP; SeCV-1
(Extasy, The.) CBEP; ReIE
"Where, like a pillow on a bed," *sel.* MemP
Ecstasy, The. C. S. Lewis. BoPe
Ecstasy. Eric Mackay. VA
Ecstasy. Duncan Campbell Scott. CaP
Ecstasy. Arthur Symons. UnTE
Ecstasy. Rachel Annand Taylor. GoTS; SiSw
Ecstasy. W. J. Turner. CH; POTE
Esctatic bird songs pound. Dawn. William Carlos Williams. MAP; MoAB; MoAmPo; PoPl
Eddi, priest of St. Wilfrid. Eddi's Service. Kipling. BoPe; OnSP
Eddington's universe goes phut. Richard Tolman's Universe. Leonard Bacon. ImOP
Eddi's Service. Kipling. BoPe; OnSP
Eddystone Light, The. *Unknown.* StPo
Eden. Milton. *Fr.* Paradise Lost, IV. DiPo; FaBoEn ("Thus was this place.") ATP
Eden. F. R. Scott. TwCaPo
Eden. Thomas Traherne. AnAnS-1; MeP; PoEL-2; SCEP-1; SeCV-2; TrGrPo
Eden Bower. Dante Gabriel Rossetti. MaVP; PoVP
Eden-Gate. Sydney Dobell. OBVV
Eden: Or One View of It. Theodore Spencer. LiTM; NePA
Edgar, *sel.* Thomas Rymer.
Wit Predominant. SeCL
Edgar A. Guest Considers "The Old Woman Who Lived in a Shoe" and the Good Old Verities at the Same Time. Louis Untermeyer. FiBHP; WhC
(Edgar A. Guest Considers "The Good Old Woman Who Lived in a Shoe" and the Good Old Truths Simultaneously. PoPl
(Just Home.) StaSt
Edgar Allan Poe. Robert H. Barlow. FiSC
Edgar Allan Poe. Clifford Lanier. PoRL
Edgar Guest/ Is never at his best. The Editor's Private Cocktail Party. Oscar Williams. PP; SiTL
Edge, The. Louise Glück. YAP
Edge, The. Lola Ridge. AnAmPo; NP; OnYI
Edge of Day, The. Laurie Lee. NYBP; ToPo
Edge of the World, The. Mary Fanny Youngs. BrR
Edges of the stones are sharp, The. The Builder. Caroline Giltinan. HBMV
Edi be thu, Hevene Quene. In Praise of Mary. *Unknown.* MeEL
Edict. Harold Vinal. NYTB
Edinburgh. Arthur Guiterman. WhC
Edinburgh. Alfred Noyes. HBV; HT
Edinburgh Spring. Norman MacCaig. NMP
Edison. Robinson Jeffers. AmPP (3d ed.)
Edith. William Ellery Channing. AA; HBV
Edith and Harold. Arthur Gray Butler. OBVV
Edith Cavell. George Edward Woodberry. HBMV
Edith, the silent stars are coldly gleaming. Edith. William Ellery Channing. AA; HBV
Editor sat in his easy chair, The. The Editor's Tragedy. St. John Emile Clavering Hankin. CenHV
Editor sat with his head in his hands, The. He Came to Pay. "Parmenas Mix." BOHV
Editor Whedon. Edgar Lee Masters. *Fr.* Spoon River Anthology. CMoP; CrMA; NP; OxBA
Editorial Poem on an Incident of Effects Far-Reaching. Russell Atkins. NBP
Editor's Private Cocktail Party, The. Oscar Williams. SiTL
Edgar Guest, *sel.* PP
Editor's Tragedy, The. St. John Emile Clavering Hankin. CenHV
Editor's Wooing, The. "Orpheus C. Kerr." BOHV
Edlesborough. Anne Ridler. NeBP
Edmund Burke. Goldsmith. *Fr.* Retaliation. InvP; OBEC; SeCeV
Edmund Campion. Sister Mary St. Virginia. JKCP (1955 ed.)
Edmund Clerihew Bentley. William Jay Smith. PV
Edmund Davie 1682, Annagram. Benjamin Tompson. SCAP
Edmund Pollard. Edgar Lee Masters. *Fr.* Spoon River Anthology. AnFE; APA; CoAnAm; ErPo
Edmund's Song. Sir Walter Scott. *See* Brignall Banks.
Edom o' Gordon. *Unknown.* HBV; OBB; OBEV (1st ed.); OxBB
(Captain Car; or, Edom o Gordon.) BaBo; EnLit; ESPB (A, B, F, *and* H *vers.*); OAEP; TOP; ViBoFo (A *and* B *vers.*)
Edouard. Ogden Nash. NePA; SiTL
Educated Love Bird, The. Peter Newell. FiBHP
Education. Arthur Guiterman. MaRV
Education. Don L. Lee. BALP
Education. Josephine Miles. FiMAP

Education of Nature, The. Wordsworth. *See* Three Years She Grew.
Edward. *Unknown.* AnFE; AtBAP; ATP; BaBo (A, B, *and* C *vers.*); BEL; BoLiVe; CABA; CaFP; CBEP; CBV; CH; ELP; EnLi-1; EnLit; ESPB; FosPo; GoTS; HBV; HoPM (A *and* B *vers.*); ILP; NoP (B *vers.*); OAEP; OBB; OBEV; OuHeWo; OxBS; PoEL-1; PoIE; StP; TOP; TrGrPo; UnPo (1st ed.); ViBoFo (A *and* B *vers.*)
(Edward, Edward.) BBV; BuBa; EnRP; ExPo; LiTB; LiTG; MaC; OnSP; OxBB; PAn; PG (1955 ed.); PoPo; PoRA; PoSa; SeCeV; ShBV-3; TreFS; WHA
"Edward back from the Indian Sea." Neglectful Edward. Robert Graves. BrPo; MoBrPo; NeMA
Edward, Edward. *Unknown.* *See* Edward.
Edward Edwards was a castaway sealer. Keith Sinclair. *Fr.* The Ballad of Halfmoon Bay. AnNZ
Edward Elgar. C. Day Lewis. MuSP
Edward Gray. Tennyson. OBVV
Edward Lear. W. H. Auden. InvP; ML
Edward Lear in February. Christopher Middleton. TwCP
Edward Millington. Richard Church. HaMV
Edward Plantagenet / (Can you imagine it). Important People. Louis Untermeyer, *and others.* StaSt
Edward the Confessor,/Slept under the dresser. Important People. Louis Untermeyer, *and others.* RIS; StaSt
Edward the Second, *sels.* Christopher Marlowe.
"I must have wanton poets, pleasant wits," *fr.* I, i. ViBoPo
"Look for rebellion, look to be depos'd," *fr.* II, ii. PoFr
Edward the Third, *sels.* *Unknown.* LO
"Thou hear'st me say that I do dote on thee."
"Whether is her beauty by her words divine?"
Edward the Third had seven sons. The Ballad of Banners (1944). John Lehmann. MoBS
Edwards' great millstone and rock. Jonathan Edwards in Western Massachusetts. Robert Lowell. MaPo (1969 ed.)
Edwin and Angelina. Goldsmith. *Fr.* The Vicar of Wakefield, *ch.* 8. CEP; OTPC
Edwin Booth. Alice Brown. HBV
Edwin the Fair, *sel.* Sir Henry Taylor.
Wind in the Pines, The. VA
Eeka, Neeka. Walter de la Mare. WaKn
Eel, The. Walter de la Mare. ShM
Eel, The. Robert Lowell, *ad. fr. the Italian of* Eugenio Montale. NaP
Eel, The. Evan Morgan. CAW
Eel, The. Ogden Nash. FaBV; FaPON
Eel, the North Sea Siren, The. The Eel. Robert Lowell. NaP
Eemis-Stane, The. "Hugh MacDiarmid." NeBP
E'en as a lovely flower. Du bist wie eine Blume. Heine, *tr. by* Kate Kroeker. AWP; JAWP; WBP
E'en as the Flowers Do Wither. *Unknown.* EG; OBSC
E'en in thy native regions, how I blush. Praise of the Pudding. Joel Barlow. *Fr.* The Hasty Pudding. AnNE
E'en [*or* Even *or* Ev'n] like two little bank-dividing brooks. My Beloved Is Mine, and I Am His [*or* A Divine Rapture *or* A Mystical Ecstasy]. Francis Quarles. *Fr.* Emblems. GTSL; HBV; LiTL; LO; MeLP; OBEV; OBS; TDP; TrGrPo
Een Napoli. T. A. Daly. PoMa
E'en Such Is Time. Sir Walter Ralegh. *See* Conclusion, The.
E'en this, Lord, didst thou bless. Insomnia. John Banister Tabb. TrPWD
Eena, meena, mina, mo. *See* Eenie, meenie, minie, mo.
Eenie, meenie, mackeracka. *Unknown.* OxNR
Eenie, meenie, minie [*or* miney], mo. *Unknown.* FaPON; RIS
(Eena, meena, mina, mo.) OxNR; SiTL
Eenity, feenity, fickety, feg. *Unknown.* OxNR
Eeny, meeny, miney, mo. The Counting Man. William Vaughn Moody. PoMS
Eeny, weeny, winey, wo. *Unknown.* OxNR
E'er I begin, I must premise. Fable II: The Vulture, the Sparrow, and Other Birds. John Gay. EiCP
Eerily Sweet. Elizabeth J. Coatsworth. ChBR
Ees, twer at Liady-Day, ya know. Liady-Day an' Ridden House. William Barnes. OBRV
Ef I had 'bout—fo'ty-five dollahs. John Henry (D *vers.*). *Unknown.* ViBoFo
Ef I had wings like Noah's [*or* Norah's] dove. Dink's Sing. *Unknown.* ABF; OxBoLi; SiTL
Ef I'd knowed dat my cap'n was blin'. Tie-tamping Chant. *Unknown.* ABF
Ef you strike a thorn or rose. Keep a-Goin'! Frank L. Stanton. OHFP; WBLP
Effect of Example, The. John Keble. HBV; HBVY; MaRV
Effect of Love, The. Thomas Campion. MeWo
Effect of Military Music on a Welfare-Worker. Laurence Whistler. MuSP
Effect of Snow, The. Robert Finch.
"I have seen the snow like a mirage impending," III. ACV
Effective Prayer. St. Luke, XI: 9-13, Bible, *N.T.* TreFT
Efficient Wife's Complaint, The. Confucius, *tr. fr. Chinese by* Ezra Pound. *Fr.* Airs of Pei. CTC
Effie. Sterling A. Brown. BANP
Effigy, The. Guido Cavalcanti, *tr. fr. Italian by* Hubert Creekmore. LiTW
Effigy. Georgia Lee McElhaney. CoPo
Effigy of a Nun. Sara Teasdale. MAP; MoAmPo; NP
Effort, The. John Newton. SoP
Effort at Speech between Two People. Muriel Rukeyser. MoAB; MoAmPo; TrGrPo (rev. ed.); TrJP; TwCP; WOW
Effortlessly Democratic Santa Fe Trail. Martha Baird. PoPl
Eftsoons they heard a most melodious sound. The Bower of Bliss [*or* Gather the Rose]. Spenser. *Fr.* The Faerie Queene, II. FaBoEn; LoBV; OBSC; UnS; ViBoPo; WHA
Eftsoons they saw an hideous host array'd. Sea Monsters. Spenser. *Fr.* The Faerie Queene, II. ChTr
Egan O Rahilly. *Unknown, tr. fr. Irish by* James Stephens. CBEP; OBMV; SeCePo
Egeria, sweet creation of some heart. Byron. *Fr.* Childe Harold's Pilgrimage, IV. ViBoPo
Egg, The. Laura E. Richards. MPB; TiPo (1952 ed.)
Egg-and-Dart. Robert Finch. OBCV
Egg and the Machine, The. Robert Frost. CABA; MAP; MoAmPo; MWA-2
Egg for Easter, An. Irene F. Pawsey. BoTP
Egg is smooth and very pale, The. The Inefficacious Egg. Roy Bishop. HBMV
Eggleston was a taxi-driver. Cynical Portraits. Louis Paul. InMe
Eggs. Herbert Asquith. BrR
Eggs for Breakfast. Irene F. Pawsey. BoTP
Eggs from a chain store grocery. One No. 7. John Frederick Frank. GoYe
Eggstravagance, An. Oliver Wendell Holmes. *See* Limericks: "Reverend Henry Ward Beecher, The."
Egidio of Coimbra (A.D. 1597). Thomas Walsh. JKCP
Egloga Quinta: "Some doleful thing there is at hand." Barnabe Googe. ReIE
Egloga Secunda: "My beasts, go feed upon the plain." Barnabe Googe. ReIE
Eglogs of the Poet B. Mantuan Carmelitan, The, *sel.* Mantuan, *tr. fr. Latin by* George Turberville.
Second Egloge Entituled Fortunatus, The. ReIE
Eglogue to Mr. Johnson, An. Thomas Randolph. *See* Eclogue to Mr. Johnson, An.
Ego. Philip Booth. TwCP
Ego. A. Kirby Congdon. NYTB
Ego. Norman MacCaig. GTBS-P
Ego Dominus Tuus. W. B. Yeats. CMoP; NP
Ego Sum. Gelett Burgess. InMe
Egoism. W. Craddle. FiBHP; WhC
Egoist, The. Anna Wickham. FaBoTw
Egoist Dead, The. Elizabeth Brewster. CaP
Ego's Dream. Alfred Kreymborg. MAPA
Egotism. Edward Sandford Martin. AA
Egrets. Max Eastman. AnEnPo
Egrets. Judith Wright. GoJo
Egypt. Hilda Doolittle ("H. D."). HBMV
Egypt. Zulfikar Ghose. NYTB
Egypt Left Behind. John Nelson Darby. SoP
Egyptian banks, an avenue of clay. Flighting for Duck. William Empson. MoPo
Egyptian Lotus, The. Arthur Wentworth Hamilton Eaton. AA
Egyptian Passage, An. Theodore Weiss. CoPo
Egyptian Serenade. George William Curtis. HBV
Egyptian tombs hold priceless things. Tombs. Louise Webster. ChIP
Egyptians say, The, The Sun has twice. Samuel Butler. *Fr.* Hudibras, II, 3. ImOP

Egypt's Might Is Tumbled Down. Mary Elizabeth Coleridge. CH; MemP; POTE
Eheu Fugaces. "Thomas Ingoldsby." NBM; OxBoLi
Eidola. Samuel Daniel. *See* Are They Shadows?
Eidolon. Robert Penn Warren. FiMAP; TDP
Eidólons. Walt Whitman. AmePo
Eies look off theires no beeholdinge. *At. to* Francis Beaumont. SeCSL
Eight Aspects of Melissa. Lawrence Durrell. NeBP
Adepts, The, *sel.* ErPo
Visitations. MoBrPo (1962 ed.)
Eight Bells, *with music. Unknown.* SaSa
Eight bells! Eight bells! their clear tone tells. All's Well! William Allen Butler. HBV
Eight-Cylinder Man. Florence Ripley Mastin. PoPo
Eight-Day Clock, The. Alfred Cochrane. HBV
Eight days went by, eight days. The Wanderer: Soothsay. William Carlos Williams. TwAmPo
Eight fingers. The Difference. Laura E. Richards. HBV; HBVY; PPL
Eight Henry, heir indubitate of York and Lancaster. William Warner. *Fr.* Albion's England. TuPP
Eight hours' work, eight hours' play. Rhymes to Remember. *Unknown.* StaSt
Eight lines of clergymen converged. Colonel B. Constance Carrier. NePoAm-2
8 May 1967. Sister Mary Norbert Körte. ThO
Eight Melons. Malcolm Cowley. TwAmPo
Eight Months Old. Marion Strobel. NP
Eight Oars and a Coxswain ("Eight oars compel"). Arthur Guiterman. SD
Eight o'Clock. A. E. Housman. BrPo; CABA; CBV; CMoP; ExPo; InPo; LoBV; MoAB; MoBrPo; NoP; PoAn; PoIE; POTE; ReMP; ShBV-4; TrGrPo; WePo
Eight o'clock;/ The postman's knock! The Postman. Christina Rossetti. *Fr.* Sing-Song. GaP; GFA; PCH; RIS; SAS; TiPo
Eight of swords, a woman, The. Poem for Martha. Alex Raybin. ThO
Eight Sandbars on the Takano River. Gary Snyder. CoPo
Eight Volunteers. Lansing C. Bailey. PAH
Eight years old, crouched in a corner, eyeing the others askance. Party. Constance Carrier. NePoAm-2
Eighteen. Sister Mary Honora. NePoAm-2
1880. Christina Rossetti. *Fr.* Valentines to My Mother. DD
1885. Christina Rossetti. *Fr.* Valentines to My Mother. BoChLi; DD
1887. A. E. Housman. A Shropshire Lad, I. CoBMV; MaPo (1969 ed.); NAMP; PoAn; PoVP; ReMP; UnPo
1811. Wordsworth. *See* Here Pause: The Poet Claims at Least This Praise.
1805. Robert Graves. ChMP; EvOK; FaBoCh; HaMV; LoGBV
Eighteen hundred and ninety-one. Ain't Workin' Song. *Unknown.* OuSiCo
Eighteen-ninety. E. Richard Shipp. PoOW
1898-1899. Rupert Hughes. For Decoration Day, II. AA
1894 in London. Charles Spear. AnNZ
1801. Wordsworth. *See* I Grieved for Buonaparté.
1861-1865. Rupert Hughes. For Decoration Day, I. AA
18,000 Feet. Ed Roberson. PoNe (1970 ed.)
Eighteenth Century Lady. Rose O'Neill. NYTB
Eighteenth of October, The. The Fire of Frendraught. *Unknown.* ESPB; OBB; OxBB; ViBoFo
Eighteenth Song, The: "New year hath come in sight, The." Hadewijch, *tr. fr. Dutch by* A. J. Barnouw. LiTw
Eighth Air Force. Randall Jarrell. ILP; MiAP; MoVE; PoCh; ReMP
Eighth child of an eighth child, your wilful advent. Birth of a Great Man. Robert Graves. NYBP
Eighth Eclogue, The. Michael Drayton. *See* Cassamen and Dowsabel.
Eighth Elegy, *sel.* Muriel Rukeyser.
Children's Elegy. FiMAP
Eighth Pastoral of Virgil, The. Vergil, *tr. fr. Latin by* Dryden. *Fr.* Eclogues. EiCP
Eighth Sonnet, The. Sir Philip Sidney. *See* Astrophel and Stella: Eighth Song.
Eighth Street West. Rachel Field. ChBR; SiSoSe
Eighty and nine with their captain. The Charge by the Ford. Thomas Dunn English. PAH
Eighty years ago a woman passed. Tomorrow Is a Birthday. Gwendolen Haste. GoYe
Eighty-four acre campus. Data for Accreditation. Sister Mary Maura. JKCP (1955 ed.)
Eileen Aroon. Gerald Griffin. AnIV; GoBC; HBV; OBEV (1st ed.); OBVV; PCD
(Aileen Aroon.) IrPN; OnYI
"When like the rising day," *sel.* OBEV (new ed.)
Eileen Aroon. Carrol O'Daly. *tr. fr. Middle Irish or fr. Late Middle Irish by* George Sigerson. OnYI
Eileen of four. The Clock's Song. Rose Hawthorne Lathrop. AA; JKCP
Eily, Eily,/ my bonnie wee lass. Hushing Song. "Fiona Macleod." MoSiPe
Einar Tamberskelver. Longfellow. Tales of a Wayside Inn: The Musician's Tale. Pt. 1. xx. AmPP (4th ed.): YT
Eine Kleine Nachtmusik. Robert E. Hayden. PoNE
Eingang (Prelude). Rainer Maria Rilke. *See* Initiation.
Einstein. Archibald MacLeish. AnFE; APA; CMoP; CoAnAm; MoPo; TwAmPo
"He lies upon his bed," *sel.* ImOP
Einstein among the Coffee-Cups. Louis Untermeyer. WhC
Eire. William Drennan. OnYI
Eisenhower's Visit to Franco, 1959. James Wright. NaP; NMP
Either, over the shoulder enjoy leaning. Don't. Against the Grain. Michael Brownstein. ANYP; YAP
Either she was foul, or her attire was bad. Shameful Impotence [*or* The Impotent Lover]. Ovid. Amores, III, vii. ErPo; UnTE
Either to keep the thinking in. Country Ways. Marcia Masters. *Fr.* Impressions of My Father. GoYe
"Ej Blot til Lyst." William Morton Payne. AA
El Aghir. Norman Cameron. FaBoTw
(Green, Green Is El Aghir.) MoBS
El Alamein Revisited. Roy Macnab. PeSA
El Camino Verde. Paul Blackburn. CoPo
El Capitan-General. Charles Godfrey Leland. AA; HBV; YaD
El Emplazado. William Henry Venable. PAH
El Greco. E. L. Mayo. HoPM; MiAP
El Greco. C. A. Trypanis. NYTB
El Greco: Espolio. Earle Birney. MoCV; PeCV (1967 ed.)
El Gusano. Irving Layton. PeCV (1967 ed.)
El-Hajj Malik El Shabazz. Monologue. Alicia L. Johnson. WSL
El Hombre. William Carlos Williams. CABA; CMoP; LiTA
El-Painter's Daughter, The. Milton Kessler. NYTB
El Vaquero. Lucius Harwood Foote. AA
Elaine, Nini, Sylvia, Marjorie, Theda. A Postcard. Edwin Denby. ANYP
Elaine the fair, Elaine the lovable. Lancelot and Elaine. Tennyson. *Fr.* Idylls of the King. PoVP; ViPo; ViPP
Elaine's Song. Tennyson. *Fr.* Idylls of the King: Lancelot and Elaine. FaBoEn
(Song of Love and Death, The.) OBNC
El-a-noy, *with music. Unknown.* AS; TrAS
Elbow. Coleman Barks. *Fr.* Body Poems. QAH
Elbowing its neighbours. The Minotaur. Eldon Grier. PeCV
Elbows in wine-slops, news of the ocean isles. Cipangu. William Hart-Smith. *Fr.* Christopher Columbus. PoAu-2
Elden-Hole. Charles Cotton. *Fr.* The Wonders of the Peak. PeRV
Elder Brother, The (Poem for All Good and Loyal Dogs). Elma Dean. NeMA
Elder Brother, The, *sel.* John Fletcher.
Beauty Clear and Fair, *fr.* III, v. BEL; CBEP; HoPM; LO; OAEP; OBEV; SeCL; SeEP; ViBoPo
(Beauty Cleere and Fair.) AtBAP
(Song: "Beauty clear and fair.") OBS
Elder Edda, The, *sels. Unknown, tr. fr. Icelandic.*
Beginning and the End, The, *abr., tr. by* Henry Adams Bellows. LiTW
Counsels of Sigrdrifa, *tr. by* William Morris *and* Eiríkur Magnússon. AWP
First Lay of Gudrun, The, *tr. by* William Morris *and* Eiríkur Magnússon. AWP; JAWP; WBP
Hell-Ride of Brynhild, The, *tr. by* William Morris *and* Eiríkur Magnússon. OuHeWo
Lay of Thrym, The, *tr. by* Henry Adams Bellows. LiTW; OuHeWo
Short Lay of Sigurd, The, *tr. by* William Morris *and* Eiríkur Magnússon. EnLi-1

(Lay Called the Short Lay of Sigurd, The.) OuHeWo
(Lay of Sigurd, The.) AWP
Voluspo, *tr. by* Henry Adams Bellows. AWP
"Elder Father, though thine eyes." The Holy of Holies. G. K. Chesterton. BoPe; FaChP; MoRP; TRV; WGRP
Elder folk shook hands at last, The. The Meeting. Whittier. AmPP (3d ed.)
Elder Tree. Conrad Aiken. AP
Elder Tree, The. *Unknown.* ChTr
Elders at Their Services Begin, The. J. V. Cunningham. StP
(Epigram.) NePoAm; PIA
(Two Epigrams, I.) SiTL
Elderly Gentlemen, The. George Canning. BOHV; NA
Elders and officers line the returning road. Good-bye to the People of Hang-chow. Po Chü-i. LiTW
Elder's Reproof to His Wife, An. 'Abdillaahi Muuse, *tr. fr. Somali by* B. W. Andrzjewski *and* I. M. Lewis. TTY
Eldorado. Poe. AmePo; AmPP; AnFE; AP; APA; AWP; CoAnAm; CoBA; FaBoBe; FaBoCh; HBV; HT; InPo; LaNeLa; LoGBV; MWA-1; NePA; NoP; OTPC (1946 ed.); OxBA; PoMa; PoPo; PTK; RePo; RIS; StaST; TDP; WaKn; WiR; YT
Eleazar Wheelock. Richard Hovey. WhC
Elected Kaiser, burgher and a knight. Charles the Fifth and the Peasant. Robert Lowell. MiAP
Elected Knight, The. *Unknown. tr. fr. Danish by* Longfellow. AWP; JAWP; WBP
Elected Silence. Siegfried Sassoon. MoBrPo
Elected Silence, sing to me. The Habit of Perfection. Gerard Manley Hopkins. ACP; BoLiVe; BoPe; BrPo; CAW; CoBMV; EnLit; ForPo; ILP; JKCP; LiTB; LiTG; MoAB; MoBrPo; NoP; OAEP (2d ed.); OBEV (new ed.); OBMV; PoeP; PoIE; PoRA; PoVP; TrGrPo; UnS, 1 *st.*; ViBoPo; VP
Election, The. Robert Pack. CoPo
Election Address, An. James Kenneth Stephen. NBM
Election Day (Newark, New Jersey). LeRoi Jones. BF
Election Reflection. M. Keel Jones. PV
Electra. Francis Howard Williams. AA
Electric car jerks, The. In the Tube. Richard Aldington. WePo
Electric Sign Goes Dark, An. Carl Sandburg. HBMV
Electric Storm. Michael C. Martin. WaP
Electrical Storm. Elizabeth Bishop. WIRo
Electronic Tape Found in a Bottle. Olga Cabral. WOW
Elegiac. Mimnermus, *tr. fr. Greek by* E. F. Watling. LiTW
Elegiac. James Gates Percival. AA
(It Is Great for Our Country to Die.) HBV
Elegiac Mood. Gordon Bottomley. *Fr.* Night and Morning Songs. NP
Elegiac Sonnet. Charlotte Smith. *See* Sonnet Written at the Close of Spring.
Elegiac Stanzas, Suggested by a Picture of Peele Castle, in a Storm. Wordsworth. BEL; CABL; ChER; EnRP; EPN; ERoP-1; HBV; MBW-2; MERP; MyFE; NoP; OAEP; OBNC; OBRV; PeER; PoFS; TOP
(Nature and the Poet.) GTBS; GTBS-D; GTBS-P; GTBS-W; GTSE; GTSL
Elegiac Verses. Wordsworth. PoeP
Elegiack Verse, on . . . Mr. Elijah Corlet, An. Nehemiah Walter. SCAP
Elegie: Autumnall, The. John Donne. *See* Autumnal, The.
Elegie: Death. John Donne. MaMe
Of a Death in Winter, II, *sel.* BoW
Elegie: "Goe stop the swift-wing'd moments in their flight." William Habington. AnAnS-2
Elegie: Going to Bed. John Donne. *See* Going to Bed.
Elegie: His Picture. John Donne. *See* His Picture.
Elegie, An: "Let me be what I am, as Virgil cold." Ben Jonson. PoEL-2; SeCP
Elegie, An: "Love, give me leave to serve thee, and be wise." Thomas Randolph. MePo
Elegie: "Natures lay ideot, I taught thee to love." John Donne. *See* Elegy: "Nature's lay idiot. . ."
Elegie: On His Mistris. John Donne. *See* On His Mistress.
Elegie: Perfume, The. John Donne. Elegies, IV. SeCP
Elegie, An: "Though beautie be the marke of praise." Ben Jonson. *See* Elegy, An: "Though Beauty . . ."
Elegie, An: "'Tis true, I'm broke! Vowes, oathes, and all I had." Ben Jonson. AnAnS-2
Elegie: To His Mistris Going to Bed. John Donne. *See* Going to Bed.
Elegie Made by Mr. Aurelian Townshend in Remembrance of the Ladie Venetia Digby, An. Aurelian Townshend. AnAnS-2; SeCP
Elegie on His Mistris. John Donne. *See* On His Mistress.
Elegie on Mrs. Boulstred. John Donne. MaMe
Elegie on the Death of a Mad Dog, An. Goldsmith. *See* Elegy on the Death of a Mad Dog, An.
Elegie on the Deploreable Departure of the Honered and Truely Religious Chieftain John Hull, An. John Saffin. SCAP
Elegie on the L. C. John Donne. *See* Elegy on the L. C.
Elegie on the Lady Jane Pawlet, Marchion: of Winton, An. Ben Jonson. SeCP
Elegie on the Lady Marckham. John Donne. MaMe
Elegie upon that Reverend . . . Mr. Thomas Shepard, An. Urian Oakes. SCAP
Elegie Upon the Death of His Owne Father, An. Richard Corbett. AnAnS-2
Elegie upon the Death of the Deane of Pauls, Dr. John Donne, An. Thomas Carew. AnAnS-2; MeLP; MePo; OBS; SCEP-2; SeCP; SeCV-1
(Elegy upon the Death of Doctor Donne, Dean of Paul's, An.) PP; StP
(Elegy upon the Death of the Dean of Paul's, Dr. John Donne, An.) NoP; SeEP
(Elegy upon the Death of the Dean of St. Paul's, Dr. John Donne, An.) CABA
Elegie upon the Death of the Lord Hastings, An. Sir John Denham. SeCV-1
("Reader, preserve thy peace; those busy eyes.") ReEn
Elegie upon the Untimely Death of the Incomparable Prince Henry. John Donne. MaMe
Elegies, *sels.* André Chénier, *tr. fr. French by* Arthur Symons.
"Every man has his sorrows; yet each still." AWP; JAWP; WBP
"Well, I would have it so. I should have known." AWP
"White nymph wandering in the woods by night, A." AWP; JAWP; WBP
Elegies, *sels.* John Donne.
Anagram, The, II. MaMe
Autumnal, The, IX. MaMe; NoP; PoEL-2; ReEn; SCEP-1; SeCV-1; TuPP; ViBoPo
(Elegy IX: Autumnal, The.) AtBAP; DiPo; EnL; OAEP; SeEP
Bracelet, The, XI. MaMe
Change, III. LiTG; MaMe; ViBoPo
Comparison, The, VIII. ErPo; MaMe
Dreame, The IX. MaMe
("Image of her whom I love, more then she.") MeP
Elegie: "Natures lay ideot, I taught thee to love," VII. MaMe; SeCP
(Elegy: "Nature's lay idiot, I taught thee to love.") PoeP
Elegie: "Oh, let mee not serve so, as those men serve," VI. Mame
Expostulation, The, XV. MaMe
Going to Bed, XIX. LiTB; LiTG; MaMe
(Elegie: Going to Bed.) MePo
(Elegie: To His Mistris Going to Bed.) SeCP
(Elegy XIX: Going To Bed.) EnRePo
(On Going to Bed.) EP
(To His Mistress [*or* Mistris] Going to Bed.) ErPo; NoP; ReEn; SiTL; UnTE
His Parting From Her, XII. MaMe
"O Fortune, thou'rt not worth my least exclaim," *sel.* CoBE
His Picture, V. CBEP; MaMe; MeLP; NoP; OBS; ReEn
(Elegie: His Picture.) FaBoEn; MePo
(Elegy V: His Picture.) EnRePo; SeEP
Jealosie, I. AnAnS-1; MaMe
Julia, XIII. MaMe
Love's Progress, XVIII. LiTB; LiTG; MaMe; ViBoPo
Loves Warre, XX. MaMe
On His Mistress, XVI. AnAnS-1; CABL; CBV; CLwM; LiTB; LiTG; MaMe; MeLP; MyFE; PoEL-2; ReEn; SCEP-1; SeCP; TuPP; ViBoPo
(Elegie: On His Mistris.) MePo; SeCV-1
(Elegy on His Mistress.) LoBV; SeCeV; SeEP
Perfume, The, IV. CBV; MaMe; SeCP
Tale of a Citizen and His Wife, A, XIV. MaMe
Variety, XVII. MaMe
Elegies, *sels.* Ovid, *tr. fr. Latin by* Christopher Marlowe.
"About my temples go triumphant bays," XII. RelE

Elegies (continued)
"Envy, why carpest thou my time is spent so ill," XV. CLwM; RelE
("Envy, why twit'st thou me my time's spent ill," *tr. by* Ben Jonson.) RelE
To Verse Let Kings Give Place, XV. ChTr
Elegies, *sels.* Propertius, *tr. fr. Latin.*
An Woe Is Me, I, 1, *tr. by* F. A. Wright. AWP
Hylas, I, 20, *tr. by* F. A. Wright. AWP
Prayer for His Lady's Life, fr. II, 28, *tr. by* Ezra Pound. NoP
Revenge to Come, III, 25, *tr. by* Kirby Flower Smith. AWP; JAWP; LiTW; WBP
Elegies. Philippe Thoby-Marcelin, *tr. fr. French by* Edna Worthley Underwood. PoNe
Elegies, *sel.* Tibullus, *tr. fr. Latin.*
"Let others pile their yellow ingots high," *tr. by* Charles A. Elton. LiTW
Elegies for a Passing World. Edmund Wilson. *See* House of the Eighties, A, *and* Riverton.
Elegies over John Reed. Marya Zaturenska.
Elegy of the Kremlin Bells, The. NP
Elegy: "April again and it is a year again." Sidney Keyes. FaBoMo; WaP
Elegy: Autumnal[l], The. John Donne. *See* Autumnal, The.
Elegy: "Child, your white face is chanting memories." Karel van de Woestijne, *tr. fr. Flemish by* Jethro Bithell. LiTW
Elegy: "Clear and gentle stream!" Robert Bridges. BrPo; OAEP
Elegy, An: "Down in a bed, and on a bed of down." Giles Fletcher. *Fr.* Licia. RelE
Elegy: E. W. L. E. Sissman. NYBP
Elegy: "Fled is the swiftness of all the white-footed ones." Joseph Auslander. MAP; MoAmPo (1942 ed.) NP; TrJP
Elegy: "Floods of tears well from my deepest heart, The." Immanuel di Roma, *tr. fr. Italian by* Joseph Chotzner. TrJP
Elegy: "Fond, frozen, first and only lover." Louis Johnson. AnNZ
Elegy, An: "Friend, whose unnatural early death." David Gascoyne. FaBoTw; TwCP
Elegy: "Gnu up at the zoo, The." John Hall Wheelock. NYBP
Elegy: Going to Bed. John Donne. *See* Going to Bed.
Elegy: He Complains How Soon the Pleasing Novelty Is Over. William Shenstone. OBEC
(Elegy XI.) CEP
Elegy: "Her face like a rain-beaten stone on the day she rolled off." Theodore Roethke. PoeP
Elegy: "Here, awaiting what hereafter." R. G. Howarth. MoAuPo
Elegy V: His Picture. John Donne. *See* His Picture.
Elegy: "I die for Your holy word without regret." Antonio Enríquez Gómez, *tr. fr. Spanish.* TrJP
Elegy: "I have lov'd flowers that fade." Robert Bridges. *See* I Have Loved Flowers That Fade.
Elegy: "I know but will not tell." Alan Dugan. AP
Elegy: "I stood between two mirrors when you died." William Jay Smith. NePoEA
Elegy, An: "I will not weep, for 'twere as great a sin." Henry King. AnAnS-2
(Conjectured to Be upon the Death of Sir Walter Raleigh.) EG
Elegy: "Image of her whom I love, move then she." John Donne. Elegies, X. MeP
Elegy, An: "In early winter before the first snow." E. J. Scovell. ChMP
Elegy: "In pain she bore the son who her embrace." Moses ibn Ezra, *tr. fr. Hebrew by* Solomon Solis-Cohen. TrJP
Elegy: "Jackals prowl, the serpents hiss, The." Arthur Guiterman. BOHV; InMe
Elegy, An: "Let others pile their yellow ingots high." Albius Tibullus. *See* Pastoral Elegy, A.
Elegy: "Let them bury your big eyes." Edna St. Vincent Millay. Memorial to D. C., V. AmLP, AnNE; CMoP; HBMV; InP; MAP; MoAB; MoAmPo; NeMA; NePA; OxBA; PoRA
Elegy, The: "Madam, no more! The time has come to eat." A. D. Hope. ErPo
Elegy IX: "My dear, observe the rose! though she desire it." William Bell. NePoEA
Elegy: "My father was born with a spade in his hand and traded it." John Ciardi. ToPo
Elegy: "My prime of youth is but a frost of cares." Chidiock Tichborne. ChTr; LoBV; OBSC; PoSa
(His Elegy.) PolE
'Lament the Night before His Execution, A. HBV
(Lines before Execution.) CBEP
(On the Eve of His Execution.) PG (1955 ed.); PoFS; TrGrPo
(Poem, Written on the Eve of Execution.) LiTG
(Retrospect.) ACP; GoBC
(Tichborne's Elegy.) ForPo
(Tichborne's Elegy, Written [with His Own Hand] in the Tower before His Execution, 1586.) ElL; FosPo; NoP; ReEn; TuPP
(Untimely End, The.) CoBE
(Written on the Eve of Execution.) AnFE; EG; GTBS-W; LiTB; TreFT
(Written the Night before His Execution.) ViBoPo
Elegy: "My thoughts impelled me to the resting-place." Moses ibn Ezra, *tr. fr. Hebrew by* Emma Lazarus. TrJP
Elegy: "Narrowing of knowledge to one window to a door, A." William Montgomerie. *See* Elegy for William Soutar.
Elegy: "Nature's lay idiot, I taught thee to love." John Donne. Elegies, VII. PoeP
(Elegie VII: "Nature's lay ideot, I taught thee to love.") SeCP
("Natures lay ideot, I taught thee to love.") MaMe
Elegy: "No spring nor summer beauty hath such grace." John Donne. *See* Autumnal, The.
Elegy: "Now Christendom bids her cathedrals call." William Bell. NePoEA
Elegy: "O fortunate man! who tilled the stubborn soil." Arthur Davison Ficke. NYTB
Elegy: "O snatch'd away in beauty's bloom!" Byron. *See* Oh! Snatched Away in Beauty's Bloom.
Elegy, An: "O youngest, best-loved daughter of Hsieh." Yuan Chen, *tr. fr. Chinese by* Witter Bynner. LiTW
Elegy: On Delia's Being in the Country. James Hammond. Love Elegies, VII. CEP
Elegy: "Out on the roads of sky the moon stands poised." Roy McFadden. NeIP
Elegy: "Responsible sound of the lawnmower, The." William Stafford. OPoP
Elegy: Separation of Man from God. George Barker. GTBS-W; LiTB
(Elegy: "These errors loved no less than the saint loves arrows.") FaBoTw
(Sacred Elegy V.) MoPo
Elegy, An: "Since you must go, and I must bid farewell." Ben Jonson. CLwM; EnRePo; LoBV
Elegy, An: "So frail our life, perchance tomorrow's sun." Tsurayuki, *tr. fr. Japanese by* Basil Hall Chamberlain. OnPM
Elegy: Summer House on the Mound, The. Robert Bridges. GoTL
Elegy: "These errors loved no less than the saint loves arrows." George Barker. *See* Elegy: Separation of Man from God.
Elegy: "They are lang deid, folk that I used to ken." Robert Garioch. OxBS
Elegy: "This winter eve how soft! how mild!" Richard Chenevix Trench. IrPN
Elegy: "Those reckless hosts rush to the wells." Baruch of Worms, *tr. fr. Hebrew.* TrJP
Elegy, An: "Though beauty be the mark of praise." Ben Jonson. BWP; EnRePo; ForPo; NoP; OBEV; QFR
(Elegie, An: "Though beautie be the marke of praise.") SCEP-2; SeCV-1
Elegy, An: "Though I see the white azaleas on the shore." *Unknown, tr. fr. Japanese by* Ishii *and* Obata. *Fr.* Manyo Shu. OnPM
Elegy, An: To and Old Beauty. Thomas Parnell. CEP
Elegy: To Delia. James Hammond. Love Elegies, XII. CEP
Elegy: To the Memory of an Unfortunate Lady. Pope. *See* Elegy to the Memory . . .
Elegy: "Tonight the moon is high, to summon all." William Bell. FaBoTw
Elegy: "Tumult of death, dizziness hath seized me, The." Moses Rimos of Majorca, *tr. fr. Hebrew by* Israel Abrahams. TrJP

Elegy: Unrewarded Lover, The. William Walsh. CEP
Elegy: "Waxen and the false grace of tulips, The." G. S. Fraser. NeBP
Elegy: "We eat and hear, as your kiss descends." Tony Towle. ANYP; YAP
Elegy: "We knew that he was not a model cat." Margaret E. Bruner. CIV
Elegy: "What should you know at last when spirit's." Robert Fitzgerald. AnAmPo
Elegy: "When in the mirror of a permanent tear." Gene Derwood. LiTA
Elegy: "Whenever we touched, I thought of the Lying-in Hospital." Robert Layzer. NePoEA; PoPl
Elegy: "Wood is bare, The: a river-mist is steeping." Robert Bridges. CMoP; OAEP; PoVP
Elegy against a Latter Day. Kendrick Smithyman. AnNZ
Elegy before Death. Edna St. Vincent Millay. AnFE; APA; CMoP; CoAnAm; GTBS-W; LiTA; LiTM
Elegy by Green for Byles's Cat. Joseph Green. CIV
Elegy for a Countryman. Padraic Fallon. NeIP
Elegy for a Dead Soldier. Karl Shapiro. AmPP (4th ed.); AP; CoBMV; FaPL; MiAP; OxBA; ThLM, *much abr.*; ToPo; WaaP; WaP
Elegy for a Lady. Walt Delegall. BF
Elegy for a Mis-spent Youth. Jon Stallworthy. MeWo
Elegy for a Nature Poet. Howard Nemerov. BoNaP; PP
Elegy for an Estrangement. John Holloway. NePoEA
Elegy for an Unknown Soldier. James K. Baxter. AnNZ
Elegy for Doctor Dunn. Lord Herbert of Cherbury. AnAnS-2
Elegy for Edward Thomas, *sel.* Charles Dalmon.
"Clods of battle fields are red, The." POTE
Elegy, for Father Anselm, of the Order of Reformed Cistercians, An. Helen Parry Eden. JKCP
Elegy for Helen Trent. Paris Leary. CoPo
Elegy for J. F. K. W. H. Auden. FIW
Elegy for Jane. Theodore Roethke. AmP; AmPP (5th ed.); AP; CaFP; CoAP; FiMAP; GTBS-W; LiTM (1970 ed.); MoAB; MoAmPo (1962 ed.); NePA; NoP; PoPo; TDP; TwAmPo; TwCP
Elegy for Lucy Lloyd. Llewelyn Goch, *tr. fr. Welsh by* Ernest Rhys. LiTW
Elegy for Margaret, *sel.* Stephen Spender.
"Dearest and nearest brother," VI. FaBoEn
Elegy for Margaret Howard, Lady Buckhurst. Robert Southwell. CoBE
Elegy for Minor Poets. Louis MacNeice. HaMV; ML; PP
Elegy for Mr. Goodbeare. Sir Osbert Sitwell. AnFE; MoBrPo
Elegy for My Father. Howard Moss. CoAP; LiTM (1970 ed.); NePoEA
Elegy for Our Dead. Edwin Rolfe. WaP
Elegy for the Monastery Barn. Thomas Merton. CoPo
Elegy for the Silent Voices and the Joiners of Everything. Kenneth Patchen. NaP
Elegy for Two Banjos. Karl Shapiro. AtBAP; LiTA; TrJP; WaP
Elegy for William Soutar. William Montgomerie. NeBP
(Elegy: "Narrowing of knowledge to one window to a door, A.") OxBS
Elegy in a Country Churchyard. G. K. Chesterton. CBV; EvOK; HBMV; MMA; MoBrPo; NeMA; TreFT; TrGrPo; ViBoPo; WhC
Elegy in a Firelit Room. James Wright. TwAmPo
Elegy in a Museum. Pamela Griffin. BoPe
Elegy in a Theatrical Warehouse. Kenneth Fearing. NYBP
Elegy in Memory of the Worshipful Major Thomas Leonard Esq., An. Samuel Danforth, Jr. SCAP
Elegy in Six Sonnets. Frederick Goddard Tuckerman. *Fr.* Sonnets. QFR
Elegy in the Orongorongo Valley. Hubert Witheford. AnNZ
Elegy Just in Case. John Ciardi. AtBAP; MiAP; TwAmPo; TwCP
Elegy, Montreal Morgue. Goodridge Macdonald. CaP
Elegy of the Duke of Marmalade. Luis Palés Matos, *tr. fr. Spanish by* Donald D. Walsh. LiTW
Elegy of the Kremlin Bells, The. Marya Zaturenska. *Fr.* Elegies over John Reed. NP
Elegy on a Dead Mermaid Washed Ashore at Plymouth Rock. Robert Hillyer. EtS
Elegy on a Lady, Whom Grief for the Death of Her Betrothed Killed. Robert Bridges. CoBMV; OBEV new ed.); OBVV
Elegy on a Lap Dog, An. John Gay. DiPo; HBV; PoE
Elegy on a Nordic White Protestant. John Gould Fletcher. PoNe
Elegy on Albert Edward the Peacemaker. *Unknown.* CoMu
Elegy on an Australian Schoolboy, *sel.* Zora Cross.
"O brother in the restless rest of God!" PoAu-1
Elegy on an Empty Skyscraper. John Gould Fletcher. AmP
Elegy on Ben. Jonson, An. *At to* John Cleveland, *also at. to* James Cleyton. MeLP; OBS
(On Ben Jonson.) SeEP
Elegy on Coleman. *Unknown.* ALV
Elegy on Gordon Barber, Lamentably Drowned in His Eighteenth Year. Gene Derwood. FaFP; GTBS-W; LiTG; LiTM; NePA; TwAmPo
Elegy on Herakleitos. Callimachus, *tr. fr. Greek by* Dudley Fitts. LiTW
Elegy on His Mistress. John Donne. *See* On His Mistress.
Elegy on Mrs. Mary Blaize. Goldsmith. *See* Elegy on That Glory of Her Sex, Mrs. Mary Blaize.
Elegy on My Father. Allen Curnow. AnNZ
Elegy on Shakespeare. William Basse. CBEP; OBS
(On Mr. Wm. Shakespeare.) CLwM; ElL; SeEP; ViBoPo
Elegy on That [*or* the] Glory of Her Sex, Mrs. Mary Blaize, An. Goldsmith. BOHV; CBEP; CEP; HBV; InMe; NA; NeHB; OAEP; OBEC; OnYI; TreFT
(Elegy on Mrs. Mary Blaize.) OnPP; WhC
(Mrs. Mary Blaize.) SiTL
Elegy on the Death of a Mad Dog. Goldsmith. *Fr.* The Vicar of Wakefield, *ch.* 17. BeLS; BLPA; BOHV; CBEP; CEP; FaBoBe; FaBoCh; FaFP; GN; HBV; HBVY; LBN; LiTG; LoGBV; MaC; MCCG; NA; NeHB; OAEP; OBEC; OnSP; OTD; OTPC; PoPo; PoSa; RIS; RoGo; ShM; SiTL; TreF; WaKn
(Elegie on the Death of a Mad Dog.) ALV
Elegy on the Death of Dr. Channing, *sels.* James Russell Lowell. MaRV
"Therefore I cannot think thee wholly gone."
Truth and Love Abide.
Elegy on the Death of John Keats, An. Shelley. *See* He Is Not Dead.
Elegy on the Death of Mme. Anna Pavlova, *sel.* E. H. W. Meyerstein.
"Glory and the ardour of the stage, The." UnS
Elegy on the Death of Sidney. *At. to* Sir Edward Dyer. *See* Epitaph on Sir Philip Sidney.
Elegy on the Eve. George Barker. WaaP
Elegy on the Glory of Her Sex, Mrs. Mary Blaize, An. Goldsmith. *See* Elegy on That Glory of Her Sex, Mrs. Mary Blaize, An.
Elegy on the L. C. John Donne. ATP (1953 ed.)
(Elegie on the L. C.) MaMe
Elegy on the Late King of Patagonia, An. St. John Emile Clavering Hankin. CenHV
Elegy on the Loss of U.S. Submarine S4, *sel.* H. C. Canfield.
"Entrapped inside a submarine." FiBHP
Elegy on Thyrza. Byron. *See* And Thou Art Dead, as Young and Fair.
Elegy on William Cobbett. Ebenezer Elliott. VA
Elegy, or Friend's Passion for His Astrophil, An, *sel.* Matthew Royden.
On Sir Philip Sidney, 7 *sts.* ElL
Elegy Over a Tomb. Lord Herbert of Cherbury. AnAnS-2; AtBAP; ElL; EP; FaBoEn; ForPo; MeLP; MePo; OBEV (new ed.); OBS; PoEL-2; QFR; SeEP; ViBoPo
Elegy to His Mistress. Ovid. *See* In Summer's Heat.
Elegy to Sports. David Shapiro. ANYP
Elegy to the Memory of an Unfortunate Lady. Pope. ACP, *sl. abr.*; CBEP; EiPP; FiP; HBV; LO; MBW-1; NoP; OBEC; OBEV; PeER; PoE; SeCeV
(Elegy: To the Memory of an Unfortunate Lady.) EiPP
(Verses to the Memory of an Unfortunate Lady.) CEP
Sel.
"Most souls, 'tis true, but peep out once an age." CH
Elegy upon My Best Friend, An. Henry King. AnAnS-2
Elegy upon the Death of Doctor Donne, Dean of Paul's, An. Thomas Carew. *See* Elegie upon the Death of the Deane of Pauls, Dr. John Donne, An.
Elegy upon the Death of Mr. Stanninow Fellow of Queenes Colledge, An. Richard Crashaw. MaMe
Elegy upon the Death of my Lord Francis Villiers, An. Andrew Marvell. MaMe

Elegy upon the Death of That Holy Man of God Mr. John Allen, An, *sel.* Edward Taylor.
"How are our spirituall gamesters slipt away?" PoEL-3
Elegy upon the Death of the Dean of Paul's, Dr. John Donne, An. Thomas Carew. *See* Elegie upon the Death of the Deane of Pauls, Dr. John Donne, An.
Elegy upon the Most Incomparable King Charles the First, An, *sel.* Henry King.
"Thou from th' en'throned martyrs blood-stain'd line." OBS
Elegy Written in a Country Churchyard. Thomas Gray. AnEnPo; AnFE; AtBAP; ATP; AWP; BEL; BoLiVe; CABA; CABL; CaFP; CBEP; CEP; CoBE; DiPo; EiCL; EiCP; EiPP; EnL; EnLi-2; EnLit; EnPE; EnRP; ExPo; FaBoBe; FaBoEn; FaFP; FaPL; FosPo; GN; GoTL; GTBS; GTBS-D; GTBS-W; GTSE; GTSL; HBV; HBVY; HoPM; ILP; InP; InPo; JAWP; LaA; LiTB; LiTG; LoBV; MaRV; MasP; MCCG; MyFE; NeHB; NoP; OAEP; OBEC; OBEV; OHFP; OTD; OTPC; OuHeWo; PAn; PG (1945 ed.); PIA; Po; PoAn; PoE; PoEL-3; PoFS; PoIE; PoLF; PoPo; PoSa; SeCeV; ShBV-3; StP; TDP; TIHL; TOP; TreF; TrGrPo; UnPo; ViBoPo; WBLP; WBP; WHA; WoL
Sels.
"Boast of heraldry, the pomp of power, The." LO
"Curfew tolls the knell of parting day, The." MemP; OQP; YAT
Stanzas Cancelled from the Elegy. ViBoPo
Elegy Written on a Frontporch. Karl Shapiro. MoPo
Elegy Wrote in the Tower, 1554. John Harrington. ElL
(Comparison of Life and Death, *with add. sts.*) ReIE
Element. P. K. Page. MoCV; PeCV
Element of air was out of hand, The. Interlude. Theodore Roethke. MiAP
Element that utters doves, angels and cleft flames. Air. Kathleen Raine. MoAB; MoBrPo (1962 ed.)
Elemental. George Dillon. AnAmPo
Elementary School Classroom in a Slum, An. Stephen Spender. BoLiVe (1945 ed.); CoBMV; FaBoMo; FosPo; ILP; LiTB; MoAB; MoBrPo; MoPo; OAEP (2d ed.); PoE; PPON; ReMP; TrGrPo; TwCP
Elements, The. W. H. Davies. MoBrPo; OBVV; RePo; WaKn; YT
Elements. Carolyn Wilson Link. GoYe
Elements, The. Cardinal Newman. GoBC; OBRV; PoVP; VA
(Chorus of the Elements.) OBVV
Elements, The. Oscar Williams. NAMP
Elements have merged into solicitude, The. The Racer's Widow. Louise Glück. NYBP
Elements of Grammar. Calvin C. Hernton. NBP
Elements of sight compose themselves, The. Statement. John Unterecker. ThO
Elena's Song. Sir Henry Taylor. *Fr.* Philip van Artevelde, II. OBEV; OBRV; OBVV
(Song: "Quoth tongue of neither maid nor wife.") VA
Elene, *sels.* Cynewulf, *tr. fr. Anglo-Saxon by* Richard L. Hoffman.
"Battle-fear mounted." YAT
Constantine's Vision of the Cross, *tr. by* Charles W. Kennedy. AnOE
Helena Embarks for Palestine, *tr. by* Charles W. Kennedy. AnOE
"King was frightened, The." YAT
"Ruler of warriors then called the wisest, The." YAT
"Then had passed by, in the course of years." YAT
"Then the glorious King, Constantine." YAT
"Then the wisest, before the assembly." YAT
"Thus wisely they taught the victorious King." YAT
"'To thee, Constantine, the King of Angels.'" YAT
Eleonora Duse as Magda. Laurence Binyon. SyP
Elephant, The. Herbert Asquith. BoTP; SoPo; SUS; TiPo; UTS
Elephant, The. Hilaire Belloc. BoTP; SoPo; TiPo; UTS
Elephant. N. H. Brettell. BoSA
Elephant, The. E. J. Falconer. BoTP
Elephant, The. Rachel Field. *Fr.* A Circus Garland. SoPo; StVeCh
Elephant, An. Joseph G. Francis. MPB
Elephant, The. A. E. Housman. *See* Elephant, The, or the Force of Habit.
Elephant. David McFadden. WHW
Elephant! Tom Scherman. PCD
Elephant. *Unknown, tr. fr. Hottentot.* PeSA
Elephant, The. Annette Wynne. GFA
Elephant I, The. *Unknown, tr. fr. Yoruba.* *See* Erin.
Elephant II, The. *Unknown, tr. by* C. M. Bowra. TTY
Elephant always carries his trunk, The. The Elephant's Trunk. Alice Wilkins. GFA; SoPo; TiPo
Elephant and the Bookseller, The. John Gay. *Fr.* Fables. EiCP; LoBV
Elephant and the Flea, The, *with music.* *Unknown.* TrAS
Elephant hunter, take your bow! The Elephant II. *Unknown.* TTY
Elephant Is an Odd Affair, An. Zhenya Gay. RePo
Elephant is like a wall, The. The Elephant. E. J. Falconer. BoTP
Elephant Is Slow to Mate, The. D. H. Lawrence. CBV; LiTB; LiTM; NAMP; PoPl
Elephant is very large, The. The Elephant. Annette Wynne. GFA
Elephant, or the Force of Habit, The. A. E. Housman. PV; WhC
(Elephant, The.) FaBV; PoPo
Elephant sat on some kegs, An. An Elephant. Joseph G. Francis. MPB
Elephant, the huge old beast, The. The Elephant Is Slow to Mate. D. H. Lawrence. CBV; LiTB; LiTM; NAMP
Elephant who brings death. Erin [*or* Elephant I]. *Unknown.* OA; PBA; TTY
Elephants, The. Dorothy Aldis. *Fr.* At the Circus. UTS
Elephants. Marianne Moore. FaBoMo
Elephants Are Different to Different People. Carl Sandburg. MAP; MoAmPo
Elephant's Trunk, The. Alice Wilkins. GFA; SoPo; TiPo
Elephants walking. Holding Hands. Lenore M. Link. FaPON; MoShBr; SoPo; TiPo (1952 ed.); UTS
Eletelephony. Laura E. Richards. BoChLi; FaPON; GoJo; PDV; SoPo; TiPo; YaD
Eleusis and Beethoven. John Press. MuSP
Elevated Train, The. James S. Tippett. SUS
Elevation. Baudelaire, *tr. fr. French by* Arthur Symons. AWP
Elevator car in the elevator shaft, The. A Modern Ballad. Caroline D. Emerson. BrR
Elevator Man Adheres to Form, The. Margaret Danner. PoNe (1970 ed.)
Elevator rises, Negro men, The. Poem to Negro and Whites. Maxwell Bodenheim. PoNe
Eleven. Archibald MacLeish. CMoP
Eleven men of England. The Red Thread of Honor. Sir Francis Hastings Doyle. BBV; OtMeF; PoVP
Eleventh and Last Book of the Ocean to Cynthia, The. Sir Walter Ralegh. *See* Ocean to Cynthia, The.
Eleventh Commandment, The, *sel.* John Holmes.
"When Moses came down from the mountain and the cloud." MoRP
Eleventh Hour, The. Francis St. Vincent Morris. WePo
Eleventh Property, The. Sir Thomas More. *Fr.* The Twelve Properties or Conditions of a Lover. EnRePo
Eleventh Song. Sir Philip Sidney. *See* Astrophel and Stella: Eleventh Song.
Elf and the Dormouse, The. Oliver Herford. AA; BoChLi; FaBoBe; FaPON; GFA; GoTP; HBV; HBVY; MPB; OnMSP; OTPC (946 ed.); PCH; PRWS; SoPo; SP; TiPo; TSW; TVC; UTS
Elf Child, The. James Whitcomb Riley. *See* Little Orphant Annie.
Elf-King, The. Goethe. *See* Erlking, The.
Elf-light, owl-light. Dusk in the Domain. Dorothea Mackellar. PoAu-1
Elf Singing, The. William Allingham. GoTP; StVeCh
Elfer Hill. *Unknown, tr. fr. Danish by* Robert Jamieson. AWP
Elfin Knight, An. Joseph Rodman Drake. *See* Fairy in Armor, A.
Elfin Knight, The (*diff. vers.*). *Unknown.* BaBo (A *vers.*); BuBa; ESPB; ViBoFo (A *and* B *vers.*)
(Cambric Shirt, The) BaBo, B *vers.*; BFSS, A, B *and* C *vers., with music*
("Can you make me a cambric shirt.") OxNR
(Lady Isabel and the Elf-Knight.) OBB
Lover's Tasks. CBEP

Rosemary and Thyme, *with music.* BFSS (D *vers.*)
My Plaid Awa', *sel.* CH
Elfin Pedlar, The. George Darley. *See* Nephon's Song.
Elfin People Fill the Tubes, The. Winifred M. Letts. BoTP
Elfin Plane, The. Rowena Bennett. MPB (1956 ed.)
Elfin Skates. Eugene Lee-Hamilton. OBVV
Elfin Song. Joseph Rodman Drake. *Fr.* The Culprit Fay. AA; PoMS
Elfin Wife, The. "Jake Falstaff." BoC
Eli, Eli, lama sabacthani? At the Ninth Hour. John Lancaster Spalding. *Fr.* God and the Soul. AA
Elihu. Alice Cary. PaPo
Elijah's mantle fell upon. A Little Song of Work. Sarah Elizabeth Sprouse. BLRP
Elinda's Glove. Richard Lovelace. OBS
(Ellinda's Glove.) SiSw
(Glove, The.) ALV; EG
Elinor Wylie fell in love with Shelley. A Thought in Time. Robert Hillyer. NYBP
Eliot Cass was from Boston, Mass. The Old School Tie-up. Laurence McKinney. WhC
Eliot saw much, thought he saw more. T. S. Eliot. Thomas Whitbread. NYTB
Eliot's Oak. Longfellow. AmePo
Elisa. Spenser. *Fr.* The Shepheardes Calendar: April. OBSC
("Ye daynte Nymphs, that in this blessed Brooke.") AtBAP
Elisa, or an Elegy upon the Unripe Decease of Sir Antony Irby, *sel.* Phineas Fletcher.
"My dearest Betty." ViBoPo
Elixer, The. George Herbert. AnAnS-1; BoLiVe; BoTP; FaBoCh; GN; LoGBV; MaMe; MaRV; MeP; NoP; OHIP; PCH, *st.* 1; SeCV-1; ThGo, *st.* 1; TrGrPo; WGRP
(Teach Me, My God and King.) SoP, *abr.*
Eliza. Erasmus Darwin. PaPo
Eliza and Anne were extremely distress'd. The Bird's Nest. Elizabeth Turner. OHIP; OTPC (1923 ed.)
Eliza Spaulding. Donald Burnie. PaA
Eliza Telefair. Jocelyn Macy Sloan. GoYe
Elizabeth. Valentin Iremonger. *See* Recollection in Autumn.
Elizabeth. George Brandon Saul. HBMV
Elizabeth. Sylvia Townsend Warner. MoAB; MoBrPo; NeMA
Elizabeth Ann Peabody. Ivy O. Eastwick. BrR
Elizabeth at the Piano. Horace Gregory. SiSw; UnS
Elizabeth, frigidly stretched. Recollection in Autumn [*or* Elizabeth *or* This Houre Her Vigill]. Valentin Iremonger. NeIP; OnYI; OxBI
Elizabeth her frock has torn. Think Before You Act. Mary Elliott. HBVY
Elizabeth L. H. Ben Jonson. *See* Epitaph on Elizabeth, L. H.
Elizabeth, Lizzy [*or* Elspeth], Betsy, and Bess. Mother Goose. HBV; HBVY; OTPC; OxNR; PPL; RIS
Elizabeth, my cousin, is the sweetest little girl. Mustard and Cress. Norman Gale. TVC
Elizabeth of Bohemia. Sir Henry Wotton. *See* On His Mistress, the Queen of Bohemia.
"Elizabeth the Beloved." Elizabeth. Sylvia Townsend Warner. MoAB; MoBrPo; NeMA
Elizabethan Days, *sel.* Thomas Caulfield Irwin.
"'Tis pleasant, stretched on grassy lawn." IrPN
Elizabethan Tragedy; a Footnote. Howard Moss. NePoEA
Elizabethan Week-End. Sir John Davies. CLwM
Elizabethans Called It Dying, The. James Schuyler. NeAP
Ella, fell a/ Maple tree. Picnic. Hugh Lofting. GoJo; SUS
Ellen Bawn. *Unknown,* *tr. fr. Irish by* James Clarence Mangan. IrPN
Ellen Irwin; or, The Braes of Kirtle. Wordsworth. MBW-2
Ellen McJones [*or* M'Jones] Aberdeen. W. S. Gilbert. HBV; InMe; PCD; TSW
Ellinda's Glove. Richard Lovelace. *See* Elinda's Glove.
Elliott Hawkins. Edgar Lee Masters. *Fr.* Spoon River Anthology. OxBA
Ellipse of a cry, The. The Cry. Federico García Lorca. OnPM
Ellis Park. Helen Hoyt. HBMV; NP; PoMa; SP; YT
Ellsworth. *Unknown.* PAH
Elm. Sylvia Plath. *See* Elm Speaks, The.
Elm, The. Odell Shepard. HBMV
Elm Angel. Harold Monro. FaBoMo
Elm Beetle, The. Andrew Young. LoBV
Elm is turned to crystal, The. Weather. William Meredith. NYBP
Elm lets fall its leaves before the frost, The. The Pine. Augusta Davies Webster. DD; HBV; OHIP
Elm Speaks, The. Sylvia Plath. NYBP
(Elm, The.) PoAn
Elms are bad, sinister trees. Breakwaters. Ted Walker. NYBP
Elms are proud. Bedtime. Elizabeth J. Coatsworth. ThGo
Elms of the Eastern Gate. *Unknown,* *tr. fr. Chinese by* Arthur Waley. *Fr.* Shi King. LiTW
Eloïsa to Abelard. Pope. CEP; EiCL; EiPP; EnL; EnLi-1; LoBV; MBW-1; OAEP; PAn; PoEL-3
Sels.
Eloisa. OBEC; SeCePo
Vestal, The, *br. sel.* ACP; CAW
Eloisa's Prayer for Abelard. GoBC
"How oft, when pressed to marriage." ViBoPo
Eloquent are the hills: their power speaks. The Green Lake. Michael Roberts. ChMP
Eloquent between the formal hedges. Affair of Honour. George Whalley. MoCV
Eloquent herald this, a speech-crammed babbler! An. Euripides. *Fr.* Suppliants. PoFr
Elphin knight sits on yon hill, The. The Elfin Knight (A *vers.*). *Unknown.* BaBo
Elsa Wertman. Edgar Lee Masters. *Fr.* Spoon River Anthology. OxBA
"Else a Great Prince in Prison Lies." Denise Levertov. NaP
Elsie. William Carlos Williams. *See* Pure Products of America, The.
Elsie Marley. *Unknown.* BBGG; OTPC (1923 ed.); OxNR
("Elsie Marley's grown so fine.") SAS
Elsie's House. Stanley McNail. FiSC
Elusive Maid, The. Abraham ibn Chasdai, *tr. fr. Hebrew by* Joseph Chotzner. TrJP
Elustrious dame whose vertues rare doe shine. An Acrostick on Mrs. Elizabeth Hull. John Saffin. SCAP
Elves' Dance, The. *Unknown,* *at. to* John Lyly *and to* Thomas Ravenscroft. *Fr.* The Mayde's Metamorphosis. CH; FaPON; HH; MPB; PoRh
(Fairy Dances, 2.) EIL
("Round about in a fair ring-a," *diff. vers.*) BoTP
Elvira, *sel.* George Digby, Earl of Bristol.
Song: "See, O see! /How every tree." SeCL
Elynour Rummynge. John Skelton. PoFS, *much abr.*
(Tunning of Elinour Rumming, The.) ReIE
Sels.
"And this comely dame." ViBoPo
Tunning of Elinour Rumming, The. TrGrPo
(Tunnyng of Elynour Rummyng, The.) EnPo; SiTL; StP
Elysium is as far as to. Emily Dickinson. AmPP (4th ed.); AWP; CABA; CoBA; DiPo; FaBoEn; FaPL; InPo; JAWP; MAP; MoAB; MoAmPo; NeMA; OnPM; OxBA; PoIE; WBP; WoL
Emanations. Ronald Johnson. YAP
Emancipation. Maltbie D. Babcock. *See* Death.
Emancipation. *Unknown.* BLPA
Emancipation from British Dependence. Philip Freneau. PAH
Emancipation Group, The. Whittier. LiPo
Sels.
Abraham Lincoln. SoP
"Let man be free! The mighty word." PGD
Emancipation of George Hector (a colored Turtle), The. Mari E. Evans. AmNP
Emancipators, The. Randall Jarrell. WaP
Emaricdulfe, *sel.* "E. C."
"I am enchanted with thy snow-white hands," XVII. Sonn; TuPP
"My heart is like a ship on Neptune's back," XXIX. Sonn; TuPP
"Within her hair Venus and Cupid sport them," VI. EIL; Sonn; TuPP
Embalming is so intricate these days. And Dust to Dust. Charles David Webb. NePoAm-2.
Embankment, The. T. E. Hulme. ELU; FaBoMo; GTBS-P; MoBrPo (1942 ed.)
(Fantasia of a Fallen Gentleman on a Cold Bitter Night on the Embankment.) SeCePo
Embankment before Snow. Alan Ross. POTi

Embarcation. Thomas Hardy. BrPo
Embargo, The, *sel.* Bryant.
"But quit thy meaner game, indignant Muse." CoBA
Embark as joyfully you may; be gay. For a Young Idealist: "Godspeed!" John Gilland Brunini. JKCP (1955 ed.)
Embarkation. John Gould Fletcher. Down the Mississippi, I. AmFN; HT; LiTA; NP
Embarkation, The, *abr.* Longfellow. *Fr.* Evangeline, I. PAH
Embarrassed Judge. *Unknown, tr. fr. Greek by* Louis Untermeyer. UnTE
Embarrassing Episode of Little Miss Muffet, The. Guy Wetmore Carryl. FaPON; MPB; OnMSP; RePo; StPo; TSW
Embassy of doves, An. Late. Helen Salz. GoYe
Embattled towers, the level lilied moat, The. The Fishers. Ruth Pitter. BoC
Ember Grease. Dick Gallup. ANYP
Embers of the day are red, The. Evensong. Robert Louis Stevenson. MaRV; PoVP; TreFT; TrPWD; TRV
Emblazoned bleak in austral skies. Southern Cross. Herman Melville. AnFE; CoAnAm; LiTA
Emblem of England's ancient faith. To an Oak Tree. Sir Walter Scott. *Fr.* Waverley. OBNC
Emblems, *sels.* Francis Quarles.
"Alas! fond child," I, 3. EP
"Behold thy darling, which thy lustfull care," V, 8. AnAnS-1; MEP
Delight in God Only, V, 6. MaRV
"Draw near, brave sparks, whose spirits scorn to light," I, 9. EP
Epigram: "Nay, soft and fair, good world; post not too fast," I, 11. EP
Epigram: "Paul's midnight voice prevail'd; his music's thunder," V, 10. LoBV
Epigram: "Peace, childish Cupid, peace: thy fingered eye," II, 8. EP
Epigram: "What makes thee, fool, so fat? fool, thee so bare?" I, 12. EP
"Great All in All, that art my rest, my home," IV, 3. TrPWD
"How shall my tongue expresse that hallow'd fire," V, 11. AnAnS-1; MEP
"Like to the Arctic needle, that does guide," V, 4. SeEP
My Beloved Is Mine, and I Am His; He Feedeth among the Lilies, V, 3. MeLP; MePo; OBS; TrGrPo, *abr.*
(Canticle.) FaBoEn
(Divine Rapture, A, 3 *sts.*) HBV; OBEV; TDP
("E'en like two little bank-dividing brooks," 3 *sts.*) LO
(He Is Mine, 3 *sts.*) LiTL
(Mystical Ecstasy, A, 3 *sts.*) GTSL
"My soule is like a bird; my flesh, the cage," V, 10. MeP
"Tis but a foil at best, and that's the most," II, 14. LoBV
Vanity of the World, The, II, 5. PPON
(False World, Thou Ly'st.) SeCePo; SeEP
(Wilt Thou Set Thine Eyes upon That Which Is Not?) OBS
"Why dost thou shade thy lovely face?" III, 7 SeCL; SeEP; TrPWD
(Wherefore Hidest Thou Thy Face, and Holdest Me for Thy Enemie?) MePo
"World's a floore, whose swelling heapes retaine, The," II, 7. AnAnS-1; MEP
Emblems. Allen Tate. AmPP (3d ed.); AWP; InPo
Emblems of Conduct. Hart Crane, *after* Samuel Greenberg. LiTA; LiTM (rev. ed.); NAMP; NePA
Emblems of Evening. Robert Horan. CrMA
Emblems of Love, *sels.* Lascelles Abercrombie.
Epilogue: "What shall we do for Love these days?" AnFE; HBV; OBVV
Small Fountains. CH
Hymn to Love. OBEV (new ed.); OBVV
Judith, *fr.* Pt. III.
Balkis. HBV
(Song: "Balkis was in her marble town.") MoBrPo
Vashti, *fr.* Pt. I.
Woman's Beauty. MoBrPo; PG
Emblems of Love, *sel.* Philip Ayres.
"Her name is at my tongue whene'er I speak." LO
Embraceable You. Ira Gershwin. BoLP
Embro to the Ploy. Robert Garioch. OxBS
Embryo. Mary Ashley Townsend. AA; HBV
Embryos. Marge Piercy. ThO
Emer, he is your man, now. Fand Yields Cuchulain to Emer. *Unknown.* AnIL
Emerald April, September's gold. Song of the Seasons. Blanche De Good Lofton. YeAr
Emerald cages a jungle, The. Prologue for a Bestiary. Ronald Perry. NePoEA-2
Emerald Is as Green as Grass, An. Christina Rossetti. *Fr.* Sing-Song. TiPo
(Precious Stones.) GoTP
Emeralds are singing on the grasses, The. How Many Heavens. Edith Sitwell. MoPW; MoRP
Emergency. Isabel Fiske Conant. HBMV
Emergency Maker, The. David Wagoner. NePoEA-2
Emerges daintily, the skunk. The Wood-Weasel. Marianne Moore. CMoP; OA
Emerging at midnight. Day's Affirmation. Sir Herbert Read. FaBoTw
Emerson. Amos Bronson Alcott. AA
Emerson. Mary Mapes Dodge. AA; DD; GA; PoRL
Emerson. James Russell Lowell. *Fr.* A Fable for Critics. AmPP (4th ed.); AnNE; AP; OxBA
("There comes Emerson first, whose rich words, every one.") CoBA; OuHeWo; PP
Emerson: Last Days at Concord. Horace Gregory. CMoP
Emerson was born in eighteen-three. Vital Statistics. Ettore Bella. WOW
Emigrant, The, *sel.* Alexander McLachlan.
Song: "Old England is eaten by knaves." OBCV
Emigrant, The, *sels.* Standish O'Grady.
"And first Morency, far famed water, you." CaP
Old Nick in Sorel. TDP
Winter in Lower Canada. OBCV
Emigrant from Pike, *with music.* John A. Stone. SGR
Emigrant Lassie, The. John Stuart Blackie. VA
Emigrant Song. "S. Ansky," *tr. fr. Yiddish by* Joseph Leftwich. TrJP
Emigrant's Child, The. Lyman H. Sproull. PoOW
Emigrant's Iconoclasm. Taner Baybars. NYTB
Emigrants, The; Introductory Stanzas. Thomas Pringle. BoSA
Emigration of the Fairies, The, *sel.* John Hunter-Duvar.
"First halt. They heard within a sugar patch." CaP
Emigravit. Helen Hunt Jackson. AA; AnFE; APA; CoAnAm
Emilia. Sarah N. Cleghorn. HBV; PFY
Emily Brontë. C. Day Lewis. ChMP; GTBS-P
Emily Carr. Wilfred Watson. MoCV; OBCV
Emily Geiger. *Unknown.* PAL; PoLF
Emily Hardcastle, Spinster. John Crowe Ransom. CMoP; NoP
Emily Jane. Laura E. Richards. RIS
Emily, John, James, and I. W. S. Gilbert. InMe; WhC
Emily wandered through town and folks said that she saw. Old Emily. Hyacinthe Hill. GoYe
Emily's Prayer to Diana. Chaucer. *Fr.* The Canterbury Tales: The Knight's Tale. MyFE
Emma. Goldsmith. OnYI
Emma and Eginhard. Longfellow. Tales of a Wayside Inn: The Student's Tale, Pt. III. AmPP (5th ed.); MWA-1
Emmanuel's Land. Isaac Watts. SoP
Emma's Store. Dorothy Aldis. OCS
Emmaus. Edith Lovejoy Pierce. SoP
Emmaus. Rainer Maria Rilke, *tr. fr. German by* J. B. Leishman. BoPe
Emmaus Road, The. Avis B. Christiansen. SoP
Emmonsail's Heath in Winter. John Clare. FaBoEn; PoEL-4
Emmy. Arthur Symons. HBV; OBNC; OBVV; PoVP; TreF
Emotion of Fiction, The. Roy Fuller. LiTM (1946 ed.)
Empedocles. Thomas S. Jones, Jr. AnAmPo
Empedocles on Etna. Matthew Arnold. MaVP; ViPP
Sels.
"And you, ye stars," *fr.* II. VA
Empedocles' Song, *fr.* I, ii. TOP
"Far, far from here," *fr.* I, ii. GTBS-P
(Cadmus and Harmonia.) OBVV; ViPo
(Song of Callicles, The.) FiP
"Fulness of life and power of feeling," *fr.* II. OAEP
"Is it so small a thing," *fr.* I, ii. OBEV; OBVV
Life and Thought, *fr.* II. FiP
"Noon is hot, The. When we have crossed the stream," *fr.* I, ii. EPN; PoVP
"Through the black, rushing smoke-bursts," *fr.* II. PoVP
(Apollo.) ViPo
(Callicles' Song.) ChTr; LoBV

(Song for Apollo.) FiP
(Song of Callicles [on Etna], The.) GTBS; OBEV; OBVV; ShBV-3
Emperor, The. Tu Fu, *tr. fr. Chinese by* E. Powys Mathers. AWP
Emperor Hadrian's Dying Address to His Soul. Emperor Hadrian. *See* To His Soul.
Emperor Nap he would set off, The. The March to Moscow. Robert Southey. BOHV; FOL; SiTL
Emperor of Ice-Cream, The. Wallace Stevens. AmLP; AmP; AmPP (4th ed.); AP; CABA; CaFP; CMoP; CoBMV; FaBoMo; FosPo; LiTA; MoPo; MoVE; NePA; OxBA; PoAn; PoeP; PoFS; PoIE; PoSa; TDP; ViBoPo (1958 ed.)
Emperor of the East, The, *sel.* Philip Massinger.
Song: "Why art thou slow, thou rest of trouble, Death," *fr.* V, iii. SeEP; TuPP; ViBoPo
(Death Invoked.) ACP (1952 ed.)
(Sad Song, A.) OBS; SeCL
Emperor of the Moon, The, *sel.* Aphra Behn.
Serenade: "When maidens are young, and in their spring." SeCL
Emperor of the Threefold World. Christopher Marlowe. *Fr.* Tamburlaine the Great, Pt. II, Act IV, sc. iii. TrGrPo
(Bloody Conquests of Mighty Tamburlaine, The.) ChTr
Emperors and kings! in vain you strive. The Republican Genius of Europe. Philip Freneau. AmPP (3d ed.)
Emperor's Bird's Nest, The. Longfellow. BiS; MPB
Emperor's crown and peony red. The Old Garden. Joseph von Eichendorff. LiTW
Emperor's Double, The. Robert Gittings. NYTB
Emperors of fourteen dynasties, The. The Middle Kingdom. Allen Upward. *Fr.* Scented Leaves from a Chinese Jar. NP
Empire Builder, The. John Jerome Rooney. JKCP
Empire Builders. Archibald MacLeish. Frescoes for Mr. Rockefeller's City, V. AmP; NoP; OxBA; Po; UnPo
Empire City. Dan Georgakas. ThO
Empire Is No More. Blake. *Fr.* America: A Prophecy. EnRP
"Empire to be lost or won, An!" Whitman's Ride for Oregon. Hezekiah Butterworth. PAH
Empires. Francis Burdett Money-Coutts. OBVV
Employment ("He that is weary, let him sit"). George Herbert. MaMe; OBS; OxBoCh; SeCP
Employment ("If as a flower doth spread and die"). George Herbert. AtBAP; MaMe; SCEP-1; SeCV-1
Employment. Jane Taylor. OTPC (1923 ed.); PPL
Employments of Life, The. John Gay. *See* Through All the Employments of Life.
Empress, The. Diane Wakoski. CoPo
Empress Poppaea, The. *Unknown.* PV
Emptied and pearly skulls. The Statue and the Perturbed Burghers. Denis Devlin. OnYI
Empties Coming Back. Angelo de Ponciano. BLPA
Empty birdcage hangs with open door, The. The Birdcage. Conrad Aiken. BiS
Empty carousel in a deserted park, The. The Carousel. G. C. Oden. AmNP; Kal
Empty Cradle, The. José Selgas y Carrasco, *tr. fr. Spanish by* Thomas Walsh. CAW
Empty Glen, The. R. Crombie Saunders. OxBS
Empty House. Elizabeth J. Coatsworth. FiSC
Empty House, The. Walter de la Mare. BrPo
Empty House, The. William Dean Howells. AmePo
Empty House, The. Harold Monro. BrPo
Empty House, The. Stephen Spender. NYBP; WePo
Empty Houses. Mary Colborne-Veel. BoAu
Empty Jar, The. William Stenhouse. AnNZ
Empty Life, The. Shakespeare. *See* Tomorrow and Tomorrow and Tomorrow.
Empty my heart, Lord, of daily vices. Theodore Spencer. *Fr.* Invocation. TrPWD
Empty of heart we wait amid the snow. The Mountain Lake. Richard Church. AtBAP; POTE
Empty of stars still. Fancy Fishing. James L. Weil. FiSC
Empty Purse, The. Tu Fu, *tr. fr. Chinese by* Chi Hwang Chu *and* Edna Worthley Underwood. OnPM
Empty sky, a world of heather, An. Divided. Jean Ingelow. HBV
Empty Soul, The. Walter R. Bowie. MaRV
Empty the last drop. Plunger. Carl Sandburg. BoLiVe; NeMA
Empty train, grumbling through noon, An. The El-Painter's Daughter. Milton Kessler. NYTB
Empty Vessel. "Hugh MacDiarmid." FaBoTw; OxBS
Ems Dispatch, The. Ron Padgett. ANYP
Emus. Mary Fullerton. PoAu-1
En Bateau. Paul Verlaine, *tr. fr. French by* Arthur Symons. AWP
En Garde, Messieurs. William Lindsey. AA; PFY
En ma Provence le blé est toujours vert. Ma Provence. Kenneth Koch. ANYP
En Monocle. Donald Evans. AnAmPo; NP
En Route. George Dillon. NP
En Route. E. L. Mayo. MiAP
En Route. Duncan Campbell Scott. OBCV
En route to the picnic they drive through their history. Picnic: the Liberated. M. Carl Holman. PoNe (1970 ed.)
En Voyage. Caroline Atherton Briggs Mason, *wr. at. to* Caroline Atwater Mason. HBV
(God Knows Best.) MaRV
(Whichever Way the Wind Doth Blow.) OQP; TreFS
Four Winds, The, *sel.* PCH
Enamel Girl, The. Genevieve Taggard. HBMV; MAP; MoAmPo; NP
Enamored [*or* Enamoured] Architect of Airy Rhyme. Thomas Bailey Aldrich. AA; AnAmPo; AnFE; AnNE; APA; HBV; MAP; MCCG
Enamored so of form, of calculation. Of the Mathematician. Alice Clear Matthews. GoYe
Encased in mud, and breathing valley steam. The Buffalo. Herbert Price. ACV
Enchainment. Arthur O'Shaughnessy. *See* Song: "I went to her who loveth me no more."
Enchanted Castle, The. Jeanne D'Orge. AnAmPo
Enchanted Fawn, The. *Unknown, tr. fr. Middle Irish by* Edward Gwynn. *Fr.* Dinnshenchas. OnYI
Enchanted Garden, The. Marjorie Barrows. GFA
Enchanted Heart, The. Edward Davison. HBMV
Enchanted Island, The. Luke Aylmer Conolly. OBRV
Enchanted Knight, The. Edwin Muir. MoVE
Enchanted Lyre, The. George Darley. *See* Solitary Lyre, The.
Enchanted Shirt, The. John Hay. BBV; BLPA; BOHV; GN; GoTP; MaC; OnSP; OTD; PaPo; RePo; TiPo (1952 ed.); TSW
Enchanted Spring, The. George Darley. BoNaP; NBM
Enchantment. Madison Cawein. HBV
Enchantment, The. Thomas Otway. HBV; LiTL; LO; NeHB; OBEV; SeCL; ViBoPo
Enchantment, The. Theocritus, *tr. fr. Greek by* Thomas Creech. *Fr.* Idylls. CTC
Enchantment. Tony Towle. YAP
Enchantress, touch no more that strain! Music and Memory. John Albee. AA
Encinctur'd with a twine of leaves. The Fruit Plucker [*or* Boy in the Wilderness *or* In a Moonlight Wilderness *or* Fragment, A]. Samuel Taylor Coleridge. *Fr.* The Wanderings of Cain. CH; FaBoCh; LoGBV; OBNC; OTPC (1923 ed.); SeCeV
Encircling Thee Thy holy brides. Pedro Malon de Chaide. *Fr.* The Conversion of the Magdalene. CAW
Enclosed the lacquered, coiling snake. The Zoo in the City. Sara Van Alstyne Allen. GoYe
Enclosure. John Clare. *Fr.* Remembrance. NBM
Encompass me, my lover. The Constant North. J. F. Hendry. NeBP; OxBS
Encompassed by a thousand nameless fears. As Day Begins to Wane. Helena Coleman. CaP
Encounter, The. Paul Blackburn. NeAP
Encounter. Denis Devlin. OnYI
Encounter, The. Lawrence Durrell. *Fr.* Eight Aspects of Melissa. NeBP
Encounter. Ted Hughes. ToPo
Encounter. Uys Krige, *tr. fr. Afrikaans by* Uys Krige *and* Jack Cope. PeSA
Encounter. John L'Heureux. YAP
Encounter in the Cage Country. James Dickey. TPM
Encountering God. Walt Whitman. *Fr.* Song of Myself, XLVIII. TreFT
Encouraged. Paul Laurence Dunbar. TRV
Encouragement. Paul Laurence Dunbar. YT
Encouragement for Little Children, *sel.* Jane Taylor.
God Is So Good. OTPC (1946 ed.)

Encouragement to Exile. Petronius Arbiter, *tr. fr. Latin by* Howard Mumford Jones. AWP; JAWP; WBP
Encouragements to a Lover. Sir John Suckling. *See* Why So Pale and Wan?
End, The. Walter de la Mare. OAEP (2d ed.)
End. Langston Hughes. CBV
End, The. Walter Savage Landor. *See* On His Seventy-fifth Birthday.
End, The. John Masefield. CMoP
(There, on the Darkened Deathbed.) LiTB
End, The. A. A. Milne. *See* When I Was One.
End, The. Wilfred Owen. CH; HBMV; MMA; MoVE
End, The. Wallace Rice. AA
End, The. Mark Van Doren. ViBoPo
End, The. Marguerite Wilkinson. *Fr.* Songs of an Empty House. HBMV
End has come, as come it must, The. At School-Close. Whittier. PoRL
End of a Day in the Provinces, The. Jules Laforgue, *tr. fr. French by* Margaret Crosland. SyP
End of a Fairy Tale. Jon Stallworthy. NYTB
End of a Leave, The. Roy Fuller. NeBP
End of a War, The. Sir Herbert Read. OBMV; WaP
End of an Ethnic Dream, The. Jay Wright. ThO
End of an Outing, The. Robert Mezey. TDP
End of Another Home Holiday. D. H. Lawrence. DTC; FaBoMo; MoVE
End of April, The. Robert Fuller Murray. CenHV
End of Being, The. Seneca, *tr. fr. Latin by* H. C. Leonard. MaRV; WGRP
End of Clonmacnois, The. *Unknown, tr. fr. Irish by* Frank O'Connor. KiLC
End of Day, The. W. B. Yeats. Upon a Dying Lady, IV. LiTB
End of Desire, The. Hugh McCrae. BoAV; MoAuPo
End of Dr. Faustus, The. Christopher Marlowe. *Fr.* Dr. Faustus. PoEL-2
("Ah, Faustus,/ Now hast thou but one bare hour to live.") AtBAP; BoLiVe; ChTr; FlW; MyFe; ViBoPo; YAT
(End of Faustus, The.) TrGrPo
(Faustus Faces His Doom.) TreFT
(Finale.) WHA
(Last Hour of Faustus.) ShBV-4
End of Ethnic Dream, The. Jay Wright. BF
End of everything approaches, The. Doomsday. Elinor Wylie. CrMA
End of Exploring, The. David Campbell. SeCePo
End of Faustus, The. Christopher Marlowe. *See* End of Dr. Faustus, The.
End of Fear, The. Ruth Pitter. POTE
End of February. Bañalbufar, a Brazier, Relativity, Cloud Formations & the Kindness & Relentlessness of Time, All Seen through a Window While Keeping the Feet Warm at the Same Time As. Paul Blackburn. CoPo
End of Love, The. George Meredith. *See* Modern Love: "By this he knew she wept with waking eyes."
End of Man Is Death, The. Moses ibn Ezra, *tr. fr. Hebrew by* Solomon Solis-Cohen. TrJP
End of Man Is His Beauty, The. LeRoi Jones. AmNP; BALP
End of Season. Robert Penn Warren. TwAmPo
End of Sorrow, The. Edmond Fleg, *tr. fr. French by* Humbert Wolfe. *Fr.* The Wall of Weeping. TrJP
End of Steel. Thomas Saunders. CaP
End of Summer, The. Basho, *tr. fr. Japanese by* Harold G. Henderson. RePo
End of Summer. Stanley Kunitz. AmLP; CrMA; MoAmPo (1962 ed.); PoAn
End of Summer, The. Edna St. Vincent Millay. BoNaP
End of Summer. Jean Starr Untermeyer. YT
End-of-Summer Poem. Rowena Bastin Bennett. FaPON; SiSoSe
End of the Day, The. Robert Creeley. AmPC
End of the Day, The. Duncan Campbell Scott. VA
End of the Duel, The. Rachel Annand Taylor. CAW
End of the Episode, The. Thomas Hardy. LO
End of the Flower-World (A.D. 2300). Stanley Burnshaw. AnAmPo; TrJP
End of the Parade, The. William Carlos Williams. NYBP
End of the Play, The. Thackeray. *Fr.* Dr. Birch and His Young Friends. GN; TreF; VA
End of the Season on a Stormy Day—Oban. Iain Crichton Smith. NePoEA-2
End of the Seers' Convention. Kenneth Fearing. LiTA
End of the Story, The. Terence Tiller. ChMP; NeBP
End of the Suitors, The. Homer, *tr. fr. Greek by* George Chapman. *Fr.* The Odyssey, XXII. OBS
End of the Trail. *Unknown.* SCC
End of the Way, The. Harriet Cole. BLRP
End of the Weekend, The. Anthony Hecht. LiTM (1970 ed.); NePoEA-2
End of the World, The. Jeremiah, IV: 19-26, Bible, *O.T.* PPON
End of the World, The. Gordon Bottomley. BrPo; CH; MoBrPo; MoVE
End of the World, The. Arnold Kemp. WSL
End of the World, The. Archibald MacLeish. AnEnPo; AP; CaFP; CBV; CMoP; CoBMV; HoPM; ILP; LiTM; MAP; MoAB; MoAmPo; NeMA; NePA; NP; OxBA; Po; PoIE; PoPo; PoSa; Sonn; StP; TrGrPo
End of the Year, The. Su T'ung-po, *tr. fr. Chinese by* Kenneth Rexroth. PoPl
End of Tyranny, The. Shelley. *Fr.* Prometheus Unbound. ShBV-3
End this enchantment, love, of my desires. Diella, XXXV. Richard Lynche. Sonn; TuPP
End to all I've ever had to say, An. Endpiece. *Unknown.* KiLC
End to Complacency, An. Barry Cole. HYE
End Which Comes, The. Sir Edwin Arnold. *Fr.* The Light of Asia. LoBV
End will come swiftly in an early autumn. Final Autumn. Josephine W. Johnson. NAMP; NePA
Endearments. Pierre Louys, *tr. fr. French by* Horace M. Brown. *Fr.* The Songs of Bilitis. UnTE
Endimion. John Lyly. *See* Endymion.
Endimion and Phoebe, *sels.* Michael Drayton.
Endymion's Convoy. OBSC
"In Ionia whence sprang old poets' fame." ReIE
(Phoebe on Latmus.) OBSC
Endimion Porter and Olivia. Sir William Davenant. *See* Song: "Before we shall again behold."
Ending, The. Paul Engle. NYBP
Ending. Norman Jordan. PoNe (1970 ed.)
Endless. Muriel Rukeyser. NYBP
Endless, The. *Unknown, tr. fr. Japanese. Fr.* Manyo Shu. OnPM
Endless cycle of idea and action. T. S. Eliot. *Fr.* The Rock. TRV
Endless, foolish merriment of stars, The. Nodes. Alice Corbin. NP; WGRP
Endless lanes sunken in the clay. The Trenches. Frederic Manning. MCCG
Endless line of splendor, An. Foreign Missions in Battle Array. Vachel Lindsay. MaRV; OQP
Endless mime goes on, The; new faces come. The Play. James B. Kenyon. HBV
Endless part of disintegration, The. The Wisdom of Insecurity. Richard Eberhart. NePA
Endless Self. *Unknown, at. to* Lao-tzu, *tr. fr.* Chinese by Witter Bynner. *Fr.* Tao Teh King. OnPM
Endless Song, The. Ruth McEnery Stuart. BOHV
Endless the darkly-printed tombstones rise. Edgar Allan Poe. Robert H. Barlow. FiSC
Endlessly over the water. The Sweetness of Nature. *Unknown.* KiLC
Endlessly, time-honoured irritant. Dry-Point. Philip Larkin. CMoP; NMP
End-Piece for His Book, An. Robert Herrick. *See* To His Book's End.
Ends. Robert Frost. PoIE (1970 ed.)
Endurance. Elizabeth Akers Allen. HBV; PoToHe, *abr.*
Endurance Test. Dacre Balsdon. FiBHP
Endure/ The farm? Lilacs for Remembrance. Irene Shirley Moran. PoMa
Endure what life God gives and ask no longer span. Sophocles. *Fr.* Oedipus at Colonus. DTC; OBMV
Enduring, The. John Gould Fletcher. TSW
Enduring Music, The. Harold Vinal. EtS
Endymion [a Poetic Romance], *sels.* Keats.
"And, truly I would rather be struck dumb," *fr.* I. ViBoPo
"Beneath my palm-trees, by the river side," *fr.* IV. ViBoPo

He Saw Far in the Concave Green of the Sea, *fr.* III. EtS
Here Is Wine, *fr.* II. OBRV
Hymn to Pan, *fr.* I. AtBAP; ChER; EPN; OBRV; PeER; PoEL-4
(Hymn of Pan.) ERoP-2
Life Again. SeCePo
Love and Friendship, *fr.* I. OBRV
"Muse of my native land! loftiest Muse!" *fr.* IV. EnRP
"O Moon! the oldest shades 'mong oldest trees," *fr.* III. EnRP
"O sovereign power of love! O grief! O balm!" *fr.* II. EnRP; OBNC; ViBoPo
Sleeping Youth, A, *fr.* II. SeCePo
"So she was gently glad to see him laid." BoPe
Song of the Indian Maid, *fr.* IV. OAEP; OBEV
(O Sorrow! *abr.*) CH
(Roundelay: "O Sorrow.") ATP (1935 ed.)
(Song: "O Sorrow," *shorter sel.*) LoBV
"Thing of beauty is a joy forever, A," *fr.* I. ATP; BBV (1951 ed.), *br. sel.*; BEL; BoC; BoLiVe; CoBE; CTC; EnLi-2; EnLit; EnRP; FaBV; FaFP; FiP; ILP; LiTB; LiTG; MaRV; MBW-2; MCCG; MERP; NeHB, *br. sel.*; OAEP; OBNC; OBRV; OTPC; OuHeWo; PG; PoeP; PoPl; PTK; SoP; StVeCh, *br sel.*; TOP; TreF; TrGrPo; TRV; ViBoPo; YAT
"To sorrow I bade good-morrow," *abr., fr.* IV. OBRV
Endymion. Longfellow. AA; HBV
Endymion, *sel.* John Lyly.
Song by Fairies. OAEP; ReEn; TuPP
(Fairy Song, A.) OBSC
Endymion. Edna St. Vincent Millay. *See* Oh, Sleep Forever in the Latmian Cave.
Endymion. Oscar Wilde. HBV
Endymion. Humbert Wolfe. NP
Endymion and Phoebe. Michael Drayton. *See* Endimion and Phoebe.
Endymion's Convoy. Michael Drayton. *Fr.* Endimion and Phoebe. OBSC
Enemies, The. Elizabeth Jennings. MoPW
Enemies. Agnes Lee. NP
Enemies of David, The. Dryden. *See* Achitophel.
Enemy, The. Baudelaire, *tr. fr. French by* Arthur Symons. OnPM
Enemy, The. John Waller. NeBP
Enemy forces are in wild flight, The. Defeat of the Rebels. Robert Graves. WaP
Enemy I had, whose mien, An. My Enemy. Edwin L. Sabin. OQP
Enemy of life, decayer of all kind, The. Epigram. Sir Thomas Wyatt. CBEP; FCP; SiPS
Enemy who wears, The. Fourteenth Birthday. Phyllis McGinley. NePoAm-2
Energy for a New Thang. Ernie Mkalimoto. NBP
Energy of Light, The. John Hay. NePoAm-2
Enfant perdu. Heine, *tr. fr. German by* Richard Monckton Milnes. AWP; PoFr; WoL
(Lost Child.) OuHeWo
Enfidaville. Keith Douglas. HaMV
Enflam'd with love and led by blind desires. *Unknown, tr. fr. Latin by* Charles Sackville. PeRV
Enfors we us with all our might. A Carol of St. George. *Unknown.* MeEL
Enfranchising cable, silvered by the sea. Granite and Steel. Marianne Moore. NYBP
Engagement, The. Arthur Hugh Clough. *Fr.* The Bothie of Tober-na-Vuolich, The. NBM
(Autumn in the Highlands.) GTSE
Engine. James S. Tippett. BoChLi; SoPo; SUS
Engine Driver, The. "G. S. O." BoTP
Engine Driver's Story, The. William Wilkins. BeLS
"Engine, engine, number nine." *Unknown.* RIS
Engine Failure. Timothy Corsellis. WaP
Engineer, The. A. A. Milne. RePo
Engineer pushes a button in the mountains, An. Poem. Tony Towle. ANYP
Engineers. Jimmy Garthwaite. SoPo
Engineers/ found the Great White Father dying. The Great White Father. William Witherup. QAH
Engineer's Story, The. Eugene J. Hall. PaPo
Engineer's Story, The. *Unknown.* BeLS
Engineer's Yell (University of California). *Unknown.* WhC
England. Elizabeth Barrett Browning. *Fr.* Aurora Leigh, I. VA
England. Grace Ellery Channing. AA
England. William Cowper. *Fr.* The Task, II. FiP; OBEC; TOP
(Love of England.) LoBV
England. Richard Edwin Day. AA
England. Walter de la Mare. HT
England. Kipling. *Fr.* The Return. OtMeF
England. Gerald Massey. HBV
England. George Edgar Montgomery. AA
England. Marianne Moore. CrMA; LiTA; MAP; MoAB; MoAmPo; TwAmPo
England. Cardinal Newman. ACP; CAW; GoBC; JKCP; PoVP; VA
England ("This England never did"). Shakespeare. *See* This England ("This England never did"). *Fr.* King John.
England ("This royal throne of kings"). Shakespeare. *See* This England ("This royal throne of kings"). *Fr.* King Richard II.
England. *Unknown.* CBEP; ELU; SeCL
England; an Ode ("Sea and strand"). Swinburne. ViPo
England and America, *sel.* Arthur Cleveland Coxe.
America. MC; PAH
England and America. James Kenneth Stephen. InMe
On a Rhine Steamer, *sel.* NBM
England and America in 1782. Tennyson. EPN; MC; PaA; PAH; PAL; PoFr; PoVP
England and Switzerland, 1802. Wordsworth. *See* Thought of a Briton on the Subjugation of Switzerland.
England, Arise! Edward Carpenter. PoFr
England! Awake! Awake! Awake! Blake. *Fr.* Jerusalem. NoP
("England! awake! awake! awake!) EnRP; OBRV
(Prelude.) OBNC
England, Awake Now. *Unknown.* PoFr
England, Be Glad. *Unknown.* TuPP
England, 1802 ("Great men have been among us. . ."). Wordsworth. *See* Great Men Have Been among Us.
England, 1802 ("It is not to be thought of that the flood"). Wordsworth. *See* It Is Not to Be Thought Of.
England, 1802 ("Milton! thou should'st be living at this hour"). Wordsworth. *See* London, 1802.
England, 1802 ("O Friend! I know not which way I must look"). Wordsworth. *See* Written in London, September, 1802.
England, 1802 ("When I have borne in memory what has tamed"). Wordsworth. *See* When I Have Borne in Memory.
England, I stand on thy imperial ground. At Gibraltar. George Edward Woodberry. AA; AnAmPo; GN; HBV
England in 1819. Shelley. BWP; CABA; EnLi-2 (1949 ed.); EnRP; EPN; MaPo (1969 ed.); NoP; OBRV; Sonn; StP; TrGrPo
(Sonnet: England in 1819.) CBEP; EnL; ERoP-2; FiP; OAEP; PoFS; SeCePo; SeCeV
England, look up! Thy soil is stained with blood. The Martyrdom of Father Campion. Henry Walpole. ACP; GoBC
England may mourn, as many kingdoms may. Sorrowful Verses Made on the Death of Our Most Sovereign Lady Queen Elizabeth My Gracious Mistress. Thomas Churchyard. ReIE
England, My England. W. E. Henley. EnLi-2 (1949 ed.); HBV; MoBrPo; OBEV; OBVV; OTPC (1923 ed.); PoLF; PoVP; TreF; YT
England My Mother. Sir William Watson. PoVP
England! once Europs envye now her scorne. *Unknown.* SeCSL
England Reclaimed, *sel.* Sir Osbert Sitwell.
"Sound out, proud trumpets." ViBoPo
England! The Time Is Come When Thou Shouldst Wean. Wordsworth. MBW-2; Sonn
(Sonnet.) ViBoPo
England, Unprepared for War. Mark Akenside. *Fr.* An Ode to the Country Gentlemen of England. OBEC
England, we love thee better than we know. Gibraltar. Richard Chenevix Trench. OBRV; OBVV
England, with all thy faults, I love thee still. England [*or* Love of England]. William Cowper. *Fr.* The Task, II. FiP; LoBV; OBEC; TOP
England with its baby rivers and little towns, each with its abbey or its cathedral. England. Marianne Moore. CrMA;

England (continued)
LiTA; MAP; MoAB; MoAmPo; TwAmPo
England's Darling; or, Great Britain's Joy and Hope on That Noble Prince James, Duke of Monmouth. *Unknown.* CoMu
England's Dead. Felicia Dorothea Hemans. HBV
England's Heart. Martin Farquhar Tupper. PaPo
England's Heroical Epistles, *sels.* Michael Drayton.
Henry Howard, Earl of Surrey, to the Lady Geraldine. ReEn; ReIE; TuPP
(Earl of Surrey to Geraldine, The.) OBSC
King Henry to Rosamond. OBSC
"Many there be excelling in this kind" *also in* Idea). SiCE; TuPP
England's lads are miniature men. Boy-Man. Karl Shapiro. NYBP
England's Prayer. William Blundell of Crosby. GoBC
England's Sovereigns in Verse. *Unknown.* BLPA
England's Standard. Macaulay. *Fr.* The Armada. OtMeF
England's sun was slowly setting. Curfew Must Not Ring To-night. Rosa Hartwick Thorpe. BLPA; HBV; TreF; WBLP
England's Triumph; or, The Subjects' Joy. *Unknown.* CoMu
English A. John Ciardi. ToPo
English, The. J. H. Goring. *See* Home.
"English." Dick Lourie. ThO
English Are Frosty, The. Alice Duer Miller. *Fr.* The White Cliffs. PoLF
English Ballad, on the Taking of Namur by the King of Great Britain, 1695, An. Matthew Prior. PoEL-3
"Illustrious Holland! hard would be his lot." OBRV
"Next comes the dull disciple of thy school." OBRV; PP
"Still must I hear?—shall hoarse Fitzgerald bawl." AtBAP
William Lisle Bowles. OBNC
English Bards and Scotch Reviewers, *sels.* Byron.
"Another epic! Who inflicts again." EiCP
"Behold! in various throngs the scribbling crew." EnRP; ERoP-2
English Beach Memory: Mr. Thuddock. Osbert Sitwell. NYBP
English Fog, The. John Dyer. *See* English Weather.
English Garden, The, *sel.* William Mason.
Landscape, *fr.* I. OBEC
English Gentlewoman, The, *sel.* Richard Brathwaite.
My Mistress. SeCL
English Girl, An. F. Wyville Home. VA
English Girl. *Unknown, tr. fr. Chinese by* E. Powys Mathers. OBMV
English Horn. Laurence McKinney. WhC
English in Virginia, The (April, 1607). Charles Reznikoff. SiSw
English lad, who, reading in a book, An. Keats. Lizette Woodworth Reese. AA
English Language, The, *abr.* William Wetmore Story. GN
English Liberal. Geoffrey Taylor. LiTM; SiTL
English Monsieur, The, *sel.* James Howard.
Ladies, Farewell! SeCL
English Mother, An. Robert Underwood Johnson. HBV
English Musical Instruments. Michael Drayton. *Fr.* Polyolbion, Fourth Song. MuSP
English Padlock, An. Matthew Prior. CEP; EiPP; FaBoEn; OBEC
English Poetry. Samuel Daniel. *Fr.* Musophilus; or, Defence of All Learning. OBSC
(Poetry of England, The.) CoBE
English Race, The. Defoe. *Fr.* The True-born Englishman. OBEC
English Rider, The. "Robin Hyde." AnNZ
English Schoolboy, The. John Heywood. *Fr.* The Play of the Weather. ACP
English Shell, An. A. C. Benson. VA
English sparrow, pert and free, An. A Card of Invitation to Mr. Gibbon, at Brighthelmstone. William Hayley. OBEC
English Thornton. Edgar Lee Masters. *Fr.* Spoon River Anthology. OxBA
English Weather. John Dyer. *Fr.* The Fleece, I. OBEC
(English Fog, The.) TrGrPo
English Wood, An. Robert Graves. BrPo; YT
Englishman, The. G. K. Chesterton. WhC
Englishman, The. Eliza Cook. PaPo
Englishman in Italy, The. Robert Browning. ExPo; PoEL-5; SeCePo; ViPo; ViPP
Englishmen's Victory over the Spaniards, The. *Unknown.* *See* Famous Fight at Malago, The.
Englyn. *Unknown, tr. fr. Welsh by* Gwyn Williams. *Fr.* The Black Book of Carmarthen. PrWP
Englyn on a Yellow Greyhound, An. William Barnes. OA
Englynion. *Unknown.* PrWP
Englynion to His Love. David Jones. PrWP
Engraved on the Collar of a Dog, Which I Gave to His Royal Highness. Pope. *See* Epigram: "I am His Highness' dog at Kew."
Engraved on the Collar of His Highness' Dog. Pope. *See* Epigram: "I am His Highness' dog at Kew."
Engrossed, the abandoned crickets sing. At the Grave of Cecil Rhodes. Peter Jackson. BoSA
Enigma. Joseph Auslander. NP
Enigma. Kenneth Burke. TwAmPo
Enigma, The. Richard Eberhart. NYBP; PoIE (1970 ed.)
Enigma. Catherine M. Fanshawe. *See* Riddle, A: "'Twas whispered in Heaven. . ."
Enigma. Jessie Redmond Fauset. PoNe
Enigma. Hugh McCrae. BoAV; MoAuPo; PoAu-1
Enigma, An. Poe. Sonn
Enigma. Katherine Reeves. FiSC
Enigma. R. S. Thomas. ChMP
Enigma in Altman's. Phyllis McGinley. PoMa; WhC
(Enigma for Christmas Shoppers.) PoPl
Enigma on the Letter H. Catherine Fanshawe. *See* Riddle, A: "'Twas whispered in Heaven. . ."
Enigma Variations, The. Paul Petrie. NYBP
Enigmatic moon has at long last died, The. Stevedore. Leslie M. Collins. AmNP
Enion Replies from the Caverns of the Grave. Blake. *Fr.* Vala; or, The Four Zoas. OBNC
Enitharmon Revives with Los. Blake. *Fr.* Vala; or, The Four Zoas. OBNC
(Enitharmon's Song.) ChTr
Enjoy the Good. Ecclesiastes, V: 18-20, Bible, *O.T.* TreFT
Enjoy Thy April Now. Samuel Daniel. *Fr.* A Description of Beauty. EIL; ELP; StP
Enjoy today; this hour is best. Well-packed Wisdom. Benjamin Franklin. *Fr.* Poor Richard's Almanac. StaSt
Enjoy your goods as if your death were near. The Golden Mean. Lucian, *tr. fr. Greek by* William Hay. OnPM
Enjoyable Evening in the Village near the Lake, An. Lin Ho Ching, *tr. fr. Chinese by* Max Perleberg. FIW
Enjoyment. Theognis, *tr. fr. Greek by* John Hookham Frere. AWP
Enjoyment, The. *Unknown.* ErPo
Enlightenment. Josephine Miles. FiMAP
Enlistments, The. Stephen Vincent Benét. *Fr.* John Brown's Body. ATP
Ennui. Paul Viereck. NYBP
Enoch, *sels.* Bible, Pseudepigrapha. TrJP
Seven Metal Mountains, The, LII: 6-9.
Wisdom's Plight, XLII: 1-3.
Enoch Arden. Tennyson. BeLS
Cast Your Cares on God, *sel.* MaRV; TRV
Enormous boots, thick-soled, elastic-sided. Brahms Peruses the Score of "Siegfried." Roy Fuller. MuSP
Enormous cloud-mountains that form over Point Lobos and into the sunset. Clouds of Evening. Robinson Jeffers. MAP; MoAB; MoAmPo
Enormous heads. Easy to Grow. John Giorno. ANYP
Enosis. Christopher Pearse Cranch. *See* Gnosis.
Enough. Charles G. Blanden. OQP
Enough. Bunyan. *See* Shepherd Boy's Song, The.
Enough: and leave the rest to fame. Epitaph [*or* An Epitaph upon——]. Andrew Marvell. CavP; LO; LoBV; MaMe; OBEV; SeCL
Enough for Me. Frances Ridley Havergal. SoP
Enough is as good as a feast. Rhymes to Remember. *Unknown.* StaSt
Enough Not One. Benjamin Franklin. TRV
Enough of Humble Arguments. Wordsworth. *Fr.* The Prelude. AtBAP
Enough of those who study the oblique. A Good Resolution. Roy Campbell. JKCP (1955 ed.)
Enough of Thought, Philosopher. Emily Brontë. NCEP
"Enough," she said. But the dust still rained around her. Dust. Randolph Stow. PoAu-2
Enough that you must turn your days to discs. Quatrains for a Bank Cashier. Samuel A. De Witt. PG (1955 ed.)
Enough! we're tired, my heart and I. My Heart and I. Eli-

zabeth Barrett Browning. HBV; VA
Enough! Why should a man bemoan. Per Iter Tenebricosum. Oliver St. John Gogarty. AnIL; OBMV; OxBI
Enough: you have the dream, the flame. Due North. Benjamin R. C. Low. EtS; HBMV
Enquiring fields, courtesies, The. Pastoral. Allen Tate. AP
Enquiring Soul, The. Thomas Traherne. *Fr.* Insatiableness. MaRV
("This busy, vast, inquiring soul.") VaPo
Enquiry, The. John Dyer. EiCL; OBEC
Enraging griefs, though you most divers be. October 14, 1644. Lord Herbert of Cherbury. AnAnS-2
Ensamples of Our Saviour. Robert Southwell. PoEL-2
Enslav'd, the Daughters of Albion weep. Visions of the Daughters of Albion. Blake. ERoP-1
Enslaved. Claude McKay. BALP
Entailed Farm, The. John Glassco. MoCV
Entanglement. Francis Sparshott. MoCV
Enter America at Concord's bridge. Emerson: Last Days at Concord. Horace Gregory. CMoP
Enter and learn the story of the rulers. Inscriptions at the City of Brass. *Unknown. Fr.* The Thousand and One Nights. AWP; PoFr; WaaP
Enter No (Silence Is the Blood Whose Flesh). E. E. Cummings. AP
Enter Patient. W. E. Henley. In Hospital, I. PoVP
Enter the chilly no-man's land of about. The Ghost's Leavetaking. Sylvia Plath. NePoEA-2
Enter the dream-house, brothers and sisters, leaving. Newsreel. C. Day Lewis. ILP; MoAB; MoBrPo (1950 ed.); NeMA
Enter these enchanted woods. The Woods of Westermain. George Meredith. BEL; ShBV-3; ViPo; ViPP; VP; WaKn
Entered in the Minutes. Louis MacNeice. LiTB
Entering by His Door. Richard Baxter. *See* Lord, It Belongs Not to My Care.
Entering casually the precincts of the cathedral. Alcestis in Ely. Nicholas Moore. NeBP
Entering the Body, *sel.* Stephen Berg.
Survivor, The. NaP
Enterprise. Nissim Ezekiel. ACV
Enterprise and *Boxer. Unknown.* PAH
Entertainment, The; or, Porch Verse at the Marriage of Master Henry Northly and the Most Witty Mistress Lettice Yard. Robert Herrick. HW
Entertainment to James, *sel.* Thomas Dekker.
Troynovant. ChTr; LoBV; OBSC
Enthroned above the world although he sit. Immanence. Richard Hovey. OQP; TRV; WGRP
Enthusiasm. James Clarence Mangan. IrPN
Enthusiast, The. Herman Melville. MAmP
Enthusiast, The; an Ode. William Whitehead. OBEC
Enthusiast, The; or, The Lover of Nature. Joseph Warton. CEP; EiPP; EnPE; EnRP; Po; PoEL-3
Sels.
Charms of Nature, The. OBEC; SeCePo
"Ye green-rob'd Dryads, oft' at dusky eve." FaBoEn
Entirely. Louis MacNeice. CMoP; LiTB; MoPW
Entrain airport: New York, Chicago, west. Valediction to My Contemporaries. Horace Gregory. MAP
Entrance and exit wounds are silvered clean. Recalling War. Robert Graves. CMoP; CoBMV; ForPo; LiTM (rev. ed.); MMA; WaP
Entrance into Heaven. Sara Henderson Hay. ChIP
Entrance to a Mirror. Jon Anderson. YAP
Entrance to Hell, The. Vergil, *tr. fr. Latin into Middle English by* Gawin Douglas. *Fr.* The Aeneid, VI. GoTS
Entranced, I saw a vision in the cloud. An Ode for the Fourth of July, 1876. James Russell Lowell. CoBA
Entrapped inside a submarine. H. C. Canfield. *Fr.* Elegy on the Loss of U.S. Submarine S4. FiBHP
Entreat Me Not to Leave Thee. Ruth, Bible, *O.T. See* Intreat Me Not to Leave Thee.
Entropy. Theodore Spencer. ImOP
Entry. Josephine Miles. AnAmPo
Enviable Isles, The. Herman Melville. AA; AmLP; AnAmPo; FaBoBe; MAmP
Envied by us all. Maples Leaves. Shiko. OnPM; SoPo
Envious Critick, The. William Wycherley. PeRV; PV
Envious neighbour is easy to find, An. The Description of an Envious and Naughty Neighbour. Thomas Tusser. SiCE
Envious wits, what hath been mine offence. Astrophel and Stella, CIV. Sir Philip Sidney. FCP; SiPS; Sonn; TuPP
Environs. Larry Eigner. NeAP
Envoi: "All that remains for me." Arthur Symons. UnTE
Envoi: "Earth puts her colours by." P. H. B. Lyon. BoTP
Envoi: "Fly, white butterflies, out to sea." Swinburne. *See* White Butterflies.
Envoi: "Go, dumb-born book." Ezra Pound. *See* Envoi (1919).
Envoi: "God, thou great symmetry." Anna Wickham. MoBrPo; NeMA; TrGrPo (1942 ed.)
Envoi: "I strove with none, for none was worth my strife." Walter Savage Landor. *See* On His Seventy-fifth Birthday.
Envoi: "I warmed both hands before the fire of Life." D. B. Wyndham Lewis. FiBHP
Envoi: "O seek me not within a tomb." John G. Neihardt. HBV; NP; WGRP
(Envoy.) OQP
(L'Envoi: "Seek not for me . . .") MaRV
Envoi: "Take of me what is not my own." Kathleen Raine. NeBP
Envoi (1919). Ezra Pound. *Fr.* Hugh Selwyn Mauberley. APA; CaFP; CLwM; CMoP; CoAnAm; CTC; GTBS-W; MAP; MemP; MoAB; MoAmPo; NePA; OxBA; PoIE; SeCeV (1967 ed.); UnPo (3d ed.)
Envoy: "Do you remember." W. E. Henley. BrPo
Envoy, The: "Go, litel book, go litel myn tragedie." Chaucer. *Fr.* Troilus and Criseyde, V. FiP
("Go, litel book. . .") MyFE; ViBoPo
Envoy: "Go, little book, and wish to all." Robert Louis Stevenson. *See* Go, Little Book.
Envoy: "Go, songs, for ended is our brief, sweet play." Francis Thompson. CoBE; FaBV; HBV; MoBrPo; PoVP
Envoy: "Have little care that life is brief." Bliss Carman. HBV; VA
(On the Tomb of Bliss Carman.) MaRV
Envoy: "If homely virtues draw from me a tune." James Weldon Johnson. TrPWD
Envoy: "Legend of Felix is ended, the toiling of Felix is done, The." Henry van Dyke. *Fr.* The Toiling of Felix. BLPA
Envoy: "O seek me not within a tomb." John G. Neihardt. *See* Envoi: "O seek me not . . ."
Envoy: "Sweet World, if you will hear me now." Sarah Morgan Bryan Piatt. AA
Envoy: "There's a whisper down the field where the year has shot her yield." Kipling. PoVP
Envoy: "They are not long, the weeping and the laughter." Ernest Dowson. *See* Vitae Summa Brevis Spem Nos Vetat Incohare Longam.
Envoy: "When Earth's last picture is painted and the tubes are twisted and dried." Kipling. *See* L'Envoi: "When earth's last picture. . ."
Envoy: "When you and I have played the little hour." Sir Gilbert Parker. *See* Reunited.
Envoy: "Whose furthest footstep never strayed." Richard Hovey. *Fr.* More Songs from Vagabondia. AA; HBV
Envoy to an American Lady, An. Richard Monckton Milnes. *See* Our Mother Tongue.
Envy. Edgar Daniel Kramer. PoMa
Envy. Charles *and* Mary Lamb. OTPC (1923 ed.)
Envy. Yevgeny Yevtushenko, *tr. fr. Russian by* George Reavey. FIW
Envy go weep; my Muse and I. To Envy. Sir John Davies. *Fr.* Hymns of Astraea. SiCE
Envy Goes Groping. R. D. Fitzgerald. MoAuPo
Envy of Poor Lovers, The. Austin Clarke. NMP
Envy the mad killer who lies in the ditch and grieves. Crime. Robert Penn Warren. AmP
Envy, why carpest thou my time is spent so ill. Ovid, *tr. by* Christopher Marlowe. *Fr.* Elegies. CLwM; ReIE
Envy, why twit'st thou me my time's spent ill. Ovid, *tr. by* Ben Jonson. *Fr.* Elegies. ReIE
Envying a Little Bird. Sister Gregoria Francisca, *tr. fr. Spanish by* Thomas Walsh. CAW
Eolian Harp, The. Samuel Taylor Coleridge. EnRP; ERoP-1; MBW-2; MERP
(Aeolian Harp, The.) NoP
Eos. Richard Henry Horne. *Fr.* Orion. VA
Eph Kate was a cow-punchin' boy. Salty Dogs. *Unknown.* CoSo
Ephemera. W. B. Yeats. BrPo

Ephesians, *sel.* Bible, *N.T.*
"Wherefore I ask that ye faint not at my tribulations for you," III: 13-21. BoC
Epic. Patrick Kavanagh. OxBI
Epic, The (Introduction to "Morte d'Arthur"). Tennyson. PoVP; ViPP
Epic of Gilgamesh. *Unknown.* *See* Gilgamesh.
Epicede. Donald Evans. NP
Epicedium. J. Corson Miller. DD; HBMV; PAH
Epicedium. Horace L. Traubel. AA
Epicoene; or, The Silent Woman, *sel.* Ben Jonson.
Simplex Munditiis, *fr.* I, i, *tr. fr. the Latin of* Jean Bonnefons. AWP; CoBE; EnLi-1; EnLit; GoBC; HBV; HoPM; InPo; JAWP; OBEV; TDP; TOP; WBP
(Clerimont's Song.) BoLiVe; LoBV; PoIE; SeCP; SeCV-1; SiCE; TrGrPo; VaPo
(Song: "Still to be neat, still to be dressed [*or* drest].") AnAnS-2; AnEnPo; CBV; EnRePo; LiTL; NeHB; OBS; SCEP-2; ViBoPo; YAT
(Still to Be Neat [Still to Be Dressed].) ALV; CABA; CBEP; ElL; EnL; GTBS-W; MaPo; NoP; OAEP; OuHeWo; PAn; PoE; PoFS; PoSa; SeCePo; StP; TreFT; TuPP; WHA
("Still to be neat, still to be dressed [*or* drest].") EG; ILP; LO; ReEn
(Such Sweet Neglect.) MeWo
Epicure, The ("Fill the bowl with rosy wine"). Abraham Cowley, *after the Greek of* Anacreon. CaVP; HBV; OBS; SCEP-2; SeCP
(Today Is Ours.) TrGrPo
Epicure, The ("Underneath this myrtle shade"). Abraham Cowley, *after the Greek of* Anacreon. AWP; OBEV (1945 ed.); PG; SiTL
(Another.) SeCP
("Underneath this myrtle shade.") EG
Epicure, dining at Crewe, An. Limerick. *Unknown.* CenHV; GoTP; LiBL; LiTG; LiTM (rev. ed.); SiTL; WhC
Epicure, The, Sung by One in the Habit of a Town Gallant. Thomas Jordan. *See* Careless Gallant, The.
Epicurean, The. Sir Franics Hastings Doyle. EPN; OBVV
Epicurean. William James Linton. VA
Epicurean Ode, An. John Hall. MeLP; MePo; SeEP; SiSw
("Since that this thing we call the world.") EG
Epicurean's Epitaph, An. Aubrey Thomas De Vere. VA
Epidermal Macabre. Theodore Roethke. PoeP
Epigram: "After such years of dissension and strife." Thomas Hood. HBV
(Dust to Dust.) GoTP; ShM
(Natural Tears.) FiBHP
Epigram V: "Against the guide of Truth." *Unknown, tr. fr. Hebrew. Fr.* Duel with Verses over a Great Man. TrJP
Epigram: "Alas, how soon the hours are over." Walter Savage Landor. *See* Plays.
Epigram: "Amid all triads let it be confest." Richard Garnett. OBVV
Epigram: Answer to the Parson, An. Blake. *See* Answer to the Parson, An.
Epigram: "And now you're ready who while she was here." J. V. Cunningham. ErPo
Epigram: "And what is love? Misunderstanding, pain." J. V. Cunningham. NePoAm
Epigram: "Arms and the man I sing, and sing for joy." J. V. Cunningham. NePoAm
Epigram: "Arctic raven tracks the caribou, The." Raymond Wilson. PV
Epigram: "As in smooth oil the razor best is whet." *Unknown.* HBV
Epigram: "As Thomas was cudgelled one day by his wife." Swift. *See* Abroad and at Home.
Epigram: "Avaro sick is seen to shiver." John Swanwick Drennan. IrPN
Epigram: "Beauty, a silver dew that falls in May." *Unknown. See* Beauty, a Silver Dew.
Epigram: "Because I am idolatrous and have besought." Ernest Dowson. ACP
Epigram: "Bring hemlock, black as Cretan cheese." Robert Hillyer. WhC
Epigram: Burnt Ship, A. John Donne. DiPo
Epigram: Character, A. Blake. SiTL
(Character, A.) OxBoLi
("Her whole life is an epigram, smart, smooth, and neatly penned.") ERoP-1; PeER; PV
Epigram: "Children romp within the graveyard's pale, The." Sir William Watson.
(Four Epigrams.) MoBrPo (1942 ed.)
Epigram: "'Come, come,! said Tom's father, 'at your time of life.' " Thomas Moore. *See* On Taking a Wife.
Epigram: "Cries Sue to Will, in matrimonial strife." *Unknown.* ALV
Epigram: "Cries Sylvia to a reverend Dean." Robert Dodsley. ALV
Epigram: "Damis, and author cold and weak." *Unknown.* HBV
Epigram: "Dear, my familiar hand in love's own gesture." J. V. Cunningham. PV
Epigram: Diversity of Doctors. *Unknown.* ALV
Epigram: "'Do you not wish to renounce the Devil?' " Armand Lanusse, *tr. fr. French by* Langston Hughes. PoNe; TTY
Epigram: "Eagle! why soarest thou above that tomb?" *Unknown. See* Spirit of Plato.
Epigram: "Elders at their services begin, The." J. V. Cunningham. *See* Elders at Their Services Begin, The.
Epigram: "Enemy of life, decayer of all kind, The." Sir Thomas Wyatt. SiPS
("Enemy of life, decayer of all kind, The.") CBEP; FCP
Epigram: Engraved on the Collar of a Dog, Which I Gave to His Royal Highness. Pope. *See* Epigram: "I am His Highness' dog at Kew."
Epigram: "Face that should content me wonders well, A." Sir Thomas Wyatt. *See* Description of Such a One as He Would Love.
Epigram: "Far happier are the dead, methinks, than they." *Unknown, tr. fr. Greek by* William Cowper. EnLi-1
Epigram: Fatum Supremum. *Unknown.* OBS
(Fatum Supremum.) SeCL
Epigram: "Fool and knave with different views, A." Samuel Bishop. *See* Touchstone, The.
Epigram: "For love is like a plant that clings." John Swanwick Drennan. IrPN
Epigram III: "Forgive us, son of Amram, be not wroth." *Unknown, tr. fr. Hebrew. Fr* Duel with Verses over a Great Man. TrJP
Epigram: "Frank carves very ill, yet will palm all the meats." Matthew Prior. CEP
Epigram: "Friend, on this scaffold Thomas More lies dead." J. V. Cunningham. NePoAm
Epigram: "Fruit of all the service that I serve, The." Sir Thomas Wyatt. SiPS
("Fruit of all the service that I serve, The.") FCP
Epigram, An: "Gil's history appears to me." Matthew Green. *See* Epigram, An, on the Reverend Mr. Laurence Echard's . .
Epigram: "God bless the King—I mean the faith's defender!" John Byrom. *See* Jacobite Toast, A.
Epigram: "Golden casket I designed, A." John Swanwick Drennan. IrPN
Epigram: "Good Fortune, when I hailed her recently." J. V. Cunningham. PV
Epigram: "Grateful heart for all things blesses, The." Walter Savage Landor. ALV
Epigram: "He is not drunk who, from the floor." Eugene Field. ALV
Epigram: "He who in his pocket hath no money." *Unknown.* HBV
Epigram: "Here lie I, Martin Elginbrodde." *Unknown. See* Epitaph: "Here lie I . . ." "
Epigram: "Here lies a great and mighty King." Earl of Rochester. *See* Epitaph on Charles II.
Epigram: "Here lies my wife. Eternal peace." J. V. Cunningham. NePoAm; PIA
Epigram: "Here lies my wife: here let her lie!" Dryden. *See* Epitaph Intended for His Wife.
Epigram: "Here lies New Critic who would fox us." J. V. Cunningham. MoAmPo (1962 ed.); PIA
Epigram: "How many drag the marriage chain." Royall Tyler. StP
Epigram: "How odd/ of God." W. N. Ever. *See* Chosen People, The.
Epigram: "I and His Highness' dog at Kew." Pope. ALV; EiCL; HBV; ShBV-4; TreFS
(Dogs.) GoTP
(Engraved on the Collar of a Dog, Which I Gave to His Royal

Highness.) CABA; CBEP; ChTr; LiTB; LiTG; OxBoLi; PoG; SeCeV; SiTL; StP
(Engraved on the Collar of His Highness' Dog.) WhC
(Epigram: Engraved on the Collar of a Dog, Which I Gave to His Royal Highness.) DiPo; TOP
("I am his Highness' dog at Kew.") InP
(Inscribed on the Collar of a Dog.) PCH
(On the Collar of a Dog [Presented by Mr. Pope to the Prince of Wales].) ExPo; OnPM
Epigram: "I had gone broke, and got set to come back." J. V. Cunningham. MoAmPo (1962 ed.); NePoAm; PV
Epigram: "'I hardly ever open my lips,' one cries." Richard Garnett. HBV; OtMeF
(Silence and Speech.) ALV
Epigram: "I have lost my mistress, horse, and wife." *Unknown.* ALV; EiCL
Epigram: "I held her hand, the pledge of bliss." Walter Savage Landor. *See* Test, The.
Epigram: "I loved thee beautiful and kind. Robert, Earl Nugent. ALV
(I Loved Thee.) FiBHP
Epigram: "I married in my youth a wife." J. V. Cunningham. MoAmPo (1962 ed.); PIA; PV
Epigram: "I owe, says Metius, much to Colon's care." Leonard Welsted. ALV
Epigram: "'I would,' says Fox, 'a tax devise.'" Sheridan. HBV
Epigram: "If a man who turnips cries." Samuel Johnson. *See* If the Man Who Turnips Cries.
Epigram: "If men be judged wise by their beards and their girth." Joseph Solomon del Medigo, *tr. fr. Hebrew.* TrJP
Epigram: "In Köln, a town of monks and bones." Samuel Taylor Coleridge. *See* Cologne.
Epigram: "Isn't it." Alfred Kreymborg. BoLP
Epigram: "Joe hates a sycophant. It shows." P. Dodd. ALV
(On Joe.) SiTL
Epigram: "Joy is the blossom, sorrow is the fruit." Walter Savage Landor. HBV
Epigram: "Justice walking o'er the frozen Thames, A." *Unknown.* ALV
Epigram: "King to Oxford sent a troop of horse, The." William Browne. ALV
Epigram: "Life is a jest, and all things show it." John Gay. *See* My Own Epitaph.
Epigram: "Lord Pam in the church (cou'd you think it) kneel'd down." Jonathan Swift. NCEP
Epigram: "Loud brayed an ass. Quoth Kate, 'My dear.'" *Unknown.* ALV
(Repartee.) TreFT
Epigram: "Love, like a bird, hath perch'd upon a spray." Sir William Watson. ALV
(Four Epigrams.) MoBrPo (1942 ed.)
(Love.) TrGrPo
Epigram: "Love signed the contract blithe and leal." John Swanwick Drennan. IrPN
Epigram: "Lux my fair falcon, and your fellows all." Sir Thomas Wyatt. *See* Of Such as Had Forsaken Him.
Epigram: "Man who goes for Christian resignation, The." J. V. Cunningham. NePoAm; PV
Epigram: "Metaphysic Sphynx that preys on us, The." John Swanwick Drennan. IrPN
Epigram: "Midas, they say, possessed the art of old." John Wolcot. ELU
Epigram: "Momentous to himself as I to me." Sir William Watson. AnEnPo
Epigram: "My name is Ebenezer Brown." J. V. Cunningham. PIA
Epigram: "Nay, soft and fair, good world; post not too fast." Francis Quarles. Emblems, I, 11. EP
Epigram: "No more of your titled acquaintances boast." Burns. ALV
Epigram: "No truer word, save God's, was ever spoken." Walter Savage Landor. HBV
(No Truer Word.) TreF
Epigram: "No wonder that Oxford and Cambridge profound." *Unknown.* WaPE
Epigram: "Nobles and heralds, by your leave." Matthew Prior. *See* Epitaph on Himself.
Epigram: "Of the divine and human thought." John Swanwick Drennan. IrPN
Epigram: "On parent knees, a naked new-born child." Sir William Jones. *See* Baby, The.
Epigram: On Sir Francis Drake. *Unknown.* OBS
(On Sir Francis Drake.) CBEP
Epigram: "Paul's midnight voice prevail'd; his music's thunder." Francis Quarles. Emblems, V, 10. LoBV
Epigram: "Peace, childish Cupid, peace: thy fingered eye." Francis Quarles. Emblems, II, 8. EP
Epigram: "Philosopher, whom dost thou most affect." Richard Garnett. HBV
Epigram: "Poet gathers fruit from every tree, The." Sir William Watson. *See* Poet, The.
Epigram: "'Prepare to meet the King of Terrors,' cried." Ebenezer Elliott. PeER
Epigram: "Quoth Satan to Arnold." *Unknown.* PAH
Epigram: "Readers and the hearers like my books, The." Sir John Harington, *after* Martial. *See* Critics and Cooks.
Epigram: Respice Finem. Francis Quarles. OBEV
(Human Touch, The: "My soul, sit thou.") PoToHe
(Respice Finem.) MaRV; TreFT
Epigram: "Rudely forced to drink tea, Massachusetts, in anger." *Unknown.* PAH
Epigram: "Should D——s print, how once you robb'd your brother. Pope. CEP
Epigram: "Sighs are my food, drink are my tears." Sir Thomas Wyatt. *See* Wyatt Being in Prison, to Bryan.
Epigram: "Sir, I admit your general rule." Pope, *also at. to* Matthew Prior *and to* Samuel Taylor Coleridge. FiBHP; HBV; LiTB; LiTG; SiTL; TreF
(Fool and the Poet, The.) BOHV
(Reply, A [*or* The].) GoTP
(Sir, I Admit Your General Rule.) ML
Epigram: Sir Joshua Reynolds. Blake. *See* Sir Joshua Reynolds.
Epigram: "Statue, The—Buonarroti said—doth wait." Sir William Watson. MoBrPo (1942 ed.)
Epigram: "They say your lady friends have no long life." Martial, *tr. fr. Latin by* G. A. Pott *and* F. A. Wright. ALV
Epigram: "Things that make the happier life, are these, The." Martial. *See* Means to Attain Happy Life.
Epigram: "This house, where once a lawyer dwelt." William Erskine. HBV
Epigram: "This is my curse, Pompous, I pray." J. V. Cunningham. PV
Epigram: "Thou art in danger, Cincius, on my word." Marcus Argentarius, *tr. fr. Latin by* Richard Garnett. ALV
Epigram II: "Thou fool profane, be silent!" *Unknown, tr. fr. Hebrew. Fr.* Duel with Verses over a Great Man. TrJP
Epigram I: "Thou Guide to doubt, be silent evermore." *Unknown, tr. fr. Hebrew. Fr.* Duel with Verses over a Great Man. TrJP
Epigram: "Thou swears't thou'lt drink no more." *Unknown.* *See* To Julius.
Epigram: "'Tis highly rational, we can't dispute." Richard Garnett. HBV
Epigram: "'Tis human fortune's happiest height, to be." Sir William Watson. TreFT
Epigram: To English Connoisseurs. Blake. *See* To English Connoisseurs.
Epigram: To Flaxman. Blake. *See* To Flaxman.
Epigram: To Hunt. Blake. *See* To Hunt.
Epigram: "To John I owed great obligation." Matthew Prior. ALV; CEP; FaFP; LiTG; SiTL
(More than Quit.) OnPM
(Quits.) AWP
Epigram: "Tonight, grave Sir, both my poor house and I." Ben Jonson. *See* Inviting a Friend to Supper.
Epigram: "Treason doth never prosper." Sir John Harington. *See* Of Treason.
Epigram: "Were I a king, I could command content." Edward de Vere, Earl of Oxford. *See* Were I a King.
Epigram: "What is an epigram? a dwarfish whole." Samuel Taylor Coleridge. GoTP; HBV; INP
(What Is an Epigram?) PV
Epigram: "What makes thee, fool, so fat? fool, thee so bare?" Francis Quarles. Emblems, I, 12. EP
Epigram: "'What? rise again with all one's bones.'" Samuel Taylor Coleridge. *See* Giles's Hope.
Epigram IV: "What thought ye to burn, when ye kindled the pyre." *Unknown, tr. fr. Hebrew. Fr.* Duel with Verses over a Great Man. TrJP
Epigram: "When doctrines meet with general approbation." David Garrick. HBV

Epigram: "When Eve upon the first of men." Thomas Hood, *wr. at. to* Thomas Moore. *See* Reflection, A.
Epigram: "When I am dead, I hope it may be said." Hilaire Belloc. *See* On His Books.
Epigram: "When other ladies to the shades go down." Pope. PoEL-3
Epigram: "When Pontius wished an edict might be passed." Matthew Prior. ALV
Epigram: "When the devil was sick, the devil a monk would be." *Unknown.* ALV
Epigram: "When whelmed are altar, priest and creed." Sir William Watson. WGRP
Epigram: "While life was mine, the little hour." Thomas Moore, *after the Greek.* ALV
Epigram: "Whilst [*or* While] Adam slept, Eve from his side arose." *Unknown.* ALV; HBV
Epigram: "Who hath heard of such cruelty before?" Sir Thomas Wyatt. CBEP; FCP; SiPS
Epigram: "Who killed Kildare? Who dared Kildare to kill?" Swift. HBV
Epigram: "With death doomed to grapple." Byron. HBV
Epigram: "With every wife he can, and you know why." J. V. Cunningham. PIA
Epigram: "With nought to hide or to betray." John Swanwick Drennan. IrPN
Epigram: "With women and apples both Paris and Adam." Thomas Moore. ALV
Epigram: "World of fools has such a store, The." *Unknown, tr. fr. French.* ALV
Epigram: "Yes, every poet is a fool." Matthew Prior. CEP
(Another [Epigram].) EiCL
Epigram: "You ask me how Contempt who claims to sleep." J. V. Cunningham. ELU; ErPo; NePoAm; StP
(Two Epigrams, II.) SiTL
Epigram: "You beat your pate, and fancy wit will come." Pope. *See* To a Blockhead.
Epigram: "You wonder why Drab sells her love for gold?" J. V. Cunningham. NePoAm
Epigram of Martial, Imitated. Sir Charles Hansbury Williams. *See* Come, Chloe, and Give Me Sweet Kisses.
Epigram on a Lawyer's Desiring One of the Tribe to Look with Respect to a Gibbet. Robert Fergusson. OxBS
Epigram on an Academic Visit to the Continent. Richard Porson. EiCL; OxBoLi; WhC
(Academic Visit to the Continent, An.) OnPM
(On a German Tour, *sl. diff. vers.*) FiBHP
(On an Imaginary Journey to the Continent.) PV
Epigram on Handel and Bononcini. John Byrom. CBEP; MuSP; OBEC; UnS
(Epigram on the Feuds between Handel and Bononcini.) CEP
Epigram on Marcus the Gnostic. St. Pothinus. CAW
Epigram on Milton. Dryden. *See* Lines Printed under the Engraved Portrait of Milton.
Epigram on Miltonicks. Samuel Wesley. OBEC
(Mr. J. M. S——e Catechized on His One Epistle to Mr. Pope.) EiCL
Epigram on Plutarch. Agathias Scholasticus. *See* Plutarch.
Epigram on the Death of Edward Forbes. Sydney Dobell. VA
Epigram on the Feuds between Handel and Bononcini. John Byrom. *See* Epigram on Handel and Bononcini.
Epigram on the Poor of Boston Being Employed in Paving the Streets, 1774. *Unknown.* PAH
Epigram, An, on the Reverend Mr. Laurence Echard's, and Bishop Gilbert Burnet's Histories. Matthew Green. PoE
(Epigram, An: "Gil's history appears to me.") StP
Epigram on the Toasts of the Kit-Kat Club, Anno 1716. Pope. CEP
Epigram on This Book of Epigrams, An. John Heywood. ReIE
Epigram on Tonson. Dryden. MBW-1
(Jacob Tonson, His Publisher.) ChTr
Epigram on Two Ladies. Sophia Burrell. ErPo
Epigram to King Charles for an Hundred Pounds He Sent Me in My Sickness, An. Ben Jonson. OAEP
Epigram, to the Household, An, 1630. Ben Jonson. Sonn
Epigrams (I-VIII). John Swanwick Drennan. IrPN
Epigrams. Francis Daniel Pastorius. SCAP
Epigrams. Sir Thomas Wyatt. SiPS
Epigrams on Castlereagh. Byron. ExPo
"So Castlereagh has cut his throat!—the worst," I.
"So He has cut his throat at last! He! Who?", II.
Epigrams on Priapus. *Unknown.* ErPo
Epigraph: "I give you the end of a golden string." Blake. *See* To the Christians.
Epigraph from *The Judge Is Fury.* J. V. Cunningham. QFR
Epilog: "Like the ears of the wheat." Heine. *Fr.* The North Sea. AWP; JAWP; WBP
Epilogue: "All is best, though we oft doubt." Milton. *See* All Is Best.
Epilogue: "All the people in my poems walk into the dark." Jon Silkin. PoDB
Epilogue: "At my casement I sat by night, while the wind remote in dark valleys." Aubrey Thomas De Vere. IrPN
Epilogue: "At the midnight in the silence of the sleep-time." Robert Browning. *Fr.* Asolando. BEL; BoLiVe; CoBE; EnL; EnLi-2; EnLit; EPN; FaBoEn; FaBV; FiP; GTSL; HBV; HBVY; InP; MaRV; MBW-2; OAEP; OBNC; OBVV; OHFP; OQP; OuHeWo; PoIE; PoVP; TOP; TreF; TrGrPo; VA; ViBoPo; ViPo; ViPP
Epilogue: Author to Reader. Henri Coulette. *Fr.* The War of the Secret Agents. NePoEA-2
Epilogue: "Away, for we are ready to a man!" James Elroy Flecker. *Fr.* The Golden Journey to Samarkand (*also in* Hassan). ShBV-3
Epilogue: "Carol, every violet has." Alfred Noyes. *Fr.* The Flower of Old Japan. MoBrPo
Epilogue: Credo. Arthur Symons. PoVP
Epilogue: "Cut is the branch that might have grown full straight." Christopher Marlowe. *Fr.* Dr. Faustus. ViBoPo
Epilogue: "Giver of bliss and pain, of song and prayer," *sel.* William Alexander Percy. TrPWD
Epilogue: "Have I spoken too much or not enough of love?" Richard Aldington. BrPo
Epilogue: "Heaven, which man's generations draws." Francis Thompson. *Fr.* A Judgment in Heaven. MoAB; MoBrPo
Epilogue: "I am sure this Jesus will not do." Blake. *Fr.* The Everlasting Gospel. OBRV
Epilogue: "I, too, sing America." Langston Hughes. *See* I, Too.
Epilogue: "If Luther's day expand to Darwin's year." Herman Melville. *Fr.* Clarel. AmePo; AnAmPo; AP; AWP; ImOP; MAmP
Epilogue: "Like the stalks of wheat in the fields." Heine, *tr. fr. German by* Emma Lazarus. *Fr.* The North Sea. TrJP
Epilogue: "Now my charms are all o'erthrown." Shakespeare. *Fr.* The Tempest, V, i. CTC
Epilogue: "Now the hungry lion roars." Shakespeare. *See* Now the Hungry Lion Roars.
Epilogue: "O chansons foregoing." Ezra Pound. OxBA
Epilogue: "Oh, Love—no, Love! All the noise below, Love." Robert Browning. *Fr.* Ferishtah's Fancies. ViPP
Epilogue: "'O where are you going?' said reader to rider." W. H. Auden. *See* O Where Are You Going.
Epilogue: "On the first of the Feast of Feasts." Robert Browning. ViPo
Epilogue: "Poets, like disputants, when reasons fail." Dryden. *Fr.* All for Love. DiPo
Epilogue: "Pretty task, A; and so I told the Fool." Dryden. *Fr.* Aureng-Zebe. SeEP
Epilogue: "Terence, this is stupid stuff." A. E. Housman. *See* Terence, This Is Stupid Stuff.
Epilogue: "There's something in a stupid ass." Byron. Par
Epilogue: "They who have best succeeded on the stage." Dryden. *Fr.* The Conquest of Granada, Pt. II. CEP; EiCL; EiPP; FiP; MBW-1; SeCV-2; SeEP
Epilogue: "Thus far, with rough and all-unable pen." Shakespeare. *Fr.* King Henry V. CTC
Epilogue: "Time is a thing." Stephen Spender. MoBrPo
Epilogue: "Touch him ne'er so lightly, into song he broke." Robert Browning. *Fr.* Dramatic Idyls. MBW-2; PoVP
Epilogue: "Truly, My Satan, thou art but a Dunce." Blake. *See* To the Accuser Who Is the God of This World.
Epilogue: "Virtue may unlock hell." Francis Thompson. *Fr.* A Judgment in Heaven. PoLi
Epilogue: "Well, when all is said and done." "Æ." MoBrPo
Epilogue: "What shall we do for Love these days?" Lascelles Abercrombie. *Fr.* Emblems of Love. AnFE; HBV; MoBrPo; OBVV
Small Fountains, *sel.* CH

Epilogue: "When that I was and a little tiny boy." Shakespeare. *See* When That I Was and a Little Tiny Boy.
Epilogue: "With heart at rest I climbed the citadel's steep height." Baudelaire, *tr. fr. French by* Arthur Symons. AWP
(Epilogue to Prose Poems.) OnPM
Epilogue at Wallack's, An. John Elton Wayland. AA
Epilogue for a Masque of Purcell. Adrienne Cecile Rich. NePoEA; NYBP
Epilogue of the Wandering Jew, The. Colin Newbury. AnNZ
Epilogue Spoken at Oxford by Mrs. Marshall. Dryden. ATP; CEP
(Epilogue Spoken by Mrs. Boutell.) SeCV-2
(Epilogue to the University of Oxford, 1674.) MBW-1
(To the University of Oxford, 1674.) FaBoEn
Epilogue Spoken to the King at the Opening the Play-House at Oxford, The. Dryden. EiCL
Epilogue to a Book of Verse. Arthur Guiterman. InMe
Epilogue to a Human Drama. Stephen Spender. EnLit; PIA
Epilogue to "A Midsummer Night's Dream." Shakespeare. *See* Now the Hungry Lion Roars.
Epilogue to Alun Mabon. John Ceiriog Hughes, *tr. fr. Welsh by* Sir Idris Bell. PrWP
Epilogue to Hassan. James Elroy Flecker. *See* Epilogue: "Away, for we are ready to a man!"
Epilogue to "Mithridates, King of Pontus." Dryden. OAEP
Epilogue to Prose Poems. Baudelaire. *See* Epilogue: "With heart at rest I climbed the citadel's steep height."
Epilogue to Rhymes and Rhythms. W. E. Henley. ViBoPo
Epilogue to the Breakfast Table Series. Oliver Wendell Holmes. *Fr.* The Poet at the Breakfast Table. AA
Epilogue to the Outrider. Dorothy Livesay. CaP
Epilogue to the Satires. Pope.
(One Thousand Seven Hundred and Thirty-eight, Dialogues I *and* II.) CEP; EiCL, Dialogue 1
Sels.
"Not twice a twelvemonth you appear in print," I. NoP
Satire: "Ask you what provocation I have had?" *fr.* II. OBEC
(In Defence of Satire.) CoBE
Epilogue to the University of Oxford, 1674. Dryden. *See* Epilogue Spoken at Oxford by Mrs. Marshall.
Epilogue to "Tyrannic Love." Dryden. BWP; MaPo (1969 ed.); MBW-1; OAEP; SeCV-2; ViBoPo
Epilogus: "Lo, ladies, here (if you can use it well)." George Whetstone. TuPP
Epilogus: "Thus have I waded through a worthless task." Henry Parrot. SiCE
Epiphany. Eileen Duggan. ISi
Epiphany. Reginald Heber. *See* Brightest and Best of the Sons of the Morning.
Epiphany. Eileen Shanahan. NeIP
Epiphany, The. George Strong. GoYe
Epipsychidion. Shelley. EPN; EnRP; ERoP-2
Sels.
Longest Journey, The. OtMeF
"See where she stands! a mortal shape indued." MBW-2
Seraph of Heaven. ISi
"Ship is floating in the harbour now, A." OBRV
"Spouse! Sister! Angel! Pilot of the fate." ChER
"There was a Being whom my spirit oft." EnLi-2
True Love ("She met me, stranger"). LoBV
"True Love in this differs from gold and clay." LO; OBNC
Episode, An. Muriel Earley Sheppard. IHA
Episode, An. John Addington Symonds. PoVP; VA
Episode of a Night of May. Arthur Symons. *Fr.* Scènes de la Vie de Bohème. BrPo; PeVV
Episode of the Cherry Tree. Mildred Weston. PV
Episode 17. William Carlos Williams. *Fr.* Paterson. OxBa
Epistemological Rag, The. Gray Burr. CoPo
Epistemology. Richard Wilbur. NePoEA
Epistle: "Christian, be up before the end of day." Robert Nathan. MaRV
Epistle, An: "First, last and always dearest, closest, best." A. D. Hope. PoAu-2
Epistle, An: "Karshish, the picker-up of learning's crumbs." Robert Browning. *See* Epistle, An, Containing the Strange Medical Experience of Karshish, the Arab Physician.
Epistle: "Meeting a monster of mourning wherever I go." George Barker. *See* Epistle to Dylan Thomas.
Epistle: "O Happiness! Our being's end." Pope. An Essay on Man, IV. ATP
Epistle: "Pult'ney, methinks you blame my breach of word." John Gay. EiCP
Epistle Answering to One That Asked to Be Sealed of the Tribe of Ben, An. Ben Jonson. AnAnS-2; OAEP; SCEP-2; SeCV-1; TuPP
Epistle, An, Containing the Strange Medical Experience of Karshish, the Arab Physician. Robert Browning. CABL; StJW; ViPo; ViPP; VP
(Epistle, An: "Karshish, the picker-up of learning's crumbs.") PoVP
(Epistle of Karshish, An.) EPN
(Karshish, the Arab Physician, *abr.*) WGRP
Sels.
All-loving, The. MaRV; OQP
("So, the All-Great were the All-Loving too.") ChIP; TRV
Karshish and Lazarus. GoBC
Epistle Dedicatory to Chapman's Translation of the Iliad, The, *sels.* George Chapman.
"Princes statue, A, or in marble carv'd." AtBAP
(Poetry and Learning.) OBS
"Since perfect happiness, by princes sought." CLwM; ReEn
(To the High-born Prince of Men, Henry.) ReIE
Epistle for Spring. R. Ellsworth Larsson. CAW
Epistle from Mr. Duke to Mr. Otway, An. Richard Duke. PeRV
Epistle from Mr. Pope, to Dr. Arbuthnot. Pope. *See* Epistle to Dr. Arbuthnot.
Epistle in Form of a Ballad to His Friends. Villon, *tr. fr. French by* Swinburne. AWP; LiTW; OuHeWo
Epistle of Condolence. Thomas Moore. OnYI
Epistle of Karshish, An. Robert Browning. *See* Epistle, An, Containing the Strange Medical Experience of Karshish, the Arab Physician.
Epistle of Rosamond to King Henry the Second. Michael Drayton. AnAnS-2
Epistle to a Young Friend. Burns. MCCG
(Letter to a Young Friend.) OHFP
Epistle to a Young Lady. Pope. *See* Epistle to Miss Blount, on Her Leaving the Town After the Coronation.
Epistle to Augusta. Byron. AnEnPo; EnRP; EPN
Epistle to Be Left in the Earth. Archibald MacLeish. BoLiVe (1945 ed.); CMoP; ImOP; MAP; MoAB; MoAmPo; TrGrPo
Epistle to Davie, a Brother Poet. Burns. OBEC
"Sacred lowe of weel-placed love, The," *sel.* PoG
Epistle to Dr. Arbuthnot (Prologue to the Satires). Pope. BEL; CABA; CABL; CoBE; EiPP; EnLi-1; EnLit; FosPo; LoBV, *abr.*; MBW-1; NoP; OAEP; PAn; PoE; PoEL-3; PoIE; TOP, *abr.*; WoL, *abr.*
(Epistle from Mr. Pope, to Dr. Arbuthnot, An.) CEP; EiCL
(To Dr. Arbuthnot, *abr.*) OxBoLi
Sels.
Atticus. AWP; JAWP; MaPo; OBEC; PoSa; SeCePo; WBP; WHA
(Characters from the Satires: Atticus.) InPo
("Peace to all such! but were there one whose fires.") PoFS; ViBoPo
(Portrait of Atticus.) UnPo (1st ed.)
Bufo ("Proud as Apollo on his forked hill"). OBEC
"Shut, shut the door, good John! fatigu'd, I said." HoPM
(Dire Dilemma, A.) WHA
Sporus. AWP; ChTr; JAWP; MaPo; WBP
(Characters from the Satires: Sporus.) InPo
("Let Sporus tremble—What? that thing of silk.") ViBoPo
Verbal Critics. OBEC
("Pains, reading, study, are their just pretense.") PP
Why Did I Write ("Of all mad creatures if the learn'd are right"). OBEC
"Why did I write? what sin to me unknown." ChTr; FiP, *longer sel.*; ViBoPo
"Yet let me flap this bug with gilded wings." ExPo
Epistle to Dr. Blacklock, Ellisland, 21st Oct. 1789, *abr.* Burns. OBEC
Epistle to Dylan Thomas. George Barker. LiTM (1952 ed.)
(Epistle I.) LiTM (1946 ed.); PoIE
Epistle to Elizabeth, Countess of Rutland, *sels.* Ben Jonson.
"Beautie, I know, is good, and bloud is more." FaBoEn
Power of Poets, The. WHA
Epistle to George Keats. Keats. *See* Epistle to My Brother George.
Epistle to Henry Wriothesley, Earl of Southampton. Samuel Daniel. EnRePo

Epistle to James Smith. Burns. CABL; MCCG; OBEC
(To James Smith, *sts.* 1-3.) HoPM
Epistle to John Bradshaw Esq., *sel.* Charles Cotton.
"Know then with horses twain, one sound, one lame." PeRV
Epistle to John Guthrie. Sydney Goodsir Smith. OxBS
Epistle to John Hamilton Reynolds. Keats. EPN; ERoP-2
Epistle to John Lapraik [an Old Scottish Bard]. Burns. BEL; CEP; EiCL; EiPP; EnL; EnLi-2; EnPE; EnRP; MCCG; NoP; OAEP
"I am nae poet, in a sense," *sel.* PP
Epistle to John Poins. Sir Thomas Wyatt. *See* Of the Courtier's Life.
Epistle to Miss [*or* Mrs.] Blount, on Her Leaving the Town, after the Coronation. Pope. BWP; CaFP; CBV; CEP; DiPo; PoEL-3
(Epistle to a Young Lady.) MBW-1
(To a Young Lady.) ExPo; OBEC; SeCeV; WePo
Epistle to Mr. Pope, An. George Lyttelton. Po
Epistle to My Brother George. Keats. MERP
(To My Brother George.) EnRP
Epistle to Reynolds, *sel.* Keats.
On Imagination. EPN
Epistle to Robert Earl of Oxford. Pope. EiCL
Epistle to Robert Lloyd, Esq., An. William Cowper. FiP
Epistle, An, to Sir Edward Sackville, now Earl of Dorset. Ben Jonson. NCEP
Epistle to the Gentiles. Alfred Hayes. TrJP
Epistle to the President of the Scottish Society of Antiquaries: On Being Chosen a Correspondent Member, *sel.* Alexander Geddes.
"Nor will the search be hard or long."
Epistle to the Reader. Walker Gibson. PP
Epi-Strauss-ium. Arthur Hugh Clough. ViPP
Epistrophe. LeRoi Jones. CAD; Kal; NNP; PoNe (1970 ed.)
Epitaph: "As I was, so be ye." *Unknown.* TreFS
Epitaph, An: "As shining sand-drift." Lady Margaret Sackville. HBMV
Epitaph: "Bathsheba: To whom none ever said scat." Whittier. CIV
Epitaph: "Believer he and unbeliever both." Robert Francis. PoIE
Epitaph, An: "Beneath this stone lies one good man; and when." W. H. Davies. ChMP
Epitaph: "Body of, The." Benjamin Franklin. TRV
Epitaph: "Daniel and Abigail." Miguel de Barrios, *tr. fr. Spanish.* TrJP
Epitaph: "Done to death by slanderous tongues." Shakespeare. *Fr.* Much Ado about Nothing, V, iii. CTC
("Done to death by slanderous tongues.") OBSC
Epitaph: "Dummer the shepherd sacrific'd." Cotton Mather. SCAP
Epitaph, An: "Enough; and leave the rest to fame." Andrew Marvell. OBEV
("Enough: and leave the rest to fame.") LO
(Epitaph upon ——, An.) CavP; LoBV; MaMe; SeCL
Epitaph: "Even such is Time, which takes in trust." Sir Walter Ralegh. *See* Conclusion, The.
Epitaph: "Fate to beauty still must give." Claudian, *tr. fr. Latin by* Howard Mumford Jones. AWP
Epitaph: "For this she starred her eyes with salt." Elinor Wylie. MAP; MoAmPo
Epitaph: "From out the stormy sea unto the shore." Azariah di Rossi, *tr. fr. Hebrew by* A. B. Rhine. TrJP
Epitaph, An: "Gaily I lived, as ease and nature taught." *Unknown.* *See* Gaily I Lived.
Epitaph: "He roamed half-round the world of woe." Aubrey Thomas De Vere. OBVV; PoVP
Epitaph: "Heap not on this mound." Edna St. Vincent Millay. *Fr.* Memorial to D. C. NP
Epitaph: "Her grieving parents cradled here." Sylvia Townsend Warner. MoBrPo; NeMA
Epitaph, An: "Here dead lie we because we did not choose." A. E. Housman. *See* Here Dead Lie We.
Epitaph: "Here—for they could not help but die." Philip Freneau. *Fr.* The Fading Rose. AA
Epitaph: "Here he lies moulding." Leslie Mellichamp. ShM
Epitaph: "Here lie [*or* lies] I, Martin Elginbrodde [*or* Elmrod]." *Unknown, at. to* George Macdonald. MaRV; WGRP
(At Aberdeen.) LiTG; SiTL
(Epigram.) HBV
(Epitaph in Elgin Cathedral.) MemP
(Gravestones, I.) OtMeF
(Here Lies. . .) GoTP
Epitaph I: "Here lies a man, and still no man." *Unknown, tr. fr. Hebrew.* *Fr.* Duel with Verses over a Great Man. TrJP
Epitaph, An: "Here lies a most beautiful lady." Walter de la Mare. AnFE; BoLiVe; CoBMV; LiTB; LiTM; LoBV; MoAB; MoBrPo; MoVE; NeMA; NP; OAEP (2d ed.); OBEV (new ed.); OBVV; OnPP; POTE; PTK; ShBV-3; SiTL; ViBoPo
Epitaph: "Here lies a poor woman who always was tired." *Unknown.* *See* On a Tired Housewife.
Epitaph: "Here lies a simple Jew." Sholom Aleichem, *tr. fr. Yiddish by* Joseph Leftwich. TrJP
Epitaph: "Here lies I and my three daughters." *Unknown.* TreFT
("Here lies I and my three daughters.") GoTP; SiTL; WhC
Epitaph, An: "Here lies Nachshon, a man of great renown." Isaac Benjacob, *tr. fr. Hebrew by* Joseph Chotzner. TrJP
Epitaph, An: "Here lies one who never drew." William Cowper. OTPC (1923 ed.)
Epitaph: "Here lies the body of Richard Hind." Francis Jeffrey. OxBoLi
Epitaph: "Here lies the flesh that tried." Louise Driscoll. HBMV; WGRP
Epitaph: "Here lies the poet Wolker, lover of the world." Jiri Wolker, *tr. fr. Czech by* Karl W. Deutsch. WaaP
Epitaph, An: "Here lieth under this marble ston." *Unknown.* MeEL
Epitaph: "Here rests a woman, good without pretence." Pope. *See* On Mrs. Corbet.
Epitaph: "I, an unwedded wandering dame." Sylvia Townsend Warner. MoBrPo; NeMA
Epitaph: "I, Richard Kent, beneath these stones." Sylvia Townsend Warner. MoBrPo; NeMA
Epitaph: "Implacable angel, The." Leone da Modena, *tr. fr. Hebrew.* TrJP
Epitaph: "In this marble, buried lies." Thomas Jordan. SeCL
Epitaph: Inscription from Anticyra. *Unknown. tr. fr. Greek by* Richmond Lattimore. WaaP
Epitaph: "Insured for every accident." Richard Armour. ShM
Epitaph, An: "Interred [*or* Interr'd] beneath this marble stone." Matthew Prior. CEP; EiCL; EiCP; EiPP; NoP; OBEC; PoE; PoEL-3; PoIE; YAT
Epitaph: "It seemed that he would rather hear." Edward Weismiller. PoMa
Epitaph: "It was for you that the mountains shook at Sinai." *Unknown.* TrJP
Epitaph: "John Bird, a laborer, lies here." Sylvia Townsend Warner. MoBrPo; NeMA
Epitaph, An: "Let us not think of our departed dead." Edwin Markham. *See* Our Dead.
Epitaph, An: "Life is a jest, and all things show it." John Gay. *See* My Own Epitaph.
Epitaph: "Like silver dew." A. E. Coppard. OBMV
Epitaph, An: "Like thee I once have stemm'd the sea of life." James Beattie. *See* Epitaph, Intended for Himself.
Epitaph, An: "Lovely young lady I mourn in my rhymes, A." George John Cayley. BoHV; ELU; FiBHP; HBV
Epitaph: "Man who in his life trusts in this world, A." *Unknown.* TrJP
Epitaph: "May, be thou never graced with birds that sing." William Browne. OBEV; PCD
(Epitaph in Obitum M. S., X. Maij, 1614.) OBS
(In Obitum M. S., Xo Maij, 1614.) EIL; SeCeV; SeEP
Epitaph: "Mr. Heath-Stubbs as you must understand." John Heath-Stubbs. NePoEA
Epitaph: "My brother is skull and skeleton now." William Montgomerie. OxBS
Epitaph: "Nature and Nature's laws lay hid in night." Pope. *See* Epitaph Intended for Sir Isaac Newton.
Epitaph: "O mortal folk, you may behold and see." Stephen Hawes. *Fr.* The Pastime of Pleasure, *ch.* 42. ACP; BoPe; CBEP; OBEV; OtMeF; TrGrPo
(Epitaph of Graunde Amoure.) ChTr; OBSC; SeCeV
(His Epitaph.) GoBC
("O mortal folk, you may behold and see.") MyFE
(Passetyme, The.) ViBoPo
Epitaph: "Of manners gentle, of affections mild." Pope. *See* On Mr. Gay. . .

Epitaph, An: On Elizabeth Chute. Ben Jonson. EnRePo
(Epitaph, An: "What beauty would have lovely styled.") NoP
Epitaph: On Sir Walter Rawleigh at His Execution. *Unknown.* OBS
Epitaph: "One whom I knew, a student and a poet." Alex Comfort. MoBrPo (1950 ed.)
(Poem.) SeCePo
Epitaph: "Poem in the rock and, The." R. S. Thomas. WePo
Epitaph: "Remember man, that passeth by." *Unknown. See* Epitaph and a Reply, An.
Epitaph: "Say he was sad, for there was none to love him." Robert Nathan. MoLP
Epitaph: "She was a high-class bitch and a dandy." Theodore Spencer. LiTA
Epitaph: "Shiftless and shy, gentle and kind and frail." J. C. Squire. HBMV
Epitaph: "Sir, you should [*or* shall] notice me: I am the Man." Lascelles Abercrombie. MoBrPo; POTE; ViBoPo
Epitaph: "Stone cries from the wall, The." *Unknown.* TrJP
Epitaph: "Stop, Christian passer by!—Stop, child of God." Samuel Taylor Coleridge. EnRP; EPN; ERoP-1; FiP; NoP; OAEP; OBRV; PeER
(Epitaph on Himself.) MaRV; OxBoCh
(O, Lift One Thought.) CH
Epitaph: "This is the end of him, here he lies." Amy Levy. TrJP
Epitaph, An: "This little vault, this narrow room." Thomas Carew. BEL; EnLi-1; UnPo (1st ed.)
(Epitaph on the Lady Mary Villers, An.) SeCP
(Epitaph on the Lady Villiers.) LiTL
(Other, An.) AnAnS-2; SeCV-1 SeEP
("This little vault, this narrow room.") OBEV
Epitaph: "Thou whom these eyes saw never." Robert Browning. VA
Epitaph: "Time and the World, whose magnitude and weight." Robert Southey. OBNC
Epitaph: "Time that bringes all things to light." Thomas Morton. SCAP
Epitaph, An: "Under this sod and beneath these trees." *Unknown.* MoShBr
Epitaph: "Underneath this marble stone." Abraham Cowley. EnLoPo
Epitaph: "Underneath this sable hearse." William Browne. *See* On the Countess Dowager of Pembroke.
Epitaph: "Warm summer sun." Robert Richardson, *ad. by* "Mark Twain." *See* Epitaph Placed on His Daughter's Tomb.
Epitaph: "Weep with me, all you that read." Ben Jonson. *See* Epitaph on S. P.
Epitaph, An: "What beauty would have lovely styled." Ben Jonson. *See* Epitaph, An: On Elizabeth Chute.
Epitaph, The: "When from this good world I depart." John Alexander Bouquet. MaRV
Epitaph: "When I shall be without regret." J. V. Cunningham. ELU; PoCh
Epitaph: "When you perceive these stones are wet." Sir William Davenant. ACP
Epitaph: "Within this grave do lie." *Unknown. See* Within This Grave. . . TreFT
Epitaph, The: "Write on my grave when I am dead." Katharine Tynan. WGRP
Epitaph after Reading Ronsard's Lines from Rabelais. J. M. Synge. PV
Epitaph and a Reply, An. *Unknown.* TreFS
(Epitaph: "Remember man, that passeth by.") TreFT
Epitaph. Cæcil. Boulstr. Lord Herbert of Cherbury. AnAnS-2; SeCP
Epitaph Ending in and, The. William Stafford. NaP
Epitaph for a Bigot. Dorothy Vena Johnson. PoNe
Epitaph for a Cat. Margaret E. Bruner. CIV; PoLF
Epitaph for a Concord Boy. Stanley Young. WaKn
Epitaph for a Funny Fellow. Morris Bishop. SiTL
Epitaph for a Godly Man's Tomb, An. Robert Wild. CBEP; ChTr; OxBoCh; SeCL
Epitaph for a Horseman. Michael Hamburger. NePoEA-2
Epitaph for a Judge. Benedict Jeitteles, *tr. fr. Hebrew by* Joseph Chotzner. TrJP
Epitaph for a Kitten. Miriam Vedder. CIV
Epitaph for a Lighthouse-Keeper's Horse. J. B. Morton. PV
Epitaph for a Man from Virginia City. Kenneth Porter. NePoAm-2
Epitaph for a Negro Woman. Owen Dodson. PoNe
Epitaph for a Postal Clerk. X. J. Kennedy. ShM
Epitaph for a Sailor Buried Ashore. Sir Charles G. D. Roberts. EtS; VA
Epitaph for a Timid Lady. Frances Cornford. ELU
Epitaph for a Tyrannous Governor Who Choked on Wine. Adib-i Sabir, *tr. fr. Persian by* R. A. Nicholson. LiTW
Epitaph for an American Bomber. James Bertram. AnNZ
Epitaph for Any New Yorker. Christopher Morley. ShM
Epitaph for Elizabeth Ranquet. Corneille, *tr. fr. French by* Roderick Gill. CAW
Epitaph; for Himself. Tristan Corbière, *tr. fr. French by* Joseph T. Shipley. AWP
(Epitaph for Tristan-Joachim-Edouard Corbière, Philospher, Stray, Stillborn, *tr. by* Walter McElroy.) LiTW
Epitaph for Himself. Lord Herbert of Cherbury. AnAnS-2
Epitaph for James Smith. Burns. *See* On a Wag in Mauchline.
Epitaph for John and Richard. Karl Shapiro. TwAmPo
Epitaph for Lincoln. Walt Whitman. *See* This Dust Was Once the Man.
Epitaph for Mr. Moses Levy. *Unknown.* TrJP
Epitaph for Peter Stuyvesant. Henricus Selyns. SCAP
Epitaph for the Poet. George Barker. PoIE
Epitaph for the Poet V., *sels.* Arthur Davison Ficke. HBMV
"Beauty—what is it? A perfume without name," III.
"For Beauty kissed your lips when they were young," II.
"It is ordained—or so Politian said," I.
"Peculiar ghost! great and immortal ghost," XVII.
Epitaph for the Race of Man, *sels.* Edna St. Vincent Millay.
"Before this coiling planet shall be cold," I. AmP
"Broken dike, the levee washed away, The," X. CMoP
"Here lies, and none to mourn him but the sea," XVIII. MoPo; ReMP
(Sonnet XVIII.) AtBAP
"O Earth, unhappy planet born to die," IV. AmP
"Only the diamond and the diamond's dust," XVII. MoPo
See Where Capella with Her Golden Kids, VI. MAP; MoAB; MoAmPo
("See where Capella. . .") CMoP
"When Death was young and bleaching bones were few," II. AmP
Epitaph for the Unknown Soldier. Annette Kohn. DD
Epitaph for Tristan-Joachim-Edouard Corbière, Philosopher, Stray, Stillborn. Tristan Corbière. *See* Epitaph; for Himself.
Epitaph, Found Somewhere in Space. Hugh Wilgus Ramsaur. MaRV; TRV
Epitaph from "The Great Gatsby." F. Scott Fitzgerald. ELU
Epitaph in Anticipation. Leonard Bacon. WhC
Epitaph; in Christ Church, Bristol, on Thomas Turner, Twice Master of the Company of Bakers. Francis Jeffrey. OxBoLi
Epitaph in Commendation of George Turberville, a Learned Gentleman, An. Sir John Harington. SiCE
Epitaph in Elgin Cathedral. *Unknown, at. to* George Macdonald. *See* Epitaph: "Here lie I, Martin Elginbrodde."
Epitaph in Form of a Ballad, The, Which Villon Made for Himself and His Comrades, Expecting to be Hanged Along with Them. Villon, *tr. fr. French by* Swinburne. CTC; EnLi-2; OuHeWo
(Ballad[e] of the Gibbet, *tr. by* Andrew Lang.) AWP; JAWP; WBP; WoL
(Ballade of the Hanged Men, *tr. by* Robert Fitzgerald.) LiTW
(Villon's Epitaph, *tr. by* Muriel Kittel.) AnML
Epitaph in Obitum M. S., Xo Maij, 1614. William Browne. *See* Epitaph: "May, be thou never graced with birds that sing."
Epitaph; in St. Olave's Church, Southwark, on Mr. Munday. Francis Jeffrey. OxBoLi
Epitaph in Sirmio. David Morton. PoLF
Epitaph Inscribed on a Small Piece of Marble. James Shirley. CavP
Epitaph, Intended for Himself. James Beattie. HBV
(Epitaph, An: "Like thee I once have stemm'd the sea of life.") MemP; OBEV
Epitaph Intended for His Wife. Dryden. BOHV; InMe
(Epigram: "Here lies my wife: here let her lie!") HBV
(Epitaph on His Wife.) TrGrPo; WhC
("Here lies my wife; here let her lie!") ShM; TreF

Epitaph Intended for Sir Isaac Newton. Pope. BWP; CBV; CEP; FaBoEn; ImOP; SeCeV
(Couplet on Newton.) EiCL
(Epitaph: "Nature and Nature's laws lay hid in night.") InP; TreFT
(Epitaph on Sir Isaac Newton.) FiP; ViBoPo
(Intended for Sir Isaac Newton.) OAEP; TOP
("Nature and Nature's laws lay hid in night.") ExPo
(Science.) MaRV
Epitaph of a Courtesan. Asclepiades, *tr. fr. Greek by* Dudley Fitts. LiTW
Epitaph of a Faithful Man. Robert Mezey. ELU
Epitaph of a Sailor. Leonidas of Tarentum, *tr. fr. Greek by* Dudley Fitts. LiTW
Epitaph of a Thessalian Hound. Simonides, *tr. fr. Greek by* Dudley Fitts. LiTW
Epitaph of a Young Man. *Unknown, tr. fr. Greek by* Dudley Fitts. LiTW
Epitaph of Bion. Moschus. *See* Lament for Bion, A.
Epitaph of Dionysia. *Unknown.* HBV; OBEV (new ed.); OBVV; VA
Epitaph of Eusthenes, The. Edward Cracroft Lefroy. *Fr.* Echoes from Theocritus. AWP; OBVV
Epitaph of Graunde Amoure, The. Stephen Hawes. Epitaph: "O mortal folk, you may behold and see."
Epitaph of Maister Win Drowned in the Sea, An. George Turberville. EnPo
Epitaph of Sarah Sexton. *Unknown.* TreFT
("Here lies the body. . .) WhC
Epitaph, An, of Sir Thomas Gravener, Knight. Sir Thomas Wyatt. EnRePo; OBSC; SiPS
Epitaph of the Death of Nicholas Grimald, An. Barnabe Googe. EnRePo; ReIE; SiCE; TuPP
Epitaph on a Bellows-Maker, An. John Hoskins. TuPP
Epitaph on a Bombing Victim. Roy Fuller. NeBP;; ToPo
Epitaph on a Career Woman. William Cole. PV
Epitaph on a Dentist. *Unknown.* OxBoLi; TreFS
(Dentist, A.) LiTG; TreFT; WhC
(On a Dentist.) GoTP
Epitaph on a Friend. Burns. MaRV
Epitaph on a Hare. William Cowper. BWP; FiP; HBV; HBVY; NoP; PoEL-3; PoG; RG; SeCeV; ShBV-1
(On a Hare.) BoPe
Epitaph on a Jacobite. Macaulay. *See* Jacobite's Epitaph, A.
Epitaph on a Madman's Grave. Morris Gilbert. YaD
Epitaph on a Man for Doing Nothing, An. John Hoskins. TuPP
Epitaph on a Marf. *Unknown.* PV
Epitaph on a Pessimist. Thomas Hardy. PoIE; VP
Epitaph on a Robin Redbreast, An. Samuel Rogers. OTPC (1923 ed.); PRWS
(Robin's Epitaph, A.) CBEP
Epitaph on a Sentry. L. A. G. Strong. NeMA
Epitaph on a Soldier. Cyril Tourneur. *Fr.* The Atheist's Tragedy, III, i. EIL
("His body lies interred within this mold.") SiCE
Epitaph on a Talkative Old Maid. Benjamin Franklin. WhC
Epitaph on a Tyrant. W. H. Auden. ELU
Epitaph on a Vagabond. Alexander Gray. HBMV
Epitaph on a Virgin. Robert Herrick. *See* Epitaph upon a Virgin.
Epitaph on a Waiter. David McCord. PoPo
(On a Waiter.) WhC
Epitaph on a Warthog. J. B. Morton. PV
Epitaph on a Well-known Poet. Thomas Moore. *See* Epitaph on Robert Southey.
Epitaph on a Worthy Clergyman. Benjamin Franklin. TRV
Epitaph on Achilles. *Unknown, tr. fr. Greek by* William M. Hardinge. AWP
Epitaph on an Army of Mercenaries. A. E. Housman. BrPo; CBV; CMoP; CoBMV; ForPo; GTBS; MMA; MoAB; MoVE; OBEV (new ed.); OtMeF; PoAn; PoFS; PoIE; POTE; StP; UnPo; ViBoPo; WaaP
Epitaph on an Infant. Crinagoras, *tr. fr. Greek by* John William Burgon. AWP
Epitaph on an Unfortunate Artist. Robert Graves. WhC
Epitaph on Charles II. Earl of Rochester. FiBHP; HBV; InP; OnPP; TOP; TreFS; TrGrPo; WhC
(Epigram: "Here lies a great and mighty King.") CavP
(Impromptu on Charles II.) ChTr
(King Charles II.) OnPM; ViBoPo
(King's Epitaph, The.) EnLi-1 (1949 ed.); SeCePo; SeEP
(On Charles II.) ALV; ExPo; GoTP; MemP; PoSa
Epitaph on Claudy Phillips, a Musician, An. Samuel Johnson. EiCL
(Epitaph upon the Celebrated Claudy Philips, Musician, Who Died Very Poor, An.) CBEP; OBEC; UnS
Epitaph on Clere, An. Earl of Surrey. *See* Epitaph on Thomas Clere, An.
Epitaph on Doctor Donne, Deane of Pauls, An. Richard Corbett. AnAnS-2
Epitaph on Dr. Johnson. Soame Jenyns. ELU
Epitaph on Drake. Thomas Beedome. *See* To the Noble Sir Francis Drake.
Epitaph on Elizabeth, L. H. Ben Jonson. AnAnS-2; CABA; EIL; ELP; EnL; EnLi-1 (1949 ed.); EnRePo; ForPo; InPo; NoP; OBEV; OBS; PoE; PoIE; ReEn; ReIE; SCEP-2; SeCP; SeCV-1; SeEP; TuPP; ViBoPo; WHA
(Elizabeth L. H.) TreFT
(On Elizabeth L. H.) HBV
Epitaph on Erotion. Martial. *See* Erotion.
Epitaph on Herself, An. Hetty Wright. WaPE
Epitaph on Himself. Samuel Taylor Coleridge. *See* Epitaph: "Stop, Christian passer-by!"
Epitaph on Himself. Matthew Prior. TreFS
(Epigram: "Nobles and heralds, by your leave.") HBV
(Prior's Epitaph.) TrGrPo
Epitaph on Himself. Mathurin Regnier, *tr. fr. French by* J. G. Legge. LiTW
Epitaph on Himselfe. John Donne. MaMe
Epitaph on His Deceased Friend, An. Robert Fletcher. SeCL
Epitaph on His Grandfather, An. Thomas Shipman. CBEP; SeCL
Epitaph on His Wife. Dryden. *See* Epitaph Intended for His Wife.
Epitaph on Husband and Wife Who Died and Were Buried Together, An. Richard Crashaw. *See* Epitaph upon Husband and Wife . . .
Epitaph on John Dove. Burns. InP
Epitaph on John Graham of Claverhouse, Viscount Dundee. Dryden. *See* Upon the Death of the Viscount of Dundee.
Epitaph on John Knott. *Unknown.* ChTr; ShM
Epitaph on Johnson. William Cowper. EiCP
Epitaph on King Charles I. James Graham, Marquess of Montrose. OBS
(His Metrical Vow.) OxBS; ViBoPo
(Lines on the Execution of King Charles I.) GoTS
(On the Death of Charles I.) OnPM
Epitaph on Lady Ossory's Bullfinch. Horace Walpole. ChTr; OA
Epitaph on M. H., An. Charles Cotton. PeRV
Epitaph on Maria, Lady Wentworth. Thomas Carew. *See* Maria Wentworth.
Epitaph on Master Philip Gray, An. Ben Jonson. NoP
Epitaph on Mr. John Sprat, Late Steward of Grayes-Inn. Alexander Radcliffe. PeRV
Epitaph on Mr. Robert Port. Charles Cotton. CavP
Epitaph on Mrs. Corbet, Who Died [*or* Dyed] of a Cancer in Her Breast. Pope. BWP; CEP
Epitaph on Mistress Mary Draper. Charles Cotton. CavP
Epitaph on Mistress Mary Prideaux, An. *At. to* George Morley. SeCL
Epitaph on My Dear and Ever Honoured Mother, An. Anne Bradstreet. AmPP (3d ed.)
Epitaph on My Father. Burns. MaRV
Epitaph on Queen Elizabeth, Wife of Henry VII. *Unknown.* AtBAP
Epitaph on Robert Southey. Thomas Moore. PP; SiTL
(Epitaph on a Well-known Poet.) InMe
Epitaph on S. P. [Salamon *or* Salomon *or* Salathiel Pavy], a Child of Q. El.'s [Queen Elizabeth's] Chapel (*or* Chappel], An. Ben Jonson. AnAnS-2; BEL; BWP; CABA; CBV; CoBE; EIL; EnRePo; FaBoEn; GoBC; InP; LoBV; MaPo; MePo; NoP; OAEP; OBEV; OBS; PAn; PoE; PoEL-2; PoFS; PoSa; PTK; ReEn; ReIE; SCEP-2; SeCP; SeCV-1; SeEP; TrGrPo; TuPP; UnPo (1st ed.); VaPo; ViBoPo
(Epitaph: "Weep with me, all you that read.") HBV
Epitaph on Sir Albert Morton's Wife. Sir Henry Wotton. *See* Upon the Death of Sir Albert Morton's Wife.
Epitaph on Sir Isaac Newton. Pope. *See* Epitaph Intended for Sir Isaac Newton.

Epitaph on Sir John Vanbrugh [Architect]. Abel Evans. TreFT; ViBoPo
(For Sir John Vanbrugh, Architect, 2 *ll.*) WhC
(On Sir John Vanbrugh [Architect].) FiBHP; OBEC; PV
Epitaph on Sir Philip Sidney. *At. to* Fulke Greville. AnFE; LiTB; LiTG; LoBV; OBSC; ReIE
(Another of the Same. Excellently Written by a Most Woorthy Gentleman.) SiCE, *at. to* Sir Edward Dyer
(Elegy on the Death of Sidney.) EnRePo, *at. to* Sir Edward Dyer
(Epitaph upon the Right Honorable Sir Philip Sidney, An.) FCP; TuPP
Epitaph on Sir Philip Sidney. Lord Herbert of Cherbury. SeEP
Epitaph on Sir Philip Sidney, An. James I, King of England. Sonn
Epitaph on Sir Philip Sidney. *At. to* Sir Walter Ralegh. *See* Epitaph upon the Right Honorable Sir Philip Sidney . . .
Epitaph, An, on the Admirable Dramatic Poet, William Shakespeare. Milton. *See* On Shakespeare.
Epitaph on the Countess [Dowager] of Pembroke. William Browne. *See* On the Countess Dowager of Pembroke.
Epitaph on the Duke of Grafton. *At. to* Sir Fleetwood Shepherd. PeRV
Epitaph on the Earl of Leicester. Sir Walter Ralegh. EnRePo; FOL; SiPS
Epitaph on the Earl of Strafford. John Cleveland. CavP; FosPo; MePo; OBS; SeCePo; TrGrPo
(Gravestones, II.) OtMeF
Epitaph on the Favourite Dog of a Politician. Hilaire Belloc. CoBE
Epitaph on the Lady Mary Villers [*or* Villiers] ("The Lady Mary Villers lyes"). Thomas Carew. AnAnS-2; CavP; OAEP; OBEV; SCEP-2; SeCL; SeCV-1; SeEP; ViBoPo
Epitaph on the Lady Villiers ("This little vault. . ."). Thomas Carew. *See* Epitaph: "This little vault, this narrow room."
Epitaph on the Lap-Dog of Lady Frail. John Wilkes. ALV
Epitaph on the Late King of the Sandwich Isles. Winthrop Mackworth Praed. FiBHP
Epitaph on the Marchioness of Winchester, An. Milton. CavP; OBS
Epitaph on the Monument of Sir William Dyer at Colmworth, 1641. Lady Catherine Dyer. EnLoPo
Epitaph on the Politician. Hilaire Belloc. InP; MoBrPo; NeMA; TreFT
(Epitaph on the Politician Himself.) CoBE
(On a Politician.) PV; ShM; WhC
Epitaph on the Proofreader of the Encyclopedia Britannica. Christopher Morley. ShM
Epitaph on the Tomb of Sir Edward Giles and His Wife. Robert Herrick. QFR
Epitaph on the World. Henry David Thoreau. OnPM
Epitaph on Thomas Clere. Earl of Surrey. SiPS
(Epitaph on Clere, An.) CBEP
(Norfolk Sprang Thee.) FCP; NCEP
Epitaph on Those Who Fell at the Battle of Chaeronea. Demosthenes, *tr. fr. Greek by* George Nathaniel Curzon. PoFr
Epitaph Placed on His Daughter's Tomb [by Mark Twain]. Robert Richardson, *ad. by* "Mark Twain." MaRV; TreF
(Epitaph: "Warm summer sun.") PoLF
Epitaph to a Dog. Byron. *See* Epitaph to a Newfoundland Dog.
Epitaph to a Man. Robert Reedburg. TNV
Epitaph to a Newfoundland Dog. Byron. TreFS
(Epitaph to a Dog.) BLPA
Epitaph to the Four Husbands of Miss Ivy Saunders. *Unknown.* PV; WePo
Epitaph to the Liberty of America. José Joaquín Fernández de Lizardi, *tr. fr. Spanish by* Alice Stone Blackwell. PoFr
Epitaph upon ——, An. Andrew Marvell. *See* Epitaph, An: "Enough; and leave the rest to fame."
Epitaph upon a Child, An ("Virgins promised when I died"). Robert Herrick. SeCV-1
Epitaph upon a Child that Died ("Here she lies, a pretty bud"). Robert Herrick. *See* Upon a Child That Died.
Epitaph upon a Virgin, An. Robert Herrick. OnPM; OxBoLi; PoEL-3; SeCV-1
(Epitaph on a Virgin.) EG
Epitaph upon Doctor Brooke, An. Richard Crashaw. MaMe
Epitaph upon Husband and Wife Which [*or* Who] Died and Were Buried Together, An. Richard Crashaw. LO; MaMe; MaRV; OBEV; OBS; TreFS; TrGrPo
(Epitaph on Husband and Wife, An.) LiTL
(Epitaph upon a Young Married Couple.) ELP; ILP; MaMe; OAEP; SeCePo; SeCL; SeCP; SeEP; WHA
(On a Young Married Couple.) FaBoEn
Epitaph upon Master Parsons, Organist at Westminster. *Unknown.* MuSP
Epitaph Upon Mr. Ashton a Conformable Citizen, An. Richard Crashaw. MaMe; OBS
Epitaph upon the Celebrated Claudy Philips, Musician, Who Died Very Poor, An. Samuel Johnson. *See* Epitaph on Claudy Phillips, a Musician, An.
Epitaph upon the Death of Sir Philip Sidney, Knight, Lord-Governor of Vlissing, An. Richard Barnfield. ReIE
Epitaph upon the Death of Sir William Drury, An. Barnabe Rich. ReIE
Epitaph, An, Upon the Death of the Right Reverent Father in God J. Jewel, Doctor of Divinity and Bishop of Sarisbury, Who Deceased the Twenty-second of September, 1571. Nicholas Bourman. ReIE
Epitaph upon the Right Honorable Sir Philip Sidney, An. *At. to* Fulke Greville. *See* Epitaph on Sir Philip Sidney.
Epitaph upon the Right Honorable Sir Philip Sidney, Knight, Lord Governor of Flushing, An. *At. to* Sir Walter Ralegh. FCP; ReIE; SiCE; TuPP
(Epitaph on Sir Philip Sidney.) SiPS
Epitaph upon the Worthy and Truly Vigilant, Sam. Micoe Esq., An. Alexander Radcliffe. PeRV
Epitaphium Citharistriae. Victor Plarr. AnEnPo; EnLoPo; HBMV; ViBoPo
(Stand Not Uttering Sedately.) PoRA
Epitaphium Meum. William Bradford. SCAP
Epitaphs. Gabriello Chiabrera, *tr. fr. Italian by* Wordsworth.
"Destined to war from very infancy," VI. AWP; JAWP; WBP
"Not without heavy grief of heart did he," VIII. AWP; JAWP; WBP
"O flower of all that springs from gentle blood," VII. AWP
"O thou who movest onward with a mind," III. AWP; JAWP; WBP
"Pause, courteous spirit!—Balbi supplicates," IX. AWP
"Perhaps some needful service of the state," II. AWP
"There never breathed a man, who, when his life," IV. AWP; JAWP; WBP
"True is it that Ambrosio Salinero," V. AWP
"Weep not, beloved friends! nor let the air," I. AWP; JAWP; WBP
(Francesco Ceni.) OnPM
Epitaphs. Francis Jeffrey.
"Here lies the body of Richard Hind." OxBoLi
In Christ Church. OxBoLi
In St. Olave's Church. OxBoLi
On Peter Robinson. OxBoLi; WhC
Epitaphs; for a Fickle Man. Mark Van Doren. ViBoPo
Epitaphs of the War, 1914-18. Kipling. BrPo; NoP
Sels.
Batteries Out of Ammunition. MMA; PoVP
Beginner, The. FaBoTw
Bombed in London. PoVP
Bridegroom, The. CLwM
Common Form. FaBoTw; PoVP; PV
Coward, The. FaBoTw; GTBS; OAEP (2d ed.); PoVP
Dead Statesman, A. OAEP (2d ed.); PoVP
Destroyers in Collision. PoVP
Drifter off Tarentum, A. MMA
"Equality of Sacrifice." FaBoTw; OAEP (2d ed.)
Ex-Clerk. PoVP
Grave near Cairo, A. PoVP
Refined Man, The. FaBoTw; MMA
Salonikan Grave. OAEP (2d ed.)
Servant, A. PoVP
Son, A. ChMP; PoVP
Wonder, The PoVP
Epithalamia. Thomas Lovell Beddoes. *See* Bridal Song to Amala.
Epithalamie to Sir Thomas Southwell and His Lady, An. Robert Herrick. HW
Epithalamion, An: "Haile [*or* Hail] Bishop Valentine, whose day this is." John Donne. AtBAP; HW; MaMe
Hail, Bishop Valentine, *sel.* ChTr
Epithalamion: "Haile wedded love, mysterious law, true sourse." Milton. *See* Wedded Love.

Epithalamion: "Hark, hearer, hear what I do." Gerard Manley Hopkins. AnEnPo; HW
Epithalamion: "Smile then, children, hand in hand." James Elroy Flecker. BrPo
Epithalamion: Time of the Mariage, The. John Donne. MaMe
Epithalamion: "While explosives blow to dust." W. H. Auden. HW
Epithalamion: "Wind in the street, and sadness of unknown walkers." Terence Tiller. POTE
Epithalamion: "Ye learned sisters, which have oftentimes." Spenser. AtBAP, *abr.*; BEL; BWP; CABL; EIL; EnL; EnLi-1 (1949 ed.); EnRePo; HBV; HW; ILP; LiTL; MaPo (1969 ed.); MasP; MBW-1; NoP; OAEP; OBEV; OBSC; Po; PoAn; PoEL-1; PoFS; ReEn; RelE; SeCeV; SiCE; TOP; ViBoPo; WoL
Sels.
"Ah! when will this long weary day have end." LO
"Hark how the minstrels gin to shrill aloud." WHA
"Now al is done; bring home the bride againe." FiP
Epithalamion Made at Lincolnes [*or* Lincoln's] Inn[e]. John Donne. HW; MaMe; OBS; PAn; SeCP
Epithalamion Teratos [*or* Teratus]. George Chapman. *Fr.* Hero and Leander: Fifth Sestiad. AtBAP; EiL; LoBV
(Wedding of Alcmane and Mya, The.) OBSC
Epithalamion upon the Marquis of Huntilies Marriage, An. James I, King of England. HW
Epithalamium, *sel.* W. J. Turner.
Song: "Can the lover share his soul." OBMV
Epithalamium: "Come, virgin tapers of pure wax." Richard Crashaw. HW; ReEn; ViBoPo, *sts.* 1-6
Epithalamium: "Crept side by side beyond the thresh." Vassar Miller. NePoEA
Epithalamium: "He is here, Urania's son." A. E. Housman. HW
Epithalamium: "High in the organ loft with lilied hair." Sir Edmund Gosse. OBVV
Epithalamium: "Hour is come, with pleasure crowned, The." Johannes Secundus, *tr. fr. Latin by* George Ogle. HW
Wedding Night, The, *sel.* UnTE
Epithalamium: "I saw two clouds at morning." John Gardiner Calkins Brainard. *See* I Saw Two Clouds at Morning.
Epithalamium: "Let mother earth now deck herself in flowers." Sir Philip Sidney. *Fr.* Arcadia. SiPS
(O Hymen, Long Their Coupled Joys Maintain!) HW
Epithalamium: "Rejoice,/ Ye woods and fountains." *Unknown.* SeCL
Epithalamium: "Rings of the sun rise, The." Anne Cluysenaar. HW
Epithalamium: "Sister, the bride-bed waits." Arthur Symons. FaBoTw
Epithalamium: "So you are married, girl. It makes me sad." Roy McFadden. NeIP
Epithalamium: "This body of my mother, pierced by me." Leo Kennedy. OBCV
Epithalamium: "We have found our peace." A. R. D. Fairburn. AnNZ
Epithalamium: "When the vast universal night shall cover." Edith Sitwell. HW
Epithalamium for Cavorting Ghosts. Dachine Rainer. NePoAm-2
Epithalamium for Charlotte Corday and Francis Ravaillac. Shelley. HW
Epithalamium for Gloucester, *sel.* John Lydgate.
"Howe maryages have grounde and cause be." HW
Epithalamium for Honorius and Maria, *sels.* Claudian, *tr. fr. Latin by* Maurice Platnauer *and* Virginia Tufte. HW
Hairdresser's Art, The.
Palm Tree Mates with Palm.
Preparing for the Wedding.
Epithalamium for Mary Stuart and the Dauphin of France, *abr.* George Buchanan, *tr. fr. Latin.* GoTS
Epithalamium for Murder. Seneca, *tr. fr. Latin by* Ella Isabel Harris. *Fr.* Medea. HW
Epithalamium for Stella and Violentilla, *sels.* Statius, *tr. fr. Latin by* D. A. Slater *and* Virginia Tufte. HW
Ah, Now I Know What Day This Is.
Of the Night, Let the Bridegroom Sing.
Why Do You Dally So?
Wishes for a Bridal Couple and Their Unborn Child.
Epithalamium for the Dedication of a Church. *Unknown, tr. fr. Latin by* Garrett Stewart. HW
Epithalamium on a Late Happy Marriage. Christopher Smart. HW
Epithalamium on the Lady Elizabeth and Count Palatine Being Married on St. Valentine's Day, An. John Donne. *See* Epithalamion, An: "Haile Bishop Valentine."
Epode. Ben Jonson. SeCP; SeCV-1
Epodes, *sel.* Horace, *tr. fr. Latin.*
Country Life, II, *tr. by* Dryden. AWP
("Happy the man whom bount'ous gods allow," *tr. by* Abraham Cowley.) CavP
(Revery of a Business Man, *tr. by* Dryden.) WoL
Epos. Julian Tuwim, *tr. fr. Polish by* Jack Lindsay. LiTW
Eppie Morrie. *Unknown.* ESPB; OxBB
Epping Forest. John Davidson. *Fr.* November. GTSL
Eppur Si Muove? Robert Hillyer. GoYe
Equality. Herman L. McMillan. TNV
Equality. James Shirley. *See* Glories of Our Blood and State.
Equality of Persons. John Donne. MaMe
"Equality of Sacrifice." Kipling. *Fr.* Epitaphs of the War. BrPo; FaBoTw; NoP; OAEP (2d ed.)
Equals. Louis Untermeyer. MeWo; UnTE
Equation, An. Hyam Plutzik. FiMAP
Equation. Sir Herbert Read. BrPo
Equilibrists, The. John Crowe Ransom. AmP; AnAmPo; AP; CaFP; CMoP; CoBMV; LiTM; MoAB; MoPo; MoVE; NePA; NoP; OxBA; UnPo (1st ed.)
Equinoctial. Adeline D. T. Whitney. HBV
Equinox, The. Longfellow. *Fr.* Seaweed. EtS
Equipment. Paul Laurence Dunbar. TrPWD
Equipment. Edgar A. Guest. PoToHe (new ed.)
Equity with God. Omar Khayyám, *tr. fr. Persian by* Edward Fitzgerald. *Fr.* The Rubáiyát. OnPM
("Oh Thou, who Man of baser Earth didst make.") EaLo; SeCeV
'Er name's Doreen. . . Well, spare me bloomin' days! The Intro. C. J. Dennis. WhC
Erasers. *Unknown.* PoToHe
Erasers are such handy things. Mistakes. George W. Swarberg. STF
Erasers are the nicest things! Erasers. *Unknown.* PoToHe
Erat Hora. Ezra Pound. CBV
Erce, Erce, Erce, Mother of earth. Charm for Unfruitful Land. *Unknown.* AnOE
Erd sould trymbill, the firmament sould schaik, The. Quod Dunbar to Kennedy. William Dunbar. OxBoLi
Erda. Vera Bishop Konrick. FiSC
Ere famous Winthrops bones are laid to rest. Chelmsfords Fate. Benjamin Tompson. SCAP
Ere five score years have run their tedious rounds. A Prophecy. *At. to* Arthur Lee. PAH
E're I forget the zenith of your love. To My Cosen Mrs. Ellinor Evins. George Alsop. SCAP
Ere, in the northern gale. Autumn Woods. Bryant. AnNE
Ere last year's moon had left the sky. My Bird. "Fannie Forester." AA
Ere long the clouds were gone, the moon was set. Sights and Sounds of the Night. Carlos Wilcox. AnAmPo
Ere long they come, where that same wicked wight. Despair [*or* To Be or Not to Be]. Spenser. *Fr.* The Faerie Queene, I. FaBoEn
Ere Mor the Peacock flutters, ere the Monkey People cry. The Song of the Little Hunter. Kipling. *Fr.* The Second Jungle Book. ShBV-1
Ere Murfreesboro's thunders rent the air. The Battle of Murfreesboro. Kinahan Cornwallis. PAH
Ere my heart beats too coldly and faintly. The Truants. Walter de la Mare. CMoP; InP; MoBrPo
Ere on my bed my limbs I lay. The Pains of Sleep [*or* A Child's Evening Prayer]. Samuel Taylor Coleridge. CBEP; EnRP; EPN; ERoP-1; MERP; NCEP; OAEP; OBNC; OBRV; OTPC (1923 ed.); SeCePo; SyP; TrPWD
Ere Sleep Comes Down to Soothe the Weary Eyes. Paul Laurence Dunbar. BALP; BANP; CDC; NoP; PoNe
Ere space exists, or earth, or sky. The Lord Is King. *Unknown.* TrJP
Ere the Golden Bowl Is Broken. Anna Hempstead Branch. AnAmPo; AnFE; APA; CoAnAm; MAPA
Ere the long roll of the ages end. Fainne Gael and Lae. Alice Milligan. HBV

Ere the moon begins to rise. Sleepy Song. Thomas Bailey Aldrich. GoTP
Ere the morn the East has crimsoned. Lines Suggested by the Fourteenth of February. Charles Stuart Calverley. InMe
Ere the steamer bore him Eastward, Sleary was engaged to marry. The Post That Fitted. Kipling. CenHV; HBV; OnMSP
Ere yellow Autumn from our plains retir'd. The Swallows; an Elegy. Richard Jago. CEP
Ere yet in Vergil I could scan or spell. "Hic Me, Pater Optime, Fessam Deseris." Lucy Catlin Robinson. AA
Ere yet the sun is high. The Iris. Gasetsu. MPB; TiPo
Erect in youthful grace and radiant. By the Sea of Galilee. Katharine Lee Bates. ChIP
Eremites, The. Robert Graves. LiTB
Ere-while of musick, and ethereal mirth. The Passion. Milton. MeP
Er-Heb beyond the hills of Ao-Safai. The Sacrifice of Er-Heb. Kipling. PeVV
Eride, *sel.* Trumbull Stickney.
Now in the Place Gardens, V. AnFE; CoAnAm; LiTA; NCEP; TwAmPo
Erie, The ("We were forty miles from Albany"), *with music.* *Unknown.* ABF; AS
Erie Canal ("It was a long, long trip on the Erie"). *Unknown.* ABF
Erie Canal, The ("I've got a mule, her name is Sal"). William S. Allen. ABF; AmFN; AS; IHA; OTD; RePo; TrAS, *with music*
(Low Bridge, Everybody Down, *longer vers., with music.*) ABF
Erie Canal Ballad, The. *Unknown.* ABF, *composite vers. of popular Erie Canal Songs and choruses*
Erie's raging and the gin is going low, The. The Erie Canal Ballad. *Unknown.* ABF
Erige Cor Tuum ad Me in Caelum. Hilda Doolittle ("H. D."). AP; CMoP
Erin. Kenelm H. Digby. CAW
Erin. *Unknown, tr. fr. Yoruba by* Ulli Beier. OA; PBA
(Elephant I, The, *tr. by* Gbadamosi *and* Ulli Beier.) TTY
Erinna. Antipater of Sidon, *tr. fr. Greek.* AWP, *tr. by* A. J. Butler; VA, *tr. by* Andrew Lang
Erinna to Her Friend. Erinna, *tr. fr. Greek by* Lord Neaves. OnPM
(Baucis.) AWP, *tr. by* Richard Garnett
Erith. *Unknown. See* Village of Erith, The.
Erl-King, The. Goethe, *tr. fr. German by* Sir Walter Scott. AWP; JAWP; MaC; OTPC (1946 ed.); WBP
(Elf-King, The, *tr. unknown.*) PoPo
Erlington. *Unknown.* BuBa; ESPB (A *and* B *vers.*); OBB
Ermine or blazonry, he knew them not. Andrew. Thomas William Parsons. AA
Ernest Dowson. John Hall Wheelock. HBMV
Ernest Maltravers, *sel.* Sir Edward Bulwer-Lytton.
When Stars Are in the Quiet Skies. VA
(Night and Love.) HBV
Ernest was an elephant, a great big fellow. The Four Friends. A. A. Milne. GoTP; TiPo (1959 ed.)
Eroded beach on the bay, an empty scene. Unnatural, Unusual and Unfair. James Schevill. FiMAP
Epws (Eros). Robert Bridges. CMoP; ExPo; ILP; LiTB; LO; NBM; PoEL-5; PoIE; QFR; SeCeV
Eros. Emerson. AnNE; FaBoBe; HBV
Eros. Coventry Patmore. GTSE
Eros. Swinburne. MaVP
Eros and Psyche, *sel.* Lucius Apuleius, *tr. fr. Latin by* Robert Bridges.
"His skin is brilliant with the nimble flood." LO
Eros, from rest in isles far-famed. Eros. Swinburne. MaVP
Eros, pray discard your bow. Plea to Eros. *Unknown.* UnTE
Eros Turannos. E. A. Robinson. AmLP; AnAmPo; AnFE; AnNE; AP; APA; BWP; CMoP; CoAnAm; CoBA; CoBMV; CrMA; ForPo; ILP; LiTA; LiTM (rev. ed.); MAmP; MAP; MAPA; MaPo (1969 ed.); MoAB; MoAmPo; MoPo; MoVe; NePA; NoP; NP; OxBA; PIA; PoE; PoFS; PoIE; QFR; TDP; TwAmPo
Eros under his bluish dark lashes again. Autumn Love. Ibycus. LiTW
Erosion. E. J. Pratt. CaP; CoBE; OnPM; TwCaPo
Erotica Antiqua, *sel.* L. A. MacKay.
Propertian. PeCV
Erotion. Martial, *tr. fr. Latin by* Kirby Flower Smith. AWP; JAWP; WBP; OnPM, *tr. by* Leigh Hunt
(Epitaph on Erotion, *tr. by* Leigh Hunt.) OBRV
Erotion. Swinburne. PoEL-5
Errand Imperious, The. Edwin Markham. PAL; PGD
Errantry. Robert Fitzgerald. NYBP
Erring in Company. Franklin P. Adams. BOHV; TOP
Erris Coast, 1943. Hugh Connell. NeIP
Error Pursued. H. A. Pinkerton. NePoAm; QFR
Errors of Ecstasie, *sel.* George Darley.
"Ecstasie, rash production of the thoughts." OnYI
Ersatz. Raymond Souster. PeCV
Erstwhile sinner knocked at Heaven's gate, An. The Countersign. Charles J. Quirk. CAW
Erthe oute of erthe is wonderly wroghte. Earth out of Earth. *Unknown.* MeEL
Erubescent flax curls crisp and dry, The. Smoking Flax. Mary Josephine Benson. CaP
Erudite, solemn/ The pious bird. Rev Owl. A. M. Klein. TrJP
Es fällt ein Stern herunter. Heine, *tr. fr. German by* Richard Garnett. AWP; JAWP
Es stehen unbeweglich. Heine, *tr. fr. German by* James Thomson. AWP; JAWP; WBP
Escalade. Arthur Symons. UnTE
Escapade, The. David Ignatow. PP
Escapade. Kenneth Leslie. EtS
Escape, An. Abu Nuwas, *tr. fr. Arabic by* E. Powys Mathers. ErPo
Escape, The. Emily Rose Burt. GFA
Escape. Emily Dickinson. *See* I never hear the word "escape."
Escape. Robert Graves. BrPo; ILP; MoBrPo
Escape. Daniel Whitehead Hicky. JKCP (1955 ed.)
Escape. Leonard Mann. NeLNL
Escape, The. Edwin Muir. WaP
Escape. *Unknown.* MaRV
Escape, The. Mark Van Doren. MAP; MoAmPo
Escape. Elinor Wylie. AnFE; APA; CoAnAm; GBV (1952 ed.); LiTA; MAP; MoAmPo; PFY; RePo; ThWaDe
Escape and Return. Elizabeth Jennings. NePoEA
Escape at Bedtime. Robert Louis Stevenson. BrR; GoTP; HBVY; OTPC; PCH; PoRh; PoVP; RG; TiPo; TreFS; TrGrPo; TSW
Escape from Cyclop, The. Homer, *tr. fr. Greek by* George Chapman. *Fr.* The Odyssey, IX. LiTW
Escape Me?—Never. Robert Browning. *See* Life in a Love.
Escaping from the enemy's hand. The Escape. Edwin Muir. WaP
Eschatology. Morris Bishop. WhC
Eskimo Baby, An. Lucy Diamond. BoTP
Eskimo baby, all dressed up in fur, An. Queer Habits. Corneille McCarn. GFA
Eskimo Chant: "There is joy in/ Feeling the warmth." *Unknown, tr. fr. Eskimo by* Knud Rasmussen. WHW
Eskimo, explorers state, The. The Immoral Arctic. Morris Bishop. FiBHP; WhC
Eskimo Song: "There is fear in/ Turning the mind away." *Unknown, tr. fr. Cooper Eskimo song by* W. E. Calvert. PeCV
Eskimo String-Figure Chant. *Tr. fr. Eskimo song by* E. Hope Kerr. TwCaPo
Eskimoes Again. Dick Gallup. ANYP
Esmeralda! Now we rest. Lines Written in Oregon. Vladimir Nabokov. NYBP
Especially When the October Wind. Dylan Thomas. BoPe; CABA; ChMP; DiPo; LiTB; MaPo; MoAB; MoBrPo (1950 ed.); OAEP (2d ed.); ToPo
(Poem: "Especially when the October wind.") NeBP
Essay in Defense of the Movies. Walker Gibson. NePoAm
Essay on Criticism, An. Pope. ATP; BEL; CABA; CEP; CoBE, Pts. I-II; EiCL; EiPP; EnLi-1; EnLit, Pts. I-II; MBW-1; OAEP, *abr.;* OuHeWo, Pts. I-II; PoEL-3; TOP, *abr.*
Sels.
"But most by numbers judge a poet's song," *fr.* Pt. II. AnFE; InP; PP
(Poetical Numbers.) OBEC; SeCePo
"But you who seek to give and merit fame," *fr.* Pt. I. EnL
"First follow Nature, and your judgment frame," *fr.* Pt. I. PIA; PP; YAT
(Nature and Art.) TreFT

Essay (continued)
"If wit so much from ign'rance undergo," *fr.* Pt. II. YAT
Little Learning, A, *fr.* Pt. II. ChTr; LiTB; LiTG; OBEC; PoLF; SeCePo
(Alps on Alps.) FaFP; GTBS-W
("Little learning is a dangerous thing, A.") HoPM; PG (1955 ed.); TreF; TrGrPo
"Of all the causes which conspire to blind," *fr.* Pt. II. EnL; FaBoEn; ILP; PoIE
(Pride, the Never-Failing Vice of Fools.) TreFT
"Pride, where wit fails, steps in to our defence," *fr.* Pt. II. YAT
"Regard not then if wit be old or new," *fr.* Pt. II. YAT
"Some to conceit alone their taste confine," *fr.* Pt. II. YAT
Sound and Sense ("True ease in writing comes from art, not chance," 14 *ll.*), *fr.* Pt. II. UnPo
(Craft of Verse, The, 12 *ll.*) BoLiVe
("True ease in writing comes from art, not chance.") ExPo, 12 *ll.*; TrGrPo, 22 *ll.*
"Sound must seem an echo to the sense, The," *fr.* Pt. II. PoPo
"Those rules of old discover'd, not devis'd," *fr.* Pt. I. PoFS
"'Tis hard to say, if greater want of skill," *fr.* Pt. I. FaBoEn; FiP, *abr.*; PP; WHA
"'Tis with our judgements as our watches," *fr.* Pt. I. ViBoPo
"True wit is Nature to advantage dress'd," *fr.* Pt. II. ShBV-3
Essay on Deity. Elder Olson. MoRP; NP
Essay on Lunch. Walker Gibson. NYBP
Essay on Man, An. Pope. CEP; EiCL; EiPP; MBW-1; PoEL-3, Epistles I-II
Sels.
"All are but parts of one stupendous whole," *fr.* Epistle I. WGRP
"Awake, my St. John! leave all meaner things," Epistle I. BEL; EnL; EnLi-1; NoP; OAEP; PAn; PoEL-3; TOP
"Far as creation's ample range extends," *fr.* Epistles I *and* II. ImOP
(Great Chain of Being, The.) ExPo
"For forms of government let fools contest," *fr.* Epistle III. ViBoPo
(Charity.) OBEC
"For modes of faith, let graceless zealots fight," *fr.* Epistle III. BoPe
(Faith.) WGRP
"Force first made conquest, and that conquest, law," *fr.* Epistle III. PoFr
"Heav'n from all creatures hides the book of fate," *fr.* Epistle I. ViBoPo
(Hope Springs Eternal.) OBEC
Henry St. John, Viscount Bolingbroke, *fr.* Epistle IV. OBEC
Honest Man, An, 2 *ll.*, *fr.* Epistle IV. TreF
"Honour and shame from no condition rise," *fr.* Epistle IV. PoFr; TrGrPo
(Man.) BoLiVe
(Worth Makes the Man.) MaRV
"Hope humbly then; with trembling pinions soar," *fr.* Epistle I. TrGrPo
"Hope springs eternal in the human breast," *fr.* Epistle I.
(Hope.) MaRV, 2 *ll.*; TreF, 4 *ll.*
(Pleasure of Hope, The, 4 *ll.*) ACP
"Know then thyself, presume not God to scan," Epistle II. AnFE, *fr.* II *and* IV; CaFP; DiPo; EnLi-1 (1949 ed.); EnLit; GoTL; LiTB; LiTG, *fr.* II and IV; MaPo; MaRV; MemP; OBEC; PAn; PG (1955 ed.); PoEL-3; PoIE; PoSa; SeCePo; SoP; TOP, *abr.*; TrGrPo; TRV; ViBoPo; YAT
(Lines from "An Essay on Man.") GoBC
(Man.) BoLiVe
(Paragon of Animals, The.) ACP
(Proper Study of Man, The.) TreFS
(Proper Study of Mankind, The.) FiP
(Riddle of the World.) GTBS-W
Life's Poor Play, *fr.* Epistle II. OBEC; SeCePo
("See! some strange comfort ev'ry state attend.") YAT
"Lo, the poor Indian! whose untutored mind," *fr.* Epistle I. PoIE; TreFS
'Oh Happiness! our being's end and aim," Epistle IV. ATP
O Sons of Earth, *fr.* Epistle IV. TreFT
"See some strange comfort ev'ry state attend," *fr.* Epistle II. YAT
Vice, *fr.* Epistle II. ELU; PoPl
"Whate'er the passion—knowledge, fame, or pelf," *fr.* Epistle II. TrGrPo
(Human Folly.) FiP
(Man.) BoLiVe
Whatever Is, Is Right, *fr.* Epistle I. OBEC
"What's Fame! a fancied life in other's breath," *fr.* Epistle IV. ViBoPo
"Who sees with equal eye, as God of all," *fr.* Epistle I. FaBoEn
Essay on Man. *Unknown.* PoToHe (new ed.)
Essay on Memory. Robert D. Fitzgerald. BoAV; MoAuPo
Essay on Rime, *sels.* Karl Shapiro. PP
"But poets are name-proud craftsmen; Greeks and Jews."
"There is a general idiom to all rime."
Essay on Satyr, An, *sel.* John Sheffield, Duke of Buckingham and Normanby.
Characters of the Wits, The. PeRV
Essay on Solitude. Abraham Cowley. *See* Of Solitude.
Essay on the Fine Arts, *sel.* John Trumbull.
Future of American Literature, The. AmPP (3d ed.)
Essay on the Fleet Riding in the Downes, An. "J. D." CoMu
Essay on the Genius of Pope, An, *sel.* Charles Lloyd.
"'Tis not so much, these men more forms survey." OBRV
Essence. Samuel Greenberg. MoPo; NePA
Essence of Existence, The. Chorus. Jack Kerouac. *Fr.* Mexico City Blues. NeAP
Essence of Opera, The. *Unknown, tr. fr. French by* Leigh Hunt. OnPM
Essence of Tomorrow. Alice Hansche Mortenson. SoP
Essential Beauty. Philip Larkin. PoeP
Essential oils are wrung. Emily Dickinson. AnPP (5th ed.); AP; CBEP; NoP
Essentials. Samuel Greenberg. LiTA
Essex Regiment March. George Edward Woodberry. PAH
Está Muy Caliente. George Bowering. MoCV
Estat ai en greu cossirier. Beatriz de Dia, *tr. fr. Provençal by* Paul Blackburn. ErPo
Estate, The, *sel.* Charles Brasch.
Waking by Night. AnNZ
Estella, Estella, they're cooking up Paella. Song in Praise of Paella. C. W. V. Wordsworth. FiBHP
Estevan, Saskatchewan. E. W. Mandel. PeCV
Esther. Wilfrid Scawen Blunt. *See* Esther; a Young Man's Tragedy.
Esther. Fray Angelico Chavez. GoBC
Esther; a Young Man's Tragedy, *sels.* Wilfrid Scawen Blunt.
"He who has once been happy is for aye," XL [L]. OBMV; OBNC; TrGrPo; ViBoPo
(With Esther.) OBEV; OBVV
"I will not tell the secrets of that place," XLIX. Sonn
"When I hear laughter from a tavern door," XLVI [LI]. MoBrPo (1942 ed.); NBM; OBMV; TrGrPo; ViBoPo
(With Esther.) OBEV; OBVV
"Yes, who shall tell the value of our tears," II. Sonn
Esther's Tomcat. Ted Hughes. POTi
Esthete in Harlem. Langston Hughes. BANP
Esthetic of Imitation, An. Donald Finkel. NePoEA
Esthétique du Mal. Wallace Stevens. LiTM (rev. ed.); PoDB
Sels.
"He was at Naples writing letters home." CMoP
"How red the rose that is the soldier's wound." CMoP; FaBoMo; WaP
"Life is a bitter aspic. We are not." CMoP
Esthonian Bridal Song. Johann Gottfried von Herder, *tr. fr. German by* W. Taylor. AWP; JAWP; WBP
Estranged. Walter de la Mare. FaBoEn
Estranged from beauty—none can be. Emily Dickinson. MWA-2
Estrangement. John Peter. BoSA
Estrangement. Sir William Watson. MoBrPo (1942 ed.)
Estuary. William Montgomerie. OxBS
Estuary, The. Ruth Pitter. MoVE
Estuary, The. Allen Upward. *Fr.* Scented Leaves from a Chinese Jar. NP
Estuary. Ted Walker. NYBP
Estuary is wide, The. Off Saguenay. A. G. Bailey. ACV
Esyllt. Glyn Jones. DTC
Et Cetera. Earl of Rochester. UnTE
Et Cetera. Dee Walker. GoYe
Et Dona Ferentes. Kipling. NoP
Et Mori Lucrum. John Lancaster Spalding. *Fr.* God and the Soul. AA
Et Quid Amabo Nisi Quod Aenigma Est. Stephen Sandy. NYBP

Et Sa Pauvre Chair. Alec Brock Stevenson. HBMV
Etc. Etc. Etc. Dorothy C. Parrish. TNV
Etching, An. Sister Mary Imelda. CAW
Eternal. Agnes Foley Macdonald. CaP
Eternal, The. Esaias Tegnér, *tr. fr. Swedish by* Charles Wharton Stork. LiTW
Eternal Christmas. Elizabeth Stuart Phelps Ward. ChIP; MaRV; PGD; TRV
Eternal Contour. Florida Watts Smyth. GoYe
Eternal Father, mighty God. Hawaiian National Hymn. Lilia K. Dominis. SoP
Eternal Father, Strong to Save. William Whiting. MaRV; TreFS
(For Those in Peril.) SoP
(Hymn.) NBM
Eternal Father, who hast given. God Bless Our Home. Robert Freeman. MaRV; SoP
Eternal Female groaned, The! It was heard over all the Earth. A Song of Liberty. Blake. EiPP; EnLi-2; EnRP
Eternal Founder of the sky. Hymn. James J. Donohue. JKCP (1955 ed.)
Eternal God! Maker of all. The Book. Henry Vaughan. EnL; SCEP-1; SeCV-1
Eternal God! Oh! Beatific Vision! *Unknown. Fr.* Everyman. CAW
Eternal God! O Thou that only art. Francis Quarles. *Fr.* Like to the Arctic Needle. MaRV
Eternal God omnipotent! The One. Invocation. Caelius Sedulius. *Fr.* Carmen Paschale [*or* Easter Song]. OnYI
Eternal God, our life is but. A Prayer. "Yehoash." TrJP
Eternal God, Whose Power Upholds. Henry Hallam Tweedy. MaRV
Eternal God Whose Searching Eye Doth Scan. Edwin McNeill Poteat. MaRV; TrPWD
Eternal Good ("Eternal Good which overlies"). Whittier. *Fr.* Eventide. OQP
Eternal Goodness, The ("O friends! with whom my feet have trod"). Whittier. AA; AmePo; AmPP (3d ed.); AnAmPo; AnFE; AnNE; APA; CoAnAm; CoBA; MaRV; OHFP; WGRP
Sels.
"And Thou, O Lord! by whom are seen." TrPWD
"I bow my forehead to the dust." OQP; SoP
"I know not what the future hath." BLRP, *abr.*; OQP; TreF
"I see the wrong that round me lies." SoP; TRV
Eternal Hope. *Unknown.* MaRV
Eternal Image, The. Ruth Pitter. MoBrPo
Eternal Jew, The. Jacob Cohen, *tr. fr. Hebrew by* I. M. Lask. TrJP
Eternal Justice, The. Anne Reeve Aldrich. AA
Eternal Kinship, The. Maurice E. Peloubet. GoYe
Eternal Life. Henry More. TRV
Eternal life God's Word proclaims. O Blessed Word. *Unknown.* SoP
Eternal life! What life is this, I pray? I Give unto Them Eternal Life. Edward Taylor. *Fr.* Preparatory Meditations, Second Series. MWA-1
Eternal Light! Thomas Binney. MaRV; WGRP
Eternal Light, The. William C. Fisher. SoP
Eternal Lord! Eased of a Cumbrous Load. Michelangelo, *tr. fr. Italian by* Wordsworth. TrPWD
Eternal Masculine. William Rose Benét. AWP; InPo; MAP; MoAmPo
Eternal Moment. "Katherine Hale." CaP
Eternal [*or* Eternall] Mover, whose diffused glory. Eternall Mover [*or* "D. O. M."]. Sir Henry Wotton. OxBoCh; TrPWD
Eternal Poem, An. Samuel Taylor Coleridge. BOHV
Eternal Power, of earth and air! The Doubter's Prayer. Anne Brontë. MaRV; TrPWD; WGRP
Eternal Quest, The. Job, XI: 7-8, Bible, *O.T.* (*Moulton, Modern Reader's Bible*). MaRV
(Job's Comforters.) WGRP
Eternal Question, The. D. B. Van Buren. CIV
Eternal Return, The. Robert Hillyer. NYBP
Eternal Reward, Eternal Pain. Sir Thomas More. *Fr.* The Twelve Weapons of Spiritual Battle. CoBE; EnRePo
Eternal Road, The, *sel.* Franz Werfel, *tr. fr. German by* Ludwig Lewisohn.
Ye Sorrowers. TrJP
Eternal Ruler of the ceaseless round. Hymn [*or* The Kingdom of God on Earth]. John W. Chadwick. SoP; TrPWD
Eternal Sabbath. Isaac Leibush Peretz, *tr. fr. Yiddish by* Joseph Leftwich. TrJP
Eternal Search, The. Sir William Watson. PoVP
Eternal Self, The. *Unknown, tr. fr. Sanskrit by* Charles Johnston. *Fr.* The Bhagavad-Gita. WoL
Eternal spirit/ of dead dried. Black Lotus. Alicia Ley Johnson. NBP
Eternal Spirit, Evermore Creating. Henry B. Robins. MaRV
Eternal Spirit of the chainless Mind! Sonnet on Chillon [*or* On the Castle of Chillon]. Byron. The Prisoner of Chillon, *introd. sonnet.* AnEnPo; ATP; BEL; BeLS; BoLiVe; CABL; EnLi-2; EnLit; EnRP; EPN; ExPo; FiP; GTBS; GTBS-D; GTBS-P; GTBS-W; GTSE; GTSL; HBV; ILP; InP; LiTB; LoBV; MaRV; MBW-2; MCCG; MERP; OAEP; OBRV; PoFr; PoFS; PoPl; PoPo; SeCeV; Sonn; TOP; TreFS; TrGrPo; YAT
Eternal Spirit, you/ Whose will maintains the world. A Prayer for My Son. Yvor Winters. CrMA; TrPWD
Eternal Spring, The. Milton. *See* Adam and Eve ("The birds their choir apply . . .").
Eternal time, that wastest without waste. To Time. "A. W." ElL; TuPP
Eternal [*or* Eternall] Truth, almighty, infinite. Caelica XCVII [XCVIII]. Fulke Greville. EnRePo; OBS; OxBoCh; SiCE
Eternal Values. Grace Noll Crowell. *See* Let Us Keep Christmas.
Eternal virgin, goddess true. To Astraea. Sir John Davies. *Fr.* Hymns of Astraea. SiCE
Eternal Way, The. Richard Le Gallienne. InP
Eternal Word, The. Longfellow. ChIP
Eternal word proceeding from. Verbum Supernum. *At. to* St. Ambrose. CAW
Eternall and all-working God, which wast. Michael Drayton. *Fr.* Noah's Floud. PoEL-2
Eternall God, (for whom who ever dare). Upon the Translation of the Psalmes by Sir Philip Sydney. John Donne. MaMe
Eternall Mover. Sir Henry Wotton. TrPWD, *abr.*
("D. O. M.") OxBoCh
Eternities. Norman Mailer. NYBP
Eternity ("He who bends [*or* binds] to himself a joy") Blake. AnFE; AWP; DiPo; ERoP-1; HW; InPo; LoBV; MemP; OBNC; PoG; PoIE; SoP; TrGrPo
(He Who Bends to Himself.) ShBV-4
(Great Things.) CBV; PV
("He who binds to himself a joy.") EG; LO
(Liberty.) BoLiVe
(Unquestioning.) OQP
Eternity. Emily Dickinson. *See* On this wondrous sea.
Eternity. Robert Herrick. SeCL WHA
Eternity. Sir Thomas More. EnRePO
Eternity. *Unknown.* SoP
Eternity. Henry Vaughan. *See* World, The.
Eternity encountered on the stair. Chez Madame. Sam Harrison. NeIP
Eternity is like unto a ring. Time and Eternity. Bunyan. WiR
Eternity of Love Protested. Thomas Carew. ATP; MeLP; OBS
("How ill doth he deserve a lover's name.") EG
(Song: Eternity [*or* Eternitie] of Love Protested.) SCEP-2; SeEP
Eternity of Nature. John Clare. StP
Eternity, when I think thee. Quoniam Ego in Flagella Paratus Sum. William Habington. ACP
Eternity's Low Voice. Mark Van Doren. EaLo
Ethelstan, *sel.* George Darley.
O'er the Wild Gannet's Bath. ChTr; PoEL-4
Ethereal minstrel! pilgrim of the sky! To a [*or the*] *Skylark.* Wordsworth. BEL; BoLiVe; EnLi-2; EnLit; EnRP; EPN; FaFP; GTBS; GTBS-D; GTBS-P; GTBS-W; GTSE; GTSL; HBV; HBVY; MERP; OAEP; PoIE (1970 ed.); PTK; TrGrPo
Ethics put it well, The. The Magnanimous. Ellen de Young Kay. NePoEA
Ethinthus, Queen of Waters. Blake. *Fr.* Europe. ChTr
Ethiopia Saluting the Colours [*or* Colors]. Walt Whitman. AmP; GTBS-D; PAH; PoNe
Ethnic Anthem, The ("Ethnasia will last a thousand years"). Anthony Delius. *Fr.* The Great Divide. BoSA
Ethnogenesis. Henry Timrod. AmPP (4th ed.); MAmP

Etiolated flame is now abroad. Summer Lightning. Horatio Colony. TwAmPo
Etiquette. W. S. Gilbert. BOHV; CenHV; EnLi-2; FaBoCh; FiBHP; MaC
Eton Boating Song. William Johnson Cory. ELP
'Ετώσιον ἄχθος ἀρούρης. Robert Bridges. FaBoTw; QFR
Etrick Forest is a fair forest. *See* Ettrick Forest is . . .
Etruscan Ring, An. John William Mackail. VA
Etruscan Tombs. Agnes Mary Frances Robinson. PeVV; WHA
Etruscan Warrior's Head. Helen Rowe Henze. GoYe
Etsi Omnes, Ego Non. Ernest Myers. VA
Etta Moten's Attic. Margaret Danner. Far from Africa: Four Poems, 4. AmNP
Ettrick [*or* Etrick] Forest is a fair foreste. The Outlaw Murray. *Unknown.* ESPB; OBB; OxBB
Étude Géographique. Stoddard King. AmFN; IHA; WhC
Etude Réaliste. Swinburne. GN; HBV; OuHeWo; PoVP; VA
Sels.
Baby's Eyes, A, III. TSW
Baby's Feet, A, I. FaPON; InP; TSW
Eucharist. E. Merrill Root. ChIP; OQP
Euclid. Vachel Lindsay. ImOP; NAMP; PoPo; TwAmPo; YaD
(Four Moon Poems) TSW
(Poems about the Moon.) MAPA
Euclid Alone Has Looked on Beauty. Edna St. Vincent Millay. AmPP; ATP; CMoP; HBMV; ImOP; InP; InPo; LiTG; MAP; MoAB; MoAmPo; MoVE; Sonn
(Euclid Alone.) FaBV; FaFP; MemP
(Sonnet: "Euclid alone has looked on beauty bare.") AWP; JAWP; NP; WBP
Euclid devised the trap. The Sextant. A. M. Sullivan. GoBC
Eugenia, *sel.* George Chapman.
Presage of Storme. FaBoEn
Eugenia, young and fair and sweet. Old Tityrus to Eugenia. Charles Cotton. ViBoPo
Eugenio Pacelli. Francis Neilson. GoYe
Eugenius, thy son, who guards the Rock. Dedication. Pope Eugenius III. ISi
Eulalie. Poe. EvOK; LaNeLa; Par
Eternities—now numbering six or seven. Saint Peter Relates an Incident of the Resurrection Day. James Weldon Johnson. Kal
Eulogium on Rum. Joseph Smith. LHV
Eulogy. Carolyn M. Rodgers. WSL
Eulogy for Hasdai ibn Shaprut. *Unknown, tr. fr. Hebrew by* Israel Abrahams. TrJP
Eulogy for Populations. Ron Welburn. BF
Eulogy of My House. Siegfried Sassoon. MoPW
Eulogy of the Vain Hours. Sotère Torregian. YAP
Eumares. Asclepiades, *tr. fr. Greek by* Richard Garnett. AWP; JAWP; WBP
Eumenides, *sel.* Aeschylus, *tr. fr. Greek.*
Chorus of the Furies ("Look, sisters, look!"), *tr. by* John Stuart Blackie. WoL
Eunice. John Betjeman. CMoP
Eunice in the Evening. Gwendolyn Brooks. TiPo (1959 ed.)
Euphrosyne. Matthew Arnold. MBW-2; VP
Eurasian Girl. Anthony Kerrigan. NYTB
Eureka! Alfred Denis Godley. CenHV
Euripides Alexopoulos. Edgar Lee Masters. *Fr.* New Spoon River Anthology. CMoP
Euroclydon. Abbie Huston Evans. NePoAm
Europa. William Johnson Cory. NBM
Europa. William Plomer. MoBS
Europa,/ your red-haired. For the West. Gary Snyder. NaP
Europa. Stephen Henry Thayer. AA
Europe. John Ashbery. CoPo
Europe, *sel.* Blake.
Ethinthus, Queen of Waters. ChTr
Europe, *sels.* Louis Dudek.
"Commotion of these waves, however strong, cannot disturb, The," XIX. OBCV
"Ignorant present has scribbled over the past, The," XXXI. PeCV
"Sea retains such images, The," XCV. OBCV; PeCV
Europe and America. David Ignatow. AmFN
Europe lies in ruins: a black headline story. Nineteen-hundred Forty-five (1945). Sheila Cussons. PeSA
European Shoe, The. Michael Benedikt. TwCP; YAP
Eurydice. Margaret Allonby. BoSA
Eurydice. Francis William Bourdillon. HBV; VA
Eurydice, The—it concerned thee, O Lord. The Loss of the *Eurydice.* Gerard Manley Hopkins. VP
Eurydice to Orpheus. Robert Browning. EPN
(Orpheus and Eurydice.) CTC
Eurymachus's Fancy. Robert Greene. *Fr.* Francesco's Fortunes. OBSC
Eurynome. Jay Macpherson. NMP; OBCV; PV
Eurystheus, trembling, called me to the throne. Heracles. Yvor Winters. QFR; TwAmPo
Eutaw Springs. Philip Freneau. *See* To the Memory of the Brave Americans.
Euterpe. Thomas Bailey Aldrich. Sonn
Euterpe; a Symmetric. David McCord. *Fr.* New Chitons for Old Gods. UnS
Euthymiae Raptus; or, The Teares of Peace, *sels.* George Chapman.
"And, now gives time, her states description." PoEL-2
(Learning.) SeCePo
"Thus, by the way, to human loves interring." LoBV
Eutopia. Francis Turner Palgrave. OBVV;TOP
Eutychides. E. A. Robinson, *after* Lucilius. UnS
Eutychides is dead, and what is worse. A Dead Song-Writer. Lucilius, *tr. fr. Greek by* Humbert Wolfe. WoL
Eutychides, who wrote the songs. Eutychides. E. A. Robinson, *after* Lucilius. Variations of Greek Themes, IV. UnS
Evacuation of New York by the British. *Unknown.* PAH
Evadne. Hilda Doolittle ("H. D."). MAPA
Evaluation. Elinor Lennen. OQP
Evanescence. Frederic William Henry Myers. *See* I Saw, I Saw the Lovely Child.
Evanescence. Harriet Prescott Spofford. AA
Evanescent Love. Eugene Redmond. TNV
Evangel. Jean Burden. NYTB
Evangelical vicar in want. Limerick. Ronald Arbuthnott Knox. CenHV; LiBL
Evangeline. Longfellow. AnNE; BeLS
Sels.
Church Scene, The, *fr.* Pt. I. TreF
Embarkation, The, *fr.* Pt. I. PAH
Evangeline in Acadie ("Somewhat apart from the village"), *fr.* Pt.I. AA
Finding of Gabriel, The, *fr.* Pt II. AA
"In the Acadian land, on the shores of the Basin of Minas," *fr.* Pt. I. CoBA
Lakes of the Atchafalaya, The, *fr. Pt. II. PoEL-5*
On the Atchafalaya, abr., fr. Pt. II. AA
"Talk not of wasted affection! affection never was wasted." *fr.* Pt. II. PoToHe (new ed.)
"They were approaching the region where reigns perpetual summer," *fr.* Pt. II. FaBoEn
"This is the forest primeval," Prologue. AmPP (3d ed.), *with* Pt. I; CoBA; InP; OTD
(In the Forest.) PCD
(Prelude.) MWA-1; TreF
(Primeval Forest, *abr.*) WBLP
Evangeline. Norma E. Smith. CaP
Evangelist, The. Donald Davie. NePoEA
Evangelist. Dave Etter. ThO
Evangelize! Henry Croker. BLRP; SoP
Evanthe's niplets are like lard. Niplets. *Unknown.* ErPo
Evarra and His Gods. Kipling. MoBrPo
Eva's Lament, *sel. Unknown.*
"Alas! that ever [*or* evyr] that speche was spoken [*or* spokyn]." AtBAP; EnLoPo
Evasion, An. Douglas Livingstone. PeSA
Evasion. Blanaid Salkeld. NeIP
Eve. David Gascoyne. GTBS-P
Eve. Oliver Herford. HBMV; YaD
Eve. Ralph Hodgson. AnEnPo; AnFE; BoLiVe; BrPo; CH; EnLi-2 (1949 ed.); EPN; EvOK; FaBoTw; GBV (1952 ed.); GTBS-D; HBV; HoPM; InP; LiTB; LiTM; MoAB; MoBrPo; NeMA; NP; OnMSP; OtMeF; SeCeV; TrGrPo; WePo
Eve. Milton. *Fr.* Paradise Lost, IX. OBS
Eve. Rainer Maria Rilke, *tr. fr. German by* M. D. Herter Norton. MoRP
Eve, *sel.* Charles Péguy, *tr. fr. French.*

Happy Are Those Who Have Died, *tr. by* Jessie Degen and Richard Eberhart. WaaP
Eve. Christina Rossetti. CH; GTBS-P; NBM; OxBoCh; PoEL-5; SeCeV
Animals Mourn with Eve, The, *sel.* OA
Eve. Robert L. Wolf. HBMV
Eve in Reflection. Jay Macpherson. OBCV
Eve of Agincourt, The. Shakespeare. *See* Now Entertain Conjecture of a Time.
Eve of Bunker Hill, The. Clinton Scollard. MC; PAH
(On the Eve of Bunker Hill.) DD; PEDC; PoRL
Eve of Crécy, The. William Morris. EnLi-2 (1939 ed.); OBVV; PAn; PoVP; SiSW; ViPo; ViPP
Eve of Election, *sel.* Whittier.
Indian Summer. PCH
Eve of Revolution, The, *sel.* Swinburne.
"O soul, O God, O glory of liberty." PoFr
Eve of St. Agnes, The. Keats. AtBAP; ATP; BEL; BeLS; BoLiVe; CABA; CABL; CaFP; ChER; CoBE; DiPo; DTo; EnL; EnLi-2; EnLit; EnRP; EPN; ERoP-2; ExPo; FiP, *abr.*; FosPo; GoTL; HoPM; ILP; LiTL; MasP; MBW-2; MERP; MyFE; NoP; OAEP; OBNC; OBRV; OnSP; PAn; PoAn; PoE; PoEL-4; PoIE; PoLF; SeCeV; ShBV-4; StP; TOP; TreF; TrGrPo; UnPo (1st ed.); WHA
Sels.
"Out went the taper as she hurried in." ViBoPo
"Stol'n to this paradise, and so entranced." LO
Eve of Saint John, The. Sir Walter Scott. EnRP; EPN; PoEL-4
Eve of Saint Mark, The. Keats. CH; EnRP; ERoP-2; MERP; OBRV
Eve of [the Battle of] Waterloo, The. Byron. *See* Waterloo ("There was a sound . . .").
Eve Penitent. Milton. *Fr.* Paradise Lost, X. OBS
Eve, smiling, pluck'd the apple, then. The Apple. Lady Margaret Sackville. OBVV
Eve-Song. Mary Gilmore. MoAuPo; PoAu-1
Eve to Adam ("With thee conversing, I forget all time"). Milton. *Fr.* Paradise Lost, IV. FaBoEn; TreFS; TrGrPo
(Eve Speaks to Adam.) ChTr
Eve, with her basket, was. Eve. Ralph Hodgson. AnEnPo; AnFE; BoLiVe; BrPo; CH; EnLi-2 (1949 ed.); EPN; EvOK; FaBoTw; GBV (1952 ed.); GTBS-D; HBV; HoPM; InP; LiTB; LiTM; MoAB; MoBrPo; NeMA; NP; OnMSP; OtMeF; SeCeV; TrGrPo; WePo
Evelyn. Rossiter Johnson. AA
Evelyn Hope. Robert Browning. BoLiVe; HBV; MaPo; MBW-2; OuHeWo; PoVP; TrGrPo; VA; ViPo
Evelyn Ray. Amy Lowell. MAP; MoAmPo
Even along the railway platform it was spring. We'll All Feel Gay. Winfield Townley Scott. MiAP
Even as a child, of sorrow that we give. Pride of Youth. Dante Gabriel Rossetti. The House of Life, XXIV. FaBoEn; MaVP; OBNC; PoVP; ViPo; ViPP; VP
Even as a lover, dreaming, unaware. Frederick Goddard Tuckerman. *Fr.* Sonnets. AP
Even as a man whose optics are diseased. Corporeal and Mental Vision. Thomas Wade. ERoP-2
Even as a nurse, whose child's imperfect pace. Divine Care. Francis Quarles. MaRV
Even as a young man/ I was out of tune with ordinary pleasures. Once More Fields and Gardens. Tao Yuan-ming. AWP
Even as children they were late sleepers. The Undead. Richard Wilbur. CoAP
Even as gently from the slime we drew him. Antinous. Quentin Stevenson. POTE (1959 ed.)
Even as I wandered the tropic jungle of fever. Shub-Ad. Robert H. Barlow. FiSC
Even as lame things thirst their perfection, so. To Mr. E. G. John Donne. MaMe
Even as love grows more, I write the less. Sonnets, XVI. Robert Hillyer. HBMV
Even as my hand my pen on paper lays. To His Lady, Who Had Vowed Virginity. Walter Davison. OBSC
Even as tender parents lovingly. The Child in the Street. John James Piatt. AA
Even as the Bird. E. Merrill Root. ChIP
Even as the day when it is yet at dawning. Canzone; Of His Love. Prinzivalle Doria. AWP
Even as the moon grows queenlier in mid-space. Gracious Moonlight. Dante Gabriel Rossetti. The House of Life, XX. MaVP; PoVP; ViPo; VP
Even as the needle, that directs the hour. Dependence on God. Francis Quarles. MaRV
Even as the Others Mock. Dante, *tr. fr. Italian by* Dante Gabriel Rossetti. La Vita Nuova, VII. LiTW
("Even as the others mock, thou mockest me.") AWP
Even as the raven, the crowe, and greedie kite. Donec Eris Felix Multos Numerabis Amicos. *Unknown.* EnPo
Even as the seed of the marigold. The Marigold. Allen Upward. *Fr.* Scented Leaves from a Chinese Jar. NP
Even as the shadows of the statues lengthen. Mrs. Southern's Enemy. Sir Osbert Sitwell. ViBoPo
Even as the sun with purple-colour'd face. Venus and Adonis. Shakespeare. BeLS
Even at their fairest still I love the less. A Dream of Flowers. Titus Munson Coan. AA
Even before His Majesty. Dansui, *tr. fr. Japanese by* R. H. Blyth. FIW
Even during War. Muriel Rukeyser. *Fr.* Letter to the Front. TrJP
Even for the defeated life goes on. Poland, October. Charles Brasch. *Fr.* Nineteen Thirty-nine. AnNZ
Even from themselves they are a secret. The Close Clan. Mark Van Doren. GoYe
Even, I think, when you're bathing. A Bathing Girl. Johannes V. Jensen. PoPl
Even if wars to come sleep warm and small. That Day. Mark Van Doren. WaP
Even in a palace, life may be led well! Worldly Place. Matthew Arnold. EPN; PoVP
Even in death they prosper; even in the death. Necropolis. Karl Shapiro. MoAB
Even in July it is our winter corner. Frigidaire. A. M. Klein. TwCaPo
Even in the Darkness. Helene Mullins. MoRP
Even in the Moment of Our Earliest Kiss. Edna St. Vincent Millay. ATP
Even in the Palace. Nago Okimaro, *tr. fr. Japanese by* Ishii *and* Obata. OnPM
Even in the time when as yet. The Wanderer. William Carlos Williams. MAPA; TwAmPo
Even in These Dying Leaves. Lon Woodrum. SoP
Even is come; and from the dark park, hark. A Nocturnal Sketch. Thomas Hood. BOHV; FiBHP; NBM; SiTL
Even like Two Little Bank-dividing Brooks. Francis Quarles. *See* My Beloved Is Mine and I am His.
Even my tombstone gives the truth away. A Dead Liar Speaks. Michael Lewis. GoTP
Even now/ Death sends me the flickering of powdery lids. Death Sends Me Flickering of Powdery Lids. Bilhana, *formerly at. to* Chauras. *Fr.* Black Marigolds. OnPM
Even now/ Her mouth carelessly scented as with lotus dust. Her Mouth Carelessly Scented. Bilhana, *formerly at. to* Chauras. *Fr.* Black Marigolds. OnPM
Even now/ I have a need to make up prayers, to speak. I Have a Need. Bilhana, *formerly at. to* Chauras. *Fr.* Black Marigolds. OnPM
Even now/ I have no surety that she is not Mahadevi. I Have No Surety. Bilhana, *formerly at. to* Chauras. *Fr.* Black Marigolds. OnPM
Even now/ I know my princess was happy. I Know My Princess. Bilhana, *formerly at. to* Chauras. *Fr.* Black Marigolds. OnPM
Even now/ I know that I have savoured the hot taste of life. I Know That I Have Savoured. Bilhana, *formerly at. to* Chauras. *Fr.* Black Marigolds. OnPM
Even now/ I love long black eyes that caress like silk. I Love Long Black Eyes. Bilhana, *formerly at. to* Chauras. *Fr.* Black Marigolds. OnPM
Even now/ I mind that I went round with men and women. I Mind That I Went Round with Men and Women. Bilhana, *formerly at. to* Chauras. *Fr.* Black Marigolds. OnPM
Even now/ I mind the coming and talking of wise men from towers. I Mind the Coming. Bilhana, *formerly at. to* Chauras. *Fr.* Black Marigolds. OnPM
Even now/ I mind the time of the falling of blossoms started my dream. I Mind the Time of the Falling of Blossoms. Bilhana, *formerly at. to* Chauras. *Fr.* Black Marigolds. OnPM

Even now/ I see her; far face blond like gold. I See Her. Bilhana, *formerly at. to* Chauras. *Fr.* Black Marigolds. OnPM
Even now/ I see the heavy startled hair of this reed-flute player. I See the Heavy Startled Hair. Bilhana, *formerly at. to* Chauras. *Fr.* Black Marigolds. OnPM
Even now/ I seem to see my prison walls come close. I Seem to See My Prison Walls. Bilhana, *formerly at. to* Chauras. *Fr.* Black Marigolds. OnPM
Even now/ If I see in my soul the citron-breasted fair one. If I See in My Soul. Bilhana, *formerly at. to* Chauras. *Fr.* Black Marigolds. OnPM
Even now/ If my girl with lotus eyes came to me again. If My Girl with Lotus Eyes. Bilhana, *formerly at. to* Chauras. *Fr.* Black Marigolds. OnPM
Even now/ Love is a god and Rati the dark his bride. Love Is a God. Bilhana, *formerly at. to* Chauras. *Fr.* Black Marigolds. OnPM
Even now/ My eyes that hurry to see no more are painting, painting. My Eyes That Hurry to See. Bilhana, *formerly at. to* Chauras. *Fr.* Black Marigolds. OnPM
Even now/ My thought is all of this gold-tinted king's daughter. Black Marigolds. Bilhana, *formerly at. to* Chauras. AWP; ErPo; LiTW
Even now/ She swims back in the crowning hour of love. She Swims Back in the Crowning Hour. Bilhana, *formerly at. to* Chauras. *Fr.* Black Marigolds. OnPM
Even now/ She with young limbs as smooth as flower pollen. She with Young Limbs. Bilhana, *formerly at. to* Chauras. *Fr.* Black Marigolds. OnPM
Even now/ Spread we our nets beyond the farthest rims. Spread We Our Nets. Bilhana, *formerly at. to* Chauras. *Fr.* Black Marigolds. OnPM
Even now/ The pleased intimacy of rough love. The Pleased Intimacy. Bilhana, *formerly at. to* Chauras. *Fr.* Black Marigolds. OnPM
Even now/ The stainless fair appearance of the moon. The Stainless Fair Appearance. Bilhana, *formerly at. to* Chauras. *Fr.* Black Marigolds. OnPM
Even now/ The woodcutter and the fisherman turn home. The Woodcutter and the Fisherman Turn Home. Bilhana, *formerly at. to* Chauras. *Fr.* Black Marigolds. OnPM
Even now/ When all my heavy heart is broken up. When All My Heavy Heart. Bilhana, *formerly at. to* Chauras. *Fr.* Black Marigolds. OnPM
Even now the question has changed. Speech to the Court. Walter Lowenfels. PPON
Even Numbers. Carl Sandburg. OCS
Even on clear nights, lead the most supple children. The Great Bear. John Hollander. LiTM (1970 ed.); NePoEA-2; NYBP; TwCP
"Even on the cross a man will make a prayer." The Dying Thief. J. S. Phillimore. OQP
Even Sea, The. May Swenson. WIRo
Even So. Dante Gabriel Rossetti. OBNC
Even so deep in the jungle they were not safe. The Garden of Ships. Douglas Stewart. PoAu-2
Even so distant, I can taste the grief. Deceptions. Philip Larkin. CABA; CMoP; ErPo; GTBS-P; NePoEA; NMP
"Even so" (the exulting Maiden said). Samuel Taylor Coleridge. *Fr.* The Destiny of Nations. ChER
Even-Song. *See* Evensong.
Even Such Is Man. Henry King. *See* Sic Vita.
Even Such Is Time. Sir Walter Ralegh. *See* Conclusion, The.
Even the beauty of the rose doth cast. Shadow. Walter de la Mare. CMoP
Even the bravest that are slain. The Trial by Existence. Robert Frost. CoBA
Even the dead laughter of the moon is beautiful. Cleansing. Heinrich Suso Waldeck. CAW
Even the morning is formal. The Morning Porches. Donald Hall. NePoAm-2
Even the rainbow has a body. The Rainbow. D. H. Lawrence. FIW
Even the shrewd and bitter. Prologue to "Rhymes to Be Traded for Bread." Vachel Lindsay. LaNeLa
Even the spring water. The Cutting Edge. Philip Levine. NYBP
Even the wild-ducks skimming. Not Alone. Princess Ki. OnPM
Even This Shall Pass Away. Theodore Tilton. BLPA; HBV; MaRV, *abr.*; NeHB; PTK; WGRP
(King's Ring, The.) TreFS
Even though it's raining. Others. Harry Behn. SoPo; TiPo (1959 ed.)
Even thus, methinks, a city rear'd should be. Written in Edinburgh. Arthur Henry Hallam. VA
Even to the children. The Blade of Grass Sings to the River. Leah Goldberg. TrJP
Even when your friend, the radio, is still; even when her. X Minus X. Kenneth Fearing. AmLP; WOW
Even with its own ax to grind, sometimes. The Mind, Intractable Thing. Marianne Moore. LiTM (1970 ed.); NYBP
Evenen in the Village. William Barnes. GTSE
Evening. Richard Aldington. MoBrPo; SeCePo
Evening, An. William Allingham. EnLoPo; IrPN
Evening. Harry Behn. TiPo (1959 ed.)
Evening. Byron, *after the Greek of* Sappho. *Fr.* Don Juan, III. BoLiVe; OTPC; TrGrPo
(Hesperus, 1 *st.*) OnPM
(Hesperus the Bringer, 1 *st.*) AWP; JAWP; OuHeWo; WBP
(Hymn to Hesperus.) TOP
Evening. Ch'en Tzu-ang, *tr. fr. Chinese by* W. J. B. Fletcher. OnPM
Evening. Charles Cotton. *See* Evening Quatrains.
Evening. William Cowper. *See* Winter Evening ("Come, Evening").
Evening. Robert J. Craig. SoP
Evening. Emily Dickinson. *See* Cricket sang, The, *and* She sweeps with many-coloured brooms.
Evening. George Washington Doane. *See* Softly Now the Light of Day.
Evening. Hilda Doolittle ("H. D."). CMoP; FaBoMo; LoBV; OTPC (1946 ed.); Po; YT
Evening. Wendell Phillips Garrison. *Fr.* Post-Meridian. AA
Evening, The. John Gay. *Fr.* Trivia; or, The Art of Walking the Streets of London, III: Of Walking the Streets by Night. EnLi-1 (1949 ed.)
Evening. Goldsmith. *Fr.* The Deserted Village. ShBV-2
("Sweet was the sound, when oft at evening's close.") FaBoEn
Evening, *sel.* John Keble.
"'Tis gone; that bright and orbed blaze." TrPWD
Evening. Mary Matheson. CaP
Evening. Hugh McCrae. PoAu-1
Evening. W. S. Merwin. FRC
Evening, An. Robert Mezey. NaP
Evening. Harold Monro. FaBoTw
Evening. Charles Sangster. ACV; CaP
Evening. Sappho, *tr. fr. Greek by* Sir Rennell Rodd. WoL
Evening. Edward Rowland Sill. AnAmPo
Evening. Edith Sitwell. MoBS
Evening. James Stephens. MoBrPo
Evening. Walter James Turner. HT
Evening. *Unknown.* BoTP
Evening. Victor van Vriesland, *tr. fr. Dutch by* Adrian J. Barnouw. TrJP
Evening. Robert Wallace. PoPo
Evening. James Wright. NYBP
Evening! A flight of pigeons in clear sky. The Flute. José María de Heredia. AWP
Evening, and Maidens. William Barnes. OBEV (new ed.); OBVV
Evening, and the slender sugar tongs of a bird's small voice. Dinner Guest. Oscar Williams. TwAmPo
Evening, as slow thy placid shades descend. Sonnet. William Lisle Bowles. CEP
Evening at the Farm. John Townsend Trowbridge. BBV (1923 ed.); FaPON; GN; MPB; RIS; StVeCh (1940 ed.);
(Evening on the Farm.) MoShBr
Evening Blessing, An. James Edmeston. BePJ
Evening, blue, voluptuous, of June, The. The Walk on the Beach. John Gould Fletcher. BoLP; MoLP
Evening by the Sea. Swinburne. SyP
Evening came, a paw, to the gray hut by the river. Fall Journey. William Stafford. NaP
Evening Cloud, The. "Christopher North." HBV
Evening comes early, and soon discovers. Master's in the Garden Again. John Crowe Ransom. AP
Evening comes, the fields are still, The. Bacchanalia; or, the

New Age. Matthew Arnold. PoVP
Evening comes, the sun is sunk and gone, The. The Shadow of His Wings. Gerhardt Tersteegen. SoP
Evening Contemplation. George Washington Doane. *See* Softly Now the Light of Day.
Evening Darkens Over, The. Robert Bridges. CMoP; NBM; PoEL-5
Evening Ebb. Robinson Jeffers. AmPP (3d ed.); OTPC (1946 ed.)
Evening, ending, The. Guest Lecturer. Darwin T. Turner. BALP
Evening Falls, An. James Stephens. SUS
Evening falls: earth/ divides. Unbroken. A. R. Annons. FRC
Evening falls on the smoky walls. Ballad of the Londoner. J. E. Flecker. EnLoPo
Evening falls soon in the hills across the river. The White Eagle. Nan McDonald. PoAu-2
Evening falls, The. The sunset burns. On This Sea-Floor. Ralph Gustafson. PeCV (1967 ed.)
Evening Fantasy. Friedrich Hölderlin, *tr. fr. German by* Frederic Prokosch. LiTW
Evening Gleam, The. James Devaney. MoAuPo; PoAu-1
Evening has brought its. Witnesses. W. S. Merwin. AmPC
Evening has brought the glow-worm to the green. Shepherd. Edmund Blunden. HBMV
Evening Hymn. Cecil Frances Alexander. OTPC (1923 ed.)
Evening Hymn. Sir Thomas Browne. *Fr.* Religio Medici. MaRV; OxBoCh
(Colloquy with God, A.) OBS; SeCL
Evening Hymn. Philip Doddridge. SoP
Evening Hymn. William Henry Furness. AA; FaBoBe; HBV
(Light of Stars, The.) TrPWD
Evening Hymn. John Keble. BePJ; MaRV; SoP
Evening Hymn, An, *abr.* Thomas Ken. OBS
Evening Hymn, *sel.* George Macdonald.
"O God, whose daylight leadeth down." TrPWD
Evening Hymn. Elizabeth Madox Roberts. TiPo
Evening Hymn for a Little Family, An. Ann *or* Jane Taylor. OTPC (1946 ed.)
Evening Hymn in the Hovels. Francis Lauderdale Adams. OxBS
Evening Hymn of the Alpine Shepherds. William Beattie. SoP
Evening in a Sugar Orchard. Robert Frost. WIRo
Evening in Camp. Patricia Ledward. WaP
Evening in England, An. Francis Ledwidge. MCCG
Evening in Gloucester Harbor. Epes Sargent. EtS
Evening in May. Gabriele d'Annunzio, *tr. fr. Italian by* G. A. Greene. WoL
Evening in Paradise. Milton. *Fr.* Paradise Lost, IV. FaBoEn; GN; LoBV
(Moon and the Nightingale.) ChTr
(Night Falls on Eden.) PoFS; TreFS
(Now Came Still Evening On.) PoG
("Now came still evening on, and twilight gray.") PoIE; SeEP
Evening in Summer. Valentin Iremonger. NeIP
(Time, the Faithless.') OxBI
(While the Summer Tress Were Crying.) AnIV
Evening in the Great Smokies. DuBose Heyward. HT
Evening in the Sanitarium. Louise Bogan. TwCP
Evening in the Subrubs. Stella Barnett. PV
Evening in Tyringham Valley. Richard Watson Gilder. AA
Evening is coming, The. Bed-Time. *At. to* Thomas Hood. BoTP; OTPC (1946 ed.)
Evening is coming, young men. A Debate on Marriage versus Virginity. Catullus. HW
Evening is tawny on the old/ Deep-windowed farm. Gold. Martin Armstrong. BoTP
Evening Knell, The. John Fletcher. *See* Evening Song.
Evening Landscape. Pol de Mont, *tr. fr. Flemish by* Jethro Bithell. LiTW
Evening Meal in the Twentieth Century. John Holmes. MiAP
Evening Melody. Aubrey Thomas De Vere. GoBC; HBV
Evening Music. Kendrick Smithyman. AnNZ
Evening Musicale. Phyllis McGinley. *See* Recipe for an Evening Musicale.
Evening News: St. Louis. "Luke." QAH
Evening of Russian Poetry, An. Vladimir Nabokov. NYBP
Evening of the Feast-Day, The. Giacomo Leopardi, *tr. fr. Italian by* R. C. Trevelyan. LiTW
Evening of the Visitation, The. Thomas Merton. ISi
Eveing on Howth Head. Eileen Brennan. NeIP
Evening on the Farm. John Townsend Trowbridge. *See* Evening at the Farm.
Evening on the Harbor. Virginia Lyne Tunstall. HBMV
Evening on the Moselle. Decimus Magnus Ausonius, *tr. fr. Latin by* Helen Waddell. AnEnPo; LiTW
Evening Out, The. Ogden Nash. MoAmPo (1950 ed.)
Evening: Ponte al Mare, Pisa. Shelley. CBEP; SyP
Evening Prayer. *At. to* C. Maud Battersby, *and to* Charles H. Gabriel. *See* My Evening Prayer.
Evening Prayer. Edward Benlowes. *Fr.* Theophila. FaBoEn
Evening Prayer. Arthur Fitger, *tr. fr. German by* Jethro Bithell. AWP
Evening Prayer. Robert Freeman. SoP
Evening Prayer, An. Henry W. Frost. SoP
Evening Prayer. Hermann Hagedorn. GoBC
Evening Prayer. Thomas Ken. *See* Glory to Thee This Night.
Evening Prayer, An. Laura E. Kendall. BLRP
Evening Prayer, An ("Now I lay me down to sleep"). *Unknown.* *See* Now I Lay Me Down to Take My Sleep.
Evening Prayer ("Before the ending of the day.") *Unknown.* FaChP
Evening Prayer, An ("Dear God, another day is done"). *Unknown.* STF
Evening Prayer ("Our Father, grant us to lie down in peace"). *Unknown, tr. fr. Hebrew by* Solomon Solis-Cohen. TrJP
Evening Prayer, An ("Upon my ryght syde y me leye"). *Unknown.* AtBAP
Evening Primrose. John Clare, *wr. at. to* Emily Brontë. CH; TrGrPo
("When once the sun sinks in the west.") EG
Evening Primrose, The. John Langhorne. CEP; OBEC
Evening Primrose, The. Dorothy Parker. ALV; InMe
Evening Quatrains. Charles Cotton. ChTr; ExPo; LoBV
("Day's grown old, The," *abr.*) EG
(Evening.) PoEL-3; WiR
(Summer Evening.) TrGrPo
Evening red and morning gray. Weather Signs [*or* Weather Wisdom *or* Rhymes about the Weather]. *Unknown.* FaBoBe; GoTP; HBV; HBVY; OTPC; OxNR; PPL; TreF
Evening Revery, An, *sel.* Bryant.
"Summer day is closed, the sun is set, The." AA
Evening Scene. E. J. Scovell. FaBoMo
Evening Song. Cecil Frances Alexander. DD, *abr.*; OHIP, *abr.*; OTPC (1923 ed.); TVC
Evening Song. Sherwood Anderson. NP
Evening Song. Fannie Stearns Davis. GFA; SP
Evening Song. Kenneth Fearing. CMoP
Evening Song. John Fletcher. *Fr.* The Faithful Shepherdess, II, i. GN; OTPC (1923 ed.)
(Evening Knell, The.) ElL
(Folding the Flocks.) CH
(Priest's Chant, The.) OBS
Evening Song. Edith King. BoTP
Evening Song. Sidney Lanier. AmPP (3d ed.); AP; CoBA; FaPL; NeHB; PG; TOP; TreFT
Evening Song. Jean Toomer. CDC; PoNe
Evening Song. *Unknown.* OTPC (1946 ed.)
Evening Songs. John Vance Cheney. AA
"Behind the hilltop drops the sun," IV.
"Birds have hid, the winds are low, The," I.
"It is that pale, delaying hour," II.
"Now is Light, sweet mother, down the west," III.
Evening spread its rags of melancholy, The. The Wild Swan. D. S. Savage. NeBP
Evening Star. George Barker. ELU; ErPo; PoCh
Evening Star, The. Amy Carmichael. TRV
Evening Star, The. John Clare. *See* Hesperus.
Evening Star, The. Longfellow. AnNE
Evening Star. Poe. AmP; AP; MAmP; MWA-1
Evening Star. Sappho, *tr. fr. Greek by* Virginia Tufte. HW
Evening star appears above Idalium, The. Thorns Arm the Rose. Claudian. HW
Evening star, enemy of lovers, why. Evening Star. George Barker. ELU; ErPo; PoCh
Evening star that in the vaulted skies, The. Verse Written in the Album of Mademoiselle ——. Pierre Dalcour. PoNe; TTY
Evening star that softly sheds, The. Refracted Lights. Celia Parker Wooley. WGRP

Evening Star, you bring together. Evening Star. Sappho. HW
Evening Sun, The. Emily Brontë. CH
Evening sun is shining bright, The. A Winter Shower. Harumi. OnPM
Evening takes them unawares, The. The Sisters Kastemaloff. Carlton Talbott. ALV
Evening, the sky coloured like a child's angel. Child's Poem. Kay Smith. TwCaPo
Evening Thought, An. Jupiter Hammon. PoNe
Evening traffic homeward burns. Before Disaster. Yvor Winters. HoPM; QFR
Evening Twilight. Heine. *Fr.* The North Sea. AWP; JAWP; WBP
Evening Walk, An, *sels.* Wordsworth.
"Dear Brook, farewell! Tomorrow's noon again." CoBE; EnRP
"Did Sabine grace adorn my living line." EiCP
Sunset in the Lake Country. EPN
Swans. OBEC
Evening-Watch, The. Henry Vaughan. AnAnS-1; MeP; NCEP
Evening Waterfall. Carl Sandburg. NP; OTPC (1946 ed.); TSW
Evening Wind, The. Bryant. AA; AnNE; AP; CoBA; LaNeLa
(To the Evening Wind.) MCCG
Evening without Angels. Wallace Stevens. MoPo
Evenings/ When the house is quiet. Setting the Table. Dorothy Aldis. FaPON; MPB; TiPo
Evenings in Greece, *sel.* Thomas Moore.
Two Streams, The. GoBC
Evening's Love, An, *sels.* Dryden.
After the Pangs [of a Desperate Lover], *fr.* II, i. ELP; OAEP; StP; UnTE; ViBoPo
Song: "After the pangs of a desperate lover," *fr.* II, i. FaBoEn
(Love's Fancy.) ErPo
Song, A: "Calm was the even, and clear [*or* cleer] was the sky [*or* skie]," *fr.* IV, i. CavP; CBV; CEP; MBW-1; SeCV-2
(Calm Was the Even [and Clear Was the Sky].) DiPo; MaPo; OAEP
Song, A: "Celimena, of my heart," *fr.* V, i. CavP
(Damon and Celimena.) InvP; SeCL
Song, A: "You charm'd me not with that fair face," *fr.* II, i. CavP; CEP; SeCV-2
You Charm'd Me Not [with That Fair Face]. ATP (1935 ed.); DiPo; EiCL
Evensong. Conrad Aiken. HBMV; PG
Even-Song, An. Sydney Dobell. OBVV
Evensong. Carleton Drewry. GoYe
Even-song ("Blest be the God of Love"). George Herbert. AnAnS-1; EP; FaBoEn; MaMe; MeP
Even-Song ("Day is spent, and hath his will on mee, The"). George Herbert. MaMe
Evensong. Ruth Schaumann, *tr. fr. German by* George N. Shuster. CAW
Evensong. Robert Louis Stevenson. MaRV; PoVP; TreFT; TrPWD; TRV
Evensong. George Tankervil. TRV
Evensong. Ridgely Torrence. HBV
Event, An. Edward Field. CoAP
Event, The. T. Sturge Moore. OBMV
Event, An. Richard Wilbur. TwAmPo
Event Itself, The. Hayden Carruth. WOW
Event stands clear of history, The. Against Time. Louis Untermeyer. MoAmPo (1942 ed.)
Eventide. Thomas Burbidge. VA
Eventide. Caroline Atherton Briggs Mason. MaRV; TreFS
Eventide, *sel.* Whittier.
Eternal Good. OQP
Events. George O'Neil. HBMV
Eventual Proteus. Margaret Atwood. MoCV
Ever after summer shower. Sunshine after a Shower. Thomas Warton, the Younger. *Fr.* On the Approach of Summer. OTPC
Ever and ever anon. The Road to the Bow. James David Corrothers. BANP
Ever as We Sailed. Shelley. *Fr.* The Revolt of Islam. SeCePo
Ever before my face there went. Vain Finding. Walter de la Mare. BrPo
Ever charming, ever new. John Dyer. *Fr.* Grongar Hill. SeCePo
Ever fainting with desire. Speak the Word. Charles Wesley. BePJ
Ever-fixed Mark, An. Kingsley Amis. ErPo
Ever fresh the broad creation. The Immanent God. Emerson. *Fr.* Woodnotes. MaRV
Ever just over the top of the next brown rise. On the Road. Charles G. D. Roberts. PTK
Ever let the fancy roam. Fancy [*or* The Realm of Fancy *or* To Fancy]. Keats. ATP (1935 ed.); EnLi-2; EnRP; EPN; GTBS; GTBS-D; GTBS-P; GTBS-W; GTSE; GTSL; HBV; LoBV; OBEV
Ever-living Church, The. Charles Wesley. STF
Ever On. *Unknown.* STF
Ever Since. Elizabeth J. Coatsworth. SiSoSe
Ever Since. Archibald MacLeish. NePA
Ever Since Uncle John Henry Been Dead, *with music.* *Unknown.* AS
Ever the words of the gods resound. The Words of the Gods. Emerson. *Fr.* My Garden. OQP
Ever Watchful. Ta' Abbata Sharra, *tr. fr. Arabic by* W. G. Palgrave. AWP; JAWP; WBP
Everest. Horace Shipp. HaMV
Everett. Thomas William Parsons. DD
Evergreen. Ewart Milne. OxBI
Evergreen Cemetery. Alfred Purdy. MoCV
Evergreen shadow and the pale magnolia, The. Souls Lake. Robert Fitzgerald. MoPo; TwCP
Everlasting Arms, The. Psalms, Bible, *O.T.* *See* God Our Refuge.
Everlasting Arms, The. William M. Scholfield. SoP
Everlasting Contenders, The. Kenneth Patchen. CrMA; NaP
Everlasting Gospel, The, *sels.* Blake.
Epilogue: "I am sure this Jesus will not do." OBRV
"Jesus was sitting in Moses' chair." OxBoCh
"Vision of Christ that thou dost see, The." OBRV
"Was Jesus chaste?" OBRV
Everlasting Love, The. Annie Johnson Flint. BLRP
Everlasting Memorial, The. Horatius Bonar. SoP
Everlasting Mercy, The. John Masefield. StJW
Sels.
Another Cross. MaRV
"By this the sun." GBV
"I did not think, I did not strive." BoC; SoP; TRV
"I opened the window." WGRP
"O Christ who holds the open gate." SoP; TreFS; TRV
(Ploughman, The.) AtBAP
Everlasting Rest. Shakespeare. *Fr.* Romeo and Juliet, V, iii. WHA
Everlasting to Everlasting, *sel.* Namdev, *tr. by* R. T. Gribble.
"Before all Time, before all worlds." MaRV
Everlasting universe of things, The. Mont Blanc. Shelley. EnRP; ERoP-2; MaPo; MBW-2; MERP; PIA; PP
Everlasting Voices, The. W. B. Yeats. AWP; JAWP; WBP
Every branch big with it. Snow in the Suburbs. Thomas Hardy. BoNaP; CMoP; GoJo; MoAB; MoBrPo; OBMV; PoVP; ShBV-3; ThWaDe; ViPP; VP; WePo
Every Bush New Springing. *Unknown.* NCEP; PoEL-2
Every button has a door. About Buttons. Dorothy Aldis. MoSiPe
Ev-er-y child who has the use. Geese [*or Some Geese].* *Oliver Herford.* *Fr.* Child's Natural History. FiBHP; HBV; NA
Every Day. *See also* Everyday.
Every Day. *At. to* Felix Mendelssohn *and to* Moses Mendelssohn, *tr. fr. German.* PCD; PCH
(Love the Beautiful.) TreFT
Every Day. Mary I. Osborn. BoTP
Every day. Mariale. Bernard of Cluny. CAW
Every-Day Characters, *sels.* Winthrop Mackworth Praed.
Belle of the Ball-Room, The, III. ALV; EnRP; HBV; InMe
(Belle of the Ball, The.) BOHV
("Our love was like most other loves," 2 *sts.*) ViBoPo
Portrait of a Lady in the Exhibition of the Royal Academy, V. CLwM; NBM; PoEL-4
Vicar, The, I. EnRP; InMe; NBM; OBEV (new ed.); PoEL-4
Every day is a fresh beginning. Begin Again [*or* New Every Morning]. "Susan Coolidge." MaRV; SoP; STF
Every day is Judgment Day. Judgment Day. John Oxenham. SoP; TRV
Every day now, since my wife told me to cease from writing

poems. The Guest. Pentti Saarikoski. PV
Every Day Thanksgiving Day. Harriet Prescott Spofford. DD; OHIP; PEDC
Every day that their sky droops down. Moles. William Stafford. NYBP
Every Day Thou Might Lere. *Unknown.* YAT
Remember the Day of Judgment. MeEL
Every day will be fun for me. To Betty. "E. G. B." PCH
Every Earthly Creature. John Malcolm Brinnin. LiTA
Every evening Baby goes. Trot, Trot [to Town]. Mary Frances Butts. HBV; HBVY; PPL; SAS
Every Harlem Face Is Afromanism Surviving. Edward S. Spriggs. BF
Every Home an Altar. *Unknown.* SoP
Every hour and every minute. A Vow for New Year's. Mary Carolyn Davies. OTD; PoToHe
Every lady in this land. *Unknown.* OxNR
Every late evening in the silence before sleep. A Sound in Cambridge, Mass. Ruth Whitman. NYTB
Every Man. *See also* Everyman.
Every man for himself, and God for us all. How God Will Not Do for Us. John Heywood. SiCE
Every man has his sorrows; yet each still. Elegies, 1. André Chénier. AWP; JAWP; WBP
Every morning at break of day. The Trains. "Seumas O'Sullivan." BoTP
Every morning at six o'clock, I go straight to my work. Everybody Works but Father. Charles W. McClintock. TreFS
Every morning bathing myself and shaving myself. Chandler Nicholas. Edgar Lee Masters. *Fr.* The New Spoon River. NAMP
Every morning from this home. The Heart to Carry On. Bertram Warr. PeCV
Every morning I hear the bells ringing. Hygiene Sonnet. Dick Gallup. ANYP
Every morning lean thine arms awhile. Begin the Day with God. *Unknown.* MaRV; SoP; TRV
Every morning the prisoner hears. The Prisoner. William Plomer. ChMP; PeSA
Every Morning When I Wake. Dylan Thomas. *Fr.* Under Milk Wood. LOW
Every morning when the sun. This Happy Day. Harry Behn. TiPo
Every night and every morn. Blake. *Fr.* Auguries of Innocence. PoG
Every night as I go to bed. Waltzing Mice. David McCord. RIS
Every night from eve [*or* even] till morn. To the Nightingale. Sir John Davies. *Fr.* Hymns of Astraea. OBSC; SiCE; TrGrPo
Every night I sleep. In the Trench. Leon Gellert. BoAV; MoAuPo; PoAu-1
Every night my prayers I say. Reward. Bert Leston Taylor. RIS
Every night my prayers I say. System. Robert Louis Stevenson. PoVP; RIS
Every Night When the Sun Goes In, *with music.* *Unknown.* ABF; TrAS
Every One. *See* Everyone.
Every path a green lady. Four Songs from the Book of Samuel. Eli Mandel. MoCV
Every rose on the little tree. The Little Rose Tree. Rachel Field. FaPON; SUS; TiPo
Every Soul Is a Circus, *sel.* Vachel Lindsay.
Pontoon Bridge Miracle, The, IV. LiTM (rev. ed.); LoBV; NePA
Every soul that touches yours. Making Life Worth While. "George Eliot." MaRV
Every Sunday there's a throng. Westland Row. James Stephens. HBMV
Every Thing. *See Also* Everything.
Every Thing. Harold Monro. AnEnPo; MoBrPo; NeMA
Every thought is public. Hush! Emerson. AnNE
Every thread of summer is at last unwoven. Puella Parvula. Wallace Stevens. PoFS
Every Thursday morning. The Dustman. Clive Sansom. BoTP
Every Time I Climb a Tree. David McCord. GoTP; PDV; SoPo; TiPo (1959 ed.)
Every time I come to town. *Unknown.* GoTP
Every time I run into you Luke. Any Author to Any Friend. Martial. ML
Every time I write a letter. Writing Letters. Rodney Bennett. BoTP
Every time the bucks went clattering. Earthy Anecdote. Wallace Stevens. CMoP; GoJo; ThWaDe
Every towered city, every street. Exodus from a Renaissance Gallery. Ellen M. V. Acton. GoYe
Every valley drinks. Winter Rain. Christina Rossetti. BoNaP; WiR
Every votary of love. Love's Extremes. Antonio Villegas. OnPM
Every waiting moment is a fold of sorrow. Low Tide. Lynette Roberts. NeBP
Every week of every season out of English ports go forth. An English Mother. Robert Underwood Johnson. HBV
Every woman of true royalty owns. The Secret Land. Robert Graves. BoC
Every Year. Albert G. Pike. FaChP
Every Year. *Unknown.* SoP
Every year Emily Dickinson sent one friend. Accomplished Facts. Carl Sandburg. WHA
Every year they're marching slower. The Veterans. Denis A. McCarthy. PEDC
Every year without knowing it I have passed the day. For the Anniversary of My Death. W. S. Merwin. CoAP; NaP
Everybody else, then, going. Exeunt Omnes. Thomas Hardy. QFR
Everybody loved Chick Lorimer in our town. Gone. Carl Sandburg. AmP; AnFE; APA; CoAnAm; NP; OnPP; TwAmPo
Everybody nowadays. Snail. C. Lindsay McCoy. GFA
Everybody Says. Dorothy Aldis. FaPON; MoSiPe
Everybody stands alone on the heart of the earth. And Suddenly It's Evening. Salvatore Quasimodo. OnPM
Everybody stop and listen to my ditty. Prince of Wales' Marriage. *Unknown.* CoMu
Everybody Works but Father. Charles W. McClintock. TreFS
"Everybody Works but Father" as W. S. Gilbert Would Have Written It. Arthur G. Burgoyne. FiBHP
Everybody's Homesick Soldier Boy. Jonathan Williams. HYE
Everybody's Welcome, *with music.* *Unknown.* TrAS
Everyday Things. Jean Ayer. BoTP
Everyman. Siegfried Sassoon. BoLiVe; MoBrPo
Everyman (*Old English Morality Play*). *Unknown.* BEL, *mod.*; EnLi-1; MeEV, *abr., mod. in spelling;* PoEL-1
Sels.
Desertion of Beauty and Strength, The. ACP (1952 ed.)
"Eternal God! Oh! Beatific Vision!" *br. sel., paraphrased and mod. by* George Sterling. CAW
Everyone grows younger; my thinning hair. Figures of Authority. Edward Watkins. NYBP; StP
Everyone grumbled. The sky was grey. Daddy Fell into the Pond. Alfred Noyes. FaPON; PDV; RePo
Everyone knows he's blind as a bat. The Umpire. Walker Gibson. NePoAm; SD
Everyone [*or* Every One] Sang ("Everyone suddenly burst out singing"). Siegfried Sassoon. AnFE; BoLiVe; BrPo; FaBV; GTBS; GTBS-P; GTSL; InvP; LOW; MoBrPo; NeMA; NP; OBEV (new ed.); PoPl; PoSC; RePo; TrJP; WaKn; WaP
Everyone thinks I am poisonous. The Tarantula. Reed Whittemore. CoAP
Every One to His Own Way. John Vance Cheney. AA
Everyone who is anyone is moving away. Poem. Sotère Torregian. YAP
Everyone's asleep here at Forest Knolls. Poem for Ed's Birthday. Eugene Lesser. FRC
Everything. *See also* Every Thing.
Everything. Janice Marie Gadsden. WSL
Everything fell down. Fielding Error. Robert Paul Smith. CAD
Everything has lasted till today. The Unknown Soldier. Alun Lewis. MoBrPo (1962 ed.)
"Everything in the Air Is a Bird." Barbara Guest. AmPC
Everything is black and gold. Black and Gold. Nancy Byrd Turner. SoPo; TiPo; YeAr
Everything is in the same moment. 121st Chorus. Jack Kerouac. TPM

Everything is laughing, singing. It Is a Pleasant Day. *Unknown.* BoTP
Everything is over and I'm feeling bad. My Gal Sal. Paul Dresser. TreFT
Everything is sexual at the beach. Concerning Unnatural Nature: An Inverted Form. Hollis Summers. ErPo
Everything is stopped. Stopped. Allen Polite. NNP
Everything shall be erased. Villa Sciarra; Rome. Christine Turner Curtis. GoYe
Everything That Is. Daniel Berrigan. TwAmPo
Everything, the bridges of small yellow stars, cloud sleds. Poem, to Jane Wilson on Television. James Brodey. ANYP
Everything was wrong; the local slaves wore smiles. Harpers Ferry. Selden Rodman. PoNe
Everything you own, Robert. Concerning Mme. Robert. Deems Taylor. UnTE
Everything's been different. The Birthday Child. Rose Fyleman. BiCB; FaPON; SiSoSe
Everywhere. Nancy Birckhead. RIS
Everywhere, Everywhere, Christmas Tonight. Phillips Brooks. *See* Christmas Carol, A: "Everywhere, everywhere, Christmas tonight."
Everywhere, everywhere, following me. Camerados. Bayard Taylor. BOHV; Par
Everywhere I—hanh! Goin' Home. *Unknown.* ABF
Everywhere I look the houses are coming down. "It Must All Be Done Over." John Haines. ThO
"Everywhere I Wander." Philip Whalen. FRC
Everywhere is far from somewhere else. Far from Somewhere. "Primus." WhC
Everywhere is our wilderness everywhere. George Barker. NeBP
Eve's Daughter. Edward Rowland Sill. AmePo
Eve's Lament. *Unknown, tr. fr. Middle Irish by* Kuno Meyer. OnYI
(Gaelic Fragment.) CAW
Eve's Speech to Adam. Milton. *Fr.* Paradise Lost, IV. DiPo
Eve's Temptation and Fall. Milton. *Fr.* Paradise Lost, IX. DiPo
Evicted. Beatrice M. Murphy. TNV
Eviction. Elizabeth Brewster. CaP
Eviction. William James Linton. VA
Evidence, The. Hebrews, XI: 1, Bible, *N.T.* TRV
Evidence. Thomas Curtis Clark. MaRV
Evidence. Arthur Kober. InMe
Evidence, The. John Banister Tabb. *See* Faith.
Evidence Read at the Trial of the Knave of Hearts. "Lewis Caroll." *Fr.* Alice's Adventures in Wonderland, *ch.* 12. FaFP; GTBS-P; LiTG; NBM; OxBoLi; SiTL
Evil. Arthur Rimbaud, *tr. fr. French by* Norman Cameron. WaaP
Evil Days. Boris Pasternak, *tr. fr. Russian by* Bernard Guilbert Guerney. MoRP
Evil Designs. Shakespeare. King Richard III, *fr.* I, i. TreF
(Hate the Idle Pleasures.) TrGrPo
Evil Eye, The. John Ciardi. AtBAP; MoBS
Evil has no home. Evil Is Homeless. D. H. Lawrence. MoRP
Evil in Women, The. *Unknown, tr. fr. Spanish by* Havelock Ellis. OnPM
Evil is generous, will not walk alone. Victus. Quentin Stevenson. POTE (1959 ed.)
Evil is here? That's work for us to do. Israel Zangwill. *Fr.* At the Worst. TRV
Evil Is Homeless. D. H. Lawrence. MoRP
"Evil Man, An!" Richard Beer-Hofmann, *tr. fr. German by* Ludwig Lewisohn. *Fr.* Der Graf von Charolais. TrJP
Evil spirit, your beauty haunts me still, An. Sonnet. Michael Drayton. Idea, XX. CoBE; EIL; LoBV; OAEP; OBSC; ReEn; ReIE; SiCE; TuPP
"Evil thing is honor, An" once of old. Ideal Passion, XXVIII. George Edward Woodberry. HBMV
Evil was dangled in front of him like an apple. A Man of Sense. Richard Elberhart. MiAP
Evil World, An. *Unknown, tr. fr. Middle Irish by* Standish Hayes O'Grady. OnYI
Ev'n like Two Little Bank-dividing Brooks. Francis Quarles. *See* My Beloved Is Mine, and I Am His.
Evocation. Herman Stowell King. FiSC
Evoe! Edith M. Thomas. HBV
Evolution. Thelma Parker Cox. TNV
Evolution. Rochelle Owens. CoPo
Evolution. Langdon Smith. BeLS; BLPA; FaBoBe; FaFP; HBV; TreF; YaD
Evolution. May Swenson. TrGrPo (rev. ed.)
Evolution. John Banister Tabb. AA; AmePo; AmP; AnAmPo; InP; MaRV; OQP; PFY; PoPl; TreF
Evolution. Israel Zangwill. TrJP
Ev'ry [or Every] night when the sun goes in. Every Night When the Sun Goes In. *Unknown.* ABF; TrAS
Ev'ry singing bird that in the wood rejoices. Vezzosi Augelli. Thomas Watson. TuPP
Ev'ry Time I Feel de Spirit, *with music.* *Unknown.* BoAN-1
Ev'ry time I think about Jesus. Calvary. *Unknown.* BoAN-1
"Ewa-yea! my little owlet!" Lullaby of Nokomis. Longfellow. *Fr.* The Song of Hiawatha. PCH
Ex and Squarey. *Unknown.* ChTr
Ex-Basketball Player. John Updike. NYBP; TPM
Ex-Clerk. Kipling. *Fr.* Epitaphs of the War. PoVP
Ex Libris. Arthur Upson. HBV
Ex Maria Virgine. Norbert Engels. ISi
Ex Nihilo. David Gascoyne. *Fr.* Miserere. GTBS-P; NeBP
Ex Ore Infantium. Francis Thompson. *See* Child's Prayer, A.
Exaction. John L. Sweeney. TwAmPo
"Exactly So." Lady T. Hastings. BOHV
Exaggeration. Elizabeth Barrett Browning. SoP
Exaggerator. Mark Van Doren. AnFE; CoAnAm
Exaltation. Franz Werfel, *tr. fr. German by* Edith Abercrombie Snow. TrJP
Examination of His Mistress' Perfections, The. Francis Beaumont. GoBC
Examine the mirror closely, and your face. Sunday, July 14th; a Fine Day at the Baths. Julian Symons. WaP
Examiner. F. R. Scott. PPON; TwCaPo
Example, The. W. H. Davies. AnFE; HBMV; MoBrPo; OA; POTE; TrGrPo; TSW; WHA
Example of the Praise of God for His Omnipotency, An, out of the CXIII Psalm. John Hall. ReIE
Exasperated, worn, you conjure a mansion. Desires of Men and Women. John Berryman. LiTM
Excavation, The. Max Endicoff. PoMa
Excavation for the new, The. Dedication for a Building. Alan Dugan. CAD
Excavator, explore rock from the great Ice Age. The Cave-Drawing. Vernon Watkins. LiTB
Exceeding brightness of this early sun, The. The Sun This March. Wallace Stevens. BWP
Exceeding Great Army, An. Ethan Ayer. FiSC
Exceeding sorrow. O Mors! Quam Amara Est Memoria Tua Homini Pacem Habenti in Substantiis Suis. Ernest Dowson. BrPo; GTSL; OBMV; PG; ViPP
Exceeding tall, but built so well his height. House-Surgeon. W. E. Henley. *Fr.* In Hospital. PoVP
Excelente Balade of Charitie, An. Thomas Chatterton. CEP; EiCL; EiPP; EnPE; EnRP; GoTL; LiTB; LiTG; OBEC; SeCePo; StP
Excellency of Christ. Giles Fletcher. *Fr.* Christ's Victory and Triumph, I. BePJ; MaRV; SoP; StJW; WGRP
(Christ.) FaChP
(He Is a Path.) TRV
("He is a path, if any be misled.") ChIP
Excellency of Wine, The. Roger Boyle, Earl of Orrery. SeCL
("'Tis wine that inspires.") SeEP
Excellent mistresse fairer than the moone. *Unknown.* SeCSL
Excellent New Song on a Seditious Pamphlet, An. Swift. CoMu
Excellent New Song upon His Grace Our Good Lord Archbishop of Dublin, An. Swift. CoMu
Excellent ritual of oils, of anointing. Sarcophagi. Bernard Spencer. FaBoMo
Excellent Sonnet of a Nymph, An. Sir Philip Sidney. *Fr.* Arcadia. ReIE
("Virtue, beauty, and speech did strike, wound, charm.") FCP
Excellent work, my Hugh. The Beset Wife. Robert Farren. OxBI
Excelsior. Longfellow. AmeP; FaPON; HBV; HBVY; NeHB; OnMSP; OTPC; PaPo; PoFS; WBLP

Except/ A grain of wheat. Resurrection. Esther H. Turner. SoP
Except I Love. *At. to* Robert Parry. *Fr.* The Mirror of Knighthood. EIL
Except ourselves, we have no other prayer. Without Ceremony. Vassar Miller. CoPo; MoAmPo (1962 ed.); TDP
Except the Lord Build the House. Psalms, CXXVII, Bible, *O.T.* OnPM; TreFT; TrJP; TRV
Except the smaller size. Emily Dickinson. MWA-2
Except Ye Repent. J. Franklin Pineo. ChIP
Excerpts from a "Gothic Notebook." Mario Luzi, *tr. fr. Italian by* William Fense Weaver. *Fr.* Gothic Notebook. LiTW
Excesses of God, The. Robinson Jeffers. MaRV; MoRP
Exchange, The. Samuel Taylor Coleridge. FiBHP; HBV; OAEP; WhC
Exchange. Sister Mary Dorothy Ann. GoBC
Exchange of Letters On Suicide Porpoises, An. William Brown. QAH
Exchange of Wills, An. Anna Jane Granniss. SoP
Exchanges. Ernest Dowson. OBMV
Exchanges II, The. Robert Kelly. CoPo
Exciseman, The. Burns. *See* De'il's Awa wi' the Exciseman, The.
Exclusion. Emily Dickinson. *See* Soul selects her own society, The.
Excursion, The. Tu Fu, *tr. fr. Chinese by* Florence Ayscough *and* Amy Lowell. AWP; JAWP; SD; WBP
Excursion, The, *sels.* Wordsworth.
  Despondency Corrected, *fr.* IV. EnRP
  Discourse of the Wanderer, and an Evening Visit to the Lake, *fr.* IX. EnRP
  "Diverging now (as if his quest had been)," *fr.* II. OBRV
  "From early childhood, even as hath been said," *fr.* I. BoPe
  "I have seen/ A curious child," *fr.* IV. OBRV; TreFT
    ("Curious child, A," *shorter sel.*) WGRP
    (Faith, *shorter sel.*) MaRV
    (Shells.) BoPe
  "I see around me here," *fr.* I. OBRV
    (Wanderer Recalls the Past, The.) OBNC
  "Once more to distant ages of the world," *fr.* IV. InP
  Prospectus, *fr.* I. NoP
  Ruined Cottage, The, *fr.* I. MBW-2
  Sky after Storm, *fr.* II. BoLiVe
  Solitary, The, *fr.* II. EnRP
  "Such was the Boy," *fr.* I. OBRV
    (Communion, *abr.*) MaRV
  Tale of Margaret, The, *fr.* I. ERoP-1
    (Margaret; or, The Ruined Cottage, *shorter sel.*) EnRP
  "Tenour which my life holds, The," *fr.* III. OBRV
  "'Twas summer, and the sun had mounted high," *fr.* I. EnRP
  Wanderer, The, *fr.* I. EnRP
  "Within the soul a faculty abides," *fr.* IV. OBRV
Excusation of the Auctor, The. Stephen Hawes. *Fr.* The Pastime of Pleasure. ReIE
Excuse, The. Robert Heath. SeCL
Excuse, The. Sir Walter Ralegh. FCP; SiPS
Excuse me, reader, though I now and then. To the Reader. Everard Guilpin. *Fr.* Skialetheia. ReIE; SiCE
Excuse of Absence, An. Thomas Carew. SeCP
Excuse Us, Animals in the Zoo. Annette Wynne. TiPo; UTS
Execration upon Vulcan, An. Ben Jonson. AnAnS-2; ReEn; SeCP
Execrators, The. David Galler. NMP
Execution, The. Alden Nowlan. PeCV (1967 ed.)
Execution of Alice Holt. *Unknown.* OxBoLi
Execution of Cornelius Vane, The. Sir Herbert Read. BrPo
Execution of King Charles, The. Andrew Marvell. *Fr.* An Horatian Ode upon Cromwell's Return from Ireland. AnEnPo; PoRA
Execution of Montrose, The. William Edmondstoune Aytoun. GTBS; HBV; OnMSP; VA
Executive's Death, The. Robert Bly. CoAP; FRC; NaP
Exequies, The. Thomas Stanley. AnAnS-2; MeLP; OBS; SeCL; SeEP
Exequy, The. Henry King. AnAnS-2; AtBAP; ATP; BWP; CABA; CaFP; CLwM; FaBoEn; ForPo; InvP; LoBV; MeLP; MePo; NoP; OBS; PoEL-2; QFR; ReEn; SeCePo; SeCL; SeCP; ViBoPo, *much abr.*; WHA
  (Exequy on His Wife.) LiTL, *abr.*; OBEV, *abr.*
  (Exequy, to His Matchless Never to Be Forgotten Friend, The.) EP; SeEP
  Sels.
  "Dear loss! since thy untimely fate." LO
  "Sleep on, my Love, in thy cold bed." CH; PoFS; TrGrPo
Exequy: To Peter Allt. Kildare Dobbs. OBCV
Exercise Book. Paul Dehn. WePo
Exercise in a Meadow. Jean Elliot. GoYe
Exercise in Aesthetics. Winfield Townley Scott. FiMAP
Exert thy voice, sweet harbinger of spring! To the Nightingale. Countess of Winchilsea. BWP; CEP; EiPP; PoIE
Exeunt. Richard Wilbur. BoNaP; ELU; FiMAP; PoLF; TwAmPo; WIRo
Exeunt Omnes. Thomas Hardy. QFR
Exhibit A; the edge of this long knife. Here Is Your Realism. Maxwell Bodenheim. AnAmPo
Exhortation. Louise Bogan. QFR
Exhortation. Thomas Hastings. AA
Exhortation: Summer, 1919. Claude McKay. CDC
Exhortation to Learn by Others' Trouble. Earl of Surrey. SiCE; TuPP
  (Lines to Ratclif.) SiPS
  ("My Radcliffe, when thy reckless youth offends.") FCP
Exhortation to praise God cheerefully, An. Psalm C, Bible, *O.T.* YAT
Exhortation to Prayer. William Cowper. SoP
Exhortation to Prayer. Margaret Mercer. AA
Exhortation to the Artists. Hyam Plutzik. FiMAP
Exhortation to Youth. Chaucer. *Fr.* Troilus and Criseyde, V. PoLi
  (Love Unfeigned, The.) OBEV
  ("O younge freshe [*or* yonge fresshe] folkes, he or [*or* and] she"). CAW; ExPo; LO
Exile. Audrey Beecham. NeBP
Exile, The. Margaret Benaya. NYTB
Exile, The. Gerald Bullett. POTE
Exile, The. Katherine Burton. JKCP (1955 ed.)
Exile, The. Walter de la Mare. POTE
Exile. Ernest Dowson. BrPo
Exile. Donald Hall. NePA
Exile. Heine, *tr. fr. German by* James Thomson. OnPM
Exile. Theodore Maynard. MoBrPo (1942 ed.)
Exile, The. Larry Rubin. GoYe
Exile. Virna Sheard. PeCV
Exile. Tu Fu, *tr. fr. Chinese by* Chi Hwang Chu *and* Edna Worthley Underwood. OnPM
Exile. *Unknown, tr. fr. Irish by* Frank O'Connor. KiLC
Exile. Paul Verlaine, *tr. fr. French by* Alan Conder. LO
Exile. Jennette Yeatman. GoYe
Exile at Rest, The. John Pierpont. AA
Exile from God. John Hall Wheelock. GoBC; WGRP
Exile in Nigeria. Ezekiel Mphahlele. PBA
Exile of Erin, The. Thomas Campbell. HBV
Exile Song. Morris Jacob Rosenfeld, *tr. fr. Yiddish by* Joseph Leftwich. LiTW
Exiled. Edna St. Vincent Millay. EtS; HT; PoRA
Exiled from places of honor about the Throne of Grace. Black Church on Sunday. Joseph M. Mosley, Jr. NBP
Exiled Heart, The. Maurice Lindsay. OxBS
Exiled to bowers of beauty. The Londoner in the Country. Richard Church. HaMV
Exiles. "Æ." MoBrPo
Exiles. William Hamilton Hayne. AA
Exile's Departure, The. Whittier. CoBA
Exile's Devotion, The. Thomas d'Arcy McGee. VA
Exile's Letter. Li Po, *tr. fr. Chinese by* Ezra Pound. CTC; FaBoMo; NP; OxBA; PoE; SeCeV
Exile's Return, The. Robert Lowell. AmPP (5th ed.); AP; MiAP; NePA; OxBA
Exile's Song, The. Robert Gilfillan. HBV; VA
Existentialism. Lloyd Frankenberg. FiBHP
Exit. William Stanley Braithwaite. Sandy Star and Willie Gee, III. BANP
Exit. John Gould Fletcher. InP; PoPo
Exit. Wilson MacDonald. CaP; ViBoPo
Exit. E. A. Robinson. MoAmPo
Exit. Sir William Watson. VA
Exit from Eden. Milton. *Fr.* Paradise Lost, XII. DiPo
Exit God. Gamaliel Bradford. HBMV; InMe; MaRV
Exit, Pursued by a Bear. Ogden Nash. NYBP

Exit the ribald clown. Colombine. Hugh McCrae. BoAV; NeLNL; PoAu-1
Exodus. Roy Basler. SiTL
Exodus, *sels.* Bible, *O.T.*
Child Moses, The, I: 7-II: 15. OuHeWo
Song of Moses, The, XV: 1-18. LiTW
(Lord Is a Man of War, The, XV: 3-10.) WaaP
(Then Sang Moses, XV: 1-18.) TrJP
("Then sang Moses and the children of Israel this song," XV: 1-27.) PoFr
(Triumphal Chant, XV: 1-13, 18.) TrGrPo
Ten Commandments, The. OHFP (XX: 2-16); TreF (XX: 1-17); WBLP (XX: 2-26)
Exodus, *sels.* Cædmon (?), *tr. fr. Anglo-Saxon.*
"Look! now with your eyes behold," *tr. by* Richard L. Hoffman. YAT
Parting of the Red Sea, The, *tr. by* Charles W. Kennedy. AnOE
Exodus for Oregon. Joaquin Miller. AmPP (3d ed.); FaPL
Exodus from a Renaissance Gallery. Ellen M. V. Acton. GoYe
Exodus from Egypt, The. Ezekielos of Alexandria, *tr. fr. Greek by* E. H. Gifford. TrJP
Exorcism. Oliver St. John Gogarty. AnIL
Exotic Perfume. Baudelaire, *tr. fr. French by* Arthur Symons. OnPM
(Parfum exotique.) AWP; MeWo
Expanded waters gather on the plain, Th'. The Flood. Ovid. *Fr.* Metamorphoses, I. ChTr
Expanding in the chill. Cold-Weather Love. Ronald Everson. MoCV
Expanding Universe, The. Norman Nicholson. POTi
Expanse cannot be lost. Emily Dickinson. MAmP
Expansion to Aveline's. James Brodey. ANYP
Expansive puppets percolate self-unction. The Canadian Authors Meet. F. R. Scott. ACV; OBCV; WhC
Expatriate. Mary Brown Onstott. PoMa
Expect! William Pierson Merrill. OQP
Expectans Expectavi. Charles Sorley. FaBoCh; HBMV; LoGBV; MaRV; WGRP
Expectant at the country gate the lantern. Ill. Bernard Spencer. NeBP
Expectation, The. Frederick William Faber. *Fr.* Our Lady's Expectation. ACP
Expectation. Thomas Stanley. AnAnS-2; OBS; SeCL; SeEP
(Destiny.) LoBV
Expectation. Theodore Wratislaw. VA
Expecting Him, my door was open wide. Praesto. Thomas Edward Brown. ChIP
Expedition North. John Morgan. YAP
Expedition to Wessagusset, The. Longfellow. *Fr.* The Courtship of Miles Standish, V *and* VII. PAH
Expense [*or* Expence] of spirit in a waste of shame, The [*or* Th']. Lust [*or* Past Reason Hunted]. Shakespeare. Sonnets, CXXIX. AnEnPo; AWP; BWP; CABA; CaFP; CBEP; CBV; CoBE; DiPo; EnL; EnRePo; EP; ErPo; ExPo; FaBoEn; ForPo; FosPo; GTBS-W; InPo; JAWP; LiTB; LiTG; LiTL; LO; LoBV; MaPo; MasP; NoP; OBEV; OBSC; OtMeF; PAn; PoAn; PoE; PoEL-2; PoeP; PoFS; PoIE; QFR; ReEn; ReIE; SeCePo; SeCeV; ShBV-4; Sonn; StP; TOP; TrGrPo; UnPo (3d ed.); VaPo; ViBoPo; WBP
Expenses. Adelaide Crapsey. NP; TOP
Expensive Wife, The. Judah ibn Sabbatai. *Fr.* The Gift of Judah the Woman-Hater. TrJP
Experience. J. V. Cunningham. CBV
Experience. Emerson. AmePo; AnAmPo; AnNE; LiTA; PoEL-4
Experience. Lesbia Harford. BoAu; PoAu-1
Experience. Aline Kilmer. BiCB; HBMV
Experience. Frederic W. H. Myers. *Fr.* Saint Paul. MaRV
(St. Paul Speaks.) BoC
Experience. John Boyle O'Reilly. ACP; OBVV
Experience. Dorothy Parker. BoLP; InMe; PoPl; WhC
Experience, The. Edward Taylor. *See* Preparatory Meditations: "Oh! that I always. . ."
Experience. Tennyson. *See* Challenge of Life, The.
Experience. Edith Wharton. AA
Experience now doth show what God us taught before. The Poor Estate to Be Holden for Best. *Unknown, at. to* Edward Seymour, Duke of Somerset. OBSC; SiCE; TuPP
Experience of delight would detonate us. Soft Letter. Peter Schjeldahl. YAP
Experience of writing you these love letters, The. The Ticket. John Ashbery. ANYP
"Experience, though all authority." The Wife of Bath's Prologue. Chaucer, *mod. by* Theodore Morrison. *Fr.* The Canterbury Tales. EnL
"Experience, though [*or* thogh] noon auctoritee." The Wife of Bath's Prologue. Chaucer. *Fr.* The Canterbury Tales. EnLi-1 (1949 ed.); MBW-1; OxBoLi; PoEL-1
Expert designing the long-range gun, The. Munitions Expert. W. H. Auden. MaRV
Experts at Veneers. Kenward Elmslie. ANYP
Experts on Woman. Arthur Guiterman. InMe
Expiatory chapel, chains. Jardin de la Chapelle Expiatoire. Robert Finch. PeCV
Expiration, The. John Donne. AtBAP; ATP; CBEP; EIL; MaMe; MBW-1; MeLP; MePo; SCEP-1; SeCP
("So, so, break off this last lamenting kiss.") EG
Explanation. "Josh Billings." TreFT
Explanation, An. Walter Learned. *See* In Explanation.
Explanation. Valerie Tarver. TNV
Explanation of the Grasshopper, An. Vachel Lindsay. FaPON; GFA; OTPC (1946 ed.); PCH; PoRh; SoPo; StVeCh
(Grasshopper, The.) TSW
Explanation, on Coming Home Late. Richard Hughes. ELU; ThWaDe
Explanations of Love. Carl Sandburg. LiTL; MoLP
Explanatory Epistle, An. John Banks. WaPE
Exploiter of the shadows. Fox. Clifford Dyment. HaMV; POTi
Exploration. Daniel Hoffman. CoAP; CoPo
Explorations. Louis MacNeice. ChMP; CoBMV; ILP
Explorer, The. Anthony Delius. BoSA
Explorer, The. Kipling. WHA
Explorer, The. William Plomer. BoSA
Explorers, The. Margaret Atwood. MoCV
Explosive. Start out. The Marionette. Irving Feldman. NYTB
Expostulation, An. Isaac Bickerstaffe. BoLP; FiBHP; PV
Expostulation, *sel.* William Cowper.
Where the Leprosy Begins. SoP
Expostulation, The. John Donne. Elegies, XV. MaMe
Expostulation, An. C. S. Lewis. HYE
Expostulation, The. Thomas Shadwell. *Fr.* The Squire of Alsatia. OAEP
Expostulation and Reply. Wordsworth. BEL; CBEP; EnL; EnLi-2; EnLit; EnRP; EPN; ERoP-1; HBV; MBW-2; MERP; OAEP; OBRV; PoE; UnPo
Communion with Nature, *sel.* MaRV
Exposure. Wilfred Owen. BoPe; FaBoMo; LiTM (rev. ed.); MMA; MoVE; OnHM; WaP
Express. W. R. Rodgers. MoVE
Express, The. Stephen Spender. AnFE; BBV (1951 ed.); CMoP; EnL; EnLi-2 (1949 ed.); EnLit; ExPo; GoJo; LiTM; MoAB; MoBrPo; MoVE; NAMP; NeMA; PoPl; RoGo; SeCeV; ShBV-3; TwCP; VaPo
Express Train. Karl Kraus, *tr. fr. German by* Albert Bloch. TrJP
Express Trains. MacKnight Black. PoMa
Expression. Isaac Rosenberg. MoBrPo
Expulsion from Paradise. Milton. *Fr.* Paradise Lost, XII. BEL; ChTr
("He ended and they both descend the hill.") ATP; SeEP
Exquisite face that agony must tear. The Boy Christ. Helene Mullins. StJW
Exquisite Lady. Mary Elizabeth Osborn. NePoAm-2
Exquisite painter Ko-tsu was often reproached, The. The Windmill. Allen Upward. *Fr.* Scented Leaves from a Chinese Jar. NP
Exquisite Sonnet, The. J. C. Squire. HBMV
Exquisite stillness! What serenities. Don Juan's Address to the Sunset. Robert Nichols. OBMV; POTE
Exquisite wines and comestibles. Martial in London. Mortimer Collins. ALV; BOHV; InMe
Exspecto Resurrectionem. Charlotte Mew. LO
Extasie, The. Abraham Cowley. *See* Ecstasy, The.
Extasy [*or* Extasie], The. John Donne. *See* Ecstasy, The.
Extempore Effusion upon the Death of James Hogg. Wordsworth. CBEP; ERoP-1; FiP; MBW-2; MyFE; NoP; OBRV; PeER
Extempore to Voltaire Criticising Milton. Edward Young. ViBoPo

Extempore Verses Intended to Allay the Violence of Party-Spirit. John Byrom. *See* Jacobite Toast, A.
Extempore Verses upon a Trial of Skill between the Two Great Masters of the Noble Science of Defence, Messrs. Figg and Sutton. John Byrom. OBEC
Extended Invitation. Jesse Stuart. FiSC
Extermination. Richard D'Alton Williams. OnYI
Extinguish My Eyes. Rainer Maria Rilke. *See* Put Out My Eyes, and I Can See You Still.
Extract from Addresses to the Academy of Fine Ideas, An. Wallace Stevens. GTBS-W; LiTA; LiTM (rev. ed.)
Extract the quint-essence. Francis Daniel Pastorius. SCAP
Extracts from the Rubaiyat of Omar Cayenne. Gelett Burgess. BOHV
Extraordinary Dog, The. Nancy Byrd Turner. TiPo
Extras. Richard Burton. AA
Extreme Unction. Ernest Dowson. ACP; CAW; JKCP; MoBrPo; OBMV; PeVV
Extremely Naughty Children. Elizabeth Godley. BBGG
Extremes. James Whitcomb Riley. FaPON; HBVY; MPB; PCH; PPL
Extremum Tanain. Horace, *tr. fr. Latin by* Austin Dobson. Odes, III, 10. AWP; JAWP; WBP
Exuberant, restless. West Lake. Kenneth O. Hanson. CoAP
Exultation is the going. Emily Dickinson. AmP; AmPP; AP; CABA; CBEP; CoBA; NCEP; PoeP
Exulting, The. Theodore Roethke. *Fr.* The Dying Man. PoDB
Eye, The. Michael Benedikt. YAP
Eye, The. Sophia Castro-Leon. QAH
Eye, The. Robinson Jeffers. AmLP; AP; CoBMV; CrMA; FaBoEn; GTBS-W; LiTA; LiTM; OxBA; PoPo; WaP
Eye, The. Allen Tate. LiTA
Eye, The. Eithne Wilkins. NeBP
Eye can hardly pick them out, The. At Grass. Philip Larkin. HaMV; NePoEA; PoeP; SD; WIRo
Eye drags all of winter, The. News Reel. David Ross. GoYe
Eye-flattering [*or* Fie! flattering] fortune, look thou never so fair. Fortune [*or* Lewis, the Lost Lover]. Sir Thomas More. *Fr.* Two Short Ballettes. GoBC; OBSC; PoLi; TuPP
Eye luminous, The. The Offender. Denise Levertov. NePoEA-2
Eye of Faith, The. J. J. Maxfield. SoP
Eye of Humility, The. Kay Smith. OBCV
Eye of Love, The. George Moses Horton. BALP
Eye of the Beholder, The. James Lionel Michael. BoAu
Eye of the garden, queen of flowers. To the Rose. Sir John Davies. *Fr.* Hymns of Astraea. OBSC; SiCE; TuPP
Eye of the Storm, The. *Unknown.* SoP
Eye winker. *Unknown.* OxNR
Eye with the piercing eagle's fire, An. Thaddeus Stevens. Phoebe Cary. PAH
Eyeless labourer in the night, The. Woman to Man. Judith Wright. BoAV; MoAuPo; PoAu-2
Eyelids glowing, some chill morning, The. Monet: "Les Nymphéas." W. D. Snodgrass. CoAP
Eyelids meet, The. He'll catch a little nap. In the Smoking-Car. Richard Wilbur. LiTM (1970 ed.); MoAmPo (1962 ed.); ToPo
Eyelids of eve fall together at last, The. Before Waterloo. Thomas Hardy. *Fr.* The Dynasts. MoAB; PoVP
Eyes. W. H. Davies. BrPo
Eyes. Walter de la Mare. BrPo
Eyes and Tears. Andrew Marvell. MaMe; MeP; MePo; NCEP
Eyes are lying again, posing, The. Self-Portrait. Robert Pack. CoPo
Eyes, calm beside thee (Lady, could'st thou know!). Robert Browning. Sonn
Eyes do not lie. Remainder. Frederika Blankner. GoYe
Eyes gaze no more as yet you may. *Unknown.* SeCSL
Eyes Have It, The. William Stephens. NAMP
Eyes, Hide My Love. Samuel Daniel. *Fr.* Hymen's Triumph. ElL
(Secrecy.) OBSC
Eyes I dare not meet in dreams. T. S. Eliot. *Fr.* The Hollow Men. GTBS-D
Eyes lie awake in hope of happy seinge. *Unknown.* SeCSL
Eyes like the morning star. The Colorado Trail. *Unknown.* AS; CoSo
Eyes of Children at the Brink of the Sea's Grasp, The. Josephine Jacobsen. NePoAm-2
Eyes of God, The. Hermann Hagedorn. HBMV
Eyes of God, The. "Gabriel Setoun." PPL
Eyes of Lincoln, The. Walt Mason. OQP
Eyes of My Regret, The. Angelina Weld Grimké. CDC
Eyes of Night-Time. Muriel Rukeyser. MiAP; NePA
Eyes of slain stag. In Some Seer's Cloud Car. Christopher Middleton. TwCP
Eyes of the pioneer woman are blue, The. The Pioneer Woman—In the North Country. Eunice Tietjens. AmFN
Eyes of twenty centuries, The. Judas Iscariot. Stephen Spender. MoAB; MoBrPo (1950 ed.)
Eyes of Wonder, The. Jessie Corrigan Pegis. JKCP (1955 ed.)
Eyes open to a cry of pulleys. Love Calls Us to the Things of This World. Richard Wilbur. AmPP (5th ed.); CMoP; FiMAP; MoAmPo (1962 ed.); NePA; NePoEA; PIA; PoAn; PoDB; PoRA; SeCeV (1967 ed.); ToPo; TrGrPo (rev. ed.); TwAmPo
Eyes red, the lips blue, The. The Three Seamstresses. Isaac Leibush Peretz. TrJP
Eyes rolled open this morning. Blues, for Sallie. Stanley Crouch. WSL
Eyes, side-to-side. Directions. Onitsura. SoPo
Eyes So Tristful. Diego de Saldaña, *tr. fr. Spanish by* Longfellow. AWP; JAWP; WBP
Eyes that are clear, serene. Madrigal. Gutierre de Cetina. LiTW
Eyes That Last I Saw in Tears. T. S. Eliot. InPo; ViBoPo
Eyes That Queenly Sit. Elizabeth Daryush. QFR
Eyes that weep for pity of the heart, The. Dante, *tr. fr. Italian by* Dante Gabriel Rossetti. La Vita Nuova, XIX. AWP; OuHeWo; WGRP
Eyes Up! Mary Gustafson. SoP
Eyes which were first to gaze—my reckless eyes. Love's Assize. Guido Cavalcanti. LiTW
Eyewitness. Rodney Hall. PoAu-2
Eye-Witness. Ridgely Torrence. HBMV;
Tramp Sings, The, *sel.* PFY
Ez fer War. James Russell Lowell. *Fr.* The Biglow Papers, 1st series, No. 1. PPON
War, 1*st.* MaRV
Ezekiel, *sels.* Bible, *O.T.*
Lamentation, XIX: 2-9. TrJP
Thy Mother Was like a Vine, XIX: 10-14. TrJP
Unfaithful Shepherds, XXXIV: 1-28. WoL
Ezekiel. Laurence Binyon. ChMP
"Ezekiel he came out." Erie Canal. *Unknown.* ABF
Ezekiel in the valley of Dry Bones. Ezekiel. Laurence Binyon. ChMP
Ezekiel Saw de Wheel. *Unknown.*
(Exekiel, You and Me, *with music, very diff. vers.*) AS
"Ezek'l saw de wheel, Ezek'l saw de wheel," *sel., sl. diff.* ExPo
Ezra Perrin's family, on his mother's side. A Health Note. Walter Hard. AnNE
Ezra Shank. *Unknown.* ShM
Ezry. Archibald MacLeish. MoVE

F

F is for Fiddler. W. H. Davies. MuSP
F Is the Fighting Firetruck. Phyllis McGinley. *Fr.* All Around the Town. FaPON
Fa La La. *Unknown, at. to* John Hilton. CH
(Madrigal.) SiTL
("My mistress frowns when she should play.") OxBoLi
Faberge. James Schuyler. ANYP
Fabien dei Franchi. Oscar Wilde. BrPo
Fable: "Bough will bend, the leaf will sometime fall, The. Mary Mills. NePoAm
Fable: "I led him on into the frosted wood." George O'Neil. NP
Fable, A: "In Aesop's tales an honest wretch we find." Matthew Prior. EiCL
Fable, A: Mice and Felis, The. John Kendrick. CIV
Fable: "Mountain and the squirrel, The." Emerson. AmP; AmPP (3d ed.); AnNE; BOHV; FaBV; FaFP; HBV; HBVY; InMe; LiTA; LiTG; MPB; NePA; OA; OnMSP; PG (1945 ed.);

Fable (continued)
PoPl; PoPo; PRWS; RG; SiTL; StaSt; TRV; TSW; UTS; VaPo; YaD
(Mountain and the Squirrel, The.) BeLS; BoChLi (1950 ed.); BoTP; FaBoBe; FaPON; GoJo; GoTP; LaNeLa; NeHB; OTPC; PTK; TreFT
Fable: "O the vines were golden, the birds were loud." Frederic Prokosch. LiTM (1946 ed.); WaP
Fable: "Oh, there once was a lady." Dorothy Parker. ALV
Fable: "Tale is every time the same, The." Maurice James Craig. NeIP
Fable: "There is an inevitability." Norman Harris. NYBP
Fable: "Under a dung-cake." D. J. Opperman, *tr. fr. Afrikaans by* Jack Cope. PeSA
Fable for Blackboard. George Starbuck. CaFP
Fable for Critics, A, *sels.* James Russell Lowell.
Bryant. AnNE; AP
("There is Bryant, as quiet, as cool, and as dignified.") AmePo; CoBA; MWA-1
"But what's that? a mass-meeting? No, there come in lots." AmePo
Cooper. AnNE; AP; OxBA
("Here's Cooper, who's written six volumes to show.") CoBA; MWA-1
Emerson. AmPP (4th ed.); AnNE; AP; OxBA
("But stay, here comes Tityrus Griswold, and leads on.") AmePo, *longer sel.*
("There comes Emerson first, whose rich words.") CoBA; MWA-1; OuHeWo; PP
Hawthorne. AmPP (4th ed.); AnNE; AP; OxBA
("There is Hawthorne, with genius so shrinking and rare.") CoBA; MWA-1
Holmes. AnNE
("There's Holmes, who is matchless among you for wit.") AmePo; CoBA
Irving. AnNE
("What! Irving? thrice welcome, warm heart and fine brain.") CoBA; MWA-1
Lowell. AmPP (4th ed.); AP; OxBA
(On Himself.) AA
("There is Lowell, who's striving Parnassus to climb.") AmePo; CoBA
Poe and Longfellow. AmPP (5th ed.); AnNE; AP; OxBA
("There comes Poe, with his raven, like Barnaby Rudge.") AmePo; CoBA; MWA-1
"There are truths you Americans need to be told." AmePo
To His Countrymen. AA
Whittier. AmPP (4th ed.); AnNE; AP; OxBA
("There is Whittier, whose swelling and vehement heart.") AmePo; CoBA
Fable of a Forgotten Woman. Louis Johnson. AnNZ
Fable of Acis, Polyphemus and Galatea, The, *sel.* Ovid, *tr. fr. Latin by* Dryden. *Fr.* Metamorphoses, XIII.
I Heard the Ruffian-Shepherd Rudely Blow. AtBAP
Fable of the Bees, The, *sel.* Bernard Mandeville.
Grumbling Hive, The; or, Knaves Turn'd Honest. CEP; EiCL; EiPP
Fable of the Magnet and the Churn, The. W. S. Gilbert. *Fr.* Patience. FaPON; MPB; OnMSP; OTD; RePo
Fable of the Speckled Cow. D. J. Opperman, *tr. fr. Afrikaans by* Jack Cope, Uys Krige *and* Ruth Miller. PeSA
Fable of the War, A. Howard Nemerov. NePoEA
Fable of white sea, The. Coward. Harold Lewis Cook. NP
Fable which I now present, The. The Musical Ass. Tomaso de Yriarte. BOHV
Fables, *sels.* John Gay.
Council of Horses, The. BoChLi; GN
Eagle, and the Assembly of Animals, The. EiCP
Elephant and the Bookseller, The. EiCP; LoBV
Father and Jupiter, The. EiCL
Fox at the Point of Death, The. EnLi-1 (1949 ed.); OBEC; OTPC (1923 ed.)
Hare and Many Friends, The. ATP (1935 ed.); EiCL; EiCP; EnLi-1 (1949 ed.)
(Hare with Many Friends, The.) HBV
Lion and the Cub, The. GN; HBV; OTPC (1923 ed.)
Lion, the Fox, and the Geese, The. EiCP
Man and the Flea, The. EiCL
Old Hen and the Cock, The. EiCP
Plutus, Cupid, and Time. EiCP
Poet and the Rose, The. EiCP
Shepard's Dog and the Wolf, The. OA
Shepherd and the Philosopher, The. CEP; EiCL
Sick Man and the Angel, The. CEP
Tame Stag, The. CBEP; EiCP
Turkey and the Ant, The. OTPC (1923 ed.)
Vulture, the Sparrow, and Other Birds, The. EiCP
Wild Boar and the Ram, The. EiCP; PPON
Fables for the Female Sex, *sel.* Edward Moore.
Poet, and His Patron, The, V. CEP; EiCL
Fables of Flora, The, *sel.* John Langhorne.
Evening Primrose, The. OBEC
Fabliau of Florida. Wallace Stevens. NP
Fabula. *Unknown.* CIV
Fabulists, The. Kipling. ChMP
Fabulla, sweet virgin, you have learned your lesson too well. The Too Literal Pupil. Martial. UnTE
Façade, *sels.* Edith Sitwell.
Dark Song. CMoP; FaBoTw
Drum, The; the Narrative of the Demon of Tedworth. BoW; FaBoTw
Hornpipe. GTBS-P; MoVE; SeCePo
Madame Mouse Trots. FaBoCh; LOW
Satyr in the Periwig, The. AnEnPo
Sir Beelzebub. CoBMV; HoPM; MoAB; MoBrPo
(When Sir Beelzebub.) FaBoMo
Waltz. OAEP (2d ed.)
Face, A. Robert Browning. CTC; PoVP; VA
Face, The. Anthony Euwer. *See* Limerick: "As a beauty I'm not a great star."
Face, The. Ebenezer Jones. VA
Face, A. Marianne Moore. PoCh
Face, The. Edwin Muir. ChMP; FaBoMo; GTBS-P
Face. Carl Sandburg. ReMP
Face. Jean Toomer. CDC
Face, The. Thomas Wade. ERoP-2
Face against the Pane, The. Thomas Bailey Aldrich. TreFS
Face in stone and. Portrait in Stone. Charles Tomlinson. NYTB
Face in the Mirror, The. Robert Graves. NoP
Face in the Rock Wall. Robert Kelly. YAP
Face it. The stars have their own lives and care. Twelve Gates. Lorenzo Thomas. BF
Face it—you must—and do not turn away. Autumnal. Rolfe Humphries. MoRP
Face of a Friend, The. Henry van Dyke. OQP
Face of all the world is changed I think, The. Sonnets from the Portuguese, VII. Elizabeth Barrett Browning. ATP; BEL; CoBE; CTC; EnLi-2; EnLit; EPN; HBV; OAEP; OuHeWo; TOP; ViPo
Face of Christ, The. J. Stuart Holden. SoP
Face of Helen, The. Christopher Marlowe. *See* Was This the Face.
Face of Jesus Christ, The. Christina Rossetti. *Fr.* The Descent from the Cross. BePJ
Face of Love, The. Ingrid Jonker, *tr. fr. Afrikaans by* Jack Cope. PeSA
Face of Poverty. Lucy Smith. NNP; PoNe (1970 ed.)
Face of the dragonfly, The. Chisoku, *tr. fr. Japanese by* R. H. Blyth. FIW
Face of the landscape is a mask, The. Mask. Stephen Spender. MoAB; MoBrPo; NeMA
Face of the precipice is black with lovers, The. In Defence of Humanism. David Gascoyne. LiTM (rev. ed.)
Face of the Waters, The. Robert D. Fitzgerald. BoAV; MoAuPo; PoAu-2
Face on the Floor, The. Hugh D'Arcy. *See* Face upon the Floor, The.
Face that should content me wondrous [*or* wonders] well, A. A Description of Such a One As He Would Love (*or* Epigram). Sir Thomas Wyatt. CTC; EnLoPo; FCP; OBSC; ReEn; SiCE; TuPP
Face the Nation. Allen Ginsberg. *Fr.* Wichita Vortex Sutra. NaP
Face to Face. Frances Cochrane. HBV
Face to Face. Denise Levertov. FRC; TPM
Face to Face. Adrienne Rich. LiTM (1970 ed.); NoP; TPM
Face to face in my chamber, my silent chamber, I saw her. Confessions. Elizabeth Barrett Browning. OBVV
Face to Face with Reality. John Oxenham. WBLP
Face to face with the sunflower. The Secret Joy. Mary Webb. BoTP

Face to Face with Trouble, *sel.* Margaret E. Sangster.
"Oh, face to face with trouble," *st.* 6. PoToHe
Face to the wall and behind him. The Wall. Louis MacNeice. PoIE
Face upon [*or* on] the [Barroom] Floor, The. Hugh Antoine D'Arcy, *also at. to* John Henry Titus. BeLS; BLPA; FaBoBe; FaFP; GSP; HBV; NeHB; PaPo; TreF; YaD
Faces. Lola Ridge. MAP; MoAmPo (1942 ed.)
Faces. Sara Teasdale. OCS
Faces. Walt Whitman. Po; PoEL-5
Justified Mother of Men, The, *sel.* OHIP
Faces from a Bestiary. X. J. Kennedy. NePoEA-2
Facets of the flesh require, The. Duality. Kenneth Slade Alling. AnAmPo; CAW
Facing a streetlight under batty moths. The Calculation. David Wagoner. NYBP
Facing Death. Chih Ming, *tr. fr. Chinese by* Henry H. Hart. OnPM; WoL
Facing the Gulf. Margaret L. Woods. *Fr.* The Return. HBMV
Facing the Music. Virginia Graham. MuSP
Facing the New Year. Mark Guy Pearse. BLRP
Facing the New Year. *Unknown.* PGD
Facing the sudden gulf, the silent. Facing the Gulf. Margaret L. Woods. *Fr.* The Return. HBMV
Facing the uncertain stillnesses. A Poem for Fathers. Keith Wilson. ThO
Facing Up. James Scully. WIRo
Facing West from California's Shores. Walt Whitman. MoAmPo
Fact, and an Imagination, A. Wordsworth. FOL
Faction, that ever dwells. Caelica, XXIX. Fulke Greville. EnRePo; OBSC
Factories, The. Margaret Widdemer. HBV; MaRV; NeMA; PoMa
Factory Children. Richard Burton. MaRV
Factory Girl. Maxwell Bodenheim. MAP; MoAmPo (1942 ed.)
Factory Girl, The, *with music.* *Unknown.* ABF
Factory Street in Daylight. Paul Zech, *tr. fr. German by* Thomas Riley. WoL
Factory Windows Are Always Broken. Vachel Lindsay. CrMA; FaFP; LiTA; LiTM; NAMP; NePA; OCS; PoIE; PoMa; PoPo
Facts. W. H. Davies. BrPo
Facts have no eyes. One must. Observation of Facts. Charles Tomlinson. NePoEA-2
Fade in the sound of summer music. Notes for a Movie Script. M. Carl Holman. AmNP; Kal; PoNe
Fade, then,—die, depart, and come no more. Conrad Aiken. *Fr.* Priapus and the Pool. AmLP
Faded boy in sallow clothes, A. Emily Dickinson. PoEL-5
Faded Face, The. Thomas Hardy. QFR
Faded Letter, A. William J. Fischer. CAW
Faded perfume of forgotten years, The. In a Volume of Austin Dobson. Mary Elizabeth Coleridge. PoVP
Faded Pictures. William Vaughn Moody. AP
Fading Beauty. Samuel Daniel. *See* Description of Beauty, A.
Fading Beauty. *Unknown.* PeRV; SeCL; SeEP
Fading-Leaf and Fallen-Leaf. Richard Garnett. OBVV; TOP
Fading light/ Dims the sight. Words for Army Bugle Calls: Taps. *Unknown.* TreF
Fading Rose, The, *sel.* Philip Freneau.
Epitaph: "Here—for they could not help but die." AA
Fading whistles outline our broken city, The. Poem from London, 1941. George Woodcock. NeBP
Faerie Fair, The. Florence Harrison. BoTP
Faerie Queene, The, *sel.* Robin Blaser.
"Okay a nightingale." CoPo
Faerie Queene, The, *sels.* Spenser.
Address to Venus, *fr.* IV, 10, *tr. fr. the Latin of* Lucretius, *fr.* De Rerum Natura. AnEnPo; AWP
(Prayer to Venus.) EIL
"And as she backward cast her busy eye," *fr.* III, 11.
(Be Bold.) MyFE
"And him beside rides fierce revenging Wrath," *fr.* I, 4. MyFE
"And is there care in heaven? and is there love," *fr.* II, 8. OxBoCh
(Bright Squadrons, The.) GoBC
(Guardian Angels.) OBSC
(Guardian Angels of Men.) BoC
(Heavenly Aid.) MaRV
"And nigh thereto a little Chappell stoode," *fr.* V, 6. MBW-1
"And now they nigh approachèd to the sted," *fr.* II, 12. MBW-1
Artegall and Radigund, *fr.* V, 5. OBSC
"At last he came unto a gloomy glade," *fr.* II, 7. MBW-1
"At last she chauncèd by good hap to meet," *fr.* I, 7. MBW-1
August, *fr.* VII, 7. GN
Autumn, *fr.* VII, 7. GN
Balme, *fr.* I, 11. CH
"Behold I see the haven nigh at hand," I, 12. FosPo
Behold, O Man, *fr.* II, 6. EIL
"Both roof, and floor, and walls were all of gold," *fr.* II, 7.
(Mammon's House.) MyFE
Bower of Bliss, The, *fr.* II, 12. CH; FaBoEn; FiP; LoBV; OBSC; PoEL-1
("Eftsoons they heard a most melodious sound.") UnS, 2 *sts.*; ViBoPo
(Gather the Rose.) EIL; WHA
("Thence passing forth, they shortly doe arryve.") ATP
Britomart in the House of Busirane, *fr.* III, 11-12. FiP
("There they dismounting drew their weapons bold.") MBW-1
"But the wyld man, contrarie to her feare," *fr.* VI, 4. MBW-1
"By this the dreadfull beast drew nigh to hand," *fr.* I, 11. YAT
(Death of the Dragon, The, *abr.*) WHA
"By this the northerne wagoner had set," I, 2. FosPo
Cave of Despair, The, *fr.* I, 9. LoBV
("So as they traveild, lo! they gan espy.") MBW-1
Cave of Mammon, The, *fr.* II, 7. FiP, 12 *sts.*; PoEL-1
(House of Richesse, The, 3 *sts.*) CH
("Mammon emovéd was with inward wrath,") ViBoPo, 5 *sts.*
Cymochles and Phaedria, *fr.* II, 6. OBSC
Dame Nature, *fr.* VII, 7. PoEL-1
"Deepe in the bottome of an huge great rocke," *fr.* IV, 11-12. MBW-1
Despair, *fr.* I, 9. SeCePo, *shorter sel.*
(To Be or Not to Be.) FaBoEn
("Who Travels by the Weary Wandering Way.") PoG
Dragon, The, *fr.* I, 11. SeCePo
"Forthwith he gave in charge unto his squyre," *fr.* I, 8. MBW-1
Garden of Adonis, The, *fr.* III, 6. PoEL-1
Garden of Proserpina, The, *fr.* II, 7. ChTr
"Gentle knight was pricking on the plaine, A." I, 1. ATP; BoLiVe, *abr.*; CoBE; ExPo; FosPo; MBW-1; YAT, 3 *sts.*
(Red-Cross Knight, The, 2 *sts.*) GoBC
"Great travell hath the gentle Calidore," *fr.* VI, 9. MBW-1
Happy Isle, The, *fr.* IV, 10. OBSC
"He, making speedy way through 'spersèd air," *fr.* I, 1. InP
(House of Morpheus, The.) UnPo (1st ed.)
"He there does now enjoy eternal[l] rest," *fr.* I, 9. MyFE
(Sleep after Toil.) ChTr
"Her seem'd, as she was doing sacrifize," *fr.* V, 7. MBW-1
"High time now gan it wex for Una fayre," I, 11. FosPo
House of Ate, The, *fr.* IV, 1. OBSC
House of Pride, The, *fr.* I, 4. WHA
"In these wylde deserts where she now abode." *fr.* VI, 8. MBW-1
"It was an hill placed [*or* plaste] in an open plain," *fr.* VI, 10. MBW-1
(Dance, The) TrGrPo
(Dance of the Graces, The.) OBSC
"Joyous birds shrouded in cheerful shade, The," *fr.* II, 12.
(Music at the Bower of Bliss, The.) MyFE
Kinds of Trees to Plant, *fr.* I, 1. OHIP
Legend of Sir Guyon, or of Temperance, The, II, 12, *abr.* WHA
Legend of the Knight [*or* knyght] of the Red Cross, or of Holiness, I, 1-12. BEL; EnLi-1 (1 *and* 2); OAEP; TOP (1 *and* 4)
(Invocation to the Faerie Queene, *prol.*) FiP
("Lo I the man whose Muse whilome [*or* wylome] did maske.") EnLit, *prol.*, 1-2; FosPo
"Like as an hynd forth singled from the heard," *fr.* III, 7-8. MBW-1

Faerie (continued)
"Like as the tide that comes from th' Ocean main," *fr.* IV, 3. HoPM
"Long they thus travellèd in friendly wise," *fr.* III, 1. MBW-1
"Long time they thus together traveilèd," *fr.* I, 2. MBW-1
Love, *introd. to* IV. OBSC
"Martiall Mayd stayd not him to lament, The," *fr.* III, 4. MBW-1
Masque of Cupid, The, *fr.* III, 12. PoEL-1
(Mask of Cupid, The.) OBSC
May, *fr.* VII, 7. GN; PoRL
Mermaids, The, *fr.* II, 12. ChTr
Mutability *fr.* VII, 7 *and* 8. FaBoEn; OxBoCh; PoEL-1
("When I bethinke me on that speech whyleare,") MBW-1; ReEn
Next unto Him Was Neptune Pictured, *fr.* III, 11. EtS
"Noble heart that harbours virtuous thought, The," *fr.* I, 5. ViBoPo
(Fight of the Red Cross Knight and the Heathen Sansjoy, The.) FiP
"Nought is there under heav'ns wide hollownesse," *fr.* I, 3. MBW-1
Now Strike Your Sailes Ye Jolly Mariners, *fr.* I, 12, *and* II, 6. EtS
"Now when the rosy fingered Morning faire," *fr.* I, 2. BoLiVe
"One day, nigh wearie of the yrkesome way," *fr.* I, 3. BoLiVe
Pastoral, A: "From thence into the open fields he fled," *fr.* VI, 9. OBSC
Prince Arthur, *fr.* I, 7. OBSC
"Redoubted knights, and honorable Dames," *fr.* III, 9 and 10. NoP
Malbecco and Hellenore. MaPo
Prologue: "So oft as I with state of present time," *fr.* V. PoFS
Sea Monsters, *fr.* II, 12. ChTr; FaBoEn
("Waves come rolling, and the billowes rore, The.") AtBAP
"Silly man that in the thickett lay, The," *fr.* III, 10. MBW-1
"So as they travellèd, the drouping night," *fr.* IV, 5. MBW-1
"So, forth Issew'd the Seasons of the yeare," *fr.* VII, 7.
(Seasons, *abr.*) GN
(Mask of Mutability, The.) OBSC
"So passeth, in the passing of a day," *fr.* II, 12.
(Song, The.) MyFE
Summer, *br. sel. fr.* VII, 7. GN
Tale of Calidore, The, VI, 9. StP
Temple of Venus, *fr.* IV, 10. WHA
Thames Doth the Medway Wed, *fr.* IV, 6. HW
"That celestial power, to whom the care," *fr.* II, 12. MyFE
"There Atin fownd Cymochles sojourning," *fr.* II, 5. MBW-1
Trees, *fr.* I, 1. PoG
Two Cantos of Mutabilitie, VII, 6, 7, *and* 8. ReEn; SiCE
("What man that sees the ever-whirling wheele,") MBW-1
"Waies, through which my weary steps I guyde, The," *fr.* VI, Proem. MBW-1
What if Some Little Paine the Passage Have, *br. sel. fr.* I, 9. CH
(Death.) MaRV
(Port after Stormie Seas.) EtS
"What man so wise, what earthly wit so ware," I, 7. CoBE
"Whom bold Cymochles traveiling to finde," *fr.* II, 6. MBW-1
Winter, *fr.* VII, 7. GN; OTPC
"With fawning wordes he courted her a while," *fr.* I, 6. MBW-1
"Yet goodly court he made still to his Dame," *fr.* I, 7. MBW-1
Faerie's Child, The. Thomas Caulfield Irwin. OnYI
Faeries' Song, The. Ben Jonson. *See* Gipsy Song.
Faeries's Song. W. B. Yeats. *See* Fairy Song.
Faery [*or* Faiery *or* Fairy] beam upon you, The. Gipsy Song [*or* Patrico's Song *or* The Faeries' Song]. Ben Jonson. *Fr.* The Gypsies Metamorphosed. AtBAP; BoW; FaBoCh; LoBV; LoGBV; NoP; PoRL; ReEn; SeCL; SeCV-1; SiSw; TuPP
Faery Foster-Mother, The. Robert Buchanan. VA
Faery Queen, The. Sir Walter Ralegh. *See* Vision upon This Conceit of the Faerie Queene, A.
Faery Reaper, The. Robert Buchanan. OBVV
Faery Song. John Keats. *See* Fairy Song.
Faery Song, A: "We who are old, old and gay." W. B. Yeats. POTE; ViBoPo
Faesulan Idyl. Walter Savage Landor. *See* Fiesolan Idyl, A.
Fagots blazed, the caldron's smoke, The. The Brewing of Soma. Whittier. AmePo; PoEL-4
Faht's in there? What's in There. *Unknown.* CH
Faiery beame upon you, The. *See* Faery beam upon you.
Failing blossoms, which a young plant bears, The. Upon Our Late Loss of the Duke of Cambridge. Edmund Waller. Po
Failing in business, grandfather. Attic. William Hathaway. QAH
Failure. Orrick Johns. PoMa
Failure. Mary Sinton Leitch. ChIP
Failure. Eithne Wilkins. NeBP
Failures. Arthur W. Upson. HBV; OQP; PoToHe (1941 ed.); WGRP
Fain [*or* Faine] I would, but oh, I dare not. *Unknown.* ElL; SeCSL
Fain we ask Erinn. The Incantation. *At. to* Amergin. OnYI
Fain Wold I Have a Pretie Thing. *Unknown.* EnPo
Fain would I be sleeping, dreaming. The Plaint of the Wife. *Unknown.* AWP; JAWP; WBP
Fain Would I Change That Note. *Unknown, At. to* Tobias Hume. AtBAP; CBEP; EG; ElL; ELP; LiTL; LO; OBS; PoEL-2; TuPP; ViBoPo
(Devotion.) LiTB; OBEV
(No Other Choice.) TrGrPo
(Omnia Vincit.) GoBC; GTSL
(Song: "Fain would I change that note.") HBV
(Where Truest Pleasure Is.) OnPM
Fain [*or* Faine] would I, Chloris, ere I die. A Lover's Legacy. *Unknown.* SeCL; SeCSL
Fain would I, Chloris, whom my heart adores. At Parting. *Unknown.* SeCL
Fain Would I Have a Pretty [*or* Prettie] Thing [to Give unto My Ladie]. *Unknown.* CoMu; ElL; InvP; ViBoPo
(Proper Song, A, Entitled: Fain Would I Have a Pretty Thing to Give unto My Lady.) OAEP; ReEn; SiCE; TuPP
Fain would I have thee barter fates with me. To a Seabird. Sir William Watson. VA
Fain would I hold my lamp of life aloft. Be Hopeful. Celia Thaxter. SoP
Fain would I ride with thee,/ Eivlin a rúin. Eileen Aroon. Carrol O'Daly. OnYI
Fain Would I Wed [a Fair Young Man]. Thomas Campion. TuPP; UnTE
("Fain would I wed a fair young man that night and day could please me.") ReEn
Fain would I write, my mind ashamèd is. The Song of Mary the Mother of Christ. *At. to* Henry Walpole. ISi
Fain would I write to thee, and great display. A Letter. Mu'tamid, King of Seville. LiTW
Fain Would My Thoughts. John Austin. OxBoCh
Faine I would but O I dare not. *See* Fain I would, but oh, I dare not.
Faine would I chang my maiden life. *Unknown.* SeCSL
Faine would I Cloris (ere I dye). *See* Fain would I, Chloris, ere I die.
Fainne Gael an Lae. Alice Milligan. HBV
Faint as a climate-changing bird that flies. Demeter and Persephone. Tennyson. BWP; MBW-2; ViPP
Faint as the far-down tone. The Voice of Thought. Thomas Holley Chivers. AnAmPo
Faint, faint and clear. The Wind-swept Wheat. "Madeline Bridges." AA
Faint grew the yellow buds of light. Om. "Æ." VA
Faint Heart. *See* Faintheart.
Faint Music. Walter de la Mare. FaBoCh; LoGBV
Faint shines the far moon. The Road. Nikolay Platonovich Ogarev. AWP
Faint white pillars that seem to fade. Fragment. E. A. Robinson. MAPA
Faint Yet Pursuing. Coventry Patmore. The Unknown Eros, I, xxi. OxBoCh; PoVP
Faint Heart. William James Linton. OBVV
Faint Heart. Rufinus, *tr. fr. Greek by* F. A. Wright. ErPo

Faint Heart Never Won Fair Lady. Vicente Espinel, *tr. fr. Spanish by* Sir John Bowring. OnPM
Faintheart in a Railway Train. Thomas Hardy. CTC; EnLoPo
Faintly and from Far Away. Vassar Miller. CoPo
Faintly as tolls the evening chime. A Canadian Boat Song. Thomas Moore. GoBC; HBV; OBRV; PTK
Faintly at first, and low. Symphony: First Movement. John Hall Wheelock. UnS
Faintly the ne'er-do-well. The Flute of the Lonely. Vachel Lindsay. CrMA
Fair Agnete, The. Agnes Miegel, *tr. fr. German by* Margarette Münsterberg. CAW
Fair am I, mortals, as a stone-carved dream. La Beauté. Baudelaire. AWP; JAWP; WBP
Fair Amazon of Heaven who tookst in hand. To Saint Margaret. Henry Constable. ACP; GoBC
Fair Amoret is gone astray. A Hue and Cry after Fair Amoret [*or* Amoret]. Congreve. CEP; OBEC OBEV; ViBoPo
Fair and bright assembly, A: never strode. Thomas Lovell Beddoes. *Fr.* Death's Jest Book. CTC
Fair and cruel, still in vain. Ode to Chloris. Charles Cotton. CavP
Fair and Fair. George Peele. *Fr.* The Arraignment of Paris. ElL; OBEV; ViBoPo
(Cupid's Curse.) BEL; TOP
("Fair and fair and twice so fair.") ReEn; SiCE; TuPP
(Song of Oenone and Paris.) OBSC
Fair and lovely maid, look from the shore. To Delia, XLII. Samuel Daniel. ReIE
Fair, and soft, and gay, and young. Song. Robert Gould. *Fr.* The Rival Sisters, III. CEP; SeCL; UnTE
Fair Angels pass'd by next in seemly Bands. The Annunciation. Abraham Cowley. *Fr.* Davideis. OxBoCh
Fair Annet's Song. Elinor Wylie. AmLP
Fair Annie. *Unknown.* AnFE; BaBo (A *and* B *vers.*); CH; ESPB (A, B, *and* E *vers.*); HBV; OBB, *sl. abr.*; OBEV (1st ed); OxBB; ViBoFo (A, B, *and* C *vers.*)
Fair Annie an Sweet Willie. Lord Thomas and Fair Annet (I *vers.*). *Unknown.* ESPB
Fair Annie had a costly bower. The Holy Nunnery. *Unknown.* BaBo; ESPB
Fair Annie of Lochroyan. *Unknown. See* Lass of Lochroyan, The.
Fair are the flowers and the children, but their subtle suggestion is fairer. Indirection. Richard Realf. AA; AnAmPo; AnFE; CoAnAm; HBV; MaRV; OQP
Fair as the night—when all the astral fires. A Similitude [*or* Love Sonnets, VIII]. Charles Harpur. BoAu; PoAu-1
Fair as the seven daughters of the sun. Pythagoras. Thomas S. Jones., Jr. AnAmPo
Fair as unshaded light, or as the day. *See* Faire as unshaded light. . .
Fair at Windgap, The. Austin Clarke. OnYI; SeCePo
Fair Bersabe the bright, once bathing in a well. George Gascoigne. *Fr.* The Adventures of Master F. I. ReIE
Fair blue sky, A. Breeze and Billow. Albert Durrant Watson. CaP
Fair breeze blew, the white foam flew, The. Samuel Taylor Coleridge. *Fr.* The Rime of the Ancient Mariner. PoG
Fair brow in the strict cold shrine. The Nettle, the Flower. Morton Dauwen Zabel. NP
Fair by inheritance, whom born we see. Of the Nativity of the Lady Rich's Daughter. Henry Constable. OBSC
Fair Charlotte, *with music. Unknown.* BFSS
Fair Circassian, The. Richard Garnett. HBV; OBVV; VA
Fair Cloris in a pig-stye lay. A Song to Cloris. Earl of Rochester. ErPo
Fair cousin mine! the golden days. Chivalry at a Discount. Edward Fitzgerald. HBV
Fair Cynthia mounted on her sprightly pad. Cynthia on Horseback. Philip Ayres. EnLoPo; Sonn
Fair Cynthia, all the homage that I may. Thoughts on the Sight of the Moon. Sarah Kemble Knight. SCAP
Fair daffodils [*or* Faire Daffadills], we weep to see. To Daffodils [*or* Daffadills]. Robert Herrick. AnAnS-2; AnEnPo; AtBAP; AWP; BEL; BoLiVe; BoNaP; CBEP; CBV; CoBE; EG; ELP; EnL; EnLi-1; EnLit; EP; EvOK; ExPo; FaBoCh; FaBoEn; FosPo; GBV; GN; GoJo; GTBS; GTBS-D; GTBS-P; GTBS-W; GTSE; GTSL; HBV; HBVY; InPo; JAWP; LiTB; LoBV; MaPo; NoP; OAEP; OBEV; OBS; OTPC; OuHeWo; PAn; PIA; PoE; PoEL-3; PoeP; PoFS; PoIE; PoPo; PoRA; QFR; ReEn; SCEP-2; SeCeV; SeCL; SeCP; SeCV-1; SeEP; ShBV-3; TrGrPo; ViBoPo; WBP; WePo WHA
Fair Danubie is praised for being wide. Rivers. Thomas Storer. ElL; FaBoCh
Fair Days; or, Dawns Deceitful, *br. sel.* Robert Herrick. MyFE
Fair Ellen Irwin, when she sate. Ellen Irwin; or, The Braes of Kirtle. Wordsworth. MBW-2
Fair England. Helen Gray Cone. AA
Fair Eve knelt close by the guarded gate. The Rose of Eden. Susan K. Phillips. BeLS
Fair Exchange, A. La Fontaine. UnTE
Fair eyes, sweet lips, dear heart, that foolish I. Astrophel and Stella, XLIII. Sir Philip Sidney. FCP; SiPS
Fair fa' your honest, sonsie face. Address to a Haggis. Burns. ViBoPo
Fair Fannie Moore, *with music. Unknown.* BFSS
Fair fields, proud Flora's vaunt, why is't you smile. Menaphon's Ditty. Robert Greene. OBSC
Fair Florella; or, The Jealous Lover. *Unknown. See* Jealous Lover, The.
Fair flower of fifteen springs. To His Young Mistress. Pierre de Ronsard. *Fr.* Amours de Marie. AWP; OuHeWo
Fair Flower of Northumberland, The. *Unknown.* BaBo; BuBa; ESPB, *sl. diff.*; LoEn; OBB; OxBB
Fair flower, that dost so comely grow. The Wild Honey Suckle. Philip Freneau. AA; AmLP; AmP; AmPP; AnAmPo; AP; CBEP; CoBA; HBV; LiTA; MAmP; OxBA; PoEL-4; PoIE (1970 ed.); PoLF; TrGrPo
"Fair flowery Name! in none but Thee." The Holy Name of Jesus. Richard Crashaw. CAW
Fair Friend, 'Tis True. Ben Jonson. EP
Fair girl was sitting in the greenwood shade, A. The Fairy Tempter. Samuel Lover. OTPC
Fair golden thoughts and lovely words. About Women. H. Phelps Putnam. AnFE; CoAnAm; MAP; MoAmPo (1942 ed.); TwAmPo
Fair grace of graces, muse of muses all. Henry Constable. *Fr.* Diana. Sonn; TuPP
Fair Greece! sad relic of departed worth! Byron. *Fr.* Childe Harold's Pilgrimage, II. ILP; PoFr
Fair-haired Girl, The. *Unknown, tr. fr. Modern Irish by* Sir Samuel Ferguson. OnYI
Fair Harvard. Samuel Gilman. InP
Fair Hebe. John West. HBV
Fair Helen of Kirconnell. *Unknown. See* Helen of Kirconnell.
Fair Hermeline ask'd her father dear. The Lady and the Dwarf-King. *Unknown.* BaBo
Fair Hills of Eiré, O, The! Donogh Mac-Con-Mara (Macnamara), *tr. fr. Irish by* James Clarence Mangan. IrPN; OBVV
Fair Hills of Ireland, The. *Unknown, tr. fr. Modern Irish by* Sir Samuel Ferguson. AnIV; IrPN; OBEV; OBVV; OnYI
Fair hope! our earlyer heav'n by thee. Richard Crashaw. *Fr.* M. Crashaw's Answer for Hope. FaBoEn
Fair in a morn (O fairest morn). Song of Phillida and Coridon. Nicholas Breton. TuPP
Fair Inconstant, The. Francis Thompson. GTSE
Fair Indian Lass, The. *Unknown. See* Little Mohee, The.
Fair Ines. Thomas Hood. EnRP; HBV; OBEV; OBRV; OBVV; PG (1945 ed.); TOP; UnPo (1st ed.); VA
Fair insect! that, with threadlike legs spread out. To a Mosquito. Bryant. AnNE
Fair Iris and Her Swain. Dryden. *Fr.* Amphitryon, IV, i. ViBoPo
Fair Iris I Love. Dryden. *See* Song: "Fair Iris I love, and hourly I die."
"Fair is Alexis," I no sooner said. On Alexis. Plato. AWP
Fair is each budding thing the garden shows. The Old-fashioned Garden. John Russell Hayes. AA
Fair is her body, bright her eye. Medieval Norman Song. *Unknown, tr. by* John Addington Symonds. AWP; JAWP; WBP; WoL
Fair is my dove, my loved one. Marriage Song. Judah Halevi. TrJP
Fair Is My Love. Samuel Daniel. *See* Fair is my love, and cruel as she's fair.
Fair Is My Love. Robert Greene. *See* Fair Is My Love for April in Her Face.

Fair Is My Love. Bartholomew Griffin. *See* Fair is my love that feeds among the lilies.
Fair Is My Love. *At. to* Shakespeare. The Passionate Pilgrim, VII. EIL; NoP
Fair is my love, and cruel as she's fair. To Delia, VI. Samuel Daniel. EIL; EnRePo; GTBS-W; HBV; HoPM; LiTB; LiTG; LiTL; NoP; OAEP; OBEV; OBSC; PoEL-2; ReEn; ReIE; SiCE; Sonn; TrGrPo; TuPP; ViBoPo
Fair is my Love, but not so fair as fickle. Fair Is My Love. *At. to* Shakespeare. *Fr.* The Passionate Pilgrim. EIL; NoP
Fair Is My Love for April in [*or* Is *or* April's in] Her Face. Robert Greene. *Fr.* Perimedes. EIL; HBV; ReIE; ViBoPo
Fair [*or* Faire] is my love that feeds among the lilies. Bartholomew Griffin. Fidessa, More Chaste than Kind, XXXVII. CBEP; EG; EIL; ErPo; LO; PoEL-2; SiCE; Sonn; TrGrPo; TuPP; ViBoPo
Fair [*or* Fayre] is my love, when her fair golden hairs [*or* heares]. Amoretti, LXXXI. Spenser. EIL; LiTL; NoP; PoE; Sonn
Fair is the hue of your mantle, Mary. The Mantle of Mary. Patrick O'Connor. ISi
Fair is the night and fair the day. Song from the Story of Acontius and Cydippe. William Morris. *Fr.* The Earthly Paradise: October. HBV
Fair Is the Rose. *Unknown.* EG; EIL
Fair Is Too Foul an Epithet. Christopher Marlowe. *Fr.* Tamburlaine the Great, Pt. I, Act V, sc. ii. LiTB
("Ah faire [*or* fair] Zenocrate, divine Zenocrate.") AtBAP; PoEL-2; ViBoPo
Fair Isabel, poor simple Isabel! Isabella; or, The Pot of Basil [*or* The Beginning of Love]. Keats. EnRP; MERP; UnPo (1st ed.); ViBoPo
Fair Isabel sat in her bower door. Hind Etin. *Unknown.* OxBB
Fair Isabell of Rochroyall. The Lass of Roch Royal. *Unknown.* BaBo; OxBB
Fair islands of the silver fleece. Ballade of the Southern Cross. Andrew Lang. InP
Fair isle, that from the fairest of all flowers. Sonnet—To Zante. Poe. MAmP
Fair Janet. *Unknown.* BaBo; ESPB; OBB, *abr.*; OxBB
Fair Jesu, gyide Thy straying sheep. The Straying Sheep. *Unknown.* JKCP (1926 ed.)
Fair Julia sitting by the fire. On a Spark of Fire Fixing on a Gentlewoman's Breast. Thomas Philipott. SeCL
Fair Ladies Tall Lovers. E. E. Cummings. SiSW
Fair lady Isabel sits in her bower sewing. Lady Isabel and the Elf-Knight. *Unknown.* BaBo (A *vers.*); ESPB (A *vers.*); OAEP; ViBoFo (A *vers.*)
Fair Lady of the Plains, The, *with music. Unknown.* BFSS
Fair[e] lady, when you see the grace. To One Admiring Herself in a Looking-Glass. Thomas Randolph. AnAnS-2; CLwM; LiTL; ViBoPo
Fair lady with the bandaged eye. Ode to Fortune. Fitz-Greene Halleck *and* Joseph Rodman Drake. *Fr.* The Croaker Papers. AA
Fair Lass of Islington, The. *Unknown. See* Lass of Islington, The.
Fair liberty, our soul's most darling prize. To the Heirs of the Pilgrims. Benjamin Church. PoFr
Fair little girl sat under a tree, A. Good Night and Good Morning. Richard Monckton Milnes. BoTP; OTPC; PRWS; SAS; TVC
Fair little spirit of the woodland mazes. A Dead Singer. John E. Logan. VA
Fair Lunacy! I see thee, with a crown. Mirthful Lunacy. Thomas Stoddart. *Fr.* The Death-Wake; or, Lunacy. OBNC
Fair Maid and the Sun, The. Arthur O'Shaughnessy. BeLS; VA
Fair Maid by the Seashore, The. *Unknown.* BaBo
Fair maid, had I not heard thy baby cries. To a Lofty Beauty, from Her Poor Kinsman. Hartley Coleridge. OBVV
Fair maid in a garden walking, A. A Sweetheart in the Army (A *vers.*). *Unknown.* BaBo
Fair Maid of Amsterdam, The. *Unknown.* OxBoLi
(A-Roving, *with music.*) ShS (*vers.* I); SoAmSa
Fair Maid of the Exchange, The, *sel. At. to* Thomas Heywood.
Ye Little Birds That Sit and Sing. EIL; ViBoPo
(Message, The.) HBV; OBEV (1st ed.)
Fair Maid of the Inn, The. John Gay. *See* Molly Mog.
Fair Maid of the West, The. *Unknown.* CoMu
Fair maid sat in her bower [*or* front] door, A. The False Lover Won Back [*or* The Fause Lover *or* Young John]. *Unknown.* BaBo; BuBa; CoBE; ESPB (A *vers.*); OBB
Fair maid who, [on] the first of May, The. Mother Goose. BoChLi; PCH
Fair Maiden. George Peele. *See* Song at the Well, The.
Fair maiden, fair maiden. Invocation to the Muse. Richard Hughes. MoBrPo
Fair maiden, white and red. A Voice [Speaks] from the Well. George Peele. *Fr.* The Old Wives' Tale. CBEP; FaBoCh; LoGBV; OBSC; OxBoLi; SiTL
Fair Maiden, Who Is This Bairn? *Unknown.* ISi
Fair Margaret and Sweet William, *diff. versions. Unknown.* BaBo; BFSS, *with music*; ESPB; OBB; OxBB; TOP; ViBoFo
(Sweet William.) BaBo
(Sweet William and Lady Margaret.) BFSS, *with music*
Fair Margaret [*or* Margret] was a young [*or* proud] ladye. Proud Lady Margaret. *Unknown.* ESPB (E *vers.*); OBB; OxBB
Fair Marjorie sat i her bower-door. Young Benjie. *Unknown.* ESPB
Fair Mary of Wallington. *Unknown.* ESPB (A *and* C *vers.*); OBB
(Bonny Earl of Livingston, The.) OxBB
Fair Millinger, The. Fred W. Loring. BOHV
Fair must that promised country be. The Promised Country. Speer Strahan. JKCP
Fair now is the springtide, now earth lies beholding. The Message of the March Wind. William Morris. GTBS-D; OBNC; OBVV; WiR
Fair Nymph Scorning a Black Boy Courting Her, A. John Cleveland. AnAnS-2
Fair of face, full of pride. A Lyke-Wake Song. Swinburne. PoVP
Fair, order'd lights (whose motion without noise). The Constellation. Henry Vaughan. SCEP-1; SeCV-1
Fair Oriana, Beauty's Queen. John Hilton. ReIE
Fair Oriana in the Morn. John Milton. ReIE
Fair Pamela came to town, The. Pamela in Town. Ellen M. H. Cortissoz. AA; HBV
Fair Penitent, The, *sel.* Nicholas Rowe.
Song: "Ah stay! ah turn! ah whither would you fly," *by* Congreve. AtBAP; LoBV; OBEC
Fair Phyllis. Ben Jonson. LiTL
Fair [*or* Faire] pledges of a fruitful tree. To Blossoms. Robert Herrick. BoNaP; BWP; EG; GTBS; GTBS-D; GTBS-P; GTBS-W; GTSE; GTSL; HBV; LoBV; OBEV; OBS; SCEP-2; SeCL; SeCP; SeCV-1; SeEP; UnPo (1st ed.)
Fair *Princess Royal,* The. *Unknown. See* Bold *Princess Royal,* The.
Fair proud, now tell me, why should fair be proud. Amoretti, XXVII. Spenser. Sonn
Fair rebel to thyself and Time. The Revenge. Pierre de Ronsard. AWP
Fair, Rich, and Young. Sir John Harington, *After the Latin of Martial.* EIL; PV; SeCePo
(Of a Fair Shrew.) SiCE
Fair rocks, goodly rivers, sweet woods, when shall I see peace? Echo. Sir Philip Sidney. *Fr.* Arcadia. FCP; SiPS
Fair Roslin Chapel, how divine. Roslin and Hawthornden. Henry van Dyke. AA
Fair sail shimmers, white and lonely, A. *See* Far sail shimmers . . .
Fair Salamis, the billow's roar. Chorus. Sophocles. *Fr.* Ajax. AWP; JAWP; WBP
Fair Seed-Time Had My Soul. Wordsworth. *Fr.* The Prelude, I. AtBAP; MaPo
(Childhood and School-Time) FaBoEn; OBNC
("Fair seed-time had my soul, and I grew up.") EnL; EnLi-2; ExPo; NoP; OBRV; PoEL-4
(Presences of Nature in Boyhood.) EPN
Fair, seek not to be feared, most lovely beloved. Sir Philip Sidney. FCP
Fair Selinda goes to prayers. All or Nothing. Congreve. MeWo
Fair ship, that from the Italian shore. In Memoriam A. H. H., IX. Tennyson. BoLiVe; EnLi-2; EPN; GTSL; OAEP; OBEV (1st ed.); ViPo; VP
Fair Singer, The. Andrew Marvell. CavP; CBEP; EG; EnLoPo; LiTL; LO, 2 *sts.*; MaMe; MeLP; MemP; MePo; PoEL-2; PoIE (1970 ed.); ReEn; SeCL; UnPo (3d ed.)

Fair Sou-Chong-Tee, by a shimmering brook. Story of the Flowery Kingdom. James Branch Cabell. HBMV; OnMSP; PCD
Fair star, new-risen to our wondering eyes. Bacchylides. George Meason Whicher. AA
Fair star of evening, splendor of the west. Composed by the Seaside, near Calais, August, 1802. Wordsworth. ATP; CoBE; EnLi-2; EnRP; MBW-2; MERP; OAEP; OuHeWo; PoE; Sonn; TOP; UnPo (1st ed.)
Fair stood the wind for France. Agincourt [*or* The Ballad (*or* Battle) of Agincourt *or* Ode to the Cambro-Britons.] Michael Drayton. AnFE; BEL; BeLS; CBEP; EIL; EnL; EnLi-1; EnRePo; FaBoBe; FaBoCh; FOL; GN; GoTL; HBV; LoGBV; MCCG; MemP; NoP; OAEP; OBEV; OBS; OnSP; PoRA; PTK; ReEn; ReIE; SeEP; ShBV-1; TOP; TuPP; WHA
Fair Summer Droops. Thomas Nashe. *Fr.* Summer's Last Will and Testament. EIL; LoBV; TuPP
(Waning Summer.) OBSC
Fair sun, if you would have me praise your light. Henry Constable. *Fr.* Diana. OBSC; SiCE
Fair, sweet and young, receive a prize. Song [*or* Fair, Sweet, and Young]. Dryden. LiTL; OBS; SeCL; SeEP
Fair Sylvia. *Unknown.* OBS
Fair Sylvia, cease to blame my youth. Song. Francis Atterbury. WaPE
Fair! that you may truly know. To Amoret. Edmund Waller. SCEP-2; SeCV-1
Fair the daughter known as Mary. An Old Song By New Singers (as Longfellow Might Have Done It.) A. C. Wilkie. BOHV
Fair the gift to Merlin given. Merlin's Apple-Trees. Thomas Love Peacock. *Fr.* The Misfortunes of Elphin. OBRV
Fair, the young acacia, thick with leaves. The Young Acacia. Hayyim Nahman Bialik. TrJP
Fair these broad meads—these hoary woods are grand. Canadian Boat Song. *Unknown, at. to* John Galt. BLPA; GoTS; OBEV (new ed.); OBRV; OxBS
Fair Thief, The. Charles Wyndham. HBV
Fair Thou Art. Mordecai ben Isaac, *tr. fr. Hebrew by* Herbert Loewe. TrJP
Fair tree! for thy delightful shade. The Tree. Countess of Winchilsea. BWP; CEP; CoBE; EiPP; OBEC
Fair varieties of earth, The. Life Is Love. William Johnson Fox. VA
Fair Verna! loveliest village of the west. Sweet Simplicity. Timothy Dwight. *Fr.* Greenfield Hill. AmPP
Fair Virgin,/ Vestured with the sun! Ode to the Virgin. Petrarch. *Fr.* Sonnets to Laura: To Laura in Death. ISi
Fair Virtue, the Mistress of Philarete, *sels.* George Wither.
Hence, Away, You Sirens, *also given in* Fidelia. EIL, 3 *sts.*
I Wandered Out. SeCL
(Divided Heart, The.) TrGrPo
Shall I, Wasting in Despair, *also given in* Fidelia. ALV; AnFE; BEL; BoLP; EG; EIL; EnLi-1; LiTB; LiTG; OBS; OuHeWo; PoIE; ReEn; WHA
(Author's Resolution in a Sonnet, The.) CLwM; NoP; ViBoPo
(Lover's Resolution, The.) AWP; EnLit; HBV; InMe; JAWP; LiTL; OBEV; PG; TOP; TreFS; WBP; YAT
(Manly Heart, The.) FaBV; GTBS; GTBS-D; GTBS-P; GTBS-W; GTSE; GTSL; MCCG
(Sonnet; "Shall I, wasting in despair.") SeCV-1; SeEP
(What Care I.) MeWo; TrGrPo
Stolen Kiss, A. HBV; LiTL; SeCL
(Kiss, The) UnTE
(Sonnet upon a Stolen Kiss, A.) PoIE (1970 ed.)
(Theft, The.) MeWo
Fair was the dawn, and, but e'en now, the skies. Robert Herrick. *Fr.* Fair Days; or, Dawns Deceitful. MyFE
Fair were our visions! Oh, they were as grand. In the Land Where We Were Dreaming. Daniel Bedinger Lucas. PAH
Fair would I have a pretty thing. A Pretty Thing. *Unknown.* UnTE
Fair [*or* Fayre] ye be sure, but cruel and unkind. Amoretti, LVI. Spenser. EnLit; NoP; Sonn
Fair Young Miss, The, *with music.* *Unknown.* BFSS
Fair Young Virgin Is like the Rose Untainted, The. *Unknown.* ReIE
Fair Young Wife, The. Helen Adam. FiSC
Faire and scornefull doe thy worst. *Unknown.* SeCSL
Faire Archibella to thine eyes. *Unknown.* SeCSL
Faire [*or* Fair] as unshaded light, or as the day. To the Queen, Entertain'd at Night by the Countess of Anglesey. Sir William Davenant. FaBoEn; MeLP; MePo; OBS; SeCL; SeEP
Faire daffadills, we weep to see. *See* Fair daffodils, we weep to see.
Faire eyes regard my love soe truelie tryed. *Unknown.* SeCSL
Faire, great, and good, since seeing you, wee see. To the Countesse of Salisbury. John Donne. MaMe
Faire Is My Love. Bartholomew Griffin. *See* Fair is my Love that feeds among the lilies.
Faire lady when you see the grace. *See* Fair Lady when you see the grace.
Faire pledges of a fruitfull tree. *See* Fair pledges of a fruitful tree.
Faire soule, how long shall veyles thy graces shroud? At Home in Heaven. Robert Southwell. AnAnS-1; MeP
Faire soule, which wast, not onely, as all soules bee. Obsequies to the Lord Harrington, Brother to the Lady Lucy, Countesse of Bedford. John Donne. MaMe
Faire will you then that I shall dye. *Unknown.* SeCSL
Fairer is the sea. Paul Verlaine. *Fr.* Sagesse. AWP; JAWP; WBP
Fairer than Fairest. *Unknown.* SeCL
("Fairer than fairest, if your eyes.") SeEP
Fairer than the rosy east. To Chloris. John Cobbes. SeCL
Fairest between Lincoln and Lindsey. *Unknown.* *See* When the Nightingale Sings.
Fairest day that ever yet has shone, The. The Lost. Jones Very. MAmP; PoIE; QFR
Fairest eyes (O eyes in blackness fair!), The. Sonnet III: Upon His Absence from Her. Francis Davison. ReIE
Fairest He, The. Horatius Bonar. BePJ
Fairest, how poor is your lover today! The Flower. Henrik Wergeland. LiTW
Fairest Isle. Dryden. *See* Song of Venus.
Fairest Lord Jesus. *Unknown, tr. fr. German by* E. Storrs Willis FaChP; SoP; TRV; WGRP
(Crusader's Hymn.) MaRV
(Song of the Crusaders.) BePJ
Fairest Lord Jesus, serene You lay. God Incarnate. Ruth M. Williams. BePJ
Fairest of fair, O lady mine, Venus. Prayer to Venus. Chaucer. *Fr.* The Canterbury Tales: The Knight's Tale. LiTL
Fairest of Freedom's Daughters. Jeremiah Eames Rankin. PAH
Fairest of Her Days, The. *Unknown.* EIL
Fairest of morning lights appear. Psalm for Christmas Day. Thomas Pestel. OxBoCh
Fairest of the fairest, rival of the rose. Mabel, in New Hampshire. James T. Fields. HBV
Fairest of valleys, in this full-bloomed night. In Wiltshire. Edmund Blunden. POTE
Fairest Theina let me know. *Unknown.* SeCSL
Fairest thing that shines below. Clad All in White. Abraham Cowley. *Fr.* The Mistress. SeCV-1
Fairest things are those that silent come, The. He Leads. Elisabeth Scollard. MaRV
Fairfax, Whose Name in Arms through Europe Rings. Milton. *See* On the Lord General Fairfax at the Siege of Colchester.
Fairground. W. H. Auden. NYBP
Fairies, The. William Allingham. AnEnPo; BoChLi; CBEP; CH; ChTr; DD, *abr.*; EvOK; FaBoCh; FaBV; FaPON; GBV; GFA, *abr.*; GTBS-D; HBV; HBVY; IrPN; LiTG; LoGBV; OBEV; OBVV; OnMSP; OnYI; OTPC; OxBI; PCH; PDV; PoMS; PoRh; PTK; RG; RoGo; SUS; TOP; TSW; TVC; VA; ViBoPo
(Fairy Folk, The.) GN; PaPo
(Up the Airy Mountain.) FaFP; StVeCh
Little Men, The, *br. sel.* OtMeF
Fairies. Marchette Chute. MoSiPe
Fairies. Hilda Conkling. GBV (1922 ed.); SP; TiPo
Fairies, The. Rose Fyleman. FaPON; HBMV; HBVY; MPB; OTPC (1946 ed.); SoPo; StVeCh; TSW; TVC
Fairies, The. John G. Herndon. MPB
Fairies, The. Robert Herrick. FaPON; MPB; OBS; OTPC (1946 ed.); SeEP
Fairies. Kikaku, *tr. fr. Japanese.* MPB
Fairies, The. Sybil Morford. OTPC (1946 ed.); PoRL; TVC
Fairies. Thomas Tickell. *Fr.* Kensington Garden. OBEC
Fairies, The ("Come follow, follow me"). *Unknown.* *See* Fairy Queen, The.
Fairies. Louis Untermeyer. StaSt

Fairies all received an invitation, The. Edith Sitwell. *Fr.* The Sleeping Beauty. FlW
Fairies are a charming folk, if all the tales be true, The. The Fairies. John G. Herndon. MPB
Fairies Break Their Dances, The. A. E. Housman. MoVE; PeVV
Fairies' Dance, The ("Dare you haunt our hallow'd green?"). *Unknown.* MPB
Fairies dance the livelong night, The. In the Moonlight. Norreys Jephson O'Conor. HBMV; SoPo; SUS
Fairies, fairies, come and be fed. Feeding the Fairies. *Unknown.* PPL
Fairies' Farewell, The. Richard Corbet. CBEP; LiTB; LiTG; LoGBV; OtMeF, *abr.*; PoFS; TrGrPo; UnPo (1st ed.); ViBoPo, *abr.*
(Farewell, Rewards and Fairies.) FaBoCh, *abr.*; LoBV; SiTL
(Farewell to the Fairies.) EvOK; HBV; HBVY, *abr.*; MoShBr
(Proper New Ballad, A, Intituled [*or* Entitled] The Fairies' Farewell; or, God-a-Mercy Will.) AnAnS-2; OBS; OxBoLi; PoE; ReEn; SeCL; SeCP; SeEP
Fairies Feast, The. Charles M. Doughty. CH
Fairies Have Never a Penny to Spend, The. Rose Fyleman. BoChLi; FaPON; GBV (1922 ed.); HBMV; MPB; SP
Fairies hold a fair, they say, The. The Faerie Fair. Florence Harrison. BoTP
Fairies in New Ross, The. *Unknown.* OnYI
Fairies, it is said, The. Fairies. Kikaku. MPB
Fairies' Lights. Alice Wilkins. GFA
Fairies' Lullaby, The. Shakespeare. *See* You Spotted Snakes.
Fairies of the Caldon Low, The. Mary Howitt. BeLS; HBV; HBVY; OTPC; PRWS; TVC
Fairies' Recall. Felicia Dorothea Hemans. OTPC
Fairies' Shopping, The. Margaret Deland. HBVY; PRWS
Fairies' Siege, The. Kipling. OtMeF
Fairies' Song. Thomas Randolph, *tr. fr. Latin by* Leigh Hunt. *Fr.* Amyntas. ALV; PoMS
(Fairy Song.) HBV
(Song of Fairies Robbing an Orchard.) OBRV
Fairies' Song, The. Shakespeare. *See* You Spotted Snakes.
Fairies, too, have aeroplanes, The. Fairy Aeroplanes. Anne Blackwell Payne. GFA; UTS
Fairweill. *Unknown.* OxBS
Fairy, The. *Unknown.* *See* Light-hearted Fairy, The.
Fairy Aeroplanes. Anne Blackwell Payne. GFA; UTS
Fairy and the soul proceeded, The. The Magic Car Moved on. Shelley. *Fr.* Queen Mab, I. GN
Fairy Artist, The. Nellie M. Garabrant. PCH; PoPl
Fairy band are we, A. Song. Alfred Noyes. GBV (1922 ed.)
Fairy beam upon you, The. *See* Faery beam upon you, The.
Fairy Blessing, The. Shakespeare. *See* Now the Hungry Lion Roars.
Fairy Book, The. Abbie Farwell Brown. HBV; HBVY
Fairy Book, The. Norman Gale. HBV; HBVY; OHIP; OTPC (1946 ed.); TVC
Fairy Boy, The. Samuel Lover. OTPC (1923 ed.)
Fairy Bread. Robert Louis Stevenson. GBV (1922 ed.); OTPC (1946 ed.)
Fairy Carpets. Anne Blackwell Payne. GFA
Fairy Chorus. *Unknown.* *Fr.* The Bride's Marriage-Cake. HW
Fairy Cobbler, The. A. Neil Lyons. BoTP
Fairy Dances ("By the moon we sport and play"). *Unknown.* *See* By the Moon We Sport and Play.
Fairy Dances ("Round about, round about"). *Unknown.* *See* Elves' Dance, The.
Fairy Dawn. Joseph Rodman Drake. *Fr.* The Culprit Fay. GN
Fairy Days. Thackeray. GoTP; OTPC (1946 ed.)
Fairy Dream, A. Dorothy Gradon. BoTP
Fairy! Fairy! list and mark. The Fay's Crime. Joseph Rodman Drake. *Fr.* The Culprit Fay. GN
Fairy Feet. Phyllis L. Garlick. BoTP
Fairy Fiddler, The. Nora Hopper. HBMV; ViBoPo
('Tis I Go Fiddling, Fiddling.) OxBI
Fairy Flute, The. Rose Fyleman. BoTP
Fairy Folk, The. William Allingham. *See* Fairies, The.
Fairy Folk, The. Robert Montgomery Bird. GFA; HBV; HBVY; OTPC; PRWS; TVC
Fairy Frilly. Florence Hoatson. GFA; OTPC (1946 ed.)
Fairy Frock, The. Katharine Morse. UTS
Fairy Frolic, The. *Unknown.* *See* By the Moon We Sport and Play.
Fairy Frolics. Annie Isobel Rentoul. GFA
Fairy Godmothers. Eugene Lee-Hamilton. OBVV
Fairy Harpers, The. James B. Dollard. CaP
Fairy has found a new fern ,A! A New Fern. "A." PRWS
Fairy Host, The. *Tr. fr. Irish by* Alfred Perceval Graves. AnIV
Fairy in Armor, A. Joseph Rodman Drake. *Fr.* The Culprit Fay. FaPON; GaP; GFA; OTPC; PRWS
(Elfin Knight, An.) BoTP
Fairy King, The. William Allingham. IrPN; PoMS
Fairy Land. *See* Fairyland.
Fairy Life, The. Shakespeare. *See* Ariel's Song: "Come unto these yellow sands" *and* Ariel's Song: "Where the bee sucks, there suck I."
Fairy Lough, The. "Moira O'Neill." OBVV; YT
Fairy Lover, The. Moireen Fox. AnIV
Fairy Lullaby ("You spotted snakes"). Shakespeare. *See* You Spotted Snakes.
Fairy Maimounè, The. John Moultrie. OBRV
Fairy Music. Enid Blyton. BoTP
Fairy Music. Rose Fyleman. HH; TSW
Fairy Music. Francis Ledwidge. YeAr
Fairy Nurse, The. Edward Walsh. OnYI
Fairy poet takes a sheet, The. In Fairyland. Joyce Kilmer. TSW
Fairy Queen, The. Shakespeare. *See* Over Hill, over Dale.
Fairy Queen, The ("Come follow, follow me"). *Unknown.* PCD; PCH, *abr.*; PoRh, *abr.*
(Fairies, The, *abr.*) BoTP
(Life of a Fairy, The, *abr.*) OTPC
(Old Song of Fairies, An.) RG
(Queen of Fairies, The.) ViBoPo
Fairy Ring, The. *Unknown.* BoTP
Fairy Ring, The. Andrew Young. ChTr
Fairy seed I planted, A. The Magic Vine. *Unknown.* GFA
Fairy Ship, The. "Gabriel Setoun." PoPl
Fairy Shoemaker, The. Phyllis Garlick. BoTP
Fairy Shoes. Annette Wynne. MPB (1956 ed.)
Fairy Sleep and Little Bo-Beep, The. *Unknown.* BoTP
Fairy Song, A. Elizabeth T. Dillingham. OTPC (1946 ed.); PCH
Fairy Song. Felicia Dorothea Hemans. HBVY
Fairy Song. Keats. FaPON; HBV; OTPC
(Faery Song.) CH
Fairy Song, A. John Lyly. *See* Song by Fairies.
Fairy Song. Winthrop Mackworth Praed. OBEV (1st ed.); SeCePo
Fairy Song. Thomas Randolph. *See* Fairies' Song.
Fairy Song, A. Shakespeare. *See* Over Hill, over Dale.
Fairy Song. W. B. Yeats. *Fr.* The Land of Heart's Desire. MoBrPo; OnYI
(Faeries' Song, *abr.*) GBV
(Song: "Wind blows out of the gates of the day, The.") BEL; InP; TSW
("Wind blows out of the gates of the day, The.") GTSL; ViBoPo
Fairy Songs ("Come unto these yellow sands"). Shakespeare. *See* Ariel's Song.
Fairy Songs ("Now the hungry lion roars"). Shakespeare. *See* Now the Hungry Lion Roars.
Fairy Songs ("Now, until the break of day"). Shakespeare. *Fr.* A Midsummer Night's Dream, V, ii. TrGrPo
Fairy Songs ("Over hill, over dale"). Shakespeare. *See* Over Hill, over Dale.
Fairy Songs ("Where the bee sucks"). Shakespeare. *See* Ariel's Song.
Fairy Songs ("You spotted snakes with double tongue"). Shakespeare. *See* You Spotted Snakes.
Fairy spirits of the breeze. Unwritten Poems. William Winter. AA
Fairy Story. Barbara Euphan Todd. BoC
Fairy Story. Robert Penn Warren. NYBP
Fairy Tailor, The. Rose Fyleman. PoRh; TVC
Fairy Tale, A. Kenneth Mackenzie. PoAu-2
Fairy Tale. John Frederick Nims. MiAP
Fairy Tempter, The. Samuel Lover. OTPC
Fairy Things. John Clare. BoPe

Fairy Thorn, The. Sir Samuel Ferguson. AnIV; CH; OnMSP; OnYI; PoVP; VA
Fairy Thrall, The. May Byron. HBV; HBVY; VA
Fairy Tree, The. Temple Lane. StJW
Fairy Umbrellas. Lucy Diamond. GFA
Fairy Voyage, A. *Unknown.* OTPC (1946 ed.); PCH; SoPo
Fairy Went a-Marketing, A. Rose Fyleman. BoTP; SoPo; SUS
Fairy Wings. Winifred Howard. SUS
Fairy Wood, The. Arthur Symons. *See* In the Wood of Finvara.
Fairy-Land. Poe. MWA-1; OTPC
Fairy Land. Shakespeare. *See* Over Hill, over Dale *and* You Spotted Snakes. *Fr.* A Midsummer Night's Dream.
Fairy Land. Shakespeare. *See* Ariel's Song. *Fr.* The Tempest.
Fairyland. Anne Glenny Wilson. BoAu
Fairy's Life, A. Shakespeare. *See* Ariel's Song: "Where the bee sucks."
Fairy's Reply to Saturn, The. Thomas Hood. *Fr.* The Plea of the Midsummer Fairies. OBNC
Fairy's Song [*or* Wander-Song]. Shakespeare. *See* Over Hill, over Dale.
Fais dodo, mon fils (Go to sleep, my son). Crabe dans Calalou. *Unknown.* OuSiCo
Faith. Robert Browning. *See* O Never Star Was Lost.
Faith. Robert Browning. *Fr.* Paracelsus, V. TreFT
Faith. Ada Cambridge. PoAu-1
Faith. Emma Carleton. MaRV
Faith. Elizabeth York Case. *wr. at. to* Edward Bulwer-Lytton. *See* There Is No Unbelief.
Faith ("Faith is not in understanding"). Avis B. Christiansen. SoP
Faith ("Only believe! How sweet that tender message"). Avis B. Christiansen. SoP
Faith. Preston Clark. HBMV; MaRV
Faith. Victor J. Daley. PoAu-1
Faith. Donald Earl Edwards. ChIP
Faith. Emerson. *See* Sacrifice.
Faith. Hortense Flexner. PoMa
Faith. George Herbert. MaMe
Faith. Petrus Herbert. SoP
Faith. William Dean Howells. MaRV; OQP; WGRP
(What Shall It Profit?) AA; AmePo
Faith. Hugh O. Isbell. ChIP
Faith. Maud Frazer Jackson. MaRV; SoP
Faith. Frances Anne Kemble. FaBoBe; HBV; OBVV; VA
(Trust.) MaRV; NeHB
Faith. Theodore Maynard. OQP
Faith. F. B. Meyer. OQP
Faith. John Richard Moreland. ChIP; OHIP
Faith. John Oxenham. *See* Lord, Give Me Faith.
Faith. Ray Palmer. *See* My Faith Looks Up to Thee.
Faith. Pope. *Fr.* An Essay on Man, Epistle III. WGRP
("For modes of faith, let graceless zealots fight.") BoPe
Faith. Edwin McNeill Poteat. ChIP; MaRV
Faith. James Whitcomb Riley. SoP
Faith. Margaret E. Sangster. FaChP; SoP; TRV
Faith. George Santayana. *See* O World.
Faith. Louise Morgan Sill. CAW
Faith. G. A. Studdert-Kennedy. MaRV
Faith. John Banister Tabb. TRV; WGRP
(Evidence, The.) FaChP
Faith ("Thou canst not prove the Nameless"). Tennyson. *Fr.* The Ancient Sage. MaRV
Faith ("You say, but with no touch of scorn"). Tennyson. *See* In Memoriam A. H. H.: "You say. . ."
Faith ("Faith looks across the storm"). *Unknown.* SoP
Faith ("Fear knocked at the door"). *Unknown.* TreFT
Faith ("Keep this for me"). *Unknown.* PoToHe (new ed.)
Faith. Charles Wesley. SoP
Faith. Whittier. TRV
Faith. Ella Wheeler Wilcox. BLRP; MaRV; OQP; PoToHe; SoP; TRV
Faith. Wordsworth. *See* Shells.
Faith and Freedom. Wordsworth. *Fr.* It Is Not to Be Thought Of. GN
Faith and Science. Thomas Curtis Clark. OQP
Faith and Sight. Mary Gardner Brainard. *Fr.* Not Knowing. FaChP; MaRV
Faith and Sight. Anna M. King. BLRP
Faith be noe longer coy. *Unknown.* SeCSL
Faith came singing into my room. Faith's Expulsive Power. Elizabeth Cheney. SoP
Faith for Tomorrow. Thomas Curtis Clark. PoToHe
Faith has no quarrel with science; she foreknows. Faith and Science. Thomas Curtis Clark. OQP
Faith-Healer. *Unknown.* *See* Limerick: "There was a faith-healer of Deal."
Faith Healing. Philip Larkin. PoeP
Faith, Hope, Love. Margaret Matthews. SoP
Faith, Hope and Love. *Unknown.* BLRP
Faith, I Wish I Were a Leprechaun. Margaret Ritter. FaPON; TiPo
Faith is a fine invention. Emily Dickinson. AmPP (5th ed.); CBEP; DiPo; ELU; FaBV; MoPW; OxBA
Faith is a living power from heaven. Faith. Petrus Herbert. SoP
Faith is not in understanding. Faith. Avis B. Christiansen. SoP
Faith—is the pierless bridge. Emily Dickinson. AmPP (5th ed.)
Faith looks across the storm. Faith. *Unknown.* SoP
Faith, Love, and Death. Dowell O'Reilly. BoAu
"Faith, master, whither you will." Captain Car, or Edom o Gordon (B *vers.*). *Unknown.* ESPB
Faith of a kind is what a man prefers. Comedian. Louis Johnson. AnNZ
Faith of Abraham Lincoln, The. Abraham Lincoln, *arr. by* Carl Sandburg. SoP; TRV
Faith of Christ's Freemen, The. Thomas Curtis Clark. ChIP, *abr.*; OQP
Faith of Our Fathers. Frederick William Faber. MaRV; TreFS
Fath of Our Mothers. Arthur B. Patten. MaRV
Faith on Trial, A, *sel.* George Meredith.
"Dream is the thought in the ghost." WGRP
Faith sees beyond the grave. Faith, Hope and Love. *Unknown.* BLRP
Faith Shall Build a Fairer Throne. Oliver Wendell Holmes. MaRV
(Heaven.) SoP
Faith to Each Other. *Unknown.* OQP
Faith to Understand. Philora Hintz. SoP
Faith Trembling. "Madeline Bridges." AA
Faithful, The. Jane Cooper. AmPC; NePoEA-2
Faithful Dairy Maid, The. *Unknown.* *See* Downright Country-Man, The.
Faithful Few, The. Chester E. Shuler. SoP; STF
Faithful helm commands the keel, The. At Best. John Boyle O'Reilly. AA
Faithful in My Fashion. Ernest Dowson. *See* Non Sum Qualis Eram Bonae sub Regno Cynarae.
Faithful Lover, The. Robert Pack. NePoEA
Faithful Pastor, A. *Unknown.* SoP
Faithful reports of them have reached me oft. The Isles. Sir Charles G. D. Roberts. VA
Faithful Shepherd, The. Giovanni Battista Guarini. *See* Il Pastor Fido.
Faithful Shepherdess, The, *sels.* John Fletcher.
"Come, shepherds, come!" *fr.* I, iii. EG; EIL; ErPo
Evening Song, *fr.* II, i. GN; OTPC (1923 ed.)
(Evening Knell, The.) EIL
(Folding the Flocks.) CH
(Priest's Chant, The.) OBS
God of Sheep, The, *fr.* V, v. EIL; FaBoCh; LoGBV
(To Pan.) TrGrPo
"Hail, holy earth, whose cold arms do embrace," I, i. MyFE
"Here be grapes, whose lusty blood," *fr.* I, i. ViBoPo
"Here be woods as green," *fr.* I, iii. ViBoPo
Hymn to Pan, *fr.* I, ii. OBEV
(Sing His Praises.) EG; ViBoPo
(Song: "Sing his praises.") OBS; SeEP
River God, The ("I am this fountain's god"), *fr.* III, i. BoC; TrGrPo
River God's Song, The, *fr.* III, i. FaPON; MoShBr; PCH
("Do not fear to put thy feet.") CBEP; TuPP
(Song: "Do not fear to put thy feet.") EIL; OBS; ThWaDe
Satyr's Song ("See, the day begins to break"), *fr.* IV, iv. OBS
"Shall I stray/ In the middle air," *fr.* V, v. ViBoPo
"Thou divinest, fairest, brightest," *fr.* V, v. LO
(Satyr's Farewell, The.) OBS
(Satyr's Leave-taking, The.) LoBV (2d ed.)

Faithful (continued)
"Who hath restored my sense, given me new breath," *fr.* III, i. LO
Faithful unto Death. Richard Handfield Titherington. PAH
Faithfully/ We had covered the nasturtiums. Mercy Killing. Kenneth Burke. TwAmPo
Faithfully Tinying at Twilight Voice. E. E. Cummings. NYBP
Faithless. Louis Lavater. PoAu-1
Faithless. *Unknown, tr. fr. Greek by* Louis Untermeyer. UnTE
"Faithless again!" I cry, and she replies. Infatuated. *Unknown.* UnTE
Faithless familiars. November. Elizabeth Daryush. QFR
Faithless Flowers, The. Margaret Widdemer. MPB; SP
Faithless Generation Asked a Sign, A. Molly Anderson Haley. OQP
Faithless Nelly [*or* Nellie] Gray. Thomas Hood. BOHV; EnRP; HBV; InMe; InP; NA; ShBV-2; ShM; SiTL; TOP; TreF; TSW; WePo
Faithless Sally Brown. Thomas Hood. BEL; BOHV; HBV; TreFS
Faithless Shepherdess, The. *Unknown.* GTSL; OBEV
(Adieu Love, Untrue Love.) EIL
(Philon.) OBSC
(Philon the Shepherd—His Song.) ALV
(Unfaithful Shepherdess, The.) GTBS; GTBS-D; GTBS-P; GTBS-W; GTSE
("While that the sun with his beams hot.") SiCE
Faithless Wife, The. Federico García Lorca, *tr. fr. Spanish.* ErPo, *tr. by* Robert O'Brien; LiTW, *tr. by* Rolfe Humphries
Faithlesse and fond mortality. Upon the Death of a Gentleman. Richard Crashaw. CavP; MaMe
Faith's Difficulty. Theodore Maynard. TrPWD
Faith's Expulsive Power. Elizabeth Cheney. SoP
Faith's Vista. Henry Abbey. AA
Faiths washed away. Elegies, II. Philippe Thoby-Marcelin. PoNe
Fake-out. Lawrence S. Cumberbatch. WSL
Fakir upon his bed of nails, The. Glad World. Robert D. Fitzgerald. ACV
Falce love awaye, & all my sighes send back. *Unknown.* SeCSL
Falcon, The. Wilfrid Scawen Blunt. *See* To Manon, Comparing Her to a Falcon.
Falcon, The. Richard Henry Stoddard. AA
Falcon, The. *Unknown.* ACP; FIW; FosPo; InPo; LiTB; OBB; OxBoCh; SeCeV; StP; ViBoPo
(Bereaved Maid, The.) TrGrPo
(Corpus Christi Carol, The.) ChTr; MeEL; NoP
(He Bare Him Up, He Bare Him Down.) MeEV
(Knight of the Grail, The.) OBEV (new ed.)
(Lully, Lullay [Lully, Lullay].) CBEP; PoIE
(Lully, Lulley [Lully, Lulley].) AtBAP; CH; DiPo; EG; EnPo; ExPo; ILP; LoBV; OAEP
(Over Yonder's a Park, A *vers.*) BaBo
Falcon, The. Elinor Wylie. LOW
Falcon and the Dove, The. Sir Herbert Read. BrPo; FaBoMo; POTE
Falconer of God, The. William Rose Benét. CAW; GBV (1952 ed.); HBMV; NP; PG; TreFT; WGRP
Falconry. Anne Wilkinson. MoCV; OBCV
Fall, The. William Barnes. NBM; PoEL-4
Fall, The. Sir Richard Fanshawe, *after the Spanish of* Luis de Góngora. *Fr.* Il Pastor Fido. MePo; OBS
Fall. Aileen L. Fisher. TiPo (1952 ed.); YeAr
Fall, The. Milton. *Fr.* Paradise Lost, IX. PoEL-3
Fall, The. Kathleen Raine. MoPo
Fall, The. Earl of Rochester. EnLoPo; UnTE
Fall, The. Nathaniel Wanley. SeEP
Fall Comes in Back-Country Vermont. Robert Penn Warren. NYBP
Fall Days. Marion Conger. SiSoSe
Fall gently and still, good corn. Corn Must Be Sown. Thomas Carlyle. ThGo
Fall gently, rain, on leaf and limb. Discarded Christmas Tree. Elizabeth-Ellen Long. ChBR
Fall has come, clear as the eyes of chickens, The. Silence. Robert Bly. NaP
Fall in Corrales. Richard Wilbur. CoPo; NoP; PIA; VaPo
Fall Journey. William Stafford. NaP
Fall, Leaves, Fall. Emily Brontë. ELP; EnLi-2 (1949 ed.); FaBV; LoBV; OTPC (1946 ed.); PoEL-5; ShBV-4; TrGrPo ("Fall, leaves, fall; die, flowers, away.") FaBoCh; GTBS-D; LoGBV
(Song: "Fall, leaves, fall; die, flowers, away.") NBM
Fall 1961. Robert Lowell. OPoP; TPM
Fall now, my cold thoughts, frozen fall. Lament. Laurence Binyon. MoVE
Fall of a Soul, The. John Addington Symonds. PoVP; VA
Fall of a Wall. John Donne. MaMe; RelE
Fall of Angels and of Man. *Unknown, at one time at. to* Caedmon, *mod. vers. Fr.* Genesis. PoLi
Fall of Hyperion, The. Keats. ERoP-2
Sels.
"Fanatics have their dreams, wherewith they weave," *fr.* I. EnRP; MBW-2
"Methought I stood where trees," *fr.* I. OBRV
(Dream, A.) OBNC
"None can usurp this height," *fr.* I. OBRV
Fall of J. W. Beane, The. Oliver Herford. StPo
Fall of Kings, The. Love of Nature. James Thomson. *Fr.* The Seasons: Autumn. OBEC
Fall of Llywelyn, the Last Welsh Prince, The. Beddyn Fardd, *tr. fr. Welsh by* D. M. Lloyd. FOL
Fall of Maubila, The. Thomas Dunn English. PAH
Fall of Niagara, The. John G. C. Brainard. AmePo
Fall of Princes, The, *sel.* John Lydgate.
Lat Noman Booste of Konnyng nor Vertu. AtBAP
(Transient as a Rose.) MeEL
Fall of Richmond, The. Herman Melville. MC; PAH
Fall of Rome, The. W. H. Auden. CBV
Fall of Satan, The. Roy Campbell. *Fr.* The Flaming Terrapin. BoSA
Fall of Siegfried, The, *abr. Unknown, pr. tr. fr. Middle High German by* Margaret Armour. *Fr.* The Song of the Nibelungs. WoL
Fall of Stars. George Dillon. NP
Fall of Tecumseh, The. *Unknown.* PAH
Fall of the Angels, The. Milton. *Fr.* Paradise Lost, I. FiP
("Is this the region, this the soil, the clime.") MyFE
(Satan Ponders His Fallen State.) TreFS
Fall of the City, The; a Verse Play for Radio. Archibald MacLeish. MoAmPo
Voice of the Announcer ("We are here on the central plaza"). HoPM
Voice of the Studio Announcer ("Ladies and gentlemen:/ This broadcast comes to you from the city"). HoPM
Fall of the House of Usher, The, *sel.* Poe.
Haunted Palace, The. AA; AmP; AnFE; APA; BeLS; BoLiVe; CH; ChTr; CoAnAm; HBV; LiTA; LiTG; MCCG; NePA; OBVV; OTPC; OxBA; PFY; Po; PoE; PoEL-4; SyP; TOP; TreFS; TrGrPo; ViBoPo
("In the greenest of our valleys.") AmPP
Fall of the Leaf, The. Henry David Thoreau. AmP; AP
Fall of the Plum Blossoms, The. Ranko, *tr. fr. Japanese.* TiPo
Fall of the Year. Henry Ellison. OBVV
Fall To. Howard Jones. NBP
Fall which twisted love to lust, The. In Praise of Music in Time of Pestilence. Daryl Hine. OBCV
Fallen, The. Duncan Campbell Scott. TrPWD
Fallen Angels, The ("Him the Almighty Power"). Milton. *See* Satan Defiant.
Fallen Angels ("Nine times the space that measures day and night"). Milton. *Fr.* Paradise Lost, I. DiPo
Fallen Angels, The ("Of Man's first disobedience, and the fruit"). Milton. *See* Invocation to the Heavenly Muse.
Fallen as he is, this king of birds still seems. The Dead Eagle. Thomas Campbell. EnRP
Fallen flowers seemed, The. Arakida Moritake, *tr. fr. Japanese by* I. W. Furukami. LiTW
Fallen Flyer Aged 19. David Ross. PG (1955 ed.)
Fallen? How fallen? States and empires fall. On the Defeat of a Great Man [*or* On the Defeat of Henry Clay]. William Wilberforce Lord. AA; PAH
Fallen Leaves. Kathryn Munro. CaP
Fallen Leaves. *Unknown, tr. fr. Chinese by* Arthur Waley. *Fr.* Shi King. LiTW
Fallen Majesty. W. B. Yeats. InP
Fallen pile! I ask not what has been thy fate. Netley Abbey. William Lisle Bowles. Sonn

Fallen Poplar, The. Mary Webb. InP
Fallen Rain. Richard Watson Dixon. NBM
Fallen Star, The. George Darley. AnFE; ERoP-2; HBV; OBEV
Fallen Tower of Siloam, The. Robert Graves. WaP
Fallen Tree, The. Patrick Maybin. NeIP
Fallen Tree, The. Andrew Young. BoNaP
Fallen Tree Elegy. Victor Contoski. ThO
Fallen with autumn's falling leaf. On the Death of President Garfield. Oliver Wendell Holmes. PAH
Fallen Yew, A. Francis Thompson. BrPo; MoAB; MoBrPo
Fallen Zulu Commander, The. C. M. van Den Heever, *tr. fr. Afrikaans by* Jack Cope *and* Uys Krige. PeSA
Falling. James Dickey. NYBP
Falling Asleep. Siegfried Sassoon. ILP; MCCG; MoBrPo; MoVE
Falling Asleep over the Aeneid. Robert Lowell. AP; CoBMV; CrMA; FiMAP; MoAmPo (1962 ed.); OxBA; ToPo; TwAmPo
Falling, falling leaves! October. John Murray Gibbon. PTK
Falling flower, The. Haiku. Moritake. CaFP
Falling from the ridge. Emperor Yozei, *tr. fr. Japanese by* Kenneth Rexroth. LiTW
Falling leaf and fading tree. Goodbye! George John Whyte-Melville. TreF
Falling leaf betrays the fawn, The. Late Autumn. A. M. Sullivan. GoBC
Falling Leaves. William M Runyan. FaChP
Falling of the Leaves, The. W. B. Yeats. PoPo
Falling of the night. Into the Darkness. Basho. OnPM
Falling of the Snow, The. Raymond Souster. CaP
Falling Snow. Amy Lowell. *Fr.* Chinoiseries. AnAmPo; NP; PoRA (rev. ed.)
Falling Snow. *Unknown.* BoChLi; GFA; SoPo; TiPo (1952 ed.)
Falling Star, The. Sara Teasdale. BrR; MoShBr; MoSiPe; PDV; PoRh; SoPo; StVeCh; SUS; TiPo
Fall'n, fall'n, a silent heap; her heroes all. John Dyer. *Fr.* The Ruins of Rome. OBEC
Fall'n pile! I ask not what has been thy fate. Sonnet: Netley Abbey. William Lisle Bowles. CEP
Fallow Deer at the Lonely House, The. Thomas Hardy. AWP; BWP; CH; CMoP; InPo; MoVE
Fallow Field, The. Julia C. R. Dorr. AA
Fallow Land. Eunice Clark. NAMP
Falls, The. F. D. Reeve. NYBP
Falls like a ripe pear in the storm. Definition of the Soul. Boris Pasternak. LiTW
Falls of Glomach, The. Andrew Young. OxBS
Falltime. Carl Sandburg. NP
Falmouth. W. E. Henley. *See* Home.
False Achitophel, The. Dryden. *See* Achitophel.
False and Fickle. Dryden. *See* Song: "Fair Iris I love, and hourly I die."
False bards the sacred fire pervert. The Indignation of Taliesin. Thomas Love Peacock. CBEP
False Bay. F. T. Prince. BoSA
False Country of the Zoo. Jean Garrigue. LiTM (1970 ed.)
False dawns. Hiawatha. Stephen Sandy. CoPo
False dreams, all false. Iliad. Humbert Wolfe. MoBrPo
False Enchantment. Jean Starr Untermeyer. MoAmPo (1950 ed.)
False Fox, The. *Unknown.* ChTr
False Gallop of Analogies, A. W. St. Leger. CenHV; FiBHP; WhC
False glozing pleasures, casks of happinesse. Dotage. George Herbert. MaMe
False Gods. Walter de la Mare. EaLo
False Heart, The. Hilaire Belloc. *See* For False Heart.
False-hearted Knight, The. *Unknown.* *See* Lady Isabel and the Elf-Knight.
False knave Flaccus once a bribe I gave, The. In Flaccum. Sir John Davies. TuPP
False Knight [*or* Fause Knicht] upon [*or* on] the Road, The. *Unknown.* AtBAP; BFSS; BuBa; CBEP; CH; EnSB; ESPB; OxBoLi; OxBS
(False Knight and the Wee Boy, The, *diff. vers.*) FaBoCh
False Lambkin was a mason. Lamkin (D *vers.*). *Unknown.* BaBo
False life! a foil and no more, when. Quickness. Henry Vaughan. BoC; BWP; ELP; LoBV; MaPo; MeLP; MePo; OBS; OxBoCh; ReEn; SCEP-1; SeCePo; SeCP; SeCV-1
False Linfinn. *Unknown.* *See* Lamkin.
False Love. Burns. *See* Banks o' Doon, The.
False Love. *At. to* John Lilliat. *See* Song: "When love on time and measure makes his ground."
False Love. Sir Walter Ralegh. CBEP; OBSC; SiPS
("Farewell, false Love!") LO; ReEn
(Farewell to False Love, A.) EIL; FCP
False Love. Sir Walter Scott, *Fr.* Waverley, *ch.* 9. ViBoPo
False Love and True Logic. Laman Blanchard. BOHV
False Lover, The ("The sun shines high on yonder hill"). *Unknown.* *See* False Lover Won Back, The.
False Lover, The, *with music.* *Unknown.* BFSS
False Lover Won Back, The. *Unknown.* BaBo; ESPB (A *and* B *vers.*)
(False Lover, The.) OxBB (B *vers.*)
(Fause Lover, The.) CoBE
(Young John.) BuBa; OBB (A *vers.*)
False! or Inconstancy. Congreve. *See* False Though She Be.
False Poets and True. Thomas Hood. HBV; PP; Sonn
False Security. John Betjeman. CMoP
False Sir John a-wooing came. May Colvin [*or* Colven]. *Unknown.* BuBa; MaC; OBB; OxBB; StPo; TrGrPo
False Summer, The. Marya Zaturenska. CrMA
False Though She Be [to Me]. Congreve. CBEP; HBV; MeWo; OBEV; WePo
(False! or Inconstancy.) BoLP
(Song: "False though she be to me and love.") EnLoPo; FaBoEn; LiTL; OBEC; ViBoPo
False world, good-night: since thou hast brought. To the World. Ben Jonson. EnRePo; EP; OBEV (1st ed.); QFR; SeCP
False World, Thou Ly'st. Francis Quarles. *See* Vanity of the World, The.
Falsehood. William Cartwright. OBEV
Falsehood hath so corrupted all the world. Man's Natural Element. Abu-l-Ala al-Maarri. LiTW
Falsest of fair ones, swear again. To a Perjur'd Mistress. Sir Francis Fane. PeRV
Falstaff's Lament over Prince Hal Become Henry V. Herman Melville. ViBoPo
Falstaff's Song. Edmund Clarence Stedman. AA; HBV
Faltering, fumbling. Braille. *Unknown.* OTD
Fame. Robert Browning. *Fr.* Earth's Immortalities. PoVP; PP
Fame ("From mighty wrongs to petty perfidy"). Byron. *Fr.* Childe Harold's Pilgrimage, IV. FiP
Fame. Eleanor Hollister Cantus. GoYe
Fame. Austin Dobson. *See* Fame Is a Food That Dead Men Eat.
Fame. Walter Savage Landor. PV
Fame. Sir Thomas More. EnRePo
Fame. John Banister Tabb. AA; AmLP
Fame. *Unknown.* TreFT
Fame and Fortune. Michael Drayton. *Fr.* The Legend of Robert, Duke of Normandy. OBSC
Fame and Friendship. Austin Dobson. *See* Fame Is a Food That Dead Men Eat.
Fame I am called, marvel you nothing. Fame. Sir Thomas More. EnRePo
Fame Is a Food That Dead Men Eat. Austin Dobson. GTSL; HBV
(Fame.) MoBrPo (1942 ed.)
(Fame and Friendship.) OBEV (new ed.); PoPo
Fame is the one that does not stay. Emily Dickinson. MWA-2
Fame let thy trumpet sound. A Song. Joel Barlow. AmPP (5th ed.)
Fame, like a wayward girl, will still be coy. Two Sonnets on Fame, I [*or* On Fame]. Keats. CABA; CBEP; EnLit; EnRP; Sonn
Fame should not be personified. Statue in a Blizzard. Ruth Douglas Keener. NYTB
Famed ship *California,* a ship of high renown, The. The Girls around Cape Horn. *Unknown.* SoAmSa
Fames pillar here, at last, we set. The Pillar of Fame. Robert Herrick. AnAnS-2; SCEP-2; SeCP
Fames Plant takes Root from Vertue, grows thereby. Life and Death. Edward Benlowes. *Fr.* Theophila. FaBoEn
Familiar Daemon. Roy Campbell. JKCP (1955 ed.)
Familiar Epistle, A. Austin Dobson. VA
Familiar Faces, Long Departed. Robert Hillyer. NYBP
Familiar Friends. James S. Tippett. BoChLi; BoTP; SoPo; SUS; UTS
Familiar Letter to Several Correspondents, A. Oliver Wendell Holmes. BOHV; InMe

Familiar Lines. *Unknown.* FiBHP
Familiar, year by year, to the creaking wain. The Sower. Laurence Binyon. MMA
Familiarity Breeds Indifference. Martial, *tr. fr. Latin by* Louis Untermeyer. UnTE
Familie, The. George Herbert. AnAnS-1; MaMe; MeP
Families, when a child is born. On the Birth of His Son. Su T'ung-po. AWP; JAWP; LiTW; OnPM; PV; TRV; WBP; WoL
Family, The. Donna R. Lydston. PoToHe (new ed.)
Family. *Unknown.* STF
Family, The. *Unknown, tr. fr. German by* Rose Fyleman. TiPo (1959 ed.)
Family Altar, The. Georgia B. Adams. STF
Family Court. Ogden Nash. FiBHP
Family Evening. Dan Huws. NYBP
Family Fool, The. W. S. Gilbert. *Fr.* Yeomen of the Guard. ALV; InMe; SiTL
Family Ghosts. W. H. Auden. *See* Strings' Excitement, The.
Family Goldschmitt, The. Henri Coulette. CoAP
Family History. John Maher Murphy. JKCP (1955 ed.)
Family is a little book, The. Family. *Unknown.* STF
Family Life. Allan M Laing. FiBHP
Family Matters. Günter Grass, *tr. fr. German by* Michael Hamburger. ELU
Family Meeting, The. Charles Sprague. HBV
Family Name, The. Charles Lamb. Sonn
Family of Nations, The. Willard Wattles. PAH
Family Poem. John Holloway. NMP
Family Portrait. Leonard Feeney. ISi
Family portrait not too stale to record, A. Father and Son: 1939. William Plomer. PeSA
Family Reunion, The, *sels.* T. S. Eliot. MWA-2
Chorus: "In an old house there is always listening."
Chorus: "We do not like to look out of the same window.'
Family Reunion. Hollis Summers. GoYe
Family Screams. Hy Sobiloff. TwAmPo
Family story tells, and it was told true, The. Funnel. Anne Sexton. MoAmPo (1962 ed.)
Family takes me in, The. The Guest of Our Lovely Daughter. Sandford Lyne. QAH
Family Trees. Douglas Malloch. OHIP; PEDC
Famine. Georg Heym, *tr. fr. German by* Werner Heider. LiTW
Famine once we had. New England's Growth. William Bradford. PAH
Famine Year, The. Lady Wilde. OnYI; PoFr, *abr.*
Famous Ballad of the Jubilee Cup, The. Sir Arthur Quiller-Couch. InMe; NA; OnSP; WhC; YT, *cond.*
"Famous bard, he comes, The." Visiting Poet. John Frederick Nims. PV
Famous Battle of Bumble-Bug and Bumble-Bee. *Unknown.* FTB
Famous city of Boston. Hubbub in Hub. Laurence McKinney. WhC
Famous Fight at Malago, The; or, The Englishmen's Victory over the Spaniards. *Unknown.* CoMu
Famous Flower of Serving-Men, The. *See* Lady Turned Serving-Man, The.
Famous hen's my story's theme, A. The Hen. Matthias Claudius. BOHV
Famous kingdom of the birds, The. Somewhere Is Such a Kingdom. John Crowe Ransom. CMoP; LiTA
Famous Light Brigade, The, *with music. Unknown.* ShS
Famous painter, jealous of his wife, A. The Superfluous Saddle. La Fontaine. UnTE
Famous Poet. Ted Hughes. LiTM (1970 ed.)
Famous poets with the muses nine, The. The Prologue. Alexander Barclay. *Fr.* Certain Eclogues. ReIE
Famous Sea-Fight, A. John Looke. CoMu
Famous Tay Whale, The. William McGonagall. PeVV
Famous Toast, A. Sheridan. *See* Let the Toast Pass.
Famous warriors of the antique [*or* anticke] world, The. Amoretti, LXIX. Spenser. CoBE; ReEn; SiCE
Famously she descended, her red hair. A Recollection. John Peale Bishop. LiTA; Sonn; TwAmPo
Fan, The. Serafín Alvarez Quintero *and* Joaquín Alvarez Quintero, *tr. fr. Spanish by* Thomas Walsh. OnPM
Fan, The, *sel.* John Gay.
"Rise, happy youth, this bright machine survey." ViBoPo
Fan, The. Edith Sitwell. HBMV
Fan, The. Sokan, *tr. fr. Japanese.* GFA
Fan, the Filly. Wilfrid Thorley. BoTP
Fanatics have their dreams, wherewith they weave. The Fall of Hyperion. Keats. EnRP; ERoP-2; MBW-2
Fancy, The. William Rose Benét. SD
Fancy. Keats. EnLi-2; EnRP; EPN; LoBV; OBEV
(Realm of Fancy, The.) ATP (1935 ed.); GTBS; GTBS-D; GTBS-P; GTBS-W; GTSE; GTSL
(To Fancy.) HBV
Thou Shalt See the Field-Mouse Peep, *sel.* OA
Fancy, A ("First shall the heavens want starry light"). Thomas Lodge. *Fr.* Rosalynde. EIL; LoBV; OBSC
("First shall the heavens want starry light.") SiCE
(Lover's Protestation, A.) GoBC
(Love's Protestation.) ACP
Fancy, A ("When I admire the rose"). Thomas Lodge. *See* Rose, The. *Fr.* The Life and Death of William Longbeard.
Fancy. Shakespeare. *See* Tell Me Where Is Fancy Bred.
Fancy, and I, last evening walkt [*or* walked]. To Amoret Gone from Him. Henry Vaughan. CBEP; MeLP; OBS
Fancy Concert, The. Leigh Hunt. MuSP
Fancy Dress. Dorothea Mackellar. PoAu-1
Fancy Dress. Siegfried Sassoon. BrPo
Fancy, Farewell. Sir Edward Dyer. EnRePo
Fancy Fishing. James L Weil. FiSC
Fancy from Fontenelle, A. Austin Dobson. HBV; OBVV
(Rose and the Gardener, The.) MPB
Fancy halts my feet at the way-side well, A. The Way-Side Well. Joseph Seamon Cotter, Sr. CDC; PoNe
Fancy! Nymph, that loves to lye. Grongar Hill (Pindaric version). John Dyer. EiCL
Fancy (quoth he), farewell, whose badge I long did bear. The Green Knight's Farewell to Fancy. George Gascoigne. EnRePo
Fancy, which that I have servèd long, The. The Restless Heart. Earl of Surrey. FCP; SiPS
Fancy's Home. W. H. Davies. AtBAP
Fancy's Knell. A. E. Housman. AnFE; EG; FaBoCh; MoPW; PoRA; ShBV-4
Fand, *sel.* William Larminie.
Killarney. AnIV
Fand Yields Cuchulain to Emer. *Unknown, tr. fr. Old Irish by* Séan O'Faoláin. AnIL
Fandango. "Stanley Vestal." IHA
Fane Wald I Luve. *At. to* John Clerk. OxBS
Fanny. Anne Reeve Aldrich. HBV
Fanny, *sel.* Fitz-Greene Halleck.
"Fanny was younger once than she is now." CTC
Fanny Foo-Foo was a Japanese girl. The Japanese Lovers. *Unknown.* BeLS; BLPA
Fanny's Doves ("Fanny loves"). Christina Rossetti. SAS
Fantasia. G. K. Chesterton. HBMV
Fantasia. Dorothy Livesay. MoCV; OBCV
Fantasia of a Fallen Gentleman on a Cold Bitter Night on the Embankment. T. E. Hulme. *See* Embankment, The.
Fantasia on a Wittelsbach Atmosphere. Siegfried Sassoon. MoVE
Fantastic Simile, A. Thomas Lovell Beddoes. Sonn
Fantasy. Gwendolyn B. Bennett. CDC
Fantasy. Giosuè Carducci, *tr. fr. Italian by* Asa Hughes. LiTW
Fantasy. Hugh McCrae. MoAuPo
Fantasy. Gérard de Nerval. *See* Old Tune, An.
Fantasy. Ruth Mather Skidmore. PoMS
Fantasy. Louis Untermeyer. TSW
Fantasy for Those Who Hate Their Work. Lou Lipsitz. YAP
Fantasy in Purple. Langston Hughes. BANP; CDC
Fantasy of Little Waters, A. James Scully. NYBP
Fantasy on the Resurrection. Vassar Miller. PoDB; ToPo
Fantasy under the Moon. Emmanuel Boundzekei-Dongala, *tr. fr. French by* Gerald Moore *and* Ulli Beier. TTY
Fantoches. Paul Verlaine, *tr. fr. French by* Arthur Symons. AWP; OBMV
(Puppets.) SyP
Far above us where a jay. Morning on the Lièvre. Archibald Lampman. SD
Far across hill and dale. Plum Blossoms. Basho. SUS
Far and free o'er the lifting sea. Return to New York. John Hall Wheelock. HT

Far and near, and now, from never. Beauty. Isaac Rosenberg. TrJP
Far and Wide She Went. Cædmon, *tr. fr. Anglo-Saxon. Fr.* Genesis. EtS
Far are the shades of Arabia. Arabia. Walter de la Mare. GTBS; HBMV; POTE; WHA
Far as Creation's ample range extends. The Great Chain of Being. Pope. *Fr.* An Essay on Man. ExPo; ImOP
Far as man can see. Song of the Rain Chant. *Tr. by* Natalie Curtis. AWP; JAWP; WBP
Far at sea and west of Spain. The Land of Cokaygne. *Unknown, At. to* Friar Michael of Kildare. OnYI
Far-away. George Sigerson. JKCP (1926 ed.)
Far away. Threnody. Thomas Lovell Beddoes. StP
Far away and long ago. The Snare. Edward Davison. PG (1955 ed.); ViBoPo (1941 ed.)
Far away arch-soul. Character and Talent. Jules Laforgue. OnPM
Far away beyond the glamor of the city and its strife. The Picture That Is Turned toward the Wall. Charles Graham. TreF
Far away from birds, herds, and village girls. Tear. Arthur Rimbaud. PIA
Far away in the twilight time. The Double-Headed Snake of Newbury. Whittier. AmePo
Far away is one who now is sleeping. The Clock. Francis Scarfe. NeBP
Far away under us, they are mowing on the green steps. The Beholders. James Dickey. AP
Far back when I went zig-zagging. Orion. Adrienne Rich. NoP
Far be the bookish Muses! Let them find. Invocation to the African Muse. Roy Campbell. *Fr.* The Flaming Terrapin. BoSA
Far behind him crept blackness and flickering glimmer. The Song of the Spirits. Joseph Sheridan Le Fanu. *Fr.* The Legend of the Glaive. OnYI
Far below Arles in those old days. The Aliscamp. Frédéric Mistral. CAW
Far beyond the sky-line, where the steamers go. Hot Weather in the Plains—India. E. H. Tipple. HBV
Far beyond Us. *Unknown, tr. fr. Japanese by* Ishii *and* Obata. OnPM
Far Country, The. Robert Greacen. NeIP
Far court opens for us all July, The. Prothalamion. Maxine W. Kumin. NYBP
Far Cry after a Close Call, A. Richard Howard. NYBP
Far Cry from Africa, A. Derek Walcott. ToPo; TTY
Far Cry to Heaven, A. Edith M. Thomas. AA; PFY; WGRP
Far dearer, the grave or the prison. The Glory of Patriotism. Thomas Moore. SoP
Far Distances. Henry W. Clark. OQP
Far-distant concerts and opaline sparks of our first home in the burning heat of summer. The Hydra of Birds. Nikos Engonopoulos. LiTW
Far down in the meadow the wheat grows green. Alice's Supper. Laura E. Richards. MPB
Far down the purple wood. The Constant Bridegrooms. Kenneth Patchen. CrMA; LiTM (1970 ed.); NaP
"Far enough down is China," somebody said. Digging for China. Richard Wilbur. GoJo; LOW; TwCP
Far—Far—Away. Tennyson. EPN; PoVP; ViPo
Far, far away, beyond a hazy height. October in Tennessee. Walter Malone. AA
Far, far away, I know not where, I know not how. A Dream of November. Edmund Gosse. SyP
Far, far away is Bethlehem. The Continuing Christ. W. Russell Bowie. ChIP; MaRV
Far, far down. City Afternoon. Barbara Howes. AmFN; TPM
Far far from gusty waves, these children's faces. An Elementary School Classroom in a Slum. Stephen Spender. BoLiVe (1945 ed.); CoBMV; FaBoMo; FosPo; ILP; LiTB; MoAB; MoBrPo; MoPo; OAEP (2d ed.); PoE; PPON; ReMP; TrGrPo; TwCP
Far, far from here,/ The Adriatic breaks in a warm bay. Cadmus and Harmonia [*or* The Song of Callicles]. Matthew Arnold. *Fr.* Empedocles on Etna, I, ii. FiP; GTBS-P; OBVV; ViPo
Far far the least of all, in want. The Prisoners. Stephen Spender. FaBoMo; GTBS-D; MoAB; MoBrPo
Far, far the mountain peak from me. The Christ of the Andes. Florence Earle Coates. StJW
Far, Far West, The. *Unknown.* CoSo
Far-Farers, The. Robert Louis Stevenson. BoTP
Far-fetched and dear-bought, as the proverb rehearses. A Singing Lesson. Swinburne. MuSP
Far-fetched with tales of other worlds and ways. Home from Abroad. Laurie Lee. POTi
Far Field, The. Theodore Roethke. NaP; NoP; SeCeV (1967 ed.); ToPo
Far from Africa: Four Poems. Margaret Danner.
  Dance of the Abakweta, 2. AmNP; NNP; PoNe (1970 ed.)
  Etta Moten's Attic, 4. AmNP
  Garnishing the Aviary, 1. AmNP; NNP
  Visit of the Professor of Aesthetics, The, 3. AmNP; NNP
Far from love the Heavenly Father. Emily Dickinson. MWA-2
Far from My Dearest Self. Tasso. *See* To His Mistress in Absence.
Far from Somewhere. "Primus." WhC
Far from the crowd they stood [*or* stand] apart. The V-a-s-e. James Jeffrey Roche. BOHV; HBV; LHV
Far from the deep roar of the Aegean main. Farewell. Plato, *tr. by* Charles Whibley. AWP; WBP
Far from the Heart of Culture. W. H. Auden. *Fr.* In Time of War. CMoP; WaaP
Far from the loud sea beaches. A Visit from the Sea. Robert Louis Stevenson. GN; YT
Far from the Madding Crowd. Nixon Waterman. BLPA; FaBoBe; MPB (1956 ed.); NeHB
  (Vacation.) WBLP
Far from the sea in his grey later days. "Cap'n". Arthur Wallace Peach. EtS
Far from the vulgar haunts of men. On the Same. Roy Campbell. BoSA
Far from the waves that soothed. The Lonely Shell. Martha Eugenie Perry. CaP
Far from the world, far from delight. Our Lady of the Snows. Lionel Johnson. JKCP
Far from the world, O Lord, I flee. Retirement. William Cowper. SoP
Far from thy dearest self, the scope. To His Mistress in Absence [*or* Far from My Dearest Self]. Tasso. AWP; JAWP; OnPM; WBP
Far from your native hills although you roam. To Claude McKay. Vivian L. Virtue. PoNe
Far happier are the dead, methinks, than they. Epigram. *Unknown. tr. by* William Cowper. EnLi-1
Far [*or* Farre] have I clamber'd [*or* clambred] in my mind. Hymn to Charity and Humility [*or* An Hymne in Honour of Those Two Despised Virtues]. Henry More. OBS; OxBoCh
Far I hear the bugle blow. The Day of Battle. A. E. Housman. A Shropshire Lad, LVI. OHIP; PoVP; WaaP
Far in a Western Brookland. A. E. Housman. A Shropshire Lad, LII. AnFE; AWP; BEL; EnLi-2; EPN; GTBS-D; HT; JAWP; NBM; OAEP; PoEL-5; PoVP; TOP; ViPo; WBP
Far in a wild, unknown to public view. The Hermit. Thomas Parnell. GoTL
Far in sea, west of Spain. Cokaygne. *Unknown.* AnIL
Far in the bosom of the deep. The Lighthouse. Sir Walter Scott. OTPC (1946 ed.); PCH
Far in the country of Arden. Cassamen and Dowsabel [*or* The Ballad of Dowsabell *or* The Eighth Eclogue]. Michael Drayton. *Fr.* The Shepherd's Garland. LoBV; OBSC; ReEn; TuPP; UnTE
Far in the future. Fret Not Thyself. Amy Carmichael. SoP
Far in the grim Northwest beyond the lines. Temagami. Archibald Lampman. OBCV
Far in the heavens my God retires. The Incomprehensible. Isaac Watts. CEP; WGRP
Far in the sea and west of Spain. The Land of Cockayne. *Unknown.* MeEV
Far in the woods my stealthy flute. Papageno. W. D. Snodgrass. NoP; NYBP
Far Land, The. John Hall Wheelock. WGRP
Far look in absorbed eyes, unaware, A. Magnets. Laurence Binyon. HBMV
Far moon maketh lovers wise, The. Moonlight. Walter de la Mare. EnLoPo

Far more than I was wont myself I prize. The Amulet of Love. Michelangelo. OnPM
"Far not, O maidens, shivering." The Little Ghost Who Died for Love. Edith Sitwell. MemP
Far, oh, far is the Mango island. The Constant Cannibal Maiden. Wallace Irwin. BOHV
Far Off. Ruth Rutherford. LO
Far-off/ at the core of space. Swan. D. H. Lawrence. CMoP
Far off a lonely hound. The Hounds. John Freeman. OBMV
Far-off a young state rises, full of might. Suggested Device of a New Western State [*or* Farther]. John James Piatt. AA; AmePo; AnAmPo
Far off, above the plain the summer dries. Second Air Force. Randall Jarrell. AP; CMoP; CoBMV; FiMAP; LiTM (1970 ed.); WaP
Far off, far off/ Those forests lie. Song of the Parrot. Elizabeth J. Coatsworth. StVeCh
Far off from these a slow and silent stream. *See* Farr off from these . . .
Far off I know not where you rest. Far Off. Ruth Rutherford. LO
Far off in the waste of desert sand. The Jim-Jam King of the Jou-Jous. Alaric Bertrand Stuart. BOHV
Far off is the sea, and the land is afar. Neap-Tide. Swinburne. PoVP; ViPo
Far-off mountains hide you from me, The. Absent Lover. *Unknown.* PBA
Far-off? Not far away. In the Twilight. George Cotterell. VA
Far-off Rose, A. Josephine Preston Peabody. AA
Far Off-Shore. Herman Melville. AmPP (4th ed.)
Far off the sea is gray and still as the sky. Week-End by the Sea. Edgar Lee Masters. MoAmPo
Far on the desert ridges. Wind-Song. *Tr. by* Natalie Curtis. RePo; SUS
Far Out. Robert Conquest. HYE
Far out across Carnarvon bay. The Welsh Sea. James Elroy Flecker. BrPo
Far out at sea. White Horses. Irene F. Pawsey. BoTP
Far out at sea—the sun was high. Genius. Richard Henry Horne. VA
Far out beyond the city's lights, away from din and roar. The Country Store. *Unknown.* BLPA
Far out in the hush of the mountain land. The Emigrant's Child. Lyman H. Sproull. PoOW
Far out in the wilds of Oregon. Jack Dempsey's Grave [*or* The Nonpareil's Grave]. M. J. McMahon. SCC; SD
Far out of sight forever stands the sea. The Slow Pacific Swell. Ivor Winters. CBV; ForPo; QFR
Far over the billows unresting forever. Thalatta. Willis Boyd Allen. EtS
Far [*or* Fair, *wr.*] sail shimmers, white and lonely, A. A Sail. Mikhail Lermontov. LiTW; OnPM; PoPl; WoL
Far Side of Introspection, The. Al Lee. CoAP
Far spread, below. The Story of Vinland. Sidney Lanier. *Fr.* Psalm of the West. PAH; ThLM
Far Sweeter than Honey. Abraham ibn Ezra, *tr. fr. Hebrew by* Israel Abrahams. TrJP
Far through the memory shines a happy day. The Cathedral. James Russell Lowell. AmePo; MAmP; MWA-1
Far to the east I see them in my mind. The Wise Men. Edgar Bowers. NePoEA
Far to the south, beyond the blue, there spreads. The Second Asgard. Matthew Arnold. *Fr.* Balder Dead. FiP
Far Trumpets Blowing. Louis F. Benson. TRV
Far up in the Northern country. Christmas in the North. Margaret E. Sangster. PEDC
Far up the dim twilight fluttered. The Unknown God. "*A E.*" ChMo; GTSL; MoBrPo; NeMA; TOP; WGRP
Far up the lonely mountain-side. A Georgia Volunteer. Mary Ashley Townsend. AA
Far voices. Old Song. F. R. Scott. PeCV
Far West. A. J. M. Smith. PeCV
Fara Diddle Dyno. *Unknown.* CBEP; EIL FaBoCh; LoBV
("Ha ha! ha ha! this world doth pass.") LO; OxBoLi; ViBoPo
(Madrigal.) SiTL
Faraway hands are folded and folded. The Starry Night. George Starbuck. NYBP
Fare not abroad, O Soul, to win. Quo Vadis? Myles E. Connolly. JKCP (1926 ed.); MaRV; TRV
Fare thee, O babe, fare thee well. Fare Thee Well, Babe. *Unknown.* ABF
Fare Thee Well. Byron. BLPA; EnLit; EnRP; FaFP; FaPL; HβV; MERP; OBNC; PeER; PoEL-4; TreFS
Fare Thee Well, Babe, *with music.* *Unknown.* ABF
Fare Well. Walter de la Mare. CoBMV; GTBS-D; GTBS-P; MoVE; OBEV (new ed.); POTE
Fare Ye Well, My Darlin', *with music.* *Unknown.* OuSiCo
Fare you well, green fields. A Prisoner for Life. *Unknown.* BFSS; CoSo
Fare you well, the Prince's Landing Stage. The Leaving of Liverpool. *Unknown.* ShS
Fareweel to a' our Scottish fame. Such a Parcel of Rogues in a Nation. Robert Burns. OxBS
Farewel, dear daughter Sara; now thou'rt gone. In Saram. John Cotton. SCAP
Farewel the fields of Irwan's vale. A Farewell Hymn to the Valley of Irwan. John Langhorne. *Fr.* Solyman and Almena. CEP
Farewel, too little and too lately known. *See* Farewell, too little and too lately known.
Farewel ye guilded follies, pleasing troubles. *Unknown.* MeLP
Farewele! Advent, Christemas is come. Farewell! Advent. James Ryman. MeEL
Farewell, A: "And if I did, what then?" George Gascoigne. *See* And If I Did, What Then?
Farewell, The: "And so, one day when the tide was away out." Pat Wilson. AnNZ
Farewell: "Far from the deep roar of the Aegean main." Plato, *tr. fr. Greek by* Charles Whibley. AWP; WBP
Farewell: "Farewell! Another gloomy word." Bert Leston Taylor. BOHV; TOP
Farewell: "Farewell! if ever fondest prayer." Byron. *See* Farewell! If Ever Fondest Prayer.
Farewell: "Farewell, then. It is finished." Wilfrid Scawen Blunt. The Love Sonnets of Proteus, LIII. MoBrPo (1942 ed.)
Farewell: "Farewell! thou art too dear for my possessing." Shakespeare. *See* Sonnets, LXXXVII.
Farewell: "Farewell to barn and stack and tree." A. E. Housman. *See* Farewell to Barn and Stack and Tree.
Farewell, The: "Farewell to Europe, and at once farewell." Charles Churchill. CEP
Farewell: "Farewell to the bushy clump close to the river." John Clare. NoP
Farewell, A: "Flow down, cold rivulet, to the sea." Tennyson. HBV; OTPC; PoVP; RIS
Farewell, A: "Go fetch to me a pint o' wine." Burns. *See* My Bonnie Mary.
Farewell, The: "Gone, gone—sold and gone." Whittier. AA; AWP; InPo; PoNe
Farewell, A: "Good-bye [*or* Good-by]—no [*or* nay], do not grieve that it is over." Harriet Monroe. AA; HBMV; NP
Farewell, A: "I go down from the hill in gladness." "Æ." AnIV
Farewell: "I leave the world to-morrow." Enid Derham. BoAu
Farewell, A: "I put thy hand aside." "Madeline Bridges." AA
Farewell: "It is buried and done with." John Addington Symonds. OBVV; PG (1945 ed.); VA
Farewell, The: "It was a' for our rightfu' king." Burns. CH; HBV; OBEV; ViBoPo
(It Was A' for Our Rightfu' King.) EnRP; GoTS; PeER; PoEL-4
Farewell: "Juliet, farewell, I would not be forgiven." Wilfrid Scawen Blunt. *See* Farewell to Juliet ("Juliet, farewell . . .")
Farewell, A: "Leave me O love, which reachest but to dust." Sir Philip Sidney. *See* Leave me, O Love . . .
Farewell: "Linden blossomed, the nightingale sang, The." Heine, *tr. fr. German by* John Todhunter. AWP
Farewell, The: "Methinks I draw but sickly breath." *Unknown.* OxBoCh
Farewell, A: "My fairest child, I have no song to give you," 2 *sts.* Charles Kingsley. BLPA; DD; GN; HBV, 3 *sts.*; HBVY, 3 *sts.*; NeHB; OTPC; PoVP; TreF; VA
Farewell, A: "My horse's feet beside the lake." Matthew Arnold. *Fr.* Switzerland. MBW-2; OAEP; ViPP; VP
Farewell: "Not soon shall I forget." Katharine Tynan. CH
Farewell, A: "Oft have I mused, but now at length I find." Sir Philip Sidney. EIL; EnLi-1; FCP; OBSC; ReIE; SiCE; SiPS

(Oft Have I Mused.) EnRePo
Farewell, A: "Only in my deep heart I love you, sweetest heart." "Æ." OBVV
Farewell: "Shores of my native land." Isaac Toussaint-L'Ouverture, *tr. fr. French by* Edna Worthley Underwood. PoNe; TTY
Farewell, The: "Since fate commands me hence, and I." Thomas Stanley. CavP
Farewell: "Smell of death was in the air, The." John Press. PoRA
Farewell: "Tell them, O Sky-born, when I die." Harry Kemp. HBMV
Farewell, A: "There lived a singer in France of old." Swinburne. *Fr.* The Triumph of Time. GTSL
Farewell: "Thou goest; to what distant place." John Addington Symonds. HBV
Farewell, A: "Thou wilt not look on me?" Alice Brown. HBV
Farewell, A: "Venus, take my votive glass." Matthew Prior. *See* Lady Who Offers Her Looking-Glass to Venus.
Farewell, A: "What is there left to be said?" A. R. D. Fairburn. AnNZ
Farewell: "What should I say." Sir Thomas Wyatt. GoBC; LO; OBSC; UnPo (1st ed.)
(Farewell, Unkist.) LoBV
(Revocation, A.) OBEV
(What Sould I Say.) EnRePo; NoP
("What should I say?") FCP; ReEn; SiCE; SiPS
(What Shulde I Saye.) AtBAP; PoEL-1
Farewell, A: "With all my will, but much against my heart." Coventry Patmore. The Unknown Eros, I, xvi. ACP; AnFE; EnLoPo; FaBoEn; GTBS-P; HBV; LiTL; LO; MemP; MeWo; OBEV; OBNC; OBVV; PoEL-5; PoVP; TrGrPo
Farewell!/ The hours of birth and death. A Soldier to His Wife. Liu Chi. OnPM
Farewell! a long farewell, to all my greatness. Wolsey's Farewell to His Greatness [*or* Cardinal Wolsey's Farewell *or* Farewell to All My Greatness]. Shakespeare, *and probably* John Fletcher. King Henry VIII, *fr.* III, ii. LiTB; LiTG; MaRV; OHFP; PTK; TIHL; TreF; TrGrPo
Farewell! A long farewell to all our school days. A Parody. Edith Putnam Painton. PEDC
Farewell, adieu, that courtly [*or* court-like] life. Haltersick's Song. John Pickering. *Fr.* Horestes. ElL; OBSC; ReEn; TuPP
Farewell! Advent. James Ryman. MeEL
Farewell all future hopes that guide the course. *Unknown.* SeCSL
Farewell, all my welfare. Sir Thomas Wyatt. EnPo; FCP; SiPS
Farewell and adieu to you, gay [*or* fair] Spanish ladies. Spanish Ladies. *Unknown.* AmSS; FaBoCh; LoGBV
Farewell and Hail! Thomas Curtis Clark. PGD
"Farewell!" Another gloomy word. Farewell. Bert Leston Taylor. BOHV; TOP
Farewell, Bristolia's dingy piles of brick. Last Verses. Thomas Chatterton. CBV; PoFS; TrGrPo
Farewell, but Whenever [You Welcome the Hour]. Thomas Moore. FaBoBe; HBV; NeHB; OAEP
Farewell Cariola! John Webster. *Fr.* The Duchess of Malfi. LO
Farewell Content. Shakespeare. *See* Othello's Farewell to His Career.
Farewell, dear babe, my heart's too much content. In Memory of My Dear Grandchild Elizabeth Bradstreet. Anne Bradstreet. AP; SCAP
Farewell, Dear Love! Since Thou Wilt Needs Be Gone. *Unknown.* ElL; OAEP; OBSC
Farewell, dear scenes, for ever closed to me. Lines Written on a Window-Shutter at Weston. William Cowper. EiCP
Farewell deere infante sucke from my pensive brest. *Unknown.* SeCSL
Farewell, Fair Armida. *At. to* Dryden. SeCL
Farewell, fair saint. let [*or* may] not the seas and wind. On His Mistress[e] Crossing the [*or* Going to] Sea. Thomas Cary. OBS; SeCL
Farewell false love, the oracle of lies. False Love [*or* Farewell to False Love]. Sir Walter Ralegh. CBEP; ElL; FCP; LO; OBSC; ReEn; SiPS
Farewell, farewell! but this I tell. He Prayeth Best. Samuel Taylor Coleridge. *Fr.* The Rime of the Ancient Mariner. YT
"Farewell, farewell, my pretty maid." The True Lover's Farewell. *Unknown.* AS
Farewell, farewell, poor joys, let not my hearse. John Hall. LO
Farewell—farewell to thee, Araby's daughter! The Peri's Lament for Hinda. Thomas Moore. *Fr.* Lalla Rookh. OBNC
Farewell for a While. Elizabeth Daryush. QFR
Farewell! for now a stormy morn and dark. Outward Bound. Edward Sydney Tylee. PAH
Farewell, friends! yet not farewell. Sir Edwin Arnold. *Fr.* Pearls of the Faith: After Death in Arabia. MaRV
Farewell happy fields. Satan's Speech. Milton. *Fr.* Paradise Lost, I. DiPo
Farewell has long been said; I have foregone thee. After a Parting. Alice Meynell. PoVP
Farewell Hymn to the Valley of Irwan, A. John Langhorne. *Fr.* Solyman and Almena. CEP
Farewell! I goe to sleep; but when. The Evening-Watch. Henry Vaughan. AnAnS-1; MeP; NCEP
Farewell, I say, with tearful eye. Roundel of Farewell. Villon. MeWo
Farewell! If Ever Fondest Prayer. Byron. EnRP; HBV; ViBoPo
(Farewell.) MeWo; TrGrPo
"Farewell, I'm fading!" cried. Indispensability. Arthur Guiterman. WaKn
Farewell in a Dream. Stephen Spender. MoAB; MoBrPo
Farewell, incomparable element. Hymn to Earth. Elinor Wylie. AmLP; BoLiVe; LiTM; MAP; MoAB; MoAmPo; MoPo; MoVE; NePA; NP; ReMP
Farewell is the bell. To the Hawks. Donald Justice. TDP
Farewell, Life. Thomas Hood. BEL; EnRP; EPN
(Stanzas: "Farewell, Life! my senses swim.") VA
Farewell, love, and all thy laws for ever. A Renouncing of [*or* The Lover Renounceth] Love. Sir Thomas Wyatt. BEL; EnLi-1 (1949 ed.); EnLit; EnPo; FaBoEn; FCP; LiTB; LiTL; OAEP; ReEn; ReIE; SiCE; SiPS; Sonn; StP; TOP; TrGrPo; TuPP; YAT
Farewell Mercy, farewell thy piteous grace. Lament. John Lydgate. *Fr.* Court of Sapience. PoEL-1
Farewell! my adored country; region beloved of the sun. My Last Thought. José Rizal. PoFr
Farewell, my friends, I'm bound for Canaan. Parting Friends. *Unknown.* ABF
Farewell, my more than fatherland! A Farewell to America. Richard Henry Wilde. AA
Farewell, my Muse! for, lo, there is no end. Ideal Passion, XLII. George Edward Woodberry. HBMV
Farewell, my sweete, untill I come. To Chloris. Charles Cotton. CavP
Farewell, my tender brother. Beatrice's Last Words. Shelley. *Fr.* The Cenci. FiP
Farewell, my youth! for now we needs must part. Ave atque Vale. Rosamund Marriott Watson. HBV; VA
Farewell now my lady gaye. A Farewell to His Mistress. *Unknown.* AtBAP
Farewell, O Patrick Sarsfield. *Unknown, tr. fr. Modern Irish by* James Clarence Mangan. OnYI
(Farewell to Patrick Sarsfield [Earl of Lucan], A.) AnIV; OxBI
(Patrick Sarsfield, Lord Lucan, *tr. by* Frank O'Connor.) KiLC
Farewell, O Prince, farewell, O sorely tried! Theodor Herzl. Israel Zangwill. TrJP
Farewell, O sun, Arcadia's clearest light. Sir Philip Sidney. *Fr.* Arcadia. FCP
Farewell of the Attendant Spirit. Milton. *See* To the Ocean Now I Fly.
Farewell, old California, I'm going far away. Australia and the Amazon. John A. Stone. SGR
Farewell, old year! Old and New. *Unknown.* BLRP
Farewell Patrick Sarsfield wherever you may roam. Patrick Sarsfield, Lord Lucan. *Unknown, tr. by* Frank O'Connor. KiLC
Farewell, Peace. *Unknown.* MC
Farewell, Renown! Austin Dobson. MoBrPo (1942 ed.)
Farewell, Rewards and Fairies. Richard Corbet. *See* Fairies Farewell, The.
"Farewell, Romance!" the Cave-men said. The King. Kipling. CABA; InP; PoVP
Farewell, sweet boy; complain not of my truth. Caelica,

Farewell (continued)
LXXXIV. Fulke Greville. EnRePo; EP; NCEP; OBSC; QFR; Sonn
Farewell, Sweet Dust. Elinor Wylie. AnAmPo; LiTA
Farewell, sweet Love! yet blame you not my truth. Farewell to Love. Samuel Taylor Coleridge. Sonn
Farewell, sweetest country; out of my heart, you roses. London. Manmohan Ghose. ACV
Farewell; the dark is falling on the wind. Farewell to Fields. Howard McKinley Corning. MAP; MoAmPo (1942 ed.)
Farewell the heart [*or* reign] of cruelty. A Renouncing of Hardly Escaped Love. Sir Thomas Wyatt. FCP; ReIE; SiPS
Farewell, then. It is finished. Farewell. Wilfrid Scawen Blunt. The Love Sonnets of Proteus, LIII. MoBrPo (1942 ed.)
Farewell this company. Robert Chamberlain. *Fr.* The Swaggering Damsel. TuPP
Farewell, This World. *Unknown.* EnPo; MeEL, 4 *sts.*
Farewell! thou art too dear for my possessing. Sonnets, LXXXVII. Shakespeare. AnFE; BoLiVe; BWP; CLwM; CoBE; EIL; GTBS; GTBS-D; GTBS-P; GTBS-W; GTSE; GTSL; InvP; LiTB; LiTG; MasP; MeWo; OAEP; OBEV; OBSC; PG (1955 ed.); PoAn; PoEL-2; PoeP; PoFS; QFR; ReIE; SiCE; Sonn; StP; TOP; TrGrPo; ViBoPo
Farewell, thou busy [*or* busie] world. The Retirement [*or* To Mr. Izaak Walton]. Charles Cotton. BoPe; CEP; HBV; OBS; ViBoPo
Farewell, thou child of my right hand, and joy. On My [*or* His] First Son [*or* Sonne]. Ben Jonson. AnAnS-2; AtBAP; AWP; BWP; CABA; CaFP; CoBE; DiPo; EIL; EnL; EnRePo; ExPo; FaBoEn; ForPo; FosPo; InPo; LiTB; LoBV; MaPo; NoP; OAEP; OBS; OnPM; PIA; PoE; PoEL-2; PoFS; PoIE; QFR; ReEn; ReIE; SCEP-2; SeCP; SeCV-1; SeEP; StP; TuPP; UnPo (3d ed.); WoL
Farewell, thou fertile soil that Brutus first out found [*or* found out]. Going towards Spain. Barnabe Googe. EnPo; EnRePo; ReIE; SiCE
Farewell, Thou Minstrel Harp. Sir Walter Scott. *See* Harp of the North, Farewell.
Farewell thou thing, time-past so knowne, so deare. His Fare-well to Sack. Robert Herrick. AnAnS-2; OAEP; SCEP-2; SeCP; SeCV-1
Farewell to a Fondling, A. Thomas Churchyard. *See* Lover Deceived by His Lady's Unconstancy Writeth unto Her as Followeth, The.
Farewell to Agassiz, A. Oliver Wendell Holmes. ImOP
Farewell to All My Greatness. Shakespeare, *and probably* John Fletcher. *See* Wolsey's Farewell to His Greatness.
Farewell to America, A. Richard Henry Wilde. AA
Farewell to an idea. . .A cabin stands. Wallace Stevens. *Fr.* The Auroras of Autumn. CMoP
Farewell to Anactoria. Sappho, *tr. fr. Greek by* Allen Tate. AWP; LiTW
Farewell to Arms, A. George Peele. *See* His Golden Locks. . .
Farewell to Barn and Stack and Tree. A. E. Housman. A Shropshire Lad, VIII. CMoP; EnLi-2 (1949 ed.); InPo; OAEP; PoIE; PoPo; PoVP; UnPo (3d ed.)
(Farewell.) MoAB; MoBrPo (1950 ed.)
Farewell to Bath. Lady Mary Wortley Montagu. CEP
Farewell to Bithynia. Catullus, *tr. fr. Latin by* Theodore Martin. OuHeWo
Farewell to Cuba. Maria Gowen Brooks. AA
Farewell to Cupid. Caelica, LXXXV. Fulke Greville. OBSC
Farewell to Europe, and at once farewell. The Farewell. Charles Churchill. CEP
Farewell to fair Alba, high house of the Sun. Deirdre's Farewell to Alba. *Unknown.* IrPN; OnYI
Farewell to Fál, A. Gerald Nugent, *tr. fr. Late Middle Irish by* Padraic Pearse. OnYI
Farewell to False Love, A. Sir Walter Ralegh. *See* False Love.
Farewell to Fields. Howard McKinley Corning. MAP; MoAmPo (1942 ed.)
Farewell to fields and butterflies. Garden-Song. James Branch Cabell. HBMV
Farewell to Folly, *sel.* Robert Greene.
Sweet Are the Thoughts That Savor of Content. BEL; CoBE; EG; PoToHe; ReIE; SiCE; TuPP
(Content.) EnLit; OnPM; WoL
(Maesia's Song.) CTC; HBV; OBSC; ReEn
(Mind Content, A.) EIL; ViBoPo
(Poor Estate, The.) TrGrPo
(Song: "Sweet are the thoughts that savor of content.") EnLi-1; OuHeWo; PoEL-2
Farewell to Greatness. Shakespeare, *and probably* John Fletcher. *See* Wolsey's Farewell to His Greatness.
Farewell to Han So. Tu Fu, *tr. fr. Chinese by* Chi Hwang Chu *and* Edna Worthley Underwood. OnPM
Farewell to himself. The Bride. Ruth Comfort Mitchell. HBMV
Farewell to His Mistress, A. *Unknown.* AtBAP
Farewell to Ireland. *At. to* St. Columcille, *tr. fr. Middle Irish by* Douglas Hyde. AWP; JAWP; LiTW; WBP
(Colum-Cille's Farewell to Ireland.) AnIV
Farewell to Italy. Walter Savage Landor. VA
Farewell to Juliet ("I see you, Juliet, still, with your straw hat"). Wilfrid Scawen Blunt. The Love Sonnets of Proteus, XLVII. EnLoPo
Farewell to Juliet ("Juliet, farewell. I would not be forgiven"). Wilfried Scawen Blunt. The Love Sonnets of Proteus, XXXIX. AnEnPo
(Farewell.) TrGrPo
Farewell to Juliet ("Lame, impotent conclusion to youth's dreams"). Wilfried Scawen Blunt. The Love Sonnets of Proteus, LII. ViBoPo
Farewell to Lesbia. Catullus, *tr. fr. Latin by* Robert Fitzgerald. LiTW
Farewell to Lochaber, an' farewell my Jean. Lochaber No More. Allan Ramsay. HBV
Farewell to London in the year 1715, A. Pope. CBEP; CEP
Farewell to Love. Samuel Taylor Coleridge. Sonn
Farewell to Love. John Donne. MaMe; ReEn
Farewell to My Mother. "Placido," *tr. fr. Spanish by* James Weldon Johnson. PoNe; TTY; BANP, *tr. by* Bryant
(Placido's Farewell to His Mother, *tr. by* James Weldon Johnson.) BANP
Farewell to Nancy. Burns. *See* Ae Fond Kiss.
Farewell to Narcissus. Robert Horan. NYBP
Farewell to old England for ever. Botany Bay. *Unknown.* PoAu-1
Farewell to one now silenced quite. Parted. Alice Meynell. PeVV
Farewell to Patrick Sarsfield, Earl of Lucan, A. *Unknown.* *See* Farewell, O Patrick Sarsfield.
Farewell to Poetry. Goldsmith. *Fr.* The Deserted Village. OBEC
Farewell to John Norris and Sir Francis Drake, A. George Peele. OBSC
Farewell to Sliev Morna. Lay of the Forlorn. George Darley. OnYI
Farewell to slumber! Air that has been still. Night Shower. Milton. PoMa
Farewell to Sorrow, A. Thomas Jordan. *See* Careless Gallant, The.
Farewell to Summer. George Arnold. AA; DD
Farewell to the bushy clump close to the river. Farewell. John Clare. NoP
Farewell to the Court. Sir Walter Ralegh. CBEP; EnRePo; FaBoEn; FCP; OBSC; SiPS
("Like truthless dreams, so are my joys expired.") EG; LO, 4 *ll.*; SiCE; Sonn; TuPP
Farewell to the Court, *sel.* Earl of Rochester.
"Tired with the noisome follies of the age." TrGrPo
Farewell to the Fairies. Richard Corbet. *See* Fairies' Farewell, The.
Farewell to the Farm. Robert Louis Stevenson. BoChLi (1939 ed.); BoTP; FaPON; GaP; OTPC; TiPo
Farewell to the Glen. Dante Gabriel Rossetti. The House of Life, LXXXIV. MaVP; PoVP; ViPo
Farewell to the Highlands, farewell to the North. My Heart's in the Highlands. Burns. AnEnPo; AWP; BBV; BEL; CEP; CoBE; EnRP; FaFP; GN; HBV; InPo; JAWP; LiTG; LiTL; NeHB; OTPC; RIS; StaSt; TOP; WBP
Farewell to the land where the clouds love to rest. Sir Walter Scott. *Fr.* Rob Roy. NBM
Farewell to the Muses. John Hamilton Reynolds. OBRV
Farewell to the Old Year. Eleanor Farjeon. SiSoSe
Farewell to the World, A. Ben Jonson. *See* To the World: A Farewell for a Gentlewoman, Virtuous and Noble.
Farewell to the World of Richard Bishop. *Unknown.* CoMu

Farewell to Tobacco. Charles Lamb. BOHV; NBM; OBRV; OxBoLi
Farewell to Town. Laurence Housman. HBMV
Farewell to Van Gogh. Charles Tomlinson. CMoP; GTBS-P; NMP
Farewell to Winnipeg. Roy Daniells. OBCV
Farewell to Wives, A. *Unknown.* SeCL
Farewell, [*or* Farewel] too little and too lately known. To the Memory of Mr. Oldham. Dryden. ATP; AWP; BWP; CABA; CaFP; CEP; DiPo; EiCL; EiPP; ExPo; FaBoEn; FiP; ForPo; InPo; JAWP; LoBV; MBW-1; NoP; OBS; PAn; PeRV; PIA; PoEL-3; PoIE; PP; SeCeV; SeCV-2; SeEP; StP; UnPo (1st ed.); VaPo; ViBoPo; WBP
Farewell, Ungrateful Traitor. Dryden. *Fr.* The Spanish Friar, V, i. CBEP; ELP; InPo; LiTB; LiTG; PAn; SeCL; ViBoPo
(“Farwell ungratful traytor.”) EnLoPo
(Love's Despair.) ACP
(Song: “Farewell, ungrateful traitor!”) CaVP; EiPP; FaBoEn; FiP; MBW-1; OBS; PeRV; SeCV-2; SeEP
Farewell, Unkind! Farewell! to me, no more a father! *Unknown.* EnLoPo
Farewell, Unkist. Sir Thomas Wyatt. *See* Farewell: “What should I say.”
Farewell Voyaging World! Conrad Aiken. NYBP
Farewell, whose like on earth I shall not find. Valedictory. Tennyson. GoBC
Farewell World. Sir Philip Sidney. *See* Leave Me, O Love.
Farewell, ye dungeons dark and strong. Macpherson's Farewell [*or* Defiance]. Burns. MCCG; OtMeF
Farewell, ye mountains, and ye much-loved paths. Schiller. *Fr.* The Maid of Orleans, *play.* PoFr
Farewell you everlasting hills! I'm cast. Mans Fall, and Recovery. Henry Vaughan. AnAnS-1; MeP
Farewells from Paradise. Elizabeth Barrett Browning. OBEV (new ed.); OBVV
Far-fetched and dear-bought, as the proverb rehearses. A Singing Lesson. Swinburne. HBV
Far-fetched with tales of other worlds and ways. Home from Abroad. Laurie Lee. ToPo
Farm, The. Donald Hall. LiTM (1970 ed.)
Farm, The. Jane Taylor. OTPC (1923 ed.)
Farm after farm, the schoolbus stops. Joy Meets Boy. Robert P. Tristram Coffin. OTPC (1946 ed.)
Farm Boy, The. Katharine Atherton Grimes. PoMa
Farm Boy after Summer. Robert Francis. PoIE; PoSa
Farm Cart. Eleanor Farjeon. BrR
Farm Child. R. S. Thomas. BoNaP; ChMP; FlW; WePo
Farm Couple, After Norman Rockwell. Barry Spacks. NYTB
Farm Died, The. Malcolm Cowley. *Fr.* Blue Juniata. MAP; MoAmPo (1942 ed.)
Farm Gate. Uys Krige, *tr. fr. Afrikaans by* Uys Krige *and* Jack Cope. PeSA
Farm Implements and Rutabagas in a Landscape. John Ashbery. CoAP
Farm Life. Ruth Edna Stanton. GFA
Farm near Norman's Lane, The. Mary Finnin. PoAu-2
Farm on the Great Plains, The. William Stafford. PIA; PoCh
Farm on the Links, The. Rosamund Marriott Watson. OBVV; VA
Farm Picture, A. Walt Whitman. OnPM; WoL
Farm Wife. John Hanlon Mitchell. CaP
Farm Wife. R. S. Thomas. BoPe
Farm Yard. *See* Farmyard.
Farmer. Liberty Hyde Bailey. RePo; YeAr
Farmer. Padraic Fallon. OxBI
Farmer, The. A. P. Herbert. CenHV
Farmer, The. Fredegond Shove. MMA
Farmer, The, *with music.* *Unknown.* AS
Farmer and Sailor. Plato, *tr. fr. Greek by* T. F. Higham. LiTW
Farmer and the Farmer's Wife, The. P. G. Hiebert. FiBHP
Farmer Comes to Town, The, *with music.* *Unknown.* TrAS
Farmer in Deep Thought, The. William Carlos Williams. PoeP
Farmer in the dell, The. *Unknown.* RIS
Farmer is busy, so busy, to-day, The. Haymaking. E. M. Adams. BoTP
“Farmer, is the harvest ready.” Bread. H. E. Wilkinson. BoTP
Farmer Jones's Wife, *with music.* *Unknown.* BFSS
Farmer once planted some little brown seeds, A. A Growing Rhyme. J. M. Westrup. BoTP
Farmer ploughs into ground, The. Seed. H. C. Bosman. BoSA; PeSA
Farmer Remembers Lincoln, A. Witter Bynner. HH; MAP; MoAmPo (1942 ed.)
Farmer Remembers the Somme, The. Vance Palmer. MoAuPo; PoAu-1
Farmer took [*or* say to] de boll weevil, De[*or* The]. De Ballet [*or* Ballit] of de Boll Weevil. *Unknown.* ABF; AS; IHA
Farmer turns for home, The; his team's glad tread. Pastoral. Muriel Lewis. MoAuPo
Farmer was plowing his field one day, A. The Bad-tempered Wife. *Unknown.* MaC
Farmer went trotting [*or* riding] upon [*or* on] his grey mare, A. Mother Goose. BoTP; EvOK; GFA; HBVY; OTPC; OxNR; PPL; RIS; StVeCh; TiPo
Farmer will never be happy again, The. The Farmer. A. P. Herbert. CenHV
Farmer, you were young once. Age. R. S. Thomas. ToPo
Farmers. Helene Mullins. WGRP
Farmers. William Alexander Percy. MaRV; WGRP
Farmers. *Unknown.* OtMeF
Farmer's Boy, The, *sels.* Robert Bloomfield.
“Again the year's decline.” OBRV
“Live, trifling incidents.” OBRV
Moonlight . . . Scattered Clouds. OBNC
“Yet never fam'd was he, nor foremost found.” PeER
Farmer's Boy, A. *Unknown.* MemP
Farmer's Bride, The. Charlotte Mew. ErPo; HBMV; MoAB; MoBrPo; NP; OnPP; PoRA; TrGrPo
Farmer's Curst Wife, The. *Unknown.* BaBo (A *and* B *vers.*); ESPB (A *and* B *vers.*); ViBoFo
(Bad-tempered Wife, The.) MaC
(Tee Roo, *diff. vers., with music.*) OuSiCo
Farmer's Daughter, The, *with music.* *Unknown.* BFSS
Farmer's eyes are dark; he speaks in song, The. On the Welsh Marches. Walter Stone. NYBP
Farmer's goose, who in the stubble, The. The Progress of Poetry. Swift. CABA; CBEP; EiCL; EiCP; InvP; OnYI
Farmer's Gun, The. Andrew Young. MemP; OA
Farmer's Head, The. Ron Padgett. ANYP
Farmer's heart with joy is filled when his crops are good and sound, The. The *Jamestown* Homeward Bound. *Unknown.* SoAmSa
Farmer's Ingle, The. Robert Fergusson. CEP
Farmer's Round, The. *Unknown.* OTPC (1923 ed.)
Farmer's Wife, The. Anne Sexton. LiTM (1970 ed.); NePoEA-2
Farmer's wife looked out of the dairy, The. The Rival. Sylvia Townsend Warner. BoLiVe (1939 ed.); MoAB; MoBrPo
Farmhand's Refrain. H. H. Lewis. LiTM
Farmhouse lingers, though averse to square, The [*or* A]. A Brook in the City. Robert Frost. OxBA; TSW
Farmhouse skyline, draped with trees, The. Pastoral. Alan Creighton. CaP
Farmhouses curl like horns of plenty. Blue Juniata. Malcolm Cowley. MAP; MoAmPo (1942 ed.)
Farming. *Unknown, tr. fr. Chinese by* Arthur Waley. *Fr.* Shi King. LiTW
Farms of Home Lie Lost in Even, The. A. E. Housman. MaPo
Farmyard, The. A. A. Attwood. BoTP
Farmyard. Ruth Dallas. AnNZ
Farm Yard, The. Eliza Lee Follen. OTPC (1946 ed.)
Farmyard [Song], The. *Unknown.* *See* Barnyard Song.
Farnese Hercules, The. Sacheverell Sitwell. FaBoMo; LiTM (rev. ed.)
Farr off from these a slow and silent stream. The Place of the Damned. Milton. *Fr.* Paradise Lost, II. FaBoEn
Farragut. William Tuckey Meredith. AA; DD; EtS; FaBoBe; HBV; HBVY; OnPP; PaA; PAH; ThLM
Farre have I clambred in my mind. *See* Far have I clamber'd in my mind.
Farther. John James Piatt. *See* Suggested Device of a New Western State.
Farther east it wouldn't be on the map. Midwest Town. Ruth Delong Peterson. AmFN
Farther he went the farther home grew, The. For the Grave of Daniel Boone. William Stafford. NoP; PoPl
Farther in summer than the birds. *See* Further in Summer . . .

Farther (continued)
Farther than I have been. Summit, The. Kathleen Raine. Beinn Naomh, IV. OxBS
Farther up the gorge the sea's voice fainted and ceased. All the Little Hoofprints. Robinson Jeffers. Po
Farthest from any war, unique in time. Hollywood. Karl Shapiro. AmPP (4th ed.); LiTM (1970 ed.); OxBA
Farwell, The: "Farewell fond Love, under whose childish whipp." Henry King. CavP
Farwell ungratfull traytor. *See* Farewell, Ungrateful Traitor.
Fascinating chill that music leaves, The. Emily Dickinson. AmePo
Fascination of What's Difficult, The. W. B. Yeats. BrPo; PoEL-5
Fa'se Footrage. *Unknown. See* Fause Foodrage.
Fashions are changing in the sphere. A Change of World. Adrienne Rich. TPM
Fashions in Dogs. E. B. White. FiBHP
Fast. John Tagliabue. SD
Fast Ball. Jonathan Williams. NeAP
Fast Bundled Is the Firewood. *Unknown, tr. fr. Chinese by* Arthur Waley. *Fr.* The Book of Songs. HW
Fast express for Gettysburg roared north, The. They Will Look for a Few Words. Nancy Byrd Turner. AmFN
Fast falls the snow, O lady mine. To F. C. Mortimer Collins. HBV; TreFS
Fast fly the faces through our blood-years. The Narrative of the Black Magicians. Larry Neal. BF
Fast this life of mine was dying. Life and Love. Elizabeth Barrett Browning. PoVP
Fasten the chamber! Bluebeard's Closet. Rose Terry Cooke. AA
Fasten your hair with a golden pin. He Gives His Beloved Certain Rhymes. W. B. Yeats. EG
Faster, faster,/ O Circe, Goddess. The Strayed Reveler. Matthew Arnold. LoBV; MBW-2; MyFE; ViPo; ViPP; VP
Faster than fairies, faster than witches. From a Railway Carriage. Robert Louis Stevenson. BoTP; FaPON; GFA; PDV; TiPo
Fastidious Serpent, The. Henry Johnstone. BOHV; HBV; HBVY; OTPC (1946 ed.); PPL
Fastinge supper call you this, A. *Unknown.* SeCSL
Fat black bucks in a wine-barrel room. The Congo. Vachel Lindsay. AmP; AmPP; CMoP; CoBA; FaFP; FaPL; GTBS-W; HoPM; LiTA; LiTG; MAP; MCCG; MoAB; MoAmPo; NeMA; NP; OxBA; PFY; PoMa; PoNe; PoRA; ShBV-3; TreF; WePo; WHA
Fat-buttocked Bushmen, The. Earnest A. Hooton. WhC
Fat flakes fall, The. South Cumberland, 10th May 1943. Norman Nicholson. POTi
Fat friar stroking golf balls, The. Walking along the Hudson. Donald Petersen. CoAP
Fat green frog sits by the pond. Grandfather Frog. Louise Seaman Bechtel. RePo; TiPo
Fat men go about the streets, The. Ballade of the Poetic Life. J. C. Squire. OBMV; WhC
Fat soil, full spring, sweet olive, grape of bliss. Christ's Bloody Sweat. Robert Southwell. ReIE
Fat torpedoes in bursting jackets. Fourth of July. Rachel Field. SiSoSe
Fatal Sisters, The. Thomas Gray, *after the Icelandic.* BEL; CEP; CoBE; EiCP; EiPP; EnPE; EnRP; NoP; OAEP; PeER
Fatal Spell, The. Byron. *Fr.* Childe Harold's Pilgrimage, IV. OBNC
("Oh Love! no habitant of earth thou art.") ViBoPo
Fatal Star, The. Thomas Lodge. TuPP
Fatal Wedding, The. W. H. Windom. TreFS
Fatalism. Omar Khayyám, *tr. fr. Persian by* Edward Fitzgerald. *Fr.* The Rubáiyát. MaRV
Fate. Louis James Block. AA
Fate. James Fenimore Cooper. HBMV
Fate. Emerson. ForPo
Fate. Susan Marr Spalding. AA; BBV (1951 ed.); BLPA; HBV; NeHB; PoToHe
Fate and the Younger Generation. D. H. Lawrence. OxBoLi; SiTL; WhC
Fate Defied. Adelaide Crapsey. NP; YT
Fate gave the word, the arrow sped. A Mother's Lament for the Death of Her Son. Burns. HoPM
Fate hired me once to play a villain's part. Between the Acts. Stanley Kunitz. ELU
Fate! I have Asked. Walter Savage Landor. ViBoPo
Fate, I will not ask for wealth or fame. The Higher Good. Theodore Parker. FaBoBe
Fate is strongest. Winter is coldest. Gnomic Verse from Cotton Manuscript. *Unknown.* YAT
Fate Is Unfair. Don Marquis. *Fr.* Archy Does His Part. EvOK
Fate of a Broom, The—an Anticipation. Thomas Love Peacock. CBEP
Fate of Elms, The. Robert Francis. NYTB
Fate of John Burgoyne, The. *Unknown.* PAH
Fate of King Dathi, The. Thomas Osborne Davis. OnYI
Fate of Narcissus, The. William Warner. *Fr.* Albion's England. OBSC
Fate of the Cabbage Rose, The. Wallace Irwin. FiBHP
Fate of the Oak, The. "Barry Cornwall." OHIP; OTPC (1923 ed.)
Fate of the Prophets, The. Longfellow. *Fr.* Christus; a Mystery, Pt. I. WGRP
Fate struck the hour! Lincoln. Jane L. Hardy. OHIP
Fate to beauty still must give. Epitaph. Claudian. AWP
Fate wafts us from the pygmies' shore. Gods of War. "*A* E." BEL
Fate with Devoted . . . Arthur Davison Ficke. AnEnPo
Fateful youngling of the dark and drift, A. Radium. Agnes Lee. PoMa
Fates of Men. *Unknown, tr. fr. Anglo-Saxon by* Charles W. Kennedy. AnOE
Fates of the Apostles, *sel.* Cynewulf, *tr. fr. Anglo-Saxon by* Charles W. Kennedy.
"Now I pray the man who may love this lay." AnOE
Father, The. Dorothy Scott Ballard. ChIP
Father. Paul Carroll. NeAP
Father. Arthur Davison Ficke. TrPWD
Father, The. Donald Finkel. CoPo; PIA
Father. Frances Frost. FaPON; SiSoSe; StVeCh (1955 ed.); TiPo (1959 ed.)
Father, The. Sara Henderson Hay. StaSt
Father, The. Richmond Lattimore. NePoAm-2
Father. Jean Lipkin. PeSA
Father. Robert Pack. CoPo
Father, The. George Francis Savage-Armstrong. VA
Father. Mildred Weston. PoSC
Father, A/ accused of shooting. John Giorno. *Fr.* The American Book of the Dead. ANYP
Father,/ Grant unto us true family love. A Prayer For Family Love. John S. Hoyland. MaRV
Father/ one day longer on this earth than you. My Father, My Son. John Malcolm Brinnin. NYBP
Father Abraham, *with music. Unknown.* BoAN-1
Father, and Bard revered! to whom I owe. Dedicatory Sonnet to S. T. Coleridge. Harley Coleridge. ERoP-2; Sonn
Father and I went down to camp. Yankee Doodle [*or* The Yankee's (*or* Yankey's) Return from Camp]. *Unknown.* ABF; FaFP; FaPON; HBV; MC; OxBoLi; PaA; PAH; PAL; PoFr; PoRL; SiTL; TreF; YaD
Father and Jupiter, The. John Gay. *Fr.* Fables. EiCL
Father and Son. F. R. Higgins. ACV; BoC; LiTM; OBMV; OxBI; PG (1955 ed.); POTE
Father and Son. Stanley Kunitz. PoAn; TwCP
Father and Son. Delmore Schwartz. LiTA
Father and Son: 1939. William Plomer. PeSA
Father, be praised for a white jasmine. Consolation in July. Rayner Heppenstall. NeBP
Father, between Thy strong hands Thou has bent. Prayer of a Teacher. Dorothy Littlewort. TrPWD
Father calls me William, sister calls me Will. Jest 'fore Christmas. Eugene Field. ChBR; DD; FaBV; FaFP; FaPON; HBV; HBVY; HH; OHFP; OTPC; PoLF; PTK; TreF; YT
Father, chancing to chastise. Self-Sacrifice. Harry Graham. Some Ruthless Rhymes, IV. BBGG; CenHV
Father, come home. Gather These Bones. Lewis Turco. FiSC
Father Damien. John Banister Tabb. ACP; AmP; JKCP
Father darts out on the stairs, The. Early Morning Feed. Peter Redgrove. BoC
Father, Dear Father, Come Home with Me Now. Henry Clay Work. TreF
(Come Home, Father.) PaPo; YaD
Father Does His Best, A. E. B. White. ALV; WhC
Father Father Son and Son. Jon Swan. NYBP
Father! father! where are you going? Little Boy Lost. Blake.

Fr. Songs of Innocence. CBEP; EnRP; TiPo (1952 ed.)
Father Francis. Walter Herries Pollock. VA
"Father Francisco! Father Francisco!" The Confessional. *Unknown.* UnTE
Father Gilligan. W. B. Yeats. *See* Ballad of Father Gilligan, The.
Father Grumble. *Unknown.* BaBo; ViBoFo
Father has a workshop. The Workshop. Aileen Fisher. SoPo
Father, hear us, we are praying. For Our Children. Amy Carmichael. FaChP
Father heard his children scream. The Stern Parent. Harry Graham. Some Ruthless Rhymes, I. BBGG; CenHV; ChTr; TreFT
Father, here a temple in Thy name we build. Hymn of Dedication. Elizabeth E. Scantlebury. BLRP
Father, How Wide Thy Glories Shine. Charles Wesley. TrPWD; TRV
Father! I bless thy name that I do live. In Him We Live. Jones Very. AmP; OxBA
Father, I know that all my life. Surrender. Anna L. Waring. SoP
Father, I lift my hands to Thee. Suppliant. Florence Earle Coates. TrPWD
Father, I loved you as a child, and still. The Mirror. Edgar Bowers. QFR
Father, I scarcely dare to pray. A Last Prayer [*or* A Prayer]. Helen Hunt Jackson. AA; MaRV; OQP; PCD; SoP; TrPWD; TRV
Father, I stretch my hands to Thee. Faith. Charles Wesley. SoP
Father, I will not ask for wealth or fame. The Higher Good [*or* A New Year Prayer]. Theodore Parker. AA; HBV; MaRV; PGD
Father in heaven! after the days misspent. Sonnet. Petrarch. *Fr.* Sonnets to Laura: To Laura in Life. CAW
Father in Heaven ("For flowers that bloom about our feet"). *Unknown, sometimes at. to* Emerson. *See* We Thank Thee.
Father in Heaven! from whom the simplest flower. A Prayer. Felicia Dorothea Hemans. TrPWD
Father in Heaven, give us bread. Prayer of the Unemployed. *Unknown.* MaRV
Father in Heaven! humbly before thee. A Prayer for Peace. Edward Rowland Sill. TrPWD
Father in Heaven, make me wise. A Mother's Prayer [*or* A Father Speaks]. Margaret E. Sangster. MaRV; SoP; STF; TrPWD
Father, in Thy mysterious presence kneeling. Prayer for Strength. Samuel Johnson. MaRV; SoP; TRV
Father, in Thy starry tent. Rest in Peace. Wilfred J. Funk. PoLF
Father, into Thy Hands. Thomas B. Pollock. BePJ
Father Is Coming. Mary Howitt. OTPC
Father John's bread was made of rye. Rye Bread. William Stanley Braithwaite. CDC
Father Knows, The. "F. L. H." BLRP
Father Land and Mother Tongue. Samuel Lover. HBV
Father, lead me, day by day. A Child's Prayer. *Unknown.* BLRP
Father, lead me on, I pray. Prayer for Guidance. Henry W. Frost. SoP
Father, lest I stumble in the new year. An Opening Prayer. *Unknown.* SoP
Father lighted candles for me. For Hanukkah. Hayyim Nahman Bialik. TiPo (1952 ed.)
"Father, look up and see that flag." The American Boy. *Unknown.* PEDC
Father Malloy. Edgar Lee Masters. *Fr.* Spoon River Anthology. NP; OxBA; PoPo
Father Mapple's Hymn. Herman Melville. *Fr.* Moby Dick, *ch.* 9. AmePo; EtS
(Ribs and Terrors, The.) EaLo; ViBoPo
(Whale, The.) AtBAP; PoPl; TrGrPo
Father Mat. Patrick Kavanagh. AnIL; OPoP
"In a meadow/ Beside the chapel three boys were playing football," *sel.* MoAB; NMP
Father Missouri takes his own. Foreclosure. Sterling A. Brown. PoNe
Father Molloy. Samuel Lover. BOHV; HBV
Father, Now My Prayer Is Said. William Brighty Rands. OTPC (1946 ed.)
Father of all! in Death's relentless claim. Oliver Wendell Holmes. *Fr.* A Poem: Dedication of the Pittsfield Cemetery, September 9, 1850. TrPWD
Father of all! in every age. The Universal Prayer. Pope. BEL; BoPe; CEP; EiCL; EiPP; EnLit; FaBoBe; GoBC; HBV; MaRV; OAEP; PoIE; TOP; TreFT; VaPo; WGRP
Father of eternal grace. The Image of God. Charles Wesley. SoP
Father of Heaven, and him, by whom. The Litanie. John Donne. AtBAP; MaMe; PoEL-2
"Father of Jealousy, be thou accursed from the earth!" Visions of the Daughters of Albion. Blake. ViBoPo
"Father of lakes!" thy waters bend. Lake Superior. Samuel Griswold Goodrich. AA
Father of life, with songs of wonder. Margaret L. Woods. *Fr.* The Return. TrPWD
Father of lights! what sunny [*or* sunnie] seed. Cock-crowing. Henry Vaughan. AnAnS-1; AtBAP; MaPo; MeP; MePo; SCEP-1; SeCV-1
Father of mercies, in Thy Word. O How Sweet Are Thy Words! Anne Steele. BLRP
Father of the bare boughs, and the leaves that die. Sure. Ted Robinson. MaRV
Father of the Man. Elizabeth Mabel Bryan. GoYe
Father O'Flynn. Alfred Perceval Graves. BOHV; HBV; OnYI
Father, part of his double interest. Holy Sonnets, XVI. John Donne. AnAnS-1; MaMe; MasP; MeP; OBS; SCEP-1; Sonn
Father Point in August. Leo Cox. TwCaPo
Father said, "Call him Anthony." Naming the Baby. May Richstone. BiCB
Father said that maybe. Tummy Ache. Aileen Fisher. SoPo
Father . . . —Say the *confiteor.*—I said it. The Confessor. G. G. Belli. ErPo
Father, send us for this meal. Christmas Blessing. Franklin D. Elmer, Jr. ChIP
Father Short came down the lane. *Unknown.* OxNR
Father, sitting on the side of your startled bed. D-Dawn. Margaret McGarvey. GoYe
Father Speaks, A. Margaret E. Sangster. *See* Mother's Prayer, A.
Father, Teach Me. Walter M. Lee. STF
Father! the little girl we see. Little Aglaë. Walter Savage Landor. *Fr.* Pericles and Aspasia, CXIII. VA
Father, this day,/ For our home we pray Thee. Prayer for Our Home. John S. Hoyland. MaRV
Father, this year's jinx rides us apart. All My Pretty Ones. Anne Sexton. CoPo
Father, through the dark that parts us. Ballad. Roy Fuller. ELU
Father, thy hand. Bryant. *Fr.* A Forest Hymn. TrPWD
Father! thy wonders do not singly stand. The Spirit Land. Jones Very. AmLP; AnAmPo
Father, thy word is past, man shall find grace. The Atonement. Milton. *Fr.* Paradise Lost, III. OBS
Father Time. Norman Ault. HBVY
Father to the Man. John Knight. EaLo
Father, to Thee. Frederick L. Hosmer. OQP
(Prayer in Sorrow.) SoP
Father, today I bring to Thee. A Father's Prayer. Mouzon W. Brabham. SoP
Father, too, The, does He not see and hear? A Voice. Samuel Valentine Cole. OQP
Father, unto Thee I pray. Good-Night Prayer for a Little Child. Henry Johnstone. PPL
Father was and aye shall be, The. The Trinity. *Unknown.* ACP
Father, we come not as of old. Hymn. John W. Chadwick. TrPWD
Father, We Thank Thee ("For flowers that bloom about our feet"). *Unknown, sometimes at. to* Emerson. *See* We Thank Thee.
Father, We Thank Thee. *At. to* Rebecca J. Weston. *See* Prayer, A: "Father, we thank Thee for the night."
Father: We thank Thee for laughter. Thanks for Laughter. *Unknown.* OQP
Father, we thank Thee for the night. A Prayer [*or* A Child's Prayer *or* Morning Prayer]. *At. to* Rebecca J. Weston. BoTP; MaRV; OTPC (1946 ed.); PCH; SoPo; TVC
Father, Whate'er of Earthly Bliss. Anne Steele. SoP
Father, who keepest. Domine, Cui Sunt Pleiades Curae [*or*

Father (continued)
Child's Prayer at Evening]. Sir Charles G. D. Roberts. VA
Father, whom I knew for forty years. The Gardener. John Hall Wheelock. NYBP; TwAmPo
Father, whom I murdered every night but one. Elegy for My Father. Howard Moss. CoAP; LiTM (1970 ed.); NePoEA
Father! whose hard and cruel law. The Death of Grant. Ambrose Bierce. AA
Father, Whose Will Is Life and Good. Hardwicke Drummond Rawnsley. MaRV
Father William, *parody.* "Lewis Carroll." *Fr.* Alice's Adventures in Wonderland, *ch.* 5. BiCB; BLV; BOHV; FaPL; FaPON; FiBHP; GoJo; GoTP; HBV; HoPM; InMe; LBN; LiTB; LiTG; OnPP; OTPC (1946 ed.); PDV; PoLF; PoRA; PoVP; RePo; RIS; SiTL; StaSt; TOP; TreF; TrGrPo; TSW; WaKn
(You Are Old, Father William.) ALV; BoChLi; ShBV-2; TiPo; WhC
("'You are old, Father William,' the young man said.") Par
Father William. Robert Southey. *See* Old Man's Comforts, The.
Father William. *Unknown.* BOHV; NA; SiTL
Fathered by March, the daffodils are here. Daffodils. Lizette Woodworth Reese. AA
Fatherland, The. James Russell Lowell. GN; HBV; HBVY; MaRV; OTPC; PGD; PoPl; PoRL; PTK
Fatherland Song (Norwegian National Hymn). Björnstjerne Björnson, *tr. fr. Norwegian by* William Ellery Leonard. AWP; PoFr
Fathers, The. Edwin Muir. OxBS
Fathers and Sons. *Unknown, tr. fr. Irish by* Frank O'Connor. KiLC
"Fathers are in dust, yet live to God, The." Relics of Saints. Cardinal Newman. JKCP
Father's Birthday Cake. Ada Lorraine Jex. GFA
Father's Business, The. Edwin Markham. TRV
Father's Day (—So He Says). *Unknown.* SoP
Father's Gold, The. *Unknown.* STF
Father's gone a-flailing. *Unknown.* OxNR
Father's Heart Is Touched, A. Samuel Hoffenstein. FiBHP
Father's Letter. Eugene Field. IHA
Father's Notes of Woe, A. Sir Walter Scott. *Fr.* The Lay of the Last Minstrel. OBNC
Father's Place, A. Eva Gray. SoP
Father's Prayer, A. Mouzon W. Brabham. SoP
Father's Prayer, A. *Unknown.* SoP; STF
Father's Story. Elizabeth Madox Roberts. FaPON; MPB; PoSC
Father's Testament, A. Judah ibn Tibbon, *tr. fr. Hebrew by* Israel Abrahams. TrJP
Fathoms deep beneath the wave. Mermaids and Mermen. Sir Walter Scott. *Fr.* The Pirate. EtS
Fath'r and I went down to camp. Yankee Doodle. *Unknown.* TrAS
Fatigue. Peggy Bacon. OCS
Fatigue. Hilaire Belloc. MoVE; PV; SiTL; TreFT
Fatigues. Richard Aldington. BrPo
Fatima. Tennyson. LO; SeCePo; UnTE
Fatlipped, You Formless. Kathleen Spivack. YAP
Fatness. Alan Ansen. CoAP
Fatted/ on herbs, swollen on crabapples. The Porcupine. Galway Kinnell. NaP
Fatum Supermum. *Unknown.* *See* Epigram: Fatum Supremum.
Fault, The. Edward Lucie-Smith. NePoEA-2
Fault Is Mine, The. Edith M. Lee. SoP
Fault Is Not Mine, The. Walter Savage Landor. HBV
Faun, The. Haniel Long. HBMV
Faun, The. T. Sturge Moore. FaBoTw
Faun, The. Ezra Pound. FaBoCh; FaBoTw; FlW; LoGBV
Faun Sees Snow for the First Time, The. Richard Aldington. MoBrPo
Faun-taken. Rose O'Neill. AnAmPo; HBMV
Faun Tells of the Rout of the Amazons, The. T. Sturge Moore. AnFE
Faunus, fleet-foot lover of flying wood-nymphs. To Faunus. Horace. *Fr.* Odes. LiTW
Faunus for feats of fencing bears the bell. Henry Parrot. SiCE
Fauré. Charles Causley. MuSP
Fause Foodrage. *Unknown.* ESPB (A, B *and* C *vers.*); OBB, *sl. diff.*
(Fa'se Footrage.) OxBB
Fause Knicht upon the Road, The. *Unknown.* *See* False Knight . . .
Fause Lover, The. *Unknown.* *See* False Lover Won Back, The.
Fause Sir John a-wooing came. May Colvin. *Unknown.* OBB
Faust. John Ashbery. TwCP
Faust, *sels.* Goethe, *tr. fr. German.*
Easter Chorus: "Christ is arisen," *tr. by* Arthur Cleveland Coxe. MaRV
(Easter Chorus from "Faust," *tr. by* Bayard Taylor, *abr.*) WGRP
(Easter Hymn.) ChIP
Faust Struggles with His Soul, *tr. by* C. F. MacIntyre. LiTW
"I'd open room for millions on the earth," *tr. by* F. Melian Stawell *and* Nora Purtscher-Wydenbruck. PoFr
King of Thule, The, *tr. by* James Clarence Mangan. AWP; JAWP; WBP
Lose This Day Loitering, *tr. by* John Anster. POLF
(Prologue: "Lose this day loitering, 'twill be the same story.") TRV
Prologue in Heaven, *tr. by* Shelley. AWP; JAWP; WBP
Soldier's Song, *tr. by* Bayard Taylor. AWP
Faust and the City, *sel.* Anatoli Vasilyevich Lunacharsky, *tr. fr. Russian by* L. A. Magnus *and* K. Walter.
Song of the Old Man in Chains. PoFr
Faustina hath a spot upon her face. De Naevo in Facie Faustinae. Thomas Bastard. LO
Faustina hath the fairer face. Madrigal. *Unknown.* OBSC
Faustine. Swinburne. BeLS; MaVP; PoVP; UnTE, *abr.*; ViPo; ViPP
Faustinus, Sextus, Cinna, Ponticus. Elizabethan Week-End. Sir John Davies. CLwM
Faustus. Christopher Marlowe. *See* Dr. Faustus.
Faustus. Hyam Plutzik. Horatio, III. FiMAP
Faustus Faces His Doom. Christopher Marlowe. *See* End of Dr. Faustus, The.
Faustus to Helen. Christopher Marlowe. *See* Was This the Face.
Favonius. Hubert Church. AnNZ
Favored was he as that great Genoese. A Modern Columbus. Eleanor Robbins Wilson. PoMa
"Favourite pleasure, A." Wordsworth. *Fr.* The Prelude, IV. OBRV
Fawn, The. Raymond Holden. NYTB
Fawn, The. Edna St. Vincent Millay. LaNeLa
Fawn in the Snow, The. William Rose Benét. AnAmPo; MAP; MoAmPo; OA
Fawn sleeps in the glade, A. Early Morning in a Glade. Glenn Ward Dresbach. NP
Fawnia. Robert Greene. *Fr.* Pandosto. HBV; OBEV; OBSC
("Ah, were she pitiful as she is fair.") EG; TrGrPo, *abr.*; ViBoPo
(In Praise of His Loving and Best-beloved Fawnia.) AtBAP; PoEL-2
Fawn's Foster-Mother. Robinson Jeffers. AmPP (3d ed.)
Fayned Fancye betweene the Spider and the Gowte, A, *sel.* Thomas Churchyard.
Old-Time Service. OBSC
Fayre copie of my Celia's face. To T. H. a Lady Resembling My Mistresse. Thomas Carew. AnAnS-2
Fayre is my love, when her fayre golden heares. *See* Fair is my love. . .
Fayre ye be sure, but cruell and unkind. *See* Fair ye be sure. . .
Fay's Crime, The. Joseph Rodman Drake. *Fr.* The Culprit Fay. GN
Fay's Departure, The. Joseph Rodman Drake. *See* First Quest, The.
Fay's Sentence, The ("Thou shalt seek the beach of sand"). Joseph Rodman Drake. *Fr.* The Culprit Fay. GN
Fe-Fi-Fo-Fum, *sel.* Dorothy Brown Thompson.
"I do like ogres." ShM
Fe [*or* Fee], fi, fo, fum. *Unknown.* EvOK; ExPo; OxNR; ShM
Fealty. Wolfram von Eschenbach, *tr. fr. German by* Jethro Bithell. LiTW
Fear, The. Lascelles Abercrombie. OBMV

Fear, The. Robert Frost. ATP; BeLS; MAPA; NAMP; TwAmPo
Fear, The. W. W. Gibson. BEL; GTSL; NP
Fear. Langdon Elwyn Mitchell. AA
Fear. Peter Schjeldahl. ANYP
Fear, The. Andrew Young. GTBS-D
Fear death?—to feel the fog in my throat. Prospice. Robert Browning. AnFE; BBV; BEL; BoLiVe; CBEP; CBV; CoBE; DD; DiPo; EnL; EnLi-2; EnLit; FaBoEn; FaBV; FaPL; FiP; GTBS; GTBS-W; GTSL; HBV; HBVY; ILP; InP; LiTB; LiTL; MaRV; MBW-2; MCCG; NeHB; OAEP; OBEC; OBVV; OQP; OuHeWo; PoIE; PoLF; PoRA; PoVP; SeCeV; SoP; TIHL; TOP; TreFS; TrGrPo; TRV; UnPo (1st ed.); VA; ViPo; ViPP; WGRP; YT
Fear, facing the New Year. Facing the New Year. Mark Guy Pearse. BLRP
Fear is faith in Satan. Why Then So Fearful? *Unknown.* SoP
Fear it has faded and the night. Schoolgirls Hastening. John Shaw Neilson. BoAV
Fear knocked at the door. Faith. *Unknown.* TreFT
Fear made the superior sea. Stratagem. Allen Curnow. AnNZ
Fear me, virgin whosoever. After the Pleasure Party. Herman Melville. MAmP; MWA-1; PoEL-5
Fear no longer for the lone grey birds. End of the Flower-World (A. D. 2300). Stanley Burnshaw. AnAmPo; TrJP
Fear No More the Heat o' the Sun. Shakespeare. *Fr.* Cymbeline. IV. ii. AnFE;ATP;BEL;CABA;CBEP;CH;ChTr;DiPo;CoBE;EG;EIL-;ELP;EnL;EnLi-1;EnRePo; ExPo; FaFP; ILP_ InPo; LiTB; LiTG; LoBV; MaPo; NoP; OAEP; OuHeWo; PAn; PoAn; PoE; PoeP; PoFS; PoG; PoIE; PoRA; PoSa; PTK; QFR; RoGo; SeCeV; TOP; TrGrPo; ViBoPo; WHA
(Dirge: "Fear no more the heat o' the sun.") CAW; EnLit; HBV
("Feare no more the heate o' th' sun.") AtBAP; PoEL-2; SiCE
(Fidele.) BoC; GTBS; GTBS-D; GTBS-P; GTBS-W; GTSE; MCCG; OBEV; OQP; PoPo; ShBV-4
(Fidele's Dirge.) FaBoCh; LoGBV; OBSC; WePo
(Lament for Imogen.) TreF
(Lament of Guiderius and Arviragus.) FaBoEn
(Song: "Fear no more the heat o' the sun.") AWP; CBV; CTC; FiP; ForPo; FosPo; JAWP; MemP; VaPo; WBP
(Song of the Two Brothers.) BoLiVe
Fear Not. J. Bullock. STF
Fear Not! *Unknown.* SoP
Fear Not, Dear Love. Thomas Carew. LiTL; MeWo; UnTE
(Secrecy [*or* Secresie] Protested.) AnAnS-2; OAEP; SeCP
Fear not, little flock. Poems by the Roadside. St. Luke, Bible, *N.T.* CAW
Fear not, my dear, a flame can never dye. Constancy. Sir Charles Sedley. PeRV
Fear not, my soul, in peace abide. Confidence. Avis B. Christiansen. SoP
Fear not, O little flock! the foe. Battle Hymn. Michael Altenburg. WGRP
Fear not that the whirlwind shall carry thee hence. The Eye of the Storm. *Unknown.* SoP
Fear not the despots raging. Song under Shadow. William Rose Benét. MoRP
Fear of Beasts, The. William Meredith. TPM
Fear of Death, The. Lucretius, *tr. fr. Latin.* *Fr.* De Rerum Natura. LoBV, *tr. by* Dryden
Fear of Death, The. Shakespeare. *Fr.* Measure for Measure, III, i. TreFT
Fear of Death Confounds Me, The. William Dunbar. *See* Lament for the Makaris.
Fear of Dying, The. John Holmes. MiAP
Fear of Flowers, The. John Clare. NBM; OBRV; SeCeV
("Nodding oxeye bends before the wind, The.") AnFE; EG
Fear of God, The. Robert Frost. MoRP
Fear of poetry, The, is the/fear. Reading Time: 1 Minute 26 Seconds. Muriel Rukeyser. MoPo; NePA
Fear of the Earth. Alex Comfort. MoBrPo (1950 ed.); NeBP
Fear of the Lord, The. Proverbs, I: 7, Bible, *O.T.* TrJP
Fear of Trembling, The. John Hollander. NePoEA
Fear the lights that cross the street. Suburban Lullaby. J. S. Manifold. BoAV
Feare No More the Heate o' the Sun. Shakespeare. *See* Fear No More the Heat o' the Sun.
Fearful Death. *Unknown.* MeEL
Fearful "had the root of the matter," bringing. Courage Means Running. William Empson. LiTB
Fearful Joy. Michelangelo. *See* Joy May Kill.
Fearful of beauty, I always went. The Enamel Girl. Genevieve Taggard. HBMV; MAP; MoAmPo; NP
Fearful the chamber's quiet; the veiled windows. A Development of Idiotcy. Ebenezer Jones. OBNC; PeVV
Fearless approach and puffed feather. Cold Weather Proverb. Robert Graves. CBV
Fearless follow, thou sad soul. Song. *Unknown.* SeCL
Fears. Henry W. Frost. SoP
Fears any one his bride lest she a virgin be not. Reasons for and against Marrying Widows. Henricus Selyns. SCAP
Fears in Solitude. Samuel Taylor Coleridge. EnRP; MERP
"On the green sheep-track, up the heathy hill," *sel.* OBNC
Feast, The. Nora B. Cunningham. OQP
Feast. Edna St. Vincent Millay. NP; WHA
Feast, The. David Wagoner. NePoEA-2
Feast Day, The. Amy McDonall. PCH
Feast is o'er, The. Now brimming wine. The Knight's Toast. *Unknown, at. to* Sir Walter Scott. PCD
Feast o' St. Stephen. Ruth Sawyer. OHIP
Feast of Padre Chala, The. Thomas Walsh. CAW
Feast of Saint Andrew the Apostle. Carl Bode. *Fr.* The Sacred Seasons. ToPo
Feast of Saint Brigid of Kildare, The. *At. to* St. Bridget, *tr. fr. Middle Irish by* Eugene O'Curry. CAW; OnYI
(Heavenly Banquet, The, *sl. abr., tr. by* Seán O'Faoláin.) OnYI
("I Should Like to Have a Great Pool of Ale, *tr. by* Kenneth Jackson.) AnIL
Feast of the Doll, The. Nora Archibald Smith. PPL
Feast of the Snow, The. G. K. Chesterton. HBV
Feast on Wine or Fast on Water. G. K. Chesterton. ALV
(Song of Right and Wrong, The.) OtMeF
Feast Time of the Year, The. Dora Read Goodale. OHIP; PEDC
"Feast was over in Branksome tower, The." Sir Walter Scott. *Fr.* The Lay of the Last Minstrel, I. OBRV
Feasting and Giving of Treasure in the Hall, The. *Unknown, tr. fr. Anglo-Saxon by* Richard L. Hoffman. *Fr.* Beowulf. YAT
Feasts and Revells. John Donne. MaMe
Feast's begun, The/ And the wine is done. Water Song. Solomon ibn Gabirol. TrJP
Feasts of Death, Feasts of Love. Stuart Z. Perkoff. NeAP
Feasts satiate; stars distress with height. The Amaranth. Coventry Patmore. *Fr.* The Angel in the House. LoBV (1949 ed.)
Feather. Francesco Bianco. CLwM
Feather, The. Lilian Bowes-Lyon. ChMP
Feather. Lew Sarett. NP
Feather, The. Vernon Watkins. FaBoTw; MoVE
Feather for My Cap, A. Ivy O. Eastwick. BoTP
Feather-footed and swift as a mouse. The Visitor. Rachel Field. TiPo (1952 ed.)
Feather on feather. Snow in Spring. Ivy O. Eastwick. PDV
Feather or Fur. John Becker. FaPON; RePo; TiPo (1959 ed.)
Feather River Valley, 1956. Coleman Barks. QAH
Feathered Dancers. Kenward Elmslie. ANYP; YAP
Feathered Faith. Elizabeth Cheney. *See* Overheard in an Orchard.
"Feathered fowl's in your orchard, father, A." Brown Robin (B *vers.*). *Unknown.* ESPB
Feathered [*or* Featherd] songster chaunticleer, The. Bristowe Tragedie; or the Dethe of Syr Charles Bawdin. Thomas Chatterton. CEP; EiCL; EiPP; EnRP; OBEC; OxBB
Feathered thing of silver-grey and jade, The. Dollar Bill. John Frederick Nims. MiAP
Feathers. Olive Hopegood. MoAuPo
Feathers in a fan, The. Man. Humbert Wolfe. *Fr.* Requiem. MoBrPo; POTE
Feathers of the Willow, The. Richard Watson Dixon. *See* Song: "Feathers of the Willow, The."
Feathers on a robin's breast, The. Robin. Anne Blackwell Payne. GFA
Feathers or Lead? James Broughton. NeAP

Feathers up fast, and steeples; then in clods. The Fountain. Donald Davie. GTBS-P
Featherstone's Doom. Robert Stephen Hawker. OBNC; VA
Featureless ghost under the wall cannot jerk out at us, The. Elegy for the Silent Voices and the Joiners of Everything. Kenneth Patchen. NaP
Feaver, A. John Donne. *See* Fever, A.
February. James Berry Bensel. GoTP
February. Bill Berkson. ANYP
February. John Clare. *Fr.* The Shepherd's Calendar. OBNC
(February; a Thaw.) NCEP
February. Anna Neil Gilmore. *See* February, Tall and Trim.
February, *abr.* William Morris. *Fr.* The Earthly Paradise. ViPo
February. Dorothy Una Ratcliffe. BoTP
February. D. S. Savage. NeBP
February. James Schuyler. ANYP; NeAP
February. Frank Dempster Sherman. PCH; YeAr
February. *Unknown.* PCH
("In the month of February.") BoTP
February. Adeline D. Whitney. OTD; YeAr
February. Francis Brett Young. HBMV; HBVY
February: a Thaw. John Clare. *See* February.
February Afternoon. Edward Thomas. MoPW
February Birthday. Nancy Byrd Turner. BiCB
February brings despair. At the Nadir. Gerta Kennedy. PoPl
February—fortnights, two. February. Frank Dempster Sherman. PCH; YeAr
February 14, 22 B.C. Franklin P. Adams, *after the Latin of* Horace. InMe
February, Tall and Trim. Anna Neil Gilmore. YeAr
(February.) DD
February Twelfth. Mary F. Hepburn. PCH
February 12, 1809. Gail Brook Burket. PGD
February Twilight. Sara Teasdale. FaPON; MoSiPe; PDV; SoPo; YeAr
Feckenham Men, The. John Drinkwater. GBV; GTSL
Feckless Dinner Party, The. Walter de la Mare. FaBoTw; MoPW
Fecund plantation, The. Florida Hillocks. Kenward Elmslie. ANYP
Fed Drapes. Clark Coolidge. ANYP
Fedele and Fortunio, *sels.* Anthony Munday, *ad. fr. the Italian of* Luigi Pasqualigo.
I Serve a Mistress. EIL; LO
(Fedele's Song.) OBSC
(Fidele's Song.) CBEP
"If love be like the flower that in the night." TuPP
Federal Constitution, The. William Milns. PAH
Federal Convention, The. *Unknown.* PAH
Federation of the World, The. Tennyson. *See* Prophecy. *Fr.* Locksley Hall.
Federico. Nicolás Guillén, *tr. fr. Spanish by* Ben F. Carruthers. PoNe
Fee, faw, fum! bubble and squeak! Holy-Cross Day. Robert Browning. OtMeF
Fee, fi, fo, fum. *See* Fe, fi, fo, fum.
Feed. Raymond Knister. OBCV; PeCV
Feed/ Upon anticipation as you sow the seed. Harvest Time. Star Powers. GoYe
Feed on my sheep, my charge, my comfort feed. Sir Philip Sidney. *Fr.* Arcadia. FCP
Feed, silly sheep, although your keeper pineth. Chloris, III. William Smith. Sonn; TuPP
Feed Still Thyself. Sir Walter Ralegh. NCEP
Feeding, The. Joel Oppenheimer. NeAP
Feeding Ducks. Norman MacCaig. OxBS
Feeding the Fairies. *Unknown.* PPL
Feeding the Lions. Norman Jordan. BOLo; NBP
Feeding the Robin. *Unknown.* *See* Come Hither, Sweet Robin.
Feel for your bad fall how could I fail. A Sympathy, a Welcome. John Berryman. NYBP
Feel like a Bird. May Swenson. TrGrPo (rev. ed.)
Feel of Fineness, The. John Hazard Wildman. NYTB
Feel of the friendly prairies, the softening shadows of night, The. Across Illinois. John Stoltze. PoMa
Feel so low-down an' sad Lawd. Friendless Blues. Mercedes Gilbert. TrAS
Feeling, Faith and Fact. *Unknown.* SoP
Feeling hunger and cold, feeling. Sensuality. Kenneth Slessor. NeLNL
Feeling it with me. Walking on Water. James Dickey. NePoEA-2
Feeling my face has the terrible shine of fish. Element. P. K. Page. MoCV; PeCV
Feeling the useless arm. Hospital Observation. Julian Symons. WaP
Feelings are perceived as vague as limbs in my dismembered past. At Eighty-seven. Dachine Rainer. NePoAm
Feelings of a Republican on the Fall of Bonaparte. Shelley. AnEnPo; Sonn
Feelings of a Very Light Negro as the Confrontation Approaches. Pearl Cleage. WSL
Feet. Dorothy Aldis. BoChLi; SUS
Feet. Mary Carolyn Davies. *See* Seeking.
Feet. "Harry." TiPo (1959 ed.)
Feet. Irene Thompson. BoTP
Feet and faces tingle. Finland. Robert Graves. BrPo
Feet o' Jesus. Langston Hughes. NP
Feet of Clay. Phyllis C. Michael. SoP
Feet of Judas, The. George Marion McClellan. BANP; PoNe
Feet of the rats, The. Four Preludes on Playthings of the Wind, IV. Carl Sandburg. AmLP; AnAmPo; AnFE; BoLiVe; CoAnAm; CoBA; InP; MAP; MoAB; MoAmPo; NePA; NP; SeCeV
Feet of the Young Men, The. Kipling. GBV; OtMeF; PoRL
Feigned Courage. Charles *and* Mary Lamb. GN
Felicia Ropps. Gelett Burgess. BBGG; FaPON; GaP; TiPo
Felicity. Thomas Traherne. SCEP-1
Felicity. Isaac Watts. OxBoCh
Felis sedit by a hole. A Fable: The Mice and Felis. John Kendrick. CIV
Félise. Swinburne. BeLS
Felix Infelix! Cat unfortunate. Ode to a Bobtailed Cat. *Unknown.* BOHV; CIV
Felix Randal. Gerard Manley Hopkins. BrPo; CaFP; CBV; DiPo; EnL; EnLi-2 (1949 ed.); EnLit; FaBoEn; FaBoMo; FosPo; GTBS-D; GTBS-P; GTBS-W; InPo; LiTB; LiTM; MaPo; MoAB; MoBrPo; MoPo; NAMP; NoP; OAEP; OBEV (new ed.); OBNC; PIA; PoeP; PoRA; PoVP; ReMP; RoGo; Sonn; StP; ViPo; VP
Fell far but the barn (came) up and smacked me. Fed Drapes. Clark Coolidge. ANYP
Feller I Know, A. Mary Austin. AmFN; FaPON; GaP
Feller isn't thinkin' mean, A. Out Fishin'. Edgar A. Guest. PoLF
Fellow-Citizens. Verner von Heidenstam, *tr. fr. Swedish by* Charles Wharton Stork. PoPl
"Fellow citizens, we cannot escape history." Lincoln Portrait. Aaron Copland. MaRV
Fellow-creatures. Ruth Pitter. NYTB
Fellow in a market town, A. The Razor Seller. "Peter Pindar." BOHV; HBV; InMe
Fellow near Kentucky's clime, A. John Thompson's Daughter. Phoebe Cary. BOHV
Fellow-Passengers. Frank Wilmot. BoAu
Fellows in Arms! whose Bliss, whose chiefest Good. Cato's Address to His Troops in Lybia. Lucan. *Fr.* Pharsalia, IX. OBEC
Fellows up in Personnel, The. The Perforated Spirit. Morris Bishop. FiBHP; PoPo
Fellowship, The. Katharine Lee Bates. OQP
Fellowship. Elinor Lennen. ChIP
Fellowship. *Unknown.* BLPA
Fellowship of Prayer, The. Nancy Byrd Turner. BePJ
Felo de Se. Richard Hughes. OBMV
Female Dancer. James Camp. Sonn
Female Frailty, *sel.* Philip Freneau.
Song of Thyrsis. AA; AnFE; APA; CoAnAm; HBV; LiTA; OnPM; ViBoPo
Female Glory. Richard Lovelace. MyFE
Female God, The. Isaac Rosenberg. FaBoTw
Female Husband, Who Had Been Married to Another Female for Twenty-one Years, The. *Unknown.* CoMu
Female is fertile, and discipline, The. Praise for Sick Women. Gary Snyder. NeAP
Female of the Species, The. Kipling. BLPA; HBV; OtMeF; TreFS
Female Phaeton, The. Matthew Prior. HBV
Female Smuggler, The, *with music.* *Unknown.* AmSS

Female Warrior, The. *Unknown.* ShS
Femina contra Mundum. G. K. Chesterton. MoRP
Feminine. H. C. Bunner. AA
Feminine Arithmetic. Charles Graham Halpine. BOHV
Femme et chatte. Paul Verlaine, *tr. fr. French by* Arthur Symons. AWP; JAWP; WBP; CIV, *tr. by* Ashmore Wingate
(Woman and Cat, *tr. by* Arthur Symons.) OnPM [*wr. at. to* Baudelaire]; WoL
Femme Fatale. Vincent Starrett. FiSC
Fence, A. Carl Sandburg. AmP; InP
Fence or an Ambulance, A. Joseph Malins. BLPA
Fenceposts wear marshmallow hats, The. Snow [*or* On a Snowy Day]. Dorothy Aldis. PDV; TiPo
Fence-walker, balancer, your devil-may-care. Divination by a Cat. Anthony Hecht. StP
Fence Wire. James Dickey. NYBP
Fences. Rebecca McCann. PoMa
Feral Pioneers, The. Ishmael Reed. PoNe (1970 ed.)
Ferdinand De Soto lies. The Distant Runners. Mark Van Doren. LiTA; LiTM; LoGBV; MAP; MoAmPo; NePA
Ferdinando and Elvira; or, The Gentle Pieman. W. S. Gilbert. BOHV; FiBHP; LBN; NA
Fergus and the Druid. W. B. Yeats. CoBE
Feri's Dream. Frances Cornford. BoC
(Little Dog, The.) RIS
Dogs, *st.* 1. ThGo
Ferishtah's Fancies, *sel.* Robert Browning.
Epilogue: "Oh, Love—no, Love! All the noise below, love." ViPP
Ferment of New Wine, The. Elizabeth Barrett Browning. *Fr.* Aurora Leigh, I. VA
Fern. Ted Hughes. NYBP
Fern Hill. Dylan Thomas. AtBAP; CABA; ChMP; CMoP; CoBMV; DiPo; EnL; EvOK; FaBoEn; FaBV; FosPo; GoJo; GTBS-D; GTBS-P; LiTB; LiTM; LoGBV; MaPo; MasP; MoAB; MoBrPo (1950 ed.); MoPo; MoPW; MoVE; NeMA; NoP; OAEP (2d ed.); PAn; PIA; Po; PoAn; PoLF; PoPl; PoRA; PrWP; RoGo; ShBV-4; ThWaDe; ToPo; TrGrPo (rev. ed.); TwCP; ViBoPo (1958 ed.); WaKn; WePo
(Under the Apple Boughs.) BoC
Fern House at Kew. Paul Dehn. ChMP
Fern Song. John Bannister Tabb. PRWS
Ferries ply like shuttles in a loom, The. This Is My Hour. Zoë Akins. HBV
Ferry, The. George Henry Boker. AA
Ferry Hinksey. Laurence Binyon. HBV
Ferry Me across the Water. Christina Rossetti. *Fr.* Sing-Song. ChTr; GaP; GoJo; PDV; PoRh; SUS
(Boatman, The.) PCH
(Ferryman, The.) BoTP; SoPo
Ferry Ride, *sel.* Selma Robinson.
Bus Ride. FaPON
Ferry-Boats. James S. Tippett. GFA; SoPo; SUS; TiPo
Ferryman, The. Christina Rossetti. *See* Ferry Me across the Water.
Fertile and rank and rich the coastal rains. Advent. Brother Antoninus. NeAP
Fertile Muck, The. Irving Layton. OBCV; PeCV (1967 ed.)
Fescennine Verses in Honor of the Marriage of the Emperor Honorius, *sel.* Claudian, *tr. fr. Latin by* Maurice Platnauer *and* Virginia Tufte.
Sing, Woods and Rivers All. HW
Fest. Puritatis. Aubrey Thomas De Vere. *Fr.* May Carols. PoVP
Festal Board, The. *Unknown.* BLPA; TreFS
Festal Song. William Pierson Merrill. *See* Rise Up, O Men of God!
Feste Burg ist unser Gott, Ein. Martin Luther. *See* Mighty Fortress Is Our God, A.
Feste's Songs. Shakespeare. *Fr.* Twelfth Night. *See* Come Away, Come Away, Death *and* O Mistress Mine *and* When That I Was...
Festival. The. Robert Eyres Landor. *Fr.* The Impious Feast, III. OBRV
Festival, The. Frederic Prokosch. LiTA; LiTM (1946 ed.); WaP
Festival in Tuscany. William Force Stead. POTE
Festoons of Fishes. Alfred Kreymborg. HBMV
Festubert: The Old German Line. Edmund Blunden. MMA
Festum Nativitatis. Aubrey Thomas De Vere. *Fr.* May Carols. IrPN
Festus, *sels.* Philip James Bailey.
Aim of Life, The. OQP
(Country Town, A, 4 *ll.*) PoToHe (new ed.)
(We Live In Deeds.) MaRV
Helen's Song. VA
"I loved her for that she was beautiful." LO
(My Lady.) OBVV
Lucifer and Elissa. VA
Poet, The. VA
Youth, Love and Death. VA
Fetching Cows. Norman MacCaig. FIW
Fetching the Wounded. Laurence Binyon. MMA
Fete, A. Larry Eigner. NeAP
Fête Champêtre. Kenneth Allott. POTE
Fêtes, Fates. John Malcolm Brinnin. LiTA
Fetish-woman crossed the stage, The. The Lady from Harlem. Malcolm Cowley. NP
Feud. Lew Sarett. AnAmPo; MAP
Feuerzauber. Louis Untermeyer. NP; TrJP
Fever, A. John Donne. DiPo; MyFe, *st.* 6
(Feaver, A.) MaMe; SCEP-1
Fever. "Klabund," *tr. fr. German by* Babette Deutsch *and* Avrahm Yarmolinsky. OnPM
Fever Monument, The. Richard Brautigan. FRC
Fever 103° Sylvia Plath. NMP
Feverish room and that white bed, The. White Heliotrope. Arthur Symons. PeVV
Few are my books, but my small few have told. Lovely Dames. W. H. Davies. SiSw
Few cities of the heroes still remain. Mycenae. Alphaeus. OnPM
Few Days, *with music. Unknown.* ABF
Few days after, A. Death of a Bird. Jon Silkin. NePoEA
Few days ago, A. A Wife Talks to Herself. Stephen Berg. NaP
Few hours remain. Darkness is big, is surly. New Words for an Old Song. Babette Deutsch. NePoAm
Few hours since, the radiant sun was standing, A. The Gloaming. Henry W. Frost. SoP
Few, in the days of early youth. The World I Am Passing Through. Lydia Maria Child. AA; HBV
Few leaves stay for a while on the trees, A. The Last Leaf. Harry Behn. RePo
Few Lines to Fill up a Vacant Page, A. John Danforth. SCAP
Few long-hoarded pennies in his hand, A. Pennies. Joyce Kilmer. CAW
Few men of hero-mould. John Bright. Francis Barton Gummere. AA
Few miles from, A. Chugachimute I Love the Name. Rochelle Owens. CoPo
Few more miles and a few more tears, A. Pilgrimage. Henry W. Frost. SoP
Few more windy days, A. Song. Helen Dudley. NP
Few More Years Shall Roll, A. Horatius Bonar. SoP
Few names tell it all, A. Names. Lisel Mueller. TPM
Few short words on the subject, A. What Poetry Is for Me. Johnie Scott. WSL
Few Things Can More Inflame. C. Day Lewis. OBMV
Few Wholly Faithful. *Unknown.* BePJ
Few will acknowledge all they owe. Daniel Defoe. Walter Savage Landor. NCEP
Fewer Books, More Salad. Thomas Hood. *See* To Minerva.
Fey. *Unknown. Fr.* The Battle of Otterbourne. OtMeF
Fhairshon swore a feud. The Massacre of the Macpherson. William Edmondstoune Aytoun. CenHV; ChTr; OtMeF; VA
Fiametta. John Peale Bishop. LiTA; LiTL; TwAmPo
Fiammetta. Boccaccio, *tr. fr. Italian by* Dante Gabriel Rossetti. GoBC
(Sonnets.) AWP; JAWP; WBP
Fiat Lux. Lloyd Mifflin. AA; AnAmPo; PFY
"Fiat!"—The flaming word. The Annunciation. John Banister Tabb. ISi
Fib Detected, A. Catullus, *tr. fr. Latin by* John Hookham Frere. AWP
Fichtenbaum steht einsam, Ein. Heine, *tr. fr. German by* James Thomson. AWP; JAWP; OuHeWo; WBP
(Pine Tree, The, *st.* 1, *tr. by* Sidney Lanier.) PCH
Fickle Hope. Harrison Smith Morris. AA

Fickle Seat Whereon Proud Fortune Sits, The. Robert Greene. *Fr.* Morando, the Tritameron of Love. ReIE
Fiction, A. "A. W." TuPP
Fiction. Charles Sprague. *Fr.* Curiosity. AA
Fiddle, The. Neil Munro. BoTP
Fiddle and the Bow, The. Humbert Wolfe. BoPe
Fiddle me away Little Man. Coaxing a Fairy Fiddler. Monica Shannon. BoChLi
Fiddlededee. Eliza Lee Follen. SAS
Fiddle-de-dee!/ Grasshoppers three. High June. Catherine A. Morin. BoTP
Fiddle-de-dee, fiddle-de-dee. *Unknown.* OTPC; RIS; SiTL
Fiddler, A. Walter de la Mare. LOW; UnS
Fiddler, The. Thomas Hardy. MuSP
Fiddler, The. Edna Valentine Trapnell. HBMV
Fiddler and his wife, The. *Unknown.* OxNR
Fiddler Jones. Edgar Lee Masters. *Fr.* Spoon River Anthology. AmP; CMoP; LiTA; LoGBV; NP; OxBA; TDP; TrGrPo; UnS
Fiddler knows what's brewing, The. The Fiddler. Thomas Hardy. MuSP
Fiddler of Dooney, The. W. B. Yeats. BEL; DiPo; FaBoCh; HBV; InP; LoGBV; NeMA; OBVV; PoMa; PoPo; TiPo; UnS; YT
Fiddler's Green. Theodore Goodridge Roberts. CaP
Fiddlers' Green. Margaret Widdemer. YT
Fiddles were playing and playing, The. Across the Door. Padraic Colum. HBV
Fidele. William Collins. *See* Song from Shakespeare's "Cymbeline," A.
Fidele [*or* Fidele's Dirge]. Shakespeare. *See* Fear No More the Heat o' the Sun.
Fidele and Fortunio. Anthony Munday. *See* Fedele and Fortunio.
Fidelia, *sels.* George Wither.
Hence, Away, You Sirens! *also given in* Fair Virtue. EIL, 3 *sts.*
Shall I, Wasting in Despair, *also given in* Fair Virtue. ALV; AnFe; BEL; BoLP; EG; EIL; EnLi-1; LiTB; LiTG; OBS; OuHeWo; PoIE; WHA
(Author's Resolution, The.) CLwM; NoP; ViBoPo
(Lover's Resolution, The.) AWP; EnLit; HBV; InMe; JAWP; LiTL; OBEV; PG; TOP; TreFS; WBP; YAT
(Manly Heart, [The].) FaBV; GTBS; GTBS-D; GTBS-P; GTBS-W; GTSE; GTSL; MCCG
(Sonnet: "Shall I, wasting in despair.") SeCV-1; SeEP
(What Care I.) MeWo; TrGrPo
Fidelis. Adelaide Anne Procter. BLPA; FaBoBe; NeHB
Fidelity. D. H. Lawrence. Po
Fidelity. Thomas Lodge. *See* Love Guards the Roses of Thy Lips.
Fidelity. Trumbull Stickney. AnFE; CoAnAm; LiTA; TwAmPo
Fidelity. Wordsworth. PeER
Fidelity and love are two different things, like a flower and a gem. Fidelity. D. H. Lawrence. Po
Fidessa, More Chaste than Kind, *sels.* Bartholomew Griffin.
"Arraign'd, poor captive at the bar I stand," V. ReIE; SiCE; Sonn; TuPP
"Care-charmer sleep, sweet ease in restless misery," XV. ReEn; ReIE; SiCE; Sonn; TuPP
(Sleep.) OBSC
"Compare me to the child that plays with fire," XIII. SiCE; Sonn; TuPP
"Fair is my love that feeds among the lilies," XXXVII. EG; LO; SiCE; Sonn; TuPP; ViBoPo
(Fair Is My Love.) CBEP; PoEL-2
(My Love.) TrGrPo
(Sonnet: "Fair is my love that feeds among the lilies.") EIL; ErPo
"Fly to her heart; hover about her heart," XXIII. ReEn; ReIE; SiCE; TuPP
(Her Heart.) MeWo; TrGrPo
"I have not spent the April of my time," XXXV. ReEn; SiCE; Sonn; TuPP
(Sonnet.) EIL
(Youth.) OBSC
"I see, I hear, I feel, I know, I rue," XLVII. ReIE
"If great Apollo offered as a dower," LIV. ReIE; Sonn; TuPP
"Striving is past, Ah, I must sink and drown," XXIV. ReIE
"Tell me of love, sweet Love, who is thy sire?" XLIII. TuPP
"Venus and [*or* with] young Adonis sitting by her," III. ReIE; ViBoPo, *sl. diff.*
"Work, work apace, you blessed sisters three," LI. SiCE; TuPP
Fie, Chloris! 'Tis silly to sigh thus in vain. To Chloris. *At. to* Dr. Waldren. SeCL
Fie, fie, I loathe to speak; wilt thou, my lust. Out of an Old Poet. Barnabe Googe. EP
Fie, Fie on Blind Fancy! Robert Greene. *Fr.* Greene's Groatsworth of Wit. EIL
(Lamilia's Song.) OBSC
Fie,fie upon her! Portrait of Cressida. Shakespeare. *Fr.* Troilus and Cressida, IV, v. TrGrPo
Fie! flattering fortune, look thou never so fair. *See* Eye-flattering fortune, look thou never so fair.
Fie (*or* Fye) foolish Earth, think you the heaven wants glory. Love's Glory. Fulke Greville. Caelica, XVI. EnRePo; LO; OBSC; PoEL-1; ReIE; SiCE; Sonn; TuPP
Fie on Love. Francis Beaumont. AnEnPo
Fie on Sinful Fantasy! Shakespeare. *Fr.* The Merry Wives of Windsor, V, v. ViBoPo
Fie on these Lydian tunes which blunt our sprights. Everard Guilpin. *Fr.* Skialetheia. SiCE
Fie, Pleasure, Fie! George Gascoigne. EIL, *sl. abr.*; InvP
Fie, school of Patience, fie! Your lesson is. Astrophel and Stella, LVI. Sir Philip Sidney. FCP; ReEn; SiPS
Fie upon hearts that burn with mutual fire. Against Fruition. Sir John Suckling. ErPo; SCEP-2
Field and Forest. Randall Jarrell. NoP
Field Daisy, The. Jane Taylor. BoTP
(Daisy, The.) PCH; PPL
Field Flower, A. James Montgomery. *See* Daisy, The.
Field-Flower. Francis Thompson. PoVP
Field Flowers. Thomas Campbell. OTPC (1923 ed.)
Field Full of Folk, The ("In a summer season"). William Langland. *See* Prologue: "In a somer sesun . . ."
Field Full of Folk, A ("What this mountain betokens"). William Langland. *See* Holy Church.
Field-Glasses. Andrew Young. CBEP; ChMP; GTBS-P
Field in sunshine is a field, A. Psalm of the Fruitful Field. A. M. Klein. WHW
Field-Mouse, The. Enid Blyton. BoTP
Field Mouse, The. "Fiona Macleod." FaPON; GBV; MoShBr
Field of Autumn. Laurie Lee. LiTM (1970 ed.); POTi; ToPo
Field of Folk, The. William Langland. *See* Prologue: "In a somer sesun . . ."
Field of Glory, The. E. A. Robinson. CMoP; HBV; MAP; MoAmPo
Field of golden wheat there grows, A. Harvest Song. Richard Dehmel. AWP; JAWP; LiTW; WBP
Field of Light, A. Theodore Roethke. LiTM (1970 ed.); PoeP; ToPo; TwCP
Field of Long Grass. A. J. M. Smith. BoLP
Field of oats, field of rye, corn-field,—these the three. Three Fields. Adolf Heyduk. LiTW
Field of Talavera, The. Thomas Hardy. *Fr.* The Dynasts, Pt. II, Act IV, sc. iv. CMoP
Fields of Tears. *Unknown, tr. fr. Russian by* W. R. S. Ralston. OnPM
Field of the Grounded Arms, The. Fitz-Greene Halleck. PoEL-4
Field of Waterloo, The. Thomas Hardy. *See* Before Waterloo.
Field-Path, The. Charles Swain. OBVV
Field Sports. Pope. *Fr.* Windsor Forest. OBEC; SeCePo
Fielding Error. Robert Paul Smith. CAD
Fields Abroad with Spangled Flowers, The. *Unknown.* ChTr
Fields are chill; the sparse rain has stopped, The. Clearing at Dawn. Li Po. AWP; JAWP; WBP
Fields Are Full, The. Edward Shanks. POTE
Fields Are Spread, The. Elizabeth J Coatsworth. PoRh
(The Moon.) RePo
Fields are wrapped in silver snow, The. The Christmas Present. Patricia Hubbell. PDV
Fields at Evening. David Morton. AnAmPo; HBMV
Fields from Islington to Marybone, The. Blake. *Fr.* Jerusalem. ChTr; ERoP-1; OBNC; OBRV
(Prelude: "Fields from Islington to Marybone, The.") OBNC
(To the Jews.) PeER
Fields grow dim, The; the somber mills. Twilight. Gerald Gould. MoBrPo (1942 ed.)

Fields of France are filled with weeping, The. To Becky in France. John Arey. LO
Fields of November, The. Mark Van Doren. WIRo
Fields were silent, and the woodland drear, The. In the Dark. Mary Potter Thacher Higginson. AA
Fiend's Weather. Louise Bogan. MoVE
Fierce and brooding holocaust of faith, The. Two Poems on the Catholic Bavarians. Edgar Bowers. PoCh
Fierce burns our fire of driftwood; overhead. Night in Camp. Herbert Bashford. AA
Fierce exulting worlds, the motes in rays, The. Love. Alexander Smith. OBEV (1st ed.)
Fierce is the flame of the vengeance of Erin. O'Neill's War Song. Michael Hogan. OnYI
Fierce is the wind tonight. The Viking Terror. *Unknown.* AnIL; OnYI
Fierce luster of sun on sea, the gulls. The Purse—Seine. Paul Blackburn. CoPo
Fierce Mars I bid a glad farewell. New Mexico and Arizona. George Canterbury. PoOW
Fierce musical cries of a couple of sparrowhawks hunting on the headland, The. Birds. Robinson Jeffers. AP; CoBMV; TwAmPo
Fierce passions discompose the mind. Contentment. William Cowper. CEP
Fierce unrest seethes at the core, A. Unrest. Don Marquis. HBMV; MaRV; OQP; PoFr
Fierce Was the Wild Billow. Anatolius, *tr. fr. Greek by* John Mason Neale. FaChP; MaRV
(Christ in the Tempest.) SoP
(Jesus, Deliverer.) BePJ
Fierce wrath of Solomon. The Burning of the Temple. Isaac Rosenberg. FaBoMo; TrJP
Fiery bitter blue it burns. The Bird of Paradise. Laura Benét. PFY
Fiery cross against the night, A. Two Crosses. Addie M. Hedrick. ChIP
Fiesolan Idyl. Walter Savage Landor. EnRP; OAEP; SeCePo; VA
(Faesulan Idyl.) OBRV
Fife and Drum. Dryden. *See* Instruments, The.
Fife Tune. John Manifold. BoAV; ExPo; FaFP; GoJo; GTBS-W; LiTB; LiTL; LiTM; LoGBV; ShBV-3; SiTL; WaaP; WaP
Fifine at the Fair, *sels.* Robert Browning.
"And so I somehow-nohow played." Par
Householder, The. LO
Fifteen. William Stafford. CAD
Fifteen Acres, The. James Stephens. BoTP; GBV (1952 ed.); ShBV-2
Fifteen churches lie here. At Dunwich. Anthony Thwaite. MoBS
Fifteen day of July, The. Lord Willoughby. *Unknown.* CoMu; TuPP
Fifteen Days of Judgement, The. Sebastian Evans. NBM
Fifteen foresters in the Braid alow. Johnie Cock (B *vers.*). *Unknown.* ESPB
"Fifteen men on the dead man's chest." Derelict [*or* the Buccaneers *or* The Dead Men's Song]. Young E. Allison. ABF; AnAmPo; BBV; BLPA; EtS; FaBoBe; FaFP; HBMV; MCCG; NeHB; OnMSP; TreFS
Fifteen or twenty feet below. The Anchorage. Pat Wilson. AnNZ
Fifteen Poems of My Heart, *sel.* Juan Chi, *tr. fr. Chinese by* Jerome Ch'ên *and* Michael Bullock.
"Once I dressed up." FIW
Fifteen Rubaiyat. Omar Khayyám, *tr. fr. Persian by* Edward Fitzgerald. *See* Bird of Time, The.
Fifteen Ships on George's Banks. *Unknown.* BaBo
Fifteen Years Past. Tom Veitch. ANYP
15th Raga: For Bela Lugosi. David Meltzer. NeAP
Fifth Birthday Gift. Marjorie Lederer. BiCB
Fifth Choir of Angelicals. Cardinal Newman. *See* Praise to the Holiest in the Height.
Fifth Day. R. D. Fitzgerald. MoAuPo
Fifth Elegy. Alex Comfort. FaBoMo
Fifth from the north wall, The. The Cross of Gold. David Gray. AA
Fifth Ode of Horace, The ("Quis multa gracilis"). Horace. *See* To Pyrrha.
Fifth of May, The—Napoleon. Alessandro Manzoni, *tr. fr. Italian by* William Dean Howells. *Fr.* Ode. CAW
Fifth Philosopher's Song. Aldous Huxley. MoBrPo (1942 ed.); SiTL
Fifth Sense, The. Patricia Beer. MoBS
Fifth Sunday after Easter. Thomas Kinsella. NMP
Fiftieth Birthday. Peter Viereck. NYTB
Fiftieth Birthday of Agassiz, The. Longfellow. ImOP
Manuscripts of God, The, *sel.* MaRV; SoP
Fifty Faggots. Edward Thomas. BrPo; MoAB; MoBrPo
Fifty leagues, fifty leagues—and I ride, and I ride. D'Artagnan's Ride. Gouverneur Morris, Jr. AA
Fifty, not having expected to arrive here. Journey toward Evening. Phyllis McGinley. GoYe; NYBP
"Fifty stories more to fall." Rhyme of Rain. John Holmes. OCS; WaKn
Fifty wizards working in the wind. A Poem to Explain Everything About a Certain Day in Vermont. Genevieve Taggard. NYBP
Fifty years and three. Our Happy Home. *Unknown.* ThGo
Fifty Years, 1863-1913. James Weldon Johnson. BANP; PoFr; PoNe
Fifty Years Spent. Struthers Burt. HBMV
Fig for care, A, why should we spare? *Unknown.* SeCL
Fig for Momus, A, *sel.* Thomas Lodge.
To a Dear Friend Lately Given Over to Covetousness. SiCE
Fig for St. Denis of France, A. St. Patrick of Ireland, My Dear! William Maginn. BOHV; InMe
Fig for those by law protected, A. Drinking Song. Burns. *Fr.* The Jolly Beggars. PoFr; TrGrPo
Fig-tree, a falling woolshed, a filled-in well, A. Mullabinda. David Rowbotham. PoAu-2
Fight. Jean Jaszi. RePo
Fight. *Unknown.* FaFP; LiTG; SiTL
Fight at Dajo, The. Alfred E. Wood. PAH
Fight at Nevadaville, The. *Unknown.* PoOW
Fight at San Jacinto, The. John Williamson Palmer. DD; PaA
(Fight at the San Jacinto, The.) AA
Fight at Sumter, The. *Unknown.* PAH
Fight at the Bridge, The. Macaulay. *Fr.* Lays of Ancient Rome: Horatius. MaC; OtMeF
Fight at the San Jacinto, The. John Williamson Palmer. *See* Fight at San Jacinto, The.
Fight in the Centre, The. Macaulay. *Fr.* The Lays of Ancient Rome: Battle of the Lake Regillus. OtMeF
Fight of Paso Del Mar, The. Bayard Taylor. BeLS
Fight of the *Armstrong* Privateer, The. James Jeffrey Roche. PAH
Fight of the Red Cross Knight and the Heathen Sansjoy, The. Spenser. *Fr.* The Faerie Queene, I, 5. FiP
("Noble heart that harbours virtuous thought, The.") ViBoPo
Fight over the Body of Keitt, The. *Unknown.* PAH
Fight that was no fight is over, The. The Bride. L. A. G. Strong. POTE
Fight the Good Fight. John S. B. Monsell. MaRV
Fight with a Water-Spirit. Norman Cameron. HaMV
Fight your little fight, my boy. Dont's. D. H. Lawrence. LiTB; LiTM; OxBoLi
Fighter, The. S. E. Kiser. BLPA
Fighting Failure, The. Everard Jack Appleton. HBV; YaD
Fighting-Man, A. Joseph Campbell. OnYI
Fighting McGuire. William Percy French. CenHV
Fighting nature of the intellect, The. Vast Light. Richard Eberhart. CMoP; NMP
Fighting Race, The. Joseph I. C. Clarke. AA; AmePo; BLPA; DD; HBV; LHV; MC; OnYI; PaA; PAH; PFY; YaD
Fighting South of the Castle. *Unknown, tr. fr. Chinese by* Arthur Waley. AWP; JAWP; WaaP; WBP
(Fighting South of the Ramparts.) FIW; LiTW
Fighting *Téméraire,* The. Sir Henry Newbolt. BBV (1923 ed.); HBV
Fighting Words. Dorothy Parker. InMe; NAMP
Fights, The. Milton Acorn. MoCV
Figmental mannequin, Turk's-head for the trap. To the Eternal Feminine. Tristan Corbière. ErPo
Figs from Thistles. Edna St. Vincent Millay. *See* First Fig.
Figure for an Apocalypse. Thomas Merton. CrMA
Figure it out for yourself, my lad. Equipment. Edgar A. Guest. PoToHe (new ed.)
Figurehead, The. Léonie Adams. NP
Figure-Head, The. Crosbie Garstin. EtS; StPo

Figurehead. Dorothy Paul. EtS
Figures in the fields against the sky! Poems. Antonio Machado, *tr. by* John Dos Passos. AWP; JAWP; LiTW; WBP
Figures of Authority. Edward Watkins. NYBP; StP
Figures on the Frieze, The. Alastair Reid. ErPo; NYBP
File into yellow candle light, fair choristers of King's. Sunday Morning, King's Cambridge. John Betjeman. BoC; EaLo; POTi
Filing-cabinet of human lives, A. Apartment House. Gerald Raftery. AmFN; OCS; PoMa
Filipino Hombre, A, *with music.* *Unknown.* AS
Fill a boul of lusty wine. Anacreontick. Charles Cotton. PeRV
Fill a glass with golden wine. Echoes, VII. W. E. Henley. ViBoPo
Fill All My Vision. Avis B. Christiansen. SoP
Fill and Illumined. Joseph Ceravolo. ANYP
Fill, comrades, fill the bowl right well. Ohnáwa. John Hunter-Duvar. *Fr.* De Roberval. VA
Fill fill the bowele the lusty wyne will dye. *Unknown.* SeCSL
Fill, fill the goblet full with sack! Song in a Siege. Robert Heath. CavP; OBS
Fill High the Bowl. John Keble. OxBoCh
Fill, kind misses, fill the bowl. Heat. Anacreon. UnTE
Fill me a mighty bowl. A Bacchanalian Verse. Robert Herrick. BEL
Fill me, boy, as deep a draught. Temperate Drinking. Anacreon. OnPM
Fill Me Now. E. R. Stokes. SoP
"Fill me this glass—it is antique Venetian." The Toast. Charles Warren Stoddard. CAW
Fill the Bowl, Butler! *Unknown.* *See* How! Butler, How!
Fill the bowl with rosy [*or* rosie] wine. The Epicure [*or* Today Is Ours]. Abraham Cowley. CavP; HBV; OBS; SCEP-2; SeCP; TrGrPo
Fill the Bumper Fair. Thomas Moore. HBV
Fill the cup, and again cry, again, again. To Heliodora. Meleager, *tr. by* Dudley Fitts. LiTW
Fill the piazza with blue water. Venetian Scene. Anne Ridler. NMP
Fill up your glass, O comrade true. The Pioneer. Eugene Field. PoOW
Fill your bowl with roses: the bowl, too, have of crystal. Chiaroscuro; Rose. Conrad Aiken. MAPA
Filled is Life's goblet to the brim. The Goblet of Life. Longfellow. MWA-1
Filled with weariness and pain. Singing My Doubts Away. *Unknown.* BePJ
Filling Station. Elizabeth Bishop. NYBP
Filling Station. A. M. Klein. TwCaPo
Filling Station. E. Merrill Root. PoMa
Filling the mind. The Clouds. William Carlos Williams. MoPo
Filthy, sick, and dying. Security. Robert Tucker. PPON
Fin de Siècle. Edmund Vance Cooke. BLPA
Fin de Siècle. Newton Mackintosh. NA
Fin de Siècle. *Unknown.* BOHV
Final Armistice, The. Frank B. Cowgill. OQP
Final Autumn. Josephine Winslow Johnson. NAMP; NePA
Final Chorus: "All is best, though we oft doubt." Milton. *See* All Is Best.
Final Chorus: "Bellies bitter with drinking." Archibald MacLeish. *Fr.* Panic. MAP; MoAmPo
Final Chorus from Hellas, The: "Victorious wrong, with vulture scream." Shelley. EnLi-2
Final Chorus from Hellas: "World's great age begins anew, The." Shelley. *See* Chorus: "World's great age begins anew, The."
Final Dirge. *Unknown.* *See* Lyke-Wake Dirge, A.
Final Faith, The. George Sterling. CAW
Final, finger-printed page is flipped, The. First Reader (Fifth Reading). Gladys McKee. JKCP (1955 ed.)
Final Green, The. Leah Bodine Drake. NePoAm
Final Hunger, The. Vassar Miller. LiTM (1970 ed.); ToPo
Final Inch, The. Emily Dickinson. *See* 'Twas like a maelstrom, with a notch.
Final Lesson, The. Arthur Stringer. MaRV
Final Man, The. Basil McFarlane. PoNe
Final Mystery, The. Sir Henry Newbolt. WGRP
Final Poem. Robert Bhain Campbell. MoPo; NePA
Final secret that two lovers shared, The. Speak This Kindly to Her. Robert Bagg. NePoAm-2
Final Soliloquy, The. Colin Thiele. *Fr.* Burke and Wills. NeLNL
Final Soliloquy of the Interior Paramour. Wallace Stevens. BWP; PoIE
"Final Status Never Ascertained." Lloyds Registry. Merrill Moore. MAP; MoAmPo (1942 ed.)
Final Struggle, The. Louis James Block. *Fr.* The New World. PAH
Final Struggle, The. Caroline Sprague Smith. SoP
Final Thoughts on the Weather in England during 1953. David Daiches. SiTL
Final Toast, The. Tom Veitch. ANYP
Final Victory, The. Shelley. *See* Demogorgon's Song.
Final Word, The. Dom Moraes. BoPe; MemP; NePoEA-2
Finale. A. P. Herbert. *Fr.* Perseverance; or, Half a Coronet. InMe
Finale. Douglas Le Pan. TwCaPo
Finale. Christopher Marlowe. *See* End of Dr. Faustus, The.
Finale. James Picot. BoAV
Finale. Carl Sandburg. *Fr.* Slabs of the Sunburnt West. NeMA
Finale: Presto. Peter Davison. CoPo
Finality broods upon the things that pass. A Walk by the Charles. Adrienne Cecile Rich. NePoEA; NYBP
Finally, among the bottles shining. The Lady in the Barbershop. Raphael Rudnick. NYBP
Finally, brethren, whatsoever things are true. Think on These Things. Philippians, Bible, *N.T.* TreFT
Finally, from your house, there is no view. Water Island. Howard Moss. CoAP; NePoEA-2; NYBP; TDP
Finches, The. Philip Murray. NePoAm
Finches, The. Thomas W. Shapcott. PoAu-2
Find, The. Francis Ledwidge. SP
Find a Role, Define a Role. Raymond Turner. WSL
Find a Way. John Godfrey Saxe. *See* Where There's a Will There's a Way.
Find me a lonely cave. Song. *Unknown.* SeCL
Finding Francesca full of tears, I said. Obituary. Thomas William Parsons. AA; HBV; HBVY
Finding is the first act. Emily Dickinson. AP; CABA; MoVE; MWA-2
Finding of Gabriel, The. Longfellow. *Fr.* Evangeline, Pt. II. AA
Finding of the Táin, The. Robert Farren. CoBE
Finding the feathers of a bird. A Dead Bird. Andrew Young. BiS
Finding Them Lost. Howard Moss. CoAP; NYBP
Finding those beams, which I must ever love. Absence. Sir Philip Sidney. FCP; SiPS
Finding You. Mary Dixon Thayer. CAW
Fine Clay. Winifred Shaw. MoAuPo; PoAu-1
Fine Day, A. Michael Drayton. *Fr.* The Muses' Elysium. BoTP; GN; OTPC; PCH
(Lines: "Clear had the day been.") LoBV
(Sixth Nymphal [*or* Sixt Nimphall], The.) OBS; TuPP
Fine delight that fathers thought, The; the strong. To R. B. Gerard Manley Hopkins. CBEP; CMoP; CoBMV; GTBS-P; InvP; ML; PoVP; ViPP
Fine Flowers in the Valley. *Unknown.* *See* Cruel Mother, The.
Fine gold is here; yea, heavy yellow gold. The House of Colour. Francis Sherman. *Fr.* The Deserted City. CaP
Fine Knacks for Ladies. *Unknown.* CBEP; CH; EIL; EnRePo; EP; ForPo; LiTB; LOBV; NoP; QFR; TuPP; ViBoPo
("Fine knacks for ladies, cheap, choice, brave and new!") OBSC
(Honest Autolycus, An.) GTSL
(Pedlar, A.) OBEV; WiR
Fine Madam Would-Be, wherefore should you fear. To Fine Lady Would-Be. Ben Jonson. NoP
Fine, neat, and curious Mistress Butterfly. Idle Housewife. Samuel Rowlands. SiCE
Fine Old English Gentleman, The. *Unknown.* CH; HBV; OnPP
Fine Old English Gentleman, The; New Version. Charles Dickens. CoMu; FOL
Fine old wine and a fair young wife, A. Age and Youth. *Unknown.* UnTE

Fine rays of praise my asking rings from her. Bought. Francis Douglas Davison. NeBP
Fine Song for Singing, The. Robert Louis Stevenson. *See* Romance.
Fine, spruce young Pansa's grown a malcontent. Of Pansa. Everard Guilpin. *Fr.* Skialetheia. ReIE
Fine Thing, A. Tom Veitch. ANYP
Fine Work with Pitch and Copper. William Carlos Williams. NoP; OxBA
Fine Young Folly. William Habington. *Fr.* The Queen of Aragon, IV, i. CavP; OBS
(Song: "Fine young folly, though you were.") FaBoEn; MePo
Fine youth Ciprius is more terse and neat, The. In Ciprium. Sir John Davies, *after the Latin of* Martial. ReIE; SiCE; TuPP
Fineen the Rover. Robert Dwyer Joyce. JKCP (1926 ed.)
Finesse be first, whose elegance deplores. Six Poets in Search of a Lawyer. Donald Hall. NYBP; SiTL
Finest, biggest fish you see, The. *Unknown.* GFA
Finest English Epigram, The. Philip Doddridge. *See* Live While You Live.
Finest Thing, The. Tom Veitch. ANYP
Finest thing in London is the Bobby, The. The London Bobby. Arthur Guiterman. HT
Finest thing in the world, The. The Finest Thing. Tom Veitch. ANYP
Fingal: An Ancient Epic Poem, *sel.* James MacPherson.
"Cuthullin sat by Tura's wall." EnLi-2
Finger Folk. H. M. Thorp. BoTP
Finger of Necessity. Coleman Barks. QAH
Finger Play ("This little bunny said, 'Let's play' "). *Unknown.* BoTP
Finger Play for a Snowy Day, A. *Unknown.* BoTP
Finger Pop'in. Charles Anderson. BF
Fingernail Sunrise. Vernon Watkins. NYBP
Fingers in the Door. David Holbrook. NePoEA-2
Fingers of the light, The. Emily Dickinson. MWA-2
Fingers of the sunrise, The. Morning Challenge. Charles E. Bayley. SoP
Fingers on the holes, Johnny. A Music Lesson. Alexander Hay Japp. VA
Finicky bird of day. Owl. Gregory Corso. CBV
Finigan's Wake. *Unknown.* *See* Finnigan's Wake.
Finis. Waring Cuney. AmNP; BANP; PoNe
Finis. Walter Savage Landor. *See* On His Seventy-fifth Birthday.
Finis? Michael Lewis. MeWo
Finis. Sir Henry Newbolt. GaP; TiPo
(Day's End.) RIS
Finish Thy Work. *Unknown.* SoP
Finished Course, The. St. Joseph, of the Studium. WGRP
Finite. Power Dalton. HBMV
Finite Reason. Dryden. *See* Reason and Revelation.
Finland. Robert Graves. BrPo
Finn on the mountain found the mangled man. The Death of Dermid. Sir Samuel Ferguson. IrPN
Finnegans Wake, *sel.* James Joyce.
Ballad of Persse O'Reilly, The. LiTB; SiTL
Finnegan's Wake, *with music.* *Unknown.* TrAS
(Finigan's Wake.) BLPA
Finnigan to Flannigan. Strickland W. Gillilan. *See* Finnigin to Flannigan.
Finnigin to Flannigan. Strickland W. Gillilan. FaBoBe; StPo; TreF; YaD
(Finnigan to Flannigan.) BOHV; HBV
Fiorentina. Ernest Myers. OBVV
Fir Forest. Ethel Romig Fuller. PGD
Fir-Tree, The. Edith M. Thomas. OHIP
Fir trees taper into twigs and wear, The. Firwood. John Clare. EG; TrGrPo
Fire, The. Charles G. Bell. MoLP
Fire, The. William Burford. NePA
Fire, A. Rachel Field. GFA
Fire. Langston Hughes. NP
Fire. M. V. Woodgate. BoC
Fire. Dorothy Wellesley. OBMV
Fire,/ Fire, Lord! Fire. Langston Hughes. NP
Fire and Ice. Robert Frost. AmPP; AnFE; AnNE; APA; CABA; CaFP; CBV; CMoP; CoAnAm; CoBMV; DiPo; FaFP; GTBS-W; HBMV; ILP; LiTA; LiTM; MAP; MaPo (1969 ed.); MoAB; MoAmPo; MoVE; NePA; NP; OnPM; OxBA; PoDB; PoeP; PoPl; PoPo; SiTL; TDP; TreFS; TrGrPo; TwAmPo; ViBoPo 1958 ed.); WePo; WHA; WoL
Fire at Alexandria, The. Theodore Weiss. CoPo ; PIA
Fire at Murdering Hut. Judith Wright. ACV
Fire-Bringer, The, *sels.* William Vaughn Moody.
Pandora's Songs.
"Along the earth and up the sky." GBV
"I stood within the heart of God." AnFE; APA; CoAnAm; GBV; MAP; MoAmPo (1942 ed.); OQP; WGRP
"Of wounds and sore defeat." BBV; GBV; HBV; PFY; PTK
Fire Burial. Edgar McInnis. CaP
Fire darkens, the wood turns black, The. Song for the Sun That Disappeared behind the Rainclouds. *Unknown.* TTY
Fire Down Below, *with music.* *Unknown.* SoAmSa
Fire, Fire, Fire, Fire. Thomas Campion. PAn
Fire! Fire! said the town crier. *Unknown.* OxNR
Fire i' the Flint. The. Lucy Catlin Robinson. AA
Fire in leaf and grass, The. Living. Denise Levertov. FRC
Fire in the Heavens [and Fire Along the Hills]. Christopher J. Brennan. CoBE; MoAuPo; NeLNL; OnPM; PoAu-1
Fire in the Snow, The. Vernon Watkins. GTBS-W; LiTM (rev ed.); MoVE
Fire is burning clear and blithely, The. The Darkened Mind. James Russell Lowell. MAmP; MWA-1
Fire is out, and spent the warmth thereof, The. Dregs. Ernest Dowson. HBV; NCEP; OBMV; SeCePo; ViPP
Fire is what's precious now. Carol. Alison Boodson. NeBP
Fire-kindled satellite. Napkin and Stone. Vernon Watkins. NYBP
Fire-Logs. Carl Sandburg. NP
Fire-mist and a planet, A. Each in His Own Tongue. William Herbert Carruth. AmePo; BBV; BLPA; HBV; MaRV; NeHB; OHFP; OQP; TRV; WBLP; WGRP
Fire of Drift-Wood, The. Longfellow. AmPP (4th ed.); AP; HBV; MAmP; MWA-1; NoP; OxBA
Fire of Frendraught, The. *Unknown.* ESPB (A *and* C *vers.*); OBB; OxBB; ViBoFo
Fire of Heaven, The. Tennyson. *Fr.* Idylls of the King: Balin and Balan. EPN
Fire of heaven's eternal ray. Prayer to the Blessed Virgin. Rodriguez del Padrón. CAW
Fire of London, The, *sels.* Dryden. *Fr.* Annus Mirabilis.
"As when some dire usurper Heav'n provides." ChTr
"But ah! how unsincere are all our joys!" SeEP
"Night came, but without darkness or repose," *6 sts.* FaBoEn; FIW
Fire of Love, The. Charles Sackville. *Fr.* The Amorous Bigot (*by* Thomas Shadwell). LiTL; PeRV; SeCL; UnTE
Fire of meditation burns, The. A Praefatory Poem to the Little Book, Entituled, *Christianus per Ignem.* Nicholas Noyes. SCAP
Fire of our victims, The. The Knell. Muhammad Al-Fituri. TTY
Fire on Belmont Street. Donald Davidson. The Tall Men: Epilogue. MAP; MoAmPo (1942 ed.)
Fire on the Hearth. Rowena Bennett. RePo
Fire on the Hills. Robinson Jeffers. CMoP
Fire Pictures. Emma Rounds. MPB
Fire Place, The. E. W. Mandel. OBCV
Fire rides calmly in the air. At War. Charles Madge. FaBoMo
Fire Seven Times Tried This, The. Shakespeare. *Fr.* The Merchant of Venice, II, ix. CTC
Fire Ship, The, *with music.* *Unknown.* AmSS
Fire Song. Jason Miller. ThO
Fire Tenders, The. Grace Noll Crowell. PEDC
Fire that cancels all that is. Burning Love Letters. Howard Moss. HoPM
Fire That Filled My Heart of Old, The. James Thomson. PoVP
Fire the heather. "Adam Drinan." *Fr.* Men of the Rocks. OxBS
Fire, the Rope. Nikolai Tikhonov, *tr. fr. Russian by* Babette Deutsch. LiTW
Fire threatens, The. Hyena's Song to Her Children. *Unknown.* PeSA
Fire to see my wrongs for anger burneth, The. The Wronged Lover. Sir Philip Sidney. *Fr.* Arcadia. FCP; SiPS
Fire-Truck, A. Richard Wilbur. TPM

Fire upon the hearth is low, The. In the Firelight. Eugene Field. AA
Fire was furry as a bear, The. Dark Song. Edith Sitwell. *Fr.* Façade. CMoP; FaBoTw
Fire was slow kindling, The—it was damp wood. The Fire. Charles G. Bell. MoLP
Fire, water, woman are man's ruin. A Dutch Proverb. Matthew Prior. CEP
Fireballs and thunder augment the wailing wind. The Ides of March. Roy Fuller. PoCh
Firebombing, The. James Dickey. OPoP
Fireborn Are at Home in Fire, The. Carl Sandburg. MoAmPo (1950 ed.)
Fired Pot, The. Anna Wickham. FaBoTw; MeWo; TrGrPo (1942 ed.)
Fire-Dragon and the Treasure, The. *Unknown, tr. fr. Anglo-Saxon by* Charles W. Kennedy. *Fr.* Beowulf. AnOE
Firedrake sejant on a field of sard, A. Prenatal Fantasy. Walter H. Kerr. FiSC
Fireflies. Grace Wilson Coplen. GFA; UTS
Fireflies. Edgar Fawcett. AnAmPo HBV
Fireflies. Aileen Fisher. SoPo
Fireflies. Carolyn Hall. FaPON; GFA; HBMV; HBVY; MPB; PCH; TSW; UTS
Fireflies, The, *sel.* Charles Mair.
"How dreamy-dark it is!" OBCV
Fireflies, The. Tu Fu, *tr. fr. Chinese by* Henry H. Hart. OnPM
Fireflies/ Play hide-and-seek in the tall grass. Phosphorescence. Melville Cane. RePo
Fireflies and the stars our only light, The. The Spinning Heart. John Berryman. LiTM (1946 ed.)
Fireflies are fairies' lights. Fairies' Lights. Alice Wilkins. GFA
Fireflies flitted in those dark spots. A Beautiful Night. Naoyoshi. OnPM
Fireflies in the Corn. D. H. Lawrence. NP
Fireflies in the Garden. Robert Frost. OA
Firefly, The. Issa, *tr. fr. Japanese by* Harold G. Henderson. RePo
Firefly, The. Ogden Nash. PoPo; SiTL; WhC
Firefly. Elizabeth Madox Roberts. GFA; GoJo; OTPC (1946 ed.); PDV; PoRh; SUS; TiPo; UTS
Fire-Fly, The. John Banister Tabb. UTS
Firefly, The. Taigi, *tr. fr. Japanese by* H. G. Henderson. OnPM
Firefly. Edna D. Wood. PCH
Firefly, airplane, satellite, star. Back Yard, July Night. William Cole. BoNaP
Firefly Lights His Lamp, The. *Unknown, tr. fr. Japanese by* William N. Porter. MPB; SoPo
Firefly Song. Longfellow. *Fr.* The Song of Hiawatha, III. PCD
(Hiawatha's Childhood.) BoTP
Firefly's flame, The. The Firefly. Ogden Nash. PoPo; SiTL; WhC
Firelight. Heine, *tr. fr. German by* Sir Theodore Martin. CIV
Firelight. E. A. Robinson. CMoP; InP; NP
Firelight. Whittier. *Fr.* Snow-bound. AA
("Shut in from all the world without.") LaNeLa
Firelight flickered on the age-old beams, The. At the Ship. R. P. Lister. FiBHP
Firelight in sunlight, silver-pale. The Marriage of Heaven and Earth. Howard Nemerov. NYBP
Fireman, Save My Child. *Unknown. See* No More Booze.
Firemen are in love, The. Loves of the Public Servants. Robert Hershon. ThO
Fires. Elizabeth Fleming. BoTP
Fire's good companionable friend, A. The Winter Fire. Mary Howitt. OTPC (1923 ed.)
Fires in the dark you build; tall quivering flames. To a Very Wise Man. Siegfried Sassoon. BrPo
Fires of Driftwood. Isabel Ecclestone MacKay. CaP
Fires of war are quenched, The. Requiem. Thomas Curtis Clark. PEDC
Fire Side, The; a Pastoral Soliloquy. Isaac Hawkins Browne. *Fr.* The Founding Hospital for Wit, IV. OBEC
Fireside Kitten, The. Elizabeth J. Coatsworth. CIV
Firetail's Nest, The. John Clare. EnRP; Sonn
Firewood Hill. Dave Etter. ThO
Fireworks. Babette Deutsch. NYBP
Fireworks. James Reeves. PoSC
Firing ceased and like a wounded foe, The. Hialmar. Roy Campbell. CoBE
Firing Squad, The. Harry Mathews. ANYP
Firm as young bones, fine as blown spume, still. Paradigm. Babette Deutsch. TrJP
Firm Belief. *Unknown.* PoToHe (new ed.)
Firm in the good brown earth. Planting a Tree. Nancy Byrd Turner. RePo; YeAr
Firm of Happiness Limited, The. Norman Cameron. FaBoTw
Firm resolve of Silas Sharp, The. Patience. E. E. Nott-Bower. WhC
Firmament Displays on High, The. Barend Toerien, *tr. fr. Afrikaans by* Barend Toerien. PeSA
Firmness. Anthony Hecht. PV
Firs' on table, nex' on de wall. Railroad Bill. *Unknown.* ABF
First/ it's not heat prostration. Woman par Excellence. Rochelle Owens. CoPo
First a word was fuzzy, and was nothing. Words. Richard Eberhart. NePA
First Aid. Peter Hopegood. NeLNL
First American Congress, The. Joel Barlow. PAH
First American Sailors, The. Wallace Rice. PAH
First and riper world of men and skill, The. Thomas Bastard. TuPP
First, and the chiefest thing by me enjoyn'd. Loyola's Instructions to His Followers. John Oldham. *Fr.* Satires upon the Jesuits. PeRV
First and the Last, The. Horatius Bonar. BePJ
First Animal, The. Victor Contoski. ThO
First Anniversary, The. John Donne. *See* Anatomie of the World, An.
First Anniversary of the Government under His Royal Highness the Lord Protector [O. C.], The. Andrew Marvell. MaMe
"Tis not a freedom that, where all command," *sel.* PoFr
First, April, she with mellow showers. The Succession of the Four Sweet Months [*or* The Four Sweet Months *or* July]. Robert Herrick. BoTP; FaPON; OTPC (1946 ed.); PCH; WiR; YeAr
First, are you our sort of a person? The Applicant. Sylvia Plath. NaP; TwCP
First Autumn, The. Marshall Schacht. MoRP; YT
First Banjo, The. Irwin Russell. *See* Fust Banjo, De.
First, Best Country, The. Goldsmith. *Fr.* The Traveller. GN
First Bible. *Unknown.* SoP
First Blood. Jon Stallworthy. TPM
First Born. Frances O'Connell Corridan. JKCP (1926 ed.)
Firstborn, The. John Arthur Goodchild. HBV
First Born, The. Oscar Williams. GTBS-W
First born of Chaos, who so fair didst come. Hymn to Light. Abraham Cowley. AtBAP; MeLP; MePo; OBS; SCEP-2; SeCV-1; SeEP
First Brutus, The, *sel.* Vittorio Alfieri, *tr. fr. Italian by* Edgar Alfred Bowring.
"What do we hear? What majesty, what force," *fr.* I, ii. PoFr
First came the primrose. A Chanted Calendar [*or* Procession of the Flowers]. Sydney Dobell. *Fr.* Balder. BoC; BoTP; DD; GBV; GN; GTSE; HBV; HBVY; OBEV; OTPC; RG
First Chorus, The. George Gascoigne. *Fr.* The Glass of Government. Po
First Christmas, The. St. Luke, Bible, *N.T. See* Adoration of the Shepherds, The.
First Christmas, The. Norah M. Holland. ChrBoLe
First Christmas, The. Emilie Poulsson. OHIP; PCH
First Christmas, The. *Unknown.* HH
First Christmas Night of All. Nancy Byrd Turner. BiCB; PEDC
First Citizen. James Jeffrey Roche. *Fr.* Washington. PGD
First cold showers pour, The. The Monkey's Raincoat. Basho. SoPo
First comes a fence, then the mouth of an alley. The Hold-Up. David Wagoner. TPM
First come I. My name is Jowett. Henry Charles Beeching. *Fr.* The Masque of Balliol. CenHV
First comes January. The Farmer's Round. *Unknown.* OTPC (1923 ed.)
First Communion. José Asunción Silva, *tr. fr. Spanish by* Thomas Walsh. CAW
First Concerns. Abbie Huston Evans. NP

First concoction perfited, The. *Unknown.* SeCSL
First Confession. X. J. Kennedy. NePoEA-2
First Corinthians, *sels.* Bible, *N.T.*
Charity, XIII. ShBV-4; StVeCh
(Gospel of Love, The.) OuHeWo
(Greatest of These, The, *abr.*) TrGrPo
(Greatness of Love, The, *tr. by* James Moffatt.) MaRV
(Love.) TRV
(Love Is Patient.) TIHL
(Love the Indispensable and Crowning Grace.) PG (1955 ed.)
(St. Paul on Charity.) TreF
("Though I speak with the tongues of men and of angels.") LO
Death's Conqueror, XV: 20, 21, 53, 55. MaRV
Mystery of Death, The, XV: 51-58. BBV (1951 ed.)
Spiritual Gifts, XII: 1-XIII: 13. WoL
Ye Are the Temple of God,III: 16-17. TreFT
First Corncrake. John Hewitt. NeIP
First Cycle of Love Poems (I-V). George Barker. MoPo
Sels.
"My joy, my jockey, my Gabriel," V. ErPo; MoAB; MoBrPo (1950 ed.); MoPW
(Love Poem) NeBP
"Then like the ship at rest in the bay," IV.
(Love Poem.) FaBoMo
1st Dance—Making Things New—6 February 1964. Jackson MacLow. CoPo
First Dandelion, The. Walt Whitman. NePA; TSW
First Date. John Frederick Nims. CBV
First Day, The. Christina Rossetti. Monna Innominata, II. EnLi-2; FaBoBe; HBV; LiTL; LO; MeWo
("I wish I could remember that first day.") Sonn; ViPo; VP
First Day, The. Neil Weiss. NYTB
First day he had gone, The. A Space in the Air. Jon Silkin. NePoEA; TrJP
First day of Christmas, The. The Twelve Days of Christmas. *Unknown.* ChBR; FaFP; LiTL; OxBoLi; OxNR; RePo; SiTL; TreFT
First Day of Creation, The. Milton. *Fr.* Paradise Lost, VII. OxBoCh
First day of spring in the year ninety-three, The. Reynard the Fox. *Unknown.* OnYI
First Day of Teaching. Bonaro W. Overstreet. TrPWD
First Day of the First Week, The. Joshua Sylvester. *Fr.* Du Bartas His Divine Weeks. Po
First day of Yole have we in mind, The. Sing We Yule. *Unknown.* MeEL
First day she passed up and down through the Heavens, The. Laura Waits for Him in Heaven. Petrarch, *pr. tr. by* Synge. *Fr.* Sonnets to Laura: To Laura in Death. OBMV
First-Day Thoughts. Whittier. AmPP; NoP; SoP
Sel.
His Strength. FaChP; SoP
First day's night had come, The. Emily Dickinson. AmPP (4th ed.); LiTA; LiTM (rev. ed.); MWA-2; OxBA
First Death in Nova Scotia. Elizabeth Bishop. CoAP; NYBP
First Departure. Frances Frost. SiSoSe
First did I fear, when first my love began. Licia, XX. Giles Fletcher. SiCE; Sonn; TuPP
First Division Marches, The. Grantland Rice. PaA; PAL; YaD
First drink a health, this solemn night. Hands All Round. Tennyson. PoFr
First Elegy [for the Dead in Cyrenaica.] Hamish Henderson. ChMP; OxBS
First Epistle of the Second Book of Horace [Imitated], The. Pope. CEP; EiCL; MBW-1
(To Augustus.) EiPP
Sels.
Court of Charles II. OBEC
Ideals of Satire, The. FiP
Poet's Use, The. OBEC
First, erected ironworks in a spiry hollow. Charles Madge. *Fr.* Poem by Stages. BoSA
First Essay on the Art of the U.S. Ron Welburn. BF
First face of light, The. 8 May 1967. Sister Mary Norbert Körte. ThO
First Fathers, The. Robert Stephen Hawker. OBVV
First Fig. Edna St. Vincent Millay. AmP; FaFP; InP; PC; PoLF
(Figs from Thistles.) FaBV
(My Candle.) MemP; OtMeF
(My Candle Burns at Both Ends.) SiTL
First Fight. Then Fiddle. Gwendolyn Brooks. BP; PoNe (1970 ed.)
First Flame. Samuel Daniel. *See* Early Love.
First Flight. Robert P. Tristram Coffin. PoMa
First follow Nature, and your judgment frame. Pope. *Fr.* An Essay on Criticism, I. PIA; PP; TreFT; YAT
First Footsteps. Swinburne. NeHB
First, for effusions due unto the dead. Upon His Sister in Law. Robert Herrick. SeEP
First Friend, The. Kipling. *Fr.* Just-so Stories. MPB
First Frost. Edwin Curran. HBMV; TSW
First Fruits in 1812. Wallace Rice. MC
(Firstfruits in 1812.) PAH
First Geography. Gladys McKee. JKCP (1955 ed.)
First get out the map and look at the country. The Subject of the Bishop's Miracle. John Philip. BoAV
First good joy our Mary had, The. The Twelve Good Joys. *Unknown.* OBB
First Grandchild. M. Whitcomb Hess. JKCP (1955 ed.)
First gray smoke of daylight blurs, The. Sunrise. Rowena Bennett. TiPo (1959 ed.)
First Grief, The. Felicia D. Hemans. *See* Child's First Grief, The.
First halt. They heard within a sugar patch. John Hunter-Duvar. *Fr.* The Emigration of the Fairies. CaP
First Harp-Player, The. Humbert Wolfe. MuSP
First he rushed over to a. The Visitor. Mary Ellen Solt. QAH
First hear the story of Kaspar the rosy-cheeked. Fraulein Reads Instructive Rhymes. Maxine W. Kumin. NYBP
First hour was a word the color of dawn, The. Spring Morning —Santa Fé. Lynn Riggs. HT
First I am frosted. Mary Austin. *Fr.* Rhyming Riddles. TiPo
First I looked on, after a long time far from home, The. American Change. Allen Ginsberg. CABL; NoP
First I ritual. The Madman Goes to a Party. Dick Lourie. ThO
First I salute this soil of the blessed, river and rock! Pheidippides. Robert Browning. PoVP
First I saw a landscape fair. "Barry Cornwall." *Fr.* A Vision. OBRV
First I would have a face exactly fair. How to Choose a Mistress. Edmund Prestwich. CLwM
First Impressions. Alfred Grant Walton. PoToHe (new ed.)
First in a carriage. *Unknown.* OxNR
First in the fight, and first in the arms. Zollicoffer. Henry Lynden Flash. PAH
First in the North. The black sea-tangle[d] beaches. The Mythical Journey [*or* Journey]. Edwin Muir. ILP; MoVE; OxBS
First Invasion of Ireland, The. John Montague. NMP; OPoP
First it was a pretty flower, dressed in pink and white. Riddle. *Unknown, at. to* Christina Rossetti. OTPC (1946 ed.); SoPo
First It Was Singing. Jon Silkin. NePoEA; PoDB
First John, *sel.* Bible, *N.T.*
Brotherhood, II: 9-11, IV: 20-21. TreFT
First joy through eye and limb. First Joy. Vernon Watkins. ChMP
First king was Pharamond, The; after him came. Kings of France. Mary W. Lincoln. BLPA
First Kings, *sel.* Bible, *O.T.*
Solomon Judges between Two Women Disputing over a Child, III: 16-27. TreFT
First Kiss, The. Norman Gale. VA
First Kiss, The. Theodore Watts-Dunton. *Fr.* The Coming of Love. HBV; VA
First Kiss of Love, The. Byron. HBV
First lambs have come, late snowfall to the hill. The Fox. Ian Serraillier. POTE
First, last and always dearest, closest, best. An Epistle. A. D. Hope. PoAu-2
First Lay of Gudrun, The. *Unknown, tr. fr. Icelandic by* William Morris *and* Eiríkur Magnússon. *Fr.* The Elder Edda. AWP; JAWP; WBP
First Leaf, The. Howard Nemerov. TwAmPo

First Lesson. Philip Booth. SD; TwCP
First Lesson. Nancy Willard. ThO
First Light. Thomas Kinsella. OPoP
First Lord's Song, The. W. S. Gilbert. *See* When I Was a Lad.
First Love. Byron. *See* 'Tis Sweet.
First Love. Charles Stuart Calverley. BOHV; FiBHP; InMe
First Love. Thomas Campion. OxBoLi
("Silly boy, 'tis full moon yet. . .") LO; SiCE
First Love. John Clare. *See* I Ne'er Was Struck.
First Love. Charles Gullans. NePoEA
First Love. Laurie Lee. ChMP; ToPo
First love is first death. There is no other. The Sequel. Delmore Schwartz. LiTM (1970 ed.)
First Love Remembered. Dante Gabriel Rossetti. PoVP
First Maccabees, *sels.* Bible, Apocrypha.
Dirge: "Her house is become like a man dishonored," II: 8-14. TrJP
Great Mourning, I: 25-28. TrJP
Judas Maccabeus, III: 1-9. TrJP
First Meditation. Theodore Roethke. *Fr.* Meditations of an Old Woman. AP
("On love's worst ugly day.") PoDB
First Meeting, The. Lord Herbert of Cherbury. AnAnS-2
First meridian, new with light, The. Academy. Sister Mary Jeremy. JKCP (1955 ed.)
First Miracle. Genevieve Taggard. HBMV
First month of his absence, The. Song. Alun Lewis. ChMP; DTC; LiTM; WaaP
First Morning of the Second World, The. Delmore Schwartz. FiMAP
First mules in America, The. Ever Since. Elizabeth J. Coatsworth. SiSoSe
First night, The/ The elopers. *Unknown.* HW
First Night of Fall and Falling Rain, The. Delmore Schwartz. NYTB
First night when I come home, as drunk as I could be. Three Nights Drunk. *Unknown.* OuSiCo
First Note. Jason Miller. ThO
First Note, Simple, The; the Second Note, Distinct. Conrad Aiken. Preludes for Memnon, X. LiTA; TwAmPo
First Nowell [the Angel Did Say], The. *Unknown.* ChrBoLe; LiTB; OTPC (1946 ed.); PTK; TreFS; ViBoPo; YaCaBo, *with music*
First o the second o the third o, The. An Autobiography. Bairam at Tunisie. LiTW
First of All My Dreams, The. E. E. Cummings. NYBP; SiSw
First of April, The. William Hone. PoRL
First of April, The. Geoffrey Johnson. PoRL
First of April, some do say, The. All Fools' Day [*or* April Fool's Day]. *Unknown.* BoTP; PCH; PoRL; SiSoSe; SoPo
First of May, The. Barbara Guest. AmPC
First of the Emigrants, The, *with music. Unknown.* ShS
First of the first. The Old Pope Is Comforted by the Thought of the Young Pompilia. Robert Browning. *Fr.* The Ring and the Book. BoC
First of the undecoded messages read, The:"Popeye sits in thunder." Farm Implements and Rutabagas in a Landscape. John Ashbery. CoAP
First Olympionique: To Hiero of Syracuse. Pindar. *See* To Hiero the Syracusan.
First or Last. Thomas Hardy. CMoP
First or Last? Margaret Veley. VA
First paint a cage. To Paint the Portrait of a Bird. Jacques Prévert. FIW
First Pastoral, The ("If We, O Dorset"). Ambrose Philips. *Fr.* Pastorals. EiCL
First Pathways. Sidney Royse Lysaght. OBVV
First Philosopher's Song. Aldous Huxley. AWP; HBMV; InPo; JAWP; WBP
First point is to love but one alone, The. The First Property. Sir Thomas More. *Fr.* The Twelve Properties or Conditions of a Lover. EnRePo
First Proclamation of Miles Standish, The. Margaret Junkin Preston. MC; PAH; YaD
First Prologue to "Secret Love; or, The Maiden Queen." Dryden. *See* Prologue to 'Secret Love; or The Maiden Queen."
First Property, The. Sir Thomas More. *Fr.* The Twelve Properties or Conditions of a Lover. EnRePo
First Pythian Ode of Pindar, The. Pindar, *tr. fr. Greek by* Arthur S. Way. Pythian Odes, I. WoL
(Power of Music, The, *tr. by* H. T. Wade-Gery *and* C. M. Bowra.) UnS, *shorter sel.*
First Quest, The. Joseph Rodman Drake. *Fr.* The Culprit Fay. AA
(Fay's Departure, The, *shorter sel.*) GN
First Rain. Zoë Akins. HBMV
First range through. James Brodey. *Fr.* Identikit. ANYP
First Reader. Paris Leary. CoPo
First Reader (Fifth Reading). Gladys McKee. JKCP (1955 ed.)
First retainer, The. A Marriage. Robert Creeley. LiTM (1970 ed.); NeAP
First rise after a low. Rules of the Road. *Unknown.* SoAmSa
First Robin, The. Lilian Leveridge. CaP
First Samuel, *sels.* Bible, *O.T.*
"And when Saul saw David go forth against the Philistine," XVII: 55-XVIII: 5. LO
David and Goliath XVI, XVII: 1-51. TreFS
Hannah's Song of Thanksgiving, II: 1-10. AWP
(Song of Hannah, The.) LiTW
First Satire of the Second Book of Horace [Imitated], The. Pope. EiCL; MBW-1
First September day was blue and warm, The. The Artist on Penmaenmawr. Charles Tennyson-Turner. OBNC
1st September 1939. W. H. Auden. *See* September 1, 1939.
First Settler's Story, The. Will Carleton. IHA
First shall the heaven[s] want starry light. A Fancy [*or* Lover's Protestation]. Thomas Lodge. *Fr.* Rosalynde. EIL; GoBC; LoBV; OBSC; SiCE
First shot out of that sling, The. After Goliath. Kingsley Amis. NePoEA-2; PoCh
First shot was fired to Wagnerian music, The. Laocoon. Don Gordon. WaaP
First Sight. Philip Larkin. BoNaP; MemP; OA
First Sight of Her and After. Thomas Hardy. PoEL-5
First Skylark of Spring, The. Sir William Watson. VA
First Snow. Marie Louise Allen. SoPo; TiPo
First Snow. Ivy O. Eastwick. TiPo
First Snow in Alsace. Richard Wilbur. AP; NoP
First Snowfall [*or* Snow-Fall], The. James Russell Lowell. AA; AnNE; BLPA; FaBoBe; GFA; HBV; MCCG; NeHB; OTD; PCD; TreF; WBLP
Sel.
"Snow had begun in the gloaming, The." FaPON; PoSC
First Song, The. Richard Burton. AA
First Song. John Donne. *Fr.* Infinitati Sacrum. MaMe
First Song. Galway Kinnell. GoJo; LiTM (1970 ed.); NePoAm; TPM; TwCP
First Song: "Doubt you to whom my Muse these notes intendeth." Sir Philip Sidney. *See* Astrophel and Stella: First Song.
First Song-Sparrow, The. *Unknown.* PCH
First Song, Sung by Two Amazons, The. Jasper Mayne. *See* Time.
First Spousal, The. Coventry Patmore. The Unknown Eros, II, ii. OBVV
First Spring Day, The. Christina Rossetti. WiR
First Spring Morning. Robert Bridges. BoNaP; BoTP; YeAr, *st.* 1
First stands the lofty Washington. Our Presidents. *Unknown.* BLPA
First station off on a cold road to the country. The Chickadees. John Hay. NePoAm-2
First Step, The. Andrew Bice Saxton. AA
First Step, The. Constantine Cavafy, *tr. fr. Greek by* Rae Dalven. ML
First Sun Day of the year. Tonight. Galway Kinnell. *Fr.* The Avenue Bearing the Initial of Christ into the New World. NaP
First Swallow, The. Charlotte Smith. DD; HBV; OTPC
First Temptation, The. Milton. *Fr.* Paradise Regained, I. OxBoCh
First Thanksgiving, The. Arthur Guiterman. DD
First Thanksgiving, The. Clinton Scollard. MC; PAH
(First Thanksgiving Day.) DD
First Thanksgiving, The. Nancy Byrd Turner. *See* First Thanksgiving of All.
First Thanksgiving Day, The. Alice Williams Brotherton. DD; OHIP

First Thanksgiving Day, The. Margaret Junkin Preston. MC; PAH; ThLM
First Thanksgiving Day. Clinton Scollard. *See* First Thanksgiving, The.
First Thanksgiving of All. Nancy Byrd Turner. FaPON; PAL; RePo; SiSoSe
(First Thanksgiving, The.) YeAr
First that we saw of the high-tone tramp, The. Broncho versus Bicycle. *Unknown.* SCC
First the artillery groaned beyond the Channel. My Sister Helen. Drummond Allison. FaBoTw
First, the middle, and the last, The. In Search of the Picturesque. William Combe. *Fr.* Dr. Syntax in Search of the Picturesque. OBRV
First the rain and then the wind. Rules of the Road. *Unknown.* SoAmSa
First, the scene endlessly diminishes. Travelling Backward. Gene Baro. NYBP
First the soul of our house left, up the chimney. Tornado. William Stafford. NaP; WIRo
First the two eyes, which have the seeing power. Sight. Sir John Davies. LoBV (2d ed.)
First the valley where the houses. Hydro Works. J. R. Hervey. AnNZ
First the yellow sea-road and the sun's. Temple Fever: Sounion. Joanne De Longchamps. NYTB
First there was the lamb on knocking knees. Dylan Thomas. *Fr.* Altarwise by Owl-Light, III. CMoP; CoBMV; LiTM; MasP
First, there's the Bible. The Hundred Best Books. Mostyn T. Pigott. BOHV; InMe
First, there's the courtship. Verses versus Verses. Marvin Bell. YAP
First they dress in green. *Unknown.* OTPC (1946 ed.)
First They Slaughtered the Angels, *sel.* Lenore Kandel. WOW
First thing, I think, is a keen sense, The. Juan Belmonte, Torero. Donald Finkel. NePoEA
First thing that I remember was Carlo tugging away, The. Asleep at the Switch. George Hoey. BeLS; PaPo
First Things First. W. H. Auden. NePoAm-2; NYBP
First Things First. "M. E. H." SoP
First Three, The. Clinton Scollard. MC; PAH
First Time, The. Karl Shapiro. ErPo
First time he came to see me, The. Naomi (Omie) Wise (B *vers.*) *Unknown.* BaBo
First time he kissed me, he but only kissed. Sonnets from the Portuguese, XXXVIII. Elizabeth Barrett Browning. BLPA; CTC; FaBoBe; HBV; NeHB; PoPl; VA; ViBoPo; ViPo
First time I saw little Weevil he was on the western plain. The Ballad [*or* Ballet] of the Boll Weevil. *Unknown.* ThLM; ViBoFo (A *vers.*)
First time I saw you, The. Peasant and Geisha Songs. *Unknown.* LiTW
First time I went to Frisco, I went upon a spree, The. Off to Sea Once More [*or* Jack Wrack]. *Unknown.* ABF; ShS, *vers.* I
First time that I dreamed, we were in flight, The. The Lesson. W. H. Auden. FaBoMo
First time that the sun rose on thine oath, The. Sonnets from the Portuguese, XXXII. Elizabeth Barrett Browning. ViBoPo; ViPo
First time the emperor Han, The. The Word. Allen Upward. *Fr.* Scented Leaves from a Chinese Jar. NP
First to Throw a Stone. *Unknown.* STF
First Tooth, The. Charles *and* Mary Lamb. OTPC (1923 ed.)
First Tooth, The. William Brighty Rands. HBV; HBVY
First Travels of Max. John Crowe Ransom. MAP; MoAmPo
First, two white arms that held him very close. Act V (Midnight). Thomas Bailey Aldrich. PFY
First Vision, The. Tadhg Dall O'Huiginn, *tr. fr. Late Middle Irish by* the Earl of Longford. AnIL
First Voyage of John Cabot, The. Katharine Lee Bates. MC; PAH
First Warm Days. Edwin Denby. GTBS-W; LiTM
First was a gray-beard Peter, The. The Three Peters. Molly Michaels. RIS
First was the world as one great cymbal made. Musicks [*or* Music's] Empire. Andrew Marvell. MaMe; MuSP; SCEP-2
First when Maggie was my care. Whistle O'er the Lave o't. Burns. CEP; OxBS
First William the Norman, then William his son. History Lesson. *Unknown.* OxNR; RIS
First Winter's Day. Dorothy Aldis. SoPo
First Woman's Lament. Brenda Chamberlain. NeIP
(Lament: "My man is a bone ringèd with weed.") NeBP
First Words before Spring. Louis Untermeyer. MAP
First World War. Kenneth Slade Alling. NePoAm
First Year, The, *sel.* E. J. Scovell. FaBoMo
"Before she first had smiled or looked with calm."
First you bite your fingernails. American Rhapsody (4). Kenneth Fearing. MoAmPo; TrGrPo (1942 ed.)
First, you think they are dead. Lobsters in the Window. W. D. Snodgrass. NYBP; PoIE (1970 ed.)
First young lady all around in town. Swing on the Corner. *Unknown.* TrAS
First Zeppelin, The. James S. Tippett. GFA
Firstborn. *See* First born.
Firste fader and findere of gentilesse, The. Gentilesse. Chaucer. NoP
Firstë stock [*or* stok], father [*or* Fader] of gentilesse. Gentilesse. Chaucer. AWP; CBEP; MaPo
Firstfruits in 1812. Wallace Rice. *See* First Fruits in 1812.
Firstlings of grief, The. The Reapings. Theodore Weiss. NMP
Firwood. John Clare. TrGrPo
("Fir trees taper into twigs and wear, The.") EG
Fish, The. Elizabeth Bishop. ExPo; FiMAP; GoJo; GoTP; LiTM (rev. ed.); MiAP; MoAB; MoAmPo (1950 ed.); NeMA; NePA; PIA; Po; PoPl; PoPo; TrGrPo (rev. ed.); TwAmPo; ViBoPo (1958 ed.)
Fish, The. Rupert Brooke. BoC
Sel.
"In a cool curving world he lies." OA
Fish, The. Paul Eluard, *tr. fr. French by* Glauco Cambon. OnPM
Fish, The. Ralph Gustafson. OBCV
Fish, The. Marianne Moore. AmPP (5th ed.); AnFE; APA; CoAnAm; MAP; MoAB; MoAmPo; MoVE; OxBA; TwAmPo
Fish. W. W. E. Ross. MoCV; PeCV
Fish. William Jay Smith. RePo
Fish. Emily Townsend. NYBP
Fish. John Unterecker. ThO
Fish and Bird. Rosemary Brinckman. BoTP
Fish and the Man, The. Leigh Hunt. Fr. The Fish, the Man, and the Spirit. RoGo
Fish Answers, A. Leigh Hunt. *Fr.* The Fish, the Man, and the Spirit. BoC; FiBHP; OA
Fish are folded, The. The Root. Francis Maguire. JKCP (1926 ed.)
Fish bones walked the waves off Hatteras. Cottonmouth Country. Louise Glück. CoAP; YAP
Fish Country at Bonneville, The. William Stafford. AmFN
Fish Crier. Carl Sandburg. AmFN; OxBA; WoL
Fish-Day. Mazie V. Caruthers. CIV
Fish dripping, A. Fish. W. W. E. Ross. MoCV; PeCV
Fish-eye. Milton Bracker. NYTB
Fish (fly-replete, in depth of June). Heaven. Rupert Brooke. AnFE; BrPo; EPN; ExPo; GTBS-D; GTBS-W; HoPM; ILP; LiTB; LiTM; MemP; MoBrPo; PoE; PoRA; POTE; SeCeV; ShBV-4; SiTL; WaKn; WGRP
Fish Food. John Wheelwright. AnFE; CoAnAm; LiTA; TwAmPo
Fish has laid her succulent eggs. Vicissitudes of the Creator. Archibald MacLeish. NePA; VaPo
Fish-Hawk, The. John Hall Wheelock. AnAmPo; EtS; HBMV
Fish in River. *Unknown, tr. fr. Anglo-Saxon by* Charles W. Kennedy. *Fr.* Riddles. AnOE
Fish in the Unruffled Lakes. W.H. Auden. AtBAP; ChMP; CMoP; GTBS-D; MaPo; TDP
(Song: "Fish in the unruffled lakes.") MoAB; MoBrPo (1950 ed.)
Fish Story, A. Henry A. Beers. BOHV
Fish, the Man, and the Spirit, The. Leigh Hunt. ATP; CBV; ChTr; EnRP; EPN; NBM; OBEV (new ed.); PoEL-4; SeCePo; ViBoPo
Sels.
Fish Answers, A. BoC; FiBHP; OA
(Fish to Man.) MoShBr
To a Fish. BoC; FiBHP; OA
(Fish and the Man, The.) RoGo
Fish took a notion, A. Tip-Toe Tale. Dixie Willson. GFA
Fish wade, The/ through black jade. The Fish. Marianne Moore. AnFE; APA; CoAnAm; MAP; MoAB; MoAmPo; MoVE; OxBA; TwAmPo

Fish, when he's exposed to air, The. Autres Bêtes, Autres Moeurs. Ogden Nash. NAMP
Fish with the Deep Sea Smile, The. Margaret Wise Brown. PDV
Fisher, The. Roderic Quinn. BoAV; PoAu-1
Fisher, The. William Renton. WePo
Fisher, in your bright bark rowing. The Fisherman. *Unknown.* FaPON
Fisher was casting his flies in a brook, A. The Microscopic Trout and the Machiavelian Fisherman. Guy Wetmore Carryl. WhC
Fisher lad, A (no higher dares he look). Eclogue III. Phineas Fletcher. *Fr.* Piscatorie Eclogues. SeCV-1
Fisher-Maiden, The. Heine. *See* Oh Lovely Fishmaiden.
Fisher-maids at Shika, The. No Spare Time. Ishikawa Kimiko. OnPM
Fisherman, The. Abbie Farwell Brown. EtS; FaPON; GaP
Fisherman, The. Leonidas of Tarentum, *tr. fr. Greek by* Andrew Lang. AWP
Fisherman, The. David McCord. PDV; TiPo (1959 ed.)
Fisherman, The. Jay Macpherson. PeCV
Fisherman. Sacheverell Sitwell. AtBAP
Fisherman, The. Douglas Stewart. ACV
Fisherman, The. *Unknown, tr. fr. Portuguese by* Anne Higginson Spicer. FaPON
Fisherman, The. W.B. Yeats. BWP; CMoP; CoBMV; MaPo (1969 ed.); MBW-2; NoP; NP; SD; ShBV-4
Fisherman goes out at dawn, The. The Fisherman. Abbie Farwell Brown. EtS; FaPON; GaP
Fisherman Husband. Brenda Chamberlain. *See* Second Woman's Lament.
Fisherman lived on the shore, A. How a Fisherman Corked Up His Foe in a Jar. Guy Wetmore Carryl. PoMS
Fisherman Speaks, A. Scharmel Iris. ChIP
Fisherman's Blunder Off New Bedford, Massachusetts. Annemarie Ewing. NePoAm-2
Fisherman's Chant, The. Sir F. C. Burnand. BOHV
Fisherman's Hymn, The. Alexander Wilson. AA; EtS
Fisherman's Luck. W. W. Gibson. EtS
Fisherman's Son. Charles Bruce. CaP
Fisherman's Song, The. Thomas D'Urfey. ALV
Fishermen. James A. Emanuel. BP
Fishermen, The. Theocritus, *tr. fr. Greek by* Charles Stuart Calverley. Idyll XXI. AWP
Fishermen, The. Emile Verhaeren, *tr. fr. French by* Jethro Bithell. WoL
Fishermen, The. Whittier. EtS
Fishermen say, when your catch is done, The. The Sea Wolf. Violet McDougal. FaPON; MPB
Fishermen will relate that in the South. The Lord of the Isle. Stefan George. AWP; JAWP; WBP
Fishermen's Weather. *Unknown. See* When the wind is in the east.
Fishers. Albert Reginald Gold. ChIP; OQP
Fishers, The. Josephine Preston Peabody. StJW
Fishers, The. Ruth Pitter. BoC
Fishers. Edwin Meade Robinson. LHV
Fishers, The. Brian Vrepont. MoAuPo
Fisher's Apology, A. *Unknown, tr. fr. Latin by* Arthur Johnstone. GoTS
Fisher's Boy, The. Henry David Thoreau. AA; AnAmPo; AnNE; ChTr
Fishers in the Night. Beulah May. ChIP
Fisher's Life, The. *Unknown.* ChTr; EtS
Fisher's Widow, The. Arthur Symons. HBV; PoMa
Fishes, The. Mrs. Motherly. SAS
Fishes, The. *Unknown. See* Boston Come-All-Ye, The.
Fishes. Humbert Wolfe. *Fr.* Kensington Gardens. RIS; StaSt
Fishes and the Poet's Hands, The. Frank Yerby. AmNP; PoNe (1970 ed.)
Fishes' Heaven. Rupert Brooke. *See* Heaven.
Fishes swim in water clear. *Unknown.* OxNR
Fishes, swimmers, boats. The Fish. Paul Eluard. OnPM
Fishing. Dorothy Wellesley. BoC; OBMV
Fishing. Wordsworth. *Fr.* The Prelude. SD
Fishing. Keith Wright. NYTB
Fishing Boats in Martigues. Roy Campbell. PeSA
Fishing boats out on the deep sea. Hopes and Memories. Giovanni Pascoli. OnPM
Fishing Fleet, The. Lincoln Colcord. HBMV
Fishing for sticklebacks, with rod and line. Sir Francis Burnand. PV
Fishing, if I, a fisher, may protest. De Piscatione. Thomas Bastard. TuPP
Fishing in the Australian Alps. Ernest G. Moll. WhC
Fishing Pole, The. Mary Carolyn Davies. FaPON; GFA; OTPC (1946 ed.)
Fishing Season. Val Vallis. PoAu-2
Fishing Song, A. William Brighty Rands. CenHV
Fishing Village. Louis Dudek. *Fr.* Provincetown. MoCV
Fishmarket closed, the fishes gone into flesh, The. Galway Kinnell. *Fr.* The Avenue Bearing the Initial of Christ into the New World. NaP
Fishwife sits by the side, The. Ireland, Mother of Priests. Shane Leslie. JKCP
Fishy-fishy in the brook. *Unknown.* GoTP
Fit of Rhyme [*or* Rime] Against Rhyme [*or* Rime], A. Ben Jonson. AnAnS-2; InvP; NoP; PAn; PoEL-2; PoFS; PP; SCEP-2; SeCP; SeCV-1; TuPP
Fit of Something against Something, A. Alan Ansen. PP
Fit Only for Apollo. Francis Beaumont. *See* Shake Off Your Heavy Trance.
Fit theme for song, the sylvan maid. Madam Hickory. Wilbur Larremore. AA
Fits of Candor. Dick Gallup. ANYP
Fitz Adam's Story. James Russell Lowell. AmePo; AmPP (5th ed.); MWA-1
Five, The. Swift. *See* Riddle, A: "We are little airy creatures."
Five Ages, The. Hesiod, *tr. fr. Greek by* Jack Lindsay. *Fr.* Works and Days. LiTW
Five-and-thirty black slaves. The Key-Board. Sir William Watson. HBV
Five Arabic Verses in Praise of Wine. *Unknown, tr. fr. Arabic by* Hartwig Hirschfeld. TrJP
Five Bells. Kenneth Slessor. BoAV; MoAuPo; OnHM; PoAu-2; PoRA; SeCePo
Five Best Doctors, The. O. S. Hoffman. PoToHe (new ed.)
Five Birds Rise. William Hayward. NYBP
Five broken loaves beside the sea and thousands fed. Broken Things. Bob Jones, Jr. SoP
Five Carols for Christmastide. Louise Imogen Guiney. ISi
"Five cents a glass!" Does anyone think. Price of a Drink. Josephine Pollard. PaPo
Five-Day Rain, The. Denise Levertov. NeAP
Five Days Old. Francis Webb. PoAu-2
Five Degrees South. Francis Brett Young. EtS
Five dollars a day is a white man's pay, way. A Dollar and a Half a Day. *Unknown.* TrAS
Five English Poets. Dante Gabriel Rossetti. PoVP
Sel.
John Keats. EPN
Five Epigrams. J. V. Cunningham. UnTE
Five Epigrams. Donald Hall. NePoAm-2
Five Eyes. Walter de la Mare. UTS
Five fearless knights of the first renown. The First American Sailors. Wallace Rice. PAH
Five-fingered Maple, The. Kate Louise Brown. BoTP
Five fives this year my years. The Conviction. J. M. Synge. SyP
Five geese deploy mysteriously. Bas-Relief. Carl Sandburg. CrMA
Five gleaming crows. In Air. Peter Clarke. PBA
Five Grand Odes, *sel.* Paul Claudel, *tr. fr. French by* John Hay.
"Blessed be your name, my God." OnHM
Five harsh black birds shining in bronze came crying. A Japanese Vase Wrought in Metals. Marjorie Allen Seifert. NP
Five Hours, (and who can do it less in?). The Lady's Dressing Room. Swift. ErPo; NCEP
Five-in-June. Lysbeth Boyd Borie. BiCB
Five Joys of Mary, The. *Unknown.* MeEL
Five Kernals of Corn. Hezekiah Butterworth. DD; MC; PAH
Five kings rule o'er the Amorite. The Ballad of the Battle of Gibeon. G. K. Chesterton. YT
Five kittens in the haymow. Kittens. Catherine Parmenter. CIV
Five Little Brothers. Ella Wheeler Wilcox. BoTP
Five Little Chickens. *Unknown.* GFA; GoTP; OTPC (1946 ed.); PDV; SAS
(Chickens, The.) FaPON; UTS
(Wishes.) BoTP

Five Little Fairies, The. Maud Burnham. HBVY; OTPC (1946 ed.); PCH; PPL
Five little monkeys. The Monkeys and the Crocodile. Laura E. Richards. BoChLi; FaPON; ShM; SoPo; SUS; TiPo; UTS
Five Little Princesses, The. Laura E. Richards. GaP
Five little pussy-cats, invited out to tea. The Cats' Tea-Party. Frederic E. Weatherly. OTPC (1946 ed); SAS; TiPo
Five Little Sisters Walking in a Row. Kate Greenaway. MoShBr
(Five Sisters.) BoTP
Five little squirrels. *Unknown.* RIS
Five Lives. Edward Rowland Sill. AnAmPo; AnFE; AnNE; APA; CoAnAm
Five long clangs from the house-clock nigh. The Shiver. Thomas Hardy. InPo
Five men over the parapet, with a one-star loot in charge. The Patrol. J. H. Knight-Adkin. MCCG
Five Minutes. Norman Nicholson. POTi
Five minutes, five minutes more, please. Bedtime. Eleanor Farjeon. SoPo; TiPo
Five mites of monads dwelt in a round drop. Five Lives. Edward Rowland Sill. AnAmPo; AnFE; AnNE; APA; CoAnAm
Five oxen, grazing in a flowery mead. On a Seal. Plato. AWP; JAWP; WBP; WoL
Five Peas on a Barrelhead. Lew Sarett. PoMa
Five Poems from Mexico. Denise Levertov. PoAn
Five Prayers. Blanche Edith Baughan. BoAu
Five Reasons [for Drinking], The. Henry Aldrich. *See* Reasons for Drinking.
Five Roses. Jacinto Verdaguer, *tr. fr. Spanish by* Thomas Walsh. CAW
Five score years the birds have flown. Failure. Orrick Johns. PoMa
Five Serpents. Charles Burgess. NePoAm-2
Five Sisters. Kate Greenaway. *See* Five Little Sisters Walking in a Row.
Five Smooth Stones. Stella Benson. MoBrPo (1942 ed.)
Five Songs, *sel.* W. H. Auden. *See* Orators, The.
Five Songs. David Shapiro. ANYP
Five Souls. W. N. Ewer. MaRV; OQP
Five Stanzas on Perfection. George Jonas. PeCV (1967 ed.)
Five Students, The. Thomas Hardy. CMOP; ExPo; GTBS-P; PoEL-5
Five summer days, five summer nights. The Blue-Fly. Robert Graves. CMoP; ILP; MoVE; NYBP
Five thousand followed him for fish and loaves. Calvary. Hugh Robert Orr. ChIP
Five thousand souls are here, and all are bounded. Troopship in the Tropics. Alun Lewis. WaP
Five thousand years have fled, let us suppose. The Archaeologist of the Future. Leonard Bacon. WhC
Five Towns on the B. and O. Carl Sandburg. OnPM; WoL
Five Vignettes. Jean Toomer. BALP
Five Visions of Captain Cook. Kenneth Slessor. BoAV
Sels.
"Flowers turned to stone! Not all the botany." PoAu-2
"Two chronometers the captain had." NeLNL
(Two Chronometers.) MoAuPo; SeCePo
Five Voyages of Arnor, The. George Mackay Brown. NePoEA-2
Five Wines. Robert Herrick. BOHV
Five workmen hired here to shovel dirt. Workmen. Herbert Morris. NePoAm-2
Five years ago (says story) I lov'd you. Love. Abraham Cowley. PoFS
Five years have passed; five summers, with the length. Lines Composed [*or* Written] a Few Miles above Tintern Abbey [*or* Tintern Abbey]. Wordsworth. BEL; BoLiVe; BWP; CABA; CABL; CaFP; CBV; ChER; CoBE; DiPo; EnL; EnLi-2; EnLit; EnRP; EPN; ERoP-1; ExPo; FaPL; FiP; ForPo; GoTL; HBV; ILP; InP; LiTB; LoBV; MaPo; MasP; MBW-2; MERP; NoP; OAEP; OBNC; OBRV; OuHeWo; PAn; PeER; PIA; PoAn; PoE; PoEL-4; PoeP; PoFS; PoIE; SeCePo; SeCeV; StP; TOP; TreFS; TrGrPo; UnPo (1st ed.); WHA
Five Years Old. Marie Louise Allen. BiCB
Five Years Old. Lysbeth Boyd Borie. BiCB; SiSoSe
Fix'd were their habits; they arose betimes. Jonas Kindred's Household. George Crabbe. *Fr.* The Frank Courtship. FaBoEn
Fixture, A. May Swenson. NYBP
Flag, The. George H. Boker. HH
Flag, The. Henry Lynden Flash. MC
Flag The. Edward A. Horton. HH
Flag, The. Lucy Larcom. DD; HH
Flag, The. James Jeffrey Roche. PaA; PAH
Flag, The. Shelley Silverstein. PoSC
Flag Goes By, The. Henry Holcomb Bennett. AA; BBV; DD; FaBoBe; FaFP; FaPON; GN; HBV; HBVY; HH; NeHB; OHFP; PaA; PAL; PCD; PEDC; PGD; PoRL; PTK; RePo; SiSoSe; TiPo (1952 ed.); TreF; WBLP; YaD
Flag o' My Land. T. A. Daly. HH
Flag of Peace, The. Charlotte Perkins Gilman. NeHB; OQP
Flag of the *Constellation,* The. Thomas Buchanan Read. EtS; PaA
Flag of the fearless-hearted. Our Flag. Margaret E. Sangster. PEDC
Flag of the Free. Walter Taylor Field. HH
Flag of the heroes who left us their glory. Union and Liberty. Oliver Wendell Holmes. OHIP
Flag Song. Lydia Avery Coonley Ward. MPB; OTPC (1946 ed.); PoRL; YeAr
(Song for Flag Day, A.) HH; PEDC
Flag Speaks, The. Emily Greene Balch. PGD
Flag We Fly, The. Aileen Fisher. YeAr
Flagpole Sitter, The. Donald Finkel. CoAP
Flags. Gwendolyn Brooks. *See* Love Note II: Flags.
Flags of all sorts. Things We Dreamt We Died For. Marvin Bell. CoAP; YAP
Flags of war like storm-birds fly, The. The Battle Autumn of 1862. Whittier. MC; PAH
Flail. Power Dalton. HBMV
Flailed from the heart of water in a bow. Ballade for the Duke of Orléans. Richard Wilbur. TDP
Flame, The. Ezra Pound. CoAnAm
Flame at the core of the world. Song. Arthur Upson. HBV
Flame-flower, Day-torch, Mauna Loa. Lines to a Nasturtium (a Lover Muses). Anne Spencer. AmNP; CDC; PoNe
Flame-Heart. Claude McKay. AmNP; BALP; BANP; CDC; NoP; PoNe
Flame-like limbs, tortured green. El Greco. C. A. Trypanis. NYTB
Flame of God. Amy Carmichael. *See* Deliver Me.
Flame of the spirit, and dust of the earth. This Is the Making of Man [*or* The Making of Man]. Priscilla Leonard. MaRV; OQP
Flame out, you glorious skies. The Dead Heroes. Isaac Rosenberg. MoBrPo; TrGrPo (1942 ed.)
Flame went flitting through the wood, A. The Scarlet Tanager. Mary Augusta Mason. AA
Flame-wing'd seraph spake a word, The. Poeta Nascitur. Thomas Ashe. VA
Flames. E. Merrill Root. PoMa
Flames. Sara Teasdale. OTD
Flaming Banners. Bhartrihari, *tr. fr. Sanskrit by* Arthur W. Ryder. OnPM
Flaming Creatures. Kenward Elmslie. ANYP
Flaming Heart, The. Richard Crashaw. AnAnS-1; CAW; GoBC; LiTB; LoBV; MaMe; MeP; OxBoCh; PoEL-2; ReEn; SCEP-1; SeCePo; SeCL; SeCV-1
Sels.
"Live here, great heart; and love and dy and kill." OBS
(Upon the Book and Picture of the Seraphicall Saint Teresa.) AtBAP
"O Heart! the equal poise of love's both parts." EG; TrGrPo
"O sweet incendiary! show here thy art." PoFS; SeEP
"O Thou undaunted daughter of desires!" CoBE; WHA
(Upon the Book and Picture of the Seraphical Saint Teresa.) OBEV
Flaming sighs that boil within my breast, The. Sir Thomas Wyatt. FCP
Flaming Terrapin, The, *sels.* Roy Campbell.
Fall of Satan, The. BoSA
Invocation to the African Muse. BoSA
"Maternal Earth stirs redly from beneath." MoBrPo
Noah. BoSA
Out of the Ark's Grim Hold. OA
Flamingo, The. Lewis Gaylord Clark. BOHV; NA

Flamingos, The. Rainer Maria Rilke, *tr. fr. German by* Jessie Lemont. OnPM
Flamingo's Egg, A. Terence Heywood. BoSA
Flammonde. E. A. Robinson. AmPP; AnAmPo; BoLiVe; CMoP; CoBA; InP; LiTA; LiTM (rev. ed.); MAPA; SeCeV; TIHL; TOP; UnPo (1st ed.)
Flannan Isle. W. W. Gibson. CH; GoTL (1949 ed.); MoVE; OBVV; PoRA; ShBV-2; StPo; TOP; WePo
Flap, flap, the captive bird in the cage. The Scholar in the Narrow Street. Tso Ssu. AWP; JAWP; WBP
Flap my sole, bim bam. Bim Bam. Dorothy Rosenberg. PoNe (1970 ed.)
Flapper. D. H. Lawrence. BoLP
Flared down from broken cloud the calipered light. Winfield Townley Scott. Bermuda Suite, V. FiMAP
Flash, The. James Dickey. FRC
Flash Crimson. Carl Sandburg. MAP; MoAmPo
Flash forth, thou sun. An Easter Carol. Christina Rossetti. PCH
Flash Frigate, The, *with music.* *Unknown.* AmSS
Flash Jack from Gundagai. *Unknown.* PoAu-1
Flash of light across the night, A. Ulric Dahlgren. Kate Brownlee Sherwood. PAH
Flash of lightning does not satisfy thirst, A. Modern Love Songs. Faraah Nuur. TTY
Flash—The Fireman's Story. Will Carleton. BBV; PoRL
Flashing and golden pageant of California, The. Walt Whitman. *Fr.* Song of the Redwood-Tree. HT
Flashing of an arc that bright and briefly, The. Flying Fish. Katherine Kelley Taylor. EtS
Flashlight, A/ looking through the empty. Brain. Coleman Barks. *Fr.* Body Poems. QAH
Flash-Lights. Mary Aldis. NP
Flat as to an eagle's eyes. The Nuptials of Attila, *abr.* George Meredith. PeVV
Flat on the bank I parted. The Trout. John Montague. NMP; OPoP
Flat on the grey steel bulkhead arch her curves. Pin-up Girl. Louis O. Coxe. WAP
Flat One, A. W. D. Snodgrass. AmPC; AP; LiTM (1970 ed.); NePoEA-2; PoCh
Flat River Girl. *Unknown.* *See* Jack Haggerty.
Flat rock is the best for taking off, A. A Swim off the Rocks. Howard Moss. TDP
Flathouse Roof, The. Nathalia Crane. YT
Flattered Flying Fish, The. E. V. Rieu. PDV; ShM
Flattered Lightning Bug, The. Don Marquis. *Fr.* Archy and Mehitabel. StPo
Flatterer (like a Wrastler) stoupeth low, A. Of a Flatterer. John Davies of Hereford. *Fr.* Wit's Bedlam. SiCE
Flattery. Swift. TreFT
("'Tis an old maxim in the schools.") PV
Flaunt of the sunshine I need not your bask. Song of Myself, XL. Walt Whitman. TrGrPo
Flavia the least and slightest toy. Written on [*or* in] the Leaves of a [White] Fan. Francis Atterbury. SeCL; SeEP
Flavia's a Wit, has too much sense to pray. Characters of Women: Flavia, Atossa, and Cloe. Pope. *Fr.* Moral Essays: Epistle II. OBEC
Flavius, If Your Girl Friend. Catullus, *tr. fr. Latin by* Horace Gregory. ErPo
Flavor the speaking of this one. Not to Forget Miss Dickinson. Marshall Schacht. LiTM
Flawless His Heart. James Russell Lowell. *Fr.* Ode for the Fourth of July, 1876. MC; PAH
Flaws cling to flesh as dews cling to a rose. Fantasy on the Resurrection. Vassar Miller. PoDB; ToPo
Flax. Ivan Alekseyevich Bunin, *tr. fr. Russian by* Babette Deutsch *and* Avrahm Yarmolinsky. AWP; JAWP; WBP
Flax Flower, The. Mary Howitt. PRWS
Fle fro the pres and dwelle with sothefastnesse. *See* Flee from the press. . .
Flea, The. John Donne. AnAnS-1; ATP; CABA; CBEP; EnLP; ForPo; HoPM; LiTB; LiTG; LiTL; MaMe; MePo; PAn; Po; PoAn; ReEn; ReIE; SCEP-1; SeCP; SeCV-1; SiTL; TDP; TrGrPo; TuPP
Flea, The. Roland Young. PoPl; WaKn; WhC
(Happy Bounding Flea, The.) SiTL
Flea and a fly got caught [*or* flew up] in a flue, A. The Flea and the Fly. *Unknown.* FaPON; WhC
Flea and a fly in a flue, A. Limerick. *Unknown.* GoTP; LiBL; LiTG; TiPo (1959 ed.); WhC
Fleas, The. Augustus De Morgan. *See* Great Fleas.
Fleckno, an English Priest at Rome. Andrew Marvell. MaMe; SeEP
Fled are those times, when, in harmonious strains. George Crabbe. *Fr.* The Village. PoSa
Fled is the blasted verdure of the fields. James Thomson. *Fr.* The Seasons: Autumn. OAEP
Fled is the swiftness of all the white-footed ones. Elegy. Joseph Auslander. MAP; MoAmPo (1942 ed.); NP; TrJP
Fledgling Bard and the Poetry Society, The, *much abr.* George Reginald Margetson. BANP
Fledgling Robin, A. Leonard Feeney. JKCP (1926 ed.)
Fledglings. Thomas Lake Harris. AA
Flee from the crowd and dwell with truthfulness. Ballade of Good Counsel, *mod.* Chaucer. TrGrPo
Flee from [*or* Fle fro] the press [*or* pres] and dwell[e] with soothfastness. Balade de Bon Conseyl [*or* Ballad of Good Counsel *or* Truth]. Chaucer. ACP; AWP; BEL; CAW; CBEP; GoBC; LiTG; MaPo; MeEL; MyFE; NoP; PAn; PoIE; PoLi; TrGrPo; ViBoPo
Flee on Your Donkey. Anne Sexton. NYBP
Fleece, The, *sels.* John Dyer.
"Ah gentle shepherd, thine the lot to tend," *fr.* Bk. I. PoEL-3
British Commerce, *fr.* Bk. IV. OBEC
English Weather, *fr.* Bk. I. OBEC
(English Fog, The.) TrGrPo
Nation's Wealth, A, *fr.* Bk. III. OBEC
Wool Trade, The, *fr.* Bk. III. OBEC; SeCePo
Fleeing from threatened flood, they sailed. The First Invasion of Ireland. John Montague. NMP; OPoP
Flees he tok and goth to Bote, The. John Gower. *Fr.* Confessio Amantis: Jason and Medea. AtBAP
Fleet and fair. Gazelles and Unicorn. John Gray. *Fr.* The Long Road. ChTr
Fleet astronomer can bore, The. Vanity [*or* Vanitie] (1). George Herbert. EP; MaMe; MePo; NoP; ReEn; SCEP-1; SeCV-1
Fleet at Santiago, The. Charles E. Russell. MC; PAH
Fleet, fleet and few, ay, fleet the moments fly. Two Sonnet-Songs, II. Frank T. Marzials. VA
Fleet ships encountering on the high sea. Good Ships. John Crowe Ransom. TPM
Fleet Street. Arthur Adams. BoAu
Fleet Street. Shane Leslie. OnYI
Fleet Street! Fleet Street! Fleet Street in the morning. A Song of Fleet Street. Alice Werner. HBV
Fleet with flags arrayed, A. A Ballad of the French Fleet. Longfellow. AA; HBV; MC; PAH
Fleeting life is a human pen. Human Pens. Stanley Elster Wilkin. SoP
Fleeting Restlessness. Juana de Ibarbourou, *tr. fr. Spanish by* Elizabeth du Gué Trapier. LiTW
Fleggit Bride, The. "Hugh MacDiarmid." OxBS
Flemish Madonna, A. Charles Wharton Stork. HBMV
Flesh. Mary Fullerton. PoAu-1
Flesh, The. Tiroux Yamanaka, *tr. fr. Japanese by* Katue Kitasono. LiTW
Flesh and the Spirit, The. Anne Bradstreet. AmP; AmPP; AnAmPo; AnFE; AP; APA; CoAnAm; LiTA; MAmP; NePA; OxBA; SCAP
Flesh, I have knocked at many a dusty door. Sonnet. John Masefield. GTSL; LiTM; MoBrPo; SeCePo
Flesh is sad, alas, The! and all the books are read. Sea-Wind. Stéphane Mallarmé, *tr. by* Arthur Symons. AWP; JAWP; SyP; WBP
Flesh is sad, alas, The, and I've read all the books. Sea Winds. Stéphane Mallarmé, *tr. by* Patricia Terry. OnPM
Flesh is sad but there are books unread, The. Charles Madge. *Fr.* Poem by Stages. BoSA
Flesh Is Weak, The. Stanton A. Coblentz. PoMa
Flesh-Scraper, The. Andrew Young. ELU
Flesh will heal and pain will fade. Claire Richcreek Thomas. PoToHe (new ed.)
Fletcher, though some call it thy fault, that wit. Upon the Dramatick Poems of Mr. John Fletcher. William Cartwright. OBS
Fleur de Lys. Rayner Heppenstall. WaP
Fleurette. Robert W. Service. TIHL
Flickering of incessant rain. Irradiations, V [VII]. John

Gould Fletcher. AnFE; APA; MAP; MAPA; NePA; TwAmPo
Flickering-sputtering-speaking-stuttering-strutting. Visions. . . Leaders. Clarence Franklin. BF
Flies. Dorothy Aldis. UTS
Flies, The. Merrill Moore. AnAmPo; AnEnPo
Flies in the buttermilk, skip to my Lou. Skip to My Lou. *Unknown.* TrAS
Flies on Shit. Quincy Troupe. WSL
Flies walk on ceilings. Flies. Dorothy Aldis. UTS
Flight. Madison Cawein. AA
Flight, The. C. Day Lewis. *Fr.* A Time to Dance. FaBoMo; MoVE, *longer sel.*
(Flight to Australia, *longer sel.*) CMoP; ShBV-3
Flight. Hazel Hall. AnAmPo; MAP; MoAmPo (1942 ed.)
Flight. Barbara Howes. NYBP
Flight. George Johnston. WHW
Flight, The. Lloyd Mifflin. AA; AnAmPo; HBV
Flight, The. Theodore Roethke. *Fr.* The Lost Son. TrGrPo (rev. ed.)
Flight. James Tate. OCS
Flight, The. Sara Teasdale. BoLP; HBMV; MAP; MoAmPo; NP; WHA
Flight. Harold Vinal. FaPON; FiSC; GA; MPB; WaKn
Flight. William Walden. NYTB
Flight. Lawrence Whistler. POTE
Flight from Glory, A. Eugene Lee-Hamilton. VA
Flight from the Convent, The. Theodore Tilton. AA
Flight into Darkness. Ralph Gustafson. PeCV
Flight into Egypt, The. W. H. Auden. *Fr.* For the Time Being. OAEP (2d ed.); OxBA
Flight into Egypt, The. Longfellow. *Fr.* Christus; a Mystery, Pt. II. OBVV
Flight into Egypt, The. Peter Quennell. LiTB; LiTM
Flight into Egypt, The. Robert Southwell. MeP
Flight into Egypt, The. *Unknown.* *Fr.* Cursor Mundi. CoBE
Flight is but the preparative. The Vision. Thomas Traherne. PeRV
Flight of Love. Shelley. *See* Lines: "When the lamp is shattered."
Flight of Malzah, The. Charles Heavysege. *Fr.* Saul, a Drama. VA
Flight of the Arrow, The. Richard Henry Stoddard. AA
(Arrow, The.) MaRV
Flight of the Birds, The. Edmund Clarence Stedman. GN
Flight of the Duchess, The, *sels.* Robert Browning. PCH
Gypsies.
North Country, The.
Flight of the Earls, The. *Unknown, tr. fr. Early Modern Irish by* Robin Flower. AnIL
Flight of the Geese, The. Sir Charles G. D. Roberts. PeCV; VA
Flight of the Goddess, The. Thomas Bailey Aldrich. HBV
Flight of the Heart, The. Dora Read Goodale. AA
Flight of the Roller-Coaster. Raymond Souster. ACV; PeCV; WHW
Flight of the Sparrows. Marya Zaturenska. TPM
Flight of the Spirit. Felicia Dorothea Hemans. Sonn
Flight of the War-Eagle, The. Obadiah Cyrus Auringer. AA
Flight of the Wild Geese. William Ellery Channing. PFY
Flight of Wild Geese, A. Harold Stewart. MoAuPo
Flight of Youth, The. Richard Henry Stoddard. AA; HBV; MaRV; OQP
(There Are Gains for All Our Losses.) OTD
Flight-Sergeant Foster flattened Gloucester. Paul Dehn. PV
Flight Shot, A. Maurice Thompson. AA; AnAmPo
Flight to Australia. C. Day Lewis. *See* Flight, The.
Flight to the City. William Carlos Williams. AnAmPo
Flighting for Duck. William Empson. MoPo
Flights. Robert Mezey. TDP
Fling forth the triple-colored flag to dare. The Need of the Hour. Edwin Markham. PaA; PAL
Fling it from mast and steeple. Our Flag. Margaret Elizabeth Sangster. PEDC
Fling out the banner! let it float. The Banner of the Cross. George Washington Doane. BePJ
Flinging its arc of silver bubbles, quickly shifts the moon. Down the Mississippi, III: Full Moon. John Gould Fletcher. HT; LiTA; NP
Flint and the Steel, The. Tomás de Iriarte, *tr. fr. Spanish.* BoChLi
Flintlike, her feet struck. Night Walk [*or* Hardcastle Crags]. Sylvia Plath. GoYe; NYBP
Flippantly/ In the cinemas past sleep. Before Dawn. Horace Hamilton. NYBP
Flirt, The. W. H. Davies. EnLoPo
Flitch of Dunmow, The. James Carnegie, Earl of Southesk. HBV; VA
Flitting, The, *sel.* John Clare.
"I've left my own old home of homes." OBRV
Flo was fond of Ebenezer. The Tides of Love. T. A. Daly. InMe; PoPl; WhC; YaD
Float, little bark, down yonder stream. Drifting. John Francis O'Donnell. IrPN
Floated in the cove. The Boat. Robert Kelly. CoPo
Floating, a floating, A. The Night Bird [*or* A Myth]. Charles Kingsley. GN; OTPC (1946 ed.); VA
Floating, face up, on the open. Queer's Song. Richard Howard. *Fr.* Gaiety. ErPo
Floating Island, The. Ruth Miller. BoSA
Floating Island, The, *sel.* William Strode.
Song: "My limbs I will fling," *fr.* I, iii. SeCL
Floating Old Man, The. Edward Lear. *See* There was an old man in a boat.
Floating with your head back. Choosing. Coleman Barks. QAH
Flock of Evening, The. Odell Shepard. HBMV
Flock of crows high from the Northland flies, A. Autumn. Detlev von Liliencron. AWP; JAWP; WBP
Flock of Guinea Hens Seen from a Car, A. Eudora Welty. NYBP
Flock of keys I had feeding out of my hand, A. Improvisation. Boris Pasternak. Po
Flock of merry singing-birds were sporting in the grove, A. The O'Lincoln [*or* O'Lincon] Family. Wilson Flagg. HBV; HBVY; OTPC
Flock of sheep that leisurely pass by, A. To Sleep. Wordsworth. BoLiVe; EnRP; EPN; GBV; GTBS; GTBS-D; GTBS-P; GTBS-W; GTSE; GTSL; HBV; InPo; MBW-2; MyFE; OBRV; PoFS; ShBV-4; Sonn; TrGrPo; ViBoPo
Flodden. Sir Walter Scott. *Fr.* Marmion, VI. FOL; PoFr
(Battle, The.) EnRP; PoEL-4
("But as they left the dark'ning heath.") ELP
Flodden Field. *Unknown.* ESPB
Floella. *Unknown.* *See* Jealous Lover, The.
Flogged Child. Joseph Joel Keith. FiSC
Flood. Ethel Anderson. NeLNL
Flood. Mary Grant Charles. GoYe
Flood. James Joyce. MoBrPo
Flood, The. Ovid, *tr. fr. Latin by* Dryden. *Fr.* Metamorphoses, I. ChTr
Flood, The. Andrew Young. ChMP
Flood of Years, The. Bryant. AA
Flood Tide. Stephen Vincent Benét. PFY
Flood-Tide, The. E. J. Pratt. CBV
Floodtide. Askia Muhammad Touré. PoNe (1970 ed.)
Flood-tide below me! [*or* Flood-tide of the river, flow on!] I see [*or* watch] you face to face! Crossing Brooklyn Ferry. Walt Whitman. AmePo; AmPo; AmPP; AP; ATP; CABA; CABL; CoBA; DiPo; LiTA; MAmP; MWA-1; PoIE
Flood was down in the Wilga swamps, three feet over the mud, The. How the Fire Queen Crossed the Swamp. Will H. Ogilvie. PoAu-1
Flooded fold of sarcenet, A. The End of Desire. Hugh McCrae. BoAV; MoAuPo
Floods and gales. Et Cetera. Dee Walker. GoYe
Floods Clap Their Hands, The. Psalms, XCVIII, Bible, *O.T.* TrGrPo
(O Sing unto the Lord a New Song.) TrJP
(Sing unto Jehovah.) BLRP
(Sing unto the Lord.) StaSt
Floods come o'er the meadow leas, The. Song. John Clare. PeER
Floods of tears well from my deepest heart, The. Elegy. Immanuel di Roma. TrJP
Flood-Time on the Marshes. Evaleen Stein. AA
Flooer o the Gean. George Campbell Hay. OxBS
Floor Is Dirty, The. Edward Field. NeAP
(Dirty Floor, The.) CoAP

Floorless Room, The. Gelett Burgess. *See* I Wish That My Room Had a Floor.
Flora MacDonald and the King, *with music*. *Unknown*. BFSS
Flora hath been all about. Pastoral I. Nicholas Breton. *Fr.* The Passionate Shepherd. TuPP
Flora's Flower. *Unknown*, *tr. fr. Latin by* John Addington Symonds. UnTE
Flora's Lamentable Passion. *Unknown*. CoMu
Florence. Walter Savage Landor. SeCePo
Florence. Robert Lowell. NoP
Florence; Design for a City. Elizabeth Jennings. HaMV
Florence MacCarthy's Farewell to His English Love [*or* Lover]. Aubrey Thomas De Vere. IrPN; NBM
Florence Vane. Philip Pendleton Cooke. AA; HBV
Florent and the Loathly Hag. John Gower, *tr. fr. Middle English by* Muriel Bowden. *Fr.* Confessio Amantis. MeEV
Florida. Elizabeth Bishop. AmP; TwCP
Florida Hillocks. Kenward Elmslie. ANYP
Florida Road Workers. Langston Hughes. GoSl; MAP; MoAmPo
Florin to the willing guard, A. The Rosy Bosom'd Hours. Coventry Patmore. EnLoPo
Florist Rose, The. Robert Graves. AtBAP; CBV
Flos Florum. Arthur Joseph Munby. VA
Flos Lunae. Ernest Dowson. OBMV; PeVV; ViPP
Floss won't save you from an abyss. Emily Dickinson. LiTA; NePA
Flounder, born erect, preversely turns, The. Fish-eye. Milton Bracker. NYTB
Flour-barrels, cracker-boxes, cans, The. The Wolf. Donald Davidson. AnAmPo
Flour Fritters. *Unknown, tr. fr. Chinese by* Isaac Taylor Headland PCH
Flour [*or* Flower] of England, fruit of Spain. Mother Goose. HBV; HBVY; OTPC; OxNR; PPL; RIS; SiTL
Flourishing and gaily springing wight, The. His Admonition to Greene's Companions. Gabriel Harvey. *Fr.* Greene's Memorial, or, Certain Funeral Sonnets. ReIE
Flow down, cold rivulet, to the sea. A Farewell. Tennyson. HBV; OTPC; PoVP; RIS
Flow Forth, Abundant Tears. *Unknown*. EnRePo
Flow Gently, Sweet Afton. Burns. AWP; BEL; EnLit; FaBoBe; FaFP; HBV; InPo; JAWP; TOP; WBP
(Afton Water.) BoNaP; CEP; EiPP; ILP; InP; OAEP; PG; PoIE
(Sweet Afton.) BoLiVe; CABA; EnLi-2; EnRP; GTBS-W; LiTB; LiTG; LiTL; MeWo; SiTL; TreF; TrGrPo
Flow [*or* Flowe], my teares! fau [*or* falle] from your springs. Lachrimae. *Unknown*. AtBAP; SeCSL
Flow Not So Fast. *Unknown*. EnRePo; QFR; ReIE; ViBoPo
Flow, O My Tears! *Unknown*. ElL
Flow on forever, in thy glorious robe. Niagara. Lydia Huntley Sigourney. AmLP
Flowe, my teares! falle from your springes. *See* Flow, my teares! fau from your springs.
Flower, The. Lee Wilson Dodd. HBMV
Flower, The. George Herbert. AnAnS-1; AtBAP; AWP; BoC; BWP; ELP; EP; FaBoEn; InPo; MaMe; MeP; MePo; NoP; OBS; OxBoCh; PoAn; PoEL-2; ReEn; SCEP-1; SeCP; SeCV-1
"And now in age I bud again," *sel.* CBEP
Flower, The. John Holmes. LiTL
Flower, The. *At. to* Samuel Speed. OxBoCh; SeCL
Flower, The. Tennyson. HBV; InP; PoVP; VA
Flower, The. Robert Penn Warren. PoPl
Flower, The. Henrik Wergeland, *tr. fr. Norwegian by* Charles Wharton Stork. LiTW
Flower, A,/ A willow. The Poem of Ten "Ones." Hô P'ei Yü. FlW
Flower Arrangement. Samuel Yellen. NYTB
Flower-Cart Man, The. Rachel Field. OCS; SiSoSe; SoPo
Flower Chorus. *Unknown*, *wr. at. to* Emerson. BoTP; PCH, 2 *sts.*
Flower-fed Buffaloes, The. Vachel Lindsay. AmFN; ATP; ChTr; CMoP; ExPo; FaPON; GoJo; LoBV; LoGBV; MAP; MoAmPo; MPB; PoIE; PoSa; PPON; RePo; ShBV-1; ThWaDe; WaKn
Flower for a Professor's Garden of Verses. Irwin Edman. InMe
Flower Given to My Daughter, A. James Joyce. BoPe; OBMV; PoPl; ReMP
Flower Herding on Mount Monadnock. Galway Kinnell. NaP
Flower—I never fancied; jewel—I profess you! Magical Nature. Robert Browning. PoVP
Flower in the Crannied Wall. Tennyson. BBV (1951 ed.); BEL; BoLiVe; BoNaP; CBV; DiPo; EnLi-2 (1949 ed.); EnLit; FaBV; FaFP; FaPON; GTBS-W; InP; LiTB; LiTG; MaRV; MaVP; MC; MCCG; MPB; OQP; OTPC (1946 ed.); OuHeWo; PoIE; PoPl; PoPo; PoVP; PTK; TOP; TreFS; TrGrPo; TRV; VA; ViPo; WGRP; YAT; YT
(Fragment.) BLPA; NeHB
Flower in the Sea, The. Malcolm Cowley. NP
Flower Is Looking, A. Harold Monro. Strange Meetings, X. MoBrPo
Flower Market, The. Po Chü-i, *tr. fr. Chinese by* Arthur Waley. PPON; WoL
Flower of Beauty, The. George Darley. *See* Song: "Sweet in her green dell the flower of beauty slumbers."
Flower of England, fruit of Spain. *See* Flour of England, fruit of Spain.
Flower of Exile. Max Dunn. BoAV
Flower of Flame, The, *sel.* Robert Nichols.
"Before I woke I knew her gone." OBMV
Flower of Liberty, The. Oliver Wendell Holmes. DD; HBVY; MC; PoRL
Flower of Love. Claude McKay. BALP
Flower of Mullein, A. Lizette Woodworth Reese. MAP; MoAmPo; NeMA
Flower of Old Japan, The, sel. Alfred Noyes.
Epilogue: "Carol, every violet has." MoBrPo
Flower of "The Living Desert." Mary Winter. NYTB
Flower of the dust am I: for dust will flower. Eagle Sonnets, VII. Clement Wood. HBMV
Flower of the medlar. A Pastoral. Théophile Marzials. HBV; VA
Flower of the moon! The Night-blooming Cereus. Harriet Monroe. AA
Flower of the shining Summer. The Pearly Everlasting. Ernest Fewster. CaP
Flower of This Purple Dye. Shakespeare. *Fr.* a Midsummer Night's Dream, III, ii. CTC
Flower of Virtue is the heart's content, The. Sonnet of Virtue. Folgore da San Geminiano. AWP; JAWP; WBP
Flower of youth, in the ancient frame. Judith. William Young. AA
Flower petals tall. From Summer Hours. Albert Samain. AWP; JAWP; WBP
Flower-Seller, The. Eleanor Farjeon. BoTP; PCH
Flower-Seller, The. William Young. *Fr.* Wishmakers' Town. AA
Flower-seller's fat, The, and she wears a big shawl! The Flower-Seller. Eleanor Farjeon. BoTP; PCH
Flower-strewn Graves. Samuel Francis Smith. MaRV
Flower, that I hold in my hand. Tuberose. Louis James Block. AA
Flower that smiles to-day, The. Mutability. Shelley. BEL; EnLi-2; EnLit; EnRP; EPN; FaBoEn; HBV; MERP; NoP; OBNC; PoPo; TOP; ViBoPo; YAT
Flower Tokens. *Unknown*. *See* Hearts and Lace Paper.
Flower unblown: a book unread, A. The New Year. Horatio Nelson Powers. OQP; PoRL; PoToHe
Flower was offered to me, A. My Pretty Rose Tree. Blake. *Fr.* Songs of Experience. PoeP
Flowering almond tree. Almond Blossom in Wartime. Stephen Spender. ACV
Flowering Currant. Patrick MacDonogh. ErPo
Flowering Forest, The. Edith Sitwell. SiSw
Flowering Past, The. Malcolm Lowry. NYTB
Flowering Urn, The. Laura Riding. FaBoMo; LiTA
Flowering without End. Stefan Zweig, *tr. fr. German by* Eden Paul *and* Cedar Paul. *Fr.* Jeremiah. TrJP
Flowers. Harry Behn. FaPON
Flowers. Thomas Hood. HBV; OTPC; VA
Flowers, The. Kipling. OBVV
Flowers. Longfellow. DD, *abr*; HBV
Flowers. Stéphane Mallarmé, *tr. fr. French by* John Gray. SyP
Flowers, The. William Brighty Rands. OBEV (1st ed.); OBVV
Flowers. Arthur Rimbaud, *tr. fr. French by* Oliver Bernard. FlW

Flowers ("Out, Alas!"). Shakespeare. *Fr.* The Winter's Tale, IV, iii. UnPo (1st ed.)
Flowers, The. Robert Louis Stevenson. FaPON; MPB
Flowers, The. *Unknown.* OTPC (1923 ed.)
Flowers all are sleeping, The. Little Sandman's Song. *Unknown.* RIS
Flowers are shadowed, the palace darkens. A Night Vigil in the Left Court of the Palace. Tu Fu. LiTW
Flowers by the Sea. William Carlos Williams. AmLP; AnEnPo; CMoP; ExPo; GoJo; MoAB; MoAmPo; Po; PoeP; SeCeV (1967 ed.)
Flowers: Calabria. George Amabile. YAP
Flowers do better here than peas and beans. All Things Are a Flowing. R. P. Blackmur. TwAmPo
Flowers: For Heliodora. Meleager, *tr. fr. Greek by* Dudley Fitts. SiSw
Flowers for Luis Bunuel. Stuart Z. Perkoff. NeAP
Flowers for our dead! For Our Dead [*or* Memorial Day]. Clinton Scollard. HH; PEDC
Flowers for the Altar. Digby Mackworth Dolben. GoBC
Flowers for the Brave. Celia Thaxter. OHIP
Flowers for you, O Glory's son, war's prey! Unknown Soldier. Alta Booth Dunn. PGD
Flowers from clods of clay and mud? A Mystery. "Gabriel Setoun." PPL
Flowers from the earth have arisen, The. Nature's Easter Music. Lucy Larcom. OHIP
Flowers hast thou in thyself, and foliage. Sonnet: To His Lady Joan, of Florence. Guido Cavalcanti. AWP; JAWP; WBP
Flowers have gone to bed, The. The Sandman. *Unknown.* BOL
Flowers I pass have eyes that look at me, The. Man in Harmony with Nature. Jones Very. AP
Flowers I Would Bring. Aubrey Thomas De Vere. HBV; IrPN; VA
Flowers in a Garden. Christopher Smart. ThGo
Flowers in a Meadow, The. Frances Cornford. ThGo
Flowers in bud on the trees, The. On the Death of a New Born Child. Mei Yao Ch'en. NaP
Flowers in the Valley. *Unknown.* AtBAP; OnMSP; OxBoLi; SiSw
Flowers in the ward. For a Hemiplegic. Walter Lowenfels. WOW
Flowers left thick at nightfall in the wood. In Memoriam: Easter 1915. Edward Thomas. GTBS-P; PoIE
Flower's Name, The. Robert Browning. Garden Fancies, I. ACV; CTC; EnLi-2 (1949 ed.); GTBS-D; HBV
"Flowers nodding gaily, scent in air." A Duet. T. Sturge Moore. OBEV; OBVV
Flowers of Apollo, The. Hildegarde Flanner. HBMV
Flowers of Darkness. Frank Marshall Davis. AmNP; IDB; PoNe
Flowers of Perdita, The. Shakespeare. *Fr.* The Winter's Tale, IV, iii. FiP
(Flowers of Middle Summer.) YeAr
("Here's flowers for you.") PoG
Flowers of Politics, The, I ("This is the huge dream of us that we are heroes"). Michael McClure. NeAP
Flowers of Politics, The, II ("Only what is heroic and courageious moves our blood"). Michael McClure. NeAP
Flowers of Sion, *sels.* William Drummond of Hawthornden.
Change Should Breed Change. OBEV; OxBoCh
"Good that never satisfies the mind, A." Sonn
Flowers of Snow. Tsurayuki, *tr. fr. Japanese by* Basil Hall Chamberlain. OnPM
Flowers of the field, The. "The Hawthorn Hath a Deathly Smell." Walter de la Mare. AtBAP; BrPo
Flowers of the Forest, The. Alison Cockburn. OBEC
Flowers of the Forest, The. Jane Elliot. CH; EiPP; FaBoCh; GoTS; OBEC; OxBS
(Lament for Flodden, A.) GTBS; GTBS-D; GTBS-P; GTBS-W; GTSE; GTSL; HBV; LiTG; OBEV; ShBV-3; WePo
Flowers of the Sea. Yasuhide, *tr. fr. Japanese by* Basil Hall Chamberlain. OnPM
Flowers of the willow-herb are wool. Seed-Time. George Meredith. VP
Flowers rejoice when night is done. Matins. Henry van Dyke. MaRV
Flowers shall hang upon the palls. Death. John Clare. ERoP-2; GTBS-P; PeER
Flowers—that have died upon my Sweet. A Song of Angiola in Heaven. Austin Dobson. HBV
Flowers that in thy garden rise, The. Song. Sir Henry Newbolt. FaBoTw
Flowers there are, partaking. Tapers. Frances Angevine Gray. FiSC
Flowers through the window. Nantucket. William Carlos Williams. OxBA; TDP
Flowers turned to stone! Not all the botany. Kenneth Slessor. *Fr.* Five Visions of Captain Cook. PoAu-2
Flowers upon the rosemary spray, The. The Rosemary Spray. Luis de Góngora. AWP; LiTW
Flowers upon your lips and hands. Love Poem. Maurice James Craig. NeIP
Flowers whirl away, The. Prime Minister Kintsune, *tr. fr. Japanese by* Kenneth Rexroth. OnPJ
Flowers without Fruit. Cardinal Newman. EPN
Flowing robe of words you weave, The. The Lethal Thought. Mary Boyd Wagner. GoYe
Flowing Summer, The, *sels.* Charles Bruce. CaP
Attic, The.
Dreaming Trout, The.
Hayfield, The.
Flown Soul, The. George Parsons Lathrop. AA
Fluid the world flowed under us. The Automobile. Percy MacKaye. AnAmPo
Flush or Faunus. Elizabeth Barrett Browning. BoC; NBM
Flush with the pond the lurid furnace burned. The Steam Threshing-Machine. Charles Tennyson-Turner. OBNC; PoVP
Flushed with the hope of high desire. My Hero; to Robert Gould Shaw. Benjamin Brawley. BANP; PoNe
Flushing Meadows, 1939. Daniel Hoffman. CoPo
Flute, The. Hilali, *tr. fr. Persian by* Emerson. OnPM
Flute, A. Nobutsuna, *tr. fr. Japanese by* Asataro Miyamori. OnPM
Flute, The. Joseph Russell Taylor. AA
Flute, The; a Pastoral. José Maria de Heredia, *tr. fr. French by* Herbert C. Grierson. AWP
Flute begins to falter, to fidget, to fret, The. Evening Music. Kendrick Smithyman. AnNZ
Flute-Man, The. Mary Oliver. TDP
Flute of Daphnis, The. Edward Cracroft Lefroy. Echoes from Theocritus, XXIII. AWP; OBVV
Flute of May, The. Harry Woodbourne. GoYe
Flute of the Lonely, The. Vachel Lindsay. CrMA
Flute Players. Jean-Joseph Rabéarivelo, *tr. fr. French by* Langston Hughes. PBA
Flute-Priest Song for Rain, *sel.* Amy Lowell.
"Whistle under the water." UnS
Flutesong willow winding weather. World War. Richard Eberhart. WaP
Fluttered Wings. Christina Rossetti. VA
Fluttering Leaves. Rodney Bennett. BoTP
Fluttering spread thy purple pinions. Lines by a Person of Quality. *At. to* Pope *and to* Swift. InMe; NA
Fluttering swarm, A. Blossoms and Storm. Sadaiye. OnPM
Flux of night is power and will, slid, The. Nightflight and Sunrise. Geoffrey Dutton. BoAV
Fly, The. Philip Ayres. CavP
Fly, The. Blake. *Fr.* Songs of Experience. BoLiVe; CBEP; DiPo; EiPP; EnL; GoTP; MaPo; OTPC (1923 ed.); PoSa; TrGrPo; YAT
Fly, The. Walter de la Mare. MemP
Fly, The. Barnabe Googe. *See* Once Musing as I Sat.
Fly, The. Ogden Nash. FaPON
Fly, The. William Oldys. *See* On a Fly Drinking Out of His Cup.
Fly, The. Karl Shapiro. CoBA; LiTM; MiAP; MoVE; NePA; TwAmPo
Fly, The. Theodore Tilton. RIS
Fly and a flea in a flue, A. *See* Flea and a fly in a flue.
Fly away, away, swallow. Full Valleys. F. R. Scott. CaP
Fly away, fly away over the sea. The Swallow. Christina Rossetti. *Fr.* Sing-Song. CoBE; GoTP; OTPC (1946 ed.); PoVP;StVeCh; SUS
Fly-away Horse, The. Eugene Field. GoTP; PTK
Fly Back to Christ. Charles Wesley. BePJ
Fly Caught in a Cobweb, A. Richard Lovelace. SCEP-2; SeCP
Fly down, Death: Call me. Madboy's Song. Muriel Rukeyser. MoAmPo; TrJP

Fly, envious Time, till thou run out thy race. On Time. Milton. BoC; BWP; CABA; DiPo; GTBS-W; LiTB; LiTG; LoBV; MaPo; MeP; MePo; OBEV; OBS; OxBoCh; PoE; PoPo; SeCeV; StP; TRV
Fly far from me. Iena's Song. Charles Mair. *Fr.* Tecumseh. VA
Fly-fishing. John Gay. *Fr.* Rural Sports. SD
Fly, fly, my friends, I have my death wound; fly. Astrophel and Stella, XX. Sir Philip Sidney. FCP; MaPo; PAn; ReIE; SiPS; TuPP
Fly, fly! The foe advances fast. Henry Cotton. EG
Fly, fly, you happy shepherds, fly! Philira [*or* Song]. Sir John Vanbrugh. *Fr.* The Provoked Wife. SeCL; SeEP
Fly from the press and dwell with sothfastness. *See* Flee fro the prees...
Fly from the World. *Unknown.* NCEP
Fly Hence Shadows. John Ford. *Fr.* The Lover's Melancholy, V, i. OnPM; SeCL; ViBoPo
(Dawn.) OBEV
(Song: "Fly hence, shadows, that do keep.") LoBV
Fly in December. Robert Wallace. NYBP
Fly, Love, That Art so Sprightly. *Unknown.* NCEP
Fly, merry muse, unto that merry town. Ad Musam. Sir John Davies. ReIE; SiCE
Fly, Muse, thy wonted themes, nor longer seek. If Pope Had Written "Break, Break, Break." J. C. Squire. CenHV
Fly, Roadster, fly! Song for a Blue Roadster. Rachel Field. FaPON; TiPo (1950 ed.)
Fly Soft, Ye Gentle Hours. *Unknown.* SeCL
Fly to her heart, hover about her heart. Her Heart. Bartholomew Griffin. Fidessa, More Chaste than Kind, XXIII. MeWo; ReEn; ReIE; SiCE; TrGrPo; TuPP
Fly to Jesus. Charles Wesley. BePJ
"Fly to the mountain! Fly!" Conemaugh. Elizabeth Stuart Phelps Ward. PAH
Fly, white butterflies, out to sea. White Butterflies [*or* Envoi]. Swinburne. FaPON; GoJo; MPB; OTPC; PCD; PCH; PDV; StaSt; SUS; UTS
"Fly with me then to all's and the world's end." The World's End. William Empson. CoBMV; MoVE; ToPo
Flycatchers. Robert Bridges. MoVE; POTE
Flye, flye, flye from the world, O fly, thou poor distrest. Fly from the World. *Unknown.* NCEP
Flye That Flew into My Mistris Her Eye, A. Thomas Carew. AnAnS-2
Flyer's Fall. Wallace Stevens. MoAB
Flying. Kaye Starbird. PDV
Flying. J. M. Westrup. BoTP
Flying above California. Thom Gunn. ToPo
Flying Blossoms. W. H. Davies. BrPo
Flying Bum, The: 1944. William Plomer. DTC
Flying Cloud, The. *Unknown.* ABF, *with music*; AmSS, *with music*; BaBo; IHA; ShS (2 *vers.*), *with music*; SoAmSa, *with music*; ViBoFo, *with music*
Flying Crooked. Robert Graves. FaBoMo; FIW; LiTM (rev. ed.); OA; TwCP
Flying Dutchman, The. Charles Godfrey Leland. PoMS
Flying Dutchman, The. A. M. Sullivan. EtS
Flying Dutchman, The, *with music. Unknown.* ShS
Flying Fish, The. Jack Cope. PeSA
Flying Fish. Mary McNeill Fenollosa. AA
Flying Fish, The. John Gray. ChTr; LoBV; OBNC
Flying Fish. J. Corson Miller. EtS
Flying Fish. Katherine Kelley Taylor. EtS
Flying Flowers. Mrs. Motherly. SAS
Flying,—flying beyond all lower regions. A Poet's Hope. William Ellery Channing. AmePo
Flying Foxes and Others. Kay Boyle. AnAmPo
Flying from Greece to see Moscow's dancing girl. Ciampino. Edwin Denby. ANYP
Flying in plane's rib. New York City. George Abbe. GoYe
Flying Inn, The, *sel.* G. K. Chesterton.
Wine and Water. ACP (1952 ed.); CenHV; FiBHP; GoBC; HBMV; InMe; LiTM; MoBrPo; ShBV-4; ViBoPo
Flying Islands of the Night, The, *sel.* James Whitcomb Riley.
Dwainie. AA
Flying Lesson, The. Petrarch, *tr. fr. Italian by* Agnes Tobin. Sonnets to Laura: To Laura in Death, LXXIV. CAW
Flying sea-bird mocked the floating dulse, The. The Sea-Weed. Elisabeth Cavazza Pullen. AA
Flying Tailor, The. James Hogg. Par
Flying to Christ. *Unknown.* SoP
Flying Trapeze, The. George Leybourne. *See* Man on the Flying Trapeze, The.
Flying Wheel, The. Katharine Tynan. WGRP
Flying word from here [there, *wr.*] and there, A. The Master. E. A. Robinson. AmP; GTBS-W; HBV; HH; InP; LiPo; LiTA; LiTG; LiTM (rev. ed.); MAP; MoAB; MoAmPo; NeMA; NP; OHIP; OTPC (1946 ed.); PaA; PFY; PoRL
Flynn of Virginia. Bret Harte. PTK
Flyting o'Life and Daith, The. Hamish Henderson. OxBS
Flyting of Dumbar and Kennedie, The, *sel.* William Dunbar.
"Iersch brybour baird, vyle beggar with thy brattis." AtBAP
Fo' a yeah or mo' on this roof I'se layed. The Signal Fire. Aeschylus. *Fr.* Agamemnon. CTC
Foal. Mary Britton Miller. PDV
Foal. Vernon Watkins. FaBoMo
Foam. *Unknown, tr. fr. Spanish by* Havelock Ellis. OnPM
Foam and Fangs. Walter Parke. BOHV
Foam of leaves applauds the crimson signal, A. House Plant. Winthrop Palmer. SiTL
Focus of eyes, focus of arrows. Sebastian. Gene Baro. PoDB
Focus of That Face, The. Edwin McNeill Poteat. ChIP
Foe at the Gates, The. John Dickson Bruns. PAH
Foe unconsecrated entered my courts, The. Lament to Nana of Erech. *Unknown.* LiTW
Foe Within, The. Longfellow. MaRV
Foeda Est in Coitu. Petronius Arbiter. *See* Doing a Filthy Pleasure Is.
Foes in plenty we shall meet. Hearts Courageous. John Oxenham. MaRV
Foes to our race! if ever ye have known. Critics. George Crabbe. PP
Foetus. Phyllis Haring. PeSA
Fog. Laurence Binyon. SyP
Fog, The. Robert P. Tristram Coffin. CrMA
Fog, The. W. H. Davies. OCS; TiPo (1959 ed.); WaKn
Fog. Louis Ginsberg. NeMA
Fog. Kenneth Patchen. NaP
Fog. John Reed. AnEnPo
Fog ("Fog comes, The/ On little cat feet"). Carl Sandburg. AmPP; AnEnPo; AP; BoChLi; CoBa; FaBV; FaFP; FaPON; GFA; GoTP; HBMV; FIW; LaNeLa; MAP; MCCG; MoAB; MoAmPo; MPB; NeMA; PoMa; PoPl; PoPo; PoRh; PTK; SoPo; SP; StVeCh; SUS; TiPo; TSW; WoL; YT
Fog comes in with a big sound, The. The Sounding Fog. Susan Nichols Pulsifer. PDV
Fog got him first. One, Two, Three. Samuel L. Albert. NePoAm-2
Fog is freezing on the trees and shrubs, The. White Dusk. Marion Margaret Boyd. HBMV
Fog rolls in across the fields of heather, The. New England Fog. Gertrude Callaghan. JKCP (1955 ed.)
Fog, the Magician. Melville Cane. MoSiPe
Foggy, Foggy Dew. *Unknown.* AS, *with music*; DTC; LiTB; LiTG; OxBoLi; PoG; SiTL
(Foggy Dew, The, *diff. vers.*) CoMu; ELP; UnTE (2 *vers.*)
(Weaver, The, *with music.*) AS
Fog-Horn. George Herbert Clarke. CaP
Fog-Horn. W. S. Merwin. NMP
Foghorn in Horror. Muriel Rukeyser. FiMAP
Foibles. Harold Bond. YAP
Foil, The. George Herbert. MaMe
Foil'd [*or* Foiled] by our fellow men, depress'd [*or* depressed], outworn. Immortality. Matthew Arnold. EPN; FiP; MaRV; PoVP
Foiled Reaper, The. William Kean Seymour. HBMV
Fold upon fold of light. Sunset. Edwin Muir. BoPe
Folded Flock, The. Wilfrid Meynell. CAW; GoBC; JKCP; TrPWD
Folded Power. Gladys Cromwell. HBMV; NP
Folded Skyscraper, A, *sel.* William Carlos Williams.
"Saloon is gone up the creek, The." AnAmPo
(Hemmed-in Males.) MoVE; PoRA (rev. ed.); PoSa
Fol-de-rol and riddle ma-ree. Spring Ring-Jingle. Michael Lewis. RIS
Folding a Shirt. Denise Levertov. NeBP
Folding the Flocks. John Fletcher. *See* Evening Song.
Foliage, *sel.* W. H. Davies.
Sweet Stay-at-Home. AtBAP; CH; GTBS; HBMV; POTE

Foliage. Felicia Dorothea Hemans. OBRV
Foliage of Vision. James Merrill. MoPo
Folk of the Air, The. W. B. Yeats. *See* Host of the Air, The.
Folk remedy, A. Skull. Coleman Barks. *Fr.* Body Poems. QAH
Folk Song: "At the boarding house where I live." *Unknown.* ShM
Folk-Song: "Back she came through the trembling dusk." Louis Untermeyer. HBV; MeWo
Folk Song: "Hat you loved, the damask-trimmed reed-hat, The." *Unknown, tr. fr. Japanese by* Arthur Waley. LiTW
Folk Song: "Swallow comes, The! She comes, she brings." *Unknown, tr. fr. Greek.* PCH
Folk Song from Fukushima. *Unknown, tr. fr. Japanese by* Geoffrey Bownas *and* Anthony Thwaite. FIW
Folk Songs. *Unknown, tr. fr. Spanish by* Havelock Ellis.
"Let the rich man fill his belly." LiTW; OnPM
"My father was a sailor." LiTW
(Sailors.) OnPM
(Spanish Folk Song.) AWP
Folk Tale. P. Mustapää, *tr. fr. Finnish by* Richard Impola. HW
Folk Tune. Richard Wilbur. AmFN; OnHM
Folk who lived in Shakespeare's day, The. Guilielmus Rex. Thomas Bailey Aldrich. AA; AnNE
Folk Wisdom. Thomas Kinsella. TwCP
Folks ain't got no right to censuah othah folks about dey habits. Accountability. Paul Laurence Dunbar. AnAmPo; PoLF; YaD
Folks and Me. Lucile Crites. WBLP
Folks at home half the time are thinkin' about dirt, The. Soap, the Oppressor. Burges Johnson. PoLF
Folks, I Give You Science! Al Graham. WhC
Folks Need a Lot of Loving. Strickland Gillilan. BLPA; MaRV; TRV; WBLP
(Need of Loving.) PoToHe
Folkways. Isabella Gardner. SiTL
Folkways of Sodom, The. "E. W." SiTL
Foller de Drinkin' Gou'd, *with music. Unknown.* ABF
Follow. Thomas Campion. *See* Follow Thy Fair Sun.
Follow a shadow [*or* shaddow], it still flies you. Song: That Women Are but Men's Shadows [*or* Follow a Shadow *or* The Shadow *or* Women Men's Shadows]. Ben Jonson. ALV; AtBAP; CBEP; EIL; EnLit; FaBoEn; HBV; LiTL; NoP; OBEV; OBS; PoIE; ReIE; SCEP-2; SeCP; ViBoPo; WBLP
Follow back from the gull's bright arc and the osprey's plunge. Water Ouzel. William H. Matchett. CoAP; NePoEA; NYBP; PoCh
Follow, follow. Thomas Campion. EnLoPo
Follow, follow me into the South. Ballad. Marjorie Allen Seiffert. HBMV
Follow Jesus. *Unknown.* STF
Follow Me! Eliza Lee Follen. PPL
Follow Me. Longfellow. PGD
"Follow Me." Joseph Fort Newton. OQP
Follow Me. John Oxenham. *See* Lord, I Would Follow.
Follow Me! Sheldon Shepard. ChIP
Follow Me! *Unknown.* SoP
"Follow Me 'Ome." Kipling. OAEP (2d ed.)
Follow my Bangalorey Man. *Unknown.* OxNR
Follow, poet, follow right. W. H. Auden. *Fr.* In Memory of W. B. Yeats. TRV
Follow That Stagecoach. Diane Wakoski. YAP
Follow the Christ. Tennyson. *Fr.* Idylls of the King: Gareth and Lynette. ChIP; MaRV
Follow the crowds to where the turnstiles click. The Game. Dannie Abse. PrWP
Follow the Gleam. Tennyson. Merlin and the Gleam, IX BBV; MaRV; OTPC (1946 ed.); PoRL; TreFT
Follow the Leader. Harry Behn. SoPo
Follow the long snake. Desert River. Patricia Benton. GoYe
Follow the ribs of my thought, lines. Cactus. Terence Heywood. BoSA
Follow Thy Fair Sun [Unhappy Shadow]. Thomas Campion. BoPe; BWP; CBEP; EIL; ELP; EnLi-1; EnLoPo; EnRePo; LiTB; LO; LoBV; NoP; OBSC; UnPo; ViBoPo
(Devotion.) OBEV
(Follow.) CH
(Followe Thy Faire Sunne.) AtBAP; PoEL-2; SiCE
(In Imagine Pertransit Homo.) GTSL
(Song from a Booke of Ayres, A.) BoW
Follow Your Saint [Follow with Accents Sweet]. Thomas Campion. AtBAP; CBEP; CLwM; EG; EIL; EnL; EnLoPo; EnRePo; EP; ExPo; FaBoEn; ForPo; InPo; LO; MeWo; NoP; OBSC; PAn; PoE; ReEn; ReIE; SeCePo; TrGrPo; TuPP; VaPo; ViBoPo
(Devotion, 2.) OBEV
Follow the bird in the long forest where it cried. In Her Song She Is Alone. Jon Swan. NYBP
Follower, A. Daisy Conway Price. ChIP
Following. Joseph Conder. SoP
Following. Henry W. Frost. SoP
Following across the moors a sound of bells. The Pansy and the Prayer-Book. Matilda Barbara Betham-Edwards. OBVV
Following Father Home. John Talman. SoP
Following forbidden streets. The Wraith-Friend. George Barker. OBMV
Following the Army to the North. Li-I. *tr. fr. Chinese by* Robert Payne. OnPM
Following the Sun. Jascha Kessler. AmPC
Followis How Dumbar Wes Desyr to Be ane Freir. William Dunbar. OAEP
Folly hath now turned out of door. Mandrake's Song. Thomas Lovell Beddoes. *Fr.* Death's Jest Book, I, i. NBM; PeER
Folly of Being Comforted, The. W. B. Yeats. AnIL; AnIV; BoPe; BrPo; BWP; GTBS; GTSL; MBW-2; NoP; Po; PoE; ViPo (1962 ed.)
Folly of Brown, The. W. S. Gilbert. InMe
Fond Affection, *with music. Unknown.* AS
Fond affection, hence, and leave me! Song. *At. to* Robert Parry. *Fr.* The Mirror of Knighthood. EIL
Fond credos, wooden ecstasies! The Stranger. Adrienne Rich. CoPo
Fond, frozen, first and only lover. Elegy. Louis Johnson. AnNZ
Fond love, deliver up thy bow. Ode to Cupid. Charles Cotton. CavP
Fond Love, No More. Thomas Forde. *Fr.* Love's Labyrinth. SeCL
Fond man, Musophilus, that thus dost spend. Poet and Critic. Samuel Daniel. *Fr.* Musophilus. OBSC; ReIE; SiCE; TuPP
Fond man, that canst beleeve her blood. Celia Bleeding, to the Surgeon. Thomas Carew. AnAnS-2; SeCP
Fond maydes, take warninge while you may. *Unknown.* SeCSL
Fond men! whose wretched care the life soon ending. Song. Phineas Fletcher. *Fr.* Brittain's Ida. EIL
Fond nymphs, from us true passion learn. In Derision of a Country Life. Edward Ravenscroft. *Fr.* The Italian Husband. SeCL
Fond scenes which delighted my youthful existence. The Exile's Departure. Whittier. CoBA
Fond woman, which would'st have thy husband die. Jealosie. John Donne. Elegies, I. AnAnS-1; MaMe
Fond words have oft been spoken to thee, Sleep. To Sleep. Wordsworth. Sonn
Fond Youth. Samuel Rogers. *Fr.* Human Life. OBRV
Fondly, too curious Nature, to adorn. On the Marriage of a Beauteous Young Gentlewoman with an Ancient Man. Francis Beaumont. LiTL; ViBoPo
Fone sayes, those mighty whiskers he do's weare. Upon Fone a School-Master, Epigram. Robert Herrick. AnAnS-2
Font in the Forest, The. Léonie Adams. CrMA
Fontenoy. Thomas Osborne Davis. HBV; OnYI
Fontenoy, 1745. Emily Lawless. AnIV; PoFr
Food. Marchette Chute. OCS
Food. Ruby Weyburn Tobias. OQP
Food and Drink. Louis Untermeyer. MAP; MoAmPo
Food for Fire, Food for Thought. Robert Duncan. NeAP
Food for Thought. Michael Lewis. RIS
Food of Love, The. Shakespeare. *See* If Music Be the Food of Love.
Fool, The. Padraic Pearse. OnYI
Fool—/ Killer lurks between the branches of every tree. The Book of Percival. Jack Spicer. CoPo
Fool, a fool, A! I met a fool i' the forest. Motley's the Only Wear [*or* A Worthy Fool]. Shakespeare. *Fr.* As You Like It, II, vii. TreFT; TrGrPo
Fool and False. *Unknown, tr. fr. Sanskrit by* Arthur W. Ryder. *Fr.* The Panchatantra. AWP; JAWP; WBP

Fool and [a] knave with different views, A. The Touchstone [*or* Epigram]. Samuel Bishop. ALV; HBV; MeWo
Fool and the Poet, The. Pope. *See* Epigram: "Sir, I admit your general rule."
Fool by the Roadside, The. W. B. Yeats. MoVE
Fool Hath Said in His Heart, The. Psalms, XIV, Bible, *O.T.* OnPM; TrJP
Fool of Love, The. *Unknown, tr. fr. Russian by* Louis Untermeyer. UnTE
Fool of Nature, stood with stupid eyes, The. The Power of Love. Dryden. *Fr.* Cymon and Iphigenia. OBS
Fool Song. Cornel Lengyel. GoYe
Fool, take up thy shaft again. Song. Thomas Stanley. EnLoPo
Fool there was and he made his prayer, A. The Vampire [as Suggested by the Painting by Philip Burne-Jones]. Kipling. BLPA; EnLit; HBV; NeHB
Fool there was, and she lowered her pride, A. A Women's Answer to "The Vampire." Felicia Blake. BLPA; NeHB
"Fool Tom" Jackson. Stonewall Jackson. Stephen Vincent Benét. OTD
Fooles, they are the onely nation. *See* Fools, they are the only nation.
Foolish boy forebeare and flee. *Unknown.* SeCSL
Foolish Child. *Unknown, tr. fr. Akan by* J. B. Danquah. PBA
Foolish Emily and Her Kitten. Adelaide O'Keeffe. OTPC (1923 ed.)
Foolish Flowers. Rupert Sargent Holland. GFA; OTPC
Foolish I, why should I grieve. Of Maids' Inconstancy. Richard Brathwaite. *Fr.* A Strappado for the Devil. ElL
Foolish Leander. Mateo Vázquez de Leca, *tr. fr. Spanish by* Sir John Bowring. OnPM
Foolish little maiden bought a foolish little bonnet, A. What the Choir Sang about the New Bonnet. M. T. Morrison. BLPA
Foolish man, by flesh and fancy led, The. Psalm XIV. *Paraphrased by* Sir Philip Sidney. FCP
Foolish man who boasts that he is able, The. Boastful Husbandman. *Unknown.* UnTE
Foolish Miller, The. *Unknown.* UnTE
Foolish prater, what dost thou. The Swallow. Abraham Cowley. BEL; CoBE; OBEV; SeCL; TOP
Foolish Proverb. *Unknown, tr. fr. Greek by* Louis Untermeyer. UnTE
("Mockery murders love, they say, and she.") MeWo
Foolish rhythm turns in my idle head, A. A Tune. Arthur Symons. BoLP; MuSP; OBNC
Foolish useless man who had done nothing, A. Brummell at Calais. John Glassco. MoCV; PeCV (1967 ed.)
Foolish Woman, A. Proverbs, IX: 13-18, Bible, *O.T.* TrGrPo
Foolish young fellow named Hyde, A. *Unknown.* GoTP
Fools. Ben Jonson. *See* Nano's Song.
Fool's Adventure, The, *sel.* Lascelles Abercrombie.
Seeker, The. WGRP
Fools Gaze at Painted Courts. Michael Drayton. *Fr.* Polyolbion, Song 18. ChTr
Fools have said/ That knowledge drives out wonder. Alfred Noyes. *Fr.* Watchers of the Sky. MaRV
Fools in Love's College. John Lyly. *See* O Cupid! Monarch over Kings.
Fools may pine, and sots may swill. Double Ballade of Life and Fate. W. E. Henley. PoVP
Fools of Forty-nine, The. John A. Stone. CoSo; SGR
Fool's Prayer, The. Edward Rowland Sill. AA; AmePo; AnNE; BeLS; FaBoBe; HBV; LHV; MAP; MaRV, *abr.*; MoAmPo (1942 ed.); NeHB; OHFP; OnMSP; OTD; PFY; PG; PoLF; TIHL; TreF; WBLP; WGRP
"'Tis not by guilt the onward sweep," *sel.* TrPWD
Fool's Preferment, A, *sel.* Thomas D'Urfey.
I'll Sail upon the Dog-Star. CBEP; FaBoCh; LoGBV; OxBoLi
Fool's Revenge, The, *sel.* Tom Taylor. Jester and His Daughter, The. VA
Fools [*or* Fooles] they are the only [*or* onely] nation. Nano's Song [*or* Fools *or* Song]. Ben Jonson. *Fr.* Volpone, I, ii. AnAnS-2; BoLiVe; ElL; InvP; LoBV; TrGrPo; TuPP
Fool's Tongue, A. John Heywood. SiCE
Foot, Fin or Feather. Christopher Smart, *paraphrased from* Psalm CXLVII, Bible, *O.T.* OA
Foot of death has printed on my chest, The. The Shudder. Donald Hall. NYBP
Foot Soldiers. John Banister Tabb. HBV; HBVY; PPL
Foot still, and nothing to go. Call It Goofus. Bill Berkson. ANYP
Football. Walt Mason. SD
Football and Rowing—an Eclogue. Alfred Denis Godley. CenHV
Football Field; Evening. J. A. R. McKellar. NeLNL
Football Player, A. Edward Cracroft Lefroy. VA
Football Song. Sir Walter Scott. SD
Footfall, The. Amy Carmichael. *See* Do We Not Hear Thy Footfall.
Footfall there, A/ Suffices to upturn to the warm air. At Ecelin. Robert Browning. *Fr.* Sordello. MyFE
Foot-hills called us, green and sweet, The. On the Height. Eunice Tietjens. HBMV; NP
Footnote. Anthony Delius. PeSA
Footnote, A. Stephen Spender. FaBoTw
Footnote to a Famous Lyric, A. Louise Imogen Guiney. AA
Footnote to History. Elizabeth J. Coatsworth. SiSoSe
Footnote to John II: 4. R. A. K. Mason. AnNZ
Footnote to Tennyson. Gerald Bullett. FiBHP
Footpath Way, The. Shakespeare. *See* Jog On, Jog On.
Footpath Way, The. Katharine Tynan. HBV
Footpath would have been enough, A. The Entailed Farm. John Glassco. MoCV
Footprints now on bread or cake. To a Child with Eyes. Mark Van Doren. LOW; PCH
Footprints of the Heart-of-the-Daybreak! Heart-of-the-Daybreak. Eugene Marais. PeSA
Footsloggers. Ford Madox Ford. NP
Footsteps. Hazel Hall. HBMV
Footsteps, The. Paul Valéry, *tr. fr. French by* C. Day Lewis. LiTW
Footsteps of a hundred years, The. The Founders of Ohio. William Henry Venable. MC; PaA; PAH; ThLM
Footwear. May Justus. SoPo; YeAr
For a Birthday. Elaine V. Emans. BiCB
For a Blind Beggar's Sign. Clemente Biondi, *tr. fr. Italian by* Roderick Gill. CAW
For a Bum Seen Walking the Rails. Dan Gillespie. QAH
For a cap and bells our lives we pay. June Weather [*or* June]. James Russell Lowell. *Fr.* The Vision of Sir Launfal: Prelude to Part First. AA; DD; GN
For a Child. Fannie Stearns Davis. FaPON; MPB
For a Child. Denis Glover. AnNZ
For a Child Expected. Anne Ridler. LiTM; MoVE; NeBP; SeCePo
For a Child Named Katherine. Louise Townsend Nicholl. SP
For a Child Who Died. Joseph G. E. Hopkins. JKCP (1955 ed.)
For a Child's Drawing. Anton Vogt. AnNZ
For a Christening. Anne Ridler. MoPo
For a Christening. Vernon Watkins. MoRP
For a Cock. Eleanor Farjeon. *See* Cock, The.
For a College Yearbook. J. V. Cunningham. CBV
For a Copy of Theocritus. Austin Dobson. HBV; VA
For a day and a night Love sang to us, played with us. At Parting. Swinburne. HBV; ViBoPo
For a Dead Kitten. Sara Henderson Hay. CIV; StaSt
For a Dead Lady. E. A. Robinson. AmLP; AmPP (4th ed.); AnFE; AnNE; AP; APA; BWP; CMoP; CoAnAm; CoBMV; FaBoEn; ForPo; GTBS-D; GTBS-W; InP; InvP; LiTA; LiTM; MAmP; MAP; MAPA; MaPo (1969 ed.); MoAB; MoAmPo; OxBA; PoEL-5; PoRA; ReMP; TreFT; TwAmPo; VaPo; ViBoPo; WHA
For a Dewdrop. Eleanor Farjeon. HBVY; YT
For a Far-out Friend. Gary Snyder. NeAP
For a Fountain. "Barry Cornwall." OBEV (new ed.); OBVV (Inscription for a Fountain.) OBRV
For a Girl in Love. Florence Hynes Willette. GoBC
For a God that would smile like a child. Without More Weight. Giuseppe Ungaretti. PoPl
For a good decade. The Drunk in the Furnace. W. S. Merwin. CBV; LiTM (1970 ed.); NePoEA-2; TwCP
For a Grotto. Mark Akenside. *See* Inscription for a Grotto.
For a Happy Girl. Philip Dow. QAH
For a heavy long time on the long green bough. Apple and Mole. Donald Davidson. MAP; MoAmPo (1942 ed.)
For a Hemiplegic. Walter Lowenfels. WOW
For a hundred years I lived with coal in the mine. Ostrava. Petr Bezruc. LiTW

For a Junior School Poetry Book. Christopher Middleton. FIW
For a Lady I Know. Countee Cullen. Four Epitaphs, 4. AmNP; GoSl; IDB; Kal; PoNe; ShM
(Four Epitaphs, 4.) CDC
(Lady I Know, A.) MAP; MaRV; MoAmPo; TRV
For a Lamb. Richard Eberhart. CMoP; FiMAP; LiTM (1970 ed.); MiAP; NoP; TDP
For a Little Lady. Fred Saidy. InMe
For a maiden sweetness, and for strength of men. John Oxenham. *Fr.* A Little Te Deum of the Commonplace. TRV
For a man that is almost blind. Mock Medicine. *Unknown.* MeEL
For a Marriage of St. Catherine. Dante Gabriel Rossetti. SiSw
For a Materialist. Adelaide Love. MaRV; OQP
For a minute, daughter, for an afternoon. The Prevention of Stacy Miller. Peter Miller. MoCV
For a Mocking Voice. Eleanor Farjeon. CH; PoMS; TiPo (1959 ed.)
For a Mouthy Woman. Countee Cullen. ShM
For a Musician. George Wither. *Fr.* Hallelujah. MuSP; OBS
(To a Musician, *wr. at. to* William Austin.) OxBoCh
For a name unknown. Why. Bliss Carman. OBEV; OBVV
For a Nativity. Lisel Mueller. NePoAm-2
For a New Home. Rosa Zagononi Marinoni. PoToHe
For a Parting. Keith Sinclair. AnNZ
For a Patriot. Shakespeare. King Henry VIII, *fr.* III, ii. PGD
For a Pessimist. Countee Cullen. PoMa; ShM
For a Poet. Countee Cullen. GoSl; PoNe; TTY
(I Have Wrapped My Dreams in a Silken Cloth.) MoSiPe
For a Poetry Reading to Which No One Came. Larry Rubin. FiSC
For a Second Marriage. James Merrill. NePoEA
(Upon a Second Marriage.) HW
For a shape, and a bloom, and an air, and a mien. Song. Edward Moore. WaPE
For a Son's Marriage. Martial, *tr. fr. Latin by* Garrett Stewart. HW
For a Statue of Chaucer at Woodstock. Mark Akenside. SeCePo
For a swarm of bees: take earth, throw it down with your right. Charm: Against a Swarm of Bees. *Unknown.* YAT
For A' That an' A' That ("That bonniest lass that ye meet neist"). *At. to* Robert Burns. CoMu; UnTE
For A' That and A' That, *parody.* Shirley Brooks. Par
For A' That and A' That ("Is there for honest poverty"). Burns. *See* Man's a Man for A' That, A.
For a thing done, repentance is no good. Past Help [*or* Sonnet: He Is Past All Help]. Cecco Angiolieri da Siena. AWP; OnPM
For a thousand years, you, African, suffered like a beast. Dawn in the Heart of Africa. Patrice Lumumba. PBA; TTY
For a Valentine. Mary Elizabeth Newell. PCH
For "A Venetian Pastoral" by Giorgione. Dante Gabriel Rossetti. PoVP; ViBoPo
(Venetian Pastoral, A.) VA
For a Very Old Man, on the Death of His Wife. Jane Cooper. NePoEA-2
For a Virgin Lady. Countee Cullen. MAP; MoAmPo
For a War Memorial. G. K. Chesterton. MMA
For a Wife in Jizzen. Douglas Young. OxBS
For a Wine Festival. Vernon Watkins. NYTB
For a Wordfarer. Rolfe Humphries. ML
For a Young Idealist: "Godspeed!" John Gilland Brunini. JKCP (1955 ed.)
For aa da scraimin stars at hing. Gallow Hill. William J. Tait. OxBS
For Adonis I am crying, for Adonis' beauty dead. Bion. *Fr.* Lament for Adonis. LiTW
For adoration, David's psalms. Christopher Smart. *Fr.* A Song to David. AnFE
For adoration seasons change. Adoration. Christopher Smart. *Fr.* A Song to David. FaBoEn
For age is opportunity no less. Longfellow. *Fr.* Morituri Salutamus. PoToHe (new ed.)
For All Blasphemers. Stephen Vincent Benét. AtBAP; OxBA
For All Fanatics. Samuel Butler. *Fr.* Hudibras, I, 1. PoFr
For all her quiet life flowed on. Whittier. *Fr.* The Friend's Burial. MaRV
For All in Pain. Amy Carmichael. TRV
For All Ladies of Shalott. Aline Kilmer. NP
For all life's beauties, and their beauteous growth. For Beauty, We Thank Thee [*or* We Thank Thee]. John Oxenham. BLRP; PGD
For All Sorts and Conditions. Norman Nicholson. EaLo
For All That Ever Has Been Ours. Ziche Landau, *tr. fr. Yiddish by* Marie Syrkin. LiTW
For, all that from her springs, and is ybredde. Mutability. Spenser. *Fr.* The Faerie Queene, VII. FaBoEn
For all that God in mercy sends. Give Thanks [*or* Thanks for Everything *or* For Everything Give Thanks]. Helena Isabella Tupper. BLRP; SoP; TreFT; WBLP
For all the beauties of the day. Grace at Evening. Edgar A. Guest. TrPWD
For all the beauty of the world, dear Lord. We Thank Thee. Phyllis C. Michael. SoP
For all Thy blessings given there are many to thank Thee Lord. A Thanksgiving. Annie Johnson Flint. SoP
For all the gracious gifts in harvests fair. Thanksgiving Day. John Kendrick Bangs. TrPWD
For all the saints who from their labors rest. Funeral Hymn [*or* For All the Saints]. William Walsham How. MaRV; WGRP
For all the vision that took fire this night. Burning Bush. Martin Feinstein. TrJP
For all the wonders of this wondrous world. John Oxenham. *Fr.* A Little Te Deum of the Commonplace. PGD
For all things beautiful, and good, and true. Thanksgiving. John Oxenham. BLRP; OQP; WBLP
For all those beaten, for the broken heads. Litany for Dictatorships. Stephen Vincent Benét. AmPP; AnEnPo; NAMP; OxBA; PoFr
For all Thy ministries. John Oxenham. *Fr.* A Little Te Deum of the Commonplace. TRV
For all Thy ministries. We Thank Thee [Lord]. John Oxenham. PGD; WBLP
For all true words that have been spoken. Thanksgiving. Margaret E. Sangster SoP; TRV
For All Who Need ("For all who watch tonight.") *Unknown.* MaRV
(Tonight.) SoP
For all your days prepare. Preparedness. Edwin Markham. FaFP; MAP; MoAmPo; NeMA; OQP; YT
For an Age of Plastics. Plymouth. Donald Davie. NePoEA-2
For an Autograph. James Russell Lowell. InP
Sels.
"Greatly begin! though thou have time." MCCG
"Life is a leaf of paper white." MaRV
For an Autumn Festival, *sel.* Whittier.
Harvest Hymn, *sts.* 5-12. OHIP, *abr.*; PoRL
("Once more the liberal year laughs out," *abr.*) PGD
For an Emigrant. Randall Jarrell. OxBA
For an Epitaph at Fiesole. Walter Savage Landor. OBRV; OBNC
TOP; VA
(His Epitaph.) OBVV
For an Eskimo. Annie Charlotte Dalton. CaP
For an Ex-Far East Prisoner of War. Charles Causley. POTi
For an Hour. Winfred Ernest Garrison. OQP
For an Old Man. Norbert Engels. JKCP (1955 ed.)
For an understanding heart, I pray. Heart Prayer. Enola Chamberlin. SoP
For Angus MacLeod. Iain Crichton Smith. OxBS
For Ann Scott-Moncrieff. Edwin Muir. GTBS-P
(To Ann Scott-Moncrieff.) SiSw
For Anne. Leonard Cohen. BoLP; ELU; PoCh
For Anne Gregory. W. B. Yeats. CMoP; DiPo; DTC; ExPo; FaBoMo; FaFP; ForPo; GTBS-W; InPo; LiTL; LiTM; LoBV; LoPo; PoSa; SeCeV; SiTL; TDP
For Annie. Poe. AmP; AmPP; AnFE; AP; APA; CoAnAm; HBV; LiTA; LO; MWA-1; NePA; OBEV; OBVV; OxBA; TreFS
For Any Beachhead. M. K. Joseph. AnNZ
For any golfer of resource. The Crow and the Nighthawk. Watson Kirkconnell. CaP
For Any Member of the Security Police. Josephine Jacobsen. NePoAm
For April Showers. Emily Rose Burt. GFA
For Artaud. Michael McClure. NeAP
For Arvia. E. A. Robinson. BiCB; TSW
For at the window of my house. She of the Impudent Face. Proverbs, Bible, *O.T.* TrJP

For aught that ever I could read. The Course of True Love. Shakespeare. *Fr.* A Midsummer Night's Dream, I, i. WHA
For August, be your dwelling thirty towers. Sonnets of the Months: August. Folgore da San Gemignano. AWP; CTC
For auld lang syne, my dear. *See* Should auld acquaintance be forgot.
For authorities whose hopes. The Paper Nautilus. Marianne Moore. CBV; FaBoMo
For Autumn. Eleanor Farjeon. ThGo
For beauty being the best of all we know. The Growth of Love, VIII. Robert Bridges. PoVP
For beauty I am not a star. *See* As a beauty I'm not a great star.
For Beauty kissed your lips when they were young. Epitaph for the Poet V., II. Arthur Davison Ficke. HBMV
For Beauty, We Thank Thee. John Oxenham. PGD
(We Thank Thee.) BLRP
For Black Poets Who Think of Suicide. Etheridge Knight. BP
For Brian Priestman. F. R. Scott. TwCaPo
For Britons, chief. British Commerce. James Thomson. *Fr.* Liberty, IV. OBEC
For Brother Malcolm. Edward S. Spriggs. CAD
For C. Philip Whalen. NeAP
For C. K. at His Christening. Daniel Lawrence Kelleher. NeIP
For certain he hath seen all perfectness. Dante. La Vita Nuova, XVII. AWP
For Charlie's Sake. John Williamson Palmer. HBV
For Charlotte Brontë. Emily Dickinson. *See* All overgrown by cunning moss.
For Christmas. Dorothy Aldis. ChBR; UTS
For Christmas. Rachel Field. ChBR; GaP
For Christmas Day. Eleanor Farjeon. ChBR; TiPo (1952 ed.)
For Christmas Day. Francis Kinwelmersh. ReIE
For Christmas-Day. Charles Wesley. CEP
"For Christ's sweet sake, I beg an alms." James Russell Lowell. *Fr.* The Vision of Sir Launfal, Pt. II. WGRP
For City Spring. Stephen Vincent Benét. PoPl
For Communion with God, *sel.* Thomas Shepherd.
"Alas, my God, that we should be." TrPWD
(Alas, My God, *longer sel.*) OxBoCh
For Crethis' store of tales and pleasant chat. Crethis. Callimachus, *tr. by* Richard Garnett. AWP
For Crow Jane. LeRoi Jones. FRC
For Danny whistling slowly. Feed. Raymond Knister. OBCV; PeCV
For dawn, wind/ off the river. For Crow Jane. LeRoi Jones. FRC
For days and days I've climbed a tree. Contemplation. John Alden Carpenter. RIS
For days gold-bright. Song of Thanksgiving. John Richard Moreland. PGD
For days these curious cardboard buds have lain. Gunpowder Plot. Vernon Scannell. FIW
For de Lawd. Lucille Clifton. TwCP
For Death by Choice. Pearl Cleage. WSL
For death must come, and change, and, though the loss. Immutabilis. Alice Learned Bunner. Vingtaine, II. AA
For Decoration Day. Rupert Hughes. AA
For dedy liif, my livy deth I wite. Come, Death—My Lady Is Dead. *At. to* Charles of Orleans. MeEL
For Deeper Life. Katharine Lee Bates. TrPWD
For Demerara bound with cod she flies. Escapade. Kenneth Leslie. EtS
For Denise McNair. Colette Inez. QAH
For Dinah, the Adeneys' Cat. Anne Wilkinson. PeCV
For do but note a wild and wanton herd. The Power of Music. Shakespeare. *Fr.* The Merchant of Venice, V, i. GN
For Dr. and Mrs. Dresser. Margaret Avison. MoCV; PeCV (1967 ed.)
For doing good to all. No Regrets. *Unknown.* SoP
For Doreen. Donald Davie. NMP
For E. McC. Ezra Pound. SD
For each new morning with its light. Thanksgiving. Emerson. PCH
For each of us a different path to God. Pilgrimage. Blanche Shoemaker Wagstaff. MaRV
For each one body that i' th' earth is sown. The Resurrection Possible and Probable. Robert Herrick. ILP; PAn
For each true deed is worship; it is prayer. True Work Is Worship. Edwin Markham. *Fr.* The Angelus. MaRV
For Eager Lovers. Genevieve Taggard. AnAmPo; NP
For ease and for dispatch the morning's best. On Walking the Streets by Day [*or* The Morning]. John Gay. *Fr.* Trivia; or, The Art of Walking the Streets of London, II. EnLi-1 (1949 ed.); TOP
For Easter. Frances Ridley Havergal. OQP
(Easter Prayer.) SoP
For Easter-Day. Charles Wesley. *See* Easter Hymn.
For Echo is the soul of the voice exerting itself in hollow places. The Instruments. Christopher Smart. WiR
For Elizabeth Madox Roberts. Janet Lewis. QFR
For England. J. D. Burns. BoAu
For England, in Grateful Appreciation, *sel.* Anton Vogt.
"I was five when we moved to England, and the strange voices." AnNZ
For England, when with fav'ring gale. Heaving the Lead [*or* The Leadsman's Song *or* By the Deep Nine]. *At. to* J. [*or* W.] Pearce *and to* Charles Dibdin. ChTr; EtS; HBV
For Eros II. Audrey Wurdemann. MoLP
For Evening. Sabine Baring-Gould. *See* Now the Day Is Over.
For Ever. *See* Forever.
For every bird there is this last migration. The Death of the Bird. A. D. Hope. PoAu-2
For Every Day. Frances Ridley Havergal. *See* Lord, Speak to Me.
For Every Evil. *Unknown.* EvOK
For every evil under [*or* ill beneath] the sun. Mother Goose. GoTP; HBV; HBVY; OTPC; OxNR; PPL
For every hill I've had to climb. Friendly Obstacles. *Unknown.* MaRV; SoP
For every houre that thou wilt spare mee now. Loves Usury. John Donne. MaMe; SCEP-1; SeEP
For Every Man. Max I. Reich. STF
For every parcel I stoop down to seize. The Armful. Robert Frost. CMoP
For every sip the Hen says grace. Grace. Walter de la Mare. ThGo
For every thing that moves and lives. Foot, Fin or Feather. Christopher Smart. OA
For Everything Give Thanks. Helena Isabella Tupper. *See* Give Thanks.
For everything is sacred, poetry. Islwyn. *Fr.* The Storm. PrWP
For Exmoor. Jean Ingelow. OBEV (new ed.); OBVV
For eyes he waves greentipped. Slug in Woods. Earle Birney. CaP; OBCV; PeCV; TDP
For False Heart. Hilaire Belloc. MoBrPo
(False Heart, The.) FaBoCh; HBMV; LoGBV
For February Twelfth. Muriel M. Gessner. RePo; YeAr
For feelings come and feelings go. God's Unchanging Word. Martin Luther. SoP
For flowers so beautiful and sweet. We Thank Thee. Mattie M. Renwick. HH; OTPC (1946 ed.); PEDC
For flowers that bloom about our feet. We Thank Thee [*or* Father, We Thank Thee *or* Spring Prayer]. *Unknown, at. to* Emerson. BoTP; HH, *abr.*; SoP; SoPo; TreFT
For Fog and Fate no charm is found. Destroyers in Collision. Kipling. *Fr.* Epitaphs of the War. PoVP
For Forgiveness. John Donne. *See* Hymn to God the Father, A.
For Forms of Government let fools contest. Charity. Pope. *Fr.* An Essay on Man. OBEC; ViBoPo
For forty years, for forty-one. This Dim and Ptolemaic Man. John Peale Bishop. CrMA; ImOP; LiTA; LiTM (rev. ed.); NePA
For forty years I shunned the lust. For a Virgin Lady. Countee Cullen. MAP; MoAmPo
For Fran. Philip Levine. PoCh
For France two grenadiers held their way. The Grenadiers. Heine. OuHeWo
For Frantz Fanon. Robert L. Terrell. WSL
For from my cradle you must know that I. Michael Drayton. *Fr.* To My Most Dearly Loved Friend, Henry Reynolds, Esq. PP
For Futures. Josephine Miles. FiMAP
For G. W. W. Gibson. LO
For George Santayana. Robert Lowell. NoP

For giving me' desire. Desire. Thomas Traherne. LO; OxBoCh
For glowing autumn's brimming yield. We Thank Thee! Thomas Curtis Clark. PGD
For God hath not given us the spirit of fear. Second Timothy, Bible, *N.T.* TiPo (1952 ed.)
For God, our God is a gallant foe. Ballad for Gloom. Ezra Pound. LiTM (rev. ed.); MAP; MoAmPo; NeMA; NePA; OBVV
For God So Loved. Barbara C. Ryberg. FaChP
For God So Loved the World. Georgia Harkness. ChIP
"For God So Loved the World." Robert Whitaker. OQP
For God so loved the world, that he gave his only begotten Son. St. John, Bible, *N.T.* LO
For God, the Lord of earth and Heaven. For God So Loved. Barbara C. Ryberg. FaChP
For God While Sleeping. Anne Sexton. CABA; NePoEA-2; PoDB
For Godsake [*or* God's sake] hold your tongue, and let me love. The Canonization. John Donne. AnAnS-1; ATP; BEL; BoLiVe; BWP; CABA; CaFP; CBEP; CBV; CoBE; DiPo; ElL; EnL; EnLi-1 (1949 ed.); EnLoPo; EnRePo; EP; ForPo; FosPo; GTBS-W; GTSE; LiTB; LiTG; LiTL; LoBV; MaMe; MaPo; MasP; MBW-1; MePo; NoP; OBS; PAn; Po; PoAn; PoE; PoEL-2; PoeP; PoFS; PoIE; ReEn; ReIE; SCEP-1; SeCePo; SeCeV; SeCP; SeCV-1; SeEP; StP; TDP; TOP; TrGrPo; TuPP; UnTE; VaPo; ViBoPo
For God's sake, let us be men. Let Us Be Men. D. H. Lawrence. MoPW
For God's sake, let us sit upon the ground. *See* For heaven's sake. . .
For God's sake mark that fly. Nulla Fides. Patrick Carey. SeEP
For Good Luck. Juliana Horatia Ewing. FaPON; OTPC (1946 ed.); PRWS
(Little Kings and Queens of the May.) BoTP
For government, though high, and low, and lower. The Commonwealth of the Bees. Shakespeare. King Henry V, *fr.* I, ii. GN
For grazing innocence a salad. Poets in Africa. Roy Campbell. ACV
For greeting, de Gaulle nods once. De Gaulle Nods Once. Eugene Brooks. NYTB
For Guillaume Apollinaire. William Meredith. CoAP
For H is a spirit and therefore he is God. Instrument Rhimes. Christopher Smart. *Fr.* Jubilate Agno. MuSP
For half a month, it has rained without cease. On a Puppy. Feng Chih. LiTW
For Hani, Aged Five, That She Be Better Able to Distinguish a Villain. Gene Baro NYBP
For Hanukkah. Hayyin Nahman Bialik. TiPo (1952 ed.)
For Haroun Al Raschid. Abu'l-Atahija, *tr. fr. Arabic by* Herbert Howarth *and* Ibrahim Shukrallah. LiTW
For Harry and June. Ray Mathew. NeLNL
For hasty word and secret sin. Prayer at Eventide. *Unknown.* SoP
For Having Thee. Francis X. Connolly. JKCP (1955 ed.)
For He Had Great Possessions. Richard Middleton. HBV
For He laid the foundations of the earth. Praise the Lord, O My Soul! *Fr.* Psalm CIV, Bible, *O.T.* ThGo
For he was of that stubborn crew. For All Fanatics. Samuel Butler. *Fr.* Hudibras. PoFr
For he was wounder amiabill. Squire Meldrum at Carrickfergus. Sir David Lindsay. *Fr.* The Historie of Squyer William Meldrum. OxBS
For heaven's [*or* God's] sake, let us sit upon the ground. Of the Death of Kings. Shakespeare. King Richard II, *fr.* III, ii. ChTr; HoPM; PoFr
For her gait, if she be walking. The Complete Lover [*or* Song]. William Browne. CLwM; HBV; LiTL; OBEV
For Her Heart Only. *Unknown.* ElL
("Only, sweet Love, afford me but thy heart.") LO
For Her Love I Cark and Care. *Unknown.* CBEP
For Her on the First Day Out. Robert Bagg. NePoAm-2
For Her Sake. Alastair Reid. PoPl
For here lies Juliet, and her beauty makes. Thus with a Kiss I Die [*or* Here Lies Juliet]. Shakespeare. *Fr.* Romeo and Juliet, V, iii. FaFP; TreFS; TrGrPo
For Hettie. LeRoi Jones. CBV; NeAP
For him, it seems, everything was molten. The Laughing Hyena, by Hokusai. D. J. Enright. TwCP
For Him, who, lost to ev'ry Hope of Life. Apology for Vagrants. John Langhorne. *Fr.* The Country Justice. OBEC
For him who must see many years. Early Death and Fame. Matthew Arnold. MBW-2
For him who sought his country's good. Washington's Monument. *Unknown.* OHIP; PAH
For Hire. Morris Jacob Rosenfeld, *tr. fr. Yiddish by* Rose Pastor Stokes *and* Helena Franks. LiTW
For his mind, I doe not care. Another Ladyes Exception Present at the Hearing. Ben Jonson. *Fr.* A Celebration of Charis. AnAnS-2; SeCP
For His Own Epitaph. W. B. Yeats. *Fr.* Under Ben Bulben. AnFE
For His Own Tomb-Stone. Matthew Prior. TOP
For his religion it was fit. The Religion of Hudibras [*or* The Presbyterian]. Samuel Butler. *Fr.* Hudibras, I, 1. BOHV; FaBoEn; FOL; InMe; LoBV; ViBoPo
For His Sake. Annie Denman. BePJ
For Hope. Richard Crashaw. GTBS-W; LiTB; ViBoPo
(Answer for Hope.) MeLP
(M. Crashaw's Answer for Hope.) MaMe; OBS; SCEP-1; SeCV-1
(Richard Crashaw's Answer; for Hope.) LiTG
"Fair hope! our earlyer heav'n by thee," *sel.* FaBoEn
For hours the princess would not play or sleep. The Yak. Virna Sheard. CaP; PeCV; WHW
For hours without stopping. Unchanged. Martial. WoL
For how long known this boundless wash of light. Summer Beach. Frances Cornford. ChMP
For human nature Hope remains alone. Hope. Theognis. AWP; JAWP; WBP
For I am not without authority in my jeopardy. Christopher Smart. *Fr.* Jubilate Agno. EiCP; EiPP; NCEP
For I am rightful fellow of their band. Mentors. Gwendolyn Brooks. Kal; PoNe
For I Am Sad. Don Marquis. BOHV
For I dip [*or* dipped] into the future, far as human eye could see Prophecy [*or* Federation of the World]. Tennyson *See also* I dipt into the future... *Fr.* Locksley Hall. GTBS-W; PGD; PoLF; TreF; TRV; WBLP.
For I Have Done a Good and Kindly Deed. Franz Werfel, *tr. fr. German by* Edith Abercrombie Snow. TrJP
For I have learned / To look on Nature. I Have Felt a Presence [*or* Lines Written above Tintern Abbey]. Wordsworth. *Fr.* Lines Composed a Few Miles above Tintern Abbey. BBV; MaRV; OQP
For I have loved [*or* lov'd] the rural walk through lanes. The Rural Walk. William Cowper. *Fr.* The Task, I. EnRP; TOP
For I learn as the years roll onward. Lessons of the Year. *Unknown.* BLRP
For I Must Sing of All I Feel and Know. James Thomson. PoVP
For I saw the field full of folk that before I described. The Confession of the Deadly Sins. William Langland. *Fr.* The Vision of Piers Plowman. MeEV
For I say, through the grace given unto me. The Duties of Man. Romans, Bible, *N.T.* TreF
For I the Ballad Will Repeat. Shakespeare. *Fr.* All's Well That Ends Well, I, iii. ViBoPo
For I was a gaunt grave councillor. La Fraisne. Ezra Pound. NP; PG
For I Will Consider My Cat Jeoffry. Christopher Smart. *See* My Cat Jeoffry.
For I would walk alone. Communion with Nature. Wordsworth. *Fr.* The Prelude, II. OBRV; TOP
For if the shaft of destiny hath quit. The Great Poet. Mu'tamid, King of Seville. LiTW
"For if your boone be askeable." Thomas Cromwell. *Unknown.* ESPB
For I'm called Little Buttercup—dear Little Buttercup. Little Buttercup. W. S. Gilbert. *Fr.* H.M.S. Pinafore. TreFS
For in and out, above, about, below. Omar Khayyám, *tr. by* Edward Fitzgerald. *Fr.* The Rubáiyát. TRV
For infants time is like a humming shell. O Dreams, O Destinations. C. Day Lewis. MoPo
For Inspiration. Michelangelo, *tr. fr. Italian by* Wordsworth. CAW; GoBC; SoP; WGRP
(Prayer for Inspiration, A.) OQP

For (continued)
(To the Supreme Being.) AWP; JAWP; LiTW; TrPWD; TRV; WBP
For Instruction. Vassar Miller. ToPo
For Irma During April. Tony Towle. YAP
For James Dean. Frank O'Hara. NeAP
For Jan. John Wieners. CoPo
For Jane Kane, Whom We Knew in Our Young Marriages. Bink Noll. ToPo
For Janice and Kenneth to Voyage. Frank O'Hara. ANYP
For January I give you vests of skins. Sonnets of the Months: January. Folgore da San Geminiano. AWP
For Jeriann's Hands. Marge Piercy. ThO
For Jillian of Berry she dwells on a hill. Jillian of Berry [*or* Merry-thought's Song]. *At. to* Francis Beaumont. *Fr.* The Knight of the Burning Pestle (*by* Beaumont and Fletcher). ElL; OBS
For Jim, Easter Eve. Anne Spencer. AmNP; PoNe
For John Keats [Apostle of Beauty]. Countee Cullen. Four Epitaphs, 2. AmNP; Kal
(Four Epitaphs, 2.) CDC
For Johnny. John Pudney. HaMV; WePo
For July in Siena, by the willow-tree. Of The Months: July. Folgore da San Geminiano. AWP
For just a brief while every day. Rendezvous. Mary Scott Fitzgerald. PoToHe (new ed.)
For Justice. Bernard Freeman Trotter. PTK
For K. R. on Her Sixtieth Birthday. Richard Wilbur. ML
For Karen. Daniel Hughes. NYTB
For Kathleen, Gone on a Brief Journey. Jack Marshall. YAP
For Kayak Magazine. Lou Lipsitz. YAP
For Keats and the Florentine Night. Gerta Kennedy. NYTB
For knighthood is not in the feats of war. The True Knight [*or* True Knighthood]. Stephen Hawes. *Fr.* The Pastime of Pleasure. ACP; AnEnPo; OBEV; TrGrPo
For Lee. A. X. Nicholas. WSL
For Life I Had Never Cared Greatly. Thomas Hardy. BEL; CMoP; EnLit; HBMV; LiTM (rev. ed.); PoVP
For life, with all it yields of joy and woe. Truth. Robert Browning. *Fr.* A Death in the Desert. MaRV; OQP; TRV
For lighter, whiter skin in just ten days. Brainwashing Dramatized. Don Johnson. PoNe (1970 ed.)
For lo! the board with cups and spoons is crowned. Pope. *Fr.* The Rape of the Lock. ViBoPo
For lo! the living God doth bare his arm. Democracy. Harriet Monroe. *Fr.* Commemoration Ode. AA
For [*or* And] lo! the sea that fleets about the land. The Dancing Sea [*or* The Sea Danceth]. Sir John Davies. *Fr.* Orchestra. ChTr; EtS
For, Lo, the Winter Is Past. Song of Solomon, II: 10-13, Bible, *O.T.* TreF
("For, lo, the winter is past," II: 11-12.) PDV; SUS; TiPo
(Lo, the Winter Is Past.) FaPON (11-13); ShBV-3 (11-12)
(Spring, 11-12.) PCD; PCH
(Time of the Singing of Birds, The.) ThGo
(Winter Is Past, The, 11-12.) SoPo; YeAr
For, Lord, the Crowded Cities Be. Rainer Maria Rilke, *tr. fr. German by* Ludwig Lewisohn. AWP; JAWP; TrJP; WBP
For Louise, Age 17. Irving Layton. PeCV
For love he offered me his perfect world. Gift to a Jade. Anna Wickham. ELU; NP
For love—I would. The Warning. Robert Creeley. NeAP
For Love is like a plant that clings. Love. John Swanwick Drennan. IrPN
For Love of Appin. Jessie Mackay. AnNZ
For love of lovely words, and for the sake. Skerryvore. Robert Louis Stevenson. ILP
For Lover Man, and All the Other Young Men Who Failed to Return from World War II. Mance Williams. NNP
For love's sake, kiss me once again. Begging Another, on Colour of Mending the Former [*or* The Kiss]. Ben Jonson. *Fr.* A Celebration of Charis. AnAnS-2; AtBAP; LO; OAEP; PoEL-2; SeCP; StP; TuPP; UnTE
For Love's Sake Only. Elizabeth Barrett Browning. *See* Sonnets from the Portuguese: "If thou must love me, let it be for naught."
For Lucas Cranach's Eve. Adelaide Crapsey. QFR
For M——. Bruce Williamson. NeIP
For M. S. Singing Frühlingsglaube in 1945. Frances Cornford. UnS
For Mack. A. X. Nicholas. WSL
For Malcolm X. Margaret Walker. BP
For Malcolm's eyes, when they broke. A Poem for Black Hearts. LeRoi Jones. BP; IDB
For Man to Act. Thomas Traherne. *Fr.* Christian Ethics. OxBoCh
For man to tell how human life began. Adam, First Man of Men. Milton. *Fr.* Paradise Lost, VIII. MaPo
For man's unceasing quest for God. The Quest Eternal. Alice M. Pullen. MaRV
For many a year I've watched the ships a-sailing to and fro. The Ships. J. J. Bell. BoTP
For many and many a year. Enemies. Agnes Lee. NP
For many blessings I to God upraise. Nature and the Child. John Lancaster Spalding. *Fr.* God and the Soul. AA
For many, many days together. Riding Together. William Morris. ViPo; ViPP; WaKn
For many thousand ages. Es stehen unbeweglich. Heine. AWP; JAWP; TrJP; WBP
For many unsuccessful years. Against Modesty in Love. Matthew Prior. ErPo
For Maria at Four. John Becker. BiCB
For Marian Anderson. Frederick Bock. NYTB
For Martha's Kitchen. Fay Inchfawn. OQP
For Mary. Kenneth Rexroth. PoPl
For Mary McLeod Bethune. Margaret Walker. PoNe
For Me. William R. Newell. SoP
For Me ("Amid a rabble cry"). *Unknown.* SoP
For Me ("Under an eastern sky"). *Unknown.* ChIP; OQP
For me, for me, two horses wait. The Wizard's Funeral. R. W. Dixon. ELP; GTBS-D; LoBV; PeVV
For me, I know nought; nothing I deny. Byron. *Fr.* Don Juan, XIV. OBRV
For me one silly task is like another. Cassandra. Louise Bogan. MAP; NP
For me the jasmine buds unfold. Song [*or* The World Is Mine]. Florence Earle Coates. AA; HBV; PoMa
For me, the naked and the nude. The Naked and the Nude. Robert Graves. NYBP; SiTL
For me there is no dismay. The Poet. C. Day Lewis. OxBI
For metaphors of man we search the skies. Sir William Watson. InP
For Miriam. Kenneth Patchen. MeWo; ToPo
For Mr. X I've Only Mischief. Joan de Guilhade, *tr. fr. Portuguese by* William M. Davis. AnML
For modes of faith, let graceless zealots fight. Faith. Pope. *Fr.* An Essay on Man. BoPe; WGRP
For mony lang year I ha'e heard frae my grannie. The Hazlewood Witch. Richard Gall. EBSV
For Morn, my dome of blue. A Child's Prayer. Siegfried Sassoon. BoTP
For morning sun and evening dew. Thanksgiving. Arthur Ketchum. STF
For mother-love and father-care. We Thank Thee. *Unknown.* FaPON; MPB; OTPC (1946 ed.)
For Mother on Father's Day. James Tate. YAP
For much imaginary work was there. Shakespeare. *Fr.* The Rape of Lucrece. MyFE
For Music. Byron. *See* Stanzas for Music: "There be none of beauty's daughters."
For My Ancestors. Rolfe Humphries. PoRA (rev. ed.)
For My Brother. Owen Dodson. *See* Poems for My Brother Kenneth.
For My Brother. Thomas Merton. InPo; TreFS
For My Brother. Su T'ung-po, *tr. fr. Chinese by* Yang Chising. WhP
For My Contemporaries. J. V. Cunningham. CoAP; PoSa; PP
For My Daughter. Weldon Kees. CoAP
For My Daughter. W. B. Yeats. *Fr.* Prayer for My Daughter. MoRP
For My Father. Rachel Field. InMe
For My Father. Paul Potts. FaBoTw
For my first twenty years, since yesterday. *See* For the first twenty years, since yesterday.
For My Funeral. A. E. Housman. BoPe; CMoP; TrPWD; ViBoPo
For My Grandfather. Francis Webb. BoAV
For My Grandmother. Countee Cullen. Four Epitaphs, 1. AmNP; CDC; GoSl; MAP; MoAmPo
For My Mother. Iain Crichton Smith. OxBS

For My Newborn Son. Sydney Goodsir Smith. ACV
For My Own Monument. Matthew Prior. CEP; EiCP; HBV; LoBV; OBEC; OBEV
For my part, I'le not meddle with the cause. Homer. *Fr.* The Odyssey. CTC
For My People. Margaret Walker. AmNP; BALP; IDB; Kal; MoRP; NoP; PoFr; PoNe
For My Shakespeare Class. Vonna Hicks Adrian. NYTB
For My Sister, Contemplating Divorce. Marvin Bell. TDP
For my sister's sake. Hitomaro. *Fr.* Manyo Shu. AWP; LiTW
For My Son. Antoni Boguslawski, *tr. fr. Polish by* L. E. Gielgud. PoFr
For My Son. John Frederick Nims. MiAP
For my soul engaged in far matters. Three Sections from "Anabasis." "St.-J. Perse." *Fr.* Anabasis. LiTW
For My Students, Returning to College. John Williams. NePoAm-2
For My thoughts are not your thoughts. My Thoughts Are Not Your Thoughts. Isaish, Bible, *O.T.* TrJP
For My Twenty-fifth Birthday in Nineteen Forty-one. John Ciardi. WaP
For my unborn son. Two Poems, II. Robert J. Abrams. NNP
For My Wife. Julian Symons. NeBP; WaP
For Nature daily through her grand design. Frederick Goddard Tuckerman. *Fr.* Sonnets. AP; MAmP
For nature then/ (The coarser pleasures of my boyish days). Wordsworth. *Fr.* Lines Written a Few Miles above Tintern Abbey. ACV
For Nicholas, Born in September. Tod Perry. NYBP
For Nijinsky's Tomb. Frances Cornford. UnS
For No Good Reason. Peter Redgrove. NMP
For no man wist who was best. The Round Table. Robert Mannying. ACP
For noble minds, the worst of miseries. Poverty. Theognis. AWP; JAWP; OnPM; WBP
For Now. W. S. Merwin. CoPo; NaP
For now are wider ways, profounder tides. The Deeper Seas. Henry Bellamann. EtS
For now, love thou, I rede, Christ, as I thee tell. Richard Rolle. *Fr.* Love Is Life. ACP; CAW
For now too nigh/ Th' Archangel stood. Their Banishment. Milton. *Fr.* Paradise Lost, XII. SeCePo
For, O America, our country!—land. America. Arlo Bates. *Fr.* The Torch-Bearers. AA; PaA; PAL
For once in a dream or trance I saw the gods. Edwin Muir. BoPe
For Once, Then, Something. Robert Frost. AnFE; AP; BWP; CoAnAm; ForPo; PoFS
For one carved instant as they flew. Sea Gulls. E. J. Pratt. EtS; TwCaPo
For one copper. Another [Beggar Poem]. Issa. PoFr
For One in Doubt. Charles Wesley. Three Hymns, 3. WaPE
For One Lately Bereft. Margaret E. Bruner. PoToHe
For one long term, or e'er her trial came. Inscription: For the Door of the Cell in NewGate where Mrs. Brownrigg, the 'Prentice-Cide, Was Confined Previous to Her Execution. George Canning and John Hookham Frere. Par
For One Moment. David Ignatow. TPM
For one month afterwards the eye stays true. Departure. Kingsley Amis. NePoEA
For One Who Is Serene. Margaret E. Bruner. PoToHe (new ed.)
For One Who Would Not Be Buried in Westminster Abbey. Pope. ACP (1926 ed.)
For One Who Would Not Take His Life in His Hands. Delmore Schwartz. NAMP
For openers, the Federal Government. How to Change the U. S. A. Harry Edwards. NBP
For others she may not be fair. Mother. Thomas Curtis Clark. PGD
For Our Children. Amy Carmichael. FaChP
For Our Dead. Clinton Scollard. HH
(Memorial Day.) PEDC
For "Our Lady of the Rocks." Dante Gabriel Rossetti. MaVP
(Our Lady of the Rocks.) OxBoCh
"For our martyr'd Charles I pawn'd my plate." The Old Cavalier. Sir Francis Hastings Doyle. VA
For Our Sakes. Oscar Wilde. PGD
For our sore-shattered Jewish life. For All That Ever Has Been Ours. Ziche Landau. LiTW
For Our Women. Larry Neal. BF
For over forty years I'd paid it atlas homage. Hammerfest. W. H. Auden. PoAn
For Palm Sunday. Henry Hart Milman. OQP
(Ride On in Majesty.) VA
For pastime, often those who sail the deep. The Albatross. Baudelaire. OnPM
For Paul Laurence Dunbar. Countee Cullen. Four Epitaphs, 3. AmNP; BALP; CDC; GoSl; Kal
For people/ on trial. Perambulator Poems, II. David McCord. WhC
For Perfect Peace. Charles Wesley. BePJ
For physic and farces. David Garrick, the Actor, to Sir John Hill, a Physician Who Wrote Plays. David Garrick. TreFT
For Pity, Pretty Eyes, Surcease. Thomas Lodge. ElL; ReIE; SiCE
(Armistice.) OBSC
For pleasing Arts behold her matchless charms. The Future of American Literature. John Trumbull. *Fr.* Essay on the Fine Arts. AmPP (3d ed.)
For "Poems of Two." Lynn Strongin. ThO
For Poets. Al Young. WSL
For Poki. A. X. Nicholas. WSL
For Posterity. Kathleen Raine. NeBP
For raiment and for daily bread. Thanksgiving. Odell Shepard. PEDC
For Randolph Bourne. James Oppenheim. AnAmPo
For Real. Jayne Cortez. WSL
For reasons any. Irapuato. Earle Birney. PeCV (1967 ed.); PoAn
For Remembrance. Basil Ebers. DD; HH
For Rhoda. Delmore Schwartz. *See* Time Is the Fire.
For right is right, since God is God. Right Is Right. Frederick William Faber. SoP; TRV; WBLP
For Righteousness' Sake. Whittier. AmePo; PoEL-4
For rigorous teachers seized my youth. Matthew Arnold. *Fr.* Stanzas from the Grande Chartreuse. ViBoPo
For road-mates and companions he chose twelve. On the Road. John Oxenham. StJW
For Robert Frost, *sel.* Galway Kinnell.
"I saw you once on the TV." PP
For St. Bartholomew's Eve. Malcolm Cowley. NAMP
For Sale, a Horse. Charles Edward Taylor. AA
For Sale or Rent. *Unknown.* PoToHe (new ed.)
For Sapphire, My Sister. Alice H. Jones. WSL
For Saturday. Christopher Smart. *Fr.* Hymns for the Amusement of Children. EiCP
(Hymn for Saturday.) CBEP
(Lark's Nest, A.) FaBoCh; LoGBV
For Saundra. Nikki Giovanni. TNV; TTY
For Scotland's and for freedom's right. Bruce and the Spider. Bernard Barton. BeLS
For seeing, a/ brightness within. A New Light. William Hawkins. MoCV
For Sergeant Fetta. Ed Sanders. ANYP
For seven long years I courted Nancy. The Wild Miz-Zou-Rye. *Unknown.* ABF
"For shame!" cries Cypris as she sees. Indignant Protest. *Unknown.* UnTE
For shame! deny that thou bear'st love to any. Sonnets, X. Shakespeare. MasP
For shame, for shame, Oxonians all! Written at Oxford: On Stealing the Body of a Girl for Dissection. *Unknown.* StP
For shame thou everlasting wooer. The Antiplatonick. John Cleveland. AnAnS-2; MePo; SeCP
For shame your green-wood fires then smother. The Maid's Answer. *Unknown.* PeRV
For shamefast harm of great and hateful need. Sir Thomas Wyatt. FCP
For she is a vapour/ of the power of God. Wisdom. Bible, Apocrypha (*Douay vers.*). ISi
For sheer urbanity, I deem. Song of Fairly Utter Despair. Samuel Hoffenstein. CIV
For Sheila. Margaret Allonby. BoSA
For Simone Weil. Sister M. Thérèse. MoRP
For, Singing Till His Heaven Fills. George Meredith. *Fr.* The Lark Ascending. VA
For Sir John Vanbrugh, Architect. Abel Evans. *See* Epitaph on Sir John Vanbrugh.

For sixty days and upwards. Vicksburg—a Ballad. Paul Hamilton Hayne. AA; MC; PAH
For Sleep or Death. Ruth Pitter. TrPWD; WePo
For Sleep When Overtired. Sarah N. Cleghorn. OQP
For Snow. Eleanor Farjeon. CH; TiPo
For so long/ We looked into mirrors and hated what we saw. Us. Julius Lester. WOW
For Soldiers. Humphrey Gifford. CH; ElL; SiCE; TuPP
For Some Poets. Mae Jackson. BOLo
For some, the sea. Bathing Song. Anne Ridler. NYBP
For some time. *Unknown.* HW
For Steve. Earle Birney. WaP
For Strength. Rabindranath Tagore. *See* Prayer for Strength.
For such as you, I do believe. The Mother in the House. Hermann Hagedorn. DD; HBMV; OHIP; PoRL; PoToHe
For summer rain, and winter's sun. A Thanksgiving. John Kendrick Bangs. MaRV
For summer's bloom and autumn's blight. Hymn. Josiah Gilbert Holland. *Fr.* Bitter-sweet. TrPWD
For Sunday's play he never makes excuse. The Lout. John Clare. NBM
For sunlit hours and visions clear. Gratitude. Clyde McGee. BLRP; OQP
For T. S. E. Only. Hyam Plutzik. FiMAP
For ten miles the mountains rise. The Farm by the Lake. Chu Hsi. OnPC
For ten years I never left my books. After Passing the Examination. Po Chü-i. Po
For that He Looked Not upon Her. George Gascoigne. ElL
For that lovely face will fail. Persuasions to Love. Thomas Carew. LiTL; ViBoPo
For the Anniversary of My Death. W. S. Merwin. CoAP; NaP
For the Antigone. Andras Hamori. NYTB
For the Baptist[e]. William Drummond of Hawthornden. GoTS; HBV; LoBV; OBS; OxBoCh; SeEP
(Baptist, The.) TrGrPo
(Saint John Baptist.) CBEP; EaLo; GTBS-D; GTBS-P; GTBS-W; GTSE; GTSL; OBEV; OnPP
For the Barbers. Joel Oppenheimer. CoPo
For the Beauty of the Earth. Folliott Sandford Pierpoint. MaRV; SoP
For the Bed at Kelmscott. William Morris. *See* Inscription For An Old Bed.
For the Bicentenary of Isaac Watts. Norman Nicholson. EaLo
For the Blind. Martha Snell Nicholson. SoP
For the Book of Love. Jules Laforgue, *tr. fr. French by* Jethro Bithell. AWP; ErPo; LiTW
For the brother who slumbers the city wails. Hymn to Tammuz. *Unknown.* LiTW
For the Candle Light. Angelina W. Grimké. CDC; PoNe
For the child, fascinated by prints and maps. The Voyage. Baudelaire. LiTW
For the Conjunction of Two Planets. Adrienne Cecile Rich. ImOP
For the Dancer, Fred Herko. Jack Marshall. YAP
For the days when nothing happens. Thanksgiving. Margaret E. Sangster. BLRP
For the Death of Anton Webern Particularly. Nathaniel Tarn. MuSP
For the Depressed. Julian Symons. WaP
For the dim regions whence my fathers come. Outcast. Claude McKay. AmNP; BALP; BP
For the discipline of sorrow. Let Us Give Thanks. "Marianne Farningham." PEDC
For the doubling of flowers is the improvement of the gard'ner's talent. Christopher Smart. *Fr.* Jubilate Agno. EiCP
For the dream unfinished. Plain-Chant for America. Katherine Garrison Chapin. PAL; PoFr
For the Earth God. *Unknown, tr. fr. Dahomean song by* Frances Herskovits. EaLo
For the Eightieth Birthday of a Great Singer. Edward Shanks. UnS
For the Existentialists. Winthrop Palmer. NYTB
For the Fallen. Laurence Binyon. AnFE; GTBS; InP; MaRV; OBEV (new ed.); PoFr; POTE; ShBV-3; WePo
"They went with songs to the battle," *sel.* ViBoPo
For the Feast of Giordano Bruno. Swinburne. PoFr; ViPo
For the feast of trumpets should be kept up. Christopher Smart. *Fr.* Jubilate Agno. UnS
For the few hours of life allotted me. Prayer. *Tr. fr. Latin by* Abraham Cowley. PoFr
For the first man to climb the hill. Pioneers. *Unknown.* MaRV
For the first Monday of my week. In the Cemetery of the Sun. Wilfred Watson. PeCV
For the first ten years I fell. A Report. Ruth Fainlight. HYE
For the first time. Three. Roger Aplon. YAP
For the first time the only. Rescue. James Tate. YAP
For the [*or* my] first twenty years [*or* yeares], since yesterday. The Computation. John Donne. ATP (1935 ed.); DiPo; MaMe; OAEP; TuPP
For the Fly-Leaf of a School-Book. Norman Cameron. OxBS
For the fount of life eternal. The Joys of Paradise. St. Augustine. CAW
For the Gifts of the Spirit. Edward Rowland Sill. TrPWD
For the gladness here where the sun is shining. Our Prayer of Thanks. Carl Sandburg. NP; TRV
For the Grave of Daniel Boone. William Stafford. NoP; PoPl
For the great red rose of sunset. Sunset. Amy Carmichael. FaChP
For the Greek & Latin are not dead languages. Christopher Smart. Jubilate Agno, XIX. NCEP
For the happy/ there is song of angels. Heaven. Cynewulf. *Fr.* Christ. PoLi
For the hay and the corn and the wheat that is reaped. Giving Thanks. *Unknown.* PEDC
For the Hearne and Duck. *Unknown.* NCEP
For the heart, willing and not willing. The Clovers. Jean Garrigue. MoPo
For the Holy Family by Michelangelo. Dante Gabriel Rossetti. GoBC
For the kingdom of heaven is as a man traveling into a far country. The Parable of the Talents. St. Matthew, Bible, *N.T.* EnLi-1
For the Lady Olivia Porter; a Present upon a New-Years Day. Sir William Davenant. MeLP; MePo; OBS
For the last time Beowulf uttered his boast. Beowulf and Wiglaf Slay the Dragon. *Unknown.* *Fr.* Beowulf. AnOE
For the Letter Which Signifies God. Christopher Smart. *Fr.* Jubilate Agno. AtBAP
For the lifting up of mountains. Mountains. Lucy Larcom. WBLP
For the long nights you lay awake. To Alison Cunningham. Robert Louis Stevenson. PoVP
For the Lost Generation. Galway Kinnell. NePoAm; PPON
For the Magdalene. William Drummond of Hawthornden. AtBAP; LoBV; PoEL-2
For the Magi. J. Patrick Walsh. JKCP (1955 ed.)
For the Marriage of Faustus and Helen (I-III). Hart Crane. AP; NePA
"Capped arbiter of beauty in this street," III. FaBoMo; LiTM
For the Marsh's Birthday. James Wright. NYBP
For the Master's Use. *Unknown.* BLRP
(Watered Lilies, The.) BLPA; SoP
For the Nativity. John Heath-Stubbs. BoPe
For the Nativity of Our Lord ("O than the fairest day"). William Drummond of Hawthornden. StJW
For the New Railway Station in Rome. Richard Wilbur. NePoEA; PoDB
For the New Year. Robert Creeley. NaP
For the New Year. Edwin Markham. OQP
For the New Year. Norman Nicholson. NeBP; POTi
For the Nightly Ascent of the Hunter Orion over a Forest Clearing. James Dickey. TwCP
For the 90th Birthday of Sibelius. James Kirkup. MuSP; POTi
For the One Who Would Take Man's Life in His Hands. Delmore Schwartz. FiMAP; LiTA; LiTM; MiAP; MoAB; MoAmPo; MoVE; NePA; ThLM; WaP
For the outside leagues of liberty. Sidney Lanier. *Fr.* The Symphony. PoFr
For the palace that lies desolate. We Sit Solitary. *Unknown.* TrJP
For the past three days she had been wandering, and following. Charles Péguy. *Fr.* The Passion of Our Lady. ISi
For the Peace of Jerusalem. Charles Wesley. BePJ
For the Picture, "The Last of England." Ford Madox Brown. VA
"For the pleasures of the many." Variations, Calypso and Fugue

on a Theme of Ella Wheeler. John Ashbery. ANYP
For the poor body that I own. Garadh. Padraic Colum. OnYI; PG (1955 ed.)
For the precision that dares hardly look. To the Precision. Richard Brathwaite. *Fr.* A Strappado for the Devil. SiCE
For the Princess Hello. David Shapiro. ANYP
For the Rain It Raineth Every Day. Robert Graves. NYBP
For the Record. George Jonas. MoCV
For the Record. R. S. Thomas. BoPe
For the Right Honorable Lucy, Countess of Huntingdon, 1649. Thomas Pestel. ReEn
For the rosebud's break of beauty. Lucy Larcom. *Fr.* A Thanksgiving. TrPWD
For the Sake o' Somebody. Burns. *See* For the Sake of Somebody.
For the sake of a weathered gray city set high on a hill. Perugia. Amelia Josephine Burr. HBV
For the Sake of [*or* o'] Somebody. Burns. AtBAP; WePo
For the sea, too, has its roads. "Through the Dear Might of Him That Walked the Waves." John Heath-Stubbs. BoPe
For the second shot. The Zen Archer. James Kirkup. EaLo
For the Sexes. Blake. *See* Gates of Paradise, The.
For the Sin. *Unknown*, *tr. fr. Hebrew*. TrJP
For the Sisters of the Hôtel Dieu. A. M. Klein. WHW
For the Slender Beech and the Sapling Oak. Thomas Love Peacock. *See* Song: "For the tender beech and the sapling oak."
For the sole edification. A Credo. Thackeray. HBV
For the Sun Declined, *sel.* Yitzhak Lamdan, *tr. fr. Hebrew by* Simon Halkin.
"Where am I, O awesome friend?" TrJP
For the sun that shone at the dawn of spring. A Song of Thanks. Edward Smyth Jones. BANP
For the tender [*or* slender] beech and the sapling oak. Song [*or* The Greenwood Tree *or* The Oak and the Beech]. Thomas Love Peacock. *Fr.* Maid Marian. GTSE; OHIP; OTPC; PRWS
For the Time Being; a Christmas Oratorio, *sels.* W. H. Auden.
Advent. OAEP (2d ed.)
"Come to our well-run desert." TRV
Dialogue between Mary and Gabriel. ISi
Flight into Egypt, The, I-IV. OAEP (2d ed.); OxBA
After Christmas, III. MoAB; MoBrPo (1950 ed.)
(Well, So That Is That.) LiTA
Chorus: "He is the Way," IV. AnFE
(He Is the Way.) EaLo; MaRV
Fugal-Chorus from "For the Time Being," ("Great is Caesar"). LiTM (rev. ed.); NePA; SeCeV
Herod. OnHM
If, on Account of the Political Situation. LiTA; WaP
"Our Father, whose creative Will." TrPWD
Powers and Times Are Not Gods. MoRP
For the Truth. Edward S. Spriggs. BF; BP
For the Union Dead. Robert Lowell. AmPP (5th ed.); CoAP; FRC; LiTM (1970 ed.); MaPo (1969 ed.); NaP; NMP; NoP; PoAn; PoeP; SeCeV (1967 ed.); TDP; TwCP
For the Unknown Seamen of the 1939-45 War Buried in Iona Churchyard. Iain Cricthon Smith. BoPe
For the wealth of pathless forests. A Thanksgiving. Lucy Larcom. OHIP
For the West. Gary Snyder. NaP
For the whole world before thee is as a little grain of the balance. Wisdom of Solomon, Bible, Apocrypha. BoC
For "The Wine of Circe"; a Picture by Edward Burne-Jones. Dante Gabriel Rossetti. ATP (1953 ed.); MaVP; NoP; PoVP
For the Word Is Flesh. Stanley J. Kunitz. AnAmPo; NP
For the Youngest. Charles Wesley. *See* Gentle Jesus.
For the youth they gave and the blood they gave. The Debt. Theodosia Garrison. DD; PEDC
For Thee. *Unknown.* FaChP
For thee a crown of thorns I wear. Any Father to Any Son. Francis Burdett Money-Coutts. OBVV
For thee a stead was builded. The Grave. *Unknown.* ACP
For thee I shall not die. I Shall Not Die for Thee. *Unknown*, *tr. by* Douglas Hyde. AnIL; OxBI
For thee, little boy, will the earth pour forth gifts. Vergil. *Fr.* Eclogues. PoPl
For thee, O dear dear Country! Jerusalem the Golden. Bernard of Cluny, *tr. by* John Mason Neale. *Fr.* De Contemptu Mundi. HBV; OBVV; WGRP
For Them. Eleanor Farjeon. ChBR; ThGo
For Them All. John Hall Wheelock. HBMV; TSW
For them, O God, who only worship Thee. Worship. William Wilberforce Lord. AA
For them the Ceylon diver held his breath. The Proud Florentines. Keats. *Fr.* Isabella; or, The Pot of Basil. PoFr
For them the sun shines ever in full might. Life after Death. Pindar. EaLo
For there are two heavens, sweet. Two Heavens. Leigh Hunt. GN
For they are dead. Respect for the Dead. Laura Riding. LiTA
For they who fashion songs must live too close to pain. Weltschmerz. Frank Yerby. AmNP
For thirdly he works it upon stretch with the forepaws extended. Christopher Smart. Jubilate Agno, XX. NCEP
For thirty year, come herrin'-time. The Skipper-Hermit. Hiram Rich. EtS
For thirty years what madness I have known. The Masters of the Heart Touched the Unknown. Delmore Schwartz. FiMAP
For this agility chance found. "The Age Demanded." Ezra Pound. *Fr.* Hugh Selwyn Mauberley. NoP
For This Child I Prayed. J. Harold Gwynne. SoP
For This Is Wisdom. "Laurence Hope." *Fr.* The Teak Forest. PoLF; TreFT
(Wisdom?) OtMeF
For this one thing above all I would be praised as man. Chorus from "King Oedipus." Sophocles. *Fr.* Oedipus Rex. LiTW
For this peculiar tint that paints my house. My House. Claude McKay. CDC
For this present, hard. Woodnotes, I. Emerson. AnNE
"For this same night att [Bucklesfeildberry]." Little Musgrave and Lady Barnard (B *vers.*). *Unknown.* ESPB
For this she starred her eyes with salt. Epitaph. Elinor Wylie. MAP; MoAmPo
For this the ancient stars were hurled. Evolution. Israel Zangwill. TrJP
For This, the Tide. Val Vallis. BoAV
For this true nobleness I seek in vain. Sonnet. James Russell Lowell. CoBA
For This World, *sel.* Walter Rauschenbusch.
For This Universe. OQP
For this your mother sweated in the cold. To Jesus on His Birthday. Edna St. Vincent Millay. LiTG; MaRV; StJW; TrGrPo
For Thomas Hardy. Jane Cooper. AmPC
For those given to voyages: these roads. Muriel Rukeyser. *Fr.* The Cornfield. FiMAP
For Those in Peril. William Whiting. *See* Eternal Father, Strong to Save.
For those my unbaptizèd rhymes [*or* rhimes]. His Prayer for Absolution. Robert Herrick. AnAnS-2; EnL; EnLi-1 (1949 ed.); MaRV; OxBoCh; ReEn; SCEP-2; SeCV-1; TOP; TrPWD; TRV
For those that never know the light. The Children of the Night. E. A. Robinson. AmPP (4th ed.); NePA; OxBA
For Those Who Died. Thomas Curtis Clark. PGD
For Those Who Fail. Joaquin Miller. MaRV; OQP; PoToHe; TSW
For those who fell at Thermopylae. The Thermopylae Ode. Simonides. WaaP
For those who had the power. C. Day Lewis. *Fr.* A Time to Dance. FaBoMo; POTE
For those who place their blooms on new-made graves. Time's Hand Is Kind. Margaret E. Bruner. PoToHe
For thou art founded in the eternal fact. George Edward Woodberry. *Fr.* My Country. PoFr
For Though the Caves Were Rabitted. Henry David Thoreau. FaBoEn; PoEL-4; VaPo
For though the giant ages heave the hill. Strength—Human. Tennyson. *Fr.* Ode on the Death of the Duke of Wellington. SoP
For though, with men of high degree. Leaders, Old Style. Sir Walter Scott. *Fr.* Marmion. OtMeF
For thoughts that curve like winging birds. I Yield Thee Praise. Philip Jerome Cleveland. TrPWD; TRV
For three years, diabolus in the scale. Mauberley, II. Ezra

For (continued)
Pound. *Fr.* Hugh Selwyn Mauberley. NoP; NP
For three years, out of key with his time. E. P. Ode pour l'Election de Son Sepulchre. Ezra Pound. Hugh Selwyn Mauberley, I. AmPP; AP; CABA; CMoP; CoBMV; CrMA; FaBoEn; FaBoMo; ILP; LiTA; LiTG; LiTM (rev. ed.); MasP; MoAmPo (1962 ed.); MoPo; MoVE; NePA; OxBA; PoIE; PP; SeCeV; UnPo (3d ed.)
For Thy Sweet Love. Shakespeare. *See* Sonnets, XXIX.
For to Admire. Kipling. MoBrPo
For to love her for her looks lovely. Sir Thomas Wyatt. FCP
For Transient Things. James A. S. McPeek. OQP
For trewthe [*or* treuthe] telleth that love is triacle of hevene [*or* to abate sinne]. The Incarnation. William Langland. *Fr.* The Vision of Piers Plowman. OBEV (new ed.); PoEL-1
For Tu Fu. Feng Chih, *tr. fr. Chinese by* Chu K'an. LiTW
For twenty minutes between the end of storm. Green and Red and Darkness. Winfield Townley Scott. FiMAP
For twenty years and more surviving. Widows. Edgar Lee Masters. MoAmPo
For Two Girls Setting Out in Life. Peter Viereck. MiAP
For unto us a child is born. Prince of Peace. Isaiah, Bible, *O.T.* BoPe
For Us. Charlotte Perkins Gilman. OQP
For us, born into a world. Overtures to Death. C. Day Lewis. CMoP
For us like any other fugitive. Another Time. W. H. Auden. MemP; OxBA
For us, the dead, though young. The Unreturning. Clinton Scollard. DD; PAH
For Vicki at Seven. Sydney King Russell. BiCB
For WGF Who Was Told He Didn't Publish Enough to Be Promoted to Associate Professor. Lou Lipsitz. YAP
For want of a nail, the shoe was lost. Mother Goose. FaBoBe; GoTP; HBV; OTPC; OxNR; PPL; SiTL; TreFT
For want of will in woe I plain. Sir Thomas Wyatt. FCP; SiPS
For wars his life and half a world away. A Lullaby. Randall Jarrell. FiMAP
For we are all Christ's creatures, and by his coffer are we wealthy. Love We as Brothers. William Langland. *Fr.* The Vision of Piers Plowman. PoLi
For We Are Thy People. *Unknown.* TrJP
For we the mighty mountain plains have trod. The Sacraments of Nature. Aubrey Thomas De Vere. ACP; CAW
For weal or woe I will not flee. That Heart My Heart. *Unknown.* NoP
For weeks and weeks the autumn world stood still. How One Winter Came in the Lake Region. Wilfred Campbell. CaP; OBCV; PeCV; TDP
For wha ere had a lealer luve. Brown Adam. *Unknown.* ESPB (B *vers.*)
For what emperor. Bowl. Wallace Stevens. NP
For what is freedom, but the unfettered use. Samuel Taylor Coleridge. *Fr.* The Destiny of Nations. EnRP
For what is knowledge duly weighed? Christina Rossetti. *Fr.* The Convent Threshold. LO
For what the World admires I'll wish no more. The Resolve. Mary, Lady Chudleigh. OBEC
For what we owe to other days. Exit. E. A. Robinson. MoAmPo
For whatever is let go. May Song. Wendell Berry. AP
For whatever, it could. The Chance. Robert Creeley. FRC
For when it dawn'd—they dropp'd their arms. Coleridge. *Fr.* The Rime of the Ancient Mariner. UnS
For when the One Great Scorer comes. Grantland Rice. *Fr.* Alumnus Football. MaRV
For whiles I mark this weak and wretched world. George Gascoigne. *Fr.* The Steel Glass. ReIE; SiCE; TuPP
For Whitsunday. Francis Kinwelmersh. SiCE
For who can longer hold? when every press. Prologue. John Oldham. *Fr.* Satires upon the Jesuits. CEP; SeCV-2
For who shall change with prayers or thanksgivings. Swinburne. *Fr.* Anactoria. AtBAP
For who that leans on His right arm. He Upholds. Martin Luther. FaChP
For Whom, Pyrrha? Horace. *See* To Pyrrha.
"For Whom the Bell Tolls." Gavin Ewart. WaP
For why should we the busy soul believe. Sir John Davies. *Fr.* The Immortality of the Soul. ViBoPo
For why the gains doth seldom quit the charge. Seven Sonnets in Sequence, VI. George Gascoigne. Sonn
For William Edward Burghardt DuBois on His Eightieth Birthday. Bette Darcie Latimer. PoNe
For winter's rains and ruins are over. Spring Song. Swinburne. PCD
For wisdom, which is the worker of all things, taught me. Wisdom. Wisdom of Solomon, Bible, Apocrypha. BoC
For X. Louis MacNeice. Trilogy for X, I. EnLoPo ("When clerks and navvies fondle.") ErPo
For Ye Shall Go out with Joy. Isaiah, LV: 6-12, Bible, *O.T.* TreFT
For years he pried among the strata. A Geologist's Epitaph. Jane W. Stedman. WhC
For years I sought the Many in the One. The Quest. Eva Gore-Booth. MaRV; OQP
For years I thought I knew, at the bottom of the dream. The Meeting. Louise Bogan. NePoAm-2; NYBP
For years I've heard. Poem. Robin Blaser. NeAP
For years I've prayed, and yet I see no change. Shall I Pray On? Edith L. Mapes. SoP
For years I've read the books on how to. A Little Bow to Books on How To. Irwin Edman. WhC
For years the scenes bustled. A Poem About Baseballs. Denis Johnson. QAH
For years we live solitary in the soul's hermitage. From Desert to Metropolis. Sister Mary Estelle. JKCP (1955 ed.)
For You. Ted Berrigan. ANYP
For you/ I will be a ghetto jew. The Genius. Leonard Cohen. MoCV
For You. Carl Sandburg. MAP; MoAmPo; MoRP; WaKn
For You. Anne Waldman. YAP
For you I search my reference books in vain. De Fesch. James Reeves. MuSP
For You, Mother. Hilda Conkling. HH
For You, My Son. Horace Gregory. MAP; MoAmPo
For You O Democracy. Walt Whitman. AmePo; CoBA; PaA; PoFr; StaST; TrGrPo
For you Time past could not forget. Hymn to Proust. Gavin Ewart. NYBP
For you who are seeking to serve with your best. In His Service. Clarence E. Clar. STF
For your music, Perot, all the shepherds have praise. The Wager. Pierre de Ronsard. *Fr.* Pastoral Song for the Nuptials of Charles, Duke of Lorraine. HW
For Zion's sake will I not hold my peace. Isaiah, Bible, *O.T.* PoFr; TrJP
Foray, The. Sir Walter Scott. EPN
Foray of Con O'Donnell [A.D. 1495], The, *sels.* Denis Florence MacCarthy.
Irish Wolf-Hound, The. VA
"'Now, by Columba!' Con exclaimed." OnYI
Forbear, bold youth; all's heaven here. To One [*or* An Answer to Another] Persuading a Lady to Marriage. Katherine Philips. CavP; OBEV
Forbear to ask me why I weep. Cloe Jealous. Matthew Prior. CEP; EiPP
Forbearance. Avis B. Christiansen. SoP
Forbearance. William Cowper. MaRV
Forbearance. Emerson. AA; AmePo; AmPP (3d ed.); AnAmPo; AnNE; BBV (1923 ed.); BoLiVe; CoBA; GN; HBV; HBVY; LaNeLa; LiTA; MCCG; MPB; OnPM; OQP; OTPC; PCD; PoRL; TreFT; TrGrPo; ViBoPo; WGRP; YT
Forbearance. Della Adams Leitner. STF
Forbeare fond swaine I cannot love. *Unknown.* SeCSL
Forbidden, The. Phyllis Haring. PeSA
Forbidden Drink. Robert Lovett. WhC
Forbidden Fruit. Charles Cotton. PeRV
Forbidden Fruit ("Heaven is what I cannot reach!"). Emily Dickinson. *See* Heaven is what I cannot reach!
Forbidden fruit a flavor has. Emily Dickinson. AnNE; MWA-2
Forbidden Lure, The. Fannie Stearns Davis. HBV
Forby Sutherland. George Gordon M'Crae. VA
Force. "Nikolai Maksimovich Minski," *tr. fr. Russian by* Babette Deutsch. LiTW
Force. Edward Rowland Sill. AA
Force first made conquest, and that conquest, law. Pope. *Fr.* An Essay on Man, Epistle III. PoFr
Force of Illusions. Wallace Stevens. NYTB
Force of Prayer, The, *sel.* Wordsworth.
"Oh! there is never sorrow of heart." MaRV

Force of Snow. Colette Inez. QAH
Force of snow and furious hail is sent, The. The Constitution of Athens. Solon. PoFr
Force That through the Green Fuse Drives the Flower, The. Dylan Thomas. ATP (1953 ed.); CABA; CBEP; CBV; CMoP; CoBMV; DiPo; ExPo; FosPo; ILP; ImOP; InPo; LiTB; LiTM; MaPo; MoAB; MoBrPo; MoPo; MoVE; NeMA; NoP; OAEP (2d ed.); PG (1945 ed.); Po; PoAn; PoE; PoIE; ReMP; ToPo; UnPo (3d ed.); ViBoPo
(Poem.) NeBP
Forced Bridal, The. *Unknown.* PaPo
Forced Entry. Jack Marshall. YAP
Forced Music, A. Robert Graves. MoBrPo
Forced Recruit, The. Elizabeth Barrett Browning. PoVP
Forced to the towns by rain on an August afternoon. Homage to Arthur Waley. Roy Fuller. ML
Forcing a Way. *Unknown.* NA
Forcing House. Theodore Roethke. AtBAP
Ford Madox Ford. Robert Lowell. PoCh; TwCP
Ford o' Kabul River. Kipling. FaBoTw; PeVV
Fore-royal furled, I pause and I stand, The. Making Land. Thomas Fleming Day. EtS
Forebearance. "Owen Meredith." PCD
Forebears. Monk Gibbon. NeIP
Forebears. Elizabeth Riddell. BoAV
Foreboding. Grant Code. FiSC
Foreboding, A. "Violet Fane." VA
Foreboding, The. Robert Graves. ChMP; ELP; GTBS-D; StP
Foreboding. Hazel Hall. HBMV
Foreboding. *Unknown, tr. fr. Japanese by* Ishii *and* Obata. *Fr.* Manyo Shu. OnPM
Foreboding sudden of untoward change. By the Conemaugh. Florence Earle Coates. PAH
Forecast, A. Archibald Lampman. VA
Forecast. Josephine Miles. CrMA
Forecast. Sydney King Russell. FiSC
Foreclosure. Sterling A. Brown. PoNe
Foreclosure. Mark Van Doren. CrMA
Forefather, The. Richard Burton. AA
Forefathers. Edmund Blunden. ChMP; OBEV (new ed.); OBMV; POTE
Forefathers' Song. *Unknown. See* New England's Annoyances.
Forehead. Coleman Barks. *Fr.* Body Poems. QAH
Foreign Affairs. Stanley Kunitz. LiTM (1970 ed.); NYBP; TwAmPo
Foreign Children. Robert Louis Stevenson. BoChLi; BoTP; GaP; GFA; GoJo; MPB; OTPC (1946 ed.); RIS; SUS
Foreign Gate, The, *sel.* Sidney Keyes.
Were I to Mount beyond the Field, V. MoPo
Foreign Land, The. Coventry Patmore. The Angel in the House, II, ix, 2. HBV
(Woman.) OBVV
Foreign Lands. Robert Louis Stevenson. BoTP; GFA; HBV; HBVY; MPB; OTPC; PCH; PoVP; RIS; TiPo (1952 ed.); TVC; VA
Foreign Missions in Battle Array. Vachel Lindsay. MaRV; OQP
Foreign Ruler, A. Walter Savage Landor. PoFr; TreFT; ViBoPo
(Foren Ruler, A.) PV
Foreign Songsters. James Miller. *See* Italian Opera.
Foreign Summer. W. S. Merwin. AmPC
Foreigner Comes to Earth on Boston Common, A. Horace Gregory. EaLo
Foren Ruler, A. Walter Savage Landor. *See* Foreign Ruler, A.
Forenoon, The. Christopher Middleton. *Fr.* Herman Moon's Hourbook. NePoEA-2
Forenoon and afternoon and night. Life. Edward Rowland Sill. BLRP; MaRV; OQP; TRV
Forensic Jocularities; the History of a Case Shortly Reported by a Master in Chancery. *Unknown.* OxBoLi
Forepledged. John Lancaster Spalding. AA
Forerunners. Emerson. AA; AmePo; AnNE; OBEV (new ed.); OBVV; OxBA
Forerunners, The. George Herbert. AnAnS-1; MaMe; MeP; MePo; NoP; ReEn
Forerunners. Alexander Smith. *Fr.* A Life-Drama. VA
Foreseen for so many years: these evils, this monstrous violence. May-June, 1940 [*or* Battle]. Robinson Jeffers. AmPP; LiTA; LiTM (rev. ed.); MoAB; MoAmPo; NePA; StP; WaP
Foreseen in the vision of sages. America. Bayard Taylor. *Fr.* The National Ode. . .July 4, 1876. AA; PAL; PoFr
Forest. Harriet Gray Blackwell. GoYe
Forest. Jean Garrigue. LiTM
Forest, The. Dorothy Quick. FiSC
Forest, The. Paul Zech, *tr. fr. German by* Glauco Cambon. OnPM
Forest-Bird, The. W. J. Turner. POTE
Forest Boat Song. Richard Clyde Ford. IHA
Forest dim and grand, with mile on mile, A. Peacefulness. Henry W. Frost. SoP
Forest Fire, The. Arthur W. Monroe. PoOW
"Forest folk," The. Strawberries Mit Cream. Rochelle Owens. CoPo
Forest Glade, The. Charles Tennyson Turner. VA
Forest Hymn. Bryant. AA; AmePo; AmP; AmPP; AnNE; AP; CoBA; MWA-1; TOP
"Father, thy hand," *sel.* TrPWP
Forest Lake, A. Charles Tennyson Turner. PeER
Forest Leaves in Autumn. John Keble. *See* November.
Forest Maid, The. Bryant. OBVV
Forest Meditation, A. Bernice Hall Legg. PGD
Forest nuns, who sheltered us and healed, The. Krankenhaus of Leutkirch. Richmond Lattimore. NYBP
Forest of Arden, The. Michael Drayton. *Fr.* Polyolbion: The Thirteenth Song. SeEP
Forest Shapes. Donald Wandrei. FiSC
Forest so much fallen from what she was before, The. The Thirteenth Song. Michael Drayton. *Fr.* Polyolbion. SeCePo
Forest Song. William Henry Venable. PEDC
Forest was fair and wide, The. Tristrem and the Hunters. *At. to* Thomas of Erceldoune. *Fr.* Sir Tristrem. OxBS
Foresters, The, *sel.* Tennyson.
Song: "There is no land like England," *fr.* II, i. VA
Forester's Song. A. E. Coppard. FaPON; MPB
Forests. Walter de la Mare. CMoP
Forest's afire, The! October's Song. Eleanor Farjeon. PoSC
Forests are made for weary men. Leading. Mary Carolyn Davies. MaRV
Forest's Queen, The. Philip Massinger. GoBC
Foretelling of Cathbad the Druid at Deirdre's Birth, The. *Unknown, tr. fr. Middle Irish by* Lady Augusta Gregory. LiTW
Fore Thought. May Sarton. MoLP
"Forever." Charles Stuart Calverley. ALV; InMe; WhC
Forever. John Boyle O'Reilly. CAW; HBV; MaRV; OnYI; OQP; WGRP, *abr.*
For Ever. William Caldwell Roscoe. *See* Parting.
Forever am I conscious, moving here. The Undiscovered Country. Thomas Bailey Aldrich. AA
Forever and a Day. Thomas Bailey Aldrich. HBV; LHV
Forever at his side to walk. Emily Dickinson. CoBA
Forever Dead. Sappho, *tr. fr. Greek by* William Ellery Leonard. AWP; JAWP; LiTW; WBP
Forever dear, forever dreaded Prince. The Author to Queen Elizabeth, in Praise of Her Reading. Sir John Harington. SiCE
For ever, fortune, wilt thou prove. James Thomson. CBEP; GTBS; GTBS-D; GTBS-P; GTBS-W; GTSE; GTSL
Forever in Advent. Motif from the Second Shepherd's Play. Sister Mary Maura. JKCP (1955 ed.)
Forever in My Dream and in My Morning Thought. Henry David Thoreau. PoEL-4
Forever let there be shouting sisters. In a Harlem Store Front Church. Clarence Reed. BF
Forever Mexicans 'tis prostrate here. Epitaph to the Liberty of America. José Joaquín Fernández de Lizardi. PoFr
For-ever Morning. Laura Riding. LiTA
Forever on Thanksgiving Day. Wilbur D. Nesbit. PEDC
Forever over now, forever, forever gone. The Cameo. Edna St. Vincent Millay. LiTA; MAP; MoAmPo
Forever; 'tis a single word! "Forever." Charles Stuart Calverley. ALV; InMe; WhC
Forever we are eating up Thy bread. Refreshment. George Edward Hoffman. ChIP
Foreword, A: "Child! do not throw this book about." Hilaire Belloc. *See* Dedication on the Gift of a Book to a Child.
Forge, The. Oliver St. John Gogarty. AnIV
Forget. John Donne. *See* If Poisonous Minerals, and If That Tree.

Forget. *Unknown.* STF
Forget each kindness that you do as soon as you have done it. The Best Memory Course. *Unknown.* STF
Forget everything I said, forget it. Against Art. David Mus. YAP
Forget It. Judd Mortimer Lewis. PoLF; WBLP, *abr.*
Forget not bees in winter, though they sleep. Bee-Master. V. Sackville-West. HaMV
Forget Not Yet [the Tried Intent]. Sir Thomas Wyatt. AnFE; AtBAP; CBEP; EiL; EnLi-1 (1949 ed.); EnLit; EnRePo; FCP; GoBC; GTSE; HBV; MaPo; NoP; OAEP; OBEV; Po; PoAn; PoE; PoIE; ReEn; ReIE; ShBV-3; SiCE; SiPS; TuPP; YAT
(Lover Beseecheth His Mistress Not to Forget His Steadfast Faith and True Intent, The.) LO; TOP; ViBoPo
(Steadfastness.) OBSC
(Supplication, A.) GTBS; GTBS-D; GTBS-P; GTBS-W; GTSL; WoL
Forget six counties overhung with smoke. The Earthly Paradise: Prologue. William Morris. BEL; EPN; ViPo; ViPP
Forget the dead, this time. There Are Children in the Dusk. Bertram Warr. PeCV
Forget the old year's sorrows, forget its lonely days. Forget. *Unknown.* STF
Forget the past and live the present hour. Live in the Present [*or* Today]. Sarah Knowles Bolton. MaRV; OQP
Forget the slander you have heard. Just Forget. Myrtle May Dryden. WBLP
Forget the tube of bark. Very Tree. Stanley J. Kunitz. NP
Forget Thee? John Moultrie. BLPA; FaBoBe; NeHB
"'Forget thee?'—If to dream by night and muse on thee by day," *sel.* PoToHe (new ed.)
Forget them not, O Christ, who stand. Our Missionaries. Margaret E. Sangster. MaRV
Forget thine anguish. Meditations. Solomon ibn Gabirol. TrJP
Forget this rotten world; and unto thee. John Donne. *Fr.* Of the Progress of the Soul. FaBoEn
Forgetful Pa. Edgar A. Guest. IHA; PoRL
Forgetfulness. Maxwell Bodenheim. MAPA
Forgetfulness. Sosei, *tr. fr. Japanese by* Basil Hall Chamberlain. OnPM
Forget-me-not, The. *Unknown.* BoTP
Forget-me-not Day. Nan Terrell Reed. HH
Forgettin'. "Moira O'Neill." HBV
Forgetting God. J. E. Harvey. STF
Forgetting I am alive, the tent comes over me. The Jewel. James Dickey. TPM
Forging boldly ahead. The Bay Fight. Henry Howard Brownell. PAH; PAP
Forging of the Anchor, The. Sir Samuel Ferguson. HBV; IrPN; PoVP
Forgive. Lalia Mitchell Thornton. BePJ
Forgive. Whittier. MaRV; OQP
Forgive!/ And tell me that sweet tale. Francis Burdett Money-Coutts. *Fr.* A Little Sequence. OBVV
Forgive and Forget. "Totius," *tr. fr. Afrikaans by* Anthony Delius. PeSA
Forgive, fair creature, form'd to please. Song. *Unknown.* EiCL
Forgive Me. Dilys Laing. WOW
Forgive Me. *Unknown.* SoP
Forgive me for neglecting to show you. Forgive Me. Dilys Laing. WOW
Forgive me if I speak possessively of him. To a New Daughter-in-Law. *Unknown.* PoToHe (new ed.)
Forgive me, Lord, for careless words. Forgive Me. *Unknown.* SoP
Forgive me, Lord, that I allow. Too Busy. Avis B. Christiansen. SoP
Forgive me, Lord, the callow things I say. Finale. James Picot. BoAV
Forgive Me, Sire. Norman Cameron. GTBS-P; OxBS
Forgive me that I love you as I do. Incompatibility. Aubrey Thomas De Vere. IrPN; Sonn
Forgive me that I pitch your praise too low. Apology for Understatement. John Wain. NePoEA-2; ToPo
Forgive Me When I Whine. *Unknown.* STF
Forgive, O Lord, My Little Jokes on Thee. Robert Frost. EaLo; LiTM (1970 ed.)
Forgive, O Lord, our severing ways. Forgive. Whittier. MaRV; OQP
"Forgive them, for they know not what they do!" Abraham Lincoln. Edmund Clarence Stedman. LiPo; PAH
Forgive Us, O Lord. T. S. Eliot. *Fr.* Murder in the Cathedral. EaLo
Forgive us, son of Amram, be not wroth. Epigram III. *Unknown.* *Fr.* Duel with Verses over a Great Man. TRJP
Forgive what I give you. Through nightmare and cinders. To Mary—A Dedication. Louis MacNeice. BoPe
"Forgive yourself" is part of the command. Insubordination. Margaret Evelyn Singleton. ChIP
Forgiven? Jeannette Bliss Gillespy. Cameos, II. AA
Forgiven. A. A. Milne. SoPo
Forgiven. Margaret E. Sangster. PoToHe
Forgiveness. Lois Duffield. SoP
Forgiveness. Henry Francis Lyte. BePJ; SoP
Forgiveness. Elizabeth Sewell. EaLo
Forgiveness. Whittier. AmPP (3d ed.); MaRV
Forgiveness Lane. Martha Dickinson Bianchi. AA; PCD
Forgiveness of Sins. Samuel John Stone. SoP
Forgiveness of Sins a Joy Unknown to Angels. Augustus Lucas Hillhouse. AA
Forgotten City, The. William Carlos Williams. LiTA; NePA; PoPl
Forgotten Countersign, The. Corinne Roosevelt Robinson. OQP
Forgotten Dreams. Edward Silvera. PoNe
Forgotten Grave, The. Austin Dobson. VA
Forgotten Man, The. Edwin Markham. PoLF
Forgotten Objects on a Beach. Patricia Excell. BoAV
Forgotten People, *sel.* Rex Ingamells.
"No more the smoke-wisp signal climbs; no more." BoAu
Forgotten Rock, The. Richard Eberhart. NePA
Forgotten soldier, in the winter grass. Trooper Temple Pulvermacher. William Branford. BoSA
Forgotten Star, The. Thomas Curtis Clark. PGD
Forlorn and white. White Symphony. John Gould Fletcher. AnFE; APA; CoAnAm; MAPA
Forlorn One, The. "Thomas Ingoldsby." BOHV
Forlornly. Heine. *See* Mein Liebchen, wir sassen zusammen.
Form. Polly Chase Boyden. NP
Form. Eva Gore-Booth. MaRV
"Form Fours." Frank Sidgwick. WhC
Form Is Delight. Ernst Stadler, *tr. fr. German by* Glauco Cambon. OnPM
Form of Adaptation, A. Robert Creeley. AmPC
Form of awe he was—and yet it seemed, A. Satan. Michael Madhusudan Dutt. ACV
Form of Epitaph, A. Laurence Whistler. GTBS-P
Form of Women, A. Robert Creeley. AmPC; NaP
Form 1040A. Phyllis Eleanor Armstrong. SiTL
Form Was the World. Maurice English. NYBP
Formal Lyric. W. J. Turner. FaBoTw
Forme of Prayer, A. Francis Quarles. MePo
Formed long ago, yet made today. Riddles [*or* A Bed]. Mother Goose. HBV; HBVY; OTPC; OxNR; RIS
Former Barn Lot. Mark Van Doren. FaBV; LOW; MAP; MoAmPo; PDV; PoPl
Former Beauties. Thomas Hardy. At Casterbridge Fair, II. BEL; EnLi-2 (1949 ed.); EnLit; OBMV; OBNC; PoVP
"Formerly a Slave." Herman Melville. PoNe
Formosae Puellae. Herbert P. Horne. VA
Forms, *sel.* Theodore Enslin.
"Things being what they are do not imply necessity." CoPo
Forms of the Human. Richard Eberhart. FiMAP
Formula. Carolyn J. Ogletree. TNV
Forsake me not thus, Adam, witness heav'n. Eve Penitent. Milton. *Fr.* Paradise Lost, X. OBS
Forsaken, The. Hamilton Aïdé. VA
Forsaken. Zalman Schneour, *tr. fr. Yiddish by* Joseph Leftwich. TrJP
Forsaken, The. Duncan Campbell Scott. CaP; TwCaPo
"Once in the winter," *sel.* WHW
Forsaken [*or* Forsaken Bride]. *Unknown.* *See* Waly, Waly.
Forsaken Garden, A. Swinburne. BoLiVe; CBEP; EPN; FaBoEn; GTBS; GTBS-D; GTBS-P; GTSL; HBV; InP; LiTB; LiTG; LoBV; MaVP; NoP; OBNC; OBVV; PAn; PIA; PoE; PoFS; PoVP; ShBV-4; StP; TOP; VA; VaPo; ViPo; VP; WHA

Forsaken Lover, The. Sir Thomas Wyatt. *See* Lover, The, Showeth How He Is Forsaken. . .
Forsaken Maiden's Lament, A. *Unknown.* SeCePo
("Were it undo that is y-do.") EnPo
Forsaken Merman, The. Matthew Arnold. ATP (1935 ed.); BBV (1923 ed.); BEL; BeLS; BoLiVe; CBEP; EnL; EnLi-2; EnLit; EPN; EtS; FaBoCh; FiP; ForPo; GBV (1922 ed.); GN; GTBS; GTBS-D; GTSL; HBV; LoEn; LoGBV; MaVP; MBW-2; MCCG; MPB; NoP; OAEP; OBEV (1st ed.); OBVV; OnSP; OTPC; OuHeWo; PAn; PoVP; RG; ShBV-1; TOP; VA; ViBoPo; ViPo; ViPP; VP; WHA; YAT; YT
"Children dear, was it yesterday," *sel.* BoTP
Forsaken of all comforts but these two. Upone Tabacco. Sir Robert Aytoun. OxBS
"Forsaking all"—You mean. The Word. Margaret Avison. MoCV
Forsaking the Course. Jonathan Cott. YAP
Fort Bowyer. Charles L. S. Jones. PAH
Fort by the oak trees there, The. The Fort of Rathangan. *At. to* Berchan. ChTr
Fort Duquesne. Florus B. Plimpton. PaA; PAH
Fort McHenry. *Unknown.* MC, *abr.*; PAH
Fort of Rathangan, The. *Unknown, at. to* Berchan, *tr. fr. Irish by* Kuno Meyer. CH; FaBoCh; LoGBV; OxBI; ChTr, *tr. unknown*
Forth from earth's opened side. The Magnolia Tree. Hubert Witheford. AnNZ
Forth from its scabbard, pure and bright. The Sword of Robert Lee. Abram Joseph Ryan. JKCP; PaA; PoRL
Forth from the east, up the ascent of Heaven. Matthew Arnold. *Fr.* Balder Dead. PeVV
Forth from the glittering spirit's peace. Love in Action. Coventry Patmore. *Fr.* The Angel in the House, II, x. EG
Forth in shining phalanx marching from the shrouding mists of time. Gods and Heroes of the Gael. Eleanor Rogers Cox. JKCP
Forth rushed from envy sprung and self-conceit. Protest against the Ballot. Wordsworth. EPN
Forth sped thy gallant sailors, blithe and free. Gloriana's England. Archibald T. Strong. *Fr.* Sonnets of the Empire. BoAu
Forth, to the alien gravity. The Launch. Alice Meynell. PeVV
Forth welling from the breast of sapphire lakes. Easter Song. Leo Alishan. CAW
Forth went the candid man. The Candid Man. Stephen Crane. War Is Kind, IX. MAP; MoAmPo
Forthfaring. Winifred Howells. AA
Forthwith he gave in charge unto his squyre. Spenser. *Fr.* The Faerie Queene, I. MBW-1
Fortitude. Reinmar von Zweter, *tr. fr. German by* Jethro Bithell. LiTW
Fortitude; a Young Man of Egypt and Valerian. Richard Edwards. ReIE
Fortitude of the North, The. Herman Melville. AmePo
Fortnight before Christmas gypsies were everywhere, A. The Gypsy. Edward Thomas. NoP
Fortress, The. Anne Sexton. LiTM (1970 ed.); ToPo
Fortress of hope, anchor of faithful zeal. Barnabe Barnes. *Fr.* A Divine Century of Spiritual Sonnets. TuPP
Fortù, Fortù, my beloved one. The Englishman in Italy. Robert Browning. ExPo; PoEL-5; ViPo; ViPP
Fortunate are the feet of the swallow. Song. W. J. Turner. LO
Fortunate bridegroom. Congratulations. Sappho. HW
Fortunate father, blessed ancestor. To the Father of the Bride. Tasso. HW
Fortunate Isles, The. Joaquin Miller. WGRP
Fortunate Isles and Their Union, The, *sel.* Ben Jonson.
Chorus: "Spring all the Graces of the age," *also in* Neptune's Triumph. OBS; SeCL
Fortunate One, The. Harriet Monroe. AA
Fortunati Nimium. Thomas Campion. *See* Jack and Joan.
Fortunatus Nimium. Robert Bridges. BrPo; PoP
(Nimium Fortunatus.) MoAB; MoBrPo
Fortunatus the R. A. ("Fortunatus the portrait-painter got twenty sons"). Nicarchus, *tr. fr. Greek by* Dudley Fitts. LiTW
Fortune. Thomas Dekker. *See* Fortune and Virtue.
Fortune. Lawrence Ferlinghetti. *Fr.* Pictures of the Gone World. CAD; OCS
Fortune. Charles Madge. MoPW
Fortune. Sir Thomas More. *Fr.* Two Short Ballettes. GoBC; PoLi
(Lewis, the Lost Lover.) OBSC; TuPP
Fortune ("The Lady Fortune is both friend and foe"). *Unknown.* ACP
Fortune. Sir Thomas Wyatt. OBSC
Fortune and Men's Eyes. Shakespeare. *See* Sonnets, XXIX.
Fortune and Virtue. Thomas Dekker. *Fr.* Old Fortunatus. GoTL
(Fortune.) OBSC
(Fortune Smiles.) AtBAP
Fortune for Mirabel. Horace Gregory. TwAmPo
Fortune has brought me down—her wonted way. His Children [*or* He Thinks of His Children]. Hittan of Tayyi. *Fr.* Hamasah. AWP; JAWP; LiTW; WBP
Fortune, in power imperious. Of Fortune. Thomas Kyd. *Fr.* Cornelia. ElL
Fortune is stately, solemn, proud, and high. Of Fortune. Sir Thomas More. CoBE
Fortune made up of toyes and impudence. Part of an Ode of Horace Paraphras'd by the Duke of Buckingham, 1680. George Villiers, Duke of Buckingham. PeRV
Fortune Smiles. Thomas Dekker. *See* Fortune and Virtue.
Fortune-Teller, A. Witter Bynner. HBMV
Fortune Teller, The. John Holmes. NePoAm-2
Fortune-Teller, The. Matthew Prior. CEP
Fortunes of Nigel, The, *sel.* Sir Walter Scott.
"'Twas when fleet Snowball's head was waxen gray," *fr. ch.* 15. NBM
Fortune's Treachery. Judah Halevi, *tr. fr. Hebrew by* Solomon Solis-Cohen. TrJP
Fortune's Wheel. Lord De Tabley. OBVV; PoVP; VA
Forty-five Years since the Fall of the Ch'ing Dynasty. Philip Whalen. NeAP
Forty full-grown products of the old hand-in-hands. Psychology Class. Elizabeth K. Campbell. TwCaPo
Forty-gun frigate from Baltimore came, A. Paul Jones. *Unknown.* ViBoFo
Forty-Niner Tells His Story, A. *Unknown.* IHA
Forty Singing Seamen. Alfred Noyes. AnFE; BBV; BEL; BoChLi; GBV; OnMSP; ShBV-1; StPo; TOP
Forty teeth have I complete. The Strange Teeth. Nancy Birckhead. RIS
Forty Viziers saw I go. The Fair Circassian. Richard Garnett. HBV; OBVV; VA
Forty Years After. H. H. Porter. BOHV
Forty Years Ago. John Perreault. ANYP
Forty Years Ago. *Unknown, at. to* Francis Huston, *to* Dill Armor Smith, *and to* A. J. Gault. HBV
(Twenty Years Ago.) BFSS, *with music*; BLPA
Forty years back, when much had place. George Meredith. Thomas Hardy. EPN
Forty years he has pursued his love. Professor of Medieval Balladry. Sister Mary Maura. JKCP (1955 ed.)
Forty Years On. Edward Ernest Bowen. HBV
Forward. Edna Dean Proctor. HBV
Forward lay sunlight silver on the sea. The Waterspout. William Hart-Smith. *Fr.* Christopher Columbus. PoAu-2
Forward rush by the lamp in the gloom, A. The Contretemps. Thomas Hardy. CMoP; LiTM (rev. ed.)
Forward, then, ye jades! Christopher Marlowe. *Fr.* Tamburlaine the Great. ViBoPo
Forward violet thus did I chide, The. Sonnets, XCIX. Shakespeare. EG; EnLi-1; OAEP; OBSC
Forward with Christ. Carlton Buck. SoP
Forward young woman, Miss Chaos, A. The Trumpeter. *Unknown.* CoMu
Forward youth that would appear, The. An Horatian Ode upon Cromwell's Return from Ireland. Andrew Marvell. AnAnS-1; BEL; BWP; CABL; EP; FosPo; GTBS; GTBS-D; GTBS-P; GTBS-W; GTSE; GTSL; HBV; LoBV; MaMe; MaPo; MePo; NoP; OBEV; OBS; PAn; PoAn; PoEL-2; SCEP-2; SeCP; SeCV-1; SeEP; TOP; UnPo (1st ed.)
Forza D'Agrò. Edwin Denby. ANYP
Fossil, The. John Lyle Donaghy. NeIP
Fossil. Paul Engle. ReMP
Fossils, The. Galway Kinnell. NYBP
Fossils. James Stephens. OnYI
Fo'ty acres jes' fo' me! Freedom in Mah Soul. David Wadsworth Cannon, Jr. PoNe
Foul canker of fair virtuous action. To Detraction [I Present My

Foul (continued)
Poesie]. John Marston. *Fr.* The Scourge of Villany. LoBV; OBSC; ReIE; SiCE; TuPP
Foul fa [*or* 'a] the breast first treason bred in! Hobie Noble. *Unknown.* BaBo; ESPB; OBB; OxBB; ViBoFo
Foul Shot. Edwin A. Hoey. OTD
"Found." Dante Gabriel Rossetti. PoVP
Found a family, build a state. Fragments of a Lost Gnostic Poem of the Twelfth Century. Herman Melville. MWA-1; NoP; PoEL-5; ViBoPo
Found in the garden dead in his beauty. The Burial of the Linnet. Juliana Horatia Ewing. PRWS
Found in the Woods. Irene F. Pawsey. BoTP
Found in Thee. *Unknown.* SoP
Foundation of Faith. John Drinkwater. MoRP
Foundation waits, The (will rise). A Weekday. Larry Eigner. CoPo
Foundations. Henry van Dyke. TRV
Foundered Tram, The. Harold Monro. BrPo
Founder's day. Robert Bridges. OBVV
Founders of Ohio, The. William Henry Venable. MC; PaA; PAH; ThLM
Founding of Bolton Priory, The. Wordsworth. OTPC
Foundling Hospital for Wit, The, *sel.* Isaac Hawkins Browne. Fire Side, The; a Pastoral Soliloquy, *fr.* IV. OBEC
Fount of Mary's joy, The. The Son of God. Charles L. O'Donnell. JKCP
Fount there is, doth overfling, A. At the Fountain. Marcabrun. AWP; JAWP; WBP
Fountain, The. Donald Davie. GTBS-P
Fountain, The. Rose Fyleman. GFA
Fountain. Elizabeth Jennings. BoC; PoCh
Fountain, The. James Russell Lowell. BoTP; GoTP; OTPC; PCH; PRWS; PTK; RG
Fountain, The. Mu'tamid, King of Seville, *tr. fr. Arabic by* Dulcie L. Smith. AWP; JAWP; WBP
Fountain, The. A. J. M. Smith. CaP
Fountain, The. Wordsworth. EnRP; FosPo; GTBS; GTBS-D; GTBS-P; GTBS-W; GTSE; GTSL; MBW-2; OBRV; SeCePo
Fountains at the Tomb, The. Nicias, *tr. fr. Greek by* Charles Merivale. AWP; JAWP; WBP
Fountain blows its breathless spray, The. Irradiations, VI [VIII]. John Gould Fletcher. AnFE; APA; MAPA; TwAmPo
Fountain flows, but where the bowl, The. The Broken Bowl. Jones Very. AP
Fountain is dry at the Plaza, The. The Lady Is Cold. E. B. White. HT
Fountain of Bandusia, The. Horace. *See* To the Fountain of Bandusia.
Fountain of fire whom all divide. I Seek Thee in the Heart Alone. Herbert Trench. WGRP
Fountain of pity now with pity flow. Psalm LVI. Countess of Pembroke. EP
Fountain of sorrow, inn of cursed ire. Sonnet. Petrarch. Sonnets to Laura: To Laura in Life, CVII. PoFr
Fountain of Sweets! Eternal Dove! Whit Sunday. Joseph Beaumont. OxBoCh
Fountain of Tears, The. Arthur O'Shaughnessy. OBEV (1st ed.); OBVV; PoVP
Fountain of the Fairies, The. Robert Southey. OTPC
Fountain of Youth, The. Hezekiah Butterworth. PAH
Fountain Opened, The. William Cowper. *See* Praise for the Fountain Opened.
Fountains, The. W. R. Rodgers. MoVE
Fountains ("Proud fountains, wave your plumes"). Sir Osbert Sitwell. MoBrPo
Fountains ("This night is pure and clear as thrice refinèd silver"). Sacheverell Sitwell. MoBrPo
Fountains and the garden, The. Song for Music. G. S. Fraser. ChMP
Fountains mingle with the river, The. Love's Philosophy. Shelley. AtBAP; BLPA; BoLP; CoBE; EnLi-2 (1949 ed.); EnLit; EnRP; EPN; FaBoBe; FaBV; GTBS; GTBS-D; GTBS-P; GTBS-W; GTSE; GTSL; HBV; HoPM; LiTG; LiTL; MERP; MeWo; NeHB; OAEP; OBRV; PG; PoFS; PoIE; PoToHe (new ed.); TOP; TreFT; TrGrPo; UnTE; ViBoPo; WePo
Fountains of fire, The. Henry Rago. *Fr.* A Sky of Late Summer. NMP
Fountains that frisk and sprinkle. Ballade Made in the Hot Weather [*or* Made in the Hot Weather]. W. E. Henley. AnFE; GN; MoBrPo
Founts of Song, The. "Fiona Macleod." WGRP
Four. Elise Gibbs. BiCB
Four, The. Geoffrey Grigson. WaP
Four Ages of Man, The. W. B. Yeats. MoRP
Four an twenty noblemen they rode thro Banchory fair. Glenlogie; or, Jean o Bethelnie. *Unknown.* ESPB
Four and Eight. ffrida Wolfe. BiCB; BoTP; SiSoSe
Four-and-eighty years are o'er me; great-grandchildren sit before me. The Battle of Monmouth. Thomas Dunn English. PAH
Four and twentieth Day of May, The. The Swimming Lady; or, A Wanton Discovery. *Unknown.* ErPo; UnTE
Four and twenty bonny boys. Sir Hugh; or, The Jew's Daughter [*or* Hugh of Lincoln]. *Unknown.* BaBo (A *and* B *vers.*); CH; EnSB; ESPB (A *and* C *vers.*); OxBB; ViBoFo (A *vers.*)
Four-and-twenty Highland men. Eppie Morrie. *Unknown.* ESPB; OxBB
Four-and-twenty ladies fair/ Was playing at the ba. Bonny Baby Livingston (C *vers.*). *Unknown.* ESPB
Four and twenty laides fair, all being at a ball. Lord Banner. *Unknown.* BaBo
Four-and-twenty nobles rode [*or* rade] to the King's hall [*or* ha']. Glenlogie. *Unknown.* BuBa; OBB
Four and twenty nobles sits in the king's ha. Glenlogie; or, Jean o Bethelnie (B *vers.*). *Unknown.* ESPB
Four and twenty tailors went to kill a snail. Mother Goose. OTPC (1923 ed.); OxNR
Four Arms Have I. *Unknown.* OTPC (1946 ed.)
Four arms, two necks, one wreathing. Song. *Unknown.* ElL
Four be the things I am wiser to know. Inventory. Dorothy Parker. AnAmPo; PoPo
Four Birds. *Unknown.* ChTr
Four Blessings, The. *Unknown, tr. fr. Greek by* Thomas Moore. OnPM
Four boards of the coffin lid, The. After Death. Swinburne. PeVV
Four bright candles. Cake. Miriam Clark Potter. BiCB
Four bright pennies in a purse of brown. Penny Problem. John Farrar. GaP
Four Brothers, The, *sel.* Carl Sandburg.
Man-Hunt, The. OQP
Four Calls, The. Lydia Hadley. SoP; STF
Four children on a rumbling cart. Tinker's Moon. Ewart Milne. OnYI
Four Corners to My Bed. *Unknown.* *See* Matthew, Mark, Luke, and John.
Four days the earth was rent and torn. Bombardment. Richard Aldington. MMA
Four Deer, The. Mary Hoxie Jones. GoYe
Four Dogs. *Unknown.* SoP
Four Ducks on a Pond. William Allingham. IrPN; OTPC (1946 ed.); OxBI; ThWaDe; WePo
(Memory, A.) HBVY; OBVV; YT
Four Epigrams. John Owen, *tr. fr. Latin by* Thomas Harvey. PrWP
Bed, The.
King Arthur's Round Table.
Of Labienus.
To Polla.
Four Epitaphs. Countee Cullen. AmNP; CDC
Sels.
For a Lady I Know, 4. GoSl; IDB; Kal; PoNe; ShM
(Lady I Know, A.) MAP; MaRV; MoAmPo; TRV
For John Keats, Apostle of Beauty, 2. Kal
For My Grandmother, 1. GoSl; MAP; MoAmPo
For Paul Laurence Dunbar, 3. BALP; GoSl; Kal
Four feet up, under the bruise-blue. Small Woman on Swallow Street. W. S. Merwin. CoAP
Four Folk-Songs in Hokku Form. *Unknown, tr. fr. Japanese by* Lafcadio Hearn. LiTW
"All things change, we are told," 3.
"If with my sleeve I hide the faint color of the dawning sun," 4.
"Things never changed since the Time of the Gods," 1.
"Thinking tomorrow remains," 2.
Four for Sir John Davies. Theodore Roethke. AP; CoBMV; FiMAP; MoAmPo (1962 ed.); ReMP

Sels.
Dance, The, I. CrMA; NePoAm; UnS
Partner, The, II. NePA; NePoAm
Vigil, The, IV. PoDB
Four Friends, The. A. A. Milne. GoTP; TiPo (1959 ed.)
Four Friends. Leo Ward. GoBC
Four gallant ships from England came. The Battle of Stonington on the Seaboard of Connecticut. Philip Freneau. PAH
Four Glimpses of Night. Frank Marshall Davis. AmNP; PoNe
"Four good dogs dead in one night." Poisoned Lands. John Montague. NMP
Four great gates has the city of Damascus. Gates of Damascus. James Elroy Flecker. AnFE; BrPo; HBMV
Four great walls have hemmed me in. Four Walls. Blanche Taylor Dickinson. CDC
Four hooves rang out and now are still. Early Waking. Léonie Adams. LiTM (1970 ed.); MoVE
Four horizons cozen me. Shooting the Sun. Amy Lowell. MoAmPo (1950 ed.)
Four horsemen rode out from the heart of the range. The Bushrangers. Edward Harrington. PoAu-1
400-Meter Freestyle. Maxine W. Kumin. SD
Four hundred urgent springs and ripened summers. Pierre de Ronsard. Miriam Allen DeFord. HBMV
Four hundred years ago a tangled waste. Columbian Ode. Paul Laurence Dunbar. PoRL
Four is too big for his breeches. Four. Elise Gibbs. BiCB
Four Kantian Lyrics. Charles Tomlinson. OPoP
Four Kinds of Wading. Mildred D. Shacklett. GFA
Four-Leaf Clover. Wesley Curtright. GoSl
Four-Leaf Clover. Ella Higginson. AA; FaPON; HBV; OTPC (1946 ed.)
Four-Leaf Clover, The. Monica Shannon. BrR
Four-legg'd Elder, The; or, A Horrible Relation of a Dog and an Elder's Maid. Sir John Birkenhead. CoMu
Four-legg'd Quaker, The. *Unknown.* CoMu
Four Legs, Two Legs, Three Legs. William Empson. MoPo; ToPo
Four Letters and Certain Sonnets, *sel.* Gabriel Harvey.
Due Commendation of the Quipping Autor, A. RelE
Four Little Foxes. Lew Sarett. FaPON; GoTP; NP; OTD; PCD; PDV; PoMa; PoSC; PTK; RePo; WaKn; YeAr
Four little girls. Birmingham Sunday. Langston Hughes. PoNe (1970 ed.)
Four little sunbeams came earthward one day. The Four Sunbeams. "M. K. B." TVC
Four little white doves. Cuatro Palomitas Blancas. *Unknown.* ABF
Four Lovely Sisters ("Four lovely spinsters, sisters to a king"). C. A. Trypanis. ELU
Four Marys, The, *with music. Unknown.* BFSS
(Mary Hamilton's Last Goodnight.) ViBoFo
Four Men of God. Edgar A. Guest. OHFP (1958 ed.)
Four men stood by the grave of a man. Alexander the Great. *Unknown.* CH
Four miles at a leap, over the dark hollow land. Health. Edward Thomas. SeCePo
Four o'clock, four o'clock, four o'clock. Cow Time. Monica Shannon. SiSoSe
Four of us went to the woods one day. Jack-in-the-Pulpit. Rupert Sargent Holland. OTPC; StVeCh (1940 ed.)
Four or five coppers in his box! The Misery of the Beggars at the Gate of Zenkoji. Issa. PoFr
4 Part Geometry Lesson, A. Robin Blaser. NeAP
Four-Paws. Helen Parry Eden. BoTP; HBMV
Four pelicans went over the house. Pelicans. Robinson Jeffers. MAP; MoAmPo
Four Pets. Christina Rossetti. *Fr.* Sing-Song. PPL
("Pussy has a whiskered face.") TiPo
Four Poems. Antonio Machado. *See* Poems.
Four Poems for April. Louis Adeane. NeBP
Four pointes, my will, or I hence departe. A Last Will and Testament. *Unknown.* MeEL
Four Prayers. *Unknown, tr. fr. Modern Irish by* Eleanor Hull. OnYI
Sels.
I Lie Down with God. AnIV
I Rest With Thee, O Jesus. JKCP (1926 ed.)
Sacred Trinity, The ("Three folds of the cloth"). JKCP (1926 ed.)
Four Preludes on Playthings of the Wind. Carl Sandburg. AmLP; AnAmPo; AnFE; AP; BoLiVe; CMoP; CoAnAm; CoBA; InP; MAP; MoAB; MoAmPo; NePA; NP; SeCeV
Four P's, The, *sel.* John Heywood.
Palmer, The. ACP; CAW
Four Quartets, *sels.* T. S. Eliot.
Burnt Norton. AnFE; AtBAP; CABL; CMoP; CoAnAm; LiTG; LiTM (rev. ed.); MoAB; MoAmPo (1950 ed.); MoPo; PAn; PoE; TwAmPo
"Garlic and sapphires in the mud," II. GTBS-W
"Words move, music moves," V. UnS (12 *ll.*); ViBoPo (1958 ed.)
Dry Salvages, The. CABA; LiTB; MaPo; NoP; OxBA; SeCePo; SeCeV
"Lady, whose shrine stands on the promontory," IV. ISi
"To communicate with Mars, converse with spirits," V. AmPP; ATP (1953 ed.)
"Where is there an end of it, the soundless wailing," II. FaBoTw
East Coker. ChMP; FaBoMo; MoVE; NePA
Little Gidding. ExPo; FaBoEn; GTBS-P; OAEP (2d ed.); PoIE; SeCeV (1967 ed.)
"Ash on an old man's sleeve," II. FaBoTw; GTBS-W; PoFS
Dove, The, IV. BoC
"We shall not cease from exploration," V. ImOP
Four Quartz Crystal Clocks. Marianne Moore. AmPP (5th ed.); ImOP; TwCP
Four Questions Addressed to His Excellency the Prime Minister. James P. Vaughn. AmNP
Four rows of jaw teeth. Cowboy Boasting Chants. *Unknown.* ABF
Four sails of the mill, The. Lubber Breeze. T. Sturge Moore. CH
Four Saints in Three Acts, *sel.* Gertrude Stein.
"Pigeons on the grass alas." CrMA
Four Scarlet Berries. Mary Vivian. BoTP
Four Seasons. Rowena Bennett. SiSoSe; TiPo (1959 ed.)
Four seasons fill the measure of the year. The Human Seasons. Keats. CoBE; EnRP; FaFP; GTBS; GTBS-D; GTBS-P; GTBS-W; GTSE; GTSL; HBV; OBRV; PG (1955 ed.); PoPo; WiR; YAT
Four Seasons of the Year, The. Anne Bradstreet. SCAP
Spring, *sel.* AnNE
Four sharp scythes sweeping—in concert keeping. A Day in Ireland. *Unknown, tr. by* Michael Cavanagh. AnIV
Four Sheets to the Wind and a One-Way Ticket to France. Conrad Kent Rivers. AmNP, *diff. vers.*; IDB; NNP; PoNe (1970 ed.)
Four Sides to a House. Amy Lowell. NP; PoRA
4 sniffs & I'm high. Aether. Allen Ginsberg. CoPo
Four Songs from the Book of Samuel. Eli Mandel. MoCV
Four Sonnets to Helen. Pierre de Ronsard. *See* Sonnets pour Hélène.
Four Sonnets to Orpheus. Rainer Maria Rilke. *See* Sonnets to Orpheus.
Four Stanzas Written in Anxiety. George Jonas. MoCV
Four stiff-standers. A Riddle. *Unknown.* ChTr; OxNR
Four Stories. David Shapiro. ANYP
Four straight brick walls, severely plain. The Quaker Graveyard. Silas Weir Mitchell. AA
Four Sunbeams, The. "M. K. B." TVC
Four Sweet Months, The. Robert Herrick. *See* Succession of the Four Sweet Months.
Four Things. Proverbs, XXX: 24-28, Bible, *O.T.* FaPON; GoTP
Four Things. *Unknown.* MaRV; SoP; TRV
Four Things. Henry van Dyke. AA; BBV; GoTP; HBV; HBVY; MaRV; PCD; PoLF; PoToHe (new ed.); SoP; TreF; TRV
(Four Things to Do.) OQP; WBLP
Four things in any land must dwell. Four Things. *Unknown.* MaRV; SoP; TRV
Four Things to Do. Henry van Dyke. *See* Four Things.
Four III. E. E. Cummings. WePo
Four times the sun had risen and set; and now on the fifth day. Embarkation. Longfellow. *Fr.* Evangeline. PAH
Four tiny folk. Less Lonely. Alfred Kreymborg. AnAmPo
Four trees upon a solitary acre. Emily Dickinson. AP; PoEL-5
Four Walls. Blanche Taylor Dickinson. CDC

Four-way winds of the world have blown, The. Strike the Blow. "F. McK." PAH
Four Winds, The. Shane Leslie. OnYI
Four Winds, The. Longfellow. *Fr.* The Song of Hiawatha. AnNE
Four Winds, The. Charles Henry Luders. AA; HBV
Four Winds, The. Caroline Atherton Briggs Mason. *Fr.* En Voyage. PCH
Four Winds, The. Frank Dempster Sherman. TVC
Four Winds. Sara Teasdale. HBV
Four Wonders, The. *Unknown.* TuPP
Four Years. Dinah Maria Mulock Craik. HBV
Four years!——and didst thou stay above. Geist's Grave. Matthew Arnold. HBV; PoVP; VA
Four years old when the blackberries come! Hal's Birthday. Lucy Larcom. BiCB
Four Years Only. *Unknown, tr. fr. Greek by* Robert Guthrie MacGregor. OnPM
Four young men, of a Monday morn. The Prize of the Margaretta. Will Carleton. PAH
Four Zoas, The. Blake. *See* Vala; or, The Four Zoas.
Foure horses fierce, as red as flaming fire. The Lunar Valley of Lost Things. Ariosto. *Fr.* Orlando Furioso, XXXIV. LiTW
Foure teeth thou had'st that ranck'd in goodly state. Out of Martiall. Richard Crashaw. MaMe
Fourscore Years. *Unknown.* SoP
Fourteen, a sonneteer thy praises sing. A Sonnet upon Sonnets. Burns. Sonn
Fourteen July 1956. Laurence D. Lerner. BoSA; PeSA
Fourteen small broidered berries on the hem. What the Sonnet Is. Eugene Lee-Hamilton. HoPM; OBVV; Sonn; VA
Fourteen Ways of Touching the Peter. George MacBeth. FIW
Fourteenth Birthday. Phyllis McGinley. NePoAm-2
Fourteenth of July had come, The. La Tricoteuse. George Walter Thornbury. BeLS
Fourteenth Street. Tony Towle. YAP
Fourth Act. Robinson Jeffers. LiTA; WaP
Fourth Book of Sibylline Oracles, The, *sel.* *At. to* "The Jewish Sibyl," *tr. fr. Greek by* Bohn.
There Is a City. TrJP
Fourth Cycle of Love Poems, *sel.* George Barker.
Love Poem: "Less the dog begged to die in the sky." NeBP
Fourth day came, but not a breath of air, The. Byron. *Fr.* Don Juan, II. ChER
Fourth Day's Battle, The. Dryden. *Fr.* Annus Mirabilis. OBS
Fourth Eclogue, The. Vergil, *tr. fr. Latin by* James Laughlin. *Fr.* Eclogues. LiTW
Sels.
"For thee, little boy, will the earth pour forth gifts." PoPl
Sibylline Prophecy, The, *tr. by* Roderick Gill. CAW; ISi, *tr. wr. at. to* Thomas Walsh
Fourth Egloge of Alexander Barclay, The, Entituled Codrus and Minalcas, Treating of the Behavior of Rich Men against Poets. Alexander Barclay. ReIE
Fourth Eglogue, The, *abr.* George Wither. *Fr.* The Shepheards Hunting. SeCV-1
Fourth Napoleon, *sel.* J. A. R. McKellar.
Love in a Cottage. PoAu-2
Fourth of July. Marchette Chute. SiSoSe
Fourth of July. Rachel Field. SiSoSe
Fourth of July. S. S. Gardons. AmPC
Fourth of July, The. John Pierpont. AnNE; DD; HH; MC; OTPC (1946 ed.); PAH; PAL; PoRL; YeAr
4th of July he stormed a nest, The. War Story. George Starbuck. TDP
Fourth of July Night. Dorothy Aldis. SiSoSe; TiPo
Fourth of July Ode. James Russell Lowell. HH; PoRL; TSW
Fourth of July Song. Lois Lenski. SiSoSe
Fourth of July, they say, sir. Young America. Carolyn Wells. DD
Fourth Satire of Dr. John Donne, Dean of St. Paul's, Versified, The. Pope. *Fr.* Imitations of Donne. MBW-1
Fourth Song, The, *sel.* Michael Drayton. *Fr.* Polyolbion.
"Mongst whom, some there were bards, that in their sacred rage." PrWP
Fourth Song: "Only joy, now here you are." Sir Philip Sidney. *See* Astrophel and Stella: Fourth Song.
Fourth Station. Paul Claudel, *tr. fr. French by* Sister Mary David. ISi
Fourth Station. Padraic Colum. ISi
Fourth Station. William A. Donaghy. ISi
Fourth Station. Ruth Schaumann, *tr. fr. German by* William J. Brell. ISi
Foweles in the frith. Fowls in the Frith. *Unknown.* NCEP
Fower oufant wivies stude. The Wee May o' Caledon. Lewis Spence. ACV
Fowler, The. W. W. Gibson. HBMV
Fowls in the Frith. *Unknown.* CBEP; NCEP
(I Live in Great Sorrow.) MeEL
Fox. Clifford Dyment. HaMV; POTi
Fox, The. Edsel Ford. NYTB
Fox, The. Phoebe Hesketh. HaMV
Fox, The. R. Williams Parry, *tr. fr. Welsh by* Gwyn Williams. PrWP
Fox, The. Kenneth Patchen. AnAmPo
Fox, The. I. L. Salomon. NYTB
Fox, The. Marjorie Somers Scheuer. GoYe
Fox, The. Ian Serraillier. POTE
Fox, The. Charles Tomlinson. OPoP
Fox, The (*diff. versions*). *Unknown.* BaBo; GFA; StPo
(Ballad of the Fox.) GoTP; OTPC (1946 ed.)
(Fox Jumped Up on a Moonlight Night, The.) OTPC (1923 ed.)
("Fox jumped up one winter's night, A.") OxNR
(Fox Walked Out, The, *with music, A and B vers.*) BFSS
(Fox Went Out One Frosty Night, The.) BLPA
(Hungry Fox, The, *with music.*) FTB
(Visit from Mr. Fox, A.) StVeCh
Fox, almost with hunger dying, A. The Fox and the Grapes. La Fontaine. OnPM
Fox and Goose. F. Hey. SAS
Fox and the Bust, The. La Fontaine, *tr. fr. French by* Elizur Wright. OnPM
Fox and the cat, as they travell'd one day, The. The Virtuous Fox and the Self-righteous Cat. John Cunningham. OnMSP
Fox and the Grapes, The. La Fontaine, *tr. fr. French by* Elizur Wright. OnPM
Fox and the Grapes, The. Joseph Lauren. GoTP; RIS
Fox at the Point of Death, The. John Gay. *Fr.* Fables. EnLi-1 (1949 ed.); OBEC; OTPC (1923 ed.)
Fox at your neck and snakeskin on your feet, A. Leaving Something Behind. David Wagoner. CoAP
Fox Awakes, The. John Masefield. *Fr.* Reynard the Fox. MoVE
Fox [he] came lolloping, lolloping, The. Hunting Song. Donald Finkel. CoAP; MoBS; NePoEA
Fox came up by Stringer's Pound, The. Midnight. John Masefield. BrPo
Fox drags its wounded belly, The. January. R. S. Thomas. ELU
Fox flees the farm in a red rogue dazzle. For Hani, Aged Five, That She Be Better Able to Distinguish a Villain. Gene Baro. NYBP
Fox-Hunters, The. Ebenezer Elliott. PeER
Fox, in heaven's trap that gleams, A. The Stars Go By. Lilian Bowes-Lyon. ChMP
Fox, in life's extreme [*or* extream] decay, A. The Fox at the Point of Death. John Gay. *Fr.* Fables. EnLi-1 (1949 ed.); OBEC; OTPC (1923 ed.)
Fox Jumped Up on a Moonlight Night, The. *Unknown. See* Fox, The.
Fox jumped up one winter's night, A. *Unknown.* OxNR
Fox knew well that, before they tore him, The. John Masefield. *Fr.* Reynard the Fox. OtMeF
Fox may steal your hens, Sir, A. John Gay. *Fr.* The Beggar's Opera. CEP
Fox Rhyme, The. Ian Serraillier. ELU
Fox set [*or* went] out in [a] hungry plight, The. The Fox [*or* A Visit from Mr. Fox *or* The Hungry Fox]. *Unknown.* FTB; GFA; StVeCh
Fox Walked Out, The. *Unknown. See* Fox, The.
Fox went out on a [*or* one] chilly night, A. The Fox [*or* Ballad of the Fox]. *Unknown.* GoTP; StPo
Fox Went Out One Frosty Night, The. *Unknown. See* Fox, The.
Foxes among the Lambs. Ernest G. Moll. BoAu

Foxes have holes in the ground, The. Hard Trials. *Unknown.* ABF
Foxglove bells, with lolling tongue, The. Foxgloves. Mary Webb. BoTP
Foxglove by the cottage door, The. Four and Eight. ffrida Wolfe. BiCB; BoTP; SiSoSe
Foxgloves. Ted Hughes. LOW
Foxgloves. Mary Webb. BoTP
Foxhole for the Night, A. John Quinn. BoAV
Foxtail Pine. Gary Snyder. CoPo; NaP
Foxtrot from a Play. W. H. Auden. LiTM
Fra Bank to Bank. Mark Alexander Boyd. *See* Sonnet: "Fra bank to bank, fra wood to wood, I rin."
Fra Carmelo's Morning Sacrifice. Gervase Toelle. JKCP (1955 ed.)
Fra Lippo Lippi. Robert Browning. BEL; BoLiVe; CABL; CTC; EnL; EnLi-2; EnLit; EPN; MaPo (1969 ed.); MaVP; MBW-2; NoP; OAEP; OtMeF; PAn; PoVP; ViBoPo; ViPo; ViPP; VP
Fra Pandolf, have you tried to reproduce. Technique. Burnham Eaton. GoYe
Fra whaur in fragrant wuds ye bide. Spring on the Ochils. J. Logie Robertson. OBVV
Frae great Apollo, poet, say. The Poet's Wish; an Ode. Allan Ramsay. CEP; EiPP
Frae nirly, nippin', Eas'lan' breeze. Ille Terrarum. Stevenson. OxBS
Fragile affirmations of the springtime, The. April. Francis Sweeney. JKCP (1955 ed.)
Fragment: Abyss of War, The. Wilfred Owen. POTE
Fragment: "As if stone Caesar shook." Hugh McCrae. BoAV
Fragment: "Breath of life imbued those few dim days, The." Jessie Redmond Fauset. CDC
Fragment: "Bury him deep. So damned a work should lie." Thomas Lovell Beddoes. ELU
Fragment: "Cataract, whirling to the precipice, The." John Clare. BoNaP
Fragment, A: "Could I remount the river of my years." Byron. ERoP-2
Fragment: "Encinctur'd with a twine of leaves." Samuel Taylor Coleridge. *See* Fruit Plucker, The.
Fragment: "Faint white pillars that seem to fade." E. A. Robinson. MAPA
Fragment: "Flower in the crannied wall." Tennyson. *See* Flower in the Crannied Wall.
Fragment: Furl of Fresh-leaved Dog-Rose Down, The. Gerard Manley Hopkins. AtBAP
Fragment: "He that but once too nearly hears." Coventry Patmore. *Fr.* The Victories of Love. NBM
Fragment, A: "His eye was stern and wild—his cheek was pale and cold as clay." *Unknown.* BOHV
Fragment, A: "I cannot find my way to Nazareth." Yvor Winters. PoIE
Fragment, A: "I saw the Sibyl at Cumae." Dante Gabriel Rossetti. PeVV
Fragment: "I strayed about the deck, an hour, to-night." Rupert Brooke. BrPo
Fragment: "I walk'd [*or* walked] along a stream for pureness rare." Gervase Markham, *at. to* Christopher Marlowe. CTC; LoBV; OBSC
Fragment: "I would to heaven that I were so much clay." Byron. *Fr.* Don Juan. CTC; FiP; ILP; OAEP; PeER
Fragment: "Language has not the power to speak what love indites." John Clare. ERoP-2; NBM; PoEL-4
Fragment: "Mary, I believ'd you quick." Thomas Hood. NBM
Fragment: "Mountain summits sleep, The. Alcman, *tr. fr. Greek by* Thomas Campbell. AWP; JAWP; WBP
(Sleep upon the World.) ChTr
Fragment: "Near where the riotous Atlantic surge." William Allingham. IrPN
Fragment: "Pity, Religion has so seldom found." William Cowper. *Fr.* Table Talk. WGRP
Fragment: Rain. Shelley. ChER
Fragment: "Repeat that, repeat." Gerard Manley Hopkins. *See* Cuckoo, The.
Fragment: "Strike, churl; hurl, cheerless wind, then; heltering hail." Gerard Manley Hopkins. NAMP
Fragment: "There is a river clear and fair." Catherine Fanshawe. *See* Fragment in Imitation of Wordsworth.
Fragment: "Though decked the tray." Jami. *Fr.* Baharistan. CIV
Fragment, A: To Music. Shelley. BoLiVe; MuSP
(Music.) TrGrPo
Fragment: To the Moon. Shelley. *See* Moon, The ("Art thou pale. . .").
Fragment: "Ukraina is sad for that she has no place to dwell in." *Unknown, tr. fr. Ukrainian by* Florence Randal Livesay. PoFr
Fragment: "Walk with thy fellow-creatures: note the hush." Henry Vaughan. TRV; WGRP
Fragment: "What is poetry? Is it a mosaic." Amy Lowell. WGRP
Fragment: "Wing'd seeds with decaying wings, The." William Allingham. IrPN
Fragment: "You see/ Nestled into a hollow of the downs." William Allingham. *Fr.* By the Way. IrPN
Fragment from "Clemo Uti—the Water Lilies." Ring Lardner. FiBHP
Fragment in Imitation of Wordsworth. Catherine Fanshawe. HBV
(Fragment: "There is a river clear and fair.") ALV; Par
(Imitation of Wordsworth, An.) BOHV
Fragment of a Greek Tragedy. A. E. Housman. CenHV; Par
Fragment of a Sleep-Song. Sydney Dobell. VA
Fragment of a Sonnet. Pierre de Ronsard, *tr. fr. French by* Keats. AWP; JAWP; OuHeWo; WBP
Fragment of an Agon. T. S. Eliot. LiTB
Fragment of an Anti-Papist Ballad. *Unknown.* CoMu
Fragment of an Ode to Maia [Written on May Day, 1818]. Keats. EnRP; ERoP-2; MBW-2; OAEP; OBEV; OBRV; PeER; PoEL-4
(To Maia.) EPN
Fragment of Chorus of a "Dejaneira." Matthew Arnold. MBW-2; ViPP
Fragment of Death. Villon. *See* Fragment on Death.
Fragment of Sappho. Sappho. *See* To a Bride.
Fragment on Death. Villon, *tr. fr. French by* Swinburne. CTC; OuHeWo; PeVV
(Fragment of Death.) AWP
Fragment 113: "Not honey." Hilda Doolittle ("H. D."). *See* Not Honey.
Fragment Thirty-Six. Hilda Doolittle ("H. D."). CMoP; OxBA
(Hesperides—Fragment Thirty-six.) NP
Fragments. Emerson. *See* Music.
Fragments. W. B. Yeats. PoeP
Fragments from Italy, *sel.* John Ciardi.
"Nona Domenica Garnaro sits in the sun." ToPo
Fragments Intended for the Dramas, *sel.* Thomas Lovell Beddoes.
Beautiful Night, A. ChER; LoBV
Fragments of a Lost Gnostic Poem of the Twelfth Century. Herman Melville. MWA-1; NoP; PoEL-5; ViBoPo
Fragments on Nature and Life. Emerson. TOP
Atom from Atom, *sel.* ImOP
("Atom from atom yawns as far.") TiPo (1959 ed.)
Fragments on the Poet and the Poetic Gift, *sels.* Emerson.
"If bright the sun, he tarries." PP
"Pale genius roves alone." TOP
Fragmentum. Petronius Arbiter. *See* Doing a Filthy Pleasure Is.
Fragoletta. Swinburne. UnTE
Fragoletta, blessed one! Songs for Fragoletta, I. Richard Le Gallienne. HBV
Fragonard. Ogden Nash. RePo
Fragrance. Ruth Gibbs Zwall. SoP
Fragrance drifts through our thoughts of Him. Incense. Leslie Savage Clark. ChIP
Fragrant prayer upon the air, A. A Poem to Be Said on Hearing the Birds Sing. *Unknown, tr. fr. Irish by* Douglas Hyde. AnIV; AWP; JAWP; WBP
Fragrant silence filled the purple air, A. The Rosary. Sister Maura. ISi
Fragrant Thy Memories. "Judah," *tr. fr. Hebrew by* Herbert Loewe. TrJP
Frail children of sorrow, dethroned by a hue. Hope. Georgia Douglas Johnson. CDC
Frail Hands. Lucia Trent. FiSC
Frail Life! in which, through mists of human breath. Life and Death. Sir William Davenant. *Fr.* The Christians Reply to the Philosopher. BoC; FaChP; OBS

Frail Sleep, that blowest by fresh banks. To Sleep. Percy MacKaye. HBMV
Frail sound of a tunic trailing, A. Poems. Antonio Machado, *tr. fr. Spanish by* John Dos Passos. AWP; JAWP; LiTW; WBP
Frail the white rose and frail are. A Flower Given to My Daughter. James Joyce. BoPe; OBMV; PoPl; ReMP
Frail, wistful guardian of the broom. The Sweeper. Agnes Lee. HBMV; NP; QFR
Frailly, frailly stands the lone bamboo. Blues #8. *Unknown.* HW
Frailtie. George Herbert. *See* Frailty.
Frailty, The. Abraham Cowley. CavP
Frailty. George Herbert. OxBoCh
(Frailtie.) MaMe
Frailty and Hurtfulness of Beauty, The. Earl of Surrey. *See* Brittle Beauty.
Frailty of Beauty, The. "J. C." *Fr.* Alcilia. EIL
Frailty, Thy Name Is Woman. Shakespeare. *Fr.* Hamlet, I, ii. TrGrPo
(Hamlet Broods over the Death of His Father.) TreFS
Frainchman he don't lak to die in de fall. On Meesh-e-gan. *Unknown.* ABF; TrAS
Framed by a silken fringe, in strange accord. The Tapestry. Stefan George. LiTW
Framed in the cavernous fire-place sits a boy. An Old Thought. Charles Henry Luders. AA
Framed in the front of forlorn hope past all recovery. His Good Name Being Blemished, He Bewaileth. Edward de Vere, Earl of Oxford. ReIE
Framed in the sedan windows, the tall triangular faces. Giraffes. N. H. Brettell. BoSA
Framework-Knitters Lamentation, The. *Unknown.* CoMu
Framework-Knitters Petition, The. C. Briggs. CoMu
France. Goldsmith. *Fr.* The Traveller. OBEC
France. Elliott Napier. BoAu
France. Wordsworth. *See* French Revolution, The.
France; an Ode. Samuel Taylor Coleridge. ATP; BEL; EnLi-2 (1949 ed.); EnRP; EPN; ERoP-1; MBW-2; MERP; OAEP; PoFr, *abr.*; StP; TOP
"Ye Clouds! that far above me float and pause," *sel.* PoG
France! It is I answering. Republic to Republic. Witter Bynner. PAH
France lured me forth, the realm that I had crossed. Residence in France. Wordsworth. *Fr.* The Prelude, IX, *and* X. MBW-2
Frances. John Gill. ThO
Frances Harris's Petition. Swift. *See* To Their Excellencies the Lords Justices of Ireland, the Humble Petition of Frances Harris.
Francesca da Rimini. Dante, *tr. fr. Italian by* Dante Gabriel Rossetti. *Fr.* Divina Commedia: Inferno. EPN
Francesca da Rimini/ Lived in a chiminey. Important People. Louis Untermeyer, *and others.* StaSt
Francesco Ceni. Gabriello Chiabrera, *tr. fr. Italian by* Wordsworth. *See* Epitaphs.
Francesco's Fortunes, *sels.* Robert Greene.
Eurymachus's Fancy. OBSC
Penitent Palmer's Ode, The. LoBV; OBSC
Francis Beaumont's Letter from the Country to Jonson. Francis Beaumont. *See* Master Francis Beaumont's Letter to Ben Jonson.
Francis, my brother, in the clear, wide morning. Boy Playing an Organ. Francis Sweeney. GoBC
Francis' New Jig. George Attowell. ReIE
Francis Parkman. Ernest Kroll. NYTB
Franciscan Aspiration. Vachel Lindsay. *See* St. Francis.
Franciscan Dream, A. Enid Dinnis. CAW
Francisco Coronado rode forth with all his train. Quivira. Arthur Guiterman. PAH; PFY
Frangipanni. *Unknown.* NA
Frank carves very ill, yet will palm all the meats. Epigram. Matthew Prior. CEP
Frank Courtship, The, *sel.* George Crabbe.
Jonas Kindred's Household. FaBoEn; OBNC
("Grave Jonas Kindred, Sybil Kindred's sire," *longer sel.*) OBRV
Frankie and Johnny [*or* Johnnie]. *Unknown.* AmPP (3d ed.); AS, *with music*; ATP; BeLS; FaFP; LiTG; LiTL; NeHB; OxBoLi; SiTL; TrAS, *with music*; TreF; TrGrPo; UnPo; YaD
(Frankie and Albert, *with music.*) ABF (A *and* B *vers.*); AS; BaBo (A *and* B *vers.*); ViBoPo (A *and* B *vers.*)
(Frankie Blues, *with music.*) AS
(Josie, *diff. vers., with music.*) AS
(Sadie, *diff. vers., with music.*) AS
Frankie's Trade. Kipling. EtS
Franklin Square. William Carlos Williams. TDP
Franklin's Crew, *with music. Unknown.* SoAmSa
Franklin's Tale, The. Chaucer. *Fr.* The Canterbury Tales. CABL; MBW-1; OAEP
Frankly, I prefer the blue. Sentimental Lines to a Young Man Who Favors Pink Wallpaper, While I Personally Lean to the Blue. Margaret Fishback. FiBHP
Frascati's. Aldous Huxley. InPo; ViBoPo
"Frater Ave atque Vale." Tennyson. ChTr; EPN; GTBS-P; MaPo (1969 ed.); MBW-2; NoP; PoVP; ViPo
Fraternitas. Confucius, *tr. fr. Chinese by* Ezra Pound. *Fr.* Deer Sing. CTC
Fraternity. Anne Reeve Aldrich. AA
Fraternity. John Bainster Tabb. HBV
Fratri Dilectissimo. John Buchan. OtMeF
Frau Bauman, Frau Schmidt, and Frau Schwartze. Theodore Roethke. CoAP; MoAB; NePoAm; NYBP
Fraud, a forger, and informer, too, A. A Bad Joke. Martial. UnTE
Fraudulent perhaps in that they gave. Swans. Lawrence Durrell. FaBoMo; MoBrPo (1962 ed.); SeCePo
Fräulein Reads Instructive Rhymes. Maxine W. Kumin. NYBP
Fray began at the middle gate, The. A Ballad of Orleans. Agnes Mary Frances Robinson. HBV; VA
Freak Show, The. Nancy Willard. ThO
Freckles/ tickle your nose. Bits and Pieces. Gregory J. Ford. TNV
Freckles numberless as stars on my forehead. My Portrait. Moishe-Leib Halpern. TrJP
Fred. Eleanor Farjeon. OnPP
Fred. David McCord. TiPo (1959 ed.)
Fred Apollus at Fava's. Nicholas Moore. ErPo; NeBP
Fred likes creatures. Fred. Eleanor Farjeon. OnPP
"Fred, where is north?" West-running Brook. Robert Frost. AmP; AP; DiPo; MAP; MoAB; MoAmPo; NoP
Freddie [*or* Freddy] and the Cherry Tree ("Freddie saw some fine [*or* nice] ripe cherries"). Ann Hawkshaw. OTPC (1923 ed.); SAS
Freddy the Rat Perishes. Don Marquis. *Fr.* Archy and Mehitabel. OCS
Frederick Douglass. Paul Laurence Dunbar. BALP
Frederick Douglass. Robert Hayden. AmNP; IDB; Kal; NoP; PoNe; TTY; WOW
Fredericksburg. Thomas Bailey Aldrich. PaA; PAH; PAP; PFY
Fredome. John Barbour. *See* Freedom.
Free America. *At. to* Joseph Warren. PAP; PoFr
Free are the Muses, and where freedom is. Breath on the Oat. Joseph Russell Taylor. HBV; PAH
Free at las'—free at las'. I Thank God I'm Free at Las'. *Unknown.* BoAN-2
Free Enterprise. Clyde McGee. *See* Cross Makers.
Free evening fades, outside the windows fastened with decorative iron grilles, The. Evening in the Sanitarium. Louise Bogan. TwCP
Free Fantasia on Japanese Themes. Amy Lowell. MAP; MoAmPo
Free I have my own self-reliance. I Drift in the Wind. Ingrid Jonker. PeSA
Free Martin. Peter Hopegood. BoAV
Free Men. Struthers Burt. PoFr
Free Nation, A. Edwin Markham. MaRV; TRV
Free Parliament Litany, A. *Unknown.* OxBoLi
Free Thoughts on Several Eminent Composers. Charles Lamb. MuSP; OBRV; OxBoLi
Free to look at fact. To the New Women. John Davidson. PoVP
Free us, safe God. Libera Nos a Malo. Eric Bruno. JKCP (1955 ed.)
Free Will and God's Foreknowledge. Milton. *Fr.* Paradise Lost, III. ExPo
Free-Will and Predestination. Maurice Evan Hare. *See* Limerick: "There once was a man who said: 'Damn!'"
Free Wine on Communion Day. Linwood D. Smith. TNV
Free Woman, The. Theodosia Garrison. HBMV

Freed dove flew to the Rajah's tower, The. The Dove of Dacca. Kipling. GN
Freedom. Joan Agnew. BoTP
Freedom. John Barbour. *Fr.* The Bruce. FaBoCh; GoTS; LoGBV; OBEV; TrGrPo
("A! fredome is a noble thing!") PoFr; ViBoPo
(Fredome.) OxBS
Freedom. Joel Barlow. *See* To Freedom.
Freedom. Emerson. PoFr
Freedom. Abraham ibn Ezra, *tr. fr. Hebrew by* Solomon Solis-Cohen. TrJP
Freedom ("Are we, then, wholly fallen? Can it be"). James Russell Lowell. PaA
Freedom. Leonard Mann. NeLNL
Freedom. Georgi Efimovich Nechayev, *tr. fr. Russian by* George Z. Patrick. PoFr
Freedom, *sel.* Charles Péguy, *tr. fr. French by* Julian Green.
"Such is the mystery of man's freedom, says God." PoFr
Freedom. Clara Smith Reber. OTD
Freedom. "Jan Struther." POTE
Freedom. Rabindranath Tagore. PoFr
Freedom ("O thou so fair in summers gone"). Tennyson. PoVP
Freedom ("Of old sat Freedom"). Tennyson. *See* Of Old Sat Freedom on the Heights.
Freedom ("I am not strong"). *Unknown.* PGD
Freedom all winged expands. Emerson. Voluntaries, II. PoFr
Freedom and Faith went wooing for a soul. The Rivals. Robert Whitaker. OQP
Freedom and Love. Thomas Campbell. GTBS; GTBS-D; GTBS-P; GTBS-W; GTSE
(Song: "How delicious is the winning.") HBV
Freedom called them up—up they rose. The Gallant Fifty-one. Henry Lynden Flash. PAH
Freedom, farewell! Or so the soldiers say. Port of Embarkation. Randall Jarrell. MiAP
Freedom for the Mind. William Lloyd Garrison. AA; FaBoBe
Freedom from fear is the freedom I claim for you, my Motherland! Freedom. Rabindranath Tagore. PoFr
Freedom has a thousand charms to show. William Cowper. *Fr.* Table Talk. PoFr
Freedom I never saw in words. After Bombardment. John Pudney. WaP
Freedom in Mah Soul. David Wadsworth Cannon, Jr. PoNe
Freedom is a breath of air. Freedom. Clara Smith Reber. OTD
Freedom is a hard-bought thing. Song of the Settlers. Jessamyn West. FaPON
Freedom is more than a word, more than the base coinage. The *Nabara.* C. Day Lewis. HaMV
Freedom is the finest gold. Ode to Freedom. Thomas of Strengnaes. PoFr
Freedom, New Hampshire. Galway Kinnell. NaP
Freedom of the Press, The. Henrik Arnold Wergeland, *tr. fr. Norwegian by* Elias Gordon. PoFr
Freedom, one of the greatest blessings of Heaven. Battle Hymn of the Chinese Revolution (1912). *Unknown.* PoFr
Freedom, Our Queen. Oliver Wendell Holmes. PEDC
Freedom the Goddess. Arthur Wilberforce Jose. BoAu; PoFr
Freedom's first champion in our fettered land! Garrison. Amos Bronson Alcott. AA; PoFr
Freedom's Hero. Byron. *See* Sonnet on Chillon.
Freedom's War Song. Thomas Chatterton. *Fr.* Goddwyn. PoFr
(Ode to Liberty.) TrGrPo
Freeing your folded wings from girlhood's cell. Flights. Robert Mezey. TDP
Freely Espousing. James Schuyler. ANYP; NeAP
Freely the dead bracken breaks to your stride. Argenteuil County. Peter Dale Scott. MoCV
Freeman and Wild, two young hot gallants. The Two Friends. John Dennis. PeRV
Freeman once of London made a Knight, A. Dupliciter Beatus. Henry Parrot. SiCE
Freeway. William Witherup. QAH
Freight Boats. James S. Tippett. BrR; FaPON; GFA; MPB; StVeCh (1955 ed.)
Freight Train, The. Rowena Bennett. PDV; RePo
Freighter. Bruce Ruddick. CaP
Freighter, gay with rust, The. Jews at Haifa. Randall Jarrell. MoAmPo (1950 ed.)
Freighting from Wilcox to Globe. *Unknown.* CoSo
French and Russian they matter not. A Chant [*or* Hymn] of Hate against England. Ernst Lissauer. HBV; OtMeF
French and the Spanish Guerrillas, The. Wordsworth. WaaP
(Sonnet: French and Spanish Guerrillas, The.) ChER
French bus halts on the Plateau of Antiques, The. A Visit to Van Gogh. Charles Causley. PoCh
French Clock. Hortense Flexner. HBMV
French Cookery. Thomas Moore. *Fr.* The Fudge Family in Paris. OBRV
French guns roll continuously, The. The Iron Music. Ford Madox Ford. HBMV
French Lisette; a Ballad of Maida Vale. William Plomer. ErPo; LiTM (rev. ed.); SiTL
French Peasants. Monk Gibbon. HaMV; NeIP; OxBI; POTE
French Poets. Aram Saroyan. ANYP
French Revolution, The, *sels.* Blake.
"Dead brood over Europe, the cloud and vision descends over cheerful France, The," *fr.* I. EiPP
"Noise of trampling, the wind of trumpets, The," *fr.* I. ChER
French Revolution, The. Erasmus Darwin. PoFr
French Revolution, The. Wordsworth. *Fr.* The Prelude, XI. FiP; FOL; TOP
(France.) MBW-2
("Oh! pleasant exercise of hope and joy!") EnLi-2; OBRV
(Residence in France Continued.) PoEL-4
Frenchman's Ball, The, *with music.* *Unknown.* OuSiCo
Frend, farly nocht; an caus is to complene. Gawin Douglas. *Fr.* Prologues to the Aeneid, X. OxBoCh
Fresco-Sonnets to Christian Sethe. Heine, *tr. fr. German by* John Todhunter. AWP; JAWP; WBP
Frescoes for Mr. Rockefeller's City. Archibald MacLeish. UnPo
Sels.
Burying Ground by the Ties, III. AmPP (4th ed.); MAP; MoAmPo; NAMP; WoL
Empire Builders, V. AmP; NoP; OxBA; Po
Landscape as a Nude, I. AmPP (4th ed.); CMoP
Oil Painting of the Artist as the Artist, IV. NAMP; OnHM
Wildwest, II. ReMP
Frescoes that crumble, marbles bullet-scarred. The Fault. Edward Lucie-Smith. NePoEA-2
Fresh Air. Kenneth Koch. NeAP; PP
Fresh Air, The. Harold Monro. CH
Fresh, bright bloom of the daffodils, The. April Fantasie. Helen Mackay Hutchinson Cortissoz. AA
Fresh Cheese and Cream. Robert Herrick. UnTE
Fresh clad from heaven in robes of white. In My Own Album. Charles Lamb. CBEP; OBRV
Fresh from His Fastnesses. W. E. Henley. PoVP
Fresh from the dewy hill, the merry year. Song. Blake. CoBE; EiPP; EnLit; EnRP
Fresh in the flush light gleam. The Sorrow of Unicume. Sir Herbert Read. BrPo; ChMP
Fresh light from a morning sky blocked through clouds. Light. Carol Coates. CaP
Fresh Morning, A. J. C. Squire. WhC
Fresh morning gusts have blown away all fear. Sonnet: To a Young Lady Who Sent Me a Laurel Crown. Keats. EnRP
Fresh Paint. Boris Pasternak, *tr. fr. Russian by* Babette Deutsch. PoPl; TrJP
Fresh palms for the Old Dominion! The Battle of Charlestown. Henry Howard Brownell. PAH
Fresh Spring. Elizabeth Daryush. QFR
Fresh spring, the herald of love's mighty king. Spenser. Amoretti, LXX. AWP; BEL; BWP; CABA; ChTr; EIL; EnLit; FaBoEn; HBV; JAWP; LiTB; LiTL; NoP; OBEV; OBSC; OnPM; PoFS; ReEn; ReIE; SeCeV; SiCE; Sonn; StP; TOP; ViBoPo; WBP
Fresh Start, The. Anna Wickham. ViBoPo
Fresh with all airs of woodland brooks. With a Copy of Herrick. Sir Edmund Gosse. VA
Freshet, A. Antiphilus of Byzantium, *tr. fr. Greek by* Sir William Marris. LiTW
Freshly the cool breath of the coming eve. The Healing of the Daughter of Jairus. Nathaniel Parker Willis. StJW
Freshmen. Barry Spacks. NYBP
Fret not because thy place is small. In a Small Place. Annie Johnson Flint. FaChP

Fret Not Thyself. Amy Carmichael. SoP
Fret not thyself because of evil doers. Psalm XXXVII, Bible, *O.T.* BLRP, *par. by* Charles Frederic Sheldon; TiPo (1952 ed.); TreFT; WoL
Fret not thyself, if thou do see. Psalm XXXVII, Bible, *O.T.*, *par. by* Sir Philip Sidney. FCP
Fret of Father Carty, The. Joseph I. C. Clarke. JKCP (1926 ed.)
Fret on fond Cupid, curse thy feeble bow. *Unknown.* SeCSL
Freya's Spinning Wheel. Adam Oehlenschläger, *tr. fr. Danish by* Charles W. Stork. LiTW
Friar, The. Julian del Casal. *tr. fr. Spanish by* Thomas Walsh. CAW; WHL
Friar, The. Thomas Love Peacock. *See* Friar's Hunting Song.
Friar and the Fair Maid, The. *Unknown. See* As I Lay Musing.
Friar Complains, A. *Unknown.* MeEL
Friar in the Well, The. *Unknown. See* As I Lay Musing.
Friar Laurence's Cell. Shakespeare. Romeo and Juliet, II, vi. GoBC
Friar Lubin. Clément Marot, *tr. fr. French by* Longfellow. AWP; WoL
(Ballade of a Friar, *tr. by* Andrew Lang.) HBV
Friar of Genoa, The. Scharmel Iris. JKCP
Friar of Orders Gray, The. John O'Keeffe. *Fr.* Merry Sherwood. BOHV; OnYI; OxBI
Friar of Orders Gray [*or* Grey], The. *Unknown.* ACP, *abr.*; CAW; CEP; GoBC; HBV; OBEC; WHL, *abr.*
Friar of Orders Grey, The. Dante Gabriel Rossetti. GoBC
(Old Song Ended, An.) PoVP
Friar of Orders Grey, The. Shakespeare. *See* How Should I Your True Love Know?
Friars? All the four orders, I found them there. Friars. William Langland. *Fr.* The Vision of Piers Plowman. PPON
Friars' Enormities. *Unknown.* MeEL
Friar's Hunting Song. Thomas Love Peacock. *Fr.* Maid Marian. GoTP
(Friar, The, 4 *ll.*) SD
Friar's Tale, The. Chaucer. *Fr.* The Canterbury Tales. EnLi-1 (1949 ed.), *mod. by* Edwin M. Everett; PoAn, *orig. and mod. vers.*
Friction. Esther Pinch. PoMa
Friday. Sir Walter Scott. BoTP
Friday came and the circus was there. The Circus. Elizabeth Madox Roberts. FaPON; GFA; MPB; SoPo; UTS
Friday night's dream on a Saturday told. Old Superstitions. Mother Goose. HBVY; TreF
Friday; or, The Dirge. John Gay. *Fr.* The Shepherd's Week. BWP; CEP; EiCP; EiPP
Blouzelinda's Funeral, *sel.* OBEC
Friend, A. Lionel Johnson. HBV; JKCP
Friend, A. Marguerite Power. FaFP; SiTL
Friend, A. Santob de Carrion. TrJP
Friend, A. Sir Thomas Noon Talfourd. *Fr.* Ion. PoToHe
Friend, A. *Unknown.* PoToHe (new ed.)
Friend Advises Me to Stop Drinking, A. Mei Yao Ch'en, *tr. fr. Chinese by* Kenneth Rexroth. HoPM
Friend and Lover. "Madeline Bridges." AA; HBV
Friend and lover mine. Song. Dinis, King of Portugal. CAW
Friend Cato. Anna Wickham. MoBrPo
Friend Cheng is too proud to serve the world. To Cheng on His Deposal. Tu Fu. OnPM
Friend, coming in a friendly wise. If Any Be Pleased to Walk into My Poor Garden. Francis Daniel Pastorius. SCAP
Friend, for your epitaphs I'm griev'd. On One Made Long Epitaphs. Pope. ALV
Friend, I have lost the way. The Way. Edwin Muir. LOW; SiSw
Friend, I have watched you down the mountain. A Parting. Wang Wei. LiTW
Friend, if the mute and shrouded dead. Love and Death. Catullus. AWP; JAWP; WBP
Friend, in my mountain-side demesne. To a Gardener. Robert Louis Stevenson. AnEnPo
Friend, in place of dark red wine, receive. Poem To Be Cast into the Sea in a Bottle. James Kirkup. BoPe
Friend in the Garden, A. Juliana Horatia Ewing. BoTP; FaPON; GFA; MPB; OTPC (1946 ed.); StVeCh; TVC; UTS
Friend, never give up. Grace Sufficient. Charles E. Bayley. SoP
Friend of Humanity and the Knife-Grinder, The. George Canning *and* John Hookham Frere. CEP; HBV; OBEC; Par; TOP
(Knife-Grinder, The.) BOHV; InMe
(Sapphics.) EiCL; FOL
Friend of mine was married to a scold, A. All's Well that Ends Well. *Unknown.* BOHV; FaFP; SiTL
Friend of Ronsard, Nashe, and Beaumont. On a Birthday. J. M. Synge. ChTr; OBMV
Friend of Sinners. Richard Burnham. BePJ
Friend of Souls. *Unknown.* BePJ
Friend of the Fourth Decade, The. James Merrill. NYBP
Friend of the wise! and teacher of the good! To William Wordsworth. S. T. Coleridge. EnRP; ERoP-1; MBW-2; PeER
Friend, on this scaffold Thomas More lies dead. Epigram. J. V. Cunningham. NePoAm
Friend or Stranger. Bhartrihari, *tr. fr. Sanskrit by* Paul Elmer More. OnPM
Friend or Two, A. Wilbur D. Nesbit. PoLF
Friend! Poor, foolish blossom. Beauty. Peter Hille. AWP
Friend sent me the other day, A. Two Homes. Martha Snell Nicholson. FaChP
Friend sparrow, do not eat, I pray. Basho, *tr. fr. Japanese by* Curtis Hidden Page. AWP
Friend That Sticketh Closer Than a Brother, A. John Newton. SoP
Friend, there be they on whom mishap. Contentment. Charles Stuart Calverley. ALV
Friend, though thy soul should burn thee, yet be still. The Truth. Archibald Lampman. CaP
Friend, when I think of your delicate feminine face. On the Death of an Acquaintance. Oscar Williams. *Fr.* Variations on a Theme. LiTA; NePA
Friend Who Just Stands By, The. B. Y. Williams. PoLF; PoToHe
Friend, whose unnatural early death. An Elegy. David Gascoyne. FaBoTw; TwCP
Friend writes me from the temperate zone, A. Termites. Charles G. Bell. NePoAm-2
Friend, you are grieved that I should go. Creeds. Karle Wilson Baker. HBMV; WGRP
Friend, you seem thoughtful. I not wonder much. A Sea Dialogue. Oliver Wendell Holmes. EtS
Friendless and faint, with martyred steps and slow. Calvary. E. A. Robinson. AmePo; AnNE; ChIP; CoBA; MaRV; MoAmPo; NeMA; PoDB; PoPo; Sonn; StJW; TreFS
Friendless Blues, *with music.* Mercedes Gilbert. TrAS
Friendly Address, A. Thomas Hood. PoEL-4
Friendly Beasts, The. *Unknown.* BiCB; ChBR; ChrBoLe; FaPON; OnMSP; PoSC; SiSoSe; SoPo
Friendly Blight, The. Aubrey Thomas De Vere. IrPN
Friendly cow all red and white, The. The Cow. Robert Louis Stevenson. BoChLi; BrPo; FaPON; GFA; MPB; OTPC (1946 ed.); PoVP; PPL; RIS; SAS; SoPo; StVeCh; SUS; TiPo; UTS
Friendly Debate between the Country Farmer and His Buxome Wife, A. *Unknown. See* New Married Couple, The.
Friendly Faces of Old Sorrows, The. Karle Wilson Baker. OQP
Friendly Obstacles. *Unknown.* MaRV; SoP
Friendly People. John G. Herndon. MPB
Friends. Abbie Farwell Brown. HBV; HBVY
Friends. Thomas Curtis Clark. PoToHe
Friends. A. E. Housman. A Shropshire Lad, LVIII. SeCePo
("When I came last to Ludlow.") PoVP
Friends. Lionel Johnson. GoBC
Friends. E. V. Lucas. HBV
Friends. John Perreault. ANYP
Friends. L. G. Warner. OTPC (1946 ed.)
Friends!/ I come [*or* came] not here to talk. Rienzi to the Romans. Mary Russell Mitford. *Fr.* Rienzi. PoFr; TreFS
Friends and Enemies. *At. to* Ali Ben Abu Taleb, *tr. fr. Persian by* Emerson. OQP
(Friends and Foes.) OnPM
(From the Persian.) AnNE
(Make Friends.) MaRV; TRV
Friends and loves we have none, nor wealth nor blest abode. The Seekers. John Masefield. BoPo; HBV; MaRV; OQP; WGRP
Friends are always those. Friends. John Perreault. ANYP

Friends Beyond. Thomas Hardy. CoBMV; GTBS-P; MaPo; OBEV (new ed.); OBVV; PoVP
Friends Beyond. Frederick L. Hosmer. MaRV
Friend's Burial, The. Whittier. OBVV
Sels.
"For all her quiet life flowed on." MaRV
In Earthen Vessels. BLRP; SoP
Friends Departed. Henry Vaughan. *See* They Are All Gone.
Friends Drinking Together. Lady Otomo of Sakanoe, *tr. fr. Japanese by* Ishii *and* Obata. OnPM
Friend's Greeting, A. Edgar A. Guest. BLPA
Friends! hear the words my wandering thoughts would say. On Southey's Death. Walter Savage Landor. TOP
Friends I Am Like You Tied. A. B. Spellman. BF
Friends in Paradise. Henry Vaughan. *See* They Are All Gone.
Friends! in this world of hurry. Charles Kingsley. OTD
Friends, my heart is half aweary. The Old Times Were the Best. James Whitcomb Riley. FaFP
Friends of His Youth, The. W. B. Yeats. *Fr.* A Man Young and Old. AtBAP
Friends of my heart: O worker at the frieze. Words for Artificers. Claude F. Koch. JKCP (1955 ed.)
Friends of the Muse, to you of right belong. The Strong Heroic Line. Oliver Wendell Holmes. AA
Friends Old and New. Joseph Parry. OQP
(New Friends and Old Friends.) BLPA; NeHB; PoToHe; TreFT
Friends, Romans, countrymen, lend me your ears. Antony's Oration [*or* Speech]. Shakespeare. *Fr.* Julius Caesar, III, ii. FOL; LiTB; PoPl; PTK; TreF; TrGrPo
Friend's Song for Simoisius, A. Louise Imogen Guiney. PFY
Friends, whom she lookt [*or* look'd] at blandly from her couch. Walter Savage Landor. *Fr.* Pericles and Aspasia: Myrtis. OBRV; VA
Friendship. Robert Blair. *Fr.* The Grave. OBEC
Friendship. Robert Bridges. *Fr.* The Testament of Beauty. MaRV
Friendship. Byron. *See* To Thomas Moore.
Friendship. Cervantes, *tr. fr. Spanish by* Peter Motteux. OnPM
Friendship. Hartley Coleridge. *See* To a Friend.
Friendship. Samuel Taylor Coleridge. *See* Broken Friendship.
Friendship. Dinah Maria Mulock Craik. BLPA; NeHB; PoToHe (new ed.)
Friendship ("A ruddy drop of manly blood"). Emerson. AmPP (3d ed.)
Friendship. Henry W. Frost. SoP
Friendship, The. Robert Mezey. NaP
Friendship. Sadi, *tr. fr. Persian by* L. Cranmer-Byng. *Fr.* The Gulistan. AWP; JAWP; WBP
Friendship. *Unknown.* PoToHe
Friendship after Love. Ella Wheeler Wilcox. CBV
(Friendship.) PoToHe
Friendship in Fashion, *sel.* Thomas Otway.
Song: "How blest he appears." SeCL
Friendship is constant in all other things. Beauty Is a Witch. Shakespeare. *Fr.* Much Ado about Nothing, II, i. TrGrPo
Friendship is in loving rather than in being lov'd. Friendship. Robert Bridges. *Fr.* The Testament of Beauty. MaRV
Friendship Is Love without His Wings. Byron. TreFT
Frienship, like love, is but a name. The Hare and [*or* with] Many Friends. John Gay. *Fr.* Fables. ATP (1935 ed.); EiCL; EiCP; EnLi-1 (1949 ed.); HBV
Friendship needs no studied phrases. Friendship. *Unknown.* PoToHe
Friendships. Mary Edith Halladay. SoP
Friendship's Mystery. Katherine Philips. ViBoPo
Frieze, A. John Peale Bishop. MoPo
Frieze of warm bronze that glides with catlike movements. The Stevedores. John Gould Fletcher. *Fr.* Down the Mississippi, V. HT; LiTA; NP
Frigate Pelican, The. Marianne Moore. InvP
Frightened Face. Marion Strobel. HBMV
Frightened Flower. William J. Harris. BOLo
Frightened Lover's Sleep, The. Jay Wright. BF
Frightened Ploughman, The. John Clare. PoEL-4
Frigidaire. A. M. Klein. TwCaPo
Fringed Gentian. Emily Dickinson. *See* God made a little gentian.
Fringed Gentians. Amy Lowell. BrR; FaPON; MPB; OTD; SP
Fringéd vallance of your eyes advance, The. Song [*or* A Good-Morrow]. Thomas Shadwell. *Fr.* Timon of Athens. SeCL; ViBoPo
Fringed with coral, floored with lava. Christmas Island. Katharine Lee Bates. HBMV; HBVY; TSW
Fringilla Melodia, The. Henry Beck Hirst. AA
Fringing cypress forests dim. Sassafras. Samuel Minturn Peck. AA
Frippery. Horace. *See* Persian Fopperies.
Frisky as a lambkin. The Lovable Child. Emilie Poulsson. HBV; MPB
Frisky Lamb, A. Christina Rossetti. *Fr.* Sing-Song. BoTP
Frithiof's Saga, *sels.* Esaias Tegnér, *tr. fr. Swedish by* Longfellow.
Frithiof's Farewell. AWP; JAWP; WBP
Frithiof's Homestead. AWP
Frog, The. Hilaire Belloc. BoChLi; BoHV; FaBoBe; FaBV; FaPON; FiBHP; GoJo; HBV; InMe; MoShBr; MPB; NA; RePo; TSW
Frog, The. Rose Fyleman. BoTP
Frog, The. *Unknown.* MoShBr; SiTL; TreFT; WhC; YaD
Frog and the Bird, The. Vera Hessey. BoTP
Frog and the Golden Ball, The. Robert Graves. NoP
Frog and the Mouse, The. *Unknown.* *See* Frog Went a-Courting.
Frog beneath the juniper, The. The Question in the Cobweb. Alastair Reid. WaKn
Frog He Would a-Wooing Go, A. *Unknown.* *See* Frog Went a-Courting.
Frog Prince, The. Stevie Smith. PoG
Frog under you, A. The Wife. Denise Levertov. ErPo; MeWo
Frog Went a-Courting [*or* Courtin']. *Unknown.* ABF, *with music*; BLPA; FTB, *with music*; GoTP; IHA; TrAS, *with music*
(Frog and the Mouse, The.) WiR
(Frog He Would a-Wooing Go, A.) OnMSP; OTPC
(Froggy Went a Courting, *with music.*) BFSS
(Frog's Courtin', The.) RIS
(Love-sick Frog, The.) OxNR
(Mister Frog Went a-Courting, *with music.*) AS
Frogs, The, *sel.* Aristophanes, *tr. fr. Greek.*
"Let us hasten—let us fly." MaRV
Frogs. Louis Simpson. TDP
Frog's a very funny thing, A. Spring Wish. John Farrar. GFA
Frogs at School. George Cooper. BoChLi; GFA; StVeCh (1940 ed.); UTS
(Twenty Froggies.) OTPC; PCH; PPL
Frog's Courtin', The. *Unknown.* *See* Frog Went a-Courting.
Frogs jump. Jump or Jiggle [*or* Jingle]. Evelyn Beyer. SoPo; TiPo
Frogs' Singing-School, The. E. T. Carbell. SoPo
Frogs Who Wanted a King, The ("The frogs were living happy as could be"). Aesop, *ad. fr. Greek by* Joseph Lauren. GoTP; MaC; RIS; StaSt
Frolic. "Æ." BoTP; FaPON; GTSL; MoBrPo; OTPC (1946 ed.)
Frolic Mariners of Devon, The. William Browne. *Fr.* Britannia's Pastorals, II, Song iii. ChTr
Frolic[k]some Farmer, The. *Unknown.* CoMu; UnTE
Frolicsome Parson Outwitted, The. *Unknown.* CoMu
From a branch the bird called. The Bird. Max Michelson. NP
From a Bus. Malaika Ayo Wangara. NBP
From a Car-Window. Ruth Guthrie Harding. HBMV
From a Childhood. Rainer Maria Rilke, *tr. fr. German by* C. F. MacIntyre. SiSw; TrJP
From a Chinese Vase. Winifred Welles. MAP
From a Churchyard in Wales. *Unknown.* FiBHP
("This spot is the sweetest I've seen in my life.") ShM; WhC
From a city window, 'way up high. Motor Cars. Rowena Bennett. FaPON; GFA; PoMa; SoPo; TiPo
From a Full Heart. A. A. Milne. BOHV; InMe
From a golden step. Flowers. Arthur Rimbaud. FIW
From a granite rib of rock off Viareggio. Off Viareggio. Kenneth Pitchford. CoPo
From a hillslope I look on the wet fields flattening before me. Daphne. Claire McAllister. TwAmPo

From a Hint in the Minor Poets. Samuel Wesley. CBEP; OBEC
From a junto that labor with absolute power. Emancipation from British Dependence. Philip Freneau. PAH
From a land of milk and honey. Weeping and Singing. César Tiempo. MoRP
From a little seed/ A flower grows. Little Things. Eileen Mathias. BoTP
From a magician's midnight sleeve. Late Air. Elizabeth Bishop. FiMAP; PoPl
From a mountain top a poet looked down. The Poet. Seumas O'Brien. JKCP (1926 ed.)
From a mountainside. Landscape, by Ch'êng Sui. James Kirkup. *Fr.* Seven Pictures from China. BoPe; POTi
From a Munster vale they brought her. The Dying Girl. Richard D'Alton Williams. OnYI
From a Porthole in the Ice. William Vincent Sieller. NYTB
From a pot of wine among the flowers. Drinking Alone with the Moon. Li Po. LiTW
From a poverty-shadowed life. Imagined Happiness. Erik Axel Karlfeldt. LiTW; PoPl
From a Railway Carriage. Robert Louis Stevenson. BoTP; FaPON; GFA; PDV; TiPo
From a Street Corner. Eleanor Hammond. HBMV
From a train window hypnotized. Moving Along. William Hunt. YAP
From a Venetian Sequence. Adèle Naudé. PeSA
From "A Vigo-Street Eclogue." Sir Owen Seaman. WhC
From a village up the Hudson. The Dark Girl Dressed in Blue. *Unknown.* BeLS
From a vision red with war I awoke and saw the Prince. The New Day. Fenton Johnson. BANP
From a window high over the factory. February. Bill Berkson. ANYP
From a Woman to a Greedy Lover. Norman Cameron. Three Love Poems, I. ELU; FaBoTw; GTBS-P
From a wreck of tree in the wash of night. Speak with the Sun. David Campbell. ACV; NeLNL; SeCePo
From all division let our land be free. Australian Federation. William Gay. BoAu; PoFr
From all eternity the Beloved unveiled His beauty in the solitude of the unseen. The Song of Mystic Unity. Jami. LiTW
From All Peoples, *sel.* Nathan Alterman, *tr. fr. Hebrew by* Simon Halkin.
"When our children cried in the shadow of the gallows." TrJP
From All That Dwell below the Skies. Isaac Watts. SoP; TRV
From all that terror teaches. Litany. G. K. Chesterton. OtMeF
From all the livid east or piercing north. James Thomson. *Fr.* The Seasons: Winter. YAT
From All the Queens. Iwan Goll, *tr. fr. French by* Iwan Goll. OnPM
From all the rest I single out you, having a message for you. To One Shortly to Die. Walt Whitman. CBEP
From All These Events. Stephen Spender. LiTB; NAMP
From All Uneasy Passions Free. John Sheffield, Duke of Buckingham. SeCL
From all vain pomps and shows. He That Doeth the Will. Longfellow. ChIP
From almost naught to almost all I flee. On the Calculus. J. V. Cunningham. PoIE; QFR
From an Ecclesiastical Chronicle. John Heath-Stubbs. HYE
From an Irish-Latin Macaronic. Geoffrey Taylor. NeIP
From an Old Maid. Vassar Miller. ToPo
From an Upland Valley. Richard Church. MoBrPo (1942 ed.)
From ancient Edens long forgot. A White-Throat Sings. Walter Prichard Eaton. DD; HBMV
From Ancient Fangs. Peter Viereck. LiTA; MiAP
From Another Room. Gregory Corso. NeAP
From Arranmore the weary miles I've come. Mavrone. Arthur Guiterman. BOHV; FiBHP; InMe
From art, from nature, from the schools. In Memoriam A. H. H., XLIX. Tennyson. EnLi-2; EPN; ViPo; VP
From Battle Clamour. Samuele Romanelli, *tr. fr. Hebrew by* Nina Davis Salaman. TrJP
From being anxious or secure. John Donne. *Fr.* The Litany. EnLit; MBW-1; OxBoCh
From bending always over bars, his glance. The Panther. Rainer Maria Rilke. ReMP
From Bethlehem Blown. Mary Sinton Leitch. PGD
From Bethlehem to Calvary. Meredith Nicholson. ChIP; PGD
From Bethlehem to Calvary. Christ and the Winds. John Banister Tabb. StJW
From Bethlehem to Calvary the Savior's journey lay. From Bethlehem to Calvary. Meredith Nicholson. PGD
From Beyond. Lucia Trent. PGD
From bill to breast a snake. Swan. Edward Lowbury. GTBS-P
From blacked-out streets. Crystal Night. Denise Levertov. *Fr.* During the Eichmann Trial. NMP
From blackhearted water colder. Castles and Distances. Richard Wilbur. FiMAP
From blue to dusk and the lights came. A Window, a Table, on the North. Ralph Gustafson. PeCV
From body's self the body. Body's Freedom. Helen Neville. NePA
From Boston harbor we set sail. Boston. *Unknown.* SoAmSa
From Break of Day. *Unknown. tr. fr. Chinese by* Henry H. Hart. WoL
(Workman.) OnPM
From breakfast on through all the day. The Land of Nod. Robert Louis Stevenson. GoTP; MPB (1956 ed.); PoVP; VA
From Brescia swiftly o're the bord'ring plain. Sir William Davenant. *Fr.* Gondibert. CEP
From British novels a thrill I get. Britannia Rules of Orthography. "Firth." InMe; WhC
From Brooklyn, over the Brooklyn bridge, on this fine morning. Invitation to Miss Marianne Moore. Elizabeth Bishop. ML; MoVE; TwAmPo
From Burton the Anatomist. Maurice James Craig. NeIP
From buses beached like an invasion fleet. Port Authority Terminal: 9 A.M. Monday. Chad Walsh. PPON
From Calvary a cry was heard. Calvary's Cry. John William Cunningham. BePJ
From camp to camp, through the foul womb of night. Before Agincourt. Shakespeare. *Fr.* King Henry V, *prologue. to* Act IV. ChTr
From child to youth; from youth to arduous man. The Heart of the Night. Dante Gabriel Rossetti. The House of Life, LXVI. EPN; MaVP; PoVP; TOP; ViPo
From Childhood's Hour. Poe. *See* Alone.
From church to Boule's hop on Sunday they'll away. Boule's Hop. *Unknown.* IHA
From Citron-Bower. Hilda Doolittle ("H. D."). AP
From Clee to heaven the beacon burns. 1887. A. E. Housman. A Shropshire Lad, I. CoBMV; MaPo (1969 ed.); NAMP; PoAn; PoVP; ReMP; UnPo; ViPo
From Country to Town. Hartley Coleridge. *See* 'Tis Strange to Me.
From dark the striped muscles sprang. "God's First Creature Was Light." Winifred Welles. ImOP
From Dark to Light. S. Weir Mitchell. *See* Vespers.
From darkened eyes no tears are falling. The Weavers. Heine. PoFr
From dawn to dark they stood. "Our Left." Francis Orrery Ticknor. MC; PAH
From Dawn to Noon. Dante Gabriel Rossetti. The House of Life, LXXX. MaVP; PoVP; ViPo
From day to day/ The calcium in our cells grows less and less. Leningrad: 1943. Vera Inber. *Fr.* The Pulkovo Meridian. WaaP
From day to day lamenting, lingering on. Mortal Grief. Francisco de Figueroa. OnPM
From Death then is there no relief? Death the Great. Elis Wyn o Lasynys. LiTW
From depth of sin and from a deep despair. Psalm CXXX. *Par. by* Sir Thomas Wyatt. FCP
From Desert to Metropolis. Sister Mary Estelle. JKCP (1955 ed.)
From dewy dreams, my soul, arise. James Joyce. Chamber Music, XV. HW
From Disciple to Master. Monk Gibbon. AnIV
From Distant Lands. Peter Hellings. MoWP
From Dover to Dunkirk. Edwin John Pratt. *Fr.* Dunkirk. PTK
From Drogheda all along the coast, the Irish sea. Back to Dublin. R. A. D. Ford. CaP; MoCV

From Dublin soon to London spread. Swift. *Fr.* Verses on the Death of Dr. Swift. ViBoPo; WHA
From dusk till dawn the livelong night. Betsy's Battle Flag. Minna Irving. DD; MC; PAH; PEDC; PoRL
From dust I rise. Thomas Traherne. *Fr.* The Salutation. FaBoEn
From early childhood, even as hath been said. Wordsworth. *Fr.* The Excursion. BoPe
From east and south the holy clan. The Bishop of Rum-Ti-Foo. W. S. Gilbert. CenHV; PoVP
From Eastertide to Eastertide. A Ballad of a Nun. John Davidson. BeLS; EnLit; HBMV; MoBrPo; OnMSP; PoVP
From England to California I went. Roll, *Julia*, Roll. *Unknown.* ShS
From eve to morn, from morn to parting night. On His Own Agamemnon and Iphigeneia. Walter Savage Landor. OBRV
From every point they gaily come. A Dance at the Ranch. *Unknown.* SCC
From every quarter came the night confounding. Burial at Sea. E. J. Pratt. *Fr.* The *Roosevelt* and the *Antinoe.* CaP
From every stormy wind that blows. The Mercy-Seat. Hugh Stowell. SoP
From every warlike city. Macaulay. *Fr.* Lays of Ancient Rome: The Battle of Lake Regillus. PoG
From fairest creatures we desire increase. Sonnets, I. Shakespeare. AtBAP; CTC; EG; FaBoEn; LiTB; LiTL; MasP; OAEP; OBSC; SiCE; TrGrPo
From falling leaf to falling leaf. October. Dollie Radford. VA
From falsehood and error. A Prayer. Digby Mackworth Dolben. GoBC
From Far. A. E. Housman. *See* From Far, from Eve and Morning.
From Far Away. William Morris. OHIP, *st.* 1
From far away, from far away. My Letter. Grace Denio Litchfield. AA
From far away we come to you. From Far Away. William Morris. OHIP
From Far, from Eve and Morning. A. E. Housman. A Shropshire Lad, XXXII. AnEnPo; BoPe; CMoP; MemP; MoBrPo; NBM; NeMA; PoEL-5; PoVP; ViPo
From far she watched his wanderings, and sighed. Seven Sad Sonnets, IV. Mary Aldis. HBMV
From far she's come, and very old. Age in Youth. Trumbull Stickney. MAP; MoAmPo (1942 ed.); NCEP
From fear to fear, successivley betrayed. Reflection from Rochester. William Empson. ToPo
From feast and song the simple cowherd crept. Cædmon. Thomas S. Jones, Jr. InP
From Feathers to Iron, *sels.* C. Day Lewis.
Now She Is like the White Tree-Rose. FaBoTw; MoBrPo
"Now the full throated daffodils." ViBoPo
From Fortune's frowns and change removed. Old Damon's Pastoral. Thomas Lodge. OBSC; SiCE
From Fortune's Reach. Robert Southwell. EP
From Four Lakes' Days. Richard Eberhart. MiAP
From France, desponding and betray'd. On the British Invasion. Philip Freneau. PAH
From frozen climes, and endless traks [*or* tracts] of snow. To the Earl of Dorset. Ambrose Philips. CEP; LoBV; OBEC
From furrows of the spring. Edict. Harold Vinal. NYTB
From Generation to Generation. William Dean Howells. AA; PFY
From Generation to Generation. Sir Henry Newbolt. FaBoTw
From Gestures to the Dead. John Wheelwright. MoVE
From Ghoulies and Ghosties. Litany for Halloween. *Unknown.* PoRL; PoSC; ShM; SiSoSe; SoPo
From giant oaks, that wave their branches dark. Vegetable Loves. Erasmus Darwin. *Fr.* The Botanic Gardens: The Loves of the Plants. OBEC; SeCePo
From Gloucester Out. Edward Dorn. CoPo
From God to God. Vergil, *tr. fr. Latin by* F. W. H. Myers. MaRV
From God's lofty City/ my Lady looks down. Lady of Lidice. Fray Angelico Chavez. ISi; JKCP (1955 ed.)
From gods of other men, fastidious heart. False Gods. Walter de la Mare. EaLo
From going always over bars his glance. The Panther. Rainer Maria Rilke. PoPl
From gold to gray. Indian Summer. Whittier. *Fr.* Eve of Election. PCH
From golden dawn to purple dusk. The March of Humanity. J. Corson Miller. HBMV
From gossamer illusion. Middle-aged Quixote. Louise Crenshaw Ray. JKCP (1955 ed.)
From Grant's grave Galena. Old Dubuque. Dave Etter. AmFN
From Greenland to Iceland. *Unknown.* FaFP; SiTL
From Greenland's Icy Mountains. Reginald Heber. HBV; OTPC; SoP; TreF; WGRP
From groves of spice. Cradle-Song [*or* Hindu Cradle Song]. Sarojini Naidu. BoTP; BrR; FaPON; MoSiPe; MPB
From Halifax station a bully there came. Halifax Station. *Unknown.* PAH
From harmony, from heavenly [*or* heav'nly] harmony. A Song for St. Cecilia's Day. Dryden. AtBAP; ATP; AWP; BEL; BoLiVe; BWP; CABA; CBEP; CBV; CEP; DiPo; EiCL; EiPP; EnL; EnLi-1 (1949 ed.); EnLit; ExPo; FaBoEn; FosPo; GoBC; GTBS; GTBS-D; GTBS-P; GTBS-W; GTSE; GTSL; HBV; ILP; InPo; JAWP; LiTB; LiTG; MaPo; MasP; MBW-1; MuSP; OAEP; OBEV; PAn; Po; PoEL-3; PoIE; PoLi; SeCV-2; SeEP; TOP; TreFT; TrGrPo; UnS; WBP
From Heals and Harrods come her lovely bridegrooms. Made in Heaven. Peter Porter. PPON
From heart to heart, from creed to creed. The Stream of Faith. William Channing Gannett. OQP; WGRP
From Heaven High I Come to You, *with music.* John Sterling. YaCaBo
From heaven his spirit came, and robed in clay. The Soul of Dante [*or* On Dante Alighieri]. Michelangelo. GoBC; OnPM
From Heaven I fall, though from earth I begin. Whiter than White. Swift. RIS
From Heaven's Gate to Hampstead Heath. The Ballad of Hampstead Heath. James Elroy Flecker. MoBrPo
From heavy dreams fair Helen rose. William and Helen. Sir Walter Scott, *after* Bürger. EnRP; OAEP
From hence began that plot; the nation's curse. Dryden. *Fr.* Absalom and Achitophel, Pt. I. PeRV
From her bed's high and odoriferous roome. Homer. *Fr.* The Odyssey. CTC
From here, the quay, one looks above to mark. The Harbour Bridge. Thomas Hardy. TDP
From here through tunnelled gloom the track. The Railway Junction. Walter de la Mare. CBEP; ChMP
From here to there,/ To Washington Square. *Unknown.* OxNR
From hill to hill he harried me. War. Arthur Stringer. TwCaPo
From hills that echo strangely clear. Reincarnation. Lloyd Frank Merrell. ChIP
From his brimstone bed at break of day. The Devil's Thoughts [*or* The Devil's Walk on Earth]. Robert Southey *and* Samuel Taylor Coleridge. BOHV; OxBoLi; PoMS; PV
From His Canadian Home. *Unknown.* IHA
From his flock stray'd Coridon. Robert Greene. EG
From his garden bed our Lord. The Harvesting of the Roses. Menahem ben Jacob. TrJP
From his shoulder Hiawatha. Hiawatha's Photographing. "Lewis Carroll." CenHV; FiBHP
From his small city Columbus. Voyage. Josephine Miles. LiTM (1970 ed.)
From hollows of a tree. Fable of the Speckled Cow. D. J. Opperman. PeSA
From Holy, Holy, Holy ones. The Lancashire Puritane. *Unknown.* CoMu
From house to house he goes. A Lane [*or* An Irish Riddle]. *Unknown.* BoTP; OTPC (1946 ed.); PCH; RIS
From hunger and cold who lives more free. Song of the Beggars. Richard Brome. *Fr.* A Jovial Crew. SeCL
From hunting whores and haunting play. A Letter to Lord Middleton. Sir George Etherege. CavP
From ignominious sleep, where age on age. To Italy. Giovanni Guidiccioni. PoFr
From immaculate construction to half death. The Man from the Top of the Mind. David Wagoner. NePoEA-2
From inland ledges I had dreamed this bay. At the Battery Sea-Wall. Clifford James Laube. GoYe
From its blue vase the rose of evening drops. An Evening in England. Francis Ledwidge. MCCG
From its thin branch high in the autumn wind. Leaf Movement. Arthur Davison Ficke. MAP; NP

From ivory towers they come. Soul. Austin Black. NBP
From Java, Sumatra, and old Cathay. A Ship Comes In. Oliver Jenkins. EtS; PCH
From keel to fighting top, I love. Manila Bay. Arthur Hale. PAH
From Killybegs to Ardara is seven Irish miles. A Road of Ireland. Charles L. O'Donnell. HBMV
From Le Havre. Charles G. Bell. NePoAm
From learned Florence, long time rich in fame. Henry Howard, Earl of Surrey, to [the Lady] Geraldine. Michael Drayton. *Fr.* England's Heroical Epistles. OBSC; ReEn; RelE; TuPP
From Leo rain the Leonids. Night in November. David McCord. NYTB
From Lewis, Monsieur Gerard came. Yankee Doodle's Expedition to Rhode Island. *Unknown.* PAH
From Life. Brian Hooker. HBV; OnPP
From little signs, like little stars. Honoria's Surrender. Coventry Patmore. *Fr.* The Angel in the House. VA
From Liverpool to Frisco a-rovin' I went. Row, Bullies, Row. *Unknown.* SoAmSa
From loud sound and still chance. Baroque Comment. Louise Bogan. CrMA
From low to high doth dissolution climb. Mutability. Wordsworth. *Fr.* Ecclesiastical Sonnets. BWP; CABA; EG; EnLi-2; EnRP; EPN; ERoP-1; ExPo; LiTB; MBW-2; NoP; OBRV; OQP; PeER; PoE; PoEL-4; SeCeV; Sonn; StP
From many a field with patriot blood imbued. Decoration Day. George Hurlbut Barbour. OHIP
From Many a Mangled Truth a War Is Won. Clifford Dyment. POTi
From Matlock Bath's half-timbered station. Matlock Bath. John Betjeman. NYBP
From me, my Dear, O seek not to receive. What Was a Cure for Love? Thomas Godfrey. AnAmPo
From meadows with the sheep so shorn. The Ruined Chapel. Andrew Young. POTE
From mental mists to purge a nation's eyes. New Morality. George Canning, J. H. Frere, *and others.* CEP
From Mexico there's just come a strange new decree. De Mexico ha venido. *Unknown.* TrAS
From mighty wrongs to petty perfidy. Fame. Byron. *Fr.* Childe Harold's Pilgrimage. FiP
From miles away/ the whole. News. Vern Rutsala. WOW
From morn to midnight, all day through. Expectans Expectavi. Charles Sorley. FaBoCh; HBMV; LoGBV; MaRV; WGRP
From mountains covered deep with snow. Chipeta's Ride. John W. Taylor. PoOW
From My Arm-Chair. Longfellow. BLPA
From My Diary, July 1914. Wilfred Owen. CoBMV; FaBoMo; LiTM (rev. ed.); MoAB; MoBrPo
From my grief on Fál's proud plain I sleep. Geoffrey Keating. *Fr.* My Grief on Fál's Proud Plain. OnYI
From My High Love. Kenneth Patchen. MoAmPo (1950 ed.)
From my mother's sleep I fell into the State. The Death of the Ball Turret Gunner. Randall Jarrell. AP; CaFP; CBV; CMoP; CoBMV; ELU; ExPo; FiMAP; ILP; LiTM (1970 ed.); MiAP; MoAmPo (1950 ed.); NMP; NoP; OxBA; PoPl; PoPo; SeCeV (1967 ed.); ShBV-3; UnPo (3d ed.); WaaP; WaP
From My Rural Pen. T. S Watt. FiBHP
From My Thought. Daniel Smythe. GoYe
From my wind-blown book I look. Spring. W. R. Rodgers. AnIL
From My Window. Mary Elizabeth Coleridge. OBNC
From My Window. Mother M. Columba. WHL
From my window, facing South. The Autumn House. George M. Brady. OnYI
From my window I can see. The Open Sea. Dorothea Mackellar. BoAu
From my years young in dayes of youth. Epitaphium Meum. William Bradford. SCAP
From mysteries of the Past. To the Modern Man. John Hall Wheelock. HBMV
From naked stones of agony. Spirit's House. Sara Teasdale. *Fr.* Interlude: Songs Out of Sorrow. OQP
From nature doth emotion come, and moods. Imagination and Taste, How Impaired and Restored. Wordsworth. *Fr.* The Prelude, XII *and* XIII. MERP
From Nazareth. Margaret E. Sangster. ChIP
From near the sea, like Whitman my great predecessor, I call. Ode: Salute to the French Negro Poets. Frank O'Hara. NeAP; PoNe (1970 ed.)
From Nether Dark the Seed. Stefan George, *tr. fr. German by* Babette Deutsch *and* Avrahm Yarmolinsky. OnPM
From Nevada's hoary ridges, from stormy coasts of Maine. Benny Havens, Oh! ——OBrien. ABF
From noise of scare-fires rest ye free. The Bell Man. Robert Herrick. CBEP; CH; OBS; PCD
From noiseful arms, and acts of prowess done. The Holy Grail. Tennyson. *Fr.* Idylls of the King. MBW-2; PoVP; ViPo; ViPP
From Nothing Strange. Gustav Davidson. FiSC
From now on kill America out of your mind. Millions Are Learning How. James Agee. NAMP; PoPl
From Oberon in fairyland. Robin Goodfellow [*or* The Mad-Merry Pranks of Robin Good-Fellow]. *Unknown.* CBEP; FaBoCh; SeCL; SeEP; ViBoPo
From off a hill whose concave wombe reworded. A Lover's Complaint. Shakespeare. NCEP
From old Fort Walla Walla and the Klickitats. In the Oregon Country. William Stafford. AmFN
From one shaft at Cleator Moor. Cleator Moor. Norman Nicholson. FaBoTw; NeBP; POTi
From one unused in pomp of words to raise. To Benjamin West. Washington Allston. AnAmPo
From one Word are all things, and this one all things speak. Thomas à Kempis, *tr. fr. Latin.* BoC
From Orford Ness to Shingle Street. Dawn on the East Coast. Alun Lewis. FaBoMo
From our hidden places. The Others. "Seumas O'Sullivan." AnIV; GBV; HBMV; NP; OxBI
From our low seat beside the fire. The Call. Charlotte Mew. ChMP
From out a book into my lap. A Withered Rose. "Yehoash." TrJP
From out Cologne there came three kings. The Three Kings of Cologne. Eugene Field. StJW
From out his castle on the sand. The Sea-King. L. Frank Tooker. EtS
From out its womb it weaves with care. Vowel Englyn to the Spider. *Unknown.* LiTW
From out my deep, wide-bosomed West. Rejoice. Joaquin Miller. PAH
From out of a wood did a cuckoo fly. The Birds. *Unknown.* ChrBoLe
From out of the North-land his leaguer he led. Saint Leger. Clinton Scollard. PAH
From out our crowded calendar. Memorial Day. McLandburgh Wilson. DD; MaRV
From out the earth I dig this plant, an herb of most effectual power. Charm to Quell a Rival. *Unknown.* *Fr.* The Rig-veda. LiTW
From out the Glow the Wrath of Heaven Spoke. Stefan George, *tr. fr. German by* Babette Deutsch *and* Avrahm Yarmolinsky. OnPM
From out the grave of one whose budding years. The Lachrymatory. Charles Tennyson Turner. VA
From out the kitchen window. Belinda's Window. Margaret Widdemer. PEDC
From out the Queen's Highcliffe for weeks at a stretch. Margate, 1940. John Betjeman. NoP
From out the South the genial breezes sigh. The Mother. *Tr. by* George Barrow. OHIP
From out the stormy sea unto the shore. Epitaph. Azariah di Rossi. TrJP
From Paumanok Starting I Fly Like a Bird. Walt Whitman. CoBA
From Pembroke's princely dome, where mimic Art. Sonnet: Written after Seeing Wilton-House. Thomas Warton, the Younger. Sonnets, V. OBEC
From Pent-up Aching Rivers. Walt Whitman. AP; CABA; ViBoPo
From plains that reel to southward, dim. Heat. Archibald Lampman. CaP; OBCV; PeCV; VA
From Plane to Plane. Robert Frost. MoAmPo (1950 ed.)
From pleasure of the bed. The Chambermaid's Second Song. W. B. Yeats. ErPo
From plum-tree and cherry. Flowering Currant. Patrick MacDonogh. ErPo
From point A a wind is blowing to point B. After the Broken Arm. Ron Padgett. ANYP

From Potomac to Merrimac. Edward Everett Hale. PAH
Merrimac Side, and Agiochook, III.
Potomac Side, I.
Signal Fires, II.
From prayer that asks that I may be. Deliver Me [*or* Make Me Thy Fuel]. Amy Carmichael. FaChP; SoP; STF
From prehistoric distance, beyond clocks. Street Fight. Harold Monro. FaBoTw
From purest wells of English undefiled. James Russell Lowell. Whittier. DD
From Romany to Rome. Wallace Irwin. HBV
From Santiago, spurning the morrow. The Destroyer of Destroyers. Wallace Rice. PAH
From Sappho's Death: Three Pictures by Gustave Moreau. T. Sturge Moore. SyP
From shadows of rich oaks outpeer. The Pike. Edmund Blunden. AnFE; LiTM (1970 ed.); MoVE; ShBV-3
From shadowy stratas of his mind. Intuition. R. H. Grenville. FiSC
From shores of Senegal, from Lake Omandaba. O My Swallows! Ernst Toller. TrJP
From Slavery to Slavery. Sadi, *pr. tr. fr. Persian by* Sir Edwin Arnold. *Fr.* The Gulistan. OuHeWo
From sluggish sleep and slumber. The Bellman's Good-Morrow. *Unknown.* PoLi
From snows packed on barren mountains. Imperial Valley, Calif. Jascha Kessler. NYTB
From Soil Somehow the Poet's Word. Kenneth Leslie. OBCV
From Solitude to Solitude towards Life. Paul Eluard, *tr. fr. French by* Stephen Spender *and* Frances Cornford. LiTW
From some sweet home, the morning train. The School Girl. William Henry Venable. AA
From something in the trees. For the New Year. Robert Creeley. NaP
From song and dream forever gone. Elegiac Mood. Gordon Bottomley. *Fr.* Night and Morning Songs. NP
From Spiralling Ecstatically This. E. E. Cummings. PoDB
From stainless steel basins of water. The Operation. W. D. Snodgrass. CBV; StP; ToPo
From Stirling [*or* Sterling] castle we had seen. Yarrow Unvisited. Wordsworth. BEL; EnLi-2; EnRP; GTBS; GTBS-D; GTBS-P; GTBS-W; GTSE; GTSL; HBV; MERP; PoRA
From stone to arrow, sling-shot, gun. No Curtain. F. R. Scott. NYTB
From Stone to Steel ("From stone to bronze, from bronze to steel"). E. J. Pratt. PeCV
From "Suite in Prison." Richard Eberhart. NYTB
From summer and the wheel-shaped city. Washington Cathedral. Karl Shapiro. MiAP
From Summer Hours. Albert Samain, *tr. fr. the French by* Jethro Bithell. AWP; JAWP; WBP
From Susquehanna's farthest springs. The Indian Student; or, Force of Nature. Philip Freneau. AmPP (4th ed.); OxBA
From that elemental land. To the Ancestral North. James Kirkup. POTi
From that last acre on oblivion's heap. Mother Goose Up to Date: Edna St. Vincent Millay Exhorts Little Boy Blue. Louis Untermeyer. MoAmPo
From that time forth, Authority in France. France. Wordsworth. The Prelude, XI. ERoP-1
From the age of the gods. Separation. Empress Kogyoku. OnPM
From the ageless garden plot of Time he came. Christmas Rose. Margaret Evelyn Singleton. ChIP
From the Antique. Christina Rossetti. EnLoPo
From the Arabic; an Imitation. Shelley. CBEP; HBV
("My faint spirit was sitting in the light.") OBEV
From the Ballad of Evil. N. P. van Wyk Louw, *tr. fr. Afrikaans by* Anthony Delius. PeSA
From the Ballad of Two-Gun Freddy. Walter R. Brooks. SoPo
From the basement of an opportunist's slave ship. A Splib Odyssey. Quency Troupe. WSL
From the Beaumont Series. Dick Gallup. ANYP
From the besieged Ardea all in post. The Rape of Lucrece. Shakespeare. BeLS
From the bonny bells of heather. Heather Ale. Robert Louis Stevenson. AnEnPo; ShBV-1; VA
From the borders of the swamp I sang. To C. T. C. Joseph Bennett. LiTM (rev. ed.)
From the Bridge. Keats. *Fr.* I Stood Tip-Toe. PCH
From the bustle of liveried soldiers. Café Scene. Saunders Lewis. PrWP
From the cassowary's beak come streaks of light. Morning at Arnheim. William Jay Smith. NePoEA
From the Chuck Wagon. *Unknown.* ABF
From the commandant's quarters on Westchester height. Aaron Burr's Wooing. Edmund Clarence Stedman. PAH
From the confusion of estranging years. For Elizabeth Madox Roberts. Janet Lewis. QFR
From the cool and dark-lipped furrows. The Earth Breath 'Æ." BEL
From the Country to the City. Elizabeth Bishop. CrMA
From the cross uplifted high. Come and Welcome. Thomas Haweis. BePJ
From the crowded belfry calling. Bega. Marjorie Pickthall. CaP
From the Crystal. Sidney Lanier. BePJ
From the dark mood's control. The Recovery. Edmund Blunden. CBEP; MoBrPo; MoPW
From the Dark Tower. Countee Cullen. BALP; BANP; CDC; IDB; Kal; LiTM (1970 ed.); NeMA; PoNe
From the dark tower which is a ship's mast. Stroke of One. Jorge Carrera Andrade. OnPM
From the dark woods that breathe of fallen showers. The Zebras. Roy Campbell. AnFE; BoSA; GTBS-D; LiTB; LiTM; MoBrPo; MoPW; ReMP; ShBV-4; ViBoPo
From the Day-Book of a Forgotten Prince. Jean Starr Untermeyer. HBMV; TSW
From the dead hand I take the bow he wielded. Funeral Hymn. *Unknown. Fr.* The Rigveda. LiTW
From the depth of the dreamy decline of the dawn. Nephelidia. Swinburne. *Fr.* The Heptalogia. ALV; BOHV; EnLi-2 (1941 ed.); HBV; HoPM; InMe; NA; OAEP; Par; PeVV; PoFS; PoVP; ViPo; VP
From the desert I come to thee. Bedouin Song. Bayard Taylor. AA; AmePo; AmP; AnAmPo; BBV; BoLP; FaBoBe; GBV; HBV; MCCG; NeHB; PaPo; PFY; TreFT
From the Domain of Arnheim. Edwin Morgan. HYE
From the drear North, a cold and cheerless land. The Heritage. Edward Bliss Reed. EtS
From the drear wastes of unfulfilled desire. Disappointment. Thomas Stephens Collier. AA
From the Duck-Pond to the Carousel. Muriel Rukeyser. FiMAP
From the dull confines of the drooping west. His Return[e] to London. Robert Herrick. AnAnS-2; EnLit; MaPo (1969 ed.); SeEP
From the dusk forest or the dark'ning strand. Perdita. John Swanwick Drennan. IrPN
From the elm-tree's topmost bough. Robin's Come. William Warner Caldwell. DD; HBVY
From the Embassy. Robert Graves. TPM
From the end of a thin string taped on my ceiling. Two Fish Cosmologies. Dick Lourie. ThO
From the ends of the earth, from the ends of the earth. Fairy Chorus. *Unknown. Fr.* The Bride's Marriage-Cake. HW
From the far horizon, and breaking in triumph towards him. Henry Reed. *Fr.* The Place and the Person. GTBS-D
From the far-off Rocky Mountains, where they meet the eastern Hills. The Gathering on the Plains. William T. Butler. PoOW
From the first circle I made my descent. Inferno. Dante. *Fr.* Divina Commedia. EnLi-1
From the first cry. First It Was Singing. Jon Silkin. NePoEA; PoDB
From the first shock of leaves their alliance. Park Poem. Paul Blackburn. CoPo
From the Flats. Sidney Lanier. AmP; CoBA; NePA; OxBA
From the flotsam of a city street we built the Swinging Stair. The Swinging Stair. Nathalia Crane. YT
From the forest of night. Lunar Moth. Robert Hillyer. OA
From the forests and highlands. Hymn of Pan. Shelley. AtBAP; EnRP; ERoP-2; ExPo; FaBoCh; HBV; LoGBV; MBW-2; MemP; MyFE; OAEP; OBEV; OBRV; PoEL-4; PoIE; RG; SeCeV
From the four corners of the earth. Carl Sandburg. *Fr.* The People, Yes, Sec. I. CMoP
From the Gallows Hill to the Tineton Copse. John Mansfield. *Fr.* Reynard the Fox, II. NAMP
From the Garden of Heaven. Hafiz, *tr. fr. Persian by* Gertrude L. Bell. LiTW

From the geyser ventilators. Business Girls. John Betjeman. WePo
From the gray woods they come, on silent feet. The Dancers. Babette Deutsch. HBMV
From the great Atlantic Ocean. The Wabash Cannonball. *Unknown.* TreFT
From the Greek Anthology ("Bill Jupp lies 'ere"). L. A. G. Strong. WhC
From the grey wicket of the morn. John Francis O'Donnell. *Fr.* To Spring. IrPN
From the Gulf. Will H. Ogilvie. BoAu; PoAu-1
From the hag [*or* hagg] and hungry [*or* hungrie] goblin. Tom o' Bedlam's Song [*or* Tom o'Bedlam]. *Unknown.* AnFE; AtBAP; BoW; CBEP; ChTr; EG; EnSB; EvOK; FosPo; HBV; HoPM; InvP; LiTB; LiTG; MemP; OtMeF; OxBoLi; PoEL-2; PoFS; PoSa; PTK; SeCeV; SeEP; SiTL; StP; TrGrPo; ViBoPo; WiR
From the halls of Montezuma. The Marines' Hymn [*or* Song]. *Unknown, at. to* L. Z. Phillips. PAL; PoRL; TreF; YaD
From the Harbor Hill. Gustav Kobbé. HBV
From the heart of a flower. Leave It to Me Blues. Joel Oppenheimer. CoPo
From the heart of the mighty mountains strong-souled for my fate I came. The Song of the Colorado. Sharlot Mabridth Hall. HBV
From the high deck of Santa Fe's El Capitan. A Siding Near Chillicothe. Richard Lattimore. AmFN
From the high terrace porch I watch the dawn. On a View of Pasadena from the Hills. Yvor Winters. QFR
From the Highest Camp. Thom Gunn. Sonn; TwCP
From the Hills of Dream. "Fiona Macleod." MoSiPe
From the hodge porridge. The Farmer's Wife. Anne Sexton. LiTM (1970 ed.); NePoEA-2
From the island aquamarine. Index (8). Gill Orlovitz. ToPo
From the Kei to Umzimkulu. Jim. Perceval Gibbon. BoSA
From the laurel's fairest bouth. The Battle of Valparaiso. *Unknown.* PAH
From the lone sheiling of the misty island. Scotland Yet. *Unknown, at. to* John Galt. *Fr.* Canadian Boat Song. OtMeF
From the madding crowd they stand apart. The V-a-s-e. James Jeffrey Roche. AmePo; BOHV; HBV; LHV
From the misty shores of midnight, touched with splendors of the moon. Tennyson [*or* In Lucem Transitus, October, 1892]. Henry van Dyke. AA; InP
From the moors and the tors of old England. Americans All. Minna Irving. PEDC
From the mountains to the sea. Georgia. Robert Loveman. PoRL
From the mouth of the Harlem Gallery. Lamda. Melvin B. Tolson. PoNe (1970 ed.)
From the Night of Forebeing, *abr.* Francis Thompson. OBVV OtMeF
From the night storm sad wakes the winter day. November Morning. Edmund Blunden. WePo
From the North the populated breeze. A Book for Christmas. Margaret Allonby. BoSA
From the ocean filled with sand inside of me. Man with a Furnace in His Hand. Lance Jeffers. BF
From the oracular archives and the parchment. Altarwise by Owl-Light, IX. Dylan Thomas. CMoP; CoBMV; LiTM; MaSP; Sonn
From the Parthenon I learn. Willard Wattles. HBMV
From the Persian. *At. to* Ali Ben Abu Taleb, *tr. by* Emerson. *See* Friends and Enemies.
From the place where I was sitting. El Gusano. Irving Layton. PeCV (1967 ed.)
From the Rain Down. Rhina P. Espaillat. GoYe
From the Recesses. Sir John Bowring. SoP; VA
From the Rio Grande's waters to the icy lakes of Maine. Buena Vista. Albert Pike. PAH
From the Roof. Denise Levertov. NoP
From the roof the night's the color. Night in Boston. Jim Harrison. ThO
From the sad eaves the drip-drop of the rain. Desolate. Sydney Dobell. CBEP; NBM; OBNC
From the Sea. Sara Teasdale. MoLP
From the sea of heaven the waves of cloud arise. The Moon's Ship. Hitomaro. OnPM
From the shieling that stands by the lone mountain river. War Song of O'Driscol. Gerald Griffin. OnYI
From the soft dyke-road, crooked and waggon-worn. Haying. John Frederic Herbin. CaP; PeCV
From the solitary desert. The Bewildered Arab. Jami, *tr. fr. Persian by* Edward Fitzgerald. *Fr.* Salámán and Absál. WoL
From the south they came, Birds of War. Ojibwa War Songs. *Unknown.* AWP; JAWP; WBP
From the Spanish. Tony Towle. ANYP; YAP
From the starry heav'ns descending. Christmas Carol. J. R. Newell. BLRP
From the start of Life. The Solar Road. Francis Carlin. JKCP
From the Station House. Galway Kinnell. *Fr.* The Avenue Bearing the Initial of Christ into the New World. NMP
From the tattered banana tree after months of waiting. Banana. Charles G. Bell. ErPo; NePoAm-2
From the temple to your home. Connubii Flores, or the Well-Wishes at Weddings. Robert Herrick. HW
From the thick cover of unknowningness. On the Curve-Edge. Abbie Huston Evans. NYBP
From the thin slats of the Venetian blinds. Underwood. Howard Moss. NePA; NePoEA-2; PP; TwCP
From the time of our old Revolution. That Things Are No Worse, Sire. Helen Hunt Jackson. OHIP
From the time when Nature in her furious fancy. The Giantess. Baudelaire. OnPM
From the top of a bridge. The River Is a Piece of Sky. John Ciardi. PDV; PoPl; SoPo
From the top of high Caucasus. Tom of Bedlam. *Unknown.* SiTL
From the top of the bluff, where the wind blows free. The Edge of the World. Mary Fanny Youngs. BrR
From the tragic-est novels at Mudie's. Dora versus Rose. Austin Dobson. ALV; BOHV
From the Train. Marjorie Wilson. BoTP
From the tug the shore crops are merely blurry wilderness. Flaming Creatures. Kenward Elmslie. ANYP
From the Turkish ("The chain I gave was fair to view"). Byron. HBV
From the unseen world descends. In the Secret Rose Garden. Sa'd ud-din Mahmud Shabistari. LiTW
From the uttermost part of the earth. I Waste Away. Isaiah, Bible, *O.T.* TrJP
From the vast caverns of old ocean's bed. Philip Freneau. *Fr.* The Beauties of Santa Cruz. AmPP (4th ed.)
From the window. Doughtry Long, Jr. TNV
From the Window Down. Louis O. Coxe. NYBP
From the years. Things Kept. William Dickey. NYBP
From Thee all skill and science flow. The Great Physician. Charles Kingsley. MaRV
From Thee to Thee. Solomon ibn Gabirol, *tr. fr. Hebrew by* Israel Abrahams. EaLo; TrJP
From their folded mates they wander far. Black Sheep. Richard Burton. AA; HBV
From them no words come. The White Chrysanthemum. Ryota. OnPM
From thence into the open fields he fled. A Pastoral. Spenser. *Fr.* The Faerie Queene, VI, 9. OBSC
From these high [*or* hie] hilles as when a spring doth fall. Comparison of Love to a Streame Falling from the Alpes. Sir Thomas Wyatt. FaBoEn; FCP
From thick clouds over the black Warrumbungles. Flood. Ethel Anderson. NeLNL
From thicket, thrush. Thrush for Hawk. John Fandel. NYTB
From this balcony. The Lace Curtains. Lewis Mac Adams. ANYP
From this carved chair wherein I sit to-night. The Voice of D. G. R. Sir Edmund Gosse. VA
From this far, late-come country that still keeps. Gordon Childe. David Martin. PoAu-2
From this high quarried ledge I see. The Mountain over Aberdare. Alun Lewis. ACV
From this hospital bed. The Injury. William Carlos Williams. AP
From this hundred-terraced height. The Centennial Meditation of Columbia. Sidney Lanier. PAH
From this low-lying valley, oh, how sweet. Two Points of View. Lucian B. Watkins. BANP
From this quaint cabin window I can see. By the Pacific. Herbert Bashford. AA
From This There's No Returning. Jean Garrigue. TwAmPo

From this tower room above the wall. Cups of Illusion. Henry Bellamann. HBMV
From this valley they say you are going. The Red River Valley. *Unknown.* AS; BFSS; CoSo; FaBoBe; FaFP; TrAS; TreFS
From thorax of storm the voices of verbs. Three Memorial Sonnets, II. George Barker. WaP
From Titian's "Bacchanal" in the Prado at Madrid. T. Sturge Moore. QFR
From Tomorrow On. *Unknown, tr. fr. Yiddish by* Joseph Leftwich. TrJP
From troubles of the world. Ducks. Frederick Williams Harvey. BoC; YT
From Tuscan[e] came my lady's worthy race. Description and Praise of His Love Geraldine. Earl of Surrey. FCP; OAEP; ReEn; ReIE; SiCE; SiPS; TuPP
From twig to twig the spider weaves. Outer and Inner. George Meredith. PrWP
From twigs of visionary boughs. Prophet and Fool. Louis Golding. HBMV
From unremembered ages we. Chorus of Spirits. Shelley. *Fr.* Prometheus Unbound. LoBV
From Venice Was That Afternoon. Jean Garrigue. LiTA
From Virgin's womb this day to us did spring. For Christmas Day. Francis Kinwelmersh. ReIE
From wars and plagues come no such harms. To a Coquet Beauty. John Sheffield, Duke of Buckingham and Normanby. CEP
From Water-Tower Hill to the brick prison. Point Shirley. Sylvia Plath. NoP
From way down south on the Rio Grande. Down South on the Rio Grande. *Unknown.* CoSo
From what dripping cell, through what fairy glen. A Drunkard to His Bottle. Joseph Sheridan Le Fanu. OnYI
From what I am, to be what I am not. Return. Vassar Miller. ToPo
From what proud star I know not, but I found. The Giant Puffball. Edmund Blunden. FaBoTw
From whence arrived the praying mantis? The Praying Mantis. Ogden Nash. PV
From where I lingered in a lull in March. Evening in a Sugar Orchard. Robert Frost. WIRo
From where I sit, I see the stars. Midnight. Archibald Lampman. OBCV; PeCV
From where the sun. For Death by Choice. Pearl Cleage. WSL
From White's and Will's. Song. Ambrose Philips. CEP
From Whitsuntide to Whitsuntide. A Ballad of a Bun. Sir Owen Seaman. CenHV
From whose white summits was this wind released. The Storm at Nightfall. Morton Dauwen Zabel. NP
From Wibbleton to Wobbleton is fifteen miles. *Unknown.* OxNR
From Wicklow to the throb of dawn. Sea Dawn. Francis Hackett. AnIV
From William Tyndale to John Frith. Edgar Bowers. NePoEA; QFR
From within/ Slight rain seems to purr. Rain on a Cottage Roof. Freda Laughton. OnYI
From wounds and death they rest—this bow and quiver. Dedication. *Unknown.* OnPM
From Wynyard's Gap the livelong day. A Trampwoman's Tragedy. Thomas Hardy. AtBAP; BeLS; HBMV; MOVE; OBNC
From yonder wood, mark blue-eyed Eve proceed. Progress of Evening. Walter Savage Landor. OBNC
From Yorktown on the fourth of May. The Gallant Fighting "Joe." James Stevenson. PAH
From you, Beethoven, Bach, Mozart. Dead Musicians. Siegfried Sassoon. BrPo
From you have I [*or* I have] been absent in the spring. Sonnets, XCVIII. Shakespeare. AWP; BEL; BoC; BWP; ChTr; DiPo; ElL; EnLi-1; InPo; JAWP; LiTB; LiTG; NoP; PoAn; ReEn; ReIE; SiCE; TOP; ViBoPo; WBP
From you, Ianthe, little troubles pass. Walter Savage Landor. *Fr.* Ianthe. BoLiVe; OBEV; OBNC; OnPM; PTK; TrGrPo; ViBoPo
From you, Rose, I do not like. Rondeau for You. Mário de Andrade. TTY
Front Street. Howard Moss. NYBP
Frontier, The. Jon Anderson. YAP
Frontier, The. Donald Hall. CBV
Frontier, The. John Masefield. NP
Frontispiece. May Swenson. CoAP; NePoEA
Frost. W. H. Davies. BoNaP
Frost, The. Emily Dickinson. *See* Apparently with no surprise.
Frost. Ethel Romig Fuller. GFA
Frost, The. Hannah Flagg Gould. BLPA; HBV; HBVY; NeHB; PTK; RIS; TVC
(Jack Frost.) DD; OTPC; PRWS
Frost. John Hewitt. NeIP
Frost. George Johnston. WHW
Frost. E. J. Pratt. WHW
Frost. Edith M. Thomas. AA
Frost and snow, frost and snow. Ariel. David Campbell. NeLNL; PoAu-2
Frost at Midnight. Samuel Taylor Coleridge. BEL; BoC; BWP; CABA; CABL; CBEP; CBV; EnLi-2; EnRP; EPN; ERoP-1; FaBoEn; FiP; FosPo; ILP; LoBV; MaPo (1969 ed.); MBW-2; MERP; NoP; OAEP; OBNC; OBRV; PAn; PeER; PoE; PoEL-4; PoIE; ShBV-4; StP; VaPo
All Seasons Shall Be Sweet, *sel.* BoTP
Frost at Night. James Thomson. *Fr.* The Seasons: Winter. OBEC
Frost at Sea. William Diaper. *Fr.* Nereides; or, Sea-Eclogues. BeR
Frost called to water "Halt!" Hard Frost. Andrew Young. BoNaP; MoVE
Frost came in the night and stole my world, A. A Hard Frost. C. Day Lewis. HaMV
Frost Fancy, A. Richard Le Gallienne. OTPC (1946 ed.)
Frost flowers on the window glass. A Valentine. Eleanor Hammond. GFA; RePo; TiPo; YeAr
Frost has sealed/ The still December field. Tree in December. Melville Cane. MAP; MoAmPo
Frost in the air and music in the air. The Waits. John Freeman. BoTP
Frost is an elf. Frost. Ethel Romig Fuller. GFA
Frost is here, The. Winter. Tennyson. PCH
Frost is out, and in the open fields, The. October. Jones Very. AnNE
Frost is tight upon the land. Now in the Time of This Mortal Life. Norman Nicholson. NeBP
Frost-King, The. Mary Mapes Dodge. DD
Frost-locked all the winter. Spring. Christina Rossetti. OBNC
Frost looked forth one still, clear night, The. The Frost [*or* Jack Frost]. Hannah Flagg Gould. BLPA; DD; HBV; HBVY; NeHB; OTPC; PRWS; PTK; RIS; TVC
Frost-Morning. William Alexander, Archbishop of Armagh. IrPN
Frost moved up the window-pane, The. Frost. E. J. Pratt. WHW
Frost on my window. Frost. George Johnston. WHW
Frost Pane, The. David McCord. BrR; RePo; RIS; StaSt; StVeCh
Frost performs its secret ministry, The. Frost at Midnight. Samuel Taylor Coleridge. BEL; BoC; BWP; CABA; CABL; CBEP; CBV; EnLi-2; EnRP; EPN; ERoP-1; FaBoEn; FiP; FosPo; ILP; LoBV; MaPo (1969 ed.); MBW-2; MERP; NoP; OAEP; OBNC; OBRV; PAn; PeER; PoE; PoEL-4; PoIE; ShBV-4; StP; VaPo
Frost shall freeze; fire melt wood. Maxims [*or* Gnomic Lines]. *Unknown.* AnOE; LiTW
Frost Spirit, The. Whittier. HBV; PCH
Frost To-Night. Edith M. Thomas. MCCG; PCD
Frost was never seen, The. Emily Dickinson. MAmP
Frost will bite us soon, The. Harvest-Home Song. John Davidson. VA
Frostbite. Conrad Aiken. PoPo; SiTL
Frosted over with cold flakes. First Winter's Day. Dorothy Aldis. SoPo
Frosted Pane, The. Charles G. D. Roberts. HBV
Frosty Christmas Eve, A. Noel: Christmas Eve, 1913. Robert Bridges. LiTB; MoVE; OxBoCh; PoEL-5
Frosty Day, A. Lord De Tabley. LoBV
Frosty Night, A. Robert Graves. CH; MoAB; MoBrPo; MoBS; MPB
Frosty, the bite of the autumn air. Blessing the Hounds. Mary Winter. GoYe
Froude informs the Scottish youth. William Stubbs. CenHV

Frowardness of the Elect in the Work of Conversion, The. Edward Taylor. SCAP
Frowned the Laird, on the Lord: "So, redhanded I catch thee?" Muckle-Mouth Meg. Robert Browning. HBV; MeWo; OtMeF; PoVP; VA
Frowning Cliff, The. Herbert Asquith. BrR
Frowning fates have taken hence, The. A Dead Child[e]. Lucian. EnLi-1; LiTW
Frowning, the mountain stronghold stood. The Lost Colors. Elizabeth Stuart Phelps Ward. AA; HBV; HBVY
Frowning, the owl in the oak complained him. Owl against Robin. Sidney Lanier. LaNeLa
Frozen City, The. Howard Nemerov. FiMAP
Frozen Fire. Floris Clarke McLaren. CaP
Frozen Girl, The. Seba Smith. *See* Young Charlotte.
Frozen ground is broken, The. In February. P. A. Ropes. BoTP
Frozen Heart, The. Robert Herrick. CavP
Frozen Hero, The. Thomas H. Vance. NYBP
Frozen Ocean, The. Viola Meynell. CH
Frugal crone, whom praying priests attend, The. The Ruling Passion. Pope. *Fr.* Moral Essays, Epistle I. BOHV
Frugal snail, with forecast of repose, The. The Housekeeper [*or* The Snail]. Vincent Bourne, *tr. by* Charles Lamb. GN; GoTP; HBV; MoShBr; OTPC; PoLF
Fruit. Ruth Miller. BoSA
Fruit. *Unknown, tr. fr. Spanish by* Havelock Ellis. OnPM
Fruit breaks on the summer mouth. The Garden. George M. Brady. NeIP
Fruit of all the service that I serve, The. Epigram. Sir Thomas Wyatt. FCP; SiPS
Fruit of the Flower. Countee Cullen. PoLF; PoNe
Fruit of the goodly tree, leaves of the palm tree. The Hut. Avigdor Hammeiri. LiTW
Fruit of the orchard is over-ripe, Elaine, The. Lancelot. Arna Bontemps. CDC
Fruit of the Tree, The. David Wagoner. NYBP
Fruit Plucker, The. Samuel Taylor Coleridge. *Fr.* The Wanderings of Cain. CH; SeCeV
(Boy in the Wilderness.) OTPC (1923 ed.)
(Fragment, A: "Encinctured with a twine of leaves.") OBNC
(In a Moonlight Wilderness.) FaBoCh; LoGBV
Fruit Rancher, The. Lloyd Roberts. CaP
Fruit-tree's branch by very wealth, The. The Penalty of Virtue. *Unknown. Fr.* The Panchatantra. AWP; PoFr
Fruit white and lustrous as a pearl. The Lychee. Wang I. FaBoCh
Fruitful Earth Drinks Up the Rain. Thomas Stanley, *after the Greek of* Anacreon. OnPM
(All Things Drink.) AWP
Fruitful was the land, rich its pastures, flowing with milk and honey. Psalm of the Singing Grave. Alexander Janta. LiTW
Fruitionless. Ina Donna Coolbrith. AA
Fruits of Experience. James Broughton. SiTL
Fruits of War, The. George Gascoigne. ReIE
Fruits of Warre Is Beggery, The. *Unknown. See* Maunding Souldier, The.
Frustra. Shakespeare. *See* Take, O Take Those Lips Away.
Frustrate. Louis Untermeyer. HBMV; InMe; YaD
Frustrated Male. Hughes Mearns. *Fr.* Later Antigonishes. InMe; SiTL
Frustration. Elizabeth Daryush. QFR
Frustration, a Heritage. Thelma Parker Cox. TNV
Frutta di Mare. Geoffrey Scott. ChTr; EtS; OBMV; SiSw
Fryar was walking in Exeter-street, A. The Crafty Miss of London; or, The Fryar Well Fitted. *Unknown.* CoMu; OxBB
Fryar Well Fitted, The. *Unknown. See* Crafty Miss of London, The.
Fu I. Ezra Pound. PIA
Fuchsia Hedges in Connacht. Padraic Colum. GoBC
Fudge Family in Paris, The, *sels.* Thomas Moore.
French Cookery. OBRV
Miss Biddy Fudge to Miss Dorothy. NBM
Fugal-Chorus from "For the Time Being" ("Great is Caesar"). W. H. Auden. *Fr.* For the Time Being. LiTM (rev, ed.); NePA; SeCeV
Fugitive Slaves, The. Jones Very. AP
Fugitive Slave's Apostrophe to the North Star, The. John Pierpoint. AA
Fugitives, The. Florence Wilkinson Evans. OQP
Fugitives, The, *st.* 1. Shelley. PCH
Fugue. Constance Carrier. GoYe
Fugue, A, *sel.* Hubert Church.
"There was a music throbbed athwart the street." AnNZ
Fugue. Harold Lewis Cook. NP
Fugue. R. A. K. Mason. OnPM
Fuimus Troes, *sels.* Jasper Fisher.
Morisco, A. SeCL; TuPP
(Song: Morisko, A.) SeEP
Song to a Viol. LO; SeCL
("So the silver-feathered swan.") SeEP; TuPP
Fulani Cattle. John Pepper Clark. PBA
Fulfill, O gracious God, to-day. Pentecost. Adelbert Sumpter Coats. TrPWD
Fulfillment. Helene Johnson. CDC; PoNe
Fulfillment. Vassar Miller. NePoEA-2
Fulfillment. Duke of Newcastle. *See* Love's Matrimony.
Fulfillment. William A. Muhlenberg. WGRP
Fulfillment. Charlotte Newton. OQP
Fulfillment, The. Delmore Schwartz. FiMAP
Fulfillment. Eunice Tietjens. *See* Psalm to My Belovèd.
Fulfilment. Elsa Barker. *Fr.* The Spirit and the Bride. HBMV
Fulfilment. Louis V. Ledoux. HBMV
Fulfilment. Robert Nichols. HBMV
Full clear and bright this Christmas night range fields of Heaven fire-sown. Christmas Rede. Jane Barlow. OBVV
Full Cycle. John White Chadwick. PAH
Full early in the morning. *Unknown.* BoTP
Full faith I have she holds that rarest gift. Modern Love, XXXII. George Meredith. ViPo; VP
Full Fathom Five. A. R. D. Fairburn. AnNZ
Full fathom [*or* fadom] five thy father lies. Ariel's Song [*or* A Sea Dirge]. Shakespeare. *Fr.* The Tempest, I, ii. AnEnPo; AnFE; AtBAP; ATP; AWP; BEL; BoLiVe; CABA; CaFP; CBEP; CBV; ChTr; DiPo; EG; ElL; ELP; EnLi-1; EtS; EvOK; ExPo; FaBoCh; FaBoEn; FlW; ForPo; FosPo; GN; GoJo; GTBS; GTBS-D; GTBS-P; GTBS-W; GTSE; GTSL; HBV; HoPM; ILP; InPo; JAWP; LiTB; LiTG; LoBV; LoGBV; MaPo; MCCG; NeHB; NoP; OAEP; OBEV; OBSC; OTPC; OuHeWo; PAn; PIA; PoEL-2; PoeP; PoIE; PoRA; PTK; SeCePo; SeCeV; ShBV-1; SiCE; ThWaDe; TOP; TreFT; TrGrPo; ViBoPo; WBP; WHA; YAT
Full forty days he pass'd, whether on hill. The First Temptation. Milton. *Fr.* Paradise Regained, I. OxBoCh
Full happy is the man who comes at last. The Year's End. Timothy Cole. HBV
Full Heart, The. Robert Nichols. BoNaP; HBMV
Full-Hearted Men! Paul Martin. SoP
Full in her glory, she as Tirzah fair. The Prophet Jeremiah and the Personification of Israel. *At. to* Eleazar ben Kalir. TrJP
Full is my sorrow now that you are dead. The Atheist Buries His Son. Abu'l-Atahija. LiTW
Full knee-deep lies the winter snow. The Death of the Old Year. Tennyson. DD; HBV; HH; OTPC; PoSC
Full Life, A. Carphyllides, *tr. fr. Greek by* Lord Neaves. OnPM
Full life, sweet rest, great love that cannot cease. Four Friends. Leo Ward. GoBC
Full little knowest thou, that hast not tried. At Court. Spenser. *Fr.* Mother Hubberds Tale. PoFr
Full many a century it crept, the child. The Silkworm. Marco Girolamo Vida. *Fr.* De Bombycibus. CAW
Full many a dreary hour have I past. Epistle to My Brother George. Keats. EnRP; MERP
Full many a fiend did haunt this house of rest. An Imitation of Spenser. John Armstrong. WaPE
Full many a glorious morning have I seen. Sonnets, XXXIII. Shakespeare. ATP; AWP; BEL; BoLiVe; BWP; CBEP; CoBE; EG; ElL; EnL; EnLi-1; FaBoEn; FaFP; HBV; ILP; InPo; JAWP; LiTB; LiTG; LoBV; NoP; OAEP; OBSC; OtMeF; OuHeWo; PoRA; ReEn; ReIE; SeCePo; SeCeV; SiCE; Sonn; TOP; TreFS; TrGrPo; UnPo (1st ed.); ViBoPo; WBP
Full many a project that never was hatched. Humpty Dumpty. Adeline D. T. Whitney. *Fr.* Mother Goose for Grown Folks. HBV
Full many a sinful notion. Apple-Pie and Cheese. Eugene Field. LHV
Full many are the centuries since the days. Assurance. Ida Norton Munson. PGD

Full many lift and sing. Negro Poets. Charles Bertram Johnson. BANP
Full merrily rings the millstone round. Song of the Elfin Miller. Allan Cunningham. OTPC (1946 ed.)
Full Moon. Clifford Bax. POTE
Full Moon. Walter de la Mare. AtBAP; BoNaP; TiPo
Full Moon. John Gould Fletcher. Down the Mississippi, III. HT; LiTA; NP
Full Moon. Robert Graves. FaBoEn; POTE
Full Moon. Robert Hayden. Kal
Full Moon. Galway Kinnell. NePoAm-2.
Full Moon. V. Sackville-West. MoBrPo (1942 ed.); MoShBr
Full Moon. Sappho, *tr. fr. Greek by* William Ellery Leonard. AWP; JAWP; WBP
Full Moon. Sara Teasdale. *See* Full Moon; Santa Barbara.
Full Moon. Elinor Wylie. CrMA; MAP; MoAB; MoAmPo
Full moon easterly rising, furious, The. A Love Story. Robert Graves. AtBAP; CMoP; FaBoTw; LiTB; MoVE
Full moon floods the vast Pacific tides. Dawn at Flying-Fish Point. Clement B. Christesen. BoAu
Full moon is partly hidden by cloud, The. A Fable of the War. Howard Nemerov. NePoEA
Full Moon; New Guinea. Karl Shapiro. MiAP; PoPo
Full moon on the Colosseum, The. Colosseum. Harold Norse. TrJP
Full moon. Our Narragansett gales subside. Dream Song 61. John Berryman. CoAP
Full moon rising on the waters of my heart. Evening Song. Jean Toomer. CDC; PoNe
Full Moon; Santa Barbara. Sara Teasdale. BrR
(Full Moon.) TSW
Full night. The moon has yet to rise. Sodom. Herman Melville. *Fr.* Clarel. AmPP (5th ed.)
Full nineteen centuries have passed since then. A Call to Pentecost. Inez M. Tyler. BLRP
Full of Grace exceedingly. Hymn of the Angels and Sibyls. Gil Vicente. CAW
Full of her long white arms and milky skin. The Equilibrists. John Crowe Ransom. AmP; AnAmPo; AP; CaFP; CMoP; CoBMV; LiTM; MoAB; MoPo; MoVE; NePA; NoP; OxBA; UnPo (1st ed.)
Full of Joy Do Not Know, The; They Need Not. Richard Eberhart. NoP
Full of rebellion, I would die. Nature. George Herbert. MaMe; OAEP
Full of the Moon. Karla Kuskin. PDV
Full of wrath was Hiawatha. The Hunting of Pau-Puk-Keewis. Longfellow. *Fr.* The Song of Hiawatha. CoBA
Full oft beside some gorgeous fane. The Mother. Sara Coleridge. OBVV
Full oft of old the islands changed their names. Epitaph on an Infant. Crinagoras. AWP
Full Redemption. John Wesley. SoP
Full Sea Rolls and Thunders, The. W. E. Henley. EtS
Full soon the Queen this crafty sleight 'gan smell. Vergil, *tr. by* the Earl of Surrey. *Fr.* The Aeneid, IV. EnLit
Full Swing Circus. Clive Matson. ThO
Full Valleys. F. R. Scott. CaP
Full Well I Know. Hartley Coleridge. NCEP
"Full well I know—my friends—ye look on me." Sonn
Full well it may be seen. Sir Thomas Wyatt. FCP; SiPS
Full well, my gentle sir, I know. To an Artful Theatre Manager. Lorenzo da Ponte. *Fr.* Il Capriccio Dramatico. TrJP
Full winter; and the lusty woodman brings. Midwinter. Oscar Wilde. *Fr.* Humanitad. PCH
Fuller and Warren. *Unknown.* BeLS; CoSo, *with music*; ViBoFo
(Ye Sons of Columbia, *with music.*) BFSS
Fulness of life and power of feeling. Matthew Arnold. *Fr.* Empedocles on Etna. OAEP
Fulness of Time, The. James Stephens. MemP
Fumes from all kinds, The. Coming down Cleveland Avenue. James Tate. YAP
Fun in a Garret. Emma C. Dowd. GFA; SUS; TiPo
Fun on the Beach. Alice Wilkins. GFA
Fun with Fishing. Eunice Tietjens. FaPON; GaP
Fundament Is Shifted, The. Abbie Huston Evans. MoRP; NYBP
Fundisi. Ruth Miller. BoSA
Funebrial Reflections. Ogden Nash. ImOP
("Among the anthropophagi.") CenHV
Funeral. Murray Bennett. GoYe
Funeral, The. Walter de la Mare. CMoP; MoVE
Funeral[l], The. John Donne. AnAnS-1; ATP; AWP; BWP; CABA; CBEP; CoBE; DiPo; EnLi-1 (1949 ed.); EnLoPo; EnRePo; InPo; JAWP; LiTL; LO; MaMe; MBW-1; MeLP; MeP; NoP; OBEV; OBS; PoE; PoEL-2; PoRA; ReEn; SCEP-1; SeCP; SeCV-1; SeEP; TOP; TuPP; WBP
Funeral, The. Donald Hall. Sonn
Funeral. Vyacheslav Ivanov, *tr. fr. Russian by* Babette Deutsch. OnPM
Funeral, The. "M. J.," *tr. fr. Polish by* A. Glanz-Leyeless. TrJP
Funeral, The. Stephen Spender. CMoP; MoAB; MoBrPo; NAMP; PoAn
Funeral Dirge for Marcello. John Webster. *See* Call for the Robin Redbreast.
Funeral Elegy on the Death of His Very Good Friend, Mr. Michael Drayton. Sir Aston Cokayne. OBS
Funeral Elogy, upon . . . Mrs. Anne Bradstreet, A. John Norton. SCAP
Funeral gent led us, The. Choosing Coffins. Raymond Souster. MoCV
Funeral Home, The. Robert Mezey. AmPC; LiTM (1970 ed.)
Funeral Hymn. William Walsham How. WGRP
(For All the Saints.) MaRV
Funeral Hymn. *Unknown, tr. fr. Sanskrit by* Arthur A. Macdonnell. *Fr.* The Rigveda. LiTW
Funeral in Hungary. Kay Boyle. AnEnPo
Funeral of Martin Luther King, Jr., The. Nikki Giovanni. BOLo; TNV
Funeral of Napoleon I. Sir John H. Hagarty. CaP
Funeral of Philip Sparrow, The. John Skelton. *Fr.* Phyllyp Sparowe. ACP
Funeral of Time, The. Henry Beck Hirst. AA
Funeral of Youth, The: Threnody. Rupert Brooke. FaBoTw; SeCeV
Funeral Oration for a Mouse. Alan Dugan. AP
Funeral Pyre, The. *Unknown, tr. fr. Anglo-Saxon by* Charles W. Kennedy. *Fr.* Beowulf. AnOE
Funeral Rites of the Rose, The. Robert Herrick. CABA; OBEV; PoSa
Funeral Song ("Urns and odors, bring away"). Fletcher *and* Shakespeare. *Fr.* The Two Noble Kinsmen, I, v. AtBAP; ChTr; UnPo (1st ed.)
(Dirge of the Three Queens.) OBEV
(Song.) BoW
(Urns and Odours Bring Away!) ElL; SiCE
Funeral Song ("Now we are left out"). *Unknown, tr. fr. Sotho by* Dan Kunene *and* Jack Cope. PeSA
Funerall Rites of the Rose, The. Robert Herrick. AnAnS-2
Funeral Song upon the Decease of Annes, His Mother, A. Nicholas Grimald. ReIE; TuPP
Funeral [*or* Funerall] stone, A. To Laurels. Robert Herrick. ExPo; SeCV-1
Funeral Toast. Stéphane Mallarmé, *tr. fr. French by* Hubert Creekmore. LiTW
Funerall, The. John Donne. *See* Funeral, The.
Funerall Song, A: "Come to me, grief, for ever." *Unknown.* CH
Funerall stone, A. *See* Funeral stone, A.
Funiculi, Funicula. Luigi Denza. TreFT
Funnel. Anne Sexton. MoAmPo (1962 ed.)
Funniest sight that ever I saw, The. *Unknown.* GoTP
Funniest Thing in the World, The. James Whitcomb Riley. PPL
Funny Face, *sel.* Ira Gershwin.
Babbitt and the Bromide, The. ALV
Funny Fantasies Are Never so Real as Oldstyle. Lawrence Ferlinghetti. *Fr.* A Coney Island of the Mind. ErPo
Funny, how Felicia Ropps. Felicia Ropps. Gelett Burgess. BBGG; FaPON; GaP; TiPo
Funny how it come about! The Cowboy and the Maid. *Unknown.* SCC
Funny old lady named Borgia, A. *Unknown.* WhC
Funny Old Man and His Wife, The. *Unknown.* SoPo; SUS
Funny old person of Slough, A. Limerick. *Unknown.* RIS
Funny, solemn, little old grey owl. Yearning. Alfred Kreymborg. MAPA
Funny the Way Different Cars Start. Dorothy W. Baruch. FaPON

Funny thing is that he's reading a paper, The. The Sandwich Man. Ron Padgett. ANYP
Fur-cloaked boyars plotting in the hall, The. A Performance of "Boris Godunov." Robert Conquest. MuSP
Fürchte Nichts, geliebte Seele. Heine, *tr. fr. German by* Louis Untermeyer. ALV
(Precaution.) ALV
Furies, The. Aeschylus. *See* Eumenides.
Furious gun, in his [most] raging ire, The. The Lover Compareth His Heart to the Overcharged Gun. Sir Thomas Wyatt. FCP; ReIE
Furious prisoner of the womb, The. An Argument—Of the Passion of Christ. Thomas Merton. CrMA
Furius and Aurelius, Catullus's comrades. Farewell to Lesbia. Catullus. LiTW
Furius, my small estate, my charming villa. Cataclysm. Catullus. LiTW
Furl of fresh-leaved dog-rose down, The. Fragment. Gerard Manley Hopkins. AtBAP
Furl that banner, for 'tis weary. The Conquered Banner. Abram Joseph Ryan. AA; DD; FaPL; HBV; JKCP; PaA; PAH; PEDC; TreF
Furlough in heart and hand, the soldier at last walks. No Furlough. Stephen Stepanchev. WaP
Furnace is of stone and clay, A. The Fire Place. E. W. Mandel. OBCV
Furnace of Colors, The. Vernon Watkins. NYBP
Furnished Lives. Jon Silkin. NePoEA-2; NMP; PoDB
Furnished room beyond the stinging of, A. Good-bye for a Long Time. Roy Fuller. NeBP
Furniture. Phyllis Harris. NYBP; TPM
Furniture Man, The. Dick Gallup. ANYP
Furniture of a Woman's Mind, The. Swift. BWP; CaFP; CEP; PoIE
Furred from the farmhouse. Winter Saturday. Earle Birney. TwCaPo
Furry Bear. A. A. Milne. SoPo; StVeCh (1955 ed.); TiPo (1959 ed.)
Furry coat has the bear to wear, A. The Pig's Tail. Norman Ault. BoTP
Furry Home, The. J. M. Westrup. BoTP
Further Advice to a Painter. Andrew Marvell. MaMe
Further Fables for Our Times, *sel.* James Thurber.
Morals. FaBV
Further [*or* Farther] in summer than the birds. Emily Dickinson. AmPP (5th ed.); AP; ForPo; LiTA; MAmP; MaPo (1969 ed.); MWA-2; NoP; PIA; PoAn; PoEL-5; PoSa; QFR
Further Instructions. Ezra Pound. AnAmPo; NP; TwCP
Further than this we may not know. Foundation of Faith. John Drinkwater. MoRP
Furthest stars recede, The. The Expanding Universe. Norman Nicholson. POTi
Furtive lights that herald dawn, The. Dawn amid Scotch Firs. "Fiona Macleod." SyP
Fury of Aerial Bombardment, The. Richard Eberhart. AmP; CMoP; ExPo; HoPM; ILP; LiTA; LiTM (1970 ed.); MiAP; NMP; Po; PoIE; PoPo; ToPo; TwCP; UnPo (3d ed.); WaP
Fury of taunt was followed by fury of blow, The. E. J. Pratt. *Fr.* Brébeuf and His Brethren, XII. PeCV; TwCaPo
Fuscara or the Bee Errant. John Cleveland. AnAnS-2
Fuscus, the man of life upright [*or* upright life] and pure. Integer Vitae [*or* To Aristius Fuscus]. Horace, *tr. by* Sir Theodore Martin. *Fr.* Odes. EnLi-1; OuHeWe
Fussy. Laura E. Richards. MPB
Fust Banjo, De. Irwin Russell. *Fr.* Christmas-Night in the Quarters. AA; BLPA; HBV; IHA; PFY
(First Banjo, The.) BOHV; LHV
Futile Sacrifice. Murray Skinner. ChIP
Futile to chide the stinging shower. Perspectives. Dudley Randall. AmNP
Futility. Mary S. Hawling. PoMa
Futility. Wilfred Owen. AtBAP; CBEP; ChMP; CMoP; CoBMV; FaBoMo; GTBS-D; GTBS-P; LiTM; LO; MMA; MoAB; MoBrPo; MoPW; NeMA; NoP; OAEP (2d ed.); PoE; SeCePo; TrGrPo
Future, The. Matthew Arnold. GTBS; OAEP; PoVP; ViPo
Future, The. George Frederick Cameron. OBCV
Future, The. Edward Cane. SoP
Future, The. James Oppenheim. TrJP
Future, The. Edward Rowland Sill. AnNE; HBV
Future lies, The/ With those whose eyes. The Goal and the Way. John Oxenham. PGD
Future of American Literature, The. John Trumbull. *Fr.* Essay on the Fine Arts. AmPP (3d ed.)
Future of the Classics, The. *Unknown.* BOHV
Future Simple. I. A. Richards. NYTB
Fuzzy fellow without feet, A. The Secret. Emily Dickinson. RIS
Fuzzy-Wuzzy. Kipling. BEL; BrPo; EnLi-2 (1949 ed.); EnLit; HBV; MCCG; MoBrPo; PoVP; StaSt; TrGrPo; VA; ViPP; YT
Fuzzy Wuzzy, Creepy Crawly. Lillian Schulz Vanada. SoPo; SUS; TiPo
Fuzzy Wuzzy was a bear. *Unknown.* GoTP
Fye awaye fye what meane you by this. *Unknown.* SeCSL
Fye foolish Earth, thinke you the heaven wants glory. *See* Fie! foolish earth, think you. . .

G

G. Hilaire Belloc. FiBHP
GI. Raymond Roseliep. FiSC
G. K. Chesterton. Humbert Wolfe. TrJP
G stands for Gnu, whose weapons of defense. G. Hilaire Belloc. FiBHP
Gaberlunzie Man, The. *Unknown, at. to* James IV, King of Scotland. EnSB; GoTS; OxBB; OxBS
Gabriel. Willard Wattles. HBMV
Gabriel, fram Hevene King. The Annunciation. *Unknown.* MeEL
Gabriel, Gabriel, come blow your horn! Trumpet for Yuletide. Louis J. Sanker. JKCP (1955 ed.)
Gabriel had gathered moss. The Crèche. Carol Ryrie Brink. ChrBoLe
Gabriel John. *Unknown.* CBEP
Gabriel Meets Satan. Milton. *Fr.* Paradise Lost, IV. LoBV
Gae bring my guid auld harp ance mair. Scotland Yet. Henry Scott Riddell. HBV
Gaelic, The. Blanche Mary Kelly. CAW
Gaelic Christmas, A. Liam P. Clancy. ISi
Gaelic Folk Song ("All day long o'er the ocean I fly"). *Unknown, tr. fr. Gaelic.* GFA
Gaelic Fragment: "I am Eve." *Unknown. See* Eve's Lament.
Gaelic Litany to Our Lady, The. *Unknown, tr. fr. Old Irish by* Eugene O'Curry. CAW; ISi
Gaelic Lullaby. *Unknown.* GFA
(Lullaby: "Hush! the waves are rolling in.") SAS
(Old Gaelic Lullaby.) PRWS
Gaffer Gray. Thomas Holcroft. HBV
Gage d'Amour, A. Austin Dobson. VA
Gaiety, *sel.* Richard Howard.
Queer's Song. ErPo
Gaiety of Descendants. Douglas Newton. NeBP
Gaiety of three winds is a game of green, The. White Goat, White Ram. W. S. Merwin. NePoEA; PoDB; TwAmPo
Gaily [*or* Gayly] bedight/ A gallant knight. Eldorado. Poe. AmePo; AmPP; AnFE; AP; APA; AWP; CoAnAm; CoBA; FaBoBe; FaBoCh; HBV; HT; InPo; LaNeLa; LoGBV; MWA-1; NePA; NoP; OTPC (1946 ed.); OxBA; PoMa; PoPo; PTK; RePo; RIS; StaSt; TDP; WaKn; Wir; YT
Gaily I Lived. *Unknown.* ELU
(Epitaph, An: "Gaily I lived, as ease and nature taught.") ExPo
Gain of Losses, The. Sadie Louise Miller. SoP
Gain without gladness. Liadain. *Unknown.* KiLC
Gal I Left behind Me, The ("I struck the trail in seventy-nine"), *with music. Unknown.* ABF; CoSo
Gal I Left behind Me, The ("If ever I travel"). *Unknown.* ABF
Galactic Lovepoem. Adrian Henri. HYE
Galactic probe seven thousand and four. Report Back. John Cotton. HYE
Galante Garden, I. Juan Ramón Jiménez, *tr. fr. Spanish by* H. R. Hays. PoPl
Galatea Again. Genevieve Taggard. WHA
Galatea and Pygmalion. Robert Graves. PIA
Galathea [*or* Gallathea], *sel.* John Lyly.
Song of Diana's Nymphs, A. OBSC
(Cupid's Indictment.) EIL

Gale day where the straight masts perform, A. The Wind Harbour. Norman Levine. PeCV
Gale had passed, but chilling was the air, The. Circumstance without Pomp. John Kendall. WhC
Gale in April. Robinson Jeffers. AmPP; CMoP; MAP; MoAB; MoAmPo; NeMA
Gale of August, '27, The, *with music.* George Swinamer. ShS
Galilean. Margielea Stonestreet. ChIP
Galilee Shore. Allen Ginsberg. FRC
Galileo Galilei. William Jay Smith. PoCh
Gall is the taste of life when we. Good Friday. Vincent Holme. ChIP
Gallant and gay in their doublets gray. The Swallows. Sir Edwin Arnold. DD; PoRL
Gallant Château. Wallace Stevens. MAP; MoAB; MoAmPo
Gallant Fifty-one, The. Henry Lynden Flash. PAH
Gallant Fighting "Joe," The. James Stevenson. PAH
Gallant Fleet, The. John Hunter-Duvar. *Fr.* De Roberval. VA
Gallant foeman in the fight, A. Robert E. Lee. Julia Ward Howe. DD; MC; PAH; PoRL
Gallant Highwayman, The. James De Mille. WHW
Gallant laird of Lamington, The. Katharine Jaffray (B *vers.*). *Unknown.* ESPB
Gallant Ship, The. Sir Walter Scott. BoTP
Gallant Youth, who may have gained, The. Yarrow Revisited. Wordsworth. EnLi-2; EnRP; MERP
Gallantly within the Ring. John Hamilton Reynolds. SD
Gallants attend and hear a friend. The Battle of the Kegs [*or* British Valor Displayed]. Francis Hopkinson. PaA; PAH
Gallathea. John Lyly. *See* Galathea.
Galleons in sea-pomp sails. An Armada of Thirty Whales. Daniel G. Hoffman. NePA
Gallery, The. Andrew Marvell. AnAnS-1; MaMe; MeLP; OBS; ReEn; SeEP; SiSw
Galley, The. Sir Thomas Wyatt. *See* Lover Compareth His State to a Ship in Perilous Storm Tossed on the Sea, The.
Galley of Count Arnaldos, The. Longfellow. *See* Secret of the Sea, The.
Galley-Slave, The. Kipling. BEL; BrPo; PeVV
Galliass, The. Walter de la Mare. FaBoTw
Gallon of gas at a gaudy igloo, A. The Danger at Funny Junction. Marvin Bell. YAP
Gallop apace, you fiery-footed steeds. Come, Gentle Night. Shakespeare. *Fr.* Romeo and Juliet, III, ii. HW
Gallop, Gallop to a Rhyme. Monica Shannon. SiSoSe
Gallop of Fire, A. Marie E. J. Pitt. PoAu-1
Galloping Randy Dandy O! *with music.* *Unknown.* SoAmSa
Gallow Hill. William J. Tait. OxBS
Gallows, The. Edward Thomas. ChMP; GTBS-D; HaMV; LiTB; MoAB; MoBrPo; PoE; UnPo (3d ed.)
Gallows and Cross. J. E. H. MacDonald. CaP
Gallows in my garden, The, people say. A Ballade of Suicide. G. K. Chesterton. ALV; BOHV; FiBHP; HBV; InMe; JKCP (1955 ed.)
Gallows Tree, The. F. R. Higgins. OnYI
Gallows Tree, The. *Unknown.* *See* Maid Freed from the Gallows, The.
Galoshes. Rhoda W. Bacmeister. BrR; SoPo; TiPo
Galway. Donagh MacDonagh. NeIP
Galway. Louis MacNeice. OxBI
Galway. Mary Devenport O'Neill. NeIP; OxBI
Galway Bay. George Barker. FaBoMo
Galway Races. *Unknown.* OxBoLi; SD
Galymaufery, A. William Turner. *See* Turners Dish of Lentten Stuffe.
Gamarra is a dainty steed. The Blood Horse. "Barry Cornwall." GN; HBV; OTPC; VA
Gambler, The ("A gambler's life I do admire"), *with music.* John A. Stone. SGR
Gambler. G. A. Studdert-Kennedy. ChIP; MaRV
Gambler, The. *Unknown.* ViBoFo
Gamblers, The. Anthony Delius. BoSA; PeSA
Gambler's Blues (St. James Infirmary Blues), *with music.* *Unknown.* TrAS
(Those Gambler's Blues, A *and* B *vers.*, *with music.*) AS
(St. James Infirmary.) TreFT
Gambler's Repentance, The. Gerald, Baron of Offaly. AnIV
Gambol. Dennis Trudell. QAH
Gamboling Man, The. *See* Roving Gambler, The.
Game, The. Dannie Abse. PrWP
Game, The. Walker Gibson. NePoAm-2
Game, The. Conrado Nalé Roxlo, *tr. fr. Spanish by* Milton Ben Davis. OnPM
Game, The. Winfield Townley Scott. AnAmPo
Game at Salzburg, A. Randall Jarrell. MiAP
Game of Cards, A. Elizabeth Jennings. NYTB
Game of Consequences, A. Paul Dehn. ErPo; FiBHP
Game of Cricket, The. Hilaire Belloc. FiBHP
Game of Dice, A. *Unknown,* *tr. fr. Greek by* Louis Untermeyer. UnTE
Game of Glass, A. Alastair Reid. NePoEA; PoCh
Game of Life, The. John Godfrey Saxe. BLPA; NeHB
Game of Tag, A. *Unknown.* PCH
(Playful Crickets, The.) RIS
Game Out of Hand. Allison Ross. GoYe
Game Resumed. Richmond Lattimore. NYBP
Game was ended, and the noise, The. Football. Walt Mason. SD
Gamesters All. DuBose Heyward. HBMV; InP
Gammer Gurton's Needle, *sel.* *At. to* William Stevenson.
Back and Side Go Bare, Go Bare. BEL; EG; EnLi-1; FosPo; InvP; LiTB; OAEP; PoRA; ReEn; SiCE; TOP; TuPP; ViBoPo
(Drinking Song.) WiR
(I Cannot Eat but Little Meat.) ExPo
(In Praise of Ale.) TrGrPo
(Jolly Good Ale [and Old].) HBV; NoP; OBEV; SeCeV; SiTL; TDP
(Of Jolly Good Ale and Old.) ElL
(Song of Ale, A.) AnFE; OBSC; UnPo (1st ed.)
Gampta, my little grey sister. The Desert Lark. Eugene Marais. PeSA
Gandhi. Angela Morgan. OTD
Gang of labourers on the piled wet timber, A. Morning Work. D. H. Lawrence. MoAB; MoBrPo (1950 ed.)
Ganga. Thomas Blackburn. MoBS
Gangan my lane amang the caulkstane alps. Ice-Flumes Owregie Their Lades. Douglas Young. SeCePo
Gangrene. Philip Levine. AmPC
Ganymede. Witter Bynner. AnFE; CoAnAm
Gar, The. Charles G. Bell. AmFN
Garadh. Padraic Colum. OnYI; PG (1955 ed.)
García Lorca. Louis Dudek. MoCV
García Lorca. In Memory of García Lorca. Eldon Grier. PeCV
Garçon! You—you. The Hero of the Commune. Margaret Junkin Preston. AA
Garden, The. Esther Antin. *Fr.* On Our Farm. RIS
Garden, The. Joseph Beaumont. OBS; OxBoCh; SeCL; SeEP
Garden, The. George M. Brady. NeIP
Garden, A. Thomas Edward Brown. *See* My Garden.
Garden, The, *sel.* Abraham Cowley.
Great Diocletian. ChTr
Garden, The. William Cowper. The Task, III. CEP; EiCL; EiPP; EnPE
Garden, The. Digby Mackworth Dolben. GoBC
Garden, The. Hilda Doolittle ("H. D."). AnFE; APA; AtBAP; CoAnAm; CoBA; LiTA; MAPA; NP; TwAmPo
Heat, *sel.* AP; CMoP; MAP; MoAmPo; NeMA; OxBA; PoIE; PoPo; TSW; UnPo; WHA
Garden, The. Caroline Giltinan. HBMV
Garden, The. Nicholas Grimald. PoLi; ReIE
Garden, The ("How vainly men themselves amaze"). Andrew Marvell. AnAnS-1; AnEnPo; AtBAP; ATP; AWP; BEL; BWP; CABA; CABL; CaFP; CBEP; CBV; CoBE; DiPo; EnL; EnLi-1; EP; ExPo; FaBoEn; ForPo; FosPo; HBV; InPo; InvP; JAWP; LiTB; LoBV; MaMe; MaPo; MasP; MeLP; MemP; MeP; MePo; NoP; OAEP; OBS; OuHeWo; PAn; PIA; Po; PoAn; PoE; PoEL-2; PoFS; PoIE; PoLF; PoRA; PoSa; QFR; ReEn; SCEP-2; SeCePo; SeCeV; SeCL; SeCP; SeCV-1; SeEP; StP; TOP; TrGrPo; UnPo (1st ed.); VaPo; ViBoPo; WBP; WHA
(Thoughts in a Garden.) GTBS; GTBS-D; GTBS-P; GTBS-W; GTSE; GTSL; LiTG; OBEV; TreFT
(Thoughts in a Summer Garden.) BoC
Sels.
"Here at the fountain's sliding foot," 1 *st.* YT
"What wondrous life is this I lead!" BoNaP; CH, 4 *sts.*; ChTr, 3 *sts.*
Garden, A ("See how the flowers, as at parade"). Andrew Marvell. *Fr.* Upon Appleton House. CEP; HBV; OBEV

Garden (continued)
(Upon Appleton House.) TrGrPo
Garden, The. Edgar Lee Masters. NP
Garden, The. Milton. *Fr.* Paradise Lost, IV. MaPo (1969 ed.)
Garden, The. Belle F. Owens. ChIP
Garden, The. Rose Parkwood. WGRP
Garden, The. Ezra Pound. AWP; CABA; InPo; JAWP; LiTA; MoAB; MoAmPo (1950 ed.); NoP; NP; PoIE; TwCP; WBP
Garden, A. Shelley. *See* Sensitive Plant, The.
Garden, The. James Shirley. CavP; OBS
Garden, The. Marvin Solomon. NePoAm
Garden, The. Joshua Sylvester. CBEP
Garden, The. Jones Very. AmP; AP; MAmP; OxBA
Garden, The. Oscar Wilde. *See* Le Jardin.
Garden, The. William Carlos Williams. PoDB
Garden and Cradle. Eugene Field. AA
Garden at St. John's, The. May Swenson. NePoEA; PoPl
Garden beds I wandered by, The. A Conservative. Charlotte Stetson. AA; AmePo; HBV
Garden bower in bower, A. God's Mother. Laurence Housman. ISi
Garden by Moonlight, The. Amy Lowell. NP; PFY; TOP; YT
Garden by the Sea, A. William Morris. *See* I Know a Little Garden-Close.
Garden called Gethsemane, The. Gethsemane. Kipling. FaBoTw
Garden cannot move, The. Mortally. James Kirkup. NeBP
Garden Fairies. Philip Bourke Marston. VA
Garden Fancies, *sels.* Robert Browning.
The Flower's Name. ACV; CTC; EnLi-2 (1949 ed.); GTBS-D; HBV
Sibrandus Schafnaburgensis. CTC; EnLi-2 (1949 ed.)
Garden flew round with the angel, The. The Pleasures of Merely Circulating. Wallace Stevens. LiTA; LOW; OnHM
Garden gives good food, and ayd for leaches cure, The. The Garden. Nicholas Grimald. PoLi
Garden in Chicago, A. Karl Shapiro. PoIE
Garden is a lovesome thing, God wot, A! My Garden. Thomas Edward Brown. DD; EnLit; FaBV; GBV; GoTP; GTSL; HBV; HBVY; MaRV; NeHB; OBEV; OBVV; OQP; OTPC (1946 ed.); PoFS; PoLF; PoVP; SoP; TOP; TreF; TRV; WBLP; WGRP; YT
Garden is a royal court, The. Jester Bee. Frank Dempster Sherman. UTS
Garden is very quiet tonight, The. Dusk Song. William H. A. Moore. BANP
Garden like a chalice-cup, A. Mary. Eleanor Downing. JKCP
Garden-Lion. "Evelyn Hayes." ChTr
Garden Lyric, A. Frederick Locker-Lampson. HBV
Garden now is sealed and dead, The. The Garden. Belle F. Owens. ChIP
Garden of a London House, The. Brian Jones. FIW
Garden of Adonis, The. Spenser. *Fr.* The Faerie Queene, III, 6. PoEL-1
Garden of Amour, The. Guillaume de Lorris, *tr. fr. French by* Chaucer. *Fr.* The Romance of the Rose. PoEL-1
Garden of Bamboos, The. E. Powys Mathers, *tr. fr. street song of Annam.* BoLP
Garden of Boccaccio, The. Samuel Taylor Coleridge. EPN
Garden of Eden, The. Genesis, II: 4-III: 24, Bible, *O.T.* EnLi-1; OuHeWo
Garden of Epicurus, The. George Meredith. ATP (1953 ed.); EPN
Garden of Gethsemane. Boris Pasternak, *tr. fr. Russian by* Bernard Guilbert Guerney. MoRP
Garden of God, The. "Æ." WGRP
Garden of Love, The. Blake. *Fr.* Songs of Experience. AWP; CABA; CBEP; DiPo; EiCL; EnLi-2 (1949 ed.); EnLoPo; EnRP; ERoP-1; ExPo; FaBV; FosPo; InPo; JAWP; LiTB; LiTG; LiTL; LO; LoBV; MeWo; NoP; OAEP; PoE; PoFS; PoIE; SeCeV; StP; TOP; VaPo; ViBoPo; WBP
Garden of Olives, The. Rainer Maria Rilke, *tr. fr. German by* M. D. Herter Norton. MoRP
Garden of Proserpina, The. Spenser. *Fr.* The Faerie Queene, II, 7. ChTr
Garden of Proserpine, The. Swinburne. AnFE; AWP; BoLiVe; CoBE; DiPo; EnL; EnLi-2; EnLit; ExPo; FaBV; ForPo; HBV; InP; InPo; LiTB; LiTG; MaVP; NoP; OBNC; OuHeWo; PAn; PeVV; PG (1945 ed.); PIA; PoAn; PoE; PoEL-5; PoFS; PoIE; PoPl; PoRA; PoVP; SeCePo; SeCeV; TreFT; TrGrPo; ViBoPo; ViPo; ViPP; VP
Sels.
Proserpine. ChTr
("Pale, beyond porch and portal.") FaBoEn
Swan Song. OtMeF
Garden of Shadow, The. Ernest Dowson. FaBoEn; HBV; OBNC
Garden of Ships, The. Douglas Stewart. PoAu-2
Garden of Shushan! Before the Feast of Shushan. Anne Spencer. BANP
Garden of the Holy Souls, The. Harriet Eleanor Hamilton King. *Fr.* Hours of the Passion. ACP; JKCP (1926 ed.)
Garden Party, The. Hilaire Belloc. DTC; MoVE
Garden Party, The. Donald Davie. NePoEA
Garden Party. Mary Mills. NePoAm
Garden Party. Sir Herbert Read. BrPo
Garden Path, The. Charlotte Druitt Cole. GFA
Garden Path, A. May Justus. PCH
Garden Prayer, A. Thomas Walsh. OQP
Garden Puzzle. Gray Burr. CoPo
Garden Seat, The. Thomas Hardy. GoJo
Garden-Song. James Branch Cabell. HBMV
Garden Song, A. Austin Dobson. BoNaP; GTSE; HBV; LoBV; OBEV; OBNC; OBVV; TOP
Garden Song. Arthur Guiterman. MoSiPe
Garden Song, A. Thomas Moore. *See* Child's Song, A.
Garden Song: "I wonder where I may gather some sweet pretty flowers." *Unknown, ad. fr. Maya Indian.* PCH
Garden That I Love, The. Florence L. Henderson. HBV
Garden under Lightning. Leonora Speyer. PFY
Garden Where There Is No Winter, The. Louis James Block. AA
Garden within was shaded, The. Thisbe. Helen Gray Cone. AA
Garden Year, The. Sara Coleridge. FaBoBe; HBV; HBVY; MPB; PCH; PPL; PTK; StVeCh; TreFT; TSW
(Calendar, A.) GoTP
("January brings the snow.") TiPo
(Months, The.) DD; OTPC; RePo; RIS; StaSt
Gardener, The. Evelyn Eaton. GoYe
Gardener. Emerson. *Fr.* Quatrains. MWA-1; OxBA
Gardener, The. Laurence Housman. TrPWD
Gardener, The. Sidney Keyes. ChMP; MoAB; MoBrPo (1962 ed.)
Gardener, The. Lucy Fitch Perkins. PCH
Gardener, The. Po Chü-i. *See* Planting Flowers on the Eastern Embankment.
Gardener, The. Arthur Symons. BoNaP; HBV; HBVY; MPB; OTPC; TreFS
Gardener, The, *sels.* Rabindranath Tagore.
Bird, The, LXVII. LiTW; PoPl
From "The Gardener," LXXXIV. NP
In the Dusky Path of a Dream, LXII. OBMV
Yellow Bird Sings, The, XVII. OBMV
Gardener, The. *Unknown.* BaBo, *sl. abr.*; CBEP; ESPB, *sl. abr.*; OBB
Gardener, The. John Hall Wheelock. NYBP; TwAmPo
Gardener and the Mole, The. Walter Savage Landor. OA
Gardener at Thirty, The. Jascha Kessler. AmPC
Gardener does not love to talk, The. The Gardener. Robert Louis Stevenson. HBV; HBVY; MPB; OTPC; TreFS
Gardener had watcht a mole, A. The Gardener and the Mole. Walter Savage Landor. OA
Gardener has pretty blooms, The. Stanzas for the Harp. *Unknown.* PrWP
Gardener in his old brown hands, The. The Gardener. Arthur Symons. BoNaP
Gardener Janus Catches a Naiad. Edith Sitwell. MoAB; MoBrPo
Gardener of Eden and Gethsemane. Unearth. Alfred Barrett. GoBC
Gardener standing by, The. *Unknown.* LO
Gardener stands in his bower-door, The. The Gardener. *Unknown.* BaBo; CBEP; ESPB; OBB
Gardener to the Magdalene, A. Diversity. Everard V. Thompson. BePJ
Gardener, Tobias Baird, A. The Headless Gardener. Ian Serraillier. BoC

Gardeners, The. Asa Benveniste. HYE
Gardeners, The. David Ignatow. NYTB
Gardener's Cat, The. Patrick R. Chalmers. CIV; HBMV; HBVY
Gardener's Song, The. "Lewis Carroll." *Fr.* Sylvie and Bruno. EvOK; HBV; OTPC
(He Thought He Saw.) GBV (1952 ed.), 7 *sts.*; HBVY, 6 *sts.*
(He Thought He Saw a Banker's Clerk.) LBN; NA, 5 *sts.*
("He thought he saw an elephant," 5 *sts.*) EnLi-2
(Mad Gardener's Song, The, 9 *sts.*) FiBHP, 7 *sts.*; NBM; PoRh; SiTL; TreFS, 6 *sts.* WiR
(Some Hallucinations, 7 *sts.*) BOHV
(Strange Wild Song, A, 7 *sts.*) StVeCh
Gardening. John Keble. OTPC
Gardening. Dabney Stuart. NYTB
Gardens. *Unknown.* OQP
Gardens Are All My Heart. Eve Triem. GoYe
Garden's grillwork gate, The. Plainness. Jorge Luis Borges. NYBP
Gardens No Emblems. Donald Davie. LiTM (1970 ed.); NePoEA-2
Gardens of the Sea, The. George Sterling. EtS
Garden's Queen, The. John Reynolds. *See* Nosegay.
Garden's quit with me, The: as yesterday. The Garden. Joseph Beaumont. OBS; OxBoCh; SeCL; SeEP
Gardin was, by mesuring, The. The Garden of Amour. Guillaume de Lorris, *tr. by* Chaucer. *Fr.* The Romance of the Rose. PoEL-1
Gareth and Lynette, *sel.* Tennyson. *Fr.* Idylls of the King.
Follow the Christ, 4 *ll.* MaRV
("Man am I grown, a man's work must I do.") ChIP
Garfield's Murder. *Unknown.* *See* Charles Guiteau.
Garfield's Ride at Chickamauga. Hezekiah Butterworth. PAH
Gargantua. Hervey Allen. MAP; PFY
Gargoyle in the Snow, The. Kathleen Millay. PoMa
Garibaldi Hymn, The. Luigi Mercantini, *tr. fr. Italian.* WBLP
Garland, The. Matthew Prior. SeCL
Garland, The. Henry Vaughan. AnEnPo
Garland and the Girdle, The. Michelangelo, *tr. fr. Italian by* John Addington Symonds. AWP
Garland fades on Heliodora's brow, The. Heliodora's Garland. Meleager, *tr. by* Robert Guthrie MacGregor. OnPM
Garland for a Storyteller. Jessie Farnham. GoYe
Garland for Heliodora, A. Meleager, *tr. fr. Greek by* "Christopher North." AWP; EnLi-1; JAWP; OuHeWo; WBP
(Wreath for Heliodora.) OnPM
Garland of Peacock Feathers, A. Dafydd ap Gwilym. BoPe
Garland of Recital Programs, A. Franklin P. Adams. InMe
Garland of the Blessed Virgin Marie, The. "B. I." Ben Jonson. *See* Ghyrlond of the Blessed Virgin Marie, The.
Garland Sunday. Padraic Colum. GoYe
Garlande of Laurell, The, *sels.* John Skelton.
To Mistress [*or* Maystres] Isabel[l] Pennell. AtBAP; CBEP; EnPo; FlW; LiTG; LiTL; LO; OBEV (new ed.); OBSC; OxBoLi; PoEL-1; PoFS; PoIE; SeCeV; StP; TrGrPo; TuPP; ViBoPo; YAT
("By Saint Mary, my lady.") EG
(In Praise of Isabel Pennell.) CH
To Mistress Margaret Hussey. ACP; AnFE; AtBAP; CBEP; DiPo; EnLoPo; GN; GoBC; GoJo; HBV; HoPM; InPo; LiTL; LoBV; NoP; OBEV; OBSC; OTPC (1923 ed.); PG (1955 ed.); PoEL-1; PoIE; PoRA; PoSa; ReEn; SeCeV; SiCE; ThWaDe; TreFT; TrGrPo; TuPP; ViBoPo
(Merry Margaret.) GoTP; RIS
(Mistress Margaret Hussey.) FaBoCh; LoGBV
To Mistress Margaret Tilney. MeEL
To Mistress Margery Wentworth. CBEP; EnLoPo; EnRePo; LoBV; OBEV; OBSC; TrGrPo; ViBoPo
("With margerain gentle.") EG
To My Lady Mirriel Howard. LoBV
Garlands fade that Spring so lately wove, The. Sonnet Written at the Close of Spring [*or* Elegiac Sonnet]. Charlotte Smith. FaBoEn; OBEC
Garlic. Justin Richardson. PV
Garlic and sapphires in the mud. T. S. Eliot. *Fr.* Four Quartets: Burnt Norton. GTBS-W
Garlic's taste is briefest pleasure. Garlic. Justin Richardson. PV
Garment. Langston Hughes. GoSl
Garment of Good Ladies, The. Robert Henryson. ACP, *mod. and abr.*
(Garmont of Gude Ladies, The.) GoTS
Garnishing the Aviary. Margaret Danner. Far from Africa, 1. AmNP; BP; NNP
Garnyvillo. Edward Lysaght. IrPN
Garret, The. Pierre Jean de Béranger, *tr. fr. French by* Thackeray. HBV
Garret, The. Ezra Pound. NP; PoPl
Garrison. Amos Bronson Alcott. AA; PoFr
Garrison ("The storm and peril"). Whittier. GA
Garrison Town. Emanuel Litvinoff. WaP
Garrisons pent up in a little fort. Sonnet of Brotherhood. R. A. K. Mason. AnNZ
Garrulous old man who once had owned, The. Under the Casuarina. Elizabeth Riddell. PoAu-2
Garryowen. *Unknown.* OnYI
Gas flaring on the yellow platform; voices running up and down. The Night-Ride. Kenneth Slessor. NeLNL
Gas sigh invert balk. Mangrove in Crome. Clark Coolidge. ANYP
Gas was on in the Institute, The. A Shropshire Lad. John Betjeman. MoBS; ShBV-4
Gasco, or the Toad. Günter Grass, *tr. fr. German by* Jerome Rothenberg. ELU
Gascoigne's Arraignment. George Gascoigne. *See* Arraignment of a Lover, The.
Gascoigne's De Profundis. George Gascoigne. TuPP
Gascoigne's Good Morrow. George Gascoigne. EnRePo; SiCE; TuPP
Gascoigne's Good-Night. George Gascoigne. ReEn; ReIE; SiCE
Gascoigne's Lullaby [*or* Lullabie]. George Gascoigne. *See* Lullaby of a Lover, The.
Gascoigne's Memories, *sels.* George Gascoigne.
"Common speech is, spend and God will send, The," III. EnRePo; EP
(Magnum Vectigal Parcimonia.) EnPo
"In haste, post haste," IV. EnRePo; Sonn
"Vain excess of flattering fortune's gifts, The," II. EnRePo
Gascoigne's Passion. George Gascoigne. *See* Passion of a Lover, The.
Gascoigne's Praise of His Mistress. George Gascoigne. EnRePo
Gascoigne's Woodmanship. George Gascoigne. *See* My Worthy Lord, I Pray You.
Gascon Punished, The ("A Gascon, being heard one day to swear"). La Fontaine. UnTE
Gasoline makes game scarce. Written on the Stub of the First Paycheck. William Stafford. *Fr.* The Move to California. PoAn
Gaspar Becerra. Longfellow. AnNE
Gaspara Stampa. William Rose Benét. HBMV
Gastronomic Guile of Simple Simon, The. Guy Wetmore Carryl. GoTP; YT
Gate, The. Edwin Muir. CMoP; LiTM (rev. ed.)
Gate at the End of Things, The. *Unknown.* BLPA
Gate of the Year, The, *sel.* M. Louise Haskins.
"And I said to the man who stood at the gate." FaChP; MaRV; TreFS; TRV; WePo
(God Knows.) SoP
Gates. Sister Mary Madeleva. GoBC
Gates and Doors. Joyce Kilmer. ChrBoLe; GBV (1952 ed.); HBV; HBVY
Gates are open on the road, The. The Seekers. Charles Hamilton Sorley. WGRP
Gates clanged and they walked you into jail, The. The Conscientious Objector. Karl Shapiro. AmPP (4th ed.); OxBA
Gates fly open with a pretty sound, The. Under the Hill. Daryl Hine. MoCV
Gates of Damascus. James Elroy Flecker. AnFE; BrPo; HBMV
Gates of Dreamland, The. "Æ." *See* Carrowmore.
Gates of Paradise, The. Blake.
(For the Sexes; the Gates of Paradise.) LiTB; PoEL-4
Sels.
To the Accuser Who Is the God of This World. NoP; PeER; TrGrPo; UnPo; ViBoPo
(Epilogue: "Truly, my Satan, thou art but a dunce.") CABA; EiCL; ERoP-1; FaBoEn; OBNC
Gates of the Rockies. James Daugherty. RePo
Gates of the Year, The. John Mervin Hull. STF

Gates to England, The. Marjorie Wilson. BoTP
Gateway, The. A. D. Hope. ErPo; UnTE
Gather all the sweet of May. Song for Youth. Dana Burnett. MPB
Gather for festival. Hilda Doolittle ("H. D."). *Fr.* Songs from Cyprus. MAP; MoAmPo
Gather the garlands rare to-day. Memorial Day. Cy Warman. DD; HH
Gathas, *sel.* *At. to* Zoroaster, *tr. fr. Persian.* *Fr.* The Avesta.
Zorcaster Devoutly Questions Ormazd, *tr. by* A. V. Williams Jackson. WGRP
(Sacred Book, The, *tr. by* A. V. Williams Jackson.) AWP
Gather all kindreds of this boundless realm. The Poet. Cornelius Mathews. AA
Gather the Rose. Spenser. *See* Bower of Bliss, The.
Gather the stars if you wish it so. Stars, Songs, Faces. Carl Sandburg. FIW; OTD
Gather These Bones. Lewis Turco. FiSC
Gather up the ribbons, give the 'orn a toot! The Phantom Mail Coach. L. O. Welcome. PoMS
Gather Us In. George Matheson. OQP
Gather, ye brave sons of Ukadi Awaka! Moon Song. Chuba Nweke. PBA
Gather Ye Rose-Buds [While Ye May]. Robert Herrick. *See* To the Virgins, to Make Much of Time.
Gather Ye Roses. Robert Louis Stevenson. TreFT
Gather ye soap-suds while ye may. Counsel to Girls. Archibald Stodart-Walker. *Fr.* The Moxford Book of English Verse. CenHV
Gathering, The. E. J. Pratt. *Fr.* Towards the Last Spike. MoCV; OBCV
Gathering, The. Sir Walter Scott. *Fr.* The Lady of the Lake. OBNC
Gathering, The. Herbert B. Swett. PAH
Gathering Leaves. Robert Frost. LOW; RePo
Gathering on the Plains, The. William T. Butler. PoOW
Gathering Song of Donald the Black [*or* Donald Dhu *or* Donuil Dhu]. Sir Walter Scott. *See* Pibroch of Donuil Dhu.
Gathering Sticks on Sunday. Norman Nicholson. POTi
Gathering, tall, a wave in a vicious sea. Heart's Desire. John Peter. BoSA
Gathering the echoes of forgotten wisdom. Odes, III. George Santayana. AmePo; AnAmPo; AnFE; APA; CoAnAm; TwAmPo
Gatineaus, The. James Wreford Watson. CaP
Gaudeamus Igitur. *Unknown, tr. fr. Latin by* John Addington Symonds. *Fr.* Carmina Burana. HBV; WoL
Gauge. Peter Schjeldahl. YAP
Gauger walked with willing foot, The. A Song of the Road. Robert Louis Stevenson. BrPo; OTPC (1946 ed.); PoVP; YT
Gauley Bridge is a good town for Negroes, they let us stand around. George Robinson: Blues. Muriel Rukeyser. FiMAP
Gauls Sacrifice Their Prisoners, The. C. M. Doughty. *Fr.* The Dawn in Britain. FaBoTw
Gaunt and relentless wolf, possessed, A. The Inhuman Wolf and the Lamb sans Gene. Guy Wetmore Carryl. ALV; AmePo
Gaunt-built woman and her son-in-law, A. Polonius and the Ballad-Singers. Padraic Colum. NP
Gaunt in gloom. Nightpiece. James Joyce. SyP
Gaunt in the midst of the prairie. Chicago. John Boyle O'Reilly. PAH
Gaunt man, Abraham Lincoln, woke one morning, The. Stephen Vincent Benét. *Fr.* John Brown's Body. LiPo
Gaunt, rueful knight, on raw-boned, shambling hack. Don Quixote. Craven Langstroth Betts. AA
Gautama. Thomas S. Jones, Jr. AnAmPo
Gautama in the Deer Park at Benares. Kenneth Patchen. NaP
Gave My Life for Thee. Frances Ridley Havergal. VA
Gay, The. "Æ." OBMV; POTE
Gay and audacious crime glints in his eyes. In the Vices. Donald Evans. HBMV; NP
Gay belles of fashion may boast of excelling, The. The Needle. Samuel Woodworth. GN; HBV
Gay citizen, myself, and thoughtful friend. Allen Tate. More Sonnets at Christmas, IV. LiTA; NePA
Gay Feast. Pushkin, *tr. fr. Russian by* Babette Deutsch. OnPM
Gay Florimel, of generous birth. A Song. *Unknown.* WaPE
Gay, gay, gay, gay. Remember the Day of Judgment. *Unknown.* MeEL
Gay go up and gay go down. The Bells of London [*or* London Bells]. *Unknown.* BoTP; BrR; ChTr; EvOK; HBV; HBVY; LiTB; LiTG; OTPC; OxBoLi; OxNR; PCH; PoRA; PPL; SiTL
Gay Goshawk [*or* Goss-Hawk], The. *Unknown.* BaBo; BuBa; CABL; EnLit; ESPB (A *and* E *vers.*); GN; HBV; OBB; OxBB; RG; TOP
Gay, guiltless pair. The Winged Worshippers. Charles Sprague. AA; HBV
Gay Head. Neilson Abeel. HT
Gay hussars, The—I love them all. Song of the Vivandière. Heine. UnTE
Gay jolly cowboy is up with the sun. Up the Trail. *Unknown.* CoSo
Gay little Dandelion. Little Dandelion. Helen Barron Bostwick. DD; HBV; HBVY; OTPC (1923 ed.); PRWS
Gay little Girl-of-the-Diving-Tank. At the Carnival. Anne Spencer. BANP; CDC; Kal; PoNe
Gay Old Hag, The. *Unknown.* IrPN
Gay Robin Is Seen No More. Robert Bridges. BoTP
Gay sea-plants familiar were to her, The. Sea-nurtured. Jean Ingelow. EtS
Gayly bedight, a gallant knight. Eldorado. Poe. *See* Gaily Bedight.
Gaze not at me, my poor unhappy bird. Ode to Mother Carey's Chicken. Theodore Watts-Dunton. VA
Gaze not on swans, in whose soft breast. Beauty Extoll'd [*or* On His Mistress]. *Unknown, at. to* Henry Noel *and to* William Strode. ChTr; ELP; LO; OBS; PoEL-2
Gaze not on thy beauties pride. Good Counsel to a Young Maid. Thomas Carew. AnAnS-2; CavP; CBEP; OBS
Gaze Not on Youth. *Unknown.* NCEP
Gazelle, A. Richard Henry Stoddard. AA
Gazelles, The. T. Sturge Moore. BrPo; OBMV
Gazelles and Unicorn. John Gray. *Fr.* The Long Road. ChTr
Gazeteer of Newfoundland. Michael Harrington. CaP
Gazing at the Moon while Journeying Homewards. Otomo Yakamochi, *tr. fr. Japanese by* Ishii *and* Obata. OnPM
Gean trees drive me to love, The. The Name Like a River. W. S. Graham. FaBoTw
Gebir, *sels.* Walter Savage Landor.
"But Gebir when he heard of her approach," *fr.* I. OBRV
"Long awaited day at last approached, The," *fr.* V il. OBRV
Masar, *fr.* V. LoBV
("Once a fair city, courted then by Kings," *shorter sel.*) OBRV
Nymph, The, *fr.* I.
(Tamar and the Nymph.) VA
(Tamar's Wrestling.) EnRP
Sea-Nymph's Parting, The. FaBoEn
Shepherd and the Nymph, The. OBNC; PeER
Gee, But There's Class to a Man Like That. Charles A. Jones. OTD
Gee Ho, Dobin. *Unknown.* CoMu
Gee I Like to Think of Dead. E. E. Cummings. HoPM
Gee-up Dar, Mules. Edwin Ford Piper. YaD
Gee up, Neddy, to the fair. *Unknown.* OxNR
Geeandess. William Cole. PV
Geese. Oliver Herford. *Fr.* Child's Natural History. HBV
(Some Geese.) FiBHP; VA
Geese, geese,/ Very white geese. Goosegirl's Song. *Unknown, tr. fr. Czech.* PCH
Geese in Autumn. *Unknown, tr. fr. Japanese by* Basil Hall Chamberlain. OnPM
Geese in lofty flight recross, The. The Spring. Chang Chungsur. OnPM
Geese in the Running Water. Raymond Holden. MAP; MoAmPo (1942 ed.)
Gehazi. Kipling. OtMeF
Geist's Grave. Matthew Arnold. HBV; PoVP; VA
Gellatley's Song to the Deerhounds. Sir Walter Scott. *See* Hie Away.
Gem and the Flower, The. Pope. *Fr.* Moral Essays, Epistle I. OBEC
Gem of all isthmuses and isles that lie. Sirmio. Catullus. AWP; JAWP; WBP
Gem of the crimson-colour'd even. To the Evening Star [*or* Caroline, II]. Thomas Campbell. GTBS; GTBS-D; GTBS-P; GTBS-W; GTSE; GTSL; OBNC; TRV

Gemini and Virgo. Charles Stuart Calverley. WhC
"And, if you asked of him to say," *sel.* FiBHP
Gemlike Flame, The. R. P. Lister. FiBHP
Gems and jewels let them heap. In a Garret. Herman Melville. MWA-1
Genau'r Glyn, Tywyn, each day from these to Rhys's halls. Ode to Rhys ap Maredudd of Tywyn. Dafydd Nanmor. PrWP
Genealogical Reflection. Ogden Nash. ALV
Genealogy of a Mermaid. Morris Weisenthal. NYTB
General, The. Siegfried Sassoon. BrPo; ELU; FaBV; FiBHP; LiTM (1970 ed.); MMA; MoVE; OxBoLi
(Leaders, New Style.) OtMeF
General Armstrong, The. *Unknown.* PAH
General Communion, A. Alice Meynell. JKCP
General Custer Versus the Titanic. Richard Brautigan. FRC
General dashed along the road, The. The General's Death. Joseph O'Connor. AA
General Eclipse, The. John Cleveland. AnAnS-2
General Galliéni. Robert Hillyer. PG (1955 ed.)
General Howe's Letter. *Unknown.* PAH
General John. W. S. Gilbert. GoTP; NA
General Joseph Warren's Address. John Pierpont. *See* Warren's Address.
General knows, The. His maps. Desert Fox. R. H. W. Dillard. TDP
General Mist of Error, A. John Webster. *See* Hark, Now Everything Is Still.
General Prologue, The. Chaucer. *See* Canterbury Tales, The: Prologue.
General Public, The. Stephen Vincent Benét. ML
General Store. Rachel Field. BoChLi; GaP; MPB (1956 ed.); SoPo; StVeCh (1955 ed.); SUS
General Summary, A. Kipling. HBV
General William Booth Enters [into] Heaven. Vachel Lindsay. AmLP; AmPP; ATP; BoC; CMoP; CoBA; FaBoMo; HBV; ILP; InPo; LiTA; LiTM; MAP; MaRV; MoAB; MoAmPo; MoPo; NP; OxBA; ReMP; SeCeV; TOP; TreFS; TrGrPo; WGRP
Generalization. Joseph Capp. *See* Man Is a Fool.
General's Death, The. Joseph O'Connor. AA
Generation Gap, The. Ruby C. Saunders. WSL
Generations, The. George M. Brady. OnYI
Generations. Robert Clark. PoAu-2
Generosity. Virginia Brasier. StVeCh (1955 ed.)
Generosity. *Unknown,* *tr. fr. Irish by* Frank O'Connor. KiLC
Generous Creed, A. Elizabeth Stuart Phelps Ward. WGRP
Generous man will not deny, The. An Elegy on the Late King of Patagonia. St. John Emile Clavering Hankin. CenHV
Generous Years, The. Stephen Spender. PoCh
Genesis, *sels.* Bible, *O.T.*
Abraham and Isaac, XXII: 1-13. EnLi-1 (1949 ed.); OuHeWo
Adam and Eve, II: 7-III: 23. TreFT
After the Flood Went Down, God Said, VIII: 22, IX: 12. ThGo
"And when Joseph came home," XLIII: 26-31. LO
Creation, The ("When God set about to create heaven and earth," *tr. by* Phraim Avigdor Speiser). FlW (I: -II: 4); TreF (I: 1-II: 3); WoL (I: 1-III: 24)
("In the beginning God created the heaven and the earth," I: 1-31.) ImOP
Garden of Eden, The, II: 4-III: 24. EnLi-1; OuHeWo
"I will put enmities," III: 15, *Douay vers.* ISi
Joseph and His Brethren, XXXVII: 3-36, XXXIX: 1-XLVI: 30. OuHeWo
Noah and the Flood, VI: 5-VIII: 22. OuHeWo
Rainbow, The, IX: 12-16. BoC
"Thus the heavens and the earth were finished," II:1-III: 13. LO
Genesis, *sel.* Charles Brasch.
Discovery, The. AnNZ
Genesis, *sels.* Cædmon *tr. fr. Anglo-Saxon.*
Approach of Pharaoh, The, tr. by C. W. Kennedy. ACP; WaaP
(Coming of Pharaoh, The.) CAW
Fall of Angels and of Man, *mod. vers.* PoLi
Far and Wide She Went. EtS
"Here the Eternal Lord, protector of all creatures," *tr. by* Richard L. Hoffman. YAT
"Murky waves/ Covered over the children of evil," *tr. by* Richard L. Hoffman. YAT
Noah's Flood, *tr. by* C. W. Kennedy. AnOE; BEL
Temptation and Fall of Man, The, *tr. by* C. W. Kennedy. AnOE
"Then spoke the Lord," *tr. by* Richard L. Hoffman. YAT
Genesis. Geoffrey Hill. ACV; NePoEA
Genesis. John Hall Ingham. AA
Genesis. Ray Mathew. NeLNL
Genesis, *sel.* Delmore Schwartz.
You Are a Jew! TrJP
Genesis. Elizabeth Sewell. ML
Genesis. A. M. Sullivan. JKCP (1955 ed.)
Genesis. Jules Alan Wein. TrJP
Genesis of Butterflies, The. Victor Hugo, *tr. fr. French by* Andrew Lang. AWP; JAWP; WBP
Genesis of Vowels. James Broughton. CrMA
Geneva. Alastair Reid. NYBP
Genius, The. Leonard Cohen. MoCV
Genius. R. J. P. Hewison. FaFP; SiTL
Genius. Richard Henry Horne. VA
Genius. Edward Lucas White. AA; WGRP
Genius in Beauty. Dante Gabriel Rossetti. The House of Life, XVIII. EnLit; InP; MaVP; OAEP; PoVP; TOP; ViPo; VP
Genius Loci. Margaret L. Woods. HBV; OBEV; OBVV
Genius of ancient Greece! whose faithful steps. Invocation to the Genius of Greece. Mark Akenside. *Fr.* The Pleasures of Imagination, I. OBEC
Genius of Death, The. George Croly. HBV
Genius, that power which dazzles mortal eyes. Success. C. C. Cameron. PoToHe (new ed.)
Gen'ral, The! one of those brave old commanders. The Old General. Sir Charles Hanbury Williams. *Fr.* Isabella. OBEC
Genteel in personage. A Maiden's Ideal of a Husband [*or* The Maid's Husband]. Henry Carey. *Fr.* The Contrivances. HBV; WaPE
Gentian. Elizabeth Green Crane. AA
Gentian sleeps in waters, The. Symphony in Blue. Raymond F. Roseliep. ISi
Gentian weaves her fringes, The. Emily Dickinson. MaPo; PoRA
Gentilesse. Chaucer. AWP; CBEP; NoP
Gentill butler, bell ami. Fill the Bowl, Butler! *Unknown.* MeEL
Gentle Air, thou breath of lovers. A Sigh. Countess of Winchilsea. CEP
Gentle Alice Brown. W. S. Gilbert. BOHV; FiBHP; InMe; NA; OnSP
Gentle and generous, brave-hearted, kind. The Comfort of the Trees. Richard Watson Gilder. OTD; PAH
Gentle and grave, in simple dress. Wordsworth. Francis Turner Palgrave. VA
Gentle, at last, and as clean as ever. Grandfather in the Old Men's Home. W. S. Merwin. LiTM (1970 ed.)
Gentle Beasts, The. *Unknown,* *tr. fr. Slovakian by* Leclaire Alger. ChrBoLe
Gentle Check, The. Joseph Beaumont. SeCL
Gentle, cheerful ticking of a clock, The. Quiet Days. Mildred T. Mey. PoToHe (new ed.)
Gentle Cock, The. *Unknown.* *See* I Have a Gentle Cock.
Gentle Craft, The, *sels.* Thomas Deloney.
Song: "Primrose in the green forest, The." TiPo (1959 ed.); ViBoPo
Would God That It Were Holiday! ElL
Gentle Echo on Woman, A. Swift. ALV; BOHV; FiBHP; LiTG; LiTL; OnYI; SiTL
Gentle Hill, The. Salvatore Quasimodo, *tr. fr. Italian by* Allen Mandelbaum. PoPl
Gentle Jane once chanced to sit. The Swift Bullets. Carolyn Wells. ShM
Gentle Jesus [Meek and Mild]. Charles Wesley. MaRV; OTPC; OxBoCh; TreFS
(For the Youngest.) SoP
Gentle Knight was pricking on the plaine, A. The Red Cross Knight. Spenser. *Fr.* The Faerie Queene, I. ATP; BoLiVe; CoBE; ExPo; FosPo; GoBC; MBW-1; YAT
Gentle Lady, do not sing. James Joyce. *Fr.* Chamber Music. MoLP
Gentle Mary, noble maiden, give us help! Prayer to the Virgin. *Unknown.* OnYI

Gentle milk jug blue and white, The. The Milk Jug. Oliver Herford. HBMV; HBVY; PCH; TSW; UTS
"Gentle, modest little flower." To Phoebe. W. S. Gilbert. BOHV; InMe; InP
Gentle Name. Selma Robinson. BiCB; MoShBr; MoSiPe
Gentle Nymphs, Be Not Refusing. William Browne. *Fr.* Britannia's Pastorals, I. ElL; ViBoPo
Gentle Park, A. Moss Herbert. GoYe
Gentle Reminders, *abr.* Goethe, *tr. fr. German by* F. Melian Stawell *and* Nora Purtscher-Wydenbruck. PoFr
Gentle River, Gentle River. *Unknown, tr. fr. Spanish by* Thomas Percy. AWP; JAWP; LiTW; WBP
Gentle Shepherd, The, *sels.* Allan Ramsay.
Dainty Sang, A. OBEC
My Peggy [Is a Young Thing]. CoBE; EiCL; GN, *abr.* HBV; OTPC (1923 ed.), *abr.*; OxBS
(Peggy.) OBEV; ViBoPo
Sang: "My Peggy is a young thing.") CEP; LoBV; OBEC
"Gentle Sleep, if you will take him." The North Wind and the Child. *Unknown.* PCH
Gentle Snorer, The. Mona Van Duyn. NePA
Gentle, soft-voiced herringdove, The. The Herringdove. Kenyon Cox. RIS
Gentle squire would gladly entertain [*or* intertain], A. Satire. Joseph Hall. *Fr.* Virgidemiarum. ReIE; SiCE; TuPP; ViBoPo
Gentle Storm. Martha Banning Thomas. PoMa
Gentle thought there is will often start, A. La Vita Nuova, XXVI. Dante. AWP; JAWP; OuHeWo; WBP
Gentle Touch, A. *Unknown, at. to* Lao-tzu, *tr. fr. Chinese by* Witter Bynner. *Fr.* Tao Teh King. OnPM
Gentle Wind, A. Fu Hsüan, *tr. fr. Chinese by* Arthur Waley. AWP
Gentle Word, A. *Unknown.* PoToHe (new ed.)
Gentleman, The. Menahem ben Judah Lonzano, *tr. fr. Hebrew by* A. B. Rhine. TrJP
Gentleman cam oure the sea, A. The Cruel Brother (B *vers.*). *Unknown.* ESPB
Gentleman in Oils. Harold Vinal. FiSC
Gentleman of City fame, A. A Discontented Sugar Broker. W. S. Gilbert. PCD
Gentleman of Fifty Soliloquizes, A. Don Marquis. HBMV
Gentleman of the Old School, A. Austin Dobson. EnLit; HBV
Gentleman with polished hair, A. The Clean Gentleman. George Abbe. FiSC
Gentleman's Garden, The. Barbara L. Greenberg. QAH
Gentlemen and ladies, I pray you lend an ear. Colonel Sharp. *unknown.* BaBo
Gentlemen of the High Command. Ogden Nash. *Fr.* Heil, Heilige Nacht! MaRV
Gentlemen who boss the age. Ballade in a Bad Temper. Louis MacNeice. PoFr
Gentleness of rain was in the wind, The. Fragment: Rain. Shelley. ChER
Gentlest Lady, The. Dorothy Parker. ISi
Gentlie, gently prethee tyme. *Unknown.* SeCSL
Gently a little breeze begins to creep. Arques—Afternoon. Arthur Symons. PoVP
Gently Death came to him and bent to him asleep. Close Up the Ranks. Edward S. Van Zile. PEDC
Gently dip, but not too deep. The Song at the Well [*or* The Voice from the Well *or* Celanta at the Well of Life]. George Peele. *Fr.* The Old Wives' Tale. ChTr; ELP; ExPo; FaBoEn; LoBV; SeCeV; ThWaDe
Gently!—gently!—down!—down! Chorus of Spirits. George Darley. *Fr.* Sylvia; or, The May Queen. OnYI; VA
Gently He Draweth. *Unknown.* BePJ
Gently I stir a white feather fan. In the Mountains on a Summer Day. Li Po. AWP; FlW; SD
Gently I wave the visible world away. The Absinthe Drinker. Arthur Symons. BrPo; FaBoTw
Gently, Johnny My Jingalo. *Unknown.* UnTE
Gently, Lord, O gently lead us. In Sorrow. Thomas Hastings. AA; HBV; SoP
Gently o gently without fright. *Unknown.* SeCSL
Geoffrey Chaucer. E. C. Bentley. *Fr.* Clerihews. PV
Geographers. Sebastian Brant, *tr. fr. German by* Alexander Barclay. *Fr.* The Ship of Fools. ACP
Geographers, The. Karl Shapiro. OxBA
Geography. G. K. Chesterton. *Fr.* Songs of Education. HBMV
Geography. Eleanor Farjeon. BrR; FaPON
Geography. Kenneth Koch. AmPC
Geography; A Song. Howard Moss. CAD; PV
Geography of This Time. Archibald MacLeish. PG (1945 ed.)
Geologic. Patric Dickinson. POTi
Geologist's Epitaph, A. Jane W. Stedman. WhC
Geometry. Alfred Kreymborg. AnAmPo
Geordie. *Unknown.* BaBo (A, B, *and* C *vers.*); ESPB (A *and* D *vers.*); OxBB
George. Hilaire Belloc. FiBHP; YT
(George Who Played with a Dangerous Toy. . .) GoTP
George. Dudley Randall. BP; Kal
George Aloe and the *Sweepstake*, The. *Unknown.* BaBo; ESPB; ViBoFo
(*George-Aloe,* The.) OBB
George and Martha Washington/ Are smiling in our hall. Picture People. Rowena Bennett. MPB (1956 ed.); YeAr
George and the Chimney-Sweeper. Adelaide O'Keeffe. OTPC (1923 ed.)
George Britton, *with music.* *Unknown.* CoSo
George Collins, *with music.* *Unknown.* BFSS
George Crabbe. E. A. Robinson. AmePo; AmPP (4th ed.); AP; CoBA; CoBMV; LiTA; LiTM (rev. ed.); MAmP; MAP; MaPo (1969 ed.); ML; MoAB; MoAmPo; MoVE; NAMP; NePA; NoP; OxBA; PoEL-5; PP
George Gray. Edgar Lee Masters. *Fr.* Spoon River Anthology. TOP
George-Hector. The Emancipation of George-Hector (a Colored Turtle). Mari E. Evans. AmNP
George, it is thy genius innated. To George Chapman. Thomas Freeman. SiCE
George Levison. William Allingham. IrPN
George lives in an apartment. Radiator Lions. Dorothy Aldis. MPB; SoPo; UTS
George loved the cause of freedom, but reproved. George Crabbe. *Fr.* Tales of the Hall. PoFr
George Meredith. Thomas Hardy. EPN
George Moses Horton, Myself. George Moses Horton. Kal
George Robinson; Blues. Muriel Rukeyser. FiMAP
George Sand. Dorothy Parker. FiBHP
George the First was always reckoned. The Georges. Walter Savage Landor. ChTr; FiBHP
George the Fourth in Ireland. Byron. OBRV
George the Third. E. C. Bentley. *Fr.* Clerihews. FiBHP; OxBoLi; PV
George the Third. Byron. *Fr.* The Vision of Judgment. FiP
George Towle. Tony Towle. ANYP
George Turbervile in Praise of the Translator of This Book. George Turberville. ReIE
George Villiers, Duke of Buckingham. Dryden. *See* Zimri.
George Washington. Rosemary Benét *and* Stephen Vincent Benét. FaPON; MaC
George Washington ("Only a baby, fair"). *At. to* Eliza Cook. MPB; OHIP; PEDC
George Washington. John Hall Ingham. AA; HH; OHIP; OTD; PAH; PAL
George Washington. Francesca Falk Miller. PEDC
George Washington. Shelley Silverstein. PoSC
George Washington. James S. Tippett. RePo; YeAr
George Washington ("In seventeen hundred thirty-two"). *Unknown, at. to* M. Alice Bryant. HH
George Washington Absent from His Country. Diane Wakoski. YAP
George Whalen. *Unknown.* *See* Whalen's Fate.
George Who Played with a Dangerous Toy, and Suffered a Catastrophe of Considerable Dimensions. Hilaire Belloc. *See* George.
Georges, The. Walter Savage Landor. ChTr; FiBHP
Georgey Porgey, pudding and pie. *See* Georgie Porgie. . .
Georgia. Robert Loveman. PoRL
Georgia Boy, *with music.* *Unknown.* OuSiCo
Georgia Dusk. Jean Toomer. AmNP; AnAmPo; BP; CDC; Kal; LA; MAP; PoNe
Georgia Land, *with music.* *Unknown.* OuSiCo
Georgia Towns. Daniel Whitehead Hicky. AmFN
Georgia Volunteer, A. Mary Ashley Townsend. AA
Georgiad, The, *sel.* Roy Campbell.

"Hail, Mediocrity, beneath whose spell." MoBrPo
Georgics, The, *sels.* Vergil, *tr. fr. Latin.*
"Am I to tell you next of the storms and stars of autumn?" *fr.* I, *tr. by* C. Day Lewis. FlW
Chariot Race, The, *fr.* III, *tr. by* Smith Palmer Bovie. SD
Honey-Farm, The, *abr., fr.* IV, *tr. by* Dryden. WoL
"Next I come to the manna, the heavenly gift of honey," *fr.* IV, *tr. by* C. Day Lewis. FlW
Prelude: "What makes a plenteous harvest," *tr. by* Dryden. AWP
"Then are the trackless copses alive with the trilling of birds," *fr.* II, *tr. by* C. Day Lewis. FlW
"Until Jove let it be, no colonist," I, *tr. by* Robert Fitzgerald. LiTW
We Have Paid Enough Long Since in Our Own Blood, *tr. by* Richmond Lattimore. WaaP
"What makes a plenteous harvest, when to turn," *fr.* I, *tr. by* Dryden. EiCP
Georgie, *with music.* *Unknown.* BFSS
Georgie Allen ("Georgie's mother came to him"), *with music.* *Unknown.* BFSS
Georgie Porgie. Franklin P. Adams. HBMV
Georgie Porgie [*or* Georgey Porgey], pudding and pie. Mother Goose. BoChLi; OxNR; RIS; SiTL
Géorgiques Chrétiennes, *sel.* Francis Jammes, *tr. fr. French by* George N. Shuster.
"This day, O Father, give us daily bread." CAW
Geraint and Enid. Tennyson. *See* Idylls of the King.
Gerald kissed me when he left. Another Cynical Variation. "Helen." InMe
Geraldines, The, *sel.* Thomas Osborne Davis.
"Geraldines, The! the Geraldines!—'tis full a thousand years." IrPN
Geraldine's Daughter, The. Egan O'Rahilly, *tr. fr. Modern Irish by* James Clarence Mangan. AnIL; OnYI
"Beauty all stainless, a pearl of a maiden, A," *sel.* IrPN
Geraldine's Garden. John Francis O'Donnell. IrPN
Geraldines, The! the Geraldines!—'tis full a thousand years. Thomas Osborne Davis. *Fr.* The Geraldines. IrPN
Geranium, The. Leonard Feeney. TIHL
Geranium, The. Theodore Roethke. CoAP; PoeP
Geranium, The. Sheridan. ErPo; UnTE
Geranium, houseleek, laid in oblong beds. Poem. John Gray. SyP
Geranium Man, The. Zulfikar Ghose. NYTB
Gerard de Nerval. In a Warm Chicken House. James Wright. NYTB
Geriatric Whore, The. Pete Winslow. PV
Germ, The. Ogden Nash. CenHV; MoShBr
German Eyes. Robert Hershon. ThO
German Fatherland, The. Ernst Moritz Arndt, *tr. fr. German.* HBV
German Prisoners. Joseph Johnston Lee. MaRV
German singers! sing and praise. The Tendency. Heine. PoFr
German Slumber Song. Karl Simrock. *See* Go to Sleep.
Germans live in Germany, The. Home [*or* The English]. J. H. Goring. MoShBr; SiTL
Germany has lots of meat. Looking at the Map of the World. Gregory Corso. CBV
Germinal. "Æ." MoBrPo; OBEV (new ed.); OBMV
Geron and Histor. Sir Philip Sidney. *Fr.* Arcadia. SiPS
Geron, whose moldy memory corrects. In Gerontem. Sir John Davies. ReIE
Geronimo. Ernest McGaffey. AA; PAH; ThLM
Gerontion. T. S. Eliot. AmPP; AnAmPo; AnFE; AP; APA; BWP; CABA; CABL; CBV; ChMP; CMoP; CoAnAm; CoBA; CoBMV; DiPo; ExPo; FaBoEn; ForPo; FosPo; GTBS-P; GTBS-W; ILP; LiTA; LiTM; LoBV; MAP; MAPA; MaPo; MoAmPo (1942 ed.); MoPo; NAMP; NePA; OAEP (2d ed.); OxBA; PoE; PoFS; PoIE; POTE; ReMP; SeCePo; SeCeV; StP; TwAmPo
Gerry's Rocks. *Unknown.* *See* Jam on Gerry's Rocks, The.
Gert Swasey. Winfield Townley Scott. FiMAP
Gertrude and Gulielma, sister-twins. Elegy in Six Sonnets. Frederick Goddard Tuckerman. *Fr.* Sonnets. AP; MAmP; QFR
Gertrude's Prayer. Kipling. FaBoEn
Gest of Robyn Hode, A. *Unknown.* ESPB; OxBB
(Little Geste of Robin Hood and His Meiny, A.) OBB
Robin Hood's End, Fytte VIII. GoTL
Gesture. Winifred Welles. HBMV; MaRV
Gesture by a Lady with an Assumed Name, A. James Wright. LiTM (1970 ed.)
Gesture of a gift is adequate, The. If You Have Nothing. Jessica Powers. JKCP (1955 ed.)
Gesture the gesture the gesture the gesture, The. Michael McClure. Hymn to St. Geryon, I. NeAP
Get a Transfer. *Unknown.* BLPA; WBLP
Get away, they're all gone. Chops Are Flyin. Stanley Crouch. NBP
"Get down, get down, loving Henry," she said. Loving Henry. *Unknown.* BaBo
Get Hence Foule Griefe. Sir Philip Sidney. *Fr.* Arcadia. AtBAP; PoEL-1
(Contentment.) SiPS
Get into the Boosting Business. *Unknown.* WBLP
Get it right or let it alone. Morals. James Thurber. *Fr.* Further Fables for Our Time. FaBV
Get on board, little chillun. The Gospel Train. *Unknown.* TrAS
Get out of the way of my dignity. All Praise. Stanley Crouch. WSL
Get ready your money and come to me. *Unknown.* OxNR
Get Somebody Else. *At. to* Paul Laurence Dunbar. BLRP; MaRV; TRV
(Too Busy.) WBLP
Get Somewhere. A. B. Simpson. FaChP
Get thee a ship well rigged and tight. In Praise of Fidelia. Mildmay Fane, Earl of Westmorland. SeCL
Get thee behind me. Even as, heavy-curled. "Retro me, Sathana!" Dante Gabriel Rossetti. The House of Life, XC. MaVP; NoP; PoVP; ViPo
Get There If You Can and See the Land You Once Were Proud to Own. W. H. Auden. NAMP
Get this now! Index to a Black Cartharsis. Richard W. Thomas. BF
Get Up and Bar the Door. *Unknown.* ATP; BaBo; BEL; BFSS, *with music*; BoChLi; BoLiVe; EnL; EnLi-1; EnLit; EnSB; ESPB (A *and* B *vers.*); GoTP; GoTS; MaC; NoP; OBB; OnMSP; OxBS; PDV; PoIE; StPo; TiPo (1952 ed.); TrGrPo; VaPo; ViBoPo
Get up at once, now, Margaret May! Eggs for Breakfast. Irene F. Pawsey. BoTP
Get Up, Blues. James A. Emanuel. AmNP; BOLo
Get up, Get up. *Unknown.* FiBHP
Get up, get up for shame, the blooming morn. Corinna's Going a-Maying. Robert Herrick. AnAnS-2; AtBAP; ATP; BEL; BoLiVe; BoNaP; CABA; CBEP; CBV; CLwM; CoBE; DD; DiPo; EnL; EnLi-1; EnLit; ExPo; FosPo; GN; GTSL; HBV; MaPo; NoP; OAEP; OBEV; OBS; OTPC (1923 ed.); OuHeWo; PAn; PIA; Po; PoAn; PoEL-3; PoeP; PoFS; PoIE; PoRL; ReEn; SCEP-2; SeCeV; SeCP; SeCV-1; SeEP; TOP; TreFT, *abr.*; TrGrPo; UnPo (1st ed.); WHA
"Get up, get up, Lord Douglas," she cried. Lord William and Lord Douglas. *Unknown.* BFSS
"Get up, get up, pretty Polly," he says. Pretty Polly. *Unknown.* UnTE
Get up, get up, you lazy-head. Get Up, Get Up. *Unknown.* FiBHP
Get Up, Jack! John, Sit Down! *Unknown.* ABF
Get up, little boy, you are sleeping too long. Sleepy Harry. *Unknown.* OTPC (1923 ed.)
Get up, little sister, the morning is bright. Early Rising. Lady Flora Hastings. OTPC (1923 ed.)
"Get up, our Anna dear, from the weary spinning wheel." The Fairy Thorn. Sir Samuel Ferguson. AnIV; CH; OnMSP; OnYI; PoVP; VA
Get You Gone. Sir Charles Sedley. ELP
Gethsemane. M. Betham-Edwards. BePJ
Gethsemane. Arna Bontemps. CDC
Gethsemane. Annette von Droste-Hülshoff, *tr. fr. German by* George N. Shuster. CAW
Gethsemane. Kipling. FaBoTw
Gethsemane. Edmund Leamy. JKCP; OQP
Gethsemane. William Bingham Tappan. *See* 'Tis Midnight; and on Olive's Brow.
Gethsemane. Charles Russell Wakeley. OQP
Gethsemane. Ella Wheeler Wilcox. MaRV; OQP; SoP
Gethsemane, Illinois. Martin S. Allwood, *tr. fr. Swedish by* Martin S. Allwood. LiTW
Gethsemane's Gift. Katherine Brégy. MaRV; StJW

Gettin' Born. Anthony Euwer. PoPl; WhC
Getting Back. Dorothy Brown Thompson. SiSoSe
Getting blue lips from standing out there in the cold, I twice. At Midnight. Joel Sloman. ThO
Getting Drunk with Daughter. Robert Huff. NePoEA-2
Getting It Together. Shirley Staples. WSL
Getting On. Stephen Sandy. CAD
Getting Out of Bed. Eleanor Farjeon. SiSoSe
Getting Short. David Hilton. QAH
Getting Through. James Merrill. NYBP
Getting Through. Robert P. Tristram Coffin. AnNE
Getting through with the world. Approach to a City. William Carlos Williams. CAD; PoRA (rev. ed.)
Getting Up. Lilian McCrea. BoTP
Getting Up Ahead of Someone (Sun). Frank O'Hara. ANYP
Getting Up Early. Robert Bly. NaP
Getting up Early on a Spring Morning. Po Chü-i, *tr. fr. Chinese by* Arthur Waley. FIW
Gettysburg. James Jeffrey Roche. MC; PaA; PAH
Gettysburg. Edmund Clarence Stedman. PAH
Gettysburg Ode, The, *sel.* Bayard Taylor.
Lincoln at Gettysburg. PAH
("After the eyes that looked.") OHIP
Ghaisties. Robert Garioch. NeBP
Ghaists, The: a Kirk-yard Eclogue. Robert Fergusson. OxBS
Ghastly, ghoulish, grinning skull. To a Skull. Joshua Henry Jones. BANP
Ghazal of Isa Akhun Zada. *Unknown, tr. fr. Pushtu by* E. Powys Mathers. PG (1945 ed.)
Ghazals. Adrienne Rich. NoP
Ghazel of Absence, A. Gerrit Lansing. CoPo
Gheluvelt. Robert Bridges. BrPo
Ghetto. Yvette Johnson. TNV
Ghetto, The, *sels.* Lola Ridge.
"Lights go out." MAP; MoAmPo (1942 ed.)
"Old Sodos no longer makes saddles." MAP; MoAmPo (1942 ed.)
"Sallow dawn is in the sky, A." MAP; MoAmPo (1942 ed.)
Ghetto-born, depression-bred. The Ark. Irving Feldman. AmPC
Ghetto Lovesong—Migration. Carole Gregory. NBP
Ghost. Witter Bynner. AnFE; CoAnAm
Ghost. Clark Coolidge. ANYP
Ghost, The. Hilary Corke. NYBP
Ghost, The. W. H. Davies. BrPo
Ghost, The. Walter de la Mare. BrPo; ChMP; CLwM; CMoP; ELP; EnLoPo; HaMV; HBMV; LiTM (1970 ed.); MoAB; MoBrPo; MoP; MoVE; OAEP (2d ed.); POTE
Ghost. R. H. Grenville. FiSC
Ghost, The. Robert Lowell, *after the Latin of* Sextus Propertius. AtBAP; MoVE; POTE (1959 ed.)
Ghost. John V. A. Weaver. HBMV
Ghost, The. James Wright. FiSC
Ghost Crabs. Ted Hughes. HYE
Ghost-Flowers. Mary Potter Thacher Higginson. AA
Ghost-grey the fall of night. Robin, A. Walter de la Mare. BiS; ChTr; CMoP
Ghost in the Cellarage, The. John Heath-Stubbs. NeBP
Ghost is someone, A: death has left a hole. The Ghost. Robert Lowell. AtBAP; MoVE; POTE (1959 ed.)
Ghost Lake's a dark lake, a deep lake and cold. The Skater of Ghost Lake. William Rose Benét. PoPo
Ghost Night. Lizette Woodworth Reese. HBMV
Ghost of a little white kitten, The. The Little Cat Angel. Leontine Stanfield. BLPA; CIV
Ghost of a mouldy larder is one thing, A; whiskery bread. Corposant. Peter Redgrove. NePoEA-2
Ghost of Abel, The. Blake. ERoP-1
Ghost of an Education, The. James Michie. NYBP
Ghost of Ninon would be sorry now, The. Veteran Sirens. E. A. Robinson. AnAmPo; AnNE; BoLiVe; OnHM; QFR
Ghost of the Buffaloes, The. Vachel Lindsay. *See* Ghosts of the Buffaloes, The.
Ghost Pet. Horatio Colony. GoYe
Ghost shall come gloating in its grief, The. The Soul to the Body. *Unknown.* PoLi
Ghost That Jim Saw, The. Bret Harte. PoMS; ShM
Ghost, that loved a lady fair, A. The Phantom-Wooer [*or* Phantom-Lover]. Thomas Lovell Beddoes. CBV; EnRP; ERoP-2; LO; OBRV; PeER; TrGrPo; ViBoPo; WiR
Ghost to Come. Margaret Widdemer. FiSC
Ghost-Town Saloon: Winter. Joseph Payne Brennan. FiSC
Ghost-Yard of the Goldenrod, The. Bliss Carman. TwCaPo
Ghostesses. *Unknown.* ChTr
Ghostly Crew, The, 2 *versions, with music. Unknown.* ShS
Ghostly Father, The. Peter Redgrove. MoBS; NePoEA-2
Ghostly Reaper. Harold Vinal. FiSC
Ghostly Tree. Léonie Adams. MAP; MoAB; MoAmPo
Ghostries. Henry Cholmondeley-Pennell. CIV
Ghosts. J. R. Ackerley. POTE
Ghosts. Robert Bridges. FaBoTw
Ghosts. Winifred Adams Burr. FiSC
Ghosts. Brian Hooker. PFY
Ghosts. Elizabeth Jennings. MemP; NePoEA-2
Ghosts, The. Longfellow. *Fr.* The Song of Hiawatha, XIX. LoBV
Ghosts. Ethna MacCarthy. NeIP
Ghosts. R. K. Munkittrick. AA; YT
Ghosts. Henri Charles Read, *tr. fr. French by* Alan Conder. LO
Ghosts. Alastair Reid. FiSC; NYBP
Ghosts, Fire, Water. James Kirkup. BoPe; POTi
Ghost's Lament, The. *Unknown.* BuBa
Ghost's Leavetaking, The. Sylvia Plath. NePoEA-2
Ghosts' Moonshine, The. Thomas Lovell Beddoes. LO
Ghosts of flowers went sailing, The. Changelings. Mary Potter Thacher Higginson. AA
Ghosts of the Buffaloes, The. Vachel Lindsay. AnAmPo; AnEnPo; MAP; MoAmPo; NePA; RG
(Ghost of the Buffaloes, The.) CoBA; RePo
Ghosts of the Dead. Besmilr Brigham. ThO
Ghosts of the early earth! Hopi Ghosts. William Haskell Simpson. *Fr.* In Arizona. NP
Ghost's Promenade, The. Thomas Caulfield Irwin. IrPN
Ghost's Song, The. *Unknown. See* Cauld Lad of Hilton, The.
Ghosts' Stories. Alastair Reid. NePoEA-2
Ghosts there must be with me in this old house. Solitude. Walter de la Mare. CMoP; FaBoEn
Ghoul Care. Ralph Hodgson. AnEnPo; MoBrPo
Ghoulies and Ghosties. *Unknown. See* Litany for Halloween.
Ghoulish Old Fellow in Kent, A. Morris Bishop. ShM
Ghyrlond of the Blessed Virgin Marie, The. Ben Jonson. ISi
(Garland of the Blessed Virgin Marie, The. "B.I.") SeCL
Giacobbe Finelli so funny, O! My! Da Comica Man. T. A. Daly. StaSt
Giant came to me when I was young, A. The Lost Genius. John James Piatt. AA
Giant firefly, A. The Firefly. Issa. RePo
Giant flagons in a row—flashing in the sun. Filling Station. E. Merrill Root. PoMa
Giant Norway spruce from Podunk, its lower branches bound, The. December. James Schuyler. ANYP
Giant Puffball, The. Edmund Blunden. FaBoTw
Giant Thunder. James Reeves. BoNaP
Giant wink in a clown's cheek, The. Phaeton. Eli Mandel. PeCV (1967 ed.)
Giantess. Baudelaire, *tr. fr. French.* ErPo, *tr. by* Karl Shapiro; OnPM, *tr. by* Arthur Symons
Giant's Cake, A. Evelina San Garde. BoTP
Giant's Tomb in Georgian Bay. "Katherine Hale." CaP
Giaour, The, *sel.* Byron.
"Clime of the unforgotten brave!" PoFr
Giardino Pubblico. Sir Osbert Sitwell. ChMP
Gib and gibbet, these shall be my signs. The Hanged Thing. Walter H. Kerr. FiSC
Gibberish. Mary Elizabeth Coleridge. MoVE
Gibbs, *sel.* Muriel Rukeyser.
"It was much later in his life he rose." ImOP
Gibraltar. Wilfrid Scawen Blunt. ACP; GTSL; HBV; OBEV; OBVV; OTPC (1923 ed.); VA
Gibraltar. Richard Chenevix Trench. OBRV; OBVV
Giddinesse. George Herbert. MaMe
Giddy Maid, The. John Clare. Sonn
Gideon at the Well. Geoffrey Hill. NePoEA
"Gie corn to my horse, mither." The Mother's Malison; or, Clyde's Water (B *vers.*). *Unknown.* ESPB
Gi'e me a lass with a lump of land. Give Me a Lass. Allan Ramsay. CEP; CoBE
Gie the Lass Her Fairin'. Burns. CoMu; ErPo
Gife Langour. Lord Darnley. OxBS
Gift, The. "Æ." HBMV
Gift, The. Margaret E. Bruner. PoToHe

Gift, The. Bliss Carman. PTK
Gift, The. John Ciardi. LiTM (1970 ed.); NMP
Gift. Carol Freeman. PoNe (1970 ed.)
Gift, The. George Newell Lovejoy. *See* Mother, The
Gift, A. Amy Lowell. NP
Gift, The. Laura Spencer Portor. PEDC; StJW
Gift, The. *Unknown, tr. fr. German.* SAS
Gift, The. William Carlos Williams. MoRP; NePoAm-2; PoPl
Gift, The. Keith Wilson. ThO
Gift from the cold and silent Past! The Norsemen. Whittier. PAH
Gift of a Mirror to a Lady. David Wagoner. NePoAm-2
Gift of a Skull, The. John Skelton. *See* Upon a Dead Man's Head.
Gift of Flowers, A. Leonard Feeney. WHL
Gift of God, The. E. A. Robinson. AnAmPo; AP; CoBMV; MAP; MAPA; MaPo (1969 ed.); MoAB; MoAmPo; OxBA; TwAmPo
Gift of God, A. *Unknown.* STF
Gift of Great Value, A. Robert Creeley. NaP
Gift of Judah the Woman-Hater, The, *sel.* Judah ibn Sabbatai.
Expensive Wife, The. TrJP
Gift of Song, The. Anthony Hecht. NYBP
Gift of Song, The. Horace, *tr. fr. Latin by* Christopher Smart. Odes, IV, 3. LiTW
Gift of Speech, The. Sadi, *tr. fr. Persian by* L. Cranmer-Byng. *Fr.* The Gulistan. AWP; LiTW
Gift of the living God to mortal man. Peace Universal. Anna H. Thorne. PEDC; PoRL
Gift of Water, The. Hamlin Garland. AA; AnAmPo
Gift of Work, The. Edwin Markham. DD
Gift Outright, The. Robert Frost. AmFN; AmLP; AmP; AmPP (4th ed.); AP; CoBMV; CMoP; CrMA; FaBoEn; InPo; LiTM; LoGBV; MaPo; MoAB; MoAmPo (1950 ed.); MWA-2; NoP; OxBA; PAL; PoeP; PoIE; PoPo; RePo; SeCeV (1967 ed.); WaKn; WaP
Gift to a Jade. Anna Wickham. ELU; NP
Gift to Be Simple, The. Howard Moss. ImOP; MoRP; TwCP
Gifts. Helen Wieand Cole. ChIP; OQP
Gifts. Mary Elizabeth Coleridge. PoVP
Gifts. Mary Edgar Comstock. OQP
Gifts. Hazel Harper Harris. BiCB
Gifts. Emma Lazarus. TrJP; WGRP
Gifts. Sister Mary of the Visitation. WHL
Gifts. Chauncey R. Piety. PGD
Gifts, The. Odell Shepard. ChrBoLe
Gifts. James Thomson. *See* Give a Man a Horse He Can Ride.
Gifts of God, The. George Herbert. *See* Pulley, The.
Gifts of God, The. Jones Very. AA
Gifts of heav'n my foll'wing song pursues, The. The Honey-Farm. Vergil, *tr. by* Dryden. *Fr.* Georgics. WoL
Gifts of the Animals to Man, The. Sir Philip Sidney. *Fr.* Arcadia. OA
Gifts Returned [*or* Return'd]. Walter Savage Landor. BOHV; OBVV
Gifts that to our breasts we fold, The. Recompense. Nixon Waterman. HBV
Gifts without Season. Joseph Auslander. MaRV
Gigantic beauty of a stallion, fresh and responsive to my caresses, A. Walt Whitman. *Fr.* Song of Myself, XXXII. PDV
Gigha. W. S. Graham. FaBoMo; NeBP
Gil Brenton. *Unknown.* BaBo; ESPB; OxBB
Gil Morrice. *Unknown.* OxBB
Gil, the Toreador. Charles Henry Webb. AA
Gila Monster Route, The. L. F. Post *and* Glenn Norton. ABF; SCC
Gilded with leaf-thick paint; a steady. Cock-Pheasant. Laurie Lee. POTi
Gilderoy was a bonnie boy. My Handsome Gilderoy. *Unknown.* AtBAP; CH
Gilead. Mary Brennan Clapp. OQP
Giles Collin he said to his mother one day. Lady Alice (C *vers.*) *Unknown.* ESPB
Giles Collins he said to his old mother. Lady Alice (B *vers.*). *Unknown.* ESPB
Giles Corey. *Unknown.* PAH; ThLM
Giles Corey of the Salem Farms, *sels.* Longfellow.
Prologue: "Delusions of the days that once have been." PAH
Trial, The. PAH
Giles Corey was a wizard strong. Giles Corey. *Unknown.* PAH
Giles's Hope. Samuel Taylor Coleridge. BOHV
(Epigram: "'What? rise again with all one's bones.'") HBV
Giles Johnson, Ph.D. Frank Marshall Davis. Kal
Gilgamesh, *abr. Tr. fr. Babylonian tablets by* William Ellery Leonard. WoL
Sels.
Gilgamesh Laments the Death of Engidu. LiTW
Seduction of Engadu. ErPo
Gill Morice stood in stable-door. Childe Maurice. *Unknown.* ESPB (D *vers.*); ViBoFo
Gillespie. Sir Henry Newbolt. PeVV; ShBV-1
Gillian, *parody. Unknown.* BOHV
Gilliflower [*or* Gillyflower] of Gold, The. William Morris. AnFE; PoVP; TOP; VA; ViPo; WHA
Gilly Silly Jarter. *Unknown.* OxNR
Gil's history appears to me. An Epigram, on the Reverend Mr. Laurence Echard's, and Bishop Gilbert Burnet's Histories. Matthew Green. PoE; StP
Gimboling. Isabella Gardner. ErPo
Gimme Dat Ol'-Time Religion, *with music. Unknown.* BoAN-1
Gimme de Banjo, *with music. Unknown.* ShS
"Gimme my scalet tie." Bangkolidye. Barry Pain. BOHV
Gimme Yo' Han', *with music. Unknown.* BoAN-2
Gin a body meet a body. Comin' thro' the Rye. Burns. *See also* Comin' through the rye, poor body. FaFP; LiTB; LiTG; LiTL; TreF.
Gin a body meet a body. Rigid Body Sings [*or* In Memory of Edward Wilson]. James Clerk Maxwell. BOHV; Par; WhC
Gin a body meet a body. Comin' through the Rye. *Unknown.* WBLP
Gin by Pailfuls. Sir Walter Scott. ChTr
Gin I were on my milkwhite steed. The Bents and Broom. *Unknown.* OxBB
Gin is white, for a white while. White Chimes. Alfred Starr Hamilton. QAH
Gin the Goodwife Stint. Basil Bunting. CTC
Gineral B. is a sensible man. *See* Guvener B. is a sensible man.
Ginevra. Samuel Rogers. *Fr.* Italy. BeLS; PoLF
Ginevra, *sel.* Shelley.
"She is still she is cold." ChER
Gingerbread Man, The. Eva Rowland. GFA
Gingham dog and the calico cat, The. The Duel. Eugene Field. BeLS; BoChLi; CenHV; FaBoBe; FaFP; FaPON; GFA; HBV; HBVY; MoShBr; NeHB; OHFP; OnMSP; OnSP; OTPC (1946 ed.); PoLF; PoPl; PoRA; PTK; SoPo; StVeCh; TiPo; TreF; UTS; YT
Gingilee. Moishe-Leib Halpern, *tr. fr. Yiddish by* Joseph Leftwich. TrJP
Gioconda. Thomas McGreevy. OnYI
Giorno dei Morti. D. H. Lawrence. BrPo; POTE; SeCePo; ShBV-4
Giotto, I have not found. To Giotto. Wesley Trimpi. NePoEA
Giotto's Campanile. Guy Butler. PeSA
Giotto's Campanile. Thomas O'Hagan. JKCP
Giotto's Tower. Longfellow. CoBA
Giovinette, che fate all' amore. Lorenzo da Ponte, *tr. fr. Italian by* Natalie MacFarren. *Fr.* Don Giovanni. TrJP
Gipsies. *See also* Gypsies.
Gipsies ("The gipsies seek wide sheltering woods again"). John Clare. ChTr
Gipsies ("The snow falls deep; the forest lies alone"). John Clare. CH; NBM; PoEL-4; ShBV-2
(Gipsy Camp, The.) ChTr
(Gypsies.) CBEP; NoP
Gipsies, The. "Richard Scrace." CaP
Gipsies came to lord Cassilis' gate, The. Johnny Faa, the Lord of Little Egypt. *Unknown.* EnSB
Gipsies came to our good lord's gate, The. *See* Gypsies came to our good lord's gate, The.
Gipsies came to the good Squire's gate, The. *Unknown.* LO
Gipsies lit their fires by the chalk-pit anew, The. The Idlers. Edmund Blunden. BoTP; CH
Gipsies Metamorphosed, The. Ben Jonson. *See* Gypsies Metamorphosed, The.

Gipsies passed her little gate, The. *See* Gypsies passed her little gate, The.
Gipsies seek wide sheltering woods again, The. Gipsies. John Clare. ChTr
Gipsy Camp, The. John Clare. *See* Gypsies ("The snow falls deep").
Gipsy Girl, The. Ralph Hodgson. EnLit; MCCG; MoBrPo
(Gypsy Girl, The.) POTE
Gipsy Jane. William Brighty Rands. BoTP; FaPON
(Gypsy Jane.) SoPo; TiPo
Gipsy Laddie, The. *Unknown.* *See* Wraggle Taggle Gipsies, The.
Gipsy Man. Dorothy King. BoTP
Gipsy Queen. John Alexander Chapman. OBEV (new ed.)
Gipsy Song ("The faery beam upon you"). Ben Jonson. *Fr.* The Gypsies Metamorphosed. FaBoCh; LoGBV; NoP; SeCL
(Faeries' Song, The.) SeCV-1
("Fairy beam upon you, The.") ReEn; TuPP
(Jackman's Song, The.) AtBAP
(Patrico's Song.) BoW; LoBV
(Song: "Faiery beame upon you, The.") SiSw
(Wish, A.) PoRL
Gipsy Song ("To the old, long life and treasure"). Ben Jonson. *Fr.* The Gypsies Metamorphosed. SeCL
Gipsy Trail, The. Kipling. HBV; HT; InP; PoRA
Gipsy Vans. Kipling. OtMeF
Gipsy's Warning, The. *Unknown.* BeLS
Giraffe, The. Geoffrey Dearmer. WePo
Giraffe, The. Nikolai Gumilev, *tr. fr. Russian by* Y. Hornstein. LiTW
"Listen:/ There roams, far away, by the waters of Clead," *sel.* FaPON
Giraffe, The. Marvin Solomon. NePoAm-2
Giraffe. *Unknown, tr. fr. Hottentot.* PeSA
Giraffe and the Woman, The. Laura E. Richards. PDV
Giraffe and Tree. W. J. Turner. CH
Giraffes. N. H. Brettell. BoSA
Giraffes, The. Roy Fuller. ChMP; NeBP
Girandole. Dorothy Donnelly. NYBP
Gird on Thy Sword. Robert Bridges. GTBS
Gird up thy loins now like a man; I will demand of thee. Out of the Whirlwind. Job, Bible, *O.T.* AWP; JAWP; WBP
Girl, A. Edwin Denby. BoLP
Girl, A. Babette Deutsch. HBMV
Girl, A. Viola Meynell. MoBrPo (1942 ed.)
Girl. Dom Moraes. NePoEA-2
Girl, A. Ezra Pound. BoLP; MAP; MoAB; MoAmPo; MoPW; NeMA
Girl and Butterfly. Edith Sitwell. MoPW
Girl and Her Fawn, The. Andrew Marvell. *Fr.* The Nymph Complaining for the Death of Her Fawn. BoTP; OTPC (1923 ed.)
(Girl Describes Her Fawn, The.) GTSL
(Nymph and Her Fawn, The.) FaBoCh; LoGBV
Girl and the Cuckoo, The. *Unknown, tr. fr. Russian by* W. R. S. Ralston. OnPM
Girl Asleep. Raymond Souster. TwCaPo
Girl at the Seaside. Richard Murphy. NMP; OPoP
Girl Athletes. Haniel Long. HBMV
Girl awaiting her lover is not more still with fear, A. Night Alert. Alison Boodson. NeBP
Girl Betrayed. Hedylos, *tr. fr. Greek by* Dudley Fitts. LiTW
Girl, could you once regain. Could You Once Regain. Kendrick Smithyman. AnNZ
Girl Describes Her Fawn, The. Andrew Marvell. *See* Girl and Her Fawn, The.
Girl grown woman fire mother of fire. Waterlily Fire. Muriel Rukeyser. OPoP
Girl Help. Janet Lewis. QFR
Girl hustles her islands of pure flesh, The. For Jan. John Wieners. CoPo
Girl I Left behind Me, The ("The dames of France"). Thomas Osborne Davis. AmSS, *with music;* FaBoBe; FaFP; HBV; OnYI; TreF
Girl I Love, The. *Unknown, tr. fr. Modern Irish by* Jeremiah Joseph Callanan. IrPN; OnYI
Girl I Took to the Cocktail Party, The. Trevor Williams. FiBHP
Girl in a Library, A. Randall Jarrell. FiMAP
Girl in a Nightgown. Wallace Stevens. OxBA
Girl in a Window, A. James Wright. ErPo
Girl in the Carriage, The. *Unknown, tr. fr. Chinese by* Arthur Waley. *Fr.* Shi King. LiTW
Girl in the lane, The. *Unknown.* OxNR
Girl in the sand, The. Nude Kneeling in Sand. John Logan. ErPo
Girl in the Subway. Sydney King Russell. StaSt
Girl in the tea shop, The. The Tea Shop. Ezra Pound. WePo
Girl Is a Girl, A. Phyllis C. Michael. SoP
Girl is twirling a parasol, A. Snapshot. John Fuller. NePoEA-2
Girl of All Periods, The. Coventry Patmore. VA
Girl of Cadiz, The. Byron. BWP
Girl of Pompeii, A. Edward Sandford Martin. AA; HBV
Girl of the Future, feared of all. A "Dresscessional." Carolyn Wells. WBLP
Girl on the dime, The. Inner Ear. Coleman Barks. *Fr.* Body Poems. QAH
Girl on the Milk-white Horse, The. Rachel Field. *Fr.* A Circus Garland. SoPo
Girl of the musing mouth. Statuette: Late Minoan. C. Day Lewis. EnLit; OxBI
Girl of the Red Mouth. Martin MacDermott. HBV; JKCP (1926 ed.); OnYI
Girl of three cows don't crow! Showing Off. *Unknown.* KiLC
Girl of whom in olden days, The. A Maiden. Kageki. OnPM
Girl on the Milk-white Horse, The. Rachel Field. *Fr.* A Circus Garland. StVeCh
Girl Skipping Rope in Flushing, A. Stephen Stepanchev. NYTB
Girl Takes Her Place among the Mothers, The. Marya Zaturenska. HBMV
Girl to Soldier on Leave. Isaac Rosenberg. MMA
Girl today, dreaming, A. Auf dem Wasser zu Singen. Stephen Spender. EnLoPo
Girl Walking. Charles G. Bell. ErPo; NePoAm-2
Girl who weighed many an oz., A. *Unknown.* GoTP
Girl with Doves. Stephen Gray. PeSA
Girl with eyes like dying flowers. Lullaby. Max Harris. BoAV; MoAuPo
Girl with Long Dark Hair. Stephen Gray. PeSA
Girl with the Afro, The. Bob Bennett. BF
Girls, The. Siasconset Song. Philip Booth. NePoAm; StP
Girls and boys come out to play. Mother Goose. BoTP; BrR; MPB (1956 ed.); OTPC; PPL; StVeCh; TiPo
Girls and Soldiers Singing. Leonard Mann. BoAu
Girls are laughing with the boys and gaming by the fire, The. Hallows' E'en. Winifred M. Letts. DD
Girls around Cape Horn, The, *with music.* *Unknown.* SoAmSa
Girl's far treble, muted to the heat, The. Milkmaid. Laurie Lee. ChMP; FaBoTw
Girls Going to the Fair. William Allingham. IrPN
Girls in Spring. Owari, *tr. fr. Japanese by* Ishii *and* Obata. OnPM
Girl's Lamentation, The. William Allingham. IrPN; SeCePo, *sl. abr.*
Girl's Mood, A. Lizette Woodworth Reese. HBMV
Girls' Names. Eleanor Farjeon. BiCB; SUS; TiPo
Girls on the Yueh River. Li Po, *tr. fr. Chinese.* ChTr
Girls scream,/ Boys shout. School's Out. W. H. Davies. BoC; OBMV; POTE
Girl's Song, A. Aubrey De Vere. GTBS-D
Girl's Song, A. Katharine Tynan. OnYI
Girl's Song. Marya Zaturenska. TPM
Girl's Treasures, A. *Unknown, tr. fr. Greek by* Lord Neaves. OnPM
Girl's voice in the night troubled my heart, A. Going Over. Sir Charles G. D. Roberts. TwCaPo
Girod Street Cemetery; New Orleans. Harry Morris. GoYe
Girondins, The. Alexandre Dumas, *tr. fr. French by* John Oxenford. *Fr.* Le Chevalier de Maison Rouge. PoFr
Girt in dark growths, yet glimmering with one star. Sleepless Dreams. Dante Gabriel Rossetti. The House of Life, XXXIX. MaVP; OAEP; PoVP; ViPo; VP
Girt in my guiltless gown, as I sit here and sew. A Woman's Answer. *At. to* the Earl of Surrey. FCP; SiPS
Girt Woak Tree That's in the Dell, The. William Barnes. HBV; PoVP
(Oak Tree, The.) OBVV

Girt wold house o' mossy stuone, The. The Old House. William Barnes. OBVV
Girtonian Funeral, A. *Unknown.* Par
Gisli, the Chieftain, *sel.* Isabella Valancy Crawford.
Song of the Arrow, The. OBCV; PeCV (1967 ed.)
Git Along, Little Dogies, *Unknown.* *See* Whoopee Ti Yi Yo, Git Along, Little Dogies.
Git on Board, Little Chillen, *Unknown.* *See* Gospel Train, The.
Git yer [*or* yo] little sage hens ready. At a Cowboy Dance [*or* Idaho Cowboy Dance]. James Barton Adams. ABF; HBV; IHA; PoOW; RePo; SCC
Gita Govinda, The, *sels.* Jayadeva, *tr. fr. Sanskrit.*
Hymn to Vishnu, *tr. by* Sir Edwin Arnold. AWP
"Sandal and garment of yellow and lotus garlands upon his body of blue," *tr. by* George Keyt. ErPo
Song: "Low whispers the wind from Malaya," *tr. by* Sir Edwin Arnold. LiTW
Gitanjali, *sels.* Rabindranath Tagore.
"Day after day," LXXVI. OBMV
"Have you not heard his silent steps?" XLV. WGRP
"Here is thy footstool," X. MaRV; WGRP (X-XI)
"I have got my leave," XCIII. BoC; OBMV
"I was not aware of the moment," XCV. NP
"If it is not my portion," LXXIX. BoC; OBMV
"Let this be my parting word," XCVI. MoRP
"On the day when the lotus bloomed," XX. NP
"On the slope of the desolate river," LXIV. OBMV
"This is my prayer to Thee," XXXVI.
(For Strength.) MoRP
(Prayer for Strength.) MaRV
"Thou art the sky and thou art the nest as well," LXVII. BoPe; OBMV
"Thou hast made me known to friends," LXIII. NP
(When One Knows Thee.) OQP
"Thy gifts to us mortals fulfil all our needs," LXXV. InP
"Where the mind is without fear," XXXV. PoFr
Gittin'-up Hollers. *Unknown.* CoSo
Giuseppe Caponsacchi. Robert Browning. *Fr.* The Ring and the Book. PoVP; VP
Giuseppe, da barber, ees greata for "mash." Mia Carlotta. T. A. Daly. InMe; MAP; MoAmPo (1942 ed.); NeMA; ShBV-3; TreFS; WhC
Giv but to things their tru esteem. Right Apprehension. Thomas Traherne. PoEL-2
Give. "Madeline Bridges." *See* Life's Mirror.
Give a Man a Horse He Can Ride. James Thomson. Sunday up the River, XV. EnLi-2; EnLit; GTSL; PoVP
(Gifts.) BBV; HBV; OBEV; OBVV; TOP; TreF
Give a Message, Pulpit! Lon Woodrum. SoP
Give a Rouse. Robert Browning. Cavalier Tunes, II. EnLi-2; EnLit; PoVP; ShBV-1; ViPo
(Cavalier Tune, A.) BoLiVe
Give a rouse, then, in the Maytime. A Stein Song. Richard Hovey. *Fr.* Spring. AmePo; AnAmPo; HBV; MAP; MoAmPo (1942 ed.); NeMA; PFY
Give All to Love. Emerson. AmePo; AmP; AmPP (4th ed.); AnAmPo; AnEnPo; AnFE; AnNE; AP; APA; AWP; CLwM; CoAnAm; FaBoEn; FaFP; HBV; InPo; JAWP; LiTA; LiTL; LO; MWA-1; NePA; OBEV; OBVV; OxBA; PAn; PCD; PFY; PG (1955 ed.); PoE; PoEL-4; PoLF; PoPo; TOP; TreFS; TrGrPo; ViBoPo; WaKn, *abr.;* WBP
Give as you would if an angel. How to Give. *Unknown.* BLRP
Give away her gowns. Chorus. Edna St. Vincent Millay. *Fr.* Memorial to D. C. NP
Give Beauty All Her Right. Thomas Campion. CLwM; OBSC; ReEn; SiCE; TuPP; ViBoPo
(Beauty Is Not Bound.) MeWo; TrGrPo
Give Ear, O Ye Heavens. Deuteronomy, Bible, *O.T.* *See* Blessed of the Lord Be His Land.
Give ear to my prayer, O God; and hide not thy self. Psalm LV, Bible, *O.T.* AWP
Give ear, ye British hearts of gold. Rodney's Glory. Owen Roe O'Sullivan. OnYI
Give Ear, Ye Heavens. Deuteronomy, XXXII: 1-43, Bible, *O.T.* TrJP
Give ear you lusty gallants. A Famous Sea-Fight. John Looke. CoMu
Give freely to the friend thou hast. Koina ta ton Philon. John Addington Symonds. OBVV
Give her but a least excuse to love me! Song. Robert Browning. *Fr.* Pippa Passes. EPN; GTBS; GTSL; ViBoPo
Give him, Lord, eyes to behold the truth. Prayer for a Priest. *Unknown.* WHL
Give him the darkest inch your shelf allows. George Crabbe. E. A. Robinson. AmePo; AmPP (4th ed.); AP; CoBA; CoBMV; LiTA; LiTM (rev. ed.); MAmP; MAP; MaPo (1969 ed.); ML; MoAB; MoAmPo; MoVE; NAMP; NePA; NoP; OxBA; PoEL-5; PP
Give honor and love forever more. Peter Cooper. Joaquin Miller. AA
Give honor unto Luke Evangelist. Old and New Art: St. Luke the Painter. Dante Gabriel Rossetti. The House of Life, LXXIV. GoBC; MaVP; PoVP; ViPo
Give, if thou canst, an alms; if not, afford. Robert Herrick. *Fr.* Alms. MyFE
Give life its full domain and feed the soul. Of Wonder. Mary Gilmore. BoAV; NeLNL
Give Love To-Day. Ethel Talbot. HBV
Give me a battle to fight. A Battle Cry. Lee Shippey. MaRV
"Give me a fillet, Love," quoth I. Love and Life. Julie Mathilde Lippmann. AA; HBV
Give me a chair. Song of the Poor Man. *Unknown.* TTY
Give Me a Gentle Heart. Percy Thomas. OQP
Give me a girlie (if one I needs must meet). Women. William Cartwright. ELU; ErPo
Give me a golden pen, and let me lean. On Leaving Some Friends at an Early Hour. Keats. MERP
Give me a good digestion, Lord. A Prayer [*or* An Ancient Prayer]. Thomas Harry Basil Webb. BBV (1951 ed.); BLPA; FaBoBe; NeHB; PoMa; PoToHe (new ed.); SoP; TreFS
Give me a harsh land to ring music from. This Land. Ian Mudie. BoAu
Give me a heart where no impure. To Castara. William Habington. AnAnS-2
Give me a home in the far, far West. The Far, Far West. *Unknown.* CoSo
Give Me a Kiss. *Unknown.* UnTE
Give me a kiss from those sweet lips of thine. An Incomparable Kiss. *Unknown.* InvP; SeCL; SeEP
Give Me a Lass [with a Lump of Land]. Allan Ramsay. CEP; CoBE
Give me a man that is not dull. His Desire. Robert Herrick. CABA; CBV; OAEP
Give me a mask, I'll join the masquerade. Heine. Fresco Sonnets to Christian Sethe, 2. AWP; JAWP; WBP
"Give me a new idea," I said. See God in Everything. A. E. Finn. SoP
Give me a nobler, wider sphere. Anno 1829. Heine. LiTW
Give me a race that is run in a breath. The Hundred-Yard Dash. William Lindsey. AA
Give me a spirit that on [this] life's rough sea. The Master Spirit. George Chapman. *Fr.* The Conspiracy of Charles, Duke of Byron. EtS; MyFE; ViBoPo
Give me a spoon of oleo, Ma. Domestic Science. *Unknown.* WBLP
Give Me Ale. *Unknown.* *See* In Praise of Ale.
Give me black souls. African Heaven. Frank Parkes. ACV
"Give me but two brigades," said Hooker. The Battle of Lookout Mountain. George Henry Boker. MC; PAH
Give me fortune, give me health. Thomas Middleton. *Fr.* The Widow. TuPP
Give me full-hearted men, who love their Lord. Full-Hearted Men! Paul Martin. SoP
Give me, give me Buriano. Bacchus's Opinion of Wine, and Other Beverages. Francesco Redi. *Fr.* Bacchus in Tuscany. AWP
Give Me Hard Tasks. *Unknown.* SoP
Give me hunger. At a Window. Carl Sandburg. FaBoBe; HBMV; MoLP; NP; PCD; PoToHe; TrPWD
Give me, in this inconstant ebb and flow. Seaward Bound. Alice Brown. TrPWD
Give Me Jesus, *with music.* *Unknown.* BoAN-1
Give me kisses! Do not stay. To Lesbia. John Godfrey Saxe. HBV; UnTE
Give Me Leave. "A. W." *See* Petition to Have Her Leave to Die.
Give me leave to rail at you. A Song. Earl of Rochester. EG
Give Me More Love, or More Disdain. Thomas Carew. *See* Mediocrity in Love Rejected.

"Give me my bow," said Robin Hood. The Death of Robin Hood. Eugene Field. StPo
Give me my harp, and let me sing a song. Deirdre. Sir Samuel Ferguson. *Fr.* Deirdre. IrPN
Give me, my love, that billing kiss. The Kiss. Thomas Moore. BoLP; EnLoPo
Give me my robe, put on my crown. Death of Cleopatra. Shakespeare. *Fr.* Antony and Cleopatra, V, ii. AtBAP; FiP; MemP; TreFS; TrGrPo
Give me my scallop shell of quiet. The Passionate Man's Pilgrimage [*or* His Pilgrimage *or* The Pilgrimage]. Sir Walter Ralegh. AnFE; AtBAP; BBV (1951 ed.); BEL; BoPe; CABA; CAW; CBEP; ChTr; CoBE; DTC; EG; ElL; EnLit; EnRePo; EP; FaPL; FCP; HBV; ILP; LiTB; LoBV; MePo; NoP; OAEP; OBEV; OBSC; OxBoCh; PoAn; PoE; PoEL-2; PoFS; PoIE; PoRA; ReEn; SeCePo; SiCE; SiPS; TOP; TreFS; TrGrPo; TRV; TuPP; ViBoPo; WePo; WGRP; YAT
Give Me My Self. Michael Drayton. *See* Idea: "You're not alone when you are still alone."
Give me my sword./ Who's there? Shakespeare. *Fr.* Macbeth, II, i. MyFE
Give Me My Work. George Whetstone. ElL
Give me no mansions ivory white. The Desire. Katharine Tynan. HBV; TSW
Give Me Not Tears. Rose Hawthorne Lathrop. AA
Give me, O friend, the secret of thy heart. Rosa Rosarum. Agnes Mary Frances Robinson. HBMV; VA
Give me, O God, the understanding heart. The Understanding Heart. Georgia Harkness. MaRV
Give me, O indulgent Fate! The Petition for an Absolute Retreat. Countess of Winchilsea. OBEC; PoEL-3; TrGrPo
Give me, O Lord, a vision of eternity. A Vision of Eternity. Avis B. Christiansen. SoP
Give me of every language, first my vigorous English. The English Language. William Wetmore Story. GN
Give me of love my love to prove. H. G. Andrews. LO
"Give me of your bark, O Birch Tree!" Hiawatha's Sailing [*or* Hiawatha's Canoe]. Longfellow. *Fr.* The Song of Hiawatha. BBV; PCH; StVeCh (1940 ed.)
Give me one kiss. To Dianeme. Robert Herrick. FaBoBe; LiTL; NeHB
Give me some music.—Now, good morrow, friends. Shakespeare. Twelfth Night, II, iv. MyFE
Give Me Strength. *Unknown.* FaChP
Give me strength, Lord, just for today. This Day That's Mine. Theresa Gamble Head. SoP
Give me that man, that dares bestride. Herrick's [*or* His] Cavalier. Robert Herrick. GoJo; PoFr
Give me the avowed, the erect, the manly foe. The Candid Friend. George Canning. TreFS; TreFT
Give me the bird of Paradise, though dying. The Captive Bird of Paradise. Ruth Pitter. SiSw
Give me the dance of your boughs, O Tree. Song to a Tree. Edwin Markham. FaPON; MPB
Give me the darkest corner of a cloud. Sonnet. R. W. Dixon. LO
Give Me the Eyes. Walter Savage Landor. EPN
Give me the faith that asks not "Why?" A Prayer. *Unknown.* SoP
Give me the harp of epic song. Odes of Anacreon, *tr. by* Thomas Moore. OuHeWo
Give me the hills and wide water. The Hills and the Sea. Wilfred Campbell. CaP
Give me the hills, that echo silence back. The Silent Ranges. Stephan Moylan Bird. HBMV
Give me the lowest place: not that I dare. The Lowest Place. Christina Rossetti. EnLi-2; MaRV; SoP; TrPWD; ViPo
Give me the merchants of the Indian mines. Mine Argosy from Alexandria. Christopher Marlowe. *Fr.* The Jew of Malta, I, i. ChTr; LO
Give Me the Old. Robert Hinckley Messinger. *See* Winter Wish, A.
Give me the priest these graces shall possess. The Priest of Christ. Thomas Ken. SoP; TRV
Give me the room whose every nook. The Library. Frank Dempster Sherman. AA
"Give me the salt spray in my face." What the Red-haired Bo'sun Said. Charles H. Souter. PoAu-1
"Give me the sky." Ilo Orleans. RIS
Give Me the Splendid Silent Sun. Walt Whitman. AA; AmePo; AmPP (3d ed.); BoLiVe; BoNaP; FaPON; MaPo; MoAmPo (1950 ed.); PG (1945 ed.); TSW
Give Me the Sun. Sister Miriam. JKCP (1955 ed.)
Give me this day a faith not personal. Allen Tate. More Sonnets at Christmas, III. LiTA; LiTM; NePA; WaP
Give Me Three Grains of Corn, Mother. Amelia Blanford Edwards. AS, *abr., with music;* BLPA
Give me thyself! It were as well to cry. Thyself. John Addington Symonds. *Fr.* Stella Maris. PoVP; VA
Give me to be Thy child, and learn for ever at Thy knee. Amor Dei. *Unknown.* BoC
Give Me Thy Heart. Adelaide Anne Procter. ACP; CAW; GoBC
Give me thy joy in sorrow, gracious Lord. Thy Joy in Sorrow. Chauncey Hare Townshend. VA
Give me to die unwitting of the day. Mors Benefica. Edmund Clarence Stedman. AA
Give me truths. Blight. Emerson. AmePo; AP; CDC; NoP
Give Me Thy Heart. Adelaide Anne Procter. SoP
Give me white paper! Columbus. Edward Everett Hale. DD; HH; MC; PAH
Give me wide walls to build my house of life. Wide Walls. *Unknown.* PoToHe (new ed.)
Give me work to do. A Prayer. *Unknown.* PGD
Give me work to do, Dear Lord. Work Motive. Carlton Buck. SoP
Give me your hand old Revolutionary. The Centenarian's Story. Walt Whitman. CTC
Give me your poppies. Choros. Hilda Doolittle ("H. D."). *Fr.* Morpheus. FaBoMo
Give me your tired, your poor. Inscription on The Statue of Liberty. Emma Lazarus. *Fr.* The New Colossus. PaA; PoFr; PoRL; PTK
Give Me Your Whole Heart. *Unknown, tr. fr. Sanskrit by* Swami Prabhavananda *and* Christopher Isherwood. *Fr.* The Bhagavad-Gita. MaRV
Give money me, take friendship whoso [or he who] list. Of Money. Barnaby Googe. CBV; ElL; EnRePo; EP; ForPo; NoP
Give My Heart a Song. Anna M. Gilleland. STF
Give no pity because my feet. Blind. Fanny Crosby. MaRV
Give No White Flower. Brenda Chamberlain. NeIP
Give not our blankets, tax-fed Squire, to him. Ebenezer Elliott. *Fr.* The Year of Seeds. Sonn
Give Our Conscience Light. Aline Badger Carter. ChIP; TrPWD
Give over to high things the fervent thought. To Lovers of Earth: Fair Warning. Countee Cullen. CDC
Give pardon, blessèd soul, to my bold cries. On the Death of Sir Philip Sidney [*or* To Sir Philip Sidney's Soul]. Henry Constable. ElL; GoBC; OBEV; OBSC; SeCePo
Give patient care to something I man saye. Admonition to Montgomerie. James I, King of England. OxBS
Give place all ye that doth rejoice. Sir Thomas Wyatt. FCP; SiPS
Give place, ye ladies, and be gone. John Heywood. *See* Give place, you ladies. . .
Give Place, Ye Lovers. Earl of Surrey. *See* Praise of His Love, A.
Give place, you [*or* ye] ladies, and be gone. A Praise of His Lady [*or* A Description of a Most Noble Lady]. John Heywood, *wr. at. to* Thomas Heywood. CoBE; ElL; HBV; OBEV; OBSC; SiCE; TuPP; ViBoPo
Give Thanks. Helen Isabella Tupper. BLRP
(For Everything Give Thanks.) TreFT
(Thankful Hearts.) SoP
(Thanks for Everything.) WBLP
Give thanks, O heart, for the high souls. Edwin Markham. *Fr.* Conscripts of the Dream. PGD
Give Them the Flowers Now. Leigh M. Hodges. WBLP
Give to barrows, trays and pans. Art. Emerson. AmePo; MAmP
Give to Caesar. Richard Crashaw. MaMe
Give to imagination some pure light. Modern Love, XXXVIII. George Meredith. ViPo; VP
Give to me the life I love. The Vagabond. Robert Louis Stevenson. AnFE; BBV; BrPo; GTSL; HBV; HBVY; HT; MCCG; OnPP; OTPC (1946 ed.); PoMa; PoPo; PoRL; ShBV-1; TreFT; ViBoPo
Give to the Living. Ida Goldsmith Morris. WBLP

Give to the Winds Thy Fears. Paul Gerhardt, *tr. fr. German by* John Wesley. SoP; TRV
(Courage.) WGRP
Give unto the Lord, O ye mighty. Psalm XXIX, Bible, *O.T.* AWP; OnPM; PoPo
Give us a good digestion, Lord. A Prayer. *Unknown.* STF
"Give us a song!" the soldiers cried. The Song of the Camp. Bayard Taylor. AA; BeLS; GN; HBV; HBVY; OTPC; WBLP
(Song in Camp, The) BBV (1923 ed.)
Give us a virile Christ for these rough days! A Virile Christ. Rex Boundy. ChIP; MaRV; OQP; TRV; WGRP
Give us a watchword for the hour. Evangelize! Henry Croker. BLRP; SoP
Give us a wrack or two, Good Lard. The Wreckers' Prayer. Theodore Goodridge Roberts. OBCV; PeCV
Give us from dawn to dark. The Bush. James Lister Cuthbertson. BoAu
Give Us Great Dreams. Marie LeNart. OQP
Give us Jesus Christ, the Carpenter. Comrade Christ. Verne Bright. ChIP; OQP
Give Us Men! Edward Henry Bickersteth. BLPA; MaRV
Give Us Men. Josiah Gilbert Holland. *See* God Give Us Men.
Give us our daily bread. Our Daily Bread. Adelaide Anne Procter. JKCP
Give Us Sober Men. Walter E. Isenhour. STF
"Give Us This Day Our Daily Bread." Maltbie D. Babcock. MaRV; SoP; TRV
(Our Daily Bread.) OQP
Give us time. Town. Alfred Starr Hamilton. QAH
Give Way. Donald Finkel. NePoEA-2; PPON
Give Way! Charlotte Perkins Gilman. WGRP
Give way to the man coming at you. Give Way. Donald Finkel. NePoEA-2; PPON
Give Way, Ye Gates. Theodore Roethke. FiMAP; NMP; OPoP
Give ye good-den. Wait's Carol. Barbara Young. MoSiPe
Giveaway, The. Phyllis McGinley. PoRA
Given a roof, and a taste for rations. Life in Laconics. Mary Mapes Dodge. BOHV
Given in marriage unto thee. Emily Dickinson. MWA-2
Given, not lent. Unto Us a Son Is Given. Alice Meynell. ChIP; GTBS; JKCP; MoRP; OQP; PoRL; StJW
Given Over. Thomas Woolner. VA
Given the "Cat," it was not only that he ran. The Cat-o'-Nine-Tails. John Blight. BoAV; NeLNL
Given this light. Ostia Antica. Anthony Hecht. NePA
Givenchy village lies a wreck, Givenchy church is bare. A Song of the Old Days. Patrick MacGill. MaRV
Giver of All. Christopher Wordsworth. MaRV
(Giving to God.) SoP; VA
Giver of bliss and pain, of song and prayer. William Alexander Percy. *Fr.* Epilogue: "O God, author of song." TrPWD
Giver of good and perfect gifts. Prayer at a Wedding. Charles Carroll Albertson. SoP
Giver of Life, The. *Unknown, tr. fr. Dahomean song by* Frances Herskovits. EaLo
Giving. William F. Kirk. MaRV
Giving. Adelaide Anne Procter. SoP
Giving. *Unknown.* PoToHe
(Life's Joy.) STF
Giving a Heart. *Unknown. See* Popular Songs of Tuscany.
Giving and Forgiving. Thomas Grant Springer. PoToHe
Giving and Taking. James Kirkup. EaLo
Giving-In, The. Jon Anderson. YAP
Giving In, The. Marvin Bell. YAP
Giving oneself to the dentist or doctor who is a good one. The Kind of Act of. Robert Creeley. NeAP
Giving Thanks. *Unknown.* PEDC
Giving to God. Christopher Wordsworth. *See* Giver of All.
Glabrous girl and hispid boy, The. and W. Craddle. WhC
Glacier, The. Louis MacNeice. AnFE
Glacier song in the keen wind of April. Mozart. Charles Higham. MuSP
Glad and blithe mote ye be. A Hymn of the Incarnation. *Unknown.* MeEL
Glad, but not flush'd with gladness. Swinburne. *Fr.* Before the Mirror. OBEV (new ed.)
Glad day. W. Graham Robertson. HBV
Glad Day. Louis Untermeyer. TrJP
Glad Earth. Ella C. Forbes. YeAr
Glad harvest greets us, The; brave toiler for bread. Song of the Harvest. Henry Stevenson Washburn. OHIP
Glad Home-coming, The. A. B. Simpson. SoP
Glad that I live am I. A Little Song of Life [*or* A Song of Life, *or* The Sun and the Rain]. Lizette Woodworth Reese. BrR; FaPON; HBMV; MPB; OTD; PoMa; ThGo; TiPo (1959 ed.); TreFT
Glad Tidings from the King of Kings. Charles Coffin, *tr. fr. Latin by* John Chandler. BePJ
Glad Time Is at His Point Arrived. Ben Jonson. *Fr.* Masque of Hymen. HW
Glad World. Robert D. FitzGerald. ACV
Glad Young Chamois, The. Burges Johnson. TSW
Gladde Things. *Unknown.* TiPo (1952 ed.)
Glade, The. Edward Shanks. LO
Gladness of the May, The. Wordsworth. YeAR
Gladstone. Julian Symons. WaP
Gladstone was still respected. Yeux Glauques. Ezra Pound. *Fr.* Hugh Selwyn Mauberley. CMoP; MoAmPo (1962 ed.)
Glamor of regret is on the brown, A. The Captains. Walter Adolphe Roberts. PoNe
Glamour on the phanton shore, A. At Les Eboulements. Duncan Campbell Scott. VA
Glance, The. George Herbert. AnAnS-1; MaMe; MeP
Glance at the Album, A. Gray Burr. CoPo
Glance behind the Curtain, A, *sel.* James Russell Lowell.
Labor. MaRV
Work. PEDC; PoSC
Glasgerion. *Unknown.* BaBo (A *and* B *vers.*); ESPB (A *and* B *vers.*); OBB; OxBB; ViBoFo
Glasgow Peggie. *Unknown.* BaBo; ESPB
Glasgow Street. William Montgomerie. OxBS
Glass. Robert Francis. PP
Glass antique, 'twixt thee and Nell. Nell Gwynne's Looking Glass. Laman Blanchard. HBV; VA
Glassblower, The. Geoffrey Johnson. NYTB
Glass Blower, The. James Scully. NYBP; TwCP
Glass Bubbles, The. Samuel Greenberg. LiTA; NePA
Glass Dialectic. Howard Nemerov. WaP
Glass falls lower, The. Sad Green. Sylvia Townsend Warner. MoBrPo
Glass Houses. E. A. Robinson. MoRP
Glass of Beer, A. James Stephens, *after the Irish of* David O'Bruaidar. AnFE; CBEP; CMoP; DTC; ExPo; FiBHP; LiTM; OBMV; SeCePo; ShBV-4; SiTL; TreFT; WhC
(Righteous Anger.) AnIV; LiTW; MoAB; MoBrPo; PoPL
Glass of Government, The, *sel.* George Gascoigne.
First Chorus, The. Po
Glass of Water, The. Wallace Stevens. AP; AtBAP; CABA; CoBMV; MoAB; MoAmPo (1950 ed.); MoPo; OxBA
Glass Poem. Karl Shapiro. PoIE
Glass tells, The. The wood. Autumn. Stan Rice. QAH
Glass Town, The. Alastair Reid. NYBP
Glass was the street, in tinsel peril. Emily Dickinson. OxBA
Glasses are raised, the voices drift into laughter, The. Pub. Julian Symons. LiTB; LiTM; WaP
Glauce. Aubrey Thomas De Vere. IrPN
Glaucopis. Richard Hughes. OBMV
Glaucous-Gull's Death, The. Daniel James O'Sullivan. NeIP
Glaucus. Sidney Keyes. FaBoMo
Glaukos, why is it you and I are honored beyond all men. Sarpedon to Glaukos. Homer, *tr. by* Richmond Lattimore. *Fr.* The Iliad, XII. WaaP
Gleam of gold in gloom and grey, A. Allegra Agonistes. Grace Fallow Norton. NP
Gleam of the camp fires of emigrant trains, The. The Land We Adore. *Unknown.* SGR
Gleaming in silver are the hills! Washed in Silver. James Stephens. ELU
Gleaner, The. Vivian L. Virtue. PoNe
Glee for King Charles. Sir Walter Scott. *Fr.* Woodstock, *ch.* 20. CoBE; EPN
Glee for Winter, A. Alfred Domett. DD; HBV; VA
Glee—The Ghosts. Thomas Love Peacock. *Fr.* Melincourt. ViBoPo
Glee—the great storm is over. Emily Dickinson. MWA-1
Glen-Almain, the Narrow Glen. Wordsworth. GTSL
Glen of Silence, The. "Hugh MacDiarmid." NeBP
Glenara. Thomas Campbell. HBV
Glenaradale. Walter Chalmers Smith. OBEV (new ed.); OBVV; PeVV
Glenarm. John Lyle Donaghy. NeIP

Glenfinlas; or, Lord Ronald's Coronach. Sir Walter Scott. GoTL
Glenkindie. William Bell Scott. HBV; VA
Glenlogie; or Jean o' Bethelnie, *diff. versions.* *Unknown.* BuBa; ESPB; GN; HBV; OBB
Glenn Miller and I were heroes. Chorus. Jack Kerouac. *Fr.* Mexico City Blues. NeAP
Glens, The. John Hewitt. NeIP
Glide gently, thus for ever glide. Remembrance of Collins. Wordsworth. PeER
Glide Soft, Ye Silver Floods. William Browne. *Fr.* Britannia's Pastorals. ElL
Gliding over Hialeah, we wave goodbye. High. John Perreault. ANYP
Glimpse. Pearl Cleage. WSL
Glimpse, A. Frances Cornford. OBMV
Glimpse, The. George Herbert. MaMe
Glimpse, A. Walt Whitman. AmPP (4th ed.); MWA-1; NePA; OxBA
Glimpse in Autumn. Jean Starr Untermeyer. StVeCh (1940 ed.); TSW
Glimpse of a Plain Cap, The. *Unknown,* *tr. fr. Chinese by* Arthur Waley. *Fr.* Shi King. LiTW
Glimpse of Beauty, A. Chien Liang Tse, *tr. fr. Chinese by* Henry H. Hart. OnPM
Glimpse of Glory, A. *Unknown.* SoP
Glimpse of the Body Shop, A. Stephen Berg. NaP
Glimpse of Time, A. Laurence Binyon. AnFE
Glimpse through an interstice caught, A. A Glimpse. Walt Whitman. AmPP (4th ed.); MWA-1; NePA; OxBA
Glimpses. Roy Helton. HBMV
Glimpses #xii, *sel.* Lawrence McGaugh.
"Old man walks to me, The." BOLo
Glints of the Year—from a Window. Thomas Caulfield Irwin. IrPN
Glion!—Ah, twenty years, it cuts. Obermann Once More. Matthew Arnold. EPN; PoEL-5; PoVP
Glistering high in the midnight sky the starry rockets soar. Dewey and His Men. Wallace Rice. PAH
Glitter of Pebbles. Dom Moraes. ACV
Glittering leaves of the rhododendrons, The. Green Symphony. John Gould Fletcher. AnFE; APA; CoAnAm; MAP; MAPA; MoAmPo; MoVE
Glittering roofs are still with frost, The. A January Morning. Archibald Lampman. ACV; OBCV
Glittering shows of Flora's dames, The. A Proper Ditty. *Unknown.* ReIE
Gloaming. Robert Adger Bowen. HBV
Gloaming, The. Henry W. Frost. SoP
Gloire de Dijon. D. H. Lawrence. BrPo; CMoP; ELP; EnLoPo; ErPo; OAEP (2d ed.)
Gloom of death is on the raven's wing, The. The Raven. E. A. Robinson. AWP; JAWP; LiTW; UnS; WBP
Gloom that breathes upon me with these airs, The. A Dark Day. Dante Gabriel Rossetti. The House of Life, LXVIII. MaVP; PoVP; ViPo
Glooms of the live-oaks, beautiful-braided and woven. The Marshes of Glynn. Sidney Lanier. AA; AmePo; AmPP; AnFE; AP; ATP; CoAnAm; CoBA; HBV; LiTA; LiTG; MAmP; MAP; MCCG; NeMA; NePA; OxBA; PG (1933 ed.); PoIE; PoMa; TOP; TreFT; WGRP; WHA
Gloomy and dark art thou, O chief of the mighty Omahas. To the Driving Cloud. Longfellow. ChTr; FaBoEn; MWA-1; Po; PoEL-5
Gloomy grammarians in golden gowns. Of the Manner of Addressing Clouds. Wallace Stevens. AnFE; APA; CoAnAm; QFR
Gloomy hulls, in armour grim, The. The *Temeraire.* Herman Melville. WaaP
Gloomy night before us flies, The. Jefferson and Liberty. *Unknown.* TrAS
Gloomy night embraced the place. A Hymn of the Nativity. Richard Crashaw. *Fr.* In the Holy Nativity. ViBoPo
Gloomy Night Is Gathering Fast, The. Burns. MCCG
Gloomy with wind and driving cloud, the night. Leaving Troy. Thomas Caulfield Irwin. IrPN
Gloria in Excelsis. *Unknown.* WGRP
Gloria, Laus, et Honor. *Unknown.* WHL
Gloria Mundi. Siegfried Sassoon. MoPW
"Gloria Patri," The. John Heywood. ACP
Gloriana's England. Archibald T. Strong. *Fr.* Sonnets of the Empire. BoAu
Glories of Our Blood and State, The. James Shirley. BWP; CavP; CBEP; ChTr; EG; ExPo; ILP; InvP; LiTG; NoP; OBS; PG; PoRA; ReEn; SeEP; TrGrPo; TuPP; ViBoPo; WaaP; YT *Fr.* Ajax and Ulysses.
(Death the Leveller.) FosPo; GTBS; GTBS-D; GTBS-P; GTBS-W; GTSE; GTSL; LiTB; LoBV; MaRV; MemP; OBEV; OtMeF; PoLi; PPON; SeCeV; ShBV-4
(Death's Final Conquest.) HBV
(Dirge, A.) ACP; AnFE; AWP; BEL; EnLit; InPo; JAWP; PoEL-2; TOP; TreFT; WBP
(Equality.) AnEnPo
(Of Death.) SeCL; WHA
(Our Blood and State.) GoBC
(Song.) CBV; FaBoEn
Glories of the world sink down in gloom, The. Sic Transit. Joseph Mary Plunkett. ACP
Glories of the world struck me, made me aria, once, The. The Dream Songs, XXVI. John Berryman. NaP
Glories, Pleasures. John Ford. *Fr.* The Broken Heart, V, III. ViBoPo
(Broken Heart, A.) OnPM
(Dirge: "Glories, pleasures, pomps, delights, and ease.") LoBV
("Glories, pleasures, pomps, delights, and ease.") TuPP
(Song: "Glories, pleasures, pomps, delights, and ease.") OBS
Glorious day when we stand in His presence. A Wonderful Day. A. H. Dixon. SoP
Glorious Game, The. Richard Burton. HBMV
Glorious Gift of God, The. Benjamin Beddome. BePJ
Glorious God, The. Jami, *tr. fr. Persian by* F. Hadland Davis. OnPM
Glorious image of the Maker's beauty, The. Amoretti, LXI. Spenser. SiCE; Sonn
Glorious Mystery. Avis B. Christiansen. SoP
Glorious Name, The. Amos R. Wells. BePJ
Glorious people vibrated again, A. Ode to Liberty. Shelley. BEL; MBW-2
Glorious sun went blushing to his bed, The. Sonnets to Idea, IV. Michael Drayton. Idea's Mirrour, XXV. OBSC
Glorious Survivors, The. A. E. Coppard. FaBoTw
Glorious the day when in arms at Assunpink. Assunpink and Princeton. Thomas Dunn English. MC; PAH
Glorious the Sun in Mid Career. Christopher Smart. *Fr.* A Song to David. FaBoCh; LiTG; LoGBV
Glorious Things of Thee Are Spoken. John Newton. MaRV; SoP; WGRP
Glorious tree is the gray old oak, A. The Oak. George Hill. HH
Glorious Twelfth, The. Robert Greacen. NeIP
Glorious Victory of Navarino, The! *Unknown.* CoMu; FOL
Glorious with scars and rents the battle-banners rise. The Great Cross of Mercy. Theodosia Garrison. PEDC
Glory. D. H. Lawrence. POTE
Glory. Marianne Moore. NYBP
Glory, The. Edward Thomas. POTE
Glory and Enduring Fame. William Gilmore Simms. Sonn
Glory and honor and fame and everlasting laudation. Sherman. Richard Watson Gilder. AA
Glory and loveliness have passed away. To Leigh Hunt, Esq. [*or* Dedication to Leigh Hunt]. Keats. EnRP; OBNC; Sonn; ViBoPo
Glory and the ardour of the stage, The. E. H. W. Meyerstein. *Fr.* Elegy on the Death of Mme Anna Pavlova. UnS
Glory be to God for dappled things. Pied Beauty. Gerard Manley Hopkins. AnEnPo; AnFe; AtP (1953 ed.); AWP; BoLiVe; BrPo; BWP; CABA; CaFP; CBV; CLwM; CMoP; CoBE; CoBMV; DiPo; EaLo; EnL; EnLi-2 (1949 ed.); EnLit; FaBoEn; FaBoMo; FaFP; FlW; GoJo; GoTP; GTBS; GTBS-D; GTBS-P; GTBS-W; ILP; InPo; InvP; LiTB; LiTG; LiTM; MaPo; MaRV; MemP; MoAB; MoBrPo; MoRP; MoVE; NAMP; NeMA; NoP; OAEP (2d ed.); OBEV (new ed.); OBMV; OBNC; PAn; PG (1955 ed.); PoAn; PoDB; PoeP; PoPl; PoPo; PoRA; PoVP; ReMP; ShBV-3; SoP; StP; ThWaDe; TIHL; TreFS; TrGrPo; TRV; ViBoPo; ViPo; ViPP; VP; WaKn; WePo
Glory be to God on high, and on earth peace, good-will towards

men. Gloria in Excelsis. *Unknown.* WGRP
Glory, Glory to the Sun. John Alford. HBMV
Glory Hallelujah! or, John Brown's Body. *Unknown,* *at. to* Charles Sprague Hall. *See* John Brown's Body.
Glory in the Commonplace. Elizabeth Barrett Browning. *Fr.* Aurora Leigh, VII. MaRV
Glory is of the sun, too, and the sun of suns. Glory. D. H. Lawrence. POTE
Glory of and Grace in the Church, The. Edward Taylor. *Fr.* God's Determinations. AnNE; AP; NoP
Glory of Christmas, The. V. P. Drake. SoP
Glory of Early Rising, The. Frank Sidgwick. WhC
Glory of God, The. Psalms, XIX, Bible, *O.T.* *See* Heavens Declare the Glory of God, The.
Glory of God in Creation, The. Thomas Moore. MaRV; OHIP
(Thou Art, O God, *sl. abr.*) TrPWD
Glory of God Revealed in Jesus, The. Second Corinthians, IV: 6, Bible, *N.T.* MaRV
"Glory of Him who moves all things soe'er, The." Dante's Heaven. Dante. *Fr.* Divina Commedia: Paradiso. BoC
Glory of Lincoln, The. Thomas Curtis Clark. PGD
Glory of Love is brightest when the glory of self is dim, The. The True Apostolate. Ruby T. Weyburn. BLRP
Glory of Motion, The. R. St. John Tyrwhitt. VA
Glory of Nature, The. Frederick Tennyson. OBNC
Glory of Patriotism, The. Thomas Moore. SoP
Glory of soundless heaven, wheel of stars. Valediction. John Hall Wheelock. NePoAm
Glory of the beauty of the morning, The. The Glory. Edward Thomas. POTE
Glory of the Day Was in Her Face, The. James Weldon Johnson. BANP; CDC; IDB; PoNe
Glory of the Grass, The. Claire Wallace Flynn. StJW
Glory of the sunset and the night, The. Youth. Preston Clark. HBMV
Glory of Toil, The. Edna Dean Proctor. PGD
Glory of warrior, glory of orator, glory of song. Wages. Tennyson. EPN; OAEP; OQP; PoVP
Glory of Women. Siegfried Sassoon. MMA
Glory, praise, and honor. Gloria, Laus, et Honor. *Unknown* WHL
Glory Road, De. Clement Wood. HBMV; IHA; PFY; YaD
Glory to God and to God's Mother chaste. Sonnet: To Dante Alighieri. Giovanni Quirino. AWP; OnPM
Glory to God in Heaven, Glory! Glory to the Corn! *Unknown.* OnPM
Glory to God who made a man like this! To a Happy Warrior. Wilfrid Scawen Blunt. AnEnPo
Glory to Osiris, the Prince of Everlastingness. He Singeth a Hymn to Osiris, the Lord of Eternity. *Unknown.* *Fr.* Book of the Dead. AWP
Glory to the Corn! *Unknown,* *tr. fr. Russian by* W. R. S. Ralston. OnPM
Glory to the Name of Jesus! A. B. Simpson. BePJ
Glory to Thee [My God] This Night. Thomas Ken. BePJ
(Evening Prayer.) MaRV
Glory to Them. Anderson M. Scruggs. MaRV; OQP
Glory Trail, The. Badger Clark. IHA; SCC; StPo
Glo'ster girls they have no combs. The Codfish Shanty. *Unknown.* SoAmSa
Gloucester Harbor. Elizabeth Stuart Phelps Ward. AA
Gloucester Moors. William Vaughn Moody. AmPP; AP; ATP; FaPL; HBV; HT; MAP; MoAmPo (1942 ed.); OxBA; PFY; TOP; TreFT; WHA
"This earth is not the steadfast place," *sel.* PoFr; WGRP
Glove, The. Harold Bond. NYBP; YAP
Glove, The. Robert Browning. PoVP; StP
Glove, The. Ben Jonson. *Fr.* Cynthia's Revels, IV, i. ElL
Glove, The. Richard Lovelace. *See* Elinda's Glove.
Glove and the Lions, The. Leigh Hunt. BeLS; EnLit; FaPON; GN; HBV; HBVY; HoPM; MaC; OnSP; OTPC; PCD; PoMa; PTK; StP; TreF; WBLP
Glow and the glory are plighted, The. A Nice Correspondent. Frederick Locker-Lampson. HBV
Glow of the restaurant is faked, the dream, The. Reality. Raymond Souster. CaP
Glow-worm, The. Edward Shanks. WHA
Glow-Worm, The Wordsworth. LO
(Among All Lovely Things My Love Had Been.) MyFE
Glowworm in a garden prayed, A. A Very Minor Poet Speaks. Israel Valle. BLPA
Glow-worm-like the daisies peer. Summer. John Davidson. BoNaP
Glow-worm sings her bed-time prayers, The. She-Goat and Glow-Worm. Christian Morgenstern. OA
Glow-Worms, The. Ann Hawkshaw. OTPC (1923 ed.)
Glow-Worms. P. A. Ropes. BoTP
Gluggity Glug. George Colman. *Fr.* The Myrtle and the Vine.
Glugs abide in a far, far land, The. Joi, the Glug. C. J. Dennis. NeLNL
Gluskap's Hound. T. G. Roberts. WHW
Glut on the Market, A. Patrick Kavanagh. *See* Pegasus.
Glutton, The. Robert Graves. CMoP
Glutton, The. William Langland. *See* Glutton and Bat the Brewer.
Glutton. Samuel Rowlands. SiCE
Glutton, The. Karl Shapiro. CBV
Glutton and Bat the Brewer. William Langland. *Fr.* The Vision of Piers Plowman, Passus 5. CoBE
(Glutton, The.) ACP
Glycerin. Frank Lima. ANYP
Glycine's Song. Samuel Taylor Coleridge. *Fr.* Zapolya, II, i. OBEV; OTPC (1946 ed); PoPl; PTK
(Song: "Sunny shaft did I behold, A") BoTP; LO; PoSC
(Sonny Shaft, A.) CEP
Glyph. *Unknown,* *tr. fr. Washoe-Paiute by* Mary Austin. LiTA
Gnarled Riverina Gum-Tree, A. Ernest G. Moll. PoAu-2
Gnarly and bent and deaf's a pos'. Zeke. L. A. G. Strong. MoBrPo
Gnat, The. Joseph Beaumont. CBEP; LoBV; OBS
Gnat. Rosalie Moore. GoTP
Gnat, be my messenger, and fly. To a Gnat. *Unknown.* UnTE
Gnome, The. Harry Behn. FaPON; PDV; SoPo; TiPo (1959 ed.)
Gnomic Lines. *Unknown.* *See* Maxims (Exeter Book).
Gnomic Verse from Cotton Manuscript. *Unknown,* *See* Maxims (Cotton MS.). *tr. fr. Anglo-Saxon by* Richard L. Hoffman.
Gnomic Verses. Blake. *Poems indexed separately by titles and first lines.*
Gnosis. Christopher Pearse Cranch. AmePo; AnAmPo; HBV; ILP
(Enosis.) PoIE
(Stanza from an Early Poem.) AA; AmLP
(Thought.) WGRP
Γνῶθι σεαυτόν—and is this the prime. Self-Knowledge. Samuel Taylor Coleridge. ERoP-1; SeCePo
Gnu up at the zoo, The. Elegy. John Hall Wheelock. NYBP
Gnu Wooing, The. Burges Johnson. HBVY
Go and ask Robin to bring the girls over. Vision by Sweetwater. John Crowe Ransom. AP; CMoP; CoBMV; CrMA; FaBoMo; MoAB; OxBA
Go and Catch a Falling Star. John Donne. *See* Song: "Go and catch a falling star."
Go & choose what sport you will. *Unknown.* SeCSL
Go and dig my grave both long and narrow. Dig My Grave. *Unknown.* OuSiCo
Go and lightly tread. Hermes of the Ways. *Unknown.* OnPM
Go and spy on the sheep. The Good Shepherd. Keidrych Rhys. NeBP
Go and tell Aunt Nancy. The Old Grey Goose. *Unknown.* ChTr
"Go ask Papa," the maiden said. Proposal. *Unknown.* TreFS
Go back, dark blood, to the springs from which you came. The Dream and the Blood. Louis Untermeyer. UnTE
Go back from pistons to the plod of hooves. The Return. Lloyd Frankenberg. NYTB
Go back now; pause to mark. Horizon Thong. George Abbe. GoYe
Go, bear him in thine arms. Shakespeare. *Fr.* King John, IV, iii. PoG
Go bow thy head in gentle spite. To a Lily. James Matthew Legaré. AA; AnAmPo
"Go break to the needy sweet charity's bread." How Long Shall I Give? *Unknown.* BLRP

Go Bring Me Back My Blue-eyed Boy, *with music.* *Unknown.* AS
(London City, *diff. vers.*) AS
"Go bring the captive, he shall die." Hezekiah Butterworth. PAH
Go, burning sighs, unto the frozen heart. The Lover Sendeth Sighs to Move His Suit. Sir Thomas Wyatt. LiTL
Go burrow in your hole. To a Mole. Louise Darcy. NYTB
Go By. Tennyson. *See* Come Not, When I Am Dead.
Go call a careful painter, let him show. Of the French Kings Nativity. Benjamin Harris. SCAP
Go count the stars! Counting. Fenton Johnson. AmNP
Go, Crystal Tears. *Unknown.* ReIE
Go, Cupid, and my sweetheart tell. A Valentine. Eugene Field. PoRL
Go, daughters of Zion. The Death of Tammuz. Saul Tchernichowsky. TrJP
Go dig a hole in the meadow. Darling Cora. *Unknown.* TrAS
Go Down Death (A Funeral Sermon). James Weldon Johnson. AmNP; AnAmPo; MaRV; TRV
Go Down Moses. *Unknown.* AmPP; BoAN-1, *with music;* EaLo; TrAS, *with music;* TreF
Go down, O ruddy sun! Help Us, Moon! *Unknown.* OnPM
Go Down, Ol' Hannah, *diff. versions.* *Unknown.* OuSiCo, *with music;* TTY
Go down to Kew in Lilac-Time. Alfred Noyes. *Fr.* The Barrel Organ. BoTP
Go Down, You Little Red Rising Sun, *with music.* *Unknown.* OuSiCo
Go, dumb-born book. Envoi (1919). Ezra Pound. *Fr.* Hugh Selwyn Mauberley. AmPP (5th ed.); APA; CaFP; CLwM; CMoP; CoAnAm; CoBMV; CTC; GTBS-W; LiTA; LiTM (rev. ed.); MAP; MemP; MoAB; MoAmPo; MoPo; NePA; OxBA; PoIE; SeCeV (1967 ed.); UnPo (3d ed.)
Go Far; Come Near. Walter de la Mare. CoBMV
Go Fetch to Me a Pint o' Wine. Burns. *See* My Bonnie Mary.
Go Fly a Saucer. David McCord. ImOP
"I've seen one flying saucer,"*sel.* FaPON
Go, for they call you, shepherd, from the hill. The Scholar-Gipsy. Matthew Arnold. AnFE; BEL; BWP; CABA; ChTr; EnL; EnLi-2; EnLit; EPN; FaBoEN; FiP; GoTL; GTBS; HBV; ILP; LoBV; MaPo; MasP; MaVP; MBW-2; NoP; OAEP; OBEV; OBNC; OBVV; Po; PoAn; PoE; PoEL-5; PoFS; PoVP; SeCeV; ShBV-4; TOP; UnPo (1st ed.); ViBoPo; ViPo; ViPP; VP
Go, Forget Me. Charles Wolfe. HBV
Go forth, my son. Benediction. Georgia Douglas Johnson. GoSl
"Go Forward." "A. R. G." BLRP
Go from me; I am one of those who fall. Mystic and Cavalier. Lionel Johnson. MoBrPo; SeCePo; ViPP
Go from Me [Yet I feel That I Shall Stand]. Elizabeth Barrett Browning. Sonnets from the Portuguese, VI. DiPo; EPN; GBV; GTSL; HBV; MaRV; MemP; OBEV; OBVV; PG (1955 ed.); PoVP; SoP; TreFS; TrGrPo; VA; ViBoPo; ViPo
(Nevermore Alone.) MaRV
Go from the east to the west, as the sun and the stars direct thee. Arthur Hugh Clough. *Fr.* Hope Evermore and Believe! MaRV
Go, gentlemen, every man unto his charge. Shakespeare. King Richard, III, *fr.* V, iii. FOL
"Go get me some of your father's gold." Pretty Polly. *Unknown.* AS
Go Get the Axe, *with music.* *Unknown.* AS; TrAS
Go get the third johnny head and touch it north. Sis Joe. *Unknown.* OuSiCo
Go get water, water is good to drink. Hymn for Water. Merrill Moore. TrGrPo (1942 ed.)
Go, glorious sun. To The Sun. Pattericke Jenkyn. SeCL
Go, go quaint follies, sugared [*or* queint follies, sugred] sin. Idle Verse. Henry Vaughan. AtBAP; OAEP
Go, happy book, and let my Candia see. To His Mistress; Sending Her the Arcadia. Thomas Beaumont. SeCL
Go, happy Rose, and, interwove [*or enterwove].* *To the Rose. Robert Herrick. HBV; OBS; SeCP*
Go, Hart. *Unknown.* *See* Go, Heart, unto the Lamp of Light.
Go! Heart, Hurt with Adversity. *Unknown.* MeEL
Go, Heart, unto the Lamp of Licht. *Unknown.* GoTS
(Go, Hart.) OxBS
Go I must; when I am gone. To His Tomb-Maker. Robert Herrick. SeCV-1
Go, I will shut the windows. Allienation. Harry Kemp. HBMV
Go idle lines unpolished rude and base. Thomas Watson. *Fr.* The Tears of Fancy. Sonn
Go inside a stone. Stone. Charles Simic. YAP
Go, intercept some fountain in the vein. Upon the Death of the Lord Hastings. Andrew Marvell. MaMe; ReEn
"Go into the highways." Compel Them to Come In. Leonard Dodd. BLRP
Go, labor on; spend and be spent. Zeal in Labor. Horatius Bonar. SoP
Go, let the fatted calf be kill'd. The Welcome. Abraham Cowley. *Fr.* The Mistress. SeCV-1
Go, litel book [*or* bok], go litel my tragedie [*or* myn tregedie]. The Envoy. Chaucer. *Fr.* Troilus and Criseyde. FiP; MyFE; ViBoPo
Go! little bill, and command me hertely. She Saw Me in Church. *Unknown.* MeEL
Go! little bill, and do me recommende. A Love Letter. *Unknown.* MeEL
Go, Little Book. Robert Louis Stevenson. InP; MoBrPo; NeMA; PoRA
(Envoy: "Go, little book, and wish to all.") HBV; MemP; PoRL; TreFT; YT
(Wishes.) OBEV (new ed.); OBVV
Go, little book, and leave me still in doubt. Epilogue to a Book of Verse. Arthur Guiterman. InMe
Go, little book, and to the world impart. To His Book (1691). William Walsh. CEP; CLwM
Go, little book, and wish to all. Go, Little Book [*or* Envoy *or* Wishes]. Robert Louis Stevenson. HBV; InP; MemP; MoBrPo; NeMA; OBEV (new ed.); OBVV; PoRA; PoRL; TreFT; YT
Go, little book: thyself present. To His Book. Spenser. *Fr.* The Shepheardes Calendar. CLwM; ReIE SiCE
Go, little quair. L'Envoy: To His Book. John Skelton. EnRePo
Go Little Ring. *Unknown.* CBEP
Go look in yonder cottage, all deserted and alone. Fair Fannie Moore. *Unknown.* BFSS
Go, lovely boy! to yonder tower. Verses Written during the War, 1756-1763. Thomas Osbert Mordaunt. CBEP; OBEC
Go, Lovely Rose. Edmund Waller. ALV; ATP; AWP; BEL; CaFP; CBEP; CoBE; CTC; EG; EnLi-1; EnLit; EnLoPo; FosPo; GTBS; GTBS-D; GTBS-P; GTBS-W; GTSE; GTSL; HBV; ILP; InPo; JAWP; LiTL; LO; MemP; MeWo; OAEP; OBEV; OuHeWo; PG (1945 ed.); PoAn; PoE; PoFS; PoRA; PoSa; ReEn; SCEP-2; SeCeV; SeCL; StP; TOP; TrGrPo; ViBoPo; WBP; WHA
(Song: "Go [*or* Goe] Lovely Rose.") AnAnS-2; AtBAP; BWP; CABA; CavP; CBV; CEP; CLwM; ELP; ExPo; FaBoEn; ForPo; GoJo; LoBV; MePo; NeHB; NoP; OBS; PoEL-3; PoIE; SeCP; SeCV-1; SeEP; UnPo (3d ed.)
Go, loving [*or* lovely] woodbine, clip with lovely grace. On a Pair of Garters. Sir John Davies. CBEP; EG; SiPS
Go, Magi, on Your Way. *Unknown, tr. fr. French by* Edward Bliss Reed. ChrBoLe
Go make thy garden fair as thou canst. Gardens. *Unknown.* OQP
Go Michael, of Celestial Armies Prince. War in Heaven (The First Battle). Milton. *Fr.* Paradise Lost, VI. ExPo
Go, Muse, unto the Bower. Nicholas Breton. ReIE
Go, my flock, go get you hence. Astrophel and Stella: Ninth Song. Sir Philip Sidney. FCP; SiPS
Go, my songs, seek your praise from the young and from the intolerant. Ité. Ezra Pound. MAP; MoAB; MoAmPo; PP; TwAmPo
Go, my songs, to the lonely and the unsatisfied. Commission. Ezra Pound. CBV; TwCP
Go, Nightly Cares. *Unknown.* EnRePo
Go Not, Happy Day. Tennyson. Maud, Pt. I, xvii. LiTL; OBVV; TOP
(Song: "Go not, happy day.") ATP
Go not into the lofty house. The Lofty House. John Gould Fletcher. MAP; MoAmPo

Go not, my soul, in search of Him. The Indwelling God. Frederick Lucian Hosmer. MaRV; OQP; WGRP
Go not to the hills of Erin. The Wind on the Hills. Dora Sigerson Shorter. HBMV; JKCP
Go not too frequently thy friends to see. Advice to Bores. Abraham ibn Chasdai. TrJP
Go not too near a house of rose. Emily Dickinson. BoLiVe; MAP; MoAB; MoAmPo; MWA-2; NeMA; PoAn
Go now; and with some daring drugg. Temperance, or the Cheap Physitian. Richard Crashaw. MaMe; SeCV-1
Go Now, My Song. Andrew Young. ChTr
Go Out. Eileen Mathias. BoTP
Go out, good ships, across the tide. Ships. Nancy Byrd Turner. SoPo; SUS
Go patter to lubbers and swabs, do ye see. Poor Jack. Charles Dibdin. BeLS; HBV
Go, Piteous Heart. John Skelton. *See* Unfriendly Fortune.
Go, Ploughman, Plough. Joseph Campbell. HBMV; MPB
Go, Pretty Child. Robert Herrick. *See* To His Saviour, a Child; a Present by a Child.
Go, pretty page, with the dimpled chin. The Age of Wisdom. Thackeray. *Fr.* Rebecca and Rowena. ALV; HBV; VA
Go, roads, to the four quarters of our quiet distance. The Evening of the Visitation. Thomas Merton. ISi
Go roll a prairie up like cloth. The Merry Miner. *Unknown.* IHA; RePo; StVeCh
Go, Rose. John Gay. CBEP
Go, Rose, and in her golden hair. To a Rose. Frank Dempster Sherman. AA
Go, Sad Complaint. Charles d' Orléans. *See* Ballade: "O! sely anker, that in thy celle."
Go sad or sweet or riotous with beer. The Old Women. George Mackay Brown. NePoEA-2; OxBS
Go saddle up my milk-white steed. Geordie (C *vers.*). *Unknown.* BaBo
Go seek her out all courteously. James Joyce. Chamber Music, XIII. HW
Go seeker, if you will, throughout the land. Burning in the Night. Thomas Wolfe. AmFN
Go, Silly Worm. Joshua Sylvester. CBEP; ElL
(Omnia Somnia.) OBS
Go Sleep, Ma Honey. Edward D. Barker. AA
Go Slow. Langston Hughes. LiTM (1970 ed.)
Go, smiling souls, your new-built cages break. *See* Goe smiling souls. . .
Go, songs, for ended is our brief, sweet play. Envoy. Francis Thompson. CoBE; FaBV; HBV; MoBrPo; PoVP
Go, soul [*or* Goe, soule], the body's [*or* bodies] guest. The Lie [*or* The Soul's Errand]. Sir Walter Ralegh. AtBAP; CBEP; ChTr; CTC; EnLi-1 (1949 ed.); EnRePo; EP; ExPo; FCP; ForPo; HBV; InvP; LiTB; MasP; NoP; PoEL-2; PoFr; OAEP; OBSC; PoFS; PoIE; PPON; QFR; ReEn; SeCeV; SiCE; SiPS; SiTL; TreFT; TrGrPo; TuPP; ViBoPo; WGRP; WoL
Go, speed the stars of thought. Intellect. Emerson. OnPM
"Go steal your father's weight in gold." Lady Isabel and the Elf-Knight (B *vers.*) *Unknown.* ViBoFo
Go, stir the brazier coals, my child. The Brazier Coals. Miguel de Unamuno. *Fr.* Domestic Scenes. LiTW; OnPM; WoL
Go Take the World. Jay Macpherson. MoCV; OBCV
Go tell Amynta gentle swain. A Song. Dryden. *Fr.* Sylvoe. CavP
Go tell Aunt Rhody [*or* Aunt Nancy *or* old Nancy]. The Old Gray Goose. *Unknown.* ABF; FTB; LaNeLa
Go tell the Spartans, thou that passest by. Thermopylae [*or* Inscription to Spartans Dead at Thermopylae]. Simonides, *tr. by* William L. Bowles. AWP; JAWP; TreF; WBP
Go Tell Them that Jesus Is Living. *Unknown.* BePJ; SoP
Go ter sleep, go ter sleep. Go to Sleepy. *Unknown.* TrAS
Go, Thames, and tell the busy town. Written at Mr. Pope's House at Twickenham. George Lyttelton. CEP
Go, the rich Chariot instantly prepare. The Muse. Abraham Cowley. BEL; Po
Go, then, and join the murmuring city's throng. To a Friend. William Lisle Bowles. Sonn
Go then, my dove, but now no longer mine. Cotton Mather. SCAP
Go thou and seek the House of Prayer! Written on a Sunday Morning. Robert Southey. BEL
Go Thou, That Vainly Dost Mine Eyes Invite. Henry King. SeCL
Go thou thy way, and I go mine. Mizpah. Julia A. Baker. BLPA; FaBoBe; NeHB; OQP
Go Thou to Rome. Shelley. *Fr.* Adonais. ChTr
Go through the gates with closed eyes. Close Your Eyes! Arna Bontemps. AmNP; CDC; Kal; PoNe
Go thy waies since thou wilt goe. *Unknown.* SeCSL
Go thy way, eat thy bread with joy, and drink thy wine with a merry heart. Live Joyfully. Ecclesiastes, Bible, O.T. TreFS
Go to Bed. *Unknown.* ChTr
("Go to bed first.") OxNR; PPL; RIS
Go to bed early—wake up with joy. *Unknown.* BoTP
Go to bed late. *Unknown.* OxNR
Go to bed, Tom. *Unknown.* OxNR
Go to Dark Gethsemane. James Montgomery. ChIP; SoP
(Christ Our Example in Suffering.) HBV
Go to him, ah, go to him, and lift your eyes aglow to him. To Her—Unspoken. Amelia Josephine Burr. HBV
"Go to jail. Go directly to jail. Do not pass go. Do not collect $ 200.00." The Book of Merlin. Jack Spicer. CoPo
Go to Sleep. Karl Simrock, *tr. fr. German by* Louis Untermeyer. RIS
(German Slumber Song.) GoTP
Go to sleep, McKade. Evening Song. Kenneth Fearing. CMoP
Go to sleep, my son. *See* Fais dodo, mon fils.
Go to sleep—though of course you will not. A Goodnight. William Carlos Williams. MoAB; MoAmPo
Go to Sleepy, *with music.* *Unknown.* AS, *longer vers.*; TrAS
Go to the Ant. Proverbs, Bible, *O.T.* *See* Reproof, A.
Go to the Shine That's on a Tree. Richard Eberhart. FiMAP; UnS
Go to the western gate, Luke Havergal. Luke Havergal. E. A. Robinson. AA; AmePo; AmP; AmPP; AP; AWP; CaFP; CoBA; CoBMV; CrMA; ForPo; ILP; InPo; JAWP; LiTA; LiTM (rev. ed.); MAmP; MAP; MoAB; MoAmPo; MoPo; MoVE; NePA; PFY; Po; PoDB; PoEL-5; PoIE; PoRA; QFR; SiSw; TreFT; UnPo (3d ed.)
Go up unto the mountain of blessing. Up, Then Down. *Unknown.* SoP
Go, Valentine, and tell that lovely maid. Robert Southey. Sonn
"Go, wash thyself in Jordan—go, wash thee and be clean!" Naaman's Song. Kipling. OtMeF
Go way, Eadie, you dirty dog. Eadie. *Unknown.* OuSiCo
Go 'way, fiddle! folks is tired o'hearin' you a-squawkin'. De Fust [*or* The First] Banjo. Irwin Russell *Fr.* Christmas Night in the Quarters. AA; BLPA; BOHV; HBV; IHA; LHV; PFY
Go 'Way f'om Mah Window. *Unknown.* ABF AS
"Go way, go way," says she, "young man." The Six Questions. *Unknown.* BFSS
Go when the morning shineth. Secret Prayer. John Cross Belle. STF
Go Where Glory Waits Thee. Thomas Moore. OBNC; TreFS
Go with your tauntings, go. Song. John Clare. OBRV
"Go ye." Who—Me? Joan Suisted. SoP
"Go ye into the highways.". Compel Them to Come In. Leonard Dodd. BLRP
Go you, O winds that blow from north to south. To Pandora [*or* Sonnet]. Alexander Craig. ElL; Sonn; TuPP
Goal, The. Frank W. Gunsaulus. MaRV
Goal, The. Ella Wheeler Wilcox. MaRV; OQP
Goal and the Way, The. John Oxenham. PGD
Goal of Intellectual Man, The. Richard Eberhart. MoPo
Goat, The. *Unknown.* *See* Goat and the Three Red Shirts, The.
Goat, The. Roland Young. WhC
Goat and the Three Red Shirts, The. *Unknown.* GSP
(Goat, The.) PoLF
Goat Milkers, The. John Stevens Wade. ThO
Goat month, when piñones are gathered, The. The Months of the Tribe. Howard McCord. YAP
Goat Paths, The. James Stephens. AnIV; AWP; BoPe; CH; GoJo; JAWP; LiTB; OA; OxBI; PG; PoDB; UnPo (3d ed.); WBP; WHA
Goat was nibbling on a vine, A. The Vine and the Goat. Aesop. AWP
Goatherd, The. Grace Hazard Conkling. GaP; TiPo
Goat-herd follows his flock, The. Juan Quintana. Alice Corbin. HBMV; NP

Goats. C. E. S. Wood. AnEnPo
Goblet of Life, The. Longfellow. MWA-1
Goblin, The. Rose Fyleman. BoTP; TiPo
Goblin Feet. J. R. R. Tolkien. FaPON; PoMS
Goblin has a wider mouth, The. How to Tell Goblins from Elves. Monica Shannon. FaPON; TiPo
Goblin, A, lives in our house, in our house, in our house. The Goblin. Rose Fyleman. BoTP; TiPo
Goblin lives in the chimney place, A. Fire on the Hearth. Rowena Bennett. RePo
Goblin marked his monarch well, The. The First Quest [*or* The Fay's Departure]. Joseph Rodman Drake. *Fr.* The Culprit Fay. AA; GN
Goblin Market. Christina Rossetti. AnFE; AtBAP; DTo; GoTL; OAEP; OnSP; PAn; PoVP; ViPo; VP
"Morning and evening," *sel.* BoTP
Goblinade, A. Florence Page Jaques. TiPo
Goblins on the doorstep. This Is Halloween. Dorothy Brown Thompson. BrR; TiPo; YeAr
Goblin's Song, The. James Telfer. ChTr
God. Gamaliel Bradford. MaRV; TRV; WGRP
God. Catherine Cate Coblentz. OQP
God. Emerson. *Fr.* Woodnotes, Pt. II. OQP
God, *sel.* Alexander McLachlan.
"Hail, Thou great mysterious Being!" CaP
God. Harold Monro. *Fr.* Dawn. WGRP
God. Isaac Rosenberg. MoPo
God. John Banister Tabb. MaRV; TreFT
God. James Cowden Wallace. *See* God the Omniscient.
God!/ glad I'm black. Blue Black. Bloke Modisane. PBA
God, a god sits on my hearth, A. The God on the Hearth. Katharine Tynan. BoPe
God, a man at Yale, adopted a monkey. Monkey. Josephine Miles. FiMAP; LiTM (1970 ed.)
God above, for man's delight, The. A New Ballade of the Marigolde [*or* The Marigold]. William Forrest. CoMu; PoLi
God Alone Suffices. St. Theresa of Avila. *See* Lines Written in Her Breviary.
God and I in space alone. Illusion. Ella Wheeler Wilcox. WGRP
God and Man. Samuel Hazo. ELU
God and Man. S. A. Nagel. MaRV
God and the devil in these letters. The Postman's Bell Is Answered Everywhere. Horace Gregory. MoAmPo; MoVE; NYBP
God and the devil still are wrangling. For a Mouthy Woman. Countee Cullen. ShM
God and the Fairies, be true, be true! For a Child Named Katherine. Louise Townsend Nicholl. SP
God and the Holy Ghost. D. H. Lawrence. MoRP
God and the Soldier. *Unknown.* TreFS
God and the Soul, *sels.* John Lancaster Spalding.
At the Ninth Hour. AA
Et Mori Lucrum. AA
Nature and the Child. AA
Starry Host, The. AA; HBV
Void Between, The. AA
God and the Strong Ones. Margaret Widdemer. HBMV; PoFr; SoP
God and Yet a Man, A? *Unknown.* NoP
("God and yet a man, A?") EnPo
(The Divine Paradox.) MeEV; PoIE
(Wit Wonders.) MeEL
God Answers Prayer. Eliza M. Hickok. *See* This I Know.
God appears, and God is Light. Blake. *Fr.* Auguries of Innocence. TRV
God approached dissolves into the air, The. Doctrinal Point. William Empson. AtBAP; ToPo
God! ask me not to record your wonders. Scholfield Huxley. Edgar Lee Masters. *Fr.* Spoon River Anthology. LiTA; MoPo; TrPWD
God bade me go when I would stay. His Way. *Unknown.* SoP
God bade the birds break not the silent spell. The Thrush. Laura Benét. HBMV
God banish from your house. Benediction. Stanley Kunitz. MoRP
God be here, God be there. *Unknown.* OxNR
God Be in My Head. *Unknown.* *Fr.* Sarum Primer. BoC; EaLo; MaRV; OxBoCh; PoLi; TRV
(God with Us.) TreFT
(Hymnus.) ChTr
(Knight's Prayer, The.) BoTP
(Mihi Adhaerere Deo Bonum Est.) PG (1955 ed.)
God be merciful unto us, and bless us. Let the Nations Be Glad. Psalm LXVII, Bible, *O.T.* FaPON; OnPM
God be praised. Working with God. "George Eliot." *Fr.* Stradivarius. MaRV; TRV
God be thanked the place is here. Joseph and the Shopkeeper. *Unknown.* ChrBoLe
God be with the night that's gone! The Vanished Night. Niall MacMurray. KiLC
God be with thee, my belovèd,—God be with thee! A Valediction. Elizabeth Barrett Browning. HBV
God Be with You. *Unknown.* PoToHe (new ed.)
God be with you in the Springtime. Through the Year. Julian S. Cutler. BLPA
God be with you in your need! Resurgat. A. S. Cripps. BoSA
God Be with You till We Meet Again. J. E. Rankin. TreFS
God behind the Veil. Jami, *tr. fr. Persian by* F. Hadland Davis. OnPM
God, bless all little boys who look like Puck. Blessing on Little Boys. Arthur Guiterman. TrPWD
God Bless America. Irving Berlin. PTK; TreFT
God bless my little kitchen. A Kitchen Prayer. M. Petersen. STF
God bless my little one! how fair. My Little One. Edgar Fawcett. SoP
God bless our country's emblem. Our Country's Emblem. *Unknown.* WBLP
God bless our dear United States. The People's Prayer. Amos R. Wells. SoP
God Bless Our Home. Robert Freeman. MaRV; SoP
God bless our meat. *Unknown.* OxNR
God Bless Our Native! *Sts.* 1-2, Siegfried A. Mahlmann, *tr. fr. German by* Charles Timothy Brooks *and* John S. Dwight; *st.* 3, William E. Hickson. MaRV
(Our Country, *sts.* 1-2.) SoP
(Our Native Land, *sts.* 1-2.) PEDC
God bless pawnbrokers. Pawnbrokers. Marguerite Wilkinson. HBMV
God bless the craft of Clanranald. Birlinn Chlann-Raghnaill. Alexander MacDonald. GoTS
God bless the field and bless the furrow. The Robin's Song. *Unknown, at. to* C. Lovat Fraser. BoTP; MoShBr
God Bless the Flag. *Unknown.* PoRL
God bless the King—I mean the Faith's defender. A Jacobite Toast [*or* Extempore Verses *or* A Toast *or* Which Is Which]. John Byrom. BOHV; HBV; OBEC; OtMeF; ViBoPo
"God bless the man who first invented sleep!" Early Rising. John Godfrey Saxe. AnNE; BOHV; HBV; InMe; PoLF; WhC
God bless the master of this house,/ The mistress also. Christmas Carol [*or* Good-Bye *or* A Grace]. *Unknown.* BoTP; BrR; ChBR; MoShBr; OHIP; OxNR; RePo; SiSoSe; StVeCh; TiPo; YaCaBo
God bless the master of this house, and all that are therein. The Singers in the Snow. *Unknown.* OHIP
God bless thee and keep thee thro' the coming days. A New Year's Wish. "J. H. S." BLRP
God bless this food, and bless us all. *Unknown.* BLRP
God Bless This House ("God bless this home and those who love it"). *Unknown.* SoP
God bless this house from thatch to floor. *Unknown.* OxNR
God Bless You. *Unknown.* PoToHe
God Bless You, Dear, To-Day! John Bennett. AA; HBV
God bless your house this holy night. This Holy Night. Eleanor Farjeon. ChBR
God braced me with His firm hand. The Tool of Fate. "Yehoash." TrJP
God breathe a blessing on. Bestiary. A. M. Klein. OBCV
God broke the years to hours and days. As Thy Days So Shall Thy Strength Be. "George Klingle." BLRP; TRV
God broke upon this upturned field; trees. Body of a Rook. David Wevill. MoCV
God! but this rain-sweet greenness shakes the heart. Soon with the Lilac Fades Another Spring. Patrick MacDonogh. OxBI
God called the nearest angels who dwell with Him above. The Two Angels. Whittier. AA

God came to Abram. Ballad of the Trial of Sodom. Vernon Watkins. MoRP
God Cares. Helen Annis Casterline. BLRP
God Cares. "Marianne Farningham." BLRP
(He Careth.) SoP; WBLP
God cares! How sweet the strain. God Cares. Helen Annis Casterline. BLRP
God Comforts. *Unknown.* SoP
God conceived the world, that was poetry. God's Work. Charlotte Cushman. TreFT
God counts the sorrows of his saints. God Comforts. *Unknown.* SoP
God counts time not by minutes nor by days. In His Sight. Anna R. Baker. OQP
God created his image. Fill and Illumined. Joseph Ceravolo. ANYP
God Does Do Such Wonderful Things. Angela Morgan. TRV
God Doeth All Things Well. *Unknown.* STF
God Don't Like It, *with music.* *Unknown.* OuSiCo
God don't want no coward soldiers. God's Goin' to Set This World on Fire (B *vers.*). *Unknown.* AS
God doth dwell in men, from th' blessed seats, A. In Consort to Wednesday, Jan. 1st, 1701. Richard Henchman. SCAP
God doth not bid thee wait. Wait Patiently for Him. Frances Ridley Havergal. SoP
God dreamed—the suns sprang flaming into place. Creation. Ambrose Bierce. AA; LHV; PFY
God ever keeps a watchful eye. God's Symphony. Phyllis C. Michael. SoP
God Everywhere. Abraham ibn Ezra, *tr. fr. Hebrew by* "D. E. de L." TrJP
God fashioned the ship of the world carefully. The Black Riders, VI. Stephen Crane. AP
God fills my being to the brim. Doxology. Jessica Powers. JKCP (1955 ed.)
God for You, A. Marion Strobel. NP
God-forgotten. Thomas Hardy. BEL; PoVP; TOP; ViPo (1962 ed.); VP
God gave all men all earth to love. Sussex. Kipling. HT; ViPP
God gave His children memory. Roses in December. G. A. Studdert-Kennedy. BLPA
God gave me eyes that I might thrill. My Wealth. Frank St. Way. SoP
God gave my son in trust to me. My Son. James D. Hughes. BLPA
God gave my world to me. My World. Chauncey R. Piety. MaRV; OQP
God gave the pig. Ode of Lament. Randolph Jeck. WhC
God girt her about with the surges. New Zealand. William Pember Reeves. BoAu
God, give me back the simple faith. A Prayer for Faith. Margaret E. Sangster. PoToHe
God Give Me Joy. Thomas Curtis Clark. OQP
God, give me love! I do not only pray. A Prayer for Love. Elsa Barker. OQP
God, give me speech, in mercy touch my lips. The Unutterable Beauty. G. A. Studdert-Kennedy. TrPWD
God, give me sympathy and sense. Prayer. Margaret Bailey. SoP; TRV
God Give to Men ("God give the yellow man"). Arna Bontemps. BANP; CDC; PoNe (1970 ed.)
God Give Us Men! Josiah Gilbert Holland. BLPA; NeHB; OQP; PaA; PAL; PoRL; TreF; WBLP
(Day's Demand, The.) MaRV
(Give Us Men.) SoP
(Wanted.) BoPo; PoMa; TrPWD; TRV
God give us women, women of such mould. Lest We Lack True Men. *Unknown.* SoP
God give you faith this coming year! Invocation for the New Year. Margaret D. Armstrong. STF
"God give you peace!" Your happy lay. Joculator Domini. Sister Mary John Frederick. GoBC
God gives not kings the style of gods in vain. The Argument of the Book. James I, King of England. Sonn
God gives so much of beauty. Early Summer Thought. Marie J. Post. SoP
God gives them sleep on ground, on straw. Roger Williams. SCAP
God gives to you another year. The New Year. *Unknown.* STF
God gives us joy that we may give. Giving [*or* Life's Joy]. *Unknown.* PoToHe; STF
God, God, be lenient her first night there. Prayer for a Very New Angel. Violet Alleyn Storey. BLPA; TreFS
God grant me privacy. Morning Prayer. Nissim Ezekiel. ACV
God grant that all who watch today. A Shining Hope. Julia H. Thayer. OQP
God grant that I may never be. Prayer in April. Sara Henderson Hay. MaRV; OQP; TrPWD
God grant thee thine own wish, and grant thee mine. John Donne. MaMe
God, grant to us Thy blessed Gift again. Bartimeus. Laura Simmons. ChIP
God grant us wisdom in these coming days. A New Earth. John Oxenham. MaRV
God granted, God denies. Frustration. Elizabeth Daryush. QFR
God 'graves cryptic script with inexorable pen. Palimpsest. Hyman Edelstein. CaP
God had called us, and we came. The Blue-Flag in the Bog. Edna St Vincent Millay. AnAmPo
God has a way of making flowers grow. In Desert Places. Sister Mary Madeleva. GoTP
God has His best thing for the few. God's Best [*or* His Best]. Albert Benjamin Simpson. SoP; STF
God has His times: No power of man. On Time with God. C. D. Nutter. STF
God has no end of material. Little Things. *Unknown.* STF
God has power, A. But can a mere man follow. The Poet. Rainer Maria Rilke. OnHM
"God has so many singing birds." The Last Song. Eileen Duggan. CAW
God Has Spoken. Paul Verlaine, *tr. fr. French by* John Gray. *Fr.* Sagesse. SyP
(My God Has Spoken.) CAW
God Has Time. Ruth M. Williams. SoP
God hath been patient long. In eons past. The Harvest Waits. Lloyd Mifflin. HBV
God hath not promised. What God Hath [*or* Has] Promised. Annie Johnson Flint. BLRP; FaChP; MaRV; SoP; STF; TRV; WBLP
God hath two wings, which he doth ever move. Mercy and Love. Robert Herrick. PoPo; SeCV-1
God, He called John while he was a-writin'. John Was a-Writin'. *Unknown.* OuSiCo
God He rejects all prayers that are sleight. Prayers Must Have Poise. Robert Herrick. LiTB
God Hears Prayer. Ethel Romig Fuller. *See* Proof.
God help the homeless ones who lack this night. Midnight. Margaret E. Sangster. SoP
God help us all to do our part. A Prayer for Mother. *Unknown.* SoP
God, help us see beyond mere race or creed. Prayer for Brotherhood. Viney Wilder. OTD
God Hide the Whole World in Thy Heart. Emerson. *Fr.* Woodnotes, II. OQP
God Holds the Key. J. Parker. SoP
God, how I envy you these great oak roots. A Jew Walks in Westminster Abbey. Aubrey Hodes. TrJP
God, How I Hate You. Arthur Graeme West. MMA
God! how they plague his life, the three damned sisters. The Little Brother. James Reeves. DTC
God, I am traveling out to death's sea. Valley of the Shadow. John Galsworthy. MaRV; OHIP; TrPWD
God I had forgotten how. New York—Albany. Lawrence Ferlinghetti. PoCh
God I love thee in Thy robe of roses. Zebaoth. Else Lasker-Schüler. TrJP
God! I will pack, and take a train. The Old Vicarage, Grantchester. Rupert Brooke. WePo
God, if this were enough. If This Were Faith [*or* If This Were Enough]. Robert Louis Stevenson. BrPo; MaRV; OBNC; OQP; TrPWD; WGRP
God in heaven above, A. The Nativity. Henry W. Frost. SoP
God, in His ages past the dawn of days. Niagara. Edward F. Garesché. JKCP

God, in His infinite wisdom. Acceptance. Langston Hughes. NePoAm-2
God in the Gospel of His Son. God Speaks Through the Bible. Thomas Cotterill. SoP
God in the Nation's Life. *Unknown.* BLRP; WBLP
God in Whom We Trust, The. *Unknown.* STF
God in wrath, A. The Black Riders, XIX. Stephen Crane. AP; NoP
God Incarnate. Ruth M. Williams. BePJ
God Is. Phyllis C. Michael. SoP
God is a distant—stately lover. Emily Dickinson. AmePo; NoP
God is a proposition. Third Enemy Speaks. C. Day Lewis. *Fr.* The Magnetic Mountain. EaLo
God Is at the Anvil. Lew Sarett. HBMV; MaRV; TRV; WGRP
God Is at the Organ. Egbert Sandford. MaRV; OQP
God is beauty. God. Catherine Cate Coblentz. OQP
God is before me, He will be my guide. Why Fear? *Unknown.* SoP
God is coming! Apocalypse. Edith Lovejoy Pierce. MoRP
God Is Faithful. Frances Ridley Havergal. BLRP
God is great and God is good. *Unknown.* BLRP
God Is Here. Madeleine Aaron. MaRV; OQP
God Is in Every Tomorrow. Laura A. Barter Snow. BLRP; SoP; STF
God, is it sinful if I feel. A Prayer. Mary Dixon Thayer. HBMV; TrPWD
God, Is, Like, Scissors. José Garcia Villa. EaLo
God Is Love. Sir John Bowring. FaBoBe; MaRV; NeHB
God is my sheepherd; therefore I can lack nothing. Psalm XXIII, Bible, *O.T.* *Fr.* The Bishops' Bible. ReIE
God Is My Strong Salvation. James Montgomery. MaRV
God Is Near. Oswald J. Smith. SoP
God is never sure He has found. Walking the Wilderness. William Stafford. NaP
God Is Nigh. *Unknown.* TRV
God Is Not Dumb. James Russell Lowell. *Fr.* Bibliolatres. MaRV; OQP; WGRP
God Is One. Panatattu. MaRV
(Unity of God, The.) WGRP
God is One and Alone, and there is none other with him. The One God. *Unknown, tr. fr. Egyptian by* E. A. Wallis Budge. MaRV
God is our refuge and strength. Psalm XLVI, Bible, *O.T.* AWP; MaRV; OnPM; TreFT; TrGrPo; TRV; WGRP
God is our refuge, our strong tow'r. Psalm XLVI, Bible, *O.T., par. by* George Sandys. SoP
God is praise and glory. Psalm of Battle. *Unknown.* *Fr.* The Thousand and One Nights. AWP; JAWP; WBP
God is returned to Earth. Vision: Second Psalm. Clive Matson. ThO
God is shaping the great future of the Islands of the Sea. The Islands of the Sea. George Edward Woodberry. MC; PAH
God Is So Good. Jane Taylor. OTPC (1946 ed.)
God is still glorified. Building in Stone. Sylvia Townsend Warner. MoBrPo
God is the Most High. Muhammedan Call to Prayer. Bilal. TTY
God is the Old Repair Man. The Old Repair Man. Fenton Johnson. AmNP
God is the refuge of His saints. A Refuge and Present Help. Isaac Watts. SoP
God Is There. Walter E. Isenhour. STF
God is very near to me. Presence. Mary E. McCullough. MaRV
God Is with Me. Oswald J. Smith. STF
God Is Working His Purpose Out. A. C. Ainger. BLRP
God, keep a clean wind blowing. A Clean Wind Blowing. *Unknown.* FaChP
God, keep all claw-denned alligators. Prayer for Reptiles. Patricia Hubbell. PDV
God keep my heart attuned to laughter. As I Grow Old. *Unknown.* FaChP; MaRV; OQP
God Keep You. "Madeline Bridges." AA; MaRV
God keep you safe, my little love. My Little Love. Charles B. Hawley. HBV
God Keeps His Word. Phyllis C. Michael. SoP
God Knew. Phyllis C. Michael. SoP
God knew what lay before us. The Best for Us. Olive H. Burnett. STF
God Knoweth. Mary G. Brainard *and* P. P. Bliss. SoP
God Knoweth Best. Emily Donaghy. SoP
God Knoweth Best. *Unknown.* WBLP
(Your Father Knoweth.) BLRP
God Knows. Minnie Louise Haskins. *Fr.* The Gate of the Year. SoP
God Knows. *Unknown.* SoP
God Knows Best. Caroline Atherton Briggs Mason. *See* En Voyage.
God knows how many nights upon her bed. Old Maid. J. U. Nicholson. HBMV
God knows it, I am with you. To a Republican Friend, 1848. Matthew Arnold. EPN; MBW-2; PoFr; PoVP; Sonn; ViPP
God knows, not I, the reason why. Faith. Margaret E. Sangster. FaChP; SoP; TRV
God Knows the Answer. F. B. Whitney. STF
God Knows What He's About. Dale Martin Stone. *See* Shaping of a Disciple, The.
God laid upon my back a grievous load. The Cross a Crown. Amos R. Wells. SoP
God lay dead in heaven. The Black Riders, LXVII. Stephen Crane. AmPP (5th ed.); AP
God Leads the Way. Cleanthes, *tr. fr. Greek by* C. C. Martindale. EaLo
God, let me be a giver. Let Me Be a Giver. Mary Carolyn Davies. PoToHe
God—let me be aware. Awareness. Miriam Teichner. FaChP; MaRV; OQP
God let me find the lonely ones. Prayer for a Day's Walk. Grace Noll Crowell. PoToHe
God, let me flower as I will! Let Me Flower as I Will. Lew Sarett. TrPWD
God! let never soe old a man. Old Robin of Portingale. *Unknown.* ESPB; OBB
God, let our sons this Holy Night. This Holy Night. Gertrude Hanson. ChIP
God, listen through my words to the beating of my heart. Prayer. Marguerittе Harmon Bro. TrPWD
God love you. A Poem for the Old Man. John Wieners. NeAP
God love you now, if no one else will ever. Ode for the American Dead in Korea. Thomas McGrath. NePoEA; PoPl
God loved the world of sinners lost. Love for All. Mrs. M. Stockton. SoP
God Lyaeus. John Fletcher. *Fr.* The Tragedy of Valentinian, V, viii. OBEV
("God Lyaeus, ever young.") OnPM; TuPP; ViBoPo
(Song to Bacchus.) BEL; TOP
God made a little gentian. Emily Dickinson. AA; FaBV
God made bees, and bees made honey. Old Lesson. *Unknown.* TreFT
God made Him birds in a pleasant humour. The Making of Birds. Katherine Tynan. BiS; DD; HBMV; JKCP; OxBI
God made my cathedral. Worship. Ruth Furbee. MaRV
God made my lady lovely to behold. How My Song of Her Began. Philip Bourke Marston. HBV; VA
God made my mother on an April day. My Mother. Francis Ledwidge. HBMV; OHIP
God made the bees. *Unknown.* GoTP
God Made the Country. William Cowper. *Fr.* The Task, I. FiP; PoEL-3
("God made the country, and man made the town.") AnFE; EnRP
(Town and Country.) FaBoEn
God made the wicked Grocer. The Song against Grocers. G. K. Chesterton. CenHV
God made thee perfet, not immutable. Milton. *Fr.* Paradise Lost V. PoFr
God made, they say, the country. City Lights. Karle Wilson Baker. PCD
God made trees. *Unknown.* LO
God make my life a little light. A Child's Prayer [*or* A Child's Hymn]. Matilda Betham-Edwards. OTPC; PRWS; TVC
God-Maker, Man, The. Don Marquis. HBV; WGRP
Sels.
"As the skull of man." OQP
"Yes, nothing seems changeless, but Change." MaRV
God Makes a Path. Roger Williams. MaRV; PAH; SoP; TRV; WGRP
God makes not good men wantons, but doth bring. Good Men Afflicted Most. Robert Herrick. LiTB
God makes sech nights, all white an' still. The Courtin'.

James Russell Lowell. *Fr.* The Biglow Papers. AA; AmePo; AmPP; AnNE; BeLS; BOHV; CoBA; HBV; IHA; InMe; LHV; MCCG; OBVV; StVeCh (1940 ed.); TreFS; YT
God meant me to be hungry. God's Will. Mildred Howells. HBV
God Meets Me in the Mountains. Badger Clark. OQP
God Moves in a Mysterious Way. William Cowper. *See* Light Shining Out of Darkness.
God Moves on the Water, *with music.* *Unknown.* OuSiCo
God Must Be Like That. Kenneth W. Sollitt. SoP
God must have loved the silence, for he laid. Silence. Mavis Clare Barnett. OQP
God never would send you the darkness. The Better Way. *Unknown.* SoP
God of a Universe within Whose Bounds. Katharine L. Aller. MaRV
God of Abraham, God of Isaac, God of Jacob. Fire. M. V. Woodgate. BoC
God of Abraham, of Isaac, and of Jacob. *Unknown,* *tr. fr. Yiddish by* Olga Marx. TrJP
God of All Comfort. *Unknown.* SoP
(God of Comfort.) STF
God of all power and might. Cecil Arthur Spring-Rice. *Fr.* In Memoriam, A. C. M. L. TrPWD
God of Comfort, The. *Unknown.* *See* God of All Comfort.
God of Fair Beginnings, The. The Song of Diego Valdez. Kipling. OtMeF
God of Galaxies, The. Mark Van Doren. ImOP; MoRP
God of Grace and God of Glory. Harry Emerson Fosdick. MaRV
God of grave nights. A Chant Out of Doors. Marguerite Wilkinson. SP; TrPWD
God of light and blossom. Prayer. James P. Mousley. GoYe
God of Love, The—ah, benedicite! The Cuckoo and the Nightingale. Thomas Clanvowe, *tr. by* Wordsworth. MeEV
God of love among the silent flowers, A. The Moment of the Rose. Dunstan Thompson. LiTA
God of love my shepherd is. Twenty-third Psalm. *Unknown, at. to* George Herbert. CBV; MaMe; SeCSL
God of men of gentle grace. Thanksgiving. Grenville Kleiser. SoP
God of Mercy. Evening Prayer. Robert Freeman. SoP
God of Might, God of Right. *Unknown.* TrJP
God of Music dwelleth out of doors, The. Music. Edith M. Thomas. HBV
God of my life! What songs of praise. A Hymn of Praise, on a Recovery from Sickness. Benjamin Colman. SCAP
God of One More Chance, The. *Unknown.* SoP
God of our boyhood, whom we yield. Boy's Prayer. A. B. Ponsonby. MaRV
God of our fathers, known of old. Recessional [*or* Lest We Forget]. Kipling. AWP; BBV; BEL; BLPA; BLRP; BoLiVe; BrPo; CABA; EnLi-2; EnLit; EPN; FaBV; FaFP; GN; GTBS; GTBS-W; GTSL; HBV; HBVY; InP; InPo; JAWP; LiTB; LiTM; MaRV; MCCG; MoBrPo; NeHB; NeMA; OAEP (2d ed.); OBEV; OBNC; OBVV; OHFP; OQP; PoE; PoMa; PoVP; PTK; SoP; TOP; TreF; TrGrPo; TRV; TSW; ViBoPo; ViPP; WBLP; WBP; WGRP; WHA; YAT; YT
God of our fathers, whose almighty hand. National Hymn. Daniel C. Roberts. PaA; PAL
God of our fathers, with bowed heads we come. The War at Home. Willard Wattles. OQP
God of Our Life through All the Circling Years. Hugh Thomson Kerr. MaRV
God of our lives, O hear our prayer. Reconsecration. Dorothy Gould. PGD
God of Sheep, The. John Fletcher. *Fr.* The Faithful Shepherdess, V, v. ElL; FaBoCh; LoGBV
(To Pan.) TrGrPo
God of Summer—I have seen. Touring. David Morton. TrPWD
God of the Earth, the Sky, the Sea. Samuel Longfellow. MaRV; TRV
(God, through All and in You All.) TrPWD
God of the Gallant Trees. "A. W. C." SoP
God of the glowing love, making men brothers. A World-Nation. Earl B. Marlatt. MaRV
God of the Granite and the Rose. A Prayer. Elizabeth Doten. *Fr.* Reconciliation. OQP; TrPWD
God of the Living, The. John Ellerton. *See* Living unto Thee.
God of the Meridian. Keats. StP
God of the Nations. Walter Russell Bowie. MaRV; TrPWD
God of the Nations. John Haynes Holmes. MaRV
God of the Nebulae. Amy Carmichael. FaChP
God of the Open Air, *sel.* Henry van Dyke.
These Are the Gifts I Ask. FaBoBe; NeHB; OQP; TreFT
God of the Prophets. Denis Wortman. MaRV
God of the seasons, hear my parting prayer. The Old Year's Prayer. Minna Irving. PGD
God of the sky, enthroned in azure blue. A Prayer for Aviators. Norman E. Richardson. MaRV
God of the Strong, God of the Weak. Richard Watson Gilder. *See* Hymn: "God of the strong . . ."
God of the vineyard's royal store. The Husbandman. Frances Beatrice Taylor. CaP
God of the World. Israel Najara, *tr. fr. Hebrew by* Israel Abrahams. TrJP
God of things that are, The. Altruism. David Starr Jordan. OQP
God of us who kill our kind! A Prayer of the Peoples. Percy MacKaye. TrPWD, 3 *sts.*; WGRP
God of Visions. Emily Brontë. *See* Plead for Me.
God of War, The. Aeschylus, *tr. fr. Greek.* *Fr.* Agamemnon. PPON
God of War, Money Changer of Dead Bodies, The. Aeschylus, *tr. fr. Greek by* Richmond Lattimore. *Fr.* Agamemnon. WaaP
God of winds, when thou art growne. *Unknown.* SeCSL
God on the Hearth, The. Katharine Tynan. BoPe
God, Our Dwelling Place. Psalms, XC, Bible, *O.T.* MaRV (*Moulton, Modern Reader's Bible*).
(Psalm XC.) AWP
God Our Father. Frederick William Faber. WGRP
There's a Wideness in God's Mercy, *sel.* ThGo, *abr.*; TRV; WBLP, *abr.*
(All-embracing, The.) BLRP; TRV
(God's Mercy.) MaRV
(Heart of the Eternal, The.) OQP
Hymn: "There's a wideness in God's mercy." NBM
God Our Help. *Unknown.* OxBoCh
God Our Refuge. Psalms, XCI, Bible, *O.T.* MaRV (Moulton, Modern Reader's Bible)
(Everlasting Arms, The, *Moulton, Modern Reader's Bible.*) WGRP
("He that dwelleth in the secret place of the Most High.") AWP; WoL
(Mighty Fortress, A.) TrGrPo
God Our Refuge. Richard Chenevix Trench. MaRV; OxBoCh; TreFT
(If There Had Anywhere Appeared.) TrPWD
God, patient of beginnings. A Prayer for the New Year. Violet Alleyn Storey. TrPWD
God pity all the brave who go. God's Pity. Louise Driscoll. MaRV; WGRP
God, pity broken little families. A Prayer for Broken Little Families. Violet Alleyn Storey. PoToHe
God pity eyes that have not seen the dawn. This Is the Tragedy. Helen Frazee-Bower. MaRV
God Pity Him. *Unknown.* STF
God Ploughed. William C. Gannett. SoP
God pours for me His draught divine. Thanks from Earth to Heaven. John Hall Wheelock. HBMV
God Praised for His Goodness and Truth. Isaac Watts. SoP
God Prays. Angela Morgan. MaRV; WGRP
"And the Lord God whispered and said to me," *sel.* OQP
God prosper long our gracious King. An Ode for the New Year. *At. to* John Gay. OxBoLi
God prosper long our noble king. Chevy Chase [*or* The Hunting of the Cheviot]. *Unknown.* BaBo (B *and* C *vers.*); BFSS; EnLi-1 (1949 ed.); ESPB (B *vers.*); GN; HBV; OAEP; TOP; ViBoFo
God Provides. St. Matthew, VI: 26-34, *abr.* Bible, *N.T.* BLRP
God Replies. Job, XXXVIII: 2-41, Bible, *O.T.* TrGrPo
God rest that Jewy woman. Song for the Clatter-Bones. F. R. Higgins. AnIL; LiTB; LiTM; OBMV; OnYI; OxBI; SiTL
God Rest Ye Merry, Gentleman. Dinah Maria Mulock Craik. GN; HH; OHIP; OTPC; PCH, 2 *sts.*; SoP
God Rest You Merry, Gentlemen. *Unknown.* DD; FaFP; HBV;

God (continued)
HBVY; LiTB; MaRV, 4 *sts.*; PTK; TreFS; ViBoPo; YaCaBo, *with music*
God rest you, merry Innocents. A Carol for Children. Ogden Nash. EaLo
God rest you, rest you, rest you, Ireland's dead! To the Dead of '98. Lionel Johnson. HBV
God rules above in Heaven. Rulers. *Unknown.* OnPM
God Said, "I Made a Man." José Garcia Villa. AnFE; CoAnAm; TwAmPo
God said, Let there be light! and there was light. At the Sunrise in 1848. Dante Gabriel Rossetti. PoVP
God Said: Let There Be Sky. James J. Donohue. JKCP (1955 ed.)
God Save Elizabeth. Francis Turner Palgrave. HBV
God save great George our King. God Save the King. *Unknown, at. to* Henry Carey. OBEC
God Save Ireland. Timothy Daniel Sullivan. OnYI
God save our gracious King,/ Long live our noble King. God Save the King. *Unknown, at. to* Henry Carey. HBV; MaRV; TreFS; WBLP
God save our gracious Queen. God Save the Queen. *Unknown.* PTK
God, save our land from that unblessed sedateness. Of Greatness in Teaching. Leslie Pinckney Hill. MaRV
God Save Our President. Francis de Haes Janvier. PaA; PAH; PAL
God Save the Flag. Oliver Wendell Holmes. FaFP; OHFP
God Save the King. *Unknown, at. to* Henry Carey. HBV; MaRV, *st.* 2 *by* William E. Hickson; OBEC, *sl. diff.*; TreFS; WBLP, *sl. diff.*
God save the King, that King that sav'd the land. Benjamin Harris. SCAP
God Save the Nation. Theodore Tilton. AA
God Save the People. Ebenezer Elliott. *See* When Wilt Thou Save the People?
God Save the Queen (*Canadian vers.*). *Unknown.* PTK
God Save the Rights of Man! Ode. Philip Freneau. AmPP (3d ed.); AP; CoBA; PoFr
God Scatters Beauty. Walter Savage Landor. EnRP; EPN
God-seeking. Sir William Watson. WGRP
God send the Devil is a gentleman. The Knight Fallen on Evil Days. Elinor Wylie. MAP; MoAmPo
God send the land deliverance. The Death of Parcy Reed. *Unknown.* BaBo (B *vers.*); ESPB; OBB
God send us a little home. A Prayer for a Little Home. Florence Bone. BLPA; FaBoBe; FaFP; MaRV; NeHB; OQP; PCH; SoP; TreFT
God SendUs Men. Frederick J. Gillman. MaRV
"God send us men with hearts ablaze, *sel.*" TRV
God send us peace, and keep red strife away. At Fredericksburg. John Boyle O'Reilly. MC; PAH
God send us wit to banish far. Peace in the World. John Galsworthy. MaRV; PoLF
God sends his teachers unto every age. Rhoecus. James Russell Lowell. MCCG
God sent his singers upon earth. The Singers. Longfellow. SoP
God sent us here to make mistakes. Mistakes. Ella Wheeler Wilcox. PoToHe
God shield ye, comrades of the road! The Blooming of the White Thorn. Edith M. Thomas. ChrBoLe
God Shows in Your Face. *Unknown.* *See* It's in Your Face.
God sought to give the sweetest thing. A Mother. *Unknown.* SoP
God Sour the Milk of the Knacking Wench. Alden Nowlan. MoCV; PeCV (1967 ed.)
God spake three times and saved Van Elsen's soul. Van Elsen. Frederick George Scott. HBV; VA
God Speaks in All Religions. Thomas Lake Harris. MaRV
God Speaks Through the Bible. Thomas Cotterill. SoP
God speed the year of jubilee. The Triumph of Freedom. William Lloyd Garrison. PoFr
God spoke! and from the arid scene. The Birth of the Flowers. Mary Mcneil Fenollosa. OQP
God spoke once that made your girdle fall, The. Daphne. Selden Rodman. PoNe
God spreads a book before my eyes. God's Book. Edgar Daniel Kramer. OQP
God spreads a carpet soft and green. The Welcome. Arthur Powell. OQP
God strengthen me to bear myself. The Battle Within [*or* Who Shall Deliver Me?]. Christina Rossetti. MaRV; OxBoCh; TRV
God That Doest Wondrously. Moses ibn Ezra, *tr. fr. Hebrew by* Solomon Solis-Cohen. TrJP
God, That Madest All Things. *Unknown.* NoP
God, that madest Earth and Heaven. Vespers. Reginald Heber. SoP
God, that mad'st her well regard her. Dieu Qu'il la Fait. Charles d'Orléans. AWP
God that stopped the sun on high, The. Watch and Pray. Martin Luther. SoP
God the Architect. Harry Kemp. HBMV; MaRV; TRV; WGRP
(To God, the Architect.) TrPWD
God, the Artist. *Unknown, at. to* Angela Morgan. BLPA; PoToHe (new ed.)
God the Holy Spirit. Prayer to the Holy Spirit. E. Margaret Clarkson. SoP
God, the Omnipotent. Henry F. Chorley *and* John Ellerton. MaRV
God the Omniscient. *At. to* James Cowden Wallace, *also to* John Aikman Wallace. BLRP
(God.) SoP; WGRP
(Prayer Moves the Hand that Moves the World, *diff. vers.*) STF
God, thou great symmetry. Envoi. Anna Wickham. MoBrPo; NeMA; TrGrPo (1942 ed.)
God, Thou Hast Made the World Beautiful. Theodosia Pearce. SoP
God, though this life is but a wraith. Prayer. Louis Untermeyer. GoTP; MAP; MaRV; MoAmPo; NeMA; OQP; PoFr; PoMa; StaSt; TOP; TrJP; WGRP; YT
God thought to give the sweetest thing. The Mother [*or* The Gift]. George Newell Lovejoy. DD; PGD
God through All and in You All. Samuel Longfellow. *See* God of the Earth, the Sky, the Sea.
God, to get the clay that stayed me. William Baylebridge. *Fr.* Life's Testament. PoAu-1
God to Man. *Fr.* The Talmud. TrJP
God, to whom we look up blindly. Bayard Taylor. *Fr.* The Poet's Journal. TrPWD
God took a fit of Paradise-wind. Field-Flower. Francis Thompson. PoVP
God Understands. *Unknown.* SoP
God Uses Broken Things. Eva Gray. SoP
God walks in my garden. In a Garden. Martha Snell Nicholson. SoP
God Wants a Man. *Unknown.* BLRP
God wants our best. He in the far-off ages. What Shall We Render. *Unknown.* BLRP
God wants the boys, the merry, merry boys. Who Wants the Boys and Girls? *Unknown.* SoP
God Was in Christ. Second Corinthians, V: 18-21, Bible, *N.T.* TRV
God watches o'er us all the day. The Eyes of God. "Gabriel Setoun." PPL
God, we don't like to complain. Caliban in the Coal Mines. Louis Untermeyer. HBV; MAP; MaRV; MoAmPo; NeMA; PDV; PoMa; PoPl; PoPo; TreFS; TrJP; TRV; WePo
God, what a day it is to be abroad! Out-of-doors. Robert Whitaker. TrPWD
God, what a world, if men in street and mart. True Brotherhood. Ella Wheeler Wilcox. OQP; WBLP
God, when you thought of a pine tree. God, the Artist. *At. to* Angela Morgan. BLPA; PoToHe (new ed.)
God, who commanded the light to shine out of darkness. The Glory of God Revealed in Jesus. Second Corinthians, Bible, *N.T.* MaRV
God who created me. Prayers [*or* A Boy's Prayer]. Henry Charles Beeching. BoTP; GN; MaRV; OBEV; OBVV; OTPC (1946 ed.); PoRL; SD; VA
God, who devisedst man who then devised. Prayer for the Age. Myron H. Broomell. TrPWD
God who formed the mountains great, The. All Nature Has a Voice to Tell. J. Gilchrist Lawson. BLRP
God, who had made you valiant, strong and swift. Maurice Baring. *Fr.* In Memoriam, A. H. CAW
God who had such heart for us, The. The Cool Gold Wines of Paradise. Robert Farren. AnIV; SeCePo

God, Who Hath Made the Daisies. E. P. Hood. OHIP
God Who Hides, The. Francis Quarles. *See* Why Dost Thou Shade Thy Lovely Face?
God, who made man out of dust. The Continuing City. Laurence Housman. WGRP
God who made New Hampshire, The. Ode Inscribed to W. H. Channing. Emerson. ViBoPo
God, who through ages past. New Dreams for Old. Thomas Curtis Clark. OQP
God, Who Touchest Earth With Beauty. Mary S. Edgar. FaChP
(Camp Hymn.) SoP; TRV
(Prayer-Poem, A.) BLRP
(Youth's Prayer, A.) MaRV
God, Whom Shall I Compare to Thee? Judah Halevi, *tr. fr. Hebrew by* Alice Lucas. TrJP
God whose goodness filleth every clime, The. Chorus. Racine. *Fr.* Athalie. CAW; WGRP
God, whose kindly hand doth sow. Francis Ledwidge. *Fr.* A Dream of Artemis. TrPWD
God Will Answer. "M. E. B." SoP
God will have all, or none; serve Him, or fall. Neutrality Loathsome [*or* "Ye Cannot Serve God and Mammon"]. Robert Herrick. LiTB; PoFr
God will never fail us. God Is Faithful. Frances Ridley Havergal. BLRP
God will not change; the restless years may bring. Changeless [*or* In Whom Is No Variableness]. Edith Hickman Divall. MaRV; OQP
God will not let my field lie fallow. The Ploughman. Karle Wilson Baker. WGRP
God Wills It. Richard F. Grady. JKCP (1955 ed.)
God wills no man a slave. The man most meek. Washington. James Jeffrey Roche. MC; PAH
God with His million cares. Dawn and Dark. Norman Gale. TSW; VA
God with honour hang your head. At the Wedding March. Gerard Manley Hopkins. HW; PoLi
God with Us. Nancy Byrd Turner. ChIP; OQP
God with Us. *Unknown.* *See* God Be in My Head.
God Within Yet Above. Sir Lewis Morris. MaRV
God works in His garden, I'm told, ev'ry day. God's Garden. Phyllis C. Michael. SoP
God would come, the god would go, The. Man Is God's Nature. Richard Eberhart. EaLo; MoRP
God ye hear not, how shall ye hear me? John Knox's Indictment of the Queen. Swinburne. *Fr.* Bothwell. VA
God, You Have Been Too Good to Me. Charles Wharton Stork. MaRV; TrPWD; WGRP
God. You need not make for me. Sunsets. Florence Boyce Davis. OQP
God, you've so much to do. Idleness. Andrew Young. POTE
Godamighty Drag, *with music.* *Unknown.* OuSiCo
Goddess, The. Théodore de Banville, *tr. fr. French by* Stuart Merrill. OnPM
Goddess, The. Thom Gunn. ToPo
Goddess, The. Denise Levertov. AP; LiTM (1970 ed.); NeAP; PoCh
Goddess, The. Kathleen Raine. FaBoTw
Goddess azure-mantled and aureoled. Our Lady. Robert Bridges. ISi
Goddesse, I do love a girle. A Short Hymne to Venus. Robert Herrick. CavP
Goddesses' Glory, The. *Unknown.* SeCL
Goddis sonne is borne. A Cause for Wonder. *Unknown.* MeEL
Goddwyn, *sel.* Thomas Chatterton.
Freedom's War Song. PoFr
(Ode to Liberty.) TrGrPo
Gode sire, pray ich thee. I Am from Ireland. *Unknown.* MeEL
Godfrey Gordon Gustavus Gore. William Brighty Rands. BBGG; BoChLi; BoTP; FaPON; GaP; HBVY; MPB; TiPo; TSW
(Reformation of Godfrey Gore, The.) HBV; OnPP; OTPC
Godfrey of Bulloigne. Tasso. *See* Jerusalem Delivered.
Godiva. Tennyson. BeLS, *sl. abr.*; HBV; PoVP
Godlike beneath his grave divinities. The Druid. John Banister Tabb. AA
Godlike Heart. Goethe, *tr. fr. German by* John S. Dwight. OnPM
Go-d'ling, *with music.* *Unknown.* BFSS
Godly and the Ungodly, The. Psalms, I, Bible, *O.T.* TreF
(Blessed Is the Man.) EnLi-1
(Psalm I.) AWP; JAWP; WoL
(Tree and the Chaff, The, *Moulton, Modern Reader's Bible.*) WGRP
Godly Casuistry. Samuel Butler. *Fr.* Hudibras, II, 2. OBS
Godly Girzie. Burns. CoMu; ErPo; UnTE
Godmother. Phyllis B. Morden. BrR; MoSiPe; SoPo
Godmother. Dorothy Parker. PoRA
Gododdin, *sel.* Aneirin, *tr. fr. Welsh by* Thomas Gray.
"To Cattraeth's vale in glittering row." PrWP
Godolphin Horne. Hilaire Belloc. CenHV; DTC; RIS; StaSt
Gods, The. W. S. Merwin. NaP
Gods. Whitman. AnAmPo
God's Acre. Blanche Edith Baughan. BoAu
God's Acre. Witter Bynner. AnEnPo
God's-Acre. Longfellow. HBV; MWA-1; PoRL
God's Aftermath. Frances Brook. SoP
God's a-Gwineter Trouble de Water, *with music.* *Unknown.* BoAN-2
God's Aid implored: the sum of all proposed. The First Day of the First Week. Joshua Sylvester. *Fr.* Du Bartas: His First Week or Birth of the World. Po
God's Altar. Emerson. MaRV
Gods and furies now depart. On Reading the *Metamorphoses.* George Garrett. NePoAm-2
Gods and Heroes of the Gael. Eleanor Rogers Cox. JKCP
God's angry man, His crotchety scholar. The Thunderer. Phyllis McGinley. EaLo
Gods are happy, The. The Strayed Reveller to Ulysses. Matthew Arnold. *Fr.* The Strayed Reveller. OBEV (new ed.)
Gods Are Mighty, The. N. P. van Wyk Louw, *tr. fr. Afrikaans by* Jack Cope. PeSA
God's Autographs. William L. Stidger. SoP
God's Bank Ain't Busted Yet! Alice P. Moss. SoP
God's Best. Avis B. Christiansen. SoP
God's Best. Albert Benjamin Simpson. SoP
(His Best.) STF
God's blessing lead us, help us! *At. to* St. Colman. *Fr.* Hymn against Pestilence. OnYI
God's Blessing on Munster. *At. to* St. Patrick, *tr. fr. Old Irish by* Whitley Stokes. OnYI
God's blessing rest upon you. An Easter Prayer. *Unknown.* SoP
God's body is all space. Essay on Deity. Elder Olson. MoRP; NP
God's Book. Edgar Daniel Kramer. OQP
God's Call. *Unknown.* STF
God's child in Christ adopted—Christ my all. On His Baptismal Birthday. Samuel Taylor Coleridge. MaRV
Gods' Consort, The. *Unknown.* MuSP
God's Controversy with New-England. Michael Wigglesworth. SCAP
God's Dark. John Martin. MaRV; PoLF
God's deathless plaything rolls an eye. Leviathan. Louis Untermeyer. GoTP
God's Determinations, *sels.* Edward Taylor.
Accusation of the Inward Man, The. LiTA
Christs Reply. MAmP; MWA-1; PoEL-3
Glory of and Grace in the Church Set Out, The. AmPP (5th ed.); AnNE; AP
God's Selecting Love in the Decree. PoEL-3
Joy of Church Fellowship [Rightly Attended], The. AmP; AmPP; AP; CBEP; MAmP; MWA-1; OxBA
Our Insufficiency to Praise God Suitably for His Mercy. LiTA
Outward Man Accused, The. LiTA
Preface, The: "Infinity, when all things it beheld." AmLP; AmPP; AP; ILP; MAmP; MWA-1; OxBA; SCAP
Souls Groan to Christ for Succour, The. MAmP; PoEL-3
God's Dominion and Decrees. Isaac Watts. CEP; OBEC
God's Dream. William Norris Burr. OQP
God's Dreams. Thomas Curtis Clark. OQP
God's Education. Thomas Hardy. MoRP
God's Eternal Now. Gerhard Tersteegan. FaChP
God's Eye Is on the Sparrow. Bertha Meyer. STF
"God's First Creature Was Light." Winifred Welles. ImOP
God's Funeral. Thomas Hardy. PoDB; WGRP
God's Garden. Richard Burton. OQP; TRV

God's Garden. Dorothy Frances Gurney. *See* Lord God Planted a Garden, The.
God's Garden. Phyllis C. Michael SoP
God's Gardener. Phyllis C. Michael. SoP
God's Gift. Enola Chamberlin. SoP
God's Glory. Psalms, XIX, Bible, *O.T.* *See* Heavens Declare the Glory of God, The.
God's Goin' to Set This World on Fire (A *and* B *vers., with music*). *Unknown.* AS
God's Goodness. C. D. Martin. WBLP
God's Grandeur. Gerard Manley Hopkins. AnFE; AWP; BoC; BrPo; BWP; CABA; CaFP; CBV; CMoP; CoBE; DiPo; EnLi-2; EnLit; ExPo; FaChP; FaFP; ForPo; FosPo; GTBS-D; GTBS-W; ILP; InPo; InvP; LiTB; LiTG; LiTM; LoBV; MaPo; MoAB; MoBrPo; MoPo; MoRP; MoVE; NoP; OBNC; OxBoCh; PAn; PeVV; PG (1955 ed.); Po; PoDB; PoE; PoeP; PoIE; PoLi; PoPo; PoVP; ReMP; SeCeV; Sonn; SoP; StP; TDP; TIHL; TreFT; TrGrPo; ViPP; VP
God's Harp. Gustav Falke, *tr. fr. German by* Ludwig Lewisohn. AWP; JAWP; WBP
Gods have heard me, Lyce, The. Revenge. Horace. Odes, IV, 13. AWP; WoL
Gods Have Heard My Vows, The. *Unknown.* EnRePo
Gods have not ordained hunger to be our death, The. To Liberality. *Unknown.* *Fr.* Vedic Hymns: Rig-Veda. PoFr
Gods have taken alien shapes upon them, The. Exiles. "Æ." MoBrPo
Gods I am pent in a cockroach. The Wail of Archy. Don Marquis. *Fr.* Archy and Mehitabel. FiBHP
God's Ideal Mother. Cora M. Pinkham. STF
God's in His Heaven: He never issues. Ninth Philosopher's Song. Aldous Huxley. ViBoPo
God in Vietnam. Eugene Redmond. NBP
God's Instrument. Sir William Herschel. OTD
God's Judgment [*or* Judgement] on a Wicked Bishop. Robert Southey. EnRP; HBV; HBVY; OBRV; OnMSP; OTPC (1923 ed.)
(Bishop Hatto.) ChTr; StPo
(Bishop Hatto and the Rats.) PaPo
God's Key. *Unknown.* STF
(He Keeps the Key.) SoP
God's lark at morning I would be! A Little Page's Song. William Alexander Percy. HBV
God's Little Mountain. Geoffrey Hill. BoPe; NePoEA
God's Love. *Unknown.* BLRP
God's love endureth forever. What More Can You Ask. Helen Steiner Rice. FaChP
God's Mercy. Frederick William Faber. *See* There's a Wideness in God's Mercy.
God's Mother. Laurence Housman. ISi
God's Mothers. Douglas Malloch. PEDC
Gods of Africa regard me, The. Distance. Anthony Delius. PeSA
Gods of fortune had quit my abode, The. Bonnie Black Bess. *Unknown.* BFSS
Gods of Hellas, gods of Hellas. The Dead Pan. Elizabeth Barrett Browning. PoVP; ViPo
Gods of the Dana, The. Leah Bodine Drake. FiSC
Gods of the Earth Beneath, The. Edmund Blunden. BrPo
Gods of the Nile, should this stout fellow here. A Grave near Cairo. Kipling. *Fr.* Epitaphs of the War. PoVP
Gods of War. "Æ." BEL
God's Pay. *Unknown.* STF
God's Pity. Louise Driscoll. MaRV; WGRP
God's pity on poor kings. Poor Kings. W. H. Davies. HBV
God's Plan. "Susan Coolidge." *Fr.* Commonplaces. MaRV
God's plan made a hopeful beginning. Limerick. *Unknown.* LiBL
God's Plans. May Riley Smith. BLRP; MaRV
God's Plans. *Unknown.* *See* He Will Silently Plan for Thee.
God's Plow of Sorrow. Robert Clarkson Tongue. SoP
God's Precepts Perfect. Psalms, XIX: 7-9, Bible, *O.T.* BLRP
God's Presence. Frederick William Faber. SoP
God's Presence Makes My Heaven. Oswald J. Smith. STF
God's Promises. *Unknown.* BLRP
God's Provident Love. Horace C. Carlisle. SoP
God's Residence. Emily Dickinson. *See* Who has not found the heaven below.
God's revelation of Himself may be. The Revelation. Leslie Clare Manchester. OQP
God's Road is all uphill. A Poet's Proverb. Arthur Guiterman. MaRV
God's rod doth watch while men do sleep; and then. The Rod. Robert Herrick. LiTB
God's Saints. Henry Vaughan. SoP; TRV
("God's Saints are shining lights.") ThGo
God's Selecting Love in the Decree. Edward Taylor. *Fr.* God's Determinations. PoEL-3
God's Speech to Job. Robert Frost. *Fr.* A Masque of Reason. OnHM
God's spice I was, and pounding was my due. The Martyrdom of Mary, Queen of Scots. Robert Southwell. *Fr.* At Fotheringay. ACP
God's Sunshine. John Oxenham. WBLP
God's Symphony. Phyllis C. Michael. SoP
God's Thanks to Job. Robert Frost. *Fr.* A Masque of Reason. MoRP
Gods, The! The Gods! D. H. Lawrence. CMoP
God's Trails Lead Home. John R. Clements. BLRP
God's Treasure. "A. M. N." SoP; STF
God's Two Dwellings, *sel.* Thomas Washbourne.
Humility ("Though Heaven be high"). MaRV
God's Unchanging Word. Martin Luther, *tr. fr. German.* SoP
God's Unspeakable Gift. Mrs. Macey P. Sealey. BePJ
God's View of Service. Robert Browning. *See* All Service Ranks the Same with God.
God's Virtue. Barnabe Barnes. BoPe
God's Way. Horatius Bonar. *See* Thy Way, Not Mine.
God's Way. Dorothy Clarke Wilson. MaRV
God's Way Is Perfect. Avis B. Christiansen. SoP
God's Ways. Albert C. Stewart. SoP
God's Ways. *Unknown.* MaRV
God's Ways and Mine. Grace Canfield Halladay. SoP
God's Ways Are Strange. Margaret E. Bruner. PoToHe
God's ways are ways of pleasantness. God's Ways. Albert C. Stewart. SoP
Gods, what a sun! I think the world's aglow. A Summer Day in Old Sicily. Edward Cracroft Lefroy. Echoes from Theocritus, V. OBVV
Gods who own Olympus as dwelling-place, The. The Five Ages. Hesiod. *Fr.* Works and Days. LiTW
God's Will. Charles E. Guthrie. BLRP
God's Will. Mildred Howells. HBV
God's Will. Robert Munger. AA
God's Will. Alice Nevin. BLRP
God's Will. Oswald J. Smith. SoP
God's Will. *Unknown.* SoP
(Message of the New Year, The. OQP
God's Will. *Unknown.* SoP
God's Will for Us. *Unknown.* BLRP; WBLP
God's will in me. God's Will. Alice Nevin. BLRP
God's Will Is Best. Thelma Curtis. STF
God's Will Is Best. *Unknown.* BLRP
God's will is better than our will. God's Will Is Best. Thelma Curtis. STF
God's Word. John Clifford. *See* Anvil, The—God's Word.
God's Work. Charlotte Cushman. TreFT
God's works are good. The Acorn and the Pumpkin. La Fontaine. BoChLi
God's World. Mildred Keeling. BLRP
God's World. Edna St. Vincent Millay. CMoP; CoBA; FaBoBe; FaBV; GoTP; HBV; MAP; MCCG; MoAmPo; MoRP; NP; PoPl; PoSC; RePo; TSW; YT
God's Youth. Louis Untermeyer. PFY
Godspeed. Harriet Prescott Spofford. EtS
Godspeed. Whittier. Sonn
Goe, and catche a falling starre. John Donne. *See* Song: "Go and catch a falling star."
Goe & seeke some other love. *Unknown.* SeCSL
Goe bidd the swan in silence dye. *Unknown.* SeCSL
Goe empty joyes. *Unknown.* SeCSL
Goe happy Rose, and enterwove. *See* Go, happy Rose, and, interwove.
Goe! hunt the whiter ermine! and present. For the Lady Olivia Porter; a Present upon a New-Years Day. Sir William Davenant. MeLP; MePo; OBS
Goe little book, and once a week shake hands. Ad Librum. Samuel Danforth, Jr. SCAP
Goe little booke: thy selfe present. *See* Go little book. . .
Goe lovely Rose. *See* Go Lovely Rose.

Goe now; and with some daring drugg. *See* Go now! and with some daring drug.
Goe, pale-fac't paper, to my deare. The Letter. John Tatham. CavP
Goe [*or* Go] smiling soules, your new built cages breake. To the Infant Martyrs. Richard Crashaw. MaMe; NoP; SCEP-1; SeCV-1
Goe solitary wood, and henceforth be. On the Death of a Nightingale. Thomas Randolph. AnAnS-2
Goe soule the bodies guest. *See* Go, soul, the body's guest.
Goe stop the swift-wing'd moments in their flight. Elegie. William Habington. AnAnS-2
Goe thou gentle whispering wind. A Prayer to the Wind. Thomas Carew. AnAnS-2; SCEP-2
Goe thow my soule to thy desired rest. *Unknown.* SeCSL
Goe thy waies and turne no more. *Unknown.* SeCSL
Goes through the mud. *Unknown.* OxNR
Goethals, the Prophet Engineer. Percy MacKaye. PoRL; StVeCh
"Man went down to Panama, A," *sel.* OTD
Goethe and Frederika. Henry Sidgwick. HBV
Goethe in Weimar sleeps, and Greece. Memorial Verses. Matthew Arnold. BWP; CABA; FiP; HBV; MaPo (1969 ed.); MBW-2; OAEP; PoVP; PP; VA; ViPo; ViPP
Goethe said that 'twixt embraces. Not Lotte. Katherine Hoskins. ErPo
Goin' down the road, Lawd. Bound No'th Blues. Langston Hughes. AmNP
Goin' Down to Town, *with music.* *Unknown.* AS
Goin' hikin'?/ git in! A Ride in a Blue Chevy from Alum Cave Trail to Newfound Gap. Jonathan Williams. NYTB
Goin' Home, *with music.* *Unknown.* ABF
Goin' up the River, *with music.* *Unknown.* TrAS
Going, The. W. W. Gibson. NP
(To Rupert Brooke.) GTSL
Going, The. Thomas Hardy. ELP; FaPL; LiTB; MaPo; PoeP; StP; UnPo (3d ed.); ViPP
Going. Robert Kelly. CoPo
Going. Philip Larkin. CMoP; ToPo
Going. James Schuyler. ANYP
Going about our business day by day. War. J. C. Hall. HaMV
Going abruptly into a starry night. Starlight. William Meredith. NePoEA
Going a-Maying. Robert Herrick. *See* Corinna's Going a-Maying.
Going and Staying. Thomas Hardy. CMoP
Going a-Nutting. Edmund Clarence Stedman. *See* Autumn Song.
Going Back Again. "Owen Meredith." EvOK; FiBHP
Going Back to School. Stephen Vincent Benét. LaNeLa
Going down Hill on a Bicycle. Henry Charles Beeching. BBV (1951 ed.); HBV; HBVY; OBEV; OBVV; OTPC (1923 ed.)
(Bicycling Song.) GN
Going down the Mountain. Valentin Iremonger. NeIP
(Descending.) EnLoPo
Going down the old way. Song. Margaret Widdemer. HBMV
Going down to town. Lynchburg Town. *Unknown.* OuSiCo
Going for Water. Robert Frost. HBMV; NP
Going from us at last. The Escape. Mark Van Doren. MAP; MoAmPo
Going home by lamplight across Boston Common. A Revivalist in Boston. Adrienne Cecile Rich. EaLo
Going Home with Jesus. Walter E. Isenhour. STF
Going In to Dinner. Edward Shanks. OBMV
Going in trains up north against the north. Ski Train. Patrick Anderson. TwCaPo
Going into Breeches. Charles *and* Mary Lamb. OTPC; PRWS
Going my way of old. Marriage. W. W. Gibson. HBV; MaRV
Going of the glade-boat, The. The Load of Sugar-Cane. Wallace Stevens. NP
Going on six thousand years. After Six Thousand Years. Victor Hugo. WaaP
Going out, those bold days. Autumn. W. R. Rodgers. NeBP
Going Over. Sir Charles G. D. Roberts. TwCaPo
Going, the wild things of our land. The Passing of the Buffalo. Hamlin Garland. StVeCh
Going thru cases and cases. The Sculptors. Alfred Purdy. PeCV (1967 ed.)
Going to Bed. Marchette Chute. BoChLi (1950 ed.); PDV
Going to Bed. John Donne. Elegies, XIX. AnAnS-1; LiTB; LiTG; MaMe
(Elegie: Going to Bed.) MePo
(Elegie XIX: To His Mistris Going to Bed.) SeCP
(Elegy XIX: Going to Bed.) EnRePo
(On Going to Bed.); EP
(To His Mistress [*or* Mistris] Going to Bed.) ErPo; NoP; ReEn; SiTL; UnTE
Going to Bed at Night. Adelaide O'Keeffe. OTPC (1923 ed.)
Going to Boston, *with music.* *Unknown.* ABF
Going to Church. Coventry Patmore. *Fr.* The Angel in the House, I, X. LoBV; PeVV
Going to him! Happy letter! Tell him. Emily Dickinson. CoBA; DiPo
Going to Mass by the heavenly mercy. Mary Hynes. Anthony Raftery. KiLC
Going to Mass Last Sunday. Donagh MacDonagh. NeIP; OxBI
Going to Pittsburgh. Dennis Trudell. QAH
Going to School. Karl Shapiro. TrJP
Going to sing about Emily. Microcosmos, XXV. Nigel Heseltine. NeBP
Going to Sleep. George Rostrevor Hamilton. MemP
Going to sleep, I cross my hands on my chest. Death. William Knott. YAP
Going to Sleep in the Country. Howard Moss. PoCh; StP
Going to the Chappell. John Donne. MaMe
Going to the Dogs. *Unknown.* TreFS
Going to the Fair. James Whitcomb Riley. IHA
Going to the Warres [*or* Wars]. Richard Lovelace. *See* To Lucasta, on Going to the Wars.
Going Too Far. Mildred Howells. OnMSP; TiPo
Going towards Spain. Barnabe Googe. EnRePo; ReIE; SiCE
Going up for the jump shot. The Poet Tries to Turn in His Jock. David Hilton. QAH
Going up is pleasant. I tips your chin. The Contraption. May Swenson. TPM
Going Up to London. Nancy Byrd Turner. GaP; HBMV
Golagros and Gawane, *sel.* *Unknown.*
"Thai passit in thare pilgramage." OxBS
Gol-darned Wheel, The. *Unknown.* CoSo, *with music*; IHA; PoMa
Gold. Martin Armstrong. BoTP
Gold. Thomas Hood. *Fr.* Miss Kilmansegg and Her Precious Leg. MaRV OQP; WBLP
(Her Moral.) VA
Gold. Glyn Jones. NeBP
Gold,/ Silver. *Unknown.* OxNR
Gold and all this werdis win. Crucified to the World. *Unknown.* MeEL
Gold and black regent-bird, The. Regent-Bird and Girl. Clem Christesen. MoAuPo
Gold and frankincense and myrrh. Three Gifts. Edward Judson Hanna. ChIP; OQP
Gold and iron are good. Politics. Emerson. AmePo; MWA-1
Gold-armoured ghost from the Roman road, The. The Youth with Red-gold Hair. Edith Sitwell. FaBoTw; MoVE
Gold as an infant's humming dream. Long Summer. Laurie Lee. BoNaP; ToPo
Gold as the hair of fairy-story queens. Lincolnshire Remembered. Frances Cornford. HaMV
Gold Coast Customs, *sel.* Edith Sitwell.
"One fantee wave." OBMV
Gold-colored skin of my Lebanese friends, The. A Trip to Four or Five Towns. John Logan. AmPC; CoAP
Gold crocus reaches up, The. The Crocus. Walter Crane. PCH
Gold for the crown of Mary. A Song of Colours. Theodore Maynard. JKCP
Gold! gold! gold! gold! Gold [*or* Her Moral]. Thomas Hood. MaRV; OQP; VA; WBLP
Gold-headed Finn has ridden away. The Last Pagan Mourns for Dark Rosaleen. Joseph Payne Brennan. FiSC
Gold-headed rose for bees to sup. The Flowers in a Meadow. Frances Cornford. ThGo
Gold in the hills, gold in the rocks. Arrowtown. Denis Glover. AnNZ
Gold in the Mountain. Herman Melville. NoP

"Gold is for the mistress—silver for the maid." Cold Iron. Kipling. OnMSP
Gold Is the Son of Zeus: Neither Moth nor Worm May Gnaw It. "Michael Field." OBMV
Gold I've none, for use or show. Lyrick for Legacies. Robert Herrick. OBS
Gold Lake and Gold Bluff. John A. Stone. SGR
Gold locks, and black locks. The Barber's. Walter de la Mare. GaP; GoJo; MPB; PCH; SoPo; SUS
Gold of a ripe oat straw, gold of a southwest moon. Falltime. Carl Sandburg. NP
Gold of heaven, The. Love. Tom Dent. NNP
Gold-of-Ophir Roses. Grace Atherton Dennen. AA
Gold of the tangled wilderness of wattle. Wattle and Myrtle. James Lister Cuthbertson. BoAu
Gold on her head, and gold on her feet. The Eve of Crecy. William Morris. EnLi-2 (1939 ed.); OBVV; PAn; PoVP; SiSw; ViPo; ViPP
Gold, red and green flies. Near Dusk. Joseph Auslander. FaPON; OTPC (1946 ed.)
Gold-Seekers, The. Hamlin Garland. AA; FaBoBe; MC; YaD
Gold Seekers, The. Marion Muir Richardson. PoOW
Gold Seeker's Song, The. *Unknown.* PoOW
Gold tane from the king's harbengers. Robin Hood and Queen Katherine. *Unknown.* BaBo; ESPB (A *and* B *vers.*)
Gold That Fell on Danae, The. Horatio Colony. TwAmPo
Gold-tinted Dragon, The. Karla Kuskin. SoPo
Gold Wings across the Sea. William Morris. *Fr.* Golden Wings AtBAP
(Song: "Gold wings across the sea!") LoBV
(Song of Jehane du Castel Beau, The.) ChTr
Gold, with an innermost speck. Street Lamps. D. H. Lawrence. BoPe
Goldbrown upon the sated flood. Flood. James Joyce. MoBrPo
Golden Age, The. Robert Conquest. HYE
Golden Age, The. Ernest Francisco Fenollosa. AA
Golden Age, The, *sel.* Thomas Heywood.
Hymn to Diana. EIL
("Hail beauteous Dian, queen of shades.") SiCE
Golden Age, The. Tasso. *See* Pastoral, A: "Oh happy golden age."
Golden Apples, The. William Morris. *Fr.* The Earthly Paradise: December. EPN
Golden as your singing-note. Amber Beads. Audrey Alexandra Brown. CaP
Golden Ball, The. *Unknown.* *See* Maid Freed from the Gallows, The.
Golden bee a-cometh, A. A Merry Bee. Joseph Skipsey. OBVV
Golden Bird, The. Rex Ingamells. PoAu-2
Golden Bough. Helen Hoyt. HBMV
Golden Bough, The. Vergil, *tr. fr. Latin by* Dryden. *Fr.* The Aeneid, VI. PeRV
Golden Bough. Elinor Wylie. MAP; MoAmPo
Golden Calf. Norman MacCaig. OxBS
Golden Carol, The. *Unknown.* OHIP
Golden casket I designed, A. Epigram. John Swanwick Drennan. IrPN
Golden City of St. Mary, The. John Masefield. GTSL; HT; MCCG
Golden cloud slept for her pleasure, A. The Mountain. Mikhail Lermontov. AWP; JAWP; WBP
Golden Cobwebs. Rowena Bennett. ChBR
Golden Cord, The. John Oxenham. *See* Prayer A: "Through every minute of this day."
Golden cradle under you, and you young, A. He Meditates on the Life of a Rich Man. Douglas Hyde. OBMV
Golden crocus reaches up, The. The Crocus. Walter Crane. OTPC (1946 ed.); SoPo
Golden eagle swooped out of the sky, The. Salmon Drowns Eagle. Malcolm Lowry. MoCV; OBCV; TwCaPo
Golden Echo, The. Gerard Manley Hopkins. *See* Leaden Echo and the Golden Echo, The.
Golden Elegy, The. Leopold Staff, *tr. fr. Polish by* Watson Kirkconnell. LiTW
Golden eve is all astir, The. Theme. James Stephens. ACV; POTE
Golden Falcon. Robert P. Tristram Coffin. CAW
Golden Fish, The. George Arnold. HBV
Golden Gates. *Unknown.* ShM
Golden gates of Sleep unbar, The. A Bridal Song. Shelley. OBRV
Golden Gift, The. Earl of Surrey. Po
("Golden gift that nature did thee give, The.") FCP; SiPS
Golden gilliflower [*or* gillyflower] today, A. The Gilliflower [*or* Gillyflower] of Gold. William Morris. AnFE; PoVP; TOP; VA; ViPo; WHA
Golden girl / in a golden gown. College Formal: Renaissance Casino. Langston Hughes. BALP
Golden Glove, The. *Unknown.* MaC
Golden Gullies of the Palmer, The. *Unknown.* PoAu-1
Golden hair that Gulla wears, The. Bought Locks. Martial. AWP; JAWP; LiTW; OuHeWo; WBP; WoL
Golden Heart, The. Witter Bynner. HBMV
Golden Hour, The. Thomas Moore. *Fr.* Lalla Rookh. OBNC
Golden Journey to Samarkand, The. James Elroy Flecker. HBMV; HT
Sels.
Epilogue to Hassan ("Away, for we are ready to a man,") *also fr.* Hassan. ShBV-3
Golden Road, The ("We are the Pilgrims, master,") *also fr.* Hassan. OtMeF
"We who with songs beguile your pilgrimage," Prologue. BrPo; GoJo; GTBS; OBMV
Golden Legend, The, *sel.* Longfellow.
This Is Indeed the Blessed Mary's Land. ISi
Golden lemon is not made, The. A Song for the Spanish Anarchists. Sir Herbert Read. ChMP
Golden Mean, The. Horace. *See* To Licinius.
Golden Mean, The. Lucian, *tr. fr. Greek by* William Hay. OnPM
Golden Mean, The. Earl of Surrey. SiPS
("Of thy life [*or* lyfe], Thomas, this compass well mark.) EnPo; FCP
Golden Mile-Stone, The. Longfellow. PoEL-5
Golden Month, The. Marion Doyle. YeAr
Golden Net, The. Blake. ERoP-1; SiSW
Golden pallor of voluptuous light, A. The Mocking-Bird. Paul Hamilton Hayne. AmPP (3d ed.)
Golden Road, The. James Elroy Flecker. *Fr.* Hassan. OtMeF
Golden-Robin's Nest, The. John White Chadwick. AA
Golden Rod, The. Frank Dempster Sherman. BoChLi; FaPON
Golden Room, The. W. W. Gibson. POTE
Golden rose the house, in the portal I saw. Apparuit. Ezra Pound. APA; CoAnAm; TwAmPo
Golden Rowan. Bliss Carman. VA
Golden Rule, The. James Wells. STF
Golden Sequence, The Pope Innocent III, *tr. fr. Latin.* CAW
Golden Sestina, The. Giovanni Pico della Mirandola, *tr. fr. Italian by* Ezra Pound. LiTW
Golden Silences. Christina Rossetti. NBM
Golden Slumbers [Kiss Your Eyes]. Thomas Dekker, *and others.* *Fr.* The Pleasant Comedy of Patient Grissell. CH; ELP; HBV; OTPC; PoE; ReEn; ShBV-4; SiCE; TuPP; ViBoPo
(Cradle Song: "Golden slumbers kiss your eyes.") OBSC; TrGrPo
(Lullaby: "Golden slumbers kiss your eyes.") EIL; LoBV
Golden Sorrow, A. Martial, *tr. fr. Latin by* Paul Nixon. LiTW
Golden spider of the sky, The. Solar Myth. Genevieve Taggard. MAP; MoAmPo
Golden spring redeems the withered year, The. Robert Hillyer. Sonnets, II. HBMV
Golden Spurs. Virginia Scott Miner. PoRL; SiSoSe; StaSt
Golden Spurs, The. *Unknown,* *tr. fr. Greek by* Louis Untermeyer. UnTE
Golden stars give warmthless fire, The. Christmas and Ireland. Lionel Johnson. JKCP
Golden Stockings. Oliver St. John Gogarty. OxBI
Golden strand that weaves through tapestry, A. The Father's Gold. *Unknown.* STF
Golden sun is garish, The. Rain. Frances Shaw. HBMV
Golden sun that brings the day, The. In Praise of the Sun. "A. W." CTC; OBSC; SiCE
Golden Tacks. Mildred D. Shacklett. GFA
Golden Targe, The. William Dunbar. *See* Goldyn Targe.
Golden Text, The. George Frederick Cameron. VA
Golden through the golden morning. The Return. Eleanor Rogers Cox. PAH

Golden trees of England, The. The Jungle Trees. Marjorie Wilson. BoTP
Golden-tressed Adelaide. "Barry Cornwall." VA
Golden Vanity, The. *Unknown.* BaBo (C *vers.*); CBEP; CH; ELP; FaBoCh; OBB, *mod.*; OnSP; ShBV-1; SoAmSa, *with music*; ViBoFo; WiR
(Golden Vanitie, The.) EnSB
(Goulden Vanitie, The.) AtBAP
(Low-down, Lonesome Low, The, *with music, diff. vers.*) OuSiCo
(Sir Walter Raleigh Sailing in the Low-Lands, *diff. vers.*) OxBoLi
(Sweet Trinity, The, A *and* B *vers.*) BaBo; ESPB
Golden Wedding, The. David Gray. FaBoBe; HBV
Golden Wedding, *sel.* Alan Mulgan.
"Breaking a line of pines, a wide white gate." ACV
Golden Wedding. William W. Pratt. MaRV
Golden Whales of California, The, *sel.* Vachel Lindsay.
"Yes, I have walked in California." AtBAP
Golden-winged, silver-winged. Birds of Paradise. Christina Rossetti. VP
Golden Wings. William Morris. OBNC; WHA
Sels.
Ancient Castle, An. SeCePo
("Midways of a walled garden.") ChTr
Gold Wings across the Sea. AtBAP
Song: "Gold wings across the sea!" LoBV
(Song of Jehane du Castel Beau, The.) ChTr
Golden world is past, saith some, The. Of the Golden World. Thomas Howell. SiCE; TuPP
Goldenhair. James Joyce. Chamber Music, V. BoTP; ChTr; HBMV; MoSiPo; RePo
("Lean out of the window.") BOLP; HW; LOW
(Song: "Lean out of the window.") POTE
Goldenrod. Elaine Goodale Eastman. HBV
Goldenrod [*or* Golden-rod] is yellow, The. September [Days Are Here]. Helen Hunt Jackson. BoChLi; FaPON; GoJo; GoTP; MPB; OTD; OTPC (1946 ed.); PEDC; PoLF; PoRL; PRWS; TiPo (1959 ed.); YeAr
Goldfinch, A. Walter de la Mare. BiS
Goldfinches. Keats. GN
Goldfish, The. Audrey Alexandra Brown. CaP
Goldfish, The. William F. Kirk. LHV
Goldfish. Harold Monro. BrPo
Goldfish. Howard Nemerov. NYTB
Goldfish on the Writing Desk. Max Brod, *tr. fr. German by* Babette Deutsch *and* Avrahm Yarmolinsky. LiTW; TrJP
Goldfish Wife, The. Sandra Hochman. NYBP
Goldsmith's Wife, The. *Unknown, tr. fr. Irish by* Frank O'Connor. KiLC
Goldyn [*or* Golden] Targe, The. William Dunbar. OxBS; SiCE
Sels.
"O reverend Chaucere, rose of rethoris all." PP
Poet's Dream, The. PoEL-1
Golf Links, The. Sarah N. Cleghorn. FaFP; InMe; LiTM; PoPl; PoPo; PPON; SiTL
(Golf Links Lie So Near the Mill, The.) HBMV; PoLF
(Quatrain.) MaRV; NAMP
Golfers. Irving Layton. SD
Golgotha. X. J. Kennedy. NYBP
Golgotha. Frederic L. Knowles. OQP
Golgotha. Katherine Greenleaf Pedley. ChIP
Golgotha. John Hall Wheelock. MoRP
Golgotha Is a Mountain. Arna Bontemps. AmNP; CDC; PoNe
Golgotha's Cross. Raymond Kresensky. ChIP; OQP
Golotha's journey is an ancient way. Crucifixion. Hugh O. Isbell. ChIP; PGD
Goliath and David. Louis Untermeyer. TrJP
Goliath of Gath. Phillis Wheatley. BALP
Goliathus goliathus, the one banana. The Zoo. Gilbert Sorrentino. NeAP
Goll's Parting with His Wife. *Unknown, tr. fr. Early Modern Irish by* Eoin MacNeill. AnIL
Golly, How Truth Will Out. Ogden Nash. LiTA; LiTM; MoAmPo
Gondibert, *sels.* Sir William Davenant.
"By what bold passion am I rudely led," *fr.* I, 3. FaBoEn; OBS
"From Brescia swiftly," II, 5. CEP
"Of all the Lombards, by their trophies knowne," *fr.* I, 1. SeCV-1
Praise and Prayer, *fr.* I, 6. GoBC; OBEV
"To streets (the people's region) early fame," II, ii. SeEP
Gondoliers, The, *sels.* W. S. Gilbert.
Duke of Plaza-Toro, The. ALV; FaPON; FiBHP; OnPP; PCD
Grand Inquisitor's Song, The. OnMSP
There Lived a King. FiBHP; StPo; WhC
(King Goodheart.) ALV; InMe
Gone. Mary Elizabeth Coleridge. HBV; OBEV (new ed.); OBNC; OBVV; OQP; TOP
Gone. Walter de la Mare. GoJo
Gone, A. Larry Eigner. NeAP
Gone. Adam Lindsay Gordon. BoAu
Gone. Carl Sandburg. AmP; AnFE; APA; CoAnAm; NP; OnPP; TwAmPo
Gone, The. Jesse Stuart. FiSC
Gone are the coloured princes, gone echo, gone laughter. The Ruin. Richard Hughes. OBMV; POTE
Gone are the days when my heart was young and gay. Old Black Joe. Stephen Collins Foster. FaFP; IHA; TreFS
Gone are the sensuous stars, and manifold. Chaucer. Benjamin Brawley. BANP
Gone are those three, those sisters rare. The Three Sisters. Arthur Davison Ficke. HBV; MAP
Gone art thou? gone, and is the light of day. To the Dead. William Bell Scott. VA
Gone away Blues. Thomas McGrath. WOW
Gone Boy. Langston Hughes. NePoAm-2
Gone down in the flood, and gone out in the flame. The Sinking of the Merrimac[k]. Lucy Larcom. MC; PAH
Gone—faded out of the story, the sea-faring friend I remember? Pasa Thalassa Thalassa. E. A. Robinson. EtS; LaNeLa
Gone Forward. Margaret Junkin Preston. DD
Gone! Gone! Forever Gone. Gerald Griffin. OnYI
Gone, gone—sold and gone. The Farewell. Whittier. AA; AWP; InPo; PoNe
Gone, I say, and walk from church. The Truth the Dead Know. Anne Sexton. MoAmPo (1962 ed.); NePoEA-2; ToPo
Gone in the Wind. James Clarence Mangan, *after the German of* Friedrich Rückert. ACP; CAW, *abr.*; CBEP; GoBC; IrPN; MaRV; OBVV; OnYI; OxBI; PoLi; SeCePo
Gone is the city, gone the day. The Right Kind of People. Edwin Markham. BLPA; PoPo; PoToHe; StaSt
Gone Is Youth. Salamah, Son of Jandal. *Fr.* The Mufaddaliyat. AWP
Gone, my white tangible angel falling. Four Poems for April, IV. Louis Adeane. NeBP
Gone the three ancient ladies. Frau Bauman, Frau Schmidt, and Frau Schwartze. Theodore Roethke. CoAP; MoAB; NePoAm; NYBP
Gone were but the winter. Spring Quiet. Christina Rossetti. BiS; BoNaP; BoTP; CH; EG; GTBS-P; LoBV; PoEL-5; ThGo; ThWaDe
Gone Were But the Winter Cold. Allan Cunningham. *See* Spring of the Year, The.
"Gone West." G. A. Studdert Kennedy. OQP
Gone while your tastes were keen to you. For E. McC. Ezra Pound. SD
"Goneys an' gullies an' all o' the birds o' the sea." Sea-Change. John Masefield. AtBAP; FaBoTw; OBMV
Good Advice. Thomas Carew. MeWo
Good Advice. Christina Rossetti. *See* Seldom "can't."
Good Advice. *Unknown, ad. fr. German by* Louis Untermeyer. *Fr.* Proverbs. RIS (1952 ed.); TiPo
(Old German Mottos: Advice.) StaSt
Good aged Bale, that with thy hoary hairs. To Doctor Bale. Barnabe Googe. EnRePo; EP; ReIE; TuPP
Good and Bad. James Stephens. MoBrPo; NeMA
Good and Bad. *Unknown.* *See* Charity.
Good and bad and right and wrong. Good and Bad. James Stephens. MoBrPo; NeMA
Good and Bad Children. Robert Louis Stevenson. BBGG; FaBoCh; FaFP; HBV; HBVY; LoGBV; NBM; OTPC (1923 ed.); PoVP; ThGo; TreF
Good and Bad Luck. John Hay, *after* Heine. ALV; BOHV; InMe
Good & Bad Wives. *Unknown.* CoMu
Good and Clever. *Unknown.* SoP
Good and great God, can I not think[e] of thee. To Heaven. Ben Jonson. AnAnS-2; BWP; EnRePo; EP; ExPo; ForPo; LiTB;

Good (continued)
LoBV; OBS; OxBoCh; PIA; PoIE; QFR; ReIE; SCEP-2; SeCeV; SeCP; TrPWD; UnPo
Good and great God! How should I fear. No Coming to God without Christ. Robert Herrick. OxBoCh; TRV
Good are attracted by men's perceptions, The. Motto to the Songs of Innocence & of Experience. Blake. ERoP-1
Good as gold, fine as. Jigsaw. John Stevens Wade. ThO
Good, better, best. *Unknown.* OxNR
Good Bishop, The. *Unknown, tr. fr. German by* William Taylor. CAW; WGRP
Good Bishop Valentine. Eleanor Farjeon. PoSC
Good Boy, The, *with music. Unknown.* AS
Good bread,/ Good meat. Grace. *Unknown.* SiTL
Good brother Philip, I have borne you long. To a Sparrow. Sir Philip Sidney. Astrophel and Stella, LXXXIII. FCP; SiPS
Good-by. Margaret E. Bruner. PoToHe
Good-by, A. Ednah Proctor Clarke. AA
Good-by. Grace Denio Litchfield. PoToHe
Good-by. Christina Rossetti. VA
Good-by and Keep Cold. Robert Frost. *See* Good-bye and Keep Cold.
Good-by can be a happy word. Good-by. Margaret E. Bruner. PoToHe
Good-by er Howdy-do. James Whitcomb Riley. CTC
Good-by [*or* Good-bye], good-by, to summer! Robin Redbreast [*or* A Child's Song.]. William Allingham. BiS; BoChLi; DD; FaBoBe; HBV; HBVY; MoShBr; MPB; OTPC; PEDC; PRWS; TVC; UTS; WePo
"Good-by," I said to my conscience. Conscience and Remorse. Paul Laurence Dunbar. MaRV
"Good-by in fear, good-by in sorrow." Good-by. Christina Rossetti. VA
Good-by Liza Jane, *with music. Unknown.* AS
Good-by, Mother, *with music. Unknown.* ABF
Good-by: nay, do not grieve that it is over. *See* Good-bye—no, do not grieve. . .
Good-by [*or* Good-bye], Old Paint, *with music. Unknown.* ABF; CoSo; TrAS
(Old Paint, *with music.*) BFSS
Good-by, Pretty Mama, *with music. Unknown.* ABF
Good-by, schoolhouse! Good-by, books! Camp Chums. Rose Waldo. MPB
Good-by, the tears are in my eyes. Rondel. Villon. AWP; JAWP; WBP
Good-by to my pals of the prairie. The Dying Cowboy of Rim Rock Ranch. *Unknown.* CoSo
Good-by, Young Man, Good-by. A. E. Housman. *See* Oh, See How Thick the Goldcup Flowers.
Goodbye, The. Guillaume Apollinaire, *tr. fr. French by* Glauco Cambon. OnPM
Good-bye. Walter de la Mare. FaBoEn; NoP
Good-bye. Emerson. AmePo; AnAmPo; AnNE; CoBA; FaFP; FaPL; HBV; LiTA; MAmP; MaRV; PG (1945 ed.); PoToHe (new ed.); TreF; YT
(Good-bye, Proud World.) WGRP
In the Woods, *sel.* OQP
Goodbye. William Knott. YAP
Good-bye ("God bless the master of this house"). *Unknown. See* Christmas Carol: "God bless the master. . ."
Goodbye! George John Whyte-Melville. TreF
Goodbye./ Incredulously the laced fingers loosen. Curtain. Helen Spalding. POTE
Goodbye/ Until such time as bobolinks do dine. To Janet. Ralph Pomeroy. NYBP
Good-bye and Keep Cold. Robert Frost. GoTP
(Good-by and Keep Cold.) CMoP
Good-bye, Brother, *with music. Unknown.* AS
Good-bye, Fare You Well, *with music. Unknown.* AmSS; SoAmSa
Good-bye for a Long Time. Roy Fuller. NeBP
Good-bye, good-bye to summer! *See* Good-by, good-by to summer!
Goodbye, lady in Bangor, who sent me. The Correspondence School Instructor Says Goodbye to His Poetry Students. Galway Kinnell. CBV
Goodbye, little Bonny, goodbye. Little Bonny. *Unknown.* OuSiCo
Good-bye, little desk at school, good-bye. Vacation Time. Frank Hutt. BoTP
Good-bye My Fancy! Walt Whitman. AnFE; AP; APA; CoAnAm; CoBA; FaFP; LiTA; MAmP; MaPo (1969 ed.); MWA-1; PG (1945 ed.)
Goodbye, My Love, Goodbye, *with music. Unknown.* SoAmSa
Good-bye [*or* Good-by]—no [*or* nay], do not grieve that it is over. A Farewell. Harriet Monroe. AA; HBMV; NP
Goodbye Now; or, Pardon My Gauntlet. Ogden Nash. FiBHP
Good-bye Now, Plato and Hegel. Louis MacNeice. *Fr.* Autumn Journal. OnHM
Good-bye now to the streets and the clash of wheels and locking hubs. A Teamster's Farewell. Carl Sandburg. CoBA
Good-bye, Old Paint. *Unknown. See* Good-by, Old Paint.
Good-bye, Proud World. Emerson. *See* Good-bye.
Goodbye sting and all my columbines. Homage to Max Jacob. Ron Padgett. ANYP
Goodbye to Regal. Daniel Huws. NYBP
Goodbye to Serpents. James Dickey. NYBP
Goodbye to the Aegean. On the Athenian Dead at Ecbatana. Plato. PoPl
Good-bye to the People of Hang-chow. Po Chü-i, *tr. fr. Chinese by* Arthur Waley. LiTW
Goodbye, Winter. Prognosis. Louis MacNeice. CMoP; OxBI
Goodbyes and griefs come here to join the world. Railway Station. John Hay. WaP
Good Christian Men, Rejoice, *with music. Unknown, tr. fr. Latin by* John Mason Neale. YaCaBo
Good Christian Reader judge me not. God's Controversy with New-England. Michael Wigglesworth. SCAP
Good Christians. Robert Herrick. LiTB
Good Christians all attend unto my ditty. A Ballad of the Strange and Wonderful Storm of Hail. *Unknown.* CoMu
Good Christians all, both great and small. The Avondale Mine Disaster. *Unknown.* BaBo; ThLM; ViBoFo
Good Companion, The. Belle F. Owens. ChIP
Good Company. Karle Wilson Baker. FaPON; HBV; OQP; WGRP
Good Company. Henry VIII, King of England. *See* Pastime with Good Company.
Good Company, Fine Houses. John Newlove. PeCV (1967 ed.)
Good Counsel. James I, King of Scotland. ACP
Good Counsel to a Young Maid. Thomas Carew. AnAnS-2; CavP; CBEP; ErPo
(Good Counsell to a Young Maid.) OBS
Good Creatures, Do You Love Your Lives. A. E. Housman. PeVV
Good Creed, A. *Unknown.* PoToHe
Good dame looked from her cottage, The. The Leak in the Dike. Phoebe Cary. FaFP; FaPON; OnSP; OTPC; PaPo; StVeCh (1940 ed.); TreF
Good dame Mercy with dame Charite, The. The Seven Deadly Sins. Stephens Hawes. *Fr.* The Pastime of Pleasure. PoEL-1
Good Day, The. Henry Howarth Bashford. HBV
Good day, good day. In Honour of Christmas. *Unknown.* MeEL
Good days/ I'm out. Perambulator Poems, VII. David McCord. WhC
Good Day's Work, A. Naomi Replansky. WOW
Good Dobbin. Ann *or* Jane Taylor. SAS
Good Earth, The. *Unknown, tr. fr. Greek by* William Hay. OnPM
Good Eating Song, A. William Cartwright. *Fr.* The Ordinary. SeCL
Good English Hospitality. Blake. *Fr.* An Island in the Moon. CoMu
(Mayors, The.) CH
Good Expectations. *Unknown, tr. fr. Greek by* Lord Neaves. OnPM
Good Farmer, The. *Unknown, tr. fr. Greek by* Hodgson *and* Bland. OnPM
Good father, I have sent for you because. The Merry Little Maid and Wicked Little Monk. *Unknown.* ErPo
Good Father John O'Hart. The Priest of Coloony. W. B. Yeats. OnYI
Good flat earth. . .and not so very high, The. Two Mountains Men Have Climbed. Pauline Starkweather. GoYe
Good folk [*or* folke], for gold or hire [*or* hyre]. The Crier [*or* Cryer]. Michael Drayton. ElL; InvP; OAEP; PoEL-2; SeEP; TuPP; WhC
Good folks ever will have their way. The Doctor's Story. Will M. Carleton. BLPA

Good for Nothing Man, *sels.* Kenneth Pitchford.
Blues Ballad. CoPo
Jacqueline Gray. CoPo
Onion Skin, The. CoPo
Pickup in Tony's Hashhouse. CoPo; ErPo
Young Buck's Sunday Blues. CoPo
Good Fortune. Heine, *tr. fr. German by* Louis Untermeyer. BLPA
Good Fortune, when I hailed her recently. Epigram. J. V. Cunningham. PV
Good frend for Jesus sake forbeare. Inscription on Stone over Shakespeare's Grave. *Unknown.* TreFS
Good Friday. George Herbert. MaMe; SCEP-1
Good Friday. Vincent Holme. ChIP
Good Friday. Alice B. Jurica. ChIP
Good Friday. Edgar Daniel Kramer. OQP
Good Friday, *sel.* John Masefield.
Madman's Song, The. ACV
"Wild duck, stringing through the sky, The." BoC
Good Friday. Lizette Woodworth Reese. OQP
Good Friday. Christina Rossetti. ChIP; MaRV; PoEL-5; SoP; StJW; TRV; VP
Good Friday. Girolamo Savonarola. ChIP; OQP
Good Friday. A. J. M. Smith. CaP; MaRV; StJW
Good Friday. Martha Provine Leach Turner. MaRV; OQP
Good Friday (Christ made a trance on Friday view). *Unknown.* ChTr
Good Friday (O heart, be lifted up; O heart be gay). *Unknown.* BoC
Good Friday. Henry Vaughan. *See* Passion, The.
Good Friday Evening. Christina Rossetti. PGD
Good Friday in My Heart. Mary Elizabeth Coleridge. PGD
Good Friday Night. William Vaughn Moody. APA; StJW
Good Friday [*or* Goodfriday], 1613. Riding Westward. John Donne. AnAnS-1; AtBAP; ATP (1953 ed.); DiPo; EnRePo; ExPo; MaMe; MBW-1; MeLP; MeP; MePo; NoP; OBS; OxBoCh; PAn; Po; PoEL-2; PoIE; ReEn; SCEP-1; SeCP; SeCV-1; SeEP; StP; TuPP
Good Friday; the Third Nocturn. Peter Abelard, *tr. fr. Latin by* Helen Waddell. LiTW
Good Friday was the day. The Martyr. Herman Melville. AmePo; LiPo; PoEL-5; PoFr; PoIE; TrGrPo
"Good from a Book." Elizabeth Barrett Browning. *See* Reading.
Good Girl, The. Elizabeth Turner. Mrs. Turner's Object-Lessons, VIII. OTPC
Good girls are down from the Bronx, The. Greenwich Village Saturday Night. Irving Feldman. AmPC
Good glory, give a look at Sporting Beasley. Sporting Beasley. Sterling A. Brown. Kal
Good God/ a 3 & 1/2 inch bony. Ed Sanders. *Fr.* Toe Queen Poems. ANYP
Good God of scholar, simpleton, and sage! Grace; before Reading Emily Brontë's Poems. Johnstone G. Patrick. TrPWD
Good God, What a Night That Was. Petronius Arbiter, *tr. fr. Latin by* Kenneth Rexroth. ErPo; LiTW
Good gray [*or* grey] guardians of art, The. Museum Piece. Richard Wilbur. CMoP; MiAP; NePA; PoIE; PoPl; TDP
Good, Great Man, The. Samuel Taylor Coleridge. EPN; HBV
(Complaint.) WhC
Good Green Bus. Rachel Field. BrR
Good Ground, The. Virginia Moore. YT
Good heaven, I thank thee since it was designed. On Myself. Countess of Winchilsea. TrGrPo
Good Hope. Emerson. OnPM
Good Hour, The. Louise Driscoll. HBMV
Good Hours. Robert Frost. OTD; RG; SiSw
Good house, and ground whereon, A. The Salt Garden. Howard Nemerov. FiMAP; NePoEA
Good Humor Man, The. Phyllis McGinley. MoShBr
Good husband and housewife, now chiefly be glad. Christmas Husbandly Fare. Thomas Tusser. SiCE; TuPP
Good in Everything. Shakespeare. *See* Uses of Adversity, The.
Good in graves as heavenly seed are sown, The. The Christians Reply to the Phylosopher. Sir William Davenant. MeLP
Good in Ill. William Henry Burleigh. SoP
Good Inn, The. Herman Knickerbocker Viele. *Fr.* The Inn of the Silver Moon. HBV
Good intent of God became the Christ, The. The Christ. John Oxenham. TRV
Good is an orchard, the saint saith. Of an Orchard. Katharine Tynan. GoBC; HBV; OBVV; WGRP
Good Joan, The. Lizette Woodworth Reese. FaPON; MoShBr; MPB; TiPo (1952 ed.); WHL
Good Junipero the Padre slowly read the king's commands. The Discovery of San Francisco Bay. Richard Edward White. PAH
Good King Wenceslas. *Unknown, tr. fr. Latin by* John Mason Neale. BBV (1923 ed.); ChrBoLe; HBV; HBVY; OHIP; OnMSP; OTPC; PoRL; PTK; YaCaBo, *with music*
Good Kosciusko, thy great name alone. To Kosciusko. Keats. MERP; PoFr
Good ladies, ye [*or* you] that have your pleasure in exile. The Lady Again Complains. Earl of Surrey. FCP; SiPS
Good Lady. A Negro Peddler's Song. Fenton Johnson. AmNP
Good little boys should never say. Politeness. Elizabeth Turner. HBV; HBVY
Good Little Girl, The. A. A. Milne. BBGG
Good Lord, behold this dreadfull enemy. The Souls Groan to Christ for Succour. Edward Taylor. *Fr.* God's Determinations. MAmP; PoEL-3
Good Lord gave, the Lord has taken from me, The. The Mother's Prayer. Dora Sigerson Shorter. HBV
Good Lord Graeme is to Carlisle gane. *See* Gude Lord Graeme is. . .
Good Lord Nelson had a swollen gland, The. A Ballad of the Good Lord Nelson. Lawrence Durrell. ErPo; LiTM; OnHM; SiTL
"Good lord of the land, will you stay thane." Lord Maxwell's Last Goodnight. *Unknown.* BaBo; ESPB; OxBB
Good Luck. Oliver St. John Gogarty. JKCP (1926 ed.)
Good luck is the gayest of all gay girls. Good and Bad Luck. John Hay. ALV; BOHV; InMe
Good luck to the milkman. The Milkman. "Seumas O'Sullivan." GaP; SUS
Good Man, The. *Unknown. Fr.* The Talmud. TrJP
Good Man in Hell, The. Edwin Muir. MoBrPo (1962 ed.); MoRP
Good man was ther of religioun, A. The Good [*or* Poor] Parson [*or* The Parish Priest]. Chaucer. *Fr.* The Canterbury Tales: Prologue. ACP; CAW; GOBC; MaRV; PoLi; WGRP
Good manners may in seven words be found. Of Courtesy. Arthur Guiterman. OTD; TiPo
Good Master and Mistress. *Unknown.* EvOK
Good master, you and I were born. A Decanter of Madeira, Aged 86, to George Bancroft, Aged 86. S. Weir Mitchell. AA; ViBoPo
Good Men Afflicted Most. Robert Herrick. LiTB
"Good men and true! in this house who dwell." The Croppy Boy. William B. McBurney. OnYI
Good Mr. Peeps or Peps or Pips. The Gospel of Mr. Pepys. Christopher Morley. InMe
Good Moolly Cow, The. Eliza Lee Follen. PPL
Good Morning. Joanna Baillie. OTPC (1923 ed.)
(Wake, Lady!) HBV
Good Morning. Robert Browning. *See* Year's at the Spring, The.
Good Morning. Rose Fyleman. BoTP
Good Morning. Muriel Sipe. SoPo; SUS; TiPo
Good-Morning. *Unknown.* SAS
Good morning, Algernon: Good morning, Percy. On Mundane Acquaintances. Hilaire Belloc. ELU; FiBHP; MoVE
Good morning all. Clipping. Tom Veitch. ANYP
Good Morning, America! Harry Kemp. PEDC
Good Morning, America, *sel.* Carl Sandburg.
"Code arrives, A; language; lingo; slang." ReMP
Good morning, daddy! Dream Boogie. Langston Hughes. AmPP (5th ed.)
Good morning, Father Francis. *Unknown.* OxNR
"Good-morning; good-morning!" the General said. The General. Siegfried Sassoon. BrPo; ELU; FaBV; FiBHP; LiTM (1970 ed.); MMA; MoVE; OtMeF; OxBoLi
Good morning, Life—and all. A Greeting. W. H. Davies. MoBrPo; MoRP; NeMA; WaKn
Good morning, Lords and Ladies, it is the first of May. May Day. *Unknown.* RIS
Good Morning Love! Paul Blackburn. NMP

"Good morning, Merry Sunshine." Merry Sunshine. *Unknown.* MPB
Good morning, Mistress and Master. *Unknown.* OxNR
Good morning to the day; and, next, my gold. Ben Jonson. *Fr.* Volpone, I, i. AtBAP
Good morning, to You, Almighty God. Kaddish. Levi-Yitzhok of Berditchev. TrJP
Good morning to you and good morning to you. Good Morning. Rose Fyleman. BoTP
Good morning to you, Lord of the world! Invocation. Levi Isaac of Berditshev. EaLo
Goodmorning with Light. John Ciardi. WaP
Good-Morrow, The. John Donne. AnAnS-1; AnFE; AtBAP; AWP; BoLiVe; CABA; CBEP; CBV; DiPo; EIL; EnL; EnLoPo; EnRePo; ExPo; FaBoBe; FaBoEn; FaBV; FosPo; GTBS-W; HBV; HoPM; InPo; InvP; LiTB; LiTG; LiTL; LoBV; MaMe; MaPo; MBW-1; MeLP; MemP; MePo; OBS; Po; PoAn; PoE; PoEL-2; PoeP; PoFS; PoIE; PoRA; ReEn; SCEP-1; SeCeV; SeCP; SeCV-1; SeEP; StP; TreFT; TrGrPo; TuPP; UnTE; ViBoPo
("I wonder, by my troth, what thou and I.") EG
Good-Morrow. Thomas Heywood. *See* Pack, Clouds, Away.
Good-Morrow, A. Thomas Shadwell. *See* Song: "Fringéd vallance of your eyes advance, The."
"Good-morrow, friend," so spoke, upon a day. The Caterpillar and the Butterfly. José Rosas Moreno. OnPM
"Good morrow, gallant Lover!" St. Valentine's Way. Eleanor Farjeon. MemP
"Good morrow, little rose-bush!" The Sweet, Red Rose. Mary Mapes Dodge. BiCB
"Good morrow, my lord!" in the sky alone. Sir Lark and King Sun. George Macdonald. *Fr.* Adela Cathcart. HBV; HBVY; OTPC
Good Morrow. 'Tis Saint Valentine's Day. Shakespeare. *See* Tomorrow Is Saint Valentine's Day.
Good morrow to the day so fair. The Mad Maid's Song. Robert Herrick. AWP; BoLiVe; CH; EG; EnLoPo; InPo; LoBV; OBEV; PoeP; PoFS; SeCL; SeCV-1; SeEP; TrGrPo; ViBoPo; WiR
Good morrow to you both. Shakespeare. *Fr.* King Lear, II, iv. AtBAP
Good Morrow to You, Valentine. *Unknown.* OxNR; PCH
Good Muse, rock me asleep. A Sweet Pastoral [*or* To His Muse]. Nicholas Breton. LO; OBSC; SiCE
Good my King, in your garden close. The King's Ballad. Joyce Kilmer. HBV
Good Name, A. Shakespeare. *Fr.* Othello, III, iii. FaFP; OTPC (1946 ed.); TreFS
("Good name in man and woman, dear my lord.") OTD; YAT
Good name is better than precious oil [*or* ointment], A. The Better Path. Ecclesiastes, Bible, *O.T.* TreFS; TrJP
Good-natur'd Man, The, *sel.* Goldsmith.
Prologue: "Prest by the load of life, the weary mind," *by* Samuel Johnson. LoBV
Good neighbor, tell me why that sound. The Neighbors of Bethlehem. *Unknown.* OHIP
Good neighbors, dear, be cautious. Allalu Mo Wauleen. *Unknown.* AnIV
Good News from New-England. *At. to* Edward Johnson. SCAP
Good news. It seems he loved them after all. A Song about Major Eatherly. John Wain. CABL; ToPo
Good news to tell! The Corner. Walter de la Mare. BiCB
Good Night. Ruth Ainsworth. BoTP
Good-Night. Joanna Baillie. OTPC (1923 ed.)
Good-Night. Hester A. Benedict. HBV
Good-Night, The. John Donne. MaMe
Good Night. Bernard Isaac Durward. JKCP (1926 ed.)
Good Night! Eleanor Farjeon. ThGo
Good-Night. Henry W. Frost. SoP
Good Night. Thomas Hood. GaP; MPB (1956 ed.); SiSoSe; SoPo
Good Night. Victor Hugo, *tr. fr. French.* BoTP; FaPON; GFA; OQP; OTPC (1946 ed.); PCH; SiSoSe; SoPo; SUS; TiPo
Good Night. S. Weir Mitchell. HBV; MaRV
Good Night. John Nichol. OBVV
Good Night. Dorothy Mason Pierce. BrR; SiSoSe; TiPo (1952 ed.)
Good-Night, A. Francis Quarles. OBS; SeCL; SeEP; TrGrPo
Good-Night. Shelley. HBV; LiTL; ViBoPo
Good Night! John Banister Tabb. ThGo
Good Night. Jane Taylor. BoChLi; HBV; HBVY; OTPC; PPL; SAS, *st.* 1
Good-Night. Edward Thomas. NoP
Good-Night. Nancy Byrd Turner. OQP
Goodnight, A. William Carlos Williams. MoAB; MoAmPo
Good night,/ Sleep tight. Night Blessing [*or* Hush Rhymes]. *Unknown.* HBVY; PCH; SAS
Good-Night? ah! no; the hour is ill. Good-Night. Shelley. HBV; LiTL; ViBoPo
Good Night and Good Morning. Richard Monckton Milnes. BoTP; CPN; OTPC (1923 ed.); PRWS; SAS; TVC
Good-Night, Babette! Austin Dobson. HBV; OBVV; PoVP; VA
Good night, big world. Back to the Ghetto. Jacob Glatstein. TrJP
Good-night, dear friend! I say good-night to thee. Good-Night. Hester A. Benedict. HBV
Good night. Ensured release. Alta Quies. A. E. Housman. SeCeV
Good night, God bless you. *Unknown.* OxNR
Good Night! Good Night! John Holmes. PoToHe
Good night! Good night!/ Far flies the light. Good Night. Victor Hugo. BoTP; FaPON; GFA; OTPC (1946 ed.); PCH; SiSoSe; SoPo; SUS; TiPo
Good-night! Good-night! Far from us day takes its flight. Good Night. Victor Hugo. OQP
Good-night. Good-night. Ah, good the night. Good Night. S. Weir Mitchell. HBV; MaRV
Good night, good rest. Ah! neither be my share. A Night Watch. *Unknown.* OBSC
Good-night! I have to say good-night. Palabras Cariñosas. Thomas Bailey Aldrich. AA; HBV; InP
Good night: it is scribbled on the panels. Finale. Carl Sandburg. *Fr.* Slabs of the Sunburnt West. NeMA
Good night, my Love, may gentle rest. Ode. Charles Cotton. ViBoPo
Good-Night, or Blessing, The. Robert Herrick. ALV
Good-Night Prayer for a Little Child. Henry Johnstone. PPL
"Good Night," Says the Owl. Lady Erskine-Crum. BoTP
"Good night, Sir Rook," said a little Lark. The Lark and the Rook. *Unknown.* OTPC (1923 ed.); PRWS
"Good-night, sleep well!" we say to those we love. Good-Night. Nancy Byrd Turner. OQP
Good night, sweet repose. *Unknown.* OxNR
Goodnight to the Season. Winthrop Mackworth Praed. ALV; InvP; OBNC; OxBoLi; PoEL-4
Good oars, for Arnold's sake. Pax Paganica. Louise Imogen Guiney. AA
Good of the Chaplain to enter Lone Bay. Billy in the Darbies. Herman Melville. *Fr.* Billy Budd. AmePo; AmPP (4th ed.); AtBAP; CBEP; ExPo; LoBV; MAmP; OxBoLi; PoEL-5
Good Ol' Mountain Dew, *with music.* *Unknown.* ABF
Good Old Days of '50, '1, and '2, The. J. Riley Mains. SGR
Good old Mother Fairie. To Mother Fairie. Alice Cary. OTPC (1946 ed.); PCH
Good old negro in the slums of the town, A. The Congo, III. Vachel Lindsay. AmPP; CoBA; LiTA; LiTG; MAP; MCCG; MoAmPo; NeMA; NP; OxBA; PFY; PoMa; PoNe; TreF; WHA
Good Old Rebel. Innes Randolph. *See* Rebel, The.
Good Parson, The. Chaucer, *mod. by* H. C. Leonard. *Fr.* The Canterbury Tales: Prologue. BoPe; MaRV; WGRP
(Parish Priest, The) PoLi
("Parson of a country town was he, The," *mod. vers. by* H. C. Leonard.) TRV
(Poor Parson, The.) ACP; CAW
(Poure Persoun, The.) GoBC
Good pastry is vended. LouLou and Her Cat. Frederick Locker-Lampson. ALV
Good people all, of every sort. Elegy on the Death of a Mad Dog. Goldsmith. *Fr.* The Vicar of Wakefield. ALV; BeLS; BLPA; BOHV; CBEP; CEP; FaBoBe; FaBoCh; FaFP; GN; HBV; HBVY; LBN; LiTG; LoGBV; MaC; MCCG; NA; NeHB; OAEP; OBEC; OnSP; OTD; OTPC; PoPo; PoSa; RIS; RoGo; ShM; SiTL; TreF; WaKn
Good people all, with one accord. An Elegy on That [*or* the] Glory of Her Sex, Mrs. Mary Blaize. Goldsmith. BOHV; CBEP; CEP; HBV; InMe; NA; NeHB; OAEP; OBEC; OnPP; OnYI; SiTL; TreFT; WhC

Good people attend now, and I will declare. Man's Amazement. *Unknown.* CoMu
Good people, come and listen, a sad story I will tell. The Gale of August, '27. George Swinamer. ShS
Good people come buy/ The fruit that I cry. A New Song of an Orange. *Unknown.* CoMu
Good people draw near as you pass along. Alphabetical Song on the Corn Law Bill. *Unknown.* OxBoLi
Good people draw neare,/ If a ballad you'l heare. A Lampoon. *Unknown.* PeRV
Good people, give attention, a story you shall hear. Lord Delamere. *Unknown.* ESPB
Good people give attention, and listen for a while. The Queen's Dream. *Unknown.* PeVV
Good people, I pray now attend to my muse. The Lord Chancellours Villanies Discovered; or, His Rise and Fall in the Four Last Years. *Unknown.* CoMu
Good people, what, will you of all be bereft. A Ballad on the Taxes. Edward Ward. OxBoLi; PPON; SiTL
Good Play, A. Robert Louis Stevenson. FaPON; GFA; MoShBr; MPB; OTPC; StVeCh (1940 ed.); TiPo
Good reader! if you e'er have seen. Nonsense. Thomas Moore. BOHV; InMe; NA
Good reason thou allow. Of the Clock and the Cock. George Turberville. EnRePo
Good Reasons. Keith Preston. WhC
Good Resolution, A. Roy Campbell. JKCP (1955 ed.)
Good Rich Man, The. G. K. Chesterton. DTC
Good Samaritan, The. St. Luke, X: 25-37, Bible, *N.T.* TreF
Good Shepherd, The. St. John, X, Bible, *N.T.* TreFS (7-18); WoL (1-30)
Good Shepherd, The. J. Harold Gwynne. BePJ
Good Shepherd, The. Lope de Vega, *tr. fr. Spanish by* Longfellow. BePJ; CAW
Good Shepherd, The. Keidrych Rhys. NeBP
Good Shepherd, The. Christina Rossetti. ChIP
Good Shepherd, The. Dorothy Ann Thrupp. SoP
Good Shepherd, The. Clyde Edwin Tuck. BePJ
Good shepherd, tell this youth what 'tis to love. Shakespeare. *Fr.* As You Like It, V, ii. LO
Good Shepherd with the Kid, The. Matthew Arnold. BoPe; PoVP
Good Ships. John Crowe Ransom. TPM
Good Sir, Whose Powers Are These? Shakespeare. *Fr.* Hamlet, IV, iv. WaaP
Good stout tankard at a Rhineland inn, A. Der Heilige Mantel von Aachen. Benjamin Francis Musser. ISi
Good struggles with evil, youth with age. The Maker Alone Knows. *Unknown.* PoLi
Good Susan, Be as Secret as You Can. *Unknown.* ErPo; SeCSL
Good sword and a trusty hand, A. The Song of the Western Men [*or* and Shall Trelawny Die?]. Robert Stephen Hawker. ACP (1926 ed.); CBEP; EnRP; EvOK; FOL; GoBC; GTBS; GTSL; HBV; OBNC; OBRV; OBVV; OtMeF; PaPo; PoFr; RoGo; ShBV-1; VA
Good Thanksgiving, A. "Marian Douglas." PoLF; SoP; TVC
Good that never satisfies the mind, A. William Drummond of Hawthornden. *Fr.* Flowers of Sion. Sonn
Good Thoughts. Katherine Maurine Haaff. PoToHe (new ed.)
Good Tidings. Luke, IV: 18-19, Bible, *N.T.* MaRV
Good Tidings. *Unknown.* PCH
Good Tidings of Great Joy! Cecil Frances Alexander. *See* Once in Royal David's City.
Good Tidings of Great Joy to All People. James Montgomery. *See* Angels, from the Realms of Glory.
Good Timber. Douglas Malloch. SoP
Good Time Coming, The. Charles Mackay. PaPo
Good time is coming, I wish it were here, A. When Santa Claus Comes. *Unknown.* ChBR
Good Times. Lucille Clifton. TwCP
Good, to forgive. La Saisiaz: Prologue. Robert Browning. PoVP
Good to hide, and hear 'em hunt. Emily Dickinson. MWA-2
Good toll-gate keeper, kindle a light! Halt and Parley. George Herbert Clarke. CaP
Good Town, The. Edwin Muir. CMoP
Good Tradition, The. *Unknown, tr. fr. Early Modern Irish by* Robin Flower. AnIL
Good we[e] must love, and must hate ill. Community [*or* Communitie]. John Donne. MaMe; Po
Good-wif [*or* Good Wyf] was ther of biside [*or* bisyde] Bathe, A. A Wife of Bath [*or* Seven Pilgrims]. Chaucer. *Fr.* The Canterbury Tales: Prologue. ATP; TrGrPo
Good Wife, The. Proverbs, XXXI: 10-31, Bible, *O.T.* TrGrPo
(Virtuous Wife, The.) MaRV
(Virtuous Woman, The.) TrJP; TRV, *abr.*
Good Wish. *Unknown, tr. fr. Gaelic by* Alexander Carmichael. FaBoCh; LoGBV
Good woman, don't love the man. Parasite. Alfred Kreymborg. NP
Good wood. Food for Fire, Food for Thought. Robert Duncan. NeAP
Good Wyf was ther of bisyde Bathe, A. *See* Good-wif was ther of biside Bathe, A.
Good, your worship, cast your eyes. The Maunding Souldier; or, The Fruits of Warre Is Beggery. Martin Parker. CoMu; WaaP
Goodby. *See* Good-by.
Goodbye. *See* Good-bye.
Goode friend for Iesus sake forbeare. Inscription in a Library. W. G. Wendell. WhC
Goodfriday, 1613. Riding Westward. John Donne. *See* Good Friday, 1613. Riding Westward.
Goodly host one day was mine, A. Mine Host of "The Golden Apple." Thomas Westwood. DD; GN; OHIP; OTPC
Goodness gracious sakes alive! Tardiness. Gelett Burgess. BBGG
Goodness of Age. *Unknown, tr. fr. Japanese by* Ishii *and* Obata. OnPM
Goody Blake and Harry Gill. Wordsworth. BEL; MERP
"Oh! what's the matter? what's the matter?" *sel.* Par
Goody Bull and her daughter together fell out. The World Turned Upside Down. *Unknown.* PAH
Goody O'Grumpity. Carol Ryrie Brink. FaPON; GaP; RePo
Goodyear, I'm glad and grateful to report. To Sir Henry Goodyear. Ben Jonson. NoP
Goops they lick their fingers, The. Table Manners. Gelett Burgess. BBGG
Goose, The. Tennyson. BOHV; GBV (1952 ed.)
Goose and Gander. *Unknown. See* Gray Goose and Gander.
Goose Fish, The. Howard Nemerov. CaFP; CMoP; FiMAP; LiTM (1970 ed.); NePoEA; NMP; NoP
Goose Girl, The. Dorothy Roberts. CaP
Goosegirl's Song. *Unknown, tr. fr. Czech.* PCH
Goose is yellow on the breath, The. The First Swallow. Charlotte Smith. DD; HBV; OTPC
Goose that laid the golden egg, The. Ars Poetica. X. J. Kennedy. ErPo; PP; PV
Gooseberries. Stephen Berg. NaP
Goosepimples. Coleman Barks. PV
Goosey, goosey gander,/ Who stands yonder? *Unknown.* OxNR
Goosey Goosey Gander—by Various Authors. William Percy French. CenHV
Goosey, goosey, gander, where [*or* whither] shall I [*or* we] wander? Mother Goose. BoChLi; HBV; OTPC; OxNR; PPL; RIS; SiTL
Gorbo and Batte. Michael Drayton. *Fr.* The Shepherd's Garland, Eclogue IX. LoBV
("Gorbo, as thou camest this way.") ViBoPo
(Ninth Eclogue, The.) OAEP; TuPP
(Sheepheards Daffadill, The.) FaBoEn
(Shepherd's Daffodil, The.) ElL
Gordian Knot, The. *At. to* Thomas Tomkis. *Fr.* Lingua. ElL; UnTE
Gordon. Ernest Myers. VA
Gordon Childe. David Martin. PoAu-2
Gorgeous in their beauty. Of Silk Is Her Fishing-Line. *Unknown. Fr.* The Book of Songs. HW
Gorilla lay on his back, The. Au Jardin des Plantes. John Wain. FIW; NePoEA-2
Gorgio Lad. Amelia Josephine Burr. HBMV
Gorse. Helen Foley. POTE
Gorse, The. W. W. Gibson. AtBAP
Goshen! Edgar Frank. MaRV; OQP
Gospel According to St. John, The. Bible, *N.T. See* St. John.
Gospel According to St. Luke, The. Bible, *N.T. See* St. Luke.
Gospel According to St. Mark, The. Bible, *N.T. See* St. Mark.
Gospel according to St. Matthew, The. Bible, *N.T. See* St. Matthew.
Gospel According to You, The. *Unknown.* BLRP; SoP; STF

Gospel of Labor, The. Henry van Dyke. TRV
Sels.
"But I think the king of that country comes out from his tireless host." WGRP
"This is the gospel of labor, ring it, ye bells of the kirk!" OQP; WBLP
Gospel of Love, The. First Corinthians, Bible, *N.T.* *See* Charity.
Gospel of Mr. Pepys, The. Christopher Morley. InMe
Gospel of Peace, The. James Jeffrey Roche. PAH
Gospel Train, The. *Unknown.* GoSl; PCH; TrAS, *with music*
(Git on Board, Little Chillen, *with music.*) BoAN-1
Gosport Tragedy, The (A *and* B *vers.*) *Unknown.* BaBo
Gossamer, The. Charlotte Smith. ViBoPo
Gossip. Lexie Dean Robertson. MoSiPe
Gossips, The. Nathalia Crane. MAP
"Got any boys?" the marshal said. The Puzzled Census-Taker. John Godfrey Saxe. HBV
Got Dem Blues, *with music.* *Unknown.* AS
Got my hands on the gospel plow. Keep Your Hands on That Plow. *Unknown.* OuSiCo
Got up and dressed up. Chorus. Jack Kerouac. *Fr.* Mexico City Blues. NeAP
Got up one morning, went out to plow. Tee Roo. *Unknown.* OuSiCo
Gotham, *sel.* Charles Churchill.
"Happy, thrice happy now the savage race." PoFr
Gothic. Jean Starr Untermeyer. AnAmPo
Gothic Church, A. At one end of an aisle. A Crucifix. Paul Verlaine. *Fr.* Amour. SyP
Gothic Landscape. Irving Layton. TrJP
Gothic looks solemn, The. On Oxford. Keats. Par
Gothic Notebook, *sel.* Mario Luzi, *tr. fr. Italian by* William Fense Weaver.
Excerpts from a "Gothic Notebook" ("Once more the stars of love cross"). LiTW
Gothic Tale, A. William Witherup. QAH
Goulden Vanitie, The. *Unknown.* *See* Golden Vanity, The.
Gourd and the Palm, The. *Unknown, tr. fr. Persian by* Charles Mackay. OTPC
Gourd-Heads, The. William D. Barney. FiSC
Gouty Merchant and the Stranger, The. Horace Smith. BeLS; BOHV
Government gave Simeon Clay, The. And/Or. Clarence Day. WhC
Government Injunction [Restraining Harlem Cosmetic Co.]. Josephine Miles. FiMAP; PoNe
Government Official. Paul Dehn. WaP
Governor your husband lived so long, The. John Berryman. *Fr.* Homage to Mistress Bradstreet. AmP; MoVE; TwAmPo
Gowden Locks of Anna, The. Burns. *See* Anna.
Gowk, The. William Soutar. GoTS; NeBP
Gown, The. Mary Carolyn Davies. HBMV
Gown which I do use to wear, The. The Image of Death. Robert Southwell. ViBoPo
Goya. Conrad Aiken. AmLP
Goyng towardes Spayne. Barnaby Googe. EnPo
Grace. Walter de la Mare. ThGo
Grace. Emerson. AmPP; CoBA; MWA-1; NoP; TrPWD
Grace. George Herbert. MaMe; SeCV-1
Grace ("Here a little child I stand"). Robert Herrick. *See* Grace for a Child.
Grace, A. Thomas Tiplady. SoP; TrPWD; TRV
(Prayer for the Presence of Christ, A.) ChIP; MaRV
Grace, A ("God bless the master of this house"). *Unknown.* *See* Christmas Carol: "God bless the master of this house."
Grace ("Good bread/ Good meat"). *Unknown.* SiTL
Grace. Richard Wilbur. LiTA
Grace after Meals. *Unknown, tr. fr. Hebrew by* Alice Lucas. TrJP
Grace Ananne [*or* GraceAnAnne]. Lysbeth Boyd Borie. BiCB; RePo
Grace and beauty has the maid. Song. Gil Vicente. LiTW
Grace and Thanksgiving. Elizabeth Gould. BoTP
Grace at Evening. Edgar A. Guest. TrPWD
Grace at Evening. Edwin McNeill Poteat. ChIP; TrPWD; TRV
Grace before Meat. Robert Herrick. *See* Grace for a Child.
Grace; before Reading Emily Brontë's Poems. Johnstone G. Patrick. TrPWD
Grace before Sleep. Sara Teasdale. MoRP; TrPWD
Grace for a Child. Robert Herrick. AWP; BEL; EnLi-1; FaPON; InPo; JAWP; LoBV; MoShBr; OAEP; PoRA; RIS; ThWaDe; TOP; TrGrPo; ViBoPo; WBP
(Another Grace for a Child.) AnAnS-2; CABA; CaFP; CavP; GoJo; InvP; OBS; OxBoCh; PoeP; ReEn; SCEP-2; SeCV-1; SeEP
(Child's Grace, A.) BoTP; EaLo; FaBoCh; LiTB; LoGBV; OBEV; OTPC; SeCeV; TreFS
(Grace.) OtMeF
(Grace before Meat.) ChTr
("Here a little child I stand.") EG; PoG; ThGo
Grace for a Spring Morning in the Mountains. Esther Davis Langdon. RoKL
Grace for Children ("What God gives, and what we take"). Robert Herrick. OxBoCh
Grace for Gardens. Louise Driscoll. TrPWD
Grace for Grace. Mark Guy Pearse. OQP
Grace for Light. "Moira O'Neill." PoRh; SP; WHL
Grace for the Noonday Meal. William L. Stidger. SoP
Grace for Theology. William Langland. *See* Theology.
Grace full of grace, though in these verses here. Henry Constable. *Fr.* Diana. OBSC
Grace of the Way. Francis Thompson.
"Now of that vision I, bereaven," *sel.* MoAB; MoBrPo
Grace Sufficient. Charles E. Bayley. SoP
Grace that never can be told. All Needs Met. J. H. Sammis. BLRP
Grace to be born and live as variously as possible. Ted Berrigan. ANYP
Grace to Do Without. *Unknown.* SoP
Grace to Share. Carlton Buck. SoP
Graceful Acacia. Walter Savage Landor. PoEL-4
Graceful and sure with youth, the skaters glide. The Skaters. John Williams. NePoAm-2; SD
Graceful as acorus or lotus flower. Aliter. Confucius. *Fr.* Songs of Ch'en. CTC
Graceful Bastion, The. William Carlos Williams. NYBP
Gracefullest leaper, the dappled fox-cub. Young Reynard. George Meredith. HoPM
Graces help the goddess dress her hair, The. The Hairdresser's Art. Claudian. *Fr.* Epithalamium for Honorius and Maria. HW
Graces sought some holy ground, The. On Aristophanes. Plato, *tr. by* Lord Neaves. OnPM
Gracious and the Gentle Thing, The. Robert P. Tristram Coffin. OA
Gracious, Divine, and most omnipotent. Barnabe Barnes. *Fr.* A Divine Century of Spiritual Sonnets. SiCE
Gracious Lady:/ Simple as when I asked your aid before. Prayer to the Virgin of Chartres. Henry Adams. AmePo; CAW; GoBC; ISi; MWA-2
Gracious Living. *Unknown.* SoP
Gracious Moonlight. Dante Gabriel Rossetti. The House of Life, XX. MaVP; PoVP; ViPo; VP
Gracious Mother of our Redeemer, for ever abiding. Alma Redemptoris Mater. *At. to* Hermanus Contractus. ISi
Gracious Spirit. Thomas Toke Lynch. SoP
(Holy Spirit, Dwell with Me.) MaRV
Gracious Spirit o'er this earth presides, A. Wordsworth. *Fr.* The Prelude, V. OBRV
Gracious Time, The ("Some say that ever 'gainst that season comes"). Shakespeare. *Fr.* Hamlet, I, i. ChrBoLe; GN
(Christmas.) ChTr
(Hallowed Season, The.) MaRV
("It faded on the crowing of the cock.") MyFE
("Some say that ever 'gainst that season comes.") ChIP; TiPo (1952 ed.)
Gracius and Gay. *Unknown.* SeCePo
Grackle, The ("Grackle's voice is less than mellow, The"). Ogden Nash. PV
Gradatim. Josiah Gilbert Holland. DD; FaFP; HBV; HBVY; MaRV; OHFP; OQP; TIHL; TreFS; WGRP
Graduates are going forth, The. At Graduating Time. *Unknown.* DD; PEDC; PoRL
Graecinus (well I wot) thou told'st me once. In Love with Two. Ovid. MeWo
Graeme and Bewick. *Unknown.* *See* Bewick and Graham.
Graf von Charolais, Der, *sel.* Richard Beer-Hofmann, *tr. fr. German by* Ludwig Lewisohn.
"Evil Man, An!" TrJP
Graffiti. Edward Field. CoPo

Graffiti Poet, The. Nancy Willard. WOW
Grail, The. Sidney Keyes. FaBoTw
Grain Elevator. A. M. Klein. CaP; TwCaPo
Grain of Rice, A. Francis Reginald Scott. PeCV
Grain of Salt, A. Wallace Irwin. BOHV; HBV; WhC
Grains of corn were planted, The. Story of the Corn. K. Fisher. BoTP
Gramercy, Death, as you've my love to win. Sonnet: He Argues His Case with Death. Cecco Angiolieri. AWP
Grammar in a Nutshell. *Unknown.* HBVY; TreFS
(Grammar in Rhyme.) HBV; OTPC
Grammar of Love, The. Martial, *tr. fr. Latin by* J. A. Pott *and* F. A. Wright. ALV
Grammarian's Funeral, A. Robert Browning. AnFE; BEL; BoLiVe; CoBE; DiPo; EnLit; EPN; GTBS; HBV; LoBV; MaRV, *sl. abr.*; MaVP; MBW-2; OAEP; PoE; PoVP; TOP; ViPo; ViPP; VP; WGRP
Grammars and the spellers, The. Vacation Time. Margaret E. Sangster. DD
Gramophone, The. James Reaney. CaP; TwCaPo
Grampa Schuler. Ruth Suckow. HBMV
Grampy Sings a Song. Holman F. Day. BOHV
Grand attempt some Amazonian dames, A. On a Fortification at Boston Begun by Women. Benjamin Tompson. PAH; SCAP
Grand Canal. Alan Ross. POTi
Grand Canyon of the Colorado, *sel.* John Gould Fletcher.
Clouds across the Canyon. HT
Grand Chorus of Birds. Aristophanes. *See* Chorus of Birds.
Grand Cortège, The. Christopher Brennan. MoAuPo
Grand Duke, The, *sel.* W. S. Gilbert.
Out of Sorts. ALV
Grand Finale. Sara King Carleton. FiSC
Grand Inquisitor's Song, The. W. S. Gilbert. *Fr.* The Gondoliers. OnMSP
Grand Match, The. "Moira O'Neill." HBMV
Grand old Duke of York, The. Mother Goose. BoTP; SoPo; TiPo
Grand Opening of the People's Theatre. O. J. Goldrick. PoOW
Grand Opera. James Reeves. MuSP
Grand red sun has glistened in, The. Morning. Hugh McCrae. BoAV
Grand republic's poet is, The. Edwin Denby. ANYP
Grand road from the mountain goes shining to the sea, The. The Little Waves of Breffny. Eva Gore-Booth. AnIV; HBV; HBVY; HT; OnYI; StaST; TSW; YT
Grand Ronde Valley, The. Ella Higginson. AA
Grand State of Maine. State of Maine Song. Roger Vinton Snow. PoRL
Grandeur of Ghosts. Siegfried Sassoon. AnFE; HaMV; MoBrPo; OBMV
Grandeur of this earthly round, The. Plato to Theon. Philip Freneau. AA
Grandeurs of Mary, The. Frederick William Faber. JKCP
Grandfa' Grig/ Had a pig. *Unknown.* OxNR; SiTL
Grandfather Frog. Louise Seaman Bechtel. RePo; TiPo
Grandfather Gabriel. Robert Penn Warren. AnAmPo
Grandfather in the Old Men's Home. W. S. Merwin. LiTM (1970 ed.)
Grandfather Watts's Private Fourth ("Grandfather Watts used to tell us boys"). H. C. Bunner. PoSC; StPo; TiPo (1959 ed.)
Grandfather wrote from Valley Forge. Prophecy in Flame. Frances Minturn Howard. AmFN
Grandfather's Clock. Henry Clay Work. FaFP; NeHB; TreF
Grandfather's Ghost. Joseph Payne Brennan. FiSC
Grandiloquent Goat, The. Carolyn Wells. MoShBr
Grandma told me all about it. The Minuet. Mary Mapes Dodge. OHFP
Grandmamma's Birthday. Hilaire Belloc. ELU; FiBHP; PoPl
Grandmither, Think Not I Forget. Willa Cather. HBV
Grandmother, The. Elizabeth Madox Roberts. GaP; MPB
Grandmother and Child. Ruth Dallas. AnNZ
Grandmother and Grandson. W. S. Merwin. NePoEA-2
Grandmother's Garden. Miriam Ott Munson. GFA
Grandmother's mother: her age, I guess. Dorothy Q. Oliver Wendell Holmes. AA; AmPP (3d ed.); AnNE; AP; CoBA; HBV; InMe; OnPP; TreFS
Grandmother's Old Armchair. *Unknown.* BLPA
Grandmother's Story of Bunker Hill Battle. Oliver Wendell Holmes. GoTP; PAH; PAP
Grandmother's Visit. William Wise. RePo
Grandpa died on his vacation. Poor Grandpa. R. C. O'Brien. ShM
Grandpa Dropped His Glasses. Leroy F. Jackson. GaP
Grandpa Is Ashamed. Ogden Nash. PV
Grandpapa. Harry Graham. WhC
Grandparents. Robert Lowell. LiTM (1970 ed.); ToPo
Grandser. Abbie Farwell Brown. HBMV
Grandson, The. James Scully. NYBP
Grania. *Unknown, tr. fr. Irish by* Frank O'Connor. KiLC
Granite and Cypress. Robinson Jeffers. AmPP (5th ed.); AnAmPo
Granite and Steel. Marianne Moore. NYBP
Granite cliff on either shore, A. The Brooklyn Bridge. Edna Dean Proctor. MC; PAH
Granite Mountain, The. Lew Sarett. HBMV
"Granny, I saw a witch go by," Halloween. Marie A. Lawson. SiSoSe; TiPo (1959 ed.)
Grant at Appomattox. Gertrude Claytor. GoYe
Grant it, Father. Petition. Eleanor Slater. TrPWD
Grant, Lord, that through the printed page. Call to Conflict. *Unknown.* STF
Grant me, dear Lord, the alchemy of toil. Suppliant. Alan Sullivan. CaP
Grant me, indulgent Heaven! a rural seat. The Choice. Nahum Tate. MemP
Grant me sweet Christ the grace to find. The Hermitage. *Unknown, at. to* St. Manchan of Lemanaghan in Offaly. KiLC
Grant me the great and solemn breath withdrawn. Invocation and Prelude. Stefan George. AWP
Grant me to share the common, human lot. The Common Lot. Adelbert Sumpter Coats. TrPWD
Grant, O regal in bounty, a subtle and delicate largess. Hymn to the Sea. Sir William Watson. EtS
Grant the gray cat. Coexistence. Marie Syrkin. NYTB
Grant us the knowledge that we need. Henry van Dyke. *Fr.* The Builders. TrPWD
Granted, we die for good. Table Talk. Wallace Stevens. NoP
Grape Hill, The. Endre Ady, *tr. fr. Hungarian by* Cornell Lengyel. OnPM
Grape is ripened, tilled the field, The. Quiet. Giuseppe Ungaretti. PoPl
Grape-gathering. Abraham Shlonsky, *tr. fr. Hebrew by* I. M. Lask. TrJP
Grapes. Sister Maris Stella. GoBC
Grapes. Pushkin, *tr. fr. Russian by* Babette Deutsch. OnPM
Grapes. *Unknown, tr. fr. Greek by* Alma Strettel. AWP
Grapes are ripe, the frost is near, The. Pastoral X. Robert Hillyer. LOW
Grapes Making. Léonie Adams. MoVE; NePA; UnPo (3d ed.)
Grapes of Wrath, The. Christopher Morley. WhC
Grapevine, The. John Ashbery. ANYP
Grapevine, The. Zoe Kincaid Brockman. GoYe
Grape-Vine Swing, The. William Gilmore Simms. AnAmPo; HBV
Graph. William Carlos Williams. CBV
Grasp. Jules Supervielle, *tr. fr. French by* Glauco Cambon. OnPM
Grass, The. George Bowering. MoCV
Grass, The. Emily Dickinson. *See* Grass so little has to do, The.
Grass. Kathleen Fraser. YAP
Grass. John Holmes. MiAP
Grass. Carl Sandburg. AmPP; AWP; BBV (1951 ed.); BoLiVe; FaBV; JAWP; MAP; MaRV; MCCG; MoAB; MoAmPo; MoVE; NeMA; NoP; NP; OHFP; OxBA; PoLF; PoMa; PoPl; PoPo; TrGrPo; WaaP; WBP; WHA
Grass. Mary Morison Webster. PeSA
Grass. Walt Whitman. Song of Myself, VI. GTBS-W; LiTG; NePA
("Child, A, said, *What is the grass?*") AtBAP; BBV (1951 ed.); BoLiVe; InP; MaPo; PG (1955 ed.); TrGrPo
(From "Walt Whitman.") PFY
(Leaves of Grass, *fr.* VI *and* XX.) AA
(What Is the Grass?) PCD, *abr.;* PCH: TSW
Grass afield wears silver thatch. A Frosty Day. Lord De Tabley. LoBV
Grass and Milk. Alfonso Gatto, *tr. fr. Italian by* Glauco Cambon. OnPM
Grass creeps everywhere, The. Enough. Charles G. Blanden. OQP
Grass Fingers. Angelina Weld Grimké. CDC

Grass grows long in the meadow, The. July Meadow. Louise Driscoll. YeAr
Grass grows profusely in the temple courts. Old Temple in Mountains. Chang Chi. OnPM
Grass grows slowly up the hill, The. The Undiscouraged God. *Unknown.* MaRV
Grass hath such a simple faith, The. Grass. Mary Morison Webster. PeSA
Grass hung wet on Rydal banks, The. With Wordsworth at Rydal. James Thomas Fields. AA
Grass is beneath my head, The. In the Garden. F. S. Flint. NP
Grass is green, the sky is blue, The. Spring Song of a Super-Blake. Louis Untermeyer. HBMV
Grass is half-covered with snow, The. Snowfall in the Afternoon. Robert Bly. NMP
Grass is short and newly yellow-green, The. Return to Lane's Island. William H. Matchett. PoPl
Grass is tougher than steel. Pilgrim. A. M. Sullivan. JKCP (1955 ed.)
Grass is very green, my friend, The. A Unison. William Carlos Williams. PoIE; SeCeV
Grass of fifty Aprils hath waved green, The. On the Proposal to Erect a Monument in England to Lord Byron. Emma Lazarus. AA
Grass of levity. An Inscription [*or* Mortality]. *Unknown.* CBEP; EIL
Grass on the Mountain, The. *Tr. fr. Paiute Indian by* Mary Austin. AmFn; AWP; FaPON; JAWP; WBP
Grass people bow, The. To Turn Back. John Haines. BoNaP
Grass singed and low. Chickory. Zerubavel Gal'ed. TrJP
Grass so little has to do, The. The Grass. Emily Dickinson. FaPON; GFA; GN; HBVY; OTPC; RePo; YT
Grass still is pale, and spring is yet only a wind stirring, The. Only the Wind Says Spring. Helen Janet Miller. GoTP
Grass that is under me now, The. The Dying Lover. Richard Henry Stoddard. HBV
Grass! That's my grass. Grass. Kathleen Fraser. YAP
Grass-Tops. Witter Bynner. MAP; MoAmPo (1942 ed.); NP
Grasse-Hopper, The. Richard Lovelace. *See* Grasshopper, The.
Grasse: The Olive Trees. Richard Wilbur. NYBP; PoAn
Grasses are clothed, The. Divine Abundance. *Unknown.* BLRP
Grasshopper, The. *At. to* Anacreon, *tr. fr. Greek by* Abraham Cowley. AWP; EnLi-1; GoTP; HBV; HBVY; JAWP; OTPC (1923 ed.); SCEP-2; SeCV-1; WBP; WiR
Grasshopper, The. Vachel Lindsay. *See* Explanation of the Grasshopper, The.
Grasshopper, The. Richard Lovelace. AnAnS-2; AtBAP; BWP; CBV; FaBoEn; LoBV; MeLP; MePo; NoP; OBEV, *sts.* 1-3; OBS; Po; SCEP-2; SeCePo; SeCL; SeCV-1; SeEP
(Ode: Grasshopper, The.) ReEn
Grasshopper, A. Richard Wilbur. CBV; NoP
Grasshopper and the Cricket, The. Keats. *See* On the Grasshopper and the Cricket.
Grasshopper, grasshopper, hop-o-the grasses. Grasshopper Hop-o-the Grasses. Grace Taber Hallock. RePo
Grasshopper Green. *Unknown.* BoChLi (1950 ed.); BoTP; FaPON; GFA; HBVY; MPB; OTPC (1946 ed.); PCH; SoPo; UTS
Grasshopper Hop-o-the Grasses. Grace Taber Hallock. RePo
Grasshopper once had a game of tag, A. A Game of Tag [*or* The Playful Crickets]. *Unknown.* PCH; RIS
Grasshopper, the grasshopper, The. An Explanation of the Grasshopper [*or* The Grasshopper]. Vachel Lindsay. FaPON; GFA; OTPC (1946 ed.); PCH; PoRh; SoPo; StVeCh; TSW; UTS
Grasshopper, your fairy [*or* tiny] Song. Earth. John Hall Wheelock. AnFE; APA; CoAnAm; HBMV; InP; LiTA; MAP; MoAmPo; MoRP
Grasshoppers, The. Dorothy Aldis. PTK; UTS
Grasshoppers four a-fiddling went. Rilloby-Rill. Sir Henry Newbolt. HBVY
Grasshopper's Song, The. Hayyim Nahman Bialik, *tr. fr. Hebrew by* Jessie Sampter. FaPON; YeAr
Grateful heart for all things blesses, The. Epigram. Walter Savage Landor. ALV
Gratefulnesse. Geroge Herbert. *See* Our Prayer.
Gratiana Dancing [*or* Dauncing] and Singing. Richard Lovelace. AnAnS-2; CavP; CBEP; CLwM; LiTL; LoBV; MeLP; MePo; OAEP; OBS; ReEn; SCEP-2; SeCL; SeCV-1; SeEP
Gratitude. William Cornish. *See* Pleasure It Is.
Gratitude. Jane Crewdson. FaChP
Gratitude. Mikhail Lermontov, *tr. fr. Russian by* Babette Deutsch. LiTW; OnPM
Gratitude. Clyde McGee. BLRP; OQP
Gratitude. Margaret E. Sangster. MaRV; SoP
Gratitude. Shakespeare. King Henry VI, Pt. II, *fr.* II, i. MaRV
Gratitude. Christopher Smart. *Fr.* Hymns for the Amusement of Children. EiCP
Gratitude for Work. John Oxenham. *See* Sacrament of Work, The.
Gratulatory Elegy of the Peaceable Entry of King James, A. Sir John Harington. SiCE
Gratulatory to Mr. Ben Johnson for His Adopting of Him to Be His Son, A. Thomas Randolph. AnAnS-2; OBS
Grave, The. Robert Blair. BEL; CEP, *abr.*; EiPP; EnRP, *abr.* *Sels.*
Friendship. OBEC
"See yonder hallow'd fane! the pious work." ViBoPo
(Church and Church-yard at Night.) OBEC
"While some affect the sun, and some the shade." CoBE; EnPE
Grave. Waring Cuney. PoNe
Grave, The. John Lyle Donaghy. NeIP
Grave, The. T. Gwynn Jones, *tr. fr. Welsh by* Ernest Rhys. LiTW
Grave, A. Marianne Moore. AnAmPo; CABA; CMoP; CrMA; ExPo; FaBoEn; ForPo; LiTA; MoPo; MoVE; PoFS; PoIE; SeCeV; UnPo (3d ed.)
(Graveyard, A.) NP
Grave, A. John Richard Moreland. HBMV; OQP
Grave, The ("For thee a stead was builded"). *Unknown, tr. fr. Anglo-Saxon.* ACP
Grave, The ("When the turf is thy tower"). *Unknown. See* When the Turf Is Thy Tower.
Grave, The. Yvor Winters. MoVE
Grave and the Rose, The. Victor Hugo, *tr. fr. French by* Andrew Lang. AWP; JAWP; WBP
Grave but ends the struggle, The—Follows then. The Triumph. William Gilmore Simms. Sonn
Grave came to him, at his wish, before, The. Dr. Donne. Kenneth Slade Alling. NePoAm
Grave Charge in Mayfair Bathroom Case. Headline History. William Plomer. FOL; SiTL
Grave fops my envy now beget. Love's Slavery. John Sheffield. CEP
Grave in Hollywood Cemetery, Richmond, A. Margaret Junkin Preston. AA
Grave in Ukraine, A. Saul Tchernichowsky, *tr. fr. Hebrew by* L. V. Snowman. TrJP
Grave Jonas Kindred, Sybil Kindred's sire. George Crabbe. *Fr.* The Frank Courtship. OBRV
Grave near Cairo, A. Kipling. *Fr.* Epitaphs of the War. PoVP
Grave of Arthur, The. G. K. Chesterton. JKCP (1955 ed.)
Grave of Hipponax, The. Edward Cracroft Lefroy. Echoes from Theocritus, XXX. AWP; JAWP; WBP
Grave of Keats, The. Oscar Wilde. PoVP
Grave of King Arthur, The. Thomas Warton, the Younger. CEP; EnRP; GoTL
Grave of Love, The. Thomas Love Peacock. CH; GTBS; GTBS-D; HBV; OBEV
(Beneath the Cypress Shade.) EnRP; OBRV
Grave of Rury, The. Thomas W. H. Rolleston. AnIL; AnIV; IrPN; OnYI
Grave Piece. Richard Eberhart. ReMP
Grave said to the Rose, The. The Grave and the Rose. Victor Hugo. AWP; JAWP; WBP
Grave seems only six feet deep, A. A Grave. John Richard Moreland. HBMV; OQP
Grave-Tree, The. Bliss Carman. CaP
Grave wise man that had a great rich lady, A. Of an Heroical Answer of a Great Roman Lady to Her Husband. Sir John Harington. ErPo
Gravedigger, The. Bliss Carman. BoNaP; CP; MAP; MoAmPo (1942 ed.)
Grave-Digger's Song. Alfred Austin. *Fr.* Prince Lucifer. VA
Gravel Path, The. Laurence Alma-Tadema. PPL
Gravel-Pit Field, The. David Gascoyne. NeBP
Graveled vacant lot. Newport North-Window View. Philip Whalen. FRC

Gravelly Run. A. R. Ammons. CoAP
Gravely she goes about her little duties. The Elfin Wife. "Jake Falstaff." BoC
Graven on the Palms of His Hands. Charles Wesley. BePJ
Graven Thoughts. Sir Philip Sidney. *Fr.* Arcadia. SiPS
Graves. Carl Sandburg. AnEnPo
Graves at Inishbofin. Richard Murphy. NYTB
Graves by the river must have melted in, The. An Exceeding Great Army. Ethan Ayer. FiSC
Grave's Cherub, The. Sydney Clouts. PeSA
Graves of a Household, The. Felicia Dorothea Hemans. HBV; WBLP
Graves of Infants. John Clare. ERoP-1; OBVV
Graves! Where in dust are laid our dearest hopes! Vigilantius, or a Servant of the Lord Found Ready. Cotton Mather. SCAP
Gravestones, I ("Here lie I, Martin Elginbrodde"). *Unknown, at. to* George Macdonald. *See* Epitaph: "Here lie I. . ."
Gravestones, II ("Here lies wise and valiant dust"). John Cleveland. *See* Epitaph on the Earl of Stafford.
Gravestones, III ("Betwixt the stirrop and the ground"). *Unknown.* OtMeF
Gravestones. Vernon Watkins. ChMP
Graveyard, The. Hayyim Nahman Bialik, *tr. fr. Hebrew by* Bertha Beinkinstadt. TrJP
Graveyard. Robert P. Tristram Coffin. AmFN
Graveyard, The. Jane Cooper. NePoEA-2
Graveyard, A. Marianne Moore. *See* Grave, A.
Graveyard Rabbit, The. Frank Lebby Stanton. AA; LHV
Gray. *See also* Grey.
Gray and blue, the boy ghosts with guns are in the spring woods. Codicil for Pvt. John Hogg's Will. Winfield Townley Scott. FiMAP
Gray cat, very willful, took a notion once to wander, A. The Resolute Cat. Nancy Byrd Turner. RIS
Gray clouds against a leaden sky. Easter Morning. Winfred Ernest Garrison. ChIP
Gray despair/ Was on the old mare. The Old Mare. Elizabeth J. Coatsworth. MAP; MoAmPo
Gray distance hid each shining sail. Jubilate. George Arnold. EtS
Gray Dove's Answer, The. Frederic Edward Weatherly. TVC
Gray financier in a thin black auto, A. Dead Snake. William Jay Smith. NePoAm-2
Gray fur collars on a steel limb. Golgotha. X. J. Kennedy. NYBP
Gray [*or* Grey] Goose and Gander. *Unknown.* OxBoLi; OxNR (Goose and Gander.) ChTr
Gray grassy hill, A. Prairie Spring. Edwina Fallis. SUS
Gray, gray [*or* Grey, grey] is Abbey Asaroe, by Ballyshanny [*or* Belashanny] town. Abbey Asaroe. William Allingham. OnYI; OxBI
Gray haunted eyes, absent-mindedly glaring. The Face in the Mirror. Robert Graves. NoP
Gray hulk of the granary uplooms against the sky, The. A Harvest Song. Edwin Markham. PEDC
Gray Matter. Ford Madox Ford. MoBrPo (1942 ed.)
Gray Nights. Ernest Dowson. PoVP; Sonn
Gray [*or* Grey] o'er the pallid links, haggard and forsaken. The Farm on the Links. Rosamund Marriott Watson. OBVV; VA
Gray owl sings f'um de chimbly top, De. A Plantation Ditty. Frank Lebby Stanton. AA; HBV; LHV
Gray Plume, The. Francis Carlin. HBMV
Gray-robed wanderer in sleep. Meeting. Arthur Davison Ficke. NP
Gray sea and the long black land, The. *See* Grey sea. . .
Gray Shore. James Rorty. EtS
Gray Squirrel, The. Humbert Wolfe. GoJo; MoBrPo; NeMA
Gray steel, cloud-shadow-stained. Watch the Lights Fade. Robinson Jeffers. CMoP
Gray Swan, The. Alice Cary. BeLS; BLPA; GN
Gray swept the angry waves. How the *Cumberland* Went Down. S. Weir Mitchell. MC; PAH
Gray the vacant circle of the sea, The. Bermuda Suite. Winfield Townley Scott. MiAP
Gray tide flows and flounders in the rocks, The. At Sainte-Marguerite. Trumbull Stickney. LiTA; MoVE; NCEP; OxBA; TwAmPo
Gray waves rock against the gray sky-line, The. When Nature Hath Betrayed the Heart That Loved Her. Sophie Jewett. AA
Gray Weather. Robinson Jeffers. CMoP
Gray whales are going south, The: I see their fountains. Ocean. Robinson Jeffers. AP; CoBMV
Gray [*or* Grey] Winter hath gone, like a wearisome guest. September in Australia. Henry C. Kendall. BoAu; OBVV; PoAu-1; VA
Grayport Legend, A. Bret Harte. *See* Greyport Legend, A.
Greasy sky-line where the grey, A. The Sailor. Goodridge MacDonald. CaP
Greasy snow remnants. Seasons. Hayden Carruth. NYTB
Greasy water surely polluted by this time. Habitat. Jack Anderson. ThO
Great, A. E. E. Cummings. NYBP
Great, A/ man. A Great. E. E. Cummings. NYBP
Great A, little a. Mother Goose. OxNR; RIS
Great A was alarmed at B's bad behaviour. *Unknown.* OxNR
Great Adventure, The. Henry David Thoreau. HBV; OBVV
Great Adventurer, The. *Unknown. See* Love Will Find Out the Way.
Great Ali, the Sultan, I've heard. The Poem on Spring. Arthur Guiterman. LHV
Great All in All, that art my rest, my home. Francis Quarles. *Fr.* Emblems. TrPWD
Great Amazon of God behold your bread. For Mary McLeod Bethune. Margaret Walker. PoNe
Great and Mighty Wonder, A, *with music.* St. Germanus, *tr. fr. Greek by* John Mason Neale. YaCaBo
Great and mighty wonder, A! Peace on Earth. Anatolius. BePJ; CAW
Great are like the maskers of the stage, The. The Fox and the Bust. La Fontaine. OnPM
Great Argument. Omar Khayyám. *See* Worldly Wisdom.
Great Art Thou, O Lord. St. Augustine, *tr. fr. Latin.* MaRV
Great Auk's Ghost, The. Ralph Hodgson. MoShBr; PoPl; PV; ShM; WhC
Great Bear, The. John Hollander. LiTM (1970 ed.); NePoEA-2; NYBP; TwCP
Great Bell Roland, The. Theodore Tilton. PAH
Great big, black bull came tearin' down the mountain. Tearin' Out-a Wilderness. *Unknown.* ABF
Great big dog. The Tale of a Dog and a Bee. *Unknown.* BoTP
Great Black Crow, The. Philip James Bailey. BOHV
Great blue ceremony of the air, The. Mary and the Bramble. Lascelles Abercrombie. OBMV
Great Blue Heron, The. Carolyn Kizer. CoAP; FRC; NePoEA-2; PIA
Great brass bell of austerity. Sousa. Edward Dorn. CoPo
Great Breath, The. "Æ." EPN; MoBrPo; OBEV; OBMV; OxBI; VA; WGRP; WHA
Great Britain through the Ice. Charles Tennyson Turner. Sonn
Great Britain's Joy and Hope on That Noble Prince James, Duke of Monmouth. *Unknown. See* England's Darling.
Great Brown Owl, The. Ann Hawkshaw. OTPC (1923 ed.)
Great Central Railway, Sheffield Victoria to Banbury. John Betjeman. NYBP
Great Chain of Being, The. Pope. *Fr.* An Essay on Man, Epistle I. ExPo
("Far as creation's ample range extends.") ImOP
Great Charles, among the holy gifts of grace. An Epigram to King Charles for an Hundred Pounds He Sent Me in My Sickness. Ben Jonson. OAEP
Great Chinese Dragon, The. Lawrence Ferlinghetti. ToPo
Great Christ, generous Lord, a grace I seek. The Fall of Llywelyn, The Last Welsh Prince. Beddyn Fardd. FOL
Great Churches. *Unknown.* STF
Great City. Harold Monro. NP
Great Commandment, The. St. Matthew, XXII: 34-40, Bible, *N.T.* TreFT
Great, creaking worm. The Elevated Train. James S. Tippett. SUS
Great Creator from His Work Returned, The. Milton. *Fr.* Paradise Lost, Bk. VIII, *ll.* 565-601. TreFT
Great Cross of Mercy, The. Theodosia Garrison. PEDC
Great cup tumbled, ringing like a bell, The. The Grail. Sidney Keyes. FaBoTw
Great Day. *Unknown.* BoAN-2, *with music*
Great Day, The. W. B. Yeats. CMoP

Great Destiny the Commissary of God. The Progress of the Soul. John Donne. OxBoCh
Great Diocletian. Abraham Cowley. *Fr.* The Garden. ChTr
Great Discovery, The. Eleanor Farjeon. PoSC
Great Divide, The, *sels.* Anthony Delius. BoSA
"And round these men spread the sub-tropic latitudes," II, 33.
"But stricken with the high cafard, the town," II, 7.
Ethnic Anthem, The, II, 11.
"Let's say, the Opposition knows the ring," II, 29.
"Oh, Jack St James can always cut a dash," II, 31.
"Ocean, with a calm sardonic titter, The," II, 3.
Great Divide, The. Lew Sarett. HBMV
Great dream stinks like a whale gone aground. Why the Soup Tastes Like the Daily News. Marge Piercy. ThO
Great Duke of Wellington, The. E. C. Bentley. *Fr.* Clerihews. CenHV
Great earth itself, The. The Endless. *Unknown. Fr.* Manyo Shu. OnPM
Great Emperor Otto, The. E. C. Bentley. *Fr.* Clerihews. PV
Great-enough both accepts and subdues. Phenomena. Robinson Jeffers. OxBA
Great eucalypti, black amid the flame. The Grave. Yvor Winters. MoVE
Great events, we often find. The Power of Littles. *Unknown.* TreFT
Great Farewells, The. Amanda Benjamin Hall. GoYe
Great Farm. Philip Booth. PoPl
"Great father Alighier, if from the skies." To Dante. Vittorio Alfieri. AWP; JAWP; WBP
Great fear is expected to flash, The. Shrouds and Away. Alfred G. Bailey. PeCV
Great Fight, A. Robert Henry Newell. BOHV
Great Figure, The. William Carlos Williams. QFR
Great Fire, The. Dryden. *Fr.* Annus Mirabilis. FiP
Great Fleas ("Great fleas have little fleas"). Augustus De Morgan. ALV; WaKn; WhC
(Fleas, The.) LiTG; SiTL
(On Fleas.) TreFS
Great Fortune is an hungry thing. Chorus. Aeschylus. *Fr.* Agamemnon. AWP; JAWP; WBP
Great Friend. Henry David Thoreau. MAmP; PoEL-4
Great Frost, The. John Gay. *Fr.* Trivia; or, The Art of Walking the Streets of London. OBEC; SeCePo
Great Gawd, I'm Feelin' Bad, *with music.* *Unknown.* AS
Great Giver of my lovely green in Spring. Autumn. Amy Carmichael. FaChP
Great Giver of the open hand. Four Prayers. *Unknown.* OnYI
Great God! William Roscoe. SoP
Great God-a'mighty, *with music.* *Unknown.* ABF
Great God! beneath whose piercing eye. Great God! William Roscoe. SoP
Great God, how short's mans time; each minute speaks. Meditations for July 19, 1666. Philip Pain. SCAP
Great God, I Ask Thee for No Meaner Pelf. Henry David Thoreau. *See* My Prayer.
Great God of Hope, how green Thy trees. Hope. Amy Carmichael. FaChP; TRV
Great God of Nations, now to Thee. Hymn of Gratitude. *Unknown.* BLRP
Great God Pan, The. Elizabeth Barrett Browning. *See* Musical Instrument, The.
Great God, that bowest sky and star. Hymn for the Church Militant. G. K. Chesterton. OxBoCh
Great God, Thou giver of all good. *Unknown.* BLRP
Great God: within whose simple essence. To God the Father. Henry Constable. GoBC; PoLi
Great goddesse to whose throne in Cynthian fires. The Shadow of Night. George Chapman. AtBAP; NCEP; PoEL-2; ReIE
Great gold apples of night, The. People. D. H. Lawrence. BrPo
Great, good, and just, could I but rate. Epitaph on King Charles I [*or* His Metrical Vow *or* Lines on the Execution of King Charles I]. James Graham, Marquess of Montrose. GoTS; OBS; OnPM; OxBS; ViBoPo
Great-Granddad, *with music.* *Unknown.* CoSo
Great-Grandmother, The. Robert Graves. DTC; MoPW
Great-grandmother talks by the hour to me. Irish Grandmother. Katherine Edelman. AmFN; SiSoSe
Great, grey caravans moving in the night. Caravans. Hal Borland. MoSiPe
Great Grey Plain, The. Henry Lawson. BoAu
Great Grey Water, The. E. J. Brady. BoAu
Great Guest Comes, The. Edwin Markham. *See* How the Great Guest Came.
Great-Heart. Kipling. HBV
Great Heart. John Oxenham. *See* Where Are You Going, Great-Heart?
Great Heart is dead, they say. Promotion. John Oxenham. MaRV
Great heart, who taught thee so to die. Epitaph: On Sir Walter Rawleigh at His Execution. *Unknown.* OBS
Great Heav'n! how frail thy Creature Man is made! Love and Reason. Matthew Prior. *Fr.* Solomon, II. OBEC
Great Herod on his golden throne. The Little Christmas Donkey. Geraldine Farrar. StJW
Great Hunger, The, *sel.* Patrick Kavanagh.
"Health and wealth and love he too dreamed of in May." MoAB
Great Hunt, The. Carl Sandburg. MoLP; NP
Great Idealist, The. Jami, *tr. fr. Persian. LiTW, tr. by* E. H. Whinfield; OnPM, *tr. by* F. Hadland Davis
Great is Caesar: He has conquered Seven Kingdoms. Fugal-Chorus. W. H. Auden. *Fr.* For the Time Being. LiTM (rev. ed.); NePA; SeCeV
Great is my beauty, like a dream of stone. To Beauty. Baudelaire. EnLi-2
Great is she, born in serfdom. The Revolution. Filip Stepanovich Shkulev. PoFr
Great is the folly of a feeble braine. The Love-Sicke Poet [*or* Satire]. Joseph Hall. *Fr.* Virgidemiarum. FaBoEn; ReIE
Great is the rose. Tadmor: Song. Nathalia Crane. MAP; MoAmPo (1942 ed.)
Great is the sun, and wide he goes. Summer Sun. Robert Louis Stevenson. MoBrPo
Great is the tumult of men's anger grown. From Bethlehem Blown. Mary Sinton Leitch. PGD
Great is thy worke in wildernesse, Oh man. Mr. Eliot Pastor of the Church of Christ at Roxbury. Edward Johnson. SCAP
Great Jehovah speaks to us, The. The Old Testament [*or* Names and Order of the Books of the Old Testament]. Thomas Russell. BLPA; TreFS
Great Jehova's working word effecting wondrously, The. Good News from New-England. *At. to* Edward Johnson. SCAP
Great jewels glitter like a wizard's rain. On Broadway. George Sylvester Viereck. OQP
Great Julius was a cuckold & may I. *Unknown.* SeCSL
Great King Sun is out in the cold. Snowdrops. W. Graham Robertson. OTPC; PPL
Great King, the Sovereign [*or* Sov'raigne] Ruler of this land. To His Late Majesty, Concerning the True Form of English Poetry. Sir John Beaumont. OBS; SeEP
"Great lady, were you Helen long ago?" Helen—Old. Isabel Ecclestone Mackay. CaP
Great Lakes Suite, The. James Reaney. WHW
Great Leo roared at my birth. Anniversaries. Donald Justice. TDP
Great Lover, The. Rupert Brooke. BEL; BoLiVe; BrPo; EnLit; FaFP; HoPM; LiTB; LiTM; MCCG; MoBrPo; NeMA; PoMa; PoRA (rev. ed.); TIHL; TreF; TrGrPo; WaP; WePo
"These I have loved," *sel.* NAMP; ShBV-2
Great Macedon, that out of Persia chased, The. In Praise of Wyatt's Psalms. Earl of Surrey. FCP; SiPS
Great Magicians, The. C. Day Lewis. EaLo
Great Man, A. Goldsmith. NA
Great Man. B. S. Johnson. ELU
Great Man, The. Eunice Tietjens. NP; WGRP
Great Master Dreamer. Charles Buxton Going. *See* Columbus.
Great master of the poet's art! John Greenleaf Whittier. Phoebe Cary. DD
Great masters of the commonplace, The. *See* Greater masters of the commonplace, The.
Great Men Have Been among Us. Wordsworth. EnRP; MBW-2; MERP; PoEL-4
(England, 1802, III.) HBV; OBEV
("Great men have been among us; hands that penned.") Sonn

Great men have lived. There Lived a Man. Thomas Curtis Clark. ChIP
Great Michelangelo, with age grown bleak. Michelangelo's Kiss. Dante Gabriel Rossetti. The House of Life, XCIV. MaVP; PoVP; ViPo
Great Misgiving, The. Sir William Watson. HBV; OBEV (1st ed.); OBVV
Great moral of my next set of, The. Naval Engagement. Tom Veitch. ANYP
Great Mother Nature! teach me, like thee. George Meredith. *Fr.* Ode to the Spirit of Earth in Autumn. EPN
Great Mourning. First Maccabees, I: 25-28, Bible, Apocrypha. TrJP
Greater Mystery, The. John Myers O'Hara. HT
Great names of the great captains gone before. Canada to England. Marjorie Pickthall. PoFr
Great Nature clothes the soul, which is but thin. The Soul's Garment. Margaret Cavendish, Duchess of Newcastle. OxBoCh; SeCePo; SeCL
Great Nature Is an Army Gay. Richard Watson Gilder. HBV
Great Oak. Bennett Chapple. HH
Great Ocean! strongest of creation's sons. Ocean. Robert Pollok. *Fr.* The Course of Time. EtS
Great Offence, The. Abu Nuwas, *tr. fr. Arabic by* E. Powys Mathers. LiTW
Great Osmond knows not how he shall be known. Satire. Joseph Hall. *Fr.* Virgidemiarum. ReIE
Great Overdog, The,/ That heavenly beast. Canis Major. Robert Frost. *Fr.* A Sky Pair. MAP; MoAB; MoAmPo
Great Pacific railway, The. The Railroad Cars Are Coming. *Unknown.* AmFN; AS; BrR; FaPON; MPB
Great Panjandrum [Himself], The. Samuel Foote. FaBoCh; LoGBV; MoShBr; Par; PoLF; RIS; WhC
Great Pax Whitie, The. Nikki Giovanni. WSL
Great Physician, The. Charles Kingsley. MaRV
Great Physician, The. Sadi, *tr. fr. Persian by* Sir Edwin Arnold. *Fr.* The Bustan. AWP; OuHeWo
Great Poet, The. Mu'tamid, King of Seville, *tr. fr. Arabic by* Dulcie L. Smith. LiTW
Great Powers Conference. Edith Lovejoy Pierce. PGD
Great Prince of heaven, begotten of that King. To God the Son. Henry Constable. OBSC
Great princes have great playthings. Playthings. William Cowper. WaaP
Great Redeemer Lives, The. Anne Steele. BePJ
Great Republic goes to war, The. War. Grace Ellery Channing. AA
Great River, The. Henry van Dyke. TrPWD
Great roads the Romans built that men might meet. What Shall Endure? Ethelyn M. Hartwich. OQP
Great Round-up, The. *Unknown. See* Cowboy's Dream, The.
Great Ruler of the earth and skies. Thanksgiving for National Peace. Anne Steele. SoP
Great Sassacus fled from the eastern shores. Death Song. Alonzo Lewis. PAH
Great Scarf of Birds, The. John Updike. NYBP
Great sea, The. Man and the Sea. Tu Hsün Hao. OnPM
Great sea dog, fighter in the great old way! Hawke. Archibald T. Strong. *Fr.* Sonnets of the Empire. BoAu
Great sea-roads to England, The. The Gates to England. Marjorie Wilson. BoTP
Great Shepherd of the Sheep. Charles Wesley. BePJ
Great ship spreads her wings, her plumes are flying, The. Godspeed. Harriet Prescott Spofford. EtS
Great Silence. Sister Mary St. Virginia. JKCP (1955 ed.)
Great Silkie of Sule Skerry [*or* Skerrie], The. *Unknown.* BaBo (A *and* B *vers.*); BuBa; ChTr; ESPB; FaBoCh; OBB; ViBoFo (A *vers.;* B *vers., with music*)
(Silkie o' Sule Skerrie, The.) EtS
Great Sir, having just had the good luck to catch. Copy of an Intercepted Despatch. Thomas Moore. NBM
Great Sled-Makers, The. Kenneth Patchen. ToPo
Great Society, The. Robert Bly. CAD
Great Society, The. John Haines. ThO
Great soft downy snow storm like a cloak, The. The Snow Storm. Ethelwyn Wetherald. VA
Great son of night! come from thine ebon cell. On Morpheus. *Unknown.* SeCL
Great soul, thou sittest with me in my room. To the Spirit of Keats. James Russell Lowell. Sonn
Great soul, to all brave souls akin. The Star. Marion Couthouy Smith. DD; PAH
Great Sovereign of the earth and sea. Europa. Stephen Henry Thayer. AA
Great Spaces. Howard Moss. TwCP
Great Spirit of the speeding spheres. Hymn. John Haynes Holmes. TrPWD
Great spirits now on earth are sojourning. Addressed to Haydon [*or* To Haydon]. Keats. EnRP; MBW-2; MERP; OBNC; PeER; Sonn
Great Statue of the General Du Puy, The. Wallace Stevens. LiTA
Great, still shape, alone, A. Ireland. John James Piatt. AA
Great stone frog doorstop, The. Glenn Pritchard. NYTB
Great stone hearth is gone, The. Fire. Dorothy Wellesley. OBMV
Great Strafford! worthy of that name, though all. On the Earl of Strafford's Trial and Death. John Denham. LoBV
Great streets of silence led away. Emily Dickinson. AtBAP
Great Summons, The. Chu Yuan, *tr. fr. Chinese by* Arthur Waley. AWP; LiTW
Great sun sinks behind the town, The. To an Ungentle Critic. Robert Graves. HBMV; InMe
Great Swamp Fight, The. Caroline Hazard. PAH
Great swart cheek and the gleam of tears, A. The Washer Woman. Otto Leland Bohanan. BANP
Great Sword Bearer, The, only knows just when he'll wound my heart—not I. The Conclusion of the Whole Matter. Ridgely Torrence. *Fr.* The House of a Hundred Lights. AA; HBV
Great tempest rages on the plain of Ler, A. Song of the Sea. *Unknown, at. to* Rumann MaColmain. OnYI
Great Things. Blake. *See* Eternity.
Great Things. Thomas Hardy. GTBS-P; GTSL; MoVE; TreFT
Great things are done when men and mountains meet. Gnomic Verses [*or* Couplet]. Blake. CBV; PV; TrGrPo
Great thoughts in crude, unshapely verse set forth. On Reading. Thomas Bailey Aldrich. AA
Great Time, A. W. H. Davies. AnFE; ExPo; LiTB; MemP; MoBrPo; MoVE; MPB; POTE; WePo; WHA; YT
Great Tom. Richard Corbet. OxBoLi
Great Towers of Steel. Eleanor Foote Soderbeck. PoMa
Great toy-maker, light-bringer, patient, A. Edison. Robinson Jeffers. AmPP (3d ed.)
Great travell hath the gentle Calidore. Spenser. *Fr.* The Faerie Queene, VI. MBW-1
Great trees in the south. Home. *Unknown.* OuHeWo
Great truths are dearly bought. The common truth. How We Learn. Horatius Bonar. HBV
Great unequal conflict past, The. Occasioned by General Washington's Arrival in Philadelphia, on His Way to His Residence in Virginia. Philip Freneau. PAH
Great Venus, Queene of Beautie and of grace. Address to Venus. Lucretius, *tr. by* Spenser. *Fr.* De Rerum Natura *and fr.* The Faerie Queene. AnEnPo; AWP; EIL
Great Victory, The. R. V. Gilbert. BLRP
Great Virginian, The. James Russell Lowell. *Fr.* Under the Old Elm, VII. PGD
Great Voice, The. Clinton Scollard. MaRV
Great Voices, The. Charles Timothy Brooks. HBV
Great Wager, The. G. A. Studdert-Kennedy. ChIP
Great Wave, The: Hokusai. Donald Finkel. PoPl
Great whale is a fish, The. The Whale's Nature. *Unknown. Fr.* The Bestiary. MeEV
Great Wheel, The. "Hugh MacDiarmid." OxBS
Great while ago, there was a school-boy, A. Old Grey [*or* Gray] Squirrel. Alfred Noyes. PoMa
Great White Father, The. William Witherup. QAH
Great, wide, beautiful, wonderful world. The Wonderful World [*or* The World *or* The Child's World]. William Brighty Rands. BoChLi; BoTP; DD; FaPON; GFA; HBV; HBVY; MPB; OBVV; OHIP; OTPC; PCH; PRWS; StVeCh (1940 ed.); TIHL; TiPo (1959 ed.); TreFT; TVC
Great wind blowing, raging sea, A. Comforted. Amy Carmichael. SoP; TRV
Great wind sweeps, A. Wild Weather. Katharine Lee Bates. PGD
Great winds may blow now. Knocking at the Door. John Freeman. HBMV
Great without pomp, without ambition brave. Tribute to Washington. *Unknown.* OHIP

Great worm of the north, in whose footsteps we tread, The. The City in the Throes of Despair. Tony Towle. ANYP
Great wrong I do, I can it not deny. Amoretti, XXXIII. Spenser. ReEn; ReIE
Great Yahweh fingered through His Bible. Apocrypha. X. J. Kennedy. PV
Great you call Demosthenes. Self-Portrait. Moses Mendelssohn. TrJP
Great Zeus, beset by love and lechery. Matter of Taste. *Unknown.* UnTE
Great Zimbabwe. Peter Jackson. BoSA
Greata Stronga Man, Da. T. A. Daly. YT
Greater and taller than our minds can figure them. Prose Poem: The Angels. Théodore de Banville. OnPM
Greater Cats, The. V. Sackville-West. *Fr.* King's Daughter. GTBS-D; OBMV; POTE; ShBV-4
("Greater cats with golden eyes, The.") LO
Greater Gift, The. Margaret E. Bruner. PoToHe (new ed.)
Greater Glory, The. Myra Brooks Welch. MaRV
Greater Guilt, The. John Richard Moreland. ChIP
Greater Love. Wilfred Owen. ACV; AtBAP; BoLiVe; BrPo; CBV; CMoP; EnLi-2 (1949 ed.); EnLoPo; FaBoMo; FaFP; GTBS-P; GTBS-W; LiTB; LiTG; LiTM; LO; MasP; MoAB; MoBrPo; NAMP; OAEP (2d ed.); SeCeV; ViBoPo; WaaP; WaP
Greater Love Hath No Man. St. John, XV: 13-16, Bible, *N.T.* TreFT
Greater [*or* Great] masters of the commonplace, The. Staff-Nurse: Old Style. W. E. Henley. *Fr.* In Hospital. InP; PoVP
Greater Music, The. Theodore Weiss. NePoAm-2
Greater Trial, The. Countess of Winchilsea. TrGrPo
Greater world is water, The. The Tower. Mark Van Doren. MoPo
Greatest, The. Marion Brown Shelton. MaRV
Greatest Battle That Ever Was Fought, The. Joaquin Miller. MaRV; NeHB; OQP; TreF
Greatest bore is boredom, The. *Unknown.* CenHV
Greatest City, The. Walt Whitman. OCS; RePo
Greatest Event, The. *Unknown.* SoP
Greatest Gift, The. Blanche Edith Baughan. BoAu
Greatest imposition that the public ever saw, The. Humbug Steamship Companies. John A. Stone. SGR
Greatest kings do least command content, The. Another, of Another Mind. *Unknown.* TuPP
Greatest Loss, The. Frances Brown. MaRV
Greatest of These, The. First Corinthians, Bible, *N.T.* *See* Charity.
Greatest of virtues is humility. Against Women's Fashions. John Lydgate. ACP
Greatest Person in the Universe, The. Daniel L. Marsh. BLRP
Greatest poem ever known, The. To a Child. Christopher Morley. BiCB; HBMV
Greatest Work, The. Ray M. Johnson. MaRV; OQP
Greatly begin! though thou have time. James Russell Lowell. *Fr.* For an Autograph. MCCG
Greatly instructed I shall hence depart. The Sum of Wisdom. Milton. *Fr.* Paradise Lost, XII. MaPo
Greatly shining,/ The autumn moon floats in the thin sky. Wind and Silver. Amy Lowell. MAP; MoAmPo; NeMA
Greatness ("He took castle and towns"). Thomas Love Peacock. *Fr.* Crotchet Castle: Llyn-y-Dreiddiad-Vrawd, *ch.* 16. OtMeF
Greatness. *Unknown.* OBS
Greatness of Love, The. First Corinthians, Bible, *N.T.* *See* Charity.
Greatness Passing By. John Drinkwater. MaRV
Greatness, Warmth, and human insight. A Chromium-plated Hat; Inlaid with Scenes from Siegfried. Howard Nemerov FiMAP
Greaty-great Grannie. Lysbeth Boyd Borie. GaP
Grecian Kindness. Earl of Rochester. PeRV
Grecian Muse, to earth who bore, The. California. Thomas Lake Harris. AA
Grecian tulip and the gothic rose, The. Poem. Terence Tiller. POTE
Greco, El. *See* El Greco.
Greece. Robert Browning. *Fr.* Cleon. OtMeF
(Cleon.) ViPo
Greece. Byron. *Fr.* Childe Harold's Pilgrimage, II. OBRV
Greece was; Greece is no more. "The White City." Richard Watson Gilder. PAH
Greed. *Unknown.* OxNR
Greedy Fox and the Elusive Grapes, The. Aesop, *ad. fr. Greek by* Louis Untermeyer. MaC
Greedy Jane. *Unknown.* HBVY
Greedy Little Pig, The. Irene F. Pawsey. BoTP
Greedy little sparrow. Birds in the Garden. *Unknown.* ThGo
Greedy Lover, Pause Awhile. Sir Albertus Morton. TuPP
Greedy Piggy That Ate Too Fast, The. Eliza Grove. OTPC (1923 ed.)
Greek Architecture. Herman Melville. MWA-1; NoP
Greek Children's Song. *Unknown.* *See* Children's Song, The.
Greek Epigram. Ezra Pound. MAP; MoAB; MoAmPo; NeMA
Greek Excavations. Bernard Spencer. ChMP
Greek Fathers, The. Cardinal Newman. JKCP
Greek Folk Song; a Cyprian Woman. Margaret Widdemer. *See* Cyprian Woman, A; Greek Folk Song.
Greek Gift, A. Austin Dobson. *Fr.* Rose-Leaves. MoBrPo (1942 ed.)
Greek Idyl, A. Mortimer Collins. VA
Greek ship/ Sails on the sea, A. The Couple. Sandra Hochman. NYBP
Greek War-Song ("Sons of the Greeks, arise!"). *Unknown, tr. fr. Greek by* Byron. FOL; PoFr
Greeks were wrong who said our eyes have rays, The. Lamarck Elaborated. Richard Wilbur. AP; NePoEA; NoP
Green. John Gray, *after* Paul Verlaine. SyP
Green. D. H. Lawrence. ELU; MoBrPo; NeMA; NP
Green. Paul Verlaine, *tr. fr. French by* C. F. MacIntyre. LiTW
Green afternoon serene and bright, along my street you sail away. A City Afternoon. Edith Wyatt. LiTM (1946 ed.); NP
Green and growing thorn-tree, A. Forgive and Forget. "Totius." PeSA
Green and Pleasant Land, A. John Peale Bishop. PoPl
Green and Red and Darkness. Winfield Townley Scott. FiMAP
Green and red lights flank the inlet mouth. Iceland in Wartime. Alan Ross. POTi
Green and silent spot, amid the hills, A. Fears in Solitude. Samuel Taylor Coleridge. EnRP; MERP
Green and the Black, The. Anthony Bailey. NYBP
Green are the tussocks of the marsh-grass springing. Yellow. Kenton Kilmer. GoYe
Green are the woods where the lovers wander. Green Woods. Elizabeth J. Coatsworth. FiSC
Green arsenic smeared on an egg-white cloth. L'Art, 1910. Ezra Pound. OxBA
Green as a seedling the one lane shines. City Traffic. Eve Merriam. OCS; PDV
Green Automobile, The. Allen Ginsberg. NoP
Green Autumn Stubble, The, *Tr. fr. Irish by* Patrick Browne. OxBI
Green be the turf above thee. On the Death [*or* Elegy in Memory] of Joseph Rodman Drake. Fitz-Greene Halleck. AA; AmePo; AmLP; BLPA; DD; FaPL; HBV; MaRV; OBVV; PAH; PoEL-1; TreFS
Green blood fresh pulsing through the trees. April—and Dying. Anne Reeve Aldrich. AA
Green-blue ground, The. On Gay Wallpaper. William Carlos Williams. MAP; MoAB; MoAmPo
Green, blue, yellow and red. The One. Patrick Kavanagh. MoBrPo (1962 ed.)
Green Branches. "Joan Ramsay." MaRV
Green Broom. *Unknown.* ALV; CH; LoEn; OnSP; StPo
(Broom, Green Broom.) LiTB; LiTG; OxBoLi; PoRA (rev. ed.); SiTL
Green Bus, The. James S. Tippett. GFA
Green Candles. Humbert Wolfe. HBMV; MoBrPo; NeMA; PoMS
Green catalpa tree has turned, The. April Inventory. W. D. Snodgrass. AP; CABA; CoAP; LiTM (1970 ed.); NePoEA; PoPl; TwCP
Green cheese, yellow laces. *Unknown.* OxNR
Green Coconuts. Lawrence Durrell. FaBoMo
Green corn waving in the dale, The. The Windmill. Robert Bridges. NoP
Green Cornfield, A. Christina Rossetti. BoTP; PoG
(Skylark, The.) GoTP
Green Councillors. Howard McKinley Corning. NP

Green Door, The. Leah Bodine Drake. BiCB
Green Dryad's Plea, The. Thomas Hood. *Fr.* The Plea of the Midsummer Fairies. OBNC
Green elm with the one great bough of gold, The. October. Edward Thomas. ChMP; MoVE; POTE
Green Estaminet, The. A. P. Herbert. HBMV
Green eye—and a red—in the dark, A. The Train. Mary Elizabeth Coleridge. BoTP
Green Eye of the Yellow God, The. J. Milton Hayes. BLPA; PaPo
Green-eyed Care. Old Cat Care. Richard Hughes. OBMV; ShBV-1; ThWaDe
Green Fiddler, The. Rachel Field. BoChLi; StPo
Green Fields of England! Arthur Hugh Clough. Songs in Absence, IV. OAEP
Green for April, pink for June. The Best Time of All. Nancy Byrd Turner. GFA
Green Frog at Roadstead, Wisconsin. James Schevill. FRC
Green gardens in Laventie! Home Thoughts in Laventie. Edward Wyndham Tennant. DaBS; HBMV
Green Gnome, The. Robert Buchanan. StPo
Green-Gown, The. *Unknown.* CoMu
Green grape, and you refused me. Brief Autumnal. *Unknown.* LiTW
Green Grass. *Unknown.* CH; OxBoLi
("A dis, a dis, a green grass.") BoTP; LO; OxNR
Green Grass and White Milk. Winifred Welles. TiPo
Green Grass Growing. Patrick Evans. NeBP
Green Grass Growing All Around, The. *Unknown.* HBVY; MoShBr; MPB
Green grass growing upward splits the concrete pavement. Green Grass Growing. Patrick Evans. NeBP
Green grass is bowing, The. To Ellen at the South [*or* The Wind in the Grass]. Emerson. BoTP; LaNeLa
Green, green, and green again, and greener still. Conrad Aiken. Sonn
Green, green, I want you green. Somnambulistic Ballad. Federico García Lorca, *tr. by* Roy Campbell *and* Mary Campbell. LiTW; OnHM
Green, Green Is El Aghir. Norman Cameron. *See* El Aghir.
Green, green is my love. Somnambulant Ballad. Federico Garcia Lorca. *tr. by* Warren Carrier. ReMP
Green grew the reeds and pale they were. Symbols. Vance Thompson. AA
Green Grow the Lilacs. *Unknown.* BFSS, *with music;* TreFT
Green Grow the Rashes. Burns. BEL; CABA; CEP; CTC; EiCL; EiPP; EnLi-2 (1949 ed.); EnPE; ErPo; FaFP; LiTG; LiTL; PoE; PoIE; ViBoPo; WHA
(Green Grow the Rashes, O.) ALV; EiCP; EnLit; EnRP; HBV; LiTB; OBEC; SeCePo; SiTL; UnTE
(Song: "Green grow the rashes.") AWP; EnLi-2 (1939 ed.); InPo; JAWP; TOP; WBP
Green Grow the Rashes ("Green grow the rashes, O"). *Unknown.* CoMu
Green Grow the Rushes, O ("I'll sing you twelve O"). *Unknown.* OxBoLi; SiTL
Green Groweth the Holly. Henry VIII, King of England. NoP; TrGrPo; TuPP
(As the Holly Groweth Green.) ViBoPo
(Holly.) CTC; OBSC
(Song: "As the holly groweth green.") FlW
Green Grows the Laurel (A *vers., with music*). *Unknown.* BFSS
Green Hills of Africa, The. Roy Fuller. BoSA
Green hobgoblin, A. A Goblinade. Florence Page Jaques. TiPo
Green, humped, wrinkled hills, The: with such a look. The Green Hills of Africa. Roy Fuller. BoSA
Green Hunters, The. Florence M. Wilson. AnIV
Green, in the wizard arms. The Banshee. John Todhunter. OnYI; VA
Green Inn, The. Theodosia Garrison. HBMV
Green is the night, green kindled and apparelled. The Candle a Saint. Wallace Stevens. PoRA; Sonn
Green is the plane-tree in the square. A London Plane-Tree [*or* A Plane-Tree]. Amy Levy. OBVV; VA; WePo
Green Isle of Lovers, The. Robert Charles Sands. AA
Green Jade Plum Trees in Spring. Ou Yang Hsiu, *tr. fr. Chinese by* Kenneth Rexroth. NaP
Green Knight's Farewell to Fancy, The. George Gascoigne. EnRePo
Green Lady, The. Charlotte Druitt Cole. BoTP
Green Lake, The. Michael Roberts. ChMP
Green lane now I traverse, where it goes, The. John Clare. *Fr.* Summer Images. OBRV
Green Leaf, The. Louis Zukofsky. CoPo
Green Leaves All Turn Yellow, The. James Kenney. IrPN
Green leaves panting for joy with the great wind rushing through. A Summer Day. Henry Charles Beeching. VA
"Green leaves, what are you doing." The Five-fingered Maple. Kate Louise Brown. BoTP
Green level of lily leaves, A. To Paint a Water Lily. Ted Hughes. PP
Green light floods the city square, The. Sunken Evening [in Trafalgar Square]. Laurie Lee. LiTM (1970 ed.); NYBP; POTi; ToPo
Green Linnet, The. Wordsworth. AtBAP; CBEP; EnRP; EPN; ERoP-1; GTBS; GTBS-D; GTBS-P; GTBS-W; GTSE; GTSL; HBV; OTPC; PeER
Green Lions. Douglas Stewart. AnNZ
Green little boy in a green little way, A. Verdancy. *Unknown.* ShM
Green Little Shamrock of Ireland, The. Andrew Cherry. DD; HBV; MPB; PoRL
(Shamrock, The.) HH
Green little vaulter in the sunny grass. To [*or* on] the Grasshopper and the Cricket. Leigh Hunt. EnLi-2; EnRP; EPN; GBV (1922 ed.); GN; GoTP; HBV; OBNC; OTPC (1946 ed.); PCD; Sonn
Green Mistletoe! Winter. Walter de la Mare. ChTr; MoVE; OBMV; YeAr
Green morning of indolence one hedge beyond, A. Morning in the Park. John Ciardi. MiAP
Green Moth. Winifred Welles. BoChLi (1950 ed.); FaPON; StVeCh; TiPo; UTS
Green Mountain Boy. Florida Watts Smyth. GoYe
Green Mountain Boys, The. Bryant. AnNE; MC; PAH; PoPl
Green mwold on zummer bars do show. Tokens. William Barnes. NBM; PoEL-4
Green of the cedars is unlike, The. Poem for Good Friday. D. G. Jones. PeCV (1967 ed.)
Green Place, A. William Jay Smith. RePo
Green Rain. Mary Webb. BoNaP; CH; FaPON
Green River. Bryant. AmPP (4th ed.); AP; CoBA; OxBA
Green River, The. Lord Alfred Douglas. BMC; HBMV; MoBrPo (1942 ed.); OBEV (new ed.); OBVV; PoVP
Green road lies this way, The. El Camino Verde. Paul Blackburn. CoPo
Green Roads, The. Edward Thomas. POTE
Green rushes with red shoots. Plucking the Rushes. *Unknown.* OnPM; ShBV-4; WoL
Green rustlings, more than regal charities. Royal Palm. Hart Crane. AP; CMoP; MAP; MoAB; MoAmPo; NoP; PoIE; TDP; TrGrPo
Green-shadowed people sit, or walk in rings. Spring. Philip Larkin. ACV; MoBrPo (1962 ed.)
Green Shepherd, The. Louis Simpson. NePoEA; NYBP
Green-Sickness Beauty, The. Lord Herbert of Cherbury. AnAnS-2
Green silk, or a shot silk, blue. The River. Donald Davie. NYTB
Green Singer, The. Shaw Neilson. BoAu
Green slated gables clasp the stem of the hill. Pot Geranium, The. Norman Nicholson. POTi
Green Snake, when I hung you round my neck. To the Snake. Denise Levertov. AmPP (5th ed.); LiTM (1970 ed.); NePoEA-2; PoIE; ToPo
Green Song. Philip Booth. BoNaP
Green spider wine, just mellowed. Cozy. T'ao Ch'ien. OnPM
Green spires of the forest, The. A Forest Meditation. Bernice Hall Legg. PGD
Green Spring receiveth. The Great Summons. Chu Yuan. AWP; LiTW
Green spring tide has risen, until its crest, The. Spring in England. Charles Buxton Going. HBMV
Green star Sirius. Winter Dawn. D. H. Lawrence. BrPo
Green Stream, A. Wang Wei, *tr. fr. Chinese by* Witter Bynner *and* Kiang Kang-hu. SD

Green Sunday. Katue Kitasono, *tr. fr. Japanese by* Katue Kitasono. LiTW
Green Symphony. John Gould Fletcher. AnFE; APA; CoAnAm; MAP; MAPA; MoAmPo; MoVE
Green Things Growing. Dinah Maria Mulock Craik. DD; FaFP; GN; HBV; HBVY; OHIP; OTPC
Green Valley. Dorothy Vena Johnson. PoNe
Green Valley, The. Sylvia Townsend Warner. MoBrPo (1950 ed.)
Green Wall My Grave. Martin Seymour-Smith. MoPW
Green were the willows. Returning Spring. Joseph von Eichendorff. CAW
Green! What a world of green! My startled soul. June Rapture. Angela Morgan. HBMV
Green Willow, The. *Unknown. See* The Complaint of a Lover Forsaken of His Love.
Green Willow Is My Garland, A. John Heywood. CoBE
("All a green willow, willow, willow.") ElL
Green willows are for girls to study under. Heresy for a Classroom. Rolfe Humphries. PoMa
Green Woods. Elizabeth J. Coatsworth. FiSC
Green World Two. Miriam Waddington. PeCV (1967 ed.)
Greenaway. John Betjeman. POTi
Greene, garlanded with February's few flowers. The Many. Swinburne. *Fr.* Sonnets on English Dramatic Poets (1590-1650). PoVP
Greene the Cony-catcher, of this dream the autor. A Due Commendation of the Quipping Autor. Gabriel Harvey. *Fr.* Four Letters and Certain Sonnets. ReIE
Greene's Groatsworth of Wit, *sels.* Robert Greene.
"Deceiving world, that with alluring toys." SiCE
Fie, Fie on Blind Fancy! ElL
(Lamilia's Song.) OBSC
Palinode, A. OBSC
"What meant the Poets in invective verse." LO
Greene's Memorial; or, Certain Funeral Sonnets, *sels.* Gabriel Harvey.
His Admonition to Greene's Companions. ReIE
His Apology of His Good Father. ReIE
Greene's Mourning Garment, *sels.* Robert Greene.
Hexametra Alexis in Laudem Rosamundi. ElL; PoEL-2; TuPP
In Praise of Rosamund. AtBAP
Shepherd's Wife Song, The. ElL; EnLit; HBV; LoBV; OBSC; PG; PTK; ReEn; SiCE; TOP; TuPP; ViBoPo
("Ah what is love? It is a pretty thing.") EG
Greene's Orpharion, *sel.* Robert Greene.
Cupid Abroad Was Lated. TuPP
Greene's Vision, *sel.* Robert Greene.
Description of Sir Geoffrey Chaucer, The. AnFE; CTC; OBSC
(Sir Geoffrey Chaucer.) FaBoCh; LoGBV; WePo
Greenest of grass in the long meadow grows, The. June. Jane G. Stewart. BoTP
Greenfield Hill, *sels.* Timothy Dwight.
"And when new regions prompt their feet to roam." Po
Church and School. AmPP (3d ed.)
Sweet Simplicity. AmPP
Two Ways of Visiting. AmPP (4th ed.)
Greenfields. John Newton. *See* How Tedious and Tasteless the Hours.
Greenland Fishery, The. *Unknown.* OBB; SoAmSa, *with music*
(Greenland Whale Fishery, The.) BaBo; OuSiCo, *with music*; ViBoFo *with music*
(Whale, The,) AmSS, *with music*; ChTr
Greenhouse, The. James Merrill. TwAmPo
Greenhouse at Delaware Park moves me, The. Fish. John Unterecker. ThO
Greenland Whale Fishery, The. *Unknown. See* Greenland Fishery.
Greenland Winter, A. Lucy Diamond. BoTP
Greenness. Angelina Weld Grimké. CDC
Greens, *with music. Unknown.* AS
Greensleeves. *Unknown, at. to* Clement Robinson. CBEP; MeWo, *abr.*; PoIE; UnTE
(Lady [*or* Ladie] Greensleeves.) AtBAP; PoEL-2
(New Courtly Sonnet of the Lady Greensleeves, A.) ElL; FaBoCh, *abr.*; LoGBV; OAEP; OBSC; ReEn; ReIE; SiCE; TuPP
Greensleeves and pudding pies. *Unknown.* LO
Greensleeves was all my joy. Greensleeves [*or* A New Courtly Sonnet of the Lady Greensleeves]. *Unknown. See also* Alas, my Love! you do me wrong. CBEP; ElL; FaBoCh; LoGBV; OAEP; OBSC; PoIE; ReEn; ReIE; SiCE; TuPP.
Greenwich Observatory. Sidney Keyes. MoAB; MoBrPo (1962 ed.)
Greenwich Village Saturday Night. Irving Feldman. AmPC
Greenwood fawn at the hidden brook, The. Song for the Greenwood Fawn. I. L. Salomon. GoYe
Greenwood Tree, The. Thomas Love Peacock. *See* Song: "For the tender beech and the sapling oak."
Greenwood Tree, The. Shakespeare. *See* Under the Greenwood Tree.
Greer County. *Unknown.* ABF; CoSo, *with music*
(Hurrah for Greer County.) BFSS
Greet All Equally. Macedonius, *tr. fr. Greek by* Lord Neaves. OnPM
Greeting, A. W. H. Davies. [Charles Kingsley *wr.*] MoBrPo; MoRP; NeMA; WaKn
Greeting, The. W. W. Gibson. POTE
Greeting, A. Philip Bourke Marston. VA
Greeting. *Unknown. See* May Day Carol, A.
Greeting. Ella Young. AnIV
Greeting from England. *Unknown.* PAH
Greeting of the Roses, The. Hamlin Garland. AA
Greetings for Two. James W. Foley. IHA
Greetings of the Season. Hilaire Belloc. SiTL
Gregory Griggs. Laura A. Richards. OxNR; SoPo
"Gregory," his dam would chide." Little Gregory. Theodore Botrel. CAW
Greife com away and doe not thou refuse. *Unknown.* SeCSL
Grenada. Mikhail Svetlov, *tr. fr. Russian by* Alexander Kaun. WaaP
Grenadier. A. E. Housman. EG; OBMV
Grenadiers, The. Heine, *tr. fr. German by* Sir Theodore Martin. OuHeWo
Grenadiers of Austria are proper men and tall, The. Cremona. Sir Arthur Conan Doyle. HBV
Grene groweth the holy. Love Ever Green. *At. to* King Henry VIII. MeEL
Grenstone River. Witter Bynner. PFY
Grevus is my sorow. Unkindness Has Killed Me. *Unknown.* MeEL
Grey. *See also* Gray.
Grey. Archibald T. Strong. BoAu
Grey and Green. Arthur Symons. *Fr.* At Dieppe. PeVV
Grey brick upon brick. Dublin. Louis MacNeice. ACV; OxBI
Grey Brother. U. M. Montgomery. BoTP
Grey clouds sink. Rain Falls on Ioannina. Marge Piercy. ThO
Grey Cock, The (A *and* B *vers.*) *Unknown.* BaBo; ELP, *diff. vers.*
(Grey Cock, The; or, Saw You My Father?) ESPB
Grey Company, The. Jessie Mackay. BoAu
Grey countries and grim empires pass away. Morning in the North-West. Arthur Stringer. CaP
Grey crystal skies. The Bridges. Arthur Rimbaud. FlW
Grey dawn—and lucent star that slowly paled. Faith, Love, and Death. Dowell O'Reilly. BoAu
Grey Day, A ("Grey drizzling mists. . ."). William Vaughn Moody. AnFE; APA; CoAnAm
Grey day left the dusk in doubt, The. Winter Night. Robert Fitzgerald. PoPl
Grey dust runs on the ground like a mouse, The. Dust. P. A. Ropes. BoTP
Grey Eye Weeping, A. Egan O'Rahilly, *tr. fr. Modern Irish by* Frank O'Connor. AnIL; KiLC; OBMV; OxBI
Grey-faced Spirit! let us sit. Thomas Caulfield Irwin. *Fr.* Antique Glimpses. IrPN
Grey Friar, The. Thomas Love Peacock. ALV
Grey girl who had not been singing stopped, The. New Year's Eve. John Berryman. LiTM (1970 ed.); NMP
Grey goat grazed on the hill, The. Grey Brother. U. M. Montgomery. BoTP
Grey Goose, The. *Unknown.* ABF, *with music*; WaKn
Grey goose and gander. *See* Gray Goose and Gander.
Grey, grey is Abbey Asaroe, by Belashanny town. *See* Gray, gray is Abbey Asaroe, by Ballyshanny town.
Grey-green stretch of sandy grass, The. At Dieppe: Grey and Green. Arthur Symons. PeVV; SyP
Grey Hair, The. Judah Halevi, *tr. fr. Hebrew by* Joseph Chotzner. TrJP
Grey horse, Death, in profile bears the young Titus, The. The

Polish Rider. Derek Walcott. ToPo
"Grey Horse Troop," The. Robert William Chambers. HBV; PAH
Grey in the sky and blue against the trees. Journey. Sam Harrison. NeIP
Grey lichens, mid thy hills of creeping thyme. Fairy Things. John Clare. BoPe
Grey Linnet, The. James McCarroll. CaP
Grey, low ceiling, sough of sea wind along forest. The Lairdless Place. Kate Rennie Archer. GoYe
Grey o'er the pallid links. *See* Gray o'er. . .
Grey pussy-willows. Slumber in Spring. Elizabeth Gould. BoTP
Grey [*or* Gray] sea and the long black land, The. Meeting at Night. Robert Browning. BoLiVe; BoLP; CaFP; CBEP; CBV; DiPo; ELP; EnL; EnLi-2; EnLit; EPN; FaBoEn; FaBV; FiP; GBV (1952 ed.); GTBS-D; GTBS-W; GTSL; HBV; InPo; InvP; JAWP; LiTL; MaVP; MBW-2; MeWo; MCCG; OAEP; OBEV; OBNC; PAn; PCD; PeVV; PG (1955 ed.); PoAn; PoFS; PoPl; PoPo; PoRA; PoVP; SeCePo; ShBV-3; TOP; TreFT; TrGrPo; UnPo (3d ed.); VA; ViBoPo; ViPo; ViPP; WBP; WePo
Grey Selchie of Sule Skerry, The. *Unknown.* OxBB
Grey Squirrels, The. William Howitt. TVC
Grey was the morn, all things were grey. A Bit of Colour. Horace Smith. BoTP
Grey Winter hath gone, like a wearisome guest. *See* Gray Winter. . .
Grey Wolf, The. Arthur Symons. BrPo; FaBoTw
Grey woods within whose silent shade. The Ocean Wood. Lord De Tabley. CBEP
Greyer than the tide below, the tower. Homage to Jack Yeats. Thomas McGreevy. OBMV
Greyhound skims the boulevard, The. Dog over Snow. Marion Strobel. NP
Greyport Legend. Bret Harte. EtS
(Grayport Legend, A.) GN
Grief. Elizabeth Barrett Browning. AnFE; CBEP; GTBS-D; GTSL; HBV; LoBV; OBEV; OBNC; OBVV; PoLF; PoVP; StP; TrGrPo; ViPo
Grief. Victor Contoski. ThO
Grief. Albert Ehrenstein, *tr. fr. German by* Glauco Cambon. OnPM
Grief. George Herbert. MaMe
Grief. D. H. Lawrence. NP
Grief Ago, A. Dylan Thomas. AtBAP
Grief and God. Stephen Phillips. WGRP
Grief, find the words; for thou hast made my brain. Astrophel and Stella, XCIV. Sir Philip Sidney. FCP; ReEn; SiPS
Grief hath been known to turn the young head gray. The Young Gray Head. Caroline Anne Bowles. BeLS
Grief-in-Idleness. Thomas Lovell Beddoes. *Fr.* Early Fragments. AtBAP
Grief is a mouse. Emily Dickinson. MWA-2
Grief may have thought it was grief. They Were Welcome to Their Belief. Robert Frost. AtBAP
Grief of a Girl's Heart, The. *Unknown. See* Donall Oge.
Grief of Joy, The, *sel.* George Gascoigne.
"Grief of joy in worthy wise to write, The." ReEn
Grief of Love, The. *Unknown, tr. fr. Arabic by* Wilfrid Scawen Blunt. AWP
Grief Plucked Me Out of Sleep. Jill King. PeSA
Grief that is but feigning, The. The Valley of Vain Verses. Henry van Dyke. HBV
Griefs for Dead Soldiers. Ted Hughes. BoPe; POTi
Griesly Wife, The. John Manifold. ATP (1953 ed.); MoBrPo (1950 ed.); MoBS
Grievance. Amy Lowell. ViBoPo (1941 ed.)
Grievance, A. James Kenneth Stephen. HBV; Par
Grieve Not, Dear Love. John Digby, Earl of Bristol. SeCL
Grieve Not for Beauty ("Almost the body leads the laggard soul"). Witter Bynner. *Fr.* The New World. NP
Grieve Not for Me. *Unknown.* ShM
Grieve Not, Ladies. Anna Hempstead Branch. AnAmPo; FaFP; HBV
Grieve Not the Holy Spirit. George Herbert. AnAnS-1; MaMe; MeP
Grieve not too much, my Albius, since Glycera is no longer. It Always Happens. Horace. Odes, I, 33. UnTE
Grieved though I am to see the man depart. Conditions in Rome. Juvenal, *tr. by* William Gifford. Satires, III. EnLi-1
Grieving mother stood in the square, The. Stabat Mater. Jozef Wittlin. PoFr
Grievous folly shames my sixtieth year, A. Hafiz. *Fr.* Odes. AWP
"Grill me some bones," said the Cobbler. At the Keyhole. Walter de la Mare. DTC; MoAB; MoBrPo
Grim and Gloomy. James Reeves. RePo
Grim Cotton Mather. Cotton Mather. Stephen Vincent Benét. ThLM
Grim death took little Jerry. *Unknown.* WhC
Grim in my little black coat as the sleazy beetle. Tom, Tom, the Piper's Son. John Crowe Ranson. ViBoPo
Grim messenger of God. Malachi. Earl Marlatt. MoRP
Grim visor'd cavalier! Rides silently mischance. Le Chevalier Malheur. Paul Verlaine. *Fr.* Sagesse. SyP
Grinder, who serenely grindest. Lines on Hearing the Organ. Charles Stuart Calverley. CenHV; FiBHP; InMe; NBM
Grinding yoke from Israel's neck he tore, The. Eulogy for Hasdai ibn Shaprut. *Unknown.* TrJP
Grindstone, The. Robert Frost. PoE
Gripped in a crossbow's teeth. The Prisoner. Marcos Ana. BoPe
Grisaille. Terence Heywood. BoSA
Grisaille with a Spot of Red. Samuel Yellen. NePoAm-2
Griselda ("Griselda is greedy, I'm sorry to say"). Eleanor Farjeon. GoTP
Griselda's dead, and so's her patience. Patient Griselda. Chaucer, *mod. by* Edward Hodnett. *Fr.* The Canterbury Tales: The Clerk's Tale. PoRA
Grisette Dines. Antoinette Deshoulières, *tr. fr. French.* CIV
Grisilde is deed, and eek hire pacience. Truth. Chaucer. PoG
Grizzled trapper of the log stockade, The. The Oregon Trail. William Rose Benét. PaA
Grizzly. Bret Harte. AA; AnAmPo; OA
Grizzly Bear. Mary Austin. FaPON; GoJo; PDV; SoPo; TiPo
Grizzly Bear is huge and wild, The. Infant Innocence. A. E. Housman. CenHV; ChTr; DTC; FaBoCh; FaFP; LiTB; LiTM; LoGBV; OxBoLi; SiTL
Groaning Board, The. "Pink." InMe
Groatsworth of Wit. Robert Greene. *See* Greene's Groatsworth of Wit.
Grocer and the Gold-Fish, The. Wilfrid Thorley. BrR
Grocery Store Cat, The. Margaret E. Bruner. CIV
Groggy fighter on his knees, The. Athletes. Walker Gibson. SD
Groined by deep glens and walled along the west. The Glens. John Hewitt. NeIP
Grongar Hill. John Dyer. CEP; ChTr; EiCL, 2 *vers.*; EiPP; EnRP; GoTL; LoBV; OBEC; PoE; PoEL-3; TOP
Sels.
"Below me trees unnumber'd rise." FaBoEn
"Ever charming, ever new." SeCePo
"O may I with myself agree." TrGrPo
"Old castles on the hill arise." ViBoPo
Groping along the tunnel, step by step. The Rear-Guard. Siegfried Sassoon. ACV; BoLiVe; MCCG; MoBrPo; NeMA; WaP
Gross sun squats above, The. Song. Dom Moraes. NePoEA-2
Grotesque! Otomo Tabito, *tr. fr. Japanese by* Ishii *and* Obata. OnPM
Grotesque Love-Letter, A. *Unknown.* MeEL
Grotesque, the line of trees, pronged. Outside. Phyllis Harris. ThO
Grotesques. Robert Graves. CMoP
Sels.
"Dr. Newman with the crooked pince-nez." DTC
"Sir John addressed the Snake god in his temple." DTC
Grotesques, *sels.* Don Marquis.
"I sometimes think that I will," III. FiBHP
"Was it fancy, sweet nurse, " I. FiBHP
Grotto, The. Francis Scarfe. NeBP
Groun' Hog. *Unknown. See* Ground Hog.
Groundhog, The. Richard Eberhart. AmLP; AmP; AnFE; CABA; CBV; CMoP; CoAnAm; DTC; ExPo; FaBoMo; FaFP; GTBS-W; ILP; LiTA; LiTG; LiTM; MasP; MiAP; MoAB; MoAmPo (1962 ed.); MoPo; MoVE; NePA; PG

Groundhog (continued)
(1955 ed.); PoIE; PoSa; ReMP; SeCeV; StP; ToPo; TwAmPo; UnPo (3d ed.); WaP
Groundhog Day. Marnie Pomeroy. OTD; PoSC
Ground Hog, *with music.* *Unknown.* TrAS, *with music*
(Groun' Hog, *longer vers., with music.*) ABF
Ground I walk'd on felt like air, The. The Secret of the Nightingale. Roden Noel. VA
Ground is white with snow, The. Resolution. Ted Berrigan. ANYP
Ground lives out its days as a landscape of refusal, The. Oklahoma Plates. Randy Blasing. YAP
Ground of contradictions, where motif, A. The Cemetery Is. Audrey McGaffin. NePoAm-2
Ground Swell. G. Stanley Koehler. NePoAm-2
Ground-Swell, The. E. J. Pratt. CaP
Ground twitches and the noble head, The. The Second Coming. Dannie Abse. NMP
Ground was all covered with snow one day, The. The Snowbird's Song. Francis C. Woodworth. PPL; SAS
Group of jolly cowboys, discussing plans at ease, A. When the Work's All Done This Fall. *Unknown.* *at. to* D. J. O'Malley *or* D. J. White. AS; BFSS; CoSo; IHA
Group of Verse, A. Charles Reznikoff. NP
Grouped nightly at the cold, accepted wall. The Cocky Walkers. Mervyn Peake. POTE; ShBV-4
Grove, The. Edwin Muir. LiTM (rev. ed.); MoPo
Grove and Building. Edgar Bowers. NePoEA
Grove beyond the Barley, The. Alden Nowlan. MoCV
Grove of Colonus, The. Sophocles, *tr. fr. Greek by* Walter Headlam. *Fr.* Oedipus at Colonus. WoL
Grover Cleveland. Joel Benton. DD; PAH
Groves are down, The. Logging, XIV. Gary Snyder. *Fr.* Myths & Texts. NaP
Groves of Blarney, The. Richard Alfred Millikin. CBEP; HBV; IrPN; OnYI, *with add. verse by* Francis Sylvester Mahoney; OxBI; OxBoLi
Groves of Eden, vanish'd now so long, The. Pope. *Fr.* Windsor Forest. BEL; OBEC
Groves were God's first temples, The. A Forest Hymn. Bryant. AA; AmePo; AmP; AmPP; AnNE; AP; CoBA; MWA-1; TOP
Grow in Hope and Grace. Barbara Anne Baker. TNV
Grow old along with me! Rabbi Ben Ezra. Robert Browning. ATP (1935 ed.); BVV (1951 ed.); BEL; BiCB; CoBE; EnLi-2; EnLit; EPN; FaBV; FaFP; FiP; GTBS; GTBS-W; GTSL; HBV; LiTG; MaRV; MasP; MaVP; MBW-2; MCCG; OAEP; OBNC; OBVV; OQP; OTD; OuHeWo; PoFS; PoPl; PoToHe; PoVP; SoP; TOP; TreFT; TRV; UnPo (1st ed.); ViPo; ViPP; VP; WGRP; YT
Grow weary if you will, let me be sad. Lesbia. Richard Aldington. NP; PoLF
Growing. Frances Frost. BiCB
Growing. *Unknown.* MaRV
Growing Clean. Donald Green. WSL
Growing Gray. Austin Dobson. HBV
Growing in the Vale. Christina Rossetti. *Fr.* Sing-Song. BrR; GFA; RIS; TiPo
(Sweet Daffadowndilly.) BoChLi
Growing need to be moving around it to see it, The. A View of the Brooklyn Bridge. William Meredith. MoVE
Growing Old. Matthew Arnold. EnLi-2; EnLit; FaFP; FiP; HBV; MaVP; MBW-2; OuHeWo; PoEL-5; PoVP
Growing Old. Karle Wilson Baker. *See* Let Me Grow Lovely.
Growing Old. Rose Henderson. BiCB; BoChLi (1950 ed.)
Growing Old. Walter Learned. HBV
Growing Old. *Unknown, tr. fr. Irish by* Frank O'Connor. ErPo; KiLC
(Autumn.) OBMV
Growing Old. Rollin J. Wells. *See* As We Grow Older.
Growing Old. Ella Wheeler Wilcox. *See* Interlude.
Growing old but not retiring. Ever On. *Unknown.* STF
Growing Older. Rollin J. Wells. *See* As We Grow Older.
Growing Rhyme, A. J. M. Westrup. BoTP
Growing River, The. Rodney Bennett. BoTP
Growing Smiles. *Unknown.* PoLF
Growing Up. Harry Behn. BiCB; PDV; SiSoSe; SoPo
Growing Up. Arthur Guiterman. BiCB
Growing Up. A. A. Milne. BiCB; ThGo
Growing Up. *Unknown.* BiCB
Growing Up. Edna Kingsley Wallace. BiCB; MoSiPe
Growltiger's Last Stand. T. S. Eliot. FaBoCh; LoGBV; OnSP; RoGo
Grown Old in Love from Seven till Seven Times Seven. Blake. EiCL
Grown sick of war, and war's alarms. On the British King's Speech. Philip Freneau. PAH
Grown-ups. Rose Fyleman. HH
Grownups. William Wise. TiPo (1959 ed.)
Grows within me slippery. "A New Flower—Pure and Untorn." Sister Mary Norbert Körte. ThO
Growth, The. Marvin Bell. YAP
Growth can sit there from. Regenesis. Ron Welburn. NBP
Growth of Lorraine, The. E. A. Robinson. NP
Growth of Love, The, *sels.* Robert Bridges.
"All earthly beauty hath one cause and proof," XXXV. PoVP
"Come gentle sleep, I woo thee: come and take," XLVIII. Sonn
"For beauty being the best of all we know," VIII. PoVP
"I will be what God made me, nor protest," LXII. PoVP
"My lady pleases me and I please her," XXX. Sonn
"O flesh and blood, comrade to tragic pain," XXI. Sonn
"O weary pilgrims, chanting of your woe," XXIII. MoAB; MoBrPo; PoVP
"This World is unto God a work of art," XVI. PoVP
"Very names of things beloved are dear, The," IV. PoVP
"Whole world now is but the minister, The," III. Sonn
"Winter was not unkind because uncouth," X. Sonn
"World comes not to an end, The: her city hives," L. Sonn
"World still goeth about to show and hide, The," XX. PoVP
Growth of raw power brings you to one knee, The. Lost in a Corridor of Power. Michael Brownstein. ANYP
Growth of Sym, The. C. J. Dennis. ACV
Gr-r-r — there go, my heart's abhorrence. Soliloquy of the Spanish Cloister. Robert Browning. ATP; BEL; BoLiVe; CABA; CaFP; CBV; DiPo; DTo; EnL; EnLi-2; EnLit; EPN; ExPo; ForPo; ILP; LiTB; MaVP; MBW-2; NoP; OAEP; OtMeF; PAn; PeVV; PIA; PoAn; PoE; PoIE; PoVP; SeCeV; ShBV-4; TDP; TOP; TrGrPo; UnPo (1st ed.); ViPo; ViPP; VP
Grub Street Recessional, A. Christopher Morley. InMe
Grubber's Day. Jay G. Sigmund. AnAmPo
Grumble Family, The. Unknown. WBLP
Grumbling Hive, The: or, Knaves Turn'd Honest. Bernard Mandeville. *Fr.* The Fable of the Bees. CEP; EiCL; EiPP
Grumbling Truck, The. Rowena Bennett. MPB (1956 ed.)
Grunto lies groaning of a grievous gout. Olim Haec Meminisse Juvabit. Henry Parrot. SiCE
Gryll eates, but ne're sayes grace; to speak the troth. Upon Gryll. Robert Herrick. AnAnS-2
Gryll Grange, *sel.* Thomas Love Peacock.
Love and Age. HBV; OBEV; OBNC; ViBoPo
Gryphon Sighted in an Iowa Flyway, A. N. G. Westerfield. NYTB
Guadalupe. Grace Hazard Conkling. NP
Guadalupe, W. I. Nicholás Guillén, *tr. fr. Spanish by* Anselm Hollo. TTY
Guard. Michael C. Martin. WaP
Guard of the Sepulcher, A. Edwin Markham. StJW; WGRP
(Guard at the Sepulcher.) SoP
Guard Thy Tongue. Alice M. Barr. STF
Guarded Wound, The. Adelaide Crapsey. AnAmPo; NP
Guardian. Alfred Starr Hamilton. QAH
Guardian Angel, The. Robert Browning. GoBC; HBV; PoVP
Guardian Angel. Cardinal Newman. GoBC
Guardian Angels. Spenser. *Fr.* The Faerie Queene, II, 8. OBSC
("And is there care in heaven?") OxBoCh
(Bright Squadrons, The.) GoBC
(Guardian Angels of Men.) BoC
(Heavenly Aid.) MaRV
Guardian Angels of the Creatures. Blake. *See* Night.
Guardian of All. *Unknown, tr. fr. Arabic by* Sir Edwin Arnold. OnPM
Guardian of Hill and Woodland. Horace, *tr. fr. Latin by* John Conington. OnPM
Guardians, The. Geoffrey Hill. NePoEA-2
Guardians, The. Dom Moraes. BoPe
Guardianship. Georgia Douglas Johnson. GoSl
Guarding the cattle on my native hill. The Sling. Roy Campbell. BoSA

Guarding the doors of the Hispanic Society. The Spanish Lions. Phyllis McGinley. NYBP
Gude and Godlie Ballatis, The, *sel.* *Unknown.*
Till Christ. OxBS
Gude [*or* Good] Lord Graeme is to Carlisle gane. Graeme and Bewick [*or* The Bewick and the Graeme]. *Unknown.* CBEP; EnSB; OxBB
Gude Lord Scroope's to the hunting [*or* huntin] gane. Hughie Grame [*or* Hughie the Graeme]. *Unknown.* ESPB (C *vers.*); OBB
Gude Wallace. *Unknown.* BaBo; ESPB (A *and* G *vers.*)
Gudrun of old days. The First Lay of Gudrun. *Unknown.* *Fr.* The Elder Edda. AWP; JAWP; WBP
Guerdon, The. John James Piatt. AA
Guerdon of the Sun, The. George Sterling. HBMV
Guerilla. Floyce Alexander. QAH
Guerilla Camp. Keith Wilson. TPM
Guerrilla Handbook, A. LeRoi Jones. FRC
Guess what I have gone and done. My Invention. Shel Silverstein. PV
Guess who is this creature. A Song to the Wind. Taliesin. FaBoCh
Guessing Song. Henry Johnstone. OTPC (1946 ed.); PRWS
Guest, The. Wendell Berry. AP; TPM
Guest, The. Harriet McEwen Kimball. AA
Guest, The. Harold Monro. BoPe; NeMA
Guest, The. Pentti Saarikoski, *tr. fr. Finnish by* Anselm Hollo. PV
Guest, The. Dennis Trudell. QAH
Guest, The. *Unknown.* *See* Yet If His Majesty, Our Sovereign Lord.
Guest came from faraway, A. Poem. *Unknown.* HW
Guest for whom I did not care had an utterly uncanny flair, A. Lines Scratched in Wet Cement. Ethel Jacobson. ShM
Guest Lecturer. Darwin T. Turner. BALP
Guest of Our Lovely Daughter, The. Sandford Lyne. QAH
Guests. *Unknown.* *See* Yet If His Majesty, Our Sovereign Lord.
Guests, The. Louis Zukofsky. CoPo
Guid-by, auld ba'! Fu' mony a year. A Scot's Farewell to His Golf Ball. James J. Montague. LHV; PoMa
Guidance ("How wonderful to lay my hand"). Avis B. Christiansen. SoP
Guidance ("There is a tender hand that guides me"). Avis B. Christiansen. SoP
Guide, The. Dawn Finlay. SoP
Guide me, O thou great Jehovah. The Christian Pilgrim's Hymn [*or* Arglwydd Arwain]. William Williams. BLRP; PrWP; SoP; WGRP
Guide, O Christ, this little hand. *Unknown.* ThGo
Guido. Robert Browning. The Ring and the Book, XI.
"You never know what life means till you die," *sel.* OAEP
Guido, I would that Lapo, thou, and I. Sonnet: To Guido Cavalcanti. Dante. AWP; JAWP; WBP
Guidwife when your guidman's from home. Could You Do That? Burns. UnTE
Guild's Signal. Bret Harte. PaPo
Guilielmus Rex. Thomas Bailey Aldrich. AA; AnNE
Guilt Redeemed. Arnold Kemp. WSL
Guilt unavowed is guilt in its extreme. Error Pursued. H. A. Pinkerton. NePoAm
Guilty. Marguerite Wilkinson. MaRV; OQP; TRV
Guilty Father to His Daughter, A. James Schevill. FiMAP; Po
"Guilty or Not Guilty?" *Unknown.* BeLS; BLPA
Guinea. Jacques Roumain, *tr. fr. French by* Langston Hughes. PoNe; TTY
Guinea-Pig, The. *Unknown.* *See* There Was a Guinea-Pig.
Guinevere. Tennyson. *Fr.* Idylls of the King. EnLit; EPN; YAT
"I made them lay their hands in mine and swear," *sel.* TRV
Guiseppe, da barber, ees greata for mash. Mia Carlotta. Thomas Daly. WePo
Guitar, The. Gail Dusenbery. ThO
Guitar Lament for a Mountain Boy. Carl De Suze. CaFP
Guitarist Tunes Up, The. Frances Cornford. ELU; MuSP
Gulbeyaz. Byron. *Fr.* Don Juan, V. PoEL-4
Gulf between us and the brutes, The. Jigsaw III. Louis MacNeice. HaMV
Gulf of Mexico. Alfonso Reyes, *tr. fr. Spanish by* J. B. Trend. OnHM
Gulf Stream, The. Henry Bellamann. EtS
Gulf Stream. "Susan Coolidge." AA; EtS
Gulf-Weed. Cornelius George Fenner. EtS
Gulistan, The. *sels.* Sadi, *tr. fr. Persian.*
Alas. *tr. by* L. Cranmer-Byng. AWP; WoL
Courage, *tr. by* Sir Edwin Arnold. AWP; JAWP; OnPM; WBP
Friendship, *tr. by* L. Cranmer-Byng. AWP; JAWP; WBP
From Slavery to Slavery, *pr. tr. by* Sir Edwin Arnold. OuHeWo
Gift of Speech, The, *tr. by* L. Cranmer-Byng. AWP; LiTW
He Hath No Parallel, *tr. by* L. Cranmer-Byng. AWP; LiTW
Help, *tr. by* Sir Edwin Arnold. AWP; JAWP; OnPM; WBP
Hyacinths to Feed Thy Soul. BLPA; FaBoBe; MaRV; NeHB
Love's Last Resource, *tr. by* L. Cranmer-Byng. AWP; LiTW
Mesnevi, *tr. by* L. Cranmer-Byng. AWP; JAWP; LiTW; WBP
On the Deception of Appearances, *tr. by* L. Cranmer-Byng. AWP; LiTW
Purgatory May Be Paradise, *pr. tr. by* Sir Edwin Arnold. OuHeWo
Sooth-Sayer, The, *tr. by* Sir Edwin Arnold. AWP
Take the Crust, *tr. by* L. Cranmer-Byng. AWP
Wealth, *tr. by* Sir Edwin Arnold. AWP; OuHeWo
Wrestler, The, *pr. tr. by* Sir Edwin Arnold. OuHeWo
Gull. William Jay Smith. TiPo (1959 ed.)
Gull. Dabney Stuart. NYTB
Gull Decoy, The, *with music.* Larry Gorman. ShS
Gull Goes Up, A. Léonie Adams. WHA
Gull Lake set in the rolling prairie. At Gull Lake: August, 1810. Duncan Campbell Scott. OBCV
Gull rides on the ripples of a dream, A. Theodore Roethke. A Walk in Late Summer. OA; PoDB
Gull shall whistle in his wake, the blind wave break in fire, The. The Voortrekker. Kipling. HBV
Gull, up close, A. Seagulls. John Updike. StP
Gulling Sonnets, *sels.* Sir John Davies.
"As when the bright cerulean firmament," II. Sonn
"Hardness of her heart and truth of mine, The," IV. Sonn; TuPP
"Into the middle temple of my heart," VII. Sonn
"Lover, under burthen of his [mistress'] love, The," I. ElL; Sonn; TuPP
"Mine eye, mine ear, my will, my wit, my heart," V. Sonn
"My case is this: I love Zepheria bright," VIII. Sonn; TuPP
"Sacred muse that first made love divine, The," VI. Sonn; TuPP
To His Good Friend, Sir Anthony Cooke, *introduction.* Sonn; TuPP
"To Love, my lord, I do knight's service owe," IX. Sonn
"What eagle can behold her sunbright eye," III. Sonn
Gulliver. Kenneth Slessor. ACV; BoAV
Gulls. Stanley Snaith. POTE
Gulls. Wallace Stevens. NoP
Gulls. William Carlos Williams. FaBoEn; OxBA; TwAmPo
Gulls and Dreams. Lionel Stevenson. CaP
Gulls spiral high above. Dayley Island. Frederick Seidel. CoPo
Gulls, that live by the water and hang around docks. Random Reflections on a Cloudness Sunday. John Hall Wheelock. NePoAm
Gulls when they fly move in a liquid arc. A Gull Goes Up. Léonie Adams. WHA
Gully, The, *sels.* Frank Wilmot.
"If I could take your mountains in my heart," X. BoAV; NeLNL
"Looking from the hut door one dawn in June," II. BoAV; NeLNL
"Now I have touched your soil I will go back," XIII. NeLNL
"There breaks upon my sight," VII. BoAV; NeLNL
Gum-Gatherer, The. Robert Frost. MWA-2
Gun explodes them, The. The Sprinters. Lee Murchison. SD
Gun full swing the swimmer catapults and cracks, The. 400-Meter Freestyle. Maxine W. Kumin. SD
Gun, the trap, the axe are borne, The. Revenge of the Hunted. R. A. D. Ford. MoCV
Gunga Din. Kipling. BBV; BEL; BoPe; BrPo; EnLi-2 (1949 ed.); EnLit; FaFP; FaPL; HBV; LiTB; LiTM (rev. ed.); MCCG; MoBrPo; NeMA; OnMSP; PoMa; PoPl; PoPo; PoVP; ShBV-2; TreF; WePo; YAT
Gunnar in the Pit of Adders. William Morris. *Fr.* The Story of Sigurd the Volsung, IV. PoVP; ViPo
Gunner, The. Francis Webb. BoAV

Gunners move like figures in a dance, The. Drunken Gunners. M. K. Joseph. AnNZ
Gunpowder Plot. Vernon Scannell. FIW
Guns and knives aren't enough. Circled by a Horsefly. Helen G. Quigless. TNV
Guns are hushed, The. On every field once flowing. The Rear Guard. Irene Fowler Brown. PAH
Guns in the Grass, The. Thomas Frost. MC; PAH
Guns know what is what, but underneath, The. Memories of a Lost War. Louis Simpson. NePoAm
Guns of war are silent, The. The Golden Day. Arthur Wallace Peach. PEDC
Guns spell money's ultimate reason, The. Ultima Ratio Regum. Stephen Spender. BBV (1951 ed.); EnLi-2 (1949 ed.); FaFP; LiTB; LiTM; MaRV; SeCePo; WaaP; WaP
Gup, Scot! John Skelton. OxBoLi
Guppy, The. Ogden Nash. WePo
Gus; the Theatre Cat. T. S. Eliot. CenHV
Gusts of the sun race on the approaching sea. Of Thomas Traherne and the Pebble Outside. Sydney Clouts. BoSA
Gusty and raw was the morning, a fog hung over the sea. The Fight of Paso Del Mar. Bayard Taylor. BeLS
Gusty morns are here, The. To a Dog's Memory. Louise Imogen Guiney. AnAmPo
Gut eats [*or* eates] all day, and lechers all the night. On Gut. Ben Jonson. AnAnS-2; EP; NoP
Guthlac, *sel.* Cynewulf, *tr. fr. Anglo-Saxon.*
Death of Saint Guthlac. ACP
Gutted of station, noise alone. Crow Country. Kenneth Slessor BoAV
Guvener [*or* Gineral] B. is a sensible man. What Mr. Robinson Thinks. James Russell Lowell. *Fr.* The Biglow Papers,1st Series, No. III. AA; AmePo; AmPP; AnNE; BOHV; HBV; IHA; InMe; LHV; PAH; TOP; YaD
Guy Fawkes Day. *Unknown.* FOL
("Please to remember.") OTPC (1923 ed.); OxNR
Guy Mannering, *sels.* Sir Walter Scott.
Nativity Chant, The. ChTr; FaBoCh; LoGBV
Twist Ye, Twine Ye! Even So, *fr. ch.* 3. EnRP; TOP
Wasted, Weary, Wherefore Stay, *fr.* ch. 27. EnRP
Gwalia Deserta, *sel.* Idris Davies.
"O what can you give me?" DTC
G'way an' quit dat noise, Miss Lucy. When Malindy Sings. Paul Laurence Dunbar. MCCG; NoP; PoNe
Gwel uwchlaw cymylau amser. Islwyn, *tr. fr. Welsh by* Gwyn Williams. PrWP
Gwine to Alabamy, *with music.* *Unknown.* TrAS
Gwine to harness in the morning soon, soon. Gwineter Harness in de Mornin' Soon. *Unknown.* ABF
Gwine Up, *with music.* *Unknown.* BoAN-1
Gwineter Harness in de Mornin' Soon, *with music.* *Unknown.* ABF
Gwineter Ride Up in de Chariot Soon-a in de Mornin, *with music.* *Unknown.* BoAN-2
Gwinter Sing All along de Way, *with music.* *Unknown.* BoAN-1
Gyges ring they bear[e] about them still, A. Lovers How They Come and Part. Robert Herrick. ATBAP; LO; OxBoLi; PoEL-3
Gymnastic Clock, The. Mary Carolyn Davies. TVC
Gypsies. *See also* Gipsies.
Gypsies. Robert Browning. *Fr.* The Flight of the Duchess. PCH
Gypsies. John Clare. *See* Gipsies ("The snow falls deep. ").
Gypsies. Rachel Field. BoTP; PoRh
Gypsies [*or* Gipsies] came to our good lord's gate. The Gypsy Laddie [*or* Johnie Faa]. *Unknown.* BaBo (A *vers.*); BuBa; ESPB
Gypsies came to our Lord's yett, The. Johny Faa. *Unknown.* OxBB
Gypsies in the Wood. *Unknown.* DTC; OxBoLi
("My mother said that I never should.") BoTP; FaBoCh; LoGBV; OxNR; SiTL
Gypsies Metamorphosed, The, *sels.* Ben Jonson.
All Your Fortunes We Can Tell Ye. ChTr
Gipsy Song ("The faery beam upon you"). FaBoCh; LoGBV; NoP; SeCL
(Faeries' Song, The.) SeCV-1
("Fairy beam upon you, The.") ReEn; TuPP
(Jackman's Song, The.) AtBAP
(Patrico's Song.) BoW; LoBV
(Song: "Faiery beame upon you, The.") SiSw
(Wish, A.) PoRL
Gipsy Song ("To the old, long life and treasure"). NoP; SeCL
Gypsies on the March. Baudelaire, *tr. fr. French by* Arthur Symons. OnPM
Gypsies passed her little gate, The. The Dreamers. Theodosia Garrison. GaP; HBMV
Gypsies' Road, The. Dora Sigerson Shorter. OBVV
Gypsies they came to [my] lord Cassilis' yett [*or* gate]. The Gypsy Laddie [*or* Jackie Faa *or* Johnny Faa]. *Unknown.* AtBAP; BaBo (B *vers.*); ChTr; ESPB (B *vers.*); ViBoFo (A *vers.*)
Gypsy, The. Eleanor Farjeon. GBV (1952 ed.)
Gypsy, The. Ezra Pound. ThWaDe
Gypsy, The. Edward Thomas. NoP
Gypsy, a gypsy, A/ Is what I'd like to be. Being Gypsy [*or* Being a Gypsy.] Barbara Young. BrR; SoPo; TiPo (1952 ed.)
Gypsy Children. Rachel Field. GaP
Gypsy Countess, The. *Unknown.* OBB
Gypsy Daisy came riding o'er the plain, The. The Gypsy Laddie (C *vers.*). *Unknown.* BaBo
Gypsy Davy. *Unknown.* *See* Wraggle Taggle Gipsies, The.
Gypsy Girl, The. Henry Alford. HBV; OTPC
Gypsy Girl, The. Ralph Hodgson. *See* Gipsy Girl, The.
Gypsy-Heart. Katharine Lee Bates. HBMV
Gypsy Heart, The. Harry Noyes Pratt. PoMa
Gypsy Jane. William Brighty Rands. *See* Gipsy Jane.
Gypsy Laddie, The. *Unknown.* *See* Wraggle Taggle Gipsies, The.
Gypsy lives on Kithurst, A. The Gypsy. Eleanor Farjeon. GBV (1952 ed.)
Gypsy passed me with a song, A. Songs of the Plains, III. Glenn Ward Dresbach. NP
Gypsy's Malison, The. Charles Lamb. Sonn
Gypsy's Window, The. Denise Levertov. ToPo
Gyres, The. W. B. Yeats. GTBS-P

H

H. Baptisme ("Since, Lord, to thee/ A narrow way and little gate"). George Herbert. *See* Holy Baptism.
H. Baptisme ("As he that sees a dark and shadie grove"). George Herbert. MaMe; SCEP-1
H. Communion, The ("Not in rich furniture, or fine aray"). George Herbert. AnAnS-1; MaMe; MeP
H. Communion, The ("O gratious Lord, how shall I know"). George Herbert. MaMe
H. L. A. L.; with penknife deep embedded. The Happy Hour. Sylvia Lynd. LO
H.M.S. Pinafore, *sels.* W. S. Gilbert.
British Tar, The. ALV
I Am the Captain of the Pinafore. TreFT
I Am the Monarch of the Sea. TreFT
It Was The Cat. CIV
Little Buttercup. TreFS
When I Was a Lad. PoPo
(First Lord's Song, The.) TreFS
(Ruler of the Queen's Navee, The.) DiPo
(Sir Joseph's Song.) CoBE; LiTB; SiTL
H. Scriptures, The. George Herbert. *See* Holy Scriptures, The.
H. Scriptures. Henry Vaughan. *See* Holy Scriptures.
H——, thou return'st from Thames, whose naiads long. An Ode on the Popular Superstitions of the Highlands of Scotland. William Collins. EiCL; EiCP; EiPP
H: W: in Hiber: Belligeranti. John Donne MaMe
H. W. L. John Nichol. VA
H was an indigent hen. Limerick. Bruce Porter. NA
Ha! are there wood-ghosts in this solitude. La Belle Sauvage. John Hunter-Duvar. *Fr.* De Roberval. OBCV
Ha ha! ha ha! this world doth pass. Fara Diddle Dyno. *Unknown.* CBEP; EIL; FaBoCh; LO; LoBV; OxBoLi; SiTL; ViBoPo
Ha! now you think you've cheated me. Oh, no! John Dancer. LO
Ha! Posanes, by my loss of peace tis shee! *Unknown.* SeCSL
Ha! sir, I have seen you sniffing and snoozling. The Faun. Ezra Pound. FaBoCh; FaBoTw; FIW; LoGBV
Ha' we lost the goodliest fere o' all. Ballad of the Goodly Fere.

Ezra Pound. CAW; CMoP; FOL; FosPo; HBV; LiTA; LiTM; MAP; MoAB; MoAmPo; MoBS; NePA; NP; PoRA; PoSa; TrGrPo
Ha! whare [*or* whaur *or* where] ye gaun, ye crowlin [*or* crawlin'] ferlie? To a Louse. Burns. BLPA; CEP; CoBE; EiCL; EnL; EnLit; EnRP; FaFP; ILP; InvP; LiTB; LiTG; OAEP; OxBS; PAn; Po; PoE; PoPo; SeCeV; SiTL; TreF; ViBoPo; WoL; YAT
Haarlem Heights. Arthur Guiterman. PAH
Habakkuk, *sel.* Bible, *O.T.*
O Lord, How Long Shall I Cry, I: 2-II: 20. LiTW
Habana. Julian Bond. NNP
Habeas Corpus. Helen Hunt Jackson. AA; AnAmPo; WGRP
"Ah, well, Friend Death," *sel.* OHIP
Habeas Corpus Blues, The. Conrad Aiken. NYBP
Habit, The. *At. to* Berton Braley. SCC
(Once You Git the Habit.) CoSo
Habit of Perfection, The. Gerard Manley Hopkins. ACP; BoLiVe; BoPe; BrPo; CAW; CoBMV; EnLit; ForPo; ILP; JKCP; LiTB; LiTG; MoAB; MoBrPo; NoP; OAEP (2d ed.); OBEV (new ed.); OBMV; PoeP; PoIE; PoRA; PoVP; TrGrPo; ViBoPo; VP
"Elected Silence, sing to me" *sel.* UnS
Habitat. Jack Anderson. ThO
Habitations. Hilaire Belloc. PV
Habits of the Hippopotamus. Arthur Guiterman. FaBV; FiBHP; RePo; TiPo (1959 ed.)
Habitué. Helen Frith Stickney. GoYe
Hack and Hew. Bliss Carman. CaP; HBV; VA
Had a great ride boss. Artists Shouldn't Have Offspring. Don Marquis. *Fr.* Archys Life of Mehitabel. CrMA
Had a Little Fight in Mexico, *with music.* *Unknown.* OuSiCo
Had birds no season for their precious songs. Music's Tragedy. W. H. Davies. MuSP
Had Cain been Scot, God would have changed his doom. On Scotland. John Cleveland. BOHV; PV
Had Christ rebuffed me as he did that mother. The Syro-Phoenician Woman. *Unknown.* StJW
Had Gadya—a Kid, a Kid. *Unknown, tr. fr. Hebrew* TrJP
Had God no other heart but this. The Jelly Fish. Robert P. Tristram Coffin. CAW
"Had he and I but met." The Man He Killed. Thomas Hardy. BrPo; CBV; CMoP; CoBE; CoBMV; EnL; FaFP; GTBS-W; ILP; InP; LiTB; LiTM; MoAB; MoBrPo; NP; OQP; OTD; PoIE; PoPl; PoPo; TreF; UnPo; VP; WaaP; WHA
Had he been at home, he would have slept. On Seeing a Dead Man. Prince Shotoku. OnPM
Had he but spar'd his tongue and pen. Swift. *Fr.* Verses on the Death of Dr. Swift. FaBoEn
Had he not breathed his breath. The Deathless Tale. Charles Hanson Towne. ChIP; StJW
Had I a Golden Pound. Francis Ledwidge. AnIV; EnLit; JKCP
Had I a man's fair form, then might my sighs. To——. Keats. Sonn
"Had I a thousand hearts, I'd raise." Love to My Lord. Louisa Van Plattenhaus. BePJ
Had I a thousand lives to live. Consecration. Anna Hoppe. BePJ
Had I a thousand souls with which to love thee. Infinity of Wishes. *Unknown.* OnPM
Had I a trumpet, and that trumpet fames. *Unknown.* SeCSL
Had I a voice of steel to tune my song. Giles Fletcher. *Fr.* Christ's Victory and Triumph: Christ's Triumph after Death. LoBV
Had I an hundred mouths, as many tongues. O Tempora! O Mores! Thomas Freeman. SiCE
Had I been there that cruel day. Crucifixion. Carl S. Weist. ChIP
Had I been worthy of the love you gave. Troilus and Cressida. Aubrey Thomas De Vere. IrPN
Had I but lived a hundred years ago. At Lulworth Cove a Century Back. Thomas Hardy. ChMP
Had I but plenty of money, money enough and to spare. Up at a Villa—Down in the City. Robert Browning. BEL; CBEP; EnLi-2 (1949 ed.); EnLit; EPN; GTBS-P; HBV; InP; MBW-2; PoRA; PoVP; SeCeV; TOP; ViPo; ViPP; WoL
Had I had an inn at Bethlehem. Lineage. Robert Farren. CoBE
Had I, my father, the persuasive voice. Euripides, *tr. fr. Greek.* *Fr.* Iphigenia in Aulis. EnLi-2
Had I not seen him by a swerve of eye. Heron in Swamp. Frances Minturn Howard. GoYe
Had I plantation of this isle, my lord. Shakespeare. *Fr.* The Tempest, II, i. PoFr
Had I that haze of streaming blue. In Phaeacia. James Elroy Flecker. HBMV
Had I the Choice. Walt Whitman. PP
Had I the heavens' embroidered cloths. Aedh [*or* He] Wishes for the Cloths of Heaven. W. B. Yeats. BoPe; CMoP; MoBrPo; NeMA; OBEV (new ed.); OBVV; OTD; SP
Had I the power. The Queen's Song. James Elroy Flecker. BrPo; HBV
Had I the power to cast a bell. A Bell. Clinton Scollard. AA
Had Life remained one whole. Unit. Mary Fullerton. BoAV
Had Lucan hid the truth to please the time. To the Translator of Lucan's Pharsalia. Sir Walter Ralegh. FCP; SiPS
Had Sacharissa lived when mortals made. At Penshurst. Edmund Waller. AnAnS-2; NoP; OAEP; PoFS; ReEn; SCEP-2; SeCV-1
Had she but liv'd in Cleopatra's age. On the Dutchess of Portsmouth's Picture. *At. to* Dryden. PeRV
Had she come all the way for this. The Haystack in the Floods. William Morris. AnEnPo; ATP (1935 ed.); BEL; BeLS; CABA; EnL; EnLi-2; EnLit; EPN; ExPo; GTBS; HoPM; ILP; LiTL; LoBV; NBM; NoP; OAEP; OBNC; OuHeWo; PAn; PeVV; PoE; PoEL-5; PoRA; PoVP; SeCeV; ShBV-3; StP; ViPo; ViPP; WHA
Had Sorrow Ever Fitter Place. Samuel Daniel. *Fr.* Hymen's Triumph. AtBAP; ElL
(Sorrow.) OBSC
Had There Been Peace. Edith Lovejoy Pierce. ChIP
Had there been peace there never had been riven. Dedication. Drummond Allison. FaBoTw
Had this effulgence disappeared. Composed upon an Evening of Extraordinary Splendor and Beauty. Wordsworth. EnRP; MBW-2; PoE
Had Those That Dwell in Error Foul. Ben Jonson. *Fr.* The Second Mask, Which Was of Beauty. TuPP
Had two little cottages out on the green. Larrie O'Dee. William O. Fink. BOHV; HBV
Had we a difference with some petty isle. John Fletcher. *Fr.* Bonduca. PoFr
"Had we a king," said Wallace then. Gude Wallace. *Unknown.* BaBo; ESPB
Had we but world enough, and time. To His Coy Mistress. Andrew Marvell. AnAnS-1; AnFE; AtBAP; ATP; AWP; BoLiVe; BWP; CABA; CaFP; CavP; CBEP; CBV; CEP; CLwM; CoBE; DiPo; EG; ELP; EnL; EnLi-1 (1949 ed.); EnLit; EnLoPo; EP; ErPo; ExPo; FaBoEn; FaBV; FaFP; ForPo; FosPo; GTBS-W; HBV; HoPM; ILP; InPo; InvP; JAWP; LiTB; LiTG; LiTL; LO; LoBV; MaMe; MaPo; MasP; MeLP; MeP; MePo; MeWo; NeHB; NoP; OAEP; OBEV; OBS; OtMeF; PAn; PIA; PoAn; PoE; PoEL-2; PoFS; PoIE; PoLF; PoPl; PoRA; PoSa; ReEn; SCEP-2; SeCePo; SeCeV; SeCL; SeCP; SeCV-1; SeEP; ShBV-4; SiTL; StP; TDP; TreFT; TrGrPo; UnPo; UnTE; VaPo; ViBoPo; WBP; WHA; YAT
Had West followed up her fine opening lead. Aram Saroyan. ANYP
Had you been strong I would have dared. Award. Gertrude Callaghan. JKCP (1955 ed.)
Had you but herd her sing. *Unknown.* SeCSL
Hadad, *sel.* James Abraham Hillhouse.
Demon-Lover, The. AA
Hadn't heard of the atom bomb. The Seals in Penobscot Bay. Daniel Hoffman. TwCP
Hadn't I been. Distance. Robert Creeley. CoPo
Hadst thou not simplicity, how should. Birth of Christ. Rainer Maria Rilke. MoRP
"Haec Est Domus Dei et Porta Coeli." Sister Maria del Rey. JKCP (1955 ed.)
Haec Fabula Docet. Robert Frost. PoeP
"Haec Olim Meminisse Iuvabit." Deems Taylor. InMe
Hag, The. Robert Herrick. BEL; EnL; FaBoCh; GoTP; LoGBV; OTPC; PoeP; PoSC; SeEP; WiR; YAT
Hag, The. Ted Hughes. CBV

Hag and the Slavies, The. La Fontaine, *tr. fr. French by* Edward Marsh. AWP
Hag is astride, The. The Hag. Robert Herrick. BEL; EnL; FaBoCh; GoTP; LoGBV; OTPC; PoeP; PoSC; SeEP; WiR; YAT
Hagar. Francis Lauderdale Adams. OxBS
Hagar. Elisabeth Eybers, *tr. fr. Afrikaans by* Elisabeth Eybers. PeSA
Hagen of Trony went to Kriemhild. The Fall of Siegfried. *Unknown. Fr.* The Song of the Nibelungs. WoL
Haggadah. Abraham M. Klein. TrJP
Hagiograph. Rayner Heppenstall. NeBP
Hai! daughter of the thundercloud. Dance-Song of the Lightning. *Unknown.* PeSA
Haidee ("It was the cooling hour"). Byron. *See* Juan and Haidee.
Haidee ("One of the two, according to your choice"). Byron. *Fr.* Don Juan, IV. SeCePo
Haikai. Issa, *tr. fr. Japanese by* Max Bickerton. PoFr
Haiku: "Ancient pond, The." Basho, *tr. fr. Japanese by* Donald Keene. CaFP
(Haiku: "Old Pond, An," *tr. by* Kenneth Rexroth.) LiTW
(Old Pond, The, *tr. unknown.*) SoPo
Haiku: "Falling flower, The." Moritake, *tr. fr. Japanese by* Babette Deutsch. CaFP
Haiku: "I wonder in what fields today." Kaga no Chiyo. *See* On Her Child's Death.
Haiku: "In my life." Issa, *tr. fr. Japanese by* Kenneth Rexroth. LiTW
Haiku: "Long, long river, The." Boncho, *tr. fr. Japanese by* Kenneth Rexroth. LiTW
Haiku: "New moon in the sky." Basho, *tr. fr. Japanese by* Nobuyuki Yuasa. Po
Haiku: "No one spoke." Ryota, *tr. fr. Japanese by* Kenneth Rexroth. LiTW
Haiku: "Old Pond, An." Basho. *See* Haiku: "Old Pond, An.
Haiku: "On this road." Basho, *tr. fr. Japanese by* Kenneth Rexroth. LiTW
Haiku: "Pine trees explode, The." "Luke." QAH
Haiku: "World of dew, The." Issa, *tr. fr. Japanese by* Donald Keene. CaFP
Hail, aged God who lookest on thy Father. He Prayeth for Ink and Palette That He May Write. *Unknown. Fr.* Book of the Dead. AWP
Hail and beware the dead who will talk life until you are blue. A Newly Discovered "Homeric" Hymn. Charles Olson. NeAP
Hail and Farewell. Anne Higginson Spicer. HBMV
Hail and farewell! Lo, I am the last of a glorious fleet of sail. The Last Gloucesterman. Gordon Grant. EtS
Hail and farewell to those who fought and died. The Dead. John Le Gay Brereton. BoAu
Hail be thou, holie hearbe. Old English Charm Song. *Unknown.* CAW
Hail, beauteous Dian, queen of shades. Hymn to Diana. Thomas Heywood. *Fr.* The Golden Age. ElL; SiCE
Hail! beauteous lands that crown the Southern Seas. Canto Twenty-third. George Canning *and* John Hookham Frere. *Fr.* The Progress of Man. CEP
Hail, beauteous stranger of the grove [*or* wood]! To the Cuckoo [*or* Ode: To the Cuckoo]. Michael Bruce, *revised by* John Logan. DD; EiCL; EiPP; HBV; OBEC; OTPC; ViBoPo
Hail, Bishop Valentine, whose day this is. *See* Haile Bishop Valentine. . .
Hail, blessed virgin, full of heavenly grace. On the Infancy of our Saviour [*or* The Child Jesus]. Francis Quarles. OBS; OxBoCh; SeCePo; SeCL; StJW
Hail, blissfulest maiden. On the Annunciation. *Unknown.* ISi
Hail, blushing goddess, beauteous Spring! Esther Vanhomrigh. LO
Hail, bright morning beam! The Dream. Francis Burdett Money-Coutts. OBVV
Hail! Christ's pure body—born of the Holy Virgin. To Our Lord in the Sacrament. St. Anselm. CAW
Hail, Columbia! Joseph Hopkinson. AA; FaBoBe; FaFP; HBV; MC; PaA; PAH; PAL; PEDC; PoFr; TreFS; YaD
Hail curious wights, to whom so fair. To the Virtuosos. William Shedstone. EiCL
Hail, Day of Days! In Peals of Praise. Fortunatus, *tr. fr. Latin.* BePJ
Hail, door, to husband and to father dear. Dialogue with a Door. Catullus. UnTE
Hail, Fair Morning. *Unknown, tr. fr. Late Middle Irish by* Standish Hayes O'Grady. *Fr.* The Life of St. Cellach of Killala. OnYI
Hail falls pitterpat, The. Hail on the Pine Trees. Basho. MPB
Hail, Father! whose creating call. Hymn to God the Father. Samuel Wesley. OxBoCh
Hail, favour'd casement!—where the sight. In Search of the Picturesque. William Combe. *Fr.* Dr. Syntax in Search of the Picturesque. OBRV
Hail, Freedom! thy bright crest. A New National Hymn. F. Marion Crawford. HH; PAH
Hail, gladdening Light, of his pure glory poured. Hymn for the Lighting of the Lamps. *Unknown, at. to* St. Athenogenes. CAW
Hail, glorious edifice, stupendous work! Loyal Effusion. Horace Smith *and* James Smith. OBRV
Hail, God revived in glory. Hymn to Horus. Mathilde Blind. OBVV
Hail, great Apollo! guide my feeble pen. The British Lyon Roused. Stephen Tilden. PAH
Hail, guest! We ask not what thou art. America Greets an Alien [*or* Welcome over the Door of an Old Inn]. *Unknown.* PAL; PGD; PoToHe (new ed.)
Hail! Hail! Hail! A Dance Chant. *Unknown, tr. by* E. S. Parker. WGRP
Hail, hail to thy blessed name, O Mary. Hymn to Mary [*or* Salutation]. Zerea Jacob. CAW; ISi
Hail, happy Britain, Freedom's blest retreat. Prophecy. Gulian Verplanck. MC
Hail, happy day, when, smiling like the morn. To the Right Honourable William, Earl of Dartmouth. Phillis Wheatley. AmPP (5th ed.); PoFr
Hail hi'roglyphick state machin. Daniel Defoe. *Fr.* A Hymn to the Pillory. NCEP
Hail! Ho!/ Sail! Ho! A Sea Song from the Shore. James Whitcomb Riley. BoTP; GaP; PRWS; TiPo; TVC
Hail, holy earth, whose cold arms do embrace. John Fletcher. The Faithful Shepherdess, I, i. MyFE
Hail, Holy Light. Milton. *Fr.* Paradise Lost; III. ExPo; FiP; GTBS-W; LoBV; ShBV-4; WHA
("Hail holy light! offspring of Heav'n first-born.") AtBAP; ATP; FosPo; InP; MBW-1; OAEP; PoIE; SeEP; ViBoPo
(Hymn to Light.) FaBoEn
(Invocation to Light, The.) MaPo (1969 ed.)
(Light.) LiTB; OBEV; OBS
Hail, holy Queen. Salve Regina. *Unknown.* WHL
Hail, Jesus! Charles Wesley. FaChP
Hail, Jesus' Virgin-Mother ever blest. Votive Ode. Erasmus. ISi
Hail! King I thee call. A Lyric from a Play. *Unknown.* MeEL
Hail, Liberty! a glorious word. Charles Churchill. *Fr.* The Duellist. PoFr
Hail, Maiden Root. Caelius Sedulius, *tr. fr. Latin by* Raymond F. Roseliep. *Fr.* Carmen Paschale. ISi
Hail Man! Angela Morgan. WGRP
Hail Mary full of grace! Prelude of the New Testament. St. Luke, Bible, *N.T.* (*Douay vers.*). CAW
Hail Matrimony, made of love. Blake. *Fr.* An Island in the Moon. ERoP-1
Hail me Diogenes underground, O Stranger, and pass by. Epitaph of a Young Man. *Unknown.* LiTW
Hail, Mediocrity, beneath whose spell. Roy Campbell. *Fr.* The Georgiad. MoBrPo
Hail! meek-eyed maiden, clad in sober grey. Ode to Evening. Joseph Warton. ATP; UnPo (1st ed.); WaPE
Hail, Mighty Rum! how wondrous is thy pow'r! Eulogium on Rum. Joseph Smith. LHV
Hail, mildly pleasing Solitude. Hymn on Solitude. James Thomson. CEP; EiPP; OBEC
Hail! Minnesota! Truman E. Rickard *and* Arthur Upson. PoRL
Hail, most high, most humble one! The Himn, O Gloriosa Domina. Richard Crashaw. MaMe
Hail! Mother-Maid, unmatched since time was born. Salutations: To Mary, Virgin. *Unknown.* ISi
Hail, Mother most pure! Salve, Virgo Florens. *Unknown. Fr.* The Little Office of the Immaculate Conception. WHL
Hail, Mother of the Savior. Adam of Saint Victor, *tr. fr. Latin by* Digby S. Wrangham. ISi

Hail, native Language, that by sinews weak. At a Vacation Exercise. Milton. OBS; PP
Hail, O most worthy in all the world! Advent Lyrics, IX. *Unknown.* *Fr.* Christ, 1. AnOE
Hail, O Queen of heaven enthroned! Ave Regina. *Unknown.* WHL
Hail, old October, bright and chill. Old October. Thomas Constable. HBV
Hail, old patrician trees, so great and good! Of Solitude [*or* Essay on Solitude]. Abraham Cowley. OBS; SeCL; SeEP; ViBoPo
Hail on the Pine Trees. Basho, *tr. fr. Japanese.* MPB
Hail, Poesie! thou nymph reserv'd! Sketch. Burns. EiCL
Hail, St. Michael with the long spear! A Satire on the People of Kildare. *Unknown, at. to* Friar Michael of Kildare. OnYI
Hail [*or* Haile], sister springs! The Weeper [*or* Saint Mary Magdalene]. Richard Crashaw. AnAnS-1; AtBAP; EP; MaMe; MeLP; MeP; MePo; OBEV; PoFS; ReEn; SCEP-1; SeCP; SeCV-1; SeEP; ViBoPo
Hail, sons of generous valor. To the Defenders of New Orleans. Joseph Rodman Drake. DD; PAH
Hail! South Dakota. Deecort Hammitt. PoRL
Hail Sovereign Queen of secrets who hast power. *At. to* Shakespeare. *Fr.* The Two Noble Kinsmen. PoEL-2
Hail, Star of the Sea. Star of the Sea. Richard Webb Sullivan. ISi
Hail [*or* Haile *or* Hale] sterne superne! Hail in eterne. Ballad [*or* Ballat] of Our Lady. William Dunbar. ACP; CAW; MeEL; OxBS
Hail, sword of Carroll! Oft hast thou been in the great woof of war. The Song of Carroll's Sword. *At. to* Dallan MacMore. OnYI
Hail, Sympathy! thy soft idea brings. William Lisle Bowles. Byron. *Fr.* English Bards and Scotch Reviewers. OBNC
Hail the choice groom. To the Choice Bridegroom. Judah Halevi. HW
Hail! the Glorious Golden City. Felix Adler. WGRP
(City of Our Hopes, The.) MaRV
Hail, thou great God in thy Boat. He Embarketh in the Boat of Ra. *Unknown.* *Fr.* Book of the Dead. AWP
Hail, Thou great mysterious Being! Alexander McLachlan. *Fr.* God. CaP
Hail, Thou Head! Bernard of Clairvaux, *tr. fr. Latin.* BePJ
Hail, thou long-expected Jesus. Hail Jesus! Charles Wesley. FaChP
Hail thou most sacred venerable thing. Hymn to Darkness. John Norris. GTSL; MePo; OBS; OxBoCh
Hail, Thou Once Despised Jesus! John Bakewell. BePJ
Hail, Thou star of ocean. Ave, Maris Stella. *Unknown.* WHL
Hail, thou who shinest from the Moon. He Establisheth His Triumph. *Unknown.* *Fr.* Book of the Dead. AWP; JAWP; WBP
Hail to Hobson! Hail to Hobson! hail to all the valiant set. The Men of the *Merrimac.* Clinton Scollard. PAH
Hail to the brightness of Zion's glad morning. The Latter Day. Thomas Hastings. AA
Hail to the Chief, Who in Triumph Advances! Sir Walter Scott. *See* Boat Song.
Hail to the Headlong! the Headlong Ap-Headlong! Chorus. Thomas Love Peacock. *Fr.* Headlong Hall. OBRV; PeER
Hail to the land whereon we tread. New England. James Gates Percival. AA
Hail to the Lord's Anointed. The King Eternal. James Montgomery. MaRV
Hail to the planting of Liberty's tree. American Independence. Alfred Billings Street. PEDC
Hail to the sage divine of Milan's plains. On Hearing That Torture Was Suppressed Throughout the Austrian Dominions. John Bampfylde. Sonn
Hail to thee, beautiful, mighty, and golden! Deirdre's Song at Sunrise. Sister Maura. CaP
Hail to thee, blithe spirit. To a Skylark [*or* Ode to a Skylark *or* To the Skylark]. Shelley. AnFE; AtBAP; ATP; BEL; BoLiVe; CoBE; DD; DiPo; EnL; EnLi-2; EnLit; EnRP; EPN; ERoP-2; FaBoBe; FaBV; FaFP; FaPON; GBV; GN; GTBS; GTBS-D; GTBS-P; GTBS-W; GTSE; GTSL; HBV; HH; InP; InvP; LiTB; LiTG; LoBV; MBW-2; MCCG; MPB; MERP; MyFE; NoP; NP; OAEP; OBEV; OBNC; OBRV; OHFP; OTD; OTPC; OuHeWo; PoFS; PoIE; PoLF; PTK; RoGo; ShBV-4; TOP; TreFS; TrGrPo; VaPo; WHA
Hail to theé, gallant foe. Cervera. Bertrand Shadwell. PAH
Hail to thee, monarch of African mountains. Kilimandjaro. Bayard Taylor. AmP
Hail to thee, our Savior's mother! Hail, Mother of the Savior. Adam of Saint Victor. ISi
Hail to thee, true body, sprung. Ave Verum Corpus Natum. *Unknown.* WHL
Hail to thy living light. Ode to Morning. William Mason. WaPE
Hail, Vermont! Josephine Hovey Perry. PoRL
Hail Wedded Love! Jay Macpherson. MoCV
Hail [*or* Haile] wedded love, mysterious law, true source. Wedded Love [*or* Their Wedded Love]. Milton. *Fr.* Paradise Lost, IV. HW; MaPo (1969 ed.); OBS; SeCePo
Hail, ye indomitable heroes, hail! The Crimean Heroes. Walter Savage Landor. ALV
Haile [*or* Hail] Bishop Valentine, whose day this is. An Epithalamion [*or* Hail, Bishop Valentine]. John Donne. AtBAP; ChTr; HW; MaMe
Haile from the dead, or from eternity. Lines on a Purple Cap Received as a Present from My Brother. George Alsop. SCAP
Haile gracefull morning of eternall daye. Sonnet. William Alabaster. AnAnS-1; MeP
Haile great Redeemer, man, and God, all haile. A Hymne to Our Saviour on the Crosse. George Chapman. PoEL-2
Haile, sister springs. *See* Hail, sister springs!
Haile, sterne superne. *See* Hail, sterne superne.
Haile wedded love, mysterious law, true source. *See* Hail wedded love, mysterious law, true source.
Haill! Quene of Heven and steren of blis. A Little Hymn to Mary. *Unknown.* MeEL
Hair. Gelett Burgess. *See* I'd Rather Have Fingers than Toes.
Hair. Remy de Gourmont, *tr. fr. French by* Jethro Bithell. AWP; ErPo
Hair long, cheekbones high. Three Dreams. James Michie. NePoEA-2
Hair Ribbons. *Unknown.* BiCB
Hair—silver-gray. Face. Jean Toomer. CDC
Haircut. William Packard. CAD
Haircut. Karl Shapiro. FiMAP; MoPo; MoVE; TwCP
Hairdresser's Art, The. Claudian, *tr. fr. Latin by* Maurice Platnauer *and* Virginia Tufte. *Fr.* Epithalamium for Honorius and Maria. HW
Hair-dressing. Louis Untermeyer. UnTE
Hairless and worse than leathery, the skin. Corrib: An Emblem. Donald Davie. PoCh
Hairless beast in old clothes. Citizen. Louis Grudin. NePA
Hair's Breadth, The. Nicholas Moore. NeBP
Hairy Dog, The. Herbert Asquith. BoChLi; FaPON; PDV; SoPo; StVeCh; SUS; TiPo; UTS
Hairy was here. News from the Cabin. May Swenson. NMP; NYBP
Haitches! Edwina May. SiTL
Hakluyt Unpurchased. Franklin McDuffee. EtS
Halcyon, *sel.* Hilda Doolittle ("H.D.").
"I'm not here/ everything's vague." MAP; MoAmPo
Halcyon Days. Walt Whitman. NePA; OxBA
Hale John Spratt, The—oft called for shortness Jack. An Idyll of Phatte and Leene. *Unknown.* BOHV
Hale, sterne superne! Hale, in eterne. *See* Hail, sterne superne. . .
Haleluiah, or Britan's Second Remembrancer. George Wither. *See* Hallelujah. . .
Half. Hawley Truax. NYBP
Half a bar, half a bar. Village Choir. *Unknown.* BOHV
Half a dozen white loaves lie. The Loaves. Ronald Everson. WHW
Half a league, half a league. The Charge of the Light Brigade. Tennyson. BBV; BEL; BeLS; BLPA; FaBoBe; FaBV; FaFP; FaPON; FOL; GN; HBV; HBVY; HoPM; MaC; MaVP; MCCG; NeHB; OHFP; OnSP; OTD; OTPC; PaPo; PCD; PeVV; PoPl; PoVP; PTK; ShBV-1; TOP; TreF; VA; WBLP; YAT
Half-asleep, The. Thomas Wade. OBEV (1st ed.)
Half-awake and half-dozing. At Memphis Station. Johannes V. Jensen. WoL

Half awake in my Sunday nap. Three Green Windows. Anne Sexton. NYBP
Half baked potato named Sue, A. Limerick. George Libaire. LiBL
Half-Bent Man. Richard Eberhart. NYBP
Half-blown Rose, The. Samuel Daniel. *See* To Delia: "Look, Delia, how we esteem the half-blown rose."
Half-Breed Girl, The. Duncan Campbell Scott. CaP
Half close your eyelids, loosen your hair. He Thinks of Those Who Have Spoken Evil of His Beloved. W. B. Yeats. CLwM; CTC; ELU
"Half-cracked" to Higginson, living. "I Am in Danger—Sir." Adrienne Rich. ML
Half Door, The. "Seumas O'Sullivan." AnIV
Half-door, hall door. Purgatory. W. B. Yeats. CMoP
Half doun the hill, whaur [*or* where] fa's the linn. The Gowk. William Soutar. GoTS; NeBP
Half-ended melodies are purer. Variation. Bill Berkson. YAP
Half fish, half fallen angel, none of you. The Mermaid at Zennor. John Heath-Stubbs. FaBoMo
Half-heard. Christopher Koch. PoAu-2
Half hidden by trees, the sheer roof of the barn. The Barn. Stephen Spender. HaMV
Half-hidden in a graveyard. The Stranger. Walter de la Mare. BrPo; MoVE
Half Holiday. Olive Enoch. BoTP
Half-holiday for the burial, A. Of course, they punish. Black Spring. Robert Lovell, *ad. fr. Russian of* Innokenti Annensky. NaP
Half Horse and Half Alligator. Samuel Woodworth. *See* Hunters of Kentucky, The.
Half Hours with the Classics. H. J. DeBurgh. BOHV; InMe
Half kneeling yet, and half reclining. The Queen's Vespers. Aubrey Thomas De Vere. VA
Half in the dim light from the hall. To——. William Stanley Braithwaite. BALP
Half-Light. Jean Percival Waddell. CaP
Half loving-kindliness, and half disdain. To My Cat. Rosamund Marriott Watson. VA
Half-Mast. Lloyd Mifflin. PAH
Half-mast the flag, and let the bell be tolled. Theodore Roosevelt. Samuel Valentine Cole. PEDC
Half-moons of her calves eclipse, The. Notes on a Girl. Peter Kane Dufault. ErPo
Half of a clasping of the hands. Half. Hawley Truax. NYBP
Half of Life, The. Friedrich Hölderlin, *tr. fr. German by* Frederic Prokosch. LiTW
(Life Half Lived, *tr. unknown.*) ChTr
Half of my life is gone, and I have left. Mezzo Cammin. Longfellow. AmePo; AmPP (3d ed.); CBEP; CoBA; ILP; NoP
Half of your book is to an index grown. Half Your Book. Swift. StP
Half past nine—high time for supper. In Praise of Cocoa, Cupid's Nightcap. Stanley J. Sharpless. ErPo; FiBHP
Half past seven in the morning. His Majesty the Letter-Carrier. Emanuel Carnevali. AnAmPo
Half Sigh. *Unknown, tr. by* Miriam Koshland. PBA
Half squatter, half tenant (no rent). Manuelzinho. Elizabeth Bishop. NYBP
Half the time they munched the grass, and all the time they lay. Cows. James Reeves. PoSC
Half-Tide Ledge. R. P. Blackmur. AnFE; CoAnAm; TwAmPo
Half-waking. William Allingham. VA
Halfway. Maxine W. Kumin. GoYe
Half way along the sloping earth. Socrates Prays a Day and a Night. George O'Neil. AnAmPo
Halfway Down. A. A. Milne. FaPON; TiPo (1959 ed.)
Half-Way Knowledge. Bhartrihari, *tr. fr. Sanskrit by* Paul Elmer More. OnPM
Halfway up the Hemlock valley turnpike. Emilia. Sarah N. Cleghorn. HBV; PFY
Half-world's width divides us, The; where she sits. Divided. David Gray. AA
Half Your Book. Swift. StP
Halibut Cove Harvest. Kenneth Leslie. CaP
Halifax Station. *Unknown.* PAH
Hall clock, metal teethed to metal, The. Contract. Frederick Nicklaus. NYTB
Hallelu-u-u, Hallelu, O, my Lord. Death Come to My House He Didn't Stay Long. *Unknown.* BoAN-2
Halleluja!/ What sound is this across the dark. A Christmas Eve Choral. Bliss Carman. ISi
Hallelujah. Psalms, CXLVI, Bible, *O.T.* TrJP
Hallelujah! A. E. Housman. FiBHP; PV; ShM
Hallelujah! *Unknown.* BoAN-1, *with music*
Hallelujah. George Wither. *See* Hallelujah; or, Britain's Second Remembrancer.
Hallelujah!/ Praise God in His Sanctuary. The Closing Doxology. Psalm CL, Bible, *O.T.* (Smith-Goodspeed *tr.*) MaRV
Hallelujah!/ Praise the Lord from the Heavens. A Hallelujah Chorus. Psalm CXLVIII, Bible, *O.T.* (Smith-Goodspeed *tr.*). MaRV
Hallelujah./ Praise the Lord, O my soul. Hallelujah. Psalm CXLVI, Bible, *O.T.* TrJP
Hallelujah./ Praise ye the Lord from the heavens. Praise Ye the Lord. Psalm CXLVIII, Bible, *O.T.* TrJP
Hallelujah; a Sestina. Robert Francis. PoCH
Hallelujah! an' a hallelujah! Hallelujah! *Unknown.* BoAN-1
Hallelujah, Bum Again. *Unknown.* *See* Hallelujah, I'm a Bum.
Hallelujah Chorus, A. Psalms, CXLVIII, Bible, *O.T.* (Smith-Goodspeed *tr.*). MaRV
Hallelujah, I'm a Bum, *with music.* *Unknown.* AS, *sl. abr.*; TrAS
(Hallelujah, Bum Again.) ABF
Hallelujah; or, Britain's Second Remembrancer, *sels.* George Wither.
For a Musician. MuSP; OBS
(To a Musician, *wr. at. to* William Austin.) OxBoCh
Hymne I: General Invitation to Praise God, A. SeCV-1
Hymn L: Rocking Hymn, A. SeCV-1
(Lullaby, A: "Sweet baby, sleep; what ails my dear.") OxBoCh, *abr.* [*wr. at. to* William Austin]
When We Are upon the Seas. BEL
"Hallelujah!" was the only observation. Hallelujah! A. E. Housman. FiBHP; PV; ShM
Hallo My Fancy. William Cleland. *and others.* CH; OxBoLi
(Hollo, My Fancy, *sl. diff.*) SeCL
Halloo to man, the pleasuring, lording creature. So, Man? Gene Derwood. NePA
Hallow days o' Yule are come, The. The Wife of Usher's Well (B *vers.*). *Unknown.* ESPB
Hallow-Fair. Robert Fergusson. OxBS
Hallow the threshold, crown the posts anew! On the Queen's Return from the Low Countries. William Cartwright. MePo; OBEV
Hallowed be the Ordainer of/ the world! A Little Prayer. Paul Goodman. LiTA
Hallowed be the Sabbaoth. Epitaphs. Francis Jeffrey. OxBoLi
Hallowed Ground. Thomas Campbell. BLPA; HBV; MaRV, *abr.*
Hallowed Places. Alice Freeman Palmer. HBV
Hallowed Season, The. Shakespeare. *See* Gracious Time, The.
Hallowe'en. Harry Behn. FaPON; GBV (1952 ed.) OTD; PDV; PoSC; RePo; SiSoSe; StVeCh (1955 ed.); TiPo; YeAr
Hallowe'en. Joel Benton. DD; OTPC (1946 ed.); PoRL
Hallowe'en. Burns. OBEC, *abr.*
Hallowe'en. Molly Capes. MoSiPe
Hallowe'en. Arthur Cleveland Coxe. DD
Hallowe'en. Frances Frost. TiPo (1959 ed.)
Halloween. Marie A. Lawson. SiSoSe; TiPo (1959 ed.)
Hallowe'en. John Mayne. HBV
Hallowe'en. Anna Medary. GFA
Halloween. Marnie Pomeroy. PoSC
Hallowe'en. Virna Sheard. DD
Hallowe'en. *Unknown.* OTPC (1946 ed.)
("Hey how for Hallowe'en!") FaBoCh; LoGBV
(Witches, The.) ChTr
Hallowe'en Helen Wing. GFA
Halloween Concert. Aileen Fisher. SiSoSe
Hallowe'en Indignation Meeting. Margaret Fishback. PoSC
Hallowe'en Memory, A. Christopher Morley. LHV
Hallowe'en's the time for nuts. Hallowe'en. Anna Medary. GFA
Hallows' E'en. Winifred M. Letts. DD
Halls of fame are open wide, The. Fame. *Unknown.* TreFT
Hallucination, I. Arthur Symons. SyP
Halo. R. N. Currey. PeSA

Hal's Birthday. Lucy Larcom. BiCB
Halt, The. Josephine Miles. ELU; FiMAP
Halt and Parley. George Herbert Clarke. CaP
Halt looks into the eyes of the halt and looks away, The. The Halt. Josephine Miles. ELU; FiMAP
Halted against the shade of a last hill. Spring Offensive. Wilfred Owen. BrPo; GTBS-P; LiTB; MoVE
Haltersick's Song. John Pickering. *Fr.* Horestes. OBSC
("Farewell, adieu, that courtly life.") ReEn; TuPP
(Song: "Farewell, adieu, that court-like life!") ElL
Halways sound your Haitches. Haitches! *Unknown.* SiTL
Ham and eggs, Lord, pork and beans. I Got to Roll. *Unknown.* OuSiCo
Hamadan is my native place. A Blessed Spot. Abulfadhel Ahmed. OnPM
Hamadryad, The. Walter Savage Landor. *Fr.* The Hellenics. EnRP; EPN; TOP; VA
Hamasah, *sel.* Hittan of Tayyi, *tr. fr. Arabic by* Sir Charles Lyall.
His Children. AWP; JAWP; LiTW; WBP
Hamatreya. Emerson. AmePo; AmP; AmPP; AnNE; AP; CoBA; FaBoEn; MAmP; MWA-1; NoP; OxBA; PAn; PoE; PoEL-4; SeCeV; WoL
Hambone and the Heart, The. Edith Sitwell. OBMV
Hame came our goodman. Our Goodman. *Unknown.* BaBo; EnLi-1; ESPB; ViBoFo (A *vers.*)
Hame, Hame, Hame. Allan Cunningham. CH; HBV; OBEV; OBRV; OTPC
("Hame, hame, hame, hame fain wad I be," *first* 6 *ll.*) LO
(Loyalty, *abr.*) GN
Hamelin Town's in Brunswick. The Pied Piper of Hamelin. Robert Browning. BBV; BeLS; BoChLi; BOHV; FaBoBe; FaBoCh; FaFP; GN; GoTP; GSP; HBV; HBVY; LoGBV; MBW-2; OnSP; OtMeF; OTPC; PoE; PoVP; RG; RIS; ShBV-1; StVeCh; TiPo (1952 ed.)
Hamilcar Barca. Roger Casement. JKCP (1926 ed.)
Hamilton. Marie E. J. Pitt. BoAu
Hamilton Greene. Edgar Lee Masters. *Fr.* Spoon River Anthology. OxBA
Hamlet, *sels.* Shakespeare.
"But looke where sadly the poore wretch comes reading," *fr.* II, ii. AtBAP
Death of Hamlet, *fr.* V, ii. FiP
Frailty, Thy Name Is Woman, *fr.* I, ii. TrGrPo
(Hamlet Broods over the Death of His Father.) TreFS
Good Sir, Whose Powers Are These? *fr.* IV, iv, *abr.* WaaP
Gracious Time, The ("Some say that ever 'gainst that season comes"), *fr.* I, i. ChrBoLe; GN
(Christmas.) ChTr
(Hallowed Season, The.) MaRV
("It faded on the crowing of the cock.") MyFE
("Some say that ever 'gainst that season comes.") ChIP; TiPo (1952 ed.)
Hamlet's Instructions to the Players, *fr.* III, ii. TreFS
"How all occasions do inform against me," *fr.* IV, iv. HoPM
"How now? what noise is that?" *fr.* IV, v. AtBAP
"I am thy fathers spirit," *fr.* I, v. AtBAP
"Is she to bee buried in Christian buriall," *fr.* V, i. AtBAP
"Let four captains/ Bear Hamlet, like a soldier, to the stage," *fr.* V, ii. MyFE
"Now Hamlet, where's Polonius?" *fr.* IV, iii. AtBAP
"O what a noble mind is here o'erthrown," *fr.* III, i.
(Shakespeare Gallery, A: Hamlet.) MaC
"O, what a rogue and peasant slave am I!" *fr.* II, ii. MemP; TreFT
Ophelia's Death, *fr.* V, i. ChTr
Ophelia's Songs, *fr.* IV, v.
And Will He [*or* A'] Not Come Again? EG; InPo; PoEL-2; ViBoPo
(Ophelia's Songs, 2.) AnFE; TrGrPo
"He is dead and gone, lady." LO
How Should I Your True Love Know. EG; EnLoPo; InPo; LiTB; LiTG; LiTL; PoRA; QFR; ViBoPo
(Frair of Orders Grey, The.) GoBC
(Ophelia's Song.) ChTr; OBSC
(Ophelia's Songs, 1.) AnFE; TrGrPo
(Song: "How should I your true love know.") CH
Tomorrow Is [*or* Good Morrow, 'Tis] Saint Valentine's Day. EnLoPo; InPo; PV; ViBoPo
(Ophelia's Song.) UnTE
(Saint Valentine's Day.) LiTB; LiTG
(Song: "Tomorrow [*or* Good morrow] is Saint Valentine's day.") FaPON; HH; MPB; SiSoSe
Polonius' Advice to Laertes, *fr.* I, iii. BBV; OHFP; OQP; PoPl
("And these few precepts in thy memory.") MasP
(Be True, 3 *ll.*) PCD; PCH
(Polonius' Advice to His Son.) MaRV; TreF
(Polonius to Laertes.) GN
("There,—my blessing with you!") OTD
(This above All.) TrGrPo; TRV, 3 *ll.*
(To Thine Own Self Be True.) FaFP; LiTB; LiTG
"Rugged Pyrrhus, he whose sable arm, The," *fr.* II, 2. Par
"To be, or not to be, that is the question," *fr.* III, i. AtBAP; DiPo; FaFP; FiP; GTBS-W; HoPM; LiTB; LiTG; MasP; MemP; OTD; PoPl; PoSa; TrGrPo; WHA; YAT
(Hamlet Contemplates Death.) MaRV
(Hamlet Contemplates Suicide.) TreF
(Hamlet's Soliloquy.) NeHB; PTK; WBLP
(Soliloquy from "Hamlet.") OHFP; OQP
"What a piece of work is man!" *fr.* II, ii. InP
(Man.) TreF
"Where is the beauteous Majesty of Denmark?" *fr.* IV, v. AtBAP
"Who's there?" *fr.* I, i, iv, *and* v. ExPo
"Why, let the stricken deer go weep," 4 *ll., fr.* III, ii. CoBE
Witching Time of Night, The. *fr.* III, ii. TreFT
Hamlet Ballytullagh, small and old, The. Ballytullagh. William Allingham. *Fr.* Laurence Bloomfield in Ireland. IrPN
Hamlet of A. MacLeish, The, *sel.* Archibald MacLeish.
"Night after night I lie like this listening." AnAmPo
Hamlet's Instructions to the Players. Shakespeare. *Fr.* Hamlet, III, ii. TreFS
Hamlet's Soliloquy. Shakespeare. *See* To Be or Not to Be.
Hamlet's Soliloquy Imitated. Richard Jago. SiTL
Hammam Name, The. James Elroy Flecker. BrPo; FaBoTw
Hammer, The. Clark Coolidge. ANYP
Hammer, The. Carl Sandburg. PoPo
Hammer/ struck my nail, The. Almanac. May Swenson. NYBP
Hammer and Anvil. Samuel Valentine Cole. PoLF
Hammer Man, *with music.* *Unknown.* AS
Hammer Song. *Unknown.* ABF
Hammered to the serenity of copper. Bronze. Derek Walcott. ToPo
Hammerfest. W. H. Auden. PoAn
Hammers, The. Ralph Hodgson. GoJo; MoBrPo; PoIE; PoMa; POTE; YT
Hammers and Anvil. John Clifford. *See* Anvil, The—God's Word.
Hammerstroke and. The Murdered Girl Is Found on a Bridge. Jane Hayman. NYBP
Hammock swings responsive as a sail, The. Siesta. Samuel Hazo. NYTB
Ha'nacker Mill. Hilaire Belloc. HBMV; MoBrPo
Hand, The. Irving Feldman. AmPC
Hand, The. Ebenezer Jones. OBVV
Hand, A. Bernard Spencer. NeBP
Hand and Foot, The. Jones Very. AmLP; AP; MAmP; NePA; OxBA; PoEL-4; QFR; Sonn
Hand at Callow Hill Farm, The. Charles Tomlinson. NePoEA-2
Hand in Hand, a Child and I. *Unknown.* SoP
Hand in hand they dance in a row. The Clothes-Line. Charlotte Druitt Cole. BoTP
Hand in Hand with Jesus. Barbara Cornet Ryberg. SoP
Hand is to the plough an' the e'e is to the trail, The. For Love of Appin. Jessie Mackay. AnNZ
Hand-Mirror, A. Walt Whitman. CBEP; CBV; MAmP; MWA-1; OxBA; TDP
Hand of Douglas is his own, The. Marmion and Douglas. Sir Walter Scott. *Fr.* Marmion. OtMeF
Hand of Labor. Lilburn H. Townsend. PEDC
Hand of Lincoln, The. Edmund Clarence Stedman. AA; LiPo; OHIP; PGD
Hand of the copper boy pours tea. Café Tableau. May Swenson. ErPo
Hand that binds the star, The. His Hand. Henry Jerome Stockard. FaChP
Hand That Held It, The. W. G. Elmslie. SoP; TRV
Hand That Rocks the Cradle Is the Hand That Rules the World, The. William Ross Wallace. FaFP; PoLF; TreF; WBLP

Hand (continued)
(What Rules the World.) DD; OHIP; OTPC (1946 ed.), 8 *ll.*; PoRL, 8 *ll.*
Hand That Signed the Paper Felled a City, The. Dylan Thomas. GTBS-W; HaMV; InPo; LiTM; MemP; MoAB; MoBrPo; MoPo; MoRP; NoP; POTE; SeCePo; TrGrPo (rev. ed.); WaP
Hand that swept the sounding lyre, The. On a Dead Poet. Frances Sargent Osgood. AA
Handel, Bendel, Mendelssohn. A Rhyme for Musicians. E. Lemke. BOHV
Handful came to Seicheprey, A. Seicheprey. *Unknown.* PAH
Handful here, that once was Mary's earth, The. Her Epitaph. Thomas William Parsons. AA; HBV
Handful of Dust, A. James Oppenheim. TrJP
Handful of old men walking down the village street, A. Memorial Day. Theodosia Garrison. DD; MPB; OHIP; PEDC; PoSC
Handfuls. Carl Sandburg. AP; NP
Handiwork of God, The. *Unknown. See* Nature's Creed.
Handle a large kingdom with as gentle a touch as if you were cooking a small fish. A Gentle Touch. *Unknown, at. to* Lao-tzu. *Fr.* Tao Teh King. OnPM
Hands. Dorothy Aldis. SUS
Hands. Frederick Cloud. LaNeLa
Hands, The. Anthony Euwer. *Fr.* The Limeratomy. HBMV
Hands. Donald Finkel. CoAP
Hands. W. W. Gibson. PoMa
Hands. Margaret Lathrop Law. PoMa
Hands, The. Denise Levertov. NeAP
Hands. Louis Untermeyer. AnAmPo; MoLP
Hands-across-the-Sea Poem, The. J. C. Squire. HBMV
Hands All Round. Tennyson. PoFr
Hands and Eyes. Louis MacNeice. PoDB
Hands and lit faces eddy to a line. The Night Journey. Rupert Brooke. BrPo
Hands must touch and handle many things, The. The New Man. Jones Very. AP
Hands of beggars peddle cigarets, The. Cante Hondo. Ellen de Young Kay. NePoEA
Hands of Christ, The. Leslie Savage Clark. ChIP; MaRV
Hands of Christ. Francisco E. Estrello, *tr. fr. Spanish by* H. M. Sein. ChIP
Hands of Christ, The. His Hands. John Richard Moreland. ChIP; MaRV; OQP; SoP; TRV
Hands of God, The. D. H. Lawrence. MoRP
Hands of the King are soft and fair, The. The Way of the World. James Jeffrey Roche. CAW; ChIP; JKCP; WBLP
Hands on a Card-Table. Polly Chase Boyden. NP
Hands they were made to assist, The. The Hands. Anthony Euwer. *Fr.* The Limeratomy. HBMV
Hands we sign our names with touch this trinket. Antique. John Stevens Wade. NYTB
Handsel Ring, The. George Houghton. AA
Handsome boy! Folk Song from Fukushima. *Unknown.* FIW
Handsome? I hardly know. Her profile's fine. A Countrywoman of Mine. Elaine Goodale Eastman. AA
Handsome one, white-black checkered son of the water. The Muscovy Drake. E. A. S. Lesoro. PeSA
Handsome Young Airman, The. *Unknown. See* Dying Airman, The.
Handsome young gent down in Fla., A. *Unknown.* SiTL
Handsome young noble of Spain, A. *Unknown.* GoTP
Handwriting on the Wall, The. Knowles Shaw. BLPA
Handy Andy, *sel.* Samuel Lover.
Widow Machree. HBV; VA
Handy dandy. *Unknown.* OxNR
Handy high and handy low. So Handy. *Unknown.* ShS
Handy Spandy, Jack-a-dandy. Mother Goose. GaP; OTPC; PCH; RIS; SoPo
Hang a small bugle cap on, as big as a crown. The Beau's Receipt for a Lady's Dress. *Unknown.* CoMu
Hang at my hand as I write now. Verses for a First Birthday. George Barker. *Fr.* Second Cycle of Love Poems. MoAB; MoBrPo (1950 ed.)
Hang it all, Ezra Pound, there is only the one sestina! Sestina. Donald Hall. NePoEA
Hang it all, Robert Browning. Canto II. Ezra Pound. AmPP (4th ed.); AP; AtBAP; CoBMV; MoAB; MoAmPo (1962 ed.), NePA; OxBA; TwAmPo
Hang Me among Your Winds. Lew Sarett. MaRV
Hang On. David Hilton. QAH
Hang on! Cling on! No matter what they say. Keep Your Grit. *Unknown.* STF
Hang Out the Flags. James S. Tippett. SiSoSe
Hang sorrow, cast away care. Song. *Unknown.* OBS
Hang thee, vile North Easter. Another Ode to the North-East Wind. *Unknown.* Par
Hang to Your Grit! Louis E. Thayer. *Fr.* Keep Your Grit. WBLP
Hang up those dull and envious fools. In Defense of Their Inconstancy. Ben Jonson. ReEn; SeCP
Hang up your weaponed wit. J. V. Cunningham. QFR
Hange golden sleepe uppon hir eye-lids faire. *Unknown.* SeCSL
Hanged Thing, The. Walter H. Kerr. FiSC
Hanging, The. J. E. H. MacDonald. OBCV
Hanging from the beam. The Portent. Herman Melville. AmePo; AmPP; AP; CaFP; CBEP; ExPo; MAmP; MWA-1; NoP; OxBA; PoEL-5; PoFS; TDP; WiR
Hanging Johnny, *with music.* *Unknown.* AmSS; ShS; SoAmSa
Hanging Limb, The. *Unknown.* IHA
Hanging Man, The. Sylvia Plath. CBV
Hanging of Billy Budd. Keith Wilson. ThO
Hanging of the Crane, The, *sel.* Longfellow.
New Household, A, *fr.* Pt. I. GN
Hanging Out the Linen Clothes, *with music.* *Unknown.* AS
Hangman, *with music.* *Unknown.* AS
Hangman at Home, The. Carl Sandburg. CMoP
Hangman, hangman, slack up on your rope. Sweetheart, sweetheart can you give me any hope. Hangman. *Unknown.* AS
Hangman's Tree [*or* Song], The. *Unknown. See* Maid Freed from the Gallows, The.
Hangman's Tree. Lillian Zellhoefer White. AmFN
Hangover. Philip H. Rhinelander. WhC
Hangsaman. *Unknown. See* Maid Freed from the Gallows, The.
Hangtown Gals, *with music.* John A. Stone. SGR
Hannah Armstrong. Edgar Lee Masters. *Fr.* Spoon River Anthology. LiPo
Hannah Bantry, in the pantry. *Unknown.* OxNR; RIS; SiTL
Hannah Binding Shoes. Lucy Larcom. GN; HBV
Hannah Dustin. Louis O. Coxe. TwAmPo
Hannah's Song of Thanksgiving. First Samuel, II: 1-10, Bible, *O.T.* AWP
(Song of Hannah, The.) LiTW
Hannibal and Scipio, *sel.* Thomas Nabbes.
"Beauty no more the subject be." TuPP
(Song.) SeCL
Hannibal crossed the Alps! When Hannibal Crossed the Alps. Eleanor Farjeon. FOL
Hanrahan and Cathleen the Daughter of Hoolihan, *sel.* W. B. Yeats.
Red Hanrahan's Song about Ireland. ACV; BEL; CMoP; FaBoCh; FaBoMo; LoGBV; OnYI; OxBI
Hans Breitmann's Party [*or* Barty]. Charles Godfrey Leland. BOHV; CenHV; HBV; LHV
Hans Christian Andersen. Sir Edmund Gosse. VA
Hans Christian Andersen in Central Park. Hy Sobiloff. PoPl
Hansel and Gretel, *sel.* Adelheid Wette, *tr. fr. German.*
Witch's Ride, The. PCH
Hansom Cabbies. Wilfrid Thorley. HBMV
Han'som stranger? Yes, she's purty, an' ez peart ez she kin be. The Engineer's Story. Eugene J. Hall. PaPo
Han'some night, with the trees snow-white, A. The Second Settler's Story. Will Carleton. IHA
Hanukkah Hymn. *Unknown.* TreFT
Hap. Thomas Hardy. AWP; CABA; CMoP; CoBMV; EaLo; EnLi-2 (1949 ed.); InPo; JAWP; MoBrPo; OAEP (2d ed.); PoAn; PoDB; PoE; PPON; Sonn; ViPo; ViPP; WBP
Hap which Paris had as due for his desert, The. Gascoigne's Praise of His Mistress. George Gascoigne. EnRePo
Hapless lover's heart is of his wooing weary, The. The Mock Caliph. *Unknown. Fr.* The Thousand and One Nights. EnLi-1
Happened like this: it was hot as hell. The Death of the Craneman. Alfred Hayes. LiTA; NAMP; WaP
Happened that the moon was up before I went to bed. Mockery. Katherine Dixon Riggs. BrR; MPB; SP
Happening. Edwin Honig. NePA

Happie is he, that from all businesse cleere. The Praises of a Countrie Life. Ben Jonson. SeCP
Happier, I would surely be. The Unfortunate Male. Kalonymos ben Kalonymos. *Fr.* The Touchstone. TrJP
Happier than green-kirtled apple-trees. Forgetfulness. Maxwell Bodenheim. MAPA
Happiest Day, the Happiest Hour, The. Poe. AmPP (4th ed.); NePA; OxBA
(Happiest Day, The.) GTBS-W; LiTA
Happiest Heart, The. John Vance Cheney. AA; AnAmPo; AnFE; APA; CoAnAm; HBV; HBVY; MaRV; OQP; PoMa; TreFS; WGRP
Happiest life that here we have, The. To Master Henry Cobham of the Most Blessed State of Life. Barnabe Googe. SiCE
Happiest Mortals Once Were We, The. George Granville. SeCL
(Song: To Myra.) CEP
Happiness. Horace, *See* Happy the Man. *par. by* Dryden.
Happiness. Walter E. Isenhour. STF
Happiness. Priscilla Leonard. BLPA; NeHB; PoToHe (new ed.)
Happiness. A. A. Milne. BoC; TiPo
Happiness. Carl Sandburg. OxBA; WoL
Happiness. *Unknown.* SoP
Happiness. Anna E. Wimmer. SoP
Happiness amidst Troubles. Immanuel di Roma, *tr. fr. Italian by* Joseph Chotzner. TrJP
Happiness an Art. Edward Young. *Fr.* Night Thoughts, VIII. OBEC
Happiness Betrays Me. Helen Hoyt. NP
Happiness Dependent on Ourselves. Goldsmith. *Fr.* Traveller. OBEC
Happiness Found, *sel.* Augustus M. Toplady.
"Lord, it is not life to live." MaRV; OxBoCh; TrPWD
Happiness in the Trees. Joseph Ceravolo. ANYP
Happiness is like a crystal. Happiness. Priscilla Leonard. BLPA; NeHB; PoToHe (new ed.); SoP
Happiness Makes Up in Height for What It Lacks in Length. Robert Frost. MoAB; MoAmPo; MoPo
Happiness of 6 A.M. Harvey Shapiro. NYBP
Happy Any Way. Richard Baxter. *See* Lord, It Belongs Not to My Care.
Happy are men who yet before they are killed. Insensibility. Wilfred Owen. ChMP; CMoP; ExPo; FaBoTw; GTBS-W; LiTB; LiTM; MMA; MoAB; OAEP (2d ed.); SeCeV; StP; WaP
Happy are they and charmed in life. Memorials on the Slain at Chickamauga. Herman Melville. AA
Happy are those who can relieve. Sir Herbert Read. *Fr.* Ode: Written during the Battle of Dunkirk, May, 1940. MaRV
Happy Are Those Who Have Died. Charles Péguy, *tr. fr. French by* Jessie Degen *and* Richard Eberhart. *Fr.* Eve. WaaP
Happy Beggarman, The. *Unknown.* OnYI
Happy bit hame this auld world would be, A. We Are Brethen A'. Robert Nicoll. HBV
Happy Bounding Flea, The. Roland Young. *See* Flea, The.
Happy boy, happy boy. Youth in Arms. Harold Monro. NP
Happy Britannia. James Thomson. *Fr.* The Seasons: Summer. OBEC; SeCePo
Happy Change, The. William Cowper. EiPP
(Olney Hymns.) CEP
Happy Child, The. W. H. Davies. AtBAP; POTE
Happy Child, A. Kate Greenaway. BoTP; OTPC; PPL
Happy choristers of air [*or* aire]. A Pastoral[l] Hymn[e]. John Hall. EG; MeLP; OBS; OxBoCh; SeCL; TrPWD
Happy Christmas, A. Frances Ridley Havergal. BLRP
Happy Christmases, *sels.* John Francis O'Donnell. IrPN
"Down looked the moon, but looked no more."
"In the December weather, grey and grim."
"'Twas summer time, the radiant world of June."
Happy, Cleora, was the time. Upon Cleora's Marriage and Retirement. Pope. EiCL
Happy Countryman, The. Nicholas Breton. *See* Merry Country Lad, The.
Happy Day. Philip Doddridge. SoP
Happy day at Whitsuntide, A. The Castle Ruins. William Barnes. VA
Happy Death. John Freeman. HBMV
Happy Ending. Harry Silleck Grannatt. StaSt
Happy Farmer, The. Tse Nan, *tr. fr. Chinese by* Henry H. Hart. OnPM
Happy Farmer, The. "David Grayson." *See* Argument with a Millionaire, An.
Happy grave, thou dost enshrine. An Epitaph on Mistress Mary Prideaux. *At. to* George Morley. SeCL
Happy, Happy Country Swains. *Unknown.* SeCL
Happy have we met. Old Toast. *Unknown.* WePo
Happy He. *Unknown.* ElL
Happy Heart, The. Thomas Dekker, *and others. Fr.* The Pleasant Comedy of Patient Grissell, I, i. GTBS; GTBS-D; GTBS-P; GTBS-W; GTSE; GTSL; HBV; MemP; WoL
(Art Thou Poor?) TOP; ViBoPo
("Art thou poor, yet hast thou golden slumbers?") EG; OAEP; SiCE; TuPP
(Basket-Maker's Song, The.) OBSC; ThWaDe; TrGrPo
(Content.) BBV (1923 ed.); EnLi-1
(O Sweet Content.) AtBAP; BEL; ShBV-2
(Sweet Content.) CH; ElL; EnLit; LoBV; OBEV; OtMeF; PG; TreFT; WHA
Happy Hen, The. James Agee. ErPo
Happy Home, The. *Unknown.* SoP
Happy Hour, The. Mary Frances Butts. DD
Happy Hour, The. Sylvia Lynd. LO
Happy Husbandman, The; Country Innocence. *Unknown.* CoMu
Happy Hyena, The. Carolyn Wells. *See* Limerick: "There once was a happy hyena."
Happy Insect, what can be. The Grasshopper. Abraham Cowley, *after* Anacreon. AWP; EnLi-1; GoTP; HBV; HBVY; JAWP; OTPC (1923 ed.); SCEP-2; SeCV-1; WBP; WiR
Happy Insensibility. Keats. *See* Stanzas: "In a Drear-nighted December."
Happy Is England. Keats. MERP
Happy is he who journeys everywhere. Returning Home. Joachim du Bellay. LiTW
Happy Is the Country Life. *Unknown.* OBS
Happy Is the Man. Psalms, I Bible, *O.T.* TrJP
Happy Is the Man That Findeth Wisdom. Proverbs, III, Bible, *O.T.* TreF (11-18); TrJP (13-18)
Happy is the man who loves the woods and waters. Beatus Vir. Richard Le Gallienne. HBMV; OHIP
Happy is the man whom Thou hast set apart. Psalm. "Yehoash." TrJP
Happy Islands, The. Isabel Maud Peacocke. BoAu
Happy Isle, The. Spenser. *Fr.* The Faerie Queene, IV, 10. OBSC
Happy Life, The. Martial. *See* Means to Attain a Happy Life, The.
Happy Life, The, *sel.* William Thompson.
"Book, A, a friend, a song, a glass." ViBoPo
Happy Life, The. Sir Henry Wotton. *See* Character of a Happy Life, The.
Happy Lifetime to You. Franklin P. Adams. InMe
Happy lover who has come, A. In Memoriam A. H. H., VIII. Tennyson. EnLi-2; EPN; ViPo; VP
Happy Man, The. Gilles Ménage. BOHV
Happy Man, A. E. A. Robinson, *after the Greek of* Carphyllides. AWP; JAWP; LiTW; WBP
Happy me! O happy sheepe. Psalme Twenty-three, *par. by* George Herbert. Bible, *O.T.* MaMe
Happy men that lose their heads, The. Fantasia. G. K. Chesterton. HBMV
Happy Miner, The. John A. Stone. SGR
Happy Miner, The. *Unknown.* CoSo; IHA, *abr.*
Happy Mortal, who these treasures share, The. Island of the Blest. Pindar. *Fr.* Olympic Odes, II. OBEC
Happy mother stalk of corn, A. Baby Corn. Lydia Avery Coonley Ward. GFA; PRWS
Happy Myrtillo. Henry Carey. SeCePo
Happy New Year! Happy New Year! *Unknown.* PoSC
Happy Night, The. John Sheffield, Duke of Buckingham and Normanby. UnTE
Happy Night, The. J. C. Squire. HBMV
Happy Oxen in a Stall. Annette Wynne. ChrBoLe
Happy people die whole, they are all dissolved in a moment. Post Mortem. Robinson Jeffers. MAP; MoAmPo; MoPo; TrGrPo
Happy road that brought me here, The. Shankill. Eileen Shanahan. NeIP

Happy Sheep, The. Wilfrid Thorley. GFA; PCH; SoPo
Happy Shepherdess, The. *Unknown, tr. fr. Provençal by* Willard Trask. CLwM
Happy Song-sparrow, that on woodland side. The Fringilla Melodia. Henry Beck Hirst. AA
Happy Songs. Blake. *See* Piping down the Valleys Wild.
Happy Swain, The. Ambrose Philips. EnLoPo
Happy that company who are intoxicated with each other's speech. Cliques and Critics. Sa'ib of Isfahan. LiTW
Happy that first white age when we. Metrum V. Henry Vaughan. PPON
Happy the dead! Consolation in War. Lewis Mumford. NYBP
Happy the feeling from the bosom thrown. Sonnet: To ——. Wordsworth. ChER
Happy the hare at morning, for she cannot read. The Cultural Presupposition [*or* Culture]. W. H. Auden. CABA; MaPo; MoPW
Happy the Home. *Unknown.* SoP
Happy the home when God is there. The Happy Home. *Unknown.* SoP
Happy the home where Jesus' name. Happy the Home. *Unknown.* SoP
Happy the Man. Horace, *par. fr. Latin by* Dryden. *Fr.* Odes, III, 29. MaRV
(Happiness, 4 *ll.*) TreF
("Happy the man, and happy he alone.") OTD; PeRV
(To Maecenas, *longer sel.*) PoFr
(Today and Tomorrow, 4 *ll.*) GoTP
Happy the Man. Pope. *See* Ode on Solitude.
Happy the man, and happy he alone. Happy the Man [*or* Imitation of Horace *or* To Maecenas]. Horace, *par. by* Dryden. *Fr.* Odes, III, 29. GoTP; MaRV; OTD; PeRV; PoFr; TreF
Happy the man who free from care and strife. The Beggar and Poet. Samuel Wesley. PeRV
Happy the man, who his whole time doth bound. The Old Man of Verona. Claudian, *tr. by* Abraham Cowley. AWP; JAWP; WBP; WoL
Happy the man, who on the mountain-side. After Reading Homer. Digby Mackworth Dolben. GoBC
Happy the man who, safe on shore. The Hurricane. Philip Freneau. AmPP (4th ed.); AP; CoBA
Happy the man who so hath Fortune tried. Of Temperance in Fortune. Richard Watson Dixon. *Fr.* Mano; a Poetical History. VA
Happy the man who, void of cares and strife. The Splendid Shilling; an Imitation of Milton. John Philips. BOHV; CEP; EiCL; EiPP; Par
Happy the man whom bount'ous Gods allow. Horace. Epodes, II. CavP
Happy the man, whose wish and care. Ode on Solitude [*or* Solitude *or* The Quiet Life *or* The Contented Man *or* Happy the Man]. Pope. ALV; ATP; AWP; BoLiVe; BoPe; CBEP; CEP; DiPo; EG; EiCL; ExPo; FaFP; FiP; FlW; GoBC; GTBS; GTBS-D; GTBS-P; GTBS-W; GTSE; GTSL; HBV; HBVY; InMe; InPo; InvP; JAWP; MaRV; MBW-1; MCCG; NeHB; NoP; OAEP; OBEC; OnPP; OTPC (1923 ed.); PG (1955 ed.); PoE; PoFS; PoIE; PoPl; PoPo; PoRA; PoToHe; SeCeV; SeCL; TreFS; TrGrPo; ViBoPo; WBP
Happy the nations of the moral North! Donna Julia. Byron. *Fr.* Don Juan. PoEL-4
Happy the stark bare wood on the hill of Bree! The Triad of Things Not Decreed. Alice Furlong. AnIV
Happy they who die for the earth which also dies. Happy Are Those Who Have Died. Charles Péguy. WaaP
Happy think a lifetime a short stage, The. Time as Variable. Lucian. OnPM
Happy those early days [or dayes], when I. The Retreat[e]. Henry Vaughan. AnAnS-1; AtBAP; ATP; AWP; BEL; BoC; BoLiVe; BWP; CABA; CAW; CBEP; CoBE; EG; EnL; EnLi-1; EnLit; ExPo; FaBoEn; GTBS; GTBS-D; GTBS-P; GTBS-W; GTSE; GTSL; HBV; InPo; InvP; JAWP; LiTB; LiTG; LO; LoBV; MaPo; MeLP; MeP; MePo; NoP; OAEP; OBEV; OBS; PAn; PoAn; PoEL-2; PoFS; PoIE; PoRA; ReEn; SCEP-1; SeCePo; SeCeV; SeCL; SeCP; SeCV-1; SeEP; StP; TOP; TreFT; TrGrPo; UnPo (1st ed.); ViBoPo; WBP; WHA
Happy Thought. Robert Louis Stevenson. BoTP; FaBoBe; HBV; HBVY; InP; OTPC; PoVP; RIS; SAS; TiPo; TreFS
Happy Thought. Bert Leston Taylor. RIS
Happy, thrice happy now the savage race. Charles Churchill. *Fr.* Gotham. PoFr
Happy, thrice happy times in silver age! Desiderium. Phineas Fletcher. *Fr.* The Purple Island, I. OBS
Happy Time, A. *Unknown. See* Limerick: "There was a young fellow named Hall."
Happy Too Much. Boethius, *tr. fr. Latin by* Elizabeth I, Queen of England. *Fr.* Consolation of Philosophy. CTC
Happy Townland, The. W. B. Yeats. ThWaDe
Happy Tree, The. Gerald Gould. MoBrPo (1942 ed.); WGRP
Happy Ulysses, The. Joachim du Bellay, *tr. by* G. K. Chesterton. *See* Heureux qui, comme Ulysse, a fait un beau voyage.
Happy verses! that were prest. To Ethelinda. Christopher Smart. CLwM
Happy View, A. C. Day Lewis. CMoP
Happy Wanderer, The. Percy Addleshaw. OBVV; VA
Happy Warrior, The. Sir Herbert Read. MMA
Happy Warrior, The. Wordsworth. *See* Character of the Happy Warrior.
Happy Were He. Earl of Essex. EIL
(Content.) OBSC
(Passion, A.) TuPP
(Wish, A.) GTSL
Happy, who like Ulysses or that lord. Heureux qui, comme Ulysse, a fait un beau voyage [*or* The Happy Ulysses *or* Translation from Du Bellay]. Joachim du Bellay, *tr. by* G. K. Chesterton. *Fr.* Regrets. AWP; InP; WoL
Happy Wind. W. H. Davies. OTPC (1946 ed.); RIS; StaSt; TSW
Happy Woman, A. Agathias, *tr. fr. Greek by* Lord Neaves. OnPM
Happy World, The. William Brighty Rands. OTPC (1946 ed.); PCH; PPL
(Brown Bee.) StVeCh (1940 ed.)
Happy ye leaves! when as those lily [*or* lilly] hands. Amoretti, I. Spenser. ATP; BEL; CoBE; EnLi-1; EnLit; LoBV; MaPo (1969 ed.); Po; PoAn; ReEn; ReIE; SiCE; Sonn
Happy: yea, happy for ever and aye! Fulfilment. Louis V. Ledoux. HBMV
Happy youth, that shalt possesse. To My Cousin (C. R.) Marrying My Lady (A.). Thomas Carew. AnAnS-2; SeCP
Happyest lyfe that here we have, The. To Master Henrye Cobham, of the Most Blessed State of Lyfe. Barnaby Googe. EnPo
Harald, the Agnostic Ale-loving Old Shepherd Enemy of the Whisky-drinking Ploughmen and Harvesters, Walks over the Sabbath Hill to the Shearing. George Mackay Brown. NePoEA-2
Harangue on the Death of Hayyim Nahman Bialik. César Tiempo, *tr. fr. Spanish by* Donald Devenish Walsh. TrJP
Harbingers. Basho, *tr. fr. Japanese by* Harold G. Henderson. PoPl; RePo
Harbingers are come, The. See, see their mark. The Forerunners. George Herbert. AnAnS-1; MaMe; MeP; MePo; NoP; ReEn
Harbor, The. Winifred M. Letts. PoMa
Harbor, The. Carl Sandburg. CBV; CoBA; NP; PoPl
Harbor Dawn, The. Hart Crane. *Fr.* The Bridge: Powhatan's Daughter. AmP; LiTA; MoPo; NePA; OxBA
Harbor wears a look of space, The. Little Steamboat. Oscar Williams. PoPl
Harbour. Harold Monro. BoPe
Harbour Bridge, The. Thomas Hardy. TDP
Harbour Whistles. H. P. Lovecraft. HYE
Hard above all things mortal is. Love's Fragility. Alan Porter. POTE
Hard aport! Now close to shore sail! Adrian Block's Song. Edward Everett Hale. PAH
Hard as hurdle arms, with a broth of goldish flue. Harry Ploughman. Gerard Manley Hopkins. FaBoMo; VP
Hard blue winds of March, The. The Three Winds. Laurie Lee. FaBoMo; POTi
Hard by a Crystal Fountain. Thomas Morley. ReIE
Hard by the Indian lodges, where the bush. The Corn Husker. Pauline Johnson. CaP
Hard by the lilied Nile I saw. A Crocodile. Thomas Lovell Beddoes. *Fr.* The Last Man. AnFE; CBV
Hard by the Wildbrooks I met Mary. Meeting Mary. Eleanor Farjeon. BiCB
Hard coming we had of it, A. The Poets. David Wevill. PP

Hard Country. Philip Booth. CoAP
Hard Daddy. Langston Hughes. BANP
Hard from the southeast blows the wind. Elizabeth J. Coatsworth. TiPo (1952 ed.)
Hard Frost, A. C. Day Lewis. HaMV
Hard Frost. Andrew Young. BoNaP; MoVE
Hard harted faire, if thou wilt not consent. *Unknown.* SeCSL
Hard is the stone, but harder still. The Image-Maker. Oliver St. John Gogarty. BoPe; OBEV (new ed.); OBMV; PoRA
Hard it is, very hard. The Choice of the Cross. Dorothy L. Sayers. *Fr.* The Devil to Pay. MaRV
Hard Lines. Tom Robinson. BiCB
Hard Lovers, The. George Dillon. AnAmPo
Hard Luck. Langston Hughes. NP
Hard on a high flower comes the sun. The Energy of Light. John Hay. NePoAm-2
Hard pomegranates split wide. Pomegranates. Paul Valéry, *tr. by* Herman Salinger. LiTW
Hard Rock Returns to Prison from the Hospital for the Criminal Insane. Etheridge Knight. BP
Hard Rows to Hoe. Daniel Henderson. PaA
Hard sand breaks, The. Hermes of the Ways. Hilda Doolittle ("H. D."). LiTA; NP
Hard Times ("Come listen awhile"). *Unknown.* ABF
Hard Times in the Country, *with music. Unknown.* OuSiCo
Hard tin bird was my lover, A. Weathercock. Elizabeth Jennings. NePoEA
Hard to Be a Nigger. *Unknown.* ABF
Hard to exert the tuneful voice. The Shrimp. Moses Browne. WaPE
Hard Travelin'. Woody Guthrie. WOW
Hard Trials, *with music. Unknown.* ABF
Hard Weather. George Meredith. EPN; Po; ViPP
Hard-working Miner, The, *with music. Unknown.* ABF
Hardcastle Crags. Sylvia Plath. GoYe
Harden Now Thy Tired Heart. Thomas Campion. NCEP
Hardening into Print. Richard Eberhart. NoP
Harder Task, The. *Unknown.* BLRP; MaRV
Harder Task. Katherine L. Ramsdell. SoP
Hardest headlands, The/ Gravel down. La Rose des Vents. Richard Wilbur. MiAP
Hardly a shot from the gate we storm'd. Badminton. Sir Alfred Comyn Lyall. *Fr.* Studies at Delhi. OBVV; PeVV
Hardly Think I Will, *with music. Unknown.* ABF
Hardness of her heart and truth of mine, The. Gulling Sonnets, IV. Sir John Davies. Sonn; TuPP
Hardship of Accounting, The. Robert Frost. FaBoCh; FaFP; LoGBV; WhC
Hare, The. Walter de la Mare. TiPo
Hare, The. Stanley Snaith. HaMV
Hare and Many Friends, The. John Gay. *Fr.* Fables. ATP (1935 ed.); EiCL; EiCP; EnLi-1 (1949 ed.)
(Hare with Many Friends, The.) HBV
Hare Drummer. Edgar Lee Masters. *Fr.* Spoon River Anthology. TOP
Hare has only the hound to fear, The. Death. Arthur MacGillivray. JKCP (1955 ed.)
Hare-hunting. William Somerville. *Fr.* The Chace, II. OBEC
Hare with Many Friends, The. John Gay. *See* Hare and Many Friends, The.
Harebells in June. Annette Wynne. SUS
Hares at Play. John Clare. CBEP; OA
Hares on the Mountain. *Unknown.* CBEP; ErPo; UnTE
Hark. John Webster. *See* Hark, Now Everything Is Still.
Hark! ah, the nightingale. Philomela. Natthew Arnold. AtBAP; BEL; BoLiVe; BWP; EnL; EnLi-2; EnLit; GTBS; GTBS-D; GTSE; GTSL; HBV; ILP; InP; MaPo; MaVP; MBW-2; MCCG; OAEP; OBEV; PIA; PoFS; PoIE; PoVP; SeCeV; TOP; UnPo (1st ed.); VA; ViPo; ViPP; VP; WHA
Hark, All You Ladies That Do Sleep! Thomas Campion. OAEP; PoE; ReIE
(Hark, All You Ladies.) EiL; TuPP
(Harke, Al You Ladies That Do Sleep.) PoEL-2
(In the Dark What the Day Doth Forbid.) UnTE
(Proserpina.) OBSC
Hark, already you can hear the working song. Sonnets to Orpheus, Pt. II, XXV. Rainer Maria Rilke. OnPM
Hark at the lips of this pink whorl of shell. Quatrain. Frank Dempster Sherman. AA
Hark Back. Richard Eberhart. ToPo
Hark, Celia, hark! but lay thou close thine ear. The Secret. *Unknown.* SeCL
Hark! do I hear again the roar. Columbus Dying. Edna Dean Proctor. MC; PAH
Hark! even here, into the chambers of the Palace. Even in the Palace. Nago Okimaro. OnPM
Hark! from yon covert, where those tow'ring oaks. Hare-hunting. William Somervile. *Fr.* The Chace, II. OBEC
Hark, happy lovers, hark! A Kiss. William Drummond of Hawthornden. EIL
Hark Hark. *Unknown.* Po
Hark! hark! down the century's long reaching slope. Yorktown Centennial Lyric. Paul Hamilton Hayne. PAH
Hark hark how Bellona thunders. *Unknown.* SeCSL
Hark, hark! the advent cry again. The Prince of Peace. Edward Henry Bickersteth. BePJ
Hark! hark! The dogs do bark. Mother Goose. BoChLi; GaP; HBVY; OTPC; OxNR; PCH; Po; RIS; SiTL; TiPo
Hark! Hark! the Lark. Shakespeare. *Fr.* Cymbeline, II, iii. AnFE; AtBAP; ATP; BEL; BoTP; CBEP; CH; ChTr; CoBE; DiPo; EnL; EnLi-1 (1949 ed.); EnLit; EnRePo; ExPo; FaBoCh; FaBV; FaFP; FaPON; HBV; ILP; InP; InPo; LiTB; LiTG; LoBV; LoGBV; NoP; OTPC; OuHeWo; PoIE; PTK; SeCeV; SiCE; TOP; TreF; TrGrPo; ViBoPo; WHA
(Aubade.) OBEV; ShBV-3
(Morning Song, A.) GN; PCH
(Morning Song for Imogen, A.) AnEnPo
(Song: "Hark! hark! the lark at heaven's gate sings.") AWP; CLwM; EIL; FiP; JAWP; WBP
(Song of the Musicians.) BoLiVe
(Song to Imogen.) EG; OBSC
(Three Songs.) UnPo (1st ed.)
Hark! hark! the merry warder's horn. A Hawking Party in the Olden Time. Mary Howitt. OTPC (1923 ed.)
Hark! hark! to the wind! 'Tis the night, they say. Hallowe'en. Virna Sheard. DD
Hark! heard ye the signals of triumph afar? Thomas Pringle. *Fr.* The Caffer Commando. ACV
Hark, hearer, hear what I do. Epithalamion. Gerard Manley Hopkins. AnEnPo; HW
Hark! how all the welkin rings. For Christmas-Day. Charles Wesley. CEP
Hark, how chimes the Passing Bell. The Passing Bell. James Shirley. ACP
Hark, how my Celia, with the choice. Celia Singing. Thomas Carew. OAEP
Hark [*or* Hearke], how the birds do sing. Man's Medley. George Herbert. MaMe; ViBoPo
Hark how the Duke of Lorraine comes. The Victory in Hungary. Thomas Shadwell. *Fr.* The Squire of Alsatia. SeCL
Hark how the Lyrick Choristers o' th' wood. To Clarestella on St. Valentines Day Morning. Robert Heath. OBS
Hark how the minstrels gin to shrill aloud. Spenser. *Fr.* Epithalamion. WHA
Hark how the mower Damon sung. Damon the Mower. Andrew Marvell. *See* Heark how the mower. . .
Hark how the passing bell. Upon a Passing Bell. Thomas Washbourne. SeCL
Hark, I hear the bells of Westgate. Westgate-on-Sea. John Betjeman. OxBoLi
Hark I hear the cannons roar. A Carrouse to the Emperor, the Royal Pole, and the Much-wronged Duke of Lorrain. *Unknown.* CoMu
Hark! I hear the tramp of thousands. The Reveille. Bret Harte. GN; HBV; MC; OHIP; OtMeF; OTPC (1946 ed.); PaA; PAH; PAL; PoRL
Hark! in the still night. Who goes there? Sixteen Dead Men. Dora Sigerson Shorter. ACP; OnYI
Hark! My Beloved! The Song of Solomon, II: 8-13, Bible, *O.T.* TrJP
Hark, my Flora! Love doth call us. A Song of Dalliance. William Cartwright. ErPo
Hark, My Soul. John Austin. OxBoCh
Hark, My Soul! It Is the Lord. William Cowper. *See* Lovest Thou Me?
Hark [*or* Hearke], Now Everything Is Still. John Webster. *Fr.* The Duchess of Malfi, IV, ii. BEL; CBEP; CenL; EIL; HW; LoBV; NoP; OBS; QFR; SeCePo; SiCE; TuPP; ViBoPo
(Dirge, A: "Hark, now everything is still.") CBEP EnLi-1
(General Mist of Error, A.) OnPM

Hark (continued)
(Hark.) CH
(Shrouding of the Duchess of Malfi, The.) OBEV
(Summons to Execution.) FaBoEn
Hark! of a matchless vision would I speak. The Dream of the Rood. *Unknown.* StJW
Hark! one saith: "Proclaim!" All Flesh Is Grass. Isaiah, Bible, *O.T.* TrJP
Hark, Reader! wilt be learn'd i' th' wars? To My Truly Valiant, Learned Friend, Who in His Book Resolv'd the Art Gladiatory into the Mathematics. Richard Lovelace. PoEL-3
Hark! she is call'd, the parting hour [*or* houre] is come. On [*or* In] the Glorious Assumption of Our Blessed Lady [*or* On the Assumption]. Richard Crashaw. AnAnS-1; ISi; LoBV; MaMe; MeP; OBS; PoLi
Hark! 't is the voice of the mountain. The Battle of Eutaw. William Gilmore Simms. PAH
Hark! the awful cries I hear. The Cries! *Unknown.* SoP
Hark! the cock crows, and yon bright star. The New Year. Charles Cotton. CEP; GoTL; OBS
Hark! the cock proclaims the morning. St. Matthias. Christopher Smart. *Fr.* Hymns and Spiritual Songs. EiCP
Hark! the flow of the four rivers. Farewells from Paradise. Elizabeth Barrett Browning. OBEV (new ed.); OBVV
Hark! the glad sound! the Saviour comes. The Prince of Peace [*or* The Saviour Comes]. Philip Doddridge. MaRV; SoP
Hark! the Herald Angels Sing. Charles Wesley. MaRV; OBEV; OTPC (1946 ed), *st.* 1; PCH, *st.* 1; PTK; TreFS; YaCaBo, *with music*
(Nativity, The.) BLRP
Hark the herald angels sing, *parody.* Sir Thomas Beecham. PV
Hark, the herald angels sing, *parody.* Paul Dehn. PV
Hark the herald angels sing. Abdication Street Song. *Unknown.* PV
Hark the herald angels sing. On Dean Inge. Humbert Wolfe. ChTr
Hark! the Mavis. Burns. *See* Ca' the Yowes to the Knowes.
Hark! the tiny cowslip bell. Spring Has Come. *Unknown.* BoTP
Hark! the Vesper Hymn Is Stealing. Thomas Moore. EnRP
Hark! The Voice of Jesus Calling. Daniel March. SoP
Hark! the voice of love and mercy. It Is Finished. Jonathan Evans. BePJ
Hark! They cry! I hear by that. Yolp, Yolp, Yolp, Yolp. *Unknown.* ElL; OA
Hark! 'tis Freedom that calls, come, patriots, awake! A Song. *Unknown.* PAH
Hark! 'tis the twanging horn! O'er yonder bridge. The Winter Evening [*or* The Postman]. William Cowper. The Task, IV. CoBE; EiPP; EnLi-2; EnLit; FiP; OAEP; SeCePo; TOP
Hark to the story of poor Romeo! Romeo and Juliet. Fred Newton Scott. InMe
Hark to the story of Willie the Weeper. Willie the Weeper. *Unknown.* TrAS
Hark to the whimper of the sea-gull. The Sea-Gull. Ogden Nash. FaFP; LiTM; NePA; PoPo; SiTL
Hark what a sound, and too divine for hearing. Frederick W. H. Myers. *Fr.* Saint Paul. FaChP
Hark! . . . what booming. Arcana Sylvarum. Charles De Kay. AA
Hark what, now loud, now low, the pining flute complains. The Flute. Hilali. OnPM
Hark you such sound as quivers? Kings will hear. November. Mahlon Leonard Fisher. HBV; PFY
Hark! Young Democracy from sleep. Young Democracy. Bernard O'Dowd. BoAu; PoAu-1 *abr.*
Harke, Al You Ladies That Do Sleep. Thomas Campion. *See* Hark, All You Ladies That Do Sleep!
Harke, harke, me thinkes I heer love saye. *Unknown.* SeCSL
Harke how the nightingale displayes. *Unknown.* SeCSL
Harke newes, O envy, thou shalt heare descry'd. Julia. John Donne. Elegies, XIII. MaMe
Harke shee is called, the parting houre is come. *See* Hark! she is call'd . . .
Harke this lesson. *Unknown.* SeCSL
Harlackenden, among these men of note Christ hath thee seated. Among These Troopes of Christs Souldiers, Came . . . Mr. Roger Harlackenden. Edward Johnson. SCAP
Harlaw. Sir Walter Scott. *Fr.* The Antiquary, *ch.* 40. EnLi-2
(Red Harlaw.) OxBB
Harlem. Jean Brierre, *tr. fr. French by* John F. Matheus. PoNe; TTY
Harlem ("Here on the edge of hell.") Langston Hughes. CAD
Harlem ("What happens to a dream deferred"). Langston Hughes. AmPP (5th ed.); NoP; PoNe (1970 ed.); TPM
(Dream Deferred.) LiTM (1970 ed.); OCS
(Lennox Avenue Mural.) AmNP
Harlem Dancer, The. Claude McKay. BALP; BANP; MAP
Harlem Freeze Frame. Lebert Bethune. BF
Harlem Gallery, *sels.* Melvin B. Tolson.
"Night John Henry is born an ax, The." TTY
"Strange but true is the story." Kal
(Sea Turtle and the Shark, The.) BP
Harlem in January. Julia Fields. CAD
Harlem Night Song. Langston Hughes. OCS
Harlem Shadows. Claude McKay. AmPP (5th ed.); BANP; PoNe
Harlem '67. Clarence Reed. BF
Harlem Sweeties. Langston Hughes. LiTM (1970 ed.); NoP; PoNe; TTY
Harlem. Where once I trailed the rivers edge. The Invaders. Clarence Reed. BF
Harlequin of Dreams, The. Sidney Lanier. AA; AP
Harley, the nation's great support. Horace, Epistle VII, Book I, Imitated. Swift. CEP
Harlot's Catch. Robert Nichols. ErPo; FaBoTw
Harlot's House, The. Oscar Wilde. MoBrPo; PoVP; StP; SyP; ViPP
Harmonie du soir. Baudelaire, *tr. fr. French by* Lord Alfred Douglas. AWP; JAWP; WBP
Harmonious Heedlessness of Little Boy Blue, The. Guy Wetmore Carryl. MPB; YT
(Little Boy Blue.) ALV
Harmony. Thomas Grant Springer. PoToHe
Harmony of the Church, The, *sels.* Michael Drayton. ReIE
Most Excellent Song Which Was Salomon's, The.
Song of Jonah in the Whale's Belly, The.
Harnet and the Bittle, a Wiltshire Tale, The ("A harnet zet in a hollur tree"). J. Y. Akerman. ChTr
Harold at Two Years Old. Frederic W. H. Meyers. HBMV
Harold Bates, who lives next door. Neighbors. "Lennox." InMe
Harold the Dauntless, *sel.* Sir Walter Scott.
'Tis Merry in Greenwood. FaPON; MPB; OHIP
Harold the Valiant. Mary Elizabeth Hewitt Stebbins. AA
Harold's Song. Sir Walter Scott. *See* Rosebelle.
Haroun Al-Rachid for Heart's-Life. *Unknown, tr. fr. Arabic by* E. Powys Mathers. *Fr.* The Thousand and One Nights. AWP
Haroun, the Caliph, through the sunlit street. Power. Thomas Stephens Collier. AA
Haroun's Favorite Song. *Unknown, tr. fr. Arabic by* E. Powys Mathers. *Fr.* The Thousand and One Nights. AWP
"Harp and carp, Thomas!" she said. *Unknown.* *Fr.* Thomas the Rhymer. LO
Harp in the Rigging. Hamish Maclaren. EtS
Harp Music. Rolfe Humphries. UnS
Harp of Alfred, The. G. K. Chesterton. *Fr.* The Ballad of the White Horse. MoVE
Harp of David, The. Jacob Cohen, *tr. fr. Hebrew by* Sholom J. Kahn. TrJP
Harp of David, The. "Yehoash," *tr. fr. Yiddish by* Alter Brody. TrJP
Harp of Sorrow, The. Ethel Clifford. HBV; WGRP
Harp of the North. Sir Walter Scott. The Lady of the Lake: Prologue. EnLi-2 (1949 ed.); ILP
(Chase, The.) EnRP
("Harp of the North! that mouldering long hast hung".) OAEP; ViBoPo
Harp of the North, Farewell. Sir Walter Scott. The Lady of the Lake: Epilogue. CoBE
(Farewell, Thou Minstrel Harp.) OBNC
(Harp of the North.) BEL; EPN
("Harp of the North, farewell! The hills grow dark.") ViBoPo
Harp of the Wind, The. Frances Shaw. NP
Harp Song of the Dane Women. Kipling. *Fr.* Puck of Pook's

Hill. AtBAP; FaBoEn; OAEP (2d ed.); OBNC; OtMeF; PoRA; POTE; SeCePo; ShBV-3
Harp That Once through Tara's Halls, The. Thomas Moore. ACP; AnFE; AnIL; ATP (1935 ed.); BEL; CoBE; EnLi-2; EnLit; EnRP; EPN; GN; LiTG; NeHB; OAEP; OBNC; OnYI; OxBI; PG; PoFr; PoLF; PTK; RoGo; TreF; ViBoPo; YAT
Harp You Play So Well, The. Marianne Moore. *See* That Harp You Play So Well.
Harpalus' Complaint [of Phillida's Love]. *Unknown.* OBSC; TuPP; ViBoPo
Harpe is an instrumente of swete molodye, The. The Lekingfelde Proverbs. *Unknown.* MuSP
Harper, The. Thomas Campbell. CBEP; NCEP
(Irish Harper and His Dog, The.) CH; MPB
(My Dog Tray.) GoTP
(Poor Dog Tray.) PTK
Harper, The. *Unknown, tr. fr. Early Modern Irish by* Frank O'Connor. AnIL; KiLC
Harper draws his golden string, The. An Etching. Sister Mary Imelda. CAW
Harper of Chao, The. Po Chü-i, *tr. fr. Chinese by* Arthur Waley. MoPW; UnS
Harpers' Farm, The. Dorothy Aldis. RIS
Harpers Ferry. Selden Rodman. PoNe
Harpooning, The. Ted Walker. WIRo
Harps Hung Up in Babylon. Arthur Colton. WGRP
(Harps in Babylon.) PFY
Harried we were, and spent. The Waradgery Tribe. Mary Gilmore. BoAV; NeLNL; PoAu-1
Harriet and the Matches. Heinrich Hoffmann. *See* Dreadful Story of Pauline and the Matches, The.
Harriet Beecher Stowe. Paul Laurence Dunbar. AA; AmePo; DD; Kal
Harriet Hutch. Nonsense Verses. Laura E. Richards. RIS
Harriet Simper Has Her Day. John Trumbull. *Fr.* The Progress of Dulness. AmPP (4th ed.)
Harriet Tubman. Margaret Walker. PoNe
Harrington Barn Dance, The. *Unknown.* CoSo
Harrow Grave in Flanders, A. Marquess of Crewe. HBV
Harrowing of Hell, The ("After sharp showers . . ."). William Langland. *Fr.* The Vision of Piers Plowman. BoPe
Harrowing of Hell, The ("Voice, A, loud in that light. . .") William Langland, *mod. by* Nevill Coghill. *Fr.* The Vision of Piers Plowman. BoC
Harrowing of Hell, The. Rainer Maria Rilke, *tr. fr. German by* J. B. Leishman. BoPe
Harrowing of Hell, The. *Unknown.* ACP; CAW
Harry Carey's General Reply, to the Libelling Gentry, Who Are Angry at His Welfare. Henry Carey. HBV
Harry Dunne, 2 *vers., with music. Unknown.* ShS
Harry, Harry, hobbillschowe! The Manere of the Crying of ane Playe. William Dunbar. AtBAP
Harry Lorrequer, *sel.* Charles Lever.
Pope, The. BOHV
(Pope He Leads a Happy Life, The.) HBV
Harry Pearce. David Campbell. NeLNL; PoAu-2
Harry Ploughman. Gerard Manley Hopkins. FaBoMo; VP
H——y P——tt. *Unknown.* CoMu
Harry, whose tuneful and well measur'd [*or* well-measured] song. To Mr. H. Lawes [*or* To My Friend Mr. Henry Lawes] on His Airs [*or* Sonnet]. Milton. AWP; InPo; JAWP; LoBV; MuSP; NoP; OBS; Sonn; WBP
Harry Wilmans. Edgar Lee Masters. *Fr.* Spoon River Anthology. PPON; WOW
Harsh bray and follow, The. Two Kitchen Songs. Edith Sitwell. CMoP
Harsh Country, The. Theodore Roethke. TDP
Harsh cry the crows. The Solitary. Nietzsche. AWP
Harsh entry I had of it, Grasud, A. Missionary. D. M. Thomas. HYE
Harshness of gorse darkens the yellow cliff-edge. A View of Rangitoto. Charles Brasch. AnNZ
Hart and Hare. *Unknown. See* Hart he loves the high wood, The.
Hart Crane. Robert Creeley. AP
Hart Crane. Julian Symons. LiTM (1946 ed.)
Hart he loves the high wood, The. *Unknown.* FaBoCh; LoGBV; OxNR
(Hart and Hare.) CBEP
Hart-Leap Well. Wordsworth. BeLS; MyFE
Hart's Castle. Gawin Douglas. *Fr.* King Hart. AtBAP; PoEL-1
Harun Omar and Master Hafiz. Puella Mea. E. E. Cummings. CLwM
Harvard. Robert Lowell. NoP
Harvard Commemoration Ode, The. James Russell Lowell. *See* Ode Recited at the Harvard Commemoration, July 21, 1865.
Harvest. Horatius Bonar. FaChP
Harvest, The. Alice Corbin. BoTP
Harvest. Ellen Mackay Hutchinson Cortissoz. AA; HBV
Harvest. Eva Gore-Booth. HBMV; OQP; WGRP
Harvest. M. M. Hutchinson. BoTP
Harvest. Thomas Nashe. *Fr.* Summer's Last Will and Testament. OBSC
Harvest. Carl Sandburg. WIRo
Harvest. Gene Shuford. GoYe
Harvest. Edith Sitwell. OAEP (2d ed.)
Harvest. John Addington Symonds. PoVP
Harvest and Consecration. Elizabeth Jennings. NePoEA-2
Harvest and the Tempest, The. Lon Woodrum. SoP
Harvest Dust. Winifred Welles. MAP
Harvest Elves, The. Wilfrid Thorley. BrR
Harvest Home. Henry Alford. MaRV; SoP; WGRP
Harvest Home. W. M. L. Fay. FaChP
Harvest Home. Arthur Guiterman. YeAr
Harvest Home. Frederick Tennyson. OBVV
Harvest Home. Theocritus, *tr. fr. Greek by* Charles Stuart Calverley. Idylls, VII. AWP
Harvest-Home Song. John Davidson. VA
Harvest Hymn. Whittier. *Fr.* For an Autumn Festival. OHIP, *abr.*; PoRL
("Once more the liberal year laughs out," *abr.* PGD
Harvest Moon, The. Longfellow. AP; GN; MAmP
Harvest Moon. Josephine Miles. FiMAP
Harvest Moon. Ryota, *tr. fr. Japanese by* Harold G. Henderson. RePo
Harvest of the Sea, The. John McCrae. EtS
Harvest of Time, The. Harold Trowbridge Pulsifer. HBMV
Harvest shall flourish in wintry weather, The. Merlin's Prophecy. Blake. ERoP-1
Harvest Song. Richard Dehmel, *tr. fr. German by* Ludwig Lewisohn. AWP; JAWP; LiTW; WBP
Harvest Song. Dan Georgakas. ThO
Harvest Song. Ludwig Hölty, *tr. fr. German by* Charles T. Brooks. AWP; JAWP; WBP; WoL
Harvest Song, A. Edwin Markham. PEDC
Harvest Song. *Unknown.* 2 ("Boughs do shake and the bells do ring, The.") OxNR BoTP
Harvest Sunset. Carl Sandburg. TSW
Harvest Time. Star Powers. GoYe
Harvest Time. G. A. Watermeyer, *tr. fr. Afrikaans by* Guy Butler, Uys Krige *and* Jack Cope. PeSA
Harvest to Seduce, A. Melville Cane. NYBP; PG (1955 ed.)
Harvest Waits, The. Lloyd Mifflin. HBV
Harvester's Song ("All ye that lovely lovers be"). George Peele. *Fr.* The Old Wives' Tale. TrGrPo
Harvesters—they say themselves, The. The Harvest Elves. Wilfrid Thorley. BrR
Harvesting. Selma Robinson. InMe
Harvesting of the Roses, The. Menahem Ben Jacob, *tr. fr. Hebrew.* TrJP
Harvests. Marie de L. Welch. PoFr
Harvey Girls invaded Kansas that spring, The. The Dustbowl. Kenward Elmslie. ANYP
Harvey Logan, *with music. Unknown.* OuSiCo
Harvey, the happy above happiest men. To the Right Worshipful, My Singular Good Friend, Master Gabriel Harvey, Doctor of the Laws. Spenser. ReIE
Has a love of adventure, a promise of gold. The Whaleman's Song. *Unknown.* EtS
Has any one seen my fair. Cressid. Nora Perry. AA
Has anybody seen my Mopser? The Bandog. Walter de la Mare. BrPo; EvOK; TiPo
Has anybody seen my mouse? Missing. A. A. Milne. MoShBr; PDV
Has auld Kilmarnock seen the dell? Tam Samson's Elegy. Burns. PoEL-4
Has no one seen my heart of you? Thomas Lovell Beddoes. EG
Has not altered. Spenser's Ireland. Marianne Moore. GTBS-W; LiTA; LiTG; LiTM (rev. ed.); MasP; NePA; OxBA

Has (continued)

Has not the night been as a drunken rose. The Drunken Rose. Amarou. AWP

Has someone seen Christ in you today? Christ in You. *Unknown.* STF

Has Sorrow Thy Young Days Shaded? Thomas Moore. OxBI

Has Summer Come without the Rose? Arthur O'Shaughnessy. See Song: "Has summer come without the rose?"

"Has the Marquis La Fayette." A New Song. Joseph Stansbury. PAH

Has there any old fellow got mixed with the boys? The Boys. Oliver Wendell Holmes. CoBA; HBV; WBLP

Hasbrouck and the Rose. H. Phelps Putnam. AnFE; CoAnAm; MoVE; OxBA; TwAmPo; ViBoPo

Hassan, *sels.* James Elroy Flecker.
Epilogue: "Away, for we are ready to a man," *also fr.* The Golden Journey to Samarkand. ShBV-3
(Golden Journey to Samarkand: Epilogue.) HBMV; HT
Golden Road, The ("We are the Pilgrims, Master"), *fr.* V, ii, *also fr.* The Golden Journey to Samarkand. OtMeF
Hassan's Serenade, *fr.* I, ii. OBEV (new ed.)
"Thy dawn, O Master of the world, thy dawn," *fr.* II, ii. OtMeF; WePo
War Song of the Saracens, *fr.* III, iii. FaBV: FOL; MoBrPo; OBVV; OtMeF; ShBV-2; WHA

Hast Never Come to Thee an Hour. Walt Whitman. CBEP

Hast thee harsh verse, as fast as thy lame measure. To Mr. T. W. John Donne. MaMe

Hast thou a charm to stay the morning-star. Hymn before Sunrise, in the Vale of Chamouni. Samuel Taylor Coleridge. BEL; EnRP; ERoP-1; HBV; MaRV; MCCG; MERP; OAEP; OxBoCh; TOP; WGRP

Hast Thou a Cloud? *Unknown.* SoP

Hast thou a cunning instrument of play. Preparation. Thomas Edward Brown. OBEV (new ed.); OBVV; TOP

Hast thou a heritage. In Shadow. Caroline Hazard. GoBC

Hast thou a lamp, a little lamp. The Lamp. Sarah Pratt Greene. AA

Hast Thou Considered Job's Wife? Esther Archibald. SoP

Hast thou entered into the treasures of the snow? The Treasures. Job, Bible, *O.T.* BoW

Hast thou given the horse strength [*or* his might]? The Horse [*or* The War-Horse]. Job, Bible, *O.T.* ChTr; FaPON; GoTP; InP; ShBV-2; TrGrPo

Hast thou heard Him, seen Him, known Him? Captured. *Unknown.* SoP

Hast Thou Heard the Nightingale? Richard Watson Gilder. AA

Hast thou named all the birds without a gun? Forbearance. Emerson. AA; AmePo; AmPP (3d ed.); AnAmPo; AnNe; BBV (1923 ed.); BoLiVe; CoBA; GN; HBV; HBVY; LaNeLa; LiTA; MCCG; MPB; OnPM; OQP; OTPC; PCD; PoRL; TreFT; TrGrPo; ViBoPo; WGRP; YT

Hast thou no right to joy. Ode on Conflicting Claims. Richard Watson Dixon. VA

Hast thou not known? hast thou not heard? They That Wait upon the Lord [*or* Power from God]. Isaiah, Bible, *O.T.* BoC; TreFT; TRV

Hast Thou Not Seen an Aged Rifted Tower. Hartley Coleridge. EnRP; PeER

"Hast thou ony greencloth." Robin Hood's End. *Unknown.* A Gest of Robyn Hode, Fytte VIII. GoTL

"Hast thou seen that lordly castle." The Castle by the Sea. Ludwig Uhland. AWP; JAWP; WBP

Hast thou seen the down in the air? A Song to a Lute [*or* A Song]. Sir John Suckling. *Fr.* The Sad One. AnAnS-2; EnLoPo; ReEn; SCEP-2; SeEP; TrGrPo

Hast Thou Spoken, Blessed Master? Avis B. Christiansen. SoP

"Hast thou then nought wiser to bring." The Catechism. Walter de la Mare. CMoP

Hast thou then survived. Address to My Infant Daughter. Wordsworth. EvOK; Par

Hast thou within a care so deep? Sanctuary. *Unknown.* SoP

Haste Not, Rest Not. Goethe, *tr. fr. German.* MaRV; OQP, *abr.*

Haste, Sylvia, haste, my charming maid! The Invitation. Thomas Godfrey. AnFE; APA; CoAnAm

Haste thee, Nymph, and bring with thee. Mirth, with Thee I Mean to Live. Milton. *Fr.* L'Allegro. FaBV; OTPC (1946 ed.); YT

Haste thee, Winter, haste away. Old Song. *Unknown.* PCH

Haste to the Wedding. Alex Comfort. ErPo

Haste, ye purple gleams of light. An African Song. Thomas Chatterton. LoBV

Hasten. The countenance of the year is hardened, the face wan, drawn. After Tschaikowsky. Wallace Gould. AnAmPo

Hastening on, the wanderer strode. The Wanderer. "Yehoash." TrJP

Hastings Mill. Cicely Fox Smith. HBV; WaKn

Hasty Pudding, The. Joel Barlow. AmPP; AP; CoBA *sels.*
Pudding Prepared and Eaten, The, *fr.* III. AnNE
"Let the green succatash with thee contend," *fr.* I. LoGBV
"Ye Alps audacious, thro' the Heavens that rise," I. OxBA
Praise of the Pudding, *fr.* I. AnNE

Hasty sin of the young after a dance, The. Living in Sin. Austin Clarke. ELU

Hat Bar. Mildred Weston. FiBHP

Hat Given to the Poet by Li Chien, The. Po Chü-i, *tr. fr. Chinese by* Arthur Waley. AtBAP; BoW

Hat you loved, the damask-trimmed reed-hat, The. Folk Song. *Unknown.* LiTW

Hatched in a rasping darkness of dry sand. Letter IV. William Empson. LiTB

Hate! Pavel Antokolsky, *tr. fr. Russian by* Babette Deutsch. TrJP

Hate. Herbert E. Palmer. POTE

Hate. James Stephens. MoAB; MoBrPo; NP; OBVV; TSW

Hate and debate Rome through the world hath spread. In Roman. Sir John Harington. PV

Hate and love, hate and love; circles still remain. Triangle. Roslyn Greer. TNV

Hate and the Love of the World, The. Max Ehrmann. PoToHe (new ed.)

Hate, be a faithful prop, and find. Hate! Pavel Antokolsky. TrJP

Hate blows a bubble of despair into. E. E. Cummings. Sonn NeAP

Hate is only one of many responses. Poem. Frank O'Hara.

Hate me or love, I care not, as I pass. The Unicorn. Ruth Pitter. LO; MoBrPo; MoVE

Hate me, or love, my Helen, as you list. Four Sonnets to Helen, 2. Pierre de Ronsard. *Fr.* Sonnets pour Hélène. LiTW

Hate only will I love. Love and Hate. *Unknown.* KiLC

Hate-Song, A. Shelley. EnLoPo

Hate the Idle Pleasures. Shakespeare. See Evil Designs.

Hate Whom Ye List. Sir Thomas Wyatt. EnRePo; EP; TuPP ("Hate whom ye list, for I care not.") FCP; SiCE; SiPS

Hater he came and sat by a ditch, A. A Hate-Song. Shelley. EnLoPo

Hath aged winter, fledg'd with feathered raine. An Elegy upon the Death of Mr. Stanninow Fellow Queenes Colledge. Richard Crashaw. MaMe

Hath any loved you well, down there. Song from "Chartivel" [*or* Sarrazine's Song]. Marie de France, *tr. by* Arthur O'Shaughnessy. *Fr.* Chartivel. AWP; EnLoPo; HBV; JAWP; LiTW; PoVP; WBP

Hath God, who freely gave you his own Son. To the Rev'd Mr. Jno. Sparhawk on the Birth of His Son. Samuel Sewall. SCAP

Hath not the dark stream closed above thy head. The Tears of the Poplars. Edith M. Thomas. AA; AnAmPo

Hath not the morning dawned with added light? Ethnogenesis; Written during the Meeting of the First Southern Congress. . .1861. Henry Timrod. AmPP (4th ed.); MAmP; OxBA

Hath onely anger an omnipotence. Upon the Asse That Bore Our Saviour. Richard Crashaw. MaMe

Hath the rude laugh of Boreas frighted thee. To a Mayflower. William E. Marshall. CaP

Hath this world, without me wrought. Questionings. Frederic Henry Hedge. HBV

Hath woman then no rights, presumptuous Paine? The Rights of Women. William Cowper. CBEP

Hatikvah—a Song of Hope. Naphtali Herz Imber, *tr. fr. Hebrew by* Henry Snowman. TrJP

Hatred. Gwendolyn B. Bennett. AmNP; BANP; CDC

Hatred and greed and pride shall die. He Shall Speak Peace. Thomas Curtis Clark. OQP; WBLP

Hatred and vengeance, my eternal portion. Lines Written dur-

ing a Period of Insanity [*or* Lines Written under the Influence of Delirium]. William Cowper. AtBAP; FiP; InPo; NoP; PeER; PoEL-3
Hatred eternal, furious revenging. Sapphics upon the Passion of Christ. *Unknown.* RelE
Hatred of Men with Black Hair. Robert Bly. FRC; NaP
Hats off!/ Along the street there comes. The Flag Goes By. Henry Holcomb Bennett. AA; BBV; DD; FaBoBe; FaFP; FaPON; GN; HBV; HBVY; HH; NeHB; OHFP; PaA; PAL; PCD; PEDC; PGD; PoRL; PTK; RePo; SiSoSe; TiPo (1952 ed.); TreF; WBLP; YaD
Hattage. A. P. Herbert. FiBHP
Hatteras Calling. Conrad Aiken. BoNaP
Hatters, The. Nan McDonald. PoAu-2
Haughty Aspen, The; a German Legend. Nora Archibald Smith. ChrBoLe
Haughty Snail-King, The. Vachel Lindsay. LOW
Haughty they said he was, at first, severe. Whom We Revere. James Russell Lowell. *Fr.* Under the Old Elm. PGD
Haul Away, Joe, *with music.* *Unknown.* AmSS; ShS, 2 *vers.*; SoAmSa
(Haul Away, My Rosy, *with music.*) *OuSiCo*
Haul on the Bowline, *with music.* Unknown. AmSS; ShS; SoAmSa
Haul on the rope. Make the high bell lean. To the Bell-Ringer. Robert Farren. OnYI
Haul up the flag, you mourners. Elegy for Two Banjos. Karl Shapiro. AtBAP; LiTA; TrJP; WaP
Haulage. E. E. Nott-Bower. WhC
Haunch of Venison, The. Goldsmith. CEP
Haunted Country. Robinson Jeffers. OxBA
Haunted Garden, The. Henry Treece. NeBP
Haunted House, The. Robert Graves. OxBI
Haunted House, The. Thomas Hood. AnEnPo, *abr.*; SeCePo; WePo; WiR
Sels.
"Centipede along the threshold crept, The." ERoP-2
"No human figure stirr'd, to go or come." MyFE
"Unhinged the iron gates half open hung." NBM
Haunted House, The. George Sylvester Viereck. AnAmPo
Haunted Houses. Longfellow. AnNE
Haunted Oak, The. Paul Laurence Dunbar. BANP; Kal
Haunted Odysseus; the Last Testament. Horace Gregory. MoVE
Haunted Palace, The. Poe. *Fr.* The Fall of the House of Usher. AA; AmePo; AmLP; AmP; AnFE; AP; APA; BeLS; BoLiVe; CH; ChTr; CoAnAm; HBV; LiTA; LiTG; MAmP; MCCG; MWA-1; NePA; OBVV; OTPC; OxBA; PFY; Po; PoE; PoEL-4; SyP; TDP; TOP; TreFS; TrGrPo; WiR; ViBoPo
("In the greenest of our valleys.") AmPP
Haunter, The. Thomas Hardy. AtBAP; ChMP; GTBS-D; QFR
Haunting Fingers. Thomas Hardy. MaPo
Haunts me the lugubrious shape. Half-Bent Man. Richard Eberhart. NYBP
Haunts of the Halcyon, The. Charles Henry Luders. AA
Havana Dreams. Langston Hughes. GoSl; PoNe
Have Angleworms attractive homes? An Alphabet. Charles E. Carryl. LBN
Have-at a Venture. *Unknown.* CoMu; ErPo
Have Courage, My Boy, to Say, No. *Unknown.* STF
Have courage, O my comradry of dreamers! The Dreamers. Sydney Jephcott. BoAu
Have dark Egyptians stolen thee away. Mimma Bella, I. Eugene Lee-Hamilton. HBV; Sonn
Have done with care, my hearts! aboard amain. A Farewell to Sir John Norris and Sir Francis Drake. George Peele. OBSC
Have done, you men and women all! The Animals in the Ark. *Unknown.* *Fr.* The Deluge. ChTr
Have fair fallen, O fair, fair have fallen, so dear. Henry Purcell. Gerard Manley Hopkins. MuSP; UnS; ViPP
Have Faith. Edward Carpenter. WGRP
Have Faith in God. Joe Budzynski. STF
Have Gentlemen perhaps forgotten this? A Poet Speaks from the Visitors' Gallery. Archibald MacLeish. NYBP
Have, have ye no regard, all ye. His Saviour's Words Going to the Cross. Robert Herrick. StJW
Have I? Jessie Cannon Eldridge. SoP
Have I a hundred years since or. John Landless Leads the Caravan. Iwan Goll. TrJP
Have I a wife? Bedam I have! The Brewer's Man. L. A. G. Strong. DTC; ELU; FiBHP; WhC
Have I caught my heavenly jewel. Stella Sleeping. Sir Philip Sidney. Astrophel and Stella: Second Song. FCP; SiPS
Have I Done My Best for Jesus? Edwin Young. STF
Have I Found Her? *Unknown.* ElL; EnRePo
Have I nocht made ane honest shift. Sir David Lindsay. *Fr.* The Satire of the Three Estates. GoTS
Have I spoken too much or not enough of love? Epilogue. Richard Aldington. BrPo
Have I watcht the winters nyght. *Unknown.* SeCSL
Have little care that life is brief. Envoy [*or* On the Tomb of Bliss Carman]. Bliss Carman. HBV; MaRV; VA
Have mercy upon me, O God, after thy great goodness. Psalm LI, Bible, *O.T.* LiTW
Have patience; it is fit that in this wise. Sonnets, IX. George Santayana. WGRP
Have Pity, Grief. Peter Hausted. *Fr.* The Rival Friends. EG; SeCL
("Have pity, grief, I cannot pay.") TuPP
(Song, The: "Have pity (Grief) I can not pay.") SeEP
Have pity on us, Power just and severe. Prayer. John Hall Wheelock. EaLo; NePoAm; NYTB
Have pity, pity, friends, have pity on me. Epistle in Form of a Ballad to His Friends. Villon. AWP; LiTW; OuHeWo
Have Sky. Lewis MacAdams. ANYP
Have the poets left a single spot for a patch to be sewn? Mu'allaqa. Antar. TTY
Have the rocks on the hillside voices. In Palestine. George W. Carlin. ChIP
Have the swallows come? The Swallows. Patric Dickinson. ChMP
Have Thine Own Way, Lord! Adelaide A. Pollard. SoP
Have we not all, amid life's petty strife. No Star Is Ever Lost. Adelaide Anne Procter. MaRV
Have We Not Seen Thy Shining Garment's Hem? Amy Carmichael. SoP; TRV
Have we seen her, The New City, O my brothers, where she stands. The New City. Marguerite Wilkinson. MaRV; OQP; PEDC
Have we, then lost the war. "Separate Peace." Harrison S. Morris. MC
Have ye beheld (with much delight). Upon the Nipples of Julia's Breast. Robert Herrick. ErPo; LiTL; UnTE; ViBoPo
"Have ye founded your thrones and altars, then." A Parable. James Russell Lowell. PGD
Have ye heard of our hunting, o'er mountain and glen. The Hunters of Men. Whittier. AnAmPo
Have ye seen the morning sky. The Happy Swain. Ambrose Philips. EnLoPo
Have you a desire to see. Of His Mistress. Peter Hausted. *Fr.* The Rival Friends. EG; SeCL; TuPP
Have you a gold cup. The Question. Robert Duncan. NeAP
Have you and I today? Transforming Friendship. *Unknown.* SoP
Have you any gooseberry wine. Mazilla and Mazura. *Unknown.* ChTr
Have you any room for Jesus. Room for Jesus. Barbara H. Staples. STF
Have you any work for a tinker, Mistris. *Unknown.* OBS
Have You Been at Carrick? *Tr. fr. Irish by* Edward Walsh. AnIV
Have you been at Garnyvillo? Garnyvillo. Edward Lysaght. IrPN
Have you been at sea on a windy day. A Windy Day. Winifred Howard. FaPON
Have you been catching of fish, Tom Noddy? Tit for Tat. Walter de la Mare. UTS
"Have you been to your dinner, Jimmy Random, my son." Jimmy Random, My Son. *Unknown.* BFSS
"Have you been with the king to Rome." The Palatine. Willa Cather. HBMV; InP; NP
Have you come to the Red Sea place in your life. At the Place of the Sea [*or* Red Sea Place in Your Life]. Annie Johnson Flint. BLPA; BLRP; FaChP; OQP; SoP; STF
Have you commited all to God? Our Times Are in His Hands. Mary D. Freeze. STF
"Have you cut the wheat in the glowing field." Thanksgiving. Amelia E. Barr. PEDC
Have you dug the spill. Harlem Sweeties. Langston Hughes. LiTM (1970 ed.); NoP; PoNe; TTY

Have you ever asked yourselves—ladies, ladies. Gert Swasey. Winfield Townley Scott. FiMAP
Have you ever been down to my countree. The Land Where I Was Born. Shaw Neilson. BoAu
Have you ever head of the Sugar-Plum Tree? The Sugar-Plum Tree. Eugene Field. FaFP; HBV; HBVY; MPB; OTPC (1946 ed.); PCH; SoPo; TreF
Have you ever heard that a tailor was ill? The Tailor. Joseph Leftwich. TrJP
Have you ever heard the tapping of the fairy cobbler men. The Fairies. Sybil Morford. OTPC (1946 ed.); PoRL; TVC
Have you ever heard the wind go "Yooooo"? The Night Wind. Eugene Field. FaPON
Have you ever in your life seen a Possum play possum? Opossum. William Jay Smith. GoTP; TiPo (1959 ed.)
Have you ever sat by the r. r. track. Empties Coming Back. Angelo De Ponciano. BLPA
Have you ever seen the dawn. Ballad of Hope and Fear. Charles Madge. FaBoMo
Have you ever seen the moon. Have You Seen It. Lula Lowe Weeden. CDC
Have you ever tried to get along. The Other Person's Place. Donald H. Hover. STF
Have You Forgotten God? *Unknown.* SoP
Have you forgotten yet? Aftermath. Siegfried Sassoon. AnFE; BrPo; GTSL; MaRV; MCCG; MoBrPo; NeMA; TrJP; ViBoPo; WaP
Have you found your life distasteful? My Sun Sets to Rise Again. Robert Browning. *Fr.* At the Mermaid. MaRV
Have you gazed on naked grandeur, where there's nothing else to gaze on. The Call of the Wild. Robert W. Service. CaP
Have you got a brook in your little heart? Emily Dickinson. BoLP; FaBV; LiTL
Have you had a kindness shown? Pass It On. Henry Burton. BLRP; MaRV; SoP
Have you had your tonsils out? The New Neighbor. Rose Fyleman. GaP; SoPo; TiPo
Have you heard of Millington? Edward Millington. Richard Church. HaMV
Have you heard of one Humpty Dumpty. The Ballad of Persse O'Reilly. James Joyce. *Fr.* Finnegans Wake. LiTB; SiTL
Have you heard of our fighting Twenty-first. The Dash for the Colors. Frederick G. Webb. BeLS
Have you heard of the dreadful fate. The Ashtabula Disaster. Julia Moore. EvOK
Have you heard of the manly turning taken. The Day of Inverlochy. Iain Lom. GoTS
Have you heard of the quaint people. Strawberries in November. John Shaw Neilson. PoAu-1
Have you heard of the Sugar-Plum Tree? *See* Have you ever heard of the Sugar-Plum Tree?
Have you heard of the terrible family They. "They Say." Ella Wheeler Wilcox. WBLP
Have you heard of the wonderful one-hoss-shay. The Deacon's Masterpiece; or, The Wonderful "One-Hoss-Shay." Oliver Wendell Holmes. *Fr.* The Autocrat of the Breakfast-Table. AmePo; AmP; AmPP; AnNE; AP; BBV (1923 ed.); BeLS; BOHV; CoBA; FaBoBe; FaFP; HBV; HBVY; InMe; LHV; LiTA; LoGBV; MoShBr; NePA; OHFP; OnSP; OTPC; OxBA; PaPo; Po; PoIE; PoLF; PoRA; PTK; RIS; SiTL; StPo; StVeCh; TreF; WBLP; YaD; YT
Have you heard the blinking toad. The Song of the Toad. John Burroughs. FaPON
Have you heard the Master's call? The Master's Call. Oswald J. Smith. SoP; STF
Have you heard the story that gossips tell. John Burns of Gettysburg. Bret Harte. HBV; LHV; MC; OHIP; PaA; PAH; PAL; PAP
Have you heard the tale of the Aloe plant. The Aloe Plant. Henry Harbaugh. BLPA
Have you heard the voice of Jesus? Christ's Call. *Unknown.* SoP
Have you hearkened the eagle scream over the sea? The Irish Hurrah. Thomas Osborne Davis. OnYI
Have You Lost Faith? *Unknown.* WBLP
Have you mark'd but the fall of the snow. The Triumph. Ben Jonson. *Fr.* The Celebration of Charis. PG
"Have you news of my boy Jack?" My Boy Jack. Kipling. OtMeF
Have you no weathervane? Straws. Elizabeth Coatsworth. AmFN
Have you not fallen asleep to strong men's rowing. The Rowers. Laura Benét. FiSC; GoYe
Have you not heard his silent steps? Rabindranath Tagore. *Fr.* Gitanjali. WGRP
Have you not heard of Monsieur Maximus. Henry Parrot. SiCE
Have you not heard the poets tell. Baby Bell. Thomas Bailey Aldrich. HBV
Have you not in a chimney seen. A Description of Maidenhead. Earl of Rochester. UnTE
Have you not noted, in some family. The Birth-Bond. Dante Gabriel Rossetti. The House of Life, XV. HBV; MaVP; OAEP; PoVP; Sonn; ViPo; VP
Have you not read. Despite and Still. Robert Graves. CBEP
Have you not seen them fighting for the lead. The Chariot Race. Vergil. *Fr.* Georgics. SD
Have you noticed the docile appeal. Letter from a State Hospital. Frank Mundorf. GoYe
Have you observed the wench in the street. The Wench in the Street. *Unknown.* CBEP; OBS
Have you read in the Talmud of old. Sandalphon. Longfellow. AmPP (3d ed.); AnNE
Have You Seen [but] a Bright Lily Grow. Ben Jonson. *Fr.* A Celebration of Chari . MemP; OTPC (1923 ed.)
("Have you seen but a bright lily grow.") EG; FaBoCh; LoGBV; ReEn
(So Sweet Is She.) GN
(So White, So Soft, So Sweet.) MeWo; TrGrPo; UnTE
(Triumph, The.) PG, 8 *ll.*
Have you seen an apple orchard in the spring? The Apple Orchard in the Spring. William Martin. GN; OTPC
"Have you seen Hugh." The King of Connacht. *Unknown.* KiLC
Have You Seen It. Lula Lowe Weeden. CDC
Have you seen the lights of London, how they twinkle, twinkle, twinkle. Parliament Hill. H. H. Bashford. BrR; MPB; SP
Have you seen walking through the village. Mollie McGee. Edgar Lee Masters. *Fr.* Spoon River Anthology. NP
Have you sometimes, calm, silent let your tread aspirant rise. Heard on the Mountain. Victor Hugo. AWP
Have you time for a story. Charity Overcoming Envy. Marianne Moore. NYBP
Have You Watched the Fairies? Rose Fyleman. SoPo; SP; TiPo
Haven. Donald Jeffrey Hayes. AmNP; PoNe
Haven and last refuge of my pain, The. Last Refuge. Michelangelo. AWP; LiTW
Haven't got no special likin' fur the toney sorts o' play. Cowboy versus Broncho. James Barton Adams. SCC
Haverhill, 1640-1890. Whittier. MAmP
Having a wheel and four legs of its own. The Grindstone. Robert Frost. PoE
Having a Wonderful Time. D. B. Wyndham Lewis. FiBHP
Having attained success in business. Robert Whitmore. Frank Marshall Davis. Kal; PoNe
Having been tenant long to a rich Lord. Redemption. George Herbert. AnAnS-1; BWP; CABA; EaLo; EP; ExPo; GTBS-W; LiTB; LiTG; MaMe; MaPo (1969 ed.); MeLP; MePo; NoP; OBS; PoE; PoSa; SCEP-1; SeCeV; SeCP; SeCV-1; SeEP; Sonn; StJW
Having been whipped through Paradise. The Great Society. John Haines. ThO
Having bitten on life like a sharp apple. Aubade. Louis MacNeice. ViBoPo
Having both daughters at home does not give me. Homecoming. Aaron Kramer. NYTB
Having Climbed to the Topmost Peak of the Incense-Burner Mountain. Po Chü-i, *tr. fr. Chinese by* Arthur Waley. SD
Having come to this place. This Place in the Ways. Muriel Rukeyser. MiAP
Having eliminated his dear brother. Cainsmorning. Dom Moraes. MemP
Having enough plowshares. Bucolic. W. S. Merwin. NMP
Having finished the Blue-plate Special. In Schrafft's. W. H. Auden. MaPo
Having inherited a vigorous mind. My Descendants. W. B. Yeats. Meditations in Time of Civil War, IV. CABL; LiTB; PIA

Having interr'd her infant-birth. An Ode Upon a Question Moved, Whether Love Should Continue for Ever? Lord Herbert of Cherbury. AnAnS-2; MeLP; MePo; OBS; SeCP; SeEP
Having lived a Coney Island life. A Coney Island Life. James L. Weil. AmFN
Having Lost My Sons, I Confront the Wreckage of the Moon. James Wright. CoAP; FRC
Having New England Fathers. John Holmes. PG (1955 ed.)
Having no father anymore, having got up. The Homecoming of Emma Lazarus. Galway Kinnell. NaP
Having passed over the world. The Last Frontier. John Gould Fletcher. InPo
Having put on new fashions, she demands. A Woman Too Well Remembered. Louis Simpson. NoP
Having put yourself on the way. Spirits, Dancing. Arthur Gregor. NYBP
Having reached my boiling point. Ghetto. Yvette Johnson. TNV
Having read the inscriptions. Wang Peng's Recommendation for Improving the People. Paul Eldridge. ShM
Having scrubbed away the gray sweat. Old Michael. George M. Brady. NeIP
Having so rich a treasury, so fine a hoard. The Daisy. Marya Zaturenska. MoAmPo
Having split up the chaparral. The Wide Land. A. R. Ammons. TwCP
Having squandered my years to follow that wake beyond the elm. Mystery. Claire McAllister. TwAmPo
Having taken her slowly by surprise. A Pause for Breath. Ted Hughes. NYBP
Having taken offence with the society of my friends at Damascus. From Slavery to Slavery. Sadi. *Fr.* The Gulistan. OuHeWo
Having this day my horse, my hand, my lance. Astrophel and Stella, XLI. Sir Philip Sidney. AnFE; ATP; BEL; CLwM; CoBE; EG; EnL; EnLit; EnRePo; FCP; ILP; MaPo (1969 ed.); NoP; OAEP; OBSC; PoFS; ReEn; ReIE; SiCE; SiPS; Sonn; TOP; TuPP; YAT
Having used every subterfuge. A Renewal. James Merrill. PoPl
Hawaii! sea-girt land! Our Native Land. Kalakaua, King of the Hawaiian Island. PoRL
Hawaiian Hilltop. Genevieve Taggard. PoMa
Hawaiian National Hymn. Lilia K. Dominis, *tr. fr. Hawaiian by* H. L. Sheldon. SoP
Hawicks' Crossing. Jane Stuart. FiSC
Hawk, The. Sydney Clouts. BoSA
Hawk, The. Raymond Knister. OBCV
Hawk, The. W. B. Yeats. AtBAP; FlW
Hawk broods earthward, The. The Hawk. Sydney Clouts. BoSA
Hawk in the Rain, The. Ted Hughes. ACV; ToPo
Hawk or shrike has done this deed. Whimper of Sympathy. George Meredith. EPN
Hawk Remembered. J. Phoenice. NYTB
Hawk Roosting. Ted Hughes. GTBS-P; LiTM (1970 ed.); NePoEA-2; NMP; OA; POTi; TwCP
Hawk with heavy-lidded eyes, The. The Last Summer. Vivian Smith. PoAu-2
Hawkbit, The. Sir Charles G. D. Roberts. HBV
Hawke. Sir Henry Newbolt. BBV
Hawke. Archibald T. Strong. *Fr.* Sonnets of the Empire. BoAu
Hawkesyard. Sister Mary Benvenuta. JKCP (1926 ed.)
Hawking. Michael Drayton. *Fr.* Polyolbion, Twentieth Song. SD
Hawking for the Partridge. Thomas Ravenscroft. NCEP; OxBoLi
Hawking Party in the Olden Time, A. Mary Howitt. OTPC (1923 ed.)
Hawks. James Stephens. HBMV; NP
Hawk's Way. Ted Olson. HoPM
Hawthorn, The. *Unknown.* ChTr
"Hawthorn Hath a Deathly Smell, The." Walter de la Mare. AtBAP; BrPo
Hawthorn Hedge, The. Judith Wright. PoAu-2
Hawthorn Tree, The. Willa Cather. HBMV
Hawthorne. Amos Bronson Alcott. AA; DD
Hawthorne. Longfellow. CBEP; CoBA; MAmP; NCEP; PoEL-5
Hawthorne. James Russell Lowell. *Fr.* A Fable for Critics. AmPP (4th ed.); AnNE; AP; OxBA
("There is Hawthorne, with genius so shrinking and rare.") CoBA
Hay Appeareth, The. Proverbs, XXVII: 25, Bible, *O.T.* FaPON
Hay Harvest. Patrick R. Chalmers. BoTP
Hay for the Horses. Gary Snyder. FRC; NaP
Hay! hay! by this day. The Scholar Complains. *Unknown.* MeEL
Hay, house-dust, or the fur from cats. Allergy. Walker Gibson. NePoAm
Hay is for horses. *Unknown.* OxNR
Hay nonny no! *See* Hey Nonny No!
Hay! Now the Day Dawis. Alexander Montgomerie. *See* Night Is Near Gone, The.
Hay-Time. C. M. Lowe. BoTP
Haytime. Irene F. Pawsey. BoTP
Haycocks stand along the fence, The. Peggy Considers Her Grandmothers. Josephine Pinckney. NP
Haydn—Military Symphony. Keith Douglas. MuSP
Haydn: The Horn. Daniel Berrigan. TwAmPo
Hayfield, The. Charles Bruce. *Fr.* The Flowing Summer. CaP
Hayfield. Aileen Fisher. RePo
Hayfoot; strawfoot; the illiterate seasons. Wessex Guidebook. Louis MacNeice. HaMV; PoIE
Haying. John Frederic Herbin. CaP; PeCV
Haying before Storm. Muriel Rukeyser. WIRo
Hayle holy-land wherin our holy lord. Uppon the First Sight of New England. Thomas Tillam. SCAP
Hayll [*or* Haylle], Comly and Clene. *Unknown.* *Fr.* The Second Shepherds' Play. AtBAP; BoW; OBEV (new ed.); OxBoLi
Hayloft, The. Robert Louis Stevenson. GFA; PCH; TSW
Haymakers, rakers, reapers and mowers. Country Glee. Thomas Dekker *and* John Ford. *Fr.* The Sun's Darling. ELP; OBSC; ViBoPo
Haymakers' Song, The. Alfred Austin. VA
Haymaking. E. M. Adams. BoTP
Haymaking. A. P. Graves. BoTP
Haymaking. Edward Thomas. AnFE; BrPo; MoAB; MoBrPo; SeCePo
Haymow, The. Luella Markley Mockett. BrR
Hay's Wharf. Richard Church. HaMV
Hayseed, *with music.* *Unknown.* AS
Hayseed. Theodore Weiss. TwAmPo
Haystack in the Floods, The. William Morris. AnEnPo; ATP (1935 ed.); BEL; BeLS; CABA; EnL; EnLi-2; EnLit; EPN; ExPo; GTBS; HoPM; ILP; LiTL; LoBV; NBM; NoP; OAEP; OBNC; OuHeWo; PAn; PeVV; PoE; PoEL-5; PoRA; PoVP; SeCeV; ShBV-3; StP; ViPo; ViPP; WHA
Hazard. Nils Petersen, *tr. fr. Danish by* R. P. Keigwin. LiTW
Hazard of Loving the Creatures, The. Isaac Watts. CEP; EiPP
(Where-e'er My Flatt'ring Passions Rove.) OxBoCh
Haze. Buson, *tr. fr. Japanese by* Harold G. Henderson. RePo
Haze. Carl Sandburg. OnHM
Haze. Henry David Thoreau. *Fr.* A Week on the Concord and Merrimack Rivers. AmePo; AmPP (3d ed.); BWP; CoBA; InPo; NoP; PoPl
(Woof of the Sun [Ethereal Gauze].) AnNE; AP; OnPM; ViBoPo
Haze, char, and the weather of All Souls'. In the Elegy Season. Richard Wilbur. FiMAP; MoAB; NePoEA; NYBP
Haze on the far horizon, A. Autumn. William Herbert Carruth. MPB
Haze upon the meadow, The. What Is Winter? Edmund Blunden. ChMP; GTBS-D
Hazlitt Sups. Katharine Day Little. GoYe
He. Lawrence Ferlinghetti. NeAP
He. Stanley Kunitz. CrMA
He Abjures Love. Thomas Hardy. OBNC
He, above the rest/ In shape and gesture proudly eminent. Milton. *Fr.* Paradise Lost, I. InP
He all that time among the sewers of Troy. Troy. Edwin Muir. CMoP
He always comes on market days. The Balloon Man. Rose Fyleman. BoTP; SoPo; SUS
He always has something to grumble about. A Chip on His Shoulder. *Unknown.* BLPA; WBLP

He always was one for a jeer and a jest. Epitaph for a Funny Fellow. Morris Bishop. SiTL
He and his, unwashed all winter. The Native. W. S. Merwin. NePoEA-2; PoRA (rev. ed.)
He and I. Dante Gabriel Rossetti. The House of Life, XCVIII. MaVP; NBM; PoVP; ViPo
He and She. Sir Edwin Arnold. BLPA
(She and He.) HBV
He and She. Eugene Fitch Ware. BOHV; PoLF; YaD
He Approacheth the Hall of Judgment. *Unknown, tr. fr. Egyptian by* Robert Hillyer. *Fr.* Book of the Dead. AWP; JAWP; WBP
He arose from the dead. New Crucifixion. Thomas Curtis Clark. ChIP
He Asketh Absolution of God. *Unknown, tr. fr. Egyptian by* Robert Hillyer. *Fr.* Book of the Dead. AWP
He ate and drank the precious words. Emily Dickinson. AA; AmPP; AP; BBV (1951 ed.); InP; NeMA; PoFr; RePo
He bade a seaworthy. Beowulf's Voyage to Denmark. *Unknown. Fr.* Beowulf. FIW
He Bare Him Up, He Bare Him Down. *Unknown. See* Falcon, The.
He beats us out upon the anvil of the days. The Master Blacksmith. Arnold Andrews. OQP
He, behind the straight plough, stands. Ploughman at the Plough. Louis Golding. HBMV; OHIP
He, being one, rules over all and everything. *Unknown. Fr.* The Upanishads. PoFr
He Biddeth Osiris to Arise from the Dead. *Unknown, tr. fr. Egyptian by* Robert Hillyer. *Fr.* Book of the Dead. AWP
He Bids His Beloved Be at Peace. W. B. Yeats. See Michael Robartes Bids His Beloved Be at Peace.
He bites upon the mouth her mouth has cut. Adam—the First Kiss. Hal Porter. ACV
He blessed is who neither loosely treads. Psalm I. *Paraphrased by* Sir Philip Sidney. FCP
He blessed is who with wise temper can. Psalm XLI. *Paraphrased by* Sir Philip Sidney. FCP
He Bloomed among Eagles. David Ross. PG (1955 ed.)
He bore the brunt of it so long. His Deaths. Haniel Long. NP
"He Bringeth Them unto Their Desired Haven." Lewis Frank Tooker. HBV
He brought a Grecian queen, whose youth and freshness. Portrait of Helen. Shakespeare. *Fr.* Troilus and Cressida, II, ii *and* IV, i. TrGrPo
He brought a light so she could see. Strains of Sight. Robert Duncan. NMP; OPoP
He brought a lily white. To His Mother. John Banister Tabb. *Fr.* The Child. AA
He brought a team from Inversnaid. The Man from Inversnaid. Robert Fuller Murray. SD
He brought them from the muddy creek. Boy and Tadpoles. Louis Untermeyer. YT
He built a house; time laid it in the dust. The Greatest Work. Ray M. Johnson. MaRV; OQP
He built a kingdom with his heart and brain. Resurrection and Ascension. Earl D. Todd. ChIP
He built no temple, yet the farthest sea. The Man Christ. Therese Lindsey. BePJ; ChIP; MaRV; TRV
He burned no fiery cross. His Cross. Marguerite Wilkinson. OQP
He burst from bed. Boy's Day. Ruth Evelyn Henderson. BiCB
He by no means flies straight at petunia. The Bee and the Petunia. Katherine Hoskins. ErPo
He calleth to me out of Seir, Watchman, what of the night? Watchman, What of the Night. Isaiah, Bible, *O.T.* AWP
He Came. *Unknown.* SoP
He came,/ striding. Paul Bunyan [*or* A Legend of Paul Bunyan]. Arthur S. Bourinot. AmFN; FaPON; TwCaPo
He came, a youth, singing in the dawn. Paul Laurence Dunbar. James David Corrothers. BANP; PoNe
He came all so still. Carol [*or* An Ancient [Christmas] Carol]. *Unknown. See also* I Sing of a Maiden. BoTP; DD; HBV; HBVY; OHIP; PCH; PTK; RG.
He came and took me by the hand. The Mystery. Ralph Hodgson. BoLiVe; CAW; CH; HBV; MaRV; MoAB; MoBrPo; NeMA; NP; OQP; SoP; WGRP
He came back from the gray dust. The Prodigal. Lon Woodrum. SoP
He came from hills to comfortable plains. The Mountaineer. Robert Nathan. TrJP
He came from Malta; and Eumelus says. A Maltese Dog. Tymnes. FaBoCh; LoGBV; TiPo (1959 ed.)
He came from out the void. *See* He came out the void.
He came from the North, and his words were few. The Man of the North Countrie. Thomas D'Arcy McGee. OnYI
He came in silvern armor, trimmed with black. Sonnet I. Gwendolyn B. Bennett. AmNP; CDC; PoNe
He came not as the princes born to rule. Lincoln. Clyde Walton Hill. PEDC; PGD
He came not in the red dawn. The Adventurer. Odell Shepard. HBMV
He came out [*or* from out] the void. Roosevelt. Robert H. Davis. HH; PEDC
He came—the infant Christ of God. The Christ of God. Russell E. Kauffman. BePJ
He came to be The Light. It Was Not Strange. Esther Lloyd Hagg. PGD
He came to call me back from death. Eurydice. Francis William Bourdillon. HBV; VA
He came to earth one blue-skied day. Christ in the Street. Jay G. Sigmund. ChIP; SoP
He came to her from out eternal years. The Spouse of Christ. D. A. Casey. JKCP
He came to me in his swift course. *Unknown. Fr.* Sweeney the Mad. OnYI
He came to me last night, as if there had never. The Druggist. Larry Rubin. FiSC
He came to my desk with quivering lip. The [*or* A] New Leaf. Kathleen Wheeler. BLRP; MaRV; OQP; PGD; PoToHe; SoP; STF; WBLP
He Came to Pay. "Parmenas Mix". BOHV
He came to sing some olden songs. The Old Singer. Eden Phillpotts. MuSP
He came to the desert of London town. William Blake. James Thomson. CBEP; HBV; OAEP; OBVV; PoVP
He came to you, for in His gentle voice. He Came. *Unknown.* SoP
He Came Too Late. Elizabeth Bogart. AA
He Came Unlook'd For. Sara Coleridge. *Fr.* Phantasmion. OBRV; VA
(Song: "He came unlook'd for, undesir'd.") CBEP; OBVV
He came with roses in his mouth. Joy o' Living. Amanda Benjamin Hall. HBMV
He Can. *Unknown.* SoP
He can hear the owl's flight in daylight. Blind Man. Michael Hamburger. NePoEA-2
He cannot as he came depart. Influence. John Banister Tabb. PoMa
He cannot be complete in aught. On a Sense of Humor. Frederick Locker-Lampson. BOHV; InP
He Cannot Heal. *At. to* Lillian R. Dickson. SoP
(Stigmata, *at. to* Edwin McNeill Poteat.) MaRV
He captured light and caged it in a glass. And Yet Fools Say. George S. Holmes. OTD
He Cares. "Susan Coolidge." MaRV
He Cares. Kabir, *tr. fr. Hindi.* MaRV
He Cares. Phyllis C. Michael. SoP
He Cares. Owen C. Salway. STF
He Careth. "Marianne Farningham." *See* God Cares.
He carved the red deer and the bull. In the Caves of Auvergne. W. J. Turner. HBMV; POTE
He casts a sheep's eye at her: a strange eye-spread. Of a Sheep's Eye. John Heywood. SiCE; TuPP
He caught his chisel, hastened to his bench. The Death of Azron. Alice Wellington Rollins. AA
He ceas'd, but while he spake, Rustum had risen. The Combat. Matthew Arnold. *Fr.* Sohrab and Rustum. VA
He ceased; and Satan stayed not to reply. Satan Views the World. Milton. *Fr.* Paradise Lost, II. WHA
He Charges Her To Lay Aside Her Weapons. Pierce Ferriter, *tr. fr. Late Middle Irish by* the Earl of Longford. AnIL; LiTW; OnYI
"He chases shadows," sneered the British [*or* Bristol] tars. The First Voyage of John Cabot. Katharine Lee Bates. MC; PAH
He cherished a girl who was pure as snow. A Man's Love. Tove Ditlevsen. LiTW

He chose the sea, mother, emancipator. The Man Who Wanted to Be a Seagull. J. R. Hervey. AnNZ
He clasps the crag with crooked [*or* hooked] hands. The Eagle. Tennyson. BEL; BoLiVe; BoTP; CaFP; CBEP; CBV; CH; DiPo; EG; EnL; ExPo; FaBoCh; FaPON; FiP; GN; GoJo; GoTP; GTBS-D; GTBS-P; GTSL; HBV; LoGBV; MaPo (1969 ed.); MBW-2; MemP; MyFE; NoP; OAEP; OTPC; PCD; PCH; PDV; PoIE; PoMa; PoPo; PoVP; PTK; RIS; SeCePo; SeCeV; ShBV-1; StaSt; StP; SUS; SyP; TDP; ThWaDe; TreFT; TrGrPo; UnPo (3d ed.); UTS; VaPo; ViPo; ViPP; WePo; WiR; YT
He climbed up the candlestick. The Mouse. *Unknown.* PCH
He climbed up the peak. High Brow. Robert Fitch. SD
He Climbs a Hill and Turns His Face. Lionel Wiggam. PoMa
He closed the Bible carefully, putting it down. The Slaver. Stephen Vincent Benét. *Fr.* John Brown's Body. AmPP
He Comes Among. George Barker. OBMV
He comes; and fawn and branch and moon delight. *Unknown. Fr.* The Mock Caliph. EnLi-1
He comes down to the shadow. Heron. Ted Walker. NYBP
He comes—he comes—the Frost Spirit comes! The Frost Spirit. Whittier. HBV; PCH
He comes in the night! He comes in the night! Santa Claus. *Unknown.* BoTP; ChBR; HBVY; HH; PEDC; PRWS; TVC
He comes, the happy warrior. Sinfonia Eroica. Alice Archer James. AA
He comes, the old one, his shabby cap askew. Old Man with a Mowing Machine. May Carleton Lord. GoYe
He comes with herald clouds of dust. Superior Nonsense Verses. *Unknown.* NA
He comes with western winds, with evening's wandering airs. Emily Brontë. *Fr.* The Prisoner. BoC; ELP; GTBS-D
He comes! Yohewah! the Great Spirit, comes. Charles Mair. *Fr.* Tecumseh. PeCV
He Cometh. Judah Halevi, *tr. fr. Hebrew by* Emma Lazarus. TrJP
He Cometh Forth into the Day. *Unknown, tr. fr. Egyptian by* Robert Hillyer. *Fr.* Book of the Dead. AWP; JAWP; WBP
He Cometh Late. *Unknown.* OQP
He cometh, O bliss! He Cometh. Judah Halevi. TrJP
He Comforts Himself. Christopher Morley. *Fr.* Translations from the Chinese. EvOK
He Commandeth a Fair Wind. *Unknown, tr. fr. Egyptian by* Robert Hillyer. *Fr.* Book of the Dead. AWP
He compares his beloved to a snake. Microcosmos, VII. Nigel Heseltine. NeBP
He Could Have Found His Way. Kathleen Dalziel. PoAu-1
He could not die when trees were green. The Dying Child. John Clare. CBEP; EnRP; FlW; NCEP; TrGrPo
He could not separate the thought. Country Church. Robert P. Tristram Coffin. MaRV
He could not tell the way he came. The Way. William Stanley Braithwaite. Sandy Star and Willie Gee, IV. BANP
He could not win you easily, your death. In Memory of Robin Hyde, 1906-39. Charles Brasch. AnNZ
He could raise scruples dark and nice. Sir Hudibras. Samuel Butler. *Fr.* Hudibras. UnPo (1st ed.)
He could see the little lake. The Lake. James Stephens. AnEnPo; MoBrPo
He could sing sweetly on a string. Orpheus. Elizabeth Madox Roberts. MAP; MoAmPo
He couldn't hear their roar. Drowned Sailor. Neufville Shaw. CaP
He crawleth here. He crepyth there. The Caterpillar. Alfred Noyes. BoPe
He crawls along the mountain walls. On the Heights. Lucius Harwood Foote. AA
He crawls to the cliff and plays on the brink. The Sea-Child. Eliza Cook. VA
He cried aloud to God: "The men below." Genius. Edward Lucas White. AA; WGRP
He crouches, and buries his face on his knees. The Last of His Tribe. Henry Kendall. PoAu-1; VA
He cut a sappy sucker from the muckle rodden-tree. The Whistle. Charles Murray. GoTS; OxBS; ShBV-1
He debated whether. Arthur Ridgewood, M.D. Frank Marshall Davis. Kal
He Declares That Albeit He Were Imprisoned in Russia, Yet His Mind Was at Liberty and Did Daily Repair to His Friend. George Turberville. TuPP
He deemed his task a solemn one. Priest and Pagan. Albert Durrant Watson. CaP
He Defendeth His Heart against the Destroyer. *Unknown, tr. fr. Egyptian by* Robert Hillyer. *Fr.* Book of the Dead. AWP
He did not come to judge the world, he did not come to blame. His Name. Dora Greenwell. ChIP
He did not come to woo U Nu. Just Dropped In. William Cole. FiBHP; GoJo; PoPl
He Did Not Know. Harry Kemp. WGRP
He did not wear his scarlet coat. The Ballad of Reading Gaol. Oscar Wilde. AnFE; BeLS; BrPo; DTo; EnLi-2; EnLit; FaPL; LiTG; HBV; MoBrPo; OBMV; OBNC; OnYI; OtMeF; PoVP; TreF
He didn't know much music. The Mocking-Bird. Frank L. Stanton. AA
He Didn't Oughter. A. P. Herbert. ALV; FiBHP
He didn't want to do it with skill. Lion & Honeycomb. Howard Nemerov. PP
He died! and with him perished all that men hold dear. Hope. *Unknown.* ChIP; OQP; SoP
He Died for Me. George Washington Bethune. BePJ
He died for me, my Saviour, He. It Was for Me. Eva Gray. STF
He died for me: what can I offer him? Not Yours but You. Christina Rossetti. ChIP; MaRV
He died in attempting to swallow. The Death of Polybius Jubb [*or* Limerick]. Roy Campbell. LiBL; LiTG; SiTL; WhC
"He died," saith the cross, "My very name." The Cross and the Tomb. Annie Johnson Flint. STF
He "Digesteth Harde Yron." Marianne Moore. CMoP
He dines alone surrounded by reflections. Witch Doctor. Robert Hayden. AmNP
He disappeared in the dead of winter. In Memory of W. B. Yeats. W. H. Auden. ACV; ATP (1953 ed.); BoLiVe (1945 ed.); CABA; CMoP; CoBMV; EnL; FaFP; FosPo; GTBS-W; HoPM; InPo; LiTB; LiTM; MaPo; MasP; ML; MoAB; MoBrPo; MoVE; NePA; OAEP (2d ed.); OnHM; PAn; Po; PoFS; PoIE; PP; ReMP; StP; TDP; TrGrPo; UnPo (3d ed.); ViBoPo (1958 ed.)
He discovers himself on an old airfield. The Old Pilot's Death. Donald Hall. TPM
He does not die that can bequeathe. Duncton Hill. Hilaire Belloc. GoBC
He does not hear the struck string. Music God. Mark Van Doren. UnS
He does not lead me year by year. Step by Step. Barbara C. Ryberg. STF
He does not think that I haunt here nightly. The Haunter. Thomas Hardy. AtBAP; ChMP; GTBS-D; QFR
He does remember. Back to the bloom. Wedlock. Barbara L. Greenberg. QAH
He doesn't know when it was that the last door closed. After Some Day of Decision. Reed Whittemore. NePoEA
He Doeth All Things Well. Anne Brontë. MaRV; TRV
He doeth well who doeth good. Best of All. *Unknown.* WBLP
He drank strong waters and his speech was coarse. Kipling. *Fr.* Plain Tales from the Hills. PV
He dreamed of lovely women as he slept. Undergraduate. Merrill Moore. ErPo
He drew a circle that shut me out. Outwitted. Edwin Markham. AnAmPo; BLPA; ELU; MAP; MaRV; MCCG; MoAmPo; NeMA; OQP; PoPo; PoToHe; TreFT; TRV
He dropt a tear on Susan's bier. Susan. Frederick Locker Lampson. BOHV
He drowsed and was aware of silence heaped. The Death-Bed. Siegfried Sassoon. LiTM (1970 ed.); MMA; MoVE; POTE
He dumped her in the wheelbarrow. Wheelbarrow. Eleanor Farjeon. FiBHP
He dwelt among 'Apartments let." Jacob. Phoebe Cary. BOHV; InMe
He earns the oblivion of book and shelf. Without Sleep. Glenway Wescott. NP
He either fears his fate too much. The Touch. James Graham. *Fr.* My Dear and Only Love. OtMeF
He Embarketh in the Boat of Ra. *Unknown, tr. fr. Egyptian by* Robert Hillyer. *Fr.* Book of the Dead. AWP
He ended, and they both descend the hill. The Expulsion from

He (continued)
Paradise. Milton. *Fr.* Paradise Lost, XII. ATP; BEL; SeEP
He ended; and thus Adam last replied [*or* reply'd]. The Retreat from Paradise. Milton. *Fr.* Paradise Lost, XII. CoBE; MyFE; PoEL-3
He entered the shop. Birthday Gift. Ethel Barnett de Vito. BiCB
He entered with the authority of politeness. The Southerner. Karl Shapiro. FiMAP; NYBP; PoNe
He Entereth the House of the Goddess Hathor. *Unknown. tr. fr. Egyptian by* Robert Hillyer. *Fr.* Book of the Dead. AWP
He enters, and mute on the edge of a chair. In the Study. Thomas Hardy. *Fr.* Satires. of Circumstance. PoPo
He Establisheth His Triumph. *Unknown, tr. fr. Egyptian by* Robert Hillyer. *Fr.* Book of the Dead. AWP; JAWP; WBP
He ever warred with freedom and the free. Byron. *Fr.* The Vision of Judgment. PoFr
He Expecteth. *Unknown.* SoP
He Falls. William A. Donaghy. *Fr.* The Stations of the Cross. JKCP (1955 ed.);
He feared the dark, his parents knew. On the Staircase. Wade Wellman. FiSC
He Fears His Good Fortune. Thomas Hardy. VP
He fears the tiger standing in his way. The Drunkard. Philip Levine. NePoEA-2
He fed them generously who were his flocks. μητις... οὐ τις William DeWitt Snodgrass. Sonn
He feels small as he awakens. The Awakening. Robert Creeley. NeAP
He fell, a slave of tinsel honour. On the Death of Pushkin. Mikhail Yurevich Lermontov. PoFr
He Fell among Thieves. Sir Henry Newbolt. BBV; HBV; HBVY; OBEV; OBVV; OnMSP; PoMa; ShBV-3
He fell from the roof. News. Louis Dudek. *Fr.* Provincetown. MoCV
He fell into blue. Abstract Painter. Gerta Kennedy. NYTB
He felt the wild beast in him between whiles. Modern Love, IX. George Meredith. ViPo; VP
He finds that talk of music, books and art is. A Man of Culture. A. S. J. Tessimond. HaMV
.He first deceas'd: she for a little tried [*or* tri'd]. Upon [*or* On] the Death of [*or* Epitaph on] Sir Albert Morton's Wife. Sir Henry Wotton. AnAnS-2; CBEP; CLwM; EnLoPo; OBEV; OBS; OnPM; SeCP; SeEP; TDP; TreFT; TrGrPo; ViBoPo; WePo; WoL
He fixed his hat Kildare-side on. Light Shoes. Patrick Kelly. JKCP (1926 ed.)
He followed her up, he followed her down. Pretty Polly. *Unknown.* BFSS
He followed the pair to Pawtucket. *See* But he followed the pair. . .
He found a formula for drawing comic rabbits. Epitaph on an Unfortunate Artist. Robert Graves. WhC
He found a woman in the cave. Thalaba and the Magic Thread. Robert Southey. *Fr.* Thalaba the Destroyer. SeCePo
He found her by the ocean's moaning verge. Modern Love, XLIX. George Meredith. BEL; EnLi-2; HBV; OAEP; PoE; ViPo; VP
He found life a pattern. Paul. Earl B. Marlatt. OQP
He found me sitting among flowers. Song. Aubrey Thomas De Vere. IrPN
He from the wind-bitten North with ship and companions descended. A Drifter off Tarentum. Kipling. *Fr.* Epitaphs of the War. MMA
He fumbles at your soul. Emily Dickinson. AmePo
He gathered cherry-stones, and carved them quaintly. An Art Master. John Boyle O'Reilly. AA
He gathered for His own delight. Ere the Golden Bowl Is Broken. Anna Hempstead Branch. AnAmPo; AnFE; APA; CoAnAm; MAPA
He gathers data. The Statistician. Charles Wharton Stork. PoMa
He Gave Himself for Me. *Unknown.* STF
He gave his card. How many times have I. Contact. Dorothy Livesay. CaP
He gave his life upon a [*or* the] cross. His Garments. Esther Lloyd Hagg. ChIP; PGD
"He gave the little wealth he had." Swift. *Fr.* Verses on the Death of Dr. Swift. ViBoPo
He gave the solid rail a hateful kick. The Egg and the Machine. Robert Frost. CABA; MAP; MoAmPo; MWA-2
He gave the world, in darkness pent. The Tragedy. Thomas Curtis Clark. ChIP
He gave us all a good-bye cheerily. Messmates. Sir Henry Newbolt. CH; HBV; MCCG; PeVV; ShBV-2
He gazed at her with his whole soul. Dark Eyes at Forest Hills. I. L. Martin. SD
He girded on his shining sword. The Quest of the Purple Cow. Hilda Johnson. BOHV
He Gives His Beloved Certain Rhymes. W. B. Yeats. EG
He Gives Nothing. James Russell Lowell. *Fr.* The Vision of Sir Launfal, Pt. I. MaRV
He gives to me His wondrous grace. This Blessed Christ of Calvary. *Unknown.* STF
He giveth me treasures of darkness. Treasures of Darkness. Sarah Faris. SoP
He Giveth More [Grace]. Annie Johnson Flint. BLRP; FaChP; SoP; STF; TRV; WBLP
He Giveth Peace! Georgia B. Adams. SoP
"He giveth quietness." O Elder Brother. Thy Peace. Emily Huntington Miller. FaChP
He Goes Before. J. Danson Smith. SoP
He goes the circle of the world. Golden Falcon. Robert P. Tristram Coffin. CAW
He grew!/ From tiny babe to sturdy boy and vigorous man. The Son of Man. Dorothy J. Langford. BePJ
He grew where waves ride nine feet high. In Memoriam: Roy Campbell. R. N. Currey. ACV; BoSA; PeSA
He grinds the clover at its root. Eight-Cylinder Man. Florence Ripley Mastin. PoPo
He grins a little as they drive him by. Dog in a Car. David McCord. RePo
He had a coat of Christendom as Holy Church teaches. The Average Man. William Langland. *Fr.* The Vision of Piers Plowman. PoLi
He had a falcon on his wrist. Love Me, Love My Dog. Isabella V. Crawford. WHW
He had a whim and laughed it out. Laughing It Out. William Stanley Braithwaite. Sandy Star and Willie Gee, II. BANP
He had awaited me. A Meeting. Daniel Hoffman. CoPo
He had been long t'wards mathematicks. Portrait of Sidrophel [*or* Sir Sidrophel, the Conjuror *or* The Character of Sydrophel]. Samuel Butler. *Fr.* Hudibras. FaBoEn; PeRV; PoEL-3
He had been singing—but I had not heard his voice. The Quiet Singer. Charles Hanson Towne. HBV
He had been stuttering, by the edge. Hart Crane. Robert Creeley. AP
He had driven half the night. Hay for the Horses. Gary Snyder. FRC; NaP
He had fought for the wrong causes. Suicide. Louis MacNeice. DTC
He had his beer. *Unknown.* WhC
He Had His Dream. Paul Laurence Dunbar. MaRV
He had his son with him, a fine young Squire. The Squire. Chaucer. *Fr.* The Canterbury Tales. WePo
He had in his hand a red plant. Meeting by the Gjulika Meadow. Geoffrey Grigson. WaP
He had no pact with time: his mind was ever. Toward Avernus. Harold Vinal. FiSC
He had no royal palace. A Christmas Verse. "Kay." BoTP
He had not reckoned on a visitor. Death Was a Woman. Sydney King Russell. GoYe
He had played by the cottage fire. The Ballad of the Fiddler. "Seumas O'Sullivan." MPB
He had played for his lordship's levee. The Child Musician. Austin Dobson. MuSP
He Had Served Eighty Masters. Lesbia Harford. PoAu-1
He had the plowman's strength. Lost in France; Jo's Requiem. Ernest Rhys. POTE
He hangs between his wings outspread. The Eagle. Andrew Young. ELU; WePo
He has a drooping winged moustache. Texas Types—"The Bad Man." William Lawrence Chittenden. PoOW
He has come! the skies are telling. Incarnation. Edwin Markham. SoP
He has come the way of the fighting men and fought by the rules of the game. The Fighting Failure. Everard Jack Appleton. HBV; YaD

He has come to report himself. The Missing Person. Donald Justice. NYBP; TPM
He has come to such a pitch. Lines for an Eminent Poet and Critic. Patric Dickinson. POTi; PV
He has conned the lesson now. Fairy Song. Winthrop Mackworth Praed. OBEV (1st ed.); SeCePo
He has dust in his eye, a fan for a wing. My What-Is-It. Robert Frost. RIS
He Has Fallen from the Height of His Love. Wilfrid Scawen Blunt. The Love Sonnets of Proteus, XIV. ViBoPo
He has fashioned the stars and the moons to the music. Imagery. Harindranth Chattopadhyaya. ACV
He has observ'd the golden rule. Blake. PV; TrGrPo
He has outsoared the shadow of our night. Shelley. *Fr.* Adonais. BoC; PeER; PoSa
He has solved it—Life's wonderful problem. Laurels and Immortelles. *Unknown.* BLPA
He has stolen from the cat his agile grace. Prose Poem: Harlequin. Théodore de Banville. OnPM
He Hath No Parallel. Sadi, *tr. fr. Persian by* L. Cranmer-Byng. *Fr.* The Gulistan. AWP; LiTW
He hath no place to rest his head. Judaeus Errans. Louis Golding. TrJP
He heard, and dreamed the night-wind on. Muse-haunted. Hugh McCrae. PoAu-1
He Heard Her Sing, *sel.* James Thomson.
"And thus all-expectant abiding I waited not long." VA
He Hears with Gladdened Heart the Thunder. Robert Louis Stevenson. TreFT
He held no dream worth waking; so he said. On the Death of Robert Browning. Swinburne. A Sequence of Sonnets on the Death of Robert Browning, VII. EnLit; EPN; PoVP
He held the lamp each Sabbath day. A Faithful Pastor. *Unknown.* SoP
He held the lamp of Truth that day. The Hand That Held It. W. G. Elmslie. SoP; TRV
He hides his heart. Sightings I. Jerome Rothenberg. CoPo
He hides within the lily. Consider the Lilies. William Channing Gannett. MaRV; WGRP
He Holdeth Fast to the Memory of His Identity. *Unknown, tr. fr. Egyptian by* Robert Hillyer. *Fr.* Book of the Dead. AWP; JAWP; WBP
He Hopes That Time Will Render Her More Merciful. Petrarch, *tr. fr. Italian by* Robert Guthrie MacGregor. Sonnets to Laura: To Laura in Life, XI. EnLi-1; OuHeWo
He huffs from the north. March Wind. Maud E. Uschold. YeAr
He Inspects His Armory. Hyam Plutzik. FiMAP
He invented a rainbow but lightning struck it. Bushed. Earle Birney. MoCV; OBCV; PeCV
He is a bird round which a trap closes. The Holy Man. *Unknown.* *Fr.* The Devil's Tribute to Moling. OnYI
He is a hat and coat. Neighbour. J. R. Hervey. AnNZ
He is a heart. A Love Song. *Unknown.* AnIL
He is a man—magnanimous broad brow. Christ before Pilate. George Herbert Clarke. StJW
He is a man who thinks. Shh! The Professor Is Sleeping. John Morris. CABA
He Is a New Creature. Edward Taylor. *See* Preparatory Meditations: "Daintiest draught thy pensill. . ."
He Is a Path. Giles Fletcher. *See* Excellency of Christ.
He is a portion of the loveliness. Shelley. *Fr.* Adonais. MemP
He is a roguish little elf. Dandelion. Kate L. Brown. TVC
"He is a sinner," you are pleased to say. Self-Righteousness. John Byrom. MaRV
He is a timid man. Childhood Ambition. David Hilton. QAH
He is a tower unleaning. But how will he not break. Vaunting Oak. John Crowe Ransom. NoP; OxBA
He is alive with pain: His body lifts. The Crucifixion. John W. Lynch. JKCP (1955 ed.)
He is always standing there. My Policeman. Rose Fyleman. BoChLi; SoPo; TiPo
He Is Buried. William A. Donaghy. *Fr.* The Stations of the Cross. JKCP (1955 ed.)
He Is Coming. Gladys M. Gearhart. STF
He Is Coming. *Unknown.* FaChP
He is coming! He is coming! His Return. "D. N. R." SoP
He is coming, my long desired lord. The River of Heaven. *Unknown.* *Fr.* Manyo Shu. AWP; LiTW
He is coming, O my spirit! with His everlasting peace. He Is Coming. *Unknown.* FaChP
He is daily with us, loving, loving, loving. "Daily with You." Annie Johnson Flint. BLRP
He is dead and gone, lady. Ophelia's Songs. Shakespeare. *Fr.* Hamlet, IV, v. LO
He is dead, the beautiful youth. Killed at the Ford. Longfellow. AP; BBV; OHIP
He Is Declared True of Word. *Unknown, tr. fr. Egyptian by* Robert Hillyer. *Fr.* Book of the Dead. AWP; JAWP; WBP
He is firm and strong. Oriki Erinle. *Unknown.* PBA; TTY
He is found with the homeless dogs. Kid. Robert Hayden. CAD
He is gliding on her like a block of ice. The Welder. Frank Lima. ANYP
He is gone before thee, carrying His cross, and He died for thee. The Royal Way of the Holy Cross. Thomas à Kempis. BoC
He is gone: better so. We should know who stand under. The Deserter from the Cause. Gerald Massey. VA; YT
He is gone on the mountain. Coronach. Sir Walter Scott. *Fr.* The Lady of the Lake, III. AnFE; BEL; CH; EnLi-2 (1949 ed.); EnLit; EnRP; EPN; GTBS; GTBS-D; GTBS-P; GTBS-W; GTSL; HBV; InP; OAEP; OBRV; OHIP; PCD; PoRA; ShBV-1; TOP; TreFS; TrGrPo; ViBoPo; WHA; WiR; YAT
He is having his hair cut he is only. Haircut. William Packard. CAD
He is here, Urania's son. Epithalamium. A. E. Housman. HW
He is just plain drunk. "I Am a Sioux Brave," He Said in Minneapolis. James Wright. ELU
He Is like the Lotus. *Unknown, tr. fr. Egyptian by* Robert Hillyer. *Fr.* Book of the Dead. AWP; EaLo; JAWP; WBP
(Death as a Lotus Flower, *tr. by* Ulli Beier.) TTY
He Is like the Serpent Saka. *Unknown, tr. fr. Egyptian by* Robert Hillyer. *Fr.* Book of the Dead. AWP
He is made one with Nature: there is heard. Shelley. *Fr.* Adonais. WGRP
He Is Mine. Francis Quarles. *See* My Beloved Is Mine, and I Am His.
He is murdered upright in the day. Vaticide. Myron O'Higgins. IDB; OnHM
He Is My Countryman. Antoni Slonimski, *tr. fr. Polish by* Frances Notley. TrJP
He Is My Refuge. *Unknown.* SoP
He is no friend who in thine hour of pride. Friendship. Sadi. *Fr.* The Gulistan. AWP; JAWP; WBP
He Is Near! Horatius Bonar. SoP
He is not a brother to me. The Brother. Semyon Yakovlevich Nadson. TrJP
He Is Not Dead. James Whitcomb Riley. *See* Away.
He Is Not Dead. Shelley. *Fr.* Adonais. MaRV
(Against Oblivion.) TreFS
(Elegy on the Death of John Keats, An.) OBNC
("Peace, peace! he is not dead, he doth not sleep.") FaBoEn; LO
He Is Not Dead. Sir Thomas Wyatt. CBEP
("He is not dead that sometime hath a fall.") FCP
He is not dead,/ Your son, your dear beloved son. Joseph Auslander. *Fr.* He Is Risen. MaRV
He is not dead nor liveth. The Buried Child. Dorothy Wellesley. Deserted House: Epilogue. DTC; GTBS-D; OBMV
He is not drunk who, from the floor. Epigram. Eugene Field. ALV
He is not great who gives to others law. William Wycherley. *Fr.* To the Duke of Buckingham, a Man of a Great Mind, Reduc'd to a Little Fortune. PeRV
He is not here, the old sun. No Possum, No Sop, No Taters. Wallace Stevens. AmP; MoVE; OxBA; PoeP; PoFS
He is not John, the gardener. A Friend in the Garden. Juliana Horatia Ewing. BoTP; FaPON; GFA; MPB; OTPC (1946 ed.); StVeCh; TVC; UTS
He Is Not Risen. W. S. Handley Jones. MaRV
He is not the wise man, who comes. The Imbecile. Donald Finkel. NePoEA-2
He is older than the naval side of British history. Chief Petty Officer. Charles Causley. POTi

He is one of the prophets come back. He. Lawrence Ferlinghetti. NeAP
"He Is Our Peace." Molly Anderson Haley. PGD
He is quick, thinking in clear images. In Broken Images. Robert Graves. PoIE
He Is Risen, *sel.* Joseph Auslander. MaRV
"He is not dead,/ Your son, your dear beloved son."
He Is Risen. Annie Johnson Flint. FaChP
He Is Risen. John Oxenham. ChIP
He is risen! Earth awakes. He Is Risen. Annie Johnson Flint. FaChP
He is running like a wasp. Pole Vault. Shiro Murano. SD
He is set so hye. John Skelton. *Fr.* Why Come Ye Nat to Courte? FOL
He is Shaka the unshakable. Shaka, King of the Zulus. *Unknown.* PBA; TTY
He is sleeping, soundly sleeping. A Departed Friend. Julia A. Moore. FiBHP
He is so small, he does not know. Six Weeks Old. Christopher Morley. BiCB
He is stark[e] mad, who ever say[e]s. The Broken Heart. John Donne. AtBAP; DiPo; ILP; LiTL; MaMe; PoFS; ReEn; SCEP-1; TuPP
He is that fallen lance that lies as hurled. A Soldier. Robert Frost. CBV; ILP; MoPo; NePA; PoPo; SeCeV; ThLM; WaaP; WaP
He is the Ancient Wisdom of the World. The Holy Child. Charles Carroll Albertson. ChIP; MaRV; StJW
He is the despots' despot. All must bide. The Dance of Death. Austin Dobson. HBV; TOP
He is the happy wanderer who goes. The Happy Wanderer. Percy Addleshaw. OBVV; VA
He Is the Lonely Greatness. Madeleine Caron Rock. CAW; CH; ChIP
He Is the Propitiation for Our Sin. Edward Taylor. *See* Preparatory Meditations: "Still I complain. . ."
He is the Star of the Morning. Star of the Morning. D. V. Johnstone. BePJ
He Is the Truth. Ilse L. Schlaitzer. SoP
He Is the Way. W. H. Auden. *See* Chorus: "He is the Way."
He is to weet a melancholy carle. Spenserian Stanzas on Charles [Armitage] Brown [*or* A Portrait]. Keats. BOHV; InMe
He is truly the only One. The Only One. Jo Gardner. BePJ
He isn't all Indian. Our Hired Man (and His Daughter, Too). Monica Shannon. FaPON
He isn't woolly, he isn't sweet. Lower Animals. Alan Anderson. PCD
He Jests at Scars [That Never Felt a Wound]. Shakespeare. *Fr.* Romeo and Juliet, II, ii. BoC; LiTB; LiTG; LiTL; MasP
(Balcony Scene, The.) TreF
(Living Juliet, The.) TrGrPo
He jumped, seeing an island like a hand. Hart Crane. Julian Symons. LiTM (1946 ed.)
He Keeps the Key. *Unknown.* *See* God's Key.
He kept his mouth forever. The Source. Phyllis Harris. ThO
He kept them pointed straight ahead. The Caravels of Columbus. Elias Lieberman. PEDC (1949 ed.)
He killed and kept. The Thoroughgoing. Josephine Miles. FiMAP
He killed the noble Mudjokovis. The Modern Hiawatha. George A. Strong. *Fr.* The Song of Milkanwatha. BOHV; FaPON; FiBHP; HBV; InMe; LiTG; MoShBr; NA; TreFS; WhC; YaD
He Kindleth a Fire. *Unknown,* *tr. fr. Egyptian by* Robert Hillyer. *Fr.* Book of the Dead. AWP
He kissed her on the face and the crew began to roar. Up She Goes. *Unknown.* SoAmSa
He knelt beside her pillow, in the dead watch of the night. Asleep. William Winter. AA
He knew how Roman legions looked, for he. The Fog. Robert P. Tristram Coffin. CrMA
He knew not that the trumpet he had blown. David Livingstone. *Unknown.* MaRV
He knew what hunger a man can feel. Bread. Leslie Savage Clark. ChIP
He knocks upon your door. Boy at the Door. Louis J. Sanker. JKCP (1955 ed.)
"He Knoweth Not That the Dead Are Thine." Mary Elizabeth Coleridge. ELU; OBNC; PoVP
(Weapon, The.) MemP
He Knoweth the Souls of the East. *Unknown,* *tr. fr. Egyptian by* Robert Hillyer. *Fr.* Book of the Dead. AWP
He Knoweth the Souls of the West. *Unknown,* *tr. fr. Egyptian by* Robert Hillyer. *Fr.* Book of the Dead. AWP; JAWP; WBP
He Knows. E. Margaret Clarkson. SoP
He knows celebrites . . . or else he lies. Savage Portraits. Don Marquis. HBMV
He knows, he loves, he cares. The Best Choice. *Unknown.* SoP; STF
He knows it all—the winding path. He Knows. E. Margaret Clarkson. SoP
He knows not bit nor bridle, his nostrils are flaming. The Neighing North. Annie Charlotte Dalton. CaP
He Knows the Way. *Unknown.* STF
He knows when shadows come my way. Because He Was Tempted. *Unknown.* STF
He knows why certain sycophants adore him. Portrait. Sydney King Russell. PoMa
He laughed derision when his foes. Heart-Hurt. *Unknown.* TreFT
He Laughed Last. Francis Whiting Hatch. WhC
He lay, and those who watched him were amazed. The Sprig of Lime. Robert Nichols. GTBS-P; POTE
He lay in the middle of the world, and twitcht. The Dream Songs, LIII. John Berryman. OPoP
He lay in's armour; as if that had been. A Soldier's Death. Cyril Tourneur. *Fr.* The Atheist's Tragedy. SeCePo
He lay upon his dying bed. The Sword of Bunker Hill. William Ross Wallace. PEDC
He Leadeth Me. Joseph H. Gilmore. BLRP; MaRV; WBLP; WGRP
He Leadeth Me. *Unknown, at. to* H. H. Barry. BLRP; SoP
(On the Twenty-third Psalm, *abr.*) MaRV; OQP; TRV
He Leads. Elisabeth Scollard. MaRV
He Leads. Graf von Zinzendorf, *tr. fr. German.* SoP
He leads His own beside and in and through. Symphony of the Soul. Carlton Buck. SoP
He leads us on. Through the Maze. *Unknown.* BLRP
He leads us on by paths we did not know. He Leads. Graf von Zinzendorf. SoP
He Leads Us Still. Arthur Guiterman. OHIP; OQP
He leant at the door. The Unfrocked Priest. Joseph Campbell. AnIL; OnYI
He leaves unplowed his furrow. Here's to the Ranger! *Unknown.* CoSo
He led me out to water, as you may understand. The Messenger Song. *At. to* John Calhoun. ShS
He left his hose, his Hannah, and his love. To the Memory of a Young Man. *Unknown.* WhC
He left his pants upon a chair. The Mistake. Theodore Roethke. NePoAm-2; UnTE
He left me exposed on a hill of woman, my mother. Oedipus at San Francisco. Donald Finkel. CoPo
He left the land of youth, he left the young. Herodotus in Egypt. Andrew Lang. PoVP
He left two children, who for virtue, wit. Of Sir Philip Sidney. Sir John Beaumont. GoBC
He lies beside her in the bed. Narcissus. Thomas M. Disch. HYE
He lies here. See the bush. His Epitaph. Frederick William Ophel. BoAu
He lies low in the levelled sand. At the Grave of Walker. Joaquin Miller. AA; AnAmPo; AnFE; APA; CoAnAm
He lies on the grass, looking up at the sky. Deaf and Dumb. "A." PRWS
He lies unloosened of his white clothes. A Dead Man. *Unknown.* OnPM
He lies upon his bed. Archibald MacLeish. *Fr.* Einstein. ImOP
He Lifted from the Dust. Helen Rogers Smith. BePJ
He lifts his hopeful eyes at each new tread. Lost Dog. Frances Rodman. PoRL
He Lived a Life, *sel.* H. N. Fifer.
"What was his creed?" PoToHe (new ed.)
He Lived amidst th' Untrodden Ways. Hartley Coleridge. *See* On Wordsworth.
He lived at Dingle Bank—he did. At Dingle Bank. Edward Lear. WhC
He lived in a cave by the seas. Double Ballade of Primitive

Man [*or* Ballade of Primitive Man]. Andrew Lang *and* Edward Burnett Tylor. ATP; BOHV; CenHV
He lived in that past Georgian day. A Gentleman of the Old School. Austin Dobson. EnLit; HBV
He lived one hundred and five. *Unknown.* WhC
He Lives. Samuel Medley. SoP
He lives among a dog. The Child. Donald Hall. NePoEA-2
He Lives at Last. Lucile Lippitt. MaRV
He Lives! He Lives to Bless! Dorothy Conant Stroud. STF
He lives, he wakes—'tis Death is dead, not he. One with Nature. Shelley. *Fr.* Adonais. MaRV
He Lives Long Who Lives Well. Thomas Randolph. WBLP
He lives, the great Redeemer lives. The Great Redeemer Lives. Anne Steele. BePJ
He lives, who last night flopped from a log. Burning. Galway Kinnell. CoAP
He lives within the hollow wood. The Charcoal-Burner. Sir Edmund Gosse. OBVV
He Liveth Long Who Liveth Well. Horatius Bonar. HBV; HBVY
(Who Liveth Well.) FaChP; MaRV
He loathed his bond, but could not stir. Maurice Hewlett. *Fr.* The Song of the Plow, V. PoFr
He looks like a fat little old man. Dead Seal. Alfred Purdy. MoCV
He looks not holy; simple in his belief. The Modern Saint. Richard Burton. OQP
He look't and saw what numbers numberless. The Parthians. Milton. *Fr.* Paradise Regained, III. OBS
"He lost his life"—yet was the reach. For Any Beachhead. M. K. Joseph. AnNZ
He loved her, having felt his love begin. The Contrast. Helen Gray Cone. AA
He loved the brook's soft sound. The Peasant Poet. John Clare. ERoP-2; OBNC; WGRP
He Loves and He Rides Away. Sydney Dobell. OBNC
He loves me. *Unknown.* OxNR
He loves not well whose love is bold! The Queen. William Winter. HBV
He lying spilt like water from a bowl. Poem. Alison Boodson. ErPo; NeBP
He made a place in his dream for the pines to grow. Farmyard. Ruth Dallas. AnNZ
He made honest doors. Integrity. William L. Stidger. ChIP; OQP
He made no history, even. Elegy for a Countryman. Padraic Fallon. NeIP
He Made the Night. Lloyd Mifflin. HBV
He made them and He called them good. Address to the Crown. Charles L. O'Donnell. GoBC
He Made Us Free. Maurice Francis Egan. AA JKCP
He makes himself comfortable. 1st Dance—Making Things New—6 February 1964. Jackson MacLow. CoPo
He makes sweet music who, in serious lines. Sir John Beaumont. *Fr.* To His Late Majesty, Concerning the True Form of English Poetry. PP
He Maketh Himself One with Osiris. *Unknown, tr. fr. Egyptian by* Robert Hillyer. *Fr.* Book of the Dead. AWP
He Maketh Himself One with the God Ra. *Unknown, tr. fr. Egyptian by* Robert Hillyer. *Fr.* Book of the Dead. AWP
He Maketh Himself One with the Only God, Whose Limbs Are the Many Gods. *Unknown, tr. fr. Egyptian by* Robert Hillyer. *Fr.* Book of the Dead. AWP; JAWP; WBP
He Maketh No Mistake. A. M. Overton. SoP; STF
He, making speedy way through 'spersèd air. The House of Morpheus. Spenser. *Fr.* The Faerie Queene, I. InP; UnPo (1st ed.)
He may be six kinds of a liar. Loyalty. Berton Braley. BLPA
He Meditates on the Life of a Rich Man. Douglas Hyde, *tr. fr. Modern Irish by* Lady Gregory. OBMV
He meets, by heavenly chance express. The Lover. Coventry Patmore. *Fr.* The Angel in the House, I. PoVP
He mends the shoes. Cobbler. Peggy Bacon. OCS; PoMa
He Met Her at the Green Horse. Peter Levi. NePoEA-2
He might have Built a palace at a word. Renunciation. Richard Chenevix Trench. SoP
He might have won the highest guerdon that heaven to earth can give. Saturninus. Katherine Eleanor Conway. AA; JKCP
He mightn't have had wherewith to buy. Last Mathematician. Hyman Edelstein. CaP
He mounted the rostrum. Stravinsky. Julian Cooper. MuSP
He Mourns for the Change That Has Come upon Him and His Beloved, and Longs for the End of the World. W. B. Yeats. Po
He Must Do It. Oswald J. Smith. SoP
He must needs go through Samaria. Living Water. Ruth M. Williams. BePJ
He must not laugh at his own wheeze. The Humorist. Keith Preston. ALV; EvOK; HBMV; WhC
He ne'er had seen one earthly sight. The Blind Highland Boy. Wordsworth. OTPC
He never completed his History of Ephesus. On a Certain Scholar. W. Craddle. SiTL; WhC
He never gave me a chance to speak. After the Quarrel. Adam Lindsay Gordon. OBVV
He never heard of Newton's law. The Rigger. Washington Jay McCormick. WhC
He never knew what made him feel so sure. The Shape of Fear. Sydney King Russell. FiSC
He never lives to tell. Calenture. Alastair Reid. NYBP
He never made parade of tooth or claw. A Ranger. Badger Clark. SCC
He never made the dive—not while I watched. The Springboard. Louis MacNeice. ChMP
He never saw a tree, they say. Mozart. Jane Mayhall. NYTB
He Never Smiled Again. Felicia Dorothea Hemans. HBV
He never spoke a word to me. Simon the Cyrenian Speaks. Countee Cullen. AmNP; BBV (1951 ed.); MAP; MaRV; MoAmPo; NeMA; OQP; PoNe; StJW; TTY
He never thought an honour done him. Swift. *Fr.* Verses on the Death of Dr. Swift. PoFr
He never used to notice me. The Policeman. Marjorie Seymour Watts. PCH; TiPo
He Never Will Forget. "M. G. H." STF
He nothing common did or mean. King Charles upon the Scaffold. Andrew Marvell. *Fr.* An Horatian Ode upon Cromwell's Return from Ireland. ChTr
He, of his gentleness. In the Wilderness. Robert Graves. EaLo; OxBI
He often came and stood outside my door. The Lonely Dog. Margaret E. Bruner. PoToHe
He often spoke of things of home. Son of Man. Leslie Savage Clark. ChIP
He often would ask us. The Choirmaster's Burial. Thomas Hardy. DTC; MuSP
He on a lean, ill-favored beast is set. The Death of Edward. Michael Drayton. *Fr.* Mortimeriados. ReIE
He, on whose natal hour you glance. The Gift of Song. Horace, *tr. by* Christopher Smart. Odes, IV, 3. LiTW
He only is worthy of freedom who honors the freedom of others. Jan Kollar. *Fr.* The Daughter of the Slava. PoFr
He or she that hopes to gain. Song. *Unknown.* SeCL
He Ought to Know! *with music.* John A. Stone. SGR
He Overcometh the Serpent of Evil in the Name of Ra. *Unknown, tr. fr. Egyptian by* Robert Hillyer. *Fr.* Book of the Dead. AWP
He passed beyond the utmost realm of stars. The Challenger. Donald Wandrei. FiSC
He past; a soul of nobler tone. In Memoriam A. H. H., LX. Tennyson. EPN; ViPo; VP
He paused a moment by the sea. The Flood-Tide. E. J. Pratt. CBV
He paused on the sill of a door ajar. The Newcomer's Wife. Thomas Hardy. PoFS; VP
He paused: the listening dames again. Sir Walter Scott. *Fr.* The Lay of the Last Minstrel, IV. OBRV
He paweth in the valley and rejoiceth in his strength. The Horse. Job, Bible, *O.T.* StaSt
He Persuadeth His Friend from the Fond Affects of Love. Thomas Churchyard. ReIE
He picks up what he thinks is. My Father: October 1942. William Stafford. NaP
He placed a prayer wheel where the wild winds dance. Orisons. Edwin McNeill Poteat. OQP
He planked down sixpence and he took his drink. Henry Turnbull. W. W. Gibson. ELU; FaBoTw
He played by the river when he was young. Washington. Nancy Byrd Turner. FaPON; MPB; SoPo; TiPo; YeAr
He played with a toy they bought. Don't Break It. Joseph Ceravolo. ANYP

He plays across the centuries. Master Musician. Margaret Evelyn Singleton. ChIP
He plays for all the little side-streets, while. The Street Musician. *Unknown.* TSW
He poises a moment and looks at the earth far under. Parachute. Stanley Snaith. HaMV
He polished snubs till they were regnant art. In the Gentlemanly Interest. Donald Evans. NP
He Praises Her Hair. *Unknown, tr. fr. Late Middle Irish by* the Earl of Longford. AnIL
He Praises His Wife When She Has Left [*or* Had Gone from] Him. *Unknown, tr. fr. Late Middle Irish by* Robin Flower. AnIL; OxBI
He prayed by the stone. Resignation. William L. Stidger. ChIP
He prayed for strength that he might achieve. Blessed [*or* How God Answers]. *Unknown.* MaRV; OQP; SoP
He Prayeth Best. Samuel Taylor Coleridge. *Fr.* The Rime of the Ancient Mariner, VII. FaPON, 1 *st.*; GoTP, 1 *st.*; MaRV, 4 *sts.*; PCH, 1 *st.*; StVeCh, 1 *st.*
("He prayeth best, who loveth best," 1 *st.*). LO; TRV; YT
(He Prayeth Well, 6*ll.*) BoTP; SoP; ThGo
He Prayeth for Ink and Palette That He May Write. *Unknown, tr. fr. Egyptian by* Robert Hillyer. *Fr.* Book of the Dead. AWP
He Prayeth Well. Samuel Taylor Coleridge. *See* He Prayeth Best.
He preached upon "breadth" till it argued him narrow. Emily Dickinson. AmePo; AmP; AmPP; AP; CABA; CBV; NoP; PoE
He pulled a flower. Ballad. Leonard Cohen. PeCV
He put away his tiny pipe. Spring Cricket. Frances Rodman. FaPON; SiSoSe
He put his acorn helmet on. A Fairy in Armor [*or* The Fay Arms Himself *or* An Elfin Knight]. Joseph Rodman Drake. *Fr.* The Culprit Fay. BoTP; FaPON; GaP; GFA; OTPC; PRWS
He quickly [*or* Pigwiggen] arms him for the field. The Arming of Pigwiggen [*or* Pigwiggen Prepares for the Fight with King Oberon]. Michael Drayton. *Fr.* Nymphidia. BoTP; GN; MoShBr; OTPC
He ran right out of the woods to me. The Story of the Baby Squirrel. Dorothy Aldis. TiPo
He ran the course and as he ran he grew. Innocence. Thom Gunn. LiTM (1970 ed.); NePoEA-2; ToPo
He raped her. Ripped the filaments from her skull. The Head-Rape. D. M. Thomas. HYE
He reached the West in a palace car where the writers tell us the cowboys are. The Disappointed Tenderfoot. Earl Alonzo Brininstool. SCC
He reaches Weymouth—treads the Esplande. The Royal Tour. "Peter Pindar." OxBoLi
He Remembers Forgotten Beauty. W. B. Yeats. *See* Michael Robartes Remembers Forgotten Beauty.
He Renounceth All the Effects of Love. Thomas, Lord Vaux. EnRePo
He replied to his own question, and with the unmannered. A Meditation on John Constable. Charles Tomlinson. NePoEA-2
He rested in the cool, that traveller. The African Tramp. Geoffrey Haresnape. PeSA
He rides at their head. The College Colonel. Herman Melville. AA; AmePo; MWA-1
He rides no dashing charger in the tournament of life. The Knight. Sister Maryanna. WHL
He rises and begins to round. The Lark Ascending. George Meredith. CABL; CoBE; EnLi-2; EPN; LoBV; OA; OAEP; PoVP; WiR
He rises from his guests, abruptly leaves. Ghost. Witter Bynner. AnFE; CoAnAm
He roamed half-round the world of woe. Epitaph. Aubrey Thomas De Vere. OBVV; PoVP
He riseth up early in the morning. The Mighty Hunter. Mrs. J. B. Worley. PoLF
He rocked the boat. Ezra Shank. *Unknown.* ShM
He rode at furious speed to Broken Edge. Temper in October. V. L. Edminson. BoPe
He rose as mediator strong. The Risen Lord. H. J. McKinnell. SoP
He rubbed his eyes and wound the silver horn. Little Boy Blue. John Crowe Ransom. LiTM; TwAmPo
He Ruleth Not Though He Reign [*or* Raigne] over Realms That Is Subject to His Own Lusts. Sir Thomas Wyatt. *See* If Thou Wilt Mighty Be.
He runs before the wise men. He. Stanley Kunitz. CrMA
He said a real revolution. Brother Malcolm: Waste Limit. Clarence Major. BP
He said, "Awake my soul, and with the sun." Barthélémon at Vauxhall. Thomas Hardy. UnS
He said his legs were stiff and sore. Autumn Fields. Elizabeth Madox Roberts. BrR
He said how much he had died for the sake. Li Po. Floyce Alexander. QAH
He said: I am a parson, but I take. Fishing in the Australian Alps. Ernest G. Moll. WhC
He said, "I will forget the dying faces." In Acceptance Lieth Peace. Amy Carmichael. FaChP; MaRV
He Said: "If in His Image I Was Made." Trumbull Stickney. AnFE; APA; CoAnAm; LiTA; TwAmPo
He Said That He Was Not Our Brother. John Banim. OnYI
He Said the Facts. Merrill Moore. CrMA
He said: "The shadows darken down." Ballad. May Kendall. HBV
He said: "Wilt thou go with me?" The Soul's Response. Annie Clarke. SoP
He sang above the vineyards of the world. The Singing Man. Josephine Preston Peabody. HBV; PoFr
He sang an old song. The Kilkenny Boy. Eileen Shanahan. NeIP
He sang at his bench in Nazareth. Carpenter. Leslie Savage Clark. ChIP
He sang of God—the mighty source. The Catholic Amen. Christopher Smart. *Fr.* A Song to David. GBV; GoBC; GTBS-W; GTSL; LiTG; TRV
He sang of joy; whate'er he knew of sadness. A Hero. Florence Earle Coates. OHIP
He sang of life, serenely sweet. The Poet. Paul Laurence Dunbar. Kal
He sang one song and died—no more but that. The Singer of One Song. Henry Augustin Beers. AA
He sang so wildly, did the boy. Mother's Love. Thomas Burbidge. VA
He sang the airs of olden times. The Blind Psalmist. Elizabeth Clementine Kinney. AA
He sang, too. Crucifixion. Earl Marlatt. ChIP
He sat above it, watching it recede. Utrillo's World. John Glassco. PeCV (1967 ed.)
He sat alone upon an ash-heap by. Love. Nicholas Moore. ErPo
He sat among the woods; he heard. Aesop. Andrew Lang. VA
He sat at the dinner table. Just like a Man. *Unknown, at. to* Lizzie M. Hadley. BoTP
He sat by a fire [*or* furnace] of seven-fold heat. The Refiner's Fire. *Unknown.* BLRP; SoP
He sat in a wheeled chair, waiting for dark. Disabled. Wilfred Owen. BrPo; CMoP; LiTM (rev. ed.); MMA; NAMP; WaP
He sat one winter 'neath a linden tree. A Minor Poet. Alexander Smith. *Fr.* A Life-Drama. VA
He sat the quiet stream beside. A Greek Idyl. Mortimer Collins. VA
He sat upon the rolling deck. Sailor. Langston Hughes. GoSl
He Satisfies. Frederick William Faber. BePJ
He saves the sheep, the goats he doth not save. The Good Shepherd with the Kid. Matthew Arnold. BoPe; PoVP
He saw beneath the bughouse wall. Solo for Bent Spoon. Donald Finkel. NePoEA-2
He Saw Far in the Concave Green of the Sea. Keats. *Fr.* Endymion. EtS
He saw her from the bottom of the stairs. Home Burial. Robert Frost. AmPP; AnFE; AnNE; AP; APA; BoLiVe; CoAnAm; CoBMV; MAPA; MaPo; StP; TwAmPo
He saw his white walls shining in the sun. Lambro's Return. Byron. *Fr.* Don Juan, III. OBRV
He saw it clearly and clairvoyant bright. Blueprint. D. B. Steinman. GoYe
He saw it last of all before they herded in the steerage. Teresina's Face. Margaret Widdemer. HBMV; NP
He saw the Word that spake it. This Is My Body. John Donne. ChIP
He says, *My reign is peace*, so slays. A Foreign [*or* Foren] Ruler. Walter Savage Landor. PoFr; PV; TreFT; ViBoPo

He says no with his head. The Dunce. Jacques Prévert. FIW
He says we are beggars. Margaret Randall. *Fr.* Retracing Paul Blackburn's Transit. WOW
He scanned it, staggered, dropped the loop. Emily Dickinson. PoEL-5
He scans the world with calm and fearless eyes. The New Negro. James Edward McCall. CDC; OTD
He scarce had ceas'd [*or* ceas't] when the superior Fiend. Satan and the Fallen Angels [*or* The Superior Fiend]. Milton. *Fr.* Paradise Lost, I. LiTB; MaPo; OBS; SeCePo
He scarce had finished, when such murmur filled. Beelzebub Rises to Speak. Milton. *Fr.* Paradise Lost, II. UnPo (1st ed.)
He seeks the mountains where the olives grow. The Transfiguration. James M. Hayes. JKCP
He seemed to know the harbour. The Shark. E. J. Pratt. WHW
He Sees His Beloved. James I, King of Scotland. *Fr.* The Kingis Quair. PoEL-1
(Coming of Love, The, *shorter sel.*) GoTS
He sees the rosy apples cling like flowers to the bough. The Fruit Rancher. Lloyd Roberts. CaP
He sees them pass. Once. Eric N. Batterham. CH
He Sees Through Stone. Etheridge Knight. BALP; NBP
He seized me round the waist and kissed my throat. Charleston in the 1860s. Adrienne Rich. CoAP
He Sent a Man before Them, Even Joseph, Who Was Sold. Edward Taylor. *See* Preparatory Meditations: "All dull, my Lord. . ."
He sent men out to preach the living Word. The Teacher. Hildegarde Hoyt Swift. ChIP; MaRV; OQP
He sent so many. Manhattan Epitaphs: Lawyer. Alfred Kreymborg. OCS
He Sent Them Out. Lon Woodrum. SoP
He Shall Bear the Glory. William Blane. SoP
He shall not hear the bittern cry. Thomas MacDonagh. Francis Ledwidge. AnIV; OnYI; OxBI
He Shall Speak Peace. Thomas Curtis Clark. OQP; WBLP
He Shall Speak Peace unto the Nations. Lila V. Walters. BePJ; FaChP; WBLP
He Shot at Lee Wing. *Unknown.* ShM
He Singeth a Hymn to Osiris the Lord of Eternity. *Unknown, tr. fr. Egyptian by* Robert Hillyer. *Fr.* Book of the Dead. AWP
He Singeth in the Underworld. *Unknown, tr. fr. Egyptian by* Robert Hillyer. *Fr.* Book of the Dead. AWP; JAWP; WBP
He sipped at a weak hock and seltzer. The Arrest of Oscar Wilde at the Cadogan Hotel. John Betjeman. CMoP; DTC; InvP; LiTM (rev. ed.); MoBrPo (1962 ed.); SiTL
He sits above the clang and dust of Time. The Sovereign Poet. Sir William Watson. PoVP; WGRP
He sits at the foot of Golgotha. Lament for a Poor Poet. Myles Connolly. CAW
He sits in silence on his porch at night. An Old Habitant. Frank Oliver Call. *Fr.* A Sonnet Series of French Canada. CaP
He sits over the glimmering coal. The Old Age Pensioner. Joseph Campbell. AnIL
He sleeps at last—a hero of his race. A Dead Soldier. George Edgar Montgomery. AA
He sleeps on the top of a mast. The Unbeliever. Elizabeth Bishop. FiMAP; LiTA
He slurs his fingers on the strings. The Sitar Player. Julian Cooper. MuSP
He snuggles his fingers. After Winter. Sterling A. Brown. GoSl; PoNe
He sought Australia's far-famed isle. The Digger's Grave. Sarah Welch. VA
He sought the mountain and the loneliest height. Jesus Praying. Hartley Coleridge. MaRV; StJW
He sought the old scenes with eager feet. The Return. John Burroughs. MaRV
He sought the sea; His footsteps press the dry. Christ Quiets the Tempest. Caelius Sedulius. *Fr.* Carmen Paschale. OnYI
He speaks not well who doth his time deplore. The Heroic Age. Richard Watson Gilder. AA; OHIP
He Spends Time in Southern California. Jonathan Cott. YAP
He spoke; and Sohrab kindled at his taunts. The Death of Sohrab. Matthew Arnold. *Fr.* Sohrab and Rustum. WHA
He spoke; and Sohrab smiled on him, and took/ The spear. The Death of Sohrab. Matthew Arnold. *Fr.* Sohrab and Rustum. FiP
He spoke of poetry: his lips had shrunk. The Pure Poet. Roy Fuller. ToPo
He spoke of undying love. The Talker. Benjamin Appel. TrJP
He sported round the watery world. Jonah and the Whale [*or* The Whale and Jonah]. Viola Meynell. EtS; MemP; MoBrPo (1942 ed.)
He Standeth at the Door. Arthur Cleveland Coxe. HBV
He stands and walks as if his knees were tensed. Eastern Shore. Charles Bruce. PeCV
He stands big-shouldered and august. The Iron Horse. Israel Newman. PoMa
He started out to sing of labor. Portrait of a Poet. Edgar Lee Masters. *Fr.* Jack Kelso. ATP
He stayed: and was imprisoned in possession. W. H. Auden. *Fr.* In Time of War. CMoP; EnLit
He steps down from the dark train, blinking; stares. Ten Days Leave. W. D. Snodgrass. MoAmPo (1962 ed.); UnPo (3d ed.)
He stood a moment at the edge. Life or Death. Glenn Ward Dresbach. *Fr.* In Western Mountains. HBMV
He stood a soldier to the last right end. Ben Jonson. *Fr.* To the Immortal Memory and Friendship of that Immortal Pair, Sir Lucius Cary, and Sir Henry Morison. CoBE
He stood, a worn-out city clerk. Peace. Charles Stuart Calverley. NBM; WhC
He stood alone within the spacious square. James Thomson. *Fr.* The City of Dreadful Night, IV. AnFE; EnLi-2; WiR
He stood among a crowd at Dromahair [*or* Drumahair]. The Man Who Dreamed of Faeryland [*or* Fairyland]. W. B. Yeats. CMoP; OAEP (2d ed.); ViPo (1962 ed.)
He stood and call'd his legions, angel forms. The Summons. Milton. *Fr.* Paradise Lost, I. WHA
He stood, and heard the steeple. Eight o'Clock. A. E. Housman. BrPo; CABA; CBV; CMoP; ExPo; InPo; LoBV; MoAB; MoBrPo; NoP; PoAn; PoIE; POTE; ReMP; ShBV-4; TrGrPo; WePo
He stood aside from his playmates. The Upward Place. Helen M. Wilson. SoP
He stood at the crossroads all alone. My Chum. *Unknown.* SoP
He stood before the Sanhedrim. Religion and Doctrine. John Hay. MaRV; StJW; WGRP
He stood in the pulpit. The Pastor. William C. Summers. STF
He stood on his head by the wild seashore. His Mother-in-Law. Walter Parke. BOHV; FiBHP
He stood up in our khaki with the poise. Gee-up Dar, Mules. Edwin Ford Piper. YaD
He stood upon a slope of Olivet. And Thou Would'st Not! Winifred Stoddard LeBar. ChIP
He stood upon the coast of County Clare. St. Enda. Laurence Lerner. PeSA
He stoops above the clumsy snare. The Snare. Patrick MacDonogh. NeIP
He strangely gazes up. Vessels. Francis Carlin. JKCP (1955 ed.)
He strides across the grassy corn. The Scarecrow. Andrew Young. FaBoTw
He stripped five of our women. What Pablo Picasso Did in "Les Demoiselles d'Avignon." John Robert Colombo. PeCV (1967 ed.)
He strode along the chapel aisle. Sabbath Reflection. Denis Wrafter. NeIP
He struggled to kiss her. She struggled the same. Old-fashioned Love [*or* An Original Love-Story]. *Unknown.* BoLP; MaC
He stumbled home from Clifden fair. High and Low. James H. Cousins. HBMV; OnYI; OxBI
He stumbles silver-haired among his bees. The Veteran. Edmund Blunden. BrPo
He surely is not built for speed. The Rhinocerostrich. Kenyon Cox. *Fr.* Mixed Beasts. RIS
He swings down like the flourish of a pen. Skier. Robert Francis. SD
He Takes My Hand. Louis Paul Lehman, Jr. SoP
He talked, and as he talked. The Story-Teller. Mark Van Doren. LOW

He tasted love with half his mind. In Memoriam A. H. H., XC. Tennyson. EPN; ViPo; VP
He taught me all the mercy, for he show'd me all the sin. Tennyson. *Fr.* The May Queen. ChIP
He telleth the stars in their number. Omnipotence. Mabel Brown Denison. SoP
He tells me in Bangkok he's robbed. Baby Villon. Philip Levine. CoAP; NaP
He that believeth on me, believeth not on me. The Light of the World. St. John, Bible, *N.T.* WoL
He that but once too nearly hears. Fragment. Coventry Patmore. *Fr.* The Victories of Love. NBM
He that buys land buys many stones. Advice. *Unknown.* CBV
He that can trace a ship making her way. The Heart Is Deep. Roger Wolcott. SCAP
He that cannot chuse but love. Selfe Love. John Donne. MaMe
He that could so well express those frantic fits. In Ariostum Orlandi Furiosi Autorem. John Heath. SiCE
He That Doeth the Will. Longfellow. ChIP
He that dwelleth in the secret place of the Most High. God Our Refuge [*or* The Everlasting Arms *or* A Mighty Fortress]. Psalm XCI, Bible, *O.T.* AWP; MaRV; TrGrPo; WGRP; WoL
He that fights and runs away. *Unknown.* TreF
He that for fear his Master did deny. To St. Peter and St. Paul. Henry Constable. ReEn; Sonn; TuPP
He that from dust of worldly tumults flies. Of True Liberty. Sir John Beaumont. OBS; PoFr
He that had come that morning. Ballad of John Cable and Three Gentlemen. W. S. Merwin. CoAP; NePoEA
He That Has and a Little Tiny Wit. Shakespeare. *Fr.* King Lear, III, ii. ViBoPo
He That Has Light Within. Milton. *Fr.* Comus. MaRV
He that hath made his refuge God. My Trust. *Unknown.* SoP
He that hath such acuteness, and such wit. On Mr. Francis Beaumont (Then Newly Dead). Richard Corbet. OBS
He that holds fast the golden mean. Moderation. Horace. *Fr.* Odes. PoToHe (new ed.)
He that intends to take a wife. The Wife-Hater. *Unknown.* CoMu
He that is by Mooni now. Mooni. Henry Clarence Kendall. OBEV; OBVV
He That Is Down. Bunyan. *See* Shepherd Boy's Song, The.
He that is grown to wisdom hurries not. Sonnet: Of Moderation and Tolerance. Guido Guinicelli. AWP; JAWP; WBP
He that is in the battle slain. Fight. *Unknown.* FaFP; LiTG; SiTL
He that is one. Trinity Sunday. George Herbert. MaMe
He That Is Slow to Anger. Proverbs, XVI: 32, Bible, *O.T.* FaPON; TiPo (1952 ed.)
He that is weary, let him sit. Employment. George Herbert. MaMe; OBS; OxBoCh; SeCP
He that leadeth men must be just. The Leader. Second Samuel, Bible, *O.T.* PCH
He that lies at the stock. Rock, Ball, Fiddle. *Unknown.* CBEP; CH; OxBoLi; OxNR; SiTL
He That Loves. Sir Philip Sidney. ErPo
He That Loves a Rosy Cheek. Thomas Carew. *See* Disdain Returned.
He that Loves a Rosy Cheek. Heinrich von Rugge, *tr. fr. German by* Jethro Bithell. AWP; JAWP; WBP
He that loves and fears to try. He That Loves. Sir Philip Sidney. ErPo
He That Marries a Merry Lass. *Unknown.* ALV; SiTL
He that meddleth with all thing may shoe the gosling. Of Common Meddlers. John Heywood. SiCE
He That Never Read a Line. *Unknown, tr. fr. Old Irish by* Robin Flower. AnIL
He that of such a height hath built his mind. To the Lady Margaret, Countess of Cumberland [*or* The High Mind]. Samuel Daniel. AnEnPo; LoBV; OBSC; ReIE; SiCE; TuPP
He that owns wealth, in mountain, wold, or waste. Wealth. Sadi. *Fr.* The Gulistan. AWP; OuHeWo
He That Regards the Precious Things of Earth. Moses Ibn Ezra, *tr. fr. Hebrew by* Solomon Solis-Cohen. *Fr.* The World's Illusion. TrJP
He that ruleth over men must be just. The Leader. Second Samuel, Bible, *O.T.* PCD
He that saith he is in the light, and hateth his brother. Brotherhood. First John, Bible, *N.T.* TreFT
He that sweareth. Advice. Hugh Rhodes. GoTP
He that to God's law doth cling. Freedom. Abraham ibn Ezra. TrJP
He that will be a lover in every wise. Three Things Jeame Lacks. *Unknown.* MeEL
He that will court a wench that is coy. Song. *Unknown.* ErPo
He that will not love, must be. Not to Love. Robert Herrick. OAEP
He that will not reason is a bigot. Reason. *Unknown.* TreF
He that would catch and catching hold. *Unknown.* SeCSL
He That Would Thrive. *Unknown.* OTPC; OxNR; PPL
(Country Saying.) RIS
(Proverbs.) HBV
(Rules of Behavior.) HBVY
He the Wind that's ever moving. Hymn to the Wind God. *Unknown.* *Fr.* Song of Quetzalcoatl. LiTW
He there does now enjoy eternal rest. Sleep after Toil. Spenser. *Fr.* The Faerie Queene, I, 9. ChTr; MyFE
He—They—We. John Oxenham. ChIP
He Thinks of His Past Greatness When a Part of the Constellations of Heaven. W. B. Yeats. DTC; OAEP (2d ed.); PoEL-5
He Thinks of Those Who Have Spoken Evil of His Beloved. W. B. Yeats. CLwM; CTC; ELU
He thought he kept the universe alone. The Most of It. Robert Frost. CABA; CaFP; CrMA; FosPo; MaPo; MoPo; NePA; PIA; PoIE; PoSa
He thought he saw an Elephant [*or* a Buffalo]. The [Mad] Gardener's Song. "Lewis Carroll." *Fr.* Sylvie and Bruno. BoHV; EnLi-2; EvOK; FiBHP; GBV (1952 ed.); HBV; HBVY; LBN; MemP; NA; NBM; OTPC; PoRh; SiTL; StVeCh; TreFS; WiR
He thought, in his great weariness, to mount. Nightmare. R. H. Grenville. FiSC
He thought to quell the stubborn hearts of oak. Buonaparte. Tennyson. PoVP; Sonn
He throws. The Chipmunk. Millen Brand. NYTB
He toiled and saved his earnings every day. Life's Illusion. Alexander Louis Fraser. OQP
He told himself and he told his wife. The Riddle. Ralph Hodgson. PoPl; WhC
He told his life story to Mrs. Courtly. Autumn. Stevie Smith. ELU
He told the barmaid he had things to do. Dodona's Oaks Were Still. Patrick MacDonogh. NeIP
He, Too, Loved Beauty. Edwin McNeill Poteat. ChIP
He took a thousand islands and he didn't lose a man. Dewey in Manila Bay. Richard Voorhees Risley. DD; MC; PAH
He took castle and towns; he cut short limbs and lives. Greatness. Thomas Love Peacock. *Fr.* Crotchet Castle, *ch.* 16. OtMeF; PV
He took her fancy when he came. Takings [*or* What He Took]. Tom Hood. BOHV; CoMu
He took his wig off, with his sleeve. The Clown: He Dances in the Clearing by Night. Ramon Guthrie. NMP; OPoP
He Took My Place. Horatius Bonar. BePJ
He took the great harp wearily. The Songs of Guthrum and Alfred. G. K. Chesterton. *Fr.* The Ballad of the White Horse. HBV
He took the quaint cup in unpractised hands. Poor Fool. Evan V. Shute. CaP
"He touched her hand, and the fever left her." The Master's Touch. *Unknown.* SoP
He touches, and the wheel of time goes round. Hurdy-Gurdy Man in Winter. Vernon Watkins. NYBP
He travels after a winter sun. Tilly. James Joyce. PoIE
He treads no more the paths of Galilee. The Christ of the World's Highway. Dorothy Clarke Wilson. MaRV
He trembled for us. O Theophilus. Margaret Allonby. BoSA
He Tries Out the Concords Gently. "Eduard Bagritsky," *tr. fr. Russian by* C. M. Bowra. TrJP
He tripp'd up the steps with a bow and a smile. The Jacobite on Tower Hill. George Walter Thornbury. VA
He turned his field into a meeting-place. W. H. Auden. *Fr.* In Time of War. PoPl
He turned his pale face to the wall. Barbara Ellen. *Unknown.* IHA
He Understands the Great Cruelty of Death. Petrarch, *pr. tr. fr. Italian by* J. M. Synge. *Fr.* Sonnets to Laura: To Laura in Death. OBMV

He unto whom thou art so partial. Post-Obits and the Poets. Martial, *tr. by* Byron. AWP; JAWP; OuHeWo; WBP
He Upholds. Martin Luther. FaChP
He used me today. The Gardener. Evelyn Eaton. GoYe
He used to dream of things he'd do. The Dreamer. Thomas Nunan. WBLP
He usually managed to be there when. Because He Liked to Be at Home. Kenneth Patchen. NaP; ToPo
He Visits a Hospital. Rolfe Humphries. AnAmPo
He wakens from the clover rick. The Sun-Witch to the Sun. George Howe. NYBP
He wakes to a confused dream of boats, gulls. Murphy in Manchester. John Montague. NMP
He walked among the alders. Birds flew down. Cowper. Norman Nicholson. ML
He walked those mountains wild, and lived within that nook. Gonzalo de Berceo. *Fr.* Life of San Millan. CAW
He walked through the woods. The Walk. W. W. E. Ross. PeCV; SD
He walked up and down the street 'till the shoes fell off his feet. Tramp, Tramp, Tramp, Keep on a-Tramping. *Unknown.* AS
He Walketh by Day. *Unknown, tr. fr. Egyptian by* Robert Hillyer. *Fr.* Book of the Dead. AWP; JAWP; WBP
He walks amid the wordly, yet in his heart afar. The Poet. William Rooney. JKCP (1926 ed.)
He Walks at Peace. *Unknown, tr. fr. Chinese. Fr.* Tao Teh King. TRV
He walks beside me every day. My Companion. Joyce Ramage. BePJ; SoP
He walks still upright from the root. The Hewel, or Woodpecker [*or* The Woodpecker]. Andrew Marvell. *Fr.* Upon Appleton House. BiS; ChTr
He walks, the enchanter, on his sea of glass. Antichrist. Edwin Muir. EaLo
He walks where clean lakes lie. The Contemplative. Sister M. Thérèse. MoRP
He wanders over the wild countryside. The Donkey. P. R. Kaikini. ACV
He was a big two-fisted brute. Bucko-Mate. Samuel Schierloh. GoYe
He was a gentle lobster. The Lobster and the Maid. Frederic Edward Weatherly. OTPC
He was a good man. Wake Cry. Waring Cuney. BANP
He was a man as hot as whiskey. Andrew Jackson. Martha Keller. AmFN; GoTP; MaC
He was a man who, with his hand. To a Mate. Roland Robinson. NeLNL
He was a rat, and she was a rat. An Old Rat's Tale [*or* What Became of Them?]. *Unknown.* BoTP; GFA
He was a reprobate I grant. The Deceased. Keith Douglas. FaBoTw
He was a singer caroling in dark. Countee Cullen. Eugene T. Maleska. PoNe (1970 ed.)
He was a wizard's son. A Love Story. Oliver Herford. PoMS
He was a worthy citizen of the town. Fire on Belmont Street. Donald Davidson. *Fr.* The Tall Men. MAP; MoAmPo (1942 ed.)
He Was Alone. Lois Duffield. SoP
He was an arrogant cat, My Lord. My Lord's Motoring. Vincent Starrett. CIV
He was as loyal as them all—and more. Peeping Tom. Francis Hope. ErPo
He was as old as old could be. Danny Murphy. James Stephens. BoTP; RoGo
He was as the morning star in the midst of a cloud, and as the moon at the full. Ecclesiasticus, Bible, Apocrypha. BoC
He was at Naples writing letters home. Esthétique du Mal. Wallace Stevens. CMoP; LiTM (rev. ed.); PoDB
He was born blind with the snow on a winter's day. Charles. Leonard Clark. FIW
He was born in Alabama. Of DeWitt Williams on His Way to Lincoln Cemetery. Gwendolyn Brooks. PoNe
He was born in Deutschland, as you would suspect. The Progress of Faust. Karl Shapiro. DiPo; MoAB; NYBP; OnHM
He was brought up out of the sea. Lifesaver. Elizabeth Riddell. NeLNL
He was caught in the whirlpool of dismay. The Whirlpool. *Unknown.* PoToHe (new ed.)
He was found by the Bureau of Statistics to be. The Unknown Citizen. W. H. Auden. CABA; CBV; ChMP; LiTA; LiTM; MaPo (1969 ed.); MoAB; MoRP; NePA; NYBP; PoPo; PoRA; PPON; ShBV-4; SiTL; TreFT
He was going to be all that a mortal could [*or* should] be—tomorrow. Tomorrow [*or* Do It Now]. *Unknown.* SoP; STF
He was in Cincinnati, she in Burlington. A Couple. Carl Sandburg. ReMP
He was in logic a great critic. The Presbyterian Knight [*or* Portrait of Hudibras *or* The Metaphysical Sectarian]. Samuel Butler. *Fr.* Hudibras, I. AtBAP; MeLP; OBS; OxBoLi; PoEL-3; SiTL
He was in love with truth and knew her near. Walt Whitman. Harrison Smith Morris. AA; DD
He was just a lonely cowboy. Cowboy Jack. *Unknown.* CoSo
He was like the Lord drunk. Alcoholic. F. D. Reeve. NYBP
He was lost!—not a shade of doubt of that. Little Lost Pup. Arthur Guiterman. BBV (1951 ed.); PCD; TreFS
He was lovelier than white birch. The Mad Lover. Speer Strahan. CAW
He was no dreamer, dwelling in a cloud. The Man of Galilee. Hildegarde Hoyt Swift. ChIP
He was no good. Somewhere. Black Jess. Peter Kane Dufault. NYBP
He was no stranger to salty tears, he. The World's Lone Lover. J. R. Perkins. ChIP
He was not bad, as emperors go, not really. Two Pieces after Suetonius. Robert Penn Warren. NoP
He was not only my friend and my lover. Second Woman's Lament [*or* Fisherman Husband]. Brenda Chamberlain. NeIP; PrWP
He Was Not Willing. Lucy R. Meyer. STF
He was now alone. The lovers had wandered across. Poet and Goldsmith. Vernon Watkins. PoCh
He was, of course, the first. End of a Fairy Tale. Jon Stallworthy. NYTB
He was of stature tall. Wordsworth. *Fr.* The Prelude, IV. SyP
He was one who followed. Sailor Man. H. Sewall Bailey. EtS
He was only a common puncher, such as the punchers were. Panhandle Cob. *At. to* H. D. Maclachlan. CoSo
He was only a lavender cowboy. The Lavender Cowboy. *Unknown.* CoSo
He was protuberant behind, before. Johnson on Pope. David Ferry. PP
He was put out of Eden. The Exile. Katherine Burton. JKCP (1955 ed.)
He was sitting on the doorstep as I went strolling by. The Road to Vagabondia. Dana Burnet. OTD
He was six years old, just six that day. A Little Boy's Vain Regret. Edith M. Thomas. AA
He was such a curious lover of shells. Full Fathom Five. A. R. D. Fairburn. AnNZ
He was Chairman of the Guild. The Meeting of the Clabberhuses. Sam Walter Foss. BOHV
He was the half-wit of that prairie town. Village Portrait. Thomas W. Duncan. MoSiPe
He was the North, the South, the East, the West. Lincoln. Maurice Thompson. PEDC
He was the player and the played upon. The Dead Musician. Charles L. O'Donnell. CAW; JKCP
He was the slave of ambition. The Mills of the Gods. *Unknown.* BLPA
He was the word that spake it. This Is My Body [*or* The Sacrament]. John Donne. OQP; TRV
He was the youngest son of a strange brood. Otto. Theodore Roethke. PoeP; ToPo
He was their servant—some say he was blind. W. H. Auden. *Fr.* In Time of War. CMoP
He was, through boyhood's storm and shower. A Dedication. G. K. Chesterton. FiBHP
He wasn't handsome or young or even clever, but oh. On Don Juan del Norte, Not Don Juan Tenorio del Sur. Alan Dugan. ErPo
He watched the spring come like a gentle maid. To One Who Died in Autumn. Virginia McCormick. HBMV
He watched the stars and noted birds in flight. W. H. Auden. *Fr.* In Time of War. CMoP

He weakened outwardly. His skin. The Death of Hoelderlin. Paul Oppenheimer. NYTB
He wears a big hat, big spurs, and all that. The Cowboy. *Unknown.* MaC; SCC
He wears a tattered coat of dreams. Love's Growing Pains. James Gallagher. JKCP (1955 ed.)
He went into the bush, and passed. The Waif. A. C. Smith. VA
He went out to their glorious/ war. The Summons. James Laughlin. ExPo; LiTA
He went so blithely on the way. The Blithe Mask. Dollett Fuguet. MaRV; TRV
He went there. Poem of the Conscripted Warrior. "Rui Nogar." TTY
He went to the wood and caught it. *Unknown.* OxNR
He went up under the gray foliage. The Garden of Olives. Rainer Maria Rilke. MoRP
He whistled soft whistlings I knew were for me. In the Park. Helen Hoyt. HBMV
He Who Ascends to Mountain-Tops. Byron. *Fr.* Childe Harold's Pilgrimage, III. OQP
(Isolation of Genius, The.) WBLP
He who binds [*or* bends] to himself a joy. Eternity [*or* Liberty *or* Unquestioning]. Blake. AnFE; AWP; BoLiVe; DiPo; EG; ERoP-1; HW; InPo; LO; LoBV; MemP; OBNC; OQP; PoG; PoIE; SoP; ShBV-4; TrGrPo
He who but yesterday would roam. Epitaph for a Sailor Buried Ashore. Sir Charles G. D. Roberts. EtS; VA
He who did most, shall bear most; the strongest shall stand the most weak. Robert Browning. *Fr.* Saul. TRV
He who died at Azan sends. After Death in Arabia. Sir Edwin Arnold. *Fr.* Pearls of the Faith. HBV; VA; WGRP
He who died on Calvary. A Thought. Margaret E. Sangster. SoP; TRV
He Who Feels Punctured. *Unknown, at. to* Lao-tzu, *tr. fr. Chinese by* Witter Bynner. *Fr.* Tao Teh King. OnPM
He who first met the Highlands' swelling blue. The Highlands' Swelling Blue. Byron. *Fr.* The Island. OBRV
He Who Forsakes the Clerkly Life. *Unknown, tr. fr. Late Middle Irish by* Standish Hayes O'Grady. *Fr.* The Life of St. Cellach of Killala. OnYI
He who had learned for thirty years to ride. The Drag-Irons. E. J. Pratt. CBV
He who has a thousand friends has not a friend to spare. Friends and Enemies [*or* From the Persian *or* Make Friends]. *At. to* Ali Ben Abu Taleb, *tr. by* Emerson. AnNE; MaRV; OnPM; OQP; TRV
He Who Has Lost All. David Diop, *tr. fr. French by* Anne Atik. TTY
He who has lost soul's liberty. Soul's Liberty. Anna Wickham. MoBrPo
He who has never known hunger. Elizabeth J. Coatsworth. TiPo
He who has no hands. Orator. Emerson. AnNE; OxBA
He who has once been happy is for aye. With Esther. Wilfrid Scawen Blunt. *Fr.* Esther. OBEV; OBMV; OBNC; OBVV; TrGrPo; ViBoPo
He who has rolled his pants up to his knee. Crossing a Creek. Herbert Clark Johnson. PoNe
He who has toiled and bought for himself books. Proverbs. Samuel ha-Nagid. TrJP
He who hath led will lead. Rest on Him [*or* The Unfailing One]. Frances Ridley Havergal. BLRP; FaChP
He Who Hath Loved. Walter Malone. AA
He who hath never warred with misery. Epistle to Henry Wriothesley, Earl of Southampton. Samuel Daniel. EnRePo
He who hung on Calvary's tree. Wondrous Son of God. Berniece Goertz. STF
He who in his pocket hath no money. Epigram. *Unknown.* HBV
He who is both brave and bold. Faint Heart Never Won Fair Lady. Vicente Espinel. OnPM
He who is the Bread of Life, began His ministry hungering. Remember. *Unknown.* SoP
He who knows not, and knows not that he knows not. Arabian Proverb [*or* He Who Knows]. *Unknown.* BLPA; GoTP; NeHB; TreF
He who knows not what thing is Paradise. Ballata of Myrrha's Eyes [*or* Three Ballate]. Angelo Poliziano. AWP; LiTW
He who learns to love his wrath. In the Mood of Blake. William Soutar. HaMV
He who looks from the outside into an open window. Prose Poem: The Windows. Baudelaire. OnPM
He Who Loves the Ocean. Mary Sinton Leitch. PoMA
He who mangold-patch doth hoe. A Purpose of Amendment. Helen Parry Eden. JKCP
He who of Rankine sang, lies stiff and dead [*or* deid]. Lines on the Author's Death [*or* On the Author]. Burns. CBEP; PV
He, who once was my brother, is dead by his own hand. Justice Is Reason Enough. Diane Wakoski. CoPo
He who plants a tree. Plant a Tree. Lucy Larcom. DD; HBVY; OHFP; PGD; WBLP
He who saved Ankoma Oh nature. Prelude to Akwasidae. *Unknown.* TTY
He who sees. The Wise. *Unknown, tr. by* Sir Edwin Arnold. *Fr.* Bhagavad-Gita. OQP
He who sits from day to day. Lines on a Bill of Mortality, 1790. William Cowper. OxBoCh
He who walks through the meadows of Champagne. The Cathedral of Rheims. Emile Verhaeren. CAW
He Who was bodiless, having heard the bidding secretly in his soul. The Akathistos Hymn. *Unknown.* ISi
He who would climb the heights of tone. Behold This Dreamer. Elizabeth Bartlett. NePoAm-2
He who would echo Horace' lays. Horace. John Osborne Sargent. AA
He who would great in science grow. The Second Ode in the Third Book of Horace, Imitated. Walter Titley. EiCL
He who would valiant be. A Pilgrim's Song. John Bunyan. *Fr.* The Pilgrim's Progress. SoP
He who writ this, not without pains and thought. Prologue to Secret Love; or, The Maiden Queen. Dryden. MBW-1; PeRV; SeCV-2; SeEP
He Whom a Dream Hath Possessed. Shaemas O'Sheel. AnIV; HBV; HBVY; JKCP; MaRV; OQP; TRV; WGRP
He whom you see to walk in so much state. The Dude. Martial. OnPM
He whose active thoughts disdain. Loves Heretick. Thomas Stanley. CavP
He will come;/ I know not when or how. The Superman. Albert Bigelow Paine. MaRV
He Will Give Them Back. "George Klingle." BLRP; SoP
He will insist on. The Bath. Joel Oppenheimer. NeAP
He Will Never Fail. H. H. Savage. SoP
He will not come, and still I wait. A Little Boy in the Morning. Francis Ledwidge. MCCG; OnYI
He Will Not Fail. *Unknown.* SoP
He Will Silently Plan for Thee. *Unknown at. to* E. Mary Grimes. SoP
(God's Plans.) BLRP
He Will Watch the Hawk. Stephen Spender. *See* Discovered in Mid-Ocean.
He willed, and Heaven's blue arch vaulted the air. The Shadows Worship. *Unknown.* OnPM
He willed to lack; He willed to bear. Mater Christi. Aubrey Thomas De Vere. *Fr.* May Carols. PoVP
He Wishes for the Cloths of Heaven. W. B. Yeats. *See* Aedh Wishes for the Cloths of Heaven.
He Wishes He Might Die and Follow Laura. Petrarch, *pr. tr. fr. Italian by* J. M. Synge. *Fr.* Sonnets to Laura: To Laura in Death. OBMV
He with body waged a fight. The Four Ages of Man. W. B. Yeats. MoRP
He wooed me sweet and he wooed me strong. Waltz. Ruth Forbes Sherry. FiSC
He Wore a Crown of Thorns. Alice Mortenson. BePJ
He wore his coffin for a hat. For a Pessimist. Countee Cullen. PoMA; ShM
He Worked. J. N. Scholes. ChIP
He would burn his books and gladly die. An Aged Writer. Roy McFadden. NeIP
He would declare and could himself believe. Never Again Would Birds' Song Be the Same. Robert Frost. CrMA; ForPo; NoP; Sonn
He Would Have His Lady Sing. Digby Mackworth Dolben. CAW; GoBC
(Heaven.) BoC
He Would Not Stay for Me. A. E. Housman. WePo
He writes from the provinces: It is. Reply to the Provinces. Galway Kinnell. NYBP
He wrote a final poem down. Then died. Lecture Note: Eli-

zabethan Period. Geoffrey Grigson. PV
He wrote in the sand . . . the wind-blown sands. Men Have Forged. Jay G. Sigmund. OQP
He Wrote to the Same Friend from Excester This Sonnet Following. George Gascoigne. ReIE
He Wrote unto a Scottish Dame Whom He Chose for His Mistress in the French Court as Followeth. George Gascoigne. ReIE
He wrote upon his heart. Inscription. Donald Jeffrey Hayes. CDC
He wrought at one great work for years. A Ballad of Heaven. John Davidson. BeLS; EnLit; PoVP; VA
He wrought with patience long and weary years. The Artist. Arthur Grissom. AA
Head and Bottle. Edward Thomas. BrPo
Head and Heart. C. D. B. Ellis. LiTM; SiTL
Head bumper. *Unknown.* OxNR
Head Byzantine or from, The. Resting Figure. Denise Levertov. TDP; ToPo
Head Couples. William H. Matchett. NYBP
Head-downward hung the bat. Viewpoints. Arthur Guiterman. UTS
Head I bear, The—the Eagle of Gal. The Lament for Urien. *Unknown. Fr.* The Red Book of Hergest. OBMV
Head in a cloud Moses stands. Moses. Sydney Tremayne. OxBS
Head, my Lord, an honourable piece, An. Meditation. Edward Taylor. *Fr.* Preparatory Meditations, Second Series. MeP
Head next to mine but turned aside, you lie. Sonnet: Head Next to Mine. Carl Bode. ToPo
Head of Medusa. Marya Zaturenska. MoAmPo
Head-Rape, The. D. M. Thomas. HYE
Head-Stone, The. William Barnes. *See* Readen ov a Head-Stwone.
Head that once was crowned with thorns, The. The Cross and the Crown [*or* The Victor]. Thomas Kelly. FaChP; MaRV; TRV
Head the ship for England! Homeward Bound. William Allingham. FaBoBe; HBV; HBVY
Head thrusts in as for the view, A. All Revelation. Robert Frost. BWP; CABA; MoPo; NePA
Headless Gardener, The. Ian Serraillier. BoC
Headless Phantoms, The. *Unknown, tr. fr. Early Modern Irish by* Eoin MacNeill. AnIL
Headless squirrel, some blood, A. A Day Begins. Denise Levertov. FRC; NaP
Headless, without an arm, a figure leans. On a Cast from an Antique. George Pellew. AA
Headlights raced; The, the moon, death-faced. The Child on the Curbstone. Elinor Wylie. OCS
Headline History. William Plomer. FOL; SiTL
Headlong Hall, *sels.* Thomas Love Peacock.
 Chorus: "Hail to the Headlong!" OBRV; PeER
 In His Last Binn Sir Peter Lies. EnRP
 (Song). OBRV; ViBoPo
Heads of strong old age are beautiful, The. Promise of Peace. Robinson Jeffers. AP; BoLiVe; CoBMV; GTBS-W; LiTA; LiTM (rev. ed.); MAP; MoAB; MoAmPo; NePA
Heads round the table disagree, The. The Trial. Dannie Abse. ACV
Headsong. Joseph Bennett. LiTM (rev. ed.); NePA
Headwaiter says, The. In This Hotel. Emanuel Carnevali. AnAmPo; NP; SiSw
Heal us, Emmanuel, here we are. Jehovah-Rophi. William Cowper. EiCP
Healed of My Hurt. Herman Melville. AmPP (5th ed.)
Healer, The. Whittier. MaRV; SoP, *abr.*
 "So stood the holy Christ," *sel.* PGD
Healin' Waters, *with music. Unknown.* ABF
Healing. Abraham Reisen, *tr. fr. Yiddish by* Joseph Leftwich. LiTW; TrJP
Healing of the Daughter of Jairus, The. Nathaniel Parker Willis. StJW
Healing of the Leper, The. Vernon Watkins. FaBoTw
Healing the Wound. Heine, *tr. fr. German by* Louis Untermeyer. UnTE
Health, A. Edward Coote Pinkney. AA; AmePo; AnAmPo; FaPL; HBV; InP; SeCePo; TreFS
Health and wealth and love he too dreamed of in May. Patrick Kavanagh. *Fr.* The Great Hunger. MoAB
Health at the Ford, A. Robert Cameron Rogers. AA; FaBoBe
Health Counsel. Sir John Harington. TreFT
Health enough to make work a pleasure. A Wish for the New Year. Phillips Brooks. STF
Health from the lover of the country, me. To Fuscus Aristus. Horace. AWP; JAWP; WBP
Health! I seek thee;—dost thou love. Robert Bloomfield. *Fr.* Shooter's Hill. OBNC
Health is a jewel, true; which when we buy. John Heath. SiCE
Health Note, A. Walter Hard. AnNE
Health of Body, Dependent on Soul. Jones Very. WGRP
Health to great Gloster—from a man unknown. The Dedication to the Sermons. Charles Churchill. QFR
Health unto His Majesty, A. *Unknown, at. to* Jeremy Savile. ChTr
 (His Majesty's Health.) SeCL
Healthy Spot, A. W. H. Auden. EnLit
Heap Cassia, Sandal-Buds and Stripes. Robert Browning. *Fr.* Paracelsus, Pt. IV. GTSL; MyFE; OBRV; PoVP
 (Song: "Heap cassia, sandal-buds, and stripes.") AnFE; OBEV; WHA
Heap high the board with plenteous cheer and gather to the feast. Thanksgiving. Alice Williams Brotherton. PGD
Heap not on this mound. Epitaph. Edna St. Vincent Millay. *Fr.* Memorial to D. C. NP
Heap of Rages, The. W. H. Davies. BrPo
Heap of stones lay at his command, A. His Passion. George Conrad Pullman. ChIP
Heap on more wood!—the wind is chill. Christmas in the Olden Time [*or* Old Christmas-Tide]. Sir Walter Scott. *Fr.* Marmion. ChBR; DD; GN; GoBC; MPB; OTPC; PCH; PoRL; PTK; SiSoSe; TiPo
Heaps on Heaps. Matthew Concanen. *Fr.* A Match at Football. SD
Hear, d'you hear? One blast. Witching Hour. Norma Farber. FiSC
Hear, Father, hear thy faint afflicted flock. Hymn of the Waldenses. Bryant. AnNE; SoP
Hear! hear! Lilian's Song. George Darley. OBNC
Hear! hear! hear! The Mocking Bird. Richard Hovey. TSW
Hear how my friend the robin sings! In the Snow. W. H. Davies. POTE
Hear, Lord, hear. The Leper Cleansed. John Collop. TrGrPo
Hear me as if thy eares had palate, Jack. An Ode in the Praise of Sack. *Unknown.* OBS
Hear me, my warriors: my heart is sick and sad. War. Chief Joseph. PGD
Hear me [*or* Heare mee], O God! A Hymn [*or* Hymne] to God the Father. Ben Jonson. AnAnS-2; EnRePo; FosPo; GoBC; MaRV; MePo; NoP; OBS; OxBoCh; ReEn; SCEP-2; SeCP; SeCV-1; TrPWD
Hear me, O hear me when I call. Psalm IV. *Paraphrased by* Sir Philip Sidney. FCP
"Hear me, ye elders, look upon me!" Gilgamesh Laments the Death of Engidu. *Unknown.* LiTW
Hear Me Yet. *Unknown.* ElL
Hear, my belovèd, an old Milesian story! Catullan Hendecasyllables. Samuel Taylor Coleridge. PoG
Hear my prayer, O Lord, hear my request. Psalm CXLIII. *Paraphrased by* Sir Thomas Wyatt. FCP
Hear my voice, Birds of War. Ojibwa War Songs. *Unknown.* AWP; JAWP; WBP
Hear, nature, hear; dear goddess, hear! King Lear Condemns His Daughter. Shakespeare. *Fr.* King Lear, I, iv. TreFT
"Hear, noble suitors! ye who throng these halls." The Return of Ulysses. Homer. *Fr.* The Odyssey, XXI. BBV (1923 ed.); OBS
Hear now, O Soul, the last command of all. The Final Mystery. Sir Henry Newbolt. WGRP
Hear now this fairy legend of old Greece. James Russell Lowell. *Fr.* Rhoecus. AA
Hear, O Israel! André Spire, *tr. fr. French by* Stanley Burnshaw. TrJP
Hear, O Israel. Shema Yisrael. *Unknown.* TrJP
Hear, O Israel, Jehovah, the Lord our God is one. Israel. Israel Zangwill. TrJP
Hear, O Israel, the commandments of life. The Path of Wisdom. Baruch, Bible, Apocrypha. TrJP
Hear, O Self-Giver, infinite as good. Thysia, XXXVII. Morton Luce. AA

Hear! O Trees that gird our camp! Taking of the Name. *Unknown, tr. fr. Omaha Indian.* PCH
Hear, Sweet Spirit. Samuel Taylor Coleridge. *See* Invocation, An: "Hear, sweet spirit."
Hear that crickley, crackley static. Static. Gertrude Van Winkle. GFA
Hear the carols. Know It Is Christmas. Lois Snelling. BiCB
Hear the fluter with his flute. The Amateur Flute. *Unknown.* Par
Hear the geysers in the highlands. Iceland's Song. Grímur Thomsen. LiTW
Hear the legend of the Admen. The Legend of the Admen. Everett W. Lord. BLPA
Hear the mellow wedding bells. Poe. *Fr.* The Bells. PoPL
Hear the sledges with the bells. The Bells. Poe. AA; AmePo; AmPP (3d ed.); BBV; CoBA; FaFP; FaPL; FaPON; GN; HBV; LiTA; NeHB; NePA; OHFP; OTPC; PCD; PCH; PG (1945 ed.); PoLF; PoPo; PTK; ShBV-1; TreF; WBLP
Hear the sound. Listen. Charles Patterson. NBP
Hear the Voice of the Bard (*Introd. to* Songs of Experience). Blake. CBEP; ELP; GTBS-D; OBEC
(Bard, The) TRV; WGRP
(Hear the Voice.) OBEV
(Introduction: "Hear the voice of the Bard!") BWP; EiPP; EnPE; EnRP; ERoP-1; LoBV; OAEP; PeER; PoEL-4; PoeP
(Introduction to "Songs of Experience.") ExPo
(Poet's Voice, The.) ChTr
Hear the Word of the Lord. Isaiah, I: 10-23, Bible, *O.T.* TrJP
Hear the word that Jesus spake. A Lost Word of Jesus. Henry Van Dyke. WGRP
Hear then what to my mind/ Deliberate thought presents. Euripides. *Fr.* Iphigenia in Aulis. EnLi-2
Hear this, O ye that would swallow the needy. O Ye That Would Swallow the Needy. Amos, Bible, *O.T.* TrJP
Hear through the morning drums and trumpets sounding. Jackson at New Orleans. Wallace Rice. DD; PAH
Hear Us, in This Thy House. Philip Doddridge. BePJ
Hear what Claudius suffered: When his wife knew he was asleep. Juvenal. *Fr.* Satires, VI. ErPo
Hear what Highland Nora said. Nora's Vow. Sir Walter Scott. BOHV
Hear, Ye Ladies [That Despise]. John Fletcher. *Fr.* The Tragedy of Valentinian. ElL; ELP; LiTG; OBEV; ViBoPo
("Hear ye ladies that despise.") OAEP
(Mighty Love.) TrGrPo
(Power of Love.) HBV; UnTE
(Song: "Heare ye Ladies that despise.") PoEL-2
Hear ye virgins, and I'll teach. To Virgins. Robert Herrick. UnTE; ViBoPo
"Hear your sovereign's proclamation." Soliloquy of a Water-Wagtail. James Montgomery. OTPC (1923 ed.)
Heard. Henry W. Frost. SoP
. . . heard him gladly. Waldere I. *Unknown.* AnOE
Heard in a Violent Ward. Theodore Roethke. ML; PoeP
Heard on the Mountain. Victor Hugo, *tr. fr. French by* Francis Thompson. AWP
"Heard say that four times four is eight." A Footnote. Stephen Spender. FaBoTw
Heard ye eer of the silly blind harper. The Lochmaben Harper. *Unknown.* ESPB; OBB
Heard ye how the bold McClellan. How McClellan Took Manassas. *Unknown.* PAH
Heard ye not yet of Captain Ferdinand? Henry Parrot. SiCE
Heard ye of Nimrud? Cities fell before him. Nimrud and the Gnat. *Unknown.* OnPM
Heard ye that thrilling word. Dirge for Ashby. Margaret Junkin Preston. PAH
Heard ye the thunder of battle. Trafalgar. Francis Turner Palgrave. BeLS; FaBoBe
Heäre, The. William Barnes. VA
Heare mee, O God! *See* Hear me, O God!
Heares non but onelie I. *Unknown.* SeCSL
Hearing: hearing: hearing. Spring Poem. Colleen Thibaudeau. TwCaPo
Hearing him, the birds came in a crowd. Saint Francis and the Birds. Roy McFadden. OxBI
Hearing how tourists, dazed with reverence. Terrible Beauty. Kingsley Amis. ErPo; NePoEA-2; PV
Hearing I ask from the holy races. The Beginning and the End [*or* Voluspo]. *Unknown.* *Fr.* The Elder Edda. AWP; LiTW
Hearing, I Saw. P. D. Cummins. MemP
Hearing Men Shout at Night on MacDougal Street. Robert Bly. CAD
Hearing of Harvests Rotting in the Valleys. W. H. Auden. MoAB; MoBrPo
(Paysage Moralisé.) LiTB
Hearing one saga, we enact the next. Remembering the 'Thirties. Donald Davie. NePoEA; PP
Hearing our voices raised. Looking On. Anthony Thwaite. NePoEA-2
Hearing Russian Spoken. Donald Davie. GTBS-P; NePoEA-2
Hearing Steps. Charles Simic. YAP
Hearing That His Friend Was Coming Back from the War. Wang Chien, *tr. fr. Chinese by* Arthur Waley. LiTW
Hearing the Early Oriole. Po Chü-i, *tr. fr. Chinese by* Arthur Waley. UnS
Hearing the Wind at Night. May Swenson. BoNaP; WIRo
Hearing your words, and not a word among them. Edna St. Vincent Millay. CMoP
Heark how she laughs aloud. Lucasta Laughing. Richard Lovelace. PoEL-3
Heark, how the birds do sing. *See* Hark, how the birds . . .
Heark [*or* Hark] how the mower Damon sung. Damon the Mower. Andrew Marvell. AnAnS-1; BWP; MaMe; SCEP-2
Heark, my Flora! Love doth call us. A Song of Dalliance. William Cartwright. ALV
Hearke, Now Everything Is Still. John Webster. *See* Hark, Now Everything Is Still.
Hearken!—now the hermit bee. The Quiet Enemy. Walter de la Mare. BrPo; CMoP
Hearken the stirring story. The Fall of Maubila. Thomas Dunn English. PAH
Hearken, thou craggy ocean pyramid! To Ailsa Rock. Keats. EnRP; OBNC
Hearken to me, gentlemen. King Estmere. *Unknown.* BuBa; ESBP; OBB; OxBB
Hears Not My Phillis, How the Birds. Sir Charles Sedley. CavP
(Knotting Song, The.) SeCL
(Phillis Knotting.) OBS
(Song: "Hears not my Phillis [*or* Phyllis] how the birds.") EnLoPo; SeCV-2; SeEP
Hearse Song, The *Unknown.* ABF, *with music*; AS (A *and* B *vers.*); DTC; OxBoLi
Hearse was the oven of the crematory, The. The Funeral. "M. J." TrJP
Hear'st thou, my soul, what serious things. Dies Irae. Thomas of Celano, *tr. by* Richard Crashaw. AWP; MaMe; OuHeWo
Heart. Coleman Barks. *Fr.* Body Poems. QAH
Heart. MacKnight Black. AnAmPo
Heart, The. Stephen Crane. *See* In the Desert.
Heart, The. Michael Drayton. SeEP
Heart, The. Harvey Shapiro. HoPM
Heart, The. Jacob Steinberg, *tr. fr. Hebrew by* Harry H. Fein. TrJP
Heart, The, *sels.* Francis Thompson.
"Heart you hold too small, The," I. OBMV
"O nothing, in this corporal earth of man," Ii. AnFE; BoLiVe; MemP; OBMV
(All's Vast.) MoAB; MoBrPo; Sonn
(Correlated Greatness.) GTBS-P
Heart, The. *Unknown, ad. fr. French by* Louis Untermeyer. MaC
Heart-affluence in discursive talk. In Memoriam A. H. H., CIX. Tennyson. EPN; ViPo; VP
Heart and Mind. Edith Sitwell. AtBAP; ChMP; FaBoTW; GTBS-D; MoPo; OAEP (2d ed.); Po; TwCP
Heart and service to you proffered, The. Sir Thomas Wyatt. FCP; SiPS
Heart and Will. William James Linton. VA
Heart asks pleasure first, The. Emily Dickinson. AmPP (5th ed.); AnNE; AP; CBEP; CMoP; InPo; MAP; MoAB; MoAmPo; NoP; OnPM; OxBA; PoIE; PoSa; TrGrPo
Heart can set its boundaries, The. Boundaries. Jessica Powers. JKCP (1955 ed.)
Heart Exchange. Sir Philip Sidney. *See* My True Love Hath My Heart.
Heart for All Her Children. Albert J. Hebert, Jr. ISi
Heart free, hand free. Sic Vita. William Stanley Braithwaite. BANP; OQP

Heart Has Its Reasons, The. *Unknown.* GoBC
Heart, Have No Pity on This House of Bone. Edna St. Vincent Millay. AmPP
Heart-Hurt. *Unknown.* TreFT
Heart-Hushings. *Unknown.* SoP
Heart in Brahma, The. Bhartrihari, *tr. fr. Sanskrit by* Paul Elmer More. OnPM
Heart Is a Strange Thing, The. Minnie Case Hopkins. OQP
Heart Is Bethlehem, The. Gertrude Hanson. ChIP
Heart is cold that has not chilled, The. Gilead. Mary Brennan Clapp. OQP
Heart Is Deep, The. Roger Wolcott. SCAP
Heart, it is time. The fruitful summer yields. Autumn. Rainer Maria Rilke, *tr. by* James McAuley. MoAuPo
Heart Knoweth Its Own Bitterness, The. Aline Kilmer. NP
Heart leaps with the pride of their story, The. The Fleet at Santiago. Charles E. Russell. MC; PAH
Heart longs for a pickax, The. Wintering in the Heartlands. William Hunt. YAP
Heart Looks On, The. Leonora Speyer. NP
Heart must always come again to home. The Heart's Wild Geese. Henry Treece. WaP
Heart of a Child, The. *Unknown.* SoP
Heart of a Girl Is a Wonderful Thing, The. *Unknown.* BLPA
Heart of a Woman, The. Georgia Douglas Johnson. BANP; CDC; PoLF; PoNe
Heart of All the Scene, The. Emerson. *Fr.* Woodnotes, I. AA
Heart of Earth, let us be gone. Song of the Wulfshaw Larches. Ernest Rhys. VA
Heart of flaming sulphur, flesh of tow, A. Beauty and the Artist. Michelangelo. PoFr
Heart of God, The. W. E. Littlewood. BePJ
Heart of Light. David Campbell. BoAV
Heart of Light, The. Winifred Welles. NP
Heart of Midlothian, The, *sels.* Sir Walter Scott.
  Proud Maisie, *fr. ch.* 38. AtBAP; CBEP; CH; ChTr; CoBE; EnLi-2; EnLit; EnRP; EPN; ERoP-1; GoTS; GTSL; HBV; ILP; InP; LoBV; NBM; OAEP; OBEV; OBRV; OTPC (1923 ed.); OxBS; PoE; PoEL-4; PoPo; SeCePo; SeCeV; ShBV-1; StP; TrGrPo; UnPo
    (Madge Wildfire Sings.) OBNC
    (Pride of Youth.) GTBS; GTBS-D; GTBS-P; GTBS-W
    ("Proud Maisie is in the wood.") EG; FaBoCh; LoGBV
Heart of My Heart. *Unknown.* HBV
Heart of my heart, the world is young. Unity. Alfred Noyes. HBV; InP
Heart of Oak. David Garrick. HBV; OBEC; OxBoLi
Heart of Oak. Charles Henry Luders. AA
Heart of the city. The Market. Gary Snyder. *Fr.* Mts. & Rivers. CoPo
Heart-of-the-Daybreak. Eugene Marais, *tr. fr. Afrikaans by* Jack Cope and Uys Krige. PeSA
Heart of the Eternal, The. Frederick W. Faber. *See* There's a Wideness in God's Mercy.
Heart of the Night, The. Dante Gabriel Rossetti. The House of Life, LXVI. EPN; MaVP; PoVP; TOP; ViPo
Heart of the soft, wild rose. Two Questions. William Stanley Braithwaite. BALP
Heart of the Tree, The. H. C. Bunner. DD; HH; OHFP; OHIP; OQP; OTD; PGD
Heart of the Woman, The. W. B. Yeats. GTSL; POTE
Heart of the Woods. Wesley Curtright. GoSl; PoNe
Heart of the World, The. Nahman of Bratzlav, *tr. fr. Yiddish by* Joseph Leftwich. TrJP
Heart on the Hill, The. Petrarch, *tr. fr. Italian by* C. B. Cayley. Sonnets to Laura: To Laura in Life, CCV. AWP
Heart oppress'd with desperate thought. Sir Thomas Wyatt. SiPS
Heart Prayer. Enola Chamberlin. SoP
Heart Recalcitrant, The. Leonora Speyer. PG
Heart shall not be satisfied, The. Fellow-creatures. Ruth Pitter. NYTB
Heart soars up like a bird, The. The Flight of the Heart. Dora Read Goodale. AA
Heart speaks and you are spooked, A. Diamond. Michael Brownstein. YAP
Heart Specialist. Elias Lieberman. ImOP
Heart-summoned. Jesse Stuart. FiSC; GoYe
Heart That Weeps, A. Oswald J. Smith. SoP; STF
Heart to Carry On, The. Bertram Warr. PeCV
Heart to Praise Thee, A. George Herbert. *See* Our Prayer.
Heart, we will forget him! Emily Dickinson. AA; LiTL; ViBoPo
Heart Wish. Henry W. Frost. SoP
Heart Wounds. Claire Richcreek Thomas. PoToHe (new ed.)
Heart you hold too small and local thing, The. The Heart. Francis Thompson. OBMV
Heartbeat of Democracy. Virginia Brasier. StVeCh (1955 ed.)
Heart-Break. Henry W. Frost. SoP
Heartbreak House. Patric Dickinson. POTi
Heartbreak Road. Helen Gray Cone. HBMV
Hearth. Peggy Bacon. FaPON; MPB
Hearth of Urien, The. Llywarch the Aged, *tr. fr. Welsh by* William Barnes. ChTr
Hearth Song. Robert Underwood Johnson. YeAr
Hearthside Story. X. J. Kennedy. CoPo
Hearthstone. Harold Monro. OBMV
  (At Home, Alone with the Dog.) BoC
Heart's Anchor, The. William Winter. PoToHe
Hearts and Lace Paper. *Unknown.* PCH
  (Flower Tokens.) RIS
  ("Lilies are white,/Rosemary's green.") BoTP; OxNR
Hearts are pumping, The—feel!—the air. Air Shaft. Ian Healy. Poems from the Coalfields, I. PoAu-2
Heart's Compass. Dante Gabriel Rossetti. The House of Life, XXVII. EPN; MaVP; Po; PoVP; ViPo; VP; WHA
Heart's Content. *Unknown.* HBV; OTPC (1923 ed.); PoLF
Heart's Country, The. Florence Wilkinson Evans. FaChP
Hearts Courageous. John Oxenham. MaRV
Heart's Desire. Omar Khayyám, *tr. by* Edward Fitzgerald. *Fr.* The Rubáiyát. MeWo
Hearts's Desire. John Peter. BoSA
Heart's Desire Is Full of Sleep, The. Ruth Pitter. BoPe
Heart's-Ease. Walter Savage Landor. EnRP; VA
Heart's-ease, an herb that sometimes hath been seen. On His Mistress' Garden of Herbs. *Unknown.* SeCL
Hearts good and true. Written in a Little Lady's Little Album. Frederick William Faber. HBV; HBVY
Heart's Haven. Kendall Banning. MaRV
Heart's Haven. Dante Gabriel Rossetti. The House of Life, XXII. EPN; MaVP; OAEP; PoVP; Sonn; ViPo; VP
Heart's Hope. Dante Gabriel Rossetti. The House of Life, V. EnLit; EPN; HBV; MaVP; PoVP; ViPo; VP
Hearts, like Doors. *Unknown.* OTPC; PPL
  ("Hearts, like doors, will open with ease.") OxNR
  (Politeness.) PCH
  (Rules of Behavior.) HBV; HBVY
Heart's Low Door, The. Susan Mitchell. HBMV
Heart's Music. *Unknown.* OBEV (new ed.)
Heart's Needle. W. D. Snodgrass. CoPo
  Sels.
  "Child of my winter, born," I. AmPC; MoAmPo (1962 ed.); PIA
  "Easter has come around," VI. AmPC; NePoEA; NMP; OPoP; PIA
  "Here in the scuffled dust," VII. NePoEA; NMP; OPoP
  "I get numb and go in," IX. AmPC; PIA
  "I thumped on you the best I could," VIII. NePoEA
  "Late April and you are three; today," II. NePoEA; PIA
  "No one can tell you why," IV. NePoEA; PIA
  "Vicious winter finally yields, The." X. AmPC; NePoEA; PIA
  "Winter again and it is snowing," V. AmPC; AP; NoP
Heart's Not Yet a Neighbour, The. Mary Fullerton. NeLNL
Hearts of the everlasting-flowers, The. By Momba Tracks. Roderic Quinn. NeLNL
Heart's Poverty. Gloria T. Stein. JKCP (1955 ed.)
Hearts Proof, The. James Buckham. BLRP; OQP; WBLP
Heart's Summer, The. Epes Sargent. AA
Hearts Were Made to Give Away. Annette Wynne. PoRL; TiPo (1959 ed.)
Heart's Wild-Flower. William Vaughn Moody. TOP
Heart's Wild Geese, The. Henry Treece. WaP
Heartsearch. Evelyn K. Gibson. STF
Heat. Anacreon, *tr. fr. Greek by* Abraham Cowley. UnTE
Heat. Hilda Doolittle ("H. D."). The Garden, II. AP; CMoP; MAP; MoAmPo; NeMA; OxBA; PoIE; PoPo; TSW; UnPo; WHA
Heat. John Gould Fletcher. *Fr.* Down the Mississippi, II. HT; LiTA; NP
Heat. Archibald Lampman. CaP; OBCV; PeCV; VA
Heat. Kenneth Mackenzie. PoAu-2
Heat, The. Gertrude Stein. AtBAP

Heat and burden of the day. Prayer on Entering Church. Bertha Gerneaux Woods. SoP
Heat is past that did me fret, The. The Lover Deceived by His Lady's Unconstancy Writeth unto Her as Followeth [*or* A Farewell to a Fondling]. Thomas Churchyard. EIL; ReIE; TuPP
Heat the furnace hot. To the New Men. John Davidson. EPN; PoVP; TOP
Heated Minutes, The. Louis MacNeice. CBV
Heath, The. Thomas Boyd. OnYI
Heathen and the Infants, The. Michael Wigglesworth. *Fr.* The Day of Doom. AmPP (3d ed.)
Heathen Are Come into Thine Inheritance, The. Psalms, LXXIX, Bible, *O.T.* TrJP
Heathen Chinee, The. Bret Harte. *See* Plain Language from Truthful James.
Heathen Hymn, A. Sir Lewis Morris. MaRV
"I praise Thee not, with impious pride, *sel.* TrPWD
Heathen Pass-ee, The. A. C. Hilton. CenHV
Heather, The. Steen Steensen Blicher, *tr. fr. Danish by* Charles Wharton Stork. LiTW
Heather, The. Neil Munro. OBVV
Heather Ale. Robert Louis Stevenson. AnEnPo; ShBV-1; VA
Heave at the windlass!—Heave O, cheerly, men! Windlass Song. William Allingham. BBV (1923 ed.); GN; OTPC
Heave Away, 2 *versions, with music. Unknown.* ShS
Heave Away ("Heave away, heave away, I'd rather court a yellow gal"), *with music. Unknown.* ABF; AS; TrAS
Heave Away (We're All Bound to Go), *with music. Unknown.* SoAmSa
(We're All Bound to Go.) AmSS, *diff. vers.*
Heave away, Rio! Rio Grande, *vers.* I. *Unknown.* ShS
Heave of mighty shoulders to the yoke, A. A Yoke of Steers. DuBose Heyward. NP
Heaven. Sir Henry William Baker. SoP
Heaven. Martha Dickinson Bianchi. AA; HBV
Heaven. Rupert Brooke. AnFE; BrPo; EPN; ExPo; GTBS-D; GTBS-W; HoPM; ILP; LiTB; LiTM; MemP; MoBrPo; PoE; PoRA; POTE; SeCeV; SiTL; TOP; WaKn; WGRP
(Fishes' Heaven.) ShBV-4
Heaven. Cynewulf. *Fr.* Christ. PoLi
Heaven. Digby Mackworth Dolben. *See* He Would Have His Lady Sing.
Heaven. Edwin Hatch. MaRV
Heaven. George Herbert. AnAnS-1; BoLiVe; MaMe; MeP; SeCP; TrGrPo
Heaven. Oliver Wendell Holmes. *See* Faith Shall Build a Fairer Throne.
Heaven. Langston Hughes. *See* Heaven; the City Called Heaven.
Heaven. Philip Levine. NaP
Heaven. John Milton. *Fr.* Paradise Lost, III. OBS
Heaven ("Heaven is closed"). *Unknown, par. fr. German by* Louis Untermeyer. UnTE
Heaven ("Think of—/ Stepping on shore"). *Unknown.* PoLF
Heaven. Clarence A. Vincent. OQP
Heaven. Isaac Watts. SoP; WGRP
(Prospect of Heaven Makes Death Easy, A.) EiCL; EiPP; NoP; OBEC
("There is a land of pure delight.") ELP
Heaven above is softer blue. Possession. Wade Robinson. BLRP; FaChP; SoP; TRV
Heaven and Earth. James I, King of England. ChTr
(Sonnet: "Azured vault, the crystal circles bright, The.") EIL; SeCePo
Heaven and Earth. Frederic Thompson. CAW
Heaven and earth and all that hear me plain. A Protest. Sir Thomas Wyatt. FCP; OBSC; SiPS
Heaven and Hell. Omar Khayyám. *See* Soul Is All, The.
Heaven and Hell. James Kenneth Stephen. CenHV
Heaven from all creatures hides the book of fate. *See* Heav'n from all creatures hides. . .
Heaven has different signs to me. Emily Dickinson. PoIE
Heaven hath no rage like love to hatred turned. William Congreve. *Fr.* The Mourning Bride, III, viii. TreF
Heaven-Haven. Gerard Manley Hopkins. ACP; BoLiVe; BrPo; CaFP; CAW; CoBE; DiPo; EnL; EnLi-2; FaBoEn; GoBC; ILP; LoBV; MemP; MoAB; MoBrPo; NeMA; OAEP; OBEV (new ed.); OBNC; PoeP; PoSa; PoVP; TrGrPo; ViBoPo; VP; WaKn; WePo
(Nun Takes the Veil, A.) BoPe
Heaven in My Hand. Raymond Kresensky. OQP
Heaven is/ The place where. Heaven; the City Called Heaven. Langston Hughes. GoSl; TiPo
Heaven is a fine place, a fine place entirely. In a Low Rocking-Chair. Helen Coale Crew. HBMV
Heaven is closed, proclaims the preacher. Heaven. *Unknown.* UnTE
Heaven Is Heaven. Christina Rossetti. *See* Skylark and Nightingale.
Heaven is in my hand, and I. A Blackbird Suddenly. Joseph Auslander. MaRV; MPB; PoRL; RePo; TiPo
Heaven is lovelier than the stars. Driftwood. Trumbull Stickney. HBV
Heaven is mirrored, Love, deep in thine eyes. Aidenn. Katrina Trask. AA
Heaven Is Not Far. Christina Rossetti. OxBoCh
Heaven is not reached at a single bound. Gradatim. Josiah Gilbert Holland. DD; FaFP; HBV; HBVY; MaRV; OHFP; OQP; TIHL; TreFS; WGRP
Heaven is open every day. The Way to Heaven. Charles Goodrich Whiting. AA
Heaven is what I cannot reach! Emily Dickinson. AnNE; MAmP
Heaven, O Lord, I Cannot Lose. Edna Dean Proctor. AA
Heaven of Animals, The. James Dickey. AP; CoAP; FRC; LiTM (1970 ed.); ToPo
Heaven Overarches [Earth and Sea]. Christina Rossetti. HBV
Heaven shall forgive you bridge at dawn. Ballade d'une Grande Dame. G. K. Chesterton. OxBoLi
Heaven sinc thou art the only place of rest. *Unknown.* SeCSL
Heaven: the City Called Heaven. Langston Hughes. GoSl (Heaven). TiPo
Heaven Tree. Henry Morton Robinson. JKCP (1955 ed.)
Heaven, which man's generations draws. Epilogue. Francis Thompson. *Fr.* A Judgment in Heaven. MoAB; MoBrPo
Heaven Will Protect the Working Girl. Edgar Smith. FaFP; TreF
"You may tempt the upper classes," *sel.* FiBHP
Heaven won't have to do with its multitudes. The Saints. Robert Creeley. NMP
Heavenborn Helen, Sparta's queen. Troy Town. Dante Gabriel Rossetti. MaVP; PoVP; ViPo; ViPP; VP
Heavenlie Visitor, A. *Unknown. See* Yet If His Majesty, Our Sovereign Lord.
Heavenly Aid. Spenser. *See* Guardian Angels.
Heavenly Archer, bend thy bow. Dust to Dust. Walter de la Mare. TrPWD
Heavenly Banquet, The. *At. to* St. Bridget. *See* Feast of Saint Brigid of Kildare, The.
Heavenly bay, ringed round with cliffs and moors, The. In Guernsey. Swinburne. ATP (1935 ed.); PoVP
Heavenly Breeze, The. George Burgess. BePJ
Heavenly City, The. Stevie Smith. FaBoTw
Heavenly City, The. *Unknown. See* New Jerusalem, The.
Heavenly Father, bless this food. Table Graces, or Prayers. *Unknown.* BLRP
"Heavenly Father," take to thee. Emily Dickinson. AmePo; PoEL-5; PoIE
Heavenly frame sets forth the fame, The. Psalm XIX. *Paraphrased by* Sir Philip Sidney. FCP
Heavenly Friend, A. Paul Tucker. BePJ
Heavenly Grass. Tennessee Williams. PoPl
Heavenly Humor, The. David Shapiro. ANYP
Heavenly Jerusalem, The. Giles Fletcher. *Fr.* Christ's Victory and Triumph. OxBoCh
Heavenly Pilot, The. Cormac, *tr. fr. Old Irish by* George Sigerson. *Fr.* Book of Leinster. CAW; OnYI
Heavenly Rhetoric, The. Shakespeare. *See* Did Not the Heavenly Rhetoric of Thine Eye.
Heavenly Stranger, The. Ada Blenkhorn. BLRP
Heavenly Tree Grows Downward, The. Gerrit Lansing. CoPo
Heavenly Vision, The. Avis B. Christiansen. SoP
Heavens, The. Psalms, XIX, Bible, *O.T. See* Heavens Declare the Glory of God, The.
Heavens, The. Joseph Addison. *See* Spacious Firmament on High, The.
Heavens Above and the Law Within, The. Psalms, XIX, Bible, *O.T. See* Heavens Declare the Glory of God, The.

Heaven's angry face is scowling, The. Winter Evening. Pushkin. WoL
Heavens Are Our Riddle. Herbert Bates. AA
Heavens are the mind of God, the systems are His word, The. Omnipresence. Stanton A. Coblentz. MaRV
Heavens are wroth—the thunder's rattling peal, The. Written in a Thunderstorm. John Clare. ERoP-2
Heavens bright lamp, shine forth some of thy light. George Alsop. SCAP
"Heavens Declare the Glory of God, The." Helen Steiner Rice. FaChP
Heavens Declare the Glory of God, The. Psalms, XIX, Bible, *O.T.* FaPON (1-3); MaRV (1-6); PoG; TreF; TRV
(Glory of God, The.) TrJP
(God's Glory.) TrGrPo
(Heavens, The, 1-4.) ChTr
(Heavens Above and the Law Within, The, *Moulton, Modern Reader's Bible.*) WGRP
(Heavens Declare, The.) ShBV-1
("Heavens doe declare, The," Bay Psalm Book.) SCAP
(Nineteenth Psalm.) WBLP
(Psalm XIX.) AWP; InP (1-4); JAWP; OuHeWo; WoL
Heavens Declare Thy Glory, Lord, The. Isaac Watts. TreFT
(Thy Word.) SoP
Heavens first in tune I'll set, The. Love Sets Order in the Elements. Thomas Nabbes. *Fr.* Microcosmus. UnS
Heaven's Last Best Work. Pope. *Fr.* Moral Essays, Epistle II. OBEC
Heaven's Magnificence. William Augustus Muhlenberg. AA
Heaven's mercy shines, wonders and glorys meet. The Mercies of the Year. John Danforth. SCAP
Heaven's Mould, The. William Cavendish, Duke of Newcastle. LO; SeCL
Heaven's power is infinite: earth, air, and sea. Baucis and Philemon. Ovid. *tr. by* Dryden. *Fr.* Metamorphoses. WoL
Heavens rejoyce in motion, why shoud I, The. Variety. John Donne. Elegies, XVII. MaMe
Heavens themselves, the planets and this center, The. On Degree. Shakespeare. *Fr.* Troilus and Cressida, I, iii. ExPo; ImOP
Heavens! what a goodly prospect spreads around. Happy Britannia. James Thomson. *Fr.* The Seasons: Summer. OBEC; SeCePo
Heavenward. Lady Nairne. HBV
Heavier the Cross. Benjamin Schmolke, *tr. fr. German.* BePJ
Heaviest Cross of All, The. Katherine Eleanor Conway. AA; JKCP
Heaviest of Flowers, the Head. Philip Larkin. ToPo
Heaving Roses of the Hedge Are Stirred, The. Richard Watson Dixon. CH
(Winter Will Follow.) GTBS-D; GTBS-P
Heaving the Lead. *At. to* J. [*or* W.] Pearce *and to* Charles Dibdin. EtS
(By the Deep Nine.) ChTr
(Leadsman's Song, The. HBV
Heav'n and beautye are aly'de. *Unknown.* SeCSL
Heav'n Boun' Soldier, *with music. Unknown.* BoAN-1
Heav'n from all creatures hides the book of fate. Hope Springs Eternal. Pope. *Fr.* An Essay on Man, Epistle I. OBEC; ViBoPo
Heavy Bear Who Goes with Me, The. Delmore Schwartz. The Repetitive Heart, IX. AmLP; AnAmPo; CBV; CrMA; FiMAP; LiTA; LiTG; LiTM; MiAP; MoPo; MoVE; NePA; PIA; ReMP; TrJP; TwCP; UnPo (3d ed.)
Heavy bus slows, New York my ride. Edwin Denby. ANYP
Heavy carnations and the small ancestral pinks. The Feel of Fineness. John Hazard Wildman. NYTB
Heavy cart rumbles, A. Kuroyanagi Shoha, *tr. fr. Japanese by* Geoffrey Bownas *and* Anthony Thwaite. FIW
Heavy contact now is o'er, The. War Poem. Richard West. FOL
Heavy glacier and the terrifying Alps, The. Long Lines. Paul Goodman. NMP
Heavy hangs the raindrop. The Two Children [*or* A. E]. Emily Brontë. NBM; PoEL-5
Heavy-hearted. Judah Al-Harizi, *tr. fr. Hebrew.* TrJP
Heavy Heavy Heavy. John Malcolm Brinnin. NYBP
Heavy heavy lies over our head. Game Out of Hand. Allison Ross. GoYe
Heavy hours are almost past, The. Song. George Lyttelton. WaPE
Heavy-hipted Woman, The, *with music. Unknown.* ABF
Heavy mists have crept away, The. Mark. Ernest McGaffey. AA
Heavy of heart and light of purse. Ditty. William Gibson. NYTB
Heavy smells of Spring, The. Jack. Louis Golding. TrJP
Heavy sounds are over-sweet, The. City-Storm. Harold Monro. MoBrPo
Heavy with length of days, summer continues. The Visitor. Michael Goldman. WIRo
Heavy yellow spider, The. Street. Alan Brown. TwCaPo
Hebe. James Russell Lowell. AA; AnFE; AnNE; APA; CoAnAm; HBV
Hebrew girl, with flaming brow, The. Magdalen. James Ryder Randall. JKCP
Hebrew Melodies, *sels.* Heine, *tr. fr. German.*
By the Waters of Babylon, *tr. by* Charles Godfrey Leland. TrJP
Come, O Friend, to Greet the Bride, *after the Hebrew of* Solomon Halevi Alkabez, *tr. by* Louis Untermeyer. TrJP
Hebrews, *sel.* Bible, *N.T.*
Evidence, The, XI: 1. TRV
Hebrews. James Oppenheim. MAP; MoAmPo (1942 ed.); TrJP
Hecatomb to His Mistress, The. John Cleveland. AnAnS-2
Hecatompathia; or, Passionate Century of Love, *sels.* Thomas Watson.
Come Gentle Death! EIL; SiCE
If Cupid Were a Child. TuPP
"Love is a sour delight, a sug'red grief." ReIE
"My heart is set him down, twixt hope and fears." ReIE
My Love Is Past. TuPP
(Here Lieth Love.) EIL
(Love's Grave.) OBSC
Some That Report. TuPP
"Time wasteth years, and months, and hours." SiCE
(Time.) OBSC
To the Author. *By* George Peele. ReIE
"When first these eyes beheld with great delight." ReIE
"Where tender love had laid him down to sleep." ReIE
"Ye stately dames, whose beauties far excel." ReIE
"Ye captive souls of blindfold Cyprian's boat."
(My Love Is Past.) ReIE
Hector. Valentin Iremonger. NeIP; OxBI
Hector and Andromache. Homer. *See* Parting of Hector and Andromache, The.
Hector Protector was dressed all in green. Mother Goose. HBV; HBVY; MoShBr; OTPC; OxNR; RIS
Hector, the captain bronzed, from single fight. Geoffrey Scott. *Fr.* The Skaian Gate. OBMV
Hector to Andromache. Homer. *See* Parting of Hector and Andromache, The.
He'd had enough of lying in the furze. The Ghostly Father. Peter Redgrove. MoBS; NePoEA-2
He'd have given me rolling lands. The Choice. Dorothy Parker. BoLP
He'd have the best, and that was none too good. The Very Rich Man. Dorothy Parker. PoPo
He'd never married, so when he got sick. Only the Moonlight. Paul Engle. TDP
He'd never wrung the. Husband, The. Barbara L. Greenberg. QAH
He'd Nothing but His Violin. Mary Kyle Dallas. AA, *abr.*; HBV
He'd play, after the bawdy songs and blues. When de Saints Go Ma'chin' Home. Sterling A. Brown. AmNP
He'd take a human life as soon as he would take a drink. A Tough Cuss from Bitter Creek. James Barton Adams. PoOW
Hedge between, A/ Keeps friendship green. Country Proverbs. *Unknown.* StaSt
Hedge of trees surrounds me, A. The Scribe. *Unknown.* AnIL OnYI
Hedge Schoolmasters, The. Seumas MacManus. CAW
Hedgehog, The. John Clare. *Fr.* The Shepherd's Calendar. OA; SeCeV
Hedgehog, The. Edith King. BoTP
Hedgehog and His Coat, The. Elizabeth Fleming. BoTP
Hedgehog, from his hollow root, The. The Hedgehog. John Clare. *Fr.* The Shepherd's Calendar. OA

Hedgehog hides beneath the rotten hedge, The. The Hedgehog. John Clare. SeCeV
Hedgehog is a little beast, The. The Hedgehog. Edith King. BoTP
Hedge-Row Story, The. Lilian Bowes-Lyon. POTE
Hedgerows are wiser than I, The. Easter Thought. Leo Cox. CaP
Hee ended, or I heard no more, for now. The Creation of Woman. Milton. *Fr.* Paradise Lost, VIII. PeRV
Hee That Loves a Rosie Cheeke. Thomas Carew. *See* Disdain Returned.
Hee that would write an epitaph for thee. An Epitaph on Doctor Donne, Deane of Pauls. Richard Corbett. AnAnS-2
Heed the old oracles. The Undersong. Emerson. *Fr.* Woodnotes, II. AA
Heedless she strayed from note to note. The Waiting Chords. Stephen Henry Thayer. AA
Heedless that now the mists of spring arise. Wild Geese. Ise. OnPM
Heeeyyysoouul/ siss-ters. This Poem for Black Women. Reginald Lockett. BF
Heere is better then the open ayre, take it thankfully. Shakespeare. *Fr.* King Lear, III, vi. AtBAP
Hegel. LeRoi Jones. CoPo
Hegemon to Praxinoe. Walter Savage Landor. PeEr
Heigh! brother mine, art a-waking or a-sleeping? Les Belles Roses sans Mercie. Arthur Shearly Cripps. OBVV
Heigh Ho! Jean Ingelow. *See* Seven Times Four.
Heigh-ho, April! Eleanor Farjeon. PoRh
Heigh ho! daisies and buttercups. Seven Times Four [*or* Maternity *or* Heigh Ho!]. Jean Ingelow. *Fr.* Songs of Seven. GBV (1922 ed.); HBV; OHIP
Heigh ho! my heart is low. *Unknown.* OxNR
Heigh-ho on a Winter Afternoon. Donald Davie. NePoEA-2
Heigh-ho, what shall a shepheard doe. James Shirley. *Fr.* The Triumph of Beautie Song. ErPo
Heigh in the hevynnis figure circulere. The Kingis Quair. James I, King of Scotland. OxBS
Heigh-o, weigh-o. *Unknown.* ThGo
"Heigho," yawned one day King Francis. The Glove. Robert Browning. PoVP; StP
Height of the highest mountain, The. My Saviour's Love for Me. William C. Fisher. SoP
Height of the Ridiculous, The. Oliver Wendell Holmes. AA; ALV; AmePo; AnNE; BBV (1951 ed.); BOHV; FaFP; FiBHP; HBV; LHV; MCCG; MoShBr; MPB; NeHB; OTD; OTPC (1946 ed.); PoPl; SiTL; StVeCh; TreFT; WhC; YaD
Heights, The. Longfellow. *Fr.* The Ladder of St Augustine. TreF
Heilige Nacht. Joseph Mohr. *See* Silent Night.
Heimdall. Harold Vinal. FiSC
Heimkehr, Die, *sels.* Heine, *tr. fr. German by* Ezra Pound.
"Multilated choir boys, The." AWP
(Choir Boys, The.) LiTW
"Tell me where thy lovely love is." AWP
"This delightful young man." AWP
Heine's Grave. Matthew Arnold. PoVP
Heinrich Heine. Ludwig Lewisohn. TrJP
Heir and Serf. Don Marquis. HBMV
Heir of Linne, The. *Unknown.* BaBo; BuBa; ESPB (A *and* B *vers.*); OBB
Heir of Vironi, The, *sel.* Isaac Pocock.
Song: "Oh! say not woman's love [*or* heart] is bought." HBV (8th ed.)
Heiress and Architect. Thomas Hardy. PoVP; ViPo (1962 ed.)
Heirloom. A. M. Klein. OBCV; PeCV; TrJP
Heirs of great yesterdays, be proud with me. To My Countrymen. Robert Underwood Johnson. OQP
Hektor and Andromache. Homer. *See* Parting of Hector and Andromache, The.
Hektor to Andromache. Homer. *See* Parting of Hector and Andromache, The.
Hélas! Oscar Wilde. AnIV; BrPo; GTSL; MoBrPo; PoVP; Sonn; UnTE; ViPP
Held on the slightest of bamboo poles. Ode to the Chinese Paper Snake. Richard Eberhart. CrMA
Helen. "Susan Coolidge." AA
Helen. Hilda Doolittle ("H. D."). FaBoTw; LiTM (1970 ed.); MAP; MoAmPo; MoVE
Helen, *sel.* Euripides, *tr. fr. Greek.*
"Soul of the deceased, although it live, The." MaRV
Helen. Mary Lamb. *Fr.* John Woodvil; a Tragedy (*by* Charles Lamb). OBRV
Helen. Christopher Marlowe. *See* Was This the Face.
Helen. Edward A. U. Valentine. AA
Helen and Corythos. Walter Savage Landor. *Fr.* Corythos. LoBV
Helen and Hermia. Shakespeare. *Fr.* A Midsummer-Night's Dream, III, ii. GN
Helen Grown Old. Janet Lewis. QFR
Helen, had I known yesterday. Release. D. H. Lawrence. CMoP
Helen Hunt Jackson. Ina Donna Coolbrith. AA
Helen Keller. Edmund Clarence Stedman. AA
Helen of Kirconnell [*or* Kirkconnell]. *Unknown.* AnFE; AWP; BBV (1923 ed.); CBEP; CH; ELP; GoTS; HBV; ILP; InPo; LiTB; LiTG; LoBV; MemP; OBB; OBEV; SeCeV; TreFT; UnPo (1st ed.)
(Fair Helen.) FaFP; GBV (1922 ed.); GTBS; GTBS-D; GTBS-P; GTBS-W; GTSE; GTSL; INP; LiTL; ViBoPo; WePo
("Fair Helen of Kirconnel.") OTPC
Helen of Troy. Shakespeare. *Fr.* Troilus and Cressida, IV, i. TreFT
Helen of Tyre. Longfellow. SiSw
Helen—Old. Isabel Ecclestone Mackay. CaP
Helen, the Sad Queen. Paul Valéry, *tr. fr. French by* Joseph T. Shipley. AWP; CAW; JAWP; WBP
(Hélène, *tr. by* Janet Lewis.) Po
Helen, thy beauty is to me. To Helen. Poe. AA; AmePo; AmP; AmPP; AnAmPo; AnFE; AP; APA; AtBAP; ATP; AWP; BoLiVe; BoLP; CABA; CaFP; CBEP; CBV; CH; ChTr; CLwM; CoAnAm; CoBA; DD; EG; ExPo; FaBoBe; FaBoEn; FaBV; FaFP; FaPL; GTBS-D; GTBS-W; GTSE; HBV; HBVY; HoPM; ILP; InP; InPo; InvP; JAWP; LaNeLa; LiTA; LiTG; LiTL; LoBV; MAmP; MCCG; MemP; MeWo; MWA-1; NeHB; NePA; NoP; OBEV; OBRV; OtMeF; OTPC; OuHeWo; OxBA; PFY; PG (1945 ed.); Po; PoEL-4; PoFS; PoIE; PoLF; PoPo; PoRA; PTK; SeCeV; StP; TIHL; TOP; TreF; TrGrPo; TSW; UnPo (1st ed.); VaPo; ViBoPo; WBP
Helen Was Just Slipped into Bed. Matthew Prior. EiCP
(On the Same.) EiCL
(Reasonable Affliction, A.) StP
Helena Embarks for Palestine. Cynewulf, *tr. fr. Anglo-Saxon by* Charles W. Kennedy. *Fr.* Elene. AnOE
Hélène. Paul Valery. *See* Helen, the Sad Queen.
Helen's lips are drifting dust. Love Triumphant. Frederic Lawrence Knowles. HBV; TreFT
Helen's Song. Philip James Bailey. *Fr.* Festus. VA
Helga. Carl Sandburg. NP; TSW
Helicopter bee fines down, The. Honey. Ruth Miller. BoSA
Heliodora's Garland. Meleager, *tr. fr. Greek by* Robert Guthrie MacGregor. OnPM
Heliodore. John Daniel Logan. CaP
Heliodore ("Pour wine"). Meleager, *tr. fr. Greek by* Andrew Lang. OBVV
(To Heliodora, *tr. by* Dudley Fitts.) LiTW
Heliodore Dead. Meleager, *tr. fr. Greek by* Andrew Lang. VA
Helios. Joel Elias Spingarn. AA
Heliotrope. Harry Thurston Peck. AA; HBV
Hell. Abraham Cowley. *Fr.* Davideis, I. OxBoCh
("Beneath the silent chambers of the earth.") SeEP
Hell. Milton. *Fr.* Paradise Lost, II. OBS
Hell and Heaven. *Unknown.* ABF, *with music*; OxBoLi; SiTL
Hell-bound Train, The. *Unknown, at. to* J. W. Pruitte. BeLS; BLPA; CoSo, *with music*
Hell Gate. A. E. Housman. UnPo
Hell-Gate of Soissons, The. Herbert Kaufman. GSP
Hell in Texas. *At. to* John R. Steele. ABF, *with music*; BLPA; CoSo, *with music*
Hell-Ride of Brynhild, The. *Unknown, tr. fr. Icelandic by* William Morris *and* Eiríkur Magnússon. *Fr.* The Elder Edda. OuHeWo
Hell with universities, The. For WGF Who Was Told He Didn't Publish Enough to Be Promoted to Associate Professor. Lou Lipsitz. YAP
Hellas, *sels.* Shelley.
Chorus: "Darkness has dawned in the East." EnRP
Chorus: "Life may change, but it may fly not." EnRP; EPN

Chorus: "O Slavery! thou frost of the world's prime." PoFr
Chorus: "Victorious wrong, with vulture scream."
(Final Chorus from "Hellas.") EnLi-2
Chorus; "World's great age begins anew, The." AtBAP; EnRP; ERoP-2; ExPo; FaBoEn; HBV; InPo; LoBV; MyFE; OAEP; PoE; PoEL-4; SeCeV; TOP; WoL
(Final Chorus.) BEL; BoLiVe; EnLit; OBRV; PoFS; SeCePo
(Hellas.) ChTr; EPN; OBEV; ShBV-4
(New World, A.) TrGrPo
(World's Great Age Begins Anew, The.) AWP; FiP; JAWP; NoP; PoIE; TreFS; WBP
Chorus: "Worlds on worlds are rolling ever." EnRP; OAEP
(Worlds on Worlds Are Rolling Ever.) NoP; PoFS
"Power from the unknown God, A." StJW
Hellenics, The, *sel.* Walter Savage Landor.
Hamadryad, The. EnRP; EPN; TOP; VA
Iphigenia and Agamemnon. BEL; BeLS; EnLi-2; EPN
(Iphigenia.) EnRP
Proem. ViBoPo
(On the Hellenics.) BEL; EnRP; EPN
Ternissa! You Are Fled! ExPo; GTSE; LoBV; PoEL-4; SeCeV
(Ternissa.) FaBoEn; OBNC
(On Ternissa's Death.) ELP
Hello. Gregory Corso. WOW
Hello! Louise Ayres Garnett. SiSoSe
Hello America let's tell the truth! To the National Arts Council. Peter Schjeldahl. ANYP
Hello Blackness. Arnold Kemp. WSL
Hello, Central, what's the matter with this line? The Hesitating Blues. W. C. Handy. GoSl
Hello dar, Miss Melerlee! Miss Melerlee. John Wesley Holloway. BANP; PoNe
Hello, Girls. *Unknown.* *See* Kansas Boys.
Hello, Somebody, *with music.* *Unknown.* ShS
Hello there, Walt! To Walt Whitman. Tom MacInnes. CaP
Hell's Bells. Margaret Fishback. ShM
Hell's Pavement. John Masefield. BrPo
Helmet and rifle, pack and overcoast. The Battle. Louis Simpson. TPM
Helmet Orchid. Douglas Stewart. BoAV
Helmsman, The. Hilda Doolittle ("H. D."). AnAmPo; CMoP; OxBA
Helmsman, The; an Ode. J. V. Cunningham. MoVE
Heloise and Abelard. Pope. *See* Eloisa to Abelard.
Helot, The, *sel.* Isabella Valancy Crawford.
"Who may quench the god-born fire." PeCV
Help. Sadi, *tr. fr. Persian by* Sir Edwin Arnold. *Fr.* The Gulistan. AWP; JAWP; OnPM; WBP
Help. Whittier. Sonn
Help for a patriot distressed, a spotless spirit hurt. "Cleared." Kipling. PeVV
Help-Givers, The. Laurence Housman. MaRV
Help, Good Shepherd. Ruth Pitter. OxBoCh
Help! Help!/ What's to do? Trouble at the Farm. Ivy O. Eastwick. BoTP
Help me! help me! now I call. To His Mistresses. Robert Herrick. ErPo; SCEP-2; SeCP; UnTE
Help me to help your life. Letter to P. Robert Friend. NYBP
Help me to hold the vision undefiled. The Scribe's Prayer. Arthur Guiterman. TrPWD
Help Me to Live! Charles Gabriel. *See* My Evening Prayer.
Help me to make this working day. Invocation. Francesca Falk Miller. PEDC
Help Me to Seek. Sir Thomas Wyatt. FCP; InvP; ReIE; SiCE; TuPP
(Rondeau: "Help me to seek, for I lost it there.") Po; SiPS
Help me to spend. Steward of God. Martha Snell Nicholson. FaChP
Help me to suffer when I most would spare. Remembering Calvary. Ethel Fanning Young. OQP
Help Me Today. Elsie Robinson. PoToHe
Help One Another. G. F. Hunting. PCH
Help, oh! my Lord, anoint mine eyes to see. Meditation CXIII [*or* I Am the Root and Offspring of David]. Edward Taylor. *Fr.* Preparatory Meditations, Second Series. MAmP; MWA-1
Help Us, Moon! *Unknown,* *tr. fr. Russian by* W. R. S. Ralston. OnPM
Help Us to Live. John Keble. *See* As We Pray.
Help Wanted. Franklin Waldheim. BLPA
Helpe O helpe kinde Abraham & send. *Unknown.* SeCSL
Helper, The. Cecil Frances Alexander. SoP
Helper, The. Phillips Brooks. *See* Our Burden Bearer.
Helping Hand, A. Georgia B. Adams. STF
Helping the Handicapped. Emily Dickinson. *See* If I can stop one heart from breaking.
Helpless am I indeed. "Labourers Together with God." Lucy Alice Perkins. BLRP
Helpless, condemned, yet still for mercy croaking. Mazeppa. Roy Campbell. AnFE
Helpless is God in struggling with that star. The Birth of Lucifer. John Gould Fletcher. MAP; MoAmPo
Helvellyn. Sir Walter Scott. PeER
Hem and Haw. Bliss Carman. HBV; MAP; MaRV; MoAmPo (1942 ed.); NeMA; PoPo
Hem of His Garment, The. Anna Elizabeth Hamilton. TrPWD
He-man, the sea-man, The. Pickup in Tony's Hashhouse. Kenneth Pitchford. *Fr.* Good for Nothing Man. CoPo; ErPo
Hemisphere could float upon, A. History Class. Robert Finch. TwCaPo
Hemlock, The. Emily Dickinson. *See* I think the hemlock likes to stand.
Hemlock Mountain. Sarah N. Cleghorn. HBV
Hemmed-in Males. William Carlos Williams. *Fr.* A Folded Skyscraper. MoVE; PoRA (rev. ed.); PoSa
("Saloon is gone up the creek, The.") AnAmPo
Hemorrhage, The. Stanley Kunitz. WaP
Hen, The. Matthias Claudius, *tr. fr. German.* BOHV
Hen, The. Oliver Herford. LBN; NA
Hen and the Oriole, The. Don Marquis. *Fr.* Archy and Mehitabel. EvOK; FiBHP
Hen Overboard. Robert P. Tristram Coffin. RePo
Hen remarked to the mooley cow, The. Art. *Unknown.* BLPA
Hen Roost Man, The. Ruth McEnery Stuart. BOHV
Hen to herself said one beautiful day, "Cluck, cluck," The. Cluck, Cluck. *Unknown.* FTB
Hen with the Golden Eggs, The. La Fontaine, *tr. fr. French by* Elizur Wright. OnPM
Hence All You Vain Delights. John Fletcher. *See* Melancholy.
Hence away, nor dare intrude! Inscription on a Grot. Samuel Rogers. *Fr.* The Pleasures of Memory. OBEC
Hence, Away, You Sirens! George Wither. *Fr.* Fidelia *and also* Fair Virtue. EIL, 3 *sts.*
Hence childish boy too long have I. *Unknown.* SeCSL
Hence, flames and darts! ye amorous sighs, hence! The Honeymoon. Henry Luttrell. *Fr.* Advice to Julia. OBRV
Hence flattring hopes. Cease longing and give ore. *Unknown.* SeCSL
Hence, hence, profane; soft silence let us have. A Dirge upon the Death of the Right Valiant Lord, Bernard Stuart. Robert Herrick. SeCV-1
Hence, hence prophane, and none appeare. Another New-Yeeres Gift, or Song for the Circumcision. Robert Herrick. SCEP-2
Hence, hence unhallowed ears and hearts more hard. Democritus Platonissans; or, An Essay upon the Infinity of Worlds out of Platonick Principles. Henry More. SeCV-2
Hence, loathèd Melancholy. L'Allegro. Milton. AnFE; AWP; BEL; BoLiVe; CABA; CBEP; CoBE; EnL; EnLi-1; EnLit; FaFP; FiP; GN; GTBS; GTBS-D; GTBS-P; GTBS-W; GTSE; GTSL; HBV; HoPM; ILP; InPo; LiTB; LiTG; LoBV; MaPo; MasP; MBW-1; MCCG; MyFE; NoP; OBEV; OBS; OuHeWo; PoE; SeCePo; SeCeV; ShBV-3; TOP; TreFS; TrGrPo; ViBoPo; WHA; WoL
Hence prophane grim man, nor dare. To Death, Castara Being Sicke. William Habington. AnAnS-2
Hence, rude Winter! crabbed old fellow. Glee for Winter. Alfred Domett. DD; HBV; VA
Hence These Rimes. Bert Leston Taylor. FiBHP
Hence two miles east, does a fourth wonder lye. Elden-Hole. Charles Cotton. *Fr.* The Wonders of the Peak. PeRV
Hence, vain deluding joys. Il Penseroso. Milton. AWP;

Hence (continued)
BoLiVe; CABA; CBEP; CEP; EiCP; EnL; EnLi-1; EnLit; FiP; GTBS; GTBS-D; GTBS-P; GTBS-W; GTSE; GTSL; HBV; HoPM; ILP; InPo; LiTB; LiTG; MaPo; MasP; MBW-1; MyFE; NoP; OBEV; OBS; OuHeWo; Po; PoE; SeCeV; ShBV-3; TOP; TrGrPo; UnPo (1st ed.); ViBoPo; WHA
Hence vaine delights beegone, tempte mee noe more. *Unknown.* SeCSL
Hence with Passion, Sighs and Tears. Thomas Heywood. *Fr.* A Maidenhead Well Lost. SeCL
Hence, ye profane! I hate you all. The Profane. Abraham Cowley. AWP
Hence, ye profane; mell not with holy things. Joseph Hall. *Fr.* Virgidemiarum. SiCE
Henceforth, from the Mind. Louise Bogan. LiTA; MoPo; MoVE; NePA; QFR
"Henceforth I learn, that to obey is best." Exit from Eden. Milton. *Fr.* Paradise Lost. DiPo
Henchman, The. Whittier. CLwM; HBV; OBEV (new ed.); OBVV
Hendecasyllabics. Swinburne. SyP
Hengest Cyning. Jorge Luis Borges, *tr. fr. Spanish by* Norman Thomas di Giovanni. NYBP
Henley on Taieri. Charles Brasch. AnNZ
"Henry Heine"—'tis here! Heine's Grave. Matthew Arnold. PoVP
Henry and King Pedro clasping. The Death of Don Pedro. *Unknown.* AWP
Henry and Mary. Robert Graves. BrPo; GoJo; LOW
Henry before Agincourt: October 25, 1415. John Lydgate. CH
Henry C. Calhoun. Edgar Lee Master. *Fr.* Spoon River Anthology. AmP; LiTA; LiTM (rev. ed.); NP
Henry VIII. Eleanor *and* Herbert Farjeon. OnPP; StPo
Henry VIII. Shakespeare *and probably* John Fletcher. *See* King Henry VIII.
Henry V. Shakespeare. *See* King Henry V.
Henry V at [*or* before] Harfleur. Shakespeare. *See* Once More unto the Breach.
Henry V to His Soldiers. Shakespeare. *See* Once More unto the Breach.
Henry Fifth's Address to His Soldiers. Shakespeare. *See* Once More unto the Breach.
Henry I to the Sea. Eugene Lee-Hamilton. PeVV
Henry IV, Pt. I. Shakespeare. *See* King Henry IV, Pt. I.
Henry IV, Pt. II. Shakespeare. *See* King Henry IV, Pt. II.
Henry Green. *Unknown.* BaBo
Henry hates the world. What the world to Henry. The Dream Songs, LXXIV. John Berryman. NaP
Henry Howard, Earl of Surrey, to [the Lady] Geraldine. Michael Drayton. *Fr.* England's Heroical Epistles. ReEn; ReIE; TuPP
(Earl of Surrey to Geraldine.) OBSC
Henry Hudson's Quest. Burton Egbert Stevenson. HBV; MC; PAH; PAL
Henry James. Robert Louis Stevenson. OBNC
Henry James/ (Whatever his other claims). Jacobean. Clifton Fadiman. FiBHP
Henry King. Hilaire Belloc. BBGG; CenHV; DTC; HBMV; ShM; TSW
Henry Martin [*or* Martyn]. *Unknown.* BaBo; CBEP; ESPB (A *and* E *vers.*); ViBoFo (A *vers.*;B *vers., with music*)
Henry Purcell. Gerard Manley Hopkins. MuSP; UnS; ViPP
Henry St. John, Viscount Bolingbroke. Pope. *Fr.* An Essay on Man. OBEC
Henry VI, Pt. I. Shakespeare. *See* King Henry VI, Pt. I.
Henry VI, Pt. II. Shakespeare. *See* King Henry VI, Pt. II.
Henry VI, Pt. III. Shakespeare. *See* King Henry VI, Pt. III.
Henry Spaulding. Donald Burnie. PaA
Henry the Eighth. Shakespeare *and probably* John Fletcher. *See* King Henry VIII.
Henry the Fifth. Shakespeare. *See* King Henry V.
Henry the Fourth, Pt. I. Shakespeare. *See* King Henry IV, Pt. I.
Henry the Fourth, Pt. II. Shakespeare. *See* King Henry IV, Pt. II.
Henry the Second keepeth (with much care). The Epistle of Rosamond to King Henry the Second. Michael Drayton. AnAnS-2
Henry the Sixth, Pt. I. Shakespeare. *See* King Henry VI, Pt. I.
Henry the Sixth, Pt. II. Shakespeare. *See* King Henry VI, Pt. II.
Henry the Sixth, Pt. III. Shakespeare. *See* King Henry VI, Pt. III.
Henry to Rosamond. Michael Drayton. AnAnS-2
Henry Turnbull. W. W. Gibson. ELU; FaBoTw
Henry Wadsworth Longfellow. Austin Dobson. DD; HBV
Henry Ward Beecher. *At. to* Oliver Wendell Holmes. *See* Limerick: "Reverend Henry Ward Beecher, The"
Henry Ward Beecher. Charles Henry Phelps. AA
Henry was a young [*or* worthy] king. Henry and Mary. Robert Graves. BrPo; GoJo; LOW
Henry Was a Worthy King. *Unknown.* MoShBr
Henry's Confession. John Berryman. The Dream Songs, LXXVI. NaP
Henry's Lament. Samuel Daniel. *Fr.* The Complaint of Rosamond. OBSC
Hens, The. Elizabeth Madox Roberts. FaPON; GoJo; GoTP; HBMV; MPB; PDV; PoRh; SoPo; SP; StVeCh; SUS; TiPo; TSW; UTS
Hen's Nest. John Clare. OA; Sonn
Hep-Cat Chung, 'ware my town. Confucius. *Fr.* Songs of Cheng. CTC
Heptalogia, The, *sels.* Swinburne.
Higher Pantheism in a Nutshell, The, *parody.* ALV; BOHV; HBV, *abr.*; NA; Par; PeVV; PoVP; SiTL; ViPo; ViPP; VP
John Jones. NA; OAEP
Nephelidia. ALV; BOHV; EnLi-2 (1949 ed.); HBV; HoPM; InMe; NA; OAEP; Par; PeVV; PoFS; PoVP; ViPo; VP
Sonnet for a Picture. OAEP; VP
Her, a Statue. Thomas Stoddart. OBNC
Her Absent Lord, *sel.* Ugga Byan, *tr. fr. Arakanese by* Maurice Collis.
"This is a colder winter than last year." LiTW
Her aged hands are worn with works of love. To One Being Old. Langdon Elwyn Mitchell. AA
Her angel looked upon God's face. The Eternal Image. Ruth Pitter. MoBrPo
Her Answer. John Bennett. AA; BLPA; NeHB
Her Apotheosis. Thomas Hardy. ViPP
Her Apparrelling. John Donne. MaMe
Her arms across her breast she laid. The Beggar Maid. Tennyson. BeLS; BoTP; HBV; OnMSP; OTPC; PoVP
Her arms first cradled me with mother love and care. My Mother. Samuel N. Wilson. PEDC
Her Beauty. Max Plowman. HBMV
Her Beauty. Shakespeare. *See* Sonnets, CVI.
Her beauty smoothed earth's furrowed face. The Tokens. Francis Thompson. *Fr.* Daisy. OtMeF
Her black eyes are made of beads. The Old Doll. Wilhelmina Seegmiller. MPB
Her blue dress lightly. The Dress. Christopher Middleton. NMP
Her blue eyes they beam and they twinkle. Winny. William Allingham. OTPC
Her body is not so white as. Queen-Ann's-Lace. William Carlos Williams. AmPP (5th ed.); AP; MAP; MoAB; MoAmPo; NoP; TDP
Her breast is cold; her hands how faint and wan! Virtue. Walter de la Mare. MMA
Her Bright Smile, *with music.* J. C. Carpenter. SoAmSa
Her Careful Distinct Sex Whose Sharp Lips Comb. E. E. Cummings. ErPo
Her casement like a watchful eye. Balder's Wife. Alice Cary. AA; AnAmPo
Her chariot ready straight is made. Queen Mab's Chariot. Michael Drayton. *Fr.* Nymphidia. OBS; OTPC; PCH
Her cheeks are hot, her cheeks are white. Bianca. Arthur Symons. PeVV; UnTE
Her Choice. Mattie Lee Hausgen. GFA
Her Commendation. Francis Davison. OBSC
(Madrigal: "Some there are as fair to see to.") EIL
(Commendation of Her Beauty, Stature, Behavior, and Wit.) TuPP
Her Confirmation. Selwyn Image. VA
Her Courage. W. B. Yeats. Upon a Dying Lady, VI. LiTB
Her Courtesy. W. B. Yeats. Upon a Dying Lady, I. LiTB
Her cruel hands go in and out. A Maiden and Her Hair. W. H. Davies. BrPo

Her curving bosom images. Bodily Beauty. George Rostrevor Hamilton. HBMV
Her Dairy. Peter Newell. NA; PCH
Her day out from the workhouse-ward, she stands. The Ice. W. W. Gibson. EPN
Her Dead Brother. Robert Lowell. NePoEA
Her Death. Thomas Hood. *Fr.* Miss Kilmansegg and Her Precious Leg. VA
Her Death and After. Thomas Hardy. PoVP; ViPo (1962 ed.)
Her Decision. James K. Baxter. Cressida, XI. AnNZ
Her deed and her name will be lost. On a Dead Teacher. Gerald Raftery. JKCP (1926 ed.)
Her Dilemma. Thomas Hardy. BrPo; Po
Her dimpled cheeks are pale. A Southern Girl. Samuel Minturn Peck. AA
Her drooping flowers dabble upon. Betty by the Sea. Ronald McCuaig. BoAV
Her drooping wrist, her arm. Piano Recital. Babette Deutsch. NePoAm
Her Dwelling-Place. Ada Foster Murray. HBV
Her Epitaph. Thomas William Parsons. AA; HBV
Her Eyes. John Crowe Ransom. LiTM (rev. ed.); NePA; PoPl
Her eyes are homes of silent prayer. In Memoriam A. H. H., XXXII. Tennyson. EPN; TOP; ViPo; VP
Her eyes are like forget-me-nots. To a Little Girl. Gustav Kobbé. HBV
Her eyes be like the violets. Anne. Lizette Woodworth Reese. AA
Her eyes? Dark pools of deepest shade. Portrait. George Leonard Allen. CDC
Her eyes flood lickes his feets faire staine. She Began to Wash His Feet with Teares. Richard Crashaw. MaMe
Her eyes have seen the monoliths of kings. Three Sonnets on Oblivion. George Sterling. HBV
Her eyes hold black whips. Dorothy. Alfred Kreymborg. AnAmPo
Her eyes long hollowed out to pits of shadow. The Worshiper. Vassar Miller. NePoEA-2
Her eyes that might be filled with wishes. Thenot Protests. "C. N. S." InMe
Her eyes the glow-worm lend thee. The Night-Piece, to Julia. Robert Herrick. AnAnS-2; AnFE; AtBAP; ATP; BEL; BoTP; CBV; CoBE; EG; ELP; EnLi-1 (1949 ed.); EnLit; FaPL; FosPo; HBV; ILP; InvP; LiTB; LiTL; LoBV; MaPo; MeWo; NeHB; NoP; OAEP; OBEV; OBS; OTPC; PCD; PoEL-3; PoeP; PoFS; PoIE; PoRA; ReEn; SCEP-2; SeCeV; SeCL; SeCP; SeCV-1; SeEP; ShBV-2; TOP; TreFT; UnTE; VaPo; WHA
Her face has made my life most proud and glad. Of His Lady's Face [*or* Sonnet]. Jacopo da Lentino. AWP; OnPM
Her Face, Her Tongue, Her Wit. *At. to* Sir Arthur Gorges *and to* Sir Walter Ralegh. CBV; ReIE
(Sonet, A.) SiCE
Her face is hushed in perfect calm. A Child's Portrait. William James Dawson. VA
Her face like a rain-beaten stone on the day she rolled off. Elegy. Theodore Roethke. PoeP
Her face was very fair to see. Our Sister. Horatio Nelson Powers. HBV
Her face wrinkles out like tree rings in a cut-off stump. The Old Peasant Woman at the Monastery of Zagorsk. James Schevill. NMP
Her failing spirits with derisive glee. Helen and Corythos. Walter Savage Landor. *Fr.* Corythos. LoBV
Her fair eyes, if they could see. Written in My Lady Speke's Singing-Book. Edmund Waller. CavP
Her Fair Inflaming Eyes. Thomas Campion. LiTL
Her Fairness, Wedded to a Star. Edward J. O'Brien. FaBoBe; HBMV; JKCP (1926 ed.)
Her Faith. Hilaire Belloc. *See* Because My Faltering Feet.
Her father loved me: oft invited me. Othello and Desdemona. Shakespeare. *Fr.* Othello, I, iii. BoC; TreF
Her Favorites. Mattie Lee Hausgen. PCH; PoPl
Her feet beneath her petticoat. The Bride. Sir John Suckling. *Fr.* A Ballad upon a Wedding. MeWo; TrGrPo
Her fingers shame the ivory keys. Amy Wentworth. Whittier. BeLS
Her First-born. Charles Tennyson Turner. VA
Her First Song. James K. Baxter. Cressida, V. AnNZ
Her Friends Bring Her a Christmas Tree. W. B. Yeats. Upon a Dying Lady, VII. LiTB
Her gait detached her from the moving throng. The Beautiful Negress. Ruth Pitter. MoVE
Her gentlewomen, like the Nereids. Shakespeare. *Fr.* Antony and Cleopatra, II, ii. MemP
Her Gifts. Dante Gabriel Rossetti. The House of Life, XXXI. HBV; MaVP; PoVP; VA; ViPo; VP
Her glance swung my body. Meeting. William Saphier. AnAmPo
Her Great Secret. Strickland Gillilan. PEDC
Her grieving parents cradled here. Epitaph. Sylvia Townsend Warner. MoBrPo; NeMA
Her Hair. Sir Robert Chester. *Fr.* Love's Martyr. EIL
Her hair the net of golden wire. So Fast Entangled [*or* Her Hair]. *Unknown.* EG; LiTL; MeWo; TrGrPo
Her hair upgathered thus behind the neck. Doric. Angelos Sikelianos. ErPo
Her hair was a waving bronze and her eyes. Disappointment. John Boyle O'Reilly. ACP; OnYI
Her hair was tawny with gold, her eyes with purple were dark. A Court Lady. Elizabeth Barrett Browning. BeLS; HBV; VA
Her hand a goblet bore for him. The Two. Hugo von Hofmannsthal. AWP; JAWP; WBP
Her hand which touched my hand she moved away. On a Hand. Hilaire Belloc. BoLP; ELU
Her Hands. Anna Hempstead Branch. *Fr.* Songs for My Mother. MPB
(My Mother's Hands.) DD
(Song for My Mother, A: Her Hands.) OHIP; RG
(Songs for My Mother: Her Hands.) HH; OnPP; PoRL; YT
Her hands are cold, her face is white. Under the Violets. Oliver Wendell Holmes. *Fr.* The Professor at the Breakfast Table. AA
Her hands have much/ Of Christlike touch. Mother—a Portrait. Ethel Romig Fuller. PGD
Her health is good. She owns to forty-one. Occupation: Housewife. Phyllis McGinley. Sonn
Her Heards Be Thousand Fishes. Spenser. *Fr.* Colin Clout's Come Home Again. ChTr
Her Heart. Bartholomew Griffin. Fidessa, More Chaste than Kind, XXIII. MeWo; TrGrPo
("Fly to her heart, hover about her heart.") ReEn; ReIE; SiCE; TuPP
Her heart is like her garden. My Mother's Garden. Alice E. Allen. BLPA; FaBoBe; NeHB
Her heart she locked fast in her breast. The Secret Combination. Ellis Parker Butler. BOHV
Her Heaven. Dante Gabriel Rossetti. The House of Life: True Woman, LVIII. EPN; MaVP; ViPo
Her Horoscope. Mary Ashley Townsend. AA
Her house is become like a man dishonored. Dirge. First Maccabees, Bible, Apocrypha. TrJP
Her I pursued across the Southern Sea. The Albatross. John Biram. NYTB
Her Immortality. Thomas Hardy. ViPo (1962 ed.)
Her Initials. Thomas Hardy. InP
Her Irish maids could never spoon out mush. Mary Winslow. Robert Lowell. AnNE; ILP; MiAP; MoVE
Her ivory hands on the ivory Keys. In the Gold Room. Oscar Wilde. SyP
Her Kind. Anne Sexton. CoAP; LiTM (1970 ed.); ToPo; TwAmPo; TwCP
Her Kisses. Thomas Lovell Beddoes. *Fr.* Early Fragments. AtBAP
("Her kisses are/ Soft as a snow-tuft in the dewless cup.") LO
Her Last Lines. Emily Brontë. *See* Last Lines: "No coward soul is mine."
Her laughter was infectious: so, some found. The Ecstasies of Dialectic. Howard Nemerov. FiMAP; TwAmPo
Her Letter. Bret Harte. CoBA; HBV; InP; PoLF; YT
Her life is in the marble! yet a fall. Her, a Statue. Thomas Stoddart. OBNC
Her Lips. Walter Savage Landor. NeHB
(Song: "Often I have heard it said.") HBV
Her Lips ("Her lips they are redder than coral"). *Unknown.* LiTG
Her Lips. *Unknown.* LiTL
("Lady, when I behold the roses sprouting"). EG
Her lips' remark was: "Oh, you kid!" Servant Girl and Grocer's

Her (continued)
Boy. Joyce Kilmer. LHV; YaD
Her lips they are redder than coral. Her Lips. *Unknown.* LiTG
Her lips were so near. In [*or* An] Explanation. Walter Learned. AA; ALV; HBV
Her Little Boy. *Unknown.* PEDC
Her Little Feet. W. E. Henley. BOHV
Her little hot room looked over the bay. Sanary. Katherine Mansfield. AnNZ
Her Love. Dante Gabriel Rossetti. The House of Life, LVII. EPN; MaVP; ViPo
Her love is like an island. Mother's Love [*or* My Mother's Love]. *Unknown.* OQP; SoP; STF
Her love is true I know. True Love. Waring Cuney. CDC
Her loved I most,/ By thee that's lost. To His Rival. Michael Drayton. ReEn
Her loveliness stirred my circumstances. Moved by Her Music. Richard Gillman. NePoAm-2
Her lute hangs shadowed in the apple-tree. A Sea-Spell. Dante Gabriel Rossetti. SyP
Her Man Described by Her Owne Dictamen. Ben Jonson. *Fr.* A Celebration of Charis. AnAnS-2; AtBAP; SCEP-2; SeCP
Her master gave the signal, with a look. Sweet Nature's Voice. Arthur Joseph Munby. *Fr.* Susan; a Poem of Degrees. VA
Her Merriment. W. H. Davies. EnLoPo
Her Mood around Me. Brewster Ghiselin. LiTL
Her Moral. Thomas Hood. *See* Gold.
Her Mother. Alice Cary. OHIP
Her Mother. Worral G. Sonastine. SoP
Her mother died when she was young. Kemp Owyne [*or* Oweyne]. *Unknown.* BaBo; BEL; BoLiVe; BuBa; CBEP; CoBE; EnLi-1 (1949 ed.); EnSB; ESPB; OBB; SeCeV; TOP; ViBoFo
Her mother has advised Mariushka. Mariushka's Wedding Song. *Unknown.* HW
Her mother watched her closely, yet one day. The Surprise. *Unknown.* UnTE
Her Mouth. Richard Aldington. BrPo
Her Mouth Carelessly Scented. Bilhana, *formerly at. to* Chauras, *tr. fr. Sanskrit by* E. Powys Mathers. *Fr.* Black Marigolds. OnPM
Her mouth is a crushed flower. Her Mouth. Richard Aldington. BrPo
Her mouth is fragrant as a vine. Cleopatra. Swinburne. BeLS
Her Music. Martha Dickinson Bianchi. AA
Her Name. Walter Savage Landor. *See* Well I Remember How You Smiled.
Her name, cut clear upon this marble cross. The Actress. Dorothy Parker. PoPo
Her name is at my tongue whene'er I speak. Philip Ayres. *Fr.* Emblems of Love. LO
Her name, Melissa, means she is a bee. Melissa. *Unknown.* UnTE
Her Name upon the Strand. Spenser. *See* Amoretti, LXXV.
Her name was Ate, mother of debate. The House of Ate. Spenser. *Fr.* The Faerie Queene, IV. OBSC
Her name was Dilliki Dolliki Dinah. A Ballad of China. Laura E. Richards. RePo
Her name was Marian Claribel Lee. The Ballad of Sir Brian and the Three Wishes. Newman Levy. FiBHP
Her Nativity. Robert Southwell. MeP
Her of your name, whose fair inheritance. To the Lady Magdalen Herbert. John Donne. MaMe
"Her Pa committed suicide." Such a Pleasant Familee. Wallace Irwin. ShM
Her Passing. William Drummond of Hawthornden. *See* Madrigal: "Beauty, and the life, The."
Her patience is infinite. The problems of a Writing Teacher. David Ray. NePoEA-2
Her Pedigree. Arthur Davison Ficke. Sonnets of a Portrait Painter, IX. HBMV
Her Perfections. Sir Philip Sidney. *See* What Tongues Can Her Perfections Tell?
Her Picture. Ellen Mackay Hutchinson Cortissoz. AA
Her Pity. Philip Bourke Marston. VA
Her Polka Dots. Peter Newell. NA
Her Powder Box. William F. Stead. NYTB
Her Praise. W. B. Yeats. Po
Her Praises. Anthony Scoloker. EIL
Her pretty feet. Upon Mistress Susanna Southwell, Her Feet [*or* Upon Her Feet]. Robert Herrick. EnLi-1; PoFS; ViBoPo
Her Race. W. B. Yeats. Upon a Dying Lady, V. LiTB
Her Rambling. Thomas Lodge. *See* My Mistress When She Goes.
Her Reply. Sir Walter Ralegh. *See* Nymph's Reply to the Shepherd, The.
Her Rival for Aziza. *Unknown, tr. fr. Arabic by* E. Powys Mathers. *Fr.* The Thousand and One Nights. AWP
Her Sacred Bower. Thomas Campion. *See* Where She Her Sacred Bower Adorns.
Her sails are strong and yellow as the sand. The Clipper. Thomas Fleming Day. EtS
Her Scarf *á la* Bardot. Twice Shy. Seamus Heaney. TwCP
Her seas and mountains made. The Weaving of the Wing. Ralph Hodgson. BrPo
Her Second Song. James K. Baxter. Cressida, IX. AnNZ
Her seem'd, as she was doing sacrifize. Spenser. *Fr.* The Faerie Queene, V. MBW-1
Her Shadow. Elisabeth Cavazza Pullen. AA
Her sight is short, she comes quite near. Jenny Wren. W. H. Davies. BiS; MoBrPo; StaSt
Her significance lies. Portrait. Jeanne D'Orge. AnAmPo
Her skin is like dusk on the eastern horizon. Jean Toomer. *Fr.* Karintha. KaL
Her skin is so white as a lily, an' each. Padraic Colum. LO
Her Skin Runs—White Stripes. Don Shea. QAH
Her smock was of the holland fine. A Ballet Song of Mary. Elizabeth Madox Roberts. MAP; MoAmPo; NP
Her son—albeit the Muse's livery. An Orson of the Muse. George Meredith. EPN
Her soul is a select district. Paysage Choisi. Francis Sparshott. MoCV
Her Strong Enchantments Failing. A. E. Housman. CBEP; FaBoTw; MoPW; PeVV; ShBV-4
Her suffering ended with the day. A Death-Bed. James Aldrich. AA; HBV
Her Sweet Voice. Thomas Carew. *See* Celia Singing ("You that think. . .").
Her talk was all of woodland things. The Wife from Fairyland. Richard Le Gallienne. HBV
Her tears fell with the dews at even. Tennyson. *Fr.* Mariana. LO
Her thoughts are like a flock of butterflies. From Life. Brian Hooker. HBV; OnPP
Her toe first in that water. First Date. John Frederick Nims. CBV
Her Triumph. Ben Jonson. *See* Triumph of Charis, The.
Her veil was artificial flowers and leaves. Christopher Marlow. *Fr.* Hero and Leander. HoPM
Her voice did quiver as we parted. On Fanny Godwin. Shelley. ChER; FaBoEn; OBNC
Her voice was like the song of birds. A Child. Richard Watson Gilder. AA
Her washing ended with the day. The Wife. Phoebe Cary. BOHV
Her Way. William Rose Benét. HBMV
Her ways were gentle while a babe. Elizabeth Oakes Smith. *Fr* The Sinless Child. AA
Her whole life is an epigram, smart, smooth, and neatly pen'd. Epigram: A Character [*or* A Character]. Blake. ERoP-1; OxBoLi; PeER; PV; SiTL
Her Window. Richard Leigh. CavP; SeCL; SeEP
Her Words. Anna Hempstead Branch. *See* Song for My Mother, A: Her Words.
Her world is all aware. She reads. For Her Sake. Alastair Reid. PoPl
Her wraithful turnings and her soft answers head/ Me off. Soft Answers. Robert Bagg. UnTE
Heracles. Yvor Winters. QFR; TwAmPo
Heraclitus. William Johnson Cory, *paraphrased fr. the Greek of* Calimachus. AWP; CBEP; ELU; EnLi-1; GTBS; GTBS-D; GTSE; GTSL; HBV; JAWP; ML; OBEV; OBNC; OBVV; OuHeWo; PCD; PoRA; SeCePo; ShBV-4; TOP; TreF; VA; ViBoPo; WBP; WePo; WoL
Heraclitus in the West. Charles G. Bell. NePoAm
Herakles Archer. Morton Dauwen Zabel. NP
Herald. Josephine Miles. FiMAP
Herald Crane, The. Hamlin Garland. HBV

Heralds of Christ, who bear the King's commands. Missions. Laura S. Copenhaver. SoP
Heralds of dawn are blowing at the last star, The. The Masked Ball. Wilson MacDonald. MaRV
Herb-Leech, The. Joseph Campbell. AnIL; OnYI
Herbivorous Thoreau, The. Alimentary. Clifton Fadiman. PV
Herbs and Simples. Martha Keller. FiSC
Herdbell—meek evening remote, The. Grass and Milk. Alfonso Gatto. OnPM
Herd Boy, The. Haniel Long. HBMV
Herd Boy, The. Lu-Yu, *tr. fr. Chinese by* Arthur Waley. ChTr; FlW
Herdboys shout unseen among the rocks, The. The Death of Chiron. J. P. McAuley. BoAV
Herdmen, The. *Unknown. See* Quiet Life, The.
Herds, The. W. S. Merwin. FRC; NaP; NYBP
Herds are gathered in from plain and hill, The. Who's That Calling So Sweet? ——Deveen. SCC
Herds of carrots cross the river. The New Sound. Roger Aplon. YAP
Herdsman, The. Theocritus, *tr. fr. Greek by* C. S. Calverley. Idylls, IV. AWP
Here. Philip Larkin. OPoP
Here. R. S. Thomas. GTBS-P
Here/ High on the hill. Song of the Hill. Edith Lodge. GoYe
Here/ Lyes a peer. Epitaph on the Duke of Grafton. *At. to* Sir Fleetwood Shepherd. PeRV
Here/ We quench/ Our thirst. Hat Bar. Mildred Weston. FiBHP
Here/ With my beer. Beer. George Arnold. TreFT
Here a little child I stand. Grace for a Child [*or* Another Grace for a Child *or* A Child's Grace]. Robert Herrick. AnAnS-2; AWP; BEL; BoTP; CABA; CaFP; CavP; ChTr; EaLo; EG; EnLi-1; FaBoCh; FaPON; GoJo; InPo; InvP; JAWP; LiTB; LoBV; LoGBV; MoShBr; OAEP; OBEV; OBS; OtMeF; OTPC; OxBoCh; PoeP; PoG; PoRA; ReEn; RIS; SCEP-2; SeCeV; SeCV-1; SeEP; ThGo; ThWaDe; TOP; TreFS; TrGrPo; ViBoPo; WBP
Here a Nit-Wit Lies. Patrick Barrington. WhC
Here a pretty baby lies. Upon a Child. Robert Herrick. LoBV; NoP; OBEV; OBS; SeCV-1; TrGrPo
Here, a sheer hulk, lies poor Tom Bowling. Tom Bowling [*or* Poor Tom *or* The Sailor's Epitaph]. Charles Dibdin. AmSS; CBEP; EtS; HBV; OBEC; OxBoLi
Here a solemn [*or* solemne] fast we keep[e]. An Epitaph upon [*or* on] a Virgin. Robert Herrick. EG; OnPM; OxBoLi; PoEL-3; SeCV-1
Here, above,/ cracks in the buildings are filled with battered moonlight. The Man-Moth. Elizabeth Bishop. LiTA; LiTM (1970 ed.); MiAP; MoAB; MoAmPo (1950 ed.); PoCH
Here Æthelstan the king, of earls the lord. The Battle of Brunanburh. *Unknown.* EnLi-1 (1949 ed.)
Here all is sunny, and when the truant gull. Skerryvore: The Parallel. Robert Louis Stevenson. ILP
Here all the summer could I stay. Teignmouth. Keats. PeER
Here alone in the night between wind and water. Companions. Margaret Widdemer. FiSC
Here Am I. *Unknown.* SoP
Here am I,/ Little jumping Joan. Mother Goose. OxNR; TiPo
Here am I among elms again—ah, look. Riverton. Edmund Wilson. *Fr.* Elegies for a Passing World. AnFE; CoAnAm
Here am I now cast down. Ex Nihilo. David Gascoyne. GTSB-P; NeBP
Here am I, this carrot eating. In Common. Gene Derwood. NePA; PoPl
Here among long-discarded cassocks. Diary of a Church Mouse. John Betjeman. BoC; POTi
Here Ananias lies because he lied. F. W. MacVeagh. WhC
Here and near as the hands of the sea. The Inland Sea. Howard Sergeant. ToPo
Here and Now, *sel.* Bliss Carman.
Where Is Heaven? GoTP; MaRV; OQP
Here and Now. Catherine Cater. AmNP; PoNe
Here and There. Johann Peter Lange, *tr. fr. German by* Jane Borthwick. SoP
Here and there, Freedom is an empty name. Svatopluk Cech. *Fr.* Songs of the Slave. PoFr
Here are cakes for thy body. The Other World. *Unknown. Fr.* Book of the Dead. AWP; JAWP; WBP
Here are crocuses, white, gold, grey! O Dear Me! Walter de la Mare. TiPo
Here, are five letters in this blessed Name. The Ghyrlond of the Blessed Virgin Marie. Ben Jonson. ISi; SeCL
Here are old trees, tall oaks and gnarled pines. The Antiquity of Freedom. Bryant. AA; AnNE; AP; CoBA; TOP
Here are sweet peas, on tiptoe for a flight. Sweet Peas. Keats. *Fr.* I Stood Tip-Toe upon a Little Hill. GN; MPB (1956 ed.); PCH
Here are the lady's knives and forks. *Unknown.* OxNR
Here are the ragged towers of vines. The Labourer in the Vineyard. Stephen Spender. NeBP
Here are the Schubert Lieder. Now begin. For M. S. Singing Frühlingsglaube in 1945. Frances Cornford. UnS
Here are three ways to get your answer to me. Answer. Merrill Moore. NeMA
Here are two helmets, stamped. The War Museum at Nagasaki. Charles Higham. NYTB
Here are we for the last time face to face. L'Envoi. William Morris. *Fr.* The Earthly Paradise. EnLi-2; PoVP; ViPo
Here, as a bare, unlichened wall, the Castle front goes up. At Ferns Castle. Padraic Colum. NePoAm
Here as I sit by the Jumna bank. The Hindu Ascetic. Sir Alfred Comyn. *Fr.* Studies at Delhi. OBVV
Here, as it were, in the heart of roaring Rome. Wild Cats. Vachel Lindsay. MAP; MoAmPo
Here at my earthly station set. The Stationary Journey. Edwin Muir. POTE
Here at my hand here at my heart lie still. First Cycle of Love Poems, II. George Barker. MoPo
Here at right of the entrance this bronze head. A Bronze Head. W. B. Yeats. LiTB; MBW-2
Here, at the airport, waiting. At the Airport. John Malcolm Brinnan. MoAB
Here at the atomic crack-end. A Vision in Hollywood. Allen Ginsberg. FRC
Here, at the beginning of the new season. Meditation on the BMT. Paul Blackburn. CoPo
Here at the center of the turning year. New Year. Stephen Spender. AWP
Here at the country inn. The Forefather. Richard Burton. AA
Here at the crossroads is the night so black. The Lynching Bee. William Ellery Leonard. PoNe
Here at the fountain's sliding foot. Andrew Marvell. *Fr.* The Garden. YT
Here at the frozen crossroads of the city. Waiting. Alan Hodge. LO
Here at the roots of the mountains. Rapids at Night. Duncan Campbell Scott. CaP
Here at the Stable Door. Sister Mary Paulinus. JKCP (1955 ed.)
Here at the Vespasian-Carlton, it's just one. Boom! Howard Nemerov. LiTM (1970 ed.); PoDB
Here at the village crossing. The Call. Daniel Corkery. OnYI
Here at the wayside station, as many a morning. The Wayside Station. Edwin Muir. FaBoTw; MoVE
Here at the wharves is payment for a loathing. Matthew. Sister Margaret Theresa. JKCP (1955 ed.)
Here at this sudden age of mine. An Autumn Walk. Witter Bynner. GoYe
Here Awa', There Awa'. *Unknown.* OBS
Here, awaiting what hereafter. Elegy. R. G. Howarth. MoAuPo
Here be grapes, whose lusty blood. The Satyr. John Fletcher. *Fr.* The Faithful Shepherdess, I, i. ViBoPo
Here be rural graces, sylvan places. Wild Cherry Tree. Edmund Blunden. BrPo
Here be woods as green. John Fletcher. *Fr.* The Faithful Shepherdess, I, iii. ViBoPo
Here Beginneth the Pastime of Pleasure. Stephen Hawes. *Fr.* The Pastime of Pleasure. SiCE
Here begins the sea that ends not till the world's end. On the Verge. Swinburne. *Fr.* A Midsummer Holiday, III. PoVP
Here beside dwelleth. The Magician and the Baron's Daughter. *Unknown.* MeEL
Here beside my Paris fire, I sit alone and ponder. Retrospect. Agnes Mary Frances Robinson. OBVV

Here between lunch and teatime, and days and hours between. Lines to Dr. Ditmars. Kenneth Allan Robinson. ImOP; PoMa
Here betwixt Ass and Oxen Mild, *with music.* *Tr. fr. French by* Winifred Douglas. YaCaBo
Here blew winter once with the snowstorms spurning. The Enchanted Heart. Edward Davison. HBMV
Here blooms the flower. Sir Philip Sidney. Eleanor *and* Herbert Farjeon. OnPP
Here bring your purple and gold. Flowers for the Brave. Celia Thaxter. OHIP
Here busy and yet innocent lyes dead. On the Death of a Monkey. Thomas Heyrick. MePo
Here by the baring bough. Autumn in King's Hintock Park. Thomas Hardy. PoVP
Here by the grey north sea. A Northern Vigil. Bliss Carman. OBEV (new ed.); OBVV; PeCV
Here by the moorway you returned. Your Last Drive. Thomas Hardy. OBNC
Here by the rose-tree. Love in Jeopardy. Humbert Wolfe. NeMA
Here, by the shore, a carven figure shows. The Living Statue. *Unknown.* UnTE
Here by the windy docks I stand alone. E. A. Robinson. Octaves, XXIII. ILP
Here, by this crumbling wall. Butterflies. Alfred Noyes. BoC
Here by this midland lake, the sand-shored water. Paul Engle. *Fr.* America Remembers. NAMP
Here by this well at noon He sat. Samaritan Woman. Mother Francis d'Assisi. JKCP (1955 ed.)
Here Caelia for thy sake I part. To the Mutable Fair. Edmund Waller. AnAnS-2; SeCP
Here, Charmian, take my bracelets. Cleopatra. William Wetmore Story. AA
Here Cleita sleeps. You ask her life and race? The Monument of Cleita. Edward Cracroft Lefroy. Echoes from Theocritus, XXIX. AWP, JAWP, WBP
Here clove the keels of centuries ago. The Salt Flats. Sir Charles G. D. Roberts. CaP
Here come Charles and Madeleina my child. Pounds and Ounces. Michael Brownstein. ANYP
Here come real stars to fill the upper skies. Fireflies in the Garden. Robert Frost. OA
Here come the line-gang pioneering by. The Line-Gang. Robert Frost. FIW
Here Come Three Merchants a-Riding, *with music.* *Unknown.* TrAS
Here comes a candle to light you to bed. Mother Goose. OTPC (1946 ed.)
Here comes a girl so damned shapely. Girl Walking. Charles G. Bell. ErPo; NePoAm-2
Here Comes a Lusty Wooer. *Unknown.* CH; OxNR
(Lily Bright and Shine-a.) AtBAP
(Old Rhyme.) LO
Here comes another, bumping over the sage. Tumbleweed. David Wagoner. BoNaP
Here comes Kate Summers who, for gold. The Bird of Paradise. W. H. Davies. AtBAP; BrPo; MoVE
Here comes my lady with her little baby. *Unknown.* OxNR
Here comes the elephant. The Elephant. Herbert Asquith. BoTP; SoPo; SUS; TiPo; UTS
Here comes the Marshall. The Proclamation. Longfellow. *Fr.* John Endicott. PAH
Here comes the shadow not looking where it is going. Sire. W. S. Merwin. CoAP; NaP
Here Comes the Thief. Hazel Hall. MAP; MoAmPo (1942 ed.)
Here comes the wind, with a noise and a whirr. Wind Song. *Unknown.* GFA
Here, Cyprian, is my jeweled looking-glass. To Aphrodite; with a Mirror. Aline Kilmer. HBMV
Here damsel sits disconsolate. Wrote in the Banquetting-House in Grayes-Inn-Walks. Alexander Radcliffe. PeRV
Here Dead Lie We [Because We Did Not Choose]. A. E. Housman. ELU; InPo; OtMeF; PoLF
(Epitaph: "Here dead lie we because we did not choose.") MoVE
Here dear [*or* deare] Iölas lies. Iölas' Epitaph. William Drummond of Hawthornden. AtBAP; PoEL-2
Here did sway the eltrot flow'rs. Times o' Year. William Barnes. BoNaP
Here dock and tare. In the Grave No Flower. Edna St. Vincent Millay. CrMA
Here doth Dionysia lie. Epitaph of Dionysia. *Unknown.* HBV; OBEV (new ed.); OBVV; VA
Here een Noo Yorka, where am I. Een Napoli. T. A. Daly. PoMa
Here ends this cycle of my poems for you. Ballade. Karl Shapiro. MeWo
Here enter not vile bigots, hypocrites. The Inscription Set upon the Great Gate of Theleme. Rabelais. *Fr.* Gargantua. PoFr
Here even experts can. Ragout Fin de Siècle. Erich Kästner. ErPo
Here, ever since you went abroad. Absence. Walter Savage Landor. OBEV (1st ed.); TOP
Here falls no light of sun nor stars. Richard Hovey. *Fr.* Taliesin. AA
Here first the day does break. Her Window. Richard Leigh. CavP; SeCL; SeEP
Here Followes Some Verses upon the Burning of Our House. Anne Bradstreet. *See* Upon the Burning of Our House.
Here Followeth the Songe of the Death of Mr. Thewlis. *Unknown.* CoMu
Here Folowith Divers Balettis and Dities Solacious, Devised by Master Skelton, Laureate. John Skelton. *See* Lullay, Lullay.
Here—for they could not help but die. Epitaph. Philip Freneau. *Fr.* The Fading Rose. AA
Here, from laborious art, proud towns, ye rose. On Catania and Syracuse Swallowed Up by an Earthquake. Anne Seward. Sonn
Here from the brow of the hill I look. The Old Mill. Thomas Dunn English. AA
Here from the field's edge we survey. Highway: Michigan. Theodore Roethke. TDP
Here further up the mountain slope. The Birthplace. Robert Frost. LoGBV
Here goes a man of seventy-four. Seventy-four and Twenty. Thomas Hardy. WhC
Here goes my lord. Mother Goose. SAS
Here halt we our march, and pitch our tent. The Green Mountain Boys. Bryant. AnNE; GA; MC; PAH
Here has my salient faith annealed me. Key West. Hart Crane. CMoP
Here hath been dawning. To-Day. Thomas Carlyle. HBV; HBVY; OQP; WGRP
Here Have I Dwelt. *Unknown.* MeEV
Here he can sleep, far inland from the sea. No Gull's Wings. Paul Engle. PoMa
Here he is of course. It was his best. Rastignac at 45. Thom Gunn. TDP; TPM
Here he lets go the struggling imp, to clutch. Shakespeare. Thomas Hood. *Fr.* The Plea of the Midsummer Fairies. OBRV
Here he lies moulding. Epitaph. Leslie Mellichamp. ShM
Here helms and swords are made of chalices. On Rome in the Pontificate of Julius II. Michelangelo. PoFr
Here, here I live with what my board. His Content in the Country. Robert Herrick. EnLit; SCEP-2; SeCV-1; SeEP
Here honest Micoe lies, who never knew. An Epitaph upon the Worthy and Truly Vigilant, Sam. Micoe Esq. Alexander Radcliffe. PeRV
Here, houses close their sleepy window eyes. Arizona Village. Robert Stiles Davieau. AmFN
Here houses rise so straight and tall. Tall City. Susan Nichols Pulsifer. OCS
Here I Am. Nancy Birckhead. RIS
Here I Am. Ann Morrissett. BoLP
Here I Am. Abraham Sutzkever, *tr. fr. Yiddish by* Joseph Leftwich. TrJP
Here I am, an industry without chimneys. The Perfection of Dentistry. Marvin Bell. CoAP; YAP
Here I am, an old man in a dry month. Gerontion. T. S. Eliot. AmPP; AnAmPo; AnFE; AP; APA; BWP; CABA; CABL; CBV; ChMP; CMoP; CoAnAm; CoBA; CoBMV; DiPo; ExPo; FaBoEn; ForPo; FosPo; GTBS-P; GTBS-W; ILP; LiTA; LiTM; LoBV; MAP; MAPA; MaPo; MoAmPo (1942 ed.); MoPo; NAMP; NePA; OAEP (2d ed.); OxBA; PoE; PoFS; PoIE; POTE; ReMP; SeCePo; SeCeV; StP; TwAmPo

Here I am born a brilliant mistake from infinity. Penicillin. Frank Lima. ANYP
Here I am, sprouted to my full height. Here I Am. Abraham Sutzkever. TrJP
Here I am with my rabbits. *Unknown.* OxNR
Here I come creeping, creeping everywhere. The Voice [*or* Song] of the Grass. Sarah Roberts Boyle. AA; BoTP, *wr. at. to* Leigh Hunt; DD; HBV; HBVY; PCH; PRWS
Here I drone in this human hive. The Landlubber's Chantey. James Stewart Montgomery. HBMV
Here I have dwelt with more and less. Here Have I Dwelt. *Unknown.* MeEV
Here I Lie. Marguerite George. FiSC
Here I lie asleep. The Absence. Denise Levertov. NaP
Here I lie at the chancel door. Four Country Epitaphs. *Unknown.* GoTP
Here I lie outside the chancel door. Outside the Chancel Door. *Unknown.* ShM
Here I ligg, Sydney Slugabed Godless Smith. Under the Eildon Tree. Sydney Goodsir Smith. OxBS
Here I Sit Alone. *Unknown.* OxBoCh
Here, I stood by the pole. Tic. Vito Hannibal Acconci. YAP
Here I'd come when weariest! Ballade of His Choice of a Sepulcher [*or* Of His Choice of a Sepulcher]. Andrew Lang. PoVP; VA
Here if you please, is a Whirligig. Whirligig Beetle. C. Lindsay McCoy. GFA
Here in a distant place I hold my tongue. Egan O Rahilly. *Tr. by* James Stephens. CBEP; OBMV; SeCePo
Here, in a field. In a Field. Robert Pack. NePoEA-2
Here in a garden sung for two. Youth Autumnal. Raymond Roseliep. JKCP (1955 ed.)
Here in a quiet and dusty room they lie. The Seed Shop. Muriel Stuart. BoNaP; GoTP; GoTS; MemP; NP; POTE
Here in a world whose heaven is powder-white. Unreasoning Heart. Louis Untermeyer. MAP; MoAmPo (1942 ed.)
Here, in cool grot and mossy cell. Inscription: On a Tablet against a Root-House. William Shenstone. EiPP
Here in Katmandu. Donald Justice. CoAP
Here in life's chaos make no foolish boast. The Nail-torn God. Edwin Markham. MaRV
Here in my curving hands I cup. This Quiet Dust. John Hall Wheelock. AnEnPo; MAP; MoAmPo; WHA
Here in my hands a small cold-chisel. The Little Chisel. N. P. van Wyk Louw. PeSA
Here in my head, the home that is left for you. Burning the Letters. Randall Jarrell. MiAP; MoAB; MoAmPo (1950 ed.)
Here, in my rude log cabin, few poorer men there be. The Battle of New Orleans. Thomas Dunn English. PAH; PAP; ThLM
Here, in my snug little fire-lit chamber. Alone by the Hearth. George Arnold. HBV
Here In My Workshop. *Unknown.* FaChP
Here in our aging district the wood pigeon lives with us. All Morning. Theodore Roethke. NaP; NoP
Here in the Cloisters a fourth dimension evolves. The Cloisters. Samuel Yellen. NePoAm
Here in the country's heart. The Country Faith. Norman Gale. BoTP; HBV; OBEV (new ed.); OBVV; OQP; OTPC; VA; WGRP
Here in the dark, O heart. Second Best. Rupert Brooke. MoBrPo; OBVV
Here in the dark what ghostly figures press! In Tesla's Laboratory. Robert Underwood Johnson. AA
Here, in the field, last year. Compensation. Gerald Gould. HBMV
Here in the furnace city, in the humid air they faint. Manhattan. Charles Hanson Towne. SoP
Here in the German. Disenchanted. Louis Untermeyer. GoTP
Here in the green scooped valley I walk to and fro. The Green Valley. Sylvia Townsend Warner. MoBrPo (1950 ed.)
Here in the marshland, past the battered bridge. A Harrow Grave in Flanders. Marquess of Crewe. HBV
Here, in the midnight of the solemn wood. Marquette on the Shores of the Mississippi. John Jerome Rooney. CAW; JKCP
Here in the midnight, where the dark mainland and island. Night Hymns on Lake Nipigon. Duncan Campbell Scott. CoBE; OBCV
Here in the minster tower. Tudor Church Music. Sylvia Townsend Warner. UnS
Here, in the most Unchristian basement. The Men's Room in the College Chapel. W. D. Snodgrass. MoAmPo (1962 ed.)
Here in the newspaper—the wreck of the East Bound. It's Here in the. Russell Atkins. AmNP
Here in the pine shade is the nest of night. Night and the Pines. Duncan Campbell Scott. OBCV
Here in the quiet of my room. Prayer of an Unemployed Man. W. C. Ackerly. MaRV; PoToHe
Here, in the sand, where someone laid him down. Cruciform. Winifred Welles. LO; NYBP; POTE
Here in the scuffled dust. W. D. Snodgrass. Heart's Needle, VII. NePoEA; NMP; OPoP
Here in the self is all that man can know. Sonnet. John Masefield. *Fr.* Sonnets ("Long long ago"). AWP; BoPe; JAWP; WBP
Here in the uplands. Scotland. Alexander Gray. GoTS; OxBS
Here, in the withered arbor, like the arested wind. Statue and Birds. Louise Bogan. MAP; MoAB; MoAmPo
Here in their health and youth they're sitting down. Schoolgirl on Speech-Day in the Open Air. Iain Crichton Smith. NePoEA-2
"Here in this corner, ladies and gentlemen." The Wrestling Match. Robert Penn Warren. AnAmPo
Here in this dark and radiant glade, wearing the sun's. The Blessed Received in Paradise. James Kirkup. BoPe
Here in this great house in the barrack's square. The Hambone and the Heart. Edith Sitwell. OBMV
Here in this inland garden. Alien. Archibald MacLeish. EtS
Here in this leafy place. Before Sedan. Austin Dobson. MoBrPo (1942 ed.); NeMA; PeVV; TreFS
Here, in this little Bay. Magna Est Veritas [*or* Truth]. Coventry Patmore. *Fr.* The Unknown Eros. AnFE; CAW; CoBE; GoBC; GTBS-P; MaRV; MemP; OBEV (new ed.); OBNC; OBVV; OnPM; OQP; PG (1945 ed.); PoVP; TreFT; TrGrPo
Here in this narrow room there is no light. Prothalamium. A. J. M. Smith. CaP
Here in this room where first we met. As She Feared It Would Be. Lilla Cabot Perry. Meeting after Long Absence, I. AA
Here in this sequestered [*or* sequester'd] close. A Garden Song. Austin Dobson. BoNaP; GTSE; HBV; LoBV; OBEV; OBNC; OBVV; TOP
Here in this shabby house at dead of night. Foreboding. Grant Code. FiSC
Here in this simple house his presence clings. House in Springfield. Gail Brook Burket. PGD
Here in this windy place. Green Councillors. Howard McKinley Corning. NP
Here in this world of fog like amethyst. Fog. Louis Ginsberg. NeMA
Here is a coast; here is a harbor. Arrival at Santos. Elizabeth Bishop. FiMAP; OPoP
Here is a ditch of dead and hopeless water. The Dead Water. Wen Yi-tuo. LiTW
Here is a face that says half-past seven. Clocks. Carl Sandburg. CrMA
Here is a fat animal, a bear. Self-Portrait, as a Bear. Donald Hall. TPM
Here is a house with a pointed door. A Little Finger Game. E. J. Falconer. BoTP
Here is a long and silent street. The Street. Octavio Paz. OCS
Here is a place that is no place. Madhouse. Calvin C. Hernton. IDB; Kal; NNP; PoNe (1970 ed.)
Here is a place you've never been. Rod Slemmons' Dream. William Hathaway. QAH
Here is a poem. Gertrude Stein. *Fr.* Land of Nations. AtBAP
Here is a quiet room! Meditation. Donald Cox. MaRV
Here is a riddle most abstruse. Riddle. *Unknown.* SiTL
Here is a room with heavy-footed chairs. The Nature of an Action. Thom Gunn. ACV; NePoEA
Here is a sack, a gunny sack. The Metal Checks. Louise Driscoll. NP
Here is a ship you made. The Ship. J. F. Hendry. NeBP
Here is a story shall stir you! Stand up, Greeks dead and gone. Echetlos. Robert Browning. ViPo

Here is a symbol in which. Rock and Hawk. Robinson Jeffers. MoVE; OxBA
Here Is a Toast That I Want to Drink. Walter Lathrop. PoLF
Here is a woman whom a man can greet. Charioteer. Witter Bynner. AnFE; CoAnAm
Here is a world which slowed the hands of time. Okefenokee Swamp. Daniel Whitehead Hicky. AmFN
Here Is a Wound That Never Will Heal. Edna St. Vincent Millay. TOP
Here is an apple. Like your little breast. Apple Offering. *Unknown.* UnTE
Here is another dream, another forgetting, another doorway. Radio. A. S. J. Tessimond. HaMV
Here is another poem in a picture. Untitled. Daryl Hine. TwCP
Here is cruel Psamtek, see. The Story of Cruel Psamtek. *Unknown.* NA
Here is dominion for peace. Country Reverie. Carol Coates. CaP
Here is fresh matter, poet. Church and State. W. B. Yeats. CMoP
"Here is Honor, the dying knight." The Soul Speaks. Edward H. Pfeiffer. HBMV
Here is how I eat a fish. Eating Fish. George Johnston. WHW
Here is Israel. Pictures at an Exhibition. Nathan Rosenbaum. GoYe
Here is Kit Logan with her love-child come. Kit Logan and Lady Helen. Robert Graves. HBMV
Here is little Effie's head. Portrait. E. E. Cummings. AnAmPo
Here is Martin's round house. Free Martin. Peter Hopegood. BoAV
"Here is my heart; it's clean." Refusal. Raymond Kresensky. OQP
Here is my last good-bye. Before Exile. Louise Mack. BoAu
Here is my love to you, flag of the free, and flag of the tried and true. A Song for the Flag. Denis A. McCarthy. PEDC
Here is no golden-crowned, celestial queen. A Flemish Madonna. Charles Wharton Stork. HBMV
Here is no peace, although the air has fainted. Innocent Landscape. Elinor Wylie. OxBA
Here is no shadow but cloudshadow and nightshadow. Hide in the Heart. Lloyd Frankenberg. AnFE; CoAnAm; LiTA
Here is no tragedy. Christopher La Farge. *Fr.* Prologue, Each to the Other. AnAmPo
Here is no tryst for love. The Wrung Heart. Jack Lindsay. MemP
Here is nothing, and nothing there. Nothing and the Soul. Bhartrihari. OnPM
Here is one leaf already gone from green. The First Leaf. Howard Nemerov. TwAmPo
Here is refinement's start. Rice Fields. Basho. OnPM
Here is the ancient floor. The Self-Unseeing. Thomas Hardy. FaBoEn; GTBS-D; MoBrPo; MoPW; NoP; OBNC; PoeP; ViPP; VP
Here is the church, and here is the steeple. *Unknown.* OxNR
Here is the crab tree. The Crab Tree. Oliver St. John Gogarty. AnIL; OxBI
Here is the Dog. Since time began. The Dog. Oliver Herford. FaBV
Here is the fern's front, unfurling a gesture. Fern. Ted Hughes. NYBP
Here is the fix: an hour of time crossed over. Despair in Seascape. Richmond Lattimore. TwAmPo
Here is the grackle, people. Fable for Blackboard. George Starbuck. CaFP
Here is the haven: pain touched with soft magic. Hospital. Wilfred Funk. PoToHe
Here is the hinge of history—the hour. The Nativity. E. Merrill Root. ChIP
Here is the house, in readiness for you. To the New Owner. Lucile Hargrove Reynolds. PoToHe
Here is the ice that girdles joyless ocean. Cross Section of a Landscape. Donald Davidson. MAP; MoAmPo (1942 ed.)
Here is the island but I do not know. Crusoe. Floris Clark McLaren. PeCV; TwCaPo
Here is the long-bided hour: the labor of years is accomplished. Work. Pushkin. AWP; JAWP; WBP
Here is the place my Lord, good my Lord enter. Shakespeare. *Fr.* King Lear, III, iv. AtBAP
Here is the place; right over the hill. Telling the Bees. Whittier. AmePo; AmPP (3d ed.); AnNE; AP; AWP; CoBA; GBV (1952 ed.); HBV; InP; InPo; LaNeLa; PFY; PoIE; TOP
Here Is the Place Where Loveliness Keeps House. Madison Cawein. HBV; PFY
Here is the rose you planted long ago. For an Old Man. Norbert Engels. JKCP (1955 ed.)
Here is the same familiar land. Thoughts upon a Walk with Natalie, My Niece, at Houghton Farm. Harold Trowbridge Pulsifer. HBMV
Here is the soundless cypress on the lawn. The Nightingale near the House. Harold Monro. HBMV; MoBrPo
Here is the spinner, the orb weaver. The Orb Weaver. Robert Francis. OA; PPON
Here is the Spring where waters flow. The Incomparable Treasure. *Unknown.* FaChP
Here is the stream again under the rainbow. Tchicaya U Tam'si. *Fr.* Debout. PBA
Here Is the Tale, *parody.* Anthony C. Deane. BOHV; InMe; NA
(Ballad of Jack and Jill, The.) YT
(Jack and Jill—as Kipling Might Have Written It.) CenHV
Here is the tale of Carrousel. The Ballad of a Barber. Aubrey Beardsley. SyP
Here is the train!/ Here is the train! The Holiday Train. Irene Thompson. BoTP
Here is the Truth in a little creed. Quatrain [*or* A Creed]. Edwin Markham. ChIP; MaRV; OQP
Here is the way the white man's heaven felt. On a Picture by Pippin, Called "The Den." Selden Rodman. PoNe
Here is the Will of Cathaeir Mor. The Testament of Cathaeir Mor. *Unknown.* *Fr.* Book of Rights. OnYI
Here is the yoke, with arrow and share nearby. The Laborer. José Maria de Heredia. AWP; JAWP; WBP
Here is this silver crucifix, to recall. Crucifix. Elder Olson. MoRP
Here is thy footstool and there rest thy feet where live the poorest. Rabindranath Tagore. *Fr.* Gitanjali. BoPe; MaRV; WGRP
Here Is Wine. Keats. *Fr.* Endymion, II. OBRV
Here Is Wisdom. James Larkin Pearson. PoNC
Here Is Your Realism. Maxwell Bodenheim. AnAmPo
Here it comes! Here it comes! Circus Parade. James S. Tippett. UTS
Here it comes sparkling. The Cataract of Lodore. Robert Southey. BOHV; GN; HBV; OTPC; WBLP
Here its like that. Blue Tanganyika. Lebert Bethune. BF
Here I've got you, Philip Desmond, standing in the marketplace. In the Market Place. John Francis O'Donnell. *Fr.* Limerick Town. IrPN; NBM
Here Jack and Tom Are Paired with Moll and Meg. George Meredith. Modern Love, XVIII. CBV; InvP; NBM; PoEL-5; ViPo; VP
Here Johnson is laid. Have a care how you walk. A Postscript to "Retaliation." Austin Dobson. PoVP
Here Johnson lies—a sage, by all allowed. Epitaph on Johnson. William Cowper. EiCP
Here Keats and Shelley heard. Piazza di Spagna. Willard M. Grimes. GoYe
Here lapped in hallowed slumber Saon lies. Saon of Acanthus. Callimachus. AWP; TRV
Here lay a fair fat land. Culbin Sands. Andrew Young. GTBS-P; OxBS
Here let my Lord hang up his conquering lance. The Celestial City. Giles Fletcher. *Fr.* Christ's Victory and Triumph. OBS
Here let the brows be bared. At the Tomb of Washington. Clinton Scollard. DD; MC; OHIP; PEDC
Here let thy clemency, Persephone, hold firm. Prayer for His Lady's Life. Propertius, *tr. by* Ezra Pound. *Fr.* Elegies, II, 28. NoP
Here let us leave him; for his shroud the snow. On a Grave at Grindelwald. Frederic William Henry Myers. VA
Here lie Ciardi's pearly bones. Elegy Just in Case. John Ciardi. AtBAP; MiAP; TwAmPo; TwCP
Here lie I, Martin Elginbrodde. Epitaph [*or* At Aberdeen *or* Epigram]. *Unknown, at. to* George Macdonald. GoTP; HBV; LiTG; MaRV; MemP; OtMeF; SiTL; WGRP
Here lie, I, Timon; who, alive, all living men did hate. Timon's

Epitaph. Callimachus, *tr. by* Shakespeare. AWP; JAWP; WBP
Here lie my husbands One Two Three. Epitaph to the Four Husbands of Miss Ivy Saunders. *Unknown.* PV; WePo
Here lie the remains of Thomas Wood*hen*. On Thomas Wood-cock. *Unknown.* WhC
Here Lies . . . Michael Lewis. YT
Here Lies. . . *Unknown, at. to* George Macdonald. *See* Epitaph: "Here lie I, Martin Elginbrodde."
Here lies/ A worthy matron of unspotted life. Epitaph on My Dear and Ever Honoured Mother, An. Anne Bradstreet. AmPP (3d ed.)
Here lies a bard, Hipponax—honored name! The Grave of Hipponax. Edward Cracroft Lefroy. Echoes from Theocritus, XXX. AWP; JAWP; WBP
Here lies a clerk who half his life had spent. *See* Here lies the clerk . . .
Here lies a Dog: may every Dog that dies. Epitaph on the Favourite Dog of a Politician. Hilaire Belloc. CoBE
Here lies a frigid man whom men deplore. A Man Whom Men Deplore. Alfred Kreymborg. HBMV
Here lies a great and mighty King. Epigram [*or* The King's Epitaph *or* On Charles II]. Earl of Rochester. CavP; PoSa; SeCePo; SeEP. *See also* Here lies our Sovereign Lord the King.
Here Lies a Lady. John Crowe Ransom. AnAmPo; AnFE; AWP; BWP; CMoP; CoAnAm; CoBMV; EvOK; ForPo; HBMV; InPo; InvP; LiTM; MAP; MoAB; MoAmPo; NAMP; NeMA; PoRA; PTK; TwAmPo; VaPo
Here lies a little bird. A Bird's Epitaph [*or* On a Little Bird]. Martin Armstrong. BiS; CH; POTE
Here lies a little boy who made believe. A Dreamer. Arthur Guiterman. PoMa
Here lies a man, and still no man. Epitaph I. *Unknown. Fr.* Duel with Verses over a Great Man. TrJP
Here lies a man much wronged in his hopes. On a Rope Maker Hanged. William Browne. CavP
Here lies a man who was killed by lightning. At Great Torrington, Devon. *Unknown.* ShM; SiTL
Here lies a most beautiful lady. An Epitaph. Walter de la Mare. AnFE; BoLiVe; CoBMV; LiTB; LiTM; LoBV; MoAB; MoBrPo; MoVE; NeMA; NP; OAEP (2d ed.); OBEV (new ed.); OBVV; OnPP; POTE; PTK; ShBV-3; SiTL; ViBoPo
Here lies a piece of Christ; a star in dust. An Epitaph for a Godly Man's Tomb. Robert Wild. CBEP; ChTr; OxBoCh; SeCL
Here lies a poor woman who was always tired. On a Tired Housewife [*or* Epitaph]. *Unknown.* EvOK; TreF; WePo
Here Lies a Prisoner. Charlotte Mew. MoBrPo
Here lies a simple Jew. Epitaph. Sholom Aleichem. TrJP
Here lies a woman—known to me, and you. R. I. P. "Jan Struther." InMe
Here lies a wretched corse. Shakespeare. *Fr.* Timon of Athens. MyFE
Here lies an aged corpse, which late. An Epitaph on His Grandfather. Thomas Shipman. CBEP; SeCL
Here lies, and none to mourn him but the sea. Sonnet XVIII. Edna St. Vincent Millay. *Fr.* Epitaph for the Race of Man. AtBAP; MoPo; ReMP
Here lies Archeanassa of Kolophon, whose face. Epitaph of a Courtesan. Asclepiades. LiTW
Here lies at rest, unknown to fame. A Mongrel Pup. Nancy Byrd Turner. PoMa
Here Lies Bill. Oliver Herford. WhC
Here lies, but seven years old, our little maid. Afraid. Walter de la Mare. ThGo
Here lies Cock Robbin dead and cold. The Death and Burial of Cock Robbin. *Unknown.* OxBoLi; SiTL
Here lies David Garrick, describe me who can. David Garrick. Goldsmith. *Fr.* Retaliation. CBEP; OBEC; SeCeV
Here lies Eunikides. The tomb. Sepulchral Imprecation. Crinagoras. LiTW
Here lies father, mother, sister, and I. In a Staffordshire Churchyard [*or* Four Country Epitaphs]. *Unknown.* GoTP; WhC
Here lies Fred. On Prince Frederick. *Unknown.* GoTP; OxBoLi; TreFS; WhC
Here lies hee, whom the tyrants rage. Epitaph on Mr. Robert Port. Charles Cotton. CavP
Here lies I [*or* me] and my three daughters. Epitaph. *Unknown.* GoTP; SiTL; TreFT; WhC
Here lies John Auricular. *Unknown.* WhC
Here lies John Bun. On John Bun [*or* John Bun]. *Unknown.* GoTP; ShM; WhC
Here lies John Coil. John Coil. *Unknown.* ShM
Here lies John Goddard, maker of bellows. An Epitaph on a Bellows-Maker. John Hoskins. TuPP
Here lies John Hill, a man of skill. *Unknown.* WhC
Here lies John Knott. Epitaph on John Knott. *Unknown.* ChTr; ShM
Here lies Johnny Cuncapod. *Unknown.* WhC
Here lies Johnny Pidgeon. Epitaph on John Dove. Burns. InP
Here lies [*or* lyes] Jonson [*or* Johnson] with the rest. Upon Ben Jonson. Robert Herrick. BEL; NoP; OAEP; OBS; SCEP-2; SeCV-1
Here lies Judge A——, he's done with legal tort. Epitaph for a Judge. Benedict Jeitteles. TrJP
Here Lies Juliet. Shakespeare. *See* Thus with a Kiss I Die.
Here lies Lester Moore. At Boot Hill in Tombstone, Arizona. *Unknown.* ShM
Here lies magnanimous humility. Upon the Tomb of the Most Reverend Mr John Cotton. Benjamin Woodbridge. SCAP
Here lies me and my three daughters. *See* Here lies I and my three daughters.
Here lies Mr. Chesterton. G. K. Chesterton. Humbert Wolfe. TrJP
Here lies my gude and gracious Auntie. *Unknown.* WhC
Here Lies My Wife. Dryden. *See* Epitaph Intended for His Wife.
Here lies my wife. At Leeds. *Unknown.* PV; WhC
Here lies my wife. Eternal peace. Epigram. J. V. Cunningham. NePoAm; PIA
Here lies my wife: here let her lie! Epitaph Intended for [*or* on] His Wife [*or* Epigram]. Dryden. BOHV; HBV; InMe; ShM; TreF; TrGrPo; WhC
Here lies Nachshon, a man of great renown. An Epitaph. Isaac Benjacob. TrJP
Here lies, neatly wrapped in sod. Epitaph for a Postal Clerk. X. J. Kennedy. ShM
Here lies New Critic who would fox us. J. V. Cunningham. MoAmPo (1962 ed.); PIA
Here lies Nolly Goldsmith. David Garrick. BEL
Here lies old Hobson, Death hath broke his girt. On the University Carrier [Who Sickn'd in the Time of His Vacancy]. Milton. FaBoCh; LoGBV; MePo
Here lies old Jones. *Unknown.* WhC
Here lies one blown out of breath. Merideth [*or* On a Man Named Merideth]. *Unknown.* GoTP; WhC
Here lies one Box within another. *Unknown.* WhC
Here lies one who for medicine would not give. *Unknown.* WhC
Here lies one who never drew. An Epitaph. William Cowper. OTPC (1923 ed.)
Here lies our good Edmund, whose genius was such. Edmund Burke. Goldsmith. *Fr.* Retaliation. InvP; OBEC; SeCeV
Here lies our Sovereign Lord the King. Epitaph on Charles II [*or* King Charles II *or* On Charles II *or* The King's Epitaph]. Earl of Rochester. ALV; EnLi-1 (1949 ed.); ExPo; FiBHP; GoTP; HBV; InP; MemP; OnPM; OnPP; TOP; TreFS; TrGrPo; ViBoPo; WhC *See also* Here lies a great and mighty King.
Here lies poor Burton. A Brewer. *Unknown.* WhC
Here lies poor Ned Pardon, from misery freed. On a Bookseller. Goldsmith. PV
Here lies poor stingy Timmy Wyatt. *Unknown.* SiTL; WhC
Here lies resting, out of breath. Little Elegy [for a Child Who Skipped Rope]. X. J. Kennedy. CaFP; CBV; CoAP; ELU; GoJo
Here lies returned to clay. *Unknown.* WhC
Here lies Richard Dent. On Richard Dent, Landlord. *Unknown.* GoTP
Here lies Robert Trollope. On a Newcastle Architect. *Unknown.* WhC
Here lies Sam Johnson: reader have a care. Epitaph on Dr. Johnson. Soame Jenyns. ELU
Here lies the best and worst of fate. Epitaph on the Duke of Buckingham. James Shirley. CavP
Here lies the body of Ann Mann. *Unknown.* WhC
Here lies the body of Anna. In Memory of Anna Hopewell. *Unknown.* ShM

Here lies the body of Cassie O'Lang. Cassie O'Lang. *Unknown.* ShM
Here lies the body of Henry Round. *Unknown.* WhC
Here lies the body of Jonathan Near. *Unknown.* WhC
Here lies the body of Jonathan Pound. Four Country Epitaphs. *Unknown.* GoTP
Here lies the body of Jonathan Stout. *Unknown.* WhC
Here lies the body of Mary Anne Lowder. Mary Anne Lowder. *Unknown.* WhC
Here lies the body of Michael Shay. On Stubborn Michael Shay. *Unknown.* GoTP
Here lies the body of Richard Hind. Epitaph. Francis Jeffrey. OxBoLi
Here lies the body of Sarah Sexton. Epitaph of Sarah Sexton. *Unknown.* TreFT; WhC
Here lies the body of this world. Epitaph on the World. Henry David Thoreau. OnPM
Here lies the [*or* a] clerk who half his life had spent. The Volunteer. Herbert Asquith. MMA; OtMeF
Here lies the Devil—ask no other name. On a Lord. Samuel Taylor Coleridge. FiBHP; PV
Here lies the flesh that tried. Epitaph. Louise Driscoll. HBMV; WGRP
Here lies the lighthouse-keeper's horse. Epitaph for a Lighthouse-Keeper's Horse. J. B. Morton. PV
Here lies the man Richard. *Unknown.* WhC
Here lies the man was born, and cried. An Epitaph on a Man for Doing Nothing. John Hoskins. TuPP
Here lies the mother of children seven. *Unknown.* WhC
Here lies the noble warrior that never blunted sword. Epitaph on the Earl of Leicester. Sir Walter Ralegh. EnRePo; FOL; SiPS
Here lies the peerless paper lord, Lord Peter. On Peter Robertson. John Gibson Lockhart. SiTL
Here lies the poet, deaf and dumb. Lines for a Dead Poet. David Ferry. ML; PP
Here lies the poet Wolker, lover of the world. Epitaph. Jiri Wolker. WaaP
Here lies the preacher, judge, and poet, Peter. On Peter Robinson. Francis Jeffrey. *Fr.* Epitaphs. OxBoLi; WhC
Here lies the Reverend Jonathan Doe. On the Reverend Jonathan Doe. *Unknown.* ChTr
Here lies the ruined cabinet. An Epitaph on His Deceased Friend. Robert Fletcher. SeCL
Here lies the sacred bones. Upon His House. Andrew Marvell. MaMe
Here lies the street of the three balls. To an Avenue Sport. Helen Johnson Collins. PoNe
Here lies the woven garb he wore. The Robe of Grass. John Le Gay Brereton. BoAu
Here lies [*or* lyes], to each her parent's ruth. On My First Daughter. Ben Jonson. AnAnS-2; EnRePo; EP; LoBV; OBS; NoP; PoFS; ReIE; SeCP; SeCV-1; SeEP
Here lies what's left. On Leslie Moore. *Unknown.* GoTP
Here lies (where all at peace may be). A Recluse. Walter de la Mare. BoPe
Here lies, whom hound did ne'er pursue. Epitaph on a Hare. William Cowper. BoPe; BWP; FiP; HBV; HBVY; NoP; PoEL-3; PoG; RG; SeCeV; ShBV-1
Here lies Will Smith—and, what's something rarish. On Will Smith. *Unknown.* SiTL
Here lies wise and valiant dust. Epitaph on the Earl of Strafford [*or* Gravestones]. John Cleveland. CavP; FosPo; MePo; OBS; OtMeF; SeCePo; TrGrPo
Here lieth he who never aught. In Tumulum Avari. John Weever. SiCE
Here lieth Hercules the Second. John Baynham's Epitaph. Thomas Dermody. OnYI
Here Lieth Love. Thomas Watson. *See* My Love Is Past.
Here lieth one, who did most truly prove. [Another] On the Oxford Carrier. Milton. BOHV; CABA; NA
"Here lieth one whose name was writ on water." On Keats. Shelley. ML
Here lieth under this marble ston. An Epitaph. *Unknown.* MeEL
Here like the maze of our bewilderment. Seafront. Laurie Lee. POTi
Here lith the fresshe flowr of Plantagenet. Epitaph on Queen Elizabeth, Wife of Henry VII. *Unknown.* AtBAP
Here lived the soul enchanted. Poe's Cottage at Fordham. John Henry Boner. AA
Here love the slain with love the slayer lies. The Play of "King Lear." Sir William Watson. VA
Here luxury's the common lot. The light. Grasse: The Olive Trees. Richard Wilbur. NYBP; PoAn
Here lyes Charles the first the Great. *Unknown.* SeCSL
Here lyes Jonson with the rest. *See* Here lies Jonson with the rest.
Here lyes, to each her parents' ruth. *See* Here lies . . .
Here may the band, that now in triumph shines. The Heavenly Jerusalem. Giles Fletcher. *Fr.* Christ's Victory and Triumph. OxBoCh
Here meet together the prefiguring day. The Passover in the Holy Family. Dante Gabriel Rossetti. GoBC; MaVP
Here 'mid these leafy walls. Woodland Worship. Ethelwyn Wetherald. CaP
Here morning in the ploughman's songs is met. Ploughman Singing. John Clare. BoPe
Here must I be forever intimate. The Spirit. Lon Woodrum. SoP
Here must wee rest; and where else shóuld wee rest? A Serious and a Curious Night-Meditation. Thomas Traherne. SeCP
Here my chameleon muse herself doth change. To His Good Friend, Sir Anthony Cooke. Sir John Davies. *Fr.* Gulling Sonnets. Sonn; TuPP
Here, Nancy, let me take your hand. To a Child. Norreys Jephson O'Connor. HBMV
Here Nature holds as in a hollowed hand. The Skylark's Nest. R. H. Long. BoAu; PoAu-1
Here! No sweetness trips so well as here. Bird Song. John Hay. NePoAm-2
Here, no woman, nor man besides. Man in a Room. William Carlos Williams. NP
Here not the flags, the rhythmic. Neutrality. Sidney Keyes. MoAB; MoBrPo (1962 ed.)
Here nothing warns. Dante Gabriel Rossetti. *Fr.* Jenny. NBM
Here now once more I lie. Tenth Reunion. Edward Steese. GoYe
Here, O lily-white lady mine. The Handsel Ring. George Houghton. AA
Here, O my Lord, I see Thee face to face. Horatius Bonar. *Fr.* This Do in Remembrance of Me. TrPWD
Here of a truth the world's extremes are met. At the Grave of Dante Gabriel Rossetti. Mackenzie Bell. VA
Here often, when a child I lay reclined. Lines. Tennyson. CABA; StP
Here on my breast have I bled! Ojibwa War Songs. *Unknown.* AWP; JAWP; WBP
Here, on our native soil, we breathe once more. Composed in the Valley near Dover. Wordsworth. MERP
Here on our rock-away horse we go. Johnny's By-low Song. Laura E. Richards. BoChLi
Here on the arid shoulder. The Broom. Giacomo Leopardi. WoL
Here on the edge of hell. Harlem. Langston Hughes. CAD
Here on the flyleaf of the garish day. I Would Define My Love. Jessica Powers. JKCP (1955 ed.)
Here on the mellow hill. Autumn Scene. Basil Dowling. BoNaP
Here on the mountain-pass. On the Heights. Matsuo Basho. OnPM
Here on the ridge where the shrill north-easter trails. The Ridge, 1919. W. W. Gibson. POTE
Here, on these hills, no sense of loneliness. Whence Cometh My Help. P. L. Montgomery. OQP
Here on this open, ancient book. Diary of a Raccoon. Gertrude Ryder Bennett. GoYe
Here, on this rock, and on this sterile soil. The Pilgrim Fathers. John Boyle O'Reilly. PEDC
Here, on this sunny shore, in simpler days. By an Ancient Sea. Thomas Curtis Clark. ChIP
Here once the evenings sobbed. The Pear-Tree. Iwan Goll. TrJP
Here, or not many feet from hence. Certain True Woords Spoken Concerning One Benet Corbett. Richard Corbett. AnAnS-2; SeCP
Here Pause: The Poet Claims at Least This Praise. Wordsworth. EnRP; EPN
(1811.) PoFr
Here pause: these graves are all too young as yet. Shelley. *Fr.* Adonais. MyFE

Here penned within the human fold. The Human Fold. Edwin Muir. LiTM (rev. ed.)
Here Pilate's Court is. The Stations of the Cross. Padraic Colum. GoBC
Here ploughshares rot and farmers. Garrison Town. Emanuel Litvinoff. WaP
Here poise, like flowers on flowers, the butterflies. At the Grave of Champernowne. John Albee. HBV
Here rage the furies that have shaped the world. Land's End (Point Lobos, California). Stanton A. Coblentz. EtS
Here rest in peace the bones of Henry Reece. History of Peace. Robert Graves. HBMV
Here rest the relics of a friend below. Tray's Epitaph. "Peter Pindar." TreFS
Here rests a woman, good without pretense. Epitaph on Mrs. Corbet, Who Died of a Cancer in Her Breast. Pope. BWP; CEP
Here Reynolds is laid, and to tell you my mind. Sir Joshua Reynolds. Goldsmith. *Fr.* Retaliation. OBEC; SeCePo
Here richly, with ridiculous display. Epitaph on the Politician [*or* On a Politician]. Hilaire Belloc. CoBE; InP; MoBrPo; NeMA; ShM; TreFT; WhC
Here room and kingly silence keep. By the Pacific Ocean. Joaquin Miller. AA; AnAmPo; MAP; MoAmPo (1942 ed.)
Here rounds our ring, the wheel of earth's horizon. Rings in a Roundness. Carleton Drewry. NYTB
Here shall remain all tears for lovely things. To Song. Thomas S. Jones, Jr. HBV
Here She Goes and There She Goes. James Nack. BOHV
Here She Is. Mary Britton Miller. TiPo (1959 ed.)
Here she lies, a pretty bud. Upon a Child That Died [*or* Epitaph upon a Child That Died]. Robert Herrick. CavP; ForPo; MaRV; NoP; OBEV; PoeP; SeCV-1; SeEP; StP
Here she lies, in bed of spice. Upon a Maid. Robert Herrick. ChTr; FaBoCh; LoGBV; OxBoLi; SeEP
Here She Stands. Jean-Joseph Rabéarivelo, *tr. fr. French by* Miriam Koshland. PBA
Here She Was Wont to Go! and Here! and Here! Ben Jonson. *Fr.* The Sad Shepherd. CLwM; ILP; TuPP
(Aeglamour's Lament.) CH
Here, Shock, the pride of all his kind, is laid. On His Dog. John Gay. ALV
Here sit a shepherd and a shepherdess. The Green Shepherd. Louis Simpson. NePoEA; NYBP
"Here sits the Lord Mayor." The City Show. Eleanor Farjeon. GaP
Here sits the Lord Mayor. Mother Goose. ExPo; HBV; HBVY; OTPC (1923 ed.); OxNR; PPL; SAS
Here Skugg Lies Snug. Benjamin Franklin. SiTL; WhC
(On Skugg.) GoTP
Here something stubborn comes. Seed Leaves. Richard Wilbur. BoNaP
Here sown to dust lies one that drave. A Dead Warrior. Laurence Housman. HBMV
Here sparrows build upon the trees. My Early Home. John Clare. BoTP; HBV; OTPC (1923 ed.); PoLF
Here stand I. On the London Fire's Monument. George Villiers, Duke of Buckingham. PeRV
Here stands a good apple tree. Apple-howling Songs. *Unknown.* OTPC (1923 ed.); PCH
Here stillness sounds like echoes in a tomb. In a Museum. Babette Deutsch. HBMV
Here stood a lofty church—there is a steeple. Pleasant Delusion of a Sumpteous Citty. Sarah Kemble Knight. SCAP
Here take my picture; though I bid farewell. His Picture [*or* Elegy V]. John Donne. Elegies, V. CBEP; EnRePo; FaBoEn; MaMe; MeLP; MePo; NoP; OBS; ReEn; SeEP
Here that old humpback, Tintoretto, tells. La Creazione Degli Animali. John Malcolm Brinnin. NYTB
Here the big stars roll down. Spoken through Glass. Eithne Wilkins. NeBP
Here the crow starves, here the patient stag. Rannoch by Glencoe. T. S. Eliot. Landscapes, IV. FaBoEn; LoGBV
Here the Eternal Lord, protector of all creatures. Cædmon (?). *Fr.* Genesis. YAT
Here the Frailest Leaves of Me. Walt Whitman. AP
Here the gallows, there the cord. Among Foes. Nietzsche. PoFr
"Here the hangman stops his cart." The Carpenter's Son. A. E. Housman. A Shropshire Lad, XLVII. BoLiVe; CoBMV; MoAB; MoBrPo; NeMA; PoAn; PoVP; VaPo
Here the hills are earth's bones. Asian Desert. Dorothy Wellesley. OBMV
Here the horse-mushrooms make a fairy ring. The Fairy Ring. Andrew Young. ChTr
Here the human past is dim and feeble and alien to us. Haunted Country. Robinson Jeffers. OxBA
Here the jack-hammer jabs into the ocean. Colloquy in Black Rock. Robert Lowell. AnNE; AP; CoBMV; FiMAP; MiAP; MoAB; MoAmPo (1950 ed.); Po; PoDB; ReMP
Here the oceans twain have waited. Panama. James Jeffrey Roche. MC; PAH; PoRL
Here the Stem Rises. Daniel Berrigan. TwAmPo
Here the tide of summer thrusts its last. August. Norman Nicholson. POTi
Here the tides flow. Newfoundland. E. J. Pratt. TwCaPo
Here the Trace. Boris Pasternak, *tr. fr. Russian by* Babette Deutsch. LiTW
Here the tram crashes to a stop. La Perouse. William Hart-Smith. BoAu
Here the white-ray'd anemone is born. In a Spring Grove. William Allingham. IrPN
Here the young lover, on his elbow raised. The Corner of the Field. Frances Cornford. BoLP; ELU
Here, then, we stand on the Canadian shore. John Hunter-Duvar. *Fr.* De Roberval. CaP
Here they all come to die. The Country of a Thousand Years of Peace. James Merrill. PoCh
Here they are. The soft eyes open. The Heaven of Animals. James Dickey. AP; CoAP; FRC; LiTM (1970 ed.); ToPo
Here they gallop pak, pak. To the Lady of Ch'i. *Unknown. Fr.* The Book of Songs. HW
Here they give me greeting. A Changeling Grateful. Josephine Preston Peabody. AA
Here they went with smock and crook. Forefathers. Edmund Blunden. ChMP; OBEV (new ed.); OBMV; POTE
Here through our little world of outward sense. Eternal Moment. "Katherine Hale." CaP;
Here to the leisured side of life. The Lamplighter. "Seumas O'Sullivan." OxBI
Here to this wide black earth, which, aeons past. Peat-Cutters. Geoffrey Johnson. HaMV
Here toil the striplings, who should be a-swarm. Factory Children. Richard Burton. MaRV
Here under Heaven ringed. Northern Light. L. A. G. Strong. POTE
Here under leafy bowers. Under Leafy Bowers. Judah Al-Harizi. TrJP
Here under this sod and under these trees. Solomon Pease. *Unknown.* WhC
Here war is simple like a monument. W. H. Auden. *Fr.* In Time of War. EnLit
Here was I with my arm and heart. Too Late. Robert Browning. PoVP
Here was the sound of water falling only. The Owl. Robert Penn Warren. MAP; MoAmPo
Here we are all, by day; by night we are hurled. Dreams. Robert Herrick. SeEP
Here we are, gentlemen; here's the whole gang of us. At Your Service; the Panama Gang. Berton Braley. BLPA
Here we are, if you have any more. Thomas Middleton. *Fr.* The Changeling, V, iii. AtBAP; PoEL-2
Here we bring new water. A New Year Carol. *Unknown.* AtBAP; BoTP; CH; FlW; OxBoLi; PoSC; ThWaDe
Here we broached the Christmas barrel. The House of Hospitalities. Thomas Hardy. MoPW
Here we can observe the superior mirages. Traveller's Guide to Antarctica. Adrien Stoutenburg. NYBP
Here We Come a-Caroling. *Unknown.* FaPON; MPB; TiPo (1952 ed.)
Here we come again, again, and here we come again! Child's Carol. Eleanor Farjeon. RePo
Here We Come a-Haying. Eunice Close. BoTP
Here We Come a-Piping. *Unknown.* BoTP; CH; ExPo; HH; OTPC (1946 ed.); PoRh; SiSoSe; TiPo (1959 ed.)
Here We Come a-Wassailing, *with music. Unknown.* YaCaBo
(Wassail Song, The.) OHIP; PoSC
Here we come a-whistling through the fields so green. Twelfth Night Carol. *Unknown.* PCD; PCH; PoRL

Here we come gathering nuts an' may. Nuts an' May. *Unknown.* EvOK
Here we dance Looby Loo. Looby Loo. *Unknown.* SoPo
Here we go a-walking, so softly, so softly. Walking Song. Charles Williams. BoTP
Here we go dancing jingo-ring. *Unknown.* OxNR
Here we go in a flung festoon. The Road Song of the Bandar Log. Kipling. *Fr.* The Jungle Book. BoPe; OAEP (2d ed.)
Here we go round ring by ring. *Unknown.* OxNR
Here we go up, up, up. *Unknown.* BoTP; OTPC; SAS
Here we halt our march, and pitch our tent. The Green Mountain Boys. Bryant. PoPl
Here We Have Idaho. Harry A. Powell. PoRL
"Here we stan' on the Constitution, by thunder!" The Debate in the Sennit. James Russell Lowell. *Fr.* The Biglow Papers. HBV; PAH
Here were planes. But everything else was gone. Wendling. Coman Leavenworth. *Fr.* Norfolk Memorials. LiTA
Here, west of winter, lies the ample flower. Prayer for This Day. Hildegarde Flanner. TrPWD
Here, when precipitate Spring with one light bound. *See* Here, where precipitate Spring . . .
Here, when the Greeks, by strength of heart and hand. The Deliverer, Jove. *Unknown.* OnPM
Here where by all All Saints invoked are. A Letter to the Lady Carey, and Mrs. Essex Riche, from Amyens. John Donne. MaMe
Here where each road-worn one. The Stirrup Cup. Aline Kilmer. CAW
Here, where fecundity of Babel frames. Babylon and Sion (Goa and Lisbon). Luís de Camoes. AWP; WoL
Here, where my father lies under the ornamental plum. Churchyard of St. Mary Magdalene, Old Milton. John Heath-Stubbs. NePoEA
Here where no increase is. Supplication. Josephine Johnson. TrPWD
Here, where our Lord once laid his head. Upon the Sepulchre of Our Lord. Richard Crashaw. MaMe
Here, where [*or* when] precipitate Spring with one light bound. A Fiesolan [*or* Faesulan] Idyl. Walter Savage Landor. EnRP; OAEP; OBRV; SeCePo; VA
Here, where summer slips. The Red and the Green. Anne Wilkinson. MoCV
Here, where the baby paddles in the gutter. Lean Street. G. S. Fraser. NeBP; OxBS
Here, where the breath of the scented-gorse floats through the sun-stained air. Breton Afternoon. Ernest Dowson. OBNC
Here where the dead lie hidden. Hide-and-Seek. Robert Francis. PoIE; PoSa
Here where the fields lie lonely and untended. A Deserted Home. Sidney Royse Lysaght. CH
Here, where the night is clear as sea-water. Lament for a Sailor. Paul Dehn. WaP
Here, where the pale grass struggles with each wind. A Decayed Monastery. Thomas Dermody. OnYI
Here where the pirate chieftains sailed. The Caribbean. Stephanie Ormsby. PoNe
Here where the season swiftly turns. Exile. Theodore Maynard. MoBrPo (1942 ed.)
Here where the sunlight. The White Peacock. "Fiona Maclead." PoVP; VA
Here where the taut wave hangs. Life's Circumnavigators. W. R. Rodgers. AnIV; FaBoMo; GTBS-P; OxBI
Here where the wind is always north-north-east. New England. E. A. Robinson. AmP; CABA; CBV; FaBoEn; ForPo; InPo; MAP; MoAB; MoAmPo; MoVE; NoP; OxBA; VaPo; WhC
Here, where the world is quiet. The Garden of Proserpine. Swinburne. AnFE; AWP; BoLiVe; CoBE; DiPo; EnL; EnLi-2; EnLit; ExPo; FaBV; ForPo; HBV; InP; InPo; LiTB; LiTG; MaVP; NoP; OBNC; OuHeWo; PAn; PeVV; PG (1945 ed.); PIA; PoAn; PoE; PoEL-5; PoFS; PoIE; PoPl; PoRA; PoVP; SeCePo; SeCeV; TreFT; TrGrPo; ViBoPo; ViPo; ViPP; VP
Here where under earth is head. Etsi Omnes, Ego Non. Ernest Myers. VA
Here, where Vespasian's legions struck the sands. Embarcation. Thomas Hardy. BrPo
Here where we are, wrapped in the afternoon. Obligations. Jane Cooper. AmPC; NePoEA-2
Here where you left me alone. Letter from Slough Pond. Isabella Gardner. ELU
Here will we rest us, under these. The Flight into Egypt. Longfellow. *Fr.* Christus; a Mystery. OBVV
Here, with my beer I sit. Beer. George Arnold. AA
Here you have sky high one wall. Moonrise in City Park. Josephine Miles. FiMAP
Here you see old Tom Moore. The Days of '49. Charles Rhodes. SGR
Here! You sons of the men. English Thornton. Edgar Lee Masters. *Fr.* Spoon River Anthology. OxBA
Hereafter. Harriet Prescott Spofford. HBV
Hereafter. Rosamund Marriott Watson. VA
Heredity. Thomas Bailey Aldrich. AA; AnAmPo; MAP; PFY
Heredity. Thomas Hardy. CBEP; CTC; ImOP; MoPW
Heredity. Lydia Avery Coonley Ward. HBV
Here's a body—there's a bed! Good Night. Thomas Hood. GaP; MPB (1956 ed.); SiSoSe; SoPo
Here's a clean year. A New Year. Mary Carolyn Davies. OQP; YeAr
Here's a guessing story. What Is It? H. E. Wilkinson. BoTP
Here's a hand to the boy who has courage. Our Heroes. Phoebe Cary. BLPA
Here's a Health to Them That's Awa'. Burns. HBV; PoFr
Here's a health unto His Majesty. A Health unto His Majesty [*or* His Majesty's Health]. *Unknown, at. to* Jeremy Savile. ChTr; SeCL
Heres a jolly couple O the jolly jolly couple. *Unknown.* SeCSL
Here's a knocking indeede. Shakespeare. *Fr.* Macbeth, II, iii. AtBAP
Here's a land where all are equal. Creede. Cy Warman. PoOW
Here's a large one for the lady. *Unknown.* OxNR
Here's a little mouse) and. Four III. E. E. Cummings. WePo
Here's a mellow cup of tea, golden tea! The Poets at Tea, 7. Barry Pain. Par
Here's a moccasin track in the drifts. The Chase. *Unknown.* SCC
Here's a [to the] Poor Widow from Babylon. *Unknown.* BoTP; OTPC; OxNR
Here's a present for Rose. A Greek Gift. Austin Dobson. *Fr.* Rose-Leaves. MoBrPo (1942 ed.)
Here's a song. Scel Lem Duib, *Tr. fr. Irish by* Brian O Nolan. OxBI
Here's a song of praise for a beautiful world. The Beautiful World. W. L. Childress. OHIP
Here's a summer, heavy and hard. Elegy for Lucy Lloyd. Llewelyn Goch. LiTW
Here's Abbey Way: here are the rooms. The Chrysanthemum Show. C. Day Lewis. MoVE
Here's an adventure! What awaits. On Opening a New Book. Abbie Farwell Brown. YeAr
Here's an example from/ A butterfly. The Example. W. H. Davies. AnFE; HBMV; MoBrPo; OA; POTE; TrGrPo; TSW; WHA
Here's another day, dear. Glad Day. W. Graham Robertson. HBV
Here's Christianity again! On the Reported New Outbreak of Christianity. James H. McCabe. JKCP (1955 ed.)
Here's Cooper, who's written six volumes to show. Cooper. James Russell Lowell. *Fr.* A Fable for Critics. AnNE; AP; CoBA; MWA-1; OxBA
Here's Finiky Hawkes. Black Your Shoes, Your Honour? *Unknown.* OxNR; PCH
Here's flowers for you. The Flowers of Perdita [*or* Flowers of Middle Summer]. Shakespeare. *Fr.* The Winter's Tale, IV, iii. FiP; PoG; YeAr
Here's good wind, here's sweet wind. Song of the Full Catch. Constance Lindsay Skinner. *Fr.* Songs of the Coast Dwellers. CaP
Here's no more news, than virtue, I may as well. To Sir Henry Wo[o]tton [*or* Verse-Letter: To Sir Henry Wootton]. John Donne. EP; MaMe; TuPP
Here's pretty conduct, Hugh O'Rourke. To Tomas [*or* Tomaus] Costello at the Wars. *At. to* Tomas O'Higgins, *tr. by* Frank O'Connor. AnIV; KiLC
Here's shade and comfort by this towering tree. Christmas 1942. Eric Irvin. BoAV; PoAu-2

Here's Sulky Sue. *Unknown.* OxNR
Here's the garden she walked across. The Flowers's Name. Robert Browning. *Fr.* Garden Fancies. ACV; CTC; EnLi-2 (1949 ed.); GTBS-D; HBV
Here's the golden cup all bossy with satyrs and saints. Melting of the Earl's Plate. George Walter Thornbury. VA
Here's the mail, sort it quick. A Sure Sign. Nancy Byrd Turner. PCH; SoPo; TiPo
Here's the mould of a musical bird long passed from light. In a Museum. Thomas Hardy. UnS
Here's the spot. Look around you. Above on the height. Caldwell of Springfield. Bret Harte. PAH
Here's the tender coming. The Press-Gang. *Unknown.* ChTr
Here's to good old Boston. *See* And this is good old Boston.
Here's to him that grows it. The Haymakers' Song, The. Alfred Austin. VA
Here's to Nelson's Memory. Robert Browning. ViPo
Here's to New Haven and Boston. To New Haven and Boston. Walter Foster Angell. TreFS
Here's to the home that was never, never ours! Song of the Drift Weed. Jessie Mackay. BoAu
Here's to the Maiden. Sheridan. *See* Let the Toast Pass.
Here's to the man who invented stairs. Stairs. Oliver Herford. FiBHP; InMe; RePo; WhC
Here's to the man with the leather lung. My Candidate. Norman H. Crowell. YaD
Here's to the men who lose! To the Men Who Lose. George L. Scarborough. BLPA
Here's to the passing cowboy, the plowman's pioneer. A Cowboy Toast. James Barton Adams. SCC
Here's to the poor widow from Babylon. *Unknown.* *See* Here's a poor widow from Babylon.
Here's to the Ranger! *Unknown.* CoSo
Here's to the red of it. Toast to the Flag, A. John Jay Daly. PAL; PoLF
Here's to the town of New Haven. On the Democracy of Yale [*or* New Haven]. Frederick Scheetz Jones. BOHV; HBV; TreFS; WhC; YaD
Here's to the white carnation. The White Carnation. Margaret E. Sangster. PEDC
Here's to the year that's awa'! The Year That's Awa'. John Dunlop. HBV
Here's to thee, old apple tree. Apple-howling Songs. *Unknown.* OTPC (1923 ed.); OxNR; PCH
Here's to those who love us. Toast. *Unknown.* SiTL
Here's to ye absent lords, may they. A Toast. *Unknown.* ALV; WhC
Here's to you and here's to me. A Toast. *Unknown.* PV
Here's to you, belov'd Rhode Island. Rhode Island. T. Clarke Brown. PoRL
Here's to your eyes. Toast. Frank Horne. BANP; PoNe
Here's tropic flora. Hotel Lobby. Mildred Weston. WhC
Here's two or three jolly boys. *Unknown.* OxNR
Here's witts extraction morall and divine. One Presenting a Rare Book to Madame Hull. John Saffin. SCAP
Heresy for a Classroom. Rolfe Humphries. PoMa
Heretic, The. Bliss Carman. WGRP
Heretics All. Hilaire Belloc. ACP (1952 ed.)
Hereto I come to view a voiceless ghost. After a Journey. Thomas Hardy. AtBAP; BWP; ChMP; CMoP; DTC; ELP; EnLoPo; FaBoEn; GTBS-D; GTBS-P; MoPW; MoVE; OBNC; PoEL-5
Heretse! Baboon. *Unknown.* PeSA
Hereunder Jacob Schmidt who, man and bones. Immortal Helix. Archibald MacLeish. CBV
Heriot's Ford. Kipling. PoRA
Heritage. Gwendolyn Bennett. AmNP; BANP
Heritage. Countee Cullen. AmNP; BALP; BANP; MAP; MoAmPo; NoP; PoNe; TTY
What Is Africa to Me? *sel.* FaBV
Heritage, The. James Russell Lowell. HBV; HBVY; OTPC
Heritage. Claude McKay. PoNe
Heritage, The. Edward Bliss Reed. EtS
Heritage. A. M. Sullivan. JKCP (1955 ed.)
Heritage of hopes and fears, An. The Soul. Madison Cawein. AA
Herman Altman. Edgar Lee Masters. *Fr.* Spoon River Anthology. OxBA
Herman Melville. W. H. Auden. GTBS-W; LiTA; LiTM (rev. ed.); NePA; OAEP (2d ed.); OxBA
Herman Moon's Hourbook, *sels.* Christopher Middleton. NePoEA-2
Abasis.
Ant Sun, The.
Forenoon, The.
Ode on Contemplating Clapham Junction.
Pointed Boots.
Waterloo Bridge.
Hermann and Dorothea, *sel.* Goethe, *tr. fr. German.*
"All is changing now—it seems as though all must be parted," *tr. by* F. Melian Stawell *and* Nora Purtscher-Wydenbruck. PoFr
Hermaphroditus. Swinburne. SyP
Hermatic Poems. Elias Ashmole. LO
Hermes of the Ways. Hilda Doolittle ("H. D."). LiTA; NP; OnPM
Hermes Trismegistus. Hilda Doolittle ("H. D.") *Fr.* A Tribute to the Angels. FaBoTw
"Herminius! Aulus greets thee." The Death of Herminius. Macaulay. *Fr.* Lays of Ancient Rome: The Battle of Lake Regillus. OtMeF
Herminius's Horse. Macaulay. *Fr.* Lays of Ancient Rome: The Battle of Lake Regillus. PoG
Hermione. "Barry Cornwall." OBVV
Hermit, The. "Æ." BEL; PoVP
Hermit, The. James K. Baxter. AnNZ
Hermit, The. W. H. Davies. BrPo; MoBrPo
Hermit, The. Hsü Pên. *tr. fr. Chinese by* Henry H. Hart. FlW
Hermit, The. Howard Moss. NePoAm
Hermit, The. Thomas Parnell. GoTL
Hermit, The. *At. to* Sir Walter Ralegh. *See* Like to a Hermit.
Hermit, The. Ruth Silcock. NYTB
Hermit Advises a Monk When Things Are Bleak Indeed, A. William Hathaway. QAH
Hermit Hoar. Samuel Johnson. PV; ViBoPo
(Imitation in the Style of Thomas Gray.) CLwM
Hermit, sick of scabby cities, The. The Hermit. Ruth Silcock. NYTB
Hermitage, The. *unknown, at. to* St. Manchan of Lemanaghan in Offaly, *tr. fr. Irish by* Frank O'Connor. KiLC
Hermit's Song, The. *Unknown.* *See* Wish of Manchin of Liath, The.
Hermogenes's Song. Ben Jonson. *Fr.* The Poetaster. PoIE
Hermotimus. William Edmondstoune Aytoun. OBVV
Hern flew east, the hern flew west, The. *See* Heron flew east. . .
Herndon. S. Weir Mitchell. PAH
Hero, The. Ambrose Bierce. OQP; PoRL
Hero, A. Florence Earle Coates. OHIP
Hero, The. Roy Fuller. FaBoMo
Hero, The. Leroy F. Jackson. SiSoSe
Hero, The. Marianne Moore. *Fr.* Part of a Novel, Part of a Poem, Part of a Play. CMoP; OnHM; OxBA; TwAmPo
Hero, The. Robert Nicoll. HBV; VA
Hero, The. Sir Henry Taylor. VA
Hero, The. George Woodcock. TwCaPo
Hero and Holy Man. Peter Fellowes. QAH
Hero and Leander. John Donne. MaMe; ReIE
Hero and Leander, *sels.* Thomas Hood. EnRP
Death of Leander, The.
Scylla's Lament.
Hero and Leander. Christopher Marlowe (First *and* Second Sestiads), *completed by* George Chapman. CABA (First *and* Second Sestiads); NoP (First *and* Second Sestiads); OBSC (First *and* Second Sestiads); ReEn (First *and* Second Sestiads); ReIE (First *and* Second Sestiads); TuPP (First *and* Second Sestiads)
Sels.
Bridal Song, *fr.* Fifth Sestiad. Chapman. OBEV
("O come, soft rest of cares! come, Night!") EG
(Song: "O come, soft rest of cares, come, Night!") ViBoPo
"By this, Leander, being near the land," *fr.* Second Sestiad. Marlowe. ErPo
Epithalamion Teratus, *fr.* Fifth Sestiad. Chapman. AtBAP; ElL; LoBV
(Wedding of Alcmane and Mya, The.) OBSC
"Her veil was artificial flowers and leaves," *fr.* First Sestiad. Marlowe. HoPM
Hero the Faire, *fr.* First Sestiad. Marlowe. FaBoEn; WHA
It Lies Not in Our Power to Love or Hate, *fr.* First Sestiad. Marlowe. BoLiVe; TrGrPo; WHA

Hero (continued)
(Love at First Sight.) FaBoEn; MeWo; TreFT
(Who Ever Loved, That Loved Not at First Sight?) FaFP; LiTB; LiTG; LiTL
"O Hero, Hero, thus he cry'de full oft," *fr.* Second Sestiad. Marlowe. AtBAP
"On Hellsepont, guilty of true love's blood," *fr.* First Sestiad. Marlowe. AnFE, *sel.*; AtBAP; LoBV, *sel.*; OAEP; OBSC; PoEL-2; SeCePo; SiCE
"On this feast day, O cursèd day and hour," *fr.* First Sestiad. Marlowe. ViBoPo
Repentance, *fr.* Third Sestiad. Chapman. OBSC
"She stay'd not for her robes, but straight arose," *fr.* Second Sestiad. Marlowe. UnTE
Hero and Leander. Joseph S. Newman. FiBHP
Hero Cockroach, The. Don Marquis. *See* Archy Experiences a Seizure.
Hero Entombed, I. Peter Quennell. FaBoMo; LiTB
Hero first thought it, The. Truth. "Æ." AnIL; GTSL; MoBrPo; TOP
Hero in the Land of Dough, A. Robert Clairmont. WaKn; WhC
Hero Leaves His Ship, The. Barbara Guest. AmPC
Hero of Bridgewater, The. Charles L. S. Jones. PAH
Hero of the Commune, The. Margaret Junkin Preston. AA
Hero Song. Robert Duncan. CrMA
Hero the Fair[e]. Christopher Marlowe. *Fr.* Hero and Leander, First Sestiad. FaBoEn; WHA
Hero-Worship. William Bell Scott. VA
Herod. W. H. Auden. *Fr.* For the Time Being. OnHM
Herod, *sel.* Stephen Phillips.
Benediction: "Now unto Him who brought His people forth." MaRV
Herod by his great cruelty. Christ Brought Home. *Unknown.* PoLi
Herod sitting on his throne. The Children's Ghosts. Winifred M. Letts. HBMV
Herod the King came sounding through. In Galilee. Jessie Mackay. AnNZ
Hérodiade, *sel.* Stéphane Mallarmé, *tr. fr. French by* Arthur Symons.
"To mine own self I am a wilderness." SyP
Herodotus in Egypt. Andrew Lang. PoVP
Herod's Suspicions. Richard Crashaw. StJW
Heroes. Edna Dean Proctor. HBV
Heroes, The. Louis Simpson. NePoAm
Heroes. Walt Whitman. *Fr.* Song of Myself. AA
Heroes, and kings! your distance keep. For One Who Would Not Be Buried in Westminster Abbey. Pope. ACP (1926 ed.)
Heroes out of music born. The Farnese Hercules. Sacheverell Sitwell. FaBoMo; LiTM (rev. ed.)
Heroes paused upon the plain, The. The Byrnies. Thom Gunn. NePoEA-2
Heroic Age, The. Richard Watson Gilder. AA; OHIP
Heroic good, target for which the young. Faint yet Pursuing. Coventry Patmore. OxBoCh; PoVP
Heroic soul, in homely garb half hid. Lincoln. John Townsend Trowbridge. PGD
Heroic [*or* Heroique] Stanzas, Consecrated to the Glorious Memory of His Most Serene and Renowned Highnesse, Oliver, Late Lord Protector of This Common-Wealth. Dryden. CEP; SeCV-2
Heroic Vengeance. Milton. *Fr.* Samson Agonistes. OBS
Heroicall Epistle. John Donne. MaMe
Heroics. Elinor Wylie. CoBA
Heroism ("Ruby wine is drunk"). Emerson. AtBAP; ViBoPo
Heroism ("So nigh is grandeur to our dust"). Emerson. *See* Duty.
Heroism. Lizette Woodworth Reese. MaRV
Heron. Philip Booth. NePoEA
Heron, The. John Lyle Donaghy. NeIP
Heron, The. Edward Hovell-Thurlow. HBV
Heron, The. Theodore Roethke. BiS; FosPo; MiAP; PDV
Heron, The. *Unknown.* EnSB
(Knight in the Bower, The, *sl. diff.*) ChTr
Heron, The. Brian Vrepont. MoAuPo
Heron. Ted Walker. NYBP
Heron, The. Vernon Watkins. ChMP; GTBS-P; TwCP; UnPo (3d ed.)
Heron-billed pale cattle-birds, The. At Algeciras—a Meditation upon Death. W. B. Yeats. NoP
Heron cries in sorrow, The. Ki no Tsurayuki, *tr. fr. Japanese by* I. W. Furukami. LiTW
Heron [*or* Hern] flew east, the heròn [*or* hern] flew west, The. The Heron [*or* Knight in the Bower]. *Unknown.* ChTr; EnSB
Heron in Swamp. Frances Minturn Howard. GoYe
Heron is harsh with despair. Song. Brenda Chamberlain. NeBP; NeIP
Heron stands in water where the swamp, The. The Heron. Theodore Roethke. BiS; FosPo; MiAP; PDV
Heron That Liked Crab-Meat, The. *Unknown,* *tr. fr. Sanskrit by* Arthur W. Ryder. *Fr.* The Panchatantra. OuHeWo
Herons. Robin Blaser. NeAP
Herons, The. Francis Ledwidge. *See* Ardan Mór.
Herons. *Unknown.* *tr. fr. Japanese.* SUS
Hero's daughter, Leinster's loveliest! All Gold. *Unknown.* KiLC
Hero's Lamp. Dante Gabriel Rossetti. The House of Life, LXXXVIII. MaVP; PoVP; ViPo
Herrick, hello. To the Author of Hesperides and Noble Numbers. Mark Van Doren. ML
Herrick's Cavalier. Robert Herrick. PoFr
(His Cavalier.) GoJo
Herring. Kenneth Rexroth. *Fr.* A Bestiary. HoPM
Herring, The. Sir Walter Scott. BOHV
("Herring loves the merry moonlight, The.") FaBoCh; LoGBV
(Oyster, The.) RIS
Herring is prolific, The. Herring. Kenneth Rexroth. *Fr.* A Bestiary. HoPM
Herring loves the merry moonlight, The. The Herring [*or* The Oysters]. Sir Walter Scott. BOHV; FaBoCh; LoGBV; RIS
Herring-run was over, The. The long days. The Hayfield. Charles Bruce. *Fr.* The Flowing Summer. CaP
Herring Weir, The. Sir Charles G. D. Roberts. PeCV
Herringdove, The. Kenyon Cox. *Fr.* Mixed Beasts. RIS
Herrings. Swift. *Fr.* Verses for Fruitwomen. AnIV; OnYI
Hers is the clean apron, good for fire. Farm Wife. R. S. Thomas. BoPe
Hers was a small room. Paneled in Pine. Marguerite George. FiSC
Hers was a world of chowders, stews. Island Cook. William Goodreau. NYTB
Herself. John Holmes. HoPM; MiAP
Herself. Dante Gabriel Rossetti. The House of Life, LVI. EPN; MaVP; ViPo
Herself a Rose Who Bore the Rose. Christina Rossetti. ISi
Herself hath given back my life to me. Love Song. *Unknown.* LiTW
Herself listening to herself, having no name. Herself. John Holmes. HoPM; MiAP
Hertha. Swinburne. BEL; EnLi-2; EPN; HBVY; MaVP; OAEP; OBEV (1st ed.); PoVP; TOP; VA; ViPo; ViPP; VP
Hervé Riel. Robert Browning. BEL; BeLS; FaBoBe; GN; HBV; MCCG; OnMSP; OtMeF; OTPC (1946 ed.); PoVP; TOP
He's a blockhead who wants a proof of what he can't perceive. Blake. EiCL
He's a little dog, with a stubby tail. Bum. W. Dayton Wedgefarth. BLPA
He's a-choppin' in de new groun'. Great God-a'mighty. *Unknown.* ABF
He's been sick. Waiting for Lunch. Joseph Cardarelli. QAH
He's bought a bed and a table too. Mary Ann. Joseph Tabrar. BoLP; PV
He's Come! The Saviour Has Come! Alice Mortenson. BePJ
He's Coming. Mark Van Doren. FaBV
He's dead/ the dog won't have to. Death. William Carlos Williams. OxBA
He's dead. Into the vault and out. Lying in State. Adrian Mitchell. ELU
He's gone./ I do not understand. The Going [*or* To Rupert Brooke]. W. W. Gibson. GTSL; NP
He's gone, and all our plans. To His Love. Ivor Gurney. MMA
He's Gone Away, *with music.* *Unknown.* AS; TrAS
He's gone to school, wee Hughie. Wee Hughie. Elizabeth Shane. HBMV

He's helping me now—this moment. This Moment. Annie Johnson Flint. BLRP
He's Jus' de Same Today, *with music*. *Unknown*. BoAN-1
He's my doll! A Kiss. *Unknown*. KiLC
He's no small prince who every day. Abraham Cowley. *Fr.* Upon Liberty. PeRV
He's nothing much but fur. A Kitten. Eleanor Farjeon. TiPo
He's off somewhere. Zombie. Joseph Cardarelli. QAH
He's on my front porch rapping. The Businessman of Alicante. Philip Levine. NaP
He's out stuck in a bird's craw. Maitreya the Future Buddha. Gary Snyder. *Fr.* Myths & Texts: Burning. NaP
He's sentenced, 'tis too late. Man New Made. Shakespeare. *Fr.* Measure for Measure, II, ii. GoBC
He's slight and old and sits up timidly. Old Man of Tennessee. John Hay. NePoAm-2
He's struttin' sho ernuff. De Drum Majah. Roy Garfield Dandridge. BANP
He's such a wanderer in his thoughts. The Wanderer. Amanda Benjamin Hall. HBMV
He's the Man for Me, *with music*. John A. Stone. SGR
Hesiod, 1908. Alexander Mair. GoTS; SiSw
Hesitating Blues, The. W. C. Handy. GoSl
Hesperia. Swinburne. OBNC; OBVV; VA
Hesperides ("I sing of brooks, of blossoms, birds and bowers"). Robert Herrick. *See* Argument of His Book, The.
Hesperides, The. Tennyson. MBW-2; PAn; SyP; ViPP
Hesperides—Fragment Thirty-six. Hilda Doolittle ("H. D."). *See* Fragment Thirty-six: "I know not what to do."
Hesperus. Byron. *See* Evening.
Hesperus. John Clare. ERoP-2; GTBS-P
(Evening Star, The.) ChTr
Hesperus' Hymn [*or* Song] to Cynthia. Ben Jonson. *See* Hymn to Diana.
Hesperus Sings. Thomas Lovell Beddoes. *See* Poor Old Pilgrim Misery.
Hesperus the Bringer. Byron. *See* Evening.
Hesperus! the day is gone. Hesperus [*or* The Evening Star]. John Clare. ChTr; ERoP-2; GTBS-P
Hesperus with the host of heaven came. Joseph Blanco White. *Fr.* Night and Death. MyFE
Hester. Charles Lamb. EnRP; GTBS; GTBS-D; GTBS-P; GTBS-W; GTSE; GTSL; HBV; LoBV; OBEV; OBRV; OTPC (1923 ed.); PoE
"Springy motion in her gait, A," *sel.* LO
Hester MacDonagh. Jeannette Slocomb Edwards. GoYe
Heterodoxy, A. Lord Dunsany. OnYI
"Heureux Qui Comme Ulysse." John Manifold. WaaP; WaP
Heureux qui, comme Ulysse, a fait un beau voyage. Joachim du Bellay, *tr. fr. French by* G. K. Chesterton. *Fr.* Regrets. AWP
(Happy Ulysses, The, *tr. by* G. K. Chesterton.) WoL
(Returning Home, *tr. by* William Stirling.) LiTW
(Translation from Du Bellay: "Happy, who like Ulysses or that lord," *tr. by* G. K. Chesterton.) InP
Hewel, or Woodpecker, The. Andrew Marvell. *Fr.* Upon Appleton House. ChTr
(Woodpecker, The.) BiS
Hex on the Mexican X, A. David McCord. FiBHP
Hexameter and Pentameter. *Unknown*. ChTr
Hexametra Alexis in Laudem Rosamundi. Robert Greene. *Fr.* Greene's Mourning Garment. ElL; PoEL-2; TuPP
(In Praise of Rosamund.) AtBAP
Hey, all you children. The Lord's Name Be Praised! *Unknown*. ThGo
Hey, Betty Martin! *Unknown*. AS, *with music*; ExPo
Hey! Crackerjack—jump! Dolphins in Blue Water. Amy Lowell. LaNeLa; TSW
Hey Derry Derry. Thomas Dekker. *See* Cold's the Wind.
Hey, Diddle, Diddle. Mother Goose. SoPo
Hey diddle diddle,/ And hey diddle dan! *Unknown*. OxNR
Hey diddle diddle,/ The physicists fiddle. Paul Dehn. *Fr.* Rhymes for a Modern Nursery. FiBHP
Hey [*or* Hi *or* High *or* Sing hey], diddle, diddle,/ the cat and the fiddle. Mother Goose. BoChLi; FaBoBe; FaFP; HBV; HBVY; HoPM; LiTG; OTPC; OxBoLi; OxNR; PCH; PPL; RIS; SAS; SiTL; StVeCh; TiPo
Hey diddle diddle, the cat and the fiddle,/ Bombers come with the moon. Maturity. J. Elgar Owen. WaP
Hey diddle, dinkety, poppety, pet. Mother Goose. BoTP; OTPC (1923 ed.); OxNR; PPL
Hey diddle dout,/ My candle's out. *Unknown*. OxNR
Hey ding a ding. *Unknown*. OxNR
Hey, dorolot, dorolot! *Unknown*. OxNR
"Hey, down a down!" did Dian sing. A Nymph's Disdain of Love. *Unknown*. ElL; SiCE; TuPP
Hey ho, care away, let the world pass. *Unknown*. *Fr.* The Trial of Treasure. TuPP
"Hey, I've found some moneywort." Kids. Witter Bynner. MPB
Hey, Joe! Cigarette! Cioccolat'! Cigarette for the Bambino. Gavin Ewart. WaP
Hey, Johnnie Cope, are ye wauking yet? Johnnie Cope. Adam Skirving. OxBS
Hey, laddie, hark, to the merry, merry lark. The Sky-Lark's Song. John Bennett. *Fr.* Master Sky-Lark. AA
Hey, little yellow boy. From a Bus. Malaika Ayo Wangara. NBP
Hey, my kitten, my kitten. Mother Goose. OTPC; OxNR; PPL; SAS
Hey, my lad, ho, my lad! Welcome to the New Year. Eleanor Farjeon. MoSiPe; YeAr
Hey! My Pony! Eleanor Farjeon. FaPON
Hey Nonny! Charles Kingsley. *Fr.* Dolcino to Margaret. OBVV
Hey Nonny No. Marguerite Merington. AA
Hey Nonny No! *Unknown*. CH; ChTr; EG; ElL; EnLi-1; LoBV; OBEV; TrGrPo; ViBoPo
(Carpe Diem.) PoFr
(Round, A.) FaBoCh; LoGBV
Hey! now, now, now. Welcome! Our Messiah. *Unknown*. MeEL
Hey! Now the Day Dawns! Alexander Montgomerie. *See* Night Is Near Gone, The.
Hey rub-a-dub, three maids in a tub. *Unknown*. SAS
Hey, rub-a-dub-dub [ho! rub-a-dub], three men in a tub. Mother Goose. GaP; SiTL
Hey! That's the wrong goal post, traitor. "Liberalissimo." Hart Leroi Bibbs. BF
Hey! the little postman. The Postman. Laura E. Richards. SoPo; TiPo
Hey there poleece. Poem to a Nigger Cop. Bobb Hamilton. BF; TTY
"Hey, troly, loly lo, maid, whither go you?" Pastourelle. *Unknown*. LO; OBSC
Hey, Wully Wine. *Unknown*. CH
Hey, you swelled-up turkey feller! November's Come. Joseph C. Lincoln. RePo
Heyhow for Hallowe'en. Hallowe'en [*or* The Witches]. *Unknown*. ChTr; FaBoCh; LoGBV; OTPC (1946 ed.)
Heywood goes down, saith Davie, sickerly. Thomas Bastard. SiCE
Heywood, th' old English epigrammatist. Ad Modernos Epigrammatistas. John Heath. SiCE; TuPP
Heywood was held for epigrams the best. Tempus Edax Rerum. Henry Parrot. SiCE
Heywood, which did in epigrams excel. In Haywodum. Sir John Davies. ReIE; SiCE; TuPP
Hi! diddle diddle. *See* Hey, diddle, diddle.
Hi! Hi! Hi! Hi! The Blue Duck. Lew Sarett. NP
Hi! hi! hi! hi! The Witch's Ride. Adelheid Wette. *Fr.* Hansel and Gretel. PCH
Hi hiana hu/ Our songs commence. Harvest Song. Dan Georgakas. ThO
Hi! Just you drop that! Stop, I say. Up the Spout. Swinburne. BOHV
"Hi!" said the blackbird, sitting on a chair [*or* swinging on the air]. The Birds' Courting Song. *Unknown*. TrAS
Hi! we shout with voice ecstatic. Roundel in the Rain. *Unknown*. FiBHP
Hi-yo, the boatsmen row. *Unknown*. LaNeLa
Hialmar. Roy Campbell. CoBE
Hialmar Speaks to the Raven. Leconte de Lisle, *tr. fr. French by* James Elroy Flecker. AWP; SyP
Hiawatha. Longfellow. *See* Song of Hiawatha, The.
Hiawatha. Stephen Sandy. CoPo
Hiawatha and Mudjekeewis. Longfellow. The Song of Hiawatha, IV. AnNE
Hiawatha's Brothers. Longfellow. *Fr.* The Song of Hiawatha, III. BoTP; PCH

Hiawatha's (continued)
(Hiawatha's Chickens, *br. sel.*) PCH
Hiawatha's Canoe. Longfellow. *See* Hiawatha's Sailing.
Hiawatha's Childhood. Longfellow. The Song of Hiawatha, III. AnNE; BoChLi, *sel.*; BoTP, *sel.*; FaBV; FaPON, *sel.*; GFA, *sel.*; MPB, *sel.*; OHFP, *sel.*; PoRh, *sel.*; RePo; RIS, *abr.*; ShBV-1, *sel.*; StVeCh, *sel.*; TiPo, *sel.*; TreF, *sel.*; WBLP, *sel.*
Hiawatha's Fishing. Longfellow. *Fr.* The Song of Hiawatha, VIII. PoG
Hiawatha's Mittens. *Unknown.* ShBV-1
Hiawatha's Photographing. "Lewis Carroll." CenHV; FiBHP
Hiawatha's Sailing. Longfellow. The Song of Hiawatha, VII. BBV; PCH, *sel.*
(Hiawatha's Canoe.) OHIP, *sel.*; StVeCh (1940 ed.), *abr.*
Hiawatha's Wooing. Longfellow. The Song of Hiawatha, X. BeLS; TreFS
Hibernalia. Jessica Nelson North. NP
Hibiscus on the Sleeping Shores. Wallace Stevens. NP
Hiboux, Les. Baudelaire. AWP; JAWP; WBP
Hic, Hoc, the Carrion Crow. *Unknown.* OxBoLi
Hic Jacet. Louise Chandler Moulton. AA; AnAmPo; AnFE; APA; CoAnAm
"Hic Me, Pater Optime, Fessam Deseris." Lucy Catlin Robinson. AA
"Hic Vir, Hic Est." Charles Stuart Calverley. NBM; OxBoLi
Hiccup, sniccup. *Unknown.* RIS
Hick-a-more, hack-a-more. Mother Goose. BoChLi; OxNR; TiPo (1952 ed.)
Hickety, pickety, i-silicity. *Unknown.* OxNR
Hickety, pickety, my black hen. *See* Higgledy, Piggledy . . .
Hickok rests by Calamity Jane. Lay of the Last Frontier. Harold Hersey. PoOW
Hickory, dickory, dock. Mother Goose. BoChLi; FaBoBe; FaFP; HBV; HBVY; OTPC; OxNR; PCH; PoPl; PPL; RIS; SAS; SiTL; SoPo; StVeCh (1940 ed.); TiPo
Hicks's Farewell, *with music.* *Unknown.* BFSS
Hid by the august foliage and fruit. To a Chameleon. Marianne Moore. GoYe; PoPl
Hid in a maze of quaintly-fashioned things. A Wedgwood Bowl. Frances Beatrice Taylor. CaP
Hidden. ffrida Wolfe. TVC
Hidden Fires. *Unknown,* *tr. fr. Japanese by* Basil Hall Chamberlain. OnPM
Hidden Flame, The. Dryden. *See* Song: "I feel a flame within. . ."
Hidden in Light. Frances Ridley Havergal. SoP
Hidden in wonder and snow, or sudden with summer. Laurentian Shield. F. R. Scott. OBCV
Hidden Joys. Laman Blanchard. VA
Hidden Line, The. Joseph Addison Alexander. BLPA; NeHB
Doomed Man, The, 2 *sts.* MaRV
Hidden lovers' woes. His Own True Wife. Wolfram von Eschenbach. AWP; JAWP; WBP; WoL
Hidden Mermaids, The. Walter de la Mare. *See* Mermaids, The.
Hidden strength, A. Chastity. Milton. *Fr.* Comus. OBS
Hidden Tide, The. Roderic Quinn. BoAu
Hidden Treasure. *Unknown.* FaChP
Hidden Truth, The. Jami, *tr. fr. Persian.* LiTW, *tr. by* E. H. Whinfield; OnPM, *tr. by* F. Hadland Davis
Hidden Weaver, The. Odell Shepard. WGRP
Hidden Years, The. Allen Eastman Cross. ChIP
Hide, Absolon. Chaucer. CBEP
(Lady without Paragon, A.) MeEL
Hide and Seek. "Robin Christopher." RIS; StaSt
Hide and Seek. Phyllis Drayson. BoTP
Hide-and-Seek. Robert Francis. PoIE; PoSa
Hide from me all lovely things. All Lovely Things. Richard Aldington. NeMA
Hide, happy damask, from the stars. Serenade. Henry Timrod. HBV
Hide in the Heart. Lloyd Frankenberg. AnFE; CoAnAm; LiTA
Hide not, hide not. The Rousing Canoe Song. Hermia Harris Fraser. CaP; WHW
Hide not thy love and myne shal bee. Pure Simple Love. Aurelian Townshend. AnAnS-2; SeCP
Hide of a leopard and hide of a deer. The Giraffe. Geoffrey Dearmer. WePo
Hide of milk-and-honey. Cow. Harold Massingham. FlW
Hide of My Mother, The. Edward Dorn. NeAP
Hide, Oh, Hide Those Hills. John Fletcher *and others.* *Fr.* The Bloody Brother, V, ii. ViBoPo
Hide this one night thy crescent, kindly Moon. To the Moon. Pierre de Ronsard. *Fr.* Amours de Marie. AWP
Hidesong. Aig Higo. TTY
Hiding. Dorothy Aldis. BoChLi; FaPON; MPB; RIS; SoPo; SUS; TiPo
Hiding the Skeleton. George Meredith. *See* Modern Love: "At dinner she is hostess, I am host."
Hiding tuft, a green-barked yew-tree, A. The Hermit's Song. *Unknown.* KiLC
Hie Away! Sir Walter Scott. *Fr.* Waverley, *ch.* 12. BoTP; MoShBr; MPB; OTPC; PCD; PCH; PRWS; ViBoPo
(Gellatley's Song to the Deerhounds.) OBRV
(Hie Away, Hie Away.) EnRP; TiPo
Hie, hie, says Anthony. Mother Goose. OxNR; RIS
Hie prudence, and wirking mervelous, The. The Preiching of the Swallow. Robert Henryson. OxBS
Hie sits oor king in Dumfermline. Sir Patrick Spens (C *vers.*). *Unknown.* BaBo
Hie to the market, Jenny come trot. *Unknown.* OxNR
Hie upon Hielands [*or* High upon Highlands]. Bonnie [*or* Bonny] George [*or* James] Campbell [*or* Ballad]. *Unknown.* AWP; BaBo (B *vers.*); BEL; BoLiVe; CBEP; CH; ELP; EnLit; EnRP; ESPB; GoTS; HBV; InPo; NoP; OBB; OxBB; OxBoLi; PCD; PoPo; ViBoPo
Hierarchie of the Blessed Angels, *sel.* Thomas Heywood.
Search for God, The ("I sought Thee . . ."), *abr.* MaRV; OxBoCh
("I sought Thee round about, O Thou my God.") WGRP
Hierusalem, [My Happy Home]. *Unknown.* *See* New Jerusalem, The.
Higamus hogamus/ Gloria Vanderbilt. Poor Kid. William Cole. PV
Higgledy-piggledy/ Andrea Doria. Last Words. John Hollander. PV
Higgledy-piggledy/ Dorothy Richardson. The Lower Criticism. John Hollander. PV
Higgledy-piggledy/ Franklin D. Roosevelt. Danish Wit. John Hollander. PV
Higgledy-piggledy/ Ludwig van Beethoven. Wrath. John Hollander. PV
Higgledy-piggledy/ Ludwig van Beethoven. E. William Seaman. PV
Higgledy-piggledy/ Mme. de Maintenon. Firmness. Anthony Hecht. PV
Higgledy-piggledy/ Thomas A. Edison. Progress. Sally Belfrage. PV
Higgledy-piggledy here we lie. *Unknown.* OxNR
Higgledy, piggledy [*or* Higgleby, piggleby *or* Hickety, pickety], my black [*or* fat] hen. Mother Goose. BoChLi; BoTP; FaBoBe; HBV; OTPC; OxNR; PCH; RIS; SoPo; StVeCh; TiPo
Higgledy, piggledy! see how they run! Kate Greenaway. TiPo
Higglety, Pigglety, Pop! Samuel Goodrich. OxNR
High. John Perreault. ANYP
High. Kathleen Spivack. YAP
High/ in your room. The Belongings. Theodore Enslin. CoPo
High/ Up/ Over the top. The Grasshoppers. Dorothy Aldis. PTK; UTS
High above all a cloth of state was spred. The House of Pride. Spenser. *Fr.* The Faerie Queene, I, 4. WHA
High above hate I dwell. Sanctuary. Louise Imogen Guiney. AA
High adventure/ And bright dream. Maps. Dorothy Brown Thompson. BrR; TiPo
High amid/ Gothic rocks the altar stands. Sus Specie Aeternitatis. Robert Hayden. AmPP (5th ed.)
High and inscrutable the old man stood. The Death of Haidee. Byron. *Fr.* Don Juan, IV. WHA
High and Low. James H. Cousins. HBMV; OnYI; OxBI
High and Low. Dora Read Goodale. PRWS
High and Low. John Banister Tabb. BrR
High and mighty lord of Glendare, The. The Cricket's Story. Emma Huntington Nason. HBV; HBVY
High and proud on the barnyard fence. Chanticleer. John Farrar. GFA; PCH; SoPo; TiPo; UTS
High and solemn mountains guard Rioupéroux. Rioupéroux. James Elroy Flecker. OBEV (new ed.); OBVV
High Barbaree, The. Laura E. Richards. CIV; SoPo; SUS

High Barbaree, The, *with music.* *Unknown.* AmSS; OuSiCo; SoAmSa; ViBoFo
(High Barbary.) BaBo
High bare field, A, brown from the plough. The Potato Harvest. Sir Charles G. D. Roberts. CaP
High-born Helen, round your dwelling. Helen. Mary Lamb. OBRV
High Bridge above the Tagus River at Toledo, The. William Carlos Williams. CTC
High Brow. Robert Fitch. SD
High ceilingd and the double mirrors. Bubbs Creek Haircut. Gary Snyder. FRC
High Chin Bob. *Unknown.* SCC
High cockalorum diddledum! Direct Song. Eve Merriam. UnTE
High Country Weather. James K. Baxter. AnNZ
High diddle diddle. *See* Hey diddle diddle.
High diddle ding, did you hear the bells ring? *Unknown.* OxNR
High Dive. William Empson. AtBAP
High Diver. Robert Francis. NePoAm; SD
High Flight. John Gillespie Magee, Jr. BBV (1951 ed.); FaFP; FaPON; MaC; MaRV; OTD; PGD; POTE; SoP; TreFS; TRV; WaKn
High Germany. Edward Shanks. OBMV
High Germany. *Unknown.* CBEP; FOL; WaaP
High grace, the dower of queens. Her Gifts. Dante Gabriel Rossetti. The House of Life, XXXI. HBV; MaVP; PoVP; VA; ViPo; VP
High grew the snow beneath the low-hung sky. The Axe [*or* The Axe of the Pioneer]. Isabella Valancy Crawford. CaP; VA
High Hill, The. Clinton Scollard. MaRV
High in the afternoon the dove. Kendrick Smithyman. *Fr.* Considerations of Norfolk Island. AnNZ
High in the air exposed the slave is hung. Two Poems Concerning the Slave Trade, II. Robert Southey. Sonn
High in the breathless hall the minstrel sate. Song at the Feast of Brougham Castle. Wordsworth. EnRP
High in the dark the moon rides white. Serenade. Paul Fearon. CIV
High in the heavens a single star. The Christmas Star. Nancy Byrd Turner. MaRV
High in the heaven's azure hemisphere. The Kingis Quair. James I, King of Scotland. MeEV
High in the noon's bright bowl of blue. Feather. Lew Sarett. NP
High in the organ-loft with lilied hair. Epithalamium. Sir Edmund Gosse. OBVV
High in the pine-tree. The Turtle-Dove's Nest. *Unknown.* BoTP; HBVY; OTPC (1923 ed.); SAS
High in [*or* on] the top of an old pine tree. The Little Doves. *Unknown.* PPL; SAS
High June. Catherine A. Morin. BoTP
High Kingdom. Howard Sergeant. ToPo
High-Life Low-Down. Justin Richardson. PV
High-lying, sea-blown stretches of green turf. The Beds of Fleur-de-Lys. Charlotte Perkins Gilman. AA
High Midnight was garlanding her head, The. Moonlight. Jacques Tahureau. AWP
High Mind, The. Samuel Daniel. *See* To the Lady Margaret, Countess of Cumberland.
High mounted on an ant Nanus the tall. On Nanus Mounted Upon an Ant. Richard Crashaw. MaMe
High Noon at Midsummer on the Campagna ("High noon,/ And from the purple-veiled hills"). "Fiona Macleod." PoVP
High o'er his moldering castle walls. A Voice from the Invisible World. Goethe. AWP; JAWP; WBP
High o'er the Poop the Audacious Seas Aspire. William Falconer. EtS
High on a banyan tree in a row. Monkey. William Jay Smith. TiPo (1959 ed.)
High on a bright and sunny bed. The Poppy. Jane Taylor. OTPC; TVC
High on a gorgeous seat, that far out-shone. Pope. *Fr.* The Dunciad, II. AtBAP
High on a leaf-carv'd ancient oaken chair. The Old Baron. Thomas Miller. VA
High on a mountain's highest ridge. Wordsworth. *Fr.* The Thorn. Par
High on a pole, he labors in the sky. Lineman. Gerald Raftery. PoMa
High on a ridge of tiles. Maurice James Craig. NeIP
High on a shelf we keep the books you had. For a Child Who Died. Joseph G. E. Hopkins. JKCP (1955 ed.)
High on a throne of royal state, which far. Milton. *Fr.* Paradise Lost, II. AtBAP; CoBE; EnL; EnLi-1; EnLit; FosPo; MBW-1; SeEP
High on the bold, gray granite shelf. The Stationed Scout. Lyman H. Sproull. PoOW
High on the dove-cot. Doves. E. J. Falconer. BoTP
High on the Mountain of Sunrise where standeth the Temple of Sebek. He Knoweth the Souls of the West. *Unknown.* *Fr.* Book of the Dead. AWP; JAWP; WBP
High on the rim edge of the Argentine. Christ in the Andes. Carl John Bostelmann. ChIP
High on the southern wall the clock. The Nursery. Conrad Aiken. *Fr.* The Coming Forth by Day of Osiris Jones. LOW
High on the top of an old pine-tree. *See* High in the top . . .
High on the top of Ararat alone. Noah. Roy Campbell. *Fr.* The Flaming Terrapin. BoSA
High over Mecca Allah's prophet's corpse. Dissatisfaction with Metaphysics. William Empson. CMoP
High overhead. Looking Up at Airplanes, Always. Rolfe Humphries. RePo
High, pale, imperial places of slow cloud. Upper Air. Frank Ernest Hill. AnAmPo; MAP; MoAmPo (1942 ed.)
High Pitched Whale. Clark Coolidge. ANYP
High Place, A. Eithne Wilkins. NeBP
High Place at Marib, The. Grant Code. FiSC
High Priest, The. *Unknown,* *tr. fr. Hebrew by* Arthur Davis. TrJP
High Priz'd Harlot, The. *Unknown.* *See* Penurious Quaker, The.
High Resolve. *Unknown.* PoToHe
High Sailboat, The. Salvatore Quasimodo, *tr. fr. Italian by* Creighton Gilbert. LiTW
High sheriff tol' de deputy, "Go out an' bring me Laz'us." Po' Laz'us. *Unknown.* ABF
High-speed metal snake switches its tail, A. The Chief of the West, Darkling. David Knight. MoCV
High-spirited friend. An Ode [*or* Noble Balm]. Ben Jonson. BWP; OBEV
High steward of thy vines. John Day. *Fr.* The Parliament of Bees. ViBoPo
High stretched upon the swinging yard. Disguises. Thomas Edward Brown. WGRP
High Summer. Jascha Kessler. AmPC
High summer's sheen upon all things. The Web. Theodore Weiss. CoAP
High the vanes of Shrewsbury gleam. The Welsh Marches. A. E. Housman. A Shropshire Lad, XXVIII. FaBoTw; PoVP; ViPo
High thoughts and noble in all lands. The Human Touch. Richard Burton. BLPA; OQP
High Tide. Jean Starr Untermeyer. MoAmPo; NeMA; TSW
High Tide, And. Doug Palmer. ThO
High Tide at Gettysburg, The. Will Henry Thompson. AA; BeLS; BLPA; FaBoBe; HBV; MC; OTD; PaA; PAH; PAL; PaPo; PFY; PoFr; TreFS
High Tide on the Coast of Lincolnshire, The (1571). Jean Ingelow. BeLS; GBV; GN; GTBS; GTBS-D; GTSL; HBV; NBM; OBVV; OnMSP; OtMeF; PaPo; ShBV-3; TOP; VA
Calling the Cows Home, *sel.* ThGo
High time now gan it wex for Una fayre. Spenser. *Fr.* The Faerie Queene, I. FosPo
High-toned Old Christian Woman, A. Wallace Stevens. AP; CBV; CMoP; CoBMV; MoVE; PoeP; PoFS
High towered the palace and its massive pile. Palace of the Gnomes. Maria Gowen Brooks. *Fr.* Zophiel. AA
High trees grieve like the sea's water, The. In Wicklow. Rhoda Coghill. NeIP
High up among the mountains, through a lovely grove of cedars. Bears. Arthur Guiterman. PoRA
High up are the angels with best quality wings. Cosmogony. David Daiches. LiTM
High up in the courts of heaven today. A Little Dog-Angel. Norah M. Holland. PoLF
High up on the lonely mountains. A Night with a Wolf. Bayard Taylor. GoTP
High upon Highlands. *See* Hie upon Hielands.
High upon the gallows tree swung the noble-hearted three. God

High (continued)
Save Ireland. Timothy Daniel Sullivan. OnYI
High upon the hillside where the shadows play. Skippets, the Bad One. Christine E. Bradley. BoTP
High walls and huge the body may confine. Freedom for the Mind. William Lloyd Garrison. AA; FaBoBe
High Way and a Low, A. John Oxenham. *See* Ways, The.
High Wedlock Then Be Honoured. Shakespeare. *Fr.* As You Like It, V, iv. HW
High Wheat Country. Elijah L. Jacobs. AmFN
High Wind, The. *Unknown.* *See* Wind, The.
High Wind at the Battery. Ralph Pomeroy. NYBP
High wisdom holds my wisdom less. In Memoriam A. H. H., CXII. Tennyson. EPN; ViPo; VP
High-yellow of my heart, with breasts like tangerines. The Peasant Declares His Love. Emile Roumer. ErPo; LiTW; PoNe; TTY
Highbridge, *with music.* *Unknown.* AS
Higher ("The shadows of night were a-comin' down swift"). *Unknown.* FiBHP
Higher Calling, The. W. M. Czamanske. STF
Higher Catechism, The. Sam Walter Foss. WGRP
Sels.
"And what is faith? OQP
Nature and Religion. OQP
Higher Command, The. Sophocles, *tr. fr. Greek.* *Fr.* Antigone. MaRV
Higher Good, The. Theodore Parker. AA; FaBoBe; HBV; MaRV
(New Year Prayer, A.) PGD
Higher Ground. Johnson Oatman, Jr. FaChP
Higher Loyalty, The. Shakespeare, *and probably* John Fletcher. King Henry VIII, *fr.* III, ii. MaRV
(Ambition, *abr.*) TrGrPo
Higher Pantheism, The. Tennyson. BEL; BoPe; EnLi-2; EPN; HBV; MaRV; MaVP; PoVP; TRV; ViPo; ViPP; VP; WGRP
Higher Pantheism in a Nutshell, The, *parody.* Swinburne. *Fr.* The Heptalogia. ALV; BOHV; HBV, *abr.*; NA; Par; PeVV; PoVP; SiTL; ViPo; ViPP; VP
Higher than a house,/ higher than a tree. Mother Goose. OxNR; PPL; SoPo; TiPo
Higher than heaven they sit. The Hope of the World. Sir William Watson. WGRP
Higher that the cedar tree under the heavens do grow, The. Of the Mean Estate. Thomas, Lord Vaux. SiCE
Highest Divinity. *Unknown,* *tr. fr. Hebrew by* Israel Zangwill. TrJP
Highest Fruit, The. Sappho, *tr. fr. Greek by* Ralph Marcus. OnPM
Highest of Immortals bright. Indra, the Supreme God. *Unknown.* *Fr.* The Rigveda. AWP
Highest queen of state. Honour, Riches, Marriage Blessing. Shakespeare. *Fr.* The Tempest, IV, i. HW
Highest Wisdom, The. Jacopone da Todi, *tr. fr. Italian by* Mrs. Theodore Beck. CAW
Highland Cattle, *sel.* Dinah Maria Mulock Craik.
"Down the wintry mountain." GN; OTPC
Highland Laddie, *with music.* *Unknown.* ShS; SoAmSa
Highland Mary. Burns. AnFE; ATP (1935 ed.); AWP; BEL; BoLiVe; CEP; EiPP; EnLi-2; EnLit; EnRP; FaPL; GTBS; GTBS-D; GTBS-P; GTBS-W; GTSE; GTSL; HBV; InP; InPo; JAWP; OAEP; OBEC; OBEV; OuHeWo; TOP; TreFS; TrGrPo; ViBoPo; WBLP; WBP
(Ye Banks, and Braes, and Streams Around.) EiCL
Highland Tinker, The. *Unknown.* CoMu
Highlandmen hae a' come down, The. The Lady of Arngosk. *Unknown.* ESPB
Highlands, The. Henry W. Frost. SoP
Highlands of Hudson! ye saw them pass. The Storming of Stony Point. Arthur Guiterman. MC; PAH
Highlands' Swelling Blue, The. Byron. *Fr.* The Island. OBRV
Highly beloved and intimate was he. Ten of Chaucer's People: A Greedy Friar. Chaucer. *Fr.* The Canterbury Tales. PoSa
Highly Educated Man, The, *with music.* *Unknown.* ABF
Highmindedness, a jealousy for good. Addressed to Haydon. Keats. CBEP; MERP
Highroad's barren scar, A. Autumn Dawn. Antonio Machado. PoPl
Highty, tighty, paradighty, clothed in green. Riddle. *Unknown.* ChTr; OxNR
Highway, The. Louise Driscoll. HBV
Highway, The. William Channing Gannett. WGRP
Highway: Michigan. Theodore Roethke. TDP
Highway, since you my chief Parnassus be. Astrophel and Stella, LXXXIV. Sir Philip Sidney. ElL; EnRePo; FCP; GTBS-W; GTSL; ILP; LiTB; LiTG; OAEP; OBEV; OBSC; ReEn; SiPS
Highway to Nowhere. Grant Code. FiSC
Highwayman, The. Alfred Noyes. ATP; BBV; BEL; BeLS; BoLP; EnLit; FaBV; FaFP; FaPON; GoTP; GSP; GTSL; HBV; HBVY; InP; LoEn; MaC; MCCG; OHFP; OnSP; PCD; PoLF; PoMa; PoPo; ShBV-2; TIHL; TOP; TreFS; TSW; YT
Highwayman's Ghost, The. Richard Garnett. StPo
Highwaymen, The. John Gay. *See* Let Us Take the Road.
Highways and Byways. John Vanderbilt. PCD
Highways run in figure of the rood, The. November. Emile Verhaeren. WoL
Hike, The. Neil Weiss. SD
Hiking Poem/ High Sierra. Lew Welch. FRC
Hilas, o Hilas, why sit we mute. *See* Hylas, O Hylas! why sit we mute.
Hill, The. Rupert Brooke. BoLP; EnLit; GTSL; HBV; LiTL; MeWo; MoBrPo; MoLP; OTD; POTE; Sonn; ViBoPo; WePo
Hill, A. Anthony Hecht. CoAP; NYBP
Hill, The. Horace Holley. WGRP
Hill, The. Edgar Lee Masters. *Fr.* Spoon River Anthology. AmLP; AmP; CMoP; ExPo; LiTA; LiTM; NePA; NP; OxBA; ReMP; SeCeV; ViBoPo
Hill, The/ Where the maiden is hiding. Metal Hoe Hill. *Unknown.* *Fr.* Kojiki. HW
Hill above the Mine, The. Malcolm Cowley. NAMP; PoPl
Hill-born, The. Struthers Burt. MaRV
Hill-born. W. W. Gibson. NP
Hill cedars and piñons, The. In the Desert. Alice Corbin. NP
Hill Farmer Speaks, The. R. S. Thomas. GTBS-P; HaMV
Hill full, a hole full, A. Mother Goose. SoPo; TiPo
Hill of Intrusion, The. W. S. Graham. NePoEA
Hill People. Harriet Gray Blackwell. AmFN
Hill people turn to their hills. The Heart's Country. Florence Wilkinson. FaChP
Hill Pines Were Sighing, The. Robert Bridges. EG; ExPo; OAEP
Hill Summit, The. Dante Gabriel Rossetti. The House of Life, LXX. MaVP; NoP; PoVP; ViPo
Hill Top. *See* Hilltop.
Hill was cool and silent, The. The Christian Camp. Artemisia E. Strout. SoP
Hill was flowing with sheep, The. Pastoral. Marion Stroebel. NP
Hill Wife, The. Robert Frost. CMoP; NoP; NP
Sels.
Impulse, The. AWP; LiTM; LO; NePA
Loneliness. FaBoEn
Oft-repeated Dream, The. PG (1945 ed.)
Hill-Woman, A. John Farrar. OnPP
Hill-billy, hill-billy come to buy. Pedlar. Confucius. *Fr.* Wei Wind. CTC
Hillcrest. E. A. Robinson. AP; CoBMV; FaBoEn; MAmP; MoAB; OxBA; PIA; PoIE
Hilloo, hilloo, hilloo, hilloo! Snowshoeing Song. Arthur Weir. VA
Hills, The. Berton Braley. MCCG
Hills. Hilda Conkling. GBV; PCH; StaSt; StVeCh
Hills, The. Frances Cornford. MoBrPo
Hills, The. Rachel Field. GFA; RePo
Hills. Arthur Guiterman. HBVY; MaRV; PoMa; RePo; YT
Hills and rivers of the lowland country, The. A Protest in the Sixth Year of Ch'ien Fu (A.D. 879). Ts'ao Sung. FaBV; LiTW; MoPW; OnPM; PoFR
Hills and the Sea, The. Wilfred Campbell. CaP
Hills are calling me from care and reason, The. Bright Abandon. Tessa Sweazy Webb. GoYe
Hills are going somewhere, The. Hills. Hilda Conkling. GBV; PCH; StaSt; StVeCh
Hills are high in Caribou, The. The Yellow Witch of Caribou. Clyde Robertson. PoOW
Hills are Tipped with Sunshine, The. Christina Rossetti. PoVP
Hills are verdigris and sallow, The. Bi-focal. Hal Porter. BoAV
Hills are white, but not with snow, The. An Orchard at Avignon. Agnes Mary Frances Robinson. HBV
Hills are wroth, The; the stones have scored you bitterly. To

a Young Girl Leaving the Hill Country. Arna Bontemps. CDC; Kal
Hills fill the first of twelve frames. The Page of Illustrations. Peter Schjeldahl. ANYP
Hills Keep Holy Ground, The. Hellene Seaman. MaRV
Hills moved. I watched their shadows. Beetle on the Shasta Daylight. Shirley Kaufman. NYBP
Hills o' My Heart. "Ethna Carbery." HBV
Hills of autumn drop, The. Kakinomoto no Asomi Hitomaro, *tr. fr. Japanese by* I. W. Furukami. LiTW
Hills of Cualann, The. Joseph campbell. AnIV
Hills of Pomeroy, The. Ewart Milne. NeIP
Hills of Rest, The. Albert Bigelow Paine. HBV; MaRV; OQP; WGRP
Hills of Rome, resound with solemn hymn, The. Ah, Now I Know What Day This Is. Statius. *Fr.* Epithalamium for Stella and Violentilla. HW
Hills of Sewanee, The. George Marion McClellan. BANP
Hills step off into whiteness, The. Sheep in Fog. Sylvia Plath. NaP
Hill's Summit, The. Dante Gabriel Rossetti. *See* Hill Summit, The.
Hills that had been lone and lean, The. The Consecration of the Common Way. Edwin Markham. StJW
Hills turn hugely in their sleep, The. Prothalamion: Second Section. Robert Hillyer. MAP; MoAmPo
Hills Were Made for Freedom, The. William Goldsmith Brown. PoFr
Hills yet hills, and still the yellow town, The. Naples Again. Arthur Freeman. NYBP
Hillside. Alexander Craig. PoAu-2
Hillside Farmer, A. John Farrar. HBMV
Hillside Pause. Catharine Morris Wright. GoYe
Hillside Thaw, A. Robert Frost. CMoP; DiPo; ExPo; StP; TSW
Hill-Side Tree. Maxwell Bodenheim. MAP; MAPA; MoAmPo (1942 ed.)
Hillsides were of rushing, silvered water, The. Gioconda. Thomas McGreevy. OnYI
Hilltops. Leslie Savage Clark. ChIP
Him Evermore I Behold. Longfellow. SoP; TRV
Him not the golden fang of furious heaven. Sonnet. Edna St. Vincent Millay. AtBAP
Him on his throne and glorious. The Fifth of May—Napoleon. Alessandro Manzoni. *Fr.* Ode. CAW
Him the Almighty Power/ Hurl'd headlong flaming. Satan Defiant [*or* The Fallen Angels]. Milton. *Fr.* Paradise Lost, I. AnFE; FaBoEn; MyFE; WHA
Him: the Roach. Harold Bond. YAP
Himalaya. Po Fei Huang. NYTB
Himn, The, O Gloriosa Domina. Richard Crashaw. MaMe
Himne for the Circumcision Day of Our Lord, An. Richard Crashaw. MaMe
Himself, *sel.* Edwin John Ellis.
"At Golgotha I stood alone." OBMV
Himself He Could Not Save. Avis B. Christiansen. SoP
"Himself on the wood there," says one. Cross Talk. Cyril Cusack. NYTB
Hind, The. Sir Thomas Wyatt, *after the Italian of* Petrarch. OBSC; SeCeV; TrGrPo
(Sonnet: "Whose list to hunt, I know where is an hind.") SiPS
(Whoso List to Hount.) AtBAP; PoEL-1
(Whoso List to Hunt [I Know Where Is an Hind].) BWP; CABA; CBEP; EnPo; EnRePo; FCP; ForPo; FosPo; InvP; MaPo; NoP; PAn; PIA; PoIE; ReEn; Sonn; TuPP
Hind and the Panther, The, *sels.* Dryden.
"But, gratious God, how well dost thou provide," *fr.* I. TrPWD
(Church's Testimony, The.) ACP; CAW
(Confession of Faith.) UnPo (1st ed.)
(Conversion: "But, gracious God, how well dost thou provide.") PoLi
Church of England, The, *fr.* I. OBS
Conversion ("Be vengeance wholly left to pow'rs divine"), *fr.* III. ACP; CAW
(World Well Lost, The.) PoLi
(Worldly Vanity.) FiP
"Dame, said the Panther, times are mended well," II. PoEL-3
King James II, *fr.* III. ACP
"Milk-white Hind, Immortal and unchanged, A," *fr.* I. CEP; CoBE; EiPP; SeCV-2; SeEP
(Churches of Rome and of England, *much abr.*) ACP
"Of all the tyrannies of human kind," *fr.* I. PoFr
"One evening, while the cooler shade she sought," *fr.* I. PoEL-3
"One in herself not rent by schism, but sound," *fr.* II. SeEP
(Catholic Church, The.) OBS
Presbyterians, The, *fr.* I. OBS
Private Judgment Condemned, *fr.* I. OBS
(Prayer, A: "What weight of ancient witness can prevail.") FiP
"To this the Panther, with a scornfull smile," *fr.* III. SeCV-2; SeEP
Hind Etin. *Unknown.* BaBo (A *vers.*); ESPB (A *and* B *vers.*); OxBB
(Hynd Etin.) BuBa; OBB
(Lady and the Dwarf King, The, B *vers.*) BaBo
Hind Horn. *Unknown. See* Hynd Horn.
Hindoo died—a happy thing to do, A. Paradise; a Hindoo Legend. George Birdseye. BOHV; HBV
Hinds of Kerry, The. William S. Wabnitz. GoYe
Hindu Ascetic, The. Sir Alfred Comyn Lyall. Studies at Delhi. OBVV
Hindu Cradle Song. Sarojini Naidu. *See* Cradle Song: "From groves of spice."
Hinky Dinky [Parlee-Voo]. *Unknown. See* Mademoiselle From Armentières.
Hint from Herrick, A. Thomas Bailey Aldrich. HBV
Hint from Voiture. William Shenstone. EnLoPo
Hint to the Wise, A. Pringle Barret. HBVY; PCH
Hinted Wish, A. Martial, *tr. fr. Latin by* Samuel Johnson. AWP; JAWP; OuHeWo; WBP; LiTW, *tr. by* Francis Lewis
(Legacy, A, *tr. by* Samuel Johnson.) OnPM
Hints on Pronunciation for Foreigners. "T. S. W." FIW
Hints on Writing Verse. Jack Mitchell. *See* Ballad of the Sailor Ben.
Hinty, minty, cuty, corn. Counting-out Ryhmes. *Unknown.* FaPON
Hinx, minx, the old witch winks. *Unknown.* OxNR
Hippety hop to the barber shop. Mother Goose. SoPo; TiPo
Hippity Hop to Bed. Leroy F. Jackson. GFA; TiPo
Hippocrene. Amy Lowell. MoLP
Hippolytus, *sels.* Euripides, *tr. fr. Greek.*
Chorus: "Could I take me to some cavern for mine hiding," *tr. by* Gilbert Murray. BoPe; ShBV-4
(Longing.) PCD
(O For the Wings of a Dove.) AWP; JAWP; WBP
No More, O My Spirit, *tr. by* Hilda Doolittle ("H. D."). AWP
Hippopotamothalamion. John Hall Wheelock. FiBHP; NePoAm-2
Hippopotamus, The. Hilaire Belloc. FiBHP; PoPl; ShBV-2; UTS; WhC
("I shoot the Hippopotamus.") CenHV
Hippopotamus, The. Georgia Roberts Durston. GFA; TiPo; UTS
Hippopotamus, The. T. S. Eliot. AmPP; AnAmPo; AWP; HoPM; LiTB; LiTM (1946 ed.); NAMP; OBMV; PoDB; PoPl; PoSa
Hippopotamus, The. Oliver Herford. NA
Hippopotamus, The. Ogden Nash. FaBV
Hippopotamus had a bride, A. Hippopotamothalamion. John Hall Wheelock. FiBHP; NePoAm-2
Hippopotamus is strong, The. Habits of the Hippopotamus. Arthur Guiterman. FaBV; FiBHP; RePo; TiPo (1959 ed.)
Hir bowgy cheekes been as softe as clay. A Description of His Ugly Lady. Thomas Hoccleve. MeEL
Hiram Hover. Bayard Taylor. BOHV
"Hiram, I think the sump is backing up." Mending Sump. Kenneth Koch. NeAP; PV
Hireling's wages to the priest are paid, A. Poet *vs.* Parson. Ebenezer Elliott. Sonn
Hiroshige. Mark M. Perlberg. NYBP
Hiroshima. Murray Noss. PoPo
Hiroshima. Margaret Rockwell. PPON
Hiroshima Crewman. Dan Georgakas. ThO
Hiroshima Lullaby, A. Joseph Langland. PPON
His Admonition to Greene's Companions. Gabriel Harvey. *Fr.* Greene's Memorial; or, Certain Funeral Sonnets. ReIE
His Age. Robert Herrick. SeCP

His age drawn out behind him to be watched. Old Man. Elizabeth Jennings. NePoEA-2
His Answer to a Question. Robert Herrick. ReEn
His Apology of His Good Father. Gabriel Harvey. *Fr.* Greene's Memorial; or, Certain Funeral Sonnets. ReIE
His Appointment. Edith Lillian Young. *See* Disappointment—His Appointment.
His are the generous days that balance. The Generous Years. Stephen Spender. PoCh
His Are the Thousand Sparkling Rills. Cecil Frances Alexander. OxBI
His are the whitenesses of soul. A Friend. Lionel Johnson. HBV; JKCP
His art is eccentricity, his aim. Pitcher. Robert Francis. CaFP; NePoAm; PP; SD
His art—the medium at war with craft. The Prisoner. Irwin Stark. NYTB
His Ballad of Agincourt. Michael Drayton. *See* Agincourt.
His Banner over Me. Gerald Massey. HBV; VA; WGRP
His bark/ The daring mariner shall urge far o'er. Prophecy. Luigi Pulci. *Fr.* Il Morgante maggiore. PAH
His bees went very far that night. Bees before Winter. Merrill Moore. RIS
His Being Was in Her Alone. Sir Philip Sidney. ELP
His Best. Albert Benjamin Simpson. *See* God's Best.
His Birth. Phillips Brooks. SoP
His blood on my arm is warm as a bird. Prayer for Messiah. Leonard Cohen. OBCV
His body doubled/ under the pack. On the Swag. R. A. K. Mason. AnNZ
His body is smashed. The Crucifix. Sir Herbert Read. BrPo
His body lies interred within this mould. Epitaph on a Soldier. Cyril Tourneur. *Fr.* The Atheist's Tragedy. EIL; SiCE
His body lies upon the shore. Richard Somers. Barrett Eastman. AA
His Book. Alice Hansche Mortenson. SoP
His Books. Robert Southey. *See* My Days among the Dead Are Past.
His bridle hung around the post. Horse. Elizabeth Madox Roberts. RePo; TiPo (1959 ed.); UTS
His broad-brimmed hat pushed back with careless air. Vaquero. Joaquin Miller. AA; PFY
His brother said that pain was what he knew. Traction: November 22, 1963. Howard Moss. AmFN
His Camel. Alqamah, *tr. fr. Arabic by* Sir Charles Lyall. *Fr.* The Mufaddaliyat. AWP; JAWP; WBP
His car was worth a thousand pounds and more. One Poet Visits Another. W. H. Davies. DTC; FaBoTw
His Cavalier. Robert Herrick. *See* Herrick's Cavalier.
His cedar paddle, scented, red. The Lily Bed. Isabella Valancy Crawford. PeCV
His Charge to Julia at His Death. Robert Herrick. SeCV-1
His cheeks grow red from the candle heat. The Altar Boy. Leonard Feeney. WHL
His cherished woods are mute. The stream glides down. At Chappaqua. Joel Benton. AA
His Children. Hittan of Tayyi, *tr. fr. Arabic by* Sir Charles Lyall. *Fr.* Hamasah. AWP; JAWP; LiTW; WBP
His childhood he gave to a public which had none. Marcel Proust. William Jay Smith. NYTB
His chosen comrades thought at school. What Then? W. B. Yeats. CMoP; POTE
His classic studies made a little puzzle. Don Juan's Education. Byron. *Fr.* Don Juan. WHA
His claw against the world, he prowls athwart. Othello: Tomcat. Laura Simmons. CIV
His collar is frayed, and his trousers unpressed. Shabby Old Dad. Anne Campbell. PoToHe (new ed.)
His Coming. Ivy M. Fordham. SoP
His Complaint against Love and Fortune. Nicholas Breton. ReIE
His Content in the Country. Robert Herrick. EnLit; SCEP-2; SeCV-1; SeEP
His Creed. Robert Herrick. ILP; SeCeV; WePo
His Cross. Marguerite Wilkinson. OQP
His day closes like a dry mouth. David Hilton. QAH
His Deaths. Haniel Long. NP
His Defense against the Idle Critic. Michael Drayton. ReIE
His delicate fingers, moving among the roses. The Utopia of Lord Mayor Howard. Randolph Stow. PoAu-2
His Delight. Meilir ap Gwalchmai, *tr. fr. Welsh by* H. Idris Bell. LiTW
His Desire. Robert Herrick. CABA; CBV; OAEP
His desires, growing. Black Man's Feast. Sarah Webster Fabio. PoNe (1970 ed.)
His Despair. Thomas Beaumont. SeCL
His Discourse with Cupid. Ben Jonson. *Fr.* A Celebration of Charis. AnAnS-2; SCEP-2; SeCP
His echoing axe the settler swung. The Settler. Alfred Billings Street. AA; FaBoBe; MC; PAH
His Ejaculation to God. Robert Herrick. SeCV-1
His Elegy. Chidiock Tichborne. *See* Elegy: "My prime of youth is but a frost of cares."
His Epitaph. Richard Crashaw. MaMe
His Epitaph. John Gay. *See* My Own Epitaph.
His Epitaph. Stephen Hawes. *See* Epitaph: "O mortal folk, you may behold and see."
His Epitaph. Walter Savage Landor. *See* For an Epitaph at Fiesole.
His Epitaph. Frederick William Ophel. BoAu
His Epitaph. Sir Walter Ralegh. *See* Conclusion, The.
His Excellency, *sels.* W. S. Gilbert.
Played-out Humorist, The. BOHV
Practical Joker, The. BOHV
His Excellency, General Washington (1775). Phillis Wheatley. Kal; PoNe
His Excuse for Loving. Ben Jonson. *Fr.* A Celebration of Charis. AnAnS-2; EnRePo; PoEL-2; QFR; SCEP-2; SeCP; SeCV-1; SeEP; TuPP
His eye was stern and wild,—his cheek was pale and cold as clay. Fragment. *Unknown.* BOHV
His eyes are big and soft and bright. Young Flash the Deer. Thornton Burgess. RePo
His eyes are closed. They are closed. His Eyes are closed. The Mummy. Vernon Watkins. MoPo; NeBP
His eyes are quickened so with grief. Lost Love. Robert Graves. AWP; CH; ChMP; FaBoCh; ILP; JAWP; LoGBV; MemP; MoAB; MoBrPo; NoP; POTE; WBP
His eyes can be quite old and stern. Father. Mildred Weston. PoSC
His eyes grow hot, his words grow wild. The Wise Woman. Louis Untermeyer. ALV; HBMV
His eyes had altered since he'd looked on death. Emmaus. Edith Lovejoy Pierce. SoP
His eyes saw all things in the symmetry. Coleridge. Aubrey Thomas De Vere. GoBC
His Face. Florence Earle Coates. OHIP
His face? I know not whether it be fair. The Surgeon's Hands. Ida Norton Munson. OQP
His Face Is Forever. *Unknown*, *tr. fr. Arabic by* Sir Edwin Arnold. OnPM
His face is truly of the Roman mould. A Character. Charlotte Fiske Bates. AA
"His face shone" she said. A Death. Elizabeth Jennings. NMP; OPoP
His face was glad as dawn to me. Shule, Shule, Shule, Agrah! "Fiona Macleod." OBVV; PoVP
His face was the oddest that ever was seen. The Strange Man. *Unknown.* FaPON; MPB; OTPC (1946 ed.); StVeCh (1940 ed.)
His falchion flashed along the Nile. The Exile at Rest. John Pierpont. AA
His Farewell to His Unkind and Unconstant Mistress. Francis Davison. EIL; OBSC
His Fare-well to Sack. Robert Herrick. AnAnS-2; OAEP; SCEP-2; SeCP; SeCV-1
His father gave him a box of truisms. The Truisms. Louis MacNeice. PoIE
His father's steel, piercing the wholesome fruit. King Honor's Eldest Son. Elinor Wylie. CoBA
His feet were shod with music and had wings. Milton. Lloyd Mifflin. AA
His fingers wake, and flutter; up the bed. Conscious. Wilfred Owen. MMA
His flaggy wings when forth he did display. The Dragon. Spenser. *Fr.* The Faerie Queene. SeCePo
His followers had fled like frightened sheep. The Crowning Wonder. John Oxenham. StJW
His footprints have failed us. Dead in the Sierras. Joaquin Miller. AA; PFY

His fourscore years and five. Whittier. Margaret E. Sangster. AA; DD
His friend the watchman was still awake. A Leave-taking. Arno Holz. AWP; JAWP; WBP
His friends he loved. His direst earthly foes. Sir William Watson. InP
His friends went off and left Him dead. The Resurrection. Jonathan Henderson Brooks. AmNP; CDC; PoNe
His Further Resolution. *Unknown.* HBV
His Garments. Esther Lloyd Hagg. ChIP; PGD
His gaze, going past those bars, has got so misted. The Panther. Rainer Maria Rilke. FIW
His generous bearing was a new invention. W. H. Auden. *Fr.* In Time of War. CMoP
His Gift and Mine. Edith B. Gurley. BLRP
His gift knew what he was—a dark disordered city. Matthew Arnold. W. H. Auden. MaPo (1969 ed.)
His glory, by whose might all things are moved. Paradise. Dante, *tr. by* Henry F. Cary. *Fr.* Divina Commedia. OuHeWo
His Glory Tell. Horatius Bonar. BePJ
His Golden Lock[e]s [Time Hath to Silver Turned]. George Peele. *Fr.* Polyhymnia. AtBAP; ElL; EnRePo; LoBV; NoP; PoE; PoIE; PoSa; ReEn; ReIE; TuPP; ViBoPo; WHA
(Farewell to Arms, A.) AnFE; BoC; CoBE; EG; EnLi-1; HBV; MemP; OBEV; PoRA
(Old Knight, The.) CBEP; ChTr; OBSC; TrGrPo
(Sonet, A: "His golden lockes, Time hath to silver turn'd.") FaBoEn; PoEL-2; SiCE
(Sonnet, A: "His golden locks time hath to silver turn'd.") ELP
His Good Name Being Blemsihed, He Bewaileth. Edward de Vere, Earl of Oxford. ReIE
His gospel sounds in every wind that sings. Communion Hymn. William Gay. ChIP
His Grace! impossible! what dead! A Satirical [*or* Satyrical] Elegy on the Death of a Late Famous General, 1722. Swift. CABA; CBV; EiCL; ExPo; FOL; FosPo; HoPM; PAn; PoEL-3; SeCeV; StP
His grace is sufficient. Sufficiency. Avis B. Christiansen. SoP
His Grace of Marlborough, legends say. Tradition of Conquest. Sara Morgan Bryan Piatt. AA
His graceful swag blocks catch the eye. The Destruction of Bulfinch's House. Stephen Sandy. CoPo
His Grange, or Private Wealth. Robert Herrick. AnAnS-2; GoJo; NoP; OAEP; OTPC (1923 ed.); SCEP-2; SeCV-1; SeEP; YAT
(His Grange, His Private Wealth.) EnLit
("Though clock/ To tell how night.") EG
His Great Love on High. Michelangelo. *See* On the Brink of Death.
His haire was blacke, and in small curls did twine. Christ's Victorie on Earth. Giles Fletcher. *Fr.* Christ's Victory and Triumph. SeCV-1
His hammer falls with rhythmic, Titan grace. The Riveter. Margaret E. Sangster. PEDC
His Hand. Henry Jerome Stockard. FaChP
His Hand Shall Cover Us. Isaac ben Samuel of Dampière, *tr. fr. Hebrew by* Nina Davis Salaman. TrJP
His Hands. John Richard Moreland. ChIP; MaRV; OQP; SoP; TRV
His hands were pierced, the hands that made. The Wounds of Jesus. Cecil J. Allen. SoP
His hands worked ceaselessly at the coverlet. Testament. Sister M. Thérèse. MoRP
His harp, whereon was al his gle. *Unknown.* *Fr.* Sir Orfeo. AtBAP
His head split in four parts. Promenade. David Ignatow. TrJP
His headstone said. The Funeral of Martin Luther King, Jr. Nikki Giovanni. BOLo; TNV
His hearing left him twenty years ago. Old Farmer Alone. Robert P. Tristram Coffin. MoLP
His heart, to me, was a place of palaces. I Have Been through the Gates. Charlotte Mew. MeWo; MoAB; MoBrPo; TrGrPo
His heart was in his garden; but his brain. Frederick Goddard Tuckerman. *Fr.* Sonnets. AP
His heart was light, and all the living day. Canadian Farmer. Genevieve Bartole. CaP
His Heart Was True to Poll. F. C. Burnand. HBV
(True to Poll.) BOHV
His Hirsute Suit. Frank Sidgwick. WhC
His holly hair, his berry eye are here. Nativity. W. R. Rodgers. NeBP
His home a speck in a vast universe. Microcosm. Bertram Dobell. OBVV
His home is on the heights; to him. The Poet. Edwin Markham. WGRP
His hope undone, now raves the impious king. The Slaughter of the Innocents by Order of King Herod. Caelius Sedulius. *Fr.* Carmen Paschale [*or* Easter Song]. OnYI
His hottest love and most delight. The Happy Hen. James Agee. ErPo
His house is a haven where fingers dare. Heart Specialist. Elias Lieberman. ImOP
His house was never short of bake-meat pies. Ten of Chaucer's People: A Gluttonous Rich Man. Chaucer. *Fr.* The Canterbury Tales. PoSa
His Immortality. Thomas Hardy. CMoP
His Incomparable Lady. Earl of Surrey. *See* Praise of His Love, A.
His iron arm had spent its force. Death and General Putnam. Arthur Guiterman. OnSP; PoMS; TIHL
His Is the Way. Thomas Curtis Clark. ChIP
His kiss is sweet, his word is kind. The Boatman of Kinsale. Thomas Osborne Davis. VA
His Lachrimae or Mirth, Turned to Mourning. Robert Herrick. SCEP-2; SeCV-1; SeEP
His Lady's Cruelty. Sir Philip Sidney. *See* Astrophel and Stella: Sonnets, XXXI.
His Lady's Death. Pierre de Ronsard, *tr. fr. French by* Andrew Lang. *Fr.* Amours de Marie. AWP
His Lady's Eyes. Fulke Greville. *See* You Little Stars That Live in Skies.
His Lady's Hand. Sir Thomas Wyatt. *See* O Goodly Hand.
His Lady's Might. Philippe Desportes. *See* Those Eyes Which Set My Fancy on Afire.
His Lady's Tomb. Pierre de Ronsard, *tr. fr. French by* Andrew Lang. *Fr.* Amours de Marie AWP; JAWP; WBP
His lamp, his bow, and quiver laid aside. Cupid Turned Plowman. Moschus. AWP; OnPM
His landlocked dreams were rainbow-tides that ran. Old Voyager. Walter Blackstock. GoYe
His last days linger in that low attic. The Old Jockey. F. R. Higgins. AnIV; GTBS-D; OBMV; OxBI
His Last Sonnet. Keats. *See* Bright Star! Would I Were Steadfast As Thou Art.
His Last Week. Elinor Lennen. PGD
His Laureate. Joyce Kilmer. StJW
His legs bestrid the ocean: his rear'd arm. Shakespeare. *Fr.* Antony and Cleopatra, V, ii. MemP
His Letanie, to the Holy Spirit. Robert Herrick. *See* His Litany to the Holy Spirit.
His life is in the body of the living. The Soul and Body of John Brown. Muriel Rukeyser. MoAmPo
His Life Is Ours. Dorothy Conant Stroud. STF
His life was gentle, and the elements. The Perfect Tribute. Shakespeare. *Fr.* Julius Caesar, V, v. MaRV
His life was private; safely led, aloof. A Characterization. Sir Henry Taylor. VA
His Litany to the Holy Spirit. Robert Herrick. DTC; ELP; EnLi-1; HBV; InPo; MaPo; NoP; OAEP; OxBoCh; PAn; PoE; PoeP; PoLF; QFR; SeCePo; SeCL; SeEP; UnPo (1st ed.)
(His Letanie, to the Holy Spirit.) AnAnS-2; OBS; SCEP-2; SeCV-1
(In The Hour of My Distress.) MaRV
(Litany to the Holy Spirit.) CoBE; EnLit; OBEV; PoFS
His little son of twelve years old Philippus here has laid. Dead Boy. Callimachus. OnPM
His Living Monument. Minna Irving. PGD
His locks were wild, and wild his eye. Taking Long Views. May Kendall. CenHV
His Love. *Unknown.* SoP
His Majesty. Theron Brown. AA
His Majesty the Letter-Carrier. Emanuel Carnevali. AnAmPo
His Majesty's Health. *Unknown, at. to* Jeremy Savile. *See* Health Unto His Majesty, A.
His malice was a pimple down his good. Three around the Old Gentleman. John Berryman. AP
His memory control stop being broken. Mad Actor. James L. Montague. NYTB

His Metrical Prayer; on the Eve of His Own Execution. James Graham, Marquess of Montrose. *See* Verses Composed on the Eve of His Execution.
His Metrical Vow; on the Death of King Charles I. James Graham. *See* Epitaph on King Charles I.
His mind dove down from the stars and curled in his head. Old Talk. Winfield Townley Scott. FiMAP
His Mistress. Earl of Rochester. *See* Mistress, The; a Song.
His most kind sister all his secrets knew. Repentance. George Chapman. *Fr.* Hero and Leander, Third Sestiad. OBSC
His mother dear, Cupid offended late. Astrophel and Stella, XVII. Sir Philip Sidney. FCP; SiPS
His Mother in Her Hood of Blue. Lizette Woodworth Reese. ISi; OHIP
His Mother-in-Law. Walter Parke. BOHV; FiBHP
His mother's fondness wrought his father's frown. Jacob and the Angel. Brother Antoninus. MoRP
His Mother's Joy. John White Chadwick. AA
His Mother's Service to Our Lady. Villon, *tr. fr. French by* Dante Gabriel Rossetti. AWP; CAW; CTC; ISi; LiTW
His Mother's Wedding Ring. George Crabbe. *See* Marriage Ring, A.
His mouth babbling under the earphones. Boy in the Lamont Poetry Room, Harvard. D. G. Jones. PeCV (1967 ed.)
His mouth is open. Man in the Street. William Brown. QAH
His mower whirred cut grass like dust. Lawn and Light. James Applewhite. *Fr.* Steps from the Stream. YAP
His murderers met. Their consciences were free. Easter Eve. James Branch Cabell. HBMV; MaRV
His Muse Speakes to Him. William Habington. AnAnS-2
His naked skin clothed in the torrid mist. The Serf. Roy Campbell. BoSA; CBV; GTBS-P; LiTB; LiTM; MoBrPo; NAMP; OBMV; ReMP; TrGrPo (1942 ed.)
His Name. Charles Poole Cleaves. OQP
His Name. Dora Greenwell. ChIP
His Name at the Top. *Unknown.* STF
His name it is Pedro-Pablo-Ignacio-Juan-/ Francesco García y Gabaldon. A Feller I Know. Mary Austin. AmFN; FaPON; GaP
"His name shall be Wonderful." This Babe for whom. And His Name Shall Be Called Wonderful. Martha Snell Nicholson. BePJ; SoP
His name, they told me afterwards, was Able. In Memory of My Uncle Timothy. Alastair Reid. NePoEA-2
His name was Chance, Jack Chance, he said. Ballad of a Strange Thing. Phelps Putnam. MAP; MoAmPo (1942 ed.); MoVE; OxBA
His name was Heimdall and it was a name. Heimdall. Harold Vinal. FiSC
His name, when uttered, thrills the world. Theodore Roosevelt. William W. Peavyhouse. HH
His name yields the richest perfume. Nothing to Wish or to Fear. John Newton. BePJ
His nose is short and scrubby. My Dog. Marchette Chute. FaPON; MoSiPe; PDV; SoPo; TiPo
His overalls hung on the hook by his hat, and I noticed his pockets were bulging out fat. Treasures. *Unknown.* PoToHe (new ed.)
His Own Epitaph. John Gay. *See* My Own Epitaph.
His Own True Wife. Wolfram von Eschenbach, *tr. fr. German by* Jethro Bithell. AWP; JAWP; WBP; WoL
His pads furring the scarp's rime. The Snow-Leopard. Randall Jarrell. LiTM (1970 ed.); MoPo; TwCP
His Parting from Her. John Donne. Elegies, XII. MaMe; OBS
"O Fortune, thou'rt not worth my least exclaim," *sel.* CoBE
His Parting with Mrs. Dorothy Kennedy, *sel.* Robert Herrick.
"Prithee (lest maids should censure thee)." MyFE
His Passion. George Conrad Pullman. ChIP
His Petition to Queen Anne of Denmark (1618). Sir Walter Ralegh. SiPS
(Petition to the Queen.) FCP
His petticoats now George cast off. George and the Chimney-Sweeper. Adelaide O'Keeffe. OTPC (1923 ed.)
His Picture. John Donne. Elegies, V. CBEP; MaMe; MeLP; NoP; OBS; ReEn
(Elegie: His Picture.) FaBoEn; MePo
(Elegy V: His Picture.) EnRePo; SeEP
His Pilgrimage. Sir Walter Ralegh. *See* Passionate Man's Pilgrimage, The.
His Plan. *Unknown.* STF
His Plan for Me. Martha Snell Nicholson. STF
His Poetry His Pillar. Robert Herrick. EnL; EnLit; LoBV; MyFE, *abr.*; QFR; SeCL; SeEP
(His Poetrie His Pillar.) AnAnS-2; FaBoEn; OBS; SCEP-2; SeCP
("Only a little more.") EG
"His policy," do you say? Mr. Johnson's Policy of Reconstruction. Charles Graham Halpine. PAH
His Prayer for Absolution. Robert Herrick. AnAnS-2; EnL; EnLi-1 (1949 ed.); MaRV; OxBoCh; ReEn; SCEP-2; SeCV-1; TOP; TrPWD; TRV
His Prayer to Ben Jonson [*or* Johnson]. Robert Herrick. AnAnS-2; BoLiVe; CavP; EnL; EnLit; ILP; MaPo (1969 ed.); ML; NoP; OAEP; OBS; OxBoLi; PoSa; PP; ReEn; SCEP-2; SeCeV; SeCV-1; SeEP; TrGrPo; UnPo
His Presence. Patrick Brontë. SoP
His Presence. Dale Schulz. STF
His Presence Came like Sunrise. Ralph S. Cushman. *See* Secret, The.
His presence is wealth. His Presence. Patrick Brontë. SoP
His Pride/ Had cast him out from Heaven. Satan. Milton. *Fr.* Paradise Lost, I. TreFT, *ll.* 36-75; TrGrPo
His Promises. Martha Snell Nicholson. BePJ
His proper name was Peter Sweet. The Reformed Pirate. T. G. Roberts. WHW
His Purposes. *Unknown.* FaChP
His Quest. Lewis Frank Tooker. AA
His radiant fingers so adorning. Dawn. George B. Logan, Jr. HBV
His Request to Julia. Robert Herrick. OBS; SeEP
His Return. "D. N. R." SoP
His Return[e] to London. Robert Herrick. AnAnS-2; EnLit; MaPo (1969 ed.); SeEP
His Reward. Sir Thomas Wyatt. *See* With Serving Still.
His Sailing from Julia. Robert Herrick. PoEL-3
His Salvation. Bernard of Clairvaux, *tr. fr. Latin by* Anthony W. Boehm. SoP
His Saviour's Words Going to the Cross. Robert Herrick. StJW
His sense of Dignity [*or* worth] is strong. My Pompous Friend. Lawrence Emerson Nelson. PoMa
His shadow monstrous on the palace wall. Oedipus. Thomas Blackburn. FaBoTw
His Shield. Marianne Moore. DTC; LiTM; NePA; TwAmPo
His shoulder did I hold. Any Saint. Francis Thompson. MoBrPo
His sight from ever gazing through the bars. The Panther. Rainer Maria Rilke. LiTW
His skin is brilliant with the nimble flood. Lucius Apuleius. *Fr.* Eros and Psyche. LO
His softest feathers winter thither sent. The Snow. Joseph Beaumont. StJW
His Son. Callimachus, *tr. fr. Greek by* G. B. Grundy. AWP; JAWP; WBP
His son meant something that he couldn't name. A Spring Night. Robert Beloof. PoPo
His songs were a little phrase. Of [*or* On] a Poet Patriot. Thomas MacDonagh. AnIV; CAW; HBMV; OnYI; OxBI; PoFr; TSW
His soul extracted from the public sink. The Scurrilous Scribe. Philip Freneau. AA
His soul fared forth (as from the deep home-grove). Samuel Taylor Coleridge. Dante Gabriel Rossetti. Five English Poets, 3. PoVP
His soul stretched tight across the skies. Preludes, IV. T. S. Eliot. AnAmPo; BoLiVe (1945 ed.); CoBA; InP; LiTA; NoP; OBMV; ReMP; UnPo
His soul to god! on a battle-psalm! Albert Sidney Johnston. Francis Orrery Ticknor. PAH
His Sovereignty. Kalonymos ben Moses of Lucca, *tr. fr. Hebrew by* Nina Davis Salaman. TrJP
His speckled pastures dipped to meet the beach. Biography. Charles Bruce. CaP; PeCV
His spirit in smoke ascended to high heaven. The Lynching. Claude McKay. BALP; BANP; IDB
His spirit lives; he died and is alive. Alive for Evermore. Amos Niven Wilder. MaRV
His Statement of the Case. James Herbert Morse. AA
His stature was not very tall. The Description of Sir Geoffrey

Chaucer. Robert Greene. *Fr.* Greene's Vision. AnFE; CTC; FaBoCh; LoGBV; OBSC; WePo
His Strength. Whittier. *Fr.* First-Day Thoughts. FaChP; SoP
His tail is remarkably long. The Kangarooster. Kenyon Cox. *Fr.* Mixed Beasts. RIS; TiPo
His Task—and Ours. Dorothy Gould. PGD
His Tears to Thamasis. Robert Herrick. OAEP
His the pardon, ours the sin. It Is Finished. Horatius Bonar. BePJ
His Throne Is with the Outcast. James Russell Lowell. ChIP
His tongue was touched with sacred fire. Henry Ward Beecher. Charles Henry Phelps. AA
His Trees. Mark Van Doren. AnFE; CoAnAm
His triumphs of a moment done. On the Departure of the British from Charleston. Philip Freneau. PAH
His trousers are torn, rolled up to the knee. The Teacher Sees a Boy. Margaret Morningstar. STF
His unregarded grave here Piron has. Epitaph. Alexis Piron. PAH
His vigil was the stars; his eyes were bright. Nox Ignatiana. James J. Daly. CAW; JKCP
His was the Word that spake it. Queen Elizabeth Tudor, as a Girl, on Trial for Heresy. *Unknown.* PoG
His Way. *Unknown.* FaChP; SoP
His way in farming all men knew. At Marshfield. William Cleaver Wilkinson. *Fr.* Webster, an Ode. AA
His weary glance, from passing by the bars. The Panther. Rainer Maria Rilke. OA; OnPM
His well shaped ears were chestnut brown and they. The Huckster's Horse. Julia Hurd Strong. GoYe
His Wife's Wedding Ring. George Crabbe. *See* Marriage Ring, A.
His wild heart beats with painful sobs. The Happy Warrior. Sir Herbert Read. MMA
His Will Be Done. Annie Johnson Flint. BLRP
His Will Be Done. Lucy M. Waelty. SoP
His Winding Sheet. Robert Herrick. AnFE; HBV; OBEV
His window is over the factory flume. Widow Brown's Christmas. John Townsend Trowbridge. BeLS
His Wisdom. Nicholas Breton. *Fr.* The Strange Fortunes of Two Excellent Princes. ALV; OBSC
(I Would Thou Wert Not Fair [or I Were Wise].) ElL; InvP
His Wish to God. Robert Herrick. AnAnS-2; BoPe; OxBoCh
His Word Is Powerful. H. H. Savage. SoP
His words were magic and his heart was true. Uncle Ananias. E. A. Robinson. AnNE; BoLiVe (1945 ed.); LaNeLa; MaPo; MoAmPo (1950 ed.); NePA; NoP
His work all done, two of my soldiers more. The Escape from Cyclop. Homer. *Fr.* The Odyssey, IX. LiTW
His work is done; his toil is o'er. Faithful unto Death. Richard Handfield Titherington. PAH
His work well done, the leader stepped aside. First Citizen. James Jeffrey Roche. PGD
His Youth. John Oxenham. StJW
Hist, but a word, fair and soft! Master Hugues of Saxe-Gotha. Robert Browning. MuSP
Hist, hist, ye winds, ye whispering wavelets hist. Two Sonnet-Songs, I. Frank T. Marzials. VA
Hist, oh hist. Thomas Lovell Beddoes. EG
Historic be the Survey of our kind. Society. George Meredith. EPN
Historic Moment, An. William J. Harris. BOLo
Historic, sidelong, implicating eyes. La Gioconda, by Leonardo Da Vinci, in the Louvre. "Michael Field." PeVV
Historic Time. Robert Eyres Landor. *Fr.* The Impious Feast, VIII. OBRV
Historical Incidents. Clarence Day. InMe
Historie of Squyer William Meldrum, The, *sel.* Sir David Lindsay.
Squire Meldrum at Carrickfergus. OxBS
History. Laurence Binyon. POTE
History. Emerson. AmLP
Informing Spirit, The, *sel.* AWP; InPo; WGRP
(History.) BBV (1951 ed.)
(No Great, No Small.) MaRV
History. Robert Fitzgerald. MoVE
History. D. H. Lawrence. BrPo
History. "Paul Tanaquil." HBMV
History, A. John Williams. NePoAm-2
History among the Rocks. Robert Penn Warren. Kentucky Mountain Farm, III. MAP; MoAmPo; MoVE
History, and nature, too, repeat themselves, they say. Same Old Story. Harry B. Smith. BOHV
History Class. Robert Finch. TwCaPo
History Lesson, A. Miroslav Holub, *tr. fr. Czech by* George Theiner. FIW
History Lesson. *Unknown.* RIS
("First William the Norman.") OxNR
History Lesson. Mark Van Doren. NYBP
History of a Literary Movement. Howard Nemerov. NePoEA; PP
History of blacklife is put down in the motions, The. The Sound of Afroamerican History Chapt I. S. E. Anderson. BF
History of Communications and a Running Account, The. Pien Chih-lin, *tr. fr. Chinese by* Pien Chih-lin. LiTW
History of Education. David McCord. WhC
History of France. Kenward Elmslie. ANYP
History of Horestes, The. John Pickering. *See* Horestes.
History of King Richard II, *sel.* Nahum Tate.
Love's Delights. SeCL
History of Peace, A. Robert Graves. HBMV
History of Prince Edward Island, The. Larry Gorman. ShS
History of Psychotherapy, The. Jon Anderson. YAP
History of the Flood, The. John Heath-Stubbs. FIW; MoBS
History of the Insipids, The, *sel.* Earl of Rochester.
Charles the Second. FOL
History of the Modern World. Stanton A. Coblentz. PGD
History of the U.S., The. Winifred Sackville Stoner. BLPA; TreF; YaD
History of the World as Pictures, The. Nancy Sullivan. CoPo
Hit. W. W. Gibson. MCCG; NP
Hit at the Times, A. A. O. McGrew. PoOW
Hit wes upon a Scere-thorsday that ure loverd aros. Judas. *Unknown.* BaBo; ESPB; OBB; ViBoFo
Hitch up my buggy, saddle up my black mare. I'm a Stranger Here. *Unknown.* OuSiCo
Hitchhiker. Jack Marshall. NYBP
Hither haste, and gently strew. Song. Thomas Lovell Beddoes. EG
Hither Hither Love. Keats. PeER
Hither, Strephon, Chloe, Phyllis. A Woodland Revel. Clarence Urmy. HBMV
Hither, thither, little feet. Behind the Door. Bert Leston Taylor. LHV
Hither thou com'st: the busy [*or* busie] wind all night. The Bird [*or* To a Bird after a Storm *or* After the Storm]. Henry Vaughan. AnAnS-1; AtBAP; BoC; LoBV; MeP; OBEV (new ed.); PoEL-2; SCEP-1; SeCL; SeCV-1; TRV
Hither where tangled thickets of the acacia. The Babiaantje. F. T. Prince. ACV; BoSA; ChMP; MoBrPo (1962 ed.)
Hitherto. Mary Gorges. SoP
Hitherto and Henceforth. Annie Johnson Flint. BLRP
Hitherto Hath the Lord Helped. *Unknown.* BLRP
(O thou of Little Faith.) SoP
Hitherto the Lord hath helped us. Hitherto and Henceforth. Annie Johnson Flint. BLRP
Hitler Dwarf, The. Dick Lourie. ThO
Hit's a mighty fur ways up de Far'well Lane. My Honey, My Love. Joel Chandler Harris. *Fr.* Uncle Remus and His Friends. AA; FaBoBe
Hit's agittin mighty late w'en de guinny hins squall. Plantation Play Song. Joel Chandler Harris. *Fr.* Uncle Remus, His Songs and His Sayings. MCCG
Hits and Runs. Carl Sandburg. SD
Hitty Pitty within the wall. *Unknown.* OxNR
Hm Hm my Lord! Hm. Po' Mourner's Got a Home at Las'. *Unknown.* BoAN-2
Hm Mos' done toilin' here. Mos' Done Toilin' Here. *Unknown.* BoAN-2
Ho, a song by the fire! Dartmouth Winter-Song. Richard Hovey. AA
Ho, all you cats in all the street. Cat's Meat. Harold Monro. OBMV; TSW
Ho! are you there, Bill Hawkins. Bloody Bill. D. M. Ross. AnNZ
Ho, boys, ho. for California, O. The Banks of Sacramento. *Unknown.* AS
Ho, boys, is you right? Tie-Shuffling Chant. *Unknown.* ABF
Ho! broder [*or* brother] Teague, dost hear de decree. Lilli Burlero [*or* Lilliburlero *or* A New Song]. Thomas, Lord

Ho (continued)
Wharton. CoMu; OxBoLi; ViBoFo
Ho! brother Teague, dost hear de decree? *See* Ho! broder Teague. . .
Ho! burnish well, ye cunning hands. Song of the Mariner's Needle. C. R. Clarke. EtS
Ho! City of the gay. The Return of Napoleon from St. Helena. Lydia Huntley Sigourney. AA
Ho! Cupid calls, come Lovers, come. Cupids Call. James Shirley. ErPo
Ho, Everyone That Thirsteth. Isaiah LV: 1-3, 6-7, Bible, *O.T.* MaRV
Ho, Everyone That Thirsteth. A. E. Housman. MaPo (1969 ed.)
Ho! for California! *with music.* Jesse Hutchinson. SGR (Sacramento, *abr., with music.*) TrAS
Ho! for Pike's Peak, where gold is found. Song for the Pike's Peaker. *Unknown.* PoOW
Ho, for taxis green or blue. Taxis. Rachel Field. FaPON; GFA; MPB; PoRh; SoPo; StVeCh (1940 ed.); TiPo
Ho! for the blades of Harden! The Blades of Harden. Will H. Ogilvie. *Fr.* Whaup o' the Rede. GoTS
Ho, for the Pirate Don Durk of Dowdee! Pirate Don Durk of Dowdee. Mildred Plew Meigs. BoChLi; GaP; PCD; PDV; PoRh; SoPo; TiPo
Ho! he exclaim'd, King George of England standeth in judgement! The Absolvers. Robert Southey. *Fr.* A Vision of Judgement. EnRP
Ho Ho Ho Caribou. Joseph Ceravolo. ANYP
Ho! Ho! The fine fellow. Camden Magpie. Hugh McCrae. PoAu-1
Ho! Ho' Yes! Yes! It's very all well. Ballade of Soporific Absorption. J. C. Squire. InMe
Ho! is there any will ride with me. Sir Giles' War-Song. William Morris. PoVP; ViPo
"Ho!" laughs the Winter. March. Arthur Guiterman. YeAr
Ho, let her rip—with her royal clew a-quiver. In the Trades. Cicely Fox Smith. EtS
Ho! pony, Down the lonely road. Army Correspondent's Last Ride. George Alfred Townsend. AA
Ho, Moeris! whether [*or* wither] on thy way so fast. Lycidas and Moeris. Vergil. Eclogues, IX. AWP; FosPo
Ho! Persephone brings flowers, to them. The Old Men. Irving Feldman. TwCP
Ho, pretty page, with the dimpled chin. The Age of Wisdom [*or* Love at Two Score]. Thackeray. *Fr.* Rebecca and Rowena. ALV; HBV; PoVP; VA; WhC
"Ho, Rose!" quoth the stout Miles Standish. The First Proclamation of Miles Standish. Margaret Junkin Preston. MC; PAH; YaD
"Ho, sailor of the sea!" "How's My Boy?" Sydney Dobell. EtS; GN; HBV; OHIP; VA
"Ho There, Death!" *Unknown.* *tr. fr. Russian by* W. R. S. Ralston. OnPM
"Ho, there! Fisherman, hold your hand!" The Second Mate. Fitz-James O'Brien. AA
Ho! who comes here along with bagpiping and drumming? The Morris Dance. *Unknown.* MuSP; SiCE
"Ho! why dost thou shiver and shake." Gaffer Gray. Thomas Holcroft. HBV
Ho! wind of the far, far prairies! The Call of the Plains. Ethel MacDiarmid. SCC
Ho! woodsmen of the mountainside! A Cry to Arms. Henry Timrod. PAH
Ho! workers of the old time styled. The Shoemakers. Whittier. AmPP (4th ed.); AnNE; CoBA
Hoar-Frost. Amy Lowell. *Fr.* Chinoiseries. AnAmPo; NP; PoRA (rev. ed.)
Hoarded Grapes. *Unknown,* *tr. fr. Greek by* Louis Untermeyer. UnTE
Hoarded Joy. Dante Gabriel Rossetti. The House of Life, LXXXII. MaVP; PoVP; ViPo
Hoary mountains seem gray and cold, The. At Timber Line. Frank H. Mayer. PoOW
Hob, shoe, hob; hob, shoe, hob. *Unknown.* OxNR
Hob the Elf. Norman M. Johnson. BoTP
Hobbes clearly proves that every creature. Critics [*or* A Rhapsody on Poetry]. Swift. *Fr.* On Poetry; a Rhapsody. OBEC; PP; SeCePo
Hobbie Noble. *Unknown.* *See* Hobie Noble.
Hobbledy Hops. *Unknown.* OTPC (1946 ed.)
Hobby Horse, The. *Unknown,* *tr. fr. French.* PCH
Hobie [*or* Hobbie] Noble. *Unknown.* BaBo; ESPB; OBB; OxBB; ViBoFo
Hobnelia, seated in a dreary vale. Thursday; or, The Spell. John Gay. *Fr.* The Shepherd's Week. CEP; EiPP; PoEL-3
Hobson and His Men. Robert Loveman. PAH
Hoc Cygno Vinces. Henry Hawkins. ACP
Hoc Est Corpus. Alex Comfort. LiTB; LiTM; POTE
Hoccleve's Humorous Praise of His Lady. Thomas Hoccleve. OAEP
(Description of His Ugly Lady, A.) MeEL
Hoccleve's Lament for Chaucer and Gower, *abr.* Thomas Hoccleve. *Fr* De Regimine Principum. OAEP
Hoch! Der Kaiser. Alexande! Macgregor Rose. *See* Kaiser & Co.
Hock-Cart, or Harvest Home, The. Robert Herrick. AnAnS-2; NoP; OAEP; OBS; OTPC (1923 ed.); PoE; PoeP; ReEn; SCEP-2; SeCP; SeCV-1; SeEP; StP
"Come sons of Summer, by whose toil," *sel.* ViBoPo
Hoddley, poddley, puddle and fogs. *Unknown.* OxNR
Hoddy doddy. *Unknown.* OxNR
Hodge the Cat. "Susan Coolidge." CIV
Hoffer. Wordsworth. FOL
Hog Butcher for the World. Chicago. Carl Sandburg. AmPP; AP; CMoP; CoBA; FaBV; HBMV; HT; InP; LiTM (rev. ed.); LoGBV; MAP; MoAB; MoAmPo; MoVE; NePA; NoP; NP; OxBA; PoIE; PoPl; TOP; TreF; ViBoPo (1958 ed.); YaD
Hog-Eye, *with music.* *Unknown.* AS
Hog-Eye Man, The, *with music.* *Unknown.* AS; SoAmSa
Hog Meat. Daniel Webster Davis. BANP
Hog Rogues on the Harricane, *with music.* *Unknown.* OuSiCo
Hogamus, Higamus. *Unknown.* ELU
Hogger on his death-bed lay, A. The Dying Hogger. *Unknown.* AS; IHA
Hogwash. Robert Francis. PoIE (1970 ed.)
Hohenlinden. Thomas Campbell. BeLS; CBEP; CH; ChTr; EnRP; FaBoCh; FOL; GN; GTBS; GTBS-D; GTBS-P; GTBS-W; GTSE; GTSL; HBV; OBNC; OBRV; OnMSP; RoGo; TreF; WaaP; WBLP; WePo; WHA
(Battle of Hohenlinden.) OTPC (1923 ed.); PaPo
Hokey, pokey, whisky, thum. *Unknown.* OxNR
Hokku: "Bits of song—what else?" Yone Noguchi. NP
Hokku: "Cry of the cicada, The." Basho, *tr. fr. Japanese by* W. G. Aston. InP
Hokku: "I thought I saw the fallen leaves." Arakida Moritake, *tr. fr. Japanese by* Yone Noguchi. InP
Hokku: in the Falling Snow. Richard Wright. IDB
Hokku: "Wayside cherry tree, A." Basho, *tr. fr. Japanese by* William N. Porter. InP
Hokku Poems. Richard Wright. AmNP
Hol' de Win' Don't Let It Blow, *with music.* *Unknown.* BoAN-2
"Hold." Patrick R. Chalmers. HBV
Hold, are you mad? you damned confounded dog. Tyrannic Love: Epilogue. Dryden. BWP; MaPo (1969 ed.); MBW-1; OAEP; SeCV-2; ViBoPo
Hold Back Thy Hours Dark Night. Beaumont *and* Fletcher. *See* Bridal Song ("Hold back thy hours").
Hold cruell love oh hold I yeild. *Unknown.* SeCSL
Hold fast to dreams. Dreams. Langston Hughes. BoChLi (1950 ed.); GoSl
Hold Fast Your Dreams. Louise Driscoll. BiCB; BLPA; FaBoBe; FaPON; HBMV; MPB; NeHB; SoPo; TiPo
Hold hard, Ned! Lift me down once more, and lay me in the shade. The Sick Stockrider. Adam Lindsay Gordon. ACV; BoAu; FOL; OBVV; PoAu-1; VA
Hold Hard, These Ancient Minutes. Dylan Thomas. CoBE
Hold her softly, not for long. At a Child's Baptism. Vassar Miller. GoJo; NYTB
Hold High the Torch. *Unknown.* MaRV
Hold high the woof, dear friends, that we may see. On a Piece of Tapestry. George Santayana. AA
Hold, hold your hand, hold; mercy, mercy, spare. A Sonnet on Sir William Alexander's Harsh Verses. James I, King of England. Sonn
Hold how you may what masks to hide your dreaming. Music. Anne Ryan. CAW
Hold it up, show it, bring the torch! Cassandra's Epithalamium. Euripides. *Fr.* The Trojan Woman. HW
Hold it up sternly—see this it sends back (who is it, is it

you?). A Hand-Mirror. Walt Whitman. CBEP; CBV; MAmP; MWA-1; OxBA; TDP
Hold, Men, Hold! *Unknown.* ChBR
Hold my breath as there's a sound on the stairs. Poem. Joel Sloman. ThO
Hold my rooster, hold my hen. Precious Things. *Unknown.* GoSl; TTY
Hold not your lips so close—dispense. The Kiss. Thomas Shipman. CLwM
Hold On, Abraham. *Unknown.* ABF
Hold on, hold on, while yet ye can. Spring Song. Aubrey Thomas De Vere. IrPN
Hold out yo' light you heav'n boun' soldier. Heav'n Boun' Soldier. *Unknown.* BoAN-1
Hold the phone. Navel. Coleman Barks. *Fr.* Body Poems. QAH
Hold Thou Me Fast. Christina Rossetti. BePJ
Hold Thou My Hands. William Canton. ThGo
Hold up your head. *Unknown.* OxNR
"Hold your hand, Lord Judge," she says. The Maid Freed from the Gallows. *Unknown.* ESPB (I *vers.*)
Hold your mad hands! for ever on your plain. Two Poems Concerning the Slave Trade, I. Robert Southey. Sonn
Hölderlin. Delmore Schwartz. MoRP
Holdfast, The. George Herbert. MaMe
Holding. Washington Gladden. *See* Ultima Veritas.
Holding a beggar's child. Meditation. Toyohiko Kagawa. MaRV; SoP; TRV
Holding a stone which has no voice. Sad Love and Sad Song. Homei Iwano. LiTW
Holding apoise in air. The Links of Chance. Edward Rowland Sill. PFY
Holding Hands. Lenore M. Link. FaPON; MoShBr; SoPo; TiPo (1952 ed.); UTS
Holding his body steady, the three upper parts erect. Yoga. *Unknown.* *Fr.* The Upanishads. OnPM
Holding its huge life open to the sky. To My Friends. Stephen Berg. NaP; NYBP
Holding-Paddock. William Hart-Smith. AnNZ
Holding the distance up before his face. The Traveller. W. H. Auden. ReMP; SyP
Holding the naked body I had bought. A Bought Embrace. G. S. Fraser. WaP
Holding this egg. First Lesson. Nancy Willard. ThO
Holding to God. Robert Herrick. *See* To God ("Lord, I am like the mistletoe").
Hold-Up. Louis MacNeice. CBV
Hold-Up, The. David Wagoner. TPM
Hole in the head where the bullet, The. On a Very Young, Very Dead Soldier. Richard Gillman. NePoAm
Hole in the Sea, The. Marvin Bell. NYBP
Holes, The. Stephen Berg. NaP; NYBP
Holes in my arms. For Real. Jayne Cortez. WSL
Holes in the Sky, *sel.* Louis MacNeice.
"And man is a spirit." TRV
Holiday. John Davidson. OBVV
Holiday ("Festo quid potius die"). Horace, *tr. fr. Latin by* Louis Untermeyer. Odes, III, 28. AWP; JAWP; WBP
Holiday. Henry Dawson Lowry. OBVV
Holiday, A. Lizette Woodworth Reese. AA
Holiday. Adrienne Cecile Rich. MoLP
Holiday. Ella Young. TiPo (1952 ed.)
Holiday, holiday, on the very first day of the year, year. Little Mathie Grove. *Unknown.* BaBo
Holiday in Reality. Wallace Stevens. NePA; OxBA
Holiday Task, A. Gilbert Abbot à Beckett, *also at. to* Barclay Philips. NA
(Polka Lyric, A.) BOHV
Holiday Train, The. Irene Thompson. BoTP
Holidays. Longfellow. MPB (1956 ed.); PoToHe (new ed.) 3*ll.*
Holidays in Childhood. Clifford Dyment. BoPe; POTi
Holier Night. Leslie Savage Clark. ChIP
Holiest of all holidays are those, The. Holidays. Longfellow. MPB (1956 ed.); PoToHe (new ed.)
Holiness[e] on the head. Aaron. George Herbert. MaMe; MeLP; MePo; OAEP; OBS; PoFS; SCEP-1
Holland. Barbara Jane Provost. PCH
Holland, that scarce deserves the name of land. The Character of Holland. Andrew Marvell. CABL; ChTr; MaMe
Hollo, My Fancy! William Cleland, *and others.* *See* Hallo My Fancy.
Hollow eyes of shock remain, The. Two Years Later. John Wieners. CoPo
Hollow heads turn toward the picket fence. 250 Willow Lane. Joseph Joel Keith. FiSC
Hollow Land, The, *sel.* William Morris.
"Christ keep the Hollow Land." AtBAP; ChTr
(Song.) NBM; PoEL-5; ThWaDe
Hollow Men, The. T. S. Eliot. AP; APA; BoLiVe (1945 ed.); CoAnAm; CoBE; CoBMV; DiPo; EnL; ForPo; LiTA; LiTM; MAP; MAPA; MBW-2; MoAB; MoAmPo; NAMP; NeMA; OBMV; PAn; PIA; Po; PoPl; POTE; TwAmPo
"Eyes I dare not meet in dreams," *sel.* GTBS-D
Hollow reed against his lips, A. The Reed-Player. Archibald MacLeish. HBMV; PTK
Hollow sea-shell which for years hath stood, The. Sea-Shell Murmurs. Eugene Lee-Hamilton. VA
Hollow shell of a house, The. The House. Henry Treece. MaRV
Hollow winds begin to blow, The. Signs of Rain. Edward Jenner. BLPA; BoNaP; OTPC; PRWS; RIS
Holly, The. Walter de la Mare. CMoP
Holly, The. Henry VIII, King of England. *See* Green Groweth the Holly.
Holly, The. Edith King. ChBR
Holly against Ivy. *Unknown.* MeEL
Holly and Ivy ("Holly and ivy made a great party"). *Unknown.* CBEP
(Carol in Praise of the Holly and Ivy.) OHIP
Holly and the Ivy, The. ("The holly and the ivy,/ When they are both full grown"). *Unknown.* CH; ChTr; ELP; OxBoCh; PoLi; YaCaBo, *with music*
Holly and Ivy ("Holy stond in the hall"). *Unknown.* *See* Nay, Ivy, Nay.
Holly Bough, The. Charles Mackay. *See* Under the Holly Bough.
Holly Fairies. Aileen Fisher. ChBR
Holly standeth [*or* Holy stond] in the hall fair to behold. Nay, Ivy, Nay [*or* Holly and Ivy]. *Unknown.* CBEP; CH; MeEL
Holly! the holly! oh, twine it with bay, The. The Christmas Holly. Eliza Cook. OTPC (1946 ed.); PRWS
Holly Tree, The. Robert Southey. EnRP; HBV
Holly wreath that now, The. A Christmas Carol. Fred Cogswell. ACV
Hollyhock, A. Frank Dempster Sherman. AA
Hollyhock with crimson bells, The. Proud Hollyhock. Marguerite Buller. BrR
Hollyhocks, The. Craven Langstroth Betts. AA
Hollyhocks are blooming in schoolyards. Prairie Summer. Dave Etter. ThO
Hollyhocks are ten feet tall, The. Wet Summer. May Williams Ward. GoYe
Hollywood. Don Blanding. YaD
Hollywood. Karl Shapiro. AmPP (4th ed.); LiTM (1970 ed.); OxBA
Hollywood . . . Hollywood . . ./ Fabulous Follywood. Hollywood. Don Blanding. YaD
Holmes. James Russell Lowell. *Fr.* A Fable for Critics. AnNE
("There's Holmes, who is matchless among you for wit.") AmePo; CoBA
Holstenwall. Sidney Keyes. FaBoTw
Holy Angels, The, *abr.* *Unknown.* WHL
Holy angels and blest. The Madonna, to Her Sleeping Child [*or* A Christmas Cradlesong]. Lope de Vega. ChrBoLe; PoPl
Holy Baptism ("As he that sees a dark and shadie grove"). George Herbert. *See* H. Baptisme.
Holy Baptism ("Since, Lord, to thee/ A narrow way and little gate"). George Herbert. HBV
(H. Baptisme.) MaMe; SCEP-1; SeCV-1
(Holy Baptisme.) PoEL-2
Holy bereth beris. Holly against Ivy. *Unknown.* MeEL
Holy Bible, Book Divine. John Burton. BLRP; SoP; WBLP
Holy Book, The. M. D. Clayburn. SoP
Holy boy, The/ Went from his mother. Children of Love. Harold Monro. MoBrPo
Holy Child, The. Charles Carroll Albertson. ChIP; MaRV; StJW
Holy Children boldly stand, The. Nativity Ode. St. Cosman. CAW
Holy Church. William Langland, *tr. fr. Middle English.*

Holy (continued)
Fr. The Vision of Piers Plowman, Passus I. MeEV
(Field Full of Folk, A, *mod. by* Grover Cronin, Jr.) CoBE
(Holy Church Speaks, *mod. by* Henry W. Wells.) PoLi
Holy City, The. W. Russell Bowie. MaRV
Holy City, The. Frederic Edward Weatherly. BLRP; WBLP
Holy Communion. George Herbert. *See* H. Communion.
Holy Communion. Speer Strahan. JKCP
Holy Communion, The. Henry Vaughan. AnAnS-1; MeP
Holy Confessor, blessed in the merit. Sancte Confessor. Rhabanus Maurus. CAW
Holy Cross. *Unknown.* ACP; CAW
(Hymn to the Cross, A.) MeEL
(Steadfast Cross.) NoP
Holy-Cross Day. Robert Browning. OtMeF
Holy Earth, The, *sel.* John Hall Wheelock.
In the Immense Cathedral. MoRP
Holy Eclogue, The. Sister Francisca Josefa del Castillo, *tr. fr. Spanish by* Thomas Walsh. CAW
Holy Eucharist, The. Pedro Calderón de la Barca, *tr. fr. Spanish by* Richard Chenevix Trench. CAW
Holy Fair, The. Burns. BEL; CEP; EiCL; EiCP; EiPP; EnRP; OAEP
Holy Family. Muriel Rukeyser. MoAmPo
Holy Father, cheer our way. Light at Evening. R. H. Robinson. SoP
Holy Field, The. Henry Hart Milman. OxBoCh
Holy Fortitude. Isaac Watts. SoP
Holy Ghost, *with music. Unknown.* OuSiCo
Holy Ghost, Dispel Our Sadness. Paul Gerhardt, *tr. fr. German by* J. C. Jacobi *and* A. M. Toplady. SoP
Holy God, We Praise Thy Name. Clarence Walworth. TreFT
Holy God, we praise Thy name. Hymn of Thanksgiving. *Unknown.* WHL
Holy Grail, The. Tennyson. *Fr.* Idylls of the King. MBW-2; PoVP; ViPo; ViPP
Holy Hill, A. "Æ." AWP; JAWP; WBP
Holy, Holy, Holy. Reginald Heber. FaChP; HBV; MaRV; OHIP; OTPC; SoP; TreFT
(Thrice Holy.) WGRP
Holy, holy, holy, Lord. Adoration. Henry W. Frost. SoP
Holy, holy, holy Lord unnamed. Sonnet. William Alabaster. MeP
Holy Innocents, The. Robert Lowell. ATP (1953 ed.); InPo; InvP; MoAB; MoAmPo (1950 ed.); NePoEA; PoAn; PoDB; PoeP; TDP; ToPo
Holy Innocents, The. Prudentius, *tr. fr. Latin by* H. T. Henry. CAW
Holy Innocents. Christina Rossetti. HBV; HBVY
Holy Jesus, Thou art born. Dedication. Victoria Saffelle Johnson. GoBC; TrPWD
Holy Land. Richard Watson Gilder. StJW
Holy Land of Walsingham, The. Benjamin Francis Musser. ISi
Holy Land of Walsinghame, The. *Unknown, at. to* Sir Walter Ralegh. *See* As You Came from the Holy Land.
Holy Light. John Hall Wheelock. LiTM (1946 ed.); PG (1955 ed.)
Holy Light Equally Lights. William M. Hoffman. ThO
Holy Lullaby. *Unknown.* GoTP
Holy Man, The. *Unknown, tr. fr. Old Irish by* Whitley Stokes *and* John Strachan. *Fr.* The Devil's Tribute to Moling. OnYI
Holy Matrimony. John Keble. HBV; MaRV; VA
Holy Matrimony. Maybell Whiting Leal. SoP
Holy monk, concealed from man, The. St. Philip in Himself. Cardinal Newman. GoBC
Holy Name of Jesus, The. Richard Crashaw. CAW
Holy Nation, A. Richard Realf. *Fr* Of Liberty and Charity. PoFr
Holy Nativity of Our Lord God. Richard Crashaw. *See* In the Holy Nativity of Our Lord God.
Holy Night. Nathaniel A. Benson. CaP
Holy night that Christ was born, The. The Ox. John Gray. GBV (1952 ed.)
Holy Nunnery, The. *Unknown.* BaBo; ESPB
Holy of England! since my light is short. On First Entering Westminster Abbey. Louise Imogen Guiney. AA
Holy of Holies, The. G. K. Chesterton. BoPe; FaChP; MoRP; TRV; WGRP
Holy Office, The. James Joyce. FaBoTw; SiTL
Holy Ones, the Young Ones, The. Chayyim Zeldis. TrJP
Holy Order. J. B. Boothroyd. FiBHP
Holy Places. Herbert D. Gallaudet. MaRV
Holy Poems (I-III). George Barker. MoPo
Holy Poet, I have heard. John Hall Wheelock. *Fr.* Thanks from Earth to Heaven. TrPWD
Holy-Rood come forth and shield. The Old Wives Prayer. Robert Herrick. SeCV-1
Holy Rose, The. Vyacheslav Ivanovich Ivanov, *tr. fr. Russian by* Babette Deutsch *and* Avrahm Yarmolinsky AWP; JAWP; WBP
Holy Saturday. John Banister Tabb. MaRV; StJW
Holy Satyr. Hilda Doolittle ("H. D."). MAP; MoAmPo
Holy Scriptures, The. George Herbert. MaMe; SCEP-1
Holy Scriptures, I, The, *sel.* AnAnS-1; MeP
Holy Scriptures. Henry Vaughan. AnAnS-1; MeP
Holy Sonnets. John Donne. AnAnS-1; MaMe; MasP; MeP; SCEP-1; Sonn
Sels.
"As due by many titles I resign[e]," II. AnAnS-1; MaMe; MasP; MeP; MePo; OBS; PIA; SCEP-1; SeEP; Sonn
"At the round earths imagin'd [*or* imagined] corners, blow," VII. AnAnS-1; AnEnPo; AtBAP; ATP (1953 ed.); BWP; CABA; CBEP; CBV; CoBE; DiPo; EaLo; EnRePo; EP; ExPo; FaBoEn; FlW; ForPo; FosPo; ILP; InPo; LiTB; LiTG; LoBV; MaMe; MaPo; MasP; MBW-1; MeLP; MeP; MePo; MyFE; NoP; OAEP; OBS; OxBoCh; PAn; PIA; Po; PoAn; PoEL-2; PoFS; PoIE; QFR; ReEn; SCEP-1; SeCeV; SeCP; SeCV-1; SeEP; ShBV-4; Sonn; StP; TDP; TreFT; TuPP; VaPo; ViBoPo; YAT
(Blow Your Trumpets, Angels.) ChTr
"Batter my heart, three person'd God; for, you," XIV. AnAnS-1; AnEnPo; AnFE; BoLiVe; BWP; CABA; CaFP; CBEP; CBV; DiPo; EaLo; EnL; EnRePo; EP; ExPo; FaFP; ForPo; FosPo; GoBC; GTBS-W; ILP; LiTB; LiTG; MaMe; MaPo; MaRV; MasP; MBW-1; MeLP; MeP; MePo; NoP; OAEP; OBS; OxBoCh; PAn; PIA; Po; PoAn; PoE; PoEL-2; PoeP; PoFS; PoIE; ReEn; SCEP-1; SeCePo; SeCeV; SeCP; SeCV-1; SeEP; Sonn; StP; TDP; TreFT; TrGrPo; TrPWD; TuPP; VaPo
"Death be not proud, though some have called thee," X. AnAnS-1; AnEnPo; AnFE; AtBAP; BoLiVe; BWP; CABA; CaFP; CBEP; CBV; ChTr; CoBE; DiPo; ElL; EnL; EnRePo; ExPo; FaBoEn; FaBV; FaFP; ForPo; GoBC; GTBS-W; HBV; ILP; InPo; InvP; LiTB; LiTG; LoBV; MaMe; MaPo; MasP; MBW-1; MeLP; MeP; MePo; MyFE; NoP; OAEP; OBS; OnPM; PAn; PG (1955 ed.); Po; PoAn; PoE; PoEL-2; PoeP; PoFr; PoFS; PoIE; PoPo; PoRA; PoSa; PPON; ReEn; SCEP-1; SeCeV; SeCP; SeCV-1; SeEP; Sonn; SoP; StP; TDP; TIHL; TreFS; TrGrPo; TRV; TuPP; ViBoPo; WHA; YAT
(Death.) ATP; BEL; BoC; EnLi-1; EnLit; FaChP; MaRV; OBEV; ShBV-4; TOP; UnPo (1st ed.)
"Father, part of his double interest," XVI. AnAnS-1; MaMe; MasP; MeP; OBS; SCEP-1; Sonn
"I am a little world made cunningly," V. AnAnS-1; CABA; CBV; EnL; EnRePo; MaMe; MaPo (1969 ed.); MasP; MeP; MyFE; NoP; OBS; OxBoCh; PIA; ReEn; SCEP-1; SeCP; SeEP; Sonn; StP
"If faithfull[l] soules be alike glorifi'd," VIII. AnAnS-1; MaMe; MasP; MeP; NoP; OBS; SCEP-1; SeEP; Sonn
"If poisonous [*or* poysonous] mineral[l]s' and if that tree," IX. AnAnS-1; AnEnPo; AtBAP; ATP (1953 ed.); CABA; EnRePo; EP; ExPo; GTBS-W; LiTB; MaMe; MaPo; MasP; MeP; MePo; NoP; OBS; PoAn; PoEL-2; PoeP; PoIE; ReEn; SCEP-1; SeCP; Sonn; TuPP; UnPo
(Forget.) WHA
"O might those sigh[e]s and tear[e]s returne againe," III. AnAnS-1; AnEnPo; MaMe; MasP; MeP; OBS; SCEP-1; SeEP; Sonn
"Oh my blacke soule! now thou art summoned," IV. AnAnS-1; MaMe; MasP; MeP; MePo; MyFE; OBS; SCEP-1; Sonn
"Oh, to vex me, contraries [*or* contraryes] meet in one," XIX. AnAnS-1; EP; MaMe; MasP; MBW-1; MeP; NoP; PoEL-2; SCEP-1; Sonn
(Devout Fits.) SeCePo
(Inconstancy.) MaRV
"Show me dear[e] Christ, thy spouse, so bright and clear," XVIII. AnAnS-1; ExPo; ILP; MaMe; MasP; MBW-1; MeLP; MeP; NoP; OAEP; OBS; SCEP-1; SeEP; Sonn; TuPP
"Since she whom I lov'd hath paid [*or* payd] her last debt,"

XVII. AnAnS-1; MaMe; MaPo; MasP; MeP; MePo; OAEP; SCEP-1; SeEP; Sonn
"Spit in my face you Jews, and pierce my side,"XI. AnAnS-1; MaMe; MasP; MeP; OBS; OxBoCh; SCEP-1; SeEP; Sonn
"This is my play's [*or* playes] last scene, here heavens appoint," VI. AnAnS-1; AnEnPo; LoBV; MaMe; MasP; MeLP; MeP; MePo; MyFE; OAEP; OBS; OxBoCh; PoFS; SCEP-1; SeCP; SeEP; Sonn; TuPP
"Thou hast made me, and shall thy worke decay?" I. AnAnS-1; AnEnPo; BWP; EG; EnRePo; EP; FaBoEn; MaMe; MaPo; MasP; MBW-1; MeLP; MeP; NoP; OAEP; OBS; OxBoCh; PAn; Po; PoEL-2; PoFS; SCEP-1; SeCP; SeEP; Sonn
"What if this present were the world's last night?", XIII. AnAnS-1; ExPo; GTBS-W; LiTB; MaMe; MaPo; MasP; MBW-1; MeLP; MeP; OAEP; OBS; SCEP-1; SeCeV; SeEP; Sonn; TuPP
"Why are wee by all creatures waited on?" XII. AnAnS-1; CABA; MaMe; MaPo; MasP; MeP; OBS; PoEL-2; SCEP-1; Sonn; TuPP
"Wilt thou love God, as he thee! then digest," XV. AnAnS-1; MaMe; MasP; MeP; OBS; SCEP-1; Sonn
Holy Spirit, The. Harriet Auber. MaRV
Holy Spirit, The. Evelyn Underhill. BoC
Holy Spirit, Dwell with Me. Thomas Toke Lynch. *See* Gracious Spirit.
Holy Spirit, Lead Me. *Unknown.* STF
Holy Spring. Dylan Thomas. WaP
Holy Star, The. Bryant. *See* Christmas.
Holy stillness, beautiful and deep, A. A Summer Noon at Sea. Epes Sargent. EtS
Holy stond in the hall. *See* Holly standeth in the hall fair to behold.
"Holy Supper is kept, indeed, The." James Russell Lowell. *Fr.* The Vision of Sir Launfal. TRV
Holy Thursday ("Is this a holy thing to see"). Blake. *Fr.* Songs of Experience. CEP; CoBE; EiPP; EnL; EnLi-2 (1949 ed.); EnPE; EnRP; ERoP-1; ILP; NoP; OAEP; PeER; PoE; PoeP; PoIE; StP
Holy Thursday (" 'Twas on a Holy Thursday"). Blake. *Fr.* Songs of Innocence. BoC; CBEP; CEP; CH; CoBE; DiPo; EiCL; EiPP; EnL; EnPE; EnRP; ERoP-1; HBV; MemP; NoP; OAEP; OBEC; OTPC; PeER; PoE; PoeP; PoFS; PoIE; StP; YAT
Holy Thursday. Leonard McCarthy. JKCP (1955 ed.)
Holy Tide, The. Frederick Tennyson. OBEV; OBVV
Holy tides are being written, The. Karezzas, Cuntras, Cockturnes, Manshrieks, Carrioncries. William Knott. YAP
Holy Transportations, *sel.* Charles Fitzgeffrey.
Take Frankincense, O God. ChTr
Holy Viaticum Comes to Me, The. Giovanni Prati, *tr. fr. Italian by* Florence Trail. CAW
Holy virtue of living, the soul's delight, The. A Hymn of Form. Gordon Bottomley. BrPo
Holy Week. Phoebe Smith Bachelder. ChIP
Holy Week. Robert Whitaker. ChIP; MaRV
Holy Well, The. *Unknown.* BaBo; FaBoCh; LoGBV; OBB; OxBoCh
Holy Willie's Prayer. Burns. BEL; BOHV; CEP, *sl. abr.*; EiCL; EiPP; EnL; EnPE; EnRP; FosPo; GoTS; NoP; OxBoLi; OxBS; PeER; PoE; PoEL-4; TOP, *abr.*; VaPo; ViBoPo
Holyday. Emily Brontë. *See* Little While, a Little While, A.
Homage. Kenneth Fearing. CMoP
Homage. Helen Hoyt. AnAmPo
Homage. Gustave Kahn, *tr. fr. French by* Jethro Bithell. TrJP
Homage. George O'Neil. AnAmPo
Homage (Diptych, 2). R. J. Schoeck. GoYe
Homage of War. Bruce Williamson. NeIP
Homage to Aesop. Chana Faerstein. NYTB
Homage to Arthur Waley. Roy Fuller. ML
Homage to Arthur Waley. Weldon Kees. NaP
Homage to change that scatters the poppy seed. Rondeau. Ronald Bottrall. MoVE
Homage to Charles Laughton. Gil Orlovitz. ToPo
Homage to Circe. Horace Gregory. MoAmPo (1950 ed.)
Homage to Diana. Sir Walter Ralegh. *See* Praised Be Diana's Fair and Harmless Light.
Homage to Ezra Pound. Gilbert Highet. Par
Homage to Ghosts. Jean Garrigue. TwAmPo
Homage to Hieronymus Bosch. Thomas McGreevy. OnYI
Homage to J. S. Bach. John Heath-Stubbs. BoPe; MuSP
Homage to Jack Yeats. Thomas McGreevy. OBMV
Homage to John Coltrane, *sel.* John Sinclair.
"John Coltrane can do this for us." WOW
Homage to Literature. Muriel Rukeyser. NAMP
Homage to Max Jacob. Ron Padgett. ANYP
Homage to Mistress Bradstreet. John Berryman. TwAmPo
Sels.
"Governor your husband lived so long, The." AmP; MoVE
"When by me in the dusk my child sits down." CrMA; ReMP
Homage to Mürren. Morton Dauwen Zabel. NP
Homage to Our Leaders. Julian Symons. NeBP
Homage to Sextus Propertius, *sels.* Ezra Pound.
Me Happy, Night, Night Full of Brightness. ErPo; InvP
"Now if ever it is time to cleanse Helicon." CrMA
"Shades of Callimachus, Coan ghosts of Philetas." CMoP; MoAB; MoVE; OxBA; PP
"When, when, and whenever death closes our eyelids." MoAB; OBMV
"Who, who will be the next man to entrust his girl to a friend?" FaBoMo
Homage to Texas. Robert Graves. LiTB
Homage to the British Museum. William Empson. CMoP; FaBoMo; LiTM (rev. ed.); MoAB; MoBrPo (1962 ed.); NoP
Homage to the Empress of the Blues. Robert E. Hayden. PoNe
Homage to the Philosopher. Babette Deutsch. ImOP; TrJP
Homage to the Weather. Michael Hamburger. NMP; OPoP
Homage to thee, O Ra, at thy tremendous rising! The Dead Man Ariseth and Singeth a Hymn to the Sun. *Unknown. Fr.* Book of the Dead. AWP; JAWP; WBP
Homage to Vaslav Nijinsky. James Kirkup. UnS
Homage to William Cowper. Donald Davie. NePoEA
Home. Sybil Leonard Armes. FaChP
Home, The. Susan Axelrod. QAH
Home. Anna Letitia Barbauld. *See* Come, Says Jesus' Voice.
Home. Joseph Beaumont. *See* House and Home.
Home. Stephen Chalmers. HBMV
Home. Robert Frost. *Br. sel. fr.* The Death of the Hired Man. MaRV; TRV
(Home Defined.) TreF
Home. W. W. Gibson. HBMV
Home. J. H. Goring. MoShBr
(English, The.) SiTL
Home. Dora Greenwell. HBV
Home. Edgar A. Guest. BLPA; FaBoBe; OHFP; TreF; YaD
Home. June Brown Harris. PoToHe (new ed.)
Home. Verner von Heidenstam, *tr. fr. Swedish by* Charles W. Stork. PoPl
Home. W. E. Henley. GN; HBV; PoLF
(Falmouth.) MoBrPo
Home. George Herbert. MaMe
Home. Nellie Womack Hines. PoToHe
Home. Martha Snell Nicholson. STF
Home. Edward Rowland Sill. AnNE; HBV
Home, The. Rabindranath Tagore. GoJo
Home ("A melancholy little man"). *Unknown.* HBV
Home ("Great trees"). *Unknown, tr. fr. Chinese by* Witter Bynner *and* Kiang Kang-hu. OuHeWo
Home. Henry van Dyke. SoP; STF
Home!/ My very heart's desire is safe. Home. Nellie Womack Hines. PoToHe
Home again? Spendthrift. I. A. Richards. PoPl
Home and Mother. Mary Mapes Dodge. BOHV
Home at Last. G. K. Chesterton. *Fr.* The House of Christmas. OQP; TRV; WGRP
Home! at the word, what blissful visions rise. Home, Sweet Home, with Variations, IV [V]. H. C. Bunner. BOHV; CenHV; InMe
Home-Bound. Henry W. Frost. SoP
Home-bound ship stood out to sea, The. The Mystery of Cro-a-tàn. Margaret Junkin Preston. PAH
Home Burial. Robert Frost. AmPP; AnFE; AnNE; AP; APA; BoLiVe; CoAnAm; CoBMV; MAPA; MaPo; StP; TwAmPo
Home comes a lad with the bonnie hair. The Pipes o' Gordon's Men. J. Scott Glasgow. HBV
Home-coming. Léonie Adams. HBMV; MAP; MoAmPo; NeMA; TSW

Homecoming, The. James K. Baxter. AnNZ
Home-coming. Albert Ehrenstein, *tr. fr. German by* Babette Deutsch *and* Avram Yarmolinsky. TrJP
Home-coming. "Isobel Hume." HBMV
Homecoming. Aaron Kramer. NYTB
Homecoming. Karl Shapiro. MiAP
Homecoming. *Unknown.* AnIV
Homecoming. Peter Viereck. CoAP
Homecoming. Theodore Weiss. TwAmPo
Homecoming in Storm. Bernice L. Kenyon. EtS
Homecoming—Massachusetts. John Ciardi. NYBP
Homecoming of Emma Lazarus, The. Galway Kinnell. NaP
Homecoming of the Sheep, The. Francis Ledwidge. EnLit; HBMV; YT
Home, Dearie, Home, *with music. Unknown.* AmSS; SoAmSa
Home Dedication. *Unknown.* FaChP
Home Defined. Robert Frost. *See* Home.
Home did I say, ye homeless? Not to ye. Lyttelton Harbour, VIII. D'Arcy Cresswell. AnNZ
Home Fire, The. Orrick Johns. HBMV
Home for Senior Citizens, the heath, The. After Seeing "Lear." Marie Syrkin. NYTB
Home for the aged opens its windows in May, The. Next Door. Richard Wilbur. NoP
Home from Abroad. Laurie Lee. POTi; ToPo
Home from Guatemala, back at the Waldorf. Arrival at the Waldorf. Wallace Stevens. PP
Home from the observatory. Stella. Charles Henry Crandall. AA
Home from the Wars. Hsüeh T'ao, *tr. fr. Chinese by* Henry H. Hart. OnPM
Home from the wars trudged a poor sailor. The Sailor's Return. *Unknown.* SaSa
Home has been a tree-house all. Dreamside Bestiary. Harold Bond. YAP
Home, home from the horizon far and clear. At Night [*or* To W. M.]. Alice Meynell. BoPe; CH; GoBC; HBV; LiTL; OBVV
Home, home—where's my baby's home? Anne Hutchinson's Exile. Edward Everett Hale. PAH
Home, in War-Time. Sydney Dobell. VA
Home is a temple when the prayer. Home. Sybil Leonard Armes. FaChP
Home Is So Sad. Philip Larkin. NoP
Home is the place where, when you have to go there. Home [*or* Home Defined]. Robert Frost. *Fr.* The Death of the Hired Man. MaRV; TreF; TRV
Home is the sailor, home from the sea. R. L. S. A. E. Housman. NoP
Home Is Where There's [*or* There Is] One to Love Us. Charles Swain. BLPA; FaBoBe; MaRV; NeHB; PoToHe
Home Leave. Barbara Howes. TwCP
Home Means Nevada. Bertha Raffetto. PoRL
Home No More Home to Me. Robert Louis Stevenson. CH
Home of Aphrodite. Euripides, *tr. fr. Greek by* Gilbert Murray. *Fr.* Bacchae. AWP
Home of my heart, I sing of thee! Michigan, My Michigan. Mrs. Henry F. Lyster. PoRL
Home of the Naiads, The. John Armstrong. *Fr.* The Art of Preserving Health, II. OBEC
Home of the Percy's high-born race. Alnwick Castle. Fitz-Greene Halleck. AA
Home of the Soul. Ellen M. Huntington Gates. BLRP
Home on the Range, A. *Unknown.* CoSo (A *and* B *vers., with music*); FaBoBe; MPB; PoRL; TreFS
(Oh, Give Me a Home Where the Buffalo Roam.) FaFP; SiTL
Home Prayer, A. *Unknown. See* Lord of all Pots and Pans and Things.
Home Revisited: Midnight. John Ciardi. NYBP
Home should have a wife, a cat, A. The Curtain Poem. Edwin Brock. NMP
Home Song. Longfellow. GN; OTPC
(Song: "Stay, stay at home, my heart, and rest.") HBV
Home, Sweet Home. John Howard Payne. *Fr.* Clari, the Maid of Milan. AA; BLPA; FaBoBe; FaFP; FaPL; HBV; MaRV; NeHB; OTPC; PaPo; TreF; WBLP
Home, Sweet Home: "We were lying on a prairie on Slaughter's ranch one night." *Unknown.* CoSo
Home, Sweet Home, with Variations, *parody.* H. C. Bunner. BOHV; CenHV; InMe
Home they brought her sailor son. The Recognition. William Sawyer. HBV
Home They Brought Her Warrior Dead. Tennyson. *Fr* The Princess, Pt. V. BEL; EnLi-2; EPN; HBV; MaRV; OTPC; PoVP; TreFS; TrGrPo; ViPP
(Home They Brought.) BoLiVe
(Lyrics from "The Princess.") OuHeWo
(Songs from "The Princess.") OAEP; ViPo
Home, thou return'st from Thames, whose Naiads long. Ode on the Popular Superstitions of the Highlands of Scotland. William Collins. CEP; EnPE; EnRP; OAEP; OBEC
Home Thoughts. Guy Butler. BoSA
Home Thoughts. Denis Glover. AnNZ
Home Thoughts. Claude McKay. GoSl
Home Thoughts. Carl Sandburg. MoLP
Home Thoughts. Odel Shepard. HBMV
Home Thoughts from Abroad. Robert Browning. AnEnPo; AnFE; AWP; BBV; BEL; BoLiVe; BoNaP; BoTP; CBEP; CBV; CoBE; DiPo; EG; EnLi-2 (1949 ed.); EnLit; FaBoBe; FaBoEn; FaBV; EPN; FaFP; FaPON; FiP; GBV (1922 ed.); GTBS; GTBS-W; GTSL; HBV; HBVY; HT; ILP; InPo; JAWP; LiTB; LiTG; MaVP; MBW-2; MCCG; MemP; NeHB; NoP; OAEP; OBEV; OBNC; OBVV; OtMeF; OTPC; PCH, *st.* 1; PoFS; PoIE; PoLF; PoPo; PoRA; PoVP; SeCeV; ShBV-2; TOP; TreF; TrGrPo; VA; ViPo; ViPP; VP; WBP; WHA; YAT; YT
(April in England.) GN
Home-Thoughts from France. Isaac Rosenberg. MMA
Home Thoughts, from the Sea. Robert Browning. AWP; BEL; CaFP; CBEP; EnLi-2 (1949 ed.); FaBoCh; FiP; GTBS; GTSL; ILP; InP; InPo; JAWP; MaVP; MBW-2; OAEP; OBEV; OBVV; OTPC; PoVP; ShBV-2; TOP; ViPo; ViPP; WBP
Home Thoughts in Laventie. Edward Wyndham Tennant. HBMV
Home to me is laughter. Home. June Brown Harris. PoToHe (new ed.)
Home to Sermio. Catullus, *tr. fr. Latin by* Leigh Hunt. OnPM
(Home to Sirmio, *tr. by* Sir Theodore Martin.) OuHeWo
(Return to Sirmio, *tr. by* Horace Gregory.) LiTW
Home Town. W. D. Snodgrass. CBV; ToPo
Home Truths from Abroad. *Unknown.* Par
Home Winner, The. Gene Lindberg. PoOW
Home without a Bible, A. Charles D. Meigs. WBLP
Homecoming. *See* Home Coming.
Homeland, The. Emile Cammaerts, *tr. fr. French by* Witter Bynner. PoFr
Homeland, The. Hugh Reginald Haweis. BLRP
Homeland, The. Sir Cecil Spring-Rice. *See* I Vow to Thee, My Country.
Homeland, The! Oh, the Homeland! The Homeland. Hugh Reginald Haweis. BLRP
Homeless! Despised and Rejected. Katharine Lee Bates. OQP
Homeless man goes, even on life's sunniest slope. Lines. William Hurrell Mallock. ACP (1926 ed.); JKCP (1926 ed.)
Homely Meats. John Davies. *See* Author Loving These Homely Meats, The.
Home-Made Peach Ice Cream. Sandford Lyne. QAH
Homemaker, The. E. Margaret Clarkson. SoP
Homeowners unite. The Firebombing. James Dickey. OPoP
Homer. Albert Ehrenstein, *tr. fr. German by* Babette Deutsch *and* Avrahm Yarmolinsky. TrJP
Homer. Dick Gallup. ANYP
Homer of moly and nepenthe sings. Of Tabacco. Sir John Davies. ReIE
Homer was a vinous Greek who loved the flowing bottle. Chantey of Notorious Bibbers. Henry Morton Robinson. InMe
Homeric Hymns, *sels. Unknown, tr. fr. Greek.*
Homeric Hymn to Neptune, *tr. by* George Chapman. EtS
Hymn to Aphrodite. LiTW, *abr., tr. by* Jack Lindsay
Hymn to Athena, *tr. by* Shelley. AWP
Hymn to Castor and Pollux, *tr. by* Shelley. AWP
Hymn to Earth the Mother of All, *tr. by* Shelley. AWP; JAWP; WBP

Hymn to Mercury, *abr., tr. by* Shelley. LiTW
(Hymn to Selene, *tr. by* Shelley.) AWP
Hymn to the Moon, *tr. by* Shelley. LiTW
To Mars, *tr. by* George Chapman. LoBV
Homeric Unity. Andrew Lang. HBV
Home's not merely four square walls. Home Is Where There Is One to Love Us. Charles Swain. BLPA; FaBoBe; MaRV; NeHB; PoToHe
Homes of England, The. Felicia Dorothea Hemans. PaPo
("Stately homes of England, The," *st.* 1.) WhC
Homes of the Cliff Dwellers. Stanley Wood. PoOW
Homesick. Dorothy Frances McCrae. BoAu
Homesick? and yet your country walks. To Henry Vaughan. A. J. M. Smith. OBCV
Homesick Blues. Langston Hughes. CDC; MAP; MoAmPo; NeMA; PoPl; WaKn
Home-Sickness. Justinus Kerner, *tr. fr. German by* James Clarence Mangan. AWP; JAWP; WBP
Home-Sickness. Hedwig Lachmann, *tr. fr. German by* Jethro Bithell. TrJP
Homestead—Winter Morning. Mary Ballard Duryee. GoYe
Homeward. Li Pin, *tr. fr. Chinese by* Herbert A. Giles. OuHeWo
Homeward Bound, The. Bill Adams. EtS
Homeward Bound. William Allingham. FaBoBe; HBV; HBVY
Homeward Bound. James Brodey. ANYP
Homeward Bound, *sels.* Heine, *tr. fr. German.*
And When I Lamented, *tr. by* Emma Lazarus. TrJP
Dearest Friend, Thou Art in Love, *tr. by* Emma Lazarus. TrJP
Du bist wie eine Blume, *tr. by* Kate Kroeker. AWP; JAWP; WBP; OuHeWo, *tr. by* Sir Theodore Martin
(Thou Seemest like a Flower, *tr. by* Emma Lazarus.) TrJP
(Translated Way, The, *tr. by* Franklin P. Adams.) BOHV
I, a Most Wretched Atlas, *tr. by* Emma Lazarus. TrJP
Mortal, Sneer Not at the Devil, *tr. by* Emma Lazarus. TrJP
Thou Hast Diamonds, *tr. by* Emma Lazarus. TrJP
Homeward Bound. D. H. Rogers. AnNZ; BoAu; EtS
Homeward Bound. Robert Southey. EtS
Homeward Bound. L. Frank Tooker. EtS
Homeward Bound, 3 *vers., with music.* *Unknown.* ShS
Homeward Bound ("To Pensacola town we'll bid adieu"), *sl. diff., with music.* AmSS
Homeward Bound. George Edward Woodberry. Wild Eden, XXV. AA
Homeward bound and ready for sea. Canso Strait. *Unknown.* ShS
Homeward Journey, The. L. Aaronson. FaBoTw; TrJP
Homing. Arna Bontemps. CDC
Homing, The. John Jerome Rooney. AA
Homing Heart, The. Daniel Henderson. HBMV
Homing Pigeons. Ted Walker. NYBP
Homing Swallows. Claude McKay. TSW
Homo Faber: the Shell Game. Marge Piercy. ThO
Homo Factus Est. Digby Mackworth Dolben. *See* Come to Me, Beloved.
Homoeopathic Soup. *Unknown.* BOHV
Homunculus et la Belle Etoile. Wallace Stevens. MAP; MoAB; MoAmPo
Honest and a perfect man, An. Destiny. John Fletcher. *Fr.* Upon an Honest Man's Fortune. MaRV
Honest Autolycus, An. *Unknown.* *See* Fine Knacks for Ladies.
Honest Doubt. Robert Weston. MaRV
Honest Fame. Pope. *Fr.* The Temple of Fame. OBEC
Honest John and William Relief. John A. Stone. SGR
Homest Lover/ whosoever. The Art of Love. Sir John Suckling. LO
Honest Man, An. Pope. *Br. sel. fr.* An Essay on Man, Epistle IV. TreF
Honest man here lies at rest, An. Epitaph on a Friend. Burns. MaRV
Honest Man's Fortune, The. John Fletcher. *See* Upon an Honest Man's Fortune.
Honest Miner, An, *with music.* John A. Stone. SGR
Honest Mr. Robin. Eleanor Hammond. GFA
Honest regular work Dick Daring gave up. A Shining Night; or, Dick Daring, the Poacher. *Unknown.* CoMu
Honest Stradivari made me. The Violin's Complaint. William Roscoe Thayer. AA
Honest Whore, The, *sels.* Thomas Dekker.
"Like an ill husband, though I knew the same," *fr.* Pt. II. LO
"Patience, my lord! why, 'tis the soul of peace," *fr.* Pt. I. ViBoPo
Honest William, an easy and good-natured fellow. The Brewer's Coachman. William Taylor. WaPE
Honest, Wouldn't You? *Unknown.* WBLP
Honesty. Horatius Bonar. *See* Be True.
Honesty. Sir Thomas Wyatt. OBSC
(Of Dissembling Words.) SiCE
(Throughout the World.) CBEP; ELU
("Troughout the world, if it were sought.") FCP
Honesty at a Fire. J. C. Squire. FiBHP
Honesty, little slut, must you insist. To the Contemporary Muse. Edgar Bowers. ELU
Honey. Melville Cane. NYTB
Honey. Ruth Miller. BoSA
Honey/ When de man. Sister Lou. Sterling A. Brown. AmNP; GoSl; PoNe
Honey & Water. Medieval Christ Speaks on a Spanish Sculpture of Himself. Rochelle Owens. CoPo
Honey Bear. Elizabeth Lang. BoTP
Honeybee, The. Helen Bevington. NYTB
Honey Bee. C. Lindsay McCoy. GFA
Honey Bee, The. Don Marquis. PoPl; PoPo; SiTL; WhC
Honey-Bee. Lucy Fitch Perkins. SUS
Honey bee is sad and cross, The. The Honey Bee. Don Marquis. PoPl; PoPo; SiTL; WhC
"Honey Bee," its habitat, The. Honey Bee. C. Lindsay McCoy. GFA
Honey Dew Falls from the Tree. John Clare. AtBAP; PoIE
Honey Dripping from the Comb. James Whitcomb Riley. AA
Honey-Farm, The, *abr.* Vergil, *tr. fr. Latin by* Dryden. *Fr.* Georgics, IV. WoL
Honey-flowers to the honey-comb. Chimes. Dante Gabriel Rossetti. OBNC
Honey for the Heart. Louis J. Sanker. JKCP (1955 ed.)
Honey from silkworms who can gather. Lines to a Critic. Shelley. CBEP; EPN; MERP
Honey from the Lion. Leah Bodine Drake. NePoAm
Honey-hued beauty, you are. Black Lady in an Afro Hairdo Cheers for Cassius. R. Ernest Holmes. WSL
Honey in the horn! I brought my horse from the water. The Valley Harvest. Harold Lenoir Davis. NP
Honey in the lion's mouth. The Holy Eucharist. Pedro Calderón de la Barca. CAW
Honey-Mead. *Unknown,* *tr. fr. Anglo-Saxon by* Charles W. Kennedy. *Fr.* Riddles. AnOE
Honey mist on a day of frost in a dark oak wood, A. The Cooleen. Douglas Hyde. OBVV
Honey! My mouth is full of it. Soundings. Kathleen Fraser. YAP
Honey, peppe , leaf-green limes. Jamaica Market. Agnes Maxwell-Hall. PoNe; TTY
Honey, see dat jay-bird dah. Settin' on de Fence. *Unknown.* WBLP
Honey, Take a Whiff on Me. *Unknown.* ABF, *with music*; LiTM; OxBoLi; SiTL
Honey-tongued [*or* tong'd] Shakespeare. when I saw thine issue. Ad Gulielmum Shakespeare. John Weever. ReIE; SiCE; TuPP
Honey, trus' der Lawd a bit, an' doan fohgit to smile. Trus' an' Smile. B. Y. Williams. BLRP
Honeybee. *See* Honey Bee.
Honeymoon. Samuel L. Albert. GoYe
Honey-Moon, The. Walter Savage Landor. BOHV
Honeymoon, The. Henry Luttrell. *Fr.* Advice to Julia. OBRV
Honey-moon is very strange, The. The Honey-Moon. Walter Savage Landor. BOHV
Honeymooners, The. Yu Ch'ien, *tr. fr. Chinese by* David Rafael Wang. HW
Honeysuckle, The. Dante Gabriel Rossetti. CBEP; PoVP; SyP
Honolulu and Back. John Logan. AmPC
Honour. Ada Cambridge. BoAu
Honor and Desert. Coventry Patmore. The Angel in the House, II, iv, 1. FaPL; HBV
Honor [*or* Honour] and shame from no condition rise. Worth Makes the Man [*or* Man]. Pope. *Fr.* An Essay on Man, Epistle IV. BoLiVe; MaRV; PoFr; TrGrPo

Honor and truth and manhood. Things That Endure. Ted Olson. WBLP
"Honor be to Mudjekeewis!" The Four Winds. Longfellow. *Fr.* The Song of Hiawatha. AnNE
Honour Corruption Villainy Holiness. E. E. Cummings. NoP
Honour Dishonoured. Wilfrid Scawen Blunt. *See* Prison Sonnet.
Honor Done to Poets of Old and Modern Poets, The. Thomas Heywood. CLwM
Honor in chief, our oath is to uphold. Chorus Primus. Fulke Greville. *Fr.* Mustapha. OBS
Honor invoked, no man may save his hide. As Always. James Gallagher. JKCP (1955 ed.)
Honor is flashed off exploit, so we say. In Honor of St. Alphonsus Rodriguez [*or* St. Alphonsus Rodriguez]. Gerard Manley Hopkins. ForPo; PoIE
Honour is so sublime perfection. To the Countesse of Bedford [*or* Verse Letter to the Countess of Bedford]. John Donne. MaMe; MBW-1; MeLP
Honor, Joy ("Honoure, joy, healthe, and pleasaunce") Charles d'Orleans. NoP
Honour, Riches, Marriage Blessing. Shakespeare. *Fr.* The Tempest, IV, i. HW
"Honor," said the man. Definitions. Joseph Joel Keith. PoToHe (new ed.)
Honour the leaves, and the leaves of life. The Holy Well. *Unknown.* BaBo
Honour with Age. Walter Kennedy. OxBS
Honora, should that cruel time arrive. To Honora Sneyd, April 1773. Anna Seward. Sonn
Honourable Entertainment Given to the Queen's Majesty in Progress at Elvetham, 1591, *sels.* Nicholas Breton, *and others.*
  Phillida and Corydon [*or* Coridon]. Nicholas Breton. HBV; OBEV; ReEn; TuPP; UnTE; ViBoPo
    (In the Merry Month of May.) EG; MeWo; PoSa
    (Pastoral, A.) TrGrPo
    (Phyllida and Corydon.) ElL; OAEP; OBSC; ReIE; SeCePo
    (Ploughman's Song, The.) ALV; LiTL; OBSC
    (Plowman's Song, The.) FaBoEn; SiCE
  With Fragrant Flowers We Strew the Way. Thomas Watson. ElL
    (Ditty of the Six Virgins, The.) OBSC; SiCE
Hon. Mr. Sucklethumbkin's Story. "Thomas Ingoldsby." *Fr.* Ingoldsby Legends. OBRV
Honorable the City Clerk, The: Dear Sir. Letter to the City Clerk. Frederick A. Wright. FaFP
"Honored [*or* Honoured] I lived erewhile with honored men." Prison Sonnet [*or* Honour Dishonoured]. Wilfrid Scawen Blunt. CAW; OBMV
Honoria's Surrender. Coventry Patmore. *Fr.* The Angel in the House, I, xii. VA
Honors. Jean Ingelow. OQP
Honours that the people give always, The. The Thespians at Thermopylae. Norman Cameron. ChMP; GTBS-P
Hooded anemones darken the Sunday morning February market. The Anemones of Collioure. John Unterecker. ThO
Hooded figure followed me, A. A Masque of Life and Death. Witter Bynner. AnAmPo
Hoof-beat on the early air. Indictment. Margaret Tod Ritter. AnAmPo
Hoof Dusk. Carl Sandburg. Po
Hook for Leviathan, A. Norman Cameron. ChMP
Hooker's Across. George Henry Boker. PAH
Hoopoe. George Darley. *Fr.* Nepenthe. OBNC
  ("Solitary wayfarer!") OBRV
Hoopskirt, The. John Gould Fletcher. LaNeLa
Hoosen Johnny. *Unknown.* AS, *with music*; FaPON
Hop, a skip, and off you go, A! Dancing. Eleanor Farjeon. StVeCh (1955 ed.)
Hop, hop, hop, nimble as a top. My Little Pony. *Unknown.* SAS
Hop-o-My-Thumb. *Unknown.* *Fr.* Ballads on Napoleon. CoBE
Hop-poles stand in cones, The. The Midnight Skaters. Edmund Blunden. ExPo; FaBoTw; GoJo; GTBS-D; GTBS-P; MoBrPo; POTE; WePo
Hop Up, My Ladies, *with music.* *Unknown.* OuSiCo
Hope. William Lisle Bowles. EnRP
Hope. Gamaliel Bradford. HBMV
Hope, A. Anne Brontë. MaRV
Hope. Amy Carmichael. FaChP; TRV
Hope. Abraham Cowley. *See* Against Hope.
Hope, *sel.* William Cowper.
  "Though clasp'd and cradled in his nurse's arms." PoEL-3
Hope. Sir Richard Fanshawe. *Fr.* Il Pastor Fido. CBEP; OBS
Hope. Goldsmith. *Fr.* The Captivity; an Oratorio, II. OBEC; TreFT
  "Hope, like a gleaming taper's light," *sel.* MaRV
Hope. George Herbert. FosPo; MaMe; PoEL-2
Hope. William Dean Howells. AA
Hope. Randall Jarrell. MoAB; MoAmPo (1950 ed.)
Hope. Georgia Douglas Johnson. CDC
Hope. Howard McCord. YaP
Hope. Anna Blake Mezquida. MaRV; TRV
Hope ("Hope springs eternal in the human breast"). Pope. *Fr.* An Essay on Man, Epistle I. MaRV, 2 *ll.*; TreF, 4 *ll.*
  (Pleasure of Hope, The, 4 *ll.*) ACP
Hope. William Shenstone. *Fr.* A Pastoral Ballad. OBEC
  (Shepherd's Home, The.) GN
  "My banks they are furnish'd with bees," *sel.* BoNaP
Hope. Phillips Stewart. CaP
Hope. Sarah Wingate Taylor. JKCP (1955 ed.)
Hope. Theognis, *tr. fr. Greek by* John Hookham Frere. AWP; JAWP; WBP
Hope ("He died!"). *Unknown.* ChIP; OQP; SoP
Hope ("Life has conquered"). *Unknown, tr. fr. Irish by* Frank O'Connor. KiLC
Hope ("Soft as the voice"). *Unknown.* MaRV
Hope. Oscar Wilde. *Fr.* The Ballad of Reading Gaol. MaRV
Hope and Despair. Lascelles Abercrombie. HBV; OBMV
Hope and Faith. Isaac Leibush Peretz, *tr. fr. Yiddish by* Henry Goodman. TrJP
Hope and Fear. Swinburne. EPN; FaBoBe; HBV; PoVP; VA
Hope, art thou true, or dost thou flatter me? Astrophel and Stella, LXVII. Sir Philip Sidney. FCP; ReEn; SiPS
Hope Evermore and Believe. Arthur Hugh Clough. BEL; EPN; PoVP; WGRP
  "Go from the east to the west," *sel.* MaRV
Hope for Miracles. Wolfram von Eschenbach, *tr. fr. German by* Jethro Bithell. LiTW
Hope humble then; with trembling pinions soar. Pope. *Fr.* An Essay on Man, Epistle I. TrGrPo
Hope I Dreamed of, The. Christina Rossetti. *See* Mirage.
Hope in Death. Samuel Crossman. SoP
Hope in Him While Thou Livest. Kabir, *tr. fr. Hindi.* MaRV
Hope is a crushed stalk. Dark Testament. Pauli Murray. AmNP
Hope is a subtle glutton. Emily Dickinson. DiPo
Hope Is a Tattered Flag. Carl Sandburg. *Fr.* The People, Yes. NAMP
Hope is the thing with feathers. Emily Dickinson. AmP; AmPP (4th ed.); CBEP; DiPo; GBV (1952 ed.); GTBS-D; MoAB; MoAmPo (1950 ed.); MoShBr; NeMA; OxBA; PG
Hope, is this thy hand. Fickle Hope. Harrison Smith Morris. AA
Hope, like a gleaming taper's light. Hope. Goldsmith. *Fr.* The Captivity; an Oratorio. MaRV; OBEC; TreFT
Hope, like the hyena [*or* hyaena], coming to be old. Henry Constable. *Fr.* Diana. EnLoPo; OBSC; SiCE; Sonn
Hope! Not distant is the Springtime. Hope and Faith. Isaac Leibush Peretz. TrJP
Hope of Our Hearts. Sir Edward Denny. BePJ; SoP; STF
Hope of the Coming of the Lord, The. Major Whittle. SoP
Hope of the World, The. Sir William Watson. WGRP
Hope of Truth grows stronger, day by day, The. Sub Pondere Crescit. James Russell Lowell. MaRV
Hope Overtaken. Dante Gabriel Rossetti. The House of Life, XLII. MaVP; PoVP; ViPo; VP
Hope Springing Up. John Wesley. BePJ
Hope Springs Eternal ("Heav'n from all creatures hides the book of fate"). Pope. *Fr.* An Essay on Man, Epistle I. OBEC
  ("Heav'n from all creatures hides the book of fate.") ViBoPo
Hope springs eternal in the human breast. Hope [*or* The Pleasure of Hope]. Pope. *Fr.* An Essay on Man, Epistle I. ACP; MaRV; TreF
Hope was faced alone. Don A. Mizell. WSL
Hope we not in this life only. Not in Vain. *Unknown.* BLRP
Hope, whose weak being ruined is. Against Hope [*or* Hope *or*

On Hope]. Abraham Cowley. *Fr.* The Mistress. GTBS-W; LiTB; LiTG; LoBV; MaMe; MeLP; MePo; OBS; SCEP-1; SeCV-1
Hopeless Desire Soon Withers and Dies. "A. W." OBSC; ReIE
Hopeless Love. *Unknown, tr. fr. Irish by* Sir Samuel Ferguson. IrPN
Hopes and Memories. Giovanni Pascoli, *tr. fr. Italian by* Glauco Cambon. OnPM
Hope's Forecast. Ethel Romig Fuller. RePo
Hopes grimly banished from the heart. Exiles. William Hamilton Hayne. AA
Hope's Song. Francis Carlin. HBMV
Hope's Song. *Unknown.* SoP
Hopi Ghosts. William Haskell Simpson. *Fr.* In Arizona. NP
Hoping all the time. *Unknown. Fr.* Kokin Shu. AWP
Hopping Frog. Christina Rossetti. UTS
Hoppity. A. A. Milne. FaBV; TiPo
Hoppity Toads. Aileen Fisher. RePo
Hora Christi. Alice Brown. HBV; MaRV; TrPWD; WGRP
Horace. John Osborne Sargent. AA
Horace, Book V, Ode III. Charles Larcom Graves. CenHV
Horace, Epistle VII, Book I, Imitated and Addressed to the Earl of Oxford. Swift. CEP
Horace, for whom I entertain. Two Garden Scenes. Charles Burgess. NePoAm-2
Horace Greeley. Edmund Clarence Stedman. DD
Horace Paraphrased. Isaac Watts. LoBV; UnPo (3d ed.)
Horace the Wise. Morrie Ryskind. HBMV
Horace to Pyrrha. Horace. *See* To Pyrrha.
Horae Canonicae, *sels.* W. H. Auden.
Prime. CMoP; MaPo (1969 ed.); PoDB
Sext. PoDB
Horas Tempestatis Quoque Enumero; the Sundial. John Hollander. NePoEA
Horat. Ode 29. Book 3. Paraphras'd in Pindarique Verse. Horace. *See* To Maecenas.
Horatian Epode to the Duchess of Malfi. Allen Tate. FaBoMo
Horatian Ode upon Cromwel[l]'s Return from Ireland, An. Andrew Marvell. AnAnS-1; BEL; BWP; CABL; EP; FosPo; GTBS; GTBS-D; GTBS-P; GTBS-W; GTSE; GTSL; HBV; LoBV; MaMe; MaPo; MePo; NoP; OBEV; OBS; PAn; PoAn; PoEL-2; SCEP-2; SeCP; SeCV-1; SeEP; TOP; UnPo (1st ed.)
Sels.
Execution of King Charles, The. AnEnPo; PoRA
King Charles upon the Scaffold, *sl. shorter.* ChTr
"So restless Cromwell could not cease." ViBoPo
Horatian Variation. Leonard Bacon. NYBP
Horatians, The. W. H. Auden. NYBP
Horatio, *sels.* Hyam Plutzik. FiMAP
Faustus, III.
Ostler, The, II.
Horatio, of ideal courage vain. Feigned Courage. Charles *and* Mary Lamb. GN
Horatius [at the Bridge]. Macaulay. *Fr.* Lays of Ancient Rome. BBV, *abr.*; BeLS; FaBoCh, *abr.*; FaFP; FOL, *abr.*; GSP, *abr.*; HBV; HBVY; LoGBV, *abr.*; MCCG; OHFP, *abr.*; PoLF; ShBV-1; TIHL, *sl. abr.*; TreF
(How Horatius Kept the Bridge.) PTK
Sels.
Fight at the Bridge, The. MaC; OtMeF
"Then out spake brave Horatius." PoFr, 5 *sts.*
Horch, horch, die Bell am Backdoor ringt! Morning Song. Kurt M. Stein. FiBHP
Horestes, *sel.* John Pickering.
"Farewell, adieu, that courtly life." ReEn; TuPP
(Haltersick's Song.) OBSC
(Song: "Farewell, adieu that court like life!") ElL
Horizon Thong. George Abbe. GoYe
Horizons. Rebecca McCann. PoMa
Horizons. Clinton Scollard. OQP
Horizons cannot nourish me. Derricks and Rainbows. Joseph Auslander. PoMa
Horizon's hatred smites Magellan. Magellan. Allen Curnow. AnNZ
Horizontal World. Thomas Saunders. CaP
Horn, The. Léonie Adams. AnAmPo; InPo; MAP; MoAB; MoAmPo
Horn. James Hayford. NePoAm-2
Horn, The. James Reaney. OBCV; PeCV
Horn, A. *Unknown, tr. fr. Anglo-Saxon. Fr.* Riddles. AnOE, *tr. by* Charles W. Kennedy; OuHeWo, *tr. by* Stith Thompson
Horned Owl, The. "Barry Cornwall." OTPC
Horner, aroused, looks up again. Variations on a Theme. Joseph G. E. Hopkins. JKCP (1955 ed.)
Hornets. C. Lindsay McCoy. GFA
Hornets build in plaster-dropping rooms, The. Abandoned. Madison Cawein. YT
Hornpipe. Edith Sitwell. *Fr.* Façade. GTBS-P; MoVE; SeCePo
Horns of Elfland, The. Tennyson. *See* Bugle Song.
Horns to Bulls Wise Nature Lends. Thomas Stanley, *after* Anacreon. *See* Beauty.
Horny-goloch is an awesome beast, The. *Unknown.* FaBoCh
Horologe, The. Clark Ashton Smith. FiSC
Horologium, *sel. Unknown. tr. fr. Greek by* G. R. Woodward.
Mother of God, The. ISi
Horoscope. J. V. Cunningham. NePoAm; PoIE
Horror. Peter Baum, *tr. fr. German by* Jethro Bithell. AWP
Horror Movie. Howard Moss. NePoEA-2; SiTL
Horrors of Civil War, The. Horace, *tr. fr. Latin by* Stephen Edward De Vere. WoL
Hors d'Oeuvre. Deems Taylor, *tr. fr. French.* UnTE
Horse, The. Job, XXXIX, Bible, *O.T.* FaPON (19-21, 24-25); GoTP (19-25); StaSt (21-25); TrGrPo (19-25)
("Hast thou given the horse his might?" XXXIX: 19-XL: 2.) InP
(Hast Thou Given the Horse Strength? XXXIX: 19-25.) ChTr
(War Horse, The, XXXIX: 19-25.) ShBV-2
Horse. Jim Harrison. WIRo
Horse, The. Philip Levine. CoAP
Horse. Elizabeth Madox Roberts. RePo; TiPo (1959 ed.); UTS
Horse, The. Naomi Royde-Smith. FiBHP; LiTM; SiTL
("I know two things about the horse.") CenHV
Horse, A. Shakespeare. *Fr.* Venus and Adonis. ExPo
Horse, The. Shakespeare. King Henry V, *fr.* III, vii. GoTP
Horse, The. William Carlos Williams. OA
Horse and a flea and three blind mice, A. *Unknown.* FaFP; SiTL
Horse and hattock. The Witch's Broomstick Spell. *Unknown.* ChTr
Horse and mule live 30 years, The. Liquor & Longevity. *Unknown.* LiTG; SiTL; WhC
Horse & Rider. Wey Robinson. SD; WhC
Horse breaks glass, A. Horses. Myra Von Riedemann. OBCV
Horse can't pull while kicking, A. Horse Sense. *Unknown.* BLPA; NeHB; TreFT; WBLP
Horse-Chestnut Time. Kaye Starbird. PDV
Horse Chestnut Tree, The. Richard Eberhart. AtBAP; CaFP; CMoP; CrMA; FiMAP; LiTM (1970 ed.); MoAB; MoAmPo (1962 ed.); NePA; NePoAm; Po; PoDB; PoPl; PoPo; ToPo
Horse in a Field. Walter de la Mare. HBMV
(To K. M.) BoC
Horse leans on a wooden fence, A. The Ache. Lewis Mac Adams. YAP
Horse moves, The. The Horse. William Carlos Williams. OA
Horse Named Bill, The, *with music. Unknown.* AS
Horse of poetry nibbles, The. The Invitation. Donagh MacDonagh. OnYI
Horse Race. Richard Brautigan. FRC
Horse Sense. *Unknown.* BLPA; NeHB; TreFT; WBLP
Horse Show, The. William Carlos Williams. CMoP
Horse Thief, The. William Rose Benét. BBV (1951 ed.); HBMV; MAP; MoAmPo; OnMSP; TSW
Horse would tire, A. Elizabeth J. Coatsworth. TiPo
Horse Wrangler, The, *with music.* D. J. O'Malley. CoSo
(Tenderfoot, The,) AS
Horseman, The. Walter de la Mare. GoJo; SoPo; SUS; TiPo (1959 ed.)
Horseman riding, A. Woodcut. R. N. D. Wilson. OxBI
Horsemen, The. Gene Baro. NePoEA-2
Horsepower crops Araby for pasture. Mordent for a Melody. Margaret Avison. ACV
Horses. Richard Armour. PoPl; WhC
Horses, The. Ted Hughes. BoPe; POTi; WIRo
Horses, The ("Barely a twelvemonth after"). Edwin Muir.

Horses (continued)
ACV; BoPe; CMoP; HaMV; MoBrPo (1962 ed.); NMP; PoIE; PoSa
Horses ("Those lumbering horses in the steady plough"). Edwin Muir. CMoP; FaBoCh; LoGBV; MoVE; SeCePo
Horses. Myra von Riedemann. OBCV
Horses. Dorothy Wellesley. ChMP; OBMV; ShBV-4
Horses, The. Keith Wilson. ThO
Horses and Men in the Rain. Carl Sandburg. PoLF
Horses Chawin' Hay. Hamlin Garland. StVeCh
Horses of Marini, The. Tania van Zyl. PeSA
Horses of summer. Day Dream. Nancy Cardozo. MeWo
Horses of the Sea, The. Christina Rossetti. *Fr.* Sing-Song. FaPON; GFA; GoJo; PCD; PoRh; SUS; UTS
Horses on the Camargue. Roy Campbell. AtBAP; BoC; GTBS-P; OA; PeSA; POTE; SeCePo; ShBV-3
Horses, resigned to their black plague of flies. Drought. Geoffrey Johnson. HaMV
Horses, the pigs, The. Familiar Friends. James S. Tippett. BoChli; BoTP; SoPo; SUS; UTS
Horses were ready, the rails were down, The. Where the Pelican Builds. Mary Hannay Foott. PoAu-1
Horseshoe, The. Edna St. Vincent Millay. *See* Wonder Where This Horseshoe Went.
Horseshoes they hammer which turn on a swivel. Gypsies. Robert Browning. *Fr.* The Flight of the Duchess. PCH
Hos Ego Versiculos. Francis Quarles. *Fr.* Argalus and Parthenia. OBS; SeEP *See also* Man's Mortality, *sl. diff. vers. at. to* Simon Wastell, *fr.* Microbiblion.
(Like as the Damask Rose.) LoBV
Hosanna. Thomas Traherne. PoEL-2; SCEP-1; SeCV-2
Hosanna for the Lord's Day, An. Isaac Watts. SoP
Hosea Biglow's Lament. James Russell Lowell. *See* Mr. Hosea Biglow to the Editor of the Atlantic Monthly.
Hospice of the Word. Brother Antoninus. ToPo
Hospital. Wilfred Funk. PoToHe
Hospital. G. C. Millard. PeSA
Hospital, A. Alfred Noyes. PoPl
Hospital Barge at Cérisy. Wilfred Owen. CBEP
Hospital for Defectives. Thomas Blackburn. GTBS-P
Hospital for sick and needy Jews, A. The New Jewish Hospital at Hamburg. Heine. TrJP
Hospital Observation. Julian Symons. WaP
Hospital Prison Ship, The. Philip Freneau. *Fr.* The British Prison Ship. AmPP (5th ed.)
Hospital Waiting-Room, The. W. H. Davies. BrPo; CBEP
Hospital Ward (of this Generation). George Rostrevor Hamilton. POTE
Hospital Window, The. James Dickey. CoPo
Hospitality. John Banister Tabb. PPL
Hospitality in Ancient Ireland. *Unknown, tr. fr. Middle Irish by* Kuno Meyer. OnYI
Host and Guest. Henry W. Clark. OQP
Host is riding from Knocknarea, The. The Hosting of the Sidhe. W. B. Yeats. PoeP
Host of the Air, The. W. B. Yeats. BrPo; CH; LoEn; OnYI; PoVP; SeCeV; ViPo (1962 ed.)
(Folk of the Air, The.) VA
Hostess' Daughter, The. Ludwig Uhland, *tr. fr. German by* Margarete Münsterberg. AWP; JAWP; WBP
(From the German of Uhland, *tr. by* James Weldon Johnson.) CDC
Hostia. Irving Layton. PV
Hosting of the Sidhe, The. W.B. Yeats. PoeP
Hosts, The. George M. Brady. NeIP
Hosts of Faery, The. *Unknown, tr. fr. Middle Irish by* Kuno Meyer. OnYI
Hot Cake. Shu Hsi, *tr. fr. Chinese by* Arthur Waley. AtBAP; BoW; FIW; MoBrPo (1942 ed.)
Hot cross buns, hot cross buns;/ One a penny poker. *Unknown.* OxNR
Hot-cross buns! Hot-cross buns!/ One a penny, two a penny. Mother Goose. BoTP; GaP; OTPC; OxNR; PCH; SoPo
Hot Flame of My Grief, The. Moses ibn Ezra, *tr. fr. Hebrew by* Solomon Solis-Cohen. TrJP
Hot Ir'n! S. Omar Barker. PoOW
Hot mice feeding in red, The. Paul Klee. John Haines. ThO
Hot midsummer night on Water Street, A. Hot Night on Water Street. Louis Simpson. TDP; TwCP
Hot muffins and crumpets too. Come Buy My Nice Muffins. *Unknown.* PCH
"Hot night makes us keep our bedroom windows open, The." Robert Lowell. MaPo (1969 ed.)
Hot Night on Water Street. Louis Simpson. TDP; TwCP
Hot September sun shone down on the wide and peaceful bay, The. The Wide Open Spaces. Oscar H. Lear. InMe
Hot Stuff. Edward Botwood. PAH
Hot sun [*or* sunne], cool fire, tempered with sweet air. Bethsabe's Song [*or* Bethsabe Bathing]. George Peele. *Fr.* David and Bethsabe. AtBAP; ATP; CBEP; ElL; EnRePo; ExPo; InPo; LO; LoBV; NoP; OBSC; OxBoLi; PoEL-2; SeCeV; SiCE; TrGrPo; TuPP
Hot through Troy's ruin Menelaus broke. Menelaus and Helen. Rupert Brooke. SeCePo
Hot Time in the Old Town, A. Joe Hayden. YaD
Hot Weather. Dorothy Aldis. GFA
Hot Weather in the Plains—India. E. H. Tipple. HBV
Hot-Weather Song, A. Don Marquis. HBMV; RePo; StVeCh; WhC; YaD
Hotel, The. Harriet Monroe. AnAmPo; NP
Hotel Continental. William Jay Smith. WaP
Hotel de l'Univers et Portugal. James Merrill. MoAB; NePoAm; NePoEA-2
Hotel Lobby. Mildred Weston. WhC
Hotel Paradiso e Commerciale. John Malcolm Brinnin. NYBP; PoCh; TwCP
Hotel Transylvanie. Frank O'Hara. NeAP
Hottentot, The. Thomas Pringle. OBRV
Hottentot Tot, The. Newman Levy. RIS
(Midsummer Fantasy.) PoSC
Hould lingell hould the coblers silken twyne. *Unknown.* SeCSL
Hound, The. Babette Deutsch. HBMV
Hound, The. Sidney Lanier. *Fr.* The Jacquerie. AA; PFY; PoMS
(Song for "The Jacquerie.") MAP; MoAmPo (1942 ed.)
Hound, A. Simonides, *tr. fr. Greek by* F. L. Lucas. WoL
Hound of Heaven, The. Francis Thompson. ACP; AnFE; ATP; BEL; BoLiVe; BrPo; CAW; CoBE; EnL; EnLi-2; EnLit; EPN; FaBV; FaFP; FaPL; GoBC; GoTL; GTBS-W; GTSL; HBV; ILP; JKCP; LiTB; LiTM; LoBV; MaRV; MasP; MCCG; MoAB; MoBrPo; OAEP; OBMV; OtMeF; OxBoCh; PoE; PoEL-5; PoIE; PoLi, *abr.*; PoVP; SeCePo; SeCeV; SoP; TIHL; TOP; TreF, *br. sel.*; TrGrPo; TRV; UnPo (1st ed.); ViBoPo; ViPP; WGRP; WHA
Sels.
"Now of that long pursuit." FaChP
Our God Finds Us. BoC
Hound Voice. W. B. Yeats. POTE; SyP
Hound was cuffed, the hound was kicked, The. The Hound [*or* Song for "The Jacquerie"]. Sidney Lanier. AA; MAP; MoAmPo (1942 ed.); PFY; PoMS
Hound yellow, light of tread—the cunning foe. An Englyn on a Yellow Greyhound. William Barnes. OA
Hounded Lovers, The. William Carlos Williams. MoLP; NYBP; TrGrPo
Hounded slave that flags in the race, The. The Wounded Person. Walt Whitman. *Fr.* Song of Myself. PoNe
Hounds, The. Patric Dickinson. ChMP
Hounds, The. John Freeman. OBMV
Hounds are all out, and the morning does peep, The. The Huntsman's Rouse. Henry Carey. SeCePo
Hounds of Spring, The. Swinburne. *See* When the Hounds of Spring.
Hounds of the Soul, The. Louis Ginsberg. TrJP
Hounds, The. The great man's dream. The stone. The Hounds. Patric Dickinson. ChMP
Hour after hour the cards were fairly shuffled. Whist. Eugene Fitch Ware. PoLF
Hour by Hour. "George Klingle." OQP
Hour ere sudden sunset fired the west, An. Beaumont and Fletcher. Swinburne. *Fr.* Sonnets on English Dramatic Poets (1590-1650). PoVP
Hour-Glass, The. Ben Jonson. CBEP; EnLoPo; EnRePo; GTBS-W; LiTB; LiTG; PIA; SeCP; SiTL
Hour Glass, The. Edward Quillinan. OBRV
Hour-glass whispers to the lion's paw [*or* roar], The. Our Bias. W. H. Auden. AtBAP; CMoP; NoP
Hour is come, with pleasure crowned, The. Epithalamium. Johannes Secundus. HW
Hour Is Late, The. Ida Norton Munson. ChIP
Hour Is Late, The. Winfield Townley Scott. FiMAP

"Hour is late, The," the shepherds said. The Shepherd Left Behind. Mildred Plew Meigs. ChBR
Hour is starry, and the airs that stray, The. Lines Written at Geneva; July 16, 1824. Thomas Lovell Beddoes. ERoP-2
Hour of Death, The. Felicia Dorothea Hemans. HBV; LoBV; OBNC
Hour of Death, The. *Unknown. Fr.* The Seafarer. PoLi
Hour of Good, a day of Ill, An. Three Proverbs. James Clarence Mangan, *after the Ottoman.* IrPN
Hour of Magic, The. W. H. Davies. MoBrPo; NeMA
Hour of Peaceful Rest, The. William Bingham Tappan. AA; HBV
Hour of Prayer, The. Georgia B. Adams. STF
Hour of Prayer, The. Charlotte Elliott. SoP; STF
Hour of sight, The. Still Life. Kathleen Raine. NeBP
Hour suggested offerings, The. Ceremony. Joanne De Longchamps. NYTB
Hour told by the owl and the moon, The. Lament for Better or Worse. Gene Baro. FiSC; NePoEA-2
Hour was on us, The; where the man? Lincoln. John Vance Cheney. DD; OHIP; PEDC
Hour which might have been yet might not be, The. Stillborn Love. Dante Gabriel Rossetti. The House of Life, LV. EnLi-2; EPN; MaVP; PoVP; ViPo; VP
Hour with Thee, An. Richard Chenevix Trench. *See* Prayer: "Lord, what a change within us."
Hourly I Die. Dryden. *See* Song, A: "Fair Iris I love, and hourly I die."
Hours, The. John Peale Bishop. MoVE; OxBA
Hours before dawn we were woken by the quake. Aubade. William Empson. FaBoTw; LiTB; ToPo
Hours Continuing Long, Sore and Heavy-Hearted. Walt Whitman. MWA-1
Hours I Remember Lonely and Lovely to Me. Thomas Caulfield Irwin. IrPN
Hours I spent with thee, dear heart, The. The Rosary. Robert Cameron Rogers. AA; FaBoBe; HBV; TreF; WBLP
Hours of Idleness. Byron. *See* Tear, The.
Hours of Prayer. Julia Biebesheimer. SoP
Hours of Sleep. *Unknown.* GoTP
Hours of Sleepy Night, The. Thomas Campion. *Fr.* The Mountebank's Mask. ElL
(Dismissal.) OBSC
Hours of the Day, The. George Dillon. NP
Hours of the Passion, *sel.* Harriet Eleanor Hamilton King.
Garden of the Holy Souls, The. ACP; JKCP (1926 ed.)
Hours of the Passion, *sel.* William of Shoreham.
"At Prime Jesus was y-led." ACP; CAW
Hours of the Passion, The. *Unknown.* MeEL
Hours of the Planets, The. Charles Madge. FaBo
"Now English eyes the cancerous sun behold!" *sel.* BoSA
Hours Rise Up Putting Off Stars and It Is, The. E. E. Cummings. CAD; CMoP; OxBA
(Impression.) MAP; MoAmPo
Hours stand around the clock. Life Studies. Peter Schjeldahl. ANYP
House. Robert Browning. DiPo; MBW-2; OAEP; PoVP; PP; ViPo
(House: A Reply.) CLwM
House, The. Robert Creeley. CoPo
House, A, *sel.* Ford Madox Ford.
"I am the House," Pt. I. MoBrPo (1942 ed.)
House, The. Paula Nelson. GoYe
House. Carl Sandburg. CMoP
House, The. Winfield Townley Scott. MiAP
House, The. Henry Treece. MaRV
House, The. Tania van Zyl. PeSA
House: A Reply. Robert Browning. *See* House.
House and Grounds, A. Leigh Hunt. CBEP; OBRV
House and hollow; village and valley-side. Winter Encounters. Charles Tomlinson. LiTM (1970 ed.)
House and Home. Joseph Beaumont. OBS
(Home.) GoTL
House and Home. Victor Hugo, *tr. fr. French.* MaRV; SoP; TRV
House and Land. Allen Curnow. ACV; AnNZ
House and Shutter. Lewis Turco. PoPl
House and the Road, The. Josephine Preston Peabody. TreFT
House Beautiful, The. Robert Louis Stevenson. PoVP
House Blessing, A. William Cartwright. ChTr
House Blessing. Arthur Guiterman. BrR; MaRV; TiPo; TrPWD
House by the Side of the Road, The. Sam Walter Foss. AmePo; BLPA; FaBoBe; FaFP; HBV; HBVY; MaRV; NeHB; OHFP; OQP; OTD; SoP; TIHL; TreF; TRV; WBLP; WGRP
House Carpenter. *Unknown. See* Demon Lover, The.
House Cat, The. Annette Wynne. StVeCh
House Cleaning. Nicholas Lloyd Ingraham. SoP
House Demolished. Charles Malam. PoMa
House Divided, A. Michael Ondaatje. MoCV
House Fear. Robert Forst. *Fr.* The Hill Wife. NP
House frames hang like spider webs, The. Construction. Patricia Hubbell. OCS
House full, a hole full, A. *Unknown.* OxNR
House Guest. Elizabeth Bishop. NYBP
House had gone to bring again, The. The Need of Being Versed in Country Things. Robert Frost. FaBoEn; OxBA; PoeP; PoSa
House in Denver. Thomas Hornsby Ferril. AmFN
House in Springfield. Gail Brook Burket. PGD
House in St. Petersburg. Stanley Burnshaw. SiSw
House in Taos, A. Langston Hughes. CDC
House in the Green Well, The. John Hall Wheelock. MoAmPo (1962 ed.)
House in Wartime, A. Richard Church. POTE
House is built of logs and stone, A. House and Home. Victor Hugo. MaRV; SoP; TRV
House is crammed, The: tier beyond tier they grin. "Blighters." Siegfried Sassoon. FaBoTw; MMA; MoVE
House Is Not the Home, The. Walter Isenhour. SoP
House is so quiet now, The. The Vacuum. Howard Nemerov. NePoEA
House lies vacant now, forbear to knock, The. Miser. Gordon LeClaire. CaP
House like a man all lean and coughing, A. Even Numbers. Carl Sandburg. OCS
House my earthly parent left, The. The Cottage. Jones Very. OxBA
House Not Made with Hands, A. Arthur Cleveland Coxe. *See* O Where Are Kings and Empires Now.
House of a Hundred Lights. The, *sels.* Ridgely Torrence.
Carpe Diem. AA
Compensation. AA
Conclusion of the Whole Matter, The. AA; HBV
Young Lovers, The. AA
Youth and Age. AA
House of Ate, The. Spenser. *Fr.* The Faerie Queene, IV, 1. OBSC
House of Broken Swords, The, *sel.* William Hervey Woods.
Prayer of Beaten Men, The. HBV
House of Cards, The. Christina Rossetti. *Fr.* Sing-Song. OTD; PCH; PoPl
House of cards, house of dreams. After G. de Nerval. Lewis MacAdams. YAP
House of Christmas, The. G. K. Chesterton. BoPe; FaChP; GoBC; HBV; HBVY; MaRV; MoBrPo; MoRP; TSW
Home at Last, *sel.* BoPe; FaChP; OQP; TRV; WGRP
House of Colour, The. Francis Sherman. *Fr.* The Deserted City CaP
House of Dust, The, *sels.* Conrad Aiken.
Portrait of One Dead, Pt. III, vi. HBMV; NP; WHA
House of Falling Leaves, The. William Stanley Braithwaite. PoLF; PoNe
House of Fire. Theodore Weiss. CoPo
House of God, The. Isaac Watts. SoP
House of God and Gate of Heaven. "Haec Est Domus Dei et Porta Coeli." Sister Maria del Rey. JKCP (1955 ed.)
House of Hospitalities, The. Thomas Hardy. MoPW
House of Life. Dorothy Quick. FiSC
House of Life, The. Dante Gabriel Rossetti. MaVP; PoVP; ViPo
Sels.
Ardour and Memory, LXIV. MaVP; PoVP; ViPo
Autumn Idleness, LXIX. ILP; MaVP; PoVP; ViPo; ViPP
Barren Spring, LXXXIII. FaBoEn; MaVP; NoP; OBNC; PoEL-5; PoVP; Sonn; VaPo; ViPo
Beauty's Pageant, XVII. MaVP; PoVP; ViPo; VP
Birth-Bond, The, XV. EmBrPo; HBV; MaVP; OAEP; PoVP; Sonn; ViPo; VP
Body's Beauty, LXXVIII. ATP (1953 ed.); EnL; HBV; ILP; MaVP; PAn; PoVP; Sonn; TrGrPo; ViPo; ViPP

House (continued)
Bridal Birth, II. MaVP; OAEP; PoVP; Sonn; ViPo; VP
Broken Music, XLVII. MaVP; PoVP; VA; ViPo; VP
Choice, The, LXXI-LXXIII. ATP; BEL; EnL; EnLi-2; GTBS-P; HBV; MaVP; MyFE; OBVV; PoVP; TOP; ViBoPo; ViPo
"Eat thou and drink," LXXI. WHA
"Think thou and act," LXXIII. OBEV (new ed.); OHIP; WHA
Cloud and Wind, XLIV. MaVP; PoVP; ViPo; VP
Dark Day, A, LXVIII. MaVP; PoVP; ViPo
Dark Glass, The, XXXIV. EPN; HBV; MaVP; PoVP; TOP; VA; ViPo; VP
Day of Love, A, XVI. MaVP; PoVP; ViPo; VP
Death-in-Love, XLVIII. MaVP; PoVP; SyP; ViPo; VP
Death's Songsters, LXXXVII. MaVP; PoVP; ViPo
Equal Troth, XXXII. MaVP; PoVP; ViPo; VP
Farewell to the Glen, LXXXIV. MaVP; PoVP; ViPo
From Dawn to Noon, LXXX. MaVP; PoVP; ViPo
Genius in Beauty, XVIII. EnLit; InP; MaVP; OAEP; PoVP; TOP; ViPo; VP
Gracious Moonlight, XX. MaVP; PoVP; ViPo; VP
He and I, XCVIII. MaVP; NBM; PoVP; ViPo
Heart of the Night, The, LXVI. EPN; MaVP; PoVP; TOP; ViPo
Heart's Compass, XXVII. EPN; MaVP; Po; PoVP; ViPo; VP; WHA
Heart's Haven, XXII. EPN; MaVP; OAEP; PoVP; Sonn; ViPo; VP
Heart's Hope, V. EnLit; EPN; HBV; MaVP; PoVP; ViPo; VP
Her Gifts, XXXI. HBV; MaVP; PoVP; VA; ViPo; VP
Hero's Lamp, LXXXVIII. MaVP; PoVP; ViPo
Hill Summit, The, LXX. MaVP; NoP; PoVP; ViPo
Hoarded Joy, LXXXII. MaVP; PoVP; ViPo
Hope Overtaken, XLII. MaVP; PoVP; ViPo; VP
Inclusiveness, LXIII. EnLi-2; MaVP; NBM; NCEP; PoVP; SyP; VA; ViPo
Kiss, The, VI. MaVP; Sonn; VP
("What smouldering senses in death's sick delay.") PoVP; UnTE; ViPo
Known in Vain, LXV. EnLi-2; MaVP; PoVP; ViPo
Lamp's Shrine, The, XXXV. MaVP; PoVP; ViPo; VP
Landmark, The, LXVII. EPN; MaVP; NBM; PoVP; ViPo
Last Fire, XXX. MaVP; PoVP; ViPo; VP
Life-in-Love, XXXVI. MaVP; PoVP; ViPo; VP
Life the Beloved, XCVI. MaVP; PoVP; ViPo
Lost Days, LXXXVI. EnL; EnLi-2; EnLit; EPN; GoBC; MaRV; MaVP; MemP; NCEP; OAEP; PoVP; TOP; ViPo; ViPP; WHA
Lost on Both Sides, XCI. GTSL; MaVP; NoP; PoVP; SeCePo; ViPo; ViPP
Love and Hope, XLIII. MaVP; PoVP; ViPo; VP
Love Enthroned, I. CoBE; MaVP; OBNC; PoVP; ViPo; VP
Love-Letter, The, XI. MaVP; PoVP; ViPo; VP
Love-Moon, The, XXXVII. MaVP; PoVP; ViPo; VP
Love-Sweetness, XXI. BEL; EnLit; EPN; MaVP; OAEP; PoVP; TOP; ViPo; VP
Lovers' Walk, The, XII. MaVP; OAEP; PoVP; TOP; ViPo; VP
Love's Baubles, XXIII. MaVP; PoVP; ViPo; VP
Love's Fatality, LIV. MaVP; PoVP; ViPo; VP
Love's Last Gift, LIX. MaVP; PoVP; ViPo; VP
Love's Lovers, VIII. MaVP; PoVP; ViPo; VP
Love's Testament, III. MaVP; PoVP; VP
("O thou who at Love's hour.") ViPo
Lovesight, IV. BEL; BoLiVe; CoBE; EnLi-2; EnLit; EPN; FaBoEn; GTBS-D; GTBS-P; GTSL; HBV; MaVP; OAEP; OBNC; OBVV; PoVP; TOP; TrGrPo; VA; ViBoPo; ViPo; ViPP; VP; WHA
Memorial Thresholds, LXXXI. MaVP; PoVP; ViPo
Michelangelo's Kiss, XCIV. MaVP; PoVP; ViPo
Mid-Rapture, XXVI. BEL; FaBoBe; HBV; MaVP; OAEP; PoE; PoVP; TOP; ViPo; VP
Monochord, The, LXXIX. MaVP; PoVP; ViPo
Moonstar, The, XXIX. MaVP; PoVP; ViPo; VP
Morrow's Message, The, XXXVIII. GTSE; MaVP; PoVP; ViPo; VP
Newborn Death, XCIX-C. MaVP; PoVP; ViPo
Nuptial Sleep, VI (A). LoBV; MaVP; PoVP; ViPo; ViPP; VP
Old and New Art, LXXIV-LXXVI.
Husbandman, The, LXXVI. MaVP; PoVP; ViPo
Not As These, LXXV. MaVP; PoVP; ViPo
St. Luke the Painter, LXXIV. GoBC; MaVP; PoVP; ViPo
One Hope, The, CI. BEL; EnLi-2; EnLit; EPN; HBV; MaVP; PoVP; ViPo; ViPP
Parted Love, XLVI. MaVP; PoVP; ViPo; VP
Passion and Worship, IX. MaVP; PoVP; ViPo; VP
Portrait, The, X. MaVP; OAEP; PoVP; ViPo; VP
Pride of Youth, XXIV. FaBoEn; MaVP; OBNC; PoVP; ViPo; ViPP; VP
"Retro me, Sathana!" XC. MaVP; NoP; PoVP; ViPo
Secret Parting, XLV. MaVP; PoVP; ViPo; VP
Severed Selves, XL. MaVP; PoVP; SyP; ViPo; VP
Silent Noon, XIX. BEL; BoLiVe; EnLi-2; EnLit; EPN; GTBS-D; HBV; ILP; LiTL; LO; MaVP; MeWo; NoP; OAEP; OBNC; PAn; PoEL-5; PoVP; Sonn; TrGrPo; ViPo; ViPP; VP; WHA; YAT
Sleepless Dreams, XXXIX. MaVP; OAEP; PoVP; ViPo; VP
Song-Throe, The, LXI. MaVP; PoVP; ViPo
Sonnet, The ("A sonnet is a moment's monument"), *introd.* BEL; CoBE; EnL; EnLi-2; EnLit; EPN; GTBS-W; HBV; ILP; InP; NoP; OAEP; PoVP; PP; Sonn; StP; TOP; ViBoPo; ViPo; ViPP; VP
(Introduction.) YAT
(Introductory.) VA
Soul-Light, XXVIII. CoBE; MaVP; PoVP; ViPo; VP
Soul's Beauty, LXXVII. CoBE; EnLit; MaVP; OAEP; OBEV (new ed.); OBVV; PAn; PoVP; ViPo; ViPP
Soul's Sphere, The, LXII. MaVP; PoVP; ViPo
Stillborn Love, LV. EnLi-2; EPN; MaVP; PoVP; ViPo; VP
Sun's Shame, The, XCII-XCIII. MaVP; PoVP; ViPo
Superscription, A, XCVII. BEL; CBEP; EnL; EnLi-2; EnLit; FaBoEn; GTBS-P; HBV; LO; MaVP; NoP; OBNC; PoEL-5; PoVP; SeCePo; TOP; VA; ViPo; ViPP; WHA; YAT
Supreme Surrender, VII. MaVP; PoVP; ViPo; VP
Through Death to Love, XLI. MaVP; PoVP; SyP; ViPo; VP
Transfigured Life, LX. MaVP; PoVP; ViPo
Trees of the Garden, The, LXXXIX. MaVP; PoVP; ViPo
True Woman, LVI-LVIII.
Her Heaven, LVIII. EPN; MaVP; PoVP; ViPo; VP
Her Love, LVII. EPN; MaVP; PoVP; ViPo; VP
Herself, LVI. EPN; MaVP; PoVP; ViPo; ViPP; VP
Vain Virtues, LXXXV. EnLi-2; HBV; MaVP; PoVP; ViPo; ViPP
Vase of Life, The, XCV. MaVP; PoVP; SyP; ViPo
Venus Victrix, XXXIII. MaVP; PoVP; ViPo; VP
Willowwood, XLIX-LII. MaVP; OAEP; PoVP; ViPo; VP
"I sat with Love upon a woodside well," XLIX. HBV; PoEL-5; Sonn; WHA
"O ye, all ye that walk in Willowwood," LI. ViPP
Winged Hours, XXV. EPN; MaVP; PoVP; ViPo; VP
Without Her, LIII. CBEP; CoBE; GTBS-W; MaVP; NCEP; OBNC; PoEL-5; PoVP; Sonn; VA; ViBoPo; ViPo; VP
Youth's Antiphony, XIII. MaVP; PoVP; TOP; ViPo; VP
Youth's Spring-Tribute, XIV. MaVP; PoVP; ViPo; VP
House of Life, The. Katharine Tynan. BoPe
House of Lords, The. W. S. Gilbert. *See* House of Peers, The.
House of Many Mansions, The. Oswald J. Smith. SoP
House of Morpheus, The. Spenser. *Fr.* The Faerie Queene, Bk. I, 1. UnPo (1st ed.)
("He, making speedy way through 'spersèd air.") InP
House of Night, The, *sels.* Philip Freneau.
"By some sad means, when Reason holds no Sway." AmPP; PoEL-4
Death. AP
Death's Epitaph, *br. sel.* AA
"Trembling I write my dream, and recollect." AnFE; APA; CoAnAm
House of Pain, The. Florence Earle Coates. HBV; OQP
House of Peers, The. W. S. Gilbert. *Fr.* Iolanthe. InMe
(House of Lords, The.) TrGrPo
(Song: "When Britain really ruled the waves.") InP
House of Pride, The. William J. Dawson. MaRV; PoToHe
House of Pride, The. Spenser. *Fr.* The Faerie Queene, I, 4. WHA
House of Richesse, The. Spenser. *See* Cave of Mammon, The.
House of Sleep, The. John Gower. *Fr.* Confessio Amantis: Ceix and Alceone. AtBAP
House of sleepers—I, alone unblest, A. Insomnia. Edith M. Thomas. AA
House of Splendour, The. Ezra Pound. InPo
House of the Eighties, A. Edmund Wilson. AnFE; CoAnAm

House of the Mouse, The. Lucy Sprague Mitchell. SoPo; TiPo
House of the Trees, The. Ethelwyn Wetherald. CaP; OQP; VA
House of Wisdom, The (" Wisdom hath builded her house"). Proverbs, IX: 1-6, Bible, *O.T.* TrGrPo
House of Yesterday. Walter Shedlofsky. FiSC
House on Maple Hill, The. Stanley McNail. FiSC
House on the Hill, The. E. A. Robinson. AA; AnNE; CoBA; FaPON; GoJo; HBMV; InP; LaNeLa; MAP; MoAmPo; MPB; OTD; PCD; PG; PIA; PoSa; PTK; TDP; TreFT; TrGrPo; TSW; WHA; YT
House or a Home, A. J. H. Sykes. SoP
House Plant. Winthrop Palmer. SiTL
House ringed round with trees and in the trees, A. Asylum. John Freeman. OBMV
House Sonnet. Elinor Wylie. *See* I Hereby Swear That to Uphold Your House.
House-Surgeon. W. E. Henley. *Fr.* In Hospital. PoVP
House That Jack Built, The. Samuel Taylor Coleridge. *See* On a Ruined House in a Romantic Country.
House that Jack Built, The. *Unknown.* SoPo
House That Was, The. Laurence Binyon. MoBrPo
House, though you've harboured grave-yards full of lives. Eulogy of My House. Siegfried Sassoon. MoPW
House-Top, The. Herman Melville. AP; LiTA; MAmP; MWA-1; NCEP; NoP; TDP
House was crammed from roof to floor, The. At the Pantomime. Oliver Wendell Holmes. AnNE
House was lonely, all dark and bare, The. House of Life. Dorothy Quick. FiSC
House was shaken by a rising wind. Brainstorm. Howard Nemerov. NoP; ToPo
House-Weary. Ian Drag. OQP
House where I was born, The. The Doves. Katharine Tynan. AnIV; AWP; JAWP; WBP
House with coarse stuccoed, The. The House. Tania van Zyl. PeSA
House with Nobody in It, The. Joyce Kilmer. BLPA; MPB; SP; StVeCh
House, you are done. Consecration of the House. W. S. Fairbridge. NeLNL; PoAu-2
Housed in each other's arms. Song for a Marriage. Vassar Miller. HW; ToPo
Housefronts rough with brick proffer. Birthday, with Leaves. James Applewhite. YAP
Houseful, a roomful, A. *Unknown.* RIS
Household Gods. J. H. Macnair. PoMa
Householder, The. Robert Browning. *Fr.* Fifine at the Fair. LO
Householder is Goathooves, A. The Faun. T. Sturge Moore. FaBoTw
Housekeeper, The. Vincent Bourne, *tr. fr. Latin by* Charles Lamb. GN; HBV; OTPC; PoLF
(Snail, The.) GoTP; MoShBr
House-Mates. Leon Gellert. MoAuPo
Housemates. Odell Shepard. MoRP
Houses ("Houses are faces"). Aileen Fisher. SoPo
Houses, The, *sels.* "Robin Hyde." AnNZ
"Adolicus; that's a creeper rug, its small," III.
"Section and brick and grass," VI.
Houses, an embassy, the hospital. Days of 1964. James Merrill. CoAP; NoP
Houses and rooms are full of perfumes, the shelves are crowded with perfumes. Song of Myself, II. Walt Whitman. TrGrPo
Houses are haunted, The. Disillusionment of Ten o'Clock. Wallace Stevens. AmP; CMoP; CrMA; ForPo; FosPo; LOW; OxBA; PoIE; PoPo; PoSa
Houses, churches, mixed together. A Description of London. John Banks. WaPE
Houses Have Open Eyes. Paul Zech, *tr. fr. German by* Glauco Cambon. OnPM
Houses in a row, houses in a row. Squares and Angles. Alfonsina Storni. OCS
Houses of men are on fire, The. The Seventh Hell. Jerome Rothenberg. CoPo; NMP
Houses Should Have Homes to Live In. David Ross. PG (1933 ed.)
Housewife, The. Catherine Cate Coblentz. BLRP; ChIP; FaChP; SoP; StJW; TrPWD; TRV
Housewife, The. W. W. Gibson. NP
Housewife. Josephine Miles. FiMAP
Housewife called out with a frown, A. *Unknown.* GoTP
Housewifery. Edward Taylor. AmP; AmPP; AnNE; DiPo; GTBS-W; ILP; LiTA; NePA; NoP; StP; TDP
(Huswifery.) AP; CBV; EaLo; FaBV; ForPo; FosPo; MAmP; MWA-1; SCAP
Housewife's Prayer, The. Blanche Mary Kelly. GoBC; JKCP; WHL
Hover about us. The Ghosts of the Dead. Besmilr Brigham. ThO
Hover o'er me, Holy Spirit. Fill Me Now. E. R. Stokes. SoP
Hovering and huge, dark, formless sway, The. The Virgin Mary. Edgar Bowers. NePoEA; QFR
How. S. J. Marks. NYBP
How? *Unknown.* STF
How a Cat Was Annoyed and a Poet Was Booted. Guy Wetmore Carryl. CIV; MAP; MoAmPo (1942 ed.)
How a Fisherman Corked Up His Foe in a Jar. Guy Wetmore Carryl. PoMS
How a Girl Was Too Reckless of Grammar by Far. Guy Wetmore Carryl. BOHV; FiBHP
How a Poet's Soul Comes into Play. Robert Browning. *Fr.* Sordello. MyFE
How about an oak leaf. Poem. James Schuyler. ANYP
How all men wrongly death to dignify. The Wisdom of Old Jelly Roll. A. J. M. Smith. PeCV (1967 ed.)
How all occasions do inform against me. Shakespeare. *Fr.* Hamlet, iv. HoPM
How all's to one thing wrought! On a Piece of Music. Gerard Manley Hopkins. UnS
How am I hitched. Suffering. Albert Ehrenstein. TrJP
How amiable are thy tabernacles, O Lord of hosts! Psalm LXXXIV, Bible, *O.T.* TRV
How Amiable Are Thy Tabernacles! Bryant. *See* Dedication: "Thou whose unmeasured temple stands."
How and When and Where and Why. Phyllis Gotlieb. WHW
How Annandale Went Out. E. A. Robinson. AmP; AP; CBV; CoBMV; HBMV; ILP; MAP; MoAB; MoAmPo
How are our Spirituall Gamesters slipt away? Edward Taylor. *Fr.* An Elegy upon the Death of That Holy Man of God Mr. John Allen. PoEL-3
How Are the Mighty Fallen. Second Samuel, Bible, *O.T.* *See* David's Lament.
How Are Thy Servants Blest. Addison. OxBoCh
(Ode: "How are thy servants blest, O Lord!") OBEC; TrPWD
How Are You? Arthur Guiterman. *See* Of Tact.
"How are you boy." The WhenIwas. Dick Lourie. *Fr.* Calls on the Dream Telephone. ThO
How Are You, Dear World, This Morning? Horace Traubel. TrJP
"How Are You, Sanitary?" Bret Harte. PaA; PAP
How, as a spider's web is spun. To Jessie's Dancing Feet. William DeLancey Ellwanger. AA
How, as we peer into tanks at these lives. Where The Manatee Plays and the Manta Ray Flutters. Harold Witt. NYTB
How avarice loseth all. The Hen with the Golden Eggs. La Fontaine. OnPM
How Bateese Came Home. William Henry Drummond. IHA
How Beastly the Bourgeois Is. D. H. Lawrence. ChTr; LiTM; PoIE; SiTL
How beauteous is the bond. The Peau de Chagrin of State Street. Oliver Wendell Holmes. AP
How beautiful! from his blue throne on high. The Ocean. George D. Prentice. EtS
How beautiful is a woman whose avarice is over. Woman without Fear. George Dillon. AnEnPo
How beautiful is genius when combined. Sacred Poetry. John Wilson. WBLP
How beautiful is night! Night [*or* Night in the Desert]. Robert Southey. *Fr.* Thalaba the Destroyer. GN; OTPC
How beautiful is the rain! Rain in Summer. Longfellow. BBV (1923 ed.); BoChLi; BoTP; GN; OTPC; PCH; PoG; RIS
How beautiful it was, that one bright day. Hawthorne. Longfellow. CBEP; CoBA; DD; MAmP; NCEP; PoEL-5
How beautiful the earth is still. Anticipation. Emily Brontë. OBNC
How beautiful this hill of fern swells on! Stanzas. John Clare. *Fr.* Child Harold. OBNC

How beautiful to live as thou didst live! Tennyson. Florence Earle Coates. AA
How Beautiful upon the Mountains. Isaiah, LII: 7-10, Bible, *O.T.* TrJP
How beautiful, white and hard, are the teeth of this dead man. Don Juan Muses. John Heath-Stubbs. MoPW
How, best of kings, dost thou a scepter beare! To King James. Ben Jonson. OAEP
How Big Was Alexander? Elijah Jones. BLPA
How blessed [*or* blest] is he, who leads a country life. To My Honored Kinsman, John Dryden [*or* Driden], of Chesterton. Dryden. MBW-1; OBS; SeEP
How blessed [*or* blest] thy creature is, O God. The Happy Change. William Cowper. CEP; EiPP
How blessed [*or* blest] was the created state. The Fall. Earl of Rochester. EnLoPo; UnTE
How blessèd were Judean hills Noel. Gail Brook Burket. PGD
How blest are lovers in disguise! Song. George Farquhar. *Fr.* Love and a Bottle. SeCL
How blest art thou, canst love the countrey, Wroth. To Sir Robert Wroth. Ben Jonson. SeCV-1
How blest he appears. Song. Thomas Otway. *Fr.* Friendship in Fashion. SeCL
How blest is he, who leads a country life. *See* How blessed is he . . .
How blest the Maid whose heart—yet free. The Three Cottage Girls. Wordsworth. HBV
How Blest the Righteous. Anna Letitia Barbauld. SoP
How blest thy creature is, O God. *See* How blessed thy creature is. . .
How blest was the created state. *See* How blessed was the created state.
How blind men are! We surely cannot know. Understanding. H. W. Bliss. PoToHe
How bravely Autumn paints upon the sky. Written in a Volume of Shakespeare. Thomas Hood. Sonn
"How brent is your brow, my Lady Elspat!" Lady Elspat. *Unknown.* ESPB
How Brer Tarrypin Learned to Fly. Joel Chandler Harris. TSW
How brief that holy hour they knew. Magi. Leslie Savage Clark. ChIP
How bright on the blue. The Kite. Harry Behn. FaPON; RePo; TiPo (1959 ed.)
How brim-full of nothing's the life of a Beau. The Life of a Beau. James Miller. OBEC
How burn the stars unchanging in the midnight skies. New Year. John J. Moment. MaRV
How busie are the sonnes of men? Roger Williams. SCAP
How, Butler, How! *Unknown.* ViBoPo
(Fill the Bowl, Butler.) MeEL
How calm and proud that lady, Nefertiti, walked. Lady and Crocodile. Charles Burgess. NePoAm-2
How calm, how beautiful, comes on. The Golden Hour. Thomas Moore. *Fr.* Lalla Rookh. OBNC
"How came that blood on thy coat-lap?" The Dead Brother. *Unknown.* EnSB
How came the noble Timon to this change? Shakespeare. *Fr.* Timon of Athens, IV, iii. MyFE
How came this troubled one to stray. Boy in the Wind. George Dillon. MAP; MoAmPo (1942 ed.)
How can a girl with such a big belly be so desirable? Mrs Loewinsohn &c. Ron Loewinsohn. NeAP
How can a man's life keep its course. Lao-tzu. *Fr.* Tao Teh King. WaKn
How can I cease to pray for thee? Prayer for One Dead. Julia C. R. Dorr. OQP
How Can I Doubt? Phyllis C. Michael. SoP
How can I dread you, O portentous wise. The Woman with the Baby to the Philosopher. Frances Cornford. PoMa
How can I ever doubt God is? How Can I Doubt? Phyllis C. Michael. SoP
How can I get through that innocence? Joy. Michael Benedikt. YAP
How can I hinder or restrain my soul. Love-Song. Rainer Maria Rilke. MeWo
How Can I Keep From Singing? *sel.* Robert Lowry. FaChP
"What though my joys and comforts die?" TRV
How Can I Keep My Maidenhead. Burns. ErPo; UnTE
How Can I Sing? *Unknown.* MaRV
How can I sing light-souled and fancy-free. Two Lyrics, 2. Lorenzo de' Medici, *tr. fr. Italian by* John Addington Symonds. AWP; JAWP; WBP
How Can I Smile. Florence B. Hodgson. BLRP
How can I tell them what it was I saw. Lincoln's Dream. Ridgely Torrence. LiPo
How can I tell which days have yielded fruit? Days. Eliot Kays Stone. OQP
How can I tell you. How. S. J. Marks. NYBP
How can I, that girl standing there. Politics. W. B. Yeats. CMoP; PoPo; POTE; StP
How can I then return in happy plight. Sonnets, XXVIII. Shakespeare. OBSC
How can I, who cannot control. Blind Steersmen. Francis Ernest Kobina Parkes. PBA
How can it be that I forget. Recollection. Anne Reeve Aldrich. AA
How Can Man Die Better. Tyrtaeus, *tr. fr. Greek by* T. F. Higham. WaaP
How can my Muse want subject to invent. Sonnets, XXXVIII. Shakespeare. EnLit; ReEn; Sonn
How can one e'er be sure. Lady Horikawa. *Fr.* Hyaku-Nin-Isshu. AWP; JAWP; WBP
How can one tell what Love may be about. Psychoanalysis. Ewart Gavin. NYBP
How can our minds and bodies be. Grace before Sleep. Sara Teasdale. MoRP; TrPWD
How can she catch the sunlight. Questions. Lord Thomson of Cardington. OtMeF
How can snow sifting so fine. Snow. John Kelleher. ELU
How can that tree but withered be. Song. *Unknown.* EIL
How can the cripple get, in running race, the game? The Lover in Distress Exclaimeth against Fortune. *Unknown.* ReIE
How can the heart for sea and stone. On a Memory of Beauty. G. S. Fraser. FaBoMo; NeBP
How Can the Heart Forget Her. Walter Davison. HBV, OBEV; PG
(At Her Fair Hands.) EIL; LiTL; LO; WHA
(Ode: "At her fair hands.") OBSC
(Ode II: Dialogue between Him and His Heart, A.) SiCE
How can the tree but waste and wither away. No Pleasure without Some Pain [*or* Death in Life]. Thomas, Lord Vaux. EIL; EnRePo; OBSC; SiCE; TuPP
How Can They Honor Him? Anderson M. Scruggs. *See* Christmas, 1930.
How can we find? how can we rest? Thoughts on the Shape of the Human Body. Rupert Brooke. BrPo
How Can You? Maxine Stevens. STF
"How can you, friend?" the Swedish say. How Do You Do? H. Bedford-Jones. WBLP
"How can you live in Goshen?" Goshen! Edgar Frank. MaRV; OQP
How can you smile when pain is everywhere. Beauty. Mary Craig Sinclair. OQP
How carefully she does her mouth. Artist. Ernestine Mercer. InMe
How changed is here each spot man makes or fills. Thyrsis. Matthew Arnold. EnLi-2; EnLit; FiP; GTSL; ILP; MaVP; MBW-2; NoP; OAEP; OBEV (new ed.); OBNC; OBVV; PAn; PoAn; PoE; PoVP; StP; TOP; ViPo; ViPP; VP
How charming is this little spot. To Mrs. Boteler. Mary Chandler. WaPE
How clear, how keen, how marvellously bright. November 1. Wordsworth. EPN
How Clear, How Lovely Bright. A. E. Housman. More Poems, XVI. MaPo
How close the white-ranked crosses stand. Armistice. Charles Buxton Going. DD; HBMV; PEDC
How cold are thy baths, Apollo! Jugurtha. Longfellow. AA; AP; CoBA; MWA-1
How Collingbourne was Cruelly Executed for Making a Foolish Rhyme. William Baldwin. NCEP
How Come? David Ignatow. CAD
How comely glisten the rounded cheeks. Fatness. Alan Ansen. CoAP
How comes it, Flora, that, whenever we. The Queen of Hearts. Christina Rossetti. PeVV
"How comes that blood all over your shirt?" Edward (B *vers.*). *Unknown.* HoPM; ViBoFo
How cool beneath this stone the soft moss lies. Epitaph for a

Negro Woman. Owen Dodson. PoNe

How cool the cattle seem. Cattle. *Unknown.* SoPo

How Could I Face the Future? Alma Hoellein. SoP

How could I know. The Dance Called David. Theodore Weiss. CoPo

How could I love you more? Prelude. Richard Aldington. BrPo

How could the love between Thee and me sever? Two Songs, 2. Kabir. LiTW

How could they think women a recreation? Don Giovanni on His Way to Hell. Jack Gilbert. NMP

How Could We, Beforehand, Live in Quiet. Nikolai Gumilev, tr. fr. *Russian* by Jeannette Eyre. WaaP

How could you be so happy, now some thousand years. Note to Wang Wei. John Berryman. ML; NYBP

How could you dream mere body's eloquence. A Prophecy. Christopher Levenson. ErPo

How Could You Know? Ben Ray Redman. PoMa

How countlessly they congregate. Stars. Robert Frost. MAmP

How courteous is the Japanese. The Japanese. Ogden Nash. InMe; WhC

How Creatures Move. *Unknown.* GFA

How crowded is the heavenly House of Light. For Those Who Died. Thomas Curtis Clark. PGD

How cruel they! the cause of all. Crusts. Walter Shea. ChIP

How cruels love when shees too kinde. *Unknown.* SeCSL

How Cyrus Laid the Cable. John Godfrey Saxe. MC; PaA; PAH

How D.D. swaggers, M.D. rolls! Epigram: Diversity of Doctors. *Unknown.* ALV

How dare one say it? The Unexpress'd. Walt Whitman. NePA; PP

How dare we deem that in this age. Empires. Francis Burdett Money-Coutts. OBVV

How dare we look askance at these two men. Simon and Judas. Kenneth W. Porter. OQP

How Dear to Me the Hour. Thomas Moore. CoBE

How dear to my heart are the grand politicians. The Old Hokum Buncombe. Robert E. Sherwood. InMe

How dear to my [*or* this] heart are the scenes of my childhood. The Old Oaken Bucket [*or* The Bucket]. Samuel Woodworth. AA; AmePo; BLPA; FaBoBe; FaFP; FaPON; HBV; NeHB; OTPC (1946 ed.); PaPo; PTK; TreF; WBLP

How Death Came. *Unknown, tr. fr. Hottentot* by W. H. I. Bleek. PeSA; TTY

How Death Comes. *Unknown.* MeEL

How deep is his duplicity who in a flash. High Diver. Robert Francis. NePoAm; SD

How delicately they are wild. Egrets. Max Eastman. AnEnPo

How delicious is the winning. Freedom and Love. Thomas Campbell. GTBS; GTBS-D; GTBS-P; GTBS-W; GTSE

How delightful, at sunset, to loosen the boat! The Excursion. Tu Fu. AWP; JAWP; SD; WBP

How delightful to meet Mr. Hodgson! Lines to Ralph Hodgson Esqre. T. S. Eliot. MaPo (1969 ed.)

How desolate!/ Ah! now forlorn. Solitude. Thomas Traherne. OBS; SeEP

How did he know our age. A Bach Cantata. Margaret Stanley-Wrench. MuSP

How did he know, the young sky-rover. Wings. Blanche W. Schoonmaker. DD

How Did He Live? Ernest Crosby. OQP

(Life and Death.) MaRV

How did it happen that we quarreled? Words! Words! Jessie Fauset. CDC

How did the Devil come? When first attack? Norfolk. John Betjeman. ChMP

How did the party go in Portman Square? Juliet. Hilaire Belloc. BoLP; ELU; EnLoPo; MemP; WePo

How did you come to me, my sweet? To a Child Who Inquires. Olga Petrova. BLPA

How Did You Die? Edmund Vance Cooke. BLPA; MaRV; OHFP; OTD

How did you feel, you libertarians. Jacob Godbey. Edgar Lee Masters. *Fr.* Spoon River Anthology. LiTA

"How did you know her?" Story from Russian Author. Peter Redgrove. NePoEA-2

How do I know that God is good? I don't. Faith. G. A. Studdert-Kennedy. MaRV

How do I know that you will come again? Surety. Lizette Woodworth Reese. MAP; MoAmPo

How do I love thee? Let me count the ways. Sonnets from the Portuguese, XLIII. Elizabeth Barrett Browning. AnFE; ATP; BBV (1951 ed.); BEL; BoC; BoLP; CBV; CoBE; CTC; EnLi-2; EnLit; EPN; FaBoBe; FaBV; FaFP; FaPL; GTBS; GTBS-W; GTSL; HBV; HoPM; ILP; InP; LiTB; LiTG; LiTL; LO; MaRV; MeWo; OAEP; OQP; OTD; OuHeWo; PG; Po; PoFS; PoLF; PoMa; PoPl; PoPo; PoRA; PoRL; PoToHe (new ed.); PTK; ShBV-4; SoP; TIHL; TreF; TrGrPo; TRV; UnPo; VA; ViBoPo; ViPo; WHA; YAT; YT

How do I love you? I do not know. Song. Irene Rutherford McLeod. HBV

How do robins build their nests? What Robin Told. George Cooper. FaPON; GFA; MPB; TiPo

How do the daughters. How the Daughters Come Down at Dunoon. Henry Cholmondeley-Pennell. BOHV

How do the pussy-willows grow? Spring Questions. Clara Doty Bates. PPL

How Do You Do? H. Bedford-Jones. WBLP

How Do You Do? *Unknown.* ChTr

How do you do, little Frankie Pankie? Baby on Her Travels. *Unknown.* SAS

"How do you do?" Will asked of me. Lines on a Certain Friend's Remarkable Faculty for Swift Generalization. Max Beerbohm. PV

How do you know it is time to bloom. Creative Force. Maude Miner Hadden. GoYe

How do you know that May has come. May-Day at Sea. John F. Finerty. EtS

How do you know that the pilgrim track. The Year's Awakening. Thomas Hardy. CMoP

How do you like to go up in a swing. The Swing. Robert Louis Stevenson. BoChLi; FaBoBe; FaFP; GFA; GoJo; MPB; NeHB; OPTC; PCH; PDV; SoPo; StVeCh; SUS; TiPo; TreF

How Do You Live? *Unknown. See* Sermons We See.

How does a person get to be a capable liar? Golly, How Truth Will Out. Ogden Nash. LiTA; LiTM; MoAmPo

How does a spider ever weave. The Spider Web. Mattie Lee Hausgen. GFA

How Does My Garden Grow? Ed Stone. WOW

How Does the Soul Grow? "Susan Coolidge." MaRV

"How does the water come down at Lodore?" The Cataract of Lodore. Robert Southey. BOHV; GN; HBV; OTPC; PoPo; PTK; TreFS; WBLP

How does your patient, doctor? A Mind Diseased. Shakespeare. *Fr.* Macbeth, V, iii. TreFT

How dost thou wear and weary out thy days. Chorus. Samuel Daniel. *Fr.* The Tragedie of Philotas. OBSC

How doth the city sit solitary, that was full of people. The Misery of Jerusalem. Lamentations, Bible, *O.T.* AWP; LiTW

How doth the jolly little spider. The Spider. A. P. Herbert. RIS

How Doth the Little Busy Bee. Isaac Watts. FaPON; HBV; HBVY; HoPM; OTPC; PPL; TreF; TVC

(Against Idleness and Mischief.) CBV; CEP; NeHB; OBEC; PaPo; Par; PoFS; YAT

(Bee, The.) GoTP

(Busy Bee, The.) PCH

(Little Busy Bee.) SoPo; StVeCh

How Doth the Little Crocodile, *parody.* "Lewis Carroll." *Fr.* Alice's Adventures in Wonderland, *ch.* 2. BoChLi; CBV; FaBoCh; FaFP; FaPON; LoGBV; MoShBr; MPB; OTPC (1946 ed.); Par; ShM; SoPo; TiPo; TreFS; WaKn; WhC; YAT; YT

(Crocodile, The.) EnLi-2 (1949 ed.); GFA; GoTP; HoPM; PoFS; TrGrPo

How dreamy-dark it is! Charles Mair. *Fr.* The Fireflies. OBCV

How dry time screaks in its fat axle-grease. The Crucifix. Robert Lowell. NoP

How dumb the vanished billions who have died! Omnia Exeunt in Mysterium. George Sterling. NP; WGRP

How D'y'-do and Good-by. William Robert Spencer. OTPC (1923 ed.)

How Each Thing save the Lover in Spring Reviveth to Pleasure. Earl of Surrey. ReIE; Sonn

("When Windsor walls sustain'd my wearied arm.") EnPo; FCP; SiPS

How Easily Men's Cheeks are Hot with Wrath! Verner von Heidenstam, *tr. fr. Swedish* by Charles W. Stork. LiTW; PoPl

How (continued)
How easily the ripe grain. The Widow. W. S. Merwin. NYBP
How erring oft the judgment in its hate. English Weather [*or* The English Fog]. John Dyer. *Fr.* The Fleece. OBEC; TrGrPo
How Excellent Is Thy Name! Eva Gray. SoP
How fades that native breath. Sweets That Die. Langdon Elwyn Mitchell. AA
How fair is youth that flies so fast! Then be happy, ye who may. Triumph of Bacchus and Ariadne. Lorenzo de' Medici. *Fr.* Carnival Songs. CTC
How falls it, oriole, thou hast come to fly. To an Oriole [*or* Oriole]. Edgar Fawcett. GoTP; HBV; OTPC
How Far? Vassar Miller. CoPo
How Far Is It Called to the Grave? *Unknown.* BLPA
"How far is it to Babylon?" The Road to Babylon. Margaret A. Wilson. HBMV
How Far Is It to Bethlehem? Frances Chesterton. BoTP; DD; HBMV; HBVY; MaRV; YaCaBo, *with music*
"How far is it to Bethlehem Town?" How Far to Bethlehem. Madeleine Sweeny Miller. BLPA; MaRV; NeHB; OQP
How far is it to peace, the piper sighed. Our Lady Peace. Mark Van Doren. WaP
"How far is St. Helena from a little child at play?" A St. Helena Lullaby. Kipling. AtBAP; FaBoCh; FOL; MoVE; OAEP (2d ed.); OBMV; OtMeF; PoEL-5; POTE; ShBV-2; ViPP
How far they throw their cheer, their gracious glow. At Christmastide. Laura Simmons. PGD
How Far to Bethlehem? Madeleine Sweeny Miller. BLPA; MaRV; NeHB; OQP
"How fared you when you mortal were?" After. Ralph Hodgson. MoBrPo
How fares it with the happy dead? In Memoriam A. H. H., XLIV. Tennyson. EnLi-2; EPN; OBEV (1st ed.); ViPo; VP
How fast the Marian death-list is unrolled! Latimer and Ridley. Wordsworth. FOL
How fast they fly—these passing years. Dwell in the Depths. J. E. Dean. SoP
How fell sage Helen? through a swain like thee. A Countryman's Wooing. Theocritus. *Fr.* Idylls. ErPo
How felt the land in every part. Washington's Vow. Whittier. OHIP
How fevered is the man, who cannot look. Two Sonnets on Fame, II [*or* On Fame]. Keats. EnL; EnLit; EnRP; EPN; NCEP
How few, of all the hearts that loved. The Wanderer from the Fold. Emily Brontë. EnLit
How fierce in its loyalties the beat of the heart. Coronary Thrombosis. William Price Turner. OxBS
How Firm a Foundation. "K.," *perhaps* Robert Keene, *sometimes at. to* George Keith. MaRV; SoP; TreFT; WGRP
How fit our well-rank'd feasts doe follow. Upon the Powder Day. Richard Crashaw. MaMe
How fond are men of rule and place. The Lion and the Cub. John Gay. *Fr.* Fables. GN; HBV; OTPC (1923 ed.)
How fond, how fierce, your arms to me would cling. The Reconciliation. Horace. *Fr.* Odes. MeWo
How foolishly I loved. Poema Morale. Charles Gullans. NePoEA
How frail/ Above the bulk. Niagara. Adelaide Crapsey. MAP; MoAmPo (1942 ed.)
How frail is mortal love. Mortal Love. Basil Dowling. AnNZ
How fresh, O Lord, how sweet and clean. The Flower. George Herbert. AnAnS-1; AWP; BoC; BWP; ELP; EP; FaBoEn; InPo; MaMe; MeP; MePo; NoP; OBS; OxBoCh; PoAn; PoEL-2; ReEn; SCEP-1; SeCP; SeCV-1
How full the glittering shops are now. Through a Shop Window. Eleanor Farjeon. ChBR; GaP
How funny you are today New York. Steps. Frank O'Hara. ANYP; FRC
How gay those bulks that tattered. Ship Bottom. Richmond Lattimore. NePoAm-2
How gentle and how friendly seem. Gulls. Stanley Snaith. POTE
How gentle God's commands! Trust God. Philip Doddridge. SoP; TRV
How gently sings my soul and whets its wings. Laurence Dakin. *Fr.* Tancred, III, i. CaP
How Glorious Is Thy Name. Psalms, VIII, Bible, *O.T.* *See* What Is Man?
How glows each patriot bosom that boasts a Yankee heart. The *United States* and *Macedonian*. *Unknown.* PAH
How God Answers. *Unknown.* *See* Blessed.
How God must love a friendly home. The Christian Home. Gail Brooks Burket. SoP
How God Speeds the tax-bribed plough. Drone *v.* Worker. Ebenezer Elliott. NBM
How God Will Not Do for Us. John Heywood. SiCE
How Goes the Night? *Unknown, tr. fr. Chinese by* Helen Waddell. *Fr.* Shi King. AWP; JAWP; WBP
How good to hear your voice again. The Priest Rediscovers His Psalm-Book. *Unknown.* KiLC
How good to lie a little while. Friends. Abby Farwell Brown. HBV; HBVY
How goodly are thy tents, O Jacob. Balaam's Blessing. Numbers, Bible, *O.T.* TrGrPo
How grace this hallowed day? Christmas. Henry Timrod. MAmP
How Grand Amour Walked in a Meadow and Met with Fame Environed with Tongues of Fire. Stephen Hawes. *Fr.* The Pastime of Pleasure. ReIE
How grandly glow the bays. On the Death of Francis Thompson. Alfred Noyes. OBVV
How Gray the Rain. Elizabeth J. Coatsworth. SoPo; TiPo
How Great My Grief. Thomas Hardy. BrPo
How great the tale, that there should be. Consecration. Murdoch O'Daly. JKPC (1926 ed.)
How Great unto the Living Seem the Dead! Charles Heavysege. CaP
How green the earth, how blue the sky. The Settlers. Laurence Housman. HBV; OBVV
How green the green at Salem is. The Burial of Terror. Carl Bode. ToPo
How happy a thing were a wedding. On Marriage [*or* The Bachelor's Song]. Thomas Flatman. ELU; EnLoPo; FiBHP; WhC
How happy art thou & I. *Unknown.* SeCSL
How happy could I be with either. John Gay. *Fr.* The Beggar's Opera, II, xiii. ViBoPo
How happy I can be with my love away! The Absence. Sylvia Townsend Warner. MoBrPo
How happy in his low degree. Country Life [*or* Revery of a Business Man]. Horace, *tr. by* Dryden. AWP; WoL
How happy is he born and taught. The Character of a Happy Life [*or* The Happy Life]. Sir Henry Wotton. AnAnS-2; DD; EIL; FaPL; GTBS; GTBS-D; GTBS-P; GTBS-W; GTSE; GTSL; HBV; HBVY; LiTB; LiTG; MaRV; MCCG; MyFE; OBEV; OBS; OTPC (1923 ed.); PCD; PoFr; PoIE; PoPo; SeEP; ShBV-2; SoP; StaSt; TOP; TreF; TrGrPo; ViBoPo
How happy is the blameless vestal's lot! The Vestal. Pope. *Fr.* Eloisa to Abelard. ACP; CAW
How happy is the little stone. Emily Dickinson. AmP; AmPP; AnNE; MWA-2; NeMA; NePA; TSW
How happy the holly-tree looks, and how strong. The Holly. Edith King. ChBR
How Happy the Little Birds. *Unknown, tr. fr. Modern Irish by* Padraic Pearse. OnYI
How Happy the Lover. Dryden. *Fr.* King Arthur, IV, i. LoBV; OnPM; ViBoPo
(Song.) SeEP
(Song to a Minuet.) SeCL
How Happy the Soldier. *Unknown.* LoGBV
How happy to be a fish. Fish and Bird. Rosemary Brinckman. BoTP
How happy were good English faces. The Women's Complaint to Venus. *Unknown.* PeRV
How happy were my days, till now. Song. Isaac Bickerstaffe. *Fr.* Love in a Village, I. OBEC
How Happy's That Lover. *Unknown.* SeCL
How happy's the prisoner that conquers his fate. Drinking Song. *Unknown.* SeCL
How hard for unaccustomed feet. In the Time of Trouble. Leslie Savage Clark. TrPWD
How hard is my fortune. The Convict of Clonmel [*or* Clonmala]. *Unknown, tr. by* Jeremiah Joseph Callanan AnIL; AnIV; IrPN; NBM; OnYI; OxBI; SD
How hard the year dies: no frost yet. Intercession in Late October. Robert Graves. MoAB

How Hardly I Conceal'd My Tears. Anne Wharton. CavP
How has king Heav'n adorn'd the happy land. Italy and Britain. Addison. *Fr.* A Letter from Italy. OBEC
How hath the oppressor ceased! Downfall of the Tyrant. Isaiah, Bible, *O.T.* TrGrPo
How haughty was thy mien. Dante. *Fr.* Divina Commedia: Purgatorio. PoFr
How have I bin religious? what strange good. To Fletcher Reviv'd. Richard Lovelace. OBS
How have I labored? Ortus. Ezra Pound. LiTA; NePA; NP
How have we fallen from our high estate. The Offering. Olive Cecilia Jacks. MaRV
How He Saved St. Michael's. Mary A. P. Stansbury. BLPA
How He Saw Her. Ben Jonson. *Fr.* A Celebration of Charis. AnAnS-2; EnRePo; QFR; OAEP; SCEP-2; SeCP; SeCV-1
"I beheld her, on a day," *br. sel.* AtBAP
How he survived them they could never understand. The Jew Wrecked in the German Cell [*or* The Diaspora]. W. H. Auden. LiTA; WaP
How heavy do I journey on the way. Sonnets, L. Shakespeare. ReEn; ReIE; SiCE
How! Hey! It is non les. *Unknown.* EnPo
How high Thou art! our songs can own. The Mediator. Elizabeth Barrett Browning. TrPWD
How history repeats itself. Can't. Harriet Prescott Spofford. DD; MC; PAH
How Homer Should Have Written the Iliad. Edwin Meade Robinson. *Fr.* Limericised Classics. HBMV
How Horatius Kept the Bridge. Macaulay. *See* Horatius at the Bridge.
"How, how," he said. "Friend Chang," I said. The Chinese Nightingale. Vachel Lindsay. AmPP (3d ed.); HBMV; LiTM (rev. ed.); MAP; MAPA; MoAmPo; NePA; NP; OnSP
How I am harnessed. Grief. Albert Ehrenstein. OnPM
How I am held within a tranquil shell. The Woman with Child. Freda Laughton. OnYI
How I Brought the Good News from Aix to Ghent (or Vice Versa). R. J. Yeatman *and* W. C. Sellar. FiBHP; OnMSP; WhC
How I Came to Rule the World. Marvin Bell. YAP
How I do love thee, Beaumont, and thy Muse. To Francis Beaumont. Ben Jonson. OAEP; OBS; SeEP; TuPP
How I forsook/ Elias and Pisa after, and betook. Giovanni Battista Guarini, *tr. by* Sir Richard Fanshawe. *Fr.* Il Pastor Fido. AWP
How I Love You. John Godfrey Saxe. NeHB
How I loved/ Witness, ye days and nights. Dryden. *Fr.* All for Love, II. LO
"How I should like a birthday!" said the child. Stevenson's Birthday. Katherine Miller. AA
How I was caught. The Missed Train. Thomas Hardy. MaPo
How I would be some night-creature of God. "In the Most Lightsome Darkness." Sister Mary Norbert Körte. ThO
How ill doth he deserve a lover's name. Eternity of Love Protested [*or* Song]. Thomas Carew. ATP; EG; MeLP; OBS; SCEP-2; SeEP
How in Heaven's name did Columbus get over. Columbus. Arthur Hugh Clough. AmFN; DD; MC; PoSC
How Infinite Are Thy Ways. William Force Stead. *Fr.* Uriel. OBMV
("I thought the night without a sound was falling.") TrPWD
How insane was Majnun. Self-Love. Shams Tabrez. OnPM
How instant joy, how clang. Love: Two Vignettes, I. Robert Penn Warren. MeWo
How is man parcell'd out? how ev'ry hour? The Tempest. Henry Vaughan. AnAnS-1; MeP
How is it I can eat bread here and cut meat. Evening Meal in the Twentieth Century. John Holmes. MiAP
How is it proved? The Great Wager. G. A. Studdert-Kennedy. ChIP
How is it, when death comes, the simple things. Remembrance. John Bunker. JKCP (1955 ed.)
How is 't, my Soul, that thous giv'st eyes their sight. To My Soul in Its Blindness. Phineas Fletcher. OxBoCh; SeCL
How Is the Gold Become Dim. Lamentations, IV: 1-5, Bible, *O.T.* ChTr
How It Strikes a Contemporary. Robert Browning. CABL; CTC; GTBS-P; MaVP; MBW-2; NoP; PoVP; PP; ViPo; ViPP
How Jack Found That Beans May go Back on a Chap. Guy Wetmore Carryl. ALV; HoPM; MAP; MoAmPo (1942 ed.)
How Jacke Cade Traiterously Rebelling agaynst His Kyng, Was for His Treasons and Cruell Doinges Wurthely Punyshed. *At. to* William Baldwin. *Fr.* A Mirror for Magistrates. SiCE
How joyous his neigh. Song of the Horse. *Unknown, tr. fr. Navajo Indian.* AWP; JAWP; WBP
How joyously the young sea-mew. The Sea-Mew. Elizabeth Barrett Browning. HBV; OTPC
How kind is night. Nox Benigna. William Pember Reeves. AnNZ
How large that thrush looks on the bare thorn-tree. Winter. Dante Gabriel Rossetti. CBEP; FosPo
How large unto the tiny fly. The Fly. Walter de la Mare. MemP
How larger is remembrance than desire! Ebbtide at Sundown. "Michael Field." CAW
How late the assassins ply their trade tonight. Nausea. E. L. Mayo. MiAP
How life and death in Thee. Upon the Savior's Tomb [*or* To Our Blessed Lord upon the Choice of His Sepulchre]. Richard Crashaw. ACP; MaMe; SCEP-1; StJW
How lightly leaps the youthful chamois. The Glad Young Chamois. Burges Johnson. TSW
How like a marriage is the season of clouds. Cloud Country. James Merrill. NePoEA
How like a well-kept garden is your soul. Moonlight. Paul Verlaine. SyP
How like a winter hath my absence been. Sonnets, XCVII. Shakespeare. ATP; AWP; BEL; CABA; CBEP; CLwM; DiPo; ElL; EnLi-1; EnLoPo; EnRePo; FaBoEn; GTBS; GTBS-D; GTBS-P; GTBS-W; GTSL; JAWP; LiTG; MeWo; NoP; OBEV; OBSC; PAn; PoeP; PoFS; PoRA; ReIE; Sonn; TOP; TrGrPo; VaPo; WBP
How like an angel came I down! Wonder. Thomas Traherne. AnAnS-1; AtBAP; CBEP; CH; LiTB; LiTG; LoBV; MeP; NoP; PoE; PoIE; SCEP-1; SeCePo; SeCeV; SeCL; SeCP; SeCV-2; SeEP; StP; TrGrPo; WHA
How like her! But 'tis she herself. In the Mile End Road. Amy Levy. VA
How like the breath of love the rustling breeze. The Moon in September. Kashiprosad Ghose. ACV
How like the consummation and despair. A Photograph of Isadora Duncan. Robert E. Hayden. PoNe
How like the leper, with his own sad cry. The Buoy-Bell. Charles Tennyson Turner. EtS; PeVV; Sonn; VA
How Like You This? Sir Thomas Wyatt. *See* Lover Showeth How He Is Forsaken of Such as He Sometime Enjoyed, The.
How Lillies [*or* Lilies] Came White. Robert Herrick. AnAnS-2; PoeP; SCEP-2
("White though ye be, yet, lilies, know.") EG
How little fades from earth when sink to rest. Shakespeare. John Sterling. VA
How little it costs if we give it a thought. Much for Little. *Unknown.* SoP
How living are the dead! Immortal. Florence Earle Coates. MaRV
How long ago she planted the hawthorn hedge. The Hawthorn Hedge. Judith Wright. PoAu-2
How long, dear sleeper, must I wait. The Vigil. T. Sturge Moore. POTE
How long false hope, wilt thou mislead myne eyes. *Unknown.* SeCSL
How long, great God, how long must I. The Aspiration. John Norris. LoBV; OxBoCh
How Long Has Trane Been Gone? Jayne Cortez. WSL
How long have I been lying asleep. A Drinking Bout. Liu Chia. OnPM
How long I pleaded I can never guess. Long Pursuit. *Unknown.* UnTE
How long I sailed, and never took a thought. Hartley Coleridge. Sonn
How long in his damp trance young Juan lay. Don Juan and Haidée. Byron. *Fr.* Don Juan. TOP
How long it seems to me since that mild April night. Seaward. Celia Thaxter. AA
How long I've loved thee, and how well. Love's Wisdom. Margaret Deland. AA

How long must we two hide the burning gaze. United. Paulus Silentiarius. AWP
How long, O lion, hast thou fleshless lain? The Lion's Skeleton. Charles Tennyson Turner. NBM; OA; VA
How long, O Lord, shall I forgotten be? Psalm XIII. *Paraphrased by* Sir Philip Sidney. FCP
How long, O Lord, to wait. The Old Pastor. John Banister Tabb. AmP
How long, O sister, how long. The Bells at Midnight. Thomas Bailey Aldrich. PAH
"How long shall fortune faile me now." The Earl of Westmoreland. *Unknown.* ESPB
How Long Shall I Give. *Unknown.* BLRP
How long shall I pine for love? Pining for Love. Francis Beaumont. BoLP
How long shall this like dying life endure. Amoretti, XXV. Spenser. EnRePo; Sonn
How long shall you and I be bound? Water Whirligigs. D. J. Opperman. PeSA
How long she waited for her executioner! Head of Medusa. Marya Zaturenska. MoAmPo
How long sometimes a day appears. Eternity. *Unknown.* SoP
How long this giant hugged and spanned. Windmill on the Cape. William Vincent Sieller. GoYe
How Long This Night Is. *Unknown.* MeEL
How long this way: that everywhere. Two Songs on the Economy of Abundance. James Agee. MAP; MoAmPo
How Long till April? Maurice C. Fields. JKCP (1955 ed.)
How long until the war's end sets you free? Longing. "Michael Lewis." *Fr.* Cherry Blossoms. UnTE
How long will ye slumber? when will ye take heart. Rallying Song. Callinus, *tr. by* H. N. Coleridge. PoFr
How long with vain complaining. Questo di Verde. Thomas Watson. TuPP
How long, young men, unsoldiered, disregarding. A Call to Action. Callinus, *tr. by* T. F. Higham. WaaP
How look'd your love, sweet Shepherd, yestereven. The Orchard by the Shore; a Pastoral. Elinor Sweetman. OBVV
How lost is the little fox at the borders of night. Night of Wind. Frances M. Frost. FaPON; TiPo
How loudly and how surely the musician plays! The Musician. R. P. Lister. UnS
How lovely are the faces of. Marked for His Own. Pauline Prosser-Thompson. SoP
How lovely are the tombs of the dead nymphs. Panope. Edith Sitwell. MoAB; MoBrPo; NP
How lovely are the waters of Babylon. R. N. Currey. *Fr.* Ultimate Exile. BoSA
How lovely are these swans. The Swans. Andrew Young. MoBrPo (1942 ed.); POTE; WePo
How lovely are thy dwellings fair! Psalm LXXXIV. Milton. TrPWD
How Lovely Are Thy Tabernacles. Psalms, LXXXIV: 1-5, Bible, *O.T.* TrJP
How lovely is the heaven of this night. A Beautiful Night [*or* Lines]. Thomas Lovell Beddoes. *Fr.* Fragments Intended for the Dramas. ChER; LoBV; NBM
How lovely is the silence of green, growing things. Let All the Earth Keep Silence. Lucy A. K. Adee. OQP
How lovely is the sound of oars at night. Boats at Night. Edward Shanks. CH; FlW; MCCG; POTE
How lovely it was, after the official fright. The Phenomenon. Karl Shapiro. CMoP; NMP; NYBP
How lovely the elder brother's. Brothers. Gerard Manley Hopkins. OAEP
How Low Is the Lowing Herd. Walt Kelly. FiBHP
How low when angels fall their black descent. The Promise in Disturbance. George Meredith. Modern Love: Prologue. ViPo; VP
How McClellan Took Manassas. *Unknown.* PAH
How McDougal Topped the Score. Thomas E. Spencer. PoAu-1
How many a father have I seen. In Memoriam A. H. H., LIII. Tennyson. BEL; EnLi-2; EPN; OAEP; TOP; ViPo; VP
How many a thing which we cast to the ground. Modern Love, XLI. George Meredith. EnLit; HBV; ViPo; VP
How many a time have I. Swimming. Byron. *Fr.* The Two Foscari. GN
How Many Bards Gild the Lapses of Time. Keats. EnRP; EPN; MERP
How many blessed groups this hour are bending. Sabbath Sonnet. Felicia Dorothea Hemans. Sonn
How many buds, how many sticky butts. Spring. Boris Pasternak. LiTW
How many buttons are missing today? Nobody Knows but Mother. Mary Morrison. BLPA
How many colors here do we see set. The Spectrum. Cosmo Monkhouse. VA
How many dawns, chill from his rippling rest. To Brooklyn Bridge [*or* Proem]. Hart Crane. *Fr.* The Bridge. AmP; AmPP; AP; CABA; CBV; CMoP; CoBMV; CrMA; DiPo; ExPo; FaBoEn; GTBS-W; HT; ILP; LiTA; LiTM; MoAB; MoAmPo (1950 ed.); MoPo; NePA; NoP; OxBA; PIA; PoDB; PoE; PoIE; PoPl; ReMP; SeCeV; TDP; ThLM
How many days has my [*or* the] baby to play? Mother Goose. BoTP; OTPC (1946 ed.); OxNR; PPL; TiPo
How many days to Christmas? Counting the Days. James S. Tippett. ChBR
How many drag the marriage chain. Epigram. Royall Tyler. StP
How many equal with the Argive queen. The Power of Poets. Ben Jonson. *Fr.* Epistle to Elizabeth, Countess of Rutland. WHA
How many Excedrin'd you take? Five? Trailer Park. Lewis MacAdams. ANYP
How Many Foolish Things. Michael Drayton. *See* How Many Paltry, Foolish, Painted Things.
How many have pretended to love. Cock. Anthony Ostroff. NYTB
How Many Heavens. Edith Sitwell. MoPW; MoRP
How many humble hearts have dipped. To a Post-Office Inkwell. Christopher Morley. InP; PoLF
How many kisses do I ask. To Anne. Sir William Stirling-Maxwell. HBV
How many kisses, Lesbia, you ask. Ad Lesbiam. Catullus, *tr. by* Niall Sheridan. OxBI
How many lives, made beautiful and sweet. Giotto's Tower. Longfellow. CoBA
How many miles [is it] to Babylon [*or* Barley Bridge]? Mother Goose. BoTP; CBEP; ExPo; FaBoCh; LoGBV; MoShBr; OxBoLi; OxNR; PCH; SiTL
How many million Aprils came. Blue Squills. Sara Teasdale. HBMV
How Many New Years Have Grown Old. *Unknown.* EIL
How many niggers did you say were out there? Auditions. Ruby C. Saunders. WSL
How Many Nights. Galway Kinnell. CBV; NaP
How many of the body's health complain. Soul-Sickness. Jones Very. AP
How many of us ever stop to think. Music. *Unknown.* MaRV
How many paltry, foolish, painted things. Sonnet. Michael Drayton. Idea, VI. BWP; CBEP; EIL; EnLoPo; EnRePo; InP; LoBV; NoP; OBSC; ReEn; ReIE; SiCE; TuPP
How many pipes have dittied unto thee. April. John Francis O'Donnell. IrPN
How many pounds does the baby weigh. Weighing the Baby. Ethel Lynn Beers. HBV; PoToHe (new ed.)
"How many?" said our good Captain. Sea Ballad. Sydney Dobell. *Fr.* Balder. VA
How Many Seconds in a Minute? Christina Rossetti. SiSoSe
How many strive to force a way. Forcing a Way. *Unknown.* NA
How many summers, love. The Poet's Song to His Wife. "Barry Cornwall." HBV; VA
How many suns have blazed and died within. Musings of an Insomniac. Edith Ogutsch. FiSC
How many thousand of my poorest subjects. The Cares of Majesty [*or* Soliloquy on Sleep]. Shakespeare. King Henry IV, Pt. II, *fr.* III, i. FiP; LiTB; TreF
How many thousands never heard the name. Samuel Daniel. *Fr.* Musophilus. PP
How Many Times? Thomas Lovell Beddoes. *Fr.* Torrismond. ELP; MeWo
How Many Times Do I Love Thee, Dear? Thomas Lovell Beddoes. *See* Song: "How many times do I love thee, dear?"
How many times these low feet staggered. Emily Dickinson.

AmPP (5th ed.); AP; CABA; MaPo; MWA-2; NoP; PoEL-5; ReMP
How many times they do come (if you will receive it). Care in Heaven. John Heath-Stubbs. BoPe
How many verses have I thrown. Verses Why Burnt. Walter Savage Landor. VA
How Many Voices. Walter Savage Landor. EPN
How Many Ways. John Masefield. *Fr.* Sonnets ("Long long ago"). LiTB
("How many ways, how many times.") WGRP
How many ways can you bring me ten? Making Tens. M. M. Hutchinson. BoTP
How Marigolds Came Yellow. Robert Herrick. ChTr
How marvellous and fair a thing. Springtime in Cookham Dean. Cecil Roberts. HBMV
How may I sing, unworthy I. Maria Immaculata. Condé Benoist Pallen. JKCP
How may the beauty of bright birds atone. Terror in Beauty. M. Eugenie Perry. TwCaPo
How memory cuts away the years. Autumn. Jean Starr Untermeyer. HBMV; MAP; MCCG; MoAmPo; NeMA; PFY
How monarchs die is easily explained. On a Royal Demise. Thomas Hood. FiBHP; PV
How most unnatural-seeming, yet how proper. Sirocco at Deyá. Robert Graves. MoVE
How most unworthy, echoing in mine ears. Frederick Goddard Tuckerman. *Fr.* Sonnets. AP
How mournful seems, in broken dreams. Not Lost, but Gone Before. Caroline Elizabeth Sarah Norton. BLRP; PaPo; WBLP
How Much I Owe. Robert Murray McCheyne. SoP
How much living have you done? The Poet Speaks. Georgia Douglas Johnson. AmNP
How Much Longer Will I Be Able to Inhabit the Divine Sepulcher. John Ashbery. NeAP
How much more. The Process. Robert Kelly. CoPo
How much, preventing God, how much I owe. Grace. Emerson. AmPP; CoBA; MWA-1; NoP; TrPWD
How much the heart may bear and yet not break! Endurance. Elizabeth Akers Allen. HBV; PoToHe
How much we pay to say, "*Je suis.*" Samuel Hoffenstein. *Fr.* As the Crow Flies. WhC
How much wood would a woodchuck chuck. If a Woodchuck Would Chuck. *Unknown.* FaPON; StVeCh (1955 ed.); TiPo
How Music's Made. Dilys Laing. ELU
How mutable is every thing that here. Meditations for July 26, 1666. Philip Pain. SCAP
How, my dear Mary,—are you critic-bitten? The Witch of Atlas. Shelley. ERoP-2
How My Songs of Her Began. Philip Bourke Marston. HBV; VA
How my thoughts betray me! A Prayer for Recollection. *Unknown.* KiLC
How natural the way that they have greeted each other. The Inner Significance of the Statues Seated outside the Boston Public Library. Walter Conrad Arensberg. AnAmPo
How near am I now to a happiness. Thomas Middleton. *Fr.* Women Beware of Women. LO
How near me came the hand of Death. A Widow's Hymn. George Wither. LO; OBEV
How Nice. Mary Dixon Thayer. GFA
How nice it is to eat! Beautiful Meals. T. Sturge Moore. BoTP
How nice to be a local swan. Sitting Pretty. Margaret Fishback. PoLF
How No Age Is Content. Earl of Surrey. EIL; LiTB; LoBV; SiCE; TuPP
(Laid in My Quiet Bed.) CH; EnRePo; FCP; InvP
(Youth and Age.) SiPS
How now could body-soul's symbol be this. The White Rat. Marguerite Young. MoPo
How now my noble cossin—what in blacke! John Webster. *Fr.* The White Devil, III, ii. AtBAP
How now, spirit? whither [*or* whether] wander you? Puck and the Fairy. Shakespeare. *Fr.* A Midsummer Night's Dream, II, i. AtBAP; GN
How now? what noise is that? Shakespeare. *Fr.* Hamlet, IV, v. AtBAP
How odd/ Of God. Epigrams, III [*or* The Chosen People]. W. N. Ewer. ALV; OtMeF; SiTL
How of the Virgin Mother Shall I Sing? Ennodius, *tr. fr. Latin.* *Fr.* Hymnus Sanctae Mariae. ISi
How oft against the sunset sky or moon. Wild Geese. Frederick Peterson. HBV; HBVY; OTPC (1923 ed.)
How oft am I for rhyme to seek? Swift. *Fr.* To Dr. Delany. PP
How oft amid the heaped and bedded hay. Written in July, 1824. Mary Russell Mitford. OBRV
How oft do they their silver bowers leave. The Ministering Angels. Spenser. *Fr.* The Faerie Queene, II, iii. OBSC
How Oft Has the Banshee Cried. Thomas Moore. AnIV; AWP; JAWP; WBP
How oft have I my dear and cruel foe. Sir Thomas Wyatt. FCP
How oft I dream of childhood days, of tricks we used to play. Rosie Nell. *Unknown.* AS
How oft I prayed to hold her in my arms. Faint Heart. Rufinus. ErPo
How oft in schoolboy-days, from the school's sway. Frederick Goddard Tuckerman. *Fr.* Sonnets. MAmP; Sonn
How oft I've watch'd thee from the garden croft. Orion. Charles Tennyson Turner. VA
How oft some passing word will tend. Our Mother. *Unknown.* PEDC
How oft when men are at the point of death. Romeo's Last Words. Shakespeare. *Fr.* Romeo and Juliet, V, iii. AtBAP; FiP; MemP
"How oft, when pressed to marriage." Pope. *Fr.* Eloïsa to Abelard. ViBoPo
How oft, when thou, my music, music play'st. Sonnets, CXXVIII. Shakespeare. EIL; EnLi-1 (1949 ed.); EnLit; ILP; MemP; ReEn; ReIE
How Often. Ben King. BOHV; HBV
How often does a man need to see a woman? The Word Made Flesh. W. J. Turner. OBMV
How often, for some trivial wrong. Retaliation. Margaret E. Bruner. PoToHe
How often have I now outwatched the night. John Addington Symonds. *Fr.* Stella Maris. PoVP
How often have we known a dog to be. Beyond the Grave. Margaret E. Bruner. PoToHe
How often I turn round. The Fear. Andrew Young. GTBS-D
How often in the summer-tide. Across the Fields to Anne. Richard Burton. HBV
How often should we think of this, that we. Meditations for August 1, 1666. Philip Pain. SCAP
How Often Sit I. Arthur Hugh Clough. *Fr.* Blank Misgivings of a Creature Moving About in Worlds Not Realized. EPN
("How often sit I, poring o'er.") GTBS-D
How often, these hours, have I heard the monotonous crool of a dove. The Dove. Walter de la Mare. CBV
How often we neglect a friend. Atonement. Margaret E. Burner. MaRV; PoToHe
How often we overslept. Adhesive: for Earlene. Robert Hass. YAP
How Old Are You? *At. to* Edward Tuck *and to* H. S. Fritsch. PoLF; PoToHe
(Age.) BiCB; PoRL
"How old art thou?" said the garrulous gourd. The Gourd and the Palm. *Unknown.* OTPC
How Old Brown Took Harper's Ferry. Edmund Clarence Stedman. HBV; MC; OnMSP; PaA; PAH; PAP; PoNe
(John Brown of Osawatomie.) PFY; PoFr
"How old is God? Has He grey hair?" S. M. B. Piatt. *Fr.* Questions of the Hour. MemP
How Old Is My Heart. Christopher Brennan. *Fr.* The Wanderer. BoAV; PoAu-1
How old is thirty-six, about? Prattle. John Ciardi. BiCB
How old may Phillis [*or* Phyllis] be, you ask. Phillis's [*or* Phyllis's] Age. Matthew Prior. BOHV; CEP; EiCL; EnLoPo
How Old Ought I to Be? *Unknown.* SoP
How old was Mary out of whom you cast. Charlotte Mew. *Fr.* Madeleine in Church. LO; MoAB; MoBrPo
How One Winter Came in the Lake Region. Wilfred Campbell. CaP; OBCV; PeCV; TDP
How Paddy Stole the Rope. *Unknown.* BLPA
How passionately I will my life away. Living. William Dean Howells. AmePo
How peaceable it seems for lonely men. The Crow. John Clare. WePo

How pitiful are little folk. Creeds. Willard Wattles. HMBV; InP; MaRV; OQP
How pitiful is her sleep. In Memory of Kathleen. Kenneth Patchen. MoAmPo
How placid, how divinely sweet. Meandering Wye. Robert Bloomfield. *Fr.* The Banks of Wye. OBNC
How plain soe'er the house or poor the guests. The King. Mary Frances Butts. OQP
How pleasant, as the sun declines, to view. Sunset in the Lake Country. Wordsworth. *Fr.* An Evening Walk. EPN
How pleasant is Saturday night. Saturday Night. *Unknown.* SAS
How Pleasant Is This Flowery Plain. *Unknown.* OBS
How pleasant it is that always. Song. Florence Smith. BLPA
How pleasant the life of a bird must be. Birds in Summer. Mary Howitt. HH; MPB; OTPC; PRWS
How Pleasant to Know Mr. Lear. Edward Lear. CBEP; ChTr; FiBHP; GoTP; ML; WhC
(Author of the "Pobble," The.) OTPC
(By Way of Preface.) GTBS-P; InvP; NBM; OnPP; OTD; OxBoLi; PoEL-5; PoSa
(Lines to a Young Lady.) InMe; NA
(Mr. Lear.) RIS
(Self Portrait.) ShBV-4
(Self-Portrait of the Laureate of Nonsense.) FaBoCh; SiTL
How pleased within my native bowers. Song: The Landskip [*or* The Landscape]. William Shenstone. CBEP; CEP; OBEC; SeCePo
How poor, how rich, how abject, how august. Man. Edward Young. *Fr.* Night Thoughts. MaRV
How prone we are. Prayer. Connie Calenberg. SoP
How prone we are to sin; how sweet were made. "And Forgive Us Our Trespasses." Aphra Behn. MeWo; PeRV
How provoked you get. Names (For Mother). Elwyn Chauncey West. DD
How pure, and frail, and white. The Annunciation. Adelaide Anne Procter. JKCP
How pure at heart and sound in head. In Memoriam A. H. H., XCIV. Tennyson. CoBE; EPN; ViPo; VP
How pure the hearts of lovers as they walk. Prothalamium. May Sarton. HW; NePoAm
How quickly doth the reader pass away. Ad Lectorem. Thomas Bastard. SiCE; TuPP
How quiet the day is. The Leaf. John Williams. NePoAm-2
How quietly in ruined state. Aix-la-Chappelle, 1945. Edgar Bowers. NePoEA
How ran lithe monkeys through the leaves! Monkeys. Joaquin Miller. *Fr.* With Walker in Nicaragua. OA; PCH
How rare to be born a human being! Hunting, XVI. Gary Snyder. *Fr.* Myths & Texts. NaP
How Red the Rose That Is the Soldier's Wound. Wallace Stevens. *Fr.* Esthétique du Mal. CMoP; FaBoMo; WaP
(Soldier's Wound, The.) WaaP
How rewarding to know Mr. Smith. Mr. Smith. William Jay Smith. FiBHP
How rich, O Lord! how fresh thy visits are! Unprofitablenes. Henry Vaughan. AnAnS-1; AtBAP; MeP; SCEP-1; SeCV-1
How rich the wave, in front, imprest. Lines Written Near Richmond, upon the Thames, at Evening. Wordsworth. EiCL; OBEC
How richly, with ridiculous display. On a Politician. Hilaire Belloc. PV
How Robin Hood Rescued the Widow's Sons. *Unknown.* *See* Robin Hood and the Widow's Three Sons.
How Roses Came Red. Robert Herrick. BEL; CavP; ChTr; EnL; PoeP
How rough the sea! On Izumo Cliff. Basho. OnPM
How sad doth Dives look? how deep he groans? The Death of Dives. Richard Baxter. *Fr.* Madness. PeRV
How sad if, by some strange new law. Suppose. Anne Reeve Aldrich. HBV
How sad it is to be a woman! Woman. Fu Hsüan. WoL
How sad the note of that funereal drum. On the Death of Commodore Oliver Hazard Perry. John G. C. Brainard. PAH
How sad's a scorch'd lovers fate. *Unknown.* SeCSL
How Samson Bore Away the Gates of Gaza. Vachel Lindsay. MoRP; NP
How say you? Let us, O my dove. Robert Browning. *Fr.* Two in the Campagna. BoLP
How see you Echo? When she calls I see. Echo. Viscountess Grey of Fallodon. CH; GBV (1922 ed.)
"How seldom, friend! a good great man inherits." The Good Great Man [*or* Complaint]. Samuel Taylor Coleridge. EPN; HBV; WhC
How Shall a Man Fore-Doomed. Three Sonnets, II. Hartley Coleridge. NCEP
How shall come the kingdom holy. An Affirmation. Minot Judson Savage. MaRV
"How shall I a habit break?" A Builder's Lesson. John Boyle O'Reilly. PoLF; PoToHe (new ed.)
How shall I address Thee, O God? how shall I praise thee? *Unknown.* *Fr.* Nanak and the Sikhs. WGRP
How shall I array my love? The Question. Frederick Goddard Tuckerman. AP
"How shall I be a poet?" Poeta Fit, Non Nascitur. "Lewis Carroll." NBM
How Shall I Build. Wilfrid Scawen Blunt. CAW; JKCP
How Shall I Ever Come to Any Good? Winfield Townley Scott. CBV; FiMAP
"How shall I find it, and which way lies?" The Pathway to Paradise. Ozora Stearns Davis. OQP
How shall I follow Him I serve? Following. Joseph Conder. SoP
How shall I forsake wisdom? In Praise of Wisdom. Solomon ibn Gabirol. TrJP
How shall I guard my soul so that it be. The Song of Love. Rainer Maria Rilke. AWP
How shall I keep April. Foreboding. Hazel Hall. HBMV
How shall I paint thee?—Be this naked stone. The River Duddon, III. Wordsworth. MERP
How shall I plead my cause, when you, my judge. Cleopatra and Antony. Dryden. *Fr.* All For Love, II. FiP
How shall I report. *See* Howe shall I report.
How shall I speak of doom, and ours in special. Tales from a Family Album. Donald Justice. NePoEA-2; TwAmPo
How shall I tell the measure of my love? Thysia, XLV. Morton Luce. HBV
How shall my tongue expresse that hallow'd fire? Francis Quarles. *Fr.* Emblems. AnAnS-1; MeP
How shall the bayonet and bomb. Design for Peace. Janet Norris Bangs. PGD
How shall the river learn. Max Schmitt in a Single Scull. Richmond Lattimore. NePoAm-2
How shall the wine be drunk, or the woman known? A Voice from under the Table. Richard Wilbur. AmPP (5th ed.); NePoEA; SeCeV (1967 ed.); ToPo
How shall we adorn. Angle of Geese. N. Scott Momaday. QFR
How shall we answer? And Rest in a Flame. Francis Maguire. JKCP (1955 ed.)
How Shall We Honor Lincoln. Thomas Curtis Clark. PoToHe (1941 ed.)
How Shall We Honor Them? Edwin Markham. OQP; PGD
How shall we keep it. Nineteen Twenty-six. Wilson MacDonald. MaRV
How shall we know it is the last good-bye? The Last Good-by. Louise Chandler Moulton. AA
How shall we please this Age? To Nysus. Sir Charles Sedley. PeRV
How shall we praise the magnificence of the dead. Tetélestai. Conrad Aiken. CMoP; LiTA; LiTM (rev. ed.); MAP; MAPA; MoAB; MoAmPo; PoDB
How Shall We Rise to Greet the Dawn? Sir Osbert Sitwell. WGRP
How shall we summon you? Hymn to Chance. Phelps Putnam. TwAmPo; WoL
How she grew old happened in fine-darned places. The People, II. "Robin Hyde." AnNZ
How She Resolved to Act. Merrill Moore. MAP; MeWo; MoAmPo; NeMA
How shocking the stocking that matches the pink. Color Blind. Carol Paine. PV
How Should I Be So Pleasant? Sir Thomas Wyatt. FCP; LoBV; SiPS
(Betrayal.) OBSC
How should I find speech. Person, or a Hymn on and to the Holy Ghost. Margaret Avison. PeCV (1967 ed.)
How should I love my best? Madrigal. Lord Herbert of Cherbury. AnAnS-2; PoEL-2; SeCP; ViBoPo
How should I praise thee, Lord! how should my rymes. The Temper. George Herbert. AnAnS-1; AtBAP; FosPo;

MaMe; MeP; MePo; NoP; OBS; OxBoCh; PoEL-2; PoFS; SCEP-1; SeCL; WHA
How should I praise theise sug'red plenties. *Unknown.* SeCSL
How Should I Your True Love Know. Shakespeare. *Fr.* Hamlet, IV, v. EnLoPo; InPo; LiTB; LiTG; LiTL; PoRA; QFR; ViBoPo
(Ophelia's Song.) ChTr; OBSC
(Ophelia's Songs, 1.) AnFE; TrGrPo
(Song.) CH
"How should I your true love know." The Friar of Orders Grey, 3 [*or* An Old Song Ended]. Dante Gabriel Rossetti. GoBC; PoVP
How should the world be luckier if this house. Upon a House Shaken by the Land Agitation. W. B. Yeats. CMoP
How shril are silent tears? when sin got head. Admission. Henry Vaughan. AnAnS-1; MeP
How sick I get. Father. Paul Carroll. NeAP
How silent comes the water round that bend. Minnows [*or* From the Bridge]. Keats. *Fr.* I Stood Tiptoe. GN; MyFE; PCH
How silent lurks this perfect anarchist. Arachnida, Female. Aletha Humphreys. FiSC
How sits this citie, late most populous. The Lamentations of Jeremy. John Donne. MaMe
How Sleep the Brave. William Collins. CBEP; DD; GN; HBV; HBVY; HH; OBEV; OtMeF; OTPC; TreF
(Ode: "How sleep the brave, who sink to rest.") CBV; EiCP; ELP; LoBV; NeHB; PoFr; ViBoPo
(Ode Written in 1746.) GTBS; GTBS-D; GTBS-P; GTBS-W; GTSE; ShBV-3; TrGrPo; WHA
(Ode Written in the Beginning of the Year 1746.) ATP; AWP; BEL; BWP; CEP; CoBE; EiCL; EiPP; EnL; EnLi-2; EnPE; EnRP; ExPo; InPo; JAWP; NoP; OAEP; OBEC; OuHeWo; PoE; PoEL-3; PoFS; SeCeV; TOP; WBP
(Sleep of the Brave, The.) OHIP
"How Sleep the Brave." Walter de la Mare. TOP
How sleep the brave who sink to rest. On a Watchman Asleep at Midnight. James Thomas Fields. CenHV
How slight a thing may set one's fancy drifting. Honey Dripping from the Comb. James Whitcomb Riley. AA
How slow they are awakening, these trees. Plain Fare (Night Thoughts on Crossing the Continent by Bus). Daryl Hine. CBV; CoAP
How slow time moves when torment stops the clock! The Conclusion. Delmore Schwartz. TwAmPo
How slowly creeps the hand of Time. The Churchyard. Robert Buchanan. HBV; VA
How slowly I sucked off. Ed Sanders. ANYP
How slowly learns the child at school. Citizenship; Form 8889512, Sub-Section Q. G. K. Chesterton. OxBoLi
How slowly moves the snail, that builds. Wild Oats. W. H. Davies. ACV
How slowly the hours pass. You Will Grieve. Guillaume Apollinaire. OnPM
How small a tooth hath mined the season's heart! Frost. Edith M. Thomas. AA
"How smooth's your brow, my lady Elspat!" Lady Elspat. *Unknown.* BuBa
How soon a mighty throne can fall. Sovereignty. Leslie Savage Clark. ChIP
How soon, alas, the hours are over. Plays. Walter Savage Landor. HBV; VA
How soon doth man decay! Mortification. George Herbert. AnAnS-1; MaMe; MeP; MePo; OAEP; PoFS; SeCP; ViBoPo
How Soon Hath Time. Milton. *See* On His Having Arrived at the Age of Twenty-three.
How sound are ye sleeping, comrades. Bitter Question. Arthur R. Macdougall, Jr. PGD
How splendid in the morning glows. Hassan's Serenade. James Elroy Flecker. *Fr.* Hassan. OBEV (new ed.)
How spoke the King, in his crucial hour victorious? King of the Belgians. Marion Couthouy Smith. PAH
How Stands the Glass Around? James Wolfe. PAH
How startling to find the portraits of the gods. Mythological Sonnets, XVI. Roy Fuller. ErPo; Sonn
How stately stand yon pines upon the hill. Spring to Winter. George Crabbe. *Fr.* The Ancient Mansion. ChTr
How steadfastly she worked at it! The Cradle. Austin Dobson. VA
How still. Sea Calm. Langston Hughes. LOW
How still, how happy! These are words. Emily Brontë. OBNC
How still, how very still the air is. The Unwilling Guest; an Urban Dialogue. Horace Gregory. CrMA
How still it is here in the woods. Solitude. Archibald Lampman. BoNaP; CBEP; ExPo; OBCV; PeCV
How still the day is, and the air how bright! By the Wood. Robert Nichols. ChMP; HBMV; MMA; NP
How Still the Hawk. Charles Tomlinson. LiTM (1970 ed.)
How still the morning of the hallow'd day! Sunday Morning. James Grahame. *Fr.* The Sabbath. OBRV
How still the room is! But a while ago. In Death. Mary Emily Bradley. AA
How still the sea! behold; how calm the sky! The Sixth Pastoral [*or* Pastoral Landscape]. Ambrose Philips. *Fr.* Pastorals. CEP; OBEC
How still this quiet cornfield is to-night! August, 1914. John Masefield. HBV
How straight it flew, how long it flew. Seaside Golf. John Betjeman. PoPl; SD
How strange and pitiful that man. Values. Leslie Savage Clark. ChIP
How strange it is that, in the after age. Praeterita ex Instantibus. William Douw Lighthall. VA
How strange it is to wake. The Shadow of Night. Coventry Patmore. CH
How strange it seems! These Hebrews in their graves. The Jewish Cemetery at Newport. Longfellow. AmP; AmPP; AnNE; AP; ForPo; HT; MAmP; MWA-1; NoP; OxBA; PoE; PoIE (1970 ed.); PPON
How Strange Love Is, in Every State of Consciousness. Delmore Schwartz. MoLP
How strange that grass should sing. Quatrains. Gwendolyn B. Bennett. CDC
How strange the sculptures that adorn these towers! Divina Commedia, II. Longfellow. AmePo; AmP; AmPP; AnAmPo; AnFE; AnNE; AP; APA; CoAnAm; CoBA; DiPo; GoBC; ILP; MWA-1; NePA; NoP; OuHeWo; OxBA; PoE; PoFS; Sonn; SeCeV; TOP
How strange to awake in a city. Hearing Men Shout at Night on MacDougal Street. Robert Bly. CAD
How strange to think of giving up all ambition! Watering the Horse. Robert Bly. NaP
How subtle-secret is your smile! Oscar Wilde. *Fr.* The Sphinx. MoBrPo; UnTE
How sweet and lovely dost thou make the shame. Sonnets, XCV. Shakespeare. CBEP; EP; MasP; PoeP; ReEn; TrGrPo
How sweet and silent is the place. Communion Hymn. Alice Freeman Palmer. MaRV; TrPWD
How Sweet I Roamed from Field to Field. Blake. *See* Song: "How sweet I roamed from field to field."
How sweet is harmless solitude! Solitude. Mary Molineux. CavP
How sweet is the shepherd's sweet lot! The Shepherd. Blake. *Fr.* Songs of Innocence. BoPe; BoTP; CBEP; EiPP; EnRP; ExPo; GaP; GoTP; HBV; LoBV; OBEC; OTPC; PoRh; ThWaDe; TiPo (1959 ed.); TOP; TVC
How sweet it is, at first approach of morn. Oliver Goldsmith, the Younger. *Fr.* The Rising Village. OBCV
How sweet only to delight in lambs and laugh by streams. Sonnet. Rex Warner. LO
How sweet the answer echo makes. Echo [*or* Echoes]. Thomas Moore. CBEP; ELP; GoBC; GTBS; GTBS-D; GTBS-P; GTBS-W; GTSL; OxBI
How sweet the harmonies of afternoon! The Blackbird. Frederick Tennyson. HBV; VA
How sweet the moon is climbing heaven's hill! Moonlight. Edward Moxon. OBRV
How Sweet the Moonlight Sleeps upon This Bank! Shakespeare. *Fr.* The Merchant of Venice, V, i. BoC; MemP; PoG; TreFS; TrGrPo
(In Tune with the Infinite.) MaRV
(Moonlight.) OHFP
(Sweet Harmony.) MuSP
How Sweet the Name of Jesus Sounds. John Newton. *See* Name of Jesus, The.
How sweet the tuneful bells' responsive peal! Sonnet: At Ostend [*or* At Ostend *or* The Bells of Ostend]. William Lisle Bowles. EnRP; ERoP-1; OBEC; Sonn
How Sweet Thy Precious Gift of Rest. Menahem ben Makhir of Ratisbon, *tr. fr. Hebrew by* Herbert Loewe. TrJP
How sweet to wear a shape of snow. Duck in Central Park. Frances Higginson Savage. GoYe

How sweet, when weary, dropping on a bank. Summer. John Clare. BoNaP
How sweetly doth My Master sound! My Master! The Odour. George Herbert. AnAnS-1; MaMe; MeP; OBS
How sweetly on the autumn scene. The Hawkbit. Sir Charles G. D. Roberts. HBV
How sweetly on the wood-girt town. Pentucket. Whittier. MC; PAH
How sweetly sings this stream. Laurence Dakin. *Fr.* Pyramus and Thisbe, III, iii. CaP
How swiftly it dries. Burial Song. *Unknown.* WoL
How Tedious and Tasteless the Hours. John Newton. SoP
(Greenfields.) AS
How tender the heart grows. Nightfall. Una Marson. PoNe
How tenderly the evening creeps between. Evening. Hugh McCrae. PoAu-1
How terrible their trust, the little leaves. April, 1942. Mark Van Doren. WaP
How that vast heaven intitled First is rolled. Sonnet. William Drummond of Hawthornden. ElL
How the Abbey of Saint Werewulf Juxta Slingsby Came by Brother Fabian's Manuscript. Sebastian Evans. PeVV
How the Babes in the Wood Showed They Couldn't Be Beaten. Guy Wetmore Carryl. RIS
How the blithe lark runs up the golden stair. The Skylark. Frederick Tennyson. GN; HBV
How the body burns and races. Homage to Aesop. Chana Faerstein. NYTB
How the Consolations of Philosophy Worked Out in Actual Practice. Anthony Haden-Guest. HYE
How the Crow-Hen Killed the Black Snake. *Unknown, tr. fr. Sanskrit by* Arthur W. Ryder. *Fr.* The Panchatantra. OuHeWo
How the *Cumberland* Went Down. Silas Weir Mitchell. MC; PAH
How the Daughters Come Down at Dunoon. Henry Cholmondeley-Pennell. BOHV
How the Fire Queen Crossed the Swamp. Will H. Ogilvie. PoAu-1
How the Flowers Grow. "Gabriel Setoun." MPB; SoPo
How the Friends Met. James Tate. PIA
How the Froggies Go to Sleep, *sel.* J. K. Nutting.
Little, Wee Froggies, The. SAS
How the Grain Grows. *Unknown, tr. fr. Russian by* W. R. S. Ralston. OnPM
How the Great Guest Came. Edwin Markham. BeLS; BLPA
(Great Guest Comes, The.) WBLP
How the greenest of wheat rang gold at his birth! For My Son. John Frederick Nims. MiAP
How the Helpmate of Blue-Beard Made Free with a Door. Guy Wetmore Carryl. InMe
How the Kite Learned to Fly. *Unknown. See* How the Little Kite Learned to Fly.
How the Leaves Came Down. "Susan Coolidge." DD; HBV; HBVY; MPB; OTPC; PRWS; TVC
How the leaves sing to the wind! In the Golden Birch. Jane Elizabeth Gostwycke Roberts. VA
How the Little Kite Learned to Fly. *Unknown, at. to* Katharine Pyle. HBV; HBVY; OTPC; TVC
(How the Kite Learned to Fly.) GFA
How the Lover Perisheth in His Delight, As the Fly in the Fire. Sir Thomas Wyatt. Sonn
("Some fowls there be that have so perfect sight.") FCP
How the Money Rolls In. *Unknown. See* My Sister She Works in a Laundry.
How the moon triumphs through the endless nights. James Thomson. *Fr.* The City of Dreadful Night. GTSL
How the mountains talked together. A Farewell to Agassiz. Oliver Wendell Holmes. ImOP
How the Old Horse Won the Bet. Oliver Wendell Holmes. AnNE
How the people held their breath. Jesse James. *Unknown.* ATP
How the red road stretched before us, mile on mile. Independence. Nancy Cato. PoAu-2
How the swift river runs bright to its doom. At the Leap of the Waters. Edward F. Garesché. JKCP
How the waters closed above him. Emily Dickinson. PoEL-5
How the Waters Come Down at Ladore. Robert Southey. *See* The Cataract of Ladore.
How the Women Will Stop War. Aristophanes, *tr. fr. Greek by* B. B. Rogers. *Fr.* Lysistrata. WaaP
How they are provided for upon the earth. Beginners. Walt Whitman. AA
How They Bite. *Unknown.* SD
How They Brought the Good News from Ghent to Aix. Robert Browning. BBV (1923 ed.); BEL; BeLS; BoChLi; EnLi-2 (1949 ed.); FaBoBe; FaFP; GN; GoTP; HBV; HBVY; HoPM; MBW-2; MCCG; MemP; OnSP; OTPC; PAn; PaPo; PCD; PeVV; PoPo; PoVP; PTK; RoGo; ShBV-1; StVeCh; TiPo (1952 ed.); TOP; TreF; VA; ViPo; ViPP; WePo
How They Came from the Blue Snows. Arnold Kenseth. PPON
How They Do It. J. C. Squire. *See* Poor Old Man, The.
How they have learned the secrets of the ether! The Patient Scientists. Bertha Gerneaux Woods. MaRV; OQP
How They Made the Golem. John R. Colombo. MoCV
How They Sleep. *Unknown.* PPL
How Thomas Wolsey Did Arise unto Great Authority and Government, His Maner of Life, Pompe, and Dignity, and How Hee Fell Downe into Great Disgrace, and Was Arrested of High Treason. Thomas Churchyard. *Fr.* A Mirror for Magistrates. SiCE
How those loose rocks got piled up here like this. 18,000 Feet. Ed Roberson. PoNe (1970 ed.)
How Time Consumeth All Earthly Things. *Unknown. See* Proper Sonnet, A, How Time Consumeth. . .
How time reverses. For My Contemporaries. J. V. Cunningham. CoAP; PoSa; PP
How to Ask and Have. Samuel Lover. *See* Ask and Have.
How to Be Happy. *Unknown.* BLPA
How to Catch Tiddlers. Brian Jones. FIW
How to Catch Unicorns. William Rose Benét. HBMV; TSW
How to Change the U. S. A. Harry Edwards. NBP
How to Choose a Mistress. Edmund Prestwich. CLwM
How to Eat Watermelons. Frank L. Stanton. BOHV
How to explain that on the day. Irreconcilables. Arthur Gregor. NYBP
How to Forget. Rebecca Foresman. PoToHe (new ed.)
(If.) WBLP
How to Get There. Frank O'Hara. FRC
How to Give. *Unknown.* BLRP
How to Go and Forget. Edwin Markham. HBMV
How to keep—is there any any, is there none such. The Leaden Echo and the Golden Echo. Gerard Manley Hopkins. BrPo; CMoP; CoBMV; DTC; EnLi-2 (1949 ed.); FaFP; GTBS-D; GTBS-P; GTBS-W; LiTB; LiTM; LoBV; MasP; MoAB; MoBrPo; MoVE; OAEP (2d ed.); OBMV; OBNC; PAn; PoDB; ViPo; VP
How to Kill. Keith Douglas. ChMP
How to Know the Wild Animals. Carolyn Wells. *See* How to Tell the Wild Animals.
How to Make a Man of Consequence. Mark Lemon. BOHV
How to Raise a Son. Martial, *tr. fr. Latin by* L. R. Lind. LiTW
How to Read Me. Walter Savage Landor. VA
How to Recognize a Snark. "Lewis Carroll." *Fr.* The Hunting of the Snark, II. MPB
("Come, listen, my men, while I tell you again.") BOHV
(Snark, The.) TSW
How to Succeed. Arnold Kemp. WSL
How to Tell Goblins from Elves. Monica Shannon. FaPON; TiPo
How to Tell Juan Don from Another. Gardner E. Lewis. FiBHP
How to Tell the Top of a Hill. John Ciardi. SoPo
How to Tell the Wild Animals. Carolyn Wells. FaFP; FaPON; FiBHP; HBVY; MaC; MPB; RePo; TiPo; TSW; UTS
(How to Know the Wild Animals.) GoTP
How to the Singer Comes the Song? Richard Watson Gilder. WGRP
How to Treat Elves. Morris Bishop. FiBHP; PoPl
How to Walk in a Crowd. Robert Hershon. ThO
How to win her. A Serious Poem. Ernest Walsh. ErPo
How to Write a Letter. Elizabeth Turner. MoShBr; OTPC (1923 ed.)
How tranquil is the life. The Life Removed. Luis de León. WoL
How true it is when I am sad. Work. John W. Thompson. PoToHe (new ed.)
How Tuesday Began. Kathleen Fraser. NYBP
How uneasy is his life. The Joys of Marriage. Charles Cotton. BOHV; InMe

How Unhappy a Lover Am I. Dryden. *Fr.* The Conquest of Granada, Pt. II. SeCL

How unhappy (though unmarried) is an uncle who, bereft. Horace, Book V, Ode III. Charles Larcom Graves. CenHV

How unpleasant to meet Mr. Eliot! Lines for Cuscuscaraway and Mirza Murad Ali Beg. T. S. Eliot. FiBHP; MaPo (1969 ed.); ML; PoPl

How vainly men themselves amaze. The Garden [*or* Thoughts in a Garden]. Andrew Marvell. AnAnS-1; AnEnPo; AtBAP; ATP; AWP; BEL; BoC; BoLiVe; BWP; CABA; CABL; CaFP; CBEP; CBV; CoBE; DiPo; EnL; EnLi-1; EP; ExPo; FaBoEn; ForPo; FosPo; GTBS; GTBS-D; GTBS-P; GTBS-W; GTSE; GTSL; HBV; InPo; InvP; JAWP; LiTB; LiTG; LoBV; MaMe; MaPo; MasP; MeLP; MePo; MemP; MeP; NoP; OAEP; OBEV; OBS; OuHeWo; PAn; PIA; Po; PoAn; PoE; PoEL-2; PoFS; PoIE; PoLF; PoRA; PoSa; QFR; ReEn; SCEP-2; SeCePo; SeCeV; SeCL; SeCP; SeCV-1; SeEP; StP; TOP; TreFT; TrGrPo; UnPo (1st ed.); VA

How vastly pleasing is my tale. Blessings on Doneraile. Patrick O'Kelly. OnYI

How very modern once they were. The Modernists. Tom MacInnes. CaP

How very sad it is to think. Poor Brother. *Unknown.* NA

How Violets Came Blue. Robert Herrick. EnL

How warm this woodland wild Recess! Recollections of Love. Samuel Taylor Coleridge. ChER

How was November's melancholy endear'd to me. Robert Bridges. *Fr.* The Testament of Beauty. MoVE

How was this I did not see. The Faded Face. Thomas Hardy. QFR

How was thy mother a lioness. Lamentation. Ezekiel, Bible, *O.T.* TrJP

How wasteful, as they say, is Nature. Love. Walker Gibson. NePoAm-2

How We Beat the Favo[u]rite. Adam Lindsay Gordon. OtMeF; PeVV; VA

How We Became a Nation. Harriet Prescott Spofford. PAH

How We Built a Church at Ashcroft. Jack Leahy. PoOW

How We Burned the *Philadelphia.* Barrett Eastman. PaA; PAH

How we dally out our days! Upon our Vain Flattery of Ourselves that the Succeeding Times Will Be Better than the Former. Robert Gomersal. SeCL

How We Heard the Name. Alan Dugan. CaFP; CoAP; NMP

How We Learn. Horatius Bonar. HBV

How We Logged Katahdin Stream. Daniel G. Hoffman. MaC

How We Need the Secret Peace. Avis B. Christiansen. SoP

How well (dear brother) art thou called Stone? To My Reverend Dear Brother M. Samuel Stone. John Cotton. SCAP

How well her name an Army doth present. Ana(Mary Army)-gram. George Herbert. CABA; MaMe; SCEP-1

How Well for the Birds. *Unknown, tr. fr. Irish by* Frank O'Connor. KiLC

How well I know what I mean to do. By the Fireside. Robert Browning. MBW-2; NoP

How well my eyes remember the dim path! Elegy: The Summer House on the Mound. Robert Bridges. GoTL

How well you served me above ground. Spirit's Song. Louise Bogan. NYBP

How—When—Where. John Oxenham. MaRV

How wild, how witch-like weird that life should be! The Wonder of It. Harriet Monroe. NP

"How will he hear the bell at school?" Mutterings over the Crib of a Deaf Child. James Wright. PoPl; StP

How will you manage. Crossing the Mountain Alone. Princess Daihaku. *Fr.* Manyo Shu. AWP; JAWP; WBP; WoL

How wisely Nature did decree. Eyes and Tears. Andrew Marvell. MaMe; MeP; MePo; NCEP

How witty's ruin! how importunate. John Donne. *Fr.* The First Anniversary. ReEn

How wonderful and unspeakable. The Moon. Edith Södergran. LiTW

How wonderful is Death. Shelley. *Fr.* The Daemon of the World. PeER

How wonderful to lay my hand. Guidance. Avis B. Christiansen. SoP

How Wondrous Are Thy Works. Henry Ustic Onderdonk. SoP

How would the centuries long asunder. Hero-Worship. William Bell Scott. VA

How wretched is he borne or taught. *Unknown.* SeCSL

How wretched is the state wee all are in. *Unknown.* SeCSL

How you gwine ter git ter de Promise Lan'. De Promise Lan'. John Richard Moreland. IHA

Howard Lamson. Edgar Lee Masters. *Fr.* The New Spoon River. NAMP; ViBoPo

Howdy, Honey, Howdy! Paul Laurence Dunbar. PoLF

Howe maryages have grounde and cause be. John Lydgate. *Fr.* Epithalamium for Gloucester. HW

Howe [*or* How] shall I report. Maystress Jane Scroupe [*or* The Commendations of Mistress Jane Scrope]. John Skelton. *Fr.* Phyllyp Sparowe. EG; OBSC; ViBoPo

Howe'er it be, it seems to me. Nobility. Tennyson. *Fr.* Lady Clara Vere de Vere. OTPC (1946 ed.)

Howe'er [*or* Howe'r] 'tis well, that while [*or* whilst] mankind. To the Honorable Charles Montague, Esq. Matthew Prior. EiCP; PeRV

Hower is come in which I must resigne, The. *Unknown.* SeCSL

However dry and windless. Bamboo. William Plomer. PeSA

However gracefully/ the spare leaves of the fig tree. Casa d'Amunt. Alastair Reid. NePoEA

However the battle is ended. An Inspiration. Ella Wheeler Wilcox. WGRP

However they talk, whatever they say. Motto. *Unknown.* Fr. Proverbs. RIS; TiPo

Howl. Allen Ginsberg. AmP; NeAP (I-II)

Sels.

"I saw the best minds of my generation destroyed by madness." NaP

"What sphinx of cement and aluminum bashed open their skulls." PoCh

Howl. Richard Wilbur. AmPP (5th ed.)

Howle, howle, howle, howle: O you are men of stones. Shakespeare. *Fr.* King Lear, V, iii. AtBAP

Howling storm is brewing, a. The Storm. Heine. AWP; JAWP; WBP

"How's My Boy?" Sydney Dobell. CH; EtS; GN; HBV; OHIP; VA

"How's your father?" came the whisper. Conversational. *Unknown.* ALV; BoLP; FiBHP

Hoyda, hoyda, jolly rutterkin. Rutterkin. William Cornish. PoMS

Hub, The. Oscar Williams. MaRV

Hub for the Universe, A. Walt Whitman. Song of Myself, XLVIII. FaFP

("I have said that the soul is not more than the body.") CoBA; TrGrPo

(I Hear and Behold God in Every Object.) MoRP

Hubbub in Hub. Laurence McKinney. WhC

Hubbubing down the dale. A Royal Pickle. Carlton Talbott. ALV

Huckleberry Hunting, *with music. Unknown.* ShS; SoAmSa

Hucksters haggle in the mart, The. For a War Memorial. G. K. Chesterton. MMA

Huckster's Horse, The. Julia Hurd Strong. GoYe

Huddled in your house. Guerrilla. Floyce Alexander. QAH

Huddled there on the sidewalk is heartbreak. Evicted. Beatrice M. Murphy. TNV

Hudibras, *sels.* Samuel Butler.

"Egyptians, they say, The Sun has twice," *fr.* II, 3. ImOP

Godly Casuistry, *fr.* II, 2. OBS

Hudibras the Sectarian ("Beside he was a shrewd philosopher"), *fr.* I, 1. SeCePo

"In Mathematicks he was greater," *fr.* I, 1. ImOP

"Marriage is but a beast, some say," *fr.* III, 1. PeRV

Presbyterian Church Government, *fr.* I, 3. OBS

Presbyterian Knight [and Independent Squire] ("He was in logic a great critic"), *abr., fr.* I, 1. OBS

(Hudibras, the Presbyterian Knight, *abr.*) OxBoLi; SiTL

(Metaphysical Sectarian, The.) MeLP

(Portrait of Hudibras.) AtBAP; PoEL-3

("He could raise scruples dark and nice"). UnPo (1st ed.)

Religion of Hudibras, The, *fr.* I, 1. BOHV; InMe

(Art of Love, The.) FaBoEn

(For All Fanatics.) PoFr

("For his religion it was fit.") LoBV; ViBoPo

(Presbyterian, The.) FOL

Hudibras (continued)
(Sir Hudibras's Religion.) FaBoEn
Sidrophel, the Rosicrucian Conjurer, *fr.* II, 3. OxBoLi
"Sir Hudibras his passing worth," *fr.* I, Argument. FosPo
Portrait of Sidrophel, *fr.* II, 3. PoEL-3
(Character of Sydrophel, The.) PeRV
(Sir Sidrophel, the Conjuror.) FaBoEn
This sturdy Squire, he had, as well," *fr.* I, 1. ViBoPo
"When civil fury [*or* dudgeon] first grew high," *fr.* I, 1. CEP; EiPP; FosPo; SeCV-2; SeEP; TOP; ViBoPo
Hudson, The. George Sidney Hellman. AA
Hue and Cry after Cupid, The, *sel.* Ben Jonson.
Beauties, Have Ye Seen This Toy. OAEP; TuPP
(Cupid.) BOHV, *abr.*; InMe
(Venus' Runaway.) HBV; ReEn
Hue and Cry after Fair Amoret, A. Congreve. CEP; OBEC; OBEV
(Amoret.) ViBoPo
Hues of the rich unfolding morn. Morning. John Keble. OBRV
Huesca. John Cornford. ChMP
(Poem.) POTE
Hug Me Tight. John Kendall. WhC
Hug Your Hunger, Brother. Ryah Tumarkin Goodman. NYTB
Huge and alert, irascible yet strong. A Toast to Our Native Land. Robert Bridges ("Droch"). MC; PAH; PAL
Huge Leviathan, The. Spenser. *Fr.* Visions of the World's Vanity. ChTr
Huge red-buttressed mesa over yonder, The. Rain in the Street. John Gould Fletcher. Arizona Poems, VI. NP
Huge through the darkened street. The Dray. Laurence Binyon. SyP
Huge, viewless, ocean into which we cast. To Silence. Thomas Lovell Beddoes. Sonn
Huge wound in my head began to heal, The. The Wound. Thom Gunn. NePoEA
Hugging the ground by the lilac tree. Man and Beast. Clifford Dyment. POTi
Hugh Maguire. *At. to* Eochadh O'Hussey. *See* O'Hussey's Ode to the Maguire.
Hugh of Lincoln. *Unknown.* *See* Sir Hugh; or, The Jew's Daughter.
Hugh Selwyn Mauberley (Life and Contacts). Ezra Pound.
I-XII and Envoi; AmPP (5th ed.); AP; CABA: *Complete with* Mauberley I-V; CoBMV; LiTA; LiTM (rev. ed.); MasP; MoPo
Sels.
"Age Demanded, The" ("For this agility chance found"). NoP
"Age demanded an image, The." CMoP; InPo; MoAmPo (1962 ed.); PoIE
"Beneath the sagging roof." MoAmPo (1962 ed.); PoIE
Brennbaum. MoAmPo (1962 ed.)
"Conservatrix of Milésien." CMoP
"'Daphne with her thighs in bark.'" CMoP
Envoi (1919). APA; CaFP; CLwM; CMoP; CoAnAm; CTC; GTBS-W; MAP; MemP; MoAB; MoAmPo; NePA; OxBA; PoIE; SeCeV (1967 ed.); UnPo (3d ed.)
E. P. Ode pour l'Election de Son Sepulchre. CMoP; CrMA; FaBoEn; ILP; MoAmPo (1962 ed.); MoVE; NePA; OxBA; PoIE; PP; SeCeV; UnPo (3d ed.)
(Pour l'Election de Son Sepulchre.) FaBoMo; LiTG
"For three years, diabolus in the scale." NoP; NP
Medallion. NoP; SeCeV (1967 ed.)
Mr. Nixon. CMoP; MoAmPo (1962 ed.)
"Scattered Moluccas." NoP
"Siena Mi Fé; Disfecemi Maremma." CMoP; MoAmPo (1962 ed.)
"Tea-rose gown, etc. The." CMoP; FaBoMo; ILP; LiTG; MoAmPo (1962 ed.); MoVE; NePA; OxBA; SeCeV; UnPo (3d ed.)
"There died a myriad." CBV; CMoP; FaBoMo; ILP; LiTG; MoAmPo (1962 ed.); MoVE; NePA; NP; OxBA; PoIE; SeCeV; UnPo (3d ed.); WaaP
"These fought in any case." CMoP; FaBoMo; LiTG; MoAmPo (1962 ed.); MoVE; NePA; NP; OxBA; PoIE; PoSa; SeCeV; ThLM; UnPo (3d ed.); WaaP
"Turned from the 'eau-forte." NoP
Yeux Glauques. CMoP; MoAmPo (1962 ed.)
Hugh Spencer's Feats in France (A *and* B *vers.*). *Unknown.* ESPB
Hugh was a cabbage. Vegetable Fantasies. Helen Hoyt. RIS
Hughie at the Inn. Elinor Wylie. NYBP
Hughie Grame (A *and* C *vers.*). *Unknown.* ESPB
(Hughie Graham.) OxBB
(Hughie the Graeme.) OBB
Hughley Steeple. A. E. Housman. A Shropshire Lad, LXI. PoVP; ViPo; VP
Huguenot, A. Mary Elizabeth Coleridge. OBVV; PoVP
"Hullo!" S. W. Foss. PaPo
("W'en you see a man in woe.") CenHV
Hull's Surrender. *Unknown.* PAH
Humaine Cares. Nathaniel Wanley. *See* Human Cares.
Human Abstract, The. Blake. *Fr.* Songs of Experience. DiPo; EiPP; EnRP; ERoP-1; MaPo; PoEL-4
Human Being Is a Lonely Creature, The. Richard Eberhart. FiMAP; NePoAm
Human Cares. Nathaniel Wanley. SeCL
(Humaine Cares.) OBS
Human contours are so easily lost, The. The Human Form Divine. Kathleen Raine. CMoP
Human Cylinders. Mina Loy. AnAmPo
Human Fold, The. Edwin Muir. LiTM (rev. ed.)
Human Folly. Pope. *Fr.* An Essay on Man, Epistle II. FiP
(Man.) BoLiVe
("Whate'er the passion—knowledge, fame, or pelf.") TrGrPo
Human Form Divine, The. Kathleen Raine. CMoP
Human Frailty. William Cowper. HBV
Human Frailty. Philip Freneau. AnAmPo
Human Greatness. Edwin Barclay. PBA
Human hand lying on my hand, The. A Hand. Bernard Spencer. NeBP
Human Happiness. Dryden. *Fr.* The Indian Emperor, IV, i. FiP
Human Heart, The. Frank Carleton Nelson. PoToHe (new ed.)
Human Image, The, *sel.* Blake.
London ("There souls of men are bought and sold"). ChTr
Human Instinct, A. Christopher Morley. *Fr.* Translations from the Chinese. EvOK
Human Life. Matthew Arnold. EPN; MBW-2; VP
Human Life [on the Denial of Immortality]. Samuel Taylor Coleridge. ChER; ERoP-1; NoP
Human Life. Aubrey Thomas De Vere. HBV; JKCP; OnYI; VA
(Sad Is Our Youth.) MaRV
Human Life. W. H. Malloch. ACP (1926 ed.); JKCP (1926 ed.); OQP
Human Life, *sels.* Samuel Rogers.
Another and the Same. OBNC
Fond Youth. OBRV
Man's Going Hence. OBNC
Human Life; on the Denial of Immortality. Samuel Taylor Coleridge. *See* Human Life.
Human Mind, The. Ai Shih-te, *tr. fr. Chinese by* William C. White. TrJP
Human Outlook, The. John Addington Symonds. *See* Loftier Race, A.
Human Pens. Stanley Elster Wilkin. SoP
Human Plan, The. Charles Henry Crandall. AA
Human race, The/ To you, means such a child or such a man. "Where There is no Vision." Elizabeth Barrett Browning. *Fr.* Aurora Leigh, II. MaRV
Human Race Comes to Be Judged, The. Cynewulf. *See* Last Judgment, The.
Human Races, The. R. P. Lister. FiBHP
Human Seasons, The. Keats. CoBE; EnRP; FaFP; GTBS; GTBS-D; GTBS-P; GTBS-W; GTSE; GTSL; HBV; OBRV; PoPo; WiR
(Four Seasons Fill the Measure.) PG (1955 ed.)
Human Soul. René Maran, *tr. fr. French by* Mercer Cook. TTY
Human Soul Speaks, The. William Langland, *mod. by* Henry W. Wells. *Fr.* The Vision of Piers Plowman. PoLi
Human Things. Howard Nemerov. BoNaP; StP; ToPo
Human Touch, The. Richard Burton. BLPA; OQP
Human Touch, The. Spencer Michael Free. FaBoBe; MaRV; NeHB; PoToHe
Human Touch, The. Helen King. PoToHe
Human Touch, The. Francis Quarles. *See* Epigram: Respice Finem.
Human will, that force unseen, The. Will. Ella Wheeler Wilcox. BLPA
Humane Mikado, The. W. S. Gilbert. *Fr.* The Mikado. ALV; SiTL

(Let the Punishment Fit the Crime.) PoVP
(Mikado's Song, The.) LiTB
(My Object All Sublime.) TreFT
Humane Thought. Rebecca McCann. YaD
Humanitad, *sels.* Oscar Wilde.
Joy. PCH
Midwinter. PCH
Humanitarian, The, *sel.* Angela Morgan.
"Seeing how the world suffered and bled." OQP
Humanity. William Cowper. *See* Heedless Cruelty.
Humanity. Richard Watson Dixon. EPN; OBVV; OQP; VA
Humanity, in whom the best. Summum Bonum. Abu-l-Ala al-Maarri. LiTW
Humanity struggles on and is blind. Lore. Edna Ethel Davis. ChIP
Humble-Bee, The. Emerson. AA; AmePo; AmPP; AnNE; GN; HBV; HBVY; LaNeLa; LHV; OTPC; OxBA
"Burly dozing humble-bee," *sel.* FaPON
Humble boon was soon obtain'd, The. Sir Walter Scott. *Fr.* The Lay of the Last Minstrel. OBRV
Humble Bumble Bee, The. Vachel Lindsay. UTS
Humble, Lord, my haughty spirit. Prayer for Humility. Henry Francis Lyte. SoP
Humble Petition of Frances Harris, The. Swift. *See* To Their Excellencies the Lords Justices of Ireland, the Humble Petition of Frances Harris.
Humble Petition of Poor Ben to the Best of Monarchs, Masters, Men, King Charles, The. Ben Jonson. PP
Humble Pomp. Robert Southwell. *See* New Prince, New Pomp.
Humble Service. Lillian G. Heard. STF
Humble springs of stately Plimouth Beach, The. Upon the Springs Issuing out from the Foot of Plimouth Beach. Samuel Sewall. SCAP
Humble Springs of Stately Sandwich Beach, The. Samuel Sewall. SCAP
Humble we must be, if to heaven we go. Humility. Robert Herrick. GoTP; WePo
Humble Wish, The. *Unknown.* EiCL
Humble Yo'self de Bell Done Ring, *with music.* *Unknown.* BoAN-2
Humbly Showeth./ That I went to warm my self in Lady Betty's Chamber. *See* That I went to warm my self. . .
Humbug Steamship Companies *with music.* John A. Stone. SGR
Humbug Steamship Companies. *Unknown.* IHA
Humilitie. George Herbert. *See* Humility.
Humility. Robert Browning. PoVP
Humility [*or* Humilitie]. George Herbert. EP; MaMe
Humility. Robert Herrick. GoTP; WePo
Humility. *Unknown.* SoP
Humility. Thomas Washbourne. *Fr.* God's Two Dwellings. MaRV
Humming bee purrs softly o'er his flower, The. The Cricket. Frederick Goddard Tuckerman. MAmP; NoP; QFR
Hummingbird, The. Emily Dickinson. *See* Route of evanescence, A.
Humming Bird, The. Mary Howitt. OTPC; PCH
Humming Bird, The. Harry Hibbard Kemp. FaPON; HBMV; MPB
Humming-Bird. D. H. Lawrence. BWP; CMoP; GTBS-D; LiTB; LiTM; MoPW; SeCePo
Hummingbird. Violet Alleyn Storey. PoMa
Humming-bird, The! the humming-bird! The Humming Bird. Mary Howitt. OTPC; PCH
Humming Stair, The. Joseph Payne Brennan. FiSC
Humor of Tobacco and the Rest, The. Henry Parrot. SiCE
Humoresque. Alice Corbin. NP
Humorist, The. Keith Preston. ALV; EvOK; HBMV; WhC
Humour Out of Breath, *sel.* John Day.
Ditty, A: "Peace, peace, peace, make no noise." EIL
Humorous Verse. Abu Dolama, *tr. fr. Arabic by* Raoul Abdul. TTY
Humours of Donnybrook Fair, The. Charles O'Flaherty, *wr. at. to* Viscount Dillon. OnYI
(Donnybrook Jig, The.) BOHV
Humours of Donnybrook Fair, The. *Unknown.* OnYI
Hump-backed and rugged, blue on blue. For My Father. Rachel Field. InMe
Hump, the Escalator. Dorothy Faubion. BrR
Humpty Dumpty. Adeline D. T. Whitney. *Fr.* Mother Goose for Grown Folks. HBV
Humpty Dumpty Dickery Dan. The Gingerbread Man. Eva Rowland. GFA
Humpty, dumpty, diddle-dum-dee! *Unknown.* SAS
Humpty Dumpty has country cousins. Easter Eggs. *Unknown.* GFA
Humpty Dumpty sat on a wall. Mother Goose. BoChLi; CaFP; ExPo; FaBoBe; HBV; HBVY; OTPC; OxBoLi; OxNR; PCH; PPL; RIS; SiTL; StVeCh
Humpty Dumpty sat on the wall. Mother Goose (circa 2054). Irene Sekula ShM; SiTL
Humpty Dumpty's Recitation. "Lewis Carroll." *Fr.* Through the Looking-Glass. BOHV; ChTr; FiBHP; GoTP; NBM; PeVV; SiTL
(Humpty Dumpty's Song.) GTBS-P; OnMSP; OxBoLi; SAS
Hunc, Said He. *Unknown.* *See* Lady Who Loved a Swine, The.
Hunchback, The. Robert Friend. NYTB
Hunchback Girl: She Thinks of Heaven. Gwendolyn Brooks. Kal
Hunchback in the Park, The. Dylan Thomas. DiPo; FaBoTw; LiTM; MoAB; MoBrPo (1950 ed.); MoPW; NeMA; NoP; PoIE; ToPo; TwCP
Hunchback on the corner, with gum and shoelaces, The. Pursuit. Robert Penn Warren. CrMA; FiMAP; LiTA; MoAmPo (1962 ed.); MoPo; NePA; PoFS; ReMP; TwAmPo; TwCP
Hunchèd camels of the night, The. An Arab Love Song. Francis Thompson. AWP; EG; MemP; MeWo; MoAB; MoBrPo; OtMeF; POTE; YT
Hunder pipers canna blaw, A. Calvinist Sang. Alexander Scott. OxBS
Hundred autumns he has wheeled, A. Crow. Mark Van Doren. OA
Hundred Best Books, The. Mostyn T. Pigott. BOHV; InMe
Hundred Collars, A. Robert Frost. YaD
Hundred-dollar cats, the sixty, The. Pet Shop. Robert Sward. ELU
Hundred mares, all white, A! their manes. The Mares of the Camargue. Frédéric Mistral. *Fr.* Mirèio. AWP; PoPl
Hundred Noble Wishes, A. Charles Francis Richardson. MaRV
Hundred slag piles north of us, A. Two Poems about President Harding, II. James Wright. AmPC
Hundred strange things, A. Ghost Night. Lizette Woodworth Reese. HBMV
Hundred-sunned Phenix. George Darley. *See* Phoenix, The.
Hundred Tartars shall attend on thee, A. Tamburlaine's Love. Christopher Marlowe. *Fr.* Tamburlaine the Great. ShBV-4
Hundred thousand Northman, A. Wait for the Wagon. *Unknown.* PAH
Hundred thousand souls a day, A. A Missionary Cry. A. B. Simpson. SoP
Hundred warblers in the nearest aching gap, An. Warblers. Marsden Hartley. AnFE; CoAnAm
Hundred-Yard Dash, The. William Lindsey. AA
Hundred Years Ago, A, *with music.* *Unknown..* AS
Hundred Years from Now, A. Mary A. Ford. BLPA
Hundred years from now, dear heart, A. In a Rose Garden. John Bennett. BLPA; FaBoBe; HBV; NeHB
Hundred years is a very long time, A. A Hundred Years Ago. *Unknown.* AS
Hundred Years on the Eastern Shore, A (D *vers. of* A Long Time Ago). *Unknown.* SoAmSa
Hundred Years to Come, A. Hiram Ladd Spencer, *wr. at. to* William Goldsmith Brown. HBV
Hundreds of birds are singing in the square. Marché aux Oiseaux. Richard Wilbur. FiMAP
Hundreds of stars in the pretty [*or* deep blue] sky. Our Mother [*or* Only One Mother *or* Mother]. George Cooper. AA; BoTP; FaPON; HH; MPB; OHIP; OTD; OTPC; PCH; PPL; SiSoSe
Hundredth Psalm, The (Metrical Version). William Kethe. OtMeF; SoP
(Old Hundredth.) MaRV
(Scotch Te Deum.) WGRP
Hundreth good points of good husbandry, A. Thomas Tusser. ReIE
Hundreth suns—in course but not in kind, A. He Wrote to the

Hundreth (continued)
Same Friend from Excester This Sonnet Following. George Gascoigne. ReIE
Hung be the heavens with black, yield day to night! A King Is Dead. Shakespeare. King Henry VI, Pt. I, *fr.* I, i. ChTr
Hung between thief and thief. Improperia. Francis Sparshott. MoCV
Hunger. Laurence Binyon. POTE
Hunger. Mary Carolyn Davies. AnAmPo
Hunger. Emily Dickinson. *See* I had been hungry all the years.
Hunger. Hazel Hall. NP
Hunger, The. Shirley Kaufman. QAH
Hunger. John Perreault. YAP
Hunger. Arthur Rimbaud, *tr. fr. French by* Edgell Rickword. AWP
Hunger. *Unknown, tr. fr. Yoruba by* Ulli Beier. PBA; TTY
Hunger, and sultry heat, and nipping blast. The French and the Spanish Guerrillas [*or* Sonnet]. Wordsworth. ChER; WaaP
Hunger is a/ Poet's Bread. Poet's Bread. Sister Mary Philip. GoBC
Hunger makes a person climb up to the ceiling. Hunger. *Unknown.* PBA; TTY
Hunger was loneliness, betrayed. Bread. R. S. Thomas. BoC
Hungering Hearts. *Unknown.* PoToHe
Hungering on the gray plain of its birth. A Lion Named Passion. John Hollander. NePoEA-2
Hungry, The. Caroline Giltinan. OQP; SoP
Hungry China, *sel.* Cha Liang-cheng, *tr. fr. Chinese by* Cha Liang-cheng.
"I see Hunger watching at every house door." LiTW
Hungry Fox, The. *Unknown. See* Fox, The.
Hungry Grass, The. Donagh MacDonagh. NeIP; OxBI
Hungry Heart, The. Edna St. Vincent Millay. TSW
Hungry old man from the Rhine, A. New Limericks. *Unknown.* StaSt
Hungry Waves, The. Dorothy Aldis. RePo
"Hungry winter, this winter." To Hell with It. Frank 'Hara. NeAP
Hunt, The. Babette Deutsch. AnAmPo
Hunt, The. Louis Kent. WaKn
Hunt. Melvin Walker La Follette. NePoEA
Hunt, The. Harriet Prescott Spofford. AA
Hunt, The. *Unknown.* CoMu
Hunt, hunt again. If you do not find it, you. Fairy Story. Robert Penn Warren. NYBP
Hunt in the Black Forest, A. Randall Jarrell. CoAP
Hunt Is Up, The. William Gray. CH; OTPC (1923 ed.)
(King's Hunt Is Up, The.) TuPP
Hunt is up, the hunt is up, The Song of the Hunt. John Bennett. *Fr.* Master Sky-Lark. AA
Hunt of Sliabh Truim, The, *sel.* *Unknown, tr. fr. Late Middle Irish.*
"'One day that we mustered on Sliabh Truim.'" OnYI
Hunt was up, the hunt was up, The. The Capture of Edwin Alonzo Boyd. Peter Miller. MoCV
Hunted. Una Marson. PoNe
Hunted City, The, *sel.* Kenneth Patchen.
"Little hill climbs up to the village and puts its green hands, The." NaP
Hunted hare seeks out some dark retreat, The. Hunted. Una Marson. PoNe
Hunter, The. Ogden Nash. EvOK; SD
Hunter, The. Walter James Turner. HBMV
Hunter, The. Eleanor Glenn Wallis. NePoAm-2
Hunter of huntsmen bred, The. The Lament of Quarry. Léonie Adams. NP
Hunter of the Prairies, The. Bryant. AA
Hunter Trials. John Betjeman. FiBHP; MemP
Hunters, The. Ruth Temple Lindsay. JKCP
Hunters in the Snow: Brueghel. Joseph Langland. LiTM (1970 ed.); NePoEA
Hunter's Moon. Stephen Sandy. NYBP
Hunters of Kentucky, The. Samuel Woodworth. PAH; TrAS, *abr., with music*
(Hunters of Kentucky, The; or Half Horse and Half Alligator, *with music.*) AS
Hunters of Men, The. Whittier. AnAmPo
Hunter's Prayer. *Unknown, tr. fr. Hottentot.* PeSA
Hunter's Song, The. William Basse. SeCL
Hunter's Song, The. "Barry Cornwall". BBV (1923 ed.); GN; OTPC, *abr.*; VA
Hunter's Song. Sir Walter Scott. *Fr.* The Lady of the Lake, VI. NBM; OA
(Toils Are Pitched, The.) EnRP
Hunters were oot on a Scottish hill. The Day of the Crucifixion. "Hugh MacDiarmid." PV
Hunting, *sels.* Gary Snyder. *Fr.* Myths & Texts. NaP
"All beaded with dew," VII.
"How rare to be born a human being," XVI.
"Out the Greywolf valley," XII.
"Swallow-shell that eases birth, The," IV.
This Poem Is for Bear, VI.
This Poem Is for Birds, III.
This Poem Is for Deer, VIII.
Hunting. "Yehoash," *tr. fr. Yiddish by* Isidore Goldstick. TrJP
Hunting after Gold. John A. Stone. SGR
Hunting of Cupid, The, *sels.* George Peele.
Coridon and Melampus' Song. TuPP
(Song of Coridon and Melampus.) OBSC
What Thing Is Love? EIL; ELP; EnRePo; OAEP; ReEn; SeCePo; TuPP; UnTE
(Love.) OBSC
Hunting of Pau-Puk-Keewis, The. Longfellow. *Fr.* The Song of Hiawatha, XVII. CoBA
Hunting of the Cheviot, The. *Unknown. See* Chevy Chase.
Hunting of the Gods, The. Walter Wasse. OxBoLi; SeCL
Hunting of the Snark, The. "Lewis Carroll." FiBHP, *much abr.*; MasP; NA, *much abr.*; OBNC; OnMSP; PoEL-5; SiTL
Sels.
Baker's Tale, The, III. BoChLi; PoVP
How to Recognize a Snark, *fr.* II. MPB
("Come, listen, my men, while I tell you again.") BOHV
(Snark, The.) TSW
("We have sailed many months," *abr.*) NA
Landing, The, I WhC
Hunting Season. W. H. Auden. CBV
Hunting Song. Samuel Taylor Coleridge. *Fr.* Zapolya, Pt. II, Act IV, sc. i. OTD; PRWS; ThWaDe
(Up, Up! Ye Dames and Lasses Gay!) BoTP; OTPC
Hunting Song. Thomas D'Urfey. *Fr.* The Marriage-Hater Match'd, II, i. SeCL
(Brother Solon's Hunting Song.) CavP
(Solon's Song.) CEP; SeEP
Hunting Song. Henry Fielding. *See* A-Hunting We Will Go.
Hunting Song. Donald Finkel. CoAP; MoBS; NePoEA
Hunting Song. Richard Hovey. *Fr.* King Arthur. HBV
Hunting Song. Sir Walter Scott. CoBE; EnLi-2; EnLit; EnRP; EPN; EvOK; GN; GTBS; GTBS-D; GTBS-P; GTBS-W; GTSE; GTSL; InP; LiTG; OAEP; OTPC; RG; SD; TOP; TrGrPo; WiR
Hunting-Song. *Unknown, tr. fr. Navaho Indian song by* Natalie Curtis. AWP; JAWP WBP
Hunting Song, The. *Unknown.* TuPP
Hunting Song, A. Paul Whitehead. *Fr.* Apollo and Daphne. EiCL; OBEC; OxBoLi
Hunting Tribes of Air and Earth, The. Sir Walter Scott. *Fr.* Rokeby, III. OA
Man the Enemy of Man. WBLP
Huntress, The. George Johnston. WHW
Huntsman, The. John Wheelwright. CrMA
Huntsman's Rouse, The. Henry Carey. SeCePo
Huntsmen, The. Walter de la Mare. CenHV; HBMV; InP; SiSoSe; StVeCh; TiPo
Huntswoman-moon was my mother, The. The Singing Huntsman. Witter Bynner. MAP; MoAmPo (1942 ed.)
Hurdy-Gurdy Days. Martha Haskell Clark. MPB
Hurdy-Gurdy Man, The. Elizabeth Fleming. BoTP
Hurdy-Gurdy Man in Winter. Vernon Watkins. NYBP
Hurdy-gurdy, public piano of the past, The. The Road from Election to Christmas. Oscar Williams. NAMP
Hurl down the nerve-gnarled body hurtling head. The Final Hunger. Vassar Miller. LiTM (1970 ed.); ToPo
Hurled back, defeated, like a child I sought. Earthborn. Peter McArthur. CaP
Hurly, hurly, roon the table. Two Graces. *Unknown.* FaBoCh; LoGBV
Hurlygush. Maurice Lindsay. OxBS

Hurrah! for a day with the farmer. A Day at the Farm. "L. J." BoTP
Hurrah for Greer County. *Unknown.* *See* Greer County.
Hurrah for revolution and more cannon-shot! The Great Day. W. B. Yeats. CMoP
Hurrah for the choice of the nation! Lincoln and Liberty. F. A. Simpson. AS; TrAS
Hurrah for the Lachlan. The Shearer's Song. *Unknown.* PoAu-1
Hurrah! the seaward breezes. The Fishermen. Whittier. EtS
Hurrahing in Harvest. Gerard Manley Hopkins. BoC; BoNaP; BrPo; CBEP; ChTr; CMoP; FlW; InvP; LO; MoAB; MoBrPo; MoPo; MoVE; PoeP; PoIE; PoVP; ViPo (1962 ed.); VP
Hurricane, The. Hart Crane. AmP; AP; CMoP; CoBMV; MoAB; MoAmPo; OxBA
Hurricane, The. Philip Freneau. AmPP (4th ed.); AP; CoBA
Hurricane, The. Luis Palés Matos, *tr. fr. Spanish by* Alida Malkus. FaPON
Hurricane, The. William Carlos Williams. PoeP
Hurricane at Sea, A. May Swenson. WIRo
Hurrier, The. Harold Monro. MoBrPo
Hurry Me Nymphs. George Darley. *Fr.* Nepenthe. NBM
(Lines: "Hurry me Nymphs! O, hurry me.") HoPM
"Hurry!" said the leaves. A Summer Shower. *Unknown.* BoTP
Hurry the baby as fast as you can. Making a Man. Nixon Waterman. BLPA
Hurry to bless the hands that play. The Players Ask for a Blessing on the Psalteries and on Themselves. W. B. Yeats. PoDB; UnS
Hurry Tomorrow. Ivy O. Eastwick. BiCB
Hurry, worry, unwary. Old Amusement Park. Marianne Moore. NYBP
Hurrying Away from the Earth. Robert Bly. NaP; WOW
Hurrying Brook, The. Edmund Blunden. BoNaP
Hurt/ u worried abt a. To All Sisters. Sonia Sanchez. BF
Hurt Hawks. Robinson Jeffers. AmP; AmPP; AP; AtBAP; BoLiVe; CMoP; CoBA; CoBMV; DiPo; LiTA; LiTM (1970 ed.); MAP; MoAB; MoAmPo; MoVE; NeMA; NoP; NP; OxBA; PoPo
Hurt No Living Thing. Christina Rossetti. *Fr.* Sing-Song. FaPON; PCH; PDV; PoRL; RIS; SiSoSe; SoPo; ThGo
Hurt was the Nation with a mighty wound. Lincoln. Paul Laurence Dunbar. LiPo; OQP
Husband, The. Donald Finkel. ELU
Husband, The. Leon Gellert. BoAu
Husband, The. Barbara L. Greenberg. QAH
Husband and Heathen. Sam Walter Foss. BOHV
Husband and Wife. Arthur Guiterman. PoToHe (new ed.)
Husband and Wife. Edward Harry William Meyerstein. LO
Husband Betrayed. John Crowe Ransom. TwAmPo
Husband of Poverty, The, *sel.* Henry Neville Maugham.
Knight of Bethlehem, A. ChIP; MaRV; OQP
(Song: "There was a Knight of Bethlehem.") BoTP
Husband to a Wife, A. Robert Louis Stevenson. *See* My Wife.
Husbandman, The. Dante Gabriel Rossetti. The House of Life, LXXVI. MaVP; ViPo
Husbandman, The. Frances Beatrice Taylor. CaP
Husbandry. William Hammond. SeCL
Husbands and Wives. Miriam Hershenson. OCS
Husbands and Wives ("Husbands would never go whoring"). *Unknown, tr. fr. Greek by* Louis Untermeyer. UnTE
Husband's Message, The. *Unknown, tr. fr. Anglo-Saxon.* AnOE, *tr. by* Charles W. Kennedy; EnLit, *tr. by* Harold S. Stine
Husband's Petition, The. William E. Aytoun. BOHV
Hush! Emerson. AnNE
Hush! Frances Ridley Havergal. SoP
Hush!/ With sudden gush. Overflow. John Banister Tabb. PTK
Hush, All Ye Sounds of War. William H. Draper. ChIP; MaRV
Hush! Did you hear. Chopin. Eleanour Norton. HBMV
Hush dove the summer. Lullaby. Miriam Waddington. CaP
Hush had fallen on the birds, A. The Young Calves. Robert P. Tristram Coffin. StVeCh (1955 ed.); TiPo
Hush! hear you how the night wind keens around the craggy reek? A Lay of the Famine. *Unknown, at. to* Rosa Mulholland. OnYI
Hush, Hush. Mani Leib, *tr. fr. Yiddish by* Joseph Leftwich. TrJP
Hush, hush,/ Nobody cares! Now We Are Sick. J. B. Morton. PV
Hush, hush, do not speak. Hush, Hush. Mani Leib. TrJP
Hush, hush, little baby. Evening. *Unknown.* BoTP
Hush is over all the teeming lists, A. Frederick Douglass. Paul Laurence Dunbar. BALP
Hush, Li'l Baby, *with music.* *Unknown.* OuSiCo
Hush, little baby, don't say a word. *Unknown.* OxNR
Hush, lullay,/ Your treasures all. Lullaby. Léonie Adams. AmLP; BoLiVe (1939 ed.); MAP; MoAB; MoAmPo; NeMA
Hush, my baby, do not cry. *Unknown.* OxNR
Hush! my baby, or soon you will hear. Weeng; an Indian Slumber Song. Lew Sarett. GaP
Hush, my dear, lie still and slumber. A Cradle Hymn [*or* A Cradle Song]. Isaac Watts. BoChLi; CEP; EiPP; HBV; LoBV; NoP; OBEC; OBEV; OTPC; OxBoCh; PoEL-3; PRWS; SoPo; SUS; ThGo; TreFS
Hush, new baby, bob-cats creep. Lullaby for Peregrine. Robert P. Tristram Coffin. RePo
Hush! not a whisper! Oars, be still! The Coracle Fishers. Robert Bloomfield. *Fr.* The Banks of Wye. OBNC
Hush Now. Dorothy C. Parrish. TNV
Hush now, my little one, and sleep. Christmas Lullaby. Ulrich Troubetzkoy. YeAr
Hush! oh ye billows. Hymn. Joseph Sheridan Le Fanu. *Fr.* Beatrice. OnYI
Hush Song. Elizabeth Shane. MoSiPe
Hush, Suzanne! The Mouse in the Wainscot. Ian Serraillier. PDV
Hush, the waves are rolling in. Gaelic Lullaby [*or* Old Gaelic Lullaby]. *Unknown.* GFA; PRWS; SAS
Hush thee, my babby [*or* baby], lie still with thy daddy. Hush Rhymes—English and Scotch. *Unknown.* OTPC; OxNR; PPL
Hush! With a sudden gush. Overflow. John Banister Tabb. CAW; HBV
Hush, woman, do not speak to me! The Tryst after Death. *Unknown.* LiTW; OnYI, *abr.*
Hush ye! Hush ye! My babe is sleeping. At Even. Frederic Manning. NP
Hush your prayers, 'tis no saintly soul. Requiem. Conal O'Riordan. HBV
Husha, oh, husha. Jewish Lullaby. Louis Untermeyer. RIS
Hush-a-ba birdie, croon, croon. *Unknown.* OxNR
Hush-a-baa, baby,/ Dinna mak' a din. *Unknown.* OxNR
Hush-a-by, baby,/ Your name is so lovely. Italian Lullaby. *Unknown.* FaPON
Hushaby, don't you cry. All the Pretty Little Horses. *Unknown.* ABF; OxBoLi
Hush-a-bye a baa lamb. *Unknown.* OxNR
Hush-a-bye, baby,/ The beggar shan't have 'ee. *Unknown.* OxNR
Hush-a-bye [*or* Rock-a-bye], baby, on [*or* in] the tree top. Mother Goose. HBVY; OTPC (1923 ed.); OxNR; PPL; RIS; SAS; StVeCh; TiPo (1959 ed.)
Hush-a-bye, baby, they're gone to milk. *Unknown.* OxNR
Hush-a-bye, baby, thy cradle is green. *See* Rock-a-bye, baby, thy cradle is green.
Hush'd is each busy shout. Prelude. A. C. Benson. OBVV
Hush'd Be the Camps To-Day. Walt Whitman. *Fr.* Memories of President Lincoln. DD; LiPo; MC; OHIP
Hushed are the pigeons cooing low. The Christmas Silence. Margaret Deland. ChrBoLe; OHIP; PRWS
Hushed by the Hands of Sleep. Angelina W. Grimké. CDC
Hushed in the smoky haze of summer sunset. Sunset; St. Louis. Sara Teasdale. HT; PoMa
Hushed to inaudible sound the deepening rain. The Tea-Tree and the Lyrebird. Roland Robinson. NeLNL; PoAu-2
Hushed was the courtyard of the temple. The Cicada. Ou-yang Hsiu. AWP
Hushed with broad sunlight lies the hill. Beaver Brook. James Russell Lowell. CoBA
Husheen the herons are crying. Lullaby. "Seumas O'Sullivan." GBV; OnYI
Hushie ba, burdie beeton. *Unknown.* OxNR
Hushing Song. "Fiona Macleod." MoSiPe
Hushoo! hushoo! tiny King. St. Bridget's Lullaby. Dorothy Una Ratcliffe. CAW
Huskers, The, *sel.* Whittier.

Huskers (continued)
Corn Song, The. GN; OHIP; OTPC
Husky Hi. Rose Fyleman. TiPo
Hustle and Grin. *Unknown.* WBLP
Hustler, it's over, The. I Watch. Clive Matson. ThO
Huswifery. Edward Taylor. *See* Housewifery.
Hut, The. Avigdor Hammeiri, *tr. fr. Hebrew by* Jacob Sloan. LiTW
Hut, The. Hilda Van Stockum. BrR
Hut, and a tree, A. Diogenes. Max Eastman. HBV; OQP
Hut in the bush of bark or rusty tin, The. The Hatters. Nan McDonald. PoAu-2
Hut near Desolated Pines. Alistair Campbell. AnNZ
Huts that stand like plaited baskets. Village and Factory. Alexander Ilyich Bezymensky. TrJP
Huzza for our liberty, boys. Terrapin War. *Unknown.* PAH
Huzza! Hodgson, we are going. Lines to Mr. Hodgson. Byron. ERoP-2; PoE
Huzza Huzza for Admiral Byrd. Admiral Byrd. Ogden Nash. InMe; YaD
Huzza, my Jo Bunkers! no taxes we'll pay. A Radical Song of 1786. St. John Honeywood. PAH
Hy-Brasail, the Isle of the Blest. Gerald Griffin. *See* O Brazil, the Isle of the Blest.
Hyacinth for Edith, A. A. J. M. Smith. TwCaPo
Hyacinths to Feed Thy Soul. Sadi, *tr. fr. Persian. Fr.* The Gulistan. BLPA; FaBoBe; MaRV; NeHB; TRV
Hyaku-Nin-Isshu, *sels. Tr. fr. Japanese by* Curtis Hidden Page. AWP; JAWP; WBP
"Day will soon be gone, The." Fujiwara No Michinobu.
"How can one e'er be sure." Lady Horikawa.
"I would that even now." Princess Shoku.
"Like a great rock, far out at sea." Lady Sanuki.
Hybrid Villanelle on a Line of Li Po, A. William Witherup. QAH
Hybris, Nemesis, One, Two, Three. Alicia Ostriker. StP
Hyd [*or* Hyde], Absolon, thy gilte tresses clere. Balade [*or* Of His Lady]. Chaucer. *Fr.* The Legend of Good Women. AtBAP; AWP; ChTr; EG; ExPo; FiP; InPo; JAWP; LiTG; LoBV; OBEV; PIA; SeCeV; WBP
Hydeous hole al vaste, withouten shape, An. Thomas Sackville, Earl of Dorset. *Fr.* Induction to "A Myrrour for Magistrates." EnPo
Hyder Iddle. *Unknown.* BOHV; NA; OxNR
Hydra of Birds, The. Nikos Engonopoulos, *tr. fr. Modern Greek by* Kimon Friar. LiTW
Hydraulic Ram, The. Charles Tennyson Turner. NBM
Hydro Works. J. R. Hervey. AnNZ
Hydrogen Dog and the Cobalt Cat, The. Frederick Winsor. ShM
Hydrographic Report. Frances Frost. EtS
Hyena ("My father came in the darkness"). *Unknown, tr. by* George Economou. TTY
Hyena ("You who make your escape from the tumult"). *Unknown, tr. fr. Hottentot.* PeSA
Hyena's Song to Her Children. *Unknown, tr. fr. Hottentot.* PeSA
Hygiene Sonnet. Dick Gallup. ANYP
Hygienist, in your dental chair. Ode to a Dental Hygienist. Earnest A. Hooton. FiBHP; WhC
Hyla Brook. Robert Frost. AnFE; AnNE; APA; BoNaP; CoAnAm; MAPA; TwAmPo
Hylas. Propertius, *tr. fr. Latin by* F. A. Wright. Elegies I, 20. AWP
Hylas, O Hylas [*or* Hilas, o Hilas]! why sit we mute. Chloris and Hylas [*or* Hilas]. Edmund Waller. SeCL; SeCV-1
Hylas, the world's perceptual scene. Equation. Sir Herbert Read. BrPo
Hymen, *sel.* Hilda Doolittle ("H. D.").
Never More Will the Wind. SiSw; TrGrPo
(Hymen.) ViBoPo
Where Love Is King. HBMV
Hymen ("Hymen, god of marriage-bed"). Joseph Rutter. *Fr.* The Shepherd's Holiday. SeCL
Hymen hath together tyed. *Unknown.* SeCSL
Hymenaei, *sel.* Ben Jonson.
Angel Describes Truth, An II. OBS
Hymeneall Dialogue, An. Thomas Carew. AnAnS-2; SeCP
Hymen's Triumph, *sels.* Samuel Daniel.
Constancy. OBSC
Early Love. ErPo
(First Flame.) BoLP
Eyes, Hide My Love. EIL
(Secrecy.) OBSC
Had Sorrow Ever Fitter Place. AtBAP; EIL
(Sorrow.) OBSC
Love Is a Sickness. AtBAP; BEL; CBEP; CBV; ELP; FosPo; LiTG; LiTL; LO; LoBV; NoP; OAEP; OBEV; PG; PoEL-2; PoIE; SiCE; TreFS; TuPP; ViBoPo
(Love.) EIL; OBSC
(Song: "Love is a sickness.") HBV
Hymettus' bees are out on filmy wing. The Sunflower to the Sun. Mary Elizabeth Hewitt Stebbins. AA
Hymn: "Abide with me; fast falls the eventide." Henry Francis Lyte. *See* Abide with Me.
Hymn: "Ah, what are strength and beauty?" Synesius, *tr. fr. Greek by* Roderick Gill. CAW
Hymn: "At morn, at noon, at twilight dim." Poe. ISi
(Hymn of the Angelus.) CAW
Hymn: "Brightest and best of the sons of the morning." Reginald Heber. NBM
Hymn: "Britannia's sons, though slaves ye be." John Bramwich. PoFr
Hymn: "By the rude bridge that arched the flood." Emerson. *See* Concord Hymn.
Hymn: Crucifixus pro Nobis. Patrick Carey. *See* Crucifixus pro Nobis.
Hymn: "Dear Lord, Whose serving-maiden." Josephine Preston Peabody. TrPWD
Hymn, A: "Drop, drop, slow tears." Phineas Fletcher. CBEP; EIL; LoBV; SeEP
(Hymne, An: "Drop, drop, slow tears.") OBS
(Litany, A.) AtBAP; BoC; BoW; OBEV; OxBoCh
Hymn: "Eternal Father, strong to save." William Whiting. *See* Eternal Father. . .
Hymn: "Eternal Founder of the sky." James J. Donohue. JKCP (1955 ed.)
Hymn: "Eternal Ruler of the ceaseless round." John White Chadwick. TrPWD
(Kingdom of God on Earth, The.) SoP
Hymn: "Father, we come not as of old." John White Chadwick. TrPWD
Hymn: "For Summer's bloom and Autumn's blight." Josiah Gilbert Holland. *Fr.* Bitter-sweet. TrPWD
Hymn, A: "From all that terror teaches," *abr. sel.* G. K. Chesterton.
Litany. OtMeF
Hymn: "God of the strong, God of the weak," *abr.* Richard Watson Gilder. TrPWD
(God of the Strong, God of the Weak, *abr.*) MaRV
Hymn: "Great Spirit of the speeding spheres.] John Haynes Holmes. TrPWD
Hymn: "He sendeth sun, he sendeth shower." Sarah Flower Adams. VA
Hymn: "Hush! oh ye billows." Joseph Sheridan Le Fanu. *Fr.* Beatrice. OnYI
Hymn, A: "Hymn of glory let us sing, A." The Venerable Bede. *See* Hymn of Glory Let Us Sing, A.
Hymn: "It was the winter wild." Milton. *Fr.* On the Morning of Christ's Nativity. WHA, *sts.* 1-23
Hymn, A: "Lead gently, Lord, and slow." Paul Laurence Dunbar. MaRV; TrPWD
(Hymn, A, after Reading "Lead, Kindly Light.") TRV
Hymn: "Lead us, heavenly Father, lead us." James Edmeston. *See* Prayer to the Trinity.
Hymn: "Lord, by whose breath all souls and seeds are living." Andrew Young. EaLo
Hymn, A: "Lord, give them freedom who are weak." Nikolai Alekseyevich Nekrasov, *tr. fr. Russian by* Frances Cornford *and* E. P. Salaman. LiTW
Hymn: "Lord, with glowing heart I'd praise thee." Francis Scott Key. TrPWD
Hymn, A: "Loving Shepherd of thy sheep." Jane E. Leeson. ThGo
Hymn: "Mighty fortress is our God, A." Martin Luther. *See* Mighty Fortress Is Our God, A.
Hymn: "My God, I love thee, not because." St. Francis Xavier. *See* My God, I Love Thee.
Hymn: "New every morning is thy love." John Keble. NBM
Hymn: "Now let us praise the Keeper of the Heavenly Kingdom." Cædmon. *See* Hymn of the World's Creator, The.

Hymn: "Now the day is over." Sabine Baring-Gould. *See* Now the Day Is Over.
Hymn: "O Christ, the glorious crown." Philip Howard. ACP; CAW
Hymn, A: "O fly, my soul! What hangs upon." James Shirley. *See* O Fly My Soul.
Hymn, A: "O God of earth and altar." G. K. Chesterton. HBMV; InP; TreFT; TrPWD
(O God of Earth and Altar.) MaRV
(Prayer: O God of earth and altar.") WGRP
Hymn: "O God, Who guid'st the fate of nations." Gunnar Wennerberg, *tr. fr. Swedish by* Charles W. Stork. PoFr
Hymn: "O li'l' lamb out in de col'." Paul Laurence Dunbar. AA
Hymn: "O Thou who camest from above." Charles Wesley. OBEC; SeCePo
(Oh Thou Who Camest from Above.) TrPWD
Hymn: "O world of love and beauty." George Edward Hoffman. MaRV
Hymn: "Once again thou flamest heavenward, once again we see thee rise." Tennyson. *Fr.* Akbar's Dream. PoVP
Hymn: "Queen and huntress chaste and fair." Ben Jonson. *See* Hymn to Diana.
Hymn: "Rise, crowned with light, imperial Salem, rise!" Pope. *See* Rise, Crowned with Light.
Hymn L: Rocking Hymn, A. George Wither. *Fr.* Hallelujah; or, Britain's Second Remembrancer. SeCV-1
(Lullaby, A: "Sweet baby, sleep; what ails my dear.") OxBoCh, *abr. [wr. at. to* William Austin]
Hymn: "Since without Thee we do no good." Elizabeth Barrett Browning. TrPWD
Hymn: "Sing, my tongue, the Saviour's glory." St. Thomas Aquinas, *tr. fr. Latin by* Edward Caswall. CAW; WGRP
(Pange Lingua Gloriosa, *abr.*) WHL
Hymn: "Slant of sun on dull brown walls, A." Stephen Crane. *See* Slant of Sun, A.
Hymn: "Spacious firmament on high, The." Addison. *See* Spacious Firmament on High, The.
Hymn: "There's a wideness in God's mercy." Frederick William Faber. *See* There's a Wideness in God's Mercy.
Hymn: "These, as they change, Almighty Father, these." James Thomson. *See* Hymn on the Seasons, A.
Hymn: "Thou God of all, whose presence dwells." John Haynes Holmes. TrPWD
Hymn: "Thou hidden love of God, whose height." John Wesley. CEP; OBEC
Hymn: "When all thy mercies, O my God." Addison. *See* When All Thy Mercies.
Hymn: "When by the marbled lake I lie and listen." Wathen Mark Wilks Call. OBVV
Hymn: "When storms arise." Paul Laurence Dunbar. FaChP; SoP; TrPWD; TRV
Hymn: "When winds are raging o'er the upper ocean." Harriet Beecher Stowe. PoToHe
(Peace.) FaChP
Hymn: "Whilst I beheld the neck o' the dove." Patrick Carey. SeCL
Hymn: "Words of hymns abruptly plod, The." Louise Townsend Nicholl. EaLo
Hymn: "Ye golden Lamps of Heav'n, farewel." Philip Doddridge. CEP; OBEC
(Ye Golden Lamps of Heaven.) OxBoCh
Hymn, A, after Reading "Lead, Kindly Light." Paul Laurence Dunbar. *See* Hymn, A: "Lead gently, Lord, and slow."
Hymn against Pestilence, *sel.* *At. to* St. Colman, *tr. fr. Old Irish by* Whitley Stokes *and* John Strachen.
"God's blessing lead us, help us!" OnYI
Hymn before Sunrise, in the Vale of Chamouni. Samuel Taylor Coleridge. BEL; EnRP; ERoP-1; HBV; MaRV; MCCG; MERP; OAEP; OxBoCh; TOP; WGRP
Hymn for a Household. Daniel Henderson. ChIP; HBMV; MaRV; OQP; StJW
Hymn for Atonement Day. Judah Halevi, *tr. fr. Hebrew by* Solomon Solis-Cohen. TrJP
Hymn for Canada, A. Albert Durrant Watson. CaP
Hymn for Christmas. Felicia Dorothea Hemans. GN; OTPC, *sts.* 1-2
Hymn for Christmas Day. John Byrom. MaRV; OBEC; PoEL-3
(Christians, Awake, Salute the Happy Morn, *with music.*) YaCaBo
Hymn for Christmas Day, A. Thomas Chatterton. MaRV; OTPC (1923 ed.)
Hymn for conquering Martyrs raise, The. Hymnum Canentes Martyrum. The Venerable Bede. CAW
Hymn for Family Worship, A. Henry Alford. SoP
Hymn for Lanie Poo, *sel.* LeRoi Jones.
Each Morning. IDB; NNP
Hymn for Laudes; Feast of Our Lady, Help of Christians. *Unknown, tr. fr. Latin by* Sister Maura. ISi
Hymn for Laudes; Feast of Our Lady of Good Counsel. *Unknown, tr. fr. Latin by* Sister Maura. ISi
Hymn—for My Brother's Ordination. Longfellow. SoP
Hymn for Pentecost. James Clarence Mangan. CAW; JKCP
Hymn for St. John's Eve. *Unknown, tr. fr. Latin at. to* Dryden. AWP
Hymn for Saturday. Christopher Smart. *See* For Saturday.
Hymn for Second Vespers; Feast of the Apparition of Our Lady of Lourdes. *Unknown, tr. fr. Latin by* Raymond F. Roseliep. ISi
Hymn for the Church Militant. G. K. Chesterton. OxBoCh
Hymn for the Day. "Gabriela Mistral," *tr. fr. Spanish by* James H. McLean. MaRV
Hymn for the Dedication of a Church. Andrews Norton. AA
Hymn for the Eve of the New Year. Abraham Gerondi, *tr. fr. Hebrew by* Solomon Solis-Cohen. TrJP
Hymn for the Feast of the Annunciation. Aubrey Thomas De Vere. ISi
Hymn for the Lighting of the Lamps. *Unknown, at. to* St. Athenogenes, *tr. fr. Greek by* John Keble. CAW
Hymn for the Nativity of My Savior, A. Ben Jonson. *See* Hymne on the Nativitie of My Saviour, A.
Hymn for the New Age, A. William Steward Gordon. MaRV; OQP
Hymn for the Sixteenth Sunday after Trinity. Henry Hart Milman. VA
Hymn for the Slain in Battle. William Stanley Braithwaite. BALP
Hymn for Water. Merrill Moore. TrGrPo (1942 ed.)
Hymn from the French of Lamartine, *sel.* Whittier.
"O Thou who bidst the torrent flow." TrPWD
Hymn in Adoration of the Blessed Sacrament. Richard Crashaw. *See* Hymn of Saint Thomas in Adoration of the Blessed Sacrament, The.
Hymn in Honor of Love, An. Spenser. ReIE
Hymn in Honour of Beauty, An. Spenser. *See* Hymne in Honour of Beautie, An.
Hymn in Praise of Neptune, A. Thomas Campion. GTSL; OBEV
(Hymne in Prayse of Neptune, A.) EtS
(Neptune.) OBSC
Hymn of Adam, The. Joost van den Vondel. *See* Adam's Hymn in Paradise.
Hymn of Apollo. Shelley. EnL; EnLit; EnRP; HBV; MBW-2; OAEP; OBRV
(Hymn to Apollo.) ERoP-2
Hymn of At-One-Ment. John Haynes Holmes. MaRV
Hymn of Cleanthes, The. Cleanthes. *See* Hymn to Zeus.
Hymn of Creation. *Unknown, tr. fr. Sanskrit by* Arthur A. Macdonnell. *Fr.* The Rigveda. LiTW
Hymn of Dedication. Elizabeth E. Scantlebury. BLRP
Hymn of Form, A. Gordon Bottomley. BrPo
Hymn of Glory Let Us Sing, A. The Venerable Bede, *tr. fr. Latin by* Elizabeth Charles. BePJ
(Ascension Hymn.) MaRV
(Hymn, A.) WGRP
Hymn of Gratitude. *Unknown.* BLRP
Hymn of Hate, The. Joseph Dana Miller. PGD
Hymn of Hate against England, A. Ernst Lissauer. *See* Chant of Hate against England, A.
Hymn [*or* Hymne] of Heavenly Love, An. Spenser. ReIE; StJW
Hymn of Joy. Henry van Dyke. MaRV; TRV
(Adoration.) SoP
Hymn of Labor. Henry van Dyke. SoP; TRV
(Jesus, Thou Divine Companion.) MaRV
Hymn of Love. St. Francis Xavier. WHL
Hymn of Man. Swinburne. PoVP
"Thou and I and he are not gods made men for a span," *sel.* WGRP
Hymn of Marriage. Burns. *See* John Anderson, My Jo.
Hymn of Nature, A. Robert Bridges. YeAr

Hymn of Pan. Keats. *See* Hymn to Pan.
Hymn of Pan. Shelley. AtBAP; EnRP; ERoP-2; ExPo; FaBoCh; HBV; LoGBV; MBW-2; MemP; MyFE; OAEP; OBEV; OBRV; PoEL-4; PoIE; RG; SeCeV
Hymn of Peace, A. Ernest Bourner Allen. MaRV
Hymn of Praise. Robert Robinson. SoP
Hymn of Praise, on a Recovery from Sickness, A. Benjamin Colman. SCAP
Hymn of praise to Ra, A, when he riseth in the Eastern part of heaven. Hymn to Ra. *Unknown.* OuHeWo
Hymn of Saint[e] Thomas in Adoration of The Blessed Sacrament, The. Richard Crashaw. MaMe; OBS; PoLi
(Hymn in Adoration of the Blessed Sacrament.) MeLP
Hymn of Sivaite Puritans. *Unknown.* WGRP
Hymn of Thanksgiving, A. Wilbur D. Nesbit. OHIP
Hymn of Thanksgiving. *Unknown.* WHL
Hymn of the Angels and Sibyls. Gil Vicente, *tr. fr. Spanish by* Thomas Walsh. CAW
Hymn of the Angelus. Poe. *See* Hymn: "At morn, at noon, at twilight dim."
Hymn of the Blessed Virgin, The. St. Luke, Bible, *N.T.* *See* Magnificat, The.
Hymn of the City. Bryant. AmePo
Hymn of the Earth. William Ellery Channing. AA; AnNE
Hymn of the Holy Cross, The. Richard Crashaw. StJW
(Vexilla Regis, the Hymn of the Holy Crosse.) MaMe
Hymn of the Incarnation, A. *Unknown.* MeEL
Hymn of the Moravian Nuns of Bethlehem. Longfellow. PAH
Hymn of the Nativity. Richard Crashaw. *See* In the Holy Nativity of Our Lord God.
Hymn of the New World. Percy MacKaye. PEDC; PoRL
Hymn of the Resurrection, A. William Dunbar. *See* Of the Resurrection of Christ.
Hymn of the Soviet Union. Sergei Mikhalkov *and* El-Registan, *tr. fr. Russian by* Louis Untermeyer. PoFr
Hymn of the Unemployed. Thomas Tiplady. MaRV
Hymn of the Waldenses. Bryant. AnNE; SoP
Hymn of the West. Edmund Clarence Stedman. HBV; PaA; PAH
(Hymn to the West.) TrPWD
Hymn of the World Within, The. Psalms, CIII, Bible, *O.T.*
(Moulton, *Modern Reader's Bible.*) WGRP
(Psalm CIII.) AWP; JAWP
Hymn of the World Without. Psalms, CIV, Bible, *O.T.*
(Moulton, *Modern Reader's Bible.*) WGRP
(Psalm CIV.) OHIP, *sel.*
Hymn of the World's Creator, The. Cædmon, *tr. fr. Anglo-Saxon.* CAW
(Creation, The.) PoLi
(Hymn: "Now let us praise the Keeper of the Heavenly Kingdom.") YAT
Hymn of Touch, A. Gordon Bottomley. BrPo
Hymn of Trust. Oliver Wendell Holmes. *Fr.* The Professor at the Breakfast Table, *ch.* 11. AA; MaRV; NeHB; SoP; TrPWD
Hymn of Trust, A. Nettie M. Sargent. BLRP
Hymn of Unity, A. Robert Freeman. OQP
Hymn of Unity. *Unknown, tr. fr. Hebrew by* H. M. Adler. TrJP
Hymn of Victory: Thutmose III. Amon-Re, *tr. fr. Egyptian by* James Henry Breasted. WaaP
Hymn of Weeping. Amittai ben Shefatiah, *tr. fr. Hebrew by* Nina Davis Salaman. TrJP
Hymn on Solitude. James Thomson. CEP; EiPP; OBEC
Hymn on the Morning of Christ's Nativity. Milton. *Fr.* On the Morning of Christ's Nativity. OBEV; OtMeF, *abr.*; StJW
(On the Morning of Christ's Nativity.) FiP
Sels.
Hymn: "It was the winter wild," *sts.* 1-23. WHA
Magi, The, 2 *ll.* ChTr
Peaceful Night, The, *sts.* 5-7. ChrBoLe
("But peaceful was the night," *sts.* 5-13.) FaBoCh; LoGBV
"Shepherds on the lawn, The." BoC
Hymn on the Omnipresence, An. John Byrom. CEP; TrPWD
Hymn on the Seasons, A. James Thomson. *Fr.* The Seasons. EiCP; EnRP; OxBoCh; PoE
(Hymn: "These, as they change, Almighty Father, these.") CEP; EiPP
Hymn Sung as by the Shepherds, A. Richard Crashaw. *Fr.* In the Holy Nativity of Our Lord God. GoBC
(Shepherd's Hymn, The.) BoC
(Shepherds' Hymn: "We saw thee in thy balmy nest.") ACP; CAW; TrGrPo, 3 *sts.*
(Shepherds Hymn Their Saviour, 2 *sts.*) EG
(Verses from the Shepherds' Hymn.) OBEV
Hymn Sung at the Completion of the Concord Monument. Emerson. *See* Concord Hymn.
Hymn to Adversity. Thomas Gray. CEP; EiPP; EnRP; GTBS; GTBS-D; GTBS-P; GTBS-W; GTSE; GTSL; OBEC; StP
Hymn to Amen Ra, the Sun God. *Unknown, tr. fr. Egyptian by* Frank Lloyd Griffith. WGRP
Hymn to Aphrodite. *Unknown, tr. fr. Greek by* Jack Lindsay. *Fr.* Homeric Hymns. LiTW, *abr.*
Hymn to Apollo. Shelley. *See* Hymn of Apollo.
Hymn to Athena. *Unknown. Fr.* Homeric Hymns. AWP
Hymn to Castor and Pollux. *Unknown. Fr.* Homeric Hymns. AWP
Hymn to Chance. H. Phelps Putnam. TwAmPo; WoL
Hymn to Charity and Humility. Henry More. OxBoCh
(Hymne in Honour of Those Two Despised Virtues, Charitie and Humilitie, An.) OBS
Hymn [*or* Hymne] to Christ, at the Authors Last Going into Germany, A. John Donne. AnAnS-1; AnEnPo; DiPo; EnRePo; FaBoEn; LiTB; LiTG; MaMe; MBW-1; MeLP; MeP; MePo; OAEP; OBS; OxBoCh; Po; SCEP-1; SeCV-1; SeEP; TuPP; ViBoPo; WoL
Hymn to Christ the Saviour. Clement of Alexandria. *See* Earliest Christian Hymn ("Curb for stubborn steed.")
Hymn to Colour [*or* Color]. George Meredith. OBNC; PoVP
Hymn to Comus. Ben Jonson. *Fr.* Pleasure Reconciled to Virtue. ElL; OAEP
(Hymn to the Belly.) SeCePo; SiTL
(Song: To Comus.) SeEP
Hymn to Contentment, A. Thomas Parnell. CEP; EiPP; OBEC
Hymn to Cynthia. Ben Jonson. *See* Hymn to Diana.
Hymn to Darkness. John Norris. GTSL; MePo; OBS; OxBoCh
Hymn to Diana. Catullus, *tr. fr. Latin by* Sir Richard Jebb. AWP
Hymn to Diana. Thomas Heywood. *Fr.* The Golden Age. ElL
("Hail, beauteous Dian, queen of shades.") SiCE
Hymn to Diana. Ben Jonson.. *Fr.* Cynthia's Revels, V, vi. AnFE; AWP; BEL; BoLiVe; ChTr; ElL; EnLi-1 (1949 ed.); EnLit; EnRePo; GTBS; GTBS-D; GTBS-P; GTBS-W; GTSE; GTSL; InPo; JAWP; MemP; PoRA; QFR; RG; SeCP; ShBV-4; TOP; TrGrPo; WBP; WHA; WiR
(Hesperus' Hymn to Cynthia.) LoBV; SeCV-1
(Hesperus' Song.) GN
(Hymn [*or* Hymne], The: "Queen[e] and huntress[e], chaste, and fair[e].") AnAnS-2; AtBAP; PoEL-2; SCEP-2; ViBoPo; YAT
(Hymn to Cynthia.) MaPo (1969 ed.); SeCePo
(Queen[e] and Huntress[e].) CABA; CBEP; EnL; NoP; OAEP; PAn; TuPP
(Queen[e] and Huntress[e], Chaste and Fair[e].) CH; EG; ILP; OBEV; OBC; PoE; ReEn; SiCE
(Song: To Cynthia.) HBV
(To Diana.) OTPC
Hymn to Earth. Elinor Wylie. AmLP; BoLiVe; LiTM; MAP; MoAB; MoAmPo; MoPo; MoVE; NePA; NP; ReMP
Hymn to Earth the Mother of All. *Unknown, tr. fr. Greek by* Shelley. *Fr.* Homeric Hymns. AWP; JAWP; WBP
Hymn to God in Time of Stress, A. Max Eastman. TrPWD
Hymn [*or* Hymne] to God My God, in My Sickness[e]. John Donne. AnAnS-1; AtBAP; BoC; BWP; CABA; ChTr; DiPo; DTC; EnL; EnRePo; EP; FaBoEn; GoBC; LoBV; MaMe; MaPo; MasP; MBW-1; MeLP; MeP; MePo; NoP; OAEP; OBS; OxBoCh; PoEL-2; PoIE; ReEn; SCEP-1; SeCL; SeCP; SeCV-1; SeEP; TDP; TrPWD, *abr.*; TuPP
"Since I am comming to that Holy roome," *sel.* UnS
Hymn [*or* Hymne] to God the Father, A. John Donne. AnFE; AtBAP; AWP; BEL; BoC; CaFP; CoBE; DiPo; EaLo; EnLi-1; EnLit; EnRePo; EP; ForPo; FosPo; GoBC; GTSE; HBV; InPo; JAWP; LiTB; LiTG; LoBV; MaMe; MaRV; MBW-1; MeLP; MePo; OBEV (1st ed.); OBS; OxBoCh; PAn; PG (1945 ed.); Po; PoAn; PoE; PoEL-2; PoeP; PoFS; PoIE; PoPo; PoRA; ReEn; SCEP-1; SeCeV; SeCL; SeCP; SeCV-1; SeEP; ShBV-4; TDP; TOP; TreFT; TrGrPo; TrPWD; TuPP; ViBoPo; WBP
(For Forgiveness.) WGRP
(To Christ.) AnAnS-1; MeP

("Wilt thou forgive that sin where I begun.") EG
Hymn [*or* Hymne] to God the Father, A. Ben Jonson. AnAnS-2; EnRePo; FosPo; GoBC; MaRV; MePo; NoP; OBS; OxBoCh; ReEn; SCEP-2; SeCP; SeCV-1; TrPWD
Hymn to God the Father. Samuel Wesley. OxBoCh
Hymn to Her Unknown. Walter James Turner. LiTL; LiTM; OBMV
Hymn to Hesperus. Byron. *See* Evening.
Hymn to Horus. Mathilde Blind. OBVV
Hymn to Intellectual Beauty. Shelley. AnEnPo; AnFE; BEL; BoLiVe; CoBE; EnL; EnLi-2; EnLit; EnRP; EPN; ERoP-2; ILP; MBW-2; MERP; NoP; OAEP; OBNC; OBRV; OuHeWo; PIA; Po; PoAn; PoE; PoFS; TOP; UnPo (1st ed.)
Hymn to Jesus, A. Richard of Caistre. MeEL
Hymn to Labor. Angela Morgan. MaRV
Hymn to Light. Abraham Cowley. AtBAP; MeLP; MePo; OBS; SCEP-2; SeCV-1; SeEP
Hymn to Light. Milton. *See* Hail, Holy Light.
Hymn to Love. Lascelles Abercrombie. *Fr.* Emblems of Love. OBEV (new ed.); OBVV
Hymn to Marduk, *sels.* *Unknown,* *tr. fr. Assyrian.* WGRP
"O Marduk, lord of countries, terrible one."
"O mighty, powerful, strong one of Ashur."
Hymn to Marriage, for Manlius and Junia. Catullus, *tr. fr. Latin by* Virginia Tufte. HW
Hymn to Mary, A. William Dunbar. *See* Ballad of Our Lady.
Hymn to Mary. Zerea Jacob, *tr. fr Abyssinian [or* Amharic] by Father Baetman. CAW
(Salutation.) ISi
Hymn to Mary, A. *Unknown.* *See* Hymn to the Virgin, A.
Hymn to Mercury, *abr.* *Unknown,* *tr. fr. Greek by* Shelley. *Fr.* Homeric Hymns. LiTW
Hymn to Moloch. Ralph Hodgson. HBMV
Hymn to My God in a Night of My Late Sicknesse, A. Sir Henry Wotton. AnAnS-2; MeLP; MePo; OBS
(It Is Finished.) BePJ
Hymn to Night. Melville Cane. MAP; MoAmPo
Hymn to Night, A. Max Michelson. NP; TrJP
Hymn to Night. *Unknown,* *tr. fr. Sanskrit by* R. T. H. Griffith. *Fr.* The Rigveda. LiTW
Hymn to No One Body, A. James Palmer Wade. NAMP
Hymn to Pan. John Fletcher. *Fr.* The Faithful Shepherdess, I, ii. OBEV
(Sing His Praises.) EG; ViBoPo
(Song: "Sing his praises that doth keep.") OBS; SeEP
Hymn to Pan. Keats. *Fr.* Endymion, I. AtBAP; ChER; EPN; OBRV; PeER; PoEL-4
(Hymn of Pan.) ERoP-2
Hymn to Poverty, A. Edward Moore. WaPE
Hymn to Priapus. D. H. Lawrence. CMoP; CoBMV; MoAB; OBMV
Hymn to Proserpine. Swinburne. BEL; EnL; EnLi-2; EPN; MaVP; OAEP; OBNC; OBVV; PAn; PoAn; PoEL-5; PoVP; SeCeV; ViPo; ViPP; VP
Sels.
"I have lived long enough, having seen one thing, that love hath an end." FOL
"Thou hast conquered, O pale Galilean." WHA
Wilt Thou Yet Take All. UnPo (1st ed.)
Hymn to Proust. Gavin Ewart. NYBP
Hymn to Ra. *Unknown,* *pr. tr. fr. Egyptian by* E. A. Wallis Budge. *Fr.* Book of the Dead. OuHeWo
Hymn to St. Geryon, *sel.* Michael McClure.
"Gesture the gesture the gesture the gesture, The," I. NeAP
Hymn to Saint Teresa. Richard Crashaw. *See* Hymn to the Name and Honor of the Admirable Saint Teresa, A.
Hymn to Satan, *abr.* Giosuè Carducci, *tr. fr. Italian by* Leonard Bacon. PoFr
Hymn to Science. Mark Akenside. CEP; PoEL-3
Hymn to Selene. *Unknown.* *See* Hymn to the Moon.
Hymn to Tammuz. *Unknown,* *tr. fr. Babylonian by* Stephen Langdon. LiTW
Hymn to the Belly. Ben Jonson. *See* Hymn to Comus.
Hymn to the Blessed Virgin. *Unknown.* *See* Hymn to the Virgin, A.
Hymn to the Creation. Addison. *See* Spacious Firmament on High, The.
Hymn to the Cross, A. *Unknown.* *See* Holy Cross.
Hymn to the Guardian Angel. J. Corson Miller. JKCP (1926 ed.)
Hymn to the Holy Cross. Venantius Fortunatus. *See* Vexilla Regis.
Hymn to the Holy Spirit. *At. to* Charlemagne, *tr. fr. Latin by* Edward Caswall. SoP
Hymn to the Holy Spirit. Richard Wilton. OxBoCh
Hymn to the Moon. *Unknown,* *tr. fr. Greek by* Shelley. *Fr.* Homeric Hymns. LiTW
(Hymn to Selene.) AWP
Hymn to the Morning, An. Mary Leapor. WaPE
Hymn to the Name and Honor [*or* Honour] of the Admirable Saint[e] Teresa, A. Richard Crashaw. FaBoEn; LoBV; MaMe; NoP; OAEP; OBEV, *abr.*; OBS; PoEL-2; PoFS; ReEn; SCEP-1; SeCL; SeCV-1, *abr.*; SeEP
(Hymn to St. Teresa.) ACP; CABL; MeLP; MePo; OxBoCh; WGRP
(In Memory of the Vertuous and Learned Lady Madre de Teresa.) AnAnS-1; MaMe; MeP
"O how oft shalt thou complain," *sel.* PoLi
Hymn to the Night. Longfellow. AA; AmePo; AmLP; AmP; AmPP; AnAmPo; AnEnPo; AnFE; AnNE; AP; APA; CoAnAm; ExPo; HBV; HBVY; LaNeLa; LoBV; NePA; OTPC; OuHeWo; OxBA; PoFS; StVeCh (1940 ed.); TOP; TreFS; TrGrPo; ViBoPo; WHA
Hymn to the Night, II. "Novalis," *tr. fr. German by* Mabel Cotterell. *Fr.* Hymns to the Night. LiTW
Hymn to the North Star. Bryant. OTPC
Hymn to the Perfect. Edith Lovejoy Pierce. ChIP
Hymn to the Pillory, A, *sel.* Daniel Defoe.
"Hail hi'roglyphick state machin." NCEP
Hymn to the Sea, A. Richard Henry Stoddard. EtS
Hymn to the Sea. Sir William Watson. EtS
Hymn to the Seal. Stevie Smith. PoG
Hymn to the Spirit of Nature. Shelley. *See* Life of Life.
Hymn to the Sun. Ikhnaton (Amenhotep IV), *tr. fr. Egyptian.* LiTW, *tr. by* T. Eric Peet; TTY, *tr. by* J. E. Manchip White; WoL, *tr. by* J. H. Breasted
Hymn to the Sun. William Alexander Percy. TrPWD
Hymn to the Sun. Michael Roberts. FaBoCh; LoGBV
Hymn to the Sunrise. *Unknown.* NA
Hymn to the Victorious Dead. Hermann Hagedorn. PEDC
Hymn to the Virgin. Sir Walter Scott. *Fr.* The Lady of the Lake, III. EnRP; GoBC
(Ave Maria.) ISi
Hymn to the Virgin, A. *Unknown.* OBEV
(Hymn to Mary, A.) MeEL
(Hymn to the Blessed Virgin.) CAW
(Of On That Is So Fayr and Bright.) BEL
(Of One That Is So Fair and Bright.) CoBe; ISi
(Prayer to the Virgin.) EnLit
(Song to Our Lady.) PoLi
(Song to the Virgin, A.) SeCePo
Hymn to the Virgin Mary. Conal O'Riordan, *tr. fr. Irish by* Eleanor Hull. ISi
Hymn to the Volunteers of the Republic, *sel.* César Vallejo, *tr. fr. Spanish.*
"Battles? No! Agonies! And before the agonies." PoFr
Hymn to the West. Edmund Clarence Stedman. *See* Hymn of the West.
Hymn to the Wind God. *Unknown,* *tr. fr. Aztec by* John Hubert Cornyn. *Fr.* Song of Quetzalcoatl. LiTW
Hymn to the Winds. Joachim du Bellay, *tr. fr. French by* Andrew Lang. AWP; WoL
Hymn to Tsui-Xgoa. *Unknown,* *tr. fr. Hottentot.* PeSA
Hymn to Varuna, God of Fire and Light. *Unknown,* *tr. fr. Sanskrit by* R. T. H. Griffith. *Fr.* The Rigveda. LiTW
Hymn to Venus. Edith Sitwell. FaBoMo
Hymn to Vishnu. Jayadeva. *Fr.* The Gita Govinda. AWP
Hymn to Zeus. Aeschylus. *Fr.* Agamemnon. WGRP
Hymn to Zeus. Cleanthes, *tr. fr. Greek by* Edward Hayes Plumptre. WGRP
(Hymn of Cleanthes, The, *tr. by* James Adam.) MaRV
Hymn Tunes, The. Edward Lucie-Smith. MuSP
Hymn Written after Jeremiah Preached to Me in a Dream. Owen Dodson. AmNP; Kal
Hymn Written for the Two Hundredth Anniversary of the Old South Church, Beverly, Massachusetts. Lucy Larcom. OHIP
Hymnal: "Bringer of sun, arrower of evening, star-begetter and moon-riser." Harold Vinal. TrPWD
Hymne, An: "Drop, drop, slow tears." Phineas Fletcher. *See* Hymn, An: "Drop, drop, slow tears."

Hymne I: Generall Invitation to Praise God, A. George Wither. *Fr.* Hallelujah; or Britain's Second Remembrancer. SeCV-1
Hymne, The: "Queene, and Huntresse, chaste, and faire." Ben Jonson. *See* Hymn to Diana.
Hymne for the Epiphanie, A. Richard Crashaw. *See* In the Glorious Epiphanie of Our Lord God.
Hymne [*or* Hymn] in Honour of Beautie [*or* Beauty], An. Spenser. SiCE
Sels.
"Ah whither, Love, wilt thou now carrie mee?" ReEn
Beauty ("What time this world's great workmaster did cast"). OBSC
(Soul Is Form, *abr.*) GoBC
Hymne in Honour of Those Two Despised Virtues, Charitie and Humilitie, An. Henry More. *See* Hymn to Charity and Humility.
Hymne in Prayse of Neptune, A. Thomas Campion. *See* Hymn in Praise of Neptune, A.
Hymne of Heavenly Beautie [*or* Beauty], An, *sel.* Spenser.
"But whoso may, thrice happy man him hold." WGRP
Hymne of Heavenly Love, An. Spenser. *See* Hymn of Heavenly Love, An.
Hymne of the Ascension, An. William Drummond of Hawthornden. OBS
(Song of the Ascension, *abr.*) SeCL
Hymne of the Nativity, Sung as by the Shepheards, An. Richard Crashaw. *See* In the Holy Nativity of Our Lord God.
Hymne on the Nativitie of My Saviour, A. Ben Jonson. SCEP-2; ScCV-1
(Hymn for the Nativity of My Savior, A.) StJW
Hymne to Christ, at the Authors Last Going into Germany, A. John Donne. *See* Hymn to Christ . . .
Hymne to God My God, in My Sicknesse. John Donne. *See* Hymn to God, My God, in My Sickness.
Hymne to God the Father, A. John Donne. *See* Hymn to God the Father, A.
Hymne to God the Father, A. Ben Jonson. *See* Hymn to God the Father, A.
Hymne to Our Saviour on the Crosse, A. George Chapman. PoEL-2
Hymne to the Saints, and to Marquesse Hamylton, An. John Donne. MaMe
Ὕμνος Ἄυμνος (Hymnos Ahymnos). Arthur Hugh Clough. EPN; PoVP; ViPP
(O Thou Whose Image.) TrPWD
Hymns and Spiritual Songs, *sels.* Christopher Smart.
Nativity of Our Lord, The. EiCP; LoBV; PoEL-3
(Christmas Day, *sts.* 6-9.) ChTr
St. Mark. EiCP
St. Matthias. EiCP
Hymns for the Amusement of Children, *sels.* Christopher Smart.
For Saturday. EiCP
(Hymn for Saturday.) CBEP
(Lark's Nest, A.) FaBoCh; LoGBV
Gratitude. EiCP
Long-Suffering of God. EiCP
Mirth. EiCP
Hymns of [*or* to] Astraea, *sels.* Sir John Davies.
Of Astraea. SiCE; TrGrPo; TuPP
To Astraea. SiCE
To Envy. SiCE
To the Lark. SiCE
To the Nightingale. OBSC; SiCE; TrGrPo
To the Rose. OBSC; SiCE; TuPP
To the Spring. EIL; SiCE; TuPP
Hymns of Praise. Psalms, VIII, XV, XIX, XXIII, XXIV, XCV, CXXI, Bible, *O.T.* OuHeWo
Hymns of the Marshes, *sel.* Sidney Lanier.
Sunrise. AA; PoEL-5
"Tide's at full, The: the marsh with flooded streams," *shorter sel.* FaBoEn
Hymns to Astraea. Sir John Davies. *See* Hymns of Astraea.
Hymns to the Night, *sel.* "Novalis," *tr. fr. German by* Mabel Cotterell.
Hymn to the Night, II. LiTW
Hymnum Canentes Martyrum. The Venerable Bede, *tr. fr. Latin by* John Mason Neale. CAW
Hymnus: "God be in my hede." *Unknown.* *See* God Be in My Head.
Hymnus ad Patrem Sinensis. Philip Whalen. FRC
Hymnus in Noctem. George Chapman. *Fr.* The Shadow of Night. PoEL-2; ReIE, *abr.*
"All you possessed with indepressed spirits." TuPP
"Great Goddesse to whose throne in Cynthian fires." AtBAP
Hymnus Sanctae Mariae, *sel.* Ennodius, *tr. fr. Latin.*
How of the Virgin Mother Shall I Sing? ISi
Hynd Etin. *Unknown.* *See* Hind Etin.
Hynd [*or* Hynde] Horn. *Unknown.* BuBa; GN; LoEn; OBB; OxBB
(Hind Horn.) ATP; BaBo (A *and* B *vers.*); EP, *sl. abr.*; ESPB (A *and* G *vers.*); NoP; TOP; ViBoFo
Hyperion; a Fragment. Keats. EnRP; EPN; ERoP-2
Sels.
"Apollo then, with sudden scrutiny and gloomless eyes," *fr.* III. OBRV
"As when upon a trancéd summer-night," *fr.* I. ViBoPo
"But one of the whole mammoth-brood," *fr.* I. OBRV
"Deep in the shady sadness of a vale," *fr.* I. ATP, *sel.*; BEL; ChER; ExPo, *sel.*; FaBoEn, *sel.*; FiP; InP, *br. sel.*; MBW-2; MyFE, *fr.* I *and* II; OAEP; OBRV, *sel.*; PeER; PoEL-4
(Saturn, *sel.*) LoBV; OBNC; TrGrPo
(Saturn Fallen, *sel.*) AnEnPo
Den of the Titans, The, *fr.* II. WHA
Hyperion's Arrival, *fr.* II. OBRV
(Hyperion and Saturn.) SeCePo
"Just at the self-same beat of Time's wide wings," *fr.* II. OBRV
(Bruised Titans, The.) OBNC
"O leave them, Muse," *fr.* III. ViBoPo
Hyperion: a Vision. Keats. *See* Fall of Hyperion, The.
Hyperion's Arrival. Keats. *Fr.* Hyperion, II. OBRV
(Hyperion and Saturn.) SeCePo
Hyperion's clear star is not yet risen. Dawn-Song to Waken the Lovers. *Unknown.* LiTW
Hypocrisy. Samucl Butlcr. BOHV
Hypocrite, The. Kalonymos ben Kalonymos, *tr. fr. Hebrew by* Joseph Chotzner. *Fr.* The Touchstone. TrJP
Hypocrite Auteur. Archibald MacLeish. AmPP (5th ed.); MoVe; NePA
Hypocrite is strange of race, A. The Hypocrite. Kalonymos ben Kalonymos. *Fr.* The Touchstone. TrJP
Hypsithilla, ask me over. An Invitation to an Invitation. Catullus. ErPo
Hyssop. Walter de la Mare. BoC
Hysteria. Chu Shu Chen, *tr. fr. Chinese by* Kenneth Rexroth. NaP

I

I. Thomas Creeley. FRC
I. E. E. Cummings. NYBP
"I." Louis Golding. TrJP
I/ am going to rise. Vive Noir! [*or* Stretchin' Out]. Mari Evans. BOLo; WOW; WSL
I/ Have arrived. Status Symbol. Mari Evans. IDB
I/ have heard the Word. For Frantz Fanon. Robert L. Terrell. WSL
I/ never/ guessed any. I. E. E. Cummings. NYBP
I/ saw/ the/ dragonfly. By a Rich Fast Moving Stream. John Tagliabue. ELU
I/ seek/ integration. The New Integrationist. Don L. Lee. BOLo
I;/ Thou. The Little Poem of Life. John Oxenham. TRV
"I/ Through/ Blue/ Sky/ Fly." The Aeronaut to His Lady. Frank Sidgwick. WhC
I/ want you/ to listen. Kenneth Patchen. *Fr.* The Journal of Albion Moonlight. NaP
I/ Why? The Shortest Poem in the World. Eli Siegel. SiTL
I/ wonder why. Tom Poole. BOLo; NBP
I, a Justified Sinner. Arnold Price. NYTB
I, a Most Wretched Atlas. Heine, *tr. fr. German by* Emma Lazarus. *Fr.* Homeward Bound. TrJP
I, a slave, chained to an oar of poem. Stoic. Lawrrence Durrell. NYBP
I a tender young maid have been courted by many. My Thing Is My Own. *Unknown.* CoMu

I abide and abide and better abide. Sonnets, VI. Sir Thomas Wyatt. EnLoPo; FCP; SiPS
I Accept. Harold Trowbridge Pulsifer. HBMV; OQP
I 'ad no education, and my pile. A Ballade of Any Father to Any Son. J. C. Squire. WhC
I adjure you, O daughters of Jerusalem. The Song of Solomon, Bible, *O.T.* LiTW
I admire the artificial art of the East. Where the Grizzly Dwells. James Fox. SCC
I admire the driven, those who rise from choice. Cinema, at the Lighthouse. Henri Coulette. *Fr.* The War of the Secret Agents. NePoEA-2
I adore Thee humbly, O Thou hidden God. Adoro Te Devote. St. Thomas Aquinas. WHL
I advocate a semi-revolution. A Semi-Revolution. Robert Frost. LiTM; SiTL
I advocate a total revolution. A Total Revolution. Oscar Williams. LiTM; SiTL
I affirm. Perambulator Poems, III. David McCord. WhC
I ain't afeard [*or* afraid] uv snakes, or toads, or bugs, or worms, or mice. Seein' Things. Eugene Field. BoChLi; HBV; HBVY; MAP; MoAmPo (1942 ed.); MPB; NeMA; OTPC; PoMa; RIS; TreF
I ain't been long in this here army. Rookie's Lament. *Unknown.* ABF
I ain't got no father. Poor Lonesome Cowboy. *Unknown.* ABF; AS; CoSo; TiPo
I ain't no wagon, ain't no dray. I'm a Round-Town Gent. *Unknown.* GoSl
I Almost Did—Very Nigh—Had Not God Stopped the Lie. Elizabeth Turner. *See* Rebecca's After-Thought.
I almost never say my prayers. Devotions. Elinor L. Norcross. OQP
I, Alphonso, live and learn. Alphonso of Castile. Emerson. AP
I always eat peas with honey. Peas. *Unknown.* SiTL
I always feel sorry. Hoppity Toads. Aileen Fisher. RePo
I always hope Father is going to play. Newspaper. Aileen Fisher. SoPo
I always knew the Ural Mountains glowed. The Mineral Collection. Abbie Huston Evans. NP
I always like the summer. Knoxville, Tennessee. Nikki Giovanni. BOLo
I always liked to go to bed. A Song for My Mother—Her Stories. Anna Hempstead Branch. OHIP
I always loved this solitary hill. L'Infinito. Giacomo Leopardi. AWP; JAWP; WBP
I always loved to call my lady Rose. Madrigal. *Unknown.* ElL
I always remember your beautiful flowers. Pad, Pad. Stevie Smith. ELU
I always say I won't go back to the mountains. Sourdough Mountain Lookout. Philip Whalen. NeAP
I always see—I don't know why. The Knowledgeable Child. L. A. G. Strong. OBMV
I always shout when Grandma comes. Afternoon with Grandmother. Barbara A. Huff. FaPON
I always struggled for things beyond my reach. Like the Prime Mover. Mehdi Ali Seljouk. ACV
I always wanted/ A little carved bowl. The Little Carved Bowl. Margaret Widdemer. BrR; YT
I always wanted a red balloon. Tragedy. Jill Spargur. BLPA
I always was afraid of Somes's [*or* Soame's] Pond. Atavism. Elinor Wylie. AnEnPo; FiSC; HBMV; NP
I Am. John Clare. BoPe; CBEP; EnRP; ERoP-2; FaBoEn; GTBS-P; GTBS-W; LiTB; NBM; NoP; OBNC; PeER; PG; PoE; PoEL-4; PoIE; PoPl; PoSa; TrGrPo; WHA
(I Am: Yet What I Am Who Cares or Knows.) InvP
(Written in Northampton County Asylum.) GTSE; GTSL; OBEV; OBVV; ViBoPo
I Am. Hilda Conkling. FaPON; NP; TiPo
I am/ A clam! Nirvana [*or* A Clam]. *Unknown.* BOHV; StaSt
I am a bold cowboy, from Midland I came. The Lovesick Cowboy. Charles A. Bobston. CoSo
I am a bold fellow. The Young Dandelion. Dinah Maria Mulock Craik. DD; GoTP; MPB; RePo
I am a boy. A Young David: Birmingham. Helen Morgan Brooks. PoNe (1970 ed.)
I Am a Brisk and Sprightly Lad. *Unknown.* AmSS
I am a broken-hearted milkman, in grief I'm arrayed. Polly Perkins. *Unknown.* BoLP; DTC; ELP; OxBoLi
I am a composite being. I Am the Flag. Lawrence M. Jones. PAL; PGD
I am a copper wire slung in the air. Under a Telephone Pole. Carl Sandburg. PoPo
I am a cowboy by my trade. A Wild Rattling Cowboy. *Unknown.* CoSo
I Am a Cowboy in the Boat of Ra. Ishmael Reed. NBP; NoP
I am a downright country-man, both faithful (aye) and true. The Downright Country Man; or, The Faithful Dairy Maid. *Unknown.* CoMu
I am a faire maide, if my glasse doe not flatter. The Wooing Maid. Martin Parker. CoMu
I am a fisherman casting. Surface Fishing. W. R. Moses. NYTB
I am a friar of orders gray. The Friar of Orders Gray. John O'Keeffe. BOHV; OnYI; OxBI
I am a frog. The Frog Prince. Stevie Smith. PoG
I am a gentelman in a dustcoat trying. Piazza Piece. John Crowe Ransom. AP; BWP; CBEP; CBV; CoBMV; ErPo; FosPo; InPo; MAP; MoAB; MoAmPo; MoPW; MoVE; NeMA; OxBA; PG (1955 ed.); Po; PoIE (1970 ed.); PoSa; SiSw; Sonn; TreFT; TrGrPo
I am a goddess of the ambrosial courts. Artemis Prologizes. Robert Browning. AnEnPo; LoBV (2d ed.)
I am a gold lock. Mother Goose. PPL
I am a happy Christmas wind. Ballad of the Happy Christmas Wind. Sister Mary Madeleva. ChrBoLe
I am a happy miner, I love to sing and dance. The Happy Miner. John A. Stone. IHA; SGR
I am a hearthrug. Midsummer Madness. *Unknown.* BOHV
I am a jolly shanty boy. Bung Yer Eye. *Unknown, at. to* Stewart Edward White. ABF; IHA; RePo
I am a jolly young fellow. The Jolly Driver. *Unknown.* CoMu; UnTE
I am a jovial collier lad, and blithe as blithe can be. Down in a Coal Mine. J. B. Geoghegan. TreFS
I am a jovial marriner, our calling is well known. The Jovial Marriner; or The Sea-Man's Renown. John Playford. CoMu
I am a kind of farthing dip. Self Portrait. Robert Louis Stevenson. CBV; SeCePo
I am a lady. Small Sad Song. Alastair Reid. NYBP
I am a lamp, a lamp that is out. She Warns Him. Frances Cornford. Two Poems, I. EnLoPo
I am a lean bird, and sinewy. The Vulture. Israel Kafu Hoh. ACV
I am a little boy. Feet. "Harry." TiPo (1959 ed.)
I Am a Little Church (No Great Cathedral). E. E. Cummings. MoRP; NePoAm-2
I am a little music box. A Music Box. Abbie Farwell Brown. PPL
I am a little thing. Do You Guess It Is I? Eliza Lee Follen. OTPC (1946 ed.); PPL
I am a little world made cunningly. Holy Sonnets, V. John Donne. AnAnS-1; CABA; CBV; EnL; EnRePo; MaMe; MaPo (1969 ed.); MasP; MeP; MyFE; OBS; NoP; OxBoCh; PIA; ReEn; SCEP-1; SeCP; SeEP; Sonn; StP
I am a lone, unfathered chick. Orphan Born. Robert J. Burdette. BOHV
I am a lonely woodland lake. The Lake. John Banister Tabb. AmP
I am a lover yet was never loved. *Unknown.* SeCSL
I am a man defeated in his loins. Beggar to Burgher. A. R. D. Fairburn. AnNZ
I am a man now. Here. R. S. Thomas. GTBS-P
I am a man of war and might. A Soldier. Sir John Suckling. SeCV-1
I am a man who knew Abe Lincoln well. The Man from Sangamon, at Gettysburg. Eleanor G. R. Young. OQP
I am a man with no ambitions. The Advantages of Learning. Martial. ErPo
I am a miner. The light burns blue. Nick and the Candlestick. Sylvia Plath. CoAP
I am a Mormon bishop and I will tell you what I know. The Mormon Bishop's Lament. *Unknown.* CoSo
I am a most superior person. Henry Charles Beeching. *Fr.* The Masque of Balliol. CenHV
I am a native of the land of Erin. A Convict's Lament on the Death of Captain Logan. *Unknown.* PoAu-1

I Am a Negro. Muhammad Al-Fituri, *tr. fr. Arabic by* Halim El-Dabh. TTY
I Am a Parcel of Vain Strivings Tied [*or* Sic Vita]. Henry David Thoreau. AnNe; AP; CLwM; FaBoEn; GTBS-W; MAmP; NoP; PoEL-4
(Sic Vita.) AmePo; AmPP (4th ed.); MWA-1; NePA; OxBA
I am a part of all that I have met. The Challenge of Life [*or* Experience]. Tennyson. *Fr.* Ulysses. MaRV; OQP; TRV
"I am a passion; I am a flame." Song. Gustavo Adolfo Bécquer. Rimas, XI. OnPM
I am a peevish student I. Melancholia. *Unknown.* NA
"I am a poor girl, and my fortune is bad." The Wagoner's Lad (A *vers.*). *Unknown.* BaBo
"I am a poor unhappy boy." Whittington and His Cat. *Unknown.* CIV
I am [*or* I'm just] a poor wayfaring stranger. Poor Wayfaring Stranger [*or* Over Jordan]. *Unknown.* BFSS; OuSiCo; TrAS
I am a poor workman as rich as a Jew. Contentment; or, The Happy Workman's Song. John Byrom. CEP; OBEC
I am a poore & harmless mayde. *Unknown.* SeCSL
I am a pretty wench. *Unknown.* OxNR
I am a quiet gentleman. The Tired Man. Anna Wickman. HBMV; MeWo; NP; ViBoPo (1941 ed.); YT
I am a reek and a rambling one. The Reek and the Rambling Blade. *Unknown.* OuSiCo
I am a roving cowboy off from the Western plains. The Black Tail Range. *Unknown.* CoSo
I am a roving gambler, I've gambled all around. The Roving Gambler. *Unknown.* ABF; AS; TrAS
I am a roving traveler and go from town to town. The Gamboling Man. *Unknown.* AS
I am a sea-shell flung. Frutta di Mare. Geoffrey Scott. ChTr; EtS; OBMV; SiSw
I am a shepherd—I have hated. The Sheep Herd. Sister Mariella. ChrBoLe; WHL
I am a shipwrecked sailor's tomb; a peasant's there doth stand. One to All Men. Plato. OnPM
I am a shoemaker by my trade. The Shoemaker. *Unknown.* TrAS
I am a sincere man. José Martí. *Fr.* Simple Verses. TTY
"I Am a Sioux Brave," He Said in Minneapolis. James Wright. ELU
I am a soul in the world: in. The Invention of Comics. LeRoi Jones. AmNP; FRC
I am a stern old bachelor. The Old Bachelor. William J. Smith. ABF
I am a strange contradiction; I'm new and I'm old. *See* I'm a strange contradiction. . .
I am a stranger in the land. Death. *Unknown.* BLPA
I am a sundial, and I make a botch. On a Sundial. Hilaire Belloc. PV
I am a tongue for beauty. Not a day. Eagle Sonnets, XIX. Clement Wood. HBMV
I am a tramp by the long trail's border. Vachel Lindsay. *Fr.* The Santa-Fé Trail. LaNeLa
I am a tree of time, a swaying shadow. Tree of Time. K. D. Sethna. ACV
I am a trombone. By the chinaberry tree. New Oreleans. Hayden Carruth. AmFN
I am a vaquero by trade. Pinto. *Unknown.* CoSo
I am a very little girl. Little Phillis. Kate Greenaway. BiCB
I am a very personable man. A New Shakespeare. Andrew Lang. CenHV
I am a walking fire, I am all leaves. Emanations. Ronald Johnson. YAP
I am a wandering, bitter shade. What's in a Name? Helen F. More. PAH
I am a wandering cowboy, from ranch to ranch I roam. The Wandering Cowboy. *Unknown.* CoSo
I am a weakling. God, who made. The Weakling. Arthur Adams. BoAu
I am a weaver by my trade. Wil the Merry Weaver, and Charity the Chamber-Maid; or, A Brisk Encounter between a Young-man and His Love. *Unknown.* CoMu
I am a white falcon, hurrah! The Falcon. Richard Henry Stoddard. AA
I Am a Wild Young Irish Boy, *with music.* *Unknown.* ShS
I am a willow-wren. Netted Strawberries. Gordon Bottomley. AtBAP
I am a woman—therefore I may not. A Woman's Thought. Richard Watson Gilder. HBV
I am a young girl. Young Girl: Annam. Padraic Colum. LOW
I am a young jolly brisk sailor. Tarpauling Jacket. *Unknown.* DTC; OxBoLi; PeVV
I am a youthful lady, my troubles they are great. Victory. *Unknown.* CoMu
I am adrift in a desert where too much sun. Desert Shipwreck. Barbara Leslie Jordan. GoYe
I am Aeolus, who keep. Aeolus. Rolfe Humphries. RePo
I am afraid of silence. The Voice. Sister Maris Stella. GoBC
I am afraid to own a body. Emily Dickinson. LiTA; MWA-2
I Am Aladdin. Robert Carlton Brown. AnAmPo
I Am Alone ("I am alive to loneliness"). V. Bhanot. ACV
I am all bent to glean the golden ore. Madrigal: To His Lady Selvaggia Vergiolesi. Cino da Pistoia. AWP; JAWP; WBP
I am all the way from Buffalo. Ballad of the Erie Canal. *Unknown.* ABF; IHA
I am all Thine, Beloved. Exchange. Sister Mary Dorothy Ann. GoBC
I Am Almost Asleep. Eldon Grier. MoCV; PV
I Am an American. Elias Lieberman. FaPON; MaRV; OTD; PaA; PAL; PoLF; TIHL; TreFT
I am an ancient jest! Ballad [*or* Ballade] of the Primitive Jest. Andrew Lang. BOHV; HBV
I am an ancient reluctant conscript. Old Timers. Carl Sandburg. AnAmPo; NP; YaD
I am an inter-citian, I am Black as you can see. Making of a Militant. Yillie Bey (William Manns, II). TNV
I am an old man now. Ossian. Joseph Payne Brennan. FiSC
I am an unadventurous man. De Gustibus. St. John Emile Clavering Hankin. CenHV
"I am an urn of anger," cried the bull. The Bull. Freda Laughton. NeIP
I am Andrew Cecil Bradley. Cecil Arthur Spring-Rice. *Fr.* The Masque of Balliol. CenHV
I am anxious after praise. Egoism. W. Craddle. FiBHP; WhC
I am approaching. Past dry. Loot. Thom Gunn. ErPo; NePoEA-2
I am ardorous, I am dark. Rimas. Gustavo Adolfo Bécquer. CAW
"I am as brown as brown can be." The [Bonny] Brown Girl. *Unknown.* BaBo (A *vers.*); ELP; ESPB; OBB; OxBB
I am as I am and so will I be. Sir Thomas Wyatt. CBEP; FCP; SiPS
I Am as Light as Any Roe. *Unknown.* ViBoPo
("To onpreise womene it were a shame.") LO
(Women Are Worthy.) MeEL
I am, as you know, Walter Llywarch. Walter Llywarch. R. S. Thomas. OPoP
I am ashamed before the earth. Therefore I Must Tell the Truth. Torlino. ExPo
I am ashamed through this thick husk of clay. Sonnet. George Henry Boker. *Fr.* Sonnets: a Sequence on Profane Love. AmePo
I am at sea, sort of. The slime is coral. Some idiot's. The Pier in Berkeley. Stan Rice. QAH
I am beautiful as a dream of stone, but not maternal. Beauty. Baudelaire. OnPM
I am beginning to alter. Poem. Bernadette Mayer. ANYP
I am bereavement, gloom and desolation. El Desdichado. Gérard de Nerval. LO
I am bewildered still and teased by elves. Tricksters. William Rose Benét. HBMV
I am black and I have seen black hands. I Have Seen Black Hands. Richard Wright. PoNe
I am broken by the tumult of the years. Old Joyce. Seán Jennett. NeIP
"I am busy," said the sea. Day. Sir Cecil Spring-Rice. BoTP
I am but clay in thy hands; but thou art the all-loving artist. I in Thee, and Thou in Me. Christopher Pearse Cranch. HBV
I am called Childhood. In play is all my mind. Childhood. Sir Thomas More. EnRePo; NCEP; TuPP
I am caught in an iridescent spider-web. The Web. Witter Bynner. *Fr.* Chapala Poems. NP
I am cold and alone. The Boy Fishing. E. J. Scovell. HaMV; ThWaDe
I am come home again. Home-coming. "Isobel Hume." HBMV

I am come of the seed of the people, the people that sorrow. The Rebel. Padraic Pearse. PoFr
I am come to make thy tomb. John Webster. *Fr.* The Duchess of Malfi. ChTr
I am coming, little maiden. Spring Is Coming. Mary Howitt. PEDC
I am concerned because my mind. Ballade to My Psychoanalyst. Kenneth Lillington. FiBHP
I am confident. More Truth and Light. John Robinson. TRV
I am confirm'd a woman can. Verses. Sir John Suckling. CavP
I am constantly wounded. Rumor Laetalis. *Unknown, at. to* Peter Abelard. LiTW
I am content, I do not care. Careless Content. John Byrom. CEP; HBV; LO, 2 *sts.*; OBEC
I am content with latticed sights. Late Winter. Hazel Hall. HBMV
I am contented by remembrances. Retractions, II. James Branch Cabell. HBMV
I am Count Orlo come to say farewell. Orlo's Valediction. Jon Manchip White. NePoEA
"I am," cried Apollo—when Daphne he wooed. To Apollo Making Love. Bernard le Bovier de Fontenelle. WaPE
I am custodian of close things. When Senses Fled. John Woods. CoPo
I am dangerous. Scissor-Man. George MacBeth. OPoP
I Am Dark and Fair to See. *Unknown.* LO; UnTE
I am dead, Horatio. Wretched queen, adieu! Death of Hamlet. Shakespeare. *Fr.* Hamlet, V, ii. FiP
I am desolate,/ Bereft by bitter fate. Love's Despair. Diarmad O'Curnain. OnYI; OxBI
I am desolate in dimension. The Pomegranate Circus. Richard Brautigan. FRC
I am Don Juan, curst from age to age. Don Juan Declaims. James Elroy Flecker. OnPP
I am dreaming about trains, perhaps. Lines Written in Objection, or, The Limpopo Express. Phillip Hey. YAP
I am driven mad with the printed word. Am Driven Mad. Allen Polite. NNP
I am driving; it is dusk; Minnesota. Driving toward the Lac Qui Parle River. Robert Bly. NaP
I am dying, Egypt, dying. Antony to [*or* and] Cleopatra. William Haines Lytle. AA; BeLS; BLPA; HBV; NeHB; OnPP; TreF
I am dying, Egypt, dying. Death of Antony. Shakespeare. *Fr.* Antony and Cleopatra, IV, xv. FiP; MemP
I am enamoured, and yet not so much. Sonnet: He Will Not Be Too Deeply in Love [*or* Not Too Deeply in Love]. Cecco Angiolieri da Siena. AWP; OnPM
I am enchanted with thy snow-white hands. Emaricdulfe, XVII. "E. C." Sonn; TuPP
"I am escaped," he said, when none pursued. Peter Grimes. George Crabbe. *Fr.* The Borough, Letter XXII. MemP
I am Eve, great Adam's wife. Eve's Lament [*or* Gaelic Fragment]. *Unknown.* CAW; OnYI
I am exceedingly rich. Cat. "Jan Struther." GoTP
I am far frae my hame, an' I'm weary often whiles. My Ain Countree. Mary Augusta Demarest. HBV; WGRP
I am featly-tripping Lee. Henry Charles Beeching. *Fr.* The Masque of Balliol. CenHV
I am fevered with the sunset. The Sea Gypsy [*or* Gipsy]. Richard Hovey. AmePo; BBV; EtS; FaPON; GBV; GoTP; HBV; HBVY; MCCG; OQP; PDV; RePo; StaSt; TIHL; TreFS; TSW; YT
I am fish. Fish. Emily Townsend. NYBP
I am fond of the late poet Sir John Suckling. Brief Lines in Not So Brief. Ogden Nash. ML
I am forever haunted by one dread. Vale. Maurice Baring. JKCP (1955 ed.)
I am Forgetfulness. I am that shadow. Another Altar. Edmund Blunden. MoPW
I am four monkeys. The Tree. Alfred Kreymborg. HBMV; PoPl; TSW
I Am Frightened. Gerald Gould. MoBrPo (1942 ed.)
I Am from Ireland. *Unknown. See* Irish Dancer, The.
I am from Ireland. Dispossessed Poet. Monk Gibbon. OnYI
I am full of grief, and the tear runs from my eye. Five Arabic Verses in Praise of Wine, IV. *Unknown.* TrJP
I Am Fur from My Sweetheart. *Unknown.* CoSo
I am gai. I am poet. I dvell. Vers Nonsensiques. George Du Maurier. HBV
I am gentle with the strong. From Solitude to Solitude towards Life. Paul Eluard. LiTW
I am Giuletta, the bird woman. I married. The Freak Show. Nancy Willard. ThO
I Am Glad Daylong. William Stanley Braithwaite. *See* Rhapsody.
I am glad I met you on the edge. A Childhood. Stephen Spender. NeBP
I am glad that I am not to-day. Something to Be Thankful For. Clara J. Denton. HH
I am coming, I am coming! The Voice of Spring. Mary Howitt. OTPC (1923 ed.); PRWS
I am glad to think/ I am not bound to make the world go right. I Will Trust. Jean Ingelow. MaRV
I am going far away, far away unto the home. The Miner's Farewell. Mart Taylor. SGR
I am going home with Jesus. Going Home with Jesus. Walter E. Isenhour. STF
I am going out West, partner. Po' Laz'us. *Unknown.* OuSiCo
I am going to market. Marketing. E. J. Falconer. BoTP
I am grown haggard and forlorn, from dreams. The Making of the Soul of Man. Upton Sinclair. OQP
I Am Ham Melanite. William Millett. GoYe
I Am He That Walks [with the Tender and Growing Night]. Walt Whitman. *Fr.* Song of Myself, XXI. AtBAP; ChTr; ExPo; MCCG; TSW
I am he who burst the guarded gate. Boast of Masopha. Z. D. Mangoaela. PeSA
I am hearing the shape of the rain. In the Mountain Tent. James Dickey. PoAn
I am here again. I Would Be a Painter Most of All. Len Chandler. NBP
I am here, I have traversed the tomb, I behold thee. He Cometh Forth into the Day. *Unknown. Fr.* Book of the Dead. AWP; JAWP; WBP
I am here, the other elsewhere, the silence seems to live. Shadows. Paul Claudel. CAW
I am His Highness' dog at Kew. Epigram [*or* Engraved on the Collar of a Dog]. Pope. ALV; CABA; CBEP; ChTr; DiPo; EiCL; ExPo; GoTP; HBV; InP; LiTB; LiTG; OnPM; OxBoLi; PCH; PoG; SeCeV; ShBV-4; SiTL; StP; TOP; TreFS; WhC
"I am Holy Chruch," she said, "and you should know me." Holy Church Speaks. William Langland. *Fr.* The Vision of Piers Plowman. PoLi
I am home in heaven, dear ones. Safely Home. *Unknown.* STF
I am Huxley, blond and merry. John Bowyer Buchanan Nichols. *Fr.* The Masque of Balliol. CenHV
I am immortal! I know it! I feel it! Dryad Song. Margaret Fuller. AA; WGRP
I Am in Christ. Frances Rhoads La Chance. SoP
"I Am in Danger—Sir." Adrienne Rich. ML
I am in love with a man. Belgravia. Barbara Guest. AmPC
I Am in Love with High Far-seeing Places. Arthur Davison Ficke. Sonnets of a Portrait Painter, XIII. NP; OQP (View from Heights.) HBMV
I am in love with the laughing sickness. Zizi's Lamanet. Gregory Corso. NeAP
I am in love with the sea, but I do not trust her yet. The Sea-Captain. Gerald Gould. EtS
I am in the old room across from the synagogue. The Old Room. W. S. Merwin. NYBP
I am inside someone. An Agony. As Now. LeRoi Jones. AmPP (5th ed.); BALP; LiTM (1970 ed.); OPoP
I am inside the box. Ceremonies. Ann Stanford. HW
I Am Ireland. Padraic Pearse, *tr. fr. Irish by* Lady Gregory. OBMV
I am jealous: I am true. My Share of the World. Alice Furlong. HBV; OBVV
I am Juniper and I am wicked. Juniper. Eileen Duggan. CAW
I am Jesu that cum to fight. Undo Your Heart. *Unknown.* MeEL
I am just on my way tomb. Oracle. E. L. Mayo. MiAP
I am just seventeen years and five months old. Pompilia. Robert Browning. The Ring and the Book, VII. MaVP; MBW-2; OAEP; PoVP; ViPo; ViPP
I am just two and two, I am warm, I am cold. A Riddle. William Cowper. HBV

I am kind to my neighbors. No Empty Hands. Michael Brownstein. ANYP
I am Lake Superior. The Great Lakes Suite. James Reaney. WHW
I am less patient than this horse. Man and Beast. Francis Meynell. MoBrPo (1942 ed.)
I am like a flag unfurled in space. Presaging. Rainer Maria Rilke. AWP; JAWP; TrJP; WBP
I am like a scrub oak tree. Scrub Oak. E. Merrill Root. MAP
I am like bound because of Abraham's knife. Microcosmos, LVI. Nigel Heseltine. NeBP
I am living for the moment. O Blessed Moment. Avis B. Christiansen. SoP
I am living more alone now than I did. The Last Chapter. Walter de la Mare. CMoP; MoBrPo
I Am Lonely. "George Eliot." *Fr.* The Spanish Gypsy. GN; HBV
I Am Long Weaned. Brother Antoninus. NMP
I am looking rather seedy now while holding down my claim. The Little Old Sod Shanty. *Unknown.* AS; CoSo; IHA
I am lying in thy tomb, love. Lament. Roden Noel. VA
"I am made to sow the thistle for wheat, the nettle for a nourishing dainty." Song of Enion [*or* The Price of Experience]. Blake. *Fr.* Vala; or, The Four Zoas. EnRP; ERoP-1
I am making songs for you. A God for You. Marion Strobel. NP
I am mature, a man child. Chicago. Sherwood Anderson. NP
I am meaning to inundate you with light. Sonnet for the Broken Windows. Anne Waldman. YAP
"I am Miss Catherine's book" (the album speaks). The Pen and the Album. Thackeray. VA
I Am Monarch of All I Survey. William Cowper. *See* Verses Supposed to Be Written by Alexander Selkirk. . .
I am my ancient self. The Pilgrim. Richard Wightman. WGRP
I Am My Beloved's. The Song of Solomon, VII: 11-14, Bible, *O.T.* TrJP
I Am My Beloved's, and His Desire Is towards Me. Francis Quarles. *See* Like to the Arctic Needle.
I am my mammy's ae bairn. I'm O'er [*or* Owre] Young to Marry Yet. Burns. EiCL; LO; UnTE; ViBoPo
I am nae poet, in a sense. Burns. *Fr.* Epistle to J. Lapraik. PP
I am no brazen face to hale the Lord. Rabbi Yom-Tob of Mayence Petitions His God. A. M. Klein. TrJP
I am no gentleman, not I! The Working Man's Song. John Stuart Blackie. VA
I am no poet who can set. Patric Dickinson. LO
I am no shepherd of a child's surmises. Montana Pastoral. J. V. Cunningham. MoAmPo (1962 ed.); PoIE
I Am No Subject unto Fate. *Unknown.* OBS
I am no trumpet, but a reed. Sympathy. Elizabeth Barrett Browning. *Fr.* A Reed. SoP
I am nobody. Hokku Poems. Richard Wright. AmNP
I am not a handsome man. Eclipse. Ed Roberson. PoNe (1970 ed.)
I am not a metaphor or symbol. The Distant Drum. Calvin C. Hernton. BOLo; NNP; TTY
I am not a painter, I am a poet. Why I Am Not a Painter. Frank O'Hara. ANYP; NeAP
I am not afraid in April. White Fear. Winifred Welles. HBMV
I am not anyone in particular. No One in Particular. John Perreault. ANYP; YAP
"I am not as these are," the poet saith. Old and New Art: Not As These. Dante Gabriel Rossetti. The House of Life, LXXV. MaVP; PoVP; ViPo
I Am Not Bound to Win. Abraham Lincoln. TRV
I am not bred and born New Englander. Late Comer. Fanny de Groot Hastings. GoYe
I am not concern'd to know. True Riches. Isaac Watts. OBEC
I Am Not Lazy. Mari Evans. WSL
I am not moved to love Thee, O my Lord. To Christ Crucified. *Unknown, tr. by* Thomas Walsh. CAW; OnPM
I am not of those fierce, wild wills. My Political Faith. George Frederick Cameron. PeCV
I am not of those miserable males. Modern Love, XX. George Meredith. EnLit; ViPo; VP
I am not one who much or oft delight. Personal Talk. Wordsworth. BEL; CABA; DiPo; EnRP; EPN; InPo; MyFE
I am not poor, but I am proud. Thought. Emerson. AmePo; AmPP (3d ed.); CoBA
I am not resigned to the shutting away of loving hearts. Dirge without Music. Edna St. Vincent Millay. AnNE; BoLiVe; CMoP; GTBS-W; LiTA; LiTG; LO; MoRP; NePA; NP; PG; PPON; TrGrPo
I am not skilled to understand. My Saviour. Dora Greenwell. SoP
I am not strong till Thou hast clasped my hand. Freedom. *Unknown.* PGD
I am not sure that earth is round. Certainty Enough. Amelia Josephine Burr. HBMV
I Am Not the Constant Reader. Michael Brownstein. ANYP
I am not the master of my fate. Jesus, the Master of My Fate. *Unknown.* SoP
"I am not treacherous, callous, jealous, superstitious." A Face. Marianne Moore. PoCh
I am not what I was yesterday. The Butterfly. Alice Archer James. AA
I am not wiser for my age. Climacteric. Emerson. MWA-1
I Am Not Worthy That Thou Should'st Come Under My Roofe. Richard Crashaw. MaMe
I am not yet born; O hear me. Prayer before Birth. Louis MacNeice. GTBS-P; LiTB; OAEP (2d ed.); TwCP
I am not you. Africa's Plea. Roland Tombekai Dempster. PBA; TTY
I am not your God. African Easter. Abioseh Nicol. PBA
I am numb from world-pain. A Little Swirl of Vers Libre. Thomas R. Ybarra. BOHV
"I am of a band of highwaymen." Cole Younger. *Unknown.* BFSS
I Am of Ireland. *Unknown.* *See* Irish Dancer, The.
"I Am of Ireland." W. B. Yeats. CMoP; LiTB; NAMP; OnYI
I am of little worth and poor, apart. Song of Loneliness. Judah Halevi. TrJP
I am old and blind! Milton's Prayer for Patience. Elizabeth Lloyd Howell. SoP; TRV
I am of old and young, of the foolish as much as the wise. Walt Whitman. Song of Myself, XVI. CoBA
I am of Shropshire, my shins be sharp. A Shropshire Lad. *Unknown.* ChTr
I am of value to men, variously am found. *Unknown.* *Fr.* Riddles. EnLit
I am off down the road. Goblin Feet. J. R. R. Tolkien. FaPON; PoMS
I am old and blind! Milton's Prayer. Elizabeth Lloyd Howell. AA; MaRV; WGRP
I am one man, worshipping silk knees. Poem. William Knott. YAP
I am one of a band of outlaws, Cole Younger is my name. Cole Younger. *Unknown.* BeLS
I am one of those troubled hearts. Human Soul. René Maran. TTY
I am only one. Lend a Hand. Edward Everett Hale. SoP; TRV
I am out on the wind. Changeling. Leah Bodine Drake. PoMS
I am, outside. Incredible panic rules. The Dream Songs, XLVI. John Berryman. NaP
I am part of the seas and stars. Kinship. Edward H. S. Terry. MaRV; OQP
I Am Partly Moon. Vincente Huidobro, *tr. fr. Spanish by* Joseph Staples. LiTW
I am picking wild grapes last year. The Winemaker's Beat-étude. Alfred Purdy. MoCV
I am poor and old and blind. Belisarius. Longfellow. PoEL-5; WiR
I am poor brother Lippo, by your leave! Fra Lippo Lippi. Robert Browning. BEL; BoLiVe; CABL; CTC; EnL; EnLi-2; EnLit; EPN; MaPo (1969 ed.); MaVP; MBW-2; NoP; OAEP; OtMeF; PAn; PoVP; ViBoPo; ViPo; ViPP; VP
I am put high over all others in the city today. Killers. Carl Sandburg. MoVE
I am Queen Anne, of whom 'tis said. Queen Anne. *Unknown.* ChTr
I am quite sure He thinks that I am God. Bishop Doane on His Dog "Cluny." William Croswell Doane, *wr. at. to* George Washington Doane. BBV (1951 ed.); BLPA; FaBoBe; NeHB

I Am Raftery [or Raferty]. Anthony Raftery, *tr. fr. Modern Irish by* Douglas Hyde. AnIV; AnIL, *tr. by* James Stephens; AWP; JAWP; LiTW; OnYI (*incl. tr. by* James Stephens); SeCePo; WBP
I Am Ready Not Onely to Be Bound But to Dye. Richard Crashaw. MaMe
I am remembering in the long ago. *Unknown. Fr.* The Dream of the Rood. ACP
I am reminded, by the tan man who wings. The Elevator Man Adheres to Form. Margaret Danner. PoNe (1970 ed.)
I am returned, my fair, but see. The Retreat. Charles Cotton. CBEP; SeCL
I am riding on a limited express, one of the crack trains of the nation. Limited. Carl Sandburg. AmP; LoGBV; MAP; MoAB; MoAmPo; NeMA; OxBA
I am rooted in the wall. Snapdragon. Cardinal Newman. GoBC
I Am Rose. Gertrude Stein. LiTM; NePA; SiTL; TrJP
I am round and very small. Pablo. Grace Hazard Conkling. GaP
I am Saint John on Patmos of my heart. Holy Poems, I. George Barker. MoPo
I am saved, but is self buried? Saved, But—. *Unknown.* SoP; STF
I am silver and exact. I have no preconceptions. Mirror. Sylvia Plath. NYBP
I am singing to you. Killers. Carl Sandburg. NP
I am sitting here. The Poor Girl's Meditation. *Unknown, tr. by* Padraic Colum. OBMV
I am sitting in Mike's Place trying to figure out. One Thousand Fearful Words for Fidel Castro. Lawrence Ferlinghetti. CoPo
I am sleepy, I'm tired, and I'm hungry and dry. Qu'avec vous, oui, belle blonde. *Unknown.* OuSiCo
I am smiling tonight not really. Smiles. Peter Schjeldahl. ANYP
I am so empty and so incomplete. Fulfilment. Elsa Barker. *Fr.* The Spirit and the Bride. HBMV
I Am So Far from Pitying Thee. *Unknown.* NCEP
I Am So Glad and Very. E. E. Cummings. CMoP
I am so little and grey. The Prayer of the Mouse. Carmen Bernos de Gasztold. PDV
I am so little that the gods go by. The Common Lot. Lizette Woodworth Reese. NP
I am so lost. Narihira, *tr. fr. Japanese by* Kenneth Rexroth. LiTW
I am so old a king that I remember. The Old King. John Heath-Stubbs. NePoEA
I am so out of love through poverty. Sonnet: Of Why He Would Be a Scullion. Cecco Angiolieri da Siena. AWP
I am so passing rich in poverty. Sonnet: He Jests concerning His Poverty. Bartolomeo di Sant' Angelo. AWP
I am so tired and weary. Supplication. Joseph Seamon Cotter, Jr. BANP; CDC; PoNe
I am so weak, dear Lord, I cannot stand. Enough for Me. Frances Ridley Havergal. SoP
I am sorry that Che Guevara is dead. Che Guevara Is Dead. Peter Schjeldahl. ANYP
I am sorry to speak of death again. Poetics against the Angel of Death. Phyllis Webb. MoCV
I am soul in the world: in. The Invention of Comics. LeRoi Jones. LiTM (1970 ed.)
I am standing on the threshold of eternity at last. On the Threshold. *Unknown.* BLPA
I am standing upon the seashore. The Ship. *Unknown.* PoLF
I am startled by comparisons. The Wizard's New Meeting. Peter Redgrove. HYE
I am still far away. Folk Tale. P. Mustapää. HW
I am still hurt, Plin. A Letter for Allhallows. Peter Kane Dufault. NYBP
I Am Still Rich. Thomas Curtis Clark. PoToHe
I am strange here and often I am still trying. Evening. W. S. Merwin. FRC
I am sure this Jesus will not do. Epilogue. Blake. *Fr.* The Everlasting Gospel. OBRV
I am surprised to see. Letter Written on a Ferry While Crossing Long Island Sound. Anne Sexton. CoAP; NYBP; TwCP
I am surrounded by armies, I have sent them word. Note in Lieu of a Suicide. Donald Finkel. CoPo
I am telling you a number of half-conditioned ideas. Sunday Evening. Barbara Guest. NeAP
I am that Adam who, with snake for guest. The Exile. Walter de la Mare. POTE
I am that exile. Bellbuoy. Sol Funaroff. WOW
I am that man who with a luminous look. Brevities. Siegfried Sassoon. MoPW; PoLF
I am that man with helmet made of thorn. For an Ex-Far East Prisoner of War. Charles Causley. POTi
I am that serpent-haunted cave. The Pythoness. Kathleen Raine. FaBoMo; MoBrPo (1962 ed.); ViBoPo (1958 ed.)
I am that which began. Hertha. Swinburne. BEL; EnLi-2; EPN; HBVY; MaVP; OAEP; OBEV (1st ed.); PoVP; TOP; VA; ViPo; ViPP; VP
I am the American heartbreak. American Heartbreak. Langston Hughes. AmPP (5th ed); LiTM (1970 ed.)
I am the ancient Apple-Queen. Pomona. William Morris. WiR
I Am the Autumn. Itzig Manger, *tr. fr. Yiddish by* Joseph Leftwich. TrJP
I am the black centipede, the rusher with a black nose. Praises of the Train. Demetrius Segooa. PeSA
I Am the Blood. Isaac Rosenberg. MoBrPo
I Am the Bread of Life. St. John VI: 35-40, Bible, *N.T.* TreFS
I am the captain of my soul. An Awful Responsiblity. Keith Preston. PoPl; WhC
I Am the Captain of the Pinafore. W. S. Gilbert. *Fr.* H. M. S. Pinafore. TreFT
I Am the Cat. Leila Usher. BLPA
I am the cat of cats. I am. The Cat of Cats [*or* The Kitten Speaks *or* Kitty: What She Thinks of Herself]. William Brighty Rands. *Fr.* The White Princess. CIV; MoShBr; RIS
I am the chaunt-rann of a Singer. The Poet. Padraic Fiacc. NeIP
I am the Child. The Child's Appeal. Mamie Gene Cole. MaRV; OQP
I am the child by the Yangtse running. Child of the World. Edna L. S. Barker. GoYe
I am the cock with armored feet. The Song of the Beasts. Anthony Hecht. CBV
I Am the Cross. William L. Stidger. ChIP
I am the dancer of the wood. The Spirit of the Birch. Arthur Ketchum. *Fr.* Legends for Trees. MPB; OHIP; SP
I am the dark cavalier; I am the last lover. The Dark Cavalier. Margaret Widdemer. HBMV; PFY
I Am the Darker Brother. Langston Hughes. *See* I, Too, Sing America.
I am the Dean of Christ Church, Sir. Cecil Arthur Spring-Rice. *Fr.* The Masque of Balliol. CenHV
I am the dog world's best detective. The Bloodhound. Edward Anthony. GoTP
I Am the Door. Richard Crashaw. MaMe; OAEP
I Am the Door. *Unknown.* OQP
I am the family face. Heredity. Thomas Hardy. CBEP; CTC; ImOP; MoPW
I am the farmer, stripped of love. The Hill Farmer Speaks. R. S. Thomas. GTBS-P; HaMV
I am the first, of all the rancorous men. The Tree at Post 4. Kenneth Mackenzie. MoAuPo
I am the first that ever lov'd. Love Speaks at Last. Lord Herbert of Cherbury. AnAnS-2
I Am the Flag. Lawrence M. Jones. PAL; PGD
I am the flower of the field. Canticle of Canticles (The Song of Solomon), Bible, *O.T. (Douay vers.).* ISi
I am the flute of Daphnis. On this wall. The Flute of Daphnis. Edward Cracroft Lefroy. Echoes from Theocritus, XXIII. AWP; OBVV
I am the gay Nasturtium. The Nasturtiums. *Unknown.* GFA
I am the ghost of Shadwell Stair. Shadwell Stair. Wilfred Owen. FaBoTw
I Am the Gilly of Christ. Joseph Campbell. AnIL; OnYI
I am the god of things that burrow and creep. The Gods of the Earth Beneath. Edmund Blunden. BrPo
I am the God Thor. The Challenge of Thor. Longfellow. *Fr.* Tales of a Wayside Inn: The Saga of King Olaf. AmPP (4th ed.)
I am the great Professor Jowett. *Unknown.* FiBHP; PV
I am the great sun. This hour begins. Canticle of the Sun Dancing on Easter Morning. John Heath-Stubbs. BoPe

I (continued)
I am the house! Ford Madox Ford. *Fr.* A House. MoBrPo (1942 ed.)
I am the key that parts the gates of Fame. Death. Florence Earle Coates. HBV; OQP
I am the lamp that Flaccus gave his love. Faithless. *Unknown.* UnTE
I am the land of their fathers. The Recall. Kipling. BoPe; NoP; POTE; PoVP
I Am the Last. Edward Shillito. OQP
(One Love.) MaRV
I am the little ass of Christ. The Ass Speaks. Katharine Tynan. MaRV
I am the little New Year, ho, ho! The New Year. *Unknown.* BoTP
I am the Lord of Light, the self-begotten youth. He Maketh Himself One with the God Ra. *Unknown.* *Fr.* Book of the Dead. AWP
I am the Lord thy God. The Ten Commandments. Exodus, Bible, *O.T.* OHFP; WBLP
I am the luring Vivien. Woman. Zora Cross. BoAu
I am the lute. If you wish to write. The Lute. Rainer Maria Rilke. OnPM
I am the magical mouse. The Magical Mouse. Kenneth Patchen. LOW
I am the maiden in bronze set over the tomb of Midas. Cleobulus' Epitaph. Simonides. PoPl
I am the man in the middle, the rare achievement. The Sandwich Man. Louis Johnson. AnNZ
I am the man that hath seen affliction. Affliction. Lamentations, Bible, *O.T.* TrJP
I am the man who looked for peace and found. War Poet. Sidney Keyes. MemP
I Am the Monarch of the Sea. W. S. Gilbert. *Fr.* H.M.S. Pinafore. TreFT
I am the mother of fair love. Ecclesiasticus, Apocrypha, Bible (*Douay vers.*). ISi
I am the mother of sorrows. The Paradox. Paul Laurence Dunbar. Kal
I Am the Mountainy Singer. Joseph Campbell. AnIL; GoBC; HBMV; JKCP; MCCG; MoBrPo
I am the mown grass, dying at your feet. Moritura. Margaret Gilman Davidson. AA
I am the New Year, and I come to you pure and unstained. The New Year. J. D. Templeton. OQP; PGD
I am the nor'west air nosing among the pines. Time. Allen Curnow. AnNZ
I am the old woman of Beare. The Old Woman of Beare. *Unknown.* AnIL
I Am the Only Being [Whose Doom]. Emily Brontë. NCEP; ViBoPo, 2 *sts.*
I am the past and the present, and I bear. Book of the Dead. *Unknown.* LiTW
I Am the People, the Mob. Carl Sandburg. AmPP; OxBA; PoPo
I Am the Poet Davies, William. W. H. Davies. CBEP; MoPW
I am the poet of the body and I am the poet of the soul. Walt Whitman. Song of Myself, XXI. CoBA; SeCeV; TrGrPo
I Am the Pony in the Central Park Zoo. John Perreault. YAP
I am the prince in the field. He Maketh Himself One with Osiris. *Unknown.* *Fr.* Book of the Dead. AWP
I am the pure lotus. He Is like the Lotus [*or* Death as a Lotus Flower]. *Unknown.* *Fr.* Book of the Dead. AWP; EaLo; JAWP; TTY; WBP
I am the pure, the true of word, triumphant. He Defendeth His Heart against the Destroyer. *Unknown.* *Fr.* Book of the Dead. AWP
I am the pure traveler. He Entereth the House of the Goddess Hathor. *Unknown.* *Fr.* Book of the Dead. AWP
I am the queen Herodias. Swinburne. *Fr.* The Masque of Queen Bersabe. AtBAP
I am the queerest sort of boy the world has ever seen. The Contrary Boy. Gaston V. Drake. BBGG
I am the reality of things that seem. Poetry. Ella Heath. HBV; WGRP
I am the Reaper. W. E. Henley. Echoes, V. OBNC; OQP
"I Am the Resurrection and the Life," Saith the Lord! Robert Stephen Hawker. GoBC
I am the rooftree and the keel. Tapestry Trees. William Morris. BoNaP; FaPON; MPB; OHIP
I Am the Root and Offspring of David. Edward Taylor. *See* Preparatory Meditations: "Help, oh! my Lord, anoint. . ."
I Am the Rose of Sharon. Song of Solomon, II, Bible, *O.T.* ChTr
(Song of Songs, II.) GBV, *abr.*; PG
I Am the Rose of Sharon. Edward Taylor. *See* Preparatory Meditations: "Lord, art thou at the table. . ."
I Am the Rose of Sharon. Catherine Winkworth. BePJ
I am the saint at prayer on the terrace. Childhood, IV. Arthur Rimbaud. *Fr.* Illuminations. PoPl
I am the serpent fat with years. He Is like the Serpent Saka. *Unknown.* *Fr.* Book of the Dead. AWP
I am the seventh son of the son. Malcolm X—an Autobiography. Larry Neal. BF
I am the shadow in the shadow of the wicker. Home Revisited: Midnight. John Ciardi. NYBP
I am the singer who, of late, put by. Portico. Rubén Darío. CAW
I am the sister of him. Little. Dorothy Aldis. FaPON; SUS; TiPo
I am the sombre wake. I Am the Wake. Iwan Goll. OnPM
I am the son of the mountain. Son of the Mountain. Eifion Wyn. PrWP
I am the spirit astir. Autochthon. Sir Charles G. D. Roberts. CaP; VA
I am the spirit of the morning sea. Ode. Richard Watson Gilder. AA
I am the stage, impassive, mute and cold. Nature. Alfred de Vigny. AWP; JAWP; WBP
I Am the Stars' Bugging-Device. William Knott. YAP
I am the teacher of athletes. Walt Whitman. Song of Myself, XLVII. CoBA
I am the tomb of Crethon; here you read. The Tomb of Crethon. Leonidas of Tarentum. AWP; JAWP; WBP
I am the torch, she saith, and what to me. Modern Beauty. Arthur Symons. EnLit; HBV; MoBrPo; PoVP
I am the true vine, and my Father is the husbandman. The True Vine. St. John, Bible, *N.T.* WoL
I am the trumpet blown by time. The Trumpet. Ilya Ehrenburg. TrJP
I am the Turquoise Woman's son. The War God's Horse Song. *Unknown.* LiTA; LoGBV
I am the unnoticed, the unnoticeable man. The Man in the Bowler Hat. A. S. J. Tessimond. HaMV; POTE
I am the very model of a modern college president. The Very Model of a Modern College President, *parody.* Harold A. Larrabee. WhC
I am the very model [*or* pattern] of a modern Major General. The Modern Major-General [*or* Major-General's Song]. W. S. Gilbert. *Fr.* The Pirates of Penzance. CoBE; InMe; NBM; OnPP; PCD
I am the Virgin; from this granite ledge. The Wayside Virgin. Langdon Elwyn Mitchell. AA
I am the voice of the uplands ringing from hill to hill. The Peace Call. Edgar Lloyd Hampton. PEDC
I Am the Wake. Iwan Goll, *tr. fr. French by* Claire Goll. OnPM
"I Am the Way." Alice Meynell. ACP; CAW; GoBC; JKCP; MaRV; OBMV; OQP; PoVP; TRV
I Am the Wind. Zoë Akins. HBV; NP; TOP
I am the wind which breathes upon the sea. The Mystery. *At. to* Amergin. OnYI; OxBI
I am the witness who dwelleth in the soul of all. The Witness. Sri Ananda Acharya. ACV
I am the woman-drawer. The Song of the Woman-Drawer. Mary Gilmore. PoAu-1
I am thin as nail parings. Light as dandruff. Embryos. Marge Piercy. ThO
I Am Thinking of Chicago and of What Survives. Lou Lipsitz. YAP
I am thinking tonight of the days that are gone. The Plain Golden Band. *At. to* Joe Scott. ShS
I am this fountain's god. The River God. John Fletcher. *Fr.* The Faithful Shepherdess, III, i. BoC; CLwM; TrGrPo
I am, thow woost, yet of thy compaignye. Chaucer. *Fr.* The Canterbury Tales: The Knight's Tale. PoG
I am thy fathers spirit. Shakespeare. *Fr.* Hamlet, I, v. AtBAP
I am thy fugitive, thy votary. To the Lord Love. "Michael Field." OBMV
I am Thy grass, O Lord! Trust. Lizette Woodworth Reese. AA

"I am thy soul, Nikoptis. I have watched." The Tomb at [*or* of] Akr Çaar. Ezra Pound. APA; CoAnAm; TwAmPo
I am tired of city sounds. Discovery. Catherine Parmenter. OQP
I am tired of cursing the Bishop. Crazy Jane on the Mountain. W. B. Yeats. AtBAP; CMoP
I am tired of echoes in the old house. It Is Time to Build. Elias Lieberman. MaRV
I am tired of planning and toiling. The Cry of the [*or* a] Dreamer. John Boyle O'Reilly. BLPA; NeHB; OnYI; TreFS
I Am Tired of the Wind. Gordon Bottomley. POTE
"I am tired of this barn!" said the colt. The Barn. Elizabeth J. Coatsworth. AnNE; BiCB; ChBR; GoTP; SoPo; UTS
I am tired of work; I am tired of building up somebody else's civilization. Tired. Fenton Johnson. BANP; IDB; Kal; PoLF; PoNe; TTY
I am to follow her. There is much grace. Modern Love, XLII. George Meredith. ViBoPo; ViPo; VP
I am told, sir, you're keeping an eye on your wife. The Careful Husband. *Unknown, tr. by* the Earl of Longford. OnYI; OxBI
I am too near, too clear a thing for you. A Flower of Mullein. Lizette Woodworth Reese. MoAmPo; NeMA
I Am Trusting Thee. Frances Ridley Havergal. SoP
I am trying to decide to go swimming. The Wind Is Blowing West. Joseph Ceravolo. ANYP
I Am 25. Gregory Corso. CoPo
I am 25 years old. My Poem. Nikki Giovanni. BOLo; TNV
I am 20 years old and holding on. After Les Fleurs (Paul Eluard). Anne Waldman. YAP
I am two fools [*or* fooles], I know. The Triple Fool. John Donne. CoBE; DiPo; MaMe; OAEP; Po; PP; SCEP-1
I am type of singleness. Artemis. Dulcie Deamer. PoAu-1
I am unable, yonder begger cries. A Lame Begger. John Donne. MaMe; TuPP
I am unjust, but I can strive for justice. Why I Voted the Socialist Ticket. Vachel Lindsay. MoAmPo (1962 ed.)
I am up early. The box-elder leaves have fallen. Getting Up Early. Robert Bly. NaP
I am valued by men, fetched from afar. Honey-Mead. *Unknown. Fr.* Riddles. AnOE
I am very fond of the little ribs of women. Vincent McHugh. *Fr.* Talking to Myself. ErPo
I Am Waiting, *sel.* Lawrence Ferlinghetti.
"I am waiting for my case to come up." PoPl; WOW
I am waiting for. A Black Poetry Day. Alicia Loy Johnson. BOLo
I am waiting for my case to come up. Lawrence Ferlinghetti. *Fr.* I Am Waiting. PoPl; WOW
I am waiting for the coming of the Bridegroom in the air. The Glad Home-coming. A. B. Simpson. SoP
I am waiting for the dawning. Waiting for the Dawning. *Unknown.* BLRP
I am walking a trail. Intimidations of an Autobiography. James Tate. YAP
I am watching them churn the last milk. The Mad Yak. Gregory Corso. CoPo
I Am Weary of Being Bitter. Arthur Davison Ficke. NP
I am weary of lying within the chase. Ballade de Marguerite. *Unknown.* AWP; JAWP; WBP
I am weary of the garden. Said the Rose. George H. Miles. BLPA
I Am What You Make Me. Franklin K. Lane. PGD
I am who the trail took. Exploration. Daniel Hoffman. CoAP; CoPo
I am willowy boughs. I Am. Hilda Conkling. FaPON; NP; TiPo
"I Am with Thee." Ernest Bourner Allen. BLRP
I Am with You Alway. Edwin Henry Nevin. BePJ
I am within as white as snow. Riddle. *Unknown.* ChTr
I am without a single doubt. The Perfect Child. Molly Michaels. RIS
I am worn out with dreams. Men Improve With the Years. W. B. Yeats. BWP; MBW-2
I am writing at the request of. Alafia. Odaro (Barbara Jones). BF
I am writing near the lamp. It's fine weather. Pleasant stillness. Promenades and Interiors. François Coppée. CAW
I am yesterday. I am gone from you forever. Yesterday. Frank Crane. OQP
I am yesterday, today and to-morrow. He Walketh by Day. *Unknown. Fr.* Book of the Dead. AWP; JAWP; WBP
I am: yet what I am none cares or knows. I Am [*or* Written in a Northampton County Asylum]. John Clare. BoPe; CBEP; EnRP; ERoP-2; GTBS-P; GTBS-W; FaBoEn; GTSE; GTSL; InvP; LiTB; NBM; NoP; OBEV; OBNC; OBVV; PeER; PG; PoE; PoEL-4; PoIE; PoPl; PoSa; TrGrPo; ViBoPo; WHA
I Am Your Brook. Iwan Goll, *tr. fr. French by* Claire Goll. OnPM
I Am Your Loaf, Lord. David Ross. GoYe
I Am Your Wife. *Unknown.* PoToHe (new ed.)
I, an ambassador of Otherwhere. From the Embassy. Robert Graves. TPM
I, an old man. Girl and Butterfly. Edith Sitwell. MoPW
I, an old woman in the light of the sun. An Old Woman. Edith Sitwell. CoBMV; MoPo
I, an old woman whose heart is like the Sun. Harvest. Edith Sitwell. OAEP (2d ed.)
I, an unwedded wandering dame. Epitaph. Sylvia Townsend Warner. MoBrPo; NeMA
I and my cousin Wildair met. Praise-God Barebones. Ellen Mackay Hutchinson Cortissoz. AA
I and my sisters three. Victorian Song. John Farrar. GoYe
I and my white Pangur. The Monk and His Pet Cat. *Unknown, tr. by* W. Stokes, J. Strachan, *and* K. Meyer. CH; OnYI
I and Pangur Bán my cat. Pangur Bán [*or* The White Cat and the Student]. *Unknown, tr. by* Robin Flower. AnIL; FaBoCh; LoGBV; OA; OnYI; OxBI; RIS
I, Angelo, obese, black-garmented. Angelo Orders His Dinner. Bayard Taylor. BOHV; Par
I approach with such. Something. Robert Creeley. NaP
I arise from dreams of thee. Indian Serenade [*or* Lines to an Indian Air]. Shelley. AnFE; ATP; AWP; BEL; BoLiVe; BoLP; EnLi-2; EnLit; EnRP; ExPo; FaBoBe; FaPL; FiP; GTBS; GTBS-D; GTBS-P; GTBS-W; GTSE; GTSL; HBV; HoPM; InPo; JAWP; LiTB; LiTG; LiTL; LoBV; MCCG; MERP; MeWo; NeHB; OAEP; OBEV; OBRV; OuHeWo; PG; PoAn; PoPl; TOP; TreF; TrGrPo; UnPo (1st ed.); UnTE; ViBoPo; WBP
I arise in the east in all my immensity. The Lord of the East. Chu Yuan. *Fr.* The Nine Songs. LiTW
I arise to-day. The Deer's Cry [*or* St. Patrick's Breastplate]. *At. to* St. Patrick. AnIL; AnIV; CAW; OnYI; WGRP; WHL
I, Arnor the red poet, made. The Five Voyages of Arnor. George Mackay Brown. NePoEA-2
I arose swiftly that night, for I heard a knock at my door. The Future. James Oppenheim. TrJP
I Arrive in Madrid. Al Young. WSL
I ask but one thing of you, only one. To a Friend. Amy Lowell. PoLF
I ask good things that I detest. Prayer. Robert Louis Stevenson. TrPWD
I ask, in truth, what right was given to me. Words. Sir Thomas Herbert Parry-Williams. PrWP
I ask no heaven till earth be Thine. Here Am I. *Unknown.* SoP
I ask no kind return of [*or* in] love. Prayer for Indifference. Fanny Greville. LO; OBEC; OBEV
I ask not how thy suffering came. Fraternity. Anne Reeve Aldrich. AA
I ask not that my bed of death. A Wish. Matthew Arnold. EPN; HBV; PoVP
I ask not wit, nor beauty do I crave. The Humble Wish. *Unknown.* EiCL
I ask thee not to withhold grief. A Morning Prayer. Betty Perpetuo. SoP; STF
I ask thee, whence those ashes were. A Question. *Unknown.* CBEP; SeCL
I ask thy aid, O potent rum! Resentments Composed because of the Clamor of Town Topers Outside My Apartment. Sarah Kemble Knight. SCAP
I ask, who will buy a poem? Who Will Buy a Poem? Mahon O'Heffernan. AnIL
I ask you, my friend. Success. Wang Chi. WoL
I ask you this. Prayer. Langston Hughes. CDC; EaLo
I ask'd my dear friend, Orator Prig. Blake. EiCL
I Asked a Thief [to Steal Me a Peach]. Blake. CABA; CBEP;

I (continued)
ERoP-1; ExPo; NoP; OBNC; PeER; PIA; PoeP; SeCeV; StP; ViBoPo
(Angel, The.) LiTB; LiTG; SiTL
I asked for bread; God gave a stone instead. Prayer. *Unknown.* OQP; SoP
I asked for bread! Life led me to a plain. The Quest. Chester B. Emerson. OQP
I asked for grace to lift me high. God's Ways. *Unknown.* MaRV
I asked for just a crumb of bread. More Than We Ask. Faith Wells. BLRP
I Asked for Peace. Digby Mackworth Dolben. BoPe; OxBoCh
(Requests.) MaRV; TrPWD
(Within Thy Heart.) FaChP
I asked for something to eat. Something to Eat. Tom Veitch. ANYP
I asked [God] for strength, that I might achieve. Prayer of an Unknown Confederate Soldier [*or* Prayer Answered]. *Unknown.* STF; TreFT
I asked her, "Is Aladdin's Lamp." The Sorceress. Vachel Lindsay. PDV
I asked her why she didn't. Girl with Long Dark Hair. Stephen Gray. PeSA
I asked if I got sick and died, would you. A Question. J. M. Synge. ELU; MoBrPo; OBMV; OBVV; OxBI
I asked if I should pray. Mohini Chatterjee. W. B. Yeats. MoRP
I Asked My Fair, One Happy Day. Gotthold Ephraim Lessing, *ad. fr. German by* Samuel Taylor Coleridge. HBV
(By What Sweet Name.) MeWo
I Asked My Mother. *Unknown.* MoShBr
("I asked my mother for fifty [*or* fifteen] cents.") FaFP; GoTP; SiTL; TiPo
(Nursery Rhymes.) OxBoLi
I asked my soul where springs the ill-omened seed. Forgetfulness. Sosei. OnPM
I asked no other thing. Emily Dickinson. MaPo; MemP; OxBA
I asked of Echo, t' other day. Echo. John Godfrey Saxe. AnNE; BOHV
I Asked of My Harp. Sir Walter Scott. CBV
I asked of Time to tell me where was Love. Love. Jones Very. AP
I asked philosophy how I should. Hermatic Poems. Elias Ashmole. LO
I asked professors who teach the meaning of life. Happiness. Carl Sandburg. OxBA; WoL
I asked the heaven of stars. Night Song at Amalfi. Sara Teasdale. MAP; MeWo; MoAmPo; NeMA
I asked the holly, "What is your life if. . .?" Trees. Ted Hughes. NYBP
I asked the Lord that I might grow. Prayer Answered by Crosses. John Newton. FaChP; STF
I asked the Lord to let me do. Service. *Unknown.* SoP
I asked the New Year [*or* Master] for a [*or* some] motto [*or* message] sweet. God's Will [*or* Message of the New Year, The]. Charles E. Guthrie. BLRP; OQP; SoP
I asked the New Year, "What am I to do." Questioning. Grace Noll Crowell. DD
I asked the roses as they grew. Transformed. D. Weston Gates. STF
I ate at Ostendorff's, and saw a dame. Traümerei at Ostendorff's. "William Laird." HBMV
I ate my fill of army bread. The Air Sentry. Patrick Barrington. CenHV
I attended school and I liked the place. Values in Use. Marianne Moore. NePoAm-2
I awoke happy, the house. The Revelation. William Carlos Williams. MoLP
I awoke in the Midsummer not to call night. Moonrise. Gerard Manley Hopkins. MoAB; MoBrPo; SeCePo
I awoke only to hear the dull clobbing of the wind. Night Shore. Barry O. Higgs. PeSA
I bade my Lady think what she might mean. Modern Love, XL. George Meredith. ViPo; VP
I bargained with Life for a penny. My Wage. Jessie Belle Rittenhouse. BLPA; NeHB; PoMa; PoToHe (new ed.)
I bear an unseen burden constantly. The Burden of Love. "Owen Innsley." AA
I Bear, in Sign of Love. Francis Andrewes. *Fr.* Shepherdess' Valentine. BiS
I began in Ohio. Stages on a Journey Westward. James Wright. AmPC; NaP
I bear the scourge of just Rhamnusia. Proemium in Librum Primum. John Marston. *Fr.* The Scourge of Villainy. ReIE
I Beat the Drum. Jan Greshoff, *tr. fr. Dutch by* A. J. Barnouw. PoFr
I Been a Bad, Bad Girl, *with music.* *Unknown.* OuSiCo
I been 'buked an' I been scorned. Hell and Heaven. *Unknown.* SiTL
I beg the pardon of these flowers. With Lilacs. Charles Henry Crandall. AA
I beg you come to-night and dine. The Menu. Thomas Bailey Aldrich. HBV
I begin through the grass once again to be bound to the Lord. Reconciliation. "Æ." MoRP; OBMV; OxBI; PoVP
I beheld her, on a day. How He Saw Her. Ben Jonson. *Fr.* A Celebration of Charis. AnAnS-2; AtBAP; EnRePo; OAEP; QFR; SeCP; SeCV-1
I, Being Born a Woman. Edna St. Vincent Millay. ALV
(Sonnet: "I, being born a woman and distressed.") ErPo
I, being Protestant, can never bow. To Mary, Mother of Christ. Una W. Harsen. ChIP
I Believe. J. B. Lawrence. BLRP
I Believe. Saul Tchernichowsky, *tr. fr. Hebrew by* Reginald V. Feldman. TrJP
(Credo, *tr. by* Maurice Samuel.) LiTW
I believe a leaf of grass is no less than the journey-work of the stars. Miracles. Walt Whitman. Song of Myself, XXXI. AmPP; AnFE; CoAnAm; CoBA; LiTA; MAP; MaRV; MoAmPo; NeMA; OQP; OxBA; PDV; PG (1955 ed.); SeCeV; TiPo; TrGrPo; TRV; YT
I believe if I should die. Creed. Mary Ashley Townsend. BLPA; FaBoBe; NeHB
I believe in human kindness. A Creed. Norman Macleod. WGRP
I believe in the brook as it wanders. Nature's Creed [*or* The Handiwork of God]. *Unknown.* MaRV; OHIP; TRV
I believe in the God of my garden, the God of the trees. A Creed in a Garden. Newman Flower. MaRV
I believe in the ultimate justice of fate. Credo. Georgia Douglas Johnson. BALP
I believe it! 'Tis thou, God, that givest, 'tis I who receive. Robert Browning. *Fr.* Saul. ChIP; StJW
I believe. That is to say. I Believe. J. B. Lawrence. BLRP
I believe the will of God prevails. The Faith of Abraham Lincoln. Abraham Lincoln. SoP; TRV
I Believe Thy Precious Blood. John Wesley. BePJ
I bend above the moving stream. Solitude and the Lily. Richard Henry Horne. OBVV; VA
I Bended unto Me. Thomas Edward Brown. PoSC; PoVP
I bent in the deep of night. The Pedigree. Thomas Hardy. CoBMV
I bent my ears to a lily's cup. Mother Love. Janie Alford. PGD
I bent to lift a comrade from the water. Ecce Homo. John Ackerson. MaRV
I bent unto the ground. The Voice of God. James Stephens. WGRP
I bequeath my turtle dove. *Unknown.* EG
I Bid You Keep Some Few Small Dreams. Helen Frazee-Bower. MoSiPe
I bid you, mock not Eros. Of a Child That Had Fever. Christopher Morley. PFY
I Bind My Heart. Lauchlan MacLean Watt. MaRV; TRV
I bind myself [*or* unto myself] to-day. St. Patrick's Breastplate [*or* The Breastplate of Saint Patrick]. *At. to* St. Patrick. *Fr.* The Deer's Cry. BBV; FaBoCh; LoGBV; MaRV; OxBI; TRV
I bind the Soul that fathered me. The Hanging. J. E. H. MacDonald. OBCV
I bleed Sebastian's brother on the ground. Holy Poems, II. George Barker. MoPo
I bless the fates that I may toil. Blessing of Toil. Samuel Ellsworth Kiser. PEDC
I bless Thee, Lord, because I grow. Paradise. George Herbert. BoLiVe; MaMe; SeCP; TrGrPo
I bless Thee, Lord, for sorrows sent. Made Perfect Through Suffering. Samuel Johnson. SoP

I Bless This Man. Pindar, *tr. fr. Greek by* Richmond Lattimore. *Fr.* Nemean Odes. SD
I bloom but once, and then I perish. Il Fior degli Eroici Furori. John Addington Symonds. VA
I Blow My Pipes. Hugh McCrae. PoAu-1
I Bore with Thee, Long, Weary Days. Christina Rossetti. *See* "Love of Christ Which Passeth Knowledge, The."
I bought a gay-roofed house upon a sunny hill. Only Heaven Is Given Away. Rose Darrough. MaRV
I bought me a cat and the cat pleased me. *See* I had a cat. . .
I bought me a Parrot in Trinidad. Parrot. William Jay Smith. RePo
I bow, I scrape, I doff my hat. Unrequited Love on the Back Piazza. Margaret Fishback. CIV
I bow my forehead to the dust. Whittier. *Fr.* The Eternal Goodness. OQP; SoP
I bow my head in sorrow. Regret. Mabel Murray. SoP
I break my bread. There are the great gold fields. Bread the Holy. Elizabeth J. Coatsworth. MoRP
I break my smooth, full loaf of warm white bread. Whatsoever I Do. Mary Louise Hector. GoBC
I breathe (sweet Ghib:) the temperate ayre of Wrest. To My Friend G.N. from Wrest. Thomas Carew. AnAnS-2
I breathed enough to take the trick. Emily Dickinson. MWA-2
I Breathed into the Ash. Roland Robinson. BoAV
I bring an unaccustomed wine. Emily Dickinson. TDP
I bring fresh showers for the thirsting flowers. The Cloud. Shelley. ATP; BEL; BoLiVe; CBEP; ChER; EnL; EnLi-2; EnLit; EnRP; EPN; ERoP-2; FaPON; GN; GTBS-W; HBV; ImOP; InP; LiTB; LiTG; MBW-2; MCCG; MERP; MPB; NoP; OAEP; OBRV; OHFP; OTPC; OuHeWo; PCH; PoE; PoEL-4; PoIE; RePo; RG; RIS; SeCeV; StaSt; TOP; TreF; TrGrPo; ViBoPo
I bring my sins to Thee. To Thee. *Unknown.* BePJ
I Bring to You as Offering Tonight. Emile Verhaeren, *tr. fr. French by* Jethro Bithell. AnEnPo
I bring ye love. What will love do? Upon Love, by Way of Question and Answer. Robert Herrick. NoP; Po
I bring you all my olden days. To-Day. Benjamin R. C. Low. HBV
I bring you the scent of the earth on my body. The Faun. Haniel Long. HBMV
I bring you with reverent hands. A Poet to His Beloved. W. B. Yeats. BrPo; MoLP
I brocht my love a cherry. Auld Sang. William Soutar. OxBS
I broider the world upon a loom. The Loom of Dreams. Arthur Symons. PoVP
I broke my heart because of you, my dear. Literary Love. Harry Kemp. HBMV
I Broke My Trust with God. *Unknown.* SoP
I broke one day a slender stem. A Spray of Honeysuckle. Mary Emily Bradley. AA
I Broke the Spell that Held Me Long. Bryant. AmePo; AmPP (3d ed.)
I, Brotachus, came not hither. Man of Crete. J. R. Hervey. AnNZ
I built a chimney for a comrade old. Two at a Fireside. Edwin Markham. OQP; TRV
I built a hut in a little wood. My Hut. E. Mathias. BoTP
I built a snare one day and sought to capture. Trap. Walter H. Kerr. FiSC
I Built My Hut. Tao Yuan-ming, *tr. fr. Chinese by* Arthur Waley. AWP
I built my soul a lordly pleasure-house. The Palace of Art. Tennyson. BEL; EnLi-2; MaVP; OAEP; PoVP; UnPo (1st ed.); ViPo; ViPP; VP
I Buried the Year. W. Luff. STF
I buried you deeper last night. To a Persistent Phantom. Frank Horne. AmNP; BANP; CDC
I Burn for England with a Living Flame. Gervase Stewart. WaaP
(Poem: "I burn for England with a living flame.") WaP
I burn no incense, hang no wreath. Votive Song. Edward Coote Pinkney. AA; AnFE; APA; CoAnAm
I burn, yet am I cold; I am a-cold, yet burn. Barnabe Barnes. *Fr.* Parthenophil and Parthenophe. PoIE
I burne, and cruell you, in vaine. Song: To My Mistris, I Burning in Love. Thomas Carew. AnAnS-2; SCEP-2; SeCP
"I burned, I wept, I sang; I burn, sing, weep again." Gaspara Stampa. William Rose Benét. HBMV
I Burned My Candle at Both Ends. Samuel Hoffenstein. ELU; FiBHP
I burned my life that I might find. The Alchemist. Louise Bogan. AWP; MAP; MoAmPo
"I busy too," the little boy. A World to Do. Theodore Weiss. SiSw
I Call and I Call. Robert Herrick. ChTr
I call her my Krishna flower. Krishnakali. Rabindranath Tagore. ACV
I call my years back, I, grown old. The Days. Theodosia Garrison. HBMV
I call no Goddess to inspire my strains. Sonnet to Robert Graham. Burns. Sonn
I call on you, Quetzalcoatl, Plumed Serpent. On the President's State Visit to Mexico. Jack Marshall. YAP
I call that parent rash and wild. The Velvet Hand. Phyllis McGinley. TreFT
I Call the Old Time Back. Whittier. Mabel Martin: Proem. ViBoPo
I called him to come in. Evening. James Wright. NYBP
I called out of mine affliction. Jonah's Prayer. Jonah, Bible, *O.T.* TrJP
I Called Them Trees. Gerald William Barrax. YAP
I called to gray squirrel. Conversation. Anne Robinson. SUS
I came across her browsing on a slope. Cow Dance. Bruce Beaver. PoAu-2
I came across my cousin. The Wood Frog. John Hay. NYTB
I Came a-Riding. Reinmar von Zweter, *tr. fr. German by* Jethro Bithell. AWP
I came as a shadow. Nocturne Varial. Lewis Alexander. PoNe
I came before the water. Mussel Hunter at Rock Harbor. Sylvia Plath. NYBP
I came [*or* I come] from Alabama. Oh! Susanna. Stephen Collins Foster. FaFP; PaA; RIS; StaSt; TrAS; TreF
I came from England into France. The Journey into France. *Unknown.* CoMu
I came from far for thee. "This Do in Remembrance of Me." *Unknown.* STF
I Came from Salem City. John Nichols. *See* I Come from Salem City.
I came from somewhere. Poem of the Future Citizen. José Craveirinha. TTY
I came from Tigris' sandy plain. The Three Wise Men. John Finley. ChIP; OQP
I came here with a young girl. The Cemetery at Academy, California. Philip Levine. NYBP
I came, I saw, and was undone. The Thraldome. Abraham Cowley. *Fr.* The Mistress. SCEP-2; SeCV-1
I came in light that I might behold. A Parable of the Spirit. John Arthur Goodchild. VA
I came into the city and none knew me. An Upper Chamber. Frances Bannerman. HBV; OBEV
I came on a happy shepherdess. The Happy Shepherdess. *Unknown.* CLwM
I came on them yesterday (merely by chance). Pussy Willows. Rowena Bastin Bennett. GFA
I came out into the wet night. Tree in the Rain. James Applewhite. YAP
I came out singing. To Come Out Singing. Jon Silkin. PoDB
I came to a great door. The Beast. Theodore Roethke. AmLP
I came to God in prayer, I asked for health. Faith to Understand. Philora Hintz. SoP
I Came to Jesus. George White. STF
I came to look, and lo! The Fall of the Plum Blossoms. Ranko. TiPo
I came to the crowded Inn of Earth. The Inn of Earth. Sara Teasdale. LiTA
I came to the door of the House of Love. Song. Alfred Noyes. HBV
I Came to the New World Empty-Handed. Hildegarde Hoyt Swift. AmFN
I came to the well-loved house. Frail Hands. Lucia Trent. FiSC
I Came to This Country in 1865, *with music.* *Unknown.* OuSiCo
I came [*or* come] to town de udder night. Old Dan Tucker. Daniel Decatur Emmett. ABF; TrAS
I came to you with a greeting. Morning Song. Afanasi Afanasievich Fet. AWP

"I came to your church last Sunday." Where Were You? *Unknown.* SoP
I came upon it unaware. Honey from the Lion. Leah Bodine Drake. NePoAm
I came upon the children at their play. The Lonely Child. Ernest Briggs. NeLNL
I came upon them by a strip of sea. The Net-Menders. Brian Vrepont. BoAV; PoAu-2
I can but name thee, and methinks I call. To His Honoured Kinsman Sir William Soame. Robert Herrick. AtBAP; BoW
I Can Climb Our Apple Tree. Jessie Orton Jones. RePo
I can close my eyes and see Him. The Last Day. Lola Derosier. STF
I can hear banjos. Slave Quarter. Carl Carmer. MoSiPe
I can imagine, in some otherworld. Humming-Bird. D. H. Lawrence. BWP; CMoP; GTBS-D; LiTB; LiTM; MoPW; SeCePo
I can imagine quite easily ending up. Plains. W. H. Auden. NePA
I can love both faire and browne. The Indifferent. John Donne. AnAnS-1; ATP (1935 ed.); BEL; CABA; DiPo; EG; EnL; EnLit; MaMe; NoP; OAEP; OuHeWo; PoeP; ReEn; ReIE; SCEP-1; SeCV-1; TOP; TuPP; UnTE
"I" Can Never Be a Great Man, An. Stephen Spender. OBMV
I can never remake the thing I have destroyed. Shards. Aline Kilmer. PFY
I can preserve your letters, not your love. Ceremony. Vassar Miller. NePoEA
I can remember flowers at your hand. Ad Matrem, in Caelis. Charles L. O'Donnell. WHL
I can remember looking cross-lots from. House in Denver. Thomas Hornsby Ferril. AmFN
I can remember our first meeting. To Madame A. P. Kern. Pushkin. LiTW
I can remember our tears [*or* sorrow], I can remember our laughter. Memory. Helen Hoyt. NP; PoLF
I can see a picture. Pictures. F. Ann Elliott. BoTP
I can see from the window a little brown house. The Sunset Garden. Marion St. John Webb. TVC
I can see him. The Last Democrat. D. J. Enright. NMP
I can see outside the gold wings without birds. The Clear Air of October. Robert Bly. NaP
I can sing of myself a true song. The Seafarer. *Unknown.* PoRA (rev. ed.)
I can support it no longer. Flower Herding on Mount Monadnock. Galway Kinnell. NaP
I can survive on ears the huskers leave. Hibernalia. Jessica Nelson North. NP
I can take the wildest bronco in the tough old woolly West. The Gol-darned Wheel. *Unknown.* CoSo; IHA; PoMa
I can tell a true story about myself. *Unknown. Fr.* The Seafarer. YAT
I Can Trust. *Unknown.* SoP
I canna tell what has come ower me. Ich Weiss Nicht, Was Soll es Bedeuten. Heine, *tr. by* Alexander MacMillan. AWP
I cannot always feel his greatness. The Great Man. Eunice Tietjens. NP; WGRP
I cannot be hurt anymore. Image. Henry Dumas. BOLo
I Cannot Believe That I Am of Wind. Samuel Greenberg. LiTA
I cannot bring a world quite round. Wallace Stevens. *Fr.* The Man with the Blue Guitar. CMoP
I cannot brook thy gaze, belovèd bird. Mother Carey's Chicken. Theodore Watts-Dunton. OBVV
I cannot but ask, in the park and the streets. Arthur Hugh Clough. *Fr.* Spectator ab Extra, III. NBM; OxBoLi; PeVV
I cannot but believe, though you were dead. The Old Nurse. Frances Cornford. MemP
I cannot, but God can. Not I, but God. Annie Johnson Flint. STF
I cannot but remember. When the Year Grows Old. Edna St. Vincent Millay. YT
I cannot call my mistress fayre. *Unknown.* SeCSL
I cannot call you as lovely as you were. Reunion. Paul Dehn. PV
I Cannot Change as Others Do. Earl of Rochester. *See* Constancy.
I cannot choose but think upon the time. Brother and Sister. "George Eliot." GN
I cannot dance upon my toes. Emily Dickinson. UnS
I cannot do it alone. Jesus and I [*or* We Two]. Dan Crawford. BLRP; FaChP; SoP; TRV
I cannot do the big things. Big and Little Things. Alfred H. Miles. OTPC (1923 ed.)
I cannot dry my eyes when I think of the distant time. Microcosmos, LVII. Nigel Heseltine. NeBP
I Cannot Eat but Little Meat. *At. to* William Stevenson. *See* Back and Side Go Bare, Go Bare.
I cannot find my way: there is no star. Credo. E. A. Robinson. AmePo; AmPP; AnNE; AP; CMoP; CoBA; GTBS-W; ILP; LiTM (rev. ed.); MaRV; MoAmPo; NeMA; NePA; OQP; OxBA; TreFT; WGRP
I cannot find my way to Nazareth. A Fragment. Yvor Winters. PoIE
I cannot find thee! Still on restless pinion. The Quest [*or* Who by Searching Can Find Out God?]. Eliza Scudder. MaRV; TrPWD; WGRP
I cannot follow them into their world of death. Chrysothemis. Henry Reed. MoVE
I cannot forget/ The sight of that straight young neck. Kevin Barry. Terence Ward. OnYI
I cannot forget my Joe. A Poor French Sailor's Scottish Sweetheart. William Johnson Cory. VA
I Cannot Forget with What Fervid Devotion. Bryant. AmPP (3d ed.); CoBA
I cannot give you much or ask you much. To a Friend. Jean Valentine. TPM
I cannot give you the Metropolitan Tower. Parting Gift. Elinor Wylie. LOW; OxBA
I cannot guess her face or form. Mater Desiderata. Winthrop Mackworth Praed. OBVV
I cannot hear thy voice with others' ears. To the Canary Bird. Jones Very. AP
I cannot hold, I cannot, I, indure. Satire II. John Marston. *Fr.* The Scourge of Villainy. ReIE
I cannot hold my peace, John Keats. To John Keats, Poet. At Springtime. Countee Cullen. BANP; CDC
I cannot live nor die. The Ghost. James Wright. FiSC
I cannot live with you. Emily Dickinson. AmP; AmPP (4th ed.); AnNE; AP; CBEP; DiPo; FaPL; MeWo; MoAB; MoAmPo; NoP; OxBA; PoEL-5; PoeP; PoIE
I cannot look above and see. The Clouds. William Croswell. AA
I cannot love thee as I ought. In Memoriam A. H. H., LII. Tennyson. BEL; EnLi-2; EnLit; EPN; OAEP; ViPo; VP
I cannot make him dead! My Child. John Pierpont. AA
I cannot move. Malcolm. Welton Smith. BF
I cannot ope mine eyes. Mattens. George Herbert. AnAnS-1; MaMe; MeP; TrPWD
I cannot praise the Doctor's eyes. On Hearing a Lady Praise a Certain Rev. Doctor's Eyes. George Outram. BOHV; TreFT
I cannot pray, as Christians use to pray. Credo. "Seumas O'Sullivan." OnYI
I cannot put the Presence by, of Him, the Crucified. The Voice of Christmas. Harry Kemp. HBV; MaRV; OQP
"I cannot quite remember. . .There were five." The Messages. W. W. Gibson. InP; MCCG; OHIP
I cannot reach it; and my striving eye. Childhood. Henry Vaughan. OxBoCh; SCEP-1; SeEP
I cannot rise. Earth-bound. Henry W. Frost. SoP
I cannot roam the woods this year. To This Lilac-Scented Room. Alice Hansche Mortenson. SoP
I cannot say, and I will not say. Away [*or* He Is Not Dead]. James Whitcomb Riley. BLRP; MaRV; NeHB; TreFT; TRV; WGRP
I cannot say, beneath the pressure of life's care. Amen. Frederick G. Browning. BLRP
I cannot say why. The Queen in Parliament, 1941. A. P. Herbert. OnPP
I cannot see/ Why men should turn from Thee. My Lord. Martha Snell Nicholson. BePJ; SoP
I cannot see fairies. Fairies. Hilda Conkling. GBV (1922 ed.); SP; TiPo
I cannot see the features right. Tennyson. In Memoriam, A. H. H., LXX. EnL; EPN; FosPo; LiTB; PoEL-5; ViPo; VP
I cannot see, with my small human sight. I Can Trust. *Unknown.* SoP
I Cannot Sing the Old Songs. Charlotte Alington Barnard. TreF
I cannot sing the old songs. Songs without Words, *parody.* Robert J. Burdette. BOHV

I cannot sing to thee as I would sing. Ecstasy. Eric Mackay. VA
I cannot skill of these thy wayes. Justice. George Herbert. MaMe
I cannot sleep in the weight of the year. Letter from the Great Society. Morton Marcus. YAP
I cannot sleep; the beautiful Lynnhaven. The River. Mary Sinton Leitch. HBMV
I cannot sleepe, my eyes ill neighbouring lids. John Marston. *Fr.* The Malcontent. PoEL-2
I cannot spare water or wine. Mithridates. Emerson. AP
I cannot speak to crowds. This I Can Do. H. T. Lefevre. STF
I cannot take these poor. Said the Innkeeper. Myles Connolly. SoP; TRV
I cannot tell, not I, why she. Poem. Walter Savage Landor. ERoP-1
I cannot tell their wonder nor make known. Ships. John Masefield. NP
I cannot tell what charms my lady finds. Sonnet. George Henry Boker. *Fr.* Sonnets: a Sequence on Profane Love. AmePo
I cannot tell what's coming o'er me. Loreley. Heine. OuHeWo
I cannot tell who loves the skeleton. La Bella Bona Roba. Richard Lovelace. AtBAP; CavP; FosPo; PIA; PoEL-3; SeCP
I cannot tell why this imagined. The Loreley. Heine. GoTP
I cannot tell you how I love. Post-Impressionism. Bert Leston Taylor. BOHV; HBMV; InMe
I cannot tell you how it was. May. Christina Rossetti. EG; VP
I cannot tell you now. The Great Hunt. Carl Sandburg. MoLP; NP
I cannot think of any word. Old Saul. Lizette Woodworth Reese. MAP; MoAmPo
I cannot think of Paradise a place. Paradise. Charles G. Blanden. OQP
I cannot think of them as dead. My Dead [*or* Friends Beyond]. Frederick Lucian Hosmer. MaRV; WGRP
I cannot think or [*or* nor] reason. Acceptance [*or* Comrades of the Cross]. Willard Wattles. HBMV; OQP
I cannot think that you have gone away. To My Father. Iris Tree. HBMV
I cannot turn from Jesus. I Turn to Jesus. Oswald J. Smith. STF
I cannot view the bloom upon the rose. Blind. Norman V. Pearce. MaRV; PoToHe
"I cannot wash my dog," she said. An Insectarian. John Banister Tabb. UTS
I Cannot Wash My Eye without an Eyecup. *Unknown.* PV
I cannot wax ecstatic with the throng. Holy Week. Robert Whitaker. ChIP; MaRV
I can't be talkin' of love, dear. Song. Esther Mathews. FaFP; LiTL; LiTM; NePA; SiTL
"I can't come in, Lady Margie," he said. Young Hunting (C *vers.*). *Unknown.* BFSS
I can't get 'em up, I can't get 'em up. Words for Army Bugle Calls: Reveille. *Unknown.* TreF
I Can't Have a Martini, Dear, but You Take One. Ogden Nash. PoRA (rev. ed.)
I can't live blossoming drunk. The Book of Wild Flowers. Joseph Ceravolo. ANYP
I can't remember where I'd been. The Green Door. Leah Bodine Drake. BiCB
I can't ridge it back again from char. Death of the Kapowsin Tavern. Richard Hugo. PIA
I can't sleep tonight, can you? Gooseberries. Stephen Berg. NaP
I can't stand Willy wet-leg. Willy Wet-Leg. D. H. Lawrence. CMoP
I Can't Think What He Sees in Her. A. P. Herbert. FiBHP
I care not for the idle state. Odes of Anacreon. *Tr. by* Thomas Moore. OuHeWo
I Care Not for These Ladies. Thomas Campion. BWP; CABA; ErPo; LiTL; NoP; OAEP; OBSC; ReIE; ViBoPo
(When We Court and Kiss.) MeWo; UnTE
(Amarillis.) HBV
(Amaryllis.) EG; EIL
I care not, Fortune, what you me deny. Indifference to Fortune. James Thomson. *Fr.* The Castle of Indolence. OBEC
I care not that the storm sways all the trees. The Goal. Frank W. Gunsaulus. MaRV
I care not tho it be. Superstition. John Norris. PeRV
I care not what the sailors say. Crazy Jane Reproved. W. B. Yeats. AtBAP; CMoP
I carried a burden of bitterness. Japanese Cherries. Katherine Brégy. JKCP (1926 ed.)
I Carried with Me Poems. Gail Dusenbery. ThO
I carry boulders across the day. The Words. Gene Fowler. ThO
"I carry my death within me." My Death. A. J. M. Smith. OBCV
I carry my keys like a weapon. To Nowhere. David Ignatow. CAD
I carry the great Singing-Book. The Illuminated Canticle. Florence Wilkinson Evans. PFY
I cast from me the medications. Loneliness. Franz Werfel. TrJP
I cast my cloud off, and appear myself. John Fletcher. *Fr.* Rule a Wife and Have a Wife. MyFE
I cast my nets in many streams. Poet Songs, II. Karle Wilson Baker. HBMV
I cast these lyric offerings at your feet. Sonnets to Miranda, V. Sir William Watson. HBV
I Catcha da Plenty of Feesh, *with music. Unknown.* AS; TrAS
I Catherine am a Douglas born. The King's Tragedy. Dante Gabriel Rossetti. EPN; PoVP; TOP; ViPo
I caught a tremendous fish. The Fish. Elizabeth Bishop. ExPo; FiMAP; GoJo; GoTP; LiTM (rev. ed.); MiAP; MoAB; MoAmPo (1950 ed.); NeMA; NePA; PIA; Po; PoPl; PoPo; TrGrPo (rev. ed.); TwAmPo; ViBoPo (1958 ed.)
I caught this morning morning's minion. The Windhover. Gerard Manley Hopkins. ACP; AnFE; AtBAP; ATP (1953 ed.); BoC; BrPo; BWP; CABA; CaFP; CAW; CBV; CMoP; CoBE; CoBMV; DiPo; EaLo; EnL; EnLi-2 (1949 ed.); EnLit; ExPo; FaBoEn; FaBoMo; ForPo; FosPo; GTBS-P; ILP; InvP; LiTB; LiTM; LoBV; MaPo; MoAB; MoBrPo; MoPo; MoPW; MoVE; NoP; OAEP; OBNC; PAn; PIA; Po; PoAn; PoDB; PoE; PoEL-5; PoeP; PoIE; PoPl; PoRA; PoVP; ReMP; SeCeV; ShBV-4; StP; SyP; TDP; TreFT; UnPo (3d ed.); VaPo; ViPo; ViPP; VP
I caught you grazing on my knee. To a Flea in a Glass of Water. D. A. Greig. PeSA
I Cease Not from Desire. Hafiz, *tr. fr. Persian by* Gertrude Lowthian Bell. *Fr.* Odes. AWP; WoL
I celebrate myself, and sing myself. Song of Myself. Walt Whitman. AA; AmePo; AmP; AmPP; AnFE; AP; APA; ATP (1935 ed.); CoAnAm; CoBA; FaBoBe; LiTA; MAmP; MAP; MoAmPo; MWA-1; NeMA; NePA; OxBA; PoFS; PoIE; PP; TrGrPo; ViBoPo; WHA
I chanced upon an early walk to spy. The Orchard and the Heath. George Meredith. OBNC
I, Chang P'ing-tzu, had traversed the Nine Wilds and seen their wonders. The Bones of Chuang Tzu. Chang Heng. AtBAP; AWP
I Change. Witter Bynner. HBMV
I change, and so do women too. Written on a Looking-Glass. *Unknown.* HBV
I charge you, lady young and fair. He Charges Her To Lay Aside Her Weapons. Pierce Ferriter. AnIL; LiTW; OnYI
I charge you, O winds of the West. Mathilde Blind. *Fr.* Love in Exile. TrJP; VA
I charm thy life. Kehama's Curse. Robert Southey. *Fr.* The Curse of Kehama. LoBV; OBNC; OBRV
I chatter over stony ways. Tennyson. *Fr.* The Brook. GFA
I choose at random, knowing less and less. An Old Atheist Pauses by the Sea. Thomas Kinsella. ELU
"I choosed my love at the bonny yates of Gight." Geordie (B *vers.*). *Unknown.* BaBo
I chopped down the house that you had been saving to live in next summer. Variations on a Theme by William Carlos Williams. Kenneth Koch. PV
I claim the right of knowing whom I serve. Manhood. Oliver Wendell Holmes. *Fr.* Wind-Clouds and Star-Drifts. AP
I clasp the hand of Love Divine. I Take, He Undertakes. A. B. Simpson. SoP
I climb the hill: from end to end. In Memoriam A. H. H., C. Tennyson. EnLi-2; EPN; PoEL-5; TOP; ViPo; VP
I climb the tower of Ste. Anne des Monts. The Bells of Ste. Anne des Monts. Leo Cox. CaP

I climb to the tower-top and lean upon broken stone. I See Phantoms of Hatred and of the Heart's Fullness and of the Coming Emptiness. W. B. Yeats. Meditations in Time of Civil War, VII. CABL; LiTB; PIA
I climb'd a hill, whose summit crown'd with wood. An Essay on the Fleet Riding in the Downes. "J. D." CoMu
I climb'd the dark brow of the mighty Helvellyn. Helvellyn. Sir Walter Scott. PeER
I climbed a hill as light fell short. The Song of Honour. Ralph Hodgson. AtBAP; CAW; GTSL; LiTB; MemP, *abr.*; MCCG; MoBrPo; OtMeF; TSW
I climbed the hill when the first wild swans were thrown. Dry Time. Norma Davis. NeLNL
I climbed the mountain to pick mawu. Up the Mountain to Pick Mawu. *Unknown.* HW
I climbed the stair in Antwerp church. Antwerp and Bruges. Dante Gabriel Rossetti. PIA
I climbed the winding stairway. The Chimes. *Unknown.* SoP
I climbed through woods in the hour-before-dawn dark. The Horses. Ted Hughes. BoPe; POTi; WIRo
I climbed towards you on a ray of moonlight. Fantasy under the Moon. Emmanuel Boundzekei-Dongala. TTY
I climbed up on the merry-go-round. Merry-go-round. Dorothy Walter Baruch. BrR; MPB (1956 ed.); SoPo; StVeCh; SUS; TiPo
I cling and swing. The Fifteen Acres. James Stephens. BoTP; GBV (1952 ed.); ShBV-2
I clink my castanet. A Starling's Spring Rondel. James Cousins. HBV; HBVY
I Close Her Eyes. Heine, *tr. fr. German by* Louis Untermeyer. UnTE
I closed another chapter. My Book of Life. Frances Humphrey. STF
I Closed My Door to the World. Emilio Prados, *tr. fr. Spanish by* Eleanor L. Turnbull. OnPM
I closed my eyes, and heard your voice recall. On a Lady Singing Lawes's Music to Milton's Ode on the Nativity. J. C. Squire. MuSP
I Closed My Eyes To-Day and Saw. William Force Stead. OBMV; POTE
I closed my hands upon a moth. Beware. Dora Sigerson Shorter. GTSL
I Closed My Shutters Fast Last Night. Georgia Douglas Johnson. PoNe
I Come Again. Afanasi Afanasievich Fet, *tr. fr. Russian by* Frances Cornford *and* Esther Polianowsky Salaman. LiTW
I come among the peoples like a shadow. Hunger. Laurence Binyon. POTE
I come back to the geography of it. Letter 27. Charles Olson. CoPo
I come dis night to sing an' pray. Oh, Yes! Oh Yes! Wait 'til I Git on My Robe. *Unknown.* BoAN-2
I come from Alabama. *See* I came from Alabama.
I come from busy haunts of men. The Cynic of the Woods. Arthur Patchett Martin. VA
I come from Castlepatrick, and me heart is on me sleeve. Me Heart. G. K. Chesterton. OtMeF
I come from good olde Boston. On the Aristocracy of Harvard. *At. to* Samuel C. Bushnell. BOHV *See also* Boston Toast, A.
I come from haunts of coot and hern. The Brook [*or* The Song of the Brook *or* The Brook's Song]. Tennyson. BoChLi; BoNaP; BoTP; EPN; FaBoBe; FaBV; FaFP; FaPON; GN; GoJo; GTBS; HBV; HBVY; MCCG; MemP; MPB; OTPC; PCH; PoVP; PTK; RIS; ShBV-2; TreF
I come from nothing, but from where. A Song of Derivations [*or* The Modern Poet]. Alice Meynell. MaRV; PoVP; VA; WGRP
I Come from Salem City. *Unknown,* *at. to* John Nichols. AmSS, *with music*
(Marching Song of the California Gold Rush, The.) OTD
(Oh California.) SGR, *with music*
I come from Salem County. Cowboy Song. Charles Causley. NePoEA; PoRA (rev. ed.); PoSa; POTi
I come from the city of Boston. Boston. *At. to* Samuel C. Bushnell. LiTM; OxBoLi; SiTL. *See also* Boston Toast, A.
I come from the rose-grove, mother. The Rose Song. Gil Vicente, *tr. by* John Bowring. OnPM
I come from woods enchaunted. Dream Song. Richard Middleton. HBV
I come! I come! ye have called me long. The Voice of Spring. Felicia Dorothea Hemans. OTPC (1946 ed.)
I come in the little things. Immanence. Evelyn Underhill. MaRV; StJW
I come like a comet ablaze, like the sun when the dawn is awaking. Revolution. "Basil Dahl." PoFr
I come more softly than a bird. Mary Austin. *Fr.* Rhyming Riddles. BoNaP; SoPo; TiPo
I come of a mighty race. Hebrews. James Oppenheim. MAP; MoAmPo (1942 ed.); TrJP
I come of the seed of the people, the people that sorrow. The Rebel. Padraic Pearse. OnYI
I Come to Bury Caesar. Shakespeare. *See* Antony's Oration.
I Come to Supplicate. Simeon ben Isaac ben Abun of Mainz, *tr. fr. Hebrew by* Nina Davis Salaman. TrJP
I come to the garden alone. In the Garden. C. Austin Miles. TreFT
I come to thee, O God long since forgot. Before the Statue of Apollo. Saul Tchernichowsky. TrJP
I come to town de udder night. *See* I came to town de udder night.
I come to visit thee agen. To a Cyclamen. Walter Savage Landor. VA
I come to work as well as play. The March Wind. *Unknown.* GFA
I come today to high Pichencha's brow. Words of the Last Inca. José Eusebio Caro. PoFr
I come unto you, forgotten god of the ages. Before a Statue of Apollo. Saul Tchernichowsky. LiTW
"I come your sin-rid souls to shrive." Father Francis. Walter Herries Pollock. VA
I cough a lot (sinus?) so I. Getting Up Ahead of Someone (Sun). Frank O'Hara. ANYP
I could believe that I am here alone. Solipsism. George Santayana. AnFE; APA; CoAnAm
I could divide a leaf. Propositions. Phyllis Webb. MoCV
I could eat it! Kobayashi Issa, *tr. fr. Japanese by* R. H. Blyth. FIW
I Could Give All to Time. Robert Frost. MoRP
I could have painted pictures like that youth's. Pictor Ignotus. Robert Browning. CTC; PoVP; ViPo; ViPP
I could have stemmed misfortune's tide. The Wife. Anna Peyre Dinnies. AA
I could have wept and howled. Song of the Unloved. *Unknown.* PeSA
I could know. Childhood. Louis Ginsberg. RIS
I could love her with a love so warm. The World Is a Mighty Ogre. Fenton Johnson. AmNP
I could love thee till I die. The Platonic Lady. Earl of Rochester. UnTE
I could make you songs. Song. Dorothy Dow. HBMV
I could never ask you. Leyland King. WSL
I could never have the power. Beaumont *and* Fletcher. *Fr.* The Maid's Tragedy. TuPP
I could not be so well content. A Cowboy Song. *Unknown.* SCC
I could not choose but gaze; a fascination. Shelley. *Fr.* The Revolt of Islam. ChER
I could not dig: I dared not rob. A Dead Statesman. Kipling. *Fr.* Epitaphs of the War. OAEP (2d ed.); PoVP
I could not even think. Rapunzel. William Morris. PoVP
I could not, ever and anon, forbear. The Solitary. Wordsworth. *Fr.* The Excursion, II. EnRP
I could not keep love down. The Power of Love. *Unknown.* *Fr.* The Thousand and One Nights. LiTW
I could not leave Thee, Christ! For when I tried. The Disciple. Dwight Bradley. ChIP; OQP
I could not look on Death, which being known. The Coward. Kipling. *Fr.* Epitaphs of the War. FaBoTw; GTBS; OAEP (2d ed.); PoVP
I could not see You with my eyes. Sight and Insight. Eleanor Slater. TrPWD
I Could Not Sleep for Thinking of the Sky. John Masefield. Lollingdon Downs, V. ChMP; FIW; GTBS-W; LiTM (rev. ed.); MemP
(Sonnet.) LiTG
I Could Not though I Would. George Gascoigne. PoEL-1
I could not understand the sudden quiet. The Quiet. W. W. Gibson. BEL
I could resign that eye of blue. To Cloe. Thomas Moore, *after* Martial. AWP; OuHeWo; UnTE
I could ride the Disneyland sky ride forever. He Spends Time in Southern California. Jonathan Cott. YAP
I Could Take. Hayden Carruth. NYTB

I could take the Harlem night. Juke Box Love Song. Langston Hughes. IDB
I could tell you. Impasse. Langston Hughes. LiTM (1970 ed.)
I could wish to be dead! The Tragic Mary Queen of Scots. "Michael Field." OBMV
I Couldn't Hear Nobody Pray, *with music*. *Unknown*. BoAN-1
I couldn't help weeping with delight. Styx River Anthology. Carolyn Wells. BOHV
I couldn't touch a stop and turn a screw. Thirty Bob a Week. John Davidson. CABL; FaBoTw; FaFP; LiTB; LiTG; LiTM (rev. ed.); NBM; OBNC; OxBS; PoFr; PoVP; TIHL
I couldn't wait. My childhood angered me. The Wise Child. Edward Lucie-Smith. NYTB
I count it true which sages teach. In Memoriam Technicam. Tom Hood. BOHV
I Count My Time by Times That I Meet Thee. Richard Watson Gilder. AA
I count up in this song of cheer. A Thanksgiving Rosary. Edwin Markham. PEDC
I counted the shapes. Before the Coming of Winter. Dennis Schmitz. YAP
I courted pretty Polly the live-long night. Pretty Polly. *Unknown*. OuSiCo
I crave an ampler, worthier sphere. Anno 1829. Heine. AWP; JAWP; WBP; WoL
I crave, dear Lord. Ike Walton's Prayer. James Whitcomb Riley. AA
I craved for flash of eye and sword. Dreams. Israel Zangwill. TrJP
I creature being mad. A Poem of Margery Kempe. Howard Nemerov. FiMAP
I crept through the house like a ghost. Spectre. Sydney King Russell. FiSC
I cried over beautiful things knowing no beautiful thing lasts. Autumn Movement. Carl Sandburg. NP
I cried unto God with my voice, even unto God with my voice. Psalm LXXVII, Bible, *O.T.* AWP
I cross a weedy meadow. Thistle, Yarrow, Clover. Kenneth Porter. NePoAm
I crossed over the county line. Crossing the County Line. Elizabeth Randall-Mills. GoYe
I crossed the furze-grown table-land. Dartmoor. Coventry Patmore. NBM
I crossed the gangway in the winter's raining. Stowaway. Bill Adams. EtS
I Cry, Love! Love! Theodore Roethke. MoVE
I cry my matches at Charing Cross. Charing Cross. *Unknown*. CBEP
I cry out war to those who spend their utmost. Stormy Nights. Robert Louis Stevenson. BrPo
I cry to the mountains; I cry to the sea. We Whom the Dead Have Not Forgiven. Sara Bard Field. PGD
I cry to thee from Jonah, Lord. And there. Circe Undersea. George MacBeth. HYE
I Cry to You as I Pass Your Windows. Christopher Brennan. *Fr.* The Wanderer. PoAu-1
I cry you mercy, sir, I knew you not. Henry Parrot. SiCE
I cry your mercy—pity—love,—aye, love! To Fanny. Keats. CLwM; ERoP-2; EnRP; MeWo; Sonn; TrGrPo; UnTE
I curse the time, wherein these lips of mine. Thomas Watson. LO
I cursed the puddle when I found. The Puddle. Eden Phillpotts. HBMV
I curst thee oft, I pity now thy case. Astrophel and Stella, XLVI. Sir Philip Sidney. FCP; SiPS
I cut a branch from the cherry-tree and take to the road again. Road Song. Louis Untermeyer. StaSt
I cut the stuff. A Spin. Jonathan Williams. PoNC
I dance and dance! Another faun. The Dancers. "Michael Field." VA
I dance and dance [*or* sing] without any feet. Spells. James Reeves. PoMS
"I dance on all the mountains." This Poem Is for Deer. Gary Snyder. Myths & Texts: Hunting. NaP
I dance on your paper. Jack o' the Inkpot. Algernon Blackwood. BoTP
I Danced before I Had Two Feet. Max Dunn. BoAV; PoAu-2
I dar nat telle how that the fressh repeir. Thomas Hoccleve. *Fr.* La Male Regle de T. Hoccleve. EnPo
I dare but sing of you in such a strain. Sonnets to Miranda, III. Sir William Watson. HBV
I dare not ask a kisse. To Electra. Robert Herrick. ALV; BEL; CavP; EG; EnLit; HBV; HoPM; LoBV; OBEV; OBS; PG (1945 ed.); PoeP; SeCV-1; YAT
I dare not ask your very all. Your Tears. Edwin Markham. HBMV
I Dare Not Be Defeated. *Unknown*. SoP
I dare not choose my lot. Choose Thou for Me. Horatius Bonar. SoP
I Dare Not Pray to Thee. Maurice Baring. TrPWD
I dare not slight the stranger at my door. The Trimmed Lamp. Laura Simmons. ChIP; MaRV
I dare not think that thou art by, to stand. Infinity. Philip Henry Savage. AA
I, dark in light, exposed. Milton. *Fr.* Samson Agonistes. TrGrPo
I deal in wisdom, not in dry desire. Supper with Lindsay. Theodore Roethke. ML
I deemed thy garments, O my Hope, were grey. Hope Overtaken. Dante Gabriel Rossetti. The House of Life, XLII. MaVP; PoVP; ViPo; VP
I delight in this naethingness. De Profundis. "Hugh MacDiarmid." SeCePo
I despise my friends more than you. To an Enemy. Maxwell Bodenheim. NP; TrJP
I destroyed the first cat we had. Catastrophe. Edwin Brock. NMP
I devise to end my days—in a tavern drinking. The Jovial Priest's Confession. Leigh Hunt. BOHV
I did but crave that I might kiss. The Slight. Thomas Flatman. LO; PeRV; SeCL
I did but look and love awhile. The Enchantment. Thomas Otway. HBV; LiTL; LO; NeHB; OBEV; SeCL; ViBoPo
I did but prompt the age to quit their clogs. On the Detraction Which Followed upon My Writing Certain Treatises [*or* On the Same *or* Second Sonnet on "Tetrachordon"]. Milton. ATP; ExPo; MaPo; MBW-1; NoP; PAn; PoFr; SeCeV; Sonn; TOP
I did not choose thee, dearest. It was Love. To Manon, on His Fortune in Loving Her. Wilfred Scawen Blunt. The Love Sonnets of Proteus, III. GTSL; OBEV (1st ed.)
I did not come to kiss her for she was kiss herself. All of Her. Samuel L. Albert. NePoAm-2
I did not cry at all. Song of the Captured Woman. James Devaney. PoAu-1
I did not cut myself this hollow reed. It Is the Reed. Sister Maris Stella. GoBC
I did not know she'd take it so. Under the Mistletoe. Countee Cullen. GoSl
I did not know, the day I nailed. Resurrection. Lloyd Frank Merrell. ChIP
I Did Not Know the Truth of Growing Trees. Delmore Schwartz. LiTM (1970 ed.)
I did not know you then. The Blinded Soldier to His Love. Alfred Noyes. PoPl
I did not live until this time. To My Excellent Lucasia, on Our Friendship. Katherine Philips. CavP; EG; LO; MeLP; OBS; SeCL; SeEP
I did not look upon her eyes. Penumbra. Dante Gabriel Rossetti. PoVP
I Did Not Lose My Heart [in Summer's Even]. A. E. Housman. LiTM; MaPo; VP
I did not make the conditions of my life whereby. Desire. Kathleen Raine. MoPo
I did not question anything. Finite. Power Dalton. HBMV
I did not see the crown. Faith. Donald Earl Edwards. ChIP
I did not see the iris move. A Matter of Life and Death. Anne Ridler. MoLP
I did not see the pachyderms. The Circus. E. B. White. InMe
I did not think, I did not strive. John Masefield. *Fr.* The Everlasting Mercy. BoC; SoP; TRV
I did not think that I should find them there. The Clerks. E. A. Robinson. AA; AnNE; CABA; MAP; MAmP; MaPo (1969 ed.); MoAB; MoAmPo; MoVE; NeMA; PIA; PoEL-5
I did not think to find You there. Christ in Woolworth's. Teresa Hooley. ChIP; StJW
I did not want to be old Mr. Uncle Dog: the Poet at 9. Robert Sward. CoAP; CoPo
I did not want to die. I wanted you. Sacco Writes to His Son. Alun Lewis. DTC

I did not want to go. Speaking: The Hero. Felix Pollak. WOW
I didn't get much sleep last night. Underwear. Lawrence Ferlinghetti. CoPo
I Didn't Like Him. Harry B. Smith. BOHV
I didn't like the way he went away. The Smile. Robert Frost. *Fr.* The The Hill Wife. NP
I didn't make you know how glad I was. A Servant to Servants. Robert Frost. BWP; CMoP
I didn't mean to hurt you, firefly. Firefly. Edna D. Wood. PCH
I Die Alive. Robert Southwell. ReIE; SiCE
I Die, Being Young. David Gray. *Fr.* In the Shadows. VA
"I Die Daily." Phil. J. Fisher. MaRV
I die for Your holy word without regret. Elegy. Antonio Enríquez Gómez. TrJP
I die, no matter what I do I die. Sestina. Richard Eberhart. FiMAP; TDP
I died, and they looked in my head: 2 plus 2. Natural Causes. Winfield Townley Scott. LiTL
I died for beauty—but was scarce. Emily Dickinson. AmePo; AnFE; AnNE; AP; APA; AWP; CBV; CoAnAm; DiPo; FaFP; GTBS-W; ILP; InPo; LiTA; LiTM; MAP; MAPA; MasP; MoAB; MoAmPo; MoVE; NCEP; NoP; OnPM; PoPo; TreFT; TwAmPo; WHA
(Beauty and Truth.) NeMA
I died from mineral and plant became. Resurgence. Jalal ed-Din Rumi. LiTW
I died; they wrapped me in a shroud. A Dream of Death. "Owen Innsley." AA
I Died True. Beaumont *and* Fletcher. *See* Aspatia's Song.
I dig in the soft earth all. The Negatives. Philip Levine. NePoEA-2
I dined with a friend in the East, one day. The Sunbeam. *Unknown.* NA
I dipped into the future, far as human eye could see. Federation of the World. Tennyson. *Fr.* Locksley Hall. PoRL.
See also For I dipt...
I discover, at the grotto's rear, another. A Cave. James Kirkup. BoPe
I discovered the United Nations night building. Poem from Deal. David Shapiro. ANYP
I do affirm that thou hast saved the race. Delay. Charlotte Fiske Bates. AA
I do be thinking God must laugh. Boys. Winifred M. Letts. HBMV
I do be thinking, lassie, of the old days now. The Shoogy-Shoo. Winthrop Packard. HBV
I do believ. Thomas Traherne. *Fr.* Solitude. FaBoEn
I do believe that die I must. His Creed. Robert Herrick. ILP; SeCeV; WePo
"I do believe the world is swinging toward the light." Swinging toward the Light. Georgia Harkness. MaRV
I do but ask that you be always fair. Edna St. Vincent Millay. Sonn
I do but look and love awhile. *See* I did but look and love awhile.
I do come about the copse. The Fairy Frolic. John Lyly. PCH
"I do complain and can find no release." Love Dialogue. *Unknown.* CoBE
I do confess, in many a sigh. Lying. Thomas Moore. BOHV; FiBHP
I Do Confess Thou Art Sae Fair. Burns. CBEP
I do confess thou 'rt smooth and fair. To His Forsaken Mistress [*or* Inconstancy Reproved]. *At. to* Sir Robert Ayton. EIL; ErPo; HBV; LiTL; LO; OBEV; OBS; SeCePo
I do like ogres. Dorothy Brown Thompson. *Fr.* Fe-Fi-Fo-Fum. ShM
I do not always know what lies before me. God Doeth All Things Well. *Unknown.* STF
I do not ask/ That crowds may throng the temple. The Parson's Prayer. Ralph Spaulding Cushman. MaRV; STF
I do not ask a truce. Prayer. Peter Gething. OQP
I do not ask for any crown. My Kingdom. Louisa May Alcott. MaRV
I do not ask for earthly store. The Eye of Faith. J. J. Maxfield. SoP
I do not ask for golden mists. Beauty for Ashes. Martha Snell Nicholson. SoP
I do not ask for love, ah! no. Lethe. Georgia Douglas Johnson. CDC
I do not ask—for you are fair. The Complaisant Swain. Ovid. AWP
I do not ask, O Lord, that life may be. Per Pacem ad Lucem. Adelaide Anne Procter. MaRV; SoP; TrPWD; VA
I do not ask, O Lord, that Thou shouldst shed. Lead Me. Adelaide A. Proctor. FaChP
I do not ask that God will keep all storms away. The All-sufficient Christ. Bernice W. Lubke. BLRP
I do not ask that I may steer. My Prayer. Annie Johnson Flint. SoP
I do not ask that you repay. A Mother's Reward. Ona Freeman Lathrop. MaRV
I Do Not Ask Thee, Lord. *Unknown.* BLRP
I do not ask Thee, Lord, for outward sign. Jesus Himself. Henry Burton. BLRP; SoP
I do not ask Thee, Lord, that all my life may be. I Do Not Ask Thee, Lord. *Unknown.* BLRP
I do not ask Thee straightway to appear. Supplication. Edith Lovejoy Pierce. TrPWD
I do not believe this room. A Game of Glass. Alastair Reid. NePoEA; PoCh
I do not care for kisses. 'Tis a debt. The Pleasures of Love. Wilfrid Scawen Blunt. HBV
"I do not care for noise and flags," I said. The Parade. Mary Esther Badley. PEDC
I do not count the day. What the Grecian Earns. Kenneth Patchen. ToPo
I do not count the hours I spend. Waldeinsamkeit. Emerson. AmPP (3d ed.); AP; HBV; MWA-1; WGRP
I do not despise you priests, all time, the world over. Walt Whitman. Song of Myself, XLIII. CoBA
I do not dread an alter'd heart. A Foreboding. "Violet Fane." VA
I do not fear/ To walk the lonely road. Apprehension. James Anderson Fraser. MaRV; OQP
I do not fear to die. The Fear. W. W. Gibson. BEL; GTSL; NP
I do not fear to lay my body down. Exile from God. John Hall Wheelock. GoBC; WGRP
I do not fear to tread the path that those I love long since have trod. My Creed. Jeannette L. Gilder. WGRP
I Do Not Fear Tomorrow. Phyllis C. Michael. SoP
I do not go, my dear, to storm. On Going to the Wars. Earle Birney. WaP
I do not grudge them; Lord, I do not grudge. The Mother. Padraic Pearse. OnYI
I do not here, upon this humorrous stage. To the Right Worthy and Judicious Favorer of Virtue, Maister Fulke Greville. Samuel Daniel. *Fr.* Musophilus. ReIE; SiCE
I do not hold with him who thinks. Thoughts on the Cosmos. Franklin P. Adams. HBMV
I do not know how I shall look. More Letters Found near a Suicide. Frank Horne. BANP
I do not know how wide the spaces are. This Only Do I Know. *Unknown.* BePJ
I do not know, I cannot see. Confidence. *Unknown.* BLRP
I do not know if the world has lied. What I'm Doing Here. Leonard Cohen. PeCV (1967 ed.)
I do not know much about gods; but I think that the river. The Dry Salvages. T. S. Eliot. *Fr.* Four Quartets. CABA; LiTB; MaPo; MBW-2; MWA-2; NoP; OxBA; SeCePo; SeCeV
I do not know the depths of love. This I Know. Grace M. Watkins. SoP
I do not know what. Antique Carved Figures. Raymond E. F. Larsson. JKCP (1955 ed.)
I do not know what next may come. This I Know [*or* The Best for Me]. E. Margaret Clarkson. SoP; STF
I do not know why. It is not only. The Double Tree. Winfield Townley Scott. PoPl
I do not lack for Jack or Joan. Me. Hughes Mearns. *Fr.* Later Antigonishes. InMe
I do not like my garden, but I love. The Garden. Edgar Lee Masters. NP
I do not like the other sort. An Ulsterman. "Lynn Doyle." OnYI
I do not like thee, Doctor Fell. Thomas Brown. *See* I Do Not Love Thee, Doctor Fell .
"I do not like to go to bed." Sleepy Harry. Ann *or* Jane Taylor. SAS

I Do Not Love Thee. Caroline E. S. Norton. GTBS; GTSL; HBV; OBEV; WePo
I do not love thee/ So I'll not deceive thee. Love's Story. John Clare. PeER
I Do Not Love Thee, Doctor Fell. Thomas Brown, *after the Latin of* Martial. GoTP; MoShBr; RIS; WhC
(Doctor Fell.) ChTr; FaFP; LiTG; SiTL; TreFT
("I do not like thee, Doctor Fell.") OxNR
(No Reason Why.) OnPM
(Non Amo Te.) AWP; ImOP; JAWP; WBP
I do not love thee! No! I do not love thee! I Do Not Love Thee. Caroline E. S. Norton. GTBS; GTSL; HBV; OBEV; WePo
I Do Not Love to See Your Beauty Fire. John Hall Wheelock. HBMV
I do not love to wed. The Poet Loves a Mistress, but Not to Marry. Robert Herrick. ALV; CavP; ErPo
I do not mind symbolism. Symbolism. Karen Swenson. NYTB
I do not need the skies'/ Pomp. All Flesh. Francis Thompson. BrPo
I do not own an inch of land. A Strip of Blue. Lucy Larcom. AA; HBV; MaRV; OQP; OTPC; WGRP
I do not pity the old men, fumbling after. Pity. Babette Deutsch. WHA
I do not pray for peace nor ease. Prayer for Pain. John G. Neihardt. HBV; NP; PFY; TrPWD; WGRP
I do not say this. "Your Need Is Greater than Mine." Theodore Enslin. CoPo
I do not see the sense of my toil putting thoughts in a dying tongue. Dain do Eimhir, LV. Sorley Maclean. NeBP
I do not sleep at night. Night-Piece. Raymond Richard Patterson. CAD
I do not thank Thee, Lord. Thanks Be to God. Janie Alford. MaRV; PGD; PoToHe
I do not think that skies and meadows are. Reciprocity. John Drinkwater. NeMA; NP
I do not think the ending can be right. But That Is Another Story. Donald Justice. CoAP; NePoEA-2
I do not understand. The Unknown. E. O. Laughlin. BLPA
I do not understand the world, father. On the Subject of Poetry. W. S. Merwin. PP
I do not want a gaping crowd. When I Am Dead. James Edward Wilson. PoLF
I do not want to be your weeping woman. Poem. Alison Boodson. NeBP
I do not want to turn away. Two Poems, I. Robert J. Abrams. NNP
I do not weep for Aprils. Compensate. Patrick D. Moreland. InP
I do not wish to know. After the Persian. Louise Bogan. NePoAm; NYBP
I do not wish to see my sins more plain. The True Need. Thomas Curtis Clark. OQP
I do not wish you joy without a sorrow. A Birthday Wish. Dorothy Nell McDonald. PoToHe (new ed.)
I do your will, yet cherish still the wish. Two Lovers in the Toils of Honor. Corneille. *Fr.* The Cid. LiTW
I doe but name thee Pembroke, and I find. To William Earle of Pembroke. Ben Jonson. SCEP-2; SeCP
I doe confess I love thee. *Unknown.* SeCSL
I doe confesse that thou art faire. *Unknown.* SeCSL
I Done Done What Ya' Tol' Me to Do, *with music.* *Unknown.* BoAN-1
I done try to go to church, I done go for court. One Wife for One Man. Frank Aig-Imoukhuede. PBA
I don't appwove this hawid waw. Swell's Soliloquy. *Unknown.* FiBHP
I don't believe in 'ristercrats. My Sort o' Man. Paul Laurence Dunbar. AmNP
I don't believe the sleepers in this house. A Cabin in the Clearing. Robert Frost. TDP
I don't go much on religion. Little Breeches. John Hay. AA; AmPP (3d ed.); BeLS; BOHV; CoBA; FaBoBe; GoTP; HBV; PaPo; StaSt; TreFS; TSW
I don't hate your color. Explanation. Valerie Tarver. TNV
I don't know any greatest treat. The Parterre. E. H. Palmer. BOHV; NA
I don't know any more what it used to be. A Girl. Edwin Denby. BoLP
I don't know how he came. Ossawatomie. Carl Sandburg. CMoP; OxBA; PFY
I don't know how it was. Mystery. "Yehoash." TrJP
I don't know how you died. The Singer. James Danner. BF
I don't know somehow it seems sufficient. Gravelly Run. A. R. Ammons. CoAP
I don't know who they are. The Pointed People. Rachel Field. FaPON; MPB
I don't like bees. Bees. Marchette Chute. BoChLi (1950 ed.)
I Don't Like No Railroad Man, *with music.* *Unknown.* AS
(Railroaders and Hobos.) OuSiCo
"I don't like the look of little Fan, mother." Little Fan. James Reeves. PoMS
I don't like the man who doesn't sleep, says God. Sleep. Charles Péguy. TIHL
I don't look back; God knows the fruitless efforts. We See Jesus. Annie Johnson Flint. BLRP
I Dont Mean to Tell You Her Name. *Unknown.* *See* Lovely Village Fair, The.
I don't mind eels. The Eel. Ogden Nash. FaBV; FaPON
I don't operate often. When I do. The Dream Songs, LXVII. John Berryman. NaP
I don't remember anything of then, down there around the magnolias. Ode to Michael Goldberg's Birth and Other Births. Frank O'Hara. NeAP
I don't say that the Fates were actuated. The Poet. H. C. Bosman. BoSA
I don't think it important. The Beast Section. Welton Smith. BF
I Don't Want Any More Visitors. Ingrid Jonker, *tr. fr. Afrikaans by* Ingrid Jonker. PeSA
I don't want none of your weevily wheat. Weevily Wheat. *Unknown.* TrAS
I Don't Want to Be a Gambler, *with music.* *Unknown.* AS
I Don't Want to Play in Your Yard. Philip Wingate. TreFT
I dote the baple buds are swellig. Kerchoo! Margaret Fishback. PoSC
I Dote upon Myself. Walt Whitman. *Fr.* Song of Myself, XXIV. AnEnPo
I Doubt A Lovely Thing Is Dead. Neil Tracy. CaP
I doubt if ten men in all Tilbury Town. E. A. Robinson. *Fr.* Captain Craig. PoEL-5
I doubt if the wind in your boots. Stiles. John Pudney. NYBP
I doubt if you knew. The Rescue. John Logan. CMoP; NYBP
I doubt not God is good, well-meaning, kind. Yet Do I Marvel. Countee Cullen. AmNP; AnAmPo; BANP; BP; CDC; IDB; NP; PoNe; TTY
I dragged my feet [*or* flesh] through desert gloom. The Prophet. Pushkin. AWP; JAWP; WBP; WGRP
I drank at every vine. Feast. Edna St. Vincent Millay. NP; WHA
I dreaded that first robin, so. Emily Dickinson. AmPP (5th ed.); AnAmPo; AP; CBEP; MAP; MoAmPo
I Dream a World. Langston Hughes. AmNP; BP
I dream now of green places. In the Third Year of War. Henry Treece. WaP
I dream of a red-rose tree. Women and Roses. Robert Browning. EPN; ViBoPo
I dream of Jeanie with the light brown hair. Jeanie with the Light Brown Hair. Stephen Collins Foster. FaFP; FaPL; TrAS; TreF
I dream of journeys repeatedly. The Far Field. Theodore Roethke. NaP; NoP; SeCeV (1967 ed.); ToPo
I dream of nude policemen investigating. The Nude Republic. John Perreault. ANYP
I dream of you, to wake: would that I might. Monna Innominata, III. Christina Rossetti. ViPo; VP
I dream you naked on a float, blown up. Poem for a Dead Aunt. Barbara L. Greenberg. QAH
I dream'd I saw a little brook. A Vision of Children. Thomas Ashe. VA
I Dream'd in a Dream. Walt Whitman. AP; MaRV
I dream'd that, as I wander'd by the way. *See* I dreamed that, as I wandered by the way.
I dream'd that I walk'd in Italy. Going Back Again. "Owen Meredith." EvOK; FiBHP
I dream'd that I woke from a dream. Song. George Macdonald. VA
I dream'd there would be Spring no more. In Memoriam A. H. H.,

I (continued)
LXIX. Tennyson. EPN; OAEP; ViPo; VP
I dream'd this mortal part of mine. The Vine. Robert Herrick. CavP; ErPo; UnTE
I dream'd we both were in a bed. *See* I Dreamed we both. . .
I dreamed a dream last night, when all was still. Reality. Angela Morgan. WGRP
I dreamed a dream next Tuesday week. My Dream. *Unknown.* BOHV; GoTP; NA; SiTL
I dreamed a dream the other night. *See* I dreamt a dream. . .
I dreamed a dream the other night, when everything was still. Prospecting Dream. John A. Stone. SGR
I dreamed a dream! what can it mean? *See* I dreamt a dream. . .
I dreamed a dreary dream this night. The Braes of Yarrow. *Unknown.* ESPB; OxBB; ViBoFo
I dreamed all my fortitude screamed. Letter across Doubt and Distance. M. Carl Holman. AmNP; PoNe
I dreamed I held/ A sword against my flesh. Lady Kasa, *tr. fr. Japanese by* Kenneth Rexroth. LiTW
I dreamed I passed a doorway. The Unknown Belovèd, John Hall Wheelock. HBMV
I dreamed I saw that ancient Irish Queen. Chivalry. "Æ." MoRP; ViBoPo
I dreamed I was a barber; and there went. The Barber. John Gray. SyP
I dreamed I was a cave-boy. The Cave-Boy. Laura E. Richards. FaPON
I Dreamed Last Night of My True Love. *Unknown. See* Locks and Bolts.
I Dreamed My Love. *Unknown.* UnTE
I dreamed my love came in my sleep. Lowlands, *vers.* I. *Unknown.* AmSS
I dreamed of him last night, I saw his face. The Dead Poet. Lord Alfred Douglas. CLwM; HBMV; MoBrPo (1942 ed.); PoVP; ViBoPo
I dreamed of war-heroes, of wounded war-heroes. The Heroes. Louis Simpson. NePoAm
I dreamed one man stood against a thousand. Graves. Carl Sandburg. AnEnPo
I dreamed one night I came. A Heterodoxy. Lord Dunsany. OnYI
I dreamed Ted Williams. Dream of a Baseball Star. Gregory Corso. SD
I dreamed [*or* dream'd] that, as I wandered by the way. The Question [*or* A Dream of the Unknown]. Shelley. CH; EnRP; EPN; FiP; GTBS; GTBS-D; GTBS-P; GTBS-W; GTSE; GTSL; HBV; MemP; MyFE; OBEV; OBRV; PeER
I dreamed that dead, and meditating. The Weed. Elizabeth Bishop. MoPo
I dreamed that God was Silence. Air was dead. Ebenezer Elliott. *Fr.* The Year of Seeds. Sonn
I dreamed that I. Slings. Rubén Darío. PoFr
I dreamed that I was dead and crossed heavens. A Dream. Helen Hunt Jackson. AnFE; APA; CoAnAm
I Dreamed That in a City Dark As Paris. Louis Simpson. CoAP; NePoEA
I dreamed that one had died in a strange place. A Dream of Death. W. B. Yeats. POTE
I dreamed that stone by stone. The Temple. Tennyson. OQP
I dreamed that the sky was tight and. Two Dreams. Clarence Franklin. BF
I dreamed that when I died a jukebox played. Death of a Jazz Musician. William Jay Smith. NePoAm-2
I dreamed the Fairies wanted me. Crab-Apple. Ethel Talbot. BiCB; PCH; TiPo
I dreamed the Saviour came to be. Interceding. Opal Lenore Gibbs. BePJ
I dreamed there was an Emperor Antony. Cleopatra's Lament. Shakespeare. *Fr.* Antony and Cleopatra, V, ii. UnPo
I dreamed two spirits came—one dusk as night. The Two Spirits. James Benjamin Kenyon. AA
I dreamed [*or* dream'd] we both were in a bed. The Vision [to Electra]. Robert Herrick. ALV; SCEP-2; SeCP; UnTE
I dreamt [*or* dreamed] a dream the other night. Lowlands [Away]. *Unknown.* ChTr; LO; OxBoLi; SoAmSa
I dreamt a dream; till morning light. Arthur Hugh Clough. *Fr.* Dipsychus, Pt. I, sc. v. OAEP
I dreamt [*or* dreamed] a dream! what can it mean? The Angel. Blake. *Fr.* Songs of Experience. CH; EiPP; EnRP
I dreamt her sensual proportions. The Death of Venus. Robert Creeley. AmPC; StP
I dreamt I came to a kind inn. A Kind Inn. George Dillon. GoYe
I dreamt I climbed to a high, high plain. The Pitcher. Yüan Chen. AWP; JAWP; WBP
I Dreamt I Dwelt in Marble Halls. Alfred Bunn. *Fr.* The Bohemian Girl. TreFS
I Dreamt I Saw Great Venus. Bion, *also at. to* Moschus, *tr. fr. Greek by* Leigh Hunt. OnPM
(Dream of Venus, A.) AWP
I dreamt. I saw three ladies in a tree. The Three Ladies. Robert Creeley. NeAP
I dreamt I was in love again. The One before the Last. Rupert Brooke. OBVV
I dreamt it! such a funny thing. What the Prince of I Dreamt. Henry Cholmondeley-Pennell. NA
I dreamt last night of you, John-John. John-John. Thomas MacDonagh. AnIV; AWP; HBMV; JAWP; OnYI; OxBI; WBP
I dreamt not that love's way. W. W. Gibson. *Fr.* Marriage. LO
I dreamt that I dwelt in marble halls. I Dreamt I Dwelt in Marble Halls. Alfred Bunn. *Fr.* The Bohemian Girl. TreFS
I dreamt that with a bullet in my side. The Triple Dream. Mikhail Lermontov. LiTW
I dreamt the other night I was in Heaven. Assimilation. Irving Feldman. AmPC
I dressed my father in his little clothes. The Boat. Robert Pack. CoAP; NePoEA-2; TPM
I drew it from its china tomb. A Dead Letter. Austin Dobson. HBV; PoVP; VA
I drew the blind on Christmas Morn. Red Sky at Morning. Gilbert Thomas. LO; TreFS
I Drift in the Wind. Ingrid Jonker, *tr. fr. Afrikaans by* Jack Cope. PeSA
I drink of the ale of Southwark, I drink of the ale of Chepe. The Maltworm's Madrigal. Austin Dobson. HBV
I drink to your glory my god. The Scorner. Tchicaya U'-Tamsi. TTY
I, driven, deeper driven in the glade. Tree Purge. George Rostrevor Hamilton. POTE
I dropped my pen—and listened to the wind. Sonnet: Composed While the Author Was Engaged in Writing a Tract Occasioned by the Convention of Cintra. Wordsworth. ChER
I dropped my sail and dried my dripping seines. Mass at Dawn. Roy Campbell. PeSA
I dropped my wad. Limericised Classics, V: Spoon River Anthology. Edwin Meade Robinson. HBMV
I drove up to the graveyard, which. The Soul Longs to Return Whence It Came. Richard Eberhart. AmP; CBV; CMoP; ExPo; LiTM; ToPo
I drown in the drumming ploughland, I drag up. The Hawk in the Rain. Ted Hughes. ACV; ToPo
I du believe in Freedom's cause. The Pious Editor's [*or* The Candidate's] Creed. James Russell Lowell. *Fr.* The Biglow Papers, 1st Series, No. VI. AmePo; AnNE; BOHV; TOP; YaD
I dug, beneath the cypress shade. The Grave of Love [*or* The Cypress *or* Beneath the Cypress Shade]. Thomas Love Peacock. CH; CLwM; EnRP; GTBS; GTBS-D; HBV; OBEV (1st ed.); OBRV
I dug you/ off red and brown. To the "JFK" Quintet. Al Fraser. BF
I dwell apart. The Hermit. Hsü Pên. FIW
I dwell in grace's court. Content and Rich. Robert Southwell. OBSC; SiCE
I dwell in Possibility. Emily Dickinson. AP; MAmP; OxBA; PP
I dwells in the herth and I breathes in the hair. Travesty of Miss Fanshawe's Enigma. Horace Mayhew. BOHV
I dwelt alone. Eulalie [A Song.] Poe. EvOK; LaNeLa; Par
I dwelt in a city enchanted. The City of Prague. William Jeffery Prowse. CenHV
I dyed my rooms in candle glow. The Heart Is Bethlehem. Gertrude Hanson. ChIP
I eagerly await your miniature, wish the artist would hurry. Letter to My Wife. Keidrych Rhys. WaP
I Eat My Peas with Honey. *Unknown.* CenHV; EvOK
(Peas.) FaPON; RePo

I edged back against the night. High Tide. Jean Starr Untermeyer. MAP; MCCG; MoAmPo; NeMA; TSW
I empty myself of the names of others. The Remains. Mark Strand. NYBP
I encountered the crowd returning from amusements. Resolution of Dependence. George Barker. FaBoTw; LiTB; LiTM (rev. ed.)
I enter and as I enter all is abandoned. Microcosmos, I. Nigel Heseltine. NeBP
I enter, and I see thee in the gloom. Divina Commedia, III [*or* Sonnets]. Longfellow. AmePo; AmP; AmPP; AnAmPo; AnFE; AnNE; AP; APA; CoAnAm; CoBA; GoBC; ILP; MWA-1; NePA; NoP; OuHeWo; OxBA; TOP
I entered a vast cathedral. Worship. Bob Jones, Jr. BePJ
I, entrance door to Tarpeia's house, swung open, once. The Complaint of Tarpeia's Door. Propertius. Elegies, I, 16. LiTW
I Entreat You, Alfred Tennyson. Walter Savage Landor. OAEP
I envy./ This secret. Envy. Yevgeny Yevtushenko. FlW
I envy e'en the fly its gleams of joy. Written in Prison. John Clare. ERoP-2
I envy every flower that blows. A Lover's Envy. Henry van Dyke. HBV
I envy no mans rest. *Unknown.* SeCSL
I envy not Endymion now no more. Sonnet. Earl of Stirling. Aurora, XXIX. ElL; Sonn
I envy not in any moods. In Memoriam A. H. H., XXVII [*or* Lost Love]. Tennyson. BEL; CoBE; EnL; EnLi-2; EnLit; EPN; FaBoEn; GTSL; HBV; LiTB; LiTG; LiTL; MaRV; OAEP; OBNC; OuHeWo; TOP; TreFS; ViPo; VP
I envy not the lark his divine song. Invention. Sir William Watson. HBV
I envy not the sun. Aspiration. John Banister Tabb. LO
I even I know the Eastern Gate of Heaven. He Knoweth the Souls of the East. *Unknown. Fr.* Book of the Dead. AWP
I, even I, will always. Psalm XXXIV. *Paraphrased by* Sir Philip Sidney. FCP
I Explain. Stephen Crane. War Is Kind, VI. AA; AmP
("I explain the silvered passing of a ship at night.") AP
I fain would be a sculptor of the soul. Sculptor of the Soul. Toyohiko Kagawa. MaRV
I falter where I firmly trod. The Larger Hope. Tennyson. *Fr.* In Memoriam A. H. H., LV. MaRV
I fasted for some forty days on bread and buttermilk. The Pilgrim. W. B. Yeats. PoSa
I favor most in flowers the shyest ones. Noctiflora. Maurice Lesemann. NP
I fear, I fear the rarity. Death by Rarity. Marguerite Young. LiTA
I Fear No Power a Woman Wields. Ernest McGaffey. AA; HBV
I fear not henceforth death. William Drummond of Hawthornden. LO
I fear one minute more than twenty years. Pinwheel. Dilys Laing. NYTB
I fear that Puck is dead—it is so long. The Death of Puck. Eugene Lee-Hamilton. HBMV; OBVV
I fear the headless man. The Lover's Ghost. Louis Simpson. FiSC
I Fear Thy Kisses, Gentle Maiden. Shelley. GTBS; GTBS-D; GTBS-P; GTBS-W; GTSE; HBV; LiTL
(To ——.) EnRP; EPN; GTSL; InPo; ViBoPo
I fear to love thee, Sweet, because. To Olivia. Francis Thompson. MoBrPo
I fear to me such fortune be assign'd. Sonnet. William Drummond of Hawthornden. NCEP
I feast on the grape hill. The Grape Hill. Endre Ady. OnPM
I Feed a Flame Within [Which So Torments Me]. Dryden. *See* Song: "I feed a flame within. . ."
I feel a breath from other planets blowing. Rapture. Stefan George. AWP; JAWP; WBP
I feel a newer life in every gale. May. J. G. Percival. BoTP
I feel a poem in my heart to-night. Embryo. Mary Ashley Townsend. AA; HBV
I feel an air from other planets flowing. Transport. Stefan George. LiTW
I Feel I Am. John Clare. ERoP-2; SeCePo
I feel it when the game is done. Footnote to Tennyson. Gerald Bullett. FiBHP
I Feel Like My Time Ain't Long ("I feel like"), *with music. Unknown.* BoAN-2
I Feel Like My Time Ain't Long ("Oh, de hearse keep a-rollin'"), *with music. Unknown.* OuSiCo
I feel myself in need. George Moses Horton, Myself. George Moses Horton. Kal
I feel myself like the flame. The Candle Flame. Janet Lewis. CrMA
I feel remorse for all that Time has done. Love's Remorse. Edwin Muir. LiTL
I feel ridiculous. Put Down. Léon Damas. TTY
I feel so exceedingly lazy. A Hot-Weather Song. Don Marquis. HBMV; RePo; StVeCh; WhC; YaD
I feel that in the days gone by. In Days Gone By. Ida M. Mills. BoTP
I feel the breath of the summer night. A Summer Night. Elizabeth Stoddard. AA
I feel the far-off cry of spring. Essence of Tomorrow. Alice Hansche Mortenson. SoP
I feel the spring far off, far off. Spring in War-Time. Sara Teasdale. OHIP
I feel towards God just as a woman might. Spiritual Passion. George Barlow. OBVV
I feel very sorry for/ Toys not played with. Not Any More. Dorothy Aldis. BoChLi
I felt a cleavage [*or* cleaving] in my mind. Emily Dickinson. DiPo; OxBA
I felt a funeral, in my brain. Emily Dickinson. AmPP (5th ed.); AnFE; AP; APA; CABA; CMoP; CoAnAm; DiPo; ExPo; ForPo; InPo; LiTA; MAmP; MAPA; MasP; MWA-2; OxBA; PIA; PoEL-5; PoeP; PoRA; TwAmPo
I Felt a Spirit of Love Begin to Stir. Dante, *tr. fr. Italian by* Dante Gabriel Rossetti. *Fr.* La Vita Nuova. AWP; JAWP; WBP
I felt my heart beat like an engine high in the air. Depression. Robert Bly. FRC; NaP
I felt my spirit leap, and look at thee. To——, M. D. Leigh Hunt. Sonn
I felt no tremor and I caught no sound. The White Dust. W. W. Gibson. MoBrPo; NeMA
I felt the chill of the meadow underfoot. The Quest of the Orchis. Robert Frost. AmePo
I felt the lurch and halt of her heart. Lightning. D. H. Lawrence. CMoP; LiTL; MoAB; MoBrPo; UnTE
I felt the world a-spinning on its nave. The Last Journey. John Davidson. *Fr.* The Testament of John Davidson. GoTS
I fight a battle every day. The Fighter. S. E. Kiser. BLPA
I Fights Mit Sigel! Grant P. Robinson. BLPA
I fill this cup to one made up of loveliness alone. A Health. Edward Coote Pinkney. AA; AmePo; AnAmPo; HBV; FaPL; InP; TreFS
I find it normal, passing these great frontiers. Manchouli. William Empson. CoBMV
I find many dishes. The History of Psychotherapy. Jon Anderson. YAP
I find no peace, and all my war is done. Description of the Contrarious Passions in a Lover [*or* Love's Inconsistency]. Petrarch, *tr. by* Sir Thomas Wyatt. Sonnets to Laura: To Laura in Life, CIV. AWP; DiPo; EnLi-1 (1949 ed.); FCP; JAWP; LiTB; LiTL; OAEP; OuHeWo; PoAn; PoFS; PoIE; ReEn; ReIE; SiPS; Sonn; TrGrPo; TuPP; WBP
I first adventure, with foolhardy might. Prologue. Joseph Hall. *Fr.* Virgidemiarum. ReEn; ReIE; SiCE; ViBoPo
I first informed them that we were to fly. Ulysses and the Sirens. Homer. *Fr.* The Odyssey. ReEn
I first tasted under Apollo's lips. Evadne. Hilda Doolittle ("H. D."). MAPA
I first would have him understand. On His Garden Book. Francis Daniel Pastorius. SCAP
I fix[e] mine eye on thine, and there. Witchcraft by a Picture. John Donne. MaMe; PoFS
I fled Him, down the nights and down the days. The Hound of Heaven. Francis Thompson. ACP; AnFE; ATP; BEL; BoLiVe; BrPo; CAW; CoBE; EnL; EnLi-2; EnLit; EPN; FaBV; FaFP; FaPL; GoBC; GoTL; GTBS-W; GTSL; HBV; ILP; JKCP; LiTB; LiTM; LoBV; MaRV; MasP; MCCG; MoAB; MoBrPo; OAEP; OBMV; OtMeF; OxBoCh; PoLi; PoIE; PoE; PoEL-5; PoVP; SeCePo; SeCeV; SoP; TIHL; TOP; TreF; TrGrPo; TRV; UnPo (1st ed.); ViBoPo; ViPP; WGRP; WHA

I flew my kite. Kite. David McCord. PDV
I fling my soul to the air like a falcon flying. *See* I flung my soul. . .
I fling myself against the ground. The Good Ground. Virginia Moore. YT
I fling out fear and discontent. House Cleaning. Nicholas Lloyd Ingraham. SoP
I Flung Me Round Him. Roden Noel. *Fr.* The Water-Nymph and the Boy. HBV; OBEV (1st ed.); OBVV
I flung [*or* fling] my soul to the air like a falcon flying. The Falconer of God. William Rose Benét. CAW; GBV (1952 ed.); HBMV; MaRV; NP; TreFT; WGRP
I follow from my window down. From the Window Down. Louis O. Coxe. NYBP
I Follow, Lo, the Footing. Ben Jonson. LiTL
I followed a barbed-wire fence. Holding-Paddock. William Hart-Smith. AnNZ
I followed each detour. The Slow Race. Andrew Young. MemP
I followed my Duke ere I was a lover. Sir Richard's Song. Kipling. OtMeF
I followed once a fleet and mighty serpent. A Subterranean City [*or* Lines]. Thomas Lovell Beddoes. HoPM; NBM; StP
I followed, splendid season. Trouble at Sea. Thomas Prys. PrWP
I followed where they led. His Throne Is with the Outcast. James Russell Lowell. ChIP
I fonde there freris alle the foure ordres. William Langland (?). *Fr.* The Vision of William Concerning Piers the Plowman. YAT
I, for long days a stranger. Petition. Clinton Scollard. MaRV
I for thy sake was pierced with heavy sorrow. Good Friday. Girolamo Savonarola. ChIP; OQP
I forgot my Lord in the summertime. Forgetting God. J. E. Harvey. STF
I found a ball of grass among the hay. Mouse's Nest. John Clare. CBV; ChTr; ExPo; LiTB; LoBV; SeCeV
I found a dimpled spider, fat and white. Design. Robert Frost. AmLP; AP; BWP; CABA; CaFP; CBV; CMoP; CoBMV; CrMA; ForPo; ILP; MaPo (1969 ed.); NoP; Po; PoAn; PoDB; PoeP; PoIE; PoPo; SeCeV; Sonn
I found a flower in a desolate plot. The Black Wall-Flower. Frances Ann Kemble. VA
I found a flower in the wood. Wood Flower. Richard Le Gallienne. HBMV
I Found a Horseshoe, *with music.* *Unknown.* AS
I found a little beetle, so that Beetle was his name. Forgiven. A. A. Milne. SoPo
I found a little brown purse. Found in the Woods. Irene F. Pawsey. BoTP
I found a little fairy flute. Fairy Music. Enid Blyton. BoTP
I found a little old elfin man. The Dandelion. Katharine Pyle. DD
I found a pigeon's skull on the machair. Perfect. Glyn Jones, *arr. by* "Hugh MacDiarmid." FIW; NeBP
I found a torrent falling in a glen. The Torrent. E. A. Robinson. MaPo; NePA
I found a yellow flower in the grass. A Summer Sanctuary. John Hall Ingham. AA
I found at daybreak yester morn. Medieval Norman Songs, V. *Unknown, tr. by* John Addington Symonds. AWP; JAWP; WBP
I found far culled from fragrant field and grove. The Stranger's Gift. Jones Very. AmePo
I Found God. Mary Afton Thacker. MaRV; SoP; TRV
I found God in the dawning. Omnipresent. Frank G. Weaver. SoP
I Found Her Out There. Thomas Hardy. CH; CMoP; LO; MoVE; PoEL-5
I found him drowned on the rock that night. Sea Dirge. Tom Scott. ACV
I found Him in the shining of the stars. Arthur's Disillusionment. Tennyson. *Fr.* Idylls of the King. TreFS
I found him openly wearing her token. A Conquest. Walter Herries Pollock. OBVV; VA
I found in dreams a place of wind and flowers. A Ballad of Life. Swinburne. HBV; MaVP; PoVP
I found in Innisfail the fair. Aldfrid's Itinerary through Ireland. *Unknown.* OnYI
I found it in a legendary land. On Discovering a Butterfly. Vladimir Nabokov. NYBP
I found myself one day all, all alone. Ballata, I. Angelo Poliziano. AWP
I found no beauty on the mountain heights. Beauty. Joel Elias Spingarn. HBMV
I found ten kinds of wild flowers growing. Late October. Sara Teasdale. PoSC; YeAr
I found that ivory image there. Crazy Jane Grown Old Looks at the Dancers. W. B. Yeats. AtBAP; CMoP; PoeP
I found the phrase [*or* words] to every thought. Emily Dickinson. AA; AmPP (5th ed.); AnFE; APA; CoAnAm; TOP
"I found the place last winter." Eric's voice. The Dreaming Trout. Charles Bruce. *Fr.* The Flowing Summer. CaP
I found the task that I had dreaded so. The Dreaded Task. Margaret E. Bruner. PoToHe
I found Thee in my heart, O Lord. Edward Dowden. *Fr.* New Hymns for Solitude. TrPWD
I found them lying on the shore. The Dolls. Frederic Prokosch. LiTM (1946 ed.)
I found them there today. Mementos, II. W. D. Snodgrass. AmPC; NePoEA-2
I found you fluttering. Caught by Chance. T. W. Ramsey. HaMV
I found you in a newspaper. Idea of a Swimmer. Jean-Richard Bloch. TrJP
I found your Horace with the writing in it. On First Looking into Loeb's Horace. Lawrence Durrell. LiTM (1970 ed.); ToPo
I, François Villon, ta'en at last. Would I Be Shrived? Villon. BLPA
I freeze, I freeze, and nothing dwels. The Frozen Heart. Robert Herrick. CavP
I gaed to spend a week in Fife. The Annuity. George Outram. BOHV; HBV; PeVV
I gat your letter, winsome Willie. To William Simpson of Ochiltree. Burns. MCCG; OxBS
"I gather my poems out of the heart of the clover." The Poet's Harvesting. Charles J. O'Malley. CAW
I gather thyme upon the sunny hills. Immalee. Christina Rossetti. BoNaP; ThWaDe
I gather where I hope to gain. *Unknown.* SeCSL
I gathered a red anemone. Anemone. Dawn Finlay. SoP
I gathered marble Venus in my arms. A Parable for Poetasters. Oliver St. John Gogarty. WhC
I gave a beggar from my scanty store. The True Gift. *Unknown.* ChIP; MaRV
I gave birth to the sun. Two Mad Songs. Emmett Jarrett. *Fr.* Design for the City of Man. ThO
I Gave Her Cakes; I Gave Her Ale. *Unknown.* AtBAP; TreFS
(Cakes and Ale.) FaFP; SiTL
("I gave her cakes; [and] I gave her ale.") EG; LO
I Gave My Life for Thee. Frances Ridley Havergal. SoP; VA
I gave my love a cherry without a stone. Captain Wedderburn's Courtship (B *vers.*). *Unknown.* ViBoFo
I Gave My Love a Gay Gold Ring, *with music.* *Unknown.* BFSS
I gave myself to him. Emily Dickinson. CBEP; FaBV; FaPL
I gave the people freedom clear. Rule of Fair Play. Solon, *tr. by* Henry Nelson Coleridge. PoFr
I gave to Hope a watch of mine: but he. Hope. George Herbert. FosPo; MaMe; PoEL-2
I gave you immortality and what did you give me? Dain do Eimhir, XIX. Sorley Maclean. NeBP
I gaze into the heavens. The Greatest Event. *Unknown.* SoP
I gaze upon the beauty of the stars. The Beauty of the Stars. Moses ibn Ezra. TrJP
I gaze, where August's sunbeam falls. Newark Abbey. Thomas Love Peacock. OBNC
I gaze with grief upon our generation. A Thought. Mikhail Yurevich Lermontov. AWP; WoL
I gazed, and lo! Afar and near. Battle of Somerset. Cornelius C. Cullen. PAH
I gazed sadly from my window. Evanescent Love. Eugene Redmond. TNV
I gazed upon her picture. The Picture. Heine. OnPM
I Gazed upon the Cloudless Moon. Emily Brontë. ChTr
I gazed upon the glorious sky. June. Bryant. AA; CoBA; HBV

I Gazed Within. Emily Brontë. ViBoPo
I gently touched her hand: she gave. I Pressed Her Rebel Lips. *Unknown.* ErPo
I get my degree. Lawd, Dese Colored Chillum. Ruby C. Saunders. WSL
I get numb and go in. W. D. Snodgrass. Heart's Needle, IX. PIA
I give more praise to Troy's redoubt. On Troy. Oliver St. John Gogarty. WhC
I give my hand back to its place. Setting Out. Jack Marshall. YAP
I Give My Heart to Thee. *Unknown, tr. fr. Latin by* Ray Palmer. BePJ
I Give My Soldier Boy a Blade. William Maginn. HBV; PAH
(Soldier-Boy, The.) VA
I give my word on it. There is no way. Still and All. Burns Singer. NePoEA-2; OxBS
I Give Thanks. Grace Fallow Norton. NP
I give the praise to Christ alone. Flowers in a Garden. Christopher Smart. ThGo
I give thee thanks, Adonai! My Soul in the Bundle of Life. *Unknown. Fr.* The Dead Sea Scrolls. TrJP
I give thee treasures hour by hour. Then. Rose Terry Cooke. HBV
I give these flowers and fruits, these leafy sprays. Green. Paul Verlaine. LiTW
I Give unto Them Eternal Life. Edward Taylor. *See* Preparatory Meditations: "Eternal life! What life is this. . ."
I give you a house of snow. The Dove of New Snow. Vachel Lindsay. MAP; MoAmPo
I give you a land of sun and flow'rs, and summer the whole year long. Oklahoma. Harriet Parker Camden. PoRL
I give you horses for your games in May. Of the Months: May. Folgore da San Geminiano. AWP
I give you meadow-lands in April, fair. Of the Months: April. Folgore da San Geminiano. AWP
I give you my hand. Microcosmos, VIII. Nigel Heseltine. NeBP
I give you now Professor Twist. The Purist. Ogden Nash. FiBHP; GoJo; MoAmPo (1950 ed.); MoShBr; NeMA; PV; ShM; TreFT
I Give You Thanks My God. Bernard Dadié, *tr. fr. French by* Donatus Ibe Nwoga. TTY
I Give You the End of a Golden String. Blake. *See* To the Christians.
I give you this Bible and more to take. Inscription on the Flyleaf of a Bible. Dannie Abse. TrJP
I glance from humble toil and see. Kitchen Window. J. E. H. MacDonald. CaP; TwCaPo
I gnarled me where the spinster tree. Waterwall Blues. Howard Moss. MoPo; NePA
I go about dumbfoundedly, and show a dullard's glance. The Glorious Game. Richard Burton. HBMV
I Go Alone. Amy L. Person. SoP
I Go by Road. Catulle Mendès, *tr. fr. French by* Alice Meynell. AWP; JAWP; TrJP; WBP
I go digging for clams once every two or three years. Clamming. Reed Whittemore. NoP; NYBP
I go down from the hill in gladness. A Farewell. "Æ." AnIV
I go downhill some days to a little room. Oldest Cemetery. Mark Van Doren. FiSC
I go down to Dupont Street. Chinatown Chant. Tom Maclnnes. CaP
I Go Fishin'. Richard S. Powell. IHA
I go North to cold, to home, to Kinnaird. Kinnaird Head. George Bruce. NeBP
I go not where I will but must. The Journey. John T. McFarland. OQP
I go out like a ghost. Home Town. W. D. Snodgrass. CBV; ToPo
I go out to Totem Street. Knock on Wood. Henry Dumas. BF
I go separately. Santa Fe Trail. Barbara Guest. NeAP
I go through hollyhocks. Las Trampas U.S.A. Charles Tomlinson. TwCP
I go to concert, party, ball. My Rival. Kipling. OnPP
I go to knit two clans together. The Wedding of the Clans. Aubrey Thomas De Vere. AnIL; IrPN
I Go to Prove My Soul. Robert Browning. *See* In His Good Time.
I Go to This Window. E. E. Cummings. NAMP
I go with earth, experiencing light. Time in the Sun. Louise Townsend Nicholl. NePoAm-2
I, God, that all the world have wrought. Noah's Flood. *Unknown.* BEL
I got a cross. Shout All over God's Heaven. *Unknown.* IHA
I got a friend named Percy. Percy/68. Glenn Myles. NBP
I Got a Gal at the Head of the Holler. *Unknown. See* Sourwood Mountain.
I Got a Home in-a Dat Rock, *with music.* *Unknown.* BoAN-1
I Got a Letter from Jesus, *with music.* *Unknown.* AS
I got a robe, you got a robe. All God's Chillun Got Wings. *Unknown.* BoAN-1; SiTL; TreFS
I got a valentine from Timmy. Valentine. Shelley Silverstein. PoSC
I got acquainted with. Pete the Parrot and Shakespeare. Don Marquis. ML
I got high/ last night. Sinner. Norman Jordan. BF
I got me flowers to straw [*or* strew] Thy way. George Herbert. *Fr.* Easter. AtBAP; BoC; BoTP; CH; EG; FaBoCh; FaBoEn; LoGBV; OBEV; OBS; OHIP; PCH; TrGrPo; TRV
I got pocketed behind 7X-3824. Ambition. Morris Bishop. AmFN
I got so I could hear his name. Emily Dickinson. AmePo; CMoP; CoBA; ReMP
I Got the Blues. *Unknown.* TTY
I got those little white schoolhouse blues. Little White Schoolhouse Blues. Florence Becker Lennon. PoNe (1970 ed.)
I Got to Roll, *with music.* *Unknown.* OuSiCo
I got up in the night. The Riverman. Elizabeth Bishop. NYBP
I got up one mornin' jes' 'bout four o'clock. Stagolee (B *vers.*). *Unknown.* BaBo; ViBoFo
I gotta lov' for Angela. Between Two Loves. T. A. Daly. BOHV; MAP; MoAmPo (1942 ed.); PoMa; StVeCh (1940 ed.)
I grant indeed that fields and flocks have charms. Truth in Poetry. George Crabbe. *Fr.* The Village. SeCePo
I grant thou wert not married to my Muse. Sonnets, LXXXII. Shakespeare. CBEP
I Grant Your Eyes Are Much More Bright. *At. to* John Bulteel. SeCL
I grazed the green as I fell. Summer. P. K. Page. PeCV
I greet my love with wine and gladsome lay. Sabbath, My Love. Judah Halevi. TrJP
I greet thee, my Redeemer sure. Salutation to Jesus Christ. John Calvin. MaRV; SoP; WGRP
I greet you, son, with joy and winter rue. Muse in Late November. Jonathan Henderson Brooks. PoNe
I grew a rose within a garden fair. Promise. Paul Laurence Dunbar. NoP
I grew up in the schoolrooms of the Dakotas. The Graffiti Poet. Nancy Willard. WOW
I grieve about my fellow-men. Wednesday. "Elspeth." WhC
I grieve, and dare not show my discontent. Elizabeth, Queen of England. LO
I grieve to think of you alone. Prescience. Donald Jeffrey Hayes. PoNe
I grieve when I think on the dear happy days of my youth. Draherin O Machree. *Unknown.* AnIV
I Grieved for Buonaparté. Wordsworth. EnRP; MBW-2; MERP; Po
(1801.) Sonn
I grieved to learn 'twas just a myth. Still Undaunted. George B. Ryan. CIV
I grow a white rose. José Martí. *Fr.* Simple Verses. TTY
I grow old under an intensity. Mirror. James Merrill. CoAP; NePoEA-2; TwAmPo
I guess I'm bad as I can be. Incorrigible. Burges Johnson. PoMa
I guess it is ever green. Evergreen Cemetery. Alfred Purdy. MoCV
I guess my political point of view. Middle-Man. William H. Matchett. TPM
I guess there is a garden named. The Mirror Perilous. Alan Dugan. LiTM (1970 ed.); TwCP
I guess today. John Plans. Dorothy Mason Pierce. BiCB
I. H. B. William Winter. AA

I ha' seen them 'mid the clouds on the heather. The White Stag. Ezra Pound. LOW
I had a beginning but shall have no end. Stone Angel. Anne Ridler. EaLo
I Had a Black Man. *Unknown.* OxBoLi
I had [*or* bought me] a cat and the cat pleased me. Barnyard Song [*or* The Farmyard]. *Unknown.* BFSS; OxNR; SoPo; TrAS
I had a dog/ Whose name was Buff. *Unknown.* OxNR
I had a dog and his name was Blue. Old Blue. *Unknown.* SD
I had a dog like a love. Penny Trumpet. Raphael Rudnik. NYBP
I Had a Dove. Keats. BiS; CH; OTPC; PoG
(Dove, The.) HBV
(Song: "I had a dove, and the sweet dove died.") FaPON; PRWS; ThWaDe
I had a dream. A wondrous thing. Spring and Death. Gerard Manley Hopkins. BrPo; FosPo; NoP; SyP
I had a dream last night, I dreamed. Andre. Gwendolyn Brooks. RePo; TiPo (1959 ed.)
I had a dream the other night. Rainbow Willow. *Unknown.* BFSS
I had a dream, which was not all a dream. Darkness. Byron. EnRP; EPN; ERoP-2; ILP; LiTB; MBW-2; OAEP; PoEL-4
I Had a Duck-billed Platypus. Patrick Barrington. CenHV; FiBHP
(Diplomatic Platypus, The.) ShBV-4
I had a feeling in my neck. Mumps. Elizabeth Madox Roberts. FaPON; GaP; MPB; SoPo; TSW
I had a friend: or thought I had a friend. The Mantis Friend. Vincent McHugh. NePoAm-2
I had a garden where for sunless days. The Music of a Friend. Louis V. Ledoux. OQP
I had a good teacher. Education. Don L. Lee. BALP
I had a heart as good as gold. The Golden Heart. Witter Bynner. HBMV
I Had a Hippopotamus. Patrick Barrington. CenHV
I had a little bird. The Orphan's Song. Sydney Dobell. CH; ELP; GTBS-D; OBNC; OTPC; PPL
I had a little cow/ Hey diddle, ho diddle! *Unknown.* OxNR
I had a little dog and his name was Blue Bell. *Unknown.* OxNR; SAS
I had a little dog, and my dog was very small. Feri's Dream [*or* The Little Dog]. Frances Cornford. BoC; RIS; ThGo
I Had a Little Doggy. *Unknown.* BoChLi; MPB; OTPC
("I had a little Doggy that used to sit and beg.") PPL; SAS
I had a little hen, the prettiest ever seen. Mother Goose. BoTP
I had a little hobby horse. Mother Goose. BoChLi; BoTP; GFA; OxNR; SiTL
I had a little horse, his name was Dappled Grey. *Unknown.* OxNR
I had a little husband. Mother Goose. BoTP; EvOK; ExPo; FaFP; HBV; HBVY; OTPC; OxNR; PPL
I had a little moppet. *Unknown.* OxNR
I had a little nag. *Unknown.* OxNR
I had a little nut-tree; nothing would it bear. Mother Goose. BoChLi; BoTP; CBEP, 2 *sts.*; CH; ExPo; GBV (1952 ed.); LiTG; MoShBr; OTPC; OxBoLi; OxNR; PoRh; PPL; RIS; SiTL; SoPo, 3 *sts.*; StVeCh; TiPo (1952 ed.)
I had a little pony. Mother Goose. BoChLi; BoTP; GFA; OTPC; OxNR; PCH; PPL; RIS; SiTL; SoPo; StVeCh; TiPo (1959 ed.)
I had a little pussy. Catkin. *Unknown.* GFA; MPB
I had a little snowball once. *Unknown.* GFA
I had a little sorrow. The Penitent. Edna St. Vincent Millay. ALV; BOHV; YaD
I had a little wife. *Unknown.* OxNR
I had a lovely bottle, bottle-blue. One Man's Goose; or, Poetry Redefined. George Starbuck. PP
I had a mother who read to me. The Reading Mother. Strickland Gillilan. BLPA
I had a nickel and I walked around the block. *Unknown.* SiTL
I Had a Part. David F. Nygren. SoP
I had a penny. Market Square. A. A. Milne. TiPo (1959 ed.)
I had a rich old great-aunt. Legacy. Nancy Byrd Turner. BrR; MoSiPe
I had a silver buckle. The Buckle. Walter de la Mare. BrR; PoRh; PTK
I had a silver penny. Nursery Rhyme of Innocence and Experience. Charles Causley. GoJo; POTi; WePo
I had a sudden vision in the night. The Ladder. Leonora Speyer. HBMV; PG
"I had a true love, but she left me." The Quaker's Wooing. *Unknown.* AS
I had a true love, if ever a girl had one. The Tri-colored Ribbon. Peadar Kearney. OnYI
I had a true-love, none so dear. Fortune's Wheel. Lord De Tabley. OBVV; PoVP; VA
I had a vision at last. Euripedes Alexopoulos. Edgar Lee Masters. *Fr.* New Spoon River Anthology. CMoP
I had a vision; was it in my sleep? Arthur Hugh Clough. *Fr.* Dipsychus, Pt. II, sc. vii. PoVP
I had a vision when the night was late. The Vision of Sin. Tennyson. PoVP; ViPo; ViPP
I had a wife, but she is gone. The Drunkard. Fenton Johnson. AnAmPo
I had a willow whistle. The Piper. Rachel Field. PoRh
I had almost grown grey before my time. Resurgent. Richard Linn Edsall. JKCP (1955 ed.)
I had ambition, by which sin. Ambition. W. H. Davies. MoBrPo; TrGrPo
I had an image of the bright, bare day. Pearl Diver. William Rose Benét. AnAmPo
I had an uncle once who kept a rock in his pocket. I've Got a Home in That Rock. Raymond Patterson. PoNe (1970 ed.)
I had approached, like other youths, the shield. The Poet and the French Revolution. Wordsworth. *Fr.* The Prelude, XI. EPN
I had as lief be embraced by the porter at the hotel. Two Figures in Dense Violet Light [*or* Night]. Wallace Stevens. CLwM; MAP; MoAB; MoAmPo; OnPM
I had asked you to try again. Christmas, Ibiza, 1966. Thomas Hanna. QAH
I had been hungry, all the years. Emily Dickinson. AmePo; CoBA; LiTA; LiTM (rev. ed.); MAP; MoAmPo; NeMA
I had been ill; and when I saw. Recovery from Mental Illness. H. C. Bosman. BoSA
I Had but Fifty Cents. *Unknown.* BeLS; BLPA; TreF
I had come to the house, in a cave of trees. Medusa. Louise Bogan. AWP; HoPM; InPo; MAP; MoAB; MoAmPo; MoPo; MoVE
I had expected. To Stephen Spender. Timothy Corsellis. WaP
I had finished my dinner. An Easy Decision. Kenneth Patchen. LOW; ToPo
I had for my winter evening walk. Good Hours. Robert Frost. OTD; RG; SiSw
I had forgotten how to pray. When I Had Need of Him. S. E. Kiser. BLRP
I had found the secret of a garret-room. The Poets. Elizabeth Barrett Browning. *Fr.* Aurora Leigh, I. VA
I had four brothers over the sea. Perrie, Merrie, Dixi, Domini. *Unknown.* BFSS
I had gone broke, and got set to come back. Epigram. J. V. Cunningham. MoAmPo (1962 ed.); NePoAm; PV; QFR
I had gone fruitless and defenceless, Lady. A Nun to Mary, Virgin. Sister Mary St. Virginia. ISi
I had gone to see a fortune teller. Dream Poem #3. Craig Sterry. QAH
I had just gone to bed. Three Lyrics, III. Petronius Arbiter. LiTW
I had ma clothes cleaned. Dressed Up. Langston Hughes. GoSl
I had my birth where stars were born. My Birth. Minot Judson Savage. AA; WGRP
I had never before held death, pale and polished, in my hands. The Captain of the Oberon. Francis Webb. *Fr.* A Drum for Ben Boyd. ACV; NeLNL
I had no God but these. Christ and the Pagan. John Banister Tabb. CAW; JKCP
I had no thought of violets of late. Sonnet. Alice Dunbar Nelson. BANP; CDC; PoNe
I had no time to hate, because. Emily Dickinson. LiTL; PoLF
I had not known what life might be. The Lesson. Sister Mary Eleanore. JKCP (1955 ed.)
I had not minded walls. Emily Dickinson. AWP; CABA; InPo; MWA-2
I had not seen my son's dear face. San Lorenzo Giustiniani's Mother. Alice Meynell. HBV

I had not thought to have unlockt my lips. Temperance and Virginity. Milton. *Fr.* Comus. OBS
I had over-prepared the event. Villanelle: the Psychological Hour. Ezra Pound. CTC; NP
I had returned from dreaming. Dream. Witter Bynner. MoLP; NP
I had seen, as dawn was breaking. La Nuit Blanche. Kipling. MoBrPo
I had the nicest Christmas list. His Name at the Top. *Unknown.* STF
I had thought of putting an. Prayer. Isabella Maria Brown. NNP; PoNe (1970 ed.)
I had three friends. Three Friends. *Unknown.* PBA
I had to kick their law into their teeth in order to save them. Negro Hero. Gwendolyn Brooks. Kal
I had to laugh. Montana Wives. Gwendolen Haste. AmFN; OTD
I had to shoot a fox today. If he. The Fox. Edsel Ford. NYTB
I had two pigeons bright and gay. *Unknown.* OxNR
I had walked life's way [*or* path] with an easy tread. I Met the Master [Face to Face]. *Unknown.* BePJ; BLRP; PoLF; SoP; STF
I had watched the ascension and decline of the moon. W. J. Turner. *Fr.* The Seven Days of the Sun. OBMV
I had written him a letter which I had, for want of better. Clancy of The Overflow. Andrew Barton Paterson. BoAu; PoAu-1
I had written to Aunt Maud. Waste [*or* Aunt Maud]. Harry Graham. LiTG; MoShBr; ShM; SiTL
I Hae a Wife o' My Ain. Burns. EiCL; EiCP
I Hae Laid a Herring in Saut. James Tytler. BOHV
I hae seen great anes and sat in great ha's. My Ain Fireside. Elizabeth Hamilton. FaBoBe; HBV
I haf von funny leedle poy. Yawcob Strauss. Charles Follen Adams. BOHV; PaPo
I hafe set my hert so hye. I Have Set My Heart So High. *Unknown.* CoBE
I hail from high in the alkali. When West Comes East. Corey Ford. InMe
I hailed me a woman from the street. My Madonna. Robert W. Service. BLPA
I hailed the bus and I went for a ride. Bus Ride. Selma Robinson. *Fr.* Ferry Ride. FaPON
"I hardly ever ope my lips," one cries. Epigram [*or* Silence and Speech]. Richard Garnett. ALV; HBV; OtMeF
I hardly suppose I know anybody who wouldn't rather be a success than a failure. Kindly Unhitch That Star, Buddy. Ogden Nash. LiTA; LiTM; PoPl
I hate/ To wait. What Literature Needs. John Holmes. InMe
I hate a prologue to a story. The Duke of Benevento. Sir John Henry Moore. CEP; OBEC
I hate and love—the why I cannot tell. Love's Unreason. Catullus, *tr. fr. Latin.* OuHeWo
I hate and love. Why? You may ask but. Odi et Amo. Catullus, *tr. by* Ezra Pound. CTC
I hate, and yet I love thee too. To Lesbia. Catullus, *tr. by* Abraham Cowley. PoPl
I hate my beauty in the glass. Thomas Hardy. *Fr.* The Beauty. LO
"I hate my verses, every line, every word." Love the Wild Swan. Robinson Jeffers. AnFE; CoAnAm; MAP; MoAB; MoAmPo; PoFr; Sonn; TwAmPo
"I hate successful people," you declare. What's Hard. Laurence Lerner. NePoEA-2
I hate that drum's discordant sound. The Drum [*or* Retort on the Foregoing *or* Ode]. John Scott of Amwell. CBEP; EiCL, OBEC; OBEV (new ed.); PPON; ViBoPo
I hate the cunning mantis, lean, mimetic. Notes for a Bestiary. Terence Heywood. LiTM
I hate the Cyclic poem, nor approve. Uncommon. Callimachus. OnPM
I hate the dreadful hollow behind the little wood. Maud. Tennyson. MBW-2; OAEP; PoVP; ViPo; ViPP; VP
I hate the man who builds his name. The Poet and the Rose. John Gay. *Fr.* Fables. EiCP
I hate the very noise of troublous man. Love and Solitude. John Clare. PeER
I hate thee, Death! Mors, Morituri Te Salutamus. Francis Burdett Money-Coutts. OBVV
I Hate Their Empty Shows. Horace. *See* Persian Fopperies.
I hate those pants that mother makes. The Small Boy's Loquitur. *Unknown.* CH
I hate those potent madmen, who keep all. John Crowne. BoC
I hate to be a kicker. Explanation. "Josh Billings." TreFT
I Hate to See You Clad. Paul Verlaine, *tr. fr. French by* Louis Untermeyer. UnTE
I hate to sing your hackneyed birds. A Panegyric on Geese. Francis S. Mahony. OnYI
I hate to spend the night. Thanks Just the Same. *Unknown.* PoLF
I hate to talk about it, 'cause. Little Danny Donkey. Helen Cowles LeCron. GFA
I hated a fellow-man long ago. Hate. Herbert E. Palmer. POTE
I hated thee, fallen tyrant! I did groan. Feelings of a Republican on the Fall of Bonaparte. Shelley. AnEnPo; Sonn
"I hates to think of dyin'," says the skipper to the mate. The Worried Skipper. Wallace Irwin. BLPA
I Have a Blue Piano. Else Lasker-Schüler, *tr. fr. German by* Ralph Manheim. TrJP
I have a bookcase, which is what. Shake, Mulleary, and Goethe. H. C. Bunner. ALV; AnAmPo; BOHV; FiBHP; InMe
I have a boy of five years old. Anecdote for Fathers. Wordsworth. EnRP
I have a brother. Envy. Edgar Daniel Kramer. PoMa
I have a companion of infinite worth. My Bible and I. M. H. Knobloch. SoP
I have a copper penny and another copper penny. Logic. *Unknown.* BOHV; PCH
I have a cup of common clay. The Common Things. Barbara Young. OQP
I have a dog. Notice. David McCord. SoPo
I have a dog,/ His name is Jack. My Doggie. C. Nurton. BoTP
I have a dream for you, Mother. For You, Mother. Hilda Conkling. HH
I have a feeling for those ships. The Stone Fleet. Herman Melville. EtS
I have a fifth of therapy. Interview with Doctor Drink. J. V. Cunningham. NMP
I Have a Friend. Anne Spencer. CDC
I have a friend so kind and true. My Friend. Marjorie Lorene Buster. STF
I have a Friend so precious. The Precious Friend. *Unknown.* SoP
I have a friend who would give a price for those long fingers all of one length. Snakes, Mongooses, Snake-Charmers and the Like. Marianne Moore. CMoP; ExPo
I have a funny Airedale dog. My Airedale Dog. W. L. Mason. GFA; SoPo; UTS
I have a garden of my own. Child's Song [*or* A Garden Song]. Thomas Moore. BoNaP; GoBC; OxBI; SUS; ViBoPo
I Have a Gentle Cock [*or* Cok *or* Cook]. *Unknown.* CBEP; EnPo; NCEP; NoP; SeCePo; ViBoPo
(Gentle Cock, The.) OxBoLi
(I Have a Noble Cock.) MeEL; MeEV
I have a golden ball. A Rune of Riches. Florence Converse. BoTP; SUS
I Have a Goodly Heritage. Psalms, XVI: 5-9, Bible, *O.T.* TreFT
I have a grief. Agitato Ma Non Troppo. John Crowe Ransom. OxBA
I have a Gumbie Cat in mind, her name is Jennyanydots. The Old Gumbie Cat. T. S. Eliot. GoTP
I have a heart that cries to God. And with No Language but a Cry. Amos Niven Wilder. MaRV
I have a kindly neighbor, one who stands. The Kindly Neighbor. Edgar A. Guest. MaRV; PoToHe
I have a king who does not speak. Emily Dickinson. MAPA; TwAmPo
I Have a Life with Christ to Live. John Campbell Shairp. MaRV
I have a little bed. My Bed. Lucy Sprague Mitchell. SoPo
I have a little home amidst the city's din. The Complacent Cliff-Dweller. Margaret Fishback. PoLF
I have a little house. My Little House. J. M. Westrup. BoTP
I have a little inward light, which still. The Inward Light. Henry Septimus Sutton. WGRP
I have a little kinsman. The Discoverer. Edmund Clarence Stedman. AA; HBV

I have a little pussy. Catkin [*or* Little Gray Pussy]. *Unknown.* GFA; MPB; OTPC; SoPo; TiPo
I have a little shadow that goes in and out with me. My Shadow. Robert Louis Stevenson. FaBoBe; FaBV; FaPON; GFA; HBV; HBVY; LiTG; MPB; NeHB; OTD; OTPC; PCH; PDV; PoVP; RIS; SoPo; StVeCh; TiPo; TreF
I have a little sister, she is only two years old. My Little Sister. *Unknown.* OTPC (1923 ed.)
I have a little sister, they call her Peep, Peep. Mother Goose. BoChLi; BoTP; OTPC (1946 ed.); OxNR; RIS; StVeCh; TiPo
I have a little valentine. My Valentine. Mary Catherine Parsons. SoPo; TiPo (1952 ed.)
I have a little wat'ring pot. Thirsty Flowers. Arthur A. Knipe. GFA
"I have a love I love too well." The Sacrilege. Thomas Hardy. DTo
I have a mackintosh shiny brown. Chestnut Buds. Evelyn M. Williams. BoTP
I have a mistress, for perfections rare. A Devout Lover. Thomas Randolph. EG; HBV; HoPM; LiTL; OBEV
I have a mother gone to glory. The Other Shore. *Unknown.* ABF
I have a name, a little name. Pet Name. Elizabeth Barrett Browning. HBV
I Have a Need. Bilhana, *formerly at. to* Chauras, *tr. fr. Sanskrit by* E. Powys Mathers. *Fr.* Black Marigolds. OnPM
I Have a New Garden. *Unknown.* MeEL
I have a new umbrella. My New Umbrella. M. M. Hutchinson. BoTP
I Have a Noble Cock. *Unknown.* *See* I Have a Gentle Cock.
I have a notion that the world is round. John Wain. *Fr.* A Boisterous Poem about Poetry. PP
I have a pair of boots so rare. The Sandman. *Unknown.* RIS
I have a picture in my room in which. Intaglio. Henri Coulette. NePoEA; PoCh
I have a pretty little flow'r. Francis Daniel Pastorius. SCAP
I have a proved, unerring guide. The Unerring Guide. Anna Shipton. BLRP
I Have a Rendezvous with Death. Alan Seeger. BBV; BLPA; CDC; DD; FaBV; FaFP; FaPL; HBV; InP; LiTM; MaRV; MCCG; NeHB; NeMA; NP; OHFP; OTD; PaA; PFY; PoMa; PoPl; PTK; ThLM; TIHL; TOP; TreF; ViBoPo; WaP; YT
(Rendezvous, The.) OtMeF; WGRP
I Have a Rendezvous with God. *Unknown.* SoP
I have a rendezvous with God. My Rendezvous with God. Anne M. Waite. SoP
I Have a Rendezvous with Life. Countee Cullen. MaRV; OQP
I have a river in my mind. Six o'Clock. Owen Dodson. PoNe
I Have a Roof. Ada Jackson. TrPWD
I have a room where into no one enters. Memory. Christina Rossetti. OBNC
"I have a ship in the North Countrie." The Sweet Trinity; or, The Golden Vanity (B *vers.*). *Unknown.* BaBo
I have a smiling face, she said. The Mask. Elizabeth Barrett Browning. CBEP; OBNC; OBVV
I Have a Son. Emory Pottle. PEDC
I have a story fit to tell. The Strong Swimmer. William Rose Benét. PoNe
I have a strain of a departed bard. Forerunners. Alexander Smith. *Fr.* A Life-Drama. VA
I have a suit of new clothes in this happy new year. When I Think of the Hungry People. O-Shi-O. MaRV; TRV
I have a surprise for you, Mother. For You, Mother. Hilda Conkling. HH
I have a thousand pictures of the sea. Muna Lee. Sonnets, IV. HBMV
I have a treasure which I prize. The Quiet Mind. *Unknown.* SoP
I have a tree, a graft of love. Arbor Amoris. Villon. AWP
I have a tree in my arm. Maze. Richard Eberhart. AnAmPo; NoP
I have a vague remembrance. The Challenge. Longfellow. AP
I have a white cat whose name is Moon. Moon. William Jay Smith. PDV
I have a white dog. My Dog, Spot. Rodney Bennett. BoTP
I have a wife of my own. Nobody. Burns. LiTL
I have a wrought-iron father. Photograph: Mother and Father: 1930. Bert Lee. WOW
I have a young love. The Sailor. Sylvia Townsend Warner. OBMV
I Have a Young Sister. *Unknown.* CH; MeEL; NoP; PoIE
(I Have [*or* Haue] a Yong Suster.) EnPo; ExPo; PoEL-1; SeCeV
(Love without Longing.) OxBoLi
I have abjured the flesh, and I. Two against One. *Unknown.* UnTE
I have achieved. That which the lonely man. The Seeker. Lascelles Abercrombie. *Fr.* The Fools' Adventure. WGRP
I Have Always Found It So. Birdie Bell. BLRP
I have always had one lode-star, now. My Lode-Star. Robert Browning. *Fr.* Pauline. MaRV
I have an arrow that will find its mark. Emerson. WhC
I Have an Orchard. Christopher Marlowe *and* Thomas Nashe. *Fr.* The Tragedy of Dido. ChTr
I have an uncle I don't like. Manners. Mariana Griswold Van Rensselaer. FaPON; HBMV; HBVY; MPB
I have an understanding with the hills. After Sunset. Grace Hazard Conkling. AnAmPo; EPN; HBMV; MaRV; MoRP; YT
I Have Approached. Alan Paton. PeSA
I have assumed a conscious sociability. Garden Party. Sir Herbert Read. BrPo
I have awakened. Getting It Together. Shirley Staples. WSL
I have awakened from the unknowing to the knowing. For William Edward Burghardt DuBois on His Eightieth Birthday. Bette Darcie Latimer. PoNe
I have baptized thee Withy, because of thy slender limbs. To ——? Richard Dehmel. AWP
I have been,/ Three separate times, in war. James Harold Manning. *Fr.* What Is Truth? CaP
I have been a censor for fifteen months. Censorship. Arthur Waley. WaP
I Have Been a Forester. *Unknown.* CBEP
I have been a snob to-day. Threnody. Alfred Kreymborg. MAPA
I have been abus'd of late/ by some of the poets crew. The Scolding Wives Vindication; or, An Answer to the Cuckold's Complaint. *Unknown.* CoMu
I have been asked to write a poem about. A Non Poem about Vietnam. Carolyn M. Rodgers. WSL
I have been busy writing a terribly critical. Notes on a Certain Terribly Critical Piece. Reed Whittemore. PP
I have been cherish'd and forgiven. Lines. Hartley Coleridge. NBM; PoEL-4
I have been dreaming all a summer day. Dreams. Victor J. Daley. PoAu-1
I have been figuring that in a way. The Time Is Today. John Farrar. GoYe
I have been given my charge to keep. The Fairies' Siege. Kipling. OtMeF
I have been here before. Sudden Light. Dante Gabriel Rossetti. CBEP; CTC; ELP; FaBoEn; GTBS-D; InP; LO; LoBV; MeWo; NBM; NoP; OAEP; OBNC; Po; PoLF; PoVP; TrGrPo; VA
I have been here. Dispersed in meditation. Agnosco Veteris Vestigia Flammae. J. V. Cunningham. QFR; TwAmPo
I have been in a marine aquarium and I have seen. The Marine Aquarium. Louis Dudek. *Fr.* Atlantis. MoCV
I have been in love, and in debt, and in drink. The Mad Lover. Alexander Brome. CBEP
I have been in this bar. The Man Who Married Magdalene: Variation on a Theme by Louis Simpson. Anthony Hecht. CoPo
I have been long away. In the Hospital. Dilys Laing. NYTB
I have been one acquainted with the night. Acquainted with the Night. Robert Frost. AmP; AP; BWP; ChTr; CMoP; CoBMV; DiPo; ForPo; InP; LiTM; MaPo; MemP; MoAmPo (1962 ed.); MWA-2; NePA; NP; OCS; PDV; PIA; PoeP; PoFS; PoG; PoIE; PoLF; PoSa; Sonn; TDP; TPM; TwCP
I have been profligate of happiness. To Olive. Lord Alfred Douglas. OBEV (new ed.); OBVV
I have been searching for some metaphor. Traveler. Sister Mary Thérèse. JKCP (1955 ed.)
I have been so great a lover. The Great Lover. Rupert Brooke. BEL; BoLiVe; BrPo; EnLit; FaFP; HoPM; LiTB;

LiTM; MCCG; MoBrPo; NeMA; PoMa; PoRA (rev. ed.); TIHL; TreF; TrGrPo; WaP
I have been so misused by chaste men with one wife. Ship near Shoals. Anna Wickham. HBMV
I have been sure of three things all my life. Clement Wood. Eagle Sonnets, III. HBMV
I Have Been through the Gates. Charlotte Mew. MeWo; MoAB; MoBrPo; TrGrPo
I have been through the valley of weeping. God of [All] Comfort. *Unknown.* SoP; STF
I have been to market, my lady, my lady. *Unknown.* SAS
I have been treading on leaves all day until I am autumn-tired. A Leaf-Treader. Robert Frost. MAP; MoAmPo; PoeP
I have been urged by earnest violins. Music. Wilfred Owen. MuSP
I have been walking today. Furnished Lives. Jon Silkin. NePoEA-2; NMP; PoDB
I have been warned. It is more than thirty years since I wrote. But I Am Growing Old and Indolent. Robinson Jeffers. AP
I have been watching crows and now it is dark. New Moon in November. W. S. Merwin. PoIE (1970 ed.)
I have been wondering. A Letter. Anthony Hecht. NYBP; StP
I have been young, and now am not too old. Report on Experience. Edmund Blunden. CBEP; FaBoEn; FaBoTw; GTBS-P; LO; MoPW; OBMV; POTE
"I have beene all day looking after." The Witches' Song. Ben Jonson. CH
I have begun to die. The Sentry. Alun Lewis. DTC
I have believed too long in one thing. March Weather. Jon Swan. NYBP
I have berries purple-blue. Invitation. Ella Young. BoChLi (1950 ed.)
I have blown, sir,/ Hard for your worship. Ben Jonson. *Fr.* The Alchemist. LO
I have borne the anguish of love, which ask me not to describe. Odes, XI. Hafiz. AWP; JAWP; OuHeWo; WBP
I have breakfast, dinner, tea. *Unknown.* ThGo
I have broken the rainbow. Pamphlet. Luis Muñoz Marín. PoFr; WoL
I have brought berries on a grape-leaf. Keepsake from Quinault. Dorothy Alyea. GoYe
I have brought the wine. This Is My Love for You. Grace Fallow Norton. HBV
I have builded my house; deep, deep have I digged in the earth. Achievement. Berta Hart Nance. MaRV
I Have Built Myself, with Honour and Dignity. "St. J. Perse," *tr. fr. French by* T. S. Eliot. *Fr.* Anabasis. AtBAP
I have buried her under a stone. The Stationmaster's Lament. Jerome Rothenberg. CoPo
I have but one story. Summer Is Gone. *Unknown.* AnIL; PoPl
I Have Cared for You, Moon. Grace Hazard Conkling. HBMV
I have carried for five years. The Return. Jon Silkin. NePoEA-2
I have carried my pillow to the windowsill. Summer near the River. Carolyn Kizer. CoAP
I Have Cast the World. Yone Noguchi. NP
I have caught a glimpse of glory. A Glimpse of Glory. *Unknown.* SoP
I have closed fast my window. The Weeping. Federico Garcá Lorca. OnPM
I have closed the door on doubt. Closing the Doors. Irene Pettit McKeehan. MaRV; OQP
I have come again, gentlemen and ladies. Spring Song. Theodore Spencer. AnFE; CoAnAm; TwAmPo
I have come back again. The Return of the Native. Harley Matthews. PoAu-2
I have come back from the mountains. The Silent Places. Harold M. Hildreth. OQP
I have come down to the garden. At the Place of the Romans Baths. "Richard Scrace." CaP
I have come far enough. A Form of Women. Robert Creeley. AmPC; NaP
I have come from pride all the way. Dawns. Alfred Kreymborg. MAP
I have come into the desert. Charles Erskine Scott Wood. *Fr.* The Poet in the Desert. NP
I have come on the River of Yellow Flowers. A Green Stream. Wang Wei. SD
I have come to catch birds. The Bird Catcher. *Unknown.* TTY
I have come to the borders of sleep. Lights Out. Edward Thomas. BrPo; FlW; GTBS-D; MMA; NoP; POTE
I have come to the quiet place. The Quiet Place. George A. McCauliff. JKCP (1955 ed.)
I have come to where the world drops off. Visit to a Hospital. Jean Valentine Chace. GoYe
I have come very far, Lord. In my time. William Byrd. Sidney Keyes. MuSP
I have committed many errors. The Visit. William Carlos Williams. PoeP
I have consider'd it; and find. The Resolve. Henry Vaughan. AnAnS-1; MeP; NCEP
I have consider'd it, and find. The Reprisal. George Herbert. AnAnS-1; EP; MaMe; MeP; OAEP; SCEP-1
I have continued to seek her. The Constant Lover. Louis Simpson. NYBP
I have courage and hardihood. Besieged. Zalman Schneour. TrJP
I have darker hair. Turk. Sam Cornish. BF
I have desired to go. Heaven-Haven. Gerard Manley Hopkins. ACP; BoLiVe; BoPe; BrPo; CaFP; CAW; CoBE; DiPo; EnL; EnLi-2; FaBoEn; GoBC; ILP; LoBV; MemP; MoAB; MoBrPo; NeMA; OAEP; OBEV (new ed.); OBNC; PoeP; PoSa; PoVP; TrGrPo; ViBoPo; VP; WaKn; WePo
I have discovered a country. Connais-tu le Pays? Richard Shelton. NYBP
I have discovered finally to-day. The Silent Pool. Harold Monro. BrPo
I have done all I could. The Tree and the Lady. Thomas Hardy. MoAB; MoBrPo
I have done it again. Lady Lazarus. Sylvia Plath. NaP
I have done my bit of carving. The Old Figurehead Carver. H. A. Cody. EtS
I have done one braver thing. The Undertaking. John Donne. AnFE; BoLiVe; CBEP; MaMe; MePo; ReEn; SCEP-1; SeEP; TuPP
I have done the deed. Didst thou not hear a noise? Macbeth Does Murder Sleep. Shakespeare. *Fr.* Macbeth, II, ii. FiP
I have done with being judged. Robert Browning. *Fr.* The Ring and the Book. OAEP
I have driven North after midnight, machined. Poem for My Thirty-second Birthday. John Ciardi. MiAP
I have drunk ale from the Country of the Young. He Thinks of His Past Greatness When a Part of the Constellations of Heaven. W. B. Yeats. DTC; OAEP (2d ed.); PoEL-5
I Have Eate My Hony Comb with My Hony. Edward Taylor. *See* Preparatory Meditations: "Oh, Angells stand agastard . . ."
I have eaten/ the plums. This Is Just to Say. William Carlos Williams. AmP; FlW; ForPo; GoJo; PIA; PoIE
I have eaten all my words. The Lost Language. Irving Feldman. AmPC
I have eaten apples and have kissed your lips. Fleeting Restlessness. Juana de Ibarbourou. LiTW
I have entreated care to cut the thread. Dan Bartholmew's Dolorous Discourses. George Gascoigne. EnRePo
I have fallen in love with American names. American Names. Stephen Vincent Benét. AmFN; AmP; BoLiVe (1945 ed.); HT; InP; LaNeLa; LoGBV; NP; OxBA; PG; TreFT; WaKn; YaD
I Have Felt a Presence. Wordsworth. *Fr.* Lines Composed a Few Miles above Tintern Abbey. MaRV
I have felt the thrill of passion in the poet's mystic book. The Ultimate Joy. *Unknown.* BOHV
"I have finished another year," said God. New Year's Eve. Thomas Hardy. MoBrPo
I have floated far too long on the surface of the wave. The Eel. Evan Morgan. CAW
I have followed you model. Ode to a Model. Vladimir Nabokov. PoPl
I have forgotten you as one forgets at dawning. Words. Helen Morgan Brooks. NNP; PoNe (1970 ed.)
I have found God on a high hill alone, alone. Discovery. Raymond Kresensky. OQP
I Have Found It! L. M. Hearn. SoP

I Have Found Out a Gift for My Fair. William Shenstone. *Fr.* A Pastoral Ballad. BiS
I have found out a gig-gig-gift. An Invitation to the Zoological Gardens. *Unknown.* BOHV
I Have Found Such Joy. Grace Noll Crowell. PoToHe (new ed.)
I have found the perfect treasure. I Have Found It! L. M. Hearn. SoP
I have four loves, four loves are mine. My Estate. John Drinkwater. HBMV
I have gathered luss/ At the wane of the moon. The Herb-Leech. Joseph Campbell. AnIL; OnYI
I Have Golden Shoes. Lesbia Harford. MoAuPo
I have gone back in boyish wonderment. Return. Sterling A. Brown. BALP; CDC
I have gone far from my beloved ones. Jerusalem the Dismembered. Uri Zvi Greenberg. *Fr.* Jerusalem. TrJP
I have gone out, a possessed witch. Her Kind. Anne Sexton. CoAP; LiTM (1970 ed.); ToPo; TwAmPo; TwCP
I have gone out and seen the lands of Faery. Dreams within Dreams. "Fiona Macleod." PoVP
I have gone past all those times when the poets. In Memory of Leopardi. James Wright. NaP
I have got a new-born sister. Choosing a Name. Mary Lamb. HBV; OTPC (1923 ed.)
I have got her. Fujiwara no Kamatari, *tr. fr. Japanese by* Arthur Waley. LiTW
I Have Got My Leave. Rabindranath Tagore. *Fr.* Gitanjali, XCIII. BoC; OBMV
I have great faith in this boy. Students. Haniel Long. AnAmPo
I have great need that the Saint grant help. Cynewulf. *Fr.* Juliana. AnOE
I have grown past hate and bitterness. Nationality. Mary Gilmore. BoAV; NeLNL; PoAu-1
I have grown tired of routine work. Afternoon in a Church. Raymond Kresensky. ChIP
I have grown tired of sorrow and human tears. In the Wood of Finvara [*or* The Fairy Wood]. Arthur Symons. BoC; MoBrPo; NeMA; PoVP
I have grown tired of you. To Alfred. Frank Horne. *Fr.* Letters Found near a Suicide. BANP
I have grown used to the retreat of seasons. Lady Anne Bathing. Anthony Delius. PeSA
I have had courage to accuse. The Crowning Gift. Gladys Cromwell. HBMV; MAP; NP
I have had enough. I gasp for breath. Sheltered Garden. Hilda Doolittle ("H. D."). PG
I have had enough of women, and enough of love. Wanderer's Song. Arthur Symons. MoBrPo; ViBoPo
I have had playmates, I have had companions. The Old Familiar Faces. Charles Lamb. AWP; BLPA; CBEP; EnLit; EPN; FaBoBe; FaFP; GTBS; GTBS-D; GTBS-P; GTBS-W; GTSE; GTSL; HBV; JAWP; LiTG; NBM; NeHB; OBEV; OBRV; PCD; PG; PoPl; PoSa; TOP; TreF; ViBoPo; WBP; YAT
I have had to learn the simplest things. Maximus, to Himself. Charles Olson. NeAP; NMP; OPoP
I have halted my horse by the tree of the doves. Song. "St.-J. Perse." *Fr.* Anabasis. LiTW
I Have Heard ("I have heard the stirring chorus"). *Unknown.* FiBHP
I have heard/ He does not bestow horses for poems. A Miserly Patron. *Unknown.* AnIL
I have heard a lady this night. Bewitched. Walter de la Mare. PoMS
I have heard a mother bird. Welcome to Spring. Irene Thompson. BoTP
I have heard echoes and seen visions of you. Jerked Heartstrings in Town. Emily B. C. Jones. HBMV
I have heard how in Ohio. Coal for Mike. Bertolt Brecht. PoPl
I have heard ingenuous Indians say. Roger Williams. SCAP
I have heard nothing. Annunciation. Ruth Gilbert. *Fr.* The Blossom of the Branches. ACV
I have heard of fish. The Sun. Anne Sexton. NYBP
I have heard song through the leaves. Marginalia for Pentecost. Leo L. Ward. JKCP (1955 ed.)
I have heard talk of bold Robin Hood. Robin Hoods's Golden Prize [*or* Robin Hood and the Two Priests]. *Unknown.* BaBo; BuBa; ESPB; OBB
I have heard that a certain princess. The Jonquils. Allen Upward. *Fr.* Scented Leaves from a Chinese Jar. NP
I have heard that hysterical women say. Lapis Lazuli. W. B. Yeats. ChMP; CMoP; CoBMV; DTC; FaBoTw; ForPo; FosPo; GTBS-W; ILP; LiTB; LiTM; MaPo (1969 ed.); MoPo; MoVE; NoP; OAEP (2d ed.); PoIE; PP
I have heard the curlew crying. Wild Geese. Katharine Tynan. GoTP
I have heard the pigeons of the Seven Woods. In the Seven Woods. W. B. Yeats. CMoP; LoBV
I have heard the stirring chorus. I Have Heard. *Unknown.* FiBHP
"I have heard the sunset song of the birches." War Is Kind, VII. Stephen Crane. AP; MWA-2
I have heard them in the night. The New-born. Helen Hoyt. NP
I have hoped, I have planned, I have striven. Unsubdued. Samuel Ellsworth Kiser. MaRV; PoToHe
I have humped my bluey in all the States. My Old Black Billy. Edward Harrington. PoAu-1
I have in my house. My House. Jane W. Krows. SoPo
I have it in my heart to serve God so. Sonnet: Of His Lady in Heaven. Jacopo da Lentini. AWP; JAWP; WBP
I have just arrived across the plains. Emigrant from Pike. John A. Stone. SGR
I have just come down from my father. The Hospital Window. James Dickey. CoPo
"I have just come from the salt, salt sea." The House Carpenter. *Unknown.* AS
I have just seen a beautiful thing. The Black Finger. Angelina W. Grimké. AmNP; PoNe
I have known life's hunger. Hunger. Hazel Hall. NP
I have known many men, and many men. Dedicatory. Mary Gilmore. BoAV
I have known nights rain-washed and crystal-clear. Wisdom. Frank Yerby. AmNP
I have known one bound to a bed by wrist and ankle. The Choice. Hilary Corke. NYBP
I have known the inexorable sadness of pencils. Dolor. Theodore Roethke. AmP; AmPP (5th ed.); AP; CABA; CoBMV; FiMAP; ILP; LiTM (1970 ed.) MoVE; NMP; PoeP; PoIE; PoSa; PPON
I have known the silence of the stars and of the sea. Silence. Edgar Lee Masters. LaNeLa; MAP; MoAmPo; NP; PoMa; PoToHe (new ed.)
I have known the strange nurses of kindness. But I Do Not Need Kindness. Gregory Corso. CoPo; NeAP
I have known two worlds. T. S. Eliot. *Fr.* The Rock. OxBoCh
I have known what it is to love. Love. Darwin T. Turner. BALP
I Have Labored Sore. *Unknown.* NoP
I have laied these sheetes you bad me on the bed. Shakespeare. *Fr.* Othello, IV, iii. AtBAP
I have lain in the sun. Fortunatus Nimium [*or* Nimium Fortunatus]. Robert Bridges. BrPo; MoAB; MoBrPo
I have learned/ To look on nature. Wordsworth. *Fr.* Lines Composed a Few Miles above Tintern Abbey. TRV
I have learned the blessed secret. The Blessed Secret. Albert Simpson Reitz. SoP
I have learned the wondrous secret. Abiding. A. B. Simpson. SoP; STF
I have led a good life, full of peace and quiet. The Good Boy. *Unknown.* AS
I have led her home, my love, my only friend. Tennyson. *Fr.* Maud. BEL; ChER; ELP; FiP; GTBS-D; PoEL-5
I have left a basket of dates. The Little Sister of the Prophet. Marjorie Pickthall. HBV
I have lifted my eyes to the strength of the hills. His Name. Charles Poole Cleaves. OQP
I Have Lived and I Have Loved. *Unknown, at. to* Charles Mackay. HBV
I have lived and worked in Pennsylvania. Steel. Henri De-Witt Saylor. PoMa
I have lived in important places, times. Epic. Patrick Kavanagh. OxBI
I Have Lived Long Enough. Shakespeare. *Fr.* Macbeth, V, iii *and* V, ii. TrGrPo
I have lived long enough, having seen one thing, that love hath an end. Hymn to Proserpine. Swinburne. BEL; EnL; EnLi-2; EPN; FOL; MaVP; OAEP; OBNC; OBVV; PAn; PoAn; PoEL-5; PoVP; SeCeV; ViPo; ViPP; VP
I have lived long enough: my way of life. I Have Lived Long

Enough. Shakespeare. *Fr.* Macbeth, V, iii *and* V, ii. TrGrPo
I Have Longed to Move Away. Dylan Thomas. CBV
I have looked at this photograph. Rescue. Dabney Stuart. NYBP
I Have Looked Inward, *sels.* Don Marquis. PFY
"I rose . . . I rose . . .," VIII.
"There was a locked door," IV.
I have lost, and lately, these. Upon the Loss of His Mistresses. Robert Herrick. AnAnS-2; BEL; EnLi-1 (1949 ed.); OAEP; ReEn; SCEP-2; SeCV-1; SeEP
I have lost her, I know. Mother. Daniel Lawrence Kelleher. NeIP
I have lost my Love to-day. Heart-Break. Henry W. Frost. SoP
I have lost my mistress, horse, and wife. Epigram. *Unknown.* ALV; EiCL
"I have lost my portmanteau." The Bishop and His Portmanteau. *Unknown.* ALV
I Have Lost My Shoes. Constantino Suasnavar, *tr. fr. Spanish by* Muna Lee. *Fr.* Numbers. FaPON
I have loved colours [*or* colors], and not flowers. Amends to Nature. Arthur Symons. GTSL; HBMV; PoVP; YT
I Have Loved England. Alice Duer Miller. *Fr.* The White Cliffs. PoLF
I Have Loved Flowers That Fade. Robert Bridges. EG; GoJo; GTBS; GTBS-D; LO; MoAB; MoBrPo; PoVP
(Elegy: "I have lov'd flowers that fade.") VA
I have loved large cities, capitals of the world. The Master City. Rose J. Orente. GoYe
I have loved so many violent loves. Declaration at Forty. Judson Crews. UnTE
I have loved to-night; from love's last bordering steep. The Happy Night. J. C. Squire. HBMV
I have loved two things deeply: the earth and silence. A Pioneer of Monaro. Francis Webb. MoAuPo
I have lyric aspiration. The Curse of Faint Praise. Irwin Edman. InMe
I have made a sirventes against the city of Toulouse. Sirventes. Paul Blackburn. NeAP
I have made, too, one of the most delicate, dainty similes. George Villiers, Duke of Buckingham. *Fr.* The Rehearsal. Par
I have marked, as on the heather now I strayed. As on the Heather. Reinmar von Hagenau. AWP
I have met them at close of day. Easter, 1916. W. B. Yeats. BrPo; BWP; CABA; ChMP; CMoP; CoBMV; DiPo; FaBoMo; LiTM; MaPo (1969 ed.); MBW-2; MoAB; NoP; OxBI; PIA; PoAn; PoeP; PoFS; PoIE; SeCeV; ShBV-4
I have mislaid the torment and the fear. Success. William Empson. ToPo
I have neither plums nor cherries. Nicholas Breton. EG
I have never been rich before. To My Friend. Anne Campbell. PoToHe
I have never seen God's face. Have I? Jessie Cannon Eldridge. SoP
I have never seen him, this invisible member of the panel, this thirteenth juror. The People vs. the People. Kenneth Fearing. MoAmPo (1950 ed.)
I have never seen volcanoes. Emily Dickinson. PoEL-5
I have new shoes in the Fall-time. New Shoes. Alice Wilkins. GFA; SUS; TiPo
I have no ale. The Muse. W. H. Davies. BrPo
I have no answer for myself or thee. Learned to Trust. William Cowper. SoP
I have no brother,—they who meet me now. Thy Brother's Blood. Jones Very. AP; MAmP; PoEL-4; QFR
I have no care for systematic theology. Eschatology. Morris Bishop. WhC
I have no chill despondence that I am. Farewell to the Muses. John Hamilton Reynolds. OBRV
I have no dog, but it must be. My Dog. John Kendrick Bangs. BLPA; FaBoBe; MPB; OTD; OTPC (1946 ed.); StVeCh; UTS
I have no ears or eyes. The Tugged Hand. W. H. Davies. MoPW
I have no faith in Heaven. Religion. Heine. LiTW
I have no folded flock to show. The Battle-Flag of Sigurd. Dora Greenwell. OBVV
I have no happiness in dreaming of Brycelinde. Under the Moon. W. B. Yeats. EG; HT
I have no life but this. Emily Dickinson. MeWo
I have no more gold. Advent. John Gould Fletcher. MAP; MaRV; MoAmPo
"I have no name." Infant Joy. Blake. *Fr.* Songs of Innocence. BiCB; CBEP; EiPP; EnLi-2; EnLit; FaPON; GoJo; GoTP; GTSL; HBV; HBVY; LoBV; MaPo (1969 ed.); MemP; NeHB; OTPC; PoeP; PoLF; PRWS; SiSoSe; ThWaDe; TiPo (1952 ed.); ViBoPo
I have no natural craving for the name. Creon. Sophocles. *Fr.* Oedipus Rex. PoFr
"I have no penny," quoth Piers, "pullets to buy." William Langland. *Fr.* The Vision of Piers Plowman. MyFE
I have no solid horse to share with Joan. Joan of Arc, 1926. Virginia Moore. YT
I have no strength nor substance, yet I shake. Here I Am. Nancy Birckhead. RIS
I Have No Surety. Bilhana, *formerly at. to* Chauras, *tr. fr. Sanskrit by* E. Powys Mathers. *Fr.* Black Marigolds. OnPM
I have no temple and no creed. After the Order of Melchisedec. Robert Norwood. MaRV
I have no thing that is mine sure. Serenader. George Dillon. NP
I have no wings, but yet I fly. Mary Austin. *Fr.* Rhyming Riddles. SoPo; TiPo
I have no wit, no words, no tears. A Better Resurrection. Christina Rossetti. FaChP; HBV; OxBoCh; PoVP; StJW; TrPWD; ViPo; VP
I have no word to match with its white wonder. Of Wounds. Sister Mary Madeleva. ISi
I have no words—alas!—to tell. Poe. *Fr.* Tamerlane. LO
I have not been as Joshua when he fought. Three Helpers in Battle. Mary Elizabeth Coleridge. EaLo
I have not come here to talk. The Beggar on the Beach. Horace Gregory. NMP
I have not gathered gold. To Death. Padraic Pearse. AnIV
I have not loved the world, nor the world me. The Poet and the World. Byron. *Fr.* Childe Harold's Pilgrimage. OBRV; SeCePo
I have not needed you for thirteen years. Father. Robert Pack. CoPo
"I have not sought Thee, I have not found Thee." Love Is Strong as [*or* Stronger than] Death. Christina Rossetti. LO; MaRV
I have not spent the April of my time. Sonnet [*or* Youth]. Bartholomew Griffin. Fidessa, More Chaste than Kind, XXXV. ElL; OBSC; ReEn; SiCE; Sonn; TuPP
I have not told my garden yet. Emily Dickinson. AA; TOP
I have not used my darkness well. Squall. Stanley Moss. CoAP
I have not where to lay my head. Mountain Song. Harriet Monroe. HBV; NP
I have nothing new ask of you. Another Year Come. W. S. Merwin. NYBP
I have oft wondred, why thou didst elect. Madam Gabrina, or the Ill-Favourd Choice. Henry King. CavP
I have often played with man, saith the Lord. Charles Péguy. *Fr.* The Mystery of the Innocent Saints. CAW
I have often wisht to love; what shall I do? The Request. Abraham Cowley. AnAnS-2
I Have Overcome the World. Laura Simmons. ChIP
(World Conqueror.) MaRV
I have picked this heatherstalk. The Goodbye. Guillaume Apollinaire. OnPM
I have praised many loved ones in my song. Mother. Theresa Helburn. FaPON; HBV; OHIP; TSW
I have put my days and dreams out of mind. The Triumph of Time. Swinburne. ViBoPo
I have read, in some old, marvellous tale. The Beleaguered City. Longfellow. MWA-1
I have received jewels of conspicuous beauty. Egan O'Rahilly. *Fr.* On a Pair of Shoes Presented to Him. OnYI
I have refused to shut. Autumn Testament. Dennis Schmitz. YAP
I have renounced already that hope. I renounce the sudden Whole. Spring Song. Rayner Heppenstall. NeBP
I have said that the soul is not more than the body. A Hub for the Universe [*or* I Hear and Behold God in Every Object]. Walt Whitman. Song of Myself, XLVIII. CoBA; FaFP; MoRP; TrGrPo
I have seen. The Hammer. Carl Sandburg. PoPo
I have seen/ A curious child. Shells [*or* Faith]. Wordsworth.

I (continued)

Fr. The Excursion, IV. MaRV; OBRV; TreFT

I have seen a gum-tree. Flesh. Mary Fullerton. PoAu-1

I have seen a lovely thing. Blight. Arna Bontemps. BANP

I have seen all the works that are done under the sun. All Is Vanity. Ecclesiastes, Bible, *O.T.* TRV

I have seen an old faith falter. And the Greatness of These. J. R. Perkins. OQP

I have seen an old street weeping. La Rue de la Montagne Sainte-Geneviève. Dorothy Dudley. HBMV

I have seen beauty where light stabs the hills. Sonnets of a Portrait Painter, XVI. Arthur Davison Ficke. AnAmPo

I Have Seen Black Hands. Richard Wright. PoNe

I have seen dawn and sunset on moors and windy hills. Beauty. John Masefield. BEL

I have seen daylight turn cadaverous. Storm. Ruth Pitter. BoPe

I have seen death too often to believe in death. A Journey Ends. Don Blanding. MaRV

I have seen enough: ugliness. Knowing All Ways, including the Transposition of Continents. Charles Olson. FRC

I Have Seen Higher, Holier Things than These. Arthur Hugh Clough. *See* Tò Kahóv.

I have seen in the Virginia forest. Apparition. John Peale Bishop. MoVE

I have seen it standing up grey. The Belfry. R. S. Thomas. BoPe

I have seen lace-makers in Madeira. Grisaille. Terence Heywood. BoSA

I have seen many things. Miser. Harold Vinal. MCCG

I have seen men binding their brothers in chains. The Hate and the Love of the World. Max Ehrmann. PoToHe (new ed.)

I have seen morning break within his eyes. Dereliction. Edward Shillito. ChIP

I have seen much to hate here—much to forgive. The White Cliffs. Alice Duer Miller. OtMeF

I have seen, O desolate one, the voice has its tower. Bell Tower. Léonie Adams. AmLP; MAP; MoAmPo; MoPl

I have seen old ships sail like swans asleep. The Old Ships. James Elroy Flecker. AnFE; BoPe; BrPo; CH; CLwM; EnLit; EtS; EvOK; FOL; GTBS-D; GTSL; HT; MoBrPo; MoVE; OBMV; OtMeF; PoRA; POTE; RoGo; ShBV-3; WHA

I have seen Our Lady in Ireland, being carried in procession in May. Heart for All Her Children. Albert J. Hebert, Jr. ISi

I have seen tall chimneys without smoke. Drought [*or* Soliloquy]. Frederick E. Laight. CaP; OBCV

I have seen the Birds of Paradise. The Birds of Paradise. John Peale Bishop. GoJo

I Have seen the light coming up over the town, like ash. Overture to Strangers. Phyllis Haring. PeSA

I have seen the proudest stars. To One Unknown. Helen Dudley. NP

I Have Seen the Robins Fall. Louis Dudek. CaP

I have seen the smallest minds of my generation. Problem in Social Geometry—the Inverted Square! Ray Durem. NBP

I have seen the snow like a mirage impending. The Effect of Snow, III. Robert Finch. ACV

I have seen them at many hours. Moths. Julia Fields. PoNe (1970 ed.)

I have seen you, O king of the dead. In the Desert. Alice Corbin. NP

I have seen you suffer in the midst of winters. Harlem. Jean Brierre. PoNe; TTY

I have seen your feet gilded by morning. Metamorphoses of M. John Peale Bishop. ErPo

I Have Set My Heart So High. *Unknown.* CoBE

I have ships that went to sea. Ships at Sea. Robert Barry Coffin. EtS

I have shut my little sister in from life and light. The Factories. Margaret Widdemer. HBV; MaRV; NeMA; PoMa

I have sinned; I have betrayed the innocent blood. Dorothy L. Sayers. *Fr.* The Just Vengeance. BoC

I have so many faults myself. What I See in Me. *Unknown.* STF

I have some dainty pussies here. Pussy Willows. Mary E. Plummer. GFA; MPB

I have sometimes thought how it would have been. World I Have Not Made. Elizabeth Jennings. ACV

I have sought beauty through the dust of strife. The Final Lesson. Arthur Stringer. MaRV

I have sought long with steadfastness. Songs and Lyrics, XXXIX. Sir Thomas Wyatt. EnRePo; EP; FCP; SiPS

I Have Sought Thee Daily. Solomon ibn Gabirol, *tr. fr. Hebrew by* Israel Zangwill. LiTW

I have sown beside all waters in my day. A Black Man Talks of Reaping. Arna Bontemps. AmNP; BANP; CDC; IDB; Kal; PoNe

I have sown upon the fields. The Idle Flowers. Robert Bridges. BoNaP; ChTr

I have spoken with the dead. Communion. Hildegarde Flanner. NP

I have spot-resistant trousers. Summer Song. W. W. Watt. FiBHP

I have spread wet linen. Today. Ethel Romig Fuller. PoToHe (new ed.)

I have stayed [*or* stay'd] too long from your grave, it seems. At Her Grave. Arthur O'Shaughnessy. PoVP; VA

I have stolen the sun from the moon's black mouth. Titan's Lament. Alex Raybin. ThO

I have stretched ropes from belfry to belfry. Arthur Rimbaud. *Fr.* Phrases. FIW

I have studied many times. George Gray. Edgar Lee Masters. *Fr.* Spoon River Anthology. TOP

"I have subdued at last the will to live." The Sanyassi. Philip Gilbert Hamerton. VA

I have sung, to deceive the evil-sounding clock of time. Jean Cocteau. *Fr.* Plain Song. PoPl

I have sunk to the cold weary depths of despair! Mourning. Josephine Van Fossan. STF

I have swallowed my nearest and dearest. Midtown Poem. Robert Hershon. ThO

I have taken that vow. The Red-haired Man's Wife. James Stephens. HBMV; MoBrPo; OBVV

I have taken the lash of today like a cowed animal. Diary of a Nondescript. Garrett Oppenheim. NYTB

I have taken the woman of beauty. The Bear's Song. *Tr. by* Constance Lindsay Skinner. AWP; JAWP; WBP

I have tasted heaven's manna. Satisfaction. Avis B. Christiansen. SoP

I have the greatest fun at night. The Quilt. Mary Effie Lee Newsome. CDC

I have the shells now in a leather box. Elizabeth Jennings. BoPe

I have this deal of death about my hands. Blood. Ray Bremser. NeAP

I have this to say, if I can say it. Before Sentence Is Passed. R. P. Blackmur. LiTA

I have thought long this wild wet night that brought no rest. A Sleepless Night. Egan O'Rahilly. AnIL; KiLC

I have thought of beaches, fields. Bundles. Carl Sandburg. MAP; MoAmPo

I have thought very much about heat. The Heat. Gertrude Stein. AtBAP

I have threatened Theology a thousand times over. Theology [*or* Grace for Theology]. William Langland. *Fr.* The Vision of Piers Plowman. GoBC; PoLi

I have three candles in my room. Candle-lighting Song. Arthur Ketchum. HBMV

I have thrown wide my window. Midnight. Michael Roberts. OBMV; POTE

I have tied my humpback behind my mother. Homage to Charles Laughton. Gil Orlovitz. ToPo

I Have to Have It. Dorothy Aldis. SoPo

I have to live with myself, and so. Myself. Edgar A. Guest. BLPA; MaRV; NeHB; OQP

I have to thank God I'm a woman. The Affinity. Anna Wickham. HBMV; MoBrPo

I have told you in another poem, whether you've read it or not. My Burial Place. Robinson Jeffers. AP

I have tossed hours upon the tides of fever. Bout with Burning. Vassar Miller. LiTM (1970 ed.); MoAmPo (1962 ed.); NePoEA; PIA; TDP; ToPo

I have travelled my land, my heart big with pride. Song of an Australian. Flexmore Hudson. BoAu

I have travelled sometime up and down our coast. Gazeteer of Newfoundland. Michael Harrington. CaP

I Have Twelve Oxen. *Unknown.* ChTr
(Song: "I have twelve oxen that be fair and brown.") ThWaDe
(Twelve Oxen.) CH; RePo

I have two dashing, prancing steeds. Steeds. Paul Hiebert. WHW
I have two friends. The Twins. Kathryn Jackson. BiCB
I have two friends—two glorious friends—two better could not be. The Two Friends. Charles Godfrey Leland. AA; AmePo
I have two servants. Blue Persian. Isabella Fiske Conant. CIV
I have two sons and a son-in-law. The Frenchman's Ball. *Unknown.* OuSiCo
I have two sons, Wife. Two Sons. Robert Buchanan. VA
I have waked, I have come, my beloved! I might not abide. Sunrise. Sidney Lanier. AA
I have walked a great while over the snow. The Witch. Mary Elizabeth Coleridge. GTBS-D; NCEP; PoVP
I have walked always in a veil. Imprisoned. Eunice Tietjens. HBMV
I have walked and prayed for this young child an hour. W. B. Yeats. *Fr.* A Prayer for My Daughter. ViBoPo; WoL
I have wandered like a sheep that's lost. Thomas Heywood. *Fr.* The Cherubim. WGRP
I have wasted nothing. O Lord, I have saved. The Miser. Laura Bell Everett. OQP
I have watch'd thee with rapture, and dwelt on thy charms. Lines: Addressed to——on the 29th of September, When We Parted for the Last Time. *Unknown.* BOHV
I have watched a thousand days. Salonikan Grave. Kipling. *Fr.* Epitaphs of the War, 1914-18. OAEP (2d ed.)
I have watched you dancing. Theme Brown Girl. Elton Hill Abu Ishak. NBP
I have wept a million tears. The Man to the Angel. "Æ." OBVV; VA
I have wished a bird would fly away. A Minor Bird. Robert Frost. CMoP; LOW
I have with fishing-rod and line. The Wounded Hawk. Herbert Palmer. FaBoTw; HaMV
I have within me such a dream of pain. Vision of a Past Warrior. Peter La Farge. WOW
I have within my hand some lilies of the valley. Lilies of the Valley. Jo Gardner. BePJ
I have worshipped in churches and chapels. My Altar [*or* At My Mother's Knee]. John H. Styles, Jr. MaRV; STF
I have woven shrouds of air. The Earth-Spirit. William Ellery Channing. AnNE; PFY
I Have Wrapped My Dreams in a Silken Cloth. Countee Cullen. *See* For a Poet.
I have written high school teachers down Savants. Chant Royal from a Copydesk. Rufus Terral. InMe
I haven't a palace. Any Bird. Ilo Orleans. RIS
I haven't got a cent. Penny Whistle Blues. E. H. L. Island. InMe
I, having loved ever since I was a child a few things, never having wavered. Modern Declaration. Edna St. Vincent Millay. MoLP
I, he, who whileom sate and sung in cage. Robert Wild. *Fr.* Iter Boreale. PeRV
I hear a bull blaring. Near Midnight. Norman MacCaig. OPoP
I hear a cricket at my window sill. Touch. Joseph Auslander. MAP; MoAmPo (1942 ed.)
I hear a mouse. The Mouse. Elizabeth J. Coatsworth. PCD; RIS; SUS; UTS
I Hear a River. Trumbull Stickney. NCEP
I hear a rumour and a shout. Athletic Code. George Santayana. AmePo
I hear a sudden[*or* the sullen] cry of pain! The Snare. James Stephens. BoTP; CH; CMoP; HBMV; MoSiPe; OxBI; PDV; PoRL; ShBV-1; TiPo; UTS; YT
I hear a whisper in the heated air. Ceylon. A. Hugh Fisher. HBV
I hear a young girl singing. Beside the Blackwater. Norreys Jephson O'Conor. HBMV
I hear again the tread of war go thundering through the land. Albert Sidney Johnston. Kate Brownlee Sherwood. MC; PAH
I hear along our street. Christmas Carols. Gui Barozai, *par. by* Longfellow. BoTP
I Hear America Griping. Morris Bishop. AmFN
I Hear America Singing. Walt Whitman. AmePo; AmFN; AWP; BBV (1951 ed.); BoChLi (1950 ed.); FaBoBe; FaBV; FaFP; FaPON; GoTP; LiTA; LoGBV; MAP; MoAmPo; MPB; NeHB; NeMA; PaA; PAL; PCD; PCH; PDV; PoFr; PoFS; PoMa; PoPl; PoPo; PoSC; PTK; StVeCh; TIHL; TiPo (1952 ed.); TreFS; TrGrPo; YaD
I Hear an Army [Charging upon the Land]. James Joyce. Chamber Music, XXXVI. AnIV; AWP; CBV; ExPo; JAWP; JKCP (1926 ed.); LiTL; LiTM; MoBrPo; NAMP; OxBI; PoRA; POTE; ShBV-4; SyP; ViBoPo; WBP
I Hear and Behold God in Every Object. Walt Whitman. *See* Hub for the Universe.
I hear and behold God in every object, yet understand God not in the least. Walt Whitman. *Fr* Song of Myself. WGRP
I Hear and See Not Strips of Cloth Alone. Walt Whitman. WaaP
I hear enormous noises in the night. March Winds. Cecil Francis Lloyd. CaP
I hear footsteps over my head all night. The Walker. Arturo Giovannitti. AnAmPo; PoFr
I hear in my brain all New England echoing down and around me. New England Suite. Charles Philbrick. TwAmPo
I hear in my heart, I hear in its ominous pulses. The Wild Ride. Louise Imogen Guiney. AA; CAW; HBV; JKCP; MAP; MoAmPo (1942 ed.); PFY
I Hear It Said. Barbara Young. BLPA; NeHB
I hear it singing, singing sweetly. Hope's Song. *Unknown.* SoP
I Hear It Was Charged against Me. Walt Whitman. AmePo; LiTA; MAP; MCCG; MoAmPo; PoPo
I hear leaves drinking rain. The Rain. W. H. Davies. BoTP; EnLit; PCH; POTE; RIS; TiPo
I hear many voices. To Adhiambo. Gabriel Okara. PBA
I hear no voice, I feel no touch. Evening Song. *Unknown.* OTPC (1946 ed.)
I hear of late, but hold it very strange. To a Dear Friend Lately Given Over to Covetousness. Thomas Lodge. *Fr.* A Fig for Momus. SiCE
I Hear Some Say. Michael Drayton. *See* Idea: "I hear some say, 'This man is not in love.' "
I hear ten thousand voices singing. Praise. *Unknown.* SoP
I hear the angels marching. October of the Angels. James J. Daly. WHL
I hear the beat. The Talking Drums. KoJo Gyinaye Kyei. PBA
I hear the bells at eventide. End of the Day. Duncan Campbell Scott. VA
I hear the clock in the half gloom. Refuge. John Thompson. BoAu
I Hear the Crane. Joshua Sylvester. *Fr.* Du Bartas His Divine Weeks. OA
I hear the cries of evening, while the paw. The Cries of Evening. Stephen Spender. NoP
I hear the engine pounding. The Ways of Trains. Elizabeth J. Coatsworth. BoChLi (1950 ed.); SoPo; TiPo
I hear the halting footsteps of a lass. Harlem Shadows. Claude McKay. AmPP (5th ed.); BANP; PoNe
I hear the little black cricket. The Cricket and the Star. Mary Effie Lee Newsome. GoSl
I hear the low wind wash the softening snow. The Flight of the Geese. Sir Charles G. D. Roberts. PeCV; VA
I hear the man downstairs slapping the hell out of his stupid wife again. The .38. Ted Joans. NNP
I hear the night hanging down in white holes. Masterindex: 23. Gil Orlovitz. ToPo
I hear the noise about thy keel. In Memoriam A. H. H., X. Tennyson. EnLi-2; EPN; GTSL; OAEP; OBEV (1st ed.); ViPo; VP
I hear the robins singing in the rain. On a Gloomy Easter. Alice Freeman Palmer. MaRV; OHIP
I hear the shadowy horses, their long manes a-shake. Michael Robartes Bids [*or* He Bids] His Beloved Be at Peace. W. B. Yeats. BrPo; Po; SyP
I hear the sullen cry of pain! *See* I hear a sudden cry of pain!
I hear the voice of the bells. My New Year Prayer. *Unknown.* STF
I Hear the Wave. *Unknown, tr. fr. Middle Irish by* Eugene O'Curry. OnYI
I hear the wind a-blowing. Mad Song. Hester Sigerson. AnIV
I hear the wings, the winds, the river pass. Out of Doors. Walter Conrad Arensberg. AnAmPo
I Hear the Woodlands Calling. Madison Cawein. TSW
I hear them grinding, grinding through the night. Machines. Daniel Whitehead Hicky. PoMa

I hear them say, "By all this stir." The Right above the Wrong, 1857. William Cox Bennett. PoFr
I hear voices praising Tshombe. Hatred of Men with Black Hair. Robert Bly. FRC; NaP
I Hear You. Shirley Kaufman. QAH
I hear you call. The Call of the River Nun. Gabriel Okara. PBA
I hear you, Little bird. Joy of the Morning. Edwin Markham. AA; FaPON; HBV; MPB; PoRL
I hear you, little spirit, in the bushes. To Puck. Beatrice Llewellyn Thomas. HBMV
I heard a/ Couple of fleas. Archy, the Cockroach, Speaks. Don Marquis. *Fr.* Certain Maxims of Archy. FaPON
I heard a bird at break of day. Overtones. William Alexander Percy. DD; HBMV; HBVY; MaRV
I heard a bird at dawn. The Rivals. James Stephens. BiS; BoTP; FaPON; GTBS-D; InvP; MoVE; OBEV (new ed.); OBMV; OTPC (1946 ed.); PoPl; PoRh; SP; UTS
I Heard a Bird Sing. Oliver Herford. MoSiPe; OTD; PDV; PoLF; SiSoSe; SoPo; TiPo (1952 ed.); YeAr
I heard a bluebird in the field today. The Bluebird. *Unknown.* SoP
I heard a brooklet gushing. Whither? Wilhelm Müller. AWP
I heard a cow low, a bonnie cow low. The Queen of Elfland's Nourrice. *Unknown.* ESPB; FaBoCh; OBB
I heard a cry in the night from a far-flung host. Memorial Day. William E. Brooks. HH; MaRV; OQP; PAL; PEDC; PGD; PoRL
I heard a fly buzz—when I died. Emily Dickinson. AmePo; AmLP; AmPP (4th ed.); AnFE; AP; APA; CABA; CBV; CMOP; CoAnAm; CoBA; DiPo; ExPo; ForPo; GTBS-W; ILP; InPo; LiTA; LiTM; MAmP; MAPA; MasP; MoAB; MoAmPo; MoPW; MoVE; MWA-2; NePA; NoP; OxBA; PIA; PoAn; PoE; PoeP; PoFS; PoIE; PoRA; ReMP; SeCeV; TDP; TwAmPo
I heard a halloo in the wood. Adventure. Mary Fullerton. BoAV
I heard a herald's note announce the coming of a king. Rex Mundi. David Gascoyne. ChMP
I heard a horseman. The Horseman. Walter de la Mare. GoJo; SoPo; SUS; TiPo (1959 ed.)
I Heard a Linnet Courting. Robert Bridges. BrPo; GTBS-W; LiTB; LiTM; MemP; OA; OBMV; PoPo
(Linnet, The.) LiTL; OBEV (new ed.)
I heard a man explaining. Barabbas Speaks. Edwin McNeill Poteat. MaRV
I heard a mouse. The Mouse. Elizabeth J. Coatsworth. BoTP; FaPON; MoShBr; MoSiPe; OTPC (1946 ed.); PCD; RIS; SoPo; SUS; TiPo; UTS
I Heard a Noise. *Unknown.* EnRePo; InvP; TuPP
(Shadow, A.) ElL
I heard a red-winged black-bird singing. A June Day. Sara Teasdale. YeAr
I heard a small sad sound. The To-be-forgotten. Thomas Hardy. PoVP
I Heard a Soldier. Herbert Trench. AnFE; CH; HBV
I heard a thousand blended notes. Lines Written in Early Spring [*or* Written in Early Spring *or* What Man Has Made of Man]. Wordsworth. ACV; BEL; CBEP; CoBE; EnLi-2; EnLit; EnRP; EPN; ERoP-1; GTBS; GTBS-D; GTBS-P; GTBS-W; GTSE; GTSL; HBV; ILP; MaRV; MBW-2; MCCG; OAEP; OBRV; PeER; PG; PoE; PoLF; PoMa; PoPo; StP; TOP; TreFT; TRV
I heard a voice at evening softly say. Day by Day. Julia Harris May. BLRP; MaRV
I heard a voice say "Look into your heart." Christopher Hassall. *Fr.* Soliloquy to Imogen. LO
I heard a voice so softly calling. Life's Cross. *Unknown.* SoP
I heard a voice that cried, "Make way for those who died!" The March. J. C. Squire. HBMV; OHIP; PoSC
I heard a woman's voice that wailed. In Ruin Reconciled. Aubrey Thomas De Vere. IrPN
I Heard a Young Man Saying. Julia Fields. NNP
I Heard an Angel Singing. Blake. CBEP; RIS
I heard an angel speak last night. Prologue. Elizabeth Barrett Browning. PoVP
I heard an ignorant crow call, "Life is now." Old Snapshot. Ronald Everson. MoCV
I heard an old farm-wife. The Son. Ridgely Torrence. HBMV; InP; InvP; MAP; MoAmPo (1942 ed.); NP; PFY; WaKn
I heard an old farmer talk one day. The Rainfall Follows the Plough. *Unknown.* SoP
I heard, as if I had no ear. Emily Dickinson. MWA-2
I Heard Christ Sing. "Hugh MacDiarmid." ACV
I Heard de Preachin' of de Word o' God, *with music.* *Unknown.* BoAN-2
I heard from Rémon, Rémon. Rémon. *Unknown.* TrAS
I heard him faintly, far away. The Corn Crake. James H. Cousins. OnYI
I heard him in the autumn winds. Life in Death. Ellice Hopkins. PeVV
I heard how, to the beat of some quick tune. The Dancer. Sadi. *Fr.* The Bustan. AWP; JAWP; OuHeWo; WBP
I heard in the night the pigeons. No Child. Padraic Colum. AnFE; OBMV; POTE
I Heard It in the Valley. Annette Wynne. MoSiPe
I heard it whispered in the cryptic streets. The Cryptic Streets. Abu-l-Ala al-Maarri. LiTW
I heard last night a little child go singing. Juliet of Nations. Elizabeth Barrett Browning. *Fr.* Casa Guidi Windows. VA
I heard men saying, Leave hope and praying. The Voice of Toil. William Morris. AnFE; CoBE; EPN; HBV; PoVP
I heard my ancient sea-blood say. A Life. George Edward Woodberry. EtS
I heard my love was goint to Yang-chou. A "Tzu-yeh" Song. *Unknown.* OnPM
I heard no sound of wild feet. Enigma. Katherine Reeves. FiSC
I heard no sound where I stood. The Sleeping House. Tennyson. *Fr.* Maud. FaBoEn; OBNC
I heard of a man. Poem. Leonard Cohen. ELU
I heard of gold at Sutter's Mill. When I Went Off to Prospect. John A. Stone. SGR
I heard one who said: "Verily." Cassandra. E. A. Robinson. AmPP; CMoP; ExPo; LiTA; LiTM (rev. ed.); MaPo; NePA; NP; OxBA; PoFr; PPON; SeCeV
I heard or seemed to hear the chiding Sea. Seashore [*or* Sea-Shore]. Emerson. AmPP (4th ed.); AnAmPo; EtS; LiTA; MAmP; OxBA
I heard that Faustus oftentimes rehearses. Of Faustus, a Stealer of Verses. Sir John Harington. SiCE; TuPP
I heard that you ask'd for something to prove this puzzle the New World. To Foreign Lands. Walt Whitman. AmPP (3d ed.)
I heard the bells across the trees. Victory Bells. Grace Hazard Conkling. HBV; MC; PaA; PAH
I heard the bells of Bethlehem ring. Birds of Bethlehem. Richard Watson Gilder. AA
I Heard the Bells on Christmas Day. Longfellow. *See* Christmas Bells.
I heard the carping [*or* herde a carpyng] of a clerk. Robyn and Gandeleyn [*or* Robin and Gandelyn]. *Unknown.* BaBo; EnSB; ESPB; OBB; OxBB
I heard the centuries tick slowly. Soul's Adventure. Stanley J. Kunitz. NP
I heard the dogs howl in the moonlight night. A Dream. William Allingham. OxBI; VA
I heard the farm cocks crowing loud, and faint, and thin. Daybreak in a Garden. Siegfried Sassoon. BoTP
I heard the Father say, "Go teach." Teaching, I Am Taught. Hazel M. Lindsey. SoP
I heard the hymn of being sound. Ralph Hodgson. *Fr.* the Song of Honour. LO
I heard the old, old men say. The Old Men Admiring Themselves in the Water. W. B. Yeats. CMoP; FaBoCh; GoJo; LoGBV; ViPo (1962 ed.)
I Heard the Old Song. B. W. Vilakazi. *tr. fr. Zulu.* PeSA
I heard the Poor Old Woman say. Lament for the Poets: 1916. Francis Ledwidge. AnIV; AWP; JAWP; JKCP (1926 ed.); OnYI; OxBI; WBP
I heard the pulse of the besieging sea. To S. C. Robert Louis Stevenson. PeVV
I Heard the Ruffian-Shepherd Rudely Blow. Ovid, *tr. fr. Latin by* Dryden. *Fr.* Metamorphoses, XIII: The Fable of Acis, Polyphemus and Galatea. AtBAP
I heard the sighing of the reeds. In Ireland: By the Pool at the Third Rosses. Arthur Symons. OBNC
I heard the singing of a thrush. Country Lane. Margaret Stanion Darling. FiSC

I heard the snowflakes whisper in the still dark night. Snowflakes. Ruth M. Arthur. BoTP
I heard the song of the breath. The Song of the Breath [*or* A Song of Breath]. Stephen Vincent Benét. *Fr.* John Brown's Body. AmP; MoVE
I heard the sparrows shouting "Eat, eat." In the Night Fields. W. S. Merwin. AP; PoCh
I heard the trailing garments of the Night. Hymn to the Night. Longfellow. AA; AmePo; AmLP; AmP; AmPP; AnAmPo; AnEnPo; AnFE; AnNE; AP; APA; CoAnAm; ExPo; HBV; HBVY; LaNeLa; LoBV; NePA; OTPC; OuHeWo; OxBA; PoFS; StVeCh (1940 ed.); TOP; TreFS; TrGrPo; ViBoPo; WHA
I heard the verdict, stern and grim. Injustice. Sheldon Shepard. ChIP
I heard the virgins sigh, I saw the sleeke. Obsequies to the Lady Anne Hay. Thomas Carew. AnAnS-2
I Heard the Voice of Jesus Say. Horatius Bonar. BePJ; MaRV; SoP
(Voice from Galilee, The.) HBV; VA
I heard the wild beasts in the wood complain. Mundus Morosus [*or* The World Morose]. Frederick William Faber. ACP; CAW; NBM; OBVV
I heard the wild geese flying. Wild Geese. Elinor Chipp. FaPON; HBMV; MPB; RePo; TiPo
I heard the wind all day. Watching by a Sick-Bed. John Masefield. NP
I heard the wind coming. Hearing the Wind at Night. May Swenson. BoNaP; WIRo
I heard thee, joyous votary. To a Robin. T. A. Daly. JKCP
I heard them in their sadness say. Dust. "Æ." HBMV; OQP; WGRP
I heard them say, "Her hands are hard as stone." Her Beauty. Max Plowman. HBMV
I heard—'twas on a morning, but when it was and where. Singing Water. Rudolph Chambers Lehmann. HBMV
I heard two workers say, "This chaos/ Will soon be ended." Idiom of the Hero. Wallace Stevens. OxBA
I heard under a ragged hollow wood. The Ragged Wood. W. B. Yeats. ViPo (1962 ed.)
I Heard You Solemn-Sweet Pipes of the Organ. Walt Whitman. CBEP; NePA; OxBA
I heare the whistling plough-man all day long. On the Plough-Man. Francis Quarles. OBS
"I heeard da ole folks talkin' in our house da other night." Why Adam Sinned. Alex Rogers. BANP
I held a jewel in my fingers. Emily Dickinson. WHA
I Held a Lamb. Kim Worthington. SoPo; TiPo (1959 ed.)
I held her hand, the pledge of bliss. The Test [*or* Epigram]. Walter Savage Landor. *Fr.* Ianthe. ALV; HBV; VA
I held it truth, with him who sings. In Memoriam A. H. H., I. Tennyson. BEL; BoLiVe; CoBE; DiPo; EnL; EnLi-2; EnLit; EPN; HBV; LiTB; LiTG; MBW-2; NoP; OAEP; OBNC; OQP; ViPo; VP
I held you. Eventual Proteus. Margaret Atwood. MoCV
I helped a little lame dog. My Little Dog. Pearl Forbes MacEwen. BoTP
I herde a carpyng of a clerk. *See* I heard the carping of a clerk.
"I hereby bequeath to the Bide-a-Wee Home all people." Lines in Dispraise of Dispraise. Ogden Nash. NAMP
I Hereby Swear That to Uphold Your House. Elinor Wylie. *Fr.* One Person. NePA; Sonn
(House Sonnet.) LiTL
(Sonnet from "One Person.") LiTA; MAP; MoAB; MoAmPo
(Sonnets from "One Person.") NP; OxBA
I hesitate to write about the spring. The Faithful Lover. Robert Pack. NePoEA
I hid behind a green bead curtain. Mad Willow Lover. Pamela Millward. FRC
I hid my heart. The Robber. Ivy O. Eastwick. SiSoSe
I hid my heart in a nest of roses. A Ballad[e] of Dreamland. Swinburne. EPN; HBV; ILP; PoVP
I Hid My Love [When Young]. John Clare. *See* Secret Love.
I hide myself within a flower. Emily Dickinson. LiTL
I hoe and I plow. Farmer. Liberty Hyde Bailey. RePo; YeAr
I Hoed and Trenched and Weeded. A. E. Housman. A Shropshire Lad, LXIII. InP; LiTM (rev. ed.); MoAB; MoBrPo; PoPo; PoVP; TrGrPo; UnPo (3d ed.); ViPo
I hold a letter in my hand. A Poem for the Meeting of the American Medical Association. Oliver Wendell Holmes. PoEL-5
I hold as faith. *Unknown.* SeCSL
I hold Helvellyn in my fingers, here. Thomas Gray in Patterdale. Norman Nicholson. ACV
I Hold Him Happiest. Menander, *tr. fr. Greek.* TreFT
I hold him, verily, of mean emprise. Canzone: He Perceives His Rashness in Love. Guido Guinicelli. AWP; JAWP; WBP
I hold him wise and well y-taught. Discretion. *Unknown.* CBEP
I hold in my hands. Look Closely. Morton Marcus. YAP
I hold it truth, with him who sings. *See* I held it truth. . .
I hold my honey and I store my bread. My Dreams, My Works, Must Wait till after Hell. Gwendolyn Brooks. NoP
"I hold no cause worth my son's life," one said. Mothers of Men. Amelia Josephine Burr. OQP
I hold no dream of fortune vast. Success. Edgar A. Guest. TreF
I hold that Christian grace abounds. My Creed. Alice Cary. WGRP
I hold that when a person dies. A Creed. John Masefield. HBMV; MoRP; WGRP
I hold the splendid daylight in my hands. Litany. George Campbell. PoNe
I hold you at last in my hand. The Butterfly. Alice Freeman Palmer. HBV; MaRV
I honor the land that gave me birth. Brothers. George E. Day. MaRV
I hope and fear, I pray and hold my peace. Phyllis, XXXV. Thomas Lodge. Sonn
I hope for nothing better than your smile. Alley Cat. Frank Stevens. CIV
I hope he doesn't see me walking past his bed. Letter. Alexander Bergman. TrJP
I hope, I fear, resolved, and yet I doubt. Sonnet. Earl of Stirling. Aurora, LXVIII. Sonn
I hope I'm fond of much that's good. Rotten Row. Frederick Locker-Lampson. ALV
I hope there is a resurrection day. Resurrection. Harry Kemp. HBV
I hope when I am dead that I shall lie. Oblivion. Jessie Redmond Fauset. BANP; PoNe
I hope when you're yourself and twice my age. Metaphor for My Son. John Holmes. MiAP
I hoped that he would love me. The Kiss. Sara Teasdale. HBV
I hoped that with the brave and strong. He Doeth All Things Well. Anne Brontë. MaRV; TRV
I hung my verses in the wind. The Test. Emerson. AA; PP
I hurried down a busy street. "One of the Least of These." Lois Duffield. SoP
I idle stand that I may find employ. The Idler. Jones Very. AA; HBV
I idly cut a parsley stalk. On a Midsummer [*or* Midsummer's] Eve. Thomas Hardy. FaBoTw; GTSL
"I, if I perish, perish"—Esther spake. Monna Innominata, VIII. Christina Rossetti. ViPo; VP
I imagine him still with heavy brow. Beethoven's Death Mask. Stephen Spender. MuSP; UnS
I imagine that these thousand. The Descent. James Tate. YAP
I imagine the midnight moment's forest. The Thought-Fox. Ted Hughes. NePoEA-2; NYBP
I implore thy pity, Thou, the unique, I adore. De Profundis Clamavi. Baudelaire. SyP
I, in My Intricate Image. Dylan Thomas. LiTB
I, in My Pitiful Flesh. Glenway Wescott. NP
I in the Grayness Rose. Stephen Phillips. EnLit
In in Thee, and Thou in Me. Christopher Pearse Cranch. HBV
I in these flowery meads would be. The Angler's Wish. Izaak Walton. *Fr.* The Compleat Angler. HBV; SeCL
I inhabited the wake of a long wave. The Wave. W. S. Merwin. FRC
I intended a handspring. Triolet. Margaret Hoover. PCD
I intended an ode. "Urceus Exit." Austin Dobson. *Fr.*

I (continued)
Rose-Leaves. ATP (1935 ed.); BoPe; GTSL; HBV; MoBrPo (1942 ed.); OBEV; PTK; TOP
I invoke the land of Ireland. Invocation to Ireland [*or* Aimirgin's Invocation]. *At. to* Amergin. AnIV; OnYI
I jabbed a jack-knife in my thumb. My Sore Thumb. Burges Johnson. HBVY
I jes' don' know ef de kohn'll grow. De Good Lawd Know My Name. Frank Lebby Stanton. WBLP
I Johon Schep, som tyme Seynte Marie prest of/ York. Sermon to the Rebels at Blackheath. John Ball. PoFr
I, Jones, Soldier, *sel.* Joseph Schull.
"Sound smashes through the dark. It is a wall." TwCaPo
I joy, deare mother, when I view. The British Church. George Herbert. AnAnS-1; MaMe; MeP; PoE
I joy not in no earthly bliss. The Quiet Mind. *Unknown.* OBSC; SiCE
I joy to see how in your drawen work. Amoretti, LXXI. Spenser. MaPo (1969 ed.); SiCE
I just knew it when we swept. Elizabeth Barrett Browning. *Fr.* Aurora Leigh, VII. PeVV
I just said I didn't know. Parachutes, My Love, Could Carry Us Higher. Barbara Guest. NeAP
I just turned a pan. Another Day. Isabella Maria Brown. PoNe (1970 ed.)
I keep a pair of lovers in my pocket. Keepsake. Victor Contoski. ThO
I keep kings secret, monstrous underground. Daedalus to Icarus. Louis Coxe. NYTB
"I keep my diamond necklace in a pond of sparkling water." Fabergé. James Schuyler. ANYP
I keep pushing this. The Prophets. Richard Shelton. NYBP
I keep reaching back for the magic of those first few days. Reaching Back. Saundra Sharp. WSL
I keep seeing/ landscapes. Archer. Lynn Strongin. ThO
I keep thinking of isolated Long Island estates. Blueprint. Joel Sloman. ThO
I keep thinking that there is. The Frightened Lover's Sleep. Jay Wright. BF
I keep Three Wishes Ready. Annette Wynne. MoSiPe; PDV; SoPo; TiPo (1952 ed.)
I keep walking around myself, mouth open with amazement. Immoral. James Oppenheim. HBV
I Keep Wondering. Hilda Conkling. PFY
I kenning through astronomy divine. Meditation VIII. Edward Taylor. *Fr.* Preparatory Meditations, First Series. AmP; AmPP; AP; AtBAP; LiTA; MAmP; NoP; OxBA; PoEL-3; SCAP; StP
I kept my answers small and kept them near. Answers. Elizabeth Jennings. NePoEA; PoDB
I kept neat my virginity. Song. Glyn Jones. NeBP
I killed a robin. The little thing. Remorse. Sydney Dayre. DD
I killed them, but they would not die. The Immortals. Isaac Rosenberg. FaBoTw; MMA; TrJP
I Kilt er Cat. Virginia Frazer Boyle. CIV
I kind of like the playful porpoise. The Porpoise. Ogden Nash. RePo
I kiss my hand to you. To the Lighted Lady Window. Marguerite Wilkinson. CAW; ISi; WHL
I kiss you good-bye, my darling. The Virgin Mother. D. H. Lawrence. ViBoPo
I kissed a kiss in youth. Scintilla. William Stanley Braithwaite. AmNP; BANP; CDC
I kissed my darling at the zoo. The Prodigy. A. P. Herbert. EvOK
I Kissed You. *Unknown.* BLPA
I kissed you in the dead of dark. The Accusation. James Wright. AmPC
I kneel beside you quietly, my son. Cradle Song of a Celtic Queen. James Edward Tobin. JKCP (1955 ed.)
I kneel not now to pray that Thou. A Prayer. Harry Kemp. HBV; MaRV; WGRP
I kneel on Holy Thursday with the faithful worshipping. The Mother of the Rose. James M. Hayes. JKCP
I kneel to pray. My Prayer. Mark Guy Pearse. OQP; SoP
I knelt to pray, but not for long. No Time. *Unknown.* SoP
I knelt to pray when day was done. The Way I Pray. Whitney Montgomery. SoP
I knew a black beetle, who lived down a drain. Nursery Rhymes for the Tender-hearted, IV. Christopher Morley. HBMV; YaD
I knew a boor—a clownish card. The Folly of Brown. W. S. Gilbert. InMe
I Knew a Boy Who Ran with the Dogs. Nancy Willard. ThO
I knew a boy who took long walks. Stalky Jack. William Brighty Rands. BoTP; RIS
I Knew a Boy with Hair like Gold. Melvin Walker La Follette. NePoEA-2
I Knew a Cappadocian. A. E. Housman. FiBHP
I knew a little Serval cat. Never Get Out! John Galsworthy. OtMeF
I knew a man with a terrible obsession. Myth. Ned O'Gorman. TwAmPo
I knew a man without a heart. Queer Poem. Malcolm Lowry. NYTB
I knew a most superior camper. The Bunyip and the Whistling Kettle. John Manifold. LiTB; LiTM; NeLNL; PoAu-2; PoMS; SiTL; WaP
I knew a much-loved mariner. "He Bringeth Them unto Their Desired Haven." Lewis Frank Tooker. HBV
I knew a simple soldier boy. Suicide in Trenches. Siegfried Sassoon. BrPo; MMA
I Knew a Woman [Lovely in Her Bones]. Theodore Roethke. AmPP (5th ed.); CABA; CBV; ErPo; LiTM (1970 ed.); MeWo; MoAmPo (1962 ed.); NePA; NePoAm-2; NoP; PoeP; PoIE; SeCeV (1967 ed.); StP; ToPo; TwAmPo; TwCP; UnPo (3d ed.); UnTE; TrGrPo (rev. ed.)
I knew an old lady. Antique Shop. Carl Carmer. FaPON; MoSiPe; RePo
I knew an old wife lean and poor. The Goose. Tennyson. BOHV; GBV (1952 ed.)
I knew her first as food and warmth and rest. My Mother. Amelia Josephine Burr. DD; HBMV
I knew his face the moment that he passed. The One. Everard Jack Appleton. MaRV
I knew his house by the poplar trees. Norah. Zoë Akins. HBV
I knew, I felt (perception unexpressed). The Development of Man. Robert Browning. *Fr.* Paracelsus. EPN
I knew once,/ In your embrace. Poem about Waking. David Ferry. NePoAm-2
I knew quite well that some day. Narihira, *tr. fr. Japanese by* I. W. Furukami. LiTW
I knew she lay above me. The White Jessamine. John Banister Tabb. HBV
I knew that Disaster. Disaster. James Clarence Mangan. IrPN
I knew that you were coming, June. June. Douglas Malloch. OTD; YeAr
I knew the dignity of the words. My Grandfather's Funeral. James Applewhite. YAP
I knew the man. I see him as he stands. Lincoln. George Henry Boker. *Fr.* Our Heroic Times. DD; MC; OHIP
I knew Thee not, Thou wounded Son of God. Knowledge through Suffering. George Wallace Briggs. MaRV
I knew this Master Host would hold me in. Extended Invitation. Jesse Stuart. FiSC
I knew you forever and you were always old. Some Foreign Letters. Anne Sexton. MoAmPo (1962 ed.); PoCh; TqPo
I knew you long before great motors buzzed. Big Thompson Canon. Jean Milne Gower. PoOW
I knock again and try [again] the key. A Pagan Reinvokes the Twenty-third Psalm. Robert L. Wolf. HBMV; TrPWD
I knock at the door of a romance. Federico. Nicolás Guillén. PoNe
I Know. Elsa Barker. HBMV
I Know. *Unknown.* STF
I know/ Not these my hands. Amaze. Adelaide Crapsey. QFR
I know/ I saw/ a spooky witch. October Magic. Myra Cohn Livingston. PDV
I know/ Where the wind flowers blow! Song from "April." Irene Rutherford McLeod. SUS
I know a bank where[on] the wild thyme blows. A Violet Bank [*or* Titania's Bower *or* Where the Wild Thyme Blows]. Shakespeare. *Fr.* A Midsummer Night's Dream, II, i. BoNaP; FaPON; OTPC (1946 ed.); PCH; PRWS; PTK; RePo; TrGrPo
I know a barber. Edward Anthony. *Fr.* Oddity Land. TiPo (1959 ed.)

I know a barn in Breckenridge on the Blue. Old Men on the Blue. Thomas Hornsby Ferril. PoOW
I know a boy who went to meet the morning. Morning. Dorothy Hamilton Gallagher. SiSoSe
I know a city on a hill, a mountain's castled crown. Assisi. Alfred Noyes. GoBC
I know a country of bright ànonymous beaches. [In] Memory of Lake Superior. George Dillon. MAP; MoAmPo (1942 ed.)
I know a dog called Isaac. Three Dogs. E. C. Brereton. BoTP
I know a flower of beauty rare. The Lay of the Captive Count. Goethe. AWP
I know a flower so sweet and fair. I Am the Rose of Sharon. Catherine Winkworth. BePJ
I know a funny little man. Mr. Nobody. *Unknown.* BoTP; FaPON; GaP; HBVY; MPB (1956 ed.); OTPC; PoMS; StVeCh
I know a garden with three strange gates. The Last Gate. Stella Mead. BoTP
I know a girl who for present purposes let us call by the name of Emily. I Want to Sit Next to Emily. Ogden Nash. BOHV
I know a girl with teeth of pearl. "Wouldn't You Like to Know." John Godfrey Saxe. HBV
I know a green grass path that leaves the field. The Green River. Lord Alfred Douglas. HBMV; MoBrPo (1942 ed.); OBEV (new ed.); OBVV; PoVP
I know a Jew fish crier down on Maxwell Street. Fish Crier. Carl Sandburg. AmFN; OxBA; WoL
I know a little butterfly with tiny golden wings. The Butterfly. Margaret Rose. BoTP
I know a little clock shop. The Clock Shop. Jeannette C. Shirk. GFA
I know a little creature. An Autumn Riddle. *Unknown.* OTPC (1946 ed.)
I know a little cupboard. The Cupboard. Walter de la Mare. BrR; FaPON; PCH; PoRh; SoPo; TiPo
I Know a Little Garden-Close. William Morris. *Fr.* The Life and Death of Jason, IV. AtBAP; CH; EG; GTSE; PoE; ViBoPo; ViPo; ViPP
(Garden by the Sea, A.) CLwM; OBNC; PoEL-5; PoVP
(Nymph's Song to Hylas, The.) HBV; OBEV; TOP
I know a little garden path. A Hint to the Wise. Pringle Barret. HBVY; PCH
I know a little island. Aloha. William Griffith. HBMV
I know a little zigzag boy. The Zigzag Boy and Girl. *Unknown.* GFA
I Know a Lovely Lady Who Is Dead. Struthers Burt. HBMV
I Know a Man. Robert Creeley. AmPC; CoPo
I know a moon door in the Forbidden City. Moon Door. Mary Kennedy. BoLP
I know a Mount, the gracious Sun perceives. Rudel to the Lady of Tripoli. Robert Browning. LoBV; OtMeF; PoVP
I know a mountain, lone it lies. The Granite Mountain. Lew Sarett. HBMV
I Know a Name. *Unknown.* BLRP; MaRV; OQP; SoP
I know a place. A Boy's Place. Rose Burgunder. PDV
I know a place. Deep in the Woods. Mildred D. Shacklett. GFA
I know a place all fennel-green and fine. A Green Place. William Jay Smith. RePo
I know a place, in the ivy on a tree. The Bird's Nest. John Drinkwater. EvOK; PDV; SoPo; StVeCh
I know a place that holds the Sky. The Upside-down World. Hamish Hendry. BoTP
I know a place where summer strives. Emily Dickinson. NePA
I know a place where the sun is like gold. Four-Leaf Clover. Ella Higginson. AA; FaPON; HBV; OTPC (1946 ed.)
I know a renegade hotel. Traveler's Rest. Ogden Nash. InMe
I know a road that leads from town. The Road to the Pool. Grace Hazard Conkling. HBMV
I Know a Secret. Christopher Morley. MPB
I know a secret, such a one. The Serf's Secret. William Vaughn Moody. HBV
"I know a solemn secret to keep between ourselves." The Elfin People Fill the Tubes. Winifred M. Letts. BoTP
I know a soul that is steeped in sin. I Know a Name! *Unknown.* BLRP; MaRV; OQP; SoP
I know a spot where love delights to dream. Sacred Grove. Edward Cracroft Lefroy. *Fr.* Echoes from Theocritus. AWP
I know a story, fairer, dimmer, sadder. My Babes in the Wood. Sarah Morgan Bryan Piatt. AA
I know a tavern in the town. Table for One. John Holmes. WhC
I know a thing that's most uncommon. On a Certain Lady at Court. Pope. ALV; CEP; HBV; OAEP; OBEC; OBEV
I know a town tormented by the sea. Galway. Mary Devenport O'Neill. NeIP; OxBI
I know a wasted place high in the Alps. Two Poems on the Catholic Bavarians. Edgar Bowers. PoCh
I know a way. The Song in the Dell. Charles Edward Carryl. AA
I know a wind-swept hill where all day long. Silentium Altum. Blanche Mary Kelly. CAW
I know, although when looks meet. Crazy Jane and Jack the Journeyman. W. B. Yeats. AtBAP; CMoP
I know an ice handler who wears a flannel shirt. Ice Handler. Carl Sandburg. OxBA
I know an old house, grey with years. Opening Door. Winifred Adams Burr. FiSC
I know an old lady who swallowed a fly. The Old Lady Who Swallowed a Fly. *Unknown.* ShM
I know, as my life grows older. Whatever Is—Is Best. Ella Wheeler Wilcox. BLPA; TreFS
I know, baby: as you fear. To a Dog Barking at Night. Francis Maguire. NYTB
I know best what moan to make. Lament for One's Self. Ruth Pitter. BoPe
I know, blue modest violets. Violets. *Unknown.* BoTP
I know but will not tell. Elegy. Alan Dugan. AP
I Know de Lord's Laid His Hands on Me, *with music. Unknown.* BoAN-2
I know derisive men and women. Aboriginal Sin. John Hay. NePoAm-2
I know four winds with names like some strange tune. Weather Words. David McCord. ImOP
I Know He Is Real. *Unknown.* STF
I know her story-telling eye. The Eye of Love. George Moses Horton. BALP
I know him, February's thrush. The Thrush in February. George Meredith. OBNC
I know him now, not now to know demanding. Nunc Scio, Quid Sit Amor. L. A. MacKay. OBCV
I know how it would be . . . a rainy moon. After Storm. David Morton. HBMV
I know how poems come. Poems. Hilda Conkling. NP
I know how to hold. How to Go and Forget. Edwin Markham. HBMV
I Know I Am but Summer to Your Heart. Edna St. Vincent Millay. AmPP; CMoP
(Sonnet: "I Know I am but summer to your heart.") HBMV
I Know I Am Deathless. Walt Whitman. *Fr.* Song of Myself, XX. MaRV
I know I have a lot of faults. Let Me Look at Me. Bessie June Martin. STF
I know I have been humiliated and insulted unbearably. I Am the Stars' Bugging-Device. William Knott. YAP
I know, I know where violets blow. God's Will. Robert Munger. AA
I know I look the kind of dolt. To a Junior Waiter. A. P. Herbert. FiBHP
I know I shall remember. The Cathedral of St. Louis. Carl Carmer. MoSiPe
I know I smell. But everyone does, somewhat. Colloquy with Cockroach. Robert Penn Warren. CBV
I know it is my sinne, which locks thine eares. Church-Lock and Key. George Herbert. AnAnS-1; MaMe; MeP
I know it must be winter (though I sleep). Winter Sleep. Edith M. Thomas. AA
I know it will not ease the smart. Edith and Harold. Arthur Gray Butler. OBVV
I know, Justine, you speak me fair. Justine, You Love Me Not! John Godfrey Saxe. HBV
I know, Lord, Thou hast sent Him. Mary at Nazareth. Cale Young Rice. StJW
I know lots of men who are in love. I Never Even Suggested It. Ogden Nash. FiBHP; LiTA; LiTL; LiTM; PoLF; SiTL

I know mine own, our Shepherd says. The Good Shepherd. J. Harold Gwynne. BePJ
I Know Moonlight, *with music*. *Unknown.* AS (Group of Negro Songs, A.) NAMP
I know my body's of so frail a kind. Man [*or* I Know Myself a Man]. Sir John Davies. *Fr.* Nosce Teipsum. ChTr; EIL; WHA
I Know My Love. *Unknown.* AnIV
I Know My Princess. Bilhana, *formerly at. to* Chauras, *tr. fr. Sanskrit by* E. Powys Mathers. *Fr.* Black Marigolds. OnPM
I know my soul hath power to know all things. Man [*or* The Vanity of Human Learning]. Sir John Davies. *Fr.* Nosce Teipsum. MaRV; OBEV
I Know Myself a Man. Sir John Davies. *See* Man.
I know no sleep you do not stand beside. The Unborn. Judith Wright. MoAuPo
I know no song to sing you. Stars and Silence. *Unknown.* OnPM
I know not, but God knows. But God. Annie Johnson Flint. SoP
I know not but in every leaf. Fraternity. John Banister Tabb. HBV
I know not by what methods rare. This I Know [*or* Prayer *or* God Answers Prayer]. Eliza M. Hickok. BLRP; FaChP; SoP; STF
I know not how it may be with others. Old Furniture. Thomas Hardy. MoVE
I know not how that Bethlehem's Babe. Our Christ. Harry Webb Farrington. BePJ; MaRV; OQP; SoP; STF; TRV
I know not how to call you light. To La Sanscoeur. William Caldwell Roscoe. VA
I know not how to speak to thee, girl (damselle?). Love Song. Reed Whittemore. AmFN
I know not if from uncreated spheres. Michelangelo, *tr. fr. Italian by* George Santayana. AWP
I know not if I love her overmuch. Sonnets after the Italian. Richard Watson Gilder. HBV
I know not if tomorrow's way. Tomorrow's Way. *Unknown.* SoP
I know not in what watch He comes. He Is Near! Horatius Bonar. SoP
I know not of what we pondered. Companions. Charles Stuart Calverley. BOHV; HBV; NA; PoVP; TOP; TSW; VA
I know not Seville. Seville. L. D'O. Walters. HBMV
I know not that the men of old. The Men of Old. Richard Monckton Milnes. GTBS; GTSL; OBEV (new ed.); OBVV
I know not too well how I found my way home in the night. Robert Browning. *Fr.* Saul. LoBV
I know not what awaits me. God Knoweth. Mary G. Brainard *and* P. P. Bliss. SoP
I know not what my health will be. I Know. *Unknown.* STF
I know not what shall befall me: God hangs a mist o'er my eyes. Mary Gardiner Brainard. *Fr.* Not Knowing. TRV
I know not what spell is o'er me. Lorelei. Heine. TrJP
I know not what the future hath. Whittier. *Fr.* The Eternal Goodness. BLRP; OQP; TreF
I know not what the future holds. The Future. Edward Cane. SoP
I know not what to do. Fragment Thirty-Six [*or* Hesperides]. Hilda Doolittle ("H. D."). CMoP; NP; OxBA
I know not what will befall me: God hangs a mist o'er my eyes. Not Knowing. Mary Gardiner Brainard. AA
I know not when this tiresome man. The Sundowner. John Shaw Neilson. PoAu-1
I know not where my steps may lead. He Knows the Way. *Unknown.* STF
I Know Not Whether I Am Proud. Walter Savage Landor. EnRP
I know not whether laws be right. In Prison. Oscar Wilde. *Fr.* The Ballad of Reading Gaol. ACP (1926 ed.); MaRV; OQP; SoP
I Know Not Why. Morris Rosenfeld. AA
I Know Not Why, but All This Weary Day. Henry Timrod. AmP
I know not why I yearn for thee again. Dreams of the Sea. W. H. Davies. EtS
I know not why my pathway leads. This Peace He Gives. Alice Hansche Mortenson. SoP
I know not why my soul is rack'd. Changed. Charles Stuart Calverley. ALV; FiBHP
I know not why or whence he came. The Deserter. Joseph S. Cotter, Jr. CDC
I know now. I Thought It Was Tangiers I Wanted. Langston Hughes. PoNe (1970 ed.)
I know now. It has been him. Him: the Roach. Harold Bond. YAP
I Know on a Night Overcast. Hayyim Nahman Bialik, *tr. fr. Hebrew by* Jacob Sloan. LiTW
I know seven mice. Edward Anthony. *Fr.* Oddity Land. TiPo (1959 ed.)
I know, Sister, that solitude. To a Severe Nun. Thomas Merton. CoPo
I know so well this turfy mile. Greenaway. John Betjeman. POTi
I know some lonely houses off the road. Emily Dickinson. AnEnPo; CBEP; MoAB; MoAmPo (1950 ed.); NoP; OxBA; PFY; PoE; PoMS; PoRA; TDP; WaKn; YT
I Know Something Good about You. *Unknown.* BLPA; PoToHe
I know that all beneath the moon decays. William Drummond of Hawthornden. Sonn
I know that any weed can tell. Song. Louis Ginsberg. TrJP
I know that behind these walls is the city, over these rooftops is the sun. Foghorn in Horror. Muriel Rukeyser. FiMAP
I know that Christ died long ago. Bethlehem's Babe. Henry W. Frost. SoP
I know that Europe's wonderful, yet something seems to lack. Henry van Dyke. *Fr.* America for Me. MaRV
I know that every note and chord of woe. Sonnet. George Henry Boker. *Fr.* Sonnets: a Sequence on Profane Love. AmePo
I know that face! Daphne. Bliss Carman. OBCV
I know that He exists. Emily Dickinson. AmePo; AmPP; AnFE; APA; CoAnAm; ILP; NoP
I know that he is ten years old. The Difference. Eleanor A. Chaffee. BiCB
I Know That I Am a Great Sinner. Purohit. OBMV
I know that I can trust the Lord. He Cares. Phyllis C. Michael. SoP
I know That I Have Savoured. Bilhana, *formerly at. to* Chauras, *tr. fr. Sanskrit by* E. Powys Mathers. *Fr.* Black Marigolds. OnPM
I Know That I Must Die Soon. Else Lasker-Schüler, *tr. fr. German by* Ralph Manheim. TrJP
I know that I shall meet my fate. An Irish Airman Foresees His Death. W. B. Yeats. AnEnPo; CABA; CoBMV; EnL; EnLi-2 (1949 ed.); FaBoCh; FaBoMo; GoJo; GTBS-P; ILP; LiTG; LiTM (rev. ed.); LoGBV; MaPo (1969 ed.); MMA; MoAB; MoBrPo; OBMV; OnPM; OtMeF; PAn; PoFr; PoPl; PoPo; TrGrPo; WaaP; WaP; WoL
I know that if thou please thou canst provide. George Wither. *Fr.* Brittan's Remembrancer. SeCV-1
I Know that My Redeemer Lives. Charles Wesley. PoFr; SoP; TreFS
I know that my Redeemer lives. He Lives. Samuel Medley. SoP
I know that my Redeemer lives & I. *Unknown.* SeCSL
I Know that My Redeemer Liveth. Virginia Frazer Boyle. BePJ
I know that my Redeemer liveth—but out of the depths of time. The Redeemer. "Fiona Macleod." WGRP
I know that there are dragons. Serious Omission. John Farrar. RIS; UTS
I know that these poor rags of womanhood. Afterwards. "Violet Fane." HBV; OBVV; VA
I know that this my crying, like the crying. Night. Hayyim Nahman Bialik. AWP; LiTW
I know that this was Life—the track. In Memoriam A. H. H. XXV. Tennyson. EnLi-2; EPN; TOP; ViPo; VP
I know that to the winds my reason is cast! The Conquest of Love. Racine. *Fr.* Phèdre. LiTW
I know the bottom, she says. I know it with my great tap root. The Elm Speaks. Sylvia Plath. NYBP; PoAn
I know the hedge in Briar Lane. I Must Away. May Sarson. BoTP

I know the injured pride of sleep. Night and Morning. Austin Clarke. AnIL MoAB; NeIP
I know the mind that feels indeed the fire. William Cowper. *Fr.* Table Talk. PP
I know the month, I know the week. First Born. Frances O'-Connell Corridan. JKCP (1926 ed.)
I know the night is near at hand [*or* drawing near]. Vespers [*or* Evening *or* From Dark to Light]. S. Weir Mitchell. MaRV; OQP; WGRP
I know the road to Jericho. The Jericho Road. Edwin McNeill Poteat. ChIP; MaRV
I know the ships that pass by day. The Lights. J. J. Bell. BoTP
I know the sky will fall one day. Child's Song. Gerald Gould. BoTP
I know the song that the bluebird is singing. The Bluebird. Emily Huntington Miller. GFA; MPB; OTPC (1946 ed.); PRWS
I know the thing that's most uncommon. On a Certain Lady at Court. Pope. ALV; BoLiVe; CBEP; CEP; CoBE; EiCL; EnLit; HBV; OAEP; OBEC; OBEV; TrGrPo
I Know the Trusty Almanac. Emerson. *Fr.* May-Day. BiS
I know the ways [*or* wayes] of learning; both the head. The Pearl. George Herbert. AnAnS-1; EP; FaBoEn; MaMe; MeP; MePo; OxBoCh; PoEL-2; ReEn; SCEP-1; SeCP; SeCV-1
I know there are some fools that care. The Deformed Mistress. Sir John Suckling. ErPo
I know that there shall dawn a day. Reverie. Robert Browning. OHIP
I know three things must always be. Three Things. *Unknown.* SoP
I know 'tis sordid, and 'tis low. The Frailty. Abraham Cowley. CavP
I know to God, full of myght. Confiteor. *Unknown.* CoBE
I know two things about the horse. The Horse. Naomi Royde-Smith. CenHV; FiBHP; LiTM; SiTL
I know two women. The Wife. Robert Creeley. AmPC; AP; CBV; ToPo
I know very well, goddess, she is not beautiful. Calypso's Island. Archibald MacLeish. MoAB; NoP
I know very well what I'd rather be. Rathers. Mary Austin. FaPON
I know well this body of mine. Vain Wish. Otomo Yakamochi. OnPM
I know what beer is. Beer and Skittles. Diana Barrett. StaSt
I know what mother's face is like. The Blind Child. *Unknown.* MaRV; SoP
I know what the caged bird feels, alas! Sympathy. Paul Laurence Dunbar. AmNP; CDC; IDB; PoNe
I know what will happen, sweet. You and I. Timothy Daniel Sullivan. JKCP (1926 ed.)
"I know what you're going to say," she said. Candor. H. C. Bunner. HBV
I know when milk does flies contain. All Things Except Myself I Know. Villon. BOHV
I know, where Hampshire fronts the Wight. "Hold". Patrick R. Chalmers. HBV
"I know where I'd get." Padraic Colum. *Fr.* Asses. LOW
I Know Where I'm Going. *Unknown.* AnIV; ELP; IrPN; LO; MoShBr; OnYI; PG (1955 ed.); ViBoPo
(I Know Who I Love.) MeWo
(Irish Song.) AtBAP
I know where is a thief, and long hath been. Ad Eandem. Thomas Bastard. SiCE
I know where the wind flowers blow. Song from "April." Irene Rutherford McLeod. SUS
I Know Who I Love. *Unknown.* *See* I Know Where I'm Going.
I know why lilies ring their bells. Secret. Esther Hull Doolittle. YeAr
I know, within my mouth, for bashful fear. Love's Despair. Richard Lynche. *Fr.* Diella. EIL
I know you after sixty years. Two of You. Mark Van Doren. UnPo (1st ed.)
I know. You cannot keep your passion hid. Dostoievsky to a Young Communist. Daniel J. Honan. JKCP (1955 ed.)
I know you, rider, gonna miss me when I'm gone. Woman Blue. *Unknown.* ABF
I know you: solitary griefs. The Precept of Silence. Lionel Johnson. ACP (1926 ed.); CAW; HBV; MemP; MoBrPo; PoToHe (1941 ed.); PoVP; SoP; ViBoPo; ViPP
I know you, wife. To My Wife. Peter Firth. BoPe
I know your barren belief—that a rose will grow. For a Materialist. Adelaide Love. MaRV; OQP
I knowed a man, which he lived in Jones. Thar's More in the Man Than Thar Is in the Land. Sidney Lanier. AmePo; AP; CoBA
I labored long, I strove with might and main. Of Impatience Which Brings All Our Gains to Nothing. Jacopone da Todi. CAW
I lack in service, lack in love. To Holy Jesus. Princess Philipa. CAW
I lack the braver mind. Confession of Faith. Elinor Wylie. AnAmPo; AnFE; APA; CoAnAm; MAP; MoAmPo
I Laid Me Down upon a Bank. Blake. CBEP; EiCL; EnLoPo; ERoP-1
(Poems from MSS.) ViBoPo
I laid me down upon the shore. Pre-Existence. Frances Cornford. HBMV; POTE; WaKn
I laid my haffet on Elfer Hill. Elfer Hill. *Unknown.* AWP
I laid my wife beneath this stone. *Unknown.* WhC
I Lais whose laughter was scornful in Hellas. Dedication of a Mirror. Plato, *tr. by* Dudley Fitts. LiTW
I lak on summer ev'ning, w'en nice cool win' is blowin'. Ole Tam on Bord-a Plouffe. William H. Drummond. PTK
I laks yo' kin' of lovin'. Long Gone. Sterling A. Brown. BALP; BANP; CDC
I landed on Iona's holy isle. Iona. Frederick Tennyson. GoBC
I lang hae thought, my youthfu' friend. Epistle to a Young Friend. Burns. MCCG; OHFP
I late the Roman youth's lou'd prayse and pride. Alexias, the Complaint of the Forsaken Wife of Sainte Alexis. Richard Crashaw. MaMe
I lately lived in quiet case. Love Is Like a Dizziness. James Hogg. BOHV; HBV; InMe
I lately lost a preposition. The Naughty Preposition. Morris Bishop. FiBHP; NYBP; PV
I Lately Vowed [but 'Twas in Haste]. John Oldmixon. ErPo; HBV
I laugh and sing, but cannot tell. To Lucasta. Richard Lovelace. OBS
I laugh at each dull bore, taste's parasite. Heine. Fresco-Sonnets to Christian Sethe, 1. AWP; JAWP; WBP
I laugh that you should be so busy to pick up morsels. Chopsticks. Yüan Mei. FIW
I laughed at the lovers I passed. Terenure. Blanaid Salkeld. NeIP
I laved my hands. Lost for a Rose's Sake. *Unknown.* AWP; JAWP; WBP
I lay among the ferns. Edward Carpenter. *Fr.* Among the Ferns. OQP
I lay and speculated on the impact of a bullet. Terror. Thomas O'Brien. NeIP
I lay beside you . . . on your lips the while. The Haunted House. George Sylvester Viereck. AnAmPo
I lay down with my love and there was song. Armorial. Ralph Gustafson. ACV; MoCV; PeCV (1967 ed.)
I lay face-downward on the grass. The Barrier. Louis Lavater. MoAuPo
I lay i' the bosom of the sun. Palabras Grandiosas. Bayard Taylor. *Fr.* The Echo Club. BOHV
I lay in my tent at mid-day. The Crossing at Fredericksburg. George Henry Boker. PAH
I lay in silence, dead. A woman came. Another Way. Ambrose Bierce. AA; LHV
I lay me down, but down is deep. Nap. Mark Van Doren. TwAmPo
I lay me down to sleep. In the Hospital. Mary Woolsey Howland. HBV; MaRV
I lay me down to sleep, with little thought or care. Rest. *Unknown.* SoP
I Lay My Lute beside Thy Door. Clarence Urmy. HBMV
I Lay My Sins on Jesus. Horatius Bonar. BePJ; SoP
I lay on Delos of the Cyclades. The Ship. Lloyd Mifflin. AA
I lay upon the summer grass. The Oracle. Arthur Davison Ficke. HBV
I lay with my heart under me. Cicada. Adrien Stoutenburg. NYBP
I lean on a lighthouse rock. Girl at the Seaside. Richard Murphy. NMP; OPoP

I leaned out of [*or* my] window, I smelt the white clover. Songs of Seven: Seven Times Three. Jean Inglow. GBV (1922 ed.); HBV; PoLF

I leant [*or* leaned] upon a coppice gate. The Darkling Thrush. Thomas Hardy. AnFE; ATP (1953 ed.); BoLiVe; BrPo; BWP; CaFP; CBV; CMoP; CoBE; CoBMV; DiPo; EvOK; ForPo; EnL; EnLi-2 (1949 ed.); EPN; ExPo; FaFP; GTBS-W; GTSL; HBMV; ILP; InP; LiTB; LiTG; LiTM; MaPo (1969 ed.); MasP; MoAB; MoBrPo; MoPo; NeMA; NoP; OAEP; OBEV (new ed.); OBNC; OBVV; PAn; PG (1955 ed.); PoAn; PoDB; PoeP; PoFS; PoIE; PoSa; POTE; PoVP; ReMP; RoGo; SeCeV; ShBV-4; StP; TreFT; TrGrPo; ViPo; ViPP; VP; WaP

I learn, as the years roll onward. Life's Lessons. *Unknown.* BLRP; PoLF; SoP; STF

I learn'd his greatness first at Lavington. Cardinal Manning. Aubrey Thomas De Vere. JKCP; VA

I learned today the world is round. The Road to China. Olive Beaupré Miller. MPB

I leave behind me the elm-shadowed square. Outward Bound. Thomas Bailey Aldrich. AA; EtS

I leave mortality, and things below. The Ecstasy [*or* The Extasie]. Abraham Cowley. AnAnS-2; Po; SeCP

I leave the world to-morrow. Farewell. Enid Derham. BoAu

I leave thee, beauteous Italy! no more. Farewell to Italy. Walter Savage Landor. VA

I leave their fields. The Long Night Home. Charles F. Gordon. NBP

I leave thy praises unexpress'd. In Memoriam A. H. H., LXXV. Tennyson. EPN; ViPo; VP

I leave with unreverted eye the towers. Florence. Walter Savage Landor. SeCePo

I leave you in your garden. To Yvor Winters, 1955. Thom Gunn. GTBS-P

I led him on into the frosted wood. Fable. George O'Neil. NP

I left a lei, Lady. Lady of Peace. Fray Angelico Chavez. ISi

I left the land where men with Nature dwelling. From Country to Town. Hartley Coleridge. PeER

I left the little birds. "Adieu." John Clare. FlW

I left the streets of Galway town. The Tramp's Song. Mary Devenport O'Neill. AnIV

I left thee last, a child at heart. Rosalind's Scroll. Elizabeth Barrett Browning. *Fr.* The Poet's Vow. HBV; OBEV (1st ed.)

I left you once in madness and disgrace. To His Mother. Heine. OnPM

I let the smoke out of the windows. Complex Autumnal. Carolyn Kizer. FRC

I Lie Down with God. *Tr. fr. Modern Irish by* Eleanor Hull. *Fr.* Four Prayers. AnIV
(Four Prayers.) OnYI

I lie in the hay. Swallow Tails. Tom Robinson. FaPON

I lie sleepless in the half light. Peace, like a Lamb. Leonard Clark. WePo

I lie under the crust of the night singing. Pregnant Woman. Ingrid Jonker. PeSA

I lie upon my bed and hear and see. The Largest Life. Archibald Lampman. CaP

I lift mine eyes against the sky. I Know Not Why. Morris Rosenfeld. AA

I lift mine eyes and all the windows blaze. Divina Commedia, V[*or* On Translating the "Divina Commedia" *or* Sonnets on the Divina Commedia, V]. Longfellow. AmePo; AmP; AmPP; AnAmPo; AnFE; AnNE; AP; APA; CoAnAm; CoBA; GoBC; ILP; NePA; NoP; OuHeWo; OxBA; SeCeV; Sonn; TOP

I lift my cap to beauty. A Song of the Road. Fred G. Bowles. MaRV; OQP

I lift my eyes, but I cannot see. A Seeker in the Night. Florence Earle Coates. TrPWD

I Lift My Gaze. John Hall Wheelock. MaRV

I lift my head from lowly bed. Moschatel. Daniel James O'Sullivan. NeIP

I lift my heart to Thee, O God. Thankful Heart. F. W. Davis. STF

I lift my heavy heart up solemnly. Sonnets from the Portuguese, V. Elizabeth Barrett Browning. TOP; VA; ViPo

I lift the Lord on high. Père Lalement. Marjorie Pickthall. CaP; OBCV; PeCV; TwCaPo

I lift these hands with iron fetters banded. South Carolina to the States of the North. Paul Hamilton Hayne. PAH

I lift this sumach-bough with crimson flare. Torch-Light in Autumn. John James Piatt. AA

I like a church; I like a cowl. The Problem. Emerson. AA; AmePo; AmP; AmPP; AnAmPo; AnNE; AP; AWP; CoBA; HBV; JAWP; LiTA; MAmP; MaRV; MWA-1; NePA; NoP; OuHeWo; OxBA; TOP; WBP; WGRP

I like a half day on one day. Page IX. Gertrude Stein. WaKn

I like a look of agony. Emily Dickinson. AP; CBEP; MWA-2; NCEP; NoP; OnPM; PoeP; ReMP

I like a mouse. Wild Animals. Elizabeth Fleming. StVeCh

I like a road that leads away to prospects white and fair. The Best Road of All. Charles Hanson Towne. HBMV; OQP

I Like Americans. Edna St. Vincent Millay. YaD

I like best. Of Man and Nature. Horace Mungin. BOLo

I like best those crotchety ones. The Odd Ones. Ruth Suckow. MCCG

I like blowing bubbles, and swinging on a swing. Things I Like. Marjorie H. Greenfield. BoTP

I Like Christmas. James S. Tippett. ChBR

I like coffee, I like tea. *Unknown.* FaFP; SiTL

I like days. December. Aileen Fisher. SiSoSe

I like her gentle hand that sometimes strays. Richard Watson Gilder. *Fr.* Sonnets after the Italian. HBV

I Like House Cleaning. Dorothy Brown Thompson. BrR; FaPON

I Like It When It's Mizzly. Aileen Fisher. PDV

I Like Little Pussy. Jane Taylor. CIV; FaBoBe; GFA; HBV; HBVY; PPL
(I Love Little Pussy.) FaPON; OTPC; OxNR, *abr.*; PCH; SoPo; TiPo, *st.* 1
("I love little pussy, her coat is so warm, *st.* 1.") RIS
(Little Pussy.) GoTP
(Pussy, *abr.*) SAS

I like men./ They stride about. Men. Dorothy E. Reid. NeMA; StaSt

I Like My Body [When It Is with Your]. E. E. Cummings. *Fr.* Sonnets — Actualities. ErPo; LiTG; Sonn; UnTE

I like nature strained through a town. City Nature. Esther Pinch. PoMa

I like not lady-slippers. Tiger-Lilies. Thomas Bailey Aldrich. GN; GoTP

I like not tears in tune, nor do I prize. On the Memory of Mr. Edward King [Drown'd in the Irish Seas]. John Cleveland. AnAnS-2; OBS; SeCP; SeEP

I like old houses, with steps that sag. Old Houses. Jennie Romano. PoToHe (new ed.)

I like our house because it is so big and old. Our House. Nellie Burget Miller. GFA

I like that ancient Saxon phrase, which calls. God's-Acre. Longfellow. HBV; MWA-1; PoRL

I like that old, kind legend. The Little Mud-Sparrows; Jewish Legend. Elizabeth Stuart Phelps Ward. ChrBoLe

I like the Chinese laundryman. Mar Quong, Chinese Laundryman. Christopher Morley. MPB

I like the clouds. Summer Sky. Ruth McKee Gordon. TiPo (1959 ed.)

I like the fall. The Mist and All. Dixie Willson. BrR; FaPON; MPB; SoPo; YeAr

I like the hunting of the hare. The Old Squire. Wilfrid Scawen Blunt. HBV; OBEV (new ed.); OBVV; SD; VA

I like the man who faces what he must. The Inevitable. Sarah Knowles Bolton. AA; MaRV; OQP; PCD; WGRP

I like the people who keep shops. Shops. Winifred M. Letts. MoSiPe

I like the story of the circus waif. The Road. Herbert Morris. NePoAm-2

I like the tangled brakes and briers. Days Like These. Ella Elizabeth Egbert. PoMa

I like the town on rainy nights. Rainy Nights. Irene Thompson. BoTP

I like the whistle of trains at night. Trains at Night. Frances Frost. BrR; TiPo

I like the wide and common road. The Knapsack Trail. Edwin Osgood Grover. OQP

I like the woods. Autumn Woods. James S. Tippett. BoChLi; SUS; TiPo

I like to chase the fireflies. Fireflies. Grace Wilson Coplen. GFA; UTS

I like to find. Pleasures. Denise Levertov. AP; NeAP
I like to go to the stable after supper. White Cat. Raymond Knister. WHW
I like to have a home life in the house. Gertrude Stein. *Fr.* Afterwards. LOW
I like to look at the blossomy track of the moon upon the sea. Main Street. Joyce Kilmer. JKCP
I like to look for bridges. Bridges. Rhoda W. Bacmeister. SoPo
I like to look out of my window and see. Rain. Helen Wing. GFA
I like to move. There's such a feeling. Moving. Eunice Tietjens. GaP; TiPo
I like to play close by my father's den. Are You There? Strickland Gillilan. PoToHe (new ed.)
I Like to Quote. Mitchell D. Follansbee. PoPl; WhC
I like to ride in a tramcar. Travelling. Dorothy Gradon. BoTP
I like to ride in my uncle's plane. Flying. Kaye Starbird. PDV
I like to see/ The spotted clown. The Clown. Dorothy Aldis. PDV
I like to see a thing I know. New Sights. *Unknown.* BoTP
I like to see it lap the miles. Emily Dickinson. AmLP; AmPP; AP; CABA; CaFP; CBEP; CoBA; DiPo; FaBV; FaPON; LiTA; LiTG; LiTM (rev. ed.); LoGBV; MAP; MCCG; MoAB; MoAmPo; MoShBr; MoVE; MPB; MWA-2; NoP; OxBA; PCD; PDV; PoE; PoeP; PoPo; RePo
I like to see the airplane and hear the buzzing sound. The Airplane. Annette Wynne. GFA
I like to see the eager-faced old woman. An Old Woman with Flowers. Agnes Lee. NP
I like to see the patience of a leafless tree. A Leafless Tree. Ann Louise Thompson. OQP
I like to see the wind. Hayfield. Aileen Fisher. RePo
I Like to Sing Also. John Updike. FiBHP
I like to sit and watch my cat. Sport for Gods. Jewell Bothwell Tull. CIV
I like to sit here by the hearth. Movies in the Fire. Mildred D. Shacklett. GFA
I like to think/ That, long ago. Snowdrops. Mary Vivian. BoTP
I like to walk. Crows. David McCord. PDV; TiPo (1959 ed.)
I like to wear my party frock. Best. Rose Fyleman. BrR
I like you, Mrs. Fry! I like your name! A Friendly Address. Thomas Hood. PoEL-4
I Liked but Never Loved Before. *Unknown.* SeCL
I liked to walk in the river meadows. The Midnight Court. Brian Merriman. KiLC
I linger on the flathouse roof, the moonlight is divine. The Flathouse Roof. Nathalia Crane. YT
I 'listed at home for a lancer. Lancer. A. E. Housman. EnLit; MoBrPo
I listen and my hand thy letter presses. An Old Woman's Answer to a Letter from Her Girlhood. Susan L. Emory. CAW
I listen, and the mountain lakes. Maybe Alone on My Bike. William Stafford. NYBP
I listen to the agony of God. The Agony of God. Georgia Harkness. MaRV
I listen'd to the music broad and deep. Love and Music. Philip Bourke Marston. VA
I listened, there was not a sound to hear. Full Moon; Santa Barbara. Sara Teasdale. BrR; TSW
I listened to a man and he. Psychometrist. James Stephens. POTE
I listened to the Phantom by Ontario's shore. The Poet. Walt Whitman. *Fr.* By Blue Ontario's Shore. MoAmPo (1950 ed.)
I little know or care. Forever and a Day. Thomas Bailey Aldrich. HBV; LHV
I live all alone, and I am a young girl. The Garden of Bamboos. *Tr. by* E. Powys Mathers. BoLP
I live among the grasses. The Field-Mouse. Enid Blyton. BoTP
I live among workers. Living among the Toilers. Henri Percikow. OCS
I live for the good of my nation. Old Rosin, the Beau. *Unknown.* CoSo
I live for those who love me. What I Live For. George Linnaeus Banks. BLPA; FaBoBe; MaRV; NeHB; PoToHe (new ed.); TreFS
I Live in Great Sorrow. *Unknown.* *See* Fowls in the Frith.
I live in hope some day to see. A Bird in the Bush. Lord Kennet. PV
I live in my wooden legs and O. Where I Live in This Honorable House of the Laurel Tree. Anne Sexton. TwAmPo
I live in the town. The Town Child. Irene Thompson. BoTP
I live in this house, walls being plastered. Keep Me Still, for I Do Not Want to Dream. Larry Eigner. NeAP
I live invisible (in my whole sky). Too Bright a Day. Norman MacCaig. GTBS-P
I live, sweet love, whereas the gentle wind. Licia, XXVI. Giles Fletcher. SiCE; TuPP
I live: this much I know; and I defy. Immortality. Willis Fletcher Johnson. OQP
I live with myself each livelong day. Myself. Edwin C. Swanson. SoP
I lived a life without love, and saw the being. The Mirage. Oscar Williams. CrMA; LiTL; LiTM; NePA
I lived among great houses. The Statesman's Holiday. W. B. Yeats. AtBAP; CMoP
I lived here nearly 5 years before I could. Chicago Poem. Lew Welch. FRC; NeAP
I lived in a dry well. Wells. Donald Hall. NMP
I Lived in a Town, *with music.* *Unknown.* TrAS
I Lived My Days Apart. Siegfried Sassoon. *See* Mystic as Soldier, A.
I lived to tell the truth, and truth was wrong. Laocoon. Donald Hall. NePoAm-2
"I lived with Mr. Punch, they said my name was Judy." Variations. Randall Jarrell. MiAP
I lived with Pride; the house was hung. The House of Pride. William J. Dawson. MaRV; PoToHe
I lived with visions for my company. Sonnets from the Portuguese, XXVI. Elizabeth Barrett Browning. BEL; CoBE; EnLi-2; EnLit; OAEP; TOP; VA; ViPo
I loathe, abhor, detest, despise. Dried Apple Pies. *Unknown.* BLPA
I loathe that I did love. The Aged Lover Renounceth Love [*or* Image of Death]. Thomas Vaux. EIL EnPo; EnRePo; EP; GoTL; OAEP; OBSC; PoEL-1; PoLi; ReEn; SiCE; TuPP
I loathe the very thought of her. Morning Star. James J. Galvin. ISi
I loathed you, Spoon River. I tried to rise above you. Archibald Higbie. Edgar Lee Masters. *Fr.* Spoon River Anthology. InP; NP
I loed you for yir kindness. The Deean Tractorman, Clear. Edith Anne Robertson. OxBS
I loitered weeping with my bride for gladness. Lyrics. James Agee. MAP; MoAmPo; PoPl
I long for the black ink. Florence. Robert Lowell. NoP
I long for the land that is not. The Land That Is Not. Edith Södergran. HW
I long have had a quarrel set with Time. The Two Highwaymen. Wilfrid Scawen Blunt. MoBrPo(1942 ed); OBEV(1st ed.)
I long not now, a little while at least. Protest. Countee Cullen. CDC
I long to be the wanton breeze. Lovesick. *Unknown.* UnTE
I long to know/ How my dear mistress fares. George Chapman. *Fr.* Bussy d'Ambois, V, iii. ViBoPo
I long to talk[e] with some old lovers ghost. Love's Deity [*or* Deitie]. John Donne. AnAnS-1; ATP; AWP; BEL; DiPo; EIL; EnLi-2; EnLit; EnRePo; ILP; InPo; LiTB; LiTG; LiTL; MaMe; MaPo; MBW-1; MemP; MePo; OAEP; OuHeWo; PoE; PoeP; ReEn; SCEP-1; SeCePo; SeCP; SeCV-1; SeEP; TOP; TuPP; WBP; WHA
I longed for peace and quiet. Peace. Avis B. Christiansen. SoP
I longed to walk along an easy road. Longing. *Unknown.* SoP
I look at the crisp golden-thread hair. Canzone: His Portrait of His Lady. Fazio degli Uberti. AWP
I look at the mirror, this body. The Poet's Reflection. Tony Connor. CBV
I look at the sun, and I think of the power. Through His Name. *Unknown.* SoP
I look at the swaling sunset. In Trouble and Shame. D. H. Lawrence. BoPe; OBMV
I Look Down. Po Chü-i, *tr. fr. Chinese by* Arthur Waley. OnPM
I Look Forward. Claire Goll, *tr. fr. French by* Claire Goll. OnPM

I Look into My Glass. Thomas Hardy. BrPo; CABA; CBEP; EG; LO; MoPW; NoP; POTE
I look into the Stars. Jane Draper. HBMV
I Look Not Back. Annie Johnson Flint [*also at. to* J. H. Hunt]. BePJ
(I Look Up.) SoP
I look on the specious electrical light. A Rhyme about an Electrical Advertising Sign. Vachel Lindsay. InP
I look out at the white sleet covering the still streets. Sleet Storm on the Merritt Parkway. Robert Bly. CBV
I look out into the yonder. Last Call. Langston Hughes. NePoAm-2
I look to Thee in ev'ry need. The Christian Life. Samuel Longfellow. SoP; WGRP
I Look Up. J. H. Hunt. *See* I Look Not Back.
I look up and see. Late Harvest. James Tate. YAP
I Look Up Hotels. Constantino Suasnavar, *tr. fr. Spanish by* Muna Lee. *Fr.* Numbers. OnPM
I look upon my native city's wall. Death Warnings. Francisco de Quevedo y Villegas. CAW
I look upon the world—and she resembles a garden. The End of Man Is Death. Moses ibn Ezra. TrJP
I look upon thy happy face. To a Child. George Edgar Montgomery. AA
I look with awe upon the human race. Two Somewhat Different Epigrams, II. Langston Hughes. NePoAm-2
I look on kingship in high pines. Exile. Jennette Yeatman. GoYe
I lookd upon my true loves eye. *Unknown.* SeCSL
I looked across and beyond the churned-up lake. A Dream. Hugh Connell. NeIP
I Looked and Saw History Caught. A. B. Spellman. NBP
I looked and saw your eyes. Three Shadows. Dante Gabriel Rossetti. HBV; PoVP; ViBoPo
I looked far back into other years, and lo, in bright array. Mary, Queen of Scots. Henry Glassford Bell. BeLS; BLPA; FaBoBe
I looked for Christ on Madison Street. Christ on Madison Street. Raymond Kresensky. ChIP
I looked for Heaven, high on a hill. Heaven in My Hand. Raymond Kresensky. OQP
I looked for him everywhere. A Child Asleep. Elizabeth Madox Roberts. AnAmPo
I looked for that which is not, nor can be. A Pause of Thought. Christina Rossetti. FaBoEn; OBNC
I looked from my window this morning and found. Winter Feathers. Mildred D. Shacklett. GFA
I looked here. The Black Riders, VIII. Stephen Crane. AP
I looked in my heart while the wild swans went over. Wild Swans. Edna St. Vincent Millay. CMoP; MAP; MoAmPo
I looked in the first glass. The Three Mirrors. Edwin Muir. PoIE
I Looked in the Mirror. Beatrice Schenk de Regniers. PDV
I looked into a lake and saw a forest. Playmates. Lillian Everts. GoYe
I looked into my body. X-Ray. Leonora Speyer. ImOP
I looked into my heart to write. Summer Song. George Barker. ChMP; FaBoTw; GTBS-D; ToPo
I looked like Abraham Lincoln. Elliott Hawkins. Edgar Lee Masters. *Fr.* Spoon River Anthology. OxBA
I looked on that prophetic land. Presences Perfected. Siegfried Sassoon. MoBrPo
I looked one night and there Semiramis. A Look into the Gulf. Edwin Markham. AA
I Looked Out into the Morning. James Thomson. Sunday up the River, I. OAEP; PoVP; ViBoPo
I looked over Jordan, and what did I see. Swing Low, Sweet Chariot. *Unknown.* ABF, *with music*; AmPP; AmFN; BoAn-1, *with music*; FaPON; GoSl; InP; LoGV; MaRV
I looked to find Spring's early flowers. The Lament of the Flowers. Jones Very. MAmP; OxBA
I looked Up from My Writing. Thomas Hardy. MMA
I looked upon the dreary waste. The Message of the Bells. Thomas Curtis Clark. PGD
I looked upon the earth: it was a floor. Our Lady in the Middle Ages. Frederick William Faber. ACP; CAW; ISi
I lost a World—the other day! Emily Dickinson. DiPo
I lost my heart the other day. *Unknown.* SeCSL
I lost my mare in Lincoln Lane. *Unknown.* OxNR
I lost my sense of sin. Hope. Howard McCord. YAP
I Lost the Love of Heaven. John Clare. CBEP; ELP; GTBS-D; LoBV
(Vision, A.) ChTr; ERoP-2; GTBS-P; NCEP; OBNC; PeER
I Love a Flower. Robert Nichols. ChMP
I Love a Flower. *At. to* Thomas Phillipps. MeEL
I Love a Hill. Ralph Hodgson. BrPo
I love a lass as fair as ere was seen. Of a Mistress. Sir Aston Cokayne. CavP; SeCL
I love a noble lady, the reason why is clear. I Serve. Meinloh von Sevelingen. OnPM; WoL
I love a prayer-book. A Girl's Mood. Lizette Woodworth Reese. HBMV
I Love a Tree. Ralph Spaulding Cushman. SoP
I Love All Beauteous Things. Robert Bridges. BoTP; BrPo; CMoP; ExPo; HBMV; HBVY; MemP; PoVP; ShBV-4; SoP
(To L. B. C. L. M.) OAEP; ViBoPo
I love all shining things. Shining Things. Elizabeth Gould. BoTP
I love all waves and lovely water in motion. Five Degrees South. Francis Brett Young. EtS
I love, and he loves me again. A Nymph's Passion [*or* A Nymph's Secret]. Ben Jonson. CLwM; EnLit; OBEV (new ed.)
I Lov'd Thee Once. Sir Robert Ayton. *See* I Loved Thee Once.
I love and worship thee in that thy ways. Madonna Natura. "Fiona Macleod." WGRP
I love as though I were not born to die. Samis Idyll. Dachine Rainer. NePoAm
I love at early morn, from new-mown swath. John Clare. *Fr.* Summer Images. CBEP; ChTr; EG
I love at eventide to walk alone. Summer Moods. John Clare. OTD
I love but dare not show it for why. *Unknown.* SeCSL
I Love but Thee. Heine. *tr. fr. German by* Louis Untermeyer. AWP
I love contemplating—apart. Napoleon and the British Sailor. Thomas Campbell. BeLS
I love daffodils. Spring Song. Hilda Conkling. GBV (1922 ed.); HH; MPB; PoSC; TSW
I love every stock and stone. An American in England. Elinor Wylie. HT
"I love, I love, and whom love ye?" I Love a Flower. *Unknown at. to* Thomas Phillipps. MeEL
I love it, I love it; and who shall dare. The Old Arm-Chair. Eliza Cook. ATP; OTPC (1923 ed.); PaPo; WBLP
I Love Little Pussy. Jane Taylor. *See* I Like Little Pussy.
I love little pussy, her coat is so warm. The Wild Home-Pussy. Emma Rounds. RIS
I Love Little Willie *with music.* *Unknown.* ABF
I Love Long Black Eyes. Bilhana, *formerly at. to* Chauras, *tr. fr. Sanskrit by* E. Powys Mathers. *Fr.* Black Marigolds. OnPM
I love loved [*or* lovyd] and so doth she. Sir Thomas Wyatt. EnPo; FCP; SiPS
I love my country with a singular love. My Country. Mikhail Lermontov. LiTW
I love my friend—but love my ease. The Citizen and the Red Lion of Brentford. Christopher Smart. NCEP
I love my God, but with no love of mine. Adoration [*or* By Thy Life I Love]. Mme Guyon. FaChP; MaRV; SoP; STF; TRV; WGRP
I love my hour of wind and light. Swallow Flight. Sara Teasdale. NP
I Love My Jean. Burns. *See* Of A' the Airts.
I love my Lady; she is very fair. My Beautiful Lady. Thomas Woolner. OBVV; VA
I love my lady with a deep purple love. Imagiste Love Lines. *Unknown.* BOHV
I Love My Life, but Not Too Well. Harriet Monroe. *See* Love Song.
I love my little gowns. "Vanity, Saith the Preacher." Josephine Preston Peabody. InP
I love my little son, and yet when he was ill. The Two Parents. "Hugh MacDiarmid." FaBoTw
I Love My Love. Helen Adam. NeAP
I Love My Love. Charles Mackay. NeHB
I Love My Love in the Morning. Gerald Griffin. ACP; GoBC; IrPN; OnYI
I love my prairies, they are mine. My Prairies. Hamlin Garland. FaPON

I love my queer cellar with its dusty smell. The Cellar. Hilda Conkling. PCH
I love not Colorado. Westward Ho. *Unknown.* CoSo
I love not thy perfections. When I hear. Depreciating Her Beauty. Wilfrid Scawen Blunt. The Love Sonnets of Proteus. OBMV
I love not wine; yet if thou'ldst make. Leave a Kiss within the Cup. Agathias Scholasticus. WoL
I love Octopussy, his arms are so long. The Octopussycat. Kenyon Cox. *Fr.* Mixed Beasts. FaPON; RIS; SoPo; TiPo
I love old gardens best. A Charleston Garden. Henry Bellamann. PoLF
I love old maps made long ago. Old Maps. Eunice Tietjens. BrR
I love old mothers—mothers with white hair. Dear Old Mothers [*or* Old Mothers]. Charles S. Ross. OQP; PGD; PoToHe (new ed.); SoP
I love our old pear tree. The Pear Tree. E. Elizabeth Longwell. BrR
I love people. Perspective. Victor Contoski. ThO
I love Russia; and Isadora in her dance. Sergey Yesenin Speaking Isadora Duncan. William Knott. YAP
I love sea words. Sea Words. Mary Sinton Leitch. EtS
I love seahorses, teddybears, African violets. Mad Sonnet 11. Michael McClure. FRC
I love sixpence, jolly [*or* pretty] little sixpence. Mother Goose. OTPC; OxNR
I love snow and all the forms. Shelley. *Fr.* Song: "Rarely, rarely, comest thou." TiPo (1959 ed.)
I Love the Beginning of All Rain. Geoffrey Scott. POTE
I Love the Blue Violet. John Clare. AtBAP
I love the chalice and the pyx. God Speaks in All Religions. Thomas Lake Harris. MaRV
I love the church that Jesus bought. Not on Sunday Night. *Unknown.* STF
I love the days of long ago. My Africa. Michael Dei-Anang. PBA
I love the evenings, passionless and fair, I love the evens. A Sunset. Victor Hugo. AWP; JAWP; WBP
I love the festive board. Gay Feast. Pushkin. OnPM
I love the fitful gust that shakes. Autumn. John Clare. BoTP; EG; GTBS-D; PCH
I love the hoss from hoof to head. The Kentucky Thoroughbred. James Whitcomb Riley. ELU
I love the jocund dance. Song. Blake. EG; EiPP
I love the little winding lanes. Lanes in Summer. Malcolm Hemphrey. BoTP
I love the locust tree. The Library. William Carlos Williams. *Fr.* Paterson, Bk. III. AtBAP
I love the luminous poison of the moon. A Sapphic Dream. George Moore. SyP
I love the man who dares to face defeat. Courage. Ozora Stearns Davis. OQP
I love the name of Christ the Lord, the Man of Galilee. The Christ of Common Folks. George T. Liddell. OQP
I love the old melodious lays. Proem. Whittier. AA; AmPP; AnNE; AP; CoBA; HBV; NePA; NoP; OxBA
I love the sacred Book of God. The Sacred Book. Thomas Kelly. SoP
I love the secret place of prayer. The Secret Place of Prayer. Georgia B. Adams. STF
I love the sound of the horn in the deep, dim woodland. The Sound of the Horn. Alfred de Vigny. AWP; JAWP; WBP
I love the stony pasture. The Deserted Pasture. Bliss Carman. HBV
I love thee and I love thee not. The Reason Why. Thomas Lovell Beddoes. OBRV
I love thee, Avon! though thy banks have known. The Avon. Henry Jacobs. AnNZ
I love thee, Baby! for thine own sweet sake. To Ianthe. Shelley. ATP
I love thee, Betty. *Unknown.* OxNR
I love thee, dear, for what thou art. To a Plain Sweetheart. T. A. Daly. JKCP
I love thee for thy ficklenes. *Unknown.* SeCSL
I Love Thee, Gracious Lord. C. C. Cox. BePJ
I Love Thee, Lord. Connie Calenberg. BePJ
I love thee, Mary, and thou lovest me. The Chemist to His Love. *Unknown.* BOHV; InMe
I love thee not, Sabidius. To Sabidius. Martial. DiPo; TuPP
I love Thee, O most gracious Lord. I Love Thee, Gracious Lord. C. C. Cox. BePJ
I love thee, pious ox, through whom my heart. The Ox. Giosuè Carducci. WoL
I love thee when thy swelling buds appear. The Tree. Jones Very. AnAmPo; AnNE; DD; GN; GoTP; HBV; OHIP; PEDC; PoRL; PoSC
I love them—and I hearken. The Carillon. Rosalia Castro de Murguía. CAW
I love this white and slender body. The White and Slender Body. Heine. UnTE
I love those spirits. Débris. Lola Ridge. NP
I Love Thy Kingdom, Lord. Timothy Dwight. MaRV
(Psalm CXXXVII.) AmePo
(Love to the Church.) AA; HBV; SoP
I love Thy Word, O God. The Word of God. J. Harold Gwynne. STF
I love to dwell upon the thought. Thoughts of Him. Georgia Adams. SoP
I love to go to see Aunt Flo. Farm Life. Ruth Edna Stanton. GFA
I love to hear the autumn crows go by. Autumn Evening. John Clare. ThWaDe
I love to hear the little bird. The Bird. Samuel Hoffenstein. FiBHP; PV
I Love to Hear the Story. Emily Huntington Miller. SoP
I love to hear the train go by. 'Spress! Jimmy Garthwaite. GFA
I love to hear thine earnest voice. To an Insect. Olive Wendell Holmes. HBV; HBVY; OTPC; StaSt; TreF
I love to lie awake and hear. Raindrops. Isla Paschal Richardson. GFA
I love to lie under the lemon. Fantasy. Hugh McCrae. MoAuPo
I Love to Love. Marion Ward. ATP
I love to peep out on a summer's morn. Summer Morning. John Clare. CBEP; PoSC
I love to rise in a summer morn. The Schoolboy. Blake. *Fr.* Songs of Experience. BoNaP; CBEP; CH; FaBoCh; FlW; GTBS-D; PeER
I love to see boards lying on the ground in early spring. Old Boards. Robert Bly. NaP
I love to see the old heath's withered brake. Emmonsail's Heath in Winter. John Clare. FaBoEn; PoEL-4
I love to see the man, a long-lived child. Manhood. Henry David Thoreau. MWA-1
I love to see, when leaves depart. Autumn. Roy Campbell. GTBS-P; JKCP (1923 ed.); MoBrPo; OBMV; POTE; TrGrPo (1942 ed.)
I Love to Steal Awhile Away. Phoebe H. Brown. SoP
(Private Devotions.) AA; AmePo
I love to step inside a church. Within the Gates. David W. Foley. MaRV
I love to stretch. Summer Morning. Charles Simic. YAP
I Love to Tell the Story. Katherine Hankey. TreFT
I love to think of things I hate. The Complete Misanthropist. Morris Bishop. FiBHP; SiTL
I love to think this fragrant air. Winds of Eros. "Æ." HBMV
I love to wander through the woodlands hoary. October. S. W. Whitman. BoTP
I Love You. Ella Wheeler Wilcox. BLPA; FaBoBe
I love you,/ Not only for what you are. Love. *Unknown, at. to* Roy Croft. BLPA; FaBoBe; MaRV; NeHB; PoToHe (new ed.); SoP; TIHL; TreFT; TRV
I love you and hate you, but if I can tell. Love and Hate. Catullus. OnPM
I love you as a stranded ship the beach. Enigma. Kenneth Burke. TwAmPo
I Love You Dear. William Allingham. PCH
I love you first because your face is fair. V-Letter. Karl Shapiro. AP; CoBMV; FiMAP; MiAP; MoLP; NYBP; ThLM; TrJP; WaP
I love you for you brownness. To a Dark Girl. Gwendolyn B. Bennett. BANP; CDC
I love you, great new Titan! Soldier: Twentieth Century. Isaac Rosenberg. ChMP; MMA
I love you more than the gilder his gilding. Token. Peggy Bacon. PV

"I love you, mother," said little John. Which Loved Best? "Joy Allison." HH; OHIP; PEDC; WBLP
"I love you, my Lord!" Triolet. Paul T. Gilbert. BOHV; PV
I love you, ox, who pour into my heart. The Ox. Giosuè Carducci. OnPM
I love you, pretty maid, for you are young. Glauce. Aubrey Thomas De Vere. IrPN
"I love you, sweet: how can you ever learn." Youth's Antiphony. Dante Gabriel Rossetti. The House of Life, XIII. MaVP; PoVP; TOP; ViPo; VP
I love you—Titan lover. Girl to Soldier on Leave. Isaac Rosenberg. MMA
I Love You Truly. Carrie Jacobs Bond. TreFS
I love you well, my steel-white dagger. Dagger. Mikhail Yurevich Lermontov. AWP; JAWP; WBP
I love your hands. Your Hands. Angelina Weld Grimké. CDC
I love your lips when they're wet with wine. I Love You. Ella Wheeler Wilcox. BLPA; FaBoBe
I Loved a Lass. George Wither. CH; EnLi-1; HBV; LO; OBEV; PG; UnTE
(Love Sonnet, A.) CLwM; EIL; LiTL; OBS; SeEP; ViBoPo
I loved a love—a royal love. Ireland. Edmund Leamy, Sr. JKCP
I loved a woman. The stars fell from heaven. Ezra Pound. *Fr.* Near Périgord. NP
I loved her for that she was beautiful. My Lady. Philip James Bailey. *Fr.* Festus. LO; OBVV
I loved her, one/ Not learned, save in gracious household ways. Tennyson. *Fr.* The Princess. PGD
I loved him not; and yet now he is gone. The Maid's Lament. Walter Savage Landor. *Fr.* the Citation and Examination of William Shakespeare. GTBS; HBV; OBEV; OBNC; OBRV; OBVV; VA
I loved him three storms ere he loved me again. Love's Flight. Else Lasker-Schüler. TrJP
I Loved, I Love You. Byron. LiTL
I loved my lord, my black-haired lord, my young love. The Magnet. Ruth Stone. MoAmPo (1962 ed.); NePA
I Loved Thee. Robert, Earl Nugent. *See* Epigram: "I loved thee beautiful and kind."
I Loved Thee, Atthis, in the Long Ago. Bliss Carman. CaP
I loved Thee late. Delay. Saint Augustine. SoP
I loved thee long and dearly. Florence Vane. Philip Pendleton Cooke. AA; HBV
I Loved [*or* Lov'd] Thee Once. Sir Robert Ayton. LiTL; OBS; ViBoPo
(On a Woman's Inconstancy.) EIL
(To an Inconstant.) HBV
(To an Inconstant One.) OBEV; QFR
I loved Theotormon. Visions of the Daughters of Albion. Blake. ERoP-1
I loved you first: but afterwards your love. Monna Innominata, IV. Christina Rossetti. ViPo; VP
I Loved You Once. Pushkin, *tr. fr. Russian by* Dudley Randall. AmNP
I, Lysidus, equestrian, offer these. The Golden Spurs. *Unknown.* UnTE
I. M. H. Maurice Baring. ACP (1952 ed.)
I. M. Margaritae Sorori. W. E. Henley. *See* Margaritae Sorori.
I. M.—R. T. Hamilton Bruce. W. E. Henley. *See* Invictus.
I made a footing in the wall. Byron. *Fr.* The Prisoner of Chillon. OBRV
I made a loaf of bread. The White Bird. Roy McFadden. ACV; NeIP
I made a pilgrimage to find the God. Revelation. Edwin Markham. MaRV; OQP; WGRP
I made a posy [*or* posie], while the day ran by. Life. George Herbert. AnAnS-1; BWP; CBEP; EG; EP; HBV; LiTB; MaMe; MeLP; MeP; MePo; NoP; OBS; PoFS; SeCeV; SeCL; SeCP; SeCV-1; SeEP
I made a song for my dear love's delight. A Song's Worth. Susan Marr Spalding. AA
I made a song one morning. Merchandise. Amy Lowell. LaNeLa; MAPA
I made a vow once, one only. Make No Vows. Grace Fallow Norton. NP
I made an armament to overcome. Against Publishing Satires. Colin Ellis. MemP
I made another garden, yea. Song. Arthur O'Shaughnessy. PoVP
I made believe fly. Make Believe. Harry Behn. RePo
I made god upon god. Pygmalion. Hilda Doolittle ("H. D."). WGRP
I made me in a sterile hospital. To Myself on the Occasion of My Twenty-First Century. John Brunner. HYE
I made my fire of little sticks. Little Sticks. Eric Rolls. PoAu-2
I made my song a coat. A Coat. W. B. Yeats. CMoP; GTBS-W; LiTG; LiTM (rev. ed.); ML; PoEL-5
I made myself as a tree. March Hares. Andrew Young. HaMV; MoVE; POTE
I made new speech for you—a secret tongue. Language. Winifred Welles. NP
I made the cross myself whose weight. A Little Parable. Anne Reeve Aldrich. AA; HBV; MaRV
I made the valley mine. Going to Sleep. George Rostrevor Hamilton. MemP
I made them lay their hands in mine and swear. Their Conscience as Their King. Tennyson. *Fr.* Idylls of the King: Guinevere. MaRV; TRV
I made up my mind in early day. The Mexico Trail. *Unknown.* BFSS
I made up my mind to change my way. The Trail to Mexico. *Unknown.* AS, *with music*; CoSo; IHA
I, Maister Andro Kennedy. The Testament of Mr. Andro Kennedy. William Dunbar. OxBS
I make a pact with you, Walt Whitman. A Pact. Ezra Pound. AmPP (5th ed.); CBEP; CBV; ELU; LiTA; ML; MoPW; NePA; OxBA; Po; PoPl
I Make Fallout Too. Thomas Hanna. QAH
I make his crescent fill or lack. Emily Dickinson. CoBA
I make man's ancient food. Bread. Nancy Keesing. PoAu-2
I make my shroud but no one knows. Song. Adelaide Crapsey. AmLP; AnAmPo; HBV; MAP; MoAmPo (1942 ed.); NP; TOP
I make no question of your right to go. Sonnets, III. Muna Lee. HBMV
I make not my division of the hours. Patrick Moloney. Sonnets —Ad Innuptam, I. BoAu
I many times thought peace had come. Emily Dickinson. AmP; AmPP
I marked a cross upon a lonely spot. Traditions. Ramón Campoamor. OnPM
I marked all kindred powers the heart finds fair. Love Enthroned. Dante Gabriel Rossetti. The House of Life, I. CoBE; MaVP; OBNC; PoVP; ViPo; VP
I marked the slow withdrawal of the year. In Memorabilia Mortis. Francis Sherman. CaP
I married in my youth a wife. Epigram. J. V. Cunningham. MoAmPo (1962 ed.); PIA; PV
I married me a wife in the month of June. Risselty Rosselty. *Unknown.* DiPo
I marry'd a wife of late. Keep a Good Tongue in Your Head. Martin Parker. CoMu
I Marvel at the Ways of God. E. B. White. WhC
I marvel not Bassanio was so bold. Portia. Oscar Wilde. BrPo
I marvell'd why a simple child. Only Seven. Henry S. Leigh. BOHV; HBV
I mastered pastoral theology, the Greek of the Apostles. The Minister. Fenton Johnson. AnAmPo; Kal
I, Maximus of Gloucester, to You. Charles Olson. FRC; LiTM (1970 ed.); NeAP
I may as well. The Retired Pork-Butcher and the Spook. G. E. Farrow. BOHV
I may be dead to-morrow, uncaressed. For the Book of Love. Jules Laforgue. AWP; ErPo; LiTW
I may be fast, I may be loose. Apologia. Herbert Farjeon. PV
I may be silent, but. Silent, But. Tsuboi Shigeji. FIW
I may be smelly and I may be old. The River God. Stevie Smith. FaBoTw
I May, I Might, I Must. Marianne Moore. ELU; PoPo; RePo
I may never be as clever as my neighbor down the street. Dad's Greatest Job. *Unknown.* STF
I may not claim. Host and Guest. Henry W. Clark. OQP

I may not keep the heights I gain. For an Hour. Winfred Ernest Garrison. OQP
I may not put my finger forth. Faith. John Richard Moreland. OHIP
I may not touch the hand I saw. A Separation. William Johnson Cory. OBNC
I may not venture to your door. I Send Our Lady. Sister Mary Thérèse. ISi
I may speak with the tongues of men and of angels. The Greatness of Love. First Corinthians, Bible, *N.T., tr. by* James Moffatt. MaRV
I mean/ the fiddleheads have forced their babies. May 10th. Maxine W. Kumin. BoNaP; NYBP
I meant not to defend the scapes of any. Apology for Loose Behavior. Ovid. *Fr.* Amores. UnTE
I Meant to Do My Work Today. Richard Le Gallienne. GoTP; MPB; OTD; PoMa; SP; StaSt; TiPo
(Called Away.) SoPo; SUS
I meant to scrub my floors. My Man Was Here Today. Ruby C. Saunders. WSL
I measure every grief I meet. Emily Dickinson. MAP; MoAB; MoAmPo
I measured myself by the wall in the garden. Day Dreams, or Ten Years Old. Margaret Johnson. BLPA
I meditate upon a swallow's flight. Coole Park, 1929. W. B. Yeats. MBW-2; OBMV; OxBI; PoeP
I meet thy pensive, moonlight face. A Lost Love. Henry Francis Lyte. GTSL
I meet you in an evil time. An Eclogue for Christmas. Louis MacNeice. FaBoMo; MoPo; MoVE; OBMV
I met a child upon the moor. On the Moor. Cale Young Rice. HBV
I met a Jack-o'-Lantern, Hallowe'en. Smiling. Dixie Willson. GFA
I met a lady from the South who said. New Hampshire. Robert Frost. AmPP (4th ed.)
I met a little cottage girl. We Are Seven. Wordsworth. BLPA; EPN; GN; HBV; WBLP
I met a little Elf-man, once. The Little Elf [*or* Elfman]. John Kendrick Bangs. AA; BiCB; BoChLi; BoTP; FaBoBe; GaP; GFA; GoTP; HBV; HBVY; MPB; OTPC (1946 ed.); PCH; PDV; PRWS; SoPo; SP; TiPo; WaKn
I met a man as I went walking. Puppy and I. A. A. Milne. BoTP; FaPON; PDV; SoPo; TiPo
I met a man in older lands. On the Safe Side. Lord Dunsany. OxBI
I met a man in South Street, tall. Cutty Sark. Hart Crane. *Fr.* The Bridge. AmPP; FaBoMo; LiTA; NP
I met a man mowing. Hay Harvest. Patrick R. Chalmers. BoTP
I met a man the other day. The Counselor. Dorothy Parker. InMe
I met a ragged man. The Song. Theodore Roethke. AP; CrMA; FiMAP
I met a sad girl in our town. Poem. Keith Sinclair. ACV
I met a seer. The Book of Wisdom. Stephen Crane. *Fr.* The Black Riders. CoBA; HoPM; MAP; MoAmPo
I met a seer. Eidólons. Walt Whitman. AmePo
I met a toad. Warty Bliggens, the Toad. Don Marquis. *Fr.* Archy and Mehitabel. FiBHP
I met a traveller from an antique land. Ozymandias Revisited. Morris Bishop. ALV
I met a traveler [*or* traveller] from an antique land. Ozymandias [of Egypt]. Shelley. ATP; AWP; BEL; BeLS; BoLiVe; CABA; CaFP; CBEP; CBV; CH; CLwM; CoBE; DiPo; EnL; EnLi-2; EnLit; EnRP; EPN; ERoP-2; ExPo; FaBoBe; FaBoCh; FaBoEn; FaFP; FiP; ForPo; GoTP; GTBS; GTBS-D; GTBS-P; GTBS-W; GTSE; GTSL; HBV; HBVY; HoPM; HT; ILP; InP; InPo; JAWP; LoBV; LoGBV; MaPo; MaRV; MBW-2; MCCG; MERP; MyFE; NeHB; NoP; OAEP; OBNC; OTD; OTPC (1946 ed.); OuHeWo; PAn; PG (1955 ed.); Po; PoAn; PoE; PoFS; PoG; PoIE; PoLF; PoPo; PoRA; PoSa; PTK; RoGo; SeCeV; ShBV-3; Sonn; StP; SyP; TDP; TIHL; TOP; TreF; TrGrPo; UnPo (1st ed.); WaKn; WBP; WHA; YAT
I met an elf-man in the woods. How to Treat Elves. Morris Bishop. FiBHP; PoPl
I met an honest man today. Alien. William Price Turner. OxBS
I Met at Eve. Walter de la Mare. HBMV
I met ayont the cairney. Empty Vessel. "Hugh MacDiarmid." FaBoTw; OxBS
I Met by Chance. Heine, *tr. fr. German by* John Todhunter. AWP
I met four guinea hens today. Life. Alfred Kreymborg. ELU
I met God in the morning. The Secret [*or* His Presence Came Like Sunrise]. Ralph Spaulding Cushman. BLRP; FaChP; MaRV; SoP; STF; TRV
I met her as a blossom on a stem. The Dream. Theodore Roethke. AmP; MoVE; NoP; NYBP
I Met Her in the Garden Where the Praties Grow, *with music. Unknown.* AS
I met her on the Umbrian Hills. The Lady Poverty. Evelyn Underhill. CAW; HBV
I met him again, he was trudging along. I Fights Mit Sigel! Grant P. Robinson. BLPA
I met Louisa in the shade. Louisa. Wordsworth. EnRP
I met Murder on the way. Shelley. *Fr.* The Masque of Anarchy. PoG
I met ol' Satan on the way. Hell and Heaven. *Unknown.* OxBoLi
I met Poetry, an old prostitute walking. Moral Story II. David Wright. ChMP; PeSA
I met the Bishop on the road. Crazy Jane Talks with the Bishop. Yeats. AtBAP; CABA; CBV; CMoP; CoBMV; DiPo; ErPo; ExPo; ILP; LiTG; LiTM (rev. ed.); OAEP (2d ed.); PAn; PoeP
I met the boss; he wanted me to go. On the Trail to Idaho. *Unknown.* CoSo; PoRL
I met the boy from Donegal, sez I, "Come here a minute." Sheskinbeg. Elizabeth Shane. HBMV
I met the Love-Talker one eve in the glen. The Love-Talker. "Ethna Carbery." AnIV; CH; OnYI; OxBI
I Met the Master [Face to Face]. *Unknown.* BePJ; BLRP; PoLF; SoP; STF
I met the yawning of my appetite. The North of Wales. Herbert Morris. NePoAm-2
I met three children on the road. Three Children near Clonmel. Eileen Shanahan. OnYI; OxBI
I met with a country lass. The Thankful Country Lass; or, The Jolly Batchelor Kindly Entertained. *Unknown.* CoMu
I met with a jovial girl. The Roaring Lad and the Ranting Lass; or, A Merry Couple Madly Met. *Unknown.* CoMu
I met with Death in his country. Lord Dunsany. Songs from an Evil Wood, III. MoBrPo (1942 ed.)
I met with the girls coming from afar off. Love-Song of the Water Carriers. *Unknown.* PeSA
I met you often when you were visiting princes. On Meeting Li Kuei-Nien down the River. Tu Fu. LiTW
I mid the hills was born. Harold the Valiant. Mary Elizabeth Hewitt Stebbins. AA
I might be better busied; I grant so. Ad Zoilum. John Heath. TuPP
I might have climbed up Calvary. A Follower. Daisy Conway Price. ChIP
I might have said a word of cheer. If I Had Known. Mary Virginia Terhune. SoP
I might have touched you where you lay. Quarrel. Jean McDougall. GoBC; JKCP (1955 ed.)
I might not, if I could. Lines by a Medium. *Unknown.* NA
I might—unhappy word—oh me, I might. Astrophel and Stella, XXXIII. Sir Philip Sidney. FCP; OBSC; ReEn; SiPS; Sonn; TuPP
I mind as 'ow the night afore that show. The Chances. Wilfred Owen. MMA
I mind, love how it ever was this way. Bed-Time. Ralph M. Jones. HBMV
I mind me in the days departed. The Deserted Garden. Elizabeth Barrett Browning. HBV; OBEV (1st ed.)
I Mind That I Went Round with Men and Women. Bilhana, *formerly at. to* Chauras, *tr. fr. Sanskrit by* E. Powys Mathers. *Fr.* Black Marigolds. OnPM
I Mind the Coming. Bilhana, *formerly at. to* Chauras, *tr. fr. Sanskrit by* E. Powys Mathers. *Fr.* Black Marigolds. OnPM
I Mind the Time of the Falling of Blossoms. Bilhana, *formerly at. to* Chauras, *tr. fr. Sanskrit by* E. Powys Mathers. *Fr.* Black Marigolds. OnPM

I mingle with your bones. The One Lost. Isaac Rosenberg. MoBrPo
I miss the polished brass, the powerful black horses. On the Road to Woodlawn. Theodore Roethke. FiMAP
I miss you in the morning, dear. Miss You. *Unknown.* PoToHe (new ed.)
I miss you now. To Mareta. Herschell Johnson. WSL
I missed him when the sun began to bend. Lost and Found. George Macdonald. FaChP; MaRV; OQP; StJW; TRV; WGRP
I Mix in Life. Samuel Taylor Coleridge. CBEP
I mock thee not, though I by thee am mockèd. To Flaxman [*or* Epigram]. Blake. OxBoLi; SiTL
I mourn for Adonis—Adonis is dead. Bion's Lament for Adonis. Bion, *tr. by* Elizabeth Barrett Browning. ATP
I mourn not those who lose their vital breath. Better to Be Brave. Lucillius. OnPM
I mourn "Patroclus," whilst I praise. My Last Terrier. John Halsham. HBV
I move amid your throng, I watch you hold. Sonnets to Miranda, VI. Sir William Watson. HBV
I moved, to keep the moon. On Aesthetics, More or Less. Peter Kane Dufault. NYBP
I Mun Be Married a Sunday. Nicholas Udall. *Fr.* Ralph Roister Doister. EIL
I Murder Hate by Field or Flood. Burns. CBEP; NCEP (Lines on War.) CBV
I must/ Not trust. Anacreontike. Robert Herrick. SCEP-2
I Must and I Will Get Married, *with music.* *Unknown.* TrAS
I Must Away. May Sarson. BoTP
I must be dreaming through the days. Experience. Lesbia Harford. BoAu; PoAu-1
I must be flattered. The imperious. Modern Love, XXVIII. George Meredith. ViPo; VP
"I must be going, no longer staying." The Grey Cock. *Unknown.* ELP
I must be mad, or very tired. Meeting-House Hill. Amy Lowell. AmPP (3d ed.); LoGBV; MAP; MoAmPo; NeMA; NP; OxBA; PFY; PoRA (rev. ed.)
I Must Complain, Yet Do Enjoy My Love. *At. to* Thomas Campion. EP
("I must complayne she doth enjoye my love," *diff. vers.*) SeCSL
I must confess that often I'm. *Time* Like an Ever-rolling Stream. P. G. Wodehouse. FiBHP
I must depart, but like to his last breath. Parted Souls. Lord Herbert of Cherbury. AnAnS-2; SeCP
I must explain why it is that at night. Still Life. Reed Whittemore. CoAP
I must go back to a vest again, to a winter vest with sleeves. April. Godfrey Fox Bradby. ShBV-1
I must go back to the small place. Resolve. Vassar Miller. TPM
I must go down to the seas again, to the lonely sea and the sky. Sea Fever. John Masefield. BEL; BoChLi; BoLiVe; CMoP; EnLi-2 (1949 ed.); EnLit; EtS; FaBoBe; FaBV; FaPON; GBV; GTBS; GTSL; HBV; HBVY; MCCG; MoAB; MoBrPo; MPB; NeHB; NeMA; OBVV; OHFP; OTD; OtMeF; OTPC (1946 ed.); PCD; PDV; PoLF; PoMa; PoPl; PoPo; RePo; RG; ShBV-1; SP; StVeCh; TIHL; TiPo; TOP; TreF; TrGrPo; WHA; YAT; YT
I Must Go Walk the Wood[s]. *Unknown.* CBEP; MeEL
I Must go Walk the Wood So Wild. *Unknown.* NCEP (Wood So Wild, The.) WiR
I must have passed the crest a while ago. The Long Hill. Sara Teasdale. HBMV; LiTA; LiTM; MAP; MoAmPo; PoPl
I must have wanton poets, pleasant wits. Christopher Marlowe. *Fr.* Edward the Second, I, i. ViBoPo
I must laugh and dance and sing. Youth. Aline Thomas. MPB
I Must Light a Candle. Gertrude Hanson. ChIP
I must needs say, were thou mine own brother. Aliud. Thomas Freeman. TuPP
I must not gaze at them although. The Barrier. Claude McKay. BANP
I must not grieve my Love, whose eyes would read. To Delia, XLVIII. Samuel Daniel. EIL; HBV; OBEV
I must not say that thou wast true. Euphrosyne. Matthew Arnold. MBW-2; VP
I Must Not Tease My Mother. Lydia Huntley Sigourney. OTPC (1923 ed.)
I must not think of thee; and, tired yet strong. Renouncement. Alice Meynell. AnFE; BoLP; BoPe; CAW; EnLit; GTSL; HBV; LiTL; LO; MeWo; MoBrPo; OBEV; OBMC; OBNC; OBVV; PoVP; Sonn; TOP; TreFT; VA; ViBoPo
I must not throw upon the floor. The Crust of Bread. *Unknown.* HBV; HBVY; OTPC (1923 ed.)
I must possess you utterly. Possession. Richard Aldington. MoBrPo
I must remember. Shelley Silverstein. PoSC
I must remember to dismiss. Nature Study, After Dufy. Helen Bevington. NYBP
I must tell you. The Grass. George Bowering. MoCV
I Must, Varus, Tell You. Catullus, *tr. fr. Latin by* Peter Whigham. ML
I, my dear, was born to-day. On My Birthday, July 21. Matthew Prior. OBEV
I myself like the climate of New York. The Climate. Edwin Denby. ANYP
I myself saw furious with blood. Aeneas at Washington. Allen Tate. AP; LiTA; MoPo; MoVE; NePA; OxBA
"I myself will now go home and see." Homer. *Fr.* The Iliad, VI. ReIE
I nebber see de like since I beeen born. Johnny Come Down to Hilo. *Unknown.* ABF; SoAmSa
I need a little stick when I. I Have to Have It. Dorothy Aldis. SoPo
I need a strength to keep me true. My Need. *Unknown.* STF
I Need No Sky. Witter Bynner. EaLo
I Need Not Go. Thomas Hardy. DTC; EG; OBEV (new ed.); OBVV
I need not leave the jostling world. The Shut Door. *Unknown.* SoP
I need not shout my faith. Thrice eloquent. Silence. Charles Hanson Towne. MaRV; OQP; TRV; WGRP
I need not your needles, they're needless to me. The Baker's Reply to the Needle Peddler. *Unknown.* OxNR; SiTL
I need so much the quiet of your love. At Nightfall. Charles Hanson Towne. BLPA; FaBoBe; NeHB; PoToHe (new ed.)
I Need Thee. George Macdonald. FaChP; MaRV
I Need Thee. Frederick Whitfield. BePJ
I Need Thee, Precious Jesus. *Unknown.* BePJ
I need Thee, precious Jesus! I Need Thee. Frederick Whitfield. BePJ
I Need Wide Spaces. *Unknown.* SoP
I Needed the Quiet. Alice Hansche Mortenson. SoP
I ne'er could any luster see. Air. Sheridan. *Fr.* The Duenna. HBV
I ne'er deserved the glorious name of poet. Of His Muse. Sir John Harington. SiCE
I Ne'er Was Struck. John Clare. ELP (First Love.) ChTr; EnLoPo; NoP
I never asked you to be perfect—did I? The Imperfect Lover. Siegfried Sassoon. BrPo
I never build a song by night or day. My Comrade. Edwin Markham. AA
"I never can do it," the little kite said. How the Little Kite Learned to Fly. *Unknown.* GFA; HBV; HBVY; OTPC; TVC
I never can rest when hills are before me. The Mount of Blessing. William M. Runyan. FaChP
I never crossed your threshold with a grief. The Closed Door. Theodosia Garrison. BLPA; PoToHe
I never cut my neighbor's throat. Guilty. Marguerite Wilkinson. MaRV; OQP; TRV
I never did on cleft Parnassus dream. Prologue to the First Satire. Persius. *Fr.* Satires. AWP
I never drank of Aganippe well. Astrophel and Stella, LXXIV. Sir Philip Sidney. CABA; EnRePo; FCP; OBSC; ReEn; ReIE; SiCE; SiPS; Sonn; TuPP
I never even hear. Whistles. Rachel Field. GFA; StVeCh (1955 ed.); TiPo
I Never Even Suggested It. Ogden Nash. FiBHP; LiTA; LiTL; LiTM; PoLF; SiTL
I never forget a face. You're So Kind. Groucho Marx. SiTL
I never gave a lock of hair away. Elizabeth Barrett Browning. Sonnets from the Portuguese, XVIII. HBV; VA
I never got a telegram before. Telegram. William Wise. TiPo (1959 ed.)
I never had a happier time. One Saturday. "Marian Douglas." AA
I never had a piece of toast. James Payn. CenHV

I never had walked quite so far. Alone. Joseph Paget-Fredericks. StVeCh
I never have got the bearings quite. The Flag. James Jeffrey Roche. PaA; PAH
I never have had a look at the sea. Recompense. Grace Noll Crowell. PCD
I never have seen the snow so white. Christmas Birthday. Grace Ellen Glaubitz. BiCB; SiSoSe
I never hear it ring without. The Door-Bell. Charlotte Becker. PoToHe (new ed.)
I never hear that one is dead. Emily Dickinson. MoVE
I never hear the word "escape." Emily Dickinson. CMoP; NCEP; NeMA
"I never hurt maid in all my time." The Death of Robin Hood. *Unknown.* ViBoPo
I Never Knew. Glenn E. Wagoner. STF
I never knew a kangaroo. Pockets. Rowena Bennett. RePo
I Never Knew a Night So Black. John Kendrick Bangs. MaRV; OTD; PoToHe
I never knew before/ The meaning of this love. Thomas Lovell Beddoes. *Fr.* Death's Jest Book. LO
I never knew how words were vain. Rain. Kenneth Slade Alling. HBMV
I never knew Jews could show such. Nationalism. Dan Simmons. WSL
I never knew the earth had so much gold. Feuerzauber. Louis Untermeyer. NP; TrJP
I never knew the old, brown violin. The Old Violin. Dorothy M. Barter-Snow. SoP
I never knew what real peace meant. I Never Knew. Glenn E. Wagoner. STF
I never laie me downe to rest. *Unknown.* SeCSL
I never like the fellow's plan. The Down-Pullers. Walter E. Isenhour. STF
I never look upon the sea. Aunt Zillah Speaks. Herbert Palmer. FaBoTw
I never look'd that he should live so long. John of Launoy. Sir Henry Taylor. *Fr.* Philip van Artevelde. VA
I never lost as much but twice. Emily Dickinson. AmePo; AP; CBV; MAP; MoAB; MoAmPo; MWA-2
I never loved your plains! Hills. Arthur Guiterman. HBVY; MaRV; PoMa; RePo; YT
I never muse upon my lady's grace. George Edward Woodberry. Ideal Passion, XXV. HBMV
I never played the Moor. Unfriendly Witness. George Starbuck. CBV
I never prayed for Dryads, to haunt the woods again. An Invocation. William Johnson Cory. HBV; OBVV
I never quite know/ How the Pooka looks. Shape-Changer. Ella Young. BoChLi (1950 ed.)
I never *quite* saw fairy-folk. Very Nearly. Queenie Scott-Hopper. FaPON; MPB; OTPC (1946 ed.); SoPo; TVC
I never read of any enforceable regulation. Because Sometimes You Can't Always Be So. Kenneth Patchen. NaP
I never realized God's birth before. Robert Browning. *Fr.* The Ring and the Book. ChIP
I never really like this cat though she is. V is for Victory, as You Can Plainly See. Marsden Hartley. LiTM
I never reared a young gazelle. 'Twas Ever Thus. Henry S. Leigh. BOHV; HBV
I never saw a man who looked. Oscar Wilde. *Fr.* The Ballad of Reading Gaol. PoFr
I never saw a moor. Emily Dickinson. AA; AmePo; AmPP; AnNE; AP; ATP; BBV; CBEP; CBV; CoBA; DiPo; EvOK; FaFP; FaPON; GN; GoTP; GTBS-W; HBV; LiTA; LiTM (rev. ed.); MAP; MaRV; MoAB; MPB; MWA-2; NeMA; NePA; OQP; OTD; OTPC; PoLF; PoPl; PoPo; PTK; SP; TIHL; TiPo (1952 ed.); TOP; TreF; TrGrPo; TRV; WGRP
I never saw a puppy that. Hot Weather. Dorothy Aldis. GFA
I never saw a Purple Cow. The Purple Cow. Gelett Burgess. BOHV; CenHV; FaFP; FaPON; FiBHP; HBV; HBVY; InP; LBN; LiTM; NA; NeHB; NePA; PDV; PoLF; PoPl; SiTL; SoPo; StaSt; TiPo; TreFS; TSW; YaD
"I never saw a Purple Cow." Diversions of the Re-echo Club. Carolyn Wells. BOHV
I never saw my father old. A Celebration. May Sarton. NePoAm 2
I never saw the morning till to-day. Chariot. Witter Bynner. HBMV
I never saw you, madam, lay [*or* sawe my ladye laye] apart. The Cornet [*or* Complaint That His Ladie. . .Kept Her Face Always Hidden from Him.] Earl of Surrey. FCP; OBSC; PoEL-1; PoIE; SiPS
I never see the colored boats of night. The Age of Sheen. Dorothy Hughes. NYBP
I never see the newsboys run. Fleet Street. Shane Leslie. OnYI
I Never See the Red Rose. John Masefield. *Fr.* Sonnets ("Long long ago"). CMoP; EnLi-2 (1949 ed.); InP (Sonnet: "I never see the red rose crown the year.") GoYe
I never see upon a hill. Symbols. John Richard Moreland. ChIP; PGD
I never set my two eyes on a head was so fine as your head. A Translation from Walther von der Vogelweide. J. M. Synge. MoBrPo
I Never Shall Love the Snow Again. Robert Bridges. BrPo; CH; CMoP; FaBV; OAEP
I never speak a word. Mary Austin. *Fr.* Rhyming Riddles. TiPo
I never stoop'd so low, as they. Negative Love. John Donne. MaMe; ReEn; SCEP-1
I never swung a staff and deep, oh deep. Sonnet. Roy Daniells. PeCV
I never thought that youth would go. Youth. Jessie B. Rittenhouse. HBMV
I never wander where the bord'ring reeds. Fly-fishing. John Gay. *Fr.* Rural Sports. SD
I never was attached to that great sect. The Longest Journey. Shelley. *Fr.* Epipsychidion. OtMeF
I never watch the sun set a-down the Western skies. Visions. Edmund Leamy. BBV; GBV (1922 ed.); JKCP
I never went to Mamble. Mamble. John Drinkwater. WePo
I never will complain of my dear husband, Mrs. Henn. He Didn't Oughter. A. P. Herbert. ALV; FiBHP
I notic'd how the spent and speechless year. Time Lags Abed. D'Arcy Cresswell. AnNZ
I notified the Chasm Inspector about. A Chasm. Michael Silverton. PV
I, now at Carthage. He, shot dead at Rome. *Vale* from Carthage (Spring, 1944.) Peter Viereck. LiTM (1970 ed.); MiAP; MoAmPo (1950 ed.); PoPo
I now mean to be serious—it is time. Lady Adeline Amundeville. Byron. *Fr.* Don Juan. PoEL-4
I now remembered slowly how I came. The Journey. Yvor Winters. MoVE
I now think[e], Love is rather deaf[e], then blind. My Picture Left in Scotland. Ben Jonson. AnAnS-2; EnRePo; ForPo; LiTL; MePo; PIA; PoEL-2; QFR; SeCP; SeCV-1
I nursed it in my bosom while it lived. Memory. Christina Rossetti. OBNC
I objurgate the centipede. The Centipede. Ogden Nash. FaPON
I observe: "Our sentimental friend, the moon!" Conversation Galante. T. S. Eliot. HBMV; MAP; MoAmPo (1942 ed.)
I, Oedipus, the club-foot, made to stumble. Oedipus. Edwin Muir. CMoP
I offer Thee. Praise to Thee [*or* Rune of Praise]. *Unknown.* FaChP; WHL
I offer wrong to my beloved Saint. Caelica, XVIII. Fulke Greville. NCEP
I offered the donkey. Ilo Orleans. RIS
I oft have heard men say there be. William Browne. LO
I oft have heard of Lydford law. Lydford Journey. William Browne. CavP
I oft stand in the snow at dawn. Don Marquis. *Fr.* To a Lost Sweetheart. FiBHP
I often have been told. The *Constitution* and the *Guerrière.* *Unknown.* PAH
I often have to wonder. Snoring. Aileen Fisher. SoPo
I often have wondered how women love men. Green Grows the Laurel. *Unknown.* BFSS
I often in the evening meet with birds. Black Spirit. Tom Poots. FiSC
I often picture you among the flowers. Mother. Sister M. Eulalia. WHL
I often say my prayers. Do I Really Pray? [*or* Prayer]. John Burton. MaRV; SoP; STF
I often say to my sad heart. Prose Poem: The Irremediable. Emile Hennequin. OnPM

I often see a puffy toad. The Proud Toad. Grace Taber Hallock. RePo
I often see flowers from a passing car. A [*or* The] Passing Glimpse. Robert Frost. InP; NeMA
I often sit and wish that I. A Wish [*or* A Kite]. Frank Dempster Sherman. BoChLi (1950 ed.); PCH; SoPo; TiPo; TVC
I Often Think of Writing Home, *with music.* John A. Stone. SGR
I often wander on the beach. The Old Swimmer. Christopher Morley. SD
I often wish I were King. If I Were King. A. A. Milne. RePo
I often wish that I had been alive. God's Youth. Louis Untermeyer. PFY
I often wonder as the fairy-story. The Lucky Marriage. Thomas Blackburn. GTBS-P
I often wonder how it is. My Playmate. Mary I. Osborn. BoTP
I on Hesiod idly browsing. Reading Hesiod. Marcus Argentarius. WoL
I on my horse, and Love on me, doth try. Astrophel and Stella, XLIX. Sir Philip Sidney. FCP; NoP; ReEn; SiPS
I once conjectur'd that those tygers hard. Seaconk or Rehoboths Fate. Benjamin Tompson. SCAP
I once had a gal and I loved her well. When I Was a Brave Cowboy. *Unknown.* CoSo
I once had a sweet little doll, dears. The Lost Doll [*or Song].* *Charles Kingsley. Fr.* The Water Babies. FaPON; MoShBr; MPB; OTPC; PaPo; PRWS; SoPo; TiPo; TVC
I once had money and a friend. Money and a Friend. *Unknown.* BLPA; NeHB
I once in happy times. The Dove. William Barnes. BiS
I once may see, when years shall [*or* may] wreck my wrong. To Delia, XXXIV [*or* Beauty's Glass]. Samuel Daniel, *after* Philippe Desportes. ONPM; ReIE
I once possessed this happiness: to bind. The Master of Time. Jan van Nijlen. LiTW
I once thought that snowflakes were feathers. Snowflakes. Marchette Chute. PDV
I once was a guest at a nobleman's wedding. The Nobleman's Wedding. William Allingham. IrPN
I Once Was a Maid. Burns. *Fr.* The Jolly Beggars. OxBoLi; SiTL; UnTE
I once was a stranger to grace and to God. Jehovah Tsidkenu—The Lord Our Righteousness. Robert Murray McCheyne. SoP
I once wrote a letter as follows. The Invoice. Robert Creeley. AmPC; FRC
I Only Am Escaped Alone to Tell Thee. Howard Nemerov. CoAP; NePA
I only have a little time. Only a Little Time. *Unknown.* SoP
I only keep this voice to give to anything afraid of me. William Knott. YAP
I only kissed her hand. A Possibility. Carolyn Wells. ALV
I only knew one poet in my life. How It Strikes a Contemporary. Robert Browning. CABL; CTC; GTBS-P; MaVP; MBW-2; NoP; PoVP; PP; ViPo; ViPP
I open my family magazine, pretty. Card Burning in Central Park. William Hathaway. QAH
I open my scuttle at night and see the far-sprinkled systems. Walt Whitman. *Fr.* Song of Myself. PFY
I opened the old, old Bible. The Old, Old Bible. Marianne Farmingham. SoP
I opened the window wide and leaned. John Masefield. *Fr.* The Everlasting Mercy. WGRP
I ordered this, this clean wood box. The Arrival of the Bee Box. Sylvia Plath. NaP; TPM
I Ought to Weep. *Unknown.* MeEL
I owe, says Metius, much to Colon's care. Epigram. Leonard Welsted. ALV
I own John Graydon's place. John Graydon. Wilson MacDonald. ACV; CaP
I owned a little boat a while ago. The Master of My Boat [*or* The Boat]. Joseph Addison Richards, *wr. at. to* George Macdonald. MaRV; OQP; SoP
I pace the sounding sea-beach and behold. Milton. Longfellow. AA; AmePo; AmLP; AmP; AmPP; AP; AWP; InPo; MAmP; MWA-1; NePA; NoP; StP; TOP; TrGrPo
I paced alone on the road across the field. The Home. Rabindranath Tagore. GoJo
I paid a man at Martinmas. The Plowman. Burns. UnTE
I paint so ill, my peece had need to bee. With a Picture Sent to a Friend. Richard Crashaw. MaMe
I Paint What I See. E. B. White. LiTM; NAMP; NYBP; PoFr
I painted her a gushing thing. Disillusioned. "Lewis Carroll." CenHV
I painted on the roof of a skycraper. People Who Must. Carl Sandburg. OCS; PDV; SAS
I paints and paints. Shirley Brooks. CenHV
I park the car half in the ditch and switch off and sit. Stealing Trout. Ted Hughes. NYBP
I Pass a Lighted Window. Clement Wood. HBMV
I pass all my hours in a shady old grove. Song. *At. to* Charles II, King of England. SeCL
I Pass in Silence. John Clare. BoLP
I pass my days among the quiet places. Hallowed Places. Alice Freeman Palmer. HBV
I pass the vale. I breast the steep. Onward and Upward. John Charles Earle. MaRV
I passed a tomb among green shades. Her Rival for Aziza. *Unknown. Fr.* The Thousand and One Nights. AWP
I passed a wood of beech trees yesterday. Beech Trees. Sister Mary Madeleva. BBV (1951 ed.)
I passed along the water's edge below the humid trees. The Indian upon God. W. B. Yeats.. MoBrPo; ViPo (1962 ed.); WGRP
I passed by a garden, a little Dutch garden. A Little Dutch Garden. Harriet Whitney Durbin. OTPC (1946 ed.)
I passed beside the reverend walls. *See* I past beside the reverend walls.
I passed by the beach. Three Poems from the Japanese, I. Yamabe no Akahito, *tr. fr. Japanese by* Kenneth Rexroth. HoPM
I passed by the house of the young man who loves me. Love Song. *Unknown.* TTY
I passed Olympus in the night. Tourist. Mark Van Doren. NePoAm-2
I passed through the gates of the city. Life and Nature. Archibald Lampman. PeCV
I past [*or* passed] beside the reverend walls. In Memoriam A. H. H., LXXXVII. Tennyson. CoBE; EPN; OAEP; ViPo; VP
I pause, amidst the clamor of the swiftly moving days. Stock-Taking. Joan Suisted. SoP
I pause not now to speak of Raleigh's dream. John Smith's Approach to Jamestown. James Barron Hope. MC; PAH
I paused in a garden alley of cypress and rose, resembling Paradise. Last Things. Kathleen Raine. NYBP
I paused last eve beside the blacksmith's door. *See* Last eve I passed beside a blacksmith's door.
I Peeled Bits of Straw. John Clare. PeER
(Bits of Straw.) WiR
I peeped through the window. *Unknown.* OxNR
I, per se I, I sing on. Carol on Corfu. Lawrence Durrell. MemP
I perceive the cow's slightly. Life in the Country. Michael Silverton. ELU
I picked a primrose, pale as death. Phyllis M. Lubbock. LO
I picked fresh mint. My Garden. Norah Hussey. BoTP
I picked up my mother. Ishikawa Takuboku, *tr. fr. Japanese by* Kenneth Rexroth. LiTW
I picked up six black stones on the beach today. Runes. Emmett Jarrett. ThO
I picked up the clod. The Clod. Edwin Curran. HBMV
I picture her there in the quaint old room. Dreaming in the Trenches. William Gordon McCabe. AA
I pitch my tent on this camp ground, few days, few days. Few Days. *Unknown.* ABF
I pitched my day's leazings in Crimmercrock Lane. The Dark-eyed Gentleman. Thomas Hardy. MoAB; MoBrPo; PoeP; PoIE
I pitied one whose tattered dress. The Vesture of the Soul. "*AE.*" ACV
I pity the slender Mother-maid. The Lonely Crib. Leonard Feeney. WHL
I placed/ my hand. Misunderstanding. Irving Layton. PV
I placed a jar in Tennessee. Anecdote of the Jar. Wallace Stevens. AmPP (5th ed.); AP; CaFP; CBV; CMoP; CoBMV; ExPo; FosPo; GTBS-W; LiTA; MaPo (1969 ed.); MoAB; MoAmPo; MoVE; NePA; OxBA; PAn; PoAn; PoeP; PoIE; VaPo

I planted beans at the foot of the Southern Mountain. Planting Beans. T'ao Ch'ien. OnPM
I Planted Little Trees To-day. James B. Carrington. PEDC
I Planted My Bright Paradise. Alexandr Blok, *tr. fr. Russian by* Michael Daly. HW
"I play for Seasons, not Eternities!" Modern Love, XIII. George Meredith. EPN; FaBoEn; OBNC; PoIE; Sonn; ViPo; VP
I play it cool. Motto. Langston Hughes. PoNe (1970 ed.)
I play my garden is a church. An Easter Surprise. Leona Covey. GFA
I play the Masonic Funeral March. Birmingham. Julia Fields. PoNe (1970 ed.)
I played a game of baseball, I belong to Casey's Nine. Slide, Kelly, Slide. J. W. Kelly. FaFP; TreFS
I played I was two polar bears. The Bear Hunt. Margaret Widdemer. FaPON; MPB; UTS
I Played on the Grass with Mary. Ernest Walsh. ErPo
I played with you 'mid cowslips blowing. Love and Age. Thomas Love Peacock. *Fr.* Gryll Grange. HBV; OBEV; OBNC; ViBoPo
"I Pledge Allegiance." Valerie Tarver. TNV
I pluck the white hibiscus. Mr. A. E. Housman on the Olymic Games, *parody.* E. V. Knox. WhC
I plucked a honeysuckle where. The Honeysuckle. Dante Gabriel Rossetti. CBEP; PoVP; SyP
I plucked a throstle from the throat of God. The Thrush. Timothy Corsellis. LiTM; WaaP; WaP
I plucked a willow switch. The Willow Switch. Douglas Gibson. NYTB
I plucked pink blossoms from mine apple-tree. An Apple Gathering. Christina Rossetti. BoLP; OBNC; PoVP
I plucked the berry from the bush, the brown nut from the tree. William Motherwell. *See* I've plucked the berry. . .
I, Pluto. Tilottama Daswani. ACV
I ply with all the cunning of my art. The Craftsman. Marcus B. Christian. PoNe
I ponder how He died, despairing once. Before an Old Painting of the Crucifixion. N. Scott Momaday. QFR
I Ponder on Life. Max Ehrmann. PoToHe (new ed.)
I pop my whip, I bring the blood. Ox-driving Song. *Unknown.* OuSiCo
I Praise. Rainer Maria Rilke, *tr. fr. German by* Jessie Lemont. OnPM
I praise a snakeskin or a stone. Snakeskin and Stone. Keith Douglas. NePoEA
I praise the Frenchman, his remark was shrewd. William Cowper. *Fr.* Retirement. BLPA; NeHB
I Praise the Tender Flower. Robert Bridges. EG
I praise Thee not, with impious pride. Sir Lewis Morris. *Fr.* A Heathen Hymn. TrPWD
I praise those ancient Chinamen. Hymnus ad Patrem Sinensis. Philip Whalen. FRC
I pray attend unto this jest. The Fair Maid of the West. *Unknown.* CoMu
I pray for courage to receive the light. A Blind Man Prays. Catherine Baird. SoP
I pray for you, and yet I do not frame. A Prayer. Mary Dixon Thayer. MaRV
I pray! My little body and whole span. Supplication of the Black Aberdeen. Kipling. BLPA
I pray not for the joy that knows. A Prayer. Marion Franklin Ham. TrPWD
"I pray," said Rolfe, "a word." Ungar and Rolfe. Herman Melville. *Fr.* Clarel. OxBA
I pray that you may never have. I Bid You Keep Some Few Small Dreams. Helen Frazee-Bower. MoSiPe
I pray the prayer the Easterners do. Salaam Alaikum. *Unknown.* PoLF
I pray thee, Dante, shouldst thou meet with Love. Sonnet: To Dante Alighieri (He Mistrusts the Love of Lapo Gianni). Guido Cavalcanti. AWP
I Pray Thee Leave, Love Me No More. Michael Drayton. *See* To His Coy Love.
I pray Thee O Lord. A Prayer. Julian Tuwim. TrJP
I Pray You. Thomas Moore. *Fr.* Odes to Nea. OBNC; OBRV
I pray you all give [*or* gyve] your audience [*or* audyence]. Everyman. *Unknown.* BEL; EnLi-1; MeEV; PoEL-1
I pray you, in your letters. Shakespeare. *Fr.* Othello, V, ii. InP
I pray you, let us roam no more. I Pray You. Thomas Moore. *Fr.* Odes to Nea. OBNC; OBRV
I pray you what's asleep? As the Day Breaks. Ernest McGaffey. AA
I pray you've finished. Candy Bar. Tom Vietch. ANYP
I prayed for help, I prayed for strength. Thou Art My Victory. Avis B. Christiansen. SoP
I prayed for strength, and then I lost awhile. The Answered Prayer. Annie Johnson Flint. STF
I prayed, "Lord, take away the pain." Remembrance. Grace V. Watkins. SoP
I prayed then to the beam, blithe in mood. The Poet Prays to the Cross. *Unknown.* *Fr.* The Dream of the Rood. PoLi
I prayed to see the face of God. The Back of God. J. R. Perkins. MaRV; OQP
I preached as never sure to preach again. A Preacher's Urgency. Richard Baxter. *Fr.* Love Breathing Thanks and Praise. MaRV; TRV
I prepare for night changes. Michyle White. WSL
I press [*or* presse] not to the quire, nor dare I greet. To My Worthy Friend Mr. [*or* Master] George Sands [on His Translation of the Psalmes]. Thomas Carew. AnAnS-2; MeLP; MePo; OBS; SCEP-2; SeCV-1; SeEP
I Pressed Her Rebel Lips. *Unknown.* ErPo
I prethee, Clodius, tell me what's the reason. To Clodius. Everard Guilpin. *Fr.* Skialetheia. ReIE
I prethee let my heart alone. Song. Thomas Stanley. AnAnS-2; ViBoPo
I Prithee Send Me Back My Heart. Sir John Suckling. EnLit; SeCL
(Send Back My Heart.) MeWo
(Song: "I prithee send me back my heart.") HBV; LiTL; SCEP-2; SeEP; ViBoPo
(To My Love.) ALV
I prithee spare me, gentle boy. Song. Sir John Suckling. BWP
I prithee Sweet to me be kind. *Unknown.* SeCSL
I proclaim Thee great and wonderful. Psalm. Murilo Mendes. MoRP
I, proclaiming that there is. The Dancer at Cruachan and Cro-Patrick. W. B. Yeats. UnS
I Promise Thee. Amy Carmichael. SoP
I promise you by the harsh funeral. Burns Singer. *Fr.* Sonnets for a Dying Man. NePoEA-2
I promised Sylvia to be true. Song: I Promised Sylvia. Earl of Rochester. CavP; SeCePo
I purposed once to take my pen and write. Prefatory Sonnet. Henry Kendall. BoAV
I put him on the train in Albury. Returned Soldier. E. G. Moll. MoAuPo
I put my hand upon her toe. Gentley, Johnny My Jingalo. *Unknown.* UnTE
I put my hand upon my heart. Head and Heart. C. D. B. Ellis. LiTM; SiTL
I put my hat upon my head. A Second Stanza for Dr. Johnson. Donald Hall. ShM
I Put My Hat upon My Head. Samuel Johnson. StP
(Hats and the Man.) FiBHP
I put my nickel. Midnight Raffle. Langston Hughes. OCS
I put the idols by. I left the place. Idols of Imagination. Richard Eberhart. FiMAP
I put those things there.—See them burn. The Song of the Demented Priest. John Berryman. MoPo
I put thy hand aside, and turn away. A Farewell. "Madeline Bridges." AA
I quarreled with my brother. The Quarrel. Eleanor Farjeon. FaPON
I question not God's means or ways. God Knows the Answer. F. B. Whitney. STF
"I quite realized," said Columbus. Clerihews. E. C. Bentley. FiBHP; OnPP
I raced west away from the dawn. Thaba Bosio. S. D. R. Sutu. PeSA
I rage, I melt, I burn. Recitativo. John Gay. *Fr.* Acis and Galatea. EiCL
I, Rain[e]y Betha, 22. Plaint. Charles Henri Ford. AtBAP; MoVE; PPON
I raise my cup and invite. Moon, Flowers, Man. Su T'ung-po. NaP
I raised a dog and his name was Blue. Old Blue. *Unknown.* OuSiCo
I raised a great hullabaloo. Limerick. *Unknown.* PDV

I raised my eyes aloft, and I beheld. One World. Dante. *Fr.* Divina Commedia: Paradiso. MaRV; TRV
I ran for a catch. A Cricket Triolet. Coulson Kernahan. CenHV; WePo
I ran from the prison house but they captured me. The Prison House. Alan Paton. PeSA
I ran out in the morning, when the air was clean and new. Autumn Morning at Cambridge. Frances Cornford. HBMV; MoVE; OBVV; PoRA (rev. ed.)
I rang them up, while touring Timbuctoo. To Someone Who Insisted I Look Up Someone. X. J. Kennedy. PV
I reached that waterhole, its mud designed. The Dancers. Roland E. Robinson. ACV
I reached the highest place in Spoon River. Henry C. Calhoun. Edgar Lee Masters. *Fr.* Spoon River Anthology. AmP; LiTA; LiTM (rev. ed.); NP
I read an impatient man. To a Western Bard Still a Whoop and a Holler Away from English Poetry. William Meredith. PP
I read, before my eyelids dropped [*or* dropt] their shade. A Dream of Fair Women. Tennyson. BEL; OBRV; ViPo
I read how Troilus served in Troy. A Comparison of His Love with the Faithful and Painful Love of Troilus to Cressid. *Unknown.* ReIE
I read in Dante how that hornèd light. S. S. *Lusitania.* Matthew Arnold. CBEP
I read last night of the Grand Review. A Second Review of the Grand Army. Bret Harte. HBV; MC; PAH
I read last night with many pauses. Troy. Robin Flower. SeCePo
I read my sentence steadily. Emily Dickinson. NePA; QFR
I read once more this care-worn, patient face. On a Picture of Lincoln. John Vance Cheney. PGD
I read poems taken from old Indian tongues. To the Poets of India. F. R. Scott. NYTB
I read somewhere that a swan, snow-white. The Watch of a Swan. Sarah Morgan Bryan Piatt. AA
I read the marble-lettered name. A Grave in Hollywood Cemetery, Richmond. Margaret Junkin Preston. AA
I read with varying degrees. Edna St. Vincent Millay. *Fr.* Journal. ImOP
I reade in ancient times of yore. The Map of Mock-Begger Hall. *Unknown.* CoMu
I really take it very kind. Domestic Asides; or, Truth in Parentheses. Thomas Hood. EnRP
I reason, earth is short. Emily Dickinson. OnPM
I rebel/ Not because of poverty. Why I Rebel. Robert J. Sye. TNV
I recall, before the banks. By the Bridge. Ted Walker. NYBP
I reckon I git your drift, gen'ts. Banty Tim. John Hay. MAP; MoAmPo (1942 ed.)
I reckon the first day I saw those eyes. To Calista. Charles Cotton. LO
I reckon—when I count at all. Emily Dickinson. MAmP; MAP; MoAmPo; PP
I recognized him by his skips and hops. Pan and the Cherries. Paul Fort. AWP; PoMS
I recollect a nurse call'd [*or* called] Ann. A Terrible Infant. Frederick Locker-Lampson. ALV; BOHV; FiBHP; HBV; InMe; TreFS; WhC
I recollect in early life. My First Love. Harry Graham. FiBHP
I recommend for plain dis-ease. Convalescence, VII. David McCord. WhC
I regret that before people can be reformed they have to be sinners. Piano Tuner, Untune Me That Tune. Ogden Nash. UnS
I regretted the arrival of my death. What Profit? Immanuel di Roma. TrJP
I Remember. Denis Glover. AnNZ
I Remember. Thomas Hood. *See* I Remember, I Remember.
I Remember. Mae Jackson. BOLo
I remember,/ There lived a Spanish Princess of our name. Thomas Heywood. *Fr.* A Challenge for Beauty. LO
I remember a dug-out in the backyard as children. Reflections upon a Recurrent Suggestion by Civil Defense Authorities That I Build a Bombshelter in My Backyard. Reed Whittemore. PoCh
I remember a house where all were good. In the Valley of the Elwy. Gerard Manley Hopkins. BoPe; BWP; EG; InPo; LiTG; PoIE; ViBoPo
I remember, as if it were yesterday. One and One. C. Day Lewis. OAEP (2d ed.); UnS
I remember distinctly the tired tumult of my urges. Journey to a Parallel. Bruce McM. Wright. PoNe
I remember ever so long. Tragic Memory. *Unknown.* *Fr.* Manyo Shu. OnPM
I remember how I lay. Two Taverns. Edwin Markham. TSW
I remember how we stood. The Last Corn Shock. Glenn Ward Dresbach. FaPON
I Remember, I Remember. Thomas Hood. BEL; BLPA; CBEP; ELP; EnLi-2 (1949 ed.); EnLit; EnRP; FaBoBe; FaBV; FaFP; FaPON; GoTP; HBV; ILP; LiTB; LiTG; MaRV; MyFE; NeHB; OBRV; PG (1945 ed.); PoEL-4; PRWS; StP; TreF
(I Remember.) CH; MPB (1956 ed.); OTPC; PCD; PoG
(Past and Present.) GTBS; GTBS-D; GTBS-P; GTBS-W; GTSE; GTSL; ShBV-1; TRV
I Remember, I Remember. Philip Larkin. PoeP
I remember, I remember, ere my childhood flitted by. As to the Weather. *Unknown.* BOHV
I remember, I remember, when once I used to mine. California as It Is and Was. John A. Stone. SGR
I remember it well; 't was a morn dull and gray. Macdonald's Raid. Paul Hamilton Hayne. PAH
I remember now how first I knew what death was. Original Sin. Alexander Laing. NYBP
I remember or remember hearing. Once Upon a Great Holiday. Anne Wilkinson. WHW
I remember paddocks opening green. I Remember. Denis Glover. AnNZ
I remember the Chillicothe ball players. Hits and Runs. Carl Sandburg. SD
I remember the dread with which I at a quarter past four. False Security. John Betjeman. CMoP
I remember the lowering wintry morn. The Risks of the Game. Adam Lindsay Gordon. OtMeF
I remember the neckcurls, limp and damp as tendrils. Elegy for Jane. Theodore Roethke. AmP; AmPP (5th ed.); AP; CaFP; CoAP; FiMAP; GTBS-W; LiTM (1970 ed.); MoAB; MoAmPo (1962 ed.); NePA; NoP; PoPo; TDP; TwAmPo; TwCP
I remember them, man and wife, in their little car. Couple. Walter Stone. NYBP
I remember Wednesday was the day. Two Lean Cats. Myron O'Higgins. PoNe
I remember when I saw for the first time. Oxford. Richard Aldridge. NYTB
I remember your hair. Marian at Tassajara Springs. William Witherup. QAH
I, Remembering. Roger Mais. PoNe
I renounce the blindness of the magazines. A Prayer to Escape from the Market Place. James Wright. NaP
I resent great instruments. Independence. Mary Fullerton. BoAV
I reside at [the] Table Mountain, and my name is Truthful James. The Society upon the Stanislaus. Bret Harte. AA; BeLS; BOHV; GSP; HBV; InMe; MaC; SiTL
I resign! Song of Resignation. Yehuda Amichai. NYBP
I Rest with Thee, O Jesus. *Unknown,* *tr. fr. Modern Irish by* Eleanor Hull. *Fr.* Four Prayers. JKCP (1926 ed.)
(Four Prayers.) OnYI
I rested on the breezy height. Above St. Irénée. Duncan Campbell Scott. VA
I, restless in the military train. City by Night. Vittorio Sereni. OnPM
I retrace your path in my bare feet. Letter from a Wife. S. Carolyn Reese. PoNe (1970 ed.)
I return the bitterness. Transformation. Lewis Alexander. CDC; PoNe
I Return unto Zion. Zechariah, VIII: 3-5, Bible, *O.T.* TrJP
I, Richard Kent, beneath these stones. Epitaph. Sylvia Townsend Warner. MoBrPo; NeMa
I ride/ the "A" train. Riding the "A". May Swenson. CAD
I Ride an Old Paint, *with music.* *Unknown.* AS; TrAS
I ride on the mountain tops, I ride. The Joy of the Hills. Edwin Markham. PoMa
I Ride the Great Black Horses of My Heart. Robert Nathan. MAP
I ride through a dark, dark land by night. Ichabod! Thy [*or* The] Glory Has Departed. Ludwig Uhland. AWP; IrPN

I rise, & greive. *Unknown.* SeCSL
I rise at 2 A.M. these mornings. The Feral Pioneers. Ishmael Reed. PoNe (1970 ed.)
I rise from the earth, I fall from on high. Everywhere. Nancy Birckhead. RIS
I rise in the dawn, and I kneel and blow. The Song of the Old Mother. W. B. Yeats. AnIV; BEL; GTSL; LOW; MCCG; MoBrPo; NeMA; PoPo; VA
I 'rived in the camp, and all I could see. Burns's Log Camp. *Unknown.* ShS
I rode a dream motorcycle. The Dream Motorcycle. Pete Winslow. PV
I rode a line on the open range. The Old Cowboy. *Unknown.* CoSo
I rode across a valley range. The Old Cowman. Badger Clark. SCC
I rode in Montana and old Idaho. Up the Trail. *Unknown.* CoSo
I rode my horse to the hostel gate. Both Less and More. Richard Watson Dixon. LoBV
I rode one evening with Count Maddalo. A Conversation. Shelley. *Fr.* Julian and Maddalo. ERoP-2
I rose at night, and visited. The Unborn. Thomas Hardy. CMoP
I rose. . . .I rose. . . Don Marquis. *Fr.* I Have Looked Inward. PFY
I rose not from my knees and called on her for comfort. The Maiden Meed. *At. to* William Langland. *Fr.* The Vision of Piers the Plowman, Passus 2. CoBE
I rose up when the battle was dead. Comrades. Laurence Housman. HBV
I row in my boat in the twilight, half-purple, half-grey, overhead. John Francis O'Donnell. *Fr.* In the Twilight. IrPN
I rub my head and find a turtle shell. The Neo-Classical Urn. Robert Lowell. NoP
I rue the day, a rueful day I trow. Thursday; or, The Spell. John Gay. *Fr.* The Shepherd's Week. CEP
I rush to your dwelling. Pursuit. Juljan Tuwim. TrJP
I said: All now complete! Twelve by the Clock. Jorge Guillén. WoL
I said, "I have shut my heart." Over the Roofs. Sara Teasdale. NP
I said I splendidly loved you; it's not true. Sonnet. Rupert Brooke. CBEP
I said, "I will find God," and forth I went. Seeking God. Edward Dowden. MaRV; WGRP
I said: "I will take heed to my ways." Lord, Make Me to Know Mine End. Psalm XXXIX, Bible, *O.T.* TrJP
I said, "I will walk in the fields." *See* I said, "Let me walk in the fields."
I said I would have my fling. The Price He Paid. Ella Wheeler Wilcox. WBLP
I said I'd let life battle it out. In the Garden. Peter Fellowes. QAH
I said, in drunken pride of youth and you. Challenge. Sterling A. Brown. CDC
I said in haste, the sun shines not to-day! Misunderstanding. Henry W. Frost. SoP
I said in my heart, "I am sick of four walls and a ceiling." Richard Hovey. *Fr.* Spring. BBV (1951 ed.); PoMa; RePo
I said: "Let me walk [*or* I will walk] in the fields." Obedience [*or* What Christ Said]. George Macdonald. BePJ; BLRP; ChIP; FaChP; HBV; MaRV; OQP; OTPC; SoP; TreFT; TRV; WGRP
I said: "My heart, now let us sing a song." A Wedding-Song. John White Chadwick. AA
I said: "Nay, pluck not,—let the first fruit be." Hoarded Joy. Dante Gabriel Rossetti. The House of Life, LXXXII. MaVP; PoVP; ViPo
I Said Sometimes with Tears. Samuel Crossman. OxBoCh
I said, "Sweet Master, hear me pray." The Blessed Task. Harriet McEwen Kimball. BePJ
I said: "The desert is so wide!" Overanxious. *Unknown.* SoP
"I," said the duck, "I call it fun." Who Likes the Rain? Clara Doty Bates. BoTP; GFA; OTPC (1946 ed.); PCH; PPL; TiPo
I said: "The flowers in this light are beautiful." Blind Geronimo. Bill Berkson. ANYP
I said—Then, dearest, since 'tis so. The Last Ride Together. Robert Browning. BEL; BoLiVe; EnLi-2; FiP; GTSL; HBV; LiTB; LoBV (1949 ed.); MaVP; OAEP; OBEV; OBVV; OuHeWo; PoEL-5; PoVP; UnPo (1st. ed.); ViPP; VP; WHA
I said, "This horse, sir, will you shoe?" Logical English. *Unknown.* BOHV
I Said, This Misery Must End. Christopher J. Brennan. *Fr.* Pauca Mea. BoAu; BoAV; NeLNL; PoAu-1
I said to Death: "Supposing it were true." Dancing Partners. Philip Child. CaP
I said to Heart, "How goes it?" Heart replied. For [*or* The] False Heart. Hilaire Belloc. FaBoCh; HBMV; LoGBV; MoBrPo
I said to heaven that glowed above. Odes, XII. Hafiz, *tr. by* Emerson. AWP; OuHeWo
I said to her, darling, I said. Vivamus, Mea Lesbia. Catullus, *tr. by* Frank O. Copley. StP
I said to Lettice, our sister Lettice. Lettice. Dinah Maria Mulock Craik. HBV
I said to Life, "How comes it." The Gift. Bliss Carman. PTK
I Said to Love. Thomas Hardy. ViPo; VP
I said to my baby. Same in Blues. Langston Hughes. NoP
I said to my companion, this is walking. Victoria Market. Francis Brabazon. BoAV
I said to my friend. "But I marched with you." This Scenery. Leo Connellan. WOW
I said to my Heart, between sleeping and waking. Chloe. Charles Mordaunt, Earl of Peterborough. CEP; OBEC
I said to myself almost in prayer. A Trial Run. Robert Frost. WePo
I said to myself one morning. Waking. Annie Higgins. ELU
I said to Sorrow's awful storm. The Soul's Defiance. Lavinia Stoddard. AA
I Said to the Leaf. Carleton Drewry. MoRP
I said to the man who stood at the gate of the year. *See* And I said to the man. . .
I said: "Within the garden trimly bordered." Inspiration. E. V. Knox. CenHV
"I said, 'You're right!' At last they've found." Asylum. David R. Clark. PPON
I sail over the ocean blue. I Catcha da Plenty of Feesh. *Unknown.* AS; TrAS
I sail the sea, I walk the land. George Crabbe. *Fr.* The World of Dreams. PeER
I sail'd from the Downs in the *Nancy.* The Tar for All Weathers. Charles Dibdin. OTPC (1923 ed.)
I sailed in my dreams to the Land of Night. Fantasy. Gwendolyn B. Bennett. CDC
I sang a canto in a canton. Country Words. Wallace Stevens. NYTB
I sang as one. The Conflict. C. Day Lewis. AnEnPo; EnLit; FaBoMo; LiTB; LiTM; MoAB; MoBrPo
I sang the songs of red revenge. Homer. Albert Ehrenstein. TRJP
I sat alone with my conscience. Conscience [and Future Judgment]. Charles William Stubbs. BLPA; MaRV
I Sat among the Green Leaves. Marjorie L. C. Pickthall. HBMV; PTK
I sat, and held the book upon my knees. The Poet Considers Perfection. Elizabeth Virginia Raplee. MaRV
I sat at Berne, and watched the chain. Below the Heights. William Herries Pollock. VA
I sat at my loom in silence. The Weaver. *Unknown.* BLRP
I sat before my glass one day. The Other Side of a Mirror. Mary Elizabeth Coleridge. CBEP
I sat beside the red stock route. Harry Pearce. David Campbell. NeLNL; PoAu-2
I sat beside the streamlet. Remember or Forget. Hamilton Aïdé. HBV; VA
I sat by the granite pillar, and sunlight fell. Commemoration. Sir Henry Newbolt. FaBoTw; OBVV
I sat here this morning, detached, summoning up, I think. The Deviator. Bertram Warr. OBCV
I sat in the cold limbs of a tree. The Man in the Tree. Mark Strand. YAP
I sat in the school of sorrow. The School of Sorrow. Harold Hamilton. BLRP
I sat me down upon a green bank-side. Bronx. Joseph Rodman Drake. AmePo; AnAmPo
I Sat Me Weary on a Pillar's Base. James Thomson. *See* Sphinx, The.

I sat on my haunches while she lined the grave. Burial. Richard C. Raymond. NYTB
I sat one night beside a blue-eyed girl. Categorical Courtship. *Unknown.* BOHV; CIV
I sat unsphering Plato ere I slept. The Fall of a Soul. John Addington Symonds. PoVP; VA
I sat upon a windy mountain height. Sunset on the Cunimbla Valley, Blue Mountains. Douglas Brooke W. Sladen. VA
I sat with Doris, the shepherd maiden. Doris; a Pastoral. Arthur Joseph Munby. HBV; VA
I sat with her, and spoke right goldenly. The Lady of Life. Thomas Michael Kettle. ACP; JKCP (1926 ed.)
I sat with Love upon a woodside well. Willowwood 1. Dante Gabriel Rossetti. The House of Life, XLIX. HBV; MaVP; OAEP; PoEL-5; PoVP; Sonn; ViPo; VP; WHA
I sat with one I love last night. Last Night. George Darley. HBV; OnYI
I saw/ Your hands on my lips like blind needles. Pirouette. Audre Lorde. NNP
I saw a bee, I saw a flower. The Bee-Orchis. Andrew Young. ChTr
I saw a boy in a black-jack wood. The Maul. Mary E. Nealy. MC
I saw a boy with eager eye. The Two Boys. Mary Lamb. CBEP; OBRV
I saw a brown squirrel to-day in the wood. Mr. Squirrel. V. M. Julian. BoTP
I saw a bus marked XANADU. Thoughts. Roy Davis. WhC
I saw a certain sailorman who sat beside the sea. All at Sea. Frederick Moxon. BOHV
I Saw a Chapel All of Gold. Blake. CABA; CBEP; EiCL; EnRP; LiTB; LiTG; PoeP; TDP
I saw a cherry weep, and why? The Weeping Cherry. Robert Herrick. AtBAP; WePo
I saw a dead man's finer part. His Immortality. Thomas Hardy. CMoP
I Saw a Delicate Flower Had Grown Up 2 Feet High. Henry David Thoreau. MAmP
I saw a dog. Ilo Orleans. RIS
I saw a donkey. The Donkey. *Unknown.* BiCB
I saw a fair [*or* faire] maiden. Lullay My Liking [*or* A Lullaby of the Nativity]. *Unknown.* EG; ELP; MeEL
I saw a famous man eating soup. Soup. Carl Sandburg. RePo
I Saw a Fish-Pond All on Fire. *Unknown.* ChTr; OxNR
I saw a fly within a bead. A Trapped Fly [*or* The Amber Bead]. Robert Herrick. ChTr; PoeP; WiR
I saw a frieze on whitest marble drawn. Ecstasy. W. J. Turner. CH; POTE
I Saw a Ghost. Joan Boilleau. TiPo
I saw a Gnome. The Gnome. Harry Behn. FaPON; PDV; SoPo; TiPo (1959 ed.)
I saw a great barge. The Barge. Rose Fyleman. BrR
I saw a grown girl coming down. Glenn Ward Dresbach. Songs of the Plains, I. NP
I saw a holly sprig brought from a hurst. A Vision of the World's Instability. Richard Verstegan. EIL
"I saw a light," Columbus said. Light in the Darkness. Aileen Fisher. YeAr
I saw a little snail [*or* a snail]. Little Snail. Hilda Conkling. FaPON; GFA; MPB; PoRh; TiPo; TVC; UTS
I saw a little squirrel. A Little Squirrel. *Unknown.* TiPo
I Saw a Maiden. *Unknown.* ISi
I Saw a Man. Stephen Crane. *See* I Saw a Man Pursuing the Horizon.
I saw a man at the dawn of day. The Drunkard's Doom. *Unknown.* ABF
I saw a man, by some accounted wise. Erastus Wolcott Ellsworth. *Fr.* What Is the Use? AA
I saw a man come down to the furious sea. The Antagonist. David Ferry. NePoAm-2
I Saw a Man [Pursuing the Horizon]. Stephen Crane. The Black Riders, XXIV. AmePo; AmPP (5th ed.); AP; CoBA; HoPM; LiTA; LiTM (1970 ed.); LoGBV; MAP; MoAmPo; NeMA; NePA; OTD
I saw a man whose face was white as snow. The Uninfected. E. L. Mayo. MiAP
I saw a marble shaft gleam white. The Washington Monument. Alma Adams Wiley. PEDC
I Saw a Monk of Charlemain [*or* Charlemaine]. Blake. *Fr.* Jerusalem. EnRP; OBRV
(Monk, The.) LoBV
I saw a mountain. I Keep Wondering. Hilda Conkling. PFY
I Saw a New World. William Brighty Rands. NBM; VA
I Saw a Peacock [with a Fiery Tail]. *Unknown.* CBEP; CH; ChTr; FaBoCh; ImOP; LiTG; LoGBV; OxBoLi; OxNR; PoMS; SiTL
(Ambiguous Lines, *longer vers.*) BOHV
(Not So Impossible.) GoTP
I saw a people rise before the sun. Yom Kippur. Israel Zangwill. TRJP
I Saw a Phoenix in the Wood Alone. Petrarch, *tr. by* Spenser. *Fr.* The Visions of Petrarch. ChTr; EnLi-1
I saw a picture once by Angelo. An Unpraised Picture. Richard Burton. AA
I saw a poor old woman on the bench. By the Saltpétrière. Thomas Ashe. VA
I saw a proud, mysterious cat. The Mysterious Cat. Vachel Lindsay. ChTr; FaPON; GoJo; MPB; PoRh; SoPo; SP; StVeCh; TiPo; UTS
I saw a querulous old man, the tobacconist of Eighth Street. The Tobacconist of Eighth Street. Richard Eberhart. MiAP; ToPo
I saw a shadow on the ground. The Sky. Elizabeth Madox Roberts. GFA; MAP; MoAmPo
I saw a ship a-sailing. Mother Goose. BoChLi; BoTP; FaBoBe; GFA; HBV; HBVY; MoShBr; MPB; OTPC; OxNR; PCH; PoPl; PoRh; PPL, *sl. diff. vers.*; RIS; SAS; SoPo; StVeCh; TiPo
I saw a ship a-sailing. Romance. "Gabriel Setoun." BoTP; OTPC; PRWS
I saw a ship a-sailing, a-sailing, a-sailing. An Old Song Re-sung. John Masefield. ExPo; EvOK; LiTB
I saw a ship of martial build. The Berg. Herman Melville. AmP; AmPP (5th ed.); AP; AtBAP; CBEP; LiTA; PoEL-5; MAmP; MWA-1; NoP; PoFS
I saw a sickly cellar plant. The Incentive. Sarah N. Cleghorn. HBMV
I saw a silvery creature scurrying. Riddle #29: The Moon and the Sun. *Unknown.* CaFP; GoJo
I saw a slowly-stepping train. God's Funeral. Thomas Hardy. PoDB; WGRP
I saw a snail. *See* I saw a little snail.
I Saw a Stable. Mary Elizabeth Coleridge. OxBoCh; TRV
I saw a star slide down the sky. The Falling Star. Sara Teasdale. BrR; MoShBr; MoSiPe; PDV; PoRh; SoPo; StVeCh; SUS; TiPo
I saw a staring virgin stand. Two Songs from a Play, I. W. B. Yeats. *Fr.* The Resurrection. CABA; CMoP; CoBMV; ExPo; FaBoTw; FosPo; ILP; LiTB; MBW-2; MoPo; NoP; PAn; PoDB; PoFS; PoIE; SeCeV; UnPo
I saw a stately lady. The Stately Lady. Flora Sandstrom. BoTP
I saw a stranger yestreen. The Rune of Hospitality. Unknown. CAW; WHL
I Saw a Sweet and Silly Sight. *Unknown, at. to* John Brackley. ISi
I saw a terrible river. The Sin; a Definition. Francis Maguire. JKCP (1955 ed.)
I saw a thing, and stopped to wonder. The Pine Bough. Richard Aldridge. NePoAm; PoSC
I saw a Tiger's golden flank, The Lion and the Lamb. Elinor Wylie. CoBA
I saw a tiny pebble fall. What Price. Lulu Minerva Schultz. GoYe
I saw a Vision yesternight. To the State of Love, or the Senses Festival. John Cleveland. AnAnS-2; MePo
I saw a vulture in the sky. Life and Death. W. J. Turner. FaBoTw
I saw a white bird once. Akiko Yosano, *tr. fr. Japanese by* Kenneth Rexroth. LiTW
I saw a woman in a green field. The Postures of Love, I. Alex Comfort. NeBP
I saw a wonder as I came along. The Shepherds. Sophie Jewett. ChrBoLe
I saw a worm, with many a fold. Psyche. Jones Very. AP
I saw a young snake glide. Snake. Theodore Roethke. NYBP; OA; PoeP; PoPl; TDP
I saw a youth and maiden on a lonely city street. Take Back Your Gold. Louis W. Pritzkow. TreF
I saw a youth go forth one day. Youth and Truth. Walter E. Isenhour. SoP

I saw again the spirits on a day. Bethesda. Arthur Hugh Clough. PoVP

I saw along each noisy city street. Christmas Trees. Violet Alleyn Storey. StJW

I saw an aged beggar in my walk. The Old Cumberland Beggar. Wordsworth. CABL; EnRP; ERoP-1; LaA; MBW-2; MERP; PoE

I saw an ass who a bore a load. The Loaded Ass. Bhartrihari. OnPM

"I saw an elephant walking down the road." April Fool. Elizabeth J. Coatsworth. RePo; YeAr

I saw an old black man walk down the road. Black Soul of the Land. Lance Jeffers. BF

I saw an old man with a long white beard. Building of Sand. Grant Code. FiSC

I saw, and trembled for the day. A Warning. Coventry Patmore. EnLoPo

I saw, at noon, Alexa on the road. Two Fires. Meleager. OnPM

I saw autumn today. . .incipiently, on the sunset. Walter Benton. *Fr.* This Is My Beloved. UnTE

I saw between a shadow and a bough. The Ungathered Apples. James Wright. ErPo

I saw Butch. 224 Stoop. Victor Hernandez Cruz. BOLo

I saw by looking in his eyes. The Wandering Jew. E. A. Robinson. MAmP; PoDB; QFR

I saw cold thunder in the grass. Herons. Robin Blaser. NeAP

I saw dawn creep across the sky. A Summer Morning. Rachel Field. BoChLi; PDV; SoPo; StVeCh (1955 ed.); SUS; TiPo

I Saw Death Slain. William Capell. ChIP

I saw death this afternoon lurking near the tennis courts. Near the Base Line. Samuel L. Albert. NePoAm-2

I Saw Eternity. Louise Bogan. LiTA; StP

I saw eternity the other night. The World [*or* Eternity]. Henry Vaughan. AnAnS-1; AtBAP; ATP; AWP; BBV; BEL; BoLiVe; BWP; CABA; CBEP; CBV; CoBE; DiPo; EnL; EnLi-1; EnLit; EP; ExPo; FaBoEn; FaBV; FaPL; FosPo; GoTL; GTBS-W; GTSL; HBV; ILP; ImOP; InPo; LiTB; LiTG; LoBV; MaPo; MaRV; MasP; MemP; MeP; MePo; NoP; OAEP; OBEV (new ed.); OBS; OuHeWo; OxBoCh; Po; PoAn; PoE; PoEL-2; PoFr; PoFS; PoIE; ReEn; SCEP-1; SeCeV; SeCP; SeCV-1; SeEP; SoP; StP; TOP; TreFS; TrGrPo; ViBoPo; WGRP; WoL

I saw fair[e] Chloris [*or* Cloris] walk[e] alone. On Chloris [*or* a Gentlewoman] Walking in the Snow[e]. William Strode. BoC; EG; ELP; GTBS-W; HBV; NoP; OBEV; OBS; SeCL; SeEP

I saw five birds all in a cage. *Unknown. Fr.* Riddles. CoBE

I Saw from the Beach. Thomas Moore. OBNC; OxBI

I saw, from yonder silent cave. The Two Streams. Thomas Moore. *Fr.* Evenings in Greece. GoBC

I Saw God. William L. Stidger. PGD

I saw God! Do you doubt it? What Tomas [an Buile] Said in a Pub. James Stephens. AnFE; CBV; CMoP; GTSL; ILP; LiTM; MemP; MoAB; MoBrPo; NeMA; NP; PoRA (rev. ed.); TrGrPo; WGRP

I Saw God Wash the World. William L. Stidger. BLPA; MaRV; MPB (1956 ed.); OQP; SoP; TRV

I saw green banks of daffodil. E. Wyndham Tennant. TiPo (1959 ed.)

I saw her crop a rose. John Clare. EG; LO, 8 *ll.*

I saw her first abreast the Boston light. The *William P. Frye.* Jeanne Robert Foster. MC; PAH

I saw her in childhood. Agnes. Henry Francis Lyte. ATP (1935 ed.); GTSL

I saw her last night at a party. The Mourner à la Mode. John Godfrey Saxe. LHV

I saw her on the bridal night. The Forced Bridal. *Unknown.* PaPo

I saw her once, one little while, and then no more. And Then No More. Friedrich Rückert, *tr. by* James Clarence Mangan. AnIV; BLPA; IrPN

I saw her plucking cowslips. The Witch. Percy H. Ilott. BoTP

I saw her scan her sacred scroll. Alma Mater's Roll. Edward Everett Hale. AA

I saw him at a funeral in town. Perennial Mourner. Sydney King Russell. FiSC

I saw him dead, a leaden slumber lies [*or* lyes]. Andrew Marvell. *Fr.* A Poem upon the Death of Oliver Cromwell [*or* His Late Highness the Lord Protector]. ChTr; OBS; PeRV; ViBoPo

I saw him forging link by link his chain. The Slave. Jones Very. AP

"I saw him kiss your cheek!" "'Tis true." The Kiss. Coventry Patmore. *Fr.* The Angel in the House, II, viii, 3. MeWo

I saw him leave his pagan century. The Centurion. Helen Purcell Roads. ChIP

I saw him lying there—my father—with eyes. The Addict. Larry Rubin. GoYe

I saw him naked on a hill. The Shepherd Boy. Edward J. O'Brien. HBMV

I saw him once before. The Last Leaf. Oliver Wendell Holmes. AA; AmePo; AmLP; AmPP; AnAmPo; AnFE; AnNE; AP; APA; CaFP; CoAnAm; CoBA; FaBoBe; FaPON; HBV; InP; OnPP; OuHeWo; PFY; PG (1945 ed.); PoIE; PoLF; PoPo; SeCeV; SiTL; TOP; TreF; TSW; WaKn; WBLP

I saw him peeping from my lawn. Dandelion. Kate L. Brown. TVC

I saw him sitting in his door. The Philosopher. Sara Teasdale. PoToHe

I saw him steal the light away. God's Education. Thomas Hardy. MoRP

I saw him there riddled. My Brother and Me. Clarence Reed. BF

I saw him where the rose was red. The Stranger. John Richard Moreland. ChIP; OQP

I saw Him with flesh all bespred—He came from [the] East. Conquering and to Conquer [*or* The Coming of Christ]. *Unknown.* ACP

I saw his searching eyes at all the bars. The Man I Met. Joseph Payne Brennan. FiSC

I Saw, I Saw the Lovely Child. Frederic William Henry Myers. VA
(Evanescence.) OBVV

I saw in dream a dapper mannikin. Im Traum sah ich ein Männchen klein und putzig. Heine. AWP

I saw in dreams a mighty multitude. No Death. Philip Bourke Marston. VA

I saw in Louisiana a Live-Oak Growing. Walt Whitman. AP; AWP; CBEP; CoBA; GBV (1952 ed.); InPo; JAWP; LiTA; MCCG; MWA-1; NePA; NoP; OxBA; PAn; WBP

I saw in Siena pictures. Sodoma's Christ Scourged. George Edward Woodberry. StJW

I saw in the East a sign, a sign. Blues Ballad. Kenneth Pitchford. *Fr.* Good for Nothing Man. CoPo

I saw in Ulm a castle high. The Blacksmith. *Unknown.* SAS

I saw it all in Fancy's glass. The Torch of Liberty. Thomas Moore. DD; PEDC

I saw it all, Polly, how when you had call'd for sop. Poor Poll. Robert Bridges. MoPo; OxBoLi

I saw it in a shell-torn town. The Cross. Donald Earl Edwards. ChIP

I saw it light the cactus sky. Back Again from Yucca Flats. Reeve Spencer Kelley. AmFN

I saw it once where a myriad works adorn. On a Sculptured Head of the Christ. Mahlon Leonard Fisher. HBV

I saw it—pink and white—revealed. A Thought in Two Moods. Thomas Hardy. EPN

I saw Love stand. Forgiven? Jeannette Bliss Gillespy. *Fr.* Cameos. AA

I saw my face. A Coffeepot Face. Aileen Fisher. MPB

I Saw My Father. E. L. Mayo. MiAP

I Saw My Lady Weep. *Unknown.* CBEP; EG; ElL; ELP; EnLoPo; GTBS-W; HBV; LiTB; LO; OBSC; TrGrPo; ViBoPo
(In Lacrimas.) GTSL
(My Lady's Tears.) MemP; OBEV

I Saw My Life as Whitest Flame. Christopher Brennan. *Fr.* Towards the Source. PoAu-1

I saw my scattered hopes upon the floor. The Phallic Symbol. Nicholas Moore. NeBP

I saw myself leaving. Reflections. Carl Gardener. NNP

I saw Nelson at the Battle of the Nile. Limerick. *Unknown.* LiBL

I saw new worlds beneath the water lie [*or* ly]. On Leaping over

I (continued)
the Moon. Thomas Traherne. AtBAP; LiTB; LoBV; SCEP-1; SeCV-2
I saw no doctor, but, feeling queer inside. *Unknown, tr. fr. Greek by* Humbert Wolfe. ShM; WhC
I saw no way—the heavens were stitched. Emily Dickinson. AP; MWA-2
I saw not they were strange, the ways I roam. After Music. Josephine Preston Peabody. AA
I saw old autumn in the misty morn. Autumn [*or* Ode: Autumn]. Thomas Hood. ERoP-2; HBV; ILP; LiTB; NoP; OBEV; OBNC; OBRV; PCD; PeER; PoEL-4; VA; ViBoPo
I saw old Duchesses with their young loves. Vanity. Anna Wickham. FaBoTw
I saw old Time, destroyer of mankind. Time and Death. William Henry Whitworth. VA
I saw on earth another light. The Light from Within. Jones Very. WGRP
I saw on the slant hill a putrid lamb. For a Lamb. Richard Eberhart. CMoP; FiMAP; LiTM (1970 ed.); MiAP; NoP; TDP
I Saw One Hanging. *Unknown.* STF
I saw one hung upon a cross. Gallows and Cross. J. E. H. MacDonald. CaP
I saw, one sultry night above a swamp. Fireflies. Edgar Fawcett. AnAmPo; HBV
I saw only the edge. A Glance at the Album. Gray Burr. CoPo
I saw Saleianus in mourning array. A Golden Sorrow. Martial. LiTW
I saw someone by the white syringa. Ballad: White Rose. Sacheverell Sitwell. POTE (1959 ed.); SiSw
I saw that country in a dream. Wilderness Theme. Ian Mudie. PoAu-2
I saw the archangels in my apple-tree last night. The Apple-Tree. Nancy Campbell. AnIV; NP
I Saw the Beauty Go. Mary Gilmore. NeLNL
I saw the best minds of my generation. Squeal. Louis Simpson. FiBHP; Par
I saw the best minds of my generation destroyed by madness, starving hysterical naked. Howl. Allen Ginsberg. AmP; AmPP (5th ed.); NaP; NeAP
I saw the bird that can the sun endure [*or* that dares behold the sun]. Joachim du Bellay, *tr. by* Spenser. *Fr.* Visions. Sonn, two vers.
I saw the bodies of earth's men. Navigators. W. J. Turner. OBMV
I saw the city's towers on a luminous pale-gray sky. Winter-Solitude. Archibald Lampman. PeCV (1967 ed.)
I Saw the Clouds. Hervey White. HBV
I saw the Connaught Rangers when they were passing by. The Connaught Rangers. Winifred M. Letts. HBMV
I saw the Conquerors riding by. The Conquerors. Harry Kemp. AnAmPo; ChIP; HBV; MaRV
I saw the constellated matin choir. Prelude. Edmund Clarence Stedman. AA
I saw the day's white rapture. Song. Charles Hanson Towne. HBV
I saw the Devil's Darning Needle. Devil's Darning Needle. C. Lindsay McCoy. GFA
I saw the farmer plough the field. Harvest. M. M. Hutchinson. BoTP
I Saw the Figure of a Lovely Maid. Wordsworth. LO
I saw the first pear. Orchard. Hilda Doolittle ("H.D."). AnFE; APA; AtBAP; CMoP; CoAnAm; CoBA; ExPo; LiTA; LiTM (1970 ed.); MAP; MoAmPo; OxBA
I saw the fog grow thick. The Fog. W. H. Davies. OCS; TiPo (1959 ed.); WaKn
I saw the ghostesses. Ghostesses. *Unknown.* ChTr
I saw the grave of Shakespeare in a dream. Shakespeare's Mourners. John Banister Tabb. AmP
I saw the Lord Christ tonight. Inasmuch. William E. Brooks. PGD
I saw the lovely arch. The Rainbow. Walter de la Mare. SoPo; TiPo
I saw the Master of the Sun. He stood. The Sun God. Aubrey Thomas De Vere. ACP; OBVV; PoVP; Sonn
I saw the midlands. Kisses in the Train. D. H. Lawrence. CBV; MoAB; MoBrPo
I saw the moon,/ One windy night. Flying. J. M. Westrup. BoTP
I saw the moonlight before my couch. On a Quiet Night [*or* My Far-off Home]. Li Po. OnPM; WoL
I saw the object of my pining thought. Sonnet. Thomas Watson. *Fr.* The Tears of Fancy. ElL; Sonn; TuPP
I Saw the Picture. Julia Vinograd. YAP
I saw the pride of all the meadows. Narcissus. William Cowper. OTPC
I saw the Prince of Darkness, with his staff. At the Cenotaph [*or* Make Them Forget]. Siegfried Sassoon. CMoP; MaRV
I saw the ramparts of my native land. Sonnet: Death Warnings. Francisco Gomez de Quevedo y Villegas. AWP; JAWP; WBP; WoL
I saw the shapes that stood upon the clouds. London Nightfall. John Gould Fletcher. MAP; MoAmPo; NeMA
I saw the shepherd fold the sheep. The Folded Flock. Wilfrid Meynell. CAW; GoBC; JKCP; TrPWD
I saw the Sibyl at Cumae. A Fragment. Dante Gabriel Rossetti. PeVV
I saw the sky descending, black and white. Where the Rainbow Ends. Robert Lowell. AmP; AnNE; AP; CoBMV; FiMAP; MoAB; MoAmPo (1950 ed.); NePoEA; OnHM; PoeP; TrGrPo (rev. ed.)
I saw the smiling bard of pleasure. Odes of Anacreon. *Tr. by* Thomas Moore. OuHeWo
I saw the Son of God go by. The Question. Rachel Annand Taylor. ChIP; HBV; MaRV
I saw the spectre of a king. Ballad of Two Kings. Grant Code. FiSC
I saw the spiders marching through the air. Mr. Edwards and the Spider. Robert Lowell. AmP; AP; CABA; CBV; CMoP; CoAP; ILP; LiTM (1970 ed.); MaPo (1969 ed.); MoAB; MoPo; MoVE; NePoEA; PoeP; ReMP; SeCeV; ToPo; TwCP
I saw the spires of Oxford. The Spires of Oxford. Winifred M. Letts. BEL; EnLit; FaFP; HBV; InP; MaRV; MCCG; NeHB; OHFP; OnYI; PoLF; PoMa; PoRA; TIHL; TOP; TreF; WGRP
I saw the spot where our first parents dwelt. The Garden. Jones Very. AmP; AP; MAmP; OxBA
I saw the sunlit vale, and the pastoral fairy-tale. The Sunlit Vale. Edmund Blunden. CBEP; ChMP; GTBS-D; MoVE
I saw the throng, so deeply separate. A General Communion. Alice Meynell. JKCP
I saw the twinkle of white feet. Hebe. James Russell Lowell. AA; AnFE; AnNE; APA; CoAnAm; HBV
I saw the two starlings. The Manoeuvre. William Carlos Williams. LOW
I Saw the Vision of Armies. Walt Whitman. WaaP
I saw the Virtues [*or* Vertues] sitting hand in hand. Humility [*or* Humilitie]. George Herbert. EP; MaMe
I Saw the Wind Today. Padraic Colum. Reminiscence, II. GoJo; LOW
(Wind, The.) PDV; RoGo; SUS
I Saw the Winter Weaving. Jalal ed-Din Rumi, *tr. fr. Persian by* Professor Hastie. LiTW
I Saw Thee. Ray Palmer. HBV
I saw Thee in a dream, Beloved! Dream of Love. Bhai Vir Singh. OnPM
I saw thee once, and nought discerned. The Discovery. Cardinal Newman. OBRV
I saw thee start and quake. In a Dream. J. M. Synge. SyP
I saw thee when, as twilight fell. I Saw Thee. Ray Palmer. HBV
I saw them chase the Gipsies. The Gipsies. "Richard Scrace." CaP
I saw them coming in the eyeless day. And the Dead. Sean Jennett. NeBP
I saw them from our car today. The Women Toilers. Grace Bowen Evans. OQP
I saw them kissing in the shade and knew the sum of all my lore. The Young Lovers. Ridgely Torrence. *Fr.* The House of a Hundred Lights. AA
I Saw Them Lynch. Carol Freeman. BF
I saw them passing endlessly. Crucified. Patrick Dacus Moreland. StJW
I saw them shining in the sun. The Little Stones of Arlington. Barbara Young. OQP
I saw them walk that lane again. On Seeing Swift in Laracor. Brinsley MacNamara. AnIV; OxBI
I saw these dreamers of dreams go by. The Gold-Seekers.

Hamlin Garland. AA; FaBoBe; MC; YaD
I saw this day sweet flowers grow thick. The Happy Child. W. H. Davies. AtBAP; POTE
I saw this eve the wandering sun. Prodigals. Charles L. O'Donnell. HBMV
I Saw Three Ships (*diff. versions*). *Unknown.* ACP; BLPA; CAW; GoTP; HH; OBB; OTPC; OxBoCh; PRWS; RePo; WHL
(As I Sat on a Sunny Bank.) ChTr; OxBoLi; OxNR; PoPo
(As I Sat under a Sycamore Tree.) ChBr; LiTB; ViBoPo
I saw three ships come sailing by. Mother Goose. OxNR; RIS
I saw three ships go sailing by. The North Ship. Philip Larkin. FIW
I saw three withered women limp across. The Private Meeting Place. James Wright. NYBP
I saw thy beauty in its high estate. To a Magnolia Flower in the Garden of the Armenian Convent at Venice. Silas Weir Mitchell. AA
I saw Time in his workshop carving faces. Time. Frederick George Scott. VA
I saw— 'twas in a dream, the other night. Montefiore. Ambrose Bierce. AA; AnAmPo; PFY
I Saw Two Clouds at Morning. John Gardiner Calkins Brainard. HBV; PoToHe
(Epithalamium.) AA
I Saw Two Lions. Clayton Hoff. TwCaPo
I saw where in the shroud did lurk. On an Infant Dying as Soon as Born. Charles Lamb. GTBS; GTBS-D; GTBS-P; GTBS-W; GTSE; GTSL; OBEV; OBRV
I saw with open eyes. Stupidity Street. Ralph Hodgson. AtBAP; BrPo; CH; EnLit; HBV; LiTM (rev. ed.); LOW; MoAB; MoBrPo; NeMA; NP; PDV; PoFr; SiSoSe; SP; TOP; TreFS; UTS
I saw you. Glimpse. Pearl Cleage. WSL
I saw you die. Murdered Little Bird. *Unknown.* FiBHP
I saw you fall but a moment ago. Falling Leaves. William M. Runyan. FaChP
I saw you hunched and shivering on the stones. The Monkey. Nancy Campbell. NP
I saw you once on the TV. Galway Kinnell. *Fr.* For Robert Frost. PP
"I saw you take his kiss!" "'Tis true." The Kiss. Coventry Patmore. The Angel in the House, II, viii, 3. ALV; EnLoPo; FiBHP; LiTL; MemP; OBVV
I saw you toss the kites on high. The Wind. Robert Louis Stevenson. BoTP; GBV (1922 ed.); GFA; GN; HBVY; MPB; OTPC; PCH; PoIE (1970 ed.); PoVP; SoPo; StVeCh; SUS; TiPo; YT
I saw your hands lying at peace. Torchbearer. Humbert Wolfe. BoPe
I saw your hinee. *Unknown.* PV
I say/ endure the law of things. The Toad Man. Howard McCord. YAP
I Say I'll Seek Her. Thomas Hardy. QFR
I say it to comfort me over and over. The Cynic. Theodosia Garrison. HBMV
I say it under the rose. Thalia. Thomas Bailey Aldrich. AA; HBV; InMe; LHV
I say no more for Clavering. Clavering. E. A. Robinson. CrMA; HBMV; OxBA
I say now, Fernando, that on a day. Hibiscus on the Sleeping Shores. Wallace Stevens. NP
I say, old man, your horse will die. Poor Old Man. *Unknown.* SoAmSa
"I say, stranger." Between the Walls of the Valley. Elisabeth Peck. AmFN
I say that I am wise. Yet dead leaves know. Wisdom. Daniel Whitehead Hicky. OQP
I say that I think for myself, but what is this Self of mine. Heir and Serf. Don Marquis. HBMV
I say, the acknowledgment of God in Christ. Robert Browning. *Fr.* A Death in the Desert. ChIP
I say the pulpit (in the sober use). William Cowper. *Fr.* The Task. TRV
I say the whole earth, and all the stars in the sky, are for Religion's sake. The Necessity of Religion. Walt Whitman. *Fr.* Starting from Paumanok. MaRV
I say this tree is much like a man. Fallen Tree Elegy. Victor Contoski. ThO
I say to thee, do thou repeat. The Kingdom of God. Richard Chenevix Trench. WBLP
I say unto you: Cherish your doubts. Honest Doubt. Robert Weston. MaRV
I scarce believe [*or* beleeve] my love to be so pure. Loves Growth. John Donne. AnAnS-1; FosPo; GTBS-W; MaMe; MBW-1; MeP; MePo; PoeP; ReEn; SCEP-1; SeCV-1; TuPP
I Scarcely Grieve, O Nature! Henry Timrod. PoMa
I scarcely think. The Zoo. Humbert Wolfe. GBV (1952 ed.); MoShBr; WaKn
I scooped up the moon. The Moon. Ryuho. SoPo
I scooped up the moon's footprints but. Because My Hands Hear the Flowers Thinking. Kenneth Patchen. ToPo
I search/ the iridescent faces. Looking for Equality. Herman L. McMillan. TNV
I search among the plain and lovely words. Definition. Grace Noll Crowell. PoToHe (new ed.)
I search the room with all my mind. Officers' Mess (1916). Harold Monro. BrPo
I see a blind man every day. The Blind Man. Margaret E. Sangster. PoToHe
I see a dog—no stone to shy at him. Dilemma. Bhartrihari. LiTW
I see a farmer walking by himself. The Farmer. Fredegond Shove. MMA
I see a nest in the green elm-tree. The Child and the World. Kate Douglas Wiggin. PPL
I see a tiny fluttering form. The Southern Snow-Bird. William Hamilton Hayne. AA
I see a white river bird, and I see the women. By the River. Harold Lenoir Davis. NP
I see all human wits. Shakespeare. Emerson. AnNE
I see all this new matter of the snow. New Forms. Peter Redgrove. NMP
I see around me here. The Wanderer Recalls the Past. Wordsworth. *Fr.* The Excursion, I. OBNC; OBRV
I see at last our great Lamorna Cove. Lamorna Cove. W. H. Davies. BrPo
I see before me now a traveling army halting. Bivouac on a Mountain Side. Walt Whitman. AA; AmP; AP; ChTr; CoBA; MWA-1; NoP; OxBA; PAL; Po; PoLF
I see black dragons mount the sky. Shapes and Signs. James Clarence Mangan. ACV; OnYI
I See God. *Unknown.* STF
I See Her. Bilhana, *formerly at. to* Chauras, *tr. fr. Sanskrit by* E. Powys Mathers. *Fr.* Black Marigolds. OnPM
I see her dancing in the square. Danse Macabre. Antonia Y. Schwab. FiSC
I see her in the festal warmth to-night. Ursula. Robert Underwood Johnson. HBV
I see her on a lonely forest track. The Maroon Girl. Walter Adolphe Roberts. PoNe
"I see herrin'." I hear the glad cry. With the Herring Fishers. "Hugh MacDiarmid." LiTM (1970 ed.)
I see him old, trapped in a burly house. A Pauper. Allen Tate. LiTM
I see Him: on thy lap He lies. Dei Genitrix. Aubrey Thomas De Vere. IrPN
I see him sit, wild-eyed, alone. The Last Aboriginal. "Fiona Macleod." PoVP; VA
I See His Blood upon the Rose. Joseph Mary Plunkett. CAW; ChIP; GoBC; HBMV; JKCP; MaRV; MoRP; NeHB; OnYI; OQP; OxBI; PoLF; StJW; TRV; WGRP
I see Hunger watching at every house door. Cha Liang-cheng. *Fr.* Hungry China. LiTW
I see, I hear, I feel, I know, I rue. Fidessa, More Chaste than Kind, XLVII. Bartholomew Griffin. ReIE
I see in his last preached and printed booke. On John Donne's Book of Poems. John Marriott. CH
I see in you the estuary that enlarges and spreads. To Old Age. Whitman. InP
I see in your eyes. To a Certain Woman. Albert Rice. CDC
I see it. Song for the Dead, III. *Unknown.* TTY
I See My Plaint. *At. to* John Harington. EIL
I see no bird arise. My Sun-killed Tree. Marguerite Harris. GoYe
I see no equivalents. The Poet at Night-Fall. Glenway Wescott. LiTM (1946 ed.); NP
I see now, not far away, the savage pit. Recognition of Death. Joseph Payne Brennan. FiSC
I See Phantoms of Hatred and of the Heart's Fullness and of the Coming Emptiness. W. B. Yeats. Meditations in Time of

I (continued)
Civil War, VII. CABL; LiTB; PIA
I see skies more bright and blue. Sight. Cora Ball Moton. GoSl
I see that chance hath chosen me. Sir Thomas Wyatt. FCP; SiPS
I see that there it is on the beach. Memorial Service for the Invasion Beach Where the Vacation in the Flesh Is Over. Alan Dugan. NMP; TwCP
I see that wreath which doth the wearer arm. To My Dead Friend Ben: Johnson. Henry King. AnAnS-2; SeCP
I See the Boys of Summer. Dylan Thomas. LiTB
I see the cloud-born squadrons of the gale. A Storm in the Distance. Paul Hamilton Hayne. AA
I see the crowd in Pilate's hall. Our Share in Calvary. Horatius Bonar. SoP
I see the curse on gestures proud and cold. The Curse. Shelley. *Fr.* Prometheus Unbound, I. PoFr
I see the dawn e'en now begin to peer. *Unknown. Fr.* Popular Songs of Tuscany. AWP
I see the four-fold man, the humanity in deadly sleep. Blake. *Fr.* Jerusalem. PoIE
I see the golden hunter go. Bliss Carman. *Fr.* Songs of the Sea-Children. OBCV
I See the Heavy Startled Hair. Bilhana, *formerly at. to* Chauras, *tr. fr. Sanskrit by* E. Powys Mathers. *Fr.* Black Marigolds. OnPM
I see the horses and the sad streets. The Eye. Allen Tate. LiTA
I see the house. My heart thyself contain! Astrophel and Stella, LXXXV. Sir Philip Sidney. FCP; SiPS
I see the light. Waiting. Henry W. Frost. SoP
I see the map of summer, lying still. Movies for the Home. Howard Moss. NePoEA-2; NYBP
I see the moon. The Moon. *Unknown.* GoTP; OxNR; PCH; SoPo; TiPo
I see the star-lights quiver. The Flight from the Convent. Theodore Tilton. AA
I see the sun. Sometimes on My Way back down to the Block. Victor Hernandez Cruz. BOLo
I see the use; and know my blood [*or* bloud]. The Storm. Henry Vaughan. AnAnS-1; CBEP; MeP
I see the winter turned around. The Bicycle Rider. David Shapiro. ANYP
I see the wrong that round me lies. Whittier. *Fr.* The Eternal Goodness. SoP; TRV
I see the young bride move among. George Barker. *Fr.* The True Confession of George Barker. ErPo
I see thee ever in my dreams. The Karamanian Exile. James Clarence Mangan. IrPN; OBVV; PeVV
I see Thee in the distant blue. God. John Banister Tabb. MaRV; TreFT
I see thee pine like her in golden story. Coleridge. Theodore Watts-Dunton. HBV; OBVV; Sonn; VA
I see thee still! thou art not dead. A Remembrance. Willis Gaylord Clarke. AA
I see them a mother and daughter. On the Bridge of Athlone; a Prophecy. Donagh MacDonagh. OxBI
I see them,—crowd on crowd they walk the earth. The Dead. Jones Very. AA; AmePo; AnNE; AP; CBV; MAmP; OxBA
I see them nightly in my sleep. Eyes of God. Hermann Hagedorn. HBMV
I see them on my trellises and walls. Wistaria Blossoms. Charles Dalmon. *Fr.* Three Pictures. TSW
I see them working in old rectories. The Country Clergy. R. S. Thomas. BoPe; GTBS-P; PoIE
I see they're packing up once more. Tabitha Soliloquizes. Minnie Leona Upton. CIV
I see thou holdest cheap two things. On the Sultan Mahmúd. Firdausi. LiTW
I see you, a child. The Album. C. Day Lewis. ChMP; EnLoPo; FaBoEn; OxBI
I see you, angels with choirboy faces. Singing Children: Luca Della Robbia (T. H.). C. Day Lewis. MuSP
I see you did not try to save. Passing the Graveyard. Andrew Young. DTC
I see you in her bed. The Lovemaker. Robert Mezey. CABA; NePoEA-2
I see you in the silver. Arctic Tern in a Museum. Mary Effie Lee Newsome. PoNe
I see you, Juliet, still, with your straw hat. Farewell to Juliet. Wilfrid Scawen Blunt. The Love Sonnets of Proteus, XLVII. EnLoPo
I seek a being to invade. Impulses. Henri Michaux. OnHM
I seek for peace—I care not where 'tis found. Peace. John Clare. BoPe
I seek, in prayerful words, dear friend. God Bless You. *Unknown.* PoToHe
I Seek Thee in the Heart Alone. Herbert Trench. WGRP
I seem but a drudge, yet I pass any king. The Praise of Husbandry [*or* True as Thy Faith, This Riddle Thus Saith]. Thomas Tusser. SiCE; TuPP
I seem to have come to the cross-roads. The Crossroads. E. Randall. SoP
I Seem to See My Prison Walls. Bilhana, *formerly at. to* Chauras, *tr. fr. Sanskrit by* E. Powys Mathers. *Fr.* Black Marigolds. OnPM
I seen a dunce of a poet once, a-writin' a little book. Gelett Burgess. *Fr.* The Protest of the Illiterate. FiBHP
I seen her last night. A Lament. L. A. G. Strong. YT
I seize the sphery harp. I strike the strings. Enitharmon Revives with Los. Blake. *Fr.* Vala. ChTr; OBNC
I selfish and forsaken do still long for you. Deus Absconditus. Anne Ridler. FaBoMo
I sell the best brandy and sherry. O'Tuomy's Drinking Song. John O'Tuomy. OnYI
I send a garland to my love. The Lover's Posy. Rufinus. AWP; JAWP; WBP
I send, I send here my supremest kiss. His Tears to Thamesis. Robert Herrick. OAEP
I send my heart up to thee, all my heart. In a Gondola. Robert Browning. BEL; EPN; PoVP; VA; ViBoPo; ViPo
I Send Our Lady. Sister Mary Thérèse. ISi
I send thee a shell from the ocean beach. With a Nantucket Shell. Charles Henry Webb. AA
I send thee here of ribbon a whole yard. *Unknown.* LO
I send thee myrrh, not that thou mayest be. Not of Itself but Thee. *Unknown.* AWP
I send you here a sort of allegory. To ——: With the Following Poem. Tennyson. *Introd. Poem to* The Palace of Art. MBV-2; ViPo; ViPP; VP
I send you here a wreath of blossoms blown. Roses. Pierre de Ronsard. AWP; JAWP; WBP
I send you perfume fresh as dew. Perfume. *Unknown.* UnTE
I sent a letter to my love. George Barker. *Fr.* The True Confession of George Barker. FaBoTw
I sent a ring—a little band. To Helene. George Darley. OBEV (1st ed.)
I Sent for Ratcliffe. Matthew Prior. *See* Remedy Worse than the Disease, The.
I sent my Collie to the wash. Nonsense Quatrains. Gelett Burgess. CenHV
I sent my love a parcel. By Parcels Post. George K. Sims. BOHV
I sent my love two roses—one. White Flag. John Hay. HBV
I sent my Soul through the Invisible. The Soul Is All [*or* Heaven and Hell]. Omar Khayyám, *tr. by* Edward Fitzgerald. *Fr.* The Rubáiyát. MaRV; OnPM
I, Seraphion, hermit of Mount Athos. Seraphion. James K. Baxter. AnNZ
I Serve. Meinloh von Sevelingen, *tr. fr. German by* Jethro Bithell. OnPM; WoL
I Serve a Mistress. Anthony Munday, *ad. fr. the Italian of* Luigi Pasqualigo. *Fr.* Fidele and Fortunio. ElL; LO
(Fedele's Song.) OBSC
(Fidele's Song.) CBEP
I serve. With unagressive mien. Ich Dien. Susie M. Best. OQP
I served in a Great Cause. Horace L. Traubel. AA
I served my time in [*or* on] the Black Ball Line. The Black Ball Line [*or* Blow, Boys, Blow]. *Unknown.* ABF; ShS (*vers.* IV); SoAmSa
I set a charm upon your hurrying breath. A Marriage Charm. Nora Hopper. HBV
I set a jumpy mouse trap. A Change of Heart. Valine Hobbs. SiSoSe
I Set Aside. Mary Morison Webster. PeSA
I set my heart to sing of leaves. Anticipation. Lord De Tabley. ELP; GTBS-D
I shake my hair in the wind of morning. Triumph of Love. John

Hall Wheelock. MAP; MoAmPo; NP
I shake-shake. Do Not Open until Christmas. James S. Tippett. ChBR
I shall always come to find you here. Orpheus. J. F. Hendry. NeBP
"I shall arise." For centuries. Resurgam. *Unknown.* WGRP
I shall be beautiful when you come back. Transformation. Jessie B. Rittenhouse. HBMV
I shall be capricious, I shall have a whim. A Man's Woman. Mary Carolyn Davies. PoLF
"I shall be careful to say nothing at all." How She Resolved to Act. Merrill Moore. MAP; MeWo; MoAmPo; NeMA
I Shall Be Loved as Quiet Things. Karle Wilson Baker. HBMV; MCCG; MoLP
I Shall Be Married on Monday Morning. *Unknown.* ErPo
I Shall Be Satisfied. M. Behemb. BePJ
I shall be shapen. A Pair of Lovers. Jeanne Robert Foster. HBMV
I shall come back in ways I think you'll know. Unregenerate. Jacqueline Embry. HBMV
I shall come back to die. In This Dark House. Edward Davidson. OBMV
I shall come this way again. Auf Wiedersehen. Donald Jeffrey Hayes. CDC
I shall cry God to give me a broken foot. Flash Crimson. Carl Sandburg. MAP; MoAmPo
I shall foot it. The Road and the End. Carl Sandburg. NP
I shall gather myself into myself again. The Crystal Gazer. Sara Teasdale. MAP; MoAmPo; NeMA
I shall go among red faces and virile voices. Cattle Show. "Hugh MacDiarmid." GoTS; MoBrPo; OBMV
I shall go as my father went. The Tenancy. Mary Gilmore. BoAV; PoAu-1
I shall go away. And the birds will still be there. The Conclusive Voyage. Juan Ramón Jiménez. PoPl
I Shall Go Back. Edna St. Vincent Millay. AnNE; MoAmPo; NePA
(I Shall Go Back Again.) MAP
("I shall go back again to the bleak shore.") GTBS-W
I shall go by lightly. Who Goes By Lightly. Gertrude Callaghan. JKCP (1955 ed.)
I shall go down from the stark, gray-stone towers. Refuge. Hervey Allen. HBMV
I shall go forth one day to joust with death. The Last Tourney. Frederic F. Van de Water. HBMV
I shall go on the gypsies' road. The Gypsies' Road. Dora Sigerson Shorter. OBVV
I shall go out as all men go. I Accept. Harold Trowbridge Pulsifer. HBMV; OQP
I shall go out when the light comes in. Death at Daybreak. Anne Reeve Aldrich. AA; OQP
I shall hate you. Hatred. Gwendolyn B. Bennett. AmNP; BANP; CDC
I shall have a gold room. Chanson d'Or. Ann Hamilton. HBMV
I Shall Have Had My Day. Tennyson. *See* Song: "O let the solid ground."
I shall have pearls blacker than caviar. Capriccio. Babette Deutsch. HBMV; TSW
I shall have three grey poplar trees above me when I sleep. The Three Poplars. Philip Francis Little. OxBI
I shall just put away this hoarded bottle. Addict. Mabel MacDonald Carver. FiSC
I Shall Laugh Purely. Robinson Jeffers. CrMA; LiTA; LiTM (rev. ed.); WaP
I shall lie hidden in a hut. Prophecy. Elinor Wylie. AnAmPo
I shall make a song like your hair. Secret. Gwendolyn B. Bennett. CDC
I shall make a song of the Queen of Crete. The Queen of Crete. John Grimes. HBMV
I shall make offering in a new basket of marsh-grass. Intervals. Beatrice Ravenel. HBMV
I shall never forget my mother's voice singing. Now That Can Never Be Done. Sister Maris Stella. GoBC
I shall never get you put together entirely. The Colossus. Sylvia Plath. LiTM (1970 ed.); NePoEA-2
I shall not ask Jean Jacques Rousseau. Pairing-Time Anticipated. William Cowper. BOHV
I Shall Not Be Afraid. Aline Kilmer. HBMV; JKCP; NP
I shall not call for help until they coffin me. Last Lines. Egan O'Rahilly. KiLC
I Shall Not Care. Sara Teasdale. AnEnPo; HBV; MAP; MoAmPo; NeMA; PFY; PoPl; TrGrPo
I Shall Not Cry Return. Ellen M. H. Gates. HBV
I Shall Not Die. *Unknown, tr. fr. Irish by* Frank O'Connor. KiLC
I Shall Not Die for Thee. *Unknown, tr. fr. Modern Irish by* Douglas Hyde. AnIL; OxBI; CTC, *tr. by* Padraic Colum
I shall not get my poem done. Karle Wilson Baker. *Fr.* Poet Songs. HBMV
I shall not go to the autumn woods again. Disillusion. Sister Mary Edwardine. JKCP (1955 ed.)
I shall not lie to you any more. The Modern Woman to Her Lover. Margaret Widdemer. HBMV
I shall not miss the roses, fading. Grapes. Pushkin. OnPM
I Shall Not Pass Again This Way ("The bread that bringeth strength"). Ellen H. Underwood. BLRP; FaChP; MaRV; OQP; TreF; WBLP
(Service, *wr. at. to* D. S. Ford.) SoP
I Shall Not Pass This Way Again ("Through this toilsome world, alas!"). *Unknown.* BLPA; NeHB; SoP; TreFS
I Shall Not Pass This Way Again. Eva Rose York. FaFP; MaRV; OHFP; WBLP
I shall not regard my swelled head as a sign of real glory. Aimé Césaire. *Fr.* Return to My Native Land. TTY
I shall not see the faces of my friends. The Dying Reservist. Maurice Baring. HBV
I shall not see thee. Dare I say. In Memoriam A. H. H., XCIII. Tennyson. EPN; ViPo; VP
I shall not tarry over scrolls. Bethlehem. Harry Webb Farrington. OQP
I Shall Not Weep. Belle MacDiarmid. HBMV
I shall not wonder more, then. Change. Raymond Knister. CaP; OBCV; PeCV
I shall note first/ the ones I loved. The Chronicler. Alexander Bergman. TrJP
I shall recall/ As a sinister omen. Revelations. Sterling A. Brown. Kal
I Shall Remember. H. D. Carberry. PoNe
I shall remember then. Youth. Thomas S. Jones, Jr. OQP
"I shall return!" Ed Sanders. *Fr.* Toe Queen Poems. ANYP
I shall rot here with those whom in their day. In Death Divided. Thomas Hardy. DTC
I shall say, Lord, "Is it music, is it morning." Resurgam. Marjorie Pickthall. OBCV
I shall say what inordinat love is. Inordinate Love. *Unknown.* MeEL
I shall see a star tonight. Star Thought. Frances Shaw. NP
I Shall See Him. Washington Gladden. *See* Ultima Veritas.
I Shall See Them Again. E. Husband. SoP
I shall slough my self as a snake its skin. "I." Louis Golding. TrJP
I shall steal upon her. Chanson Naïve. John McClure. HBMV
I shall take flight from Death on sudden wings. The Victory. John Hall Wheelock. NP
I shall tell you. Strangers. Mark Turbyfill. NP
I shall walk down the road. Death. Maxwell Bodenheim. AnAmPo; LiTM; MAP; MAPA; MoAmPo (1942 ed.); NP; PFY; TrJP
I shall wear laughter on my lips. Hope. Anna Blake Mezquida. MaRV; TRV
I Shall Weep. Peretz Hirshbein, *tr. fr. Yiddish by* Joseph Leftwich. TrJP
I shape the vessel of my life. Misdirection. Eleanor Slater. MoSiPe
I sheath my sword. In mercy go. Victory. Aline Kilmer. MaRV
I shipped, dy'e see, in a Revenue sloop. The Darned Mounseer. W. S. Gilbert. *Fr.* Ruddigore. TSW
I shipped on board of th' *Ebenezer.* The *Ebenezer.* *Unknown.* ShS
I shiver, Spirit fierce and bold. At the Grave of Burns. Wordsworth. *Fr.* Memorials of a Tour in Scotland, 1803. BEL; EnLi-2; EnRP; MERP
I shoot the Hippopotamus. The Hippopotamus. Hilaire Belloc. CenHV; FiBHP; PoPl; ShBV-2; UTS; WhC
I shot a golf ball into the air. The Ball and the Club. Forbes Lindsay. SD

I shot an arrow into the air. A Shot at Random. D. B. Wyndham Lewis. FaFP; FiBHP; SiTL

I shot an arrow into the air. The Arrow and the Song. Longfellow. AA; AnAmPo; AnNE; BBV (1951 ed.) DD; FaFP; HBV; HBVY; MaRV; NeHB; OQP; OTPC; PG (1933 ed.); PoPl; PoToHe (new ed.); TreF

I shot an otter because I had a gun. The Shooting. Robert Pack. CoPo

I shot him where the Rio flows. Marta of Milrone. Herman Scheffauer. SCC

I shot my friend to save my country's life. The Body Politic. Donald Hall. NePoEA; TwCP

I should grieve to desperation. Anacreon to the Sophist. "B. H." InMe

I should have been delighted there to hear. The Cold Divinities. James Wright. AmPC

I should have cut my life. Eviction. Elizabeth Brewster. CaP

I should have seen the sign: "Fresh paint." Fresh Paint. Boris Pasternak. PoPl; TrJP

I should have thought. At Baia. Hilda Doolittle ("H. D."). AnFE; APA; CoAnAm; LiTA; NP; TwAmPo

I should like a great lake of ale. The Feast of Saint Brigid of Kildare. *At. to* St. Bridget. CAW; OnYI

"I should like to buy you a birthday present," said Billy to Betsy Jane. Betsy Jane's Sixth Birthday. Alfred Noyes. BiCB; SiSoSe

I should like to creep. A Mona Lisa. Angelina Weld Grimké. CDC

I Should Like to Have a Great Pool of Ale. *At. to* St. Bridget, *See* Feast of Saint Brigid of Kildare, The.

I should like to rise and go. Travel. Robert Louis Stevenson. BrPo; FaBoCh; FaPON; GoTP; HT; LoGBV; MoShBr; MPB; PoVP; StVeCh; TiPo; WaKn

I should like to see that country's tiled bedrooms. Keeping Their World Large. Marianne Moore. WaP

I should not dare to be so sad. Emily Dickinson. InPo; MWA-2

I should not say. Thomas Lovell Beddoes. *Fr.* The Second Brother, II, i. AtBAP

I should pray but my soul is stopt. At the Ocean's Verge. Ralph Gustafson. OBCV

I should rather say one prayer to the Mother of God. Preference. Daniel Sargent. ISi

I should worry, I should care. *Unknown.* ExPo

I shout my words above the blowing wind. I Sing America Now! Jesse Stuart. AmFN

I sicken of men's company. The Green Inn. Theodosia Garrison. HBMV

I sieze the sphery harp. I strike the strings. *See* I seize the sphery harp. . .

I Sigh All the Night. Edward Ravenscroft. *Fr.* The Citizen Turned Gentleman. SeCL

I Sigh, As Sure to Wear the Fruit. *Unknown.* NCEP

I sigh for the heavenly country. The Heavenly City. Stevie Smith. FaBoTw

I sighed [*or* sigh'd] and owned [*or* own'd] my love. *Unknown.* EG; GTBS-W

I sike when I singe. The Crucifixion. *Unknown.* MeEL

I sing a legend of the sea. The Captain and the Mermaids. W. S. Gilbert. YT

I Sing a Maiden. *Unknown.* *See* I Sing of a Maiden.

I sing a woofull ditty. A Ballad Call'd the Hay-Markett Hectors. *At. to* Andrew Marvell. PeRV

I Sing America Now! Jesse Stuart. AmFN

I Sing an Old Song. Oscar Williams. LiTM; NePA

I sing divine Astrea's praise. A Dialogue between Two Shepherds, Thenot and Piers, in Praise of Astrea. Countess of Pembroke. ReIE

I sing her worth and praises hy. A Description. Lord Herbert of Cherbury. AnAnS-2; SeCP

I sing no harme good sooth to any wight. A Tale of a Citizen and His Wife. John Donne. Elegies, XIV. MaMe

I sing no longer of the skies. The Song of the King's Minstrel. Richard Middleton. HBV

I Sing No New Songs. Frank Marshall Davis. PoNe

I sing not of Angelica the fair. Richard Barnfield. *Fr.* Lady Pecunia; or, The Praise of Money. ReIE

I sing not of the draper's praise, nor yet of William Wood. An Excellent New Song upon His Grace Our Good Lord Archbishop of Dublin. Swift. CoMu

I sing not old Jason, who travell'd thro' Greece. Down-Hall; a Ballad. Matthew Prior. CEP

I sing of a frigate, a frigate of fame. The Flash Frigate. *Unknown.* AmSS

I Sing of a Maiden. *Unknown.* AtBAP; BoW; BuBa; CABA; CBEP; CH; EG; ELP; ExPo; FaBoCh; GoTP; InPo; ISi; LiTB; LoGBV; MeEL; MeEV; MemP; NoP; PoAn; PoEL-1; PoIE; SeCeV; TreFS; TrGrPo; ViBoPo
(Ancient Carol, An.) PTK
(As Dew in Aprille.) FIW
(Carol: "I sing of a Maiden.") BoC; OBEV; OxBoCh; PoLi; ShBV-2; ThWaDe
(Carol to Our Lady.) CAW; GoBC
(I Sing a Maiden.) OnPM
(I Syng of a Mayden.) OAEP
("I syng of a myden that is makeles.") EnPo
(Maiden Makeles, The.) ChTr
(Two Carols to Our Lady, 1.) ACP
Ancient Christmas Carol, An, *sel.* OHIP; PCH; RG
(Carol: "He came all so still.") BoTP; DD; HBV; HBVY

I sing of autumn and the falling fruit. Ship of Death. D. H. Lawrence. DTC; MoAB; NAMP; MoBrPo (1962 ed.); ViBoPo

I sing of brooks, of blossom[e]s, birds, and bowers. The Argument of His Book. Robert Herrick. *Fr.* Hesperides. AnAnS-2; AtBAP; AWP; BEL; BoLiVe; CoBE; EnL; EnLi-1; EnLit; ForPo; HBV; HBVY; InP; InPo; InvP; MyFE; NoP; OAEP; OBS; PoE; PoEL-3; PoeP; PoIE; PoRA; ReEn; SCEP-2; SeCePo; SeCeV; SeCP; SeCV-1; SeEP; TrGrPo; ViBoPo; WHA

I sing of George Augustus Chadd. The Ballad of Private Chadd. A. A. Milne. CenHV

I sing of ghosts and people under ground. The End. Mark Van Doren. ViBoPo

I sing of men and angels, and the days. Ebenezer Elliott. *Fr.* Spirits and Men. OBRV

I sing of news, and all those vapid sheets. George Crabbe. *Fr.* The Newspaper. PPON

I Sing of Olaf [Glad and Big]. E. E. Cummings. AmP; LiTA; LiTM; NePA; PoIE; PPON; SiTL; StP; WaP

I sing of Pope. A Dialogue. Austin Dobson. PoVP

I sing of Tony Caesar, a big league arbiter of unimpeachable repute. Decline and Fall of a Roman Umpire. Ogden Nash. SD

I sing of the decline of Henry Clay. Conquistador. A. D. Hope. MoAuPo

I sing of the Good Samaritan. The Song of the Good Samaritan. Vernon Watkins. LiTM (rev. ed.)

I sing th' adventures of mine worthy wights. The Poem. Thomas Morton. SCAP

I sing the birth, was born[e] tonight. A Hymne on (*or* A Hymn for] the Nativitie of My Saviour. Ben Jonson. SCEP-2; SeCV-1; StJW

I Sing the Body Electric. Walt Whitman. CTC; MasP
Sels.
"O my body! I dare not desert the likes of you in other men and women, nor the likes of the parts of you." ErPo
"This is the female form." ErPo

I sing the civil wars, tumultuous broils. Samuel Daniel. *Fr.* The Civil Wars. ReIE

I sing the glorious power with azure eyes. Hymn to Athena. *Unknown.* *Fr.* Homeric Hymns. AWP

I sing the hymn of the conquered, who fell in the battle of life. Io Victis! William Wetmore Story. AA; HBV; MaRV; OQP; WGRP

I sing the Man, by Heav'ns peculiar grace. A Poem on Elijahs Translation. Benjamin Colman. SCAP

I sing the Man who Judah's Scepter bore. Abraham Cowley. *Fr.* Davideis, I. SCEP-2; SeEP

I Sing the Mighty Power of God. Isaac Watts. SoP; TRV

I sing the Name which none can say. To the Name above Every Name, the Name of Jesus, a Hymn [*or* On the Name of Jesus]. Richard Crashaw. AnAns-1; MaMe; MeP; SCEP-1; SeCV-1

I sing the praise of honored wars. The Soldier's Song. *Unknown.* ReEn; TuPP; WiR

I sing the progresse of a deathlesse soule. First Song. John Donne. *Fr.* Infinitati Sacrum. MaMe

I sing the simplest flower. Karl Shapiro. *Fr.* Six Religious Lyrics, I. CMoP

I sing the sofa. I, who lately sang [*or* sung]. The Sofa.

William Cowper. *Fr.* The Task. CEP; EiCP; NoP; OAEP
I sing the song of a new dawn waking. Song of the New World. Angela Morgan. HBMV; HBVY; OQP
I sing the song of the sleeping wife. Sing Song. Robert Creeley. NMP
I sing the song of the workman. The Song of Labor. Ninette M. Lowater. PEDC
I sing the uplift and the up-welling. The Redeeming Mercy. Israel Zangwill. *Fr.* Jehovah. WGRP
I sing this, to a revolving of rubber wheels. Night Letter. Tyner White. YAP
I sing to him that rests below. In Memoriam, A. H. H., XXI. Tennyson. EnL; EnLi-2; EPN; FosPo; ViPo; VP
I sing what was lost and dread what was won. What Was Lost. W. B. Yeats. POTE
I sing with myself. Duet. Leonora Speyer. HBMV
I, singularly moved. Winter. Coventry Patmore. The Unknown Eros, I, iii. LO; OBNC
I Sit Alone. Walter de la Mare. POTE
I sit alone and watch the dark'ning years. Thy Look. Spencer. SoP
I sit among my flasks and jars. The Story of the Alchemist. Eugene Williams. PCD
I Sit and Look Out. Walt Whitman. AmePo; CABA; CBEP; MaRV; OxBA; PPON
("I sit and look out upon all the sorrows of the world.") TRV
I Sit and Sew. Alice Dunbar Moore Nelson. CDC
I sit at eve within the curtain's fold. L'Angelo. Thomas Caulfield Irwin. IrPN
I sit at home and sew. Needle Travel. Margaret French Patton. HBMV
I sit beside my darling's grave. To God and Ireland True. Ellen O'Leary. VA
I sit beside the brazier's glow. Before Action. W. W. Gibson. BEL; TOP
I sit drinking wine. Percussion, Salt and Honey. Stuart Peterfreund. QAH
I sit here at the window. Poetry and Thoughts on Same. Franklin P. Adams. HBMV
I sit here dreaming. Our Beautiful West Coast Thing. Richard Brautigan. FRC
I sit in a roadside diner. September 1, 1965. Paris Leary. CoPo
I sit in an office at 244 Madison Avenue. Spring Comes to Murray Hill. Ogden Nash. FiBHP
I sit in my garden among the roses. Prisoners. Nancy Barr Mavity. HBMV
I sit in one of the dives. September 1, 1939. W. H. Auden. CMoP; CoBMV; ExPo; FaBoEn; ForPo; InPo; LiTA; LiTM; MaPo; MasP; MoAB; MoBrPo (1950 ed.); MoVE; NePA; OAEP (2d ed.); OxBA; PIA; PoFS; ReMP; SeCeV; WaP
I sit in the dusk. I am all alone. Tableau at Twilight. Ogden Nash. FiBHP
I sit in the top of the wood, my eyes closed. Hawk Roosting. Ted Hughes. GTBS-P; LiTM (1970 ed.); NePoEA-2; NMP; OA; POTi; TwCP
I sit on the back platform of the train. The Train Butcher. Thomas Hornsby Ferril. GoYe
I sit on the surge called ten stories tall. The Seesaw. Oscar Williams. LiTA; LiTG
I Sit with My Dolls. *Unknown, tr. fr. Yiddish by* Joseph Leftwich. TrJP
I sit within my room, and joy to find. The Presence. Jones Very. PoIE
I sleep and rest, my heart makes moan. Seven Times Five—Widowhood. Jean Ingelow. *Fr.* Songs of Seven. GBV (1922 ed.); HBV
I Sleep, but My Heart Waketh. The Song of Solomon, V:2-VI:3, Bible, *O.T.* TrJP
I sleep with thee and wake with thee. To Mary. John Clare. EnLoPo
I slept all day. The Birds Do Thus. Robert Frost. AmePo
I slept and dreamed that life was Beauty. Duty. Ellen S. Hooper. BLPA; HBV; NeHB; OQP; TreFS
I slept. I dreamed. I seemed to climb a hard, ascending [*or* ascended] track. Africa. *Unknown.* MaRV; SoP; StJW
I slept in a sleepy field. Airship. Hy Sobiloff. NePA
I slept in an old homestead by the sea. Chimney Swallows. Horatio Nelson Powers. HBV; OTPC (1923 ed.)
I slept on my three-legged stool by the fire. Two Songs of a Fool, II. W. B. Yeats. CMoP; OA; PoG
I slouch in bed. Two Hangovers. James Wright. AmPC
I slumbered with your poems on my breast. To E. T. Robert Frost. ML
I slump in the bucket-seat. Twink Drives Back, in a Bad Mood, from a Party in Massachusetts. George Amabile. NYBP
I smile sometimes, although my grief be great. The Passion of a Lover [*or* Gascoigne's Passion]. George Gascoigne. EnRePo; NCEP
I smile to see how you devise. A Proper Sonnet Intituled: I Smile to See How You Devise. *Unknown.* ReIE
I so love water laughter. Streams. Clinton Scollard. PoMa
I somersault just like a clown. Somersault. Dorothy Aldis. SoPo
I sometimes hold it half a sin. In Memoriam A. H. H., V. Tennyson. EnLi-2; EPN; FosPo; OAEP; OuHeWo; ViPo; VP
I Sometimes Think. *Unknown.* *See* To Be or Not to Be.
I sometimes think I'd like to be. The Best of All. Margaret G. Rhodes. BoTP
I sometimes think that I will. Don Marquis. Grotesques, III. FiBHP
I sometimes think that mountains are not worth. Praise of Engineers. James J. Donohue. JKCP (1955 ed.)
I sometimes think that never blows so red. So Red the Rose. Omar Khayyám, *tr. by* Edward Fitzgerald. *Fr.* The Rubáiyát. InP; LO; OnPM
I sometimes wonder if it's really true. Hill-born. W. W. Gibson. NP
I sometimes wonder where he lives. Echo. *Unknown.* GFA
I sorrow for youth—ah, not for its wildness (would that were dead!). Christopher Brennan. *Fr.* The Wanderer. ACV
I sought a theme and sought for it in vain. The Circus Animals' Desertion. W. B. Yeats. CMoP; DiPo; FaBoTw; LiTB; MaPo (1969 ed.); OAEP (2d ed.); PoeP; PoIE; PP
I sought for peace, but could not find. Peace [*or* On Peace]. *At. to* Samuel Speed. BoPe; OxBoCh; SeCL; SeEP
I sought for the greatness. America Is Great Because—. *At. to* Alexis de Tocqueville. TreFT
I sought Him in a great cathedral, dim. Search. Anne Marriott. MaRV; SoP; TRV
I sought Him in the still, far place where flowers blow. God's Way. Dorothy Clarke Wilson. MaRV
I sought Him where my logic led. The Search. Sara Henderson Hay. MaRV
I sought his love in sun and stars. The Search. Thomas Curtis Clark. MaRV; SoP; WGRP
I sought immortality. The Crib. Christopher Morley. BiCB
I Sought My Soul. *Unknown.* MaRV; TreFT; TRV
I sought not from thee a return. Abraham Cowley. *Fr.* The Vain-Love. LO
I sought of bishop and priest and judges. On Christians, Mercy Will Fall. *Unknown.* *Fr.* The Black Book of Carmarthen. PrWP
I Sought on Earth. George Santayana. Sonnets, I. AnEnPo
(Sorrow.) WGRP
I Sought the Living God. John Calvin Slemp. ChIP
I Sought the Lord. *Unknown.* FaChP; MaRV; TRV
(I Was Found of Thee.) SoP
I sought Thee round about, O Thou my God. The Search for God. Thomas Heywood. *Fr.* Hierarchie of the Blessed Angels. MaRV; OxBoCh; WGRP
I sought to hear the voice of God. The Voice of God. Louis I. Newman. OQP; PoToHe; SoP; TreF
I sought to hold her, but within her eyes. The Angel at the Ford. William James Dawson. VA
I Sought with Eager Hand. Allan Dowling. ErPo
I Sought You. John Hall Wheelock. BoLP
I sowed my wild oats. Song. Dom Moraes. BoPe
I sowed the seeds of love. The Seeds of Love. *Unknown, at. to* Mrs. Fleetwood Habergham. CBEP; ELP; FaBoCh; LoGBV; OxBoLi, *sl. diff.*; WiR
I span and Eve span. Eve Song. Mary Gilmore. MoAuPo; PoAu-1
I speak for each no-tongueéd tree. Sidney Lanier. *Fr.* The Symphony. ViBoPo
I Speak Not, I Trace Not, I Breathe Not Thy Name. Byron. *See* Stanzas for Music.
I speak of that great house. Beyond the Hunting Woods. Donald Justice. NePoEA; NYBP; PoPl

I speak of that lady I heard last night. The Lady's Complaint. John Heath-Stubbs. TwCP
I speak of wants, of frauds, of policies. De Subiecto Operis Sui. Thomas Bastard. SiCE
I speak this poem now with grave and level voice. Immortal Autumn. Archibald MacLeish. AP; BoLiVe (1945 ed); CMoP; CoBMV; LiTA; MAP; MoAB; MoAmPo; NeMa; NP; ReMP; SiSw; TrGrPo
I speak with a proud tongue of the people who were. Slainthe [*or* Dedication]. Patrick MacGill. AnIV; OnYI
I Spend My Days Vainly. Frank Kendon. MoBrPo (1942 ed.); POTE
I spend my sad life in sighs and in cries. To Celia. Daniel Kenrick. SeCL
I spent a night turning in bed. The Whip. Robert Creeley. NaP; NeAP; ToPo
I spent afternoons like an old man's drowsy years. The Catfish. Jack Mathews. TPM
I spent the day in a heavenly way. Katharine. Heine. UnTE
I spied a very small brown duck. Duck-Chasing. Galway Kinnell. NMP; TwCP
I spied beside the garden bed. In the Garden. Ernest Crosby. HBV; HBVY
I splash—I flop. The Lesson. Jane W. Krows. SoPo
I spoiled the day. A Wasted Day. Frances Cornford. HBMV; MoBrPo; NeMA; TSW
I spoke a word, and no one heard. A Little Word [*or* Influence]. John Oxenham. OTD; STF
I spoke to the pale and heavy-lidded woman, and said. The Pale Woman. Arthur Symons. FaBoTw
I Spoke to the Violet. John Shaw Neilson. BoAV
I spoke to thee. Orientale. E. E. Cummings. NP;PG
I spoke to you about soul today. To My Friend. Martha Snell Nicholson. SoP
I spot the hills. Theme in Yellow. Carl Sandburg. MPB; PCD; RePo; StVeCh (1955 ed.); TiPo; YeAr
I sprang to the rollocks and Jorrocks and me. How I Brought the Good News from Aix to Ghent (or Vice Versa). Robert Julian Yeatman *and* Walter Carruthers Sellar. FiBHP; OnMSP; WhC
I sprang to the stirrup, and Joris, and he. How They Brought the Good News from Ghent to Aix. Robert Browning. BBV (1923 ed.); BEL; BeLS; BoChLi; EnLi-2 (1949 ed.); FaBoBe; FaFP; GN; GoTP; HBV; HBVY; HoPM; MBW-2; MCCG; MemP; OnSP; OTPC; PAn; PaPo; PCD; PeVV; PoPo; PoVP; PTK; RoGo; ShBV-1; StVeCh; TiPo (1952 ed.); TOP; TreF; VA; ViPo; ViPP; WePo
I Spy. N. E. Hussey. BoTP
I staid the night for shelter at a farm. *See* I stayed the night. . .
I stand above a white-rimmed sea. The Sea of Peace. Ruth McEnery Stuart. MaRV
I stand alone through each long day. The Blind Peddler. Sir Osbert Sitwell. MoBrPo (1942 ed.)
I stand amid the roar. A Dream within a Dream. Poe. ChTr
I stand before your cage to make my sketch. Artist and Ape. Gordden Link. GoYe
I stand beneath the tree, whose branches shade. St. John's, Cambridge. Longfellow. OBEV
I stand beside a comrade tree. At Lanier's Grave. John Banister Tabb. AmP
I stand between the Future and the Past. Mortal and Immortal. Robert Cassie Waterston. SoP
I Stand Corrected. Margaret Fishback. PoPl; WhC
I stand here every afternoon. The Balloon Man. E. Herbert. BoTP
I stand here in the ditch, my feet on a rock in the water. The Blackberry Thicket. Ann Stanford. WIRo
I stand in my door and look over the low field[s] of Drynam. The Widow of Drynam. Patrick MacDonogh. NeIP; OnYI; OxBI
I stand in the dark light in the dark street. Birthplace Revisited. Gregory Corso. CAD; NeAP; OCS
I stand most humbly. Wisdom. Langston Hughes. TiPo
I stand on slenderness all fresh and fair. A Cut Flower. Karl Shapiro. BoNaP
I stand on the cliff and watch the veiled sun paling. The Voice of Nature. Robert Bridges. PoVP
I stand on the mark, beside the shore. The Runaway Slave at Pilgrim's Point. Elizabeth Barrett Browning. PoNe
I stand serene beside the struggling marts. Your Sanctuary. Walter Lyman French. MaRV
I stand upon the summit of my life. Thalatta! Thalatta! Joseph Brownlee Brown. AA; HBV
I stand upon the threshold of two years. Backward—Forward. *Unknown.* BLRP
I stand within the stony, arid town. The City Tree. Isabella Valancy Crawford. CaP
I stared, but not to seize. Four Kantian Lyrics. Charles Tomlinson. OPoP
I started early, took my dog. Emily Dickinson. AnAmPo; CBEP; DiPo; LiTA; LiTM (rev. ed.); NCEP; PoEL-5; ThWaDe
I started from my sleep. Frankenstein. John Robert Colombo. HYE
I started on the trail on June twenty-third. The Lone Star Trail. *Unknown.* AS
I started out with Maw and Paw. The Bank of the Arkansaw. *Unknown.* OuSiCo
I stayed [*or* staid] the night for shelter at a farm. The Witch of Coös. Robert Frost. *Fr.* Two Witches. AmP; AnNE; AP; AtBAP; CMoP; CoBMV; DiPo; ExPo; LiTM (rev. ed.); MoAB; NePA; ReMP; SeCeV (1967 ed.); ViBoPo (1958 ed.)
I steal across the sodden floor. The Dream House. Marjorie Allen Seiffert. HBMV
I step into my heart and there I meet. John Davidson. *Fr.* Thirty Bob a Week. ELU
I stepped from plank to plank. Emily Dickinson. AmePo; AP; CBV; CMoP; MAmP; Po
I stepped on the black winter seeds. Seeds. Thurmond Snyder. NNP
I still bear in mind the picture of the globe. The Philosophic Apology. Samuel Greenberg. MoPo; NePA
I still keep open Memory's chamber; still. Memory. Earl of Rosslyn. VA
I Stole Brass. *Unknown.* ChTr
I stole forth dimly in the dripping pause. Moon Compasses. Robert Frost. DiPo; MoVE
I stole the prince and I brought him here. The Grand Inquisitor's Song. W. S. Gilbert. *Fr.* The Gondoliers. OnMSP
I stole through the dungeons, while everyone slept. Alternative Endings to an Unwritten Ballad. Paul Dehn. FiBHP
I stood above the sown and generous sea. The Morality of Poetry. James Wright. PP
I Stood Alone. C. Kearnie Keegan. SoP
I stood alone at the bar of God. Crowned or Crucified. *Unknown.* SoP
I stood among the wanting many. Just Making It. Richard Thomas. PoNe (1970 ed.)
I stood and leant upon the mast. The Voyage. Heine. AWP
I stood and saw my mistress dance. Upon His Mistress [*or* M.] Dancing. James Shirley. CLwM; SeCL; SeEP
I stood at eve, as the sun went down, by a grave where a woman lies. 'Ostler Joe. George R. Sims. BeLS; BLPA; HBV; TreF
"I stood at the back of the shop, my dear." At the Draper's. Thomas Hardy. *Fr.* Satires of Circumstance. EnLi-2 (1949 ed.); MoAB; MoBrPo; NeMA; PoeP; VaPo
I stood beside a baby's bed. Beside a Baby's Bed. Walter E. Isenhour. SoP
I stood beside a hill. February Twilight. Sara Teasdale. FaPON; MoSiPe; PDV; SoPo; YeAr
I stood beside a pool, from whence ascended. Sonnet. Richard Chenevix Trench. IrPN
I stood between two mirrors when you died. Elegy. William Jay Smith. NePoEA
I stood by the window while she made the bed. North and South. Florida Watts Smyth. StaSt
I stood in a meadow. Green Valley. Dorothy Vena Johnson. PoNe
I stood in the gloom of a spurious room. Awake, My Lute. C. S. Lewis. CenHV
I stood in the ride, and the glamour. My Woodcock. Patrick Reginald Chalmers. CenHV
I stood in Venice on the Bridge of Sighs. Venice. Byron. *Fr.* Childe Harold's Pilgrimage, IV. BEL; EnRP; EPN; HBV; MBW-2; MCCG; OAEP; OBRV; ViBoPo
I stood musing in a black world. The Black Riders, XLIX. Stephen Crane. AP
I stood on a roof top and they wove their cage. On the pilots Who

Destroyed Germany in the Spring of 1945. Stephen Spender. NeBP; Po
I stood on Brocken's sovran height, and saw. Lines Written in the Album at Elbingerode. S. T. Coleridge. ERoP-1
I Stood on the Bridge. *Unknown.* LiTG
("I stood on the bridge at midnight.") •FaFP; SiTL
I stood on the bridge at midnight. The Bridge. Longfellow. CoBA; FaPL; HBV; TreF
I stood one day beside a blacksmith's door. *See* Last eve I passed beside a blacksmith's door.
I stood one day by the breezy bay. A Nautical Extravaganza [*or* Extravagance]. Wallace Irwin. GSP; StPo; StVeCh
I stood still and was a tree amid the wood. The Tree. Ezra Pound. APA; CoAnAm; CMoP; InPo; TwAmPo
I Stood Tiptoe [upon a Little Hill]. Keats. EnRP; FaPON; MERP; OTD
Sels.
"How silent comes the water round that bend." MyFE
(From the Bridge, *br. sel.*) PCH
(Minnows.) BoPe; FaPON; GN; GoTP; RIS
"I stood tiptoe upon a little hill," *first* 14 *ll.* OTPC
(Sigh of Silence, The.) GN
(Upon a Hill, 22 *ll.*) RIS; StaSt
Sweet Peas. GN; MPB (1956 ed.); PCH
I Stood upon a High Place. Stephen Crane. *Fr.* The Black Riders, IX. AmePo; AmP; AP; LiTA; NePA; PoPo
I stood upon a highway. The Black Riders, XXXIV. Stephen Crane. AP
I stood upon a hill one night. God's Autographs. William L. Stidger. SoP
I Stood upon a Star. Sara Teasdale. RePo
I stood where love in brimming armfuls bore. Love's Baubles. Dante Gabriel Rossetti. The House of Life, XXIII. MaVP; PoVP; ViPo; VP
I Stood with the Dead. Siegfried Sassoon. ChMP
I stood within the city disinterred. Shelley. *Fr.* Ode to Naples. EPN
I stood within the cypress gloom. Implora Pace. Charles Lotin Hildreth. AA
I stood within the heart of God. Pandora's Song. William Vaughn Moody. *Fr.* The Fire-Bringer. AnFE; APA; CoAnAm; GBV; MAP; MoAmPo (1942 ed.); OQP; WGRP
I stoop to gather a seabird's feather. The Feather. Vernon Watkins. FaBoTw; MoVE
I stooped to the silent earth and lifted a handful of her dust. A Handful of Dust. James Oppenheim. TRJP
I stopped deep. African in Louisiana. Kojo Gyinaye Kyei. PBA
I stopped for him. The Rabbit. John Lewisohn. PCD
I stopped in a sidestreet surplus shop, just south of Yorkville. The Cot. Grover Amen. NYBP
I stopped to pick up the bagel. The Bagel. David Ignatow. TwCP
I stopped to watch a man strike at the trunk. The Axe in the Wood. Clifford Dyment. ACV; POTE; POTi
I stopped to watch you. For a Bum Seen Walking the Rails. Dan Gillespie. QAH
I strayed about the deck, an hour, to-night. Fragment. Rupert Brooke. BrPo
I strayed along the strand with mussels strewn. Along the Strand. Alfred Mombert. TRJP
I stretched my mind until I stood. I Stood upon a Star. Sara Teasdale. RePo
I strive to live my life in whitest truth. Sonnet. George Henry Boker. *Fr.* Sonnets: a Sequence on Profane Love. AmePo
I Stroll. Peter Redgrove. NePoEA-2
I stroll on Madison in expensive clothes, sour. Summer. Edwin Denby. ANYP
I strolled along the Garfield avenue. A Second Birthday. Albert Kayper-Mensah. ACV
I strolled beside the shining sea. The Cumberbunce. Paul West. BOHV; NA
I strove, O Lord, to grasp a star for Thee. Failure. Mary Sinton Leitch. ChIP
I Strove with None. Walter Savage Landor. *See* On His Seventy-fifth Birthday.
I struck for what I deemed the right. After the Battle. George Sylvester Viereck. GoYe
I struck the board, and cried [*or* cry'd], "No more." The Collar. George Herbert. AnAnS-1; AtBAP; ATP; AWP; BEL; BoPe; BWP; CABA; CaFP; CBEP; CBV; CoBE; EaLo; EnL; EnLi-1; EnLit; ExPo; FaBoEn; FaPL; ForPo; FosPo; GTBS-W; HBV; InPo; ILP; JAWP; LiTB; LiTG; LoBV; MaMe; MaPo; MaRV; MasP; MeLP; MemP; MeP; MePo; NoP; OAEP; OBS; OuHeWo; OxBoCh; PAn; PoAn; PoE; PoEL-2; PoFS; PoIE; PoRA; ReEn; SCEP-1; SeCePo; SeCeV; SeCL; SeCP; SeCV-1; SeEP; StP; TOP; TrGrPo; UnPo (1st ed.); ViBoPo; WBP; WHA
I struck the trail in seventy-nine. The Gal I Left behind Me. *Unknown.* ABF; CoSo
I struck tomorrow square in the face. Hidesong. Aig Higo. TTY
I studied my tables over and over. A Mortifying Mistake [*or* A Little Mistake]. Anna Maria Pratt. AA; HBV; HBVY; RePo; RIS
I suddenly saw I was wrang when I felt. Deep-Sea Fishing. "Hugh MacDiarmid." SeCePo
I suffer when I sit next to Joe Brainard's painting "Bingo." Joe Brainard's Painting "Bingo." Ron Padgett. ANYP
I suffered so much from printer's errors. The Author's Epitaph. *Unknown.* FiBHP
I summon to the winding ancient stair. A Dialogue of Self and Soul. W. B. Yeats. CABA; CMoP; ExPo; FaBoMo; LiTB; LiTM; MasP; MoBrPo (1962 ed.); OAEP (2d ed.); PIA; Po; PoDB; ReMP
I sundry see, for beauty's gloss. That He Findeth Others as Fair, but Not So Faithful as His Friend. George Turberville. EIL; SiCE; TuPP
I supped where bloomed the red rose. Supper. Walter de La Mare. NYBP
I suppose it just depends on where you're raised. The Mallee Fire. Charles Henry Souter. BoAu
I suppose you have heard all the talkin'. Joaquin the Horse-Thief. John A. Stone. SGR
I supposed I knew my Bible. When I Read the Bible Through. Amos R. Wells. SoP; STF
I swallow the pill and the pill. Waves. John Perreault. YAP
I swear by swayings of that form so fair. The Mock Caliph. *Unknown.* *Fr.* The Book of a Thousand Nights and a Night. EnLi-1
I swear I begin to see the meaning of these things. Walt Whitman. *Fr.* By Blue Ontario's Shore. PoIE
I swear to the Lord. The Black Man Speaks. Langston Hughes. TreFT
I Swear to You, That Ship Never Sunk in Middle-Passage! Lawrence S. Cumberbatch. WSL
I sweare to thee I will begone. *Unknown.* SeCSL
I sweep the street and lift me hat. The Old Man at the Crossing. L. A. G. Strong. OBMV
I swept my house of life and garnished it. Perfection. Ruth Scofield Fargo. OQP
I swim in darkness, swim. Arrivals and Departures. Melvin Walker La Follette. CoPo
I Syng of a Mayden. *Unknown.* *See* I Sing of a Maiden.
I tak the Queenis Grace, thy mother. The Childhood of James V. Sir David Lindsay. *Fr.* The Complaynt of Schir David Lindesay. AtBAP
I take a comfort from my very badness. Oneness with Him. George Macdonald. MaRV
I Take 'Em and Like 'Em. Margaret Fishback. PoPl; WhC
I take four devils with me when I ride. Poem. Gervase Stewart. WaP
I Take, He Undertakes. A. B. Simpson. SoP
I take him down upon the beach. Son and Surf. Julia Hurd Strong. GoYe
I take it he doesn't think at all. The Pike. John Bruce. SD
I take it you already know. Hints on Pronunciation for Foreigners. "T.S.W." FIW
I take my chaperon to the play. The Chaperon. H. C. Bunner. AA; HBV
I take my leave with sorrow of Him I love so well. Multiplication. Joyce Kilmer. WHL
I take no books, nor I read no papers. The Gull Decoy. Larry Gorman. ShS
I take no shame that still I sing the rose. The Eternal Way. Richard Le Gallienne. InP
I take the dogs into. La Baragède. Galway Kinnell. NYBP
I take the road that bears leaves in the mountains. The Dream Again. W. W. Merwin. FRC
I take the twist-about, empty street. The Rendezvous. Bernard Spencer. GTBS-P
I Take Thee, Life. Margot Ruddock. OBMV; POTE

I take thee now to be no other. Adam. Philip Booth. MoLP
I take what never can be taken. The Poet. Haniel Long. HBMV
I takes and I paints. Poem by a Perfectly Furious Academician. *Unknown.* FiBHP
I takes up for my colored men. The Generation Gap. Ruby C. Saunders. WSL
I talk to the birds as they sing i' the morn. I Pass in Silence. John Clare. BoLP
I Talk to You. John Newlove. PeCV (1967 ed.)
I talked one midnight with the jolly ghost. All in a Garden Green. W. E. Henley. OBMV
I talked to a farmer one day in Iowa. Iowa Farmer. Margaret Abigail Walker. Kal
I talked to old Lem. Old Lem. Sterling A. Brown. IDB; PoNe; TTY
I taste a liquor never brewed. Emily Dickinson. AmePo; AmP; AmPP (4th ed.); AnAmPo; AP; ATP; CABA; CMoP; CoBa; DiPo; EvOK; FaBV; LiTA; LiTM (rev. ed.); MAmP; MAP; MaPo; MCCG; MoAmPo; MoPW; MWA-2; NeMa; NePA; NoP; OxBA; PAn; PoEL-5; PoeP; ReMP; SeCeV; TreFS
I teach-a da bird an' I blow-a da ring. The Educated Love Bird. Peter Newell. FiBHP
I teach how we cheat the young. A 4 Part Geometry Lesson. Robin Blaser. NeAP
I Tell of Another Young Death. Cesar Tiempo, *tr. fr. Spanish by* Donald Devenish Walsh. TrJP
I Tell the King. *Unknown.* SoP
I tell thee Dick where I have been. A Ballad [*or* Ballade] upon a Wedding. Sir John Suckling. AnAnS-2; AtBAP; BOHV; CABA; CABL; CavP; CBEP; CoMu; HBV; InvP; LoBV; NoP; OBS; Par; ReEn; SCEP-2; SeCeV; SeCL; SeCP; SeCV-1; SeEP; UnTE; ViBoPo
I tell thee, stationer—why never fear! To the Stationer. Thomas Freeman. SiCE; TuPP
I tell them where the wind comes from. People with Proud Chins. Carl Sandburg. PFY
I tell time. Silent in America, 5. Philip Levine. TDP
I tell yeh whut! The chankin'. Horses Chawin' Hay. Hamlin Garland. StVeCh
I tell you a poet must be free. Freedom. Leonard Mann. NeLNL
I tell you a tale to-night. The Admiral's Ghost. Alfred Noyes. BBV; PoMS; TiPo (1952 ed.)
I tell you again that I discovered silence. The Sounds of Dawn. Efraín Huerta. LiTW
I tell you, hopeless grief is passionless. Grief. Elizabeth Barrett Browning. AnFE; CBEP; GTBS-D; GTSL; HBV; LoBV; OBEV; OBNC; OBVV; PoLF; PoVP; StP; TrGrPo; ViPo
I tell you, Lesbia, life is love. Catullus to Lesbia. James Reeves. ErPo
I tell you man must. The Ascent. John Stevens Wade. ThO
I tell you that I see her still. I Only Am Escaped Alone to Tell Thee. Howard Nemerov. CoAP; NePA
I tell you there is nothing there at all. The Unexplored. Burnham Eaton. FiSC
I tell you what I dreamed last night. Christina Rossetti. *Fr.* The Convent Threshold. PeVV
I 'tend that in the garden. The Nugly Little Man. Marion St. John Webb. TVC
I thank all who have loved me in their hearts. Sonnets from the Portuguese, XLI. Elizabeth Barrett Browning. CoBE; VA; ViPo
I Thank God I'm Free at Las', *with music. Unknown.* BoAN-2
I thank the goodness and the grace. A Child's Hymn of Praise. Jane Taylor. OTPC (1923 ed.)
I thank the Lord for quiet things. Quiet Things. "I. W." OQP
I Thank Thee. F. L. Knowles. SoP
I Thank Thee (A Prayer). Dorothy Conant Stroud. SoP
I thank thee and I praise thee, O thou radiant grace. Thanksgiving. "Yehoash." TrJP
I thank Thee, dear Lord, for my eyes. Thanksgiving. *Unknown.* SoP
I thank thee, Father, once again. Thanksgiving for Thanksgiving. Amos R. Wells. PEDC
I Thank Thee, Lord. Oliver Huckel. *See* Unanswered Prayer.
I Thank Thee, Lord. Myra Brooks Welch. SoP
I thank Thee, Lord, for beauty in the little things of life. I Thank Thee (A Prayer). Dorothy Conant Stroud. SoP
I thank Thee, Lord, for cloudy weather. I Thank Thee. F. L. Knowles. SoP
I thank Thee, Lord, for quiet rest. A Child's Morning Prayer. Mary Lundie Duncan. OTPC
I Thank Thee, Lord, for Strength of Arm. Robert Davis. MaRV
I thank Thee, Lord, for this good life. For Having Thee. Francis X. Connolly. JKCP (1955 ed.)
I thank You for these gifts, dear God. Gratitude. Margaret E. Sangster. MaRV; SoP
I Thank You God. E. E. Cummings. *See* I Thank You God for Most This Amazing.
I thank you God, /For a hundred things. Ilo Orleans. RIS
I thank you, God,/ That swallows know their way. Thanksgiving. Louise Driscoll. YeAr
I Thank You God for Most This Amazing. E. E. Cummings. EaLo; MoAB; PoDB
(I Thank You God.) MoRP
I thank You, God in Heaven, for friends. In Gratitude for Friends. Maragret E. Sangster. SoP
I that am clothed with the sun. Our Lady of the Apocalypse. Sister Mary Bertrand. JKCP (1955 ed.)
I that had found the way so smooth. The Return. Jessie Fauset. CDC
I that had yearned for youth, my own, again. My Son. Douglas Malloch. MaRV
I that have beene a lover, and could shew it. A Sonnet, to the Noble Lady, the Lady Mary Worth. Ben Jonson. AnAnS-2
I that in heill wes [*or* health was] and gladnes[s]. Lament for the Makaris [*or* Makars] [*or* The Fear of Death Confounds Me]. William Dunbar. ACP; AtBAP; CBEP; ChTr; GoTS; MeEL; OAEP; OBEV; OxBS; PoEL-1; PoIE; PP; SiCE; ViBoPo
I that lived ever about you. English Girl. *Unknown, tr. by* E. Powys Mathers. OBMV
I that my slender oaten pipe in verse was wont to sound. Vergil. *Fr.* The Aeneid, I. ReIE
I that tremble at your feet. The Missive. Sir Edmund Gosse. HBV
I that Ulysses' yeres have spent. The Lover Disceived by His Love Repenteth Him. *Unknown.* EnPo
I that whilom lived secure. A Testament. *Unknown.* OBSC
I' the how-dumb-deid o the cauld hairst nicht. The Eemis-Stane. "Hugh MacDiarmid." NeBP
I, the image of godhead, who thought myself. Faust Struggles with His Soul. Goethe. *Fr.* Faust. LiTW
I, the old woman of Beare. The Old Woman of Beare [Regrets Lost Youth]. *Unknown.* KiLC; OBMV
I the Preacher was king over Israel in Jerusalem. Vanity. Ecclesiastes, Bible, *O.T.* OuHeWo
I thee advise. To One That Had Little Wit. George Turberville. EnRePo
I, then, will not restrain my mouth. Let Me Alone. Job, Bible, *O.T.* PPON
I therefore will begin: soule of the age! Ben Jonson. *Fr.* To the Memory of My Beloved, the Author, Mr. William Shakespeare: and What He Hath Left Us. ML
I think a stormless night-time shall ensue. The World's Death-Night. James Chapman Woods. VA
I think a time will come when you will understand. For My Father. Paul Potts. FaBoTw
I think about God. God. Gamaliel Bradford. WGRP
I think all this is somewhere in myself. The Room. W. S. Merwin. FRC; NaP
I think and think; yet still I fail. The Veil. Walter de la Mare. CMoP
I think before they saw me the giraffes. The Giraffes. Roy Fuller. ChMP; NeBP
I think between my cradle-bars. Ballade of Faith. Tom MacInnes. CaP
I Think Continually of Those Who Were Truly Great. Stephen Spender. AnFE; AtBAP; CaFP; EaLo; EnL; EnLit; ExPo; FaBoEn; LiTB; LiTG; LiTM; MoRP; NAMP; OAEP (2d ed.); PG (1945 ed.); PoIE; PoPl; PoRA; ReMP; TIHL; TreFT; WaP
(I Think Continually.) POTE; ShBV-4
(I Think Continually of Those.) BoLiVe; ChTr; CMoP; DiPo; GTBS-W; MaRV; MoAB; MoBrPo; NeMA; PoFr; PoFS; PoSa; PP; TrGrPo; ViBoPo (1958 ed.)
(Truly Great, The.) BoC

I think ere any early poet awed. The Masterpiece. Walter Conrad Arensberg. AnAmPo
I think flowers can see. Thoughts of a Little Girl. María Enriqueta. FaPON
I think God loves new temples built to Him. New Temples. Lexie Dean Robertson. OQP
I think God loves simplicity. Thanksgiving. Margaret E. Sangster. PEDC
I think God sang when He had made. The Star. Beatrice Redpath. CaP
I think God seeks this house, serenely white. A Country Church. Violet Alleyn Storey. OQP
I think God took the fragrance of a flower. Mothers. *Unknown.* PGD
I think he had not heard of the far towns. St. John Baptist. Arthur O'Shaughnessy. HBV
I think he would have hated this white shrine. At the Lincoln Memorial. William E. Brooks. OQP
I think I could turn and live with animals. Animals [*or* The Beasts]. Walt Whitman. Song of Myself, XXXII. AnEnPo; BoC; CBEP; FaFP; GTBS-W; HBV; LiTG; LoBV (1949 ed.); MCCG; NePA; OBVV; PDV; PG (1955 ed.); PoG; PoMa; PoPl; PPON; SiTL; TrGrPo; WGRP
I think I hear them stirring there, today. Armistice Day. Roselle Mercier Montgomery. MC; PoRL
I Think I Know No Finer Things than Dogs. Hally Carrington Brent. BBV (1951 ed.); BLPA; NeHB
I think I remember this moorland. We Have Been Here Before. Morris Bishop. EvOK; FiBHP; InMe; NYBP; WhC
I Think I See Her. Jessie Fauset. *See* Oriflamme.
I Think I See Him There. Waring Cuney. CDC
I think if I lay dying in some land. The Harbor. Winifred M. Letts. PoMa
I think if I should cross the room. Room's Width. Elizabeth Stuart Phelps Ward. AA
I think if I should wait some night in an enchanted forest. Fantasy. Ruth Mather Skidmore. PoMS
I think if I were a tree. If I. T. C. O'Donnell. GFA
I think if thou couldst know. Trust Is Best. *Unknown.* SoP
"I think I'm going to die." I tried to say. Finale: Presto. Peter Davison. CoPo
I think it better that in times like these. On Being Asked for a War Poem. W. B. Yeats. MoVE; PP
I think it is his blindness makes him so. An Afternoon in Artillery Walk. Leonard Bacon. AnAmPo; ATP
I think it is over, over. In Harbor. Paul Hamilton Hayne. AA; HBV
I think it very nice to take. Perhaps. Pringle Barret. PCH
I think little Louie will turn out a crook. Psychological Prediction. Virginia Brasier. BBGG
I think mice/ Are rather nice. Mice. Rose Fyleman. BoTP; EvOK; FaPON; MoSiPe; MPB; PDV; SoPo; StVeCh; SUS; TiPo
I Think Myself to Be Alive. Dorothy Wellesley. POTE
I think now of latitudes solitary, Asian, and velvet. In a Valley of This Restless Mind. Ewart Milne. NeIP
I think Odysseus, as he dies, forgets. Odysseus Dying. Sheila Wingfield. OxBI
I think of a flower that no eye has ever seen. Beauty. Laurence Binyon. MoBrPo
I think of all the things at school. Johnny's History Lesson. Nixon Waterman. PoLF
I think of her where she lies there on her stone couch by the Thames. The Cutty Sark. George Barker. *Fr.* Dreams of a Summer Night. FlW
I Think of Him as One Who Fights. Anna Hempstead Branch. HBMV
I think of robins. Passport beyond Tyranny. David Ross. PG (1945 ed.)
I think of the blond child on the westward train. "Nobody." John Stevens Wade. ThO
I think of the tribes: the women prized for fatness. The Tribes. Roy Fuller. BoSA; LiTM (1970 ed.); ToPo
I think of the unknowing art my watching made. Voyeur. John Edward Hardy. ErPo
I think of thee!—my thoughts do twine and bud. Sonnets from the Portuguese, XXIX. Elizabeth Barrett Browning. EPN; VA
I think of you when sun with sudden splendor. The Lover Is Near. Goethe. LiTW
I Think of Your Generation. Charles Brasch. AnNZ
I think oft times as the night draws nigh. Are All the Children In? *Unknown.* SoP; STF
I Think on Thee. Thomas Kibble Hervey. VA
I think she sleeps: it must be sleep, when low. Modern Love, XV. George Meredith. ViPo; VP
I think some saint of Eirinn wandering far. Fuchsia Hedges in Connacht. Padraic Colum. GoBC
I think something beautiful. The Sidney Greenstreet Blues. Richard Brautigan. FRC
I think sometimes of the dear little arms. The Dear Little Arms. Walter E. Isenhour. SoP
I Think That God Is Proud. Grace Noll Crowell. PoToHe
I think that God, when I was born. Ghosts. Henri Charles Read. LO
I think that I am drawing to an end. The Poets at Tea, 2. Barry Pain. Par
I think that I live in a street. For the Record. George Jonas. MoCV
I think that I shall never make. In a Garden. Donald C. Babcock. NePoAm
I think that I shall never see/ A billboard. Song of the Open Road. Ogden Nash. LiTM; NAMP; PoPo; SiTL; TreFS; WhC
I think that I shall never see/ A poem. Trees. Joyce Kilmer. BBV (1923 ed.); BLPA; DD; FaBoBe; FaFP; FaPON; HBV; HBVY; HH; InP; JKCP; MAP; MaRV; MCCG; MPB; NeHB; NeMA; NP; OHFP; OTD; OTPC (1946 ed.); PEDC; PoMa; PoPo; TreF; UnPo; WBLP; WGRP; YT
I think that I shall never ski. Winter Trees. Conrad Diekmann. SD
I think that if some faery spirit strewed. The Salesman. Robert Mezey. NePoEA
I think that life has spared those mortals much. Vigil. Faith Baldwin. MaRV
I think that look of Christ might seem to say. The Meaning of the Look. Elizabeth Barrett Browning. ChIP; MaRV; SoP; TRV
I think that man hath made no beauteous thing. To Melody. George Leonard Allen. CDC
I think that Mary Magdalene. Mary Magdalene. Leonora Speyer. HBMV; NP
I think that no one ever knew. Shoes. Louis Untermeyer. StaSt
I think that we retain of our dead friends. Remembrance. John Henry Boner. AA
I think that what he gave us most was pride. Thanksgiving, 1963. Molly Kazan. TreFT
I think the dead are tender. Shall we kiss? She. Theodore Roethke. BoLP; ErPo
I think the fairies to my christening came. Fairy Godmothers. Eugene Lee-Hamilton. OBVV
I think the gentle soul of him. Ilicet. Theodosia Garrison. PoLF
I think the ghost of Leerie. Daffodils over Night. David Morton. PCH
I think the hemlock likes to stand. Emily Dickinson. OnPM
I think the lovely shooting stars. Shooting Stars. Grace Noll Crowell. BoChLi
I think the wind is curious. Lonely Wind. Eleanor Hammond. GFA
I think they must be sorry. The Sleepy Maple Trees. Eleanor Hammond. GFA
I think thou waitest, Love, beyond the gate. The Lonely Road. Kenneth Rand. HBV
"I think" thought Sam Butler. English Liberal. Geoffrey Taylor. LiTM; SiTL
I think true love is never blind. True Love. Phoebe Cary. PoToHe
I think we are too ready with complaint. Complaints [*or* Cheerfulness Taught by Reason]. Elizabeth Barrett Browning. FaChP; PoVP
I think we can all remember when a Greaser hadn't no show. The Texas Cowboy and the Mexican Greaser. *Unknown.* SCC
I think we were the only ones who slept. Vigil in Gethsemane. Ruth Margaret Gibbs. SoP
I Think When I Read That Sweet Story of Old. Jemima Luke. MaRV; OTPC (1946 ed.); PCH
(Of Such Is the Kingdom of God.) SoP
I think when Judas' mother heard. Judas Iscariot. Countee Cullen. PoLF

I think you know, Annas, the price is low. Thirty Pieces of Silver for Jesus. Helene Mullins. StJW
"I Thirst . . ." Katherine Brégy. CAW
I thirst for God, to Him my soul aspires. The Living God. Abraham ibn Ezra. TrJP
I thought, belovèd, to have brought to you. The Gift. "Æ." HBMV
I thought he was dumb. Tortoise Shout. D. H. Lawrence. LiTM
I thought, "How terrible, if I were seen." Company. William Dean Howells. AmePo
I thought I could saw, and I thought I could plane. Carpenter. E. V. Lucas. StVeCh
I thought I heard a knock on the door. Rispetti: On the Death of a Child. Paul Heyse. PoPl
I thought I heard Him calling! Did you hear. In the Cool of the Evening. James Stephens. MemP
I thought I heard the Old Man say. Leave Her, Johnny. *Unknown.* SoAmSa
I thought I needed many things. My Need. Grace E. Troy. SoP
I thought I saw an angel flying low. Nocturne at Bethesda. Arna Bontemps. AmNP; BALP; BANP; CDC; PoNe
I Thought I Saw Stars. R. P. Lister. PV
I thought I saw the fallen leaves. Hokku. Arakida Moritake. InP
I thought I saw white clouds, but no! Lilies. Shiko. SUS; TiPo
I thought I was so tough. Tamer and Hawk. Thom Gunn. NePoEA
I thought I'd done, but that my presse took't ill. The Printer, to Her Majesty. Leon Lichfield. HW
I thought it hard that Christ should ask of me. Discipleship. Henry W. Frost. SoP
I thought it strange he asked for me. Riding through Jerusalem. Marion Susan Campbell. ChIP
I Thought It Was Tangiers I Wanted. Langston Hughes. PoNe (1970 ed.)
I thought it was the little bed. Half-Waking. William Allingham. VA
I Thought Joy Went by Me. Willard Wattles. HBMV
I thought Love lived in the hot sunshine. Where to Seek Love. Blake. *Fr.* William Bond. LO; TRV
I thought no more was needed. A Song. W. B. Yeats. AtBAP
I thought of Chatterton, the marvellous boy. Wordsworth. *Fr.* Resolution and Independence. ML
I thought of death beside the lonely sea. Life and Death. Duncan Campbell Scott. VA
I thought of happiness, how it is woven. The Work of Happiness. May Sarton. MoRP
I thought of killing myself because I am only a bricklayer. Bricklayer Love. Carl Sandburg. AmP
I thought of the mariners of Solomon. The Peacock of Java. William Jay Smith. RePo
I thought of thee, my partner and my guide. After-Thought. Wordsworth. The River Duddon, XXXIV. EnL; EnLi-2; EnRP; EPN; FaBoEn; MBW-2; OAEP; OBEV; OBNC; OBRV; PeER; SeCePo
I thought of your beauty, and this arrow. The Arrow. W. B. Yeats. EG
I thought how once Theocritus had sung. Sonnets from the Portuguese, I. Elizabeth Barrett Browning. AnFE; BEL; CoBE; EnLi-2; EnLit; EPN; GTBS; GTBS-D; GTSL; HBV; OAEP; OBEV; OBNC; OuHeWo; PoE; PoVP; TOP; TreFT; VA; ViBoPo; ViPo
I thought one spring that just for fun. The Horse Wrangler. D. J. O'Malley. CoSo (B *vers.*)
I thought that I could follow Him. There Was No Room on the Cross. *Unknown.* GoBC
I thought that I stood in His presence. In the Presence of the King! *Unknown.* SoP
I thought that Love had been a boy. *Unknown.* EnLoPo
I thought that nature was enough. Emily Dickinson. MaRV; MWA-2
I thought the night without a sound was falling. How Infinite Are Thy Ways. William Force Stead. *Fr.* Uriel. OBMV; TrPWD
I thought the winner had been found. Brooklynese Champion. Margaret Fishback. WhC
I Thought There Were Limits. D. G. Jones. MoCV
I thought they were/ wind chimes. The Bells of the Cherokee Ponies. D. A. Levy. WOW
I thought they'd be strangers aroun' me. The Curate's Kindness. Thomas Hardy. CoBMV; ILP; PoVP; VP
I thought this day to bring to thee. A Birthday Song. Richard Watson Gilder. PoRL
I thought to die that night in the solitude. The Edge. Lola Ridge. AnAmPo; NP; OnYI
I thought to meet no more, so dreary seem'd. Burial of the Dead. John Keble. OBEV (1st ed.)
I thought to pass away before, and yet alive I am. Conclusion to the May Queen and New Year's Eve. Tennyson. *Fr.* The May Queen. OTPC (1923 ed.)
"I thought you loved me." "No it was only fun." In the Orchard. Muriel Stuart. ErPo; NP
I threatned to observe the strict decree. The Holdfast. George Herbert. MaMe
I threw a penny in the air. *Unknown.* CenHV
I throw open the door. April Fourth. Robert Mezey. NaP
I thumped on you the best I could. Heart's Needle, VIII. W. D. Snodgrass. NePoEA
I thy servant, full of sighs, cry unto thee. Penitential Psalm. *Unknown.* WGRP
I tink I hear my brother say. Stars Begin to Fall. *Unknown.* AA
I to my home shall be going. The Parting of Hector and Andromache. Homer. *Fr.* The Iliad, VI. TreFS
I to My Perils. A. E. Housman. CaFP; EnLi-2 (1949 ed.); ViBoPo
I told my little boy a story. Night, Stars, Glow-Worms. H. Leivick. LiTW
I told myself in singing words. As It Was. Lila Cabot Perry. Meeting after Long Absence, II. AA
I told the sun that I was glad. The Sun. John Drinkwater. FaPON; SoPo; TiPo
I, too. Langston Hughes. AmNP; CDC; Kal; TIHL
(Epilogue: "I, too, sing America.") BALP
(I, Too, Sing America.) IDB; PoLF; PoNe
I, too, dislike it: there are things that are important beyond all this fiddle. Poetry. Marianne Moore. AmP; AmPP (5th ed.); AnFE; AP; APA; ATP (1953 ed.); CABA; CBV; CMoP; CoAnAm; CoBMV; ExPo; ILP; InPo; LiTA; LiTM; ML; MoAB; MoAmPo (1950 ed.) NAMP; NePA; NP; OxBA; PoAn; PoIE; PoPo; PoSa; PP; ReMP; SeCeV; StP; TreFT; TwAmPo; ViBoPo (1951 ed.)
I, Too, Have Known. Marguerite George. OQP
I too have suffered; yet I know. Urania. Matthew Arnold. MBW-2; VP
I Too Have Travelled. Maurice Baring. JKCP (1955 ed.)
I, Too, Know What I Am Not. Bob Kaufman. NBP
I too my shovel, pick and pan. Striking a Lead. John A. Stone. SGR
I, too, O Christ, denied you. Easter Joy. Daisy Conway Price. ChIP
I too remember, in the after years. Frederick Tennyson. *Fr.* Niobe. VA
I, too, saw God through mud. Apologia pro Poemate Meo. Wilfred Owen. ChMP; CoBE; CoBMV; LiTM (rev. ed.); MoAB; MoBrPo; NeMA; NP; PoFr
I, Too, Sing America. Langston Hughes. *See* I, Too.
I Took a Bow and Arrow. John Ciardi. EvOK
I took a day to search for God. Vestigia. Bliss Carman. CaP; MaRV; OQP; WGRP
I Took a Hansom on To-Day. W. E. Henley. HBV
I took a piece of plastic clay. A Piece of Clay [*or* Sculpture *or* The Sculptor]. *Unknown.* MaRV; OQP; PoLF; PoToHe (new ed.)
I took away three pictures. Sandhill People. Carl Sandburg. CMoP
I took her dainty eyes, as well. Villanelle of His Lady's Treasures. Ernest Dowson. HBV
I took her to the river. The Faithless Wife. Federico García Lorca. LiTW
I took Love to task. Love's Argument. Father Andrew. MaRV
I took money and bought flowering trees. Planting Flowers on the Eastern Embankment [*or* The Gardener]. Po Chü-i. BoNaP; BoPe
I took my dolly for a walk. *Unknown.* GFA

I took my girl to a fancy ball. I Had but Fifty Cents. *Unknown.* BeLS; BLPA; TreF
I took my heart in my hand. Twice. Christina Rossetti. GTSL; OBEV; OBNC; OBVV; ViBoPo
I took my oath I would inquire. The Inquest. W. H. Davies. CBEP; DTC; GTBS-P
I took my power in my hand. Emily Dickinson. MWA-2; NeMA; NePA
I took my watch beside the rose. Anne Wilkinson. *Fr.* Nature Be Damned. PeCV (1967 ed.)
I took one draught of life. Emily Dickinson. CoBA
I took the crazy short-cut to the bay. Swimmers. Louis Untermeyer. PFY
I tossed my friend a wreath of roses, wet. Gifts. Mary Elizabeth Coleridge. PoVP
I touch and recollect/ Less than the shape and shade. Tiresias' Lament. Ellen de Young Kay. NePoEA
I touch you all over. Love's Eschatology. Vassar Miller. ToPo
I touch you in the night, whose gift was you. The Science of the Night. Stanley Kunitz. MoAmPo (1962 ed.); TDP; TwCP; UnTE
I touch your face. Poems of Night. Galway Kinnell. NaP
I touched a shining mote of sand. Lyric. Philip Child. CaP
I towered far, and lo! I stood within. God-forgotten. Thomas Hardy. BEL; PoVP; TOP; ViPo (1962 ed.); VP
I traced the Circus whose gray stones incline. In the Old Theater, Fiesole. Thomas Hardy. Sonn
I Tramp a Perpetual Journey. Walt Whitman. *Fr.* Song of Myself, XLVI. OQP
I tramped the pavement, blaming [*or* cursing] God. Comrade Jesus. Ralph Cheyney. ChIP; PGD
I travel through thin jails of rain. Patrol. Ralph Pomeroy. CoPo
I travel'd thro' a land of men. The Mental Traveller. Blake. DiPo; EnRP; ERoP-1; MasP; PeER; PoEL-4
I Traveled among Unknown Men. Wordsworth. *Fr.* Lucy. AWP; BoLiVe; CBEP; EnL; EnRP; EPN; ERoP-1; FaBV; GTBS; GTBS-D; GTBS-P; GTBS-W; GTSL; ILP; InPo; JAWP; MBW-2; MERP; OAEP; OBEV; OBNC; OBRV; OuHeWo; PoFS; PTK; TOP; TrGrPo; WBP
(Lucy.) EnLi-2; EnLit; FiP; HBV; OBEV; OBNC
I Traveled with Them. Mu'tamid, King of Seville, *tr. fr. Arabic by* J. B. Trend. AWP
I travelled [*or* travell'd] on, seeing the hill, where lay. The Pilgrimage. George Herbert. AnAnS-1; ChTr; MaMe; MeP
I traversed a dominion. Mute Opinion. Thomas Hardy. CMoP; ViPo
I tread on many autumns here. Walking in Beech Leaves. Andrew Young. MoVE
I treasure in secret some long, fine hair. The Wind-Harp. James Russell Lowell. CAP
I tried but I could not remember my dream. The Hills of Pomeroy. Ewart Milne. NeIP
I tried, myself, to bring to pass. Success. Barbara E. Cornet. SoP
I tried to live by bread alone. Satisfied. Edgar Cooper Mason. BLRP
I tripped along a narrow way. Forthfaring. Winifred Howells. AA
I trod the mellow earth between the rows. Distribution. Elsie B. Purcell. PoMa
"I trow that gude ending." Bruce Consults His Men. John Barbour. *Fr.* The Bruce. GoTS
I trust I have not wasted breath. In Memoriam A. H. H., CXX. Tennyson. CoBE; EPN; ImOP; SeCePo; TOP; ViPo; VP
I try to capture rhythm. Futility. Mary S. Hawling. PoMa
I try to knead and spin, but my life is low the while. In Leinster. Louise Imogen Guiney. AA; GoBC; HBV; JKCP; OBVV; PFY
"I try to look hard-boiled, but I." Early Morning. Morris Bishop. PV
I turn my steps where the lonely road. In Dark Hour. Seumas MacManus. JKCP; WGRP
I Turn the Key. Winifred Corrigan. JKCP (1955 ed.)
I turn the page and read. At the British Museum. Richard Aldington. MoBrPo
I Turn to Jesus. Oswald J. Smith. STF
I turned an ancient poet's book. Home. Henry van Dyke. SoP; STF
I turned and gave my strength to woman. Two Generations. L. A. G. Strong. OBMV
I turned my back when in the pot they tossed. Walthena. Elisabeth Peck. AmFN
I turned to the parlor in panic. Frustrate. Louis Untermeyer. HBMV; InMe; YaD
I twined a wreath of heather white. Corona Inutilis. James Lister Cuthbertson. BoAu
I twist your arm. A Deux. William Wood. BoLP; ELU
I understand the large hearts of heroes. Heroes. Walt Whitman. *Fr.* Song of Myself. AA; PoFr
I understand what you are running for. For Eager Lovers. Genevieve Taggard. AnAmPo; NP
I upon the first creation. Gratitude. Christopher Smart. *Fr.* Hymns for the Amusement of Children. EiCP
I urged my mind against my will. The Heart Looks On. Leonora Speyer. NP
I used to curse the wind and rain. Cursing and Blessing. "Michael Lewis." *Fr.* Cherry Blossoms. UnTE
I used to have a old grey horse. Goin' Down to Town. *Unknown.* AS
I used to live on Cottonwood and owned a little farm. A Mormon Immigrant Song. *At. to* George Hicks. CoSo
I used to live on mountain top. Old Joe Clarke. *Unknown.* TrAS
I Used to Love My Garden. C. P. Sawyer. LiTG
I used to see her in the door. Paul. James Wright. NePoEA; PoPl
I used to walk on solid gr'und. To a Sea Eagle. "Hugh MacDiarmid." MoBrPo
I used to wonder. Border Line. Langston Hughes. PoCh
I Used to Wrap My White Doll Up in. Mae Jackson. BOLo
I ust to read in the novel books 'bout fellers that got the prod. Cowboy's Worrying Love. James Barton Adams. SCC
I uster own the Double D. Cyclone Blues. *Unknown.* CoSo
I Vecchi. Ezra Pound. PoIE
I venerate the man whose heart is warm. Of Preachers. William Cowper. *Fr.* The Task, II. SoP
I venture to suggest that I. An Election Address. James Kenneth Stephen. NBM
I vex my heart with fancies dim. In Memoriam A. H. H., XLII. Tennyson. EPN; ViPo; VP
I, Virgin of the Snows, have liv'd. The Jungfrau's Cry. Stopford Brooke. VA
I Vision God. *Unknown.* TTY
I Vow to Thee, My Country. Sir Cecil Spring-Rice. BoTP; ShBV-3
(Homeland, The.) MaRV
I vow'd unvarying faith; and she. Constancy. Coventry Patmore. *Fr.* The Angel in the House. OBVV
I wad ha'e gi'en him my lips tae kiss. Mary's Song. Marion Angus. LO
I wad I were where Helen lies. *See* I wish I were where Helen lies.
I wadna gi'e my ain wife. My Ain Wife. Alexander Laine. HBV; VA
I wage not any feud with Death. In Memoriam A. H. H., LXXXII. Tennyson. EnLi-2; EPN; LiTB; LiTG; PPON; TOP; ViPo; VP
I waigh not Fortunes frowne or smile. A Contented Mind. Joshua Sylvester. HBV
I wait and he does not come. *Unknown, tr. fr. Japanese by* Kenneth Rexroth. LiTW
I wait beside the fount. The Wooden Mirror. John Logan. FRC
I wait for his foot fall. Earth Trembles Waiting. Blanche Shoemaker Wagstaff. PoLF
I wait for wonder, or the weather's turn. Absent Creation. D. S. Savage. NeBP
I Wait My Lord. *Unknown, tr. fr. Chinese by* Helen Waddell. AWP; JAWP; WBP
I wait with a pencil in my hand. Waiting. James Kirkup. FIW
I waited and worked. Koheleth. Louis Untermeyer. TrJP
I waited for the train at Coventry. Godiva. Tennyson. HBV; PoVP
I waited in the little sunny room. Eve's Daughter. Edward Rowland Sill. AmePo
I Wake and Feel the Fell of Dark. Gerard Manley Hopkins.

I (continued)
BrPo; CBV; CMoP; CoBE; CoBMV; DiPo; EnLi-2; ForPo; GTBS-P; GTBS-W; ILP; LiTB; LiTG; MaPo; MoPW; NoP; OAEP; PeVV; PoDB; PoEL-5; PoeP; PoIE; PoVP; ReMP; SeCeV; StP; ViPo (1962 ed.); ViPP; VP
(Sonnet.) PoLi
(Terrible Sonnets, The, III.) MoPo
I wake and hear it raining. Morning Worship. Mark Van Doren. NePoAm-2; TwAmPo
I wake! I feel the day is near. Chanticleer. Celia Thaxter. PRWS; TVC
I wake in the morning early. Singing-Time. Rose Fyleman. SiSoSe; TiPo
I wake in the night with such uncertain gladness. The Girl Takes Her Place among the Mothers. Marya Zaturenska. HBMV
I wake late and leave. A Cardinal. W. D. Snodgrass. PP
I wake to sleep, and take my waking slow. The Waking. Theodore Roethke. AmPP (5th ed.); AP; CoAP; CoBMV; CrMA; FiMAP; LiTM (1970 ed.) MoAmPo (1962 ed.); NoP; PIA; Po; PoeP; PoPl; SeCeV (1967 ed.); TDP; ToPo; TwCP
I wake up/ and hells around me. The Clown. D. L. Graham. BF
I wake up back aching from soft bed Pat. Ted Berrigan. ANYP
I waked; the sun was in the sky. On Waking from a Dreamless Sleep. Annie Fields. AA
I Waken [*or* Wakened] to a Calling. Delmore Schwartz. PoPl; TIHL
I wakened on my hot, hard bed. The Watch. Frances Cornford. DTC; HBMV; LiTM; MoBrPo
I Wakened to a Calling. *See* I Waken to a Calling.
I walk a road—an ancient, trodden way. Another While. Morris Rosenfeld. TrJP
I walk along the crowded streets, and mark. The Mystery of Life in Christ. Elizabeth Payson Prentiss. SoP
I walk and I wonder.. Spring. Isaac Rosenberg. TrJP
I walk beside the prisoners to the road. A Camp in the Prussian Forest. Randall Jarrell. AP; CMoP; MiAP; MoAmPo (1950 ed.); NeMa
I walk down a long. A Poem for Museum Goers. John Wieners. NeAP
I walk [*or* walked] down the garden-paths. Patterns. Amy Lowell. AmPP; AnFE; AnNE; APA; ATP; AWP; BoLiVe; BoLP; CoAnAm; CoBA; FaFP; FosPo; HBV; JAWP; LiTA; MAP; MoAmPo; NeMA; NePA; NP; OnMSP; OxBA; PoFr; TOP; TreFS; TrGrPo; UnPo; WBP
I walk down the narrow. The Man in the Mirror. Mark Strand. NYBP; YAP
I walk down the Valley of Silence. The Valley of Silence [*or* Song of the Mystic]. Abram J. Ryan. JKCP; SoP
I walk, I only. Nocturn. Francis Thompson. POTE
I walk, I trust, with open eyes. Love's Reality. Coventry Patmore. *Fr.* The Angel in the House. PoVP
I walk in London. Belle Isis; Ballad of a Rose. Sacheverell Sitwell. Rosario d'Arabeschi; Poems and Rose Portraits, I. POTE
I walk in nature still alone. Great Friend. Henry David Thoreau. MAmP; PoEL-4
I walk my paint-box suburb. The clear air. Edinburgh Spring. Norman MacCaig. NMP
I walk of grey noons by the old canal. Sonnet. Thomas Caulfield Irwin. IrPN
I walk on grass as soft as wool. An Old Woman Laments in Springtime. Edith Sitwell. LO; ViBoPo
I walk on the waste-ground for no good reason. For No Good Reason. Peter Redgrove. NMP
I walk the alleys trampled through the wheat. Sensation. Arthur Rimbaud. SyP
I walk the dusty ways of life. The Troubadour of God. Charles Wharton Stork. WGRP
I walk the old frequented ways. Behind the Closed Eye. Francis Ledwidge. MCCG
I walk the purple carpet into your eye. Inside Out. Diane Wakoski. CoAP; NYBP
I walk these many rooms, wishing to trace. C. Day Lewis. BoPe
I walk through the long schoolroom questioning. Among School Children. W. B. Yeats. AnIL; ATP (1953 ed.); CABA; CaFP; ChMP; CMoP; CoBMV; DiPo; FaBoEn; ForPo; FosPo; GTBS-P; ILP; LiTB; LiTG; LiTM (rev. ed.); MaPo; MBW-2; MoAB; MoBrPo; MoVE; NoP; OAEP (2d ed.); PAn; PIA; PoAn; PoeP; PoIE; PoVP; ReMP; SeCeV; TDP; TrGrPo; UnPo
I walk upon the rocky shore. My Mother. Josephine Rice Creelman. DD; OHIP
I walk'd [*or* walked] along a stream for pureness rare. A Fragment. Gervase Markham, *at. to* Christopher Marlowe. CTC; LoBV; OBSC
I walk'd in the lonesome evening. Song [*or* Song: "Across the Sea"]. William Allingham. EnLoPo; IrPN
I walked a mile with Pleasure. Along the Road [*or* Pleasure and Sorrow]. Robert Browning Hamilton. BLPA; MaRV; NeHB; TreFS
I walked abroad in a snowy day. Soft Snow. Blake. AtBAP; BoW; CBV; ERoP-1
I walked across the park to the fever monument. The Fever Monument. Richard Brautigan. FRC
I walked alone and thinking. Sinner's Rue. A. E. Housman. PeVV
I walked alone to my Calvary. Calvary. *Unknown.* OQP
I walked along a stream for pureness rare. *See* I walk'd along...
I walked along the cedar grove. A Psalm for Moderns. Thomas P. McDonnell. JKCP (1955 ed.)
I walked amid the lilies, at the morn. The Lilies. John Francis O'Donnell. IrPN
I walked and came upon a picket fence. Wordsworthian Reminiscence. *Unknown.* BOHV; TOP
I walked beside the deep, one night of stars. Nocturne. Victor Hugo. CAW
I walked beside the evening sea. Ebb and Flow. George William Curtis. AA; HBV
I walked beside the prisoners to the road. A Camp in the Prussian Forest. Randall Jarrell. NMP
I walked by the pond. Ed Sanders. ANYP
I walked down the lane. In September. Eleanor Hammond. GFA
I walked entranced/ Through a land of Morn. King Cahal Mór of the Wine-red Hand [*or* A Vision of Connaught in the Thirteenth Century]. James Clarence Mangan. AnIL; AnIV; GoBC; IrPN
I Walked in a Desert. Stephen Crane. AmePo
I walked in loamy Wessex lanes, afar. The Pity of It. Thomas Hardy. CMoP; InP; LiTM (rev. ed.); WaP
I walked in Palestine one summer day. The Good Shepherd. Clyde Edwin Tuck. BePJ
I walked my fastest down the twilight street. Apparition. John Erskine. HBMV
I walked on the banks of the tincan banana dock. Sunflower Sutra. Allen Ginsberg. AmPP (5th ed.); CoAP; NeAP
I walked on the billows with Jesus. Hand in Hand with Jesus. Barbara Cornet Ryberg. SoP
I walked one day on a lonely road. No Greater Love. *Unknown.* STF
I Walked Out to the Graveyard to See the Dead. Richard Eberhart. MiAP; MoPo; PoIE
I walked that day out to the death-marked hill. Simon of Cyrene. Georgia Harkness. ChIP
I walked the mountains. Microcosmos, XLIII. Nigel Heseltine. NeBP
I Walked [*or* Walkt] the Other Day [to Spend My Hour]. Henry Vaughan. AnAnS-1; BoC; EnL; FaBoEn; MeP; MePo; OBS; OxBoCh; ReEn; SCEP-1; SeCL; SeEP
I walked this Easter morning in the wood. Assurance. Grace Noll Crowell. PoRL
I walked through Ballinderry in the spring-time. Lament for [the Death of] Thomas Davis. Sir Samuel Ferguson. AnIV; IrPN; NBM; OnYI; OxBI; PoFr
I walked through the woodland meadows. The Broken Pinion [*or* The Bird with a Broken Wing]. Hezekiah Butterworth. FaChP; MaRV
I walked, when love was gone. A Breath of Air. James Wright. PoPl
I walked where in their talking graves. At the British War Cemetery, Bayeux. Charles Causley. BoPe; POTE (1959 ed.); POTi
I walked with a flower. Earth, Sky. Sydney Clouts. PeSA
I Walked with My Reason. Sorley Maclean. Dain do Eimhir, XXII. LiTW
("I walked with my reason out beside the sea.") NeBP
I walked with you as far as the graineries beside the gates. Songs for a Three-String Guitar. Léopold Sédar-Senghor. PBA

I walked with you this eleventh in the coppice. November Poppies. Hilary Corke. NYBP
I Walkt the Other Day. Henry Vaughan. *See* I Walked the Other Day.
I wander aimless, to and fro. Aimless. Louis Palagyi. TrJP
I wander all night in my vision. The Sleepers. Walt Whitman. AmP; AmPP (5th ed.); MAmP; MWA-1
I wander down on Clinton street south of Polk. Clinton South of Polk. Carl Sandburg. AmFN
I wander far and unrestrained. Spring. John Alden Carpenter. RIS
I wander on as in a dream. Love Me, and the World Is Mine. David Reed, Jr. TreFT
I wander thro' [*or* through] each charter'd street. London. Blake. *Fr.* Songs of Experience. AtBAP; AWP; BWP; CABA; CaFP; CBEP; CBV; CEP; ChER; ChTr; DiPo; EiCL; EiPP; EnL; EnLi-2 (1949 ed.); EnPE; EnRP; ERoP-1; ExPo; FaBoEn; ForPo; ILP; InPo; LiTB; LO; MaPo; NoP; OBNC; OnPM; PAn; PeER; PIA; PoAn; PoE; PoEL-4; PoeP; PoFS; PoIE; PoSa; PPON; SeCePo; SeCeV; StP; TDP; UnPo; ViBoPo; WoL
I wander through a crowd of women. At Piccadilly Circus. Vivian de Sola Pinto. OBMV
I wander'd [*or* wandered] by the brookside. The Brookside. Richard Monckton Milnes. HBV; TreFS; VA
I Wandered Lonely as a Cloud. Wordsworth. AtBAP; BEL; BoNaP; BoTP; BWP; CABA; CaFP; CBV; CoBE; DiPo; EG; EnLi-2; EnLit; EnRP; EPN; ERoP-1; ExPo; HBV; HBVY; ILP; InP; LoBV; MaPo; MasP; MBW-2; MemP; MERP; NoP; OAEP; OBRV; OTPC; OuHeWo; PAn; PoE; PoeP; PoFS; PoIE; PoPl; PoPo; PoRA; RG; RoGo; SUS; ThWaDe; TOP; UnPo; ViBoPo; WHA; YAT
(Daffodils.) AnEnPo; AnFE; BLPA; BoChLi; BoLiVe; DD; FaBoBe; FaBV; FaFP; FaPON; FiP; GBV; GN; GoJo; GoTP; GTBS; GTBS-D; GTBS-P; GTBS-W; GTSE; GTSL; HoPM; LiTB; LiTG; MaRV; MCCG; MemP; MPB; NeHB; OBEV; OBNC; OHFP; PAn; PCD; PG (1945 ed.); PoMa; PoSa; SeCeV; ShBV-1; StVeCh; TreF; TrGrPo; WBLP; WePo
I wandered lonely where the pine-trees made. The Trailing Arbutus. Whittier. AnAmPo; CoBA
I wandered on through field and fold. The Ploughman. Gilbert Thomas. HBMV
I wander'd today to the hill, Maggie. When You and I Were Young, Maggie. George W. Johnson. TreF
I Wandered Out. George Wither. *Fr.* Fair Virtue, the Mistress of Philarete. SeCL
(Divided Heart, The.) TrGrPo
I wandered through Scoglietto's far retreat. Sonnet on Holy Week. Oscar Wilde. JKCP (1926 ed.)
I wandered to the village, Tom. Twenty Years Ago. *Unknown.* BFSS
I wandered up to Beaucourt; I took the river track. Beaucourt Revisited. A. P. Herbert. MMA
I wane and weary: come, thou swifter One. To the Daemon Sublimity. Clark Ashton Smith. FiSC
I want/ a love to hold. Defense Rests. Vassar Miller. MoAmPo (1962 ed.)
I Want a Girl (Just Like the Girl That Married Dear Old Dad). Will Dillon. TreFS
I want a hero: an uncommon want. Byron. *Fr.* Don Juan, I. EnL; EnLit; EnRP; MBW-2; NoP; OAEP; Po
I want a little witch cat. Witch Cat. Rowena Bennett. SiSoSe
I Want a Pasture. Rachel Field. RePo
I want a principle within. My Desire. Charles Wesley. SoP
I want a Puppy Dog. For Christmas. Dorothy Aldis. ChBR; UTS
I want an egg for Easter. An Egg for Easter. Irene F. Pawsey. BoTP
I want free life and I want fresh air. Lasca. Frank Desprez. BeLS; BLPA; FaBoBe; HBV; NeHB; SCC; TreF
I Want God's Heab'n to Be Mine, *with music.* *Unknown.* BoAN-2
I want my buddies and all my friends. Dupree (A *vers.*) *Unknown.* ViBoFo
I want my heart so cleared of self. An Exchange of Wills. Anna Jane Granniss. SoP
I Want My Time. *Unknown.* SCC
I want nothing but your fire-side now. Hearthstone [*or* At Home, Alone with the Dog]. Harold Monro. BoC; OBMV
I want the New Year's opening days. A Prayer for the New Year. *Unknown.* BLRP
I want the proved certainties. The Holy Book. M. D. Clayburn. SoP
I want to be a carpenter. Trades. Amy Lowell. OTPC (1946 ed.)
I want to be a cauliflower. The Cauliflower. John Haines. ThO
I want to be buried in an anonymous crater inside the moon. Unholy Missions. Bob Kaufman. TTY
I Want to Be Married and Cannot Tell How. *Unknown.* OnYI
"I want to be new," said the duckling. The New Duckling. Alfred Noyes. *Fr.* Touchstone on a Bus. BoTP; FaPON; MPB
I want to be ready. Walk in Jerusalem Jus' like John. *Unknown.* BoAN-2
I want to be still as a quiet hill. Be Still. Betsy W. Kline. STF
I Want to Die Easy When I Die, *with music.* *Unknown.* BoAN-2
I Want to Die While You Love Me. Georgia Douglas Johnson. AmNP; BANP; CDC; Kal
"I want to get away somewhere and re-read Proust." Problems of a Journalist. Weldon Kees. NaP
I want to go aboard my ship, and sail and sail away. The Dream Ship. W. K. Holmes. BoTP
I Want to Go Wandering. Vachel Lindsay. HT; TSW
I Want to Know. John Drinkwater. BoChLi; FaPON
I want to know, am I the only stooge. All Awry. Justin Richardson. SiTL
I want to know the language Jesus spoke. The Language Jesus Spoke. *Unknown.* SoP
I want to know why when I'm late. I Want to Know. John Drinkwater. BoChLi; FaPON
I want to learn to whistle. Whistles [*or* Whistle]. Dorothy Aldis. BoChLi (1950 ed.); GFA; TiPo (1952 ed.)
I want to remember the fallen palm. Oblivion. Ellis Ayitey Komey. PBA
I want to see the slim palm trees. Heritage. Gwendolyn B. Bennett. AmNP; BANP
I want to see the wagons in the wood. Christmas. Margaret Avison. TwCaPo
I want to sing lyrics, lyrics. How Can I Sing? *Unknown.* MaRV
I Want to Sit Next to Emily. Ogden Nash. BOHV
I want to tell you of a trip I did take. George Britton. *Unknown.* CoSo
I want to travel the common road. The Common Road. Silas H. Perkins. BLPA; FaBoBe; NeHB
I want to walk by the side of the man. Lyman Abbott. *Fr.* The Man Who Has Won. OTD
I want ye. Cowboy Boasting Chants. *Unknown.* ABF
I Want You. Arthur L. Gillom. BLPA; FaBoBe; NeHB
I want you to hear me. Don A. Mizell. WSL
I want you to stop, think and say a prayer. Formula. Carolyn J. Ogletree. TNV
I wanted a rifle for Christmas. Presents. Marchette Chute. BrR; ChBR; EvOK; SiSoSe; StVeCh
I wanted so ably. The World. Robert Creeley. NaP
I wanted the gold, and I sought it. The Spell of the Yukon. Robert W. Service. BLPA; FaBoBe; FaFP; NeHB; OTD; PoPl; TreF
I wanted this morning to bring you a gift of roses. The Roses of Sa'adi. Marceline Desbordes-Valmore. LiTW
I wanted to be. Death's Only Son. Jon Anderson. YAP
I wanted to be more human. Forms of the Human. Richard Eberhart. FiMAP
I wanted to be sure to reach you. To the Harbormaster. Frank O'Hara. ANYP; CBV; CoAP
I wanted to bring you this Jap iris. For C. Philip Whalen. NeAP
I Wanted to Die in the Desert. *Unknown.* CoSo
I wanted to harness and go. Baroness Mu Impeded in Her Wish to Help Famine Victims in Wei. Confucius. *Fr.* Yung Wind. CTC
I wanted to write. For Saundra. Nikki Giovanni. TNV; TTY
I wanted you, nameless woman of the South. Southern Cross. Hart Crane. *Fr.* The Bridge: Three Songs. LiTA

I wanted you when skies were red. Unanswered. Martha Dickinson Bianchi. AA
I war against the folly that is War. The New Mars. Florence Earle Coates. PGD
I warmed both hands before the fire of life. Envoi. D. B. Wyndham Lewis. FiBHP
I warn, like the one drop of rain. The Voice of the Void. George Parsons Lathrop. AA
"I warn ye all, ye gay ladies." Child Waters. *Unknown.* ESPB; OAEP; OBB
I warned the parents, you know. Father to the Man. John Knight. EaLo
I was a bachelor, I lived by myself. The Weaver. *Unknown.* AS
I was a boy when I heard three red words. Threes. Carl Sandburg. CMoP; OxBA; PoLF
I Was a Brook. Sara Coleridge. *Fr.* Phantasmion. OBRV
I Was a Bustle-Maker Once, Girls. Patrick Barrington. WhC
I was a child and overwhelmed: Mozart. The Corner Knot. Robert Graves. NYBP
I was a dreamer: I dreamed. The Dream-Teller. Padraic Gregory. HBMV; OnYI
I was a goddess ere the marble found me. A Statue in a Garden. Agnes Lee. HBMV; NP
I was a high-born gentleman. Gypsy Davy. *Unknown.* AS
I was a humble clerk. The African Trader's Complaint. Dennis C. Osadebay. PBA
I was a joke at dinners; aye, any would-be wit. Revenge to Come. Propertius. *Fr.* Elegies. AWP; JAWP; LiTW; WBP
I Was a Labourer. Sean Jennet. Cycle; Seven War Poems, II. OnYI
I was a lady of high renown. Jamie Douglas [*or* Lord Douglas]. *Unknown.* BaBo (A *vers.*); ESPB; OBB; OxBB; ViBoFo (A *vers.*); WHA
I was a lover of turkey and holly. Carol. Anne Wilkinson. OBCV
I was a peasant girl from Germany. Elsa Wertman. Edgar Lee Masters. *Fr.* Spoon River Anthology. OxBA
I was a peasant of the Polish plain. Five Souls. W. N. Ewer. MaRV; OQP
I was a phoebe—nothing more. Emily Dickinson. BiS
I was a Roman soldier in my prime. [A] Guard of [*or* at] the Sepulcher. Edwin Markham. SoP; StJW; WGRP
I was a scholar; seven useful springs. A Scholar and His Dog. John Marston. BoPe
I was a stricken deer, that left the herd. The Stricken Deer [*or* Self-Portrait *or* In His Mental Illness, William Cowper Finds He Is Not Alone]. William Cowper. BoC; CoBE; EnRP; FiP; LoBV; MaRV; OAEP; OxBoCh; PeER
I Was a Wandering Sheep. Horatius Bonar. *See* Lost but Found.
I was a warrior's weapon, once. Riddle #14: A Horn. *Unknown.* DiPo
I was a woman always liked spangles. Sleep, Madame, Sleep. Annemarie Ewing. NePoAm
I was a young maid truly. The Sandgate Girl's Lamentation. *Unknown.* CoMu; ELP
I was alone once, waiting. For the Marsh's Birthday. James Wright. NYBP
I was always a lover of ladies' hands! Your Hands. Ernest Dowson. UnTE
I was an elephant. Elephant! Tom Scherman. PCD
I was an English shell. An English Shell. A. C. Benson. VA
I was angry with my friend. A Poison Tree. Blake. *Fr.* Songs of Experience. AnFE; AWP; BoLiVe; BWP; CABA; CaFP; CBEP; CBV; DiPo; EG; EiCL; EnL; EnLi-2; EnLit; EnRP; ERoP-1; FaFP; GTBS-W; HoPM; InPo; JAWP; LiTB; LiTG; MaPo; NoP; OAEP; OtMeF; PoAn; PoEL-4; PoeP; PoFS; PoMS; SiSw; ToP; TreFS; TrGrPo; VaPo; WBP
I was apprenticed as a callow lad. The Stone. Walter H. Kerr. FiSC
I was asking for something specific and perfect for my city. Mannahatta. Walt Whitman. MoAmPo; OuHeWo
I was astonished by no grace. A Woman Passes the Door. George O'Neil. NP
"I was bat seven year alld." *See* "I was but seven year auld."
I Was Born Almost Ten Thousand Years Ago, *with music.* *Unknown.* AS
I was born committing suicide. Adjust, Adjust. Christopher Bursk. WOW
I was born downtown on a wintry day. Karl Shapiro. Recapitulations, I. FiMAP
I was born for deep-sea faring. A Son of the Sea. Bliss Carman. EtS
I was born in a bad slum. Plot Improbable, Character Unsympathetic. Elder Olson. NePA
I was born in Belfast between the mountain and the gantries. Carrickfergus. Louis MacNeice. AnIL; OnYI
I was born in Boston city. The Boston Burglar. *Unknown.* CoSo
I was born in Illinois. My Fathers Came from Kentucky. Vachel Lindsay. *Fr.* Alexander Campbell. AmFN; HBMV
"I was born in Indiany," says a stranger, lank and slim. Like His Mother Used to Make. James Whitcomb Riley. IHA
I was born in the town of Boston. The Boston Burglar. *Unknown.* ViBoFo
I was born on a street named Joy. Lines on His Birthday. John Logan. FRC
I was born on the prairie. Prairie. Carl Sandburg. LaNeLa; NP
I was born on the prairie. Prairie Birth. Grace Stone Coates. PaA
I was born, they say, in tears. Tears and Song. *Unknown.* OnPM
I was born under a kind star. Katharine Tynan. EG
I Was Born Upon Thy Bank, River. Henry David Thoreau. ELU; PoEL-4
I was borned and raised in east Virginia. East Virginia. *Unknown.* OuSiCo
I was broke and out of a job in the city of London. Paddy Get Back. *Unknown.* AmSS; ShS; SoAmSa
I was brought up in a rampart. The Stolen Fifer. Padraic Fiacc. NeIP
I was brought up in Sheffield, both low and high degree. The Sheffield Apprentice. *Unknown.* BFSS
"I was but [*or* bat] seven year auld [*or* alld]." The Laily Worm and the Machrel of the Sea. *Unkown.* ChTr; ESPB; InvP; LoBV; OA; OBB; OxBB; PoEL-1
I was carried to a font. Dithyramb in Retrospect. Peter Hopegood. BoAV; PoAu-2
I was confused; I cannot promise more. Sonnet XIV. Mark Van Doren. MoLP
I was descending from the mountains of sleep. Afternoon Sleep. Robert Bly. NaP
I Was Down the Field. Pamela Millward. FRC
I was driving north. Dream Poem #1. Craig Sterry. QAH
I was driving the cows and the frogs were soothsaying. Twilight. Eileen Duggan. JKCP (1955 ed.)
I was even wearier where I waited. Migrants. Ethel Anderson. BoAV
I was five when we moved to England, and the strange voices. Anton Vogt. *Fr.* For England, in Grateful Appreciation. AnNZ
I was foretold, your rebell sex. A Deposition from Love. Thomas Carew. AnAnS-2; CavP; OAEP; OBS
I Was Found of Thee. *Unknown.* *See* I Sought the Lord.
I was glad when they said unto me. Psalm CXII, Bible, *O.T.* TRV
I was going to make a boat. But That Was Yesterday. Aileen Fisher. SoPo
I was gouging beneath a group of soft. An End to Complacency. Barry Cole. HYE
I was holding my son's hand. The Scale of Things. Patric Dickinson. POTi
"I was in a hooker once," said Karlssen. Cape Horn Gospel—I. John Masefield. StPo
I was in a summery dale. The Owl and the Nightingale. *Unknown, at. to* Nicholas de Guildford. MeEV
I was in Margate last July, I walked upon the pier. Misadventures at Margate. "Thomas Ingoldsby." BOHV; HBV
I was in the boy scouts once. Butchers. Redmond Phillips. NeLNL
I was in the harbor. Resolution. "Wiolar." InMe
I was in the sand near to the seawall. The Husband's Message. *Unknown.* EnLit
I was in Vegas. Celibate and able. J. V. Cunningham. PV
I was just about to take a drink. To Hear Him Tell It. *Unknown.* SCC

I was just turned twenty-one. Harry Wilmans. Edgar Lee Masters. *Fr.* Spoon River Anthology. PPON; WOW
I was laying around town, just spending my time. The Strawberry Roan. *Unknown.* ABF
I was lost/ In doubt and fear. Lost, but Won. Henry von Schlichten. BePJ
I was lying still in a field one day. Zhenya Gay. TiPo (1959 ed.)
I Was Made Erect and Lone. Henry David Thoreau. FaBoEn; PoEL-4
I Was Made of This and This. Gertrude Robison Ross. HBMV
I was [*or* wus] mighty good lookin', when I was [*or* wus] young. Spacially [*or* Specially] Jim. Bessie Morgan. BOHV; HBV
I was milking in the meadow when I heard the Banshee keening. The Warnings. Alice Furlong. AnIV
I was near the King that day. I saw him snatch. Devotion to Duty. Siegfried Sassoon. MoPW
I was nine when my father died. Kit Carson. Arthur Guiterman. OTD
I was not, and I was conceived. Three Characteristic Epitaphs. *Unknown.* SoP
I was not asked if I should like to come. The Bewildered Guest. William Dean Howells. AmePo
I was not aware of the moment. Rabindranath Tagore. Gitanjali, XCV. NP
I was not blind,/ you must not think that I was blind. Priam. Dudley Fitts. OnHM
I was not borne to Helicon, nor dare. A Gratulatory to Mr. Ben Johnson for His Adopting of Him to Be His Son. Thomas Randolph. AnAnS-2; OBS
I was not, I was made: I was. To Be and Not to Be. *Unknown.* OnPM
I was not meant to stand in a sea-edge garden. Figurehead. Dorothy Paul. EtS
I was not sorrowful, I could not weep. Spleen. Ernest Dowson. BrPo; CBEP; MoBrPo; NCEP; SyP
I was not train'd in academic bowers. Written at Cambridge. Charles Lamb. EnRP; OBRV
I was of delicate mind. I stepped aside for my needs. The Refined Man. Kipling. *Fr.* Epitaphs of the War. FaBoTw; MMA
I was on the drive in Eighty. Silver Jack. *Unknown.* CoSo
I was once an armed warrior. Now the worthy youth. A Horn. *Unknown.* OuHeWo
I was one with woods; my body, the Earth. Brajendranath Seal. *Fr.* The Quest Eternal. ACV
I was out walking an' a-ramblin' one day. The Wild Rippling Water. *Unknown.* CoSo
I was playing golf that day. *Unknown.* FiBHP; PV
I was sat in the church of their Lord. Microcosmos, XXXV. Nigel Heseltine. NeBP
I was seventy-seven, come August. The Little Old Lady in Lavender Silk. Dorothy Parker. InMe; YaD
I was sick. Jesus Was Crucified or: It Must Be Deep. Carolyn M Rodgers. WSL
I was so chill, and overworn, and sad. Song [*or* Since I Saw My Love]. Anna Wickham. MeWo; MoBrPo; NeMA
I was spawned from the glacier. The Iceberg. Sir Charles G. D. Roberts. CaP
I was spinning with earth and a foul wind was blowing. Finger Pop'in. Charles Anderson. BF
I was stung by a man-of-war. The Lesson. Larry Rubin. GoYe
I was takin' off my bonnet. Darwinism in the Kitchen. *Unknown.* FiBHP
I was taught prayer as a child, to bend the knee. Prayer at Dawn. Diarmuid O'Shea. KiLC
I was that dancer. On the screen. Re-run. Winfield Townley Scott. FiMAP
I was that youth. Now, from myself estranged. The Revolutionary. Vernon Watkins. NYTB
I was the captain of my ship. Jason. Dom Moraes. TDP
I was the chief of the race—he had stricken my father dead. The Voyage of Maeldune. Tennyson. PoEL-5
I was the first fruits of the battle of Missionary Ridge. Knowlt Hoheimer. Edgar Lee Masters. *Fr.* Spoon River Anthology. OxBA
I was the last passenger of the day. The Bus. Leonard Cohen. CAD
I Was the Midmost. Thomas Hardy. MaPo
I was the milliner. Mrs. Williams. Edgar Lee Masters. *Fr.* Spoon River Anthology. NAMP
I was the moon. Dead. Rhoda Coghill. OnYI
I was the only child of Frances Harris of Virginia. Hamilton Greene. Edgar Lee Masters. *Fr.* Spoon River Anthology. OxBA
I was the patriarch of the shining land. John Sutter. Yvor Winters. MoAmPo (1962 ed.); MoVE; PoPl; PoSa; QFR
I was the staunchest of our fleet. The Derelict. Kipling. BrPo
"I was thinking, Mother, of that poor old horse." Reserved. Walter de la Mare. GTBS-P
I was the third man running in a race. The Service. Burges Johnson. HBMV; StaSt
I was thy Neighbour once, thou rugged Pile! Elegiac Stanzas, Suggested by a Picture of Peele Castle, in a Storm [*or* Nature and the Poet]. Wordsworth. BEL; CABL; ChER; EnRP; EPN; ERoP-1; GTBS; GTBS-D; GTBS-P; GTBS-W; GTSE; GTSL; HBV; MBW-2; MERP; MyFE; NoP; OAEP; OBNC; OBRV; PeER; PoFS; TOP
I was too ambitious in my deed. Content. Elizabeth Barrett Browning. MaRV
I was upon the high and blessed mound. Sonnet: Of [*or* At] the Grave of Selvaggia. Cino da Pistoia. AWP; JAWP; OnPM; WBP
I was walking on the sea-shore. The Seagulls. Sir John Morris-Jones. PrWP
"I was with Grant," the stranger said. The Aged Stranger. Bret Harte. AA; AmFN; LHV; MaC; MAP; MoAmPo (1942 ed.); NeMA; TreFS
I was wrong, quite wrong. Soliloquy II. Richard Aldington. BrPo; MMA
I was wrought of walnut blocks and rolled rod steel. The Springfield Calibre Fifty. Joseph Mills Hanson. PoOW
I was yesterday in Ben Dorain and in her precincts I was not at a loss. Last Leave of the Hills. Duncan Ban MacIntyre. GoTS
I was young/ when I foreswore. A Deposition by John Wilmot. Vincent McHugh. ErPo
I was young and happy and my heart was light and gay. Snagtooth Sal. Lowell O. Reese. ABF; SCC
I was young when I met the Master. When I Met Him. Sybil Leonard Armes. FaChP
I Was My Face in a Golden Vase. *Unknown.* ChBR
I washed my face in water. Riddle. *Unknown.* ChTr
I wasn't born here man. Man I Thought You Was Talking Another Language That Day. Victor Hernandez Cruz. BOLo
I Wasn't There. Lon Woodrum. SoP
I Waste Away. Isaiah, XXIV: 16-20, Bible, *O.T.* TrJP
I Watch. Clive Matson. ThO
I watch, and long have watched, with calm regret. Wordsworth. Sonn
I watch beside you in your silent room. Morton Luce. *Fr.* Thysia. HBV
I watch her fingers where they prance. Enigma. Hugh McCrae. BoAV; MoAuPo; PoAu-1
I watch her in the corner there. Arachne. Rose Terry Cooke. AA; AnAmPo
I watch the battle in the orange-grove. The Rout of San Romano. Jon Manchip White. NePoEA
I watch the curious hastened trait of twilight. Sadness, Glass, Theory. Roy Fuller. WaP
I watch the doctors walking with the nurses to and fro. The Memory. Lord Dunsany. OxBI
I watch the dung-cart stumble by. In December. Andrew Young. SeCePo
I watch the farmers in their fields. Farmers. William Alexander Percy. MaRV; WGRP
I watch the great spokes of this wheel. Beside a Balance Wheel. MacKnight Black. NP
I watch the leaves that flutter in the wind. Leaves at My Window. John James Piatt. AA
I watch them on the drill field, the awkward and the grave. The Drill. Harry Brown. WaaP
I watched a log in the fireplace burning. Flames. Sara Teasdale. OTD
I watched a man in a cafe. In a Cafe. Richard Brautigan. FRC
I watched a sail until it dropped from sight. 'Tis Life Beyond [*or* Horizon]. *Unknown.* MaRV

I watched her as she stooped to pluck. On the Brink. Charles Stuart Calverley. VA
I watched him at the banquet wait. Lazarus. A. S. Cripps. BoSA
I watched the agony of a mountain farm. The Farm Died. Malcolm Cowley. *Fr.* Blue Juniata. MAP; MoAmPo (1942 ed.)
I watched the blind attack. Snow in April. Leonora Speyer. PG (1955 ed.)
I watched the Captains. The Captains of the Years. Arthur R. Macdougall, Jr. ChIP; MaRV; OQP; TRV
I watched the hills drink the last color of light. Thought's End. Léonie Adams. MAP; MoAB; MoAmPo
I watched the Lady Caroline. Lovelocks. Walter de la Mare. MoVE
I watched the new moon fly. The Golden Bird. Rex Ingamells. PoAu-2
I watched the pretty, white sea gull. The Sea Gull. Leroy F. Jackson. GFA; UTS
I watched the sea for hours blind with sun. Sonnet. Winfield Townley Scott. MiAP
I watched the seeds come down this afternoon. At a Country Hotel. Howard Nemerov. PoRA (rev. ed.)
"I watched thee when the foe was at our side." Byron. ERoP-2
I watched them playing there upon the sand. The Castle. Sidney Alexander. PoNe
I watched them tearing a building down. Building [*or* Which Are You?]. G. K. Chesterton. PoLF; SoP
I wayed by star and planet shine. The Well-beloved. Thomas Hardy. ViPo (1962 ed.)
I wear a cloak of laughter. Cloak of Laughter. Abigail Cresson. PoToHe
I Wear a Crimson Cloak To-Night. Lois Seyster Montross. HBMV
"I wear a cross of bronze," he said. The Cross. Leon Gellert. BoAu
I wear a snow-white rose today. Love's Tribute. Lorena W. Sturgeon. PGD
I wear your kiss like a feather. Two Kisses. Stephen Spender. CMoP
I weary of these noisy nights. Away. Max Ehrmann. PoToHe
I Weep. Angelina Weld Grimké. CDC
I weep. To Gottfried Benn. Else Lasker-Schüler. OnPM
I weep a sight which was not seen. Doom Devoted. Louis Golding. HBMV
I weep, but with no bitterness I weep. Souvenir. Alfred de Musset. AWP; WoL
I weep for Adonais—he is dead! Adonais. Shelley. AtBAP; ATP; BEL; BoLiVe; CABA; ChER; EnL; EnLi-2; EnLit; EnRP; EPN; ERoP-2; FaPL; FiP; FosPo; GoTL; HBV; HoPM; LoBV; MaPo; MasP; MBW-2; MCCG; MERP; NoP; OAEP; OBRV; PAn; PoE; PoEL-4; PoIE; StP; TOP; TrGrPo; UnPo (1st ed.); ViBoPo; WHA; WoL
I weep—not as the young do. I Weep. Angelina Weld Grimké. CDC
I weep those dead lips, white and dry. Linen Bands. Vance Thompson. AA
I weep two deaths with one tear to lament. Upon Christ's Saying to Mary "Why Weepest Thou?" William Alabaster. Sonn
I weigh not fortune's frown or smile. A Contented Mind. Joshua Sylvester. HBV; PoToHe (1941 ed.)
I well remember how the race began. On Becoming Man. R. P. Lister. PV
I well remember those old times. Old Forty-nine. Mart Taylor. SGR
I Wend to Death. *Unknown.* NoP
I went across the pasture lot. The Cornfield. Elizabeth Madox Roberts. GoJo; SUS
I went a-riding, a-riding. Texas. Amy Lowell. AmFN; InP; PoMa
I went a roaming, maidens, one bright day. Angelo Poliziano. Three Ballate, 3. AWP
I went a-roaming through the woods alone. The Nightingale. John Addington Symonds. VA
I went away last August. Eat-It-All Elaine. Kaye Starbird. PDV
I went back an old-time lane. In the Fall o' Year. Thomas S. Jones, Jr. HBV
I went back to a place I knew. Remembrance. Aline Kilmer. CAW
I went by the Druid stone. The Shadow on the Stone. Thomas Hardy. QFR
I Went Down into the Desert to Meet Elijah. Vachel Lindsay. WGRP
I Went Down to the Depot, *with music.* *Unknown.* AS
I went down to the river. Life Is Fine. Langston Hughes. BP; WaKn
I went down to the river, poor boy. Bow Down Your Head and Cry. *Unknown.* CoSo
I went down to the shouting sea. Sand-between-the-Toes. A. A. Milne. TiPo (1959 ed.)
I went down town one day in a lope. Ida Red. *Unknown.* ABF
I went for a walk over the dunes again this morning. Corsons Inlet. A. R. Ammons. CoAP
I went into a public-'ouse to get a pint o' beer. Tommy. Kipling. BrPo; CABA; EnLi-2 (1949 ed.); EnLit; FaBV; MoBrPo; NeMA; NoP; PeVV; PoVP; TreFS; ViPP
I went into a sort of house. The Wheelgoround. Robert Clairmont. PoMS
I went into my grandmother's garden. *Unknown.* OxNR
I went into my stable, to see what I might see. Old Wichet. *Unknown.* StPo
I went into the fields, but you were there. You. John Masefield. MoRP
I went into the flea circus. Small Talk. Don Marquis. *Fr.* Archy Does His Part. StPo
I went on Friday afternoons. Au Tombeau de Mon Père. Ronald McCuaig. PoAu-2
I went out at the eastern gate. The Eastern Gate. *Unknown.* FIW
I Went Out into the Garden. Moses ibn Ezra, *tr. fr. Hebrew by* Solomon Solis-Cohen. LiTW; TrJP
I went out on an April morning. Morning. Sara Teasdale. NP
I went out to the farthest meadow. Love Is a Terrible Thing. Grace Fallow Norton. HBV; PFY
I went out to the hazel wood. The Song of Wandering Ængus. W. B. Yeats. BoLiVe; BoLP; BrPo; CH; CLwM; CMoP; DiPo; EnLi-2 (1949 ed.); EnLit; FaBoCh; GoJo; GoTP; InP; LoGBV; LOW; MaPo; MemP; MoAB; MoBrPo; OnSP; PG; PoEL-5; PoeP; PoMS; PoRA; PoSa; RG; SiSw; SP; TDP; ThWaDe; TiPo; ViPo (1962 ed.); WaKn; YAT
I went this morning down to where the Johnny-Jump-Ups grow. The Faithless Flowers. Margaret Widdemer. MPB; SP
I went through the market-place crying, There is no death. A. R. D. Fairburn. *Fr.* Disquisition on Death. AnNZ
I went to bat for the Lady Chatte. A Lass in Wonderland. F. R. Scott. MoCV
I went to bring. The Skippery Boo. Earl L. Newton. GoTP
I went to court last night. Puck Goes to Court. Fenton Johnson. CDC; GoSl
"I went to dances when I carried you." To My Mother. Edwin Brock. NMP
I went to dig a grave for Love. Love's Change. Anne Reeve Aldrich. AA
I went to Frankfort and got drunk. Epigram on an Academic Visit to the Continent [*or* On an Imaginary Journey to the Continent]. Richard Porson. EiCL; OnPM; OxBoLi; PV; WhC
I went to heaven. Emily Dickinson. FaBV; NePA
I went to her who loveth me no more. Enchainment [*or* Song]. Arthur O'Shaughnessy. OBNC
I went to ma daddy. Hard Daddy. Langston Hughes. BANP
I went to market and bought me a cat. An Old Rhyme. *Unknown.* BoTP
I went to Noke. *Unknown.* OxNR
I went to San Francisco. Trip: San Francisco. Langston Hughes. AmFN; GoSl
I went to school with the tutor, Law. The Teachers. C. V. Pilcher. OQP
I went to seek for Christ. The Search. James Russell Lowell. MaRV; SoP; StJW; TRV
I went to sleep smiling. Prescience. Margaret Widdemer. HBMV
I went to someone's dinner and a play. Moan in the Form of a Ballade. Maurice Baring. WhC
I went to Strasbourg, where I got drunk. On a German Tour. Richard Porson. FiBHP

I went to sup with Cinna t'other night. Of Good Sauce. Sir John Harington. SiCE
I went to tea at Elizabeth's house. A Strange Interlude. Margaret Fishback. BOHV
I went to the animal fair. Animal Fair. *Unknown.* AS; BLPA; FaBoBe; GoTP; MoShBr; SiTL; SoPo; YaD
I went to the captain with my hat in my hand. Take This Hammer. *Unknown.* OuSiCo
I Went to the City. Kenneth Patchen. PoPl
I went to the dances at Chandlerville. Lucinda Matlock. Edgar Lee Masters. *Fr.* Spoon River Anthology. CMoP; FaBV; ILP; InP; LaNeLa; LiTA; LiTL; LiTM; MAP; MCCG; MoAmPo; MoVE; NeMA; NP: OnPP; OxBA; PoPo; ReMP
I went to the fields with the leisure I got. The Frightened Ploughman. John Clare. PoEL-4
I went to the Garden of Love. The Garden of Love. Blake. *Fr.* Songs of Experience. AWP; CABA; CBEP; DiPo; EiCL; EnLi-2 (1949 ed.); EnLoPo; EnRP; ERoP-1; ExPo; FaBV; FosPo; InPo; JAWP; LiTB; LiTG; LiTL; LO; LoBV; MeWo; NoP; OAEP; PoE; PoFS; PoIE; SeCeV; StP; TOP; VaPo; ViBoPo; WBP
I went to the park. The Balloon. Karla Kuskin. PDV
I went to the place. Don't Pay. Ruby C. Saunders. WSL
I went to the toad [road, *wr.*] that lies under the wall. *Unknown.* OxNR; SiTL
I went to the wood and got it. Mother Goose. PPL, *longer vers.* RIS
I went to the Wood of Flowers. The Wood of Flowers. James Stephens. BoTP; MemP; PDV
I went to turn the grass once after one. The Tuft of Flowers. Robert Frost. AmP; AmPP; AnNE; AP; AtBAP; AWP; CBEP; CoBMV; GoYe; HBV; HBVY; InP; JAWP; LaNeLa; LiTA; MAP; MoAB; MoAmPo; MoPW; NeMA; NoP; OxBA; PC; PoPo; SeCeV; TSW; WBP
I went to worship in a house of God. Prayer in a Country Church. Ruth B. Van Dusen. TrPWD
I went up and down the streets. Doc Hill. Edgar Lee Masters. *Fr.* Spoon River Anthology. NP
I went up one pair of stairs. Just like Me. Mother Goose. BoTP; PPL
I went up to a high hill. The High Hill. Clinton Scollard. MaRV
I went up to London Town. Devilish Mary. *Unknown.* OuSiCo
I went up to the light of truth as if into a chariot. To Truth. *Unknown.* *Fr.* Solomon. WGRP
I went upstairs. Upstairs. John Stevens Wade. ThO
I went visiting Miss Melinda. Strawberry Jam. May Justus. FaPON
I wept a tear. Tears for Sale. Leonora Speyer. HBMV
I Wept as I Lay Dreaming. Heine, *tr. fr. German by* John Todhunter. AWP
I wept Theonoe's loss; but one fair child. Loss after Loss. Bianor. OnPM
I were unkind unless that I did shed. Lines on His Companions Who Died in the Northern Seas. Thomas James. SeCL
I. . .What a fine statue! Victory. Arthur B. Rhinow. MaRV
I which was once a happy wight. A Proper New Song Made by a Student in Cambridge. Thomas Richardson. TuPP
I whispered, "I am too young." Brown Penny. W. B. Yeats. BoLP; CLwM; CMoP; ELP; ExPo; FaBoCh; LoGBV
I whispered my great sorrow. The Sedges. "Seumas O'Sullivan." AnIV
I, who all my life had hurried. Epitaph for Any New Yorker. Christopher Morley. ShM
I who am dead a thousand years. To a Poet a Thousand Years Hence. James Elroy Flecker. ChTr; HBV; InP; MemP; MoBrPo; MoPW; PoRA; ShBV-4; TrGrPo (1942 ed.)
I, who am known as London, have faced stern times before. London Under Bombardment. Greta Briggs. OtMeF
I who am nothing and this tissue. Hoc Est Corpus. Alex Comfort. LiTB; LiTM; POTE
I who am street-known am also street knowing. Investigator. Miriam Waddington. CaP
I who employ a poet's tongue. Timid Lover. Countee Cullen. BANP
I who ere while the happy Garden sung. Paradise Regained. Milton. CABL
I who erst while the worlds sweet aire did draw. *Unknown.* SeCSL
I, Who Fade with the Lilacs. William Griffith. HBMV
I Who Had Been Afraid. Sister Maris Stella. GoBC
I who have favour'd many, come to be. To the Most Learned, Wise, and Arch-Antiquary, M. John Selden. Robert Herrick. SeCV-1
I who have heard solemnities of sound. The Great Voice. Clinton Scollard. MaRV
I, who have lost the stars, the sod. On a Subway Express. Chester Firkins. PFY; YaD
I, who have ridden the world. Pastoral. Willard Trask. CLwM
I—who have the healing creed. Christ in Introspect. Charlotte Brontë. MaRV
I who have walked splay-footed in hobnailed boots. Imaginary Correspondence, *parody.* Frank Sidgwick. WhC
I, who knew Circe, have come back. Ulysses in Autumn. Joseph Auslander. MAP; MoAmPo (1942 ed.)
I who love beauty in the open valleys. He, Too, Loved Beauty. Edwin McNeill Poteat. ChIP
I who love you bring. Song. Theodore Spencer. AnFE; CoAnAm; TwAmPo
I who once was free. Seguidilla. José de Valdivielso. CAW
I who was once a golden woman like those who walk. Invocation. Edith Sitwell. AtBAP
I, who was the flower of my day among the beauties. The Beautiful Woman. Tu Fu. WoL
I whom thou seest with horyloge in hand. Time. Sir Thomas More. EnRePo
I Will Accept. Christina Rossetti. OxBoCh
I will accomplish that and this. In After Days. George Frederick Cameron. CaP
I Will Arise and Go Now. Ogden Nash. WaKn
I will arise and go now, and go to Innisfree. The Lake Isle of Innisfree. W. B. Yeats. ATP; BEL; BoC; BoLiVe; BrPo; CMoP; CoBMV; DiPo; EnL; EnLi-2 (1949 ed.); EnLit; FaBV; FaFP; FaPL; FaPON; GBV; GTBS; GTBS-W; GTSL; HBV; HT; ILP; InP; LiTG; LiTM (rev. ed.); MaPo; MBW-2; MCCG; MoAB; MoBrPo; NeMA; NoP; OAEP (2d ed.); OBEV; OBVV; OnYI; OTPC (1946 ed.); PoPl; PoPo; PoRA; PoVP; RoGo; ShBV-2; SP; TDP; TOP; TreF; TrGrPo; TSW; ViPo (1962 ed.); WHA; YAT; YT
I will arise and go now, and go to Inverness. The Cockney of the North. Harry Graham. CenHV
I will arise, and leave these haggard realms. The Prodigal Son. Arthur Symons. BrPo
I will arise and to my Father go. Seeking and Finding God. John C. Earle. MaRV
I will be a lion. Wild Beasts. Evaleen Stein. MPB (1956 ed.); SoPo; UTS
I will be an old man sometime. You Talk of Going but Don't Even Have a Suitcase. John Wieners. FRC
I will be happy if but for once. Dubiety. Robert Browning. *Fr.* Asolando. MaPo (1969 ed.); MBW-2; PoVP; ViPo
I will be nice to you. Forsaking the Course. Jonathan Cott. YAP
I will be the gladdest thing. Afternoon on a Hill. Edna St. Vincent Millay. BoTP; FaPON; MPB; OxBA; PDV; SoPo; StVeCh (1955 ed.); TiPo (1952 ed.); TSW
I will be what God made me, nor protest. Robert Bridges. The Growth of Love, LXII. PoVP
I Will Believe. William H. Roberts. BLRP
I Will Bow and Be Simple. *Unknown.* EaLo
I will commit my way, O Lord, to Thee. Be Still My Heart. *Unknown.* SoP
I will consider my Cat Jeoffry. The Cat. Christopher Smart. *Fr.* Jubilate Agno. BoW
I will defy you down until my death. The Quiet Woman. Genevieve Taggard. AnEnPo; NP
I will drink, I will gamble, I will play wild again. O-Bar Cowboy. *At. to* Bill Wagon. CoSo
I will enjoy thee now. Thomas Carew. *See* Rapture, A.
I will exchange a city for a sunset. Barter. Marie Blake. PoPl; PoToHe (new ed.)
I will explain the eagle's nature. The Eagle's Nature. *Unknown, tr. fr. Middle English.* *Fr.* The Bestiary. MeEV
I will fling wide the windows of my soul. Sonnet. Robert Hillyer. HBMV
I Will Give My Love an Apple. *Unknown.* CBEP

I Will Give You. Blake. *See* To the Christians.
I will give you a golden ring. The Keys of Heaven. *Unknown.* FTB
I Will Give You a Purpose. Gregory Orr. QAH
I will give you painted shoes. Offerings. Rodrigo De Reinosa. CLwM
I will give you the end of a golden string. *See* I give you the end of a golden string.
I will go back to the great sweet mother. The Sea [*or* The Return]. Swinburne. *Fr.* Triumph of Time. BoLiVe; EtS; FaPL; GTSL; HBV; OAEP; TrGrPo; TSW
I will go down to the sea again. Sea Song. Norah Holland. CaP
I will go out and hear the strain. Macquarie Place. Robert D. Fitzgerald. PoAu-2
I will go up the mountain after the moon. Moon Folly. Fannie Stearns Davis. *Fr.* Songs of Conn the Fool. RG; SP
I will go walking on Eighth Street. Eighth Street West. Rachel Field. ChBR; SiSoSe
I Will Go with My Father a-Ploughing. Joseph Campbell. AnIL; FaPON; GaP; GoBC; JKCP; OnYI; SiSoSe; TiPo (1959 ed.)
I will go with the first air of morning. Fishing. Dorothy Wellesley. BoC; OBMV
I will grieve alone. In Response to a Rumor That the Oldest Whorehouse in Wheeling, West Virginia, Has Been Condemned. James Wright. CoAP
I Will Guide Thee. W. L. Alexander. SoP
I will have an image. Larry Eigner. CoPo
I will have few cooking-pots. Domestic Economy. Anna Wickham. NeMA
I will have one built/ Like Pompey's theatre. John Day. *Fr.* The Parliament of Bees. ViBoPo
"I will have to my supper a chicken without a bone." An Old Man's Courtship. *Unknown.* BFSS
I will hew great windows for my soul. Windows For My Soul. Angela Morgan. OQP
I will hold beauty as a shield against despair. Beauty as a Shield. Elsie Robinson. BLPA; PoToHe (new ed.)
I Will Keep Christmas. P. A. Ropes. BoTP
I will keep the fire of hope ever burning on the altar of my soul. Realization. Sri Ananda Acharya. WGRP
I will leave the dust of the city street and the noise of the busy town. The Vagrant. Pauline Slender. HBMV
I will legislate in this poem. Take Notice. Ralph Robin. NYTB
I Will Lift Up Mine Eyes unto the Hills. Psalms, CXXI, Bible, *O.T.* AWP; BBV (1951 ed.); CBEP; EnLi-1; FaPON; JAWP; OnPM; OuHeWo; PoG; TreF; TRV
(Pilgrim's Song, *Moulton, Modern Reader's Bible.*) WGRP
(Song of Trust, A.) PCD; TrGrPo
I will live in Ringsend. Ringsend. Oliver St. John Gogarty. AnIL; LiTM; OBMV
I will make a new song of the word. Paul Engle. *Fr.* Break the Heart's Anger: Prologue. PoFr
I will make a song for these States. A Song for the States. Walt Whitman. PoRL
I Will Make You Brooches. Robert Louis Stevenson. *See* Romance.
I will never buy the pig in the poke. Buying a Pig. John Heywood. SiCE
"I will never eate nor drinke," Robin Hood said. Robin Hood's Death. *Unknown.* BaBo; ESPB
I will not be reduced to what I am. Five Stanzas on Perfection. George Jonas. PeCV (1967 ed.)
I will not break the tryst, my dear. A Tryst. Louise Chandler Moulton. HBV
I will not change my horse with any that treads. The Horse. Shakespeare. *Fr.* King Henry V. GoTP
I will not change my path with you. Dreams. Philip M. Raskin. OQP
I will not comb my morning hair. Morning Hair. *Unknown.* OnPM
I will not doubt for evermore. Henry David Thoreau. *Fr.* Inspiration. MaRV
I will not doubt, though all my ships at sea. Faith. Ella Wheeler Wilcox. BLRP; MaRV; OQP; PoToHe; SoP; TRV
I will not gather the vervain sweet. Sorrow. *Unknown.* OnPM
"I will not go," he said, "for well." Infirm. Edward Sandford Martin. ALV
I will not have the mad Clytie. Flowers. Thomas Hood. HBV; OTPC (1923 ed.); VA
I will not have you think me less. A Jewish Poet Counsels a King. Santob de Carrion. TrJP
I Will Not Hurry. Ralph Spaulding Cushman. MaRV
I will not kiss you country fashion. A Calvinist in Love. Jack R. Clemo. ChMP
I Will Not Let Thee Go. Robert Bridges. AnFE; BeLS; CMoP; CoBMV; EnLoPo; FaBoBe; LiTL; OBNC; PoVP; VA
I will not look for him. A Woman's Pride. Helen Hay Whitney. AA
I will not perturbate/ Thy Paradisal state. To the Dead Cardinal of Westminster. Francis Thompson. PeVV; PoVP
I will not rail, or grieve when torpid eld. Age [*or* Sonnet—Age]. Richard Garnett. OBVV; VA
I will not say to you, "This is the Way; walk in it." To My Son. *Unknown.* PoLF; PoMa
I will not shut me from my kind. In Memoriam A. H. H., CVIII. Tennyson. EnLi-2; EPN; ViPo; VP
I will not tell her that she's fair. A Song. Matthew Coppinger. CavP
I will not tell the secrets of that place. Esther, A young Man's Tragedy, XLIX. Wilfrid Scawen Blunt. Sonn
I will not therefore minimize my prayer. Prayer and Promises. William Olney. SoP
I will not weep, for 'twere as great a sin. An Elegy [*or* Conjectured to Be upon the Death of Sir Walter Raleigh]. Henry King. AnAnS-2; EG
I will not write a poem for you. The Thought. Humbert Wolfe. BoPe
I will now address myself to the problem of writing. A Week of Doodle. Reed Whittemore. NePoEA
I will o'ertake thee, Cleopatra, and. Shakespeare. *Fr.* Antony and Cleopatra, IV, xiv. MemP
I will paint her as I see her. A Portrait. Elizabeth Barrett Browning. GN; HBV; OTPC
I will pluck from my tree a cherry-blossom wand. The Cherry-Blossom Wand. Anna Wickham. MeWo; MoBrPo; TSW
I Will Praise the Lord at All Times. William Cowper. EiCP; NoP
(Olney Hymns.) CEP
I will praise thee, O Lord, with my whole heart. I Will Sing Praise. Psalm IX, Bible, *O.T.*. FaPON
I will put Chaos into fourteen lines. Edna St. Vincent Millay. Sonn
I will put enmities/ Between thee and the woman. Genesis, Bible, *O.T.* (*Douay vers.*). ISi
"I will put upon you the Telephone Curse," said the witch. The Witch of East Seventy-second Street. Morris Bishop. NYBP
I will repudiate the lie. If a Man Die, Shall He Live Again? John Richard Moreland. ChIP; MaRV; PGD
I will rise, I will go from the places that are dark with passion and pain. Seaward. George E. Woodberry. Wild Eden, XLI. AA
I will row my boat on Muckross Lake. The Wings of Love. James H. Cousins. AnIV
"I Will Send Them Prophets and Apostles." Bryant. SoP
I will sing a song of battle. The Song of Chess. *At. to* Abraham ibn Ezra. TrJP
I will sing, I will go, and never ask me why. The Tramp Sings. Ridgely Torrence. *Fr.* Eye-Witness. PFY
I will sing, if ye will hearken. The Laird of Logie. *Unknown.* BaBo; CBEP; CH; ESPB
I will sing no more songs: the pride of my country I sang. O Bruadair. James Stephens, *after* O'Bruaidar. OxBI
I will sing of myself a song that is true. The Seafarer. *Unknown.* EnLi-1 (1949 ed.)
I Will Sing Praise. Psalms, IX, Bible, *O.T.* FaPON
I will sing unto the Lord, for he hath triumphed gloriously. Triumphal Chant [*or* The Song of Moses]. Exodus, Bible, *O.T.* LiTW; TrGrPo
I will sing unto the Lord, for He is highly exalted. Then Sang Moses. Exodus, Bible, *O.T.* TrJP
I will sing you a song full of quiet fire. Song: To a Lady with Many Names. John Wickham. JKCP (1955 ed.)
I will sing you a song of that beautiful land. Home of the Soul. Ellen M. Huntington Gates. BLRP
I will sleep. December. Ron Padgett. ANYP

I will speak of your deeds. An Oration, Entitled "Old, Old, Old, Old Andrew Jackson." Vachel Lindsay. ATP (1935 ed.); YaD

I will start anew this morning with a higher fairer creed. A New Start. *Unknown.* OQP

I Will Take Thy Hand. *Unknown.* SoP

I will teach you my townspeople. Tract. William Carlos Williams. AmP; AmPP; AP; CABL; CoBMV; ILP; LiTA; LiTM; MoAB; MoAmPo; NePA; PoeP; StP; TDP; TrGrPo; TwAmPo; TwCP; WoL

I will tell you a tale tonight. The Admiral's Ghost. Alfred Noyes. BBV

I Will Trust. Jean Ingelow. MaRV

I will trust Him, yea, I will trust. Why Should I Fear? Annie Johnson Flint. SoP

I, Willie Wastle. *Unknown.* OxNR

I winged my bird. Bert Kessler. Edgar Lee Masters. *Fr.* Spoon River Anthology. AnFE; APA; CoAnAm

I Wish. Nancy Byrd Turner. SiSoSe

I wish a cricket in a wicker boat. A Japanese Birthday Wish. Thomas Burnett Swann. GoYe

I wish all the/ mandragora. Blue Funk. Joel Oppenheimer. NeAP

I wish, because the sweetness of your passing. Wild Wishes. Ethel M. Hewitt. HBV

I wish he were the Polar Star in Heaven. Anchises. Blanaid Salkeld. OxBI

I wish, how I wish that I had a little house. The Shiny Little House. Nancy M. Hayes. BoTP; SUS

I wish I could lend a coat. Akahito. *Fr.* Manyo Shu. AWP

I wish I could remember. To a Child. David McCord. AnAmPo

I wish I could remember that [*or* the] first day. The First Day. Christina Rossetti. Monna Innominata, II. EnLi-2; FaBoBe; HBV; LiTL; LO; MeWo; Sonn; ViPo; VP

I wish I could take a quiet corner in the heart. Baby's World. Rabindranath Tagore. FIW

I wish I could tell it — how wondrous is He. I Know He Is Real. *Unknown.* STF

I wish I had a golden voice. A Mother Sings. Lois Duffield. SoP

I wish I had a great big ball. Bouncing Ball. Sara Ruth Watson. SoPo

I wish I had a man any man. Chiaroscuro. Carole Bergé. ErPo

I wish I had a penguin playmate. My Penguin Playmate. Donald E. Cooke. MPB (1956 ed.)

I wish I had an aeroplane. A Penny Wish. Irene Thompson. BoTP

I wish I had been his apprentice. The Nazareth Shop [*or* In the Carpenter Shop]. *Unknown.* ChIP; GoTP; OQP; SoP; StJW

I Wish I Had Great Knowledge or Great Art. Delmore Schwartz. FiMAP

I wish I knew geography—for that would tell me why. Lines on a Mysterious Occurrence. Alfred Denis Godley. CenHV

I wish I lived in a caravan. The Pedlar's [*or* Peddler's] Caravan. William Brighty Rands. BoChLi; BoTP; GaP; GFA; HBV; HBVY; MPB; OTPC; PCH; PRWS; RIS; SoPo; StVeCh (1940 ed.); TVC

I wish I loved the human race. The Wishes of an Elderly Man [*or* Wishes at a Garden Party]. Sir Walter Raleigh. CenHV; FaBoCh; FiBHP; LoGBV; MemP; PV; ShBV-4; SiTL; WhC

I wish I owned a Dior dress. Reflections at Dawn. Phyllis McGinley. FiBHP

I Wish I Was a Little Bird. *Unknown.* AS

I Wish I Was a Mole in the Ground. *Unknown.* ABF

I wish I was an apple, a hangin' on [*or* in] the tree. Cindy. *Unknown.* TrAS; TreFS

I Wish I Was by That Dim Lake. Thomas Moore. GoBC; PoEL-4

I wish I was in de [*or* the] land ob [*or* of] cotton. Dixie. Daniel Decatur Emmett. ABF; FaFP; FaPON; HBV; PaA; PoFr; TrAS; TreF; TrGrPo; YaD

I Wish I Was Single Again. *Unknown.* *See* When I Was Single.

I Wish I Were. *Unknown.* FaFP; OxBoLi; SiTL

I wish I were an Emperor. Wishes. F. Rogers. BoTP

I wish I were an ivory lyre. Wishes. Callistratus. OnPM

I Wish I Were by That Dim Lake. Thomas Moore. NBM

I wish I were close. Three Poems from the Japanese, III.

Yamabe no Akahito, *tr. fr. Japanese by* Kenneth Rexroth. HoPM; LiTW

I wish I were in the Dutchman's Hall. Lowlands, *vers.* III. *Unknown.* AmSS

I wish I were the little key. A Child's Wish. Abram J. Ryan. AA; CAW; JKCP

I wish I were the little man. To an Andalusian Fan. J. Rodríguez la Orden. OnPM

I wish I were where Helen lies. Helen of Kir[k]connell [*or* Fair Helen]. *Unknown.* AnFE; AWP; BBV (1923 ed.); CBEP; CH; ELP; FaFP; GBV (1922 ed.); GoTS; GTBS; GTBS-D; GTBS-P; GTBS-W; GTSE; GTSL; HBV; ILP; InP; InPo; LiTB; LiTG; LiTL; LO; LoBV; MemP; OBB; OBEV; OTPC; SeCeV; TreFT; UnPo (1st ed.); ViBoPo; WePo

I wish my enemies would go to hell. Greetings of the Season. Hilaire Belloc. SiTL

I wish my eyes were big and blue. Wishes. Edna Kingsley Wallace. MoSiPe

I Wish My Tongue Were a Quiver. L. A. Mackay. *Fr.* The Ill-tempered Lover. CaP; OBCV; SiTL

I wish no rich-refined Arabian gold. Parthenope. Barnabe Barnes. *Fr.* Parthenophil and Parthenophe. CBEP

I wish not Thasos rich in mines. Mimnermus Incert. Walter Savage Landor. PoEL-4

I wish, O son of the Living God. The Wish of Manchin of Liath [*or* The Hermit's Song]. *Unknown.* AnIL; OnYI

I wish she would not ask me if I love the kitten more than her. Concerning Love. Josephine Preston Peabody. CIV; WhC

I wish that Easter eggs would do. If Easter Eggs Would Hatch. Douglas Malloch. MPB; SoPo

I wish that I could have my wish to-night. Shakespeare. Henry Ames Blood. AA

I wish that I could understand. The Wonderer. Robert W. Service. BBV

I wish that I were rubber-skinned. Wish at Meal-Time. John Farrar. BoChLi

I Wish That My Room Had a Floor. Gelett Burgess. FiBHP; GoTP; InvP; RePo

(Floorless Room, The.) HBVY

(Limerick.) ALV; CenHV; HBV; LiBL; NA; TSW; WhC

(My Room.) PTK

I wish that there were some wonderful place. "The Land of Beginning Again." Carl F. Bruhn. SoP

I wish that there were some wonderful place. The Land of Beginning Again. Louise Fletcher Tarkington. BLPA; OQP

I wish that when you died last May. May and Death. Robert Browning. MBW-2

I wish there were some wonderful place. Louise Fletcher Tarkington. *See* I wish that there were . . .

I wish they would hurry up their trip to Mars. A Projection. Reed Whittemore. NePoEA; WaKn

I wish to make my sermon brief,—to shorten my oration. Praise of Little Women. Juan Ruiz, Archpriest of Hita. *Fr.* The Book of Good Love. AWP

I wish to tune my quivering lyre. The Bard of Love. *Unknown,* *tr. fr.* by Byron. OuHeWo

I wish we could take a statistic with more grace, beloved. Enlightenment. Josephine Miles. FiMAP

"I wish, when summer's drawing near about the end of May." I Wish. Nancy Byrd Turner. SiSoSe

I wish you all that pen and ink. Thanksgiving Wishes. Arthur Guiterman. PoSC

I wish you were a pleasant wren. Child's Talk in April. Christina Rossetti. GN; OTPC (1923 ed.)

I wish you were real! Phantasus: VI-14. Arno Holz. LiTW

I wish you'd speak to Mary, Nurse. The Game of Cricket. Hilaire Belloc. FiBHP

I wish your breast were made of glass. The Lover's Lament [B *vers.*]. *Unknown.* AS

I wished to shirk my task one day. Discovery. Benjamin Keech. PoToHe

I with the morning's love have oft made sport. Sunrise on the Sea. Shakespeare. *Fr.* A Midsummer Night's Dream, III, ii. ChTr

I with uncovered head. James Russell Lowell. *Fr.* Ode Recited at the Harvard Commemoration, July 21, 1865. OHIP

I, with Whose Colo[u]rs, Myrs Dressed [*or* Drest] Her Head.

I (continued)
Fulke Greville. Caelica, XXII. AtBAP; EG; EnRePo; InvP; PoE; QFR
(Myra.) CBEP; ElL; GTBS-W; LoBV; OBEV; OBSC
(To Myra.) LiTB; LiTG; LiTL; ViBoPo
I woke/ Just about daybreak, and fell back. Poems to a Brown Cricket. James Wright. NaP; NYBP
I woke at three; for I was bid. Going to Church. Coventry Patmore. *Fr.* The Angel in the House. LoBV; PeVV
I woke by first light in a wood. A Dream Sestina [*or* Sestina). Donald Justice. NePoEA; PIA; TDP
I woke from death and dreaming. A Shepherd's Coat. Lilian Bowes-Lyon. ChMP; GTBS-D
I woke up this mornin' 'bout four o'clock. Casey Jones (G *vers.*) *Unknown.* ViBoFo
I woke up this mornin' with the blues all round my bed. I Got the Blues. *Unknown.* TTY
I woke up with foreboding, and despair. Comfort for the Sleepless. H. C. Bradby. BoC
I woke up with morning yawning in my mouth. Dawn. Louis Dudek. PeCV
I wold fain be a clarke. The Scholar Complains. *Unknown.* MeEL
I wolde witen of sum wis wight. The World an Illusion. *Unknown.* MeEL
I won a noble fame. Sir Marmaduke's Musings. Theodore Tilton. AA
I won the prize essay at school. John Horace Burleson. Edgar Lee Masters. *Fr.* Spoon River Anthology. CrMA
I Wonder. Q. R. Hand. BF
I Wonder. Jeannie Kirby. BoTP
I wonder about the trees. The Sound of [the] Trees. Robert Frost. AnFE; APA; AtBAP; CoAnAm; MAPA; MWA-2; OxBA; PG; TwAmPo
I Wonder as I Wander. *Unknown,* *arr. by* John Jacob Niles. EaLo
I wonder by my troth, what thou, and I. The Good-Morrow. John Donne. AnFE; AtBAP; AnAnS-1; AWP; BoLiVe; CABA; CBEP; CBV; DiPo; EG; ElL; EnL; EnLoPo; EnRePo; ExPo; FaBoBe; FaBoEn; FaBV; FosPo; GTBS-W; HBV; HoPM; InPo; InvP; LiTB; LiTG; LiTL; LoBV; MaMe; MaPo; MBW-1; MeLP; MemP; MePo; OBS; Po; PoAn; PoE; PoEL-2; PoeP; PoFS; PoIE; PoRA; ReEn; SCEP-1; SeCeV; SeCP; SeCV-1; SeEP; STP; TreFT; TrGrPo; TuPP UnTE; ViBoPo
I wonder, dear, if you had been. A Conjecture. Charles Francis Richardson. AA
I wonder do you feel today. Two in the Campagna. Robert Browning. BoLiVe; ELP; EnLi-2 (1949 ed); EPN; ExPo; FaBoEn; GTBS-D; GTBS-P; HBV; MaVP; MBW-2; MeWo; NoP; OAEP; OBNC; PoEL-5; PoVP; SeCePo; SeCeV; TOP; TrGrPo; ViPo; ViPP; WHA
I wonder, Duddon, if you still remember. To the River Duddon. Norman Nicholson. FaBoMo
I wonder, have I giv'n my best to Jesus. Have I Done My Best for Jesus? Edwin Young. STF
I wonder how it happens. I Change. Witter Bynner. HBMV
I wonder how it would be here with you. Altitude. Lola Ridge. NP
I Wonder How Many People in This City. Leonard Cohen. CAD; ELU
I wonder how the organist can do so many things. The Organist. *Unknown.* BLPA
I wonder if Christ had a little black dog. The Little Black Dog. Elizabeth Gardener Reynolds. PoLF; SoP
I wonder if, sunning in Eden's vales. Ballade of the Ancient Wheeze. Nate Salsbury *and* Newman Levy. InMe
I wonder if that cypress tree. Question. Howard McKinley Corning. ChIP
I wonder if the cabbage knows. Affinity. "Ricketty Kate." MoAuPo
I wonder if the elephant. Pete at the Zoo. Gwendolyn Brooks. LOW; PDV
I wonder if the engine. Engine. James S. Tippett. BoChLi; SoPo; SUS
I Wonder If the Lion Knows. Annette Wynne. UTS
I wonder if the name is right. The Address. *Unknown.* PCH
I wonder if the old cow died or not. The Question. W. W. Gibson. BEL; MMA
I wonder if the sap is stirring yet. The First Spring Day. Christina Rossetti. WiR
I wonder if there's anywhere. Teddy's Wonderings. John Kendrick Bangs. BiCB
I wonder if they like it—being trees? Tree Feelings. Charlotte Perkins Gilman. GFA; PGD
I wonder if this new reality is going to destroy me. The Hero Leaves His Ship. Barbara Guest. AmPC
I wonder if, when Galatea woke. A Question. Edna Livingston. GoYe
I wonder in what fields today. On Her Child's Death [*or* Haiku] Kaga no Chiyo. CaFP; LiTW
I wonder in what Isle of Bliss. A Ballad of Dead Ladies. Justin Huntly M'Carthy. *Fr.* If I Were King. HBV
I wonder, James, through the whole history. To His Friend——— Henry Vaughan. PP
I wonder poet, can you take it. The Muse to an Unknown Poet. Paul Potts. FaBoTw
I wonder, since we are both travelling out. The Travelling Out. Lucile Adler. NYBP
I wonder sometimes if the soldiers lying. Song for the Heroes. Alex Comfort. MoBrPo (1950 ed.); NeBP
I wonder that the grot was bare of birds. Didymus. Eileen Duggan. JKCP (1955 ed.)
I wonder that the metal stands the test. The Anvil of God's Mercy. Anna Hamilton Wood. OQP
I wonder the way ghosts come to be . . . . Do you think there will be a ghost. Ghost to Come. Margaret Widdemer. FiSC
I wonder — were there flowers there. Were Flowers There? George William Allison. ChIP
I wonder What Became of Rand, McNally. Newman Levy. InMe; WhC
I wonder what day of the week. Untimely Thought. Thomas Bailey Aldrich. AnNE
I wonder what he charged for chairs at Nazareth. The Carpenter. G. A. Studdert-Kennedy. ChIP; OQP; StJW
I Wonder What It Feels Like to Be Drowned? Robert Graves. BrPo; MoBrPo; TSW
I wonder what my kite can see. The Kite. Pearl Forbes MacEwen. BoTP
I wonder what spendthrift chose to spill. March. Celia Thaxter. GoTP
I wonder what the Clover thinks. A Song of Clover. Helen Hunt Jackson. GN; OTPC
I wonder what your thoughts are, little Cloud. The Cloud. Oliver Herford. BOHV
I wonder where I may gather some sweet pretty flowers. Garden Song. *Unknown.* PCH
I wonder where it could of went to. Legend. John V. A. Weaver. AmFN; PFY; YaD
I wonder where the rabbits go. Tracks. John Farrar. GFA
I wonder where's the circus clown, with all his fun and noise. The Old-Time Circus Clown. Frank L. Stanton. OTD
I wonder whether the girls are mad. William Bond. Blake. MyFE; NCEP; OxBB; PeER
I wonder who is haunting the little snug café. At the Lavender Lantern. Charles Divine. HBMV
I wonder why God took such care. Anticipation. Sarah Carter Lewis. SoP
I wonder why the grass is green. I Wonder. Jeannie Kirby. BoTP
I wonder will he be gentle. The Young Bride's Dream. Rhoda Coghill. OxBI
I wondered at the mighty horse. The Overworked Horse. Gerald Gould. MoBrPo (1942 ed.)
I Won't Be My Father's Jack. *Unknown.* OxNR; UnS
"I won't go with you. I want to stay with Grandpa!" My Last Afternoon with Uncle Devereux Winslow. Robert Lowell. ForPo
I won't print and you won't see. World War III. *Unknown.* SiTL
I won't say much for the sea. On the Coast near Sausalito. Robert Hass. YAP
I work or play, as I think best. Emancipation. *Unknown.* BLPA
I work to music on the radio. The Campus. David Posner. NYBP
I worked for a woman. Madam and Her Madam. Langston Hughes. BALP

I worship thee, sweet will of God! The Will of God. Frederick William Faber. MaRV; SoP; VA
I worshipped, when my veins were fresh. Revelation. William Baylebridge. *Fr.* Life's Testament. BoAV; PoAu-1
I wot full well that beauty cannot last. To His Friend, Promising That Though Her Beauty Fade, Yet His Love Shall Last. George Turberville. CTC; OBSC; SiCE; TuPP
I wot not how the world's degenerate. Satire. Joseph Hall. *Fr.* Virgidemiarum. ReIE
I would all womankind were dead. The Lay of the Lover's Friend. William E. Aytoun. BOHV
I would ask of you, my darling. Will You Love Me When I'm Old? *Unknown.* BLPA; FaBoBe; NeHB
I Would Be a Channel. Myra Brooks Welch. SoP
I Would Be a Painter Most of All. Len Chandler. NBP
I would be as ignorant as the dawn. *See* I would be ignorant . . .
I would be dismal with all the fine pearls of the crown of a king. To a Blue Flower. John Shaw Neilson. BoAV; PoAu-1
I Would Be Great. Hattie B. McCracken. OQP
I would be His if He were anywhere. If He Were Anywhere. Cecil Hemley. PoDB
I would be ignorant [*or* as ignorant] as the dawn. The Dawn. W. B. Yeats. MaPo; MoVE; NP
I would be married, but I'd have no wife. On Marriage. Richard Crashaw. HW; MaMe; ReEn
I would be one with Thee. Communion. Loren W. Burch. ChIP
I would be only. Love Song. Iwan Goll. OnPm
I Would Be True. Howard Arnold Walter. *See* My Creed.
I would be yielded to Jesus. Yielded to Him. Connie Calenberg. SoP
I would beat out your face in brass. Face. Carl Sandburg. ReMP
I would build myself a house. Songs of the Plains, IV. Glenn Ward Dresbach. NP
I Would Comprehend Thee. Rainer Maria Rilke, *tr. fr. German by* Jessie Lemont. OnPM
I would, dear Jesus, I could break. A Prayer. John D. Long. OQP
I Would Define My Love. Jessica Powers. JKCP (1955 ed.)
I would flee from the city's rule and law. A Country Summer Pastoral. Sam Walter Foss. BOHV
I would follow Jesus. Follow Jesus. *Unknown.* STF
I Would Forgo. Hilda Doolittle ("H. D."). LO
I Would Go Back. Mary M. Curchod. ChIP
"I would go up to the gates of hell with a friend." The Utmost in Friendship. John E. McCann. TreFT
I would have gone; God bade me stay. Weary in Well-doing. Christina Rossetti. SeCePo; SoP; TrPWD; ViPo; VP
I would have my own vision. The Analysis of Love. Sir Herbert Read. FaBoMo; LiTG
I would have spared you this, Prytherch. Too Late. R. S. Thomas. NMP; POTi
I would I had been island-born. A Ballade of Islands. Lucy Catlin Robinson. AA
I would I had something to do—or to think! All in the Downs. Tom Hood. ALV; CenHV
I would I had thrust my hands of flesh. Edmund Pollard. Edgar Lee Masters. *Fr.* Spoon River Anthology. AnFE; APA; CoAnAm; ErPo
I would I had thy courage, dear. To Manon on Her Lightheartedness. William Scawen Blunt. *Fr.* The Love Sonnets of Proteus, XI. NBM; VA
I would I might forget that I am I. Sonnets, IV. George Santayana. AWP; JAWP; TOP; WBP
I would I were a bird so free. Popular Songs of Tuscany. *Unknown, tr. by* John Addington Symonds. AWP
I Would I Were a Careless Child. Byron. ERoP-2
I Would I Were Actaeon. *Unknown, at. to*——Bewe. EIL (Actaeon.) OBSC
I would I were the little flower. Valentine. Charles G. Blanden. DD
I would, if I could. *Unknown.* OxNR
I would immortalize these nymphs: so bright. L'Après-Midi d'un Faune. Stéphane Mallarmé, *tr. by* Aldous Huxley. AWP; LiTW
I would in rich and golden-colored rain. Phyllis, XXXIV. Thomas Lodge. ReEn
I would in that sweet bosom be. Chamber Music, VI. James Joyce. HW; ReMP
I would kiss the whole length of the rich black locks that grace thy neck. The Kiss. Pierre Louys. *Fr.* The Songs of Bilitis. UnTE
I would lie low—the ground on which men tread. The Earth. Jones Very. AmP; OxBA
I Would Like to Be—a Bee. Dorothy W. Baruch. BiCB
I would like to dive. The Diver. W. W. E. Ross. OBCV; PeCV; WHW
I would like to have the men of Heaven. The Heavenly Banquet. *At. to* St. Bridget. OnYI
I Would Like You for a Comrade. Edward Abbott Parry. PCH; TVC
I would live all my life in nonchalance and insouciance. Introspective Reflection. Ogden Nash. WhC
I would live for a day and a night. The Song-Maker. Anna Wickham. MoBrPo
I would live this life so well. A Creed. Edgar A. Guest. HH; PEDC
I would make a list against the evil days. A Ballade-Catalogue of Lovely Things. Richard Le Gallienne. HBMV
I would make songs for you. Songs. Babette Deutsch. HBMV
I would make you. Petition for a Miracle. David Morton. *Fr.* Boke of Two Ladies. ISi
I would not alter thy cold eyes. Flow Lunae. Ernest Dowson. OBMV; PeVV; ViPP
I Would Not Always Reason. Bryant. *Fr.* The Conjunction of Jupiter and Venus. OQP
I would not, as the light-hearts do. The Dying Year. Clyde Walton Hill. PEDC
I Would Not Ask. Grace E. Troy. STF
I would not ask Thee that my days. A Prayer for Faith. Alfred Norris. BLRP
I would not be a serving-man. Merrythought's Song. Beaumont *and* Fletcher. *Fr.* The Knight of the Burning Pestle. OBS
I would not be the moon, the sickly thing. In Dispraise of the Moon. Mary Elizabeth Coleridge. BoNaP; CH; NBM
I would not call him in, my heart decried. The Architect. Molly Anderson Haley. ChIP
"I Would Not Change for Thine." William Carlos Williams. PoeP
I would not, could I, make thy life as mine. A Vain Wish. Philip Bourke Marston. VA
I would not give my Irish wife. The Irish Wife. Thomas D'Arcy McGee. HBV; VA
I would not go to old Joe's house. Old Joe Clark. *Unknown.* ABF
I would not have a god come in. Mastery. Sara Teasdale. *Fr.* Interlude: Songs Out of Sorrow. HBV; WGRP
I Would Not Live Alway. William August Muhlenberg. AA; HBV; SoP
I would not meek in dire rebuttal. Pride and Hesitation. Cerise Farallon. UnTE
I would not paint—a picture. Emily Dickinson. MAmP; MWA-2; PoeP
I would not that immortal soul reclaim. He Lives at Last. Lucile Lippitt. MaRV
I would not wish to sit. Between Two Prisoners. James Dickey. AP; NoP
I would perpetuate these nymphs. The Afternoon of a Faun. Stéphane Mallarmé, *tr. by* C. F. MacIntyre. PIA
I would rather have one little rose. "One Little Rose" [*or* Kindness during Life]. *Unknown.* SoP; STF
I would rather ruffle leaves. Summer Lightning. T. Sturge Moore. BrPo; SyP
I would say a few words. Perhaps a Prayer. James Schevill. FiMAP
"I would," says Fox, "a tax devise." Epigram. Sheridan. HBV
I would set all things whatsoever front to back. Wyndham Lewis. *Fr.* One-Way Song. CTC
I would sit in the windows ledge. Education. Josephine Miles. FiMAP
I would take words. To Hold in a Poem. A. J. M. Smith. ACV
I would that all men my hard case might know. Behold the Deeds! H. C. Bunner. ALV; BOHV; HBV; InMe
I would that even now. Princess Shoku, *tr. fr. Japanese by* Curtis Hidden Page. *Fr.* Hyaku-Nin-Isshu. AWP; JAWP; WBP
I would that folk forgot me quite. Tess's Lament. Thomas Hardy. FaBoTw

I would that we were, my beloved, white birds on the foam of the sea! The White Birds. W. B. Yeats. EnL; VA; ViPo (1962 ed.)
I would the gift I offer here. Dedication. Whittier. *Fr.* Songs of Labor. AmPP (4th ed.); AnNE; CoBA; OxBA
I Would Thou Wert Not Fair. Nicholas Breton. *See* His Wisdom.
I would to God I were quenched and fed. The Anguish. Edna St. Vincent Millay. NeMA
I would to God, that mine old age might have. His Wish to God. Robert Herrick. AnAnS-2; BoPe; OxBoCh
I would to heaven that I were so much clay. Fragment. Byron. *Fr.* Don Juan. CTC; FiP; ILP; OAEP; PeER
I would unto my fair restore. Of Joan's Youth. Louise Imogen Guiney. AA; HBV
I would worship if I could. Great Spaces. Howard Moss. TwCP
I wouldn't coax the plant if I were you. Woman with Flower. Naomi Long Madgett. BP
I wrastled wid Satan, I wrastled wid sin. *Unknown.* NAMP
I write. He sits beside my chair. A New Poet. William Canton. HBV; VA
I write about a silly ass. Hero and Leander. Joseph S. Newman. FiBHP
I write. My mother was a Florentine. Motherless. Elizabeth Barrett Browning. *Fr.* Aurora Leigh, I. VA
I write my name as one. An Autograph. Whittier. AA
I Write Verses. Walter Savage Landor. *See* Yes, I Write Verses.
I wrote him a letter asking him for old times' sake. Hannah Armstrong. Edgar Lee Masters. *Fr.* Spoon River Anthology. LiPo
I wrote some lines once on a time. The Height of the Ridiculous. Oliver Wendell Holmes. AA; ALV; AmePo; AnNe; BBV (1951 ed.); BOHV; FaFP; FiBHP; HBV; MCCG; MoShBr; MPB; NeHB; OTD; OTPC (1946 ed.); PoPl; SiTL; StVeCh; TreFT; WhC; YaD
I wrote the postcard to you and went out. Getting Through. James Merrill. NYBP
I wrought and battled and wept, near and afar. The Last Port. Frank Wilmot. BoAu
I wrought, them like a targe of hammered gold. On His "Sonnets of the Wingless Hours." Eugene Lee-Hamilton. VA
I wus mighty good-lookin' when I wus young. *See* I was mighty good lookin' when I was young.
I yearn to bite on a colloid. Amazing Facts about Food. *Unknown.* BOHV
I years had been from home. Emily Dickinson. AmP; AmPP (4th ed.); CBEP; DiPo; OxBA; PoRA
I yield, dear enemy, nor know. La Belle Ennemie. Thomas Stanley. CavP
I Yield Thee Praise. Philip Jerome Cleveland. TrPWD; TRV
I you assure. To Mistress Margaret Tilney. John Skelton. *Fr.* The Garlande of Laurell. MeEL
Iago Prytherch his name, though, be it allowed. A Peasant. R. S. Thomas. ToPo
Iambicum Trimetrum. Spenser. ElL; OBEV (new ed.); PoEL-1; ReIE
(Iambica.) OxBoLi; SiTL
Ianthe, *sels.* Walter Savage Landor.
Do You Remember Me? EnRP; GTBS-D; OBNC; ViBoPo
(Ianthe's Question.) OBEV
"From you, Ianthe, little troubles pass." BoLiVe; OBEV; OBNC; TrGrPo
(Ianthe's Troubles.) OnPM; VA; ViBoPo
(Verses to Ianthe.) PTK
(Your Pleasures Spring like Daisies.) EPN
"Ianthe! you resolve to cross the sea!" OBNC; OBVV
(Absence.) EnRP; OBRV
"Mild is the parting year, and sweet." OBRV; PG; TrGrPo
(Autumn.) BoLiVe; OBEV (1st ed.)
"My hopes retire; my wishes as before." OBNC
(Persistence.) VA
"Part ruin'd [*or* ruined] Ilion Helen lives." AnFE; AWP; BoLiVe; CBEP; CLwM; CTC; ELP; EnLoPo; EnRP; EPN; ExPo; FaBoEn; GTBS-D; InPo; JAWP; LiTL; LO; LoBV; NoP; OAEP; OBNC; OBRV; OQP; Po; PoAn; PoE; PoEL-4; PoIE; PoRA (rev. ed.); PoSa; TreFT; TrGrPo; UnPo (1st ed.); ViBoPo; WBP
(Ianthe.) LiTB
(Verse: "Past ruined Ilion. . .") HBV; OBEV
"Proud word you never spoke, but you will speak." EnLoPo; EPN; GTBS; GTSL; OBEV; TOP; ViBoPo
(Prophecy, A.) VA
"Remain, ah not in youth alone." OBNC
Test, The. HBV; VA
(Epigram: "I held her hand, the pledge of bliss.") ALV
"Well I remember how you smiled." CBEP; FaBoEn; GTBS; LoBV; OBNC; TrGrPo; ViBoPo
(Her Name.) OBVV
Ibadan. John Pepper Clark. CAD
Ibant Obscurae. Thomas Edward Brown. OBNC
Ibbety bibbety gibbety goat. *Unknown.* ExPo
Ibbity, bibbity, sibbity, sab. *Unknown.* RIS
Iberia. Leo Kirschenbaum. UnS
Iberian God, *sel.* Antonio Machado, *tr. fr. Spanish by* Ruth Matilda Anderson.
"O master of fortunes and of poverties." PoFr
Iberian! palter no more! By thine hands. To Spain—a Last Word. Edith M. Thomas. MC
Ibycus. John Heath-Stubbs. PoCh
Icarus. Ronald Bottrall. GTBS-P
Icarus. Valentin Iremonger. NeIP; OnYI; OxBI
Icarus. Harry Lyman Koopman. AA
Icarus. Kendrick Smithyman. AnNZ
Icarus. *Unknown.* *See* Love Winged My Hopes.
Ice. Dorothy Aldis. GFA; SUS; TiPo
Ice, The. W. W. Gibson. EPN
Ice. Charles G. D. Roberts. BoNaP; ExPo; OBCV; TDP; WHW
Ice. Stephen Spender. AtBAP; FaBoMo; GTBS-P; SeCePo
Ice and Fire. Sir Edward Sherburne. CavP
Ice built, ice bound, and ice bounded. Alaska. Joaquin Miller. OTD; PAH; ThLM
Ice cannot shiver in the cold. Howard Lamson. Edgar Lee Masters. *Fr.* The New Spoon River. NAMP; ViBoPo
Ice-Cart, The. W. W. Gibson. ShBV-2
Ice-Cream Man, The. Rachel Field. BoChLi; FaPON; GaP; SiSoSe; SoPo
Ice-Floes, The. E. J. Pratt. CaP
Ice-Flumes Owregie Their Lades. Douglas Young. SeCePo
Ice Handler. Carl Sandburg. OxBA
Ice in a Stream. Liu Tsung-yuan, *tr. fr. Chinese by* Robert Payne. OnPM
Ice King, The. A. B. Demille. WHW
Ice rushes down the Indian river, The. Sudden Spring. Margaret Coulby. TwCaPo
Ice-Skaters. Elder Olson. SD
Ice Skin, The. James Dickey. NYBP
Ice tinkled in glasses. Blues and Bitterness. Lerone Bennett. NNP
Iceberg, The. W. S. Merwin. PoIE
Iceberg, The. E. J. Pratt. *Fr.* The *Titanic.* TwCaPo
Iceberg, The. Sir Charles G. D. Roberts. CaP
Icebergs. William Prescott Foster. EtS
Icebound Swans, The. *Unknown, tr. fr. Old Irish by* Sean O'-Faolain. OA
Iceland First Seen. William Morris. PoVP
Iceland in Wartime. Alan Ross. POTi
Iceland's Song. Grímur Thomsen, *tr. fr. Icelandic by* Jakobina Johnson. LiTW
Ich Am of Irlonde. *Unknown.* *See* Irish Dancer, The.
Ich Dien. Susie M. Best. OQP
Ich sterbe. . .Life ebbs with an easy flow. The End of a War. Sir Herbert Read. OBMV; WaP
Ich Weiss Nicht, Was Soll es Bedeuten. Heine. *See* Lorelei, The.
"Ich wünscht', ich wäre ein Vöglein." The Bird. Louis Simpson. NePoEA-2
Ichabod. Whittier. AA; AmePo; AmP; AmPP; AnAmPo; AnFE; AnNE; AP; APA; CBEP; CoAnAm; CoBA; DD; HBV; LiTA; OxBA; PAH; PG; Po; PoEL-4; PoIE (1970 ed.); TOP
Ichabod! Thy [*or* The] Glory Has Departed. Ludwig Uhland. *tr.fr. German by* James Clarence Mangan. AWP; IrPN
Icham of Irlaundë. The Irish Dancer. *Unknown.* EnL
Ichot a burde in boure bryht. Blow [*or* Blou] Northern[e] Wind [*or* Wynd]. *Unknown.* AtBAP; OBEV
Ichthyosaurus, The. *Unknown.* OTPC (1946 ed.)
"Ici Repose." Bernard Freeman Trotter. MaRV
Icicle finger of death, aimed, The. Digging It Out. John Hollander. AmPC

Icicles, which grow silently in the night. The Thaw. Jack Matthews. WIRo
Icker-backer. *unknown.* RIS
Ickle ockle, blue bockle. *Unknown.* OxNR
Icons. Edgar Paiewonsky. QAH
Icos. Charles Tomlinson. GTBS-P; OPoP
Icosasphere, The. Marianne Moore. ImOP
Icy cold the night was, in heaven the brilliant/ Stars. Sapphic Stanzas. Aleksandr Radishchev. LiTW
I'd a dream to-night. Mater Dolorosa [*or* The Mother's Dream]. William Barnes. CH; HBV; MaRV; MemP; OBEV; PoVP
I'd asked the grocer. The Grocer and the Gold-Fish. Wilfrid Thorley. BrR
I'd Be a Butterfly. Thomas Haynes Bayly. HBV
I'd been on duty from two till four. Stand-to; Good Friday Morning. Siegfried Sassoon. FaBoTw
I'd Choose to Be a Daisy. *Unknown.* BoTP
I'd draw all this into a fine element,—a color. The Rug. Michael McClure. NeAP
I'd fill up the house with guests this minute. A Revel. Donagh MacDonagh. NeIP
I'd Have You, Quoth He. *Unknown.* ErPo
I'd Leave. Andrew Lang. FaPON
I'd like a different dog. Dogs and Weather. Winifred Welles. FaPON; StVeCh; TiPo
I'd like a little. *Unknown.* FaFP; SiTL
I'd like a stocking made for a giant. A Christmas Wish. Eugene Field. ChBR
I'd like to/ pull. The Intelligent Sheep-Man and the New Cars. William Carlos Williams. NePoAm-2
I'd like to be a dentist with a plate upon the door. The Dentist. Rose Fyleman. GaP; SoPo; TiPo
I'd Like to Be a Lighthouse. Rachel Field. GFA; OTPC (1946 ed.); PDV; SoPo
I'd like to be a scarecrow. Summer Wish. John Farrar. GFA
I'd like to be a water-lily sleeping on the river. Water Lily. John Farrar. GFA
I'd like to be a worm. Zhenya Gay. TiPo (1959 ed.)
I'd like to be the sort of friend that you have been to me. A Friend's Greeting. Edgar A. Guest. BLPA
I'd like to be walking the cranberry road. Cranberry Road. Rachel Field. MoSiPe
I'd like to hear a sermon done. S.P.C.A. Sermon. Stuart Hemsley. FiBHP
I'd like to peddle toy balloons. The Balloon Seller. Elizabeth Fleming. BoTP
I'd like to run like a rabbit in hops. Rabbit. Tom Robinson. FaPON
I'd like to think when life is done. When Life Is Done. Edgar A. Guest. MaRV
I'd like to view the whole wide earth. Wishing. Henry W. Frost. SoP
I'd Love to Be a Fairy's Child. Robert Graves. BiCB; BoTP; FaPON; HBVY; PDV; SoPo; TSW
I'd love to give a party. A Wish. Elizabeth Gould. BoTP
I'd never dare to walk across. The Invisible Bridge [*or* Queer Quatrains]. Gelett Burgess. BOHV; NA; RIS; TreFT
I'd oft heard of this Sledburn Fair. Sledburn Fair. *Unknown.* CH
I'd often seen before. The Sheaf. Andrew Young. ChTr
I'd open room for millions on the earth. Goethe. *Fr.* Faust. PoFr
I'd rather be the ship that sails. The Ship that Sails. *Unknown.* PoToHe (new ed.)
I'd Rather Have Fingers than Toes. Gelett Burgess. BOHV; HBV; LBN; TSW
(Hair.) SiTL
(On Digital Extremities.) FaPON; HBVY
I'd rather have habits than clothes. Limerick. Gelett Burgess. NA
I'd rather have Jesus than all earth can give. My Choice. Grace B. Renfrow. BePJ
I'd rather have the thought of you. Choice. Angela Morgan. PoLF
I'd rather hear a rattler rattle. The Bloody Injians. *Unknown.* CoSo
I'd rather listen to a flute. Samuel Hoffenstein. FiBHP
I'd rather live in Bohemia than in any other land. In Bohemia. John Boyle O'Reilly. LHV
I'd rather see a sermon than hear one any day. Sermons We See [*or* The Living Sermon *or* How Do You Live?]. Edgar A. Guest. MaRV; SoP; STF
I'd "read" three hours. Both notes and text were fast a mist becoming. A Dialogue from Plato. Austin Dobson. BOHV; HBV
I'd really hate to go to bed. Bats. Mary Effie Lee Newsome. GoSl
I'd swish through the door. Pudgy. Frank Lima. ANYP
I'd watched the sorrow of the evening sky. Pine Trees and the Sky: Evening. Rupert Brooke. MCCG
I'd wave the gnats away and try. Crew Practice on Lake Bled, in Jugoslavia. James Scully. NYBP
I'd weave a wreath for those who fought. Through Fire in Mobile Bay. *Unknown, at. to* David Glascoe Farragut. PAH
I'd wed you without herds, without money, or rich array. Cashel of Munster. *At. to* William English, *tr. by* Sir Samuel Ferguson. AnIV; IrPN; OBEV; OBVV; OnYI; OxBI
Ida Red. *Unknown.* ABF
Ida, Sweet as Apple Cider. Eddie Leonard. TreFT
Idaho. John Ashbery. ANYP
Idaho Cowboy Dance, An. James Barton Adams. *See* At a Cowboy Dance.
Idbury bells are ringing. Country Thought. Sylvia Townsend Warner. MoBrPo; NeMA
Idea, *sels.* Michael Drayton.
"As in some countries, far remote from hence," L. ReIE
"As other men, so I myself do muse," IX. EnLi-1 (1949 ed.) (XII); ReEn; SiCE; Sonn; TuPP
"Bright star of beauty, on whose eye-lids sit," IV. HBV; SiCE
"Calling to mind since first my love begun", LI. EnRePo; OBSC; PoEL-2; SiCE
"Clear Anker, on whose silver-sanded shore," LIII (*also given as XIII in Idea's Mirrour*). TuPP
"Cupid, dumb idol, peevish saint of love," XXVI. EnRePo
"Cupid, I hate thee, which I'd have thee know," XLVIII. LO
Dear, [*or* Deare *or* Deere], why should you comma[u]nd me to my rest," XXXVII. EG; ElL; FaBoEn;HBV; LiTL; LO; OAEP; PoEL-2; ReEn; Sonn; TuPP; ViBoPo
(Night and Day.) LiTB; LiTG
(Sonnets to "Idea," 11.) OBSC
"Evil spirit, your beauty haunts me still, An," XX. CoBE; ElL; LoBV; OAEP; OBSC; ReEn; ReIE; SiCE; TuPP
"How many paltry, foolish, painted things," VI. BWP; ElL; EnLoPo; EnRePo; HBV (XLII); InP; LoBV; NoP; OBSC; ReEn; ReIE; SiCE; TuPP
(How Many Foolish Things.) CBEP
"I hear some say, 'This man is not in love!' " XXIV. BEL; LO; OAEP; TrGrPo
(I Hear Some Say.) MeWo
"If he from heaven that filched that living fire," XIV. NoP
"In pride of wit, when high desire of fame," XLVII. SiCE; Sonn; TuPP
"Into these loves who but for passion looks," *introd. sonnet.* BEL; HBV; NoP; TuPP; ViBoPo
(To the Reader of These Sonnets.) EnRePo; ReEn; ReIE; SiCE; Sonn
"Like an adventurous seafarer am I," I. EnLi-1 (1949 ed.); NoP; ReEn; SiCE; Sonn; TuPP
"Love once would daunce within my mistris eye," IX (1599).
(Musical Love.) MuSP
"Many there be excelling in this kind," LXXII (*last sonnet in Esdaile ed.*; *also in* England's Heroical Epistles.) SiCE; TuPP
"Methinks I see some crooked mimic jeer," XXXI. Sonn; TuPP
(Sonnet—To the Critic.) LoBV
(To the Critic.) SiCE
"My heart the anvil where my thoughts do beat," XL (*also given as XLIV in* Idea's Mirrour). HBV; ReIE
"Nothing but No and I, and I and No," V. PoEL-2
"Our flood's queen Thames for ships and swans is crowned," XXXII. NoP; TuPP
(To the River Anker.) SiCE
"Since there's no help[e], come let us kiss[e] and part," LXI. AtBAP; ATP; AWP; BEL; BoLP; BWP; CABA; CaFP; CBEP; CBV; DiPo; EG; ElL; EnL; EnLi-1; EnLit; EnLoPo; EnRePo; ExPo; FaBoEn; FaPL; ForPo; FosPo; HBV; ILP; InP; JAWP;

Idea (continued)
LO; LoBV; NoP; OAEP; OBSC; PoAn; PoE; PoEL-2; PoIE; PoSa; ReEn; ReIE; SeCePo; ShBV-4; SiCE; Sonn; TOP; TrGrPo; TuPP; ViBoPo; WBP; WePo; WHA
(Come Let Us Kiss and Part.) TreFS
(Love's Farewell). GTBS; GTBS-D; GTBS-P; GTBS-W; GTSE; GTSL
(Parting, The.) AnEnPo; HoPM; LiTB; LiTG; LiTL; MemP; OBEV; OtMeF; SeCeV
(Since There's No Help.) MeWo
(Sonnet from "Idea.") OuHeWo
"Some men there be which like my method well," XLII. SiCE; TuPP
"Some misbelieving and profane in love," XXXV. TuPP
(To Miracle.) SiCE
"Stay, speedy Time, behold, before thou pass," XVII. EnRePo; OBSC
(To Time.) SiCE
"There's nothing grieves me but that age should haste," VIII. ReEn; ReIE; SiCE
"Three sorts of serpents do resemble thee", XXX. EnRePo
"To nothing fitter can I thee compare," X. BEL; EIL; HBV; OBSC; SiCE; Sonn; TrGrPo; TuPP; ViBoPo
"Truce, gentle love, a parley now I crave," LXIII. NoP; ReIE; Sonn; TuPP
"When conquering love did first my heart assail," XXIX.
(To the Senses.) OAEP
"When first I ended, then I first began," LXII (*also given as L in* Idea's Mirrour). TrGrPo
"Whilst thus my pen strives to eternize thee," XLIV. BEL; OBSC; ReEn; SiCE; Sonn; TuPP; ViBoPo
"Why should your fair eyes with such sovereign grace," XLIII. OBSC
"Witless gallant, a young wench that wooed, A," XXI. SiCE; TuPP
"You're [*or* You] not alone when you are still alone," XI. PoEL-2; TrGrPo
(Give Me My Self.) LO
(You're Not Alone.) LiTL
Idea of a Swimmer. Jean-Richard Bloch, *tr. fr. French by* "S. P." TrJP
Idea of a University, The. David Shapiro. ANYP
Idea of Ancestry, The. Etheridge Knight. BALP
Idea of Joy. Josephine Miles. FiMAP
Idea of justice may be precious, An. Ode. Frank O'Hara. NeAP
Idea of Order at [*or,* in] Key West, The. Wallace Stevens. AmLP; AmP; AmPP; AP; BWP; CMoP; CoBMV; ForPo; ILP; MAP; MaPo (1969 ed.); MoAB; MoAmPo; MoPo; NoP; OxBA; PIA; Po; PoIE; PP; SeCeV (1967 ed.)
Idea; or, The Shepherd's Garland. Michael Drayton. *See* Shepherd's Garland, The.
Idea ran around the world, An. The Return. Muriel Rukeyser. FiMAP
Ideal, The. Baudelaire, *tr. fr. French by* Arthur Symons. SyP
Ideal. Padraic Pearse, *tr. fr. Modern Irish by* Thomas MacDonagh. AnIV; AWP; CAW; JAWP; JKCP; LiTW; NP; OnYI; WBP
Ideal, The. Francis Saltus Saltus. AA
Ideal Age for a Man, The. Monica Shannon. BiCB
Ideal Angels. John R. Colombo. MoCV
Ideal Beauty. Fernando de Herrera, *tr. fr. Spanish by* Longfellow. CAW
Ideal City, The. Washington Gladden. OQP
Ideal Husband to His Wife, The. Sam Walter Foss. BOHV; InMe
Ideal Memory. William James Dawson. VA
Ideal Passion, *sels.* George Edward Woodberry.
"Between my eyes and her so thin the screen," XXXVII. HBMV
"'Evil thing is honor,' once of old, An," XXVIII. HBMV
"Fairwell, my Muse! for, lo, there is no end," XLII. HBMV
"I never muse upon my lady's grace," XXV. HBMV
"Immortal Love, too high for my possessing," XL. HBMV; PoPo
"In what a glorious substance did they dream," XXVI. HBMV
"Oh, how with brightness hath Love filled my way," XXX. HBMV
"Why, Love, beneath the fields of asphodel," XXXIII. HBMV
Idealists. Alfred Kreymborg. PoMa; TSW
Ideality. Hartley Coleridge. VA
Ideals. Robert Greene. PoToHe (new ed.)
Ideals are the fairy oil. Emily Dickinson. MWA-2
Ideals of Satire, The. Pope. *Fr.* First Epistle of the Second Book of Horace. FiP
Idea's Mirrour, *sels.* Michael Drayton.
"Black pitchy night, companion of my woe," XLV. LoBV (LXX); OBSC; ReIE; SiCE; TuPP
"Clear Anker, on whose silver-sanded shore," XIII (*also given as LIII in* Idea). TuPP
"Glorious sun went blushing to his bed, The," XXV. OBSC
"If chaste and pure devotion of my youth," XXXVIII. OBSC; SiCE; ViBoPo
"Letters and lines, we see, are soon defaced," XXI. ReIE
"My fair, look from those turrets of thine eyes," XXXIV. OBSC; SiCE
"My heart, imprisoned in a hopeless isle," XXII. OBSC; SiCE
"My heart the anvil where my thoughts do beat," XLIV (*also given as XL in* Idea). HBV; ReIE
"Read here (sweet Maid) the story of my woe," I. OBSC; ReIE
"Stay, stay, sweet Time! Behold, or ere thou pass," VII. ReIE
"Sweet secrecy, what tongue can tell thy worth?" XLVI. SiCE; ViBoPo
To the Dear Child of the Muses and His Ever Kind Maecenas, Master Anthony Cooke, Esquire. ReIE; SiCE; TuPP
"When first I ended, then I first began," L (*also given as LXII in* Idea). TrGrPo
Ideantikit, *sels.* James Brodey. AnYP
"All these numbers, several are possibly aghast."
"First range through."
"Steamshovel, seen from afar, The."
"'The: the'/ matter-of-factness, plural."
"White sheet of paper, A."
Identity. Thomas Bailey Aldrich. AA; AnNE; MAP; PFY
Identity. Sister Mary Helen. GoBC
Identity. Elizabeth Jennings. NePoEA
Identity. Hyam Plutzik. FiMAP
Identity, known or unknown, survives. Indecision. Helen Pinkerton. QFR
Ides of March, The. Roy Fuller. PoCh
Idiom of the Hero. Wallace Stevens. OxBA
Idiot, The. Hart Crane. CBV; PoFS
Idiot, The. Adèle Naudé. PeSA
Idiot ("The idiot greens the meadows with his eyes.") Allen Tate. AnAmPo; FaBoMo; LiTA; NAMP; TwAmPo
Idle Charon. Eugene Lee-Hamilton. OBVV
Idle Chatter. Charles Cooper. BOLo
Idle chatter, rising like a fountain, The. Lèse-Majesté. Herbert S. Gorman. HBMV
Idle dayseye, the laborious wheel, The. O. Richard Wilbur. LiTA; MoPo; StP
Idle Flowers, The. Robert Bridges. BoNaP; ChTr
Idle Fyno. *Unknown.* *See* A Ha Ha Ha! This World Doth Passe.
Idle Housewife. Samuel Rowlands. SiCE
Idle Life I Lead, The. Robert Bridges. EG; LiTM; MemP
Idle poet, here and there, An. The Revelation. Coventry Patmore. *Fr.* The Angel in the House. EG; EnLoPo; GTBS-P; NBM; OBNC; PoG; ViBoPo
Idle Verse. Henry Vaughan. AtBAP; OAEP
Idleness. Silas Weir Mitchell. AA
Idleness. Andrew Young. POTE
Idler, The. Elizabeth Jennings. NcPoEA
Idler, The. Jones Very. AA; HBV
Idler holds that rose as always rose, An. The Idler. Elizabeth Jennings. NePoEA
Idlers, The. Edmund Blunden. BoTP; CH
Idleset: "Ill's the airt o the word the day." Thurso Berwick. OxBS
Idling pivot of the frigate bird, The. Man o'War Bird. Derek Walcott. TTY
Idly she yawned, and threw her heavy hair. Sonnet. George Moore. ErPo
Idmon, a dyer in purple. The Birth of Arachne, the Spider. James Schevill. FiMAP
Idol, The. Louise Driscoll. HBMV
Idolatry. Arna Bontemps. AmNP; PoNe

Idols. Richard Burton. TrPWD
Idol's Eye, The, *sel.* Harry B. Smith.
Tattooed Man, The. InMe
Idols of Imagination. Richard Eberhart. FiMAP
Idyl: "And my young sweet heart sat at board with me." Alfred Mombert, *tr. fr. German by* Ludwig Lewisohn. AWP; JAWP; WBP
Idyl, An: "Come down, O maid, from yonder mountain height." Tennyson. *See* Come Down, O Maid.
Idyl in Idleness, An. Robert Pack. NePoEA
Idyll: "At noon the sun puffed up, outsize." Francis Webb. PoAu-2
Idyll: "In Switzerland one idle day." Hugh Macnaghten. HBMV
Idyll of Phatte and Leene, An. *Unknown.* BOHV
Idyll of the Rose. Decimus Magnus Ausonius, *tr. fr. Latin by* John Addington Symonds. AWP
Idylls, *sels.* Theocritus, *tr. fr. Greek.*
Countryman's Wooing, The, XXVII, *tr. by* Charles Stuart Calverley. ErPo
Cyclops, The, XI, *tr. by* Elizabeth Barrett Browning. AWP; EnLi-1; JAWP; WBP
Death of Daphnis, The, I, *tr. by* C. S. Calverley. AWP; JAWP; WBP
(Song of the Death of Daphnis, The, *tr. by* J. H. Hallard.) EnLi-1
Enchantment, The, II, *tr. by* Thomas Creech. CTC
Fisherman, The, XXI, *tr. by* C. S. Calverley. AWP
Harvest-Home, VII, *tr. by* C. S. Calverley. AWP
Herdsman, The, IV, *tr. by* C. S. Calverley. AWP
Incantation, The, II, *tr. by* C. S. Calverley. AWP; JAWP; WBP
(Second Idyll, The, *tr. by* Jack Lindsay.) LiTW
Song of the Sleepy Bridegroom, *fr.* XVIII, *tr. by* Dryden. HW
Syracusan Women, The, *fr.* XV, *tr. by* J. M. Chapman. WoL
"There's but one stirrer-up of the crafts, Diophantes," XXI, *pr. tr. by* J. M. Edmonds. FosPo
Idylls of the King, *sels.* Tennyson.
Balin and Balan.
Fire of Heaven, The. EPN
Dedication: "These to His Memory—since he held them dear." CABA; PoVP; ViPP
Geraint and Enid.
O Purblind Race, 7 *ll.* OQP
Guinevere. EnLit; EPN; MaVP
"But I was first of all the kings who drew." GTSL; YAT
"I made them lay their hands in mine and swear." TRV
Remorse ("Shall I kill myself?") MaRV
Their Conscience as Their King. MaRV
Too Late. MaRV; OQP
We Needs Must Love the Highest, 7 *ll.* MaRV
Holy Grail, The. MBW-2; PoVP; ViPo; ViPP
Lancelot and the Grail. GoBC
"When the hermit made an end." PeVV
Lancelot and Elaine. PoVP; ViPo; ViPP
Elaine's Song. FaBoEn
(Song of Love and Death, The.) OBNC
Last Tournament, The. ViPo
"Man am I grown, a man's work must I do," 4 *ll.* ChIP
(Follow the Christ.) MaRV
Merlin and Vivien.
In Love, if Love Be Love. CABA; GTBS; GTSL; MeWo; PoEL-5; TrGrPo
(All in All.) GTBS-W; LiTB
(If Love Be Ours.) OQP
(Vivien's Song.) FaBoEn; OBNC
Passing of Arthur, The. CoBE; EPN; OBNC
(Morte d'Arthur, *incorporated in the* Idylls, *with changes, as* The Passing of Arthur.) AnEnPo; ATP; BBV; BEL; BoLiVe; EnLi-2; FaBoBe; FiP; GTSL; HBV; NoP; OAEP; OnSP; PoE; PoEL-5; TOP; UnPo (1st ed.); ViPo; WHA
"And slowly answered Arthur from the barge." GTSL
Arthur's Disillusionment. TreFS
Prayer ("[Pray for my soul] More things are wrought by prayer"), 9 *ll.* BLRP; OQP; TreF; WGRP
Prayer ("The Old order changeth, yielding place to new"). MaRV
(Prayer for the Dead.) GoBC
"Then rose the King and moved his host by night." PeVV
"Then saw they how there hove a dusky barge." VA
Pelleas and Ettarre.
"Rose, A, but one, none other rose had I." PoEL-5
(Worm within the Rose, A.) PAn
To the Queen. PoVP
Iena's Song. Charles Mair. *Fr.* Tecumseh. VA
Iersch brybour baird, vyle beggar with thy brattis. William Dunbar. *Fr.* The Flyting of Dumbar and Kennedie. AtBAP
Iesu. George Herbert. *See* Jesu.
Iesu, swete sone dere! Our Lady's Song [*or* The Virgin's Song]. *Unknown.* AtBAP; OBEV (new ed.). *See also* Jesu my sweet Son dear.
If. *See also* Ef.
If. Carolyn Sherwin Bailey. PCH
If. Daisy Moore Bynum. SoP
If. Mortimer Collins. BOHV; FiBHP; HBV; Par
If. H. C. Dodge. BOHV
If. Oswald Durand, *tr. fr. French by* Edna Worthley Underwood. PoNe
If. Rebecca Foresman. *See* How To Forget.
If. William Dean Howells. AA
If. Kipling. BBV (1951 ed.); BLPA; EnLit; FaBoBe; FaFP; FaPL; GoTP; HBV; HBVY; LiTM; MaRV; NeHB; OHFP; OTD; OtMeF; OTPC (1946 ed.); PaPo; PoMa; PTK; TIHL; TreF; TSW; WBLP; WePo
If. James Jeffrey Roche. HBV
If. P. A. Ropes. BoTP
If. Alice Todd. BoTP
If/ ice shall melt. If Ice. W. W. E. Ross. OBCV
If a body meet a body. *See* Gin a body meet a body.
If a daughter you have, she's the plague of your life. Song. Sheridan. *Fr.* The Duenna. CEP; NeHB
If a good man were ever housed in Hell. A Good Man in Hell. Edwin Muir. MoBrPo (1962 ed.); MoRP
If a feller's been a-straddle. When You're Throwed. *Unknown.* SCC
If a lad's but a lad in the heart of a town. The Ditty the City Sang. Alfred Kreymborg. NeMA
If a leaf rustled, she would start. The White Moth. Sir Arthur Quiller-Couch. VA
If a Maid Be Fair. Laura Goodman Salverson. CaP
If a man could live a thousand years. If. H. C. Dodge. BOHV
If a Man Die. Florence Hamilton. MaRV
If a Man Die, Shall He Live Again? John Richard Moreland. ChIP; MaRV; PGD
If a Man Who Turnips Cries. Samuel Johnson. *See* If the Man Who Turnips Cries.
If a man would be a soldier, he'd expect, of course, to fight. A Little Rhyme and a Little Reason. Henry Anstadt. BLRP
If a Pig Wore a Wig. Christina Rossetti. *Fr.* Sing-Song. BoChLi
If a rowdy meet a rowdy. The Rowdy. John A. Stone. SGR
If a task is once begun. Alwasy Finish [*or* Perseverance]. *Unknown.* BLPA; FaBoBe; NeHB; TreFT; WBLP
If a Woodchuck Would Chuck. *Unknown.* FaPON
("How much wood would a woodchuck chuck.") StVeCh; TiPo
If a wren can cling. Faith. F. B. Meyer. OQP
If after kirk ye bide a wee. An Angel Unawares. *Unknown.* BLRP; MaRV; TRV
"If, after obtaining Buddhahood, anyone in my land." Burning, X. Gary Snyder. *Fr.* Myths & Texts. NaP
If Ah evah git to glory, an' Ah hope to mek it thoo. Black Mammies. John Wesley Holloway. BANP
If Alcibiades kill my countrymen. Shakespeare. *Fr.* Timon of Athens, V, i. MyFE
If all a top physicist knows. After Reading a Child's Guide to Modern Physics. W. H. Auden. NYBP
If All Be True That I Do Think. Henry Aldrich. *See* Reasons for Drinking.
If all my days were summer, could I know. Revelation. Warren F. Cook. BLRP
If all our life were one broad glare. The Joy of Incompleteness. Albert Crowell. PoToHe (new ed.)
If all that love and man hath sworne. *Unknown.* SeCSL
If all the answer's to be the Sinai sort. Golden Calf. Norman MacCaig. OxBS
If all the earthe were paper white. *Unknown.* SeCL
If all the good people were clever. Good and Clever. *Unknown.* SoP

If all the grief and woe and bitterness. Planh for the Young English King. Bertrans de Born. LiTW
If all the harm that women have done. A Thought. James Kenneth Stephen. BOHV; FiBHP; VA
If all the little Christmas trees. If. Carolyn Sherwin Bailey. PCH
If All the Pens That Ever Poets Held. Christopher Marlowe. *Fr.* Tamburlaine the Great, Pt. I, Act V, sc. ii. ChTr
(Beauty.) TrGrPo
If all the seas were one sea. Mother Goose. BoTP; OTPC (1946 ed.); OxNR; Po; PPL; SiTL; SoPo; StVeCh
If all the ships I have at sea. My Ships [*or* Love Ship]. Ella Wheeler Wilcox. PoLF; SoP
If All the Skies [Were Sunshine]. Henry van Dyke. WBLP; WGRP
If all the sorrows of this weary earth. Friends. Thomas Curtis Clark. PoToHe
If all the trees in all the woods were men. Cacoëthes Scribendi. Oliver Wendell Holmes. AA; BOHV
If all the verse what I have wrote. Archys Autobiography. Don Marquis. *Fr.* Archys Life of Mehitabel. CrMA
If All the Voices of Men. Horace L. Traubel. AA
If all the women in the town were bundled up together. The Agricultural Irish Girl. *Unknown.* OnYI
If All the World. Dollie Radford. VA
If all the world and love were young. The Nymph's Reply to the [Passionate] Shepherd [*or* Answer to Marlowe *or* Reply. . .]. Sir Walter Ralegh. ATP; BWP; CABA; CaFP; CBEP; CBV; CLwM; CoBE; CTC; DiPo; ElL; EnL; EnLi-1; ExPo; FCP; FosPo; GTBS-W; HBV; HoPM; ILP; LiTB; LiTG; LiTL; LoBV; NoP; OAEP; OBEV; OBSC; OuHeWo; PAn; PG (1945 ed.); Po; PoE; PoFS; PoPo; PoSa; ReEn; ReIE; SeCePo; SeCeV; SiCE; SiPS; SiTL; StP; TOP; TreFS; TrGrPo; TuPP; UnPo (1st ed.); ViBoPo; WHA
If all the world were [*or* was] apple pie. Mother Goose. BOHV; FaFP; HBV; HBVY; NA; OTPC; PCH; PPL; RIS; SoPo
If all the world were candy. The Ambitious Mouse. John Farrar. PCH; TSW
If All the World Were [*or* Was] Paper. *Unknown.* CBEP; LiTG; LoBV; OxNR; SeCL; SiTL
(Interrogativa Cantilena.) DiPo; SeEP
If all the world were right. If All the World. Dollie Radford. VA
If all those pretty maidens were as hares on the mountain. Hares on the Mountain. *Unknown.* CBEP
If all were rain and never sun. Sun and Rain. Christina Rossetti. PPL
If Along the Highroad. *Unknown, tr. fr. Chinese by* Arthur Waley. *Fr.* Shi King. LiTW
If Amorous Faith. Petrarch, *tr. fr. Italian by* C. B. Cayley. Sonnets to Laura: To Laura in Life, CLXXXVIII. OnPM
("If amour's faith, an heart unfeigned," *tr. by* Sir Thomas Wyatt.) FCP
(Signs of Love.) AWP; JAWP; WBP
If an eagle be imprisoned. America. Henry Dumas. BOLo
If an unkind word appears. On File. John Kendrick Bangs. PoToHe (new ed.); WBLP
If, antique hateful bird. The Raven. Adrienne Rich. NePoEA-2
If any ask why there's no great She-Poet. Dedication of the Cook. Anna Wickham. MoBrPo
If Any Be Pleased to Walk into My Poor Garden. Francis Daniel Pastorius. SCAP
If any flower that here is grown. Inscription in a [*or* His] Garden. George Gascoigne. CBEP; OBSC; TrGrPo; TuPP
If any God should say. Rebirth. Kipling. GTSL; LoBV; OBNC
If any have a stone to shy. The Pebble. Elinor Wylie. MAP; MoAmPo; MoRP
If any little word of ours. A Good Creed. *Unknown.* PoToHe
If any man drew near. A Woman Homer Sung. W. B. Yeats. CLwM
If Any Man Would Come after Me. Edwin McNeill Poteat. ChIP
If any man would know the very cause. Sonnet: He Is Out of Heart with His Time. Guerzo di Montecanti. AWP
If any mourn us in the workshop, say. Batteries Out of Ammunition. Kipling. *Fr.* Epitaphs of the War. MMA; PoVP
If any question why we died. Common Form. Kipling. *Fr.* Epitaphs of the War. FaBoTw; PoVP; PV
If any sink, assure that this, now standing. Emily Dickinson. MWA-2
If any vague desire should rise. In Memoriam A. H. H., LXXX. Tennyson. EnLi-2; EPN; ViPo; VP
If any vision should reveal. In Memoriam A. H. H., XCII. Tennyson. EPN; ViPo; VP
If any wench Venus's girdle wear. Song. John Gay. *Fr.* The Beggar's Opera. PoEL-3
If any would portray thee. Before the Ikon of the Mother of God. Constantine of Rhodes. ISi
If anyone has fun. Notes on a Track Meet. David McCord. SD
If anyone long for a musical song. The Wanton Trick [*or* 'Tis but a Wanton Trick]. *Unknown.* CoMu; UnTE
If apples were pears. To My Valentine. *Unknown.* PCH; SoPo
If art and industry should doe as much. New English Canaan: Prologue. Thomas Morton. SCAP
If as a flowre doth spread and die. Employment. George Herbert. AtBAP; MaMe; SCEP-1; SeCV-1
If, as I live, I could become. If. Daisy Moore Bynum. SoP
If, as mine is, thy life a slumber be. To Mr. R. W. John Donne. MaMe
If as the winds and waters here below. The Storm. George Herbert. AnAnS-1; MaMe; MeP
If, as they tell in stories old. The Eye of the Beholder. James Lionel Michael. BoAu
If, as well may happen. Read Me, Please! Robert Graves. NYBP
If asked the day that this man dies. At a Loss. James L. Weil. GoYe
If Asked Whereon I Rest My Claim. A. Samuel Wallgren. SoP
If at this time I am Derided. The Sympathy. *Unknown.* SeCL
If aught can teach us aught, Affliction's looks. Affliction. Sir John Davies. *Fr.* Nosce Teipsum. OBSC
If aught I may have said or done. An Evening Prayer. Laura E. Kendall. BLRP
If aught [*or* ought] of oaten stop, or pastoral song. Ode to Evening [*or* To Evening]. William Collins. AnEnPo; AnFE; AtBAP; ATP; AWP; BEL; BWP; CABA; CaFP; CBEP; CBV; CEP; CoBE; EG; EiCL; EiCP; EiPP; EnL; EnLi-2; EnPE; EnRP; ExPo; FaBoBe; FaBoEn; FosPo; GTBS; GTBS-D; GTBS-P; GTBS-W; GTSE; GTSL; HBV; InP; InPo; JAWP; LiTB; LiTG; LoBV; MasP; NoP; OAEP; OBEC; OBEV; OuHeWo; PeER; PIA; Po; PoE; PoEL-3; PoFS; SeCePo; SeCeV; ShBV-4; StP; TOP; TreFT; TrGrPo; UnPo (1st ed.); ViBoPo; WBP; WHA
If aught of simple song have power to touch. The Birthday Crown. William Alexander. OBVV
If aught that stumbles in my speech. Abstemia. Gelett Burgess. NA
If Beer Cans Were Bullets. Arthur Pfister. WSL
If bees stay at home. Weather Wisdom [*or* Signs and Seasons]. *Unknown.* GoTP; OxNR; RIS; TreF
If, before being earth, the thought of sound. Anticipation. Joseph Tusiani. GoYe
If Bet bedecks herself with gems, bestirs herself when bid. Why Not? *Unknown.* WhC
If Bethlehem were here today. Christmas Morning. Elizabeth Madox Roberts. ChBR; ChrBoLe; GoTP; MAP; MaRV; MoAmPo; MPB; PCH; PoRh; PoSC; RePo; StJW; StVeCh; SUS; TSW; WHL
If blossoms could blossom. To Be Sung. Peter Viereck. FaBV
If bright the sun, he tarries. Emerson. *Fr.* Fragments on the Poet and the Poetic Gift. PP
If but One Year. *Unknown.* *See* One Year to Live.
If but some vengeful god would call to me. Hap. Thomas Hardy. AWP; CABA; CMoP; CoBMV; EaLo; EnLi-2 (1949 ed.); InP; JAWP; MoBrPo; OAEP (2d ed.); PoAn; PoDB; PoE; PPON; Sonn; ViPo; ViPP; WBP
If buttercups buzz'd after the bee. *Unknown.* LoGBV
If by dull rhymes our English must be chain'd. On the Sonnet [*or* Sonnet on the Sonnet]. Keats. CABA; ERoP-2; ILP; MBW-2; NoP; PAn; PeER; PP

If by his torturing, savage foes untraced. The Captive Escaped in the Wilds of America. Charlotte Smith. Sonn
If Candlemas Day be dry and fair. Candlemas. *Unknown.* PoRL; PoSC
If Candlemas Day be fair and bright. *Unknown.* PoSC
If care do cause men cry, why do not I complain? Earl of Surrey. FCP; SiPS
If chance assigned. Sir Thomas Wyatt. FCP; SiPS
If chaste and pure devotion of my youth. Idea's Mirrour, XXXVIII. Michael Drayton. OBSC; SiCE; ViBoPo
If childhood were not in the world. The Salt of the Earth. Swinburne. PoVP
If Christ, as thou affirmest, be of men. The Illimitable God. Robert Browning. *Fr.* A Death in the Desert. MaRV
If Christ could ever be born again. The Christmas Tree. Edward Shillito. ChIP; OQP
If Christ is mine, then all is mine. Kept Every Moment. John Roberts. SoP
If Christ Were Here To-night. Margaret E. Sangster. SoP; TRV
If Christmas brought me nothing more. A Poem for Christmas. C. A. Snodgrass. PoToHe (new ed.)
If close hauled on the starboard tack. Rules of the Road. *Unknown.* SoAmSa
If come into this world again I must. Dew on a Dusty Heart. Jean Starr Untermeyer. MAP; MoAmPo
If "compression is the first grace of style." To a Snail. Marianne Moore. CMoP; FaBoMo; OnPM
If Crossed with All Mishaps. William Drummond of Hawthornden. CBEP
If Cupid Were a Child. Thomas Watson. *Fr.* Hecatompathia; or, Passionate Century of Love. TuPP
If Cynthia Be a Queen. Sir Walter Ralegh. FCP; SiPS
If Dante mourns, there wheresoe'er he be. To One Who Had Censured [*or* A Tribute to Dante]. Boccaccio *Fr.* Sonnets. AWP; GoBC
If dead, we cease to be; if total gloom. Human Life; on the Denial of Immortality. Samuel Taylor Coleridge. ChER; ERoP-1; NoP
If dear[e] Anthea, my hard fate it be. To Anthea. Robert Herrick. OBS; SeEP
If death and time are stronger. Strong Love. A. E. Housman. OtMeF
If death is what he seeks in life he fails. The Malefic Surgeon. Gerrit Lansing. CoPo
If Doughty Deeds [My Lady Please]. Robert Graham. GoTS; GTBS; GTBS-D; GTBS-P; GTBS-W; GTSE; GTSL; OBEV
(Cavalier's Song.) HBV
(O Tell Me How to Woo Thee.) OBEC
If down his throat a man should choose. An Unsuspected Fact. Edward Cannon. BOHV; NA
If dreams, as ancient sages hold. To a Young Lady That Told Me My Fortune in the Cards. Thomas Catesby Paget. WaPE
If dumb too long the drooping Muse hath stayed. To the Earl of Warwick on the Death of Mr. Addison. Thomas Tickell. CEP; EiPP; HBV; OBEC
If duty to your country means. A Soldier's Wife to Her Husband. Liu Chi. OnPM
If Easter Be Not True. Henry H. Barstow. BLRP; MaRV; OQP; PGD; SoP; TRV
If Easter Eggs Would Hatch. Douglas Malloch. MPB; SoPo
If echoes from the fitful past. Abstrosophy. Gelett Burgess. CenHV; NA
If e'er my rhyming be at fault. Erring in Company. Franklin P. Adams. BOHV; TOP
If enemies amputate. Ego. A. Kirby Congdon. NYTB
If England were what England seems. England. Kipling. OtMeF
If ever a garden was [a] Gethsemane. For Jim, Easter Eve. Anne Spencer. AmNP; PoNe
If ever against this easy blue and silver. Interruption. Robert Graves. GTBS-W; LiTB; LiTM
If ever age. Bitten. Mark Van Doren. AnAmPo
If ever, as I struck thy strings. To His Lyre. Franklin P. Adams. LHV
If ever at Saint Peter's gate. The Plea. John Drinkwater. MoRP
If ever chance or choice thy footsteps lead. The Flying Tailor. James Hogg. Par
If ever happiness hath lodg'd with man. Consummate Happiness. Wordsworth. *Fr.* The Prelude. OBNC
If ever I dig out. Via Lucis. Charles G. Blanden. OQP
If ever I git off this warpath. That Pretty Little Gal. *Unknown.* ABF
If ever I go to Stony Town, I'll go as to a fair. Stony Town. John Shaw Neilson. BoAV; NeLNL
If ever I had dreamed of my dead name. To My Friend. Wilfred Owen. NAMP
If Ever I Marry [I'll Marry a Maid]. *Unknown.* ElL
If ever I O mighty gods have done you service true. An Epithalamion upon the Marquis of Huntilies Marriage. James I, King of England. HW
If ever I render back your heart. Song for a Slight Voice. Louise Bogan. AmLP; NP
If ever I saw blessing in the air. April Rise. Laurie Lee. BoC; FlW; GTBS-D; OnHM; POTi
If ever I should condescend to prose. Poetical Commandments [*or* Poet's Credo]. Byron. *Fr.* Don Juan. FiP; OBRV; OxBoLi; SeCePo
If ever I suspect thee of a lie. To L——. D'Arcy Cresswell. AnNZ
If ever I travel this road again. The Gal I Left behind Me. *Unknown.* ABF
"If ever I walk to church to wed." The Satin Shoes. Thomas Hardy. CoBMV
If ever I'd known Italy. If. Oswald Durand. PoNe
If ever it were time for the nation's dead to ride. Australia Day, 1942; in Memoriam W. J. Miles. Ian Mudie. BoAu
If ever Jesus has need of me. Obedience. *Unknown.* SoP
If ever man had love too dearly bought. A Lover, Disdained, Complaineth. Thomas, Lord Vaux. TuPP
If ever man might him avant. Sir Thomas Wyatt. FCP; SiPS
If ever pitty were acquainted. Another (Upon the Death of Mr. Herrys). Richard Crashaw. MaMe
If ever round our domicile you chance to be a-wandering. "Everybody Works but Father" as W. S. Gilbert Would Have Written It. Arthur G. Burgoyne. FiBHP
If ever Sorrow spoke from soul that loves. Sonnet. Henry Constable. *Fr.* Diana. ElL; SiCE
If ever the sun had thought to pass this way. Dark Corner. Graham Hough. NMP
If ever there is something nice. Five Years Old. Lysbeth Boyd Borie. BiCB; SiSoSe
If ever there lived a Yankee lad. Darius Green and His Flying-Machine. John Townsend Trowbridge. BeLS; BoChLi; BOHV; FaBoBe; HBV; HBVY; IHA; InMe; MoShBr; PoLF; StVeCh (1940 ed.); YaD
If ever there was man who justly stank. Two Poems against His Rival, 1. Catullus. LiTW
If Ever Time Shall Come. Alison Brown. PEDC
If ever two were one, then surely we. To My Dear and Loving Husband. Anne Bradstreet. AmP; AmPP; AP; CBEP; ForPo; HW; MAmP; NePA; OxBA; PoEL-3; PoLF; SCAP
If ever you go to Dolgelly. Thomas Hughes. CenHV
If Ever You Go to Dublin Town. Patrick Kavanagh. AnIL; NMP
If ever you should follow. Belden Hollow. Leslie Nelson Jennings. GoYe
If ever you should go by chance. How to Tell [*or* Know] the Wild Animals. Carolyn Wells. FaFP; FaPON; FiBHP; GoTP; HBVY; MaC; MPB; RePo; TiPo; TSW; UTS
If every home were an altar. Every Home an Altar. *Unknown.* SoP
If everyone had a flying machine. Chairoplane Chant. Nancy Byrd Turner. RIS
If Everything. Paul Engle. SiTL
If everywhere in the street. Songs, II. Denis Glover. AnNZ
If external action is effete. The Past Is the Present. Marianne Moore. PP
If faithful souls [or faithful soules] be alike glorifi'd. Holy Sonnets, VIII. John Donne. AnAnS-1; MaMe; MasP; MeP; NoP; OBS; SCEP-1; SeEP; Sonn
If fancy would favor. Sir Thomas Wyatt. FCP; SiPS
If Fathers Knew [but How To Leave]. *Unknown.* EG; ElL
If few are won to read my lays. A Song to One. T. A. Daly. YT
If Floods of Tears Could Cleanse My Follies Past. *Unknown.* EP

If flowers could speak. Nature in War-Time. Herbert Palmer. HaMV
If flowers reasoned, would they understand? Suffering. Jane W. Lauber. SoP
If for a moment only, and then ineptly. People as Flowers. Francis Maguire. JKCP (1955 ed.)
If for a woman I would die. A Song. Countess of Winchilsea. ViBoPo
If for thy self thou wilt not watch thy whore. Ovid. *Fr.* Amores, II, 19. PeRV
If Frequently to Mass. Christine de Pisan, *tr. fr. French by* J. G. Legge. PoPl
If Friday's dream is on Saturday told. Signs and Charms. *Unknown.* StaSt
If from the height of the celestial sphere. To Shakespeare. Frances Anne Kemble. Sonn
If from the public way you turn your steps. Michael [a Pastoral Poem]. Wordsworth. BEL; DiPo; EnL; EnLi-2; EnLit; EnRP; EPN; ERoP-1; GoTL; MBW-2; MERP; NoP; OAEP; PAn; PoE; ShBV-3; TOP; UnPo (1st ed.); WHA
If fruits are fed on any beast. Epitaph after Reading Ronsard's Lines from Rabelais. J. M. Synge. PV
If girls were as charming after the fact as before it. Andante, ma Non Assai. Rufinus Domesticus. ErPo; LiTW
If God can make of an ugly seed. What Can He Do with You? *Unknown.* SoP
If God compel thee to this destiny. A Thought for a Lonely Death-Bed. Elizabeth Barrett Browning. MaRV
If God ever has intended. Man Has No Smokestack. *Unknown.* STF
If God hath made this world so fair. The Earth Is Full of God's Goodness. James Montgomery. MaRV
If graver heads shall count it overlight. To the Author. George Peele. *Fr.* Hecatompathia (*by* Thomas Watson). ReIE
If Gray Had Had to Write His Elegy in the Cemetery of Spoon River Instead of in That of Stoke Poges. J. C. Squire. WhC
If great Apollo offered as a dower. Fidessa, More Chaste than Kind, LIV. Bartholomew Griffin. ReIE; Sonn; TuPP
If grief come early. First or Last. Thomas Hardy. CMoP
If grief for grief can touch thee. The Appeal. Emily Brontë. BoPe; EnLoPo; LoBV; OBNC
If gutter-puddles after rain. Dirt and Deity. Louis Ginsberg. OQP
If handycraftmen have great praise for working well. George Turbervile in Praise of the Translator of This Book (Sir Geoffrey Fenton]. George Turberville. ReIE
If He be truly Christ. Second Seeing. Louis Golding. WGRP
If He could doubt on His triumphal [*or* triumphant] cross. Calvary. William Dean Howells. AmePo; ChIP; OQP
If he could have looked ahead. In Memory of Robinson Jeffers. Eric Barker. NYTB
If He could speak, that victim torn and bleeding. The Suffering God. G. A. Studdert-Kennedy. MaRV
If he from heaven that filched that living fire. Idea, XIV. Michael Drayton. NoP
If he had not taken her to the forest. The Forest. Dorothy Quick. FiSC
If he is held in love. Joyful Prophecy. Vassar Miller. CoPo
If he play, being young and unskilful, for shekels of silver and gold. Maxim. Kipling. OtMeF
If He Should Come. Lilith Lorraine. ChIP; MaRV
If He Should Come. Edwin Markham. ChIP; OQP; SoP
If He Should Come Today. Grace E. Troy. FaChP
(What Would He Say?) SoP
If he should come tomorrow, the Meek and Lowly One. If He Should Come. Lilith Lorraine. ChIP; MaRV
If he that erst the form so lively drew. Earl of Surrey. FCP; SiPS
If He Were Anywhere. Cecil Hemley. PoDB
If he were living—dare I ask? Emily Dickinson. CoBA
If Hearts Are Dust. James Terry White. OQP
If heaven and earth were both not fully bent. His Complaint against Love and Fortune. Nicholas Breton. ReIE
If Heaven did not love wine. Drinking Alone in Moonlight. Li Po. AWP
If Heaven the grateful liberty would give. The Choice. John Pomfret. CEP; EiPP; OBEC; PoE; PoFS; TOP
If Heaven were to do again. The Peaceful Shepherd. Robert Frost. *Fr.* A Sky Pair. MAP; MoAB; MoAmPo; MoRP
If heav'n be pleased when sinners cease to sin. Elegy on Coleman. *Unknown.* ALV
If heav'n the grateful liberty wou'd give. The Choice. John Pomfret. EiCL; YAT
If He'd Be a Buckaroo, *with music. Unknown.* OuSiCo
If her neck is. Parallel Texts. Robert Kelly. CoPo
If here and now be but a timely span. Here and Now. Catherine Cater. AmNP; PoNe
If homely virtues draw from me a tune. Envoy. James Weldon Johnson. TrPWD
If humility and purity be not in the heart. T. S. Eliot. *Fr.* The Rock. TiPo
If hungry, Lord, I need bread. In Harbor. Lizette Woodworth Reese. TrPWD
If I. T. C. O'Donnell. GFA
If I/ or anybody. 306. E. E. Cummings. AnEnPo
If I/ Were a bee. I Would Like to Be—a Bee. Dorothy W. Baruch. BiCB
If I am to live or be in the studios. John Standish, Artist. Kenneth Fearing. AnAmPo
"If I ascend to heaven, thou art there." Without and Within. Norman Ault. MaRV; StJW
If I ask why/ You need not reply. The Question Is Proof. Elizabeth Bartlett. NePoAm-2
If I, athirst by a stream, should kneel. A Drifting Petal. Mary McNeil Fenollosa. AA
"If I Be Lifted Up". E. P. Dickie. *See* "And I, if I Be Lifted Up, Shall Draw All Men".
If I But Knew. Amy E. Leigh. AA
If I But Read. Martha Snell Nicholson. SoP
If I can bear your love like a lamp before me. The Lamp. Sara Teasdale. InP; MoLP
If I can do some good today. My Daily Prayer. Grenville Kleiser. BLRP; MaRV; SoP
If I can lead a man who has been blind. The Reward. Grace G. Bostwick. MaRV
If I Can Live. Helen Hunt Jackson. OTD
If I can stop one heart from breaking. Emily Dickinson. MaRV; OHFP; PoLF; PoToHe; TIHL; TreF; TRV
If I come in, you must leave the door ajar. Cat's World. Bernice Kenyon. CIV
If I could be a gipsy-boy. The Caravan. Madeleine Nightingale. BoTP; GaP; MPB
If I could be born an animal. Rebirth. Stan Rice. QAH
If I could catch that moth. Under Glass. Alfred Kreymborg. AnAmPo; MAPA
If I could choose my paradise. No and Yes. Thomas Ashe. HBV
If I could climb the garden wall. There—and Back. Rodney Bennett. BoTP
If I Could Come Again to That Dear Place. John Masefield. *Fr.* Sonnets ("Long long ago"). HBV
(Revelation.) CMoP
If I could drive steel like John Henry. Drivin' Steel. *Unknown.* AS
"If I could find a dollar." Two Ways of Giving. *Unknown.* SoP
If I could get within this changing I. John Masefield. *Fr.* Sonnets ("Long long ago"). WGRP
If I Could Grasp a Wave from the Great Sea. John Richard Moreland. EtS
If I could have/ Two things in one. Moriturus. Edna St. Vincent Millay. AnAmPo; GTBS-W; LiTA; NAMP
If I could hold within my hand. Jesus the Carpenter. Charles M. Sheldon. ChIP; MaRV; OQP; SoP
If I could I surely would. Pharaoh's Army Got Drownded. *Unknown.* AS
If I could know that here about. Evelyn. Rossiter Johnson. AA
If I could live without the thought of death. On the Shortness of Time. Wilfred Scawen Blunt. The Love Sonnets of Proteus, XCVI. MoBrPo (1942 ed.)
If I could live year-round upon this hill. In Conclusion. Abbie Huston Evans. NP
If I could look across the waste. Longing. Henry W. Frost. SoP
If I Could Meet God. Dennis Schmitz. YAP
If I could not be the girl I am. Her Choice. Mattie Lee Hausgen. GFA
If I Could Only Live at the Pitch That Is Near Madness. Richard Eberhart. FiMAP; LiTM (1970 ed.); MiAP; MoAB; PoPl; ToPo

If I could paint you, friend, as you stand there. Football Player. Edward Cracroft Lefroy. VA
If I could rise and see my father young. Gil Orlovitz. *Fr.* Art of the Sonnet. ToPo
If I could see a little fish. On the Bridge. Kate Greenaway. MCCG; MPB; SAS
If I Could Shut the Gate [against My Thoughts]. *Unknown.* ElL; HBV; LoBV; OxBoCh; SiCE
If I could smell smells with my ears. Curious Something. Winifred Welles. TiPo
If I could stand, gel, goldenly. Come Michaelmas. A. Newberry Choyce. HBMV
If I could take the beauty of the orchid. Mother. *Unknown.* SoP
If I could take your mountains in my heart. Frank Wilmot. *Fr.* The Gully. BoAV; NeLNL
If I could tell how glad I was. Emily Dickinson. MAmP
If I Could Tell You. W. H. Auden. *See* Villanelle.
If I could think how these my thoughts to leave. Sir Philip Sidney. FCP
If I Could Touch. William Stanley Braithwaite. BALP
If I could trust mine own self with your fate. Trust. Christina Rossetti. Monna Innominata, XIII. VA; ViPo; VP
If I dare pray for one. A Prayer. Vernon Watkins. MoRP; PoPL
If I deny my kinship to a man. A Gentle Park. Moss Herbert. GoYe
If I Desire. Thomas Burbidge. VA
If I did come of set intent. To Archinus. Callimachus. AWP
If I Die a Railroad Man, *with music.* *Unknown.* AS
If I dont bring you. The Couple. Joel Oppenheimer. CoPo
If I don't drive around the park. Some Beautiful Letters [*or* Observation]. Dorothy Parker. FiBHP; InMe
If I drink water while this doth last. Chorus. Thomas Love Peacock. *Fr.* Crotchet Castle. ViBoPo
If I entreat this lady that all grace. Sonnet: To a Friend Who Does Not Pity His Love. Guido Cavalcanti. AWP
If I err not, the sylvan sprites rejoice. Olympia. Boccaccio. WoL
If I Ever Have Time for Things That Matter. Vilda Sauvage Owens. BOHV
If I fail to catch the music in the gently falling rain. Alive. Nellie Goode. SoP
If I Felt Less. Morris Wintchevsky, *tr. fr. Yiddish by* Joseph Leftwich. TrJP
If I Forget Thee. Emanuel Litvinoff. TrJP
If I forswear the art divine. The Exile's Devotion. Thomas d'Arcy McGee. VA
If I Freely May Discover. Ben Jonson. *Fr.* The Poetaster, II, ii. EG; ReEn; TuPP
(Hermogenes's Song.) PoIE
(Song.) AnAnS-2; ElL
If I Go Not, Pray Not, Give Not. *Unknown.* STF
If I go to see the play. Old Stuff. Bert Leston Taylor. BOHV; HBMV; LHV
If I Got My Ticket, Can I Ride? *with music.* *Unknown.* OuSiCo
If I grieve often, thinking of the dead. To a Believer. Marjorie Pickthall. PeCV
If I Had a Boy. *Unknown.* PEDC
If I Had a Broomstick. Patrick R. Chalmers. TVC
If I had a donkey that wouldn't go. *Unknown.* OxNR
If I had a farm, an' no need to be beggin' my bread. The Beggar. H. L. Doak. HBMV
If I Had a Firecracker. Shelley Silverstein. PoSC
If I had a green automobile. The Green Automobile. Allen Ginsberg. NoP
If I had a hundred dollars to spend. The Animal Store. Rachel Field. OTPC (1946 ed.); PDV; SoPo; TiPo; UTS
If I had a son! A little child. Barren. "Rachel." TrJP
If I had a spoon. Clouds. Dorothy Aldis. SoPo
If I had a-listened what my mother said. Prison Moan. *Unknown.* OuSiCo
If I had [*or* I'd] as much money as I could spend. Mother Goose. FaFP; HBV; OTPC; OxNR
If I had been a Heathen. The Song of the Strange Ascetic. G. K. Chesterton. HBMV
If I had been in Palestine. Judge Me, O Lord! Sarah N. Cleghorn. ChIP; MaRV; StJW
If I had but one year to live. One Year to Live [*or* If but One Year]. Mary Davis Reed. PoToHe (new ed.); SoP; STF
If I Had but Two Little Wings. Samuel Taylor Coleridge. BoTP; CH; OHIP; OTPC (1923 ed.)
(Something Childish, but Very Natural.) OBRV
If I had chosen thee, thou shouldst have been. To Manon, as to His Choice of Her. Wilfred Scawen Blunt. *Fr.* The Love Sonnets of Proteus. HBV; Sonn; ViBoPo
If I had just one penny. Choice. John Farrar. BrR; SiSoSe
If I Had Known. Mary Carolyn Davies. BLPA
If I Had Known. Mary Virginia Terhune. SoP
If I had known how narrow a prison is love. Liadain to Curither. Moireen Fox. NP
If I had known what trouble you were bearing. If I Had Known. Mary Carolyn Davies. BLPA
If I had lightly given at the first. A Lodging for the Night. Elinor Wylie. ErPo
If I had met in Galilee. Devotion. Henry W. Frost. SoP
If I had never known your face at all. Sonnets to Miranda, VIII. Sir William Watson. FaBoBe; HBV
If I had only loved your flesh. Song. V. Sackville-West. HBMV
If I had peace to sit and sing. The Singer. Anna Wickham. HBMV; MoBrPo; NeMA; NP; TSW
"If I Had Prayed." M. Joyce Roder. SoP
If I Had Ridden Horses. Theodore Maynard. HBMV
If I had sat at supper with the Lord. With Me in Paradise. Alexander Harvey. ChIP
If I had sight enough. The Flesh-Scraper. Andrew Young. ELU
If I had thought thou couldst have died. To Mary. Charles Wolfe. GTSL; HBV; LO; OBEV; OBRV; ViBoPo
If I had time to find a place. Time. *Unknown.* SoP
If I had trained a gull I'd send it off to Boothbay Harbor. A Ghazel of Absence. Gerrit Lansing. CoPo
If I had wings like Noah's dove. Dink's Song. *Unknown.* ErPo
If I had wit for to indite. A Secret. *Unknown.* OBSC
If I had won my Wendy. Luck. Evan V. Shute. CaP
If I have any taste, it is hardly. Hunger. Arthur Rimbaud. AWP
If I have complained I hope I have done with it. The Gods. W. S. Merwin. NaP
"If I have eaten my morsel alone." Alone? William Alexander. SoP
If I have erred or run a course unfit. To the Right Worthy Knight Sir Fulke Greville. Samuel Daniel. EnRePo
If I have faltered more or less. The Celestial Surgeon. Robert Louis Stevenson. BBV; BoC; BrPo; EPN; GBV (1922 ed.); GoTP; HBV; HBVY; MaRV; MemP; MoBrPo; OQP; PoToHe (new ed.); PoVP; TreFS; TrGrPo; TrPWD; TRV; ViBoPo; WGRP
If I Have Lifted Up Mine Eyes to Admire. Amos N. Wilder. TrPWD
If I Have Made, My Lady, Intricate. E. E. Cummings. CMoP; FaBV; NAMP; NoP; PoRA
If I have run my course and seek the pearls. The Marathon Runner. Fenton Johnson. CDC
If I have since done evil in my life. The Sinner-Saint. Wilfrid Scawen Blunt. ACP; CAW
If I Have Sinn'd in Act. Hartley Coleridge. NCEP
If I have wounded any soul today. My Evening Prayer [*or* Help Me to Live!]. *At. to* C. Maud Battersby, *also to* Charles H. Gabriel. BLPA; FaBoBe; NeHB; OQP; SoP
If I Have Wronged You. Trumbull Stickney. NCEP
"If I hold my breath and do not speak." Ganga. Thomas Blackburn. MoBS
If I in woemen would take my delight. *Unknown.* SeCSL
If I kiss Anthea's breast. Love Perfumes All Parts. Robert Herrick. UnTE
If I Knew. Phillips Brooks. SoP
If I Knew You and You Knew Me. Nixon Waterman. *See* "To Know All Is to Forgive All."
If I knew you, and you knew me. At Church Next Sunday. *Unknown.* BLRP
If I knocked in this dead night. Threshold. Edmund Blunden. HBMV
If I lay waste and wither up with doubt. Faith [*or* What Shall It Profit?]. William Dean Howells. AA; AmePo; MaRV; OQP; WGRP
If I leave all for thee, wilt thou exchange. Sonnets from the Portuguese, XXXV. Elizabeth Barrett Browning. BEL; EnLi-2; EnLit; Sonn; TOP; VA; ViBoPo; ViPo

If I lie naked. Confession. Pearl Cleage. WSL
If I, like Solomon. O to Be a Dragon. Marianne Moore. CTC; GoYe; PoPl
If I live to be [*or* grow] old, for I find I go down. The Old Man's Wish [*or* The Wish]. Walter Pope. BoPe; CoMo; OBS; SeCL; SeEP
"If I live yet, it is for good, more love." The Old Whom God Loves. Robert Browning. *Fr.* A Death in the Desert. BoC
If I Loved You. Oscar Hammerstein, II. Po
If I make the lashes dark. Before the World Was Made. W. B. Yeats. GTBS-P
"If I may trust your love," she cried. Tantalus; Texas [*or* The Llano Estacado]. *Unknown*, *at. to* Joaquin Miller. CoSo; HBV
If I Might Choose. John Anster. OnYI
(Sonnet: "If I might choose where my tired limbs shall lie.") IrPN
If I might guess, then guess I would. Dorcas. George Macdonald. OBVV
If I might only love my God and die! If Only. Christina Rossetti. OxBoCh
If I might see another Spring. Another Spring. Christina Rossetti. VP
If I must die. Youth. George Cabot Lodge. AA
If I must go, let it be easy, slow. Improvisation on an Old Theme. Dorothy Livesay. ACV; CaP
If I must of my senses lose. Prayer. Theodore Roethke. TwCP
If I only had not chanced. Two Others, on Either Side. Edith Mirick. ChIP
If I Only Was the Fellow. Will S. Adkin. BLPA
(Just Try to Be the Fellow That Your Mother Thinks You Are.) WBLP
If I profane with my unworthiest hand. Shakespeare. *Fr.* Romeo and Juliet, II, v. Sonn
If I really, really trust Him. A Question. *Unknown.* BLRP
If I remain and fight. The Prayer of Calcas. *Unknown.* *Fr.* Troelus a Chresyd. PrWP
If I said, "Little wives." The Wives. Donald Hall. CoAP
If I See in My Soul. Bilhana, *formerly at. to* Chauras, *tr. fr. Sanskrit by* E. Powys Mathers. *Fr.* Black Marigolds. OnPM
If I seeke t'enjoy the fruit of my paine. *Unknown.* SeCSL
If I shall ever win the home in Heaven. Daniel Gray. Josiah Gilbert Holland. AA; HBV
If I should ask of him who holds. Gracious Living. *Unknown.* SoP
If I Should Cast Off This Tattered Coat. Stephen Crane. The Black Riders, LXVI. AmePo; AP
If I should choose, yea, for my life. In Nigellum. John Weever. TuPP
If I should die. Emily Dickinson. MoAB; WOW
If I should die and leave you here a while. Turn Again to Life. Mary Lee Hall. MaRV; PoLF
If I Should Die Before I Wake. Robert Mezey. *See* Bedtime Story.
If I should die out there on the battle-front. Poem to Lou. Guillaume Apollinaire. LiTW
If I should die, think only this of me. The Soldier. Rupert Brooke. *Fr.* 1914. AnFE; BBV; BEL; BoC; BoLiVe; BrPo; CBV; EnLit; EPN; ExPo; FaBoEn; FaBV; FaFP; FaPL; GTBS; GTBS-W; GTSL; InP; LiTB; LiTM; MaC; MaRV; MCCG; MoBrPo; MoVE; NeHB; NeMA; OBEV (new ed.); OTPC (1946 ed.); PoLF; PoMa; PoPl; PoPo; PoRA; POTE; ShBV-3; Sonn; TOP; TreF; TrGrPo; ViBoPo; WaP; WHA; YT
If I Should Die Tonight, *parody.* Ben King. BOHV; FiBHP; HBV; InMe; PoLF; TreFS; YaD
If I Should Die Tonight. Arabella Eugenia Smith, *wr. at. to* Robert C. V. Meyers. BLPA; HBV; TreF
If I Should Ever by Chance. Edward Thomas. FaBoCh; GoJo; GTSL; HBMV; LoGBV; MoAB; MoBrPo; MoShBr; NeMA; OBMV
If I should ever need to reach your heart. Understanding. Pauline E. Soroka. PoLF
If I should go away. Post-script for Gweno. Alun Lewis. GTBS-P; WePo
If I should labor through daylight and dark. Philosophy. Dorothy Parker. InMe
If I Should Learn, in Some Quite Casual Way. Edna St. Vincent Millay. MemP
If I should lift my look for yours to-night. Realization. Mahlon Leonard Fisher. AnAmPo
If I should live a thousand years. His Book. Alice Hansche Mortenson. SoP
If I should paint thy portrait, mother dear. My Mother. Bertha Nolan. PGD
If I should pamphleteer twenty years against royalists. To the Ghost of John Milton. Carl Sandburg. PP; ReMP
If I should pass the tomb of Jonah. Losers. Carl Sandburg. CMoP; HBMV; MAP; MoAB; MoAmPo; MoVE; NP; TrGrPo
If I should round the corner quickly. The Mythos of Samuel Huntsman. Hyam Plutzik. LiTM (1970 ed.)
If I should speak with the tongues of men and of angels. *See* Though I speak. . .
If I should touch her she would shriek and weeping. Secretary. Ted Hughes. ErPo; ToPo
If I shouldn't be alive. Emily Dickinson. CoBA; DiPo; MAPA; OnPM; PG; TwAmPo
If I speak with the tongues of men and of angels. *See* Though I speak. . .
If I stoop. Faith. Robert Browning. *Fr.* Paracelsus, V. TreFT
If I take an acorn. If. Alice Todd. BoTP
If I take my own excitement. After a Lobster Dinner and Playing like Kids on a King-Sized Bed. Roger Aplon. YAP
If I think music. Music. Hilda Conkling. HH; MPB
If I think myself. The Insidious Dr. Fu Man Chu. LeRoi Jones. CoPo
If I think of a horse wandering about sleeplessly. Night. Robert Bly. NaP
If I turn to the lady on my left, and say. Conversation. William F. Walsh. JKCP (1955 ed.)
If I walk on my hands. Trying for Solitude. Jack Lindeman. WOW
If I was drawn here from a distant place. To —— in Church. Alan Seeger. HBV
If I Was Not a Soldier. "Hugh MacDiarmid." CBV
If I were a bear. Furry Bear. A. A. Milne. SoPo; StVeCh (1955 ed.); TiPo (1959 ed.)
If I were a cassowary. *At. to* Samuel Wilberforce. CenHV
If I Were a Cat. *Unknown.* CIV
If I were a chipmunk. No Escape. Harriet L. Delafield. GoYe
If I were a cloud in heaven. Lise. Rose Terry Cooke. AA
If I were a mouse. The Furry Home. J. M. Westrup. BoTP
If I Were a Pig. Elizabeth Fleming. BoTP
If I Were a Pilgrim Child. Rowena Bennett. RePo; YeAr
If I Were a Queen. Christina Rossetti. *Fr.* Sing-Song. CoBE; GaP; PoVP; SiSoSe
If I were a tailor, I'd make it my boast. The Tradesman. *Unknown.* PCH
If I Were a Voice. Charles Mackay. TreF
If I Were an Apple. *Unknown.* BoTP
If I were asked to give a thought which in one word would speak. You Mean My Mother. *Unknown.* PEDC
If I were called in. Water. Philip Larkin. PoeP
If I Were Dead. Coventry Patmore. The Unknown Eros, I, xiv. ACP; CAW; GoBC; HBV; JKCP; OBEV (1st ed.)
If I were dead, and in my place. A Song to Amoret. Henry Vaughan. HBV; LiTL; ViBoPo
If I were dead in the desert—as you would like me to be. To a Depraved Lying Woman. Sorley Maclean. NeBP
"If I were dead, you'd sometimes say, 'Poor Child!'" If I Were Dead. Coventry Patmore. *Fr.* The Unknown Eros. ACP; CAW; GoBC; HBV; JKCP; OBEV (1st ed.)
If I were fierce, and bald, and short of breath. Base Details. Siegfried Sassoon. CBV; MemP; MMA; MoBrPo; NeMA
If I were fire I'd burn the world away. Sonnet: Of All He Would Do. Cecco Angiolieri da Siena. AWP; JAWP; OnPM; WBP
If I were God, up in the sky. A Child's Thought. Bertha Moore. PaPo
If I were hanged on the highest hill. Mother o' Mine [*or* Dedication]. Kipling. *Fr.* The Light That Failed. FaFP; MaRV; NeHB; OQP; SoP; TRV; WBLP
If I were in a fairy tale. The Duck. Edith King. BoTP; GFA; HBVY; StVeCh

If I were John and John were Me. A Thought. A. A. Milne. ThGo
If I were just a fairy small. A Fairy Voyage. *Unknown.* OTPC (1946 ed.); PCH; SoPo
If I were King, *sels.* Justin Huntly M'Carthy.
Ballad of Dead Ladies, A, *fr. ch.* 9, *par. fr. the French of* Villon. HBV
If I Were King ("All French folk, whereso'er ye be"), *fr. ch.* 2, *par. fr. the French of* Villon. HBV
If I Were King ("If I were king—ah, love, if I were king"), *introd. poem, par. fr. the French of* Villon. FaFP; PoLF; TreF
If I Were King. A. A. Milne. RePo
If I were King of France, that noble fine land. The Heather. Neil Munro. OBVV
If I were less the man, I might have kept. Two Sonnets for a Lost Love, II. Samuel A. De Witt. GoYe
If I were Lord of Tartary. Tartary [*or* Lord of Tartary]. Walter de la Mare. GaP; GoTP; HBMV; PoRh; ShBV-1; SP
If I were loved, as I desire to be. Tennyson. Sonn
If I were mild, and I were sweet. Dilemma. Dorothy Parker. InMe
If I were oh, so very small. If. P. A. Ropes. BoTP
If I were only dafter. Witter Bynner. *Fr.* Spectra: Opus 6. LiTM
If I were queen of all the land. The Chain of Princes Street. Elizabeth Fleming. PCH
If I were rich what would I do? Why Tomas Cam Was Grumpy. James Stephens. CMoP; WhC
If I Were Santa's Little Boy. Mary Carolyn Davies. DD; HH
If I were Sophocles, brave with truth. Penmanship. Tom Clark. ANYP
If I were stone dead and buried under. Felo de Se. Richard Hughes. OBMV
If I were thine, I'd fail not of endeavour. The Third Proposition. "Madeline Bridges." BOHV
If I Were to Tell of Our Labours, Our Hard Lodging. Aeschylus, *tr. fr. Greek by* Louis MacNeice. *Fr.* Agamemnon. WaaP
If I were told that I must die to-morrow. When [*or* The Last Hour]. "Susan Coolidge." HBV; SoP
If I were very sure. The Coup de Grace. Edward Rowland Sill. AA
If I were you, when ladies at the play, Sir. Tu Quoque. Austin Dobson. BOHV
If I when my wife is sleeping. Danse Russe. William Carlos Williams. CMoP
If I, who only sing, in other ways. The New Physician. Stephen Chalmers. HBMV
If I woke in Bombay it would be possible. Bombay. Josephine Miles. FiMAP
If Ice. W. W. E. Ross. OBCV
If I'd a little money. Plans. Luisa Hewitt. PCH
If I'd as much money as I could spend. *See* If I had as much money. . .
If I'd as much money as I could tell. *Unknown.* OxNR
If "ifs" and "ands." Proverbs [*or* Some Proverbs in Verse]. *Unknown.* FaBoBe; HBV
If in a picture, Piso, you should see. The Art of Poetry. Horace, *tr. by* the Earl of Roscommon. EnLi-1
If in all the world there be more woe. *See* If in the World There Be More Woe.
If, in an odd angle of the hutment. Eighth Air Force. Randall Jarrell. ILP; MiAP; MoVE; PoCh; ReMP
If in Beginning Twilight. E. E. Cummings. NYBP
If in his study he hath so much care. Antiquary. John Donne. CLwM; MaMe; TuPP
If in some far-off, future day. Epitaph for a Cat. Margaret E. Bruner. CIV; PoLF
If in that secret place. Barter. Margaret Widdemer. HBMV; WGRP
If in that Syrian garden, ages slain. Easter Hymn. A. E. Housman. CABA; CaFP; ChMP; EaLo; ILP; MaRV; MoAB; SeCeV
If in the fight my arm was strong. The Warrior to His Dead Bride. Adelaide Anne Procter. OBVV
If in the material world. The Soul Eternal. Sir John Bowring. MaRV
If, in the mind of God or book of fate. The Day. Edwin Muir. PoDB
If, in the month of dark December. Written after Swimming from Sestos to Abydos. Byron. ALV; BOHV; ERoP-2; InMe; MBW-2; NoP; OBRV; PoE
If, in the silent mind of One all-pure. In Utrumque Paratus. Matthew Arnold. MaVP; OAEP; OBNC; PoEL-5; PoVP; ViPP
If in the summer of thy bright regard. To M. William Gay. BoAu
If in the World There Be More Woe. Sir Thomas Wyatt. EG; EIL; FCP; SiPS
(Disdain.) TrGrPo
(Treizaine.) OBSC
If in the years that come such thing should be. Ideal Memory. William James Dawson. VA
If in this book dullness do chance to lurk. Ad Collegium Wintoniensem. John Heath. TuPP
If, in thy second state sublime. In Memoriam A. H. H., LXI. Tennyson. EPN; ViPo; VP
If it/ Were lighter touch. The Guarded Wound. Adelaide Crapsey. AnAmPo; NP
If it be all for nought, for nothingness. Resurrection. *Unknown.* ChIP; MaRV
If It Be Destined. Petrarch, *tr. fr. Italian by* Edward Fitzgerald. Sonnets to Laura: To Laura in Life, XI. AWP; JAWP; OnPM; WBP
If it be kindness, God, be kind. A Prayer for His Lady. Oliver St. John Gogarty. NYTB
If it be pleasant to look on, stalled in the packed serai. Certain Maxims of Hafiz. Kipling. HBV
If it be sin so dearly for to love thee. Coelia, VII. William Percy. ReIE
If it be so that I forsake thee. Sir Thomas Wyatt. FCP
If it chance your eye offend you. A. E. Housman. A Shropshire Lad, XLV. PoVP
If It Do Come to Pass. Shakespeare. *Fr.* As You Like It, II, v. ViBoPo
If it form the one landscape that we the inconstant ones. In Praise of Limestone. W. H. Auden. CABA; CMoP; CoBMV; MaPo; MoAB; MoVE; NePA; PoIE
If it had not a been for Cotton-eyed Joe. Cotton-eyed Joe. *Unknown.* ABF
If it had not been the Lord who was on our side. Psalm CXXIV, Bible, *O.T.* OnPM
If it is horrible to be burned alive by savage tribesmen. On Horror. Robert Hershon. ThO
If It Is Not My Portion. Rabindranath Tagore. *Fr.* Gitanjali, LXXIX. BoC; OBMV
If it is true that we no longer seek. The Fear of Trembling. John Hollander. NePoEA
If it is unpermissible, in fact fatal. To a Giraffe. Marianne Moore. TDP
If it must be; if it must be, O God. Sonnet. David Gray. *Fr.* In the Shadows. OxBS
If It Offend Thee. Horace Gregory. NMP
If it should come to this. A Prospect of Death. Andrew Young. DTC
If it so hap this offspring of my care. To Delia, III. Samuel Daniel. ReEn
If it so happens. No Escape. Lilith Lorraine. FiSC
If it was not slavery. Of the Cosmic-Blueprints. Sun-Ra. BF
If it wasn't for me and the likes of me. Madeline at Jefferson Market Night Court. Margaret McGovern. WhC
If it were but a wall between us. Small Song. Daniel Whitehead Hicky. MaRV
If it were done when 'tis done, then 'twere well. Vaulting Ambition [*or* The Murder Pact]. Shakespeare. *Fr.* Macbeth, I, vii. FiP; WHA
If it were less beautiful. A Song for Beauty. P. Lal. ACV
If it were not for the voice. Nakatsukasa. *Fr.* Shui Shu. AWP
If it were only a dream. The Father. George Francis Savage-Armstrong. VA
If it were only still! Pastoral. Edna St. Vincent Millay. RePo
If It Were Spring. Leonard Cohen. ACV
If it would walk at all. Shadow to Shadow. Hervey Allen. HBMV
If-itty-teshi-mow Jays. Limerick. *Unknown.* BOHV
If I've a babe in town, Babe. Belle. *Unknown.* OuSiCo
"If, Jerusalem, I Ever Should Forget Thee." Heine, *tr. fr. German by* Margaret Armour. TrJP
If Jesus Came Back Today, *sel.* Vincent Godfrey Burns.

If (continued)
"If Jesus came back today." ChIP; OQP
If Jesus came to earth again. Christ's Sympathy. Sir Edward Bulwer-Lytton. BePJ
If Jesus Came to Your House. *Unknown.* SoP; STF
If Jesus Christ is a man. The Song of a Heathen. Richard Watson Gilder. AA; BePJ; ChIP; MaRV; OQP; StJW; TRV; WGRP
If Jesus should tramp the streets tonight. If He Should Come. Edwin Markham. ChIP; OQP; SoP
If ladies' manners with their gauds agree. Against the Fantastical Attire That Many Ladies Wear Nowadays. John Davies of Hereford. SiCE
If learned in other things you be. Abraham Cowley. *Fr.* Resolved to Love. LO
If life be as a flame that death doth kill. A Rhyme of Life. Charles Warren Stoddard. HBV; MaRV
If life on earth be less than is a day. Sonnet. Joachim du Bellay. *Fr.* Olive. CAW
If life seems drab and difficult. The Bridge You'll Never Cross. Grenville Kleiser. MaRV
If life were never bitter. If. Mortimer Collins. BOHV; FiBHP; HBV; Par
If life's pleasures cheer thee. Our Rock. Francis Scott Key. BePJ; SoP; STF
If light of life outlive the set of sun. After Sunset, III. Swinburne. BEL; EPN; OQP
If Lincoln Should Return. Margaret E. Bruner. PoToHe
If little mice have birthdays. Birthday Cake. Aileen Fisher. BiCB; PDV
If livelihood by knowledge were endowed. Mesnevi. Sadi. *Fr.* The Gulistan. AWP; JAWP; LiTW; WBP
If, Lord, Thy Love for Me Is Strong. St. Teresa of Avila, *tr. fr. Spanish by* Arthur Symons. AWP; CAW; JAWP; LiTW; WBP
If, Lord, your splendid gift the Word I truly hold. Request for a Song. Julian Tuwim. LiTW
If love be life, I long to die. Dispraise of Love, and Lovers' Follies. "A. W." EIL; HBV; LO; OBSC; TrGrPo
If love be like the flower that in the night. Anthony Munday, *ad. fr. the Italian of* Luigi Pasqualigo. *Fr.* Fedele and Fortunio. TuPP
If Love Be Ours. Tennyson. *See* In Love, if Love Be Love.
If Love, for Love for Long Time Had. John Heywood. EIL (Love Continual.) CBEP
If love should count you worthy, and should deign. Decision. *Unknown.* PoToHe (new ed.)
If love were but a little thing. Song. Florence Earle Coates. HBMV
If Love Were Jester at the Court of Death. Frederic Lawrence Knowles. HBV
If love were what the rose is. A Match. Swinburne. ALV; BEL; ELP; EnLi-2; EnLit; GTBS-D; GTBS-W; GTSL; HBV; LiTL; OBVV; PG (1945 ed.); PoVP; TOP; VA
If Luther's day expand to Darwin's year. Epilogue. Herman Melville. *Fr.* Clarel. AmePo; AnAmPo; AP; ImOP; MAmP
If Man, That Angel of Bright Consciousness. Conrad Aiken. NePA
If, Marchioness, you can descry. Stanzas. Corneille. LiTW
If Mary goes far out to sea. Stately Verse. *Unknown.* FaPON; TiPo (1959 ed.)
If meadow-grass can turn to milk. Fairy Story. Barbara Euphan Todd. BoC
If medals were ordained for drinks. To a Boon Companion [*or* The Boon Companion]. Oliver St. John Gogarty. OBMV; OtMeF
If men be judged wise by their beards and their girth. Epigram. Joseph Solomon del Medigo. TrJP
If men may credit give to true reported fames. In Praise of a Gentlewoman. George Gascoigne. EnRePo; ReIE
If Merlin did not lie, come quickly, king! Cablegram. Aaron Karmer. NYTB
If Michael, leader of God's host. The Rose of Peace. W. B. Yeats. OBVV; PoDB
If mine eyes can speak to do hearty errand. Sapphics. Sir Philip Sidney. *Fr.* Arcadia. FCP; SiPS
If mine eyes do e're declare. The Soul. Abraham Cowley. AnAnS-2
If Mother Nature patches. Sewing. William H. Hayne. *Fr.* Pine Needles. GFA; OTPC (1946 ed.); PCH
If Music and Sweet Poetry. Richard Barnfield. *See* To His Friend Master R. L., in Praise of Music and Poetry.
If Music Be the Food of Love. Shakespeare. *Fr.* Twelfth Night, I, i. PoFS; UnS
(Food of Love, The.) TrGrPo
(Music.) TreFS
If my bark sink. Emily Dickinson. MaRV; TRV
If my best wines mislike thy taste. Quits. Thomas Bailey Aldrich. AA
If my body came from brutes, tho' somewhat finer than their own. Tennyson. *Fr.* By an Evolutionist. MaRV
If my books easy of digestion be. Ad Lectorem. Thomas Bastard. SiCE
If My Complaints Could Passions Move. *Unknown.* EP
If, My Darling. Philip Larkin. LiTM (1970 ed.); PoeP; ToPo
If my face could only promise that its color would remain. Face to Face. Frances Cochrane. HBV
If my feeble prayer can reach Thee. Mystic's Prayer. *Unknown.* MaRV
If my garden oak spares one bare ledge. Creed. Anne Spencer. CDC
If My Girl with Lotus Eyes. Bilhana, *formerly at. to* Chauras, *tr. fr. Sanskrit by* E. Powys Mathers. *Fr.* Black Marigolds. OnPM
If my grave becomes too painful, what should I do? Late August to Early November. William Knott. YAP
If my harsh, humble style and rimes ill-dressed. Sonnet I: Dedication of These Rimes to His First Love. Francis Davison. ReIE
If my ill-tuned rhymes content the wise. To the Ungentilized Censurer. Henry Parrot. SiCE
If my mother had never been the protected child. House in St. Petersburg. Stanley Burnshaw. SiSw
If my peculiar pulchritude in Paris seemed to please. An Intermezzo for the Fourth Act. William Allen White. InMe
If, my religion safe, I durst embrace. To Sir Henrie Savile [upon His Translation of Tacitus]. Ben Jonson. OBS; SeCV-1
If my vain soul needs blows and bitter losses. Ella Wheeler Wilcox. *Fr.* The Christian's New-Year Prayer. TrPWD
If Nancy Hanks/ Came back as a ghost. Nancy Hanks. Rosemary Benét *and* Stephen Vincent Benét. FaBV; FaPON; GBV (1952 ed.); LaNeLa; LiPo; NeMA; PoPl; RePo; SiSoSe; StVeCh (1955 ed.); TiPo
If Nature, for a favorite child. Matthew. Wordsworth. MBW-2; MERP
If Nature say to you. The Daily Grind. Fenton Johnson. AmNP
If neither brass nor marble can withstand. The Power Of Time [*or* Shall I Repine]. Swift. CBEP; NCEP; PV
If Nero lived today. Guilt Redeemed. Arnold Kemp. WSL
If no love is, O God, what fele I so? Song of Troilus [*or* Troilus Soliloquizes *or* Canticus Troili]. Chaucer. *Fr.* Troilus and Criseyde. AtBAP; AWP; EG; LO
If No One Ever Marries Me. Laurence Alma-Tadema. BiCB; GoTP; OTPC; RIS
If none but you in the world today. The Gospel According to You. *Unknown.* STF
If not now soft airs may blow. Absence. John Arthur Blaikie. VA
If now thou seest me a wreck, worn out and minished out of sight. Old Age. Al-Aswad, Son of Ya'fur. *Fr.* The Mufaddaliyat. AWP
If now unto my lips be raised. The Cup. Frederick T. Roberts. ChIP
If now you cannot hear me, it is because. The Barricades. Denise Levertov. NeBP
If, of a wretched state and all forlorn. Sonnet. Leonard Digges. LO; SeCL; SeEP
If of our life the span be not a day. Sonnet. Joachim du Bellay. *Fr.* Olive. WoL
If of thy mortal goods thou art bereft. Hyacinths to Feed Thy Soul. Sadi. *Fr.* The Gulistan. BLPA; FaBoBe; MaRV; NeHB; TRV
If of us two might only one be glad. The Greatest Gift. Blanche Edith Baughan. BoAu
If on a spring night I went by. Courage. John Galsworthy. OtMeF
If, on Account of the Political Situation. W. H. Auden. *Fr.* For the Time Being. LiTA; WaP

If on my theme I rightly think. Why I Drink. Henry Aldrich. ALV; WhC
If on the Book itself we cast our view. The Scriptures. Dryden. *Fr.* Religio Laici. OBS
If on this night of still, white cold. Faith. Hortense Flexner. PoMa
If once I could gather in song. Song. W. W. Gibson. OBVV; TOP
If once might have been, once only. Youth and Art. Robert Browning. BOHV; HBV; VA
If Once You Have Slept on an Island. Rachel Field. BrR; OTD
If one could have that little head of hers. A Face. Robert Browning. CTC; PoVP; VA
If one could only be certain beyond all question. The Anti-Symbolist. Sidney Keyes. MoPo
If one day you are walking along. The Guest. Dennis Trudell. QAH
If one should bring me this report. In Memoriam A. H. H., XIV [*or* Of One Dead]. Tennyson. EnLi-2; EPN; LiTB; LiTG; ViPo; VP
If one should tell them what's clearly seen. Crumbs or the Loaf. Robinson Jeffers. CMoP
If one were soundproof, like a well-built house. Machines—or Men. Elizabeth Newport Hepburn. PoMa
If Only. . . Rose Fyleman. StVeCh; UTS
If Only. Christina Rossetti. OxBoCh
If only a single rose is left. If Only Thou Art True. George Barlow. VA
If only I could send you one small slice. Letter from the Vieux Carre. Ethel Green Russell. GoYe
If only I'd quit fooling round with rhyme. Epistle to the Reader. Walker Gibson. PP
If only I'd some money. If Only . . . Rose Fyleman. StVeCh; UTS
If only in dreams may man be fully blest. The First Kiss. Theodore Watts-Dunton. *Fr.* The Coming of Love. HBV; VA
If only Mr. Roosevelt. E. C. Bentley. *Fr.* Clerihews. CenHV
If only once for every perjured oath. Barine the Incorrigible. Horace. Odes, II, 8. UnTE
If only once the chariot of the Morn. The Glory of Nature. Frederick Tennyson. OBNC
If only the brown leaf were gold. Generosity. *Unknown.* KiLC
If Only the Dreams Abide. Clinton Scollard. HBV
If only the phantom would stop reappearing! Faust. John Ashbery. TwCP
If Only Thou Art True. George Barlow. VA
If only we might live as we choose! To His Cousin. Martial. PoFr
If Only We Understood. *Unknown.* STF
If only, when one heard. *Unknown.* *Fr.* Kokin Shu. AWP; LiTW
If Orpheus' voice [*or* voyce] had force to breathe such music's love. Astrophel and Stella: Third Song. Sir Philip Sidney. FCP; PoEL-1; ReIE; SiPS
If other men could clearly see your moon-white face. Silent Sufferer. John Gilland Brunini. JKCP (1926 ed.)
If ought of oaten stop or pastoral song. *See.* If aught of oaten stop, or pastoral song.
If parting be decreed for the two of us. Parting. Judah Halevi. AWP; TrJP
If Peace and Silence could arise. To a Cat. Samuel Hoffenstein. CIV
If people ask me. Politeness. A. A. Milne. PoPl
If pleasures where not wastinge. *Unknown.* SeCSL
If Poisonous [*or* Poysonous] Mineral[l]s and If That Tree. John Donne. Holy Sonnets, IX. AnAnS-1; AnEnPo; AtBAP; ATP (1953 ed.); CABA; EnRePo; EP; ExPo; GTBS-W; LiTB; MaMe; MaPo; MasP; MeP; MePo; NoP; OBS; PoAn; PoEL-2; PoeP; PoIE; ReEn; SCEP-1; SeCP; Sonn; TuPP; UnPo (Forget.) WHA
If Pope Had Written "Break, Break, Break." J. C. Squire. CenHV
If possible, choose a lot. Choosing a Homesite. Philip Booth. TPM
If prating from morning to night. Prattling Swallows. Nicostratus. OnPM
If publique weal or country's claim might languish and bewail. An Epitaph upon the Death of the Right Reverent Father in God J. Jewel. Nicholas Bourman. ReIE
If radio's slim fingers can pluck a melody. Proof [*or* God Hears Prayer]. Ethel Romig Fuller. FaChP; MaRV; MoSiPe; OQP; TRV
If recollecting were forgetting. With Flowers. Emily Dickinson. AA
If rest is sweet at shut of day. A Roundel of Rest. Arthur Symons. HBV
If right be wracked and overrun. They of the Mean Estate Are Happiest. *Unknown.* SiCE
If rightly tuneful bards decide. Amoret. Mark Akenside. OBEV
If Rome can pardon sins, as Romans hold. On Rome's Pardons. *At. to* the Earl of Rochester. PeRV
If Rome so great, and in her wisest age. To Edward Allen [*or* Alleyne]. Ben Jonson. OAEP; OBS; ReIE
If Sackvile, all that have the power to doe. An Epistle to Sir Edward Sackville, now Earl of Dorset. Ben Jonson. NCEP
If sad complaint would show a lover's pain. Giles Fletcher. *Fr.* Licia. TuPP
If sadly thinking, with spirits sinking. The Deserter [*or* The Deserter's Lamentation *or* Let Us Be Merry before We Go]. John Philpot Curran. AnIV; IrPN; SeCePo; ViBoPo
If seen by many minds at once your image. By the Lake. Lawrence Durrell. *Fr.* Eight Aspects of Melissa. NeBP
If self-regard has golden wit. Five Epigrams, 3. Donald Hall. NePoAm-2
If she asks why the sun. To Jann, in Her Absence. C. J. Driver. PeSA
If She Be Made of White and Red. Herbert P. Horne. HBV; VA
If She Be Made of White and Red. Shakespeare. *Fr.* Love's Labour's Lost, I, ii. CTC
If She Be Not as Kind as Fair. Sir George Etherege. *Fr.* The Comical Revenge; or, Love in a Tub. SeCL
(Song: "If she be not as kind as fair.") CavP; CEP
If She Bees. Arthur Pfister. WSL
If She But Knew. Arthur O'Shaughnessy. HBV; VA
If she had—Well: She longed, and knew not wherefore. Oliver Wendell Holmes. *Fr.* Iris. LO
If she should die (as well suspect we may). Upon Thought Castara May Die. William Habington. *Fr.* Castara. ACP
If she should give me all I ask of her. Sonnet. George Henry Boker. *Fr.* Sonnets; a Sequence on Profane Love. AmePo
If she stood with you where the men playing. "English." Dick Lourie. ThO
If shoemakers' children are left with feet bare. Left Out. Mary Carolyn Davies. HH
If Sleep and Death be truly one. In Memoriam A. H. H., XLIII. Tennyson. EnLi-2; EPN; MaPo (1969 ed.); OBNC; ViPo; VP
If so be a toad be laid. A Charm, or an Allay for Love. Robert Herrick. FaBoCh; LoGBV
If Some Grim Tragedy. Ninna May Smith. HBMV
If someone asks you. Mitchell Donian. PoSC
If someone said, Escape. Longface Mahoney Discusses Heaven. Horace Gregory. CMoP; ExPo
If Someone, Something, somehow (as man dreams). A Musical Critic Anticipates Eternity. Siegfried Sassoon. UnS
If someone was walking across. A Confession. Robert Mezey. NaP
If sometimes I must hear good men debate. Witness of God. James Russell Lowell. *Fr.* The Cathedral. OQP
If sometimes strangeness seems on me to fall. The New House. Joseph Easton McDougall. CaP
If Spirits Walk. Sophie Jewett. AA; HBV
If stars dropped out of heaven. Christina Rossetti. *Fr.* Sing-Song. RIS
If Still They Live. Edith M. Thomas. *Fr.* The Inverted Torch. AA; OQP
If Stones Can Dream. Daniel Berrigan. JKCP (1955 ed.)
If strange things happen where she is. On Portents. Robert Graves. FaBoMo
If Suddenly a Clod of Earth. Harold Monro. *Fr.* Strange Meetings. MoBrPo
If suddenly blackness crawled. Cat's Eye. Paul Engle. PoMa
If suddenly, wonderfully, glittering among the leaves. The Daily Manna. Sara Henderson Hay. GoYe
If that I for thy sweet sake. *Unknown.* SeCSL
If that my hand, like yours, dear George, were skilled. To G. H. B. James Bayard Taylor. Sonn

If that thou hast the gift of strength, then know. The Burden of Strength. George Meredith. EPN
If that we thus are guilty doth appear. Thesis and Antithesis. Arthur Hugh Clough. ViPP
If that which warns the young beware of vice. Barnabe Rich, Gentleman Soldier, in Praise of the Author. Barnabe Rich. RelE
If the autumn ended. The Enduring. John Gould Fletcher. TSW
If the butterfly courted the bee. Topsy-turvy World. William Brighty Rands. MPB; OTPC (1946 ed.); TSW; VA
If the compass of his mind. Specialist. Theodore Roethke. PV
If the cuckoo were. The Cuckoo. Kodo. FIW
If the day looks kinder gloomy. Just Try This [*or* Just Keep on Keepin' On]. *Unknown.* STF; WBLP
If the deep night is haunted, it is I. Rendezvous. Robert Hillyer. MoLP
If the distrait verdure cleave not to the branch. Croesus in Autumn. Robert Penn Warren. AnAmPo
If the drink that satisfied. Poem. R. A. K. Mason. ACV
If the dull substance of my flesh were thought. Sonnets, XLIV. Shakespeare. CBEP; PoeP; Sonn
If the evening's red and the morning gray. A Weather Rule [*or* Weather Signs]. *Unknown.* MPB (1956 ed.); OTPC; RIS
If the French have a notion. The Island. *Unknown.* *Fr.* Ballads on Napoleon. CoBE
If the golden-crested wren. A Child's Laughter. Swinburne. BiCB
If the good God were suddenly. Paradox. Huw Menai. MaRV
If the green cedar is bitter, you can eat it. Empty Purse. Tu Fu. OnPM
If the Heart Be Homeless. Annemarie Ewing. NePoAm-2
If the Heart of a Man. John Gay. *Fr.* The Beggar's Opera, II, i. ATP (1935 ed.); CBEP; ELP
(“If the heart of a man is depress with cares.”) CEP; EnLoPo; NoP
If the lady hath any loveliness, let it die. Blackberry Winter. John Crowe Ransom. OnHM; OxBA; PoRA
If the Lord Should Come. J. R. Miller. SoP
If the lost word is lost, if the spent word is spent. T. S. Eliot. *Fr.* Ash Wednesday. OxBoCh
If the man in the moon. Gathering Sticks on Sunday. Norman Nicholson. POTi
If the [*or* a] Man Who Turnips Cries. Samuel Johnson. BOHV; TreFT; WhC
(Burlesque [of Lope de Vega].) FaFP; LiTG; SiTL
(Epigram: “If a man who turnips cries.”) HBV
(If a Man Who Turnips Cries.) OxNR
(Turnip Seller, The.) EvOK
If the moon shines. What Night Would It Be? John Ciardi. PDV
If the moon smiled, she would resemble you. The Rival. Sylvia Plath. NoP
If the oak is out before the ash. *Unknown.* OxNR
If the Owl Calls Again. John Haines. BoNaP; CoAP
If the quick spirits in your eye. Persuasions to Joy [*or* Persuasions to Enjoy *or* Song: Perswasions to Enjoy]. Thomas Carew. AnAnS-2; EnLi-1; FosPo; HBV; MePo; OBEV; SCEP-2; SeCL; SeCP; SeCV-1
If the red slayer think[s] he slays. Brahma. Emerson. AA; AmePo; AmLP; AmP; AmPP; AnAmPo; AnFE; AnNE; AP; APA; AWP; BoLiVe; BWP; CBEP; CBV; CoAnAm; CoBA; DiPo; EaLo; GTBS; GTBS-D; GTBS-W; HBV; InPo; JAWP; LiTA; LiTG; MAmP; MemP; MWA-1; NePA; NoP; OBEV; OBVV; OxBA; PFY; Po; PoAn; PoIE; PoPo; PoRA; SeCeV; ShBV-4; TreF; TrGrPo; UnPo; ViBoPo; WBP; WGRP; WHA; WoL
If the rose in meek duty. Dedication. Francis Thompson. CoBE
If the sea were one great ink-pot/ And of paper all the sky. The Lies of Men. *Unknown.* OnPM
If the sea were one great ink-pot/ And the sky of paper made. The Evil in Women. *Unknown.* OnPM
If the scorn of your bright eyne. Song. Shakespeare. *Fr.* As You Like It, IV, iii. CTC
If the Stars Should Fall. Samuel Allen. IDB; NNP
If the sudden tidings came. The World's Justice. Emma Lazarus. HBV
If the sun low down in the West, my friend. A Lady to a Lover. Roden Noel. OBVV
If the things of earth must pass. If Only the Dreams Abide. Clinton Scollard. HBV
If the truth were but known when she came at last. Lady Godiva. Edward Shanks. HBMV
If the unfortunate fate engulfing me. Farewell to My Mother. “Plácido.” BANP; PoNe; TTY
If the walls are whitewashed clean, I hope. The Church. Nancy Willard. ThO
If the way be rough with thorns and stones. My Prayer. Lucy Carruth. SoP
If the wild bowler thinks he bowls. Brahma. Andrew Lang. CenHV
If the woman in the purple petticoat. Give No White Flower. Brenda Chamberlain. NeIP
If their bee nothing new, but that which is. *See* If there be nothing new, but that which is.
If There Are Any Heavens. E. E. Cummings. MoAB; MoAmPo (1950 ed.)
If there be any one can take my place. Abnegation. Christina Rossetti. Monna Innominata, XII. VA; ViPo; VP
If there be graveyards in the heart. God Bless You, Dear, To-Day! John Bennett. AA; HBV
If there be [*or* their bee] nothing new, but that which is. Sonnets, LIX. Shakespeare. FaBoEn; ReEn
If there be some weaker one. Whittier. *Fr.* Andrew Rykman's Prayer. FaChP; MaRV; TRV
If There Be Sorrow. Mari Evans. Kal; NNP; PoNe (1970 ed.)
If there be soul in wood and strings. The Violin. E. N. da Costa Andrade. MuSP
If there exists a hell—the case is clear. To Sir Toby. Philip Freneau. AP; CoBA
If There Had Anywhere Appeared. Richard Chenevix Trench. *See* God Our Refuge.
If there is a vile, pernicious. School. James Kenneth Stephen. BOHV
If there is any life when death is over. On the Dunes. Sara Teasdale. NP
If there is any pleasure to repeat. Prayer against Love. Catullus. LiTW
If there is any way, dear Lord. A Message. Anna Nelson Reed. OQP
If there is no God for thee. To a Dog. Anna Hempstead Branch. MAP; MoAmPo (1942 ed.)
If there is righteousness. The Way to Peace. *Unknown.* SoP
If there was a broken whispering by night. Parting at Dawn. John Crowe Ransom. AnAmPo
If there were any of the sons of men. Retrospection. Hubert Church. AnNZ
If there were dreams to sell. Dream-Pedlary [*or* Dreams to Sell]. Thomas Lovell Beddoes. AnFE; AtBAP; BoTP; CBEP; CH; EG; EnRP; EPN; FaBoBe; GTBS-W; LiTB; LoBV; NeHB; OBEV; OBNC; OBRV; OBVV; OQP; OtMeF; OTPC (1946 ed.); PCD; PG (1945 ed.); PoEL-4; TOP; TreFS; TrGrPo; VA; ViBoPo; WiR; YT
If there were no past, but specious present only. Speculative Evening. Marguerite Young. LiTA
If there were, oh! an Hellespont of cream. The Author Loving These Homely Meats [*or* Homely Meats *or* Buttered Pippin-Pies]. John Davies of Hereford. ChTr; ElL; FaBoCh; LoGBV; Sonn
If there were sound, the slapping. Tall Tale God. Mark Van Doren. CrMA
If there's a fox, he said, I'll whistle the beggar. Mahony's Mountain. Douglas Stewart. PoAu-2; SeCePo
If there's a wind, we get it. Lobster Cove Shindig. Lillian Morrison. BoNaP
If there's no sun, I still can have the moon. Philosophy. John Kendrick Bangs. PoToHe (new ed.)
If there's one who often falters. First to Throw a Stone. *Unknown.* STF
If these brief lays, of Sorrow born. In Memoriam A. H. H., XLVIII. Tennyson. EnLi-2; EPN; ViPo; VP
If these clerics or commoners take Christ for their topic. Preaching and Not Doing. William Langland. *Fr.* The Vision of Piers Plowman. PoLi
If These Endure. Lilith Lorraine. PGD
If these, quoth Potus, prove not things admired. Nemo Nascitur Artifex. Henry Parrot. SiCE

If they are doomed and all that can be done. The Fate of Elms. Robert Francis. NYTB
If they hint, O Musician, the piece that you played. The Ballad of Imitation. Austin Dobson. HBV
If They Honoured Me, Giving Me Their Gifts. "Michael Field." OBMV
If They Meant All They Said. Alice Duer Miller. BOHV
If They Spoke. Mark Van Doren. ImOP
If they true bailiffs be, who for the law maintaining. On Mercenary and Unjust Bailiffs. Henricus Selyns. SCAP
If thine were wings, and in thy hand were bow. The Better Eros. Asclepiades. OnPM
If this ain't the Holy Ghost, I don't know. Holy Ghost. *Unknown.* OuSiCo
If This Be All. Anne Brontë. TrPWD
If this be all, for which I've listened long. A Word with a Skylark. Sarah Piatt. JKCP (1926 ed.)
If This Be Love. Henry Constable. *See* Diana: "To live in hell. . ."
If This Be Love. Richard Eberhart. LiTL
If this be love, to draw a weary breath. To Delia, IX. Samuel Daniel. OBSC; ReEn; SiCE; TrGrPo
If this brain's over-tempered. I've Tasted My Blood. Milton Acorn. MoCV
If this bright lily. A Song at Easter. Charles Hanson Towne. BLRP; ChIP; MaRV
If this country were a sea (that is solid rock). Pennines in April. Ted Hughes. WePo
If This Great World of Joy and Pain. Wordsworth. EPN
If This Is All. Alban Asbury. OQP
If this is peace, this dead and leaden thing. Dead Fires. Jessie Redmond Fauset. BANP; PoNe
If this life-saving rock should fail. On Middleton Edge. Andrew Young. ELU; POTE; SD
If This Little World To-night. Oliver Herford. *Fr.* The Bashful Earthquake. ShM
(Proem.) AA
If This Old Place. Mary Kolars. JKCP
If this our little life is but a day. Sonnet to Heavenly Beauty. Joachim du Bellay, *tr. by* Andrew Lang. *Fr.* Olive. AWP; CTC; JAWP; WBP
If this pale rose offend your sight. Presenting [*or* On Presenting] to a Lady a White Rose and a Red on the Tenth of June. William Somervile. CEP; OBEC
If this small human testament. Electronic Tape Found in a Bottle. Olga Cabral. WOW
If this uncertain age in which we dwell. The Lesson for Today. Robert Frost. LiTA; LiTM (rev. ed.); NePA; SiTL; WaP
If This Were Faith. Robert Louis Stevenson. BrPo; MaRV; OBNC; TrPWD; WGRP
(If This Were Enough.) OQP
"If to feel, in the ink of the slough," *sel.* PoFr
If this worlds friends might see but once. The Seed Growing Secretly. Henry Vaughan. AnAnS-1; MeP; OxBoCh; SCEP-1; SeCV-1
If thou a reason dost desire to know. To Cynthia, on Her Embraces. Sir Francis Kynaston. EG; LO; NCEP
If thou are sinful, there are thousands then. Sonnet. George Henry Boker. *Fr.* Sonnets; a Sequence on Profane Love. AmePo
If thou art merely conscious clay—ah, well. Surrender. "S. M. M." JKCP
If thou art sleeping, maiden. Song. Gil Vicente, *tr. by* Longfellow. AWP; JAWP; LiTW; WBP
If thou canst fashion no excuse. To His Friend J. H. Alexander Brome. CavP
If thou canst wake with me, forget to eate. John Ford. *Fr.* The Lover's Melancholy. PoEL-2
If thou chance for to find. To My Successor. George Herbert. MaMe
If thou didst feed on western plains of yore. To a Goose. Robert Southey. Sonn
If thou dislik'st the piece thou light'st on first. To the Soure Reader. Robert Herrick. AnAnS-2; SeCP
If thou doest not love sacke. *Unknown.* SeCSL
If thou dost bid thy friend farewell. Parting. Coventry Patmore. PoToHe
If thou dost find an house built to thy mind. To My Successor. George Herbert. MaMe
If thou dost love. *Unknown.* SeCSL
If thou dost love me as thou sayst. *Unknown.* SeCSL
If Thou Dost Need. Mary E. Kendrew. SoP
If thou hast squander'd years to grave a gem. A Charge. Herbert Trench. HBV; OBEV (new ed.); OBVV
If thou hast wisdom, hear me, Celia. Ben Jonson. *Fr.* Volpone. ViBoPo
If thou in surety safe wilt sit. Look or You Leap [*or* The Lookers-on]. Jasper Heywood. ACP (1952 ed.); ElL; SiCE; TuPP
If Thou Indeed Derive Thy Light from Heaven. Wordsworth. EnRP; OBRV
If thou must love me, let it be for naught. Sonnets from the Portuguese, XIV. Elizabeth Barrett Browning. AnFE; ATP (1935 ed.); BEL; BoLP; CoBE; CTC; EnLi-2; EnLit; EPN; FaFP; GTBS; GTBS-W; GTSE; GTSL; HBV; LiTB; LiTG; LiTL; MaRV; MemP; MeWo; OBEV; OBNC; OBVV; PG; PoPo; PoToHe (new ed.); Sonn; TOP; TreFS; TrGrPo; ViBoPo; ViPo; WHA; YAT
If Thou, O God, the Christ didst leave. Prayer of a Modern Thomas. Edward Shillito. ChIP; MaRV; PGD
If thou of fortune be bereft. Not by Bread Alone. *Unknown.* OQP; PoLF; TreFT
If thou seekest the dread throne of God on earth. On Our Lady of Blachernae. *Unknown.* ISi
If thou serve a lord of prise. A Warning to Those Who Serve Lords. *Unknown.* MeEL
If thou shouldst bid thy friend farewell. Counsel. Mollie E. Moore. HBV
If thou shouldst ever come by choice or chance. Ginevra. Samuel Rogers. *Fr.* Italy. BeLS; PoLF
If thou survive my well-contented day. Sonnets, XXXII. Shakespeare. BEL; BoLiVe; CBEP; ElL; EnL; EnLit; GTBS; GTBS-D; GTBS-P; GTBS-W; GTSE; GTSL; HBV; LiTL; ML; OBSC; PP; SiCE; TOP
If Thou Wert by My Side, My Love. Reginald Heber. HBV
If thou wert lying cold and still and white. Reconciliation. Caroline Atherton Briggs Mason. AA
If thou wilt come and dwell with me at home. Daphnis to Ganymede. Richard Barnfield. *Fr.* The Affectionate Shepherd. ElL; ThWaDe
If Thou Wilt Ease Thine Heart. Thomas Lovell Beddoes. *See* Dirge: "If thou wilt ease thine heart."
If Thou Wilt Mighty Be. Sir Thomas Wyatt. EnRePo; NoP
("If thou wilt mighty be, flee from the rage.") FCP; SiPS
(He Ruleth Not though He Reign over Realms That Is Subject to His Own Lust.) ReIE; SiCE
If thou wouldst have me speak, Lord, give me speech. The Preacher's Prayer. George Macdonald. MaRV; SoP; TRV
If Thou Wouldst Know. Hayyim Nahman Bialik, *tr. fr. Hebrew by* Harry H. Fein. TrJP
If thou wouldst learne, not knowing how, to pray. A Forme of Prayer. Francis Quarles. MePo
If thou wouldst roses scent. Francis Daniel Pastorius. SCAP
If thou would'st stand on Etna's burning brow. Our Traveller. Henry Cholmondeley-Pennell. BOHV; InMe
If thou would'st view fair Melrose aright. Melrose Abbey [*or* Sir William of Deloraine at the Wizard's Tomb]. Sir Walter Scott. *Fr.* The Lay of the Last Minstrel. OBNC; OBRV; SeCePo
If thoughts had wings. A Little Valentine. Elizabeth Winton. PCH
If through my perjured lips Thy voice may speak. A Prayer for a Preacher. Edward Shillito. TrPWD
If thus we needs must go. The Heart. Michael Drayton. SeEP
If thy mistress be too coy. *Unknown.* SeCSL
If thy sad heart, pining for human love. To Edgar Allan Poe. Sarah Helen Whitman. *Fr.* Sonnets from the Series Relating to Edgar Allan Poe. AA
If thy soul check thee that I come so near. Sonnets, CXXXVI. Shakespeare. MaPo (1969 ed.)
If tired of trees I seek again mankind. The Vantage Point. Robert Frost. CoBMV; MAmP; MaPo; OxBA
If to be absent were to be. To Lucasta, [on] Going beyond the Seas. Richard Lovelace. AnAnS-2; AtBAP; FaBoEn; GTBS; GTBS-D; GTBS-P; GTBS-W; GTSE; GTSL; HBV; ILP; LiTB; LITG; LiTL; LO; LoBV; MeLP; OAEP; OBEV; OBS; ReEn; SCEP-2; SeCL; SeCP; SeCV-1; SeEP; TreFT; ViBoPo
If to demands of others I agree. Resolving Doubts. William Dickey. ErPo

If to Die. Myrtle Romilu. BLRP
If to feel, in the ink of the slough. Robert Louis Stevenson. *Fr.* If This Were Faith. PoFr
If to grow old in Heaven is to grow young. True Woman, 3. Dante Gabriel Rossetti. The House of Life, LVIII. EPN; MaVP; PoVP; ViPo; VP
If to your twilight land of dream. In Memoriam—Leo, a Yellow Cat. Margaret Sherwood. BLPA; CIV; NeHB
If 'Trane had only seen. Doughtry Long, Jr. TNV
If transmigration e'er compel. In Praise of Gilbert White. William John Courthope. *Fr.* The Paradise of Birds. VA
If trombone music be the food of love. Miss Multitude at the Trombone. J. B. Morton. MuSP
If truth in hearts that perish. A. E. Housman. A Shropshire Lad, XXXIII. PoVP
If valour's noblest part is to die well. On Those Who Fell at Plataea. Simonides, *tr. by* Walter Leaf. PoFr
If virtue be thy guide. To the Christian Reader. Robert Southwell. SiCE
If waker care, if sudden pale color. Sir Thomas Wyatt. FCP
If wandering in a wizard's car. To Helen. Winthrop Mackworth Praed. HBV
If War Be Kind. Stephen Crane. *See* War Is Kind, I.
If War Is Right. Alice Corbin. OQP
If we are marked to die, we are enow. King Henry before the Field of Saint Crispian. Shakespeare. King Henry V, *fr.* IV, iii. BBV (1951 ed.)
If We Believed in God. Jessie Wiseman Gibbs. BLRP
If We Break Faith. Joseph Auslander. TRV
If we but knew what forces helped to mold. Plea for Tolerance. Margaret E. Bruner. PoToHe (new ed.)
If we could get the hang of it entirely. Entirely. Louis MacNeice. CMoP; LiTB; MoPW
If we could hear the voice of Lincoln saying. The Deaf. L. Lamprey. *Fr.* Days of the Leaders, 1925. BBV (1951 ed.)
If We Could Only Be! Lee Shippey. PEDC
If we could plunge to the depths of truth. Our Guiding Light. S. F. Logsdon. SoP
If we could push ajar the gates of life. God's Plans. May Riley Smith. BLRP; MaRV
If we could see below. The Foil. George Herbert. MaMe
If we could see beyond today. Beyond Today. *Unknown.* SoP
If We Didn't Have to Eat. Nixon Waterman. BOHV
"Life would be an easy matter," *sel.* FiBHP
If we dreamed that we loved Her aforetime. To San Francisco. S. J. Alexander. PAH
If we gave unto the living as we lavish on the dead. Give to the Living. Ida Goldsmith Morris. WBLP
If we give love and sympathy. The Human Touch, 2. Helen King. PoToHe
If we go walking on the streets. Angleworm. Herbert Cahoon. SiTL
If we had lived on that long-gone day. Crucifixion. Mrs. Roy L. Peifer. STF
If we have never sought, we seek Thee now. *See* If we never sought. .
If we have not learned that God's in man. For Us. Charlotte Perkins Gilman. OQP
If We Knew. May Riley Smith. BLPA
If We Knew ("If we knew the cares and crosses"). *Unknown.* MaRV
If we knew the woe and heartache. If We Knew. May Riley Smith. BLPA
If We Must Die. Claude McKay. AmNP; AmPP (5th ed.); BALP; BANP; BP; FaBV; IDB; Kal; MAP; NoP; PoNe; TTY; WOW
If we never [*or* have never] sought, we seek Thee now. Jesus of the Scars. Edward Shillito. ChIP; MaRV; OQP
If we, O Dorset, quit the city throng. The First Pastoral. Ambrose Philips. *Fr.* Pastorals. EiCL
If we raced a century over hills. Blackfeet, Blood and Piegan Hunters. James Welch. YAP
If we say it here. Responsive Reading. Pearl Cleage. WSL
If we shadows have offended. Shakespeare. *Fr.* A Midsummer Night's Dream, V, ii. OBSC
If we shall live, we live. Meeting. Christina Rossetti. LO
If we should find unfinished, incomplete. Fulfillment. Charlotte Newton. OQP
If we square a lump of pemmican. Scientific Proof. J. W. Foley. BOHV
If we, the proximate damned, presumptive blest. To Franz Kafka. Edwin Muir. BoPe
If we with earnest effort could succeed. This Were to Pray. Richard Chenevix Trench. MaRV
If what heals can bless. Come Green Again. Winfield Townley Scott. PoPl
If what I find I do not love. Resignation. Santob de Carrion. TrJP
If what we fought for seems not worth the fighting. Lines for the Hour. Hamilton Fish Armstrong. HBMV; MaRV; MC
If wheels bar up the road, where streets are crossed. Of Crossing the Streets. John Gay. *Fr.* Trivia. EnLi-1 (1949 ed.)
If When I Die. *At. to* William Fowler. ElL
If, when I kneel to pray. Prayer. Charles Francis Richardson. AA; SoP
If when my wife is sleeping. Danse Russe. William Carlos Williams. ForPo; NoP
If when the sun at noon[e] display[e]s. A Beautifull Mistress [*or* Song]. Thomas Carew. EG; OBS; SeEP
If when the wind blows. Daniel Webster's Horses. Elizabeth J. Coatsworth. AmFN; AnNE; FiSC; MAP; MoAmPo; PoMS
If wind or wave swept all away. Sustainment. *Unknown.* SoP
If wine and music [*or* musick] have the power. A Song. Matthew Prior. ATP (1935 ed.); CEP; LoBV
If wisdom, as it seems it is. J. V. Cunningham. QFR
If wisdom's height is only disenchantment. A Word to the Wise. Caroline Duer. AA
If wishes were horses, beggars would ride. Mother Goose. BoChLi; FaBoBe; HBV; OTPC; OxNR; PPL; SiTL
If wit so much from ign'rance undergo. Pope. *Fr.* An Essay on Criticism. YAT
If with complaint the pain might be expressed. Sir Thomas Wyatt. FCP; SiPS
If with exultant tread. Francis Thompson. *Fr.* Ode to the Setting Sun. OHIP
If with light head erect I sing. Inspiration. Henry David Thoreau. AA; AmPP; AnAmPo; AnFE; AnNE; APA; CoAnAm; FaBoBe; HBV; WGRP
If with my sleeve I hide the faint color of the dawning sun. Four Folk-Songs in Hokku Form, 4. *Unknown.* LiTW
If with old love of you, dear hills! I share. Composed at Rydal on May Morning, 1838. Wordsworth. PeER
If with pleasure you are viewing any work a man is doing. Do It Now. Berton Braley. BLPA; FaFP; WBLP
If Women Could Be Fair. Edward de Vere, Earl of Oxford. CoBE; ElL; OAEP; ReEn; TuPP
(If Women Would Be Fair.) LiTL
(Renunciation, A.) GTBS; GTBS-D; GTBS-P; GTBS-W; GTSE; HBV
If ye fear to be affrighted. A Charm. Robert Herrick. ChTr
If ye fear to be benighted. Another Charm. Robert Herrick. OTPC (1923 ed.)
If ye will with Mab find grace. The Fairies. Robert Herrick. FaPON; MPB; OBS; OTPC (1946 ed.); SeEP
If yet I have not all thy love. Lovers' [*or* Love's] Infiniteness[e]. John Donne. AnAnS-1; ElL; EnLi-1 (1949 ed.); FaBoEn; FosPo; GTBS-W; LiTB; LiTG; LiTL; MaMe; MaPo; MBW-1; MeLP; MeP; OBS; PoE; PoEL-2; SCEP-1; SeCP; SeCV-1; SeEP; TuPP
If yet there be a few that take delight. Prologue. Dryden. *Fr.* The Loyal General (*by* Nahum Tate). CEP; SeCV-2
If yet thine eyes (great Henry) may endure. The Epistle of Rosamond to King Henry the Second. Michael Drayton. AnAnS-2
If yo' brother done you wrong. You Fight On. *Unknown.* AS
If You. Robert Creeley. CBV; NeAP
If you a wrinkle on the sea have seene. *Unknown.* SeCSL
If you and your folks like me and my folks. *Unknown.* SiTL
If you are a gentleman. *Unknown.* OxNR; SiTL
If you are a little girl. It's a Fib. "Elspeth." ALV
If you are bound to till a soil where farms. A Letter from the Country. Howard Baker. TwAmPo
If You Are Fire. Isaac Rosenberg. ChMP
If you are merry sing away. Mirth. Christopher Smart. *Fr.* Hymns for the Amusement of Children. EiCP
If you are on the Gloomy Line. Get a Transfer. *Unknown.* BLPA; WBLP

If you are still alive when you read this. Goodbye. William Knott. YAP
If you are tempted to reveal. Three Gates. Beth Day, *after the Arabian.* BLPA; MaRV; NeHB; OQP; PoToHe; TreFS
If you ask for the cause of our national flaws. Eureka! Alfred Denis Godley. CenHV
If you ask me whence the story. Goosey Goosey Gander—by Various Authors (Longfellow's Version). William Percy French. CenHV
If You Be a Nun. Leigh Hunt. *See* Nun, The.
If you be that May Margaret. May Margaret. Théophile Marzials. HBV; VA
If you become [*or* be] a nun, dear. The Nun. Leigh Hunt. ALV; BOHV; HBV; InMe; OBRV; OBVV; PG (1945 ed.)
If You Believe. Phyllis C. Michael. SoP
If You But Knew. *Unknown.* BLPA; FaBoBe; NeHB
If you can finde a hart sweet love to kill. *Unknown.* SeCSL
If you can fry flour fritters. Flour Fritters. *Tr. by* Isaac Taylor Headland. PCH
If you can keep your head when all about you. If. Kipling. BBV (1951 ed.); BLPA; EnLit; FaBoBe; FaFP; FaPL; GoTP; HBV; HBVY; LiTM; MaRV; NeHB; OHFP; OTD; OtMeF; OTPC (1946 ed.); PaPo; PoMa; PTK; TIHL; TreF; TSW; WBLP; WePo
If you can live as youth today is living. Another If. *Unknown.* SoP
If you can make life brighter. Humble Service. Lillian G. Heard. STF
If you cannot on the ocean. Your Mission [*or* Your Field of Labor]. Ellen M. Huntington Gates. BLPA; BLRP; NeHB; SoP; TreFT
If you cannot speak like angels. Something You Can Do. *Unknown.* STF
If you can't be a pine on the top of the hill. Be the Best of Whatever You Are. Douglas Malloch. BLPA; SoP; YAD
If You Can't Eat You Got To. E. E. Cummings. CMoP
If You Come Back. Jack Cope. PeSA
If you come my way that is. Poem from Llanybri. Lynette Roberts. NeBP
If you could bring her glories back! Babylon. Ralph Hodgson. BrPo; HBMV
If you could creep out on a summer's night. A Midnight Performance. Helen Wing. GFA
If you could crowd them into forty lines! Limitations. Siegfried Sassoon. MoBrPo
If you could lie upon this berth, this berth whereon I lie. Through a Porthole. Leon Gellert. BoAu
If you could look into my heart. For a Valentine. Mary Elizabeth Newell. PCH
If you could see, fair brother, how dead beat. Prolonged Sonnet: When the Troops Were Returning from Milan [*or* Troops Returning from Milan]. Niccolo degli Albizzi. AWP; OnPM; WaaP
If you could tell me this sense of digression. Gauge.. Peter Schjeldahl. YAP
If you do love, as well as I. The Thought. Lord Herbert of Cherbury. AnAnS-2; InvP; LoBV (2d ed.); SeCL; SeEP
"If you do love me weel, Willie." Fair Janet (B *vers.*). *Unknown.* ESPB
If you don't know the kind of person I am. A Ritual to Read to Each Other. William Stafford. NePA
If you don't like my apples. Nursery Rhymes. *Unknown.* OxBoLi
If you don't quit monkeying with my Lulu. Lulu. *Unknown.* ABF; CoSo
If you evah go to Houston. The Midnight Special. *Unknown.* AS
If you ever, ever, ever meet a grizzly bear. Grizzly Bear. Mary Austin. FaPON; GoJo; PDV; SoPo; TiPo
If you ever get there. Going. Robert Kelly. CoPo
If you feel for it pressing back the glossy leaves. Orange Tree by Night. Sacheverell Sitwell. *Fr.* The Red-gold Rain. AtBAP
If you find a paddling pool. The Paddling Pool. E. M. Adams. BoTP
If you for orders, and a gown design. John Oldham. *Fr.* A Satyr Address'd to a Friend That Is About to Leave the University, and Come Abroad in the World. OBS
If you from spoyle of th'old worlds farthest end. Cales and Guyana. John Donne. MaMe
If you give me your attention, I will tell you what I am. The Disagreeable Man. W. S. Gilbert. *Fr.* Princess Ida. ALV; FiBHP; MPB; PoVP
If you go a-picnicking and throw your scraps about. Picnics. *Unknown.* BoTP
If you go down the garden path. The Garden Path. Charlotte Druitt Cole. GFA
If you go over desert and mountain. The Fountain of Tears. Arthur O'Shaughnessy. OBEV (1st ed.); OBVV; PoVP
If You Had a Friend. Robert Lewis. PoToHe (new ed.)
If you had asked of me. The Idol. Louise Driscoll. HBMV
If you had lived in that more stately time. Sonnets to Miranda, II. Sir William Watson. HBV
If you have a friend worth loving. Say It Now [*or* Seeds of Kindness]. *Unknown.* BLPA; FaFP; PoToHe; WBLP
If you have a kind word, say it. Be Kind Now. *Unknown.* SoP
If you have a tender message. Before It Is Too Late. Frank Herbert Sweet. PoToHe (new ed.)
If you have a thing to do. Do It Right. Samuel O. Buckner. WBLP
If you have a word of cheer. Tell Him So. James Arthur Edgerton. MaRV
If you have climbed a laden apple tree. Afternoon in a Tree. Sister Maris Stella. GoBC
If you have ever, like me. Please Excuse Typing. J. B. Boothroyd. FiBHP; SiTL
If you have forgotten water-lilies floating. Water-Lilies. Sara Teasdale. MAP; MoAmPo; NeMA
If you have formed a circle to go into. To God. Blake. CBV
If you have gone a little way ahead of me, call back. Call Back. *Unknown.* SoP
If you have heard a kind word spoken. Tell Him So. *Unknown.* BLPA; WBLP
If you have lost the radio beam. Any Man's Advice to His Son. Kenneth Fearing. CMoP
If You Have Made Gentler the Churlish World. Max Ehrmann. OQP
(If You Made Gentler the Churlish World.) PoToHe (new ed.)
If You Have Nothing. Jessica Powers. JKCP (1955 ed.)
If you have revisited the town, thin Shade. To a Shade. W. B. Yeats. LiTB; PoE; PoEL-5
If you have passed a dangerous place. Warn Someone. *Unknown.* SoP
If You Have Seen. Thomas Moore. BOHV
(Nonsense.) InMe; NA
If you have spoken something beautiful. If You Have Made Gentler the Churlish World. Max Ehrmann. OQP; PoToHe (new ed.)
If you have tears, prepare to shed them now. Shakespeare. *Fr.* Julius Caesar, III, ii. MemP
If you haven't any ideas. Deny Yourself. Christopher Morley. LHV; YaD
If you hear a kind word spoken. Tell Him So. *Unknown.* BLPA; WBLP
If You Keep Faith with Me. John Edward Spear. JKCP (1955 ed.)
If you listen, I'll sing you a sweet little song. My Wild Irish Rose. Chauncey Olcott. TreFT
If you love God, take your mirror between your hands and look. Song. Mahmud Djellaladin Pasha. ErPo; LiTW
If You Love Me. Samuel Hoffenstein. ALV
("If you love me, as I love you.") FiBHP
If you loved me ever so little. Satia Te Sanguine. Swinburne. PeVV
If You Love Them, Wouldn't You Like to See Them Better Off? Kuwasi Balagon. BF
If You Made Gentler the Churlish World. Max Ehrmann. *See* If You Have Made Gentler the Churlish World.
If you miss me on the picket line. *Unknown.* *Fr.* Back of the Bus. WOW
If you must draw mere beauty. Design for a Stream-lined Sunrise. Sister Mary Madeleva. GoBC; JKCP (1955 ed.)
If you never came with a pigeon rainbow purple. Sumach and Birds. Carl Sandburg. YT
If you never do anything for anyone else. The Immoral Proposition. Robert Creeley. LiTM (1970 ed.); NeAP; ToPo
If You Never Talked with Fairies. Elsie Melchert Fowler. BiCB

If you press a stone with your finger. Natural Law. Babette Deutsch. MoLP
If you promise me a rose. Promise Me a Rose. Bob Merrill. BoLP
If You See a Fairy Ring. *Unknown.* BoTP
If you see a package. Secrets. Elsie Melchert Fowler. BiCB; ChBR
If you see a tall fellow ahead of the crowd. Forget It. Judd Mortimer Lewis. PoLF; WBLP
If you shortened many a road and put a halo. Raftery's Dialogue with the Whiskey. Padraic Fallon. DTC
If you should bid me make a choice. The Windmill. E. V. Lucas. BoTP
If you should go before me, dear, walk slowly. Walk Slowly. Adelaide Love. BLPA
If You Should Lightly. Trumbull Stickney. NCEP
If you should look for this place after a handful of lifetimes. Tor House. Robinson Jeffers. AnAmPo; LoBV
If You Should Meet a Crocodile. *Unknown.* PDV; SoPo
If you should rise from Nowhere up to Somewhere. The Fear of God. Robert Frost. MoRP
If you should see a man. The Truth [*or* Voice in the Crowd]. Ted Joans. BOLo; Kal; TTY
If You Should Tire of Loving Me. Margaret Widdemer. HBMV
If you sit down at set of sun. Count That Day Lost [*or* At Set of Sun]. "George Eliot." MaRV; NeHB; OQP; OTD; PoPl; PoToHe (new ed.); TreFT; TRV
If you sneeze on [*or* Sneeze on a] Monday, you sneeze for danger. Mother Goose. EvOK; HBV; HBVY; PPL; RIS; StaSt; TreF
If you spin me around until I'm so dizzy. Six of Cups. Diane Wakoski. CoPo
If You Stick a Stock of Liquor. Newman Levy. ALV
If you strike a thorn or rose. Keep a-Goin'. Frank L. Stanton. FaFP; OHFP; WBLP
If you take the moon in your hands. The Moon in Your Hands. Hilda Doolittle ("H. D."). NYBP
If you, that have grown old, were the first dead. The New Faces. W. B. Yeats. GTBS-P; MoVE
If you think you are beaten, you are. Thinking [*or* The Man Who Thinks He Can]. Walter D. Wintle. PoLF; WBLP
If You Trap the Moment. Blake. DiPo; ERoP-1
If you wake at midnight, and hear a horse's feet. A Smuggler's Song. Kipling. *Fr.* Puck of Pook's Hill. ShBV-1
If you walk out in bus'ness ne'er so great. The Streets of London. John Oldham. *Fr.* A Satyr in Imitation of the Third of Juvenal. PeRV
If you walk slowly, out of breath, and think. Enchantment. Tony Towle. YAP
If you wander far enough. Oh No. Robert Creeley. AmPC; NaP
If you want a great revival. Pray, Christian, Pray! *Unknown.* STF
If you want to drive wrinkles from belly and brow. Eating Song. Sir Walter Raleigh. WhC
If you want to get a favor done. The Busy Man. *Unknown.* SoP
If You Want to Go a-Courting, *with music.* *Unknown.* TrAS
If you want to go to heaven. The Blood-strained Banders. *Unknown.* OuSiCo
If you want to have the kind of a church. It Isn't the Church—It's You. *Unknown.* BLPA; WBLP
If You Want to Know Where the Privates Are. *Unknown.* ABF
(Where They Were, *sl. diff.*) AS
If you want to live in the kind of a town. It Isn't the Town, It's You. R. W. Glover. BLPA
If you want to work in the kind of a church. It's You. L. A. McDonald. STF
If you wants to hear ol' Rattler moan. Ol' Rattler. *Unknown.* ABF
If you were an Eskimo baby. An Eskimo Baby. Lucy Diamond. BoTP
If you were busy being kind. How to Forget [*or* if]. Rebecca Foresman. PoToHe (new ed); WBLP
If you were coming in the fall. Emily Dickinson. AmePo; *AmPP (4th ed.); AnAmPo; AP; DiPo; FaPL; LaNeLa; MaPo (1969 ed.); OxBA; PoRA*
If you were going to get a pet. If You. Robert Creeley. CBV; *NeAP*
If you were gone afar. To Rosemary. Stephen Vincent Benet. LaNeLa
If You Were Here. Philip Bourke Marston. HBV; VA
If you were queen of bloaters. A Catch. Tom Hood. CenHV
If you were twenty-seven. Heaven. Philip Levine. NaP
"If you will answer these questions for me." The Devil's Nine Questions. *Unknown.* BFSS
If you will come on such a day. The Gardener. Sidney Keyes. ChMP; MoAB; MoBrPo (1962 ed.)
If you will listen a while I will sing you a song. *See* If you'll listen awhile. .
If you will love know such to be. *Unknown.* SeCSL
If you will tell me why the fen. I May, I Might, I Must. Marianne Moore. ELU; PoPo; RePo
If you wish to grow a lily. The Geranium. Leonard Feeney. TIHL
If you would happy company win. Titmouse. Walter de la Mare. BrPo
If you would have a good hound. The Perfect Greyhound. *Unknown.* PCH
If you would have dark themes and high flown words. Insights. Catherine Davis. NePoEA
If you would know the love which I you bear. Sir John Davies. *Fr.* Sonnets to Philomel. SiPS
If you would see him. The Eagle. James Daly. AnAmPo
If you your lips would keep from slips. Our Lips and Ears. *Unknown.* BLPA; NeHB; StaSt; TreF; WBLP
If you'd have me go on loving you. Ezra Pound. *Fr.* Impressions of François-Marie Arouet (de Voltaire). MoAB
If you'd rather not to kiss then say so then. Rebuff. Samuel L. Albert. NePoAm-2
If you'll come gather round me, I'll sing you a song. Lone Driftin' Riders. *Unknown.* CoSo
If you'll [*or* you will] listen awhile I will sing you a song. Jim Fisk. *Unknown.* AS; ViBoFo
If you'll listen awhile I'll sing you a song. The Road to Cook's Peak. *Unknown.* CoSo
If your brother has a burden. A Helping Hand. Georgia B. Adams. STF
If your friend has got a heart. Your Friend. *Unknown.* TreFT
If your miraculous DDT. Natural Selection. David Brock. TwCaPo
If your nerve, deny you. Emily Dickinson. MWA-2
If your nose is close to the grindstone rough. A Timely Warning. *Unknown.* PoMa
If you're anxious for to shine in the high aesthetic line as a man of culture rare. Bunthorne's Song [*or* The Aesthete]. W. S. Gilbert. *Fr.* Patience. ALV; EnLi-2; FiBHP; LiTB; NBM; PoVP; SiTL; VaPo
If You're Ever Going to Love Me. *Unknown.* BLPA; NeHB
If you're in London, Will'um, then I take it you're en route. To William Allen White. Edna Ferber. InMe
If you're longing for fun or enjoyment. Duffy's Hotel. *Unknown.* ShS
If You're the Man You Ought to Be. Walter E. Isenhour. STF
If you're told to do a thing. Obedience. Phoebe Cary. PCH
If you're Volunteer Artist or Athlete, or if you defend the Home. "Form Fours." Frank Sidgwick. WhC
If you're waking call me early, call me early, mother dear. New Year's Eve. Tennyson. *Fr.* The May Queen. OTPC (1923 ed.)
If you've ever been in a car. Stun. James Schuyler. ANYP
If you've got a job to do. Do It Now! *Unknown.* BLPA; FaFP; WBLP
If You've Never. Elsie M. Fowler. GFA; SoPo
If you've tried and have not won. Don't Give Up. Phoebe Cary. PCH
I'faith, sweetheart, methinks now you are in an excellent good temporality. Shakespeare. King Henry IV, Pt. II, *fr.* II, iv. MyFE
Ignorance. John Masefield. BEL
Ignorance of Death. William Empson. CMoP; CoBMV; LiTM (rev. ed.); ReMP; ToPo
Ignorance of Man, The. James Merrick. OxBoCh
Ignorant present has scribbled over the past, The. Louis Dudek. *Fr.* Europe. PeCV
Ignorant two, we glide. On Minding One's Own Business. James Wright. PoPl

Ignore dull days; forget the showers. Proverbs: Lesson from a Sun-Dial. *Unknown.* RIS; TiPo
Ignu. Allen Ginsberg. NaP
Igor's Escape. *Unknown, tr. fr. Russian by* Vladimir Nabokov. *Fr.* The Song of Igor's Campaign. FOL
Igstrawnary tail I vill tell you this veek, An. A Wofle New Ballad of Jane Roney and Mary Brown. Thackeray. BOHV
Iguanas. David Atamian. NYTB
Ike Walton's Prayer. James Whitcomb Riley. AA
"Il Est Cocu—le Chef de Gare!" H. S. Mackintosh. WhC
Il était un' bergère. *Unknown, tr. fr. French.* CIV
Il Fior degli Eroice Furori. John Addington Symonds. VA
I'l gaze no more on her bewitching face. Murdering Beauty. Thomas Carew. OAEP
Il Insonio Insonnado, *sel.* Nathaniel Whiting.
Office of Poetry, The. OBS
Il Pastor Fido, *sels.* Sir Richard Fanshawe, *after the Italian of* Giovanni Battista Guarini.
Fall, The. *After the Spanish of* Luis de Góngora. MePo; OBS
Hope. OBS
"How I forsook." AWP
Now War Is All the World About. LoBV
(Ode, An, upon Occasion of His Majesties Proclamation in the Year 1630, Commanding the Gentry to Reside upon Their Estates in the Countrey.) MePo; OBS
Of Time. SeCL
(Of Beauty.) InMe
Rose, A. *After the Spanish of* Luis de Góngora. CavP; HBV; OBEV; OBS; PoEL-2; SeCePo; SeCL; SeEP
(Rose of Life, The.) AWP
Il Penseroso. Milton. AWP; BoLiVe; CABA; CBEP; CEP; EiCP; EnL; EnLi-1; EnLit; FiP; GTBS; GTBS-D; GTBS-P; GTBS-W; GTSE; GTSL; HBV; HoPM; ILP; InPo; LiTB; LiTG; MaPo; MasP; MBW-1; MyFE; NoP; OBEV; OBS; OuHeWo; Po; PoE; SeCeV; ShBV-3; TOP; TrGrPo; UnPo (1st ed.); ViBoPo; WHA
"Sweet bird that shunn'st the noise of folly," *sel.* CH
Il pleut doucement sur la ville. Paul Verlaine, *tr. fr. French by* Ernest Dowson. AWP; BrPo; JAWP; PG (1945 ed.); WBP
(Tears and Rain.) OnPM
(Tears Fall within Mine Heart.) EnLi-2; SyP
("Tears in my heart that weeps," *tr. by* Arthur Symons.) SyP
Ile gaze no more on her betwitching face. Song: Murdring Beautie. Thomas Carew. AnAnS-2; SeCP
Ile give thee leave my love, in beauties field. Sonnet. Earl of Stirling. Aurora, XXVI. OxBS
I'le Sail upon the Dog-Star. Thomas D'Urfey. *See* I'll Sail upon the Dog-Star.
Ile sooth his plots: and strow my hate with smiles. George Chapman. *Fr.* Bussy d'Ambois, IV, ii. PoEL-2
I'le tell you a tale of my love and I. *See* I'll tell you a tale. . .
Ile weare those golden spurres upon my heeles. George Chapman. *Fr.* The Conspiracy of Charles, Duke of Byron, III, i. PoFr
Ilex Tree, The. Agnes Lee. NP
Ilford Rose Book. James Schuyler. ANYP
Iliad, The, *sels.* Homer, *tr. fr. Greek.*
Achilles Shield, *fr.* XVIII, *tr. by* George Chapman. ReEn
("This said, he left her there, and forth did to his bellows go.") TuPP
Achilles Shows Himself in the Battle by the Ships, *fr.* XVIII, *tr. by* Geroge Chapman. OBS
Achilles to Lycaon, *fr.* XXI, *tr. by* Richmond Lattimore. LiTW; WaaP
Death of Hector, The, *fr* XXII, *tr. by* George Chapman. OBS
Lamentations, The, *fr.* XXIV, *tr. by* Sir William Marris. LiTW
"Meanwhile Achilles, plung'd," *fr.* I, *tr. by* the Earl of Derby. PoPl
Nestor's Speech to Achilles and Agamemnon, *fr.* I, *tr. by* George Chapman. ReEn
Night Encampment outside Troy, *fr.* VIII, *tr. by* Tennyson. RoGo
(Trojans outside the Walls, The, *tr. by* George Chapman.) OBS
"Nor had great Hector and his friends the rampire overrun," *fr.* XII, *tr. by* George Chapman. AtBAP
"O that I were as sure to live, immortal, and sustain," *fr.* VIII, *tr. by* George Chapman. AtBAP
"O tyrant, armed with insolence and pride," *fr.* I, *tr. by* William Hyde Appleton. PoFr
Parting of Hector and Andromache, The, *fr.* VI. SeEP, *tr. by* George Chapman; TreFS, *tr. by* Willam B. Smith *and* Walter Miller
"Chief, The, reply'd: This time forbids to rest," *tr. by* Pope. ATP, *abr.*; CEP
Hector and Andromache, *tr. by* Pope. OBEC
Hektor and Andromache, *tr. by* Maurice Hewlett. LiTW
Hektor [*or* Hector] to Andromache. ReEn, *tr. by* George Chapman; WaaP, *tr. by* Richmond Lattimore
"I myself will now go home and see," *tr. by* George Chapman. ReIE
Last Parting of Hector and Andromache, The, *tr. by* Dryden. SeEP
"She with his sight made breathless haste to meet him," *tr. by* George Chapman. ViBoPo
Patroclus' Body Saved, *fr.* XVII, *tr. by* E. R. Dodds. WaaP
Priam and Achilles, *fr.* XXIV. OBEC, *tr. by* Pope; OBS, *shorter sel., tr. by* George Chapman
Pyre of Patroclus, The, *fr.* XXIII, *tr. by* Pope. OBEC
(Preparation of the Pyre for Patroclus, *shorter sel.*) UnPo (1st ed.)
Quarrel, The, *fr.* I, *tr. by* Sir William Marris. WoL
("Achilles' baneful wrath resound, O goddess that impos'd," *shorter sel., tr. by* George Chapman.) ReIE
("O Goddess! sing the wrath of Peleus' son," *tr. by* Bryant.) EnLi-1
Sarpedon's Speech, *fr.* XII, *tr. by* George Chapman. OBS
(Sarpedon to Glaukos, *shorter sel., tr. by* Richmond Lattimore.) WaaP
Thetis and Achilles, *fr.* XVIII, *tr. by* Sir William Marris. LiTW
"When every least commander's will best soldiers had obeyed," *fr.* III, *tr. by* George Chapman. ReEn
Wrath of Achilles, The, *abr., fr.* XIX, *tr. by* Bryant. BBV (1923 ed.)
Iliad. Humbert Wolfe. MoBrPo
Ilicet. Theodosia Garrison. PoLF
Ilicet. Swinburne. MaVP; PoVP
Ilion, Ilion. Tennyson. LoBV
Ill. Bernard Spencer. NeBP
Ill-advised, An/ And foolish thing. Episode of the Cherry Tree. Mildred Weston. PV
I'll be an otter, and I'll let you swim. River-Mates [*or* Otters]. Padraic Colum. AnIV; AWP; JAWP; OA; WBP
I'll Be as True. Thomas Lovell Beddoes. *Fr.* Early Fragments. AtBAP
I'll be the strongest amid you. The Strongest. "Yehoash." TrJP
I'll Be Your Epitaph. Leonora Speyer. HBMV
I'll believe than that you are dead. Then I'll Believe. B. W. Vilakazi. PeSA
I'll build a house of arrogance. Haven. Donald Jeffrey Hayes. AmNP; PoNe
I'll Build My House. Amanda Benjamin Hall. HBMV
Ill busied man! why shouldst thou take such care. My Midnight Meditation. *At. to* Henry King *and to* John King. MePo; OBS; SeCL
I'll buy you a tartan bonnet. *Unknown.* OxNR
I'll call thy frown a headsman, passing grim. To My Lady. George Henry Boker. *Fr.* Sonnets. AA
I'll carry you off. Fragment of an Agon. T. S. Eliot. LiTB
I'll Come to Thee. Robert Herrick. UnTE
Ill days and dolorous nights and years accurst. The Incubus of Time. Clark Ashton Smith. FiSC
I'll do what the raids suggest. A Boy. John Ashbery. NeAP
I'll eat when I'm hungry, I'll drink when I'm dry. Rye Whisky. *Unknown.* ABF; CoSo; GoTP; OxBoLi; SiTL
Ill fares the land, to hastening ills a prey. The Common Man. Goldsmith. *Fr.* The Deserted Village. MaRV; TreFT, 6 *ll.*; TRV
I'll find me a spruce. Christmas Tree. Aileen Fisher. ChBR; PDV
I'll frame, my Heliodora! a garland for thy hair. A Garland for Heliodora [*or* Wreath for Heliodora]. Meleager. AWP; EnLi-1; JAWP; OnPM; OuHeWo; WBP
I'll gallop away to market town. A Ballad of Riding. Marjorie Allen Seiffert. NP
I'll Give My Love a Light and Friendly Kiss. *Unknown.* *See*

I'll (continued)
Je caresserai la belle par amitié.
"I'll give thee [*or* to you] a paper of pins." Paper of Pins. *Unknown.* ABF; BFSS
I'll give you now, both great and small. The Gift. *Unknown.* SAS
I'll go into the bedroom silently and lie down between the bridegroom and the bride. Love Poem on Theme by Whitman. Allen Ginsberg. NaP
I'll go, said I, to the woods and hills. The Apostate. A. E. Coppard. OBMV
I'll Go to Bethlehem. *Unknown, tr. fr. Czecho-Slovakian by* Edward Bliss Reed. ChrBoLe
I'll go to my Love where he lies in the deep. On a Gentleman in a Late Engagement against the Turks, Was Slain and Thrown Overboard, and She Since Mad. *Unknown.* SeCL
I'll go up on the mountain top. Liza Jane [*or* Mountain Top]. *Unknown.* AS
I'll go where You want me to go, dear Lord. Think It Over. *Unknown.* SoP; STF
I'll hold my candle high, and then. High Resolve. *Unknown.* PoToHe
I'll keep a little tavern. Tavern. Edna St. Vincent Millay. GaP; OTPC (1946 ed.)
I'll kick your walls to bits, I'll die scratching a tunnel. Gulliver. Kenneth Slessor. ACV; BoAV
I'll Live in This Poor Rime. Shakespeare. *See* Sonnets, CVII.
Ill Luck. Baudelaire, *tr. fr. French by* Roy Campbell. PoPl
Ill Met by Zenith. Ogden Nash. NYBP
I'll never be a nun, I trow. Nightingale Weather. Andrew Lang. ACV
I'll Never Get Drunk Any More. *Unknown.* OnYI
I'll Never Love Thee More. James Graham, Marquess of Montrose. *See* My Dear and Only Love.
I'll not allow the birchtree. Alun Mabon's Song. John Ceiriog Hughes. WePo
I'll not believe the dullard dark. Rubric. Josephine Preston Peabody. AA
I'll not forget the warm blue night when my bold girl. A Thing Remembered. *Unknown* ErPo
I'll not weep that thou art going to leave me. Stanzas. Emily Brontë. LoBV
Ill Omens. Thomas Moore. PoEL-4
I'll praise my Maker with my breath. God Praised for His Goodness and Truth. Isaac Watts. SoP
I'll range around the shady bowers. Love for Love's Sake. Henry Carey. WaPE
I'll Remember You, Love, in My Prayers. *Unknown.* BLPA; FaBoBe; NeHB
When the Curtains of Night Are Pinned Back, *br. sel., with music.* AS
I'll [*or* I'le] Sail upon the Dog-Star. Thomas D'Urfey. *Fr.* A Fool's Preferment. CBEP; EiCL; FaBoCh; LoGBV; OxBoLi
Ill sat to be with the calm, The. Essentials. Samuel Greenberg. LiTA
I'll sing of heroes, and of kings. Love. Abraham Cowley. AWP; MemP; PG (1945 ed.)
I'll sing you a good old song. The Fine Old English Gentleman. *Unknown.* CH; HBV; OnPP
I'll sing you a new ballad, and I'll warrant if first-rate. The Fine Old English Gentleman; New Version. Charles Dickens. CoMu; FOL
I'll sing you a song/ Nine verses long. *Unknown.* OxNR
I'll sing you a song/ The days are long. *Unknown.* OxNR
I'll sing you a song, it won't take long. The Man That Wouldn't Hoe Corn. *Unknown.* IHA
I'll sing you a song, not very long. His Heart Was True to Poll [*or* True to Poll]. F. C. Burnand. BOHV; HBV
I'll sing you a song of a schooner of fame. The Loss of the *Druid. Unknown.* ShS
I'll sing you a song of peace and love. Whack Fol the Diddle. Peadar Kearney. FiBHP; OnYI
I'll sing you a song of the world and its ways. Six Feet of Earth. *Unknown.* BLPA
I'll sing you a song that has often been sung. Brigham Young. *Unknown.* CoSo
I'll sing you a song, though it may be a sad one. Sioux Indians. *Unknown.* BFSS; CoSo
I'll sing you a true song of Billy the Kid. Billy the Kid. *Unknown.* ABF; CoSo (B *vers.*); FaBoBe; ThLM
I'll sing you twelve O. Green Grow the Rushes O. *Unknown.* OxBoLi; SiTL
I'll sit down again, Steve, with your shy ghost. For Steve. Earle Birney. WaP
I'll stay where You've put me; I will, dear Lord. Where You've Put Me. *Unknown.* SoP
I'll Take You Home Again, Kathleen. Thomas P. Westendorf. TreF
I'll talk no more. Young Africa's Resolve. Dennis Osadebay. ACV
I'll teach my sons. My Sons. Ron Loewinsohn. NeAP
I'll teach thee, lovely Phillis, what love is. Phyllis, XXVI. Thomas Lodge. TuPP
I'll Tell Her. George Granville. SeCL
(Song: "I'll tell her the next time, said I.") SeEP
I'll tell my own daddy. *Unknown.* OxNR
"I'll tell St. Peter that I know." Cowboy Songs. *Unknown.* OuSiCo
I'll Tell Thee Everything I Can. "Lewis Carroll." *See* White Knight's Song, The.
I'll tell thee now (deare love) what thou shalt doe. A Valediction: of the Booke. John Donne. MaMe; SCEP-1
I'll tell you a story/ About Jack a Nory. Mother Goose. HBV; MPB (1956 ed.); OTPC; OxNR; PPL; RIS; SAS; SiTL
I'll tell you a story, a story anon. King John and the Bishop. *Unknown.* ESPB
I'll tell you a story that will thrill you. Pattonio, the Pride of the Plain. *Unknown.* CoSo
I'll [*or* I'le] tell you a tale of my love and I. The Shepherd [*or* Shepheard] and the Milkmaid. *Unknown.* CoMu; UnTE
I'll tell you how the leaves came down. How the Leaves Came Down. "Susan Coolidge." DD; HBV; HBVY; MPB; OTPC; PRWS; TVC
I'll tell you how the sun rose. Emily Dickinson. AmPP (5th ed.); AnNE; AP; BrR; FaBV; GoTP; ILP; LaNeLa; MoShBr; NeHB; PDV; PoEL-5; PRWS; RePo; SiSoSe; StaSt; StVeCh; SUS; ThWaDe; TreFS; YT
I'll tell you of a false hearted knight. The False-hearted Knight. *Unknown.* BaBo
I'll tell you of a fellow. Hardly Think I Will. *Unknown.* ABF
I'll tell you of a sailor now, a tale that can't be beat. The Story of Samuel Jackson. Charles Godfrey Leland. StPo
I'll tell you what I heard that day. Upon the Hill before Centreville. George Henry Boker. PAH
I'll tell you whence the rose did first grow red. William Strode. EG
Ill-tempered Lover, The, *sel.* L. A. MacKay.
I Wish My Tongue Were a Quiver. CaP; OBCV; SiTL
I'll Try. Ann Hawkshaw. *See* Robin Redbreasts, The.
"I'll wager, I'll wager, I'll wager with you." The Broomfield Hill (B *vers.*). *Unknown.* ESPB
I'll wake you and shake you. To the Laggards. Joseph Bovshover. TrJP
I'll Walk the Tightrope. Margaret Danner. BP; Kal
I'll Wear a Shamrock. Mary Carolyn Davies. BrR; SiSoSe; TiPo (1952 ed.); YeAr
Ill Wind, The. Jay Macpherson. MoCV
I'll wish no more thou shouldst love me. The Contented Lover. *Unknown.* SeCL
I'll wreathe my sword in myrtle bough. Patriotic Song. Callistratus. PoFr
I'll write a poem, then sink to dreams. Count William's Escapade. Guillaume de Poitiers. ErPo
I'll write, because I'll give. To Critics. Robert Herrick. PV
Illa iuventus, that is so nise. Fearful Death. *Unknown.* MeEL
Ille Terrarum. Stevenson. OxBS
Illegitimate Things. William Carlos Williams. MoAB; MoAmPo
Illi Morituri. Mary Morison Webster. PeSA
Illic Jacet. A. E. Housman. Last Poems, IV. VP
Illimitable God, The. Robert Browning. *Fr.* A Death in the Desert. MaRV
Illinois. C. H. Chamberlain. PoRL
Illness ("Sad, sad—lean with long illness"). Po Chü-i, *tr. fr. Chinese by* Arthur Waley. MoPW
Illness falls like a cloud upon. Sick Boy. Anne Ridler. NYTB
Ills I sorrow at, The. Any Human to Another. Countee Cullen. MoRP

Ill's the airt o the word the day. Idleset. Thurso Berwick. OxBS
Illuminated Canticle, The. Florence Wilkinson Evans. PFY
Illuminating lamps, ye orbs crystallite. *Unknown. Fr.* Zepheria. ReIE
Illumination for Victories in Mexico. "Grace Greenwood." PAH
Illuminations, *sels.* Arthur Rimbaud, *tr. fr. French.*
Childhood ("I am the saint at prayer on the terrace," *tr. by* Louise Varese). PoPl
Childhood ("This idol with black eyes and yellow hair," *tr. by* T. Sturge Moore). SyP
Illusion. Edmund Gosse. SyP
Illusion. Ján Rak, *tr. fr. Slovak by* Michael Flach. LiTW
Illusion. Ella Wheeler Wilcox. WGRP
Illusion forms before us like a grove. The Triumph of Death. Barbara Howes. MoAmPo (1962 ed.); NePoAm-2
Illusions. Kirk Hall. BF
Illustration, The/ is nothing to you without the application. To a Steam Roller. Marianne Moore. CMoP; MAP; MoAB; MoAmPo; OxBA; PP
Illustrious Ancestors. Denise Levertov. AmPP (5th ed.); ToPo
Illustrious Holland! hard would be his lot. Byron. *Fr.* English Bards and Scotch Reviewers. OBRV
Illustrious monarch of Iberia's soil. Columbus to Ferdinand. Philip Freneau. PAH
Illyrian woodlands, echoing falls. To E. L., on His Travels in Greece. Tennyson. SeCePo
Illyria's hair fell down. The Oracular Portcullis. James Reaney. ErPo; PeCV
I'm a bird that's free. Aretina's Song. Sir Henry Taylor. VA
I'm a blizzard from the Brazos on a tear, hear me hoot. The Bad Man from the Brazos. *Unknown.* CoSo
I'm a broken-hearted gardener, and don't know what to do. The Broken-hearted Gardener. *Unknown.* ChTr
I'm a Decent Boy from Ireland, *with music.* *Unknown.* ShS
I'm a fashionable beau, just turn'd out the newest go. The Dandy O. *Unknown.* CoMu
I'm a gay puncher, fresh from the Pecos Flat. The Pecos Puncher. *Unknown.* CoSo
I'm a gay tra, la, la. Serenade [*or* Swiss Air]. Bret Harte. LBN; NA
I'm a goin' [*or* a gwine] to tell you 'bout de comin' of de Saviour. In Dat Great Gittin' Up Mornin'. Unknown. AA; BoAN-2
I'm a grandchild of the gods. The Complaint of New Amsterdam. Jacob Steendam. PAH
I'm a gwine to tell you bout de comin' ob de Saviour. *See* I'm a goin' to tell you. . .
I'm a hammer. Announcement. James T. Stewart. BF
I'm a happy little thing. *See* I'm a pretty little thing.
I'm a happy miner, I love to sing and dance. The Happy Miner. *Unknown.* CoSo; IHA
I'm a heartbroken raftsman. Jack Haggerty. Dan McGinnis. ViBoFo
I'm a howler from the prairies of the West. The Desperado. *Unknown.* CoSo; TreFS
I'm a lean dog, a keen dog, a wild dog, and lone. Lone Dog. Irene Rutherford McLeod. FaPon; MCCG; MPB; NeMA; PDV; PoMa; SP; StVeCh (1940 ed.); TiPo; UTS
I'm a little butterfly. *Unknown.* OxNR
I'm a little Hindoo. *Unknown.* FaFP; SiTL
I'm a lonely bullwhacker. The Bullwhacker. *Unknown.* ABF; CoSo
I'm a new contradiction; I'm new and I'm old. *See* I'm a strange contradiction. . .
I'm a peddler, I'm a peddler. The Connecticut Peddler. *Unknown.* ABF
I'm a peevish old man with a penny-whistle. Beggar's Serenade. John Heath-Stubbs. ErPo; NeBP
I'm a pig, I'm a seagull. The Animals. Stephen Berg. NaP
I'm a poor lonesome cowboy. Poor Lonesome Cowboy. *Unknown.* ABF; AS
I'm a pretty [*or* happy] little thing. The Field Daisy [*or* The Daisy]. Jane Taylor. BoTP; PCH; PPL
I'm a rambler and a gambler. Rambling Gambler. *Unknown.* CoSo
I'm a rambling wretch of poverty, from Tip'ry town I came. The Son of a Gambolier. *Unknown.* AS
I'm a Round-Town Gent. *Unknown.* GoSl
I'm a rowdy cowboy just off the stormy plains. The Lone Star Trail. *Unknown.* AS
I'm a six foot t'ree from Brooklyn. Situation Normal. Hank Chernick. WhC
I'm a spent arrow shouldered from the sun. The Unknown Warrior Sings and Curses in the Street. Herbert Palmer. FaBoTw
I'm [*or* I am) a strange [*or* new] contradiction; I'm new and I'm old. A Book [*or* A Riddle: A Book]. Hannah More. GN; HH; OTPC; PoRL; PoSC
I'm a strange creature, for I satisfy women. Riddle. *Unknown.* PV
I'm a Stranger Here, *with music.* *Unknown.* OuSiCo
I'm a stranger in your city, my name is Paddy Flynn. Portland County Jail. *Unknown.* AS
I'm a very highly educated man. The Highly Educated Man. *Unknown.* ABF
I'm a young married man that is tired in life. Cod Liver Ile. *Unknown.* OuSiCo
I'm a-goin' down this road feelin' bad. I'm Goin' down This Road Feelin' Bad. *Unknown.* TrAS
I'm always told to hurry up. Going to Bed. Marchette Chute. BoChLi (1950 ed.); PDV
I'm an alley-cat. A Roving Alley-Cat. Mary Cockburn Bomke. CIV
I'm a-Rollin', *with music.* *Unknown.* BoAN-1
I'm as friendly as can be. Chickadee. Marion Mitchell Walker. GFA
I'm as restless as a willow in a windstorm. It Might as Well Be Spring. Oscar Hammerstein II. PO
I'm a-tellin' you the truth and not lying nor joking. Cheyenne. *Unknown.* CoSo
I'm beginning to lose patience. W. H. Auden. PV
I'm Black and Blue. Heine, *tr. fr. German by* John Todhunter. AWP; JAWP; WBP
"I'm bleeding. A boy, they said." Operation. Alfred Alvarez. OPoP
I'm bound away to leave you, good-bye, my love, good-bye. Goodbye, My Love, Goodbye. *Unknown.* SoAmSa
I'm bound to Alabama, Oh, roll the cotton down. Roll the Cotton Down. *Unknown.* SoAmSa
I'm bound to follow the long-horn cows. The Lone Star Trail. *Unknown.* CoSo
"I'm busy!" Too Busy? Ralph S. Cushman. SoP
I'm called by the name of a man. *Unknown.* OxNR
I'm called Little Buttercup. Little Buttercup. W. S. Gilbert. *Fr.* H.M.S. Pinafore. TreFS
I'm Captain Jinks of the Horse Marines. Captain Jinks. *Unknown, at. to* T. Maclagan. BLPA; FaFP; OnPP; TreF
I'm ceded, I've stopped being theirs. Emily Dickinson. ViBoPo
I'm comin' back and haunt you, don't you fret. Ghost. John V. A. Weaver. HBMV
I'm doubtful that he knew how well he taught. Dew-Plants. Ernest G. Moll. NeLNL
I'm down, good Fate, you've won the race. Thrown. Ralph Hodgson. HBMV
I'm dreaming now of Hally [*or* Hallie], sweet Hally, sweet Hally. Listen to the Mocking-Bird. Septimus Winner. TrAS; TreFT
I'm far frae my hame, an' I'm weary aftenwhiles. My Ain Countree. Mary Demarest. HBV; TRV; WGRP
I'm folding up my little dreams. My Little Dreams. Georgia Douglas Johnson. BANP; CDC; GoSl; PoNe
I'm fonder of carats than carrots. I Take 'Em and Like 'Em. Margaret Fishback. PoPl; WhC
I'm full of everything I do not want. Sonnet: Of the 20th June 1291. Cecco Angiolieri da Siena. AWP
I'm giving a party to-morrow at three. My Party. Queenie Scott-Hopper. BoTP
I'm Glad. *Unknown.* GFA; HBVY; OTPC (1946 ed.); WhC
(Cheerfulness.) TreFT
(I'm Glad the Sky Is Painted Blue.) SoPo
I'm glad I am living this morning. God's World. Mildred Keeling. BLRP
I'm Glad My Birthday Comes in May! Ivy O. Eastwick. BiCB
I'm glad our house is a little house. Song for a Little House. Christopher Morley. BoTP; FaPON; MPB; OTD; StVeCh; TreF; TSW
I'm glad that I/ Live near a park. The Park. James S. Tippett. BrR; SUS; TiPo
I'm glad that I am born to die. Burges. *Unknown.* ABF

I'm glad that I am not to-day. Something to Be Thankful For. Clara J. Denton. HH
I'm Glad the Sky Is Painted Blue. *Unknown.* *See* I'm Glad.
I'm glad the stars are over me. Stars. *Unknown.* GFA
I'm goin' away for to stay a little while. He's Gone Away. *Unknown.* AS; TrAS
I'm Goin' down This Road Feelin' Bad, *with music.* *Unknown.* TrAS
I'm goin' out West, down on the Rio Grande. Alice B. *Unknown.* AS
I'm goin' where them chilly winds won't [*or* don'] blow, darlin' baby. Chilly Winds. *Unknown.* OuSiCo; TrAS
I'm going by the upper road, for that. The Upper Road. Christina Rossetti. FaChP
"I'm going down," she said, tying her yellow scarf. Going down the Mountain [*or* Descending]. Valentin Iremonger. EnLoPo; NeIP
I'm going home to stop awhile. Then Hurrah for Home! John A. Stone. SGR
I'm going out! I'm tired of tables, chairs. House-weary. Ian Drag. OQP
I'm going out to clean the pasture spring. The Pasture. Robert Frost. AmLP; AmPP; AnNE; BoC; CMoP; DiPo; FaPON; GoJo; LaNeLa; MAP; MaPo (1969 ed.); MemP; MoAB; MoAmPo; MoShBr; MWA-2; NeMA; OTD; OxBA; PDV; Po; PoPl; PoRh; SoPo; SP; StVeCh; SUS; TiPo; TSW; TwCP; UTS; ViBoPo; WePo
I'm going out to dine at Gray's. Ballade of Hell and of Mrs. Roebeck. Hilaire Belloc. MoVE
I'm going softly all my years in wisdom if in pain. Babylon. Viola Taylor. HBV
I'm going to be a pirate with a bright brass pivot-gun. The Tarry Buccaneer. John Masefield. MCCG
I'm going to be just like you, Ma. A Dance for Ma Rainey. Al Young. NBP
I'm going to leave old Texas now. The Texas Song. *Unknown.* CoSo
I'm going to roll up. Jack's Blues. Robert Creeley. ToPo
"I'm going to school tomorrow, just." Patrick Goes to School. Alicia Aspinwall. MPB
I'm going to try and suit. That's the Way to Talk It. Mart Taylor. SGR
I'm going to write a letter to our oldest boy who went. Father's Letter. Eugene Field. IHA
I'm going to write a novel, hey. An Ode. John Updike. FiBHP
I'm going to write a story. The Nicest Story. Abbie Farwell Brown. HH
I'm go'n' to lay down my sword and shield. Ain' Go'n' to Study War No Mo'. *Unknown.* AS
I'm gonna preach to my diamond, hammer ring. Drive It On. *Unknown.* OuSiCo
I'm gonna take those shoes I bought you. Good-by, Pretty Mama. *Unknown.* ABF
"I'm growing old, I've sixty years." Carcassonne. Gustave Nadaud. BLPA; FaBoBe; HBV; HT; NeHB; PTK
I'm growing very big and tall. Growing Up. Edna Kingsley Wallace. BiCB; MoSiPe
I'm gwine to Alabamy, oh. Gwine to Alabamy. *Unknown.* TrAS
I'm Gwine Up to Heab'n Anyhow, *with music.* *Unknown.* BoAN-2
I'm Happiest When Most Away. Emily Brontë. SeCePo
I'm happy, Kerouac, your madman Allen's. Malest Cornifici Tuo Catullo. Allen Ginsberg. NeAP
"I'm having five minutes," he said. Five Minutes. Norman Nicholson. POTi
I'm Here. Theodore Roethke. *Fr.* Meditations of an Old Woman. CoAP; NYBP
I'm hiding, I'm hiding. Hiding. Dorothy Aldis. BoChLi; FaPON; MPB; SoPo; SUS; TiPo
I'm holdin' down the Boar's Nest, an a-cookin' for myself. Batchin'. S. Omar Barker. IHA
I'm hungry, oh so hungry! The Birds on the School Windowsill. Evelyn Dainty. BoTP
I'm in a 10der mood today. O I C. *Unknown.* SiTL; WhC
I'm in New York covered by a layer of soap foam. How Come? David Ignatow. CAD
I'm jilted, forsaken, outwitted. The Jilted Nymph. Thomas Campbell. BoLP; EnLoPo
I'm just a poor wayfaring stranger. *See* I am a poor wayfaring stranger.
I'm just the grocery store cat. The Grocery Store Cat. Margaret E. Bruner. CIV
I'm just trying to get next to myself. Resurrection. Paula Giddings. WSL
I'm king of the road! I gather. His Majesty. Theron Brown. AA
I'm learning how to dive and swim. Learning to Swim. Anna Medary. GFA
I'm like a skiff on the ocean tost. John Gay. EnLoPo
I'm longing for the forest. Home. Verner von Heidenstam. PoPl
I'm looking at your lofty head/ Away up in the air. Pikes Peak. *Unknown.* PoOW
I'm looking rather seedy now while holding down my claim. Little Old Sod Shanty. *Unknown.* BFSS
I'm lovely as a dream in stone, O mortal! Beauty. Baudelaire. LO
I'm made in sport by Nature. On an Indian Tomineios, the Least of Birds. Thomas Heyrick. PeRV
I'm makin' a road. Florida Road Workers. Langston Hughes. GoSl; MAP; MoAmPo
I'm Married. Eric Torgersen. QAH
I'm mining in a dry ravine. The Sensible Miner. John A. Stone. SGR
I'm night guard all alone tonight. I Want My Time. *Unknown.* SCC
I'm nobody! Who are you? Emily Dickinson. AmePo; AmPP (5th ed.); AnNE; BBV (1951 ed.); CBEP; DiPo; GoTP; MaC; NCEP; NeMA; PDV; PoPl; TiPo (1952 ed.); TreFS; WHA; YaD
I'm Not a Single Man. Thomas Hood. HBV
(Lines in a Young Lady's Album.) ALV
I'm not afraid of rats and mice. The Escape. Emily Rose Burt. GFA
I'm Not Alone. L. E. Dunkin. SoP
I'm not here. Halcyon. Hilda Doolittle ("H. D."). MAP; MoAmPo
I'm now arriv'd the soul desired port. Edmund Davie 1682, Annagram. Benjamin Tompson. SCAP
I'm O'er [*or* Owre] Young to Marry Yet. Burns. EiCL; UnTE; ViBoPo
("I am my mammie's ae bairn.") LO
I'm offering for sale today. A Bargain Sale. S. E. Kiser. PoToHe (new ed.)
"I'm old." Old Botany Bay. Mary Gilmore. PoAu-1
I'm on an Island. Tom Clark. ANYP
I'm only a little sparrow. The Sparrow's Song. *Unknown.* STF
I'm out to find the new, the modern school. The Fledgling Bard and the Poetry Society. George Reginald Margetson. BANP
I'm Owre Young to Marry Yet. Burns. *See* I'm O'er Young to Marry Yet.
I'm persistent as the pink locust. The Pink Locust. William Carlos Williams. PP
I'm picking my mother a present. Dandelions. Marchette Chute. BiCB
I'm pressing on the upward way. Higher Ground. Johnson Oatman, Jr. FaChP
I'm pretty old. Five-in-June. Lysbeth Boyd Borie. BiCB
I'm ready now to cat-chase those porcelain people. Imprecation for an Aesthetic Society with Newts, Warts, Waxes and Pins. Rosalie Moore. OnHM
I'm really a very unfortunate man. The Unfortunate Man. *Unknown.* BFSS
"I'm rich,"/ said/ Irish. Eternities. Norman Mailer. NYBP
I'm ridin' tonight round the dam bed-ground. Up the Trail. *Unknown.* CoSo
I'm Sad and I'm Lonely, *with music.* *Unknown.* AS; TrAS
I'm Sad and Lonely Here, *with music.* John A. Stone. SGR
I'm scared a lonely. Never see my son. Dream Song 40. John Berryman. CoAP
I'm sending you a valentine. Valentine for My Mother. Harry Lee. MPB
I'm seven years old. Middle-aged Child. Inez Hogan. BiCB
I'm Seventeen Come Sunday. *Unknown.* UnTE
I'm shouting. Spring. Karla Kuskin. PDV
I'm sick of fog and yellow gloom. Homesick. Dorothy Frances McCrae. BoAu

I'm sittin' on the stile, Mary. Lament of the Irish Emigrant. Helen Selina Sheridan. HBV; OBEV (1st ed.); OBVV; VA
I'm sitting alone by the fire. Her Letter. Bret Harte. CoBA; HBV; InP; PoLF; YT
I'm sitting here a-thinking. We've Done Our Hitch in Hell. *Unknown.* ABF
I'm sitting in the living room. Sonic Boom. John Updike. TPM
I'm sitting on the grass by the roadside. The Wheel Change. Bertolt Brecht. ELU
I'm Smith of Stoke, aged sixty-odd. Epitaph on a Pessimist. Thomas Hardy. PoIE; VP
I'm so sorry for old Adam. Old Adam. *Unknown.* AS
I'm something I have never been. Something Very Elegant. Aileen Fisher. BiCB
I'm sorry for the old wharves. The Old Wharves. Rachel Field. SoPo
I'm standing in the shade of a tree. Passage Charles Dallery. Ron Padgett. YAP
I'm Standing, Lord. Betty Stam. SoP
I'm such a quiet little ghost. The Superstitious Ghost. Arthur Guiterman. ShM
I'm sure that I like Christmas best. I Like Christmas. James S. Tippett. ChBR
I'm sure that no one ever knows. Underneath the Clothes. Madeleine Nightingale. RIS
I'm sure that Spring is on the way. Signs. Beatrice M. Murphy. GoSl
I'm taught p-l-o-u-g-h. O-U-G-H. Charles B. Loomis. BOHV
"I'm tell j'you what, thees sheeps beezness." The Sheep Beezness. S. Omar Barker. IHA
I'm thankful for the hills from whence comes help from Thee. Thankfulness. Albert Leonard Murray. SoP
I'm Thankful that My Life Doth Not Deceive. Henry David Thoreau. PoEL-4; VaPo
I'm that distinguished twice-born hero. The Death of Digenes Akritas. John Heath-Stubbs. NePoEA
I'm the gardener today. Lawn-Mower. Dorothy Baruch. SoPo; SUS
I'm the king of the castle. *Unknown.* OxNR
I'm the pert little pimpernel. Pimpernel. Charlotte Druitt Cole. BoTP
I'm the Police Cop Man, I Am. Margaret Morrison. SoPo
"I'm the sort of girl." Nausicäa. Irving Layton. ErPo
I'm the sub-average male *Time* reader. The Sub-average *Time* Reader. Ernest Wittenberg. FiBHP
I'm three years old and like to wear. Hair Ribbons. *Unknown.* BiCB
"I'm tired—oh, tired of books," said Jack. The Bookworm. Walter de la Mare. TiPo (1959 ed.)
I'm Tired of Being Scared. John Giorno. ANYP
I'm tired of Love: I'm still more tired of Rhyme. Fatigue. Hilaire Belloc. MoVE; PV; SiTL; TreFT
I'm tired of symbols, of laws divine. To My Generation. Benyamin Galai. TrJP
I'm tired of trying to think. Existentialism. Lloyd Frankenberg. FiBHP
I'm told that certain insect wives. Insect Wives. Rudolph Altrocchi. WhC
I'm too tired to trust and too tired to pray. Sleep. Ella Conrad Cowherd. SoP
Im Traum sah ich ein Männchen klein und putzig. Heine, *tr. fr. German by* Sir Theodore Martin. AWP
I'm travellin' down the Castlereagh, and I'm a station-hand. A Bushman's Song. Andrew Barton Paterson. BoAu; PoAu-1
I'm Troubled in Mind, *with music.* *Unknown.* BoAN-1
I'm up against the wall. The Wall. William Hawkins. MoCV
I'm up and down and round about. As the World Turns. Swift. OTPC (1946 ed.); RIS
I'm very, very glad indeed. The Centipede. Samuel Hopkins Adams. InMe
I'm wearin' [*or* wearing] awa', John [*or* Jean]. The Land o' [*or* of] the Leal. Lady Nairne. GTBS; GTBS-D; GTBS-P; GTBS-W; GTSE; GTSL; HBV; MaRV; MCCG; NA; OBEV; OxBS; WBLP; WGRP
I'm weary o' the rose as o' my brain. The Great Wheel. "Hugh MacDiarmid." OxBS
I'm "wife"; I've finished that. Emily Dickinson. CMoP; ViBoPo
I'm wild and wool[l]y and full of fleas. The Drunken Desperado [*or* Cowboy Boasting Chants]. Baird Boyd. ABF; ChTr; SCC
I'm Wishing the World Christmas. Annette Wynne. MoSiPe
I'm Worried Now but I Won't Be Worried Long, *with music.* *Unknown.* OuSiCo
Image. Henry Dumas. BOLo
Image, The. Roy Fuller. ChMP; GTBS-P; ToPo
Image, The. Richard Hughes. OBMV
Image, The. Sylvia Townsend Warner. BoLiVe (1939 ed.); InP
Image comes down to live as fact, and turns. The Shadowgraphs. Richmond Lattimore. NYBP
Image dance of change, An. Conclusion. Siegfried Sassoon. MoBrPo
Image from D'Orleans. Ezra Pound. FIW; LOW
Image Imagination. Elizabeth Sewell. JKCP (1955 ed.)
Image in a Lilac Tree. Terence Tiller. NeBP
Image in a Mirror. Mae Winkler Goodman. GoYe
Image in the bulb-ringed mirror. Mask. Elizabeth Cox. GoYe
Image in the Forum, The. Robert Buchanan. ChIP
Image-Maker, The. Oliver St. John Gogarty. BoPe; OBEV (new ed.); OBMV; PoRA
Image o' God, The. Joe Corrie. OxBS
Image of Death, The, *sel.* Robert Southwell.
"Gown which I do use to wear, The." ViBoPo
Image of Death, The. Thomas, Lord Vaux. *See* Aged Lover Renounceth Love, The.
Image of Delight, The. William Ellery Leonard. AnFE; APA; CoAnAm; HBMV; MAP; MoAmPo (1942 ed.)
Image of God, The. Francisco Aldana, *tr. fr. Spanish by* Longfellow. CAW; WGRP
Image of God, The. Charles Wesley. SoP
Image of her whom I love, more than she. The Dreame. John Donne. Elegies, X. MaMe; MeP
Image of Lethe, An. The Coming of War; Actaeon. Ezra Pound. CMoP; NP
Image Reach, The. Sun-Ra. BF
Image, The/ the pawnees. The Pride. John Newlove. MoCV
Imageries of dreams reveal a gracious age. The Age of a Dream. Lionel Johnson. OBMV; ViPP
Imagery. Harindranth Chattopadhyaya. ACV
Images. Richard Aldington. MoBrPo; NeMA; NP; TOP
Images. Kathleen Raine. NYBP
Images. Richard Schaukal, *tr. fr. German by* Ludwig Lewisohn. AWP
Images break upon a sad day, The. Gladstone. Julian Symons. WaP
Images of Angels. P. K. Page. MoCV
Images of J—— assail him. The Bus Trip. Joel Oppenheimer. NeAP
Imaginary Correspondence, *parody.* Frank Sidgwick. WhC
Imaginary Elegies, I-IV. Jack Spicer. NeAP
Imaginary Figures of the Virtues. Shirley Bridges. TPM
Imaginary good, or true. On Fame. John Banks. WaPE
Imaginary Iceberg, The. Elizabeth Bishop. LiTM; MoAB; MoAmPo (1950 ed.); MoVE; ReMP
Imagination. John Davidson. *Fr.* New Year's Eve. MoBrPo
Imagination. Shakespeare. *See* Lunatic, the Lover, and the Poet, The.
Imagination. Wordsworth. *Fr.* The Prelude, VI. FiP
Imagination and Taste, How Impaired and Restored. Wordsworth. *See* Prelude, The.
Imagination—here the Power so called. Imagination. Wordsworth. *Fr.* The Prelude. FiP
Imaginative Crisis, The. *Unknown.* BOHV
Imagine a road as straight as a wish. The Road. Hyam Plutzik. FiMAP
Imagine it, a Sophocles complete. The Fire at Alexandria. Theodore Weiss. CoPo; PIA
Imagine that any mind ever *thought* a red geranium! Red Geranium and Godly Mignonette. D. H. Lawrence. GTBS-P
Imagine that July morning: Cape Henry and Virginia. The Tempest. William Jay Smith. MoAmPo (1962 ed.)
Imagine the South. George Woodcock. MoCV; NeBP
Imagine them as they were first conceived. Images of Angels. P. K. Page. MoCV
Imagine what Mrs. Haessler would say. Dance of the Abakweta. Margaret Danner. Far from Africa: Four Poems, 2. AmNP; PoNe (1970 ed.)

Imagine yourself. The Sense of Comedy: I. Jay Wright. ThO
Imagined Happiness. Erik Axel Karlfeldt, *tr. fr. Swedish by* Charles Wharton Stork. LiTW; PoPl
Imagining How It Would Be to Be Dead. Richard Eberhart. FiMAP; LiTA
Imagiste Love Lines. *Unknown.* BOHV
Imbecile, The. Donald Finkel. NePoEA-2
Imitated from the Persian. Robert Southey. *See* Lord, Who Art Merciful.
Imitation. Anthony C. Deane. BOHV
Imitation in the Style of Thomas Gray. Samuel Johnson. *See* Hermit Hoar.
Imitation of Chaucer. Pope. Par
Imitation of Christ. Wilma C. Ludlow. ChIP
Imitation of Christ, *sels.* Thomas à Kempis, *tr. fr. Latin.*
Immunity. ChIP; OQP
Man Proposes. TreF
Of Love of Silence and of Solitude. TreF
Thoughts of Death, The. OuHeWo
Imitation of Faust, The. Alfred Hayes. LiTM (1946 ed.)
Imitation of Robert Browning. James Kenneth Stephen. InMe
(Sincere Flattery of R. B.) Par
Imitation of Spenser, An. John Armstrong. WaPE
Imitation of Spenser. Keats. ATP; EnRP; MBW-2
Morning, *st.* 1. GN
Imitation of Walt Whitman. "Judy." BOHV
Imitation of Wordsworth, An. Hartley Coleridge. *See* On Wordsworth.
Imitation of Wordsworth, An. Catherine Fanshawe. *See* Fragment in Imitation of Wordsworth.
Imitations of Donne, *sel.* Pope.
Fourth Satire of Dr. John Donne, Dean of St. Paul's, Versified, The. MBW-1
Immaculate Conception, The. John Banister Tabb. ISi
Immaculate Palm. Joseph Joel Keith. ISi
Immalee. Christina Rossetti. BoNaP; ThWaDe
Immanence. F. Barrie Flint. OQP
Immanence. Edmond G. A. Holmes. MaRV
Immanence. Richard Hovey. OQP; TRV; WGRP
Immanence. Thomas Durley Landels. MaRV
Immanence. Evelyn Underhill. MaRV; StJW
Immanent God, The. Emerson. *Fr.* Woodnotes, II. MaRV
Immeasurable haze. To the Holy Spirit. Yvor Winters. ForPo; MoAmPo (1962 ed.); MoVE; PoIE; QFR
Immeasurable height, The. Wordsworth. *Fr.* The Prelude. PeER
Immense plain, The. The Ruined City. Pao Chao. FlW
Immense terrestrial ball. The Sustaining Power. Anna-Modine Moran. SoP
Immensitie [*or* Immensity] cloysterd in thy deare wombe. Nativitie. John Donne. AnAnS-1; MaMe; MeP; OBS; Sonn
Immensity of music seizes me like the Sea, The! The Music. Baudelaire. SyP
Immigrant, The. Frank Kendon. MemP; MoBrPo (1942 ed.); POTE
Immigrants. Nancy Byrd Turner. AmFN
Immobile Wind, The. Yvor Winters. NP
Immolated. Herman Melville. ViBoPo
Immolation. Robert Farren. OnYI
Immoral. James Oppenheim. HBV
Immoral Arctic, The. Morris Bishop. FiBHP; WhC
Immoral Proposition, The. Robert Creeley. LiTM (1970 ed.); NeAP; ToPo
Immorality, An. Ezra Pound. CMoP; ForPo; GoJo; HBV; LiTL; LiTM; MAP; MoAB; MoAmPo; NeMA; NePA; PoPl; PoSa; SiTL
Immortal, The. Blake. *Fr.* The Book of Los, *ch.* 2. LiTB; LoBV
Immortal. Richard Church. MoBrPo (1942 ed.)
Immortal. Florence Earle Coates. MaRV
Immortal, The. Marjorie Pickthall. CaP
Immortal. Sara Teasdale. WGRP
Immortal. Mark Van Doren. MAP; MoAmPo
Immortal Aphrodite. Sappho. *See* Ode to Aphrodite.
Immortal Autumn. Archibald MacLeish. AP; BoLiVe (1945 ed.); CMoP; CoBMV; LiTA; MAP; MoAB; MoAmPo; NeMA; NP; ReMP; SiSw; TrGrPo
Immortal bard! for whom each muse has wove. An Epistle to Mr. Pope. George Lyttelton. Po
Immortal Flowers. Wallace Rice. AA
Immortal[l] Heat, O let thy greater flame. Love. George Herbert. MeP; SCEP-1; Sonn
Immortal Helix. Archibald MacLeish. CBV
Immortal Imogen, crowned queen above. The Two Swans. Thomas Hood. CH
Immortal Israel. Judah Halevi, *tr. fr. Hebrew by* Solomon Solis-Cohen. TrJP
Immortal Living. Harold Trowbridge Pulsifer. MaRV
Immortal Love. George Edward Woodberry. *Fr.* Ideal Passion. PoPo
("Immortal love, too high for my possessing.") HBMV
Immortal[l] love, authour of this great frame. Love. George Herbert. AnAnS-1; MaMe; MeP; SCEP-1; SeCV-1; Sonn
Immortal Love, forever full. Our Master. Whittier. BLRP; MaRV; SoP; StJW; TRV; WBLP; WGRP
Immortal love, too high for my possessing. Immortal Love. George Edward Woodberry. Ideal Passion, XL. HBMV; PoPo
Immortal Mind, The. Byron. WGRP
Immortal Morn. Hezekiah Butterworth. PEDC; PoRL
Immortal Nature. Erasmus Darwin. *Fr.* The Economy of Vegetation. OBEC
Immortal Newton Never Spoke. Earl of Chesterfield. InP
(On a Full-Length Portrait of Beau Marsh, *wr.* [Nash], *st.* 1 *by* the Earl of Chesterfield, *st.* 2 *by* Jane Brereton.) BOHV
Immortal Part, The. A. E. Housman. A Shropshire Lad, XLIII. MasP; MoBrPo; Po; PoVP; StP; UnPo (3d ed.)
Immortal Residue, The. Adelaide Crapsey. MaRV; MoAmPo (1942 ed.)
Immortal Spirit, The. Stephen Spender. MoRP
Immortal spirit hath no bars, The. Dawn. Frederick George Scott. CaP; MaRV; PoPl
Immortal Spirit is that single ghost, The. The Immortal Spirit. Stephen Spender. MoRP
Immortal stood frozen amidst, The. The Immortal. Blake. *Fr.* The Book of Los. LiTB; LoBV
Immortal Words. Aline Badger Carter. ChIP
Immortalis. David Morton. HBV
Immortality. "Æ." AnIV; AWP; JAWP; OBMV; VA; WBP; WGRP
Immortality. Addison. *See* Cato.
Immortality. Matthew Arnold. EPN; FiP; MaRV; PoVP
Immortality. Job, XIV: 1-2, 7-12, XIX: 25-27, Bible, *O.T. (Moulton, Modern Reader's Bible).* WGRP
Immortality. Richard Henry Dana. AA; WGRP
Immortality. Emily Dickinson. *See* It is an honourable thought.
Immortality. Samuel Greenberg. LiTA
Immortality. Arthur Sherburne Hardy. AA
Immortality. Frank Horne. BANP
Immortality. Joseph Jefferson. BLPA; NeHB
Immortality. Willis Fletcher Johnson. OQP
Immortality. Milton. *Fr.* Lycidas. MaRV
("Weep no more, woful Shepherds, weep no more.") BoC
Immortality. "Nicolai Maksimovich Minski," *tr. fr. Russian by* Babette Deutsch. TrJP
Immortality. Susan L. Mitchell. OnYI
Immortality. Frederic William Henry Myers. VA
Immortality. Lizette Woodworth Reese. AA; HBMV; HBVY
Immortality. Sir Philip Sidney. *See* Who Hath His Fancy Pleasèd.
Immortality. *Unknown, tr. fr. Greek by* William Hay. OnPM
Immortality. *Unknown.* SoP
Immortality Conferred in Vain. Theognis, *tr. fr. Greek by* J. M. Edmonds. LiTW
Immortality of the Soul, The ("For why should we the busy soul believe"). Sir John Davies. *Fr.* Nosce Teipsum. ViBoPo
Immortality of Verse, The. Pope, *after the Latin of* Horace. AWP; JAWP; WBP
(Poet, The.) CBEP
Immortality she gave, The. Emily Dickinson. BoLiVe
Immortall Heat, O let thy greater flame. *See* Immortal Heat...
Immortall Love, authour of this great frame. *See* Immortal Love, Author of This Great Frame.
Immortals, The. Isaac Rosenberg. FaBoTw; MMA; TrJP
Immortals in Exile. Arthur Davison Ficke. PFY
Immovable, unchanging. Two Songs. Heine. WoL

Immunity. Thomas à Kempis, *tr. fr. Latin. Fr.* Imitation of Christ. ChIP; OQP
Immutabilis. Alice Learned Bunner. *Fr.* Vingtaine. AA
Imogen. Sir Henry Newbolt. HBMV
Imogen—in Wales. Thomas Caulfield Irwin. IrPN
Impact of a Dollar upon the Heart, The. Stephen Crane. NoP
Impar Impares Odit. Henry Parrot. SiCE; TuPP
Impartial Law enrolled a name, The. My Name and I. Robert Graves. NYBP
Impasse. Langston Hughes. LiTM (1970 ed.)
Impassive god with baneful threatening hand. The Clock. Baudelaire. LO
Impatience. Ts'ao Ho, *tr. fr. Chinese by* Henry H. Hart. OnPM
Impatient as we were for all of them to join us. The Bungalows. John Ashbery. CoAP
Impatient Poet, The. D'Arcy Cresswell. AnNZ
Impatient with Desire. George Granville. SeCL
Impatiently she tampered with the locks. Bluebeard's Wife. Daryl Hine. ACV
Impenitent, we meet again. To Philip Levine, on the Day of Atonement. Robert Mezey. AmPC
Impenitentia Ultima. Ernest Dowson. BrPo; HBV
Imperator Augustus. Sir Rennell Rodd. VA
Imperator Victus. Hart Crane. OxBA
Imperceptively the world became haunted by her white dress. The White Dress. Marya Zaturenska. MoAmPo; TwAmPo
Impercipient, The. Thomas Hardy. MaPo; MaRV; OAEP; TrGrPo; ViBoPo; ViPo; WGRP
Imperfect Enjoyment, The. Earl of Rochester. ErPo; UnTE
Imperfect Lover, The. Siegfried Sassoon. BrPo
Imperial Adam. A. D. Hope. ErPo; MeWo; UnTE
Imperial boy had fallen in his pride, The. My Fatherland. William Cranston Lawton. AA
Imperial Consort of the Fairy King, The. Sonnet: The Wild Duck's Nest. Wordsworth. ChER
Imperial Man. James Russell Lowell. *Fr.* Under the Old Elm, VIII. PGD
Imperial Valley, Calif. Jascha Kessler. NYTB
Impertinent, we tease the weary Heaven. The Man and the Flea. La Fontaine. OnPM
Impetuous Lover, The. A. R. D. Fairburn. AnNZ
Impetuous Resolve, An. James Whitcomb Riley. BiCB
Impetuous Samuel. Harry Graham. NA
Impiety, *sel.* Helene Margaret.
"Lord, I have not time to pray." TrPWD
Impious Feast, The, *sels.* Robert Eyres Landor. OBRV
Babylon, *fr.* Bk. I.
Festival, The, *fr.* Bk. III.
Historic Time, *fr.* Bk. VIII.
Jew's Home, The, *fr.* Bk. I.
Nineveh, *fr.* Bk. V.
Sleep, *fr.* Bk. VII.
Implacable angel, The. Epitaph. Leone da Modena. TrJP
Implacable as are thy arctic floes. Russia. Elliott Napier. BoAu
Implacable woman. The Land. Dorothy Livesay. *Fr.* The Colour of God's Face. PeCV (1967 ed.)
Implicated generations made, The. Celtic Cross. Norman MacCaig. OxBS
Implicit Faith. Aubrey Thomas De Vere. *Fr.* May Carols. GoBC; MaRV
Implora Pace. Charles Lotin Hildreth. AA
Imponderable the dinosaur. Cape Hatteras. Hart Crane. *Fr.* The Bridge. LiTA
Importance of Poetry, or the Coming Forth from Eternity into Time, The. Hyam Plutzik. PP
Important People. Louis Untermeyer, *and others.* StaSt
Important Statement. Patrick Kavanagh. PoCh
Importune Me No More. Elizabeth I, Queen of England. *See* When I Was Fair and Young.
Impossibilities to His Friend. Robert Herrick. SiSw
Impossibility, The. Coventry Patmore. *Fr.* The Angel in the House. PoVP
Impossibility Motivated by Midnight. E. E. Cummings. NAMP
Impossible the years have fled away so fast! The Mice at the Door. Vincent McHugh. NePoAm-2
Impossible to Trust Women. *Unknown.* MeEL
("Whan netilles in wynter bere rosis rede.") EnPo
Impossible, you say, that man survives. The Unbelievable. Edwin Markham. MaRV
Imposture, The, *sels.* James Shirley.
O Fly My Soul, *fr.* II, ii. AtBAP; EG; OBS; OxBoCh
(Hymn, A: "O fly, my soul!"). GoBC; OBEV (1st ed.)
(Song of Nuns, A.) ACP; CAW
Piping Peace. ACP; LoBV
(Io.) OBS; SeCL
(Song: "You Virgins that did late despair.") PoEL-2
(You Virgins.) ViBoPo
Impotent Lover, The. Ovid. *See* Shameful Impotence.
Imprecation for an Aesthetic Society with Newts, Warts, Waxes and Pins. Rosalie Moore. OnHM
Impression ("Stinging/ gold swarms"). E. E. Cummings. *See* Sunset.
Impression ("The hours rise up putting off stars and it is"). E. E. Cummings. *See* Hours rise up. . .
Impression. Sir Edmund Gosse. HBV
Impression. Arthur Symons. SyP
Impression de Nuit; London. Lord Alfred Douglas. OBEV (new ed.); OBVV; PoVP
Impression de Paris. Oscar Wilde. SyP
Impression du Matin. Oscar Wilde. BrPo; CABA; CBV; MoBrPo; PoVP; SyP
Impression Japonais. Oscar Wilde. SyP
Impression: Le Réveillon. Oscar Wilde. PoVP
Impression of a Fountain. Hakushu Kitahara, *tr. fr. Japanese by* Katue Kitasono. LiTW
Impressions. Kirk Hall. BF
Impressions, *sels.* Oscar Wilde.
La Fuite de la Lune, II. Po; PoVP; SyP
Les Silhouettes, I. BrPo; Po; PoVP; SyP
Impressions of François-Marie Arouet (de Voltaire), *sel.* Ezra Pound.
"If you'd have me go on loving you." MoAB
Impressions of My Father, *sel.* Marcia Masters.
Country Ways, I. GoYe
Imprisoned, The. Robert Fitzgerald. TwCP
Imprisoned. Eunice Tietjens. HBMV
Imprisoned Revolutionist, The, *abr.* Mihran Damadian, *tr. fr. Armenian by* Alice Stone Blackwell. PoFr
Imprisoned Soul, The. Walt Whitman. *See* Last Invocation, The.
Impromptu. Francis Atterbury. WaPE
Impromptu. Thomas Gray. EiCP; HoPM; MyFE; NCEP; SeCePo
(On Lord Holland's Seat near Margate, Kent.) CABA; PeER; SeCeV
Impromptu on Charles II. Earl of Rochester. *See* Epitaph on Charles II.
Improperia. Francis Sparshott. MoCV
Improved 4-Way. Tom Veitch. ANYP
Improvisation. Alfred Kreymborg. MAP
Improvisation. Boris Pasternak, *tr. fr. Russian by* Babette Deutsch. Po
Improvisation III. Harold Silverman. TwCaPo
Improvisation on an Old Theme. Dorothy Livesay. ACV; CaP
Improvisations: Light and Snow, *sels.* Conrad Aiken.
"This girl gave her heart to me." BoLP
"When I was a boy, and saw bright rows of icicles." BoNaP
Improvising. Louise Townsend Nicholl. NePoAm-2
Impulse, The. Robert Frost. *Fr.* The Hill Wife. AWP; LiTM; LO; NePA; NP
Impulses. Henri Michaux, *tr. fr. French by* Eunice Clark. OnHM
Impulsive Dialogue. Maxwell Bodenheim. NP
In a Balcony. Robert Browning. EnLi-2 (1949 ed.); PoVP; ViPP
In a Bar near Shibuya Station, Tokyo. Paul Engle. AmFN; CAD
In a basement just off Saint-Michel. 104 Boulevard Saint-Germain. Kenneth Pitchford. NYBP
In a Bath Teashop. John Betjeman. BoC; ELU; EnLoPo
In a Bird Sanctuary. Richard Wilbur. FiMAP
In a Boat. Hilaire Belloc. ISi
In a Boat. D. H. Lawrence. BoLP
In a branch of willow hid. To a Caty-did. Philip Freneau. AA; AmP; AmPP; CoBA; LHV
In a Bye-Canal. Herman Melville. MAmP; MWA-1; PoFS
In a Cafe. Richard Brautigan. FRC
In a Cathedral City. Thomas Hardy. EnLoPo

In a cavern, in a canyon. Paul Dehn. *Fr.* Rhymes for a Modern Nursery. FiBHP; PV; ShM
In a cavern in a canyon. Oh, My Darling Clementine. *Unknown, at. to* Percy Montross. FaBoBe; FaFP; SGR; TreF
In a certain crypt-like courtroom. When Nobody Prays. Merl A. Clapper. STF
In a certain region grew a great banyan tree. The Panchatantra: How the Crow-Hen Killed the Black Snake. *Unknown, tr. by* Arthur W. Ryder. OuHeWo
In a certain town lived a merchant named Naduk. The Panchatantra: The Mice That Ate Iron. *Unknown, tr. by* Arthur W. Ryder. OuHeWo
In a chariot of light from the regions of day. Liberty Tree. Thomas Paine. MC; PAH; PoFr
In a Child's Album. Wordsworth. *See* To a Child.
In a China Shop. George Sidney Hellman. AA
In a church which is furnish'd with mullion and gable. All Saints. Edmund Yates. BOHV; HBV; SiTL
In a City Square. Eleanor Glenn Wallis. NePoAm-2
In a Class of Moral Theology. Francis Sweeney. JKCP (1955 ed.)
In a climate where. Intuition. Anthony Delius. PeSA
In a Closed Universe. James Hayford. NePoAm-2
In a cloud of time, this dust of locusts, in which we move. O Contemporaries. Louis Dudek. TwCaPo
In a [*or* the] coign of the cliff between lowland and highland. A Forsaken Garden. Swinburne. BoLiVe; CBEP; EPN; FaBoEn; GTBS; GTBS-D; GTBS-P; GTSL; HBV; InP; LiTB; LiTG; LoBV; MaVP; NoP; OBNC; OBVV; PAn; PIA; PoE; PoFS; PoVP; ShBV-4; StP; TOP; VA; VaPo; ViPo; VP; WHA
In a cool curving world he lies. The Fish. Rupert Brooke. BoC; OA
In a Convex Mirror. Rosemary Dobson. MoAuPo
In a Copy of Browning. Bliss Carman. HBMV
In a Copy of Omar Kháyyám. James Russell Lowell. AA
In a corner. Dissembler. Charles Shaw. GoYe
In a Corner of Eden. Peter Levi. NePoEA-2
In a cottage embosom'd within a deep shade. Blue Ey'd Mary. *Unknown.* CoMu
In a Cottage in Fife. *Unknown.* OxNR; RIS
In a Country Church. R. S. Thomas. ToPo
In a crack near a cupboard, with dainties provided. The Young Mouse. Jefferys Taylor. OTPC (1923 ed.)
In a Crumbling. Kenneth Patchen. ToPo
In a dark hour, tasting the Earth. Tasting the Earth. James Oppenheim. MAP; MoAmPo (1942 ed.); PFY
In a dark little crack, half a yard from the ground. The Spider and His Wife. Jane Taylor. OTPC (1923 ed.)
In a dark, silent, shady grove. Et Cetera. Earl of Rochester. UnTE
In a Dark Time. Theodore Roethke. EaLo; MoAmPo (1962 ed.); NYBP; PoAn; PoeP; TDP; ToPo
In a Day, *sel.* Augusta Davies Webster.
Deaths of Myron and Klydone, The. VA
In a dazzle of lights and goodbyes. North Star West. Earle Birney. TwCaPo
In a dear little home of tarpaulin and boards. No Thoroughfare. Ruth Holmes. BoTP
In a Desert Town. Lionel Stevenson. AmFN; StVeCh
In a Devonshire lane as I trotted along. The Devonshire Lane. John Marriott. BOHV
In a dim corner of my room for longer than my fancy thinks. The Sphinx. Oscar Wilde. PoVP; ViPP
In a dingy kitchen. Lamentations. Alter Brody. TrJP
In a dirty old house lived a Dirty Old Man. The Dirty Old Man. William Allingham. PCD
In a doomed and empty house in Houndsditch. The Vindictive Staircase; or, The Reward of Industry. W. W. Gibson. AnFE
In a Dream. J. M. Synge. SyP
In a dream I saw a beautiful island. Island of Night. Galway Kinnell. NePoAm
In a dream not long sped. Sisters. "Robin Hyde." AnNZ
In a Drear-nighted December. Keats. *See* Stanzas: "In a drear-nighted December."
In a factory building there are wheels and gearings. Our Father's Hand. Annie Johnson Flint. BLRP
In a far corner. *See* In the far corner.
In a far eastern country. The Sending of the Magi. Bliss Carman. ChrBoLe
In a far land upon a day. The Riding of the Kings. Eleanor Farjeon. ChBR; YeAr
In a far-away northern country in the placid pastoral region. The Ox-Tamer. Walt Whitman. CBEP
In a fashionable suburb of Santa Barbara. In Montecito. Randall Jarrell. CoAP; NoP; NYBP
In a Field. Robert Pack. NePoEA-2
In a Field. Doug Palmer. ThO
In a field/ I am the absence. Keeping Things Whole. Mark Strand. CoAP; YAP
In a frosty sunset. Winter in East Anglia. Edmund Blunden. WePo
In a funny little garden not much bigger than a mat. The Proud Vegetables. Mary McNeil Fenollosa. GFA
In a Garden. Donald C. Babcock. NePoAm
In a Garden. Martha Snell Nicholson. SoP
In a Garden. Swinburne. PRWS
In a Garden by Moonlight. Thomas Lovell Beddoes. *Fr.* Torrismond. VA
In a garden of shining sea-weed. The Sea Princess. Katharine Pyle. PCH; SoPo
In a garden shady this holy lady. Song [*or* Anthem for St.Cecilia's Day]. W. H. Auden. FaBoTw; TwCP
In a garden where the whitethorn spreads her leaves. Alba Innominata. *Unknown.* AWP; LiTW
In a Garret. Elizabeth Akers Allen. AA
In a Garret. Herman Melville. MWA-1
In a Gay Jar. "Feodor Sologub." *See* Amphora, The.
In a Girl's Album. Cedric Dover. WePo
In a Girls' School. David Morton. PoRL
In a Glass. Swift. RIS
In a Glass-Window for Inconstancy. Lord Herbert of Cherbury. AnAnS-2; SeCP
In a glorius garden grene. The Lily-white Rose. *Unknown.* EG; MeEL
In a Gondola. Robert Browning. BEL; EPN; PoVP; VA; ViBoPo, *abr.*; ViPo
Moth's Kiss, First, The, *sel.* AtBAP; GTSL; MeWo; OBEV; OBVV; UnTE
(Song: "Moth's Kiss, first, The.") BoLiVe; HBV; TrGrPo
In a goodly night, as in my bede I laye. Waking alone. *Unknown.* MeEL
In a gorge titanic. Ula Masondo's Dream. William Plomer. MoBS
In a green place lanced through. The Blue Heron. Theodore Goodridge Roberts. CaP; OBCV; PeCV; TDP; TwCaPo
In a grove most rich of shade. Astrophel and Stella: Eighth Song. Sir Philip Sidney. FCP; OAEP; OBSC; SiPS
In a harbour green aslepe whereas I lay. *See* In a herber green. . .
In a Hard Intellectual Light. Richard Eberhart. CMoP; FiMAP; LiTM (rev. ed.); MoVE; NoP
In a Harlem Store Front Church. Clarence Reed. BF
In a herber [*or* harbour *or* an arbour] green, asleep where as I lay. In Youth Is Pleasure [*or* Of Youth He Singeth *or* Youth]. Robert Wever. *Fr.* Lusty Juventus. CBEP; ChTr; EG; ElL; ELP; OBEV; OBSC; SiCE; TuPP
In a hidden valley a pale blue flower grows. The Valley of Pale Blue Flowers. "Fiona Macleod." PoVP
In a high valley of the hills. From an Upland Valley. Richard Church. MoBrPo (1942 ed.)
In a high wind. Hands and Eyes. Louis MacNeice. PoDB
In a hole of the heel of an old brown stocking. Stocking Fairy. Winifred Welles. FaPON; SoPo; TiPo
In a hollow of the forest. The Bomber. Brian Vrepont. BoAV
In a Hundred Years. Elizabeth Doten. BLPA
In a Lady's Album. Marcus Clarke. BoAu
In a hushed, tremendous descent. Under Oaks. James Dickey. NYTB
In a hut of mud and fire. Gautama in the Deer Park at Benares. Kenneth Patchen. NaP
In a Land. *Unknown, at. to* Lao-tzu, *tr. fr. Chinese by* Witter Bynner. *Fr.* Tao Teh King. OnPM
In a Lecture-Room. Arthur Hugh Clough. EPN; PoVP; VA; ViPo
In a Liberal Arts Building. Ruth Stone. TwAmPo
In a little piece of wood. Mr. and Mrs. Spikky Sparrow. Edward Lear. SAS
In a little white house. The Return of the Fairy. Humbert Wolfe. PoMS

In a London Square. Arthur Hugh Clough. EnLi-2; EPN; PoVP
(Put Forth Thy Leaf, Thou Lofty Plane.) ViPP
In a London Terminus. John Lehmann. AtBAP
In a Lonely Place. Stephen Crane. NoP
In a loose robe of tinsel forth [*or* tynsell foorth] she came. Corinna Bathes [*or* Natures Naked Jem]. George Chapman. *Fr.* Ovid's Banquet of Sense. FaBoEn; OBSC
In a Lovely Garden Walking. Ludwig Uhland, *tr. fr. German by* George MacDonald. AWP; JAWP; WBP
In a Low Rocking-Chair. Helen Coale Crew. HBMV
In a Meadow. John Swinnerton Phillimore. OBEV (new ed.); OBVV
In a meadow/ Beside the chapel three boys were playing football. Father Mat. Patrick Kavanagh. AnIL; MoAB; NMP; OPoP
In a melancholy fancy. *See* In melancholic fancy.
In a milkweed cradle. Baby Seeds. *Unknown.* OTPC (1946 ed.); PCH
In a minute the doctor will find out what is wrong. A Utopian Journey. Randall Jarrell. CBV; FiMAP
"In a Moment." *Unknown.* SoP
In a Moonlight Wilderness. Samuel Taylor Coleridge. *See* Fruit Plucker, The.
In a Museum. Babette Deutsch. HBMV
In a Museum. Thomas Hardy. UnS
In a Museum. Anne Elizabeth Wilson. CIV
In a nation of one hundred fine, mob-hearted, lynching, relenting, repenting millions. Bryan, Bryan, Bryan, Bryan. Vachel Lindsay. CMoP; CrMA; LiTA; OxBA; OxBoLi
In a net of mist the moon depends on the wood. Spring Song. George Brandon Saul. GoYe
In a nook/ That opened south. In May. J. M. Synge. MeWo; MoBrPo
In a palace of pearl and sea-weed. The Sea Princess. Katherine Pyle. TVC
In a Parlor Containing a Table. Galway Kinnell. ELU
In a pellucid calm of summer sunset. Mandarin on the Air. Christopher Morley. PoMa
In a pitched bed. Totem. Jon Anderson. YAP
In a plain pleasant cottage, conveniently neat. The Miller. John Cunningham. CEP; OBEC
In a pleasant place today. The Mass of the Grove. Dafydd ap Gwilym. BoPe
In a Poem. Robert Frost. PoeP; PP
In a pool of shadow floating on the sand. Asleep. Witter Bynner. *Fr.* Chapala Poems. NP
In a Prominent Bar in Secaucus [One Day]. X. J. Kennedy. PIA; PoCh; UnTE
In a Province. F. T. Prince. BoSA; MoVE
In a puddle by the roadside. Reflections. Cyrus E. Albertson. MaRV
In a race-course box behind the stand. Right Royal. John Masefield. OtMeF
In a Railway Compartment. John Fuller. NePoEA-2
In a Rented Room. Denis Johnson. QAH
In a Roman tram, where the famous Roman mob. The Thief. Stanley Kunitz. MoAmPo (1962 ed.)
In a Rose Garden. John Bennett. BLPA; FaBoBe; HBV; NeHB
In a scented wood. The Night. Helen Leuty. BoTP
In a Season of Unemployment. Margaret Avison. MoCV
In a September Night. F. Wyville Home. VA
In a shady nook one moonlit night. The Leprahaun. Robert Dwyer Joyce. OnYI; PoMS
In a shelter one night, when death was taking the air. In the Shelter. C. Day Lewis. BoC
In a shoe box stuffed in an old nylon stocking. The Meadow Mouse. Theodore Roethke. NaP; NoP; OA; PoeP; PoIE (1970 ed.); SeCeV (1967 ed.)
In a Shoreham Garden. Laurence Lerner. NePoEA-2
In a sick shade of spruce, moss-webbed, rock-fed. As It Looked Then. E. A. Robinson. CMoP; MaPo; NePA
In a slumber visional. The Vision of Mac Conglinne. *Unknown.* CAW
In a small bitterness of wind. Young Argonauts. Sheila Wingfield. SD
In a Small Place. Annie Johnson Flint. FaChP
In a snug little court as I stood t'other day. The Pleasing Constraint. Aristaenetus. ALV; ErPo
In a solitude of the sea. The Convergence of The Twain. Thomas Hardy. BrPo; BWP; CBV; CoBMV; EnL; FaBoTw; ILP; InPo; LiTB; LiTM (1970 ed.); MaPo; MoAB; MoBrPo; MoPo; MoVE; NoP; OAEP (2d ed.); PAn; PeVV; PoAn; PoeP; SeCeV; ShBV-3; ViPP; VP
In a somer sesun [*or* summer season], when softe [*or* soft] was the sonne [*or* sun *or* when the sun was softest]. Prologue [*or* The Induction *or* The Field Full of Folk]. William Langland. *Fr.* The Vision of Piers Plowman. BEL; CoBE; EnLi-1; EnLit; MeEV; PoEL-1; PoLi
In a Southern Garden. Dorothea Mackellar. BoAu
In a Southern garden Lucinda sits. The Bones of Incontention. Robert David Cohen. NYBP
In a Spring Grove. William Allingham. IrPN
In a Spring Still Not Written Of. Robert Wallace. BoNaP; PP
In a stable bare. Yuletide. Alice Furlong. JKCP
In a stable of boats I lie still. The Lifeguard. James Dickey. CoPo; NoP; NYBP
In a Staffordshire Churchyard. *Unknown.* WhC
(Four Country Epitaphs.) GoTP
In a stately hall at Brentford, when the English June was green. The Last Meeting of Pocahontas and the Great Captain. Margaret Junkin Preston. MC; PAH
In a Station of the Metro. Ezra Pound. AmP; AmPP (5th ed.); CABA; CAD; CaFP; CBV; ExPo; ForPo; InP; MAP; MoAB; MoAmPo; NeMA; NoP; OxBA; PoAn; PoIE; UnPo; VaPo
In a Storm. Harry Kemp. PFY
In a Strange House. Stanley J. Kunitz. NP
In a summer cottage. Nightmare. Anne Marx. FiSC
In a summer season, when soft was the sun. *See* In a somer sesun, when softe was the sonne.
In a Surrealist Year. Lawrence Ferlinghetti. A Coney Island of the Mind, 4. PPON
In a tabernacle of a toure [*or* tower]. *Unknown.* *Fr.* Quia Amore Langueo. ACP; CoBE; MeEL
In a tangled, scented hollow. Sleep. Lewis Frank Tooker. AA
In a temple at Kioto in far-away Japan. The Three Wise Monkeys. Florence Boyce Davis. WBLP
In a throng, a festal company. Wordsworth. *Fr.* The Prelude. OBRV
In a Time of Crisis. Lawrence Durrell. LiTM
In a Time of Pestilence. Thomas Nashe. *See* Adieu, Farewell, Earth's Bliss!
In a Town Garden. Donald Mattam. ELU; FiBHP
In a Train. Robert Bly. NaP
In a tree at the edge of the clearing. On Falling Asleep to Birdsong. William Meredith. PoCh
In a Troubled World. Stanton A. Coblentz. ChIP
In a valley, centuries ago. The Petrified Fern. Mary Lydia Bolles Branch. AA
In a Valley of This Restless Mind. Ewart Milne. NeIP
In a valley [*or* valey *or* the vale *or* the vaile] of this restless [*or* of restles] mind [*or* minde *or* mynd]. Quia Amore Langueo. *Unknown.* AtBAP; CBEP; EnLit; LiTG; LiTL; LO; NoP; OBEV; OxBoCh; PoEL-1; PoLi; WoL
In a Vermont bedroom closet. A Record Stride. Robert Frost. NePA
In a Volume of Austin Dobson. Mary Elizabeth Coleridge. PoVP
In a Warm Chicken House. James Wright. NYTB
In a week of perpetual rain. The Tray. Thomas Cole. NePoAm
In a while they rose and went out aimlessly riding. Merlin Enthralled. Richard Wilbur. CMoP; NePoEA; NYBP
In a white gully among fungus red. Native-born. Eve Langley. BoAV; NeLNL; PoAu-2
In a wife I would desire. Blake. ERoP-1
In a wild moraine of forgotten books. The Old School List. James Kenneth Stephen. CenHV
In a Wine Cellar. Victor J. Daley. PoAu-1
In a Woman's Face. Richard Church. LO
In a Wood. Thomas Hardy. *Fr.* The Woodlanders. InP; OAEP; OBNC; PoPl; ViPo (1962 ed.)
In a Wood Clearing. Wilson MacDonald. CaP
In a wood they call the Rouge Bouquet. Rouge Bouquet. Joyce Kilmer. DD; HBV; MC; PaA; PAH; PFY; PoPl; TIHL; TreFS
In a world of battlefields there came. When the Dead Men Die. Rose O'Neill. HBMV

In a world of orange serenity. The Lacemaker (Vermeer). Anne Marx. GoYe
In a world where kapok on a sidewalk looks like an "accident." Shirley Temple Surrounded by Lions. Kenward Elmslie. ANYP
In a Year. Robert Browning. AtBAP; EPN
In Absence. Tu Fu, *tr. fr. Chinese by* Herbert A. Giles. OuHeWo
In Acceptance Lieth Peace. Amy Carmichael. FaChP; MaRV
In Aesop's tales an honest wretch we find. A Fable. Matthew Prior. EiCL
In Africa. Roy Fuller. BoSA
In After Days. George Frederick Cameron. CaP
In After Days. Austin Dobson. EnLit; HBV; InP; MaRV; MoBrPo (1942 ed.); NeMA; OBEV; OBVV; OQP; PoVP; PTK; TIHL; TOP; TreFS; TSW; VA
In After Time. Richard Eberhart. MoRP
In After Time. Walter Savage Landor. VA
In after times when strength or courage fail. Buffel's Kop. Roy Campbell. ChMP; PeSA
In after years, when you look back upon. The Window. Francis Scarfe. NeBP
In agony of mind, in the west country. The Royal Military Canal. Patric Dickinson. POTi
In Air. Peter Clarke. PBA
In all góod Greek of Plato. *See* In all the good Greek of Plato.
In all happiness and peace of mind. What Followed. Josephine Miles. FiMAP
In all his life and teaching. Certainties. Kenneth W. Porter. ChIP
In all my Emma's beauties blest. Emma. Goldsmith. OnYI
In All the Argosy of Your Bright Hair. Dunstan Thompson. WaP
In all the Eastern hemisphere. The Fall of J. W. Beane. Oliver Herford. StPo
In all the four seas. The Taoist Monk. Tu Hsun Hao. OnPM
In all the good Greek of Plato. Survey of Literature. John Crowe Ransom. FaBoCh; LiTA; LoGBV; SiTL; TwCP
In All the Humors. Martial. *See* Temperament.
In all the land, range up, range down. Langley Lane. Robert Buchanan. HBV
In all the parish not a dame dared stir. Ten of Chaucer's People: The Wife of Bath. Chaucer. *Fr.* The Canterbury Tales. PoSa
In all the towns and cities fair. Thomas Winterbottom Hance. W. S. Gilbert. InMe
In All These Acts. Brother Antoninus. OPoP; ToPo
In All These Turning Lights I Find No Clue. Maxwell Anderson. *Fr.* Winterset. TreFT
In all they brood. Numbers. Agnes Lee. NP
In all this cool. Coolness in Summer. Ryusui. RePo
In all this world of visible images. Ceremony for Birth and Naming. Ridgely Torrence. MoRP
In all thy humors, whether grave or mellow. Temperament [*or* To a Capricious Friend *or* In All the Humors]. Martial. AWP; BOHV; ELU; JAWP; OnPM; WBP
In alternate measure chanting, daily sing we Mary's praise. Irish Hymn to Mary. *Unknown.* CAW
In amaze. Ode to Quinbus Flestrin. Pope. OAEP
"In America," began. The Student. Marianne Moore. TwCP
In among the silver birches winding ways of tarmac wander. Indoor Games near Newbury. John Betjeman. MoPW; MoVE
In Amorem Divinum (Hermannus Hugo). Richard Crashaw. MaMe
In Ampezzo ("In days of summer let me go"). Trumbull Stickney. TwAmPo
In Ampezzo ("Only once more and not again"). Trumbull Stickney. AnFE; APA; CoAnAm; CrMA; NCEP; TwAmPo
In Amsterdam there dwells [*or* dwelt *or* lived] a maid. The Maid of Amsterdam [*or* A-Roving]. *Unknown.* AmSS; OxBoLi; ShS; SoAmSa
In an age of fops and toys. Voluntaries, III [*or* Duty *or* So Nigh Is Grandeur]. Emerson. AnNE; CBV; HBVY; LiTA; MaRV; MWA-1; PoLF; PoPo; TreFS; YT
In an Age of Science. Thomas Curtis Clark. MaRV
In an Arbour Green. Robert Weever. *See* In Youth Is Pleasure.
In an arboure of green may. *Unknown.* SeCSL
In an Artist's Studio. Christina Rossetti. EnLi-2; NoP; OAEP
In an Autumn Wood. William Alexander Percy. HBMV
In an Editor's Office. Zoe Kincaid Brockman. PoNC
In an envelope marked. Personal. Langston Hughes. AmNP; PoNE
In an Iridescent Time. Ruth Stone. MoAmPo (1962 ed.); PoPl; TwAmPo
In an ocean, 'way out yonder. The Dinkey-Bird. Eugene Field. AA; BOHV; HBVY; LBN; NA; PFY; TreFS; TSW; UTS
In an old and ashen island. Sappho's Tomb. Arthur Stringer. CaP
In an old book at even as I read. "Ex Libris." Arthur Upson. HBV
In an old chamber softly lit. During a Chorale by César Franck. Witter Bynner. *Fr.* To Celia. AnAmPo; HBMV; NP
In an old city by the storied shores. Opportunity. Edwin Markham. OQP
In an old, dark house. Fly in December. Robert Wallace. NYBP
In an Old House. Spencer Brown. NYBP
In an old house there is always listening. Chorus. T. S. Eliot. *Fr.* The Family Reunion. MWA-2
In an old house with many fireplaces. In an Old House. Spencer Brown. NYBP
In an Old Library. Yuan Mei, *tr. fr. Chinese by* L. Cranmer-Byng. LiTW
In an Old Nursery. Patrick R. Chalmers. HBMV
In an Old Orchard. Peter Kane Dufault. NYBP
In an old print. The Lake Boats. Edgar Lee Masters. NP
In an upper room at midnight. The Love Feast. W. H. Auden. CBV; ErPo
In ancient days there lived [*or* dwelt] a Turk. Kafoozalum [*or* Kafoozelum]. *Unknown.* BELS; BLPA
In ancient time old men observed that. Of Clergymen and Their Livings. Sir John Harington. TuPP
In ancient [*or* antient] times, as story tells. Baucis and Philemon. Swift. CEP; EiCP; EiPP; GN; GoTL; GSP, *abr.*; NoP; OBEC; OTPC (1946 ed.); PAn; StPo
In ancient times the hungry gods. The Ways of the Gods. Stanton A. Coblentz. OQP
In and between the cities. Going to Pittsburgh. Dennis Trudell. QAH
In and Out. L. E. Sissman. NYBP
In and Out: Severance of Connections, 1946. L. E. Sissman. TwCP
In and out the bushes, up the ivy. The Chipmunk's Song. Randall Jarrell. PDV
In anguish we uplift. War Song. John Davidson. NBM; OBNC
In another country, black poplars shake themselves over a pond. The North Country. D. H. Lawrence. OAEP (2d ed.)
In Answer of an Elegiacall Letter upon the Death of the King of Sweden. Thomas Carew. AnAnS-2
In Answer to a Lady Who Advised Retirement. Lady Mary Wortley Montagu. OBEC
In Answer to a Question. Wilfrid Scawen Blunt. The Love Sonnets of Proteus, XXVIII. ViBoPo
In Antarctica drooping their little shoulders. The View from Here. William Stafford. ELU
In any hour the singers with mouths of gold. Two Musics. Norman McCaig. NeBP
In any medium except that of verse. One Way Song, XXIV. Wyndham Lewis. PP; SiTL
In Any Office. Amy Carmichael. FaChP
In Apia Bay. Sir Charles G. D. Roberts. PAH
In Aprell and in May. Besse Bunting. *Unknown.* EnPo; MeEL
In April. Elizabeth Akers Allen. OTPC (1946 ed.); PRWS
In April. Emily Gail Arnold. PEDC
In April. Ethelwyn Wetherald. CaP
In April/ Come he will. The Cuckoo. *Unknown.* BoTP
In April cuckoos come. Signs and Charms. *Unknown.* StaSt
In April Once, *sel.* William Alexander Percy.
Spring of God, The. OQP
In April sun the dead march played. Appomattox. MacKinlay Kantor. AnAmPo
In April, when raining is sunlight. Great Farm. Philip Booth. PoPl
In Aprile at the hicht of noon. On Seein an Aik Tree Sprent wi Galls. Robert Garioch. OxBS
In Arabia's book of fable. Princess Sabbath. Heine. TrJP

In Arcadia. Lawrence Durrell. FaBoMo; MoBrPo (1962 ed.)
In Arcady. Cosmo Monkhouse. OBVV
In Ariostum Orlandi Furiosi Autorem. John Heath. SiCE
In Arizona, *sels.* William Haskell Simpson.
  Bareback. NP
  Burdens. NP
  Hopi Ghosts. NP
  Pity Not. HBMV; NP
  Trees. NP
In Armorik, that called is Britayne. The Franklin's Tale. Chaucer. *Fr.* The Canterbury Tales. OAEP
In arrogance and vanity. Only One King. John Richard Moreland. ChIP; PGD
In Auchtermuchty there dwelt ane man. The Wife of Auchtermuchty. *Unknown.* GoTS
In August. William Dean Howells. AmePo; GN; PoRL
In Authorem. Ben Jonson. Sonn
In Autumn. Gene Derwood. NYTB
In autumn/ the barren trees'. Lost Love. Herman L. McMillan. TNV
In autumn down the beechwood path. Beech Leaves. James Reeves. RePo
In autumn pastures where a bird had flown. Autumn Bird. Howard McKinley Corning. MAP; MoAmPo (1942 ed.)
In Autumn tomboy winds begin to throw. Old Nurse Winter. Jean Starr Untermeyer. TSW
In autumpn whan the sun in Virgine. The Bowge of Court. John Skelton. ReIE
In Baalbec there were lovers. The Passing Flower. Harry Kemp. HBMV
In Babylon, where first her queen, for state. Pyramus and Thisbe. Ovid. OuHeWo
In back of our town. Gasco, or the Toad. Günter Grass. ELU
In Back of the Real. Allen Ginsberg. AmPP (5th ed.)
In Ballades things always contrive to get lost. A Ballade of Ballade-Mongers. Augustus M. Moore. BOHV
In Baltimore there lived a boy. The Boy Who Laughed at Santa Claus. Ogden Nash. BBGG; CenHV; MaC; StPo
In Barracks. Siegfried Sassoon. FaBoTw
In Battle. Wallace Stevens. NP
In battle-line of sombre gray. The Spirit of the *Maine.* Tudor Jenks. AA; MC; PAH
In Bayreuth once. Mary Desti's Ass. Frank O'Hara. ANYP
In Beatricem Praepropere Defunctam ("In Beatrice did all perfections grow"). John Heath. TuPP
In Bed We Laugh. Samuel Johnson. CBV
  (Translation of Lines by Benserade.) CABA
In Bertram's Garden. Donald Justice. ErPo; NePoEA
In Between Time (Transcience). Marsha Ann Jackson. TNV
In Beverley town a maid did dwell. The Beverley Maid and the Tinker. *Unknown.* CoMu
In Bibberley Town, *with music.* *Unknown.* SaSa
In blessèd silence vegetates the place. The Parish Church. Julio Herrera y Reissig. CAW
In blows the loitering air of spring. Spring Air. Gene Derwood. FaFP; GTBS-W; LiTL
In Bodenstown Churchyard there is a green grave. Tone's Grave. Thomas Osborne Davis. OnYI
In Bodleian and Harleian/ Lurk ambushes of grace. Our Lady of the Libraries. Sister Mary Ignatius. ISi
In bodnie (bonnie), bright and fair Scotland, where bluebells they did grow. The Paisley Officer, *vers.* II. *Unknown.* ShS
In Bohemia. John Boyle O'Reilly. LHV
In Bohemia. Arthur Symons. *See* City Nights: In Bohemia.
In borrowed boots which don't fit. Small Game. Philip Levine. AmPC
In Bowre and Field he sought, where any tuft. Eve. Milton. *Fr.* Paradise Lost, IX. OBS
In boxes lined with faded satin. Pawnshop Window. R. H. Grenville. GoYe
In, boy; go first. You houseless poverty. Poor Naked Wretches. Shakespeare. *Fr.* King Lear, III, iv. PPON
In breaking of belief in human good. Litany of the Lost. Siegfried Sassoon. MoRP
In Breughel's great picture, The Kermess. The Dance. William Carlos Williams. AmP; AmPP (5th ed.); CMoP; ExPo; GoJo; LiTM (1970 ed.); LoGBV; NoP; OxBA; PoeP; TDP
In Brittany ("In Brittany the churches"). E. V. Lucas. WHL
In Brittany ("In Brittany I lost my way"). Charles Weekes. OnYI
In Brittany. Nancy Willard. ThO
In Brittany there lived a lad. The Heart. *Unknown.* MaC
In Broad Street building (on a winter night). The Gouty Merchant and the Stranger. Horace Smith. BeLS; BOHV
In Broken Images. Robert Graves. PoIE
In Brunton Town. *Unknown.* BaBo
  (Bruton Town, *diff. vers.*) EnSB
"In Buckinghamshire hedgerows." The Icosasphere. Marianne Moore. ImOP
In Cacum. Thomas Bastard. SiCE
In Caium. Thomas Bastard. SiCE
In California/ ankle-high animals occupy the tablelands. Report from California. Lois Moyles. NYBP
In calm and cool and silence, once again. First-Day Thoughts. Whittier. AmPP; NoP; SoP
In came her sister. Lady Maisry (B *vers.*). *Unknown.* ESPB
In candent ire the solar splendor flames. Aestivation [*or* Intramural Aestivation]. Oliver Wendell Holmes. *Fr.* The Autocrat of the Breakfast-Table. AmPP; AnNE; BOHV; ChTr; InMe; NA; WhC
In careless days now dim. Native Land. Gina Ballantyne. BoAu
In Carmel Bay the people say. Abalone. *Unknown.* AS
In Carnival we were, and supp'd that night. Versailles.. Stopford Augustus Brooke. VA
In Caroline, whar I was born. Walk, Jaw-Bone. S. S. Steele. TrAS
In Cavan of little lakes. A Song of Freedom. Alice Milligan. AnIV; OnYI; PoFr
In caves emptied of their workers, turning. The Angels at Hamburg. Randall Jarrell. AmP
In Cawsand Bay lying, with the Blue Peter flying. Cawsand Bay. *Unknown.* OBB
In certain minds the strength wells. The Rich Interior Life. Richard Eberhart. MoRP
In chariot like an hibiscus flower at his side. Confucius. *Fr.* Songs of Cheng. CTC
In Cherbourg Roads the pirate lay. The Eagle and Vulture. Thomas Buchanan Read. PAH
In Cherry Lane. William Livingston. JKCP
In childhood, when with eager eyes. The Trance of Time. Cardinal Newman. OxBoCh
In childhood's pride I said to Thee. The Soul's Prayer. Sarojini Naidu. MaRV
In Childhood's unsuspicious hours. Epicurean. William James Linton. VA
In Christ. John Oxenham. *See* No East or West.
In Christ Alone. Connie Galenberg. SoP
In Christ I feel the heart of God. Our Christ. Lucy Larcom. MaRV; OQP; StJW
In Christ there is no East or [*or* nor] West. No East or West [*or* All One in Christ *or* Brothers of the Faith]. John Oxenham. BLRP; ChIP; FaChP; MaRV; OQP; SoP
In Christ We Have. *Unknown.* SoP
In Christian world Mary the garland wears! The Names. Charles Lamb. OTPC (1923 ed.)
In Christophorum. Thomas Freeman. SiCE
In Church. William Barnes. *See* Vo'k a-Comen into Church.
In Church. Thomas Hardy. Satires of Circumstance, II. DiPo; DTC; FosPo; MoAB; MoBrPo; PoDB; VaPo; VP
In Church. R. S. Thomas. BoPe
In church your grandsire cut his throat. On the Upright Judge [Who Condemned the "Drapier's" Printer]. Swift. ALV; SiTL
"In churches," said the Pardoner, "when I preach." Prologue to the Pardoner's Tale. Chaucer. *Fr.* The Canterbury Tales. EnL
In Chus. *Unknown.* TuPP
In Cicatrices Domini Jesu. Richard Crashaw. MaMe
In cinemas we sought. Sing, Brothers, Sing! W. R. Rodgers. MoAB; MoBrPo (1950 ed.)
In Ciprium. Sir John Davies, *after the Latin of* Martial. ReIE; SiCE; TuPP
In City Streets. Ada Smith. HBV; OTPC (1923 ed.)
In Clementina's Artless Mien. Walter Savage Landor. *See* Of Clementina.
In Clonmel Parish Churchyard. Sarah Morgan Bryan Piatt. AA
In clouds she shines, and so obscurely shineth. Thomas Wat-

In (continued)
son. *Fr.* The Tears of Fancy. Sonn; TuPP
In cock-wattle sunset or grey. Nostalgia. Louis MacNeice. GTBS-D; OnYI
In cold November/ the old man stood. The News Stand. Daniel Berrigan. CAD
In college once I climbed the tree. Sickle Pears. Owen Dodson. AmNP
In colleges and halls, in ancient days. Discipline in Education. William Cowper. *Fr.* The Task. CoBE
In Collins street standeth a statue tall. Gone. Adam Lindsay Gordon. BoAu
In Cologne, a town of monks and bones. Cologne. Samuel Taylor Coleridge. PV
In comes the captain's daughter, the captain of the yeos. The Boys of Wexford. *Unknown.* ELP
In coming down to Manchester to gain my liberty. The Soldier's Farewell to Manchester. *Unknown.* CoMu
In coming to the feast I found. The Horn. Léonie Adams. AnAmPo; InPo; MAP; MoAB; MoAmPo
In Commendation of George Gascoigne's Steel Glass. Sir Walter Ralegh. SiPS
(In Commendation of The Steel Glass.) FCP
In Commendation of Music. William Strode. ELP; MuSP; OBEV (new ed.)
(Commendation of Music, The.) CLwM; SeCL
In Commendation of The Steel Glass. Sir Walter Ralegh. *See* In Commendation of George Gascoigne's Steel Glass.
In Common. Gene Derwood. NePA; PoPl
In concert with the curfew bell. The Black Bird. John Hall-Stevenson. *Fr.* Makarony Fables. EiCL
In Conclusion. Abbie Huston Evans. NP
In concord then they set up hasty ways. Freighter. Bruce Ruddick. CaP
In Conjunction. Charles Madge. FaBoMo; NeBP
In Consolation. Vassar Miller. CBV; ToPo
In Consort to Wednesday, Jan. 1st, 1701. Richard Henchman. SCAP
In Controversial Foul Impureness. Arthur Hugh Clough. ViPP
(Noli Aemulari.) PoVP
In Córdoba within the drowsing Plaza. Quién Sabe? Ruth Comfort Mitchell. PoMa
In Country Sleep. Dylan Thomas. LiTB; LiTM (rev. ed.)
In court to serve, deckèd with fresh array. The Courtier's Wife. Sir Thomas Wyatt. CBV; ReIE
In Coventry. James J. Daly. CAW
In cruelty you greater are. To Francelia. Thomas Duffett. CavP
In crystal towers and turrets richly set. Content [*or* Song]. Geffrey Whitney. ACP; EIL; SiCE
In Cumberland city, as you shall all hear. Villkins and His Dinah (A *vers.*). *Unknown.* BaBo
In Cupid's school whoe'er would take degree. Ovid. *Fr.* The Art of Love. UnTE
In Cycle Repeated. Katherine Garrison Chapin. NYTB
In Cypres Sat Fair Venus by a Fount. Robert Greene. ReIE
In Cyprus springs—whereas dame Venus dwelt. Complaint of the Lover Disdained. Earl of Surrey. BEL; FCP; SiPS; Sonn
In Dacum. Sir John Davies. TuPP
In dark fens of the Dismal Swamp. The Slave in the Dismal Swamp. Longfellow. MWA-1
In Dark Hour. Seumas MacManus. JKCP; WGRP
In dark Thermopylae they lie. On Those Who Fell at Thermopylae. Simonides, *tr. by* Robert Bland. PoFr
In darkest hours I hear a voice. Jesus Is Near. Robert Cassie Waterston. BePJ
In darkest hours, in nights so drear. With Thee. Cora M. Pinkham. STF
In Darkness and Aridity. Psalms, CXXX, Bible, *O.T.* BoC
In Dat Great Gittin' Up Mornin'. *Unknown.* AA; BoAn-2, *with music*
In daylight, even. The Countershadow. Philip Booth. NYBP
In Days Gone By. Ida M. Mills. BoTP
In days long gone God spake unto our sires. The Call. Thomas Curtis Clark. PGD
In days of ease, when now the weary sword. Court of Charles II. Pope. *Fr.* To Augustus. OBEC
In days of old, when Arthur filled the throne. Chaucer. *Fr.* The Canterbury Tales: The Wife of Bath's Tale. MBW-1
In days [*or* the] of old, when Englishmen were—men. Italian Opera [*or* Foreign Songsters]. James Miller. MuSP; OBEC; UnS
In days of old when knights caught cold. Thoughts on Progress. David Daiches. SiTL
In days of old when Spenser sang. Ballade of the Goth. Sir Walter Raleigh. WhC
In days of peace my fellow-men. From a Full Heart. A. A. Milne. BOHV; InMe
In days of summer let me go. In Ampezzo, II. Trumbull Stickney. TwAmPo
In days of yore, from Britain's shore. The Maple Leaf Forever. Alexander Muir. PTK
In days when Albion's seamen knew. Sea-Birds. Fray Angelico Chavez. ISi
In days when George the Third was King. Miss Nancy's Gown. Zitella Cocke. AA
In de dead of night I sometimes. The Old Cabin. Paul Laurence Dunbar. PoLF
In de ebening by de moonlight when dis darkie's work was over. In the Evening by the Moonlight. James A. Bland. TreFS
In de Lord, in de Lord. My Soul's Been Anchored in de Lord. *Unknown.* BoAN-2
In de Mornin', *with music. Unknown.* SoAmSa
In de Vinter Time, *with music. Unknown.* AS
In dead of winter. Approximations. Robert Hayden. PoIE (1970 ed.)
In Deadly Fear. Blake. *Fr.* Jerusalem. SeCePo
In Dear Detail, By Ideal Light. William Stafford. NaP
In Death. Mary Emily Bradley. AA
In Death Divided. Thomas Hardy. DTC
In Debtor's Yard the stones are hard. Oscar Wilde. *Fr.* The Ballad of Reading Gaol. ViBoPo
In December. Andrew Young. SeCePo
In December, when the days draw to be short. Little John Nobody. *Unknown.* OxBoLi
In Decium. Sir John Davies. TuPP
In deep blue sky the sun is bright. Alfred Domett. *Fr.* Ranolf and Amohia. AnNZ
In Defence of Humanism. David Gascoyne. LiTM (rev. ed.)
In Defence of Satire. Pope. *See* Satire: "Ask you what provocation I have had?"
In Defense of Black Poets. Conrad Kent Rivers. BOLo
In Defense of Felons. Robert Mezey. NePoEA; ToPo
In Defense of Marriage. John Gill. ThO
In Defense of Metaphysics. Charles Tomlinson. MoBrPo (1962 ed.)
In Defense of Superficiality. Elder Olson. NYBP
In Defense of Their Inconstancy. Ben Jonson. ReEn; SeCP
(Another.) SeCP
In Derision of a Country Life. Edward Ravenscroft. *Fr.* The Italian Husband. SeCL
In Desert Places. Sister Mary Madeleva. GoTP
In desolation, here a lost world lies. Epitaph, Found Somewhere in Space. Hugh Wilgus Ramsaur. MaRV; TRV
In despair at not being able to rival the creations of God. Hymn to Her Unknown. Walter James Turner. LiTL; LiTM; OBMV
In dim green depths rot ingot-laden ships. Sunken Gold. Eugene Lee-Hamilton. EtS; NCEP; VA
In Dispraise of Poetry. Jack Gilbert. PP
In Dispraise of the Moon. Mary Coleridge. BoNaP; CH; NBM
In distant days of wild romance. Now and Then. Jane Taylor. OTPC (1923 ed.)
In Distrust of Merits. Marianne Moore. AmPP; AP; CoBMV; EaLo; LiTA; LiTM; MoAB; MoAmPo (1950 ed.); NePA; OxBA; PoAn; PoRL; SeCeV; TreFT; TrGrPo (rev. ed); UnPo (3d ed.); ViBoPo (1958 ed.); WaaP; WaP
In Dives' Dive. Robert Frost. TDP
In dog-days plowmen quit their toil. The Swimmer. John Crowe Ransom. PFY; SD
In Domrèmy a maid. The Maid of Arc. Gordon Bottomley. GoTL (1949 ed.)
In Doubt of Doubt. Robert Browning. *Fr.* Bishop Blougram's Apology. MaRV
In Dream. J. M. Synge. SyP
In dream, again within the clean cold hell. The Gorse. W. W. Gibson. AtBAP

In dream, body dives from a high bridge. The Invisible Craft of Evil. James Schevill. FRC
In dream I saw two Jews that met by chance. Moses and Jesus. Israel Zangwill. TrJP
In dreams a dark château. The Dark Château. Walter de la Mare. BrPo
In dreams I see the Dromedary still. The Dromedary. Archibald Y. Campbell. HBMV; PoMa; StaSt
In dreams the Daemon comes, upon the hour. The Dream-Daemon. Lin Carter. FiSC
In Dreamy Swoon. George Darley. *Fr.* Nepenthe. OBNC
("Over a bloomy land untrod.") OBRV
In Dresden, in the square one day. The Violinist. Archibald Lampman. CaP
In drooping leaves of the plane. August. Laurence Binyon. SyP
In Dublin's fair city, where the girls are so pretty. Cockles and Mussels [*or* Molly Malone]. *Unknown.* ELP; LO; MaC; OnYI
In due course of course you will be issued with. Unarmed Combat. Henry Reed. Lessons of the War, III. LiTB
In due season the amphibious crocodile. Amphibious Crocodile. John Crowe Ransom. AnAmPo
In Dulci Jubilo. John Wedderburn. *after the German* ChTr
In Dulci Jubilo. *Unknown, tr. fr. Middle High German by* Paul Crowley. CAW
In each green leaf a memory let lie. With Roses. Beatrix Demarest Lloyd. AA
In each man's heart that doth begin. Love's World. Sir John Suckling. SCEP-2; SeCV-1
In each of us you live on, the lodged seed. To Wallace Stevens. Daniel Berrigan. ML
In Earliest Spring. William Dean Howells. AA; FaBoBe; PFY
In Early Spring. Richard Aldridge. NYTB
In Early Spring. Alice Meynell. AnFE; HBV
In early spring when Samuel plows. On Our Farm. Esther Antin. RIS
In Early Summer Lodging in a Temple to Enjoy the Moonlight. Po Chü-i, *tr. fr. Chinese by* Arthur Waley. LiTW
In early winter before the first snow. An Elegy. E. J. Scovell. ChMP
In early youth, as you may guess. The Young Gazelle. Walter Parke. BOHV
In earth is a little thing. The Rule of Money. *Unknown.* PoFr
In Earthen Vessels. Whittier. *Fr.* The Friend's Burial. BLRP; SoP; TRV
In easy dialogue is Fletcher's praise. To My Dear Friend, Mr. Congreve, on His Comedy Called "The Double-Dealer." Dryden. CEP; FiP; OBS; PoE; PoEL-3
In eaves sole sparrow sits not more alone. David's Peccavi. Robert Southwell. EP
In Ed. Allen. John Weever. ReIE
In Ego with Us All. John Ciardi. ToPo
In Egypt they worshipped me. I Am the Cat. Leila Usher. BLPA
In eighteen hundred and forty-five. Greenland Whale Fishery. *Unknown.* OuSiCo
In eighteen hundred and forty one [*or* forty-wan]. Paddy [*or* Pat] Works on the Railway [*or* the Erie]. *Unknown.* ABF; TrAS
In eighteen hundred and forty-six. A-Working on the Railway. Arthur H. Clark. IHA
In eighteen hundred and sixty-one. The *Alabama, vers.* II. *Unknown.* ShS
In eighteen hundred fifty, when Gold Lake was in its prime. Gold Lake and Gold Bluff. John A. Stone. SGR
In 1846/ the burning of Nauvoo. To New Jerusalem. Dan Gillespie. QAH
In either mood, to bless or curse. Doom. Arthur O'Shaughnessy. MoBrPo (1942 ed.); OBVV
In elder times an ancient custom 'twas. Swearing. Henry Fitzsimon. ACP (1952 ed.)
In elderis dayis, as Esope can declair. The Taill of the Foxe, That Begylit the Wolf, in the Schadow of the Mone. Robert Henryson. OxBS
In England from the train you see. From the Train. Marjorie Wilson. BoTP
In England there was a lordling born. Hynd [*or* Hynde] Horn. *Unknown.* GN; OBB
In England's Green & (a Garland and a Clyster). Jonathan Williams. CoPo
In enterprise of martial kind. The Duke of Plaza-Toro. W. S. Gilbert. *Fr.* The Gondoliers. ALV; FaPON; FiBHP; OnPP; PCD
In Epitaphium Pingui Minerva Compositum. Thomas Freeman. TuPP
In Eternum [I Was Once Determed]. Sir Thomas Wyatt. BWP; FosPo; MaPo
("In eternum I was once determed.") FCP; SiPS
In Europe you can't move without going down into history. In the Yukon. Ralph Gustafson. MoCV
In Evening Air. Theodore Roethke. NYBP
In every church, in every clime. The Faithful Few. Chester E. Shuler. SoP; STF
In every leaf that crowns the plain. Faith. John Richard Moreland. OHIP
In every meanest face I see. Sons of Promise. Thomas Curtis Clark. PoToHe
In every path of timber you. Trees. *Unknown.* SoP
In every place ye may well see. What Women Are Not. *Unknown.* MeEL
In every seed to breathe the flower. Faith [*or* The Evidence]. John Banister Tabb. FaChP; TRV; WGRP
In every solemn tree the wind. Love Song from New England. Winifred Welles. HBMV; MAP; MeWo
In Every Thing Give Thanks. *Unknown.* STF
In every trembling bud and bloom. An Easter Canticle. Charles Hanson Towne. ChIP; MaRV, *abr.*; OHIP; TrPWD
In every war, strange legends circulate. Philippine Madonna. Louise Crenshaw Ray. ISi
In evil hour did Pope's declining age. On the Edition of Mr. Pope's Works with a Commentary and Notes. Thomas Edwards. Sonn
In Evil Long I Took Delight. John Newton. MaRV; OxBoCh; SoP
(Looking at the Cross.) BePJ; SoP
In ev'ry thought, in ev'ry wish I own. Joseph Howe. *Fr.* Acadia. CaP
In Excelsis. Amy Lowell. MAP; MoAmPo
In Exile. B. E. Baughan. ACV; AnNZ
In Explanation. Walter Learned. AA; HBV
(Explanation, An.) ALV
In exsilio, somewhere around Pontus. Notes to the Life of Ovid. Andras Hamori. NYTB
In extended observation of the ways and works of man. Et Dona Ferentes. Kipling. NoP
In Extremis. Fray Angelico Chavez. JKCP (1955 ed.)
In Extremis. Margaret Fishback. FiBHP
In Extremis. George Sterling. HBV
In fair Provence, the land of lute and rose. Sestina. Sir Edmund Gosse. InP
In fair Worcester City and in Worcestershire. The Gosport Tragedy (A *vers.*). *Unknown.* BaBo
In Fairyland. Joyce Kilmer. TSW
In faith, good Histor, long is your delay. Geron and Histor. Sir Philip Sidney. *Fr.* Arcadia. SiPS
In faith, I do not love thee with mine eyes. Sonnets, CXLI. Shakespeare. CBEP; MaPo; PoEL-2; TrGrPo
In faith I wot not well what to say. Sir Thomas Wyatt. FCP; SiPS
In Faith Methinks It Is No Right. Sir Thomas Wyatt. CBEP; FCP
(Resignation.) OBSC
In far forests' leafy twilight, now is stealing gray dawn's shy light. Music of the Dawn. Virginia Bioren Harrison. HBV
In far Tibet/ There live a lama. I Will Arise and Go Now. Ogden Nash. WaKn
In Fargo, North Dakota, a man. To Flood Stage Again. James Wright. FRC
In fashion as a snow-white rose, lay then. Paradiso: The Saints in Glory. Dante. *Fr.* Divina Commedia. WGRP
In Favor of One's Time. Frank O'Hara. NeAP
In February. P. A. Ropes. BoTP
In February. Henry Simpson. HBV
In February. John Addington Symonds. DD; PRWS; YeAr
In February I give you gallant sport. Of the Months, February. Folgore da San Geminiano. AWP

In February there are days. When. Dorothy Aldis. RePo; SiSoSe
In February when few gusty flakes. Groundhog Day. Marnie Pomeroy. OTD; PoSC
In February, when the sap's below. Pruning Vines. Howard McKinley Corning. MAP; MoAmPo (1942 ed.)
In fellowship of living things. A Creed. Ellen Glasgow. OQP
In fellowship Religion has its founts. George Meredith. *Fr.* The Test of Manhood. WGRP
In Festubert. Edmund Blunden. OBMV
In fiction tales we keep performing. The Collies. Edward Anthony. GoTP
In Fields of Summer. Galway Kinnell. BoNaP; WIRo
In fifty years, when peace outshines. Song-Books of the War. Siegfried Sassoon. InP
In '59 Pike's Peakers were a sight. The Pike's Peakers. Lawrence N. Greenleaf. PoOW
In five-score summers! All new eyes. 1967. Thomas Hardy. PG (1945 ed.); VP
In Flaccum. Sir John Davies. TuPP
In Flanders Fields. John McCrae. BBV; BEL; BLPA; CaP; DD; EnLit; FaBV; FaFP; GTSL; HBV; HH; InP; MaRV; MCCG; MPB; NeHB; NeMA; OBCV; OHFP; OQP; OTD; OtMeF; OTPC (1946 ed.); PaA; PAL; PCD; PeCV; PEDC; PGD; PoFr; PoMa; PoPl; PoPo; PoRL; SiSoSe; SP; StVeCh (1940 ed.); TIHL; TreF; TwCaPo; ViBoPo; YT
In Flanders Fields. *Unknown.* WBLP
In Flanders Fields the cannon[s] boom. Another Reply to "In Flanders Fields" [*or* In Flanders Fields; an Answer]. C. B. Galbreath. BLPA; HH; PAL
In Flanders fields the poppies blow. In Flanders Fields. John McCrae. BBV; BEL; BLPA; CaP; DD; EnLit; FaBV; FaFP; GTSL; HBV; HH; InP; MaRV; MCCG; MPB; NeHB; NeMA; OBCV; OHFP; OQP; OTD; OtMeF; OTPC (1946 ed.); PaA; PAL; PCD; PeCV; PEDC; PGD; PoFr; PoMa; PoPl; PoPo; PoRL; SiSoSe; SP; StVeCh (1940 ed.); TIHL; TreF; TwCaPo; ViBoPo; YT
"In Flanders fields, where poppies blow." Old Soldier Dead. Annette Kohn. HH
In Flanders Now. Edna Jaques. CaP; MaRV
In Flaundres whylom [*or* whilom] was a companye [*or* compaignye]. The Pardoner's Tale. Chaucer. *Fr.* The Canterbury Tales. BEL; CoBE; EnLit; FiP; FosPo; MBW-1; OAEP; PoEL-1; PoIE; WHA
In flowed at once a gay embroidered race. Pope. *Fr.* The Dunciad, IV. NoP
In flow'ry Japan, the home of the fan. The Feast of the Doll. Nora Archibald Smith. PPL
In fond delusion once I left thy side. A Sonnet to My Mother. Heine. TrJP
In Foreign Parts. Laura E. Richards. HBV; HBVY
In Forest Depths. Richard Henry Horne. *Fr.* Orion. VA
In forgiving mood, this sultry July afternoon. Goodbye to Regal. Daniel Huws. NYBP
In form and feature, face and limb. The Twins. Henry Sambrooke Leigh. BiCB; BOHV; CenHV; FaPON; GaP; GoTP; HBV; HBVY; MaC; OTPC (1946 ed.); PoMa; PoPl; ShM; StaSt; StVeCh (1940 ed.); TiPo; TSW; WaKn
In former days my father and mother. Cuckoo. *Unknown.* *Fr.* Riddles. AnOE
In former times, when Israel's ancient creed. Absolute and Abitofhell. Ronald Arbuthnott Knox. CenHV
In fourteen hundred and ninety-two. Christopher Columbus. Franklin Pierce Adams. InMe
In fourteen hundred and ninety-two. Christofo Columbo. *Unknown.* AmSS
In fourteen hundred and ninety-two. Moosehead Lake. *Unknown.* OuSiCo
In fourteen hundred ninety-two, Columbus sailed the ocean blue. The History of the U. S. Winifred Sackville Stoner. BLPA; TreF; YaD
In frames as large as rooms that face all ways. Essential Beauty. Philip Larkin. PoeP
In France. Frances Cornford. HBMV
In Freedom's War, of "Thirty Years" and more. Enfant Perdu [*or* Lost Child—Enfant Perdu]. Heine, *tr. by* Richard Monckton Milnes. AWP; OuHeWo; PoFr; WoL
In Freezing Winter Night. Robert Southwell. *See* New Prince, New Pomp.
In 'Frisco Bay there lay three ships. A Long Time Ago (C *vers.*). *Unknown.* SoAmSa
In front of our mouths, wherever we swim. Goldfish on the Writing Desk. Max Brod. LiTW; TrJP
In Front of the Landscape. Thomas Hardy. OBNC
In front of the sombre mountains, a faint, lost ribbon of rainbow. On the Balcony. D. H. Lawrence. BrPo
In front the awful Alpine track. Stanzas in Memory of the Author of "Obermann." Matthew Arnold. EPN; MaVP; PoVP; ViPo; ViPP
In front the horse's rump bright as a lantern. Sleighride. Patrick Anderson. CaP; OBCV
In futurity/ I prophetic see. The Little Girl Lost. Blake. *Fr.* Songs of Experience. DiPo
In Galilee. Mary Frances Butts. AA
In Galilee. Jessie Mackay. AnNZ
In gayer hours, when high my fancy run. The Bastard's Lot. Richard Savage. *Fr.* The Bastard. CBEP; OBEC
In Genesis, the world was made. Old Testament Contents. *Unknown.* BLPA
In Genoa a friar walked. The Friar of Genoa. Scharmel Iris. JKCP
In Genoa the superb O'Connell dies. The Dead Tribune. Denis Florence MacCarthy. ACP
In Gerontem. Sir John Davies. ReIE
In Gethsemane. Giles Fletcher. MaRV; StJW
In Glencullen. J. M. Synge. BiS; ELU; OBMV; OxBI; ThWaDe
In Go-Cart So Tiny. Kate Greenaway. *See* Around the World.
In God We Trust. Oswald J. Smith. SoP
In God's Eternal Studios. Paul Shivell. *Fr.* The Studios Photographic. HBV
In God's name, cheerly on, courageous friends. Shakespeare. King Richard III, *fr.* V, ii. PoFr
In going to my naked bed, as one that would have slept. Amantium Irae. Richard Edwards. CBEP; EIL HBV; LoBV; OBEV; OBSC; PoE; ReEn; ReIE; SiCE; TuPP
In Golden Gate Park that day. Lawrence Ferlinghetti. *Fr.* A Coney Island of the Mind. ToPo
In golden youth when seems the earth. Gethsemane. Ella Wheeler Wilcox. SoP
In good condition. For Sale, a Horse. Charles Edward Taylor. AA
In good King Charles's golden days. The Vicar of Bray. *Unknown.* ALV; CEP; EiCL; HBV; InvP; OBEC; OxBoLi; ViBoPo
In good old Benjamin Franklin's time. The Truth about B. F. Albert Stillman. InMe
In Good Old Colony Times, *with music.* *Unknown.* BFSS
In good old times, which means, you know. Verses Intended to Go with a Posset Dish to My Dear Little Goddaughter, 1882. James Russell Lowell. AP
In Goya's greatest scenes we seem to see. A Coney Island of the Mind, 1. Lawrence Ferlinghetti. LiTM(1970 ed.); NeAP; NMP
In Granada baths are de rigeur; therefore the freighters. The Andalusian Lute: Another Baedeker. Raymond Dipalma *and* Stephen Shrader. QAH
In Gratitude for Friends. Margaret E. Sangster. SoP
In Grato Jubilo. David McCord. UnS
In graves where drips the winter rain. The Song of the Graves. *Unknown.* OBMV
In Great Bitterness. Cino da Pistoia. *See* Sonnet: To Love, in Great Bitterness.
In great museums one learns simple things. Visit to a Museum. Arthur Davison Ficke. NYTB
In Greece the shadows slept as still. Hawaiian Hilltop. Genevieve Taggard. PoMa
In green Caledonia they ne'er were two lovers. Burns and His Highland Mary. *Unknown.* ShS
In Green Old Gardens. "Violet Fane." HBV; VA
In "green pastures?" Not always; sometimes He. *See* In "pastures green"?. . .
In greenwoods once these relics must have known. Driftwood. Richard Wilbur. FiMAP
In grey April when the bud rounded. The Flute of May. Harry Woodbourne. GoYe
In grey-haired Celia's withered arms. A Paraphrase from the French. Matthew Prior. OxBoLi

In Grief. Tennyson. *See* In Memoriam, A. H. H.: "Strong Son of God, immortal Love."
In grief and anguish of my heart my voice I did extend. The Song of Jonah in the Whale's Belly. Michael Drayton. *Fr.* The Harmony of the Church. ReIE
In grimy winter dusk. Stop. Richard Wilbur. WIRo
In groves of green trees. Black Students. Julia Fields. NBP
In Guernsey. Swinburne. ATP (1935 ed.); PoVP
In guilty night & hid in false disguise. *Unknown.* SeCSL
In Gusts of Music. Sister Davida. JKCP (1955 ed.)
In Hades. Anna Callender Brackett. AA
In haist ga hy thee to sum hoill. John Rolland. *Fr.* The Sevin Seages. OxBS
In halls of sleep you wandered by. Among Shadows. Arthur Davison Ficke. NP
In Hampton Roads, the airs of March were bland. The Attack. Thomas Buchanan Read. PAH
In Hans' old mill his three black cats. Five Eyes. Walter de la Mare. UTS
In Harbor. Paul Hamilton Hayne. AA; HBV
In Harbor. Lizette Woodworth Reese. TrPWD
In hard/ country each white. Hard Country. Philip Booth. CoAP
In Hardin County, 1809. Lulu E. Thompson. GSP; PoMa; PoSC; StPo
In Hardwood Groves. Robert Frost. AmLP; MWA-2
In Harmony with Nature. Matthew Arnold. EPN; MaRV; MBW-2; OAEP; PoIE; PoVP; ViPP
(To an Independent Preacher.) TOP
In haste, post haste, when first my wandering mind. Gascoigne's Memories, IV. George Gascoigne. EnRePo; Sonn
In having all things, and not Thee, what have I? Delight in God Only. Francis Quarles. *Fr.* Emblems. MaRV
In Haywodum. Sir John Davies. ReIE; SiCE; TuPP
In health and ease am I. Francis Davison. EG
In hearts too young for enmity there lies the way. Disarm the Hearts. Ethel Blair Jordan. PGD
In Heaven,/ Some little blades of grass. The Blades [*or* Blade] of Grass. Stephen Crane. The Black Riders, XVIII. AmP; AP; MAP; MaRV; MoAmPo; NeMA; PoPl; PoPo; TreFT
In Heaven a spirit doth dwell. Israfel. Poe. AA; AmePo; AmP; AmPP; AnAmPo; AnFE; AP; APA; AWP; BoLiVe; CoAnAm; CoBA; HBV; InPo; LiTA; MAmP; MWA-1; NePA; OxBA; PFY; PoEL-4; PoPo; RG; TDP; TreFS; TSW; WHA
In heaven a Spirit doth dwell. Israfiddlestrings, *parody. Unknown.* BOHV
In heaven-high musings and many. The Strength of Fate. Euripides, *tr.* by A. E. Housman. *Fr.* Alcestis. AWP; JAWP; WBP
In Heaven, I Suppose, Lie Down [Together]. C. Day Lewis. CMoP; MoPo
In heaven soaring up I dropt an ear. The Joy of Church Fellowship [Rightly Attended]. Edward Taylor. *Fr.* God's Determinations. AmP; AmPP; AP; CBEP; MAmP; MWA-1; OxBA; SCAP
In heaven there is a star I call my own. Sonnets. Irene Rutherford McLeod. HBMV
In heaven, too. Heard in a Violent Ward. Theodore Roethke. ML; PoeP
In Heavenly Love Abiding. Anna L. Waring. MaRV; SoP
In heav'n the blessed angels have their being. Ode VIII: That All Other Creatures Have Their Abiding in Heaven, Hell, Earth, Air, Water, or Fire; but He in All of Them. Francis Davison. ReIE
In Heavy Mind. James Agee. MAP; MoAmPo
In Hellbrunn. George Trakl, *tr. fr. German by* Werner Heider. LiTW
In her coffin, satin-shirred. A Poor Relation. Audrey McGaffin. NePoAm-2
In her desperation she opens the gas-tap. Ordinary People on Sunday. Tom Veitch. ANYP
In her ear he whispers gaily. The Lord of Burleigh. Tennyson. OTPC (1923 ed.)
In her fair cheeks two pits do lie. A Song. Thomas Carew. UnTE
In her first passion woman loves her lover. Byron. *Fr.* Don Juan. ErPo; UnTE
In her little tent Honey Bumps. Trumansburg Fair. William Hathaway. QAH
In her lone cottage on the downs. Miss Thompson Goes Shopping. Martin Armstrong. ShBV-2; WePo
In Her Song She Is Alone. Jon Swan. NYBP
In higher natures, poetic or mystical. Robert Bridges. *Fr.* The Testament of Beauty. LO
In highest Heaven, at Mary's knee. The Cherub-Folk. Enid Dinnis. CAW
In highest way of heaven the sun did ride. Astrophel and Stella, XXII. Sir Philip Sidney. FCP; OBSC; SiPS; Sonn
In Him. James Vila Blake. WGRP
In Him. Annie Johnson Flint. BLRP; SoP; TRV
In Him Confiding. William Cowper. *See* Joy and Peace in Believing.
In Him We Live. Henry More. MaRV
In Him We Live. Jones Very. AmP; OxBA
In Him Ye Are Made Full. William H. Hudnut, Sr. ChIP
In his chamber, weak and dying. A Strike among the Poets. *Unknown.* BOHV; FiBHP; PP; SiTL
In his cliff-carved tomb. Above the Nile. Horace E. Hamilton. NYTB
In His Extreme Sickness. Thomas, Lord Vaux. ReIE
In his father's face flying. Icarus. Ronald Bottrall. GTBS-P
In His Good Time. Robert Browning. *Fr.* Paracelsus. OQP
(I Go to Prove My Soul.) MaRV
In his grandmother's garden was a cake with seven candles. Seven Times One Are Seven. Robert Hillyer. BiCB
In His hands I leave tomorrow. Tomorrow. Della Adams Leitner. STF
In his last bin [*or* binn] Sir Peter lies. Song. Thomas Love Peacock. *Fr.* Headlong Hall. EnRP; OBRV; ViBoPo
In his lone cave the lion sleeps. The Lion at Noon. Victor Hugo. LiTW
In his malodorous brain what slugs and mire. God. Isaac Rosenberg. MoPo
In His Mental Illness, William Cowper Finds He Is Not Alone. William Cowper. *See* Stricken Deer, The.
In his old gusty garden of the North. Robert Louis Stevenson. Lizette Woodworth Reese. HBV
In his own image the Creator made. On Man [*or* Man]. Walter Savage Landor. NBM; OBNC; OBRV; VA
In his sea lit. The Double Play. Robert Wallace. PP; SD
In His Service. Clarence E. Clar. STF
In His Sight. Anna R. Baker. OQP
In His Steps. Katharine Lee Bates. PGD
In his tall senatorial. The Drum; the Narrative of the Demon of Tedworth. Edith Sitwell. *Fr.* Façade. BoW; FaBoTw
In his travels, the elephant. Elephant. David McFadden. WHW
In His Utter Wretchedness. John Audelay. MeEL
In Hoc Signo. Godfrey Fox Bradby. MaRV; SoP; TRV
(Kingdoms.) ChIP
In holly hedges starving birds. Christmas Eve. John Davidson. MPB; OHIP
In holy night we made the vow. Writ in Water. Meleager. OuHeWo
In Homer's time. The City. Emmett Jarrett. *Fr.* Design for the City of Man. ThO
In honnour of this heghe fest, of custume yere by yere. A Lover's New Year's Gift. John Lydgate. PoEL-1
In Honor of His Mistress. Cecco Angiolieri da Siena. *See* Sonnet: Of Love, in Honor of His Mistress Becchina.
In Honor of St. Alphonsus Rodriguez. Gerard Manley Hopkins. ForPo
(St. Alphonsus Rodriguez.) PoIE
In Honour of Christmas. *Unknown.* MeEL
In Honour of St. David's Day. *Unknown.* PrWP
In Honor of Taffy Topaz. Christopher Morley. CIV; PoMa; TiPo
In Honour of the City of London. William Dunbar. OBEV
(To the City of London.) ChTr
In Hospital. W. E. Henley. BrPo
Sels.
Apparition, XXV. BEL; EnLi-2 (1949 ed.); PoVP; TrGrPo
Before, IV. BEL; EnLi-2; MoBrPo; OuHeWo; PoVP
Casualty, XIII. PoVP
Discharged, XXVIII. PoVP
Enter Patient, I. PoVP
House-Surgeon, XVI. PoVP
Operation, V. PoVP
Pastoral, XXII. Po

In (continued)
Romance, XXI. EnLit; MC; PAH
Scrubber, XIX. PoVP
Staff-Nurse: New Style, X. NBM; PoVP
Staff-Nurse: Old Style, VIII. InP; PoVP
Vigil, VII. LoBV
Waiting, II. NBM; PoVP
In Hospital: Poona (I). Alun Lewis. DTC; MoPW; NeBP; SeCePo
In Hospital: Poona (II). Alun Lewis. DTC
In Hotels Public and Private. Ralph Pomeroy. CoPo
In Hours of Discouragement God Is Our Encouragement. Helen Steiner Rice. FaChP
In houses where no snakes are found. *Unknown.* *Fr.* The Panchatantra. LiTW
In Humbleness. Daniel G. Hoffman. NePA
In Imagine Pertransit Homo. Thomas Campion. *See* Follow Thy Fair Sun.
In Imitation of Anacreon. Matthew Prior. CEP; EiCL
(On Critics.) SeCeV
In Imitation of Pope. Isaac Hawkins Browne. *Fr.* A Pipe of Tobacco. OBEC
("Blest Leaf! whose aromatic gales dispense.") Par
In Imitation of Young. Isaac Hawkins Browne. *Fr.* A Pipe of Tobacco. OBEC
In Immemoriam. "Cuthbert Bede." NA
(In Memoriam.) BOHV
In India. Karl Shapiro. NYBP
In inexperienc'd infancy. Shadows in the Water. Thomas Traherne. AtBAP
In innocence that this could be. Three Persons. Louise Townsend Nicholl. CAW
In Ionia Whence sprang old poets' fame. Phoebe on Latmus. Michael Drayton. *Fr.* Endimion and Phoebe. OBSC; ReIE
In Ireland: By the Pool at the Third Rosses. Arthur Symons. OBNC
In Islington for the moment I reside. Important Statement. Patrick Kavanagh. PoCh
In it there is a space-ship. A Boy's Head. Miroslav Holub. FIW
In Italy, in Belgium, in France. Our Dead, Overseas. Edwin Markham. OQP
In Italy, where this sort of thing can occur. A Hill. Anthony Hecht. CoAP; NYBP
In its absence it has become beautiful. The Glove. Harold Bond. NYBP; YAP
In its going down, the moon. Poem. Robert Hogg. MoCV
In jealousy of cause and pride of plan. Autonomous. Mark Van Doren. LiTA; PG (1955 ed.)
In Jericho. *Unknown.* SiTL
In Jerusalem. *Unknown.* StJW
In Joe Brainard's collage its white arrow. Sonnet XV. Ted Berrigan. FRC
In July month, ae bonny morn. My Winsome Dear. Robert Fergusson. *Fr.* Leith Races. SeCePo
In June. Nora Perry. YeAr
In June, amid the golden fields. The Groundhog. Richard Eberhart. AmLP; AmP; AnFE; CABA; CBV; CMoP; CoAnAm; DTC; ExPo; FaBoMo; FaFP; GTBS-W; ILP; LiTA; LiTG; LiTM; MasP; MiAP; MoAB; MoAmPo (1962 ed.); MoPo; MoVE; NePA; PG (1955 ed.); PoIE; PoSa; ReMP; SeCeV; StP; ToPo; TwAmPo; UnPo (3d ed.); WaP
In June and Gentle Oven. Anne Wilkinson. MoCV; PeCV
In June I give you a close-wooded fell. Of the Months: June. Folgore da San Geminiano. AWP
In June the bush we call. The Victors. Denise Levertov. NoP
In June the early signs. For a Christening. Anne Ridler. MoPo
In Just-/ Spring When the World Is Mud. E. E. Cummings. Chansons Innocentes, I. AmLP; AmPP; CAD; FaBV; FaPON; GoTP; MAP; MoAB; MoAmPo; MoShBr; NoP; NP; PoAn; ReMP; RePo; ThWaDe
In Kalamazoo, in Kalamazoo. Why I No Longer Travel. Laura E. Richards. MPB
In Kensington Gardens. Arthur Symons. EnLoPo
In Kerry. J. M. Synge. AWP; JAWP; MoBrPo; WBP
In kirtle of myrtle the goose girl goes. The Goose Girl. Dorothy Roberts. CaP
In kohl mines and estaminets of gold. The Vole. Marvin Solomon. NePoAm-2
In Köln [*or* Köhln], a town of monks and bones. Cologne. Samuel Taylor Coleridge. ALV; BOHV; HBV; InMe; WhC
In kraals of slanting shade the herd. Buffalo. Charles Eglington. PeSA
In Lacrimas. *Unknown.* *See* I Saw My Lady Weep.
In lands I never saw, they say. Emily Dickinson. NePA
In Larch Wood/ Is a little grey pool. Larch Wood Secrets. Ivy O. Eastwick. BoTP
In late summer the wild geese. August Hail. J. V. Cunningham. PoIE; PoSa
In late winter. The Bear. Galway Kinnell. CoAP; PoIE (1970 ed.)
In Leinster. Louise Imogen Guiney. AA; JKCP; OBVV
(Song: "I try to knead and spin.") GoBC; HBV
(Song in Leinster.) PFY
In letters large upon the frame. What's in a Name? Richard Kendall Munkittrick. BOHV; InMe
In life still death is here. Media Vita. *At.to* Notker Balbulus. CAW
In life three ghostly friars were we. Glee—The Ghosts. Thomas Love Peacock. *Fr.* Melincourt. ViBoPo
In Lincolnshire, a village full of tongues. On Looking at Stubbs's Anatomy of the Horse. Edward Lucie-Smith. NePoEA-2
In little Annie's garden. Annie's Garden. Eliza Lee Follen. PPL
In little faces pinched with cold and hunger. As Ye Do It unto These. *Unknown.* ChIP; SoP
In Little Rock the people bear. The Chicago *Defender* Sends a Man to Little Rock, Fall, 1957. Gwendoyn Brooks. AmNP
In little white dresses and little white pants. The Popcorn Party. "E. R. B." GFA
In Liverpool there liv'd a man. The Big Five-Gallon Jar. *Unknown.* ShS
In Locksley town, in merry Nottinghamshire. Robin Hood's Birth, Breeding, Valor, and Marriage. *Unknown.* ESPB
In Loco. Peter Jackson. BoSA
In London city there did dwell. The Farmer's Daughter. *Unknown.* BFSS
In London city was Bicham born. Young Beichan. *Unknown.* ESPB; ViBoFo
In London City where I once did dwell, there's where I got my learning. Barbara Allen. *Unknown.* AS; BeLS
In London I never know what I'd be at. The Contrast. C. Morris. BOHV
In London once I lost my way. A Plain Direction. Thomas Hood. OTPC (1946 ed.)
In London, September, 1802. Wordsworth. *See* Written in London, September, 1802.
In London there I was bent. London Lackpenny [*or* Lickpenny]. *Unknown.* ChTr; CoMu; EnPo
In London town where I did dwell. The Butcher Boy. *Unknown.* ViBoFo
In London was young Beichan born. Young Beichan [and Susie Pye]. *Unknown.* FIW; HBV; LoEn; OBB; OnMSP
In lonely watches night by night. Requiescat. Frederick George Scott. DD; OHIP
In loopy links the canker crawls. Indifference. *Unknown.* NA
In Lord Carpenter's Country. Barry O. Higgs. PeSA
In Louisiana. Albert Bigelow Paine. AA; AmFN
In Love. David Wevill. MoCV
In Love for Long. Edwin Muir. GTBS-W; LiTM (rev. ed.); MoBrPo (1962 ed.)
In love his kingdom great two fools there be. Laura, VIII. Robert Tofte. ReIE; Sonn; TuPP
In Love, If Love Be Love. Tennyson. *Fr.* Idylls of the King: Merlin and Vivien. CABA; GTBS; GTSL; MeWo; PoEL-5; TrGrPo
(All in All.) GTBS-W; LiTB; TRV
(If Love Be Ours.) OQP
(Vivien's Song.) FaBoEn; OBNC
In love they wore themselves in a green embrace. Adolescence. P. K. Page. CaP; OBCV; TwCaPo
In love to be sure what disasters we meet. The Lover's Arithmetic. *Unknown.* OxBoLi
In love with all earth's loveliness. The Parable of the Mustard Weed. Dora Hagemeyer. StaSt
In Love with the Bears. Greg Kuzma. NYBP

In Love with Two. Ovid, *tr. fr. Latin by* Christopher Marlowe. Amores, II, 10. MeWo
In love with you I all things elce doe hate. *Unknown.* SeCSL
In loving thee thou know'st I am forsworn. Sonnets, CLII. Shakespeare. ReIE; Sonn
In loving you, sweet land, we love a thing. Sweet Land. Francis Maguire. JKCP (1955 ed.)
In lowly dale, fast by a river's side. Land of Indolence. James Thomson. *Fr.* The Castle of Indolence. EnRP; OBEC; SeCePo; ViBoPo
In Magic Words. Merrill Moore. Sonn
In Maidstone Gaol, I am lamenting. Farewell to the World of Richard Bishop. *Unknown.* CoMu
In Mantua-territory half is slough. Sordello's Birth-Place. Robert Browning. *Fr.* Sordello. MyFE
In Manus Tuas, Domine. *Unknown.* CoBE
In many forms we try. The Bohemian Hymn. Emerson. OQP; PFY; WGRP
In many places here and. Fate Is Unfair. Don Marquis. *Fr.* Archy Does His Part. EvOK
In marble halls as white as milk. Mother Goose. ChTr; HBV; HBVY; OTPC; OxNR; PPL; RIS; SiTL; StVeCh
In Marcellum. Thomas Freeman. SiCE
In March. Philip Martin. PoAu-2
In March. Wordsworth. *See* Written in March.
In March come the March winds. The March Winds. George Washington Wright Houghton. YeAr
In March I give you plenteous fisheries. Sonnets of the Months: March. Folgore da San Geminiano. AWP
In March sow thy barley, thy lond not too cold. March. Thomas Tusser. ReIE
In Marion, the honey-locust trees are falling. Two Poems about President Harding, I. James Wright. AmPC; CoAP
In martial sports I had my cunning tried. Astrophel and Stella, LIII. Sir Philip Sidney. FCP; ReEn; ReIE; SiPS
In mathematicks he was greater. Samuel Butler. *Fr.* Hudibras, I, 1. ImOP
In Mather's Magnalia Christi. The Phantom Ship. Longfellow. EtS
In matters of commerce the fault of the Dutch. Epigrams: The Dutch. George Canning. OxBoLi
In May. W. H. Davies. OBVV
In May. J. M. Synge. MeWo; MoBrPo
In May. *Unknown.* BoTP
In May, approaching the city, I. The Ritualists. William Carlos Williams. NYBP
In May I go a-walking to hear the linnet sing. In May. *Unknown.* BoTP
In May my heart was breaking. Autumn Valentine. Dorothy Parker. NeMA
In May, when Flora, the fresshe lusty quene. John Lydgate. *Fr.* The Complaint of the Black Knight. EnPo
In May, when sea-winds pierced our solitudes. The Rhodora. Emerson. AA; AmePo; AmLP; AmPP; AnAmPo; AnEnPo; AnFE; AnNE; AP; APA; AWP; BoLiVe; BoNaP; CoAnAm; CoBA; DD; FaBV; FaFP; GN; GoTP; GTSE; HBV; HBVY; ILP; InPo; JAWP; LiTA; LiTG; MAmP; MCCG; MPB; MWA-1; NeHB; NoP; OHFP; OTPC; OxBA; PoIE; SeCeV; TOP; TreFS; TrGrPo; TRV; WBP; WHA; YT
In May, when sea-winds pierced our solitudes. Variation on a Line by Emerson. W. S. Merwin. NePA
In me is a little painted square. Old Age. Maxwell Bodenheim. MAP; MoAmPo (1942 ed.)
In Me, Past, Present, Future Meet. Siegfried Sassoon. OBEV (new ed.)
In Me Two Worlds. C. Day Lewis. AnFE
In mean time flew our ships, and straight we fetched. Homer. *Fr.* The Odyssey, XII. TuPP
In Measure Time We'll Row, *with music.* *Unknown.* ShS
In Medias Res. William Stafford. StP
In melancholic [*or* a melancholy] fancy. Hallo [*or* Hollo], My Fancy! William Cleland, *and others.* CH; OxBoLi; SeCL
In Memorabilia Mortis. Francis Sherman. CaP
In Memoriam. "Max Adeler". *See* Willie.
In Memoriam. "Cuthbert Bede". *See* In Immemoriam.
In Memoriam. Frank A. Collymore. PoNe
In Memoriam. Henry W. Frost. SoP
In Memoriam. Ada Jackson. PGD
In Memoriam. Mary Lamb. *See* Parental Recollections.
In Memoriam. Lewis MacAdams. ANYP
In Memoriam. Richard Monckton Milnes. HBV
In Memoriam, A. C. M. L., *sel.* Cecil Arthur Spring-Rice. "God of all power and might." TrPWD
In Memoriam: A. C., R. J. O., K. S. John Betjeman. NYBP
In Memoriam, A. H., *sel.* Maurice Baring. "God, who had made you valiant, strong, and swift." CAW
In Memoriam A. H. H. Tennyson. EnLi-2, *abr.*; EPN; ILP, *much abr.*; MaVP; MBW-2; NoP, *abr.*; OAEP, *abr.*; PAn, *much abr.*; PoVP; ViPo; ViPP; VP
Sels.
"Again at Christmas did we weave," LXXVIII. EnL; EnLit
"And all is well, tho' faith and form," CXXVII. BEL; CoBE; HBV
"And, star and system rolling past," *fr.* Epilogue. ImOP
"Are God and Nature then at strife," *fr.* LV. TRV
"As sometimes in a dead man's face," LXXIV. LiTB; LiTG
"Be near me when my light is low," L. AnFE; AtBAP; BEL; CoBE; ELP; EnL; LiTB; LiTG; MemP; PoE; PoEL-5; PoFS; TOP
"By night we linger'd on the lawn," XCV. AnFE; EnL; FosPo; LoBV; OBNC; PoEL-5
"Calm is the morn without a sound," XI. BoLiVe; ChTr; CoBE; ELP; ExPo; FaBoEn; FiP; ForPo; FosPo; GTBS-D; LiTB; MaPo (1969 ed.); OBEV (1st ed.); OBNC; PIA; PoE; PoEL-5; PoFS; SeCeV; ShBV-4; TrGrPo
"Contemplate all this work of Time," CXVIII. BEL; CoBE; EnL; MaPo; PoFS; SeCeV; TOP
"Danube to the Severn gave, The," XIX. EnL; GTBS-P; LoBV; TOP
"Dark house, by which once more I stand," VII. BEL, *abr.*; BWP; CoBE; DiPo; EnL; EnLit; FaBoEn; FosPo; GTBS-P; LiTB; MaPo; OBNC; PoE; PoEL-5; PoIE; PoSa; SeCeV; UnPo
"Dear friend, far off, my lost desire," CXXIX. MaPo; TOP
(Truths That Never Can Be Proved, The.) MaRV
"Strange friend, past, present and to be," *br. sel.* LO
"Dip down upon the northern shore," LXXXIII. MaPo
(Spring.) HBV
"Do we indeed desire the dead," LI. AtBAP; BEL; TOP
"Doors, where my heart was used to beat," CXIX. DiPo; OBNC; PoEL-5
"Fair ship, that from the Italian shore," IX. BoLiVe; GTSL; OBEV (1st ed.)
"Her eyes are homes of silent prayer," XXXII. TOP
"How fares it with the happy dead," XLIV. OBEV (1st ed.)
"How many a father have I seen," LIII. BEL; TOP
"How pure at heart and sound in head," XCIV. CoBE
"I cannot love thee as I ought," LII. BEL; EnLit
"I cannot see the features right," LXX. EnL; FosPo; LiTB; PoEL-5
"I climb the hill: from end to end," C. PoEL-5; TOP
"I envy not in any moods," XXVII. BEL; CoBE; EnL; EnLit; FaBoEn; LiTB; LiTG; LiTL; OBNC; OuHeWo; TOP
(Lost Love.) TreFS
(Tis Better to Have Loved and Lost.) MaRV
"I falter where I firmly trod." *fr.* LV.
(Larger Hope, The.) MaRV
"I hear the noise about thy keel," X. GTSL; OBEV (1st ed.)
"I held it truth, with him who sings," I. BEL; BoLiVe; CoBe; DiPo; EnL; EnLit; HBV; LiTB; LiTG; OBNC; OQP
"I know that this was Life—the track," XXV. TOP
"I past beside the reverend walls," LXXXVII. CoBE
"I sing to him that rests below," XXI. EnL; FosPo
"I sometimes hold it half a sin," V. FosPo; OuHeWo
"I trust I have not wasted breath," CXX. CoBE; ImOP; SeCePo; TOP
"I wage not any feud with Death," LXXXII. LiTB; LiTG; PPON; TOP
"If one should bring me this report," XIV.
(Of One Dead.) LiTB; LiTG
"If sleep and death be truly one," XLIII. MaPo (1969 ed.); OBNC
"Is it, then, regret for buried time," CXVI. BEL; MaPo
"Lo, as a dove when up she springs," XII. LoBV
"Love is and was my lord and king," CXXVI. BEL; CoBE; HBV; OBEV; OBNC; SeCeV
(My Lord and King.) ChTr
"Man, that with me trod, The," *fr.* Epilogue. TRV
"My own dim life should teach me this," XXXIV. CoBE; EnL; FosPo; MaPo; SeCePo

In (continued)
(Life Shall Live for Evermore.) MaRV; OQP
"Now fades the last long streak of snow," CXV. BEL; BoC; CoBE; FaBoEn; GTBS-D; GTBS-P; MaPo; OBEV (1st ed.); OBNC; PoE; PoSa; SeCeV; ShBV-4
(Spring.) DD; HBV; YT
"Now, sometimes in my sorrow shut," XXIII. OBEV (1st ed.); TOP
"O days and hours, your work is this," CXVII. BEL; HBV; MaPo
"O living will that shalt endure," CXXXI. BEL; BoLiVe; CoBE; DiPo; EnL; EnLit; FaBoBe; ForPo; HBV; TOP
(Prayer, The: "O living will that shalt endure.") WGRP
(Truths That Never Can Be Proved, The.) MaRV
"O Sorrow, cruel fellowship," III. EnL; MaPo; TOP
"O sorrow wilt thou live with me." LIX. GTSL
"O thou that after toil and storm," XXXIII. TOP
"O true and tried, so well and long," Epilogue. HW
"O wast thou with me, dearest, then," CXXII. TOP
"O yet we trust that somehow good," LIV. AnFE; AtBAP; BEL; BoLiVe; DiPo; EaLo; EnL; EnLit; ExPo (LIV-LVI); FaPL; GTBS-W; GTSL; HBV; LiTB; LiTG; LoBV; MaPo; OBNC; OQP; OuHeWo; PoE; PoFS; PoIE; SeCeV; TOP; TrGrPo; TRV; UnPo; YAT
(Larger Hope, The.) MaRV, *fr.* LIV *and* LV; TreFS; WGRP
"Old warder of these buried bones," XXXIX. PoEL-5
"Old yew, which graspest at the stones," II. BWP; ELP; EnLi-2; EPN; FaBoEn; GTBS-D; GTBS-P; MaPo; OAEP; OBNC; PIA; PoEL-5; SeCeV; ViPo
(Yew in the Graveyard, The.) UnPo (3d ed.)
"On that last night before we went," CIII. PoEL-5
"One writes, that 'other friends remain,'" VI. BEL; MaPo (1969 ed.); PoEL-5
"Our little systems have their day," *fr.* Proem. TRV
"Path by which we twain did go, The," XXII. TOP
"Perplext in faith, but pure in deeds," *fr.* XCVI. TRV
"Ring out, wild bells, to the wild sky," CVI. BEL; BoLiVe; CoBE; DD; DiPo; EnL; EnLit; FaFP; FaPL; FaPON; FiP; GTBS; GTBS-W; GTSL; HBV HH; InP; LiTB; LiTG; MaPo; MaRV; MCCG; MemP; MPB; NeHB; OQP; OTPC; PEDC; PG (1945 ed.); PGD; PoE; PoIE; PoRL; SeCeV; ShBV-2; SoP; TiPo (1959 ed.); TOP; TreF; TrGrPo; TRV; UnPo; WiR, *fr.* CV *and* CVI; YAT
(Ring Out the Old, Ring in the New.) WBLP
"Risest thou thus, dim dawn, again," LXXII. GTBS-D; OBNC; PoEL-5
"'So careful of the type?' but no," LVI. AnFE; CoBE; DiPo; EnL; FosPo; HBV; InP; LoBV; MaPo; OBEV (1st ed.); OBNC; OuHeWo; SeCeV; TOP
"So many worlds, so much to do," LXXIII. HBV
Spring, CXV. TreFT
"Strong Son of God, immortal love," Proem [*or* Prologue]. BBV; BEL; BoLiVe; ChIP; CoBE; EnL; EnLit; FaPL; GTBS-W; HBV; LiTB; MaRV; NeHB; OQP; OuHeWo; OxBoCh; PoFS; PoIE; SeCeV; StJW; TOP; TreF; TrGrPo; TrPWD; TRV; UnPo (1st ed.); WGRP; WHA
(In Grief.) SoP
(Strong Son of God.) EaLo
"Sweet after showers, ambrosial air," LXXXVI. BEL; TOP
"That which we dare invoke to bless," CXXIV. EnL; FosPo; GTSL; WGRP
(Intuition.) MaRV
"There rolls the deep where grew the tree," CXXIII. CoBE; MaPo; SeCePo; SeCeV
"Tho' truths in manhood darkly join," XXXVI. ChIP
(Word, The.) GoBC
(Word Incarnate, The.) MaRV
"Thou comest, much wept for; such a breeze," XVII. EnLi-2; OBEV (1st ed.)
"Thy voice is on the rolling air," CXXX. DiPo; EnL; FaPL; FosPo; HBV; MaPo; PoFS; TOP; TRV; UnPo
(Truths That Never Can Be Proved, The.) MaRV
"Till now the doubtful dusk reveal'd," *fr.* XCV. GTBS-P
"Time draws near the birth of Christ, The," XXVIII. ChIP, 3 *sts.*; EnLit; PGD, 3 *sts.*; TOP
(Christmas Bells, 3 *sts.*) MaRV
(Rise, Happy Morn, 4 *sts.*, *incl.* 1 *st.* *fr.* XXX.) BePJ
(Time Draws Near, The.) OQP
"Time draws near the birth of Christ, The," CIV. EnLit; PoE
"To Sleep I give my powers away," IV. MaPo
"Tonight the winds begin to rise," XV. AnFE; FaBoEn; GTBS-D; GTBS-P; LiTB; OBEV (1st ed.); OBNC; PoEL-5; PoFS; PoSa; ShBV-4
"Unwatch'd the garden bough shall sway," CI. ELP; GTBS-D; GTBS-P; OBEV (1st ed.); OBNC; PoEL-5; SeCeV
"We leave the well-beloved place," CII. PoEL-5
"What hope is here for modern rhyme," LXXVII. CoBE; PP
"What words are these have fall'n from me," XVI. CoBE; FosPo
"When Lazarus left his charnel-cave," XXXI. MemP
"When on my bed the moonlight falls," LXVII. EnL; LoBV; NeHB; PoE; SeCePo; SeCeV; TOP
"When rosy plumelets tuft the larch," XCI. FaBoEn; OBNC; ViBoPo
"Wild bird, whose warble, liquid sweet," LXXXVIII. BEL
"Wish, that of the living whole, The," LV. AnFE; AtBAP; BEL; DiPo; EnL; EnLit; FosPo; HBV; LoBV; MaPo; OBEV (1st ed.); OBNC; OQP; OuHeWo; PoFS; SeCeV; TOP; UnPo
"Witch-elms that counterchange the floor," LXXXIX. OBNC
"With trembling fingers did we weave," XXX. CoBE; EnL; EnLit
"Yet if some voice that man could trust," XXXV. MaPo; ViBoPo
"You say, but with no touch of scorn," XCVI. BEL; EnL; EnLit; TOP
(Doubt.) WGRP
Stronger Faith, A ("Perplext in faith, but pure in deeds"), 3 *sts.* MaRV
"Yule-clog sparkled keen with frost, The," *fr.* LXXVIII. TRV
In Memoriam; Easter 1915. Edward Thomas. GTBS-P; PoIE
In Memoriam I, Elizabeth at Twenty. Richard Weber. ErPo
In Memoriam II, Elizabeth in Italy. Richard Weber. ErPo
In Memoriam: Ernst Toller. W. H. Auden. *See* In Memory of Ernst Toller.
In Memoriam F. A. S. Robert Louis Stevenson. BrPo; GTBS
In Memoriam; Francis Ledwidge. Norreys Jephson o'Connor. HBMV
In Memoriam; Ingvald Bjorndal and His Comrade. Malcolm Lowry. OBCV
In Memoriam; John Davidson. Ronald Campbell Macfie. GoTS
In Memoriam—Leo, a Yellow Cat. Margaret Sherwood. BLPA; CIV; NeHB
In Memoriam Margaritae Sorori. W. E. Henley. *See* Margaritae Sorori.
In Memoriam; Roy Campbell. R. N. Currey. ACV; BoSA; PeSA
In Memoriam S. C. W., V. C. Charles Sorley. MMA
In Memoriam S. L. Akintola. David Knight. MoCV
In Memoriam Technicam. Tom Hood. BOHV
In Memoriam—W. G. Ward. Tennyson.
(Valedictory, I.) GoBC
In Memory, *sel.* Lionel Johnson.
"Ah! fair face gone from sight, II." FaBoEn; OBNC; PoEL-5
In Memory of a Child. Vachel Lindsay. InP
In Memory of Abraham Lincoln. Oliver Wendell Holmes. LiPo
In Memory of Ann Jones. Dylan Thomas. *See* After the Funeral.
In Memory of Anna Hopewell. *Unknown.* ShM
In Memory of Arthur Winslow. Robert Lowell. AP; MiAP
Death from Cancer, *sel.* FiMAP; PoSa; TDP; TwCP
In Memory of "Barry Cornwall." Swinburne. HBV
In Memory of Boris Pasternak. Denise Levertov. NoP
In Memory of Con and Eva Gore-Booth. W. B. Yeats. *See* In Memory of Eva Gore-Booth and Con Markiewicz.
In Memory of Edward Wilson, *parody.* James Clerk Maxwell. *See* Rigid Body Sings.
In Memory of Ernst Toller. W. H. Auden. AtBAP
(In Memoriam: Ernst Toller.) NYBP
In Memory of Eva Gore-Booth and Con Markiewicz. W. B. Yeats. CABA; MBW-2; MoAB; OBMV
(In Memory of Con and Eva Gore-Booth.) OxBI
In Memory of G. K. Chesterton. Walter de la Mare. GoBC
In Memory of García Lorca. Eldon Grier. PeCV
In Memory of General Grant. Henry Abbey. AA
In Memory of James T. Fields. Whittier. OBVV
In Memory of Jane Frazer. Geoffrey Hill. NePoEA
In Memory of John Lothrop Motley. Bryant. AA
In Memory of Kathleen. Kenneth Patchen. MoAmPo
In Memory of Leopardi. James Wright. NaP
In Memory of Lewis Carroll. *Unknown.* PoRL
In memory of Maggie. On a Monument in France Which

Marks the Last Resting Place of an Army Mule. *Unknown.* ShM
In Memory of Major Robert Gregory. W. B. Yeats. AnIL; DiPo; OAEP (2d ed.); PAn; PoFS
In Memory of Marie A. Bertold Brecht, *tr. fr. German by* H. R. Hays. LiTW
In Memory of My Dear Grandchild Elizabeth Bradstreet. Anne Bradstreet. AP; SCAP
In Memory of My Feelings. Frank O'Hara. NeAP
In Memory of My Uncle Timothy. Alastair Reid. NePoEA-2
In Memory of Radio. LeRoi Jones. NeAP; NoP
In Memory of Robin Hyde, 1906-39. Charles Brasch. AnNZ
In Memory of Robinson Jeffers. Eric Barker. NYTB
In Memory of Sigmund Freud. W. H. Auden. AtBAP; CoBMV; FaBoMo; LiTB; OxBA
In Memory of the Circus Ship *Euzkera*, Wrecked in the Caribbean Sea, 1 September 1948. Walker Gibson. NePoAm
(Circus Ship *Euzkera*, The.) FiBHP
In Memory of the Spanish Poet Federico García Lorca. Thomas Merton. ML
In Memory of the Vertuous and Learned Lady Madre de Teresa. Richard Crashaw. *See* Hymn to the Name and Honor of the Admirable Saint Teresa, A.
In Memory of Two Sons. Russell Stellwagon. STF
In Memory of W. B. Yeats. W. H. Auden. ACV; ATP (1953 ed.); BoLiVe (1945 ed.); CABA; CMoP; CoBMV; EnL; FaFP; FosPo; GTBS-W; HoPM; InPo; LiTB; LiTM; MaPo; MasP; ML; MoAB; MoBrPo; MoVE; NePA; OAEP (2d ed.); OnHM; PAn; Po; PoFS; PoIE; PP; ReMP; StP; TDP; TrGrPo; UnPo (3d ed.); ViBoPo (1958 ed.)
Sels.
"Earth, receive an honoured guest." ChMP; ChTr; FaBoTw; NeMA; PG (1955 ed.)
"Follow, poet, follow right." TRV
"In the nightmare of the dark." TRV
In Memory of Walter Savage Landor. Swinburne. HBV; PoEL-5; PoFS; PoVP; VA
In Men Whom Men Condemn [as Ill]. Joaquin Miller. *Fr.* Byron. HBV; MaRV; NeMa; PoLF; OQP; TreFT
(Byron.) MAP; MoAmPo
("In men whom men condemn as ill.") OTD
(Lines.) BBV (1951 ed.)
In Merioneth, over the sad moor. Dead. Lionel Johnson. BrPo; FaBoEn; GTBS-D; OBNC; PoEL-5
In merry Scotland, in merry Scotland. Henry Martyn. *Unknown.* BaBo; CBEP; ESPB
In Mexico. Evaleen Stein. AA
In mid whirl of the dance of Time ye start. Exit. Sir William Watson. VA
In Midnights of November. A. E. Housman. PeVV
In Midst of Woods. *Unknown.* TuPP
(Blackbird, The.) ElL
In minds pure glasse when I my selfe behold. Sonnet. William Drummond of Hawthornden. OBS
In Minnesota the barns are black. William Witherup. *Fr.* Three for Robert Bly. QAH
In Misery's darkest cavern known. Samuel Johnson. *Fr.* On the Death of Mr. Robert Levet. ViBoPo
In Misty Blue. Laurence Binyon. HBMV
In mole-blue indolence the sun. The Jungle. Alun Lewis. MoPo
In Montana [a Land of Contrasts]. Washington Jay McCormick. SiTL; WhC
"In Montana, claws skim through the dawn." Experts at Veneers. Kenward Elmslie. ANYP
In Montecito. Randall Jarrell. CoAP; NoP; NYBP
In Mornigan's park there is a deer. Riddle. *Unknown.* ChTr
In morning light my damson show'd. The Plum Tree by the House. Oliver St. John Gogarty. OBEV (new ed.); PoRA
In Mortem Venerabilis Andreae Prout Carmen. Francis Sylvester Mahony. IrPN; NBM
In Moses' hand 'twas but a rod. What Is That in Thine Hand? Eva Gray. STF
In moss-prankt dells which the sunbeams flatter. Lovers, and a Reflection. Charles Stuart Calverley. BOHV; NA; WhC
In mothers womb thy fingers did me mak. A Thankful Acknowledgment of God's Providence. John Cotton. SCAP
In moving-slow he has no peer. The Sloth. Theodore Roethke. FiBHP; NePA; NePoAm; PoPo; SiTL; WaKn
In my beginning is my end. East Coker. T. S. Eliot. *Fr.* Four Quartets. ChMP; FaBoMo; MoVE; NePA
In my boat that goes. Saigyo Hoshi, *tr. fr. Japanese by* Arthur Waley. AWP
In my cave lives a solitary rat. Chez-Nous. A. G. Austin. PoAu-2
In my childhood trees were green. Autobiography. Louis MacNeice. FaBoTw; FlW
In My Craft or Sullen Art. Dylan Thomas. CaFP; ChMP; CLwM; CMoP; DiPo; GTBS-P; GTBS-W; ILP; InvP; LiTM (rev. ed.; MaPo (1969 ed.); NeBP; NoP; OAEP (2d ed.); OnHM; Po; PoSa; PP; PrWP; SeCV
In My Crib. Joseph Ceravolo. ANYP
In my dark hermitage, aloof. Stormcock in Elder. Ruth Pitter. BoC
In my ear their words are ringing. The Last Good-bye. John A. Stone. SGR
In My End Is My Beginning. Rosemary Dobson. BoAV; NeLNL
In my fancy I came upon a scene of carnage. A Thought. Michael McClure. FRC
In my father's garden, oh, beauteous, oh, fair. The Wondrous Apple Tree. *Unknown.* SaSa
In My Father's House. Robert Freeman. OQP
In My Father's House, *with music.* *Unknown.* AS
In My First Hard Springtime. James Welch. YAP
In My Garden. *Unknown.* BoTP
In my garden grows a tree. The Apple Rhyme. Madeleine Nightingale. BoTP
In my grandmother's house there was always chicken soup. A Story about Chicken Soup. Louis Simpson. NMP
In My Infancy. David Ross. PG (1955 ed.)
In my life. Haiku. Issa. LiTW
In my little garden. In My Garden. *Unknown.* BoTP
In my little log cabin. Rye Whisky. *Unknown.* ABF
In My New Clothing. Basho, *tr. fr. Japanese.* SoPo
In My Old Verses. Charles Guérin, *tr. fr. French by* Joseph T. Shipley. CAW
In My Own Album. Charles Lamb. CBEP; OBRV
In my own shire, if I was sad. A. E. Housman. A Shropshire Lad, XLI. BrPo; PoVP
In My Place. Esther Archibald. SoP; STF
In my room, the world is beyond my understanding. Of the Surface of Things. Wallace Stevens. ELU; NP
In my rudyard-kipling-simple years I read. The Thrifty Elephant. John Holmes. NYBP
In my sleep I was fain of their fellowship, fain. Sunrise. Sidney Lanier. *Fr.* Hymns of the Marshes. AA; AmePo; PoEL-5
In my stone eyes I see. What Riddle Asked the Sphinx. Archibald MacLeish. HoPM
In my sunny girlhood's vernal life. A Portrait. Joseph Ashby-Sterry. HBV; VA
In My Thirtieth Year. Archibald MacLeish. *See* L'An Trentiesme de Mon Eage.
In My Time. Edmund Blunden. MoPW
In my young days I drank a/ Lot of wine. A Friend Advises Me to Stop Drinking. Mei Yao Ch'en. HoPM
In my youth's summer I did sing of One. The Wandering Outlaw. Byron. *Fr.* Childe Harold's Pilgrimage, III. FiP
In Nakedness. Marnie Pomeroy. ErPo
In nature apt to like, when I did see. Astrophel and Stella, XVI. Sir Philip Sidney. FCP; SiPS
In "nature" there's no choice. Beyond the End. Denise Levertov. NeAP
In natures peeces still I see. A Divine Mistris. Thomas Carew. AnAnS-2
In Nazareth. Leslie Savage Clark. ChIP
In Nazareth he knew each narrow street. Sight. Ida Norton Munson. ChIP
In Nazareth, the narrow road. The Carpenter of Nazareth. George Blair. StJW
In need of time, I thought that I. New Technique. Richard Armour. PoPo
In Nets of Golden Wires. *Unknown.* EnRePo
In new romance with blackness. Again the Summoning. Lawrence S. Cumberbatch. WSL
In New Ross. Valentin Iremonger. NeIP
In New South Wales, as I plainly see. William Forster. *Fr.*

In (continued)
The Devil and the Governor. PoAu-1
In New York I got drunk, to tell the truth. A Trip to Four or Five Towns. John Logan. *Fr.* A Trip to Four or Five Towns. NMP
In Nigellum. John Weever. TuPP
In night, when colo[u]rs all to black are cast. Caelica, C. Fulke Greville. EnRePo; EP; QFR; Sonn
In 1945, when the keepers cried kaput. The Gift. John Ciardi. LiTM (1970 ed.); NMP
In nineteen-thirty-four I spent July. 1934. Donald Hall. PoPl
In 1939 the skylark had nothing to say to me. The Ninth of July. John Hollander. CoAP
In No Strange Land. Francis Thompson. AnFE; AtBAP; BoLiVe; BoPe; ChIP; GTBS; HBMV; LiTB; LiTG; MoAB; OBEV (new ed.); OQP; ShBV-4; TreFT; TrGrPo; WGRP
(Kingdom of God, The.) BrPo; CaFP; CoBE; EaLo; EPN; GoBC; GTBS-P; MaRV; MemP; OxBoCh; Po; PoIE; PoLi; POTE; PoVP; SeCeV; TRV; WoL
In no way that I chose to go. The Snow. Clifford Dyment. MoVE; POTE
In Norgum. *Unknown.* TuPP
In Normandy. E. V. Lucas. GaP
In Norway land[s] there lived a maid. The Great Silkie [*or* Grey Selchie] of Sule Skerry. *Unknown.* BaBo (A *vers.*); OxBB, *with music*; ViBoFo (B *vers., with music*)
In Nottamun Town not a soul would look up. Nottamun Town. *Unknown.* NCEP; OxBoLi; SiTL
In Nottingham there lives a jolly tanner. Robin Hood and the Tanner. *Unknown.* BaBo; ESPB; MaC
In November. Anne Reeve Aldrich. AA
In November. Archibald Lampman. OBCV
In November. Duncan Campbell Scott. VA
In November, in the days to remember the dead. St. Malachy. Thomas Merton. CoPo
In November of Catherine wheels and rockets. Dylan Thomas. Stephen Spender. ML
In numbers, and but these few. An Ode on the Birth of Our Saviour. Robert Herrick. GN; OTPC (1923 ed.)
In nuptial chamber far from feast. Wedding Song. Goethe. HW
In obedience to the imperial command. A Soldier. *Unknown.* OnPM
In Obitum Alienius. Henry Parrot. SiCE
In Obitum Ed. Spenser Poetae Prestaniss. John Weever. ReIE
In Obitum M. S., X Maii, 1614. William Browne. *See* Epitaph: "May, be thou never graced with birds that sing."
In Ocean's wide domains. The Witnesses. Longfellow. AtBAP
In October. Bliss Carman. YeAr
In October. Michael Hamburger. NePoEA
In October at midnight in the olive groves. Thoughts from Abroad. Patrick Maybin. NeIP
In October the pregnant woman walked by the river. In October. Michael Hamburger. NePoEA
In October, when they know. Winter Coats. Dorothy Aldis. RIS
In Oklahoma. Life Is Motion. Wallace Stevens. AmLP; PoeP; SD; TDP
In Old Age. Brenda Chamberlain. NYTB
In old days those who went to fight. Hearing That His Friend Was Coming Back from the War. Wang Chien. LiTW
In old Kentuck in de arternoon. Clare de Kitchen. *Unknown.* BLPA
In old Nevers, so famous for its. Vert-Vert, the Parrot. Louis Gresset. CAW
In old Pekin a monarch reigned. The Street of Doctors. Thomas Walsh. PoMa
In old time they were called the church's pillars. Of the Pillars of the Church. Sir John Harington. SiCE
In one of the Assyrian wars. Wading at Wellfleet. Elizabeth Bishop. AmP
In One of Those Excursions. Wordsworth. *Fr.* The Prelude, XIV. MaPo
(Ascent of Mount Snowdon, The.) ERoP-1
(Conclusion.) FosPo
In only thee, my timid, fleet gazelle. The Timid Gazelle. Kasmuneh. TrJP
In Orange, tree-plague has struck the mile-long groves, greased. Orange County Plague: Scenes. Laurence Liberman. CoPo
In Order To. Kenneth Patchen. NaP; Po
In order to perfect all readers. Wall, Cave, and Pillar Statements, After Asôka. Alan Dugan. CoAP
In Orknay. William Fowler. GoTS; OxBS
In Ortygia the Dawn land the old gods dwell. Ortygia. Jessie Mackay. BoAu
In other men we faults can spy. The Turkey and the Ant. John Gay. *Fr.* Fables. OTPC (1923 ed.)
In Our Boat. Dinah Maria Mulock Craik. HBV
In our country, in our country. The Merry Hay-Makers; or, Pleasant Pastime between the Young-Men and Maids in the Pleasant Meadows. *Unknown .* CoMu; ErPo
In our crazed brains words are visions. Prose Poem: Words. Emile Hennequin. OnPM
In our Durham County I am sorry for to say. The Durham Lock-out. *Unknown.* CoMu
In our fields, fallow and burdened, in grass and furrow. Christopher Fry. *Fr.* The Boy with a Cart. LiTB
In our hearts is the Great One of Avon. Jocosa Lyra. Austin Dobson. BOHV; InP
In Our Lane. *Unknown, tr. fr. Chinese by* Arthur Waley. *Fr.* Shi King. LiTW
In our Museum galleries. The Burden of Nineveh. Dante Gabriel Rossetti. MaVP; OAEP; PoVP
In our museum—we always go there on Sundays. Family Matters. Günter Grass. ELU
In our old shipwrecked days there was an hour. Modern Love, XVI [*or* Love Dies]. George Meredith. BEL; EnLi-2; GTBS; GTBS-D; HBV; LO; PoFS; SeCePo; ViPo; VP; WHA
In Our Time. Huw Menai. MaRV
In Our Time. Michael Roberts. WaP
In our town people live in rows. The Fired Pot. Anna Wickham. FaBoTw; MeWo; TrGrPo (1942 ed)
In Owenni Epigrammata. Thomas Freeman. SiCE
In Oxford town the faggots they piled. Latimer's Light. *Unknown.* TRV
In Pace. Arthur Reed Ropes. VA
In Pace in Idipsum Dormiam et Requiescam. Patrick O'Connor. CAW
In Paco town and in Paco tower. The Ballad of Paco Town. Clinton Scollard. PAH
In pain she bore the son who her embrace. Elegy. Moses ibn Ezra. TrJP
In pairs,/ as if to illustrate their sisterhood. For the Sisters of the Hôtel Dieu. A. M. Klein. WHW
In Palestine. George W. Carlin. ChIP
In Panelled Rooms. Ruth Herschberger. LiTA
("Love-grip, first excited by the eye, The.") GTBS-W
In Paradise. Arlo Bates. AA
In Parenthesis, *sel.* David Jones.
"So they would go a long while in the solid dark," III. FIW
In Paris. Thomas Macdonagh. OnYI
"In Paris, at the Louvre, there have I seen." Modern Love, XXXIII. George Meredith. ViPo; VP
In part these nightly terrors to dispel. Moonlight. . .Scattered Clouds. Robert Bloomfield. *Fr.* The Farmer's Boy. OBNC
In paschall feast, the end of ancient rite. Of the Blessèd Sacrament of the Altar. Robert Southwell. GoBC
In Passing. Roy Helton. HBMV
In passing with my mind. The Right of Way. William Carlos Williams. MoVE
In pasture where the leaf and wood. The Quest. James Wright. NYBP
In "pastures green"? [*or* "green pastures"?] Not always; sometimes He. He Leadeth Me [*or* On the Twenty-third Psalm]. *Unknown.* BLRP; MaRV; OQP; SoP; TRV
In Paths Untrodden. Walt Whitman. AP; NePA; OxBA
In peace, Love tunes the Shepherd's reed. Sir Walter Scott. *Fr.* The Lay of the Last Minstrel, III. ViBoPo
In Peblis town sum tyme, as I heard tell. *At. to* John Reid of Stobo. *Fr.* The Thre Prestis of Peblis. OxBS
In petticoat of green. Phyllis [*or* Of Phyllis]. William Drummond of Hawthornden. EIL; GN; HBV; LiTL; OTPC
In Phaeacia. James Elroy Flecker. HBMV
In Phaedram. Thomas Freeman. TuPP
In Philistia. Bliss Carman. ALV
In Philonem. Thomas Bastard. SiCE
In Piam Memoriam. Geoffrey Hill. NePoEA-2
In pious times, ere [*or* e'r] priestcraft did begin. Absalom and Achitophel, Pt. I. Dryden. CABL; CEP; EiCL; EiPP;

EnLi-1; MaPo (1969 ed.); MBW-1; NoP; OAEP; SeCV-2; SeEP; TOP
In Piranezi's rarer prints. Prelusive. Herman Melville. *Fr.* Clarel. AmPP (5th ed.)
In pity for man's darkening thought. Two Songs from a Play, II. W. B. Yeats. *Fr.* The Resurrection. CABA; CMoP; ExPo; FosPo; ILP; LiTB; MBW-2; MoPo PAn; PoDB; PoFS; PoIE; SeCeV; UnPo
In Place of a Curse. John Ciardi. CaFP; ToPo
In place where wants Apollo with his lute. An Epitaph upon the Death of Sir William Drury. Barnabe Rich. ReIE
In placid hours well-pleased we dream. Art. Herman Melville. AmPP (5th ed.); AP; CBV; MAmP; MWA-1; PoFS; PoIE; ViBoPo
In Plague Time. Thomas Nashe. *See* Adieu, Farewell, Earth's Bliss!
In Plimmerton, in Plimmerton. Threnody. Denis Glover. AnNZ
In Plymouth Town there lived a maid. A-Roving. *Unknown.* UnTE
In Polar noons when the moonshine glimmers. The Weaver of Snow. "Fiona Macleod." PoVP
In Porcum. John Heath. SiCE; TuPP
In Portugal, 1912. Alice Meynell. OxBoCh
In Postures That Call. Oscar Williams. WaP
In Praise of a Beggar's Life. "A. W." EIL, 2*sts.*; PTK; TrGrPo
(Play, Beggars, Play!) WHA
(Song in Praise of a Beggar's Life, A.) OBSC; SiCE
In Praise of a Gentlewoman [Who, though She Were Not Very Fair, Yet Was She as Hard-favored as Might Be]. George Gascoigne. EnRePo; ReIE
In Praise of a Girl. Huw Morus, *tr. fr. Welsh by* Gwyn Williams. PrWP
In Praise of Aed. *Unknown, tr. fr. Old Irish by* Robin Flower. AnIL
In Praise of Ale ("I cannot eat but little meat"). *Unknown, at. to* William Stevenson. *See* Back and Side Go Bare, Go Bare.
In Praise of Ale ("Whenas the chill sirocco blows"). *Unknown, at. to* Thomas Bonham. ALV; FaBoCh; OBS; SelL SeEP; ViBoPo
(Give Me Ale.) HBV
(Pipe and Can, 2.) OBEV
In Praise of Antonioni. Stephen Holden. NYBP
In Praise of BIC Pens. David Hilton. QAH
In Praise of Cocoa, Cupid's Nightcap. Stanley J. Sharpless. ErPo; FiBHP
In Praise of Commonplace. Sir Owen Seaman. InMe
In Praise of Country Life. Robert Chamberlain. CavP
In Praise of Diversity. Phyllis McGinley. SiTL
In Praise of Dust. Rachel Field. RePo
In Praise of Fidelia. Mildmay Fane, Earl of Westmorland. SeCL
In Praise of Gilbert White. William John Courthope. *Fr.* The Paradise of Birds. VA
In Praise of His Daphnis. Sir John Wotton. EIL
In Praise of His Lady. Matthew Grove. *Fr.* Pelops and Hippodamia. EIL
In Praise of His Love. Earl of Surrey. *See* Praise of His Love.
In Praise of His Love. Sir John Wotton. EIL
In Praise of His Loving and Best-beloved Fawnia. Robert Greene. *See* Fawnia.
In Praise of Isabel Pennell. John Skelton. *See* To Mistress Isabel Pennell.
In Praise of Ivy. *Unknown.* MeEL
In Praise of Johnny Appleseed. Vachel Lindsay. PoRL; StVeCh; TSW
In Praise of Lessius His Rule of Health. Richard Crashaw. *See* Temperance, or the Cheap Physitian.
In Praise of Limestone. W. H. Auden. CABA; CMoP; CoBMV; MaPo; MoAB; MoVE; NePA; PoIE
In praise of little children I will say. Laus Infantium. William Canton. HBV; VA
In Praise of Llamas. Arthur Guiterman. FiBHP
In Praise of Mary. *Unknown.* MeEL
In Praise of May. *Unknown, tr. fr. Old Irish by* T. W. Rolleston. AnIV; BiS (*shorter vers.*)
(Song of Finn, The, *tr. by* John O'Donovan.) OnYI
In Praise of Music in Time of Pestilence. Daryl Hine. OBCV
In Praise of Neptune. Thomas Campion. BoNaP; CBEP; WiR
In Praise of Rosamund. Robert Greene. *See* Hexametra Alexis in Laudem Rosamundi.
In Priase of the Sun. "A. W." CTC; OBSC
("Golden sun that brings the day, The.") SiCE
In praise of thee. Bean Spasms. Ted Berrigan. ANYP
In Praise of Unfamous Men. Francis Meynell. MemP
In Praise of Wisdom. Solomon ibn Gabirol, *tr. fr. Hebrew by* Solomon Solis-Cohen. TrJP
In Praise of Wyatt's Psalms. Earl of Surrey. SiPS
("Great Macedon, that out of Persia chased, The.") FCP
In Praise of Young Girls. Raymond Asquith. OtMeF
In pride of May. *Unknown.* OBSC
In pride of wit, when high desire of fame. Idea, XLVII. Michael Drayton. SiCE; Sonn; TuPP
In Prison. William Morris. AtBAP; CBEP; NBM; PeVV; PoVP
In Prison. Oscar Wilde. *Fr.* The Ballad of Reading Gaol. OQP
("I know not whether laws be right.") ACP; MaRV; SoP
In Prize. Cicely Fox Smith. WhC
In Procession. Robert Graves. TwCP
In Prospect Street, outside the Splendid Bar. Sweeney to Mrs. Porter in the Spring. L. E. Sissman. NYBP
In Provence. Jean Aicard, *tr. fr. French by* Thomas Walsh. CAW
In purest song one plays the constant fool. Infirmity. Theodore Roethke. CoAP; NYBP; PoeP
In Puritan New England a year had passed away. The First Thanksgiving Day. Alice Williams Brotherton. DD; OHIP
In pyntarris. *Unknown.* WhC
In Quietness. Grace E. Troy. SoP
In quietness and confidence. A Hymn of Trust. Nettie M. Sargent. BLRP
In quietness let me abide. In Quietness. Grace E. Troy. SoP
In Railway Halls [on Pavements near the Traffic]. Stephen Spender. CMoP; FaBoMo; NoP
("In railway halls, on pavements near the traffic.") EnLit
In rain and twilight mist the city street. This Is My Hour. Zoë Akins. HBV
In rain or shine; in heat or snow. Pushcart Row. Rachel Field. SoPo
In Rainy-gloomy Weather. John Davies of Hereford. CBEP
In Rama. George Alfred Townsend. AA
In re Solomon Warshawer. A. M. Klein. MoCV
In Reading Gaol by Reading Town. Oscar Wilde. *Fr.* The Ballad of Reading Gaol. FaFP; LiTB; PoPl
In Rebellion. J. M. Synge. SyP
In Regent's Park. Anne Ridler. POTE
In Response to a Rumor That the Oldest Whorehouse in Wheeling, West Virginia, Has Been Condemned. James Wright. CoAP
In revel and carousing. Theodosia Burr; the Wrecker's Story. John Williamson Palmer. PAH
In Richard's days, when lost his pastur'd plain. The Country Justice. John Langhorne. LaA
In right I have no power to live. The Soul's Bitter Cry. *Unknown.* WGRP
In rigorous hours, when down the iron lane. Winter. Robert Louis Stevenson. ACV; WePo
In Ringlets Curl'd Thy Tresses Flow. Mary Balfour. IrPN
In Robin Hood Cove. Marsden Hartley. AnFE; CoAnAm
In Roman. Sir John Harington. PV
In Romney Marsh. John Davidson. GoTS; GTBS; GTBS-D; HT; OBVV; POTE; ShBV-3; ViBoPo
In rooms of stone. Abandoned Copper Refinery. Dan Gillespie. QAH
In Rudionem. John Weever. SiCE; TuPP
In Rufum. Sir John Davies. ReIE
In Ruin Reconciled. Aubrey Thomas De Vere. IrPN
In ruling well what guerdon? Life runs low. The Two Old Kings. Lord De Tabley. OBEV (new ed.); OBVV; VA
In S Street trod the phantom guard. The Warrior Passes. Hubert Kelley. DD
In St. Luke's Gospel we are told. The Shifting of Peter. Longfellow. SoP
In Salamis, filled with the foaming. Troy. Euripides. WoL
In Salem seasick spindrift drifts or skips. Salem. Robert Lowell. AnNE; CABA; NePoEA; PoPo; Sonn; ToPo
In Samarcand. Laura E. Richards. PoRh

In Santa Maria del Popolo. Thom Gunn. GTBS-P; NePoEA-2; NMP; NoP; OPoP; PoIE; QFR
In Saram. John Cotton. SCAP
In Saturday Market, there's eggs a-plenty. Charlotte Mew. *Fr.* Saturday Market. FaPON
In Saturn's reign, at nature's early birth. Juvenal, *tr. fr. Latin by* Dryden. *Fr.* Satires, VI. MBW-1
In Scarlet Town where I was born [*or* bound]. Barbara Allen [*or* Bonny Barbara Allen *or* Barbara Allen's Cruelty]. *Unknown.* BFSS; DiPo; ESPB (B *vers.*); FaFP; HBV; LO; OBB; OBEV; OnSP; OTPC (1923 ed.); TreF; TrGrPo; ViBoFo (C *vers.*); ViBoPo
In scented gardens of the south. The Nightingale. Elizabeth Belloc. JKCP (1955 ed.)
In schomer, when the leves spring [*or* spryng]. Robin Hood and the Potter. *Unknown.* BaBo; ESPB
In School Days. Whittier. AA; AnNE; BLPA; CoBA; FaBoBe; MPB (1956 ed.); NeHB; OTPC (1946 ed.); PCD; PoPl; PTK; StVeCh (1940 ed.); TreF
"Still sits the schoolhouse by the road," *sel.* FaPON
In Schrafft's. W. H. Auden. MaPo
In Scotland there was a babie born. Hind Horn. *Unknown.* ATP; BaBo (A *vers.*); ESPB; NoP; TOP; ViBoFo
"In Scotland was I bred and born." Bonny Barbara Allen [*or* Ellen]. *Unknown.* BaBo (B *ver.*); Po
In Scotland, where the porridge grows. Of the Stalking of the Stag. Sir Owen Seaman. CenHV
In Scotland's realm, forlorn and bare. The Chaffinch's Nest at Sea. William Cowper. OTPC (1923 ed.)
In sea-cold Lyonesse. Sunk Lyonesse. Walter de la Mare. CoBMV; FaBoCh; LiTM (1970 ed.)
In seaboard town there was a merchant. In Brunton Town. *Unknown.* BaBo
In Search of a God. Charles Thomas. WSL
In Search of the Picturesque. William Combe. *Fr.* Dr. Syntax in Search of the Picturesque. OBRV
In season what time every growing thing. The Spider and the Fly. John Heywood. ReIE
In secreit place, this hindir nicht. The Man of Valour to His Fair Lady. William Dunbar. MeEL
In secret mountain fastnesses we stored. Sara Bard Field. *Fr.* Barabbas. PoFr
In secret place where once I stood. The Flesh and the Spirit. Anne Bradstreet. AmP; AmPP; AnAmPo; AnFE; AP; APA; CoAnAm; LiTA; MAmP; NePA; OxBA; SCAP
In seed time learn, in harvest teach, in winter enjoy. Proverbs of Hell. Blake. *Fr.* The Marriage of Heaven and Hell. AtBAP; EnLi-2
In se'enteen hunder an' forty-nine. On Andrew Turner. Burns. PV
In Senecam. John Heath. SiCE
In sensuous coil. Kings. *Unknown.* *Fr.* The Panchatantra. AWP; LiTW; PoFr
In September. Eleanor Hammond. GFA
In September. Francis Ledwidge. POTE
In Service. Winifred M. Letts. HBMV; YT
In seventeen hundred and fifty-nine. Hawke. Sir Henry Newbolt. BBV
In seventeen hundred and ninety-four. The Greenland Fishery. *Unknown.* OBB
In seventeen hundred and seventy-five. The Bombardment of Bristol. *Unknown.* PAH
In seventeen hundred thirty-two. George Washington. *Unknown, at. to* M. Alice Bryant. HH
In Severum. Sir John Davies. ReIE
In shade of death's sad tree. Sancta Maria Dolorum or The Mother of Sorrows. Richard Crashaw. MaMe
In shades we live, in shades we die. Amanda's Complaint. Philip Freneau. AP
In Shadow. Hart Crane. TwAmPo
In Shadow. Caroline Hazard. GoBC
In shadowy calm the boat. Hope. Phillips Stewart. CaP
In shantung suits we whites are cool. The Devil-Dancers. William Plomer. BoSA; PeSA
In shards the sylvan vases lie. The Ravaged Villa. Herman Melville. AP; CTC; GTBS-D; MAmP; MWA-1; PoEL-5
In Sherwood lived stout Robin Hood. *Unknown.* OBSC
In shining groups, each stem a pearly ray. Ghost-Flowers. Mary Potter Thacher Higginson. AA
In Siberia's wastes. Siberia. James Clarence Mangan. FOL; IrPN; NBM; PeER; RoGo
In Sickness. Swift. CEP; OBEC
In signe of favor stedfast still. To His Darrest Freind. John Stewart of Baldynneis. OxBS
In silence, and at night, the conscience fells. The Cardinal's Soliloquy. Sir Edward Bulwer-Lytton. *Fr.* Richelieu; or, The Conspiracy. VA
In silence stark and bitter. The Day of the Slaves. Leonard Bacon. PoFr
In silent gaze the tuneful choir among. Stanzas to Mr. Bentley. Thomas Gray. EiPP; NoP
In silent horror o'er the boundless waste. Eclogue the Second. William Collins. Persian Eclogues, II. CEP
In silent night when rest I took. Upon the Burning of Our House [*or* Verses *or* Some Verses *or* Here Followes Some Verses]. Anne Bradstreet. AmP; AmPP (4th ed.); AP; MAmP; OxBA; SCAP; TDP
In silken, milken Samarcand. In Samarcand. Laura E. Richards. PoRh
In simmer, whan aa sorts foregether. Embro to the Ploy. Robert Garioch. OxBS
In simple muslin delicately dressed. A New Orleans Balcony. Dorothy Haight. CAW
In simple wise the revelation came. Pentecost. Laura Simmons. ChIP
In simpler verse than triolets. An Old-Fashioned Poet. Ada Foster Murray. HBV
In Sleep. Richard Burton. AA
In Sligo the country was soft; there were turkeys. County Sligo. Louis MacNeice. OnYI
In slow recuperative hours. Convalescence, V. David McCord. WhC
In slumbers of midnight the sailor boy lay. The Mariner's Dream. William Dimond. BeLS; HBV
In small green cup an acorn grew. The Acorn. *Unknown.* BoTP
In smokey inns whose loft is reached by ladders. The Old Masters. Emile Verhaeren. AnEnPo
In smoky outhouses of the court of love. In the Queen's Room. Norman Cameron. *Fr.* Three Love Poems. GTBS-P
In snorts of wind, the tawny meadow. Runaway. Kim Kurt. NePoAm-2.
In Snow. William Allingham. IrPN
In sober mornings do[e] not thou rehearse. When He Would Have His Verses Read. Robert Herrick. EnL; OAEP; OBS; SCEP-2; SeCV-1; SeEP
In Sobieski's Shield. Edwin Morgan. HYE
In Soho's square mile of unoriginal sin. After the Release of Ezra Pound. Dannie Abse. NMP; OPoP
In solemn conclave vow and swear. Constitution for a League of Nations. Arthur Guiterman. InMe
In solemn pause the forest waits. The Untended Field. Robert Hillyer. AnNE
In solitary august, like a story. Passage of an August. Eithne Wilkins. NeBP
In Solitary Confinement, Sea Point Police Cells. C. J. Driver. PeSA
In Some Seer's Cloud Car. Christopher Middleton. TwCP
In some unused lagoon, some nameless bay. The Dismantled Ship. Walt Whitman. AmPP (4th ed.); CABA; CBEP; NoP; OxBA
In somer, when the shawes by sheyne. Robin Hood and the Monk [*or* Robyn Hode and the Munke]. *Unknown.* BaBo; CH; ESPB; OBB; OBEV; OxBB; ViBoFo; ViBoPo. *See also* In summer when the shaws be sheen.
In Sorrow. Thomas Hastings. AA; HBV; SoP
In sorrowes drown'd I wast my weary dayes. *Unknown.* SeCSL
In sorrow's cell I laid me down to sleep. Rosader's Sonnet. Thomas Lodge. *Fr.* Rosalynde; or, Euphues' Golden Legacy. ReIE
In Spain. Emily Lawless. AnIV
In Spain ("So feeble is the thread that doth the burden stay"). Petrarch, *tr. fr. Italian by* Sir Thomas Wyatt. FCP
In Spain ("Tagus, farewell, that westward with thy streams"). Sir Thomas Wyatt. *See* Of His Return[e] from Spain[e].
In Spain; Drinking Song. Emily Lawless. AnIV
In Spain, where the courtly Castilian hidalgo twangs lightly each night his romantic guitar. Carmen. Newman Levy. ALV; FiBHP

In speaking of a person's faults. Be Careful What You Say. Joseph Kronthal. STF
In Spirit Senses Are. "Angelus Silesius," *tr. fr. German by* Paul Carus. OnPM
In spite of a day a day lost in the heat a day. A Day Lost. Gertrude Stein. AtBAP
In spite of all the learned have said. The Indian Burying Ground. Philip Freneau. AA; AmP; AmPP; AnAmPo; AnFE; AP; APA; CBEP; CoAnAm; CoBA; ForPo; HBV; LiTA; LiTG; MAmP; NePA; NoP; OxBA; Po; PoEL-4; PoIE; PoLF; PoPl; StP; ThLM
In spite of all the solemn-hearted fools. The Joy of Love. Allan Dowling. ErPo
In Spite of All This Much Needed Thunder. Zack Gilbert. PoNe (1970 ed.)
In spite of cold and chills. Daffodils. Kikurio. SoPo; SUS; TiPo
In spite of her sniffle. The Sniffle. Ogden Nash. RePo; WePo
In spite of my efforts. Taira no Kanemori, *tr. fr. Japanese by* I. W. Furukami. LiTW
In spite of purple sky, moonless. The Night Refuses a Dreamer. Grant Code. FiSC
In spite of rice, in spite of wheat. Epigram on the Poor of Boston . . . 1774. *Unknown.* PAH
In Spite of Sorrow. Adoniram Judson. FaChP; MaRV; SoP; TRV
(Sowing and Reaping.) SoP
In Spring. Michael Lewis. *See* April Winds.
In Spring. Li Po, *tr. fr. Chinese by* Witter Bynner. LiTW
In spring I look gay. A Tree. *Unknown.* BoTP; OxNR; RIS
In Spring in Warm Weather. Dorothy Aldis. BiCB
In spring of youth [*or* youth's spring] it was my lot. The Lake: To——. Poe. AmePo; AmP; MAmP; MWA-1; OnPM
In Spring the day is early. April Winds [*or* In Spring]. Michael Lewis. StaSt; TSW
In spring, when the green gits back in the trees. When the Green Gits Back in the Trees. James Whitcomb Riley. YT
In Springfield Mountain. *Unknown. See* Springfield Mountain.
In Springtime. Samuel Taylor Coleridge. *Fr.* Work without Hope. BoTP
In Springtime. Kipling. BrPo
In springtime when the leaves are young. Seasons. Christina Rossetti. YeAr
In Stature, the Manlet was dwarfish. The Manlet. "Lewis Carroll." Par
In Stratis Viarum. Arthur Hugh Clough. PoVP
In streets, among the rocks of time and weather. The Mountains. Louis Dudek. CaP
In such a marvellous night so fair. The Night of Marvels. Sister Violante do Ceo. CAW
In Such a Night. Shakespeare. *Fr.* The Merchant of Venice, V, i. ChTr; FiP; WHA
(Divine Harmony, The.) GoBC
(Duet.) CLwM
("Moon shines bright, The: in such a night as this.") MemP
In such a night, when every louder wind. A Nocturnal Reverie. Countess of Winchilsea. BWP; CEP; EiCL; EiPP; FaBoEn; GoTL; LoBV; OBEC; PoEL-3; SeCePo
In such a spot, with radiant flowers for halo. She of the Garden. Emile Verhaeren. CAW
In Such an Age. Angela Morgan. *See* Today.
In such an armor he may rise and raid. Bronzeville Man with a Belt in the Back. Gwendolyn Brooks. IDB
In Summer. Trumbull Stickney. NCEP
In Summer. Charles Hanson Towne. HBMV
In Summer. *Unknown. Fr.* Robin Hood and the Monk [*or* Robyn Hode and the Munke]. CH
("In somer, when the shawes be sheyne.") OxBB; ViBoPo
(In the Fair Forest, 2 *sts., mod.*) BoTP
(May in the Green-Wood.) OBEV
(Morning of May, A, *mod.*) PoLi
(Robin Hood and Guy of Gisborne, *mod.*) BuBa
In summer when the shaws be [*or* are] sheen. Robin Hood and the Monk [*or* A Morning of May], *mod. Unknown.* MeEV; PoLi. *See also* In somer, when. . .
In summer when the woods are green. In the Fair Forest. *Unknown.* BoTP
In summer when the woods be bright. Robin Hood and Guy of Gisborne. *Unknown.* BuBa
In summer elms are made for me. Dilemma of the Elm. Genevieve Taggard. MAP; MoAmPo
In summer I am very glad. Playgrounds. Laurence Alma-Tadema. BoTP; HBV; HBVY; OTPC; PCH; PPL
In summer I'm disposed to shirk. The Lazy Writer. Bert Leston Taylor. ALV; PoMa
In summer, in the open air. Summer Sabbath. Jessie E. Sampter. TrJP
In summer, on the headlands. The Neckan. Matthew Arnold. GBV (1952 ed.)
In summer the garden where we played. The Crack. J. C. Hall. HaMV
In summer this town is full of rebels. The Cannery. Lucien Stryk. NYTB
In summertime it was a paradise. The Seaside. Charles Tennyson Turner. Sonn
In summertime on Bredon. Bredon Hill [*or* Summer Time on Bredon]. A. E. Housman. A Shropshire Lad, XXI. BEL; BrPo; CLwM; EnLi-2; FosPo; GBV (1952 ed.); LiTL; MeWo; MoAB; MoBrPo; NeMA; PAn; PoVP; TreF; ViPo; VP; WHA
In summer time, when leaves grew green and birds were singing. King Edward the Fourth and a Tanner of Tamworth. *Unknown.* BaBo; ESPB
In summer time, when leaves grow green/ Down a down a down. Robin Hood and the Tinker. *Unknown.* BaBo; ESPB
In summer time, when leaves grow green and flowers are fresh and gay. Robin Hood and the Curtal Friar. *Unknown.* BaBo; ESPB
In summer time, when leaves grow green, when they doe grow both green and long. The Noble Fisherman; or, Robin Hood's Perferment. *Unknown.* ESPB; OBB
In summer, when the days were long. Summer Days. Wathen Marks Wilks Call. VA
In summer, when the grass is thick, if mother has the time. The Fairy Book. Norman Gale. HBV; HBVY; OHIP; OTPC (1946 ed.); TVC
In summer when the hills are blond. January. Geoffrey Dutton. PoAu-2
In summer when the rose-bushes. Song. Edith Sitwell. NP
In Summer's Heat. Ovid, *tr. fr. Latin by* Christopher Marlowe. Amores, I, 5. CLwM
(Elegy to His Mistress.) ErPo
(Ovid's Fifth Elegy.) NCEP
In summer's mellow midnight. The Night Wind. Emily Brontë. ChER; ChTr; NCEP; OAEP; PoSa; RoGo
In sunburnt parks where Sundays lie. Cobb Would Have Caught It. Robert Fitzgerald. InvP; SD; TwCP
In sunlight on the avenue. Galway Kinnell. *Fr.* The Avenue Bearing the Initial of Christ into the New World. NMP
In sunny girlhood's vernal life. A Portrait. Joseph Ashby-Sterry. HBV; VA
In Superbum. Thomas Freeman. SiCE
In Sweet Communion. John Newton. SoP; TRV
In Switzerland one idle day. Idyll. Hugh Macnaghten. HBMV
In tabernacle Thine, O Lord, who shall remain? Psalm XV. *Paraphrased by* Sir Philip Sidney. FCP
In talking/ You are very like. To a Lady Holding the Floor. Mildred Weston. FiBHP
In tangled wreaths, in clustered gleaming stars. Yellow Jessamine. Constance Fenimore Woolson. AA; HBV
In tattered old slippers that toast at the bars. The Cane-bottomed Chair. Thackeray. HBV; OTPC; PaPo; PoVP
In taverns/ There is a rituality in the careless talk. Notes from an Ohio Tavern. Sandford Lyne. QAH
"In teacup-times!" The style of dress. A Rondeau to Ethel. Austin Dobson. VA
In tears I tossed my coin from Trevi's edge. Italian Rhapsody. Robert Underwood Johnson. HBV
In Tempestiva. Henry Longan Stuart. CAW
In temporary pain. The New God. Witter Bynner. *Fr.* The New World. WGRP
In Temptation. Charles Wesley. *See* Jesus, Lover of My Soul.
In tender May when the sweet laugh of Christ. The Puritan. Karl Shapiro. MoAmPo (1950 ed.)
In Tenebris. Thomas Hardy. FaBoEn; LiTB; NoP; SeCePo; ViPo
Sels.

In (continued)
"When the clouds' swoln bosoms," II. BrPo; CMoP; LiTM (rev. ed.)
"Wintertime nighs," I. OAEP (2d ed.); PoDB; TreFS; UnPo
In Tenebris. Sister Mary of the Visitation. JKCP (1955 ed.)
In Tennessee, the dogwood tree. Tennessee. Francis Brooks. AA
In Terra Nostra. Alan C. Tarbat. BoPe
In Tesla's Laboratory. Robert Underwood Johnson. AA
In the' olde dayes of the Kyng Arthour. The Wife of Bath's Tale. Chaucer. *Fr.* The Canterbury Tales. EnLit; MBW-1; ViBoPo
In Thankful Remembrance for My Dear Husband's Safe Arrivall Sept. 3, 1662. Anne Bradstreet. TrPWD
In that age, the great anagram of God. The Incarnation of Sirius. James McAuley. MoAuPo
In that bad year and city of your birth. For an Emigrant. Randall Jarrell. OxBA
In that building, long and low. The Ropewalk. Longfellow. AP; MAmP
In that country of thresholds we move like vandals. Papermill Graveyard. Ben Belitt. NYBP
In That Dark Cave. Shel Silverstein. ELU
In that day I had hoped for a pair of boots to guard my feet on the terrible trek. My Head on My Shoulders. Jeremy Ingalls. GoYe
In that desolate land and lone. The Revenge of Rain-in-the-Face. Longfellow. BBV; PaA; PAH
In That Dim Monument Where Tybalt Lies. Arthur Davison Ficke. HBMV
In that fell strife, when force with force engages. William Tell. Schiller. PoFr
In that final rage I saw my hair turn white. Metamorphosis. Eli Mandel. ACV
In that furious, final wake for Flannagan. The Dancers with a Hop. James Schevill. FiMAP
In that I have so greatly failed thee, Lord. So Little and So Much. John Oxenham. BLRP
In that land all Is, and nothing's Ought. Neither Here nor There. W. R. Rodgers. FaBoMo; GTBS-W; LiTB; LiTM; MoAB; MoBrPo (1950 ed.; NeBP; ViBoPo (1958 ed.)
In that land of dopy dreams, happy peaceful Philippines. Damn the Filipinos. *Unknown.* ABF
In that most wretched hovel. In the Wretched Hovel. *Unknown.* OnPM
In that new world toward which our feet are set. Compensation. Celia Thaxter. HBV
In that November off Tehuantepec. Sea Surface Full of Clouds. Wallace Stevens. AmPP (5th ed.); AnAmPo; AnFE; AP; CMoP; CoAnAm; CoBA; CoBMV; MAP; MaPo (1969 ed.); MoAB; MoAmPo; TwAmPo
In that, O Queen of queens, thy birth was free. To Our Blessed Lady [*or* To Our Lady]. Henry Constable. ACP; CAW; CoBE; GoBC; ISi; OBSC
In that proud port, which her so goodly graceth. Amoretti, XIII. Spenser. BWP; ReIE; Sonn
In that rapacious littoral now slaked by sea. Shore Birds. Vi Gale. GoYe
In that remote and solitary place. At Seeing Archbishop Williams's Monument at Carnarvonshire. Sneyd Davis. EiCL
In that rest made green by window shades. Afternoon for a Small Boy. Bink Noll. ToPo
In that so sudden summer storm they tried. Summer Storm. Louis Simpson. CBV; ErPo
In that soft mid-land where the breezes bear. Rodney's Ride. Elbridge Streeter Brooks. MC; OTPC; PAH
In that sore hour around thy bed there stood. Deliverance. William James Dawson. OBVV
In that strange city. Hunger. Mary Carolyn Davies. AnAmPo
In that town, nothing is sane but the sea. Beads from Blackpool. Anne Ridler. NMP
In the/ In the Quarter. Cultural Exchange. Langston Hughes. PoNe (1970 ed.)
In the Acadian land, on the shores of the Basin of Minas. Longfellow. *Fr.* Evangeline. CoBA
In the accident. Newlyweds' Accident, The. David Hilton. QAH
In the Age of Gold. A Little Girl Lost [*or* Children of a Future Age]. Blake. *Fr.* The Songs of Experience. CBEP; ERoP-1
In the age that was golden, the halcyon times. Pessimism. Newton Mackintosh. BOHV
In the air of the room. Rendezvous. Antonia Pozzi. OnPM
In the air there are no coral. A Song. Duncan Campbell Scott. PeCV
In the Allegheny Mountains. The Barn-Swallow. William Sargent. RIS
In the America of the dream. The Lonesome Dream. Lisel Mueller. CoAP
In the American dream it is customarily deleted. The Bush on Mount Venus. Donald Finkel. CoPo
In the American Grain, *sel.* William Carlos Williams.
Sir Walter Raleigh. OnHM
In the ancient town of Bruges. Carillon. Longfellow. *Fr.* The Belfry of Bruges. CoBA
In the Annals of Tacitus. Philip Murray. NePoAm
In the April Rain. Mary Anderson. BoTP
In the Autumn sky the clouds are thinned. After Rain. Tu Fu. OnPM
In the Azure Night. Bartolomé Galindez. CAW
In the bad old days it was not so bad. The Managers. W. H. Auden. EnLit
In the Baggage Coach Ahead. Gussie L. Davis. TreFS
In the Baggage Room at Greyhound. Allen Ginsberg. NaP
In the Barn. Josephine Pinckney. NP
In the barn the tenant Cock. Day; a Pastoral. John Cunningham. OBEC
In the Barnyard. Dorothy Aldis. RePo; UTS
In the Barn-Yard's Southerly Corner. Sir Charles G. D. Roberts. TwCaPo
In the Bay. Arthur Symons. *Fr.* Amoris Exsul. OBNC; PoVP
In the Bayou. Don Marquis. AmFN
In the Bazaars of Hyderabad. Sarojini Naidu. FaPON; GaP; MoSiPe; RePo
In the beauty of the morning. The Touch Divine. Jennie Wilson-Howell. SoP
In the Beck. Kathleen Raine. CMoP
In the Beginning. Daniel G. Hoffman. PP
In the Beginning. Harriet Monroe. AA
In the Beginning. Jenny Lind Porter. GoYe
In the Beginning. Dylan Thomas. MaPo; MoRP
In the beginning, at every step, he turned. The Sickness of Adam. Karl Shapiro. *Fr.* Adam and Eve. AmP; AP; CoBMV; FiMAP; MoAB; ReMP
In the beginning, earth gave forth, around. The Origins of Life. Lucretius. *Fr.* De Rerum Natura. LiTW
In the beginning God created the heaven and the earth. The Creation. Genesis, Bible, *O.T.* ImOP; TreF; WoL
In the beginning God created the world. T. S. Eliot. *Fr.* The Rock. OxBoCh
In the beginning nothing is congenial, not even the world. Music. Tony Towle. ANYP
"In the beginning," said the old man. Genesis. Ray Mathew. NeLNL
In the beginning the Great Spirit gave the prairie rare gifts. The Western Trail. Robert V. Carr. PoOW
In the beginning there arose the Golden Child. To the Unknown God. *Unknown.* *Fr.* The Rig-Veda. OuHeWo
In the beginning, there was nought. Creation. Alfred Noyes. GoBC; OBVV
In the beginning there were transports. Genesis. Jules Alan Wein. TrJP
In the beginning this was Self alone, in the shape of a person. The Universal Self. *Unknown.* *Fr.* The Upanishads. WoL
In the Beginning Was the. Lee Murchison. SD
In the Beginning Was the Bird. Henry Treece. LiTB; LiTM; WaP
In the beginning was the three-pointed star. In the Beginning. Dylan Thomas. MaPo; MoRP
In the Beginning Was the Word. St. John, I: 1-17, Bible, *N.T.* BoC; TreF
(Word, The, I: 1-5.) MaRV; TrGrPo
In the beginning was the Word. The Eternal Word. Longfellow. ChIP
In the beginning was the word. The Great Pax Whitie. Nikki Giovanni. WSL
In the beginning, when green came on the pasture. In the

Beginning. Jenny Lind Porter. GoYe
In the beginning will be the hand. Fantasy for Those Who Hate Their Work. Lou Lipsitz. YAP
In the Beginninging. William D. Barney. FiSC
In the bend of your mouth soft murder. Lion. May Swenson. LiTM (1970 ed.)
In the big-flaked sugar-snow. Maple Feast. Frances Frost. SiSoSe
In the bitter waves of woe. Ultima Veritas [*or* I Shall See Him *or* Holding]. Washington Gladden. FaChP; OQP; SoP
In the black furrow of a field. The Hare. Walter de la Mare. TiPo
In the Bleak Mid-Winter. Christina Rossetti. *See* Christmas Carol, A: "In the bleak mid-winter."
In the blossom-land Japan. An Old Song. "Yehoash." AWP; JAWP; LiTW; WBP
In the blue hubbub of the same-through-wealth sky. Geography. Kenneth Koch. AmPC
In the bluebell forest. Bluebells. Olive Enoch. BoTP
In the Book of Beards and Accomplishments of Men. Mustache. William M. Hoffman. ThO
In the Boston Sunday *Herald* just three lines. To an American Poet Just Dead. Richard Wilbur. ML
In the bowl of buildings alias the back yard. Milk at the Bottom of the Sea. Oscar Williams. GTBS-W; LiTA; MoPo
In the Breeze. Boris Pasternak, *tr. fr. Russian by* C. M. Bowra. TrJP
In the bright bay of your morning, O God. Prayer. Claire Goll. TrJP
In the bright season when He, most high Jove. The Golden Sestina. Giovanni Pico della Mirandola. LiTW
In the broken light, in owl weather. Colloquy. Weldon Kees. NaP; NYBP
In the broken range. About Face. Anne Waldman. YAP
In the burgeoning age of Arnaut when for God and man to be. A Fit of Something against Something. Alan Ansen. PP
In the busy street. Till He Come. "L. R." SoP
In the Cage. Robert Lowell. NoP; Sonn; SyP
In the cage my life began. Bagheera's Song. Kipling. *Fr.* The Second Jungle Book. PoFr
In the Carpenter Shop. Robert McIntyre. *See* Nazareth Shop, The.
In the Carpenter's Shop. Sara Teasdale. HBMV; StJW
In the castle of my soul. The Little Gate to God. Walter Rauschenbusch. *Fr.* The Postern Gate. MaRV; TRV
In the Catacombs. Harlan Hoge Ballard. BOHV; YaD
In the Cathedral Close. Edward Dowden. NBM; OBVV; OxBI
In the cathedral the acolytes are praying. The Habeas Corpus Blues. Conrad Aiken. NYBP
In the Caves of Auvergne. W. J. Turner. HBMV; POTE
In the Cemetery. Thomas Hardy. Sonn
In the Cemetery of the Sun. Wilfred Watson. PeCV
In the Chaotic Age. C. Day Lewis. CMoP
In the Children's Hospital. Tennyson. HBV; PoVP
In the church, fallen like dancers. Enfidaville. Keith Douglas. HaMV
In the Churchyard at Cambridge. Longfellow. AmPP (5th ed.); AP; MWA-1; PoEL-5
In the Cities. D. H. Lawrence. WePo
In the City. Humbert Wolfe. BoC
In the City. Israel Zangwill. WGRP
In the city of St. Francis. Afterwards, They Shall Dance. Bob Kaufman. PoNe (1970 ed.); TwCP
In the city of Sendai, electric cold. Sakunami. James Kirkup. POTi
In the cliff over the frog pond. The Fossils. Galway Kinnell. NYBP
In the close covert of a grove. The Geranium. Sheridan. ErPo; UnTE
In the cloud-gray mornings. Hoar-Frost. Amy Lowell. *Fr.* Chinoiseries. AnAmPo; NP
In the Coach, *sel.* Thomas Edward Brown.
Conjergal Rights. PeVV
In the coign of the cliff between lowland and highland. *See* In a coign. . .
In the coiled shell sounds Ocean's distant roar. The Tutelage. Robert Mowry Bell. AA
In the cold, cold parlor. First Death in Nova Scotia. Elizabeth Bishop. CoAP; NYBP
In the cold I will rise, I will bathe. The Lonely Death. Adelaide Crapsey. AnFE; APA; CoAnAm; MAP; MoAmPo (1942 ed.); NP
In the cold October night-time. *See* In the wild October night-time.
In the cold room. Morning at the Temple of Kobai. Edith Shiffert. NYTB
In the cold shed sharpening saws. Sixth-Month Song in the Foothills. Gary Snyder. FRC; WIRo
In the College of Surgeons. James Stephens. *See* College of Surgeons, The.
In the common round of duty. A Sure Promise. Herbert G. Tovey. SoP
In the Congo. Vachel Lindsay. *Fr.* The Congo. WePo
In the cool, impersonal room. The Egoist Dead. Elizabeth Brewster. CaP
In the Cool of the Evening. Alfred Noyes. HBV
In the Cool of the Evening. James Stephens. MemP
In the cool of twilight, now the sun has gone. My Two Daughters. Victor Hugo. LO
In the cool waters of the river. Woman. Valente Malangatana. PBA; TTY
In the copper marsh. Heron. Philip Booth. NePoEA
In the corner lot. Inventory—to 100th Street. Frank Lima. ANYP
In the corner the fire made a place. Two Women. Tania van Zyl. PeSA
In the County Tyrone, in the town of Dungannon. The Old [*or* Ould] Orange Flute. *Unknown.* MuSP; OxBoLi
In the Courts of Evil/ Borgias dine. Saint Francis Borgia; or, A Refutation for Heredity. Phyllis McGinley. NePoAm-2
In the Cove. Mary Fanny Youngs. HH
In the cowslip pips I lie. Clock-a-Clay. John Clare. CBEP; ERoP-2; FaPON; LiTB; LoBV; NBM; OBNC; PoEL-4; PoFS; SeCeV; ThWaDe; TrGrPo; WHA
In the cream gilded cabin of his steam yacht. Mr. Nixon. Ezra Pound. *Fr.* Hugh Selwyn Mauberley. CMoP; MoAmPo (1962 ed.)
In the crewel world of my grandmother. Crewel. Nancy Willard. ThO
In the crimson of the morning, in the whiteness of the noon. The Coming of His Feet. Lyman W. Allen. BLPA; MaRV; NeHB; SoP
In the Cross of Christ I Glory. Sir John Bowring. HBV; MaRV; WGRP
(The Cross.) SoP
(Towering o'er the Wrecks of Time.) BePJ
In the crowd's multitudinous mind. Crucifixion. Eva Gore-Booth. MaRV; WGRP
In the daisied lap of summer. The Season's Lovers. Miriam Waddington. MoCV; OBCV; PeCV (1967 ed.)
In the Dark. George Arnold. HBV
In the Dark. Frances Louisa Bushnell. AA
In the Dark. Mary Potter Thacher Higginson. AA
In the Dark. Sophie Jewett. TrPWD
In the dark and peace of my final bed. Little Pagan Rain Song. Frances Shaw. HBMV; NP
In the dark at first, we see things in their sleep. Girandole. Dorothy Donnelly. NYBP
In the dark caverns of the night. Poem. Henry Treece. NeBP
In the dark church of music. Vivaldi. Delmore Schwartz. NYBP
In the dark corners of buildings. White Powder! Victor Hernandez Cruz. BF
In the dark crevasses the smoke-white fish. Leviathan. Margaret R. Gould. TwCaPo
In the dark dungeons of the mind. The Praying-Mantis. Annie Charlotte Dalton. TwCaPo
In the Dark, in the Dew. Mary Newmarch Prescott. HBV
In the dark night where none could ever spy. Wasted Night. *Unknown.* UnTE
In the Dark None Dainty. Robert Herrick. CBEP; ELU
In the dark of the wood, silence. No leaf stirred. The Dark Wood. John Hall Wheelock. PG (1955 ed.)
In the dark pathways of his Gothic mind. Sketch. "Seumas O'Sullivan." AnIV
In the dark pine-wood. James Joyce. Chamber Music, XX. BoLP
In the dark room of her disinclination. Chorus for Refusal. Margaret Marks. MAP

In the Dark What the Day Doth Forbid. Thomas Campion. *See* Hark All Ye Ladies that Do Sleep.
In the dark womb where I began. C. L. M. [*or* To His Mother.] John Masefield. BoLiVe; HBV; LiTM; MoBrPo; OBVV; POTE
In the darkening church. Rufus Prays. L. A. G. Strong. MoBrPo
In the darkness deep. The Song of the Turnkey. Harry Bache Smith. AA
In the darkness east of Chicago. A Valedictory to Standard Oil of Indiana. David Wagoner. NYBP
In the darkness he sings of the dawning. The Poet. Mary Sinton Leitch. HBMV; PoMa
In the darkness, who would answer for the color of a rose. The Blind Girl. Nathalia Crane. MAP; MCCG; MoAmPo (1942 ed.)
In the Dawn. Odell Shepard. WGRP
"We are standing in the great dawn of a day they did not know," *sel.* MaRV
In the dawn I gathered cedar-boughs. Song of Whip-plaiting. Constance Lindsay Skinner. *Fr.* Songs of the Coast-Dwellers. NP
In the dawn of breaking day. With Him. Julia E. Martin. STF
In the day the sun is darkened. Lines. Stopford Augustus Brooke. IrPN
In the Days of Crinoline. Thomas Hardy. WhC
In the days of my season of salad. A Song of Renunciation. Sir Owen Seaman. CenHV
In the Days of Old. Thomas Love Peacock. *Fr.* Crotchet Castle. HBV
In the Days of Old Rameses, *with music.* *Unknown.* AS
In the days of old, when Englishmen were—men. *See* In days of old. . .
In the days of President Washington. In Praise of Johnny Appleseed. Vachel Lindsay. PoRL; TSW
In the Days of Rin-Tin-Tin. Daniel Hoffman. CoPo
In the Days of Thy Youth. Bhartrihari, *tr. fr. Sanskrit by* Arthur W. Ryder. OnPM
In the days when Arthur bold. Sir Launfal. Thomas Chester. ATP
In the Days When the Cattle Ran. Hamlin Garland. MPB; RePo
In the Day's Work. Jessie Litchfield. MoAuPo
In the dead middle of night. The Exile. Gerald Bullett. POTE
In the dead of night I heard a sound of storm. The Messiah. David Frishman. LiTW
In the dead park a bench sprawls drunkenly. End of the Season on a Stormy Day—Oban. Iain Crichton Smith. NePoEA-2
In the dean's porch a nest of clay. In the Cathedral Close. Edward Dowden. NBM; OBVV; OxBI
In the December weather, grey and grim. John Francis O'-Donnell. *Fr.* Happy Christmases. IrPN
In the Deep Channel. William Stafford. NaP
In the deep kingdom under ground. Under Ground. James Reeves. RePo
In the Deep Museum. Anne Sexton. MoAmPo (1962 ed.); ToPo
In the deep shadows of the porch. Bind-Weed. "Susan Coolidge." GN; OTPC
In the deep silent depths far away from the shore. Buried Thy Sins. *Unknown.* SoP
In the deep violet air. Chanson sans Paroles. Ernest Dowson. PoVP
In the Depths. Arthur Hugh Clough. PoVP
In the Depths of Night. Manuel Gutiérrez Nájera, *tr. fr. Spanish by* Thomas Walsh. CAW
In the depths of the Greyhound Terminal. In the Baggage Room at Greyhound. Allen Ginsberg. NaP
In the Desert. Alice Corbin. NP
In the Desert. Stephen Crane. The Black Riders, III. AmePo; AP; CrMA; LiTM (1970 ed.)
(Heart, The.) HoPM; MAP; MoAmPo; NeMA
In the deserted garden on weed-grown terraces the willows are fresh again. The Deserted Garden. Li Po. OnPM
In the deserted moon-blanch'd street. A Summer Night. Matthew Arnold. CBEP; EnLi-2; EPN; ExPo; GTBS; GTSE; GTSL; MBW-2; MCCG; NoP; OAEP; PoVP; SeCePo; SeCeV; ViPo; ViPP; VP
In the Dials. W. E. Henley. BrPo
In the dim and distant ages, in the half-forgotten days. A Soldier of Weight. John Kendall. WhC
In the Dock. Walter de la Mare. ChMP; LiTM (1970 ed.); Sonn
In the dome of my Sires as the clear moonbeam falls. Newstead Abbey. Byron. ChER
In the Doorway. Robert Browning. *Fr.* James Lee's Wife. NCEP
In the Dordogne. John Peale Bishop. AnAmPo
In the downhill of life, when I find I'm declining. To-Morrow. John Collins. GTBS; GTBS-D; GTBS-P; GTBS-W; GTSE; GTSL; HBV; TreFT
In the dream, in the charmed dream we are flying. The Eye of Humility. Kay Smith. OBCV
In the dream your face appeared in a blue light. Two Birthday Poems. Dick Lourie. ThO
In the drifting rain the cows in the yard are as black. Milking before Dawn. Ruth Dallas. ACV; AnNZ
In the drinking-well. Aunt Eliza. Harry Graham. ALV; ChTr; FaFP; MaC; NA; SiTL; WhC
In the Due Honor of the Author Master Robert Norton. John Smith. SCAP
In the Dumps. *Unknown.* NA; SiTL
In the dungeon-crypts idly did I stray. The Prisoner. Emily Brontë. AnFE; EnLi-2 (1949 ed.); OAEP
In the Dusky Path of a Dream. Rabindranath Tagore. The Gardener, LXII. OBMV
In the Dying of Daylight. Walter de la Mare. ACV
In the early crystal morning. In the Early Morning Breeze. Lawrence S. Cumberbatch. WSL
In the early days in our own wild way we hurried the time along. The Ruin of Bobtail Bend. James Barton Adams. PoOW
In the early days of my visitation. "The Visitation." Sun-Ra. BF
In the Early Hours. Dawn Finlay. SoP
In the early morning/ when the light and the sea smell come stumbling in. In Solitary Confinement, Sea Point Police Cells. C. J. Driver. PeSA
In the Early Morning Breeze. Lawrence S. Cumberbatch. WSL
In the early morning-shine. Life's Hebe. James Thomson. VA
In the Early, Pearly Morning, *sel.* "Laurence Hope." Carpe Diem. OtMeF
In the early spring, the fattening young weeds. The Spirit. Harold Lenoir Davis. NP
In the earth, the earth, thou shalt be laid. Warning and Reply. Emily Brontë. OBVV; OxBI; PoVP; VA
In the East, in the East is my heart. My Heart Is in the East. Judah Halevi. TrJP
In the east of the city. The Morning Bell of Fang T'a. Hsi P'ei Lan. OnPM; WoL
In the eastern quarter dawn breaks, the stars flicker pale. Cock-Crow Song. *Unknown.* LiTW
In the Egyptian Museum. Janet Lewis. NYBP; QFR
In the Elegy Season. Richard Wilbur. FiMAP; MoAB; NePoEA; NYBP
In the end. For the Magi. J. Patrick Walsh. JKCP (1955 ed.)
In the End of Days. Isaiah, II: 2-4, Bible, *O.T.* TrJP
In the end of the sabbath, as it began to dawn. Easter Morning. St. Matthew, Bible, *N.T.* TreF
In the enormous tragic silence of the night. Brother Dog. Luis Aníbal Sanchez. CAW
In the environs of the funeral home. The Funeral Home. Robert Mezey. AmPC; LiTM (1970 ed.); NePoEA
In the Evening. Thomas Hardy. ImOP
In the evening/ haze darkening on the hills. Another Night in the Ruins. Galway Kinnell. CoAP
In the evening/ Quiet of the country town. Tanka. Noin Hoshi. Po
In the evening/ The sun goes down. At Sunset. Ivy O. Eastwick. BoTP
In the Evening by the Moonlight. James A. Bland. TreFS
In the evening from my window. *Unknown.* SUS
In the evening, just before. For Mary. Kenneth Rexroth. PoPl
In the evening things stand no longer blind. Houses Have Open Eyes. Paul Zech. OnPM
In the evening we came back. A Light Left On. May Sarton. MoLP
In the evening when I sit alone a-dreaming. Sweet Adeline. Richard H. Gerard. TreFT

In the evening, when the world knew he was dead. In the Evening. Thomas Hardy. ImOP
In the Face of Grief. Sister Juana Inés de la Cruz, *tr. fr. Spanish by* Thomas Walsh. CAW
In the fair days when God. To Victor Hugo. Swinburne. OBVV
In the Fair Forest. *Unknown. See* In Summer.
In the Fall o' Year. Thomas S. Jones, Jr. HBV
In the Falling Deer's Mouth. Michael Levien. PoRA (rev. ed.)
In the falling snow. Hokku: in the Falling Snow. Richard Wright. IDB
In the fall-out of daisies on the rockland. Absent Daughter. Barend Toerien. PeSA
In the family drinking well. Sister Nell. *Unknown.* BBGG; FaPON
In the far and mighty West. Wyoming. Charles E. Winter. PoRL
In the far corner. The Blackbird. Humbert Wolfe. BoTP; FaPON; GoJo; HBMV; HBVY; MPB; PCH; RePo; StVeCh; SUS; TiPo; TSW; UTS
In the far north stands a pine tree, lone. The Pine Tree. Heine. PCH
In the far spaces of eternity. Harmony. Thomas Grant Springer. PoToHe
In the Far Years. Wilson MacDonald. CaP
In the Farmhouse. Galway Kinnell. WIRo
In the Fashion. A. A. Milne. RePo
In the Field. Harold Lenoir Davis. NP
In the Field. Richard Wilbur. NYBP
In the Fields. Charlotte Mew. BoNaP; MoAB; MoBrPo; POTE
(Spring.) StaSt
In the Firelight. Eugene Field. AA
In the First House. Joseph Joel Keith. GoYe
In the first rank of these did Zimri stand. Zimri. Dryden. *Fr.* Absalom and Achitophel. PoFS; SeCePo; ShBV-4; ViBoPo
In the first year of the last disgrace. News of the World II. George Barker. DTC; FaBoTw; LiTB
In the flare of rose-bed. Saint Francis. Roger Pfingston. NYTB
In the fleece of your flesh. The Moment before Conception. Eve Merriam. UnTE
In the foil-and-pastel tea room. Non-Euclidean Elegy. John Frederick Nims. MoVE
In the fold. The Little Young Lambs. Patrick Chalmers. TiPo (1952 ed.)
In the Forest. Longfellow. *See* Prologue to "Evangeline."
In the Forest. Alexander Petofi, *tr. fr. Hungarian by* Henry Phillips, Jr. LiTW
In the Forest. Oscar Wilde. SyP
In the forest there. The King of Sunshine. Michael Silverton. PV
In the "foursome" some would fain. Ballade of the Golfer in Love. Clinton Scollard. BOHV
In the full ripeness of thy beauty's prime. Pluto and Venus. *Unknown.* OnPM
In the Future. Edward Lucie-Smith. HYE
In the Garden. Ernest Crosby. HBV; HBVY
In the Garden. Emily Dickinson. *See* Bird came down the walk, A.
In the Garden. Richard Eberhart. NePoAm-2
In the Garden. Peter Fellowes. QAH
In the Garden. F. S. Flint. NP
In the Garden. C. Austin Miles. TreFT
In the Garden. John S. B. Monsell. OQP
In the Garden. Ilo Orleans. RIS
In the Garden. *Unknown.* MaRV
In the Garden at Swainston. Tennyson. OBEV (new ed.); OBNC; OBVV; PoVP; ViPo
(Valedictory, II.) GoBC
In the garden of death, where the singers whose names are deathless. In Memory of "Barry Cornwall." Swinburne. HBV
In the Garden of Eden, planted by God. Trees. Bliss Carman. DD; OHIP; PoRL
In the garden of my soul. Himalaya. Po Fei Huang. NYTB
In the garden of spring. Blossoms. Otomo Yakamochi. OnPM
In the Garden of the Lord. Helen Keller. MaRV; OQP; SoP; TRV; WGRP
In the garden there strayed/ A beautiful maid. *Unknown.* LO
In the Garden; Villa Cleobolus. Lawrence Durrell. ChMP
In the garret under the sloping eaves. The Wedding Gift. Minna Irving. BLPA
In the gathering gloom they lie. Terror. "Yehoash." TrJP
In the Gentlemanly Interest. Donald Evans. NP
In the glittering collection of paste diamonds one in particular ranks very high. Oh, Stop Being Thankful All over the Place. Ogden Nash. NePA; SiTL
In the Gloaming. James C. Bayles. NA
In the Gloaming ("In the gloaming, Oh my darling"). Meta Orred. FaFP; TreF
In the Gloaming ("In the gloaming to be roaming"), *parody.* Charles Stuart Calverley. ALV; InMe
In the gloom of whiteness. Snow. Edward Thomas. FaBoTw; MoVE
In the gloomy ocean bed. The *Kearsarge.* James Jeffrey Roche. AA; PAH
In the Glorious Assumption of Our Blessed Lady. Richard Crashaw. *See* On The Glorious Assumption. . .
In the Glorious Epiphanie of Our Lord God. Richard Crashaw. MaMe; PoEL-2; SCEP-1
(Hymne for the Epiphanie, A.) AnAnS-1; MeP
In the glow of early morning. Christ Is Coming. W. Macomber. STF
In the Gold Mines. B. W. Vilakazi. TTY
In the Gold Room. Oscar Wilde. SyP
In the golden air, the risky autumn. Piazzas. Barbara Guest. NeAP
In the Golden Birch. Jane Elizabeth Gostwycke Roberts. VA
In the Golden Morning of the World. Thomas Westwood. VA
In the golden twilight the rain. The Terrace in the Snow. Su Tung P'o. NaP
In the Good Old Summer Time. Ren Shields. TreF
In the Gorge. W. S. Merwin. AmPC
In the grass. Little Folks in the Grass. Annette Wynne. BoChLi; SP; UTS
In the Grave No Flower. Edna St. Vincent Millay. CrMA
In the gray beginning of years, in the twilight of things that began. Hymn of Man. Swinburne. PoVP
In the gray dawn they left Jerusalem. The Ascension. Edwin Markham. StJW
In the gray dawning across the white lake. Wild March. Constance Fenimore Woolson. YeAr
In the Great Green Commonwealth of Thought. John Masefield. LiTM
In the Great House, and in the House of Fire. He Holdeth Fast to the Memory of His Identity. *Unknown. Fr.* Book of the Dead. AWP; JAWP; WBP
In the Great Metropolis. Arthur Hugh Clough. PoVP; ViPP
In the great place the great house is gone from. Slave Quarters. James Dickey. NYBP
In the great world—which, being interpreted. Byron. *Fr.* Don Juan, XI. OxBoLi
In the green hedge tall and thick. June in Wiltshire. Geoffrey Grigson. WaP
In the green light of water, like the day. The Swans. Edith Sitwell. ACV; CMoP; FaBoMo; GTBS-D; MoVE
In the green quiet wood, where I was used. Mortality. Gerald Gould. MoBrPo (1942 ed.)
In the greenest growth of the Maytime. An Interlude. Swinburne. ViBoPo
In the greenest of our valleys. The Haunted Palace. Poe. *Fr.* The Fall of the House of Usher. AA; AmePo; AmLP; AmP; AmPP; AnFE; AP; APA; BeLS; BoLiVe; CH; ChTr; CoAnAm; HBV; LiTA; LiTG; MAmP; MCCG; MWA-1; NePA; OBVV; OTPC; OxBA; PFY; Po; PoE; PoEL-4; SyP; TDP; TOP; TreFS; TrGrPo; ViBoPo; WiR
In the greenhouse lives a wren. *Unknown.* OxNR
In the Greenwood. Shakespeare. *See* Under the Greenwood Tree.
In the grey wastes of dread. Horses on the Camargue. Roy Campbell. AtBAP; BoC; GTBS-P; OA; PeSA; POTE; SeCePo; ShBV-3
In the groined alcoves of an ancient tower. The Second Volume. Robert Mowry Bell. AA
In the growing haste of the world must this thing be. Sails. George Sterling. EtS
In the gutter. Beggar. F. S. Flint. MoBrPo (1942 ed.)

In the Half Light of Holding and Giving. John Wieners. CoPo
In the hall-grounds, by evening-gloom concealed. The Hydraulic Ram. Charles Tennyson Turner. NBM
In the hall, scuffling; in the cat's mouth, a dove. High. Kathleen Spivack. YAP
In the hall the coffin waits, and the idle armourer stands. Laus Deo. Sydney Dobell. OBEV (1st ed.)
In the halls, in the universities. Cripples. Kathleen Spivack. YAP
In the happier years gone by me. February 14, 22 B.C. Franklin P. Adams. InMe
In the harbour, in the island, in the Spanish Seas. Trade Winds. John Masefield. FaBoCh; OBMV; ShBV-4
In the Heart. Anna Bunston de Bary. MaRV
In the Heart of a Seed. Kate L. Brown. *See* Little Plant, The.
In the Heart of Contemplation. C. Day Lewis. FaBoMo; MoPo
In the Heart of Jesus. Murdoch O'Daly, *tr. fr. Irish by* George Sigerson. CAW
In the heart of night. The Two Houses. Thomas Hardy. NP
In the heart of the hills of life, I know. My Springs. Sidney Lanier. UnPo
In the heart of the queen anne's lace, a knot of blood. The Knot. Adrienne Rich. NoP
In the heart of the white summer mist lay a green little piece of the world. Karma. William Canton. VA
In the Hedgeback. "Hugh MacDiarmid." NeBP
In the Henry James Country. William Abrahams. WaP
In the heydays of 'forty-five. For George Santayana. Robert Lowell. NoP
In the high country people. Each to His Own Ground. John Stevens Wade. ThO
In the high, high grass of Guinée. Country Graveyard. Charles F. Pressoir. PoNe
In the high places lo! there is no light. Lighten Our Darkness. Lord Alfred Douglas. HBMV
In the high trees—many doleful winds. The Liberator. Wu Ti, *tr. fr. Chinese by* Arthur Waley. BiS
In the high turret chamber sat the sage. Death as the Fool. Frank T. Marzials. VA
In the Highlands. Robert Louis Stevenson. ACV; FaBV; GoTS; GTBS-D; HBV; MemP; OBEV; OBVV; OxBS
(In the highlands, in the country places.) BrPo; FaBoCh
In the history of the nations. Nations. Michael Brownstein. ANYP
In the hole of a heel of an old brown stocking. Stocking Fairy. Winifred Welles. BoChLi
In the hollow tree, in the old grey tower. The Owl [*or* The Horned Owl]. "Barry Cornwall." OTPC
In the Holy Nativity of Our Lord God. Richard Crashaw. BEL; CABA; CoBE; EnL; MaMe; PoEL-2; SCEP-1; SeCeV; SeCV-1; SeEP; UnPo (1st ed.)
(Holy Nativity of Our Lord God, *sl. abr.*) WGRP
(Hymn of the Nativity.) AtBAP; MeLP; OBS
(Hymne of the Nativity, Sung as by the Shepheards, An.) AnAnS-1; MaMe; MeP; MePo
(Nativity, The.) OxBoCh; PoLi
Sels.
"Gloomy night embraced the place."
(Hymn of the Nativity, A.) ViBoPo
Shepherds' Hymn: "We saw thee in thy balmy nest." ACP; BoC; CAW; TrGrPo, 3 *sts.*
(Hymn Sung as by the Shepherds, A.) GoBC
(Shepherds Hymn Their Saviour, 2 *sts.*) EG
(Verses from the Shepherds' Hymn.) OBEV
"Welcome to our wondering sight," 6 *ll.* ChIP
In the Hospital. Arthur Guiterman. MaRV; WGRP
In the Hospital. Mary Woolsey Howland. HBV; MaRV
(Rest.) SoP
In the Hospital. Dilys Laing. NYTB
In the hot valley of the never was. The Last Campaign. Geoffrey Lehmann. PoAu-2
In the Hour of Death. Richard Doddridge Blackmore. *See* Dominus Illuminatio Mea.
In the Hour of My Distress. Robert Herrick. *See* His Litany to the Holy Spirit.
In the Hour of Trial. James Montgomery. SoP
In the Hours of Darkness. James Flexner. FaPON; MPB
In the house I have a cat. The Dog and the Cat. Grace Taber Hallock. RePo
In the House of Idiedaily. Bliss Carman. OBVV; PFY
In the hush of early even. The Fugitive. John Freeman. MBP
In the Immense Cathedral. John Hall Wheelock. *Fr.* The Holy Earth. MoRP
In the inn they had no room. Easter, Day of Christ Eternal. Maurice Moore. STF
In the Interest of Black Salvation. Don L. Lee. BP; WSL
In the Interstices. Ruth Stone. ErPo
In the Isle of Dogs. John Davidson. OBNC
In the jar of apricot jam a lava sea &. Kitchen. Alden Van Buskirk. YAP
In the jolly, jolly spring. What the Toys Are Thinking. ffrida Wolfe. TiPo
In the kitchen of the old house, late. In the Old House. Donald Hall. NePoEA-2
In the land of lobelias and tennis flannels. T. S. Eliot. *Fr.* The Rock. SoP
In the Land of Magic. Henri Michaux, *tr. fr. French by* Richard Ellmann. LiTW
In the land of Tao-chou. The People of Tao-chou. Po Chü-i. ChTr
In the land of turkeys in turkey weather. Dance of the Macabre Mice. Wallace Stevens. CMoP; NePA OxBA; SeCeV
In the Land Where We Were Dreaming, *abr.* Daniel Bedinger Lucas. PAH
In the Lane. L. A. G. Strong. HaMV
In the last days. Apocalypse. Francis Ernest Kobina Parkes. PBA
In the last storm, when hawks. The Epitaph Ending in and. William Stafford. NaP
In the late evening, when the house is still. The Anodyne. Sarah N. Cleghorn. OQP
In the leafy tree-tops. Echo. Otomo Yakamochi. OnPM
In the Lecture Room. James K. Baxter. Cressida, I. AnNZ
In the Library. Elizabeth Brewster. OBCV
In the licorice fields at Pontefract. The Licorice Fields at Pontefract. John Betjeman. CMoP; NMP
In the light of the moon, by the side of the water. My Daughter Louise. Homer Greene. HBV
In the lights of this festival and my birthday. Julia Vinograd. YAP
In the Lilac-Rain. Edith M. Thomas. HBV
In the loam we sleep. Loam. Carl Sandburg. CMoP
In the lone places of my soul. Faith, Hope, Love. Margaret Matthews. SoP
In the lonesome latter years. The Promissory Note. Bayard Taylor. BOHV; HBV; Par
In the long journey out of the self. Journey to the Interior. Theodore Roethke. NaP; NYBP
In the long, sleepless watches of the night. The Cross of Snow. Longfellow. AmePo; AmP; AmPP; AnAmPo; AP; CoBA; FaPL; MAmP; MaRV; MWA-1; OxBA
In the loud waking world I come and go. Nihil Humani Alienum. Titus Munson Coan. AA
In the low house, whose thick lights. Lady Day. Padraic Fallon. NeIP
In the lower lands of day. Before Sunset. Swinburne. EG; StP
In the Lupanar at Pompeii. James Dickey. ToPo
In the Lybian desert I. Modo and Alciphron. Sylvia Townsend Warner. MoBrPo
In the manner of Klee's favorite cat, named Bimbo. Bimbo's Pome. Paul Klee. FIW
In the maple-sugar bush. March. Elizabeth J. Coatsworth. YeAr
In the Marble Quarry. James Dickey. AmFN; NoP
In the Market-Place. John Francis O'Donnell. *Fr.* Limerick Town. NBM
("Here I've got you, Philip Desmond, standing in the market-place.") IrPN
In the market-place of Bruges stands the belfry old and brown. Longfellow. *Fr.* The Belfry of Bruges. HBV; HT
In the marrow of the living. Undocumented Observations From the Letters of G. Craig Sterry. QAH
In the Master Bedroom of the White House. Dick Lourie. ThO
In the Matter of Two Men. James David Corrothers. BANP
In the Merry Month of May. Nicholas Breton. *See* Phyllida and Corydon.

In the mid-city, under an oiled sky. A Garden in Chicago. Karl Shapiro. PoIE
In the middle of the harbour. Derek Walcott. *Fr.* A Sea-Chantey. TTY
In the middle of the night. Silver Wedding. Ralph Hodgson. HBMV; TrGrPo
In the middle of the night in the next room. The Cell of Himself. Arthur Freeman. TwCP
In the middle of this life's journey. An American Takes a Walk. Reed Whittemore. MoVE
In the midmost of ocean. The Sea. Lloyd Frankenberg. AnFE; CoAnAm
In the midst of my garden. The Palm-Tree. Abd-ar-Rahman I. AWP; JAWP; WBP
In the midst of roaring cannon. "Lean Hard on Me." Clifford Lewis. SoP
In the midst of words your wordless image. The Heart. Harvey Shapiro. HoPM
In the midway of this our mortal life. Dante. *Fr.* Divina Commedia: Inferno. OuHeWo
In the milde close of an hot summers day. The Retirement. Thomas Flatman. PeRV
In the Mile End Road. Amy Levy. VA
In the Mind's Eye. Thomas Hardy. SiSW
In the Mirror. Elizabeth Fleming. BoTP
In the Mohave. Patrick Orr. BANP; LiTM
In the moment of his glory. Lincoln Slain. Edwin Markham. LiPo
In the Monastery. Norreys Jephson O'Conor. CAW
In the moneth of May when the new tender green. The Prologue. *Unknown.* ReIE
In the month of April. *Unknown.* RIS
In the month of February. February. *Unknown.* BoTP; PCH
In the Month of Green Fire. Sophie Himmell. GoYe
In the month of the long decline of roses. Hendecasyllabics. Swinburne. SyP
In the month when the Kamchatka bugbane. Going. James Schuyler. ANYP
In the Mood of Blake. William Soutar. HaMV
In the Moonlight. Thomas Hardy. NP
In the Moonlight. Norreys Jephson O'Conor. HBMV; SoPo; SUS
In the Moonlight. Kenneth Patchen. ToPo
In the Moonlight. David McKee Wright. AnNZ; BoAu
"In the moonlight evening." By Moonlight. *Unknown.* UnTE
In the moonlit room your face. Clair de Lune. Arthur Symons. SyP
In the Morgue. Israel Zangwill. TrJP
In the morn we met the proud array. The March of the Three Kings. *Unknown.* ChrBoLe
In the Morning. Paul Laurence Dunbar. GoSl
In the Morning. A. E. Housman. WePo
In the Morning. Cecilia Loftus. GFA
In the morning. The Rider. William Burford. NYTB
In the morning in the blue snow. Annual Gaiety. Wallace Stevens. MAP; MoAB; MoAmPo
In the morning, in the dark. The Night Hunt. Thomas MacDonagh. OxBI; RoGo
In the morning, in the morning. In the Morning. A. E. Housman. WePo
In the morning light trills the gay swallow. Hezekiah Butterworth. *See* In the rosy light. . .
In the morning the city. City [San Francisco]. Langston Hughes. AmFN; FaPON; GoSl; PDV
In the morning the hawk and the sun flew up together. Night and the Child. Judith Wright. SeCePo
In the morning, very early. Barefoot Days. Rachel Field. FaPON; YeAr
In the morning when I swing. My Swinging Shadow. Grace Wilson Coplen. GFA
In the morning when ye rise. A Charm. Robert Herrick. OTPC (1923 ed.)
"In the Most Lightsome Darkness." Sister Mary Norbert Körte. ThO
In the motionless haze of interior heat. Louise Townsend Nicholl. *Fr.* Recital. UnS
In the Mountain Tent. James Dickey. PoAn
In the mountains. The Guests. Louis Zukofsky. CoPo
In the mountains o' the west. The Maid o' the West. John Clare. ERoP-2
In the Mountains on a Summer Day. Li Po, *tr. fr. Chinese by* Arthur Waley. AWP; FlW; SD
In the mud of the Cambrian main. A Ballade of Evolution. Grant Allen. ATP (1935 ed.)
In the Museum. Isabella Gardner. ELU; NYBP
In the mustardseed sun. Poem on His Birthday. Dylan Thomas. DiPo; SeCeV (1967 ed.)
In the Naked Bed, in Plato's Cave. Delmore Schwartz. ExPo; FiMAP; GTBS-W; ILP; LiTA; LiTG; LiTM; MiAP; MoAB; MoAmPo; MoVE; NePA; PoDB; ReMP; TwAmPo
In the name of God advancing. Daily Work. *Unknown.* SoP
In the name of God—Who shall open. The Lord. José Maria Gabriel y Galán. CAW
In the name of Him who died. Follow Me! Sheldon Shepard. ChIP
In the Name of Jesus Christ. Claudia Cranston. HBMV
In the Name of Our Sons. Dorothy Gould. PGD
In the narrow street. Return. H. D. Garberry. PoNe
In the nativity of time. Love Made in the First Age: To Chloris. Richard Lovelace. AnAnS-2; CavP; SCEP-2; SeCP
In the negro gardens negro birds. To Eliza, Duchess of Dorset. Joseph Bennett. LiTA; NePA
In the Neolithic Age, *br. sel.* Kipling.
Wide, Wide World, The. OtMeF
In the new city of marble and bright stone. The Unknown Soldier. Conrad Aiken. *Fr.* The Soldier. WaaP; WaP
In the News. Don Shea. QAH
In the Night. Stephen Crane. *See* Peaks, The.
In the Night. Elizabeth Jennings. NePoEA; NYBP
In the night. Blues. Sonia Sanchez. BF
In the Night. James Stephens. OBMV
In the Night. *Unknown.* NA
In the Night Fields. W. S. Merwin. AP; PoCh
In the night, in the night, O my Country, the stream calls out from afar. Parvuli Ejus. Aubrey Thomas De Vere. IrPN
In the night my great swamp-willow fell. Who Guessed Amiss the Riddle of the Sphinx. James Merrill. TwAmPo
In the Night of the Full Moon. Carl Busse, *tr. fr. German by* Jethro Bithell. AWP
In the night the agile mole. The Unfortunate Mole. Mary Kennedy. GoYe
In the night the man could hear the wind walking. Harvest. Gene Shuford. GoYe
In the Night Watches. Sir Charles G. D. Roberts. PeCV
In the night when all are sleeping. The Hoopskirt. John Gould Fletcher. LaNeLa
In the nightmare of the dark. W. H. Auden. *Fr.* In Memory of W. B. Yeats. TRV
In the nook of a wood—where a pool freshed with dew. The Stranger. Walter de la Mare. OAEP (2d ed.)
In the northern hemisphere. Kangaroo. D. H. Lawrence. FlW; MoVE; OA; ShBV-4
In the numb time when foam froze. All That Is, and Can Delight. Robert Farren. OxBI
In the ocean of the sky. Hitomaro, *tr. fr. Japanese by* Arthur Waley. LiTW
In the ocean of the sky. The Moon Ship. *Unknown.* GFA
In the ocean, 'way out yonder. The Dinkey-Bird. Eugene Field. AA; BOHV; HBVY; LBN; NA; PFY; TSW; UTS
In the old age black was not counted fair. Sonnets, CXXVII. Shakespeare. CBEP; DiPo; ReIE; Sonn
In the old back streets o' Pimlico. The Rambling Sailor. Charlotte Mew. HBMV; PoRA
In the Old Churchyard at Fredericksburg. Frederick Wadsworth Loring. AA
In the Old City. Jacob Fichman, *tr. fr. Hebrew by* Sholom J. Kahn. TrJP
In the old colony days, in Plymouth the land of the Pilgrims. The Courtship of Miles Standish. Longfellow. BeLS; TreFS
In the old days (a custom laid aside). Abraham Davenport. Whittier. AMePo; AmPP; AnNE; CoBA; NoP
In the old days the white gates swung. Pastoral. Clifford Dyment. MoVE
In the old days when King Arthur ruled the nation. The Wife of Bath's Tale. Chaucer. *Fr.* The Canterbury Tales. EnL
In the old days with married women's stockings. The Libertine. Louis MacNeice. DTC
In the old deep sing-song of the sea. Old Deep Sing-Song. Carl Sandburg. FlW

In the Old House. Donald Hall. NePoEA-2
In the old, lonely park all white with frost. Sentimental Colloquy. Paul Verlaine, *tr. by* Alan Conder. LO
In the old man's eyes. Takahama Kyoshi, *tr. fr. Japanese by* Geoffrey Bownas *and* Anthony Thwaite. FIW
In the "Old South." Whittier. AA
In the Old Theater, Fiesole. Thomas Hardy. Sonn
In the one-two domestic goose one-two one-two step. Henry Beissel. *Fr.* New Wings for Icarus. MoCV
In the olive darkness of the sally-trees. The Bull. Judith Wright. PoAu-2
In the Open. Ruth Pitter. BoPe
In the open sea. Peasant and Geisha Songs. *Unknown.* LiTW
In the Orchard. Ibsen, *tr. fr. Norwegian by* Sir Edmund Gosse. AWP; JAWP; WBP
In the Orchard. James Stephens. LOW; RoGo
In the Orchard. Muriel Stuart. ErPo; NP
In the Orchard. *Unknown, tr. fr. Provençal by* Swinburne. UnTE
In the orchestra the fixed stars. Round Dance, & Canticle. Robert Kelly. CoPo
In the Oregon Country. William Stafford. AmFN
In the other gardens. Autumn Fires. Robert Louis Stevenson. GFA; SUS; TiPo; YeAr
In the pages of the past. Africa Speaks. Michael Dei-Anang. ACV
In the painkilling cold that wrapped. Snow. David Wevill. MoCV
In the palace of a certain king stood an incomparable bed. Leap and Creep. *Unknown. Fr.* The Panchatantra. OuHeWo
In the pale mauve twilight, streaked with orange. Evensong. Conrad Aiken. HBMV; PG
In the pale summertime, when far above you. Of Swimming in Lakes and Rivers. Bertolt Brecht. SD
In the palm/ the seed. A Guerrilla Handbook. LeRoi Jones. FRC
In the Paralelo a one-legged/ Man. Entered in the Minutes. Louis MacNeice. LiTB
In the Park. Rose Fyleman. StVeCh (1955 ed.)
In the Park. Helen Hoyt. HBMV
In the park I saw a stranger. Interrupted Romance. *Unknown.* UnTE
In the Past. Trumbull Stickney. MAP; MoAmPo (1942 ed.); OxBA
In the pathways of heaven. To the Memory of John Burroughs. Catherine Parmenter. PEDC; PoRL
In the Pauper's Turnip-Field. Herman Melville. PoEL-5
In the Person of Woman-kind. Ben Jonson. SCEP-2; SeCP; SeCV-1
In the Piazza at Night. Arthur Hugh Clough. *Fr.* At Venice. ViPo
In the picture the people stroll and stroll all day. Public Holiday; Paris. Joyce Horner. GoYe
In the Place of a Passage 22. Robert Duncan. FRC
In the placid summer midnight. Street Scene. W. E. Henley. BoTP
In the pleasant green garden. A [*or* The] Tea Party. Kate Greenaway. MPB; OTPC; PPL; TiPo (1952 ed.)
In the poet's vigorous fifties. Confidential. Winfield Townley Scott. ELU
In the pond in the park. Water Picture. May Swenson. BoNaP; OCS
In the Poppy Field. James Stephens. PoRA (rev. ed.)
In the Presence of the King! *Unknown.* SoP
In the prison cell I sit. Tramp, Tramp, Tramp. George Frederick Root. TreFS
In the Prison Pen. Herman Melville. MWA-1; PoEL-5
In the profound platform's floodlit aquarium. Symphony Orchestra. James Kirkup. MuSP
In the Proscenium. Gene Derwood. GTBS-W; LiTA; LiTM (rev. ed.)
(War's Clown in the Proscenium.) NePA
In the Public Garden. Marianne Moore. NoP
In the Public Gardens. John Betjeman. NYBP
In the pure soul, although it sing or pray. Eternal Christmas. Elizabeth Stuart Phelps Ward. ChIP; MaRV; PGD; TRV
In the purple light, heavy with redwood, the slopes drop seaward. Apology for Bad Dreams. Robinson Jeffers. AmP; AmPP; AnFE; AP; CoAnAm; CoBMV; ILP; LiTA; MAP; MoAB; MoAmPo; NoP; OxBA; SeCeV; TwAmPo
In the pushcart market, on Sunday. Galway Kinnell. *Fr.* The Avenue Bearing the Initial of Christ into the New World. NaP
In the Queen's Room. Norman Cameron. Three Love Poems, II. FaBoTw; GTBS-P
In the queer light, in twilight. The Young Man in April. Rupert Brooke. BoLP
In the Quiet. T. Moore Atkinson. SoP
In the quiet before cockcrow when the cricket's. Dear Men and Women. John Hall Wheelock. NYBP
In the quiet of the moments. In the Quiet. T. Moore Atkinson. SoP
In the rain that has passed by. Lost City. Ingrid Jonker. PeSA
In the rain what is there to do, what to play. From the Spanish. Tony Towle. ANYP; YAP
In the rain's push and the wind's hand. From My Thought. Daniel Smythe. GoYe
In the ranks of the Austrian you found him. The Forced Recruit. Elizabeth Barrett Browning. PoVP
In the Ravine. W. W. E. Ross. PeCV
In the red April dawn. A World Still Young [*or* Birds in April]. W. E. Henley. MeWo; YT
In the Redwood Forest. Ralph Pomeroy. CoPo
In the region where the roses always bloom. Ida, Sweet as Apple Cider. Eddie Leonard. TreFT
In the Restaurant. Thomas Hardy. Satires of Circumstance, XI. MoAB; MoBrPo
In the Rhine, in the beautiful river. A Madonna. Heine. OnPM
In the ribs of an ugly school building. Three Brown Girls Singing. M. Carl Holman. Kal
In the Ringwood. Thomas Kinsella. NMP; OxBI
In the roof. The Zoo Club. Robert Hershon. ThO
In the Room. James Thomson. OBVV; PeVV
In the room at Warm Springs. At Warm Springs. William Rose Benét. PoRL
In the roses, snuggled deep. A Surprise. Elizabeth Winton. PCH
In the rosy [*or* morning] light trills the gay swallow. The Snow-bird. Hezekiah Butterworth. PCH; PRWS
In the Round. Theodore Weiss. NMP
In the round park the old men sitting on benches. Fifth Elegy. Alex Comfort. FaBoMo
In the Royal City spring is almost over. The Flower Market. Po Chü-i. PPON; WoL
In the royal path. The Triumph of Joseph. Charles Jeremiah Wells. *Fr.* Joseph and His Brethren. VA
In the rude age, when knowledge was not rife. Another Tribute to Wyatt. Earl of Surrey. FCP; NCEP; SiPS
In the sad Southwest, in the mystical Sunland. Homes of the Cliff Dwellers. Stanley Wood. PoOW
In the sad spirit. To the Unknown Light. Edward Shanks. TrPWD
In the salt terror of the stormy sea. The City of the Soul. Lord Alfred Douglas. HBMV
In the sand I grew, by the rocky sea-wall. The Husband's Message. *Unknown.* AnOE
In the sanded desert stands a tree. The Tree in the Desert. Friedrich Hebbel. LiTW
In the Santa Clara Valley, far away and far away. On the Great Plateu. Edith Franklin Wyatt. HBMV; NP
In the scented bud of the morning—O. The Daisies. James Stephens. AnIV; AWP; JAWP; WBP
In the sea, Biscayne, there prinks. Homunculus et la Belle Etoile. Wallace Stevens. MAP; MoAB; MoAmPo
In the sea wave tosses side by side with wave. Muhammad Iqbal. *Fr.* An Invocation. ACV
In the seaport of Saint Malo 'twas a smiling morn in May. Jacques Cartier. Thomas D'Arcy McGee. CaP; PTK
In the Season. Robert Louis Stevenson. VA
In the Secret Rose Garden. Sa'd ud-din Mahmud Shabistari, *tr. fr. Persian by* Florence Lederer. LiTW
In the secret Valley of Silence. The Valley of Silence. "Fiona Macleod." PoVP
In the Selkirks. Duncan Campbell Scott. CaP
In the Seraglio. David R. Slavitt. ErPo
In the Servants' Quarters. Thomas Hardy. MoAB; MoBrPo; MoRP
In the Seven Woods. W. B. Yeats. CMoP; LoBV
In the shabby train no seat is vacant. The Refugees. Randall

Jarrell. MoAB; MoAmPo (1950 ed.)
In the shade of a tree, we two sat, him and me. Jim Haggerty's Story. *Unknown.* ABF
In the shade of the gardens, in the blue night. Midnight at Mestre. Alfonso Gatto. OnPM
In the Shade of the Old Apple Tree. Harry H. Williams. TreFT
In the shadow of a broken house. A Glimpse of Time. Laurence Binyon. AnFE
In the shadow of Old South Church the turn of spring is. A Foreigner Comes to Earth on Boston Common. Horace Gregory. EaLo
In the Shadows, *sels.* David Gray.
 Sonnet: "If it must be; if it must be, O God!" OxBS
 I Die, Being Young. VA
In the shadows of old buildings, human bodies are opened. I Am Thinking of Chicago and of What Survives. Lou Lipsitz. YAP
In the Shadowy Whatnot Corner. Robert Silliman Hillyer. NePoAm
In the shaking of a sieve the refuse remaineth. The Test of Men. Ecclesiasticus, Bible, Apocrypha. TrJP
In the shape of this night, in the still fall of snow, Father. At the New Year [*or* Before the Bells of This New Year Ring]. Kenneth Patchen. AnFE; CoAnAm; LiTM (1970 ed.); ToPo; WOW
In the Shelter. C. Day Lewis. BoC
In the Shenandoah Valley, one rider grey and one rider blue. Shenandoah. Carl Sandburg. PaA
In the Shreve High football stadium. Autumn Begins in Martins Ferry, Ohio. James Wright. NaP
In the shut drawer, even now, they rave and grieve. Packet of Letters. Louise Bogan. LiTL
In the silence that falls on my spirit. My Father's Voice in Prayer. May Hastings Nottage. BLRP
In the silence that prolongs the span. Black Jackets. Thom Gunn. CBV; TwCP
In the silent midnight watches, list—thy bosom door! He Standeth at the Door. Arthur Cleveland Coxe. HBV
In the Silent Night. Isaac Leibush Peretz, *tr. fr. Yiddish by* Joseph Leftwich. TrJP
In the six-acre field. Lost. Millen Brand. NYBP
In the sleepy forest where the bluebells. The Awakening of Dermuid. Austin Clarke. *Fr.* The Vengeance of Finn. AnIV
In the slow lapse of unrecorded afternoon. No Answer. Laurence Whistler. MoVE
In the Small Canals. John Addington Symonds. *Fr.* In Venice. PoVP
In the small New England places. Graveyard. Robert P. Tristram Coffin. AmFN
In the smoke-blue cabaret. Ecclesiastes. Morris Bishop. HBMV
In the Smoking-Car. Richard Wilbur. LiTM (1970 ed.); MoAmPo (1962 ed.); ToPo
In the smoky outhouses of the court of love. In the Queen's Room. Norman Cameron. Three Love Poems, II. FaBoTw
In the Snake Park. William Plomer. NYBP
In the Snow. W. H. Davies. POTE
In the snowing and the blowing. Nearly Ready. Mary Mapes Dodge. PRWS
In the snowy yard a baroque thermometer. Comatas. Harry Mathews. ANYP
In the soft dark night. Fireflies. Aileen Fisher. SoPo
In the sorrow and the terror of the nations. The Mother. Nettie Palmer. BoAu; PoAu-1
In the Soul Hour. Robert Mezey. NaP
In the South be drooping trees. Confucius. *Fr.* Chou and the South. CTC
In the southern land many birds sing. The South. Wang Chien. AWP
In the southern village the boy who minds the ox. The Herd Boy. Lu Yu. ChTr; FlW
In the Sprightly Month of May. Sir John Vanbrugh. *Fr.* Aesop. UnTE
In the Spring. Meleager, *tr. fr. Greek by* Andrew Lang. AWP; JAWP; WBP
In the Spring. Tennyson. *Fr.* Locksley Hall. BoNaP
In the spring garden. Otomo no Yakamochi, *tr. fr. Japanese by* Kenneth Rexroth. LiTW
In the spring of the year, in the spring of the year. The Spring and the Fall. Edna St. Vincent Millay. BoLP
In the spring, on the trees. Fluttering Leaves. Rodney Bennett. BoTP
In the spring twilight, in the colour'd twilight. An Even Song. Sydney Dobell. OBVV
In the spring when the green gits back in the trees. When the Green Gits Back in the Trees. James Whitcomb Riley. YT
In the spring, when winds blew and farmers were plowing fields. American Spring Song. Sherwood Anderson. NP
In the Spring-Time. Shakespeare. *See* It Was a Lover and His Lass.
In the squdgy river. The Hippopotamus. Georgia R. Durston. GFA; TiPo; UTS
In the Stable. Elizabeth Goudge. ChBR
In the stagnant pride of an outworn race. Santiago. Thomas A. Janvier. MC; PAH
In the States. Robert Louis Stevenson. BrPo; PoVP; VA
In the still air the music lies unheard. The Master's Touch [*or* The Touch of His Hand]. Horatius Bonar. BePJ; FaChP; HBV; MaRV; SoP; TrPWD; VA
In the still of an island evening. Island Moment. Ian Hamilton Finlay. NMP
In the Still, Star-lit Night. Elizabeth Stoddard. AA
In the stillness of the quiet hour. The Quiet Hour. Harvey E. Haver. SoP
In the Stoneworks. John Ciardi. PoDB
In the stony night move the stars' white mouths. The Postures of Love, III. Alex Comfort. NeBP
In the Storm. Stanton A. Coblentz. ChIP
In the strange city of life. Nostalgia. Walter de la Mare. CoBMV; LiTM (1970 ed.)
In the Strange Isle. Michael Roberts. FaBoMo; POTE
In the street I have just left. Charles Reznikoff. OCS
In the street I take my stand. Music in a Spanish Town (Cordoba 1936). Laurie Lee. MuSP
In the street, when they march by in short. Imaginary Figures of the Virtues. Shirley Bridges. TPM
In the street young men play ball, else in fresh shirts. People on Sunday. Edwin Denby. ANYP
In the Streets of Catania. Roger Casement. AnIV
In the Study. Thomas Hardy. *Fr.* Satires of Circumstance. PoPo
In the subtraction of my yeares. *Unknown.* SeCSL
In the Suburbs. Louis Simpson. ELU; PoIE (1970 ed.)
In the Sultan's Garden. Clinton Scollard. InP
In the summer, by the river. Peasant and Geisha Songs. *Unknown.* LiTW
In the summer even. Ballad. Harriet Prescott Spofford. HBV
In the Summer of Sixty. *Unknown.* CoSo; IHA; PoOW
In the summer palace the fireflies have lost their way. Ninth Moon. Li Ho. LiTW
In the summit of my head. Ad Majorem Hominis Gloriam. John Gould Fletcher. MAP; MoAmPo
In the sunny orchard closes. In the Orchard. Ibsen. AWP; JAWP; WBP
In the Sweet By and By. S. F. Bennett. TreFT
In the sweet shire of Cardigan. Simon Lee [the Old Huntsman]. Wordsworth. BEL; EnRP; EPN; GTBS; GTBS-D; GTBS-P; GTBS-W; GTSE; GTSL; MERP
In the sweet solitude, the Mountain's life. The Mountain. William Ellery Channing. PFY
In the Tank. Thom Gunn. CBV
In the tea rooms. For the Truth. Edward S. Spriggs. BF; BP
In the tender spreading tropical mornings. Lizard. K. E. Ingram. PoNe
In the third-class seat sat the journeying boy. Midnight on the "Great Western." Thomas Hardy. BWP; CH; CoBMV; PoG
In the third day of May. The Boy and the Mantle. *Unknown.* BaBo; ESPB; OBB; OxBB
In the third month, a sudden flow of blood. The Vow. Anthony Hecht. NePoEA; PoCh
In the Third Year of War. Henry Treece. WaP
In the tides of the warm south wind it lay. Verazzano. Hezekiah Butterworth. PAH
In the time of old sin without sadness. Variations on an Air: After Swinburne. G. K. Chesterton. InP; Par
In the Time of Trouble. Leslie Savage Clark. TrPWD

In the time of wild roses. Bab-Lock-Hythe. Laurence Binyon. MoVE; SD; WePo
In the time when herbs and flowers. Caelica Philocell. Fulke Greville. Caelica, LXXVI. OBSC
In the time when swan and swan. Waratah. Roland Robinson. PoAu-2
In the town of Athy one Jeremy Lanigan. Lanigan's Ball. *Unknown.* OxBoLi
In the Township. Denis Glover. AnNZ
In the Trades. Cicely Fox Smith. EtS
In the Train. Clifford Bax. InP
In the Train. James Thomson. *See* As We Rush, as We Rush in the Train.
In the Tree House at Night. James Dickey. NoP; PIA; ToPo
In the Trench. Leon Gellert. BoAV; MoAuPo; PoAu-1
In the Trenches. Richard Aldington. MMA
In the tub on Monday morning. Monday Morning. Helen Wing. GFA
In the Tub We Soak Our Skin. Edward Newman Horn. ELU
In the Tube. Richard Aldington. WePo
In the turret's great glass dome, the apparition, death. Siegfried. Randall Jarrell. MiAP; ReMP
In the Twilight. George Cotterell. VA
In the Twilight. James Russell Lowell. AA; HBV
In the Twilight, *sel.* John Francis O'Donnell.
"I row in my boat in the twilight, half-purple, half-gray, overhead." IrPN
In the unnavigable dusk, when. Owl. Peter Kane Dufault. NYBP
In the vaile [*or* vale] of restles mynd. *See* In a valley of this restless mind.
In the Valley of Cauteretz. Tennyson. EPN; MaPo (1969 ed.); MBW-2; OBVV; PoVP; TOP; ViPo
In the Valley of the Elwy. Gerard Manley Hopkins. BoPe; BWP; InPo; LiTG; PoIE; ViBoPo
("I remember a house where all were good.") EG
In the valley of the Pegnitz, where across broad meadowlands. Nuremberg. Longfellow. AmPP; CoBA; HBV; MWA-1
In the vast glow of sun at evening. Song before Night. Richard Dehmel. OnPM
In the Vastness, a God. *Unknown.* OQP
In the vegetarian guest-house. The Flying Bum: 1944. William Plomer. DTC
In the ventless room. Hospice of the Word. Brother Antoninus. ToPo
In the very early morning when the light was low. The Interpreter. Orrick Johns. AnAmPo; HBMV; MAP; NP; PFY
In the vestibule behind the church I saw the parson. Parson's Pleasure. Barry O. Higgs. PeSA
In the Vices. Donald Evans. HBMV; NP
In the village churchyard she lies. In the Churchyard at Cambridge. Longfellow. AmPP (5th ed.); AP; MWA-1; PoEL-5
In the village of the dead. Hunting. Gary Snyder. CoPo
In the village squares. The Unemployed. LeVan Roberts. PGD
In the vineyard of our Father. Working in the Vineyard. Thomas MacKellar. SoP
In the Virginia lowlands I was born. Lowlands, *vers.* II. *Unknown.* ShS
In the void, in the storm, in the wastelands of our hearts. Sunrise Rolland Snellings. BF
In the Water. Swinburne. *Fr.* A Midsummer Holiday. PoVP
In the wax works of Nature they strike. Note. Anthony Euwer. *Fr.* The Limeratomy. HBMV
In the Way of Peace. Lauchlan MacLean Watt. ChIP; OQP
In the way that He shall choose. Chosen Lessons. Frances Ridley Havergal. SoP
In the Web. E. L. Mayo. MiAP
In the Week When Christmas Comes. Eleanor Farjeon. ChBR; PDV; SiSoSe; TiPo (1952 ed.)
In the wet dusk silver-sweet. The Memory of Earth. "*AE.*" OBVV; PoVP
In the white-flowered hawthorn brake. Song from "Ogier the Dane" [*or* Antiphony]. William Morris. *Fr.* The Earthly Paradise. EG; OAEP; PoVP; VA; ViBoPo
In the White Giant's Thigh. Dylan Thomas. AtBAP; LiTB; RemP; ToPo
In the white moonlight, where the willow waves. The Graveyard Rabbit. Frank L. Stanton. AA; LHV
In the white of noon-day's brightness the city seems blotted out. In the Old City. Jacob Fichman. TrJP
In the wicked afternoon. Abracadabra. Dorothy Livesay. WHW
In the Wicker Fish-Trap. *Unknown. tr. fr. Chinese by* Arthur Waley. *Fr.* The Book of Songs.
In the wide and rocky pasture where the cedar trees are gray. Connecticut Road Song. Anna Hempstead Branch. HT
In the Wide Awe and Wisdom of the Night. Sir Charles G. D. Roberts. CaP
In the wild autumn weather, when the rain was on the sea. Love and Death. Rosa Mulholland. HBV; VA
In the wild [*or* cold] October night-time, when the wind raved round the land. The Night of Trafalgar [*or* The Boatman's Song *or* Trafalgar]. Thomas Hardy. *Fr.* The Dynasts. CH; ChTr; FaBoCh; MoBrPo; OBMV; OTD; PoVP; ShBV-1; WaaP
In the Wilderness. Robert Graves. BoC; CBV; CH; EaLo; GTBS-D; MoAB; MoBrPo; OxBI; SeCePo; ShBV-3
In the Wilderness. Edith Lovejoy Pierce. TrPWD
In the window of a grange. Love and Honour. Fulke Greeville. Caelica, LXXIV. OBSC
In the Wind's Eye. R. P. Blackmur. Scarabs for the Living, II. CrMA
In the winter, in the winter. The Organ Grinders' Garden. Mildred Plew Meigs. GaP; SoPo
In the winter the rabbits match their pelts to the earth. White Season. Frances M. Frost. FaPON; TiPo
In the winter time we go. White Fields. James Stephens. BoNaP; FaPON; MoShBr; PoSC; SiSoSe; SoPo; SUS
In the winter when the wet lanes hissed and sucked. Microcosmos, XXXIII. Nigel Heseltine. NeBP
In the Wood. Herbert Edwin Clarke. VA
In the Wood. Eileen Mathias. BoTP
In the Wood of Finvara. Arthur Symons. MoBrPo; NeMA; PoVP
(Fairy Wood, The.) BoC
In the Woods. Dorothy Baker. BoTP
In the Woods. Emerson. *Fr.* Good-bye. OQP
In the Woods. Frederick George Scott. ACV; CaP
In the woods my Master went. Ballad of Trees and the Master. Sidney Lanier. TreFT
In the woods the fox is no more timorous. Autumnal. Horatio Colony. TwAmPo
In the woodyard were green and dry. The Rick of Green Wood. Edward Dorn. NeAP
In the Workhouse: Christmas Day. George R. Sims. *See* Christmas Day in the Workhouse.
In the world are millions and millions of men. Angel and Stone. Howard Nemerov. NoP; NYBP
In the worst inn's worst room, with mat half-hung. Death [*or* The Duke] of Buckingham. Pope. *Fr.* Moral Essays, Epistle III. ExPo; FiP; OBEC
In the wracks [*or* wrecks] of Walsingham. A Lament for Our Lady's Shrine at Walsingham [*or* The Wreck of Walsingham]. *Unknown.* ACP; CBEP; ISi; NCEP; PoEL-2; SiCE
In the wrath of the lips that assail us. Stigmata. Charles Warren Stoddard. JKCP; TrPWD
In the wrecks of Walsingham. *See* In the wracks. . .
In the Wretched Hovel. *Unknown, tr. fr. Japanese by* Ishii *and* Obata. OnPM
In the year 1910—and I give the date without uncertainty. Versos de Montalgo. *Unknown.* AS
In the Year of Many Conversions and the Private Soul. John Ciardi. MiAP
In the year of ninety-four in the city of Mazatlán. Tragedia de Heraclio Bernal. *Unknown.* ABF
In the year since Jesus died for men. The Siege of Corinth. Byron. GoTL
In the year that king Uzziah died, I saw also the Lord. Isaiah's Angels. Isaiah, Bible, *O.T.* BoC
In the years about twenty. An Irish Love-Song. Robert Underwood Johnson. HBV
In the Year's Morning. David Ross. PG (1955 ed.)
In the years of her age the most beautiful. He Wishes He Might Die and Follow Laura. Petrarch. *Fr.* Sonnets to Laura: To Laura in Death. OBMV
In the young merry time of spring. Cornfields. Mary Howitt. OTPC (1923 ed.)

In the youth of summer. The Hills of Cualann. Joseph Campbell. AnIV
In the Yukon. Ralph Gustafson. MoCV
In their ragged regimentals. Carmen Bellicosum [*or* The Old Continentals]. Guy Humphreys McMaster. AA; ALV; DD; GN; HBV; MC; PaA; PAH; PAL; PAP
In these cold evenings, when the rain. Fear of the Earth. Alex Comfort. MoBrPo (1950 ed.); NeBP
In these days, every mother's son or daughter. Ebenezer Elliott. Sonn
In these days of indigestion. Some Little Bug. Roy Atwell. BoHV; PoLF; ShM
In these deep solitudes and awful cells. Eloïsa to Abelard. Pope. CEP; EiCL; EiPP; EnL; EnLi-1; LoBV; MBW-1; OAEP; PAn; PoEL-3
In these drear wastes of sea-born land, these wilds where none may dwell but He. Sir Richard Francis Burton. *Fr.* The Kasidah. HBV
In These Fair Vales. Wordsworth. CBEP
In these far cleaner days no armies clash. Security. Denis Glover. AnNZ
In these firm ranks a load slips from his soul. The Young Recruit. Arthur Davison Ficke. ELU
In these gay thoughts the loves and graces shine. To Miss Blount [*or* To a Young Lady], with the Works of Voiture. Pope. EiCL; PIA
In these latter days. Twentieth Century Love-Song. Richard Church. HaMV
In these long winter nights when moon doth steer. Four Sonnets to Helen, 3. Pierre de Ronsard. *Fr.* Sonnets pour Hélène. LiTW
In These Our Winter Days. C. Day Lewis. POTE
In these restrained and careful times. Impression. Sir Edmund Gosse. HBV
In these wylde deserts where she now abode. Spenser. *Fr.* The Faerie Queene, VI, 7. MBW-1
In Thin Arms. Oliver Wendell Holmes. TRV
In Thine hour of holy sadness. St. Bernard of Clairvaux. *Fr.* Of Our Lord's Passion. ChIP
In Thine Own Heart. "Angelus Silesius," *tr. fr. German.* ChIP; MaRV; TRV
In 'thirty-nine, in Poland. Children's Crusade 1939. Bertolt Brecht. MoBS
In this air. One of the Regiment. Douglas Le Pan. CaP
In this book every line has been clean. Limerick. H. I. Brock. LiBL
In this book I see your face and in your face. Frontispiece. May Swenson. CoAP; NePoEA
In this broad earth of ours. In This Earth Perfection. Walt Whitman. *Fr.* Birds of Passage. OQP
In this brown husk a dale of hawthorn dreams. Seeds. Muriel Stuart. BoC
In this brown seed, so dry and hard. Resurrection. Agnes W. Storer. ChIP; OQP
In this buff-gray cliff. Sandstone. Anne Marriott. CaP
In this café Durruti. The Midget. Philip Levine. NaP
In This City. Alan Brownjohn. CAD
In this city I loved you, where light. Chicago. Galway Kinnell. NePoAm
In this city, perhaps a street. In This City. Alan Brownjohn. CAD
In this cold monument lies one. An Epitaph on M. H. Charles Cotton. PeRV
In this cool corner where dark stars of ivy. Destroying Angel. Hilary Corke. NYBP
In this country there is neither measure nor balance. Two Campers in Cloud Country. Sylvia Plath. NYBP
In This Dark House. Edward Davidson. OBMV
In this desolation. The Soldier. Uys Krige. PeSA
In this dread hour for thee and all mankind. The Prophetic Hour. Michael Thwaites. PoFr
In This Earth, Perfection. Walt Whitman. *Fr.* Birds of Passage. OQP
In this enemy city where your winged danger. Epitaph for an American Bomber. James Bertram. AnNZ
In this factory, here the axe-grinders. University Curriculum. William Price Turner. OxBS
In this fair niche above the unslumbering sea. A Singer Asleep. Thomas Hardy. OAEP; POTE
In this fair stranger's eyes of grey. Absence. Matthew Arnold. Switzerland, VI. CBEP; MBW-2; OAEP; PoVP; ViPP; VP
In This Forest. Robert Hershon. ThO
In this friend's face I know. Time-Bomb. Earle Birney. TwCaPo
In this glass palace are flowers in golden baskets. The Lovers. Conrad Aiken. AP; NYBP
In this green chest is laid away. On a Fair Woman. Francis Burdett Money-Coutts. OBVV
In this green countryside, the flowers bloom. Palm Tree Mates with Palm. Claudian. *Fr.* Epithalamium for Honorius and Maria. HW
In this green month when resurrected flowers. Memorial Wreath. Dudley Randall. IDB; NNP; PoNe (1970 ed.)
In this green valley where the Ouse. Cowper at Olney. Sylvia Lynd. POTE
In this green world budged by the round shoulder. Merits of Laughter and Lust. Eli Mandel. PeCV (1967 ed.)
In this high pasturage, the Blunden time. The Archaeological Picnic. John Betjeman. EnLoPo
In This Hotel. Emanuel Carnevali. AnAmPo; NP; SiSw
In This Hour. Josephine W. Johnson. MoRP
In this hour of pure sunlight. Brazil. Ronald de Carvalho. WoL
In this hour of worship. Prayer. *Unknown.* SoP
In this house, she said, in this high second storey. Under. J. C. Squire. FaBoTw
In this life/ Of error, ignorance, and strife. Shelley. *Fr.* The Sensitive Plant. LO
In this little urne [*or* urn] is laid. Upon Prue [*or* Prew] His Maid. Robert Herrick. CavP; ForPo; NoP; OAEP; SeCV-1; SeEP
In this little vault she lyes. Upon a Wife That Dyed Mad with Jealousie. Robert Herrick. CavP
In this lone, open glade I lie. Lines Written in Kensington Gardens. Matthew Arnold. EnLi-2; EPN; MBW-2; PoVP; ViPo; ViPP
In this marble, buried lies. Epitaph. Thomas Jordan. SeCL
In this May-month, by grace. Asian Birds. Robert Bridges. VA
In this merry morn of May. *Unknown, tr. fr. French by* John Addington Symonds. Medieval Norman Songs, VII. AWP
In this mountain village, I have grown accustomed. The Voices of Pine Trees. Rengetsu. OnPM
In this orchestra full of vain deceit. The Changing World. Jami. OnPM
In this our English coast much blessed blood is shed. A Song of Four Priests Who Suffered Death at Lancaster. *Unknown.* ACP
In this quiet town, it is odd to discover. In New Ross. Valentin Iremonger. NeIP
In this red wine, where Memory's eyes seem glowing. Toast to Omar Khayyám. Theodore Watts-Dunton. VA
In This River. Valentin Iremonger. NeIP
In this road that I must take. Journey. Roy Daniels. MoCV
In this sad place. The Haunted Garden. Henry Treece. NeBP
In this savage place the sun stands still. Margaret Allonby. *Fr.* Lustration of the Winter Tree. BoSA
In this secluded shrine. To a Wood-Violet. John Bannister Tabb. HBV
In this shrill moon the scouts of winter ran. Isabella Valancy Crawford. *Fr.* Malcolm's Katie. PeCV
In this small character is sent. Upon a Braid of Hair in a Heart. Henry King. EnLoPo
In this squalid, dirty dooryard. The Pear Tree. Edna St. Vincent Millay. MAP; MoAmPo
In This Stern Hour. Josephine Johnson. MaRV
In this still place, remote from men. Glen-Almain, the Narrow Glen. Wordsworth. GTSL
In This Strange House. Carleton Drewry. MoRP
In this sweet book, the treasury of wit. To His Lady. Sir John Davies. SiPS
In this sweet solitude, the mountain sits. William Ellery Channing. *Fr.* The Mountain. PFY
In this the hour of new reckonings! This Hour. Oliver La-Grone. NNP; PoNe (1970 ed.)
In this the ultimate exile no man born. Ultimate Exile IV. R. N. Currey. PeSA
In this theayter they has plays. An Old Woman, outside the Abbey Theater. L. A. G. Strong. FiBHP; MoBrPo

In this time and place, where "Bread and Circuses" has. Nuremburg, U.S.A. William Knott. YAP
In this town, in the blurred and snowy dawn. Geneva. Alastair Reid. NYBP
In This Trembling Shadow. *Unknown.* TuPP
In this world a tablecloth need not be laid. Tea in a Space-Ship. James Kirkup. POTi
In this world of toil and turmoil. How We Need the Secret Place. Avis B. Christiansen. SoP
In this world (the Isle of Dreames). The White Island; or Place of the Blest. Robert Herrick. AnAnS-2; ChTr; HBV; NoP; OBS; OxBoCh; SeCL; SeEP; WiR
In This World's Raging Sea. William Drummond of Hawthornden. CBEP
(Regrat.) PoEL-2
(Regret.) AtBAP
In tholde dayes of the Kyng Arthour. *See* In th' olde dayes. . .
In those days/ When civilization kicked us in the face. The Vultures. David Diop. PBA; TTY
In those fields haunted by fear. Three Barrows Down. Jocelyn Brooke. ChMP
In those great days adventure called. Adventure. T. W. Earp. PoMa
In those old days which poets say were golden. Beer. Charles Stuart Calverley. CenHV
In those sad words I took farewell. In Memoriam A. H. H., LVIII. Tennyson. EPN; ViPo; VP
In thought that brought no rest nor peace of heart. The Sages. Adam Mickiewicz. CAW
In Three Days. Robert Browning. EPN; PoVP
In thronged procession gliding slow. The Logs. Sir Charles G. D. Roberts. ACV
In through every lattice-bar/ Where the trellis gapes ajar. Annunciation Night. Abby Maria Hemenway. *Fr.* Mary of Nazareth. ISi
In thy coach of state. A Crowned Poet. Anne Reeve Aldrich. AA
In thy fair domain. Landscape. William Mason. *Fr.* The English Garden. OBEC
In Thy garden, in Thy garden, though the rain. The Garden of the Holy Souls. Eleanor Hamilton King. *Fr.* Hours of the Passion. ACP; JKCP (1926 ed.)
In thy hammock gently sleeping. Baby Dear. Samuel Lover. OTPC (1946 ed.)
In Thy Hand. Samuel Longfellow. FaChP
In Thy Love. John Byrom. FaChP
In Thy Presence. Richard Chenevix Trench. *See* Prayer: "Lord, what a change within us one short hour."
In thy western halls of gold. Ode to Apollo. Keats. ERoP-2
In thy white bosom Love is laid. Song. John Arthur Blaikie. VA
In tight pants, tight skirts. The Young Ones, Flip Side. James A. Emanuel. Kal
In Tilbury Town did Old King Cole. Old King Cole. E. A. Robinson. HBV
In till this tyme that I of tell. Macbeth. Andrew of Wyntoun. OxBS
In Time. Robert Graves. MemP
In Time. Kathleen Raine. CMoP; NeBP
In time all undertakings are made good. In Time. Robert Graves. MemP
In time and measure perfect moves. Dupont's Round Fight. Herman Melville. MWA-1
In Time like Air. May Sarton. MoLP; NYBP
In Time like Glass. W. J. Turner. ILP; MoBrPo; NAMP; OBMV; POTE
In Time of Crisis. Ray Patterson. *See* You Are the Brave. . .
In Time of Daffodils. E. E. Cummings. PoDB
In Time of Darkness. Raymond Roseliep. FiSC
In Time of Grief. Lizette Woodworth Reese. AA; ATP (1953 ed.); PFY
In Time of Need. Katharine Tynan. TrPWD
In Time of Pestilence. Thomas Nashe. *See* Adieu, Farewell, Earth's Bliss!
In Time of Plague. Thomas Nashe. *See* Adieu, Farewell, Earth's Bliss!
In Time of Silver Rain. Langston Hughes. GoSl; SoPo; TiPo
In time of sorrow one should be. Thought for the Winter Season. Mary Elizabeth Osborn. NePoAm
In Time of Suspense. Laurence Whistler. POTE
In Time of "The Breaking of Nations." Thomas Hardy. AnEnPo; CaFP; CMoP; CoBMV; EnLi-2 (1949 ed.); EnLit; ExPo; ForPo; GTBS-W; GTSL; ILP; InP; LiTB; LiTM; LoBV; MaPo (1969 ed.); MMA; MoAB; MoBrPo; MoRP; NeMA; NoP; NP; OAEP (2d ed.); OBEV (new ed.); PoAn; PoPo; PoSa; POTE; PoVP; QFR; SeCeV; ShBV-3; TDP; TreF; VP
In Time of War, *sels.* W. H. Auden.
"And the age ended, and the last deliverer died." CMoP; ExPo; Sonn
"As a young child the wisest could adore him." CMoP
"But in the evening the oppression lifted." EnLit
"Far from the heart of culture he was used." CMoP
"He stayed: and was imprisoned in possession." CMoP; EnLit
"He turned his field into a meeting-place." PoPl
"He was their servant—some say he was blind." CMoP
"He watched the stars and noted birds in flight." CMoP
"Here war is simple like a monument." EnLit
"His generous bearing was a new invention." CMoP
"Life of man is never quite completed, The." EnLit
"So from the years the gifts were showered." CMoP
"They wondered why the fruit had been forbidden." CMoP; Sonn
"Wandering lost upon the mountains of our choice." CMoP; EnLit
In time of yore when shepherds dwelt. Olden Love-making. Nicholas Breton. DiPo; OBSC
In time the snowman always dies. Thaw. Walker Gibson. ELU; NePoAm
In time the strong and stately turrets fall. Licia, XXVIII. Giles Fletcher. ILP; ReEn; ReIE; SiCE; Sonn; TuPP
(Time.) OBSC
In Time We See That Silver Drops. Robert Greene. *Fr.* Arbasto. ReIE; SiCE
(Doralicia's Song.) LoBV; OBSC
In Time's concatenation and/ Carnal conventicle. Mortmain. Robert Penn Warren. PoCh
In times o'ergrown with rust and ignorance. Priestcraft and Private Judgement. Dryden. *Fr.* Religio Laici. OBS
In times of old, when time was young. Vanbrug's House. Swift. PP
In Tir-na'n-Og. "Ethna Carbery." JKCP
In Titum. Sir John Davies. ReIE; TuPP
In to thir dirk and drublie dayis. Meditation [*or* Meditatioun] in Winter. William Dunbar. NCEP; OxBS; SeCePo
In torrid heats of late July. Of the Book-Hunter. Andrew Lang. VA
In tottering row, like shadows, silently. By the Sea. Richard Watson Dixon. OBNC
In Town. Austin Dobson. InP
In Town. *Unknown.* ABF
In Town. David McKee Wright. ACV
In towns like ours where fifty years are just. The Yellow Cat. Leslie Nelson Jennings. FiSC
In Tribute. Vernal House. CaP
In tropical climes there are certain times of day. Mad Dogs and Englishmen. Noel Coward. CenHV; FiBHP; WhC
In Trouble and Shame. D. H. Lawrence. BoPe; OBMV
In Trust. Mary Mapes Dodge. PPL; SiSoSe
In truth how glorious was the High Priest. The High Priest. *Unknown.* TrJP
In truth, O Love, with what a boyish kind. Astrophel and Stella, XI. Sir Philip Sidney. EIL; FCP; InvP; ReEn; SiCE; SiPS
In Tuaim Inbhir here I find. The Ivy Crest. *Unknown.* AnIL
In Tumulum Abrahami Simple. John Weever. SiCE; TuPP
In Tumulum Avari. John Weever. SiCE
In Tune with the Infinite. Shakespeare. *See* How Sweet the Moonlight Sleeps upon This Bank.
In Tuscany. Eric Mackay. VA
In Tuscany, the vintage season reigns. The Vintage. Belle Cooper. GoBC
In twelve chambers the ladies, decked for the day. A Palace Poem. Hsüeh Feng. LiTW
In twice five years the "greatest living poet." Contemporary Poets. Byron. *Fr.* Don Juan, XI. OBRV
In Two Months Now. Geroge Dillon. MAP; MoAmPo (1942 ed.); PoMa
In unexperienced infancy. Shadows in the Water. Thomas Tra-

herne. EnLi-1; LiTB; MePo; NoP; OBS; PoEL-2; SCEP-1; SeCL; SeCP; UnPo (1st ed.)
In Utrumque Paratus. Matthew Arnold. MaVP; OAEP; OBNC; PoEL-5; PoVP; ViPP
In vacant intraterminal hush. Vacation Exercise. M. K. Joseph. AnNZ
In Vain. Rose Terry Cooke. AA
In vain. Irony of God. Eva Warner. ChIP
In Vain Earth Decks Herself. Moses ibn Ezra, *tr. fr. Hebrew by* Solomon Solis-Cohen. *Fr.* The World's Illusion. TrJP
In vain I look around. To the Memory of a Lady. George Lyttelton. OBEC
In vain, in vain—the all-composing Hour. Conclusion [*or* Chaos *or* The Triumph of Ignorance]. Pope. *Fr.* The Dunciad. CoBE; EnLi-1; FiP; LoBV; ViBoPo
In Vain Mine Eyes. Sir Philip Sidney. *Fr.* Arcadia. SiPS
In vain, poor Nymph, to please our youthful sight. An Elegy: To an Old Beauty. Thomas Parnell. CEP
In vain the cords and axes were prepared. William Falconer. *Fr.* The Shipwreck. OBEC
In vain thy altars do they heap. May Carol. Aubrey Thomas De Vere. CAW
In vain to me the smiling [*or* smileing] mornings shine: Sonnet on the Death of [Mr.] Richard West. Thomas Gray. BWP; CEP; EiCL; EiCP; EiPP; EnLit; EnPE; EnRP; NoP; OAEP; OBEC; PoE; PoEL-3; SeCePo; Sonn; StP; TrGrPo; ViBoPo
In Vain Today. Austin Dobson. MoBrPo (1942 ed.); YT
(To Brander Matthews.) ALV
In vain we call old notions fudge. Stealing [*or* International Copyright]. James Russell Lowell. AA; MaRV; PV; TreF
In vain with mimic skill my pencil tries. On an Unsuccessful Attempt to Draw Lord Boyle's Picture. Elizabeh Rowe. WaPE
In vain you tell your parting lover. Song. Matthew Prior. HBV
In vain your bangles cast. Abiku. Wole Soyinka. PBA
In vaine faire sorceresse, thy eyes speake charmes. To a Wanton. William Habington. AnAnS-2; SeCP
In valleys green and still. A. E. Housman. BrPo; FaBoTw
In Venice, *sels.* John Addington Symonds.
In the Small Canals. PoVP
Invitation to the Gondola, The. PoVP
In villages from which their childhoods came. The City. W. H. Auden. Sonn
In Vinculis, *sels.* Wilfrid Scawen Blunt.
Deeds That Might Have Been, The. TrGrPo
Liberty, Equality, Fraternity. PoFr
In Virgine [*or* Virgyne] the sweltry [*or* sweltrie] sun gan sheene. An Excelente Balade of Charitie. Thomas Chatterton. CEP; EiCL; EiPP; EnPE; EnRP; GoTL; LiTB; LiTG; OBEC; SeCePo; StP
In vision now I seem to see. Himself He Could Not Save. Avis B. Christiansen. SoP
In visions of the dark night. A Dream. Poe. MWA-1
In Vitam Humanam. Francis Bacon. *See* Life.
In Wakefield there lives a jolly pinder. The Jolly Pinder of Wakefield. *Unknown.* BaBo; ESPB
In warm war-sun they erupt. Mules. Ted Walker. NYBP
In Waste Places. James Stephens. CaFP; CBV; GTSL; MoAB; MoBrPo; MoVE; PoFr
(Waste Places, The.) HBV; NP
In Western Mountains, *sel.* Glenn Ward Dresbach.
Life or Death. HBMV
In Westminster Abbey. *At. to* Francis Beaumont *and to* William Basse. *See* On the Tombs in Westminster Abbey.
In Westminster Abbey. John Betjeman. CaFP; CMoP; FosPo; ILP; LiTM; POTi
In Westminster not long ago. The Ratcatcher's Daughter. *Unknown.* ChTr; OxBoLi
In wet and cloudy mists I slowly rise. Night's Song. *At. to* Sir William Davenant. *Fr.* Luminalia. SeCL
In what a glorious substance did they dream. Ideal Passion, XXVI. George Edward Woodberry. HBMV
In what a strange bewilderment do we. Morn. Helen Hunt Jackson. AA
In what dark silent grove. Cogitabo pro Peccato Meo. William Habington. CoBE
In what estate so ever I be. Timor Mortis. *Unknown.* NoP
In what far, Judean field. The Glory of the Grass. Claire Wallace Flynn. StJW
In what finite tendon dost thou rise? Spirituality. Samuel Greenberg. LiTA
In What Manner the Soul Is United to the Body. Sir John Davies. *See* Soul and the Body, The.
In what order or what degree. Be True to Your Condition in Life. John Audelay. MeEL
In what torn[e] ship soever I embark[e]. A Hymn [*or* Hymne] to Christ, at the Authors Last Going into Germany. John Donne. AnAnS-1; AnEnPo; DiPo; EnRePo; FaBoEn; LiTB; LiTG; MaMe; MBW-1; MeLP; MeP; MePo; OAEP; OBS; OxBoCh; Po; SCEP-1; SeCV-1; SeEP; TuPP; ViBoPo; WoL
In whatever galaxy. Star-gaze Poem. Sandford Lyne. QAH
In where the smoke runs black against the snow. Spring Offensive, 1941. Maurice Biggs. PoAu-2
In white splendors and red terrors my thoughts. Michael the Archangel. Michael Williams. JKCP (1955 ed.)
In whitest hour of pain the iron air. Prayer in Time of War. Henry Treece. WaP
In Whom Is No Variableness. Edith Hickman Divall. *See* Changeless.
In Whom We Live and Have Our Being. James Rhoades. MaRV
In Whose Will Is Our Peace? J. V. Cunningham. PoIE
("In whose will is our peace? Thou happiness.") QFR
In Wicklow. Rhoda Coghill. NeIP
In wild October when the low hills lie. Two States of Prayer. Thomas Merton. JKCP (1955 ed.)
In William Rufus's hall the galleries reached. Fifth Day. R. D. Fitzgerald. MoAuPo
In Wiltshire. Edmund Blunden. POTE
In Windsor Castle. Earl of Surrey. *See* Prisoned in Windsor, He Recounteth His Pleasure There Passed.
In Windsor Castle lives the king. Home Thoughts. Denis Glover. AnNZ
In Winnipeg at Christmas. Winnipeg at Christmas. Rose Fyleman. ChBR
In Winter. C. H. Bretherton. InMe
In Winter. Emily Dickinson. *See* In winter, in my room.
In Winter. Arthur Symons. BrPo
In Winter. Robert Wallace. BoNaP
In winter I get up at night. Bed in Summer. Robert Louis Stevenson. GFA; GoJo; OTD; OTPC; PCH; PoPl; PoVP; PTK; RIS; StVeCh; TreFT
In winter in my room. Emily Dickinson. AmPP (5th ed.); AP; ErPo; LiTA; MAPA; OxBA; PoE; SeCeV; TwAmPo
In Winter in the Woods Alone. Robert Frost. NoP
In winter, when it's cold out. Baseball Note. Franklin P. Adams. SD
In winter when people pay a call. Visitors. Harry Behn. SoPo
In winter, when the fields are white. Humpty Dumpty's Recitation [*or* Song]. "Lewis Carroll." *Fr.* Through the Looking-Glass. BOHV; ChTr; FiBHP; GoTP; GTBS-P; NBM; OnMSP; OxBoLi; PeVV; SAS; SiTL
In winter when the nights are long. The Beggar Wind. Mary Austin. BoNAP
In winter when the rain rain'd cauld. Tak' Your Auld Cloak about Ye. *Unknown.* OxBS
In winter, when the wind I hear. The Four Winds. Frank Dempster Sherman. TVC
In winter's just return, when Boreas gan his reign. Earl of Surrey. FCP; SiPS
In wintertime I have such fun. Quoits. Mary Effie Lee Newsome. CDC; GoSl
In winter-time we go. White Fields. James Stephens. BoTP
In Wintry Midnight, o'er a Stormy Main. Petrarch, *tr. fr. Italian by* William Barnes. ChTr
In wiser days, my darling rosebud, blown. To My Daughter Betty, the Gift of God. Thomas Michael Kettle. CAW; HBMV; JKCP (1955 ed.); OnYI
In wishing nothing we enjoy still most. Human Happiness. Dryden. *fr.* The Indian Emperor. IV. i. FiP
In wonder and time-mists. Chorus. Lord De Tabley. *fr.* Philoctetes. PoVP
In wonderment I walk to music pouring. Undersong. Mark Van Doren. PoCh
In Wonted Walks, Since Wonted Fancies Change. Sir Philip Sidney. FCP; MaPo; ReIE
(In Wonted Walks.) BWP; CABA; PoEL-1
In woods so long time bare. Cuckoo! Hilaire Belloc. MoVE

In (continued)
In woods still winter bare. Shadbush. Christina Rainsford. GoYe
In Xanadu did Kubla Khan. Kubla Khan. Samuel Taylor Coleridge. AnFE; AtBAP; ATP; AWP; BBV; BEL; BoC; BoLiVe; CABA; CaFP; CBEP; CBV; CH; ChER; ChTr; CoBE; DiPo; EG; ELP; EnL; EnLi-2; EnLit; EnRP; ERoP-1; ExPo; FaBoBe; FaBoCh; FaBoEn; FaBV; FaFP; FaPL; FiP; ForPo; GBV (1952 ed.); GN; GoJo; GTBS-W; GTSL; HBV; HoPM; HT; ILP; InP; InPo; InvP; JAWP; LiTB; LiTG; LoBV; LoGBV; MaC; MasP; MBW-2; MCCG; MemP; MERP; MyFE; NeHB; NoP; OAEP; OBEV; OBNC; OBRV; OtMeF; OTPC; OuHeWo; PAn; PG (1945 ed.); PIA; Po; PoAn; PoE; PoEL-4; PoFS; PoIE; PoPl; PoRA; PP; PTK; RG; RoGo; SeCeV; ShBV-3; StP; SyP; TDP; ThWaDe; ToP; TreFS; TrGrPo; UnPo (3 ed.); ViBoPo; WBP; WHA
In yon hollow Damon Lies. In Arcady. Cosmo Monkhouse. OBVV
In yonder grave a Druid Lies. Ode on the Death of Mr. Thomson. William Collins. CBEP; EiCL; EiCP; EiPP; OBEC; PeER; SeCePo
In yonder valley there dwelt, alone. The Mountain Sprite. Thomas Moore. OTPC
In Your Absence. Elizabeth Baxter. PoToHe (new ed.)
In your arms was still delight. Retrospect. Rupert Brooke. NP
In Your Arrogance. Lynne Lawner. ErPo
In your daily round of duties. The Golden Rule. James Wells. STF
In your ears my song. You Laughed and Laughed and Laughed. Gabriel Okara. PBA
In your face I sometimes see. To My Little Son. Julia Johnson Davis. HBMV
In your garb and outward clothing. Neatness in Apparel. Charles *and* Mary Lamb. OTPC
In your hesitant moments, remember Cornford and Fox. They Live. Randall Swingler. WaP
In your mother's apple orchard. Yvonne of Brittany. Ernest Dowson. PoVP
In your next letter I wish you'd say. Letter to New York [*or* N. Y.]. Elizabeth Bishop. LiTL; TwCP
In your presence I rediscovered my name. Your Presence. David Diop. PBA
In your silk robe I hate to see you clad. I Hate to See You Clad. Paul Verlaine. UnTE
In your watercolor, Nely Silvínová. Robert Mezey. *Fr.* Theresienstadt Poems. NaP
In Youth. Evaleen Stein. AA
In youth from rock to rock I went. To the Daisy. Wordsworth. EnRP; MERP
In youth, gay scenes attract our eyes. The Vanity of Existence. Philip Freneau. AmPP (5th ed.); AP
In youth have I known one with whom the Earth. Stanzas. Poe. MAmP
In youth I frowned. Old Woman's Song. Thomas Cole. NePoAm-2
In youth I served my time. Retirement. *Unknown.* ErPo; KiLC
In Youth, in Age. Robert Cooper. TuPP
In Youth Is Pleasure. R. Wever. *Fr.* Lusty Juventus. CBEP; ChTr; OBEV
("In a herber green asleep whereas I lay.") EG; SiCE; TuPP
(In an Arbour Green.) ELP
(Of Youth He Singeth.) EIL
(Youth.) OBSC
In youth's spring it was my lot. *See* In spring of youth it was my lot.
In Ystrad Fflur a soft breeze blows. Ystrad Fflur. T. Gwynn Jones. PrWP
In zummer, leäte at evenèn tide. The Rwose in the Dark. William Barnes. AtBAP; CBEP
Inalienable, The. Rabindranath Tagore. MemP
Inalienable/ for the humbly dying. And Then There. Frantisek Halas. LiTW
Inasmuch! William E. Brooks. PGD
Inaudible move day and night. Silence. John Lancaster Spalding. AA
Inauguration Day. Richard Watson Gilder. PoRL
Inauguration Day: January 1953. Robert Lowell. PoeP; ToPo
Inbound. Burnham Eaton. FiSC
Inbrothered ("There is a destiny"). Edwin Markham. *Fr.* A Creed. BLPA
Incantation, The. *At. to* Amergin. *See* Invocation to Ireland.
Incantation, An. Byron. *Fr.* Manfred, I, i. OBRV
Incantation, The. Theocritus, *tr. fr. Greek by* C. S. Calverley. AWP; JAWP; WBP
(Second Idyll, The, *tr. by* Jack Lindsay.) LiTW
Incantation, An. Marguerite Wilkinson. NP
Incantation for Rain. *Unknown, tr. fr. Navajo Indian by* Washington Matthews. ExPo
Incantation to Oedipus. Dryden. *Fr.* Oedipus, III, i. SiSw
(Spell, A.) WiR
Incarnate Devil. Dylan Thomas. ToPo
Incarnate for our marriage you appeared. The Marriage. Yvor Winters. HW; MoVE; QFR
Incarnate Love. Christina Rossetti. ChIP; MaRV
Incarnate Love. Wilbur Fisk Tillett. BLRP
Incarnate One, The. Edwin Muir. PoDB; PoIE
Incarnatio Est Maximum Donum Dei. William Alabaster. MePo
Incarnation, The. Giles Fletcher. StJW
Incarnation, The. William Langland. *Fr.* The Vision of Piers Plowman. PoEL-1
Incarnation. Edwin Markham. SoP
Incarnation. Edith Lovejoy Pierce. MaRV
Incarnation of Sirius, The. James McAuley. MoAuPo
Incense. Leslie Savage Clark. ChIP
Incense. Vachel Lindsay. MoRP
Incense. Louise Townsend Nicholl. NePoAm-2.
Incense, and flesh of swine, and this year's grain. To Phidyle. Horace. *Fr.* Odes. AWP
Incense of the Lucky Virgin. Robert Hayden. AmPP (5th ed.)
Incentive, The. Sarah N. Cleghorn. HBMV
Incentive, The. Martial, *tr. fr. Latin by* Louis Untermeyer. UnTE
Incentive/ born in ancient. On Riots. Cy Leslie. NBP
Inchcape Rock, The. Robert Southey. BeLS; ChTr; FaBoBe; GN; GoTP; HBV; HBVY; OBRV; OnSP; OTPC; PaPo; TreFS
Incident. Countee Cullen. BoChLi (1950 ed.); CDC; GoSl; IDB; MoSiPe; OQP; PoNe; WOW
Incident, An. Douglas Le Pan. ACV; MoCV; PeCV
Incident, An. Frederick Tennyson. GoBC
Incident at Matauri. Kendrick Smithyman. AnNZ
Incident Here and There, An. Hilda Doolittle ("H. D."). CrMA
Incident in the Early Life of Ebenezer Jones, Poet, 1828, An. John Betjeman. CMoP
Incident of French History, An. James I. Whitman. PCD
Incident of the French Camp. Robert Browning. BBV; BEL; BeLS; EnLi-2 (1949 ed.); EPN; GN; GoTP; HBV; HBVY; MAC; MaVP; MBW-2; MCCG; NeHB; OnSP; OTPC; PoPo; PoVP; PTK; RoGo; TreF; TrGrPo; TSW; VA
Incident on a Front Not Far from Castel de Sangro. Harry Brown. NYBP
Incident on a Journey. Thom Gunn. NePoEA
Incident with Lions. Sara Henderson Hay. NYTB
Incidents in Playfair House. Nicholas Moore. ErPo; NeBP
Incidents in the Life of My Uncle Arly. Edward Lear. MoShBr; NA; NBM; OxBoLi; SiTL; TrGrPo; WhC
Incipit Vita Nova. William Morton Payne. AA
Incline Thine ear, O God. Therefore, We Thank Thee, God. Reuben Grossman. TrJP
Inclusions. Elizabeth Barrett Browning. HBV; OBVV; TOP; UnTE
Inclusiveness. Dante Gabriel Rossetti. The House of Life, LXIII. EnLi-2; MaVP; NBM; NCEP; PoVP; SyP; VA; ViPo
Incognita. Austin Dobson. CenHV; PoVP
Incognita of Raphael. William Allen Butler. AA
Incognitos of masquerading moons. Festoons of Fishes. Alfred Kreymborg. HBMV
Income taxes. Taxes. Don L. Lee. BOLo
Incomparable Kiss, An. *Unknown.* SeCL; SeEP
(Give Me a Kiss from Those Sweet Lips of Thine.) InvP
Incomparable Light, The. Richard Eberhart. MoRP
Incomparable Treasure, The. *Unknown.* FaChP
Incompatibility. Aubrey Thomas De Vere. IrPN; Sonn
Incomprehensible, The. Isaac Watts. CEP; WGRP

Incomprehensible—/ O Master—fate and mystery. Sanctus. David Gascoyne. *Fr.* Miserere. NeBP
Incongruously gray he sits. Balloon Man. Hazel I. Dannecker. PoMa
Inconsistency of Women's Love. Catullus, *tr. fr. Latin by* George Lamb. OnPM
(On the Inconstancy of Women.) PV
Inconsistent. Mark Van Doren. BoLP; ELU
Inconstancy. John Donne. *See* Sonnet: "Oh, to vex me. . ."
Inconstancy Reproved. *At. to* Sir Robert Ayton. *See* To His Forsaken Mistress.
Inconvenience, An. John Banister Tabb. UTS
Incorrigible. Burges Johnson. PoMa
Incorrigible one, still groping with your eyes. Thought and the Poet. Peter Yates. ChMP
Increasing moonlight drifts across my bed, The. Fredericksburg. Thomas Bailey Aldrich. PaA; PAH; PAP; PFY
Incredulous, he stared at the amused. Vocation. W. H. Auden. CMoP
Incremation, The. Matthew Arnold. *Fr.* Balder Dead. VA
Incubus of Time, The. Clark Ashton Smith. FiSC
Incurable, an Epigram, The. Matthew Prior. EiCL
Incurables, The. Arthur Upson. AnAmPo
Incursive on the frozen snow. The Fox. I. L. Salomon. NYTB
Indecision. Helen Pinkerton. QFR
Indeed a sweet and knowing lady. Anemones for Miss Austen. Bernard Bergonzi. HaMV
Indeed I live in the dark ages! To Posterity. Bertolt Brecht. OnHM
Indeed I must confess. Platonic[k] Love. Abraham Cowley. *Fr.* The Mistress. SCEP-2; SeCV-1; SeEP
Indeed, it will soon be over, I shall be done. Intimations of Mortality. Phyllis McGinley. MoAmPo (1962); NeMA
Indeed, my Caelia, 'tis in vain. Song. Sir John Henry Moore. LO; OBEC
Indeed, Sir Peter, I could wish, I own. On Clergymen Preaching Politics. John Byrom. SeCePo
Indeed this is sweet life! my hand. No Master. W. H. Davies. PoFr
Indeed, this world is flat: as for the other, nonsense. The Cigarette. Jules Laforgue. LiTW
Indeed this very love which is my boast. Sonnets from the Portuguese, XII. Elizabeth Barrett Browning. HBV
Indeede I am studying Alcumye. John Webster. *Fr.* The White Devil, I, ii. AtBAP
Indelicate is he who loathes. Epidermal Macabre. Theodore Roethke. PoeP
Independence. Nancy Cato. PoAu-2
Independence. Adebayo Faleti, *tr. fr. Yoruba by* Bakare Gbadamosi *and* Ulli Beier. PBA
Independence. Mary Fullerton. BoAV
Independence. Roy McFadden. OxBI
Independence. Guy Mason. CaP
Indenpendence. Tobias George Smollett. *Fr.* Ode to Independence. OBEC
("Thy spirit, Independence, let me share") PoFr
Independence. Henry David Thoreau. AmPP (3d ed.); AnNE; CoBA; PoFr; TreFS
Independence Bell, July 4, 1776 (*sl. diff. versions*). *Unknown.* BLPA; DD, *abr.*; FaBoBe; PAL
(Independence Bell.) MC, *abr.*; PEDC, *abr.*
(Liberty and Independence, *sl. abr.*) TreFS
Independence Day. William Jay Smith. TwCP
Independence Day. Royall Tyler. PAH
Independence Day To-Day. Margaret E. Sangster. PEDC
Independence Square, Christmas 1783. Arthur Guiterman. PEDC
Index. Bernadette Mayer. ANYP
Index (8). Gil Orlovitz. ToPo
Index to a Black Cartharsis. Richard W. Thomas. BF
India. Florence Earle Coates. AA
India. W. J. Turner. MoBrPo; PDV
India became his jasmined youth, Goa. Roy Macnab. *Fr.* The Man of Grass. BoSA
India the Magic. H. A. Jules-Bois, *tr. fr. French by* Thomas Walsh. CAW
Indian, The. *Unknown.* *See* American Indian, The.
Indian at the Burial-Place of His Fathers, An. Bryant. CoBA; MWA-1
Indian Burying Ground, The. Philip Freneau. AA; AmP; AmPP; AnAmPo; AnFE; AP; APA; CBEP; CoAnAm; CoBA; ForPo; HBV; LiTA; LiTG; MAmP; NePA; NoP; OxBA; Po; PoEL-4; PoIE; PoLF; PoPl; StP; ThLM
Indian Children. Annette Wynne. BoChLi; GaP; GFA; MPB; OTPC (1946 ed.); PCH; SoPo; StVeCh; SUS; TiPo
Indian children squat upon the ground. Chairs. Annette Wynne. GFA
Indian Cradle Song. *Unknown.* BoChLi
Indian Dance. Frederick Niven. CaP
Indian Elephant, The. C. J. Kaberry. FiBHP
Indian Emperor, The, *sels.* Dryden.
Ah, Fading Joy, *fr.* IV, iii. ChTr; FiP; LoBV; OAEP; TreFT; ViBoPo
("Ah fading joy, how quickly art thou past?") MaPo
(Song: "Ah, fading joy, how quickly art thou past.") FaBoEn; NoP
Human Happiness, *fr.* IV, i. FiP
Indian Ghost Dance and War, The. W. H. Prather. PoOW
Indian Hunter, The. Eliza Cook. BLPA
Indian Hymn of Thanks to Mother Corn, An. *Unknown.* PCH
Indian Love Song. "Owen Meredith." VA
Indian Lullaby. Charles Myall. MPB
Indian Mohee, The, *with music.* *Unknown.* *See* Little Mohee.
Indian Mother About to Destroy Her Child, An. James Montgomery. PaPo
Indian Names. Lydia Huntley Sigourney. AmFN; FaPON; HBV; MC; MPB; OTPC; PAH; PoLF; PoRL; RePo
Indian Night Tableau. Hyman Edelstein. CaP
Indian Pipe. Richard Eberhart. TDP
Indian Pipe and Moccasin Flower. Arthur Guiterman. BrR; SUS
Indian Pipes. Winifred Welles. AnAmPo
Indian Prayer. Chief Joseph Strongwolf. TRV
Indian- Queen, The, *sel.* Sir Robert Howard *and* John Dryden.
Poor Mortals. PoIE
(Song of Aerial Spirits.) AtBAP
Indian Reservation: Caughnawaga. Abraham Klein. LiTM (1970 ed.); OBCV
Indian Serenade, The. Shelley. AnFE; ATP; AWP; BEL; BoLiVe; BoLP; EnLi-2; EnLit; EnRP; ExPo; FaPL; GTSL; HoPM; InPo; JAWP; LiTB; LiTG; LiTL; LoBV; MCCG; MERP; MeWo; OAEP; OBEV; OBRV; OuHeWo; PG; PoAn; PoPl; ToP; TreF; TrGrPo; UnPo (1st ed.); UnTE; ViBoPo; WPB
(Lines to an Indian Air.) FaBoBe; FiP; GTBS; GTBS-D; GTBS-P; GTBS-W; GTSE; HBV; NeHB
Indian Sky. Alfred Kreymborg. NP
Indian Song, An. W. B. Yeats. VA
Indian Songs. Louis Mertins. StVeCh (1955 ed.)
Rain Chant.
Prayer to the Sun God.
Indian Student, The; or, Force of Nature. Philip Freneau. AmPP (4th ed.); OxBA
Indian Summer. Wilfred Campbell. CaP; OBCV; PoPl; WHW
Indian Summer. Emily Dickinson. *See* These are the days when birds come back.
Indian Summer. A. S. Draper. YeAr
Indian Summer. William Ellery Leonard. Two Lives, Pt. III. AnAmPo; HBMV; NP; PG (1945 ed.)
Indian Summer. Susanna Strickland Moodie. CaP
Indian Summer. John Banister Tabb. AA; DD
Indian Summer. Whittier. *Fr.* Eve of Election. PCH
Indian Summer—Buffalo Summer. Winfield Townley Scott. FiMAP
Indian Summer Day on the Prairie, An. Vachel Lindsay. SoPo; StVeCh; WaKn; YT
Indian summer is with us now. Indian Summer. A. S. Draper. YeAr
Indian upon God, The. W. B. Yeats. MoBrPo; ViPo (1962 ed.); WGRP
Indian war was over, The. The Captive's Hymn. Edna Dean Proctor. PAH
Indian weed [now] withered quite, The. A Religious Use of Taking Tobacco [*or* Pipe and Can]. *Unknown,* *at. to* Robert Wisdome. EIL; HBV; OBEV; OBS; SeEP
Indian Woman, The. Walt Whitman. *Fr.* The Sleepers. PCD; PCH
Indiana. Hart Crane. *Fr.* The Bridge: Powhatan's Daughter.

Indiana (continued)
AnFE; CoAnAm; LiTA; TwAmPo
Indiana: no blustering summit or coarse gorge. Midwest. John Frederick Nims. MoVE; PoPl
Indians. John Fandel. AmFN; NYBP; RePo
Indians. Charles Sprague. *Fr.* Centennial Ode. GN
Indians chant and dance about, The. Not a Cloud in the Sky. Richard Armour. WhC
Indians Come down from Mixco, The. Miguel Angel Asturias, *tr. fr. Spanish by* Donald Devenish Walsh. FaPON
Indians count of men as dogs, The. Roger Williams. SCAP
Indian's Grave, The. George J. Mountain. CaP
Indians prize not English gold, The. Roger Williams. SCAP
Indians stole fair Annie, The. Fair Annie (C *vers.*) *Unknown.* ViBoFo
Indian's Welcome to the Pilgrim Fathers, The. Lydia Huntley Sigourney. AA; DD
Indications and tally of time, The. Walt Whitman. *Fr.* Song of the Answerer. PP
Indictment. Dorothy C. Parrish. TNV
Indictment. Margaret Todd Ritter. AnAmPo
Indifference. Louise Driscoll. PoMa
Indifference, The. Sir Charles Sedley. BWP; CEP; SeCV-2
Indifference. G. A. Studdert-Kennedy. ChIP; MaRV; OQP; PGD; SoP; TRV
(Crucifixion, The.) StJW
Indifference ("The cat is in the parlour"). *Unknown.* BOHV
Indifference ("In loopy links the canker crawls"). *Unknown.* NA
Indifference to Fortune. James Thomson. *Fr.* The Castle of Indolence, II. OBEC
Indifferent, The. Francis Beaumont. ElL; EnLit; HBV
Indifferent, The. John Donne. AnAnS-1; ATP (1935 ed.); BEL; CABA; DiPo; EnL; EnLit; MaMe; NoP; OAEP; OuHeWo; PoeP; ReEn; ReIE; SCEP-1; SeCV-1; TOP; TuPP; UnTE
("I can love both fair and brown.") EG
Indifferent, but indifferent—pshaw! he doth it not. Sir Walter Scott. *Fr.* The Monastery. NBM
Indifferent, flippant, earnest, but all bored. The Conscript. W. W. Gibson. MaRV
Indigestion of the Vampire, The. W. S. Merwin. NaP
Indignant at the fumbling wits, the obscure spite. Paudeen. W. B. Yeats. MaPo; PoEL-5
Indignant Male, An. A. B. Ross. BrR; MPB
Indignant Protest. *Unknown, tr. fr. Greek by* Louis Untermeyer. UnTE
Indignation. Victor Hugo. *tr. fr. French.* WoL
Indignation Dinner, An. James David Corrothers. BANP; PoNE
Indignation of Taliesin, The. Thomas Love Peacock. CBEP
Indirection. Richard Realf. AA; AnAmPo; AnFE; APA; CoAnAm; HBV;MaRV; OQP
Indispensability. Arthur Guiterman. WaKn
Individualist Speaks, The. Louis MacNeice. MoVE; OBMV
Indolence. Robert Bridges. BrPo
Indolence. Veron Watkins. FaBoTw
Indolent. The. Paul Verlaine. *tr. fr. French by* Arthur Symons. SyP
Indolent and kitten-eyed. Cheetah. Charles Eglington. BoSA
Indolent Gardener, The. Mary Kennedy. BoNaP
Indolent wind on the prairie. Prairie Wind. Duncan Campbell Scott. ACV
Indoor Games near Newbury. John Betjeman. MoPW; MoVE
Indra, the Supreme God. *Unknown, tr. fr. Sanskrit by* Romesh Dutt. *Fr.* The Rig-Veda. AWP
Induced Current. Herbert Mayo. PoMa
Induction, The: "In a summer season. . ." William Langland. *See* Prologue: "In a somer sesun. . ."
Induction to "The Mirror [*or* A Myrrour] for Magistrates." Thomas Sackville, Earl of Dorset. *See* Mirror for Magistrates, The.
Indulge no more may we. The End of the Episode. Thomas Hardy. LO
Indulgent giants burned to crisp. Lavish Kindness. Elinor Wylie. AtBAP; CrMA
Indwelling God, The. Frederick Lucian Hosmer. MaRV; OQP; WGRP
Inebriate of Air. Emily Dickinson. *See* I taste a liquor never brewed.
Inebriety, *sel.* George Crabbe.
Vicar, The. AnFE
Ineffable Dou, The. Sydney Goodsir Smith. OxBS
Inefficacious Egg, The. Roy Bishop. HBMV
Inert he lies on the saltgold sand. The Sunbather. Vernon Watkins. MoPo; MoVE
Inert in his chair. Drugged. Walter de la Mare. BrPo
Inertia. Audrey McGaffin. NePoAm
Inescapable romance, inescapable choice. Wallace Stevens. *Fr.* An Ordinary Evening in New Haven. ReMP
Inevitable, The. Sarah Knowles Bolton. AA; MaRV; OQP; PCD; WGRP
Inexhaustible. Israel Zangwill. TrJP
Inexorable. William Drummond of Hawthornden. *See* Madrigal: "My thoughts hold mortal strife."
Inexperience. June Breining. PoMa
Infallibility. Thomas Stephens Collier. AA
Infant-Ey, An. Thomas Traherne. *See* Infant's Eye.
Infant Innocence. A. E. Housman. ChTr; DTC; EnLi-2 (1949 ed.), *sl. diff.*; FaBoCh; FaFP; LiTB; LiTM; LoGBV; OxBoLi; PoPo; SiTL; WhC, *sl. diff.*
("Grizzly Bear is huge and wild, The.") CenHV
Infant Joy. Blake. *Fr.* Songs of Innocence. BiCB; CBEP; EiPP; EnLi-2; EnLit; FaPON; GoJo; GoTP; GTSL; HBV; HBVY; LoBV; MaPo (1969 ed.); MemP; NeHB; OTPC; PoeP; PoLF; PRWS; SiSoSe; ThWaDe; TiPo (1952 ed); ViBoPo
Infant Noah. Vernon Watkins. NeBP
Infant Sorrow. Blake. *Fr.* Songs of Experience. BoLiVe; BWP; CBEP; DiPo; EiCL; EiPP; EnL; FaBoEn; MaPo (1969 ed.); OBNC; PeER; PoEL-4; PoeP; PoFS
Infant Spring. Fredegond Shove. HBMV
Infant—wailing in nameless fear, An. Life. Ella Wheeler Wilcox. PoToHe
Infantryman, An. Edmund Blunden. ViBoPo
Infant's Eye, An. Thomas Traherne. CoBE
(Infant-Ey, An.) SCEP-1
Infants' graves [*or* gravemounds] are steps of angels, where. Graves of Infants. John Clare. ERoP-2; OBVV
Infants of Summer. Lennox Raphael. NBP
Infants' Petition, The. Michael Wigglesworth. *Fr.* The Day of Doom. AnNE
Infatuated. *Unknown, tr. fr. Greek by* Louis Untermeyer. UnTE
Infected vein, An. Freeway. William Witherup. QAH
Inferno. Dante, *tr. fr. Italian. Fr.* Divina Commedia. EnLi-1 (*fr.* V *and* XIII), *tr. by* Frances Winwar; OuHeWo, *abr. tr. by* Henry F. Cary
Sels.
Francesca da Rimini, *fr.* V, *tr. by* Dante Gabriel Rossetti. EPN
Pier delle Vigne, *fr.* XIII, *tr. by* John Ciardi. HoPM
"While I was all absorbed," *fr.* XXVIII, *tr. by* Longfellow. CAW
Infida's Song. Robert Greene. *Fr.* Never Too Late. AtBAP; OBSC
(Sweet Adon.) NoP
("Sweet Adon', dar'st not glance thine eye?") LO
Infidelity. Louis Untermeyer. NP
Infinitati Sacrum, *sel.* John Donne.
First Song. MaMe
Infinite, The. Giacomo Leopardi, *tr. fr. Italian.* LiTW, *tr. by* Kenneth Rexroth; OnPM, *tr. by* Glauco Cambon; WoL, *tr. by* R. C. Trevelyan
(Infinito, L', *tr. by* Lorna de' Lucchi.) AWP; JAWP; WBP; Po, *tr. by* John Heath-Stubbs
Infinite, The. John Boyle O'Reilly. OnYI
Infinite consanguinity it bears. Voyages, III. Hart Crane. ForPo; MoPo; MoVE; Po; PoIE
Infinite gentleness, infinite irony. Effigy of a Nun. Sara Teasdale. MAP; MoAmPo; NP
Infinite! let me not think on you. Simple Things. Paul Jean Toulet. CAW
Infinite orderliness of the natural world, The. The Spiral. John Holmes. MiAP
Infinite power essenciall, The. Mary Queen of Heaven. *Unknown.* MeEL
Infinite Power, eternal Lord. The Comparison and Complaint. Isaac Watts. TrPWD

Infinite Truth and Might! whose love. Thy Name We Bless and Magnify. John Power. BLRP
"Infinite," The. Word Horrible! at feud. Legem Tuam Dilexi. Coventry Patmore. NBM; OxBoCh; PoEL-5; PoLi
Infinitesimal James. Limerick. *Unknown.* BOHV
Infinito, L'. Giacomo Leopardi. *See* Infinite, The.
Infinity. Philip Henry Savage. AA
Infinity. Walt Whitman. *Fr.* Song of Myself, XLIV-XLV. AA
Infinity of Wishes. *Unknown,* *tr. fr. Spanish by* Sir John Bowring. OnPM
Infinity, when all things it beheld. The Preface. Edward Taylor. *Fr.* God's Determinations. AmLP; AmPP; AP; ILP; MAmP; MWA-1; OxBA; SCAP
Infir Taris. *Unknown.* ChTr; OxNR
Infirm. Edward Sandford Martin. ALV
Infirmity. Theodore Roethke. CoAP; NYBP; PoeP
Inflamed Disciple, The. Arthur Kramer. InMe
Inflatable Globe, The. Theodore Spencer. LiTA; LiTM; NePA; WaP
Inflated boys, when clergymen are odd. Memorandum for Minos. Richard Kell. ELU
Inflictis. Archibald Stodart-Walker. *Fr.* The Moxford Book of English Verse. CenHV
Influence. Joseph Morris, *wr. wr. at. to* Joseph Norris. MaRV
Influence. John Oxenham. *See* Little Word, A.
Influence. John Banister Tabb. PoMa
Influence. *Unknown.* MaRV
Influence of Natural Objects. Wordsworth. *Fr.* The Prelude, I. AWP; InPo; JAWP; LoBV; MCCG; OBRV; WBP
(Boyhood.) WHA
("Wisdom and spirit of the universe.") AtBAP
Influence of Time on Grief. William Lisle Bowles. *See* Time and Grief.
Informing Spirit, The. Emerson. *Fr.* History. AWP; InPo; WGRP
(History.) BBV
(No Great, No Small.) MaRV
Infusorial earthmounds of the Upper Amazon, The. Lost Explorer. Edmund Pennant. GoYe
Ingenious insect, but of ruthless mold. To the Spider. Thomas Russell. Sonn
Ingenious Little Old Man, The. John Bennett. FaPON; GaP
Ingenious Raconteur. Renée Haynes. PV
Ingenuities of Debt, The. Robert Frost. MWA-2
Ingle-Side, The. Hew Ainslie. HBV; OTPC (1923 ed.)
Inglorious friend! most confident I am. Sonnet to a Clam. John Godfrey Saxe. AnNE; BOHV
Ingmar Bergman's Seventh Seal. Robert Duncan. NMP
Ingoldsby Legends, The, *sels.* "Thomas Ingoldsby."
Forlorn One, The. BOHV
Hon. Mr. Sucklethumbkin's Story. OBRV
Jackdaw of Rheims, The. BOHV; HBV; OnMSP; OTPC (1923 ed.); PaPo; ShBV-1; TSW; VA
Knight and the Lady, The. BOHV
Lay of St. Cuthbert, The. OtMeF
Misadventures at Margate. BOHV; HBV
Mr. Barney Maguire's Account of the Coronation. VA
Not a Sou Had He Got. *Fr.* The Cynotaph. HBV
Ingrateful[l] Beauty Threatened. Thomas Carew. AnAnS-2; BWP; EnLi-1; EP; HBV; InvP; LO; MeLP; OBEV; OBS; SCEP-2; SeCP; SeCV-1; SeEP; TOP
(Know, Celia, since thou art so proud.") EG
Ingratitude. Shakespeare. *See* Blow, Blow Thou Winter Wind.
In-Group. Lionel Kearns. PeCV (1967 ed.)
Inhabitants of old Jerusalem, The. The Popish Plot. Dryden. *Fr.* Absalom and Achitophel. ACP
Inheritance. "Æ." EPN; PoVP
Inheritance. Marv Potter Thacher Higginson. AA
Inheritance. Alfonsina Storni, *tr. fr. Spanish by* Jessie Read Wendell. OnPM
Inheritance. *Unknown,* *tr. fr. Irish by* Frank O'Connor. KiLC
Inherited Estate, The. Thom Gunn. ToPo
Inheritors, The. Dorothy Livesay. CaP
Inhibited Persian, An. Richard Hart. CIV
Inhospitable./ Another bald. Afterwards. Edward Lucie-Smith. HYE
Inhuman Henry; or, Cruelty to Fabulous Animals. A. E. Housman. BBGG; FiBHP
Inhuman man! curse on thy barb'rous art. The Wounded Hare. Burns. OTPC
Inhuman Rain Rejoiced, The. Don Shea. QAH
Inhuman Wolf and the Lamb Sans Gene The. Guy Wetmore Carryl. ALV; AmePo
Inis Fal. *Unknown,* *tr. fr. Irish by* James Stephens. OBMV
Inisgallun. Darrell Figgis. OnYI
Initial. Arthur Boyars. NePoEA-2
Initiation. Rainer Maria Rilke, *tr. fr. German by* C. F. MacIntyre. TrJP
(Eingang [Prelude], *tr. by* M. D. Herter Norton.) Po
Injian Ocean sets an' smiles, The. For to Admire. Kipling. MoBrPo
Injunction. Blake. BoLiVe
(Gnomic Verses.) OBRV; TrGrPo
Injury, The. William Carlos Williams. AP
Injustice. Sheldon Shepard. ChIP
Ink runs from the corners of my mouth. Eating Poetry. Mark Strand. YAP
Inland City. John Crowe Ransom. CMoP
Inland Sea, The. Howard Sergeant. ToPo
Inland, within a hollow vale, I stood. Near Dover, September, 1802 [*or* Sonnet: September, 1802]. Wordsworth. ChER; EnLi-2; EnRP; MaPo; MBW-2; MERP; OAEP; TOP
Inlet, The. Louise Glück. YAP
Inmate of a mountain-dwelling. To Miss Blackett on Her First Ascent to the Summit of Helvellyn. Wordsworth. CLwM
Inmate of smoaking cots, whose rustic shed. Ode on Lyric Poetry. Sir James Marriott. Po
Inn by the Road, The. C. E. Warner. OQP
Inn of Care, The. Samuel Waddington. OBVV; VA
Inn of Earth, The. Sara Teasdale. LiTA
Inn of the Silver Moon, The, *sel.* Herman Knickerbocker Viele.
Good Inn, The. HBV
Inn That Missed Its Chance, The. Amos Russel Wells. ChrBoLe
Innate Helium. Robert Frost. ImOP
Inner Brother. Stephen Stepanchev. WaP
Inner Ear. Coleman Barks. *Fr.* Body Poems. QAH
Inner Light. Milton. *Fr.* Paradise Lost, III. MaRV
Inner Light, The. Frederic William Henry Myers. *Fr.* Saint Paul. HBV; MaRV; WGRP
Inner Man, The. Plato, *tr. fr. Greek.* PoPl
Inner Significance of the Statues Seated outside the Boston Public Library, The. Walter Conrad Arensberg. AnAmPo
Inner Silence, The. Harriet Monroe. HBMV; NP
Inner Temple Masque, The, *sels.* William Browne.
Sirens' Song. ETS; OBEV
(Siren Song.) EG
(Song of the Sirens.) ChTr; EIL
(Song of the Syrens, *sl. abr.*) OBS
("Steer hither, steer your wingèd pines.") ViBoPo
"Son of Erebus and Night." ViBoPo
Inner Vision. *Unknown,* *tr. fr. Sanskrit by* Joseph Nadin Rawson. *Fr.* The Upanishads. OnPM
Inner Vision, The. Wordsworth. GTBS; GTBS-D; GTBS-P; GTBS-W; GTSE; GTSL; HBV
(Most Sweet It Is with Unuplifted Eyes.) EnLit; EnRP; EPN; LO; TOP
Innocence. Blake. BoPe
Innocence. George S. Chappell. YaD
Innocence, The. Robert Creeley. NeAP
Innocence. Thom Gunn. LiTM (1970 ed.); NePoEA-2; ToPo
Innocence. Norman MacCaig. NMP; OPoP
Innocence. Anne Spencer. CDC
Innocence. Thomas Traherne. AnAnS-1; MeP
Innocent, The. Gene Derwood. NePA; WaP
Innocent country girl going to town, An. Advice to Country Girls. *Unknown.* UnTE
Innocent Country-Maid's Delight, The; or, A Description of the Lives of the Lasses of London. *Unknown.* CoMu
Innocent decision: to enjoy. Triple Feature. Denise Levertov. NoP
Innocent eyes not ours. All Things Wait upon Thee. Christina Rossetti. GN
Innocent Gazer, The. Lord Cutts. CavP
Innocent Landscape. Elinor Wylie. OxBA
Innocent spirits, bright, immaculate ghosts! From Generation to Generation. William Dean Howells. AA; PFY
Innocent, sweet Day is dead, The. Night and Day. Sidney

Innocent (continued)
Lanier. AA; AnAmPo; MAP; MoAmPo (1942 ed.)
Innocent Usurper, The, *sel.* John Banks.
"Sweet harmony of life, just musick flows." PeRV
Innocents, The. Jay Macpherson. OBCV
Innocents, The. *Unknown.* OBB
Innocents, The. Elinor Wylie. StJW
Innocents' Day. Norman Nicholson. POTi
Innocent's Song. Charles Causley. GTBS-P; POTi
Innominatus. Sir Walter Scott. *See* Breathes There the Man.
Innumerable Beauties. Lord Herbert of Cherbury. *See* Sonnet: "Innumerable Beauties thou white haire."
Innumerable Christ, The. "Hugh MacDiarmid." EaLo; OxBS
Innumerable Friend. May Sarton. WaKn
Inordinate Love. *Unknown.* MeEL
Inquest, The. W. H. Davies. CBEP; DTC; GTBS-P
Inquiry, The. Thomas Hardy. At Casterbridge Fair, V. BEL; EnLi-2 (1949 ed.); EnLit; PoVP
Inquisition upon Fame and Honor, An. Fulke Greville. SiCE
Inquisitive Barn. Frances Frost. BrR
Inquisitors, The. Robinson Jeffers. MoAmPo (1950 ed.)
Insatiableness. Thomas Traherne. OxBoCh
"This busy, vast, inquiring soul," *sel.* VaPo
(Enquiring Soul, The, 1 *st.*) MaRV
Insatiate, The. Johannes Secundus, *tr. fr. Latin by* John Nott. *Fr.* Basia. UnTE
"Insatiate brute, whose teeth abuse." The Small Silver-coloured Bookworm. Thomas Parnell. OnYI
Inscribed on the Collar of a Dog. Pope. *See* Epigram: "I am his Highness' dog at Kew."
Inscribed upon a Rock. Wordsworth. SyP
Inscription: For the Door of the Cell in Newgate Where Mrs. Brownrigg, the Prentice-Cide, Was Confined Previous to Her Execution. George Canning *and* John Hookam Frere. Par
Inscription, An: "Grass of levity." *Unknown.* EIL
(Mortality.) CBEP
Inscription: "He wrote upon his heart." Donald Jeffrey Hayes. CDC
Inscription: "It is not hard to tell a rose." Ann Hamilton. HBMV
Inscription: On a Tablet against a Root-House. William Shenstone. EiPP
Inscription: On the Back of a Gothic Seat. William Shenstone. EiPP
Inscription, The: "Sealed with the seal of Life, thy soul and mine." Elsa Barker. *Fr.* Spirit and the Bride. HBMV
Inscription: "Ye powers unseen, to whom the bards of Greece." Mark Akenside. CBEP; OBEC
Inscription at Mount Vernon. *Unknown.* PoRL
Inscription at the City of Brass. *Unknown.* *See* Inscriptions at the City of Brass.
Inscription by the Sea, An. *Unknown, tr. fr. Greek by* E. A. Robinson. *Fr.* The Greek Anthology. AWP; ChTr; ELU; InP; JAWP; TOP; WBP
Inscription for a Fountain. Barry Cornwall. *See* For a Fountain.
Inscription for a Fountain on a Heath. Samuel Taylor Coleridge. ERoP-1; MCCG; OAEP
Inscription for a Grotto. Mark Akenside. BWP; CEP; OBEC; PoEL-3
(For a Grotto.) SeCePo
Inscription for a Mirror in a Deserted Dwelling. William Rose Benét. MAP; MoAmPo
Inscription for a Portrait of Dante. Boccaccio, *tr. fr. Italian by* Dante Gabriel Rossetti. *Fr.* Sonnets. AWP; JAWP; WBP
(Inscription for Portrait of Dante.) OnPM
(Tribute to Dante, A.) GoBC
Inscription for a Statue of Love. Voltaire, *tr. fr. French by* Henry Carrington. LiTW
Inscription for a Tablet on the Banks of a Stream. Robert Southey. OBEC
Inscription for an Old Bed. William Morris. OBEV (new ed.); OBVV; WiR
(For the Bed at Kelmscott.) NBM; PoEL-5; PoVP
(Lines for a Bed at Kelmscott Manor.) CH
Inscription for Arthur Rackham's Rip Van Winkle. James Elroy Flecker. BrPo
Inscription for My Little Son's Silver Plate. Eugene Field. PPL
Inscription for Portrait of Dante. Boccaccio. *See* Inscription for a Portrait of Dante.
Inscription for the Entrance to a Wood. Bryant. AmLP; AmP; AmPP; AnNE; AP; CoBA; ILP; MAmP; MCCG; MWA-1; OxBA
Inscription for the Statue of Liberty. Emma Lazarus. PTK
Inscription for the Tank. James Wright. TwCP
Inscription in a Garden. George Gascoigne. CBEP; OBSC; TrGrPo
(Inscription in His Garden.) TuPP
Inscription in a Hermitage. Thomas Warton, the Younger. HBV
Inscription in a Library. W. G. Wendell. WhC
Inscription on a Chemise. *Unknown, tr. fr. Arabic by* E. Powys Mathers. *Fr.* The Thousand and One Nights. ErPo
Inscription on a Grot. Samuel Rogers. *Fr.* Pleasures of Memory. OBEC
Inscription on a Shrine near Ischl. Elizabeth, Empress of Austria-Hungary, *tr. fr. German by* Thomas Walsh. CAW
Inscription on an Altar of the Dead. Victor Contoski. ThO
Inscription on an Ancient Bell. *Unknown, tr. fr. Latin by* Fr. Bridgett. ISi
Inscription on Stone over Shakespeare's Grave. *Unknown.* TreFS
Inscription on the Cross. St. John, XIX; 19-22, Bible, *N.T.* TreFT
Inscription on the Flyleaf of a Bible. Dannie Abse. TrJP
Inscription on the Pyramid of Pepi I. *Unknown, tr. fr. Egyptian by* Lindley W. Hubbell. LiTW
Inscription on the Pyramid of Unas. *Unknown, tr. fr. Egyptian by* Lindley W. Hubbell. LiTW
Inscription on the Statue of Liberty. Emma Lazarus. *Fr* The New Colossus. PaA; PoRL
("Give me your tired, your poor.") PoFr
Inscription on the Tomb of the Lady Mary Wentworth, The. Thomas Carew. *See* Maria Wentworth.
Inscription Set upon the Great Gate of Theleme, The, *abr.* Rabelais, *tr. fr. French by* Sir Thomas Urquhart. *Fr.* Gargantua. PoFr
Inscription to Spartans Dead at Thermopylae. Simonides. *See* Thermopylae.
Inscriptions at the City of Brass. *Unknown, tr. fr. Arabic by* E. Powys Mathers. *Fr.* The Thousand and One Nights. AWP; PG (1945 ed.); PoFr, 2 *sts.*; WaaP, 3 *sts.*
Inscription at the City of Brass ("Drunkenness of youth has passed like a fever"), *sel.* LiTW
Inscriptions for the Caledonian Canal. Robert Southey. NBM
Inscriptions on Greek tombstones intrigued him. Ronald Wyn. Robert Bagg. TwAmPo
Insect or blossom? Fragile, fairy thing. The Mariposa Lily. Ina Donna Coolbrith. AA
Insect Wives. Rudolph Altrocchi. WhC
Insect world, now sunbeams higher climb, The. March. John Clare. OA
Insectarian, An. John Banister Tabb. UTS
Insects. Isidor Schneider. AnAmPo; TrJP
Insensibility. Wilfred Owen. ChMP; CMoP; ExPo; FaBoTw; GTBS-W; LiTB; LiTM; MMA; MoAB; OAEP (2d ed.); SeCeV; StP; WaP
Inside its zig-zag lines the little camp is asleep. The Magazine Fort, Phoenix Park, Dublin. William Wilkins. IrPN; SeCePo
Inside my father's close. My Father's Close. *Unknown.* AWP; PoVP
Inside of a whirlpool, The. Warning. John Ciardi. PDV
Inside of King's College Chapel, Cambridge. Wordsworth. EnLi-2; EnRP; EPN; GoBC; MaRV; MBW-2; OAEP; OBNC; OBRV; OxBoCh; PeER Ecclesiastical Sonnets, XLIII.
(Within King's College Chapel, Cambridge.) GTBS; GTBS-D; GTBS-P; GTBS-W; GTSE; GTSL
Inside Out. Diane Wakoski. CoAP; NYBP
Inside that figure rides opaque malice. The Picador Bit. Bink Noll. ToPo
Inside the house I sit alone. Meditation in Winter. Leonard Mann. BoAV
Inside the lunchroom the travelling nuns wove. Feathered Dancers. Kenward Elmslie. ANYP; YAP
Inside the Tulip. George Bowering. MoCV

Inside the veins there are navies setting forth. Waking from Sleep. Robert Bly. FRC
Inside this northern summer's fold. Siena. Swinburne. ViPo
Insidious Dr. Fu Man Chu, The. LeRoi Jones. CoPo
Insight. Lionel Kearns. PeCV (1967 ed.)
Insights. Catherine Davis. NePoEA; QFR
Insistently through sleeping—a tide of voices. The Harbor Dawn. Hart Crane. *Fr.* The Bridge: Powhatan's Daughter. AmP; LiTA; MoPo; NePA; OxBA
Insomnia. Ethna MacCarthy. NeIP
Insomnia. Dante Gabriel Rossetti. PoVP
Insomnia. John Banister Tabb. TrPWD
Insomnia. Edith M. Thomas. AA
Insomniac Poem. Ron Loewinsohn. NeAP
Insomniacs, The. Adrienne Cecile Rich. NYBP
Inspect Us. Edith Daniell. BOHV
Inspection. Wilfred Owen. WaP
Inspection, The. Frederick B. Watt. CaP
Inspector of stairs is on the stairs, The. Walk-up. W. S. Merwin. CoPo
Inspiration. Mary Fullerton. PoAu-1
Inspiration. W. W. Gibson. WGRP
Inspiration. Samuel Johnson. AA; HBV; TrPWD; WGRP
Inspiration. E. V. Knox. CenHV
Inspiration, The. James Montgomery. *See* Columbus.
Inspiration. John Banister Tabb. WGRP
Inspiration. Henry David Thoreau. AA; AmPP; AnAmPo; AnFE; AnNE; AP; APA; CoAnAm; FaBoBe; HBV; MWA-1; OxBA; WGRP, *abr.*
"I will not doubt for evermore," *br. sel.* MaRV
Inspiration ("As the hand moves over the harp and the strings speak"). *Unknown.* *Fr.* Solomon. WGRP
Inspiration, An. Ella Wheeler Wilcox. WGRP
Inspirations. William James Dawson. MaRV; WGRP
Instance, An. Alastair Reid. PP
Instans Tyrannus. Robert Browning. PoFr
Instant splendour, the swung bells that speak, The. Prothalamion. Terence Tiller. NeBP
Instantaneous ("Instantaneously!"). Vivian Ayers. NNP
Instead of/ the flower of the hawthorn. Franklin Square. William Carlos Williams. TDP
Instead of a Journey. Michael Hamburger. NYBP
Instead of being sad and hurt. Forbearance. Della Adams Leitner. STF
Instead of blushing cherry hue. Allan M. Laing. PV
Instead of incense (Blessed Lord) if wee. Nathaniel Wanley. TrPWD
Royal Presents.
Instead of Neat Inclosures. Robert Herrick. *Fr.* An Ode on the Birth of Our Saviour. ChTr
Instead of swinging from a beam. Avery Anameer. Joseph Payne Brennan. FiSC
Instead of the Puritans landing on Plymouth Rock. Thoughts for St. Stephen. Christopher Morley. ShM; WhC
Instinctively, unwittingly. Love Poem. Janet Lewis. QFR
Instruction. Hazel Hall. NP
Instruction in the Art. Philip Booth. SD
Instruction Manual, The. John Ashbery. NeAP
Instruction sore long time I bore. Charles Kingsley. CenHV
Instructions of King Cormac. Cormac, King of Cashel, *tr. fr. Irish.* PoToHe (new ed.)
Instructor said, The. Theme for English B. Langston Hughes. BALP
Instrument Rhimes. Christopher Smart. *Fr.* Jubilate Agno. MuSP
Instruments, The. Dryden. *Fr.* A Song for St. Cecilia's Day. PoPo
(Fife and Drum, 8 *ll.*) GN
Instruments, The. Christopher Smart. WiR
Insubordination. Margaret Evelyn Singleton. ChIP
Insufficient Vengeance. Martial, *tr. fr. Latin by* Louis Untermeyer. UnTE
Insult, The. Robert Layzer. NePoEA
Insult, The. *Unknown.* SCC
Insulting Beauty. Earl of Rochester. CavP
Insured for every accident. Epitaph. Richard Armour. ShM
Intaglio. Henri Coulette. NePoEA; PoCH
Intaglios. Francis Brooks. AA
On the Plains.
Tennessee.
Integer Vitae. Thomas Campion. *See* Man of Life Upright, The.
Integer Vitae. Horace, *tr. fr. Latin by* Sir Theodore Martin. Odes, I, 22. EnLi-1
(To Aristius Fuscus.) OuHeWo
Integrity. William L. Stidger. ChIP; OQP
Intellect. Emerson. OnPM
Intellect of man is forced to choose, The. The Choice. W. B. Yeats. CMoP; PoeP
Intellectual, The. Karl Shapiro. CMoP
Intelligent Sheep-Man and the New Cars, The. William Carlos Williams. NePoAm-2
Intemperance. Isaiah, V: 11-12, Bible, *O.T.* (Moulton, *Modern Reader's Bible.* MaRV
Intempestiva. Henry Longan Stuart. JKCP (1926 ed.)
Intended for Sir Isaac Newton. Pope. *See* Epitaph Intended for Sir Isaac Newton.
Intense and terrible beauty, how has our race with the frail naked nerves. Gale in April. Robinson Jeffers. AmPP; CMoP; MAP; MoAB; MoAmPo; NeMA
Inter, mitzy, titzy, tool. *Unknown.* OxNR
Inter Sodales. W. E. Henley. HBV
Interceding. Opal Leonore Gibbs. BePJ
Intercession. *Unknown.* SoP
Intercession in Late October. Robert Graves. MoAB
Intercessor, An. *Unknown,* *at. to* Frances Ridley Havergal. SoP; STF
Intercessors. Austin Clarke. NMP
Interests of a black man in a cellar, The. Black Tambourine. Hart Crane. AP; CBEP; CoBMV; NAMP; OxBA; PoNe
Interim. Clarissa Scott Delany. CDC; PoNe
Interior. Padraic Colum. ACV; MoBrPo; TSW
Interior. Marjorie Allen Seiffert. NP
Interior; the Suburbs. Horace Gregory. AnAmPo; NP
Interlude, An. John Peale Bishop. LiTA
Interlude. Maxwell Bodenheim. MAPA
Interlude. Eileen Duggan. AnNZ
Interlude, An. Robert Duncan. NoP
Interlude. Walter Savage Landor. GTBS-P
Interlude. Holger Lundbergh. PoMa
Interlude. Theodore Roethke. MiAP
Interlude, The. Karl Shapiro. MoVE
Interlude. Edith Sitwell. MoAB; MoBrPo; NeMA
Interlude ("Screams/ screams"). Welton Smith. BF
Interlude ("We never spent time in the mountains"). Welton Smith. BF
Interlude, An. Swinburne. ViBoPo
Interlude. Ella Wheeler Wilcox. HBV
(Growing Old.) BLPA
Interlude: Songs Out of Sorrow, *sels.* Sara Teasdale.
Mastery, II. HBV; WGRP
Sprits's House, I. OQP
Wisdom, IV. InP; MAP; MoAmPo
Interlude: The Casement. Christopher Brennan. PoAu-1
Intermezzo. Robert Hillyer. NePoAm
Intermezzo for the Fourth Act, An. William Allen White. InMe
Interminable ocean lay beneath, The. Sunrise at Sea. Edwin Atherstone. EtS
Intermission, Please! Irwin Edman. SiTL; WhC
Internal Cerberus, whose griping fangs. Conscience. Sir Edward Sherburne. ACP
Internal Harmony. George Meredith. EPN
International Brigade Arrives at Madrid, The. "Pablo Neruda," *tr. fr. Spanish by* Angel Flores. WaaP
International Brigade Dead. Thomas O'Brien. NeIP
International Copyright. James Russell Lowell. *See* Stealing.
International Episode, An. Caroline Duer. AA; PAH
International Hymn. George Huntington. MaRV; PoLF
Interne, The. Maxwell Bodenheim. NP
Interpretation. Sheldon Shepard. ChIP
Interpreter, The. Orrick Johns. AnAmPo; HBMV; MAP; NP; PFY
Interpreters, The. D. J. Enright. PP
Interpreters, The. Swinburne. PoEL-5
Interracial. Georgia Douglas Johnson. PoNe; TTY
Interred [*or* Interr'd] beneath this marble stone. An Epitaph. Matthew Prior. CEP; EiCL; EiCP; EiPP; NoP; OBEC; PoE; PoEL-3; PoIE; YAT
Interrogation, The. Edwin Muir. CMoP; LiTB; SeCePo

Interrogativa Cantilena. *Unknown.* *See* If All the World Were Paper.
Interrogative. Sister Mary Thérèse. MoRP
Interruption. Robert Graves. LiTB; LiTM
("If ever against this easy blue and silver.") GTBS-W
Interrupted Romance. *Unknown,* *tr. fr. Russian by* Louis Untermeyer. UnTE
Interval. Joseph Auslander. MAP; MoAmPo (1942 ed.)
Interval. Rolfe Humphries. ML
Interval of grateful shade. Evening Hymn. Philip Doddridge. SoP
Interval with Fire. Dorothy Livesay. CaP
Intervals. Robert Creeley. TPM
Intervals. Beatrice Ravenel. HBMV
Interview near Florence, An. Samuel Rogers. *Fr.* Italy. OBNC
Interview with Doctor Drink. J. V. Cunningham. NMP
Intery, mintery, cutery, corn. Mother Goose. OTPC; OxNR; PCH; PPL; StVeCh; TiPo
Intice not me with thy alluringe eye. *Unknown.* SeCSL
Intil the pit-mirk nicht we northwart sail. Artic Convoy. J. K. Annand. OxBS
Intimate Parnassus. Patrick Kavanagh. MoBrPo (1962 ed.)
Intimations of Immorality from Recollections of Early Childhood. Wordsworth. *See* Ode: Intimations of Immortality. . .
Intimations of Mortality. Phyllis McGinley. MoAmPo (1962 ed.); NeMA
Intimations of Sublimity. Wordsworth. *Fr.* The Prelude. OBNC
Intimidations of an Autobiography. James Tate. YAT
Into a gentle wildness and confusion. Sea Side. Robert Graves. MoPo
Into a little close of mine I went. Two Lyrics, 1. Lorenzo de' Medici. AWP
Into a sweet May morning. John of Hazelgreen. *Unknown.* BaBo (A *vers.*); ESPB; ViBoFo
Into a ward of the whitewashed halls. Somebody's Darling. Marie La Coste [*or* La Conte]. BLPA; DD; HBV; TreF; WBLP
Into a world where children shriek like suns. On a Child Who Lived One Minute. X. J. Kennedy. NYBP
Into azure cloudland searching. To My Distant Beloved. Alois Jeitteles. TrJP
Into Battle. Julian Grenfell. HBV; LoBV; MMA; OBEV (new ed.); OBMV; OtMeF; POTE; ShBV-3; WaaP
Into ethereal meads. Life's Testament, XII. William Baylebridge. BoAV
Into gathered movement love. The Poets of Peace and Gladness. Sister Mary Norbert Körte. ThO
Into love and out again. Theory. Dorothy Parker. BOHV
Into my closet fleeing, as the dove. Alone with God. Elizabeth Payson Prentiss. SoP
Into my eyes he loving looked. The Mirror. Judah Halevi. TrJP
Into My Heart an Air That Kills. A. E. Housman. A Shropshire Lad, XL. ChTr; CMoP; EnL; EvOK; GoJo; GTBS-W; LiTB; MasP; MoAB; MoBrPo; OAEP (2d ed.); Po; PoPo; PoVP; ViBoPo; ViPo
(Yon Far Country.) LiTM; SeCePo
Into my heart's treasury. The Coin. Sara Teasdale. HBMV; RePo; SP; TiPo (1952 ed.)
Into my room to-night came June. June Night. Hazel Hall. HBMV
Into my shoulder your head bores. Blossom. Jason Miller. ThO
Into our empty room. Their Party, Our House. Jon Swan. NYBP
Into Slumbers. John Fletcher. *See* Care-charming Sleep.
Into that stricken hour the hunted had gathered. Vaticide. Myron O'Higgins. Kal
Into the ark, by docile two and seven. Incident with Lions. Sara Henderson Hay. NYTB
Into the basin put the plums. The Christmas Pudding. *Unknown.* TiPo (1952 ed.)
Into the big-flaked sugar-snow. Maple Feast. Frances Frost. RePo
Into the bosom of the one great sea. God Is One [*or* The Unity of God]. Panatattu. MaRV; WGRP
Into the caverns of the sea. Joy Enough. Barrett Eastman. AA
Into the closed air of the slow. Sonnet XVI. Ted Berrigan. FRC
Into the crucible of life. Onwardness. Doris Hedges. CaP
Into the Dark. Edith Gilling Cherry. SoP
Into the Darkness. Basho, *tr. fr. Japanese by* H. G. Henderson. OnPM
Into the Devil tavern. The Three Troopers. George Walter Thornbury. BeLS; HBV; VA
Into the dusk and snow. A Traveller. *Unknown.* WGRP
Into the dust of the making of man. The Builders. Henry van Dyke. OQP
Into the endless dark. City Lights. Rachel Field. FaPON; GFA; PDV
Into the Fountain. The Fountain. James Russell Lowell. GoTP
Into the furnace let me go alone. Baptism. Claude McKay. AnEnPo; PoNe
Into the Glacier. John Haines. CoAP
Into the golden vessel of great song. Edna St. Vincent Millay. NP
Into the inmost temple thus I came. The Temple of Venus. Spenser. *Fr.* The Faerie Queene. WHA
Into the justice of eternity. Dante. *Fr.* Divina Commedia: Paradiso. PoFr
Into the lonely park all frozen fast. Colloque sentimental [*or* Sentimental Conversation]. Paul Verlaine. BrPo; EnLi-2; SyP
Into the middle temple of my heart. Gulling Sonnets, VII. Sir John Davies. Sonn
Into the mists of the pagan island. The Sons of Patrick. James B. Dollard. JKCP
Into the nexus a webbed hand. Fear. Peter Schjeldahl. ANYP
Into the Noiseless Country. Thomas William Parsons. AA
Into the Salient. Edmund Blunden. ViBoPo
Into the scented woods we'll go. Green Rain. Mary Webb. BoNaP; CH; FaPON
Into the shadow Kunai-mai-pa Mo. Kunai-mai-pa Mo. Ethel Anderson. PoAu-2
Into the Silent Land. Song of the Silent Land. Johann Gaudenz Salis-Seewis. AWP; HBV; JAWP; OQP; WBP
Into the Silent Places. The Old Year and the New. Annie Johnson Flint. BLRP
Into the silver night. Revelation. Sir Edmund Gosse. OBEV; OBVV
Into the skies, one summer's day. The Thought. William Brighty Rands. OBEV; OBVV
Into the slain tons of needles. By Canoe through the Fir Forest. James Dickey. NYBP
Into the street the Piper stept. Robert Browning. *Fr.* The Pied Piper of Hamelin. BoTP
Into the Sunset. S. Hall Young. OQP
(Let Me Die Working.) MaRV
Into the sunshine, full of the light. The Fountain. James Russell Lowell. BoTP; OTPC; PRWS; PTK; RG
Into the temple the gaunt old saint strode, by the Spirit led. The Light in the Temple. William Rose Benét. MoRP
Into the thick of the fight he went, pallid and sick and wan. Wheeler at Santiago. James Lindsay Gordon. PAH
Into the town of Conemaugh. The Man Who Rode to Conemaugh. John Eliot Bowen. PAH
Into the Twilight. W. B. Yeats. BEL; EPN; HBV; PoPo; PoVP; ViPo (1962 ed.)
Into the west of the waters on the living ocean's foam. Homeward Bound. George Edward Woodberry. *Fr.* Wild Eden. AA
Into the wilderness. Tempted. Katharine Lee Bates. ChIP; StJW
Into the Wind. Winfield Townley Scott. NMP
Into the wood at close of rainy day. Sonnet. Thomas Caulfield Irwin. IrPN
Into the woods my Master went. A Ballad of Trees and the Master [*or* The Cross). Sidney Lanier. AA; AmePo; AmP; AnAmPo; AP; BePJ; CAW; ChIP; CoBA; GoBC; GTBS-W; HBV; LaNeLa; LiTA; MAmP; MAP; MoAmPo (1942 ed.); OQP; OxBA; PFY; PoEL-5; PoLF; PoRL; PTK; SoP; StJW; TOP; TRV; WGRP; WHL
Into the World and Out. Sarah Morgan Bryan Piatt. HBV
Into the yard the farmer goes. Evening at the Farm. John Townsend Trowbridge. BBV; GN; MPB; RIS
Into these loves who but for passion looks. To the Reader of These

Sonnets. Michael Drayton. Idea, *introd.* Sonnet. BEL; EnRePo; HBV; NoP; ReEn; ReIE; SiCE; Sonn; TuPP; ViBoPo
Into Thy Hands. Loren W. Burch. ChIP
Into what fictive worlds can imagination. The Horatians. W. H. Auden. NYBP
Into your arms I came. To the Anxious Mother. Valente Malangatana. PBA
Intolerably sad, profound. Before the Anaesthetic; or, A Real Fright. John Betjeman. SeCePo
Intolerance. Molly Anderson Haley. MaRV
Intolerance. John Richard Moreland. ChIP
Intolerance. Winthrop Mackworth Praed. MaRV
Intoxicated Poet, The. Allen Upward. *Fr.* Scented Leaves from a Chinese Jar. NP
Intra-Political. Margaret Avison. MoCV
Intra Sepulchrum. Thomas Hardy. MaPo
Intramural Aestivation, or Summer in Town, by a Teacher of Latin. Oliver Wendell Holmes. *See* Aestivation.
Intreat [*or* Entreat] Me Not to Leave Thee. Ruth, I: 16-17, Bible, *O.T.* InP; TreF; TRV
(Address of Ruth to Naomi.) GBV (1952 ed.)
("And Ruth said, Intreat me not to leave thee.") LO
(Ruth to Naomi.) MaRV; TrGrPo
Intrepid Ricardo, The. E. C. Bentley. *Fr.* Clerihews. CenHV
Intro, The. C. J. Dennis. WhC
Introduction: "Camille St. Saëns was racked with pains." Ogden Nash. *Fr.* The Carnival of Animals. UnS
Introduction: "Forget six counties overhung with smoke." William Morris. *See* Prologue: "Forget six counties. . ."
Introduction: "Hear the voice of the Bard!" Blake. *See* Hear the Voice of the Bard.
Introduction: "Piping down the valleys wild." Blake. *See* Piping down the Valleys Wild.
Introduction: "Sonnet is a moment's monument, A." Dante Gabriel Rossetti. *See* Sonnet, The ("A sonnet is. . .").
Introduction: "'Thou beel amy, thou Pardoner,' he sayde." Chaucer. *Fr.* The Canterbury Tales: The Pardoner's Tale. FosPo
Introduction: "'Twas late in my long journey, when I had clomb to where." Robert Bridges. *Fr.* The Testament of Beauty. MoVE
Introduction and Anecdotes. "Peter Pindar." *Fr.* Bozzy and Piozzi. PoEL-3
Introduction—Childhood and Schooltime. Wordsworth. *See* Prelude, The.
Introduction of a refrain, The. 'Twixt Cup and Lip. Mark Hollis. FiBHP
Introduction to Dogs, An. Ogden Nash. GoTP; MoShBr
Introduction to "Songs of Experience." Blake. *See* Hear the Voice of the Bard.
Introduction to "Songs of Innocence." Blake. *See* Piping down the Valleys Wild.
Introduction to "The Last Fruit off an Old Tree." Walter Savage Landor. *See* On His Seventy-fifth Birthday.
Introductory. Dante Gabriel Rossetti. *See* Sonnet, The ("A Sonnet is a moment's monument").
Introspective Reflection. Ogden Nash. WhC
Introversion. Evelyn Underhill. MaRV; WGRP
Intruder, The. Carolyn Kizer. FRC; NePoEA-2
Intruder, The. James Reeves. PDV
Intrudinge hopes what make you heere. *Unknown.* SeCSL
Intuition. Anthony Delius. PeSA
Intuition. R. H. Grenville. FiSC
Intuition. Tennyson. *See* In Memoriam A. H. H.: "That which we dare invoke to bless."
Intuitive guilt and the sun's harsh light. On the Seventh Anniversary of the Death of My Father. Robert Pack. NePoEA
Inundation, The. Howard Sergeant. *Fr.* The Leaves of Europe. ToPo
Invader, The. Norman Cameron. POTE
Invaders, The. Ronald Johnson. HYE
Invaders, The. Clarence Reed. BF
Invaders, The. Jocelyn Macy Sloan. FiSC
Invalid. Audrey McGaffin. NePoAm-2
Invariably when wine redeems the sight. The Wine Menagerie. Hart Crane. AP; OxBA
Invasion. Hubert Witheford. AnNZ
Invasion of Greece, The. Jeremy Ingalls. PoFr
Invasion Song. *Unknown.* PoOW
Invasion Weather. Douglas Newton. NeBP
Invective against the Wicked of the World, An, *sel.* Nicholas Breton.
"Let but a fellow in a fox-furred gown." ViBoPo
Invented a Person. Lenore G. Marshall. GoYe
Inventin'est Man, The. "J. B. H." IHA
Inventing a story with grass. A Birth. James Dickey. FRC
Invention. Sir William Watson. HBV
Invention of Comics, The. LeRoi Jones. AmNP; FRC; LiTM (1970 ed.)
Invention of New Jersey. Jack Anderson. ThO
Inventions. Samuel Butler. *Fr.* Misscellaneous Thoughts. CBV; PV
Inventor's Wife, The. Mrs. E. T. Corbett. PoLF
Inventory, The. Burns. CABL
Inventory. Dorothy Parker. AnAmPo; PoPo
Inventory. Ellen McKay Trimmer. SoP
Inventory—to 100th Street. Frank Lima. ANYP
Inventress and virgin,/ Martyred Cecelia. Verses to St. Cecilia. David Wright. POTE (1959 ed.)
Inverberg. J. F. Hendry. NeBP
Inverey cam doun Deeside, whistlin and playin. The Baron of Brackley. *Unknown.* BaBo; ESPB; OBB
Inverse Ratio. *Unknown.* WhC
Inversnaid. Gerard Manley Hopkins. ACP; BrPo; CABA; CMoP; FaBoMo; GTBS-P; GTBS-W; LiTB; LiTG; LiTM (rev. ed.); LoBV; MoAB; MoBrPo; PeVV; PIA; PoIE; PoRA; PoVP; ShBV-3; TDP; UnPo (3d ed.)
Wildness, *last* 4 *ll.* OtMeF
Inverted Torch, The, *sels.* Edith M. Thomas.
If Still They Live. AA; OQP
Tell Me. AA
When in the First Great Hour. AA
Will It Be So? AA
Investigator. Miriam Waddington. CaP
Investment, The. Robert Frost. BWP; CMoP; OxBA
Investor's Soliloquy. Kenneth Ward. FaFP; SiTL
Invictus. W. E. Henley. AnEnPo; AnFE; BBV; BEL; BLPA; CBV; DD; EnLi-2; EnLit; FaBoBe; FaBV; FaFP; FaPL; GoTP; GTBS-W; GTSE; GTSL; HBV; HBVY; HoPM; LiTB; LiTG; LiTM (rev. ed.); MaRV; MCCG; MoBrPo; NeHB; NeMA; OBEV; OBMV; OBVV; OHFP; OQP; OTD; OtMeF; OTPC (1946 ed.); OuHeWo; PCD; PoIE; PoMa; PoPl; PoPo; PoVP; PTK; ShBV-3; TIHL; TOP; TreF; TrGrPo; TSW; WGRP; YT Echoes, IV.
(Echoes.) LoBV
(I. M.—R. T. Hamilton Bruce.) ViBoPo
(Out of the Night.) EPN
(Out of the Night that Covers Me.) GTBS; OBNC
Invincible. Sir Gilbert Parker. *Fr.* A Lover's Diary. VA
Invincible. Winnie Lynch Rockett. OQP
Invisible, The. Richard Watson Gilder. WGRP
Invisible atoms of the air, The. Three Rimas, 1. Gustavo Adolfo Bécquer. *Fr.* Rimas. LiTW
Invisible Bride, The. Edwin Markham. HBV
Invisible Bridge, The. Gelett Burgess. NA; TreFT
(Queer Quatrains.) RIS
Invisible Craft of Evil, The. James Schevill. FRC
Invisible hammers. Paces. Sophia Castro-Leon. QAH
Invisible Man, The. Conrad Kent Rivers. Kal
Invisible Painter. Alfred Dorn. FiSC
Invisible Playmate, The. Margaret Widdemer. FaPON; MPB
Invisible Trumpets Blowing. E. J. Pratt. *Fr.* Brébeuf and His Brethren. CaP
Invitation, An. Basho, *tr. fr. Japanese by* H. G. Henderson. OnPM
Invitation. Harry Behn. FaPON; SoPo
Invitation, The. Tom Buchan. ACV
Invitation. Victor Contoski. PV
Invitation, The. Thomas Godfrey. AnFE; APA; CoAnAm
Invitation, The. George Herbert. AnAnS-1; MaMe; MeP
Invitation, The. Robert Herrick. OAEP
Invitation. Solomon ibn Gabirol, *tr. fr. Hebrew by* Israel Zangwill. TrJP
Invitation. Emmett Jarrett. ThO
Invitation, The. Donagh MacDonagh. OnYI
Invitation, The. Goronwy Owen, *tr. fr. Welsh by* George Borrow. LiTW, *abr.*; PrWP
Invitation. Raymond R. Patterson. WSL
Invitation, The. Shelley. *See* To Jane: The Invitation.
Invitation. Ridgely Torrence. NP; PCH

Invitation, The. *Unknown.* OxBoCh
Invitation, The. Nathaniel Wanley. SeEP
Invitation. Ella Young. BoChLi (1950 ed.)
Invitation to a Mistress. *Unknown, tr. fr. Latin by* George F. Whicher. UnTE
Invitation to a Sabbath. Harry Mathews. ANYP
Invitation to an Invitation, An. Catullus, *tr. fr. Latin by* Gardner E. Lewis. ErPo
Invitation to Eternity. John Clare. *See* Invite to Eternity.
Invitation to Jane, The. Shelley. *See* To Jane: The Invitation.
Invitation to Juno. William Empson. AtBAP; CMoP; FaBoMo
Invitation to Lubberland, An. *Unknown.* CoBE
Invitation to Miss Marianne Moore. Elizabeth Bishop. ML; MoVE; TwAmPo
Invitation to Phyllis, An. Charles Cotton. CLwM
Invitation to Sleep. Christina Rossetti. GTSE
Invitation to the Dance. Sidonius Apollinaris, *tr. fr. Latin by* Howard Mumford Jones. AWP
Invitation to the Dance. *Unknown, tr. fr. Latin by* John Addington Symonds. UnTE
Invitation to the Gondola, The. John Addington Symonds. *Fr.* In Venice. PoVP
Invitation to the Zoological Gardens, An. *Unknown.* BOHV
Invitation to Youth. *Unknown, tr. fr. Latin by* John Addington Symonds. OnPM; UnTE
Invite to Eternity, An. John Clare. ERoP-2; NBM; OBNC; PeER
(Invitation to Eternity.) NCEP; PoEL-4
Invites His Nymph to His Cottage. Philip Ayres. EnLoPo
Invites Poets and Historians to Write in Cynthia's Praise. Philip Ayres. Sonn
Inviting a Friend to Supper. Ben Jonson, *after the Latin of* Martial. AnAnS-2; AWP; BWP; EnRePo; EP; JAWP; LiTB; LoBV; MaPo; NoP; OAEP; OBS; OxBoLi; Po; PoE; PoEL-2; ReEn; SCEP-2; SeCP; SeCV-1; SeEP; TuPP; WBP
(Epigram: "Tonight, grave Sir, both my poor house and I," *sl. abr.*) MyFE
Invocatio ad Mariam. Chaucer, *mod. vers. by* Frank Ernest Hill. *Fr.* The Canterbury Tales: The Second Nun's Tale. ISi
("Thou maid and mother, daughter of thy Son," *mod. vers.*) GoBC
(Two Invocations of the Virgin, 1.) ACP
Invocation: "American muse, whose strong and diverse heart." Stephen Vincent Benét. *Fr.* John Brown's Body. AmFN; CrMA; MPB; NP, *shorter sel.*; PaA
Invocation: "Appear, O mother, was the perpetual cry." Wilfred Watson. MoCV
Invocation: "As pools beneath stone arches take." John Drinkwater. HBMV; NP
Invocation: "Bob Southey! You're a poet—Poet laureate." Byron. *See* Dedication: "Bob Southey!. . ."
Invocation: "Come down from heaven to meet me when my breath." Siegfried Sassoon. MoBrPo
Invocation: "Earth, ocean, air, beloved brotherhood." Shelley. *See* Invocation to Nature.
Invocation: "Empty my heart, Lord of daily vices." Theodore Spencer. TrPWD
Invocation: "Eternal God omnipotent! The One." Caelius Sedulius, *tr. fr. Latin by* George Sigerson. *Fr.* Carmen Paschale. OnYI
Invocation: "Good morning to you, Lord of the world!" Levi Isaac of Berditshev, *tr. fr. Hebrew by* Olga Marx. EaLo
Invocation, An: "Hear, sweet spirit." Samuel Taylor Coleridge. *Fr.* Remorse (Osorio), III, i. OAEP
(Hear, Sweet Spirit.) ViBoPo
(Song: "Hear, sweet spirit.") MCCG
(Song from "Osorio.") TOP
(Voice Sings, A.) CAW; CH
Invocation: "Help me to make this working day." Francesca Falk Miller. PEDC
Invocation, An: "I never prayed for Dryads, to haunt the woods again." William Johnson Cory. HBV; OBVV
Invocation: "I who was once a golden woman like those who walk." Edith Sitwell. AtBAP
Invocation, An: "In the sea wave tosses side by side with wave," *sel.* Muhammad Iqbal. ACV
Invocation: "Let me be buried in the rain." Helene Johnson. AmNP; BANP; PoNe
Invocation: "Maiden, and mistress of the months and stars." Swinburne. *Fr.* Atalanta in Calydon. PoEL-5; PoVP
Invocation: "Maidens young and virgins tender." Horace, *tr. fr. Latin by* Louis Untermeyer. Odes I, 21. AWP; JAWP; WBP
Invocations: "Mother of God, mother of man reborn." Arthur J. Little. *Fr.* Christ Unconquered. ISi
Invocation: "O mother-maid! O maiden-mother free!" Chaucer, *mod. vers. by* Frank Ernest Hill. *Fr.* The Canterbury Tales: The Prioress's Tale. ISi
(O Mooder Mayde.) BoW
(Prayer to the Blessed Virgin, *shorter sel., mod. vers.*) CAW
(Two Invocations of the Virgin, 2, *mod. vers.*) ACP
Invocation: "O Thou whose equal purpose runs." Wendell Phillips Stafford. MaRV; TrPWD
Invocation: "O world watched over by the cold moon and the mindless stars." Carleton Drewry. MoRP
Invocation: "Of Man's first disobedience, and the fruit." Milton. *See* Invocation to the Heavenly Muse.
Invocation: "Phoebus, arise!" William Drummond of Hawthornden. *See* Phoebus, Arise!
Invocation: "Rarely, rarely, comest thou." Shelley. *See* Song: "Rarely, rarely, comest thou."
Invocation: "There is a poem on the way." Kathleen Raine. CMoP
Invocation: "There is no balm on earth." Gilbert Thomas. TrPWD
Invocation: "Thou, whose enduring hand once laid in sooth." Edmund Clarence Stedman. AA
Invocation, An: "To God, the everlasting, who abides." John Addington Symonds. WGRP
"O God, unknown, invisible, secure," *sel.* MaRV; TrPWD; TRV
Invocation: "Truth, be more precious to me than the eyes." Max Eastman. OQP; WGRP
(Truth.) MaRV
Invocation, An: "We are what suns and winds." Walter Savage Landor. *See* Regeneration.
Invocation and Prelude. Stefan George, *tr. fr. German by* Ludwig Lewisohn. AWP
Invocation for the New Year. Margaret D. Armstrong. STF
Invocation of Comus, The. Milton. *See* Star That Bids the Shepherd Fold, The.
Invocation of Death. Kathleen Raine. MoAB
Invocation of Peace, *sel.* "Fiona Macleod."
"Deep peace, pure white of the moon to you." BoTP
Invocation of Silence. Richard Flecknoe. SeCL
(Silence Invoked.) GoBC
Invocation to Death. Emanuel Carnevali. NP
Invocation to Fancy. Joseph Warton. *Fr.* Ode to Fancy. OBEC
Invocation to Ireland. *At. to* Amergin, *tr. fr. Old Irish by* R. A. S. Macalister *and* Eoin MacNeill. OnYI
(Aimirgin's Invocation). AnIV
(Incantation, The, *tr. by* George Sigerson.) OnYI
Invocation to Light, The. Milton. *See* Hail, Holy Light.
Invocation to Nature. Shelley. *Fr.* Alastor; or, The Spirit of Solitude. EPN
("Earth, ocean, air, beloved brotherhood!") FiP
(Invocation: "Earth, ocean, air, beloved brotherhood.") WHA
Invocation to Rain in Summer. William C. Bennett. GN
(Summer Invocation.) HBV; OTPC
Invocation to Sleep. John Fletcher. *See* Care-charming Sleep. *Fr.* The Tragedy of Valentinian.
Invocation to the African Muse. Roy Campbell. *Fr.* The Flaming Terrapin. BoSA
Invocation to the Faerie Queene. Spenser. *See* Legend of the Knight of the Red Cross.
Invocation to the Genius of Greece. Mark Akenside. *Fr.* The Pleasures of Imagination. OBEC
Invocation to the Goddess, An. David Wright. NMP
Invocation to the Heavenly Muse. Milton. *Fr.* Paradise Lost, I. TreFS
(Fallen Angels, The, *longer sel.*) WoL
(Invocation: "Of Man's first disobedience, and the fruit.") DiPo; FaBoEn; PoEL-3; PoFS
(Of Man's First Disobedience.) FiP
("Of Man's first disobedience, and the fruit.") ATP; BEL; BoLiVe; CoBE; EnL; EnLi-1; EnLit; FosPo; MBW-1; OAEP; OuHeWo; SeEP; TOP
Invocation to the Muse. Richard Hughes. MoBrPo

Invocation to the Social Muse. Archibald MacLeish. LiTM; NAMP
Invocation to the Wind. Joseph Kalar. AnEnPo
Invocation to Urania. Milton. *Fr.* Paradise Lost, VII. FiP; OBS
Invocation to Youth. Laurence Binyon. OBEV; OBVV
Invoice, The. Robert Creeley. AmPC; FRC
Inward and outward to northward and southward the beach-lines linger and curl. The Marshes of Glynn. Sidney Lanier. AA; ATP; HBV; MAP; MCCG; MoAmPo (1942 ed.); PG (1933 ed.); TOP; WGRP; WHA
Inward Life, The. *Unknown.* SoP
Inward Light, The. Henry Septimus Sutton. WGRP
Inward Morning, The. Henry David Thoreau. AmP; AmPP (3d ed.); AP; CLwM; MAmP; MWA-1; NoP
Inward Peace. Matthew Arnold. *Fr.* Lines Written in Kensington Gardens. MaRV
Io. James Shirley. *See* Piping Peace.
Io! Paean! Io! sing. Triumph of the Whale. Charles Lamb. EtS; ImOP; OBRV
Io Victis! William Wetmore Story. AA; HBV; MaRV; OQP; WGRP
"Speak, History! Who are life's victors?" *sel.* ChIP
Iolanthe, *sels.* W. S. Gilbert.
Contemplative Sentry, The. ALV; EnLi-2; FiBHP; PoVP
House of Peers, The. InMe
(House of Lords, The.) TrGrPo
(Song: "When Britain really ruled the waves.") InP
Lord Chancellor's Song ("When you're lying awake"). CoBE; NBM; PCD, *much abr.*
(Nightmare.) LiTM; OxBoLi; PoRA (rev. ed.); ShBV-3; SiTL; YT
Said I to Myself, Said I. PoVP
Susceptible Chancellor, The. ALV; PoVP
Iölas' Epitaph. William Drummond of Hawthornden. AtBAP; PoEL-2
Ion, *sel.* Sir Thomas Noon Talfourd.
Friend, A, *fr.* I, ii. PoToHe
Iona. Arthur Cleveland Coxe. AA
Iona. Frederick Tennyson. GoBC
Ione ("Ione, fifteen years have o'er you passed."). Aubrey Thomas De Vere. GTSE; IrPN
Iowa. Michael Dennis Browne. NYBP
Iowa Farmer. Margaret Abigail Walker. Kal
Ipecacuanha. George Canning. ChTr
Iphigeneia and Agamemnon ("Iphigeneia, when she heard her doom"). Walter Savage Landor. *Fr.* The Hellenics. BEL; BeLS; EnLi-2; EPN
(Iphigeneia.) EnRP
Iphigeneia in Aulis. Euripides. *See* Iphigenia in Aulis.
Iphigenia. Tennyson. *Fr.* A Dream of Fair Women. BHV
Iphigenia [*or* Iphigeneia] in Aulis, *sels.* Euripides, *tr. fr. Greek.*
Aftermath, The. *tr. by* Richmond Lattimore. WaaP
Chorus: "And Pergamos," *tr. by* Hilda Doolittle ("H. D."). AWP; LiTW
"Had I, my father, the persuasive voice." EnLi-2
"Hear then what to my mind/ Deliberate thought presents." EnLi-2
Iphione. Thomas Caulfield Irwin. EnLoPo; IrPN
Ipsa Quae. Nicholas Breton. *See* Pastoral of Phillis and Corydon, A.
Ipsey Wipsey spider. *Unknown.* OxNR
Ipsissimus. Eugene Lee-Hamilton. PeVV
Ipswich Bar. Esther Willard Bates *and* Brainard L. Bates. HBMV
I'r hen Iaith a'i Chanedon. Walter Dowding. ACV
Iram Indeed Is Gone. Omar Khayyám, *tr. fr. Persian by* Edward Fitzgerald. *Fr.* The Rubáiyát. OnPM
Irapuato. Earle Birney. PeCV (1967 ed.); PoAn
Ireland. Stephen Lucious Gwynn. HBV
Ireland. Lionel Johnson. HBV
Ireland. Walter Savage Landor. GTBS-P
(Ireland Never Was Contented.) OxBoLi
Ireland. Edmund Leamy, Sr. JKCP
Ireland, *abr.* Denis Florence MacCarthy. PoFr
Ireland. John James Piatt. AA
Ireland. Dora Sigerson Shorter. OBEV; OBVV; OxBI
Ireland. Francis Stuart. NeIP
Ireland, Mother of Priests. Shane Leslie. JKCP
Ireland Never Was Contented. Walter Savage Landor. *See* Ireland.
Ireland, O Ireland. center of my longings. Ireland. Stephen Lucius Gwynn. HBV
Ireland Weeping. William Livingston, *tr. fr. Gaelic.* GoTS
Ireland with Emily. John Betjeman. GTBS-P
Irene, do you yet remember. The Chess-Board. "Owen Meredith." HBV; OBVV; VA
Iridescent vibrations of midsummer light, The. Irradiations, II [IV]. John Gould Fletcher. AnFE; APA; MAPA; TwAmPo
Iris. "Michael Field." VA
Iris, The. Gasetsu, *tr. fr. Japanese.* TiPo
Iris, *sel.* Oliver Wendell Holmes.
"If she had—Well! She longed, and knew not wherefore." LO
Iris. *unknown, tr. fr. Japanese by* William N. Porter. MPB
Iris-flower with topaz leaves, An. At Delos. Duncan Campbell Scott. PeCV
Iris, lilac, lily, milk. Lalique. Hal Porter. PoAu-2
Iris was yellow, the moon was pale, The. Iris. "Michael Field." VA
Irises. Padraic Colum. BoNaP
Irish, The. Francis Carlin. JKCP (1926 ed.)
Irish. Edward J. O'Brien. MoSiPe; SiSoSe
Irish Airman Foresees His Death, An. W. B. Yeats. AnEnPo; CABA; CoBMV; EnL; EnLi-2 (1949 ed.); FaBoCh; FaBoMo; GoJo; GTBS-P; ILP; LiTG; LiTM (rev. ed.); LoGBV; MaPo (1969 ed.); MMA; MoAB; MoBrPo; OBMV; OnPM; OtMeF; PAn; PoFr; PoPl; PoPo; TrGrPo; WaaP; WaP; WoL
Irish Astronomy. Charles G. Halpine. HBV
Irish Council Bill, 1907, The [*parody on the* Shan Van Vocht], *sel.* Susan Mitchell.
"Is it this you call Home Rule?" OnYI
Irish Dancer, The. *Unknown.* AnIL; EnL; FaBoCh; LoGBV; OBEV (new ed.); SeCePo
(I Am from Ireland.) MeEL
(I Am of Ireland.) CBEP; OnYI
(Ich Am of Irlonde.) AtBAP; PoEL-1
Irish faults are not so very new, The. Written on the Sense of Isolation in Contemporary Ireland. Robert Greacen. NeIP
Irish Franciscan, The. Rosa Mulholland. CAW
Irish Girl's Lament, The, *with music. Unknown.* ShS
Irish Grandmother. Katherine Edelman. AmFN; SiSoSe
Irish Harper and His Dog, The. Thomas Campbell. *See* Harper, The.
Irish History. William Allingham. IrPN
Irish Hotel. David Wevill. NYBP
Irish Hurrah, The. Thomas Osborne Davis. OnYI
Irish Hymn to Mary. *Unknown.* CAW
Irish Lady, *with music. Unknown.* OuSiCo
Irish Lamentation, An. Goethe, *tr. fr. German by* James Clarence Mangan. AWP
Irish Lords. Charles H. Souter. PoAu-1
Irish Love-Song, An. Robert Underwood Johnson. HBV
Irish Lullaby: "I've found my bonny babe a nest." Alfred Perceval Graves. HBV
Irish Molly O. *Unknown.* HBV
Irish Mother in the Penal Days, The. John Banim. AnIV
Irish Peasant Girl, The. Charles Joseph Kickham. AnIV; JKCP (1926 ed.)
Irish Peasant to His Mistress, The. Thomas Moore. ACP; OBEV (1st ed.); PoFr
(Thro' Grief and thro' Danger.) AnIV
Irish poets, learn your trade. W. B. Yeats. *Fr.* Under Ben Bulben. ML
Irish Rapparees, The. Sir Charles Gavan Duffy. AnIV; PoFr; VA
Irish Riddle, An. *Unknown. See* Lane, A.
Irish Schoolmaster, The. James A. Sidey. BOHV; FiBHP
Irish Song: I Know Where I'm Going. *Unknown. See* I Know Where I'm Going.
Irish Te Deum, The. *Unknown.* WHL
Irish Wife, The. Thomas D'Arcy McGee. HBV; VA
Irish Wild-Flower, An. Sarah Morgan Bryant Piatt. AA
Irish Wish, An. *Unknown.* TreFT
Irish Wolf-Hound, The. Denis Florence McCarthy. *Fr.* The Foray of Con O'Donnell. VA
Irishman, The. James Orr. DD
Irishman and the Lady, The. William Maginn. BOHV; HBV; VA
Irishman's Christening, An. *Unknown.* OnYI

Iron Characters, The. Howard Nemerov. TDP
Iron cross is black as death and hard as human hate, The. The Three Crosses. Edmund Vance Cooke. PEDC
Iron dragon nuzzles paving crust, The. House Demolished. Charles Malam. PoMa
Iron Fare. Marjorie Allen Seiffert. NP
Iron Gate, The, *sel.* Oliver Wendell Holmes.
"As on the gauzy wings." AA
Iron Horse, The. Israel Newman. PoMa
Iron, left in the rain. Rust. Mary Caroline Davies. HBMV
Iron long time hid in our mother earth. Volucre Ferrum. John Heath. SiCE
Iron Messiah, The. Vladimir Timofeevich Kirillov, *tr. fr. Russian by* George Z. Patrick. PoFr
Iron Music, The. Ford Madox Ford. HBMV
Iron Pot proposed, An. The Earthen Pot and the Iron Pot. La Fontaine. BoChLi
Iron-red rose-leaf, tinctured with. Rose. Lewis Thompson. AtBAP
Iron, sulphur, steam: the wastes. Saratoga Ending. Weldon Kees. NaP
Iron thing coming from Pompi, from the round-house. The Train. *Unknown.* TTY
Iron-Wind Dances. Lew Sarett. Thunderdrums, V. MAP
Iron Wine. Lola Ridge. NP
Ironic: LL.D. William Stanley Braithwaite. BANP
Irony, An. Plato, *tr. fr. Greek by* Sir Alexander Croke. OuHeWo
Irony. Louis Untermeyer. NP; TrJP
Irony of God. Eva Warner. ChIP
Irradiations, *sels.* John Gould Fletcher.
"Ant, An, crawling up a grass blade," XVI. LaNeLa
"Balancing of gaudy broad pavilions, The," IV [VI]. AnFE; APA; CoAnAm; MAPA; TwAmPo
"Brown bed of earth, still fresh and warm with love," VIII [XIV]. MAPA; TwAmPo
"Flickering of incessant rain," V [VII]. AnFE; APA; CoAnAm; MAP; MAPA; MoAmPo; NePA; TwAmPo
"Fountain blows its breathless spray, The," VI [VIII]. AnFE; APA; CoAnAm; MAPA; TwAmPo
"Iridescent vibrations of midsummer light, The," II [IV]. AnFE; APA; CoAnAm; MAPA; TwAmPo
"It is evening, and the earth," XXIX. LaNeLa
"Morning is clean and blue, The," XXII. AnAmPo; MAP; MoAmPo; NePA; NP
"Not noisily, but solemnly and pale," XXI. AnAmPo; NePA; NP
"O seeded grass, you army of little men," IX [XV]. AnAmPo; MAP; MAPA; MoAmPo; NeMA; NP; PoPo TwAmPo
"Over the roof-tops race the shadows of clouds," III [V]. AnFE; AnAmPo; AP; CoAnAm; LaNeLa; MAP; MAPA; MoAmPo; NePA; NP; PFY; TwAmPo
"Spattering of the rain upon pale terraces, The," I. AnFE; APA; CoAnAm; MAPA; TwAmPo
"Today you shall have but little song from me," X [XXXII]. MAPA; TwAmPo
"Trees, The, like great jade elephants," VII [X]. MAP; MAPA; MoAmPo; NeMA; NePA; TwAmPo
Irreconcilables. Arthur Gregor. NYBP
Irregular rattle (shutters) and, An. The Master of the Golden Glow. James Schuyler. ANYP
Irregular Sonnet for a Marraige. A. K. Ramanujan. NYTB
Irresistible bacilli are at work, The. With the Most Susceptible Element, the Mind, Already Turned under the Toxic Action. Walter Benton. WaP
Irresponsive silence of the land, The. Aloof. Christina Rossetti. *Fr.* The Thread of Life. BoLiVe; FaBoEn; OBEV; OBNC; OBVV; TrGrPo; VA; YT
Irreverent Brahmin, The. Arthur Guiterman. LHV
Irrevocable. Mary Wright Plummer. WGRP
Irrigation. Ann Nolan Clark. StVeCh (1955 ed.)
Irritable Song. Russell Atkins. AmNP
Irving. James Russell Lowell. *Fr.* A Fable for Critics. AnNE
("What! Irving? thrice welcome, warm heart and fine brain.") CoBA; MWA-1
Is/ Georgia grown. My Beige Mom. Edward Spriggs. BF
Is a caterpillar ticklish? Only My Opinion. Monica Shannon. FaPON; MPB; SoPo; StVeCh (1955 ed.); TiPo
Is a condition. New England. William Carlos Williams. PoeP
I's a little Alabama coon. Little Alabama Coon. Hattie Starr. AA
Is a monstrance. The Moon Is the Number 18. Charles Olson. NMP
Is an enchanted thing. The Mind Is an Enchanting Thing. Marianne Moore. AP; CMoP; CoBMV; CrMa; InvP; MoAB; MoAmPo (1950 ed.); MoPo; OxBA; PIA; Po; ReMP; TwAmPo
"Is anybody there?" said the Traveller. *See* "Is there anybody there?"
Is Bakuba memory. Every Harlem Face Is Afromanism Surviving. Edward S. Spriggs. BF
I's boun' to see my gal to-night. On the Road. Paul Laurence Dunbar. AA
Is 5, *sels.* E. E. Cummings.
"It really must/ be nice," I. AnAmPo; YaD
My Sweet Old Etcetera, III. AnAmPo; CABA; NAMP; NePA; OxBA; PoPl; WaaP; WaP
"Poets yeggs and thirsties," II. AnAmPo
Is God Dead? Martin Radcliffe. OCS
Is God invisible? This very room. Sonnet XI. Adele Greeff. GoYe
Is Here, As If. G. Bishop-Dubjinsky. ThO
Is It a Dream? G. A. Studdert-Kennedy. MaRV; PoToHe
"Is it a dream?" I asked. To which my fellow. The Fulfillment. Delmore Schwartz. FiMAP
Is it a reed that's shaken by the wind. Calais, August, 1802. Wordsworth. MERP; Sonn
"Is it a sail?" she asked. From the Harbor Hill. Gustav Kobbé. HBV
Is It a Sin to Love Thee? *Unknown.* BLPA
Is it any better in Heaven, my friend Ford. To Ford Madox Ford in Heaven. William Carlos Williams. AmPP (5th ed.)
Is it as plainly in our living shown. On Seeing Weather-beaten Trees. Adelaide Crapsey. InP; MAP; MCCG; MoAmPo (1942 ed.); NeMA
Is it bad to have come here. Gallant Château. Wallace Stevens. MAP; MoAB; MoAmPo
Is It Because I Am Black? Joseph Seamon Cotter, Jr. BANP
Is It Because of Some Dear Grace. Louis Golding. TrJP
Is it because that lad is dead. Vision. Frank Sidgwick. MMA
Is it birthday weather for you, dear soul? Birthday Poem for Thomas Hardy. C. Day Lewis. CoBMV
Is it dirty/ does it look dirty. Song. Frank O'Hara. CAD
Is it enough? I'm Here. Theodore Roethke. *Fr.* Meditations of an Old Woman. CoAP; NYBP
Is it enough to think to-day. Memorial Day. Annette Wynne. MaRV; OHIP
Is It Far to Go? C. Day Lewis. AtBAP; GTBS-D
Is it for fear to wet a widow's eye? Sonnets, IX. Shakespeare. MasP; Sonn
Is It for This I Live? Sotère Torregian. YAP
Is it her nature or is it her will. Amoretti, XLI. Spenser. OAEP
Is it illusion? or does there a spirit from perfecter ages. A Spirit from Perfecter Ages. Arthur Hugh Clough. *Fr.* Amours de Voyage, II. EPN; OBNC
Is it indeed so? If I lay here dead. Sonnets from the Portuguese, XXIII. Elizabeth Barrett Browning. VA
Is It Morning? Is It the Little Morning? Delmore Schwartz. ELU
Is it naught? Is it naught. Cuba. Edmund Clarence Stedman. PAH
Is it not a delicious fancy. Thinking of a Master. Richard Church. HaMV
Is it not better at an early hour. On Timely Death [*or* On Living Too Long]. Walter Savage Landor. TOP; VA
Is it not by his high superfluousness we know. The Excesses of God. Robinson Jeffers. MaRV; MoRP
Is it not fine to fling against loaded dice. Hughie at the Inn. Elinor Wylie. NYBP
Is it not interesting to see. Thoughts on the Christian Doctrine of Eternal Hell. Stevie Smith. PPON
Is it not strange that men can die. Reflection. W. J. Turner. OBMV
Is It Not Sure? *Unknown.* CBEP
Is it not sure a deadly pain. *Unknown.* EG; EnLoPo
Is It Nothing to You? L. James Kindig. BePJ
"Is It Nothing to You?" May Probyn. GoBC; JKCP; OBEV (new ed.); OBVV; VA

Is it nothing to you, all ye that pass by. Is It Nothing to You? L. James Kindig. BePJ
Is It Possible. Sir Thomas Wyatt. BWP; CBEP; ELP; EnRePo; LoBV; MaPo; NoP
("Is it possible that so high debate.") FCP; SiPS
(Varium et Mutabile.) OBSC; QFR
(Ys Yt Possyble.) PoEL-1
"Is it really very far." Little Miss Pitt. William Wise. TiPo (1959 ed.)
Is It Really Worth the While? *Unknown.* BLPA
Is it serious, or funny? B. Larry Eigner. NeAP
Is it so far from thee. The Chamber over the Gate. Longfellow. AP; MAmP
Is it so small a thing. Matthew Arnold. *Fr.* Empedocles on Etna. OBEV; OBVV
Is it the beauty of the rose. The Reversible Metaphor. "Troubadour." InMe
Is it the fecundating life you see around. Stranger, Why Do You Wonder So? K. B. Jones-Quartey. PBA
Is it the horse explains the field. Man Watching. Alan Brownjohn. NYTB
Is it the hour? We leave this resting place. The Wayfarers. Rupert Brooke. MoLP
Is it the petals falling from the rose? The Dance of the Daughters of Herodias. Arthur Symons. BrPo
Is it the tinkling of mandolins which disturbs you? Little Ivory Figures Pulled with String. Amy Lowell. AnFE; APA; CoAnAm; MAPA; NAMP; TwAmPo; ViBoPo
Is it the wind of the dawn that I hear in the pine overhead? Duet. Tennyson. *Fr.* Becket. SiSw
Is it the wind, the many-tongued, the weird. The Draft Riot. Charles De Kay. PAH
Is it, then, regret for buried time. In Memoriam A. H. H., CXVI. Tennyson. BEL; EnLi-2; EPN; MaPo; OAEP; ViPo; VP
Is it this sky's vast vault or ocean's sound. The Monochord. Dante Gabriel Rossetti. The House of Life, LXXIX. MaVP; PoVP; ViPo
Is it this you call Home Rule? Susan Mitchell. *Fr.* The Irish Council Bill, 1907 [*parody on the* Shan Van Vocht]. OnYI
Is it thy will that I should wax and wane. Apologia. Oscar Wilde. PoVP
Is it thy will thy image should keep open. Sonnets, LXI. Shakespeare. LO; PoEL-2
Is it time now to go away? Death of a Vermont Farm Woman. Barbara Howes. MoAmPo (1962 ed.)
Is It True? Sarah Williams. BLPA
Is it true, then, my girl, that you mean it? Yes? H. C. Bunner. HBV
Is It True, Ye Gods, Who Treat Us. Arthur Hugh Clough. *See* "Wen Gott Betrügt, Ist Wohl Betrogen."
Is it Ulysses that approaches from the east. The World As Meditation. Wallace Stevens. BWP; MaPo (1969 ed.); MoAB; PoeP
Is It Well with the Child? Christina Rossetti. OBEV (1st ed.)
"Is John Smith within?" Mother Goose. GaP; OTPC; OxNR; RIS; SAS
Is less like that of a bean. The Manner of a Poet's Germination. José Garcia Villa. PP
Is life itself but many ways of thought? Substitution. Anne Spencer. CDC
Is Life Worth Living? Alfred Austin. OTPC (1946 ed.)
"Is life worth living? Yes, so long," *sel.* MaRV; TreFS
Is Love a Boy? *Unknown.* EnRePo; ReIE
Is Love Not Everlasting? Ronald McCuaig. BoAV
Is Love, Then, So Simple? Irene Rutherford McLeod. HBMV; WHA
Is man's destructive lust insatiable? Kyrie. David Gascoyne. *Fr.* Miserere. NeBP
Is Mary in the dairy? Where's Mary? Ivy O. Eastwick. TiPo
Is memory most of miseries miserable. Memory. Dante Gabriel Rossetti. CBEP
Is murther no sin? or a sin so cheape. To Pontius Washing His Blood-Stained Hands. Richard Crashaw. MaMe
Is My Lover on the Sea? "Barry Cornwall." EtS
Is My Team Plowing? A. E. Housman. A Shropshire Lad, XXVII. AnEnPo; AtBAP; BoLiVe; CMoP; CoBMV; EnL; ILP; LiTM (rev. ed.); MaPo; MeWo; MoAB; MoBrPo; OAEP (2d ed.); OBEV (new ed.); OnPP; OuHeWo; PG; PoPo; PoSa; PoVP; SeCeV; TrGrPo; ViPo; VP; WePo; WHA
Is not man's greatest heart's desire. Omnia Vanitas. Dugald Buchanan. GoTS
Is not one's life itself an act of daring. The Venture of Faith. Francis Greenwood Peabody. MaRV
Is not something other. Everything That Is. Daniel Berrigan. TwAmPo
Is not spendthrift of faith. Jack. Gwendolyn Brooks. TPM
Is not the body more that meat? the soul. The Soul. Hartley Coleridge. Sonn
Is not the work done? Nay, for still the scars. A Prayer for the Healing of the Wounds of Christ. Laurence Housman. MaRV
Is not thilke same a goteheard prowde. July. Spenser. *Fr.* The Shepheardes Calender. ReIE
Is not this April of our brief desire. April of Our Desire. Lola Ridge. MAP; MoAmPo (1942 ed.)
Is not this hearth, where goats now feed? The Hearth of Urien. Llywarch the Aged. ChTr
Is not thy sacred hunger of science. To Mr. B. B. John Donne. MaMe
Is patiently/ making my mask as I sleep. Death. Philip Dow. QAH
Is Praxinoa at home? The Syracusan Women. Theocritus. *Fr.* Idylls. WoL
Is seacoast fog, is starfish caught. New England Is New England Is New England. Brenda Heloise Green. GoYe
Is she/ Thoughtless of life. Nun Snow. Alfred Kreymborg. AnFE; APA; CoAnAm; MAPA; TwAmPo
Is she dead?/ She is what you would have her. John Webster. *Fr.* The Duchess of Malfi. AnFE
Is she not come? The messenger was sure. Tristram and Iseult. Matthew Arnold. PoVP; ViPo; ViPP; VP
Is she to bee buried in Christian buriall, that wilfully seekes her owne salvation? Shakespeare. *Fr.* Hamlet, V, i. AtBAP
"Is Sin, then, fair?" The Sting of Death. Frederick George Scott. OBCV; PeCV
Is situated at the foot of Chocorua. Wilbur's Garden. Walter Clark. NYTB
Is some such word. Propriety. Marianne Moore. UnS
Is something like the rest. The Politics of Rich Painters. LeRoi Jones. CoPo
Is that dance slowing in the mind of man. The Dance. Theodore Roethke. Four for Sir John Davies, I. AP; CoBMV; CrMA; FiMAP; MoAmPo (1962 ed.); NePoAm; ReMP; UnS
Is that enchanted moan only the swell. Tennyson. *Fr.* Maud. SyP
"Is that the Three-and-Twentieth, Strabo mine." The Legion. Robert Graves. BrPo
Is that you, Barnes? Now see here, friend. The Crab-Apple Crisis. George MacBeth. HYE
"Is that you, Peggy? my goodness me!" Peggy's Wedding. Thomas Edward Brown. EnLit
Is the basketball coach a homosexual lemon manufacturer? Aus einer Kindheit. Kenneth Koch. AmPC
Is the eternal voice, Coltrane is. Orishas. Larry Neal. NBP
"Is the grandson." I. Robert Creeley. FRC
Is the Moon Tired? Christina Rossetti. *Fr.* Sing-Song. BoTP; StVeCh
Is the noise of grief in the palace over the river. A Mother in Egypt. Marjorie Pickthall. CaP; HBV
Is the unexpected ring of the Cancer. Love. Gerald Jonas. PV
Is the way o'ercast with shadows? Jesus Understands. *Unknown.* BLRP
Is there a cause why we should wake the dead? The Yew-Tree. Vernon Watkins. EaLo; LiTB
Is there a great green commonwealth of Thought. Sonnet. John Masefield. *Fr.* Sonnets ("Long long ago"). ILP; LiTM; MoBrPo
Is there a madness underneath the sun. The Starred Mother. Robert Whitaker. PGD
Is there a whim-inspirèd fool. A Bard's Epitaph. Burns. EiPP; InP
Is there any season, O my soul. Hegemon to Praxinoe. Walter Savage Landor. PeER
"Is there anybody [*or* Is anybody] there?" said the Traveller. The Listeners. Walter de la Mare. AnFE; AWP; BBV (1952 ed.); BoLiVe; BrPo; CaFP; CMoP; CoBMV; EnLit; FaFP; FaPON; GTBS-D; GTBS-W; GTSL; HBV; HBVY; HoPM; ILP; InP; InvP; JAWP; LiTB; LiTM; MaC; MaRV; MemP; MoAB; MoBrPo; MoPo; MoVE; NAMP; NeMA;

Is (continued)
NP; OAEP (2d ed.); OBEV (new ed.); OBMV; OBVV; OnMSP; OtMeF; PCD; Po; PoPl; PoPo; PoRA; POTE; RePo; SeCeV; ShBV-3; ThWaDe; TOP; TreF; TrGrPo; ViBoPo; WBP; WHA
Is there anyone here who has a desire. Poor Diggings. Mart Taylor. SGR
"Is there anything." Wise Sarah and the Elf. Elizabeth J. Coatsworth. PoMS
Is there anything as I can do ashore for you. A Valediction (Liverpool Docks). John Masefield. FaBoTw; OBMV
Is there anything else that is better worth. Nothing Better. *Unknown.* STF
Is there anything I can do. The Key to Everything. May Swenson. NePoEA
Is there anything in Spring so fair. Apple Blossoms. Helen Adams Parker. BoTP
Is There for Honest Poverty. Burns. *See* Man's a Man for A' That, A.
Is there never a man in all Scotland. Johnnie Armstrong (B *vers.*). *Unknown.* ESPB
Is there no greater good than health and ease. Deliver Us From. Amelia Josephine Burr. OQP
Is there no hope? the sick man said. The Sick Man and the Angel. John Gay. *Fr.* Fables. CEP
"Is there no other way, O God?" Lean on Me. *Unknown.* SoP
Is there no place/ Left for repentance. Satan's Pride. Milton. *Fr.* Paradise Lost, IV. MaRV
Is there no secret place on the face of the earth? The Moneyless Man. Henry Thompson Stanton. BLPA
Is there no splendid Himalayan height. The Better Part. Bhartrihari. OnPM
Is there no vision in a lovely place? William Montgomerie. *Fr.* Kinfauns Castle. OxBS
Is there no voice in the world to come crying. New Dreams for Old. Cale Young Rice. HBV
Is there one desires to hear. Killarney. William Larminie. *Fr.* Fand. AnIV
Is there so small a range. Keats. *Fr.* Sleep and Poetry. BEL
Is There Some Desert. Edward Everett Hale. FaChP
Is there some problem in your life to solve? God's Key [*or* He Keeps the Key]. *Unknown.* SoP; STF
Is there still any shadow there. Memo. Kenneth Fearing. CMoP
Is this a dagger which I see before me. Macbeth's Words Before Murdering. Shakespeare. *Fr.* Macbeth, II, i. TreFS
Is this a fast, to keep? To Keep a True Lent [*or* A True Lent]. Robert Herrick. AnAnS-2; BEL; DD; EnLi-1; HBV; MaRV; OHIP; PoRL; SCEP-2; TOP; TRV
Is this a holy thing to see. Holy Thursday. Blake. *Fr.* Songs of Experience. CEP; CoBE; EiPP; EnL; EnLi-2 (1949 ed.); EnPE; EnRP; ERoP-1; ILP; NoP; OAEP; PeER; PoE; PoeP; PoIE; StP
Is this a time to be cloudy and sad. The Gladness of Nature. Bryant. DD; HBV; HBVY; OTPC
Is This Africa? Roland Tombekai Dempster. PBA
Is this dancing sunlight. Sumphony. Frank Horne. AmNP
"Is this Henry, my own true love." Love Henry. *Unknown.* BFSS
Is This Presumption? Louise H. Toness. ChIP
Is this Sir Philip Sidney, this loud clown. The Knight in Disguise. Vachel Lindsay. HBV
Is this the face that thrills with awe. The Face of Jesus Christ. Christina Rossetti. *Fr.* the Descent from the Cross. BePJ; ChIP
Is this the front—this level sweep of life. At the Front. John Erskine. HBMV
Is this the grace of God, this strange sweet calm? Peace. Frances Ridley Havergal. SoP
Is this the Lake, the cradle of the storms. Written on the Banks of Wastwater during a Calm. "Christopher North." OBRV
Is this the man by whose decree abide. Imperator Augustus. Sir Rennell Rodd. VA
Is this the night the world must burn like Troy? Like Ilium. Thomas Merton. JKCP (1955 ed.)
Is this the price of beauty! Fairest thou. Charleston. Richard Watson Gilder. PAH
Is this the region, this the soil, the clime. The Fall of the Angels [*or* Satan Ponders His Fallen State]. Milton. *Fr.* Paradise Lost, I. FiP; MyFE; TreFS
"Is this the road that climbs above and bends." The Chalk-Pit. Edward Thomas. BrPo
Is this the Seine? An Ode to Spring in the Metropolis. Sir Owen Seaman. FiBHP; WhC
Is this the street? Never a sign of life. Stormy Night. W. R. Rodgers. OxBI
Is This the Time to Halt? Charles Sumner Hoyt. MaRV (Is This the Time to Sound Retreat?) BLRP
Is this the tribute you have brought to Me. Voice in a Cathedral. Thomas Curtis Clark. ChIP
Is this to live?—to cower and stand aside. The Eleventh Hour. Francis St. Vincent Morris. WePo
Is This Your Church? *Unknown.* SoP
Is this your duty? Never lay your ear. "Man Is a Lumpe Where All Beasts Kneaded Be." C. S. Lewis. BoPe
Is thy cruse of comfort failing? Compensation. Elizabeth Rundle Charles. SoP
Is thy face like thy mother's, my fair child! Byron. *Fr.* Childe Harold's Pilgrimage, III. BEL; BoLiVe; ChER; CoBE; EnL; EnLi-2; EnLit; EnRP; EPN; ERoP-2; MBW-2; MERP; OAEP; TOP
"Is thy husband hang'd?" "He was, but he is nat." Of a Husband Hang'd. John Heywood. ReIE
"Is Thy Servant a Dog?" John Banister Tabb. JKCP
Is Time on my hands? Yes, it is. Thoughts Thought While Waiting for a Pronouncement from a Doctor, a Big Executive, the Department of Internal Revenue, or Any Other Momentous Pronouncer. Ogden Nash. SiTL
Is to love, this—to nurse a name. Poem. Rhoda Coghill. NeIP
Is true Freedom but to break. Stanzas on Freedom. James Russell Lowell. GN
"Is water nigh?" The Gift of Water. Hamlin Garland. AA; AnAmPo
Is your place a small place? Your Place. John Oxenham. BLRP; FaChP; MaRV; OQP; SoP; TRV
Isaac a ransom while he lay. Didn't Old Pharaoh Get Los'? *Unknown.* BoAN-1
Isaac and Archibald. E. A. Robinson. AmPP; MAmP; OxBA
Isabel. Sydney Dobell. OBVV
Isabel. *Unknown, tr. fr. French-Canadian by* George T. Lanigan. WHW
Isabel Jones & Curabel Lee. David McCord. GoTP
Isabel met an enormous bear. Adventures of Isabel. Ogden Nash. CenHV; MoAmPo; MoShBr; NeMA; OnMSP; PDV; ShM; TiPo (1959 ed.)
Isabel of the lily-white hand. Isabel. *Unknown.* WHW
Isabel Sparrow. Mary Oliver. NYTB
Isabella, *sel.* Sir Charles Hanbury Williams.
Old General, The. OBEC
Isabella Condemns Tyranny. Shakespeare. *Fr.* Measure for Measure, II, ii. TreFT
Isabella; or, The Pot of Basil. Keats. EnRP; MERP; ViBoPo, *much abr.*
Sels.
Beginning of Love, The. UnPo (1st ed.)
Proud Florentines, The. PoFr
"With her two brothers this fair lady dwelt." PoG
Isabelle. James Hogg. Par
Isador and Ida Strauss. E. J. Pratt. *Fr.* The *Titanic.* TwCaPo
Isaiah, *sels.* Bible, *O.T.*
All Flesh Is Grass, XL: 6-8. TrJP
"And it shall come to pass in the day that the Lord shall give thee rest," XIV: 3-19. PoFr
Behold, My Servant, LII: 13-LIII: 9. OuHeWo
"But they that wait upon the Lord shall renew their strength," XL: 31. TiPo (1952 ed.)
Comfort When Work Seems Difficult, XLI: 6-7, 9-10. BoC
Comfort Ye, Comfort Ye My People, XL: 1-11. EaLo; TrJP (1-5); WoL, XL *and* LV
(Comfort Ye My People, XL: 1-11.) TreFS
Downfall of the Tyrant ("How hath the oppressor ceased"), XIV: 4-19. TrGrPo
For Ye Shall Go out with Joy, LV: 6-12. TreFT
"For Zion's sake will I not hold my Peace," LXII: 1, 6, 10. PoFr (For Zion's Sake, 1-5). TrJP
Hear the Word of the Lord, I: 10-23. TrJP
Ho, Everyone That Thirsteth, LV: 1-3, 6-7. MaRV

How Beautiful Upon the Mountains, LII: 7-10. TrJP
I Waste Away, XXIV: 16-20. TrJP
In the End of Days, II: 2-4. TrJP
Intemperance, V: 11-12 (*Moulton, Modern Reader's Bible*). MaRV
Isaiah's Angels, VI: 1-8. BoC
Israel, My Servant, XLI: 8-16. TrJP
Let Me Sing of My Well-Beloved, V. TrJP
Messiah, The ("Behold, a virgin shall conceive"), VII: 14-25. AWP
My Thoughts Are Not Your Thoughts, LV: 8-13. TrJP
Peaceable Kingdom, The, XI:6. FaPON; LiTW (6-9)
Perfect Peace, XXVI: 3. TRV
Power from God ("Hast thou not known"), XL: 28-31. TreFT
Prince of Peace, The ("The people that walked in darkness"), IX: 2, 6-7. ChrBoLe; BoPe (6)
Proclamation ("Thus saith the Lord, the Redeemer of Israel"), *arr. fr.* XLIX. StaSt
Rod of Jesse, The, XI: 1-10. AWP; OuHeWo, XI: 1-9, LIII: 10-12
(And There Shall Come Forth, XI: 1-9.) TrJP
Song of the Harlot, XXIII: 16. TrJP
"Therefore the Lord Himself shall give you a sign," VII: 14-15, *Douay vers.* ISi
They That Wait upon the Lord, XL: 28-31. TRV
("Hast thou not known? hast thou not heard, that the everlasting God," XL: 28-31, XLIX: 13-16.) BoC
Vision of the Day of Judgment, LXIII (*Moulton, Modern Reader's Bible*). WGRP
Watchman, What of the Night? XXI: 11-15. AWP
Whom Shall One Teach, XXVIII: 9-13. TrJP
"Wilderness and the solitary place shall be glad for them, The." XXV: 1. BoPe
"Woe to thee that spoilest," XXXIII: 1-4. PoFr
"Wolf also shall dwell with the lamb, The," XI: 6-9. BoPe; PDV
Isaiah of Souillac, The. W. S. Merwin. PoDB
Isaiah, the country-boy, marched against the jazz. Babylon, Babylon, Babylon the Great. Vachel Lindsay. LiPo
Isaiah's Angels. Isaiah, VI: 1-8 Bible, *O.T.* BoC
Isaias. Bible, *O.T.* (*Douay vers.*). *See* Isaiah.
Isbrand's Song. Thomas Lovell Beddoes. *Fr.* Death's Jest Book, III, iii. PoE
(Song by Isbrand.) OBNC
(Squats on a Toad-Stool under a Tree.) InvP
I'se de niggah, I'se de niggah. The Song of Dark Waters. Roy Helton. IHA
I'se got religion an' I doan care. Mandy's Religion. Alice Corbin. *Fr.* Echoes of Childhood. PoNe
Iseult of Brittany. Matthew Arnold. Tristram and Iseult, III. PoVP
Ishmael. Herbert Edward Palmer. OBEV (new ed.); POTE
Isis Wanderer. Kathleen Raine. FaBoMo; OxBS
Island, The, *sel.* Byron.
Highlands Swelling Blue, The. OBRV
Island, The. Richard Henry Dana. *Fr.* The Buccaneer. AnNE
Island, The. Séan Jennett. JKCP (1955 ed.); NeIP; SeCePo
Island, The. Christopher Morley. HT
Island, The. Edwin Muir. PoIE
Island, The. Giuseppe Ungaretti, *tr. fr. Italian by* Creighton Gilbert. LiTW
Island, The ("If the French have a notion"). *Unknown. Fr.* Ballads on Napoleon. CoBE
Island, The. George Woodcock. MoCV; NeBP
Island, The, *sel.* Francis Brett Young.
Atlantic Charter; 1942. BBV (1951 ed.); PAL
(Atlantic Charter, A.D. 1620-1942.) AmFN; TiPo (1952 ed.)
Island Boatman's Love-Croon, The. Robert Farren. CoBE
Island Cemetery, The. W. H. Auden. NePoAm-2
Island Cook. William Goodreau. NYTB
Island Dogs ("The island crawls with dogs"). Charles G. Bell. NePoAm-2
Island Galaxy, An. John Ciardi. ToPo
Island in the Moon, An, *sels.* Blake.
Good English Hospitality. CoMu
(Mayors, The.) CH
"Hail, Matrimony, Made of Love." ERoP-1
"When Old Corruption First Begun." ERoP-1
Island lies nine leagues away, The. The Island. Richard Henry Dana. *Fr.* The Buccaneer. AnNE
Island Moment. Ian Hamilton Finlay. NMP
Island of bitter memories, thickly sown. Irish History. William Allingham. IrPN
Island of Night. Galway Kinnell. NePoAm
Island of Saints, still constant, still allied. Erin. Kenelm H. Digby. CAW
Island of shadow/ Silk of the kine. Nostalgie d'Automne. Leslie Daiken. NeIP
Island of Shadows, The. Richard Garnett. VA
Island of the Blest, The. Pindar, *tr. fr. Greek by* Gilbert West. *Fr.* Olympian Odes, II. OBEC
Island Quarry. Hart Crane. CrMA
Island that had flowered to the sun, The. The Coming of Dusk upon a Village in Haiti. Henry Rago. HoPM
Islands, The. Hilda Doolittle ("H. D."). MAP; MoAmPo; PG
Islands. Rachel Field. GFA
Islands. Ralph Pomeroy. CoPo
Islands; a Song. John Malcolm Brinnin. AnFE; CoAnAm
Islands and peninsulas, continents and capes. Geography. Eleanor Farjeon. BrR; FaPON
Islands and the mountains in the day, The. Shelley. *Fr.* The Revolt of Islam. ChER
Islands are islands though in the steady sea. Islands. Ralph Pomeroy. CoPo
Islands are subtle places, still. Islands; a Song. John Malcolm Brinnin. AnFE; CoAnAm
Islands of the Ever Living, The. *Tr. fr. Irish by* Padraic Colum. AnIV
Islands of the Sea, The. George Edward Woodberry. MC; PAH
Islands which whisper to the ambitious, The. At Epidaurus. Lawrence Durrell. LiTB; MoPo
Isle, The. Shelley. SyP
Isle of a summer sea. Cuba. Harvey Rice. PAH
Isle of Apple-Trees, The. Fritz S. Burnell. BoAu
Isle of Arran. Alastair Reid. WIRo
Isle of the [the] Long Ago, The. Benjamin Franklin Taylor. FaFP; HBV; PTK; TreFS; WBLP
(Long Ago, The.) BLPA; NeHB
Isle of Lost Dreams. "Fiona Macleod." VA
Isle of Portland, The. A. E. Housman. MoBrPo; PoVP
Isle of the Long Ago, The. Benjamin Franklin Taylor. *See* Isle of Long Ago, The.
Isle of trees full foliaged in a meadow, An. Sonnet. Thomas Caulfield Irwin. IrPN
Isled in the midnight air. The Moth. Walter de la Mare. BrPo; FaBoEn; MoVE; NoP; ShBV-3
Isles, The. Sir Charles G. D. Roberts. VA
Isles of Greece, The. Byron. *Fr.* Don Juan, III. AnFE; AWP; BEL, *longer sel.*; CBEP; ChTr; CoBE; EnLit; EPN, *longer sel.*; FaBoEn; FiP; HBV; HT, *abr.*; InPo; LiTB; MemP; OBEV; OBRV; OTPC, *sts.* 1-3; PoFr; PoIE; PTK; RoGo; SeCeV, *longer sel.*; TOP; TreFS; ViBoPo; WHA
Isles of Greece, The. Demetrios Capetanakis. GTBS-P
Isn't it. Epigram. Alfred Kreymborg. BoLP
Isn't it strange/ That princes and kings. A Bag of Tools. R. L. Sharpe. BLPA; FaChP; MaRV; NeHB; PoToHe (new ed.); TreFT; YaD
Isn't it strange some people make. Some People. Rachel Field. FaPON; PDV
Isn't she soft and still? Captive. Marion Strobel. ErPo
"Isn't the violet a dear little flower? And the daisy, too." The Lay Preacher Ponders. Idris Davies. ACV; FaBoTw
"Isn't this Joseph's son?"—ay, it is He. Jesus the Carpenter. Catherine C. Liddell. DD; HBV; VA
Isolation. Arthur Hugh Clough. *Fr.* Dipsychus, Pt. II, sc. ii. OBVV
("Where are the great, whom thou would'st wish to praise thee?") EPN
Isolation. Josephine Preston Peabody. AA; AnAmPo
Isolation of Genius, The. Byron. *See* He Who Ascends to Mountain-Tops.
Isolation: To Marguerite. Matthew Arnold. Switzerland, IV. MBW-2; PoVP; TreFT; ViPP; VP
(To Marguerite.) CBEP
Isolda was an Irish queen who always spoke in German. Tristan and Isolda. Newman Levy. InMe
Israel. Israel Zangwill. TrJP
Israel Freyer's Bid for Gold. Edmund Clarence Stedman. PAH
Israel, My Servant. Isaiah, XLI: 8-16, Bible, *O.T.* TrJP
Israeli Navy, The. Marvin Bell. YAP

Israel's Duration. Judah Halevi, *tr. fr. Hebrew by* Nina Davis Salaman. TrJP
Israfel. Poe. AA; AmePo; AmP; AmPo; AmPP; AnAmPo; AnFE; AP; APA; AWP; BoLiVe; CoAnAm; CoBA; HBV; InPo; LiTA; MAmP; MWA-1; NePA; OxBA; PFY; PoEL-4; PoPo; RG; TDP; TreFS; TSW; WHA
Israfiddlestrings. *Unknown.* BOHV
Issue of great Jove, draw near, you muses nine, The! The Garden. Nicholas Grimald. ReIE
"Issues from the hand of God, the simple soul." Animula. T. S. Eliot. AmPP; LiTB; MAP; MoAmPo (1942 ed.); MoPW; MoVE; TwAmPo
Istanbul. 21 March. I woke today. The Thousand and Second Night. James Merrill. NYBP
Isthmian Odes. Pindar. *See* Odes.
It. Richmond Lattimore. PP
It ain't gonna rain, it ain't gonna snow. Ain't Gonna Rain. *Unknown.* AS
It ain't no jive. Jacques Wakefield. WSL
It ain't no use to grumble and complain. Rain. James Whitcomb Riley. BoNaP
It ain't the failures he may meet. The Quitter. *Unknown.* BLPA; WBLP
It ain't the funniest thing a man can do. The First Settler's Story. Will Carleton. IHA
It ain't the guns nor armament. Co-operation. J. Mason Knox. BLPA; YaD
It all began so easy. Christina. Louis MacNeice. OxBI
It Always Happens. Horace, *tr. fr. Latin by* Thomas Charles Baring. Odes, I, 33. UnTE
It autumne was, and on our hemisphere. Song. William Drummond of Hawthornden. OBS
It avails not, time nor place—distance avails not. Walt Whitman. *Fr.* Crossing Brooklyn Ferry. NeMA
It baffles the foreigner like an idiom. Drug Store. Karl Shapiro. AmPP (4th ed.); CMoP; FiMAP; ILP; MoVE; OxBA; TwCP
It befell at Martynmas [*or* Marynmas]. Captain Car; or, Edom o Gordon. *Unknown.* BaBo; EnLit; ESPB (A *vers.*); OAEP; TOP; ViBoFo
It being in this life forbidden to move. The Death-Wish. Louis MacNeice. AnFE
It bends far over Yell'ham Plain. The Comet at Yell'ham. Thomas Hardy. CMoP; ExPo
It Bids Pretty Fair. Robert Frost. CaFP
It brims in the white cistern; flows. A Meditation upon the Toothache. Laurence Lerner. NePoEA-2
It came! The East Wind. George Cabot Lodge. AmePo
It came so quietly—the first gray light. Resurrection. Ida Norton Munson. ChIP
It came to pass. Brother Ass and St. Francis. John Banister Tabb. AnAmPo
It came to pass after this, that Absalom the son of David had a fair sister. Second Samuel, Bible, *O.T.* LO
It Came upon the Midnight Clear. Edmund Hamilton Sears. FaPON; MaRV; OTPC (1946 ed.); PCH, *st.* 1; TreFT; YaCaBo, *with music*
(Angels' Song, The.) AA; AmePo; BePJ; PEDC; SoP
(Christmas Carol: "It came upon the midnight clear.") PTK
(Christmas Carols.) HBV; HBVY
(Peace on Earth.) FaFP
It can be beautiful this sitting by oneself all alone. Moon-Watching by Lake Chapala. Al Young. WSL
It Can Be Done. *Unknown.* PoToHe (new ed.)
It can be so tedious, a bore. Moods of Rain. Vernon Scannell. BoNaP
It Cannot Be. David Banks Sickels. *See* Reincarnation.
It cannot be that men who are the seed. Our First Century. George Woodberry. AmePo; PAH
It cannot be Where is that mightie joy. The Temper. George Herbert. MaMe; SCEP-1
It can't be the passing of time that casts. Rip. James Wright. NaP
It chanced his lips did meet her forehead cool. Modern Love, VI. George Meredith. ViBoPo; ViPo; VP
It chanced of late, a shepherd's swain. A Fiction [*or* Cupid's Pastime]. *At. to* Francis Davison *and to* "A. W." TuPP; UnTE
It chanced one day they met. Each in surprise. Seven Sad Sonnets, VII. Mary Aldis. HBMV
It chanced that I, the other day. The Bore. Horace. *Fr.* Satires. EnLi-1; OuHeWo
It chanced to be our washing day. Oliver Wendell Holmes. *Fr.* The September Gale. FiBHP
It comes to me more and more. The Love of the Father. *Unknown.* BLRP
It comes to this. Revelation. David Meltzer. NeAP
It comes to this, in plain words. Victory. Eileen Duggan. AnNZ
It costs me never a stab nor squirm. Thought for a Sunshiny Morning. Dorothy Parker. PoMa
It Couldn't Be Done. Edgar A. Guest. BLPA; FaBoBe; FaFP; NeHB; OTD; PTK; SoP; STF; TreFS; WBLP; YaD
It crawled away from 'neath my feet. That Hill. Blanche Taylor Dickinson. CDC
It did not last; the Devil shouting Ho! J. C. Squire. ExPo
It does no good to speak of the big, blue bush. Study of Images, I. Wallace Stevens. ReMP
It does not happen. That love, removes. Audubon, Drafted. LeRoi Jones. Kal; TTY
It does not hurt. She looked along the knife. "Non Dolet." Swinburne. PoVP; ViPP
It does not make sense in terms of historical fact. Sans Souci. Lisel Mueller. NePoAm-2.
It doesn't always do to let a mug know everything. Charlie Piecan. F. Murray *and* F. Leigh. OxBoLi
It don't seem hardly right, John. Jonathan to John. James Russell Lowell. *Fr.* The Biglow Papers. CoBA; PaA; PAH; PAP
It don't take sech a lot o' laws. Code of the Cow Country. S. Omar Barker. PoOW
It dropped so low in my regard. Emily Dickinson. AmPP; CABA; CMoP; CoBA; OxBA; PoPl
It ended, and the morrow brought the task. Modern Love, II. George Meredith. BEL; EnLi-2; HBV; ILP; OAEP; ViPo; VP
It faded on the crowing of the cock. Shakespeare. *Fr.* Hamlet, I, i. MyFE
It falls, the peony. The Red Peony. Buson. RePo
It Feels Good as It Is without the Giant. Wallace Stevens. Notes toward a Supreme Fiction, VII. MoPo; NePA
It fell about a Marti[n]mas time. Barbara Allen (B *vers., with music*). *Unknown.* ViBoFo
It fell about the Lambmass tide. Bonny Lizie Baillie. *Unknown.* BaBo; ESPB
It [*or* Yt] fell about [*or* upon *or* and about *or* abowght] the Lammas tide [*or* time *or* tyde]. Otterbourne [*or* Otterburn *or* Oterborne]. *Unknown.* BaBo (B *vers.*); ESPB; FaBoCh; GoTS; HBV; OBB; OnMSP; OxBB; OxBS
It fell about the Lammas time. Lord Livingston. *Unknown.* ESPB; OxBB
It fell about the Martinmas [time]. Edom o' Gordon [*or* Captain Car]. *Unknown.* ESPB (F *and* H *vers.*); HBV; OBB; OBEV (1st ed.); OxBB; ViBoFo
It fell about the Martinmas time. Get Up and Bar the Door. *Unknown.* ATP; BaBo; BEL; BFSS; BoChLi; BoLiVe; EnL; EnLi-1; EnLit; ESPB; GoTP; GoTS; MaC; NoP; OBB; OnMSP; OxBS; PDV; PoIE; StPo; TiPo (1952 ed.); TrGrPo; VaPo; ViBoPo
It fell about the Martinmas [tyde]. Jamie Telfer in [*or* of] the fair Dodhead. *Unknown.* ESPB; OxBB
It fell in the ancient periods. Uriel. Emerson. AmePo; AnFE; AnNE; AP; APA; BWP; CoAnAm; LiTA; MAmP; MWA-1; NePA; OBEV (1st ed.); OxBA; PFY
It fell on a day and a bonny summer [*or* simmer] day. The Bonnie House of Airlie [*or* Lady Ogalbie]. *Unknown.* BaBo (A *vers.*); BFSS; BuBa; ESPB; OBB; OBEV; OxBS
It Fell on a Summer's Day. Thomas Campion. ErPo; UnTE
It fell upon a bonny simmer day. The Bonnie House o' Airlie. *Unknown.* OxBB
It Fell upon a Holy Eve. Spenser. *See* Perigot and Cuddy's Roundelay.
It fell upon a Wednesday [*or* Wodensday]. Brown Robin's [*or* Robyn's] Confession. *Unknown.* ACP; CH; ESPB; OBB; WHL
It fell upon the Lammas time. Young Ronald. *Unknown.* ESPB
It fell upon us like a crushing woe. Colonel Ellsworth. Richard Henry Stoddard. PAH
It fleeth away, my heart, quickly. Stand Fast, O My Heart. *Unknown.* LiTW

It flows through old [*or* all] hushed Egypt [*or* Aegypt] and its sands. The Nile [*or* A Thought of the Nile]. Leigh Hunt. EnRP; ERoP-1; NBM; OBNC; OBRV; ViBoPo
It follows up the hill and down. Market Day. Abigail Cresson. HBMV
It Fortifies My Soul to Know. Arthur Hugh Clough. *See* "With Whom Is No Variableness . . ."
It gets awful lonely. Lonely. Bloke Modisane. PBA
It glides and glints. July in Dutchess County. Babette Deutsch. WIRo
It grieves mee, Lord, my fancy's rusty: rub. Meditation XCII. Edward Taylor. *Fr.* Preparatory Meditations, Second Series. MAmP
It had an autumn smell. Autumn. Allen Tate. Seasons of the Soul, II. MoVE
It had to be. She from his weariness. Seven Sad Sonnets, I. Mary Aldis. HBMV
It hain't no use fer me to say. Love Lyrics of a Cowboy. R. V. Carr. SCC
It Happened. Efua Sutherland. ACV
It happened in Milan one summer night. Crushed Fender. Rosa Zagnoni Marinoni. MaRV; PoToHe (1941 ed.)
It happened on a certain day. The Ship *Rambolee.* *Unknown.* ShS
It happened, on a solemn eventide. The Walk to Emmaus. William Cowper. *Fr.* Conversation. SoP; StJW
It happened on a summer's day. The Castle Builder. La Fontaine. OTPC
It happened on a Sunday. Camp. Patrick Anderson. OBCV
It happened on an April day. Resurgam. John Richard Moreland. ChIP
It happened once, some men of Italy. The Lady of the Land. William Morris. *Fr.* The Earthly Paradise. PoVP; TOP
It happened once upon a time. James Hatley. *Unknown.* BaBo; ESPB
It Happens, Often. Edwin Meade Robinson. HBMV
It hardly seems that he is dead. A Dead Friend. Norman Gale. VA
It has all. From Gloucester Out. Edward Dorn. CoPo
It has been hours in these rooms. E. W. Mandel. *Fr.* Minotaur Poems. OBCV
It has been rumored that there are. Adjuration. Frank Belknap Long. FiSC
It has happened before. Four Preludes on Playthings of the Wind, III. Carl Sandburg. AmLP; AnAmPo; AnFE; CoBA; InP; MAP; MoAB; MoAmPo; NePA; NP; SeCeV
It has happened suddenly. Je Suis une Table. Donald Hall. NePoEA
It is/ yet almost. "Everything in the Air Is a Bird." Barbara Guest. AmPC
It Is a Beauteous Evening [Calm and Free]. Wordsworth. ATP; AWP; BoLiVe; BWP; CABA; CBEP; ChTr, 8 *ll.*; CoBE; DiPo; EnL; EnLi-2; EnLit; EnRP; EPN; ERoP-1; FaPL; FiP; ForPo; FosPo; HBV; HBVY; ILP; InPo; JAWP; LiTB; MaPo; MBW-2; MCCG; MERP; NeHB; NoP; OAEP; OuHeWo; PoAn; PoE; PoEL-4; PoeP; PoFS; PoIE; PoLF; PoPo; SeCePo; SeCeV; Sonn; TOP; TreFS; ViBoPo; WBP; WHA
(By the Sea.) EtS; GTBS; GTBS-D; GTBS-P; GTBS-W; GTSE; GTSL; TRV
(On the Beach at Calais.) TrGrPo
(On the Sea-Shore near Calais.) BEL
(Sonnet.) ChER; LoBV
It is a beauteous morning, calm and free. Country Club Sunday. Phyllis McGinley. CrMA; PoPo
It is a clever pushbutton you have, Juan Trippe. What Bright Pushbutton? Samuel Allen. PoNe (1970 ed.)
It is a cold and snowy night. The main street is deserted. Driving to Town Late to Mail a Letter. Robert Bly. BoNaP; ELU; NaP
It is a cold courage. Marigold. Louise Townsend Nicholl. RePo
It is a crude thing as it shapes up here. New Construction; Bath Iron Works. G. Stanley Koehler. NePoAm-2
It is a curious thing that you. The Kangaroo. Elizabeth J. Coatsworth. StVeCh (1955 ed.); TiPo (1952 ed.)
It Is a Distinct Pleasure. Tom Veitch. ANYP
It is a doorway to seasons; it makes. To a Dead Poet, His Book. Daniel Berrigan. ML
It is a father's place. A Father's Place. Eva Gray. SoP
It is a fearful thing to fall into the hands of the living God. The Hands of God. D. H. Lawrence. MoRP
"It is a foolish thing," said I. Tolerance. Thomas Hardy. MoRP
It is a funny thing, but true. Folks and Me. Lucile Crites. WBLP
It is a good plan, and began with childhood. Monologue of a Deaf Man. David Wright. POTE (1959 ed.)
It Is a Gracious House and Ever Was. Euripides, *tr. fr. Greek by* Dudley Fitts *and* Robert Fitzgerald. *Fr.* Alcestis. LiTW
It is a hollow garden, under the cloud. Winter Swan. Louise Bogan. AnAmPo
It is a human universe: and I. Ted Berrigan. ANYP
It is a kind of shadow. The Umbrella. Ann Stanford. NYBP
It is a land with neither night nor day. Cobwebs. Christina Rossetti. NoP
It is a lie—their priests, their pope. The Confessional. Robert Browning. OtMeF; PoVP; ViBoPo
It is a lost road into the air. An Airstrip in Essex, 1960. Donald Hall. LiTM (1970 ed.); PoCh
"It is a month, and isna mair." The White Fisher. *Unknown.* ESPB
It is a most exciting thing. The New Garden. Reginald Arkell. RePo
It is a new America. Brown River, Smile [*or* The Blue Meridian]. Jean Toomer. AmNP; PoNe (1970 ed.)
It is a pilgrim coming from the East. The Pilgrim from the East. Gustave Kahn. TrJP
It is a place where poets crowned may feel the heart's decaying. Cowper's Grave. Elizabeth Barrett Browning. HBV; OBVV; PoVP; ViPo
It Is a Pleasant Day. *Unknown.* BoTP
It is a solemn evening, golden-clear. The After-Glow. Mathilde Blind. OBNC
It is a strange, miraculous thing. Enigma in Altman's [*or* Enigma for Christmas Shoppers]. Phyllis McGinley. PoMa; PoPl; WhC
It is a sultry day; the sun has drunk. Summer Wind. Bryant. AA; AP; PoEL-4
It is a summer twilight, balmy-sweet. A Summer Twilight. Charles Tennyson-Turner. OBRV; PeER
It is a thread—a tiny, shining thread. Vision. Ida Norton Munson. ChIP
It is a whisper among the hazel bushes. The Twilight People. "Seumas O'Sullivan." OnYI
It is a willow when summer is over. Willow Poem. William Carlos Williams. NP
It is a winter night. Fever and chill. A Winter's Tale. Robert Patrick Dana. NYBP
It is a winter's tale. A Winter's Tale. Dylan Thomas. AtBAP; CMoP; FaBoMo; LiTB; SeCeV
It is a wonder foam is so beautiful. Spray. D. H. Lawrence. BoNaP
It is all a rhythm. The Rhythm. Robert Creeley. CoPo; FRC; LiTM (1970 ed.); TPM
It is all falling away, the days fall faster now. Descending. Robert Pack. NePoEA-2
It is all mountains running away in one direction. Ocean. Adrien Stoutenburg. WIRo
It is all one in Venus' wanton school. Song. John Lyly. SeCePo
It is almost as hard for friends to meet. To My Retired Friend Wei. Tu Fu. LiTW
It is always so: the declining. Returning from Harvest. Vernon Watkins. NYBP; StP
It is always the women who are the Watchers. And There Was Mary Magdalene and the Other Mary, Sitting Over against the Sepulchre. W. R. Rodgers. WePo
It is an ancient Mariner. The Rime of the Ancient Mariner. Samuel Taylor Coleridge. AnFE; AtBAP; ATP; BEL; BeLS; BoLiVe; CABA; CABL; CaFP; CBEP; CH; ChER; CoBE; DiPo; EnL; EnLi-2; EnLit; EnRP; EPN; ERoP-1; ExPo; FaBoBe; FaBoCh; FaBV; FaFP; FaPL; FiP; FosPo; GBV (1922 ed.); HBV; HoPM; ILP; LiTB; LiTG; LoGBV; MaPo; MasP; MBW-2; MCCG; MERP; NoP; OAEP; OBEV; OBNC; OBRV; OnSP; OtMeF; OTPC; OuHeWo; PAn; PeER; Po; PoAn; PoE; PoEL-4; PoFS; PoSa; PTK; RoGo; SeCeV; ShBV-2; StP; TOP; TreF; TrGrPo; UnPo (1st ed.); VaPo; ViBoPo; WePo; WHA; YAT

It is [*or* 'Tis] an honorable thought. Emily Dickinson. AP; EG; MAPA; TwAmPo
It is an illusion that we were ever alive. The Rock. Wallace Stevens. AP
It is an old belief. Beyond. John Gibson Lockhart. MaRV
It is as though some babe, that loveth hues. The Missal. Ruth Pitter. CAW
It is as true as strange, else trial feigns. Sonnet. John Davies of Hereford. EIL
It Is at Moments after I Have Dreamed. E. E. Cummings. OxBA
It is at morning, twilight they expire. After Midnight. Charles Vildrac. AWP; JAWP; WBP
It is because of the savage mystery. Matador. Richard Eberhart. NoP
It is because the sea is blue. The Great Wave: Hokusai. Donald Finkel. PoPl
It is because they troubled me. The Pupil to His Master. Fannie Stearns Davis. PFY
It is because you were my friend. Mortal Combat. Mary Elizabeth Coleridge. OBVV
It Is Becoming Now to Declare My Allegiance. C. Day Lewis. LiTM (rev. ed.)
It Is Better . . . Ecclesiastes, Bible, *O.T.* *See* Better Path, The.
It Is Better to Be Together. Ruth Miller. PeSA
It Is Better to Go into Heaven with One Eye. Richard Crashaw. MaMe
It is bleak December noon. December. Thomas Caulfield Irwin. IrPN; NBM
It is blue-butterfly day here in spring. Blue-Butterfly Day. Robert Frost. NeMA
It is borne in upon me that pain. The Human Being Is a Lonely Creature. Richard Eberhart. FiMAP; NePoAm
It is buried and done with. Farewell. John Addington Symonds. OBVV; PG (1945 ed.); VA
It is but little that remaineth. Notes of an Interview. William Johnson Cory. NBM
It is Christmas Day in the workhouse, and the cold, bare walls are bright. Christmas Day in the Workhouse [*or* In the Workhouse: Christmas Day]. George R. Sims. BeLS; BLPA; PaPo; TreF
It is Christmas in the mansion. Christmas in the Heart. *Unknown.* ChBR; MaRV; OHIP; RePo; SiSoSe
It is cold here. The Moths. W. S. Merwin. FRC
"It is cold outside, you will need a coat." The Arabian Shawl. Katherine Mansfield. *Fr.* Two Nocturnes. HBMV
It is cold without flesh, without bones. Dead in Wars and in Revolutions. Mary Devenport O'Neill. NeIP
It is colder now/ there are many stars/ we are drifting. Epistle to Be Left in the Earth. Archibald MacLeish. BoLiVe (1945 ed.); CMoP; ImOP; MAP; MoAB; MoAmPo; TrGrPo
It is common knowledge to every schoolboy. Portrait of the Artist as a Prematurely Old Man. Ogden Nash. CrMA; FaFP; LiTA; LiTM; NePA; SiTL
It is creation's morning. Now. Harriet Monroe. HBV
It is dangerous for a woman to defy the gods. Letter to My Sister. Anne Spencer. AmNP; PoNe
It is dark. The Last Bus. Mark Strand. TwCP
It is dark and lonesome here. The Lover. Richard Henry Stoddard. AA
It is dark as a cave. The Clock-Winder. Thomas Hardy. PoVP
It is dark, now, and grave. Melting Pot. Michael Echeruo. TTY
It is dawn. The horizon. Names. Jorge Guillén. LiTW
It is deep summer. Far out. There. Robert Mezey. NaP
It is difficult to imagine how vulnerable they are. The Birds. David Posner. NYBP
It is disastrous to be a wounded deer. Hello. Gregory Corso. WOW
It is done!/ Clang of bell and roar of gun. Laus Deo! Whittier. AmP; AmPP; AnNE; AP; CoBA; DD; MC; PaA; PAH; PoFr
It is early morning within this room; without. Laurence Binyon. *Fr.* Winter Sunrise. ChMP
It is easier to be angry than to pity. Humbert Wolfe. *Fr.* The Uncelestial City. BoC
It is easy enough to be pleasant. Worth While. Ella Wheeler Wilcox. BLPA; PoToHe; TreF
It is easy to mold the yielding clay. Clay Hills. Jean Starr Untermeyer. HBMV; MAP; MoAmPo (1942 ed.); NeMA; NP; PCD
It is equal to living in a tragic land. Dry Loaf. Wallace Stevens. AtBAP; CrMA; OxBA; PoRA
It is evening. One bat dances. A Soul. Randall Jarrell. CMoP
It is evening, Senlin says, and in the evening. Evening Song of Senlin. Conrad Aiken. *Fr.* Senlin; a Biography. HBMV; LOW
It is fallen! it is fallen! At Dawn. Charles Williams. FaBoTw
It is far to Assisi. The Garden. William Carlos Williams. PoDB
It Is Finished. Horatius Bonar. BePJ
It Is Finished. Jonathan Evans. BePJ
It Is Finished. Christina Rossetti. VA
It is Finished. John Hall Wheelock. MoRP
It Is Finished. Sir Henry Wotton. BePJ
It is finished! Man of Sorrows. Via Crucis, Via Lucis. T. H. Hedge. BePJ
"It is finished." The last nail. Tenebrae. David Gascoyne. *Fr.* Miserere. FaBoMo; NeBP
It is fitting that you be here. On Seeing Two Brown Boys in a Catholic Church. Frank Horne. BANP; CDC; PoNe; TTY
It is folly for any man in the world. The Praises of God. *Unknown.* AnIL
It is for us/ to praise the Lord of all. The Kingdom of God. Rab. TrJP
It is for you/ The larks sing loud. To the Wind at Morn. W. H. Davies. ELU
It is God's will that I should cast. God's Will. *Unknown.* SoP
It is good for strength not to be merciful. To a Young Artist. Robinson Jeffers. CoBA
It is good just to think about Johann Sebastian. Homage to J. S. Bach. John Heath-Stubbs. BoPe; MuSP
It is good to be out on the road, and going one knows not where. Tewkesbury Road. John Masefield. BoTP; EPN; GBV; MCCG; StaSt; TreFT; TSW
It is good to sing Thy praises and to thank Thee, O Most High. Psalm XCII, Bible, *O.T.* FaChP
It is good to strive against wind and rain. A Mood. Amélie Rives. AA
It Is Great for Our Country to Die. James Gates Percival. *See* Elegiac.
It is green, it is made of willow. The Day-Bed. Richard Eberhart. FiMAP
It is hard for those who have never known persecution. Chorus VI [*or* Why Should Men Love the Church]. T. S. Eliot. *Fr.* The Rock. LiTM; MoRP
It is hard going to the door. The Door. Robert Creeley. NaP; NeAP; ToPo
It is hard, inland. In Winter. Robert Wallace. BoNaP
It is hot today, dry enough for cutting grain. August from My Desk. Roland Flint. AmFN
It is humiliating. Wormwood. Sappho. WoL
It is I, America, calling! A Call to Arms. Mary Raymond Shipman Andrews. MC; PAH
It Is I, Be Not Afraid. A. B. Simpson. BePJ; SoP; STF
It is I that am under sorrow at this time. Another Song. William Ross. GoTS
It is impossible to find anything good. Flood. Mary Grant Charles. GoYe
It is in captivity. The Bull. William Carlos Williams. LiTM (1970 ed.); MoVE; NoP; TDP; TwCP
It is in loving—not in being loved. Christian Paradox. *Unknown.* MaRV; SoP
It is in many ways made plain to us. Retractions, V. James Branch Cabell. HBMV
It is in the rock, but not in the stone. Riddle. *Unknown.* ChTR
It is in these stones that the claviers sing. On the Death of Frank O'Hara. Sotère Torregian. YAP
It Is in Winter That We Dream of Spring. Robert Burns Wilson. AA; AmLP
It is, indeed, a pleasant thing to know. A Snowfall on Plum Trees after They Had Bloomed. Charles Dalmon. *Fr.* The Three Pictures. TSW
It Is July. Susan Hartley Swett. *See* July.
It is late afternoon at the beach; I lie on the swaying dock. "And All the While the Sky Is Falling. . ." Lora Dunetz. NePoAm

It is late afternoon. Out of my study window. Out of My Study Window. Reed Whittemore. PoPl
It is late at night and still I am losing. In Dives' Dive. Robert Frost. TDP
It is late in year. Night in the House by the River. Tu Fu. NaP
It is late last night the dog was speaking of you. Donall Oge [*or* The Grief of a Girl's Heart]. *Unknown, tr. by* Lady Gregory. BoLP; ChTr
It is leviathan, mountain and world. History. Robert Fitzgerald. MoVE
It is likely enough that lions and scorpions. Ante Mortem. Robinson Jeffers. MAP; MoAmPo; MoVE
It is little I repair to the matches of the Southron folk. At Lord's. Francis Thompson. MemP
It Is March. W. S. Merwin. NaP; PoIE (1970 ed.)
It is mellowed and soft as an apple's cheek. An Old Face. Francesca Falk Miller. PEDC
It is memory speaking, preternaturally clear. Elizabeth at the Piano. Horace Gregory. SiSw; UnS
It is midnight. Poem at Thirty. Sonia Sanchez. BF
It is midnight, my wedded. The Ghosts' Moonshine. Thomas Lovell Beddoes. LO
It is midnight; the great dwelling. Miserere. Gaspar Nuñez de Arce. CAW
It is Monday morning. The Goldfish Wife. Sandra Hochman. NYBP
It is morning, Senlin says, and in the morning. Morning Song of Senlin. Conrad Aiken. *Fr.* Senlin; a Biography. AmP; CMoP; HBMV; InP; LiTA; LiTM; MAP; MoAB; MoAmPo; NeMA; NP; OxBA; PoMa; ReMP; TrGrPo; WoL
It is most true, that eyes are formed to serve. Astrophel and Stella, V. Sir Philip Sidney. FCP; MaPo; NoP; OBSC; ReEn; SiCE; SiPS; Sonn; TuPP
It is my body leaves my love, not I. Struggling Fancies. Bhartrihari. OnPM
It is my joy in life to find. A Prayer. Frank Dempster Sherman. TreFS
It is my own door that is shut. Dialogue. John Erskine. HBMV
It is my sorrow that this day's troubles. Slievenamon. *Unknown.* KiLC
It is myself. To a Dog Injured in the Street. William Carlos Williams. LiTM (1970 ed.); MoAB; NePoAm; PP; SeCeV
It is necessary to wait until the boss's eyes are on you. Notes from a Slave Ship. Edward Field. PP
It is New Year's Day. Best Loved of Africa. Margaret Danner. PoNe (1970 ed.)
It is No Dream of Mine. Henry David Thoreau. MAmP
It is no idle fabulous tale, nor is it fayned newes. Newes from Virginia. Richard Rich. PAH
It is no longer necessary to sleep. A Man Walking and Singing. Wendell Berry. AP
It is no vulgar nature I have wived. Modern Love, XXXV. George Meredith. ViPo; VP
It is not a whirlwind rolling along the valley. The Murder of the Tsarevich Dimitri by Boris Godunov. *Unknown.* LiTW
It Is Not a Word. Sara Teasdale. NP
It is not bad. Let them play. The Bloody Sire. Robinson Jeffers. CMoP; LiTM; NePA; VaPo
It Is Not Beauty I Demand. George Darley. *See* Loveliness of Love, The.
It is not, Celia [*or* darling], in our power. To a Lady Asking [Him] How Long He Would Love Her. Sir George Etherege. CEP; EG; HBV; LiTL; LO; LoBV; MeWo; OBEV; OnPM; SeCL; SeEP; ViBoPo
It Is Not Death. Thomas Hood. *See* Death.
It Is Not Death to Die. César Malan. BePJ
(What Is Death?) SoP
It is not death so much we dread. Poem for Combatants. Alan White. MaRV
It is not death, that sometime in a sigh. Death [*or* Sonnet]. Thomas Hood. EG; ERoP-2; LoBV; OBEV; OBNC; OBRV; ViBoPo
It Is Not Death to Die. George Washington Bethune. AA
It is not easy to be less than lovers. For M——. Bruce Williamson. NeIP
It Is Not Enough. David Henderson. PPON
It is not fair to visit all. Eve. Oliver Herford. HBMV; YaD
It Is Not Far. Sara Teasdale. *See* Night.
It is not far to my place. Visit. A. R. Ammons. CoAP; TwCP
It Is Not Finished, Lord. G. A. Studdert-Kennedy. ChIP
It is not for nothing that the sun looks like a young-again old-timer. For Harry and June. Ray Mathew. NeLNL
It is not four years ago. Proffered Love Rejected [*or* The Rejected Offer]. Sir John Suckling. CavP; ErPo; NCEP; UnTE
It Is Not Growing like a Tree. Ben Jonson. *Fr.* To the Immortal Memory, and Friendship of That Noble Pair, Sir Lucius Cary, and Sir Henry Morison. AnFE; BBV (1951 ed.); BEL; CABA; ChTr; CoBE; DiPo; EnLi-1 (1949 ed.); LiTB; LiTG; OBEV; OQP; OTD; PoIE; TOP; YAT
(Noble Nature, The.) GN; GoBC; GTBS; GTBS-D; GTBS-P; GTBS-W; GTSE; GTSL; HBV; HBVY; MaRV; MCCG; OTPC; PG; PoPo; TreFT
(Oak and Lily.) BoLiVe; TrGrPo
(Proportion.) FaBoEn
(Short Measures.) WePo
It is not hard to tell of a rose. Inscription. Ann Hamilton. HBMV
It is not—I swear it by every fiery omen. Readings, Forecasts, Personal Guidance. Kenneth Fearing. MoAmPo
It is not in the books. The Three Movements. Donald Hall. NePoEA-2
It is not its air but our own awe. The Iceberg. W. S. Merwin. PoIE
It is not life upon Thy gifts to live. Life. Jones Very. AP
It Is Not Likely Now. Frances Bellerby. ChMP
It is not, Lord, the sound of many words. Henry Lok. *Fr.* Sonnets of Christian Passions. SiCE; Sonn; TuPP
It is not mine to run. Not Mine. Julia C. R. Dorr. SoP
It Is Not Only the Dead. Frank Belknap Long. FiSC
It is not raining rain to me. *See* It isn't raining rain to me.
It is not right for you to know, so do not ask, Leuconoë. Ad Leuconoen. Franklin P. Adams, *after* Horace. AWP; JAWP; WBP
It is not right to judge a man. First Impressions. Alfred Grant Walton. PoToHe (new ed.)
It is not so much where you live. How—When—Where. John Oxenham. MaRV
It Is Not So with Me. Blake. *Fr.* Vala; or, The Four Zoas. SeCePo
It is not sweet content, be sure. In the Depths. Arthur Hugh Clough. PoVP
It is not that I love thee, fairest. Love and Respect. Patherícke Jenkyn. CavP
It is not that I love you less. The Self[e]-banished. Edmund Waller. CavP; FaBoEn; MePo; OBS; SeEP
It Is Not the Deed. *Unknown.* FaChP
It is not the fear of death. Andre's Request to Washington. Nathaniel Parker Willis. MC; PAH
It is not the foreignness *per se* of heroes. Why the British Girls Give In So Easily. Nicholas Moore. WaP
It is not the still weight. The Jungle. William Carlos Williams. CABA; PoeP
It is not the young whom we find feeding the pigeons. The Pigeon-Feeders in Battery Park. Julia Cooley Altrocchi. GoYe
It Is Not to Be Thought Of. Wordsworth. EnRP; EPN; FiP; MaRV; MBW-2; PoFr; TOP
(England, 1802, IV.) HBV; OBEV
(Sonnet: "It is not to be thought of that the Flood.") ACV; LoBV; OBRV
It Is Not Too Late. Lucia Trent. PGD
It is not vertue, wisdom, valour, wit. Woman. Milton. *Fr.* Samson Agonistes. OBS
It is not you that move, but the running sand. The Eye. Eithne Wilkins. NeBP
It is now the tenth hour of this October night. October. John Bayliss. NeBP
It is of a fearless highwayman a story I will tell. Quantrell (B *vers.*) *Unknown.* CoSo
It is of a flash packet, flash packet of fame. The *Dom Pedro. Unknown.* SoAmSa
It is on the sea and under the waves of the sea. Cycle. Seán Jennett. WaP
It is only that this warmth and movement are like. The Woman in Sunshine. Wallace Stevens. MoVE
It is only the orange light that brings forth the orange in things. Fits of Candor. Dick Gallup. ANYP

It is ordained, or so Politian said. Epitaph for the Poet V., I. Arthur Davison Ficke. HBMV
It is over, it is. Poem for a Selfpitying Friend/ for Lost Loves. Sandford Lyne. QAH
It is plain now what you are. Your head has dropped. Carrion. Harold Monro. *Fr.* Youth in Arms. MMA
It is pleasant to think, just under the snow. Under the Snow. T. Hempstead. SoP
It is portentous, and a thing of state. Abraham Lincoln Walks at Midnight. Vachel Lindsay. AmFN; AmLP; AmPP; AnFE; ATP (1935 ed.); CMoP; CoAnAm; CoBA; FaBV; FaFP; FaPON; HBV; InP; LaNeLa; LiPo; LiTA; MAP; MaRV; MC; MCCG; MoAmPo; MoRP; MoVE; MPB; NAMP; NP; OHFP; OHIP; OnPP; OQP; OTD; OxBA; PaA; PAH; PAL; PEDC; PG (1945 ed.); PoPl; PoPo; PoRL; PPON; RePo; ThLM; TIHL; TreF
Is is posted in the clubrooms. SOS. Kenneth Fearing. AmP
It is queer to think that many people. The Man with the Rake. Christopher Morley. *Fr.* Translations from the Chinese. EvOK
It Is Raining. Lucy Sprague Mitchell. BrR; SoPo; TiPo
It is red. An Artist Paints Dawn. Rochelle Ratner. QAH
It is related that the Caliph Harun al-Rashid. The Mock Caliph. *Unknown, tr. by* Sir Richard Francis Burton. EnLi-1
It is said that many a king in troubled Europe. Rulers: Philadelphia. Fenton Johnson. AmFN; GoSl; PoNe
It is said the Bedouins cry, on the Syrian hills, a clear. On Syrian Hills. Richard Burton. ChIP
It is 7:53 Friday morning in the Universe. Personal Poem #7. Ted Berrigan. ANYP
It is she alone that matters. Bouquet of Belle Scavior. Wallace Stevens. MoAB; MoAmPo
It is, sir, a confest intrusion here. To My Honoured Friend Mr. George Sandys. Henry King. AnAnS-2
Is is snowing heavily again. Between Us. Stephen Berg. NaP
It Is So Long Since My Heart Has Been with Yours. E. E. Cummings. CMoP
It is so many ages now since He. Our Father. Roberta Teale Swartz. MoRP
It is so much easier to forget than to have been Mr. Whittier. Mr. Whittier. Winfield Townley Scott. CrMA; OnHM
It is so peaceful on the ceiling! Sleeping on the Ceiling. Elizabeth Bishop. MiAP
It is so sweet to know. God Understands. *Unknown.* SoP
It is some school, brick, green, a sleepy hill. An Officer's Prison Camp Seen from a Troop-Train. Randall Jarrell. WaP
It is some time since the last rainfall was heard. The Body of Summer. "Odysseus Elytis." LiTW
It is Spring and All Is Well. Charles Erskine Scott Wood. PFY
It is spring in the mountains. Written on the Wall at Chang's Hermitage. Tu Fu. HoPM; NaP
Is is springtime, to the south and north of my cottage the floods are out. The Arrival of a Guest. Tu Fu. WoL
Is is still the tallest building in the world. Looking at the Empire State Building. Ralph Pomeroy. NYTB
It is strange to think of the Annas, the Vronskys, the Pierres. Fate and the Younger Generation. D. H. Lawrence. OxBoLi; SiTL; WhC
It is strange we trust each other. Why Doubt God's Word? A. B. Simpson. BLRP
It is sublime adjustment: now. Walking Home on St Cecilia's Day. Peter Porter. MuSP
It is sweet and bitter, on the winter nights. The Cracked Bell. Baudelaire. OnPM
It Is That Bane of Self in Love. Richard Eberhart. LiTL
It is that pale, delaying hour. Evening Songs, II. John Vance Cheney. AA
It is the association after all. A Way of Looking. Elizabeth Jennings. NePoEA; PP
It is the best, erely and late. Be True to Your Condition in Life. John Audelay. MeEL
It is the bittern's solemn cry. Solitude. Frederick Peterson. AA
It is the box from which no jack will spring. The Funeral. Donald Hall. Sonn
It is the calm and solemn night! Alfred Domett. *Fr.* A Christmas Hymn. PGD
It is the cause, it is the cause, my soule. Othello and Desdemona. Shakespeare. *Fr.* Othello, V, ii. AtBAP; FiP; MemP
It is the Celestial Ennui of Apartments. Wallace Stevens. *Fr.* Notes toward a Supreme Fiction. MoPo; NePA
It is the counterpoise that minds. Noble Love. Richard Flecknoe. ACP
It is the dark of the moon. Doubled Mirrors. Kenneth Rexroth. OPoP
It is the day of all the year. *Unknown.* OxNR
It is the day when he was born. In Memoriam A. H. H., CVII. Tennyson. EnLi-2; EPN; OAEP; ViPo; VP
It is the duty of the student. Duty of the Student. Edward Anthony. GoTP
It is the East we dream of: there. The Rider. Leah Bodine Drake. NePoAm-2
It is the endless dance. Dirge. Quincy Troupe. WSL
It is the evening hour. Mary [*or* To Mary It Is the Evening Hour.] John Clare. ChTr; EnLoPo; FaBoEn; PeER
It is the fall, the eternal fall of water. The Fall. Kathleen Raine. MoPo
It is the first mild day of March. To My Sister [*or* A Change in the Year]. Wordsworth. BoTP; EnRP; MBW-2; OBRV; PoE
It is the football season once more. Vernon Scannell. *Fr.* Autumn. FlW
It is the Harvest Moon! On gilded vanes. The Harvest Moon. Longfellow. AP; GN; MAmP
It is the hour when Arno turns. A Song of Arno. Grace Ellery Channing. AA
It Is the Hush of Night. Byron. *Fr.* Childe Harold's Pilgrimage, III. LiTB
(Night.) LoBV
It is the littleness I would keep. To a Photograph. Parker Tyler. NePA
It is the memory of the peacock and the muses. Letter to R. Willard Maas. WaP
It is the midnight hour; the beauteous sea. Calm as the Cloudless Heaven. "Christopher North." EtS
It is the miller's daughter. Song. Tennyson. *Fr.* The Miller's Daughter. CBEP; EG; GTBS; GTBS-W; GTSL; HBV; LiTG; LiTL; OBEV; OBVV; TrGrPo; UnTE
It is the month of falling stars. The Month of Falling Stars. Ella Higginson. YeAr
It is the pain, it is the pain, endures. Villanelle. William Empson. ChMP; CMoP; EnLoPo; PoIE
It is the picnic with Ruth in the spring. The Picnic. John Logan. BoLP; NePoEA-2
It is the reaching out into the dark. The Moment. David Rowbotham. BoAV
It is the Reed. Sister Maris Stella. GoBC
It is the road, the chart. Faith. John Richard Moreland. ChIP
It is the same infrequent star. The Star of Calvary. Nathaniel Hawthorne. AA
It is the sea: dead calm—and the spring tide. Paris at Night. Tristan Corbière. SyP
It is the sea's edge lubbers love. Sailing, Sailing. Gray Burr. CoPo; NYBP
It is the season now to go. In the Season. Robert Louis Stevenson. VA
It is the season of the sweet wild rose. Sonnet. George Meredith. Modern Love, XLV. NBM; PoEL-5; ViPo; VP
It is the sigh of languid bliss. Wind in the Wood. Paul Verlaine. LO
It is the sinking of things. Rain. James Wright. NaP
It is the slow encroachment, word by word. Scarabs for the Living, VIII. R. P. Blackmur. TwAmPo
It is the snow-gum silently. The Snow-Gum. Douglas Stewart. PoAu-2
It is the soul that sees; the outward eyes. The Lover's Journey. George Crabbe. *Fr.* Tales. EiCL
It is the spot I came to seek. An Indian at the Burial-Place of His Fathers. Bryant. CoBA; MWA-1
It is the thirty-first of March. Peter Bell. John Hamilton Reynolds. OBNC; Par
It is the very error of the moon. Shakespeare. *Fr.* Othello, V, ii. MyFE
It is the way of a pleasant path. Green Frog at Roadstead,

Wisconsin. James Schevill. FRC
It is the white Plum Tree. 'Tis the White Plum Tree. John Shaw Neilson. BoAV; PoAu-1
It is the word pejorative that hurts. Sailing after Lunch. Wallace Stevens. MoPo
It is their way to find the surface. Poem by the Charles River. Robin Blaser. NeAP
It is there, above him beyond, behind. The Being. James Dickey. NMP
It is this deep blankness is the real thing strange. Let It Go. William Empson. PoIE
It is 3.42 A.M. on a troop train. The Kid in Upper 4. Nelson C. Metcalf. TreFS
It is Thy right to choose, my blessèd Lord. Surrender. Henry W. Frost. SoP
It Is Time. Ted Joans. Kal; NNP
"It Is Time for Action." Bob Bennett. BF
It is time for the United States to spend money on education. It Is Time. Ted Joans. Kal
It Is Time That I Wrote My Will. W. B. Yeats. The Tower, III. MBW-2; MoVE
It is time to be old. Terminus. Emerson. AA; AmePo; AmPP; AnNE; AP; AWP; CoBA; HBV; InPo; MWA-1; NoP; OuHeWo; OxBA; PoEL-4; PoIE (1970 ed.); PoLF
It Is Time to Build. Elias Lieberman. MaRV
It is time to explain myself—let us stand up. Walt Whitman. *Fr.* Song of Myself, XLIV. DiPo; MaRV
It is time to say words of good omen. Midst the Free Green Fields. Aristophanes. *Fr.* The Peace. HW
It is tiresome always to talk about weather, or think about it. The Self and the Weather. Reed Whittemore. NMP
It is told by seafarers. Told by Seafarers. Galway Kinnell. NePoAm-2
It is told, in Buddhi-theosophic schools. Transcendentalism. *Unknown.* BOHV; NA
It Is Too Late! Longfellow. *Fr.* Morituri Salutamus. PoLF (Too Late?) WBLP
It is too sudden. Flower of "The Living Desert." Mary Winter. NYTB
It Is toward Evening. *Unknown.* BePJ
It is true love because. True Love. Judith Viorst. MeWo
It is true, that even in the best-run state. The Murder of William Remington. Howard Nemerov. CoAP; CMoP
It is true that, older than man and ages to outlast him. Gray Weather. Robinson Jeffers. CMoP
It is 12:20 in New York a Friday. The Day Lady Died. Frank O'Hara. ANYP; NeAP
It is Ulysses that approaches from the east. The World as Meditation. Wallace Stevens. AP
It is unreasoning. Flat. Möbius. Phillip Hey. YAP
It is very aggravating. The Truth about Horace. Eugene Field. BOHV; InMe; InP; LHV
It is very late. Popcorn. Phillip Hey. YAP
It is very nice to think. A Thought. Robert Louis Stevenson. OTPC; PCH; PPL; ThGo
It is we, it is we. Lament. Dan Georgakas. ThO
It is well with this noble prince. The happy destiny hath come to pass. Song of the Harper. *Unknown.* LiTW
It is what he does not know. On a Squirrel Crossing the Road in Autumn, in New England. Richard Eberhart. NePA; PoCh
It is when they come with questions. Poem for the Atomic Age. Emanuel Litvinov. NeBP
It Is Winter, I Know. Merrill Moore. MAP; MoAmPo
It is written in the skyline of the city. Pact. Kenneth Fearing. CMoP
It is yourself you seek. Man Alone. Louise Bogan. NYBP
It Isn't Far to Bethlehem. Arthur R. Macdougall, Jr. PGD
It isn't hard/ to drive a car. Ilo Orleans. RIS
It isn't raining rain to [*or* for] me. April Rain [*or* Rain Song]. Robert Loveman. BoTP; DD; HBV; HBVY; MaRV; OQP; RIS; SUS; TreFT; TrJP; WBLP
It Isn't the Church—It's You. *Unknown.* BLPA; WBLP
It Isn't the Cough. *Unknown.* FaFP; LiTM; ShM; SiTL
It isn't the thing you do. The Sin of Omission. Margaret E. Sangster. BLPA; HBV; MaRV; PoToHe; SoP; TreFS; TRV
It isn't the thing you do, dear. The Thing You Leave Undone. *At. to* Adelaide Procter. FaChP
It Isn't the Town, It's You. R. W. Glover. BLPA
It joins a dark pine to another tree. Cobweb. Winifred Welles. AnAmPo
It keeps eternal whisperings around. On the Sea [*or* Sonnet on the Sea]. Keats. ATP (1935 ed.); BoLiVe; BWP; CABA; CoBE; DiPo; EnL; EnRP; EPN; ERoP-2; EtS; ExPo; GTBS-W; HBV; LiTB; MaPo; MBW-2; MCCG; NoP; PeER; PoeP; SeCePo; SeCeV; SG; Sonn; TrGrPo; ViBoPo; YAT
It later befell in the years that followed. The Fire-Dragon and the Treasure. *Unknown.* *Fr.* Beowulf. AnOE
It lies around us like a cloud. The Other World. Harriet Beecher Stowe. AA; HBV; WGRP
It Lies Not in Our Power to Love or Hate. Christopher Marlowe. *Fr.* Hero and Leander, First Sestiad. BoLiVe; TrGrPo; WHA
(Love at First Sight.) FaBoEn; MeWo; TreFT
(Who Ever Loved, That Loved Not at First Sight?) FaFP; LiTB; LiTG; LiTL
It lies not on the sunlit hill. The White Peace. "Fiona Macleod." EPN; FaBoBe; HBV; OQP; PoVP
It lifts the poor man from his cell. The Powers of Love. George Moses Horton. BALP
It little profits that an idle king. Ulysses. Tennyson. ATP; AWP; BEL; BoLiVe; BWP; CABA; CaFP; CBEP; CBV; CoBE; DiPo; EnL; EnLi-2; EnLit; EPN; ExPo; FiP; ForPo; GTSE; HBV; HoPM; ILP; InP; InPo; LiTB; LoBV; MaPo; MaVP; MBW-2; MCCG; MyFE; NoP; OAEP; OnPP; OuHeWo; PAn; Po; PoAn; PoE; PoFS; PoIE; PoPo; PoRA; PoSa; PoVP; PTK; SeCePo; SeCeV; ShBV-4; StP; TOP; TreF; TrGrPo; UnPo; VA; VaPo; ViBoPo; ViPo; ViPP; VP; WHA; YT
It looked extremely rocky for the Mudville [*or* Boston] nine that day. Casey at the Bat. Ernest Lawrence Thayer. BBV (1951 ed.); BeLS; BLPA; BOHV; FaBoBe; FaFP; GSP; HBV; IHA; InMe; LHV; MaC; NeHB; OnSP; PoRA; StPo; TIHL; TreF; YaD
It looks a piece of golden, broken glass. Onion Skin in Barn. Kenneth Slade Alling. NePoAm
It looks like any building. The Library. Barbara A. Huff. FaPON
It makes a man feel happy. Three Sweethearts. Heine. UnTE
It makes no difference abroad. Emily Dickinson. AP; DiPo
It matters not, when I am dead. Heart's Haven. Kendall Banning. MaRV
It May Be. Max Jacob, *tr. fr. French by* Wallace Fowlie. PoPl
It May Be. *Unknown.* SoP
It may be/ I'll join with thee in a most just revenge. John Webster. *Fr.* The Duchess of Malfi. PoFr
It May Be Good [Like It Who List]. Sir Thomas Wyatt. EnRePo; EP; FCP; FosPo; SiPS
It may be in the evening. It May Be. *Unknown.* SoP
It May Be Like This. Lilith Lorraine. FiSC
It may be so,—perhaps thou hast. To the Portrait of "A Gentleman." Oliver Wendell Holmes. BOHV; InMe
It May Be So with Us. John Masefield. *Fr.* Sonnets ("Long long ago"). ATP; TOP
It may be that a strange dream. It May Be. Max Jacob. PoPl
It may be that the sun was bright. Mary Shakespeare. Ada Jackson. PoMa
It may be these things never did occur. Kinnereth. "Rachel." LiTW; TrJP
It may be 'tis observ'd, I want relations. George Wither. *Fr.* The Tired Petitioner. SeCV-1
It may be when the sunlight strikes the sill. In Your Absence. Elizabeth Baxter. PoToHe (new ed.)
It may have been a sunset such as this. Plain Chant of the Hill Country. Sister Mary David. JKCP (1955 ed.)
It may indeed be fantasy [*or* phantasy], when I. To Nature. Samuel Taylor Coleridge. BWP; ERoP-1; MaRV
It May Not Always Be So; and I Say. E. E. Cummings. *Fr.* Sonnets—Unrealities. AnAmPo; FaBV; MoLP
It Means Just What It Says. A. B. Simpson. SoP (Believe the Bible.) STF
It Might as Well Be Spring. Oscar Hammerstein II. Po
It Might Have Been. Walter E. Isenhour. SoP
It might have been in the heart of a deep forest. The False Summer. Marya Zaturenska. CrMA
It Might Have Been Worse. G. J. Russell. PoToHe (new ed.)
It Moves Across. Bernadette Mayer. ANYP
"It Must All Be Done Over." John Haines. ThO
It must be done, my soul, but 'tis a strange. The Meditation. John Norris. PeRV
It must be so—Plato, thou reason'st well. Cato's Soliloquy [on

It (continued)
Immortality]. Addison. *Fr.* Cato. MaRV; OQP; TreFS; WBLP
It must be true. Poem. William Knott. YAP
It must have been for one of us, my own. Not Thou but I. Philip Bourke Marston. BLPA
It must have been one o'clock at night. To Remain. C. P. Cavafy. ErPo
It nearly cancels my fear of death, my dearest said. Cremation. Robinson Jeffers. ELU
It Never Comes. *Unknown.* SoP
It never occurred to me, never. The Meeting. Howard Moss. NYBP
It never occurred to the turtle that it should hurry. Reluctances. Harold Witt. NYTB
It Nods and Curtseys and Recovers. A. E. Housman. A Shropshire Lad, XVI. NoP; PoVP
It ofttimes has been told. The *Constitution* and the *Guerrière*. *Unknown.* AmSS; SoAmSa; ViBoFo
It once might have been, once only. Youth and Art. Robert Browning. BOHV; BoLiVe; CTC; HBV; MaPo; MBW-2; PoVP; VA; ViBoPo; ViPo
It ought to come in April. Wearing of the Green. Aileen Fisher. YeAr
"It Out-Herods Herod, Pray You Avoid It." Anthony Hecht. CoAP
It Pays. Arnold Bennett. *See* Limerick: "There was a young man of Montrose."
It Pays to Advertise. *Unknown.* TreFT
It pleased the Lord of Angels (praise His name!). A Legend of Service. Henry van Dyke. GBV (1922 ed.)
It quickned next a toyfull Ape, and so. John Donne. *Fr.* The Progresse of the Soule. PoEL-2
It rained/ Upon the tall windows. The Lime Avenue. Sacheverell Sitwell. LOW
It rained a mist, it rained a mist. The Jewish Lady [*or* The Jew's Daughter]. *Unknown.* BaBo; BFSS
It rained, it poured, it rained so hard. Sir Hugh (B *vers.*). *Unknown.* ViBoFo
It rained quite a lot, that spring. You woke in the morning. Metropolitan Nightmare. Stephen Vincent Benét. ImOP; NYBP
It rained toward day. The morning came sad and white. Colder Fire. Robert Penn Warren. *Fr.* To a Little Girl, One Year Old, in a Ruined Fortress. LiTM (1970 ed.); MoVE
It Rains. Edward Thomas. MoVE
It rains and then it rains and still it rains. Rain Inters Maggiore. Alfred Kreymborg. AnAmPo
It rains in Santiago. Madrigal to the City of Santiago. Federico García Lorca. CAD
It rains on Berwyn hills, the night draws on. The Poet's Welcome. Edward Richard. *Fr.* Pastoral Poem. PrWP
It really gives me heartfelt pain. Maria Jane. Alfred Scott-Gatty. BBGG
It Really Happened. Elizabeth Henley. BiCB
It really must. E. E. Cummings. *Fr.* Is 5. AnAmPo; YAD
It rely is ridikkelus. Bobby's First Poem. Norman Gale. MoShBr
It rests me to be among beautiful women. Tame Cat. Ezra Pound. ELU
It ripen'd by the river banks. Circumstance. Frederick Locker-Lampson. BOHV
It rises over the lake, the farms. The Kite. Mark Strand. NYBP
It Rolls On. Morris Bishop. ImOP
It rose dark as a stack of peat. Suilven. Andrew Young. OxBS
It sat between my husband and my children. Seele im Raum. Randall Jarrell. CoBMV; FiMAP
It saves the city. Málaga: Port. Paul Blackburn. OPoP
It say in de Bible. Ku Kluck Klan. Lawrence Gellert. TrAS
It Scarcely Seems Worth While. Vladislav Khodasevich, *tr. fr. Russian by* Babette Deutsch. LiTW
It seconds the crickets of the province. The Rocking Chair. A. M. Klein. CaP; PeCV
It seemed corrival of the world's great prime. A Fallen Yew. Francis Thompson. BrPo; MoAB; MoBrPo
It seemed so mad a thing to do. The Rich Young Man. Laura Simmons. ChIP
It seemed that he would rather hear. Epitaph. Edward Weismiller. PoMa
It seemed that out of the battle I escaped. Strange Meeting. Wilfred Owen. AnFE; AtBAP; BoPe; BrPo; ChMP; CMoP; CoBE; CoBMV; DTC; EnLi-2 (1949 ed.); ExPo; FaBoEn; FaBoMo; FaPL; GTBS-P; GTBS-W; ILP; LiTB; LiTM; LoBV; MMA; MoAB; MoBrPo; MoPo; MoVE; NAMP; NP; OAEP (2d ed.); PoE; PoIE; POTE; SeCeV; ShBV-4; TreFT; TrGrPo; WaaP; WaP
It seemed to be but chance, yet who shall say. May 30, 1893. John Kendrick Bangs. AA
It seemed to me in the night. The Hour Is Late. Winfield Townley Scott. FiMAP
It seemed to me when I saw her. The Torn Nightgown. Joel Oppenheimer. CoPo
It seemed too late for roses. An Autumn Rose-Tree. Michael Earls. JKCP
It seemeth such a little way to me. The Beyond. Ella Wheeler Wilcox. MaRV
It seems a certain time ago: a-maybe. One Time. Douglas Livingstone. PeSA
It seems a day. Nutting. Wordsworth. CBEP; EnRP; ERoP-1
"It seems a shame." The Last Flower. John Travers Moore. PoSC
It seems a stage. The Gypsy's Window. Denise Levertov. ToPo
It seems I have no tears left. They should have fallen. Tears. Edward Thomas. CBEP; GTBS-P; LiTB; MoPW; PoE
It seems like a dream. An Autumn Morning. *Unknown.* BoTP
It seems like a dream—that sweet wooing of old. Bachelor Hall. Eugene Field. BLPA
It seems no work of man's creative hand. Pedra [*or* Petra]. John William Burgon. BLPA; NeHB
It seems now far off and foolish, a memory. Lot Later. Howard Nemerov. NMP
It seems so simple now, that life of thine. Washington. Geraldine Meyrich. OHIP
It seems so strange that I once loved you so. Twenty Years After. Evan V. Shute. CaP
It seems so strange that man, full-blooded man. Quail. Bernard O'Dowd. BoAu
It seems that I hear that beauty who. Lament of the Lovely Helmet-Dealer. Villon. ErPo
It seems that Rome through the long roars of war. The Appian Way. Geoffrey Johnson. JKCP (1955 ed.)
It seems to me I'd like to go. Far from the Madding Crowd [*or* Vacation]. Nixon Waterman. BLPA; FaBoBe; MPB (1956 ed.); NeHB; WBLP
"It seems to me," said Booker T. Booker T. and W. E. B. Dudley Randall. BP; Kal
It seems wrong that out of this bird. A Blackbird Singing. R. S. Thomas. BoC; FIW; POTi; WePo
It semes white and is red. The Sacrament of the Altar. *Unknown.* MeEL
It settles on the lot of us. My wife. Conversation Piece. Philip Hobsbaum. NYTB
It settles softly on your things. The Dust. Gertrude Hall. AA
It shall be said I died for Coelia! Coelia, XIX [*or* Sonnet]. William Percy. EIL; ReEn; ReIE; Sonn; TuPP
It Shall Not Be Again! Thomas Curtis Clark. *See* Apparitions.
It shifts and shifts from form to form. The Name. Don Marquis. HBV
It Should Be Easy. Mark Van Doren. CrMA
It sifts from leaden sieves. Emily Dickinson. DiPo; GoTP; MWA-2; PoPl; RePo; RG
It singeth low in every heart. The Abiding Love [*or* Auld Lang Syne]. John White Chadwick. BLPA; FaBoBe; MaRV
It sings to me in sunshine. Segovia and Madrid. Rose Terry Cooke. AA
It sleeps among the thousand hills. The Unnamed Lake. George Frederick Scott. CAP; NeHB; PTK; WGRP
It snowed in spring on earth so dry and warm. Our Singing Strength. Robert Frost. AnAmPo; AtBAP; CoBA; InP
It so happens I am tired of being a man. Walking Around. "Pablo Neruda." LiTW
It softens now. April snow. The Turning. Philip Booth. NePoAm-2
It soothes the savage doubts. Apocalypse. D. J. Enright. NMP; OPoP

It sounded as if the streets were running. Emily Dickinson. NePA; NoP
It speaks in voices varying with the wind. Africa. Adèle Naudé. PeSA
It spreads, the campaign—carried on. Glory. Marianne Moore. NYBP
It stands upon a plain in far Cathay. The Tower of Genghis Khan. Hervey Allen. HT
It started as a pilgrimage. Enterprise. Nissim Ezekiel. ACV
It started into raining. Me an' My Doney-Gal. *Unknown.* CoSo
It started with an alto horn. Jazz. Frank London Brown. PoNe (1970 ed.)
It Stays. Shirley Kaufman. QAH
It stood embosom'd in a happy valley. Norman Abbey. Byron. *Fr.* Don Juan. OBRV
It stood in the cellar low and dim. The Apple-Barrel. Edwin L. Sabin. DD
It stood on a bleak country corner. The Old Brown Schoolhouse. *Unknown.* TreF
It stops the town we come through. Troop Train. Karl Shapiro. OxBA; WaaP; WaP
It suiteth well that when at table. Table Manners for the Hostess. Jean de Meun. *Fr.* The Romance of the Rose. EnLi-1
It sushes. Cynthia in the Snow. Gwendolyn Brooks. TiPo (1959 ed.)
It takes a heap o' children to make a home that's true. Edgar A. Guest Considers "The Good Old Woman Who Lived in a Shoe" [*or* Just Home]. Louis Untermeyer. FiBHP; MoAmPo; PoPl; StaSt; WhC
It takes a heap o' livin' in a house t' make it home. Home. Edgar A. Guest. BLPA; FaBoBe; OHFP; TreF; YaD
It takes a heart to make a home. To Make a Home. Lon Woodrum. SoP
It takes a little courage. The Only Way to Win. *Unknown.* WBLP
It takes a long time to hear what the sands. The Bones. W. S. Merwin. LiTM (1970 ed.); NePoEA-2
It takes a lot of letters to make up the alphabet. P's and Q's. Rupert Sargent Holland. OTPC
It takes much art. La Carte. Justin Richardson. ELU; FiBHP; SiTL
It Takes So Little. *Unknown.* SoP
It takes the broken soil to grow. God Uses Broken Things. Eva Gray. SoP
It talks and talks, but the words. The Typewriter. Mariana Griswold Van Rensselaer. GFA
It tis hir voice, deare mistress, sweetest hart. *Unknown.* SeCSL
It took the sea a thousand years. Erosion. E. J. Pratt. CaP; CoBE; OnPM; TwCaPo
It took two hours, then six. Marrakech. William M. Hoffman. ThO
It trembled off the keys—a parting kiss. Her Music. Martha Dickinson Bianchi. AA
It troubled me as once I was. Emily Dickinson. ImOP
It was a beautiful and silent day. Residence in France. Wordsworth. The Prelude, X. ERoP-1
It Was a Beauty That I saw. Ben Jonson. *Fr.* The New Inn, IV, iv. AnAnS-2; OBS; ReEn; SeCL; SeEP
(Lovel's Song.) TrGrPo
It was a big house, bleak. Order to View. Louis MacNeice. TDP
It was a blind beggar, had long lost his sight. The Blind Beggar's Daughter of Bednall Green. *Unknown.* LoEn; OBB; OTPC
It was a blue fly with wings of pomegranate gold. Blue Fly. Joaquim Maria Machado de Assis. TTY
It was a bowl of roses. A Bowl of Roses. W. E. Henley. EnLi-2; MeWo; MoBrPo; OuHeWo
It was a bright and cheerful afternoon. Summer and Winter. Shelley. BoNaP; UnPo (3d ed.)
It was a bright day and all the trees were still. Silence. W. J. Turner. MoBrPo
It was a chilly winter's night. A Winter Night. William Barnes. ChTr; OBNC; PoG
It was a close, warm, breezeless summer night. Conclusion. Wordsworth. *Fr.* The Prelude. MBW-2; PoEL-4
It was a comely young lady fair. Dark eyed Canaller. *Unknown.* OuSiCo
It was a cough that carried him off. *Unknown.* WhC
It was a dark and stormy night. The Sailor Boy. *Unknown.* ShS
It was a day of sun and rain. At Fontainebleau. Arthur Symons. VA
It was a day of turning when you came. The Turning. Philip Murray. NePoAm
It was a deliberate moment, and O. W. H. Rodgers. *Fr.* Resurrection—an Easter Sequence. ACV
It was a den where no insulting light. The Den of the Titans. Keats. *Fr.* Hyperion. WHA
It was a dismal, and a fearful night. On the Death of Mr. William Hervey. Abraham Cowley. AnAnS-2; CBEP; GTSL; OBEV; OBS; SeCP; SeCV-1; SeEP; ViBoPo
It was a dismal day when chilling rain. The Greater Gift. Margaret E. Bruner. PoToHe (new ed.)
It was a draper eminent. The Seraph and the Snob. May Kendall. CenHV
It was a dreary day in Padua. Countess Laura. George Henry Boker. BeLS
It was a dreary morning when the wheels. Residence at Cambridge. Wordsworth. The Prelude, III. MBW-2
It was a falling castle, full of drafts. For a Poetry Reading to Which No One Came. Larry Rubin. FiSC
It was a famous story, proclaim it far and wide. The Famous Light Brigade. *Unknown.* ShS
It was a fiery circus horse. The Day of the Circus Horse. T. A. Daly. RIS; UTS
It Was A' for Our Rightfu' King. Burns. *See* Farewell, The: "It was a' for our rightfu' king."
It was a friar of orders free. Song. Thomas Love Peacock. *Fr.* Maid Marian. ViBoPo
It was a friar of orders grey. The Friar of Orders Grey. *Unknown.* ACP; CAW; CEP; GoBC; HBV; OBEC; WHL
It Was a Funky Deal. Etheridge Knight. BOLo
It was a gallant highwayman. Gallant Highwayman, The. James De Mille. WHW
It was a gallant sailor man. The Two Anchors. Richard Henry Stoddard. BeLS
It was a German town that we awoke in. Long Roads. Mikhail Matusovsky. LiTW
It Was a Goodly Co. E. E. Cummings. CrMA; LiTA; LiTM; MoVE; SiTL; WaP
It was a grey day. Tom Thomson. Arthur S. Bourinot. CaP
It was a heavenly time of life. The Quest. Ellen Mackay Hutchinson Cortissoz. HBV
It was a hundred years ago. The White-footed Deer. Bryant. AnNE
It was a hungry pussy cat. A Thanksgiving Fable. Oliver Herford. HH; PRWS; UTS
It was a kind and northern face. Praise for an Urn (In Memoriam: Ernest Nelson). Hart Crane. AmP; AnFE; AP; ATP (1953 ed.); AWP; CMoP; CoAnAm; CoBMV; InPo; LiTG; LiTM (rev. ed.); MAP; MoAB; MoAmPo; MoVE; NoP; OxBA; PoE; ReMP; UnPo (3d ed.)
It was a knight in Scotland borne. The Fair Flower of Northumberland. *Unknown.* BaBo; BuBa; ESPB; LoEn; OBB; OxBB
It was a lady of the north she lov'd a gentleman. Room for a Jovial Tinker: Old Brass to Mend [*or* The Jovial Tinker]. *Unknown.* CoMu; OxBB; UnTE
It was a little captive cat. The Singing Cat. Stevie Smith. BoC
It was a long, long trip on the Erie. Erie Canal. *Unknown.* ABF
It Was a Lording's Daughter. *Unknown, at. to* Shakespeare. *Fr.* The Passionate Pilgrim. EIL
(Contentions.) HBV
It Was a Lover and His Lass. Shakespeare. *Fr.* As You Like It, V, iii. BEL; CBEP; CH; CLwM; EG; EIL; ELP; EnL; EnLi-1; EnLit; ExPo; GTBS; GTBS-D; GTBS-P; GTBS-W; GTSE; GTSL; HBV; InPo; LiTB; LiTG; LiTL; LO; LoBV; NoP; OBEV; PIA; PoRA; ShBV-1; SiCE; SiTL; TOP; UnTE; ViBoPo
(Country Song.) TrGrPo
(In the Spring-Time.) MeWo
(Love in Spring-Time.) MCCG
(Pages' Song, The.) OBSC; SeCePo
(Song: "It was a lover and his lass.") CTC; FiP; YAT
(Song of the Two Pages.) BoLiVe
(Songs from the Plays.) AWP; JAWP; WBP
It was a Maine lobster town. Water. Robert Lowell. OPoP; TDP

It was a merry time. The Courtship, Merry Marriage, and Picnic Dinner of Cock Robin and Jenny Wren. *Unknown.* HBV; OTPC; PPL
It was a mighty monarch's child. Mir traümte von einem Königskind. Heine. AWP
It was a mile of greenest grass. The Occasional Yarrow. Stevie Smith. PoG
It was a millinger most gay. The Fair Millinger. Fred W. Loring. BOHV
It was a miniature country once. Japan. Anthony Hecht. CrMA; LiTM (rev. ed.)
It was a mischievous wind that pushed him; a murderous gust that jarred young Jan from the scaffold. Monument. A. M. Sullivan. GoYe
It was a Moorish maiden was sitting by a well. The Broken Pitcher. William E. Aytoun. BOHV; InMe; PoVP
It was a mother and a maid. The Milk White Doe. *Unknown.* AWP
It was a night in winter. Clive Sansom. *Fr.* The Witnesses. FIW
It was a night of early spring. Wisdom. Sara Teasdale. AmLP; MAP; MoAmPo
It was a noble Roman. Find a Way. John Godfrey Saxe. PEDC
It was a noble Roman. On Fort Sumter. *Unknown.* MC; PAH
It was a perfect day. Sowing. Edward Thomas. HBMV; NP; POTE
It was a place that I had known before. Carcosa. Lin Carter. FiSC
It was a puritanical lad. Two Puritans [*or* Off a Puritane]. *Unknown.* CoMu; UnTE
It was a quiet way. Emily Dickinson. CoBA
It was a railway passenger. Striking. Charles Stuart Calverley. CenHV
It was a rich merchant man. The Merchant and the Fidler's Wife. *Unknown.* CoMu; OxBB
It was a robber's daughter, and her name was Alice Brown. Gentle Alice Brown. W. S. Gilbert. BOHV; FiBHP; InMe; NA; OnSP
It was a rule of Leonardo da Vinci's. Clerihews. E. C. Bentley. OnPP
It was a saying used a great while since. To Master Bastard, Taxing Him of Flattery. Sir John Harington. SiCE
It was a sergeant, old and gray. Picciola. "Orpheus C. Kerr." AA
It was a sheep—not a lamb, that strayed away. 'Twas a Sheep. . Not a Lamb. *Unknown.* SoP
It was a still autumnal day. We Walked among the Whispering Pines. John Henry Boner. AA
It was a summer [*or* summer's] evening. The Battle of Blenheim [*or* After Blenheim]. Robert Southey. BBV; BeLS; BoChLi; BOHV; EnLit; EnRP; EPN; FaBV; FOL; GN; GoTP; GTBS; GTBS-D; GTBS-P; GTBS-W; GTSE; GTSL; HBV; HBVY; InMe; MCCG; MemP; NeHB; OBNC; OBRV; OnSP; OTPC; PaPo; PoLF; PoPo; PoSa; PTK; StP; StVeCh (1940 ed.); TIHL; TOP; TreF; TrGrPo; TRV; WBLP
It was a summer's night, a close warm night. Conclusion. Wordsworth. *Fr.* The Prelude. FaBoEn; OBNC
It was a Sunday evening. The Ballad of Charlotte Dymond. Charles Causley. POTi
It was a tall young oysterman lived by the river-side. The Ballad of the Oysterman. Oliver Wendell Holmes. AmePo; AmPP; AnAmPo; AnNE; AP; BOHV; EtS; FaFP; HBV; HBVY; MCCG; MoShBr; OnSP; PCD; PTK; TreFS; YT
It was a time of trouble—executions. Chesspieces. Joseph Campbell. OxBI
It was a violent time. Wheels, racks and fires. A Mirror for Poets. Thom Gunn. LiTM (1970 ed.); ML; NePoEA
It was a waning crescent. July Dawn. Louise Bogan. NePoAm-2
It was a wasp, or an imprudent bee. The Wasp. Daryl Hine. NYBP
It was a weakness of Voltaire's. Clerihews. E. C. Bentley. OnPP
It was a wild black nicht. In the Hedgeback. "Hugh MacDiarmid." NeBP
It was a wondrous realm beguiled. Alfred Domett. *Fr.* Ranolf and Amohia. ACV
It was a worthy Lord of Lorn. *See* It was the worthy Lord of Lorn.
It was a Yule Day that Arthur lay in London. The Round Table. Layamon. *Fr.* The Brut. EnLi-1
It was about the deep of night. A Ballad of Christmas. Walter de la Mare. StJW
It was about the Martinmas time. Barbara Allan. *Unknown.* EnSB
It was after hearing the parish priest. Virgins. Francis Carlin. HBMV
It was all on a hollow day. Little Matty Groves. *Unknown.* BFSS
It was all over now. The populace. Fishers in the Night. Beulah May. ChIP
It was amusing on that antique grass. Recorders in Italy. Adrienne Rich. TwAmPo; UnS
It was an ancient Mariner. *See* It is an ancient Mariner.
It Was an April Morning. Wordsworth. MERP
It was an artless Bandar, and he danced upon a pine. Divided Destinies. Kipling. BOHV
It was an earthly place, but strangely made. To the Memory of Yale College. Phelps Putnam. AnAmPo
It Was an English Ladye Bright. Sir Walter Scott. *Fr.* The Lay of the Last Minstrel, VI. ATP
(Song of Albert Graeme.) EnRP
It was an hairy oubit, sae proud he crept alang. The Oubit. Charles Kingsley. BOHV; PoVP
It was an hill placed [*or* plaste] in an open plain. Dance of the Graces. Spenser. *Fr.* The Faerie Queene, VI, 10. MBW-1; OBSC; TrGrPo
It was an icy day. Complete Destruction. William Carlos Williams. PoeP
It was an old, old, old, old lady. One, Two, Three. H. C. Bunner. FaPON; HBV; InP; MPB; OTPC; PCH; PoLF; PRWS; TSW; TVC
It was as if Gauguin. Etta Moten's Attic. Margaret Danner. Far from Africa: Four Poems, 4. AmNP
It was as if the devil of evil had got. García Lorca. Louis Dudek. MoCV
It was as if thunder took form upon. Woman Looking at a Vase of Flowers. Wallace Stevens. CrMA; TDP
It was at dinner as they sat. The Laird of Wariston (B *vers.*). *Unknown.* ESPB
It was awful long ago. The Anxious Farmer. Burges Johnson. BoNaP
It was back in nineteen forty-two. Waist Deep in the Big Muddy. Peter Seeger. WOW
It was beside the fire that I had lit. Yea. John Crowe Ransom. Two Sonnets, I LO
It was between the night and day. Evening by the Sea. Swinburne. SyP
It was but now their sounding clamours sung. On the Crucifixion. Giles Fletcher. *Fr.* Christ's Victory and Triumph. OxBoCh
It was but the lightest word of the King. The King. Mary Elizabeth Coleridge. OBVV
It was but yesterday, my love, thy little heart beat high. Lament of Anastasius. William Bourn Oliver Peabody. AA
It was by these men's valor that wide-lawned Tegea. Epigram for the Dead at Tegea. *Unknown.* WaaP
It was by yonder thorn I saw the fairy host. The Fairy Lover. Moireen Fox. AnIV
It was Captain Pierce of the *Lion* who strode the streets of London. The First Thanksgiving [Day]. Clinton Scollard. DD; MC; PAH
It was cause for laughter of a special brand. The Fish. Ralph Gustafson. OBCV
It was Chrismus Eve. I mind hit fu' a mighty gloomy day. Chrismus on the Plantation. Paul Laurence Dunbar. IHA
It was Christmas Eve in the year fourteen. Under the Snow. Robert Collyer. AA
It was dark and frosty, pain congealed into ice. Deportation. "M. J." TrJP
It was down in a lone green valley. The Jealous Lover. *Unknown.* ShS
It was down in old Joe's barroom. Gambler's Blues [*or* Those Gambler's Blues *or* St. James Infirmary]. *Unknown.* AS; TrAS; TreFT
It was down to Red River I came. The Skew-Ball Black. *Unknown.* CoSo

It was Earl Haldan's Daughter. Ballad of Earl Haldan's Daughter. Charles Kingsley. GN; OTPC
It was early, early in one spring. Early in One Spring. *Unknown.* BFSS
It was early, early in the spring. The Croppy Boy. *Unknown.* AnIV; CBEP; OxBoLi; PoFr
It was early, early one mornin'. Stagolee. *Unknown.* TTY
It was early in the season in the spring of '63. Lunberjacks and Teamsters. *Unknown.* OuSiCo
It was early Monday morning Willie Leonard arose. Willie Leonard or the Lake of Cold Finn. *Unknown.* BaBo
It was early one mornin' as I passed St. James Hospital. Cowboy's Lament (Iron Head's Version). *Unknown.* CoSo
It was early Sunday morning in the year of sixty-four. *Kearsarge* and *Alabama.* *Unknown.* PAH
It was easy. How I Came to Rule the World. Marvin Bell. YAP
It was easy enough. Circe. Hilda Doolittle ("H. D."). PoRA (rev. ed.)
It was eight bells in the forenoon and hammocks running sleek. How They Do It. J. C. Squire. HBMV; InMe
It was eight bells ringing. The Fighting *Téméraire.* Sir Henry Newbolt. BBV (1923 ed.); HBV
It was Einar Tamberskelver. Einar Tamberskelver. Longfellow. *Fr* Tales of a Wayside Inn: The Saga of King Olaf. AmPP (4th ed.); YT
It was far in the sameness of the wood. The Demiurge's Laugh. Robert Frost. OxBA
It was for beauty like a fleet at sea. The Faun Tells of the Rout of the Amazons. T. Sturge Moore. AnFE
It Was for Me. Eva Gray. STF
It was for you that the mountains shook at Sinai. Epitaph. *Unknown.* TrJP
It was frosty winter's season. Philomela's Second Ode. Robert Greene. *Fr.* Philomela, the Lady Fitzwater's Nightingale. OBSC; SiCE
It was good to lie in the Cove. Tide Trapped. Floris Clark McLaren. TwCaPo
It was her first sweet child, her heart's delight. Her First-born. Charles Tennyson Turner. VA
It was high noon, the shining hour. J. F. K. Sister M. Stanislaus. TIHL
It was hurry and scurry at Monmouth town. Molly Pitcher. Kate Brownlee Sherwood. PAL
It was in a pleasant depot, sequestered from the rain. The Ballad of Charity. Charles Godfrey Leland. BOHV; GSP; InMe
It was in a pleasant time. Earl Mar's Daughter. *Unknown.* BuBa
It was in and about the Martinmas time. Barbara Allen [*or* Bonny Barbara Allan *or* Sir John Graeme and Barbara Allen]. *Unknown.* AWP; BaBo (A *vers.*); BoLiVe; CABA; CH; CoBE; EnLi-1 (1949 ed.); EnLit; ESPB; ForPo; InPo; JAWP; LiTB; LiTL; LoEn; NoP; OuHeWo; OxBB; OxBoLi; TOP; ViBoFo (A *vers.*); WBP
It was in October, a favorite season. Elegy for a Nature Poet. Howard Nemerov. BoNaP; PP
It was in October the woe began. The Fire of Frendraught (C *vers.*). *Unknown.* ESPB
It was in the lovely month of May. The Troubled Soldier. *Unknown.* AS
It was in the merry, merry month of May. Sweet William. *Unknown.* OuSiCo
It was in the merry month of May. The Trail to Mexico. *Unknown.* AS; IHA
It was in the month of May. Bonny Barbara Allen (C *vers.*). *Unknown.* BaBo
It was in the schooner *Ambition.* The Spring Trip of the Schooner *Ambition.* *Unknown.* ShS
It was in the town of Liverpool, all in the month of May. *Unknown.* LO
It was in the town of Waterford. The Wexford Girl. *Unknown.* ShS (*vers.* II); ViBoFo
It was in the town of Wexford. The Wexford Girl, *vers.* I. *Unknown.* ShS
It was in the Wars of the Roses white and red. The Bonnie House of Airlie (B *vers.*). *Unknown.* BaBo
It was in the year eighteen hundred and forty-nine. Sacramento, *vers.* I. *Unknown.* ShS
It was in the year of forty-four [*or* ninety-four]. The Whale. *Unknown.* AmSS
It Was in Vegas. J. V. Cunningham. UnTE
It was intill a pleasant time. Earl [of] Mar's Daughter. *Unknown.* BaBo; CH; ESPB; GN; HBV; OBB; OnSP
It was Ips, Gips, and Johnson, as I've heard many say. The Three Butchers. *Unknown.* PeVV
It was just before Custer's last fierce charge. Custer's Last Fierce Charge. *Unknown.* BFSS
It was last Monday morning as I have heard them say. Lancashire Lads. *Unknown.* CoMu
It was late in the night when the Squire came home. The Gipsy Laddie. *Unknown.* FaBoCh; LoGBV; OxBoLi; SiTL
It was laughing time, and the tall Giraffe. Laughing Time. William Jay Smith. FaPON; SoPo
It was less than two thousand we numbered. With Corse at Allatoona. Samuel H. M. Byers. PAH
It was like a church to me. The Moor. R. S. Thomas. BoPe
It was like something done in fever, when nothing fits. Walter Benton. *Fr.* This Is My Beloved. UnTE
It was Lilith the wife of Adam. Eden Bower. Dante Gabriel Rossetti. MaVP; PoVP
It was lonely in the zero dark, Admetus. Alcestis. Isabel Williams Verry. GoYe
It was long ago, but I seem to see. The Legend of the Christmas Rose. Florence Boyce Davis. PEDC
It was long ago, I yet remember. The Cross Speaks. *Unknown.* *Fr.* The Dream of the Rood. PoLi
It was Love that built the mountains. The Work of Love. Margaret E. Sangster. BLRP
It was many and many a year ago. A Po-'em of Passion. Charles Fletcher Lummis. BOHV; ShM
It was many and many a year ago. Andrew M'Crie. Robert Fuller Murray. CenHV
It was many and many a year ago. Annabel Lee. Poe. AA; AmePo; AmP; AmPP; AnFE; AP; APA; AWP; BBV; BeLS; BLPA; BoLiVe; BoLP; CH; CLwM; CoAnAm; CoBA; DiPo; EtS; FaFP; FaPL; FaPON; GoTP; GTBS-W; GTSE; HBV; HBVY; HoPM; InPo; JAWP; LiTA; LiTG; LiTL; LoEn; LoGBV; MaC; MAmP; MCCG; MemP; MPB; MWA-1; NeHB; NePA; NoP; OBEV (1st ed.); OBVV; OnMSP; OTD; OtMeF; OTPC; OuHeWo; OxBA; PCD; PG; PoFS; PoG; PoPl; PoPo; PTK; RoGo; SeCeV; StaSt; StPo; StVeCh; TOP; TreF; TrGrPo; ViBoPo; WBP; WBLP; YT
It was maybe eight o'clock. Phyllis and the Philosopher. Josephine Pinckney. NP
It was much later in his life he rose. Muriel Rukeyser. *Fr.* Gibbs. ImOP
It Was My Choice. Sir Thomas Wyatt. EnRePo; FCP; QFR; SiPS
It Was My June. Daryl Duke. TwCaPo
It was my thirtieth year to heaven. Poem in October. Dylan Thomas. BoC; CaFP; CoBMV; DiPo; EnL; GTBS-W; LiTB; LiTM (rev. ed.); MaPo; MoVE; NeBP; NoP; OAEP (2d ed.); PIA; PAn; PoIE; PoPl; PoRA; SeCePo; StP; TDP; ToPo; WePo
It was near evening, the room was cold. The Oath. Allen Tate. LiTM; OxBA
It was nearly morning when the giant. The Reason for Skylarks. Kenneth Patchen. NaP
It was night in the village of Nazareth. Annunciation Night. Katherine E. Conway. CAW; ChIP
It was night-time! God, the Father Good. What the Devil Said. James Stephens. CMoP
It was no enemy which did this wrong. The Sop. *Unknown.* StJW
It was noon when the company marched to the railroad-station. Stephen Vincent Benét. *Fr.* John Brown's Body. ThLM
It was not by vile loitering in ease. The Praise of Industry. James Thomson. *Fr.* The Castle of Indolence. OBEC
It was not death, for I stood up. Emily Dickinson. AmePo; AtBAP; CABA; CBEP; MAPA; MaPo; MasP; MoPo; NoP; NePA; PoAn; PoE; TwAmPo
It was not death to me. The Kiss of God. G. A. Studdert-Kennedy. BLRP
It was not dying: everybody died. Losses. Randall Jarrell. AmP; CoBMV; FiMAP; LiTM (1970 ed.); MoVE; OxBA; UnPo (3d ed.); WaP
It Was Not Fate. William H. A. Moore. BANP
It was not God that told us. We knew. Le Secret Humain. Archibald MacLeish. CMoP

It Was Not in the Winter. Thomas Hood. *See* Time of Roses.
It was not like your great and gracious ways! Departure Coventry Patmore. The Unknown Eros, I, viii. ACP; CoBE; FaPL; GTBS-D; GTSL; HBV; JKCP; LO; OBEV; OBNC; OBVV; PG (1945 ed.); PoLi; PoVP; SeCePo; TreFT
It was not long e're he perceiv'd the skies. Michael Drayton. *Fr.* The Moone-Calfe. PoEL-2
It was not meant for human eyes. The Combat. Edwin Muir. ChMP; CMoP; GTBS-D; LiTB; MoBrPo (1962 ed.)
It was not night, not even when the darkness came. The Annunciation. W. S. Merwin. AP
It Was Not Strange. Esther Lloyd Hagg. PGD
It was not that you said I thought you knew. Colloquial. Rupert Brooke. BrPo
It Was Not You. André Spire, *tr. fr. French by* Jethro Bithell. TrJP
It was nothing but a rose I gave her. A Sigh. Harriet Prescott Spofford. AA; HBV
It was of a sea captain that followed the sea. The Sea Captain. *Unknown.* ViBoFo
It was on a cold winter's night. When Poor Mary Came Wandering Home. *Unknown.* AS
It was on a May, on a midsummer's day. Sir Hugh; or, The Jew's Daughter (N *vers.*). *Unknown.* ESPB
It was on a merry time/ When Jenny Wren was young. Mother Goose. BoChLi (1939 ed.)
It was on a Sunday morn. The Three Butchers. *Unknown.* BFSS
It was on a Sunday morning, the church was far away. The Duff. David McKee Wright. AnNZ
It was on a Wednesday night, the moon was shining bright. Jesse James. *Unknown.* AmPP (3d ed.); AS; BeLS; FaBoBe; PoPo; UnPo; WiR; WOW; YaD
It was on a Yule Day that Arthur in London lay. The Round Table. Layamon. *Fr.* The Brut. MeEV
It was on an evning sae saft and sae clear. The Broom of Cowdenknows (B *vers.*). *Unknown.* ESPB
It was on Christmas Day. All in the Morning. *Unknown.* BiCB
It was on one Monday morning just about one o'clock. The *Titanic* (A *vers.*). *Unknown.* ViBoFo
It was on Saturday eve, in the gorgeous bright October. The Engagement [*or* Autumn in the Highlands]. Arthur Hugh Clough. *Fr.* The Bothie of Tober-na-Vuolich. GTSE; NBM
It was on the fourteenth day of January. Bold Daniels. *Unknown.* SoAmSa
It was on the seventeenth, by break of day. The Battle of Bunker Hill. *Unknown.* PAH
It was on [*or* out on] the western frontier. The Clown's Baby. "Margaret Vandegrift." PaPo; SCC
It was one afternoon when I was young. The Tale the Hermit Told. Alastair Reid. NePoEA-2
It was one fine day in the month of May. The *River Lea.* Sam Peck. SoAmSa
It was one summer's morning on the fourteenth day of May. The Mower. *Unknown.* CoMu
It was only a few short years ago. The Cowboy. *Unknown.* CoSo
It was only a kindly smile he gave. Little Things. *Unknown.* STF
It was only a tiny seed. Only a Little Thing. Mrs. M. P. Handy. PoToHe
It was only important. The Moss of His Skin. Anne Sexton. CoAP
It was only my own voice that I had heard. This One Heartshaken. Sister Maris Stella. GoBC
It was only the clinging touch. The Child. George Edward Woodberry. Wild Eden, XXX. AA
It was only two fields away from the house. In Memoriam I: Elizabeth at Twenty. Richard Weber. ErPo
It was our hard general's false treachery. Braddock's Defeat. *Unknown.* ABF
It was our love's Gethsemane, and you wept. The Dark Memory. John Hall Wheelock. LiTL
It was our room, that cold day. Window, Painted Shut. Phillip Hey. YAP
It Was Out by Donnycarney. James Joyce. Chamber Music, XXXI. MeWo
It was out on the western frontier. *See* It was on the western frontier.
It was Private Blair, of the regulars, before dread El Caney. Private Blair of the Regulars. Clinton Scollard. PAH
It was quite a day at Melrose. All the folks had come to town there. Coronation Day at Melrose. Peter Bladen. PoAu-2
It was roses, roses, all the way. The Patriot. Robert Browning. EPN; GTBS-D; MemP; PoRA; PoVP; TrGrPo; ViPP
It was running down to the great Atlantic. The Stream. Lula Lowe Weeden. CDC
It was simply a dark. The Color. John Haines. ThO
It was six foot four of my father. The Brigg. Robin Skelton. NMP
It was six men of Indostan [*or* Hindostan]. The Blind Men and the Elephant. John Godfrey Saxe. AmePo; AnNE; BBV (1951 ed.); BLPA; BoTP; FaBoBe; GoTP; GSP; HBV; HBVY; MaC; MaRV; NeHB; OnMSP; OTPC; PCD; PoToHe (new ed.); StPo; StVeCh (1940 ed.); TreF; TSW; WBLP
It was so cold the skyline seemed to splinter. Contrast. Eileen Duggan. ACV; AnNZ
It was something to see that their white was different. Holiday in Reality. Wallace Stevens. NePA; OxBA
It was something you did not know. An Air by Sammartini. Louis Dudek. OBCV
It was sometime in the P.M. of the fall of '92. Doing Railroads for *The Rocky Mountain News.* Cy Warman. PoOW
It was strange O strange. A Green and Pleasant Land. John Peale Bishop. PoPl
It was strange when I fell to the bottom of Column A. Column A. Michael Silverton. PV
It was such a bright morning. A Day in Spring [*or* Beautiful Sunday]. "Jake Falstaff." BoC; BoNaP
It was sudden. The Sea Fog. Josephine Jacobsen. NYBP
It was taken a long time ago. The Verdict. Norman Cameron. SeCePo
It was that fierce contested field when [*or* where] Chickamauga lay. Thomas at Chickamauga. Kate Brownlee Sherwood. PAH
It was the autumn of the year. Left Behind. Elizabeth Akers Allen. HBV
It was. The breach smelling of oil. First Blood. Jon Stallworthy. TPM
It was the busy hour of 4. Spring Arithmetic. *Unknown.* FiBHP
It was the calm and silent night! A Christmas Hymn. Alfred Domett. DD; GN; GTBS; HBV; OBVV; OTPC; VA; WGRP
It Was the Cat. W. S. Gilbert. *Fr.* H.M.S. Pinafore. CIV
It was the charming month of May. Chloe. Burns. GN; HBV; OTPC
It was the cooling hour, just when the rounded. Juan and Haidee. Byron. *Fr.* Don Juan. OBNC; OBRV; ViBoPo
It was the departure, the sun was risen. Farewell Voyaging World! Conrad Aiken. NYBP
It was the earth that Dante trod. About an Allegory. Walter Conrad Arensberg. AnAmPo
It was the fruit on high. Soul's Kiss. Samuel Greenberg. LiTA
It was the good ship *Billycock,* with thirteen men aboard. The Ballad of [*or* to] the *Billycock.* Anthony C. Deane. ALV; NeMA; TSW
It Was the Last of the Parades. Louis Simpson. NYBP
It was the little Isabel. Bell's Dream. Frederic Edward Weatherly. OTPC
It Was the Love of Life. Siegfried Sassoon. CMoP
It Was the Lovely Moon. John Freeman. BoNaP; POTE
It was the man from Ironbark who struck the Sydney town. The Man from Ironbark. A. B. Paterson. PoAu-1
It was the month in which the righteous maide. Prosopopoia; or, Mother Hubberd's Tale. Spenser. ReIE
It was the morning of the first of May. Popular Songs of Tuscany. *Unknown.* AWP; JAWP; WBP
It was the night before the famous day. The Death of Santa Claus. Vincent Starrett. FiSC
It was the rainbow gave thee birth. The Kingfisher. W. H. Davies. BoPe; GTBS-D; MoVE; OBEV (new ed.); POTE; ShBV-2; TSW
It was the schooner *Hesperus.* The Wreck of the *Hesperus.* Longfellow. AmePo; AnNE; ATP (1935 ed.); BeLS; BoChLi (1939 ed.); CoBA; EtS; FaBoBe; FaFP; FaPL; FaPON; GN; GSP; HBV; HBVY; NeHB; OnSP; OTPC; PAH; PaPo; TreF; WBLP

It was the season, when through all the land. The Birds of Killingworth. Longfellow. *Fr.* Tales of A Wayside Inn. OnMSP; OxBA
It was the soul of Karnaghan Buidhe. The Soul of Karnaghan Buidhe. James B. Dollard. JKCP
It was the stage driver's story, as he stood with his back to the wheelers. The Stage Driver's Story. *Unknown.* IHA
It was the Stately Southerner, that carried the Stripes and Stars. The Stately Southerner. *Unknown.* SoAmSa
It was the Sun that drew her up from the earth. Our Lady's Assumption. Sister Agnes. JKCP (1955 ed.)
It Was the Time of Roses. Thomas Hood. *See* Time of Roses.
It was the time of year. A Prehistoric Camp. Andrew Young. CBEP; MoPW
It was the time when lilies blow. Lady Clare. Tennyson. BeLS; FaPON; HBV; LoEn; OnMSP; OTPC; StPo; StVeCh
It was the time, when rest, soft sliding downe. Sonnet. Joachim du Bellay. *Fr.* Visions. AWP; OnPM; Sonn
It was the very noon of night: the stars above the fold. The Story of the Shepherd. *Unknown.* OHIP
It was the wild midnight. The Death of Leonidas. George Croly. BeLS
It was the wildest vanity. Interlude. Eileen Duggan. AnNZ
It was the winter wild. Hymn. Milton. *Fr.* On the Morning of Christ's Nativity. FiP; OBEV; OtMeF; StJW; WHA
It was the [*or* a] worthy Lord of Lorn [*or* Learne]. The Lord of Lorn and the False Steward. *Unknown.* ESPB; OBB; OxBB
It was then I dreamed. A Dream of Metals. Jack Anderson. ThO
It was then night; the sounde and quiet slepe. Vergil. *Fr.* The Aeneid, IV. PoEL-1; YAT
It was then she struck—from behind. The Wanderer; Broadway. William Carlos Williams. TwAmPo
It was there, again. Nightmare in Morganza. Joseph Joel Keith. FiSC
It was there on the hillside, no tall traveller's story. Pegasus. C. Day Lewis. AtBAP
It was this way. Rumoresque Senum Severiorum. Marcus Argentarius. ErPo; LiTW
It was three slim does and a ten-tined buck in the bracken lay. The Revenge of Hamish. Sidney Lanier. AnEnPo; AP; CoBA; HoPM; PoEL-5; TOP
It was through a mucous membrane, a kind of mouth. Lion, Leopard, Lady. Douglas Le Pan. OBCV
It was Tiny's habit. Sketches of Harlem. David Henderson. Kal; NNP; PoNe (1970 ed.)
It was too dark in the chimney corner to see. Cinderella. Cynthia Pickard. PoPl
It was too late for man. Early for God. Emily Dickinson. OnPM
It was too lonely for her there. The Impulse. Robert Frost. *Fr.* The Hill Wife. AWP; LiTM; LO; NePA; NP
It was touching when I started. Aunt Nerissa's Muffin. Wallace Irwin. FiBHP
It was twenty years ago I saw the fox. The Fox. Phoebe Hesketh. HaMV
It was upon a Lammas night. The Rigs o' Barley [*or* Corn Rigs Are Bonny *or* Song]. Burns. CBEP; EiCL; ErPo; LiTB; LoBV; OxBS; UnTE; ViBoPo
It was upon a Maundy Thursday that our Lord arose. Judas. *Unknown.* FIW
It was very early in the spring. The Croppy Boy. *Unknown.* AnI!
It was water I was trying to think of all the time. Appoggiatura. Donald Jeffrey Hayes. AmNP; PoNe
It was wet & white & swift and where I am. Snow Line. John Berryman. The Dream Songs, XXVIII. NaP
It was, when scarce had rang the morning bells. An Almanack for the Year of Our Lord 1657. Samuel Bradstreet. SCAP
It was when weather was Arabian I went. Allegory of the Adolescent and the Adult. George Barker. LiTB; MasP
It was wild. Assassination. Don L. Lee. BOLo; BP
It was winter. Christmas Star. Boris Pasternak, *tr. by* Lydia Pasternak. FIW
It was wintertime. Star of the Nativity. Boris Pasternak, *tr. by* Eugene M. Kayden. PoPl
It was worth the while of a boy to live. In the Days When the Cattle Ran. Hamlin Garland. MPB; RePo
It Was Wrong to Do This, Said the Angel. Stephen Crane. The Black Riders, LIV. AmP; AP; LiTA; NePA
It was yesterday she roller-skated down. Eighteen. Sister Mary Honora. NePoAm-2
It was young David, lord of sheep and cattle. Five Smooth Stones. Stella Benson. MoBrPo (1942 ed.)
It wasn't a sizable interruption. The Mole. William H. Matchett. WIRo
It wasn't Ernest; it wasn't Scott. Song for the Squeeze-Box. Theodore Roethke. NePoAm
It wasn't our battalion, but we lay alongside it. Sergeant-Major Money. Robert Graves. MMA
It were a double grief, if the true-hearted. Longfellow. *Fr.* Auf Wiedersehen. OQP
It were easiest to say, "The moon and lake." Sonnet. Muna Lee. NP
It were my soul's desire. The Soul's Desire. *Tr. by* Eleanor Hull. OxBI
It wes upon a Scere Thorsday that oure Lord aros. Judas Sells His Lord. *Unknown.* MeEL
It will all get explained. Blues. Bob Maxey. WSL
It will always be like this. Departure Platform. Kenneth Allott. NeBP
It will be all the same in a hundred years. In a Hundred Years. Elizabeth Doten. BLPA
It will be easy to love you when I am dead. Sonnet. Muna Lee. HBMV
It will be looked [*or* look'd] for, book[e], when some but see. To My Book[e]. Ben Jonson. AnAnS-2; EP; MaPo; OAEP; Po; ReIE; SCEP-2; SeCV-1; TuPP
It will be strange. When the Vacation Is Over for Good. Mark Strand. NYBP
It will be with us always through our lives. The Quiet Flower. Josephine W. Johnson. MoRP
It will not always be like this. A Day in Autumn. R. S. Thomas. BoNaP; WePo
It will not matter. The First Harp-Player. Humbert Wolfe. MuSP
It will not meet us where the shadows fall. "And the Life Everlasting." Percy Clough Ainsworth. MaRV
It will not stay! The robe so pearly white. The April Snow. Jones Very. AP
It will rain tonight. New Life. Joseph E. Kariuki. TTY
It will snow tomorrow. La Bohème. Dick Gallup. ANYP
It worries me to beat the band. Ain't It Awful, Mabel? John Edward Hazzard. BOHV
It would have starved a gnat. Emily Dickinson. MoVE
It would never be morning, always evening. Memory of Brother Michael. Patrick Kavanagh. MoAB; OnYI; OxBI
It wouldn't be so bad if he. In Extremis. Margaret Fishback. FiBHP
It wound through strange scarred hills, down cañons lone. The Old Santa Fé Trail. Richard Burton. PAH
It wuz one day, I believe in May, when old Si Hubbard to me did say. Si Hubbard. *Unknown.* AS; IHA
Italia, Io Ti Saluto! Christina Rossetti. LO; OBVV
Italia, mother of the souls of men. On the Monument Erected to Mazzini at Genoa. Swinburne. VA
Italia! Oh Italia! thou who hast. Italy. Vincenzo da Filicaja, *tr. by* Byron. AWP; OnPM; WoL
Italia, O Italia, upon whom. Sonnet. Vincenzo da Filicaja, *tr. by* Lorna de' Lucchi. PoFr
Italian Air, The. Lewis Mac Adams. ANYP
Italian boy that liked to play, An. Columbus. Annett Wynne. HH; MPB; TiPo
Italian Chest, An. Marjorie Allen Seiffert. HBMV
(Lorenzo's Bas-Relief for a Florentine Chest.) NP
Italian Extravaganza. Gregory Corso. CoPo; OCS
Italian Husband, The, *sel.* Edward Ravenscroft.
In Derision of a Country Life. SeCL
Italian in England, The. Robert Browning. MaVP; OAEP; PoVP; ViPo
Italian Lullaby. *Unknown, tr. fr. Italian.* FaPON
Italian Music in Dakota. Walt Whitman. AmePo; AmP
Italian Opera. James Miller. OBEC; UnS, *abr.*
(Foreign Songsters.) MuSP
Italian Poppies. Joel Elias Spingarn. HBMV
Italian Rhapsody. Robert Underwood Johnson. HBV
Italy. Byron. *Fr.* Beppo. OBRV; SeCePo
Italy. Vincenzo da Filicaja, *tr. fr. Italian.* AWP; WoL
(Italia! Oh Italia! *tr. by* Byron.) OnPM
(Sonnet: "Italia, O Italia," *tr. by* Lorna de' Lucchi.) PoFr
Italy, *sels.* Samuel Rogers.

Italy (continued)
Byron Recollected at Bologna. OBNC
(Bologna and Byron.) OBRV
Ginevra. BeLS; PoLF
Interview near Florence, An. OBNC
Italy and Britain. Addison. *Fr.* A Letter from Italy. OBEC
Itch to Etch, The. Harold A. Larrabee. WhC
Itchin, when I behold thy banks again. To the River Itchin, near Winton. William Lisle Bowles. ERoP-1
Ité. Ezra Pound. MAP; MoAB; MoAmPo; PP; TwAmPo
Ite Domum Saturae, Venit Hesperus. Arthur Hugh Clough. BEL; EnLit; EPN; PoVP; VA
(Les Vaches.) OAEP
Item. E. E. Cummings. MoAB; MoAmPo
Iter Boreale, *sel.* Robert Wild.
"I, he, who whileom sate and sung in cage." PeRV
Iter Supremum. Arthur Sherburne Hardy. AA
Ithaca. C. P. Cavafy, *tr. fr. Modern Greek by* Edward Fenton. LiTW
'Ithin the woodlands flow'ry gleaded. Linden Lea. William Barnes. GTSE
Itiskit, Itaskit, *with music. Unknown.* TrAS
(Kitty, Kitty Casket, *diff. vers., with music.*) OuSiCo
(Tisket, a Tasket, A.) RIS
It's a Beautiful Day! Alice Hansche Mortenson. SoP
It's a cage I'm building. The Cage. Eric Torgersen. QAH
It's a certain voice, it's the sound. The Homeland. Emile Cammaerts. PoFr
It's a comfort to me in life's battle. The Little Child's Fatih. Louis E. Thayer. PoToHe
"It's a damn skinny get-by." Have Sky. Lewis Mac Adams. ANYP
It's a dark and dreary season. Triolet on a Dark Day. Margaret Fishback. PoSC
It's a debatable land. The winds are variable. Helen Bevington. *Fr.* Report from the Carolinas. AmFN
It's a Far, Far Cry. Patrick MacGill. HBMV
It's a Fib. "Elspeth." ALV
It's a Gay Old World. *Unknown.* FaFP
It's a great deal better to lose than win. After Reading Certain Books. Mary Elizabeth Coleridge. EaLo
It's a great pleasure to. Many Happy Returns. Ted Berrigan. ANYP
It's a great separation my friends they have caused me. Adieu to Bon County. *Unknown.* ABF
It's a likelier requisition. Angels Adoring. Jonathan Cott. YAP
It's a lonely road through bogland to the lake at Carrowmore. Carrowmore [*or* The Gates of Dreamland]. "Æ." BEL; HBMV; HBV
It's a Long Way. William Stanley Braithwaite. GoSl
It's a long way out of the past and a long way forward. Written in a Time of Crisis. Stephen Vincent Benét. PAL
It's a Mighty Good World. Robert W. Service. OTD, 1 *st.*
It's a mournful tune the rain is making. Spinster Song. Virginia Lyne Tunstall. HBMV
It's a Queer Time. Robert Graves. MCCG; MoAB; MoBrPo; NeMA
It's a *rum*—/ Ba band. "And Now. . ." J. B. Boothroyd. FiBHP
It's a sitting-pretty, windy-city kind of a place. Tonight in Chicago. *Unknown.* AmFN
It's a strange courage. Nuances of a Theme by Williams. Wallace Stevens. CMoP; LiTA
It's a strange courage. El Hombre. William Carlos Williams. CABA; CMoP; LiTA
It's a sunny pleasant anchorage, is Kingdom Come. Port of Many Ships. John Masefield. OBMV
It's a very odd thing. Miss T. Walter de la Mare. CenHV; FaBoBe; GFA; GoJo; MoShBr; MPB (1956 ed.); PDV; PoRh; SoPo; SUS; TiPo; TSW
"It's a very warm day," observed Billy. Limerick. Tudor Jenks. BOHV
It's a warm wind, the west wind, full of birds' cries. The West Wind. John Masefield. BEL; EnLi-2 (1949 ed.); EnLit; FaFP; GTBS-W; GTSL; InP; LiTB; LiTM; MemP; MoAB; MoBrPo; PG; PoPl; TOP; TreF; TSW
Its Ain Drap o' Dew. James Ballantine. HBV
It's all a trick, quite easy when you know it. Villanelle. W. W. Skeat. FiBHP; SiTL
It's all aboard for outer space. Space Travel. Jane W. Krows. SoPo
It's all in. The Poem. William Carlos Williams. PoeP
It's all too swift; it's over all too soon. A Plea for Postponement. Petronius. UnTE
It's all very well to dream of a dove that saves. Birdwatchers of America. Anthony Hecht. CoPo
It's all very well to write reviews. Lasca. Frank Desprez. BLPA; HBV; SCC
It's an approach. Say what you like. Astrology. Tom Marshall. PeCV (1967 ed.)
It's autumn in the country I remember. Mnemosyne. Trumbull Stickney. AmePo; AnFE; CoAnAm; CrMA; LiTA; NCEP; OxBA; TDP; TwAmPo; ViBoPo (1958 ed.)
It's awf'lly bad luck on Diana. Hunter Trials. John Betjeman. FiBHP; MemP
Its blossoms dried, its glories brief. Midsummer. Hermann Hesse. LiTW
It's Christmas Day. I did not get. Otto. Gwendolyn Brooks. PDV
It's clear, Trojan cried out to Greek. Why They Waged War. John Peale Bishop. NYBP
Its cloven hoofprint on the sand. How to Catch Unicorns. William Rose Benét. HBMV; TSW
It's co-existence. A Message for the Nations of the World. Bertrand Russell. SiTL
It's cold and raw the north winds blow. The Maid That Sold Her Barley. *Unknown.* OnYI
"It's cold," said the cricket. Halloween Concert. Aileen Fisher. SiSoSe
It's cold, says Crean at the tiller. Douglas Stewart. *Fr.* Worsley Enchanted. NeLNL
It's coming, boys. In Trust. Mary Mapes Dodge. PPL; SiSoSe
Its cry is mournful. Tanka: The Cry of the Crane. Tsurayuki. InP
It's cuddle-me-time by the nursery clock. A Rock-a-bye Song. Helen Wing. GFA
It's dark in this wood, soft mocker. Praise to the End! Theodore Roethke. ToPo
It's dark out, Jack. All the Roary Night. Kenneth Patchen. LiTM (1970 ed.)
It's doing your job the best you can. Success [*or* That's Success]. Berton Braley. PoToHe; WBLP
It's easy to die 'mid the world's applause. The Greater Glory. Myra Brooks Welch. MaRV
It's easy to fight when everything's right. Carry On! Robert W. Service. HBV; MaRV
It's easy to invent a life. Emily Dickinson. AmePo
It's easy to talk of the patience of Job. Humph! Job hed nothin' to try him! The Inventor's Wife. Mrs. E. T. Corbett. PoLF
Its edges foamed with amethyst and rose. The Great Breath. "Æ." EPN; MoBrPo; OBEV; OBMV, OxBI; VA; WGRP; WHA
It's 8:54 A.M. in Brooklyn it's the 28th of July and. Ted Berrigan. ANYP
Its eyes are gray. A Sketch from the Life. Arthur Guiterman. BOHV
It's far I must be going. Via Longa. Patrick McDonough. HBMV
It's farewell to the drawing-room's civilized cry. Song for the New Year. W. H. Auden. EnLi-2 (1949 ed.)
It's fifty miles to Sittingen's Rocks. Prince Robert (B *vers.*). *Unknown.* ESPB
It's Fine Today. Douglas Malloch. *See* "Ain't It Fine Today!"
It's 5:03 A.M. on the 11th of July this morning. Personal Poem #8. Ted Berrigan. ANYP
It's foolish to bring money. Spring Market. Louise Driscoll. HBMV; HBVY
Its former green is blue and thin. The Garden Seat. Thomas Hardy. GoJo
It's forty in the shade to-day, the spouting eaves declare. Pan in Vermont. Kipling. WhC
It's four long years since I reached this land. The Lousy Miner. John A. Stone. SGR
It's full of the moon. Full of the Moon. Karla Kuskin. PDV
It's fun to clean house. I Like House Cleaning. Dorothy Brown Thompson. BrR; FaPON
It's fun to go out and buy new shoes to wear. Mary Ann Hoberman. TiPo (1959 ed.)

It's funny early spring weather, mild and washy. 3/26/66. James Schuyler. ANYP
It's funny how a little thing. Reminder. *Unknown.* STF
It's funny how often they say to me, "Jane?" The Good Little Girl. A. A. Milne. BBGG
It's gettin' bits o' posies. Sweethearts. Mary Gilmore. BoAu
It's going to come out all right—do you know? Caboose Thoughts. Carl Sandburg. AnAmPo; CMoP
It's going to rain. The Watchers. Paul Blackburn. NMP; NYBP
"It's going to rain," said Noah. His friend laughed. Noah. Hermann Hagedorn. MoRP
It's good to be back. In the Garden. Ilo Orleans. RIS
It's great to be alive and be. It's Simply Great. Sidney Warren Mase. PoToHe
It's growing evening in my soul. In Summer. Trumbull Stickney. NCEP
It's hair and dress, framing old portrait faces. Eternal Contour. Florida Watts Smyth. GoYe
It's Hard on We Po' Farmers, *with music.* *Unknown.* OuSiCo
"It's hard to be without a wage," I said. Unemployed. Ralph Cheyney. ChIP
It's hard to breathe in a tenement hall. Song of a Factory Girl. Marya Zaturenska. HBMV; NP
It's hard to know if you're alive or dead. It's a Queer Time. Robert Graves. MCCG; MoAB; MoBrPo; NeMA
It's hard to think. To a Human Skeleton. Richard Armour. WhC
It's he, it's sea. The sea is continuous; a continuous body. Sea. Bernadette Mayer. ANYP
It's Here in The. Russell Atkins. AmNP
Its ice cap, milky green. Expedition North. John Morgan. YAP
It's in Bolton Hall, and the clock strikes one. The Lay of St. Cuthbert. "Thomas Ingoldsby." OtMeF
It's in Connacht in Munster that yourself might travel wide. Kerry Cow. Winifred M. Letts. TSW
It's in Your Face. *Unknown.* PoLF
(God Shows in Your Face.) SoP
It's I've got a ship in the north country. The Golden Vanity. *Unknown.* ELP
It's Jamie rose on a May morning. James o' Broodies. *Unknown.* BFSS
It's Jim Farrow and John Farrow and little Simon, too. Jim Farrow. *Unknown.* CoSo
It's jolly/ Odd what pops into. E. E. Cummings. ThLM
It's just the little homely things. Little Things. *Unknown.* PoToHe (new ed.)
It's just the way we carry through. The Business of the Day. Patience Strong. SoP
It's kind of you to let me have my hat. Hattage. A. P. Herbert. FiBHP
It's Lamkin was a mason good. Lamkin. *Unknown.* BaBo (A *vers.*); CBEP; ESPB; FosPo; OBB; OxBB; ViBoFo
It's Little for Glory I Care. Charles James Lever. *Fr.* Charles O'Malley, the Irish Dragoon. OnYI
(Mickey Free's Song.) ALV
It's little I care what path I take. Departure. Edna St. Vincent Millay. MAP; MoAmPo
It's Little Joe, the wrangler. Little Joe, the Wrangler. *At. to* N. Howard Thorp. CoSo
It's lonely in lodgings above the street. A Lonely Man. Agnes Lee. NP
Its masts of might, its sails so free. The Wreck. John Ruskin. VA
It's Me, O Lord, *with music.* *Unknown.* BoAN-1
"It's mending worse," he said. Old Man at a Cricket Match. Norman Nicholson. HaMV; POTi
It's Midsummer Day. Haytime. Irene F. Pawsey. BoTP
It's more than just an easy word for casual good-bye. Aloha Oe. Don Blanding. PoToHe (new ed.)
It's my lunch hour, so I go. A Step Away from Them. Frank O'Hara. ANYP
Its Name Is Known. Daniel Lawrence Kelleher. NeIP
"It's narrow, narrow, make [*or* mak] your bed." Fair Annie. *Unknown.* AnFE; BaBo (A *vers.*); ESPB; OBB; ViBoFo (A *vers.*)
It's Never Easy. Phyllis C. Michael. SoP
It's no go the merry-go-round [*or* merrygoround], it's no go the rickshaw. Bagpipe Music. Louis MacNeice. ExPo; GTBS-P; ILP; LiTB; LiTM; NoP; OAEP (2d ed.); OnYI; PoE; PoSa; SeCePo; SeCeV; SiTL; ViBoPo (1958 ed.)
It's No Good! D. H. Lawrence. PV
It's no joke at all, I'm not that sort of poet. The Confession. Wen Yi-tuo. ChTr; LiTW
It's no use having good taste in Chicago. Disclaimer of Prejudice. Eli Siegel. PV
It's No Use Raising a Shout. W. H. Auden. HoPM; LiTM; OBMV; ReMP
It's not/ Your ignorance I mind. A Letter. Alex Raybin. ThO
It's not a bit windy. Toadstools. Elizabeth Fleming. BoTP
It's not a landscape from too near. Variations on a Theme from James. Donald Justice. TDP
It's not adultery, the lawyers say. Stop, Science—Stop! A. P. Herbert. FiBHP
"It's not I," said the cat. Who Is Tapping at My Window. A. G. Deming. SoPo
It's not my role to ask today. Until Eternity. Phyllis C. Michael. SoP
It's not so hard to ask You, Lord. The Harder Task. Katherine L. Ramsdell. SoP
It's not so much the things without. Happiness. Walter E. Isenhour. STF
It's not so much what you say. The Tone of Voice. *Unknown.* PoToHe (new ed.)
It's not the age,/ Disease, or accident. Apologia. David Gascoyne. ChMP
It's not the thickened midriff that I mind. So This Is Middle Age! Francis Whiting Hatch. WhC
It's not the tunes that it can play. The Old Music Box. Rachel Field. BoChLi
It's not very far to the edge of town. Adventure. Harry Behn. TiPo (1959 ed.)
It's odd to have a separate month. October. Bill Berkson. ANYP
It's of a blind beggar, and he lost his sight. The Blind Beggar of Bednall (Bethnal) Green. *Unknown.* BaBo
It's of a brisk young butcher, as I have heard 'em say. Leicester Chambermaid. *Unknown.* CoMu
It's of a fair young creature that dwelt by the sea side. Mary on the Silvery Tide. *Unknown.* ShS
It's of a famous American ship, for New York we are bound. The *Shenandoah.* *Unknown.* SoAmSa
It's of a famous [*or* fearless] highway-man a story I will [*or* now I'll] tell. Brennan on the Moor. *Unknown.* OnYI; ViBoFo
It's of a rich squire in Bristol doth dwell. Squire and Milkmaid; or, Blackberry Fold. *Unknown.* CoMu; OxBB
It's of a young lord o' the Hielands. Lizie Lindsay [*or* Donald of the Isles]. *Unknown.* ESPB; OxBB
It's of those Texas cowboys a story I'll tell. The Lone Buffalo Hunter [*or* The Texas Cowboys]. *Unknown.* CoSo
It's once I courted as pretty a lass. *Unknown.* OxNR
It's only we, Grimalkin, both fond and fancy free. The Ride to Cherokee. Amelia Walstein Carpenter. AA
It's Over a (See Just). E. E. Cummings. MoPW; OxBA
It's over, it's over! Taking Down the Tree. Aileen Fisher. RePo
It's Pleasant to Think. Elizabeth J. Coatsworth. RePo
(Sitting Here.) UTS
Its presence is not impeded by visible form. The Human Mind. Ai Shih-te. TrJP
It's primrose petals for a gown. The Fairy Frock. Katharine Morse. UTS
It's queer about my Uncle Frank. Uncle Frank. Monica Shannon. GaP
"It's queer," she said, "I see the light." The Maid Servant at the Inn. Dorothy Parker. StJW
Its quick soft silver bell beating, beating. Auto Wreck. Karl Shapiro. AmLP; CMoP; FlW; ILP; LiTM; MiAP; MoVE; NePA; PoAn; PoPl; PoPo; ReMP
It's quiet in Hell just now, it's very tame. Lament of an Idle Demon. R. P. Lister. FiBHP
It's raining again in the Southwest. Rain in the Southwest. Reeve Spencer Kelley. AmFN
It's Raining, It's Pouring. *Unknown.* OxNR; TrAS, *with music*
It's raining, it's raining. *Unknown.* OxNR
It's raining today and I'm reading about pharmacies in Paris. Les Réalités. Barbara Guest. AmPC

It's rare to see the morning breeze. The Ingle-Side. Hew Ainslie. HBV; OTPC (1923 ed.)
It's really almost past belief. Harriet and the Matches. Heinrich Hoffmann. RIS
It's right to have a little maid. Song Against Servants. Gertrude Jane Codd. JKCP (1926 ed.)
Its roof among the stars projected. Phantasus. Arno Holz. AWP; JAWP; WBP
It's seldom wise to generalize. Homage to Texas. Robert Graves. LiTB
It's Simply Great. Sidney Warren Mase. PoToHe
It's singin' in an' out. Marri'd. Mary Gilmore. BoAu
It's so cold and shiny till the birds can't hardly sing. Lines from the Blues. *Unknown.* OuSiCo
It's Somebody's Birthday. Leslie Norris. NYTB
It's spring; the City, wrapped. To His Chi Mistress. George Starbuck. NYBP
It's springtime in Donegal. Springtime in Donegal. Mabel Rose Stevenson. StVeCh
It's step her to your weev'ly wheat. Weevily Wheat. *Unknown.* AS
"It's strange," my mother said, "to think." My Mother's House. Eunice Tietjens. HBMV; NP
It's such a little thing to weep. Emily Dickinson. AmePo; AmP; AmPP
It's such a static reference; looking. Epistrophe. LeRoi Jones. CAD; Kal; NNP; PoNe (1970 ed.)
Its sudden dash from the huddled trees. The Death of a Squirrel in McKinley Park. Gerald William Barrax. Kal
It's 10 A.M. we got the jolly roger's gold. White Country. Peter Schjeldahl. ANYP
It's the anarchy of poverty. The Poor. William Carlos Williams. MoAB; MoAmPo; NeMA; NoP
It's the end of the world! The End of the World. Arnold Kemp. WSL
It's the great leap forward. The Growth. Marvin Bell. YAP
It's the long road to Guinea. Guinea. Jacques Roumain. PoNe; TTY
It's the mixture of peasantry. Peasant. Alfred Kreymborg. MAP
It's the Same the Whole World Over. *Unknown.* *See* Poor but Honest.
It's the spring. Pastoral. W. E. Henley. *Fr.* In Hospital. Po
It's the Syme the Whole World Over. *Unknown.* AS, *with music*; TrAS, *with music*; TreFS
(It's the Syme the Wide World Over.) BeLS
It's the way I conceive myself sometimes. The Horses. Keith Wilson. ThO
It's there/ in the hole of the sea. The Hole in the Sea. Marvin Bell. NYBP
It's there you'll see confectioners with sugar sticks and dainties. Galway Races. *Unknown.* OxBoLi; SD
It's Three No Trumps. Guy Innes. FiBHP
It's time again. "Earth's Holocaust." James Schuyler. ANYP
It's time for bloody Watusis to romp through the streets. Time Poem. Quentin Hill. NBP
It's time to make love. Douse the glim. Limberick. Conrad Aiken. FiBHP; SiTL
It's time to say farewell. My horse I stay. Parting. Wang Wei. OnPM
It's to possess more than the skin. Cutting the Jewish Bride's Hair. Ruth Whitman. HW
It's Tuesday morning, Cook, my dear. Backstair Ballad. David McCord. BOHV
Its unobtrusive force leaves you so free. The Catholic Faith. Kenelm H. Digby. CAW
It's very nice to think of how. A Kitten's Thought. Oliver Herford. RIS
It's Very Unwise to Kill the Goose. Philip H. Rhinelander. WhC
It's we two, it's we two, it's we two for aye. Like a Laverock in the Lift. Jean Ingelow. HBV
Its wingéd lion stands up straight to hide. Venice. Howard Moss. MoAB
It's wiser being good than bad. Robert Browning. *Fr.* Apparent Failure. MaRV
It's Wonderful. Walter E. Isenhour. STF
It's wonderful dogs they're breeding now. Tim, an Irish Terrier. Winifred M. Letts. BoC
It's wonderful how I jog. Animals Are Passing from Our Lives. Philip Levine. CoAP
It's wonderful, so wonderful. It's Wonderful. Walter E. Isenhour. STF
It's You. L. A. McDonald. STF
Itt rely is ridikkelus. Bobby's First Poem. Norman Gale. FiBHP; PV
'Ittle Touzle Head. Ray Garfield Dandridge. BANP
Itylus. Swinburne. ChTr; EnLi-2; GTBS; GTSL; HBV; NoP; OBEV; PoVP; StP; ViPo; ViPP; VP; WHA
Iulus. Eleanor Glenn Wallis. NePoAm-2
Ivan Skavinsky Skavar. *Unknown.* *See* Abdul A-Bul-Bul A-Mir.
Ivanhoe, *sels.* Sir Walter Scott.
Anna Marie, Love, Up Is the Sun, *fr. ch.* 40. ViBoPo
Rebecca's Hymn. EnRP
("When Israel . . .") ViBoPo
I've a friend, over the sea. Time's Revenges. Robert Browning. PoVP; VP
I've a humble little motto. Keep a-Pluggin' Away. Paul Laurence Dunbar. MCCG
I've a pal called Billy Peg-Leg, with one leg a wood leg. Peg-Leg's Fiddle. Bill Adams. BBV; EtS; RePo
I've a secret in my heart, sweet Marie. Sweet Marie. Cy Warman. TreFS
I've always thought Polonius a dry. Lines to His Son on Reaching Adolescence. John Logan. NePoEA-2
I've an ingle, shady ingle, near a dusky bosky dingle. Midsummer Jingle. Newman Levy. BoNaP; WhC
I've beat my way wherever any winds have blown. Once You Git the Habit. *At. to* Berton Braley. CoSo
I've been a bird of night. New Year's. Gail Dusenbery. ThO
I've been a moonshiner for sev'nteen long years. Kentucky Moonshiner. *Unknown.* AS; TrAS
I've been along the quarry road. Shells in Rock. Elizabeth Madox Roberts. AnAmPo
I've been doing some hard traveling, I thought you knowed. Hard Travelin'. Woody Guthrie. WOW
I've been in love for long. In Love for Long. Edwin Muir. GTBS-W; LiTM (rev. ed.); MoBrPo (1962 ed.)
I've been prayin' for centuries. Prayer to the White Man's God. Charles Anderson. BF
I've been thinking today. Rounded Up in Glory. *Unknown.* CoSo
I've been to California, and I haven't got a dime. Alas. *Unknown.* IHA
I've been to Palestine. John Brown. Vachel Lindsay. *Fr.* The Booker Washington Trilogy. AnAmPo; MAP; MoAmPo; NP
I've been to Red Hoss Mountain, where Field once dwelt and wrote. Old Red Hoss Mountain. Cy Warman. PoOW
I've been travlin' all de day. Ride On, Moses. *Unknown.* BoAN-1
I've been trying to fashion a wifely ideal. A Plea for Trigany. Sir Owen Seaman. BOHV
I've been upon the prairie. Bronc Peeler's Song. *Unknown.* CoSo
I've Been Workin' on the Railroad. *Unknown.* FaFP; TreF
I've borne full many a sorrow, I've suffered many a loss. The Heaviest Cross of All. Katherine Eleanor Conway. AA; JKCP
I've brought you nuts and hops. October. Christina Rossetti. *Fr.* The Months; a Pageant. BoTP
I've built a castle in the sand. Castles in the Sand. Dorothy Baker. BoTP
I've busted bronchos off and on. The Bronc That Wouldn't Bust. *Unknown.* SCC
I've chosen this title because not only do I like it. The Statue of a Libertine. Ron Padgett. YAP
I've come by the May-tree all times o' the year. The May Tree. William Barnes. LiTB; LoBV
I've come this far to freedom. Midway. Naomi Long Madgett. NNP; PoNe (1970 ed.)
I've come to give you fruit from my orchard. The Crossed Apple. Louise Bogan. NP
I've done a very frightful thing. The Liar. Rue Carpenter. RIS

I've dropped my brain—my soul is numb. Emily Dickinson. MWA-2; PoeP
I've dug up all my garden. Sowing Seeds. Ursula Cornwall. BoTP
I've eaten bitter bread. Whalin' up the Lachlan. Louis Esson. NeLNL
I've forgotten what day, but late in December. The Basilisk. Philip Child. CaP
I've found a friend whose equal. My Friend. *Unknown.* SoP
I've found a joy in sorrow. All Things in Jesus. J. Danson Smith. SoP
I've found a small dragon in the woodshed. A Small Dragon. Brian Patten. HYE
I've found my bonny babe a nest. An Irish Lullaby. Alfred Perceval Graves. HBV
I've found the place where Darkness goes. The Railway Tunnel. Queenie Scott-Hopper. TVC
I've given thee wings shall waft thee forth with ease. Immortality Conferred in Vain. Theognis. LiTW
I've got a barrow; it's a very small. My Barrow. Elizabeth Fleming. GFA
I've got a bow and arrow. Robin Hood. Rachel MacAndrew. BoTP
I've Got a Dog. Ethel M. Kelley. PCD
I've Got a Home in That Rock. Raymond Patterson. PoNe (1970 ed.)
I've got a letter, parson, from my son away out West. Billy, He's in Trouble. James Barton Adams. YaD
I've got a lovely home. Best of All. J. M. Westrup. BoTP
I've got a mule, her name is Sal. The Erie Canal [*or* Low Bridge, Everybody Down]. William S. Allen. ABF; AmFN; AS; IHA; OTD; RePo; TrAS
I've Got a New Book from My Grandfather Hyde. Leroy F. Jackson. BrR; FaPON; RePo; SiSoSe
I've got a pony. The Pony. Rachel MacAndrew. BoTP
I've Got a Rocket. *Unknown.* SiSoSe; TiPo (1959 ed.)
I've got a sister nine feet tall. 'Way Down in Cuba. *Unknown.* AmSS
I've got shoes with grown up laces. Growing Up. A. A. Milne. BiCB; ThGo
I've Got the Giggles Today. A. P. Herbert. FiBHP
I've had my share of pastime, and I've done my share of toil. The Sick Stockrider. Adam Lindsay Gordon. OtMeF
I've had you on my mind a thousand years. God's Thanks to Job. Robert Frost. *Fr.* A Masque to Reason. MoRP
I've heard it said that Sir Barnabas Beer. Endurance Test. Dacre Balsdon. FiBHP
I've heard, I've heard. Margaret Woods. BoC
I've heard the sea upon the troubled rocks. The Man Whom the Sea Kept Awake. Robert Bly. NePoEA
I've Heard Them Lilting at Loom and Belting. C. Day Lewis. OBMV
I've heard them lilting at our ewe [*or* yowe]-milking. The Flowers of the Forest [*or* A Lament for Flodden]. Jane Elliot. CH; EiPP; FaBoCh; GoTS; GTBS; GTBS-D; GTBS-P; GTBS-W; GTSE; GTSL; HBV; LiTG; OBEC; OBEV; OxBS; ShBV-3; ViBoPo; WePo
I've just come down from the mines. The Miner's Lament, III. David G. Robinson. SGR
"I've just come from a place." The Little Duck. Joso. SoPo
I've just got [in] across the plains. The Arrival of the Greenhorn. John A. Stone. RePo; SGR
I've just got here, through Paris, from the sunny southern shore. The Man Who Broke the Bank at Monte Carlo. Fred Gilbert. TreF
I've kept a haughty heart thro' grief and mirth. To My Mother. Heine. AWP; JAWP; WBP
I've kissed thee, sweetheart, in a dream at least. Sleep. Theophile de Viau. AWP
I've known a Heaven like a tent. Emily Dickinson. BoLiVe
I've known ere now an interfering branch. The Axe-Helve. Robert Frost. CABL; OxBA
I've known rivers. The Negro Speaks of Rivers. Langston Hughes. AmFN; AmNP; BANP; CDC; GoSl; IDB; NoP; PoNe; TTY
I've labored long and hard for bread. "Black Bart." PV
I've landed today in a peaceful nook. Literary Gruk. Piet Hein. LiTW
I've learned a precious secret. The Secret of the Cross. M. J. Clarkson. BePJ
I've Learned to Sing. Georgia Douglas Johnson. GoSl
I've left my own old home of homes. John Clare. *Fr.* The Flitting. OBRV
I've lived my life in careless ease. Epitaph on Himself. Mathurin Regnier. LiTW
I've Lost My ——. Harry Cholmondeley Pennell. CenHV
I've never known a dog to wag. The Dog. *Unknown.* WBLP
I've never sailed the Amazon. Rolling Down to Rio. Kipling. HT
I've never travelled for more'n a day. On the Quay. John Joy Bell. HBV
I've not sung of my country. To My Country. "Rachel." LiTW
I've not the gold of Gyges. To Himself. Anacreon. LiTW
I've noticed how the woolly lamb. All Wool. Abbie Farwell Brown. TiPo (1952 ed.)
I've oft been asked by prosing souls. A Reason to Fill My Glass. Charles Morris. HBV
I've oft been told by learned friars. An Argument. Thomas Moore. EnLoPo
I've often heard my mother say. The Unknown Color. Countee Cullen. FaPON; GoSl
I've paid for your sickest fancies; I've humoured your crackedest whim. The *Mary Gloster.* Kipling. BeLS; OtMeF
I've plucked the berry from the bush. Sing On, Blithe Bird! William Motherwell. DD; GN; HBV; HBVY; OTPC (1923 ed.)
I've put some/ Ashes in my sweet papa's bed. A Group of Negro Songs. W. C. Handy. NAMP
I've rambled and gambled all my money away. Rabble Soldier. *Unknown.* AS
I've Rambled This Country Both Earlye and Late, *with music. Unknown.* OuSiCo
I've reached the point of no return. Resolution. Carlton Buck. SoP
I've said goodbye to the three black kittens. First Departure. Frances Frost. SiSoSe
I've sailed among the Yankees, the Spaniards and Chinees. The Sailor's Way. *Unknown.* ShS
I've seen a dying eye. Emily Dickinson. AmPP (5th ed.); InPo; MAPA; NePA; OnPM; PoEL-5; PoLF; TwAmPo
I've seen caravans/ Going to the fair! Caravans. Irene Thompson. BoTP
"I've seen everything." Joso. *See* Little Duck, The.
I've seen her, I've seen her. Vision. Rose Fyleman. PCH
I've seen her pass with eyes upon the road. Una Anciana Mexicana. Alice Corbin. NP
I've seen one flying saucer. Only when. Go Fly a Saucer. David McCord. FaPON; ImOP
I've seen the moonbeam's shining light. Life. *Unknown.* PoToHe
I've seen the smiling/ Of fortune beguiling. The Flowers of the Forest. Alison Cockburn. OBEC
I've seen the Thousand Islands. Tadoussac. Charles Bancroft. BLPA
I've shore at Burrabogie, and I've shore at Toganmain. Flash Jack from Gundagai. *Unknown.* PoAu-1
I've stayed in the front yard all my life. A Song in the Front Yard. Gwendolyn Brooks. IDB
I've swum the Colorado where she runs close down to hell. The Insult. *Unknown.* SCC
I've taken my fun where I've found it. The Ladies. Kipling. ALV; EnLit; MoBrPo; TreFT; ViPP
I've Tasted My Blood. Milton Acorn. MoCV
I've taught me other tongues—and in strange eyes. To England. Byron. *Fr.* Childe Harold's Pilgrimage, IV. WHA
I've taught thee love's sweet lesson o'er. Song [*or* Romanzo to Sylvia]. George Darley. *Fr.* Sylvia; or, The May Queen. OBRV; VA
I've Thirty Months. J. M. Synge. OBMV
I've told you many a tale, my child, of the old heroic days. Madeleine Verchères. William Henry Drummond. CaP
I've traveled all around this world and Tonawanda, too. The Erie Canal Ballad. *Unknown.* ABF
I've traveled the mountains all over. He's the Man for Me. John A. Stone. SGR
I've Travelled Far in Many Lands. Hinton White. MaRV
I've tried in vain, day after day. The Promise. Mary B. Fowler. STF

I've walked along with Jesus. His Presence. Dale Schulz. STF
I've walked through all the lodgings. John Fletcher. *Fr.* The Night-Walker; or, The Little Thief. MyFE
I've wandered east, I've wandered west. Jeanie Morrison. William Motherwell. HBV; LO
I've wandered to the village, Tom, I've sat beneath the tree. Forty Years Ago [*or* Twenty Years Ago]. *Unknown.* BLPA; HBV
I've watched the clouds by day and night. Watching Clouds. John Farrar. SoPo; StVeCh
I've watched, with microscopic eye. On the Rising Generation. Howard Dietz. ALV
I've watched you now a full half-hour. To a Butterfly. Wordsworth. BWP; GoTP; HBV; OTPC; SeCeV
I've Worked for a Silver Shilling. Charles W. Kennedy. HBMV
I've worked on the Nine-Mile, likewise on the River. The Broken-down Digger. *Unknown.* PoAu-1
Ives, *sel.* Muriel Rukeyser.
"This is Charles Ives." UnS
Ivesiana. Bill Berkson. ANYP
Ivory Bed, The. Winfield Townley Scott. ErPo
Ivory, Coral, Gold, The. William Drummond of Hawthornden. *See* Madrigal: "Ivory, coral, gold, The."
Ivory Gate, The, *sel.* Thomas Lovell Beddoes.
Mighty Thoughts of an Old World, The. EG; GoJo
(Song: "Mighty thoughts of an old world, The.") SiSw
(Song of Thanatos.) ERoP-2; NBM
(Stanzas: "Mighty thought of an old world, The.") TrGrPo
(Stanzas from "The Ivory Gate.") EnRP
Ivory Gate, The. Mortimer Collins. VA
Ivory in her black, and all intent. Jesu, Joy of Man's Desiring. Robert Fitzgerald. NYBP
Ivory Masks in Orbit. K. William Kgositsile. BF
Ivory Tower, The. Robert Hillyer. NYBP
Ivry. Macaulay. FaBV; FOL; GN; HBV; HBVY; OBRV; OTPC; RG; VA
(Battle of Ivry, The.) WBLP
Ivy. Frank Dempster Sherman. MAP
Ivy and Holly. E. H. W. Meyerstein. ELU
Ivy, chefe of trees it is. In Praise of Ivy. *Unknown.* MeEL
Ivy Crest, The. *Unknown, tr. fr. Old Irish by* Robin Flower. AnIL
Ivy Crown, The. William Carlos Williams. NoP
Ivy Green, The. Charles Dickens. *Fr.* The Pickwick Papers, *ch.* 6. BoNaP; HBV; HBVY; OTPC (1946 ed.); RIS; VA
Ivy in the dungeon grew, The. Climbing to the Light. Charles Mackay. RIS
Ivy o'er the mouldering wall, The. The Sun-Dial. Thomas Love Peacock. *Fr.* Melincourt. ERoP-1; OBNC; OBRV
Ixions of the slow wheel of the day. Christ in the Hospital. Roy Campbell. BoC
Izaac Walton, Cotton, and William Oldways. Walter Savage Landor. NBM; PoEL-4
Izaak Walton to River and Brook. Eugene Lee-Hamilton. VA

J

J. A. G. Julia Ward Howe. PAH
J. Alfred Prufrock to. Said. George Starbuck. PV
J. B. H. C. Bunner. AA
J. B., *sel.* Archibald MacLeish.
Curse God and Die, You Said to Me. EaLo
J. F. K. D. L. O'Neill. OTD
J. F. K. Sister M. Stanislaus. TIHL
J. Milton Miles. Edgar Lee Masters. *Fr.* Spoon River Anthology. CrMA
J. S. Mill. E. C. Bentley. *Fr.* Clerihews. BOHV; OxBoLi; WhC
("John Stuart Mill.") FiBHP
Ja, Ja, Ja! *with music.* *Unknown.* ShS
Ja-Nez—burro with the long ears. Burro with the Long Ears. *Tr. by* Hilda Faunce Wetherill. FaPON
Jabberwocky. "Lewis Carroll." *Fr.* Through the Looking Glass, *ch.* 1. ALV; BoChLi; CABA; CaFP; CBEP; CBV; DiPo; EnLi-2 (1949 ed.); FaBoBe; FaBV; FaFP; FaPON; FiBHP; GoJo; GoTP; HBV; HoPM; InP; LBN; LiTB; LiTG; NA; NAMP; NBM; OnSP; OTPC; PeVV; PIA; PoIE; PoPl; PoPo; PoRA; PoVP; RIS; SeCeV; ShBV-2; SiTL; TiPo; TreF; TrGrPo; VaPo; WHC
Jabberwocky (as the Author of "The Faerie Queene" Might Have Written It). Junius Cooper. InMe
Jabberwocky of Authors, The. Harry Persons Taber. BOHV
Jack. Gwendolyn Brooks. TPM
Jack. Louis Golding. TrJP
Jack and Gye. *Unknown.* OxNR
Jack and His Father. John Heywood. CBV; DiPo; TuPP
Jack and Jill. Harriet S. Morgridge. *Fr.* Mother Goose Sonnets. AA
Jack and Jill—as Kipling Might Have Written It. Anthony C. Deane. *See* Here Is the Tale.
Jack and Jill went up the hill/ To fetch some heavy water. Paul Dehn. *Fr.* Rhymes for a Modern Nursery. FiBHP; PV
Jack and Jill [*or* Gill] went up the hill. Mother Goose. FaBoBe; FaFP; HBV; HBVY; OTPC; OxBoLi; OxNR; PCH; PPL; SAS; SiTL; SoPo; StVeCh; TiPo
Jack and Jille. Gillian. *Unknown.* BOHV
Jack and Joan. Thomas Campion. EnL; FaBoCh; HBV; MemP; NoP; TuPP
(Fortunati Nimium.) GTSL
("Jack and Joan they think no ill.") EG; OAEP; OBSC; ReEn; SiCE
Jack and Roger. Benjamin Franklin. ChTr
(On a Foolish Person.) CBV
(Quatrain: "Jack, eating rotten cheese, did say.") WhC
Jack Barrett went to Quetta. The Story of Uriah. Kipling. BrPo; PeVV
Jack, be nimble. Mother Goose. BoChLi; OxNR; PCH; RIS; SiTL; SoPo; StVeCh; TiPo
Jack Creamer. James Jeffrey Roche. MC; PAH
Jack Dempsey's Grave. M. J. MacMahon. SCC
(Nonpareil's Grave, The.) SD
Jack Denver died on Talbragar when Christmas Eve began. Talbragar. Henry Lawson. PoAu-1
Jack Donahoe. *Unknown.* CoSo
Jack, eating rotten cheese, did say. Jack and Roger [*or* Quatrain]. Benjamin Franklin. CBV; ChTr; WhC
Jack Ellyat Heard the Guns. Stephen Vincent Benét. *Fr.* John Brown's Body. PoLF
Jack Frenchman's Lamentation. *Unknown.* CoMu
Jack Frost. Helen Bayley Davis. GFA; MPB; SoPo
Jack Frost. Hannah Flagg Gould. *See* Frost, The.
Jack Frost. Cecily E. Pike. BoTP
Jack Frost. "Gabriel Setoun." BoTP; DD; GFA; HBV; HBVY; MPB; OTPC
Jack Frost ("When Jack Frost comes—Oh the fun"). *Unknown.* GFA
Jack Frost in the Garden. John P. Smeeton. BoTP
Jack Frost must be a caterer. Winter Treats. Mildred D. Shacklett. GFA
Jack Frost was in the garden. Jack Frost in the Garden. John P. Smeeton. BoTP
Jack Giantkiller took and struck. Driving Cross-Country. X. J. Kennedy. TwCP
Jack Haggerty. *Unknown, at. to* Dan McGinnis. ShS, *with music*; ViBoFo
(Flat River Girl, *with music.*) AS
Jack Hall, he is so small. Mother Goose. RIS
Jack his own merit sees: this gives him pride. On a Proud Fellow. *Unknown.* PV
Jack Horner ("Jack Horner was a pretty lad"). *Unknown.* OTPC; PPL
Jack-in-the-Box. Elder Olson. NePA
Jack-in-the-Pulpit. Rowena Bennett. MPB (1956 ed.)
Jack-in-the-Pulpit. Ivy O. Eastwick. YeAr
Jack-in-the-Pulpit. Rupert Sargent Holland. OTPC; StVeCh (1940 ed.)
Jack-in-the-Pulpit is preaching a sermon. Jack-in-the-Pulpit. Rowena Bennett. MPB (1956 ed.)
Jack in the pulpit, out and in. *Unknown.* OxNR
Jack Kelso, *sel.* Edgar Lee Masters.
Portrait of a Poet. ATP
Jack o' Diamonds, *with music.* *Unknown.* OuSiCo
Jack o' Diamonds; or, The Rabble Soldier, *with music.* *Unknown.* CoSo
(Rabble Soldier, *diff. vers., with music.*) AS
(Troubled Soldier, The, *diff. vers., with music.*) AS
Jack o'Lantern. Anna Chandler Ayre. SoPo
Jack o' the Inkpot. Algernon Blackwood. BoTP

Jack of Newbury, *sels.* Thomas Deloney.
"Maiden fair I dare not wed, A." ReIE
"My masters, I thank you, it's time to pack home." ReIE
Weavers' Song, The. SiCE
Jack (quoth his father) how shall I ease take? Jack and His Father. John Heywood. CBV; DiPo; TuPP
Jack Rose. Maxwell Bodenheim. HBMV
Jack Shows His Qualities and Great Good Will to Jone. Thomas Howell. ReIE; TuPP
Jack Sprat/ Had a cat. *Unknown.* OxNR
Jack Sprat [*or* Spratt] could eat no fat. Mother Goose. BoChLi; FaBoBe; FaFP; HBV; HBVY; OTPC; OxNR; PCH; PPL; RIS; SiTL
Jack Sprat's pig. Mother Goose. BrR
Jack Tar. Emile Jacot. BoTP
Jack Tar, *with music.* *Unknown.* ShS
Jack the Guinea Pig. *Unknown.* AmSS
Jack the Jolly Tar. *Unknown.* BaBo
Jack the Piper. *Unknown.* ChTr
("As I was going up the hill.") OxNR
Jack the Ripper. Allan M Laing. FiBHP
Jack Was Every Inch a Sailor. *Unknown.* WHW
Jack Wrack. *Unknown.* *See* Off to Sea Once More.
Jackals prowl, the serpents hiss, The. Elegy. Arthur Guiterman. BOHV; InMe
Jackaro, *with music.* *Unknown.* IHA
(Jackie Frazier, *with music.*) BFSS
(Lily Munro, *with music.*) OuSiCo
Jackdaw, The. Vincent Bourne, *tr. fr. Latin by* William Cowper. HBV; HBVY; OTPC (1923 ed.)
Jackdaw of Rheims, The. "Thomas Ingoldsby." *Fr.* The Ingoldsby Legends. BOHV; HBV; OnMSP; OTPC (1923 ed.); PaPo; ShBV-1; TSW; VA
Jacket So Blue; or, A Company of Boatmen, *with music.* *Unknown.* BFSS
Jackie Faa. *Unknown.* *See* Wraggle Taggle Gipsies, The.
Jackie Frazier. *Unknown.* *See* Jackaro.
Jackman's Song, The. Ben Jonson. *See* Gipsy Song ("The faery beam upon you").
Jacko the Skunk, in black and white. The Skunk. Alfred Noyes. RePo
Jack's Blues. Robert Creeley. ToPo
Jack's Fidelity. Charles Dibdin. EtS
Jack's wondrous sick, who thinks he shall go mad. Nil Perdunt Mendici. Henry Parrot. SiCE
Jackson, *with music.* *Unknown.* AS
Jackson at New Orleans. Wallace Rice. DD; PAH
Jackson is on sea, Jackson is on shore. Jackson. *Unknown.* AS
Jacky, Come Give Me Thy Fiddle. *Unknown.* OxNR; UnS
Jacob. Phoebe Cary. BOHV; InMe
Jacob. Arthur Hugh Clough. ViPP
Jacob and the Angel. Brother Antoninus. MoRP
Jacob Godbey. Edgar Lee Masters. *Fr.* Spoon River Anthology. LiTA
Jacob, hear! Jacob's Destiny. Richard Beer-Hofmann. *Fr.* Jacob's Dream. TrJP
Jacob! I do not like to see thy nose. The Pig. Robert Southey. BOHV; PeER
Jacob Tonson, His Publisher. Dryden. *See* Epigram on Tonson.
Jacobean. Clifton Fadiman. FiBHP
Jacobite on Tower Hill, The. George Walter Thornbury. VA
Jacobite Toast, A. John Byrom. OtMeF
(Epigram: "God bless the King—I mean the faith's defender.") HBV
(Extempore Verses Intended to Allay the Violence of Party Spirit.) OBEC
(Toast, A.) ViBoPo
(Which Is Which?) BOHV
Jacobite's Epitaph, A. Macaulay. GTBS; InP; OBEV; OBNC; OBVV
(Epitaph on a Jacobite.) NBM; VA; ViBoPo
Jacobite's Exile, 1746, A. Swinburne. OBVV; OtMeF
Jacobite's Farewell, A. Swinburne. PoVP; TOP
Jacob's Dream, *sel.* Richard Beer-Hofmann, *tr. fr. German by* Ida Bension Wynn.
Jacob's Destiny. TrJP
Jacob's Ladder, The. Denise Levertov. AmPP (5th ed.); CaFP; CoPo; ToPo
Jacob's Ladder. *Unknown.* MaRV
Jacopone da Todi. Matthew Arnold. *See* Austerity of Poetry.
Jacqueline Gray. Kenneth Pitchford. *Fr.* Good for Nothing Man. CoPo
Jacquerie, The, *sels.* Sidney Lanier.
Betrayal. AA
Hound, The. AA; PFY; PoMS
(Song for "The Jacquerie.") MAP; MoAmPo (1942 ed.)
Jacques Cartier. Thomas D'Arcy McGee. CaP; PTK
Jade Flower Palace. Tu Fu, *tr. fr. Chinese.* LiTW, *tr. by* Robert Payne; NaP, *tr. by* Kenneth Rexroth
Jaffar. Leigh Hunt. BeLS; HBV; OTPC
Jagg'd mountain peaks and skies ice-green. Breughel's Winter. Walter de la Mare. SeCePo
Jaguar, The. Ted Hughes. LiTM (1970 ed.); NoP; PoPl; POTE (1959 ed.); POTi; ToPo
Jahr der Seele, Das, *sel.* Stefan George, *tr. fr. German by* Daisy Broicher.
"No way too long, no path too steep." AWP
Jail would have killed me. Nathan Suffrin. Edgar Lee Masters. *Fr.* The New Spoon River. CMoP
Jake Diefer, the barrel-chested Pennsylvanian. The Enlistments. Stephen Vincent Benét. *Fr.* John Brown's Body. ATP
Jake was a dirty Dago lad, an' he gave the skipper chin. Cape Horn Gospel. John Masefield. ShBV-3
Jake's Wharf. Philip Booth. NYBP
Jam on Gerry's Rock, The. *Unknown.* AS, *with music*; BaBo; ShS, *vers.* I, *with music*; ViBoFo, *with music*
(Gerry's Rocks, *with music.*) ABF
(Jam at Gerry's Rock, The, *with music.*) BFSS
(Jam on Jerry's Rock, The, *vers.* II, *with music.*) ShS
(Young Monroe at Gerry's Rock, *with music.*) AmSS
Jam Trap, The. Charles Tomlinson. MoBrPo (1962 ed.)
Jamaica Market. Agnes Maxwell-Hall. PoNe; TTY
Jambangle/ and a black body. Blackie Speaks on Campus: Valentine for Vachel Lindsay. Stanley Crouch. BF
James and John. Cardinal Newman. SoP
James Bird, *with music.* *Unknown.* BFSS
James Garber. Edgar Lee Masters. *Fr.* Spoon River Anthology. ILP
James Grant. *Unknown.* ESPB
James Harris. *Unknown.* *See* Demon Lover, The.
James Hatley. *Unknown.* BaBo; ESPB
James Honeyman. W. H. Auden. MoBS
James Lee's Wife. Robert Browning. ViPP
Sels.
Ah, Love, but a Day, I. EPN
Among the Rocks, VII. BoLiVe
(Ancient Doctrine, The.) OBVV
("O good gigantic smile.") EPN; YT
In the Doorway. NCEP
James McCosh. Robert Bridges. AA
James Monroe. Rosemary Benét *and* Stephen Vincent Benét. OTD
James o'Broodies, *with music.* *Unknown.* BFSS
James Rigg. James Hogg. Par
James Russell Lowell ("Thou shouldst have sung the swan song for the choir"). Oliver Wendell Holmes. DD
James Russell Lowell. Whittier. DD
James Shirley. Swinburne. Sonnets on English Dramatic Poets (1590-1650), XIV. Sonn
James went to the door of the kitchen and said. Rudeness. Elizabeth Turner. OTPC (1923 ed.)
James Wetherell. E. A. Robinson. MoAmPo
James Whaland. *Unknown.* AS, *with music*; IHA
Jamestown had its starving time. Hard Rows to Hoe. Daniel Henderson. PaA
Jamestown Homeward Bound, The, *with music.* *Unknown.* SoAmSa
Jamie Douglas. *Unknown.* *See* Waly, Waly.
Jamie Telfer in [*or* of] the Fair Dodhead. *Unknown.* ESPB; OxBB
Jam-Pot, The. Kipling. HBV
Jan., Jan., is a jeweler-man. January Snow. Aileen Fisher. YeAr
Jan Kubelik. Carl Sandburg. NP
Jane and Eliza. Ann Taylor. HBV; HBVY; OnPP
Jane, Do Be Careful. Irene Page. BBGG
Jane, do you see these little dots. Silkworms. Mary Elliott. OTPC (1923 ed.)

Jane, Jane,/ Tall as a crane. Aubade. Edith Sitwell. CMoP; ExPo; InP; MoAB; MoBrPo; NeMA; NP; PoRA; TrGrPo; WePo
Jane Jones. Ben King. IHA
Jane looks down at her organdy skirt. In Bertram's Garden. Donald Justice. ErPo; NePoEA
Jane Retreat. Edwin Honig. LiTL
Jane, she could not. Man's Way. L. A. G. Strong. HBMV
Jane Smith. Kipling. HBV
Jane Was a Neighbor. *Unknown.* *See* Death of Queen Jane, The.
Jane went to Paradise. Jane's Marriage. Kipling. BoC
Jane Williams had a lover true. Shocking Rape and Murder of Two Lovers. *Unknown.* CoMu
Jane's Marriage. Kipling. BoC
Janet Waking. John Crowe Ransom. AmLP; AmP; AnAmPo; CMoP; ExPo; ForPo; MAP; MoAB; MoAmPo; PoIE; PoPo; ThWaDe
Janette's Hair. Charles Graham Halpine. HBV
Janitor Working on Threshold. Margaret Avison. PeCV (1967 ed.)
Janitor's Boy, The. Nathalia Crane. GoTP; NeMA; PoLF; StaSt
Jankin, the Clerical Seducer. *Unknown.* *See* Jolly Jankin.
Januar. By thys fyre I warme my handys. January by This Fire. *Unknown.* NCEP
January. James Applewhite. YAP
January. Elizabeth J. Coatsworth. BoChLi (1950 ed.); PoSC
January. Geoffrey Dutton. PoAu-2
January. Weldon Kees. CoAP
January. Sylvia S. Lambdin. YeAr
January. Lucy Larcom. OQP
January. "Michael Lewis." *See* Skiing Song.
January. James Russell Lowell. *See* Winter Morning, A.
January. Daniel James O'Sullivan. NeIP
January. James Reaney. *Fr.* A Suit of Nettles. OBCV; PIA
January. Frank Dempster Sherman. OTD; YeAr
January. Spenser. *See* January Eclogue.
January. R. S. Thomas. ELU
January. John Updike. PDV
January. William Carlos Williams. MAP; MoAB; MoAmPo; NP
January, angry at the whole damned town. Spleen LXXV. Baudelaire. ReMP
January, bleak and drear. January. Frank Dempster Sherman. OTD; YeAr
January brings the snow. The Garden Year [*or* The Months]. Sara Coleridge. DD; FaBoBe; GoTP; HBV; HBVY; MPB; OTPC; PCH; PPL; PTK; RePo; RIS; StaSt; StVeCh; TiPo; TreFT; TSW
January by This Fire. *Unknown.* NCEP
January cold [and] desolate. The Months. Christina Rossetti. *Fr.* Sing-Song. FaPON; RIS
January Eclogue. Spenser. *Fr.* The Shepheardes Calender. FiP
(January.) ReIE
(Januarye.) PIA
January falls the snow. Calender Rhyme. Flora Willis Watson. BoTP
January 1. Marnie Pomeroy. PoSC
January Is Here. Edgar Fawcett. YeAr
January Morning, A. Archibald Lampman. ACV; OBCV
January Night. Rafael Alberto Arrieta, *tr. fr. Spanish by* Muna Lee. OnPM
January 1940. Roy Fuller. HoPM; LiTM; OnHM; SeCePo; WaP
January sky is deep and calm, The. Reason for Not Writing Orthodox Nature Poetry. John Wain. HaMV; PP; ToPo
January Snow. Aileen Fisher. YeAr
January snowy, February flowy, March blowy. The Months. Sheridan. PCH
January sparkles. January. Sylvia S. Lambdin. YeAr
Januarye. Spenser. *See* January Eclogue.
Janus. Madeline Mason. GoYe
Japan. Anthony Hecht. CrMA; LiTM (rev. ed.)
Japan That Sank under the Sea. Satoru Sato. PoPl
Japanese, The. Ogden Nash. InMe; WhC
Japanese Birthday Wish, A. Thomas Burnett Swann. GoYe
Japanese Cherries. Katherine Brégy. JKCP (1926 ed.)
Japanese Children. James Kirkup. FIW
Japanese City. Kenward Elmslie. YAP
Japanese Fan. Margaret Veley. NBM
Japanese have funny things, The. A Rhyme Sheet of Other Lands. Hugh Chesterman. BoTP
Japanese Hokku. Lewis Alexander. CDC
Japanese Love-Song, A. Alfred Noyes. OBVV
Japanese Lovers, The. *Unknown.* BeLS; BLPA
Japanese next to me at the bar, The. In a Bar Near Shibuya Station, Tokyo. Paul Engle. AmFN; CAD
Japanese poetry. *See* Haikai; Haiku; Hokku; Hyaku-Nin-Isshu; Kokin Shu; Manyo Shu; Shui Shu; Tanka; *also individual titles and first lines.*
Japanese Vase Wrought in Metals, A. Marjorie Allen Seiffert. NP
Japanesque. Oliver Herford. FiBHP
Jar, The. Richard Henry Stoddard. AA
(Day and Night My Thoughts Incline.) HBV
Jar of cider and my pipe, A. The Sluggard. W. H. Davies. OBMV
Jar of Nations, The. A. E. Housman. *See* Oh Is It the Jar of Nations.
Jardin de la Chapelle Expiatoire. Robert Finch. PeCV
Jardin des Fleurs. Charles David Webb. NePoAm-2
Jardin du Palais Royal. David Gascoyne. MoPo
Jarring the air with rumour cool. Small Fountains. Lascelles Abercrombie. *Fr.* Emblems of Love. CH
Jasmine and the Gypsies. Fanny Howe. QAH
Jasmine sees intentions everywhere. Jasmine and the Gypsies. Fanny Howe. QAH
Jason. Anthony Hecht. CoPo
Jason. Dom Moraes. TDP
Jason and Medea. John Gower. *Fr.* Confessio Amantis, V. ACP
"Flees he tok and goth to bote, The," *sel.* AtBAP
Jason and Medea. Alun Lewis. CBEP
Javanese Dancers. Arthur Symons. PoVP; VA
Jay-bird, jay-bird, settin' on a rail. *Unknown.* GoTP
Jay Gould's Daughter, *with music.* *Unknown.* AS
Jay Hawkins. Edgar Lee Masters. *Fr.* The New Spoon River. CMoP
Jay in the Feathers of the Peacock, The. La Fontaine, *tr. fr. French by* Elizur Wright. OnPM
Jay walking! Reading the headlines! Struck down. Jay Hawkins. Edgar Lee Masters. *Fr.* The New Spoon River. CMoP
Jazz. Frank London Brown. PoNe (1970 ed.)
Jazz Band in a Parisian Cabaret. Langston Hughes. BANP; MAP; MoAmPo
Jazz band struck up Dixie, The . . . I could see. Victory in the Cabarets. Louis Untermeyer. HBMV
Jazz Coltrane Sings. Walter K. Dancy. WSL
Jazz Fantasia. Carl Sandburg. AnFE; CoAnAm; MAP; MoAB; MoAmPo; NeMA; OCS; OTD; PoNe; TwAmPo; WePo
Jazz. Muffled voices pushed behind the squeaking doors of a place. Recreation. Eric Priestley. WSL
Jazz of This Hotel, The. Vachel Lindsay. ATP; PoPl
Jazzonia. Langston Hughes. AmNP; BANP; Kal
Jazzy Vanity. Richard W. Thomas. BF
Je caresserai la belle par amitié, *with music.* *Unknown,* *tr. fr. French.* OuSiCo
Je Ne Sais [*or* Sçay *or* Scai] Quoi, The. William Whitehead. EiCL; LO; OBEC
Je ne veux de personne auprès de ma tristesse. Henri de Régnier, *tr. fr. French by* "Seumas O'Sullivan." AWP; JAWP; WBP
Je Suis une Table. Donald Hall. NePoEA
Jealosie. John Donne. Elegies, I. AnAnS-1; MaMe
Jealous Adam. Itzig Manger, *tr. fr. Yiddish by* Jacob Sonntag. TrJP
Jealous Enemy, The. Petrarch, *tr. fr. Italian by* Thomas LeMesurier. Sonnets to Laura: To Laura in Death, XLVII. LiTW
Jealous girls these sometimes were. How Marigolds Came Yellow. Robert Herrick. ChTr
Jealous, I own it, I was once. On Thomas Hood. Walter Savage Landor. PV
Jealous Lover, The (*diff. vers.*). *Unknown.* ShS, *with music*; ViBoFo
(Fair Florella or the Jealous Lover, A *and* B *vers.*) BaBo
Jealous Lovers, The. Donald Hall. NYBP
Jealous Lovers, The, *sel.* Thomas Randolph.

Charm, A. SeCL
Jealous Man, A. Robert Graves. CMoP
Jealous Man, A. *Unknown, tr. fr. Irish by* Frank O'Connor. KiLC
Jealous Wife, The. Vernon Scannell. ErPo
Jealousy. Mary Elizabeth Coleridge. EnLoPo; NBM; OBNC; PoVP
(Myrtle Bush Grew Shady, The.) CH
Jealousy. Sir William Davenant. *Fr.* The Siege of Rhodes. BoLP
("This cursed jealousy, what is't?") LO
Jealousy. *Unknown, tr. fr. Irish by* Frank O'Connor. KiLC
Jealousy. Countess of Winchilsea. SeCL
Jealousy's an awful thing and foreign to my nature. I Can't Think What He Sees in Her. A. P. Herbert. FiBHP
Jean. Burns. *See* Of A' the Airts.
Jean. Paul Potts. NeBP
Jean Desprez. Robert W. Service. GSP
Jean Richepin's Song. Herbert Trench. LiTG; LiTM (rev. ed.); OBMV; OxBI; POTE
Jeane. William Barnes. LO
Jeane's Wedden Day in Mornen. William Barnes. PoVP
Jeanie, come tie my. *See* Jennie, come tie my.
Jeanie Morrison. William Motherwell. HBV; LO
Jeanie with the Light Brown Hair. Stephen Collins Foster. FaFP; FaPL; TrAS, *with music*; TreF
Jeannette. Otto Julius Bierbaum, *tr. fr. German by* Jethro Bithell. AWP
Jeannette and Jeannot. Charles Jefferys. BLPA
Jeannie Marsh. George Pope Morris. AA
Jeat Ring Sent, A. John Donne. MaMe; PoeL-2
Jefferson and Liberty, *with music. Unknown.* TrAS
Jefferson D. H. S. Cornwell. PAH
Jefferson Davis. Walker Meriwether Bell. PAH
Jefferson Davis. Harry Thurston Peck. GA
Jefferson Highway, The. Sister Mariella. JKCP (1955 ed.)
Jehovah. Israel Zangwill. WGRP
Jehovah Buried, Satan Dead. E. E. Cummings. NePA
Jehovah-Rophi. William Cowper. EiCP
Jehovah-Shammah. William Cowper. NoP
Jehovah Tsidkenu—The Lord Our Righteousness. Robert Murray McCheyne. SoP
Jehovah's Immovable Throne. Psalms, XCIII, Bible, *O.T.* (*Moulton, Modern Reader's Bible*). WGRP
Jehu. Louis MacNeice. LiTG; LiTM (rev. ed.); MoAB; WaP
Jellicle Cats are black and white. The Song of the Jellicles. T. S. Eliot. FaBoCh; LoGBV
Jellon Grame. *Unknown.* BaBo; ESPB (A *and* B *vers.*); OBB; OxBB
Jelly Jake and Butter Bill. Leroy F. Jackson. BBGG
Jelly Fish, The. Robert P. Tristram Coffin. CAW
Jellyfish, The. Ogden Nash. FaPON
Jem writes his verses with more speed. A Rhymester. Samuel Taylor Coleridge. BOHV; PV
Jemima. *Unknown. See* There Was a Little Girl.
Jemima is my name. Mima. Walter de la Mare. BiCB; BrPo
Jennie [*or* Jeanie *or* Jenny], come tie my. Mother Goose. BoTP; BrR; OxNR; TiPo (1952 ed.)
Jennie Jenkins, *with music. Unknown.* OuSiCo
Jennifer Gentle and Rosemary. *Unknown. See* Riddles Wisely Expounded.
Jenny. Dante Gabriel Rossetti. MaVP; PoEL-5; ViPo; ViPP; VP
"Here nothing warns, *sel.*" NBM
Jenny and Johnny. Dorothy King. BoTP
Jenny and Me were engaged, you see. Pink Dominoes. Kipling. CenHV
Jenny come tie my. *See* Jennie, come tie my.
Jenny gay and Johnny grim. Jenny and Johnny. Dorothy King. BoTP
Jenny Kiss'd [*or* Kissed] Me. Leigh Hunt. ALV; BiCB; BLPA; EnLi-2; FaBoBe; FaFP; GTBS-W; HBV; InMe; LiTG; LiTL; MemP; MeWo; NeHB; OBEV; OBVV; OTPC (1946 ed.); PCD; PG (1945 ed.); PoPl; PoMa; PoRA; PTK; SiTL; TIHL; TreF
(Rondeau, A: "Jenny kiss'd me when we met.") ATP (1935 ed.); EnLit; EnRP; FaBV; GTBS; GTSL; HoPM; InP; MCCG; OnPM; PoE; TOP; ViBoPo; WePo; YAT
Jenny kiss'd me in a dream. "Such Stuff as Dreams." Franklin P. Adams. FiBHP
Jenny kiss'd me when we met. Paul Dehn. *Fr.* A Leaden Treasury of English Verse. FiBHP
Jenny White and Johnny Black. Eleanor Farjeon. FaPON
Jenny wi' the Airn Teeth. Alexander Anderson. HBV
Jenny Wren. W. H. Davies. BiS; MoBrPo; StaSt
Jenny Wren. Walter de la Mare. BiS
Jenny Wren fell sick. Mother Goose. EvOK; OTPC; OxNR; RIS
Jenny Wren's got a house. The Secret. Elizabeth Fleming. BoTP
Jenny, your mind commands. Reading the Brothers Grimm to Jenny. Lisel Mueller. NYBP
Jensen: a Slideshow. Eric Torgersen. QAH
Jephthah's Daughter. Judges, XI: 30-40, Bible, *O.T.* OuHeWo
Jephthah's Daughter, *sel.* Charles Heavysege.
"Oh, think how hard it is to die when young!" CaP
Jephthah's Daughter. Tennyson. FOL
Jephthah's Daughter. "Yehoash," *tr. fr. Yiddish by* Alter Brody. TrJP
Jerboa, The. Marianne Moore. AtBAP; CMoP; MoPo
Jeremiad. Oscar Williams. LiTA
Jeremiah, *sels.* Bible, *O.T.*
As Fowlers Lie in Wait, V: 26-31. TrJP
But Fear Thou Not, O Jacob, XLVI: 27-28. TrJP
Call for True Repentance, A, VII: 1-20. WoL
Cry of the Daughter of My People, The, VIII: 18-23. TrJP
Cursed Be the Day, XX: 14-18. TrJP
End of the World, The, IV: 19-26. PPON
O Lord, Thou Hast Enticed Me, XX: 7-10. TrJP
Oh That I Were in the Wilderness, IX: 1-10. TrJP
Peace! and There Is No Peace, VIII: 1-22. WoL
Potter and the Clay, The, XVIII: 1-11. WoL
"Therefore thus saith the Lord; Ye have not hearkened unto me," XXXIV: 17. PoFr
Jeremiah. Witter Bynner. CrMA
Jeremiah, *sels.* Stefan Zweig, *tr. fr. German by* Eden Paul *and* Cedar Paul.
Chosen of God. TrJP
Flowering without End. TrJP
Jeremiah, blow the fire. *Unknown.* OxNR
Jeremy Hobbler. *Unknown.* BoTP
Jeremy's Secrets ("Jeremy's six, so his sisters say"). Barbara E. Todd. BiCB
Jericho. Willard Wattles. HBMV
Jericho is on the inside. The Walls of Jericho. Blanche Taylor Dickinson. CDC
Jericho, Jericho, round and round the walls I go. Jericho. Willard Wattles. HBMV
Jericho Road, The. Edwin McNeill Poteat. ChIP; MaRV
Jericho's Blind Beggar. Longfellow. *See* Blind Bartimeus.
Jerked Heartstrings in Town. Emily B. C. Jones. HBMV
Jeroboam failed to do. Trusting God. Enola Chamberlin. SoP
Jeronimo's House. Elizabeth Bishop. MiAP
Jerry and Me. Hiram Rich. HBV
Jerry, Go an' Ile That Car. *Unknown.* AS, *with music*; IHA
Jerry Hall,/ He is so small. *Unknown.* OxNR; SiTL
Jerry Jones. *Unknown.* ShM
Jersey Marsh, The. David Galler. NYBP
Jerusalem. Bernard of Cluny. *See* Jerusalem, the Golden.
Jerusalem, *sels.* Blake.
"Ah! weak and wide astray," *fr. ch.* 2. OBRV
"But still the thunder of Los peals loud, and thus the thunders cry," *fr. ch.* 4. PoIE
"England! awake! awake! awake," *fr. prologue to ch.* 4. EnRP; NoP; OBRV
(Prelude: "England! awake! awake! awake!") OBNC
"Fields from Islington to Marybone, The," *fr. prologue to ch.* 2. ChTr; ERoP-1; OBRV
(Prelude: "Fields from Islington to Marybone, The.") OBNC
(To the Jews.) PeER
"I give you the end of a golden string," *fr. prologue to ch.* 4. OBRV; ShBV-4
(Epigraph: "I give you the end of a golden string.") OBNC
(I Will Give You.) OTPC (1946 ed.)
(To the Christians.) EnRP; WGRP
"I saw a monk of Charlemain[e]," *fr. prologue to ch.* 3. EnRP; OBRV

Jerusalem (continued)
(Monk, The.) LoBV
"I see the four-fold man, the humanity in deadly sleep," *fr. ch.* 1. PoIE
In Deadly Fear. SeCePo
Male & Female Loves in Beulah, *fr. ch.* 3. OBNC
"Rhine was red with human blood, The," *fr. prologue to ch.* 2. ViBoPo
"What are those golden builders doing," *fr. ch.* 1. OBRV
Written 1811, *fr. ch.* 4. MaRV; StJW
Jerusalem. Blake. *Fr.* Milton. *See* And Did Those Feet in Ancient Time.
Jerusalem. "George Eliot." SoP
Jerusalem, *sel.* Uri Zvi Greenberg, *tr. fr. Hebrew by* Charles A. Cowen.
Jerusalem the Dismembered. TrJP
Jerusalem. *Unknown. See* New Jerusalem, The.
Jerusalem Delivered [*or* Godfrey of Bulloigne], *sels.* Tasso, *tr. fr. Italian by* Edward Fairfax.
Armida, the Sorceress, *fr.* IV. EnLi-1
Crusaders Reach Jerusalem, The, *fr.* III. EnLi-1
(Crusaders Behold Jerusalem, The, *tr. by* J. H. Wiffen.) CAW
"Know, he assists the cause of God, who toils," *fr.* IV, *tr. by* J. H. Wiffen. PoFr
Pluto's Council. OBSC
Prayer Brings Rain, A. OBSC
"Sacred armies and the godly knight, The," *fr.* I. CAW
"When they had passed all those troubled ways," *fr.* XVI. TuPP
Jerusalem Delivered. Louis Untermeyer. MAP
Jerusalem, My Happy Home. *Unknown. See* New Jerusalem.
Jerusalem Street and Paradise Square. Closing Time. James Michie. NePoEA-2
Jerusalem the Dismembered. Uri Zvi Greenberg, *tr. fr. Hebrew by* Charles A. Cowen. *Fr.* Jerusalem. TrJP
Jerusalem, the Golden. Bernard of Cluny, *tr. fr. Latin by* John Mason Neale. *Fr.* De Contemptu Mundi. CAW; MaRV; WGRP
(Celestial Country, The.) GoBC, *abr.*
(Jerusalem, *abr.*) HBV; OBVV
Jerusalem, thy joys divine. The Under Song. *Unknown.* ACP
Jes' beyan a clump o' pines. The Corn Song. John Wesley Holloway. BANP
Jesous Ahatonhia. Jesse Edgar Middleton, *after* Jean de Brébeuf. CaP; ChrBoLe
Jess, a wild cowboy, loves whisky and beer. Jess's Dilemma. *Unknown.* CoSo
Jesse James. William Rose Benét. BBV (1951 ed.); InP; MAP; MoAmPo; NAMP; NeMA; StPo; ThLM; TrGrPo
Jesse James (*diff. vers.*) *Unknown.* ABF (A *vers., with music;* B *vers.*); AmFN; AmPP (3d ed.); AS; ATP; BaBo (A, B, *and* C *vers.*); BeLS; BFSS, *with music*; CoSo (A *vers., with music;* B, C, *and* D *vers.*); FaBoBe; IHA; InP; MaC; PoPo; TrAS, *wih music*; TreFS; UnPo; ViBoFo (A *and* B *vers.*); WiR; YaD
(Death of Jesse James, The.) WOW
Jesse James was a lad who [*or* that] killed many a man. Jesse James. *Unknown.* BaBo (C *vers.*); MaC; ViBoFo (A *vers.*)
Jesse James was a man, and he had a robber band. Jesse James. *Unknown.* AmFN
Jesse James was a man who killed many a man. Jesse James. *Unknown.* BFSS
Jesse James was a two-gun man. Jesse James. William Rose Benét. BBV (1951 ed.); InP; MAP; MoAmPo; NAMP; NeMA; StPo; ThLM; TrGrPo
Jesse James was one of his names, another it was Howard. Jesse James (B *vers.*). *Unknown.* BaBo; ViBoFo
Jessica's my sister. Richard Has Something to Say. Rose Fyleman. GaP
Jessie. Thomas Edward Brown. HBV; OBEV (1st ed.)
Jessie. Eugene Field. InMe
Jessie. Bret Harte. GN
Jessie, the Flower o' Dunblane. Robert Tannahill. HBV
Jess's Dilemma. *Unknown.* CoSo
Jest a-wearyin' for you. Wearyin' for You. Frank L. Stanton. HBV
Jest 'fore Christmas. Eugene Field. ChBR; DD; FaBV; FaFP; FaPON; HBV; HBVY; HH; MPB; OHFP; OTPC; PoLF; PTK; TreF; YT
Jester and His Daughter, The. Tom Taylor. *Fr.* The Fool's Revenge. VA
Jester Bee. Frank Dempster Sherman. UTS
Jester Condemned to Death, The. Horace Smith. BOHV
Jester in the Trench, The. Leon Gellert. PoAu-1
Jester shook his hood and bells, and leap'd upon a chair, The. The Jester's Sermon. George Walter Thornbury. BeLS; TreFS
Jester walked in the garden, The. The Cap and Bells. W. B. Yeats. BrPo; ChTr; FlW; GTSL; OBVV; OnMSP
Jester's Plea, The. Frederick Locker-Lampson. CenHV
Jester's Sermon, The. George Walter Thornbury. BeLS; TreFS
Jesu. George Herbert. MaMe; MeLP
(Iesu.) OBS
Jesu,/ If thou wilt make. A Page's Road Song. William Alexander Percy. TrPWD; YeAr
Jesu! by that shuddering dread which fell on Thee. Angel of the Agony. Cardinal Newman. *Fr.* The Dream of Gerontius. OxBoCh
Jesu Christ, my lemmon swete. Jesus, My Sweet Lover. *Unknown.* MeEL
Jesu Dulcis. St. Bernard of Clairvaux, *tr. fr. Latin.* CAW
Jesu, Dulcis Memoria. *At. to* St. Bernard of Clairvaux. *See* Jesus the Very Thought of Thee.
Jesu! for thy mercy endelesse [*or* for thy wondes fife]. Jesu! Send Us Peace. *Unknown.* MeEL
Jesu, I now begin. *Unknown.* BoC
Jesu [*or* Iesu] is in my heart, his sacred name. Jesu [*or* Iesu]. George Herbert. MaMe; MeLP; OBS
Jesu, Joy of Man's Desiring. Robert Fitzgerald. NYBP
Jesu, Lord, welcom thou be. A Prayer to the Sacrament of the Altar. *Unknown.* MeEL
Jesu, Lorde, that madest me. A Hymn to Jesus. Richard of Caistre. MeEL
Jesu, Lover of My Soul. Charles Wesley. *See* Jesus, Lover of My Soul.
Jesu, Maria—I am near to death. Cardinal Newman. *Fr.* The Dream of Gerontius. ACP; CoBE; EnLi-2; PoVP
Jesu, my sweet Son dear. Cradle Song of the Virgin. *Unknown.* ISi. *See also* Jesu [*or* Iesu], swete sone dere!
Jesu, no more! it is full tide. On the Bleeding Wounds of Our Crucified Lord [*or* Upon the Bleeding Crucifix]. Richard Crashaw. MaMe; SeCP; SeCV-1; TrGrPo
Jesu! Send Us Peace. *Unknown.* MeEL
Jesu, swetë sonë derë. *Unknown.* EnL.*See also* Iesu, swete sone dere! *and* Jesu, my sweet Son dear.
Jesu, that hast me dere iboght. A Devout Prayer of the Passion. *Unknown.* MeEL
Jesu! The Very Thought of Thee. *See* Jesus the very Thought of Thee.
Jesu, thie love within mee is soe maine. Sonnet. William Alabaster. AnAnS-1; MeP
Jesu, to Thee I cry and greed. *Unknown. Fr.* Jesus the Comforter. MaRV
Jesukin. *At. to* St. Ita, *tr. fr. Old Irish by* George Sigerson. CAW; OnYI
(Saint Ita's Fosterling, *tr. by* Robin Flower.) OnYI
(Vision of Ita, The, *tr. by* Whitley Stokes.) AnIL
Jesus. Francis Lauderdale Adams. OxBS
Jesus. Robert Bridges. *Fr.* The Testament of Beauty, I. MaRV
Jesus. Ray Palmer. *See* Jesus, These Eyes Have Never Seen.
Jesus ("Jesus, there is no dearer name than thine"). Theodore Parker. AA
Jesus. Ramón Pimental Coronel, *tr. fr. Spanish by* Joseph I. C. Clarke. CAW
Jesus. *Unknown.* ChIP; OQP
Jesus/ Wracked on your cross. Unity. Lloyd Frank Merrell. ChIP
Jesus—all Thy labor vast. Father, into Thy Hands. Thomas B. Pollock. BePJ
Jesus, almighty King of Blis. The Nativity. *Unknown.* MeEL
Jesus and Alexander. *Unknown.* SoP
Jesus, and didst Thou condescend. Thou Alone Canst Save. Amelia Wakeford. BePJ
Jesus—and didst Thou leave the sky. Compassion So Divine. Anne Steele. BePJ
Jesus and His Mother. Thom Gunn. CaFP; EaLo
Jesus and I. Dan Crawford. BLRP; FaChP; TRV
(We Two.) SoP
Jesus! and shall it ever be. Ashamed of Jesus [*or* Not Ashamed of Christ]. Joseph Grigg. BePJ; SoP
Jesus and the Children. St. Mark, X: 13-16, Bible, *N.T.* TreFT

Jesus and the Woman at the Well. St. John, IV: 5-26, Bible, *N.T.* TreFT
Jesus Answers the Pharisees. St. John, VIII: 12-32, Bible, *N.T.* TreFS
Jesus, at whose supreme command. The Cup of Blessing. Charles Wesley. BePJ
Jesus Bids Man Remember. *Unknown.* MeEL
Jesus bids us shine with a clear, pure light. A Candle Burning in the Night. Susan B. Warner. ThGo
Jesus Calls Us o'er the Tumult. Cecil Frances Alexander. MaRV
Jesus came, the heavens adoring. Jesus Comes on Clouds Triumphant. Godfrey Thring. BePJ
Jesus, Child and Lord. Frederick William Faber. BePJ
Jesus Christ—and We. Annie Johnson Flint. *See* World's Bible, The.
Jesus Christ the Lord. Thomas T. Lynch. *See* Thousand Years Have Come, A.
Jesus Christ the Lord. Godfrey Thring. SoP
Jesus Christ to-day is risen. Easter. Martin Luther, *tr. fr. German by* Richard Massie. SoP
Jesus Christ, who brought good news. Subversive. William Rose Benét. MoRP
Jesus Christ, who stands between. The Covenant of His Grace. Charles Wesley. BePJ
Jesus Comes on Clouds Triumphant. Godfrey Thring. BePJ
Jesus Comforts His Mother. *Unknown.* *See* Dear Son, Leave Thy Weeping.
Jesus Contrasts Man and Himself. *Unknown.* MeEL
Jesus, Deliverer. Anatolius. *See* Fierce was the Wild Billow.
Jesus doth him bimene. Jesus Contrasts Man and Himself. *Unknown.* MeEL
Jesus Eats with Sinners. St. Mark, II: 15-17, Bible, *N.T.* TreFT
Jesus, Estrella, Esperanza, Mercy. Middle Passage. Robert Hayden. AmNP; IDB
Jesus First and Jesus Last. Thomas MacKellar. BePJ
Jesus, Fountain of my days. Peace, Be Still! George Matheson. SoP
Jesus, Friend of sinners, hear. Bid Me Sin No More. Charles Wesley. BePJ
Jesus, great Shepherd of the sheep. Great Shepherd of the Sheep. Charles Wesley. BePJ
Jesus hath died that I might live. Dying that I Might Live. Charles Wesley. BePJ
Jesus Himself. Henry Burton. BLRP; SoP
Jesus His Mother meets. Fourth Station. Padraic Colum. ISi
Jesus, How Much Thy Name Unfolds. Mary Peters. BePJ
Jesus, I am far astray. Wanderer's Song. Henry W. Frost. SoP
Jesus, I Am Resting, Resting. Jean Sophia Pigott. FaChP
Jesus, I kneel down to say. Just for Jesus. Lysbeth Boyd Borie. GaP
Jesus, I Love Thy Charming Name. Philip Doddridge. BePJ
Jesus I my cross have taken. Lo, We Have Left All. Henry Francis Lyte. VA
Jesus I saw, crossing Times Square. The Flower in the Sea. Malcolm Cowley. NP
Jesus, immortal King, arise. Christ, the Conqueror. Aaron C. H. Seymour, *wr. at. to* Henry Foster Burder. BePJ
Jesus in the Temple. John Donne. *See* Temple.
Jesus, in whom the Godhead's rays. Wash Me Whiter than Snow. Charles Wesley. BePJ
Jesus Is Near. Robert Cassie Waterston. BePJ
Jesus is our common Lord. Walking with Him in White. Charles Wesley. BePJ
Jesus lead me up the mountain. Take the Supreme Climb! *Unknown.* SoP
Jesus, let Thy pitying eye. Break My Heart of Stone [*or* Prayer for Forgiveness, A]. Charles Wesley. BePJ; SoP
Jesus Lives, and So Shall I, *diff. vers.* Christian Fürchtegott Gellert, *tr. fr. German.* BePJ
(Jesus Lives.) FaChP; PGD, 2 *sts.*
(Ye Shall Live Also, 3 *sts.*, *tr. by* Frances E. Cox, *wr. at. to* Arthur Coxe.) BePJ
Jesus, Lord mickle of might. Sir Cawline. *Unknown.* OBB
Jesus [*or* Jesu], Lover of My Soul. Charles Wesley. BePJ; HBV; MaRV; NeHB; OxBoCh; TreF; WGRP
(Divine Lover, The, *sl. abr.*) BLRP
(In Temptation.) CEP; EiCL; EiPP; PoE; PoEL-3; SoP; TOP
Jesus, Master, whose I am. "Whose I Am." Frances Ridley Havergal. SoP
Jesus' mother never had no man. Conception. Waring Cuney. BANP; PoNe
Jesus, my chief pleasure. Peace and Joy in Jesus Christ. Johann Franck. BePJ
Jesus, My God and My All. Frederick William Faber. BePJ
Jesus, my Lord, attend. For Perfect Peace. Charles Wesley. BePJ
Jesus, my Lord, my chief delight! The Glorious Gift of God. Benjamin Beddome. BePJ
Jesus, my Lord, when I look upon Thee. Thy Nail-pierced Hands. Kathryn Bowsher. STF
Jesus, my one Love, behold me draw near. Scattering Flowers. St. Thérèse of Lisieux. WHL
Jesus, my Saviour, Brother, Friend. Fly Back to Christ. Charels Wesley. BePJ
Jesus, My Saviour, Look on Me! John Macduff. BePJ
Jesus! my Shepherd, Husband, Friend. John Newton. *Fr.* The Name of Jesus. TrPWD
Jesus, my strength and righteousness. Thy Conquering Name. Charles Wesley. BePJ
Jesus, My Sweet Lover. *Unknown.* MeEL
Jesus Never Fails. Walter E. Isenhour. STF
Jesus never will forget me. He Never Will Forget. "M. G. H." STF
Jesus of Nazareth. Ernest Cadman Colwell. ChIP; MaRV
Jesus of Nazareth, King of the Jews. Villanelle. A. M. Sullivan. OQP
Jesus of Nazareth Passes By. George T. Liddell. ChIP
Jesus of Nazareth Passeth By. Lydia Huntley Sigourney. BePJ; StJW
Jesus of the Scars. Edward Shillito. ChIP; MaRV; OQP
Jesus Only. Elias Nason. BePJ
Jesus Only. A. B. Simpson. BePJ
Jesus our brother, kind [*or* strong] and good. The Friendly Beasts. *Unknown.* BiCB; ChBR; ChrBoLe; FaPON; OnMSP; PoSC; SiSoSe; SoPo
Jesus' Parable of the Sower. St. Luke, VIII: 5-15, Bible, *N.T.* TreFT
Jesus Praying. Hartley Coleridge. MaRV; StJW
Jesus Prays Alone. William Bingham Tappan. *See* 'Tis Midnight; and on Olive's Brow.
Jesus, Priceless Treasure. Johann Franck, *tr. fr. German, by* Catherine Winkworth. SoP
Jesus Reassures His Mother. *Unknown.* MeEL
Jesus, Refuge of the Weary. Savonarola, *tr. fr. Latin.* MaRV
Jesus Reproaches His People. *Unknown.* MeEL
Jesus, Return. Henry van Dyke. SoP; TRV
Jesus said, "Wouldst thou love one who never died." Written 1811. Blake. *Fr.* Jerusalem. MaRV; StJW
Jesus Saviour, Pilot Me. Edward Hopper. BLRP; SoP
Jesus Shall Reign Where'er the Sun. Isaac Watts. BePJ; MaRV; SoP; WGRP, *sl. abr.*
(King Triumphant, *abr.*) BLRP; FaChP
Jesus! she's thin. She squirms in her sleep. Waking Up in the Woods. Gregory Orr. QAH
Jesus, stand beside them. A Wedding Hymn. Thomas Tiplady. MaRV
Jesus, Sun and Shield art Thou. The First and the Last. Horatius Bonar. BePJ
Jesus, sweet is love of Thee. Jesu Dulcis. St Bernard of Clairvaux. CAW
Jesus, teach me how to be. The Housewife. Catherine Cate Coblentz. BLRP; ChIP; FaChP; SoP; StJW; TrPWD; TRV
Jesus, Tender Shepherd [Hear Me]. Mary L. Duncan. *See* Child's Evening Prayer, A.
Jesus, the Blessed Agitator. The Blessed Agitator. Lucia Trent. ChIP
Jesus the Carpenter. Catherine C. Liddell. DD; HBV; VA
Jesus the Carpenter. Charles M. Sheldon. ChIP; MaRV; OQP; SoP
Jesus the Comforter, *sel.* *Unknown.*
"Jesu, to Thee I cry and greed." MaRV
Jesus, the friend of lonely, beaten folk. Mary's Son. Lucia Trent. ChIP; PGD
Jesus, the gift divine I know. The Well of Living Water. Charles Wesley. BePJ
Jesus, the Lamb of God, hath bled. Graven on the Palms of

Jesus (continued)
His Hands. Charles Wesley. BePJ
Jesus, the Lord of glory, died. Our Ever-present Guide. *Unknown.* BePJ
Jesus, the Master of My Fate. *Unknown.* SoP
Jesus the Name Most High. Charles Wesley. BePJ
Jesus, the sinner's Friend, to Thee. Flying to Christ. *Unknown.* SoP
Jesus, the Soul of Our Joys. Charles Wesley. BePJ
Jesus [*or* Jesu!] the Very Thought of Thee. *At. to* St. Bernard of Clairvaux, *tr. fr. Latin by* Edward Caswall. MaRV; SoP
(Jesu, Dulcis Memoria.) WHL
(Sweetest Name, The.) BePJ
Jesus, there is no dearer name than thine. Jesus. Theodore Parker. AA
Jesus, These Eyes Have Never Seen. Ray Palmer. MaRV
(Blessed Face, The.) BePJ
(Jesus.) SoP
Jesus, Thou Art the King. Charles Wesley. BePJ
Jesus! Thou art the sinner's Friend. Friend of Sinners. Richard Burnham. BePJ
Jesus, Thou Divine Companion. Henry van Dyke. *See* Hymn of Labor.
Jesus, Thou everlasting King. Accept Our Tribute. Isaac Watts. BePJ
Jesus, Thou Joy of Loving Hearts. *At. to* St. Bernard of Clairvaux, *tr. fr. Latin by* Ray Palmer. MaRV; SoP; WGRP
(Thou Light of Life.) BePJ
Jesus, Thou Living Bread. The Living Jesus. R. F. Pechey. SoP
Jesus, thou soul of all our joys. Jesus, the Soul of Our Joys. Charles Wesley. BePJ
Jesus, Thou source divine. The Only Name Given under Heaven. Anne Steele. BePJ
Jesus, Thy blood and righteousness. I Believe Thy Precious Blood. John Wesley. BePJ
Jesus! Thy church, with longing eyes. The Triumphs of Thy Conquering Power. William H. Bathurst. BePJ
Jesus! thy Crucifix. Emily Dickinson. MoVE
Jesus, Thy far-extended fame. Christ, the Good Physician. Charles Wesley. BePJ
Jesus, Thy Life Is Mine! *Unknown, at. to* Frances Ridley Havergal. SoP
(Prayer, A.) STF
Jesus, Thy love alone, alone Thy Love. Thy Love Alone. Horatius Bonar. FaChP
Jesus! Thy love shall we forget. Shall We Forget. William Mitchell. BePJ
Jesus to Those Who Pass By. *Unknown.* MeEL
Jesus Understands. *Unknown.* BLRP
Jesus, united by Thy grace. The Loadstone of His Love. Charles Wesley. BePJ
Jesus was a carpenter. He gladly plied. The Carpenter. Amy Bruner Almy. ChIP
Jesus Was Crucified or: It Must Be Deep. Carolyn M. Rodgers. WSL
Jesus Was a Humble Man. Raymond Kresensky. ChIP
Jesus was sitting in Moses' chair. The New Law. Blake. *Fr.* The Everlasting Gospel. OxBoCh; StJW
Jesus, we lift our souls to Thee. Bless, Dear Saviour, This Child. Thomas Beck. BePJ
Jesus, we look to Thee. Claiming the Promise. Charles Wesley. BePJ
Jesus, when from Thy Mother's clasp I see Thee go. The Unpetalled Rose. St. Thérèse of Lisieux. CAW
Jesus! When my soul is parting. Jesus First and Jesus Last. Thomas MacKellar. BePJ
Jesus, where'er thy people meet. The Place of Prayer. William Cowper. SoP
Jesus, while our hearts are bleeding. Thy Will Be Done. *Unknown.* BePJ
Jesus, who knows full well. All Our Griefs to Tell. John Newton. BePJ
Jesus, whose lot with us was cast. Jesus. *Unknown.* ChIP; OQP
Jesus, whose love rekindles dying fires. In the Way of Peace. Lauchlan MacLean Watt. ChIP; OQP
Jesus, whoso with Thee. Lauda. Girolamo Benevieni. CAW
Jesus, Won't You Come B'm-By? *with music.* *Unknown.* AS
Jesus' Wounds So Wide. *Unknown.* NoP
(Wells of Jesus Wounds, The.) MeEL
Jet form swaying in the morning mist, A. Intolerance. John Richard Moreland. ChIP
Jet Plane. A. M. Sullivan. JKCP (1955 ed.)
Jetsam, *sel.* William Vaughn Moody.
"Once at a simple turning." MAP; MoAmPo (1942 ed.)
Jew, The. Isaac Rosenberg. MoBrPo; PoFr
Jew. Karl Shapiro. ToPo
Jew of Malta, The, *sels.* Christopher Marlowe.
Mine Argosy from Alexandria, *fr.* I, i. ChTr
("Give me the merchants of the Indian mines.") LO
Song of Ithamore, The, *fr.* IV, iv. WHA
Jew to Jesus, The. Florence Kiper Frank. ChIP; HBMV; MaRV; NP; StJW; TRV; WGRP
Jew Walks in Westminster Abbey, A. Aubrey Hodes. TrJP
Jew Wrecked in the German Cell, The. W. H. Auden. WaP
(Diaspora, The.) LiTA
Jewel, The. James Dickey. TPM
Jewel, The. James Wright. CoAP; FRC
Jewel-blue electric flowers, The. Three o'Clock; Morning. Ridgely Torrence. NP
Jewel of the Secret Treasury, The. Hafiz. Odes, VI. AWP; JAWP; LiTW; WBP
Jewelled mine of the pomegranate, whose hexagons of honey, The. The Pomegranate. Louis Dudek. OBCV; PeCV
Jewels. Asayasu, *tr. fr. Japanese by* Basil Hall Chamberlain. OnPM
Jewels, The. Baudelaire, *tr. fr. French by* Paul Blackburn. ErPo
Jewels, The. Austin Clarke. MoAB
Jewish Arabic Liturgies. *Unknown, tr. fr. Arabic by* Hartwig Hirschfeld. TrJP
Jewish Cemetery at Newport, The. Longfellow. AmP; AmPP; AnNE; AP; ForPo; HT; MAmP; MWA-1; NoP; OxBA; PoE; PoIE (1970 ed.); PPON
Jewish Conscript, The. Florence Kiper Frank. OQP; TrJP
Jewish king now walks at large and sound, The. Zaph Describes the Haunts of Malzah. Charles Heavysege. *Fr.* Saul. OBCV
Jewish Lady, The. *Unknown.* *See* Sir Hugh.
Jewish Lullaby. Louis Untermeyer. RIS
Jewish Main Street. Irving Layton. CaP
Jewish May, The. Morris Rosenfeld, *tr. fr. Yiddish by* Rose Pastor Stokes *and* Helena Frank. TrJP
Jewish Poet Counsels a King, A. Santob de Carrion, *tr. fr. Spanish.* TrJP
Jews, The. George Herbert. MaMe
Jews, The. Henry Vaughan. OBS
Jews at Haifa. Randall Jarrell. MoAmPo (1950 ed.)
Jew's Daughter, The. *Unknown.* *See* Sir Hugh.
Jew's Home, The. Robert Eyres Landor. *Fr.* The Impious Feast, I. OBRV
Jezebel. Scudder Middleton. HBMV
Jezebel Jones smelled really punk. The Tale of the Skunk and Poor Jez. John Becker. RePo
Jezreel. Thomas Hardy. NoP
Jhesu cryst, myn leman swete. *Unknown.* *Fr.* A Prayer of the Five Wounds. AtBAP
Jig. C. Day Lewis. OxBI; WePo
Jig, A. Robert Greene. *See* Doron's Jig.
Jig for Sackbuts. D. B. Wyndham Lewis. ErPo
Jigsaw. John Stevens Wade. ThO
Jigsaw III. Louis MacNeice. HaMV
Jill Came from the Fair. Eleanor Farjeon. TiPo
Jillian of Berry. Beaumont *and* Fletcher. *Fr.* The Knight of the Burning Pestle. ElL
(Merrythought's Song: "For Jillian of Berry.") OBS
Jilted Funeral, The. Gelett Burgess. ShM
Jilted Nymph, The. Thomas Campbell. BoLP; EnLoPo
Jim. Hilaire Belloc. BBGG; CenHV; ChTr; HBMV; MaC; OnSP; ShBV-2; TSW
(Jim, Who Ran Away from His Nurse, and Was Eaten by a Lion.) EvOK; ShM
Jim. Perceval Gibbon. BoSA
Jim. Bret Harte. AA; BOHV; MAP; MoAmPo (1942 ed.); NeMA; WhC
Jim and Bill. Franklin P. Adams. LHV
Jim and I as children played together. Oh Lucky Jim! *Unknown.* ChTr
Jim at the Corner. Eleanor Farjeon. GaP; SoPo; SUS

Jim Bludso [of the *Prairie Belle*]. John Hay. AA; AmePo; AmPP (3d ed.); AnAmPo; BBV; BeLS; BOHV; CoBA; FaBoBe; FaFP; HBV; IHA; MaC; MCCG; MoAmPo (1942 ed.); NeMA; PaA; PaPo; PCD; PFY; PoMa; PoPo; TIHL; TreFS; YaD
Jim Bowker, he said, if he'd had a fair show. Then Ag'in. Sam Walter Foss. BOHV; HBV
Jim Desterland. Hyam Plutzik. FiSC
Jim Farrow. *Unknown.* CoSo
Jim Finley's Pig. *Unknown.* FTB
Jim Fisk. *Unknown.* AS, *with music*; ViBoFo
Jim Haggerty's Story. *Unknown.* ABF
Jim-Jam King of the Jou-Jous, The. Alaric Bertrand Stuart. BOHV
Jim Jay. Walter de la Mare. BrPo; CenHV; GaP; GoTP; HBMV; RG; RIS; SiSoSe
Jim Jones. *Unknown.* PoAu-1
Jim Porter's Shanty Song. *Unknown.* IHA
Jim says a sailor man/ He means to be. When We Are Men. E. Stella Mead. BoTP
Jim the Splitter. Henry Kendall. PoAu-1
Jim was a sailor. Jim at the Corner. Eleanor Farjeon. GaP; SoPo; SUS
Jim, Who Ran Away from His Nurse, and Was Eaten by a Lion. Hilaire Belloc. *See* Jim.
Jiminy Jiminy Jukebox! Wheatcakes! Crumbs! Mole. William Jay Smith. RePo
Jiminy Whillikers/ Admiral Samuel. George Starbuck. PV
Jimmie Randall was a-hunting, a-hunting in the dark. Molly Bawn. *Unknown.* ViBoFo
Jimmy Random, My Son. *Unknown.* *See* Lord Randal.
Jimmy the Mowdy. *Unknown.* OxNR
Jimmy's Enlisted; or, The Recruited Collier. *Unknown.* CoMu
Jimmy's Father. John Stevens Wade. ThO
Jimson lives in a new. A Call to the Wild. Lord Dunsany. OnYI
Jingle. John O'Keeffe. *See* Amo, Amas.
Jingle Bells. James S. Pierpont, *wr. at. to* John Pierpont. FaFP; TreF; YaD
Jingle, bells! jingle, bells! *Unknown.* OxNR
Jinny Git Around, *with music.* *Unknown.* OuSiCo
Jinny the Just. Matthew Prior. CABL; CEP; OBEC; OBEV (new ed.); PoEL-3
Jippy and Jimmy. Laura E. Richards. MPB; SoPo; TiPo
Jitterbug/ Is out. Bring the Soul Blocks. Victor Hernandez Cruz. CAD
Jitterbugging in the Streets. Calvin C. Hernton. BF; WOW, *abr.*
Jittery Jim. William Jay Smith. BBGG
Jo Jo, My Child. *Unknown, tr. fr. Hebrew by* Immanuel Olsvanger. TrJP
Joan of Arc. Hugh McCrae. PoAu-1
Joan of Arc, 1926. Virginia Moore. YT
Joan of Arc to the Tribunal. Anthony Frisch. CaP
Joan to Her Lady. *Unknown.* UnTE
Joan's Door. Eleanor Farjeon. BiCB
Joaquin the Horse-Thief. John A. Stone. SGR
Job, *sels.* Bible, *O.T.*
  "Behold, God is great, and we know him not," XXXVI: 26-30, 32. ImOP
  Immortality ("For I know that my vindicator liveth"), XIX: 25-27, *Moulton, Modern Reader's Bible.* WGRP
  Job's Comforters, XI: 7-10, *Moulton, Modern Reader's Bible.* WGRP
    (Eternal Quest, The, XI: 7-8, *Moulton, Modern Reader's Bible.*) MaRV
  Job's Curse, III: 3-26. AWP; JAWP; WBP
    (Job Complains.) TrGrPo
    (Let the Day Perish, III: 1-26.) TrJP
  Job's Entreaty, XIV. AWP; JAWP; WBP
    (Immortality: "Man that is born of woman," XIV: 1-2, 7-12, *Moulton, Modern Reader's Bible.*) WGRP
    (Job Cries Out, XIV.) TrGrPo
    (Job's Questions, XIV.) OuHeWo
  Let Me Alone, VII: 11-21. PPON
  Lord Gave, The, I: 20-21. TreF
  Man That Is Born of a Woman, XIV: 1-2. ChTr
  Not Flesh of Brass, VI: 1-13. TrJP
  Oh That I Knew Where I Might Find Him, XXIII: 3, 8-10. MaRV
  Of God's Great Power in the Leviathan, XLI, *abr.* PoG
  Price of Wisdom, The, XXVIII. TrGrPo
  Voice Out of the Whirlwind, The. MaRV (XXXVIII: 2-XL: 2, *Moulton, Modern Reader's Bible*); OuHeWo (XXXVIII: 2-XLII: 6)
    God Replies, XXXVIII: 2-41. TrGrPo
    "Hast thou given the horse his might?" XXXIX: 19 XL: 2. ChTr; InP
    Horse, The, XXXIX: 19-25. FaPON; GoTP; StaSt, *abr.*; TrGrPo
    (War Horse, The.) ShBV-2
    Leviathan, XLI: 1-21. TrGrPo
    Out of the Whirlwind, XL: 7-24; XLI. AWP; JAWP; WBP
    Then the Lord Answered, XXXVIII: 2-24; XXXIX. AWP; JAWP; ShBV-4 (XXXVIII: 1-11, 31-35); WBP
    Treasures, The, XXXVIII: 22-32. BoW
    Voice from the Whirlwind, The; God's Majesty, XXXVIII. PG (1955 ed.)
    "Where wast thou when I laid the foundations of the earth," ImOP (XXXVIII: 4-38, *abr.*); PoG (XXXVIII: 4-41, *abr.*)
  Where Shall Wisdom Be Found? XXVIII: 12-20, 28. TreFT
Job. Samuel Taylor Coleridge. BOHV
Job. E. W. Mandel. PeCV
Job. Elizabeth Sewell. EaLo
Job. R. S. Thomas. NYTB
Job ("O Job, Job"), *with music.* *Unknown.* OuSiCo
Job That's Crying to Be Done, The. Kipling. TRV
Jobson's Amen. Kipling. AnFE
Jock o' Dreams. Rose Fyleman. BoTP
Jock o' the Side. *Unknown.* ESPB (A *and* B *vers.*); OBB; ViBoFo
Jock of [*or* o'] Hazeldean. Sir Walter Scott. BEL; BeLS; CoBE; EnLi-2 (1949 ed.); EnLit; EnRP; EPN; GN; GTBS; GTBS-D; GTBS-P; GTBS-W; GTSE; GTSL; HBV; ILP; MCCG; OAEP; OBRV; OTPC; OxBS; PoPo; StP; TOP
Jock o' Hazeldean. *Unknown.* *See* John of Hazelgreen.
Jock o' the Side. *Unknown.* OxBB
Jock the Leg and the Merry Merchant. *Unknown.* ESPB
Jockey was a dowdy lad. Scotch Song. Thomas D'Urfey. *Fr.* The Campaigners; or, The Pleasant Adventures at Brussels. CEP
Jockie, Thine Hornpipe's Dull. *Unknown.* NCEP
Jocky said to Jenny, Jenny wilt thou do't. A Dainty Sang. Allan Ramsay. *Fr.* The Gentle Shepherd. OBEC
Jocosa Lyra. Austin Dobson. BOHV; InP
Joculator Domini. Sister Mary John Frederick. GoBC
Jodrell Bank. Patric Dickinson. POTi
Joe. David McCord. TiPo (1959 ed.)
Joe Beauchamp ees conceited man. De Baby Show. Wilson MacDonald. WhC
Joe Bowers. *Unknown, at. to* John Woodward. ABF, *with music*; ATP; BaBo; BFSS; CoSo, *with music*; SGR; TrAS, *with music*; TreFS; ViBoFo
Joe Brainard's Painting "Bingo." Ron Padgett. ANYP
Joe Dobson, *with music.* "B. A. T." FTB
Joe Green Joe Green O how are you doing today? An Old Inmate. Kenneth Mackenzie. PoAu-2
Joe Greene. Merrill Moore. WoL
Joe hates a sycophant. It shows. Epigram [*or* On Joe]. P. Dodd. ALV; SiTL
Joe saw the train but couldn't stop. *Unknown.* OTD
Joe Tinker. Amanda Benjamin Hall. HBMV
Joe Turner [Blues], *with music.* *Unknown.* AS; TrAS
Joe, you prefatory mortal. Apostrophe to a Pram Rider. E. B. White. InMe
Joe's an imp of three. Proud Motherhood. Frank Laurence Lucas. FOL
Jog On, Jog On [the Foot-Path Way]. Shakespeare. *Fr.* The Winter's Tale, IV, ii. CBEP; ChTr; EG; FaBoCh; GN; HBV; HBVY; LoGBV; OBSC; PoG; SiCE; TiPo (1952 ed.); TVC; ViBoPo
  (Autolycus' Song.) WhC
  (Foothpath Way, The.) RIS
  (Merry Heart, The.) BoTP; EIL; PCH; SiTL; TrGrPo
  (Songs of Autolycus, The.) OTPC (1923 ed.)
Johannes Agricola in Meditation. Robert Browning. MaVP; OBVV; PoVP; ViPo; ViPP
Johannes Milton, Senex. Robert Bridges. CMoP; LiTB; NAMP; PoEL-5; PoPl
Johannesburg. William Plomer. BoSA
John. Bible, *N.T.* *See* First Epistle of John *and* St. John.

John Adams. Rosemary Benét *and* Stephen Vincent Benét. PAL
John Adams lies here, of the parish of Southwell. On John Adams, of Southwell. Byron. PV
John Alcohol, my foe, John. My Foe. *Unknown.* BOHV
John and Peter and Robert and Paul. The Chemistry of Character. Elizabeth Dorney. BLPA
John Anderson. Burns. *See* John Anderson, My Jo.
"John Anderson, My Jo." Charles G. Blanden. HBV
John Anderson, My Jo ("John Anderson, my jo, John,/When we were first acquent"). Burns. AWP; BEL; BoLiVe; CABA; CaFP; CBEP; CEP; CoBE; EiCL; EiCP; EiPP; EnLi-2; EnLit; EnPE; EnRP; ErPo; FaBV; GTBS-P; InPo; JAWP; LiTL; MaRV; MCCG; NeHB; NoP; OAEP; OBEC; OBEV; OtMeF; OuHeWo; OxBS; PG; Po; PoE; PoIE; PoMa; PoSa; ShBV-1; TOP; TreFT; TrGrPo; UnTE; ViBoPo; WBP; WHA
(Hymn of Marriage.) PoToHe
(John Anderson.) GTBS; GTBS-D; GTBS-W; GTSE; GTSL; HBV; InP; LiTB; LiTG; MemP; OTPC; PoPo; PTK; WBLP
John Anderson, My Jo ("John Anderson, my jo, John/ I wonder what ye mean"). *At. to* Robert Burns. CoMu
John Anderson my jo, John. Recipe for a Marriage. Phyllis McGinley. TIHL
John B. Sails, The, *with music.* *Unknown.* AS
John Ball shot them all. *Unknown.* PPL
John Barleycorn. Burns. BOHV; EiCL; FaBoCh; HBV; LoGBV; PAn; PIA; SeCeV; ShBV-1
John Baynham's Epitaph. Thomas Dermody. OnYI
John Bird, a laborer, lies here. Epitaph. Sylvia Townsend Warner. MoBrPo; NeMA
John Bright. Francis Barton Gummere. AA
John Brown. Stephen Vincent Benét. *Fr.* John Brown's Body. WoL
John Brown. Harry Lyman Koopman. AA
John Brown. Vachel Lindsay. Booker Washington Trilogy, II. AnAmPo; MAP; MoAmPo; NP
John Brown. Edna Dean Proctor. OTD; PAH
John Brown; a Paradox. Louise Imogen Guiney. DD
John Brown and Jeanne at Fontainebleau. Students. Florence Wilkinson Evans. HBV
John Brown died on the scaffold for the slave. John Brown. Edna Dean Proctor. OTD; PAH
John Brown in Kansas settled, like a steadfast Yankee farmer. How Old Brown Took Harper's Ferry. Edmund Clarence Stedman. OnMSP
John Brown of Osawatomie. Edmund Clarence Stedman. *See* How Old Brown Took Harper's Ferry.
John Brown of Osswatomie [*or* Osawatomie] spake on his dying day. Brown of Ossawatomie [*or* Osawatomie). Whittier. AmePo; DD; HBV; MC; OTPC; PAH; ThLM
John Brown's Body, *sels.* Stephen Vincent Benét.
Battle of Gettysburg, The. BeLS
Enlistments, The. ATP
"Gaunt man, Abraham Lincoln, woke one morning, The." LiPo
Invocation: "American muse, whose strong and diverse heart." AmFN; CrMA; MPB; NP, *shorter sel.*; PaA
"It was noon when the company marched to the railroad-station." ThLM
Jack Ellyat Heard the Guns. PoLF
John Brown. WoL
John Brown's Prayer. AtBAP; NP; PoNe
Lincoln Calls for Volunteers. ATP
Love Came By from the Riversmoke. MAP; MoAmPo
Out of John Brown's Strong Sinews. WHA
Robert E. Lee. AmFN
Significance of John Brown, The. PaA
Slaver, The, Prelude. AmPP
Soliloquy of Lincoln before Manassas. PaA
Song of Breath, A. MoVE
(Song of the Breath, The.) AmP
Song of the Riders. MAP; MoAmPo
There Was a Girl I Used to Go With. LOW
Thirteen Sisters, The. TreF
"This is the hidden place that hiders know." ViBoPo
Three Elements. EaLo
John Brown's Body (*diff. versions*). *Unknown, at. to* Charles Sprague Hall *and to* Thomas Brigham Bishop. ABF, *with music*; FaFP; InP; MC; PoFr; ShS, *with music*; SiTL; TrAS, *with music*
(Glory Hallelujah! or, John Brown's Body.) PaA; PAH; ThLM
John Brown's Prayer. Stephen Vincent Benét. *Fr.* John Brown's Body. AtBAP; NP; PoNe
John Bull, Esquire, my jo John. A New Song to an Old Tune. *Unknown.* PAH
John Bull for pastime took a prance. Nongtongpaw. Charles Dibdin. BOHV; HBV
John Bun. *Unknown.* *See* On John Bun.
John Burns of Gettysburg. Bret Harte. HBV; LHV, *abr.*; MC; OHIP; PaA; PAH; PAL; PAP
John Butler Yeats. Jeanne Robert Foster. GoYe
John Cabot—out of Wilma, once a Wycliffe. Riot. Gwendolyn Brooks. BP
John Calvin whose peculiar fad. Ballade of the Heresiarchs. Hilaire Belloc. MoVE
John Charles Frémont. Charles F. Lummis. PAH
John Cherokee, *with music.* *Unknown.* SoAmSa
John Chinaman. *Unknown.* SGR
John Chinaman, My Jo, *with music.* J. W. Conner. SGR
John Chinaman's Appeal. Mart Taylor. SGR
John Coil. *Unknown.* ShM
John Coltrane—an Impartial Review. Alfred B. Spellman. NNP
John Coltrane can do this for us. John Sinclair. *Fr.* Homage to John Coltrane. WOW
John Cook had a little grey mare. *Unknown.* OxNR
John courts Perrette, but all in vain. To Promise Is One Thing, to Perform Is Another. La Fontaine. UnTE
John Dameray, *with music.* *Unknown.* ShS
John Darrow. Donald Davidson. HBMV
John Day, Frontiersman. Yvor Winters. PoSa
John Deth, *sel.* Conrad Aiken.
With Myriad Voices Grass Was Filled. OA
John Done Saw That Number, *with music.* *Unknown.* OuSiCo
John Donne's Defiance. J. R. Hervey. AnNZ
John Dory. *Unknown.* BuBa; ESPB
John Endicott, *sels.* Longfellow. PAH
Proclamation, The.
Prologue, The: "Tonight we strive to read."
John Evereldown. E. A. Robinson. AmPP (4th ed.); NePA; OxBA
John Fane Dingle by Rumney Brook. Glaucopis. Richard Hughes. OBMV
John Filson. William Henry Venable. PAH
John Fitzgerald Kennedy. John Masefield. PAL
John Frost. William Miller. PCH
John Garner's Trail Herd. *Unknown.* CoSo
John Gilpin. William Cowper. *See* Diverting History of John Gilpin, The.
John Gorham. E. A. Robinson. MAP; MAPA; MoAB; MoAmPo; NP
John Graydon. Wilson MacDonald. ACV; CaP
John Greenleaf Whittier. Phoebe Cary. DD
John Greenleaf Whittier. John Cameron Grant. DD
John Grumlie. Allan Cunningham. BoHV; HBV; PoLF
John had. Happiness. A. A. Milne. BoC; TiPo
John Hancock Otis. Edgar Lee Masters. *Fr.* Spoon River Anthology. PoFr; TOP
John Hardy. *Unknown.* BaBo (A *and* B *vers.*); TrAS, *with music*; ViBoFo (A *and* B *vers.*)
(John Harty, *diff. vers., with music.*) ABF
John Henry. *Unknown, ad. by* John Jacob Niles. AmFN
John Henry (*diff. versions*). *Unknown.* ABF, 2 *vers., with music*; AmPP (3d ed.); AS, *with music*; BaBo (A *and* B *vers.*); BeLS; FaBoBe; FaFP; GoSl; MaC; OuSiCo, *with music*; OxBoLi; PoPo; SiTL; ThLM; TiPo (1959 ed.); TrAS, *with music*; TreFT; TrGrPo; ViBoFo (A, B, C, D, E, *and* F *vers.*); WOW
("John Henry tol' his cap'n," *much abr.*) NAMP
John Henry in Harlem. M. B. Toleson. GoSl
John Henry said to his captain. John Henry. *Unknown.* TreFT
John Henry told his old captain. John Henry. *Unknown.* WOW
John Henry tol' his cap'n. John Henry. *Unknown.* AmPP (3d ed.); AS; BeLS; NAMP
John Henry was a lil [*or* little] baby. John Henry. *Unknown.* ABF; FaFP; MaC; OxBoLi; SiTL; TrGrPo
John Henry was a railroad man. John Henry (B *vers.*). *Unknown.* BaBo

John Henry was a steel drivin' man. John Henry. *Unknown.* ABF
John Henry was a very small boy. John Henry (A *vers.*). *Unknown.* ViBoFo
John Henry, who was a baby. John Henry (C *vers.*). *Unknown.* ViBoFo
John Henry's mother had a little baby. John Henry. *Unknown.* OuSiCo
John Horace Burleson. Edgar Lee Masters. *Fr.* Spoon River Anthology. CrMA
John Hoskins to His Little Child Benjamin, from the Tower. John Hoskins. TuPP
John. In the sound of that rebellious word. Ebenezer Elliott. Sonn
John is the tallest—he's ever so high. Comparison. Mary Ann Hoberman. BiCB
John James Audubon. Stephen Vincent Benét. ThLM
John-John. Thomas MacDonagh. AnIV; AWP; HBMV; JAWP; OnYI; OxBI; WBP
John Jones. Swinburne. *Fr.* The Heptalogia. NA; OAEP
John Keats. Dante Gabriel Rossetti. Five English Poets, 4. EPN
John Kinsella's Lament for Mrs. Mary Moore. W. B. Yeats. AtBAP; CMoP; DTC; LiTM; MoAB; OAEP (2d ed.); SiTL
John Knox. Iain Crichton Smith. OxBS
John Knox's Indictment of the Queen. Swinburne. *Fr.* Bothwell. VA
John Landless beside the Road. Iwan Goll, *tr. fr. French by* Claire Goll. OnPM
John Landless Leads the Caravan. Iwan Goll, *tr. fr. French by* William Carlos Williams. TrJP
John Littlehouse the redhead was a large ruddy man. The Blacksmith's Serenade. Vachel Lindsay. StPo
John Marr, *sel.* Herman Melville.
"Since as in night's deck-watch ye show." ViBoPo
John Marston. Swinburne. Sonnets on English Dramatic Poets (1590-1650), XII. Sonn
John Masefield Relates the Story of Tom, Tom, the Piper's Son, *parody.* Louis Untermeyer. MoAmPo
John Maynard. Horatio Alger, Jr. BeLS; BLPA; FaBoBe
John Milton said the world in a starry rain. A Willing Suspension. John Holmes. PoCh
John Muir on Mt. Ritter. Gary Snyder. *Fr.* Myths & Texts: Burning. FIW
John o' Dreams. Theodosia Garrison. HBMV
John O'Dwyer of the Glen. *Tr. fr. Irish by* Thomas Furlong. AnIV
John of Gaunt's Dying Speech. Shakespeare. *See* This England ("This royal throne of kings.")
John of Hazelgreen. *Unknown.* BaBo (A, B, *and* C *vers.*); BFSS (B *vers., with music*); ESPB (A *and* E *vers.*); ViBoFo
(Jock o' Hazeldean, A *vers., with music.*); BFSS
John of Launoy. Sir Henry Taylor. *Fr.* Philip van Artevelde. VA
John of Tours. *Unknown, tr. fr. French by* Dante Gabriel Rossetti. AWP; JAWP; PoVP; WBP
John Otto. W. S. Merwin. AP
John Paul Jones. Richard Watson Gilder. PoRL
John Paul Jones. Walt Whitman. *See* Old-Time Sea-Fight.
John Peel. John Woodcock Graves. CH; OxBoLi; PoG; SD
(Song: "D'ye ken John Peel with his coat so gay?") NBM
John Pelham. James Ryder Randall. AA; PAH
John Plans. Dorothy Mason Pierce. BiCB
John Popham. Robert P. Tristram Coffin. OnPP
John Quincy Adams. Stephen Vincent Benét. NAMP; PoPl
John Richard William Alexander Dwyer. Horace Smith *and* James Smith. *Fr.* The Theatre. OBRV
John Riley, *with music.* *Unknown.* OuSiCo
John Saw the Holy Number, *with music.* *Unknown.* BoAN-1
John Skelton. Robert Graves. BrPo
John Smith, fellow fine. *Unknown.* OxNR
John Smith of His Friend Master John Taylor. John Smith. SCAP
John Smith's Approach to Jamestown. James Barron Hope. MC; PAH
John Standish, Artist. Kenneth Fearing. AnAmPo
John Stuart Mill. J. S. Mill. E. C. Bentley. *Fr.* Clerihews. BOHV; FiBHP; OxBoLi; WhC
John Sutter. Yvor Winters. MoAmPo (1962 ed.); MoVE; PoPl; PoSa; QFR
John the Baptist. Louis Simpson. NePoEA
John the Pilgrim. Theodore Watts-Dunton. MaRV
John Thompson's Daughter. Phoebe Cary. BOHV
John Thomson and the Turk (A *and* B *vers.*). *Unknown.* ESPB
John Underhill. Whittier. PAH
John warns me of nostalgia. Not Wholly Lost. Raymond Souster. OBCV
John was a sort of rounder, not always true to his wife. Anecdote in Verse. Rolfe Humphries. CBV
John Was a-Writin', *with music.* *Unknown.* OuSiCo
John Wasson. Edgar Lee Masters. *Fr.* Spoon River Anthology. LaNeLa
John Webster. Swinburne. Sonnets on English Dramatic Poets (1590-1650), VII. InvP; Sonn
John Wesley Gaines. *Unknown.* ELU; FiBHP
John Wesley's Grace before Meals. John Wesley. *See* Be Present at Our Table, Lord.
John Wesley's Rule. John Wesley. HBVY; PCH; TreFT (Rule, A.) FaFP; OTD
John woke on Jan. first and felt queer. Limerick. *Unknown.* BOHV
John Woodvil; a Tragedy, *sel.* Charles Lamb.
Helen, *by* Mary Lamb. OBRV
John you are my husbandes'man you knowe. *Unknown.* SeCSL
John, you were figuring in the gay career. To John Lamb, Esq. of the South-Sea House. Charles Lamb. Sonn
John-a-Dreams and Harum-Scarum. Ballad of Low-lie-down. Madison Cawein. HBV
Johneen. Patrick J. Carroll. WHL
Johnie Armstrong. *Unknown.* BaBo; BoLiVe; EnLi-1 (1949 ed.); ESPB (A, B, *and* C *vers.*); HoPM; NoP; OBB; OxBB; PoPo; TOP; TrGrPo; UnPo; VaPo; ViBoFo (A *and* B *vers.*)
(Johnny Armstrong.) MaC; StaSt, *abr.*
"King he wrytes a luving letter, The," *sel.* PoFr
Johnie Blunt. *Unknown.* OxBB
Johnie Cock. *Unknown.* BaBo (A, B, C, *and* D *vers.*); ESPB (A, B, C, D, *and* K *vers.*); ViBoFo (A *and* B *vers.*)
(Johnie o' Cocklesmuir.) OxBB
(Johnnie of Cockerslee.) OBB
Johnie Faa. *Unknown.* *See* Wraggle Taggle Gipsies, The.
Johnie rose up in a May morning. Johnie Cock [*or* o' Cocklesmuir]. *Unknown.* BaBo (C *vers.*) OBB; OxBB; ViBoFo (B *vers.*)
Johnie Scot. *Unknown.* BaBo (A *and* B *vers.*); ESPB
Johnnie Bought a Ham, *with music.* *Unknown.* OuSiCo
Johnnie, Cock Up Your Beaver. Burns. AtBAP
Johnnie Cope. Adam Skirving. OxBS
Johnnie Courteau. William Henry Drummond. CaP; PeCV
Johnnie Crack and Flossie Snail. Dylan Thomas. *Fr.* Under Milk Wood. FaPON; GoJo; LOW; PDV
(Song: "Johnnie Crack and Flossie Snail.") FiBHP
Johnnie of Cockerslee. *Unknown.* *See* Johnie Cock.
Johnnie Norrie. *Unknown.* OxNR
Johnny. Emma Rounds. ShM
Johnny and the Highwayman, *with music.* *Unknown.* BFSS
Johnny Appleseed. Rosemary Benét *and* Stephen Vincent Benét. BoChLi (1950 ed.); MPB; OTD; OTPC (1946 ed.); TrAS, *with music*
Johnny Appleseed. Arthur S. Bourinot. CaP
Johnny Appleseed, *sel.* Vachel Lindsay.
"Johnny Appleseed, Johnny Appleseed." FaPON
Johnny Appleseed. William Henry Venable. PaA; PAH
Johnny Appleseed's Hymn to the Sun. Vachel Lindsay. MoRP
Johnny Armstrong. *Unknown.* *See* Johnie Armstrong.
Johnny Armstrong killed a calf. *Unknown.* OxNR
Johnny Boker, *with music.* *Unknown.* AmSS; ShS; SoAmSa
Johnny Cock, in a May morning. Johnie Cock. *Unknown.* BaBo (B *vers.*); ESPB (C *vers.*)
Johnny Come Down to Hilo, *with music.* *Unknown.* ABF; SoAmSa, *st.* 1
(Johnny Walk Along to Hilo, *with music.*) ShS
Johnny Dow. *Unknown.* WhC
("Wha lies here?") FiBHP; SiTL
Johnny Faa, the Gypsy Laddie. *Unknown.* *See* Wraggle Taggle Gipsies, The.
Johnny Faa, the Lord of Little Egypt. *Unknown.* *See* Wraggle Taggle Gipsies, The.
Johnny Fife and Johnny's Wife. Mildrew Plew Meigs. GaP; SoPo; TiPo
Johnny German, *with music.* *Unknown.* BFSS

Johnny had a little dove. Johnny's Farm. H. M. Adams. BoTP
Johnny he's risen up in the morn. Johnny of Cockley's Well. *Unknown.* EnSB
Johnny, I Hardly Knew Ye. *Unknown.* AnIV; EiCL; ELP; OnYI; OxBoLi; WaaP
Johnny, I Hardly Knew Ye: In Dublinese, *parody.* *Unknown.* OnYI
Johnny, I Hardly Knew Ye: In Miltonese, *parody.* Oliver St. John Gogarty. OnYI
Johnny, I Hardly Knew Ye: In Swinburnese, *parody.* Robert Yelverton Tyrrell. OnYI
Johnny McCardner, *with music.* *Unknown.* OuSiCo
Johnny made a custard. Some Cook! John Ciardi. PDV
Johnny O Dutchman, *with music.* *Unknown.* BFSS
Johnny of Cockley's Well. *Unknown.* EnSB
Johnny Raw and Polly Clark. *Unknown.* CoMu
Johnny reading in his comic. Any Day Now. David McCord. ShM
Johnny Sands. *Unknown, at to* John Sinclair. CoMu; ViBoFo
Johnny shall have a new bonnet. Mother Goose. HBV; HBVY; OTPC; OxNR
Johnny Stiles, or the Wild Mustard River, *with music.* *Unknown.* OuSiCo
Johnny, though clear mine eyes, to speculate. Johnny, I Hardly Knew Ye: In Miltonese, *parody.* Oliver St. John Gogarty. OnYI
Johnny used to find content. Johnny. Emma Rounds. ShM
Johnny Walk Along to Hilo. *Unknown.* *See* Johnny Come Down to Hilo.
Johnny Went to Church One Day. *Unknown.* BBGG
Johnny, Won't You Ramble? *with music.* *Unknown.* OuSiCo
Johnnycake, The. *Unknown.* MPB
Johnny's been on sea, Johnny's been on shore. Young Johnny. *Unknown.* BFSS
Johnny's By-low Song. Laura E. Richards. BoChLi
Johnny's Farm. H. M. Adams. BoTP
Johnny's History Lesson. Nixon Waterman. PoLF
Johnny's into England gane. McNaughtan. *Unknown.* OxBB
Johnny's the Lad I Love. *Unknown.* AnIV; OxBoLi
(As I Roved Out.) DTC
John's manners at the table. The Visitor. Katharine Pyle. BBGG
John's words were the words. After the Rain. Stanley Crouch. WSL
Johnson on Pope. David Ferry. PP
Johny Faa. *Unknown.* *See* Wraggle Taggle Gipsies, The.
Johny he has risen up i' the morn. Johnie Cock. *Unknown.* BaBo (A *vers.*); ESPB; ViBoFo (A *vers.*)
Joi, the Glug. C. J. Dennis. NeLNL
Join hands and circle to the left. Rhymed Dance Calls. *Unknown.* CoSo
Join mates in mirth to me. Two Pastorals [*or* Upon His Meeting with His Two Worthy Friends]. Sir Philip Sidney. FCP; SiCE; TuPP
Join once again, my Celia, join. Song. Charles Cotton. ViBoPo
Join with the noble-hearted. Distich. Shuraikh. TrJP
Joined the Blues. John Jerome Rooney. AA
Joke Versified, A. Thomas Moore. *See* On Taking a Wife.
Jokesmith's Vacation, The. Don Marquis. ALV; FiBHP
Jolly Batchelor Kindly Entertained, The. *Unknown.* *See* Thankful Country Lass, The.
Jolly Beggar, The (A beggar man came over the lea"), *with music.* *Unknown.* BFSS
Jolly Beggar, The ("There was a jolly beggar"), *diff. versions.* *Unknown, at. to* James, V, King of Scotland. CoMu; OxBB
Jolly Beggars, The. Burns. BEL; CEP; EiCL; EiCP; EiPP; EnRP; NoP; OAEP; PoEL-4
Sels.
I Once Was a Maid. UnTE
See the Smoking Bowl before Us. ALV, *abr.*; ATP (1935 ed.); GoTS
(Drinking Song: "Fig for those by law protected, A.") PoFr; TrGrPo
(Jolly Mortals, Fill Your Glasses.) EnLi-2 (1949 ed.)
Jolly boating weather. Eton Boating Song. William Johnson Cory. ELP
Jolly Cowboy, The, *with music.* *Unknown.* CoSo
Jolly Days. Ivy O. Eastwick. GoTL; MPB (1956 ed.)
Jolly Driver, The. *Unknown.* CoMu; UnTE
Jolly Farmer, The, *with music.* *Unknown.* BFSS
Jolly fat friar loved liquor good store, A. Gluggity Glug. George Colman. *Fr.* The Myrtle and the Vine. HBV
Jolly Good Ale and Old. *At. to* William Stevenson. *See* Back and Side Go Bare, Go Bare.
Jolly Jack. Thackeray. HBV
Jolly Jankin [*or* Jankyn]. *Unknown.* NoP; OxBoLi
(Jankin, the Clerical Seducer.) MeEL
("Kyrie, so kyrie.") EnPo
Jolly Juggler, The. *Unknown.* NoP
("Drawe me nere, draw me nere.") EnPo
(Magician and the Baron's Daughter, The.) MeEL
Jolly Lumbermen, The. *Unknown.* *See* Buffalo Skinners, The.
Jolly men at Feckenham, The. The Feckenham Men. John Drinkwater. GBV; GTSL
Jolly Miller, The. Isaac Bickerstaffe. *See* There Was a Jolly Miller.
Jolly Mortals, Fill Your Glasses. Burns. *See* See the Smoking Bowl before Us.
Jolly old clown, The. The Clown. Mary Catherine Rose. SoPo
Jolly Old Pedagogue, The. George Arnold. HBV; OnPP; TreFS
Jolly old sow once lived in a sty, A. The Three Little Pigs. Sir Alfred Scott-Gatty. BoTP
Jolly Phoebus his car to the coach-house had driven. Homecoming. *Unknown.* AnIV
Jolly Pinder of Wakefield, The. *Unknown.* BaBo; ESPB
Jolly Shepherd, The. Shakespeare. *Fr.* King Lear, III, vi. PCH
Jolly shepherd, shepherd on a hill. In Praise of His Love. Sir John Wotton. ElL
Jolly Trades-Men, The. *Unknown.* CoMu
Jolly Wagoner, The, *with music.* *Unknown.* TrAS
Jolly Wat. *Unknown.* *See* Can I Not Sing.
Jolly Woodchuck, The. Marion Edey. FaPON; PDV; TiPo
Jolly Young Sailor and the Beautiful Queen, The, *with music.* *Unknown.* ShS
Joly [Joly] Wat. *Unknown.* *See* Can I Not Sing.
Jonah, *sels.* Bible, *O.T.*
Jonah's Prayer, II: 3-11. TrJP
Jonah. Aldous Huxley. ChTr
Jonah. Randall Jarrell. MoRP
Jonah. *Unknown.* *Fr.* Patience. ACP
Jonah and the Whale. Viola Meynell. EtS; MoBrPo (1942 ed.)
Jonah and the Whale. *Unknown.* BLPA
Jonah was an immigrant, so runs the Bible tale. Darky Sunday School. *Unknown.* ABF; OxBoLi; SiTL
Jonah's Prayer. Jonah, II: 3-11, Bible, *O.T.* TrJP
Jonas Kindred's Household. George Crabbe. *Fr.* The Frank Courtship. FaBoEn; OBNC
Jonathan. Rose Fyleman. TiPo
Jonathan. "Rachel," *tr. fr. Hebrew by* L. V. Snowman. TrJP
Jonathan,/ Winesap,/ Sheep-nose. Cider Song. Mildred Weston. BoNaP
Jonathan Bing. Beatrice Curtis Brown. FaPON; GaP; OnMSP; PCD; PDV; RIS; SoPo; TiPo
Jonathan Bing Dances for Spring. Beatrice Curtis Brown. SiSoSe
Jonathan Bing Does Arithmetic. Beatrice Curtis Brown. GaP; RIS
Jonathan Bing's Tea. Beatrice Curtis Brown. WaKn
Jonathan Blake. After the Party. William Wise. FaPON
Jonathan Edwards in Western Massachusetts. Robert Lowell. MaPo (1969 ed.)
Jonathan Gee. Jonathan. Rose Fyleman. TiPo
Jonathan Gentry, *sel.* Mark Van Doren.
Tom's Sleeping Song, *fr.* III. LOW
Jonathan Houghton. Edgar Lee Masters. *Fr.* Spoon River Anthology. OxBA; TDP
Jonathan Moulton lost his wife. The Two Wives. Daniel Henderson. ShM
Jonathan to John. James Russell Lowell. *Fr.* The Bigelow Papers, 2d Series, No. II. CoBA; PaA; PAH; PAP
Jone is a wench that's painted. Upon Jone and Jane. Robert Herrick. AnAnS-2
Jones! as from Calais southward you and I. Composed near

Calais, on the Road Leading to Andres. Wordsworth. MERP
Jones's Pasture. Abbie Huston Evans. NP
Jonquils, The. Allen Upward. *Fr.* Scented Leaves from a Chinese Jar. NP
Jonquils and violets smelling sweet. Before Spring. P. A. Ropes. BoTP
Joralemon Street. Patricia Hubbell. OCS
Jordan ("When first my lines *or* verse"). George Herbert. AnAnS-1; ATP; MaMe; MeP; MePo; OBS; PoFS; PP; SCEP-1; SeCP; SeEP; VaPo
Jordan ("Who sayes [*or* says] that fictions"). George Herbert. CABA; EP; FaBoEn; LiTB; MaMe; MeLP; MePo; NoP; OBS; PAn; PIA; Po; PoAn; PoEL-2; PoFS; PP; PrWP; ReEn; SCEP-1; SeCP; SeEP; VaPo
Jorkyns was great; he labored in the City. The Tale of Jorkyns and Gertie; or, Vice Rewarded. R. P. Lister. NYBP
Jorridge and Porridge. Louise Ayres Garnett. GaP; OTPC (1946 ed.)
Joseph and His Brethen. Genesis, XXXVII: 3-36, XXXIX: 1-XLVI: 30, Bible, *O.T.* OuHeWo
Joseph and His Brethren, *sels.* Charles Jeremiah Wells. VA
Patriarchal Home, The.
Phraxanor to Joseph.
Rachel.
Triumph of Joseph, The.
Joseph and Mary. *Unknown.* *See* Cherry-Tree Carol, The.
Joseph and the Shopkeeper. *Unknown,* *tr. fr. French by* Alfred R. Bellinger. ChrBoLe
Joseph Ben Tachfin came from the Sahara. Marrakech. R. N. Currey. PeSA
Joseph, honoured from sea to sea. The Man of the House. Katherine Tynan. CAW; ChrBoLe; JKCP; WHL
Joseph Mary Plunkett. Wilfrid Meynell. ISi
Joseph Mica. *Unknown.* *See Wreck of the Six-Wheel Driver, The.*
Joseph Mickel was a good engineer. The Wreck of the Six-Wheel Driver. *Unknown.* ABF
Joseph, mild and noble, bent above the straw. Mary's Baby. Shaemas O'Sheel. CAW; HBV; HBVY; JKCP
Joseph Rodman Drake. Fitz-Greene Halleck. *See* On the Death of Joseph Rodman Drake.
Joseph Was an Old Man. *Unknown.* *See* Cherry-Tree Carol, The.
Joseph was an old man. A Carol. Lizette Woodworth Reese. StJW
Josephs Coat. George Herbert. MaMe; SCEP-1
Joseph's Suspicion. Rainer Maria Rilke, *tr. fr. German.* MoRP, *tr. by* M. D. Herter Norton; ReMP, *tr. by* Paul Engle
Joses, the Brother of Jesus. Harry Kemp. HBMV; MaRV; OQP
Joshua Fit de Battle ob Jerico [*or* of Jericho]. *Unknown.* ATP; BoAN-1; MaC; TrAS, *with music*; TrGrPo
(Group of Negro Songs, A.) NAMP
Joshua Hight. *Unknown.* ShM
Josie. *Unknown.* *See* Frankie and Johnny.
Journal, *sel.* Edna St. Vincent Millay.
"I read with varying degrees." ImOP
Journal of Albion Moonlight, The, *sels.* Kenneth Patchen. NaP
"But there is no black jaw which cannot be broken by our word."
"I/ want you/ to listen."
Journals, *sel.* Emerson.
"America, my country, can the mind." AmPP
Journey, The. Thomas Curtis Clark. MaRV
Journey, The. Aidan Clarke. BoTP
Journey. Roy Daniells. MoCV
Journey, The. Walter de la Mare. InP
Journey, The. Mary Berri Hansbrough. AA
Journey. Sam Harrison. NeIP
Journey, IV. Erik Lindegren, *tr. fr. Swedish by* Martin S. Allwood. LiTW
Journey, The. John T. McFarland. OQP
Journey, The. Scudder Middleton. HBMV
Journey, The. Edwin Muir. *See* Mythical Journey, The
Journey, The. Yvor Winters. MoVE
Journey Ends, A. Don Blanding. MaRV
Journey from New Zealand. "Robin Hyde." AnNZ
Journey into France, The. *Unknown.* CoMu
Journey of the Magi. T. S. Eliot. AmP; BoC; BWP; CABA; CaFP; CoBA; DiPo; DTC; EaLo; FaBoCh; FaBoMo; FaFP; GTBS-D; GTBS-W; ILP; InPo; LiTA; LiTM; LoGBV; MAP; MaPo; MoAB; MoAmPo; MoRP; MWA-2; NePA; NoP; OAEP (2d ed.); OBMV; PAn; PIA; PoAn; PoE; PoIE; PoPo; PoSa; ShBV-3; StJW; TIHL; TrGrPo; TwCP; UnPo (3d ed.); WePo
Journey Onwards, The. Thomas Moore. GTBS; GTBS-D; GTBS-P; GTBS-W; GTSE; GTSL; HBV; SeCePo
Journey through the Night. John Holloway. NePoEA
Journey to a Parallel. Bruce McM. Wright. PoNe
Journey to Brundusium, *abr.* Horace, *tr. fr. Latin by* William Cowper. WoL
Journey to Exeter, A, *abr.* John Gay. WoL
Journey to Golotha, The. K. Raghavendra Rao. ACV
Journey to the Interior. Theodore Roethke. NaP; NYBP
Journey toward Evening. Phyllis McGinley. GoYe; NYBP
Journeying Alone. Princess Oku, *tr. fr. Japanese by* Ishii *and* Obata. OnPM
Journeyman, The. Ralph Hodgson. AtBAP
Journeyman, The. *Unknown,* *tr. fr. Irish by* Frank O'Connor. KiLC
Journeyman Tailor, The, *with music.* *Unknown.* BFSS
Journey's End. Evelyn H. Healey. MaRV
Journey's End. Humbert Wolfe. TrJP; YT
Jove descends in sleet and snow. The Storm. Alcaeus. AWP; JAWP; OnPM; WBP
Jove for Europa's love took shape of bull. Parthenophil and Parthenophe, LXIII. Barnabe Barnes. ReEn
Jovial Beggar, The. *Unknown.* BoTP
Jovial Crew, A; or, The Merry Beggars, *sels.* Richard Brome.
"Round, a round, a round, boys, a round, A," *fr.* IV, i. TuPP
Song of the Beggars, *fr.* I, i. SeCL
Jovial Marriner, The; or, The Sea-Man's Renown. John Playford. CoMu
Jovial Priest's Confession, The. Leigh Hunt. BOHV
Jovial Shepheard's Song, The. Michael Drayton. *See* Sirena.
Jovial Tinker, The ("It was a lady of the North"). *Unknown.* *See* Room for a Jovial Tinker: Old Brass to Mend.
Jovial Tinker, The; or, The Willing Couple ("There was a Tinker liv'd of late"). *Unknown.* CoMu
Jovial Welshmen, The. *Unknown.* *See* Three Jovial Welshmen, The.
Jowls of his belly crawl and swell like the sea, The. The Glutton. Karl Shapiro. CBV
Joy. Michael Benedikt. YAP
Joy. Clarissa Scott Delany. CDC; PoNe
Joy. Sister Mary Irma. JKCP (1955 ed.)
Joy. Robinson Jeffers. CMoP; NeMA; NP
Joy. John Newton. SoP
Joy. Carl Sandburg. NP
Joy. Oscar Wilde. *Fr.* Humanitad. PCH
Joy and Dream. Goethe, *tr. fr. German by* L. R. Lind. LiTW
Joy and Peace in Believing. William Cowper. SoP; TRV
(In Him Confiding.) MaRV
Joy and Pleasure. W. H. Davies. OBMV
Joy and Sorrow. Aubrey Thomas De Vere. OQP
Joy and the soul are mates, as heart and sorrow. The Cruse. Louise Townsend Nicholl. NYBP
Joy as Old as Breathing, A. Etta May Van Tassel. JKCP (1955 ed.)
Joy, beauty, awe, supremest worship blending. At Benediction. Eleanor Rogers Cox. JKCP
Joy comes and goes; hope ebbs and flows. To Fausta. Matthew Arnold. PoVP
Joy Enough. Barrett Eastman. AA
"Joy for ever" of a beauteous thing, The. The Face. Thomas Wade. ERoP-2
Joy for the sturdy trees. Tree-planting. Samuel Francis Smith. OHIP
Joy, great joy, was the message. Joy to the World. *Unknown.* STF
Joy, I did lock thee up: but some bad man. The Bunch of Grapes. George Herbert. AnAnS-1; MaMe; MeP; SCEP-1
Joy in Insecurity. Emily Dickinson. *See* Go not too near a house of rose.
Joy in rebel Plymouth town, in the spring of sixty-four. "Albemarle" Cushing. James Jeffrey Roche. PAH
Joy in the rising of our Orient starre. Her Nativity. Robert Southwell. MeP

Joy is a fruit that will not grow. Joy. John Newton. SoP
Joy is a trick in the air. Birth-Dues. Robinson Jeffers. MAP; MoAB; MoAmPo
Joy Is Built of Little Things. Alice Hansche Mortenson. SoP
Joy is everywhere on earth. Chant of the Ninth Order of Seraphim. Inigo de Mendoza. CAW
Joy is the blossom, sorrow is the fruit. Epigram. Walter Savage Landor. HBV
Joy, joy to mortals! The rejoicing fires. Love's Triumph. Ben Jonson. EnRePo
Joy May Kill. Michelangelo, *tr. fr. Italian by* John Addington Symonds. AWP; JAWP; WBP
(Fearful Joy.) OnPM
Joy Meets Boy. Robert P. Tristram Coffin. OTPC (1946 ed.)
Joy-Month. David Atwood Wasson. HBV
Joy o' Living. Amanda Benjamin Hall. HBMV
Joy of Church Fellowship [Rightly Attended], The. Edward Taylor. *Fr.* God's Determinations. AmP; AmPP; AP; CBEP; MAmP; MWA-1; OxBA; SCAP
Joy, of flame celestial fashioned. Ode to Joy. Schiller. LiTW
Joy of Giving, The. Whittier. ChBR; OTD
Joy of Incompleteness, The. Albert Crowell. PoToHe (new ed.)
Joy of Knowledge. Isidor Schneider. TrJP
Joy of Life. Moses ibn Ezra, *tr. fr. Hebrew by* Solomon Solis-Cohen. *Fr.* The Book of Tarshish. TrJP
Joy of Life. Mary Russell Mitford. OTPC
Joy of Living, The. Robert Browning. *See* David's Song.
Joy of Love, The. Allan Dowling. ErPo
Joy of My Life! Henry Vaughan. *See* Joy of My Life! While Left Me Here.
Joy of my life! full oft for loving you. Amoretti, LXXXII. Spenser. BEL; ReIE
Joy of My Life! While Left Me Here. Henry Vaughan. SCEP-1; SeCV-1
(Joy of My Life!) BoC; OBS
Joy of the Hills, The. Edwin Markham. PoMa
Joy of the Morning. Edwin Markham. AA; FaPON; HBV; MPB; PoRL
Joy, rose-lipped dryad, loves to dwell. Thomas Warton, the Elder. *Fr.* Retirement, an Ode. ViBoPo
Joy shakes me like the wind that lifts a sail. Joy. Clarissa Scott Delany. CDC; PoNe
Joy, Shipmate, Joy! Walt Whitman. AmP; BBV (1923 ed.); DD; HBVY; MCCG; MoAmPo (1950 ed.); OHIP; PCH; TOP; TreFT
Joy so short, alas, the pain so near, The. Sir Thomas Wyatt. FCP; SiPS
Joy, the triumph, the delight, the madness, The! Shelley. *Fr.* Prometheus Unbound. AtBAP
Joy to Philip, he this day. Going into Breeches. Charles *and* Mary Lamb. OTPC (1923 ed.); PRWS
Joy to the present, hope of future ages. To James VI, King of Scotland. Sir John Harington. SiCE
Joy to the World. *Unknown.* STF
Joy to the World! The Lord Is Come, *with music.* Isaac Watts. YaCaBo
Joy to You. Francis Carlin. PFY
Joyce Kilmer. Amelia Josephine Burr. DD; HBMV
Joyful, joyful, we adore Thee. Hymn of Joy [*or* Adoration]. Henry van Dyke. MaRV; SoP; TRV
Joyful, lady, sing! To a Lady Playing and Singing in the Morning. Thomas Hardy. TOP
Joyful [*or* Joyfull] New Ballad, A. Thomas Deloney. CoMu
"O noble England," *sel.* ViBoPo
Joyful Noise, A. Donald Finkel. CoAP
Joyful Prophecy. Vassar Miller. CoPo
Joyful Wisdom, The. Coventry Patmore. The Angel in the House, I, x, 1. HBV
Joyous birds shrouded in cheerful shade, The. The Music at the Bower of Bliss. Spenser. *Fr.* The Faerie Queene, II. MyFE
Joyous morning ran and kissed the grass, The. The Wakers. John Freeman. HBMV; TSW
Joys. James Russell Lowell. BoTP
Joys of Art, The. Rachel Annand Taylor. OBVV
Joys of Childhood, *sel.* John Clare.
"Joys of childhood are full thickly sown, The." ERoP-2
Joys of Heaven, The. Thomas à Kempis, *tr. fr. Latin by* Erastus C. Benedict. CAW
Joys of Marriage, The. Charles Cotton. BOHV; InMe
Joys of Paradise. St. Augustine, *tr. fr. Latin by* Prioress Augustine. CAW
Joys of the Road, The. Bliss Carman. HBV; HBVY, *sl. abr.*; OBVV; TSW
Joy's Peak. Robert Farren. ISi
J's the Jumping Jay-Walker. Phyllis McGinley. *Fr.* All Around the Town. FaPON; TiPo (1952 ed.)
Juan and Haidee. Byron. *Fr.* Don Juan, II. EPN; MaPo, *shorter sel.*
(Haidee [and Don Juan].) OBNC; OBRV
("It was the cooling hour," *shorter sel.*) ViBoPo
Juan Belmonte, Torero. Donald Finkel. NePoEA
Juan de Juni the priest said. Aodh Ruadh O'Domhnaill [*or* Red Hugh]. Thomas McGreevy. AnIV; OBMV; OnYI; OxBI
Juan in England. Byron. *Fr.* Don Juan, XI. FiP
Juan Quintana. Alice Corbin. HBMV; NP
Juan was taught from out the best edition. Byron. *Fr.* Don Juan, I. PIA
Juana. Alfred de Musset, *tr. fr. French by* Andrew Lang. AWP; JAWP; WBP
Juanita. Joaquin Miller. AA
Juan's Song. Louise Bogan. NYBP
Jubalee, *with music. Unknown.* BoAN-2
Jubilant the music through the fields a-ringing. World Music. Frances Louisa Bushnell. AA
Jubilate. George Arnold. EtS
Jubilate Agno, *sels.* Christopher Smart.
"For I am not without authority in my jeopardy." EiCP; EiPP; NCEP
"For the doubling of flowers is the improvement of the gard'ner's talent." EiCP
"For the feast of Trumpets should be kept up that being the most direct and acceptable of all instruments." UnS
"For the Greek & Latin are not dead languages." NCEP
For the Letter s Which Signifies God. AtBAP
"For thirdly he works it upon stretch with the fore paws extended." NCEP
Instrument Rhimes. MuSP
Let Elizur Rejoice with the Partridge. PoEL-3
Let Lotan Rejoice with Sauterelle. AtBAP
Let Peter Rejoice with the Moon Fish. AtBAP
"Let Tobias bless charity with his dog." NCEP
My Cat Jeoffry. ChTR; FaBoCh; GoTP; LiTB; PoSa; SeCePo; SiTL; WiR
(Cat, The.) BoW, *abr.*
(For I Will Consider My Cat Jeoffry.) AtBAP; CTC; EiCL; EiCP; EiPP; NoP; PeER; PIA; PoEL-3; SeCeV
Rejoice in God. AtBAP
("Rejoice in God, O ye tongues; give the glory to the Lord, and the Lamb.") EiCP; EiPP
Jubilo. Allen Tate. WaP
Judaeus Errans. Louis Golding. TrJP
Judaism. Cardinal Newman. ACP
Judas. Gamaliel Bradford. OQP
Judas. Howard McKinley Corning. ChIP
Judas. Vassar Miller. MoAmPo (1962 ed.)
Judas. *Unknown.* BaBo; ESPB; FlW; OBB, 5 *sts.*; ViBoFo
Judas Iscariot. Robert Buchanan. OBVV; OxBoCh
Judas Iscariot. Countee Cullen. PoLF
Judas Iscariot. Margaret Nickerson Martin. ChIP; PGD
Judas Iscariot. R. A. K. Mason. AnNZ
Judas Iscariot. Stephen Spender. MoAB; MoBrPo (1950 ed.)
Judas Iscariot dour and dark. Descent for the Lost. Philip Child. CaP
Judas Maccabeus. First Maccabees, Bible, Apocrypha. TrJP
Judas Sells His Lord. *Unknown.* MeEL
Judas was I! Ah, the mockery! Judas Iscariot. Margaret Nickerson Martin. ChIP; PGD
Judean Hills Are Holy. William L. Stidger. ChIP; MaRV; OQP
Judg'd [*or* Judged] by my goddess' doom to endless pain. Coelia, I. William Percy. ReIE; Sonn; TuPP
Judge enforcing the obsolete law, The. W. H. Auden. TRV
Judge, judge, tell the judge. Nursery Rhymes, II. *Unknown.* OxBoLi
Judge me, O God, and plead my cause against an ungodly nation. Psalm XLIII, Bible, *O.T.* OnPM
Judge Me, O Lord! Sarah N. Cleghorn. ChIP; MaRV; StJW
Judge mildly the tasked world; and disincline. The World's Advance. George Meredith. EPN

Judge Not According to the Appearance. Christina Rossetti. TrPWD
Judge of all, judge me. Psalm XLIII. *Paraphrased by* Sir Philip Sidney. EP; FCP
Judge of modes in silks and satins, A. Harriet Simper Has Her Day. John Trumbull. *Fr.* The Progress of Dulness. AmPP (4th ed.)
Judge Roy Bean of Vinegarroon. The Law West of the Pecos. S. Omar Barker. IHA
Judge, who lives impeccably upstairs, The. Upstairs Downstairs. Hervey Allen. HBMV; PoNe
Judged by my goddess' doom to endless pain. *See* Judg'd by my goddess' doom . . .
Judged by the Company One Keeps. *Unknown, at. to* Aimor R. Dickson. BLPA; NeHB; YaD
(Company One Keeps, The.) TreFT
Judgement. George Herbert. AnAnS-1; MaMe; MeP; SeCP
Judgement in Heaven, A. Francis Thompson. *See* Judgment in Heaven, A.
Judgement of Desire, The. *Unknown.* EnPo
Judgement of God, The. William Morris. *See* Judgment of God, The.
Judges, *sels.* Bible, *O.T.*
"Awake, awake, Deborah," V: 12-28. PoFr
Jephthah's Daughter, XI: 30-40. OuHeWo
Song of Deborah, The, V: 2-31. LiTW
(Song of Deborah and Barak, The, 2-21.) AWP
(Then Sang Deborah and Barak, 1-31.) TrJP
Judges, Judges. Gene Baro. NePoEA-2
Judge's Song, The. W. S. Gilbert. *Fr.* Trial by Jury. PoVP
Judging by Appearances. Emilie Poulsson. MPB
Judging Distances. Henry Reed. Lessons of the War, II. ChMP; FaBoMo; GTBS-P; LiTB; MoAB
Judging from the pictures. *Unknown, tr. fr. Japanese by* Geoffrey Bownas *and* Anthony Thwaite. FIW
Judgment, The. Katharine Lee Bates. OQP
Judgment. William Rose Benét. AnAmPo
Judgment. Grace Ellery Channing. AA
Judgment, The. Dora Read Goodale. AA; AnAmPo
Judgment. Kenneth W. Porter. ChIP
Judgment. *Unknown.* *See* Success ("Before God's footstool to confess").
Judgment and cash and health and faith in God go wrong. But Choose. John Holmes. MiAP
Judgment and Mercy. Dorothy L. Sayers. *Fr.* The Devil to Pay, sc. iv. MaRV
Judgment Day. William Dean Howells. AA; AmePo; PFY
Judgment Day. John Oxenham. SoP; TRV
Judgment [*or* Judgement] in Heaven, A, *sels.* Francis Thompson.
"Athwart the sod which is treading for God." CoBE
Epilogue: "Heaven, which man's generations draws." MoAB; MoBrPo
Epilogue: "Virtue may unlock hell." PoLi
Judgment Is Near, The. Reginald Heber. SoP
Judgment [*or* Judgement] of God, The. William Morris. OBVV; PeVV; ViPP
Judgment of Paris, The, *sels.* Ralph Schomberg. TrJP
Ay or Nay?
Courtier's a Riddle, A.
Like Birds of a Feather.
Judgment of Paris, The, 4 *ll.* *Unknown.* *Fr.* Goddesses Three *in* Winchester College Songs. OtMeF
Judgment of the May, The. Richard Watson Dixon. OBNC
Judgment! two syllables can make. A Dooms-Day Thought. Thomas Flatman. CEP
Judicious Observation of That Dreadful Comet, A. Ichabod Wiswall. SCAP
Judith, *sel.* Lascelles Abercrombie. *Fr.* Emblems of Love, III.
Balkis. HBV
(Song: "Balkis was in her marble town.") MoBrPo
Judith, *sels.* Bible, Apocrypha.
Tyrant's Death, The, XIII: 6-15 PoFr
". . . With Timbrels," XVI: 2-21. TrJP
Judith. William Young. AA
Judith of Bethulia. John Crowe Ransom. CrMA; DTC; FaBoMo; LiTA; LiTM (rev. ed.); MoPo; NePA
Judith of Minnewaulken, *sel.* Maxwell Anderson.
Judith Remembers. WHA
Jug and a book and a dame, A. The Rubáiyát. Edwin Meade Robinson. *Fr.* Limericised Classics. HBMV
Jug, jug! Fair fall the nightingal. The Nightingale. Richard Brathwaite. *Fr.* Nature's Embassy. ElL
Jug of water in the hand, and on, A. Dawn. "Rachel." TrJP
Juggernauting trams and the prolonged, The. The Towers at Evening. Frank Wilmot. *Fr.* Melbourne and Memory. NeLNL
Juggler. Richard Wilbur. AmP; CMoP; FiMAP; LiTM (rev. ed.); MoAB; NePA; NePoEA; NYBP; PoIE
Juggling Jerry. George Meredith. BEL; BeLS; BoLiVe; EnLit; EPN; HBV; OAEP; OnPP; SeCePo; VA; ViPo; VP
(Last Words of Juggling Jerry, The.) TOP
Jugurtha. Longfellow. AA; AP; CoBA; MWA-1
Juice glass throbs against his lips, The. A Negro Judge. Frederick Seidel. CoPo
Juice of apples climbs in me, The. The Forbidden. Phyllis Haring. PeSA
Juju of My Own, A. Lebert Bethune. BF; PoNe (1970 ed.)
Juke box has a big square face, The. King Juke. Kenneth Fearing. PoPo
Juke Box Love Song. Langston Hughes. IDB
Juley, *with music.* *Unknown.* SoAmSa
Julia. John Donne. Elegies, XIII. MaMe
Julia. Robert Herrick. *See* Rock of Rubies, The.
Julia, a Novel, *sel.* Helen Maria Williams.
To Hope. OBEC
Julia and I did lately sit. Cherry-Pit. Robert Herrick. OAEP
Julia, how Irishly you sacrifice. Reproach to Julia. Robert Graves. ELU
Julia, if I chance to die. His Request to Julia. Robert Herrick. OBS; SeEP
Julia Miller. Edgar Lee Masters. *Fr.* Spoon River Anthology. MoVE
Julia, my dear, how long, I wonder. Lovers and Friends. Henry Luttrell. *Fr.* Advice to Julia. OBRV
Julia was careless, and withal. Upon Julia's Fall. Robert Herrick. UnTE
Julian and Maddalo, *sel.* Shelley.
Conversation, A. ERoP-2
Julian Grenfell. Maurice Baring. HBMV; POTE
Julian M. and A. G. Rochelle. Emily Brontë. *See* Visionary, The.
Juliana, *sel.* Cynewulf, *tr. fr. Anglo-Saxon by* Charles W. Kennedy.
"I have great need that the Saint grant help." AnOE
Juliana. *Unknown, tr. fr. Latin by* George F. Whicher. BoLP
Julia's Petticoat. Robert Herrick. AnAnS-2; PoeP
(Upon Julia's Petticoat.) UnTE
Julie Ann Johnson, *with music.* *Unknown.* ABF
Julie-Jane. Thomas Hardy. MoVE
Julie Plante, The. William Henry Drummond. *See* Wreck of the *Julie Plante,* The.
Juliet. Hilaire Belloc. BoLP; ELU; EnLoPo; WePo
(How Did the Party Go?) MemP
Juliet, farewell. I would not be forgiven. Farewell [to Juliet]. Wilfrid Scawen Blunt. The Love Sonnets of Proteus, XXXIX. AnEnPo; TrGrPo
Juliet of Nations. Elizabeth Barrett Browning. *Fr.* Casa Guidi Windows. VA
Juliet's Yearning. Shakespeare. *Fr.* Romeo and Juliet, III, ii. TreFS
Julius Caesar, *sels.* Shakespeare.
Brutus Explains Why He Murdered Caesar, *fr.* III, ii. TreFT
Cassius Poisons Brutus' Mind, *fr.* I, ii. TreFS
Cowards ("Cowards die many times before their deaths"), *fr.* II, ii. MaRV, 2 *ll.*
(Death of Cowards, The.) TreFS
(That Men Should Fear.) TrGrPo
"Friends, Romans, countrymen, lend me your ears," *fr.* III, ii. FOL
(Antony's Oration.) PoPl; TrGrPo
(Antony's Oration over Caesar's Body.) LiTB; TreF
(I Come to Bury Caesar.) WHA
("If you have tears, prepare to shed them now.") MemP
(Mark Antony's Speech.) PTK
Julius Caesar's Preference, *fr.* I, ii. TreFS
Noblest Roman, The, *fr.* V, v. PTK
"O, pardon me, thou bleeding piece of earth," *fr.* III i. MemP; TreFS

Julius (continued)
(Mark Antony's Lament.) TreFS
Perfect Tribute, The ("His life was gentle"), *fr.* V, v. MaRV
There Is a Tide [in the Affairs of Men], *fr.* IV, iii. MaRV; PoPl; TRV
(Time to Strike, The.) TreFS
Noblest Roman, The, *fr.* V, v. FaFP; TreFS
(Brutus.) GoTP
(Portrait of Brutus.) TrGrPo
(Shakespeare Gallery, A: Brutus.) MaC
Portrait of Caesar, *fr.* I, ii. TrGrPo
(Shakespeare Gallery, A: Caesar.) MaC
Julius Caesar and the Honey-Bee. Charles Tennyson Turner. NBM; OA
July, *sel.* John Clare. *Fr.* The Shepherd's Calendar.
"Loud is the summer's busy song." GoTP; OBRV
July. Spenser. *Fr.* The Shepheardes Calender. ReIE
July. Susan Hartley Swett. GN; OTPC (1946 ed.); PoRL; StVeCh (1940 ed.)
(It Is July.) OTD; YeAr
July. Thomas Tusser. ReIE
July. *At. to* Whittier. YeAr
July Dawn. Louise Bogan. NePoAm-2
July Dawn, A, *sel.* John Francis O'Donnell.
"We left the city, street and square." IrPN
July 14, at Night. Feodor Ivanovich Tyutchev, *tr. fr. Russian by* Babette Deutsch. OnPM
July ghost, aghast at the strange winter, A. Midsummer Frost. Isaac Rosenberg. MoBrPo (1950 ed.); MoPo
July in Dutchess County. Babette Deutsch. WIRo
July in Indiana. Robert Fitzgerald. NYBP
July in the Jardin des Plantes. Claire McAllister. NePA
July in Washington. Robert Lowell. NaP; TDP
July is honored with the labor of fields. Labor of Fields. Elizabeth J. Coatsworth. TiPo (1959 ed.)
July is just in the nick of time! The Mowers. Myron B. Benton. YeAr
July Meadow. Louise Driscoll. YeAr
July 19, a dog has been run over by an airplane. Horse Race. Richard Brautigan. FRC
July the first, of a morning clear, one thousand six hundred and ninety. The Boyne Water. *Unknown.* AnIV; OnYI
July the redbird (*hanh!*), redbird, Augus' the fly (*hanh!*). Don't Talk about It. *Unknown.* OuSiCo
July; the Succession of the Four Sweet Months. Robert Herrick. *See* Succession of the Four Sweet Months, The.
July the twenty-second day. The Descent on Middlesex. Peter St. John. PAH
July's dry emperies have fired a snake. Crotalus Rex. Brewster Ghiselin. MoVE
Jumbled in the Common Box. W. H. Auden. PoRA
Jumblies, The. Edward Lear. BOHV; ChTr; EnLi-2 (1949 ed.); EvOK; FaBoBe; FaFP; GFA; GoJo; HBV; HBVY; LBN; LiTB; NA; OnMSP; OtMeF; OTPC; OxBoLi; PeVV; PoE; PoRA; PoVP; RIS; SAS; SeCeV; SiTL; SoPo; TiPo; VA; WiR
Jumbo Jee. Laura E. Richards. GaP; SUS
Jump—jump—jump. The Little Jumping Girls. Kate Greenaway. FaPON; MPB; TiPo
Jump or Jiggle. Evelyn Beyer. TiPo
(Jump or Jingle.) SoPo
Jump Shooter, The. Dennis Trudell. QAH
"Jump up behind me and away we will ride." Pretty Molly. *Unknown.* BFSS
Jumpin' Judy, *with music.* *Unknown.* ABF
Juncture. Rea Lubar Duncan. PoNe (1970 ed.)
June. Bryant. AA; CoBA; HBV
June. Mary Carolyn Davies. SiSoSe; TiPo (1959 ed.)
June. Aileen Fisher. PDV
June. Nora Hopper. YeAr
June. Francis Ledwidge. HBMV; OnYI
June. Amy Levy. MeWo
June ("And what is so rare"). James Russell Lowell. *Fr.* The Vision of Sir Launfal: Prelude to Part First. BBV; DD; FaBV; GoTP; HBVY; OHFP; PoRL; PTK; StaSt
("And what is so rare as a day in June.") AmLP; FaPL
(Day in June, A.) FaPON; StVeCh
("Earth gets its price for what Earth gives us.") TreF
("For a cap and bells.") AA
(June Weather.) GN
(Now Is the High-Tide of the Year.) TreFS
(What Is So Rare as a Day in June.) FaBoBe; FaFP; NePA; TIHL
June ("Over his keys the musing organist"). James Russell Lowell. *See* Vision of Sir Launfal, The: Over His Keys.
June. Wilson MacDonald. CaP
June. Douglas Malloch. OTD; YeAr
June. Harrison S. Morris. HBV
June. William Morris. *Fr.* The Earthly Paradise. PoVP; ViPo, *abr.*
("O June, O June, that we desired so," *abr.*) ViBoPo
June. Irene F. Pawsey. BoTP
June. Theodore Harding Rand. CaP
June. James Reaney. WHW
June. Spenser. *Fr.* The Shepheardes Calender. EnLit
June. Jane G. Stewart. BoTP
June Bracken and Heather. Tennyson. EnLoPo; PoVP
June-bug's got the golden wing, The. Bedbug. *Unknown.* GoSl
June Day, A. Sara Teasdale. YeAr
"June! June! June!" A Spring Lilt. *Unknown.* PCH
June Light. Richard Wilbur. CaFP
June Morning. Hugh McCrae. BoAV; PoAu-1
June Night. Hazel Hall. HBMV
June or July—I'm not really sure—in. The Way It Is. Joe Goncalves. BF
June Rapture. Angela Morgan. HBMV
June Song of a Man Who Looks Two Ways. Leslie Daiken. NeIP
June sunlight slants across the path. Commencement. Margaret E. Sangster. PEDC
June Thunder. Louis MacNeice. ChMP; CMoP; GTBS-D; MoPo
June, too soon. Rules of the Road. *Unknown.* SoAmSa
June Twilight. John Masefield. BoPe; GoYe
June was not over. Another Way of Love. Robert Browning. PoVP
June Weather. James Russell Lowell. *See* June.
Junes were free and full, driving through tiny, The. June Thunder. Louis MacNeice. ChMP; CMoP; GTBS-D; MoPo
Jung Idea, The. "P. H." SiTL
Jungfrau's Cry, The. Stopford Brooke. VA
Jungle, The. Louis Dudek. PeCV
Jungle. Phyllis Haring. PeSA
Jungle, The. Alun Lewis. MoPo
Jungle, The, *sel.* Archibald Fleming MacLiesh.
Report. NAMP
Jungle. Mary Carter Smith. PoNe (1970 ed.)
Jungle, The. William Carlos Williams. CABA; PoeP
Jungle:/ Glaze green and red feathers, jungle. Ezra Pound. *Fr.* Canto XX. MoPo
Jungle/ takes over the garden. The Indolent Gardener. Mary Kennedy. BoNaP
Jungle Book, The, *sels.* Kipling.
Road-Song of the Bandar-Log. OAEP (2d ed.)
(Seal Lullaby.) PRWS
Jungle is the frame for the machine, The. The Bulldozer. Donald A. Stauffer. WaP
Jungle Mammy Song, *with music.* *Unknown.* AS
Jungle necklaces are hung. Here She Is. Mary Britton Miller. TiPo (1959 ed.)
Jungle Pest, The. Roland Young. BOHV
Jungle Taste. Edward S. Silvera. CDC
Jungle Trees, The. Marjorie Wilson. BoTP
Junglegrave. S. E. Anderson. WSL
Juniper. Eileen Duggan. CAW; ChBR; MoSiPe
Juniper. Laurie Lee. ChMP; NeBP
Juniper Jim. "F. Anstey." YT
Juniper, Juniper,/ Green in the snow. *Unknown.* BoTP
Juniper Tree, The. Wilfred Watson. BoLP; PeCV; WHW
Junk. Richard Wilbur. CaFP; NoP; TDP
Junk man passed the house today, The. Ol' Clothes. *Unknown.* PoToHe (new ed.)
Junk Shop, The. Henri Coulette. NYBP
Junker Schmidt. "Kozma Prutkov" (Alexsey Tolstoy *and others*), *tr. fr. Russian by* W. D. Snodgrass *and* Tanya Tolstoy. ELU
Juno, that on her head Love's livery carried. Caelica, XI. Fulke Greville. EP; NCEP
Just a few of the roses we gathered from the Isar. Roses on the Breakfast Table. D. H. Lawrence. BrPo
Just a Fishing Smack at Empson. George Barker. SiTL

Just a little nudge, he said, and then. The Door to the Future. Dick Gallup. ANYP
Just a Mile Beyond. Aileen Fisher. RePo
Just a picture of somebody's child. Somebody's Child. Louise Chandler Moulton. HBV
Just a Smack at Auden. William Empson. FaBoTw; LiTM (rev. ed.); MoBrPo (1962 ed.); SiTL; ToPo; UnPo (3d ed.)
Just a Smack at Smacking. *Unknown.* SiTL
Just a solitude. Little Air. Stéphane Mallarmé. PoPl; SyP
Just a song at twilight, when the lights are low (refrain). Love's Old Sweet Song. G. Clifton Bingham. TreF
Just a song of sunshine! Sunshine. *Unknown.* FaChP
Just a Wearyin' for You. Frank L. Stanton. *See* Wearyin' for You.
Just after Noon with Fierce Shears. Tram Combs. TwCP
Just after the Board had brought the schools up to date. Modern Ode to the Modern School. John Erskine. YaD
Just an ivy-covered cottage with a brooklet running near. All That Glitters Is Not Gold. *Unknown.* TreFT
Just & Unjust. Lord Bowen. *See* Rain It Raineth, The.
Just are the ways of God. The Transcendence of God. Milton. *Fr.* Samson Agonistes. OBS
Just a-Ridin'. Badger Clark. SCC
Just as a mother, with sweet, pious face. Providence. Vincenzo da Filicaja. CAW
Just as, from a well-blazing fire, sparks. The Universal Fire. *Unknown. Fr.* The Upanishads. OnPM
Just As I Am. Charlotte Elliott. HBV; SoP; VA
Just as I am, Thine own to be. Consecration. "Marianne Farningham." FaChP; MaRV
Just as I am—without one plea. Just As I Am. Charlotte Elliott. HBV; SoP; VA
Just as I thought I was growing old. The Prime of Life. Walter Learned. HBV
Just as I used to say. Pictures of the Gone World, Sec. 2. Lawrence Ferlinghetti. TDP; ToPo
Just as my fingers on these keys. Peter Quince at the Clavier. Wallace Stevens. AmPP (4th ed.); AnFE; AnNE; AP; APA; ATP (1953 ed.); CABA; CBV; CLwM; CMoP; CoAnAm; CoBMV; ExPo; ForPo; HBMV; ILP; InPo; LiTM; MAP; MAPA; MaPo (1969 ed.); MoAB; MoAmPo; NAMP; NP; OxBA; PAn; PoAn; ReMP; TDP; TrGrPo; TwAmPo; TwCP; UnPo (3d ed.); VaPo; ViBoPo; WoL
Just as of yore the friendly rain. Mater Dolorosa. Elliott Napier. BoAu
Just as soon as summer's done. The Weather Factory. Nancy Byrd Turner. SUS
Just as the hour was darkest. The Ballad of New Orleans. George Henry Boker. PAH
Just as the moon was fading amid her misty rings. Kriss Kringle. Thomas Bailey Aldrich. BoChLi (1939 ed.); HBVY; MPB; PEDC; TSW
Just as the school came out. The Snow. W. W. Gibson. BEL
Just as the Small Waves Came Where No Waves Were. Pamela Millward. FRC
Just as the spring came laughing through the strife. John Pelham. James Ryder Randall. AA; PAH
Just as those who gaze get higher than those who climb. The Glacier. Louis MacNeice. AnFE
Just as Thou Art. *Unknown.* FaChP
Just at the blackest bit of my depression. Dirge. Hazel Townson. PV
Just at the self-same beat of Time's wide wings. The Bruised Titans. Keats. *Fr.* Hyperion; a Fragment. OBNC; OBRV
Just Be Glad. James Whitcomb Riley. WBLP
Just because I smile and smile. Because. B. W. Vilakazi. PeSA
Just before bed. The Mother's Tale. Eleanor Farjeon. BiCB
Just before the Battle, Mother. George F. Root. TreFS
Just Beguiler. Thomas Campion. AtBAP
Just behind the Battle, Mother, *parody. Unknown.* FiBHP
Just bent on viewing cherries. Issa. Satirical Poems on Daimyos, II. PoFr
Just beyond the rainbow's rim a river ripples down. The Sleepytown Express. James J. Montague. HBMV
Just Dropped In. William Cole. FiBHP; GoJo; PoPl
Just ere the darkness is withdrawn. Sleep and His Brother Death. William Hamilton Hayne. AA
Just Exchange. Sir Philip Sidney. *See* My True Love Hath My Heart.
Just finger prints and drool. Not Writing. Joseph Cardarelli. QAH
Just Folks. Edgar A. Guest. FaFP; TreFS
Just for a handful of silver he left us. The Lost Leader. Robert Browning. BEL; EnL; EnLi-2; EnLit; EPN; FaPL; FOL; GTBS; GTBS-D; GTBS-W; GTSL; HBV; MBW-2; MCCG; ML; OtMeF; PoFr; PoFS; PoVP; TreFS; TrGrPo; VA; ViBoPo; ViPo; ViPP
Just for a space that I met her. Incognita. Austin Dobson. CenHV; PoVP
Just for Jesus. Lysbeth Boyd Borie. GaP
Just for the Ride. *Unknown.* FaFP; SiTL
Just for Today (*sl. diff. versions*). Sybil F. Partridge, *wr. at. to* Samuel Wilberforce *and to* Frederick William Faber. HBV; MaRV; OQP, *abr.*; SoP; TreF; TRV; VA, *abr.*
(To-Day.) WHL
Just 'fore Christmas. Eugene Field. *See* Jest 'fore Christmas.
Just Forget. Myrtle May Dryden. WBLP
Just Friends. Robert Creeley. NeAP
Just from Dawson, *with music. Unknown.* ABF
Just God! and these are they. Clerical Oppressors. Whittier. PAH; PPON
Just Home. Louis Untermeyer. *See* Edgar A. Guest Considers "The Old Woman Who Lived in a Shoe."
Just imagine yourself seated on a shadowy terrace. That Reminds Me. Ogden Nash. FiBHP; MeWo
Just in the gray of the dawn, as the mists uprose from the meadows. The Expedition to Wessagusset. Longfellow. *Fr.* The Courtship of Miles Standish. PAH
Just Jumbo. Eileen Mathias. BoTP
Just Keep On. Clifton Abbott. WBLP
Just Keep on Keepin' On. *Unknown. See* Just Try This.
Just like a Man. *Unknown, at. to* Lizzie M. Hadley. BoTP
Just like Me. P. W. Sinks. BLRP
Just like This. D. A. Olney. BoTP
Just look, Manetto, at that wry-mouth'd minx. Sonnet: Of an Ill-favored Lady. Guido Cavalcanti. AWP; JAWP; WBP
Just lost, when I was saved. Emily Dickinson. AmePo; AmPP (5th ed.); AP; CoBA; MWA-2
(Called Back.) AA; AnFE; APA; CoAnAm; MoAmPo;
Just Making It. Richard Thomas. PoNe (1970 ed.)
Just now/ Out of the strange. The Warning. Adelaide Crapsey. AnAmPo; InP; MAP; MCCG; MoAmPo (1942 ed.); NeMA; NP
Just now a honeybee. The Honeybee. Helen Bevington. NYTB
Just now I visited the monkeys. The Petty Officers' Mess. Roy Fuller. ChMP
Just now the lilac is in bloom. The Old Vicarage, Grantchester. Rupert Brooke. BrPo; FaBV; GoTL (1949 ed.); MoBrPo; MoVE; PoRA; ShBV-3; TOP
Just off the highway to Rochester, Minnesota. A Blessing. James Wright. AmPC; FIW; NaP; OPoP; StP; TwCP
Just One Book. *Unknown.* BLRP
Just One Signal. *Unknown.* PAH
Just one thing, O Master, I ask today. My Only Plea. Walter J. Kuhn. SoP
Just Passing. *Unknown.* BLRP
Just road choice fifty ditch. Scrip Ant. Clark Coolidge. YAP
Just short of the isthmus, the court. The Campaign: Letters from the Front. Stephen Shrader. QAH
Just Sixteen. Hsü Chien, *tr. fr. Chinese by* Henry H. Hart. OnPM
Just so it goes—the day, the night. An Ordinary Evening in Cleveland. Lewis Turco. NYBP
Just stand aside and watch yourself go by. Watch Yourself Go By [*or* A Cure for Fault-finding]. Strickland W. Gillilan. BLPA; PoToHe; WBLP
Just take a trifling handful, O philosopher! Sky-making. Mortimer Collins. BOHV
Just tell her this, Dorkas. Got it? Good. The Message. Meleager. LiTW
Just Tell Them That You Saw Me. Paul Dresser. TreFS
"Just the place for a Snark!" the Bellman cried. The Hunting of the Snark. "Lewis Carroll." FiBHP; MasP; NA; OBNC; OnMSP; PoEL-5; SiTL; WhC
Just the Same To-Day. *Unknown.* BLRP; WBLP
Just Then the Door. Merrill Moore. AnEnPo

Just think of that odd little sparrow. That Odd Little Sparrow. *Unknown.* SoP
Just to Be Glad. Merlin G. Miller. STF
Just to Be Needed. Mary Eversley. PoToHe
Just to let thy Father do. The Secret of a Happy Day. Frances Ridley Havergal. SoP
Just Try This. *Unknown.* WBLP
(Just Keep on Keepin' On.) STF
Just Try to Be the Fellow That Your Mother Thinks You Are. Will S. Adkin. *See* If I Only Was the Fellow.
Just wait upon the Lord and you will know. Trust and Wait. Oswald J. Smith. SoP
Just when each bud was big with bloom. Birth. Grace Raymond. AA
Just where the tide of battle turns. John Burns of Gettysburg. Bret Harte. HBV; LHV; MC; OHIP; PAH; PAP
Just where the Treasury's marble front. Pan in Wall Street. Edmund Clarence Stedman. AA; AmePo; AnAmPo; HBV; PFY
Justice ("I cannot skill of these thy wayes"). George Herbert. MaMe
Justice ("O Dreadfull justice"). George Herbert. MaMe
Justice Denied in Massachusetts. Edna St. Vincent Millay. CoBA; MAP; MoAmPo; WOW
Justice Is Reason Enough. Diane Wakoski. CoPo
Justice to Scotland. *Unknown.* BOHV; InMe
Justice walking o'er the frozen Thames, A. Epigram. *Unknown.* ALV
Justified Mother of Men, The. Walt Whitman. *Fr.* Faces. OHIP
Justify all those renowned generations. The Renowned Generations. W. B. Yeats. OxBoLi
Justine, You Love Me Not! John Godfrey Saxe. HBV
Justus Quidem Tu Es, Domine. Gerard Manley Hopkins. *See* Thou Art Indeed Just, Lord.
Juxta. Grover Jacoby. GoYe
Juxtaposition. Arthur Hugh Clough. *Fr.* Amours de Voyage, Canto III, vi. OBNC; VA

K

K. K. Can't Calculate. Frances Miriam Whitcher. BOHV
Kabul town's by Kabul river. Ford o' Kabul River. Kipling. FaBoTw; PeVV
Kacelyvo's slope still felt. The Last Redoubt. Alfred Austin. HBV
Kaddish. Allen Ginsberg. AmPC
"Strange now to think of you, gone without corsets & eyes," *sel.* NeAP; OPoP
Kaddish. Levi Yitzhok of Berditchev, *tr. fr. Yiddish by* Joseph Leftwich. TrJP
Kadia the Young Mother Speaks. Jessie Sampter. TrJP
Kafoozalum. *Unknown.* BeLS; BLPA
Kaiser & Co. Alexander Macgregor Rose, *sometimes at. to* Rodney Blake. BLPA; HBV
(Hoch! Der Kaiser.) BOHV
Kaiser of dis Vaterlandt, Der. Teddy unt Me unt Gott. *Unknown.* BLPA
Kalamazoo. Vachel Lindsay. HT
Kalevala, *sel.* *Unknown, tr. fr. Finnish.*
Prayer for Rain. WGRP
Kallundborg Church. Whittier. BeLS; GBV
Kallyope Yell, The. Vachel Lindsay. BoLiVe
Kalymniad, *sel.* Robert Lax.
"Call it a crescent," Pt. II. ThO
Kamal is out with twenty men to raise the Border side. A Ballad of East and West. Kipling. BEL; FaBoBe; HBV; TSW; VA
Kamaoktunga. . . I am afraid and I tremble. Manerathiak's Song. *Unknown.* WHW
Kanawâki—"By the Rapid." The Caughnawaga Beadwork Seller. William Douw Lighthall. CaP
Kane. Fitz-James O'Brien. PAH
Kangaroo, The. Elizabeth J. Coatsworth. StVeCh (1955 ed.); TiPo (1952 ed.)
Kangaroo. D. H. Lawrence. FlW; MoVE; OA; ShBV-4
Kangaroo, The. *Unknown.* SoPo
Kangaroo by Nightfall. Noel Macainsh. PoAu-2
Kangaroo has a heavy tail, The. Tails. Rowena Bennett. RePo
Kangarooster, The. Kenyon Cox. *Fr.* Mixed Beasts. RIS; TiPo
Kanheri Caves. Dom Moraes. TDP
Kansas. Vachel Lindsay. HT; TOP
Kansas Boy. Ruth Lechlitner. AmFN
Kansas Boys (*diff. versions*). *Unknown.* AS (B *vers.*); IHA, *abr.*
(Hello, Girls, A *vers., with music.*) AS
("Hello, girls, listen to my voice.") CoSo
(Mississippi Girls.) BFSS
(Texian Boys, *with music.*) CoSo
Kansas Cowboy, A, *with music.* *Unknown.* CoSo
Kansas Emigrants, The. Whittier. CoBA; MC; PaA; PAH
Kansas Line, The. *Unknown.* CoSo
Kanyariri, village of toil. The Village. Marina Gashe. PBA
Karamanian Exile, The. James Clarence Mangan, *after the Turkish* IrPN; OBVV; PeVV
Karezzas, Cuntras, Cockturnes, Manshrieks, Carrioncries. William Knott. YAP
Karintha, *sel.* Jean Toomer.
"Her skin is like dusk on the eastern horizon." Kal
Karl. Charles Spear. AnNZ
Karl, from your beachhead on that hollow island. V-Letter to Karl Shapiro in Australia. Selden Rodman. WaP
Karma. William Canton. VA
Karma. E. A. Robinson. AmPP; AnNE; AP; CMoP; CoBMV; ILP; MoAB; MoAmPo (1950 ed.)
Karolin's Song. Ben Jonson. *See* Though I Am Young.
Karoo Town. Robert Dederick. PeSA
Karshish and Lazarus. Robert Browning. *See* Epistle, An, Containing the Strange Medical Experience of Karshish, the Arab Physician.
Karshish, the Arab Physician ("Karshish, the picker-up of learning's crumbs"). Robert Browning. *See* Epistle, An, Containing the Strange Medical Experience of Karshish, the Arab Physician.
Kashmiri Song ("Pale hands I love"). "Laurence Hope." BLPA; FaBoBe; FaFP; NeHB; TreF
Kasidah, The, *sel.* Sir Richard Francis Burton.
"In these drear wastes." HBV
Kate. Helen Underwood Hoyt. RIS
Kate Kearney. Lady Morgan. BLPA; FaBoBe; NeHB
Kate o' Belashanny. William Allingham. IrPN
Kate of Aberdeen. John Cunningham. HBV
Kate rose up early as fresh as a lark. Wind's Work. T. Sturge Moore. BrPo; HBMV; HBVY
Kate Temple's Song. Mortimer Collins. HBV; VA
Kate was a pretty child. Kate. Helen Underwood Hoyt. RIS
Kathaleen Ny-Houlahan. *Unknown, tr. fr. Gaelic by* James Clarence Mangan. CoBE
(Kathleen-Ni-Houlahan.) AnIV
Katharine. Heine, *tr. fr. German by* Louis Untermeyer. UnTE
Katharine Jaffray. *Unknown.* BaBo; ESPB (A, B, *and* C *vers.*); InP; OxBB; ViBoFo (A *vers.*; B *vers., with music*)
(Katharine Johnstone.) BuBa; OBB
(Kathrine Jaffrey, *with music.*) BFSS
Katherine Milton: Died MDCLVIII. Milton. *See* On His Deceased Wife.
Kathleen Mavourneen. Louisa Macartney Crawford, *sometimes at. to* Julia Crawford. FaBoBe; HBV; PTK; TreF; VA
Kathleen-Ni-Houlahan. *Unknown.* *See* Kathaleen Ny-Houlahan.
Kath'rine Jaffrey. *Unknown.* *See* Katharine Jaffray.
Katie Lee and Willie Grey. *Unknown, at. to* Josie R. Hunt *and to* J. H. Pixley. BeLS; BLPA
Katy Dorey, *with music.* *Unknown.* OuSiCo
Katy-did. C. Lindsay McCoy. GFA
Katy's Answer. Allan Ramsay. CEP; EiPP
Katzenjammer Kids, The. James Reaney. MoCV; OBCV; PeCV; TwCaPo
Kavanagh, The. Richard Hovey. HBV; LHV
Kay Price and Stella Pajunas. Vito Hannibal Acconci. YAP
Kayak, The. *Unknown.* FaPON; GFA; OTPC (1946 ed.); PCH; RePo
Kayak Song, A. Lucy Diamond. BoTP
K'e still ripples to its banks, The. A Chinese Poem Written in B.C. 718. *Unknown.* WePo
Kearny at Seven Pines. Edmund Clarence Stedman. AA; DD;

HBV; HBVY; MC; OTPC; PaA; PAH; PAP
Kearsarge. S. Weir Mitchell. PAH
Kearsarge, The. James Jeffrey Roche. AA; PAH
Kearsarge and *Alabama.* *Unknown.* PAH
Keats. Longfellow. AmP; AP; MAmP; Sonn
Keats. William Wilberforce Lord. *Fr.* Ode to England. AA
Keats. Lizette Woodworth Reese. AA
Keats. John Banister Tabb. AmP
Keats at Teignmouth: 1818. Charles Causley. MemP; ML; POTi
Keen. Edna St. Vincent Millay. HBMV
Keen blaws the wind o'er the braes o' Gleniffer. The Braes o' Gleniffer. Robert Tannahill. OBRV
Keen, Fitful Gusts [Are Whispering Here and There]. Keats. BEL; CABA; EnLit; EnRP; GTBS-W; MaPo; MBW-2; MERP; OAEP; PAn; Sonn
(Sonnet.) PoEL-4
Keen is the wind, bare the hill, it is difficult to find shelter. Winter. *Unknown.* *Fr.* The Black Book of Carmarthen. PrWP
Keen stars were twinkling, The. To Jane. Shelley. EPN; NoP; ThWaDe
Keen Thyself, Poor Wight. Geoffrey Keating, *tr. fr. Late Middle Irish by* Padraic Pearse. OnYI
Keen was the air, the sky was very light. Garden Fairies. Philip Bourke Marston. VA
Keen winds of cloud and vaporous drift. Nocturne. Richard Garnett. OBVV
Keenan's Charge. George Parsons Lathrop. AA; BBV (1923 ed.); HBV; MC; PAH; PAP, *abr.*; PFY
Keener tempests come, The: and, fuming dun. Winter. James Thomson. *Fr.* The Seasons. EnRP; NoP; TOP; ViBoPo
Keening of Mary, The. *Unknown,* *tr. fr. Irish by* Padraic Pearse. ISi
Keep a brave spirit, and never despair. Press Onward. *Unknown.* FaFP
Keep a Good Tongue in Your Head. Martin Parker. CoMu
Keep a Poem in Your Pocket. Beatrice Schenk de Regniers. PDV; SoPo
Keep a red heart of memories. Haze. Carl Sandburg. OnHM
Keep a Stiff Upper Lip. Phoebe Cary. FaFP
Keep a-Goin'. Frank L. Stanton. FaFP; OHFP; WBLP
Keep a-Inchin' Along, *with music.* *Unknown.* BoAN-1
Keep a-Pluggin' Away. Paul Laurence Dunbar. MCCG
Keep away from roads' webs, they always lead. Direction to a Rebel. W. R. Rodgers. LiTM (rev. ed.)
Keep away, son, these lakes are salt. Advice to a Young Prophet. Thomas Merton. WOW
Keep back the one word more. Reserve. Lizette Woodworth Reese. AA
Keep Darkness. Leslie Nelson Jennings. FiSC
Keep dis in min', an' all'll go right. Don't Tell All You Know. *Unknown.* PCH
Keep heart, O comrade, God may be delayed. Walt Whitman. BBV (1951 ed.)
Keep in God's way; keep pace with evry hour. To Be Engraven on a Dial. Samuel Sewall. SCAP
Keep in the Heart the Journal [Nature Keeps]. Conrad Aiken. *Fr.* Preludes for Memnon. CMoP; NePA; OxBA
Keep It Dark. *Unknown,* *tr. fr. Zezuru by* Hugh Tracey. PBA
Keep Looking Up. Carlton Buck. SoP
Keep love a-boiling; keep soup in the pot. Recipe. *Unknown.* UnTE
Keep Love in Your Life. Thomas Curtis Clark. WBLP
Keep Me f'om Sinkin' Down, *with music.* *Unknown.* BoAN-1
Keep me from bitterness. It is so easy. Prayer in Affliction. Violet Alleyn Storey. MaRV; TrPWD
Keep me from fretting, Lord, today. Prayer. May Carleton Lord. PGD
Keep me, I pray, in wisdom's way. The Bibliomaniac's Prayer. Eugene Field. AA
Keep Me, Jesus. Keep Me. Waverly Turner Carmichael. BANP
Keep me quiet, Master. A Prayer for Peace. William Adams Brown. MaRV
Keep Me Still, for I Do Not Want to Dream. Larry Eigner. NeAP
Keep my riband, take and keep it. Elizabeth Barrett Browning. *Fr.* Catarina to Camoens. GTSE
Keep Not Thou Silence. Psalms, LXXXIII, Bible, *O.T.* TrJP
Keep On Praying. Roger H. Lyon. BLRP
Keep on Pushing. David Henderson. BF
Keep on your mask and hide your eye. *Unknown.* LO
Keep Silence, all created things. God's Dominion and Decrees. Isaac Watts. OBEC
Keep Smiling. *Unknown.* WBLP
Keep Sweet. A. B. Simpson. SoP; STF, 3 *sts.*
Keep the dream alive and growing always. Song (2). Edwin Rolfe. TrJP
Keep the Glad Flag Flying. *Unknown.* FaFP
"Keep this for me." Faith. *Unknown.* PoToHe (new ed.)
Keep this little light, O Father. A Birthday Prayer. John Finley. TrPWD
Keep Thou me ever hungry, Lord. Until He Comes. Martha Snell Nicholson. SoP
Keep Thou My Way, O Lord. Fanny Crosby. TrPWD
Keep Ye Holy Sabbath Rest. *Unknown,* *tr. fr. Hebrew by* Herbert Loewe. TrJP
Keep you these calm and lovely things. To the Liffey with the Swans. Oliver St. John Gogarty. AnIL; OxBI
Keep your copper coin, save your cup of wheat. Never Ask Me Why. Silvia Margolis. GoYe
Keep Your Grit. Louis E. Thayer. STF
Hang to Your Grit! *sel.* WBLP
Keep Your Hands on That Plow, *with music.* *Unknown.* OuSiCo
Keeper, The. Arthur Stringer. MaRV
Keepers of the Pass, The. Sir Charles G. D. Roberts. VA
Keeping On. Arthur Hugh Clough. *See* Say Not the Struggle Nought Availeth.
Keeping Store. Mary Frances Butts. GFA; OTPC (1946 ed.); PCH; PPL
Keeping the Sabbath. Emily Dickinson. *See* Some keep the Sabbath going to church.
Keeping Their World Large. Marianne Moore. WaP
Keeping Things Whole. Mark Strand. CoAP; YAP
Keeping Victory. Walter E. Isenhour. SoP; STF
Keepsake. Victor Contoski. ThO
Keepsake from Quinault. Dorothy Alyea. GoYe
Keepsake Mill. Robert Louis Stevenson. TSW
Kehama's Curse. Robert Southey. *Fr.* The Curse of Kehama. OBNC
("I charm thy life.") LoBV; OBRV
Keine Lazarovitch. Irving Layton. ACV
Keith of Ravelston. Sydney Thompson Dobell. *See* Ballad of Keith of Ravelston, The.
Kellyburnbraes. *Unknown.* OxBB
Kelpius's Hymn. Arthur Peterson. AA
Kemp Owyne [*or* Oweyne]. *Unknown.* BaBo; BEL; BoLiVe; BuBa; CBEP; CoBE; EnLi-1 (1949 ed.); EnSB; ESPB (A *and* B *vers.*); OBB, *var.*; SeCeV; TOP; ViBoFo
(Kempion.) OxBB
Ke-ni-ga Song. *Tr. fr. American Indian song by* Natalie Barnes. MPB
Kendal is dead, and Cambridge riding post. Upon His Grand-Children. Andrew Marvell. MaMe
Kenilworth, *sel.* Sir Walter Scott.
Bonny, Bonny Owl, The, *fr. ch.* 2. BiS
Kensington Gardens, *sel.* Thomas Tickell.
Fairies. OBEC
Kensington Gardens, *sels.* Humbert Wolfe. *Poems indexed separately by titles and first lines.*
Kentish hamlets gray and old. The Memory of Kent. Edmund Blunden. HBMV
Kentish Petition, The, 1701, *sel.* Defoe.
"'Tis fatal to tyrannic power, when they." PoFr
Kentish Sir Byng stood for his King. Marching Along. Robert Browning. Cavalier Tunes, I. ATP (1935 ed.); BEL; EnLi-2; EnLit; EPN; HBV; MCCG; OAEP; PoVP; ShBV-1; TOP; VA; ViPo; YT
Kenton and Deborah, Michael and Rose. Ambition. Aline Kilmer. HBMV; LHV; WHL
Kentucky Babe. Richard Henry Buck. AA; HBV
Kentucky Belle. Constance Fenimore Woolson. BeLS; BLPA; FaBoBe; GoTP; MaC; PAH; StaSt; StPo
Kentucky Birthday; February 12, 1815. Frances Frost. SiSoSe; YeAr
Kentucky Moonshiner, *with music.* *Unknown.* AS; TrAS
Kentucky Mountain Farm, *sels.* Robert Penn Warren.
Cardinal, The, IV. MoVE
History among the Rocks, III. MAP; MoAmPo; MoVE

Kentucky Philosophy. Harrison Robertson. BOHV; HBV; IHA
Kentucky Thoroughbred, The. James Whitcomb Riley. ELU
Kentucky water, clear springs: a boy fleeing. The Swimmers. Allen Tate. AP; MoAmPo (1962 ed.); MoVE
Kepe well x, and flee fro vii. Ten Commandments, Seven Deadly Sins, and Five Wits. *Unknown.* ChTr
Kept Every Moment. John Roberts. SoP
Kept for Jesus. Edith E. Cherry. BePJ
Kéramos. Longfellow. MAmP; PoEL-5, *much abr.*
(Potter's Song, The.) YT
Keraunograph. Hayden Carruth. NMP
Kerchoo! Margaret Fishback. PoSC
Kernel, The. Frank Kendon. MoBrPo (1942 ed.)
Kerry Cow, The. Winifred M. Letts. TSW
Kerry Dance, The. James Lyman Molloy. OnYI
Kerry Lads, The. Theodosia Garrison. HBMV
Kestrels, The. Sidney Keyes. FaBoMo; POTE
Kestrel wakes now to the morning air, The. Hawk Remembered. J. Phoenice. NYTB
Kettle changes its note, The. The Unknown. Denise Levertov. FRC
Kettle descants in a cosy drone, The. Satires of Circumstance. Thomas Hardy. BrPo; PoVP; VaPo
Kettle sang the boy to a half-sleep, The. Halibut Cove Harvest. Kenneth Leslie. CaP
Kevin Barry, *with music.* *Unknown.* AS
Kevin Barry. Terence Ward. OnYI
Key, The. John Oxenham. BePJ
Key-Board, The. Sir William Watson. HBV
Key into the Language of America, A; or, An Help to Language of the Natives, *sels.* Roger Williams.
Boast Not, Proud English. AmPP (4th ed.); SCAP
Courteous Pagan Shall Condemn, The. AmPP (4th ed.); SCAP
Key of the Kingdom, The. *Unknown.* *See* This Is the Key.
Key of yesterday, The. The Lost Key. Priscilla Leonard. MaRV; OQP
Key to Everything, The. May Swenson. NePoEA
Key West. Hart Crane. CMoP
Key will stammer, and the door reply, The. Week-End, II. Harold Monro. MoBrPo (1950 ed.); YT
Keyhole in the Door, The. *Unknown.* CoMu
Keys of Heaven, The. *Unknown.* *See* Paper of Pins, A.
Keys of Morning, The. Walter de la Mare. AtBAP; MoVE; NoP
Keys of the Jail, The. *Unknown.* *See* Clefs de la prison, Les.
Khamsin. Clinton Scollard. AA; PFY
Khristna and His Flute. "Laurence Hope." HBV
Khrushchev is coming on the right day! Poem. Frank O'-Hara. NeAP
Kibbutz Sabbath. Levi Ben Amittai, *tr. fr. Hebrew by* Simon Halkin. EaLo
Kick a Little Stone. Dorothy Aldis. SoPo
Kick at the rock, Sam Johnson, break your bones. Epistemology. Richard Wilbur. NePoEA
Kicking his mother until she let go of his soul. Mundus et Infans. W. H. Auden. LiTB; LiTM; MoAB; MoBrPo (1950 ed.)
Kickoff. In the Beginning Was the. Lee Murchison. SD
Kid, The, *sels.* Conrad Aiken.
Awakening, The, VII. MoVE
Proem to "The Kid" ("Where now he roves, by wood or swamp whatever"). MoAB
Kid. Robert Hayden. CAD
Kid, The. William Shenstone. OTPC (1923 ed.)
Kid Has Gone to the Colors, The. William Herschell. PoLF
Kid in the Park. Langston Hughes. OCS
Kid in Upper 4, The. Nelson C. Metcalf. TreFS
Kid March had the stuff but his style was hard. The Up-Set. Corey Ford. WhC
Kid Stuff. Frank Horne. AmNP; Kal; PoNe
Kiddy cars of little tikes. Transportation Problem. Richard Armour. WhC
Kidnapping of Sims, The. John Pierpont. PAH
Kids. Witter Bynner. MPB
Kids in the street. This Is the City. Yvette Johnson. TNV
Kid's Last Fight, The. *Unknown.* TreF
Kilbarchan now may say alas! The Life and Death of [Habbie Simson] the Piper of Kilbarchan. Robert Sempill of Beltrees. OBS; OxBS
Kilcash. *Unknown,* *tr. fr. Irish by* Frank O'Connor. KiLC; OBMV; OxBI; ThWaDe; WePo
Kilimandjaro. Bayard Taylor. AmP
Kilkenny Boy, The. Eileen Shanahan. NeIP
Kilkenny Cats, The. *Unknown.* BOHV; CIV; FaFP; LiTG; ShM; TreF
(Cats of Kilkenny, The.) GoTP
(Limerick: "There once were two cats of Kilkenny," *sl. diff.*) CenHV
Kill, The. Donald Hall. WIRo
Kill me not ev'ry day. Affliction. George Herbert. MaMe
Kill yourselves with knives and poisoned gas. Strangers Are We All upon the Earth. Franz Werfel. TrJP
Killarney. Edmund Falconer. TreFS
Killarney. Charles Kingsley. WhC
Killarney. William Larminie. *Fr.* Fand. AnIV
Killed at the Ford. Longfellow. AP; BBV; OHIP
Killed in Action. Terence Tiller. NeBP
Killer, The. *Unknown.* ABF; CoSo
Killers ("I am put high over all others in the city today"). Carl Sandburg. MoVE
Killers ("I am singing to you"). Carl Sandburg. NP
Killers are killed, their violent rinds, The. Lunch on Omaha Beach. Bink Noll. StP; ToPo
Killing. Samuel Greenberg. LiTA
Killing, The. Edwin Muir. ACV; BoPe; ChMP; MoRP; PoPl
Killing is unthinkable, The. Thinking. Thinking About the Unthinkable. Barbara Gibson. WOW
Killing No Murder. Sylvia Townsend Warner. MoBrPo
Killyburn Brae. *Unknown.* OnYI
Kilmallock. Sir Aubrey De Vere. IrPN
Kilmeny. James Hogg. *Fr.* The Queen's Wake. CABL; GBV (1922 ed.); HBV; OBEV; OBRV; OnSP, *abr.*; OtMeF, *abr.*
(Bonny Kilmeny Gaed up the Glen.) GoTS
Kilmeny. Alfred Noyes. EnLit
Kilroy. Peter Viereck. MoAmPo (1950 ed.); NeMA; ThLM
(Kilroy Was Here.) PoRA
Kimono, The. Don Gordon. WOW
Kin. Carl Sandburg. NP
Kinchinjunga. Cale Young Rice. AnAmPo; HBV
Kincora. *Unknown,* *tr. fr. Middle Irish by* James Clarence Mangan. AnIV; OnYI; OxBI
(Lamentation of Mac Liag for Kincora.) AnIL
Kind. Josephine Miles. FiMAP
Kind and True. Aurelian Townsend. CBEP
Kind Are Her Answers. Thomas Campion. AnFE; CLwM; EG; ELP; HBV; LiTL; MeWo; OBSC; SeCeV; TrGrPo
(Kinde Are Her Answers.) AtBAP; FaBoEn; PoEL-2
Kind bird, thy praises I design. The Bird. Countess of Winchilsea. EiPP
Kind country-men listen I pray. All Things Be Dear but Poor Mens Labour; or, The Sad Complaint of Poor Pople. "L. W." CoMu
Kind Deeds. Julia A. Fletcher Carney. *See* Little Things.
Kind friends, if you will listen, a story I will tell. The Sherman Cyclone [*or* Brown-eyed Lee]. *Unknown.* BFSS; CoSo
Kind friends, you must pity my horrible tale. The Dreary Black Hills. *Unknown.* ABF; CoSo
Kind gentlemen, will you be patient awhile? Robin Hood's Birth, Breeding, Valor, and Marriage. *Unknown.* ESPB
Kind Hearts. *Unknown.* HBV
Kind Heaven, assist the trembling muse. Wyoming Massacre. Uriah Terry. PAH
Kind Inn, A. George Dillon. GoYe
Kind Keeper, The. Dryden. *See* Limberham; or, The Kind Keeper.
Kind Look, The. Willard Maas. LiTM (1946 ed.)
Kind Lovers, Love On. John Crowne. *See* Song: "Kind lovers, love on."
Kind Marcus me to supper lately bade. Against Feasting. Sir John Harington. SiCE
Kind Miss, *with music.* *Unknown.* AS
Kind Mistress, The. *Unknown.* PeRV
Kind Mousie, The. Natalie Joan. BoTP
Kind of Act of, The. Robert Creeley. NeAP
Kind of an Ode to Duty. Ogden Nash. TrGrPo; UnPo (3d ed.); WhC
Kind of Dad I'd Buy, The. Helen Kitchell Evans. SoP
Kind of grass that a spit-bug chooses, The. The Spit-Bug. William H. Matchett. WaKn

Kind of heart, of beauty bright. The Rendezvous. Catullus. OnPM
Kind of like a stormy day, take it all together. A Rainy Day. Joseph C. Lincoln. OTD; RePo
Kind pity [*or* Kinde pitty] chokes my spleen[e]; brave scorn forbids. Satire [*or* Satyre] III: On Religion. John Donne. *Fr.* Satires. AnAnS-1; CABA; CABL; FosPo; MaMe; MaPo; MBW-1; MeLP; MeP; MePo; NoP; OBS; PoEL-2; ReEn; ReIE; SCEP-1; SeCP; SeCV-1; SeEP; TuPP
Kind Sir: These Woods ("Kind Sir: This is an old game"). Anne Sexton. GoYe; TPM; TwAmPo
Kind solace in a dying hour! Tamerlane. Poe. AmP; AP; MAmP
Kind voice, A, calls, "Come, little ones." Crocuses. Anna M. Platt. BoTP
Kinde Are Her Answeres. Thomas Campion. *See* Kind Are Her Answers.
Kinde pitty chokes my spleene; brave scorn forbids. *See* Kind pity chokes my spleen . . .
Kindergarten children first come forth, The. The May Day Dancing. Howard Nemerov. NYBP
Kindest and the happiest pair, The. Forbearance. William Cowper. MaRV
Kindle the Christmas brand, and then. The Ceremonies for Candlemas Day. Robert Herrick. EnLit; OAEP
Kindler of glory's embers. In Praise of Aed. *Unknown.* AnIL
Kindliest thing God ever made, The. Shade. Theodosia Garrison. MaRV; OHIP; SoP
Kindly Advice. *Unknown. See* Panther, The.
Kindly cock is the fairies' friend, The. The Cock. Rose Fyleman. UTS
Kindly I envy thy songs perfection. To Mr. R. W. John Donne. AnAnS-1; MaMe
Kindly Neighbor, The. Edgar Guest. PoToHe
"I have a kindly neighbor, one who stands," *sel.* MaRV
Kindly Screen, The. Belle Chapman Morrill. MaRV
Kindly Unhitch That Star, Buddy. Ogden Nash. LiTA; LiTM; PoPl
Kindly Vision. Otto Julius Bierbaum. AWP; JAWP; WBP
Kindly watcher by my bed, lift no voice in prayer. Music. George DuMaurier. CBEP; OBEV (new ed.; OBVV
Kindly word and a tender tone, A. A Gentle Word. *Unknown.* PoToHe (new ed.)
Kindness. Catherine Davis. NYBP
Kindness. T. Sturge Moore. OBMV
Kindness. Sylvia Plath. BoC
Kindness. *Unknown.* SoP; STF
Kindness. Ella Wheeler Wilcox. *See* Better, Wiser and Happier.
Kindness during Life. *Unknown. See* "One Little Rose."
Kindness to Animals. J. Ashby-Sterry. BOHV; InMe; NA
Kindness to Animals. Laura E. Richards. SoPo; TiPo
Kindness to Animals. *Unknown.* BoTP; GoTP; HBV; HBVY; OTPC; PPL; SoPo
Kinds of Shel-fish. William Wood. SCAP
Kinds of Trees to Plant. Spenser. *Fr.* The Faerie Queene, I, i. OHIP
Kine of My Father, The. Dora Sigerson Shorter. OnYI; OxBI
Kinfauns Castle, *sel.* William Montgomerie.
"Is there no vision in a lovely place?" OxBS
King, The. Mary Frances Butts. OQP
King, The. Mary Elizabeth Coleridge. OBVV
King, The. Kipling. CABA; InP; PoVP
"King, a flock is feeding." Montoro's Song against Count Alvaro de Luna, High Constable of Castile. Eduardo Marquina, *tr. by* Dorothea Mackellar. MoAuPo
King Alexander led the van. Allegro. "McM." InMe
King Alfred Answers the Danes. G. K. Chesterton. *Fr.* Ballad of the White Horse. OxBoCh
King Alfred sensed among his country's words. Anglo-Saxon. E. L. Mayo. MiAP
King and his knights went to church [*or* to the church went], The. The Confessions of the Seven Deadly Sins. William Langland. *Fr.* The Vision of Piers Plowman. BEL; EnLi-1 (1949 ed.)
King and Queen of Cantelon. Babylon. *Unknown.* ChTr
King and queen were riding, The. *See* King and the queen were riding, The.
King and the Clown, The. *Unknown, ad. fr. Persian by* Michael Lewis. MaC
King and the queen were riding, The. Child's Song [*or* The Naughty Blackbird]. Kate Greenaway. HBVY; OTPC (1946 ed.); PCH
King Arthur, *sels.* Dryden.
Fairest Isle, *fr.* V, i. CBEP
How Happy the Lover, *fr.* IV, i. LoBV; OnPM; ViBoPo
(Song: "How happy the lover.") SeEP
(Song to a Minuet.) SeCL
Song: "Your hay it is mowed and your corn is reap'd," *fr.* V, i. CEP; SeCV-2
Song of Venus, *fr.* V, i. LoBV; OxBoLi; PoEL-3; SeCeV
King Arthur, *sel.* Richard Hovey.
Hunting Song. HBV
King Arthur and His Round Table, *sel.* John Hookham Frere.
Bees and Monks, *fr.* Canto III. OBRV
King Arthur and King Cornwall. *Unknown.* ESPB *sl. abr.*; OBB
King Arthur, growing very tired indeed. Salad—after Tennyson. Mortimer Collins. CenHV; Par
King Arthur's Death. *Unknown.* ACP
King Arthur's Dream. *Unknown.* ACP
King Arthur's Round Table. John Owen, *tr. fr. Latin by* Thomas Harvey. *Fr.* Four Epigrams. PrWP
King Arthur's Waes-hael. Robert Stephen Hawker. ISi; JKCP; OBEV; OBVV; OxBoCh
King asked, The. The King's Breakfast. A. A. Milne. CenHV
King Berdok. *Unknown.* OxBS
King Borborigmi. Conrad Aiken. MAPA
King Bruce and the Spider. Eliza Cook. OTPC (1923 ed.); PTK; StVeCh (1940 ed.)
(Try Again.) BoTP
King but an' his nobles a', The. Brown Robin. *Unknown.* ESPB; OxBB
King Cahal Mór of the Wine-red Hand. *Tr. by* James Clarence Mangan. *See* Vision of Connaught in the Thirteenth Century, A.
King Canute, *abr.* Thackeray. OTPC
King Charles, and who'll do him right now? Give a Rouse. Robert Browning. Cavalier Tunes, II. BEL; BoLiVe; EnLi-2; EnLit; EPN; HBV; MCCG; OAEP; PoVP; ShBV-1; TOP; VA; ViPo
King Charles he is King James's son. The White Cockade. *Unknown.* OnYI
King Charles II. Earl of Rochester. *See* Epitaph on Charles II.
King Charles the First walked and talked. *Unknown.* OxNR
King Charles upon The Scaffold. Andrew Marvell. *Fr.* An Horatian Ode upon Cromwell's Return from Ireland. ChTr
King Christian. Johannes Evald, *tr. fr. Danish by* Longfellow. AWP; JAWP; WBP
King Cophetua and the Beggar Maid. Don Marquis. HBMV; InMe
King Cotton, *sel.* Sir Leo Money.
"Mills of Lancashire grind very small, The." MaRV; OQP
King Croesus carried to Apollo's sibyl. Oracle at Delphi. Robert Bagg. NePoAm-2
King David. Stephen Vincent Benét. HBMV; TCPD
King David. Walter de la Mare. UnPo (1st ed.)
King David. Heine, *tr. fr. German by* Louis Untermeyer. PoFr
King David and King Solomon. James Ball Naylor. CenHV; GoTP
King David, knowing well. An Example of the Praise of God for His Omnipotency, out of the CXIII Psalm. John Hall. ReIE
King Easter has courted her for her gowd [*or* lands]. Fause [*or* Fa'se] Foodrage [*or* Footrage]. *Unknown.* ESPB; OBB; OxBB
King Edward the Fourth and a Tanner of Tamworth. *Unknown.* BaBo; ESPB
King Edward the Third, *sels.* Blake.
"Let liberty, the charter'd right of Englishmen." PoFr
War Song to Englishmen, A. CH; WaaP
(War Song, A.) OHIP
King Edwards, *with music. Unknown.* SoAmSa
King Edwin's Feast. John White Chadwick. OTPC
King Enjoys His Own Again, The. Martin Parker. OBS
King Estmere. *Unknown.* BuBa; ESPB; OBB; OxBB
King Eternal, The. James Montgomery. MaRV
King Fisher courted Lady Bird. The King-Fisher Song. "Lewis Carroll." *Fr.* Sylvie and Bruno Concluded. RIS

King Francis was a hearty king, and loved a royal sport. The Glove and the Lions. Leigh Hunt. BeLS; EnLit; FaPON; GN; HBV; HBVY; HoPM; MaC; OnSP; OTPC; PCD; PoMa; PTK; StP; TreF; WBLP
King Goodheart. W. S. Gilbert. *See* There Lived a King.
King Hancock sat in regal state. A Song about Charleston. *Unknown.* PAH
King Harald's Trance. George Meredith. PeVV
King Hart, *sel.* Gawin Douglas.
Hart's Castle. AtBAP; PoEL-1
King has called for priest and cup, The. The Last Rhyme of True Thomas. Kipling. OtMeF
King has passed along the great highway, The. The King Passes. Anne Hunter Temple. ChIP
King has written a braid letter, The. Lord Derwentwater. *Unknown.* ESPB
King he hath been a prisoner, The. Willie o Winsbury. *Unknown.* BaBo; ESPB
King he wrytes a luving letter, The. *Unknown.* *Fr.* Johnie Armstrang. PoFr
King Henry. *Unknown.* BaBo; ESPB; OBB; OxBB
King Henry IV, Pt. II, *sels.* Shakespeare.
Cares of Majesty, The. LiTB; TreF
(Soliloquy on Sleep.) FiP
"I'faith, sweetheart, methinks now you are in an excellent good temporality," *abr.* MyFE
My Liege, I Did Deny No Prisoners, *fr.* I, iii. WaaP
(Staff Officer, The.) OtMeF
"Nay, you shall see mine orchard," V, iii. MyFE
"O my worshipful lord, an't please your grace," *fr.* II, i. LO
King Henry V, *sels.* Shakespeare.
Before Agincourt, *fr. Prologue to* IV. ChTr
(Eve of Agincourt, The.) ShBV-3
(Now Entertain Conjecture of a Time.) WaaP
"Boy, bristle thy courage up; for Falstaff he is dead," *fr.* II, iii. LO
(Commonwealth of the Bees, The.) GN
Epilogue: "Thus far, with rough and all-unable pen." CTC
Horse, The, *fr.* III, vii. GoTP
King Henry before the Field of Saint Crispian, *fr.* IV, iii. BBV (1951 ed.)
(King Henry V before the Battle of Agincourt.) PTK
"Marry, if you would put me to verses or to dance," *fr.* V, ii. LO
"O for a Muse of fire, that would ascend," *fr. Prologue to* I. MemP
Muse of Fire, A, 2 *ll.* ChTr
Once More unto the Breach, Dear Friends, Once More, *fr.* III, i. FaBV; PoSa; WaaP
(Blast of War, The.) TrGrPo
(Henry V at Harfleur.) TreF
(Henry V before Harfleur.) ShBV-2
(Henry Fifth's Address to His Soldiers.) WHA
(Henry V to His Soldiers.) PoFS
"Prithee, honey-sweet husband, let me bring thee to Staines," *fr.* II, iii. MyFE
Upon the King, *fr.* IV, i. PPON
King Henry VI, Part I, *sels.* Shakespeare.
King Is Dead, A, *fr.* I, i. ChTr
"Methinks your looks are sad, your cheer appall'd, *fr.* I, ii. FOL
King Henry VI, Pt. II, *sels.* Shakespeare.
Gratitude, 3 *ll., fr.* II, i. MaRV
Thrice Armed ("What stronger breastplate than a heart untainted!"), 4 *ll., fr.* III, ii. MaRV
King Henry VI, Pt. III, *sels.* Shakespeare.
Content ("My crown is in my heart"), 4 *ll., fr.* III, i. MaRV
("My crown is in my heart, not on my head," 3 *ll.*) PoToHe (new ed.)
King Henry VI Yearns for the Simple Life, *fr.* II, v. TreFS
King Henry VIII, *sels.* Shakespeare *and probably* John Fletcher.
Ambition ("Cromwell, I charge thee, fling away ambition"), *fr.* III, ii. TrGrPo
(Higher Loyalty, The.) MaRV
Cranmer's Prophecy of Queen Elizabeth, *fr.* V, v. WGRP
For a Patriot, 3 *ll., fr.* III, ii. PGD
Orpheus with His Lute, *fr.* III, i, *song by* Fletcher, *also at. to* Shakespeare. AtBAP; CBEP; ChTr; ElL; EnRePo; GN; OAEP; OBEV; OTPC; SiCE; TrGrPo; TuPP; ViBoPo
(Music.) FaBoCh
(Orpheus.) PoRL; UnS
(Song: "Orpheus with his lute made trees.") OBS; PoEL-2
Wolsey's Farewell to Cromwell ("Cromwell, I did not think to shed a tear"), *fr.* III, ii.
("Cromwell, I did not think to shed a tear.") InP
(Wolsey.) OTPC (1923 ed.)
(Wolsey's Regrets.) TreFS
Wolsey's Farewell to His Greatness, *fr.* III, ii. OHFP; TIHL
(Cardinal Wolsey's Farewell.) LiTB; MaRV; TreF
(Farewell to All My Greatness.) LiTG
(Farewell to Greatness.) PTK; TrGrPo
King Henry before the Field of Saint Crispian. Shakespeare. King Henry V, *fr.* IV, iii. BBV (1951 ed.)
King Henry Fifth's Conquest of France. *Unknown.* BaBo (*A and B vers.*); ESPB
King Henry VI Yearns for the Simple Life. Shakespeare. King Henry VI, Pt. III, *fr.* II, v. TreFS
King Henry to Rosamond. Michael Drayton. *Fr.* England's Heroical Epistles. OBSC
King Henry was sent for. The Death of Queen Jane (D *vers.*). *Unknown.* BaBo
King Honor's Eldest Son. Elinor Wylie. CoBA
King I saw who walked a cloth of gold, The. Cloth of Gold. F. R. Scott. MoCV
King in His Beauty, The. St. Bernard of Clairvaux, *tr. fr. Latin.* BePJ
King in His Beauty, The. James G. Deck. BePJ
King in May, The. Michael Dennis Browne. NYBP
King Is Dead, A. Shakespeare. King Henry VI, Pt. I, *fr.* I, i. ChTr
"King is gone, The," the old man said. The Deserted Kingdom. Lord Dunsany. AnIV
King is out a-hunting, The. The King's Wood. C. S. Holder. BoTP
King is sick, The. His cheek was red. *See* King was sick, The. His cheek was red.
King James and Brown. *Unknown.* ESPB
King James II. Dryden. *Fr.* The Hind and the Panther. ACP
King Jamie hath made a vow. Flodden Field. *Unknown.* ESPB
King John, *sel.* John Bale.
Wassail, Wassail. ChTr
("Wassail, wassail, out of the milk-pail.") TuPP
King John, *sels.* Shakespeare.
"Go, bear him in thine arms," *fr.* IV, iii. PoG
O Amiable Lovely Death, *fr.* III, iv. TreFT
"O, let us pay the time but needful woe," *fr.* V, vii. PoFr
This England, *fr.* V, vii. BoTP
(England, 2.) OTPC
To Gild Refinèd Gold, *fr.* IV, ii. LiTB; LiTG
(Ridiculous Excess.) TreFT
King John and Matilda, *sel.* Robert Davenport.
Requiem: "Matilda, now go take thy bed." SeCL
("Matilda, now go take thy bed.") TuPP
King John and the Abbot of Canterbury. *Unknown.* BoTP; ESPB; GN; GoTP; HBV; OBB; OnSP; OTPC; RG; StaSt; TrGrPo
(King John and the Abbot.) BoChLi; BOHV; EnSB
(King John and the Bishop.) BaBo; ESPB, *longer vers.*
King John's Castle. Thomas Kinsella. OxBI
King Juke. Kenneth Fearing. PoPo
King Lear, *sels.* Shakespeare.
Blow, Winds, *fr.* III, ii. TrGrPo; WHA
("Blow windes, and crack your cheeks; rage, blow.") AtBAP; FlW
(King Lear to the Storm.) TreFT
Cod-Piece That Will House, The, *fr.* III, ii. ViBoPo
Death of Lear, *fr.* V, iii. FiP
"Good morrow to you both," *fr.* II, iv. AtBAP
He That Has and a Little Tiny Wit, *fr.* III, ii. ViBoPo
"Heere is better then the open ayre, take it thankfully," *fr.* III, vi. AtBAP
"Here is the place my Lord, good my Lord enter," *fr.* III, iv. AtBAP
"Howle, howle, howle, howle: O you are men of stones," *fr.* V, iii. AtBAP
Jolly Shepherd, The, *fr.* III, vi. PCH
King Lear Condemns His Daughter, *fr.* I, iv. TreFT
King Lear Pledges Revenge, *fr.* II, iv. TreFT
Lear and Cordelia, ("Some officers take . . ."), *fr.* V, iii. FiP

"No, no, no, no! Come, let's away to prison," *fr.* V, iii. MemP
"No, they cannot touch me for coyning. I am the King himselfe," *fr.* IV, vi. AtBAP
Poor Naked Wretches, *fr.* III, iii. PPON
"Pray, do not mock me," *fr.* IV, vii. MemP
Take Physic, Pomp, *fr.* III, iv. TrGrPo
(Discovery of Pity.) UnPo (1st ed.)
When Priests Are More in Word, *fr.* III, ii. ViBoPo
"With hey, ho, the wind and the rain," 2 *ll., fr.* III, ii. TiPo (1952 ed.)
King Lear Condemns His Daughter. Shakespeare. *Fr.* King Lear, I, iv. TreFT
King Lear Pledges Revenge. Shakespeare. *Fr.* King Lear, II, iv. TreFT
King Lear to the Storm. Shakespeare. *Fr.* King Lear, III, ii. TreFT
King luikit owre his castle wa', The. Sir Colin. *Unknown.* OxBB
King Louis on his bridge is he. Le Père Sévère. *Unknown.* AWP; JAWP; WBP
King Midas. Howard Moss. CoAP
King Midas. Ovid, *tr. fr. Latin by* Arthur Golding. *Fr.* Metamorphoses, XI. CTC
King Midas Has Asses' Ears. Donald Finkel. NePoEA-2
King might miss the guiding star, A. Far Trumpets Blowing. Louis F. Benson. TRV
King must rule kingdom. Cities are seen from afar. Maxims (Cotton MS.). *Unknown.* AnOE
King o' Spain's Daughter, The. Jeanne Robert Foster. HBMV
King of Ai, The. Hyam Plutzik. LiTM (1970 ed.)
King of Brentford, The. Thackeray, *after* Béranger. HBV; OtMeF
King of Canoodle-Dum, The. W. S. Gilbert. CenHV
King of China's Daughter, The. Edith Sitwell. BoTP; FlW; MoBrPo; PoRh
(Two Nut Trees, 2.) CH
(Variations on an Old Nursery Rhyme.) HBMV; TSW
King of comforts! King of life! Praise. Henry Vaughan. AnAnS-1; MeP
King of Connacht, The. *Unknown, tr. fr. Irish by* Frank O'Connor. KiLC
King of Cuckooz, The. Kenneth Slessor. *Fr.* The Atlas. PoAu-2
King of Denmark's Ride, The. Caroline Norton. BBV; BeLS; GN; HBV; VA
King of Dreams, The. Clinton Scollard. HBV
King of France and four thousand men, The. *Unknown.* PPL
King of France, the king of France, The,/ with forty [*or* fifty] thousand men. Mother Goose. OxNR; RIS
King of glorie, king of peace,/ With the one make warre to cease. L'Envoy. George Herbert. *Fr.* The Church Militant. AnAnS-1; MaMe; MeP; SCEP-1
King of glorie, King of Peace,/ I will love thee. Praise. George Herbert. AnAnS-1; MaMe; MeP
King of hell came singing, The. Lucifer. Maxwell Anderson. MoRP
King of Ireland's Son, The. Nora Hopper. AnIL
King of Kings, The. Lon Woodrum. BePJ
King of Love, The. Henry W. Baker. BePJ; MaRV; SoP
(Lord Is My Shepherd, The.) ThGo
King of mercy, King of love. Begging. Henry Vaughan. AnAnS-1; MeP
"King of Morven," Carthon said, "I fall in the midst of my course." James Macpherson. *Fr.* Carthon. EnPE
King of my life, I crown Thee now. Lead Me to Calvary. Jennie Evelyn Hussey. SoP
King of stars. The Open Door. *Unknown.* KiLC
King of Sunshine, The. Michael Silverton. PV
King of the Belgians. Marion Couthouy Smith. PAH
King of the Cradle, The. Joseph Ashby Sterry. HBV
King of the Rainy Country, The. Baudelaire, *tr. fr. French by* Edna St. Vincent Millay. WoL
King of the sea, and Ruler of the shore. Dedication of a Ship. Macedonius. OnPM
King of the Wood, The. Clifford Dyment. POTi
King of Thule, The. Goethe, *tr. fr. German by* James Clarence Mangan. *Fr.* Faust. AWP; JAWP; WBP
King of Ulster, The. *Unknown, tr. fr. Irish by* Frank O'Connor. KiLC
King of waters, the sea shouldering whale, The. William Wood. SCAP
King of Yvetot, The. Pierre Jean de Béranger, *tr. fr. French by* William Toynbee. AWP; JAWP; WBP; WoL
—— *Tr. by* Thackeray. OnPP; RIS
King, oh boon for my aspiring mind, A! Another, of Another Mind. "F. M." TuPP
King Olaf's Death-Drink. Longfellow. Tales of a Wayside Inn: The Musician's Tale, Pt. I, xxi. AmPP (4th ed.)
King Olaf's Return. Longfellow. Tales of a Wayside Inn: The Musician's Tale, Pt, I, ii. AmPP (4th ed.)
King Olaf's War-Horns. Longfellow. Tales of a Wayside Inn: The Musician's Tale, Pt. I, xix. AmPP (4th ed.); PFY
King on the Tower, The. Ludwig Uhland, *tr. fr. German by* Thackeray. OBVV
King Orpheo. *Unknown.* BuBa; ESPB; OBB; OxBoLi
(King Orfeo.) OxBB
King Paladin plunged on his moon-coloured mare. Mad Marjory. Hugh McCrae. PoAu-1
King Passes, The. Anne Hunter Temple. ChIP
King Philip had vaunted his claims. A Ballad to Queen Elizabeth. Austin Dobson. ALV; GTBS; OBVV; ShBV-2
King Philip's Last Stand. Clinton Scollard. PAH
King Richard II, *sels.* Shakespeare.
Dying Men ("The tongues of dying men"), *fr.* II, i. MaRV
"For heaven's [*or* God's] sake, let us sit upon the ground," *fr.* III, ii. HoPM; PoFr
(Death of Kings, The.) TrGrPo
(Let's Talk of Graves.) DiPo
(Of the Death of Kings.) ChTr
(Richard II's Dejection.) TreFS
Perils of Darkness, *fr.* III, ii. TreFT
Richard II Banishes Bolingbroke, *fr.* I, iii. PoFS
This England, *fr.* II, i. HT; PTK; TreF; TrGrPo
(England.) OTPC
(John of Gaunt's Dying Speech, *longer sel.*) FiP
(This Blessed Plot . . . This England.) FaBV
(This Royal Throne of Kings.) ShBV-2; YAT
King Richard III, *sels.* Shakespeare.
Address of Richard III to His Army, The, *fr.* V, iii. UnPo (1st ed.)
Dream of Wrecks, A, *fr.* I, iv. ChTr
(Methought I Saw a Thousand Fearful Wrecks, *shorter sel.*) EtS
Evil Designs, *fr.* I, i. TreF
(Hate the Idle Pleasures.) TrGrPo
"Go, gentlemen, every man unto his charge," *fr.* V, iii. FOL
"In God's name, cheerly on, courageous friends," *fr.* V, ii. PoFr
"My conscience hath a thousand several tongues," *fr.* V, iii. MemP
"Why, then, 'tis time to arm and give direction," *fr.* V, iii. PoFr
King Richard hearing of the pranks. The King's Disguise and the Friendship with Robin Hood. *Unknown.* ESPB
King Robert of Sicily. Longfellow. Tales of a Wayside Inn: The Sicilian's Tale, Pt. I. AnNE; BeLS; MWA-1; OHIP; OnSP; PCD; YT
(Sicilian's Tale, The.) AP
King Rufus. Y. Y. Segal, *tr. fr. Yiddish by* A. M. Klein. WHW
King sent for his wise men all, The. W. James Reeves. ChTr
King sent his lady on the first Yule day, The. The Yule Days. *Unknown.* ChTr
King Shall Come, The. *Unknown.* SoP
King Siegfried sat in his lofty hall. The Three Songs. Bayard Taylor. StPo
King sits in Dunfermline [*or* Dumferling] town [*or* toune], The. Sir Patrick Spens [*or* Spence] *Unknown.* AnFE; AtBAP; ATP; AWP; BaBo (A *and* B *vers.*); BBV (1923 ed.); BEL; BoChLi; BuBa; CABA; CABL; CaFP; CBEP; CBV; CH; CoBE; DiPo; ELP; EnL; EnLi-1; EnLit; EnRP; EnSB; ESPB; EtS; ExPo; FaBoCh; FlW; ForPo; FosPo; GN; GoJo; GoTS; HBV; HoPM; ILP; InP; InPo; InvP; JAWP; LiTB; LoBV; LoGBV; MCCG; NoP; OAEP; OBB; OBEV; OnSP; OtMeF; OTPC (1946 ed.); OuHeWo; OxBB; OxBS; PAn; PIA; PoAn; PoEL-1; PoIE; PoMA; PoPo; PoRA; PoSa; RG; RoGo; SeCeV; ShBV-1; StP; TiPo (1952 ed.); TOP; TreF; TrGrPo; UnPo; ViBoFo (A *and* B *vers.*); ViBoPo; WBP; WHA; YAT
King Solomon and King David. *Unknown.* RIS, *diff. vers.*
King Solomon, before his palace gate. Azrael (The Spanish Jew's

King (continued)
Tale). Longfellow. *Fr.* Tales of a Wayside Inn. AnAmPo; MWA-1
King Solomon stood in the house of the Lord. The Dead Solomon. John Aylmer Dorgan. AA
King Solomon was the wisest man. A Song of Solomon. Josephine Preston Peabody. NP
King Stephen. Robert Graves. WaKn
King stood crowned, The; around in the gate. The Crowning of Arthur. Charles Williams. FaBoMo
King to Oxford sent a troop of horse, The. Oxford & Cambridge [*or* Epigram]. Sir William Browne. ALV; WhC
King Triumphant. Isaac Watts. *See* Jesus Shall Reign Where'er the Sun.
King walked in his garden green, The. The Three Singing Birds. James Reeves. PDV; PoMS
King was embarked along with a Persian slave, A. Purgatory May Be Paradise. Sadi. OuHeWo
King was frightened, The. Cynewulf. *Fr.* Elene. YAT
King was on his throne, The. The Vision of Belshazzar. Byron. FOL; GN; HBV; OnMSP; OTPC; RoGo; TOP
King was [*or* is] sick, The. His cheek was red. The Enchanted Shirt. John Hay. BBV; BLPA; BOHV; GN; GoTP; MaC; OnSP; OTD; PaPo; RePo; TiPo (1952 ed.); TSW
King was sitting on his throne, A. King Henry Fifth's Conquest of France (B *vers.*). *Unknown.* BaBo
King William and King James. *Unknown.* *See* William of Orange; or, The Battle of Boyne.
King William Was King George's Son, *with music.* *Unknown.* OuSiCo
King Winter sat in his Hall one day. Outside. Hugh Chesterman. BoTP
King with all his kingly train, The. Louis XV. John Sterling. BeLS; VA
King Witlaf's Drinking-Horn. Longfellow. CoBa; MWA-1
Kingcups. Eleanor Farjeon. GBV (1952 ed.)
Kingcups. Sacheverell Sitwell. MoBrPo
Kingdom, The. Thomas Curtis Clark. ChIP; MaRV
Kingdom. Sir Edward Dyer. *See* My Mind to Me a Kingdom Is.
Kingdom, The, *sels.* Louis MacNeice.
"Little dapper man but with shiny elbows, A." ChMP
"Under the surface of flux and of fear there is an underground movement." LiTM
Kingdom, The. Jon Swan. NYBP
Kingdom of God, The. Rab, *tr. fr. Hebrew.* TrJP
Kingdom of God, The. Francis Thompson. *See* In No Strange Land.
Kingdom of God, The. Richard Chenevix Trench. WBLP
Kingdom of God on Earth, The. John W. Chadwick. *See* Hymn: Eternal Ruler. . .
Kingdom of Heaven. Léonie Adams. MAP; MoAB; MoAmPo
Kingdom of Heaven, The. G. K. Chesterton. OQP
Kingdom of Number is all boundaries, The. W. H. Auden. *Fr.* Numbers and Faces. ImOP
Kingdom Within, The. Percy Clough Ainsworth. MaRV
Kingdoms. Godfrey Fox Bradby. *See* In Hoc Signo.
Kingdoms. Charles Oluf Olsen. OQP
Kingdoms fall in sequence, like the waves on the shore, The. The Sparrow's Skull. Ruth Pitter. EaLo
Kingdoms of the Earth go by, The. In Hoc Signo [*or* Kingdoms]. Godfrey Fox Bradby. ChIP; MaRV; SoP; TRV
Kinge Arthur lives in merry Carleile, and seemely is to see. The Marriage of Sir Gawain. *Unknown.* BaBo; ESPB; OBB
Kingfisher, The. W. H. Davies. BoPe; GTBS-D; MoVE; OBEV (new ed.); POTE; ShBV-2; TSW
Kingfisher, The. Blanche Mary Kelly. GoBC
Kingfisher, The. Andrew Marvell. *Fr.* Upon Appleton House. AtBAP; ChTr; FaBoEn
King-Fisher Song, The. "Lewis Carroll." *Fr.* Sylvie and Bruno Concluded. RIS
Kingfishers, The. Charles Olson. NeAP; OPoP
Kingis Quair [*or Quhair*], *The, abr.* James I, King of Scotland. MeEV; OxBS, *abr.*
Sels.
"Blissit mot be the heye goddis all." AtBAP
He Sees His Beloved, *longer sel.* PoEL-1
(Coming of Love, The.) GoTS
Walking under the Tour, 3 *sts.* SeCePo
"Worshipe, ye that lovers been, this May," 7 *ll.* TrGrPo
(Spring Song of the Birds.) OBEV
Kingly lyon, and the strong arm'd beare, The. William Wood. SCAP
Kingly were his rags, his uniform. The Drug Addict. Miriam Waddington. *Fr.* Three Prison Portraits. ACV
Kings, The. Louise Imogen Guiney. GoBC; HBV; MAP; MoAmPo (1942 ed.)
Kings. Joyce Kilmer. WHL
Kings. John Richard Moreland. ChIP; MaRV
Kings. *Unknown, tr. fr. Sanskrit by* Arthur W. Ryder. *Fr.* The Panchatantra. AWP; PoFr
("In sensuous coil.") LiTW
Kings/ like golden gleams. A History Lesson. Miroslav Holub. FIW
Kings and Tyrants. Robert Herrick. PoFr
Kings Are Passing Deathward, The. David Morton. OQP
King's Ballad, The. Joyce Kilmer. HBV
King's Breakfast, The. A. A. Milne. CenHV
King's College Chapel. Charles Causley. BoC; MuSP; POTi
Kings come riding home from the Crusade, The. Crusade. Hilaire Belloc. GoBC
King's Daughter, *sel.* V. Sackville-West.
Greater Cats, The GTBS-D; OBMV; POTE; ShBV-4
("Greater cats with golden eyes, The.") LO
King's Disguise, and Friendship with Robin Hood, The. *Unknown.* ESPB
King's Dochter Lady Jean, The. *Unknown.* ESPB
King's Entertainment, The, *sel.* Thomas Dekker.
Troynovant. LoBV
King's Epitaph, The. Earl of Rochester. *See* Epitaph on Charles II.
Kings from the East, The. Heine, *tr. fr. German.* ChTr; ACV; GoTS, *tr. into Scottish by* Alexander Gray
King's Highway, The. John Masefield. BLRP; TRV
King's Highway, The. John Steven McGroarty. HBV; HT
King's Hunt Is Up, The. William Gray. *See* Hunt Is Up, The.
Kings live in palaces, and pigs in sties. Habitations. Hilaire Belloc. PV
King's Missive, The. Whittier. PAH
King's most faithful Subjects we, The. England's Truimph; or, The Subjects' Joy. *Unknown.* CoMu
Kings must be dauntless; subjects will contemn. Upon Kings. Robert Herrick. PoFr
Kings of Europe, The; a Jest. Robert Dodsley. CEP
Kings of France. Mary W. Lincoln. BLPA
Kings of the earth are men of might, The. Kings. Joyce Kilmer. WHL
Kings of the East, The. Katharine Lee Bates. ChIP, *abr.*; MaRV; OQP; WGRP
King's Own Regulars, The. *Unknown.* PAH
King's poet was his captain of horse in the wars, The. Mount Badon. Charles Williams. FaBoTw
King's Quhair, The. James I, King of Scotland. *See* Kingis Quair, The.
King's Ring, The. Theodore Tilton. *See* Even This Shall Pass Away.
Kings River Canyon. Kenneth Rexroth. NaP
King's Son, The. Thomas Boyd. AnIV; OBMV; OxBI
Kings they came from out the south, The. Christmas Carol. Sara Teasdale. ChrBoLe; StJW
King's Tragedy, The. Dante Gabriel Rossetti. EPN; PoVP; TOP; ViPo
King's Visit, The. William Morris. *Fr.* The Earthly Paradise. VA
Kings' wares; and dreams; and April dusks. The Portrait of a Florentine Lady. Lizette Woodworth Reese. HBMV
Kings who without control the sceptre sway'd. George Wither. *Fr.* The Conquered King. PoFr
Kings, who would have good subjects, must. Loyalty. W. H. Davies. BrPo
King's Wood, The. C. S. Holder. BoTP
King's X. Hollis Summers. StP
King's young dochter was sitting in her window, The. The King's Dochter Lady Jean. *Unknown.* ESPB
Kingship is passing down the yellow road. Bonfire of Kings. Donald Evans. AnAmPo
Kingston Church. Thomas D'Urfey. SeCL
Kinkaiders, The. *Unknown.* AS, *with music*; CoSo
Kinmont Willie. *Unknown.* BaBo; BEL; ESPB; OBB; OxBB
Kinnaird Head. George Bruce. NeBP
Kinnereth. "Rachel," *tr. fr. Hebrew by* A. M. Klein. LiTW; TrJP

Kinsey! Thy pages studiously rehearse. Volume II (Kinsey). David Daiches. SiTL
Kinship. Sir Charles G. D. Roberts. CaP
Kinship. Edward H. S. Terry. MaRV; OQP
Kinship with the Stars. George Meredith. *Fr.* Modern Love, IV. GTBS-W
Kinsman. Jean Ingelow. MaRV
Kiph. Walter de la Mare. TiPo (1959 ed.)
Kirby with Muckby-cum-Sparrowby-cum Spinx. A Lincolnshire Tale. John Betjeman. FiSC
Kirk's Alarm, The. Burns. OxBoLi
Kiss, A. Austin Dobson. *Fr.* Rose-Leaves. ALV; EnLit; HBV; InP; MoBrPo (1942 ed.)
Kiss, A. William Drummond of Hawthornden. ElL
Kiss, The ("For love's sake, kiss me once again"). Ben Jonson. *See* Begging Another, on Colour of Mending the Former.
Kiss, The ("Oh, that joy so soon should waste"). Ben Jonson. *See* Song: "O, that joy so soon should waste."
Kiss, The. Pierre Louys, *tr. fr. French by* Horace M. Brown. *Fr.* The Songs of Bilitis. UnTE
Kiss, The. Tom Masson. BOHV
Kiss, The. Thomas Moore. BoLP; EnLoPo
Kiss, The ("My ghostly father"). Charles d'Orléans. *See* My Ghostly Father.
Kiss, The. Coventry Patmore. *Fr.* The Angel in the House, II, viii, 3. ALV; EnLoPo; FiBHP; MemP; MeWo
Kiss, The. Dante Gabriel Rossetti. The House of Life, VI. LiTL; MaVP; OBVV; PoVP; Sonn; VP; UnTE
("What smouldering senses in death's sick delay.") ViPo
Kiss, The. Siegfried Sassoon. MMA; NP
Kiss, The. Thomas Shipman. CLwM
Kiss, The. Sara Teasdale. HBV
Kiss, A ("He's my doll"). *Unknown, tr. fr. Irish by* Frank O'Connor. KiLC
Kiss, The ("O keep your kisses, young provoking girl!"). *Unknown, tr. fr. Late Middle Irish by* the Earl of Longford. OnYI; OxBI
Kiss, The. George Wither. *See* Stolen Kiss, A.
Kiss and the Cup, The. *Unknown, tr. fr. Greek by* Louis Untermeyer. UnTE
Kiss-Fest, The. Irwin Edman. InMe
Kiss her, kiss her, kiss her a thousand times. Ersatz. Raymond Souster. PeCV
Kiss I begged, A; but, smiling, she. Weeping and Kissing. Sir Edward Sherburne. SeCL; SeEP
Kiss, if you can: Resistance if she make. Ovid. *Fr.* Art of Love. ErPo
Kiss in the Rain, A. Samuel Minturn Peck. BOHV
Kiss in the Ring. *Unknown.* OxBoLi
Kiss is maypole where my seven, The. First Cycle of Love Poems, III. George Barker. MoPo
Kiss, lovely Celia, and be kind. Love's Courtship. Thomas Carew. UnTE
Kiss Me Again. Henry Blossom. TreFT
Kiss me but once, and in that space supreme. Love's Kiss. Helen Hay Whitney. AA
Kiss Me, Dear. Dryden. *See* Rondelay: "Chloe found Amyntas lying."
Kiss me softly and speak to me low. To My Love. John Godfrey Saxe. HBV
Kiss [*or* Kisse] me, sweet: the wary [*or* warie] lover. To Celia [*or* To the Same]. Ben Jonson. AnAnS-2; AWP; ElL; EnRePo; JAWP; LiTL; LO; LoBV; SCEP-2; SeCP; SeCV-1; UnTE; WBP
Kiss me then, my merry May. Medieval Norman Songs, III. *Unknown, tr. by* John Addington Symonds. AWP
"Kiss me there where pride is glistening." Aria. Delmore Schwartz. ErPo
Kiss me, though you make believe. Make Believe. Alice Cary. HBV
Kiss my grey hair, oh, my love. Healing. Abraham Reisen. LiTW; TrJP
Kiss of death by water or desire, The. Sailor. P. K. Page. ACV
Kiss of God, The. G. A. Studdert-Kennedy. BLRP
Kiss thou nor deny'st, nor givest one, A. To Polla. John Owen. *Fr.* Four Epigrams. PrWP
Kiss'd Yestreen. *Unknown.* ErPo; OtMeF
Kisse, The. Robert Herrick. CavP
Kisse me, sweet; the warie lover. *See* Kiss me, sweet; the wary lover.
Kissed me from the saddle, and I still can feel it burning. The Smoke-blue Plains. Badger Clark. YaD
Kisses. *At. to* Thomas Campion. ElL; OBSC
(Kisses Make Men Loath to Go.) LiTL; UnTE
(My Love Bound Me.) TuPP
(Song: "My Love bound me with a kiss.") HBV
Kisses. William Strode. NeHB
Kisses Desired. William Drummond of Hawthornden. EnLoPo
Kisses in the Train. D. H. Lawrence. CBV; MoAB; MoBrPo
Kisses Make Men Loath to Go. *At. to* Thomas Campion. *See* Kisses.
Kisses upon your breast, like water from a jug. Vorobyev Hills. Boris Pasternak, *tr. by* J. M. Cohen. OnHM
Kissin'. *Unknown.* BoLP; FiBHP; LiTG; LiTL; MeWo; SiTL; TreF
(Kissing's No Sin.) HBV; UnTE
Kissing. Lord Herbert of Cherbury. EnLoPo; LiTL; ViBoPo
Kissing and Bussing. Robert Herrick. OAEP
Kissing the Dancer. Robert Sward. CoPo
Kissing's No Sin. *Unknown. See* Kissin'.
Kit Carson. Arthur Guiterman. OTD
Kit Carson's Last Smoke. "Stanley Vestal." PoOW
Kit Carson's Ride. Joaquin Miller. AmPP (3d ed.); TreFS
Kit Hath Lost Her Key. *Unknown.* UnTE
Kit Logan and Lady Helen. Robert Graves. HBMV
Kit, the recording angel wrote. Kitty's "No." Arlo Bates. Conceits, II. AA
Kitchen. Alden Van Buskirk. YAP
Kitchen Clock, The. John Vance Cheney. BOHV
Kitchen fire that wakes so soon, The. Fires. Elizabeth Fleming. BoTP
Kitchen Prayer, A. M. Petersen. STF
Kitchen Window. J. E. H. MacDonald. CaP; TwCaPo
Kitchenette Building. Gwendolyn Brooks. BALP; NoP; PoNe
Kitchie-Boy, The. *Unknown.* BaBo; ESPB
Kite, The. Harry Behn. FaPON; RePo; TiPo (1959 ed.)
Kite, The. Fang Che Chai, *tr. fr. Chinese by* Henry H. Hart. OnPM
Kite. David McCord. PDV
Kite, The. Pearl Forbes MacEwen. BoTP
Kite, The. José Moreno Villa, *tr. fr. Spanish by* Eleanor L. Turnbull. OnPM
Kite, A. Frank Dempster Sherman. *See* Wish, A.
Kite, The. Mark Strand. NYBP
Kite. Hollis Summers. NYTB
Kite, A. *Unknown.* SoPo; TiPo
Kite, a sky, and a good firm breeze, A. Kite Days. Mark Sawyer. BrR; SiSoSe; TiPo
Kite and a string, A. She Would. Dixie Willson. GFA
Kite Days. Mark Sawyer. BrR; SiSoSe; TiPo
Kite Is a Victim, A. Leonard Cohen. SD
Kite of rags, A. Contrast. Issa. PoFr
Kite Poem. James Merrill. NoP; TwCP
Kite Tales. Rose Waldo. GFA
Kite, while devouring a skylark, A. The Stupid Kite. Allen Upward. *Fr.* Scented Leaves from a Chinese Jar. NP
Kites. Michael Brownstein. ANYP
Kit's conscience shall ne'er bring him in trouble. In Christophorum. Thomas Freeman. SiCE
Kit's Cradle. Juliana Horatia Ewing. CIV; SAS, *abr.*
Kitten, The. Joanna Baillie. CIV
Kitten, A. Eleanor Farjeon. TiPo
Kitten, The. Ogden Nash. FaPON; MoShBr; WhC
Kitten and Falling Leaves, The. Wordsworth. CIV, *much abr.*; PTK
Sels.
"See the kitten on the wall." PRWS, *shorter sel.*
(Kitten at Play, The.) BoTP; FaPON; MPB (1956 ed.); OTPC
(Kitten Playing with the Falling Leaves, The.) GoTP
"That way look, my infant, lo!" HBVY
Kitten and Firefly. Marie Grimes. CIV
Kitten at Play, The. Wordsworth. *See* Kitten and Falling Leaves, The.
Kitten once to its mother said, A. The Robber Kitten. *At. to* George M. Baker. CIV; FTB
Kitten Playing with the Falling Leaves, The. Wordsworth. *See* Kitten and Falling Leaves, The.
Kitten Speaks, The. William Brighty Rands. *See* Cat of Cats, The.

Kitten went a-walking, A. A Serious Question. Carolyn Wells. CIV
Kittens, The. F. Hey. SAS
Kittens. Catherine Parmenter. CIV
Kitten's Night Thoughts. Oliver Herford. BoChLi; MPB
"Kittens, now I'll find names for you." The Kittens. F. Hey. SAS
Kitten's Thought, A. Oliver Herford. RIS
Kittiwakes and cormorants go to sleep, The. Nightfall in Inishtrahull. Daniel James O'Sullivan. NeIP
Kitty. Elizabeth Prentiss. *See* Long Time Ago.
Kitty Bhan. Edward Walsh. ACP
Kitty Caught a Hornet. Leroy F. Jackson. UTS
Kitty Hawk, *sel.* Robert Frost.
But God's Own Descent. EaLo; MoRP
Kitty in the Basket. Eliza Lee Follen. SAS
Kitty, Kitty,/ Wash your paws. *Unknown.* RIS
Kitty, Kitty Casket. *Unknown.* *See* Itiskit, Itaskit.
"Kitty, Kitty, you mischievous elf." Both Sides. Mary Abigail Dodge. CIV
Kitty Neil. John Francis Waller. HBV; VA
Kitty of Coleraine. *Unknown, at. to* Charles Dawson Shanly *and to* Edward Lysaght. BOHV; HBV; MCCG; OnYI; StPo
Kitty Wants to Write. Gelett Burgess. BOHV
Kitty: What She Thinks of Herself. William Brighty Rands. *See* Cat of Cats, The.
Kitty's Laugh. Arlo Bates. Conceits, I. AA
Kitty's "No." Arlo Bates. Conceits, II. AA
Kivers. Ann Cobb. AmFN
Klaxon. James Reaney. TwCaPo
Kleptomaniac. Leonora Speyer. AnAmPo; HBMV
Klockius. John Donne. MaMe
Klondike, The. E. A. Robinson. PaA; PAH; ThLM
Klondike Miner, The. *Unknown.* IHA
Knapsack Trail, The. Edwin Osgood Grover. OQP
Knapweed. A. C. Benson. HBV; VA
Knave's a knave, A. The True Tar. Henry Carey. WaPE
Knee-Deep in June. James Whitcomb Riley. AmePo; OHFP
Knee Lunes. Robert Kelly. CoPo
Kneel down, fair Love, and fill thyself with tears. A Ballad of Death. Swinburne. MaVP; PoVP
Kneel then with me, fall worm-like on the ground. Night. George Chapman. *Fr.* The Shadow of Night. OBSC
Kneeling Camel, The. Anna Temple Whitney. BLPA; FaChP
(And So Should You.) STF
(Purpose of Prayer, The.) SoP
(Rest and Work.) MaRV
(Submission and Rest.) BLRP
Kneeling he spoke the names he loved the most. A Martyr's Mass. Alfred Barrett. GoBC; JKCP (1955 ed.)
Knell. George Chapman. MaRV
Knell, The. George Herbert. MaMe
Knell, The. Muhammad Al-Fituri, *tr. fr. Arabic by* Samir M. Zoghby. TTY
Knell nor deep minute-gun gave the world warning. Cid of the West. Edna Dean Proctor. DD
Knell of Whitehead tolls, The—his cares are past. Written in the Spring of 1785 on the Death of the Poet Laureate. Anna Seward. Sonn
Knell that dooms the voiceless and obscure, The. Survival. Florence Earle Coates. AA
Knew the Master. James Reeves. MuSP
Knew'st thou the edicts which forbade these things? The Higher Command. Sophocles. *Fr.* Antigone. MaRV
Knicht had two sons o sma fame, A. Sir Lionel (B *vers.*). *Unknown.* ESPB
Knife, The. Milton Kaplan. TrJP
Knife, The. "J. R." MoAuPo
Knife-Grinder, The. George Canning *and* John Hookham Frere. *See* Friend of Humanity and the Knife-Grinder, The.
Knife within his hand he stood, A. Chicago Idyll. E. Merrill Root. AnAmPo
Knight, A. Chaucer, *See* Canterbury Tales, The: Prologue. *mod. vers. by* Louis Untermeyer.
Knight, The. Sister Maryanna. WHL
Knight and a lady, A/ Went riding one day. *Unknown.* BoTP
Knight and a Lady Bride, A, *with music.* *Unknown.* BFSS
Knight and a lady once met in a grove, A. Sympathy. Reginald Heber. BeLS; BOHV
Knight and Shepherd's Daughter[s], The (A *and* B *vers.*). *Unknown.* BaBo; ESPB
(Knight and the Shepherd's Daughter, The.) ViBoFo
Knight and the Lady, The. "Thomas Ingoldsby." *Fr.* The Ingoldsby Legends. BOHV
Knight and the Shepherd's Daughter, The. *Unknown.* *See* Knight and Shepherd's Daughter, The.
Knight, Death, and the Devil, The. Randall Jarrell. CrMA
Knight Fallen on Evil Days, The. Elinor Wylie. MAP; MoAmPo
Knight from the world's end, The. A Dream of Governors. Louis Simpson. NYBP; PoSa
Knight had ridden down from Wensley Moor, The. Hart-Leap Well. Wordsworth. BeLS; MyFE
Knight in Disguise, The. Vachel Lindsay. HBV
Knight in the Bower, The. *Unknown.* *See* Heron, The.
Knight in the Wood, The. Lord De Tabley. NCEP; PeVV
Knight knock'd at the castle gate, The. Desire. William Cornish. EG; OBSC; SeCeV
Knight of Bethlehem, A. Henry Neville Maugham. *Fr.* The Husband of Poverty. ChIP; MaRV; OQP
(Song: "There was a Knight of Bethlehem.") BoTP
Knight of Curtesy, The, *sel.* *Unknown, tr. fr. Middle English by* Pearl London.
Eaten Heart, The. TrGrPo
Knight of Ghosts and Shadows, A. Dunstan Thompson. NePA
Knight of Liddesdale. *Unknown.* ESPB
Knight of the Burning Pestle, The, *sels.* Beaumont *and* Fletcher.
"Better music ne'er was known," *fr.* V, iii. SiCE; TuPP
Come, You Whose Loves Are Dead, *fr.* IV, iv. AtBAP; ElL; SiCE; TuPP
Jillian of Berry, *fr.* IV, v. ElL
(Merrythought's Song: "For Jillian of Berry.") OBS
Merrythought's Song: "I would not be a serving man," *fr.* IV, v. OBS
Mirth, *fr.* II, viii. ElL
("Tis mirth that fills the veins with blood.") SiCE
(Laugh and Sing.) TrGrPo
Month of May, The, *fr.* IV, v. ChTr
"Nose, nose, jolly red nose," *fr.* I, iii. FaBoCh; LoGBV
Knight of the Grail, The. *Unknown.* *See* Falcon, The.
Knight of the Holy Ghost, he goes his way. In Memory of G. K. Chesterton. Walter de la Mare. GoBC
Knight Olaf. Heine, *tr. fr. German by* Christa Wolf *and* Virginia Tufte. HW
Knight Stained from Battle, The. William Herebert. MeEL
Knight stands in the stable-door, The. Young Johnstone. *Unknown.* BaBo; ESPB
Knight there was, and that a worthy man, A. A Knight [*or* Seven Pilgrims]. Chaucer. *Fr.* The Canterbury Tales: Prologue. GoTP; MaC; TrGrPo
Knight, with Umbrella. Elder Olson. FiBHP
Knight without a Name, The. *Unknown.* WiR
Knightes Tale, The. Chaucer. *See* Knight's Tale, The.
Knightliest of the knightly race, The. The Virginians of the Valley. Francis Orrery Ticknor. AA; AnAmPo; DD; HBV; PaA; PAH
Knightly Code, The. Eustache Deschamps, *tr. fr. French by* Daniel J. McKenna. CAW
Knights Errant. Sister Mary Madeleva. CAW
Knight's Ghost, The. *Unknown.* ESPB
Knight's Leap, The. Charles Kingsley. PCD; StPo
Knight's Prayer, The. Sarum Primer. *See* God Be in My Head.
Knight's Song, The. *Unknown.* *See* Wandering Knight's Song, The.
Knight's [*or* Knightes] Tale, The. Chaucer. *Fr.* The Canterbury Tales. BEL; GoTL; TOP
Sels.
Arcite's Farewell, *mod. vers. by* John Hall Wheelock. LiTL
"Allas the Wo! Allas, the peynes stronge." LO
Emily's Prayer to Diana. MyFE
"I am, thow woost, yet of thy compaignye." PoG
Knights to Chrysola, The. Rachel Annand Taylor. OBVV
Knight's Toast, The. *At. to* Sir Walter Scott. PCD
Knight's Tomb, The. Samuel Taylor Coleridge. CBEP; EnRP; EPN; ERoP-1; FaBoCh; GN; InP; LoGBV; ShBV-1
Knightsbridge of Libya. Sorley Maclean. NeBP
Knitting is the maid o' the kitchen, Milly. The Kitchen

Clock. John Vance Cheney. BOHV
Knob and hump upon this tree. A Gnarled Riverina Gum-Tree. Ernest G. Moll. PoAu-2
Knock at the door [*or* doorie]. *Unknown.* OxNR; SAS
"Knock-me-down sermon, and worthy of Birch, A." An Old Buffer. Frederick Locker-Lampson. CenHV
Knock on the forehead. Strawberry Blond. Bill Berkson. ANYP
Knock on Wood. Henry Dumas. BF
Knocking at the Door. John Freeman. HBMV
Knolege, aquayntance, resort, favour with grace. Knowledge, Acquaintance. John Skelton. NCEP
Knot, The. Adrienne Rich. NoP
Knot, The. Henry Vaughan. ISi
Knot of Blue and Gray, A. *Unknown.* PEDC
Knot of knaves are early met together, A. Henry Parrot. SiCE
Knot which first my heart did strain, The. Sir Thomas Wyatt. FCP; SiPS
Knotting Song, The. Sir Charles Sedley. *See* Hears Not My Phyllis.
Know all to whom these few sad lines shall come. Sir Aston Cokayne. ReEn
Know, Celadon, in vain you use. Song. "Ephelia." CavP
Know Celia, (since thou art so proud). Ingrateful[l] Beauty Threatned. Thomas Carew. AnAnS-2; BWP; EG; EP; EnLi-1; HBV; InvP; LO; MeLP; OBEV; OBS; SCEP-2; SeCP; SeCV-1; SeEP; TOP
"Know, he assists the cause of God, who toils." Jerusalem Delivered, IV. Tasso. PoFr
Know I not who thou mayst be. At the Hacienda. Bret Harte. AA
Know in Vain. Dante Gabriel Rossetti. *See* Known in Vain.
Know It Is Christmas. Lois Snelling. BiCB
Know lady that my life depends. *Unknown.* SeCSL
Know That I Am God. Lon Woodrum. SoP
Know, that I would accounted be. To Ireland in the Coming Times [*or* Apologia Addressed to Ireland]. W. B. Yeats. BrPo; OxBI
Know that the age of Pyrrha is long passed. Patrick Moloney. Sonnets—Ad Innuptam, IV. BoAu
Know the world by heart. Theory of Poetry. Archibald MacLeish. AP
Know then, I was born in a strange country. To My People. Edwin Seaver. TrJP
Know Then Thyself. Pope. An Essay on Man, Epistle II. DiPo, 18 *ll.*; LiTB, *fr.* II *and* IV; LiTG, *fr.* II *and* IV; MaRV, 18 *ll.*; MemP, 18 *ll.*; OBEC, 18 *ll.*; SeCePo, 18 *ll.*
("Know then thyself, presume not Got to scan.") AnFE; *fr.* II *and* IV; CaFP, 18 *ll.*; EnLi-1 (1949 ed.); EnLit; ExPo; GoTL; MaPo; PAn; PG (1955 ed.); PoEL-3; PoIE, *longer sel.*; PoSa, 18 *ll.*; SoP, 18 *ll.*; TOP, *abr.*; TrGrPo, 18 *ll.*; TRV, 18 *ll.*; ViBoPo, 18 *ll.*; YAT
(Lines from "An Essay on Man," 18 *ll.*) GoBC
(Man, 18 *ll.*) BoLiVe
(Paragon of Animals, The, 18 *ll.*) ACP
(Proper Study of Man, The, 18 *ll.*) TreFS
(Proper Study of Mankind, The, 30 *ll.*) FiP
(Riddle of the World, 18 *ll.*) FaFP; GTBS-W
Know then with horses twain, one sound, one lame. Charles Cotton. *Fr.* Epistle to John Bradshaw Esq. PeRV
Know this./ Spent bullets die. Manifesto of the Soldier Who Went Back to War. Angel Miguel Queremel. PoFr; WaaP
Know thou, O Virgin, noble-blest. Prudentius. *Fr.* Cathemerinon. ISi
Know, 'twas well said, that spirits are too high. Sir Francis Kynaston. EG
Know Ye Not That Lovely River. Gerald Griffin. OnYI
Know ye not that ye are the temple of God. Ye Are the Temple of God. First Corinthians, Bible, *N.T.* TreFT
Know ye the land where the cypress and myrtle. The Bride of Abydos. Byron. BEL; MCCG; OAEP
Know ye the willow-tree. The Willow-Tree. Thackeray. BOHV; CenHV; HBV
Know you faire on what you looke. On Mr. G. [*or* George] Herberts Booke Intituled the Temple. Richard Crashaw. AnAnS-1; MaMe; MeP; OxBoCh; SCEP-1; SeCV-1
Know you her secret none can utter? Alma Mater. Sir Arthur T. Quiller-Couch. OBVV
Know you that land where forest shadows fold. Mignon. Goethe. *Fr.* Wilhelm Meister. LiTW
Knowed him more 'n twenty year'. Greeting for Two. James W. Foley. IHA
Knowest Thou Isaac Jogues? Francis W. Grey. CAW
Knowest thou the land where bloom the lemon trees. Mignon [*or* Mignon's Song]. Goethe. *Fr.* Wilhelm Meister. AWP; JAWP; WBP
Knowing All Ways, including the Transposition of Continents. Charles Olson. FRC
Knowing the heart of man is set to be. Samuel Daniel. *Fr.* To the Lady Margaret Countesse of Cumberland. FaBoEn
Knowing this man, who calls himself comrade. Definition. Edwin Rolfe. NAMP
Knowing too little. Three Organ Rituals for Erik Satie. Robert Kelly. YAP
Knowing What Time It Is at Night. Louise Townsend Nicholl. PG (1955 ed.)
Knowing what's possible, one knows. Empty House. Elizabeth J. Coatsworth. FiSC
Knowledge. Louise Bogan. HBMV
Knowledge. Thomas Curtis Clark. OQP
Knowledge. Frederic W. H. Myers. *Fr.* Saint Paul. OQP
("Whoso has felt the Spirit of the Highest.") FaChP; TRV
Knowledge. Frederick George Scott. VA
Knowledge. Whittier. *See* Bible, The.
Knowledge, Acquaintance. John Skelton. NCEP
Knowledge after Death. Henry Charles Beeching. OBVV; VA
Knowledge and Reason. Sir John Davies. *See* Much Knowledge, Little Reason.
Knowledge and wisdom, far from being one. Wisdom. William Cowper. *Fr.* The Task, VI. MaRV
Knowledge of Age. Margaret Avison. PeCV
Knowledge of Light, The. Henry Rago. PoCh
Knowledge Studies Others. *Unknown, at. to* Lao-tzu, *tr. fr. Chinese by* Witter Bynner. *Fr.* Tao Teh King. OnPM
Knowledge through Suffering. George Wallace Briggs. MaRV
Knowledge without Wisdom. T. S. Eliot. *See* Eagle Soars in the Summit of Heaven, The.
Knowledgeable Child, The. L. A. G. Strong. OBMV
Knowlt Hoheimer. Edgar Lee Masters. *Fr.* Spoon River Anthology. OxBA
Known in Vain. Dante Gabriel Rossetti. The House of Life, LXV. EnLi-2; MaVP; PoVP; ViPo
Known of Him. Barbara Cornet Ryberg. SoP
Known Soldier, The. Kenneth Patchen. WaaP
Known World, The. Brewster Ghiselin. MoVE
Knows he that never took a pinch. To My Nose. Alfred A. Forrester. BLPA; BOHV
Know'st thou not. Perils of Darkness. Shakespeare. *Fr.* King Richard II, III, ii. TreFT
Know'st thou not at the fall of the leaf. Autumn Song. Dante Gabriel Rossetti. ViBoPo; YAT
Know'st thou the land where the fair citron blows. Mignon. Goethe, *tr. by* Edgar A. Bowring. *Fr.* Wilhelm Meister. PoPl
Know'st thou this, souldier? "Tis a much chang'd plant." Upon the Crowne of Thorns [or Upon the Thornes Taken downe from our Lords Head Bloody]. Richard Crashaw. MaMe
Knoxville, Tennessee. Nikki Giovanni. BOLo
Kochia. Thomas Hornsby Ferril. NePoAm-2
Koheleth. Louis Untermeyer. TrJP
Κοινα τὰ τῶν Φίλων (Koina ta ton Philon). John Addington Symonds. OBVV
Kojiki, *sel.* *Unknown,* *tr. fr. Japanese by* Donald L. Philippi. Metal Hoe Hill. HW
Kokin Shu [*or* Sho], *sels.* *Tr. fr. Japanese by* Arthur Waley.
"Although it is not plainly visible to the eye." Fujiwara no Toshiyuki. AWP; JAWP; WBP
"Beloved person must I think, The." Ki no Akimine. AWP
"Did I ever think." Ono no Takamura. AWP
"Hoping all the time." *Unknown.* AWP
"If only, when one heard." *Unknown.* AWP; LiTW
"My love/ Is like the grasses." Ono no Yoshiki. AWP; LiTW
(Unknown, *tr. by* Basil Hall Chamberlain.) OnPM
"O cuckoo." *Unknown.* AWP
"Since I heard/ Faintly the voice." Mitsune. AWP
"Thing which fades, A." Ono no Komachi. AWP; JAWP
"When the dawn comes." *Unknown.* AWP
Ko-Ko's Song ("As some day it may happen that a victim must be

Ko-Ko's (continued)
found"). W. S. Gilbert. *Fr.* The Mikado. LiTB; SiTL
(They'll None of 'em Be Missed.) EnLi-2 (1949 ed.); PoVP
Ko-Ko's Song ("On a tree by a river a little tom-tit"). W. S. Gilbert. *See* Suicide's Grave, The.
Ko-Ko's Song ("There is beauty in the bellow of the blast"), *much abr.* W. S. Gilbert. *Fr.* The Mikado. PCD
Kol Nidra. Joseph Leiser. *Fr.* The Day of Atonement. AA; TrJP
Kookaburra, *sel.* T. Inglis Moore.
"Over the multiple terrors of Mars." NeLNL
"Kookoorookoo! kookoorookoo!" Christina Rossetti. *Fr.* Sing-Song. RIS
Kora for March 5th. Lewis MacAdams. ANYP
Koran, The, *sel.* Mohammed, *tr. fr. Arabic by* J. M. Rodwell.
Teaching of Mohammed, The. WoL
Kore. Robert Creeley. CoPo; NMP; OPoP
Kore. Frederic Manning. HBV; LoBV, *wr. at. to* Ezra Pound
Korea. Vincent Buckley. BoAV
Korea Bound, 1952. William Childress. AmFN
Korean Woman Seated by a Wall, A. William Meredith. NePoEA
Korf's Joke ("Korf invents a novel kind of joke"). Christian Morgenstern, *tr. fr. German by* Max Knight. ELU
Kolendy for Christmas. *Unknown, tr. fr. Polish by* Irena Dalgiewicz. CAW
Korosta Katzina Song. *Unknown, tr. fr. Hopi Indian by* Natalie Curtis. AWP; JAWP
Koskiusko. Samuel Taylor Coleridge. EnRP; Sonn
Kossuth. James Russell Lowell. FOL
Kotatsu, from which to watch, A. Issa. Satirical Poems on Daimyos, I. PoFr
Kraken, The. Tennyson. CABA; CaFP; GTBS-D; MBW-2; OBNC; OBRV; PeER; Po; PoEL-5; PoG; PoVP; SyP; VaPo; ViPP; WiR
Krankenhaus of Leutkirch, The. Richmond Lattimore. NYBP
Krazy; Reflection No. 5. "Baron Ireland." PoMa
Kree. A. C. Gordon. AA
Kris Kringle. Clinton Scollard. ChBR; GaP
Krishna. "Æ." *See* Oversoul.
Krishna, Krishna,/ Now as I look on. Considerations of Murder [*or* Debate between Arjuna and Sri Krishna]. *Unknown. Fr.* Bhagavad-Gita. LiTW; WaaP
Krishnakali. Rabindranath Tagore. ACV
Kriss Kringle. Thomas Bailey Aldrich. BoChLi (1939 ed.); HBVY; MPB; PEDC; TSW
Ku Kluck Klan, *with music.* Lawrence Gellert. TrAS
Ku Klux. Madison Cawein. AA; PAH; ThLM
Ku Li. "Robin Hyde." AnNZ
Ku! Listen! In Alahiyi you repose, O Terrible Woman. Sacred Formula to Attract Affection. *Unknown.* LiTA
Kubla Khan; or, A Vision in a Dream. Samuel Taylor Coleridge. AnFE; AtBAP; ATP; AWP; BBV; BEL; BoC; BoLiVe; CABA; CaFP; CBEP; CBV; CH; ChER; ChTr; CoBE; DiPo; ELP; EnL; EnLi-2; EnLit; EnRP; EPN; ERoP-1; ExPo; FaBoBe; FaBoCh; FaBoEn; FaBV; FaFP; FaPL; FiP; ForPo; GBV (1952 ed.); GN; GoJo; GTBS-W; GTSL; HBV; HoPM; HT; ILP; InP; InPo; InvP; JAWP; LiTB; LiTG; LoBV; LoGBV; MaC; MasP; MBW-2; MCCG; MemP; MERP; MyFE; NeHB; NoP; OAEP; OBEV; OBNC; OBRV; OtMeF; OTPC; OuHeWo; PAn; PG (1945 ed.); PIA; Po; PoAn; PoE; PoEL-4; PoFS; PoIE; PoPl; PoRA; PP; PTK; RG; RoGo; SeCeV; ShBV-3; StP; SyP; TDP; ThWaDe; TOP; TreFS; TrGrPo; UnPo (3d ed.); ViBoPo; WBP; WHA
("In Xanadu did Kubla Khan.") EG
Kukkuu, kukkuu, sounds the distant voice. Two Folk Songs, 2. *Unknown.* LiTW
Kunai-mai-pa Mo. Ethel Anderson. PoAu-2
Kung walked/ by the dynastic temple. Canto XIII. Ezra Pound. CMoP
Kupris bears trophies away. Sophocles. *Fr.* Women of Trachis. CTC
Kyng Jamy/ Jamy your joye is all go. A Ballade of the Scottyshe Kynge. John Skelton. CoMu
Kyrie. David Gascoyne. *Fr.* Miserere. NeBP
Kyrie Eleison! The Funeral of Philip Sparrow. John Skelton. *Fr.* Phyllyp Sparowe. ACP
"Kyrie, so kyrie." Jolly Jankin [*or* Jankin, the Clerical Seducer]. *Unknown.* EnPo; MeEL; NoP; OxBoLi
Kyrielle. John Payne. HBV

L

La Bagarède. Galway Kinnell. NYBP
La Bella Bona Roba. Richard Lovelace. AtBAP; CavP; FosPo; PIA; PoEL-3; SeCP
La Bella Donna della Mia Mente. Oscar Wilde. UnTE
La Belle Confidente. Thomas Stanley. FaBoEn; MeLP; MePo; OBS
La Belle Dame sans Merci. A. R. D. Fairburn. AnNZ
La Belle Dame sans Merci. Keats. AnFE; AtBAP; ATP; AWP; BBV; BEL; BeLS; BoLiVe; CABA; CBEP; CBV; CH; ChTr; CLwM; CoBE; DiPo; DTo; ELP; EnL; EnLi-2; EnLit; EnRP; ERoP-2; ExPo; FaBoBe; FaBoCh; FaFP; FiP; ForPo; FosPo; GBV; GoJo; GoTP; GTBS-D; GTBS-P; GTBS-W; GTSE; GTSL; HBV; HoPM; ILP; InP; InPo; InvP; JAWP; LiTB; LiTG; LO; LoBV; LoEn; LoGBV; MasP; MaC; MBW-2; MCCG; MemP; MERP; MyFE; NoP; OAEP; OBEV; OBMV; OBNC; OBRV; OnSP; OtMeF; OTPC (1923 ed.); PAn; PeER; PG; PIA; PoAn; PoE; PoEL-4; PoeP; PoFS; PoIE; PoPo; PoRA; PoSa; RG; SeCeV; ShBV-3; SiSw; StP; StPo; TOP; TrGrPo; TreFT; UnPo; VaPo; WaKn; WePo; WHA; WoL
(Ballad: La Belle Dame sans Merci.) ViBoPo
La Belle Ennemie. Thomas Stanley. CavP
La Belle Sauvage. John Hunter-Duvar. *Fr.* De Roberval. OBCV
La Bête Humaine. James Kirkup. NeBP
La Bohème. Dick Gallup. ANYP
La Carte. Justin Richardson. ELU; FiBHP; SiTL
La Ci Darem la Mano. John Frederick Nims. MiAP
La Condition Botanique. Anthony Hecht. NePoEA
La Corona. John Donne. AnAnS-1; MaMe; MeP; OBS; Sonn
La Creazione Degli Animali. John Malcolm Brinnin. NYTB
La Crosse at Ninety Miles an Hour. Richard Eberhart. AmFN
La Donna E Mobile. "A. K." FiBHP; InMe
La Donna E Perpetuum Mobile. Irwin Edman. FiBHP; NYBP
La Fayette. Samuel Taylor Coleridge. Sonn
La Fayette. Dolly Madison. PAL; ThLM
La Figlia Che Piange. T. S. Eliot. AWP; BoLiVe; BWP; CLwM; CoAnAm; FaBoTw; LiTA; MAP; MaPo (1969 ed.); MoAmPo (1942 ed.); MWA-2; NP; PG (1945 ed.); PoIE; POTE; ReMP; ViBoPo
La Fraisne. Ezra Pound. NP; PG (1933 ed.)
La Fuite de la Lune. Oscar Wilde. *Fr.* Impressions. Po; PoVP; SyP
La Galisse now I wish to touch. The Happy Man. Gilles Ménage. BOHV
La Gialletta Gallante; or, The Sun-burn'd Exotique Beauty. Lord Herbert of Cherbury. AtBAP
La Gioconda, by Leonardo Da Vinci, in the Louvre. "Michael Field." PeVV
La Grande Jatte; Sunday Afternoon. Thomas Cole. NePoAm
La Grisette. Oliver Wendell Holmes. AA; HBV
La Guerre. E. E. Cummings. MAP; MoAB; MoAmPo
O Sweet Spontaneous, II. AnNE; AP; BoLiVe (1945 ed.); CBV; NoP
(O Sweet Spontaneous Earth.) OxBA; TrGrPo
La' laha, il Allah! The Three Khalandeers. James Clarence Mangan. OBVV;
La Madonna di Lorenzetti. John Williams Andrews. HBMV
La Male Regle de T. Hoccleve, *sel.* Thomas Hoccleve.
"I dar nat telle how that the fressh repeir." EnPo
La Mélinite: Moulin-Rouge. Arthur Symons. PeVV; SyP
La Mer. Oscar Wilde. SyP
La Nuit Blanche. Kipling. MoBrPo
La Perouse. William Hart-Smith. BoAu
La Plata chants silver, The/ Where its glittering waters roll. Rivers of the West. "Sunset Joe." PoOW
La Preciosa. Thomas Walsh. ISi
La Prière de Nostre Dame. Chaucer. *See* A. B. C., An.
La Rose des Vents. Richard Wilbur. MiAP
La Rue de la Montagne Sainte-Geneviève. Dorothy Dudley. HBMV

La Saisiaz, *sel.* Robert Browning.
Prologue. PoVP
La Torre. Charles Olson. FRC
La Tricoteuse. George Walter Thornbury. BeLS
La Vie C'est la Vie. Jessie Redmond Fauset. BANP; CDC; PoNe
Labor. James Russell Lowell. *Fr.* A Glance behind the Curtain. MaRV
(Work.) PEDC; PoSC
Labor. Frances Sargent Osgood. PEDC; PoRL
Labor ("We have fed you all"). *Unknown.* PGD; OQP
Labor and Capital. William Dean Howells. AmePo
Labor and Love. Sir Edmund Gosse. HBV
Labor Day. Marnie Pomeroy. PoSC
Labor is wealth—in the sea the pearl groweth. Labor. Frances Sargent Osgood. PEDC; PoRL
Labor Not in Vain. *Unknown.* STF
Labor of Fields. Elizabeth J. Coatsworth. TiPo (1959 ed.)
Labor raises honest sweat. The Dignity of Labor. Robert Bersohn. PoPl; WhC
Labor Song. Denis Florence MacCarthy. *Fr.* The Bell-Founder. DD
Labor sweet that I sustained in thee, The. To the Translation of Palingenius. Barnabe Googe. EnRePo
Laborare Est Orare. Francis Albert Rollo Russell. *See* Rise!
Laboratory, The; Ancien Régime. Robert Browning. ATP; BoLiVe; OBEV (new ed.); OBVV; PoFS; PoVP; ShBV-3; ViPo; ViPP; YT
Laboratory Midnight, The. Reuel Denney. ImOP; NePA
Laboratory Poem. James Merrill. NePoEA-2; TwCP
Laborer, The. Richard Dehmel, *tr. fr. German by* Jethro Bithell. AWP; JAWP; WBP; WoL
Laborer, The. José Maria de Heredia, *tr. fr. French by* Wilfrid Thorley. AWP; JAWP; WBP
Labourer, The ("There he goes, tacking against the fields"). R. S. Thomas. BoPe; POTi
Labourer, A ("Who can tell his years, for the winds have stretched"). R. S. Thomas. ToPo
Labourer in the Vineyard, The. Stephen Spender. NeBP
Laborer, The, to the lady: Yes, there are. Madonna; 1936. John Louis Bonn. ISi
"Laborers Together with God." Lucy Alice Perkins. BLRP
Labouring man, that tills the fertile soil, The. Pains and Gains. Edward de Vere, Earl of Oxford. ElL
Labors of Hercules, The. Marianne Moore. AnAmPo; OxBA
Laburnum. Humbert Wolfe. MoBrPo
Labyrinth, The. W. H. Auden. GTBS-W; LiTA; LiTM (rev. ed.); NePA; SiTL
Labyrinth, The. Edwin Muir. CMoP; MoBrPo (1962 ed.); PoIE
Lace Curtains, The. Lewis MacAdams. ANYP
Lace Maker, The. Barbara Howes. NYTB
Lace Pedlar, The. Catherine A. Morin. BoTP
Lacedemonian Instruction. Blake. ERoP-1
Lacemaker, The (Vermeer). Anne Marx. GoYe
Lachesis. Kathleen Raine. NYBP
Lachin y Gair. Byron. OxBS
Lachrimae. *Unknown.* AtBAP
("Flow my teares fau from your springs.") SeCSL
Lachrymae. David Gascoyne. *Fr.* Miserere. AtBAP; BoW; NeBP; POTE
Lachrymae Christi. Hart Crane. ReMP
Lachrymae Musarum. Sir William Watson. *See* Lacrimae Musarum.
Lachrymatory, The. Charles Tennyson Turner. VA
Lack of Steadfastness. Chaucer. CBEP; NoP; PoLi
(Lak of Stedfastnesse.) AWP; ILP
Lackey Bill. *Unknown.* CoSo
Lacking my love, I go from place to place. Amoretti, LXXVIII. Spenser. ElL; ViBoPo
Lacking samite and sable. Christmas Carol. May Probyn. ACP; CAW; GoBC; HBMV; ISi; OBVV
Lacking Sense, The. Thomas Hardy. CMoP; PoEL-5
Lacquer Liquor Locker, The. David McCord. FiBHP; InMe
Lacrimae Musarum. Sir William Watson. HBV; VA
(Lachrymae Musarum.) PoVP
Lad came to the door at night, The. The True Lover. A. E. Housman. A Shropshire Lad, LIII. ATP; BoLiVe; LiTL; MeWo; PoVP
Lad of the Curly Locks. *Unknown, tr. fr. Irish by* Frank O'Connor. KiLC
Lad Philisides, The. A Country Song. Sir Philip Sidney. *Fr.* Arcadia. FCP; OBSC; SiPS
Lad That Is Gone, A. Robert Louis Stevenson. *See* Sing Me a Song.
Lad, you took the soul of me. Lindbergh. Angela Morgan. DD
Ladd I the dance a midsomer day. A Night with a Holy-Water Clerk. *Unknown.* MeEL
Ladder, The. Gene Baro. NePoEA-2
Ladder, The. Leonora Speyer. HBMV; PG
Ladder, flag, and amplifier. Corner Meeting. Langston Hughes. CAD
Ladder of Saint Augustine, The. Longfellow. SoP
Heights, The, *br. sel.* TreF
Ladder to Thrift, The. Thomas Tusser. ReIE; SiCE
Laddie, little laddie, come with me over the hills. A Cry from the Canadian Hills. Lilian Leveridge. BLPA
Laden with yellowing pears. The Half of Life. Friedrich Hölderlin. LiTW
Ladie Greensleeves. *Unknown.* *See* Greensleeves.
Ladie stude in her bour-door, The. Young Hunting (C *vers.*). *Unknown.* ESPB
Ladies, The. Kipling. ALV; EnLit; MoBrPo; TreFT; ViPP
Ladies' Aid, The. *Unknown.* PoLF
Ladies and gentleman:/ This broadcast comes to you from the city. Voice of the Studio Announcer. Archibald MacLeish. *Fr.* The Fall of the City. HoPM; MoAmPo
Ladies and gentleman/ Whose mother is no more. Complaint on the Oblivion of the Dead. Jules Laforgue. LiTW
Ladies at a ball. Glimpse in Autumn. Jean Starr Untermeyer. StVeCh (1940 ed.); TSW
Ladies by Their Windows. Donald Justice. TwAmPo
Ladies' Eyes Serve Cupid Both for Darts and Fire. "A. W." OBSC
Ladies, Farewell! James Howard. *Fr.* The English Monsieur. SeCL
Ladies, fly from Love's smooth tale! Good Advice. Thomas Carew. MeWo
Ladies, I do here present you. A Present to a Lady. *Unknown.* ErPo
Ladies in the Dinin' Room, *with music.* *Unknown.* OuSiCo
Ladies men admire, The, I've heard. Some Beautiful Letters: Interview. Dorothy Parker. InMe
Ladies of London, both wealthy and fair. Advice to the Ladies of London in the Choice of Their Husbands. *Unknown.* CoMu
Ladies of St. James's, The. Austin Dobson. HBV; PoRA; PoVP; VA
Ladies of the morning gauze their mouths, The. Canonical Hours. William Dickey. CoAP
Ladies rose, The. I held the door. The Dean's Consent. Coventry Patmore. *Fr.* The Angel in the House. VA
Ladies that guild the glittering noon. The General Eclipse. John Cleveland. AnAnS-2
Ladies That Have Intelligence in Love. Dante, *tr. fr. Italian by* Dante Gabriel Rossetti. La Vita Nuova, X. AWP; LiTW; OuHeWo; WoL
Ladies, though to your conquering eyes. Song. George Etherege. *Fr.* The Comical Revenge. HBV; LO; OBEV (1st ed.); OBS
Ladies, to this advice give heed. A Maxim Revised. *Unknown.* BLPA; NeHB; WBLP
Ladies, well I deem, delight. My Lady Nature and Her Daughters. Cardinal Newman. GoBC
Ladies, where were your bright eyes glancing. Imogen. Sir Henry Newbolt. HBMV
Ladies You See Time Flieth. *Unknown.* EnRePo
Lads and lasses gathering. The Willow-Boughs. Aleksandr Blok. BoTP
Lads in Their Hundreds, The. A. E. Housman. A Shropshire Lad, XXIII. ATP (1953 ed.); CoBMV; MasP; MoBrPo; Po; PoVP; UnPo (1st ed.); VP
Lad's Love. Esther Lilian Duff. HBMV
Lads of Wamphray, The. *Unknown.* BaBo; ESPB
Lads were hanging baskets, The. The May Basket. Dora Read Goodale. PCH
Lady, The. Elizabeth J. Coatsworth. InP; MaC
Lady, A. Amy Lowell. MAP; MAPA; MoAmPo; NeMA; NP
Lady,/ Baby. *Unknown.* OxNR

Lady Adeline Amundeville. Byron. Don Juan, XIII. PoEL-4
Lady Again Complains, The. Earl of Surrey. SiPS
("Good ladies, you that have your pleasure in exile.") FCP
Lady Alice. *Unknown.* ESPB (A, B *and* C *vers.*); OBB
Lady Alice, Lady Louise. The Blue Closet. William Morris. NBM; PoVP; VA; ViPo; ViPP
Lady Alice was sitting in her bower window. Lady Alice. *Unknown.* ESPB; OBB
Lady and an Ape, A. W. S. Gilbert. GBV
Lady and Crocodile. Charles Burgess. NePoAm-2
Lady and gentlemen fays, come buy! Nephon's Song [*or* The Elfin Pedlar]. George Darley. *Fr.* Sylvia. BoTP; VA
Lady and Queen and Mystery manifold. Ballade to Our Lady of Czestochowa. Hilaire Belloc. ACP (1952 ed.); ISi
Lady and the Bear, The. Theodore Roethke. GoJo
Lady and the Dwarf-King, The. *Unknown. See* Hind Etin.
Lady and the Magpie, The. *Unknown, tr. fr. Chinese by* Arthur Waley. AtBAP
Lady and the Swine, The. *Unknown. See* Lady Who Loved a Swine, The.
Lady Anne Bathing. Anthony Delius. PeSA
Lady Anne Bothwell's Lament. *Unknown. See* Balow.
Lady Anne Dewhurst on a crimson couch. Daughters of Philistia. Walter C. Smith. *Fr.* Olrig Grange. VA
Lady Apple Blossom. Apple Blossom. Kate Louise Brown. GFA; OTPC (1946 ed.)
Lady April. Richard Le Gallienne. YeAr
Lady, as I know thy power. Song to the Virgin Mary. Pero López de Ayala. CAW
Lady asks me, A. Canzone: Donna Mi Priegha. Guido Cavalcanti. CTC; LiTW
Lady Bates. Randall Jarrell. MiAP
"Lady, beside the great green wall of sea." Hymn to Venus. Edith Sitwell. FaBoMo
Lady-Bird. *See* Ladybird.
Lady-Bug. *See* Ladybug.
Lady Byron's Reply to Lord Byron's "Fare Thee Well." *Unknown.* BLPA
Lady came to a bear by a stream, A. The Lady and the Bear. Theodore Roethke. GoJo
Lady Clara V. de V., The. An Answer. Henry S. Leigh. YT
Lady Clara Vere de Vere. Tennyson. HBV; PoVP; YT
Nobility, *br. sel.* OTPC (1946 ed.)
Lady Clara Vere de Vere! The Wedding. Tom Hood. BOHV; InMe
Lady Clare. Tennyson. BeLS; FaPON; GoTP; HBV; LoEn; OnMSP; OTPC; StPo; StVeCh
Lady Comes to an Inn, A. Elizabeth J. Coatsworth. MAP; MoAmPo; NeMA; StPo
Lady Complains of Her Lover's Absence, A. Earl of Surrey. *See* Complaint of the Absence of Her Lover Being upon the Sea.
Lady Day. Padraic Fallon. NeIP
Lady Day in Harvest. Sheila Kaye-Smith. ISi
Lady Day in Ireland. Patrick J. Carroll. JKCP
Lady Diamond. *Unknown.* BaBo; ESPB
Lady, do not hold your parasol. By the Beautiful Sea. Thomas Cole. NePoAm-2
Lady Dying in Childbed, A. Robert Herrick. EG
Lady dying of diabetes, A. The Mechanical Optimist. Wallace Stevens. NAMP
Lady Elspat. *Unknown.* BuBa; ESPB; OBB
Lady Erskine sits in her chamber. Child Owlet. *Unknown.* ESPB
Lady fair, of lineage high, A. A Lady and an Ape. W. S. Gilbert. GBV
Lady farewell, whom I in silence serve. A Poem Put into My Lady Laiton's Pocket. Sir Walter Ralegh. FCP; SiPs
Lady Feeding the Cats, *sel.* Douglas Stewart.
"Shuffling along in her broken shoes from the slums." FlW
Lady Flower, *with music. Unknown.* BFSS
Lady Fortune is both friend and foe, The. Fortune. *Unknown.* ACP
Lady Franklin's Lament, 2 *vers., with music. Unknown.* ShS
Lady from Harlem, The. Malcolm Cowley. NP
Lady Geraldine's Courtship. Elizabeth Barrett Browning. DTo
Lady, giver of bread. Litany to Our Lady. Caryll Houselander. ISi
Lady Godiva. Edward Shanks. HBMV
Lady Greensleeves. *Unknown. See* Greensleeves.
Lady! helpe, Jesu! mercy. In His Utter Wretchedness. John Audelay. MeEL
Lady hold your horses, sit down in your seat. Driver Saying. Josephine Miles. FiMAP
Lady I Know, A. Countee Cullen. *See* For a Lady I Know.
Lady, I loved you all last year. A Song of Impossibilities. Winthrop Mackworth Praed. BOHV; InMe; NA
Lady, I thank thee. Look on Me with Thy Sweet Eyes. *Unknown.* MeEV
Lady, I thank thee for thy loveliness. The Moonstar. Dante Gabriel Rossetti. The House of Life, XXIX. MaVP; PoVP; ViPo; VP
Lady, I trust it is not to do harm. A Volume of Chopin. James Picot. PoAu-2
Lady, if grace to me so long be lent. He Hopes That Time Will Render Her More Merciful. Petrarch. Sonnets to Laura: To Laura in Life, XI. EnLi-1; OuHeWo
Lady, If You So Spight Me. *Unknown.* ReIE
Lady in Kicking Horse Reservoir, The. Richard Hugo. CoAP
Lady in the Barbershop, The. Raphael Rudnick. NYBP
Lady! in whose heroic port. Ode to a Lady Whose Lover Was Killed by a Ball. Byron. ERoP-2
Lady Is Cold, The. E. B. White. HT
Lady is smarter than a gentleman, maybe, A. Trial and Error. Phyllis McGinley. SiTL
Lady Isabel. *Unknown.* BaBo; ESPB
Lady Isabel and the Elf-Knight (*diff. versions*). *Unknown.* BaBo (A, B, *and* C *vers.*); ESPB (A, B, *and* H *vers.*); OAEP; OBB; ViBoFo (A *and* B *vers.*)
(False-hearted Knight, The.) BaBo
(Pretty Polly, *with music.*) BFSS (B *vers.*)
(Sweet William, A *vers., with music.*) BFSS
Lady Jane (Sapphics). Sir Arthur Quiller-Couch. FiBHP; InMe; WhC
Lady Jane was tall and slim, The. The Knight and the Lady. "Thomas Ingoldsby." *Fr.* The Ingoldsby Legends. BOHV
Lady! Lady!/ Upon Heaven-height. In a Boat. Hilaire Belloc. ISi
Lady, lady, should you meet. Some Beautiful Letters: Social Note. Dorothy Parker. BOHV; InMe
Lady Lazarus. Sylvia Plath. NaP
Lady Lost. John Crowe Ransom. AnFE; CoAnAm; MAP; MoAB; MoAmPo; NeMA; OA; PoSa; TrGrPo; TwAmPo
Lady loved a swaggering rover, A. Pirate Treasure. Abbie Farwell Brown. EtS
Lady, lovely lady. Vain and Careless. Robert Graves. LOW
Lady M. M——'s Farewel to Bath. Lady Mary Wortley Montagu. EiCL
Lady Maisdry was a lady fair. Lord Ingram and Chiel Wyet (C *vers.*). *Unknown.* ESPB
Lady Maisry. *Unknown.* BaBo (A *and* B *vers.*); ESPB (A *and* B *vers.*); OBB; OxBB; ViBoFo
Lady Maisry lives intill a bower. Thomas o Yonderdale. *Unknown.* ESPB
Lady Margaret sat in her bower-door. Prince Heathen (B *vers.*). *Unknown.* ESPB
Lady Margaret sat in her bowry all alone. Sweet William's Ghost (B *vers.*). *Unknown.* ViBoFo
Lady Margaret sits in her bower door. Hind Etin. *Unknown.* BaBo (A *vers.*); ESPB
Lady Margery May sits in her bower. Prince Heathen. *Unknown.* ESPB
Lady Mary. Henry Alford. VA
Lady Mary, blissful Dame. The Mother of God. *Unknown. Fr.* Horologium. ISi
Lady Mary Villers lyes [*or* lies], The. Epitaph on the Lady Mary Villers [*or* Villiers]. Thomas Carew. AnAnS-2; CavP; OAEP; OBEV; SCEP-2; SeCL; SeCV-1; SeEP; ViBoPo
Lady may allow me be so bold, A. Hope for Miracles. Wolfram von Eschenbach. LiTW
Lady Mine. Herbert Edwin Clarke. BOHV
Lady Moon, The. Kate Louise Brown. BoTP
Lady Moon. Kate Kellogg. PPL
Lady Moon. Richard Monckton Milnes. BoTP; MoShBr; OTPC; PCH; PRWS; SAS, *st.* 1
Lady Moon. Christina Rossetti. *See* O Lady Moon.
Lady moon is sailing, The. The Lady Moon. Kate Louise Brown. BoTP

Lady moon, lady moon, sailing so high! Lady Moon. Kate Kellogg. PPL
Lady Moon, Lady Moon, where are you roving? Lady Moon, Richard Monckton Milnes. BoTP; MoShBr; OTPC; PCH; PRWS; SAS
Lady, my lady, come from out the garden. To a Certain Lady, in Her Garden. Sterling A. Brown. CDC
Lady of Arngosk, The. *Unknown.* ESPB
Lady of Carlisle, The, *with music.* *Unknown.* OuSiCo
Lady of Castlenoire. Thomas Bailey Aldrich. BeLS; LoEn
Lady of Heaven. Guittone d'Arezzo, *tr. fr. Italian by* Dante Gabriel Rossetti. CAW
Lady of Heaven and earth, and therewithal. His Mother's Service to Our Lady. Villon, *tr. by* D. G. Rossetti. AWP; CAW; CTC; ISi; LiTW
Lady of Heaven, the mother glorified. Lady of Heaven. Guittone d'Arezzo. CAW
Lady of High Degree, A. *Unknown, tr. fr. French by* Andrew Lang. AWP
Lady of Letters. Raymond F. Roseliep. ISi
Lady of Lidice. Fray Angelico Chavez. ISi; JKCP (1955 ed.)
Lady of Life, The. Thomas Michael Kettle. ACP; JKCP (1926 ed.)
Lady of Light, I would admit a dream to you. The Buried Lake. Allen Tate. CrMA
Lady of O. James J. Galvin. ISi
Lady of Peace. Fray Angelico Chavez. ISi
Lady of Shalott, The. Tennyson. AnFE; ATP (2 *vers.*); BEL; BeLS; BoLiVe; CABL; DiPo; EnL; EnLi-2; EnLit; EPN; FaFP; FiP; FosPo; GBV; GN; GTSL; HBV; InP; LiTG; MaC; MaVP; MBW-2; MCCG; OAEP; OBEV; OBRV, *diff. vers.*; OBVV; OnSP; OTPC; PAn; PoE; PoVP; RG; SeCeV; ShBV-1; TOP; TreF; ViPo; ViPP; VP; WePo; WHA; WiR
Lady of sorrow! What though laughing blue. Grey. Archibald T. Strong. BoAu
Lady of the Lake, The, *sels.* Sir Walter Scott.
  Alice Brand, *fr.* IV. HBV; HBVY; OnMSP; OTPC (1946 ed.)
  Boat Song, *fr.* II. BEL; EnLi-2 (1949 ed.); OAEP; PeER; PoEL-4
    (Hail to the Chief Who in Triumph Advances!) EnRP
  Chase, The, *fr.* I. EnRP
  Coronach, *fr.* III. AnFE; BEL; CH; EnLi-2 (1949 ed.); EnLit; EnRP; GTBS; GTBS-D; GTBS-P; GTBS-W; GTSL; HBV; InP; OAEP; OBRV; OHIP; PCD; PoRA; ShBV-1; TOP; TreFS; TrGrPo; ViBoPo; WHA; WiR; YAT
    ("He is gone upon the mountain.") EPN
  Harp of the North. Prologue. EnLi-2 (1949 ed.); ILP; ViBoPo
    ("Harp of the North that moldering long hast hung.") OAEP
  Harp of the North, Farewell. Epilogue. CoBE
    (Farewell, Thou Minstrel Harp.) OBNC
    ("Harp of the North, farewell! The hills grow dark.") OAEP; ViBoPo
  Hunter's Song, *fr.* IV. NBM; OA
    (Toils Are Pitched, The.) EnRP
  Hymn to the Virgin, *fr.* IV. EnRP; GoBC
    (Ave Maria.) ISi
  "'Now, yield thee, or by Him who made,'" *fr.* V. OxBS
  Roderick Dhu, *fr.* V. OBRV
  "Rose is fairest when 'tis budding new, The," *fr.* IV. ViBoPo
  Soldier, Rest! [Thy Warfare O'er], *fr.* I. ATP (1935 ed.); AWP; BEL; CoBE; DD; EnLi-2; EnLit; EPN; GN; HBV; HBVY; HH; JAWP; MoShBr; OTPC (1946 ed.); PoRA; TOP; TreFS; TrGrPo; WaKn; WBP
    (Song: "Soldier, rest! thy warfare o'er.") OAEP; OBNC; OBRV
  Soldier's Song ("Our vicar still preaches that Peter and Poule"), *fr.* VI. NBM; ViBoPo
  "Time rolls his ceaseless course," *fr.* III. ViBoPo
    (Gathering, The.) OBNC
  Western Waves of Ebbing Day, The, *fr.* I. OTPC; PoEL-4
Lady of the Lake, The. *Unknown.* ShS
Lady of the Lambs, The. Alice Meynell. *See* Shepherdess, The.
Lady of the Land, The. William Morris. *Fr.* The Earthly Paradise. PoVP; TOP
Lady of the legless world I have. Notes after Blacking Out. Gregory Corso. NeAP
Lady of the Manor, The. George Crabbe. *Fr.* The Parish Register. OBNC
Lady of the manor was dressing for the ball, The. The Highland Tinker. *Unknown.* CoMu
Lady Ogalbie. *Unknown.* *See* Bonnie House o' Airlie, The.
Lady Pecunia; or, The Praise of Money, *sel.* Richard Barnfield.
  "I sing not of Angelica the fair." ReIE
Lady of the Pearls, The, *sel.* Alexandre Dumas, *tr. fr. French by* Gerard Manley Hopkins.
  "We set out yesterday upon a winter drive." TTY
Lady Poverty, The. Alice Meynell. GTSL; HBV; OBMV; PeVV; PoVP
Lady Poverty, The. Evelyn Underhill, *also at. to* Jacob Fischer. CAW; HBV
Lady Prayeth the Return of Her Lover Abiding on the Seas, The. *Unknown.* EIL
  (Seafarer, The.) OBSC
  (To Her Sea-faring Lover.) OBEV
Lady put off her fur, it was so warm in the outer office, The. Appointment in Doctor's Office. Josephine Miles. FiMAP
Lady Queen Anne she sits in the sun. *Unknown.* OxNR
Lady Ralegh's Lament. Robert Lowell. NoP
Lady, receive, receive in gracious wise. He Wrote unto a Scottish Dame. . . as Followeth. George Gascoigne. ReIE
Lady red upon the hill, A. Emily Dickinson. AA; BoNaP; HBV; LHV; OHIP
Lady Sleep. Rowena Bastin Bennett. GaP
Lady stands in her bower door, The. The Twa Magicians. *Unknown.* BaBo; ESPB; OxBB
Lady Stood, A. Dietmar von Aist, *tr. fr. German by* Jethro Bithell. AWP; LiTW
Lady, sweet, now do not frown. Joan to Her Lady. *Unknown.* UnTE
Lady, take care; for in the diamond eyes. Light and Dark. Barbara Howes. MoVE
Lady, take my broken heart. Christ and His Mother at the Cross. Jacopone da Todi. CAW
Lady That Hast My Heart. Hafiz, *tr. fr. Persian by* Gertrude L. Bell. *Fr* Odes. LiTW
  ("Lady that hast my heart within thy hand.") AWP
Lady That in the Prime. Milton. NoP; Sonn
  (To a Virtuous Young Lady.) BWP; TOP
Lady, the glass you lift has sleep's bright fever in it. Homage to Circe. Horace Gregory. MoAmPo (1950 ed.)
Lady—the lyre thou bid'st me take. To —— Jeremiah Joseph Callanan. IrPN
Lady, the meshes of your coiling hair. He Praises Her Hair. *Unknown.* AnIL
Lady, the Silly Flea. *Unknown.* NCEP
Lady! the songs of spring were in the grove. Sonnet: To the Lady Beaumont. Wordsworth. ChER
Lady, the sunlit hour is beautiful. Children. Euripides. WoL
Lady, there is a hope that all men have. William Ellery Channing. *Fr.* A Poet's Hope. AA; AnAmPo
Lady there was of Antigua, A. Limerick. Cosmo Monkhouse. HBV; TSW
Lady Thinks She Is Thirty, A. Ogden Nash. PoPl
Lady, Three White Leopards. T. S. Eliot. *Fr.* Ash Wednesday. SiSw
  ("Lady, three white leopards sat under a juniper-tree.") LO; LoBV
  (Salutation.) AnAmPo
Lady, thy soldier I would be. Ave Maria. John Jerome Rooney. JKCP
Lady to a Lover, A. Roden Noel. OBVV
Lady took exception to assertions, The. Salems of Oppression. Joseph Joel Keith. FiSC
Lady Turned Serving-Man, The. *Unknown.* OBB
  (Famous Flower of Serving-Men, The.) ESPB; OxBB
Lady up on yonder hill. Legend. Sister Mary Jeremy. JKCP (1955 ed.)
Lady Venetia Digby, The. Ben Jonson. GoBC
Lady, very fair are you. Ad Chloen, M. A. Mortimer Collins. BOHV; HBV
Lady walked by the ocean strand, The. Strand-Thistle. Gustav Falke. AWP
Lady, Was It Fair of Thee. Thomas Lovell Beddoes. HoPM
Lady, Weeping at the Crossroads. W. H. Auden. MoVE
Lady, when I behold the roses sprouting. Her Lips. *Unknown.* EG; LiTL

Lady, when we sat together. The Seamy Side of Motley. Sir Owen Seaman. InMe
Lady, when your lovely head. On a Sleeping Friend. Hilaire Belloc. POTE
Lady who intervenes, The. Virgin. Padraic Fallon. OnYI
Lady who liked to crochet, A. *Unknown.* SiTL
Lady who lived in Uganda, A. The Panda. William Jay Smith. RePo
Lady Who Loved a Swine, The, *with music.* *Unknown.* OuSiCo
(Hunc, Said He.) ChTr
(Lady and the Swine, The, *sl. diff.*) RIS
(Silver Sty, The.) Po
(There Was a Lady Loved a Swine.) StP
("There was a lady loved a swine.") OxNR
Lady Who Offers Her Looking-Glass to Venus, The. Matthew Prior, *after* Plato. CBEP; CLwM; OBEV; ViBoPo
(Farewell, A: "Venus take my votive glass.") AWP
(Lais' Mirror.) OnPM; WoL
Lady who stands on my long writing table. Leaving Ithaca. W. D. Snodgrass. AmPC
Lady, who with tender word. The Housewife's Prayer. Blanche Mary Kelly. GoBC; JKCP; WHL
Lady, whose ancestor/ Fought for Prince Charlie. The Stirrup Cup. Douglas Ainslie. ESBV; GoTS
Lady, whose shrine stands on the promontory. T. S. Eliot. *Fr.* Four Quartets: The Dry Salvages. ISi
Lady, why doth love torment you? Love's Torment. *Unknown.* UnTE
Lady Will You Come with Me into. E. E. Cummings. ThWaDe
Lady with Arrows. Margaret Marks. MAP
Lady with Technique, The. Hughes Mearns. *Fr.* Later Antigonishes. FiBHP; InMe; SiTL; WhC
Lady with the Unicorn, The. Vernon Watkins. LiTB; TwCP
Lady without Paragon, A. Chaucer. *See* Hide, Absolon.
Lady, you are with beauties so enriched. Song. Francis Davison. ElL
Lady, you think too much of speeds. Statistics. Stephen Spender. MoBrPo
Lady, your art or wit could ne'er devise. To a Lady Who Sent Me a Copy of Verses at My Going to Bed. Henry King. PP
Lady-Bird. Caroline Anne Bowles. GFA; GoTP; OTPC
Ladybird, ladybird [*or* Lady-bug, lady-bug] fly away home! Mother Goose. BoChLi (1950 ed.); CBEP; FaPON; OxNR; PCH; PoPl; PPL; RIS; SAS; SiTL; SoPo; TVC
Lady Bug. C. Lindsay McCoy. GFA
Ladybug. Raymond Souster. MoCV
Ladye Chapel at Eden Hall. Eleanor Cecilia Donnelly. JKCP
Ladye Marye! today/ Let me say my own say. The Spotless Maid. Vincent McNabb. ISi
Ladyes, you that seeme soe nice. *Unknown.* SeCSL
Lady's Complaint, The. John Heath-Stubbs. TwCP
Lady's Dressing Room, The. Swift. ErPo; NCEP
Lady's-Maid's Song, The. John Hollander. ErPo; LiTM (1970 ed.); NePoEA; TwCP
Lady's Receipt for a Beau's Dress, The. *Unknown.* CoMu
Lady's Song, The. Dryden. LoBV; MBW-1; SeCeV
Lady's Song. Milton. *See* Sweet Echo.
Lady's Third Song, The. W. B. Yeats. *Fr.* The Three Bushes. FaBoTw
Lady's Trial, The, *sel.* John Ford.
Pleasures, Beauty, Youth Attend Ye. LiTL; ViBoPo
Lady's "Yes," The. Elizabeth Barrett Browning. HBV; LiTL
Laegaire, son of the king of Connacht, was out one day. Army of the Sidhe. Lady Gregory. SP
Laetus did in his mistress' quarrel die. Thomas Bastard. TuPP
La Fayette. Samuel Taylor Coleridge. EnRP
La Fayette. Dolly Madison. PaA; PAH
Lafayette to Washington. Maxwell Anderson. *Fr.* Valley Forge. PAL
Lagoon, The. Ashton Greene. NePoAm
Laid in My Quiet Bed. Earl of Surrey. *See* How No Age Is Content.
Laid Off. Francis Webb. BoAV
Laid on Thine Altar. *Unknown.* SoP; TrPWD
Laid out for dead, let thy last kindness be. To Robin Redbreast. Robert Herrick. OBS; SeEP; TrGrPo
Laily Worm and the Machrel [of the Sea], The. *Unknown.* ChTr; ESPB; InvP; LoBV; OA; OBB; OxBB; PoEL-1
'Laine. Robert Bagg. TwAmPo
Laird, a lord, A. *Unknown.* OxNR
Laird o' Cockpen, The. Lady Nairne, 2 *added sts. by* Susan Ferrier. BeLS; BOHV; HBV; OBRV
Laird o' Drum, The. *Unknown.* ESPB
Laird o' Logie, The. *Unknown.* CBEP; CH; ESPB (A *and* B *vers.*)
(Laird of Logie, The.) BaBo
Laird o' Ochiltree Wa's, The. *Unknown.* OxBB
Laird of Bristoll's daughter was in the woods walking, The. Captain Wedderburn's Courtship. *Unknown.* BaBo (A *vers.*); ESPB
Laird of Leys is on to Edinburgh [*or* Edinbrugh], The. The Baron o [*or* of] Leys. *Unknown.* ESPB; OxBB
Laird of Logie, The. *Unknown.* *See* Laird o Logie, The.
Laird of Schelynlaw, The. John Veitch. VA
Laird of Wariston, The (A *and* B *vers.*). *Unknown.* BaBo; ESPB
(Death of Lord Warriston, The, B *vers.*) OxBB
Lairdless Place, The. Kate Rennie Archer. GoYe
Lais. Hilda Doolittle ("H. D."). MAP; MoAmPo
Lais' Mirror. Plato, *tr. fr. Greek by* Matthew Prior. OnPM; WoL
Lais Now Old. *Unknown.* EnRePo
Lak of Stedfastnesse. Chaucer. *See* Lack of Steadfastness.
Lake, The. Matthew Arnold. *See* Meeting.
Lake, The. Louis O. Coxe. MoVE; NYBP
Lake, The. Ted Hughes. NYBP
Lake, The. Alphonse de Lamartine, *tr. fr. French by* Katherine Hillard. WoL
Lake, The. Poe. *See* Lake, The: To ——.
Lake, The. James Stephens. AnEnPo; MoBrPo
Lake, The. John Banister Tabb. AmP
Lake allows an average father, walking slowly, A. Lakes. W. H. Auden. NePA; NePoAm
Lake and a Fairy Boat, A. Thomas Hood. *See* Song: "Lake and a fairy boat, A."
Lake Boats, The. Edgar Lee Masters. NP
Lake Chelan. William Stafford. NaP
Lake, The: Coda. Tom Clark. YAP
Lake comes throbbing in with voice of pain, The. A Lake Memory. Wilfred Campbell. VA
Lake Harvest. Raymond Knister. PeCV
Lake is born all of a May, A. Three Christmas Carols, I. *Unknown.* ACP
Lake is sharp along the shore, The. Lakeshore. F. R. Scott. MoCV; OBCV
Lake Isle, The. Ezra Pound. CABA; CrMA; SiTL
Lake Isle of Innisfree, The. W. B. Yeats. ATP; BEL; BoC; BoLiVe; BrPo; CMoP; CoBMV; DiPo; EnL; EnLi-2 (1949 ed.); EnLit; FaBV; FaFP; FaPL; FaPON; GBV; GTBS; GTBS-W; GTSL; HBV; HT; ILP; InP; LiTG; LiTM (rev. ed.); MaPo; MBW-2; MCCG; MoAB; MoBrPo; NeMA; NoP; OAEP (2d ed.); OBEV; OBVV; OnYI; OTPC (1946 ed.); PoPl; PoPo; PoRA; PoVP; RoGo; ShBV-2; SP; TDP; TOP; TreF; TrGrPo; TSW; ViPo (1962 ed.); WHA; YAT; YT
Lake lay blue below the hill, The. L'Oiseau Bleu (*or* The Blue Bird]. Mary Elizabeth Coleridge. BoTP; CH; PoVP; WePo
Lake Leman ("Clear, placid Leman!"). Byron. *Fr.* Childe Harold's Pilgrimage, III. MaPo; OBNC
(Night and Storm in the Alps, *abr.*) MCCG
Lake Leman ("Lake Leman woos me"). Byron. *Fr.* Childe Harold's Pilgrimage, III. PoEL-4
Lake Leman lies by Chillon's walls. Byron. *Fr.* The Prisoner of Chillon. OBRV
Lake Memory, A. Wilfred Campbell. VA
Lake, Mountain, Tree. Denis Glover. AnNZ
Lake of Gaube, The. Swinburne. PAn; PoVP
Lake of the Dismal Swamp, The. Thomas Moore. BLPA
Lake Poets, The. Byron. *Fr.* Don Juan, III. UnPo (1st ed.)
Lake Song. Jean Starr Untermeyer. AnAmPo; HBMV; MAP; MoAmPo (1942 ed.); NP; TrJP
Lake Superior. Samuel Griswold Goodrich. AA
Lake, The: To ——. Poe. AmePo; AmP; MAmP; MWA-1; OBRV; OnPM
Lake Winnipesaukee. Olive Driver. RePo
Lakes. W. H. Auden. NePA; NePoAm
Lakes. Francesco Bianco. CLwM
Lakes of astonishment break open. The Mountain Climber. Antonia Pozzi. OnPM

Lakes of surprising shape. Hunger. John Perreault. YAP
Lakes of the Atchafalaya, The. Longfellow. *Fr.* Evangeline. PoEL-5
Lakeshore. F. R. Scott. MoCV; OBCV
Lalela Zulu. *Unknown, tr. fr. Zulu.* PeSA
Lalique. Hal Porter. PoAu-2
Lalla Rookh, *sels.* Thomas Moore.
By Bendemeer's Stream, *fr.* The Veiled Prophet of Korassan. OTPC (1946 ed.); RG
(Bendemeer.) OBRV
Golden Hour, The, *fr.* The Fire-Worshippers. OBNC
Light of the Haram, The, *fr.* The Story of the Sultana Nourmahal. EnRP
Peri's Lament for Hinda, The, *fr.* The Fire-Worshippers. OBNC
Syrian Evening, A, *fr.* Paradise and the Peri. PeER
Lalla Rookh/ Is a naughty book. On Thomas Moore's Poems. *Unknown.* FiBHP; SiTL
La-la-llamas rate as mammals. In Praise of Llamas. Arthur Guiterman. FiBHP
L'Allegro. Milton. AnFE; AWP; BEL; BoLiVe; CABA; CBEP; CoBE; EnL; EnLi-1; EnLit; FaFP; FiP; GN; GTBS; GTBS-D; GTBS-P; GTBS-W; GTSE; GTSL; HBV; HoPM; ILP; InPo; LiTB; LiTG; LoBV; MaPo; MasP; MBW-1; MCCG; MyFE; NoP; OBEV; OBS; OTPC, *abr.* (1923 ed.); OuHeWo; PoE; SeCePo; SeCeV; ShBV-3; TOP; TreFS; TrGrPo; ViBoPo; WHA; WoL
Sels.
Mirth, with Thee I mean to Live. FaBV
"Haste thee, Nymph, and bring with thee." OTPC (1946 ed.); YT
Sometimes, with Secure Delight. MPB
Lalus a jolly youthfull lad. The Second Nimphall. Michael Drayton. *Fr.* The Muses Elizium. AnAnS-2
Lama, The. Ogden Nash. FaPON; FiBHP; PV; RePo; SiTL
"One-l lama, The.") FaBoCh; LoGBV
Lamarck Elaborated. Richard Wilbur. AP; NePoEA; NoP
Lamb, The. Blake. *Fr.* Songs of Innocence. AnFE; BEL; BoChLi; BoLiVe; BoTP; BWP; CABA; CaFP; CAW; CBEP; CBV; CEP; CH; CoBE; DiPo; EaLo; EiCL; EiPP; EnL; EnLi-2; EnLit; EnPE; EnRP; ERoP-1; ExPo; FaBoBe; FaBoCh; FaPON; ForPo; GoJo; GoTP; HBV; ILP; LiTB; LiTG; LoBV; LoGBV; MaPo; MaRV; MemP; MPB; NeHB; OAEP; OBEC; OTPC: OuHeWo; OxBoCh; PAn; PG (1945 ed.); PIA; PoAn; PoeP; PoFS; PoIE; PoPl; PoPo; PoRh; PRWS; RIS; SeCeV; SoP; StaSt; StVeCh (1940 ed.); SUS; TIHL; TOP; TreF; TrGrPo; TRV; TVC; UTS; VaPo; WaKn; WGRP; WHA; YAT
(Little Lamb.) StVeCh (1955 ed.)
Lamb, The. Kate Greenaway. OTPC (1923 ed.); PPL; SAS
Lamb, The. *Unknown.* OTPC (1923 ed.)
Lamb. Humbert Wolfe. MoBrPo
Lamb-Child, The. John Banister Tabb. ChBR
(When Christ Was Born.) ThGo
Lamb of God! Behold Him ready. "Thou Art Worthy." *Unknown.* SoP
Lamb of God, I look to thee. A Child's Prayer. Charles Wesley. FaChP
Lamb of God, Thy faithful promise. The Coming and the Appearing. *Unknown.* STF
Lamb of God wears a scarlet robe, The. Futile Sacrifice. Murray Skinner. ChIP
Lamb, whan the hert is laich. Whan the Hert Is Laich. Sidney Goodsir Smith. NeBP
Lambro's Return, *sl. abr.* Byron. *Fr.* Don Juan, III. OBRV
Lambs at Play. Christina Rossetti. *See* On the Grassy Banks.
Lambs in the Meadow. Laurence Alma-Tadema. PRWS
Lambs on the Green Hills Stood Gazing on Me, The. *Unknown.* AnIV
Lambs that learn to walk in snow. First Sight. Philip Larkin. BoNaP; MemP; OA
Lamda. Melvin B. Tolson. PoNe (1970 ed.)
Lame Beggar [*or* Begger], A. John Donne. MaMe; TuPP
Lame, impotent conclusion to youth's dreams. Farewell to Juliet. Wilfrid Scawen Blunt. The Love Sonnets of Proteus, LII. ViBoPo
Lame Man and the Blind Man. Waring Cuney. PoNe
Lame One, The. Sherwood Anderson. AnAmPo
Lame Soldier, The, *with music.* *Unknown.* OuSiCo
Lament: "Ban of Time there is no disobeying, The." Gelett Burgess. InMe
Lament: "Chaste maids which haunt fair Aganippe's well." William Drummond of Hawthornden. *Fr.* Tears on the Death of Meliades. LoBV
Lament: "Fall now, my cold thoughts, frozen fall." Laurence Binyon. MoVE
Lament: "Farewell Mercy, farewell thy piteous grace." John Lydgate. *Fr.* Court of Sapience. PoEL-1
Lament: "I am lying in thy tomb, love." Roden Noel. VA
Lament, A: "I seen her last night." A. G. Strong. YT
Lament: "It is we, it is we." Dan Georgakas. ThO
Lament: "Listen, children:/ Your father is dead." Edna St. Vincent Millay. PoPl; PoPo
Lament: "My man is a bone ringèd with weed." Brenda Chamberlain. *See* First Woman's Lament.
Lament, A: "My thoughts hold mortal strife." William Drummond of Hawthornden. *See* Madrigal: "My thoughts hold mortal strife."
Lament: "Nashe's old queens who bartered young and fair." Richard Wilbur. FiMAP
Lament: "Oh, everything is far." Rainer Maria Rilke, *tr. fr. German by* C. F. MacIntyre. PoPl; TrJP
Lament, A: "O world! O life! O time!" Shelley. AtBAP; BoLiVe; ChER; ChTr; EG; EnLi-2 (1949 ed.); EnLit; EnRP; EPN; GTBS; GTBS-D; GTBS-P; GTBS-W; GTSE; LoBV; MemP; OAEP; OBRV; PoPo; PoRA; TOP; TreFT; TrGrPo; WHA
(Threnos.) GTSL
Lament: "Sigh, wind in the pine." Douglas Stewart. MoAuPo
Lament: "Snows cloaked/ Mountain cliffs." Gudmundur Gudmundsson, *tr. fr. Icelandic by* Watson Kirkconnell. LiTW
Lament, A: "We who are left, how shall we look again." W. W. Gibson. MMA
Lament: "Weariness of the bones." "Pablo de Rokha," *tr. fr. Spanish by* H. R. Hays. OnPM
Lament: "What moved me, was the way your hand." Dorothy Livesay. CaP
Lament: "When I was a windy boy and a bit." Dylan Thomas. ErPo; MasP
Lament: "When the folk of my household." *Tr. fr. Irish by* Edward Walsh. OBVV
Lament: "Within my bosom stirs once more tonight." Princess Zeb-un-Nissa, *tr. fr. Persian by* Paul Whalley. LiTW
Lament: "Youth's bright palace." Denis Florence MacCarthy. JKCP (1926 ed.); OBVV
Lament, A; 1547, *abr.* Alexander Scott. CH
("Depart, depart, depart!") LO
Lament for a Dead Cow. Francis Cary Slater. BoSA; TDP
Lament for a Man Who Loved God. James Schevill. FiMAP
Lament for a Poor Poet. Myles Connolly. CAW
Lament for a Sailor. Paul Dehn. WaP
Lament for a Warrior. *Unknown, tr. fr. Sotho by* Dan Kunene *and* Jack Cope. PeSA
Lament for Adonis. Bion, *tr. fr. Greek by* John Addington Symonds. AWP; JAWP; WBP; WoL
(Bion's Lament for Adonis, *tr. by* Elizabeth Barrett Browning.) ATP
"For Adonis I am crying, for Adonis' beauty dead," *sel., tr. by* George Allen. LiTW
Lament for Art O'Leary, The. Eileen O'Leary, *tr. fr. Modern Irish by* Frank O'Connor. AnIL; KiLC
Lament for Banba. Egan O'Rahilly, *tr. fr. Irish by* James Clarence Mangan. AnIV; AWP; JAWP; WBP
Lament for Better or Worse. Gene Baro. FiSC; NePoEA-2
Lament for Bion, A. *At. to* Moschus, *tr. fr. Greek by* George Chapman. AWP; JAWP; WBP; EnLi-2, *tr. by* J. H. Halard
(Epitaph of Bion, *tr. by* Edmund Clarence Stedman.) WOL
Lament for Capt. Paton. John Gibson Lockhart. OBRV
Lament for Chaucer. Thomas Hoccleve. *Fr.* De Regimine Principum. OBEV
Lament for Corc and Niall of the Nine Hostages. *At. to* Torna, *tr. fr. Old Irish by* Sir Samuel Ferguson. OnYI
Lament for Culloden. Burns. CBEP; GTBS; GTBS-D; GTBS-P; GTBS-W; GTSE; GTSL; HBV; OBEV
(Lovely Lass o' Inverness, The.) GoTS
Lament for Daphnaida. Spenser. FiP
Lament for Flodden. Jane Elliot. *See* Flowers of the Forest, The.
Lament for Glasgerion. Elinor Wylie. AmLP

Lament for Ignacio Sanchez Mejias. Federico García Lorca. *See* Lament for the Death of a Bullfighter.
Lament for Imogen. Shakespeare. *See* Fear No More the Heat o' the Sun.
Lament for Lost Lodgings. Phyllis McGinley. NYBP
Lament for My Brother on a Hayrake. James Wright. TwAmPo
Lament for One's Self. Ruth Pitter. BoPe
Lament for O'Sullivan Beare, The. *Tr. fr. Irish by* Jeremiah Joseph Callanan. AnIV
(Dirge of O'Sullivan Bear.) IrPN; NBM
Lament for Our Lady's Shrine at Walsingham, A. *Unknown, at. to* Philip Howard, Earl of Arundel. ISi; PoEL-2
("In the wracks of Walsingham.") NCEP; SiCE
(Lament for Walsingham.) CBEP
(Wreck of Walsingham, The.) ACP
Lament for Pasiphae. Robert Graves. FaBoTw
Lament for Prytherch. R. S. Thomas. POTi
Lament for Richard Rolston. Sir Osbert Sitwell. ChMP
Lament for Seán. Daniel James O'Sullivan. NeIP
Lament for Sean MacDermott. "Seumas O'Sullivan." AnIV
Lament for Tabby. *Unknown.* CIV
Lament for the Alamo. Arthur Guiterman. AmFN; RePo
Lament for the Death of a Bullfighter. Federico García Lorca. *tr. fr. Spanish by* Warren Carrier. ReMP
(Lament for Ignacio Sanchez Mejias, *tr. by* Stephen Spender *and* J. L. Gili.) LiTW
Lament for the Death of Eoghan Ruadh O'Neill. Thomas Osborne Davis. AnIV; FOL; OxBI
(Lament for the Death of Owen Roe O'Neill.) IrPN; OnYI
Lament for the Death of Thomas Davis. Sir Samuel Ferguson. *See* Lament for Thomas Davis.
Lament for the Graham. Henry the Minstrel. *See* Wallace's Lament for the Graham.
Lament for the Great Yachts. Patric Dickinson. HaMV; POTi
Lament for the Makaris [*or* Makars]. William Dunbar. ACP; AtBAP; CBEP; ChTr; GoTS; OxBS; PP; SiCE; ViBoPo, *abr.*
(Fear of Death Confounds Me, The.) MeEL
(Lament for the Makaris Quhen He Wes Seik, The.) OAEP; PoIE
(Lament for the Makers.) OBEV; PoEL-1
"Unto the death gois all estatis, *sel.* ML
Lament for the Poets: 1916. Francis Ledwidge. AnIV; AWP; JAWP; JKCP (1926 ed.); OnYI; OxBI; WBP
Lament for the Princes of Tyrone and Tyrconnel, A. *Tr. fr. Irish by* James Clarence Mangan. AnIV
Lament for the Priory of Walsingham, A, *sel. Unknown.*
"Bitter was it, Oh to view." ChTr
Lament for the Two Brothers Slain by Each Other's Hand. Aeschylus, *tr. fr. Greek by* A. E. Housman. *Fr.* The Seven against Thebes. AWP; JAWP; WBP
Lament for the Woodlands. *Unknown, tr. fr. Irish by* Frank O'Connor. KiLC
Lament for Thomas Davis. Sir Samuel Ferguson. AnIV; PoFr, 6 *sts.*
(Lament for the Death of Thomas Davis.) IrPN; NBM; OnYI; OxBI
Lament for Thomas MacDonagh. Francis Ledwidge. *See* Thomas MacDonagh.
Lament for Tintoretta. William Collins. Three Fragments, 3. WaPE
Lament for Urien, The. *Unknown, tr. fr. Middle Welsh by* Ernest Rhys. *Fr.* The Red Book of Hergest. OBMV
Lament for Walsingham. *Unknown. See* Lament for Our Lady's Shrine at Walsingham, A.
Lament for Yellow-haired Donough, The. *Unknown, tr. fr. Irish by* Frank O'Connor. KiLC
Lament him, Mauchline husbands a'. On a Wag in Mauchline [*or* Epitaph for James Smith]. Burns. ALV; ELU; FiBHP
Lament in Autumn. Harold Stewart. PoAu-2
Lament my loss, my labor, and my pain. Sir Thomas Wyatt. FCP
"Lament not thy path of woe, O loved man." Christ to the Sufferer. *Unknown. Fr.* Andreas. PoLi
Lament of a Border Widow. *Unknown. See* Lament of the Border Widow.
Lament of a Man for His Son. *Unknown, tr. fr. Paiute Indian by* Mary Austin. AWP; JAWP; WBP; WOW
Lament of a Mocking-Bird. Frances Anne Kemble. AA; HBV
Lament of an Idle Demon. R. P. Lister. FiBHP
Lament of Anastasius. William Bourn Oliver Peabody. AA
Lament of Edward Blastock, The. Edith Sitwell. OBMV
Lament of Eve, The. *Unknown.* ACP (1952 ed.)
Lament of Granite. David Ross. PG (1945 ed.)
Lament of Guiderius and Arviragus. Shakespeare. *See* Fear No More the Heat o' the Sun.
Lament of "La Belle Heaulmière," The. Villon. *See* Complaint of the Fair Armouress, The.
Lament of Maev Leith-Dherg, The. *Unknown, tr. fr. Middle Irish by* Thomas W. H. Rolleston. OnYI
Lament of Quarry, The. Léonie Adams. NP
Lament of Saint Anne, The. *Unknown. Fr.* The Protevangelium of James. CAW
Lament of the Border Widow, The. *Unknown.* HBV; OBB; OTPC (1923 ed.) *sl. diff.*; OxBB
(Bonnie Bower.) CH
(Lament of a Border Widow.) BFSS
"My love he built me a bonny bower." LO
Lament of the Damned in Hell, The. Edward Young. OxBoCh
Lament of the Flowers, The. Jones Very. MAmP; OxBA
Lament of the Flutes. Christopher Okigbo. PBA
Lament of the Frontier Guard. Li Po; *tr. fr. Chinese by* Ezra Pound. AP; CoAnAm; CoBMV; TwAmPo; WaaP
Lament of the Irish Emigrant. Helen Selina Sheridan. HBV; OBEV (1st ed.); OBVV; VA
Lament of the Lovely Helmet-Dealer. Villon. *See* Complaint of the Fair Armouress, The.
Lament of the Mangaire Sugach. Andrew Magrath, *tr. fr. Modern Irish by* Edward Walsh. OnYI
Lament of the Scotch-Irish Exile. James Jeffrey Roche. BOHV
Lament of the Voiceless, The. Laura Bell Everett. OQP; PGD
Lament the Night before His Execution, A. Chidiock Tichborne. *See* Elegy: "My prime of youth is but a frost of cares."
Lament to Nana of Erech. *Unknown, tr. fr. Babylonian tablets by* Stephen Langdon. LiTW
Lamentable Ballad of the Bloody Brook, The. Edward Everett Hale. HBV; PAH
Lamentable Case, A. Sir Charles Hanbury-Williams. ErPo; UnTE; WaPE
Lamentable Tragedy of Locrine, The. *At. to* George Peele, *also at. to* Charles Tilney. *See* Locrine.
Lamentation, A. Thomas Campion. CH; OHIP
Lamentation. Ezekiel, XIX: 2-9, Bible, *O.T.* TrJP
Lamentation for Celin, The. *Unknown, tr. fr. Spanish by* John Gibson Lockhart. AWP; JAWP; OuHeWo; WBP
"At the gate of old Granada, when all its bolts are barred," *sts.* 1-5. PoFr
Lamentation for the Death of Sir Maurice Fitzgerald, Knight of Kerry, A. Pierce Ferriter, *tr. fr. Late Middle Irish by* James Clarence Mangan. IrPN
Lamentation for the Fall of Jerusalem. Lamentations, Bible, *O.T. See* Misery of Jerusalem, The.
Lamentation of Beckles, The. Thomas Deloney. SiCE
Lamentation of Chloris, The. *Unknown.* CoMu
Lamentation of Enion, The. Blake. *Fr.* Vala; or, The Four Zoas. OBNC
Lamentation of Mac Liag for Kincora. *Unknown. See* Kincora.
Lamentation of Nippur. *Unknown, tr. fr. Babylonian tablets by* Stephen Langdon. LiTW
Lamentation of the Old Pensioner, The. W. B. Yeats. MaPo; NoP; PeVV; PoPo; PPON
Lamentation on My Dear Son Simon, A. John Saffin. SCAP
Lamentations, *sels.* Bible, *O.T.*
Affliction, III: 1-15. TrJP
Desolation in Zion, I: 12-17. TrJP
How Is the Gold Become Dim, IV: 1-5. ChTr
Lamentation for the Fall of Jerusalem, I. LiTW
(Misery of Jerusalem, The.) AWP
Lamentations. Alter Brody. TrJP
Lamentations, The. Homer, *tr. fr. Greek by* Sir William Marris. *Fr.* The Iliad, XXIV. LiTW
Lamentations of Jeremy, The. John Donne. MaMe
Lamentations of the Fallen Angels. Cædmon (?), *tr. fr. An-*

glo-Saxon by Charles W. Kennedy. *Fr.* Christ and Satan. AnOE
Laments. *Unknown, tr. fr. Arabic by* E. Powys Mathers. *Fr.* The Thousand and One Nights. AWP; JAWP; WBP
Lami Poem ("Lami, leather nightingale"). Alden Van Buskirk. YAP
Lamia. Keats. BEL; CABL; EnLi-2; EnRP; EPN; ERoP-2; MBW-2; MERP; OAEP
Sels.
Banquet, The, *fr.* Pt. II. SeCePo
"She was a gordian shape of dazzling hue," *fr.* I. FlW
Lamilia's Song. Robert Greene. *See* Fie, fie on Blind Fancy!
L'Amitié et L'Amour. John Swanwick Drennan. IrPN
Lamkin. *Unknown.* BaBo (A, C, *and* D *vers.*); CBEP; ESPB (A, B, *and* K *vers.*); FosPo; OBB; OxBB; ViBoFo
(False Linfinn, B *vers.*) BaBo
Lamorna Cove. W. H. Davies. BrPo
Lamp, The. Sarah Pratt Greene. AA
Lamp, The. Sara Teasdale. InP; MoLP
Lamp [*or* Lampe], The. Henry Vaughan. AnAnS-1; MeP; QFR; SeCL
Lamp, The. Charles Whitehead. OBEV (new ed.); OBVV
(As Yonder Lamp.) VA
Lamp burns long in the cottage, The. There's Money in Mother and Father. Morris Bishop. FiBHP
Lamp burns sure, within, The. Emily Dickinson. LiTA
Lamp Flower, The. Margaret Cecilia Furse. BoTP
Lamp in the night, a song in time of sorrow, A. The Hope of the Coming of the Lord. Major Whittle. SoP
Lamp in the West, The. Ella Higginson. AA; HBV
Lamp must be replenished, but even then, The. Manfred. Byron. BEL; EnLi-2 (1939 ed.); EnRP; EPN; MBW-2; MERP
Lamp of Life, The. Amy Lowell. MaRV
Lamp of our feet, whereby we trace. The Bible. Bernard Barton. SoP
Lamp of Poor Souls, The. Marjorie Pickthall. HBV
Lamp once hung in an ancient town, A. The Old Lamp. *Unknown.* SoP
Lamp Posts. Helen Hoyt. YT
Lampe, The. Henry Vaughan. *See* Lamp, The.
Lamplighter, The. "Seumas O'Sullivan." OxBI
Lamplighter, The. Robert Louis Stevenson. FaFP; GaP; MPB; OTD; OTPC; PCH; PoVP; TreF; TVC
Lampoon, A. *Unknown.* PeRV
Lamps along the river, The. Estuary. William Montgomerie. OxBS
Lamps Are Burning, The. Charles Reznikoff. TrJP
Lamps burn all the night. The Fifth Sense. Patricia Beer. MoBS
Lamps inside the house, The. 2000 A.D. Beverly Connelly. FiSC
Lamp's Shrine, The. Dante Gabriel Rossetti. The House of Life, XXXV. MaVP; PoVP; ViPo; VP
Lampus extinct at last in ashes lies. In Obitum Alienius. Henry Parrot. SiCE
L'an Trentiesme de Mon Eage [*or* Age]. Archibald MacLeish. AmLP; AnFE; APA; CoAnAm; LiTM; MoVE; NePA; NP; SiSw; TwAmPo
(In My Thirtieth Year.) MAP; MoAmPo
Lana Turner has collapsed! Poem. Frank O'Hara. FRC
Lancashire Lads. *Unknown.* CoMu
Lancashire Puritane, The. *Unknown.* CoMu
Lancaster bore him—such a little town. A Hundred Collars. Robert Frost. YaD
Lancaster County Tragedy. W. Lowrie Kay. ShM
Lancelot. Arna Bontemps. CDC
Lancelot and Elaine. Tennyson. *Fr.* Idylls of the King. PoVP; ViPo; ViPP
Elaine's Song, *sel.* FaBoEn
(Song of Love and Death, The.) OBNC
Lancelot and Guinevere. Gerald Gould. HBV
Lancelot and the Grail. Tennyson. *Fr.* Idylls of the King: The Holy Grail. GoBC
Lancer. A. E. Housman. EnLit; MoBrPo
L'Ancien Régime. James Thomson. PoVP
Land, The, *sel.* Struthers Burt.
"Be not afraid, O Dead." DD; HBMV
Land, The. Kipling. MoBrPo; OnMSP; ViPP
Land, The. Dorothy Livesay. *Fr.* The Colour of God's Face. PeCV (1967 ed.)
Land, The, *sels.* V. Sackville-West.
"Shepherds and stars are quiet with the hills." ShBV-4
Spring Was Late That Year, The. AtBAP
Weed Month. MoBrPo (1942 ed.)
Winter Song. MoBrPo (1942 ed.)
Land across the Sea, A. William Morris. *Fr.* The Earthly Paradise. VA
Land beloved of horsemen, fair, The. Choral Poem. Sophocles. *Fr.* Oedipus at Colonus. LiTW
Land Dirge, A. John Webster. *See* Call for the Robin Redbreast and the Wren.
Land grew bright in a single flower, The. Christmas Carol. Sister Francisca Josefa del Castillo. CAW
Land I Came thro' Last, The. Christopher Brennan. *Fr.* The Wanderer. PoAu-1
"Land Is Ours, The." Sir Samuel Ferguson. *Fr.* Congal. IrPN
Land it is the landlord's, The. The Song of the Wage-Slave. Ernest Charles Jones. PoFr
Land lies in water; it is shadowed green. The Map. Elizabeth Bishop. LoGBV; ReMP; RePo
Land o' the Leal, The. Lady Nairne. GTBS; GTBS-D; GTBS-P; GTBS-W; GTSE; GTSL; HBV; MaRV; MCCG; NA; OBEV; OxBS; WBLP; WGRP
"Land of Beginning Again, The." Carl F. Bruhn. SoP
Land of Beginning Again, The. Louise Fletcher Tarkington. BLPA; OQP
Land of Cokaigne, The. *Unknown, tr. fr. Middle English.* CAW, *br. sel.*
(Cokaygne.) AnIL
(Land of Cockayne, The.) MeEV
(Land of Cokaygne, The, *at. to* Friar Michael of Kildare, *mod. vers. by* Russell K. Alspach.) OnYI
Land of Counterpane, The. Robert Louis Stevenson. BoChLi; BrPo; EvOK; FaBoBe; FaFP; FaPON; HBV; HBVY; ILP; MPB; NeHB; OTPC; PCH; PoPL; PoVP; RIS; SoPo; StVeCh; TreF; VA
Land of Destiny. Catherine Parmenter. PEDC
Land of Dreams, The. Blake. BeLS; CH; OBRV
Land of Dreams, The. Henry Martyn Hoyt. HBMV
Land of Dreams and Sleep, A—a poppied land! Nubia. Bayard Taylor. HBV
Land of gold! — thy sisters greet thee. California. Lydia Huntley Sigourney. MC; PAH
Land of Heart's Desire, The. Emily Huntington Miller. HBV
Land of Heart's Desire, The. W. B. Yeats. PoVP
"Wind blows out of the gates of the day, The," *sel.* FlW; HT; ViBoPo
(Faerie's Song.) GBV
(Fairy Song.) MoBrPo; OnYI
(From "The Land of Heart's Desire.") GTSL
(Song: "Wind blows out of the gates of day, The.") BEL; InP; TSW
Land of Hope and Glory. A. C. Benson. PTK
Land of Indolence. James Thomson. *Fr.* The Castle of Indolence. OBEC; SeCePo
("In lowly dale, fast by a river's side.") EnRP; ViBoPo
Land of leaning ice, A. North Labrador. Hart Crane. CMoP; FaBoMo
Land of Masters. Mikhail Yurevich Lermontov, *tr. fr. Russian by* Babette Deutsch. OnPM
Land of my birth! though now, alas! no more. William Charles Wentworth. *Fr.* Australasia. PoAu-1
Land of My Heart. William Dudley Foulke. *Fr.* Ad Patriam. PAL; PGD
Land of Nations, *sel.* Gertrude Stein.
"Here is a poem." AtBAP
Land of Nod, The. Robert Louis Stevenson. GoTP; MPB (1956 ed.); PoVP; VA
Land of Our Birth. Kipling. *Fr.* Puck of Pook's Hill. BoTP; MaRV
(Children's Song, The.) PoVP
Land of Our Fathers. Clinton Scollard. *See* Ad Patriam.
Land of running horses, fair, The. Chorus. Sophocles. *Fr.* Odeipus at Colonus. SiSw
Land of Story-Books, The. Robert Louis Stevenson. FaBoBe; FaPL; FaPON; GoTP; HBV; HBVY; MPB; NeHB; OTD; OTPC; PoVP; PRWS; TiPo; TreFS; TSW
"There, in the night, where none can spy," *sel.* YT
Land of the Empire Builders. Oregon State Song. J. A. Buchanan. PoRL

Land of the Evening Mirage, The. *Unknown, tr. fr. Sioux Indian by* A. M. Beede. WGRP
Land of the Free. Arthur Nicholas Hosking. BLPA; PaA; PAL
Land of the Free. Archibald MacLeish. AmFN
"We wonder whether the dream of American liberty," *sel.* MoAB; MoAmPo; NeMA
Land of the Free. Sister Mary Honora. NePoAm-2
Land of the masters, land of slaves, farewell. Land of Masters. Mikhail Lermontov. OnPM
Land of the mountains high. Utah, We Love Thee. Evan Stephens. PoRL
Land of the Never-ending Heart. Kenneth Patchen. ToPo
Land of the Wilful Gospel. Sidney Lanier. *Fr.* The Psalm of the West. PAH
Land of unconquered Pelayo! land of the Cid Campeador! The Surrender of Spain. John Hay. AA
Land starts dentelle, indented, The. Carta Canadensis. Ralph Gustafson. PeCV (1967 ed.)
Land, that, from the rule of kings, The. The Bartholdi Statue. Whittier. PaA; PAH; ThLM
Land that is lonelier than ruin, A. By the North Sea, I. Swinburne. PoEL-5; PoVP
Land That Is Not, The. Edith Södergran, *tr. fr. Finnish by* Erik Wahlgren *and* Martin S. Allwood. HW
Land That Man Has Newly Trod, A. Joaquin Miller. AmPP (3d ed.)
Land That We Love. Richard Watson Gilder. PaA
Land War, The. "Seumas O'Sullivan." OxBI
Land was ours before we were the land's, The. The Gift Outright. Robert Frost. AmFN; AmLP; AmP; AmPP (4th ed.); AP; CMoP; CoBMV; CrMA; FaBoEn; InPo; LiTM; LoGBV; MaPo; MoAB; MoAmPo (1950 ed.); MWA-2; NoP; OxBA; PAL; PoeP; PoIE; PoPo; RePo; SeCeV (1967 ed.); WaKn; WaP
Land was overmuch like scenery, The. Beowulf. Richard Wilbur. CrMA
Land was white, The. Riddle. *Unknown.* ChTr; OxNR
Land We Adore, The, *with music. Unknown.* SGR
Land Where Hate Should Die, The. Denis A. McCarthy. PGD
Land Where I Was Born, The. Shaw Neilson. BoAu
"Land where I was born sits by the seas, The." Paolo and Francesca. Dante, *tr. by* Byron. *Fr.* Divina Commedia: Inferno. TreFT
Land where the banners wave last in the sun. Freedom, Our Queen. Oliver Wendell Holmes. PEDC
Land Where the Columbines Grow. Arthur J. Fynn. PoOW
Land Where the Taffy Birds Grow, The. Margaret McBride Hoss. GFA
Land Which No One Knows, The. Ebenezer Elliott. *See* Plaint.
Land-Fall. George M. Brady. NeIP
Landfall in Unknown Seas. Allen Curnow. AnNZ
Landing, The. "Lewis Carroll." *Fr.* The Hunting of the Snark. WhC
Landing of the British Settlers of 1820, The, *sel.* Alex Wilmot.
"North, south, east, west, the settlers scatter wide." ACV
Landing of the Pilgrim Fathers [in New England], The. Felicia Dorothea Hemans. BeLS; BLPA; DD; FaBoBe; FaBV; FaFP; FaPL; FaPON; GN; GoTP; HBV; HBVY; HH; MaRV; MC; NeHB; OHIP; OnSP; OTPC; PaA; PAH; PAL; PaPo; PCH; PGD, *abr.*; PoFr; PoRL; SoP; ThLM; TreF; WBLP
(Pilgrim Fathers.) BoTP; PTK
Landlady. P. K. Page. CaP; TwCaPo
Landlord, landlord. Ballad of the Landlord. Langston Hughes. TPM
Landlubber's Chantey, The. James Stuart Montgomery. HBMV
Landmarch by camel and shipsail we take. Cargoes of the Radanites. Harry Alan Potamkin. TrJP
Landmark, The. Dante Gabriel Rossetti. The House of Life, LXVII. EPN; MaVP; NBM; PoVP; ViPo
Landor. John Albee. AA
Landor. Alexander Hay Japp. VA
Landrail, The. Sir Aubrey De Vere. IrPN
Land's End (Point Lobos, California). Stanton A. Coblentz. EtS
Landscape. William Cowper. *Fr.* The Task. CoBE
Landscape, A. John Cunningham. CEP
Landscape. R. N. Currey. BoSA
Landscape. John L'Heureux. YAP
Landscape. William Mason. *Fr.* The English Garden. OBEC
Landscape. Alfred W. Purdy. CaP
Landscape, The. William Shenstone. *See* Song: Landskip, The.
Landscape. Robert Wells. MemP
Landscape as a Nude. Archibald MacLeish. Frescoes for Mr. Rockefeller's City, I. AmPP (4th ed.); CMoP
(Frescoes for Mr. Rockefeller's City.) UnPo
Landscape as Metal and Flowers. Winfield Townley Scott. AmFN; GoJo; HoPM; MiAP
Landscape: Beast/ Yonder, by the eastward sea. Figure for an Apocalypse. Thomas Merton. CrMA
Landscape, brown and sere beneath the sun, The. Fear Not! *Unknown.* Sop
Landscape, by Ch'eng Sui. James Kirkup. *Fr.* Seven Pictures from China. BoPe; POTi
Landscape, Deer Season. Barbara Howes. GoJo
Landscape Lies withing My Head, The. Gervase Stewart. WaaP
Landscape near a Steel Mill. Herschel Horn. PPON
Landscape near an Aerodrome, The. Stephen Spender. AnEnPo; AnFE; CoBMV; EnLit; LiTM; MoAB; MoBrPo; MoVE; OAEP (2d ed.); PoAn; ReMP; ShBV-4; StP; WoL
Landscape of Love, The. Thomas Cole. NePoAm
Landscape of Screams. Nelly Sachs, *tr. fr. German by* Michael Roloff. NYBP
Landscape of the Heart, The. Geoffrey Grigson. LiTB; LiTM; WaP
Landscape of Violence. R. N. Currey. PeSA
Landscape sleeps in mist from morn till noon, The. John Clare. *Fr.* November. FIW
Landscape, suspended from our loins, The. Aircraft, Landing. Colin Thiele. ACV
Landscape (the landscape!) again, The: Gloucester. The Librarian. Charles Olson. CoPo
Landscape where I lie, The. Song for a Lyre. Louise Bogan. LiTA
Landscape with Children. Sister Maris Stella. JKCP (1955 ed.)
Landscape with Figures. A. R. Ammons. FRC
Landscape with Figures. Keith Douglas. NePoEA
Landscape with Figures. Theodore Enslin. CoPo
Landscape with Figures. A. R. D. Fairburn. AnNZ
Landscape with the Fall of Icarus. William Carlos Williams. TDP
Landscape with the Giant Orion, *sel.* Sacheverell Sitwell.
Orion Seeks the Goddess Diana. MoVE
Landscapes (I-V). T. S. Eliot. LoGBV
Sels.
Cape Ann, V. EvOK; GoJo; ThWaDe
New Hampshire, I. FaBoCh; GTBS-P; LoBV; LOW; NoP; PoSa; ThWaDe
Rannoch by Glencoe, IV. FaBoEn
Usk, III. CoBE; FaBoCh
Virginia, II. NoP; PoSa
Landscapes. Louis Untermeyer. HBV
Landscapes are all we get. Predator. Peter Fellowes. QAH
Landscape's private and all that it contains, The. Artillery Shoot. James Forsyth. WaP
Landskip, The. William Shenstone. *See* Song: Landskip, The.
Lane, A. *Unknown.* PCH
("From house to house he goes.") BoTP; OTPC (1946 ed.)
(Irish Riddle, An, *sl. diff.*) RIS
Lane, The. Andrew Young. HaMV
Lane County Bachelor, The, *with music. Unknown.* AS
(Starving to Death on a Government Claim.) IHA, *diff. vers.*
Lane of elms in June, A—the air. Forby Sutherland. George Gordon M'Crae. VA
Lanes in Summer. Malcolm Hemphrey. BoTP
Lang Johnny More. *Unknown.* ESPB
L'Angelo. Thomas Caulfield Irwin. IrPN
Langland's Life. William Langland, *tr. fr. Middle English. Fr.* The Vision of Piers Plowman. MeEV
Langley Lane. Robert Buchanan. HBV
Langston. Mari Evans. BOLo

Langston Hughes. Jacques Roumain, *tr. fr. French by* Edna Worthley Underwood. PoNe
Langsyne, When Life Was Bonnie. Alexander Anderson. HBV
Language, The. Robert Creeley. CoPo
Language. Winifred Welles. NP
Language has not the power to speak what love indites. Fragment. John Clare. ELU; ERoP-2; NBM; OBNC; PoEL-4
Language Jesus Spoke, The. *Unknown.* SoP
Language thou art too narrow, and too weake. Elegie: Death. John Donne. MaMe
Languages We Are, The. F. J. Bryant. NBP
Langue d'Oc, *sel.* Ezra Pound.
Alba. PoIE
Languid, and sad, and slow, from day to day. Sonnet. William Lisle Bowles. CEP
Languid lady next appears in state, The. Characters of Women. Edward Young. *Fr.* Love of Fame, the Universal Passion, Satire V. OBEC
Languish and dispaire my hart. *Unknown.* SeCSL
Languishing Moon, The. Sir Philip Sidney. *See* Astrophel and Stella: Sonnets, XXXI.
Lanigan's Ball. *Unknown.* OxBoLi
Lanky hank of a she in the inn over there, The. A Glass of Beer [*or* Righteous Anger]. James Stephen, *after* O'Bruaidar. AnFE; AnIV; CBEP; CMoP; DTC; ExPo; FiBHP; LiTM; LiTW; MoAB; MoBrPo; OBMV; PoPl; SeCePo; ShBV-4; SiTL; TreFT; WhC
L'Annunciazione. Ned O'Gorman. TwAmPo
Lantern, The. Richard Church. MoBrPo (1942 ed.)
Lantern light from deeper in the barn, A. The Fear. Robert Frost. ATP; BeLS; MAPA; NAMP; TwAmPo
Lantern out of Doors, The. Gerard Manley Hopkins. CMoP; LiTB; OxBoCh
Lanthorn is to keep the candle Light, The. Bunyan. ThGo
Lanty Leary. Samuel Lover. BOHV; BoLP; ChTr
Laocoon. Don Gordon. WaaP
Laocoon. Donald Hall. NePoAm-2
Laodamia. Wordsworth. BEL; EnRP; EPN; ERoP-1; MBW-2; OAEP
Laon and Cythna. Shelley. *See* Revolt of Islam, The.
Lao-tse. Thomas S. Jones, Jr. AnAmPo
Lao-tzu. Po Chü-i, *tr. fr. Chinese by* Arthur Waley. LiTW; OnPM; WoL
(Philosopher, The.) WhC
Lapful of Nuts, The. *Unknown, tr. fr. Irish by* Sir Samuel Ferguson. IrPN
Lapis Lazuli. W. B. Yeats. ChMP; CMoP; CoBMV; DTC; FaBoTw; ForPo; FosPo; GTBS-W; ILP; LiTB; LiTM; MaPo (1969 ed.); MoPo; MoVE; NoP; OAEP (2d ed.) PoIE; PP
"L'Apparition" of Gustave Moreau. Gordon Bottomley. BrPo
Lapping of lake water, The. Lake Song. Jean Starr Untermeyer. AnAmPo; HBMV; MAP; MoAmPo (1942 ed.); NP; TrJP
Laprairie Hunger Strike. Ronald Everson. MoCV
L'Après Midi d'une Fille aux Cheveux de Lin. Ronald McCuaig. PoAu-2
Lapsus Calami. James Kenneth Stephen. *See* To R. K.
Lapsus Linguae. Keith Preston. WhC
Lapwing. Rex Warner. ShBV-3
Lara, *sel.* Byron.
"There was in him a vital scorn of all." OBRV
Laramie Trail. Joseph Mills Hanson. PoOW
Larbowlins stout, you must turn out. Rules of the Road. *Unknown.* SoAmSa
Larch Hill. Leslie Daiken. OnYI
Larch Tree. Laurie Lee. NeBP
Larch Wood Secrets. Ivy O. Eastwick. BoTP
Larches about this retrospective town. Naseby; Late Autumn. Basil Dowling. AnNZ
Large Bad Picture. Elizabeth Bishop. MiAP; NYBP
Large glooms were gathered in the mighty fane. James Thomson. The City of Dreadful Night, XIV. OAEP
Large towns, small towns. Our Largest and Smallest Cities. Nettie Rhodes. OCS
Larger, gentler slopes of its mouth opening upon the ocean, The. The Dysynni Valley. Theodore Holmes. CoPo
Larger Hope, The. Tennyson. *See* In Memoriam A. H. H.: "Oh yet we trust. . ."
Larger Prayer, The. Ednah Dow Cheney. BLRP; MaRV; OQP; SoP; WGRP
(Prayer—Answer.) STF
Largess, The. Richard Eberhart. LiTA; LiTM (rev. ed.)
Largest Life, The. Archibald Lampman. CaP
There Is a Beauty, *sel.* MaRV
Largo. Sidney Goodsir Smith. NeBP
Largo. Dunstan Thompson. LiTA; LiTM; MoPo; WaP
Largo e mesto. W. E. Henley. *See* Out of the Poisonous East.
Lariat snaps; the cowboy rolls, The. The Closing of the Rodeo. William Jay Smith. NePoEA; RePo; SD; TwCP
Larissa. Thomas Love Peacock. *Fr.* Rhododaphne. OBRV
Lark, The. Bernart de Ventadorn, *tr. fr. Provençal by* Ezra Pound. CTC
Lark. Josephine Miles. FiMAP
Lark, The. Lizette Woodworth Reese. GFA; HBMV; OTPC (1946 ed.)
Lark, The. *Unknown.* OBS; SeCL
Lark above our heads doth know, The. A Violinist. Francis William Bourdillon. OBVV; VA
Lark and the Nightingale, The. Hartley Coleridge. OTPC (1923 ed.)
(Song: "Tis sweet to hear the merry lark.") HBV
Lark and the Rook, The. *Unknown.* OTPC; PRWS
Lark as small as a flint arrow, A. The Round Barrow. Andrew Young. SeCePo
Lark Ascending, The. George Meredith. CABL; CoBE; EnLi-2; EPN; LoBV; OAEP; PoVP; WiR; VA
"He rises and begins to round," *sel.* OA
Lark bender hair air. Clark Coolidge. ANYP
Lark he rises early, The. Break of Day. John Clare. CBEP
Lark hit us in the face with his rising sound. Lark. Josephine Miles. FiMAP
Lark in the mesh of the tangled vine, A. Kyrielle. John Payne. HBV
Lark in the Morning, The. *Unknown.* *See* As I Was a-Walking.
Lark is but a bumpkin fowl, The. The Bonny, Bonny Owl. Sir Walter Scott. *Fr.* Kenilworth. BiS
Lark is singing in the blinding sky, The. Sea-Marge [*or* Autumn]. Alexander Smith. *Fr.* A Life-Drama. GTSE; VA
Lark is up to meet the sun, The. Morning. Jane Taylor. HBV
Lark Now Leaves His Wat'ry [*or* Watery] Nest, The. Sir William Davenant. AnEnPo; CH; ChTr; EG; InvP; LO; PoRA; ReEn; SeCL; ViBoPo; WHA
(Aubade.) ATP (1935 ed.); OBEV
(Awake! Awake!) MeWo
(Morning.) ACP; HBV
(Morning Song.) TrGrPo
(Song: "Lark now leaves his wat'ry [*or* watery] nest, The.") AWP; FaBoEn; GoBC; JAWP; LiTL; MeLP; MePo; OBS; SeCV-1; SeEP; TOP; WBP
Larks. Katharine Tynan. OnYI
Lark's Grave, The. Thomas Westwood. TVC
Lark's Nest, A. Christopher Smart. *See* For Saturday.
Lark's Song, The. Blake. *See* Nightingale and Flowers.
Larkspur. John Haines. ThO
Larkspur and Hollyhock. Names. Dorothy Aldis. BoChLi; SUS
Larrie O'Dee. William W. Fink. BOHV; HBV; OTPC (1946 ed.)
Larry and Gogo love mushrooms. Making Mushrooms. Esther Antin. RIS
Larry M'Hale. Charles James Lever. *Fr.* Charles O'Malley, the Irish Dragoon. OnYI
Larry O'Toole. Thackeray. ALV
Lars Porsena of Clusium. Horatius at the Bridge [*or* How Horatius Kept the Bridge]. Macaulay. *Fr.* Lays of Ancient Rome. BBV; BeLS; FaBoCh; FaFP; FOL; GSP; HBV; HBVY; LoGBV; MCCG; OHFP; OnSP; PoLF; PTK; ShBV-1; TIHL; TreF
L'Art, 1910. Ezra Pound. OxBA
Las Trampas U. S. A. Charles Tomlinson. TwCP
Lasca. Frank Desprez. BeLS; BLPA, *sl. abr.*; FaBoBe; HBV; NeHB; SCC; TreF
Lashes of my eye are clipped away, The. Cataract. Margoret Smith. NYBP
Lass and the Friar, The. Burns, *also at. to* Earl of Rochester. *See* Lovely Lass to a Friar Came, A.
Lass in Wonderland, A. F. R. Scott. MoCV
Lass O' Gowrie. Lady Nairne. HBV
Lass of Isleworth Mill, The. Richard Wooddeson. WaPE

Lass of Islington, The. *Unknown.* CoMu
(Fair Lass of Islington, The.) OxBB
Lass of Lochroyan, The. *Unknown.* HBV; OBB; OBEV (1st ed.)
(Annie of Lochroyan.) BuBa
(Fair Annie of Lochroyan, *with music.*) AS
(Lass of Roch Royal, The.) BaBo; ViBoFo (A *vers., with music*; B *and* C *vers.*)
(Oh, Who Will Shoe Your Bonney Feet? *with music.*) BFSS
(True Lover's Farewell, The *diff. vers.*) AS
(Who Will Shoe Your Pretty Little Foot?) AS
Lass of Lynn's New Joy, for Finding a Father for Her Child, The. *Unknown.* CoMu
Lass of Mohea, The. *Unknown.* *See* Little Mohee, The.
Lass of Richmond Hill, The. James Upton. HBV
Lass of Roch Royal. *Unknown.* *See* Lass of Lochroyan, The.
Lass That Died of Love, The. Richard Middleton. HBV
Lass That Made the Bed to Me, The. Burns. InvP; UnTE
Lass there lives upon the green, A. Pastorella. *At. to* Sir Henry Sheers. SeCL
Lass, when they talk of love, laugh in their face. Love. Francis Jammes. AWP
Lassie, can ye say. For a Wife in Jizzen. Douglas Young. OxBS
Lassie, What Mair Wad You Hae? Heine, *tr. fr. German into Scottish by* Alexander Gray. GoTS; OxBS
Lassie, with the lips sae rosy. Mädchen mit dem rothen Mündchen. Heine. AWP; JAWP; WBP
Lassitude. Paul Verlaine, *tr. fr. French by* Lawrence M. Bensky. ErPo
Last Abbot of Gloucester, The. Wilfred Rowland Childe. CAW
Last Aboriginal, The. "Fiona Macleod." PoVP; VA
By Sonnet [*or* To Beatrice on All Saints' Day]. Gabriel *tr. by* Dante Gabriel Rossetti. AWP; GoBC; JAWP; OnPM; WBP
Last and greatest herald of Heaven's King, The. For the Baptist [*or* Saint John Baptist]. William Drummond of Hawthornden. CBEP; EaLo; GoTS; GTBS-D; GTBS-P; GTBS-W; GTSE; GTSL; HBV; LoBV; OBEV; OBS; OnPP; OxBoCh; SeEP; Sonn; TrGrPo
Last Antelope, The. Edwin Ford Piper. PoMa
Last Antiphon: To Mary. James J. Donohue. ISi
Last Appeal, A. Frederic William Henry Myers. MaRV; VA
Last Appendix to "Yankee Doodle," The. *Unknown.* PAH
Last April, when the winds had lost their chill. Dover Cliff. F. Wyville Home. VA
Last Ascent, The. John Lehmann. ChMP
Last autumn's chestnuts, rather *passées.* Ingenious Raconteur. Renée Haynes. PV
Last Battle, The. *Unknown, tr. fr. Old French by* C. K. Scott Moncrieff. *Fr.* The Song of Roland. LiTW
Last Boats, The. Endre Ady, *tr. fr. Hungarian by* Antal Nyerges. LiTW
Last Bowstrings, The. Edward Lucas White. AA
Last Buccaneer, The. Charles Kingsley. BeLS; EtS; GoTP; HBV; MCCG; PeVV; PoVP; ShBV-1; VA
(Old Buccaneer, The.) EvOK; FaBoBe
Last Buccaneer, The. Macaulay. EtS; HBV
Last Bus, The. Mark Strand. TwCP
Last Call. Langston Hughes. NePoAm-2
Last came Anarchy; he rode. Shelley. *Fr.* The Masque of Anarchy. PoFr
Last came, and last did go. Milton. *Fr.* Lycidas. PoFr
Last Campaign, The. Geoffrey Lehmann. PoAu-2
Last Camp-Fire, The. Sharlot Mabridth Hall. HBV
Last Cargo. Silence Buck Bellows. EtS
Last chair finally was carried out, The. The House. Paula Nelson. GoYe
Last Chance, The. Andrew Lang. SD
Last Chantey, The. Kipling. AnFE; BoLiVe; EPN; EtS; FaBoCh; GTBS; LoGBV; MoBrPo; OBVV; OtMeF; PoVP; VA
Last Chapter, The. Walter de la Mare. CMoP; MoBrPo
Last Chorus: "All is best, though we oft doubt." Milton. *See* All Is Best.
Last Chrysanthemum, The. Thomas Hardy. CMoP; LiTB; PG (1955 ed.); PoVP; ViPo (1962 ed.)
Last Coachload, The. Walter de la Mare. SeCePo
Last Communion, The. Leo Ward. CAW; GoBC
Last Confession, A. Dante Gabriel Rossetti. NCEP; ViPP
Last Confession, A. W. B. Yeats. CMoP; ELP; ErPo; LiTL; LO
Last Conqueror, The. James Shirley. *See* Victorious Men of Earth.
Last Corn Shock, The. Glenn Ward Dresbach. FaPON
Last Cup of Canary, The. Helen Gray Cone. AA; PFY
Last Day, The. Lola Derosier. STF
Last Day, The. Daniel Sargent. CAW
Last Day and the First, The. Theodore Weiss. TwCP
Last Day of the Year, The. Alexander Smart. PCH
Last Days, The. George Sterling. AnAmPo; HBMV; NP
Last Days. Elizabeth Stoddard. AA; AnAmPo
Last Days of Alice. Allen Tate. AmP; AtBAP; OxBA; TwAmPo; UnPo
Last Days of Pompeii, The, *sel.* Sir Edward Bulwer-Lytton.
Nydia's Song. OBVV
Last Defile, The. Amy Carmichael. FaChP; MaRV; TRV
Last Democrat, The. D. J. Enright. NMP
Last Easter Jim put on his blue. Easter Zunday. William Barnes. PoVP
Last Easter when my voice was lifted up. Easter. Zula Evelyn Coon. SoP
Last eve I passed [*or* I paused last eve] beside a blacksmith's door. The Anvil [of] God's Word [*or* Hammers and Anvil *or* God's Word]. John Clifford. BLPA; BLRP; FaChP; MaRV; NeHB; OQP; PoToHe (new ed.); SoP; STF; TRV; WBLP
Last Evening. Rainer Maria Rilke, *tr. fr. German.* OnPM. *tr. by* Jessie Lemont; WaaP *tr. by* C. F. MacIntyre
Last evening when I went to bed. Our Birthday. Marion Ebey. BiCB; SiSoSe
Last Fight, The. Lewis Frank Tooker. AA; FaBoBe
Last Fire. Dante Gabriel Rossetti. The House of Life, XXX. MaVP; PoVP; ViPo; VP
Last Flower, The. John Travers Moore. PoSC
Last, for December, houses on the plain. Sonnets of the Months: December. Folgore da San Gemignano. AWP
Last Frontier, The. John Gould Fletcher. InPo
Last Fruit off an Old Tree, The, *sels.* Walter Savage Landor.
On His Seventy-fifth Birthday. AmEnPo; AnFE; BEL; BoLiVe; EPN; InP; InPo; LiTB; MaRV; OAEP; PoE; SeCeV; TIHL; TOP; TreF; TrGrPo; WHA
(Dying Speech of an Old Philosopher.) FaPL; GTBS-P; NoP; ViBoPo; YAT
(End, The.) SeCePo
(Envoi.) FaBoEn
(Finis.) GTBS-W; OBEV; OBVV; OnPP
("I Strove with None.) ChTr; EG; EnRP; GTBS; GTSL; HBV; MCCG; MemP; OBNC; PoIE; PoPo; PoSa
(Introduction: "I strove with none, for none was worth my strife.") EnLi-2
(On Himself.) VA
"There falls with every wedding chime." SeCePo; VA
Last Furrow, The. Edwin Markham. AA
Last Gate, The. Stella Mead. BoTP
Last Gloucesterman, The. Gordon Grant. EtS
Last glow from the orchid candle now fails, The. A Dream of Chiangnan. Huang-fu Sung. OnPM
Last Good-by, The. Louise Chandler Moulton. AA
Last Good-bye, The. John A. Stone. SGR
Last Guest, The. Frances Shaw. HBMV; NP
Last Hero, The. G. K. Chesterton. OtMeF
Last Hill. Edith Mirick. ChIP
Last Hour, The. Ethel Clifford. HBV
Last Hour, The. "Susan Coolidge." *See* When.
Last Hour, The. Henry Augustus Rawes. CAW
Last Hour of Faustus, The. Christopher Marlowe. *See* End of Dr. Faustus, The.
Last Hunt, The. William Roscoe Thayer. AA; FaBoBe; HBV
Last Hymn, The. "Marianne Farningham." BLPA
Last Instructions to a Painter, The. Andrew Marvell. MaMe
Sels.
Dutch in the Thames, The. PeRV
Dutch in the Medway, The, *shorter sel.* OBS
Charles II. OBS
Last Invocation, The. Walt Whitman. AmP; AnFE; APA; BoLiVe; CoAnAm; GTSB-D; HBV; MAP; MaRV; MoAmPo; NeMA; OQP; OxBA; PoEL-5; SoP; TOP; TreFT; TrGrPo; TrPWD; TRV
(Imprisoned Soul, The.) OBEV; WGRP
Last Journey, The. John Davidson. *Fr.* The Testament of John Davidson. GoTS
Last Journey, The. Leonidas of Tarentum, *tr. fr. Greek by*

Charles Merivale. AWP; JAWP; WBP
Last Judgment, The. Revelation, XX: 11-XXI: 7, Bible, *N.T.* TreF
Last Judgment. Stanton A. Coblentz. MaRV
Last Judgment, The. Cynewulf, . *tr. fr. Anglo-Saxon by* Charles W. Kennedy. *Fr.* Christ. AnOE
(Human Race Comes to Be Judged, The, *diff. tr.*) PoLi
Last Judgment. John Gould Fletcher. AWP
Last June I saw your face three times. June. Amy Levy. MeWo
Last Landlord, The. Elizabeth Akers Allen. AA
Last, last of all, in this high night of dews. Lakes. Francesco Bianco. CLwM
Last Lauch. Douglas Young. OxBS; SeCePo
Last Laugh, The. Wilfred Owen. CBV
Last Leaf, The. Harry Behn. RePo
Last Leaf, The. Oliver Wendell Holmes. AA; AmePo; AmLP; AmPP; AnAmPo; AnFE; AnNE; AP; APA; CaFP; CoAnAm; CoBA; FaBoBe; FaPON; HBV; InP; LHV; MCCG; OBVV; OnPP; OuHeWo; PFY; PG (1945 ed.); PoIE; PoLF; PoPo; SeCeV; SiTL; TOP; TreF; TSW; WaKn; WBLP
Last Leap, The. Adam Lindsay Gordon. BoAu
Last Leave of the Hills. Duncan Ban MacIntyre, *tr. fr. Gaelic.* GoTS
Last Letter to the Western Civilization. D. T. Ogilvie. NBP
Last light has gone out of the world, except, The. Liberty. Edward Thomas. MoAB
Last Lines. Emily Brontë. BoC; CBEP; ChER; EnLi-2 (1939 ed.); FaBoBe; FaPL; GoBC; HBV; MaRV; MemP; NeHB; OBEV; OBVV; PeER; TrGrPo; WGRP; WHA
(Her Last Lines.) VA
(No Coward Soul [Is Mine].) EaLo; EnLi-2 (1949 ed.); EnLit; EPN; FaBoEn; FaFP; ForPo; GTBS-W; GTSL; LiTB; OAEP; OBNC; OxBI; PoEL-5; PoIE; PoVP; TreFS; TrPWD
"Though earth and man were gone," *sel.* TRV
Last Lines. "Thomas Ingoldsby." *See* As I Laye a-Thynkynge.
Last Lines, *sel.* "Owen Meredith."
"Lord! if in love, though fainting oft, I have tended thy gracious vine." TrPWD
Last Lines. Egan O'Rahilly, *tr. fr. Irish by* Frank O'Connor. KiLC
Last Lines. Sir Walter Ralegh. *See* Conclusion, The.
Last Longhorn, The. *At. to* R. W. Hall. CoSo
Last Love. Feodor Ivanovich Tyutchev, *tr. fr. Russian.* LiTW, *tr. by* Vladimir Nabokov
Last Man, The, *sel.* Thomas Lovell Beddoes.
Crocodile, A. AnFE; CBV
Last Man, The. Thomas Campbell. EnRP; OBRV
Last Man, The. Thomas Hood. OBRV
Last March, an angel of the night. A Son in December. Frank Kendon. POTE
Last Mathematician. Hyman Edelstein. CaP
Last May a Braw Wooer. Burns. EnLi-2
Last Meeting. Gwen Harwood. PoAu-2
Last Meeting of Pocahontas and the Great Captain, The. Margaret Junkin Preston. MC; PAH
Last Memory, The. Arthur Symons. HBV
Last Minstrel, The. Sir Walter Scott. *Fr.* The Lay of the Last Minstrel. TreFS
("Way was long, the wind was cold, The," *abr.*) OTPC
Last Month. John Ashbery. ANYP; CoAP
Last Mowing, The. Robert Frost. InP
Last Music, The. Lionel Johnson. PoVP
Last Night, The. Alfred Austin. PeVV
Last Night. George Darley. HBV; OnYI
Last Night. Christian Winther, *tr. fr. Danish by* Theophilus Marzials. VA
Last night a baby gargled in the throes. A Widow in Wintertime. Carolyn Kizer. NMP
Last night a sword-light in the sky. Stone Trees. John Freeman. BoNaP
Last night a wind from Lammermoor came roaring up the glen. The Raiders. Will H. Ogilvie. ShBV-2
Last night, against the wall of the moon. Roses. J. Corson Miller. CAW
Last night, ah, yesternight, betwixt her lips and mine. Non Sum Qualis Eram Bonae sub Regno Cynarae [*or* Cynara]. Ernest Dowson. AnEnPo; AnFE; AWP; BeLS; BLPA; BoLP; BrPo; BWP; CABA; CLwM; EnLi-2; EnLit; EnLoPo; FaBoBe; FaFP; FaPL; GTBS-D; GTBS-P; GTBS-W; HBV; InPo; LiTB; LiTG; LiTL; LiTM (rev. ed.); LO; MeWo; MoBrPo; NeHB; NeMA; NoP; OBEV (new ed.); OBMV; OBNC; OBVV; OtMeF; PeVV; PG; PoFS; PoPl; PoRA; PoVP; TreF; TrGrPo; UnPo; UnTE; ViBoPo; ViPP
Last night Alicia wore a Tuscan bonnet. Alicia's Bonnet. Elisabeth Cavazza Pullen. AA
Last night along the river banks. The Boats Are Afloat. Chu Hsi. NaP
Last night, among his fellow roughs. The Private of the Buffs. Sir Francis Hastings Doyle. GTBS; HBV; InP; OBEV (new ed.); OBVV; PaPo; PoVP; VA
Last night as I lay on the prairie. The Cowboy's Dream. Charles J. Finger. BFSS; CoSo; IHA; MaC; YT
Last night, as through the crowd on Market Street. Glimpses. Roy Helton. HBMV
Last night at black midnight I woke with a cry. The Ghosts of the Buffaloes. Vachel Lindsay. AnAmPo; AnEnPo; CoBA; MAP; MoAmPo; NePA; RePo; RG
Last night beneath the foreign stars I stood. Sonnet : The Common Grave. Sydney Thompson Dobell. NCEP
Last night for the first time since you were dead. To L. H. B. Katherine Mansfield. AnNZ; HBMV
Last night God barr'd the portals of the East. Holiday. Henry Dawson Lowry. OBVV
Last night I crept across the snow. Prayer. John Farrar. ChrBoLe; OTPC (1946 ed.); PoRL
Last night I did not fight for sleep. In Hospital: Poona (I). Alun Lewis. DTC; MoPW; NeBP; SeCePo
"Last night I dreamed a ghastly dream." Ballad of the Flood. Edwin Muir. MoBS
Last night I dreamed we parted once again. Frederick Goddard Tuckerman. *Fr.* Sonnets. MAmP
Last night I dreamt I saw. The Lake: Coda. Tom Clark. YAP
Last night I got to thinking, when I couldn't go to sleep. Thanksgiving Night. Wilbur Nesbit. DD; HH; PEDC
Last night I heard a *rat-tat-too.* Rain Riders. Clinton Scollard. GaP; SoPo; TiPo
Last night I heard him in the woods. The Woodpecker. Joyce Sambrook. BoTP
Last night I kissed you with a brutal might. Sonnets of a Portrait Painter, XXXVII. Arthur Davison Ficke. AnAmPo
Last night I lay a-sleeping. The Holy City. Frederick Edward Weatherly. BLRP; WBLP
Last night I looked into a dream; 'twas drawn. A Dream. Thomas Lovell Beddoes. HoPM
Last night I saw a silver road. The Silver Road. Hamish Hendry. BoTP
Last night I saw the monster near; the big. The White Monster. W. H. Davies. LiTB
Last night I saw the Pleiades again. The Pleiades. Arthur Adams. BoAu
Last night I saw you in my sleep. Bad Dreams. Robert Browning. OAEP; PoVP
Last night I saw you in the sky. Starfish. Winifred Welles. FaPON; SiSoSe
Last night I supped on lobster. The Dream. *Unknown.* OxBoLi
Last night I thought I heard the bomb fall. How Does My Garden Grow? Ed Stone. WOW
Last night I took a journey. Traveling on My Knees. Sandra Goodwin. STF
Last night I tossed and could not sleep. God Prays. Angela Morgan. MaRV; WGRP
Last night I watched my brothers play. The Brothers. Edwin Muir. GTBS-P
Last night in a land of triangles. Zalinka. Tom MacInnes. PeCV
Last night, in snowy gown and glove. At the Comedy. Arthur Stringer. HBV
Last night knives flashed. LeChien cried. The Wolves. Galway Kinnell. NePoEA-2
Last night muffles itself in cloud and goes, The. Mise en Scène. Robert Fitzgerald. NYBP
Last night my fayre resolv'd to goe. *Unknown.* SeCSL
Last night my friend—he says he is my friend. I Hear It Said. Barbara Young. BLPA; NeHB
Last night my kisses drowned in the softness of black hair. Black Hair. Muhammadji. LiTW
Last night my little boy confessed to me. Two Prayers. Andrew Gillies. BLRP; FaChP; MaRV; PoToHe; SoP; TRV
Last Night of Winter, The. Winifred Welles. NP

Last night rain fell over the scarred plateau. Dawn on the Somme. Robert Nichols. POTE
Last night returning from my twilight walk. A Ballad of Past Meridian. George Meredith. PeVV; PoVP
Last night that she lived, The. Emily Dickinson. AmePo; AmP; AmPP; AnFE; APA; CBEP; CMoP; CoAnAm; CoBA; DiPo; ExPo; ForPo; GTBS-D; ILP; LiTA; MAmP; NePA; OxBA; PIA; PoEL-5; QFR; TDP
Last night the carol-singers came. The Carol Singers. Margaret G. Rhodes. BoTP
Last night the cherry-apple was sprinkled with rain. Words for a Picture of Newlyweds. T'ang Yin. HW
Last night the cold wind and the rain blew. Sunday at the End of Summer. Howard Nemerov. BoNaP
Last night the gypsies came. Gypsies. Rachel Field. BoTP; PoRh
Last night the nightingale woke me. Last Night. Christian Winther. VA
Last night the rainbow. Moon Shadow. George Bowering. MoCV
Last night the thunder began to roll. Broadcasting. Mildred D. Shacklett. GFA
Last night the wind was up to tricks. Picking Up Sticks. Eleanor Farjeon. PCH
Last night they came across the river and. The Enemies. Elizabeth Jennings. MoPW
Last night 'twas witching Hallowe'en. The Charms. Emma A. Opper. DD
Last night when all the stars were still. Three White Birds of Angus. Eleanor Rogers Cox. HBMV
Last night, when my tired eyes were shut with sleep. A Gazelle. Richard Henry Stoddard. AA
Last night while we were fast asleep. New Year's Day. Rachel Field. SoPo; TiPo
Last night, within my dreaming. Pine Music. Kate Louise Brown. BoTP
Last night you stirred in your sleep as the night went through. Before Dawn. Elinor Chipp. HBMV
Last o' the Tinkler, The. Violet Jacob. OxBS
"Last of England, The! O'er the sea, my dear." For the Picture, "The Last of England." Ford Madox Brown. VA
Last of flowers, in tufts around. The Brilliancies of Winter. Thomas Love Peacock. PeER
Last of His Tribe, The. Henry Clarence Kendall. PoAu-1; VA
Last of last words spoken is, Good-bye, The. Good-bye. Walter de la Mare. FaBoEn; NoP
Last of October, The. Fall. Aileen L. Fisher. TiPo (1952 ed.); YeAr
Last of our steers on the board has been spread, The. The Foray. Sir Walter Scott. EPN
Last of the *Eurydice*, The. Sir Joseph Noel Paton. VA
Last of the night's quaint clan. The Badger. P. R. Chalmers. BoPe
Last of them escapes, The. Zoo, with Lamps and Chairs. David Hilton. QAH
Last out in the raining weather, a girl and I. The Day the Weather Broke. Alastair Reid. TPM
Last Pagan Mourns for Dark Rosaleen, The. Joseph Payne Brennan. FiSC
Last Pain, The. William Empson. MoBrPo (1962 ed.)
Last Parting of Hector and Andromache, The. Homer. *See* Parting of Hector and Andromache, The.
Last Plea. Jean Starr Untermeyer. TrPWD
Last Poems. A. E. Housman. *Poems indexed separately by titles and first lines.*
Last Port, The. Frank Wilmot. BoAu
Last Portage, The, *sel.* Wilson MacDonald.
"As the stars go out so let me go." MaRV
Last pose flickered, failed, The. Rain after a Vaudeville Show. Stephen Vincent Benét. MAP; MoAmPo
Last Post, The. Robert Graves. MMA
Last Prayer, A. Helen Hunt Jackson. AA; MaRV; PCD; SoP; TrPWD; TRV
(Prayer, A: "Father, I scarcely dare to pray.") OQP
Last Prayer. Christina Rossetti. *See* Before the Beginning.
Last Quarter Moon of the Dying Year, The. Jonathan Henderson Brooks. CDC
Last Rally. Clifford K. Laube. JKCP (1955 ed.)
Last Redoubt, The. Alfred Austin. HBV
Last Refuge. Michelangelo, *tr. fr. Italian by* George Santayana. LiTW
(Three Poems, 2.) AWP
Last Reservation, The. Walter Learned. AA; PaA; PAH
Last Review, The. Emily J. Bugbee. BLPA
Last Rhyme of True Thomas,/ The. Kipling. OtMeF
Last Ride Together, The. Robert Browning. BEL; BoLiVe; EnLi-2; FiP; GTSL; HBV; LiTB; LoBV (1949 ed.); MaVP; OAEP; OBEV; OBVV; OuHeWo; PoEL-5; PoVP; UnPo (1st ed.); ViPP; VP; WHA
Last Ride Together, The (from Her Point of View). James Kenneth Stephen. BOHV; CenHV; Par
Last Romantic, The. Alexander Laing. AnAmPo
Last Rose, The. John Davidson. OBEV (1st ed.)
Last Rose of Summer, The. Thomas Moore. *See* 'Tis the Last Rose of Summer.
Last Round, The. Anna Wickham. MoBrPo
Last Saturday night I called at the house. Johnny McCardner. *Unknown.* OuSiCo
Last sea-thing dredged by sailor Time from Space. Australia. Bernard O'Dowd. BoAu; NeLNL; PoAu-1
Last Sight, The. Robert Louis Stevenson. BrPo
Last Signal, The. Thomas Hardy. ML
Last, since a pinch of dust may quench the eyes. Lilith on the Fate of Man. Christopher Brennan. *Fr.* Lilith. PoAu-1
Last Snow. Andrew Young. MoBrPo (1942 ed.); POTE; StaSt
Last snow is going, The. Spring. Harry Behn. TiPo
Last Song, The. Eileen Duggan. CAW
Last Song. James Guthrie. PDV; TiPo
Last Sonnet. Keats. *See* Bright Star, Would I Were Steadfast as Thou Art.
Last Stanzas of "The Bush." Bernard O'Dowd. *Fr.* The Bush. BoAu
("Where is Australia, singer, do you know?") PoFr
Last Summer, The. Vivian Smith. PoAu-2
Last sunbeam, The/ Lightly falls from the finished Sabbath. Dirge for Two Veterans [*or* Two Veterans]. Walt Whitman. BoLiVe; GN; MoAmPo (1950 ed.); NeMA; PoEL-5
Last Supper, The. St. John, XIII: 1-XVI: 17, Bible, *N.T.* OuHeWo
Last Supper, The. Joaquin Miller. StJW
Last Supper, The. Rainer Maria Rilke, *tr. fr. German by* M. D. Herter Norton. MoRP
Last Supper, The. Oscar Williams. FaFP; GTBS-W; LiTA; LiTM; MoRP; NePA; TwAmPo
Last Temptation, The. T. S. Eliot. *Fr.* Murder in the Cathedral. TreFT
Last, the long-haired casuarina, The. Casuarina. Roland Robinson. BoAV
Last thin acre of stalks that stood, The. Immortal. Mark Van Doren. MAP; MoAmPo
Last Things. Kathleen Raine. NYBP
Last Thoughts of a Fighting Man. Frances Angermayer. *See* Conversion.
Last Time, The. Tom Veitch. ANYP
Last time, The/ I went to the library. I Called Them Trees. Gerald William Barrax. YAP
Last time I kissed her, The. Almost Ninety. Ruth Whitman. NYTB
Last time I saw Donald Armstrong, The. The Performance. James Dickey. CoAP; LiTM (1970 ed.); NePoEA-2; TDP
Last time I slept was when, The. The Last Time. Tom Veitch.
Last time I slept with the queen, The. Dylan Thomas. SiTL
Last Time I the Well Woke, The. *Unknown.* NCEP
Last to leave, The—the first to go. The First Division Marches. Grantland Rice. PaA; PAL; YaD
Last Tournament, The. Tennyson. *Fr.* Idylls of the King. ViPo
Last Tourney, The. Frederic F. Van de Water. HBMV
Last Trams, *sel.* Kenneth Slessor.
"Then, from the skeletons of trams." MoAuPo
Last Trial, The. Petrarch. *See* Set Me Where Phoebus' Heat.
Last Verses. Thomas Chatterton. CBV; PoFS; TrGrPo
Last Verses. Michael Drayton. *See* Soe Well I Love Thee.
Last Verses. William Motherwell. HBV
Last Verses. Edmund Waller. *See* Old Age.
Last Voyage, The, *sels.* Alfred Noyes. The Torch Bearers, III. GoBC
Messages, *fr.* XIII.
Strong City, The, *fr.* Dedication.

Under the Pyrenees, *fr.* Dedication.
You That Sing in the Blackthorn, *fr.* II.
Last Voyage, The. Katharine Tynan. HBMV
Last Voyage of the Fairies, The. William H. Davenport Adams. HBVY; PRWS
Last Warmth of Arnold, The. Gregory Corso. CoPo
Last week...I heard a man speak. Pride and Prejudice. Linwood D. Smith. TNV
Last Whiskey Cup, The. Paul Engle. ATP; YaD
Last wild element is mastered now, The. The Discipline of Consequences. Eileen Duggan. JKCP (1955 ed.)
Last Will and Testament, A. *Unknown.* MeEL
Last Will of the Drunk. Myra Von Riedemann. OBCV
Last winter a snowman; and after snow an iceman. Farmer. Padraic Fallon. OxBI
Last winter we were/ short of firewood. A Letter to Hitler. James Laughlin. LiTA; WaP
Last winter when the snow was deep. One Night. Marchette Chute. ChBR
Last Wish, The. "Owen Meredith." OBEV (1st ed.); OBVV
Last Word, The. Matthew Arnold. BEL; BoLiVe; CABA; CBV; EnLi-2; FaBoEn; FiP; GTBS-D; HBV; MaRV; MBW-2; MCCG; MemP; OBNC; OBVV; PG; PoEL-5; PoFS; PoRA; PoSa; PoVP; TOP; TreFT; TrGrPo; ViPo
Last Word, A. Ernest Dowson. MoBrPo; PoVP; SyP
Last Word, The. Frederic Lawrence Knowles. HBV
Last Word of a Bluebird, The. Robert Frost. FaPON; GoJo; StVeCh (1955 ed.); ThGo; TiPo
Last Words. Annette von Droste-Hülshoff, *tr. fr. German by* Margarete Münsterberg. CAW
Last Words. John Hollander. PV
Last Words, The. Maurice Maeterlinck, *tr. fr. French by* Frederick York Powell. AWP; JAWP; PoPl; WBP
Last Words before Winter. Louis Untermeyer. GoTP; MAP; MoAmPo; NeMA
Last Words; Napoleon and Wellington, *sel.* Arthur Hugh Clough.
Serve in Thy Post, 4 *ll.* PGD
Last Words of Don Henriquez, The. Zalman Schneour, *tr. fr. Yiddish by* Joseph Leftwich. TrJP
Last Words of Juggling Jerry, The. George Meredith. *See* Juggling Jerry.
Last Words on Greece. Byron. ERoP-2
Last Words to a Dumb Friend. Thomas Hardy. OAEP (2d ed.); PoFS
Last Words to Miriam. D. H. Lawrence. CoBMV
Last World, A. John Ashbery. ANYP
Last year Harold was making a boat. Holidays in Childhood. Clifford Dyment. BoPe; POTi
Last year I trod these fields with Di. Mrs. Smith. Frederick Locker-Lampson. BOHV; HBV
Last year the war was in the northeast. War. Li Po. ChTr
Last year we fought by the head-stream of the So-kan. The Nefarious War. Li Po. WoL
Last year when I accompanied you. To a Traveler. Su T'ung-po. HoPM
Lastlie stode warre in glittering armes yclad. A Vision of War. Thomas Sackville. *Fr.* Induction to "A Mirror for Magistrates." FaBoEn
Lastly came Winter Clothèd all in frize. Winter. Spenser. *Fr.* The Faerie Queene, VII, 7. GN; OTPC
Lat never a man a wooing wend. King Henry. *Unknown.* BaBo; ESPB; OBB; OxBB
Lat Noman Booste of Konnyng nor Vertu. John Lydgate. *Fr.* The Fall of Princes. AtBAP
(Transient as a Rose.) MeEL
Lat Take a Cat. Chaucer. *Fr.* The Canterbury Tales: The Manciple's Tale. ChTr
Late. Helen Salz. GoYe
Late/ a storm of birds. Again Beginning. Sophia Castro-Leon. QAH
Late Air. Elizabeth Bishop. FiMAP; PoPl
Late Annie in her bower lay. The Ballad of Late Annie. Gwendolyn Brooks. CBV
Late April and you are three; today. W. D. Snodgrass. Heart's Needle, II. NePoEA; PIA
Late as last summer. Thou Didst Say Me. Miriam Waddington. OBCV; PeCV (1967 ed.)
Late at een, drinkin' the wine. The Dowie Houms [*or* Dens] o' Yarrow [*or* The Braes o' Yarrow]. *Unknown.* BaBo; ESPB; GoTS; OBB; OBEV; OBS; OxBS
Late at night I have heard the. And If I Die before I Wake. Clay Goss. WSL
Late August, given heavy rain and sun. Blackberry-Picking. Seamus Heaney. BoNaP
Late August to Early November. William Knott. YAP
Late Autumn. William Allingham. IrPN
Late Autumn. A. M. Sullivan. GoBC
Late Autumn. Andrew Young. HaMV; MoVE
Late Comer. Fanny de Groot Hastings. GoYe
Late Corner. Langston Hughes. Kal; NePoAm-2
Late Dandelions. Ben Belitt. NYBP
Late-Flowering Lust. John Betjeman. CMoP; ErPo; NMP
Late Harvest. James Tate. YAP
Late in an evening forth as I went. Archie o' Cawfield. *Unknown.* BaBo (A *vers.*); ESPB
Late in the afternoon. Spring Burning. Patrick Roland. PeSA
Late in the afternoon the light. Crepuscular. Richard Howard. TwCP
Late, in the louring sky, red, fiery, streaks. James Thomson. *Fr.* The Seasons: Winter. FaBoEn
Late in the winter came one day. Blossom Themes. Carl Sandburg. FIW
Late into the lulling night the pickers toiled. Uneasy Peace. Edmund Blunden. BrPo
Late Lark Twitters, A. W. E. Henley. *See* Margaritae Sorori.
Late las' night I was a-makin' my rounds. Bad Man Ballad. *Unknown.* ABF
Late last night I slew my wife. Necessity. Harry Graham. ShM; WePo
Late, Last Rook, The. Ralph Hodgson. MoBrPo
Late Late. George Starbuck. PPON
Late, late: and grey day darkens into eve. Evening. Ch'en Tzu-ang. OnPM
Late, late, so late! and dark the night and chill. Too Late. Tennyson. *Fr.* Idylls of the King: Guinevere. MaRV; OQP
Late Leaves. Walter Savage Landor. HBV; OBEV (1st ed.) ("Leaves are falling, The: so am I.") EG; GTSE
Late lies the wintry sun abed. Winter-Time. Robert Louis Stevenson. GFA; GoTP; MoBrPo; StVeCh
Late Light. Edmund Blunden. EnLoPo
Late Light. Barbara Bellow Watson. NYBP
Late Massacre in Piedmont, The. Milton. *See* On the Late Massacre in Piedmont.
Late, my grandson! half the morning have I paced these sandy tracts. Locksley Hall Sixty Years After. Tennyon. EnLi-2 (1949 ed.); PoVP; ViPo
Late October. Sara King Carleton. GoYe; PoSC; YeAr
Late of the jungle, wild and dim. Billiards. Walker Gibson. NePoAm
Late Reflections. Babette Deutsch. NYBP
Late, retarding, and unsettled season, The. Autumn; an Ode. Charles Gullans. NePoEA
Late Rising. Jacques Prévert, *tr. fr. French by* Selden Rodman. CAD; OnHM
Late September sun fills the room with light. Death-Bed. A. L. Rowse. WePo
Late Snow. Issa, *tr. fr. Japanese by* Harold G. Henderson. RePo
Late Snow and Lumber Strike of the Summer of Fifty-four, The. Gary Snyder. NaP; NMP
Late snow beats, A. Faces. Lola Ridge. MAP; MoAmPo (1942 ed.)
Late Spring, A. James Scully. NYBP
Late Summer. Kinoshita Yuji, *tr. fr. Japanese by* Geoffrey Bownas *and* Anthony Thwaite. FIW
Late sun in the winter sky, The. Vision. Giosuè Carducci. OnPM
Late that mad Monday evening. Madness One Monday Evening. Julia Fields. Kal; NNP
Late tired with woe, even ready for to pine. Astrophel and Stella, LXII. Sir Philip Sidney. EnLit; FCP; HBV; ReEn; SiPS
Late Tutorial. Vincent Buckley. PoAu-2
Late 'twas in June, the fleece when fully grown. Michael Drayton. *Fr.* The Shepherd's Garland. OBSC
Late Winter. Hazel Hall. HBMV
Late Winter. J. P. McAuley. NeLNL; PoAu-2
Late Winter. Philip Henry Savage. PCH

Late Wisdom. George Crabbe. *Fr.* Reflections. HBV, *abr.*; OBEV, *abr.*; TrGrPo
("We've trod the maze of error round.") OBRV
Lately, Alas, I Knew a Gentle Boy. Henry David Thoreau. AP; MAmP
(Sympathy.) MWA-1
Lately having escaped three-kinded death. A Birth. Muriel Rukeyser. FiMAP
Lately his haunch has grown stiff. Father. Jean Lipkin. PeSA
Lately, I've become accustomed to the way. Preface to a Twenty Volume Suicide Note. LeRoi Jones. AmNP; Kal; NNP; PoNe (1970 ed.); TTY
Lately I've become religious about atoms. Metamorpho I. Joe Rosenblatt. MoCV
Lately Our Poets. Walter Savage Landor. CABA; EPN; ERoP-1; LiTB; NBM; PoEL-4
("Lately our poets loiter'd in green lanes.") GTBS-P
Later Antigonishes, *sels.* Hughes Mearns.
Alibi. InMe
Crime Note. InMe
Frustrated Male. InMe; SiTL
Lady with Technique, The. FiBHP; InMe; SiTL; WhC
Me. InMe
Reveille. InMe; SiTL
"Later," his mother said; and still those little hands. A Child Accepts. Michael Hamburger. NMP
Later Life, *sels.* Christina Rossetti.
"Before the mountains were brought forth, before," I. Sonn
"Did Adam love his Eve from first to last?" 3 *ll.*, *fr.* XV. LO
"Star Sirius and the Pole Star dwell afar," IX. VA
"This life is full of numbness and of balk," XXVI. Sonn
"To love and to remember; that is good," VII. Lo, 4 *ll.*; Sonn
"We lack, yet cannot fix upon the lack," VI. VA
Latest Decalogue, The. Arthur Hugh Clough. BEL; BOHV; CABA; CaFP; CBEP; CBV; ChTr; EnLi-2 (1949 ed.); EnLit; EPN; ExPo; FosPo; GTBS-P; HoPM; ILP; InMe; LiTG; LoBV; NBM; OAEP; OBNC; OBVV; OtMeF; PoE; PoFS; PoIE; PoVP; SiTL; TOP; TreFT; TRV; VaPo; ViBoPo; ViPo; ViPP; WGRP
Latest, earliest, of the year. Primroses. Alfred Austin. OBVV
Latet Anguis. *Unknown.* *See* You and I and Amyas.
Lather and shave. Barber's Cry. *Unknown.* TrAS
Lather as You Go. Ogden Nash. WePo
Latimer and Ridley. Wordsworth. FOL
Latimer's Light. *Unknown.* TRV
Latin. *Unknown.* ChTr
Latin Hymn. Winthrop Mackworth Praed. CoBE
Latin is a dead tongue. Latin. *Unknown.* ChTr
Latin Lullaby. *Unknown.* *See* Lullaby: "Slumber, Jesu, o'er thy dreaming."
Latin Tongue, The. James J. Daly. CAW; GoBC
Latter Day, The. Thomas Hastings. AA
Latter Day, The. Thomas, Lord Vaux. PoLi
(Bethinking Himself of His Ende, Writeth Thus.) EnPo; SiCE
Latter-Day Warnings. Oliver Wendell Holmes. *Fr.* The Autocrat of the Breakfast Table, *ch.* 1. PCD
Latter Rain, The. Jones Very. AmP; GN; OxBA
Lattice at Sunrise, The. Charles Tennyson Turner. OBVV; Sonn; VA
Laud of Saint Catherine, The. Swinburne. *Fr.* Siena. CAW
Laud to my Lord who gave thee all of loveliness. The Mock Caliph. *Unknown, Fr.* The Thousand and One Nights. EnLi-1
Lauda. Girolamo Benevieni, *tr. fr. Italian by* John Addington Symonds. CAW
Lauda Anima Mea. Psalms, CXLVI, Bible, *O.T.*, *tr. by* John Hopkins. ReIE
Lauda Sion, *much abr.* St. Thomas Aquinas, *tr. fr. Latin.* WHL
Lauda Sion Salvatorem. Richard Crashaw. MaMe
Laudate Dominum. Psalms, CL, Bible, *O.T.* ChTr
Laudate for Christmas. Prudentius, *tr. fr. Latin by* H. T. Henry. CAW
Laude, honor, praisingis, thankis infinite. The Difficulties of Translation. Gawin Douglas. *Fr.* Prologues to the Aeneid. GoTS
Lauded lilies of the field, The. Mrs. Seymour Fentolin. Oliver Herford. HBMV
Laugh and Be Merry. John Masefield. EnLit; FaFP; MoBrPo; NeMA; PoPl; TreFT
Laugh and Sing ("'Tis mirth that fills the veins with blood"). Beaumont *and* Fletcher. *See* Mirth.
Laugh, and the world laughs with you. Solitude [*or* The Way of the World]. Ella Wheeler Wilcox. AmePo; FaFP; HBV; OHFP; PaPo; PoLF; TreF; WBLP; YaD
Laugh at all my dreams, my dearest. Credo. Saul Tchernichowsky. LiTW
Laugh, Be Jolly. A. E. Housman. *See* Think No More, Lad.
Laugh is just like sunshine, A. Sunshine and Music. Ripley Dunlap Saunders. PoToHe (new ed.)
Laugh It Off. Henry Rutherford Elliot. WBLP
Laugh not fond foole cause I a face. *Unknown.* SeCSL
Laugh now but by tomorrow you may weep. After Laughter. Grace Buchanan Sherwood. GoYe
Laugh on, laugh on at all the dreams. I Believe. Saul Tchernichowsky. TrJP
Laughed at the old deliberate ways. Repression. Timothy Corsellis. WaP
Laughin' wif yo' dinnah in the cohneh ob yo' mouf. A Dixie Lullaby. Strickland W. Gillilan. LHV
Laughing and teasing. A Glimpse of Beauty. Chien Liang Tse. OnPM
Laughing Ann. A. P. Herbert. OnPP
Laughing god born of a startling answer, The. Bacchus. William Empson. PoCh
Laughing Hyena, by Hokusai, The. D. J. Enright. TwCP
Laughing It Out. William Stanley Braithwaite. Sandy Star and Willie Gee, II. BANP
Laughing knot of village maids, A. The Shaded Pool. Norman Gale. HBV; OBVV
Laughing, she flashes down the shifting tides of green. Water Sprite. Donald Wandrei. FiSC
Laughing Song. Blake. *Fr.* Songs of Innocence. BoTP; BrR; CBEP; DiPo; EiPP; EnLi-2; EnRP; GoJo; GoTP; OTPC; PCH; PoRh; PoSC; SoPo; SUS; ThWaDe; TiPo; WaKn
(When the Green Woods Laugh.) CH
Laughing Time. William Jay Smith. FaPON; SoPo
Laughing Willow, The. Oliver Herford. BOHV; HBV
Laughter. Isabella Valancy Crawford. CaP
Laughter. Olive Enoch. BoTP
Laughter. Miriam Waddington. WHW
Laughter and Death. Wilfrid Scawen Blunt. The Love Sonnets of Proteus, XCI. MoBrPo (1942 ed.); PoMa; Sonn; VA
Laughter and Tears. Tertius van Dyke. MaRV
Laughter not time destroyed my voice. The Friends of His Youth. W. B. Yeats. *Fr.* A Man Young and Old. AtBAP
Laughter of children brings. Early Supper. Barbara Howes. GoJo; PoPl
Laughter of the lesser lynx, The. The Lesser Lynx. E. V. Rieu. CenHV; FiBHP
Laughter wears a lilied gown. Laughter. Isabella Valancy Crawford. CaP
Laughter, with us, is no great undertaking. Mrs. Reece Laughs. Martin Armstrong. POTE
Launch, The. Alice Meynell. PeVV
Launch Out into the Deep. Ida Norton Munson. ChIP
Launched upon ether float the worlds secure. Authority. William Reed Huntington. AA
Laundry so near the ocean bothered Frank. Duo-tang. Kenward Elmslie. ANYP
Laundry truck, A. Calamity. F. R. Scott. PeCV (1967 ed.)
Laura. Thomas Campion. *See* Rose-cheeked Laura.
Laura, *sels.* Robert Tofte.
"As burnish'd gold, such are my sovereign's hears." ReIE
"Down from the neck unto that dainty breast." ReIE
"In love his kingdom great, two fools there be." ReIE; Sonn; TuPP
"Rich damask roses in fair cheeks do bide." ElL
"Strange is this thing! My horse I cannot make." ReIE; Sonn; TuPP
"Two winds, one calm, another fierce to see." ReIE
"Unto thy favor, which when nature formed." Sonn; TuPP
"What time with brow the loveliest gins to scowl." ReIE
"When I did part from thee the other night." ReIE
"When she was born she came with smiling eye." ReIE; Sonn; TuPP
Laura Age Eight. Ramon Guthrie. OPoP
Laura Cashdollars. Bernadette Mayer. ANYP

Laura Sleeping. Charles Cotton. CavP; ELP; FaBoEn; LoBV; OBS; SeCL; ViBoPo
Laura Sleeping. Louise Chandler Moulton. AA
Laura Waits for Him in Heaven. Petrarch, *pr. tr. fr. Italian by* J. M. Synge. *Fr.* Sonnets to Laura: To Laura in Death. OBMV
Laurana's Song. Richard Hovey. AA
Laura's Song. Oliver Madox Brown. OBVV; VA
Laureate, The. William Aytoun. Par
Laureate, The. Robert Graves. FaBoTw
Laurel-crowned Horatius. Lauriger Horatius [*or* Time's Flying]. *Unknown.* HBV; OnPM
Laurel leaf, which you this day do wear, The. Amoretti, XXVIII. Spenser. CABA; RelE
Laurel, meed of mighty conquerors, The. Trees. Spenser. *Fr.* The Faerie Queene, I, 1. PoG
Laurels and Immortelles. William Allingham. BLPA
Laurence Bloomfield in Ireland, *sel.* William Allingham.
Ballytullagh. IrPN
Laurentian Shield. F. R. Scott. OBCV
Lauriger Horatius. *Unknown, tr. fr. Latin by* John Addington Symonds. HBV
(Time's Flying.) OnPM
L'Aurore Grelottante. Peter Levi. NePoEA-2
Laus Deo. Sydney Dobell. OBEV (1st ed.)
Laus Deo! Whittier. AmP; AmPP; AnNE; AP; CoBA; DD; MC; PaA; PAH; PoFr
Laus Infantium. William Canton. HBV; VA
Laus Mariae. Sidney Lanier. Sonn
Laus Mortis. Frederic Lawrence Knowles. HBV
Laus Veneris. Louise Chandler Moulton. AA; HBV
Laus Veneris. Swinburne. MaVP; PoVP; ViPP
Laus Virginitatis. Arthur Symons. EnLoPo
Lausanne. Thomas Hardy. FaBoTw; ViPo
Lavender Bush, The. Elizabeth Fleming. BoTP
Lavender Cowboy, The, *with music. Unknown.* CoSo
Lavender's Blue. *Unknown.* CH; HH; LiTL
("Lavender's blue, diddle, diddle," *sl. diff.*) OxNR
Lavender's blue, diddle diddle. The Country Lovers. *Unknown.* UnTE
Lavender's for Ladies. Patrick R. Chalmers. HBMV
Lavengro, *sel.* George Borrow.
"Life is sweet, brother." BBBV (1951 ed.)
Lavinia. James Thomson. *Fr.* The Seasons: Autumn. OBEC
Lavish Kindness. Elinor Wylie. AtBAP; CrMA
Law, The. Samuel Butler. CBV
Law, The. Albert Haynes. NBP
Law, The. Abraham ibn Ezra, *tr. fr. Hebrew by* Alice Lucas. TrJP
Law against Lovers, The, *sel.* Sir William Davenant.
Wake All the Dead. What Ho! What Ho! CBEP; ELP; FaBoCh; LoGBV; SeCePo; SeCL
(Song: "Wake all the dead!") LoBV
Law firm commanding, A. Help Wanted. Franklin Waldheim. BLPA
Law in the Country of the Cats. Ted Hughes. ToPo
Law is the true embodiment, The. The Susceptible Chancellor. W. S. Gilbert. *Fr.* Iolanthe. ALV; PoVP
Law like Love. W. H. Auden. CaFP; CMoP; CoBMV; FaBoTw; NoP; PoFS
(Law, Say the Gardeners, Is the Sun.) MoAB; MoBrPo; TrGrPo
Law makes long spokes of the short stakes of men. Legal Fiction. William Empson. CMoP; ExPo; FaBoMo; LiTB; LiTM; MoVE; NoP; ReMP; SeCeV (1967 ed.); ToPo
Law of Averages, The. "Troubadour." FiBHP; InMe
Law of Jehovah is perfect, restoring the soul, The. *See* Law of the Lord is perfect. . .
Law of Love, The. John Oxenham. *Fr.* Chaos—and the Way Out. OQP
Law of the Jungle, The. Kipling. *Fr.* The Second Jungle Book. BoChLi; LiTB; OA; PoEL-5; PoVP; ShBV-1; VA
Law of the Lord [*or* Jehovah] is perfect, restoring the soul, The. The Law Within [*or* God's Precept Perfect]. *Fr.* Psalm XIX, Bible, *O.T.* BLRP; MaRV
Law of the Yukon, The. Robert W. Service. CaP; HBV; TreFS
Law, Say the Gardeners, Is the Sun. W. H. Auden. *See* Law like Love.
Law West of the Pecos, The. S. Omar Barker. IHA
Law Within, The. Pasalms, XIX: 7-14, Bible, *O.T., (Moulton, Modern Reader's Bible).* MaRV
Lawd, Dese Colored Chillum. Ruby C. Saunders. WSL
Lawd he thought he'd make a man, De. *See* Lord he thought he'd make a man, De.
Lawd, if I got my ticket, can I ride? If I Got My Ticket, Can I Ride? *Unknown.* OuSiCo
Lawd is dead, The. On Philosophy. Barbara Marshall. TNV
Lawlands o' Holland, The. *Unknown. See* Lowlands of Holland, The.
Lawn and Light. James Applewhite. *Fr.* Steps from the Stream. YAP
Lawn as White as Driven Snow. Shakespeare. *Fr.* The Winter's Tale, IV, iii. OAEP; OBSC; SiCE; ViBoPo
(Autolycus's Song.) LoBV
(Come Buy! [Come Buy!]) ElL; GaP
(Pedlar, The.) WiR
(Pedlar's Song.) CH
(Songs of Autolycus, The.) OTPC (1923 ed.)
Lawn-Mower. Dorothy Baruch. SoPo; SUS
Lawn Roller, The. Robert Layzer. NePoEA
Lawns darken, evening broods in the black, The. Tennyson. Alan Ansen. CoAP
Lawrence of Virtuous Father Virtuous Son. Milton. *See* To Mr. Lawrence.
Lawrence; the Last Crusade, *sel.* Selden Rodman.
"Out of the east the plane spun; over rolling." NAMP
Laws-a-massey, what have you done? Negro Reel. *Unknown.* AS
Lawsamassy, for heaven's sake. Lucy Lake. Ogden Nash. ShM
Laws are the secret avengers, The. The Avengers. Edwin Markham. MAP; MoAmPo; NeMA
Laws of God, the Laws of Man, The. A. E. Housman. EnLi-2 (1949 ed.); MoAB; MoBrPo; OxBoLi
Lawyer in Search of Six Poets. *Unknown.* SiTL
Lawyers, Bob, know too much, The. The Lawyers Know Too Much. Carl Sandburg. CMoP; HBMV; YaD
Lawyer's head to draw a crafty deed, A. Description of Cozeners. George Whetstone. TuPP
Lawyer's Invocation to Spring, The. Henry Howard Brownell. BOHV; PoLF
Lawyers Know Too Much, The. Carl Sandburg. CMoP; HBMV; YaD
Lawyers may revere that tree, The. Epigram on a Lawyer's Desiring One of the Tribe to Look with Respect to a Gibbet. Robert Fergusson. OxBS
Lay a Garland on My Hearse. Beaumont *and* Fletcher. *See* Aspatia's Song.
Lay aside phrases; speak as in the night. This Is Not Death. Humbert Wolfe. MoBrPo
Lay by your pleading, Love lies a-bleeding. *Unknown.* LO
Lay Called The Short Lay of Sigurd, The. *Unknown. See* Short Lay of Sigurd, The.
Lay Dis Body Down, *with music. Unknown.* ABF
Lay down, boys, and take a little nap. Cumberland Gap. *Unknown.* ABF
Lay down one hand before you like a tool. Scarabs for the Living, III. R. P. Blackmur. CoAnAm; TwAmPo
Lay down the axe; fling by the spade. Our Country's Call. Bryant. AnNE; MC; PaA; PAH
Lay down these words. Riprap. Gary Snyder. NeAP
Lay down your stake at play, lay down your passion. A Rule to Play. Sir John Harington. SiCE
Lay his dear ashes where ye will. President Lincoln's Grave. Caroline Atherton Briggs Mason. DD; OHIP
Lay in the house mostly living. Madness. James Dickey. NYBP
Lay It Bare. *Unknown, tr. fr. Japanese by* Ishii *and* Obata. OnPM
Lay me down beneaf de willers in de grass. A Death Song. Paul Laurence Dunbar. AA; BANP; CDC; PoLF; PoNe
"Lay me in a cushioned chair." The Ballad of the Foxhunter. W. B. Yeats. EnLit
Lay me in the woodbox. Last Will of the Drunk. Myra Von Riedemann. OBCV
Lay me in yon place, lad. The Last o' the Tinkler. Violet Jacob. OxBS
Lay me low, my work is done. Valedictory. Adam Lindsay Gordon. VA
Lay me on an anvil, O God. Prayers of Steel. Carl Sand-

Lay (continued)
burg. AnAmPo; AP; CBV; CMoP; FaPON; MAP; MoAmPo; MPB; NeMA; NP; PFY; OCS; OQP; PDV; PoMa; TrPWD; YAD
Lay me to rest in some fair spot. Traveller's Hope. Charles Granville. HBV; OBVV
Lay me to rest on yon towering height. Simpson's Rest. George S. Simpson. PoOW
Lay me to sleep in sheltering flame. The Mystic's Prayer. "Fiona Macleod." HBV; MaRV; TrPWD; WGRP
Lay not up for yourselves treasures upon earth. Treasures [in Heaven]. St. Matthew, Bible, *N.T.* GoTP; TrGrPo
Lay of Ancient Rome. Thomas R. Ybarra. BOHV; HBV; InMe; LHV; WhC
Lay of Finn, The. Unknown, *tr. fr. Anglo-Saxon by* Charles W. Kennedy. *Fr.* Beowulf. AnOE
Lay of Prince Marvan, The. *Tr. fr. Irish by* Eleanor Hull. AnIV
Lay of Sigurd, The. *Unknown.* *See* Short Lay of Sigurd, The.
Lay of St. Cuthbert, The. "Thomas Ingoldsby." *Fr.* The Ingoldsby Legends. OtMeF
St. Cuthbert Intervenes, *sel.* NBM
Lay of the Battle of Tombland, The. Dunstan Thompson. LiTA; NePA
Lay of the Captive Count, The. Goethe, *tr. fr. German by* James Clarence Mangan. AWP
Lay of the Cid, The. *Unknown.* *See* Cid, The.
Lay of the Deserted Influenzaed. Henry Cholmondeley-Pennell. BOHV; InMe
Lay of the Famine, A. *Unknown, at. to* Rosa Mulholland. OnYI
Lay of the Forlorn. George Darley. OnYI
Lay of the Laborer. Thomas Hood. DD; HH; VA
Lay of the Last Frontier. Harold Hersey. PoOW
Lay of the Last Minstrel, *sels.* Sir Walter Scott.
Breathes There the Man [with Soul So Dead], *fr.* VI. BBV; BLPA; EnRP; FaFP; HT; InP; MaRV; NeHB; OAEP; OBRV; OxBS; PGD; TreF
(Innominatus.) OBEV; PAL; TOP
(Love of Country.) OHFP; OQP; OTD; PaPo; WBLP
(My Native Land.) GN; MPB (1956 ed.); OTPC (1923 ed.); PTK; StaSt
(My Own, My Native Land.) StVeCh (1940 ed.)
(Native Land.) TrGrPo
(Patriot, The.) OBNC
(Patriotism.) PCD; PG (1945 ed.); SoP; TRV
"Call it not vain; they do not err," *fr.* V. OBRV
Dies Irae, *fr.* VI, *par. fr. the Latin* Dies Irae of Thomas of Celano. GoBC; MaRV
("Nought of the Bridal will I tell," *longer sel.*) OBRV
Fathers's Notes of Woe, A, *fr.* IV. OBNC
"Feast was over in Branksome tower, The," *fr.* I. OBRV
"He paused: the listening dames again," Interlude *after* IV. OBRV
"Humble boon was soon obtain'd, The," *fr. introd. and* I. OBRV
"If thou would'st view fair Melrose aright," *fr.* II. OBRV
(Melrose Abbey.) SeCePo
(Sir William of Deloraine at the Wizard's Tomb.) OBNC
"In peace, Love tunes the shepherd's reed," *fr.* III. ViBoPo
It Was an English Ladye Bright, *fr.* VI. ATP
(Song of Albert Graeme.) EnRP
Minstrel Responds to Flattery, The, *fr.* V. OBNC
Rosabelle, *fr.* VI. BeLS; GTBS; GTBS-D; GTBS-P; GTBS-W; GTSE; GTSL; HBV; OTPC (1923 ed.)
(Harold's Song.) EnLi-2; EnRP
Sweet Teviot, *fr.* IV. OBRV
True Love's the Gift, *fr.* V. OBRV
"Way was long, the wind was cold, The." *Introd.* OTPC
(Last Minstrel, The.) TreFS
Lay of the Levite, The. William E. Aytoun. HBV
Lay of the Love-lorn, The. William E. Aytoun *and* Sir Theodore Martin. BOHV
(Cry of the Lovelorn, The.) CenHV
Lay of the Lover's Friend, The. William E. Aytoun. BOHV
Lay of the Trilobite, The. May Kendall. CenHV
Lay of Thrym, The. *Unknown, tr. fr. Icelandic by* Henry Adams Bellows. *Fr.* The Elder Edda. LiTW; OuHeWo
Lay on the fire their ancient hold. Burning the Bee-Tree. Ruth Pitter. POTE
Lay out the minutes, row on ordered row. Time Out. Frances Westgate Butterfield. GoYe
Lay Preacher Ponders, The. Idris Davies. ACV; FaBoTw
Lay this laurel on the one. Emily Dickinson. AP; MWA-2
Lay up nearer, brother, nearer. The Dying Californian. *Unknown.* BFSS; TrAS
Lay willows under Walsingham. The Holy Land of Walsingham. Benjamin Francis Musser. ISi
Lay Your Head. Iwan Goll, *tr. fr. French by* Iwan Goll. OnPM
Lay Your Sleeping Head, [My Love]. W. H. Auden. BoLiVe (1945 ed.); ChMP; CoBMV; FaBoEn; GTBS-D; LiTB; LO; MaPo; MoAB; MoBrPo; MoPo; MoVE; PAn; PIA; PoAn; PoE; POTE; ReMP; SeCePo; UnPo (3d ed.); VaPo
(Song XI.) EnLoPo
Laye of ye Woodpeckore, Ye. Henry A. Beers. NA
Layer above layer—the moving clouds! Rain. Tu Fu. OnPM
Laying the Dust. Denise Levertov. ToPo
Laymen, The. Edgar A. Guest. SoP
Lays of Ancient Rome, *sels.* Macaulay.
Battle of Lake Regillus, The. PoG, 16 *ll.*.
Death of Herminius, The. OtMeF
Fight in the Centre, The. OtMeF
Herminius's Horse. PoG
Horatius [at the Bridge]. BBV, *abr.*; BeLS; FaBoCh. abr.; FaFP; FOL, *abr.*; GSP, *abr.*; HBV; HBVY; LoGBV; MCCG; OHFP, *abr.*; OnSP; PoLF; PTK; ShBV-1; TreF
Fight at the Bridge, The. MaC; OtMeF
"Then out spake brave Horatius." PoFr
Lazarus. A. S. Cripps. BoSA
Lazarus. *Unknown.* *See* Dives and Lazarus.
Lazily through the clear. The Goldfish. Audrey Alexandra Brown. CaP
Lazy and slow, through the snags and trees. In the Bayou. Don Marquis. AmFN
Lazy-bones, lazy-bones, wake up and peep. Nonsense Verses. Charles Lamb. BOHV; NA
Lazy deuks that sit i' the coal-neuks. *Unknown.* OxNR
Lazy laughing languid Jenny. Jenny. Dante Gabriel Rossetti. MaVP; PoEL-5; ViPo; ViPP; VP
Lazy Lou. Mary Mapes Dodge. BBGG
Lazy Mary, Will You Get Up? Maud *and* Miska Petersham. RePo
Lazy petals of magnolia-bloom flat down the sluggish river. Elegy on a Nordic White Protestant. John Gould Fletcher. PoNe
Lazy Roof, The. Gelett Burgess. BOHV; NA; TreFT
(Queer Quatrains.) RIS
Lazy sheep, pray tell me why. The Sheep [*or* The Boy and the Sheep]. Ann Taylor. BoChLi; BoTP; MPB; OTPC; PRWS; UTS
Lazy Thought, A. Eve Merriam. OCS
Lazy Writer, The. Bert Leston Taylor. ALV; PoMa
Le Christianisme. Wilfred Owen. BrPo
Le Coeur de l'Immaculée. Benjamin Francis Musser. WHL
Le Fou. Robert Creeley. FRC
Le Hore di Recreatione; or, The Pleasant Historie of Albino and Bellama, *sel.* Nathaniel Whiting.
Tinker and the Monks, The. SeCL
Le Jardin ("The lily's withered chalice falls"). Oscar Wilde. SeCePo; SyP; ViPP
(Garden, The.) PoRA
Le Jardin des Tuileries ("This winter air is keen"). Oscar Wilde. JKCP (1926 ed.)
Le Jeune Homme Caressant Sa Chimère. John Addington Symonds. OBVV; PoVP
Le Livre Est sur la Table. John Ashbery. ANYP
Le Marais du Cygne. Whittier. PAH
Le Mauvais Larron. Rosamund Marriott Watson. VA
Le Monocle de Mon Oncle. Wallace Stevens. AnAmPo; AnFE; AP; APA; CoAnAm; CoBMV; LiTM; MAPA; MoAB; NP; TwAmPo
Le Musée Imaginaire. Charles Tomlinson. NePoEA-2
Le Repos en Egypte; the Sphinx. Agnes Repplier. CAW; ISi; JKCP
(Sphinx, The.) StJW
Le Roi Est Mort. Agnes Mary Frances Robinson. OBVV
Le saltimbanque is coming with. Song for Zarathustra. Lawrence Durrell. ToPo
Le Secret Humain. Archibald MacLeish. CMoP
Le Tombeau de Pierre Falcon. James Reaney. MoCV

Lead gently, Lord, and slow. A Hymn [after Reading "Lead Kindly Light"). Paul Laurence Dunbar. MaRV; TrPWD; TRV
Lead, Kindly Light. Cardinal Newman. *See* Pillar of the Cloud, The.
Lead Me. Adelaide A. Procter. FaChP
Lead me, O God, and thou my Destiny. God Leads the Way. Cleanthes. EaLo
Lead Me On. *Unknown.* SoP
Lead Me to Calvary. Jennie Evelyn Hussey. SoP
Lead on, lead on, America. Louise Ayres Garnett. *Fr.* Song of Liberty. PGD
Lead On, O King Eternal. Ernest W. Shurtleff. MaRV
Lead us, heavenly Father, lead us. Prayer to the Trinity [*or* Hymn]. James Edmeston. HBV; NeHB; VA
Leadbelly's Chisholm Trail. *Unknown.* *See* When I Was a Cowboy.
Leade the black bull to slaughter, with the bore. Upon Master W. Montague. Thomas Carew. SeEP
Leaden Echo and the Golden Echo, The. Gerard Manley Hopkins. BrPo; CMoP; CoBMV; DTC; EnLi-2 (1949 ed.); FaFP; GTBS-D; GTBS-P; GTBS-W; LiTB; LiTM; LoBV; MasP; MoAB; MoBrPo; MoVE; OAEP (2d ed.); OBMV; OBNC; PAn; PoDB; ViPo; VP
Leaden Treasury of English Verse, A, *sels.* Paul Dehn. FiBHP
"Jenny kiss'd me when we met."
"Nuclear wind, when wilt thou blow."
Leaden-eyed, The. Vachel Lindsay. ATP; BoLiVe; CMoP; ELU; GTBS-W; LiTA; LiTM; MaRV; MemP; MoRP; NAMP; NePA; NP; PoPo; PPON
Leader, A. "Æ." HBMV
Leader, The. Hilaire Belloc. ACP (1952 ed.)
Leader, The. Second Samuel, XXIII: 3-4, Bible, *O.T.* PCD; PCH
Leader, The. Thomas Hanna. QAH
Leader, The. Dorothy Livesay. MoCV; PeCV (1967 ed.)
Leaders. *Unknown.* WBLP
Leaders, New Style; the General (1917). Siegfried Sassoon. *See* General, The.
Leaders of the Crowd, The. W. B. Yeats. EnLit; MoAB; MoBrPo; PoAn; PoPo
Leaders, Old Style. Sir Walter Scott. *Fr.* Marmion, III OtMeF
Leading. Mary Carolyn Davies. MaRV
Leading with his chin, though bristling. "Blue Is the Hero." Bill Berkson. ANYP
Leadsman's Song. *At. to* J. Pearce *and to* Charles Dibdin. *See* Heaving the Lead.
Leaf. John Hewitt. NeIP
Leaf, A. Ludwig Uhland, *tr. fr. German by* John S. Dwight. AWP; JAWP; WBP
Leaf, The. John Williams. NePoAm-2
Leaf after Leaf Drops Off. Walter Savage Landor. OQP; TRV; ViBoPo
Leaf and Soul. John Banister Tabb. PoMa
Leaf falls softly at my feet, A. A Leaf. Ludwig Uhland. AWP; JAWP; WBP
Leaf is wilting, The. Summer drains out. Junker Schmidt. "Kozma Prutkov" (Alexsey Tolstoy *and others*). ELU
Leaf-Makers, The. Harold Stewart. PoAu-2
Leaf Mirrors. James Applewhite. YAP
Leaf moved up on me, like a tattered old sailor dropped from the long winds, A. Punchinello. Hugh de Burgh. CAW
Leaf-Movement. Arthur Davison Ficke. MAP; NP
Leaf of Grass, A. Walt Whitman. *See* Miracles ("I believe a leaf of grass").
Leaf-picking, The. Frédéric Mistral, *tr. fr. Provençal by* Harriet Waters Preston. AWP; JAWP; WBP
Leaf ran at my heels, A. Companions. Adrien Stoutenburg. WIRo
Leaf-Treader, A. Robert Frost. MAP; MoAmPo; PoeP
Leaf turns, A. The Walker. Yvor Winters. NP
Leaf will wrinkle to decay, The. The Crest Jewel. James Stephens. AnIL; MoAB; MoBrPo
Leafe gold, Lord of thy golden wedge o'relaid. Meditation XVI. Edward Taylor. *Fr.* Preparatory Meditations, First Series. MAmP
Leafless are the trees; their purple branches. The Golden Mile-Stone. Longfellow. PoEL-5
Leafless, stemless, floating flower. The Butterfly. John Banister Tabb. UTS
Leafless Tree, A. Ann Louise Thompson. OQP
Leaflight to lamplight, blind with so much sight. The Brahms. Herbert Morris. NePoAm-2.
Leafy-with-love banks and the green waters of the canal. Canal Bank Walk. Patrick Kavanagh. MoBrPo (1962 ed.)
League of Love in Action, The. Edwin Markham. PEDC
League of Nations, A. Joel Barlow. *Fr.* The Columbiad, X. CoBA
("Eager he look'd. Another train of years.") AmPP (5th ed.)
(One Centred System.) AP
League of Nations, The. Mary Siegrist. MC; PAH
Leagues north, as fly the gull and auk. The *Palatine.* Whittier. EtS
Leak in the Dike [*or* Dyke], The. Phoebe Cary. FaFP; FaPON; OnSP; OTPC; PaPo; StVeCh (1940 ed.); TreF
Lean and tall and stringy are the Navajo. The Painted Desert: The Navajo. Elizabeth J. Coatsworth. AmFN
Lean back, and get some minutes' peace. Faustine. Swinburne. BeLS; MaVP; PoVP; UnTE; ViPo; ViPP
Lean close and set thine ear against the bark. Heart of Oak. Charles Henry Luders. AA
Lean coyote, prowler of the night, The. Sunrise. Charles Erskine Scott Wood. *Fr.* The Poet in the Desert. GoTP; MAP; PFY
Lean Hard. *Unknown.* FaChP; SoP
"Lean Hard on Me." Clifford Lewis. SoP
Lean in the greenhood of my fearful years. Fool Song. Cornel Lengyel. GoYe
Lean, lanky son of desert sage. To a Jack Rabbit. S. Omar Baker. IHA
Lean on Me. *Unknown.* SoP
Lean Out of the Window. Goldenhair [*or* Song]. James Joyce. Chamber Music, V. BoLP; BoTP; ChTr; HBMV; HW; LOW; MoSiPe; POTE; RePo
Lean out the window: down the street. A Man with a Little Pleated Piano. Winifred Welles. FaPON; GaP
Lean Street. G. S. Fraser. NeBP; OxBS
Lean your small head against the Spring. Walking to Dedham. David Wright. NeBP
Leander Stormbound. Sydney Goodsir Smith. OxBS
Leaners or Lifters. Ella Wheeler Wilcox. *See* Lifting and Leaning.
Leaning/ On my shoulder. Impatience. Ts'ao Ho. OnPM
Leaning against the wind across the paddock ways. Winter Westerlies. James Devaney. BoAV; MoAuPo
Leaning his chin in his small hard hands. Kentucky Birthday [February 12, 1815]. Frances Frost. SiSoSe; YeAr
Leaning out over. W. H. Auden. *Fr.* Symmetries and Asymmetries. FIW
Leap, The. James Dickey. FRC
Leap and Creep. *Unknown,* *tr. fr. Sanskrit by* Arthur W. Ryder. *Fr.* The Panchatantra. OuHeWo
Leap Before You Look. W. H. Auden. TPM
Leap for Life, A. George Pope Morris, *Also at. to* Walter Colton. *See* Main-Truck, The; or, A Leap for Life.
Leap of Roushan Beg, The. Longfellow. StVeCh
Leap out, chill water, over reeds and brakes. The River God. Sacheverell Sitwell. MoBrPo
Leap to the highest height of spring. An Early Bluebird. Maurice Thompson. AA
Leap-Year Episode, A. *At. to* Eugene Field. BoLP
Leaped at the caribou. Ho Ho Ho Caribou. Joseph Ceravolo. ANYP
Leaping Falls. Galway Kinnell. NePoAm-2
Leaping from oak to oak, tangled-up in the woods. Sacrifice of a Red Squirrel. Joseph Langland. NYBP
Leaping Laughers, The. George Barker. OBMV
Lear. Thomas Hood. VA
Lear and Cordelia ("Some officers take them away"). Shakespeare. *Fr.* King Lear, V, iii. FiP
Lear and Cordelia! 'twas an ancient tale. To England. George Henry Boker. AA; AnAmPo; HBV; OTPC
Learn if you must, but do not come to me. Glass Houses. E. A. Robinson. MoRP
Learn, lads and lasses, of my garden. Francis Daniel Pastorius. SCAP
Learn to mak your bed, Annie. Fair Annie. *Unknown.* OxBB

Learn to speak this little word. "No!" Eliza Cook. PoToHe (new ed.)
Learn to Wait. *Unknown.* PoToHe
Learned and a happy ignorance, A. Eden. Thomas Traherne. AnAnS-1; MeP; PoEL-2; SCEP-1; SeCV-2; TrGrPo
Learned Man, A. Stephen Crane. The Black Riders, XX. LiTA; MoAmPo (1950 ed.); NePA
Learned Men, The. Archibald MacLeish. MoAB; MoAmPo (1950 ed.)
Learned Mistress, A. *Unknown, tr. fr. Irish by* Frank O'-Connor. KiLC; OBMV
Learned Negro, The. *Unknown.* BOHV
Learned to Trust. William Cowper. SoP
Learning. George Chapman. *Fr.* Euthymiae Raptus; or, The Tears of Peace. SeCePo
Learning. Mary Fullerton. NeLNL
Learning. Bob Jones, Jr. SoP
Learning and dignity. Flaming Banners. Bhartrihari. OnPM
Learning by Doing. Howard Nemerov. TwCP
Learning Destiny. Herman Charles Bosman. PeSA
Learning Family. Dell Washington. WSL
Learning to Dance. Rudy Bee Graham. BF
Learning to Draw. Ann *or* Jane Taylor. SAS
Learning to Play. Abbie Farwell Brown. HH; PPL
Learning to Skate. Emilie Blackmore Stapp. GFA
Learning to Swim. Anna Medary. GFA
Least little sound sets the coyotes walking, The. Outside. William Stafford. NePoAm-2
Least of Carols, The. Sophie Jewett. ChrBoLe; OHIP
Leather Bottel, The. *Unknown, at. to* John Wade. PeRV; SeCL
Leather-skinned wrinkled old man, A. Rock Painting. Jack Cope. PeSA
L'Eau Dormante. Thomas Bailey Aldrich. HBV
Leave a Kiss within the Cup. Agathias Scholasticus, *tr. fr. Greek by* J. M. Edmonds. WoL
"Leave all and follow—follow!" The Forbidden Lure. Fannie Stearns Davis. HBV
Leave Caelia, leave the woods to chase. On His Mistris That Lov'd Hunting. *Unknown.* OBS
Leave Cancelled. Bill Berkson. ANYP
Leave go my hands, let me catch breath and see. In the Orchard. *Unknown.* UnTE
Leave God to Order. George Neumark, *tr. fr. German by* Catherine Winkworth. SoP
Leave Helen to her lover. Draw away. The White Isle of Leuce. Sir Herbert Read. FaBoTw
Leave her alone. The Seals. L. A. G. Strong. LO; POTE
Leave Her, Johnny. *Unknown.* SoAmSa, *with music.*
(Leave Her, Bullies, Leave Her, *diff. vers., with music.*) AS
(Time for Us to Leave Her, *diff. vers., with music.*) ShS
(Time to Leave Her, *diff. vers., with music.*) AmSS
Leave her now, go out and learn. To Himself. Richard Aldridge. NePoAm
Leave him alone, sweet enemy. The Lonely Traveller. Kwesi Brew. PBA; TTY
Leave him: he's quiet enough: and what matter. Here Lies a Prisoner. Charlotte Mew. MoBrPo
Leave Him Now Quiet. Trumbull Stickney. CrMA; LiTA; NCEP; TwAmPo
Leave husbandry sleeping a while, ye must do. A Digression to Hospitality. Thomas Tusser. SiCE
Leave It All Quietly to God. Psalms, LXII: 1-8, Bible, *O.T., tr. by* James Moffatt. MaRV
Leave It to Me Blues. Joel Oppenheimer. CoPo
Leave it to the ministers, and soon the church will die. The Laymen. Edgar A. Guest. SoP
Leave It with Him. *Unknown.* BLRP; SoP
Leave Lady, in Your Glass. Spenser. *See* Amoretti, XLV.
Leave, leave, converted publican! lay down. Christus Matthaeum et Discipulos Alloquitur. Sir Edward Sherburne. ACP
Leave leave to weepe Ornone, & now, move. *Unknown.* SeCSL
Leave me a little while alone. At His Grave. Alfred Austin. VA
Leave me a while, for you have been too long. Lover to Lover. David Morton. HBMV
Leave me, all sweet refrains my lip hath made. Sonnet. Lúis de Camoes. AWP; CAW; JAWP; WBP
Leave Me O Love [Which Reachest but to Dust]. Sir Philip Sidney. *Sometimes considered Sonnet CX of* Astrophel and Stella; *also in* Certain Sonnets. BWP; CABA; DiPo; EG; ElL; EnLit; EnRePo; EP; ExPo; FCP; ForPo; LiTB; LiTG; MaPo; OAEP; OxBoCh; PAn; PIA; PoAn; PoE; PoIE (1970 ed.); PoRA; PoSa; ReEn; ReIE; SeCePo; SeCeV; SiCE; Sonn; TOP; TreFT; TriL; TrPWD; TuPP; ViBoPo; WHA
(Farewell, A.) UnPo (1st ed.)
(Farewell World.) FaBoEn
(Splendidis Longum Valedico Nugis.) LO; OBEV; OBSC; SiPS
Leave now the beach, and even that perfect friendship. End of Season. Robert Penn Warren. TwAmPo
Leave off, good Beroe, now. To an Old Gentlewoman. George Turberville. CBV; EnPo; EnRePo
Leave off my sheep, it is no time to feed. Sir Philip Sidney. *Fr.* Arcadia. FCP
Leave, Philomel, to make thy moan! To Philomel. John Tatham. SeCL
Leave-taking, A. Sir Frederick Napier Broome. AnNZ
Leave-taking, A. Arno Holz, *tr. fr. German by* Jethro Bithell. AWP; JAWP; WBP
Leavetaking. Eve Merriam. PDV
Leave Taking. Milton. *Fr.* Paradise Lost, XII. FaBoEn
Leave-taking, A. Swinburne. CH; FaBoEn; HBV; MaVP; OAEP; OBNC; OBVV; PoEL-5; PoLF; PoVP; ViBoPo
("Let us go hence, my songs; she will not hear.") EG
Leavetaking ("Pass thou wild light"). Sir William Watson. HBV; PoVP
Leave tarnished sorrow, disappointment, doubt. Thought for a New Year. Gail Brook Burket. PGD
Leave the chicory where it stands. Bavarian Roadside. Leonora Speyer. NP
Leave the early bells at chime. Road-Hymn for the Start. William Vaughn Moody. MAP; MoAmPo (1942 ed.)
Leave the flurry/ To the masses. *Unknown.* WhC
Leave the How with Jesus. How? *Unknown.* STF
Leave the lady, Willy, let the racket rip. Willy and the Lady. Gelett Burgess. HBMV
Leave the Miracle to Him. Thomas H. Allan. BLRP
Leave the Thread with God. *Unknown.* BLRP
Leave the uproar! At a leap. Nature and Life. George Meredith. Po; PoIE; VP
Leave the Word Alone. Edward Marshall. NeAP
Leave these deluding tricks and shows. To a Painted Lady. Alexander Brome. CavP
Leave thine own home, O youth, seek distant shores! Encouragement to Exile. Petronius. AWP; JAWP; WBP
Leave this barren spot to me! The Beech Tree's Petition. Thomas Campbell. GTSL; HBV
Leave to the street its glare and race. Shadowed. Burnham Eaton. FiSC
Leave Train. Alan Ross. ChMP
Leave Us Religion. Blanaid Salkeld. NeIP
Leave we awhile without the turmoil of the town. Our Lady of France. Lionel Johnson. ISi
Leave your home behind, lad. The Recruit. A. E. Housman. A Shropshire Lad, III. PoVP
Leaves. William Barnes. BoNaP; ChTr
(Sonnet: Leaves.) OBNC
Leaves, The. Alice Cary. SoP
Leaves. W. H. Davies. MoBrPo
Leaves. Sara Teasdale. HBV; NP; PoPl
Leaves. Katharine Tynan. BoTP
Leaves, The. *Unknown.* BoTP
Leaves. Paul Walker. PDV
Leaves. J. M. Westrup. BoTP
Leaves/ Murmuring by myriads. From My Diary, July 1914. Wilfred Owen. CoBMV; FaBoMo; LiTM (rev. ed.); MoAB; MoBrPo
Leaves and branches, flowers and fruits are here. Green. John Gray. SyP
Leaves are always beautiful, I think. Leaves. J. M. Westrup. BoTP
Leaves are born, The; the organ man. Six in June. Mary Carolyn Davies. BiCB
Leave are dropping from the trees, The. Autumn Leaves. Margaret P. Sutphen. PCH
Leaves are fading and falling, The. The Leaves. Alice Cary. SoP

Leaves are falling, falling, The. Autumn Leaves. W. Hodgson Burnet. PoMa
Leaves are falling, The; so am I. Late Leaves. Walter Savage Landor. EG; GTSE; HBV; OBEV (1st ed.)
Leaves are fresh after the rain, The. April Showers. James Stephens. TiPo (1959 ed.)
Leaves are uncurling, The. Spring. Marchette Chute. TiPo (1959 ed.)
Leaves at My Window. John James Piatt. AA
Leaves before the Wind. May Sarton. MoLP; NePoAm
Leaves Compared with Flowers. Robert Frost. MWA-2
Leaves Do Not Mind at All, The. Annette Wynne. SoPo
Leaves Drink, The. Alice Wilkins. GFA
Leaves fall. The City of Falling Leaves. Amy Lowell. *Fr.* 1777. MAPA; SUS; TiPo; TwAmPo
Leaves fall, The. Leaves. Paul Walker. PDV
Leaves fall, fall as from far, The. Autumn. Rainer Maria Rilke, *tr. by* Jessie Lemont. OnPM
Leaves fall, fall as if from far away, The. Autumn. Rainer Maria Rilke, *tr. by* C. F. McIntyre. TrJP
Leaves had a wonderful frolic, The. The Leaves. *Unknown.* BoTP
Leaves have their time to fall. The Hour of Death. Felicia Dorothea Hemans. HBV; LoBV; OBNC
Leaves like women, interchange, The. Emily Dickinson. NoP
Leaves make a slow. Spring Rain. Harry Behn. TiPo
Leaves of autumn burning through the grey, The. Chorale for Autumn. Marya Zaturenska. NP
Leaves of Europe, The, *sels.* Howard Sergeant. ToPo
"Autumn again, the leopardlike and burning."
Inundation, The.
Man Meeting Himself.
Leaves of Grass. Walt Whitman. *See* Miracles ("I believe a leaf of grass").
Leaves of the summer, lovely summer's pride. Leaves [*or* Sonnet]. William Barnes. BoNaP; ChTr; OBNC
Leaves of the Tree of Love are fears and sighs and tears, The. The Tree of Love. Ramon Lull. CAW
Leaves, summer's coinage spent, golden are all together whirled. Lapwing. Rex Warner. ShBV-3
Leaves, the little birds, and I, The. The Little Shepherd's Song. William Alexander Percy. GFA; YeAr
Leaves, though little time they have to live, The. October Maples, Portland. Richard Wilbur. CoPo
Leaves were fading when to Esthwaite's banks. Cambridge and the Alps. Wordsworth. *Fr.* The Prelude. ERoP-1
Leaves were reddening to their fall, The. The Gray Doves' Answer. Frederic Edward Weatherly. TVC
Leaves will fall again sometime and fill, The. Sunday Morning Apples. Hart Crane. NAMP
Leaves would have been mere leaves. Invisible Painter. Alfred Dorn. FiSC
Leavetaking. *See* Leave-taking.
Leaving. "Michael Lewis," *after the Chinese. Fr.* Cherry Blossoms. UnTE
Leaving a forest of bikes. 305 Honda. Gene Fowler. ThO
Leaving Barra. Louis MacNeice. CMoP; POTE
Leaving Ithaca. W. D. Snodgrass. AmPC
Leaving Me, and Then Loving Many. Abraham Cowley. AnAnS-2
Leaving of Liverpool, The, *with music. Unknown.* ShS
Leaving Something Behind. David Wagoner. CoAP
Leaving Sunnyside behind, the high weaving clarinet. Girl Asleep. Raymond Souster. TwCaPo
Leaving the Atocha Station. John Ashbery. ANYP
Leaving the bambino home, by bus, afoot. Forza D'Agrò. Edwin Denby. ANYP
Leaving the bar slack-watered, I have left. Two Voyages. Maurice James Craig. NeIP
Leaving the House of a Friend. Basho, *tr. fr. Japanese by* Harold G. Henderson. RePo
Leaving the pond, she looks like someone I know. The End of the Outing. Robert Mezey. TDP
Leaving the viaduct on the left, and coming over the hill. St. Ursanne. Michael Roberts. LiTM
Leaving tropic parallels. Northbound. Larry Rubin. NYTB
Leaving Troy. Thomas Caulfield Irwin. IrPN
Lecompton's Black Brigade. Charles Graham Halpine. PAH
Lector Aere Perennior. J. V. Cunningham. QFR
Lectori Quomodo Legat. Thomas Freeman. SiCE
Lecture Note: Elizabethan Period. Geoffrey Grigson. PV
Lecture upon the Shadow, A. John Donne. AnAnS-1; AnEnPo; AtBAP; AWP; CABA; CaFP; DiPo; EnRePo; InPo; MaMe; OBS; PAn; Po; PoeP; ReEn; SCEP-1; SeCP; SeEP; TuPP
Lecturer's impartial prose, The. In the Lecture Room. James K. Baxter. Cressida, I. AnNZ
Leda. Hilda Doolittle ("H. D."). HBMV; InPo
Leda and the Swan. Oliver St. John Gogarty. AnIL; OnYI
Leda and the Swan. W. B. Yeats. AnIL; AtBAP; BWP; CABA; CaFP; CBV; ChMP; CMoP; CoBMV; DiPo; EnL; EnLi-2 (1949 ed.); ErPo; ExPo; FaBoEn; FosPo; GTBS-P; ILP; InPo; LiTM; MaPo; MBW-2; MoAB; MoBrPo; MoVE; NoP; OAEP (2d ed.); PAn; PIA; PoAn; PoE; PoeP; PoFS; PoIE; SeCeV; Sonn; StP; TDP; TrGrPo; VaPo
Leda in Stratford, Ont. Anne Wilkinson. MoCV
Leda, the Lost. Eda Lou Walton. AnAmPo
Lee in the Mountains. Donald Davidson. MoVE; UnPo
Lee to the Rear. John Reuben Thompson. MC; PaA; PAH
Leedle Yawcob Strauss. Charles Follen Adams. BOHV
Lee's Parole. Marion Manville. PAH
Leesome Brand. *Unknown.* BaBo (A *vers.*); ESPB (A *and* B *vers.*); OBB
(Medelwold and Sidselille, B *vers.*) BaBo
Leetla Boy, Da. T. A. Daly. HBV; YT
Leetla Giorgio Washeenton. T. A. Daly. FaPON; MPB; OTPC (1946 ed.); PoSC; TSW
Leetle Bateese. William Henry Drummond. CaP
Leezie Lindsay. *Unknown. See* Lizie Lindsay.
Lefroy in the Forest, *abr.* Charles Mair. *Fr.* Tecumseh, II, i. VA
Left Behind. Elizabeth Akers Allen. HBV
Left by his friend to breakfast alone on the white/ Italian shore. Edward Lear. W. H. Auden. InvP; ML
Left from gay behind private. High Pitched Whale. Clark Coolidge. ANYP
Left leg flung out, head cocked to the right. Poet. Karl Shapiro. AnFE; CMoP; CoAnAm; LiTM (1970 ed.); MoAB; MoAmPo (1950 ed.); ToPo; TwAmPo
Left like an unknown's breath on mirrors. Visitations. Lawrence Durrell. *Fr.* Eight Aspects of Melissa. MoBrPo (1962 ed.); NeBP
Left Out. Mary Carolyn Davies. HH
Left to himself, wherever man is found. Americans! Philip Freneau. *Fr.* Reflections. PPON
Leg, The. Karl Shapiro. MoAB; MoAmPo (1950 ed.); NeMA; TPM; TrGrPo (rev. ed.); UnPo (3d ed.)
Leg in a Plaster Cast, A. Muriel Rukeyser. MoAmPo
Leg in the Subway, The. Oscar Williams. AnFE; CoAnAm; LiTM; NePA; TwAmPo
Leg over leg. *Unknown.* OxNR
Legacie, The. John Donne. AtBAP; MaMe; SeCP; TrGrPo
Legacies. Ethelwyn Wetherald. MaRV; OQP
Legacy, The. Proverbs, IV: 1-13, Bible, *O.T.* TrJP
Legacy, The. John Donne. *See* Legacie, The.
Legacy, The. Henry King. AnAnS-2
Legacy. Gladys McKee. JKCP
Legacy, A. Martial. *See* Hinted Wish, A.
Legacy, *with music.* Thomas Moore. AS
Legacy. Nancy Byrd Turner. BrR; MoSiPe
Legacy. Ruth Winant Wheeler. ChIP
Legacy: My South. Dudley Randall. NNP; PoNe (1970 ed.)
Legal Fiction. William Empson. CMoP; ExPo; FaBoMo; LiTB; LiTM; MoVE; NoP; ReMP; SeCeV (1967 ed.); ToPo
Legem Tuam Dilexi. Coventry Patmore. The Unknown Eros, II, vi. NBM; OxBoCh; PoEL-5; PoLi
Legend. Hart Crane. CABA; InPo; MoVE; OxBA; SyP; TwAmPo
Legend. Ralph Gustafson. CaP; PeCV (1967 ed.)
Legend. Sister Mary Jeremy. JKCP (1955 ed.)
Legend, A. May Kendall. VA
Legend, A. Adelaide Anne Procter. GoBC; JKCP
Legend. Ridgely Torrence. EtS
Legend, A: "Christ, when a child, a garden made." *Unknown, at. to* Peter Ilich Tchaikovsky, *tr. fr. Russian by* Nathan Haskell Dole. ChIP; MaRV; OHIP
Legend. John Waller. NeBP
Legend. John V. A. Weaver. AmFN; PFY; YaD
Legend. John Hall Wheelock. LiTL; MoLP
Legend. Judith Wright. BoAV; FIW
Legend has sunk it where the shoreless foam. Atlantis. Stanton A. Coblentz. FiSC

Legend of Babe Jesus and the Weeders, The. *Unknown.* ChrBoLe
Legend of Boastful Bill, The. Badger Clark. SCC
Legend of Camelot, A. George Du Maurier. CenHV
Legend of Cherries, A. Charles Dalmon. HBMV; TSW
Legend of Felix is ended, the toiling of Felix is done, The. Envoy. Henry van Dyke. *Fr.* The Toiling of Felix. BLPA
Legend of Gethsemane, A. Teresa Hooley. StJW
Legend of Ghost Lagoon, The, *sel.* Joseph Schull.
Pirates' Fight, The, I *and* II, *much abr.* CaP
Legend of Good Women, The: Prologue, *sels.* Chaucer.
"And as for me, though that my wit be lite." ViBoPo
("And as for me, thogh that I can but lyte.") CH
Balade: "Hyd, Absolon, thy gilte tresses clere." AtBAP; AWP; ChTr; FiP; InPo; JAWP; LiTG; LoBV; OBEV; SeCeV; WBP
(Hyd, Absolon, Thy Gilte Tresses Clere.) ExPo
(Of His Lady, *sl. diff.*) EG
"Of all the floures in the mede." LO
"She is the clernesse and the verray light." LO
This Fresshe Flour. SeCePo
Whan That the Month of May. AtBAP
Legend of Grand Lake, The. Joseph L. Westcott. PoOW
Legend of Heinz von Stein, The. Charles Godfrey Leland. BOHV; HBV
Legend of His Lyre. Aaron Schmuller. GoYe
Legend of Lake Okeefinokee, A. Laura E. Richards. PoRh; RIS; StPo
(Legend of Okeefinokee, A.) BoChLi
Legend of Montrose, The, *sel.* Sir Walter Scott.
Annot Lyle's Song: "Birds of Omen." EnRP
Legend of Okeefinokee, A. Laura E. Richards. *See* Legend of Lake Okeefinokee, A.
Legend of Paul Bunyan. A. Arthur S. Bourinot. *See* Paul Bunyan.
Legend of Rabbi Ben Levi, The. Longfellow. Tales of a Wayside Inn: The Spanish Jew's Tale, Pt. I. AnNE; GBV (1952 ed.)
Legend of Ramapo Mountain. Jennie M. Palen. FiSC
Legend of Robert, Duke of Normandy, The, *sel.* Michael Drayton.
Fame and Fortune. OBSC
Legend of Service, A. Henry van Dyke. GBV (1922 ed.)
Legend of Sir Guyon, or of Temperance, The, *abr.* Spenser. The Faerie Queene, II, 12. WHA
Legend of Success, The Salesman's Story, The. Louis Simpson. NYBP
Legend of the Admen, The. Everett W. Lord. BLPA
Legend of the Christmas Rose, The. Florence Boyce Davis. PEDC
Legend of the Dead Lambs, The. "Owen Meredith." VA
Legend of the Dogwood Tree, The. Geraldine Farrar. StJW
Legend of the Dove, A. George Sterling. NP
Legend of the Easter Eggs, The. Fitz-James O'Brien. BeLS
Legend of the First Cam-u-el, The. Arthur Guiterman. ALV; BOHV; CenHV
Legend of the Glaive, The, *sel.* Joseph Sheridan Le Fanu.
Song of the Spirits, The. OnYI
Legend of the Knight [*or* Knyght] of the Red Cross, or of Holiness. Spenser. The Faerie Queene, I, 1-12. BEL; EnLi-1 (1 *and* 2); OAEP; TOP (1 *and* 4)
(Invocation to the Faerie Queene, *prologue.*) FiP
("Lo! I, the man whose Muse whylome did maske.") EnLit, *prologue,* 1 *and* 2; FosPo
Legend of the Northland, A. Phoebe Cary. GoTP; HBV; HBVY; OnMSP; OTPC; RIS
Legend of the Organ-Builder, The. Julia C. R. Dorr. BeLS; BLPA; FaBoBe
Legend of the Saintfoin, The. Pamela Tennant. GBV (1922 ed.)
Legend of the Tortoise, The. Pamela Tennant. GBV (1922 ed.)
Legend of the Waving Lady. Ethel Livingston. ThO
Legend of Viable Women, A. Richard Eberhart. MiAP; MoVE
Legend of Walbach Tower, The. George Houghton. PAH
Legend of Waukulla, The. Hezekiah Butterworth. PAH
Legendary Abraham. The Succession. Edwin Muir. PoDB
Legends. Eric Torgersen. QAH
Legends for Trees, *sels.* Arthur Ketchum.
Countersign. HBMV
Spirit of the Birch, The. MPB; OHIP
Legends of Christmas. Aileen Fisher. ChBR
Legends of Evil, The. Kipling. MoShBr
"This is the sorrowful story," I. MemP
Legerdemain. Kenneth Mackenzie. BoAV; PoAu-2
Legion, The. Robert Graves. BrPo
Legion of Iron, The. Lola Ridge. NAMP
Legree's big house was white and green. Simon Legree—a Negro Sermon [*or* A Negro Sermon: Simon Legree]. Vachel Lindsay. The Booker Washington Trilogy, I. AnAmPo; ATP (1935 ed.); CoBA; HBMV; InMe; LiTA; LoGBV; MAP; MoAmPo; MoVE; NAMP; NePA; PFY; ShBV-2
Legs, The. Robert Graves. FaBoMo; HaMV; LiTB; LiTM; PoSa
Legs!/ How we have suffered each other. Poem in Which My Legs Are Accepted. Kathleen Fraser. YAP
Legs being uneven, The. The Letter. Paul Blackburn. CoPo
Legs of the elk punctured the snow's crust, The. To Christ Our Lord. Galway Kinnell. TwCP; WIRo
Lehayyim, my brethren, Lehayyim, I say. Simhat Torah. Judah Leib Gordon. TrJP
Lehmann does well with Largactil. Laprairie Hunger Strike. Ronald Everson. MoCV
Leicester Chambermaid. *Unknown.* CoMu
Leichhardt in Theatre, *sel.* Francis Webb.
Room, The. PoAu-2
Leif was a man's name. Hervey Allen. *Fr.* Saga of Leif the Lucky. EtS
Leila. George Hill. AmLP
Lesiure. W. H. Davies. AnFE; AWP; BoNaP; BoTP; CH; EnLit; FaBoBe; FaFP; FaPON; GTSE; HBV; JAWP; LiTB; LiTM; MoShBr; OBEV (new ed.); OBMV; OBVV; OtMeF; PoRA (rev. ed.); PTK; RePo; SeCePo; ShBV-1; TIHL; TiPo; TOP; TrGrPo; TSW; WaKn; WBP; WePo; WHA; WoL
Leisure the serfs will not forget. Reading Tolstoy. John Peters. BoSA
Leith police dismisseth us, The. *Unknown.* OxNR
Leith Races, *sel.* Robert Fergusson.
My Winsome Dear. SeCePo
Leitrim Woman, A. Lyle Donaghy. OnYI; OxBI
Lekingfelde Proverbs, The. *Unknown.* MuSP
Lementable New Ballad upon the Earle of Essex Death, A. *Unknown.* CoMu
Lemme be wid Casey Jones. Odyssey of Big Boy. Sterling A. Brown. BANP; CDC
Lemmings, The. John Masefield. CMoP
Lemmings, The. Donald A. Stauffer. LiTG; PIA; SiTL; WaP
Lemon Sherbet. Marvin Solomon. NePoAm
Lemonade Stand. Dorothy Brown Thompson. SiSoSe
Lemons. Ted Walker. NYBP
Lemuel's Blessing. W. S. Merwin. CoPo; NYBP
Lend a Hand. Edward Everett Hale. *See* Look Up.
Lend me, a little while, the key. The Pedler. Charlotte Mew. HBMV
Lend me thy fillet, Love! The Lover's Song. Edward Rowland Sill. AA; HBV
Lend me your song, ye nightingales! The Woodland Choir. James Thomson. *Fr.* The Seasons: Spring. CoBE
Length o' days ageän do shrink, The. The Fall. William Barnes. NBM; PoEL-4
Length of Moon. Arna Bontemps. CDC; LiTM (1970 ed.); PoNe
Lengthy Symphony. Persis Greely Anderson. WhC
Lenin, *sel.* Dorothy Wellesley.
"So I came down the steps." OBMV
Leningrad: 1943. Vera Inber, *tr. fr. Russian by* Dorothea Prall Radin *and* Alexander Kaun. *Fr.* The Pulkovo Meridian. WaaP
Lenore. Poe. AA; AmP; AmPo; AmPP; AnFE; AP; APA; CoAnAm; CoBA; LiTA; MWA-1; TreFS; WHA
Lenox Avenue. Sidney Alexander. PoNe
Lenox Avenue/ by daylight. Dive. Langston Hughes. CAD
Lenox Avenue is a big street. Keep on Pushing. David Henderson. BF
Lenox Avenue Mural. Langston Hughes. *See* Harlem.
Lens. Anne Wilkinson. MoCV; OBCV; PeCV
Lens of Morning, polished sheer by sleep, The. Celestial Body. Louise Townsend Nicholl. NePoAm
Lent. Miriam LeFevre Crouse. ChIP
Lent. George Herbert. MaMe
Lent. Jane McKay Lanning. MaRV
Lent. W. R. Rodgers. AnIL; DTC; NeBP; OxBI

Lent Lily, The. A. E. Housman. A Shropshire Lad, XXIX. MPB; OHiP; PoRL; PoSC; PoVP
Lente, Lente. Ovid. *See* Slowly, Slowly.
Lenten Is Come [with Love to Toune]. *Unknown.* MeEL; ViBoPo
(Alysoun.) GoBC
(Spring.) AtBAP
(Spring Has Come.) PoLi
(Spring Has Come to Town with Love.) CABA
(Spring Song.) EnLi-1, *mod. vers.*; PoEL-1
(Spring-Tide.) OBEV
Lenten stuff is come to the town. Two Old Lenten Rhymes, I. *Unknown.* ACP; WHL
Lenton has brought us, as I understand. Two Old Lenten Rhymes, II. *Unknown.* ACP
L'Envoi: "Here are we for the last time face to face." William Morris. *Fr.* The Earthly Paradise. EnLi-2; PoVP; ViPo
L'Envoi: "My towers at last! these rovings end." Herman Melville. *See* L'Envoi: Return of the Sire de Nesle, The.
L'Envoi: "O love triumphant over guilt and sin." Frederick Lawrence Knowles. FaChP; OQP; TrPWD; TRV
L'Envoi: Return of the Sire de Nesle, The. Herman Melville. AnFE; CoAnAm; ViBoPo
(L'Envoi: "My towers at last! these rovings end.") APA
L'Envoi: "Seek not for me within a tomb." John G. Neihardt. *See* Envoi: "O seek me not within a tomb."
L'Envoi: "There's a whisper down the field where the year has shot her yield." Kipling. *See* Long Trail, The.
L'Envoi: "What is the moral? Who rides may read." Kipling. *Fr.* The Story of the Gadsbys. MoBrPo; NeMA; TrGrPo
(Winners, The.) BLPA
L'Envoi: "When earth's last picture is painted and the tubes are twisted and dried." Kipling. DD; FaFP; HBV; MaRV; OHFP; PoPl; SoP; TRV; WGRP
(Envoy.) PoVP
(When Earth's Last Picture Is Painted.) EnLit; LiTB; TreFS
L'Envoi: "Where are the loves that we loved before." Willa Cather. HBV
L'Envoi: "Who findeth comfort in the stars and flowers." Thomas Lovell Beddoes. *Fr.* Death's Jest Book. LO; OBNC
(Dedicatory Stanzas.) ERoP-2
L'Envoy: "King of glorie, king of peace." George Herbert. *Fr.* The Church Militant. AnAnS-1; MaMe; MeP; SCEP-1
L'Envoy: To His Book. John Skelton. EnRePo
L'Envoy to W. L. H. Ainsworth, Esq. Francis S. Mahony. OnYI
Leo to His Mistress. Henry Dwight Sedgwick. BLPA; CIV
Leolin and Edith. Tennyson. *Fr.* Aylmer's Field. GN
Leonardo Da Vinci's. Marianne Moore. NYBP
Leonardo's "Monna Lisa." Edward Dowden. *See* Mona Lisa.
Leonidas. George Croly. HBV
Leonora. E. A. Robinson. MaPo; NePA
Lepanto. G. K. Chesterton. AnFE; BEL; CAW; CoBE; FaBV; FOL; GoBC; GoTL (1949 ed.); HBMV; HBVY; InP; JKCP (1955 ed.); MoBrPo; NeMA; OBMV; OnSP; OtMeF; PoRA; PoTE; ShBV-3; TIHL; TreFS; WHA
Lepanto marks the spot of victory. Our Lady of the Rosary. Francis A. Gaffney. JKCP
Leper, The. Swinburne. LO
Leper, The. Nathaniel P. Willis. StJW; WGRP
Leper Cleansed, The. John Collop. TrGrPo
Leprahaun, The. Robert Dwyer Joyce. OnYI; PoMS
Leprecaun [*or* Fairy Shoemaker], The. William Allingham. PCH; RG
(Lupracaun, or Fairy Shoemaker, The.) OnYI
Leprechaun—the omadhaun!—that lives in County Clare, The. Of Certain Irish Fairies. Arthur Guiterman. PoLF
Lerians are bad: not some bad, and some not. Problem in Logic. Phocylides, *tr. by* Lord Neaves. OnPM
Les Amours. Charles Cotton. HBV
Les Ballons. Oscar Wilde. SyP
Les Belles Roses sans Mercie. Arthur Shearly Cripps. OBVV
Les Chasse-Neige. Ralph A. Lewin. FiBHP
Les Demoiselles De Sauve. John Gray. PeVV
"Le's go down to Jurdon, le's go down to Jurdon." 'Ligion So Sweet. *Unknown.* ABF
Les Halles d'Ypres. Edmund Blunden. MMA
Les Morts Vont Vite. H. C. Bunner. AA
Les Planches-en-Montagne. Michael Roberts. OBMV
Les Réalités. Barbara Guest. AmPC
Les Silhouettes. Oscar Wilde. *Fr.* Impressions. BrPo; Po; PoVP; SyP
Les Sylphides. Louis MacNeice. CoBMV
Les Vaches. Arthur Hugh Clough. *See* Ite Domum Saturae, Venit Hesperus.
Lesbia. Richard Aldington. NP; PoLF
Lesbia forever on me rails. Lesbia Railing [*or* Catullus de Lesbia]. Catullus, *tr. by* Swift. AWP; CBEP; JAWP; LiTW; WBP
Lesbia, my love, let's be gay and enjoy ourselves. The Kiss-Fest. Irwin Edman. InMe
Lesbia on Her Sparrow. William Cartwright. *See* Dead Sparrow, The.
Lesbia Railing. Catullus, *tr. fr. Latin by* Swift. AWP; JAWP; LiTW; WBP
(Catullus de Lesbia.) CBEP
(Upon Lesbia's Abuse, *tr. by* George Lamb.) OnPM
Lesbia Sewing. Harold Vinal. HBMV
Lesbia still rails at me when by. Upon Lesbia's Abuse. Catullus, *tr. by* George Lamb. OnPM
Lesbia, whom some thought a lovely creature. Lesbia's Rule of Praise. Sir John Harington. SiCE
Lesbia's Disgrace. Catullus, *tr. fr. Latin by* George Lamb. OnPM
Lesbia's Rule of Praise. Sir John Harington. SiCE
Lesbia's Vow. Catullus, *tr. fr. Latin by* Francis Hodgson. OnPM
Lèse-Majesté. Herbert S. Gorman. HBMV
Lesotho. B. Makalo Khaketla, *tr. fr. Sotho by* Dan Kunene *and* Jack Cope. PeSA
Less, less of self each day. Less of Self. *Unknown.* FaChP
Less Lonely. Alfred Kreymborg. AnAmPo
Less of Self. *Unknown.* FaChP
Less passionate the long war throws. The Long War. Laurie Lee. BoPe; POTi; ToPo
Less said the better. Missing. John Pudney. HaMV; WePo
Less than Angelic. Bats. Philip Dow. QAH
Less Than the Dust. "Laurence Hope." MeWo
Less than two hours it took the Iroquois. The Martyrdom of Brébeuf and Lalemant, 16 March 1649. E. J. Pratt. *Fr.* Brébeuf and His Brethren. OBCV
Less the dog begged to die in the sky. Love Poem. George Barker. *Fr.* Fourth Cycle of Love Poems. NeBP
Lesser griefs that may be said, The. In Memoriam A. H. H., XX. Tennyson. EnLi-2; EPN; ViPo; VP
Lesser Lynx, The. E. V. Rieu. CenHV; FiBHP
Lesser Testament, The. Villon. *See* Petit Testament, Le.
Lesson, The. W. H. Auden. FaBoMo
Lesson. Harry Behn. TiPo (1959 ed.)
Lesson, The. Sister Mary Eleanore. JKCP (1955 ed.)
Lesson, The. Jane W. Krows. SoPo
Lesson, The. Robert Lowell. NMP; NoP
Lesson, The. Edward Lucie-Smith. TwCP
Lesson, A. Christina Rossetti. RIS
Lesson, The. Larry Rubin. GoYe
Lesson, A. Wordsworth. GTBS; GTBS-D; GTBS-P; GTBS-W; GTSE; GTSL
(Small Celandine, The.) BWP; ERoP-1; HBV; OBRV; PeER
Lesson for Today, The. Robert Frost. LiTA; LiTM (rev. ed.); NePA; SiTL; WaP
Lesson from a Sun-Dial. *Unknown, ad. fr. German by* Louis Untermeyer. *Fr.* Proverbs. RIS; TiPo
Lesson from Van Gogh, A. Howard Moss. MoAB
Lesson in Detachment, A. Vassar Miller. NePoEA-2
Lesson in Handwriting, A. Alastair Reid. NYBP
Lesson of Love. Simon Browne. SoP
Lesson of Mercy, A. George Murray. VA
Lesson of the Water Mill, The. Sarah Doudney. *Fr.* The Man o' Airlie. HBV; PoToHe, *abr.*; TreFS
(Water Mill, The.) BLPA; WGRP
Lesson of Water. *Unknown, at. to* Lao-tzu, *tr. fr. Chinese by* Witter Bynner. *Fr.* Tao Teh King. OnPM
Lessons. Helen Weber. PGD
Lessons for a Boy. Samuel Taylor Coleridge. *See* Metrical Feet.
Lessons from the Gorse. Elizabeth Barrett Browning. HBV
Lessons in Limericks. David McCord. InMe
Lessons of Nature, The. William Drummond of Hawthornden. *See* Book of the World, The.
Lessons of the War (I-III). Henry Reed. LiTB; NoP

Lessons (continued)
Sels.
Judging Distances, II. ChMP; FaBoMo; GTBS-P; MoAB
Naming of Parts, I. CaFP; DTC; GoJo; HoPM; ILP; LiTM; MoAB; MoBrPo (1962 ed.); MoVE; PoPl; PoRA (rev. ed.); SeCePo; SeCeV (1967 ed.); ShBV-3; SiTL; StP; ViBoPo (1958 ed.); WaP; WePo
("Today we have naming of parts.") TrGrPo (rev. ed.)
Lessons of the Year. *Unknown.* BLRP
Lest Fools Should Fail. Piet Hein. TIHL
Lest it may more quarrels breed. Twelve Articles. Swift. BOHV; InMe
Lest men suspect your tale to be untrue. The Devil's Advice to Story-Tellers. Robert Graves. CBEP; LiTM (rev. ed.)
Lest men suspect your tale untrue. The Painter Who Pleased Nobody and Everybody. John Gay. BeLS; CEP
Lest the ripple deceive us. Winter Pond. Ben Belitt. NYBP
Lest Thou Forget. William L. Stidger. PoToHe
Lest, tortured by the world's strong sin. Desideravi. Theodore Maynard. HBMV
Lest We Forget! Kipling. *See* Recessional.
Lest we forget! The months swing into years. Armistice Night. Curtis Wheeler. HH
Lest We Lack True Men. *Unknown.* SoP
Lest you should think that verse shall die. The Immortality of Verse [*or* Poet]. Pope. AWP; CBEP; JAWP; WBP
Lester Young. Ted Joans. AmNP
Let a joy keep you. Joy. Carl Sandburg. NP
Let all men see the ruins of the shrine. Robert Hillyer. Sonnets, XIV. HBMV
Let All the Earth Keep Silence. Lucy A. K. Adee. OQP
Let all the world in ev'ry corner sing. Antiphon. George Herbert. MaMe; ThGo
Let All Things Pass Away, *sel.* W. B. Yeats.
"Rivery field spread out below, A." ChTr
Let America Be America Again. Langston Hughes. PoFr; PoNe; WOW
Let ancients boast no more. Pindarick. *At. to* the Earl of Rochester. PeRV
Let Bacchus's sons be not dismayed. Garryowen. *Unknown.* OnYI
Let baths and wine-butts be November's due. Of the Months: November. Folgore da San Geminiano. AWP
Let Be. *Unknown.* WBLP
Let Be at Last. Ernest Dowson. PoSa
Let Bourbons fight for status quo. Status Quo. Binga Dismond. PoNe
Let but a fellow in a fox-furred gown. An Invective against the Wicked of the World. Nicholas Breton. ViBoPo
Let but a thrush begin. Lyric. John Hewitt. NeIP
Let but the son of earth. The Ages of Man. *At. to* Abraham ibn Ezra. TrJP
Let but thy voice engender with the string. Upon her Voice. Robert Herrick. MuSP
Let certain holdings of stocks and bonds. Codicil. Mabel MacDonald Carver. GoYe
Let Christmas not become a thing. Christmas Prayer. Madeline Morse. PGD
Let come what will, let come what may! Consolation. Theodor Storm. ACP
Let courage stiffen. Iron Fare. Marjorie Allen Seiffert. NP
Let dainty wits cry on the Sisters nine. Astrophel and Stella, III. Sir Philip Sidney. FCP; OBSC; ReEn; ReIE; SiCE; SiPS; Sonn; TuPP
Let de peoples know (unnh). Blues for Bessie. Myron O'Higgins. PoNe
Let Deirdre be her name: harm will come through her. The Foretelling of Cathbad the Druid at Deirdre's Birth. *Unknown.* LiTW
Let Dogs Delight [to Bark and Bite]. Isaac Watts. HBVY; OTPC; ThGo; TreFS
(Against Quarrelling and Fighting.) EiCL; OBEC; SeCePo
(Quarrelling.) BLPA
Let Dreamers Wake. Lilith Lorraine. PGD
Let dull and ignorant pretenders art condemn. John Oldham. *Fr.* Upon the Works of Ben Jonson. PP
Let each man first seek out his proper totem. A Joyful Noise. Donald Finkel. CoAP
Let Elizur Rejoice with the Partridge. Christopher Smart. *Fr.* Jubilate Agno. PoEL-3
Let 'em censure: what care I? In Imitation of Anacreon [*or* On Critics]. Matthew Prior. CEP; EiCL; SeCeV
Let Erin Remember the Days of Old. Thomas Moore. EnRP; PoE
Let every corner of this day. Altars. Sybil Leonard Armes. FaChP
Let Fate do her worst; there are relics of joy. Thomas Moore. *Fr.* Long, Long Be My Heart with Such Memories Filled. TreFT
Let fate or insufficiency provide. To J. M. George Meredith. EPN
Let fickle Fortune run her blindest race. From Fortune's Reach. Robert Southwell. EP
Let folly praise that fancy loves, I praise and love that Child. A Child My Choice. Robert Southwell. CAW; GoBC; HBV; OxBoCh; PoLi; SiCE
Let foreign [*or* forrain] nations of their language boast. The Son [*or* The Sonne]. George Herbert. EP; MaMe; SeCP; Sonn
Let four captains/ Bear Hamlet, like a soldier, to the stage. Shakespeare. *Fr.* Hamlet, V, ii. MyFE
Let from its dream the soul awaken. The Coplas on the Death of His Father, the Grandmaster of Santiago. Jorge Manrique. CAW
Let God, the Lord, hear thee. Psalm XX. *Paraphrased by* Sir Philip Sidney. FCP
Let go the Limb? Leaf and Soul. John Banister Tabb. PoMa
Let Go the Peak Halyards, *frag.* *Unknown.* AmSS
Let Go the Reef Tackle, *with music.* *Unknown.* ShS
Let hammer on anvil ring. The Armorer's Song. Henry Bache Smith. AA; OHIP
Let hands be about him white, O his mother's first. The Mother and Child. Vernon Watkins. NeBP
Let happy throats be mute. Threnody. Donald Jeffrey Hayes. AmNP
Let heathen sing thy heathen praise. The Greek Fathers. Cardinal Newman. JKCP
Let Her Give Her Hand. *Unknown.* BoLP; ELP
Let her lie naked here, my hand resting. News of the World III. George Barker. AtBAP; FaBoTw; LiTB; LiTM (rev. ed.)
Let her rest. One of the Sidhe. Mary Kennedy. FiSC
Let her who walks in Paphos. Lais. Hilda Doolittle ("H. D."). MAP; MoAmPo
Let here the brow be bared. At the Tomb of Washington. Clinton Scollard. DD; MC; OHIP; PEDC
Let him alone and when he is one year older. A Young Boy. Jessica Nelson North. NP
Let him be safe in sleep. Spell of Sleep. Kathleen Raine. HaMV
Let Him Kiss me with the kisses of his mouth. The Song of Songs. Song of Solomon, Bible, *O.T.* AWP; TrGrPo; UnTE
Let Him Kiss Me with the Kisses of His Mouth. Edward Taylor. *See* Preparatory Meditations: "My onely Lord . . ."
Let Him lead thee blindfold onwards. The Blessed Journey. Gerhard Tersteegen. FaChP
Let Him Return. Leona Ames Hill. PoToHe (new ed.)
Let hoary time's vast bowels be the grave. On the Frontispiece of Isaacsons Chronologie Explained. Richard Crashaw. MaMe
Let in the wind. Kathleen Raine. *Fr.* Northumbrian Sequence. CMoP
Let It Be Forgotten. Sara Teasdale. HBMV; MAP; MoAmPo; NP; PG (1945 ed.); TrGPo
(Song.) PFY
Let it be Sabbath, Sabbath! Eternal Sabbath. Isaac Leibush Peretz. TrJP
Let it be understood that I am Don Juan Gomez! Conquistador [*or* Announcement]. Elizabeth J. Coatsworth. GoTP; MAP
Let it disturb no more at first. Fountain. Elizabeth Jennings. BoC; PoCh
Let It Go. William Empson. PoIE
Let it idly droop, or sway. The Flag. Lucy Larcom. DD; HH
Let it no longer be a forlorn[e] hope. On the Baptized Ethiopian [*or* Aethiopian]. Richard Crashaw. MaMe; NoP; SeCV-1; SeEP
Let it not be, love, underneath a roof. Golden Bough. Helen Hoyt. HBMV
"Let it not come unto you, all ye that pass by!" Desolation in

Zion. Lamentations, Bible, *O.T.* TrJP

Let it not your wonder move. His Excuse for Loving. Ben Jonson. A Celebration of Charis, I. AnAnS-2; EnRePo; PoEL-2; QFR; SCEP-2; SeCP; SeCV-1; SeEP; TuPP

Let it rain! The Engineer. A. A. Milne. RePo

Let Liberty run onward with the years. A Holy Nation. Richard Realf. *Fr.* Of Liberty and Charity. PoFr

Let liberty, the charter'd right of Englishmen. Blake. *Fr.* King Edward the Third. PoFr

Let lofty Greek and Latin go. To the Laud and Praise of a Shock Bitch. Samuel Wesley. PeRV

Let Loneliness be mute. Accuse. To Losers. George Dillon. NP

Let Lotan Rejoice with Sauterelle. Christopher Smart. *Fr.* Jubilate Agno. AtBAP

Let lovers that like honey-flies. To Cynthia on His Love after Death. Sir Francis Kynaston. SeEP

Let man be free! The mighty word. Whittier. *Fr.* The Emancipation Group. PGD

Let man's soul [*or* soule] be a sphere [*or* spheare], and then, in this. Good Friday, 1613. Riding Westward. John Donne. AnAnS-1; AtBAP; ATP (1953 ed.); DiPo; EnRePo; ExPo; MaMe; MBW-1; MeLP; MeP; MePo; NoP; OBS; OxBoCh; PAn; Po; PoEL-2; PoIE; ReEn; SCEP-1; SeCP; SeCV-1; SeEP; StP; TuPP

Let Me Alone. Job, VII: 11-21, Bible, *O.T.* PPON

Let me alone, I prithee, in this cell. Satyra Quinta. Everard Guilpin. *Fr.* Skilaletheia. SiCE; TuPP

Let me at last be laid. At Last. Sir Lewis Morris. VA

Let Me Be a Giver. Mary Carolyn Davies. PoToHe

Let me be a little kinder. My Daily Creed [*or* A Creed]. *Unknown.* FaChP; MaRV; SoP; STF; TRV

Let me be at the place of the castle. Psalm Concerning the Castle. Denise Levertov. TwCP

Let me be buried in the rain. Invocation. Helene Johnson. AmNP; BANP; PoNe

Let me be marble, marble once again. Galatea Again. Genevieve Taggard. WHA

Let me be my own fool. A Counterpoint. Robert Creeley. NeAP

Let me be the one. By Myself. Robert Frost. RIS

Let me be what I am, as Virgil cold. An Elegie. Ben Jonson. PoEL-2; SeCP

Let Me Be with Thee. Charlotte Elliott. VA

Let me Blackpeople Let me. For Lee. A. X. Nicholas. WSL

Let but do my work from day to day. Work. Henry van Dyke. *Fr.* The Three Best Things. MaRV; OQP; OTD; PoMa; PoRL; SoP; SP; TIHL; TRV

Let me but live my life from year to year. Life. Henry van Dyke. *Fr.* The Three Best Things. MaRV; OQP; SoP

Let me call a ghost. Song of Three Smiles. W. S. Merwin. CoAP

Let me close my eyes tight. Invocation to Death. Emanuel Carnevali. NP

Let me come in where you sit weeping—aye. Bereaved. James Whitcomb Riley. AA; MaRV

Let me confess that we two must be twain. Sonnets, XXXVI. Shakespeare. CBEP; OAEP

Let me die in the spring. Transmigration. Seth D. Cudjoe. ACV

Let Me Die Working. S. Hall Young. *See* Into the Sunset.

Let me discern by living faith. Discerning the Lord's Body. Carrie Judd Montgomery. STF

Let me do my work each day. A Prayer. Max Ehrmann. BLPA; FaBoBe; MaRV; NeHB; PoToHe

Let Me Enjoy ["Let me enjoy the earth no less"]. Thomas Hardy. AnFE; AWP; FaBV; HBV; InPo; JAWP; MoRP; PoVP; ViBoPo; WBP

Let me enjoy myself in drunkenness. Drinking. Hsin Ch'i-chi. LiTW

Let Me Flower as I Will. Lew Sarett. TrPWD

Let Me Go. W. H. Bucks. SoP

Let Me Go Back. Mary E. Albright. BLRP

Let Me Go Down to Dust. Lew Sarett. TrPWD

Let me go forth, and share. Ode in May. Sir William Watson. MoBrPo (1942 ed.); OBEV; OBVV; PoVP; WGRP

Let me go; my soul is weary. Let Me Go. W. H. Bucks. SoP

Let Me Go Warm. Luis de Góngora, *tr. fr. Spanish by* Longfellow. AWP; JAWP; WBP; WoL

Let me go where'er I will. Music. Emerson. AnNE; FaBV; GoTP; MaRV; OQP; WGRP

Let Me Grow. Mary Mapes Dodge. FaChP

Let Me Grow Lovely. Karle Wilson Baker. BLPA; FaBoBe; HBMV; NeHB; TrPWD (Growing Old.) OQP

Let me have a scarlet maple. The Grave-Tree. Bliss Carman. CaP

Let me have men about me that are fat. Julius Caesar's Preference. Shakespeare. *Fr.* Julius Caesar, I, ii. TreFS

Let Me Laugh. *Unknown.* SeCL

Let me lay it to you gently, Mr. Gone! Poem of Holy Madness, IV. Ray Bremser. NeAP

Let me learn now where Beauty is. Questing. Anne Spencer. CDC

Let Me Lift Jesus, Lord. Jo Gardner. BePJ

Let Me Live But from Year to Year. Henry van Dyke. *Fr.* The Three Best Things. TreFT

Let me live harmlessly; and near the brink. The Angler's Song. John Dennys. *Fr.* The Secrets of Angling. EIL; MyFE

Let me live, O Mighty Master. A Sportsman's Prayer. *Unknown.* MaRV

Let Me Live Out My Years. John G. Neihardt. HBMV; MAP; MaRV; PoMa; TreFS; YaD

Let me look and see love's. Soul-Smiles. S. E. Anderson. BF

Let Me Look at Me. Bessie June Martin. StF

Let Me Love Bright Things. A. Newberry Choyce. HBMV

Let me no more despise. A Song in Humility. Carleton Drewry. MoRP

Let Me Not Die. Edith Lovejoy Pierce. TrPWD

Let me not know how sins and sorrows glide. Prayer. James Elroy Flecker. TrPWD

Let me not pray to be sheltered from dangers. Prayer for Courage. Rabindranath Tagore. MaRV

Let me not to the marriage of true minds. Sonnets, CXVI [*or* The Marriage of True Minds *or* True Love *or* Love's Not Time's Fool]. Shakespeare. AnEnPo; AnFE; ATP; AWP; BBV; BEL; BoC; BoLiVe; BoPe; CABA; CaFP; CBEP; MemP; CLwM; CoBE; DiPo; EG; EIL; EnL; EnLi-1; EnLit; EnLoPo; EnRePo; EP; ExPo; FaBoEn; FaBV; FaFP; FosPo; GBV; GoBC; GTBS; GTBS-D; GTBS-P; GTBS-W; GTSE; GTSL; HBV; ILP; InPo; InvP; JAWP; LiTB; LiTG; LiTL; LO; LoBV; MaPo; MaRV; MasP; MCCG; MeMP; MeWo; NoP; OAEP; OBEV; OBSC; OuHeWo; PAn; PG; PIA; Po; PoE; PoEL-2; PoeP; PoIE; PoPl; PoPo; PoRA; PoSa; ReEn; ReIE; SeCePo; SeCeV; ShBV-4; SiCE; Sonn; TOP; TreF; TrGrPo; TRV; UnPo; ViBoPo; WBP; WePo; WHA

Let me now set down a picture of New England that will show it to you and explain it. Praise of New England. Thomas Caldecot Chubb. GoYe

Let Me Play the Fool. Shakespeare. *Fr.* The Merchant of Venice, I, i. TrGrPo

Let me pour [*or* powre] forth. A Valediction: of Weeping. John Donne. AnAnS-1; AtBAP; ATP; BWP; CABA; CBEP; EG; EP; MaMe; MBW-1; MeLP; MePo; NoP; OBS; PoAn; ReIE; SCEP-1; SeCP; TuPP

Let me pour upon the mind. Remember the Source. Richard Eberhart. MoRP

Let me remember on this day. Others. *Unknown.* STF

Let Me Sing of My Well-Beloved. Isaiah, V, Bible, *O.T.* TrJP

Let me sit down a minute, stranger. Down in Lehigh Valley. *Unknown.* TreF

Let me sit here by this adobe wall. Summer Comes. Edith Agnew. SiSoSe

Let Me Speak of Pure Things. Ho Chih-fang, *tr. fr. Chinese by* Chiang Shao-yi. LiTW

Let me speak, sir. Cranmer's Prophecy of Queen Elizabeth. Shakespeare *and probably* John Fletcher. King Henry VIII, *fr.* V, v. WGRP

Let me take this other glove off. In Westminster Abbey. John Betjeman. CaFP; CMoP; FosPo; ILP; LiTM; POTi

Let me tell to you the story. "Los Pastores." Edith Agnew. ChBR; GaP

Let me tell you the story of how I began. Song: Lift Boy. Robert Graves. DTC

Let me thy properties explain. On an Ill-managed House. Swift. AnIV

Let me today do something that will take. A Morning Prayer. Ella Wheeler Wilcox. MaRV; OQP; PoToHe

Let me work and be glad. A Prayer. Theodosia Garrison. TrPWD
Let men take note of her, touching her shyness. The Gift of Song. Anthony Hecht. NYBP
Let Mine Eyes See Thee. St. Teresa of Avila, *tr. fr. Spanish by* Arthur Symons. AWP; CAW; JAWP; WBP
Let mine not be the saddest fate of all. Uselessness. Ella Wheeler Wilcox. TrPWD
Let Minions Marshal Every Hair. *Unknown.* ALV
Let Mother Earth now deck herself in flowers. Epithalamium [*or* O Hymen, Long Their Coupled Joys Maintain!]. Sir Philip Sidney. *Fr.* Arcadia. HW; SiPS
Let my soul, a shining tree. Tree and Sky. Siegfried Sassoon. TSW
Let my sweet song be pleasing unto Thee. A Love Song. Judah Halevi. TrJP
Let my voice ring out and over the earth. Song. James Thomson. Sunday up the River, XVII. HBV; MaRV; OBVV; PoVP; TreFT
Let Myron muse at Nature's passing might. The Lover Extolleth the Singular Beauty of His Lady. George Turberville. ReIE
Let Nature Be Your Teacher. Wordsworth. *Fr.* The Tables Turned. MaRV
Let never a man a wooing wend. King Henry. *Unknown.* ESPB; OBB
Let no blasphemer till the sacred earth. Benediction. Mark Turbyfill. NP
Let No Charitable Hope. Elinor Wylie. AnAmPo; HBMV; InP; LiTA; LiTM; MAP; MoAB; MoAmPo; NePA; OxBA; PoE; TrGrPo; WOW
Let no man cum into this hall. Now Is the Time of Christmas. *Unknown.* MeEL
Let no man see my girl. Inconsistent. Mark van Doren. BoLP; ELU
"Let no man write my epitaph; let my grave." On the Speech of Robert Emmet. Robert Southey. PoFr
Let no one mourn his mount, upholstered bone. Epitaph for a Horseman. Michael Hamburger. NePoEA-2
Let no pirate's sword storm these veins of yours. For Her on the First Day Out. Robert Bagg. NePoAm-2
Let none but guests or clubbers hither come. Ben Jonson's [*or* Johnsons] Sociable Rules for the Apollo. Ben Jonson. SeCV-1; TuPP
Let none who have not wisdom govern you. Canzone: He Rebukes the Evil of That Time. Siciliano Inghilfredi. PoFr
Let not Chloris think, because. *Unknown.* OBSC
Let not dark nor shadows fright thee. A Song of Dalliance. William Cartwright. ALV
Let not Death boast his conquering power. On Eleanor Freeman, Who Died 1650, Aged 21. *Unknown.* OBEV (new ed.)
Let not his humble vesture make thee blind. The Poor Scholar. Abraham ibn Chasdai. TrJP
Let not old age disgrace my high desire. Old Age. Sir Philip Sidney. *Fr.* Arcadia. SiPS
Let not our hearts be busy inns. Christmas Prayer. Ralph Spaulding Cushman. MaRV
Let not our town be large, remembering. On the Building of Springfield. Vachel Lindsay. AmPP (3d ed.); InP; MoRP; NAMP; OHFP; PaA; SoP; TOP; WHA
Let not, sweet saint, let not these lines offend you. Sonnet I: He Demands Pardon for Looking, Loving, and Writing. Walter Davison. ReIE
Let not the ballad-singer's shrilling strain. Of Ballad-Singers [*or* Ballad Singers]. John Gay. *Fr.* Trivia; or, The Art of Walking the Streets of London, III. EnLi-1 (1949 ed.); MuSP
Let Not the Sluggish Sleep. *Unknown.* OxBoCh
(Song, A: "Let not the sluggish sleep.") ACP; GoBC
Let Not Thy Beauty. Aurelian Townshend. AnAnS-2
Let Not Us. *Unknown.* CBEP
Let not us that youngmen be. Youth. *Unknown.* OBSC
Let not young souls be smothered out before. The Leaden-eyed. Vachel Lindsay. ATP; BoLiVe; CMoP; ELU; GTBS-W; LiTA; LiTM; MaRV; MemP; MoRP; NAMP; NePA; NP; PoPo; PPON
Let not your heart be faint. The Peace of Christ. John Antes La Trobe. BePJ
Let Not Your Heart Be Troubled. Alice Mortenson. BePJ
Let not your heart be troubled. My Peace I Give unto You [*or* The Peace of Christ]. St. John, Bible, *N.T.* TreFS; WoL
Let nothing disturb thee/ Let nothing dismay thee. St. Teresa's Book-Mark. St. Teresa of Avila, *tr. by* E. Allison Peers. BoC
Let nothing disturb thee,/ Nothing affright thee. Lines Written in Her Breviary [*or* St. Teresa's, Book-Mark]. St. Teresa of Avila, *tr. by* Longfellow. AWP; CAW; CTC; EaLo; FaChP; MaRV; OnPM; OQP; PoEL-5; SoP; TreFT; TRV; WHL
Let now each mead with flowers be depainted. Ring Forth, Fair Nymphs, Your Joyful Songs for Gladness. Gaspar Gil Polo. *Fr.* Diana Enamorada. HW
Let now the willow weep no more. To A. E. Housman. Witter Bynner. NYTB
Let observation with extensive view. The Vanity of Human Wishes; The Tenth Satire of Juvenal, Imitated. Samuel Johnson. ATP; BEL; BWP; CABA; CEP; CoBE; EiCL; EiCP; EiPP; EnPE; LaA; LoBV; MasP; NoP; Po; PoE; PoEL-3; PoFS; TOP; UnPo (1st ed.); VaPo
Let one another this embrace. *Unknown.* LO
Let other poets treat of lofty things. The Battle between a Cock and a Capon. Thomas Heyrick. PeRV
Let other servants boast a snowy glove. Upon Scarlet and Blush-coloured Ribbands, Given by Two Ladies. James Shirley. GoBC
Let others better mold the running mass. The Sixth Book of the Aeneis [*or* The Destiny of Rome]. Vergil, *tr. by* Dryden. *Fr.* The Aeneid. PeRV; SeCV-2
Let others chaunt a country praise. London Town. Lionel Johnson. PoVP
Let others cheer the winning man. A Smile. *Unknown.* BLPA; WBLP
Let others from the town retire. Nonpareil. Matthew Prior. EnLoPo
Let others of the world's decaying tell. Sonnet. Earl of Stirling. Aurora, XCVII. EIL; Sonn
Let others pile their yellow ingots high. Pastoral Elegy [*or* An Elegy]. Albius Tibullus. AWP; LiTW
Let Others Share. Edward Anthony. GoTP
Let others sing of knights and paladins. To Delia, LII [*or* Beauty, Time, and Love]. Samuel Daniel. BEL; CoBE; EIL; EnLi-1 (1949 ed.); FaBoEn; HBV; NoP; OAEP; OBEV; OBSC; ReEn; ReIE; SiCE; Sonn; TuPP; ViBoPo
Let others sing of Mars, and of his train. To Love; a Sonnet. Philip Ayres. CEP
Let party names no more. Communion of Saints. Benjamin Beddome. SoP
Let Peter Rejoice with the Moon Fish. Christopher Smart. *Fr.* Jubilate Agno. AtBAP
Let pious Damon take his seat. Sermon in a Churchyard. Macaulay. OBRV
Let Poets chant of clouds and things. A Pure Mathematician. Arthur Guiterman. PoMa
Let pride grow big my rose, and let the cleare. On a Damaske Rose Sticking upon a Ladies Breast. Thomas Carew. AnAnS-2
Let readers say (description or abuse). The Lemmings. Donald A. Stauffer. LiTG; PIA; SiTL; WaP
Let sailors watch the waning Pleiades. Cleonicos. Edward Cracroft Lefroy. Echoes From Theocritus, XXVII. AWP; JAWP; WBP
Let schoolmasters puzzle their brain. Song [*or* The Three Jolly Pigeons.]. Goldsmith. *Fr.* She Stoops to Conquer. ELP; EnLi-1 (1949 ed.); OAEP; PoRA; ViBoPo
Let Sol his annual journeys run. Hint from Voiture. William Shenstone. EnLoPo
Let Some Great Joys Pretend to Find. Thomas Shadwell. *Fr.* The Woman-Captain. OAEP
Let Something Good Be Said. James Whitcomb Riley. MaRV
Let Sporus tremble—"What? that thing of silk." Sporus [*or* Lord Hervey]. Pope. *Fr.* Epistle to Dr. Arbuthnot. AWP; ChTr; InPo; JAWP; MaPo; ViBoPo; WBP
Let such pure hate still underprop. Love. Henry David Thoreau. AnNE
Let Swedish bosoms deep and strong. Swedish National Hymn. Karl Vilhelm August Strandberg. PoFr
Let tears be for all men, all children. Pray Pity for Bill Smith. Paul L. Grano. BoAu
Let that which is to come be as it may. John Masefield. *Fr.* Sonnets ("Long, long ago"). HBV

Let the bells of Easter toll. Easter Song. Kenneth Leslie. MoRP
Let the bells ring, and let the boys sing. Song. John Fletcher. *Fr.* The Spanish Curate, III, ii. OBS; TuPP
Let the bird of loudest lay. The Phoenix and the Turtle. Shakespeare. CABA; CBEP; CBV; EnRePo; EP; FaBoEn; GTBS-W; LiTB; LiTG; LiTL; LoBV; MaPo; MasP; MePo; MyFE; NoP; OBEV; OBSC; PoEL-2; PoeP; SeCePo; SeCeV; SiCE; StP; TDP
Let the boy try along this bayonet-blade. Arms and the Boy. Wilfred Owen. AnEnPo; BrPo; CMoP; FaFP; FosPo; GTBS-W; LiTB; LiTM; MoAB; MoBrPo; NAMP; NP; OAEP (2d ed.); PoPo; WaP
Let the bright blood flow; starve and liquidate. Song above Death. James Edward Tobin. JKCP (1955 ed.)
Let the Brothels of Paris Be Opened. Blake. FOL
Let the Catholic Church be now arrayed. Bishop Butler of Kilcash. *Unknown.* OnYI
Let the Day Perish. Job, Bible, *O.T.* *See* Job's Curse.
Let the door be open wide. Christmas Eve. Liam P. Clancy. ISi
Let the dull merchant curse his angry fate. Elegy: The Unrewarded Lover. William Walsh. CEP
Let the eye remember the loved face. The Soul Remembers. Richard Burdick Eldridge. GoYe
Let the farmer praise his grounds. The Cruiskeen Lawn. *Unknown.* HBV; OnYI
Let the Florid Music Praise. W. H. Auden. MoPo
Let the foul scene proceed. The Marionettes. Walter de la Mare. AtBAP; MMA
Let the green Succatash with thee contend. Joel Barlow. *Fr.* The Hasty Pudding. LoGBV
Let the knowing speak. Adjuration. Charles Enoch Wheeler. AmNP; PoNe
Let the leaders of nations. We Pass. Beatrice M. Murphy. TNV
Let the Light Enter. Frances E. W. Harper. PoNe
Let the lover his mistress's beauty rehearse. My Bonny Black Bess. *Unknown.* ViBoFo
Let the mad poets say whate'er they please. A Real Woman. Keats. LiTL
Let the mighty and great. An Argument with a Millionaire [*or* The Happy Farmer]. "David Grayson." GoTP; OTD
Let the mountains stand forth! Requiem. Hamilton Warren. GoYe
Let the musicians begin. At a Solemn Musick. Delmore Schwartz. MoRP; TwAmPo
Let the Nations Be Glad. Psalms, LXVII, Bible, *O.T.* FaPON (1-5)
("God be merciful unto us, and bless us.") OnPM
Let the night keep/ What the night takes. Night. William Rose Benét. MAP; MoAmPo; NeMA
Let the night weep on your hand. Admonition before Grief. Hazel Hall. NP
Let the Nile cloak his head in the clouds, and defy. On the Discoveries of Captain Lewis. Joel Barlow. AmPP (5th ed.); MC; PAH
Let the place of the solitaires. The Place of the Solitaires. Wallace Stevens. NP; SyP
Let the Punishment Fit the Crime. W. S. Gilbert. *See* Humane Mikado, The.
Let the rain kiss you. April Rain Song. Langston Hughes. FaPON; OTD; PDV; PoRh; SUS; TiPo
Let the rain plunge radiant. The Way Through. Denise Levertov. NeAP
Let the [*or* uh] revolution come. Uh. U Name This One. Carolyn M. Rodgers. TNV; WSL
Let the Rich Man Fill His Belly. *Unknown, tr. fr. Spanish by* Havelock Ellis. OnPM
(Folk Songs, 1.) LiTW
(Spanish Folk Songs.) AWP; JAWP; WBP
Let the robed kings march in the mind. A Letter from a Friend. John Morris. CABA
Let the sloughs back up and history. Spring for All Seasons. James Welch. YAP
Let the snake wait under. A Sort of a Song. William Carlos Williams. CBV; HoPM; NoP; PoIE; PP; SeCeV
Let the tale's sailor from a Christian voyage. Altarwise by Owl-Light, X. Dylan Thomas. CMoP; CoBMV; LiTM; MaSP
Let the Toast Pass. Sheridan. *Fr.* The School for Scandal, III, iii. HBV; OnYI; OxBI
(Famous Toast, A.) TreF
(Here's to the Maiden.) ALV; CBEP; ELP; LiTL; SiTL
(Song: "Here's to the maiden [*or* maid] of bashful fifteen.") CEP; NeHB; OBEC; OxBoLi; PoRA; ViBoPo
Let the toper regale in his tankard of ale. The Pipe of Tobacco. *At. to* John Usher. HBV
Let the waves of slumber billow. To a Lady Troubled by Insomnia. Franklin P. Adams. InMe
Let the wise man place his seat. The Confession of Golias. "The Archpoet of Cologne." LiTW
Let the wood be pulled. Surprised by Me. Walter Darring. NYBP
Let the youth hardened by a sharp soldier's life. Horace. Odes, III, 2. WaaP
Let Them Alone. Robinson Jeffers. AP
Let them bestow on every airth [*or* earth] a limb. Verses Composed on the Eve of His Execution [*or* On Himself *or* His Metrical Prayer]. James Graham, Marquess of Montrose. CavP; CBEP; ChTr; OBS; OxBS; SeCePo
Let them bury your big eyes. Elegy. Edna St. Vincent Millay. *Fr.* Memorial to D. C. AmLP; AnNE; CMoP; HBMV; InP; MAP; MoAB; MoAmPo; NeMA; NePA; PoRA
Let them come, come never so proudly. God Save Elizabeth! Frances Turner Palgrave. HBV
Let them devour and be devour'd! Christopher Brennan. *Fr.* The Burden of Tyre. NeLNL
Let them go by—the heats, the doubts, the strife. Oasis. Edward Dowden. OxBI
Let them lie,—their day is over. Refrigerium. Frederick Goddard Tuckerman. AP
Let them say to my Lover. Amor Mysticus. Sister Marcela de Carpio de San Félix. AWP; CAW; JAWP; LiTW; WBP
Let there be laid, when I am dead. Posthumous Coquetry. Theophile Gautier. AWP; PeVV
Let There Be Law. Mark Van Doren. MoRP
Let there be life, said God. The Power and the Glory. Siegfried Sassoon. OBMV
Let there be many windows to your soul. Progress. Ella Wheeler Wilcox. BLPA
Let there be violet dusk and a cool air. In Pace in Idipsum Dormiam et Requiescam. Patrick O'Connor. CAW
Let there be within these phantom walls. Dream House. Catherine Parmenter Newell. PoToHe
Let things touch your mind. Details. Luke Zilles. RePo
Let This Be My Parting Word. Rabindranath Tagore. *Fr.* Gitanjali. MoRP
Let those complain that feel Love's cruelty. To the Blest Evanthe. John Fletcher. *Fr.* A Wife for a Month. SeCL; SeEP
Let those love now, who never loved before. The Vigil of Venus. *Unknown.* WoL
Let those who are in favour with their stars. Sonnets, XXV. Shakespeare. CBEP; EnL; EnLi-1; OBSC; ReIE SiCE; Sonn; WoL
Let thy gold be cast in the furnace. Cleansing Fires. Adelaide Anne Procter. WGRP
Let thy soul walk slowly in thee. Silence. Samuel Miller Hageman. TRV
Let thy tears, Le Vayer, let them flow. To Monsieur de la Mothe le Vayer. Molière. AWP; JAWP; WBP
Let time and chance combine, combine. Adieu. Thomas Carlyle. HBV; OBRV; VA
Let Tobias bless charity with his dog. Christopher Smart. Jubilate Agno, III. NCEP
"Let trees be made, for Earth is bare." The Coming of the Trees. Arthur Guiterman. PEDC
Let tyrants shake their iron rods. Chester. William Billings. TrAS
Let uh revolution come. Uh. *See* Let the revolution come. Uh.
Let us abandon then our gardens and go home. Justice Denied in Massachusetts. Edna St. Vincent Millay. CoBA; MAP; MoAmPo; WOW
Let us ask ourselves some questions; for that man is truly wise. The Higher Catechism. Sam Walter Foss. WGRP
Let us ask you a few questions, without rancor. For Any Member of the Security Police. Josephine Jacobsen. NePoAm
Let us be guests in one another's house. Any Wife or Husband. Carol Haynes. BLPA; NeHB; PoToHe

Let us be like a bird for a moment perched. Wings. Victor Hugo. TRV
Let Us Be Men. D. H. Lawrence. MoPW
Let Us Be Merry before We Go. John Philpot Curran. *See* Deserter, The.
Let Us Be Off! C. Day Lewis. WoL
Let us begin and carry up this corpse. A Grammarian's Funeral. Robert Browning. AnFE; BEL; BoLiVe; CoBE; DiPo; EnLit; EPN; GTBS; HBV; LoBV; MaRV; MaVP; MBW-2; OAEP; PoE; PoVP; TOP; ViPo; ViPP; VP; WGRP
Let us begin and portion out these sweets. A Girtonian Funeral. *Unknown.* Par
Let us break bread togedder. When I Fall on My Knees. *Unknown.* BoAN-2
Let us cheer the weary traveler. Weary Traveler. *Unknown.* BoAN-1
Let Us Come Boldly. E. Margaret Clarkson. SoP
Let Us Consider Where the Great Men Are. Delmore Schwartz. *Fr.* Shenandoah. MoAB; MoAmPo
Let us dance and let us sing. The Fairy Ring. *Unknown.* BoTP
Let us deal kindly with a heart of old by sorrow torn. Saadabad. James Elroy Flecker. SeCePo
Let Us Declare! *sel.* Angela Morgan.
"Come, workers! Poets, artists, dreamers, more and more." PGD
Let us deliberately sit into design. Shapes. Mark Turbyfill. NP
Let Us Drink. Alcaeus, *tr. fr. Greek by* John Hermann Merivale. AWP
Let us drink and be merry, dance, joke, and rejoice. Careless Gallant [*or* Coronemus Nos Rosis antequam Marcescant]. Thomas Jordan. CoMu; HBV; OBEV; OxBoLi; SeCL; SeEP; SiTL
Let us drink old wine, at the sight of which I rejoice. Five Arabic Verses in Praise of Wine, I. *Unknown.* TrJP
Let us evoke no phantom throng. Armistice Day. Lucia Trent. PGD
Let Us Forget. Agnes Mary Frances Robinson. WHA
Let us forget these principalities. Innumerable Friend. May Sarton. WaKn
Let us gather us the sunshine. Scatter Seeds of Kindness. May Riley Smith. BLPA; WBLP
Let Us Give Thanks. "Marianne Farningham." PEDC
Let Us Go Down [the Long Dead Night Is Done]. Christopher Brennan. *Fr.* Towards the Source. BoAV; PoAu-1
Let us go hence, my songs; she will not hear. A Leave-taking. Swinburne. CH; EG; FaBoEn; HBV; MaVP; OAEP; OBNC; OBVV; PoEL-5; PoLF; PoVP; ViBoPo
Let us go hence: the night is now at hand. A Last Word. Ernest Dowson. MoBrPo; PoVP; SyP
"Let us go off on a candid cadenza." Lincoln. Delmore Schwartz. FiMAP
Let Us Go, Then, Exploring. Virginia Woolf. BoNaP
Let us go then, you and I. The Love Song of J. Alfred Prufrock. T. S. Eliot. AmPo; AmPP; AnFE; AP; APA; ATP (1953 ed.); AWP; BWP; CABA; CaFP; CBEP; CBV; CMoP; CoAnAm; CoBA; CoBMV; DiPo; EnL; EnLit; ExPo; ForPo; FosPo; HBMV; HoPM; ILP; InPo; LiTB; LiTM (1946 ed.); MAP; MAPA; MaPo; MBW-2; MoAB; MoAmPo; MoPW; MoVE; MWA-2; NeMA; NePA; NoP; NP; OAEP (2d ed.); PAn; PIA; Po; PoAn; PoFS; PoIE; PoRA; ReMP; SeCeV; TreFT; TrGrPo; TwAmPo; TwCP; UnPo; ViBoPo
"Let us go to the wood," said this pig. Song to Five Toes. *Unknown.* OTPC (1946 ed.); PCH
Let us hasten—let us fly. Aristophanes. *Fr.* The Frogs. MaRV
Let Us Have Peace. Nancy Byrd Turner. MaRV; OQP; OTD; PoToHe
Let us have winter loving that the heart. Winter Love. Elizabeth Jennings. NePoEA
Let Us Keep Christmas. Grace Noll Crowell. MaRV; SoP; TRV
(Eternal Values.) PoToHe (new ed.)
Let us keep splendid loyalites. Loyalties. Walter A. Cutter. OQP
Let us leave talking of angelic hosts. Sonnets from "One Person." Elinor Wylie. OxBA
Let us, Lesbia darling, still. Love Is All. Catullus, *tr. by* Sir Theodore Martin. EnLi-1; OuHeWo
Let Us Live and Love. Thomas Campion. *See* My Sweetest Lesbia.
Let us live, my wife, as we have lived, and keep. To My Wife. Ausonius. HW
Let us live, then, and be glad. Gaudeamus Igitur. *Unknown.* *Fr.* Carmina Burana. HBV; WoL
Let us make love, let us make war. Paying a Debt. Chevalier de Boufflers. OnPM
Let us, my Lesbia! live and love. To Lesbia. Catullus, *tr. by* Charles Abraham Elton. OnPM
Let us not fear for the creative word. Liberté, Egalité, Fraternité. Florence Converse. PoFr
Let us not look upon. Prayer. Witter Bynner. EaLo
Let Us Not Pretend. Ray Mathew. BoAV
"Let us not [*or* now] speak, for the love we bear one another." In a Bath Teashop. John Betjeman. BoC; ELU; EnLoPo
Let us not think of our departed dead. Our Dead [*or* An Epitaph]. Edwin Markham. MaRV; OQP
Let Us Now Praise Famous Men. Ecclesiasticus, XLIV: 1-15, Bible, Apocrypha. BoC; ChTr
(Our Fathers, XLIV: 1-15.) TrJP
(Praise of Famous Men, XLIV: 10-14.) MaRV
"Let Us Now Praise Famous Men." C. Day Lewis. CMoP
"Let us now speak, for the love we bear one another." *See* "Let us not speak. . ."
Let us play, and dance, and sing. The Vision of Delight. Ben Jonson. PoEL-2; SeCV-1
Let Us Pray. Ralph Spaulding Cushman. FaChP
Let us put by some hour of every day. Sanctuary. Clinton Scollard. MaRV; OQP
Let us put feathers. Feathers. Olive Hopegood. MoAuPo
Let us record/ The evenings when we were innocents of twenty. Winfield Townley Scott. *Fr.* Biography for Traman. ErPo
Let us remember the yellow. In the Month of Green Fire. Sophie Himmell. GoYe
Let us return from Ilium, and no more. Independence. Guy Mason. CaP
Let us ride together. Riding Song. *Unknown.* SCC
Let us rise in early morning. Risen with Healing in His Wings. St. John of Damascus. BePJ; CAW
Let Us Rise Up and Live. Francis Sherman. CaP
Let us save the babies. The Babies. Mark Strand. NYBP
Let Us See Jesus. Anna B. Warner. *See* We Would See Jesus.
Let us sit by the hissing steam radiator a winter's day, grey wind. Horses and Men in the Rain. Carl Sandburg. PoLF
Let Us Smile. Wilbur D. Nesbit. WBLP
(Smile.) SoP
Let us suppose, valleys & such ago. The Dream Songs, XV. John Berryman. NaP
Let Us Take the Road. John Gay. *Fr.* The Beggar's Opera. ATP (1935 ed.); CEP
(Highwaymen, The.) WiR
Let us take to our hearts a lesson. The Tapestry Weavers. Anson G. Chester. BLPA; BLRP; WBLP
Let us thank Almighty God. Creatrix. Anna Wickham. MoBrPo; TrGrPo (1942 ed.)
Let us thank God for unfulfilled desire. For Transient Things. James A. S. McPeek. OQP
Let us to-day. Song for Memorial Day. Clinton Scollard. OHIP
Let us tunnel/ the air. Letters to Walt Whitman. Ronald Johnson. YAP
Let us turn, now, from the rigid clocks. Subject for Prophecy. Gemma D'Auria. JKCP (1955 ed.)
Let us use time [*or* it] whilst we may. Of Time [*or* Of Beauty]. Sir Richard Fanshawe. *Fr.* Il Pastor Fido. InMe; SeCL
Let us walk in the white snow. Velvet Shoes. Elinor Wylie. CH; FaPON; GoJo; MAP; MoAB; MoAmPo; NeMA; NP; OTD; OTPC (1946 ed.); PCH; PFY; PG; PoPl; PTK; SiSoSe; SoPo; SP; StVeCh; TiPo (1952 ed.); TreFS; TrGrPo; TSW; WHA
Let us walk softly, friends. New Year's Thoughts. Lillian Gray. OQP
Let Us with a Gladsome Mind, *abr.* Milton. MaRV; SoP; TRV; WGRP
(Praise the Lord.) FaBoCh; FaChP; LoGBV
Let vain or busy thoughts have there no part. George Herbert. *Fr.* The Church Porch. TRV
Let War's Tempests Cease. Longfellow. OHIP
Let wits contest. The Posie. George Herbert. MaMe

Let Y stand for you who says. You. Kenneth Rexroth. *Fr.* A Bestiary. HoPM
Let Ye Then My Birds Alone. John Clare. *Fr.* Summer Evening. BiS
Let your hands meet. The Death of Meleager. Swinburne. *Fr.* Atalanta in Calydon. OBVV; PoVP
Let Your Pastor Know. *Unknown.* STF
Let your song be delicate. Song Be Delicate. John Shaw Neilson. BoAV; PoAu-1
Let Zeus Record, *sel.* Hilda Doolittle ("H. D.").
"Stars wheel in purple, yours is not so rare." MAP; MoAmPo
Lethal Thought, The. Mary Boyd Wagner. GoYe
Lethe. Hilda Doolittle ("H. D."). AmLP; CMoP; LiTM (1970 ed.); MAP; MoAmPo; NeMA; PG (1945 ed.); PoRA; TrGrPo; ViBoPo
Lethe. Georgia Douglas Johnson. CDC
Lethe. Edna St. Vincent Millay. PG
Letrilla; the Lord of Dollars. Francisco de Quevedo y Villegas, *tr. fr. Spanish by* Thomas Walsh. WoL
Let's Be Merry. Christina Rossetti. *Fr.* Sing-Song. FaPON
("Mother shake the cherry-tree.") PoVP; TiPo
Let's build bridges here and there. Interracial. Georgia Douglas Johnson. PoNe; TTY
Let's contend no more, Love. A Woman's Last Word. Robert Browning. BEL; BLPA; BoLiVe; CBEP; EPN; FaBoBe; FaFP; GTBS; GTBS-D; HBV; InPo; LiTL; LO; MeWo; OAEP; PoVP; TreFS; TrGrPo; UnTE; ViBoPo; ViPo
Let's count the bodies over again. Counting Small-Boned Bodies. Robert Bly. NaP
Let's enjoy, while the season invites us. Giovinette, che fate all' amore. Lorenzo da Ponte. *Fr.* Don Giovanni. TrJP
Let's Forget. Charles L. H. Wagner. PoToHe
"Let's go huntin'," says Risky Rob. Billy Barlow. *Unknown.* OuSiCo
Let's go play in the sun. Out. Nathaniel Burt. MoLP
Let's Go to Bed. *Unknown.* ChTr
Let's go to the wood, says this pig. *Unknown.* OxNR
Let's go up to the hillside today. Play Song. Peter Clarke. PBA
Let's Have a Picnic Out-of-Doors. Mary Carolyn Davies. PCH
Let's not be slow in knowing. On Calvary's Lonely Hill. Herbert Clark Johnson. PoNe
Let's not use eyes anymore. Dialogue—2 Dollmakers. Gregory Corso. NeAP
Let's play we are a tune. Invitation. Ridgely Torrence. PCH
Let's say I live here, at any rate. O'Reilly's Reply. Richard Weber. NMP
Let's say, the opposition knows the ring. Anthony Delius. *Fr.* The Great Divide. BoSA
Let's shake wild music from gray belfry chimes. Resurrection. Lady Margaret Sackville. HBMV
Let's sing a song together once. Song. Louis Simpson. NePoAm
Let's skip a few short years of hollow peace. George the Third. Byron. *Fr.* The Vision of Judgment. FiP
Let's smile and be kind—life is so short. Life Is So Short. Margaret S. Hall. STF
Let's straighten this out, my little man. To a Small Boy Standing on My Shoes While I Am Wearing Them. Ogden Nash. ALV; FiBHP
Let's talk about some unpretentious things. A Change of Subject. Daniel Sargent. JKCP (1955 ed.)
Let's talk of graves, of worms and epitaphs. The Death of Kings [*or* Richard II's Dejection]. Shakespeare. King Richard II, *fr.* III, ii. DiPo; TreFS; TrGrPo
Let's think of eggs. The Poultries. Ogden Nash. CenHV
Letter. Alexander Bergman. TrJP
Letter, The. Paul Blackburn. CoPo
Letter, A. Sophia Castro-Leon. QAH
Letter, A. Emerson. OxBA
Letter I ("You were amused to find you too could fear"). William Empson. ChMP; LiTB
Letter IV ("Hatched in a rasping darkness of dry sand"). William Empson. LiTB
Letter II ("Burned in this element"). W. S. Graham. NePoEA
Letter VI ("A day the wind was hardly"). W. S. Graham. ChMP
Letter, A. Anthony Hecht. NYBP; StP
Letter, The. John Holmes. NePoAm
Letter, The. Beatrice M. Murphy. PoNe
Letter, A. Mu'tamid, King of Seville, *tr. fr. Arabic by* Dulcie L. Smith. LiTW
Letter, The. Po Chü-i, *tr. fr. Chinese by* Arthur Waley. LoBV
Letter, A. Matthew Prior. *See* Letter to the Hon. Lady Miss Margaret Cavendish-Holles-Harley, A.
Letter, A. Sir Arthur Quiller-Couch. CenHV
Letter, A. Alex Raybin. ThO
Letter, A. Anne Ridler. LiTL; LiTM
Letter, A, *sel.* Earl of Rochester.
"Love—the most generous passion of the mind." LO
Letter I ("The midnight streets as I walk back"). Randall Swingler. WaP
Letter VIII ("On the first day of snow, my train"). Randall Swingler. WaP
Letter, The. John Tatham. CavP
Letter, The. Elizabeth Turner. Mrs. Turner's Object-Lessons, IX. OTPC (1923 ed.)
Letter, The. John Hall Wheelock. AnEnPo; LiTL
Letter across Doubt and Distance. M. Carl Holman. AmNP; PoNe
Letter Containing a Panegyric on Bath, *abr.* Christopher Anstey. The New Bath Guide, VI. OBEC
Letter for Allhallows, A. Peter Kane Dufault. NYBP
Letter for Melville 1951. Charles Olson. CoPo
Letter for You, A. Catharine M. Fanshawe. *See* Riddle, A: "'Twas whispered in Heaven, 'twas muttered in hell."
Letter from a Coward to a Hero. Robert Penn Warren. MAP
Letter from a Friend, A. John Morris. CABA
Letter from a Girl to Her Own Old Age, A. Alice Meynell. GoTL; GTBS-W; LiTB; MoBrPo; ViBoPo
Letter from a State Hospital. Frank Mundorf. GoYe
Letter from a Wife. S. Carolyn Reese. PoNe (1970 ed.)
Letter from Artemisa in the Town, to Cloe, in the Country, A. Earl of Rochester. SeCV-2
Letter from Brooklyn, A. Derek Walcott. ToPo
Letter from Italy, A. Addison. CEP
Sels.
Italy and Britain. OBEC
"O Liberty, thou goddess heavenly bright." PoFr
Letter from Mr. Ezekiel Biglow of Jaalam to the Hon. Joseph T. Buckingham, A ("Thrash away, you'll hev to rattle") James Russell Lowell. The Biglow Papers, 1st Series, No. I. AmPP; OxBA
(Mr. Hosea Biglow Speaks.) PAH
("Thrash away, you'll hev to rattle.") CoBA
(To a Recruiting Sergeant.) AnNE
War, *sel.*, 1 *st.* MaRV
Letter from Mr. Hosea Biglow to the Hon. J. T. Buckingham, A ("This kind o' sogerin' "). James Russell Lowell. The Biglow Papers, 1st Series, No. II. OxBA
"Letter from my love today, A!" A Ballad of Hell. John Davidson. ACV; AnEnPo; AnFE; HoPM; MoBrPo; PoVP; STP; WHA
Letter from Newport, A. Frederic William Henry Myers. VA
Letter from Oregon. William Stafford. NaP
Letter from Paparua. Colin Newbury. AnNZ
Letter from Rome, A. Arthur Hugh Clough. Amours de Voyage, Canto I, v. LoBV
Letter from Slough Pond. Isabella Gardner. ELU
Letter from the Caribbean, A. Barbara Howes. CoAP
Letter from the Country, A. Howard Baker. TwAmPo
Letter from the Country to a Friend in Town, A. John Oldham. PP
"'Tis endless, Sir, to tell the many ways," *sel.* PeRV
Letter from the Great Society. Morton Marcus. YAP
Letter from the South. Robert E. Hayden. PoNe
Letter from the Vieux Carre. Ethel Green Russell. GoYe
Letter from Town; the Almond Tree. D. H. Lawrence. MoPW
Letter from Underground. Ronald Everson. MoCV
Letter Is a Gypsy Elf, A. Annette Wynne. SUS
Letter of a Mother. Robert Penn Warren. MAP; MoAmPo
Letter of Advice, A. Winthrop Mackworth Praed. HBV; OBRV; OxBoLi; TOP; WhC
Letter Received, A. Emily Dickinson. *See* Way I read a letter's this, The.
Letter: The Japanese, to Her Husband at War. William Walsh. PoPl
Letter to a Friend. John Thompson. BoAV; PoAu-2

Letter to a Friend. Robert Penn Warren. MAP; MoAmPo
Letter to a Live Poet, A. Rupert Brooke. BrPo
Letter to a Poet. Robert Hass. YAP
Letter to a Teacher of English. Robert Hillyer. AnFE; CoAnAm
Letter to a Young Friend. Burns. *See* Epistle to a Young Friend.
Letter to a Young Poet. George Barker. ChMP
Letter to Alex Comfort. Dannie Abse. FaBoTw; TwCP
Letter to Anne Ridler. G. S. Fraser. OxBS
Letter to Ben Jonson. Francis Beaumont. *See* Master Francis Beaumont's Letter to Ben Jonson.
Letter to Daphnis, A. Countess of Winchilsea. EnLoPo
Letter to Duncan. Gail Dusenbery. ThO
Letter to Elsa, A. Grace Hazard Conkling. HBMV; HBVY
Letter to Her Husband, A ("Phoebus, make haste"). Anne Bradstreet. AmP; AmPP; AnFE; APA; CoAnAm; LiTA
Letter to Her Husband, Absent upon Publick Employment, A ("As loving hind that hartless wants her deer"). Anne Bradstreet. CBEP; OxBA; SCAP
Letter to Her Husband, Absent upon Public[k] Employment, A ("My head, my heart, mine eyes, my life—nay more"). Anne Bradstreet. MAmP; SCAP
Letter to His Friend Isaac, A. Judah Halevi, *tr. fr. Hebrew by* Emma Lazarus. TrJP
Letter to Hitler, A. James Laughlin. LiTA; WaP
Letter to Karl Shapiro. E. L. Mayo. MiAP
Letter to Lady Margaret Cavendish-Holles-Harley When a Child, A. Matthew Prior. *See* Letter to the Hon. Lady Miss Margaret Cavendish-Holles-Harley, A.
Letter to Lord Middleton, A. Sir George Etherege. CavP
Letter to Manlius Torquatus. Catullus, *tr. fr. Latin by* Jack Lindsay. LiTW
Letter to Maria Gisborne, *sel.* Shelley.
"You are now/ In London, that great sea, whose ebb and flow." OBRV; PeER
Letter to My Daughter. Donald Finkel. CoAP
Letter to My Sister. Anne Spencer. AmNP; PoNe
Letter to My Wife. Roy Fuller. NeBP; POTE
Letter to My Wife. Keidrych Rhys. WaP
Letter to N.Y. Elizabeth Bishop. LiTL; TwCP
Letter to P. Robert Friend. NYBP
Letter to Pasternak. Ralph Pomeroy. CoPo
Letter to R. Willard Maas. WaP
Letter to Robert Fergusson. Alexander Scott. OxBS
Letter to Robert Frost, A. Robert Hillyer. MoAmPo
Letter to Rome, A. Steven Peele. ReIE
Letter to Sara Hutchinson, A. Samuel Taylor Coleridge. *See* Dejection; an Ode.
Letter to Sir H. Wotton at His Going Ambassador to Venice. John Donne. OBS
Letter to Sir Robert Walpole, A. Henry Fielding. CEP
Letter to the City Clerk. Frederick A. Wright. FaFP
Letter to the Countess of Denbigh against Irresolution and Delay in Matters of Religion, A. Richard Crashaw. *See* To the Noblest and Best of Ladies, the Countess of Denbigh.
Letter to the Front Muriel Rukeyser. WaP
Sels.
Even during War. TrJP
To Be a Jew in the Twentieth Century. TrJP
Letter to the Hon. Lady Miss Margaret Cavendish-Holles-Harley, A. Matthew Prior. CEP; EiCP; LoBV; OBEC
(Letter, A.) SeCePo
(Letter to Lady Margaret Cavendish-Holles-Harley, When a Child, A.) OBEV; PRWS
(To a Child of Noble Birth.) OTPC (1923 ed.)
Letter to the Lady Carey, and Mrs. Essex Riche, from Amyens, A. John Donne. MaMe
Letter to the Night. Lloyd Frankenberg. AnAmPo
Letter to the World. Emily Dickinson. *See* This is my letter to the world.
Letter to Viscount Cobham. Congreve. LoBV
Letter to Wilbur Frohock, A. Daniel Hoffman. CoPo
Letter to William Carlos Williams, A. Kenneth Rexroth. OnHM; PP
Letter to Yvor Winters, A. Kenneth Rexroth. ML
Letter today, official, buff, A. Letter from Paparua. Colin Newbury. AnNZ
Letter 27. Charles Olson. CoPo
Letter 22. Charles Olson. FRC
Letter Written on a Ferry [While] Crossing Long Island Sound. Anne Sexton. CoAP; NYBP; TwCP
Letters. Bernard Spencer. NeBP; WaP
Letters, The. Tennyson. HBV
Letters and lines, we see, are soon defaced. Idea's Mirrour, XXI. Michael Drayton. ReIE
Letters are comforting to get. Convalesence, VI. David McCord. WhC
Letters at School, The. *Unknown.* OTPC (1923 ed.)
Letters [*or* Notes] Found near a Suicide. Frank Horne. AmNP; CDC; PoNe
To James, *sel.* BANP; BiCB; GoSl; Kal
Letters from Teignmouth, *sel.* Winthrop Mackworth Praed.
Our Ball. EnRP
Letters, I, your lone friend, write in sorrow, The. From William Tyndale to John Frith. Edgar Bowers. NePoEA; QFR
Letters, like blood along a weakening body. Letters. Bernard Spencer. NeBP; WaP
Letters of the Jews as strict as flames, The. The Alphabet. Karl Shapiro. MoRP
Letters she left to clutter up the desk. A Gesture by a Lady with an Assumed Name. James Wright. LiTM (1970 ed.)
Letters: To Barbara. Kathleen Fraser. YAP
Letters to Dead Imagists. Carl Sandburg. AmPP (3d ed.)
Letters to Walt Whitman. Ronald Johnson. YAP
Lettice. Dinah Maria Mulock Craik. HBV
Lettice. "Michael Field." VA
Letty's Globe. Charles Tennyson Turner. CBEP; EPN; HBV; OBEV; OBVV; PeVV; VA
Leukothea. Keith Douglas. NeBP
Levantine, A. William Plomer. OBMV
Levedy, ic thonke thee. Thanks and a Plea to Mary. *Unknown.* MeEL
Levee Camp "Holler," *with music.* *Unknown.* ABF
Levee Moan (A *and* B *vers., with music*). *Unknown.* AS
Level and the Square, The. Robert Morris. BLPA
Level ocean lies immeasurably blind, The. The Flying Fish. Jack Cope. PeSA
Level with duty, days ride a city-express across the calendar page. Coin in the Fist. Florence Kerr Brownell. GoYe
Level with the summit of that eastern mount. Eos. Richard Henry Horne. *Fr.* Orion. VA
Leveling his pole like some quixotic lance. Challenge. Samuel Hazo. SD
Leves Amores. Arthur Symons. AnEnPo; UnTE
(Your Kisses.) MeWo
Levi, thou art a load, I'll lay thee down. Dryden. *Fr.* Absalom and Achitophel, Pt. II. AtBAP; SeEP
Leviathan. Job, XLI, Bible, *O.T.* TrGrPo
(Of God's Great Power in the Leviathan.) PoG
Leviathan. Margaret R. Gould. TwCaPo
Leviathan. Jay Macpherson. MoCV
Leviathan. W. S. Merwin. NePoEA
Leviathan. Peter Quennell. POTE
"Music met Leviathan returning, A," *sel.* MoBrPo
Leviathan. Louis Untermeyer. GoTP
Leviathan; a Poem in Four Movements. Kenneth Pitchford. CoPo
Leviathan drives the eyed prow of his face. Leviathan. Peter Quennell. POTE
Lewd Love Is Loss. Robert Southwell. ACP
Lewis and Clark. Stephen Vincent Benét. RePo
Lewis Has a Trumpet. Karla Kuskin. PDV
Lewis, the Lost Lover. Sir Thomas More. *See* Fortune.
Lewti; or, The Circassian Love-Chaunt. Samuel Taylor Coleridge. MERP
(Lewti.) EnRP
Lexington. Oliver Wendell Holmes. DD; MC; PAH
Lexington. Sidney Lanier. *Fr.* Psalm of the West. PaA; PAH; PAL
Lexington. Whittier. MC; PAH
Lexington Murder, The. *Unknown.* BaBo; OuSiCo, *with music*
(Lexington Miller, The.) BaBo
Li Po. Floyce Alexander. QAH
Li Po. Ruth Gilbert. AnNZ
Liadain. *Unknown,* *tr. fr. Old Irish by* Frank O'Connor. KiLC
Liadain to Curither. Moireen Fox. NP
Liadin and Curither. *Unknown,* *tr. fr. Old Irish by* Kuno Meyer. OnYI

Liadov: "The Enchanted Lake." James Kirkup. MuSP
Liady-Day an' Ridden House. William Barnes. OBRV
Liar, The. Rue Carpenter. RIS
Liar, The. LeRoi Jones. AmPP (5th ed.)
Liar, The. *Unknown, tr. fr. Irish by* Frank O'Connor. KiLC
Liar and bragger. Peregrine. Elinor Wylie. HBMV
'Lias! 'Lias! Bless de Lawd! In the Morning. Paul Laurence Dunbar. GoSl
Libel of Divorce, A. George Gascoigne. ReEn
Libel on Doctor Delaney and a Certain Great Lord, A. Swift. NCEP
Libera Nos a Malo. Eric Bruno. JKCP (1955 ed.)
Libera Nos, Domine—Deliver us, O Lord, not only from British dependence, but also. Emancipation from British Dependence. Philip Freneau. PAH
Liberal nature did dispense. Woman's Arms. Anacreon. UnTE
"Liberalissimo." Hart Leroi Bibbs. BF
Liberals raised this in their finest hour. Norris Dam. Selden Rodman. PoNe
Liberator, The. Wu Ti, *tr. fr. Chinese by* Arthur Waley. BiS
Liberia?/ No micro-footnote in a bunioned book. Do. Melvin B. Tolson. *Fr.* Libretto for the Republic of Liberia. PoNe (1970 ed.)
Liberté, Egalité, Fraternité. Florence Converse. PoFr
Libertine, The. Aphra Behn. OBEV (1st ed.)
(Thousand Martyrs I Have Made, A.) CavP
Libertine, The. Louis MacNeice. DTC
Liberty. Blake. *See* Eternity.
Liberty. John Hay. AA; PoFr
Liberty. John Ceiriog Hughes. PoFr
Liberty. Michael Chazarian Nalbandian, *tr. fr. Armenian by* Alice Stone Blackwell. PoFr
Liberty. Leopold Staff, *tr. fr. Polish by* Watson Kirkconnell. PoFr
Liberty. Edward Thomas. MoAB
Liberty, *sel.* James Thomson.
British Commerce, *fr.* IV. OBEC
Liberty, *sel.* Wordsworth.
"Beetle loves his unpretending track, The." FiBHP; Par
Liberty. Sir Thomas Wyatt. *See* Lover Rejoiceth, The.
Liberty and Independence. *Unknown. See* Independence Bell, July 4, 1776.
Liberty Enlightening the World. Edmund Clarence Stedman. PAH
Liberty, Equality, Fraternity. Wilfrid Scawen Blunt. *Fr.* In Vinculis. PoFr
Liberty for All. William Lloyd Garrison. AA; AmePo
Liberty of the Press. Sir Aubrey De Vere. PoFr
Liberty Pole, The. John Trumbull. *Fr.* M'Fingal. AmPP (3d ed.)
Liberty Pole, The. *Unknown. Fr.* The Procession with the Standard of a Faction; a Cantata. PAH
Liberty Song, The. John Dickinson. AmPP; TrAS, *with music*
(Song of American Freedom, A.) PoFr
Liberty Tree. Thomas Paine. MC; PAH; PoFr
Librarian, The. Charles Olson. CoPo
Library, The, *sels.* George Crabbe. OBEC
Books.
Crusty Critics.
Library, The. Barbara A. Huff. FaPON
Library, The. Mary Mills. NePoAm
Library, The. Frank Dempster Sherman. AA
Library, The. William Carlos Williams. *Fr.* Paterson, III. AtBAP
Libretto for the Republic of Liberia, *sel.* Melvin B. Tolson.
Do. PoNe (1970 ed.)
Lice-Finders, The. Arthur Rimbaud. *See* Chercheuses de poux, Les.
Lice Seekers, The. Arthur Rimbaud. *See* Chercheuses de poux, Les.
Licences? Yes. Poetic licence. Ode to Himself. Sir Walter Raleigh. WhC
Licentious Person, A. John Donne. MaMe
Lichen. Mary Fullerton. PoAu-1
Licht Nichts, The. Violet Jacob. ACV
Lichtenberg. Kipling. EnLit
Licia, *sels.* Giles Fletcher.
"Are those two stars, her eyes, my life's light gone," XLIII. Sonn
Elegy, An: "Down in a bed, and on a bed of down." ReIE
"First did I fear, when first my love began," XX. SiCE; Sonn; TuPP
"I live, sweet love, whereas the gentle wind," XXVI. SiCE; TuPP
"If sad complaint would show a lover's pain," Elegie III. TuPP
"In time the strong and stately turrets fall," XXVIII. ILP; ReEn; ReIE; SiCE; Sonn; TuPP
(Time.) OBSC
"Like Memnon's rock, touched [*or* touch'd] with the rising sun," XLVII. EIL; ReEn; ReIE; SiCE; TuPP
"Love was laid down, all weary, fast asleep," IX. ReIE
"My love was mask'd and armed with a fan," XXIII. ReIE
"O sug'red talk, wherewith my thoughts do live," LII. ReIE
"Sad, all alone, not long I musing sat," I. ReIE; SiCE; Sonn; TuPP
"Seven are the lights that wander in the skies," XXV. ReEn; ReIE; SiCE; TuPP
"Whenas her lute is tuned to her voice," XXXI. TuPP
Licorice Fields at Pontefract, The. John Betjeman. CMoP; NMP
Licus, thou art deceived in saying that. To Licus. Everard Guilpin. *Fr.* Skialetheia. SiCE
Liddell and Scott; on the Completion of Their Lexicon. Thomas Hardy. OxBoLi
Liddesdale Crosiers hae ridden a race, The. The Death of Parcy Reed. *Unknown.* BaBo (A *vers.*) ESPB; OBB
Lido, The. Edmund Wilson. ErPo
Lie, The. Howard Moss. AtBAP; LiTM (1970 ed.); MoAB; NePoAm
Lie, The. Howard Nemerov. NYTB
Lie, The. Sir Walter Ralegh. AtBAP; CBEP; ChTr; CTC; EnLi-1 (1949 ed.); EnRePo; EP; ExPo; FCP; ForPo; HBV; InvP; LiTB; MasP; NoP; OAEP; OBSC; PoEL-2; PoFr; PoFS; PoIE; PPON; QFR; ReEn; SeCeV; SiCE; SiPS; SiTL; TreFT; TrGrPo; TuPP; ViBoPo; WoL, *abr.*
(Soul's Errand, The.) WGRP
Lie back, daughter, let your head. First Lesson. Philip Booth. SD; TwCP
Lie heavy on him, earth! for he. For Sir John Vanbrugh, Architect. Abel Evans. WhC
Lie low; my little one. Roman Lullaby. *Unknown.* RIS
Lie of the Land, The. Margaret Fishback. SiTL
Lie on the mats and sweat in summer. Things to Do around Kyoto. Gary Snyder. NaP
Lie on the Sand. Alistair Campbell. AnNZ
Lie on! while my revenge shall be. Revenge. Lord Nugent. PV
"Lie still, my newly married wife." The Griesly Wife. John Manifold. ATP (1953 ed.); MoBrPo (1950 ed.); MoBS
Lie still, old Dane, below thy heap. A Danish Barrow. Francis Turner Palgrave. VA
Liebesweh. Dora Wilcox. BoAu
Liefer would I turn and love. Deranged. Padraic Fiacc. NeIP
Lien, The. Adelaide Love. MoSiPe
Lier, The. John Donne. MaMe
Lies have short wings. He lies that so sings. John Davies of Hereford. SiCE
Lies of Men, The. *Unknown, tr. fr. Spanish by* Havelock Ellis. OnPM
Lies of young boys are to be heard about, or read about. Election Day (Newark, New Jersey). LeRoi Jones. BF
Lt. Cmdr. T. E. Sanderson. James Scully. TPM
Lieutenant who went out to shoot, A. Limerick. Morgan Taylor. LiBL
Life. Franklin P. Adams. InMe
Life. Francis Bacon. GTBS; GTBS-D; GTBS-P; GTBS-W; GTSE
(In Vitam Humanam.) PoIE
(Life of Man, The.) EIL; OBSC; WHA
Life. Anna Letitia Barbauld. BLPA; FaFP; HBV; MaRV, *abr.*; NeHB, *abr.*; OBEV; OBRV; TreFS, *abr.*; TRV
("Life! I know not what thou art.") GTBS; GTBS-D; GTBS-P; GTBS-W; GTSE; GTSL
Life. Horatius Bonar. OQP
Life. Charlotte Brontë. OQP
Life. Alice Brown. AA

Life. Robert Browning. *Fr.* Christmas Eve and Easter-Day. OQP
Life. "N. C." SeCL
Life. Samuel Taylor Coleridge. EnRP
Life. "Barry Cornwall." VA
Life. George Crabbe. OBEC
Life. Margaret Deland. *See* By One Great Heart.
Life. *Comp. by* Mrs. H. A. Deming. *Fr. various poems.* BOHV
Life. Emily Dickinson. *See* I asked no other thing.
Life. Paul Laurence Dunbar. AmNP; CDC
Life. Wayne Gard. OQP
Life. Amory Hare. HBMV
Life. George Herbert. AnAnS-1; BWP; CBEP; EP; HBV; LiTB; MaMe; MeLP; MeP; MePo; NoP; OBS; PoFS; SeCeV; SeCL; SeCP; SeCV-1; SeEP
(“I made a posie, while the day ran by.”) EG
Life. Frederick Lawrence Knowles. ChIP; MaRV
Life. Alfred Kreymborg. ELU
Life. Lizzie M. Little. VA
Life. Longfellow. *Fr.* The Psalm of Life. GN
Life. Nan Terrell Reed. BLPA
Life. Edward Rowland Sill. BLRP; MaRV; OQP; TRV
Life. Charles Swain. VA
Life. *Unknown, at. to* Lao-tzu, *tr. fr. Chinese by* Witter Bynner. *Fr.* Tao Teh King. OnPM
Life ("I've seen the moonbeam's shining light"). *Unknown.* PoToHe
Life ("Life is a burden; bear it"). *Unknown.* SoP
Life. Henry van Dyke. *Fr.* The Three Best Things. MaRV; OQP; SoP
Life. Jones Very. AP
Life. William Merrell Vories. MaRV; OQP
Life, *abr.* Ella Wheeler Wilcox. PoToHe
Life, A. George Edward Woodberry. EtS
Life, The. James Wright. NaP
Life, a Bubble. William Drummond of Hawthornden. *See* Madrigal: "This life, which seems so fair."
Life, a Question. Corinne Roosevelt Robinson. HBV
Life Above, the Life on High, The. St. Teresa of Avila, *tr. fr. Spanish by* Edward Caswall. WGRP
Life after Death. Pindar, *tr. fr. Greek by* Walter Headlam. EaLo
Life Again. Keats. *Fr.* Endymion. SeCePo
Life and Death. Edward Benlowes. *Fr.* Theophila. FaBoEn
Life and Death. Ernest H. Crosby. *See* How Did He Live.
Life and Death. Sir William Davenant. *Fr.* The Christians Reply to the Philosopher. BoC; FaChP; OBS
Life and Death. Lilla Cabot Perry. AA
Life and Death. Duncan Campbell Scott. VA
Life and Death. Shakespeare. *Fr.* Measure for Measure, III, i. UnPo (1st ed.)
Life and Death. W. J. Turner. FaBoTw
Life and Death for the Christian. Avis B. Christiansen. SoP
Life and Death of Habbie Simson, the Piper of Kilbarchan, The. Robert Sempill. *See* Life and Death of the Piper of Kilbarchan, The.
Life and Death of Jason, The, *sels.* William Morris.
I know a Little Garden Close, *fr.* IV. AtBAP; CH; EG; GTSE; PoE; ViBoPo; ViPo; ViPP
(Garden by the Sea, A.) PoEL-5; PoVP
(Nymph's Song to Hylas, The.) HBV; OBEV; TOP
O Bitter Sea. PoVP
(Song of the Argonauts, *abr.*) EtS
O Death, That Maketh Life So Sweet, *fr.* XII. PoVP; ViPo
"O happy seafarers are ye," *fr.* XIV. ViBoPo
Life and Death of the Piper of Kilbarchan, The. Robert Sempill. OBS
(Life and Death of Habbie Simson, the Piper of Kilbarchan, The.) OxBS
Life and Death of William Longbeard, The, *sels.* Thomas Lodge.
Fancy, A. EIL
"My mistress when she goes." EG; SiCE; TuPP
(Her Rambling.) OBSC; LoBV
(My Mistress.) TrGrPo
Rose, The. OBSC
Life and Fame. Abraham Cowley. AnEnPo; LiTG
Life and Genuine Character of Dean Swift, The. Swift. EiPP
Life and Love. Elizabeth Barrett Browning. PoVP
Life and Love. Whittier. *Fr.* Snow-Bound. BLRP; TRV
(Yet Love Will Dream.) MaRV
Life and Nature. Archibald Lampman. PeCV
Life and the Universe show spontaneity. The Positivists. Mortimer Collins. BOHV
Life and the Weaver. A. W. Dewar. BLRP; WBLP
Life and Thought. Matthew Arnold. *Fr.* Empedocles on Etna, II. FiP
Life and Thought have gone away. The Deserted House. Tennyson. PeER; VA
Life? and worth living? Life, a Question. Corinne Roosevelt Robinson. HBV
Life at last I know is terrible. What Is Terrible. Roy Fuller. WaP
Life, believe, is not a dream. Life. Charlotte Brontë. OQP
Life Boat. *See* Lifeboat.
Life by the Cabin Fire, A, *with music.* John A. Stone. SGR
Life can hold such lovely things! Thank You, God. Nina Stiles. PoToHe (new ed.)
Life contracts and death is expected. Death of a [*or* the] Soldier. Wallace Stevens. AmPP; BWP; ForPo; QFR
Life Death Does End. Gerard Manley Hopkins. *See* No Worst, There Is None.
Life did not bring me silken gowns. Red Geraniums. Martha Haskell Clark. BLPA; NeHB
Life-Drama, A, *sels.* Alexander Smith.
Forerunners. VA
Minor Poet, A. VA
Sea-Marge. VA
(Autumn.) GTSE
Life, friends, is boring. We must not say so. The Dream Songs, XIV. John Berryman. LiTM (1970 ed.) NaP; TwCP
Life from the Lifeless. Robinson Jeffers. CMoP
Life has conquered, the wind has blown away. Hope. *Unknown.* KiLC
Life has loveliness to sell. Barter. Sara Teasdale. FaBV; FaPON; MCCG; MPB; OQP; OTPC (1946 ed.); SP; TIHL; TreFS
Life holds no sweeter thing than this—to teach. No Sweeter Thing. Adelaide Love. PGD
Life! I Know Not What Thou Art. Anna Letitia Barbauld. *See* Life.
Life impaled him high on a cliff. Biography of an Agnostic. Louis Ginsberg. TrJP
Life in a day: he took his girl to the ballet. Les Sylphides. Louis MacNeice. CoBMV
Life in a Half-Breed Shack. *Unknown.* CoSo
Life in a Love. Robert Browning. GTBS; HBV; MaVP; OAEP; OBNC; OBVV; PoFS; PoVP; TOP; TrGrPo
(Escape Me?—Never.) LiTL
(Love's Pursuit, 7 *ll.*) TreFT
Life in California, *with music.* David G. Robinson. SGR
Life in Death. Ellice Hopkins. PeVV
Life in her creaking shoes. To K. de M. W. E. Henley. Echoes, XXXIV. PoVP
Life in Laconics. Mary Mapes Dodge. BOHV
Life-in-Love. Dante Gabriel Rossetti. The House of Life, XXXVI. MaVP; PoVP; ViPo; VP
Life, in one semester. Song. Charles G. Blanden. OQP
Life in the Country. Michael Silverton. ELU
Life is a bitter aspic. We are not. Wallace Stevens. *Fr.* Esthétique du Mal. CMoP
Life is a burden; bear it. Life. *Unknown.* SoP
Life Is a Dream, *sel.* Pedro Calderón de la Barca, *tr. fr. Spanish. by* Arthur Symons.
"We live, while we see the sun." AWP; JAWP; LiTW; PoFr; WBP
Life is a gift that most of us hold dear. Fin de Siècle. *Unknown.* BOHV
Life is a jest; and all things show it. My Own Epitaph [*or* His Epitaph]. John Gay. ALV; CBV; EiCL; HBV; InP; OnPM; SeCePo; SeCeV; TOP; TreFT; ViBoPo
Life is a leaf of paper white. James Russell Lowell. *Fr.* For an Autograph. MaRV
Life is a long discovery, isn't it? Discovery. Hilaire Belloc. ViBoPo
Life is a most extraordinary thing. Tomato Juice. A. P Herbert. WhC
Life is a pilgrimage, they say. Cockle-Shell and Sandal-Shoon. Herbert T. J. Coleman. CaP
Life is a poet's fable. *Unknown.* OBSC; SiCE

Life is a shepherd lad who strides and sings. Life. Amory Hare. HBMV
Life is a sorry mélange of gold and silver and stubble. Nonsense. Robert Haven Schauffler. HBMV
Life is a trifle. The New Crusade. Katharine Lee Bates. MC
Life is a woven fabric. Life and the Weaver. A. W. Dewar. BLRP; WBLP
Life Is but Loss. Robert Southwell. SiCE
Life Is Fine. Langston Hughes. BP; WaKn
Life is inadequate, but there are many real. Independence Day. William Jay Smith. TwCP
Life Is Leaving One Strange Port. Raymond Boesch. JKCP (1955 ed.)
Life is like a wayside bloom. Life. Wayne Gard. OQP
Life is long that loathsomely doth last, The. Elegy Wrote in the Tower, 1554 [*or* Comparison of Life and Death]. John Harington. ElL; ReIE
Life Is Love. William Johnson Fox. VA
Life Is More True. E. E. Cummings. WaP
Life Is Motion. Wallace Stevens. AmLP; PoeP; SD; TDP
Life is not dear or gay. The Lass That Died of Love. Richard Middleton. HBV
Life is our quest. The Way of Life. Joseph V. B. Danquah. ACV
Life is real, life is earnest. A Parody on "A Psalm of Life." *Unknown.* BLPA
Life is seldom if ever dull. Gull. William Jay Smith. TiPo (1959 ed.)
Life Is So Short. Margaret S. Hall. STF
Life Is Struggle. Arthur Hugh Clough. BEL; EnLi-2; PoVP
Life is sweet, brother. George Borrow. *Fr.* Lavengro. BBV (1951 ed.)
Life is teeming with evil snares. Where Is Your Boy Tonight? *Unknown.* PaPo
Life Is the Art of Drawing. Carolyn J. Ogletree. TNV
Life is too brief. Life. William Merrell Vories. MaRV; OQP
Life is vile. Green Sunday. Katue Kitasono. LiTW
Life isn't dreary. A Word about Woodpiles. Nancy Byrd Turner. BrR
Life-Lesson, A. James Whitcomb Riley. AA; HBV; PoLF; TreFS
Life like the billow rolls, and youthful bloom. The Heart in Brahma. Bhartrihari. OnPM
Life-long, Poor Browning. Anne Spencer. CDC; PoNe
Life may be given in many ways. James Russell Lowell. *Fr.* Ode Recited at the Harvard Commemoration. LiPo
Life May Change, but It May Fly Not. Shelley. *Fr.* Hellas. EPN
(Choruses from Hellas.) EnRP
Life met me on the threshold—young, divine. The Forgotten Countersign. Corinne Roosevelt Robinson. OQP
Life-Mosaic. Frances Ridley Havergal. TrPWD
Life Must Burn. John Hay. NePoAm
Life Not Death. Tennyson. *Fr.* The Two Voices. MaRV
Life of . . ., The. Theodore Weiss. NYBP
Life of a Beau, The. James Miller. OBEC
Life of a Fairy, The. *Unknown. See* Fairy Queen, The.
Life of Guthlac, The, *sel.* *Unknown.*
Death in Bed. PoLi
Life of itself will be cruel and hard enough. Sonnets, V. Muna Lee. HBMV
Life of Life. Johannes Edfelt, *tr. fr. Swedish by* Martin S. Allwood. LiTW
Life of Life. Shelley. *Fr.* Prometheus Unbound, II, v. CH; FiP
(Chorus: "Life of Life! thy lips enkindle.") LoBV
(Hymn to the Spirit of Nature.) GTBS; GTBS-D; GTBS-P; GTBS-W; GTSE
("Life of Life! thy lips enkindle.") AnFE; AtBAP; GTBS-P; LO; OBRV; PoEL-4; ViBoPo
Life of Man, The. Francis Bacon. *See* Life.
Life of Man, The. Barnabe Barnes. *Fr.* A Divine Century of Spiritual Sonnets. OBSC
(Blast of Wind, A, a Momentary Breath.) SiCE; Sonn; TuPP
Life of Man, The. Swinburne. *See* Before the Beginning of Years.
Life of Man, The. Lucius H. Thayer. OQP
Life of man [*or* men], The/ Is an arrow's flight. The Flight of the Arrow [*or* The Arrow]. Richard Henry Stoddard. AA; MaRV
Life of man is full of grief and sorrow, The. The Misery of Man. Alexander Craig. SeCL
Life of man is never quite completed, The. W. H. Auden. *Fr.* In Time of War. EnLit
Life of my learning, fire of all my Art. A Dedication. Mary Elizabeth Coleridge. TrPWD
Life of my life, take not so soon thy flight. To His Dying Brother, Master William Herrick. Robert Herrick. OAEP; SeCV-1
Life of Our Lady, The, *sel.* John Lydgate.
"O thoughtful herte, plunged in distresse." EnPo
Life of Our Life. Henry Burke Robins. MaRV
Life of Sabbaths here beneath, A. Thomas Traherne. *Fr.* The Third Century. AnAnS-1; MeP
Life of St. Cellach of Killala, The, *sels.* *Unknown, tr. fr. Late Middle Irish by* Standish Hayes O'Grady.
Dear Was He. OnYI
Hail, Fair Morning. OnYI
He Who Forsakes the Clerkly Life. OnYI
Life of San Millan, *sel.* Gonzalo de Berceo, *tr. fr. Spanish.*
"He walked those mountains wild, and lived within that nook," *tr. by* John Hookham Frere. CAW
Life of Service, The. Donald Davie. NYBP
Life of the Blessed, The. Luis de León, *tr. fr. Spanish by* Bryant. AWP; SoP, *abr.*
Life of the body's a cage, The. The House of Life. Katharine Tynan. BoPe
Life of the Poet, The. Philip Dow. QAH
Life on its way returns into a mist. Life. *Unknown, at. to* Lao-tzu. *Fr.* Tao Teh King. OnPM
Life on the Ocean Wave, A. Epes Sargent. AA; EtS; FaBoBe; GN; HBV; NeHB; TreFS
Life or Death. Glenn Ward Dresbach. *Fr.* In Western Mountains. HBMV
Life Owes Me Nothing. *Unknown.* OQP; PoToHe
Life (priest and poet say) is but a dream. The Dragon-Fly [*or* Lines to a Dragon Fly]. Walter Savage Landor. OBEV (new ed.); OBNC; OBRV; OBVV
Life Removed, The. Luis de León, *tr. fr. Spanish by* Aubrey F. G. Bell. WoL
Life Sculpture. George Washington Doane. BLPA; MaRV; OHFP; WBLP
(Sculptors of Life.) OQP
Life Shall Live for Evermore. Tennyson. *See* In Memoriam A. H. H.: "My own dim life . . ."
Life should be very pleasant for. Reflections on an Ideal Existence. Sara Henderson Hay. CIV
Life Studies. Peter Schjeldahl. ANYP
Life That Counts, The. "A. W. S." FaFP; SoP; WBLP
Life that is free as the bandits' of old, A. Brave Donahue. *At. to* Jack Donahue. PoAu-1
Life the Beloved. Dante Gabriel Rossetti. The House of Life, XCVI. MaVP; PoVP; ViPo
Life through Verse. Alpheus of Mitylene, *tr. fr. Greek by* Lord Neaves. OnPM
Life to Come, The. Edward Shillito. OQP
Life to the bigot is a whip. Epitaph for a Bigot. Dorothy Vena Johnson. PoNe
Life Upright, The. Thomas Campion. *See* Man of Life Upright, The.
Life was a narrow lobby, dark. For the Bicentenary of Isaac Watts. Norman Nicholson. EaLo
Life was a thorough pool of restoration. An Ancient Degree. Bernadette Mayer. ANYP
Life went whistling a catch, between the plum and the cherry. Flood Tide. . Stephen Vincent Benét. PFY
Life, where your lone candle burns. Holy Light. John Hall Wheelock. LiTM (1946 ed.); PG (1955 ed.)
Life with her weary eyes. Song. Marya Zaturenska. NMP
Life with its weariness. Song. E. Margaret Clarkson. SoP
Life within Our Forms, The. Jami, *tr. fr. Persian by* F. Hadland Davis. OnPM
Life without Passion, The. Shakespeare. *See* Sonnets, XCIV.
Life would be an easy matter. If We Didn't Have to Eat. Nixon Waterman. BOHV; FiBHP
Lifeboat, The. George R. Sims. PaPo
Lifeboat that's kept at Torquay, The. Limerick. *Unknown.* LiBL
Lifeguard, The. James Dickey. CoPo; NoP; NYBP
Lifeguard's whistle organized our swimming, The. The River. Dabney Stuart. NYBP
Lifeless solitude—an angry waste, A. On the Telescopic

Lifeless (continued)
Moon. John Swanwick Drennan. IrPN
Lifers file into the hall. In the Cage. Robert Lowell. NoP; Sonn; SyP
Life's a Dream. Pedro Calderón de la Barca. *See* Life Is a Dream.
Life's a Funny Proposition after All. George M. Cohan. PoLF
Life's a Game. *Unknown.* BLPA
Life's a veil the real has. Francis Thompson. *Fr.* An Echo of Victor Hugo. MemP
Life's all getting and giving. The Wishing-Caps. Kipling. OtMeF
Life's Angel watched a happy child at play. The Angel of Life. Richard Rowe. BoAu
Life's Brevity. Simonides, *tr. fr. Greek by* J. H. Merivale *and* Lord Neaves. OnPM
Life's burnished grail I take from him. The Potion. Winnie Lynch Rockett. ChIP
Life's Chequer-Board. John Oxenham. TRV
Life's Circumnavigators. W. R. Rodgers. AnIV; FaBoMo; GTBS-P; OxBI
Life's Common Duties. Minot Judson Savage. WBLP
Life's Common Things. Alice E. Allen. WBLP
Life's Cross. *Unknown.* SoP
Life's Evening. William Dudley Foulke. OQP; WGRP
Life's Finest Things. Bangs Burgess. OQP
Life's happiness is woven. Happiness. Anna E. Wimmer. SoP
Life's Hebe. James Thomson. VA
Life's Illusion. Alexander Louis Fraser. OQP
Life's Joy. *Unknown. See* Giving.
Life's Last Scene. Samuel Johnson. *Fr.* The Vanity of Human Wishes. OBEC, *abr.*; SeCePo
Life's Lessons. *Unknown.* BLRP; PoLF; SoP; STF
Life's Little Things. *Unknown.* STF
Life's Made Up of Little Things. Mary R. Hartman. PoToHe (new ed.)
Life's Mirror. "Madeline Bridges." BLPA; FaBoBe; MaRV; NeHB; PoToHe; TreF; WBLP
(Give.) FaChP
Life's not our own,-'tis but a loan. Life. Charles Swain. VA
Life's Parallels, A. Christina Rossetti. NBM; PoEL-5
Life's Poor Play. Pope. *Fr.* An Essay on Man, Epistle II. OBEC; SeCePo
("See! some strange comfort ev'ry state attend.") YAT
Life's Purpose. "George Eliot." *Fr.* A Minor Prophet. MaRV
Life's Purpose. James Russell Lowell. *Fr.* The Cathedral. MaRV
Life's Scars. Ella Wheeler Wilcox. BLPA
Life's sweetest joys are hidden. The Tree-Top Road. May Riley Smith. HBV
Life's Testament, *sels.* William Baylebridge.
"All that I am to Earth belongs," XI. BoAV; PoAu-1
"Brain, the blood, the busy thews, The," II. BoAV; PoAu-1
"Choir of spirits on a cloud, A," XVII. PoAu-1
"God, to get the clay that stayed me," XIII. PoAU-1
"I worshipped, when my veins were fresh," VI. BoAV; PoAu-1
"Into ethereal meads," XII. BoAV
"This miracle in me I scan," VIII. PoAu-1
Life's Uncertainty. Ecclesiastes, Bible, *O.T. See* Cast Thy Bread upon the Waters.
Lifesaver. Elizabeth Riddell. NeLNL
Lift as he will a wordless face. Defeated Farmer. Mark Van Doren. AnAmPo
Lift Every Voice and Sing. James Weldon Johnson. FaBV; GoSl; PoNe
Lift her up tenderly. Song of the Ballet. J. B. Morton. FiBHP
Lift high the roof beams, carpenters! The Bridegroom Is So Tall. Sappho. HW
Lift it high, our glorious banner. The American Flag. Lena E. Faulds. HH
Lift me above myself, I pray. Above Myself. Carlton Buck. SoP
Lift me, O God, above myself. Per Ardua ad Astra. John Oxenham. TrPWD
Lift Not the Painted Veil. Shelley. *See* Sonnet: "Lift not the painted veil."
Lift, O dark and glorious Wonder. A Hymn to God in Time of Stress. Max Eastman. TrPWD
Lift up the banner of our love. The Raising of the Flag. Condé Benoist Pallen. JKCP; OTD
Lift. . .up the drooping head. Welcome to the Prince of Ossory. William Heffernan the Blind. IrPN
Lift up thy lips, turn round, look back for love. Hermaphroditus. Swinburne. SyP
Lift up your eyes on high. Erige Cor Tuum ad Me in Caelum. Hilda Doolittle ("H. D."). AP; CMoP
"Lift up your hartes and be glad." A Cheerful Welcome. *Unknown.* MeEL
Lift up your head. Stop blood and breath. The Fawn. Raymond Holden. NYTB
Lift up Your Heads. Psalms, Bible, *O.T. See* Twenty-fourth Psalm, The.
Lift up your heads, great gates, and sing. The Ascension. Joseph Beaumont. OxBoCh
Lift Up Your Heads, O Ye Gates. Psalms, Bible, *O.T. See* Twenty-fourth Psalm, The.
Lift Up Your Heads, Rejoice! Thomas T. Lynch. WGRP
Lift Up Your Hearts! Henry Montague Butler. MaRV
Lift Up Your Hearts. Mrs. D. R. H. Goodale. FaChP
Lift up your hearts to things above. Rejoicing in Hope. Charles Wesley. SoP
Lift your arms to the stars. Love and Liberation. John Hall Wheelock. BoLP; MAP; MoAmPo
Lifted by the teaching of a Master. Peter. Earl Marlatt. MoRP
Lifters and Leaners. Ella Wheeler Wilcox. *See* Lifting and Leaning.
Lifting a tangle of roots away from the bank I found. The Basilisk. D. M. Black. HYE
Lifting and Leaning. Ella Wheeler Wilcox. BLPA; WBLP
(Leaners or Lifters.) MaRV
(Lifters and Leaners.) SoP
(Two Kinds of People.) PoToHe
Lifting my eyes from Hesiod's [great] book. Class Dismissed. *Unknown.* MeWo; UnTE
Lifting the thunder of their acclamation. Shelley. *Fr.* The Revolt of Islam. ChER
Li Fu-jen. Wu Ti, *tr. fr. Chinese by* Arthur Waley. AtBAP; BoW
("Sound of her silk skirt has stopped, The.") LO
Ligeia, *pr. tale, sel.* Poe.
Conqueror Worm, The. AA; AmePo; AmP; AnAmPo; AnFE; AP; APA; AWP; CoAnAm; CoBA; HBV; InPo; LiTA; MAmP; MWA-1; TDP
("Lo! 'tis a gala night.") AmPP
Light. Francis William Bourdillon. *See* Night Has a Thousand Eyes, The.
Light. Carol Coates. CaP
Light. Hermann Hagedorn. MoRP
Light, The. John Holloway. NePoEA
Light. George Macdonald. VA
Light. Milton. *See* Hail, Holy Light.
Light. Grace Wilkinson. OQP
Light after Darkness. Carlton Buck. SoP
Light after Darkness. Frances Ridley Havergal. SoP
(Afterwards.) BLRP
Light and Dark. Barbara Howes. MoVE
Light and Glory of the World, [The]. William Cowper. SoP; TRV
(Spirit's Light, The.) BLRP
Light and Love. Francis William Bourdillon. *See* Night Has a Thousand Eyes, The.
Light and Love, Hope and Faith. Eva Gray. STF
Light and Rejoicing to Israel. *Unknown, tr. fr. Hebrew by* Israel Abrahams. TrJP
Light as a leaping faun! Nijinsky. Doris Ferne. CaP
Light at Equinox. Léonie Adams. CrMA
Light at Evening Time. R. H. Robinson. SoP
Light beats upon me, The. Mid-Day. Hilda Doolittle ("H. D."). ViBoPo (1941 ed.)
Light became audible, that is, a child, and took the empty place. The Heavenly Humor. David Shapiro. ANYP
Light became her grace and dwelt among, The. Ballatetta. Ezra Pound. NoP
Light between the Trees. Henry van Dyke. GBV (1922 ed.)
Light beyond compare is the light I saw, The. The Incomparable Light. Richard Eberhart. MoRP
Light Breaks Where No Sun Shines. Dylan Thomas. CMoP;

EnL; ErPo; FaBoMo; LiTB; LiTL; LiTM; MoAB; MoBrPo; OAEP (2d ed.); SeCePo; ViBoPo
Light Breather, A. Theodore Roethke. NoP
Light breeze rustles the reeds, A. Night Thoughts While Travelling. Tu-Fu. NaP
Light broke in upon my brain, A. Byron. *Fr.* The Prisoner of Chillon. OBRV
Light Comes Brighter, The. Theodore Roethke. NoP
Light comes in your face, a sudden glow, A. A Question of Sacrifice. Sister M. Eulalia. WHL
Light diffusing my likeness. Legend of His Lyre. Aaron Schmuller. GoYe
Light do I see within my Lady's eyes. Ballata V. Guido Cavalcanti. CTC
Light drunkenly reels into shadow. Wet Windy Night on a Pavement. A. S. J. Tessimond. WePo
Light exists in spring, A. Emily Dickinson. ExPo; FosPo; LiTA; PAn; PoeP; PoFS; StP
Light falls gently from the dormer panes, The. On a Spring Board. Edward Cracroft Lefroy. OBVV
Light flower leaves its little core, The. The Changed Woman. Louise Bogan. HBMV
Light flows our war of mocking words, and yet. The Buried Life. Matthew Arnold. BEL; BoLiVe; BoPe; BWP; EnL; EnLi-2; EnLit; EPN; ForPo; MaVP; MBW-2; OAEP; OuHeWo; PoFS; PoVP; SeCeV; VA; ViPo; ViPP; VP
Light foot hears you and the brightness begins, The. A Poem Beginning with a Line by Pindar. Robert Duncan. NeAP; NMP
Light for the North Room. Alice Hansche Mortenson. SoP
Light from Within, The. Jones Very. WGRP
Light going out in the forehead, A. Swimming by Night. James Merrill. NYBP
Light had gone out from his vanquished eyes, A. The Dying Eagle. E. J. Pratt. ACV
Light has come again and found. Ark of the Covenant. Louise Townsend Nicholl. ImOP
Light has transformed them. Their utility gone. Apples. Lisel Mueller. NePoAm-2
Light Heart. T. Sturge Moore. POTE
Light-hearted Fairy, The. *Unknown.* BoChLi; BoTP; FaPON; GaP; MPB (1956 ed.); OTPC; PCH; SUS; TiPo (1952 ed.)
(Fairy, The.) PPL
Light-hearted I walked into the valley wood. Conversion. T. E. Hulme. FaBoMo; LoBV; MoBrPo (1942 ed.); ViBoPo
Lighthearted William. William Carlos Williams. LOW; PoSa
Light, in light breezes and a favoring sun. Watching Tennis. John Heath-Stubbs. Sonn
Light in the Darkness. Aileen Fisher. YeAr
Light in the Darkness. Cardinal Newman. *See* Pillar of the Cloud, The.
Light in the Temple, The. William Rose Benét. MoRP
Light in the window seemed perpetual, The. The Room above the Square. Stephen Spender. ChMP; CMoP
Light into the olive entered. After Greece. James Merrill. NYBP
Light is around the petals, and behind them. Looking at Some Flowers. Robert Bly. NaP
Light is like a spider, The. Tattoo. Wallace Stevens. AnFE; APA; CoAnAm; LiTA; NP
Light is made to shine in darkness. Light and Love, Hope and Faith. Eva Gray. STF
Light is music, and the first note breaks, The. Genesis. A. M. Sullivan. JKCP (1955 ed.)
Light Is Sweet, The. Ecclesiastes, XI: 7, Bible, *O.T.* FaPON
Light Left On, A. May Sarton. MoLP
"Light, light, light, my little Scotch-ee." Little Scotch-ee. *Unknown.* AS
Light, Light of My Eyes. Propertius, *tr. fr. Latin by* Ezra Pound. LiTW
Light Listened. Theodore Roethke. ToPo; UnTE
Light looked down and beheld Darkness. "And the Word Was Made Flesh." Laurence Housman. MaRV
Light Love. *Unknown, tr. fr. Japanese by* Basil Hall Chamberlain. OnPM
Light Lover. Aline Kilmer. HBMV
Light may be had for nothing. Little Candle. Carl Sandburg. GoYe
"Light! more light! the shadows deepen." Let the Light Enter. Frances E. W. Harper. PoNe
Light, my light, the world-filling light, the eye-kissing light, heart-sweetening light! A Song-Offering. Rabindranath Tagore. LiTW
Light Now Shineth, The. *Unknown.* STF
Light of Asia, The, *sels.* Sir Edwin Arnold.
End Which Comes, The, *fr.* III. LoBV
Nirvana, *fr.* VIII. VA
Light of autumn evenings falls serene, The. Autumn Evening. Feodor Ivanovich Tyutchev. OnPM
Light of Bethlehem, The. John Banister Tabb. CAW; ChIP; MaRV; PoRL
Light of dim mornings, shield from heat and cold. To Duty. Thomas Wentworth Higginson. AA; AnAmPo
Light of evening, Lissadell, The. In Memory of Eva Gore-Booth and Con Markiewicz. W. B. Yeats. CABA; MBW-2; MoAB; OBMV; OxBI
Light of Faith, The. Edgar Dupree. BLRP
Light of God is Falling, The. Louis FitzGerald Benson. MaRV; OQP
Light of Life, The. *Unknown, tr. fr. Arabic by* Sir Edwin Arnold. OnPM
Light of morning around her like a sash of glory. Petrarch for Laura. Claire McAllistair. SiSw
Light of Other Days, The. Alfred Bunn. TreFS
Light of Other Days, The. Thomas Moore. *See* Oft in the Stilly Night.
Light of our cigarettes, The. Pastel. Arthur Symons. SyP
Light of spring, The. Song. Alice Duer Miller. AA
Light of Stars, The. William H. Furness. *See* Evening Hymn.
Light of Stars, The. Longfellow. OTPC
Little Moon, The, *sel.* BoTP
Light of the eyes in the house of the crow, The. Lost Month. W. S. Merwin. AmPC
Light of the Haram, The. Thomas Moore. *Fr.* Lalla Rookh. EnRP
Light of the Soul. *Tr. fr. Latin by* Edward Caswall. BePJ
Light of the World, The. St. John, XII: 44-50, Bible, *N.T.* WoL
Light of the World. Sylvester Judd. BePJ
Light of the World. John S. B. Monsell. TrPWD
Light of the World, How Long the Quest. Edwin McNeill Poteat. MaRV
Light on Cape May, The, *with music.* *Unknown.* ShS
Light on the dark horizon, A. Go Tell Them that Jesus Is Living. *Unknown.* BePJ; SoP
Light on the Erie Canal, A. The Erie Canal Ballad. *Unknown.* ABF
Light passes, The. Evening. Hilda Doolittle ("H. D."). CMoP; FaBoMo; LoBV; OTPC 1946 ed.); Po; YT
Light Poem. Jack Marshall. YAP
Light Shining Out of Darkness. Jane Borthwick. BLRP
Light Shining Out of Darkness. William Cowper. AtBAP; BLRP; BWP; CBV; EaLo; EiCL; EiCP; EiPP; EnPE; EnRP; FaBoCh; FaChP; FaFP; FaPL; HBV; LiTB; LoGBV; MaRV; OBEC; PoE; PoEL-3; PoIE; SeCePo; SeCeV; SoP; TreF; TrGrPo; TRV; VaPo
(God Moves in a Mysterious Way.) CBEP; CoBE; ELP; FiP
(Mysterious Way, The.) STF
(Providence.) WGRP
Light Shoes. Patrick Kelly. JKCP (1926 ed.)
Light, stillness and peace lie on the broad sands. The Estuary. Ruth Pitter. MoVE
Light That Failed, The, *sel.* Kipling.
Mother o' Mine. FaFP; MaRV; NeHB; OQP; TRV; WBLP
(Mother Love.) SoP
Light that fills thy house at morn, The. The Gifts of God. Jones Very. AA
Light that labored to an early fall, The. The Lake. Louis O. Coxe. MoVE; NYBP
Light, that out of the west looked back once more. Night Thoughts in Age. John Hall Wheelock. MoVE; NYBP; PoDB
Light the first light of evening, as in a room. Final Soliloquy of the Interior Paramour. Wallace Stevens. BWP; PoIE
Light the Lamp Early. Raymond Holden. MAP; MoAmPo (1942 ed.)
Light the Lamps Up, Lamplighter. Eleanor Farjeon. CH; GaP; RIS; SiSoSe; TiPo (1959 ed.)
Light through the window. Is Here, As If. G. Bishop-Dubjinsky. ThO

Light up My world for Me. God to Man. *Fr.* The Talmud. TrJP
Light up thy homes, Columbia. Illumination for Victories in Mexico. Grace Greenwood. PAH
Light upon the Mountains, A. Henry Burton. MaRV; SoP
Light wake early in this house. Various Wakings. Vicnet Buckley. PoAu-2
Light was gone, and there wasn't a sound, The. Lost. Maurice Lesemann. NP
Light will never open sightless eyes, The. Morning. Jones Very. AnNE
Light will shine again, The; it cannot die. There Will Be Peace. Margaret Miller Pettengill. PGD
Light-winged Smoke, Icarian Bird. Henry David Thoreau. *See* Smoke.
Light-winged wilding meadowlark, The. Out of Darkness. Sister Maris Stella. JKCP (1955 ed.)
Light [*or* Cleanse] with the burning log of oak. Yule-Tide Fires. *Unknown.* PCD; PCH; PoRL
Light without a body, The. Light Poem. Jack Marshall. YAP
Light woke him, The. Today's. In the Future. Edward Lucie-Smith. HYE
Light Woman, A. Robert Browning. CLwM; HBV; PoVP
Light words they were, and lightly falsely said. Arthur Hugh Clough. VA
Light Yoke and Easy Burden, The. Charles Wesley. BePJ
"Light you down, light you down." Young Hunting (B *vers.*). *Unknown.* BFSS
Lighted city is dark, but somewhere a bus, The. The Dark City. Clifford Dyment. POTi
Lighten Our Darkness. Lord Alfred Douglas. HBMV
Lighteneth she night's darkness, ay, as an evening lamp. The Night Long. Imr El Kais. LiTW
Lighter than dandelion down. Silkweed. Philip Henry Savage. AA
Lighter than thistledown. First Snow. Ivy O. Eastwick. TiPo
Lightest foam, straightest spray. Waters of the Sea. Cecil Goldbeck. EtS
Lighthouse, The. Sir Walter Scott. OTPC (1946 ed.); PCH
Lighthouse, The. Marjorie Wilson. BoTP
Lighthouse Keeper's Offspring, The. James Broughton. CrMA
Light-House-Keeper's White-Mouse, The. John Ciardi. PDV
Lighting a spill late in the afternoon. A Winter Talent. Donald Davie. NePoEA-2
Lightless, unholy, eldritch thing. The Bat. Ruth Pitter. WePo
Lightly an ignorant boor is made content. Half-Way Knowledge. Bhartrihari. OnPM
Lightly like Music Running. Jean Garrigue. MoVE
Lightly, O lightly, we bear her along. Palanquin Bearers. Sarojini Naidu. MoSiPe
Lightly She Whipped o'er the Dales. John Mundy. ReIE
Lightly stepped a yellow star. Emily Dickinson. AP; MAP; MoAmPo; MoShBr; OxBA
Lightly the breath of the spring wind blows. By Wood and Wold. Adam Lindsay Gordon. BoAu
Lightness. Richard Wilbur. FiMAP
Lightning, The. Myron H. Broomell. CBV
Lightning. Witter Bynner. MoLP
Lightning. D. H. Lawrence. CMoP; LiTL; MoAB; MoBrPo; UnTE
Lightning bug got, A. The Flattered Lightning Bug. Don Marquis. StPo
Lightning bug has wings of gold, The. *Unknown.* OCS
Lightning flashed, and lifted, The. The Thunder-Shower. John Hall Wheelock. NP
Lightning for Atmosphere. Marya Zaturenska. TwAmPo
Lightning is local. Local Light. Millen Brand. WOW
Lightning! Lightning! Lightning! Without thunder! Flushing Meadows, 1939. Daniel Hoffman. CoPo
Lightning of a summer, The. Lady Bates. Randall Jarrell. MiAP
Lightning of the Abyss. Jules Laforgue, *tr. fr. French by* Vernon Watkins. SyP
Lightning spun your garment for the night, The. The Lights of New York. Sara Teasdale. PoMa
Light'ood Fire, The. John Henry Boner. AA
Lights, The. John Joy Bell. BoTP
Lights along the shore at night, The. The Hub. Oscar Williams. MaRV
Lights from the parlor and kitchen shone out, The. Escape at Bedtime. Robert Louis Stevenson. BrR; GoTP; HBVY; OTPC; PCH; PoRh; PoVP; TiPo; TreFS; TrGrPo; TSW
Light's Glittering Morn. John Mason Neale. OxBoCh
"Lights go out." Lola Ridge. *Fr.* The Ghetto. MAP; MoAmPo (1942 ed.)
Lights I Have Seen Before. Philip Levine. TDP
Lights in the Quarters Burnin' Mighty Dim, *with music. Unknown.* OuSiCo
Lights of a hundred cities are fed by its midnight power, The. The River of Stars. Alfred Noyes. OnMSP
Lights of heaven (which are the world's fair eyes), The. Of the Soul of Man and the Immortality Thereof. Sir John Davies. *Fr.* Nosce Teipsum. ReIE
Lights of New York, The. Sara Teasdale. PoMa
Lights of people shandle holiness. Land of the Never-ending Heart. Kenneth Patchen. ToPo
Lights of Saturday night beat golden, golden over the pillared street, The. Saturday Night. James Oppenheim. HBV; TSW
Lights Out. Edward Thomas. GTBS-D; POTE BrPo; FIW; MMA; NoP
Lights out! And a prow turned towards the South. The Race of the *Oregon.* John James Meehan. PAH
Lights out. Shades up. Girl in a Nightgown. Wallace Stevens. OxBA
Lights were red, refused to change, The. Hold-Up. Louis MacNeice. CBV
Lightship, The. Josephine Winslow Johnson. MoSiPe
'Ligion So Sweet, *with music. Unknown.* ABF
Like a bird that trails a broken wing. Prodigal. Ellen Gilbert. GoBC; MaRV
Like a black enamoured king whispered low the thunder. Dunedin in the Gloaming. Jessie Mackay. BoAu
Like a blind spinner in the sun. Spinning. Helen Hunt Jackson. HBV; OQP
Like a bread without the spreadin'. Smile. *Unknown.* BLPA; WBLP
Like a bulwark against fate. At Rest in the Blast. Marianne Moore. MoAB; MoAmPo (1950 ed.)
Like a caricature, the scraggy arms, arthritic knuckles. Der Arme Poet. Michael Roberts. ML
Like a coy maiden, ease, when courted most. Nature and God. William Cowper. *Fr.* The Task. CoBE
Like a damask rose you see. *See* Like as the damask rose you see.
Like a deaf man meshed in his endless silence. Poem. John Wain. PoCh
Like a deserted beach. The Man Closing Up. Donald Justice. CoAP
Like a dog with a bottle, fast ty'd to his tail. The Batchelors Song. Thomas Flatman. CEP; PeRV
Like a drop of water is my heart. Youth and Maidenhood. Sarah Williams. OBVV
Like a drowsy, rain-browned saint. Hill-Side Tree. Maxwell Bodenheim. MAP; MAPA; MoAmPo (1942 ed.)
Like a dry fish flung inland far from shore. Lost Anchors. E. A. Robinson. CMoP; MAmP
Like a fleet thief, this sparrow has. House and Shutter. Lewis Turco. PoPl
Like a forsaken theatre art thou. By Cobequid Bay. Alexander Louis Fraser. CaP
Like a gaunt, scraggly pine. Lincoln. John Gould Fletcher. HBMV; LaNeLa; LiPo; MoAmPo; MAP; NeMA; PaA; PoRL; SP
Like a glacier man advances. All Too Slowly. Lucia Trent. ChIP
Like a glum cricket. Flight. James Tate. OCS
Like a gondola of green scented fruits. Images. Richard Aldington. MoBrPo; NeMA; NP; TOP
Like a great rock, far out at sea. Lady Sanuki. *Fr.* Hyaku-Nin-Isshu. AWP; JAWP; WBP
Like a hidden spring. My Love-Song. Else Lasker-Schüler. TrJP
Like a hound with nose to the trail. Michaelmas. Norman Nicholson. FaBoTw; MoBrPo (1950 ed.); POTi
Like a huge python, winding round and round. Our Casuarina Tree. Toru Dutt. ACV; VA
Like a king from a sunrise-land. Days and Nights. T. Sturge Moore. HBMV
Like a Laverock in the Lift. Jean Ingelow. HBV

Like a lizard in the sun, though not scuttling. The Laureate. Robert Graves. FaBoTw
Like a lone Arab, old and blind. Love's Apparition and Evanishment. Samuel Taylor Coleridge. EnRP
Like a loose island on the wide expanse. To a Deaf and Dumb Little Girl. Hartley Coleridge. PoEL-4
Like a loud-booming bell shaking its tower. The Latin Tongue. James J. Daly. CAW; GoBC
Like a Mourningless Child. Kenneth Patchen. MoAmPo
Like a musician that with flying finger. The Master-Chord. William Caldwell Roscoe. VA
Like a painting it is set before one. The View from the Window. R. S. Thomas. BoC; POTi
Like a Pearl Dropped. Trumbull Stickney. NCEP
Like a private eye she searches. The Jealous Wife. Vernon Scannell. ErPo
Like a river glorious is God's perfect peace. Perfect Peace. Frances Ridley Havergal. SoP
Like a ship, that through the ocean wide. *See* Like as a ship.
Like a Shower of Rain. Ennius, *tr. fr. Latin by* John Wight. *Fr.* Annales. WaaP
Like a skein of loose silk blown against a wall. The Garden. Ezra Pound. AWP; CABA; InPo; JAWP; LiTA; MoAB; MoAmPo (1950 ed.); NoP; NP; PoIE; TwCP; WBP
Like a sleeping swine upon the skyline. Muckish Mountain (The Pig's Back). Shane Leslie. AnIV
Like a small gray/ coffee pot. The Gray Squirrel. Humbert Wolfe. GoJo; MoBrPo; NeMA
Like a stone toppled from an endless hill. The Fall of Satan. Roy Campbell. *Fr.* The Flaming Terrapin. BoSA
Like a tower of brass is Punch. Conrad Aiken. *Fr.* Punch, the Immortal Liar. NP
Like a wave crest. Emperor Uda. *tr. fr. Japanese by* Kenneth Rexroth. LiTW
Like a Whisper. Ethan Ayer. GoYe
Like a white cat. Moonlight. Maud E. Uschold. StVeCh (1955 ed.)
Like a White Stone. "Anna Akhmatova," *tr. fr. Russian by* Babette Deutsch. OnPM
Like a white wall whereon forever breaks. Octaves, XVIII. E. A. Robinson. ILP
Like a young child who to his mother's door. Doors. Hermann Hagedorn. AnAmPo; PFY
Like Achilles you had a goddess for mother. On Looking into E. V. Rieu's Homer. Patrick Kavanagh. ML
Like air on skin, coolness of yachts at mooring. Yachts on the Nile. Bernard Spencer. ChMP
Like all great thoughts that revolutionize. The Autostrada. Geoffrey Johnson. NYTB
Like an adventurous seafarer am I. Idea, I. Michael Drayton. EnLi-1 (1949 ed.); EtS; NoP; ReEn; SiCE; Sonn; TuPP
Like an April Day. Johan Sebastian C. Wellhaven, *tr. fr. Norwegian by* Charles Wharton Stork. LiTW
Like an arrow shot. Wine. Micah Joseph Lebensohn. LiTW; TrJP
Like an hart, the live-long day. The Relief on Easter Eve. Thomas Pestel. CBEP; OxBoCh; SeCL
Like an ill husband, though I knew the same. Thomas Dekker. *Fr.* The Honest Whore. LO
Like an invader, not a guest. Winter's Troops. Charles Cotton. *Fr.* Winter. ChTr
Like an Old Proud King in a Parable. A. J. M. Smith. OBCV
Like any grey old-timer droving dreams. The Town. David Rowbotham. PoAu-2
Like any merchant in a store. The Ticket Agent. Edmund Leamy. HBMV; PoMa; StVeCh
Like any of us—you or me. Old Man Pot. Lyon Sharman. CaP
Like apple-blossom, white and red. To Daphne. Sir Walter Besant. HBV; VA
Like April morning clouds, that pass. To William Erskine, Esq. Sir Walter Scott. Marmion, *introd. to* III. OBRV
Like architects of a sumptuous palace. Olympian Ode, VI. Pindar. *Fr.* Odes. LiTW
Like Aristaeus, seeking the secret of the bees. Bran. George H. Moorse. NYTB
Like [*or* Lyke] as a huntsman after weary chase [*or* chace]. Amoretti, LXVII. Spenser. BoLiVe; EnRePo; ForPo; ILP; NoP; PoEL-1; PoIE; OAEP; PoSa; ReEn; SeCePo; SiCE; Sonn; TrGrPo
Like [*or* Lyke] as a ship, that through the ocean wide [*or* wyde]. Amoretti, XXXIV. Spenser. AnFE; BEL; CoBE; DiPo; EnLi-1; EnLit; EtS; HBV; ILP; MaPo (1969 ed.); OBSC; PAn; PoAn; PoFS; PoIE; ReEn; ReIE; SiCE; YAT
Like as an hynd forth singled from the heard. Spenser. *Fr.* The Faerie Queene, III. MBW-1
Like as herb and tree in May. True Love. Ernest Rhys. POTE
Like as the bay, that bears on branches sweet. In Praise of His Lady. Matthew Grove. *Fr.* Pelops and Hippodamia. EIL
Like as the bird in the cage enclosed. Sir Thomas Wyatt. FCP; SiPS
Like [*or* Lyke] as the culver, on the bared bough. Amoretti, LXXXIX. Spenser. EG; MaPo (1969 ed.); Sonn
Like as the Damask Rose You See. *Unknown.* CBEP; FaBoCh; HBV; LoBV; LoGBV; OBS; SeCL; SeEP; WBLP. *See also* Like to the damask rose you see.
Like as the divers-fretchled butterfly. The Muse Reviving. Sir John Davies. SiPS
Like as the doleful dove delights alone to be. No Pains Comparable to His Attempt. William Hunnis. ReIE
Like as the Dove. Sir Philip Sidney. FCP; SiPS
Like as the dumb solsequium, with care ourcome. The Solsequium. Alexander Montgomerie. GoTS
Like as the fountaine of all light created. Incarnatio Est Maximum Donum Dei. William Alabaster. MePo
Like as the hart, athirst in desert dreary. Where Is Thy God? J. Lewis Milligan, *par. fr.* Psalm XLII, Bible, *O.T.* MaRV
Like as the hart, that lifteth up his ears. He Renounceth All the Effects of Love. Thomas, Lord Vaux. EnRePo
Like as the lark that, soaring higher and higher. Thomas William Parsons. AA
Like as the lark within the marlian's foot. The Lover Showeth His Woeful State and Prayeth Pity. *Unknown.* TuPP
Like as the lute delights or else dislikes. To Delia, LIV. Samuel Daniel. OAEP
Like as the rage of rain. The Uncertain State of a Lover. *Unknown.* EIL
Like as the swan towards her death. Sir Thomas Wyatt. FCP; SiPS
Like as the sweet red apple that ripens on high in the branches. The Highest Fruit. Sappho. OnPM
Like as the tide that comes from th' ocean main. Spenser. *Fr.* The Faerie Queene, IV. HoPM
Like as the waves make towards the pebbled shore. Sonnets, LX. Shakespeare. AnFE; ATP (1953 ed.); BEL; BoLiVe; BWP; CBEP; ChTr; CoBE; EIL; EnL; EnLi-1; EnLit; EnRePo; ExPo; FaBoEn; FaFP; GTBS; GTBS-D; GTBS-P; GTBS-W; GTSE; GTSL; HBV; LiTB; LiTL; LoBV; OBSC; Po; PoRA; ReEn; ReIE; SeCeV; ShBV-4; SiCE; Sonn; UnPo; ViBoPo
Like as the wind with raging blast. Of Love. Sir Thomas Wyatt. FCP
Like as, to make our appetites more keen. Sonnets, CXVIII. Shakespeare. CABA; CBEP; UnPo (1st ed.)
Like autumn winds that rustle in the leaves. The Old Bard Speaks. Joseph R. N. Maxwell. JKCP (1955 ed.)
Like Barbarossa's beard bright with oil. Boys in October. Irving Layton. OBCV
Like Barley Bending. Sara Teasdale. HBMV
Like Birds of a Feather. Ralph Schomberg. *Fr.* The Judgment of Paris. TrJP
Like birds when first light breaks. Children Waking: Indian Hill Station. R. N. Currey. PeSA
Like buckskin and broadcloth and strange American shillings. Tanglewood. Francis Sweeney. JKCP (1955 ed.)
Like butterflies but lately come. Beautiful Creatures Brief as These. D. G. Jones. MoCV
Like children in the market-place. Children in the Market-Place. Henry van Dyke. SoP; TRV
Like crown'd athlete that in a race has run. Landor. Alexander Hay Japp. VA
Like Crusoe with the bootless gold we stand. Experience. Edith Wharton. AA
Like Desert Woods. Thomas Lodge. SiCE; TuPP
Like Esops fellow-slaves, O Mercury. Mercurius Gallo-Belgicus. John Donne. MaMe
Like flies that summer, night would always break. Between Motions. Jerome Mazzaro. NYTB
Like Flowers We Spring. *Unknown.* CBEP; EIL

Like gods who are fêted. They Came to the Wedding. Babette Deutsch. NePoAm
Like gossamer/ On the swift breath of morn, the vessel flew. Ever as We Sailed. Shelley. *Fr.* The Revolt of Islam. SeCePo
Like gript stick. The Sermon. Richard Hughes. BoC; OBMV
Like Groping Fingers. Abraham Sutzkever, *tr. fr. Yiddish by* Joseph Leftwich. TrJP
Like hatred when a child falls. Eulogy of the Vain Hours. Sotère Torregian. YAP
Like Hermit Poor. *At. to* Sir Walter Ralegh. *See* Like to a Hermit.
Like Him, whilst friends and lovers slept. Gethsemane. M. Betham-Edwards. BePJ
Like Him Whose Spirit. Arthur Davison Ficke. NP
Like His Mother Used to Make. James Whitcomb Riley. IHA
Like Ilium. Thomas Merton. JKCP (1955 ed.)
Like intuition, starlight pierced the twelve. Starlight like Intuition Pierced the Twelve. Delmore Schwartz. MiAP
Like Jonah in the green belly of the whale. Emily Carr. Wilfred Watson. MoCV; OBCV
Like labour-laden moonclouds faint to flee. Through Death to Love. Dante Gabriel Rossetti. The House of Life, XLI. MaVP; PoVP; SyP; ViPo; VP
Like lamp of intricate stained glass which hangs. From Ancient Fangs. Peter Viereck. LiTA; MiAP
Like lemon jello in a dream. Plea Based on a Sentence from a Letter Received by the Indiana State Welfare Department. James Tate. YAP
Like Lise, moreover, my mother was white. The Black Man's Son. Oswald Durand. TTY
Like many a one, when you had gold. The Old Story. E. A. Robinson, *after* Marcus Argentarius. AWP; JAWP; LiTW; WBP
Like marble, nude, against the purple sky. The Diver. John Frederic Herbin. CaP
Like Memnon's rock, touched [*or* touch'd] with the rising sun. Licia, XLVII. Giles Fletcher. EIL; ReEn; ReIE; SiCE; TuPP
"Like men riding." Nelly Trim. Sylvia Townsend Warner. ErPo; MoAB; MoBrPo
Like mirrored paintings done by Fragonard. The Flamingos. Rainer Maria Rilke. OnPM
Like missionary priests from some bland creed. Seven Themes from the Zoo, No. 2 John Bennett. NYTB
Like moody beasts they lie along the sands. Condemned Women. John Gray. SyP
Like Mother, Like Son. Margaret Johnston Grafflin. BLPA; NeHB
(To My Son.) PoToHe (new ed.)
Like mourners filing into church at a funeral. Trees on the Calais Road. Edmund Blunden. BrPo
Like Music. John Hall Wheelock. NP
Like musical instruments. Poem. Tom Clark. ANYP
Like One I Know. Nancy Campbell. JKCP
Like one of my professors said to me. Jazz Coltrane Sings. Walter K. Dancy. WSL
Like one who'in her third widdowhood doth professe. To Mr. Rowland Woodward. John Donne. AnAnS-1; MaMe; MeP; MePo
Like Orphans. Opal Leonore Gibbs. SoP
Like pensive herds at rest upon the sands. The Accursed. Baudelaire. LiTW
Like Plimsoll lines on British hulls. Convalescence, II. David McCord. WhC
Like plump green floor plans. Rotation. Julian Bond. NNP
Like Sieur Montaigne's distinction. Golfers. Irving Layton. SD
Like silver dew are the tears of love. Epitaph. Alfred Edgar Coppard. OBMV
Like silver lamps in a distant shrine. Silver Lamps. W. C. Dix. BePJ
Like small curled feathers, white and soft. While Shepherds Watched Their Flocks by Night. Margaret Deland. DD; GN; HBVY; StJW
Like small foreign villages whose gates have been. Lewis Warsh. *Fr.* The Suicide Rates. YAP
Like smoke held down by frost. Bluebells. Patric Dickinson. BoPe; POTi
Like smoke I vanish though I burn like flame. Human Life. William H. Mallock. ACP (1926 ed.); JKCP (1926 ed.); OQP
Like snails I see the people go. From a Street Corner. Eleanor Hammond. HBMV
Like snakes of golden autumn fire. Nevada. Lawrence Gurney. GoYe
Like snooker balls thrown on the table's faded green. A Poet's Progress. Michael Hamburger. NePoEA; PP
Like Snow. Robert Graves. AtBAP
Like Snow. Omar Khayyám. *See* Worldly Hope, The.
Like so many other young men in those troubled. For Lover Man, and All the Other Young Men Who Failed to Return from World War II. Mance Williams. NNP
Like some great pearl from out the Orient. Night-Wind. Beatrix Demarest Lloyd. AA
Like some huge bird that sinks to rest. Sunset. Herbert Bashford. AA
Like some lone miser, dear, behold me stand. Morton Luce. *Fr.* Thysia. HBV
Like some old voyager out of the past. Captain's Walk; Salem. Oliver Jenkins. PoMa
Like some school master, kind in being stern. Unanswered Prayers. Ella Wheeler Wilcox. WGRP
Like some weak lords, neighbour'd by mighty kings. Astrophel and Stella, XXIX. Sir Philip Sidney. FCP; SiPS
Like souls that balance joy and pain. Sir Launcelot and Queen Guinevere. Tennyson. ACV; VA
Like South-Sea Stock, expressions rise and fall. Time's Changes. James Bramston. *Fr.* The Art of Politicks. OBEC
Like spectral hounds across the sky. Minot's Ledge. Fitz-James O'Brien. OnYI
Like Stephen Vincent Benét, I have fallen in love with American names. Ill Met by Zenith. Ogden Nash. NYBP
Like tall men with battering-plank—the colt. Letter from Underground. Ronald Everson. MoCV
Like that oldtimer who has kept by me. Homecoming. Theodore Weiss. TwAmPo
Like the clever seagull. Dancing on the Shore. Al Young. WSL
Like the crash of the thunder. Zionist Marching Song. Naphtali Herz Imber. TrJP
Like the ears of wheat in a wheat-field. Epilog. Heine. *Fr.* The North Sea. AWP; JAWP; WBP
Like the Eyes of Wolves. Nachum Yud, *tr. fr. Yiddish by* Joseph Leftwich. TrJP
Like the first seed before man's birth. The Baptism. L. Aaronson. FaBoTw
Like the ghost of a dear friend dead. Time Long Past. Shelley. EPN; HBV
Like the Idalian Queen. William Drummond of Hawthornden. *See* Madrigal: "Like the Idalian queen."
Like the idle fingers of wind caressing the forehead of God. The Falling of the Snow. Raymond Souster. CaP
Like the Prime Mover. Mehdi Ali Seljouk. ACV
Like the song of angel choirs. Jerusalem. "George Eliot." SoP
Like the soul of a stream. To a Cloud. Manuel Altolaguirre. LiTW
Like the stalks of wheat in the fields. Epilogue. Heine. *Fr.* The North Sea. TrJP
Like the steps of footsore armies. Waiting for Death. Mordecai Gebirtig. TrJP
Like the sweet apple which reddens upon the topmost bough. One Girl [*or* Beauty *or* A Young Bride]. Sappho, *tr. by* Dante Gabriel Rossetti. AWP; EnLi-1; JAWP; LiTW; OuHeWo; ViBoPo; WBP
Like the Touch of Rain. Edward Thomas. EnLoPo
Like the tribes of Israel. Sherman's in Savannah. Oliver Wendell Holmes. MC; PAH
Like the vain curlings of the watry maze. The First Anniversary of the Government under O. C. Andrew Marvell. MaMe
Like the violet which alone. Castara [*or* The Description of Castara]. William Habington. *Fr.* Castara, I. AnAnS-2 CavP; HBV; LiTL
Like thee I once have stemmed the sea of life. Epitaph, Intended for Himself. James Beattie. HBV; MemP; OBEV
Like They Say. Robert Creeley. ELU
Like This Together. Adrienne Rich. CoPo
Like those boats which are returning. Saigyo Hoshi, *tr. fr. Japanese by* Arthur Waley. AWP

Like to a baker's oven is the grave. Epitaphs. Francis Jeffrey. OxBoLi
Like to a Coin. Arlo Bates. AA
Like to a god he seems to me,/ O more than god. Sappho. Catullus, *tr. by* William Ellery Leonard. AWP; JAWP; WBP
Like to a Hermit. *At. to* Sir Walter Ralegh. PoFS; TuPP
(Hermit, The.) OBSC
(Like Hermit Poor.) SiPS
("Like to a hermit poor in place obscure.") EG; FCP; ReEn; Sonn
(Like to an Hermit Poor.) ReIE
(Poem, A: "Like to an Hermit poore in place obscure.") SiCE
(Sonnet: "Like to an hermit poor. . .") ElL
Like to Ahasuerus, that shrewd prince. The Pope. Robert Browning. *Fr.* The Ring and the Book, X. MBW-2; ViPo; ViPP
Like to an Hermit Poor. *At. to* Sir Walter Ralegh. *See* Like to a Hermit.
Like to clear in highest sphere. *See* Like to the clear. . .
Like to Diana in her summer weed[e]. Doron's Description of Samela [*or* Samela]. Robert Greene. *Fr.* Menaphon. AtBAP; ElL; HBV; LoBV; OBEV; OBSC; PoEL-2; ReIE; SiCE; TuPP; ViBoPo
Like to the Arctic Needle. Francis Quarles. Emblems, V, 4. OxBoCh
(I Am My Beloved's, and His Desire Is towards Me.) OBS
("Like to the Arctic needle, that does guide.") SeEP
"Eternal God! O Thou that only art," *sel.* MaRV
Like to the clear in highest sphere. Rosaline. Thomas Lodge. *Fr.* Rosalynde; or, Euphues' Golden Legacy. ElL; GoBC; GTBS; GTBS-D; GTBS-P; GTBS-W; GTSE; GTSL; LiTB; LiTG; LO; OBEV; OBSC; PoIE; TrGrPo; UnTE
Like to the damask rose you see. Hos Ego Versiculos. Francis Quarles. *Fr.* Argalus and Parthenia. OBS; SeEP. *See also* Like as the damask rose you see.
Like to the Falling of a Star. Henry King. *See* Sic Vita.
Like to the fatal, ominous raven which tolls. To Deloney. Everard Guilpin. *Fr.* Skialetheia. ReIE
Like to the leaf that falls. Epicedium. Horace L. Traubel. AA
Like to the leaves of the forest that bloom in the flowery season. Elegiac. Mimnermus. LiTW
Like to the marigold, I blushing close. Edward Taylor. *Fr.* Preparatory Meditations, Second Series. AnNE; SCAP
Like to the seely fly. Francis Davison. EG
Like to the Thundering Tone. Richard Corbet. BOHV; NA
Like to These Unmeasurable Mountains. Jacopo Sannazaro. *See* Lover's Life Compared to the Alps, The.
Like torn-up newsprint the nonchalant snow. 1894 in London. Charles Spear. AnNZ
Like trains of cars on tracks of plush. Emily Dickinson. AnNE; GN; MoAB; MoAmPo (1950 ed.); NeMA; OTPC
Like truthless dreams so are my joys expired. Farewell to the Court. Sir Walter Ralegh. CBEP; EG; EnRePo; FaBoEn; FCP; LO; OBSC; SiCE; SiPS; Sonn; TuPP
Like two pale stars at distance seen. St. Simon and St. Jude's Day. Cecil Frances Alexander. IrPN
Like two proud armies marching in the field. Your Beauty and My Reason. *Unknown.* OBSC; TrGrPo
Like unto Them That Dream. Psalms, CXXVI, Bible, *O.T.* TrJP
Like violets pale i' the spring o' the year. Song. James Thomson. Sunday up the River, IX. OBVV
Like Washington ("We cannot all be Washingtons."). *Unknown.* DD; HH
Like Water down a Slope. Zalman Schneour, *tr. fr. Hebrew by* Harry H. Fein. TrJP
Like water pouring from a pitcher, my mouth on your nipples! Sparrow Hills. Robert Lowell, *ad. fr. Russian of* Boris Pasternak. NaP
Likeness, A. Robert Browning. CTC; PoVP
Likeness, A. Willa Cather. HBMV
Likeness, The. William Henry Davies. MemP
Likeness has made them animal and shy. The Twins. Karl Shapiro. AnFE; CBV; CoAnAm; MiAP; MoAmPo (1950 ed.); Po; PoSa; TrJP; TwAmPo
Likeness of heaven!/ Agent of Power! The Ocean. John Augustus Shea. EtS
Li'l' Gal. Paul Laurence Dunbar. GoSl
Lilac. F. S Flint. HBMV
Lilac, The. Humbert Wolfe. FaPON; HBVY; MoBrPo; NeMA; OTPC (1946 ed.); YT
Lilac bushes were small with winter, The. Exercise in Aesthetics. Winfield Townley Scott. FiMAP
Lilac in my garden comes to bloom, The. My Garden. W. H. Davies. BoNaP
Lilac ribbon is unbound, A. Country of No Lack. Jean Starr Untermeyer. MAP; MoAmPo
Lilac Time. Piet Hein. PV
Lilacs. Hilda Conkling. NP
Lilacs. Amy Lowell. AmPP; AnAmPo; AnNE; AtBAP; LaNeLa, *abr.*; MAP; MoAmPo; MoVE; OxBA; PoRA (rev. ed.)
Lilacs are flowering, sweet and sublime. Lilac Time. Piet Hein. PV
Lilacs blossom just as sweet. Threnody. Dorothy Parker. InMe
Lilacs for Remembrance. Irene Shirley Moran. PoMa
Lilacs shall bloom for Walt Whitman. Memories of Whitman and Lincoln. James Oppenheim. LiPo
L'Ile du Levant; the Nudist Colony. Barbara Howes. NePoAm-2; PoCh
Lilian. Tennyson. HBV; PoVP
Lilian Adelaide Neilson. Clement Scott. VA
Lilian's Song. George Darley. OBNC
Lilied fields behold, The. Song of Faith. William Croswell. SoP
Lilies. Padraic Colum. NePoAm
Lilies. Don Marquis. BOHV
Lilies, The. John Francis O'Donnell. IrPN
Lilies. Shiko, *arr. by* Olive Beaupré Miller. SUS; TiPo
Lilies are white,/ Rosemary's green. Hearts and Lace Paper [*or* Flower Tokens]. *Unknown.* BoTP; OxNR; PCH; RIS
Lilies lie in my lady's bower, The. Oh! Weary Mother. Barry Pain. The Poets at Tea, VIII. NA; Par
Lilies, lilies, white lilies and yellow. Lilies. Don Marquis. BOHV
Lilies of the Field, The. Daniel Henderson. MaRV; StJW
Lilies of the Field, The. Compton Mackenzie. OBVV
Lilies of the Valley. Jo Gardner. BePJ
Lilies of the Valley. Marion Mitchell Walker. GFA
Lilies say on Easter day, The. The Song of the Lilies. Lucy Wheelock. OHIP
Lilith, *sels.* Christopher Brennan. PoAu-1
Adam to Lilith.
Anguish'd Doubt Broods over Eden, The.
Lilith on the Fate of Man.
Lilith. X. J. Kennedy. UnTE
Lilith. Dante Gabriel Rossetti. *See* Body's Beauty.
Lilith on the Fate of Man. Christopher Brennan. *Fr.* Lilith. PoAu-1
Lilium Regis. Francis Thompson. HBMV; JKCP
(Lillium Regis.) WGRP
Lille Burlero. Lord Wharton. OxBoLi
(Lilliburlero, *with music.*) ViBoFo
(New Song, A; or, Lilliburlero.) CoMu
Lilliput Levee. William Brighty Rands. CenHV; TSW
Lillium Regis. Francis Thompson. *See* Lilium Regis.
Lilly in a Christal, The. Robert Herrick. AnAnS-2; AtBAP; PoEL-3; SCEP-2; SeCP
(Lily in a Crystal, The.) PoeP; SeCePo
Lily, The. William Carlos Williams. TDP
Lily and the Rose, The. *Unknown.* *See* Maidens Came, The.
Lily Bed, The. Isabella Valancy Crawford. PeCV
Lily Bright and Shine-a. *Unknown.* *See* Here Comes a Lusty Wooer.
Lily Flower. Michael Brownstein. ANYP
Lily, Germander, and Sops-in-Wine. *Unknown.* *See* And Can the Physician Make Sick Men Well.
Lily has a smooth stalk, The. Christina Rossetti. *Fr.* Sing-Song. OuHeWo
Lily has an air, The. There's Nothing like the Rose. Christina Rossetti. PRWS
Lily in a Crystal, The. *See* Lilly in a Christal, The.
Lily in my garden grew, A. The Maiden and the Lily. John Fraser. HBV
Lily McQueen. Sara Jackson. BoLP
Lily Munro. *Unknown.* *See* Jackaro.
Lily of the Valley, The. Thomas Lovell Beddoes. EG
Lily of the West, The, *with music.* *Unknown.* BFSS

Lily of Yorrow, The. Henry van Dyke. AA
Lily on liquid roses floating. Champagne Rosée [*or* Rosé]. John Kenyon. OBEV; OBRV; OBVV; VA
Lily-Pool and the Cow, The. T. E. Brown. MemP
Lily Princess, The. *Unknown, tr. fr. Japanese by* William N. Porter. MPB
Lily-white Rose, The. *Unknown.* MeEL
Lilya, *sel.* Eysteinn Asgrímsson, *tr. fr. Icelandic by* Eiríkur Magnússon.
Author's Entreaty for His Lay. ISi
Lily's withered chalice falls, The. Le Jardin [*or* The Garden]. Oscar Wilde. PoRA; SeCePo; SyP; ViPP
Limb and Mind. John Waller. NeBP
"Limber-limbed, lazy god, stretched on the rock." Pan Learns Music. Henry van Dyke. PCH
Limberham; or, The Kind Keeper, *sel.* Dryden.
Song from the Italian, A, *fr.* III, i. CEP; SeCV-2
Limberick. Conrad Aiken. FiBHP; SiTL
Limbo. S. T. Coleridge. ERoP-1
Limbs remember blood and fire, The. Time Regained. Sir Herbert Read. FaBoMo
Limbs that erstwhile charmed your sight, The. Dear, They Have Poached the Eyes You Loved So Well. Rupert Brooke. WhC
Lime Avenue, The. Sacheverell Sitwell. LOW
Limeratomy, The. Anthony Euwer. HBMV
Sels.
Face, The. TreF
(Limerick: "As a [*or* For] beauty I'm not a great star.") BOHV; GoTP; HBV; HBVY; InvP; LiBL
(My Face.) FaFP; LiTM; NePA; SiTL; WhC
Limerick: "No matter how grouchy you're feeling." LiBL; WhC
Limericised Classics. Edwin Meade Robinson. HBMV
Limerick: "All young men should take note of the case." M. B. Thornton. LiBL
Limerick: "Amateur, driving too fast, An." Aristophanes, *ad. fr. Greek by* F. A. Wright. *Fr.* The Wasps. LiBL
Limerick: "Amorous M. A., An." *Unknown.* LiBL
Limerick: "And let the canakin clink, [clink]." Shakespeare. *Fr.* Othello, II, iii. LiBL
Limerick: "And those two young ladies of Birmingham." *Unknown. See* Limerick: "There were three young women of Birmingham."
Limerick: "Angry young husband called Bicket, An." John Galsworthy. CenHV
Limerick: "Ankle's chief end is exposiery, The." Anthony Euwer. The Limeratomy: The Ankle. HBMV
Limerick: "As a [*or* For] beauty I'm not a great star." Anthony Euwer. *Fr.* The Limeratomy. BOHV; GoTP; HBV; HBVY; InvP; LiBL
(Face, The.) HBMV; TreF
(My Face.) FaFP; LiTM; NePA; PoLF; SiTL; WhC
Limerick: "At the village emporium in Woodstock." Frederick Winsor. WhC
Limerick: "Beautiful lady named Psyche, A." *Unknown.* LiBL; LiTG; SiTL; WhC
Limerick: "Book and a jug and a dame, A." Edwin Meade Robinson. *See* Limerick: "Jug and a book and a dame, A."
Limerick: "Bottle of perfume that Willie sent, The." *Unknown.* GoTP; WhC
Limerick: "Bright little maid of St. Thomas, A." *Unknown.* HBV
Limerick: "But he [*or* He *or* Pa] followed the pair to Pawtucket." *Unknown. Fr.* That Nantucket Limerick. HBV (8th ed.); LiBL; LiTG; TreF
Limerick: "Canner, exceedingly [*or* remarkably] canny, A." Carolyn Wells. HBV; HBVY; LiBL; TSW
(Canner, Exceedingly Canny, A.) FaPON
(Two Limericks.) YaD
Limerick: "Cannibal bold of Penzance, A." *Unknown.* LiBL
Limerick: "Canny old codger at Yalta, A." *Unknown.* LiBL
Limerick: "Cautious collapsible cow, The." *Unknown.* LiBL
Limerick: "Certain young fellow, named Bobbie, A." *Unknown.* LiBL
Limerick "Certain young gourmet of Crediton, A." Charles Cuthbert Inge. CenHV; LiBL; WhC
Limerick: "Cleopatra, who thought they maligned her." Newton Mackintosh. LiBL; NA
Limerick: "Clergyman [*or* Evangelical vicar] in want, A." Ronald Arbuthnott Knox. CenHV; LiBL; OxBoLi; WhC
Limerick: "Clergyman out in Dumont, A." Morris Bishop. LiBL; WhC
Limerick: "Consider the lowering lynx." Langford Reed. CenHV
Limerick: "Dear Sir: Your astonishment's odd." *Unknown.* LiBL
Limerick: "Decrepit old gasman, named Peter, A." *Unknown.* LiBL; SiTL
(Decrepit Old Gasman, A.) FaFP
Limerick: "Eccentric old person of Slough, An." George Robey. CenHV
Limerick: "Epicure [*or* Diner while..., A], dining at Crewe, An." *Unknown.* CenHV; LiBL; LiTG; RIS; StaSt; WhC
(Epicure, An [Dining at Crewe].) GoTP; LiTM (rev. ed.); SiTL
Limerick: "Evangelical vicar in want." Ronald Arbuthnott Knox. *See* Limerick: "Clergyman in want, A."
Limerick: "Flea and a fly [*or* Fly and a flea] in a flue, A." *Unknown.* GoTP; LiBL; LiTG; TiPo (1959 ed.); WhC
Limerick: "For beauty I am not a star." Anthony Euwer. *See* Limerick: "As a beauty I'm not a great star."
Limerick: "Funny old lady named Borgia. A." *Unknown.* WhC
Limerick: "Funny old person of Slough. A." *Unknown.* RIS
Limerick: "God's plan made a hopeful beginning." *Unknown.* LiBL
Limerick: "H was an indigent hen." Bruce Porter. NA
Limerick: "Half baked potato, named Sue, A." George Libaire. LiBL
Limerick: "Hands they were made to assist, The." Anthony Euwer. The Limeratomy: The Hands. HBMV
Limerick: "He died in attempting to swallow." Roy Campbell. LiBL
(Death of Polybius Jubb, The.) LiTG; SiTL; WhC
Limerick: "He followed the pair to Pawtucket." *Unknown. See* Limerick: "But he followed. . ."
Limerick: "Hungry old man from the Rhine, A." *Unknown. See* Limerick: "There was an old man of the Rhine."
Limerick: "I raised a great hullabaloo." *Unknown.* PDV
Limerick: "I saw Nelson at the Battle of the Nile." *Unknown.* LiBL
Limerick: "'I think' thought Sam Butler." Geoffrey Taylor. LiTM
Limerick: "I wish that my room had a floor!" Gelett Burgess. *See* I Wish That My Room Had a Floor.
Limerick: "I'd rather have fingers than toes." Gelett Burgess. *See* I'd Rather Have Fingers than Toes.
Limerick: "I'd rather have habits than clothes." Gelett Burgess. NA
Limerick: "If-itty-teshi-mow Jays." *Unknown.* BOHV
Limerick: "In the wax works of Nature they strike." Anthony Euwer. The Limeratomy: Note HBMV
Limerick: "In this book every line has been clean." H. I. Brock. LiBL
Limerick: "Infinitesimal James." *Unknown.* BOHV
Limerick: "'It's a very warm day,' observed Billy." Tudor Jenks. BOHV
Limerick: "John woke on Jan. first and felt queer." *Unknown.* BOHV
Limerick: "Jug and a book [*or* Book and a jug] and a dame, A." Edwin Meade Robinson. LiBL
(Limericised Classics: The Rubaiyat.) HBMV
Limerick: "Lady there was of Antigua, A." Cosmo Monkhouse. HBV; TSW
Limerick: "Lieutenant who went out to shoot, A." Morgan Taylor. LiBL
Limerick: "Lifeboat that's kept at Torquay, The." *Unknown.* LiBL
Limerick: "Limerick packs laughs anatomical, A." *Unknown.* LiBL
(Limerick on Limericks, A.) SiTL
Limerick: "Man to whom illness was chronic, A." *Unknown.* LiBL
(Beer.) SiTL
Limerick: "Man went a-hunting at Reigate [*or* Rygate], A." *Unknown.* BOTP; RIS
Limerick: "Miss Minnie McFinney of Butte." *At. to* Carolyn Wells. LiBL; WhC
Limerick: "Mussolini's pet Marshal, Graziani." T. R. Ybarra. LiBL

Limerick: "My name's Mister Benjamin Bunny." Frederic Edward Weatherly. CenHV
Limerick: "Nice old lady named Tweedle, A." *Unknown.* LiBL
Limerick: "No matter how grouchy you're feeling." Anthony Euwer. *Fr.* The Limeratomy. LiBL; WhC
(Smile, The.) HBMV
Limerick: "Now the ears, so I always had thunk." Anthony Euwer. The Limeratomy: The Ears. HBMV
Limerick: "Now the sneeze is a joy-vent, I s'pose." Anthony Euwer. The Limeratomy: The Sneeze. HBMV
Limerick: "O God, inasmuch as without Thee." *Unknown.* LiBL
Limerick: "Pa followed the pair to Pawtucket." *Unknown.* *See* Limerick: "But he followed the pair. . ."
Limerick: "Poor benighted Hindoo, The." Cosmo Monkhouse. HBV; PCD; TSW
Limerick: "Pretty young actress, a stammerer, A." Eille Norwood. CenHV
Limerick: "Remarkable truly, is art!" Gelett Burgess. HBV
Limerick: "Reverend Henry Ward Beecher, The." *At. to* Oliver Wendell Holmes. CenHV; HBVY
(Eggstravagance, An.) PCD
(Henry Ward Beecher.) ChTr
(Limerick: "Said a great Congregational preacher.") LiBL; WhC
("Said a great Congregational preacher.") GoTP; SiTL
Limerick: "Rheumatic old man in White Plains, A." *Unknown.* LiBL
Limerick: "Said a bad little youngster named Beauchamp." *At. to* Carolyn Wells. TSW
Limerick: "Said a girl from beyond Pompton Lakes." Morris Bishop. LiBL
Limerick: "Said a great Congregational preacher." *At. to* Oliver Wendell Holmes. *See* Limerick: "Reverend Henry Ward Beecher, The."
Limerick: "Said Nero to one of his train." *Unknown.* LiBL
Limerick: "Said old Peeping Tom of Fort Lee." Morris Bishop. LiBL; WhC
Limerick: "Said the Reverend Jabez McCotton." James Montgomery Flagg. LiBL
Limerick: "She frowned and called him Mr." *Unknown.* GoTP
(She Called Him Mr.) FaPON
Limerick: "Should a plan we suggest just that minute." "R. K. B." LiBL
Limerick: "Silly young fellow named Hyde, A." *Unknown.* *See* Silly Young Fellow. . .
Limerick: "Sleeper from the Amazon, A." *Unknown.* WhC
(Sleeper from the Amazon, A.) RePo
Limerick: "Styles that at present are regnant, The." *Unknown.* LiBL
Limerick: "Then the pair followed Pa to Manhasset." *Unknown.* *Fr.* That Nantucket Limerick. LiBL; TreF
Limerick: "There is a creator named God." James Abbott McNeill Whistler. BOHV; LiBL
Limerick: "There is a wonderful family called Stein." *Unknown.* BOHV
(Limerick: "Wonderful family is Stein, A.") LiBL
Limerick: "There is a young artist called [*or* named] Whistler." Dante Gabriel Rossetti. BOHV; LiBL
Limerick: "There is a young lady whose nose/ Continually prospers and grows." Edward Lear. OTPC (1946 ed.). *See also* Limerick: "There was a young lady whose nose/ Was so long. . ."
Limerick: "There is an old he-wolf named Gambart." Dante Gabriel Rossetti. CenHV
Limerick: "There once was a bonnie Scotch laddie." *Unknown.* LiBL; WhC
Limerick: "There once was a boy of Bagdad." *Unknown.* RIS; StaSt
Limerick: "There once was a girl of New York." Cosmo Monkhouse. LiBL; NA
Limerick: "There once was a girl of Pitlochry." *Unknown.* CenHV
Limerick: "There once was a happy hyena." Carolyn Wells. PCH
Limerick: "There once was a man from Nantucket." *Unknown.* *See* Limerick: "There was an old man of Nantucket."
Limerick: "There once was a man of Bengal." *Unknown.* *See* Limerick: "There was a young man of Bengal."
Limerick: "There once was a man of Calcutta." *Unknown.* LiBL; WhC
Limerick: "There once was a man [*or* was a young man] who said: 'Damn!' " Maurice Evan Hare. CenHV; LiBL; OxBoLi
(Free-Will and Predestination.) MemP
Limerick: "There once was a man [*or* was a young man] who said, 'God.' " Ronald Arbuthnott Knox. LiBL; OxBoLi
Limerick: "There once was a man who said, 'How.' " *Unknown.* LiBL; NA
Limerick: "There once was a painter named Scott." Dante Gabriel Rossetti. CenHV
Limerick: "There once was a person of Benin." Cosmo Monkhouse. LiBL; NA
Limerick: "There once was a popular crooner." M. B. Thornton. LiBL
Limerick: "There once was a sculptor called [*or* named] Phidias." Oliver Herford. BOHV; LiBL
Limerick: "There once was an arch armadillo." Carolyn Wells. PCH
Limerick: "There once was an Ichthyosaurus." *Unknown.* OTPC (1946 ed.)
Limerick: "There once was an old man of Lyme." *Unknown, at. to* Edward Lear, *also to* Cosmo Monkhouse. NA
(Limerick: "There was an old party [*or* a young fellow] of Lyme.") LiBL; LiTG; OxBoLi
(Limerick: "There was an old person of Lyme.") CenHV
Limerick: "There once were some learned M. D.'s." Oliver Herford. BOHV; LiBL
Limerick: "There once were two cats of Kilkenny." *Unknown.* *See* Kilkenny Cats, The.
Limerick: "There was a dear lady of Eden." *Unknown.* LiBL; NA
Limerick: "There was a fair maid from Decatur." *Unknown.* LiBL
Limerick: "There was a faith-healer of Deal." *Unknown.* CenHV; LiBL; WhC
(Faith-Healer.) FaFP; SiTL
(Mind and Matter.) LiTM
("There was a faith-healer of Deal.") GoTP
Limerick: "There was a fat canon of Durham." *Unknown.* WhC
Limerick: "There was a fat man of Bombay." *Unknown.* BoChLi; RIS
Limerick: "There was a gay damsel of Lynn." *Unknown.* LiBL; NA
Limerick: "There was a good canon of Durham." William Ralph Inge. CenHV
Limerick: "There was a kind curate of Kew." *Unknown.* CenHV
Limerick: "There was a poor chap called Rossetti." Dante Gabriel Rossetti. CenHV
Limerick: "There was a princess of Bengal." Walter Parke. NA
Limerick: "There was a queer fellow named Woodin." "Cuthbert Bede." CenHV
Limerick: "There was a small boy of [*or* young man from] Quebec." Kipling. HBV; HBVY; LiBL; NA
Limerick: "There was a trim maiden named Wood." William A. Lockwood. LiBL
Limerick: "There was a young bard of Japan." *Unknown.* CenHV
Limerick: "There was a young belle of Old Natchez." Ogden Nash. LiBL
Limerick: "There was a young critic of King's." Arthur Clement Hilton. CenHV
Limerick: "There was a young curate of Hants." E. V. Knox. CenHV
Limerick: "There was a young curate of Salisbury." *Unknown, at. to* George Libaire. LiBL
Limerick: "There was a young farmer of Leeds." *Unknown.* RIS; StaSt
Limerick: "There was a young fellow called Green." *Unknown.* CenHV
Limerick: "There was a young fellow from Fife." T. R. Ybarra. LiBL
Limerick: "There was a young fellow named Clyde." *Unknown.* BOHV
Limerick: "There was a young fellow named Dice." *Unknown.* LiBL

Limerick: "There was a young fellow named Hall." *Unknown.* LiTG; WhC
(Happy Time, A.) LiTM; SiTL
Limerick: "There was a young fellow named Hatch." *Unknown.* LiBL
Limerick: "There was a young fellow named Sydney." Don Marquis. LiBL
(Young Fellow Named Sydney, A.) SiTL
Limerick: "There was a young fellow [*or* person] named Tate [*or* Tait]." *At. to* Carolyn Wells. GoTP; HBV; HBVY; LiBL; TSW; WhC
Limerick: "There was a young fellow of Ceuta." *Unknown.* CenHV
Limerick: "There was a young fellow of Lyme." *Unknown. See* Limerick: "There once was an old man of Lyme."
Limerick: "There was a young fellow of Perth." *Unknown.* RIS; StaSt; WhC
Limerick: "There was a young genius of Queens'." Arthur Clement Hilton. CenHV
Limerick: "There was a young girl of Asturias." *Unknown.* BBGG
Limerick: "There was a young girl of Lahore." Cosmo Monkhouse. HBV
Limerick: "There was a young girl of Majorca." Edward Lear. LiBL
Limerick: "There was a young gourmand of John's." Arthur Clement Hilton. CenHV
Limerick: "There was a young lady at Bingham." *Unknown.* LiBL
Limerick: "There was a young lady called Starky." *Unknown. See* Mendelian Theory.
Limerick: "There was a young lady from Joppa." *Unknown.* BOHV; LiBL
Limerick: "There was a young lady in white." Edward Lear. NBM
Limerick: "There was a young lady [*or* woman] named [*or* called] Bright." *Unknown, at. to* Arthur Buller. CenHV; LiBL; OxBoLi; WhC
(Relativity.) FaFP; ImOP; LiTM; SiTL
(Young Lady Named Bright, A.) FaPON
Limerick: "There was a young lady of Bute." Edward Lear. OTPC (1946 ed.); StVeCh
Limerick: "There was a young lady of Byde." *Unknown.* LiBL
Limerick: "There was a young lady of Corsica." Edward Lear. CenHV; ChTr
Limerick: "There was a young lady of Ealing." *Unknown.* CenHV
Limerick: "There was a young lady of Firle." Edward Lear. RePo
Limerick: "There was a young lady of Flint." *Unknown.* CenHV
Limerick: "There was a young lady of Hull." Edward Lear. MoShBr
Limerick: "There was a young lady of Kent." *Unknown.* CenHV; LiBL; SiTL
Limerick: "There was a young lady of Limerick." Andrew Lang. CenHV
Limerick: "There was a young lady of Lynn,/ Who was deep in original sin." *Unknown.* BOHV; LiBL
Limerick: "There was a young lady of Lynn/ Who was so exceedingly thin." *Unknown.* CenHV; InP; OnPP
(Young Lady of Lynn, The.) ChTr
Limerick: "There was a young lady of Milton." *Unknown.* NA
Limerick: "There was a young lady of Niger." *Unknown, at. to.* Cosmo Monkhouse. BOHV; HBV; HBVY; InP; LiBL; NA; PCD; PDV; TiPo (1959 ed.); TSW
(Not Just for the Ride.) FaFP; LiTM; SiTL
(Satisfied Tiger.) TreFT
(There Was a Young Lady of Niger.) InvP; PTK; ShM; SoPo
(Young Lady of Niger, The.) FaPoN
Limerick: "There was a young lady of Norway." Edward Lear. OTPC (1946 ed.); StVeCh; TiPo; TSW
(Young Lady of Norway, A.) FaPON
Limerick: "There was a young lady of Oakham." *Unknown.* BBGG; BOHV
Limerick: "There was a young lady of Portugal!" Edward Lear. LiTG; OxBoLi
Limerick: "There was a young lady of Riga." *Unknown.* CenHV
Limerick: "There was a young lady of Russia." Edward Lear. MoShBr
Limerick: "There was [once] a young lady of Ryde/ Who ate a green apple and died." *Unknown.* CenHV; EvOK; PDV
(There Was a Young Lady of Ryde.) ShM
Limerick: "There was a young lady of Ryde/ Whose shoe-strings were seldom untied." Edward Lear. OxBoLi; WhC
Limerick: "There was a young lady of Spain." *Unknown.* LiTG
(Young Lady of Spain, A.) LiTM
Limerick: "There was a young lady of station." "Lewis Carroll." BOHV; CenHV; GoTP
Limerick: "There was a young lady of Truro." *Unknown.* BOHV
Limerick: "There was a young lady of Twickenham." Oliver Herford. BOHV; LiBL; WhC
Limerick: "There was a young lady of Venice." *Unknown.* BOHV; LiBL
Limerick: "There was a young [*or* an old] lady of Wales." *Unknown.* NA; RIS
Limerick: "There was a young lady of Warwick." *Unknown.* ATP
Limerick: "There was a young lady of Wilts." *Unknown.* HBV
Limerick: "There was a young lady of Woosester." *Unknown.* GoTP; LiBL; WhC
Limerick: "There was a young lady whose bonnet." Edward Lear. GFA; PCH; StVeCh
Limerick: "There was a young lady whose chin." Edward Lear. BoChLi; RePo; RIS; SoPo; StaSt; TiPo
Limerick: "There was a young lady whose eyes." Edward Lear. GoJo; RIS; StaSt; TSW
Limerick: "There was a young lady whose nose/ Was so long. . ." Edward Lear. BoChLi; FaPON; RePo; SAS. *See also* Limerick: "There is a young lady whose nose/ Continually prospers. . ."
Limerick: "There was a young maid of Manila." *Unknown.* OnPP
Limerick: "There was a young maid who said, 'Why.' " *Unknown.* LiBL; NA; RIS; StaSt
Limerick: "There was a young maiden, a Sioux." *Unknown.* LiBL
Limerick: "There was a young man at St. Kitts." *Unknown. See* Limerick: "There was a young man of St. Kitts."
Limerick: "There was a young man down in Ga." *Unknown.* OnPP
Limerick: "There was a young man from Cornell." *Unknown.* BOHV
Limerick: "There was a young man from Japan." *Unknown.* LiBL; LiTM; SiTL
Limerick: "There was a young man from Quebec." Kipling. *See* Limerick: "There was a small boy of Quebec."
Limerick: "There was a young man from the city." *Unknown.* TreFT
Limerick: "There was a young man of Bengal." *Unknown.* GoTP; OxBoLi
(Limerick: "There once was a man of Bengal," *sl. diff.*) CenHV
Limerick: "There was a young man of Cohoes." Robert J. Burdette. BOHV; NA
Limerick: "There was a young man of Devizes." *Unknown, at. to* Archibald Marshall. CenHV; WhC
Limerick: "There was a young man of Fort Blain[e]y." *Unknown.* BOHV; LiBL
Limerick: "There was a young man of Hong Kong." *Unknown.* LiBL
Limerick: "There was a young man of Laconia." *Unknown.* BOHV
Limerick: "There was a young man of Madrid." *Unknown.* LiBL; WhC
Limerick: "There was a young man of Montrose." Arnold Bennett. CenHV; OxBoLi
(It Pays.) FaFP; LiTM; SiTL
Limerick: "There was a young man of Ostend." *Unknown.* BOHV; LiBL
Limerick: "There was a young [*or* an old] man of St. Bees." W. S. Gilbert. BOHV; InvP; LBN; LiBL; LiTG
(Limerick in Blank Verse, A.) LBN
(Old Man of St. Bees.) SiTL
Limerick: "There was a young man of [*or* at] St. Kitts." *Unknown.* BOHV; LiBL; NA

Limerick: "There was a young man of Sid. Sussex." Arthur C. Hilton. WhC
Limerick: "There was a young man of the Cape." *At. to* Robert Louis Stevenson. *See* Limerick: "There was an old man of the Cape."
Limerick: "There was a young man so benighted." *Unknown.* HBV; OnPP
("There was a young man so benighted.") PTK
Limerick: "There was a young man who said, 'Damn!'" Maurice Evan Hare. *See* Limerick: "There once was a man who said, 'Damn!'"
Limerick: "There was a young man who said, 'God.'" Ronald Arbuthnott Knox. *See* Limerick: "There once was a man who said, 'God.'"
Limerick: "There was a young man who said, 'Run.'" *Unknown.* LiBL
Limerick: "There was a young man who was bitten." *At. to* Walter Parke. LiBL; NA
Limerick: "There was a young monk of Siberia." *Unknown.* TreFT
Limerick: "There was a young person named Tate." *At. to* Carolyn Wells. *See* Limerick: "There was a young fellow named Tate."
Limerick: "There was a young person of Crete." Edward Lear. OTPC (1946 ed.)
Limerick: "There was a young person of Smyrna." Edward Lear. NBM; OxBoLi
Limerick: "There was a young poet of Thusis." *Unknown.* OxBoLi
Limerick: "There was a young poet of Trinity." *Unknown.* HBMV
Limerick: "There was a young woman named Bright." *Unknown.* *See* Limerick: "There was a young lady named Bright."
Limerick: "There was an Archdeacon who said." *Unknown.* OxBoLi
Limerick: "There was an auld birkie ca'ed Milton." Andrew Lang. CenHV
Limerick: "There was an old fellow of Lynn." *Unknown.* LiBL
Limerick: "There was an old Fellow of Trinity,/ A doctor well versed in Divinity." *Unknown.* CenHV; LiBL
Limerick: "There was an old fellow of Trinity/ Who solved the square root of Infinity." *Unknown.* LiBL; WhC
Limerick: "There was an old lady of Chertsey." Edward Lear. RePo
Limerick: "There was an old lady of Wales." *Unknown.* RIS
Limerick: "There was an old lady who said,/ When she found a thief under her bed." *Unknown.* RIS; SaSt
Limerick: "There was an old lady whose folly." Edward Lear. RIS; StaSt
Limerick: "There was an old man from [*or* of] Peru/ Who dreamt he was eating his shoe." *Unknown.* CenHV; LiTG; PDV
(Old Man from Peru, An.) FaFP; LiTM (rev. ed.); SiTL
Limerick: "There was an old man from the Rhine." *Unknown.* *See* Limerick: "There was an old man of the Rhine."
Limerick: "There was an old man in a barge." Edward Lear. PoVP
(Nonsense Pictures in Rhyme.) MPB
Limerick: "There was an old man in a boat." Edward Lear. BoChLi (1950 ed.); HBV; OTPC; StVeCh
(Floating Old Man, The.) WiR
Limerick: "There was an old man in a pew." Edward Lear. MoShBr
Limerick: "There was an old man in a pie." *Unknown.* BOHV
Limerick: "There was an old man in a tree." Edward Lear. BoChLi; BOHV; GoTP; HBV; InvP; LBN; LiBL; NA; OTPC; PoVP; RePo; SAS; SoPo; TiPo (1952 ed.)
(There Was an Old Man in a Tree.) SoPo
Limerick: "There was an old man in a trunk." Ogden Nash. CenHV
Limerick: "There was an old man of Bengal." "F. Anstey." CenHV
Limerick: "There was an old man of Berlin." Edward Lear. PoVP
Limerick: "There was an old man of Blackheath." *Unknown.* CenHV; PDV
Limerick: "There was an old man of Boulogne." *Unknown.* CenHV; OxBoLi
(Old Man of Boulogne, An.) LiTM; SiTL
Limerick: "There was an old man of Cape Horn." Edward Lear. TSW
Limerick: "There was an old man of Corfu." Edward Lear. RePo
Limerick: "There was an old man of Dumbree." Edward Lear. NBM
Limerick: "There was an old man of Hong Kong." Edward Lear. NBM; RePo
Limerick: "There was an old man of Ibreem." Edward Lear. RePo
Limerick: "There was an old man of Kamschatka." Edward Lear. NA
Limerick: "There was an old man of Khartoum." *Unknown.* LiBL; OxBoLi
Limerick: "There was an old man of Leghorn." Edward Lear. NA
Limerick: "There was an old man of Melrose." Edward Lear. LBN
Limerick: "There was an old man of [*or* once was a man from] Nantucket." *Unknown, at. to* Dayton Voorhees. *Fr.* That Nantucket Limerick. HBV (8th ed.); LiBL; LiTG; TreF
Limerick: "There was an old man of Peru/ Who dreamt he was eating his shoe." *Unknown.* *See* Limerick: "There was an old man from Peru."
Limerick: "There was an old man of St. Bees." W. S. Gilbert. *See* Limerick: "There was a young man of St. Bees."
Limerick: "There was an old man of Tarentum." *Unknown.* HBV; LiBL; WhC
Limerick: "There was an old [*or* a young] man of the Cape." *At. to* Robert Louis Stevenson. ATP; BOHV; LiBL
Limerick: "There was an old man of the coast." Edward Lear. CenHV; LiBL; MoShBr; PoVP; RIS; StaSt
Limerick: "There was an old man of the Dargle." Edward Lear. ChTr
Limerick: "There was an old man of the Dee." Edward Lear. RePo
Limerick: "There was an old man of The Hague." Edward Lear. EvOK
Limerick: "There was an old man of the Isles." Edward Lear. OTPC (1946 ed.); StVeCh
Limerick: "There was an old man of [*or* from] the Rhine." *Unknown.* BOHV; GoTP
(Limerick: "Hungry old man from the Rhine, A.") StaSt
Limerick: "There was an old man of the West." Edward Lear. RIS; StaSt
Limerick: "There was an old man of Thermopylae." Edward Lear. CenHV; EvOK; LBN; LiBL; NA; NBM
Limerick: "There was an old man of Tobago." *Unknown.* BOHV; LiBL; RIS
Limerick: "There was an old man of Vesuvius." Edward Lear. LiBL
Limerick: "There was an old man of Whitehaven." Edward Lear. NBM
Limerick: "There was an old man on the Border." Edward Lear. CenHV; PoVP
Limerick: "There was an old man on whose nose." Edward Lear. BoChLi
(There Was an Old Man on Whose Nose.) SoPo
Limerick: "There was an old man who said, 'Do.'" *Unknown.* FaPON; ImOP; LiBL; NA; RIS; StaSt
Limerick: "There was an old man who said 'Gee!'" *Unknown.* BOHV
Limerick: "There was an old man who said: 'How.'" Edward Lear. BoChLi; EvOK; GFA; SAS; StVeCh; TSW
Limerick: "There was an old man who said, 'Hush!'" Edward Lear. GoJo; GoTP; HBV; LiTG; NA; NBM; OTPC; OxBoLi; StVeCh
Limerick: "There was an old man who said, 'Well!'" Edward Lear. OTPC (1946 ed.); RIS; StaSt
Limerick: "There was an old man who supposed." Edward Lear. LBN; LiBL; NA; RIS; StaSt; WhC
Limerick: "There was an old man, who when little." Edward Lear. GoTP; RePo
Limerick: "There was an old man with a beard,/ Who said, 'It is just as I feared!'" Edward Lear. BoChLi; ChTr; HBV; LBN; LiBL; NA; OTPC; PDV; PoVP; RePo; SoPo; StVeCh; TiPo; TSW
(Old Man with a Beard.) FaPON

Limerick: "There was an old man with a beard,/ Who sat on a horse when he reared." Edward Lear. LiBL
Limerick: "There was an old man with a gong." Edward Lear. GoJo
Limerick: "There was an old man with a poker." Edward Lear. HBV; OTPC
Limerick: "There was an old monk of Siberia." *Unknown.* LiBL
Limerick: "There was an old party of Lyme." *Unknown. See* Limerick: "There once was an old man of Lyme."
Limerick: "There was an old person of Anerly." Edward Lear. LiBL
Limerick: "There was an old person of Bromley." Edward Lear. NBM
Limerick: "There was an old person of Burton." Edward Lear. RIS; StaSt
Limerick: "There was an old person of Dean." Edward Lear. BoChLi; MoShBr; PCH
Limerick: "There was an old person of Diss." Edward Lear. GoJo
Limerick: "There was an old person of Gretna." Edward Lear. ChTr
Limerick: "There was an old person of Hurst." Edward Lear. RePo
Limerick: "There was an old person of Ickley." Edward Lear. EvOK
Limerick: "There was an old person of Leeds." *Unknown.* WhC
Limerick: "There was an old person of Lyme." *Unknown. See* Limerick: "There once was an old man of Lyme."
Limerick: "There was an old person of Minety." Edward Lear. RePo
Limerick: "There was an old person of Shoreham." Edward Lear. NBM
Limerick: "There was an old person of Sparta." Edward Lear. BoChLi (1939 ed.)
Limerick: "There was an old person of Stroud." Edward Lear. RePo
Limerick: "There was an old person of Tring/ Who, when somebody asked her to sing." *Unknown.* LiBL; WhC
Limerick: "There was an old person of Ware." Edward Lear. BoChLi; CenHV; GoTP; LiBL; NA; PCH; PoPl; RePo
(Moppsikon Floppsikon Bear, The.) SAS
Limerick: "There was an old person of Wick." Edward Lear. NA
Limerick: "There was an old person of Woking." Edward Lear. NA
Limerick: "There was an old person whose habits." Edward Lear. BoChLi (1950 ed.); FaPON; LBN
Limerick: "There was an old soldier of Bister." *Unknown.* BOHV
Limerick: "There was an old stupid who wrote." Walter Parke. LiBL; NA
Limerick: "There was an old tailor of Bicester." *Unknown.* CenHV
Limerick: "There was an old woman of Leeds." *Unknown.* RIS
Limerick: "There was once a maiden of Siam." *Unknown.* TreFT
Limerick: "There was once a young lady of Ryde." *Unknown. See* Limerick: "There was a young lady of Ryde/ Who ate a green apple. . .
Limerick: "There were three young women of Birmingham." *Unknown.* HBV
(Limerick: "And those two young ladies of Birmingham.") LiBL
Limerick: "There's a combative artist named Whistler." Dante Gabriel Rossetti. CenHV
Limerick: "There's a Portuguese person named Howell." Dante Gabriel Rossetti. CenHV
Limerick: "There's a vaporish maiden in Harrison." Morris Bishop. LiBL; WhC
Limerick: "There's an Irishman, Arthur O'Shaughnessy." Dante Gabriel Rossetti. CenHV
(On the Poet O'Shaughnessy.) ChTr
Limerick: "These places abound in the old." George Libaire. LiBL
Limerick: "They say that I was in my youth." *Unknown.* CenHV
Limerick: "This bird is the keel-billed toucan." Howard Ketcham. LiBL
Limerick: "To smash the simple atom." Ethel Jacobson. LiTM
Limerick: "Tutor who tooted the [*or* a] flute, A." Carolyn Wells. BOHV; HBV; HBVY; LBN; LiBL; TSW; WhC
(Tutor, The.) MoShBr
(Tutor Who Tooted the [*or* a] Flute, A.) GoTP; TiPo (1959 ed.)
(Two Limericks.) YaD
Limerick: "Well, it's partly the shape of the thing." *Unknown.* WhC
Limerick: "When a jolly young fisher named Fisher." *Unknown.* LiBL
Limerick: "When that Seint George hadde sleyne ye dragone." *Unknown. See* When That St. George Had Slain His Dragon.
Limerick: "When you go to a store in Ascutney." Richard H. Field. WhC
Limerick: "When you think of the hosts without No." *Unknown.* SiTL
Limerick: "With a conscience we're able to see." Anthony Euwer. The Limeratomy: The Conscience. HBMV
Limerick: "Wonderful bird is the pelican, A." Dixon Lanier Merritt. CenHV; LiBL; LiTG
Limerick: "Wonderful family is Stein, A." *Unknown. See* Limerick: "There is a wonderful family called Stein."
Limerick: "Yes, theirs was a love that was tidal." Paul Kieffer. LiBL
Limerick: "You remember that pastoral frolic." "R. K. B." LiBL
Limerick: "Young lady of fair Mytilene, A." *Unknown.* CenHV
Limerick: "Young man on a journey had met her, A." *Unknown.* LiBL
Limerick: "Your verses, dear friend, I surmise." *Unknown.* LiBL
Limerick gets laughs anatomical, A. *See* Limerick packs laughs anatomical, A.
Limerick in Blank Verse, A. W. S. Gilbert. *See* Limerick: "There was a young man of St. Bees."
Limerick packs [*or* gets] laughs anatomical, A. Limerick [on Limericks]. *Unknown.* LiBL; SiTL
Limerick Town, *sel.* John Francis O'Donnell.
In the Market-Place. NBM
("Here I've got you, Philip Desmond, standing in the market-place.") IrPN
Limitary nature of a wall, The. Divisibility. Hyam Plutzik. FiMAP
Limitations. Siegfried Sassoon. MoBrPo
Limitations of Human Art. William Collins. Three Fragments, 2. WaPE
Limited. Carl Sandburg. AmP; LoGBV; MAP; MoAB; MoAmPo; NeMA; OxBA
Limits. Emerson. MWA-1; OA; PoEL-4
Limits. Sister Rita Agnes. JKCP (1955 ed.)
Limits of Submission, The. Faarah Nuur, *tr. fr. Somali by* B. W. Andrzjewski *and* I. M. Lewis. TTY
Limousine up to my brass facade, The. After Mardi Gras. Sister Mary Honora. NePoAm-2
Limpopo and Tugela churned. The Scorpion. William Plomer. AtBAP; BoSA; OBMV; POTE
Lincoln. George Henry Boker. *Fr.* Our Heroic Times. DD; MC; OHIP
Lincoln. John Vance Cheney. DD; OHIP; PEDC
Lincoln. Thomas Curtis Clark. HH
Lincoln. Rembrandt William B. Ditmars. HBMV
Lincoln. Paul Laurence Dunbar. LiPo; OQP
Lincoln. John Gould Fletcher. HBMV; LaNeLa; LiPo; MAP; MoAmPo; NeMA; PaA; SP
Sels.
"Like a gaunt, scaggly pine." PoRL
There Was a Darkness in This Man. PAL; PoFr
Lincoln. Florence Kiper Frank. PGD
Lincoln. Jane L. Hardy. OHIP
Lincoln. Clyde Walton Hill. PEDC; PGD
Lincoln. Julia Ward Howe. PoRL
Lincoln. Vachel Lindsay. *Fr.* The Litany of the Heroes. OHIP
Lincoln ("Nature, they say, doth dote"). James Russell Lowell. *See* Martyr Chief, The.
Lincoln ("Such was he, our Martyr-Chief"). James Russell Lowell. *See* Abraham Lincoln.
Lincoln. S. Weir Mitchell. PAH
Lincoln. Harriet Monroe. *Fr.* Commemoration Ode. AA; LiPo

Lincoln. James Whitcomb Riley. DD; LiPo; OHIP
Lincoln. Corinne Roosevelt Robinson. MaRV; OHIP
Lincoln. Delmore Schwartz. FiMAP
Lincoln. Wendell Phillips Stafford. HH
Lincoln. Maurice Thompson. PEDC
Lincoln. John Townsend Trowbridge. PGD
Lincoln. Nancy Byrd Turner. FaPON; MPB; TiPo
Lincoln. Henry Tyrrell. PEDC
(Lincoln's Way, *much abr.*) HH
(Masterful Man, The, *first* 5 *ll.*) PGD
Lincoln ("Lincoln! When men would name a man"). *Unknown.* OHIP
Lincoln?/ He was a mystery in smoke and flags. Carl Sandburg. *Fr.* The People, Yes. LiPo
"Lincoln?—/ Well, I was in the old Second Maine." A Farmer Remembers Lincoln. Witter Bynner. HH; MAP; MoAmPo (1942 ed.)
Lincoln and Liberty, *with music.* F. A. Simpson. AS; TrAS
Lincoln arose! the masterful great man. Lincoln [*or* The Masterful Man *or* Lincoln's Way]. Henry Tyrrell. HH; PEDC; PGD
Lincoln at Gettysburg. Bayard Taylor. *Fr.* The Gettysburg Ode. PAH
("After the eyes that looked.") OHIP
Lincoln Calls for Volunteers. Stephen Vincent Benét. *Fr.* John Brown's Body. ATP
Lincoln Child, The. James Oppenheim. GA, *abr.*; HBMV; MAP; MoAmPo (1942 ed.)
Lincoln, Come Back. Thomas Curtis Clark. PGD
Lincoln is not dead. He lives. Lincoln Triumphant. Edwin Markham. HH; LiPo; PEDC; PoRL
Lincoln Leads. Minna Irving. HH; OHIP
Lincoln Memorial, The. Alma Adams Wiley. PEDC
Lincoln Portrait, *abr.* Aaron Copland. MaRV
Lincoln, six foot one in his stocking feet. Lincoln Calls for Volunteers. Stephen Vincent Benét. *Fr.* John Brown's Body. ATP
Lincoln Slain. Edwin Markham. LiPo
Lincoln Statue, The. W. F. Collins. OHIP; PGD
Lincoln—the Boy. James Whitcomb Riley. LiPo
Lincoln, the Man of the People. Edwin Markham. BoChLi; HBV; HH; LiPo; MAP; MC; MCCG; MoAmPo; NeMA; OHFP; OHIP; OnPP; PaA; PAH; PAL; PFY; PoMa; PTK; TreFS; TrGrPo; YT
(Lincoln, the Great Commoner.) GN
"Color of the ground was in him, The," *sel.* MaRV; OQP; PGD
Lincoln, the man who freed the slave. A Tribute. *Unknown.* PGD
Lincoln! "Thou shouldst be living at this hour!" "Thou Shouldst Be Living at This Hour." Kenyon West. PGD
Lincoln Triumphant. Edwin Markham. HH; LiPo; PEDC; PoRL
Lincoln was a long man. Abraham Lincoln. Rosemary Benét *and* Stephen Vincent Benét. LiPo; NAMP; PoSC; TiPo; YeAr
Lincoln! When men would name a man. Lincoln. *Unknown.* OHIP
Lincoln's Birthday. John Kendrick Bangs. DD; HH; PGD
Lincoln's Birthday. Richard Henry Stoddard. *See* Abraham Lincoln.
Lincoln's Birthday—1918. John Kendrick Bangs. DD; HH
Lincoln's Dream. Ridgely Torrence. LiPo
Lincoln's Grave, *sel.* Maurice Thompson.
Prophecy, A. AA
Lincoln's Way. Henry Tyrrell. *See* Lincoln.
Lincolnshire Poacher, The. *Unknown.* CH; OnMSP; OxBoLi; SD
(Poacher, The.) WiR
Lincolnshire Remembered. Frances Cornford. HaMV
Lincolnshire Tale, A. John Betjeman. FiSC
Lindbergh. Aline Michaelis. DD
Lindbergh. Angela Morgan. DD
Linden blossomed, the nightingale sang, The. Farewell. Heine. AWP
Linden Lea. William Barnes. GTSE
Linden Tree, The. Dietmar von Aist, *tr. fr. German by* Edgar Taylor. PoPl
Line-Gang, The. Robert Frost. FIW
Line in long array where they wind betwixt green islands, A. Cavalry Crossing a Ford. Walt Whitman. AA; AmePo; AmP; AmPP; AP; BWP; CABA; CBEP; CBV; ChTr; CoBA; MaPo; MWA-1; NoP; OxBA; Po; PoPl; PoPo; RePo; StP; TDP; UnPo (3d ed.)
Line of an American Poet, The Reed Whittemore. MoVE; PPON
Line of Beauty, The. Edward Dowden. OnYI
Line of light, A! it is the inland sea. Mare Mediterraneum. John Nichol. VA
Lineage. Robert Farren. CoBE
Lineage. Margaret Walker. BOLo; Kal
Lineman. Gerald Raftery. PoMa
Lineman Calling. Josephine Miles. FiMAP
Linen Bands. Vance Thompson. AA
Liner She's a Lady, The. Kipling. FaBV
Lines, The. Randall Jarrell. CrMA
Lines: Addressed to —— on the 29th of September, When We Parted for the Last Time. *Unknown.* BOHV
Lines: "By this the sun was all one glitter." John Masefield. *Fr.* The Everlasting Mercy. GBV
Lines: "Child, A, said, '*What is the grass?*' " Walt Whitman. *See* Grass.
Lines: "Clear had the day been from the dawn." Michael Drayton. *See* Fine Day, A.
Lines: "Cold earth slept below, The." Shelley. AnEnPo; ChER; EnRP; LoBV; NCEP; SyP
(Cold Earth Slept Below, The.) PeER
Lines: "Here often, when a child I lay reclined." Tennyson. CABA; StP
Lines: "Homeless man goes, even on life's sunniest slope." William Hurrell Mallock. ACP (1926 ed.); JKCP (1926 ed.)
Lines: "How lovely is the heaven of this night." Thomas Lovell Beddoes. *See* Beautiful Night, A.
Lines: "Hurry me Nymphs! O, hurry me." George Darley. *See* Hurry Me Nymphs.
Lines: "I followed once a fleet and mighty serpent" *See* Subterranean City, A.
Lines: "I have been cherish'd and forgiven." Hartley Coleridge. NBM; PoEL-4
Lines: "In men whom men condemn as ill." Joaquin Miller. *See* In Men Whom Men Condemn.
Lines: "In the day the sun is darkened." Stopford Augustus Brooke. IrPN
Lines: "Love within the lover's breast." George Meredith. HBV
Lines: "Mine ears have heard your distant moan." J. C. Squire. WhC
Lines: "Nay, traveller! rest." Wordsworth. *See* Lines Left upon a Seat in a Yew-Tree.
Lines: "Shall earth no more inspire thee." Emily Brontë. *See* Shall Earth No More Inspire Thee?
Lines: "Slumber did my spirit seal, A." Wordsworth. *See* Slumber Did My Spirit Seal, A.
Lines: "Sun that brief December day, The." Whittier. *See* Winter Day.
Lines: "This living hand, now warm and capable." Keats. *See* Lines Supposed to Have Been Addressed to Fanny Brawne.
Lines: "Though all the Fates should prove unkind." Henry David Thoreau. *See* Though All the Fates Should Prove Unkind.
Lines: "Unwarmed by any sunset light." Whittier. *Fr.* Snow-bound. GBV
Lines: "When I am lost in the deep body of the mist on a hill." Yone Noguchi. NP
Lines: "When the lamp is shattered." Shelley. BWP; EnL; EnLi-2; EnLit; EnRP; EPN; ERoP-2; ForPo; ILP; LoBV; MaPo; MBW-2; MERP; NoP; OAEP; OBEV; OBNC; PAn; PoE; PoEL-4; TOP; VaPo; ViBoPo
(Flight of Love, The.) GTBS; GTBS-D; GTBS-P; GTBS-W; GTSE; GTSL; HBV; PoLF
(When the Lamp Is Shattered.) AnFE; BEL; BoLiVe; CBEP; CH; CoBE; EG; FiP; LiTG; MCCG; OBRV; PG; PoFS; ShBV-4; TreFT; TrGrPo; UnPo (1st ed.); WHA
Lines: "When youthful faith hath fled." John Gibson Lockhart. OBEV (new ed.); OBVV
Lines: "You drop a tear for those that die." Aubrey Thomas De Vere. IrPN
Lines Addressed to a Seagull. Gerald Griffin. OnYI
Lines Based on a 1924 Advertisement. Geoffrey Lehmann. NYTB
Lines before Execution. Chidiock Tichborne. *See* Elegy: "My prime of youth is but a frost of cares."
Lines beneath the Portrait of Milton. Dryden. *See* Lines Print-

Lines (continued)
ed under the Engraved Portrait of Milton.
Lines beyond, The. Soft Rain. Sophia Castro-Leon. QAH
Lines by a Fond Lover. *Unknown.* NA
Lines by a Medium. *Unknown.* NA
Lines by a Person of Quality. J. B. B. Nichols. VA
Lines by a Person of Quality. *At. to* Pope *and to* Swift. InMe; NA
Lines Composed a Few Miles above Tintern Abbey. Wordsworth. BEL; BoLiVe; BWP; CABA; CaFP; CBV; ChER; CoBE; DiPo; EnL; EnLi-2; EnLit; EnRP; EPN; ERoP-1; ExPo; FaPL; ForPo; GoTL; HBV; ILP; InP; LoBV; MaPo; MasP; MBW-2; MCCG; MERP; NoP; OAEP; OBNC; OBRV; OuHeWo; PAn; PeER; PIA; PoAN; PoEL-4; PoeP; PoFS; PoIE; SeCePo; SeCeV; StP; TOP; TreFS; TrGrPo; UnPo (1st ed.); WHA
(Lines Written a Few Miles above Tintern Abbey.) CABL
(Tintern Abbey.) LiTB; PoE
Sels.
"And now, with gleams of half-extinguished thought." ViBoPo
"For nature then/ (The coarser pleasures of my boyish days)." ACV
"For I have learned/ To look on nature." OQP
("I have learned/ To look on nature.") TRV
(Lines Written above Tintern Abbey.) BBV
I Have Felt a Presence. MaRV
"Sounding cataract, The/ Haunted me." BoPe; FaBoEn; WGRP
"That best portion of a good man's life," *br. sel.* PoToHe
This Prayer I Make. PoToHe
Lines Composed at Grasmere. Wordsworth. MBW-2; OBRV
Lines Composed in a Concert-Room. Samuel Taylor Coleridge. MuSP
Lines Descriptive of Thomson's Island. Benjamin Lynde. SCAP
Lines for a Bed at Kelmscott Manor. William Morris. *See* Inscription for an Old Bed.
Lines for a Dead Poet. David Ferry. ML; PP
Lines for a Drawing of Our Lady of the Night. Francis Thompson. ISi
Lines for a Feast of Our Lady. Sister Maris Stella. ISi
Lines for a Night Driver. Peter Kane Dufault. WIRo
Lines for a Sundial. Thomas Herbert Warren. OBVV
Lines for a Wedding Gift. Wesley Trimpi. NePoEA
Lines for an Eminent Poet and Critic. Patric Dickinson. POTi; PV
Lines for an Interment. Archibald MacLeish. CMoP; InP; MaRV
Lines for an Old Man. T. S. Eliot. FaBoTw; MoPW; MWA-2
Lines for Cuscuscaraway and Mirza Murad Ali Beg. T. S. Eliot. FiBHP; MaPo (1969 ed.); ML; PoPl
Lines for the Hour. Hamilton Fish Armstrong. HBMV; MaRV; MC
Lines for the Margin of an Old Gospel. Sheila Wingfield. ChMP
Lines from a Sampler. *Unknown.* ThGo
Lines from an Elegy on the Death of His Wife. Kakinomoto no Asomi Hitomaro, *tr. fr. Japanese by* Clara A. Walsh. LiTW
Lines from Catullus. Sir Walter Ralegh, *after the Latin of* Catullus. EnRePo; SiPS
("Sun may set and rise, The.") FCP
Lines from Crotchet Castle. Thomas Love Peacock. PV
Lines from Love Letters. *Unknown.* OBEV (new ed.)
(To the One I Love Most.) MeEL
Lines from the Blues. *Unknown.* OuSiCo
Lines grow slack in our hands at full high-water, The. Rock Carving. Douglas Stewart. NeLNL; SeCePo
Lines in a Young Lady's Album. Thomas Hood. *See* I'm Not a Single Man.
Lines in Dispraise of Dispraise. Ogden Nash. NAMP
Lines in Order to Be Slandered. Paul Verlaine, *tr. fr. French by* T. Sturge Moore. SyP
Lines Inscribed upon a Cup Formed from a Skull. Byron. PeER
Lines Left upon a Seat in a Yew Tree. Wordsworth. EPN; MBW-2
(Lines: "Nay, traveller! rest.") MCCG
Lines of the Lords of Tartary, The. The Pipe of Peace. F. L. Lucas. HaMV
Lines on a Bill of Mortality, 1790. William Cowper. OxBoCh
Lines on a Certain Friend's Remarkable Faculty for Swift Generalization. Max Beerbohm. PV
Lines on a Mysterious Occurrence. Alfred Denis Godley. CenHV
Lines on a Purple Cap Received as a Present from My Brother. George Alsop. SCAP
Lines on a Re-reading of Parts of the Old Testament, *sel.* Wilfred Campbell.
"Sublimity! Sublimity! I lay thee down." InP
Lines on a Young Lady's Photograph Album. Philip Larkin. EnLoPo; NoP; ToPo
Lines on Carmen Sylva. Emma Lazarus. TrJP
Lines on Hearing the Organ. Charles Stuart Calverley. CenHV; FiBHP; InMe; NBM
Lines on His Birthday. John Logan. FRC
Lines on His Companions Who Died in the Northern Seas. Thomas James. SeCL
Lines on Isabella Markham. John Harington. *See* Sonnet Made on Isabella Markham, A.
Lines on Leaving a Scene in Bavaria. Thomas Campbell. OBNC
Lines on Milton. Dryden. *See* Lines Printed under the Engraved Portrait of Milton.
Lines on Mountain Villages. "Sunset Joe." PoOW
Lines on Receiving His Mother's Picture. William Cowper. *See* On the Receipt of My Mother's Picture Out of Norfolk.
Lines on the Antiquity of Microbes. Strickland Gillilan. *See* On the Antiquity of Microbes.
Lines on the Author's Death. Burns. PV
(On the Author.) CBEP
Lines on the Back of a Confederate Note. Samuel Alroy Jonas. BLPA; PaA
Lines on the Celebrated Picture by Leonardo da Vinci, Called the Virgin of the Rocks. Charles Lamb. ISi
Lines on the Death of Bismarck. John Jay Chapman. PoEL-5
Lines on the Death of Mr. Levett. Samuel Johnson. *See* On the Death of Mr. Robert Levet, a Practiser in Physic.
Lines on the Execution of King Charles I. James Graham, Marquess of Montrose. *See* Epitaph on King Charles I.
Lines on the Loss of the *Titanic.* Thomas Hardy. *See* Convergence of the Twain, The.
Lines on the Mermaid Tavern. Keats. AWP; BEL; CoBE; DiPo; EnLi-2; EnLit; EnRP; EPN; HBV; ILP; InMe; InPo; LoBV; MERP; ML; OAEP; OBRV; OTPC (1923 ed.); PoeP; PoRA; PP; SeCeV; TOP; TreFS; ViBoPo
(Mermaid Tavern, The.) ATP; FaBoBe; GTBS; GTBS-D; GTBS-P; GTBS-W; GTSE; GTSL; InvP; PoFS
Lines on the Sea. Dilys Bennett Laing. NYBP
Lines on the Tombs in Westminster. *At. to* Francis Beaumont *and to* William Basse. *See* On the Tombs in Westminster Abbey.
Lines on the Wall of His Prison Cell. Luis de León. *See* Written on the Walls of His Dungeon.
Lines on War. Burns. *See* I Murder Hate by Field or Flood.
Lines Printed under the Engraved Portrait of Milton. Dryden. BEL; CEP; EiPP; InP; SeCeV; SeCV-2; TOP
(Epigram on Milton.) BoLiVe; EnLi-1 (1939 ed.); EnLit; MBW-1; TrGrPo
(Lines beneath the Portrait of Milton.) SeEP
(Lines on Milton.) YAT
(Portrait of Milton.) ACP
(Under the Portrait of [John] Milton.) HBV; WHA
Lines Scratched in Wet Cement. Ethel Jacobson. ShM
Lines Spoken by a Boy of Seven Years. David Everett. *See* Tall Oaks from Little Acorns Grow.
Lines Suggested by the Fourteenth of February ("Darkness succeeds to twilight"). Charles Stuart Calverley. ALV
Lines Suggested by the Fourteenth of February ("Ere the morn the East has crimsoned"). Charles Stuart Calverley. InMe
Lines Supposed to Have Been Addressed to Fanny Brawne. Keats. BoLP; ELU; ERoP-2; NCEP; OBNC
(Lines: "This living hand, now warm and capable.") ChER
(This Living Hand.) CABA; MBW-2; NoP; SyP
Lines to a Blind Girl. Thomas Buchanan Read. AA
Lines to a Critic. Shelley. CBEP; EPN; MERP
Lines to a Don. Hilaire Belloc. MoBrPo; OtMeF
Lines to a Dragon Fly. Walter Savage Landor. *See* Dragon-Fly, The.

Lines to a Lady, Who Asked of Him How Long He Would Love Her. Sir George Etherege. *See* To a Lady Asking [Him] How Long He Would Love Her.
Lines to a Man Who Thinks that Apple Betty with Hard Sauce Is Food for a Human Being. George S. Kaufman. InMe
Lines to a Movement in Mozart's E-Flat Symphony. Thomas Hardy. BoLP; ELP
Lines to a Nasturtium (a Lover Muses). Anne Spencer. AmNP; CDC; PoNe
Lines to a Young Lady. Edward Lear. *See* How Pleasant to Know Mr. Lear.
Lines to an Indian Air. Shelley. *See* Indian Serenade, The.
Lines to Dr. Ditmars. Kenneth Allan Robinson. ImOP; PoMa
Lines to Fanny, *sels.* Keats.
To Dream of Thee. MeWo
"Where shall I learn to get my peace again?" ChER
Lines to Garcia Lorca. LeRoi Jones. NNP
Lines to His Son on Reaching Adolescence. John Logan. NePoEA-2
Lines to Homo Somejerktensis. Earnest A. Hooton. WhC
Lines to Miss Florence Huntingdon. *Unknown, at. to* James De Mille. BOHV; NA
(Maiden of Passamaquoddy, The.) WhC
(Sweet Maiden of Passamaquoddy.) WHW, *abr.*
Lines to Mr. Hodgson. Byron. ERoP-2; PoE
Lines to My Father. Leslie Daiken. NeIP; OxBI
Lines to Our Elders. Countee Cullen. CDC
Lines to Ralph Hodgson Esqre. T. S. Eliot. MaPo (1969 ed.)
Lines to Ratclif. Earl of Surrey. *See* Exhortation to Learn by Others' Trouble.
Lines to the Blessed Sacrament. James Joseph Callanan. OnYI
Lines to the Unborn. Patrick D. Waddington. TwCaPo
Lines to William Linley while He Sang a Song to Purcell's Music. Samuel Taylor Coleridge. MuSP
"Lines twelve to twenty are in great dispute." Classical Criticism. George Lynde Richardson. AA
Lines with a Gift of Herbs. Janet Lewis. QFR
Lines, Written [a Few Miles] above Tintern Abbey. Wordsworth. *See* Lines Composed a Few Miles above Tintern Abbey.
Lines Written after a Battle. *Unknown.* BOHV; InMe
Lines Written after the Discovery by the Author of the Germ of Yellow Fever. Sir Ronald Ross. ImOP; MaRV
(Reply.) InP
Lines Written among the Euganean Hills. Shelley. EnRP; PoEL-4
("Many a green isle needs must be," *abr.*) GTBS
(Written among the Euganean Hills, North Italy.) GTSE, *abr.*; GTSL, *much abr.*
(Written in the Euganean Hills, North Italy.) GTBS-D; GTBS-P; GTBS-W
"'Mid the mountains Euganean," *sel.* ViBoPo
Lines Written at Cambridge, to W. R., Esquire. Phineas Fletcher. ElL
Lines Written at Geneva; July 16, 1824. Thomas Lovell Beddoes. ERoP-2
Lines Written at the Grave of Alexandre [*or* Alexander] Dumas. Gwendolyn B. Bennett. CDC; PoNe
Lines Written at the Temple of the Holy Sepulchre. George Sandys. BePJ
Lines Written during a Period of Insanity. William Cowper. FiP; InPo; NoP; PeER
(Lines Written under the Influence of Delirium.) AtBAP; PoEL-3
Lines Written in a Blank Leaf of the Prometheus Unbound. Thomas Lovell Beddoes. ERoP-2
Lines Written in a Country Parson's Orchard. Leslie Daiken. OnYI
Lines Written in a Mausoleum. Lillian Grant. GoYe
Lines Written in a Moment of Vibrant Ill-Health. Morris Bishop. WhC
Lines Written in an Album at Malta. Byron. InP
Lines Written in Dejection. W. B. Yeats. MBW-2
Lines Written in Early Spring. Wordsworth. ACV; BEL; CBEP; CoBe; EnLi-2; EnLit; EnRP; EPN; ERoP-1; HBV; MBW-2; MCCG; OAEP; OBRV; PeER; PG; PoE; PoLF; PoMa; PoPo; StP
(What Man Has Made of Man.) MaRV
(Written in Early Spring.) GTBS; GTBS-D; GTBS-P; GTBS-W; GTSE; GTSL; ILP; TOP; TreFT; TRV
Lines Written in Her Breviary. St. Teresa of Avila, *tr. fr. Spanish by* Longfellow. AWP; CAW; EaLo; MaRV; OnPM; SoP; TRV
(Alone God Sufficeth.) OQP
(Bookmark.) CTC
(God Alone Suffices.) FaChP
(St. Teresa's Book-Mark.) BoC, *tr. by* E. Allison Peers; TreFT; WHL
(Santa Teresa's Book-Mark.) PoEL-5
Lines Written in Kensington Gardens. Matthew Arnold. EnLi-2; EPN; MBW-2; PoVP; ViPo; ViPP
Calm Soul of All Things, *sel.* TRV; WGRP
("Calm soul of all things! make it mine.") TrPWD
(Inward Peace.) MaRV
Lines Written in Objection, or, The Limpopo Express. Phillip Hey. YAP
Lines Written in Oregon. Vladimir Nabokov. NYBP
Lines Written in Ridicule of Certain Poems Published in 1777. Samuel Johnson. EiPP
Lines Written in the Album at Elbingerode. Samuel Taylor Coleridge. ERoP-1
Lines Written in the Bay of Lerici. Shelley. ERoP-2
Lines Written in Windsor Forest. Pope. SiSw
Lines Written Near Richmond, upon the Thames, at Evening. Wordsworth. EiCL; OBEC
Lines Written on a Window-Shutter at Weston. William Cowper. EiCP
Lines Written on Hearing the News of the Death of Napoleon. Shelley. ChER; ERoP-2
Lines Written on November 15, 1933, by a Man Born November 14, 1881, to Another Born November 15, 1881. Clayton Hamilton. InMe
Line Written on the Antiquity of Microbes. Strickland Gillilan. *See* On the Antiquity of Microbes.
Lines Written the Night Before His Execution. Sir Walter Ralegh. *See* Conclusion, The.
Lines Written under the Influence of Delirium. William Cowper. *See* Lines Written during a Period of Insanity.
Line-up, A. *Unknown.* PCH
("One to make ready.") OxNR
Line-up for Yesterday. Ogden Nash. SD
Linger awhile upon some bending planks. Minnows. Keats. BoPe
Linger Not! Horatius Bonar. SoP
Linger not long. Home is not home without thee. The Wife to Her Husband. *Unknown.* HBV
Lingering sunset across the plain, The. The Gila Monster Route. L. F. Post *and* Glenn Norton. ABF; SCC
Lingua, *sel. At. to* Thomas Tomkis.
Gordian Knot, The. ElL
Link, The. Robert Lowth. WaPE
Link o' Day, *with music. Unknown.* TrAS
Linked to a clod, harassed, and sad. Circumstance. Thomas Bailey Aldrich. AA
Links are chance, the chain is fate, The. Mathematics of Love. Michael Hamburger. NePoEA-2
Links of Chance, The. Edward Rowland Sill. PFY
Linnet, The. Robert Bridges. *See* I Heard a Linnet Courting.
Linnet, The. Walter de la Mare. HBMV; LiTB; LoBV; NP
Linnet in a Gilded Cage, A. Christina Rossetti. UTS
Linnet in the Rocky Dells, The. Emily Brontë. *See* Song: "Linnet in the rocky dells, The."
Linnet who had lost her way, A. Tenebris Interlucentem. James Elroy Flecker. CBEP; MoBrPo
Linota Rufescens. Lyle Donaghy. OnYI
Lintie in a Cage. Alice V. Stuart. OxBS
Lion, The. Hilaire Belloc. MoBrPo; TSW; UTS
Lion, A. Joseph G. Francis. MPB
Lion. Mary Fullerton. PoAu-1
Lion, The. Mary Howitt. FaPON; OTPC
Lion, The. Vachel Lindsay. HBMV (2d ed.); InP; RePo; ShM; UTS
Lion. Mary Britton Miller. UTS
Lion, The. Ogden Nash. CenHV; MemP; ShM
Lion. Kenneth Rexroth. *Fr.* A Bestiary. HoPM
Lion. May Swenson. LiTM (1970 ed.)
Lion, The. W. J. Turner. MoBrPo; TrGrPo (1942 ed.)
Lion. *Unknown, tr. fr. Hottentot.* PeSA
Lion & Honeycomb. Howard Nemerov. PP
Lion and O'Reilly, The. Richard Weber. PPON

Lion and the Cub, The. John Gay. *Fr.* Fables. GN; HBV; OTPC (1923 ed.)
Lion and the Lamb, The. Elinor Wylie. CoBA
Lion and the Mouse, The. Jefferys Taylor. HBV; HBVY; OnMSP; OTPC; RePo
Lion and the unicorn, The. Mother Goose. BoTP; EvOK; FOL; HBV; OTPC; OxBoLi, *diff. vers.*; OxNR; PPL; SiTL
Lion at Noon, The. Victor Hugo, *tr. fr. French by* Eva Martin. LiTW
Lion Cub, of sordid mind, A. The Lion and the Cub. John Gay. GN; HBV; OTPC (1923 ed.)
Lion emerged from his lair, A. A Lion. Joseph G. Francis. MPB
Lion, even when full of mud, with burrs, The. Birds. Ruth Miller. PeSA
Lion Grown Old, The. La Fontaine, *tr. fr. French by* Elizur Wright. OnPM
Lion has a tail and a very fine tail, A. In the Fashion. A. A. Milne. RePo
Lion, he prowleth far and near, The. The Hunters. Ruth Temple Lindsay. JKCP
Lion heart, the ounce gave active might, The. The Gifts of the Animals to Man. Sir Philip Sidney. *Fr.* Arcadia. OA
Lion-House, The. John Hall Wheelock. HBMV
Lion-hunger, tiger-leap! The Way of Cape Race. E. J. Pratt. CoBE; EtS; WHW
Lion is a beast to fight, The. *See* Lion is the beast to fight, The.
Lion is a kingly beast, The. The Lion. Vachel Lindsay. HBMV (2d ed.); InP; RePo; ShM; UTS
Lion is called the king, The. Lion. Kenneth Rexroth. *Fr.* A Bestiary. HoPM
Lion is the [*or* a] beast to fight, The. Sage Counsel. Sir Arthur Quiller-Couch. CenHV; HBV; HBVY; LBN; NA
Lion, Leopard, Lady. Douglas Le Pan. OBCV
Lion, mourning, in his age, the wane, A. The Lion Grown Old. La Fontaine. OnPM
Lion Named Passion, A. John Hollander. NePoEA-2
Lion of my sun, my fiery joy. The Psalm of St. Priapus. James Broughton. ErPo
Lion of St. Mark's upon the glass, The. Her Dead Brother. Robert Lowell. NePoEA
Lion of Winter, The. Shakespeare. *See* Now the Hungry Lion Roars.
Lion over the Tomb of Leonidas, The. *Unknown, tr. fr. Greek by* Walter Leaf. AWP; JAWP; WBP
Lion roars at the Enraging Desert, The. Wallace Stevens. Notes toward a Supreme Fiction, V. MoPo; NePA
Lion sleeps with open eyes, The. Faces from a Bestiary. X. J. Kennedy. NePoEA-2
Lion standeth on a hill, The; if he hear a man hunting. The Lion's Nature. *Unknown. Fr.* The Bestiary. MeEV
Lion tamers wrestle with the lions in a cage, The. Apex. Nate Salsbury. InMe; WhC
Lion, the Fox, and the Geese, The. John Gay. *Fr.* Fables. EiCP
Lion, the lion, he dwells in the waste, The. The Lion. Hilaire Belloc. MoBrPo; TSW; UTS
Lion, thou are girt with might! The Lion. Mary Howitt. OTPC
Lion, tired with state affairs, A. The Lion, the Fox, and the Geese. John Gay. *Fr.* Fables. EiCP
Lion walks on padded paws, The. How Creatures Move. *Unknown.* GFA
Lion with the heat oppressed, A. The Lion and the Mouse. Jefferys Taylor. HBV; HBVY; OnMSP; OTPC; RePo
Lion, you were once the King. Lion. Mary Britton Miller. UTS
Lioness whelped, and the sturdy cub, The. The Eagle's Song. Richard Mansfield. DD; HBV; HBVY; MC; PaA; PAH
Lions and tigers dominate. Jungle. Mary Carter Smith. PoNe (1970 ed.)
Lion's Cub, The. Maurice Thompson. AA
Lion's Nature, The. *Unknown, tr. fr. Middle English. Fr.* The Bestiary. MeEV
Lions of the hill are gone, The. Deirdre's Lament for the Sons of Usnach. *Unknown.* IrPN; OnYI; SeCePo
Lions on the mountains I've drove them to their lairs, The. Dodge City, the End of the Trail. *Unknown.* CoSo
Lions Running over the Green. Annette Wynne. UTS
Lion's Skeleton, The. Charles Tennyson Turner. NBM; OA; VA
Lip. J. V. Cunningham. ErPo
("Lip was a man who used his head.") PV
Lip and the Heart, The. John Quincy Adams. AA; AmLP; LHV; OTD
Lip Service. Helen G. Quigless. TNV
Lip was a man who used his head. Lip. J. V. Cunningham. ErPo; PV
Lip which had once been stolid, now moving, A. Divine Love. Michael Benedikt. CoAP; YAP
Lips and Eyes. Thomas Middleton. *See* Song: "Love for such a cherry lip."
Lips hardened by winter's dumb duress. Boy with a Mouth Organ. James Kirkup. MuSP
Lips, lips, open. A Sleeping Child. Arthur Hugh Clough. PRWS
Lips of the Christ-child are like to twin leaves, The. The Christ-Child. St. Gregory of Narek. CAW
Lips of the Wise, The. Proverbs, XV: 1-5, 7-8, 15-17, Bible, *O.T.* TrGrPo
(Merry Heart, A, XV: 1, 13, 15-17.) StVeCh
("Soft answer turneth away wrath, A," XV: 1.) TiPo (1952 ed.)
Lips That Touch Liquor. George W. Young. TreFT
Lips That Touch Liquor Shall Never Touch Mine, The. Harriet A. Glazebrook. PaPo
Lips that touch wine jelly. Wine Jelly. *Unknown.* WhC
Liquid'll. Alfred Starr Hamilton. QAH
Liquids. Merrill Moore. PoMa
Liquor & Longevity. *Unknown.* LiTG; SiTL; WhC
Liquor and Love. The World Narrowed to a Point. William Carlos Williams. MoLP
Liquor don't drown. Blues. Quandra Prettyman. BOLo
Lise. Rose Terry Cooke. AA
Lis'en to de Lam's, *with music. Unknown.* BoAN-1
Lissen to my story. John Henry (B *vers.*). *Unknown.* ViBoFo
List no more the ominous din. George Darley. *Fr.* Nepenthe. OBRV
List the harp in window wailing. The Aeolian Harp. Herman Melville. AmePo; AmPP (5th ed.); AP; MAmP; MWA-1
List to an old-time lay of the Spear-Danes. Beowulf. *Unknown.* EnLi-1
List to me, as when ye heard our father. *See* Listen to me . . .
List to that bird! His song—what poet pens it? The Mocking-Bird. Ednah Proctor Clarke. AA
List to the song of the chickadee. Song of the Chickadee. *Unknown.* OTPC (1946 ed.); PCH
List while the poet trolls. The Rival Curates. W. S. Gilbert. CenHV
Listed by beauty's conquering charms. Proud Chloe's Heart. Horace. OnPM
Listen. E. E. Cummings. WaaP
Listen. Charles Patterson. NBP
Lis/ -ten/ you know what I mean. Listen. E. E. Cummings. WaaP
Listen:/ There roams, far away, by the waters of Clead. Nikolai Gumilev. *Fr.* The Giraffe. FaPON
Listen . . ./ With faint dry sound. November Night. Adelaide Crapsey. AnAmPo; FaPON; MAP; MoAmPo (1942 ed.); MPB; NeMA; NP; PFY; WePo
Listen a moment, I pray you; what was that sound that I heard. A Sign of Spring. Eben Eugene Rexford. PCH; PEDC
Listen a while, the moon is a lovely woman. Night Stuff. Carl Sandburg. NP; TSW
Listen all ye, tis the Feast o' St. Stephen. Feast o' St. Stephen. Ruth Sawyer. OHIP
Listen and I'll tell you about Willie the Weeper. Willie the Weeper. *Unknown.* ABF; BLPA
Listen, and when thy hand this paper presses. A Letter from a Girl to Her Own Old Age. Alice Meynell. GoTL; GTBS-W; LiTB; MoBrPo; ViBoPo
Listen, children:/ Your father is dead. Lament. Edna St. Vincent Millay. PoPl; PoPo
Listen, children, listen, won't you come into the night? Who Calls? Frances Clarke. HH; PoRh; SiSoSe; StaSt; TSW
Listen, David! Josephine Jacobsen. JKCP (1955 ed.)

Listen! Do you hear the winging. Angel Voices. Mary B. Stevenson. ChIP
Listen, gallants, to my words. The Commonwealth of Birds. James Shirley. GoBC
Listen here, Joe. Without Benefit of Declaration. Langston Hughes. AmNP; TTY
Listen! I will be honest with you. Walt Whitman. *Fr.* Song of the Open Road. PoFr
Listen, I will tell thee what is done in the caverns of the grave. Enion Replies from the Caverns of the Grave. Blake. *Fr.* Vala; or, The Four Zoas. OBNC
Listen! In the April rain. In the April Rain. Mary Anderson. BoTP
Listen! It is the summer's self that ambles. The Good Humor Man. Phyllis McGinley. MoShBr
Listen jealous man. A Jealous Man. *Unknown.* KiLC
Listen, lass, if you would be. Caution. *Unknown.* UnTE
Listen, listen! The small song bird. Song to Imogen (in Basic English). Richard L. Greene. WhC
Listen, lively lordings all. The Rising in the North. *Unknown.* ACP; BaBo; ESPB
Listen, Lord. James Weldon Johnson. BANP
Listen lordings both great and small. The Murder of Saint Thomas of Kent. *Unknown.* ACP
Listen, men!/ The scratching friar. Ballyhoo for a Mendicant. Carlton Talbott. AnAmPo
Listen more often. Breaths. Birago Diop. TTY
Listen, my children, and you shall hear. Paul Revere's Ride. Longfellow. *Fr.* Tales of a Wayside Inn. AmePo; AmPP (4th ed.); AnNE; BBV; BeLS; BLPA; CaFP; CoBA; DD; FaBoBe; FaBV; FaFP; FaPON; GoTP; HBV; HBVY; LoGBV; MC; NeHB; OHFP; OnSP; OTD; PaA; PAH; PAL; PAP; PaPo; PEDC; PoFr; PoRL; PTK; RePo; RIS; StPo; StVeCh; ThLM; TiPo (1952 ed.); TreF: TrGrPo; WBLP; YaD
Listen now and ye may lere. The Burgesses of Calais. Laurence Minot. ACP
Listen! Now I have come to step over your soul. Sacred Formula to Destroy Life. *Unknown.* LiTA
"Listen, now, verse should be as natural." Poetry for Supper. R. S. Thomas. POTi; ToPo
Listen now, whoever you may be. To the Faithful. Marcos Ana. BoC
Listen, Pigeon, Bend an Ear. H. W. Haenigsen. WhC
Listen. Put on Morning. W. S. Graham. FaBoTw; LiTM (1970 ed.); NMP; OPoP
Listen sweet Dove unto my song. Whitsunday. George Herbert. AtBAP; MaMe
Listen, the hay-bells tinkle as the cart. The Holy Innocents. Robert Lowell. ATP (1953 ed.); InPo; InvP; MoAB; MoAmPo (1950 ed.); NePoEA; PoAn; PoDB; PoeP; TDP; ToPo
Listen. The wind is still. Spring Thunder. Mark Van Doren. WIRo
Listen [*or* List] to me, as when ye heard our father. The Canadian Boat Song. *Unknown, at. to* John Galt. BLPA; CaP; CBEP; FaBoCh; GoTS; LoGBV; OBEV (new ed.); OBNC; OBRV
Listen to me there have. Freddy the Rat Perishes. Don Marquis. *Fr.* Archy and Mehitabel. OCS
Listen to my story— 'tis a story true. John Henry. *Unknown.* TrAS
Listen to the cicada's burning drone. The Cicada. H. M. Green. PoAu-1
Listen to the exhortation of the Dawn! The Salutation of the Dawn. *Unknown.* MaRV; PoLF; TIHL; TreFT
Listen to the kitchen clock. The Old Kitchen Clock. Ann Hawkshaw. BoTP; OTPC (1923 ed.)
Listen to the lyre! The Lyre [*or* The Enchanted Lyre]. George Darley. LO; OBVV
Listen to the Mocking-Bird. Septimus Winner. TrAS, *with music*; TreFT
Listen to the mournful drums of a strange funeral. A Strange Funeral in Braddock. Michael Gold. WOW
Listen to the Muse's lyre. Odes of Anacreon, *tr. by* Thomas Moore. OuHeWo
Listen to the People: Independence Day, 1941, *sel.* Stephen Vincent Benét.
"This is Independence Day." PoSC
Listen to the roar of your liberation! Angelos Sikelianos. *Fr.* On Death. LiTW
Listen to the song. Wandering Jack. Emile Jacot. BoTP
Listen to the story of Willie the Weeper. Willie the Weeper. *Unknown.* ABF; BeLS; BLPA; YaD
Listen to the tale. Slim Greer. Sterling A. Brown. BALP; BANP
Listen to the tawny thief. Bacchus. Frank Dempster Sherman. MAP
Listen to the water mill. The Lesson of the Water Mill [*or* The Water Mill]. Sarah Doudney. *Fr.* The Man o' Airlie. BLPA; HBV; PoToHe; TreFS; WGRP
Listen to this. Condemnation. Thich Nhat Hanh. PPON
Listen Zulus. Lalela Zulu. *Unknown.* PeSA
Listene/ secting. Clark Coolidge. ANYP
Listeners, The. Walter de la Mare. AnFE; AWP; BBV (1951 ed.); BoLiVe; BrPo; CaFP; CMoP; CoBMV; EnLit; FaFP; FaPON; GTBS-D; GTBS-W; GTSL; HBV; HBVY; HoPM; ILP; InP; InvP; JAWP; LiTB; LiTM; MaC; MaRV; MemP; MoAB; MoBrPo; MoPo; MoVE; NAMP; NeMA; NP; OAEP (2d ed.); OBEV (new ed.); OBMV; OBVV; OnMSP; OtMeF; PCD; Po; PoPl; PoPo; PoRA; POTE; RePo; SeCeV; ShBV-3; ThWaDe; TOP; TreF; TrGrPo; ViBoPo; WBP; WHA
Listener's Guide to the Birds, A. E. B. White. NYBP
Listening. Amy Lowell. PoPo
Listening. William Stafford. PIA
Listening Dryads hushed the woods, The. The Pewee. John Townsend Trowbridge. HBV; OTPC
Listening, listening; it is never still. The Märchen. Randall Jarrell. CMoP; FiMAP
Listening to a Broadcast. John Manifold. WaP
Listening to Foxhounds. James Dickey. WIRo
Listening to Handel's "Messiah". A. L. Rowse. MuSP
Listening to the Mourners. James Wright. FRC
Listeth, lordes, in good entent. Sir Thopas. Chaucer. *Fr.* The Canterbury Tales. BEL; Par
Listless beauty of the hour, The. History. D. H. Lawrence. BrPo
Listless he eyes the palisades. In the Prison Pen. Herman Melville. MWA-1; PoEL-5
Lisy's Parting with Her Cat. James Thomson. CIV
Liszt. E. C. Bentley. *Fr.* Clerihews. UnS
Litanie, The. John Donne. *See* Litany, The.
Litanies of Satan, The. Baudelaire. *See* Litany to Satan.
Litany [*or* Litanie], The. John Donne. AtBAP; MaMe; PoEL-2
"From being anxious, or secure," *sel.* EnLit; MBW-1, 2 *sts.*; OxBoCh, 4 *sts.*
Litany, A: "Drop, drop, slow tears." Phineas Fletcher. *See* Hymn, An: "Drop, drop, slow tears."
Litany: "From all that terror teaches". G. K. Chesterton. *Fr.* A Hymn. OtMeF
Litany: "I hold the splendid daylight in my hands." George Campbell. PoNe
Litany: "Oh, by Thy cross and passion." Marie LeNart. ChIP
Litany, A: "Ring out your bells." Sir Philip Sidney. *See* Ring Out Your Bells.
Litany: "When my feet have wander'd." John S. B. Monsell. VA
Litany: "When the sun rises on another day." Charles Angoff. TrPWD
Litany at [*or* of] Atlanta, A. William Edward Burghardt DuBois. BANP; CDC; PoNe
Litany for Dicatorships. Stephen Vincent Benét. AmPP; AnEnPo; NAMP; OxBA; PoFr
Litany for Halloween. *Unknown.* PoRL; SiSoSe; SoPo
(Ghoulies and Ghosties.) PoSC
(Old Cornish Litany, An.) ShM
Litany for Latter-Day Mystics, A. Cale Young Rice. WGRP
Litany for Old Age, A. Una W. Harsen. TrPWD
Litany for Peace. Leslie Savage Clark. PGD
Litany in Plague Time, A. Thomas Nashe. *See* Adieu, Farewell, Earth's Bliss.
Litany in Time of Plague, A. Thomas Nashe. *See* Adieu, Farewell, Earth's Bliss.
Litany of Atlanta, A. W. E. B. DuBois. *See* Litany at Atlanta, A.
Litany of the Dark People, The. Countee Cullen. EaLo; MaRV; MoRP; TrPWD

Litany (continued)
(Litany of the Black People.) StJW
Litany of the Heroes, *sels.* Vachel Lindsay.
Lincoln. OHIP
("Would I might rouse the Lincoln in you all.") LiPo; PoSC
"Would I might wake St. Francis in you all." MoRP
Litany of the Lost. Siegfried Sassoon. MoRP
Litany of the Rooms of the Dead. Franz Werfel, *tr. fr. German by* Edith Abercrombie Snow. TrJP
Litany to Our Lady. Caryll Houselander. ISi
Litany to Satan. Baudelaire, *tr. fr. French by* James Elroy Flecker. AWP; SyP
(Litanies of Satan, The, *tr. by* Frances Winwar.) EnLi-2
Litany to the Holy Spirit. Robert Herrick. *See* His Litany To The Holy Spirit.
Literary Dinner. Vladimir Nabokov. FiBHP
Literary Gruk. Piet Hein, *tr. fr. Danish by* Piet Hein, Stephen Schwartz, *and* Martin S. Allwood. LiTW
Literary Lady, The. Sheridan. *Fr.* The Fatal Falsehood (*by* Hannah More): Epilogue. BOHV
Literary Landscape with Dove and Poet. Phyllis McGinley. NePoAm-2
Literary Love. Harry Kemp. HBMV
Literary Squabble, A. James Robinson Planché: CenHV
Literary Zodiac. R. A. Piddington. PV
Lithe [*or* Lythe] and listen [*or* lysten], gentlemen,/ That be of free-born blood. A Gest of Robyn Hode [*or* A Little Geste of Robin Hood and His Meiny]. *Unknown.* ESPB; OBB; OxBB; YAT
Lithe and listen, gentlemen:/ Other knight of sword or pen. Holiday. John Davidson. OBVV
Lithe and long as the serpent train. The Grape-Vine Swing. William Gilmore Simms. AnAmPo
Lithe beautiful fear, A. Python. Grace Hazard Conkling. NP
Lit'le David Play on Yo' Harp, *with music.* *Unknown.* BoAN-1
Little. Dorothy Aldis. FaPON; SUS; TiPo
Little, A. George Du Maurier. *See* Little Work, A.
Little Aglae. Walter Savage Landor. *Fr.* Pericles and Aspasia, CXIII. VA
Little Ah Sid, *with music.* *Unknown.* AS
Little Air. Stéphane Mallarmé, *tr. fr. French by* Roger Fry. PoPl; SyP
Little Alabama Coon. Hattie Starr. AA
Little Alexander's dead. Obituary. "Max Adeler." DTC
Little and Brown have lost their cat. The Lost Cat. Lilian Whiting. CIV
Little and Great. Charles Mackay. HBV; HBVY; PoLF
Little and plain seem now those red brick walls. The Nation's Shrine. Alma Adams Wiley. PEDC
Little *and,* the tiny *if,* The. Alliances. Nathalia Crane. MAP
Little Angels, The. Jacopone da Todi, *tr. fr. Italian by* Anne Macdonnell. CAW
Little angels of heaven, The. "There Shall Be More Joy . . ." Ford Madox Ford. MoBrPo (1942 ed.)
Little Annie Rooney. Michael Nolan. TreF
Little Ants, The. Ann *or* Jane Taylor. SAS
Little baby, lay your head. Good Night! Jane Taylor. HBV; HBVY; OTPC; PPL; SAS
Little bat, little bat. To the Bat. Edith King. BoTP
Little Beach Bird, The. Richard Henry Dana. AA; AmLP; AnAmPo; AnFE; AnNE; APA; CoAnAm; EtS; HBV; OTPC (1923 ed.)
Little beauty that I was allowed, The. Elinor Wylie. *Fr.* One Person. Sonn
Little Bell. Thomas Westwood. GN; HBV; OTPC (1946 ed.), *sl. abr.*; TVC
Little betrothed has washed her linen, The. Whiteness. "Isobel Hume." HBMV
Little Betty Blue. Agnes Grozier Herbertson. BoTP
Little Betty Blue/ Lost her holiday shoe. Mother Goose. OxNR; SAS; StVeCh
Little Betty Pringle she had a pig. *Unknown.* OxNR
Little Big Horn. Ernest McGaffey. PAH
Little Billee. Thackeray. BOHV; CenHV; EtS; FaBoCh; GaP; HBV; HBVY; LBN; LoGBV; MPB; NA; OnSP; OTPC; PoVP; ShM; TreFS; TSW
(Three Sailors, The.) OxBB
Little Billy Breek. *Unknown.* OxNR
Little Birches. Mary Effie Lee Newsome. PoNe
Little birches, white and slim, The. The Birches. Walter Prichard Eaton. StVeCh
Little Bird, The. Walter de la Mare. BiCB; BrR
Little Bird, A. Aileen Fisher. SoPo
Little Bird, The. *Unknown, tr. by* Rolf Italiaander. PBA
Little bird flew through the dell, A. Autumn Song. Johann Ludwig Tieck. AWP
Little Bird, Go through My Window, *with music.* *Unknown.* OuSiCo
Little Bird I Am, A. Mme Guyon, *tr. fr. French.* SoP; WGRP
(Prisoner's Song, A.) MaRV
Little bird, little bird, go through my window. *Unknown.* OuSiCo
Little bird of paradise. *Unknown.* OxNR
Little bird sat on a slender limb, The. Wings. *Unknown.* SoP
Little Birdie. Tennyson. *See* What Does Little Birdie Say?
Little Birds. "Lewis Carroll." *Fr.* Sylvie and Bruno Concluded. WhC
Little Birds Are Playing, *sel.* OxBoLi
Little Birds. Jacob Sternberg, *tr. fr. Yiddish by* Joseph Leftwich. TrJP
Little Birds are dining. Little Birds. "Lewis Carroll." *Fr.* Sylvie and Bruno Concluded. WhC
Little Birds Are Playing. "Lewis Carroll." *Fr.* Little Birds. OxBoLi
Little birds in a row. Little Birds. Jacob Sternberg. TrJP
Little birds praise you, The. Cradle Carol. Eleanor Slater. MaRV
Little birds sing with their beaks. Singing. Dorothy Aldis. GFA
Little birds sleep sweetly in their soft round nests. Evening Song. Cecil Frances Alexander. DD; OHIP; OTPC (1923 ed.); TVC
Little Bird's Song, A. Margaret Rose. BoTP
Little birds trust God, for they go singing, The. Trust. Annie Johnson Flint. SoP
Little bit of blowing, A. After Winter. Carolyn Sherwin Bailey. PCH
Little bit of blowing, A. Thoughts for a Cold Day. *Unknown.* BoTP
Little black ant found a large grain of wheat, A. The Little Ants. Ann *or* Jane Taylor. SAS
Little Black Boy, The. Blake. *Fr.* Songs of Innocence. AnFE; AtBAP; AWP; BEL; BoC; CABA; CaFP; CBEP; CBV; CEP; CH; DiPo; EiPP; EnL; EnLi-2; EnLit; EnPE; EnRP; ERoP-1; ForPo; HBV; ILP; InPo; LoGBV; MyFE; NoP; OAEP; OBEC; OBEV; OBNC; OxBoCh; PAn; PoEL-4; PoeP; PoFr; PoIE; PoNe; SeCeV; TDP; TOP; TreFS; TrGrPo
Little Black Boy. Barbara Marshall. TNV
Little Black boy/ Chased down the street. Nigger. Frank Horne. BANP; CDC
Little Black Bug. Margaret Wise Brown. FaPON
Little black bull kem down de medder, De. Hoosen Johnny. *Unknown.* AS
Little Black Dog, The. Elizabeth Gardner Reynolds. PoLF; SoP
Little black dog ran round the house, The. *Unknown.* OxNR
Little Black-eyed Rebel, The. Will Carleton. FaPON; GoTP; PAH; PAP
Little Black Man with a Rose in His Hat. Audrey Wurdemann. YaD
Little Black Rose, The. Aubrey Thomas De Vere. ACP; OnYI
(Song: "Little Black Rose shall be red at last, The!") IrPN
Little Black Sheep, The. At. to Paul Laurence Dunbar, *also to* Sarah Pratt McLean Greene. *See* Sheepfol', De.
Little black thing among the snow, A. The Chimney Sweeper. Blake. *Fr.* Songs of Experience. AtBAP; BoW; BWP; CABA; CBEP; EiCL; EiPP; EnL; EnLi-2 (1949 ed.); EnLit; EnPE; ERoP-1; ForPo; PAn; PoeP; PoIE; TDP; YAT
Little Black Train, A, *with music.* *Unknown.* OuSiCo
Little blessed Earth that turns, The. O Earth, Turn! George Johnston. MoCV
Little blind girl wandering, A. The Brook. William Wilberforce Lord. AA
Little Blue Apron. *Unknown.* BoTP
Little Blue Ben, who lives in the glen. *Unknown.* OxNR
Little Blue Betty lived in a den. *Unknown.* OxNR
Little Blue Pigeon. Eugene Field. GBV (1922 ed.)
Little Blue-Ribbons. Austin Dobson. BiCB; OnPP

Little Blue Shoes. Blue Shoes. Kate Greenaway. MPB; TiPo
Little Boats of Britain, The. Sara E. Carsley. CaP
Little Bob Robin. *Unknown.* OxNR
Little body I would hold. Unborn. Irene Rutherford McLeod. HBMV
Little Bonny, *with music. Unknown.* OuSiCo
Little boots and big boots. Rubber Boots. Rowena Bennett. GFA
Little Bo-Peep/ Had lost her sheep. The Fairy Sleep and Little Bo-Peep. *Unknown.* BoTP
Little Bo-Peep has lost her sheep. Mother Goose. FaBoBe; HBV; HBVY; OTPC; OxNR; PCH; PPL; RIS; SAS; SoPo; StVeCh; TiPo
Little bo peepals. Boston Nursery Rhymes. Joseph Cook. BOHV
Little Bow to Books on How To, A. Irwin Edman. WhC
Little boy and a little girl, A. Mother Goose. PPL. *See also* There was a little boy and a little girl.
Little Boy Blue. Guy Wetmore Carryl. *See* Harmonious Heedlessness of Little Boy Blue, The.
Little Boy Blue. Eugene Field. AA; BeLS; FaFP; FaPON; HBV; HBVY; LiTG; MAP; MoAmPo (1942 ed.); NeHB; NeMA; OHFP; OTD; PaPo; PEDC; PoLF; TreF
Little Boy Blue. John Crowe Ransom. LiTM; TwAmPo
Little Boy Blue, come blow [up] your horn. Mother Goose. BoChLi; BoTP; FaBoBe; FaFP; HBV; HBVY; OTPC; OxNR; PCH; PPL; RIS; SAS; SoPo; StVeCh; TiPo
Little Boy Found, The. Blake. *Fr.* Songs of Innocence. CBEP; EnRP; TiPo (1952 ed.)
Little boy has bought a top, A. The Boy and His Top. John Hookham Frere. OTPC (1923 ed.)
Little Boy in the Morning, A. Francis Ledwidge. MCCG; OnYI
Little boy is fishing, The. The Fisherman. David McCord. PDV; TiPo (1959 ed.)
Little Boy Lost ("Father! father! where are you going?"). Blake. *Fr.* Songs of Innocence. CBEP; EnRP; TiPo (1952 ed.)
Little Boy Lost, A ("Nought loves another as itself"). Blake. *Fr.* Songs of Experience. CBEP; CEP; EnLi-2; EnLit; EnRP; OAEP; PeER; PoIE; ViBoPo
"Little Boy Lost, A." Jerome Rothenberg. CoPo
Little Boy Lost, The. Stevie Smith. FaBoTw
Little boy lost in the lonely fen. The Little Boy Found. Blake. *Fr.* Songs of Innocence. CBEP; EnRP; TiPo (1952 ed.)
Little Boy of heavenly birth, A. Out of Bounds. John Banister Tabb. JKCP; MaRV; TRV
Little boy once long ago, A. Modern Miracle. William Atherton. SoP
Little boy once played so loud, A. Extremes. James Whitcomb Riley. FaPON; HBVY; MPB; PCH; PPL
Little boy sat dreaming, A. Stars. *Unknown.* GFA
Little boy stood on the corner, A. December. Sanderson Vanderbilt. OCS
Little Boy to the Locomotive, The. Benjamin R. C. Low. HBMV
Little boy was set to keep, A. The Boy and the Wolf. John Hookham Frere. HBV; HBVY; OTPC (1923 ed.)
Little boy, well known to me, A. The New Name. *Unknown.* SoP
Little boys and little maidens. Little Catkins. Aleksandr Blok. EaLo
Little boy's first Bible, A. First Bible. *Unknown.* SoP
Little Boy's Good-Night, The. Eliza Lee Follen. OTPC (1923 ed.)
Little Boys of Texas. Robert P. Tristram Coffin. ShM; WaKn
Little Boy's Pocket, A. *Unknown.* PPL
Little Boy's Vain Regret, A. Edith M. Thomas. AA
Little Breeches. John Hay. AA; AmPP (3d ed.); BeLS; BOHV; CoBA; FaBoBe; GoTP; HBV; PaPo; StaSt, *abr.*; TreFS; TSW
Little Brother. Aileen Fisher. BiCB
Little Brother, The. James Reeves. DTC
Little Brother of the Rich, A. Edward Sandford Martin. AA; HBV
Little Brother's Secret. Katherine Mansfield. FaPON; MoSiPe; OTD; TiPo
Little Brown Baby. Paul Laurence Dunbar. BANP; NoP; PoNe
Little brown baby-bird, lapped in your nest. Lullaby of the Iroquois. Pauline Johnson. ACV
Little Brown baby wif spa'klin' eyes. Little Brown Baby. Paul Laurence Dunbar. BANP; NoP; PoNe
Little Brown Bear. Alice Wilkins. GFA
Little Brown Bobby. Laura Elizabeth Richards. SAS
Little Brown Boy. Helene Johnson. *See* Poem: "Little brown boy."
Little brown brother, oh! little brown brother. Baby Seed Song. Edith Nesbit. BoChLi; DD; FaPON; HBV; HBVY; MPB; OTPC; PCH; PRWS; SP; TVC
Little Brown Bulls, The. *Unknown.* BaBo; OuSiCo, *with music*
Little Brown Church in the Vale. William S. Pitts. TreFT
Little brown gopher explored one day, A. The Little Gopher Man. Nancy Bockius Scott. PCH
Little Brown Jug, The. *Unknown.* ABF, *with music*; FaFP; TrAS, *with music*; TreF; YaD
Little Brown Seed. Rodney Bennett. BoTP
Little brown squirrel hops in the corn, The. The Rejected "National Hymns," VII. "Orpheus C. Kerr.' BOHV; InMe
Little brown surf-bather of the mountains! The Water Ouzel. Harriet Monroe. NP; OTPC (1946 ed.)
Little Busy Bee. Isaac Watts. *See* How Doth the Little Busy Bee.
Little Buttercup. W. S. Gilbert. *Fr.* H. M. S. Pinafore. TreFS
Little by little we subtract. Observation. Samuel Hoffenstein. PoMa
Little Cabin, A. Charles Bertram Johnson. BANP
Little Calathine. *Unknown, tr. fr. Greek by* Lord Neaves. OnPM
Little Candle. Carl Sandburg. GoYe
Little care that fretted me, The. Out in the Fields with God. *Unknown, at. to* Louise Imogen Guiney *and to* Elizabeth Barrett Browning. BLPA; BLRP; DD; GoTP; HBV; HBVY; MaRV; MPB; NeHB; OQP; OTPC (1946 ed.); SoP; TreFS; TRV; WBLP; WGRP
Little Cart, The. Ch'en Tzu-lung, tr. fr. Chinese by Arthur Waley. AtBAP; FlW; LoBV
Little Carved Bowl, The. Margaret Widdemer. BrR; YT
Little Cat Angel, The. Leontine Stanfield. BLPA; CIV
Little cat played on a silver flute, A. The Boston Cats. Arthur Macy. CIV
Little caterpillar creeps, The. Cocoon. David McCord. PoPo
Little Catkins. Aleksandr Blok, *tr. fr. Russian by* Babette Deutsch. EaLo
(Willow-Boughs, The, *tr. unknown.*) BoTP
Little Chap Who Follows Me, The. *Unknown. See* Little Fellow Follows Me, A.
Little Charlie Chipmunk. Helen Cowles LeCron. FaPON; GFA; SoPo; TiPo
Little charm of placid mien. To Miss Georgiana. Ambrose Philips. WaPE
Little Child, A. Edith Shaw Brown. SoP
Little Child, The. Albert Bigelow Paine. AA; ChIP; MaRV
Little child, A. Puer Aeternus. Kathleen Raine. NYBP
Little child, A. Bethlehem of Judea. *Unknown.* BiCB; ChBR
Little Child, a joy-of-heart, with eyes, A. At Nazareth. Katharine Lee Bates. StJW
Little Child, a Limber Elf, A. Samuel Taylor Coleridge. *Fr.* Christabel. LoBV; ViBoPo
Little child at mother's knee, A. A Little Child. Edith Shaw Brown. SoP
Little child, good child, go to sleep. Evening Song. Fannie Stearns Davis. GFA; SP
Little Child of Mary. H. T. Burleigh. StJW
"Little Child Shall Lead Them, A." Phyllis C. Michael. SoP
Little Children, The. Irwin Granich. MaRV
Little Children. Mary Howitt. PRWS
Little children, never give. Kindness to Animals. *Unknown.* BoTP; GoTP; HBV; HBVY; OTPC; PPL; SoPo
Little children, yet a little while I am with you. Love One Another. St. John, Bible, *N.T.* TreFT
Little Child's Faith, The. Louis Edwin Thayer. PoToHe
Little Child's Hymn, A. Francis Turner Palgrave. VA
Little Child's Prayer, A. John Banister Tabb. *See* Child's Prayer, A.
Little Chisel, The. N. P. van Wyk Louw, *tr. fr. Afrikaans by* Jack Cope *and* Uys Krige. PeSA
Little Christ Child. Elsie M. Fowler. PoRL

Little Christ was good, and lay. Like One I Know. Nancy Campbell. JKCP
Little Christel. William Brighty Rands. PRWS
Little Christmas Donkey, The. Geraldine Farrar. StJW
Little Christmas Tree, The. "Susan Coolidge." DD; PEDC
Little Christmas tree that stands, The. What the Christmas Tree Thinks. Mary Carolyn Davies. PCH
Little City. Robert Horan. CrMA; LiTM (rev. ed.); NePA
Little Clan, The. Frederick Robert Higgins. OBMV
Little clock is friends with me, The. The Gymnastic Clock. Mary Carolyn Davies. TVC
Little Clotilda. *Unknown.* BoTP
Little Clown Puppet. Carolyn Haywood. BrR
Little cock sparrow sat on a [green] tree, A. Mother Goose. BoTP; OTPC; OxNR; SiTL
Little colt—broncho, loaned to the farm, A. The Broncho That Would Not Be Broken. Vachel Lindsay. ATP (1935 ed.); BBV (1951 ed.); LaNeLa; LiTM (rev. ed.); NePA; PFY; PTK; RoGo; YT
Little colts caper and kick up their heels. In Spring in Warm Weather. Dorothy Aldis. BiCB
Little Commodore, The. J. C. Squire. HBMV
Little Cossack, The. Laura E. Richards. PoRh
Little cottage stood alone, the pride, The. The Old Cottagers. John Clare. OBRV
Little cousin is dead, by foul subtraction, The. Dead Boy. John Crowe Ransom. CMoP; LiTA; MoPW; NoP; OxBA; TwCP
Little cousins/ play on your. Victor Hernandez Cruz. *Fr.* Cities #8. BOLo
Little cowboy, what have you heard. The Leprecaun [or Fairy Shoemaker]. William Allingham. OnYI; PCH; RG
Little Creature, The. Walter de la Mare. EvOK
Little cross, A/ To tell my loss. Robin's Cross. George Darley. OnYI
Little cross of weather-silvered wood, A. "Ici Repose." Bernard Freeman Trotter. MaRV
Little Dame Crump. *Unknown.* BoTP; FTB, *with music*; PCH
Little Dancers, The. Laurence Binyon. BoTP; CH; MoBrPo; MoVE; OBVV
Little Dandelion. Helen Barron Bostwick. DD; HBV; HBVY; OTPC (1923 ed.); PRWS
Little Dandelion, The. Lula Lowe Weeden. CDC
Little Danny Donkey. Helen Cowles LeCron. GFA
Little dapper man but with shiny elbows, A. Louis MacNeice. *Fr.* The Kingdom. ChMP
Little dark Cape girl why is it you roam? Wordspinning. Olga Kirsch. PeSA
Little David, *with music.* *Unknown.* TrAS
(Little David, Play on Yo' Harp.) GoSl
Little Day Moon. Nellie Burget Miller. GFA
Little Derwent's Breakfast, *sel.* *Unknown.*
Little Gentleman, The. HBV; HBVY
Little Dicky Dilver. *Unknown.* OxNR
"Little did I, the young one, slumber at night." The Child's Dream. *Unknown.* OnPM
Little Dirge. Jean Starr Untermeyer. HBMV
Little Disaster, The. *Unknown.* SAS
Little Dog, The. Frances Cornford. *See* Feri's Dream.
Little Dog-Angel, A. Norah M. Holland. PoLF
Little Dog Under the Wagon, The *Unknown.* PoLF
Little Dog's Day, The. Rupert Brooke. ShBV-1
Little Donkey Close Your Eyes ("Little Donkey on the hill"). Margaret Wise Brown. PDV
Little Dove. Mary's Lullaby. Ivy O. Eastwick. ChBR
Little Doves, The. *Unknown.* PPL; SAS
Little Dreams. Langston Hughes. NYTB
Little dreams of maidenhood, The. The Wife. Theodosia Garrison. HBV
Little drop of dew. A Dewdrop. Frank Dempster Sherman. PPL
Little drops of water. Little Things. Julia A. Fletcher Carney, *wr. at. to* E. C. Brewer *and to* Frances S. Osgood. BoTP; FaBoBe; FaFP; FaPON; GFA; GoTP; HBV; HBVY; NeHB; OTPC; TreF
Little Drummer, The. Richard Henry Stoddard. AA; PAH
Little Duck, The. Joso, *tr. fr. Japanese by* Harold G. Henderson. SoPo
("I've seen everything.") FlW
Little Dutch Garden, A. Harriet Whitney Durbin. OTPC (1946 ed.)
Little Dutch Gretchen sat in the kitchen. *Unknown.* SAS
Little Dutchman, The. Mary Mapes Dodge. GaP
Little Eau Pleine, The. *Unknown.* IHA
Little elbow leans upon your knee, A. Tired Mothers. May Riley Smith. HBV
Little Elegy [for a Child Who Skipped Rope]. X. J. Kennedy. CaFP; CBV; CoAP; ELU; GoJo
Little Elegy. Elinor Wylie. LOW
Little elephant was crying, The. Cradle Song of the Elephants. Adriano del Valle. FaPON; RePo
Little Elf, The. John Kendrick Bangs. AA; BiCB; FaBoBe; GaP; GFA; GoBP; GoTP; HBV; HBVY; MPB; PDV; PRWS; SP; WaKn
(Little Elf-Man, The.) BoChLi; BoTP; PCH
(Little Elfman, The.) OTPC (1946 ed.); SoPo; TiPo
Little Ellie sits alone. Romance of the Swan's Nest. Elizabeth Barrett Browning. GN; OTPC
Little enough of that wide country. The Spell of France. Edmund Blunden. POTE
Little Epithalamium. Chester Kallman. CrMA
Little Exercise. Elizabeth Bishop. CBV; CoAP; CrMA; MoAB; MoAmPo (1950 ed.); NYBP; UnPo (3d ed.)
Little face there was, A. In Rama. George Alfred Townsend. AA
Little Fair Soul, The. Menella Bute Smedley. VA
Little fairy comes at night, A. Queen Mab [*or* The Dream Fairy]. Thomas Hood. BoTP; DD; HBV; HBVY; OTPC, *abr.*; PCH; PPL; StVeCh; TVC
Little Fairy Flitabout had such a craze for fleetness. The Careless Fairy. Nancy Byrd Turner. BoChLi
Little fairy snowflakes. Santa Claus. *Unknown.* OTPC (1946 ed.); SoPo
Little Falls. Robert Hogg. MoCV
Little Family, The. *Unknown.* BaBo; BFSS, *with music*
Little Fan. James Reeves. PoMS
Little Farm, The; or, The Weary Ploughman. *Unknown.* CoMu
Little Feet. Elizabeth Akers Allen. HBV
Little feet too young and soft to walk. The Stranger's Grave. Emily Lawless. OnYI
Little Fellow Follows Me, A. *Unknown.* SoP
(Little Chap Who Follows Me, The.) PoToHe (new ed.)
(Service Supreme.) STF
Little Finger Game, A. E. J. Falconer. BoTP
Little Fir Tree, The. Margaret Rose. BoTP
Little fish that in the stream doth fleet, The. To Alexander Neville. Barnabe Googe. EnRePo; NoP
Little Fish That Would Not Do as It Was Bid, The. Ann *or* Jane Taylor. OHIP
Little fishes in a brook. *Unknown.* OxNR
Little Flag on Our House, The. William Curtis Demorest. PaA
Little Flags, The. John Clair Minot. DD; HH; PEDC
Little flock of clouds go down to rest, A. Evening Clouds. Francis Ledwidge. MPB
Little flower grew in a lonely vale, A. To Mrs. Ann Flaxman. Blake. OBRV
Little flowers came through the ground, The. At Easter Time. Laura E. Richards. BoChLi; DD; HH; MPB; OHIP; OTPC (1946 ed.)
Little flutt'rer! swifter flying. To a Hedge-Sparrow. *Unknown.* OTPC (1923 ed.)
Little fly,/ Thy summer's play. The Fly. Blake. *Fr.* Songs of Experience. BoLiVe; CBEP; DiPo; EiPP; EnL; GoTP; MaPo; OTPC (1923 ed.); PoSa; TrGrPo; YAT
Little Folks in the Grass. Annette Wynne. BoChLi; SP; UTS
Little Fox, The. Marion Edey. TiPo
Little French doll was a dear little doll, The. The Doll's Wooing. Eugene Field. RIS
Little French Lawyer, The, *sel.* John Fletcher.
Song in the Wood. EIL; ThWaDe
Little Frog, A. Alice Wilkins. GFA
Little Gal at Our House, *with music.* *Unknown.* ABF
Little Garaine. Sir Gilbert Parker. FaPON; OTPC (1946 ed.); PRWS
Little Garden, A. Amy Lowell. GBV
Little garden little Jowett made, A. *Unknown, sometimes at. to* Richard Porson. WhC
Little Garment, A. Diodorus, *tr. fr. Greek by* Lord Neaves. OnPM

Little Gate to God, The. Walter Rauschenbusch. *Fr.* The Postern Gate. MaRV, *abr.*
("In the castle of my soul.") TRV
Little gate was reached at last, The. Auf Wiedersehen. James Russell Lowell. AA; CoBA; HBV
Little General Monk. *Unknown.* OxNR
Little Gentleman, The. *Unknown.* *Fr.* Little Derwent's Breakfast. HBV; HBVY
Little Geste of Robin Hood and His Meiny, A. *Unknown.* *See* Gest of Robyn Hode, A.
Little Ghost, The. Katharine Tynan. HBV
Little Ghost Who Died for Love. Edith Sitwell. MemP
Little Ghosts, The. Thomas S. Jones, Jr. HBV
Little Gidding. T. S. Eliot. *Fr.* Four Quartets. ExPo; FaBoEn; GTBS-P; OAEP (2d ed.); PoIE; SeCeV (1967 ed.)
Sels.
"Ash on an old man's sleeve," II. FaBoTw; GTBS-W; PoFS
"We shall not cease from exploration," *fr.* V. ImOP
Little Giffen. Francis Orrery Ticknor. AA; AmePo; CoBA; DD; FaPL; HBV; MaC; MC; PaA; PAH; PCD; PTK; TreFS
Little Girl, A. Charles Angoff. GoYe
Little Girl, The. Nicholas Moore. ErPo; NeBP
Little girl, A/ Had wandered in the night. John W. Lynch. *Fr.* A Woman Wrapped in Silence. ISi
Little girl all in her garden, A. The Cowboy's Return. *Unknown.* BFSS
Little Girl, Be Careful What You Say. Carl Sandburg. FIW; GoYe
Little Girl Cat. Hy Sobiloff. TwAmPo
Little Girl Found, The. Blake. *Fr.* Songs of Experience. CBEP; DiPo
Little Girl in Bloom, A. Anne Blackwell Payne. GFA
"Little girl, little girl." Mother Goose. BoTP; OxNR
Little Girl Lost, A ("Children of the future age"). Blake. *Fr.* Songs of Experience. ERoP-1
(Children of a Future Age.) CBEP
Little Girl Lost, The ("In futurity/ I prophetic see"). Blake. *Fr.* Songs of Experience. DiPo
Little Girl, My Stringbean, My Lovely Woman. Anne Sexton. NYBP
Little Girl That Lost a Finger, The. "Gabriela Mistral," *tr. fr. Spanish by* Muna Lee. FaPON
Little Girl That Mother Used to Be. Nancy Byrd Turner. HH
Little Girl to Her Dolly, The. Ann Taylor. SAS
Little girl went for a walk, A. A Summer Walk. Elizabeth Winton. PCH
Little girl won't eat her sandwich, The. Blasting from Heaven. Philip Levine. CoAP
Little girls. Day's End. Lesbia Harford. PoAu-1
Little girls' frocks are frilly, The. Ballroom Dancing Class. Phyllis McGinley. MoShBr
Little Girl's Songs, A. Hilda Conkling. NP
Little girls that live next door, The. Grace Ananne [*or* GraceAnAnne]. Lysbeth Boyd Borie. BiCB; RePo
Little girls, through the blowing leaves. Through the Blowing Leaves. Glenn Ward Dresbach. BoC
Little goat, The. April. Ivor Winters. ELU
Little Gods, The. Abigail Cresson. PoMa
Little gold head, my house's candle. Lullaby of a Woman of the Mountain. *Unknown.* NP
Little Golden Ring, The, *with music.* *Unknown.* ShS
Little Goose, A. Eliza Sproat Turner. BOHV
Little Gopher Man, The. Nancy Bockius Scott. PCH
Little Gottlieb. Phoebe Cary. OTPC (1946 ed.); TVC
Little granite church upholds, The. Sheepstor. L. A. G. Strong. HBMV
Little gray cat was walking prettily, The. The Little White Cat. *Unknown.* OnYI
Little gray [*or* grey] hill-glade, A, close-turfed, withdrawn. Marsyas. Sir Charles G. D. Roberts. PeCV; VA
Little Gray Lamb, The. Archibald Beresford Sullivan. ChrBoLe
Little Gray Pussy. *Unknown.* *See* Catkin.
Little Gray Songs from St. Joseph's, *sels.* Grace Fallow Norton.
"My little soul I never saw," XLVII. HBV
"With cassock black, baret and book," XXX. HBV
Little gray wonder, in pride of fur. To an Enchantress. Alice Brown. CIV
Little green bird sat on a fence rail, A. Mother Goose. BoChLi
Little Green Blackbird, The. Kenneth Patchen. PoCH
Little green frog lived under a log, A. Strange Talk. L. E. Yates. BoTP
Little green frog once lived in a pool, A. The Frog. Rose Fyleman. BoTP
Little Green Orchard, The. Walter de la Mare. EvOK; MPB; TiPo (1952 ed.)
Little Green Tents. Walt Mason. OQP
Little Green Tree Blues. Langston Hughes. PoNe
Little Gregory. Theodore Botrel, *tr. fr. French by* Richard C. Savage. CAW
Little grey hill-glade, A, close-turfed, withdrawn. *See* Little gray hill-glade. . .
Little Guinever. Annie Fields. AA
Little Gustava. Celia Thaxter. BoChLi; FaPON; HBV; HBVY; PRWS
"Little Haly! Little Haly!" cheeps the robin in the tree. On the Death of Little Mahala Ashcraft. James Whitcomb Riley. AA
Little hand is knocking at my heart, A. The Return. Arthur Symons. *Fr.* Amor Triumphans. BrPo; HBMV
Little Hands. Laurence Binyon. HBV; MaRV
Little harp, at thy cry. Brechva's Harp Song. Ernest Rhys. VA
Little hedgerow birds, The. An Old Man [*or* Animal Tranquillity and Decay *or* A Sketch]. Wordsworth. BoPe; ERoP-1; FaBoCh; LoGBV
Little herdboy, sitting there. The Pilgrim and the Herdboy. Robert Buchanan. OBVV
Little Herd-Boy's Song, The. Robert Buchanan. *Fr.* The Pilgrim and the Herdboy. BoTP
Little hill climbs up to the village and puts its green hands, The. Kenneth Patchen. *Fr.* The Hunted City. NaP
Little Hobby-Horse, A. Eliza Grove. OTPC
Little hope, a lot of faith, A. Worry. George W. Swarberg. STF
Little Horned Toad. *tr. fr. Navajo Indian by* Hilda Faunce Wetherill. FaPON
Little House, The. Pierre Louys, *tr. fr. French by* Horace M. Brown. *Fr.* The Songs of Bilitis. UnTE
Little house, a quiet wife, A. The Wish. Rowland Watkyns. CavP
Little house with a broken stair, A. Promenade. Sam Cornish. BF
Little Hymn to Mary, A. *Unknown.* MeEL
Little I ask; my wants are few. Contentment. Oliver Wendell Holmes. *Fr.* The Autocrat of the Breakfast Table, *ch.* 11. AmPP (4th ed.); AnNE; AP; BOHV; HBV; InMe; OnPP; OxBA; TOP; TreF
Little, I ween, did Mary guess. His Mother's Joy. John White Chadwick. AA
Little Indian, Sioux or Crow. Foreign Children. Robert Louis Stevenson. BoChLi; BoTP; GaP; GFA; GoJo; MPB; OTPC (1946 ed.); RIS; SUS
Little Ink More or Less, A. Stephen Crane. War Is Kind, II. AmPP (3d ed.); AnAmPo
Little inmate, full of mirth. The Cricket. Vincent Bourne, *tr. by* William Cowper. HBV; HBVY; OTPC; PoLF
Little inn in Bethlehem first heard the echo of his voice, A. Echoes of Jesus. Lucile Coleman. ChIP
Little is he victor here, A. Tactic. Margaret Marks. MAP
Little is much when God is in it. Workers with Him. A. A. Rees. FaChP
Little Ivory Figures Pulled with String. Amy Lowell. AnFE; APA; CoAnAm; MAPA; NAMP; TwAmPo; ViBoPo
Little Jack Dandy-prat. *Unknown.* OxNR
Little Jack Frost. *Unknown.* GFA; PPL; SoPo
Little Jack Horner/ Sat in the corner. Mother Goose. BoChLi; FaBoBe; FaFP; FOL; HBV; HBVY; OTPC; OxNR; PCH; RIS; SAS; SiTL; SoPo
Little Jack Horner sat in the corner eying the pies all day. A Medley. Michael Lewis. TSW
Little Jack of Christ, The. St. Stephen's Word. Rayner Heppenstall. ChMP
Little Jack Pumpkin Face. *Unknown.* PCH
Little Jack Sprat/ Once had a pig. *Unknown.* OxNR
Little Jenny Wren/ Fell sick upon a time. Mother Goose. BoChLi (1950 ed.); BoTP
Little Jesus. Francis Thompson. *See* Child's Prayer, A.
Little Jesus came to town, The. A Christmas Folk-Song. Lizette Woodworth Reese. ChBR; ChrBoLe; DD; FaPON;

Little (continued)
GFA; HBMV; HBVY; MPB; OHIP; OnMSP; OTPC (1946 ed.); PoRh; PoRL; SP; StJW; SUS; ThGo; TiPo (1952 ed.); TSW; UTS
Little Jesus, little Jesus. A Child at a Creche. Alice Isabel Hazeltine. ChrBoLe
Little Jesus, sweetly sleep, do not stir. Rocking. *Unknown.* ChrBoLe
Little Jesus wast Thou shy. A Child's Prayer [*or* Little Jesus *or* Ex Ore Infantium]. Francis Thompson. BoTP; ChrBoLe; DD; FaBV; FaChP; GTSE; HBV; HBVY; MaRV; OBVV; OHIP; PoRh; PoRL; PoVP; SoP; StJW; SUS; TreFS; TRV; TSW
Little Jew lived in a little straw hut, A. Biography. Abraham M. Klein. TrJP
Little Jim. Edward Farmer. PaPo
Little Joe, the Wrangler, *with music.* *At. to* N. Howard Thorp. CoSo
Little John a Begging. *Unknown.* BaBo; ESPB (A *and* B *vers.*)
Little John Bottlejohn. Laura E. Richards. PDV; PoMS; RePo; RIS
Little John Jiggy Jag. *Unknown.* OxNR
Little John Nobody. *Unknown.* OxBoLi
Little Johnny-jump-up said. Wise Johnny. Edwina Fallis. SiSoSe; SUS; TiPo
Little Johnny Mine, The. Daisy L. Detrick. PoOW
Little Johnny Morgan. *Unknown.* OxNR
Little Johnny's Confession. Brian Patten. CAD
Little Joke. Elinor Wylie. LHV
Little Jumping Girls, The. Kate Greenaway. FaPON; MPB
("Jump—jump—jump.") TiPo
Little Katy. *Unknown.* ShM
Little King, The. Irene Gass. ChrBoLe
Little King Boggen, he built a fine hall. Mother Goose. StVeCh
Little King Pippin he built a fine hall. *Unknown.* OxNR
Little Kings and Queens of the May. Juliana Horatia Ewing. *See* For Good Luck.
Little Kittens, The. Eliza Lee Follen. GFA; TiPo; UTS
Sels.
"Where are you going,/ My little cat?" BoTP
"Where are you going,/ My little kittens?" BoTP
"Little kittens, be quiet—be quiet, I say!" A Cat to Her Kittens. Eliza Grove. OTPC (1923 ed.)
Little Kitty. Elizabeth Prentiss. *See* Long Time Ago.
Little Knight in Green, The. Katharine Lee Bates. AA
Little Lad. *Unknown.* BiCB
("Little lad, little lad.") OxNR
Little ladies, white and green. Snowdrops. Laurence Alma-Tadema. BoTP; PRWS
Little lady lairdie, The. *Unknown.* OxNR
Little lady of my heart! Ad Domnulam Suam. Ernest Dowson. HBV; PG
Little Lady Wren. Tom Robinson. FaPON; TiPo
Little Lamb. Blake. *See* Lamb, The.
Little lamb had Mary, A; sweet. An Old Song by New Singers. A. C. Wilkie. BOHV
Little Lamb Went Straying, A. Albert Midlane. OTPC (1923 ed.)
Little lamb, who made thee? The Lamb. Blake. *Fr.* Songs of Innocence. AnFE; BEL; BoChLi; BoLiVe; BoTP; BWP; CABA; CaFP; CAW; CBEP; CBV; CEP; CH; CoBE; DiPo; EaLo; EiCL; EiPP; EnL; EnLi-2; EnLit; EnPE; EnRP; ERoP-1; ExPo; FaBoBe; FaBoCh; FaPON; ForPo; GoJo; GoTP; HBV; ILP; LiTB; LiTG; LoBV; LoGBV; MaPo; MaRV; MemP; MPB; NeHB; NoP; OAEP; OBEC; OTPC; OuHeWo; OxBoCh; PAn; PG (1945 ed.); PIA; PoAN; PoeP; PoFS; PoIE; PoPl; PoPo; PoRh; PRWS; RIS; SeCeV; SoP; StaSt; StVeCh; SUS; TIHL; TOP; TreF; TrGrPo; TRV; TVC; UTS; VaPo; WaKn; WGRP; WHA; YAT *Fr.* Songs of Innocence.
Little lambkin, The, says "Ba, Ba!" Buttercup Farm. *Unknown.* SAS
Little lambs, little lambs. Baby Beds. *Unknown.* BoTP
Little lamps of the dusk. Fireflies. Carolyn Hall. FaPON; GFA; HBMV; HBVY; MPB; PCH; TSW; UTS
Little Land, The. Robert Louis Stevenson. PoVP; PRWS; SoPo; StVeCh (1955 ed.); TVC
Little Learning Is a Dangerous Thing, A. Pope. *Fr.* An Essay on Criticism, Pt. II. HoPM; PG (1955 ed.); PoLF; TreF; TrGrPo
(Alps on Alps.) FaFP; GTBS-W
(Little Learning, A.) ChTr; LiTB; LiTG; OBEC; SeCePo
Little less returned for him each spring, A. Anglais Mort à Florence. Wallace Stevens. AP
Little Lettice is dead, they say. Lettice. "Michael Field." VA
Little Libbie. Julia A. Moore. ATP
Little light is going by, A. Firefly. Elizabeth Madox Roberts. GFA; GoJo; OTPC (1946 ed.); PDV; PoRh; SUS; TiPo; UTS
Little Litany to St. Francis, A. Philip Murray. NePoAm
Little lonely child am I, A. The Moon-Child. "Fiona Macleod." CH; EtS
Little lonely girl, A. Xmas Time. Walta Karsner. ELU
Little Lord Jesus, The. *Unknown.* ChrBoLe
Little Lost Child, The. Edward B. Marks. TreFS
Little Lost Pup. Arthur Guiterman. BBV (1951 ed.); PCD; TreFS
Little Lough, The. John Hewitt. NeIP
Little Love-God, The. Meleager, *tr. fr. Greek by* Walter Headlam. AWP
Little love god lying once asleep, The. Sonnets, CLIV. Shakespeare. ReIE; Sonn
Little love, A, of heaven a little share. Sufficiency. Gleeson White. VA
Little love serves my turne. *Unknown.* SeCSL
Little Lover. Leonora Speyer. HBMV
Little Lucy Lavender. Lucy Lavender. Ivy O. Eastwick. BiCB; BoTP; SiSoSe
Little Lucy Lester. M. Steel. BoTP
Little Lullaby. Irving Feldman. NYBP
Little madness in the spring, A. Emily Dickinson. AP; MAmP
Little Maid and the Cowslips, The. John Clare. BoTP
Little maid of Astrakan, A. The Divan. Richard Henry Stoddard. AA
Little Maid of Far Japan. Annette Wynne. MPB
Little maid, pretty maid,/ Whither goest thou? Mother Goose. OxNR; PPL
Little maid upon my fan. Little Maid of Far Japan. Annette Wynne. MPB
Little maiden climbed an old man's knee, A. After the Ball. Charles Kassell Harris. TreF
Little maiden, dost thou pine. Valentine to a Little Girl. Cardinal Newman. GoBC
Little Mamma. Charles Henry Webb. BOHV
Little Man, The. Hughes Mearns. *See* Antigonish.
Little man/ Little man. Ilo Orleans. RIS
Little man in coal pit. *Unknown.* OxNR
Little Man Who Wasn't There, The. Hughes Mearns. *See* Antigonish.
Little Marine, The. *Unknown.* *See* Snapoo.
Little marsh-plant, yellow green, A. The Sundew. Swinburne. ELP; NoP; OBNC; PeVV; WePo
Little Mary Bell had a fairy in a nut. Long John Brown and Little Mary Bell. Blake. SiTL
Little Mary Cassidy. Francis A. Fahy. HBV
Little masters, hat in hand. Clover. John Banister Tabb. AA; AnAmPo; AnFE; APA; CoAnAm
Little Mathey [*or* Mathie *or* Matty] Grove [*or* Groves.] *Unknown.* *See* Little Musgrave and Lady Barnard.
Little Men, The. William Allingham. *Fr.* The Fairies. OtMeF
Little Men, The. Flora Fearne. BoTP
Little men all in a row. Little Rain Men. Ruth Anne Hussey. PCH
Little men of meadow land, The. Adventure. Nancy Byrd Turner. StVeCh (1955 ed.)
Little Milliner, The. Robert Buchanan. BeLS
Little Miss Muffet/ Crouched on a tuffet. Paul Dehn. *Fr.* Rhymes for a Modern Nursery. FiBHP; ShM
Little Miss Muffet/ Sat on a tuffet. Mother Goose. BoChLi; FaBoBe; FaFP; HBV; HBVY; OTPC; OxNR; PCH; PPL; RIS; SAS; SiTL; SoPo; StVeCh; TiPo
Little Miss Muffet discovered a tuffet. The Embarrassing Episode of Little Miss Muffet. Guy Wetmore Carryl. FaPON; MPB; OnMSP; RePo; StPo; TSW
Little Miss Pitt. William Wise. TiPo (1959 ed.)
Little Mistake, A. Anna Maria Pratt. *See* Mortifying Mistake, A.
Little Mr. Browny Bee. Browny Bee. Irene F. Pawsey. BoTP
Little Mister Polliwog. Ways of Traveling. Alice Wilkins. GFA

Little Mistress Comfort got up early one fine day. Mistress Comfort. Elizabeth Gould. BoTP
Little Mohee, The. *Unknown.* ABF, *with music*; AmSS, *with music*; BaBo
(Indian Mohee, The, *with music.*) BFSS
(Lass of Mohea, The, *with music.*) SoAmSa
Little Moon, The. Longfellow. *Fr.* The Light of Stars. BoTP
Little moon was restless in eternity, A. Night Note. James Oppenheim. MAP; MoAmPo (1942 ed.)
Little more kindness and a little less creed, A. The World Needs. *Unknown.* PoToHe (new ed.)
Little more tired at close of day, A. As We Grow Older [*or* Growing Old]. Rollin J. Wells. BLPA; PoToHe; TreFT; WBLP
Little more toward the light, A. Growing Gray. Austin Dobson. HBV
Little Morning Music, A. Delmore Schwartz. BoNaP; NYBP
Little Mother. "M. P. D." PEDC
Little Mother Maybe. *Unknown.* SAS
Little moths are creeping, The. Interior. Padraic Colum. ACV; MoBrPo; TSW
Little mountain spring I found, A. The Spring. Rose Fyleman. BrR; FaPON
Little mouse:/ Are you. Race Prejudice. Alfred Kreymborg. ELU
Little mouse in gray velvet. Mouse. Hilda Conkling. SoPo; StVeCh; TiPo
Little mouse nibbled a Limburger cheese, A. A Mouse, a Cat, and an Irish Bull. John Banister Tabb. CIV
Little Mousgrove and the Lady Barnet. *Unknown. See* Little Musgrave and Lady Barnard.
Little Mud-Sparrows, The; Jewish Legend. Elizabeth Stuart Phelps Ward. ChrBoLe
Little Musgrave and Lady Barnard. *Unknown.* BaBo (A *vers.*); CABL; ErPo; ESPB (A *and* B *vers.*); InvP; NoP OBB; ViBoFo
(Little Mathey Grove, A *vers., with music.*); BFSS
(Little Mathie Grove, B *vers.*) BaBo
(Little Matty Groves, B *vers., with music.*) BFSS
(Little Mousgrove and Lady Barnet, *diff. vers.*) OxBB
(Lord Banner, C *vers.*) BaBo
Little mushroom table spread, A. Robert Herrick. *Fr.* Oberon's Feast. OTPC (1923 ed.); ViBoPo
Little music, please, but let, A. To all Musicians. Richard Church. MuSP
Little my lacking fortunes show. Expenses. Adelaide Crapsey. NP; TOP
Little Nancy [*or* Nanny *or* Nan] Etticoat. Mother Goose. BoChLi; ChTr; HBV; HBVY; OTPC; OxNR; PCH; PPL; RIS; SiTL; SoPo; StVeCh; TiPo
Little Nellie Cassidy has got a place in town. In Service. Winifred M. Letts. HBMV; YT
Little new neighbor, have you come to be. Welcome. Rose Waldo. MPB; SoPo
Little newt, The. The Newt. David McCord. TiPo (1959 ed.)
Little Night Music, A. Felix Stefanile. FiSC
Little Nipper an' 'Is Ma, The. George Fauvel Gouraud. AA
Little noises of the house, The. During a Bombardment by V-Weapons. Roy Fuller. ToPo
Little Old Lady, The. Rodney Bennett. BoTP
Little Old Lady in Lavender Silk, The. Dorothy Parker. InMe; YaD
Little old man came in from plow, The. Dandoo. *Unknown.* BFSS
Little old man came riding by, A. *Unknown.* GoTP
Little old man lived up in a cloud, A. The Cloud House. Adrian Mott. GaP
Little old man of Derby, A. *Unknown.* OxNR
Little old man of the sea, A. The Ingenious Little Old Man. John Bennett. FaPON; GaP
Little Old Sod Shanty, The. *Unknown.* AS, *with music*; BFSS; CoSo, *with music*; IHA
Little old tailor that came from Mayo, The. The Tailor That Came from Mayo. Denis A. McCarthy. OnYI
Little old woman, A. Bramble Jam. Irene F. Pawsey. BoTP
Little old woman, A. Behind the Waterfall. Winifred Welles. PoMS; StVeCh; TiPo
Little one, come to my knee! A Story for a Child [*or* A Night with a Wolf]. Bayard Taylor. GN; HBV; HBVY; OTPC (1923 ed.); PCD; TVC
Little one sleeps in its cradle, The. Song of Myself, VIII. Walt Whitman. MaPo; TrGrPo
Little Ones, The. W. H. Davies. MaRV
Little onward lend thy guiding hand, A. Samson Agonistes. Milton. AtBAP; EnLi-1; ILP; MBW-1; PoEL-3; ViBoPo
Little or nothing said soon mended is. John Davies of Hereford. SiCE
Little Orphant Annie. James Whitcomb Riley. AA; BBGG; BoChLi; BOHV; FaFP; FaPON; HBV; HBVY; MoShBr; MPB; OTPC; PaPo; PFY; PTK; StVeCh; TiPo; TreF; TSW
(. . .Elf Child, The.) AmePo
Little owl flew through the night, The. On the Adequacy of Landscape. Wallace Stevens. PoeP
Little Pagan Rain Song. Frances Shaw. HBMV; NP
Little Page's Song, A. William Alexander Percy. HBV
Little Papoose. Hilda Conkling. FaPON; GaP
Little Parable, A. Anne Reeve Aldrich. AA; HBV; MaRV
Little park that I pass through. Ellis Park. Helen Hoyt. HBMV; NP; PoMa; SP; YT
"Little, passionately, not at all, A." Villanelle of Marguerites. Ernest Dowson. EnLi-2; MoBrPo
Little Peach, The. Eugene Field. BOHV; LBN; ShM
Little Peach, The. *Unknown.* NA
Little peach in the orchard grew, A. The Little Peach. Eugene Field. BOHV; LBN; ShM; TSW
Little Penelope Socrates. Christmas Chimes. *Unknown.* BOHV
Little People. Isaac Leibush Peretz, *tr. fr. Yiddish by* Joseph Leftwich. TrJP
Little Person, A. Brian Hooker. HBMV
Little Phillis. Kate Greenaway. BiCB
Little Pig Asleep, A. Leroy F. Jackson. BrR
Little pig lived in a sty, A. The Greedy Little Pig. Irene F. Pawsey. BoTP
Little Piggy [*or* Piggies]. Thomas Hood. BoTP; SoPo
Little pitiful, worn, laughing faces, The. The Beggars. Margaret Widdemer. NP
Little Pixie Piper went, A. Pipes and Drums. Lilian Holmes. GFA
Little Plant, The. Kate Louise Brown. DD; HH; OTPC (1946 ed.)
(In the Heart of a Seed.) RePo
Little Poem of Life, The. John Oxenham. TRV
Little Poll Parrot. *Unknown.* OxNR
Little Polly Flinders/ sat among the cinders. Mother Goose. HBV; HBVY; OTPC; OxNR; RIS; SAS
Little Ponds. Arthur Guiterman. HBMV
Little poppies, little hell flames. Poppies in July. Sylvia Plath. NaP
Little Prayer, A. Paul Goodman. LiTA
Little Prayer, A. Samuel Ellsworth Kiser. MaRV
Little Pretty Bonny Lass, A. *Unknown.* ElL; NCEP
Little pretty Nancy girl. *Unknown.* OxNR
Little pretty nightingale, [*or* Lytyll prety nyghtyngale], The. The Nightingale. *Unknown.* EG; LO; OAEP; TrGrPo
Little priest of Felton, The. *Unknown.* OxNR; PPL
Little Prince Carl he stole away. What the Lord High Chamberlain Said. Virginia Woodward Cloud. BBGG
Little Prince of long ago, A. Sons of the Kings. Joan Agnew. BiCB; BoTP
Little Prince Tatters has lost his cap! Prince Tatters. Laura E. Richards. GaP; HBV; HBVY; MPB
Little Puppy. *Tr. fr. Navajo Indian by* Hilda Faunce Wetherill. FaPON; TiPo (1959 ed.)
Little Pussy. Jane Taylor. *See* I Like Little Pussy.
Little Pussy Whitey-toes. *Unknown.* SAS
Little ragged girl, our ball-boy, A. A Game at Salzburg. Randall Jarrell. MiAP
Little Rain. Elizabeth Madox Roberts. PoRh; SoPo; SUS; TiPo (1952 ed.)
Little Rain, The. Tu Fu, *tr. fr. Chinese by* L. Cranmer-Byng. FaPON
Little Rain Men. Ruth Anne Hussey. PCH
Little Raindrops. *At. to* Ann Hawkshaw. BoTP; HBV; HBVY; OTPC (1923 ed.)
Little Rebel, The. Joseph Ashby-Sterry. VA
Little Red Hen, The. Eudora Bumstead. FTB
Little Red Lark, The. Alfred Perceval Graves. HBV
Little red lark, The/ Arises with dawn. Morning. Ivy O. Eastwick. BoTP
Little Red Ribbon, The. James Whitcomb Riley. HBV

Little Red Riding Hood. Guy Wetmore Carryl. FiBHP
Little Red Sled, The. Jocelyn Bush. PCH; SoPo; TiPo
Little Rhyme and a Little Reason, A. Henry Anstadt. BLRP
Little river twittering in the twilight, The. Bei Hennef. D. H. Lawrence. BrPo
Little Road, The. Nancy Byrd Turner. RIS; TiPo
Little road grows narrow up the hill, The. No Season for Our Season. Willard Maas. AnAmPo
Little road says, Go, The. The House and the Road. Josephine Preston Peabody. TreFT
Little road was straying, A. The Little Road. Nancy Byrd Turner. RIS
Little roads I travel, The. Nugatory. E. B. White. BOHV
Little Roads to Happiness. Wilhelmina Stitch. PoToHe (new ed.)
Little Robin red breast I hear you sing your song. Robin Red Breast. Lula Lowe Weeden. CDC
Little Robin Redbreast came to visit me. *Unknown.* OxNR
Little Robin Redbreast sat upon a tree [*or* rail]. Mother Goose. BoChLi; BoTP (2 *vers.*); GFA; GoBP; HBV; HBVY; MPB; OxNR; PPL; RIS; SAS; SiTL; StVeCh
Little room, depressing, old, A. The Tailor. "S. Ansky." TrJP
Little Rose, be not sad for all that hath. The Little Dark Rose. *Unknown.* OnYI
Little Rose Is Dust, My Dear, The. Grace Hazard Conkling. HBV; NP
Little Rose Tree, The. Rachel Field. FaPON; SUS; TiPo
Little saint best fits a little shrine, A. A Ternary [*or* Ternarie] of Littles. Robert Herrick. ALV; BOHV; BoTP; FaBoCh; GoJo; HBV; HBVY; LoGBV; MaPo; MyFE; OTPC (1923 ed.); PG (1955 ed.); PoEL-3; PoRA; WhC
Little Salamander, The. Walter de la Mare. NP
Little Saling. Olaf Baker. HBMV
Little Sally Sand, *with music.* *Unknown.* TrAS
Little Sally Waters. Mother Goose. TiPo
Little Sandman's Song. *Unknown,* *tr. fr. German by* Louis Untermeyer. RIS
Little Sarah she stood by her grandmother's bed. The Johnnycake. *Unknown.* MPB
Little Satellite. Jane W. Krows. SoPo
Little scarlet emblem, A. The Red Cross. Edna Jacques. PoRL
Little Scotch-ee, *with music.* *Unknown.* AS
Little seed lay on the ground, A. The Critic. *Unknown.* SoP
Little Senorita. Charles Divine. MPB
Little Sequence, A, *sels.* Francis Burdett Money-Coutts. OBVV
"Forgive!"
"No wonder you so oft have went."
Little Serenade. Kenton Kilmer. WHL
Little sharp vexations, The. Our Burden Bearer [*or* The Unfailing One]. Phillips Brooks. BLRP; FaChP; MaRV; SoP; TRV
Little shepherd maiden, A. Il Etait un' Bergère. *Unknown.* CIV
Little Shepherd's Song, The. William Alexander Percy. GFA; YeAr
Little ship was tossed about, The. On Top of Troubled Waters. Dorothy J. Langford. BePJ
Little ships of whitest pearl. A Mother's Song. Francis Ledwidge. EtS
Little shoes of fairies are, The. Fairy Shoes. Annette Wynne. MPB (1956 ed.)
Little shop at Nazareth, The. Carpenter's Son. Annie Johnson Flint. BePJ
Little shrivelled and humpbacked creature, The! Tim, the Fairy. Florence Randal Livesay. CaP
Little shrivelled up old woman rejoiced, The. The Despair of the Old Woman. Baudelaire. OnPM
Little Shroud, The. Letitia E. Landon. PaPo
Little Shrub Growing By, A. Ben Jonson. *See* Ask Not to Know This Man.
Little siren of the stage. To Signora Cuzzoni. Ambrose Phillips. CEP; LoBV; OBEC
Little Sister Left in Charge, The. Cecil Frances Alexander. OTPC (1923 ed.)
Little Sister of the Prophet, The. Marjorie Pickthall. HBV
Little Sister Rose-Marie. Rose-Marie of the Angels. Adelaide Crapsey. HBV
Little slender lad, toad-headed. The Ambrosia of Dionysus and Semele. Robert Graves. NYBP
Little Snail. Hilda Conkling. FaPON; GFA; MPB; PoRh; TiPo; TVC; UTS
Little snail. Snail. Langston Hughes. FaPON; GoSl; TiPo
Little snail, little snail,/ With your hard stony bed. The Snail. *Unknown.* PCH
Little snake now grieves, The. A Spring Serpent. Ivor Winters. CBV; ExPo
Little snatch of an ancient song. Of an Old Song. William E. H. Lecky. WGRP
Little snow people are hurrying down, The. Putting the World to Bed. Esther W. Buxton. TVC
Little soldiers thread the hills, The. Small Soldiers with Drum in Large Landscape. Robert Penn Warren. Mexico Is a Foreign Country, IV. FiMAP
Little Son. Georgia Douglas Johnson. CDC
Little Song, A. Duncan Campbell Scott. VA
Little Song, A. Robert Grosseteste, *tr. fr. Latin by* William de Shoreham, *mod. vers. by* F. M. Capes. ISi
Little Song in Assisi, A. George Barker. ToPo
Little Song of Life, A. Lizette Woodworth Reese. BrR; FaPON; HBMV; MPB; PoMa; SP; TiPo (1959 ed.); TreFT
(Song of Life, A.) OTD
(Sun and the Rain, The.) ThGo
Little Song of Spring, A. Mary Austin. YeAr
Little Song of Work, A. Sarah Elizabeth Sprouse. BLRP
Little Songs. Marjorie Pickthall. CaP
Little songs of summer are all gone today, The. End-of-Summer Poem. Rowena Bennett. FaPON; SiSoSe
Little Sorrow. "Marian Douglas." SAS; TVC
Little soul, like a cloud, like a feather. To His Soul. Hadrian. PoPl
Little soul, little tease, little stray. Animula Blandula Vagula. Emperor Hadrian, *tr. by* Charles Glenn Wallis. LiTW
Little sound, A. Many a Mickle. Walter de la Mare. FaBV; GTSE
Little sparrows, The. Pastoral. William Carlos Williams. TwCP
Little Spring. *Unknown.* GFA
Little Spring Flows Clear Again, The. Glenn Ward Dresbach. NP
Little Squirrel, A. *Unknown.* TiPo
Little Star, The. Vivien Jameson. SoP
Little Star. Jane Taylor. *See* Twinkle, Twinkle, Little Star.
Little Star, The ("Scintillate, scintillate"). *Unknown.* BOHV; InMe
Little star shone singly in the night, A. The Little Star. Vivien Jameson. SoP
Little stars have five sharp wings. Stars. Carolyn Hancock. RIS
Little Steamboat. Oscar Williams. PoPl
Little Sticks. Eric Rolls. PoAu-2
Little stones chuckle among the fields, The. At Toledo. Arthur Symons. BrPo
Little Stones of Arlington, The. Barbara Young. OQP
Little strokes/ Fell great oaks. Well-packed Wisdom. Benjamin Franklin. *Fr.* Poor Richard's Almanac. StaSt
Little sun, a little rain, A. The Earth and Man. Stopford Augustus Brooke. HBV; OnYI; OTPC
Little Swirl of Vers Libre, A. Thomas R. Ybarra. BOHV
Little sycamore, The. Love Song. *Unknown.* TTY
Little syren of the stage. To Seignora Cuzzoni. Ambrose Philips. EiCL
Little Talk. Aileen Fisher. FaPON
Little Talk wid Jesus Makes It Right, A, *with music.* *Unknown.* BoAN-2
Little taper set tonight. The Christmas [*or* Christ] Candle. Kate Louise Brown. OTPC (1946 ed.); PoRL; SoPo
Little Te Deum of the Commonplace, A, *sels.* John Oxenham.
"For all the wonders of this wondrous world." PGD
"For all Thy ministries." TRV
"For maiden sweetness, and for strength of men." TRV
"With hearts responsive." TrPWD
Little Tee-wee. *Unknown.* OxNR
Little Testament, The. Villon. *See* Petit Testament, Le.
Little Theocritus. Caroline Wilder Paradise. AA
Little Things. Julia A. Fletcher Carney, *Wr. at. to* E. C. Brewer *and to* Frances S. Osgood. FaBoBe; FaFP; GoTP; HBV; HBVY; NeHB, 2 *sts.*; OTPC; TreF, 2 *sts.*
(Kind Deeds.) BoTP
("Little drops of water.") FaPON, 2 *sts.*; GFA, *st.* 1
Little Things, The. Elizabeth Isler. PoToHe (new ed.)

Little Things. Orrick Johns. AnAmPo; MAP; NP; PG (1945 ed.); PoToHe (new ed.)
Little Things. Eileen Mathias. BoTP
Little Things. Maud Rose. SoP
Little Things. James Stephens. AnEnPo; EaLo; FaPON; GoJo; HBMV; MemP; MoBrPo; MPB; NeMA; PDV; PoRA (rev. ed.); SiSoSe; TiPo (1959 ed.); UTS; WePo
Little Things. Marion Strobel. HBMV; NP
Little Things ("God has no end of material"). *Unknown.* STF
Little Things ("It was only a kindly smile he gave"). *Unknown.* STF
Little Things ("It's just the little homely things"). *Unknown.* PoToHe (new ed.)
Little Things ("What will it matter in a little while"). *Unknown.* SoP
Little Things That Happen, The. Marjorie Wilson. BoTP
Little things, that run, and quail. Little Things. James Stephens. AnEnPo; EaLo; FaPON; GoJo; HBMV; MemP; MoBrPo; MPB; NeMA; PDV; PoRA (rev. ed.); SiSoSe; TiPo (1959 ed.); UTS; WePo
Little thinkest thou, poor flower. *See* Little think'st thou, poor flower.
Little thinks, in the field, yon red-cloaked clown. Each and All. Emerson. AA; AmePo; AmP; AmPP; AnNE; AP; AWP; CoBA; HBV; ILP; MAmP; MCCG; MWA-1; NePA; OHFP; OQP; OxBA; PoIE; WGRP
Little think'st [*or* thinkest] thou, poor [*or* poore] flower. The Blossom[e]. John Donne. AnAnS-1; AWP; InPo; LiTB; MaMe; MBW-1; MeLP; OBS; SCEP-1; SeCP; SeEP; UnPo (1st ed.)
Little Thomas. F. Gwynne Evans. BBGG
Little tigers are at rest, The. Tom Hood. CenHV
Little Tillie Turtle. Road Fellows. Barbara Young. BrR
Little time for laughter, A. After. Philip Bourke Marston. HBV
Little Tippler, The. Emily Dickinson. *See* I taste a liquor never brewed.
"Little toe is attractive, The." "The Time of Man." Phyllis Webb. MoCV
Little Toil of Love, The. Emily Dickinson. *See* I had no time to hate, because.
Little Tom Dogget. Colly, My Cow. *Unknown.* EvOK
Little Tom Tittlemouse,/ Lived in a bell-house. *unknown.* OxNR
Little Tommy Tacket. *Unknown.* OxNR
Little Tommy Tiddler. Paul Edmonds. BoTP
Little Tommy Tittlemouse/ Lived in a little house. *Unknown.* OxNR
Little Tommy Tucker/ Sings for his supper. Mother Goose. HBVY; OTPC; OxNR; PCH; PPL; RIS; SAS
Little too abstract, a little too wise, A. Return. Robinson Jeffers. GoYe
Little Town. Federico García Lorca, *tr. fr. Spanish by* Eleanor L. Turnbull. OnPM
Little toy dog is covered with dust, The. Little Boy Blue. Eugene Field. AA; BeLS; FaFP; FaPON; HBV; HBVY; LiTG; MAP; MoAmPo (1942 ed.); NeHB; NeMA; OHFP; OTD; PaPo; PCD; PoLF; TreF
Little Toy Land of the Dutch, The. *Unknown.* GFA; MPB; OTPC (1946 ed.)
Little Tree. E. E. Cummings. Chansons Innocentes, II. FlW; LOW; PDV; PoSC; RoGo
Little Trotty Wagtail. John Clare. BoTP; CBEP; FaPON; PCH; RIS; UnPo (3d ed.)
Little Tumescence, A. Jonathan Williams. ErPo; NeAP
Little Turtle, The. Vachel Lindsay. BoChLi; FaPON; GFA; GoJo; PCH; PDV; SoPo; StVeCh; SUS; TiPo; UTS
Little Vagabond, The. Blake. BOHV; CBEP; CEP; SeCeV; TDP
Little Valentine, A. Elizabeth Winton. PCH
Little Waves of Breffny, The. Eva Gore-Booth. AnIV; HBV; HBVY; HT; OnYI; YT
(Waves of Breffny, The.) StaSt; TSW
Little Way, A. Frank L. Stanton. AA
Little Way, A. *Unknown.* SoP
Little way below her chin, A. On Some Buttercups. Frank Dempster Sherman. AA
Little way—I know it is not far, A. A Little Way. *Unknown.* SoP
Little way, more soft and sweet, A. First Footsteps. Swinburne. NeHB
Little way to walk with you, my own, A. A Little Way. Frank L. Stanton. AA
Little, Wee Froggies, The. J. K. Nutting. *Fr.* How the Froggies Go to Sleep. SAS
Little Wee Man, The. *Unknown.* *See* Wee Wee Man, The.
Little While, A. Horatius Bonar. *See* Beyond the Smiling and the Weeping.
Little While, A. Emily Brontë. *See* Little While, a Little While, A.
Little While, A. Fanny J. Crosby. SoP
Little While, A. Don Marquis. HBV
Little While, A. Dante Gabriel Rossetti. VA; ViBoPo
Little While, a Little While, A. Emily Brontë. OAEP; OBNC; OxBI; ViBoPo
(Holyday.) NBM
(Little While, A.) EnLi-2 (1949 ed.); TreFS
"Where wilt thou go my harassed heart?" *sel.* LO
Little While I Fain Would Linger Yet, A ("A little while, my life is almost set!"). Paul Hamilton Hayne. AA; HBV
Little while my love and I, A. A May Song. "Violet Fane." OBVV; VA
Little while the tears and laughter, A. A Little While. Don Marquis. HBV
Little While to Love and Rave, A. Samuel Hoffenstein. ALV
Little while to sow in tears and weakness, A. A Little While. Fanny J. Crosby. SoP
Little Whistler, The. Frances Frost. PDV; SoPo; StVeCh (1955 ed.); TiPo
Little White Cat, The. *Unknown, tr. fr. Modern Irish by* Mrs. Costello of Tuam. OnYI
Little white clouds are racing over the sky, The. Magdalen Walks. Oscar Wilde. MoBrPo; YT
Little white face that looks into mine. Metempsychosis. Louella C. Poole. CIV
Little white feathers. Snowflakes. Mary Mapes Dodge. MPB
Little White Fox. David Rowbotham. BoAV
Little white horses are out on the sea. White Horses. Winifred Howard. BrR; SoPo; SUS; UTS
Little White Lily. George Macdonald. HBV; HBVY; MPB; OTPC; PRWS; SAS
Little white mermaidens live in the sea, The. The Mermaidens. Laura E. Richards. BrR; StVeCh (1955 ed.)
Little white prayers, The. Cologne Cathedral. Frances Shaw. NP
Little White Schoolhouse Blues. Florence Becker Lennon. PoNe (1970 ed.)
Little white snowdrop just waking up. Waiting to Grow. Frank French. PEDC
Little Wild Baby. "Margaret Vandegrift." AA; HBV
Little wild bird sometimes at my ear, A. Ballata: Of True and False Singing. *Unknown.* AWP; OnPM; UnS
Little wild birds have come flying, The. Love-Song. *Unknown.* AWP
Little Willie. Gerald Massey. PaPo
Little Willie ("Little Willie from his mirror"). *Unknown.* MoShBr; ShM
("Little Willie from his mirror.") GoTP; WhC
Little Willie ("Little Willie hung his sister"). *Unknown.* NA; TreFS
Little Willie ("Little Willie, mad as hell"). *Unknown.* ShM
Little Willie ("Little Willie, once in ire"). *Unknown.* ShM
Little Willie ("Willie saw some dynamite"). *Unknown.* FaPON
Little Willie/ Pair of skates. Golden Gates. *Unknown.* ShM
Little Willie, in the best of sashes. Tender-Heartedness. Harry Graham. ALV; NA
Little Willie's My Darlin', *with music.* *Unknown.* OuSiCo
Little Wind. Kate Greenaway. GFA; GoJo; SUS
("Little wind, blow on the hill-top.") TiPo
Little winter cottontails. The Outdoor Christmas Tree. Aileen Fisher. SiSoSe
Little Word, A. John Oxenham. OTD
(Influence.) STF
Little Word, A ("Little word in kindness spoken, A"). *Unknown.* SoP
Little Word, A ("You'd be surprised, I'm sure, to know"). *Unknown.* STF
Little Words. Benjamin Keech. PoToHe
Little words that wear silk dresses. The Words. Opal Whiteley. TSW
Little Work, A. George Du Maurier. *Fr.* Trilby, Pt. VIII.

Little (continued)
FaBoBe; HBV; NeHB; OQP; PoLF; PTK
(Little, A.) MaRV
(Little Work, a Little Play, A.) PoToHe (new ed.); TreFS
Little world of olden days is gone, The. In an Age of Science. Thomas Curtis Clark. MaRV
Little wrists. So That Even a Lover. Louis Zukofsky. CoPo
Little yellow buttercup, A. A Buttercup. *Unknown.* BoTP
Little yellow flame of fur. To a Kitten. Martha Haskell Clark. CIV
Little Young Lambs, The. Patrick Chalmers. TiPo (1952 ed.)
Little young lambs, oh! why do you stay. The Wolf and the Lambs. Ivy O. Eastwick. BoTP
Littles. Robert Herrick. *See* Ternarie of Littles, A.
Littlest door, the inner door, The. The Door. Mary Carolyn Davies. HBMV
Liu Ch'e. Ezra Pound. AP
Live-a humble, humble, Lord. Humble Yo'self de Bell Done Ring. *Unknown.* BoAN-2
Live all thy sweet life thro'. A Summer Wish. Christina Rossetti. OBNC
Live and Help Live. Edwin Markham. MaRV; OQP
Live and Love. Elizabeth Barrett Browning. *Fr.* A Drama of Exile. OQP
Live and love; live and love. Differences. Valerie Tarver. TNV
Live as you like, long as you like, secure. For Haroun Al Raschid. Abu'l-Atahija. LiTW
Live Blindly. Trumbull Stickney. AmLP; AnAmPo; AnFE; APA; CoAnAm; LiTA; NePA; TwAmPo
(Live Blindly and upon the Hour.) AmePo; MAP; MoAmPo (1942 ed.); TrGrPo
Live Christ. John Oxenham. BLRP; ChIP; OQP
Live Day by Day. *Unknown.* SoP
Live Each Day. Goethe, *tr. fr. German.* OQP
Live ever here, Lorenzo?—shocking thought! Edward Young. *Fr.* Night Thoughts. EnRP
Live for Something. Robert Whitaker. SoP
Live here, great heart; and love and dy [*or* die] and kill. Upon the Book and Picture of the Seraphicall Saint Teresa. Richard Crashaw. *Fr.* The Flaming Heart. AtBAP; OBS
Live in a Love. Robert Browning. TrGrPo
Live in the Present. Sarah Knowles Bolton. OQP
(Live Today.) MaRV
Live Jesus, live, and let it bee. The Authors Motto. Richard Crashaw. MaMe
Live Joyfully. Ecclesiastes, IX: 7-11, Bible, *O.T.* TreFS
("Live joyfully with the wife whom thou lovest.") PoG
"Live like the wind," he said, "unfettered." The Wind Bloweth Where It Listeth. Countee Cullen. NP
Live, live with me, and thou shalt see. To Phyllis [to Love and Live with Him]. Robert Herrick. AnEnPo; CavP; CLwM; LiTL; OAEP; PAn
Live long, Elisa, that the wolf of Spain. Ad Reginam Elizabetham. Thomas Bastard. SiCE
Live Not, Poor Bloom, But Perish. *Unknown.* NCEP
Live, prince of poets! Thy affections guide. Ad Gulielmum Warner. John Weever. ReIE
Live so that you. Certain Maxims of Archy. Don Marquis. InMe
Live, Spenser, ever in thy *Faerie Queene* [*or Fairy Queene*]. A Remembrance of Some English Poets. Richard Barnfield. ReIE; SiCE; TuPP
Live thy life/ Young and old. The Oak. Tennyson. EPN; FaPON; MPB; PoPl; PoVP; YT
Live Today. Sarah Knowles Bolton. *See* Live in the Present.
Live, trifling incidents, and grace my songs. Robert Bloomfield. *Fr.* The Farmer's Boy. OBRV
Live unlamenting though obscure remaining. To J. S. Collis. Ruth Pitter. OxBoCh
Live While You Live. Philip Doddridge. OxBoCh
(Dum Vivimus, Vivamus.) OBEC
(Finest English Epigram, The.) SoP
Live with me; be my wife. The Passionate Clerk to His Love. Ronald McCuaig. MoAuPo
Live with Me Still. Thomas Dekker *and* John Ford. *Fr.* The Sun's Darling. SeCL
Live you by love confined. C. Day Lewis. LO
Lived on one's back. Vigil. W. E. Henley. *Fr.* In Hospital. LoBV
Lively larke did stretche her wyng, The. The Judgement of Desire. *Unknown.* EnPo
Lively sparks that issue from those eyes, The. The Lover Describeth His Being Striken with Sight of His Love. Sir Thomas Wyatt. FCP; ReIE
Lively young turtle lived down by the banks, A. The Turtle and Flamingo [*or* The Song of the Turtle and Flamingo]. James T. Fields. BOHV; GN; HBV
Lives. Henry Reed. BoNaP; LiTB
Lives and times of Oedipus and Elektra, The. This One's on Me. Phyllis Gotlieb. MoCV
Lives he in any other world. Emily Dickinson. MWA-2
Lives in winter. Mother Goose. HBV; SoPo; TiPo
Lives of Great Men. *Unknown.* FaFP; TreFT
Lives of Great Men All Remind Us. Longfellow. *Fr.* A Psalm of Life. DD
Lives of great men all remind us/ As their pages o'er we turn. Lives of Great Men. *Unknown.* FaFP; TreFT
Lives of Gulls and Children, The. Howard Nemerov. FiMAP; NePoEA
Lives there a man with soul so dead. Whatever Is, Is Right. Laman Blanchard. BOHV
Livid Lightnings Flashed in the Clouds, The. Stephen Crane. The Black Riders, XXXIX. AmePo; AP
Livid sky on London, A. The Old Song. G. K. Chesterton. FaBoTw
Living. William Dean Howells. AmePo
Living. Denise Levertov. FRC
Living. Harold Monro. FaBoMo; LiTB; LiTM; SeCePo
Living. D. S. Savage. NeBP
Living ("To live with saints in heaven"). *Unknown.* SoP
Living ("To touch the cup with eager lips"). *Unknown.* BLPA; FaBoBe; NeHB; TreFS
Living/ is/ too much/. I Am Not Lazy. Mari Evans. WSL
"Living a life." A Man. Denise Levertov. TPM
Living among the Toilers. Henri Percikow. OCS
Living and Dying. "Michael Lewis," *after the Chinese. Fr.* Cherry Blossoms. UnTE
Living Book, The. Charlotte Fiske Bates. AA
Living Bread. Eva Weaver Sefton. BePJ
Living by the Red River. James Wright. FRC
Living Chalice, The. Susan Mitchell. HBMV
"Living Dog" and "The Dead Lion," The. Thomas Moore. OBRV
Living Flame of Love, The. St. John of the Cross, *tr. fr. Spanish by* E. Allison Peers. LiTW
(O Flame of Living Love, *tr. by* Arthur Symons.) AWP; CAW
Living God, The. Daniel ben Judah, *tr. fr. Hebrew by* Israel Zangwill. TrJP
Living God, The. Charlotte Perkins Gilman. WGRP
Living God, The. Abraham ibn Ezra, *tr. fr. Hebrew by* Alice Lucas. TrJP
Living God O magnify and bless, The. The Living God. Daniel ben Judah. TrJP
Living in a wide landscape are the flowers. Desert Flowers. Keith Douglas. FaBoTw
Living in Missouri wuz a bold, bad man. Jesse James (B *vers.*). *Unknown.* ABF
Living in retirement beyond the World. The Valley Wind. Lu Yün. OnPM
Living in Sin. Austin Clarke. ELU
Living in Sin. Adrienne Cecile Rich. NePoEa; NYBP
Living Jesus, The. R. F. Pechey. SoP
Living Juliet, The. Shakespeare. *See* He Jests at Scars . . .
Living man is blind and drinks his drop, A. W. B. Yeats. *Fr.* A Dialogue of Self and Soul. DTC
Living Memory, A. William Augustus Croffut. AA
Living? Our Supervisors Will Do That for Us! David Holbrook. NePoEA-2
Living Pearl, A. Kenneth Rexroth. LiTM (1970 ed.)
Living Sermon, The. *Unknown.* *See* Sermons We See.
Living soul, how priceless, A. A Soul. Bertha Prince Vander Ark. SoP
Living Statue, The. *Unknown, tr. fr. Greek by* Louis Untermeyer. UnTE
Living Temple, The. Oliver Wendell Holmes. *Fr.* The Autocrat of the Breakast Table, *ch.* 7. AA; AmePo; AmPP (3d ed.); AP
Living Tithe, The. Mabel Munns Charles. ChIP
Living unto Thee. John Ellerton. MaRV
(God of the Living.) WGRP

Living Water. Ruth M. Williams. BePJ
Liz-Town Humorist, A. James Whitcomb Riley. AmePo; IHA
Liza, go steep your long white hands. Spring Pastoral. Elinor Wylie. AnEnPo
Liza in the Summer Time, *with music.* *Unknown.* AS
Liza Jane, *with music.* *Unknown.* ABF, *with add. sts.*; AS
(Mountain Top, *diff. vers., with music.*) AS
Liza Lee, *with music.* *Unknown.* SoAmSa
Lizard, The. Abbie Farwell Brown. UTS
Lizard. K. E. Ingram. PoNe
Lizard. Agnes Maxwell-Hall. PoNe
Lizard Head, star-thirsty stone. To Lizard Head. Clifford J. Laube. CAW
Lizards and Snakes. Anthony Hecht. CoPo; TPM; TwCP
Lizards sprawl on the sun-baked stones, The. Iguanas. David Atamian. NYTB
Lizie Lindsay (A *and* B *vers.*). *Unknown.* ESPB
(Donald of the Isles.) OxBB
(Leezie Lindsay.) BFSS, *with music*; FaBoCh; LoGBV
Lizie Wan. *Unknown.* BaBo (A *and* B *vers.*); ESPB; ViBoFo
Lizzie Borden. *Unknown.* BOHV; ShM; TreFS
(Crimes of Lizzie Borden, The.) FaFP; LiTM; SiTL
("Lizzie Borden took an axe.") CenHV
Lizzie's Sister. *Unknown.* SiTL
Lizzy Liberty, *abr.* John Skinner. PoFr
Llama, The. Hilaire Belloc. BOHV; EvOK; FaBoCh; FiBHP; LoGBV
Llama seems a sensitive creature, The. A Snap Judgement on the Llama. Peggy Bennett. ELU
Llano Estacado, The. *Unknown.* *See* Tantalus; Texas.
Llewellyn and the Tree. E. A. Robinson. BeLS; HBMV
Lo! above the mournful chanting. Kol Nidra. Joseph Leiser. *Fr.* The Day of Atonement. AA; TrJP
Lo! all in Silence, all in Order stand. Books. George Crabbe. *Fr.* The Library. OBEC
Lo! all thy glory gone! Nekros. John Banister Tabb. AmP
Lo, as a careful housewife runs to catch. Sonnets, CXLIII. Shakespeare. CBEP; OAEP; ReEn
Lo, as a dove when up she springs. In Memoriam A. H. H., XII. Tennyson. EnLi-2; EPN; LoBV; ViPo; VP
Lo, as some bard on isles of the Aegean. The Inner Light. Frederic William Henry Myers. *Fr.* Saint Paul. MaRV; VA
Lo! as some venturer, from his stars receiving. Advent. Frederic William Henry Myers. *Fr.* Saint Paul. ChIP; MaRV; PGD
Lo! as the Potter Mouldeth. *Unknown, tr. fr. Hebrew by* Elsie Davis. TrJP
Lo, as the sun from his ocean bed rising. There She Blows! *Unknown.* EtS; SoAmSa
Lo, Collin, here the place whose pleasaunt syte. June. Spenser. *Fr.* The Shepheardes Calender. EnLit
Lo! Death has reared himself a throne. The City in the Sea. Poe. AA; AmePo; AmLP; AmP; AmPo; AmPP; AnAmPo; AnEnPo; AnFE; AP; APA; BoLiVe; CBEP; CoAnAm; CoBA; FaBoEn; ForPo; GTBS-D; HBV; ILP; LiTA; MAmP; MWA-1; NePA; NoP; OBRV; OxBA; PeER; PoE; PoEL-4; PoFS; PoIE; SiSw; TDP; TrGrPo; ViBoPo; WHA
Lo, fainter now lie spread the shades of night. Morning Hymn. Gregory the Great. CAW; WGRP
Lo, from our loitering ship a new land at last to be seen. Iceland First Seen. William Morris. PoVP
Lo! from the Livid East. James Thomson. *Fr.* The Seasons: Winter. AtBAP
("Lo! from the livid East, or piercing North.") FaBoEn; PeER
Lo! from the woodland skirting the old town. Autumn. Thomas Caulfield Irwin. IrPN
Lo, God, our God, has come! Bless the Blessed Morn. Horatius Bonar. BePJ; SoP
Lo, had begun again for her the time. William Ellery Leonard. *Fr.* Two Lives. AnEnPo
Lo, He Comes! Thomas Kelly. SoP
Lo [*or* Loe] here a little volume, but great [*or* large] book! Prayer [*or* An Ode Which Was Prefixed to a Prayer Booke *or* On a Prayer Booke Sent to Mrs. M. R.]. Richard Crashaw. AnAnS-1; HBV; MaMe; MeP; SCEP-1; SeEP
Lo, here is God, and there is God! The New Sinai. Arthur Hugh Clough. PoVP; ViPo
Lo here the faire Chariclia! in whom strove. Upon the Faire Ethiopian Sent to a Gentlewoman. Richard Crashaw. MaMe
Lo! Here the Gentle Lark. Shakespeare. *Fr.* Venus and Adonis. ChTr
Lo, here the impost of a faith entire. To Delia, LV. Samuel Daniel. Sonn; TuPP
Lo, here the state of every mortal wight. Respice Finem. Thomas Proctor. OBSC; ReIE; SiCE; TuPP
Lo! How I seek and sue to have. Sir Thomas Wyatt. FCP; SiPS
Lo! how the lark soars upward and is gone. The Death of Leander. Thomas Hood. *Fr.* Hero and Leander. EnRP
Lo, how the terraced towers, and monstrous round. No Single Thing Abides. Lucretius. *Fr.* De Rerum Natura. AWP; JAWP; PG (1945 ed.); WBP
Lo, I, a maiden knight. Petition of Youth before Battle. John Bunker. CAW
Lo, I am black, but I am comely too. The Dark Brother. Lewis Alexander. CDC
Lo, I Am Stricken Dumb. *Unknown, tr. fr. Hebrew by* Theodor H. Gaster. *Fr.* The Dead Sea Scrolls. TrJP
Lo, I am weary of all. A Cry. Herbert Edwin Clarke. VA
Lo, I Am with You Always. John Charles Earle. ChIP; MaRV; OQP
Lo, I Am with You Always. Martha Snell Nicholson. BePJ
Lo, I beheld Maurus. On Maurus the Rhetor. Palladas of Alexandria. LiTW
Lo! I have learned of the loveliest of lands. *Unknown.* *Fr.* The Phoenix. AnOE
Lo, I have opened unto you the wide gates of my being. Psalm to My Beloved [*or* Fulfillment]. Eunice Tietjens. BoLP; ErPo; PoToHe (new ed.)
Lo, I shall tell you the truest of visions. The Dream of the Rood. *Unknown, at. to* Cynewulf. EnLi-1; OuHeWo
Lo, I the man that whilom loved and lost. Caelia, I. William Browne. Sonn
Lo! I, the man whose Muse whylome did maske. The Legend of the Knight of the Red Crosse, or of Holinesse. Spenser. *Fr.* The Faerie Queene, I. BEL; EnLi-1; EnLit; FiP; FosPo; OAEP; TOP
Lo, I who erst beneath a tree. The Shepherd's Week. John Gay. EiCL
Lo! I will tell the dearest of dreams. A Dream of the Rood. *Unknown, at. to* Cynewulf. AnOE
Lo, if some pen should write upon your rafter. The Inner Light. Frederic William Henry Myers. HBV; WGRP
Lo, in a valley peopled thick with trees. The Dying Crane. Michael Drayton. OA
Lo! in Corruption's lumber room. The Fate of a Broom—an Anticipation. Thomas Love Peacock. CBEP
Lo! in the mute, mid wilderness. The Unicorn. George Darley. *Fr.* Nepenthe. ChTr; ERoP-2; FaBoEn; NBM; OBNC; OBRV; PoEL-4
Lo, in the orient when the gracious light. Sonnets, VII. Shakespeare. ReIE; SiCE
Lo! in the painted oriel of the West. The Evening Star. Longfellow. AnNE
Lo, in the sanctuaried East. Orient Ode. Francis Thompson. CoBE
Lo! in the vigils of the night, ere sped. In Whom We Live and Have Our Being. James Rhoades. MaRV
Lo! in the West, fast fades the ling'ring light. Henry Kirke White. *Fr.* Clifton Grove. OBNC
Lo! in this unlovely shell. The Chrysalis. John James Piatt. InP
"Lo, it is I, be not afraid!" James Russell Lowell. *Fr.* The Vision of Sir Launfal. OQP; TreF
Lo, it was the last supper, I leader from gutter. The Drunken Preacher's Sermon. James Reaney. *Fr.* A Suit of Nettles. PeCV (1967 ed.)
Lo, Joseph dreams his dream again. The League of Nation's. Mary Siegrist. MC; PAH
Lo, ladies, here (if you can use it well). Epilogus. George Whetstone. TuPP
Lo! Leman Sweet. *Unknown.* CoBE
Lo, Lord, Thou ridest! The Hurricane. Hart Crane. AmP; AP; CMoP; CoBMV; MoAB; MoAmPo; OxBA
Lo, Love's obeyed by all. 'Tis right. The Impossibility. Coventry Patmore. *Fr.* The Angel in the House. PoVP

Lo! 'Mid the splendor of eternal spaces. Resurrection. Angela Morgan. OQP
Lo, praise of the prowess of people-kings. Beowulf. *Unknown.* BEL
Lo Que Digo, *with music. Unknown, tr. fr. Spanish.* AS
Lo, quhat it is to lufe. *See* Lo, what it is to love.
Lo, she cometh to us from afar. Assumpta Est Maria. Liam Brophy. ISi
Lo! sun and moon, these minister for aye. Israel's Duration. Judah Halevi. TrJP
Lo, that doves. A Song for Souls under Fire. Mark Turbyfill. NP
Lo, the Day-Spring, brightest Angel. Prayer to Christ Our Lord. Cynewulf. PoLi
Lo! the foolish fell. Killing. Samuel Greenberg. LiTA
Lo, the Lilies of the Field. Reginald Heber. *See* Providence.
Lo, the moon's self! Phases of the Moon. Robert Browning. *Fr.* One Word More. ChTr
Lo, the Poor Indian. Pope. *Fr.* An Essay on Man, Epistle I. TreFS
("Lo, the poor Indian! whose untutored mind.") PoIE
Lo, the Winter Is Past. Song of Solomon, Bible, *O.T. See* For, Lo, the Winter Is Past.
Lo! there he lies, our Patriarch Poet, dead! Bryant Dead. Paul Hamilton Hayne. DD
Lo, thou, my Love, art fair. Christ to His Spouse [*or* The Beloved to the Spouse]. William Baldwin. EIL; OBSC; OxBoCh
Lo, thou the glory of the great earth. A Maiden Ring-adorned. Cynewulf. *Fr.* Christ. PoLi
Lo! through a shadowy valley. The Funeral of Time. Henry Beck Hirst. AA
Lo, thus, as prostrate, "In the dust I write." The City of Dreadful Night. James Thomson. EnLit; GoTS; OAEP; OBNC; OxBS; PoVP; ViBoPo
Lo! 'tis a gala night. The Conqueror Worm. Poe. *Fr.* Ligeia. AA; AmePo; AmP; AmPP; AnAmPo; AnFE; AP; APA; AWP; CoAnAm; CoBA; HBV; InPo; LiTA; MAmP; MWA-1; TDP
Lo—to the battle-ground of life. On the Birth of a Child. Louis Untermeyer. NeMA
Lo, upon the carpet, where. Tamerlane. Victor J. Daley. PoAu-1
Lo, Victress on the Peaks. Walt Whitman. PoIE
Lo, we have heard of the glory in days of old of the Spear-Danes. Beowulf. *Unknown, tr. by* Albert C. Baugh. EnLit
Lo! we have learned of the glory of the kings who ruled the Spear-Danes. Beowulf. *Unknown, tr. by* C. B. Tinker. EnL; OuHeWo; TOP
"Lo, We Have Left All." Henry Francis Lyte. VA
Lo, what a golden day it is! Thorgerda. John Payne. VA
Lo! what [*or* quhat] it is to love [*or* lufe]. A Rondel of Love. Alexander Scott. OBEV; OxBS
Lo, what it is to love! Sir Thomas Wyatt. FCP
Lo, what wonders the day hath brought. Snow. Elizabeth Akers Allen. HBV
Lo, when back mine eye. Thomas Campion. SiCE
Lo, when the Lord made North and South. The Rose of the World. Coventry Patmore. *Fr.* The Angel in the House. HBV
Lo, where enviousness and lies. Lines on the Wall of His Prison Cell. Luis de León. *tr. by* Thomas Walsh. CAW
Lo, where envy and where lies. Written on the walls of His Dungeon. Luis de León, *tr. by* Thomas Walsh. OnPM; TrJP
Lo, where he loometh, a hulk elephantine. Government Official. Paul Dehn. WaP
Lo! where the four mimosas blend their shade. For an Epitaph at Fiesole [*or* His Epitaph]. Walter Savage Landor. OBNC; OBRV; OBV; TOP; VA
Lo! where the rosy-bosomed Hours. Ode on the Spring. Thomas Gray. CEP; EiCP; GTBS; GTBS-D; GTBS-P; GTBS-W; GTSE; GTSL; HBV
Lo, Who Could Stand. *Unknown, tr. fr. Hebrew by* Israel Zangwill. TrJP
Lo! yon phantom army marching across Heaven. Indian Night Tableau. Hyman Edelstein. CaP
Load. John Hewitt. OnYI
Load of brushes and baskets and cradles and chairs, A. No Buyers; a Street Scene. Thomas Hardy. LiTB; NoP
Load of Hay! *Unknown.* RIS
Load of Sugar Cane, The. Wallace Stevens. NP
Loaded Ass, The. Bhartrihari, *tr. fr. Sanskrit by* Paul Elmer More. OnPM
"Loaded with benefits daily." Mercies and Blessings. *Unknown.* STF
Loaded with gallant soldiers. Ready. Phoebe Cary. PAH; PAP
Loadstone of His Love, The. Charles Wesley. BePJ
Loam. Carl Sandburg. CMoP
Loam Norton. Gwendolyn Brooks. BP
Loan of a Stall, The. James L. Duff. ISi
Loathing both seas of Life and Death. Upland of Nirvana. *Unknown.* OnPM
Loathsome mask has fallen, the man remains, The. The End of Tyranny. Shelley. *Fr.* Prometheus Unbound. ShBV-3
Loaves, The. Ronald Everson. WHW
Lob. Edward Thomas. MoVE
Lobbed ball plops, then dribbles to the cup, The. Ford Madox Ford. Robert Lowell. PoCh; TwCP
Lobster, The. *Unknown.* GoTP
Lobster and the Maid, The. Frederic Edward Weatherly. OTPC
Lobster Cove Shindig. Lillian Morrison. BoNaP
Lobster Pot, The. John Arden. ELU
Lobster Quadrille, The. "Lewis Carroll." *Fr.* Alice's Adventures in Wonderland, *ch.* 10. BoChLi; BoTP; FaPON; MoShBr; OTPC (1946 ed.); Par; PCD; PCH; PRWS; RIS; SAS; StVeCh; UTS
(Mock Turtle's Song, The.) ChTr; MPB (1956 ed); PoVP
(Quadrille, A.) EnLi-2
(Whiting and the Snail, The.) HBV; HBVY
("Will you walk a little faster?' said a whiting to a snail.") TiPo (1952 ed.)
Lobsters in the Window. W. D. Snodgrass. NYBP; PoIE (1970 ed.)
Local I'll bright my tale on, how. The Children of Greenock. W. S. Graham. FaBoTw
Local Light. Millen Brand. WOW
Local Places. Howard Moss. NePoEA-2
Local Train of Thought, A. Siegfried Sassoon. AtBAP
Localities. Carl Sandburg. AmFN; Po
Locate I/ love you. The Language. Robert Creeley. CoPo
Loch Achray was a clipper tall, The. The Yarn of the *Loch Achray.* John Masefield. InP; SeCeV; StPo
Loch Coruisk (Skye). "Fiona Macleod." SyP
Loch Lomond. *Unknown, at. to* Lady John Scott. TreFS
Lochaber No More. Allan Ramsay. HBV
Lochiel's Warning. Thomas Campbell. EnRP
Lochinvar. Sir Walter Scott. *Fr.* Marmion, V. ATP; BBV; BEL; BeLS; BoChLi; BoTP; CoBE; EnLi-2 (1949 ed.); EnLit; EnRP; EPN; EvOK; FaBoBe; FaBV; FaFP; FaPON; GN; GoTP; GoTS; GSP; HBV; InP; LoEn; MaC; MCCG; MemP; NeHB; OAEP; OBNC; OBRV; OnSP; OtMeF; OTPC; OxBS; PaPo; PCD; PoE; PoPo; PoRA; RoGo; ShBV-1; StPo; StVeCh; TIHL; TOP; TreF; WHA; YAT
(Young Lochinvar.) HBVY; RG
Lochmaben [*or* Lochmabyn] Harper, The. *Unknown.* BaBo; BuBa; ESPB; OBB, *sl. diff. vers.*; OxBB
Lochnagar cam frae the west. Katharine Jaffray (B *vers.*). *Unknown.* ViBoFo
Lock and form had first to burst. Form Is Delight. Ernst Stadler. OnPM
Lock the dairy door. *Unknown.* OxNR
Lock the Door, Lariston. James Hogg. GoTS; OxBS
Lock up, fair lids, the treasure of my heart. Sleep [*or* Sonnet]. Sir Philip Sidney. *Fr.* Arcadia. EG; EIL; OBSC; SiCE; SiPS
Lock up thy heart within thy breast alway. Volto Sciolto e Pensieri Stretti. James Clarence Mangan. IrPN
Lock your bedroom doors with terror. Admonition. John Peale Bishop. TwAmPo
Locke sank into a swoon. Fragments. W. B. Yeats. PoeP
Locked arm in arm they cross the way. Tableau. Countee Cullen. AmFN; BANP; Kal
Locked in a glossy iceland lake. Green World Two. Miriam Waddington. PeCV (1967 ed.)
Locked in the stillness of this mighty wheel. New Dynamo. Gerald Raftery. PoMa
Locks. Kenneth Koch. CoAP
Locks and Bolts, *with music. Unknown.* TrAS

(I Dreamed Last Night of My True Love, *with music.*) AS
Locks between her chamber and his will, The. Midnight. Shakespeare. *Fr.* The Rape of Lucrece. OBSC; SiCE
Locksley Hall. Tennyson. ATP (1935 ed.); BEL; CABA; CABL; DiPo; EnL; EnLi-2; EnLit; EPN; FaBoBe; FaFP; HBV; LiTG; MaVP; MBW-2; OAEP; PoVP; TOP; ViPo; ViPP; WHA
Sels.
Federation of the World, The, *abr.* MaRV
For I Dipped into the Future. PoLF
(Federation of the World.) PoRL
("For I dipt into the future, far as human eye could see.") PGD; TRV
(Prophecy.) GTBS-W; TreF; WBLP
In the Spring. BoNaP
"Slowly comes a hungry people, as a lion creeping nigher." PoFr
Locksley Hall Sixty Years After. Tennyson. EnLi-2 (1949 ed.); PoVP; ViPo
That Which Made Us, *sel.* OQP
Locomotive, The. Emily Dickinson. *See* I like to see it lap the miles.
Locomotive to the Little Boy, The. Benjamin R. C. Low. HBMV
Locrine, *sel.* *At. to* George Peele, *also at. to* Charles Tilney.
Cobbler's Song, The, *fr.* II, iii. OBSC
(Strumbo, Dorothy, Trumpart, Cobbling Shoes.) TuPP
Locust, The. *See* Coyote and the Locust, The. *Tr. fr. Zuni Indian by* Frank Cushing.
Locust drones along the drowsy noon, The. Bush Goblins. H. M. Green. BoAu
Locust Hunt, The. Philip Murray. NePoAm-2.
Locust, locust, playing a flute. The Coyote and the Locust [*or* Locust]. *Tr. by* Frank Cushing. AWP; FaPON; JAWP; RePo; SUS; WBP
Locust Tree in Flower, The. William Carlos Williams. PIA
Locusts, or Apollyonists, The, *sels.* Phineas Fletcher.
"Of Men, nay Beasts: worse, Monsters: worst of all," *fr.* I. SeCV-1; SeEP
Sin, Despair, and Lucifer, *fr.* I. OBS
Lodge Room over Simpkins' Store, The. Lawrence N. Greenleaf. PoOW
Lodged. Robert Frost. RePo
Lodgepole/ cone/ seed waits for fire. Logging, XV. Gary Snyder. *Fr.* Myths & Texts. NaP
Lodging for the Night, A. Elinor Wylie. ErPo
Lodging with the Old Man of the Stream. Po Chü-i, *tr. fr. Chinese by* Arthur Waley. AWP; JAWP; WBP
Loe here a little volume but great [*or* large] book! *See* Lo here a little volume. . .
Loe here the precious dust is laid. *See* And here the precious dust is laid.
Loeërd, thou clepedest me. Prayer for Forbearance. *Unknown.* LoBV
Loftier Race, A. John Addington Symonds. MaRV
(Church Triumphant, The) WBLP
(Human Outlook, The.) WGRP
(These Things Shall Be.) PoFr; TRV
Lofty against our Western dawn uprises Achilles. Song, Youth, and Sorrow. William Cranston Lawton. AA
Lofty House, The. John Gould Fletcher. MAP; MoAmPo
Lofty Lane. Edwin Gerard. PoAu-1
Lofty ship from Salcombe came, A. The Salcombe Seaman's Flaunt to the Proud Pirate [*or* High Barbary]. *Unknown.* ChTr; EtS
Logan at Peach Tree Creek. Hamlin Garland. MC; PAH
Logan Braes ("By Logan's streams that rin sae deep"). John Mayne. OxBS
Logging, *sels.* Gary Snyder. *Fr.* Myths & Texts.
"Again the ancient, meaningless," V. NaP
"Each dawn is clear," VIII. NaP NMP; OPoP
"Groves are down, The," XIV. NaP
"Lodgepole/ cone/ seed waits for fire," XV. NaP
"Morning star is not a star, The," I. OPoP
"Pines, under pines," IV. OPoP
"Stood straight/ holding the choker high," III. NaP; NMP
Logic. *Unknown.* BOHV; PCH
Logic is my eye. Seeing.—John Lyle Donaghy. NeIP
Logic of grammar is not genuine. The. A Sonnet for Dick Gallup. Ted Berrigan. ANYP
Logical English. *Unknown.* BOHV
Logical Song, A. *Unknown.* ErPo
Logical Vegetarian, The. G. K. Chesterton. CenHV; LiTG; SiTL
Logs, The. Sir Charles G. D. Roberts. ACV
Lohengrin. William Morton Payne. AA
L'Oiseau Bleu. Gordon Bottomley. BrPo
L' Oiseau Bleu. Mary Elizabeth Coleridge. BoTP; CH; PoVP
(Blue Bird, The.) WePo
Loitering with a vacant eye. A. E. Housman. A Shropshire Lad, LI. PoVP
Lollay, lollay, little child, why wepestou so sore? An Adult Lullaby. *Unknown.* MeEL
Lollingdon Downs, *sels.* John Masefield. LiTB (I-XV)
Choice, The, VIII. MoAB; MoBrPo
"I could not sleep for thinking of the sky," V. ChMP; GTBS-W; LiTM (rev. ed.); MemP
(Sonnet.) LiTG
"Night is on the downland, on the lonely moorland," XVIII. GoYe
(Night on the Downland.) GTBS-W; LiTM; MoBrPo; MoPo
Lollocks. Robert Graves. ChTr; DTC; EvOK; FIW; MoPW
Lolly Too-Dum, *with music.* *Unknown.* OuSiCo
Lolly Trudom, *with music.* *Unknown.* BFSS
Lollypops, The. Cordia Thomas. SoPo
Lolotte, who attires my hair. Noblesse Oblige. Jessie Fauset. CDC
London. John Betjeman. POTi
London ("I wander thro' each charter'd street"). Blake. *Fr.* Songs of Experience. AtBAP; AWP; BWP; CABA; CaFP; CBEP; CBV; CEP; ChER; DiPo; EiCL; EiPP; EnL; EnLi-2 (1949 ed.); EnPE; EnRP; ERoP-1; ExPo; FaBoEn; ForPo; ILP; InPo; LiTB; LO; MaPo; NoP; OBNC; OnPM; PAn; PeER; PIA; PoAn; PoE; PoEL-4; PoeP; PoFS; PoIE; PoSa; PPON; SeCePo; SeleV; StP; TDP; UnPo; ViBoPo; WoL
"I wander thro' each dirty street," *sel., sl. diff.* ChTr
London ("There souls of men are bought and sold"). Blake. *Fr.* The Human Image. ChTr
London. John Davidson. OBNC; StP; VA
London. Dryden. *See* New London, The.
London. F. S. Flint. MoBrPo (1942 ed.); NP
London. Manmohan Ghose. ACV
London [a Poem in Imitation of the Third Satire of Juvenal]. Samuel Johnson. EiCP; EnPE; GoTL; PoEL-3
Sel.
Poverty in London. ChTr; OBEC
("By numbers here from shame or censure free.") EnLi-1 (1949 ed.); ViBoPo
London. Peter Anthony Motteux. *See* Slaves to London.
London. Ernest Rhys. POTE
London. T. P. Cameron Wilson. HBMV
London Beautiful. Richard Le Gallienne. HT
London Bells. *Unknown.* *See* Bells of London, The.
London Bobby, The. Arthur Guiterman. HT
London Bridge. *Unknown.* CH; ChTr; OTPC; OxBoLi; PCH, 4 *ll.*
("London Bridge is broken down.") OxNR
London Bridge. Frederic Edward Weatherly. VA
London Bridge is broken down. After London. John Dynham Cornish Pellow. GTBS
London Bridge is broken [*or* falling] down. London Bridge. *Unknown.* CH; ChTr; OTPC; OxBoLi; OxNR; PCH
London Bridge is falling down, Rome's burnt, and Babylon. Spring MCMXL. David Gascoyne. MoVE
London City. *Unknown.* *See* Go Bring Me Back My Blue-eyed Boy.
London Despair. Frances Cornford. OBMV
London, 1802 ("Milton! thou should'st be living. . ."). Wordsworth. AnFE; ATP; AWP; BEL; CABA; CoBE; DiPo; EnL; EnLi-2; EnLit; EnRP; EPN; ExPo; FaBV; FiP; GTSL; ILP; InP; InPo; InvP; JAWP; LiTB; MaPo; MBW-2; MCCG; MERP; ML; NoP; OAEP; OBNC; OBRV; OuHeWo; PAn; PoAn; PoE; PoEL-4; PoeP; PoFr; PoFS; PoIE; PoPo; PoRA; SeCeV; ShBV-3; Sonn; StP; TDP; TOP; TreF; WBP; YAT
(England, 1802.) HBV; OBEV
(Milton.) PoMa
(Milton, Thou Shouldst Be Living at This Hour.) GTBS;

London (continued)
GTBS-D; GTBS-W; GTSE; WHA
(Same, The.) GTBS-P
(Sonnet: "Milton! Thou shouldst be living at this hour.") LoBV
(To Milton.) BoLiVe; TrGrPo
London, 1802 ("O Friend! I know not which way I must look"). Wordsworth. *See* Written in London, September, 1802.
London Feast. Ernest Rhys. VA
London Fete, A. Coventry Patmore. NBM; PeVV
London, Hast Thou Accused Me. Earl of Surrey. *See* Satire on London, A.
London, I heard one say, no more is fair. London Beautiful. Richard Le Gallienne. HT
London Interior. Harold Monro. BrPo
London Is a Fine Town. *Unknown.* CoMu
London is painted round them: burly railings. Street Performers, 1851. Terence Tiller. GTBS-P
London: John Lane, The Bodley Head. On the Imprint of the First English Edition of the Works of Max Beerbohm. Max Beerbohm. PV
London Lickpenny. *Unknown, wr. at. to* John Lydgate, *tr. fr. Middle English.* CoMu; EnPo; GoTL; MeEV
(London Lackpenny.) ChTr
London Mourning in Ashes. *Unknown.* FOL; PeRV
London, my beautiful. London. F. S. Flint. MoBrPo (1942 ed.); NP
London Night. Kathleen Raine. NeBP
London Nightfall. John Gould Fletcher. MAP; MoAmPo; NeMA
London, 1940. A. A. Milne. MaRV
London Plane-Tree, A. Amy Levy. VA; WePo
(Plane-Tree, The.) OBVV
London Poets. Amy Levy. OBVV
London Prentice, The. *Unknown.* CoMu; UnTE
London Rain. Louis MacNeice. NoP
London Rain. Nancy Byrd Turner. MoSiPe
London Sad London. *Unknown.* OBS
London Snow. Robert Bridges. AnFE; BoNaP; BrPo; CBV; CH; ChTr; CMoP; CoBMV; GTBS-P; GTBS-W; GTSE; LiTB; LiTG; LiTM (rev. ed.); LoBV; MoAB; MoBrPo; NBM; NoP; OBNC; Po; PoE; PoEL-5; PoIE; PoMa; PoSa; PoVP; ReMP; SeCePo; SeCeV; ShBV-3; StP; TrGrPo; WePo; WiR; YAT
London Sonnets, *sels.* Carl Bode. ToPo
City Considered as a Tulip Tree, The.
Covent Garden Market.
Who Calls the English Cold?
London Spring. Antoni Slonimski, *tr. fr. Polish by* Frances Notley. TrJP
London, the "Flower of Cities All". London. Ernest Rhys. POTE
London, thou art of townes *A per se.* In Honour of the City of London [*or* To the City of London]. William Dunbar. ChTr; OBEV
London to Folkestone. Dante Gabriel Rossetti. *Fr.* A Trip to Paris and Belgium. PeVV
London, to thee I do present the merry Month of May. The Month of May. Beaumont *and* Fletcher. *Fr.* The Knight of the Burning Pestle. ChTr
London Town. Lionel Johnson. PoVP
London Town. John Masefield. OtMeF; YAT
London Trees. Beryl Netherclift. BoTP
London under Bombardment. Greta Briggs. OtMeF
London Voluntaries. W. E. Henley. Po (I-II); PoVP
Sels.
Out of the Poisonous East, IV. SyP
(Largo e Mesto.) BrPo
Scherzando, III. BrPo
Londoner in the Country, The. Richard Church. HaMV
Londoners Gent to the King do present, The. On the Lord Mayor and Court of Aldermen, Presenting the Late King and Duke of York Each with a Copy of Their Freedoms, Anno Dom. 1674. Andrew Marvell. CoMu
London's full of statues. Temple Bar. Rose Fyleman. UTS
London's Tempe; *or,* The Field of Happiness, *sel.* Thomas Dekker.
"Brave iron! brave hammer! from your sound." TuPP
(Song of the Cyclops, The.) ShBV-1
Lone and forgotten/ Through a long sleeping. The Lonely. "Æ." AWP; JAWP; OnYI; WBP
Lone Bather. A. M. Klein. TwCaPo
Lone Buffalo Hunter, The. *Unknown.* CoSo
(Texas Cowboys, The, *same.*) CoSo
Lone crow caws from the tall dead gum, The. Sheaf-Tosser. Eric Rolls. PoAu-2
Lone Dog. Irene R. McLeod. FaPON; MCCG; MPB; NeMA; PDV; PoMa; SP; StVeCh (1940 ed.); TiPo; UTS
Lone Driftin' Riders. *Unknown.* CoSo
Lone Founts. Herman Melville. AnFE; CoAnAm; LiTA; OnPM; ViBoPo
Lone Gentleman. "Pablo Neruda," *tr. fr. Spanish by* Clayton Eshleman. ErPo
Lone heart, learning. Vigils. Siegfried Sassoon. CMoP
Lone Huntsman. Christie Jeffries. GoYe
Lone kingfisher skims the river's crest, A. The Kingfisher. Blanche Mary Kelly. GoBC
Lone-Land. John Banister Tabb. OQP
Lone, lone and lone I stand. The Myall in Prison. Mary Gilmore. BoAV; PoAu-1
Lone Man, The. *Unknown, tr. fr. Old English. Fr.* Widsith. PoLi
Lone midnight-soothing melancholy bird. The Nightingale. Edward Moxon. OBRV
Lone o'er the moors I stray'd. The Hand. Ebenezer Jones. OBVV
Lone, phallic, A—let's get. Tour de Force. Peter Kane Dufault. ErPo
Lone Prairie, The. *Unknown. See* Dying Cowboy, The ("Oh, bury me not . . .").
Lone seas are ominous. Lone Huntsman. Christie Jeffries. GoYe
Lone Star Trail, The, *diff. versions. Unknown.* AS; BFSS, *with music*; CoSo, *with music*
Lone Striker, A. Robert Frost. NoP
Lone watch of the moon over mountains old, The. Mortality. James Devaney. BoAV; PoAu-1
Loneliness. Edwin Essex. JKCP (1926 ed.); TrPWD
Loneliness. Robert Frost. *Fr.* The Hill Wife. FaBoEn; NP
("One ought not to have to care.") CMoP; NoP
Loneliness. Hashin, *tr. fr. Japanese by* Harold G. Henderson. PoPl; WoL
(No Sky at All.) SoPo
Loneliness. Franz Werfel, *tr. fr. German by* Edith Abercrombie Snow. TrJP
Loneliness lies just there beyond heartbreak. Soliloquy. Dorothy C. Parrish. TNV
Loneliness of her old age flashed clear, The. Aged Ninety Years. Wilbert Snow. AnAmPo
Loneliness of the Long Distance Runner, The. Alden Nowlan. PV
Loneliness one dare not sound, The. Emily Dickinson. MWA-2
Lonely, The. "Æ." AWP; JAWP; OnYI; WBP
Lonely. Bloke Modisane. PBA
Lonely. André Spire, *tr. fr. French by* Jethro Bithell. AWP; JAWP; TrJP; WBP
Lonely, A/ Sick old man. Taxes. Tu Hsün Hao. OnPM
Lonely and cold and fierce I keep my way. Gulf Stream. "Susan Coolidge." AA; EtS
Lonely and wild it rose. The Mysterious Music of Ocean. *Unknown.* EtS
Lonely Are the Fields of Sleep. Mary Newton Baldwin. GoYe
Lonely Beauty. Samuel Daniel. *Fr.* The Complaint of Rosamond. CTC; OBSC
Lonely-Bird, The. Harrison Smith Morris. AA
Lonely Bugle Grieves, The. Grenville Mellen. *Fr.* Ode on the Celebration of the Battle of Bunker Hill, June 17, 1825. AA
Lonely Child, The. Ernest Briggs. NeLNL
Lonely Child, The. James Oppenheim. NP
Lonely Christ, The. Edward Shillito. ChIP
Lonely Crib, The. Leonard Feeney. WHL
Lonely Death, The. Adelaide Crapsey. AnFE; APA; CoAnAm; MAP; MoAmPo (1942 ed.); NP
Lonely Dog, The. Margaret E. Bruner. PoToHe
Lonely I lay in the heather-soft hollow. The Heather. Steen Steensen Blicher. LiTW
Lonely Isle, The. Claudian, *tr. fr. Latin by* Howard Mumford Jones. AWP; JAWP; WBP
Lonely lake, a lonely shore, A. The Loon. Lew Sarett. HBMV
Lonely Land, The. A. J. M. Smith. CaP

Lonely Little question mark. Kid in the Park. Langston Hughes. OCS
Lonely, lonely lay the hill. As Rivers of Water in a Dry Place. Anna Bunston De Bary. HBMV
Lonely Lover. Robert P. Tristram Coffin. MoLP
Lonely Man, A. Agnes Lee. NP
Lonely Month, The. Ruthven Todd. NeBP
Lonely Mother, The. Fenton Johnson. GoSl; NP; PoNe
Lonely music arose and bid, A. Wrack. Irving Feldman. AmPC
Lonely Night. Sappho. *See* Alone.
Lonely o'er the dying ember. Shadows. Sebastian Evans. PrWP
Lonely pond in age-old stillness sleeps, A. Basho, *tr. fr. Japanese by* Curtis Hidden Page. AWP; JAWP; WBP
Lonely Road. Peter Abrahams. PBA
Lonely Road, The. Kenneth Rand. HBV
Lonely, save for a few faint stars, the sky. The Litttle Dancers. Laurence Binyon. BoTP; CH; MoBrPo; MoVE; OBVV
Lonely Scarecrow, The. James Kirkup. PDV
Lonely season in lonely lands, when fled, The. November. Robert Bridges. NBM; OBNC; PoEL-5
Lonely Shell, The. Martha Eugenie Perry. CaP
Lonely, sickly old man, A. Casual Lines. Su Shih. FIW
Lonely Street, The. William Carlos Williams. TDP; TwCP
Lonely student in a silent room, A. International Brigade Dead. Thomas O'Brien. NeIP
Lonely task it is to plow, A. Plowing; a Memory. Hamlin Garland. StVeCh
Lonely?—Tired?—Afraid? R. Hare. SoP
Lonely Traveller, The. Kwesi Brew. PBA; TTY
Lonely wanderer, wounded with iron, A. Shield. *Unknown. Fr.* Riddles. AnOE
Lonely way, A, and as I went my eyes. Two Infinities. Edward Dowden. VA
Lonely Wind. Eleanor Hammond. GFA
Lonely Woman, The. M. Forrest. BoAu
Lonely workman, A, standing there. In the Moonlight. Thomas Hardy. NP
Lonely? Yes, sometimes when the night is dark. Lonely?—Tired?—Afraid? R. Hare. SoP
Lonesome. Paul Laurence Dunbar. MPB; PoRL
Lonesome, dear Lord, how can I ever be. Living Bread. Eva Weaver Sefton. BePJ
Lonesome Dream, The. Lisel Mueller. CoAP
Lonesome Grove, The, *with music. Unknown.* TrAS
Lonesome Road. *Unknown. See* Long Lonesome Road.
Lonesome Water. Roy Helton. AmFN; MAP; MoAmPo; PoMS; WaKn
Lonesome? Well, I guess so! A Nevada Cowpuncher to His Beloved. *Unknown.* SCC
Long after the days and seasons, the beings and countries. Barbarian. Arthur Rimbaud. LiTW
Long after you have swung back. Losing Track. Denise Levertov. NaP; OPoP
Long ages past in Caiaphas' court. He Is the Truth. Ilse L. Schlaitzer. SoP
Long Ago, The. Benjamin Franklin Taylor. *See* Isle of Long Ago, The.
Long ago I blazed a trail. The Pioneer. Arthur Guiterman. MPB
Long ago I learned how to sleep. Wind Song. Carl Sandburg. GBV (1952 ed.); MAP; MoAB; MoAmPo; MoShBr; NeMA; TwAmPo; YT
Long ago, on a bright spring day. Old and Young. Francis William Bourdillon. VA
Long ago powerful snake when men also. The Deluge. *Unknown. Fr.* Wallam Olum. LiTA
Long ago the thunder went talking. Before Winter. Frederick R. McCreary. MAP
Long ago to a white-haired gentleman. The Hat Given to the Poet by Li Chien. Po Chü-i. AtBAP; BoW
Long ago to Thee I gave. *Unknown.* BoC
Long and gray and gaunt he lies. At the Dog Show. Christopher Morley. MoShBr; MPB
Long annoys and short contentings. Of Love. *Unknown.* SeCL
Long Are the Hours the Sun Is Above. Robert Bridges. EG; LO; NoP
Long are the years since he fell asleep. Washington. B. Y. Williams. OQP; PGD
Long as I can call to mind. A Childish Game. Reinmar von Hagenau. AWP; JAWP; WBP
Long as I was able, in the town of my birth. Harvest Moon. Josephine Miles. FiMAP
Long as thine Art shall love true love. Dear Land of All My Love. Sidney Lanier. *Fr.* The Centennial Meditations of Columbia. DD; GN; HBVY; MPB; PGD; StVeCh
Long autumn rain. An Autumn Song. Edward Dowden. ACV; OnYI
Long awaited day, The. Walter Savage Landor. *Fr.* Gebir, VII. OBRV
Long before a woman knows she's pregnant. Progression of the Species. Brian W. Aldiss. HYE
Long before he reached our age. Lines Written on November 15, 1933, by a Man Born November 14, 1881, to Another Born November 15, 1881. Clayton Hamilton. InMe
Long betwixt Love and Fear. Dryden. *Fr.* The Assignation. LiTL; SeCL; ViBoPo
("Song: Long betwixt love and fear Phillis tormented.") SeEP
Long-billed Gannets. Frances D. Emery. GoYe
Long 'bout June, when everything's. I Go Fishin'. Richard S. Powell. IHA
Long by the willow-trees. The Willow-Tree. Thackeray. BOHV; HBV; InMe
Long canoe, The. Lullaby. Robert Hillyer. FaPON; LOW
Long-closed door, oh open it again, The. Love Song. Judah Al-Harizi. LiTW; TrJP
Long days of absence, dear, I could endure. The Kind Mistress. *Unknown.* PeRV
Long Did I Toil. John Quarles. *See* My Beloved Is Mine, and I Am His.
Long Distance. William Stafford. ELU
Long Distance, 1944. James Boyd.
Long ere the morn. The Hunter's Song. William Basse. SeCL
Long-Expected One-and-twenty. Samuel Johnson. *See* Short Song of Congratulation, A.
Long fed on boundless hopes, O race of man. The Better Part. Matthew Arnold. ChIP; EPN; MaRV; PoVP; StJW; TOP; ViPP
Long Feud. Louis Untermeyer. AnAmPo; AnFE; APA; CoAnAm; MAP; MoAmPo; NeMA
Long from the lists of love I stood aloof. Omnia Vincit. Alfred Cochrane. HBV
Long Gone. Sterling A. Brown. BALP; BANP; CDC
Long Gone, *with music. Unknown.* ABF
Long grass searches the wind, The. Shearing Grass. Peter Redgrove. NePoEA-2
Long, gray moss that softly swings, The. In Louisiana. Albert Bigelow Paine. AA; AmFN
Long green swell, A. Chill of the Eve. James Stephens. CMoP; OnYI
Long had the giant-form on Gallia's plains. The French Revolution. Erasmus Darwin. PoFr
Long had we crept in cryptic. The Ecstasy. C. S. Lewis. BoPe
Long-haired kittens of Damascus, why are you playing in the streets of St. Paul? Damascus. Edna Holyroyd Yellan. CIV
Long-haired preachers come out every night. The Preacher and the Slave. *Unknown, at. to* Joe Hill. AS; PPON; TrAS
Long-haired Yak has long black hair, The. Yak. William Jay Smith. GoTP; RePo; TiPo (1959 ed.)
Long Harbour, The. Mary Ursula Bethell. ACV; AnNZ
Long has he been of that amphibious fry. Portrait of a Physician. Sir Samuel Garth. *Fr.* The Dispensary. PeRV
Long has the summer sunlight shone. Incognita of Raphael. William Allen Butler. AA
Long hast thou, friend! been absent from thy soil. Mr. Pope's Welcome from Greece. John Gay. OBEC; OxBoLi; PoEL-3
Long hath she slept, forgetful of delight. Vita Nuova. Sir William Watson. OBVV
Long have I beat with timid hands upon life's leaden door. The Suppliant. Georgia Douglas Johnson. BALP; CDC; PoNe
Long Have I Borne Much. Ovid, *tr. fr. Latin by* Christopher Marlowe. Amores, III, 10. MeWo
Long have I dreamed of love's adventure. The Spell. Medora Addison. HBMV

Long have I framed weak phantasies of Thee. ΑΓΝΩΣΤΩι ΘΕΩι (To an Unknown God). Thomas Hardy. MoPo; WGRP
Long have I loved the terrible clouds that loom. Prayer for Dreadful Morning. E. Merrill Root. TrPWD
Long have I searched the Earth for liberty. Liberty, Equality, Fraternity. Wilfrid Scawen Blunt. *Fr.* In Vinculis. PoFr
Long have I sigh'd for a calm: God grant I may find it at last! Tennyson. Maud, Pt. I, ii. SyP
Long heron feather, The. The Gray Plume. Francis Carlin. HBMV
Long, hideously long the plodding was. Babylon. Laura Benét. FiSC
Long Hill, The. Sara Teasdale. HBMV; LiTA; LiTM; MAP; MoAmPo; PoPl
Long hours we toiled up through the solemn wood. Mount Rainier. Herbert Bashford. AA
Long I followed [*or* follow'd] happy guides. Forerunners. Emerson. AA; AmePo; AnNE; OBEV (new ed.); OBVV; OxBA
Long I Have Loved to Stroll. T'ao Ch'ien, *tr. fr. Chinese by* William Acker. ChTr
Long in thy shackels [*or* shackles], Liberty. To Lucasta, from Prison. Richard Lovelace. AnAnS-2; PoFr; SCEP-2
Long is the day without Usnagh's Children. Deirdre's Lament. *Unknown.* LiTW; OnYI
Long John. Padraic Fallon. NeIP
Long John Brown and Little Mary Bell. Blake. SiTL
Long Last Mile, The. Lauchlan MacLean Watt. MaRV; SoP
Long lay the ocean-paths from man concealed. Columbus [*or* The Inspiration]. James Montgomery. *Fr.* The West Indies. PAH; PEDC
Long-legged Fly. W. B. Yeats. CaFP; CMoP; FaBoEn; FaBoTw; ForPo; LiTM; NoP; PoE; PoeP; PoIE
Long legs, crooked thighs. Mother Goose. HBV; HBVY; OTPC; OxNR; PPL; RIS
Long life to old Whalan of Waitin' a While. Whalan of Waitin' a While. J. W. Gordon. PoAu-1
Long Lines. Paul Goodman. NMP
Long lines of cliff breaking have left a chasm. Enoch Arden. Tennyson. BeLS
Long Lonesome Road, *with music.* *Unknown.* OuSiCo
(Lonesome Road, *diff. vers., with music.*) AS
(Look Down That Lonesome Road, *diff. vers., with music.*) OuSiCo
Long, Long Ago. Thomas Haynes Bayly. TreF
Long, Long Ago. *Unknown.* BrR; ChBR; DD; FaPON; GFA; MPB; OHIP; OTPC (1946 ed.); PDV; PEDC; PoSC; TiPo (1952 ed.)
(Christmas Song, A: "Winds through the olive trees.") BoTP
Long, long ago, beyond the misty space. The Celts. Thomas D'Arcy McGee. OnYI; OxBI
Long long ago on Calvary. Victory. *Unknown.* STF
Long, long ago, so I have been told. Two Mothers. *Unknown.* SoP
Long, long ago, when all the glittering earth. John Masefield. *Fr.* Sonnets ("Long long ago"). HBV
Long long ago when the world was a wild place. Bedtime Story. George MacBeth. HYE; NePoEA-2
Long, Long Be My Heart with Such Memories Filled. Thomas Moore. FaBoBe
"Let Fate do her worst; there are relics of joy," *sel.* TreFT
Long, long before the Babe could speak. At Bethlehem [*or* The Child at Bethlehem]. John Banister Tabb. *Fr.* The Child. AA; PRWS
Long, long legs, The. From the Country to the City. Elizabeth Bishop. CrMA
Long, long, long the trail. Light between the Trees. Henry van Dyke. GBV (1922 ed.)
Long, long river, The. Haiku. Boncho. LiTW
Long, long sleep, a famous sleep, A. Emily Dickinson. NCEP
Long, long time, and a long time ago, A. A Long Time Ago. *Unknown.* AmSS
Long Love That in My Thought Doth Harbor, The. Sir Thomas Wyatt. *See* Lover for Shamefastness Hideth His Desire within His Faithful Heart, The.
Long may the shamrock. The Shamrock. *Unknown.* HH
Long months He lay within the womb. Signum Cui Contradicetur. Sister Mary Angelita. GoBC; JKCP (1926 ed.)
Long Nature travailed, till at last she bore. Nature's Travail. *Unknown.* AWP
Long Night, The. Harry Bache Smith. AA
Long Night Home, The. Charles F. Gordon. NBP
Long Night Moon, The: December. Frances Frost. OTD; YeAr
Long night succeeds thy little day. Margaret Love Peacock [for Her Tombstone, 1826.] Thomas Love Peacock. OBNC; OBRV; VA
Long over, what's on the tree. To Her Body, against Time. Robert Kelly. CoPo
Long past midnight I sit here. Forsaken. Zalman Schneour. TrJP
Long poles support the branches of the orchards in New Hampshire. Apples in New Hampshire. Marie Gilchrist. BoNaP; PoMa
Long Pursuit. *Unknown, tr. fr. Greek by* Louis Untermeyer. UnTE
Long Race, The. E. A. Robinson. CrMA
Long resounding marble corridors, The, the shining parlors with shining women in them. The Hotel. Harriet Monroe. AnAmPo; NP
Long, rich breadth of Holland lace, A. Old Flemish Lace. Amelia Walstien Carpenter. AA
Long River, The. Donald Hall. NePoEA-2
Long Road, The, *sel.* John Gray.
Gazelles and Unicorn. ChTr
Long Road, The. A. E. Housman. *See* White in the Moon the Long Road Lies.
Long road and a village, A. Holy Family. Muriel Rukeyser. MoAmPo
Long Road West, The. H. H. Knibbs. IHA
Long Roads. Mikhail Matusovsky, *tr. fr. Russian by* Babette Deutsch. LiTW
Long-rolling, The,/ Steady-pouring. The Main-Deep. James Stephens. MoBrPo; OBMV; PoPo; ShBV-1; UnPo
Long scythe biting through the grain, The. The Hare. Stanley Snaith. HaMV
Long Shadow of Lincoln, The. Carl Sandburg. LiPo; MoAmPo (1950 ed.); TPM
Long since, a dream of heaven I had. Divine Compassion. Whittier. MAmP
Long since I'd ceased to care. The Parrot. W. W. Gibson. OBMV
Long since, in sore distress, I heard one pray. A Warrior's Prayer. Paul Laurence Dunbar. MaRV; OQP
Long Since Last. Ruth Miller. PeSA
Long since the first fruits have been laid. Forever on Thanksgiving Day. Wilbur D. Nesbit. PEDC
Long Small Room, The. Edward Thomas. BrPo; PoIE
Long sobbings, The. Autumn Song. Paul Verlaine. LiTW
Long-Suffering of God. Christopher Smart. *Fr.* Hymns for the Amusement of Children. EiCP
Long Summer. Laurie Lee. BoNaP; ToPo
Long Summer Day, *with music.* *Unknown.* OuSiCo
Long-tailed pig, A. *Unknown.* OxNR
Long-tailed ponies go nosing the pine-lands. Parochial Theme. Wallace Stevens. LiTA
Long the proud Spaniard. The Winning of Cales. Thomas Deloney. CoMu
Long the tyrant of our coast. On the Capture of the *Guerrière.* Philip Freneau. PAH
Long, their fixed eyes to Heaven bent. Lord Herbert of Cherbury. *Fr.* An Ode upon a Question Moved, Whether Love Should Continue for Ever? LO
Long they pine in weary woe, the nobles of our land. Kathleen-Ni-Houlahan [*or* Kathaleen Ny-houlahan]. *Tr. by* James Clarence Mangan. AnIV; CoBE
Long they thus travellèd in friendly wise. Spenser. *Fr.* The Faerie Queene, III. MBW-1
Long Time a Child. Hartley Coleridge. CBEP; EnRP; HBV; NBM; NCEP; OBRV; PoEL-4; Sonn
(Sonnet: Long Time a Child.) ERoP-2; OBNC
Long Time Ago. Elizabeth Prentiss. ABF, *sl. diff.*; GFA; TVC
(Kitty.) BoTP; MoShBr; MPB
(Little Kitty.) CIV; SAS
Long Time Ago, A. *Unknown.* AmSS, *with music*; ShS, 6 *vers., with music*; SoAmSa, *diff. vers., with music*

Long time ago, A/ I went on a journey. T'ao Ch'ien, *tr. fr. Chinese by* Arthur Waley. FaBoCh; LoGBV
Long time ago in the big city, A. Small Quiet Song. Robert Paul Smith. CAD
Long time ago, when I was a child, A. The Snow Globe. Howard Nemerov. FiMAP
Long time have human ignorance and guilt. Imagination and Taste, How Impaired and Restored. Wordsworth. The Prelude, Book XII. ERoP-1; MERP
Long time he lay upon the sunny hill. Childhood. Edwin Muir. CMoP; SeCePo
Long time in some forgotten churchyard earth of Warwickshire. Who Were before Me. John Drinkwater. OBMV
Long time, many years, we've had these wars, A. On a Certain Engagement South of Seoul. Hayden Carruth. AmFN; NMP; OPoP
Long time plain dealing in the haughty town. Plain Dealing's Downfall. Earl of Rochester. BWP; PeRV
Long time they thus together traveilèd. Spenser. *Fr.* The Faerie Queene, I. MBW-1
Long time those gay and spotted hides. Your Chase Had a Beast in View. John Peale Bishop. LiTA
Long Trail, The. Kipling. FaBV; HBV; OtMeF; ViBoPo
(Envoy: "There's a whisper down the field where the year has shot her yield.") PoVP
(L'Envoi: "There's a whisper. . .") OBEV; OBVV
Long tyme hathe Christ (long tyme I must confesse). On the Reed of Our Lord's Passion. William Alabaster. PoEL-2
Long up and down I paced the House of Pain. The Incurables. Arthur Upson. AnAmPo
Long View. Genevieve Taggard. MoAmPo
Long Voyage, The. Malcolm Cowley. AnFE; CoAnAm; GBV (1952 ed.); NePA; TwAmPo; WaKn
Long War, The. Laurie Lee. BoPe; POTi; ToPo
Long War, The. Li Po, *tr. fr. Chinese by* Cheng Yu Sun. WaaP
Long war had ended, The. The Next War. Sir Osbert Sitwell. MMA
Long was I, Lady Luck, your serving-man. Davy, the Dicer. Sir Thomas More. *Fr.* Two Short Ballettes. . . Made for His Pastime While He Was Prisoner in the Tower of London. DiPo; TuPP
Long was the great Figg by the prize fighting swains. Extempore Verses upon a Trial of Skill between the Two Great Masters of the Noble Science of Defence, Messrs. Figg and Sutton. John Byrom. OBEC
Long was the way to Bethlehem to those who sought. The Way to Bethlehem. Clinton Scollard. OQP
Long Waters, The. Theodore Roethke. NaP; NYBP
Long While, The. Omar Khayyám, *tr. fr. Persian by* Edward Fitzgerald. *Fr.* The Rubáiyát. OnPM
Long while I sought to what I might compare. Amoretti, IX. Spenser. PoE; Sonn
Long white barn, A. Riddle. *Unknown.* ChTr
Long white clouds are Morning's wash, The. Morning Clouds. Nellie Burget Miller. GFA
Long White Seam, The. Jean Ingelow. GN; HBV; OTPC; VA
Long years ago I blazed a trail. The Pioneer. Arthur Guiterman. MPB; TiPo
Long years ago I wandered here. On Recrossing the Rocky Mountains after Many Years. John Charles Frémont. PoOW
Long years, methinks, of sorrow and of care. The Cascade. Tadamine. OnPM
Long years of pleasant friendship may be broken. True to the Best. Benjamin Keech. PoToHe
Long years their cabin stood. Eviction. William James Linton. VA
Longer life, the more offence, The. Upon Consideration of the State of This Life He Wisheth Death. *Unknown.* SiCE; TuPP
Longer on this earth we live, The. Unwasted Days. James Russell Lowell. *Fr.* Under the Old Elm. MCCG
Longer to muse. Sir Thomas Wyatt. FCP; SiPS
Longest day in the year had come, The. Midsummer Night. Marion Edey. YeAr
Longest Journey, The. Shelley. *Fr.* Epipsychidion. OtMeF
Longest tyranny that ever sway'd, The. To My Honor'd Friend, Dr. Charleton. Dryden. CEP; EiCL; EiPP; EnL; MBW-1; SeCV-2; SeEP
Longface Mahoney Discusses Heaven. Horace Gregory. CMoP; ExPo
Longfellow. Craven Langstroth Betts. DD
Longfellow ("The winds have talked with him confidingly"). James Whitcomb Riley. AA; DD; PoRL
Longford Legend, A. *Unknown.* OnYI; StPo
Longing. Matthew Arnold. BoPe; CBEP; HBV; LO, *st.* 1; MBW-2; OAEP; PoLF; VP
Longing. Euripides. *See* O for the Wings of a Dove.
Longing. Henry W. Frost. SoP
Longing. Judah Halevi, *tr. fr. Hebrew by* Nina Davis Salaman. TrJP
Longing. George Herbert. AnAnS-1; MaMe; MeP; SeCV-1, *abr.*
Longing. "Michael Lewis," *after the Chinese. Fr.* Cherry Blossoms. UnTE
Longing, *sel.* James Russell Lowell.
Thing We Long For, The. OQP
Longing, The. Theodore Roethke. NaP
Longing. *Unknown.* SoP
Longing at twilight the lovesick Adam saw. The Begetting of Cain. Hyam Plutzik. FiMAP
Longing for Heaven. Anne Bradstreet. *See* As Weary Pilgrim, Now at Rest.
Longing for Home. Jean Ingelow. *See* Seven Times Seven.
Longing for Jerusalem. Judah Halevi, *tr. fr. Hebrew by* Emma Lazarus. TrJP
Longings. José Moreno Villa, *tr. fr. Spanish by* Eleanor L. Turnbull. OnPM
Lonnie said before this, "I'm." Commanding Elephants. Philip Levine. NaP
Lon's away/ Cill Garad is sad today. St. Columcille. *Fr.* On a Dead Scholar. AnIL
Looby Loo. *Unknown.* SoPo
Look, The. Elizabeth Barrett Browning. MaRV; SoP; TRV
(Lord Turned, and Looked upon Peter, The.) ChIP
Look! Arthur Hugh Clough. *See* Say Not the Struggle Nought Availeth.
Look, The. Sara Teasdale. ALV; BoLP; HBV; LiTL; LiTM; WePo
Look ahead, look astern, look the weather and the lee. The Coasts of High Barbary. *Unknown.* OnSP
Look and remember. Look upon this sky. Travelogue for Exiles. Karl Shapiro. AnFE; CoAnAm; MoAmPo (1950 ed.); NeMA; PG (1945 ed.); TrJP; TwAmPo
Look and See. Tom Robinson. BoChLi (1950 ed.)
Look at her, calm and benign. A Bronze Statuette of Kwan-yin. Charles Wharton Stork. GoYe
Look at her—there she sits upon her throne. The Turbine. Harriet Monroe. NP
Look at him there in his stovepipe hat. American Primitive. William Jay Smith. MoAmPo (1962 ed.); NePoAm; NePoEA; PoPl; PPON; TwCP
Look at it well. This was the good town once. The Good Town. Edwin Muir. CMoP
Look at Jonah embarking from Joppa, deterred by. Tom Fool at Jamaica. Marianne Moore. AP; NYBP
Look at me. Here I Am. Ann Morrissett. BoLP
Look at me 8th/ grade. Poem for 8th Graders. Sonia Sanchez. WOW
Look at me. I am Ishmael. The Old Convict. H. A. Vaughan. PoNe
Look at me with thy large brown eyes. Philip, My King. Dinah Maria Mulock Craik. HBV; VA
Look at my knees. I Wonder What It Feels Like to Be Drowned? Robert Graves. BrPo; MoBrPo; TSW
Look at Six Eggs. Carl Sandburg. *Fr.* Prairie. FaPON
Look at That Gal. Julian Bond. PoNe (1970 ed.); TTY
Look at the aeroplane. The Aeroplane. Jeannie Kirby. BoTP
Look at the eyes look from my tail. Peacock and Nightingale. Robert Finch. OBCV
Look at the fish! Fish. William Jay Smith. RePo
Look at the little darlings in the corn! Fireflies in the Corn. D. H. Lawrence. NP
Look at the stars! Look, look up at the skies! The Starlight [*or* Starlit] Night. Gerard Manley Hopkins. ACP; BoC; BrPo; BWP; CAW; DiPo; GoBC; GTBS; GTBS-P; GTBS-W; JKCP; LiTM; MoAB; MoBrPo; MoPW; MoVE; OBVV; OxBoCh; PoVP; SeCePo; ShBV-4; Sonn; ThWaDe; ViBoPo; ViPo (1962 ed.); VP; WoL
Look at this ancient house; it has survived. A House in War-

Look (continued)
time. Richard Church. POTE
Look at this red pear. The Indigestion of the Vampire. W. S. Merwin. NaP
Look at this skin—at fourscore years. Robert Barnabas Brough. *Fr.* The Marquis of Carabas. FiBHP
Look at this village boy, his head is stuffed. Farm Child. R. S. Thomas. BoNaP; ChMP; FlW; WePo
Look away now from the high lonesome hills. Admonition for Spring. L. A. MacKay. CaP; OBCV; PeCV
Look back with longing eyes and know that I will follow. The Flight. Sara Teasdale. BoLP; HBMV; MAP; NP; WHA
Look, Barker, when you wrote me I lay cringing. Mailed to G. B. Gene Derwood. NePA
Look Closely. Morton Marcus. YAP
Look [*or* Looke], Delia, how we esteem the half-blown rose. To Delia, XXXVI. Samuel Daniel. EIL; EnLit; HBV; NoP; ReEn; SeCePo; SiCE; TuPP; WHA
Look down at midnight when my strangled prayer. The Strangled Prayer. Vernon Watkins. PoIE (1970 ed.)
Look down; be still. Wonga Vine. Judith Wright. PoAu-2
Look Down Fair Moon. Walt Whitman. OnPM
Look down from the lip of the hill. The Quiet Street. Nan McDonald. NeLNL
Look down, look down. Lonesome Road [*or* Look Down That Lonesome Road]. *Unknown.* AS; OuSiCo
Look down on me, a little one. A Child's Morning Prayer. Jeannie Kirby. BoTP
Look Down That Lonesome Road. *Unknown.* *See* Long Lonesome Road.
Look down. The dead have life. Gravestones. Vernon Watkins. ChMP
Look down the long valley and there stands a mountain. Too Anxious for Rivers. Robert Frost. CBEP; MoPW
Look, Edwin! Edna St. Vincent Millay. GoJo
Look ere thou leap; nay, thou canst in no wise brook. Looking and Leaping. John Heywood. ReIE
Look, everyone, look! Easter Joy. Nancy Byrd Turner. YeAr
Look: Florentines and Umbrians have made whole. For a Nativity. Lisel Mueller. NePoAm-2
Look for Me on England. H. B. Mallalieu. WaP
Look for rebellion, look to be depos'd. Christopher Marlowe. *Fr.* Edward the Second. PoFr
Look forth and say, "Lo, on the left, from where tumultuous Moyle." "The Land Is Ours." Sir Samuel Ferguson. *Fr.* Congal. IrPN
Look forth and tell me what they do. Hammer and Anvil. Samuel Valentine Cole. PoLF
Look forward, truant, to your second childhood. The Death Room. Robert Graves. NYBP
Look from the [*or* thy] sphere of endless day. Other Sheep I Have, Which Are Not of This Fold [*or* A Prayer to Make Your Own]. Bryant. SoP; TrPWD
Look, God, I have never spoken to You. Conversion [*or* Last Thoughts of a Fighting Man]. Frances Angermayer. PGD; PoLF; TreFS
Look, Hart, That Horse You Ride Is Wood. Peter Viereck. ML
Look he comes! how tall he is! Conrad Aiken. *Fr.* Punch; the Immortal Liar. NP
"Look here," I said, "Hawk." The Shepherd and the Hawk. William Hart-Smith. AnNZ
Look: Here our bodies lie in a long, long line. But We Shall Bloom. Haim Guri. TrJP
Look Home. Robert Southwell. TuPP
(Looke Home.) AnAnS-1 MeP
Look, How Beautiful. Robinson Jeffers. MoRP
Look, how he shakes for cold! Crucifixus pro Nobis [*or* Hymn]. Patrick Carey. OxBoCh; SeCL
Look how her close defences laddered now. Apollo and Daphne. W. R. Rodgers. ErPo; LiTB
Look how it sparkles, see it greet. A Diamond. Robert Loveman. AA
Look, how the daffodils arise. John Hall. *Fr.* The Lure. LO
Look how the golden children. New Leaves. Juan Ramón Jiménez. PoPl
Look how the industrious bee in fragrant May. The Bee. Charles Fitzgeffrey. *Fr.* Sir Francis Drake. EIL
Look how the lark soars upward and is gone. False Poets and True. Thomas Hood. HBV; PP; Sonn
Look [*or* Looke] how the pale queen [*or* queene] of the silent night. A Sonnet of the Moon [*or* The Moon]. Charles Best. CH; EIL; EtS; HBV; OBSC; TuPP
Look, I Have Thrown All Right. L. A. MacKay. PeCV
Look! I stand among workbenches, hammers, furnaces, forges, and/ among a hundred comrades. We Grow Out of Iron. Aleksey Kapitonovich Gastev WoL
Look in mine eyes, Beloved! Is it true. Consummation. Elsa Barker. *Fr.* The Spirit and the Bride. HBMV
Look in my face; my name is Might-have-been. A Superscription. Dante Gabriel Rossetti. The House of Life, XCVII. BEL; CBEP; EnL; EnLi-2; EnLit; FaBoEn; GTBS-P; HBV; LO; MaVP; NoP; OBNC; PG (1955 ed.); PoEL-5; PoVP; SeCePo; TOP; VA; ViPo; ViPP; WHA; YAT
Look, in the attic, the unentered room. Before the Carnival. Thom Gunn. NePoEA
Look, in the Labyrinth of Memory. Delmore Schwartz. TrJP
Look in this cast, and know the hand. The Hand of Lincoln. Edmund Clarence Stedman. LiPo
Look in this mirror, tell me what you see. Glass Dialectic. Howard Nemerov. WaP
Look in thy glass and tell the face thou viewest. Sonnets, III. Shakespeare. BWP; CABA; EG; EnRePo; GTBS-W; LiTB; MasP; OBSC; SiCE
Look Inland Now. Percy MacKaye. JKCP (1955 ed.)
Look into the Gulf, A. Edwin Markham. AA
Look into Thy Heart. Sir Philip Sidney. *See* Astrophel and Stella, I.
Look! it is as though the sun. Fern House at Kew. Paul Dehn. ChMP
Look, it's morning, and a little water gurgles in the tap. Morning Song. Alan Dugan. CAD; CBV; ELU
Look! Look at me! Tree Birthdays. Mary Carolyn Davies. BiCB; OHIP
Look, look! Day dies and the evening has come! Amitié Amoureuse. Luc Grimard. PoNe
Look, look, my lord! Dialogue from "The Dream Queen." Bhasa. *Fr* The Dream Queen. LiTW
Look! Look! the spring is come. First Spring Morning. Robert Bridges. BoNaP; BoTP; YeAr
Look, Mother! the Mariner's rowing. The Mariner's Bride. James Clarence Mangan. IrPN
Look, my love, on the wall, and here, at this Eastern picture. Morning. Henry Reed. MoVE; NeBP
Look not in my eyes, for fear. A. E. Housman. A Shropshire Lad, XV. PoEL-5; PoVP
Look not on me with scorn because. Simon the Cyrenian Speaks. Glen Baker. ChIP
Look Not, Thou. Sir Walter Scott. *See* Lucy Ashton's Song.
Look Not to Me for Wisdom. Charles Divine. HBMV
Look not upon me, seek no more to stay me. M. Kirwan. LO
Look not upon me with such eyes, my son. Miguel de Unamuno. *Fr.* Domestic Scenes. LiTW; WoL
Look now, at this February street in April. A Street in April. Louis Dudek. OBCV
Look now, directed by yon candle's blaze. Fiction. Charles Sprague. *Fr.* Curiosity. AA
Look Now, the Hawk. Michael Parr. NYTB
Look! now with your eyes behold. *At. to* Cædmon. *Fr.* Exodus. YAT
Look nymphs, and shepherds look. Arcades. Milton. MaPo (1969 ed.)
Look off, dear Love, across the sallow sands. Evening Song. Sidney Lanier. AmPP (3d ed.); AP; CoBA; FaPL; NeHB; PG; TOP; TreFT
Look on Me with Thy Sweet Eyes. *Unknown, tr. fr. Middle English by* Mabel Van Duzee. MeEV
Look, on the topmost branches of the world. Sunday Evening in the Common. John Hall Wheelock. CLwM; HBV; MAP; MoAmPo; NP; PFY
Look on these waters, with how soft a kiss. An Aestuary. George Croly. IrPN
Look on this cast, and know the hand. The Hand of Lincoln. Edmund Clarence Stedman. AA; OHIP
Look on this maid of honour, now. Philip Massinger. *Fr.* The Maid of Honour. ACP (1952 ed.); GoBC
Look once more e're we leave this specular Mount. Athens. Milton. *Fr.* Paradise Regained, IV. OBS; SeEP; ViBoPo
Look one way and the sun is going down. The Mockingbird. Randall Jarrell. NYBP; OA
Look or You Leap. Jasper Heywood. EIL; SiCE; TuPP

(Lookers-on, The.) ACP (1952 ed.)
Look our ransomed shores around. Additional Verses to "Hail Columbia." Oliver Wendell Holmes. PAH
Look Out Below! Charles R. Thatcher. PoAu-1
Look out, boys, better wash your hands. The Marrowbone Itch. *Unknown.* OuSiCo
Look out how you use proud words. Primer Lesson. Carl Sandburg. FaPON; MAP; MoAmPo; MoShBr; PoPl; RePo; StVeCh; TSW
Look out! look out! Jack Frost. Cecily E. Pike. BoTP
Look out! Look out, boys! Clear the tracks! The Broomstick Train; or, Return of the Witches. Oliver Wendell Holmes. FaPON; MCCG; PoMS
Look out! Look out! You've spilt the ink. April Fools' Day. Marnie Pomeroy. OTD; PoSC
Look out upon the stars, my love. A Serenade. Edward Coote Pinkney. AA; AmLP; AnFE; APA; CoAnAm; HBV
Look over Yonder, *with music.* Lawrence Gellert. TrAS
Look round the habitable world, how few. The Tenth Satire of Juvenal. *Tr. by* Dryden. WoL
Look round: You see a little supper room. De Coenatione Micae. Martial. FaBoCh; LoGBV
Look, See the Cat. Nancy Price. NYTB
Look, sisters, look! Chorus of the Furies. Aeschylus. *Fr.* Eumenides. WoL
Look, Stranger, on This Island Now. W. H. Auden. *See* On This Island.
Look, sunset's all undone! Emblems of Evening. Robert Horan. CrMA
Look, the raft, a signal flying. Far Off-Shore. Herman Melville. AmPP (4th ed.)
Look, the Soldiers! Felix V. Ramos, *tr. fr. Spanish by* Muriel Rukeyser. PoFr
"Look, there's a robin." Little Brother. Aileen Fisher. BiCB
Look through this glass. The Telescope. J. C. Hall. HaMV
Look to the blowing Rose about us—"Lo." Careless Delight. Omar Khayyám, *tr. by* Edward Fitzgerald. *Fr.* The Rubáiyát. OnPM
Look to the Leaf. *Unknown, tr. fr. German by* Louis Untermeyer. UnTE
Look to This Day. *Unknown. See* Salutation of the Dawn, The.
Look Up. Edward Everett Hale. FaBoBe; FaFP; NeHB; OQP (Lend a Hand.) SoP; TreFS; TRV
Look Up. Martha Snell Nicholson. BePJ
Look up.../ From bleakening hills. Snow. Adelaide Crapsey. QFR
Look up, God's child. Perhaps Today. J. Danson Smith. SoP
Look up into the dome. Altitudes. Richard Wilbur. CMoP
Look up, languishing soul! Lo, where the fair. The Hymn of the Holy Cross [*or* Vexilla Regis]. Richard Crashaw. MaMe; StJW
"Look up," she said; and all the heavens blazed. Starlight. John White Chadwick. AA
Look up this river in the book of rivers. Border River. Alfred Goldsworthy Bailey. CaP
Look up, you loose-haired women in the field. Running Vines in a Field. H. L. Davis. AnAmPo; NP
Look upon the rainbow, and praise him that made it. Ecclesiasticus, Bible, Apocrypha. BoC
Look upward at the hill that must be climbed. Progression. Inez Clark Thorson. MaRV
Look, we don't give a hoot if Zippo-Fasteners have gone to war. Memorial to the Great Big Beautiful Self-sacrificing Advertisers. Frederick Ebright. ThLM; WaP
Look well about, ye that lovers be. The Blind Eateth Many a Fly. *Unknown.* NoP
Look what immortal floods the sunset pours. The Sea—in Calm. "Barry Cornwall." EtS
Look, wild and wide. The Sea. *Unknown.* KiLC
Look, William, how the morning mists. The Morning Mist. Robert Southey. OTPC
"Look!" you said. "Look!" Two Egrets. John Ciardi. PoPl
Look-a How Dey Done My Lord, *with music. Unknown.* BoAN-2
Looke back old Janus, and survey. A New-Yeares Gift. Thomas Carew. SCEP-2
Looke Delia how we 'steeme the half-blowne rose. *See* Look, Delia, how we esteem the half-blown rose.
Looke Home. Robert Southwell. *See* Look Home.
Looke How the Pale Queene. Charles Best. *See* Sonnet of the Moon, A.
Looke to mee faith, and looke to my faith, God. Elegie upon the Untimely Death of the Incomparable Prince Henry. John Donne. MaMe
Looke well about, ye that lovers be. Against Women. *Unknown.* MeEL
Looker-on, The. Frank Kendon. POTE
Lookers-on, The. Jasper Heywood. *See* Look or You Leap.
Lookin' for the Bully of the Town. *Unknown.* BaBo
Looking and Leaping. John Heywood. ReIE
Looking at New-Fallen Snow from a Train. Robert Bly. FRC; NaP
Looking at Sheep. R. S. Thomas. POTi
Looking at Some Flowers. Robert Bly. NaP
Looking at the Cross. John Newton. *See* In Evil Long I Took Delight.
Looking at the Empire State Building. Ralph Pomeroy. NYTB
Looking at the high-raised mini creations. Sallie Jewel. Stanley Crouch. WSL
Looking at the Map of the World. Gregory Corso. CBV
Look at the Moon on Putting out from the Shore at Nagato. *Unknown, tr. fr. Japanese by* Geoffrey Bownas *and* Anthony Thwaite. FIW
Looking away from my sin and my shame. That's Faith. S. N. Leitner. STF
Looking back across the years, O Christ, we see Thee go. Palm Sunday Hymn. "George Klingle." ChIP
Looking Backward. Martha Snell Nicholson. SoP
Looking by chance in at the open window. The Foreboding. Robert Graves. ChMP; ELP; GTBS- D; StP
Looking cautiously down they saw two men fishing. Drama. William Hart-Smith. BoAV; NeLNL
Looking Down on Mesopotamia. Mary Ursula Bethell. AnNZ
Looking for a Sunset Bird in Winter. Robert Frost. BiS
Looking for Equality. Herman L. McMillan. TNV
Looking for Jonathan. Jon Anderson. YAP
Looking for Mushrooms at Sunrise. W. S. Merwin. NaP
Looking Forward. Robert Louis Stevenson. BrPo; InP; OTPC (1946 ed.); PoVP ("When I am grown to man's estate.") CenHV
Looking from the hut door one dawn in June. Frank Wilmot. *Fr.* The Gully. BoAV; NeLNL
Looking-Glass, The. Michael Drayton. *See* So Well I Love Thee.
Looking-Glass, The. Kipling. EvOK; FaBoTw; GTSL; OBMV; OnPP
Looking Glass, The. James Shirley. LiTL; LO
Looking-Glass Pussy, The. Margaret Widdemer. UTS
Looking into my daughter's eyes I read. For My Daughter. Weldon Kees. CoAP
Looking into the man god's stone. The Carver and the Rock Are One. Besmilr Brigham. ThO
Looking into the windows that doom has broken. Sonnet. George Woodcock. NeBP
Looking north from 23rd the vast avenue. Standing on the Streetcorner. Edwin Denby. ANYP
Looking On. Anthony Thwaite. NePoEA-2
Looking on the peaceful face. A Dirge. Hisaki. OnPM
Looking one day toward the coast of France. Ballade. Charles d'Orléans. LiTW
Looking over the water shows nothing but trees. Windowed Habitations. Charles G. Bell. NePoAm-2
Looking to Jesus. *See* My Faith Looks Up to Thee.
Looking to the sea, it is a line. The Innocence. Robert Creeley. NeAP
Looking unto Jesus. Sarah Elizabeth Miles. SoP
Looking Up at Airplanes, Always. Rolfe Humphries. RePo
Looking Up at Leaves. Barbara Howes. BoNaP
Looking West. William Stafford. NYBP
Lookout, The. William Collins. EtS
Lookout watch must climb and climb, The. Crow's Nest. Richard F. Armknecht. GoYe
Looks like to me. Little Green Tree Blues. Langston Hughes. PoNe
Looks of a Lover Enamoured, The. George Gascoigne. ElL, SeCePo

Loom of Dreams, The. Arthur Symons. PoVP
Loom of Time, The ("Man's life is laid"). *Unknown.* BLPA; MaRV; NeHB
Loom of Years, The, *sel.* Alfred Noyes.
"O, woven in one wide Loom." MaRV
Loon, The. Theodore Harding Rand. CaP
Loon, The. Lew Sarett. HBMV
Loon, The. Alfred Billings Street. AA
Loons, The. Archibald Lampman. VA
Loon's Egg, The. Peter Dale Scott. MoCV
Loose eyes of an old man, The. Negroes. Maxwell Bodenheim. PoNe
Loose Saraband, A. Richard Lovelace. CavP; PoEL-3
Loot. Thom Gunn. ErPo; NePoEA-2
Loping along on the day's patrol. The Sheepherder. Lew Sarett. AmFN; FaPON; GaP
Loping and sloped with heat, face thatched and red. Drinker. Patrick Anderson. PeCV
Loppèd tree in time may grow again, The. Times [*or* Tymes] Go by Turns. Robert Southwell. ACP; CoBE; EIL; EP; FaBoEn; GoBC; GTBS-W; HBV; LiTB; LiTG; OBEV (1st ed.); OBSC; OxBoCh; PG; PoEL-2; SiCE
Lopsided with God. On the Road to Vicenza. Ralph Gustafson. CaP
Lord, The. José María Gabriel y Galán, *tr. fr. Spanish by* Thomas Walsh. CAW
Lord,/ do not be displeased. The Camel. Carmen Bernos de Gasztold. OA
Lord,/ I am the cat. The Prayer of the Cat. Carmen Bernos de Gasztold. PDV
Lord,/ I keep watch! The Prayer of the Dog. Carmen Bernos de Gasztold. TIHL
Lord, a big fat woman with the meat shakin on her bones. Big Fat Woman. *Unknown.* OuSiCo
Lord above gave man an arm of iron, The. With a Little Bit of Luck. Alan Jay Lerner. FaFP
Lord above has kept you safe, The. God Keeps His Word. Phyllis C. Michael. SoP
Lord above, in tender love, The. Thanksgiving Hymn. *Unknown.* PAH
Lord Alcohol. Thomas Lovell Beddoes. WiR
Lord Alfred Tennyson/ Lived upon venison. Important People. Louis Untermeyer, *and others.* StaSt
Lord Apollo, who has never died, The. Many Are Called. E. A. Robinson. InP; MAmP; MoVE; OxBA
Lord Arnaldos. James Elroy Flecker. StPo
Lord, art thou at the table head above. The Reflexion [*or* Reflection *or* I am the Rose of Sharon]. Edward Taylor. *Fr.* Preparatory Meditations, First Series. AmPP; AP; AtBAP; MWA-1; NePA; OxBA
Lord, art Thou wrapped in cloud. The Evening Star. Amy Carmichael. TRV
Lord, as thou wilt, bestow. Prayer. Eduard Mörike. TrPWD
Lord Banner. *Unknown.* *See* Little Musgrave and Lady Barnard.
Lord Bateman. *Unknown.* *See* Young Beichan.
Lord, behold our family here assembled. A Prayer for the Household. Robert Louis Stevenson. SoP; TRV
Lord Beichan and Susie Pye. *Unknown.* *See* Young Beichan.
Lord, Bless Our Home. Phyllis C. Michael. SoP
Lord bless thee and keep thee, The. Benediction [*or* Blessing of the Priests]. Numbers, Bible, *O.T.* ThGo; TrGrPo; TrJP
Lord, bless these sacred vows we take. Lord, Bless Our Home. Phyllis C. Michael. SoP
Lord, but it's cold and wretchedly I'm wrapped. The Second Shepherds' Play. *Unknown.* MeEV
Lord, by thy sweet & saving sign. The Office of the Holy Crosse. Richard Crashaw. MaMe
Lord, by whose breath all souls and seeds are living. Hymn. Andrew Young. EaLo
"Lord Byron" was an Englishman. Julia A. Moore. *Fr.* Sketch of Lord Byron's Life. FiBHP
Lord Caesar, when you sternly wrote. After Construing. A. C. Benson. VA
Lord, can a crumb of earth [*or* dust] the earth outweigh. Prologue. Edward Taylor. AmLP; AP; MeP
Lord, Carry Me. Christina Rossetti. SoP
Lord Chancellor's Song ("When you're lying awake"). W. S. Gilbert. *Fr.* Iolanthe. CoBE; NBM; PCD, *much abr.*
(Nightmare.) LiTM; OxBoLi; PoRA (rev. ed.); ShBV-3; SiTL; YT
Lord Chancellours Villanies Discovered, The; or, His Rise and Fall in the Four Last Years. *Unknown.* CoMu
Lord Christ, beneath Thy starry dome. Hymn for a Household. Daniel Henderson. ChIP; HBMV; MaRV; OQP; StJW
Lord Christ, My Darling Is So Dear. C. Hansen-Bay. ThGo
Lord Christ wanted a tongue one day, The. Wanted—A Messenger. *Unknown.* SoP
Lord Christ, when first thou cam'st to men. O Love That Triumphs over Loss. Walter Russell Bowie. MaRV
Lord Clive. E. C. Bentley. *Fr.* Clerihews. BOHV; MoShBr; OxBoLi; WhC
(Clive.) ShBV-3
("What I like about Clive.") CenHV
Lord, Come Away! Jeremy Taylor. *See* Christ's Coming in Triumph.
Lord, confound this surly sister. The Curse. J. M. Synge. ChTr; PV; SiTL; TreFT
Lord Delamere. *Unknown.* ESPB
Lord Derwentwater. *Unknown.* BaBo; ESPB (A *and* D *vers.*)
Lord descended from above, The. Majesty of God. Thomas Sternhold. SoP; WGRP
Lord, Dismiss Us. John Fawcett, *also at. to* Walter Shirley. SoP
Lord, do away my motes and mountains great. Meditation 49. Edward Taylor. *Fr.* Preparatory Meditations, First Series. EP
Lord, Dost Thou Look on Me. Christina Rossetti. EPN
Lord Douglas. *Unknown.* *See* Waly, Waly.
Lord Erlinton had ae daughter. Erlinton. *Unknown.* ESPB
Lord Erskine, at women presuming to rail. A Wife. Matthew Gregory Lewis, *also at. to* Sheridan. BOHV; PV
Lord Finchley. Hilaire Belloc. DTC; ELU; FiBHP; OxBoLi
Lord, for the erring thought. The Undiscovered Country [*or* A Thanksgiving *or* A Prayer]. William Dean Howells. HBV; MaRV; OQP; SoP; TrPWD; WGRP
Lord, for tomorrow and its needs. Just for Today [*or* To-Day]. Sybil F. Partridge, *wr. at. to* Samuel Wilberforce *and to* Frederick W. Faber. HBV; MaRV; OQP; SoP; TreF; TRV; VA; WHL
Lord, forgive. Prayer. Pauline Schroy. OQP
Lord frowned down from every wall, The. Childhood. Donagh MacDonagh. NeIP
Lord Gabriel, wilt thou not rejoice. Cradle Song. Josephine Preston Peabody. HBV; NP
Lord Galloway. Burns. OxBoLi
Lord Gave, The. Job, I: 20-21, Bible, *O.T.* TreF
Lord, Give Me Faith. Dwight Edwards Marvin. SoP
Lord, Give Me Faith. John Oxenham. SoP
(Faith.) MaRV
Lord, give me grace to share from day to day. Grace to Share. Carlton Buck. SoP
Lord, give me vision that shall see. Beyond the Profit of Today. *Unknown.* PoToHe (new ed.)
Lord, give them freedom who are weak. A Hymn. Nikolai Alekseyevich Nekrasov. LiTW
Lord, Give Us Bread. Phyllis C. Michael. SoP
Lord, God, forgive white Europe. Prayer for Peace: II. Léopold Sédar Senghor. TTY
Lord God, how full our cup of happiness! The Cup of Happiness. Gilbert Thomas. MaRV; TrPWD
Lord God in Paradise. Grace for Gradens. Louise Driscoll. TrPWD
Lord, God of all in life and death. Hymn for the Slain in Battle. William Stanley Braithwaite. BALP
Lord, God of love, the wedded hearts'. The Sanctum. T. A. Daly. TrPWD
Lord God of the oak and the elm. Prayer. George Villiers. TrPWD
Lord God of trajectory and blast. Man unto His Fellow Man. Norman Corwin. *Fr.* On a Note of Triumph. TrJP
Lord God Planted a Garden, The. Dorothy Frances Gurney. DD; FaBoBe; HBMV; NeHB; WGRP
(God's Garden.) MaRV
Lord God said to His angel, The: "Let the old things pass away." Revelation. John Jerome Rooney. JKCP
Lord God smiled, The. The Preachers. Norman Nicholson. NeBP

Lord God! this was a stone. The Stone. Thomas Vaughan. OBS; PrWP
Lord God whose mercy guards the virgin jungle. Asking for It. Siegfried Sassoon. MoRP
Lord Gorbals. Harry Graham. ShBV-2
Lord, grant me the gift of forbearance. Forbearance. Avis B. Christiansen. SoP
Lord, Grant Us Calm. Christina Rossetti. EPN; OxBoCh
Lord, grant us eyes to see, and ears to hear. Prayer [*or* Thou Thyself]. Christina Rossetti. ChIP; FaChP
Lord Guy. George F. Warren. BOHV
Lord had a job for me, The. Get Somebody Else [*or* Too Busy]. *At. to* Paul Laurence Dunbar. BLRP; MaRV; TRV; WBLP
Lord, hast Thou set me here. The Priest's Lament. Robert Hugh Benson. ACP
Lord hath builded for Himself, The. The Unknown God. Henry Francis Lyte. MaRV; SoP; TRV
"Lord hath need of thee, The; do thou be good." One Day at Rouen. Sister Mary Bernetta. JKCP (1955 ed.)
Lord, Have Mercy on Us. Thomas Nashe. *See* Adieu, Farewell, Earth's Bliss!
Lord Hay's Mask, *sel.* Thomas Campion. Roses. OBSC
Lord [*or* Lawd] he thought he'd make a man, De. Dese Bones Gwine to Rise Again. *Unknown.* ABF; AS; OxBoLi
Lord, Hear My Prayer. John Clare. NoP
Lord, hear my prayer, and let my cry pass. Psalm CII. *Paraphrased by* Sir Thomas Wyatt. FCP
Lord, hear my prayer when trouble glooms. Lord, Hear My Prayer. John Clare. NoP
Lord, help, it is high time for me to call. Psalm XII. *Paraphrased by* Sir Philip Sidney. EP; FCP
Lord, help me live from day to day. Others. Charles D. Meigs. MaRV; OQP; SoP; WBLP
"Lord help me," so we pray. The Three Prayers. Annie Johnson Flint. SoP
Lord Heygate. Hilaire Belloc. OxBoLi
Lord High-Bo. Hilaire Belloc. FiBHP
Lord, how can man preach thy eternall word? The Windows [*or* The Church Windows]. George Herbert. AnAnS-1; BWP; CABA; CBEP; CoBE; ILP; MaMe; MaPo; MeLP; MeP; NoP; OAEP; OBS; PAn; SeCP; SeCV-1
Lord, how couldst thou so much appease. Faith. George Herbert. MaMe
Lord, how do they increase. Psalm III. *Paraphrased by* Sir Philip Sidney. FCP
Lord, how I am all ague, when I seek. The Sinner. George Herbert. MaMe; SCEP-1; Sonn
Lord, how is Gamester chang'd! His hair close cut. On Reformed Gamester. Ben Jonson. ReIE
Lord, how reformed and quiet are we grown. Prologue. Dryden. *Fr.* Marriage à la Mode. MBW-1
Lord, How Shall I Me Complain. *Unknown.* CBEP
Lord! how this weather is cold, and I am ill happed. The Second Shepherds' Play. *Unknown.* EnLit
Lord, I am glad for the great gift of living. Prayer to the Giver. Charles Hanson Towne. OQP
Lord, I am humbled by the great. Scatheless. Marguerite Wilkinson. HBMV
Lord, I am like to [*or* the] mistletoe. To God [*or* Holding to God]. Robert Herrick. BoPe; TrPWD; TRV; WGRP
Lord, I am poor; but it becomes. I Have a Roof. Ada Jackson. TrPWD
Lord, I come, and simply resting. A Prayer. *Unknown.* SoP
Lord, I confesse my sinne is great. Repentance. George Herbert. MaMe; OAEP
Lord, I do not ask for houses of steel. Prayer of the Unemployed. Raymond Kresensky. OQP
Lord, I give thanks! Thanksgiving. Susie M. Best. TrPWD
Lord, I have fasted, I have prayed. Weakness of Nature. Richard Hurrell Froude. OBRV
Lord, I have knelt and tried to pray to-night. Communion. Edward Dowden. MaRV; TrPWD
Lord, I have laid my heart upon Thy altar. Sacrifice. George Macdonald. FaChP
Lord, I have not time to pray. Helene Magaret. *Fr.* Impiety. TrPWD
Lord, I have sinn'd, and the black number swells. The Penitent. Jeremy Taylor. OBS; OxBoCh
Lord, I Love Thy Morning. Barbara E. Cornet. SoP
Lord I love went on ahead, The. If I But Read. Martha Snell Nicholson. SoP
Lord, I my vows to Thee renew. Direct This Day. Thomas Ken. TRV
Lord, I remember, and am sore amazed. Hymn of Weeping. Amittai ben Shefatiah. TrJP
Lord, I say nothing; I profess. Christ the Man. W. H. Davies. MaRV; WGRP
Lord, I told them things they wanted to hear. Am I Running from You, Jesus? Warren Risch. SoP
Lord, I Want to Be a Christian in-a My Heart. *Unknown.* BoAn-2, *with music*
Lord, I will mean and speak thy praise. Praise. George Herbert. MaMe
Lord, I would ask for a holy year. A Prayer for the New Year. A. B. Simpson. SoP
Lord, I Would Follow. John Oxenham. SoP
(Follow Me!) ChIP; MaRV
Lord, I would own thy tender care. A Thanksgiving. Jane Taylor. ThGo
Lord, I would thank You for these things. Gifts without Season. Joseph Auslander. MaRV
"Lord, if I love Thee and Thou lovest me." Why? Christina Rossetti. Sonn
Lord! if in love, though fainting oft, I have tended thy gracious Vine. "Owen Meredith." *Fr.* Last Lines. TrPWD
Lord, If Thou Art Not Present. John Gray. CAW; TrPWD
Lord, I'm done for: now Margot. Rondeau. William Jay Smith. FiBHP
Lord, I'm just a little boy. A Child's Christmas Song. T. A. Daly. BiCB
Lord, in an age of steel and stone. A Prayer for Today. Charles Nelson Pace. MaRV; OQP
Lord in His wisdom made the fly, The. The Fly. Ogden Nash. FaPON
Lord, in mercy pardon me. A Prayer. Frances Ridley Havergal. SoP
Lord, in my silence how do I despise. Frailty [*or* Frailtie]. George Herbert. MaMe; OxBoCh
Lord, in the strength of grace. Dedication. Charles Wesley. MaRV
Lord in the Wind, The. James Picot. PoAu-2
Lord, in this day of battle. Prayer during Battle. Hermann Hagedorn. TrPWD
Lord, in this dust Thy sovereign voice. A Thanksgiving. Cardinal Newman. TrPWD
Lord, in thy name thy servants plead. Seed Time Hymn. John Keble. VA
Lord indeed is risen, The. He Is Risen. John Oxenham. ChIP
Lord Ingram and Chiel Wyet. *Unknown.* BaBo; ESPB (A, B, *and* C *vers.*); OBB
Lord Is a Man of War, The. Exodus, XV: 3-10, Bible, *O.T.* WaaP
Lord Is Good to All, The. Psalms, CXLV: 9, Bible, *O.T.* TRV
Lord, Is It I? John Philo Trowbridge. SoP
Lord Is King, The. *Unknown, tr. fr. Hebrew by* Solomon Solis-Cohen. TrJP
Lord is my friend, so I shall not be lonely, The. A One Hundred Fifty-first Psalm. Henry B. Robins. MaRV
Lord is my light and my salvation, The. My Light and My Salvation [*or* The Deliverance of Jehovah]. Psalm XXVII, Bible, *O.T.* MaRV; TreFT; WGRP
Lord is my refuge, The. He Is My Refuge. *Unknown.* SoP
Lord Is My Shepherd, The. Henry W. Baker. *See* King of Love, The.
Lord Is My Shepherd, The. Psalms, XXIII, Bible, *O.T.* EnLi-1; FaPON; MaRV; OuHeWo; StVeCh; TreF; TrJP
(Lord's My Shepherd, The, *Scottish Psalter.*) FaChP; SoP; TRV
(Protection of Jehovah, The, *Moulton, Modern Reader's Bible.*) WGRP
(Psalm of David, A.) CBV; SUS
(Psalm XXIII.) AWP; CBEP; ExPo; JAWP; OHIP; OnPM; PG (1955 ed.); PoLF; ReIE; RePo; TiPo (1952 ed.); TRV; WBLP; WoL
(Shepherd's Psalm.) PCD; PCH
(Twenty-third Psalm, The.) FaBoBe; NeHB; OTPC (1946 ed.); PoPl; PoPo; StaSt; TrGrPo
Lord Is My Shepherd, The. John Knox, *par. fr.* Psalms, XXIII, Bible, *O. T.* BePJ

Lord Is My Shepherd, The. James Montgomery. SoP
Lord is my shepherd and I do want, The. Show Me Lord Show Me. Yusef Iman. BF
Lord is my Shepherd, no want shall I know, The. The Lord Is My Shepherd. James Montgomery. SoP
Lord is risen, The. Easter Day. Henry W. Frost. SoP
Lord is the portion of mine inheritance, The. I Have a Goodly Heritage. *Fr.* Psalm, XVI Bible,* *O.T.* TreFT
Lord, It Belongs Not to My Care. Richard Baxter. MaRV; OxBoCh
(Entering by His Door, *abr.*) BePJ
(Happy Any Way.) SoP
Lord it is my chief complaint. William Cowper. *Fr.* Lovest Thou Me? TrPWD
Lord It Is Not Life to Live. Augustus Montague Toplady. *Fr.* Happiness Found. MaRV; OxBoCh; TrPWD
Lord, it is time. The summer was too long. Autumn Day. Rainer Maria Rilke, *tr. by* C. F. MacIntyre. TrJP
Lord, It's All, Almost Done, *with music.* *Unknown.* OuSiCo
Lord Jehovah Reigns, The. Isaac Watts. SoP
Lord Jesus, all my sin and guilt. Gerhardt Tersteegen. SoP
Lord Jesus Christ, my life, my light. I Shall Be Satisfied. M. Behemb. BePJ
Lord Jesus, make Thyself to me. My Prayer. *Unknown.* BePJ; BLRP; SoP
Lord Jesus, show Thyself to me. Prayer by the Open Book. E. Margaret Clarkson. SoP
Lord Jesus, Think on Me. Synesius, *tr. fr. Greek by* Allen William Chatfield. SoP
Lord Jesus, Thou hast known. A Mother's Birthday. Henry van Dyke. MaRV; OHIP
Lord Jesus! when I think of Thee. The King in His Beauty. James G. Deck. BePJ
Lord Jesus, When We Stand Afar. William Walsham How. ChIP
Lord Jesus, who would think that I am thine? Hold Thou Me Fast. Christina Rossetti. BePJ
Lord Jesus! with what sweetness and delights. Ascension-Day. Henry Vaughan. AnAnS-1; MeP; OxBoCh
Lord, judge me and my case. Psalm XXVI. *Paraphrased by* Sir Philip Sidney. FCP
Lord, Keep Me Still. *Unknown.* SoP
Lord, keep me sweet when I grow old. When I Grow Old. *Unknown.* SoP
Lord, Keep Us Steadfast in Thy Word. Martin Luther, *tr. fr. German by* Catherine Winkworth. SoP
Lord, lay the taste of Prayer upon my tongue. The Taste of Prayer. Ralph W. Seager. TrPWD
Lord, lay your fingers on. Closing Prayer. Johnstone G. Patrick. TrPWD
Lord, let me be the torch that springs to light. The Torch. Theodosia Garrison. BLPA
Lord, let me do the little things. Humility. *Unknown.* SoP
Lord, let me live like a regular man. A Prayer. Berton Braley. BLPA
Lord, let me make this rule. School Days. Maltbie D. Babcock. MaRV
Lord, let me not die until I've done for Thee. My Work. *Unknown.* MaRV
Lord, let me not in service lag. A Creed. Edgar A. Guest. HH; PEDC
Lord, let me see Thy glory. Christ, My Life. Margaret J. Lucas. SoP
Lord, let not me a worm by Thee be shent. Psalm VI. *Paraphrased by* Sir Philip Sidney. FCP
Lord, let not my religion be. A Prayer. Clarence M. Burkholder. OQP
Lord, let the angels praise thy name. Miserie. George Herbert. MaMe; PoEL-2
Lord let the house of a brute to the soul of a man, The. By an Evolutionist. Tennyson. BEL; EnLi-2; EPN; PoVP
Lord, let war's tempests cease. Let War's Tempests Cease. Longfellow. OHIP
Lord, life is good! Thanksgiving. Charles Hanson Towne. PoMa
Lord Livingston. *Unknown.* ESPB; OxBB
Lord, look upon a little child. Jane Taylor. ThGo
Lord, Lord—these miracles, the streets, all say. Stone Too Can Pray. Conrad Aiken. EaLo; MoRP
Lord, Lord to Thee. A Sailor's Prayer. George Hornell Morris. TrPWD
Lord Lovel. *Unknown.* AS, *with music*; BaBo (A *and* B *vers.*); BLPA; BoChLi; ESPB (A, B, *and* D *vers.*); FaPON; LoEn; NoP; OBB; OnSP; OTPC; PoMS; TreFS; ViBoFo (A *and* B *vers.*)
(Lord Lovel and Lady Nança Bell, *with music.*) BFSS
Lord Lundy. Hilaire Belloc. OxBoLi; ShBV-3
Lord, Make a Regular Man Out of Me. Edgar A. Guest. BLPA; NeHB
Lord, make me a man. An Apt Prayer. A. F. Thomas. SoP
Lord, Make Me an Instrument of Your Peace. St. Francis of Assisi, *tr. fr. Italian.* TreFS
(Prayer, A: "Lord, make me an instrument of Thy peace.") FaChP; PoToHe (new ed.)
(Prayer for Peace.) SoP; TIHL
(Prayer of Saint Francis of Assisi.) OTD; PoLF; PoPl
(St. Francis' Prayer.) MaRV; TRV
Lord, make me available today. Make Me Available. Florence Duncan Long. SoP
Lord, make me coy and tender to offend. Unkindness. George Herbert. EP; HBV; MaMe
Lord, Make Me Strong. Dorothy Clark Wilson. SoP
Lord, make me sensitive to the sight. Prayer. Barbara Marr. TrPWD
Lord, Make Me to Know Mine End. Psalms, XXXIX, Bible, *O.T.* TrJP
Lord, make my childish soul stand straight. A Prayer. "William Laird." HBMV
Lord, make my loving a guard for them. Mother-Prayer. Margaret Widdemer. HBMV
Lord, make my soul. The Mirror. Blanche Mary Kelly. GoBC; TrPWD
Lord, Many Times I Am Aweary Quite. Richard Chenevix Trench. BePJ; OBRV
Lord Maxwell's Last Goodnight. *Unknown.* BaBo; ESPB (A *and* B *vers.*); OBB; OxBB
Lord, may I enter this day without hurry. A Prayer for the Day. *Unknown.* SoP
Lord, may there be no moment in her life. Prayer of Any Husband. Mazie V. Caruthers. MaRV; PoToHe
Lord, mind your trees to-day! The Bushfeller. Eileen Duggan. AnNZ; JKCP (1955 ed.)
Lord, must I bear the whole of it, or none? Crucifixion. Frederick George Scott. ChIP; MaRV; OQP
Lord, my first fruits present themselves to thee. The Dedication. George Herbert. AnAnS-1; MaMe; MeP; OAEP
"Lord my Maker, forming me of clay, The." Adam's Complaint. Theophanes. SoP
Lord my pasture shall prepare, The. Pastoral Hymn. Addison. OBEC
Lord never grant me what I ask for. The Unforeseen. Conrado Nale Roxlo. LiTW; MoRP
Lord North's Recantation. *Unknown.* PAH
Lord, not for light in darkness do we pray. A Prayer. John Drinkwater. HBV; MaRV; OBVV; TrPWD; WGRP
Lord, now lettest thou thy servant depart in peace. Nunc Dimittis. St. Luke, Bible, *N.T.* WGRP; WHL
Lord, now that Spring is in the world. An Easter Prayer [*or* Easter]. Charles Hanson Towne. ChIP; OQP; SoP
Lord, Oh, hear me prayin' Lord. Oh, Hear Me Prayin'. *Unknown.* BoAN-2
Lord of All, The. Edwin Markham. CAW
Lord of All. Phyllis C. Michael. SoP
Lord of all being! throned afar. A Sun-Day Hymn. Oliver Wendell Holmes. AmePo; AnNE; InP; MaRV; SoP; TrPWD; TRV; WGRP
Lord of all growing things. Growing. *Unknown.* MaRV
Lord of All I Survey. Keith Sinclair. AnNZ
Lord of all light and darkness. At a Burial. Sir William Watson. MaRV
Lord of All Pots and Pans and Things. *Unknown, ad. fr.* Cecily Hallack. ChIP; FaChP; OQP; SOP; TRV. *See also* Divine Office of the Kitchen, The.
(Home Prayer, A.) STF
Lord of all pow'r and might. Spread the Word. Hugh Stowell. SoP
Lord of all the lore that man had found, The. Saint Thomas Aquinas. Thomas S. Jones, Jr. CAW
Lord of all, who reigned supreme, The. Adon 'Olam. *Unknown.* EaLo
Lord of Burleigh, The. Tennyson. OTPC (1923 ed.)

Lord of comfort, hope, and love. Give My Heart a Song. Anna M. Gilleland. STF
Lord of Eden. Marie de L. Welch. AnAmPo
Lord of Heaven to Earth Came Down, The. Kathryn Blackburn Peck. BePJ
Lord of Joy, The. Charles Wesley. FaChP
Lord of Life Is Risen, The. Johann Peter Lange, *tr. fr. German by* Henry Harbaugh. SoP
Lord of Lorn and the False Steward, The. *Unknown.* ESPB; OxBB
(Lord of Lorn, The, *shorter vers.*) OBB
Lord of My Heart's Elation. Bliss Carman. HBV; OBCV; TrPWD
(Veni Creator.) MaRV
Lord of my love, to whom in vassalage. Sonnets, XXVI. Shakespeare. PoFS; ReEn
Lord of my years, can life be bare. Common Blessings. Thomas Curtis Clark. TrPWD
Lord of our fathers, hear our prayer. Decoration Day Prayer. Arthur Roszelle Bemis, Jr. OQP
Lord of Rosslyn's daughter gaed through the wud her lane, The. Captain Wedderburn's Courtship. *Unknown.* ESPB (B *vers.*); ViBoFo (A *vers.*)
Lord of Sea and Earth and Air. Prayer for a Pilot. Cecil Roberts. BBV; FaPON; OTPC (1946 ed.); TrPWD
Lord of Tartary. Walter de la Mare. *See* Tartary.
Lord of the bow. In the Gorge. W. S. Merwin. AmPC
Lord of the East, The. Chu Yuan, *tr. fr. Chinese by* Shen Yuting. *Fr.* The Nine Songs. LiTW
Lord of the Far Horizons. Bliss Carman. MaRV; TrPWD
Lord of the grass and hill. Overlord [*or* Veni Creator]. Bliss Carman. CaP; MoRP; WGRP
Lord of the Isle, The. Stefan George, *tr. fr. German by* Ludwig Lewisohn. AWP; JAWP; WBP
Lord of the land. Prayer of a Patriot. Henry J. von Schlichten. BePJ; SoP
Lord of the lands, beneath Thy bending skies. A Hymn for Canada. Albert Durrant Watson. CaP
Lord of the Mountain. Navajo Prayer [*or* Prayer to the Mountain Spirit]. *Unknown.* PoRL; StVeCh; WGRP
Lord of the pots and pipkins, since I have no time to be. The Divine Office of the Kitchen. Cecily Hallack. BLRP; PoLF; TreFT
Lord of the Sabbath, hear us pray. Hear Us, in This Thy House. Philip Doddridge. BePJ
Lord of the strong, when earth you trod. Lord of Us All. Donald Hankey. MaRV
Lord of the Winds. Mary Elizabeth Coleridge. OxBoCh; TrPWD
Lord of the World, The. G. A. Studdert-Kennedy. PGD
Lord of the World. *Unknown, tr. fr. Hebrew by* D. A. de Sola. TrJP
Lord of the worlds above. The House of God. Isaac Watts. SoP
Lord of Thyself and me, through the sore grief. George Macdonald. *Fr.* Within and Without. TRV
Lord of Us All. Donald Hankey. MaRV
Lord over all! whose power the sceptre swayed. Lord of the World. *Unknown.* TrJP
Lord over life and all the ways of breath. Ernest Dowson. *Fr.* De Amore. TrPWD
Lord Pam in the church (cou'd you think it) kneel'd down. Epigram. Jonathan Swift. NCEP
Lord possessed me in the beginning of his ways, The. The Voice of Wisdom. Proverbs, Bible, *O.T.* (*Douay vers.*). ISi; TreFT
Lord, purge our eyes to see. Judge Not According to the Appearance. Christina Rossetti. TrPWD
Lord Rameses of Egypt sighed. Birthright. John Drinkwater. CH; HBV; POTE; WHA
Lord Randal. *Unknown.* AtBAP; ATP; AWP; BaBo (A, B, C, *and* D *vers.*); BEL; BoLiVe; CABA; CBEP; CoBE; DiPo; EnL; EnRP; EnSB; ESPB (A, B, *and* J *vers.*); ForPo; FosPo; GBV (1952 ed.); HBV; HoPM; ILP; InP; InPo; JAWP; LiTB; LiTG; MeWo; LoBV; NoP; OBB; OnSP; OuHeWo; OxBB; OxBS; PoIE; PoPo; SeCeV; ShBV-1; StP; TOP; TreF; TrGrPo; UnPo; ViBoFo (A, B, *and* C *vers.*); WBP
(Jimmy Random, My Son, 1 *st., with music.*) BFSS
(Lord Randall.) LiTL; MaC
(Lord Rendal.) PoG
(My Ramboling Son, *with music.*) BFSS
Lord, The, reigneth, he is apparelled with majesty. Jehovah's Immovable Throne. Psalms, XCIII, Bible, *O.T.* WGRP
Lord Ronald. *Unknown.* LoEn
Lord Ronald courted Lady Clare. Lady Clare. Tennyson. GoTP
Lord Ronald was a mighty man. Lord Ronald. *Unknown.* LoEn
Lord said, The. Pronouns. Karle Wilson Baker. TreFT
Lord Saltoun and Auchanachie. *Unknown.* BaBo; ESPB
Lord, Save Us, We Perish. Christina Rossetti. TrPWD
Lord Shaftesbury. Dryden. *See* Achitophel.
Lord, Show Me. *Unknown.* SoP
Lord, since the strongest human hands I know. In the Dark. Sophie Jewett. TrPWD
Lord, spare to them this very little child. Prayer That an Infant May Not Die. Francis Jammes. CAW
Lord, Speak to Me, that I May Speak. Frances Ridley Havergal. MaRV; SoP
(For Every Day.) BLRP
(Teacher's Prayer, A.) TRV
(Use Even Me.) FaChP
Lord, stabilize me. My legs. From "Suite in Prison." Richard Eberhart. NYTB
Lord, Take Away Pain. *Unknown.* OQP
(Pain.) MaRV
Lord that purposed for his more avail, A. Of Inclosing a Common. Sir John Harington. SiCE
Lord, the Lord my shepherd is, The. Psalm XXIII. *Paraphrased by* Sir Philip Sidney. FCP
Lord, the newness of this day. Prayer. Henry van Dyke. SoP; TRV
Lord, the Roman hyacinths are blooming in bowls. A Song for Simeon. T. S. Eliot. BoLiVe; CoBE; EaLo; LiTB; MAP; MaRV; MoAmPo (1942 ed.); OxBoCh; POTE
Lord, the snowful sky. Sailor's Carol. Charles Causley. AtBAP
Lord, Thine humble servants hear. Hymn for Atonement Day. Judah Halevi. TrJP
Lord—Thine the Day. Dag Hammarskjöld, *tr. fr. Swedish by* Leif Sjöberg *and* W. H. Auden. EaLo
Lord, this humble house we'd keep. Edgar A. Guest. *Fr.* Prayer for the Home. MaRV; TRV
Lord Thomas and Fair Annet (*diff. versions*). *Unknown.* BaBo (A *and* B *vers.*); EnLit; ESPB (A, D, *and* I *vers.*); NoP (A *vers.*); OBB; OxBB; ViBoFo (A *vers.*)
(Brown Girl, The, C *vers.*) BaBo
(Brown Girl, or Fair Eleanor, The, *with music.*) AS
(Lord Thomas and Fair Eleanor, B *vers.*) FIW
(Lord Thomas and the Brown Girl, *with music.*) BFSS
(Sir Peter's Leman, D *vers., tr. fr. Danish by* E. M. Smith-Dampier.) BaBo
Lord Thomas and Lady Margaret. *Unknown.* BaBo; ESPB
Lord Thomas he was a bold forester. Lord Thomas and Fair Annet [*or* Eleanor]. *Unknown.* BaBo; FIW
Lord Thomas is to the hunting gone. Lord Thomas and Lady Margaret. *Unknown.* BaBo
Lord Thomas Stuart. *Unknown.* BaBo; ESPB
Lord, thou art mine, and I am thine. Clasping of Hands. George Herbert. MaMe; PoEL-2
Lord, thou dost know with what implacable hand. The Calling. Luis Felipe Contardo. CAW
Lord, thou hast been our dwelling place in all generations. God, Our Dwelling Place. Psalm XC, Bible, *O.T.* AWP; EaLo; MaRV
Lord, thou hast given me a cell. A Thanksgiving to God, for His House [*or* A Thankful Heart]. Robert Herrick. AnAnS-2; BEL; BoC; ChTr; EnLi-1; EnLit; FaBoBe; HBV; InPo; MaRV; NeHB; NoP; OBS; OHIP; OQP; OTPC; PGD; Po; PoE; PoRA; PoToHe; ReEn; SCEP-2; SeCeV; SeCP; SeCV-1; SeEP; SoP; TiPo (1952 ed.); TOP; TreFT; TrPWD; UnPo (1st ed.); ViBoPo; WGRP; WoL
Lord, Thou hast made this world below the shadow of a dream. McAndrew's Hymn. Kipling. CABL; OtMeF; PoEL-5; ViPP
Lord, Thou Hast Suffered. Amy Carmichael. TRV
Lord, thou who didst teach, forgive me for teaching. The Teacher's Prayer. "Gabriela Mistral." MaRV
Lord, thus I sin, repent, and sin again. A Sinner's Lament. Lord Herbert of Cherbury. SeCP

Lord, Thy peaceful gift restore. Night-Watch Prayer. Henry van Dyke. SoP
Lord 'tis midnight. Three Phases of Africa. Francis Ernest Kobina Parkes. PBA
Lord Turned, and Looked upon Peter, The. Elizabeth Barrett Browning. *See* Look, the.
Lord Ullin's Daughter. Thomas Campbell. BBV (1923 ed.); BeLS; BoTP; EnRP; FaPON; GN; GTBS; GTBS-D; GTBS-P; GTBS-W; GTSE; GTSL; HBV; HBVY; LoEn; OBRV; OnSP; OTPC; RoGo; TreF; WBLP
Lord, very fair my lot and beautiful my story. Very Fair My Lot. Jacob David Kamzon. TrJP
Lord Vyet. A. C. Benson. OBVV
Lord, walk close beside me. Walk Close Beside Me. Roy J. Wilkins. SoP
Lord Walter's Wife. Elizabeth Barrett Browning. BeLS
Lord Waterford. *Unknown.* ChTr
Lord we have not forgotten them, the pioneers. Lord of All I Survey. Keith Sinclair. AnNZ
Lord, we thank Thee for affliction. Thank Thee, Lord. Georgia B. Adams. SoP; STF
Lord, we thank Thee for the beauty. Thanksgiving and Praise. Neva Brien. SoP
Lord! what a busy [*or* busie], restless thing. The Pursuit. Henry Vaughan. OAEP; SeCP; TrPWD
Lord, what a change within us one short hour. Prayer [*or* In Thy Presence *or* An Hour with Thee]. Richard Chenevix Trench. BePJ; BLRP; FaChP; MaRV; OQP; PoToHe; SoP; TrPWD; TRV; WBLP; WGRP
Lord what a stately piece was Man. The Fall. Nathaniel Wanley. SeEP
Lord, what am I, that with unceasing care. Tomorrow. Lope de Vega. AWP; CAW; SoP; TrPWD
Lord what is man, that he should find. Psalm VIII, Bible, *O.T. Paraphrased by* Christopher Smart. TrPWD
Lord, what is man? why should he cost you [*or* thee]? Charitas Nimia, or the Dear Bargain. Richard Crashaw. AnAnS-1; MaMe; MaRV; MeP; MePo; OxBoCh; PoFS; PoLi; ReEn; SeEP
Lord, what these weders ar cold. The Second Shepherds' Play. *Unknown.* PoEL-1
Lord, what unvalued pleasures crown'd. The Invitation. Nathaniel Wanley. OxBoCh; SeEP
Lord, when I find at last Thy paradise. She Asks for New Earth. Katharine Tynan. BoPe; HBMV
Lord, when I look at lovely things which pass. In the Fields [*or* Spring]. Charlotte Mew. BoNaP; MoAB; MoBrPo; POTE; StaSt
Lord, when on my bed I lie. A Prayer [*or* Whirring Wheels]. John Oxenham. SoP; TRV
Lord, when the sense of thy sweet grace. Song [*or* A Song of Divine Love *or* Divine Love]. Richard Crashaw. CBV; GoBC; MaMe; MaRV; PoE; SeCeV; TrPWD; ViBoPo
Lord When the Wise Men Came from Far[r]. Sidney Godolphin. MeLP; OBS
(Hymn: "Lord when the wise men came from farr.") MePo
(Wise Men and Shepherds.) OxBoCh
Lord, when they kill me, let the job be thorough. Merthyr. Glyn Jones. PrWP
Lord, when Thou seest that my work is done. After Work. John Oxenham. MaRV; TRV
Lord! when Thou wentest from this place. The Lament of Eve. *Unknown.* ACP (1952 ed.)
Lord, Where Shall I Find Thee? Judah Halevi, *tr. fr. Hebrew by* Nina Davis Salaman. TrJP
Lord, where Thou art our holy dead must be. Easter Eucharist. *Unknown.* MaRV
Lord, While for All Mankind We Pray. John R. Wreford. MaRV; TrPWD
Lord, while that Thy rage doth bide. Psalm XXXVIII. *Paraphrased by* Sir Philip Sidney. FCP
Lord, who am I to teach the way. The Teacher. Leslie Pinckney Hill. BANP; FaChP; MaRV; PoNe; SoP; TrPWD
Lord, Who Art Merciful. *Tr. fr. Persian by* Robert Southey. MaRV; TrPWD
(Imitated from the Persian.) EnRP
Lord, who createdst man in wealth and store. Easter Wings. George Herbert. AnAnS-1; ATP; CABA; ExPo; LiTB; MaMe; MaPo (1969 ed.); MeLP; MeP; MePo; NoP; OAEP; OBS; PAn; PIA; PoEL-2; PoFS; PoSa; PP; SCEP-1; SeCP; SeEP; StP; VaPo; YAT
Lord! who desirest that the sin should die. Penitence. Pedro Soto de Rojas. OnPM
Lord, who hast form'd me out of mud. Trinitie Sunday. George Herbert. MaMe
Lord, who ordainest for mankind. The Mother's Hymn. Bryant. DD; MaRV; OHIP
Lord, who shall abide in thy tabernacle? Psalm XV, Bible, *O.T.* OuHeWo
Lord Will Happiness Divine, The. William Cowper. *See* Contrite Heart, The.
Lord Will Provide, The. John Newton. SoP
Lord William; or, Lord Lundy. *Unknown.* BaBo; ESPB
Lord William and Lord Douglas, *with music. Unknown.* BFSS
Lord Willoughby. *Unknown.* CoMu; TuPP
Lord, with glowing heart I'd praise thee. Hymn. Francis Scott Key. TrPWD
Lord, with what bountie and rare clemencie. Ungratefulnesse. George Herbert. MaMe
Lord, with what care hast thou begirt us round! Sin [*or* Sinne]. George Herbert. MaMe; SCEP-1; ViBoPo
Lord, with what glorie wast thou serv'd of old. Sion. George Herbert. AnAnS-1; MaMe; MeP
Lord, you visited Paris on the day of your birth. Paris in the Snow. Léopold Sédar-Senghor. PBA
Lordinges, I wol you singen of a grotë. Sing a Song of Sixpence, *parody.* Frank Sidgwick. WhC
Lordings [*or* Lordinges], listen, and hold you still. Durham Field. *Unknown.* ESPB; OBB
Lordings, Listen to Our Lay. *Unknown, tr. fr. Anglo-Norman carol by* F. Douce. OHIP
"Lordings," quod he, "in chirches whan I preche." Prologue to the Pardoner's Tale. Chaucer. *Fr.* The Canterbury Tales. BEL; CaBL; CoBE; EnLi-1; FosPo; MBW-1; OAEP
Lordly and Isolate Satyrs, The. Charles Olson. CABL; CoAP; NeAP
Lordly Hudson, The. Paul Goodman. CoAP; NMP
Lord's Charge, The. Charles Wesley. *See* Charge to Keep I Have, A.
Lord's Day, The. Henry W. Frost. SoP
Lord's Day, A. Christopher Wordsworth. *See* O Day of Rest and Gladness.
Lords, knights, and squires, the numerous [*or* num'rous] band. To a Child of Quality, Five Years Old. Matthew Prior. CBEP; CoBE; EiCL; EiCP; EiPP; ExPo; GN; GTBS-W; HBV; InP; LiTB; OBEC; OBEV; PoEL-3; SeCeV; VaPo
Lord's lost Him His mockingbird. Mourning Poem for the Queen of Sunday. Robert Hayden. NoP
Lords' Mask, The, *sel.* Thomas Campion.
Song: To the Masquers Representing Stars. LoBV
(Stars Dance, The.) OBSC
Lord's My Shepherd, The. Psalms, XXIII, Bible, *O.T. See* Lord Is My Shepherd, The.
Lord's Name Be Praised, The! *Unknown.* ThGo
Lords of Creation, The. *Unknown.* PoLF
Lords of life, the lords of life, The. Experience. Emerson. AmePo; AnAmPo; AnNE; LiTA; PoEL-4
Lords of the Main, The. Joseph Stansbury. PAH
Lords of the Wilderness. John Leyden. OBRV
Lord's Prayer, The. St. Matthew, VI: 9-13, Bible, *N.T.* EaLo; MaRV; PoLF; TrGrPo; TRV
(Poem of the Our Father, The.) CAW
"Lordynges," quod he. *See* "Lordings," quod he . . .
Lore. Edna Ethel Davis. ChIP
Lorelei [*or* Loreley], The. Heine, *tr. fr. German.* GoTP, *tr. by* Louis Untermeyer; OuHeWo, *tr. by* Sir Theodore Martin; PoMS, *tr. by* William Ellery Leonard; TrJP, *tr. by* Emma Lazarus
(Ich Weiss Nicht, Was Soll es Bedeuten.) AWP, *tr. by* Alexander MacMillan
Lorena, *with music.* H. D. L. Webster. BFSS; BLPA
Lorenzo's Bas-Relief for a Florentine Chest. Marjorie Allen Seiffert. *See* Italian Chest, An.
Lorraine. Charles Kingsley. VA
(Lorraine Lorèe.) BBV
(Lorraine, Lorraine, Lorrèe.) PoVP
Los is by mortals nam'd Time, Enitharmon is nam'd Space. Blake. *Fr.* Milton, I. OBRV
"Los Pastores." Edith Agnew. ChBR; GaP
Lose This Day Loitering. Goethe, *tr. fr. German by* John An-

ster. *Fr.* Faust: Prologue. PoLF
(Prologue: "Lose this day loitering, 'twill be the same story.") TRV
Losers. Carl Sandburg. CMoP; HBMV; MAP; MoAB; MoAmPo; MoVE; NP; TrGrPo
Losers, The. William Young. *See* Pawns, The.
Losing a Slave-Girl. Po Chü-i, *tr. fr. Chinese by* Arthur Waley. AWP
Losing Track. Denise Levertov. NaP; OPoP
Loss. Richard Aldington. BrPo
Loss. Julia Johnson Davis. HBMV
Loss. Paul Eluard, *tr. fr. French by* Patricia Terry. OnPM
Loss. Randall Jarrell. FiMAP
Loss after Loss. Bianor, *tr. fr. Greek by* Goldwin Smith. OnPM
Loss at Sea. Callimachus, *tr. fr. Greek by* John Addington Symonds. OnPM
Loss falls from the air as the tables turn. Complaint. Joseph Bennett. LiTA; StP
Loss in Delay[s]. Robert Southwell. OBSC; SiCE
Loss of gold is much, The. Lines from a Sampler. *Unknown.* ThGo
Loss of Love, The. Countee Cullen. PoNe
Loss of something ever felt I, A. Emily Dickinson. MWA-2
Loss of the *Birkenhead,* The. Sir Francis Hastings Doyle. HBV
Loss of the *Cedar Grove,* The, *with music. Unknown.* ShS
Loss of the *Central America, with music.* John A. Stone. SGR
Loss of the *Druid,* The, *with music. Unknown.* ShS
Loss of the *Eurydice,* The. Gerard Manley Hopkins. VP
Loss of the *Ramillies,* The. *Unknown. See* Ship *Rambolee,* The.
Loss of the *Royal George,* The. William Cowper. *See* On the Loss of the *Royal George.*
Losses. Randall Jarrell. AmP; CoBMV; FiMAP; LiTM (1970 ed.); MoVE; OxBA; UnPo (3d ed.); WaP
Lost. Alfred Alvarez. NMP
Lost. Millen Brand. NYBP
Lost. Maurice Lesemann. NP
Lost. Carl Sandburg. AmPP (5th ed.); BrR; CMoP; NP; PDV; PoPl; PoPo; RePo; WHA
Lost. Celia Thaxter. PPL
Lost. *Unknown.* SoP
Lost, The. Jones Very. MAmP; PoIE; QFR
Lost Acres. Robert Graves. FaBoMo; LiTG; MoPW
Lost Anchors. E. A. Robinson. CMoP; MAmP
Lost and Found. George Macdonald. FaChP; MaRV; OQP; StJW; TRV; WGRP
Lost and Found. Edwin Muir. PoDB
Lost and Given Over. E. J. Brady. BoAu; PoAu-1
Lost at Sea. Simonides, *tr. fr. Greek by* Walter Leaf. WoL
Lost Ball, The. Lucy Sprague Mitchell. TiPo (1959 ed.)
Lost Beliefs. William Dean Howells. AmePo
Lost but Found. Horatius Bonar. HBV; VA
(I was a Wandering Sheep.) BePJ; SoP
Lost, but Won. Henry von Schlichten. BePJ
Lost Cat, The. Lilian Whiting. CIV
Lost Child. Heine. *See* Enfant perdu.
Lost Children, The. Richard Eberhart. NePoAm-2
Lost Children, The. Randall Jarrell. CoAP
Lost Chord, The. D. B. Wyndham Lewis. MuSP; WhC
Lost Chord. Adelaide Anne Procter. CAW; FaFP; HBV; MaRV; OTD; PaPo; SoP; TreF; WBLP; WGRP
Lost Christ, The. Thomas Curtis Clark. ChIP; OQP
Lost Christ, The. Franklin D. Elmer, Jr. ChIP
Lost Cities, The. Lawrence Durrell. ToPo
Lost City. Ingrid Jonker, *tr. fr. Afrikaans by* Jack Cope *and* Ruth Miller. PeSA
Lost City. Marion Strobel. NP
Lost Colors, The. Elizabeth Stuart Phelps Ward. AA; HBV; HBVY
Lost Dancer, The. Jean Toomer. BALP
Lost day. A Certain Saturday. Edith Lovejoy Pierce. ChIP
Lost Days. Dante Gabriel Rossetti. The House of Life, LXXXVI. EnL; EnLi-2; EnLit; EPN; GoBC; MaRV; MaVP; MemP; NCEP; OAEP; PoVP; TOP; ViPo; ViPP; WHA
Lost Days. Stephen Spender. NYTB
Lost days of my life until to-day, The. Lost Days. Dante Gabriel Rossetti. The House of Life, LXXXVI. MaVP; MemP; NCEP
Lost Desire. Meleager, *tr. fr. Greek by* William M. Hardinge. AWP
Lost Dog. Frances Rodman. PoRL
Lost Doll, The. Charles Kingsley. *Fr.* The Water Babies. FaPON; MoShBr; MPB; OTPC; PRWS; SoPo; TVC
("I once had a sweet little doll, dears.") TiPo
(Song: "I once had a sweet little doll, dears.") PaPo
Lost Explorer. Edmund Pennant. GoYe
Lost for a Rose's Sake. *Unknown, tr. fr. French by* Andrew Lang. AWP; JAWP; WBP
Lost Garden. "Katherine Hale." CaP
Lost Genius, The. John James Piatt. AA
Lost God, A, *sel.* Francis W. Bourdillon.
"Ah happy, who have seen." WGRP
Lost Heifer, The. Austin Clarke. OxBI
Lost Illusion, A. George Du Maurier. CenHV
Lost Illusions. Georgia Douglas Johnson. BANP
Lost in a Blizzard. Arthur W. Monroe. PoOW
Lost in a Corridor of Power. Michael Brownstein. ANYP
Lost in France. Ernest Rhys. POTE
Lost in Heaven. Robert Frost. MAP; MoAmPo
Lost in the vastness of the void Pacific. Homecoming. Karl Shapiro. MiAP
Lost Ingredient, The. Anne Sexton. CoPo
Lost is my quiet for ever. Song. *Unknown.* SeCL
Lost Jewel, A. Robert Graves. EnLoPo; NYBP
Lost Jimmie Whalen. *Unknown.* ABF, *with music*; BaBo
Lost Key, The. Priscilla Leonard. MaRV; OQP
Lost Lady, The, *sel.* Sir William Berkeley.
Where Did You Borrow That Last Sigh? SeCL; TuPP
Lost Lamb, The. Thomas Westwood. OTPC (1923 ed.); PCH
Lost Language, The. Irving Feldman. AmPC
Lost Leader, The. Robert Browning. BEL; EnL; EnLi-2; EnLit; EPN; FaPL; FOL; GTBS; GTBS-D; GTBS-W; GTSL; HBV; MBW-2; MCCG; ML; OtMeF; PoFr; PoFS; PoVP; TreFS; TrGrPo; VA; ViBoPo; ViPo; ViPP
Lost Light. Elizabeth Akers Allen. HBV
Lost Little Sister, The. William Barnes. PoEL-4
Lost! lost! Forever lost! I have betrayed. Aceldama. Longfellow. StJW
Lost! lost! lost! Advertisement of a Lost Day. Lydia H. Sigourney. WBLP
Lost Love. Robert Graves. AWP; CH; ChMP; FaBoCh; ILP; JAWP; LoGBV; MemP; MoAB; MoBrPo; NoP; POTE; WBP
Lost Love, The. Fenton Johnson. NP
Lost Love. Andrew Lang. HBV
Lost Love, A. Henry Francis Lyte. GTSL
Lost Love. Herman L. McMillan. TNV
Lost Love. Tennyson. *See* In Memoriam, A. H. H.: "I envy not in any moods."
Lost Love, The. Wordsworth. *See* She Dwelt among the Untrodden Ways.
Lost manor where I walk continually. The Pier-Glass. Robert Graves. CMoP; CoBMV; MoAB
Lost Mr. Blake, The. W. S. Gilbert. EnLi-2 (1949 ed.); InMe
Lost Mistress, The. Robert Browning. CBEP; FaBoEn; FiP; GTSE; HBV; MeWo; OBEV; OBNC; OBVV; PoVP
Lost Month. W. S. Merwin. AmPC
Lost music returns, The: a few bring it. Of the New Prosody. Brewster Ghiselin. MoVE
Lost my partner, skip to my Lou. Skip to My Lou. *Unknown.* ABF
Lost Occasion, The. Whittier. CoBA
Lost on Both Sides. Dante Gabriel Rossetti. The House of Life, XCI. GTSL; MaVP; NoP; PoVP; SeCePo; ViPo; ViPP
Lost Orchard, The. Edgar Lee Masters. CMoP; LaNeLa; MoPo
Lost Pilot, The. James Tate. CoAP; TwCP; YAP
Lost Playmate, The. Abbie Farwell Brown. HBVY
Lost Playmate, The. Walter de la Mare. *See* Autumn.
Lost Pleiad, The. Arthur Reed Ropes. BOHV
Lost Pleiad, The. William Gilmore Simms. AA
Lost Sheep, The. St. Luke, XV: 4-7, Bible, *N.T.* TreF
Lost Shepherd, The. James Thomson. *Fr.* The Seasons: Winter. CoBE
(Winter.) SeCePo
Lost Shipmate, The. Theodore Goodridge Roberts. CaP
Lost Ships. Thomas Hornsby Ferril. EtS

Lost Shoe, The. Walter de la Mare. BoChLi (1939 ed.); BrR; TSW
Lost Silvertip. J. D. Reed. NYBP
Lost Son, The. Theodore Roethke. AP; CoBMV; FiMAP; LiTM (1970 ed.); MiAP; MoPo; NePA; PIA; PoeP; ReMP; TwAmPo
Flight, The, *sel.* TrGrPo (rev. ed.)
Lost Spectacles, The. *Unknown.* BOHV
Lost—Three Little Robins. *Unknown.* DD; PEDC
Lost, tortured by the world's strong sin. Desideravi. Theodore Maynard. HBMV
Lost Tribe, The. Robert Finch. CaP
Lost Voice on This Hill. Burnham Eaton. FiSC
Lost War-Sloop, The. Edna Dean Proctor. PAH
Lost Willie. *Unknown. See* Sweet William ("Weary are the hours of a sailor boy").
Lost Word of Jesus, A. Henry van Dyke. WGRP
Lost World, A. Robert Graves. NYBP
Lost Years. Eugene Lee-Hamilton. OBVV
Lost Youth. Roger Casement. CAW; JKCP (1926 ed.)
Lot Later. Howard Nemerov. NMP
Lot of love is chosen, The. I learnt that much. Chosen. W. B. Yeats. CMoP
Lot of the old folk here, A—all that's left. Reflections in a Slum. "Hugh MacDiarmid." NMP; OPoP
Lot would be no loss, the slender stand, The. Wild Cherry. Louise Townsend Nicholl. NePoAm
Loth to depart, but yet at last, each one. The Parting Verse, the Feast There Ended. Robert Herrick. SeCV-1
Lotos-Eaters, The. Tennyson. AtBAP; BEL; BoLiVe; DiPo; EnL; EnLi-2; EnLit; EPN; ExPo; FiP; ForPo; GoTL; LiTB; MaPo; MaVP; MBW-2; MCCG; NoP; OAEP; OBRV, *abr.*; OnMSP; PAn; PIA; PoAn; PoE; PoEL-5; PoFS; PoIE; PoVP; PTK; SeCeV; ShBV-4; TOP; VA; ViPo; ViPP; VP
Sels.
Choric Song: "There is sweet music here that softer falls." GTSL; LiTG; OBNC; OuHeWo; WHA
(Choric Song of the Lotos-Eaters.) GTBS-W; ViBoPo
(Song of the Lotos-Eaters.) OBEV
(There Is Sweet Music Here.) FaBV; HT
"'Courage!' he said, and pointed toward the land." ChTr; CoBE; HBV; OTPC, *abr.*; TreFT
Lotosblume ängstigt, Die. Heine, *tr. fr. German by* James Thomson. AWP
(Lotus-Flower, The) OnPM
Lots of truisms don't have to be repeated. The Anatomy of Happiness. Ogden Nash. LiTA; LiTM; SiTL
Lottie Mae ("Lottie was a skinny child"). Stanley McNail. FiSC
Lotus Eaters, The. Floyce Alexander. QAH
Lotus Eaters, The. Tennyson. *See* Lotos-Eaters, The.
Lotus-Flower, The. Heine. *See* Lotosblume ängstigt, Die.
Lotus Leaves. Mitsukuni, *tr. fr. Japanese by* Asataro Miyamori. OnPM
Lotuses. Witter Bynner. MoLP
Loud brayed an ass. Quoth Kate, "My dear." Epigram [*or* Repartee]. *Unknown.* ALV; TreFT
Loud deep calls me home even now to feed it, The. Shelley. *Fr.* Prometheus Unbound, III, ii. ChER
Loud drums are rolling, the mad trumpets blow, The! Battle Cry. William Henry Venable. PAH
Loud is the summer's busy song. July. John Clare. *Fr.* The Shepherd's Calendar. GoTP; OBRV
Loud is the vale! the voice is up. Lines Composed at Grasmere. Wordsworth. MBW-2; OBRV
Loud mechanical voices of the sirens, The. Letter to My Wife. Roy Fuller. NeBP; POTE
Loud mockers in the roaring street. The Second Crucifixion. Richard Le Gallienne. HBV; MaRV; OBEV (1st ed.); OBVV; WGRP
Loud pianist summons from the dark, The. Melodie Grotesque. Persis Greely Anderson. WhC
Loud roared the tempest. The Requital. Adelaide Anne Procter. VA
Loud roared the winds, dark grew the night. The Old Oak Tree. *Unknown.* ShS
Loud talk in the overlighted house. Ends. Robert Frost. PoIE (1970 ed.)
Loud through the still November air. The Church of the Revolution. Hezekiah Butterworth. PAH
Loud, tumultuous and troubled world, The. Holy Night. Nathaniel A. Benson. CaP
Loud were they, loud, as they rode o'er the hill. Charm for a Sudden Stitch [*or* Charm against the Stitch]. *Unknown.* AnOE; FlW
Loudens the sea-wind, downward plunge the bows. To D'Annunzio; Lines from the Sea. Robert Nichols. OBMV
Loudest Sound in our car, The. Vacation Trip. William Stafford. PV
Loudon Hill, or, Drumclog. *Unknown.* ESPB
Loudoun's Bonnie Woods and Braes. Robert Tannahill. HBV
Lough, The. William Allingham. IrPN
Lough Bray. Standish James O'Grady. IrPN
Loughareema, Loughareema. The Fairy Lough. "Moira O'Neill." OBVV; YT
Louis XV. John Sterling. BeLS; VA
Louisa. Wordsworth. EnRP
Louisa May Alcott. Louise Chandler Moulton. AA
Louisburg. *Unknown.* PAH; ThLM
Louise, have you forgotten yet. Old Loves. Henry Murger. AWP
Louisiana Girls, *with music. Unknown.* ABF
Louisiana! Louisiana! That dear old state of ours. Song of Louisiana. Vashti R. Stopher. PoRL
Loulou and Her Cat. Frederick Locker-Lampson. ALV
Lounge Bar. James K. Baxter. Cressida, XII. AnNZ
Lourenço Marques. Charles Eglington. PeSA
Louse-Catchers, The. Arthur Rimbaud. *See* Chercheuses de poux, Les.
Louse Crept Out of My Lady's Shift, A. Gordon Bottomley. ChTr
Lousy Miner, The, *with music.* John A. Stone. SGR
Lousy Peter. Sir Osbert Sitwell. HaMV
Lout, The. John Clare. NBM
Lovable Child, The. Emilie Poulsson. HBV; MPB
Love. Sarah Flower Adams. VA
Love. Joseph Beaumont. OBS
Love. First Corinthians, Bible, *N.T. See* Charity.
Love. The Song of Solomon, VIII: 6-7, Bible, *O. T.* MaRV
("Set me as a seal upon thine heart.") LiTW
Love. Maxwell Bodenheim. NP
Love. Rupert Brooke. MoLP
Love. Robert Browning. *Fr.* Earth's Immortalities. EnLoPo; PoVP
Love ("All love at first, like generous wine"). Samuel Butler. CBEP; SeCL
Love ("Lovers like wrestlers"). Samuel Butler. ErPo
Love. Charles Stuart Calverley. ALV; FiBHP
Love. John Clare. *See* Song: "Love lives beyond the tomb."
Love. Samuel Taylor Coleridge. BEL; BeLS; ChER; EnRP; ERoP-1; GTBS; GTBS-D; GTBS-P; GTBS-W; GTSE; GTSL; HBV; LiTL; LoBV; OAEP; OBEV; TOP; TreFT
"All impulses of soul and sense," *sel.* LO
Love ("Five years ago"). Abraham Cowley. MemP; PoFS
Love ("I'll sing of heroes and of kings."). Abraham Cowley, *after the Greek of* Anacreon. AWP; PG (1945 ed.)
Love. Samuel Daniel. *See* Love Is A Sickness.
Love. Sir William Davenant. *Fr.* The Unfortunate Lovers. SeCL
Love. Tom Dent. NNP
Love. John Swanwick Drennan. IrPN
Love. Dryden. *Fr.* The Conquest of Granada, Pt. II, Act III, sc. iii. FiP
Love. Euripides, *tr. fr. Greek by* Arthur S. Way. *Fr.* Hippolytus. WoL
Love. Walker Gibson. NePoAm-2.
Love ("Immortal Heat, O let thy greater flame"). George Herbert. MeP; SCEP-1; Sonn
Love ("Immortal love, authour of this great frame"). George Herbert. AnAnS-1; MaMe; MeP; SCEP-1; SeCV-1; Sonn
Love ("Love bade me welcome; yet my soul drew back"). George Herbert. AnAnS-1; AWP; BoLiVe; BWP; CABA; CH; ChTr; EG; EnL; EnLit; EP; ExPo; FaBoEn; FaBV; ForPo; FosPo; HBV; InPo; LiTB; LO; MaMe; MaPo; MaRV; MeLP; MemP; MeP; MePo; NoP; OBEV; OBS; OxBoCh; PAn; Po; PoE; PoEL-2; PoLF; ReEn; SCEP-1; SeCePo; SeCeV; SeCL; SeCP; SeCV-1; SeEP; ShBV-4; StJW; TOP; TreFT; TrGrPo; TRV; ViBoPo; WHA
(Christ Our Lord.) BoC
(Love Bade Me Welcome.) LiTL

Love ("Thou art too hard for me in love"). George Herbert. MaMe
Love. Immanuel di Roma, *tr. fr. Italian by* Joseph Chotzner. TrJP
Love. Francis Jammes, *tr. fr. French by* Jethro Bithell. AWP
Love. Gerald Jonas. PV
Love. Ben Jonson. UnTE
Love. Toyohiko Kagawa. SoP; TRV
Love. William Langland. *See* Vision of the Holy Church, The.
Love. Gordon LeClaire. CaP
Love, *sel.* James Russell Lowell.
True Love. OQP
Love. "Hugh MacDiarmid." PoIE
Love. James Clarence Mangan. IrPN
Love. Nicholas Moore. ErPo
Love. Anthony Munday. *Fr.* Zelanto, the Fountain of Fame. OBSC
Love. John Oxenham. BLRP
Love. George Peele. *See* What Thing Is Love?
Love. Samuele Romanelli, *tr. fr. Hebrew by* A. B. Rhine. TrJP
Love. Sappho, *tr. fr. Greek by* William Ellery Leonard. AWP
Love ("Tell me where is fancy bred"). Shakespeare. *See* Tell Me Where Is Fancy Bred.
Love ("What is love? 'tis not hereafter"). Shakespeare. *Fr.* Twelfth Night, II, iii. TreFT
Love. Shelley. *See* One Word Is Too Often Profaned.
Love. Alexander Smith. OBEV (1st ed.)
Love. Spenser. The Faerie Queene, *introd. to* IV. OBSC
Love. Tasso. *See* Love, the Master of True Eloquence.
Love. Henry David Thoreau. AnNE; CBEP; OBVV; OQP
Love. Joann Ludwig Tieck, *tr. fr. German by* Herman Salinger. LiTW
Love. Thomas Traherne. SCEP-1; SeCV-2
Love. Katrina Trask. AA
Love. Herbert Trench. *See* Come, Let Us Make Love Deathless.
Love. Darwin T. Turner. BALP
Love ("I love you"). *Unknown, at. to* Roy Croft. BLPA; FaBoBe; NeHB; SoP; TIHL; TreFT; TRV
(Why Do I Love You?) PoToHe (new ed.)
"I love you,/ Not only for what you are," *sel.* MaRV
Love ("Love is a funny thing"). *Unknown.* TTY
Love ("Love was before the light began"). *Unknown, tr. fr. Arabic by* E. Powys Mathers. *Fr.* The Thousand and One Nights. AWP; LiTW
Love. Louis Untermeyer. HBMV
Love. Jones Very. AP
Love. Charles Russell Wakeley. OQP
Love. Sir William Watson. *See* Epigram: "Love, like a bird. . ."
Love a bee, that lurked among. Stung. *Unknown.* OuHeWo
Love, a Thousand Sweets Distilling. James Shirley. *Fr.* The Witty Fair One. SeCL
(Song.) SeEP
Love a woman! You're an ass. Song. Earl of Rochester. CavP; PeRV
Love above Beauty. Henry Reynolds. TuPP
Love all the senses doth beguile. Of Love. James Sandford. ElL
Love among the Manichees. William Dickey. PoCh
Love among the Ruins. Robert Browning. BEL; BoLiVe; CoBE; EnL; EnLi-2 (1949 ed.); EnLit; EPN; FaBV; GTSE; HBV; MaPo; MBW-2; MCCG; OAEP; OBEV (new ed.); OBVV; PoAn; PoEL-5; PoVP; TOP; UnPo (1st ed.); ViPo; ViPP; VP
Love and a Bottle, *sel.* George Farquhar.
Song: "How blest are lovers in disguise!" SeCL
Love and a Question. Robert Frost. MoBS
Love and Age. Thomas Love Peacock. *Fr.* Gryll Grange. HBV; OBEV; OBNC; ViBoPo
Love and Death. Catullus, *tr. fr. Latin by* H. W. Garrod. AWP; JAWP; WBP
Love and Death. Margaret Deland. AA; HBV
Love and Death. Ben Jonson. *See* Though I Am Young.
Love and Death. Rosa Mulholland. HBV VA
Love and Debt Alike Troublesome. *At. to* Sir John Suckling. AnAnS-2; CavP
Love and Discipline. Henry Vaughan. TrPWD
Love and Folly. La Fontaine, *tr. fr. French by* Bryant. AWP
Love and forgetting might have carried them. Two Look at Two. Robert Frost. AnAmPo; AP; CoBA; CoBMV; CrMA; LiTL; MAP; MoAB; MoAmPo; PoeP
Love and Fortune. Fulke Greville. Caelica, XXIX. OBSC
Love and fortune and my mind, remember. Sir Thomas Wyatt. FCP
Love and Friendship. Emily Brontë. GTBS-D
Love and Friendship. Keats. *Fr.* Endymion, I. OBRV
Love and harmony combine. Song. Blake. EnRP; LiTL
Love and Hate. Catullus. *See* Odi et Amo.
Love and Hate. Longfellow. *Fr.* Christus; a Mystery, Pt. I, 1st Interlude. MaRV
Love and Hate. *Unknown, tr. fr. Irish by* Frank O'Connor. KiLC
Love and Honour. Fulke Greville. Caelica, LXXIV. OBSC
Love and Hope. Dante Gabriel Rossetti. The House of Life, XLIII. MaVP; PoVP; ViPo; VP
Love & I of late did parte. *Unknown.* SeCSL
Love and Jealousy. Robert Greene. *See* When Gods Had Fram'd the Sweet of Women's Face.
Love and Know Not Why. *Unknown. See* Love Not Me.
Love and Law. Vachel Lindsay. OQP
Love and Liberation. John Hall Wheelock. MAP; MoAmPo
("Lift your arms to the stars.") BoLP
Love and Life. Abraham Cowley. *Fr.* The Mistress. SeEP
Love and Life. Winfred Ernest Garrison. OQP
Love and Life. Julie Mathilde Lippmann. AA; HBV
Love and Life: A Song. Earl of Rochester. BWP; CavP; CBV; CEP; CLwM; EiCL; ELP; EnLoPo; FaBoEn; HBV; LiTL; LoBV; MePo; OBEV; OBS; PeRV; PoEL-3; SeCL; SeCV-2; SeEP; TrGrPo; ViBoPo
("All my past life is mine no more.") EG
Love and Life. Henry Timrod. *Fr.* Quatorzain. OQP
Love and Lust. Isaac Rosenberg. ChMP; TrJP
Love and Marriage. Ray Mathew. PoAu-2
Love and Music. Philip Bourke Marston. VA
Love and Philosophy. George Chapman. *See* Sonnet: "Muses that sing love's sensual empery."
Love and Poverty. Elisabeth Cavazza Pullen. AA
Love and Reason. Matthew Prior. *Fr.* Solomon, II. OBEC
Love and Reason. Sir Philip Sidney. *Fr.* Arcadia. SiPS
Love and Respect. Pathericke Jenkyn. CavP
Love and Sacrifice. Bernard O'Dowd. BoAu; BoAV
Love and Sleep. Swinburne. MeWo; UnTE
Love and Solitude. John Clare. PeER
Love and the Child. William Brighty Rands. PRWS
Love and the gentle heart are one same thing. La Vita Nuova, XI. Dante. AWP; OuHeWo
Love and the Lady Lagia, Guido and I. Sonnet: On the Detection of a False Friend. Guido Cavalcanti. AWP
Love and Time. Beatrix Demarest Lloyd. AA
Love and Time. Sir Walter Ralegh. *See* Nature, That Washed Her Hands.
Love and War. Arthur Patchett Martin. VA
Love and Wine. Julianus, *tr. fr. Greek by* Lord Neaves. OnPM
Love and Wine. Thomas Shadwell. UnTE
Love and Youth. William James Linton. VA
Love, any devil else but you. Love's Exchange. John Donne. LiTL; MaMe
Love Armed. Aphra Behn. *See* Song: "Love in fantastic triumph sate."
Love, as a Warrior Lord. Ovid, *tr. fr. Latin by* the Earl of Rochester. LiTW
Love at First Sight. Christopher Marlowe. *See* It Lies Not in Our Power to Love or Hate.
Love at Large. Coventry Patmore. *Fr.* The Angel in the House. HoPM; PoVP; StP
Love at Sea. Swinburne, *after the French of* Théophile Gautier. AWP; HBV; SiSw; TOP; VA
Love at the closing of our days. Last Love. Feodor Tyutchev. LiTW
Love at the Door. Meleager, *tr. fr. Greek by* John Addington Symonds. AWP
Love at the lips was touch. To Earthward. Robert Frost. AnFE; AP; APA; BoLiVe; CABA; CoAnAm; CoBMV;

Love (continued)
GTBS-D; HBMV; InPo; LiTA; LO; MAP; MoAB; MoAmPo; MoPo; MoVE; MWA-2; NePA; NoP; OxBA; PIA; PoIE; ReMP; TwAmPo; WoL
Love at Two Score. Thackeray. *See* Age of Wisdom, The.
Love Bade Me Welcome. George Herbert. *See* Love ("Love bade me welcome").
Love Beleaguered. Katherine Garrison Chapin. MoLP
Love Bit, The. Joel Oppenheimer. CoPo
Love, born in Greece, of late fled from his native place. Astrophel and Stella, VIII. Sir Philip Sidney. FCP; SiPS; Sonn
Love born of knowledge, love that gains. George Meredith. *Fr.* The Thrush in February. FaBoEn
Love, brave vertues younger brother. Love's Horoscope. Richard Crashaw. HBV; MaMe; MeLP; OBS
Love Breathing Thanks and Praise, *sel.* Richard Baxter.
"I preached as never sure to preach again." TRV
(Preacher's Urgency, A.) MaRV
Love brought by night a vision to my bed. Lost Desire. Meleager. AWP
Love brought me to a silent grove. Upon Love. Robert Herrick. BoLiVe; TrGrPo
Love built a stately house; where Fortune came. The World. George Herbert. BEL; MaMe; OBS; SCEP-1; SeCL; SeCV-1; SeEP; StJW; TOP
Love built this shrine; these hallowed walls uprose. On Entering a Chapel. John Davidson. MaRV; OQP
Love, by sure proof I may call thee unkind. Astrophel and Stella, LXV. Sir Philip Sidney. FCP; SiPS; Sonn
Love, by that loosened hair. Song. Bliss Carman. HBV; VA
Love Calls Us to the Things of This World. Richard Wilbur. AmPP (5th ed.); CMoP; FiMAP; MoAmPo (1962 ed.); NePA; NePoEA; PIA; PoAn; PoDB; PoRA; SeCeV (1967 ed.); ToPo; TrGrPo (rev. ed.); TwAmPo
Love Came Back at Fall o' Dew. Lizette Woodworth Reese. HBV; LO
Love Came By from the Riversmoke. Stephen Vincent Benét. *Fr.* John Brown's Body. MAP; MoAmPo
Love came down at Christmas. Incarnate Love. Christina Rossetti. ChIP; MaRV
Love came into a world of hate. Yet Love Was Born. Charles Hannibal Voss. BePJ
Love can do all but raise the dead. Emily Dickinson. LiTA; MWA-2; NePA
Love Cannot Live. *Unknown.* EIL
Love-Cave, The. Seami Motokiyo, *tr. fr. Japanese by* Ernest Fenollosa. LiTW
Love chill'd with cold & missing in the skyes. *Unknown.* SeCSL
Loves Comes. Ernest Crosby. OQP
Love comes back to his vacant dwelling. The Wanderer [*or* Rondel: The Wanderer]. Austin Dobson. HBV; InP; MoBrPo (1942 ed.); TOP
Love comes laughing up the valleys. The Call. Reginald Wright Kauffman. HBV
Loves Comes Quietly. Robert Creeley. BoLP
Love Concealed. Shakespeare. *See* She Never Told Her Love.
Love Continual. John Heywood. *See* If Love, for Love of Long Time Had.
Love Dead. Heine. *See* Sag', wo ist dein schönes Liebchen.
Love demands the loving deed. Pass It On. *Unknown.* SoP
Love Dialogue. *Unknown.* CoBE
Love Dies. George Meredith. *See* Modern Love: "In our old shipwrecked days there was an hour."
Love Dirge to the Whitehouse, A. Bob Fletcher. NBP
Love Dislikes Nothing. Robert Herrick. AnAnS-2; CavP; CBEP
Love Divine. Charles Wesley, *wr. at. to* Augustus Toplady. MaRV
(Divine Love.) SoP; WGRP
Love, do not count your labor lost. Sullen Moods. Robert Graves. StP
Love doth again. Sir Thomas Wyatt. FCP; SiPS
Love, Drink and Debt. Alexander Brome. *See* Mad Lover, The.
Love drooped when beauty fled the bower. On the Death of a Recluse. George Darley. OBVV; OxBI
Love Elegies, *sels.* James Hammond.
Elegy: On Delia's Being in the Country, VII. CEP
Elegy: To Delia, XII. CEP
Love Elegy. Tobias George Smollett. WaPE
Love Enslaved. Benedetto Guidi, *tr. fr. Italian by* Thomas Moore. OnPM
Love Enthroned. Dante Gabriel Rossetti. The House of Life, I. CoBE; MaVP; OBNC; PoVP; ViPo; VP
Love Equals Swift and Slow. Henry David Thoreau. NoP
Love ere he bleeds, an eagle in high skies. Modern Love, XXVI. George Meredith. HBV; ViPo; VP
Love ever gives. Love's Prerogative [*or* Love's Aim]. John Oxenham. BLRP; SoP
Love Ever Green. *At. to* King Henry VIII. MeEL
Love-Faith. Harry Kemp. HBMV
Love Fallen to Earth. Paul Verlaine, *tr. fr. French by* Arthur Symons. SyP
Love Feast, The. W. H. Auden. CBV; ErPo
Love feeds, like Intellect, his lamp with truth. William Baylebridge. *Fr.* Love Redeemed. PoAu-1
Love, felt from far, long sought, scarce found. In the Small Canals. John Addington Symonds. *Fr.* In Venice. PoVP
Love flows not from my liver but her living. A Coronet for His Mistress Philosophy, III. George Chapman Sonn
Love for a Beautiful Lady. *Unknown.* *See* Blow, Northern Wind.
Love for a Hand. Karl Shapiro. CoAP; FiMAP; MoLP; NYBP; ToPo
Love for a Hare. Melvin Walker La Follette. NePoEA-2
Love for All. Mrs. M. Stockton. SoP
Love for Love, *sels.* Congreve.
Nymph and a Swain, A. ALV; SeCL; UnTE
(Song; Set by Mr. John Eccles.) SeEP
Soldier and a Sailor, A, *fr.* III, iv. OAEP
(Buxom Joan.) BOHV; InMe
(Song: "Soldier and a Sailor, A.") CoMu
Love for Love's Sake. Henry Carey. WaPE
Love for Patsy, A. John Thompson, Jr. GTBS-W; LiTA; LiTL; LiTM; NePA; WaP
Love for such a cherry lip. Song [*or* Lips and Eyes]. Thomas Middleton. *Fr.* Blurt, Master Constable. EG; ElL; HBV; ViBoPo
Love forged for me a golden chain. Wildness. Blanche Shoemaker Wagstaff. HBMV
Love Forsworn. Shakespeare. *See* Take, O Take Those Lips Away.
Love Found Me. Richard Chenevix Trench. MaRV
Love from a source admired. Song from the Gulf. Rolfe Humphries. MoLP
Love, from the awful throne of patient power. The Cross. Shelley. BoC
Love, give me leave to serve thee, and be wise. An Elegie. Thomas Randolph. MePo
Love gives every gift, whereby we long to live. Echoes of Love's House. William Morris. GTSL
Love gives its best. Love. John Oxenham. BLRP
Love God—/ My mother said. The Will's Love. Besmilr Brigham. ThO
Love Goes a-Hawking. Thomas Lovell Beddoes. *See* Song: "A ho! A ho!" *Fr.* The Bride's Tragedy.
Love-grip, first excited by the eye, The. In Panelled Rooms. Ruth Herschberger. GTBS-W; LiTA
Love growne proude would governe me. *Unknown.* SeCSL
Love Grows by What It Feeds On. Bhartrihari, *tr. fr. Sanskrit by* Arthur W. Ryder. OnPM
Love Guards [*or* Guides] the Roses of Thy Lips. Thomas Lodge. Phyllis, Sonnet XIII. EG; ElL; OBEV; ReEn; SiCE; Sonn; TuPP
(Fidelity.) OBSC
(To Phyllis.) ViBoPo
Love has been sung a thousand ways. Songs Ascending. Witter Bynner. *Fr.* To Celia. HBV; NP
Love has crept out of her sealèd heart. Flapper. D. H. Lawrence. BoLP
Love has gone and left me, and the days are all alike. Ashes of Life. Edna St. Vincent Millay. FaBoBe; HBV; LiTL; NP
Love has its morn, its noon, its eve, and night. Too Late. Philip Bourke Marston. OBNC
Love has its secrets, joy has its revealings. The Love Secret. *Unknown.* AWP
Love has never read the *Ave Maria.* Love. Immanuel di Roma. TrJP

Love Hath a Language. Helen Selina Sheridan. *Fr.* To My Son. HBV
Love hath great store of sweetness, and 'tis well. R. W. Dixon. *Fr.* Love's Consolation. LO
Love hath his poppy-wreath. Love in Dreams. John Addington Symonds. HBV
Love hath me brought in evil thought. A Rhyme-beginning Fragment. *Unknown.* AnIL
Love hath so long possessed me for his own. La Vita Nuova, XVIII. Dante. AWP; OuHeWo
Love he tomorrow, who loved never. The Vigil of Venus. *Unknown.* AWP; OuHeWo; UnTE
Love heeds no more the sighing of the wind. The Garden of Shadow. Ernest Dowson. FaBoEn; HBV; OBNC
Love held a harp between his hands, and lo! Love's Music. Philip Bourke Marston. VA
Love Henry. *Unknown.* *See* Young Hunting.
Love, how ignobly hast thou met thy doom! He Has Fallen from the Height of His Love. Wilfrid Scawen Blunt. The Love Sonnets of Proteus, XIV. ViBoPo
Love, how thou'rt tired out with rhyme! *See* O Love, How thou art tired out with rhyme!
Love, I am guilty of listening to hot rods. Confession. Ralph Pomeroy. CoPo
Love, I am sick for thee, sick with an absolute grief. The Grief of Love. *Unknown.* AWP
Love I have placed on you, The. Misplaced? *Unknown, tr. by* Havelock Ellis. OnPM
Love, I have warmed the car. News from the House. Michael Dennis Browne. NYBP
Love, I Marvel What You Are. Trumbull Stickney. HBV
Love I obey shoot home thy dart. *Unknown.* SeCSL
Love, I proclaim, the vagrant child. The Child Eros [*or* Love, the Vagrant]. Meleager. OnPM; WoL
Love, I should be content. Duality. Katherine Thayer Hobson. GoYe
Love, 'f a god thou art. To Cupid [*or* Madrigal: To Cupid]. Francis Davison. EG; OBSC; SiCE; TuPP
Love in a Cottage. J. A. R. McKellar. *Fr.* Fourth Napoleon. PoAu-2
Love in a Cottage. Nathaniel Parker Willis. HBV; LHV
Love in a Life. Robert Browning. CBEP; EPN; HBV; InvP; LiTL; MaVP; OAEP; OBNC; OBVV; PoVP; TOP
Love in a Tub. Sir George Etherege. *See* Comical Revenge, The.
Love in a Village, *sels.* Isaac Bickerstaffe.
Song: "How happy were my days." OBEC
There Was a Jolly Miller. GoTP; HBV; OnPP; OTPC (1946 ed.); ViBoPo
(Jolly Miller.) RIS
(Song: "There was a jolly miller once.") OBEC, *shorter sel.*; OnYI
("There was a jolly miller once," *st.* 1.) OxNR
Love in a Wood, *sel.* William Wycherley.
Song: "Spouse I do hate, A." PeRV
(Spouse I Do Hate, A.) OAEP
Love in Action. Coventry Patmore. *Fr.* The Angel in the House, II, x. EG
Love in Age. Ethel Anderson. MoAuPo
Love in Age. Charles G. Bell. NePoAm-2
Love in Dreams. John Addington Symonds. HBV
Love in Exile, *sels.* Mathilde Blind.
"Dost thou remember ever, for my sake." OBNC
"I charge you, O winds of the West. TrJP; VA
"Why will you haunt me unawares. VA
Love in Fantastic Triumph. Aphra Behn. *See* Song: "Love in fantastic truimph sate."
Love in Her Eyes Sits Playing. John Gay. *Fr.* Acis and Galatea. ELP; EnLi-1 (1949 ed.); OBEC; OnPM; ViBoPo
(Song: "Love in her eyes sits playing.") FaBoEn
Love in her sunny eyes does basking play. The Change. Abraham Cowley. *Fr.* The Mistress. AnAnS-2; BEL; CoBE; FaBoEn; LO; MeLP; MePo; OBS; ReEn; SCEP-2; SeCP; SeCV-1
Love-in-Idleness. Thomas Lovell Beddoes. LiTL; PeER; ViBoPo
Love-in-Idleness. Shakespeare. *Fr.* A Midsummer Night's Dream, II, i. TrGrPo
("That very time I saw, but thou couldst not.") MemP
Love in Jeopardy. Humbert Wolfe. NeMA
Love in May. Jean Passerat, *tr. fr. French by* Andrew Lang. AWP
Love in Men and Devils. Cecco Angiolieri da Siena. *See* Sonnet: Of Love in Men and Devils.
Love in Moonlight. Bhartrihari, *tr. fr. Sanskrit by* Paul Elmer More. LiTW
Love in My Bosom like a Bee. Thomas Lodge. *See* Rosalynde: Rosalind's Madrigal.
Love in my heart: oh, heart of me, heart of me! Song. "Fiona Macleod." AA
Love in Spring-Time. Shakespeare. *See* It Was a Lover and His Lass.
Love in the Dark, *sel.* Sir Francis Fane.
Cupid, I Scorn to Beg the Art. SeCL; SeEP
Love in the Museum. Adrienne Cecile Rich. NePoEA; NYBP
Love in the Valley. George Meredith. AnEnPo; AWP; BEL; EnL; EnLi-2; EPN; GTSL; HBV; InPo; LiTB, *abr.;* LiTG, *abr.* LiTL, 4 *sts.,* OBEV; OBVV; OnPP; *abr.,* PoVP; TOP; TreFT; 2 sts,; VaPo; ViBoPo; ViPo; VP; WHA, *abr.*
"Under yonder beech-tree single on the greensward," *sel.* ErPo, 3 *sts.*; GTBS-D, 7 *sts.*; GTBS-W, 2 *sts.*; ShBV-4, 3 *sts.*; TrGrPo, 6 *sts.*; UnTE, 4 *sts.*
Love in the Winds. Richard Hovey. AA; BoLP; HBV; MAP; MoAmPo (1942 ed.); PoMa
Love in Thy Youth. *Unknown.* HBV; ViBoPo
("Love in thy youth, fair maid; be wise.") EG; GTSL; LO
(Madrigal.) SeCL
Love in Time's Despite. Edwin Muir. LiTL
Love Indestructible. Robert Southey. *Fr.* The Curse of Kehama. OBNC
("They sin who tell us Love can die.") OBRV
Love Is a Babel. *Unknown.* CBEP
Love is a breach in the walls, a broken gate. Love. Rupert Brooke. MoLP
Love is a circle that doth restless move. Love What It Is. Robert Herrick. AnAnS-2; LO
Love is a funny thing. Love. *Unknown.* TTY
Love Is a God. Bilhana, *formerly at. to Chauras, tr. fr. Sanskrit by* E. Powys Mathers. *Fr.* Black Marigolds. OnPM
Love Is a Hunter Boy. Thomas Moore. OnYI
Love Is a Keeper of Swans. Humbert Wolfe. MoBrPo
Love Is a Law. *Unknown.* *Fr.* The Thracian Wonder. EIL
("Love is a law, a discord of such force.") TuPP
Love is a light burden that gladdeneth young and old. Richard Rolle of Hampole. *Fr.* Love Is Life. GoBC
Love is a little golden fish. The Golden Fish. George Arnold. HBV
Love is a proud and gentle thing, a better thing to own. The Door. Orrick Johns. NP
Love Is a Sickness[e]. Samuel Daniel. *Fr.* Hymen's Triumph. AtBAP; BEL; CBEP; CBV; ELP; FosPo; LiTG; LiTL; LO; LoBV; NoP; OAEP; OBEV; PG; PoEL-2; PoIE; TreFS; TuPP; ViBoPo
(Love.) EIL; OBSC
(Song: "Love is a sickness.") HBV
Love is a sour delight, a sug'red grief. Thomas Watson. *Fr.* Hecatompathia. ReIE
Love Is a Terrible Thing. Grace Fallow Norton. HBV; PFY
Love is a torment. Lay It Bare. *Unknown.* OnPM
Love is a torment, there's no question. Love's Torment. *Unknown.* UnTE
Love Is All. Catullus, *tr. fr. Latin by* Theodore Martin. EnLi-1; OuHeWo
(To Lesbia, *tr. by* Charles Abraham Elton.) OnPM
"Love is all/ Unsatisfied." Crazy Jane on the Day of Judgment. W. B. Yeats. AtBAP; CMoP
Love is an attitude—love is a prayer. What Is Love? *Unknown.* SoP
Love is and was my lord and king. In Memoriam A. H. H., CXXVI. Tennyson. BEL; ChTr; CoBE; EnLi-2; EPN; HBV; OAEP; OBEV; OBNC; SeCeV; ViPo; VP
Love Is Bitter. *Unknown, tr. fr. Zulu.* PeSA
Love is cruel, Love is sweet. Song. Thomas Macdonagh. ACP
Love Is Dead. Sir Philip Sidney. *See* Ring Out Your Bells.
Love Is Enough, *sels.* William Morris.
"Dawn talks to-day." AtBAP
"Love is enough: ho ye who seek saving." OBVV
"Love is enough: though the world be a-waning." AnEnPo; BoLP; EPN; FaBV; LiTL; NeHB; OBEV; OBVV; PoEL-5; TOP; ViBoPo; WePo

Love Is Kind. Benjamin Keech. PoToHe
Love Is Life, *sels.* Richard Rolle of Hampole.
"For now, love thou, I rede, Christ, as I thee tell." ACP; CAW, 4 *sts.*
"Love is a light burden that gladdeneth young and old," 3 *sts., mod. vers. by* Alfred Noyes. GoBC
Love Is like a Dizziness. James Hogg. BOHV; HBV; InMe
Love is like a lamb, and love is like a lion. Song: Love Is like a Lamb. Thomas Middleton. *Fr.* Blurt, Master Constable. AtBAP; BoLP
Love Is like the Wild Rose-Briar. Emily Brontë. ELP; GTBS-D
Love is lost, nor can his mother. Out of the Greeke, Cupid's Cryer. Richard Crashaw. MaMe
Love Is Love. Sir Edward Dyer. *See* Lowest Trees Have Tops, The.
Love Is More Thicker than Forget. E. E. Cummings. AnFE; CoAnAm; Po
Love is not all; it is not meat nor drink. Sonnet. Edna St. Vincent Millay. AmLP; BoLP; CMoP; MasP; MoLP; OxBA; Sonn
Love is not love which altereth. Under All Change. Josephine W. Johnson. MoRP
Love Is Not Solace. Sister Maris Stella. GoBC
Love is not true: mathematicians know. Dogma. Babette Deutsch. MoLP
Love is not worth so much. Coda. James Tate. NYBP
Love Is of God. Horatius Bonar. MaRV; SoP; TRV
Love is our argument of joy. News of the World. Anne Ridler. MoLP
Love Is Patient. First Corinthians, Bible, *N.T.* *See* Charity.
Love is sharper than stones or sticks. Ballade of Unfortunate Mammals. Dorothy Parker. ALV; BOHV; InMe
Love Is Strong. Richard Burton. AA; HBV
Love Is Strong as Death. Christina Rossetti. MaRV
(Love Is Stronger than Death.) LO
Love is that later thing than death. Emily Dickinson. LiTA; NePA
Love is that madness which all lovers have. Love. Dryden. *Fr.* The Conquest of Granada, Pt. II. FiP
Love is that orbit of the restless soul. George Henry Boker. Sonn
Love is the blossom where there blows. Wooing Song. Giles Fletcher, the Younger. *Fr.* Christ's Victory and Triumph: Christ's Victory on Earth. ElL; HBV; LO; OBEV; ViBoPo
Love is the bread that feeds the multitudes. George Edward Woodberry. *Fr.* The Roamer. MaRV
Love is the cause of war and death in battle. Affidavit in Platitudes. E. B. White. InMe
Love Is the Every Only God. E. E. Cummings. CMoP
Love is the heaven's fair aspèct. Michael Drayton. *Fr.* The Shepherd's Garland. LO
Love is the key of life and death. A Song for the Least of All Saints. Christina Rossetti. BePJ
Love is the sunne it selfe from whence. *Unknown.* SeCSL
Love is too young to know what conscience is. Sonnets, CLI. Shakespeare. CBEP; PoEL-2; ReEn
Love is witty, but not wise. A Displeasure against Love. Nicholas Breton. SiCE
Love-Joy. George Herbert. MaMe
Love-Knot, The. Nora Perry. AA; BOHV; HBV
Love laid his sleepless head. Song. Swinburne. BoLiVe; MeWo; TrGrPo
Love Laughs at Winter. *Unknown, tr. fr. Latin by* George F. Whicher. UnTE
Love Lesson, A. Clement Marot. *See* Yes and No.
Love, let us live as we have lived, nor lose. To His Wife. Decimus Magnus Ausonius. LiTW
Love-Letter, The. Dante Gabriel Rossetti. The House of Life, XI. MaVP; PoVP; ViPo; VP
Love Letter. Karl Shapiro. *See* V-Letter.
Love Letter, A. *Unknown.* MeEL
Love Letter from an Impossible Land. William Meredith. WaP
Love Letter to Elizabeth Thatcher, A. Thomas Thatcher. SCAP
Love Lies Beyond the Tomb. John Clare. PeER
Love Lies Bleeding. Christina Rossetti. FaPL
Love, lift me up upon thy golden wings. An Hymn[e] of Heavenly Love. Spenser. ReIE; StJW
Love Lifted Me. Paris Leary. CoPo
Love, light for me/ Thy ruddiest blazing torch. Deliciae Sapientiae de Amore: Hail Virgin in Virginity a Spouse. Coventry Patmore. *Fr.* To the Unknown Eros. OxBoCh; PoVP
Love Lights His Fire. W. H. Davies. CBV
Love, like a bird, hath perch'd upon a spray. Epigram [*or* Love]. Sir William Watson. ALV; MoBrPo (1942 ed.); TrGrPo
Love, like a mountain-wind upon an oak. Love. Sappho. AWP
Love like anything. Prothalamium for Bobolink and His Louisa A Poem. Gertrude Stein. HW
Love like heat and cold. Jealousy. *Unknown.* KiLC
Love, like Ulysses. Counsel. Roselle Mercier Montgomery. HBMV
Love-Lily. Dante Gabriel Rossetti. AtBAP; PoVP
Love Lives beyond the Tomb. John Clare. *See* Song: "Love lives beyond the tomb."
Love Looks to the Future. Gerald Gould. POTE
Love, love, a lily's my care. Words for the Wind. Theodore Roethke. AP; CoAP; FiMAP; PoCh
Love, love alone, cause King Edwards to leave the t'rone. King Edwards. *Unknown.* SoAmSa
Love, love, love. For Janice and Kenneth to Voyage. Frank O'Hara. ANYP
Love, love me only. Song. Robert Crawford. BoAu
Love, love today, my dear. Song. Charlotte Mew. MoBrPo
Love, love, what wilt thou with this heart of mine. Rondel: To His Mistress. Jean Froissart. AWP
Love Lyric. Max Michelson. NP
Love Lyrics. Song of Solomon, II: 8-14, Bible, *O.T.* OuHeWo
Love Lyrics of a Cowboy. R. V. Carr. SCC
Love Lyrics of Proteus, The, *sel.* Wilfrid Scawen Blunt.
Song: "Oh fly not, Pleasure," *fr.* A Rhapsody. JKCP; OBEV (1st ed.); OBVV; ViBoPo
Love Made in the First Age: To Chloris. Richard Lovelace. AnAnS-2; CavP; SCEP-2; SeCP
Love making all things else his foes. Against Love. Sir John Denham. CBEP
Love-making, The: His and Hers. Eve Merriam. UnTE
Love Me Again. *Unknown.* ElL
Love me and leave me; what love bids retrieve me? can June's fist grasp May? John Jones. Swinburne. *Fr.* The Heptalogia. NA; OAEP
Love Me and Never Leave Me. Ronald McCuaig. BoAV; MoAuPo
Love Me, and the World Is Mine. David Reed, Jr. TreFT
Love Me at Last. Alice Corbin. HBMV; NP
Love me because I am lost. Song. Louise Bogan. NP; PG (1955 ed.)
Love Me Black Woman. Arnold Kemp. WSL
"Love me, for I love you"—and answer me. Monna Innominata, VII. Christina Rossetti. Sonn; ViPo; VP
Love Me—I Love You. Christina Rossetti. *Fr.* Sing-Song. BoTP
(Mother's Song, A.) OTPC (1946 ed.)
Love Me Little, Love Me Long. *Unknown.* BLPA, *abr.*; CBEP; ElL; FaBoBe; FaFP; LiTL; NeHB; NoP; PG (1955 ed.); TreF
Love Me, Love My Dog. Isabella V. Crawford. WHW
Love me, love my dog: by love to agree. Of Loving a Dog. John Heywood. SiCE; TuPP
Love Me Not for Comely Grace. *Unknown.* *See* Love Not Me.
Love me, not with smiles, or with flutes, or with the plaited flowers. The Despairing Embrace. Pierre Louys. *Fr.* The Songs of Bilitis. UnTE
Love Me or Not. Thomas Campion. ElL; HBV; ViBoPo
Love Me Still. *Unknown.* *See* Love Not Me for Comely Grace.
"Love me, sweet girl! your love is all I ask!" Light Love. *Unknown.* OnPM
Love, Meet Me in the Green Glen. John Clare. *See* Meet Me in the Green Glen.
Love, men's honour, many ripening deeds. The Impatient Poet. D'Arcy Cresswell. AnNZ
Love, mine! seek not to grope. Ad Leuconoen. Francis Sylvester Mahony. IrPN
Love mistress is of many minds. Love's Servile Lot. Robert Southwell. ReIE; SiCE; TuPP
Love mocks us all. Then cast aside. Albi, Ne Doreas [*correctly* Doleas]. Horace. Odes, I, 33. AWP
Love-Moon, The. Dante Gabriel Rossetti. The House of Life, XXXVII. MaVP; PoVP; ViPo; VP

Love much. Earth has enough of bitter in it. Ella Wheeler Wilcox. PoToHe (new ed.)
Love must be a fearsome thing. Wood-Song. Josephine Preston Peabody. AA
Love must think in music sweetly. Love. Johann Ludwig Tieck. LiTW
"Love my heart for an hour, but my bone for a day." Street Song. Edith Sitwell. CMoP; CoBMV; MoPo; MoVE; OnHM; POTE
Love needs no pondered words. Song for Lovers. T. I. Moore. MoAuPo
Love Nest. John Sladek. HYE
Love Not. Caroline Elizabeth Sarah Norton. HBV; IrPN; OBVV; VA
Love not a loveliness too much. Ownership. Lizette Woodworth Reese. MAP; MoAmPo
Love not, love not, ye hapless sons of clay! Love Not. Caroline Elizabeth Sarah Norton. HBV; IrPN; OBVV; VA
Love Not Me [for Comely Grace]. *Unknown.* ALV; CH; ElL; ELP; FaFP; GTBS; GTBS-D; GTBS-P; GTBS-W; GTSE; GTSL; HBV; LiTB; LiTG; LiTL; LO; OBEV; PG; PoLF; SiTL; TreFT; ViBoPo
(Love and Know Not Why.) OnPM
(Love Me Not for Comely Grace.) EG; SiCE; TOP
(Love Me Still.) WePo
(Love's Unreason.) TrGrPo
Love not too much. But how. The Affliction of Richard. Robert Bridges. QFR
Love Note II: Flags. Gwendolyn Brooks. PoNe
(Flags.) AmNP
Love now no fire hath left him. Out of the Italian. Richard Crashaw. MaMe
Love, oh love, oh careless love. Careless Love. *Unknown.* AS, *with music*; BFSS; TrAS; UnTE
Love of Christ doth me constrain, The. His Love. *Unknown.* SoP
"Love of Christ Which Passeth Knowledge, The." Christina Rossetti. StJW
(I Bore with Thee, Long, Weary Days.) BePJ
Love of Country. Sir Walter Scott. *See* Breathes There the Man.
Love of England. William Cowper. *See* England.
Love of Fame, the Universal Passion, *sels.* Edward Young.
Characters of Women, *fr.* Satire V. OBEC
Satire I: "My verse is satire; Dorset, lend your ear." EiCL
Love of field and coppice, The. My Country. Dorothea Mackellar. BoAu; PoAu-1
Love of God. Amy Carmichael. SoP
Love of God, The. Bernard Rascas, *tr. fr. Provençal by* Bryant. CAW; WGRP
Love of God, The. Isaac Watts. SoP
Love of Hell, The. Abraham Burstein. TrJP
Love of man and woman is as fire, The. My Comrade. James Jeffrey Roche. AA
Love of Nature. James Thomson. *Fr.* The Seasons: Autumn. OBEC
Love of our mothers living yet. Mother Love. *Unknown.* SoP
Love of Swans, The. Leonard Mann. MoAuPo
Love of the Father, The. *Unknown.* BLRP
Love of the World Reproved, The; or, Hypocrisy Detected. William Cowper. EiCL
Love, of this clearest, frailest glass. In a Glass-Window for Inconstancy. Lord Herbert of Cherbury. AnAnS-2; SeCP
Love on a day, wise poets tell. How Violets Came Blue. Robert Herrick. EnL
Love on the Farm. D. H. Lawrence. CMoP; ErPo; FaBV; MeWo; MoAB; MoBrPo; TrGrPo
Love on the Mountain. Thomas Boyd. AnIV; BoLP; HBV; OxBI
Love Once Was like an April Dawn. Robert Underwood Johnson. HBV
Love once would daunce within my Mistris eye. Musical Love. Michael Drayton. *Fr.* Idea. MuSP
Love One Another. St. John, XIII: 33-35, Bible, *N.T.* TreFT
Love over All. *Unknown.* *See* On an Old Sun Dial.
Love Passing By. Gustavo Adolfo Bécquer, *tr. fr. Spanish by* Alice Jane McVan. OnPM
Love, Peace, and Repose! the tenderest trio. My Early Home. John Clark. HBV; OTPC (1923 ed.)
Love Perfumes All Parts. Robert Herrick. UnTE
Love Planted a Rose. Katharine Lee Bates. InP
Love Play. William Cavendish, Duke of Newcastle. ErPo
Love Poem: "Flowers upon your lips and hands." Maurice James Craig. NeIP
Love Poem: "Instinctively, unwittingly." Janet Lewis. QFR
Love Poem: "Less the dog begged to die in the sky." George Barker. *Fr.* Fourth Cycle of Love Poems. NeBP
Love Poem: "My clumsiest dear, whose hands shipwreck vases." John Frederick Nims. CBV; HoPM; MiAP
Love Poem: "My joy, my jockey, my Gabriel." George Barker. *See* My Joy, My Jockey, My Gabriel.
Love Poem: "O Golden Fleece she is where she lies tonight." George Barker. *See* O Golden Fleece.
Love Poem: "O tender under her right breast." George Barker. *See* O Tender under Her Right Breast.
Love Poem: "Oh your thighs." Judson Crews. UnTE
Love Poem: "Then like the ship at rest in the bay." George Barker. First Cycle of Love Poems, IV. FaBoMo
("Then like the ship at rest in the bay.") MoPo
Love Poem: "There is a white mare that my love keeps." Alex Comfort. The Postures of Love, II. ErPo
("There is a white mare. . .") FaBoMo
Love Poem: "When we are in love, we love the grass." Robert Bly. BoLP
Love Poem: "Where you (in this saying) lag in the waving woods." W. S. Graham. FaBoMo
Love Poem: "Written under Capricorn, a land." Chris Wallace-Crabbe. PoAu-2
Love Poem: "You say that in your eyes alone is all the world." Jiri Wolker, *tr. fr. Czech by* E. Osers *and* J. K. Montgomery. LiTW
Love Poem: "Yours is the face that the earth turns to me". Kathleen Raine. LiTB; MoAB; MoBrPo (1962 ed.); MoPo; NeBP
Love Poem-1940. Miriam Hershenson. GoYe
Love Poem on Theme by Whitman. Allen Ginsberg. NaP
Love, Reason, Hate. Sir John Suckling. NCEP
(Barley-break.) SeCV-1
Love Redeemed, *sels.* William Baylebridge.
"As fire, unfound ere pole approaches pole," LXXXVIII. PoAu-1
"Love feeds, like Intellect, his lamp with truth," XXXII. PoAu-1
"Utile canons, the set codes of priests, The," XXXIII. BoAV
"Who questions if the punctual sun unbars," LXXXII. BoAV; PoAu-1
Love Restored, *sel.* Ben Jonson.
"This motion was of love begot." UnS
Love scorch'd my finger, but did spare. Upon Love. Robert Herrick. SeCV-1
Love Secret, The. *Unknown, tr. fr. Arabic by* Wilfrid Scawen Blunt. AWP
"Love seeketh not her own," and so. The Choice of Love. Marion Wilmshurst. SoP
"Love seeketh not itself to please." The Clod and the Pebble. Blake. *Fr.* Songs of Experience. AWP; BEL; BoLiVe; CABA; CBEP; EiPP; EnL; EnLi-2; EnLit; EnLoPo; EnRP; FaBoEn; FaBV; ForPo; JAWP; LO; LoBV; MaPo (1969 ed.); OAEP; OBEC; OBNC; OnPM; OtMeF; PeER; PoAn; PoeP; TOP; TrGrPo; ViBoPo; WBP
Love Serviceable. Coventry Patmore. The Angel in the House, I, vi, 3. EnLoPo; MaRV
Love set you going like a fat gold watch. Morning Song. Sylvia Plath. CBV
Love Sets Order in the Elements. Thomas Nabbes. *Fr.* Microcosmus. UnS
Love Ship. Ella Wheeler Wilcox. *See* My Ships.
Love, should I fear death most for you or me? Cloud and Wind. Dante Gabriel Rossetti. The House of Life, XLIV. MaVP; PoVP; ViPo; VP
Love-Sight. Dante Gabriel Rossetti. *See* Lovesight.
Love signed the contract blithe and leal. Epigram. John Swanwick Drennan. IrPN
Love Sleeping. Plato, *tr. fr. Greek by* Thomas Stanley. AWP; OnPM; WoL
Love Somebody, Yes I Do, *with music.* *Unknown.* AS
Love Song. Judah Al-Harizi, *tr. fr. Hebrew by* Emma Lazarus. LiTW; TrJP
Love Song. Samuel Allen. NNP
Love Song ("Now the lusty spring is seen"). John Fletcher. *See* Love's Emblems.
Love Song ("Take, oh take those lips away"). John Fletcher.

Love (continued)
Fr. The Bloody Brother, V, ii. FaBoEn
Love Song. Iwan Goll, *tr. fr. French by* Claire Goll. OnPM
Love Song, The. Ivor Gurney. EnLoPo
Love Song, A. Judah Halevi, *tr. fr. Hebrew by* Nina Davis Salaman. TrJP
Love Song, A. W. F. Hawley. OBCV
Love-Song. Else Lasker-Schüler, *tr. fr. German by* Jethro Bithell. TrJP
Love Song. Luis de León, *tr. fr. Spanish by* Thomas Walsh. TrJP
Love Song. Denise Levertov. PoIE (1970 ed.)
Love Song. Joseph Gordon Macleod. NeBP; OnHM
Love Song. Harriet Monroe. AmLP; NP
(I Love My Life, but Not Too Well.) HBV
Love Song. Dorothy Parker. InMe; NeMA
Love Song, A. Raymond Richard Patterson. BOLo
Love Song: "Do not love me, my friend." Flavien Ranaivo, *tr. fr. French by* Miriam Koshland. PBA
Love-Song. Rainer Maria Rilke, *tr. fr. German by* Louis Untermeyer. MeWo
Love Song. Margot Ruddock. OBMV
Love Song. Lynn Strongin. ThO
Love Song. Arthur Symons. PoVP
Love-Song, A, *abr.* Thomas of Hales, *tr. fr. Middle English by* Henry S. Pancoast. MeEV
Where Is Paris and Heleyne? *orig. vers., sel.* ChTr
Love Song. Henry Treece. MaRV
Love-Song, A. W. J. Turner. OBMV
Love Song ("Beautiful is she"). *Unknown, tr. fr. Haida Indian by* Constance Lindsay Skinner. AWP; JAWP; WBP
Love Song ("Early I rose"). *Unknown, tr. fr. Papago Indian by* Mary Austin. AWP; JAWP; LiTA
Love Song, A ("He is a heart"). *Unknown, tr. fr. Old Irish by* Myles Dillon. AnIL
Love Song ("Herself hath given back my life to me"). *Unknown, tr. fr. Latin by* Helen Waddell. LiTW
Love Song ("I passed by the house of the young man who loves me"). *Unknown, tr. fr. Egyptian by* Jon Manchip White. TTY
Love Song ("The little sycamore"). *Unknown, tr. fr. Egyptian by* Jon Manchip White. TTY
Love-Song ("The little wild birds."). *Unknown, tr. fr. Russian by* W. R. S. Ralston. AWP
Love Song ("My boat sails downstream"). *Unknown, tr. fr. Egyptian by* Jon Manchip White. TTY
Love Song ("My love is a lotus blossom"). *Unknown, tr. fr. Egyptian by* Jon Manchip White. TTY
Love Song ("My loved one is unique, without a peer"). *Unknown, tr. fr. Egyptian by* Jon Manchip White. TTY
Love Song, A ("One alone, a sister without her peer"). *Unknown, tr. fr. Egyptian by* Alan H. Gardiner. LiTW
Love Song, A ("Sabina has a thousand charms"). *Unknown.* SeCL; SeEP
Love Song. Reed Whittemore. AmFN
Love Song. William Carlos Williams. MoAB; MoAmPo (1950 ed.); NP
Love-Song by a Lunatic, A. *Unknown.* NA
Love Song from New England. Winifred Welles. HBMV; MAP; MeWo
Love Song: I and Thou. Alan Dugan. AP
Love Song of Har Dyal, The. Kipling. BoPe; GBV; OtMeF
Love Song of J. Alfred Prufrock, The. T. S. Eliot. AmPP; AnFE; AP; APA; ATP (1953 ed.); AWP; BWP; CABA; CaFP; CBEP; CBV; CMoP; CoAnAm; CoBA; CoBMV; DiPo; EnL; EnLit; ExPo; ForPo; FosPo; HBMV; HoPM; ILP; InPo; LiTB; LiTM (1946 ed.); MAP; MAPA; MaPo; MBW-2; MoAB; MoAmPo; MoPW; MoVE; MWA-2; NePA; NoP; NP; OAEP (2d ed.); PAn; PIA; Po; PoAn; PoFS; PoIE; PoRA; ReMP; SeCeV; TreFT; TrGrPo; TWAmPo; TwCP; UnPo; ViBoPo
Sels.
"Let us go then, you and I," 22 *ll.* NeMA
"Yellow fog that rubs its back upon the window panes, The." PoPo
(Yellow Fog.) LOW
Love Song of Polyphemus, The. Luis de Góngora, *tr. fr. Spanish by* Frances Fletcher. *Fr.* Polyphemus and Galatea. LiTW
Love-Song of the Water Carriers. *Unknown, tr. fr. Zulu.* PeSA
Love Song Out of Nothing. Vassar Miller. NePoEA
Love Song to Eohippus. Peter Viereck. MoAmPo (1950 ed.)
Love Songs. Mina Loy. AnAmPo
Love Sonnet, A. George Wither. *See* I Loved a Lass.
Love Sonnets, VIII. Charles Harpur. *See* Similitude, A.
Love Sonnets of Proteus, The, *sels.* Wilfrid Scawen Blunt.
As to His Choice of Her, VIII. Sonn
Depreciating Her Beauty, VI. OBMV
Farewell to Juliet, *sels.*
Farewell ("Farewell, then, it is finished"), LIII. MoBrPo (1942 ed.)
Farewell to Juliet ("I see you, Juliet, still, with your straw hat"), XLVII. EnLoPo
Farewell to Juliet ("Juliet, farewell. I would not be forgiven"), XXXIX. AnEnPo
(Farewell.) TrGrPo
Farewell to Juliet ("Lame, impotent conclusion"), LII. ViBoPo
He Has Fallen from the Height of His Love, XIV. ViBoPo
In Answer to a Question, XXVIII. ViBoPo
Laughter and Death, XCI. MoBrPo (1942 ed); PoMa; Sonn; VA
On the Nature of Love, XXII. ViBoPo
On the Shortness of Time, XCVI. MoBrPo (1942 ed.)
St Valentine's Day, LV. EnLoPo; NBM; OBEV (1st ed.); OBVV; ViBoPo
To Manon, as to His Choice of Her, VIII. HBV
(As to His Choice of Her.) ViBoPo
To Manon, Comparing Her to a Falcon, II. OBVV; VA
(Falcon, The.) ACP
To Manon on Her Lightheartedness, XI. NBM; VA
To Manon, on His Fortune in Loving Her, III. GTSL; OBEV (1st ed.)
To One on Her Waste of Time, LVIII. ViBoPo
To One Who Would Make a Confession, LXII. HBV; ViBoPo
Two Highwaymen, The, LXXI. MoBrPo (1942 ed.); OBEV (1st ed.)
"Woman with a past, A," XLIX. Sonn
Love Speaks at Last. Lord Herbert of Cherbury. AnAnS-2
Love steered my course, while yet the sun rode high. Of Fiammetta Singing [*or* Fiammetta]. Boccaccio. *Fr.* Sonnets. AWP; GoBC
Love still a boy, and oft a wanton is. Astrophel and Stella, LXXIII. Sir Philip Sidney. EG; FCP; HBV; MyFE; OAEP; ReEn; SiPS; Sonn
Love Still Has Something of the Sea. Sir Charles Sedley. *See* Song: "Love still has. . ."
Love Story, A. Robert Graves. AtBAP; CMoP; FaBoTw; LiTB; MoVE
Love Story, A. Oliver Herford. PoMS
Love suffereth all things. Sacrifice. Frederic Manning. NP
Love Suffereth Long. Sara Henderson Hay. ChIP; OQP
Love, Sweet Love. Felix McGlennon. PaPo
Love-Sweetness. Dante Gabriel Rossetti. The House of Life, XXI. BEL; EnLit; EPN; MaVP; OAEP; PoVP; TOP; ViPo; VP
Love Symphony, A. Arthur O'Shaughnessy. HBV
Love-Talker, The. "Ethna Carbery." AnIV; CH; OnYI; OxBI
Love that can never be fathomed, A. In Christ We Have. *Unknown.* SoP
Love that doth reign and live within my thought. *See* Love that liveth and reigneth in my thought.
Love, that drained her, drained him she'd loved, though each. The Turtle Dove. Geoffrey Hill. NePoEA
Love, that dwarfs our life. Yamabo no Akahito, *tr. fr. Japanese by* I. W. Furukami. LiTW
Love that I had for you, my dear, The. El Amor Que Te Tenjá. *Unknown.* ABF
Love [*or* Luve] that I have [*or* hae] chosen, The. The Lowlands [*or* Lawlands] o' Holland. *unknown.* AmSS; CH; OBB
Love, that is dead and buried, yesterday. Love Lies Bleeding. Christina Rossetti. FaPL
Love That Is First and Last. Swinburne. *See* Tristram and Iseult.
Love that is hoarded, moulds at last. Song. Louis Ginsberg. MaRV; PoToHe (new ed.)
Love that liveth and reigneth [*or* doth reign and live] in my thought. Complaint of a Lover Rebuked. Petrarch, *tr. by* the Earl of Surrey. Sonnets to Laura: To Laura in Life,

CIX. AWP; BEL; CABA; CBV; CoBE; EnLi-1 (1949 ed.); EnLit; FCP; ILP; LiTW; NoP; OAEP; OnPM; PIA; ReEn; ReIE; SiCE; SiPS; Sonn; StP; TrGrPo; TuPP
Love, that long since hast to thy mighty power. An Hymn in Honor of Love. Spenser. ReIE
Love that looks still on your eyes. Song. William Browne. EG
Love that rose on stronger wings, The. In Memoriam A. H. H., CXXVIII. Tennyson. EPN; ViPo; VP
Love that the heart is feeling, The. Mouth and Eyes. *Unknown.* OnPM
Love the Beautiful. *at. to* Felix Mendelssohn *and to* Moses Mendelssohn. *See* Every Day.
Love, the Delight of All Well-thinking Minds. Fulke Greville. Caelica, I. FCP; OBSC; PoE; SiCE
Love, the Fisher. Bhartrihari, *tr. fr. Sanskrit by* Arthur W. Ryder. OnPM
Love, the great master of true eloquence. Love, the Master of True Eloquence. Tasso. AWP; OnPM
Love the Indispensable and Crowning Grace. First Corinthians, Bible, *N.T.* *See* Charity.
Love, the inevitable, here appears. Love's Tyranny. Marcus Argentarius. OnPM
Love, the Light-Giver. Michelangelo, *tr. fr. Italian by* John Addington Symonds. AWP; LiTW
Love, the Master of True Eloquence. Tasso, *tr. fr. Italian by* John Herman Merivale. OnPM
(Love.) AWP
Love—the most generous passion of the mind. Earl of Rochester. *Fr.* A Letter. LO
Love the unholy, that frost which quickens summer. Didactic Sonnet. Melvin Walker La Follette. NePoEA
Love, the Vagrant. Meleager. *See* Child Eros.
Love the Wild Swan. Robinson Jeffers. AnFE; CoAnAm; MAP; MoAB; MoAmPo; PoFr; Sonn; TwAmPo
Love, thou art absolute sole lord. A Hymn to the Name and Honor of the Admirable Saint Teresa [*or* Hymn to St. Teresa *or* In Memory of the Vertuous and Learned Lady Madre de Teresa]. Richard Crashaw. ACP; AnAnS-1; CABL; FaBoEn; LoBV; MaMe; MeLP; MeP; MePo; NoP; OAEP; OBEV; OBS; OxBoCh; PoEL-2; PoFS; ReEn; SCEP-1; SeCL; SeCV-1; SeEP; WGRP
Love, thou art best of human joys. A Song [*or* On Love]. Countess of Winchilsea. SeCL; SeEP
Love Thou Thy Land [With Love Far-brought]. Tennyson. EPN; MBW-2; PoVP; ViPo
Love through me, Love of God. Love of God. Amy Carmichael. SoP
Love, through your spirit and mine what summer eve. Last Fire. Dante Gabriel Rossetti. The House of Life, XXX. MaVP; PoVP; ViPo; VP
Love throwes more dangerous darts than death I spy. *Unknown.* SeCSL
Love thy bright monarchy I now defy. *Unknown.* SeCSL
Love thy country, wish it well. Ode [*or* Love Thy Country *or* Shorten Sail]. George Bubb Dodington. CBEP; CEP; OBEC; OBEV (1st ed.)
Love thy God and love Him only. Reality. Sir Aubrey De Vere. WGRP
Love Thyself Last. Ella Wheeler Wilcox. MaRV; SoP
Love, Time and Death. Frederick Locker-Lampson. HBV
Love to faults is always blind. Blake. *Fr.* Poems from MSS. ViBoPo
Love, to give law unto his subject hearts. *Introduction to* Penitential Psalms. Sir Thomas Wyatt. FCP
Love to God. Anna Letitia Barbauld. SoP
Love to his singer held a glistening leaf. Love's Last Gift. Dante Gabriel Rossetti. The House of Life, LIX. MaVP; PoVP ViPo; VP
Love to My Lord. Louisa Van Plattenhaus. BePJ
Love to Stephen. Elinor Wylie. ML
Love to the Church. Timothy Dwight. *See* I Love Thy Kingdom, Lord.
Love Token, The. *Unknown.* *See* Bailiff's Daughter of Islington, The.
Love took my life and thrilled [*or* thrill'd] it. Song [*or* The Surface and the Depths]. Lewis Morris. HBV; OBVV; VA
Love Triumphant, *sel.* Dryden.
Prologue to "Love Triumphant." OxBoLi; SiTL
Love Triumphant. Frederic Lawrence Knowles. HBV; TreFT
Love 20! the First Quarter Mile. Kenneth Fearing. MeWo
Love twists. The Pressures. LeRoi Jones. CBV
Love: Two Vignettes. Robert Penn Warren. MeWo
Love—uncaused, loving me. For Me. William R. Newell. SoP
Love Unchangeable. Rufus Dawes. AA
Love, under thy dominion unbending hearts bow low. Love. Euripides. WoL
Love Unfeigned, The. Chaucer. *See* Exhortation to Youth.
Love Unknown. Samuel Crossman. BoC
Love Unknown. George Herbert. MaMe; SCEP-1
Love Unlike Love. *Unknown.* MeEL
Love unreturn'd, how ere the flame. Constancye. Sidney Godolphin. MePo
Love Unsought. Emma Catharine Embury. AA
Love vs. Marriage. Jean de Meun, *tr. fr. French by* Bernard D. N. Grebanier. *Fr.* The Romance of the Rose. EnLi-1
Love wakes men, once a life-time each. Coventry Patmore. *Fr.* The Angel in the House: The Revelation. LO
Love walked alone. The Black Riders, XLI. Stephen Crane. AP
Love, wandering through the golden maze. Love Enslaved. Benedetto Guidi. OnPM
Love was before the light began. Love. *Unknown.* *Fr.* The Thousand and One Nights. AWP; LiTW
Love was laid down, all weary, fast asleep. Licia, IX. Giles Fletcher. ReIE
Love Was Once Light as Air. C. Day Lewis. *Fr.* Two Songs (Written to Irish Airs). OAEP (2d ed.)
Love was true to me. Song. John Boyle O'Reilly. ACP
Love We as Brothers. William Langland, *mod. by* Henry W. Wells. *Fr.* The Vision of Piers Plowman. PoLi
Love, we have spread the flowers here for your return. Pentecost. James Kirkup. BoPe
Love we the warmth and light of tropic lands. The Tropics. Douglas Brooke Wheelton Sladen. VA
Love well and pray for all thy dead. Pray for the Dead. Arthur Dentworth Hamilton Eaton. PoRL
Love, What Art Thou? Lady Mary Wroth. *Fr.* The Countess of Montgomery's Urania. SeCL
Love What It Is. Robert Herrick. AnAnS-2
("Love is a circle, that doth restless move.") LO
Love, when all the years are silent, vanished quite and laid to rest. Hereafter. Harriet Prescott Spofford. HBV
Love Which Is Here a Care. William Drummond of Hawthornden. OxBoCh
Love which is the most difficult mystery. Psyche with the Candle. Archibald MacLeish. MoLP
Love Who Will, for I'll Love None. William Browne. CavP; HBV (8th ed.); SeCL
Love Whom Ye List and Spare Not. *Unknown.* ReIE
Love, Whose Month Was Ever May. Ulrich von Lichtenstein, *tr. fr. German by* Jethro Bithell. AWP; JAWP; WBP
Love, why have you led me here. The Young Cordwainer. Robert Graves. MoBS
Love will die that very hour. Love vs. Marriage. Jean de Meun. *Fr.* The Romance of the Rose. EnLi-1
Love Will Find Out the Way. *Unknown.* CBEP; FaBoCh; GN, *abr.*; HBV; LiTG; LiTL; LoGBV; MeWo; OBEV; OTPC, *abr.* (1923 ed.); PCD; SeCL; TreFS; WiR
(Great Adventurer, The.) FaFP; GTBS; GTBS-D; GTBS-P; GTBS-W; GTSE; GTSL
("Over the mountains.") LO
(Truth's Integrity.) SeEP; TuPP
Love will not have me cry. Canzonetta: He Will Neither Boast nor Lament. Jacopo da Lentino. AWP
Love will outwatch the stars, and light the skies. Love's Vigil. Edwin Markham. OQP
Love Winged My Hopes. *Unknown.* EIL; TrGrPo
(Icarus.) OBEV
("Love winged my hopes and taught me how to fly.") OBSC
"And none but Love their woeful hap did rue," *sel.* LO
Love within the lover's breast. Lines. George Meredith. HBV
Love without Hope. Robert Graves. BoLP; ChTr; ELU; GTBS-P; OxBl; SiSw
Love without Longing. *Unknown.* *See* I Have a Young Sister.
Love, won or lost, is countless gain. Coventry Patmore. *Fr.* The Angel in the House, I, v, 2. LO
Love writes surrender as its due. Beauty, Too, Seeks Surrender.

Love (continued)
Jessica Powers. JKCP (1955 ed.)
Love, you have broken my wings—I cried. Answer. Leonora Speyer. PG (1945 ed.)
Love, You have struck me straight, my Lord! Resolution. Charles L. O'Donnell. GoBC; TrPWD
"Love you?" said I, then I sighed, and then I gazed upon her sweetly. Ferdinando and Elvira; or, The Gentle Pieman. W. S. Gilbert. BOHV; LBN; NA
Love Your Enemy. Yusef Iman. BF; TTY
"Love your neighbor as yourself!" Thoughts on the Commandments. George Augustus Baker, Jr. AA; HBV
Lovebirds. William Jay Smith. ErPo
Loved for themselves, too. Oft as I behold. Paul Veronese: Three Sonnets, II. Sir Samuel Ferguson. IrPN
Loved I Am, and Yet Complaine of Love. Sir Philip Sidney. *Fr.* Arcadia. PoEL-1
(Complaint of Love.) SiPS
Loved of My Soul. Israel Najara, *tr. fr. Hebrew by* Nina Davis Salaman. TrJP
Loved One, The. Joseph Hansen. NYBP
Lovelier than all the rest. With Her Beauty. Tu Fu. OuHeWo
Loveliest dawn of gold and rose. The Least of Carols. Sophie Jewett. ChrBoLe; OHIP
Loveliest of Trees [the Cherry Now]. A. E. Housman. AnFE; ATP; AWP; BEL; BoLiVe; BoNaP; BoPe; CaFP; CBV; ChTr; CMoP; CoBE; CoBMV; DiPo; ELP; EnL; EnLi-2 (1949 ed.); EnLit; FaBoBe; FaBV; FaFP; FlW; GTBS-W; GTSL; ILP; InP; InPo; JAWP; LiTB; LiTM; MasP; MoAB; MoBrPo; MPB (1956 ed.); NeMA; NoP; OAEP; OHIP; OQP; OTPC (1946 ed.); OuHeWo; PCH, *st.* 1; PoAn; PoE; PoLF; PoVP; RePo; ShBV-3; StVeCh; TDP; TIHL; TOP; TreFT; TrGrPo; TSW; ViBoPo; ViPo; VP; WBP; YAT A Shropshire Lad, II.
Loveliest of trees, the cherry now. In a Town Garden. Donald Mattam. ELU; FiBHP
Loveliest things of earth are not, The. The Forest-Bird. W. J. Turner. POTE
Lovelight. Georgia Douglas Johnson. AmNP
Lovelilts. Marion Hiil. BOHV
Loveliness. Hilda Conkling. TiPo
Loveliness. Martha Snell Nicholson. FaChP
Loveliness of Love, The. George Darley. GTBS; GTBS-D; GTBS-P; GTBS-W; GTSE
(It Is Not Beauty I Demand.) EG; ERoP-2; HBV; LiTL; OBRV; PoE
(Song, A: "It is not Beauty I demand.") OBNC; OBVV
Loveliness that dies when I forget. Loveliness. Hilda Conkling. TiPo
Lovelocks. Walter de la Mare. MoVE
Lovel's Song. Ben Jonson. *See* It Was a Beauty That I Saw.
Lovely are curves of the white owl sweeping. The White Owl. George Meredith. *Fr.* Love in the Valley. ChTr
Lovely Bed, A. Mattie Lee Hausgen. GFA
Lovely body of the dead, The. Lament for Glasgerion. Elinor Wylie. AmLP
Lovely boy, thou art not dead. Three Epitaphs upon the Death of a Rare Child of Six Years Old, II. Francis Davison. OBSC; ReIE
Lovely cherries on the tree. Adjectives. Moishe Nadir. TrJP
Lovely Chloris, though thine eyes. Love above Beauty. Henry Reynolds. TuPP
Lovely courier of the sky. Anacreon's Dove. Samuel Johnson. AWP; JAWP; WBP
Lovely dainty Spanish needle. The Spanish Needle. Claude McKay. GoSl
Lovely Dames. W. H. Davies. SiSw
Lovely days of spring have clothed the plains, The. The Round-up. Sarah Elizabeth Howard. PoOW
Lovely Delightful Song of Thy Sister, The. *Unknown, tr. fr. Egyptian by* T. Eric Peet. LiTW
Lovely Fia was the summer queen. A Mare. Kate Barnes. NYBP
Lovely form there sate beside my bed, A. Phantom or Fact. Samuel Taylor Coleridge. EnRP; ERoP-1
Lovely grapes and apples. A Tabernacle Thought. Israel Zangwill. TrJP
Lovely Green Lady, A. The Green Lady. Charlotte Druitt Cole. BoTP
Lovely hill-torrents are. Song. W. J. Turner. GoJo; MoBrPo
Lovely kind, and kindly loving. An Odd Conceit [*or* Song]. Nicholas Breton. EIL; LO; OBSC; SiCE; TuPP
Lovely lady, Christabel, The. Samuel Taylor Coleridge. *Fr.* Christabel. LO
Lovely Lady dressed in blue. To Our Lady. Mary Dixon Thayer. TreFS
Lovely lady, rein thy will. Death's Warning to Beauty. *Unknown.* AnIL
Lovely lady sat and sange, A. Mary and Her Child. *Unknown.* OxBoCh
Lovely Lass o' Inverness, The. Burns. *See* Lament for Culloden.
Lovely Lass to a Friar Came, A. Burns, *also at. to* the Earl of Rochester. CoMu
(The Lass and the Friar.) UnTE
"Lovely, lasting peace of mind!" A Hymn to Contentment. Thomas Parnell. CEP; EiPP; OBEC
Lovely, lost, italic curve, The. The Missal. Rosemary Dobson. BoAV; MoAuPo
Lovely Lucinda, blame not me. The Innocent Gazer. Lord Cutts. CavP
Lovely maid, with rapture swelling. Lines by a Fond Lover. *Unknown.* NA
Lovely Mary Donnelly. William Allingham. AnIV; GTSE; HBV; IrPN; VA
Lovely morn, A, so still, so very still. May, 1840. Hartley Coleridge. OBVV
Lovely of hair and breast and face. The Question. Norman Gale. ELU; FiBHP
Lovely Rivers and Lakes of Maine, The. George B. Wallis. BLPA
Lovely Rose Is Sprung, A. *Unknown, tr. fr. German by* Margarete Münsterberg. AWP
Lovely Semiramis. The Fan. Edith Sitwell. HBMV
Lovely Shall Be Choosers, The. Robert Frost. AmP; CoBMV; MAP; MoAB; MoAmPo; OxBA
Lovely ter of lovely eiye. Christ's Tear Breaks My Heart. *Unknown.* MeEL
Lovely Things. H. M. Sarson. BoTP
Lovely Village Fair, The; or, I Dont Mean to Tell You Her Name. *Unknown.* CoMu
Lovely was the death. A Desultory Poem, Written on the Christmas Eve of 1794. Samuel Taylor Coleridge. *fr.* Religious Musings. EnRP
Lovely Woman, A. W. H. Davies. FaBoTw
Lovely woman rolls up, A/ The delicate bamboo blind. The Night of Sorrow. Li Po. WoL
Lovely years went lightly by, The. Child's Song to Her Mother. Winifred Welles. HBMV
Lovely young lady I mourn in my rhymes, A. An Epitaph. George John Cayley. BOHV; ELU; FiBHP; HBV
Lovely young Lavinia once had Friends, The. Lavinia. James Thomson. *Fr.* The Seasons: Autumn. OBEC
Lovely Youth, The. Aneirin, *tr. fr. Welsh by* H. Idris Bell. LiTW
Lovemaker, The. Robert Mezey. CABA; NePoEA-2
Lovemusic. Carolyn Kizer. ErPo
Lover, The. Conventry Patmore. The Angel in the House, I, iii, I. PoVP
Lover, The. Richard Henry Stoddard. AA
Lover, The; a Ballad. Lady Mary Wortley Montagu. CEP; LO; OBEC
Lover Abused Renounceth Love, The, *sel.* George Turberville.
"Was never day came on my head." EIL
Lover Accusing Hys Love Her Unfaithfulnesse, The. *Unknown.* EnPo
Lover and Birds, The. William Allingham. OBVV
(Spring: The Lover and the Birds.) OBNC
Lover and Echo. Carrol O'Daly, *tr. fr. Middle Irish or fr. Late Middle Irish by* George Sigerson. OnYI
Lover and Philosopher. Sir William Davenant. *See* To a Mistress Dying.
Lover and the Belovèd, The. Ramon Lull, *tr. fr. Spanish by* Garret Strange. CAW
Lover and the Nightingale, The. *Unknown, tr. fr. Latin by* John Addington Symonds. UnTE

Lover Approving His Lady Unkind Is Forced Unwilling to Utter His Mind, A. *Unknown.* ReIE
Lover Beseecheth His Mistress Not to Forget His Steadfast Faith and True Intent, The. Sir Thomas Wyatt. *See* Forget Not Yet.
Lover Comforteth Himself with the Worthiness of His Love, The. Earl of Surrey. PoE; SiCE; TuPP
(When Raging Love.) EnRePo
("When raging love with extreme pain.") EnLoPo; EnPo; FCP; SiPS
("When ragyng love with extreme payne.") EnPo
Lover Compareth Himself to the Painful Falconer, The. *Unknown.* EnPo
Lover Compareth His Heart to the Overcharged Gun, The. Sir Thomas Wyatt. ReIE
("Furious gun in his raging ire, The.") FCP
Lover Compareth His State to a Ship in Perilous Storm Tossed on the Sea, The. Petrarch, *tr. fr. Italian by* Sir Thomas Wyatt. Sonnets to Laura: To Laura in Life, CLVI. BEL; CoBE; ElL; EnLi-1; EnLit; PoE; PoEL-1; PoFS; ReIE; Sonn; STP; TuPP
(Galley, The.) OBSC
(Lover Like to a Ship Tossed on the Sea.) EtS
(My Galley Charged with Forgetfulness.) BWP; CABA; CBEP; DiPo; EnL; EnPo; FCP; ILP; LiTB; MaPo; NoP; PAn; PoAn; ReEn; SiCE; SiPS
Lover Complaineth of His Lady's Unconstancy, The. *Unknown.* ReIE
Lover Complaineth [*or* Complayneth] the Unkindness of His Love, The. Sir Thomas Wyatt. AtBAP; BoW; ElL; EnLit; FaBoEn; OAEP; PoE; PoEL-1; PoFS; ReIE; STP; TrGrPo; TuPP; ViBoPo
(My Lute, Awake.) CABA; CaFP; CBEP; CoBE; EG; ELP; EnL; EnRePo; ILP; MaPo; NoP; PoAn; ReIE, *diff. vers.*; SiPS
("My lute awake! perform the last.") EnPo; FCP; ReEn; SiCE
(To His Lute.) OBEV; OBSC; PG; QFR
Lover Consults with Reason, The. Thomas Carew. TrGrPo
Lover Deceived by His Lady's Unconstancy Writeth unto Her as Followeth, The. Thomas Churchyard. ReIE; TuPP
(Farewell to a Fondling, A.) ElL
Lover Deceived Writes to His Lady, The, *sel.* Thomas Howell.
Who Would Have Thought. ElL
Lover Declareth His Affection, Together with the Cause Thereof, The. George Gascoigne. TuPP
Lover Describeth His Being Striken with Sight of His Love, The. Sir Thomas Wyatt. ReIE
("Lively sparks that issue from those eyes, The".) FCP
Lover Disceived by His Love Repenteth Him, The. *Unknown.* EnPo
Lover, Disdained, Complaineth, A. Thomas, Lord Vaux. TuPP
Lover divine and perfect Comrade. Gods. Walt Whitman. AnAmPo
Lover Exhorteth His Lady to Be Constant, The. *Unknown.* OBSC; TuPP
Lover Exhorteth His Lady to Take Time, While Time Is, The. George Turberville. EnRePo; ReIE
Lover Extolleth the Singular Beauty of His Lady, The. George Turberville. ReIE
Lover for Shamefastness Hideth His Desire within His Faithful Heart, The. Petrarch, *tr. fr. Italian by* Sir Thomas Wyatt. Sonnets to Laura: To Laura in Life, CIX. CoBE; ReIE; Sonn; STP; TuPP
(Long Love, The.) CBV; ILP
(Long Love That in My Thought Doth Harbor, The.) CABA; FCP; NoP; PIA; ReEn; SiCE
Lover Forsaken, The. Sir Thomas Wyatt. *See* Lover Showeth How He Is Forsaken. . .
Lover Forsaketh His Unkind Love, The. Sir Thomas Wyatt. Sonn
("My heart I gave thee, not to do it pain.") FCP
Lover Freed from the Gallows, The, *with music.* *Unknown.* BFSS
Lover Having Dreamed of Enjoying of His Love, Complaineth That the Dream Is Not either Longer or Truer, The. Sir Thomas Wyatt. BEL; CoBE; EnLi-1; ReIE; WHA
(Unstable Dream, According to the Place.) FCP; OAEP
Lover I Am, A. *Unknown.* SeCL
Lover in Distress Exclaimeth against Fortune, The. *Unknown.* ReIE
Lover in Liberty Smileth at Them in Thraldom. *Unknown.* ElL
Lover in the Praise of His Beloved and Comparison of Her Beauty, The. *Unknown.* ReIE; TuPP
Lover in Winter Plaineth for the Spring, The. *Unknown.* *See* Western Wind, When Wilt Thou Blow?
Lover is a slender, glowing urn, A. A Fantastic Simile. Thomas Lovell Beddoes. Sonn
Lover Is Near, The. Goethe, *tr. fr. German by* Werner Heider. LiTW
Lover is of colour deed and pale, The. The X Properte. Sir Thomas More. *Fr.* The XII Properties or Condicyons of a Lover. CoBE
Lover Left Alone, A. *Unknown.* MeEL
Lover Like to a Ship Tossed on the Sea, The. Sir Thomas Wyatt. *See* Lover Compareth His State to a Ship in Perilous Storm Tossed on the Sea, The.
Lover Mourns for the Loss of Love, The. W. B. Yeats. Po
Lover of all, I hold me fast by Thee. God of the Nebulae. Amy Carmichael. FaChP
Lover of child Marjory, The. A Sea Child. Bliss Carman. HBV; VA
Lover of children! Fellow heir with those. In Memory of Lewis Carroll. *Unknown.* PoRL
Lover of her body said, The. The Two Lovers. Richard Hovey. HBV
Lover of Music to his Pianoforte, A. Leigh Hunt. MuSP
Lover of swamps. To the Snipe. John Clare. NCEP; OBNC
Lover of the moorland bare, A. To K[atharine] de M[attos]. Robert Louis Stevenson. OBNC
Lover Praises His Lady's Bright Beauty, The. Shaemas O'Sheel. BoLP
Lover Rejected Complaineth, A. Edward de Vere, Earl of Oxford. ReIE
Lover Rejoiceth, The. Sir Thomas Wyatt. MeWo; TrGrPo
(Liberty.) OBSC
(Love's Snare.) LiTL
(Tangled I Was.) TuPP
(Tangled I was in love's snare.) FCP; MaPo (1969 ed.); ReEn; SiPS
Lover Rejoiceth the Enjoying of His Love, The. Sir Thomas Wyatt. FaBoEn; ReIE
("Once, as methought, Fortune me kiss'd.") CBEP; FCP; SiPS
(Promise, A.) OBSC
Lover Renounceth Love, The. Sir Thomas Wyatt. *See* Renouncing of Love, A.
Lover Sendeth Sighs to Move His Suit, The. Sir Thomas Wyatt. LiTL
Lover Showeth His Woeful State and Prayeth Pity, The. *Unknown.* TuPP
Lover Showeth [*or* Sheweth] How He Is Forsaken of Such as He Sometime Enjoyed, The. Sir Thomas Wyatt. AtBAP; CBV; ElL; ELP; FaBoEn; HoPM; OAEP; PoE; PoEL-1; PoFS; PoRA; ReIE; TrGrPo; TuPP; ViBoPo
(Forsaken Lover, The.) MeWo
(How Like You This?) SeCePo
(Lover Forsaken, The.) UnTE
(Remembrance.) OBSC; QFR
(They Flee from Me.) AnEnPo; ATP (1953 ed.); BWP; CABA; CaFP; CBEP; CBV; EG; EnL; EnRePo; ExPo; ForPo; FosPo; GTBS-W; ILP; InPo; LiTB; LoBV; MasP; NoP; PAn; PoAn; PoIE; SeCeV; SiPS; UnPo (3d ed.); VaPo
("They flee from me that sometime did me seek.") EnLoPo; EP; FCP; MaPo; PIA; ReEn; SiCE; TDP
(Vixi Puellis Nuper Idoneus.) LiTG; LiTL; LO; OBEV
Lover Sings of a Garden, The. Helen Hoyt. NP
Lover Tells of the Rose in His Heart, The. W. B. Yeats. CMoP; CoBE; EnLi-2 (1949 ed.); ViBoPo
(Aedh Tells of the Rose in His Heart.) BrPo; MoBrPo; ViPo (1962 ed.)
Lover, the lover will always remember, The. Act of Love. Nicholas Moore. NeBP
Lover Thinks of His Lady in the North, The. Shaemas O'-Sheel. HBV
Lover to His Bed, with Describing of His Unquiet State, The. Sir Thomas Wyatt, *after the Italian of* Petrarch. ReIE; TuPP
("Restful place, reviver of my smart.") FCP; SiPS
Lover to His Lady, The. *At. to* Plato, *tr. fr. Greek by* George Turberville. CTC; OBSC; TuPP
(Lover to His Lady That Gazed Much Up to the Skies, The.) SiCE

Lover to Lover. David Morton. HBMV
Lover to the Thames of London, to Favour His Lady Passing Thereon, The. George Turberville. ChTr; ElL; OBSC; RelE
Lover, under burthen of his [mistress'] love, The. Gulling Sonnets, I. Sir John Davies. ElL; Sonn; TuPP
Loverd Godd, in hondes tine. In Manus Tuas, Domine. *Unknown.* CoBE
Lovers, The. Conrad Aiken. AP; MeWo; NYBP
Lovers, The. Byron. LiTL
Lovers, The. Phoebe Cary. HBV
(Love's Moods and Tenses.) BOHV
Lovers, The. Alex Comfort. NeBP
Lovers, The. Edward Davison. LO
(Willow and Water.) PG (1955 ed.)
Lovers. Mary Fullerton. BoAV; PoAU-1
Lovers, The. W. R. Rodgers. WePo
Lovers, The. William Jay Smith. MoAmPo (1962 ed.)
Lovers. Miriam Waddington. TwCaPo
Lovers, The. Marya Zaturenska. MoAmPo
Lovers, and a Reflection. Charles Stuart Calverley. BOHV; NA; WhC
Lovers and Friends. Henry Luttrell. *Fr.* Advice to Julia. OBRV
Lovers and madmen have such seething brains. The Lunatic, the Lover, and the Poet [*or* Imagination]. Shakespeare. *Fr.* A Midsummer Night's Dream, V, i. FiP; GTBS-W; LiTB; PP
Lovers and the City, The, *sel.* M. K. Joseph.
Old Montague. AnNZ
Lover's Anger, A [*or* The]. Matthew Prior. ErPo; LO; SeCL; UnTE
(Angry Lover, The.) MeWo
Lover's Appeal, The. Sir Thomas Wyatt. *See* Earnest Suit to His Unkind Mistress Not to Forsake Him, An.
Lover's Arithmetic, The. *Unknown.* OxBoLi
Lover's Choice, The. Thomas Bedingfield. HBV
Lover's Complaint, A. Shakespeare. NCEP
Lover's Complaint, A. *Unknown, at. to* Sir Walter Ralegh. *See* As You Came from the Holy Land.
Lovers conceits are like a flattring glasse. *Unknown.* OBS
Lover's Curse, A. Meleager, *tr. fr. Greek by* Dudley Fitts. LiTW
Lovers' Death, The. Baudelaire, *tr. fr. French by* "Michael Field." SyP
Lovers' Dialogue. Sir Philip Sidney. *See* Astrophel and Stella: Eleventh Song.
Lover's Diary, A, *sels.* Sir Gilbert Parker.
Art. VA
Invincible. VA
Love's Outset. VA
Reunited. OBVV; OQP
(Envoy: "When you and I have played the little hour.") VA
Woman's Hand, A. VA
Lover's Envy, A. Henry van Dyke. HBV
Lover's Farewell, The. James Clarence Mangan. IrPN
Lovers, fast in their longing, The. March. William Everson. ErPo
Lovers, forget your love. Wind and Window-Flower. Robert Frost. YT
Lover's Ghost, The. Louis Simpson. FiSC
Lovers Go Fly a Kite, The. W. D. Snodgrass. NYBP
Lovers have poisoned themselves and died singing, The. Grand Opera. James Reeves. MuSP
Lovers How They Come and Part. Robert Herrick. AtBAP; LO; OxBoLi; PoEL-3
Lovers in the act dispense. The Thieves. Robert Graves. CBV; CMoP; GTBS-P; GTBS-W; LiTM (rev. ed.); OxBI
Lovers in Winter. Robert Graves. NYBP; Po
Lovers' Infiniteness[e]. John Donne. AnAnS-1; ElL; EnLi-1 (1949 ed.); FaBoEn; FosPo; GTBS-W; LiTB; MaMe; MaPo; MBW-1; MeLP; MeP; OBS; PoE; PoEL-2; SCEP-1; SeCP; SeCV-1; SeEP; TuPP
(Love's Infiniteness.) LiTG; LiTL
Lover's Journey, The. George Crabbe. EiCL
Lover's Lament, The ("My dearest dear, the time draws near"). *Unknown.* AS
Lover's Lament, A ("My little breath"). *Unknown, tr. fr. Tewa Indian by* H. J. Spinden. AWP; JAWP; WBP
Lover's Lane. Paul Laurence Dunbar. BANP
Lover's Legacy, A. *Unknown.* SeCL
("Faine would I Cloris ere I dye.") SeCSL
Lover's Life Compared to the Alps, The. Jacopo Sannazaro, *tr. fr. Italian by* Sir Thomas Wyatt. RelE; Sonn; TuPP
(Like to These Unmeasurable Mountains.) CABA; FCP; ReEn; SiCE
Lovers, like wrestlers, when they do not lay. Love. Samuel Butler. ErPo
Lover's Lullaby, A. George Gascoigne. *See* Lullaby of a Lover, The.
Lovers may find similitudes. The Cascade. Edgell Rickword. ChMP; FaBoTw
Lover's Melancholy, The, *sels.* John Ford.
"Cunning arts man, The/ Faltered not in a line." MyFE
Fly Hence, Shadows, *fr.* V, i. OnPM; SeCL; ViBoPo
(Dawn.) OBEV
(Song: "Fly hence, shadows, that do keep.") LoBV
"If thou canst wake with me, forget to eate," *fr.* IV, ii. PoEL-2
"Minutes are numbered by the fall of sands," *fr.* IV, iii. PoEL-2
Lover's New Year's Gift, A. John Lydgate. PoEL-1
Lovers of Marchaid, The. Marjorie Pickthall. HBV
Lovers Parted. Lesbia Harford. BoAu
Lover's Play of Words. Martial, *tr. fr. Latin by* Thomas Moore. OnPM
Lover's Posy, The. Rufinus, *tr. fr. Greek by* W. H. D. Rouse. AWP; JAWP; WBP
Lover's Prison, The. Ariosto, *tr. fr. Italian by* Leigh Hunt. OnPM
Lover's Progress, The, *sel.* John Fletcher.
Dead Host's Welcome, The, *fr.* III, i. SeCL; TrGrPo
('Tis Late and Cold.) ViBoPo
Lover's Protestation, A. Thomas Lodge. *See* Fancy, A ("First shall the heavens. . .").
Lovers, Rejoice [*or* Rejoyce]! Beaumont *and* Fletcher. *Fr.* Cupid's Revenge. ElL; FaBoEn
Lovers Relentlessly. Stanley Kunitz. TwAmPo; UnTE
Lover's Reply to Good Advice. Richard Hughes. MoBrPo
Lover's Resolution, The. George Wither. *See* Shall I, Wasting in Despair.
Lover's Song, The. Alfred Austin. OBVV
Lover's Song, The. Edward Rowland Sill. AA; HBV
Lovers' Tasks. *Unknown.* *See* Elfin Knight, The.
Lovers tread the water, lovers go. Lovers. Miriam Waddington. TwCaPo
Lovers' Walk, The. Dante Gabriel Rossetti. The House of Life, XII. MaVP; OAEP; PoVP; TOP; ViPo; VP
Lovers who must say farewell. Archibald MacLeish. *Fr.* What Must. MoLP
Lovers whose lifted hands are candles in winter. For a Child Expected. Anne Ridler. LiTM; MoVE; NeBP; SeCePo
Lover's Words, A. Vernon Watkins. DTC
Love's a hussy when you know her. You'll Know Love. F. T. Macartney. MoAuPo
Love's a Jest, *sel.* Peter Anthony Motteux.
Slaves to London. OAEP
(London.) SeCL
(Song, A: "Slaves to London, I'll deceive you.") SeEP
Love's Absence in the Spring. Abraham Cowley. *See* Spring, The.
Love's Aim. John Oxenham. *See* Love's Prerogative.
Loves Alchemy [*or* Alchymie]. John Donne. AnAnS-1; CABA; LiTL; MaMe; MePo; NoP; OAEP; ReEn; SCEP-1; SeCP; TuPP; ViBoPo
Loves and Losses of Pierrot, *sel.* William Griffith.
Pierrette in Memory. HBV
Loves and sorrows of those who lose an orchard. The Lost Orchard. Edgar Lee Masters. CMoP; MoPo
Love's Apparition and Evanishment. Samuel Taylor Coleridge. EnRP
Love's Argument. Father Andrew. MaRV
Love's Arithmetic. Sir Edward Sherburne. CavP
Love's Assize. Guido Cavalcanti, *tr. fr. Italian by* Hubert Creekmore. LiTW
Love's Autumn. John Payne. VA
Love's Baubles. Dante Gabriel Rossetti. The House of Life, XXIII. MaVP; PoVP; ViPo; VP
Love's Blindness. William James Linton. VA
Love's Bravo. Thomas Flatman. PeRV
Love's but the Frailty of the Mind. Congreve. *Fr.* The Way of the World. EnLi-1; SeCL
(Song.) SeEP

Love's Calendar. William Bell Scott. HBV
Love's Caution. W. H. Davies. ChMP
Love's Change. Anne Reeve Aldrich. AA
Love's Coming. John Shaw Neilson. BoAu; MoAuPo; PoAu-1
Love's Consolation, *sels.* Richard Watson Dixon.
"All who have loved, be sure of this from me." OBNC
"Love hath great store of sweetness, and 'tis well." LO
Love's Constancy. *Unknown.* MeWo
(Valentine Promise.) PoSC
Love's Cosmopolitan. Annie Matheson. OBVV
Love's Courtship. Thomas Carew. UnTE
Love's Cure, *sel.* Beaumont *and* Fletcher.
Turn, Turn Thy Beauteous Face Away. AtBAP
(Song.) PoEL-2
Love's Deity [*or* Deitie]. John Donne. AnAnS-1; ATP; AWP; BEL; DiPo; ElL; EnLi-1; EnLit; EnRePo; ILP; InPo; LiTB; LiTG; LiTL; MaMe; MaPo; MBW-1; MemP; MePo; OAEP; OuHeWo; PoE; PoeP; ReEn; SCEP-1; SeCePo; SeCP; SeCV-1; SeEP; TOP; TuPP; WBP; WHA
Love's delight. Winter Tryst. Ormonde de Kay, Jr. MeWo
Love's Delights. Nahum Tate. *Fr.* The History of King Richard II. SeCL
Love's Despair. Dryden. *See* Farewell, Ungrateful Traitor.
Love's Despair. Richard Lynche. *Fr.* Diella. ElL
Love's Despair. Diarmad O'Curnain, *tr. fr. Modern Irish by* George Sigerson. OnYI; OxBI
Love's Despair. Shakespeare. *See* Come Away, Come Away, Death!
Love's Diet. John Donne. ILP; MaMe; OAEP; PoFS; SCEP-1
Love's Emblems. John Fletcher. *Fr.* The Tragedy of Valentinian, II, iv. ElL; HBV; OBEV; UnTE
(Love Song.) FaBoEn
(Now the Lusty Spring.) EG; ELP; ErPo; ViBoPo
(Song.) SeEP
Loves End. Lord Herbert of Cherbury. AnAnS-2; SeCP
Love's Ending. *Unknown.* *See* Sought by the World.
Love's Entreaty. Michelangelo, *tr. fr. Italian by* John Addington Symonds. AWP
Love's Epitaph. William Cavendish, Duke of Newcastle. CBEP
Love's equinoctial gales are past. Winter. Maurice James Craig. OnYI
Love's Eschatology. Vassar Miller. ToPo
Love's Exchange. John Donne. LiTL; MaMe
Love's Extremes. Antonio Villegas, *tr. fr. Spanish by* Sir John Bowring. OnPM
Love's Fancy. Dryden. *See* After the Pangs.
Love's Fancy. Tamuke, *tr. fr. Japanese by* Ishii *and* Obata. OnPM
Love's Farewell. Michael Drayton. *See* Idea: "Since there's no help . . .")
Love's Fatality. Dante Gabriel Rossetti. The House of Life, LIV. MaVP; PoVP; ViPo; VP
Love's Fidelity. Petrarch. *See* Vow to Love Faithfully, Howsoever He Be Rewarded, A.
Love's Flight. Else Lasker-Schüler, *tr. fr. German by* Jethro Bithell. TrJP
Love's Fragility. Alan Porter. POTE
Love's Franciscan. Henry Constable. ACP; GoBC
Love's fruit in all the world is only this. Two as One. Bhartrihari. OnPM
Love's Glory. Fulke Greville. Caelica, XVI. OBSC
("Fie [*or* Fye] foolish Earth, think you the heaven wants glory.") EnRePo; LO; PoEL-1; SiCE; Sonn; TuPP
(Sonnet.) ReIE
Love's god is a boy. Cupid. *Unknown.* ElL
Love's Grave. George Meredith. *See* Modern Love: "Mark where the pressing wind."
Love's Grave. Thomas Watson. *See* My Love Is Past.
Love's Growing Pains. James Gallagher. JKCP (1955 ed.)
Love's Growth. John Donne. AnAnS-1; FosPo; GTBS-W; MeMe; MBW-1; MeP; MePo; PoeP; ReEn; SCEP-1; SeCV-1; TuPP
Love's Harmony. Shakespeare. *Fr.* Love's Labour's Lost, IV, iii. CLwM
Loves Heretick. Thomas Stanley. CavP
Loves Horoscope. Richard Crashaw. HBV; MaMe; MeLP; OBS
Love's Immaturity. E. J. Scovell. LiTB
Love's Immortality. Elsa Barker. *Fr.* The Spirit and the Bride. HBMV
Love's Inconsistency. Petrarch, *See* Description of the Contrarious Passions in a Lover. *tr. by* Sir Thomas Wyatt.
Love's Infiniteness. John Donne. *See* Lovers' Infiniteness.
Love's Insight. *Unknown.* GTSL
Love's Justification. Michelangelo, *tr. fr. Italian by* Wordsworth. AWP; JAWP; WBP
(Deathless Flower, A.) WoL
(To the Marchesana of Pescara.) CTC
Love's Kiss. Helen Hay Whitney. AA
Love's Labour Lost. Robert Tofte. *Fr.* Alba. CLwM; ElL
Love's Labour's Lost, *sels.* Shakespeare.
"But love, first learnèd in a lady's eyes," *fr.* IV, iii. PP
Did Not the Heavenly Rhetoric of Thine Eye, *fr.* IV, iii. LiTB; LiTG; Sonn
(Heavenly Rhetoric, The.) GTBS-W
(Sonnet: "Did not the heavenly rhetoric. . .") ViBoPo
If She Be Made of White and Red, *fr.* I, ii. CTC
Love's Harmony, *fr.* IV, iii. CLwM
On a Day—Alack the Day! *fr.* IV, III. ElL; ViBoPo
(Blossom.) OBEV; TDP
(Dumain's Rhymes.) OBSC
(Love's Perjuries.) GTBS; GTBS-D; GTBS-P; GTBS-W; GTSE; GTSL; HBV
(Passionate Shepherd's Song, The.) ReIE
So Sweet a Kiss, *fr.* IV, iii. ElL; InvP
"When Daisies Pied and Violets Blue," *fr.* V, ii. AnFE; CBEP; EG; EnRePo; MyFE; NoP; OBEV; OBSC; PoEL-2; PoRA; SeCeV; SiCE
(Dialogue in Praise of the Owl and the Cuckoo.) DiPo
(Song[s]: Spring and Winter.) ExPo; LoBV
(Song: "When daisies pied and violets blue.") CBV; FiP; HBV; VaPo
(Spring.) BoC; BoTP; ElL; ILP; InPo; MaPo; PAn; PoAn; PoeP; PoFS; PoIE; SeCePo; SiTL; TrGrPo; UnPo; ViBoPo
(Spring and Winter.) OBEV; ThWaDe
(Spring Song.) TreFT
(Ver and Hiems.) ALV
When Icicles Hang by the Wall, *fr.* V, ii. AnFE; ATP; BBV (1923 ed.); BEL; CaFP; CBEP; CoBE; EG; EnLi-1; EnLit; FaPON; GN; GoJo; LiTB; MyFE; OBSC; OTPC; OuHeWo; PIA; PoEL-2; PoRA; PoSa; PoSC; RoGo; SeCeV; SiCE; TOP
(Hiems.) FaBoCh; LoGBV
(Merry Note, A.) WiR
(Song: "When icicles hang by the wall.") CBV; FiP; HBV; YAT
(Songs: Spring and Winter.) ExPo
(Songs from the Plays.) AWP; JAWP; WBP
(Spring and Winter, 2.) OBEV
(To-Whit To-Who.) PoG
(Tu-Whit To-Who.) CH
(Winter.) BoC; BoNaP; ChTr; ElL; EnL; GBV (1952 ed.); GTBS; GTBS-D; GTBS-P; GTBS-W; GTSE; GTSL; ILP; InPo; LiTG; MaPo; MCCG; MPB; PAn; PCD; PCH; PoAn; PoE; PoeP; PoFS; PoIE; PoPo; PTK; RG; SeCePo; ShBV-1; TreFS; TrGrPo; UnPo; ViBoPo; WaKn; WHA
(Winter Song.) BoLiVe; FaBoEn
Love's Labyrinth, *sel.* Thomas Forde.
Fond Love, No More. SeCL
Love's Land. Isabella Valancy Crawford. CaP
Love's Language. Donagh MacDonagh. NeIP
Love's Last Gift. Dante Gabriel Rossetti. The House of Life, LIX. MaVP; PoVP; ViPo; VP
Love's Last Resource. Sadi, *tr. fr Persian by* L. Cranmer-Byng. *Fr.* The Gulistan. AWP; LiTW
Love's Lesson. Moschus, *tr. fr. Greek by* Ernest Myers. AWP
Love's Likeness. George Darley. OBVV
Love's Limit. *Unknown.* MeWo; TrGrPo
("Ye bubbling springs that gentle music makes.") EG
Love's Longing. *Unknown, tr. fr. Latin by* John Addington Symonds. UnTE
Love's Lord. Edward Dowden. HBV
Love's Lovers. Dante Gabriel Rossetti. The House of Life, VIII. MaVP; PoVP; ViPo; VP
Love's Martyr, *sels.* Sir Robert Chester. ElL
Ditty: "O holy Love, religious saint!"
Her Hair.
Love's Matrimony ("There is no happy life."). Duke of Newcastle. BoPe; SeCePo; SeCL

Love's (continued)
(Fulfillment.) MeWo
(Love's Vision.) LO
Love's Miracle. Lucy Maud Montgomery. MaRV
Love's Moods and Tenses. Phoebe Cary. *See* Lovers, The.
Love's Mortality. Richard Middleton. WHA
Love's multitudinous boneyard. Chorus. Jack Kerouac. *Fr.* Mexico City Blues. NeAP
Love's Music. Philip Bourke Marston. VA
Love's Nightingale. Richard Crashaw. *See* Two Dedicatory Poems ("Though now 'tis neither May nor June").
Love's Nobility. Emerson. *Fr.* Celestial Love. TreF
Love's Not Time's Fool. Shakespeare. *See* Sonnets, CXVI.
Loves of the Plants, The. Erasmus Darwin. *See* Botanic Garden, The.
Loves of the Public Servants. Robert Hershon. ThO
Loves of the Puppets. Richard Wilbur. CoPo
Love's Old Sweet Song. G. Clifton Bingham. FaBoBe; TreF
Love's Omnipresence. *At. to* Joshua Sylvester. *See* Were I as Base as Is the Lowly Plain.
Love's on the highroad. Song. Dana Burnet. HBV; PoMa
Love's Outset. Sir Gilbert Parker. *Fr.* A Lover's Diary. VA
Love's pallor and the semblance of deep ruth. Dante. *Fr.* La Vita Nuova. AWP; JAWP; WBP
Love's perfect blossom only blows. Courtesy. Coventry Patmore. *Fr.* The Angel in the House. OBVV
Love's Perjuries. Shakespeare. *See* On a Day—Alack the Day!
Love's Philosophy. Shelley. AtBAP; BLPA; BoLP; CoBE; EnLi-2 (1949 ed.); EnLit; EnRP; EPN; FaBoBe; FaBV; GTBS; GTBS-D; GTBS-P; GTBS-W; GTSE; GTSL; HBV; HoPM; LiTG; LiTL; MERP; MeWo; NeHB; OAEP; OBRV; PG; PoFS; PoIE; PoToHe (new ed.); TOP; TreF TrGrPo; UnTE; ViBoPo; WePo
Love's Pilgrims. Thomas Campion. OBSC
(Pilgrimage towards Loves Holy Land, A.) FaBoEn
(What Faire Pompe Have I Spide of Glittering Ladies.) AtBAP; PoEL-2
Love's Poor. Richard Le Gallienne. VA
Love's Prayer. James Whitcomb Riley. *See* Prayer Perfect, The.
Love's Prerogative. John Oxenham. BLRP
(Love's Aim.) SoP
Love's priestess, mad with pain and joy of song. Sappho. Swinburne. *Fr.* Cliffs. VA
Love's Prime. Thomas May. *Fr.* The Old Couple, III, i. SeCL
("Dear, do not your fair beauty wrong.") EG; TuPP; ViBoPo
Love's Prisoner. Mariana Griswold Van Rensselaer. HBV
Love's Progress. John Donne. Elegies, XVIII. LiTB; LiTG; MaMe; ViBoPo
Love's Progress. Theodore Roethke. FiMAP; PoeP
Love's Protestation. Thomas Lodge. *See* Fancy, A ("First shall the heavens. . .").
Love's Pursuit. Robert Browning. *See* Life in a Love.
Love's Reality. Coventry Patmore. *Fr.* The Angel in the House, I, i, 1. PoVP
Love's Rebel. Earl of Surrey. OBSC
(Complaint of a Lover That Defied Love and Was by Love After the More Tormented.) ReIE; SiCE
("When summer took in hand the winter to assail.") FCP; SiPS
Love's Remorse. Edwin Muir. LiTL
Love's Résumé. Heine, *tr. fr. German by* "J. F. C." TrJP
Love's Resurrection Day. Louise Chandler Moulton. AA; HBV
Love's Riddle, *sel.* Abraham Cowley.
Sport. SeCL
Love's Rosary. George Edward Woodberry. AA
Love's Secret. Blake. BoLiVe; EnLi-2 (1939 ed.); FaFP; GTSL; MeWo; NeHB; OBEV; OtMeF; PG; PoFS; PoSa; TrGrPo
(Never Seek to Tell Thy Love.) AnFE; BoLP; CBEP; ChER; CLwM; EG; ELP; EnL; EnLoPo; EnRP; FaBV; GTBS-D; LiTL; LO; OAEP; OBEC; OBNC; OnPM; PoE; PoEL-4; StP; TreFT
(Poems from MSS.) ViBoPo
(Song: "Never seek to tell thy love.") ExPo; LoBV
Love's Secret Name. John Arthur Blaikie. VA
Love's Servile Lot. Robert Southwell. ACP; ReIE; SiCE; TuPP
Loves She like Me? Samuel Woodworth. AA
Love's Slavery. John Sheffield, Duke of Buckingham and Normanby. CEP
Love's Snare. Sir Thomas Wyatt. *See* Lover Rejoiceth.
Love's Spite. Aubrey Thomas De Vere. HBV; VA
Love's Story. John Clare. PeER
Love's Stratagems. Donald Justice. NYBP
Love's Strength. Harriet Eleanor Hamilton King. MaRV; OQP (4 *ll.*)
Love's stricken "why." Emily Dickinson. BoLiVe
Love's Terror. *Unknown, tr. fr. Japanese by* Arthur Waley. WoL
Love's Testament. Dante Gabriel Rossetti. The House of Life, III. MaVP; PoVP; VP
("O thou who at Love's hour.") ViPo
Loves that doubted, the loves that dissembled, The. Lines by a Person of Quality. J. B. B. Nichols. VA
Love's the boy stood on the burning deck. Casabianca. Elizabeth Bishop. SiSw
Love's tongue within my heart speaks plain to thee. The Mock Caliph. *Unknown.* EnLi-1
Love's Torment ("Lady, why doth love torment you?"). *Unknown.* UnTE
Love's Torment ("Love is a torment, there's no question"). *Unknown, tr. fr. German by* Louis Untermeyer. UnTE
Love's Tribute. Lorena W. Sturgeon. PGD
Love's Trinity. Alfred Austin. OBVV
Love's Triumph. Ben Jonson. EnRePo
Love's Tyranny. Marcus Argentarius, *tr. fr. Greek by* Lord Neaves. OnPM
Love's Unreason. Catullus, *tr. fr. Latin.* OuHeWo
Love's Unreason. *Unknown. See* Love Not Me for Comely Grace.
Loves Usury. John Donne. MaMe; SCEP-1; SeEP
Love's very fleas are mine. Enter. The A, B & C of It. William Carlos Williams. PoeP
Love's Victories. James Shirley. *Fr.* Cupid and Death. GoBC
Love's Victory. Aurelian Townsend. *See* To the Countess of Salisbury.
Love's Vigil. Edwin Markham. OQP
Love's Vision. Edward Carpenter. WGRP
Love's Vision ("Dear, let us two each other spy"). Duke of Newcastle. LO, *abr.*; SeCL
Love's Vision ("There is no happy life."). Duke of Newcastle. *See* Love's Matrimony.
Loves Warre. John Donne. Elegies, XX. MaMe
Love's Wisdom. Margaret Deland. AA
Love's Witchery. Thomas Lodge. *See* My Bonny Lass, Thine Eye.
Love's without Reason. Alexander Brome. OBS; SeEP
Love's World. Sir John Suckling. SCEP-2; SeCV-1
Love's worshipers alone can know. Love and Folly. La Fontaine. AWP
Love's Young Dream. Thomas Moore. HBV; WBLP
Lovesick. *Unknown, tr. fr. Greek by* Louis Untermeyer. UnTE
Lovesick Cowboy, The. Charles A. Bobston. CoSo
Love-sick Frog, The. *Unknown. See* Frog Went a-Courting.
Love-sicke Poet, The. Joseph Hall. *Fr.* Virgidemiarum. FaBoEn
(Satire: "Great is the folly of a feeble brain.") ReIE
Lovesight [*or* Love-Sight]. Dante Gabriel Rossetti. The House of Life, IV. BEL; BoLiVe; CoBE; EnLi-2; EnLit; EPN; FaBoEn; GTBS-D; GTBS-P; GTSL; HBV; MaVP; OAEP; OBNC; OBVV; PoVP; TOP; TrGrPo; VA; ViBoPo; ViPo; ViPP; VP; WHA
Lovest Thou Me? William Cowper. HBV; OBEC
"Hark, my soul! It Is the Lord.] BePJ
"Lord it is my chief complaint," *sel.* TrPWD
Lovest Thou Me? Feed My Lambs. Philip Doddridge. SoP
Lovewell's Fight ("Of worthy Captain Lovewell I purpose now to sing"). *Unknown.* BaBo; HBV; PAH
Lovewell's Fight ("What time the noble Lovewell came"). *Unknown.* PAH
Loving and Beloved. Sir John Suckling. FaBoEn; OBS; SeEP
Loving and Liking. Dorothy Wordsworth. OTPC
Loving Ballad of Lord Bateman, The. *Unknown. See* Young Beichan.
Loving friend is Jesus, A. A Heavenly Friend. Paul Tucker. BePJ
Loving Henry. *Unknown. See* Young Hunting.

Loving in truth, and fain in verse my love to show. Astrophel and Stella, I. Sir Philip Sidney. AnFE; AWP; BEL; BWP; CABA; CBEP; CBV; CoBE; EG; EnL; EnLi-1; EnLit; FaBoEn; FCP; ForPo; GTBS-W; HBV; ILP; InPo; JAWP; LiTB; LiTG; LiTL; MaPo; MasP; NoP; OAEP; OBSC; PAn; Po; PoFS; PoIE; PP; ReEn; ReIE; SeCePo; SeCeV; SiCE; SiPS; Sonn; TOP; TreFT; TrGrPo TuPP; ViBoPo; WBP; YAT
Loving Jesus, gentle Lamb. Charles Wesley. ThGo
Loving looks the large-eyed cow. A Christmas Prayer. George MacDonald. SUS
Loving Mad Tom. *Unknown.* *See* Tom o'Bedlam's Song.
Loving man, I wearied of the ways of men. Redemption. Thomas Curtis Clark. SoP
Loving she is, and tractable, though wild. Characteristics of a Child Three Years Old. Wordsworth. ERoP-1; OBRV
Loving Shepherd of thy sheep. A Hymn. Jane E. Leeson. ThGo
Loving you, flesh to flesh, I often thought. Travel. Leonard Cohen. MeWo
Low-anchored Cloud. Henry David Thoreau. *See* Mist.
Low and mournful be the strain. Voluntaries. Emerson. AmePo
Low at Thy feet, Lord Jesus. None But Thyself. *Unknown.* FaChP
Low-backed Car, The. Samuel Lover. HBV
Low Barometer. Robert Bridges. CMoP; CoBMV; ForPo; LiTB; LoBV (2d ed.); PoIE; QFR; UnPo (3d ed.)
Low beating of the tom-toms, The. African Dance. Langston Hughes. FaPON; MoSiPe; RePo; TiPo (1952 ed.)
Low Bridge, Everbody Down. William S. Allen. *See* Erie Canal, The ("I've got a mule").
Low Doun in the Broom. *Unknown.* GoTS
Low Down Chariot, *with music. Unknown.* OuSiCo
Low-down, Lonesome Low, The. *Unknown.* *See* Golden Vanity, The.
Low! I, the man whose Muse whylome did maske. *See* Lo I the man. . .
Low in the eastern sky. To the Maiden in the East. Henry David Thoreau. MWA-1; OxBA
Low in thy grave with thee. David's Lament for Jonathan. Peter Abelard. LiTW
Low lies the land upon the sea. The Lookout. William Collins. EtS
Low, like another's lies the laureled head. Lacrimae [*or* Lachrymae] Musarum. Sir William Watson. HBV; PoVP; VA
Low moon shone on the desert land and the sage was silver white, A. Charley Lee. Henry Herbert Knibbs. WaKn
Low on his fours the Lion. Unstooping. Walter de la Mare. UTS
Low sandy beach and the thin scrub pine, The. Cape Cod. George Santayana. AmePo
Low spake the knight to the peasant maid. The Rose and the Gauntlet. "Christopher North." BeLS
Low stream by a winding track, A. Festival in Tuscany. William Force Stead. POTE
Low sun whitens on the flying squalls, The. Rounding the Cape. Roy Campbell. BoSA; PeSA
Low Tide. Lynette Roberts. NeBP
Low Tide on Grand-Pré. Bliss Carman. CaP; OBCV; PeCV
Low-voiced girls that go, The. The Invisible Bride. Edwin Markham. HBV
Low was our pretty cot: our tallest rose. Reflections on Having Left a Place of Retirement. Samuel Taylor Coleridge. EnRP; MERP; OBEC
Low whispers the wind from Malaya. A Song. Jayadeva. *Fr.* The Gita Govinda. LiTW
Lowell. James Russell Lowell. *Fr.* A Fable for Critics. AmPP (4th ed.); AP; OxBA
(On Himself.) AA
("There is Lowell, who's striving Parnassus to climb.") AmePo; CoBA
Lower Animals. Alan Anderson. PCD
Lower Criticism, The. John Hollander. PV
Lower Forms of Life. Mary Winter. GoYe
Lower him gently, gently, now, into the quiet deep. Sea Burial. Robina Monkman. EtS
Lowercase jensen, that's dangerous. Jensen: a Slideshow. Eric Torgersen. QAH
Lowering night, with muggy sultry air, A. The Stampede. Earl Alonzo Brininstool. PoOW
Lowery Cot. L. A. G. Strong. MoBrPo
Lowest Place, The. Christina Rossetti. EnLi-2; MaRV; SoP; TrPWD; ViPo
Lowest Trees Have Tops [*or* Topps], The. Sir Edward Dyer. AtBAP; CBEP; EG; EIL; EnRePo; FaBoEn; InPo; PoEL-1; PoRA; SiCE
(Love Is Love.) TrGrPo
(Modest Love, A.) BoLP; LiTG; LiTL; OBSC
Lowland hills and rivers. The War Year. Ts'ao Sung. PPON
Lowlands, *diff. versions. Unknown.* AmSS (3 *vers., with music*); ChTr; OxBoLi; ShS (3 *vers., with music*); SoAmSa (A *and* B *vers., with music*); TrAS, *with music*
("I dreamt a dream the other night.") LO
Lowlands Low, The. *Unknown.* *See* Golden Vanity, The.
Lowlands, lowlands, away [*or* hurrah], my John. Lowlands. *Unknown.* *See also* I dreamt a dream the other night. AmSS; SoAmSa; TrAS.
Lowlands o' [*or* of] Holland, The. *Unknown.* OBB; OxBB
(Lawlands o' Holland, The.) AmSS; CH
Lowly Bethlehem, *with music.* Count Zinzendorf, *tr. fr. German.* TrAS
Low'ring heaven had mask'd her in a cloud, The. Michael Drayton. *Fr.* Mortimeriados. ReIE
Lowveld, The. Charles Eglington. PeSA
Loyal Effusion. Horace Smith *and* James Smith. OBRV
Loyal General, The, *sel.* Nahum Tate.
Prologue: "If yet there be a few that take delight," *by* Dryden. CEP; SeCV-2
"Loyal hearts of London City, come, I pray, and sing my ditty." The Dutchess of Monmouth's Lamentation for the Loss of Her Duke. *Unknown.* CoMu
Loyal to country and comrades and then. February Twelfth. Mary F. Hepburn. PCH
Loyall [or Loyal] Scot, The. Andrew Marvell. MaMe
"But who considers well will find indeed," *sel. at.* to Marvell. ViBoPo
Loyalties. Walter A. Cutter. OQP
Loyalty. Berton Braley. BLPA
Loyalty. Allan Cunningham. *See* Hame, Hame, Hame.
Loyalty. W. H. Davies. BrPo
Loyalty Confin'd. Sir Roger L'Estrange. OBS
(Mr. Le Strange His Verses in the Prison at Linn.) SeCL
Loyalty Hymn. Edith Lovejoy Pierce. ChIP; MaRV
Lo-yang. Emperor Ch'ien Wen-ti, *tr. fr. Chinese by* Arthur Waley. AtBAP; AWP; JAWP; WBP
Loyola's Instructions to His Followers. John Oldham. *Fr.* Satires upon the Jesuits. PeRV
Lu Yün's Lament. Sir Herbert Read. ML
Lubber Breeze. T. Sturge Moore. CH
Lubly Fan, *with music.* Cool White. TrAS
Luca Signorelli to His Son. Eugene Lee-Hamilton. PeVV
Lucasta frown and let me die. To Lucasta: Her Reserved Looks. Richard Lovelace. SeCV-1
Lucasta Laughing. Richard Lovelace. PoEL-3
"Lucasta," said Terence O'Connor. "To Lucasta, on Going to the Wars." Edwin Meade Robinson. *Fr.* Limericised Classics. HBMV
Lucasta Weeping ("Lucasta wept, and still the bright"). Richard Lovelace. AnAnS-2; PoIE (1970 ed.)
Lucasta's World. Richard Lovelace. SCEP-2; SeCP
Lucid instant comes upon, The. Teufelsdröckh Minor. Morton Dauwen Zabel. NP
Lucifer. Maxwell Anderson. MoRP
Lucifer. Norman Cameron. MemP
Lucifer, The. Guy Glover. CaP
Lucifer. D. H. Lawrence. OAEP (2d ed.)
Lucifer. Milton. *Fr.* Paradise Lost, I. UnPo (1st ed.)
Lucifer Alone. Josephine Miles. CBV
Lucifer and Elissa. Philip James Bailey. *Fr.* Festus. VA
Lucifer at Leisure. Sister Mary Maura. JKCP (1955 ed.)
Lucifer did not wish to murder God. Lucifer. Norman Cameron. MemP
Lucifer in Starlight. George Meredith. AnEnPo; AnFE; ATP; BEL; BoLiVe; CABA; CaFP; CBEP; CBV; CH; CoBE; EnL; EnLi-2; EnLit; EPN; ExPo; ForPo; HBV; HoPM; ILP; InP; InPo; LiTB; LiTG; LoBV; MemP; OAEP; OBEV; OBNC; OBVV; PG (1955 ed.); PoEL-5; PoFS; PoIE; PoPo; PoSa; PoVP; SeCeV; ShBV-4; Sonn; TOP; TreFT; TrGrPo; UnPo; VA; ViBoPo; ViPo; ViPP; VP
Lucifer in the Train. Adrienne Cecile Rich. EaLo; NePoEA-2; TwAmPo
Lucile, *sels.* "Owen Meredith."

Lucile (continued)
Dinner Hour, The. VA
What We May Live Without. TreF
("We may live without poetry, music and art.") PoToHe (new ed.)
Lucilia, wedded to Lucretius, found. Lucretius. Tennyson. MBW-2; ViPo; ViPP
Lucilius was the man, who, bravely bold. The Art of Poetry. Nicolas Boileau. EnLi-1
Lucilla, saved from shipwreck on the seas. A Dedication. Claire McAllister. TwAmPo
Lucinda. *Unknown.* SeCL
Lucinda Matlock. Edgar Lee Masters. *Fr.* Spoon River Anthology. CMoP; FaBV; ILP; InP; LaNeLa; LiTA; LiTL; LiTM; MAP; MCCG; MoAmPo; MoVE; NeMA; NP; OnPP; OxBA; PoPo; ReMP
Lucinda wink or vaile those eyes. *Unknown.* SeCSL
Luck. W. W. Gibson. EtS; MoShBr; OBMV
Luck. Langston Hughes. MoLP
Luck. Evan V. Shute. CaP
Luck? I am upset. My dog is ill. A Rune for C. Barbara Howes. NYBP
Luck in the Square Stone, The, *sel.* H. C. Bosman.
"At the safari's end a porter." BoSA
Luck is a star. The Fireborn Are at Home in Fire. Carl Sandburg. MoAmPo (1950 ed.)
Luck of Edenhall, The. Ludwig Unland, *tr. fr. German by* Longfellow. AWP; StPo
Luckes, my fair falcon, and your fellows all. Sir Thomas Wyatt. FCP
Luckless Collings. William Collins. Three Fragments, 1. WaPE
Luckless man/ Avoids the miserable bodkin's point. Man's Anxious, but Ineffectual Guard against Death. Thomas Lovell Beddoes. ChER
Lucky Chance, The, *sel.* Aphra Behn.
Of Love, *at. to* Aphra Behn, *also to*——Ousley. SeCL
(Song: "O Love! that stronger art than wine.") LO
Lucky Coin, The. Austin Clarke. NeIP
Lucky like Cook to travel and return. "Heureux Qui Comme Ulysse." John Manifold. WaaP; WaP
Lucky live like Oedipus, The. On Luck. Mark Goldman. NYTB
"Lucky magpie, holy bird, what hateful lies you tell!" The Lady and the Magpie. *Unknown.* AtBAP
Lucky Marriage, The. Thomas Blackburn. GTBS-P
Lucky Snail, The. Winifred Welles. StVeCh (1940 ed.)
Lucky stars are for gazing upon and lying to yourself. Treasure Hunt. Art Wilson. WSL
Lucky Thing, A. Dorothy Aldis. RePo
Lucrative offices are seldom lost. Absence of Occupation. William Cowper. *Fr.* Retirement. OBEC
Lucrece and Nara. Laura Riding. FaBoMo
Lucretius. Tennyson. MBW-2; ViPo; ViPP
Lucretius could not credit centaurs. Invitation to Juno. William Empson. AtBAP; CMoP; FaBoMo
Lucretius felt the change of the world in his time. Prescription of Painful Ends. Robinson Jeffers. LiTA; MoAB; MoAmPo; OxBA
Lucy. Walter de la Mare. CMoP
Lucy, *complete, in 5 parts.* Wordsworth. EnL; EnLi-2; EnLit; EnRP; EPN; FiP; HBV; OAEP; OBEV; OBNC; OBRV; PoFS; TrGrPo
Sels.
"I traveled [*or* Travell'd] among unknown men." AWP; BoLiVe; CBEP; EnL; EnLi-2; EnLit; EnRP, EPN; ERoP-1; FaBV; FiP; GTBS; GTBS-D; GTBS-P; GTBS-W; GTSL; HBV; ILP; InPo; JAWP; MBW-2; MERP; OAEP; OBEV; OBNC; OBRV; OuHeWo; PoFS; PTK; TOP; TrGrPo; WBP
"She dwelt among the untrodden ways." AnFE; ATP; AWP; BEL; BLPA; BoLiVe; CABA; CBEP; CoBE; DiPo; EG; ELP; EnL; EnLi-2; EnLit; EnLoPo; EnRP; EPN; ERoP-1; FaBoEn; FaBV; FiP; GTSL; HBV; HBVY; ILP; InP; InPo; JAWP; LiTB; LiTG; LiTL; LoBV; MaC; MaPo; MBW-2; MCCG; MERP; NeHB; NoP; OAEP; OBEV; OBNC; OBRV; OTPC; OuHeWo; PAn; PG; PoAn; PoE; PoeP; PoFS; PoIE; PTK; ShBV-4; TOP; TreF; TrGrPo; ViBoPo; WBP; WHA
(Lost Love.) GTBS; GTBS-D; GTBS-P; GTBS-W; GTSE; PoPo
Violet, The, *sel.* PCH
"Slumber did my spirit seal, A." AnEnPo; AnFE; AWP; BEL; BoLiVe; BWP; CABA; CaFP; CBEP; CBV; DiPo; EG; ELP; EnL; EnLi-2; EnLit; EnLoPo; EnRP; EPN; ERoP-1; ExPo; FaBoCh; FaBoEn; FiP; FLW; ForPo; FosPo; GTBS; GTBS-D; GTBS-P; GTBS-W; GTSE; GTSL; HBV; ILP; InPo; InvP; JAWP; LiTB; LiTG; LiTL; LoGBV; MaPo; MBW-2; MERP; NoP; OAEP; OBEV; OBNC; OBRV; OnPM; OuHeWo; PAn; Po; PoAn; PoE; PoEL-4; PoeP; PoFS; PoIE; PoRA; SeCeV; ShBV-4; TOP; TreFS; TrGrPo; UnPo (3d ed.); ViBoPo; WBP; WePo
(Lines.) LoBV
"Strange fits of passion have I known." CBEP; CoBE; EG; EnL; EnLi-2; EnLit; EnRP; EPN; ERoP-1; FiP; HBV; ILP; LiTB; LiTG; LiTL; LO; MBW-2; MERP; OAEP; OBEV; OBNC; OBRV; PAn; PIA; Po; PoE; PoeP; PoFS; TrGrPo; ViBoPo
"Three years she grew in sun and shower." AtBAP; AWP; BEL; CBEP; EnL; EnLi-2; EnLit; EnRP; EPN; ERoP-1; FiP; FosPo; GBV; GN; HBV; HBVY; ILP; LiTL; LoBV; MBW-2; MERP; NoP; OAEP; OBEV; OBNC; OBRV; OnPP; OTPC (1923 ed.); OuHeWo; PAn; PoE; PoEL-4; PoFS; PoIE; SeCeV; TOP; TreFS; TrGrPo
(Education of Nature, The.) GTBS; GTBS-D; GTBS-P; GTBS-W; GTSE; GTSL
Lucy and Colin. Thomas Tickell. *See* Colin and Lucy.
Lucy Ashton's Song. Sir Walter Scott. *Fr.* The Bride of Lammermoor, *ch.* 3. EnRP; GoTS; OBEV; OtMeF; OxBS
(Look Not Thou.) CBEP; OBRV
Lucy Gray; or, Solitude. Wordsworth. BEL; BeLS; CH; EnRP; EPN; ERoP-1; FiP; GTSL; HBV; MBW-2; MERP; OAEP; OBRV; OnSP; OTPC; PoFS; PRWS; SeCeV; TOP; TreFS; UnPo (1st ed.)
Lucy Lake. Newton Mackintosh. BOHV; HBV
Lucy Lake. Ogden Nash. ShM
Lucy Lavender. Ivy O. Eastwick. BiCB; BoTP; SiSoSe
Lucy Locket lost her pocket. Mother Goose. BoChLi; FOL; OxBoLi; OxNR; PCH; PPL; SiTL; TiPo (1959 ed.)
Lucy McLockett. Phyllis McGinley. BiCB
Lucy, you brightness[e] of our sphere [*or* spheare], who are. To Lucy, Countess[e] of Bedford, with Mr. Donnes Satires [*or* Satyres]. Ben Jonson. AnAnS-2; OBS; ReIE; SCEP-2; SeCV-1; SeEP; TuPP
Lucy's Birthday. Thackeray. OTPC (1923 ed.)
Lucy's Canary. Adelaide O'Keeffe. OTPC (1923 ed.)
Ludmilla; an Ode on the Occasion of Her Departure from These Shores. Ernest W. Thiele. WhC
Luer, faulkners! give warning to the field! For the Hearne and Duck. *Unknown.* NCEP
Luf es lif that lastes ay, thar it in Criste es feste. A Song of the Love of Jesus. Richard Rolle of Hampole. PoEL-1
Lufoten. Quentin Stevenson, *ad. fr.* O. V. De Lubicz-Milosz. POTE (1959 ed.)
Lugubrious Whing-Whang, The. James Whitcomb Riley. BOHV; NA; YaD
Luini in porcelain! Medallion. Ezra Pound. *Fr.* Hugh Selwyn Mauberley. NoP; SeCeV (1967 ed.)
Luis de Camoes. Roy Campbell. BoSA; FaBoTw; PeSA
Luke. Bible, *N.T.* *See* St. Luke.
Luke 11. Richard Crashaw. *See* Blessed Be the Paps Which Thou Hast Sucked.
Luke Havergal. E. A. Robinson. AA; AmePo; AmP; AmPP; AP; AWP; CaFP; CoBA; CoBMV; CrMA; ForPo; ILP; InPo; JAWP; LiTA; LiTM (rev. ed.); MAmP; MAP; MoAB; MoAmPo; MoPo; MoVE; NePA; PFY; Po; PoDB; PoEL-5; PoIE; PoRA; QFR; SiSw; TreFT; UnPo (3d ed.)
Luke tells us how the boy Jesus. The Temple. Clifford Dyment. ChMP
Lull, lullaby, all is still and the sea lakes are. An Unmarried Mother Sings. F. R. Higgins. POTE
Lulla by [*or* Lullaby] baby, lulla by baby. Lullaby. John Phillip. *Fr.* Comedy of Patient and Meek Grissell. ElL; ReEn; TuPP
Lulla, My Sweet Little Baby. *Unknown.* TuPP
("Lulla, la lulla, lulla lullaby.") ReEn
Lullabie of a Lover, The. George Gascoigne. *See* Lullaby of a Lover, The.
Lullaby, The: "As through the palms ye wander." Lope de Vega Carpio, *tr. fr. Spanish by* Thomas Walsh. CAW
Lullaby: "Baby wants a lullaby." William Brighty Rands. PPL
Lullaby: "Baloo, loo, lammy, now baloo, my dear." Lady Nairne. HBV
Lullaby: "Bedtime's come fu' little boys." Paul Laurence Dunbar. BoChLi; GoSl; MPB; StVeCh (1940 ed.); TSW

Lullaby: "Beloved, may your sleep be sound." W. B. Yeats. FaBoTw; OBMV; POTE
Lullaby: "Come sleep, and with the sweet deceiving." Beaumont *and* Fletcher. *See* Come, Sleep.
Lullaby, A: "For wars his life and half a world away." Randall Jarrell. FiMAP
Lullaby: "Girl with eyes like dying flowers." Max Harris. BoAV; MoAuPo
Lullaby: "Golden slumbers kiss your eyes." Thomas Dekker, *and others. See* Golden Slumbers.
Lullaby: "Hush dove the summer." Miriam Waddington. CaP
Lullaby: "Hush, lullay,/ Your treasures all." Léonie Adams. AmLP; BoLiVe (1939 ed.); MAP; MoAB; MoAmPo; NeMA
Lullaby: "Hush! the waves are rolling in." *Unknown. See* Gaelic Lullaby.
Lullaby: "Husheen, the herons are crying." "Seumas O'Sullivan." GBV; OnYI
Lullaby: "Lay your sleeping head, my love." W. H. Auden. MaPo (1969 ed.); PoAn
Lullaby: "Long canoe, The." Robert Hillyer. FaPON; LOW
Lullaby: "Lullaby baby, lullaby baby." John Phillip. *Fr.* Comedy of Patient and Meek Grissell. EIL
("Lulla by baby, lulla by baby.") ReEn; TuPP
Lullaby: "Lullaby, lullaby,/ Shadows creep across the sky." Phyllis Garlick. BoTP
Lullaby: "Lullaby, oh, lullaby!" Christina Rossetti. *Fr.* Sing-Song. OTPC (1946 ed.); RIS
Lullaby: "My little one, sleep softly." Harriet Monroe. NP
Lullaby: "Oh, honey, li'l honey, come and lay yo' wooly head." Edmund S. Leamy. GBV (1922 ed.)
Lullaby: "O! hush thee, my darling, sleep soundly my son." *Unknown, tr. fr. Yiddish by* Alice Lucas. TrJP
Lullaby: "Puva—puva—puva." *Tr. fr. Hopi Indian by* Natalie Curtis. SUS
Lullaby: "Rockaby, lullaby, bees in the clover!" Josiah Gilbert Holland. *Fr.* The Mistress of the Manse. AA; HBV
Lullaby: "Sing lullaby, as women do." George Gascoigne. *See* Lullaby of a Lover, The.
Lullaby, A: "Sleep, child, lie quiet, let be." James Agee. OnHM
Lullaby: "Sleep, little baby, sleep and rest." Elinor Chipp. HBMV
Lullaby: "Sleep, love, sleep." Quandra Prettyman. BOLo
Lullaby: "Sleep, mouseling, sleep." Elizabeth J. Coatsworth. SiSoSe
Lullaby: "Sleep, my little baby, sleep." Samuel Hoffenstein. TrJP
Lullaby: "Sleep, sleep, lovely white soul." Walter de la Mare. GBV
Lullaby: "Slumber, Jesu, lightly dreaming." *Unknown, tr. fr. Latin by* Raymond F. Roseliep. ISi
(Latin Lullaby, *tr. by* Garrett Strange.) CAW
Lullaby: "Softly now the burn is rushing." Seumas MacManus. AnIV
Lullaby: "Sweet and low, sweet and low." Tennyson. *See* Sweet and Low.
Lullaby, A: "Sweet baby, sleep! what ails my dear." George Wither. *See* Hymn L: Rocking Hymn, A.
Lullaby: "Though the world has slipped and gone." Edith Sitwell. AtBAP; ChMP; CMoP; LiTM; POTE; WaP
Lullaby: "Upon my lap my sovereign sits." Richard Verstegan. CH; EIL; GTSL; HBV; LoBV; OBEV
(Our Blessed Lady's Lullaby.) LO
(Our Lady's Lullaby.) ACP; CAW; GoBC; ISi
(Upon My Lap My Sovereign Sits.) ViBoPo
Lullaby: "Wide as this night, old as this night is old and young as it is young." Kenneth Fearing. CMoP
Lullaby: "Wind whistled loud at the window-pane, The." William Brighty Rands. BoTP
Lullaby: "With lights for eyes, our city turns." Dom Moraes. NePoEA-2
Lullaby./ Adult and child. Songs for a Colored Singer, III. Elizabeth Bishop. PoNe
Lullaby baby, lullaby baby. *See* Lulla by baby, lulla by baby.
Lullaby for a Man-Child. Jean Starr Untermeyer. YT
Lullaby for Peregrine. Robert P. Tristram Coffin. RePo
Lullaby for Titania. Shakespeare. *See* You Spotted Snakes.
Lullaby in Bethlehem. Henry Howarth Bashford. HBV; HBVY
Lullaby, little Jesus, my little pearl. Kolendy for Christmas. *Unknown.* CAW
Lullaby, lullaby baby. Thomas Goffe. *Fr.* The Tragedy of Orestes. TuPP
Lullaby, my little one. Cradle Song. Carl Michael Bellman. FaPON
Lullaby, O Lullaby. William Cox Bennett. HBV; OTPC
Lullaby, oh lullaby! Lullaby. Christina Rossetti. *Fr.* Sing-Song. BoChLi; OTPC (1946 ed.); RIS
Lullaby of a Lover, The. George Gascoigne. EIL; EnRePo; EP; OAEP; QFR; ReIE; SiCE
(Gascoigne's Lullaby [*or* Lullabie].) PoE; PoEL-1; PoFS; PoIE; ReEn; TrGrPo; TuPP
(Lover's Lullaby, A.) HBV; OBEV
(Lullabie of a Lover, The.) EnPo
(Lullaby: "Sing lullaby, as women do.") CLwM
(Sing Lullaby, as Women Do.) InvP
Lullaby of a [*or* the] Woman of the Mountain. Padraic Pearse, *tr. fr. Modern Irish by* Thomas MacDonagh. NP; OnYI
Lullaby of an Infant Chief. Sir Walter Scott. EnRP; FaPON; GoTP; HBV; MPB; OTPC; PCH, *st.* 1; PoRh; PRWS; RIS; TVC
Lullaby of Nokomis,*abr.* Longfellow. *Fr.* The Song of Hiawatha, III. PCH
Lullaby of the Catfish and the Crab. William Rose Benét. WhC
Lullaby of the Iroquois. Pauline Johnson. ACV
Lullaby of the Nativity, A. *Unknown. See* Lullay My Liking.
Lullaby of the Woman of the Mountain. Padraic Pearse. *See* Lullaby of a Woman of the Mountain.
Lullaby, sweet baby mine!/ Mother spins the thread so fine. A Danish Cradle Song. *Unknown.* BoTP
Lullaby Town. John Irving Diller. BLPA; NeHB
Lullay, Lullay [like a Child]. John Skelton. AtBAP; PoEL-1; PoIE
(Here Folowith Divers Balettis and Ditles Salacious, Devised by Master Skelton, Laureate.) PoFS
(My Darling Dear My Daisy Flower.) EnRePo; NoP
(Sleeper Hood-winked, The.) MeEL
(With Lullay, Lullay, [like a Child].) InvP; NCEP
("With, lullay, lyke a chylde.") EnPo
Lullay, Lullay ("Lullay, lullay, litel child,/ Thu that were so sterne"). *Unknown.* OxBoCh
Lullay, lullay, la, lullay. Jesus Reassures His Mother. *Unknown.* MeEL
Lullay My Liking. *Unknown.* ELP
("I saw a faire maiden.") EG
(Lullaby of the Nativity.) MeEL
Lullay, thou little tiny child. *See* Lully, lulla, thou little tiny child.
Lulled, at silence, the spent attack. Baggot Street Deserta. Thomas Kinsella. NMP
Lulled by La Belle Dame sans Merci he lies. The Enchanted Knight. Edwin Muir. MoVE
Lully, lulla, thou little tiny child. The Coventry Carol. *Unknown.* ELP; MeEL; YaCaBo
Lully, Lullay [*or* Lulley]. *Unknown. See* Falcon, The.
Lulu, *with music. Unknown.* ABF; CoSo
(My Lulu, *diff.*) AS
Lumber Camp Song, The. *Unknown.* ShS
Lumber of a London-going dray, The. An Incident in the Early Life of Ebenezer Jones, Poet, 1828. John Betjeman. CMoP
Lumber of Spring. Anne Ridler. NYBP
Lumbering tractor rolls its panting round, The. A Melbourne Ode; the Agricultural Show, Flemington, Victoria. Frank Wilmot. BoAu
Lumberman's Alphabet, The, *with music. Unknown.* ShS
Lumbermen, The. Whittier. WoL
Lumberyak, The. William F. Kirk. IHA
Lumberyard, The. Ruth Herschberger. LiTA; LiTL; LiTM (rev. ed.)
Lumen de Lumine. Shelley. *Fr.* Adonais. GoBC
("One remains, the many change and pass, The.") InP
Luminalia, *sel. At. to* Sir William Davenant.
Night's Song. SeCL
Luminous Hands of God, The. Eleanor Kenly Bacon. OQP
Lump says that Caliban's of gutter breed. On Two Ministers of State. Hilaire Belloc. PV
Lunae Custodiens. Lin Carter. FiSC
Lunar Moth. Robert Hillyer. OA

Lunar Stanzas. Henry Coggswell Knight. BOHV; NA
Lunar Valley of Lost Things, The. Ariosto, *tr. fr. Italian by* Sir John Harington. *Fr.* Orlando Furioso, XXXIV. LiTW
Lunatic, the Lover, and the Poet, The. Shakespeare. *Fr.* Midsummer Night's Dream, V, i. DiPo; FiP; InP; MasP
(Imagination.) GTBS-W; LiTB; LiTG
("Lovers and madmen have such seething brains," *sl. longer sel.*) PP
(Tricks of Imagination, The.) TreFS
Lunch at the Coq D'or. Peter Davison. TwCP
Lunch on Omaha Beach. Bink Noll. StP; ToPo
Lunch paper sinking. Stomach. Coleman Barks. *Fr.* Body Poems. QAH
Lunchroom bus boy who looked like Orson Welles, The. They Were All like Geniuses. Horace Gregory. The Passion of M'Phail, IV. NYBP; TwAmPo
Lungs draw in the air and rattle it out again, The. Remorse. John Betjeman. MoBrPo (1962 ed.)
Lupercalia. Ted Hughes. NMP; ToPo
Lupin. Humbert Wolfe. ThGo
Lupracaun, or Fairy Shoemaker, The. William Allingham. *See* Lepracaun. . .
Lupus in Fabula. Malcolm Lowry. OBCV; PeCV
(Xochitepec.) MoCV; TDP
Lupus, you question carefully. How to Raise a Son. Martial. LiTW
Lure, The, *sel.* John Hall.
"Look, how the daffodils arise." LO
Lure, The. John Boyle O'Reilly. HBV
Lure me with lovers. Monogramania. Eve Merriam. UnTE
"Lured," little one? Nay, you've but heard. Nested. Habberton Lulham. HBV
Luscious and Sorrowful. Christina Rossetti. PoEL-5; SeCePo
Luscious lobster, with the crabfish raw, The. Kinds of Shellfish. William Wood. SCAP
Lusiads, The (Os Lusíadas), *sels.* Luís de Camoes, *tr. fr. Portuguese.*
Cape of Tempests, The, *tr. by* Sir Richard Fanshawe. LiTW
Passage to India, *abr., tr. by* J. J. Aubertin. WoL
Lust. Shakespeare. *See* Sonnets, CXXIX.
Lust in Song. Robert Graves. *See* Bards, The.
Lust is the oldest lion of them all. An Italian Chest [*or* Lorenzo's Bas-Relief for a Florentine Chest.] Marjorie Allen Seiffert. HBMV; NP
Lust of Gold, The. James Montgomery. *Fr.* The West Indies. PAH
Lustily, lustily, lustily let us sail forth. *Unknown.* *Fr.* Common Conditions. ReEn; SiCE; TuPP
Lustral sweat in its fine slow beads, The. Grave Piece. Richard Eberhart. ReMP
Lustration of the Winter Tree, *sel.* Margaret Allonby.
"In this savage place the sun stands still." BoSA
Lusty Fryer of Flanders, The. *Unknown.* CoMu
Lusty Juventus. Charles Madge. FaBoMo
Lusty Juventus, *sel.* R. Wever.
In Youth Is Pleasure. CBEP; ChTr; OBEV
("In a herber green asleep whereas I lay.") EG; SiCE; TuPP
(In an Arbour Green.) ELP
(Of Youth He Singeth.) EIL
(Youth.) OBSC
Lusty May. *Unknown.* OBEV
(May Poems.) OxBS
Lute, The. Rainer Maria Rilke, *tr. fr. German by* Jessie Lemont. OnPM
Lute and the pear are your half sisters, The. A Flock of Guinea Hens Seen from a Car. Eudora Welty. NYBP
Lute in the Attic, The. Kenneth Patchen. OnHM
Lute, no longer hang upon your peg unstirred. Song and Wine. Bacchylides. LiTW
Lute Obeys, The. Sir Thomas Wyatt. *See* Blame Not My Lute.
Lutea Allison. Sir John Suckling. ErPo
Luther B——stepped from his air-conditioned house. I Hear America Griping. Morris Bishop. AmFN
Luther, they say, was unwise. A Letter from Rome. Arthur Hugh Clough. *Fr.* Amours de Voyage. LoBV
Luther to a Bluebottle Fly (1540). Eugene Lee-Hamilton. Sonn
Luther's Hymn. Martin Luther. *See* Mighty Fortress is our God, A.
Luve that I hae chosen, The. *See* Love that I have chosen, The.
Luveli Ter of Loveli Eyghe. *At. to* Johan de Grimestone. AtBAP
Luvin wumman is a licht, A. Love. "Hugh MacDiarmid." PoIE
Lux Advenit Veneranda. Adam of St. Victor, *tr. fr. Latin by* H. T. Henry. CAW
Lux Est Umbra Dei. John Addington Symonds. VA
Lux in Tenebris. Katharine Tynan. OxBI; TrPWD
Lux in Tenebris. *Unknown.* GoBC
Lux, My Fair Falcon. Sir Thomas Wyatt. *See* Of Such as Had Forsaken Him.
Luxurious man, to bring his vice in use. The Mower against Gardens. Andrew Marvell. AnAnS-1; BWP; ILP; LiTB; MaMe; MaPo (1969 ed.); OAEP; PoEL-2; PP; ReEn; SCEP-2; SeCV-1; SeEP
Luxury, then, is a way of. Political Poem. LeRoi Jones. CoAP
Lychee, The. Wang I, *tr. fr. Chinese by* Arthur Waley. FaBoCh
Lycias. Earl of Rochester. ErPo
Lycidas. Milton. AnEnPo; AnFE; AtBAP; ATP; AWP; BEL; BoLiVe; BWP; CABA; CaFP; CBV; ChTr; DiPo; EnL; EnLi-1; EnLit; ExPo; FaBoEn; FiP; FosPo; GTBS; GTBS-D; GTBS-P; GTBS-W; ILP; InPo; JAWP; LiTB; LiTG; LoBV; MaPo; MasP; MBW-1; MCCG; MyFE; NoP; OAEP; OBEV; OBS; OuHeWo; PAn; PIA; Po; PoAn; PoE; PoEL-3; PoFS; PoIE; SeCeV; SeEP; StP; TOP; TrGrPo; UnPo; VaPo; ViBoPo; WBP; WGRP; WHA; WoL
Sels.
"And call the Vales, and bid them hither cast." WePo
Immortality. MaRV
"Last came, and last did go." PoFr
"Weep no more, woful Shepherds weep no more." BoC
"Yet once more, O ye laurels, and once more." MemP
Lycidas and Moeris. Vergil, *tr. fr. Latin by* Dryden. Eclogues, IX. AWP
(Ninth Eclogue.) FosPo
Lycidus, *sel.* Aphra Behn.
O What Pleasure 'Tis to Find. UnTE
Lycon begin—begin the mournful tale. Eclogue. William Diaper. *Fr.* Nereides; or, Sea-Eclogues. SeCePo
Lycon, the rising down that first appeared. Good Expectations. *Unknown.* OnPM
Lydford Journey. William Browne. CavP
Lydia. Lizette Woodworth Reese. AA
Lydia Is Gone This Many a Year. Lizette Woodworth Reese. CH; GBV (1952 ed.); GoJo; HBV
Lydia Pinkham, *with music.* *Unknown.* AS
Lydia Sherman, *sel.* *Unknown.*
"Lydia Sherman is plagued with rats." ShM
Lydia, why do you ruin by lavishing. Questioning Lydia. Horace, *tr. by* Louis Untermeyer. *Fr.* Odes. InP
Lyell's Hypothesis Again. Kenneth Rexroth. MoVE; OnHM
"Lyf So Short, The." William Stafford. ML
Lyf so short, the craft so long to lerne, The. The Parlement of Foules: Proem. Chaucer. FiP; MyFE; ViBoPo
Lying. Thomas Moore. BOHV; FiBHP
Lying asleep between the strokes of night. Love and Sleep. Swinburne. MeWo; UnTE
Lying at night poised between sleep and waking. East Coast—Canada. Elizabeth Brewster. CaP
Lying Awake. W. D. Snodgrass. MoAmPo (1962 ed.); NYBP
Lying by the fireside. Fire Pictures. Emma Rounds. MPB
Lying here quietly beside you. Quietly. Kenneth Rexroth. ErPo
Lying in a Hammock at William Duffy's Farm. James Wright. FRC; NaP; PIA
Lying in bed this morning, just a year. A Letter. Anne Ridler. LiTL; LiTM
Lying in State. Adrian Mitchell. ELU
Lying in the dark music. Enigma Variations, The. Paul Petrie. NYBP
Lying in the Grass. Sir Edmund Gosse. OBVV; TOP; VA
Lying in the sunshine among the buttercups. Tribute to Grass. John J. Ingalls. WBLP
Lying on your back in the chill of November. Autumn in the Plains. William Hunt. YAP

Lyk as the dum. The Solsequium. Alexander Montgomerie. OxBS
Lyke as a huntsman after weary chace. See Like as a huntsman. . .
Lyke as a ship, that through the ocean wyde. See Like as a ship. . .
Lyke as the culver on the bared bough. See Like as the culver. . .
Lyke-Wake Dirge, A. *Unknown.* AnFE; AtBAP; BuBa; CBEP; CH; ChTr; EaLo; EvOK; FaBoCh; FlW; GoBC; HBV; HoPM; LoBV; NoP; OBB; OBEV; OtMeF; OxBoCh; PoEL-1; PoLi; SeCeV; ShBV-2
(Cleveland Lyke-Wake Dirge.) EnSB
(Final Dirge.) ACP
Lyke-Wake Song, A. Swinburne. PoVP
Lynchburg Town, *with music.* *Unknown.* OuSiCo
Lynched Negro. Maxwell Bodenheim. PoNe
Lynching, The. Claude McKay. BALP; BANP; IDB
Lynching Bee, The. William Ellery Leonard. PoNe
Lynching for Skip James, A. Rudy Bee Graham. BF
Lynx. R. A. D. Ford. CaP
Lyre, The. George Darley. *See* Listen to the Lyre *and* Solitary Lyre, The.
Lyre of the sonnet, that full many a time. Written December 1790. Anna Seward. Sonn
Lyre-Bird, The. Roland Robinson. PoAu-2
Lyrebird by the damp track, frozen, The. The Makers. Nan McDonald. ACV
Lyrebirds. Judith Wright. GoJo
Lyric: "Angora anger who art in heaven." Gil Orlovitz. ToPo
Lyric: "Bird sings on a matin tree, A." Kathleen Raine. CMoP
Lyric, A: "How can I sing light-souled." Lorenzo de' Medici, *tr. fr. Italian by* John Addington Symonds. JAWP; WBP
Lyric: "I touched a shining mote of sand." Philip Child. CaP
Lyric: "Let but a thrush begin." John Hewitt. NeIP
Lyric: "Songs of adolescence, The." John Thompson. BoAu
Lyric, A: "There's nae lark loves the lift, my dear." Swinburne. HBV
Lyric: "When I am gone and green." Gil Orlovitz. ToPo
Lyric: "You would have understood me, had you waited." Ernest Dowson. *See* You Would Have Understood Me.
Lyric Barber. Liboria E. Romano. GoYe
Lyric Deed, The. John G. Neihardt. DD
Lyric from a Play, A. *Unknown.* MeEL
Lyric from "Maud." Tennyson. *See* Come into the Garden, Maud.
Lyric Love. Robert Browning. *See* O Lyric Love.
Lyric of Doubt. Donald Wandrei. FiSC
Lyrical Poem, The. Richard Garnett. VA
Lyrick for Legacies. Robert Herrick. OBS
Lyrics, *sels.* James Agee.
"I loitered weeping with my bride for gladness." MAP; MoAmPo; PoPl
"No doubt left. Enough deceiving." MAP; MoAmPo; PoPl
"Not met and marred with the year's whole turn of grief." MAP; MoAmPo; PoPl
Lyrics from "The Princess." Tennyson. *See* Princess, The.
Lysistrata, *sel.* Aristophanes, *tr. fr. Greek by* Benjamin Bickley Rogers.
How the Women Will Stop War. WaaP
Lytell Geste of Robyn Hode, A, *sel.* *Unknown.*
"Lithe and lysten, gentylmen." YAT
Lyth and listen, gentlemen. Robin Hood and the Beggar, II. *Unknown.* BaBo; ESPB
Lythe and listin, gentilmen. A Gest of Robyn Hode. *Unknown.* *See* Lithe and listen, gentlemen.
Lyttel Boy, The. Eugene Field. AA
Lyttelton Harbour, *sels.* D'Arcy Cresswell. AnNZ
"Home did I say, ye homeless? Not to ye," VIII.
"Thou bent and only motion of our lives," XXXIII.
"Ye barren hearts and bitter, steep'd in brine," XXXVIII.
Lytyll prety nyghtyngale, The. *See* Little pretty nightingale.

M

M. Edward Lear. WhC
M. Antonio Flaminio: To His Farm. John Ashmore. CLwM
M. Crashaw's Answer for Hope. Richard Crashaw. *See* For Hope.
M. Edwards' May. Richard Edwards. TuPP
(Master Edwards' May.) SiCE
(May.) OBSC
M. Francis Beaumont's Letter to Ben Jonson. Francis Beaumont. *See* Master Francis Beaumont's Letter to Ben Jonson.
M., Singing. Louise Bogan. CrMA; GoJo; LiTA; NePA
M was once a little mouse. M. Edward Lear. WhC
Ma an' Pa'd been raisin' chickens. Pa's Chickens. Homer Roberts. IHA
Ma Jesus/ Was a troubled man. Troubled Jesus. Waring Cuney. BANP; GoSl
Ma lass by munelicht fesht me frae the fail. The Deean Tractorman, Deleerit. Edith Anne Robertson. OxBS
Ma Lord. Langston Hughes. GoSl
Ma Provence. Kenneth Koch. ANYP
Mab. Ben Jonson. *Fr.* The Satyr. WiR
Mab the Mistress-Fairy. Ben Jonson. *See* Queen Mab.
Mabel, in New Hampshire. James T. Fields. HBV
Mabel, little Mabel. The Face against the Pane. Thomas Bailey Aldrich. TreFS
Mabel Martin; a Harvest Idyl, *sel.* Whittier.
I Call the Old Time Back: Proem. ViBoPo
Mac and Daisy, Carl and Marie. Hornets. C. Lindsay McCoy. GFA
Mac had a place to drink and talk downtown. McSorley's Bar. Reuel Denney. TwAmPo
Macadam, gun-gray as the tunny's belt. Van Winkle. Hart Crane. *Fr.* The Bridge. AmP; AmPP; CrMA; FaBV; LiTA; MAP; MoAB; MoAmPo; ReMP
Macaffie's Confession. *Unknown.* BeLS; CoSo, *with music*
McAndrew's Hymn. Kipling. CABL; ViPP
(M'Andrew's Hymn.) OtMeF; PoEL-5
Macaulay. Walter Savage Landor. VA
Macaulay at Tea. Barry Pain. *See* Poets at Tea, The.
Macavity; the Mystery Cat. T. S. Eliot. CenHV; EnL; HaMV; LiTM; MemP; NeMA; PoRA; RePo; ShBV-3; TiPo; WaKn
Macaw preens upon a branch outspread, A. Decoration. Louise Bogan. MAP; MoAB; MoAmPo
Macbeth. Andrew of Wyntown. OxBS
Macbeth, *sels.* Shakespeare.
"Blood hath been shed ere now, i' the olden time," *fr.* III, iv. MyFE
"Give me my sword./ Who's there?" *fr.* II, i. MyFE
"Here's a knocking indeede," *fr.* II, iii. AtBAP
"I have lived long enough; my way of life," *fr.* V, iii. TrGrPo
Macbeth Does Murder Sleep, *fr.* II, ii. FiP
(Conscience.) MaRV
("Methought I heard a voice cry, 'Sleep no more' ") MemP
(Murderers, The.) WHA
(Sleep.) TreFS
Macbeth's Words before Murdering, *fr.* II, i. TreFS
Mind Diseased, A. *fr.* V, iii. TreFT
(Remorse.) MaRV
("Canst thou not minister to a mind diseas'd.") TrGrPo; TRV, 3*ll.*
Murder Pact, The, *fr.* I, vii. WHA
(Vaulting Ambition.) FiP
O! Full of Scorpions, *fr.* III, ii. FiP
"She should have died hereafter," *fr.* V, v. MemP
"That which hath made them drunk, hath made me bold," II, ii. AtBAP; MyFE
"They met me in the day of successe," I, v. AtBAP
"Tomorrow, and tomorrow, and tomorrow." FaFP; LiTB; MasP; OQP; PG; PoPl; PTK; TrGrPo; TRV; WHA; YAT
(Empty Life, The.) MaRV
(Macbeth Learns of His Wife's Death.) TreF
(Out, Out, Brief Candle!) ChTr
(She Should Have Died Hereafter.) FiP; InP
(Tomorrow and Tomorrow.) DiPo; NeHB; UnPo
"We have scotch'd the snake, not kill'd it," *fr.* III, ii. AtBAP

Macbeth (continued)
Witches' Brew, The, *fr.* IV, i. TreFT
(Charm, The.) EIL
("Thrice the brinded cat hath mewed.") InvP; MyFE
(Witches' Charm.) SiTL
(Witches' Spell, The.) PoMS
McCullam Camp. Larry Gorman. *See* Winter of '73, The.
MacDiarmod's Daughter. Francis Carlin. HBMV
Macdonald's Raid. Paul Hamilton Hayne. PAH
McDonogh Day in New Orleans. Marcus B. Christian. AmNP; PoNe
M'Fingal, *sels.* John Trumbull.
"At once with resolution fatal," *fr.* III. AmPP (5th ed.)
Liberty-Pole, The, III. AmPP (3d ed.)
Town Meeting, The, *abr.* AnNE
MacFlecknoe; or, A Satire upon the True-Blue Protestant Poet T. S. Dryden. ATP (1953 ed.); BEL; BWP; CABA; CABL; CEP; DiPo; EiCL; EiPP; EnLi-1; EnLit; ForPo; FosPo; MaPo; MBW-1; NoP; OAEP; OxBoLi; PAn; PeRV; Po; PoAn; PoE; PoFS; PoIE; PP; QFR; SeCV-2; SeEP; SiTL; StP
"All human things are subject to decay, *sel.*" AtBAP; CoBE; ExPo; TrGrPo; ViBoPo
(Poet Shadwell, The.) FiP
(Primacy of Dullness, The.) OBS
(Shadwell.) AnFE
MacGregor's Gathering. Sir Walter Scott. AnFE; OxBS; PoFr
Machberoth, *sel.* Immanuel di Roma. *tr. fr. Hebrew by* Joseph Chotzner.
Virtue. TrJP
Macheath and Polly. John Gay. *See* Song: "Were I laid on Greenland's coast."
Machine Hand, A. Thomas Ashe. OBVV
Machine stitched rivets ravel on a tree. The Pilot in the Jungle. John Ciardi. MiAP
Machinery is enough for a scientist. James Oppenheim. *Fr.* Night. TRV
Machines. Daniel Whitehead Hicky. PoMa
Machines in haughty and presumptuous pride. Ode to Machines. Louis Ginsberg. PoMa
Machines of death from east to west. Revelation. William Soutar. HaMV
Machines—or Men. Elizabeth Newport Hepburn. PoMa
McIlrath of Malate. John Jerome Rooney. PAH
MacKenna's Dream. *Unknown.* OnYI
Mackerel skies and mares' tails. Rules of the Road. *Unknown.* SoAmSa
Mackerel sky,/ Mackerel sky. *Unknown.* OxNR
McKinley. *Unknown.* MC; PAH
McKinley Brook, *with music.* George Calhoun. ShS
McLean's Welcome. James Hogg. OxBS
MacLugach! says Finn. *Unknown.* *Fr.* The Colloquy of the Ancients. OnYI
McLuhan put his telescope to his ear. The Taste of Space. A. J. M. Smith. PV
McNaughtan. *Unknown.* OxBB
MacPhairson Clonglocketty Angus Mc Clan [*or* M' Clan]. Ellen McJones [*or* M'Jones] Aberdeen. W. S. Gilbert. HBV; InMe; PCD; TSW
Macpherson's [*or* M'Pherson's] Farewell. Burns. MCCG; OtMeF
Macquarie Place. Robert D. Fitzgerald. PoAu-2
Macrobius Mingling with Nature. Rochelle Owens. CoPo
Macrocosm. Philip Child. CaP
McSorley's Bar. Reuel Denney. TwAmPo
Mad Actor. James L. Montague. NYTB
Mad as the Mist and Snow. W. B. Yeats. AtBAP; ChTr; MBW-2
Mad Berkeley believed, with his gay cavaliers. The Burning of Jamestown. Thomas Dunn English. PAH
Mad Blake. William Rose Benét. HBMV
Mad Boy's Song. Leo Kennedy. TwCaPo
Madboy's Song. Muriel Rukeyser. MoAmPo; TrJP
Mad Day in March. Philip Levine. NYBP
Mad Dogs and Englishmen. Noel Coward. CenHV; FiBHP; WhC
Mad Farmer's Song. *Unknown.* BrR; RIS
("My father left me three acres of land.") OxNR
(Sing Ivy.) BoTP
(Three Acres of Land.) NA
Mad Gardener's Song, The. "Lewis Carroll." *See* Gardener's Song, The.
Mad girl with the staring eyes and long white fingers, The. Cassandra. Robinson Jeffers. LiTA; LiTM; NePA; VaPo; WaP
Mad Jasper. Max Harris. MoAuPo
Mad Lover, The. Alexander Brome. CBEP; SeCL; SeEP
(I Have Been in Love and in Debt.) ALV
(Love, Drink, and Debt.) OtMeF
Mad Lover, The, *sels.* John Fletcher.
Arm, Arm, Arm, Arm, *fr.* V, iv. EIL
Prayer to Venus, *fr.* V, iii. SeCL
"To the fair fields where loves eternal dwell," *fr* IV, i. MyFE
Mad Lover, The. Speer Strahan. CAW
Mad Maid's Song, The. Robert Herrick. AWP; BoLiVe; CH; EG; EnLoPo; InPo; LoBV; PoeP; PoFS; OBEV; SeCL; SeCV-1; SeEP; TrGrPo; ViBoPo; WiR
Mad Maid's Whim. Randolph Stow. ACV
Mad Margaret's Song. W. S. Gilbert. *Fr.* Ruddigore. RIS
Mad Marjory. Hugh McCrae. PoAu-1
Mad Maudlin to Find Out Tom of Bedlam. *Unknown.* SiTL
Mad Merry Pranks of Robin Good-Fellow, The. *Unknown.* *See* Robin Goodfellow ("From Oberon, in fairy land").
Mad Negro Soldier Confined at Munich, A. Robert Lowell. NMP; PoeP
Mad paper stay, and grudge not here to burne. To Mrs. M. H. John Donne. MaMe
Mad Patsy said, he said to me. In the Poppy Field. James Stephens. PoRA (rev. ed.)
Mad Poll. J. Corson Miller. JKCP (1955 ed.)
Mad Rapist of Calaveras County, The. Pete Winslow. PV
Mad Scene, The. James Merrill. CoAP
Mad Song. Blake. BEL; CBEP; CEP; EiPP; EnLi-2; EnLit; EnRP; ERoP-1; FosPo; ILP; MaPo (1969 ed.); PoE; PoEL-4; PoRA; TrGrPo
Mad Song. Hester Sigerson. AnIV
Mad Sonnet 11: "I love seahorses, teddybears, African violets." Michael McClure. FRC
Mad Sonnet 5: "Oh science, I love the touch of velvet." Michael McClure. FRC
Mad Sweeney. *Unknown.* *See* Sweeney the Mad.
Mad Willow Lover. Pamela Millward. FRC
Mad Woman of Punnet's Town, The. L. A. G. Strong. MoBrPo
Mad World, My Masters, A, *sel.* Thomas Middleton.
O for a Bowl of Fat Canary. *Also in* Alexander and Campaspe (*by* John Lyly). OnPM; ViBoPo
Mad Yak, The. Gregory Corso. CoPo
Madaket Beach. Isabel Harriss Barr. GoYe
Madam and Her Madam. Langston Hughes. BALP
Madam Gabrina, or the Ill-Favourd Choice. Henry King. CavP
Madam Hickory. Wilbur Larremore. AA
"Madam, I have come a-courting." The Quaker's Wooing. *Unknown.* BFSS
Madam Life. W. E. Henley. MoBrPo; TrGrPo
(Madam Life's a Piece in Bloom.) CaBA; NBM; PeVV
Madam Mouse Trots. Edith Sitwell. *See* Madame Mouse Trots.
Madam, no more! The time has come to eat. The Elegy. A. D. Hope. ErPo
Madam, twice through the muses grove I walkt. Upon Mrs. Anne Bradstreet Her Poems. John Rogers. SCAP
Madam, Were you but only great, there are some men. To the Excellent Pattern of Beauty and Virtue, Lady Elizabeth, Countess of Ormond. James Shirley. GoBC
Madam, withouten Many Words. Sir Thomas Wyatt. *See* To a Lady to Answer Directly. . .
Madam would speak with me? So, now it comes. Modern Love, XXXIV. George Meredith. ViPo; VP
Madam, ye ben of all beauty shrine. *See* Madame, ye ben of al beauté shryne.
Madam, you are right; the fight was a great pity. To the Woman in Bond Street Station. Edward Weismiller. LiTA; NePA; WaP
Madame d'Albert's [*or* d'Albret's] Laugh. Clément Marot, *tr. fr. French by* Leigh Hunt. ALV; AWP; JAWP; WBP
(On Her Laugh.) OnPM
Madame Dill. *Unknown.* FiBHP
Madame, for your[e] newefangelnesse. Against Women Unconstant [*or* A Ballade against Woman Inconstant]. Chaucer. CABA; NoP

Madame, had all antiquitie been lost. To Mary Lady Wroth. Ben Jonson. OBS
Madame, his grace will not be absent long. Cyril Tourneur. *Fr.* The Revenger's Tragedy. AtBAP; PoEL-2
Madame Louise sleeps well o' nights. Aux Carmélites. Katharine Tynan. OnYI
Madame Mouse Trots. Edith Sitwell. *Fr.* Façade. FaBoCh; LOW
(Madam Mouse Trots) SyP
Madame Sans Souci. *Unknown.* BOHV
Madame, withouten Many Words. Sir Thomas Wyatt. *See* To a Lady to Answer Directly. . .
Madame [*or* Madam], ye ben of al beauté shryne. To Rosamond [*or* To Rosemounde *or* Ballade to Rosamund] Chaucer. CABA; CBEP; InP; MeEL; NoP; PAn; PIA
Mädchen mit dem rothen Mündchen. Heine, *tr. fr. German by* Sir Theodore Martin. AWP; JAWP; WBP
Made in Heaven. Peter Porter. PPON
Made in the Hot Weather. W. E. Henley. *See* Ballade Made in the Hot Weather.
Made Lake, The. Louise Townsend Nicholl. NePoAm-2
Made Perfect Through Suffering. Samuel Johnson. SoP
Madeira from the Sea. Sara Teasdale. HT
Madeleine in Church, *sel.* Charlotte Mew.
"How old was Mary out of whom you cast." LO; MoAB; MoBrPo
Madeleine Verchères. William Henry Drummond. CaP
Madeline at Jefferson Market Night Court. Margaret McGovern. WhC
Mademoiselle from Armentières. *Unknown.* SiTL; SoAmSa, *with music*
(Hinky Dinky, *with music.*) TrAS
(Hinky Dinky, Parlee-Voo.) ABF; AS
Mademoiselle Richarde. Edith Sitwell. MoVE
Madge Wildfire Sings. Sir Walter Scott. *See* Proud Maisie.
Madhouse. Calvin C. Hernton. IDB; Kal; NNP; PoNe (1970 ed.)
Madly Singing in the Mountains. Po Chü-i, *tr. fr. Chinese by* Arthur Waley. CBEP; MoPW; OuHeWo
Madman, The. S. J. Pretorius, *tr. fr. Afrikaans by* Uys Krige *and* Jack Cope. PeSA
Madman, The. Constance Urdang. PoPl
Madman Goes to a Party, The. Dick Lourie. ThO
Madman Looks at His Fortune, The. Dick Lourie. ThO
Madman's Song, The. John Masefield. *Fr.* Good Friday. ACV
("Wild duck, stringing through the sky, The.") BoC
Madman's Song, The. John Webster. *See* Oh, Let Us Howl Some Heavy Note.
Madman's Song. Elinor Wylie. LOW; MAP; MoAB; MoAmPo; MoSiPe; PoRA
Madness, *sel.* Richard Baxter.
Death of Dives, The. PeRV
Madness. James Dickey. NYBP
Madness. Harry Lee. MaRV
Madness One Monday Evening. Julia Fields. Kal; NNP
Madone! my lady, I will build for thee. To a Madonna. John Gray. SyP
Madonna, A. Heine, *tr. fr. German by* James Thomson. OnPM
Madonna di Campagna. Alfred Kreymborg. HBMV
Madonna loves. Madonna Remembers. Sister Mary Edwardine. WHL
Madonna, Madonna,/ Sat by the grey road-side. Cradle-Song. Adelaide Crapsey. HBMV; ISi
Madonna Mia. Swinburne. HBV
Madonna Natura. "Fiona Macleod" WGRP
Madonna; 1936. John Louis Bonn. ISi
Madonna of the Dons. Arthur MacGillivray. ISi; JKCP (1955 ed.)
Madonna of the Empty Arms. Maurice Francis Egan. ISi
Madonna of the Evening Flowers. Amy Lowell. AmLP; MAP; MoAmPo; NeMA; TOP; TreFT
Madonna of the Exiles. James Edward Tobin. ISi
Madonna Remembers. Sister Mary Edwardine. WHL
Madonna, to Her Sleeping Child, The. Lope de Vega, *tr. fr. Spanish by* George Ticknor. ChrBoLe
(Christmas Cradlesong, A.) PoPl
Madonna's Lamp, The. Wilhelm, Prince of Sweden, *tr. fr. Swedish by* Thomas Walsh. CAW
Madonna's Lullaby. St. Alphonsus Liguori, *tr. fr. Italian by* James J. Galvin. ISi
Madrigal V: Allusion to the Confusion of Babel. Francis Davison. ReIE
Madrigal: "Ay me, alas, heigh ho, heigh ho!" *Unknown. See* Ay Me, Alas.
Madrigal: "Beautie [*or* Beauty], and the life, The." William Drummond of Hawthornden. AtBAP; ElL; PoEL-2
(Her Passing.) OBEV
Madrigal: "Beside the rivers of the midnight town." John Frederick Nims. MiAP
Madrigal: "Come let's begin to revel 't out." *Unknown.* BoTP
Madrigal A: "Crabbed age and youth." Shakespeare. *See* Crabbed Age and Youth.
Madrigal: "Dear, when I did from you remove." Lord Herbert of Cherbury. ElL
Madrigal: "Eyes that are clear, serene." Gutierre de Cetina, *tr. fr. Spanish by* L. R. Lind. LiTW
Madrigal: "Ha ha! ha ha! This world doth pass." *Unknown. See* Fara Diddle Dyno.
Madrigal: "How should I love my best?" Lord Herbert of Cherbury. AnAnS-2; PoEL-2; SeCP; ViBoPo
Madrigal: "I always loved to call my Lady Rose." *Unknown.* ElL
Madrigal: "I fear not henceforth death." William Drummond of Hawthornden. LO
Madrigal: "Ivory, coral, gold, The." William Drummond of Hawthornden. ElL
(Ivory, Coral, Gold, The.) ELP
Madrigal: "Like the Idalian queen." William Drummond of Hawthornden. ElL; ELP; FaBoEn; InvP; LiTL; NoP; OBEV; OBS; PoEL-2; SeEP; ViBoPo
(Like the Idalian queen.) ELP; GoTS; NoP; SeCePo
Madrigal: "Love in thy youth, fair maid; be wise." *Unknown. See* Love in Thy Youth.
Madrigal: Love Vagabonding. William Drummond of Hawthornden. LoBV
Madrigal: "My Love in her attire doth show her wit." *Unknown. See* My Love in Her Attire.
Madrigal: "My mistress frowns when she should play." *Unknown, See* Fa La La. *at. to* John Hilton.
Madrigal: "My mistress is as fair as fine." Thomas Ravenscroft. CH; SiTL
("My mistress is as fair as fine.") OxBoLi
Madrigal: "My thoughts hold mortal strife." William Drummond of Hawthornden. AtBAP; CBV; ElL; GTBS; GTBS-D; GTBS-P; GTBS-W; GTSE; LoBV; OBS; OnPM
(Inexorable.) OBEV
(Lament, A.) GTSL
(My Thoughts Hold Mortal Strife.) CBEP
Madrigal: "O I do love, then kiss me." Robert Jones. OxBoLi;
(O I Do Love, Then Kiss Me.) NCEP
Madrigal: "Once in an arbor was my mistress sleeping." Barnabe Barnes. *Fr.* Parthenophil and Parthenophe. TuPP
Madrigal: "Since Bonny-boots was dead, that so divinely." *Unknown. See* Since Bonny-Boots Was Dead.
Madrigal: "Sister, awake, close not your eyes." *Unknown. See* Sister, Awake!
Madrigal: "Some there are as fair to see to." Francis Davison. *See* Her Commendation.
Madrigal: "Sound of thy sweet name, my dearest treasure, The." Francis Davison. *See* Sound of Thy Sweet Name, The.
Madrigal, A: "Swans, The, whose pens as white as ivory," *sel.* Robert Greene. ViBoPo
Madrigal: "Take, O take those lips away." Shakespeare. *See* Take, O Take Those Lips Away.
Madrigal: "Tell me where is fancy bred." Shakespeare. *See* Tell Me Where Is Fancy Bred.
Madrigal: "This life, which seems so fair." William Drummond of Hawthornden. EG; ElL; NoP; LiTG; OBS; SeCePo
(Life, a Bubble.) TOP
(This Life.) CH; TrGrPo
(This Life a Bubble.) OnPM
(This Life, Which Seems So Fair.) GTBS; GTBS-D; GTBS-P; GTBS-W; GTSE; GTSL
Madrigal: "This saith my Cloris bright." *Unknown, par. fr.* Giovanni Battista Guarini. LO
Madrigal: To Cupid. Francis Davison. *See* To Cupid.
Madrigal: To His Lady Selvaggia Vergiolesi. Cino da Pistoia, *tr. fr. Italian by* Dante Gabriel Rossetti. AWP; JAWP; WBP

Madrigal: "Unhappy [*or* Unhappie] light." William Drummond of Hawthornden. AtBAP; OBS
Madrigal: "When in her face mine eyes I fix." Earl of Stirling. Aurora, Madrigal I. EIL
Madrigal: "Why dost thou haste away." Sir Philip Sidney. *Fr.* Arcadia. EG; OBSC; SiPS
Madrigal: "Your love is dead, lady, your love is dead." R. S. Thomas. ELU; EnLoPo
Madrigal de Verano. Federico García Lorca, *tr. fr. Spanish by* Paul Blackburn. ErPo
Madrigal Macabre. Samuel Hoffenstein. ShM
Madrigal to a Streetcar Token. Rafael Alberti, *tr. fr. Spanish by* Lloyd Mallan. LiTW
Madrigal to the City of Santiago. Federico García Lorca, *tr. fr. Spanish by* Norman Di Giovanni. CAD
Madroño. Bret Harte. AA
Maerchen. Walter de la Mare. CoBMV
Maesia's Song. Robert Greene. *See* Sweet Are the Thoughts That Savor of Content.
Maeve. Mervyn Peake. LO
Magalu. Helene Johnson. CDC; PoNe
Magazine Fort, Phoenix Park, Dublin, The. William Wilkins. IrPN; SeCePo
Magdalen. Henry Kingsley. HBV; MaRV; OBVV
(At Glastonbury.) MemP; PoRA
Magdalen. James Ryder Randall. JKCP
Magdalen, The. Sir Edward Sherburne. *See* And She Washed His Feet with Her Teares. . .
Magdalen at Michael's gate. Magdalen [*or* At Glastonbury] Henry Kingsley. HBV; MaRV; MemP; PoRA
Magdalen Walks. Oscar Wilde. MoBrPo; YT
Magdalene. Boris Pasternak, *tr. fr. Russian by* Bernard Guilbert Guerney. MoRP
Magellan. Allen Curnow. AnNZ
Maggie and Milly and Molly and May. E. E. Cummings. LOW; NePoAm-2
(Poem.) PoSC
Maggie Lauder. *Unknown, at. to* Francis Sempill. OBS; OxBS
Maggie's Visit to Oxford, *sel.* "Lewis Carroll."
"To Worcester gardens next." CIV
Magi. Leslie Savage Clark. ChIP
Magi, The. Milton. *Fr.* On the Morning of Christ's Nativity. ChTr
Magi, The. W. B. Yeats. BoPe; BrPo; BWP; CaFP; CMoP; CoBMV; ELU; MaPo; MBW-2; NoP; NP; PoAn; PoDB; PoIE; StP
Magi Visit Herod, The. Caelius Sedulius, *tr. fr. Latin by* H. T. Henry. *Fr.* Carmen Paschale. CAW
Magic. Hamlin Garland. NP
Magic. Shakespeare, *after the Latin of* Ovid. *Fr.* The Tempest, V, i. AWP; JAWP; WBP
Magic. Thomas Wolfe. PoPl
Magic Car Moved On, The. Shelley. *Fr.* Queen Mab, I. GN
Magic Casements. Keats. *See* Nightingale, The.
Magic Flute, The. W. D. Snodgrass. NYBP
Magic Idle Windy Spaces, The. Don Shea. QAH
Magic Lariat. Glenn Ward Dresbach. BrR
Magic Mirror, The. Henry Mills Alden. HBV
Magic Piper, The. E. L. Marsh. BoTP; SiSoSe
Magic Vine, The. *Unknown.* GFA
Magic Waves. Gertrude Van Winkle. GFA
Magic Whistle, The. Margaret Rose. BoTP
Magic Window, The. Eleanor Hammond. MPB
Magical Mouse, The. Kenneth Patchen. LOW
Magical Nature. Robert Browning. PoVP
Magically awakened to a strange, brown night. Fog. Laurence Binyon. SyP
Magician and the Baron's Daughter, The. *Unknown. See* The Jolly Juggler.
Magico prodigioso, El, *sel.* Pedro Calderón de la Barca, *tr. fr. Spanish by* Shelley.
Demon Speaks, The. CAW
Magna Charta. *Unknown.* OHFP; WBLP
Magna Est Veritas. Coventry Patmore. *Fr.* The Unknown Eros. AnFE; CAW; CoBE; GoBC; GTBS-P; MaRV; MemP; OBEV (new ed.); OBNC; OBVV; OQP; PG (1945 ed.); PoVP; TreFT
(Here, in This Little Bay.) BoNaP
(Truth.) TrGrPo
(Truth Is Great, The.) OnPM
Magnanimous, The. Ellen de Young Kay. NePoEA
Magnet, The. Thomas Stanley. MePo
Magnet, The. Ruth Stone. MoAmPo (1962 ed.); NePA
Magnet hung in a hardware shop, A. The Fable of the Magnet and the Churn. W. S. Gilbert. *Fr.* Patience. FaPON; MPB; OnMSP; OTD; RePo
Magnet Is Mistaken, The. Louis Ginsberg. NYTB
Magnet said, The: "I." Of Natural Forces. Elizabeth Chesley. NYTB
Magnetic Mountain, The, *sels.* C. Day Lewis.
Nearing Again the Legendary Isle, VI. CoBMV; FaBoTw; GTBS-W; LiTB; MoAB; MoBrPo; MoPW; NeMA; ReMP
"Tempt me no more; for I," XXIV. EnLit; NAMP
(Tempt Me No More.) AnFE; MoAB; MoBrPo; OAEP (2d ed.) OBMV; PoDB; PoFr; PoPL; POTE
Third Enemy Speaks, XXI. EaLo
"Though winter's barricade delays," XXVIII. EnLit
Magnets. Laurence Binyon. HBMV
Magnets. Countee Cullen. BALP
Magnificat, The. St. Luke, I: 46-55, Bible, *N.T.* ISi (*Douay vers.*); MaRV; WGRP; WHL
(Hymn of the Blessed Virgin.) CAW
Magnificat. Arthur Symons. UnTE
Magnificence, *sel.* John Skelton.
"So merrily singeth the nightingale!" *fr.* IV, xxix. PoFr
Magnificent strong sun! in these last days. September Sun; 1947. David Gascoyne. AtBAP; FaBoMo; POTE (1959 ed.)
Magnificent the beast! Look in the eyes. A New Idol. Laurence Binyon. PoFr
Magnolia Cemetery. Henry Timrod. *See* Ode: "Sleep sweetly in your humble graves."
Magnolia Tree, The. Hubert Witheford. AnNZ
Magnolia Tree in Summer. Sacheverell Sitwell. BoC
Magnolia's Shadow, The. Robert Lowell, *ad. fr. the Italian of* Eugenio Montale. NaP
Magnum Vectigal Parcimonia. George Gascoigne. *See* Gascoigne's Memories.
Magpie, magpie, flutter and flee. *Unknown.* OxNR
Magpie Singing His Delight, The. David Campbell. *Fr.* Bird Cage. BiS
Magpies, The. Denis Glover. AnNZ; TDP
Magpies in Picardy. T. P. Cameron Wilson. HBV; MMA; OtMeF
Magpie's Nest. Charles *and* Mary Lamb. OTPC (1923 ed.); PRWS
Magpie's Song, The. Frank S. Williamson. BoAu
Mag's Song. *Unknown. See* Orphan Girl, The.
Magus, A. John Ciardi. HYE
Magus would needs, forsooth, this other day. Henry Parrot. SiCE; TuPP
Mah man. Flies on Shit. Quincy Troupe. WSL
Mah mule is white, mah chahcoal is black. Charcoal Man. *Unknown.* TrAS
Maharani of midnight tresses, The. In the Seraglio. David R. Slavitt. ErPo
Mahmud and Ayaz; a Paraphrase on Sa'di. Sir Edwin Arnold. *Fr.* With Sa'di in the Garden. VA
Mahogany Tree, The. Thackeray. HBV; VA
Mahoney. Séan Jennett. NeIP
Mahony's Mountain. Douglas Stewart. PoAu-2; SeCePo
Maia was one, all gold, fire, and sapphire. A Legend of Viable Women. Richard Eberhart. MiAP; MoVE
Maid, The. Katherine Brégy. CAW; GoBC
Maid, The. Theodore Goodridge Roberts. HBV; MoShBr
Maid and the Palmer, The. *Unknown.* ACP; BaBo; ESPB (A *and* B *vers.*); OBS
Maid, The (and thereby hangs a tale). Sir John Suckling. *Fr.* A Ballad upon a Wedding. LO
Maid Antibia, The. Anyte, *tr. fr. Greek by* William Hay. OnPM
Maid Freed from the Gallows, The. *Unknown.* AnFE; AS (*American vers., with music*); BaBo (A *and* C *vers.*); ESPB (A *and* I *vers.*); InPo; TOP; ViBoFo (A, B, C, *and* D *vers.*)
(Gallows Tree, The, D *vers.*) BaBo
(Golden Ball, The, B *vers.*) BaBo
(Hangman Tree, The, *with music.*) BFSS
(Hangman's Tree, The.) ExPo
(Hangsaman, *with music.*) TrAS
(Maid Saved from the Gallows, The.) AWP

Maid, I dare not tell her name, A. The Nameless Maiden. *Unknown.* ErPo
Maid I Left Behind, The, *with music.* *Unknown.* ShS
Maid I Love, The. Walter Savage Landor. EPN
(Kiss, The.) OBVV
Maid in the Mill, The, *sel.* John Fletcher *and* William Rowley.
Come Follow Me, You Country Lasses. SeCL
Maid in the Rice-Fields, The. Viola Meynell. MoBrPo (1942 ed.)
Maid Marian, *sels.* Thomas Love Peacock.
For the Slender Beach and the Sapling Oak. EnRP
(Song: "For the tender beech and the sapling oak.") OHIP; PRWS
(Greenwood Tree, The.) GTSE
(Oak and the Beech, The.) OTPC
Friar, The. SD
Song: "It was a friar of orders free." ViBoPo
Maid Marjory sits at the castle gate. Medieval Norman Songs, XVII. *Unknown,* *tr. fr. French by* John Addington Symonds. AWP; JAWP; WBP
Maid Mary came to Bethlehem town. The First Christmas. Norah M. Holland. ChrBoLe
Maid Me Loved, A. Patrick Hannay. ALV; SeCL
Maid my true heart loves would not my true love be, The. Round Robin. Bhartrihari. LiTW
Maid o' the West, The. John Clare. ERoP-2
Maid of Amsterdam. *Unknown.* AmSS, *with music*
Maid of Arc, The. Gordon Bottomley. GoTL (1949 ed.)
Maid of Athens [Ere We Part]. Byron. BEL; EnLi-2 (1949 ed.); EnLit; EnRP; FaBV; FaFP; FaPL; HBV; MBW-2; MCCG; MERP; NeHB; OAEP; OuHeWo; TreF
Maid of Christ entreateth me. A Love-Song. Thomas of Hales. MeEV
Maid of Honour, The, *sel.* Philip Massinger.
"Look on this maid of honour, now," *fr.* V, ii. ACP (1952 ed.); GoBC
Maid of Kent, A. *Unknown.* OxBoLi
(There Was a Maid.) ElL
("There was a mayde cam out of Kent.") LO
Maid of Neidpath, The. Thomas Campbell. GoTS; GTBS; GTBS-D; GTBS-P; GTBS-W; GTSE
("Earl March look'd on his dying child.") GTSL
(Song.) HBV
Maid of Neidpath, The. Sir Walter Scott. BeLS; EnRP; GTBS; GTBS-D; GTBS-P; GTBS-W; GTSE; GTSL
Maid of Orleans, The (*play*), *sel.* Schiller, *tr. fr. German by* John Eliot Drinkwater-Bethune.
"Farewell, ye mountains, and ye much-loved paths," *fr.* Prologue, sc. iv. PoFr
Maid of Orleans, The (*poem*). Schiller, *tr. fr. German by* James Clarence Mangan. AWP; JAWP; WBP
Maid of the rock! though loud the flood. Taliesin and Melanghel. Thomas Love Peacock. PeER
Maid of the Sweet Brown Knowe, The. *Unknown.* AnIV; OnYI
Maid of Tottenham, The. *Unknown.* CoMu
Maid, Out of Thine Unquarried Mountain-Land. *Unknown,* *tr. fr. Greek by* G. R. Woodward. ISi
Maid Saved from the Gallows, The. *Unknown.* *See* Maid Freed from the Gallows, The.
Maid-Servant at the Inn, The. Dorothy Parker. StJW
Maid she [*or* shee] went to the well to wash[e], The. The Maid and the Palmer. *Unknown.* ACP; BaBo; ESPB; OBS
Maid That Sold Her Barley, The. *Unknown.* OnYI
Maid, where's my lawrel? Oh my rageing soul! The Enchantment. Theocritus. *Fr.* Idylls. CTC
Maid who binds her warrior's sash, The. The Brave at Home. Thomas Buchanan. *Fr.* The Wagoner of the Alleghanies. HBV; PAP
Maid who mindful of her playful time, A. The Sibyl. Thomas Gordon Hake. VA
Maid who, on the first of May, The. Old Superstitions. *Unknown.* HBVY; TreF
Maiden, The. Peter Hille, *tr. fr. German by* Jethro Bithell. AWP
Maiden, A. Kageki, *tr. fr. Japanese by* Asataro Miyamori. OnPM
Maiden, The. Rochelle Ratner. QAH
Maiden and Her Hair, A. W. H. Davies. BrPo
Maiden, and mistress of the months and stars. Atalanta in Calydon. Swinburne. PoEL-5; PoVP; ViPo
"Maiden and Mother, daughter of thine own Son." Vision of the Divine Mystery. Dante. *Fr.* Divina Commedia: Paradiso, XXXIII. LiTW
Maiden and the Lily, The. John Fraser. HBV
Maiden caught me in the wild, The. The Crystal Cabinet. Blake. CH; DiPo; ERoP-1; FaBoCh; FosPo; LoGBV; NCEP; OBNC; OBRV; PIA; PoEL-4
Maiden caught stealing a dahlia, A. Thief. *Unknown.* BBGG
Maiden City, The. Charlotte Elizabeth Tonna. HBV
Maiden Eyes. Gerald Griffin. HBV
"Maiden fair I dare not wed, A." Thomas Deloney. *Fr.* Jack of Newbury. ReIE
Maiden from the Bosphorus, A. How the Helpmate of Blue-Beard Made Free with a Door. Guy Wetmore Carryl. InMe
Maiden Gown, The. William Cavendish, Duke of Newcastle. SeCL
Maiden Hind, The. *Unknown,* *tr. fr. Danish by* E. M. Smith-Dampier. LiTW
Maiden in the Moor [*or* Mor]. *Unknown.* AtBAP; BuBa; LoBV; PoEL-1
(Maiden in the Moor Lay.) NCEP
(Maiden Lay in the Wilds, The.) MeEL
Maiden Lies in Her Chamber, A. Heine, *tr. fr. German by* Louis Untermeyer. AWP;
Maiden Makeles, The. *Unknown.* *See* I Sing of a Maiden.
Maiden Meed, The. William Langland. *Fr.* The Vision of Piers Plowman, Passus 2. CoBE
Maiden most beautiful, mother most bountiful, lady of lands. The Song of the Standard. Swinburne. PoVP
Maiden Name. Philip Larkin. GTBS-P; ToPo
Maiden of late, A. The Maid's Longing. Thomas d'Urfey. *Fr.* Pills to Purge Melancholy. SiTL
Maiden of Passamaquoddy, The. *Unknown,* *at. to* James De Mille. *See* Lines to Miss Florence Huntingdon.
Maiden once, of certain age, A. Any One Will Do. *Unknown.* BOHV
Maiden Queen, The. Dryden. *See* Secret Love; or, The Maiden Queen.
Maiden ran away to fetch the clothes, The. Deluge. John Clare. BoNaP
Maiden Ring-adorned, A. Cynewulf, *tr. fr. Anglo-Saxon by* Mother Margaret Williams. *Fr.* Christ. ISi; PoLi, *shorter sel.*
Maiden sat in an apple tree, A. The Apple Tree. Brian Vrepont. BoAu; PoAu-2
Maiden, thy checks with tears are wet. April. Robert Loveman. AA
Maiden! with the meek, brown eyes. Maidenhood. Longfellow. HBV
Maiden wooes the handsome knight, The. Sir Magnus and the Elf-Maid. *Unknown.* BaBo
Maidenhead Well Lost, A, *sel.* Thomas Heywood.
Hence with Passion, Sighs and Tears. SeCL
Maidenhood. Longfellow. HBV
Maidenhood, maidenhood. Bride's Lament. Sappho. HW
Maidens, The. *Unknown,* *tr. fr. Russian by* W. R. S. Ralston. OnPM
Maidens Came, The. *Unknown,* AtBAP; CBEP; EG; FlW; LO; PoEL-1, *longer vers.*; PoG; ViBoPo
(Bailey Beareth the Bell Away, The.) ExPo; LiTB; SeCePo, *longer vers.*; SeCeV
(Bridal Morning.) OBEV (new ed.)
(Lily and the Rose, The.) DTC; OxBoLi; StP
(Song: "Maidens came, The.") ThWaDe
(Young Girl's Song.) TrGrPo
Maiden's Complaint, The. Brian Merriman, *tr. fr. Modern Irish by* Arland Ussher. *Fr.* The Midnight Court. LiTW
Maiden's Denial, A. *Unknown.* ErPo
(Reluctant Lady, The.) UnTE
Maidens, gather not the yew. Prologue to a Saga. Dorothy Parker. InMe
Maidens have come forth, The. The Maidens. *Unknown.* OnPM
Maiden's Ideal of a Husband, A. Henry Carey. *Fr.* The Contrivances. HBV
Maidens, kilt your skirts and go. Celia's Home-coming. Agnes Mary Frances Robinson. OBEV (new ed.); OBVV; VA

Maidens rise & come away. *Unknown.* SeCSL
Maidens shall weep at merry morn. The Summer Malison. Gerard Manley Hopkins. CMoP; PoEL-5
Maidens who this bursting [*or* burning] May. A Young Man's Song. William Bell. FaBoTw; NePoEA
Maidens, why spare ye? To Cupid. Michael Drayton. ElL
Maidens young and virgins tender. Invocation. Horace. *Fr.* Odes. AWP; JAWP; WBP
Maid's Answer, The. *Unknown.* PeRV
Maids Are Simple. Thomas Campion. TuPP
Maid's Complaint, A. Thomas Campion. *See* My Love Hath Vowed He Will Forsake Me.
Maid's Complaint for want of a Dil Doul, The. *Unknown.* CoMu
Maids Conjuring Book, The. *Unknown.* CoMu
Maid's Husband, The. Henry Carey. Two Songs, 2. WaPE
Maid's Lament, The. Walter Savage Landor. *Fr.* The Citation and Examination of William Shakespeare. GTBS; HBV; OBEV; OBNC; OBRV; OBVV; VA
Maid's Last Prayer, The, *sel.* Thomas Southerne.
Though You Make No Return. SeCL
(Song, A, Set by H. Purcell, and Sung by Mrs. Hodgson.) SeEP
Maid's Longing, The. Thomas d'Urfey. *Fr.* Pills to Purge Melancholy. SiTL
Maid's Metamorphosis, The. *Unknown.* *See* Mayde's Metamorphosis, The.
Maids need no more their silver piss-pots scoure. On Melting down the Plate; or, The Piss-Pot's Farewel, 1697. *Unknown.* PeRV
Maids of Elfin-Mere, The. William Allingham. IrPN; OnYI
"Maids of Honour, The." *Unknown.* CoMu
Maids of Simcoe, The, *with music.* *Unknown.* ShS
Maid's Thought, The. Robinson Jeffers. BoLP; ErPo
Maids to bed and cover coal. The Bellman's Song. *Unknown.* DiPo; ElL; SeCePo
Maid's Tragedy, The, *sels.* Beaumont and Fletcher.
Aspatia's Song, *fr.* II, i. AWP; HBV; InPo; JAWP; OBEV; OBS; TOP; TrGrPo; WBP
(I Died True.) CH
(Lay a Garland on My Hearse.) AtBAP; ElL; ILP; InP; OAEP; SiCE; TuPP; ViBoPo; WHA
Bridal Song ("Cynthia, to thy power") *fr.* I, ii. OBEV
("Cynthia, to thy power and thee.") TuPP
Bridal Song ("Hold back thy hours"), *fr.* I, ii. ElL; ErPo; TrGrPo
("Hold back thy hours, dark Night, till we have done.") EG; ILP; UnTE; ViBoPo
"I could never have the power," *fr.* II, i. TuPP
To Bed, to Bed, *fr.* I, ii. UnTE
Mail has come from home, The. To My Friend, Grown Famous. Eunice Tietjens. HBMV
Mailed to G. B. Gene Derwood. NePA
Mailligh Mo Stor. George Ogle. IrPN
Mailman and Das Ewig Weibliche, The. James Schevill. FRC
Maimed and enormous in the air. The Feast. David Wagoner. NePoEA-2
Maimed [*or* Maim'd] Debauchee, The. Earl of Rochester. CABA; CBEP; EiCL; NCEP; PeRV; PoEL-3; UnPo (3d ed.)
(Satire: The Maimed Debauchee). EP
Main artery of fighting. War. Guillaume Apollinaire. WaaP
Main-Deep, The. James Stephens. MoBrPo; OBMV; PoPo; ShBV-1; UnPo
Main Range. James Picot. BoAu
Main-Sheet Song, The. Thomas Fleming Day. EtS
Main Street. Joyce Kilmer. JKCP
Main-Truck, The; or, A Leap for Life. George Pope Morris, *also at.* to Walter Colton.
(Leap for Life, A.) PoPo
Maine. Philip Booth. AmFN
Maine Roustabout, A. Richard Eberhart. TPM
Maine Trail, A. Gertrude Huntington McGiffert. HBV
Mainsail Haul, 2 *vers., with music.* *Unknown.* ShS
Mainspring, The. Martha Eugenie Perry. CaP
Maire My Girl. John Keegan Casey. AnIV; IrPN; JKCP (1926 ed.); OnYI
Mairgread ni Chealleadh. Edward Walsh. IrPN
Maisrie. Jessie Mackay. AnNZ
Maister and the Man, The. John Heywood. ReIE
Maitreya the Future Buddha. Gary Snyder. *Fr.* Myths & Texts: Burning. NaP
"Majestic Bird! so proud and fierce." Eagle on a Tombstone. Antipater of Sidon. OnPM
Majestic Sweetness. Samuel Stennett. BePJ; SoP, *longer vers.*
Majestic tomes, you are the tomb. Epitaph on the Proofreader of the Encyclopedia Britannica. Christopher Morley. ShM
Majesty and Mercy of God, The. Sir Robert Grant. OHIP; SoP; WGRP
Majesty of God. Thomas Sternhold. SoP; WGRP
Majesty of horns sweeps in the stagtide. In a Crumbling. Kenneth Patchen. ToPo
Major André. *Unknown.* *See* Brave Paulding and the Spy.
Major-General, The. W. S. Gilbert. *See* Modern Major-General, The.
Major-General Scott. On to Richmond. John R. Thompson. PAH
Major-General's Song. W. S. Gilbert. *See* Modern Major-General, The.
Majuba Hill. Roy Macnab. BoSA; PeSA
Makar, The. William Soutar. OxBS
Makarony Fables, *sel.* John Hall-Stevenson.
Black Bird, The, IV. EiCL
Make a joyful noise unto the Lord, all ye lands. Thanksgiving [*or* Psalm of Praise *or* Be Thankful unto Him]. Psalm C, Bible, *O.T.* BoChLi (1950 ed.); FaPON; MPB; OHIP; OnPM; PG (1955 ed.); RePo; SiSoSe; StVeCh; SUS; TiPo (1952 ed.); TRV; UnS; YAT
Make Believe. Harry Behn. RePo
Make Believe. Alice Cary. HBV
Make Friends. *At. to* Ali Ben Abu Taleb, *tr. by* Emerson. *See* Friends and Enemies.
Make haste, O God, to deliver me. Psalm LXX, Bible, *O.T.* OnPM
Make Haste, Sweet Love. Spenser. *See* Amoretti, LXX.
"Make it sweet and delicate to eat." The Eaten Heart. *Unknown.* *Fr.* The Knight of Curtesy. TrGrPo
Make me a bowl, a mighty bowl. The Cup. John Oldham. AWP; PeRV
Make me a captive, Lord. Christ's Bondservant [*or* Christian Freedom]. George Matheson. MaRV; SoP; STF; TrPWD; TRV
Make Me a Garment, *with music.* *Unknown.* OuSiCo
Make me a handle as straight as the mast of a ship. To the Blacksmith with a Spade. *Unknown.* KiLC
Make me a willow cabin at your gate. Shakespeare. *Fr.* Twelfth Night, I, v. MemP
Make me an intercessor. An Intercessor. Frances Ridley Havergal. SoP; STF
Make Me Available. Florence Duncan Long. SoP
Make me content, O Lord, with daily bread. Prayer for Contentment. Edwin McNeill Poteat. TrPWD
Make me, dear Lord, polite and kind. A [Little] Child's Prayer. John Banister Tabb. FaPON; GAP; TreF; YaD
Make me feverish, sleepless, and breathless. Prayer. "Anna Akhmatova." OnPM
Make me no vows of constancy, dear friend. Until Death. Elizabeth Akers Allen. HBV
Make me, O Lord, Thy spinning-wheel complete [*or* of use for thee]. Housewifery [*or* Huswifery]. Edward Taylor. AmP; AmPP; AnNE; AP; CBV; DiPo; EaLo; FaBV; ForPo; FosPo; GTBS-W; ILP; LiTA; MAmP; MWA-1; NePA; NoP; OxBA; SCAP; StP; TDP
Make me over, mother April. Spring Song. Bliss Carman. HBV; HBVY; VA; YT
Make Me Thy Fuel. Amy Carmichael. *See* Deliver Me.
Make me thy lyre, even as the forest is. Shelley. *Fr.* Ode to the West Wind. MaRV
Make Me Thy Mountaineer. Amy Carmichael. SoP
Make me too brave to lie or be unkind. A Prayer for Every Day. Mary Carolyn Davies. BLPA; FaBoBe; NeHB; PoToHe
Make my mortal dreams come true. Whittier. *Fr.* Andrew Rykman's Prayer. TrPWD
Make new friends, but keep the old. Friends Old and New [*or* New Friends and Old Friends]. Joseph Parry. BLPA; NeHB; OQP; PoToHe; TreFT
Make no mistake: if He rose at all. Seven Stanzas at Easter. John Updike. EaLo
Make No Vows. Grace Fallow Norton. NP

Make of my heart an upper room, I pray. A River of Grace. Molly Anderson Haley. ChIP
Make room, all ye kingdoms, in history renown'd. American Independence. Francis Hopkinson. PAH
Make room for the World-man! The World-Man. Henry Victor Morgan. OQP
Make room on our banner bright. Song of Texas. William Henry Cuyler Hosmer. PAH
Make the most of it, mood. Separation. John L. Sweeney. TwAmPo
Make Them Forget. Siegfried Sassoon. *See* At the Cenotaph.
Make this thing plain to us, O Lord! Clean Hands. Austin Dobson. TrPWD
Make three-fourths of a cross, and a circle complete. Riddles. *Unknown.* HBV; HBVY; OxNR
Make thyself known, Sibyl, or let despair. Mona Lisa [*or* Leonardo's "Monna Lisa"]. Edward Dowden. OnYI; VA
Make Us Thine. *Unknown.* FaChP
Make us Thy mountaineers. The Last Defile. Amy Carmichael. FaChP; MaRV; TRV
Make Way! Florence Crocker Comfort. PGD
Make Way for Liberty. James Montgomery. *See* Arnold von Winkelried.
Make way for the beast with chrome teeth. The Beast with Chrome Teeth. Thurmond Snyder. NNP
Make way, make way. The Stream's Song. Lascelles Abercrombie. OBMV; POTE
Make way, my lords! for Death now once again. Charles II of Spain to Approaching Death. Eugene Lee-Hamiton. VA
Make we mery bothe more and lasse. Now Is the Time of Christmas. *Unknown.* MeEL
Make we mirth. Sing We Yule. *Unknown.* MeEL
Make ye jubilation to God al the earth. Psalm XCIX, Bible, *O.T.* (*Douay vers.*). YAT
Make your cotton and make your corn. Farmers of the South. *Unknown.* OuSiCo
Maker, The. R. S. Thomas. ELU
Maker Alone Knows, The. *Unknown.* PoLi
Maker-of-Sevens in the scheme of things. The Wife-Woman. Anna Spencer. BANP
Maker of Songs. Hazel Hall. HBMV
Makers, The. David Galler. NYBP
Makers, The. Nan McDonald. ACV
Making. Phyllis Webb. PoCh
Making a Man. Nixon Waterman. BLPA
Making his advances. Tortoise Gallantry. D. H. Lawrence. CMoP
Making it, making it. Thirst Song. Denise Levertov. FRC
Making It, or Black Corruption. Donald Green. WSL
Making Land. Thomas Fleming Day. EtS
Making Life Worth While. "George Eliot." MaRV; OQP
Making Love, Killing Time. Anne Ridler. NMP
Making mountain war, here river wandered. Waitaki Dam. Denis Glover. AnNZ
Making Mushrooms. Esther Antin. RIS
Making of a Militant. Yillie Bey. TNV
Making of Birds, The. Katharine Tynan. BiS; DD; HBMV; JKCP; OxBI
Making of Man, The. John White Chadwick. AA
Making of Man, The. Priscilla Leonard. *See* This Is the Making of Man.
Making of Man, The. Tennyson. EPN
Making of Master Messerin, The. Rustico di Filippo. *See* Sonnet: Of the Making of Master Messerin.
Making of the Soul of Man, The. Upton Sinclair. OQP
Making of Viola, The. Francis Thompson. PoVP
Making our late world whole, we grow to see. Toward Harvest. Samuel French Morse. NYTB
Making Port. J. T. McKay. EtS
Making Tens. M. M. Hutchinson. BoTP
Making toast at the fireside. Misfortunes Never Come Singly [*or* Nurse]. Harry Graham. FaFP; MaC; NA; SiTL; TreFT
Malachi. Earl Marlatt. MoRP
Malachy stamped the diving decks. Superiorities. Richard Wilbur. CBV
Maladies, assembled all, The. On Dr. Crank's Victory over the Gout. Sneyd Davies. WaPE
Malady of Love Is Nerves, The. Petronius Arbiter, *tr. fr. Latin by* Howard Mumford Jones. AWP
Málaga: Port. Paul Blackburn. OPoP
Malbecco and Hellenore. Spenser. *Fr.* The Faerie Queene, III, 9 *and* 10. MaPo
("Redoubted knights, and honorable dames.") NoP
Malbrouck. Francis Sylvester Mahony, *after the French.* BOHV
Malchus. Ida Norton Munson. ChIP
Malchus' Ear. Richard Crashaw. StJW
(On St. Peter Cutting of Malchus His Eare.) MaMe
Malcolm. Kattie M. Cumbo. BOLo
Malcolm. Sonia Sanchez. BP
Malcolm. Welton Smith. BF
Malcolm./ The Saint/ behind our skulls. That Old Time Religion. Marvin E. Jackmon. BF
Malcolm Bryler. *Unknown.* SiTL
Malcolm X. Gwendolyn Brooks. BALP; BP; TTY
Malcolm X. Vernoy E. Hite. TNV
Malcolm X—An Autobiography. Larry Neal. BF
Malcolm X spoke to me and sounded you. My Ace of Spades. Ted Joans. BOLo
Malcolm's Katie, *sels.* Isabella Valancy Crawford.
"Bite deep and wide, O Axe, the tree." OBCV
"In this shrill moon the scouts of winter ran." PeCV
"South Wind laid his moccasins aside, The." OBCV
Malcontent, The, *sel.* John Marston.
"I cannot sleepe, my eyes ill neighbouring lids." PoEL-2
Malcontents, The. Dryden. *See* Zimri.
Maldive Shark, The. Herman Melville. AmP; AmPP (4th ed.); AP; CBEP; CBV; LoGBV; MAmP; MWA-1; NePA; NoP; OxBA; PoEL-5; PoFS; PoG; TDP
Male and Female. W. Craddle. WhC
Male and Female Created He Them. Aldous Huxley. ALV
Male & Female Loves in Beulah. Blake. *Fr.* Jerusalem. OBNC
Male Torso. Christopher Middleton. NePoEA-2
Malediction upon Myself. Elinor Wylie. AnAmPo
Malefic Surgeon, The. Gerrit Lansing. CoPo
Malemute Dog, A. Pat O'Cotter. BLPA
Malest Cornifici Tuo Catullo. Allen Ginsberg. NeAP
Malice and love, in their ways opposite. Caelica, XCV. Fulke Greville. SiCE
Mallee Fire, The. Charles Henry Souter. BoAu
Mallee in October. Flexmore Hudson. PoAu-2
Maltese Dog, A. Tymnes, *tr. fr. Greek by* Edmund Blunden. FaBoCh; LoGBV; TiPo (1959 ed.)
Maltworm's Madrigal, The. Austin Dobson. HBV
Malum Opus. James Appleton Morgan. NA
Malvern Hill. Herman Melville. AmPP; AP; MAmP; MC; MWA-1; PAH; TDP
Malvolio. Walter Savage Landor. Par
Malzah and the Angel Zelehtha. Charles Heavysege. *Fr.* Saul. VA
Malzah's Song. Charles Heavysege. *Fr.* Saul. OBCV
Mama Have You Heard the News? *Unknown.* *See* Casey Jones.
Mama, they're gonna give me the keys to this jail. Les Clefs de la Prison. *Unknown.* OuSiCo
Mama told me she found me a feller. Old Beard a-Shakin'. *Unknown.* BFSS
Mama writes/ "your papa's/ dad is gone." Under Your Voice, among Legends. Phyllis Harris. ThO
Mama's Advice. Kurt M. Stein. InMe
Mamba the Bright-eyed, *sel.* George Gordon McCrae.
"Day had fled, the moon arose, The." PoAu-1
Mamble. John Drinkwater. WePo
Mambo dans le Hounfort, La. Charles F. Pressoir, *tr. fr. French by* Edna Worthley Underwood. PoNe
Mamma and Nurse went out one day. The Dreadful Story of Pauline and the Matches. Heinrich Hoffmann. CIV
Mamma and Papa/ Wo-ho Lawdy. Godamighty Drag. *Unknown.* OuSiCo
Mamma gave us a single peach. The Peach. Charles *and* Mary Lamb. OTPC (1923 ed.)
Mamma, I have been in the lane to see. The Fishes. Mrs. Motherly. SAS
Mamma, let's go and see the lambs. A Visit to the Lambs. *Unknown.* OTPC (1923 ed.); SAS
Mamma, Mamma, *with music.* *Unknown.* OuSiCo
Mamma, Mamma, make me a garment. Make Me a Garment. *Unknown.* OuSiCo

Mamma, there's Rachel making hay. The Mistake. *Unknown.* PaPo
Mamma's Gone to the Mail Boat, *with music.* *Unknown.* OuSiCo
Mammon. Milton. *Fr.* Paradise Lost, I. MaRV
Mammon movèd was with inward wrath. Spenser. *Fr.* The Faerie Queene, II. ViBoPo
Mammon Marriage. George Macdonald. CBEP; NBM; OBVV
Mammon, the least erected spirit that fell. Mammon. Milton. *Fr.* Paradise Lost, I. MaRV
Mammon's House. Spenser. *Fr.* The Faerie Queene, II, 7. MyFE
Mammy Hums. Carl Sandburg. PoNe
Mamua, when our laughter ends. Tiara Tahiti. Rupert Brooke. BrPo; SeCeV
Man. Harold Lewis Cook. NP
Man, The. Stephen Crane. *See* Man Said to the Universe, A.
Man. Sir John Davies. *Fr.* Nosce Teipsum. EIL; OBEV, 2 *sts.*
(I Know Myself a Man.) ChTr
(Vanity of Human Learning, The, 2 *sts.*) MaRV
(Which is a Proud, and Yet a Wretched Thing.) WHA
Man. Samuel Greenberg. CrMA
Man. George Herbert. AnAnS-1; BoLiVe; CABA; InPo; MaMe; MaPo; MeP; MePo; NoP; OAEP; PAn; PoEL-2; SCEP-1; SeCP; SeCV-1; TrGrPo; TrPWD, *abr.*
Man. Walter Savage Landor. *See* On Man.
Man, A. Denise Levertov. TPM
Man. Pope. *See* Human Folly *and* Know Then Thyself *and* Worth Makes the Man.
Man, A. Clinton Scollard. OHIP; PEDC
Man ("What a piece of work is a man!"). Shakespeare. *Fr.* Hamlet, II, ii. TreF
("What a piece of work is man!") InP
Man. Marvin Stevens. MaRV
Man. Swinburne. *See* Before the Beginning of Years.
Man. Henry Vaughan. AnAnS-1; AnEnPo; BWP; CBEP; FaBoEn; ForPo; HBV; MeLP; MeP; MePo; OBEV (new ed.); OBS; PoEL-2; PoFS; SCEP-1; SeCV-1
Man. Humbert Wolfe. *Fr.* Requiem. MoBrPo
Man. Edward Young. *Fr.* Night Thoughts. MaRV
Man, a field, silence, A,—what is there to say? Autumn on the Land. R. S. Thomas. POTi
"Man, a man, a kingdom for a man, A!" Satire VII. John Marston. *Fr.* The Scourge of Villainy. ReIE
Man Adrift on a Slim Spar, A. Stephen Crane. AmePo; AP; CrMA; MWA-2
Man, afraid to be alive. The Cage. Martin Armstrong. PoFr; POTE
Man against the Sky, The. E. A. Robinson. AmPP; AP; APA; CMoP; CoAnAm; CoBMV; LiTA; MAP; MoVE; NAMP; OxBA; TwAmPo
Man Alone. Louise Bogan. NYBP
Man am I grown, a man's work must I do. Follow the Christ. Tennyson. *Fr.* Idylls of the King: Gareth and Lynette. ChIP; MaRV
Man Among the Seals, The. Denis Johnson. QAH
Man and a Maid, A, *with music.* *Unknown.* BFSS
Man and Beast. Clifford Dyment. POTi
Man and Beast. Francis Meynell. MoBrPo (1942 ed.)
Man and His Makers. Muriel Stuart. NP
Man and his man chanced late to be, A. The Maister and the Man. John Heywood. ReIE
Man and Nature. Robert Kelley Weeks. AA
Man and the Ascidian. Andrew Lang. HBV
Man and the Flea, The. John Gay. *Fr.* Fables. EiCL
Man and the Flea, The. La Fontaine, *tr. fr. French by* Elizur Wright. OnPM
Man and the Machine, The. E. J. Pratt. WoL
Man and the maid go side by side, The. Sunday Afternoon in Italy. D. H. Lawrence. BrPo
Man and the pitiless waters. Death-Grapple. Laura Bell Everett. OQP
Man and the Sea. Tu Hsün Hao, *tr. fr. Chinese by* Henry H. Hart. OnPM
Man and the Weasel, The. Phaedrus, *tr. fr. Latin by* Christopher Smart. AWP; OnPM
Man and Wife. Robert Lowell. AmPP (5th ed.); MaPo (1969 ed.); OPoP
Man and woman walking, A. The Feather. Lilian Bowes-Lyon. ChMP
Man-apes. Between the Karim Shahir. Rochelle Owens. CoPo
Man as He Shall Be. Rochelle Owens. CoPo
Man at Peace. Antipater of Sidon, *tr. fr. Greek by* John Addington Symonds. OnPM
Man at the moment of departure, turning, A. Ritual of Departure. Thomas Kinsella. OPoP
Man at Work. John Holmes. WhC
Man, be merry, I thee rede. Three Christmas Carols, II. *Unknown.* ACP
Man be ware ere thou be woe. Pride Is Out. *Unknown.* CBEP
Man behind the book may not be man, The. The Intellectual. Karl Shapiro. CMoP
Man Beholdeth God, A. "Angelus Silesius," *tr. fr. German by* Paul Carus. OnPM
Man bent over his guitar, The. Wallace Stevens. The Man with the Blue Guitar. CMoP; LiTA; TPM; UnS
Man, born to toil, in his labour rejoiceth. A Hymn to Nature. Robert Bridges. YeAr
Man-brained and man-handed ground-ape, The. Original Sin. Robinson Jeffers. MoAB; MoAmPo (1950 ed.); MoVE
Man by the Name of Bolus, A. James Whitcomb Riley. AA
Man by the wall snores, The. *Unknown.* *Fr.* Mad Sweeney. AnIL
Man Called Dante, I Have Heard, A. Georgiana Goddard King. HBV
Man came slowly, from the setting sun, A. Cuchulain's Fight with the Sea [*or* The Death of Cuchulain]. W. B. Yeats. AnIL; ChTr; GoTL; PoVP; ViPo (1962 ed.)
Man can build a mansion, A. What Makes a Home. *Unknown.* SoP
Man cannot look round the roadway's curve. Boundaries. Catherine Cate Coblentz. OQP
Man Carrying Bale. Harold Monro. BrPo; MoBrPo
Man Carrying Thing. Wallace Stevens. PoIE; SyP
Man-Child. Michael Breathnach. JKCP (1926 ed.)
Man Christ, The. Therese Lindsey. BePJ; ChIP; MaRV; TRV
Man Closes the Shutters, The. Lionello Fiumi, *tr. fr. Italian by* Creighton Gilbert. LiTW
Man Closing Up, The. Donald Justice. CoAP
Man comes a pilgrim of the universe. The Pilgrim. Edwin Markham. MaRV
Man Coming toward You, The. Oscar Williams. AnAmPo; AnFE; CoAnAm; LiTA; LiTM; TwAmPo
"Man coming toward you is falling forward on all fronts, The," I *and* II. NePA
Man divided into animal, A. Sun of the Center. Robert Kelly. CoPo
Man, do not despair. On the Eve of New Wars. Louis Untermeyer. MAP
Man, dreame no more of curious mysteries. Fulke Greville. Caelica, LXXXVIII [LXXXIX]. EnRePo; MePo; OBS; QFR
Man Exalted. *Unknown.* *See* Out of Your Sleep Arise and Wake.
Man feared that he might find an assassin, A. Stephen Crane. The Black Riders, LVI. MWA-2
Man Flammonde, from God knows where, The. Flammonde. E. A. Robinson. AmPP; AnAmPo; BoLiVe; CMoP; CoBA; InP; LiTA; LiTM (rev. ed.); MAPA; SeCeV; TIHL; TOP; UnPo (1st ed.)
Man! Foolish Man! On Exodus III, 14, I Am That I Am. Matthew Prior. CEP
Man fools about with self-analysis. The Collective Portrait. Robert Finch. MoCV
Man for Galway, The. Charles James Lever. OnYI
Man found a treasure, A; and, what's very strange. An Irony. Plato. OuHeWo
Man Frail and God Eternal. Isaac Watts. *See* O God, Our Help in Ages Past.
Man from Inversnaid, The. Robert Fuller Murray. SD
Man from Ironbark, The. A. B. Paterson. PoAu-1
Man from Porlock, The. Helen Bevington. EvOK
Man from Sangamon, at Gettysburg, The. Eleanor G. R. Young. OQP
Man from Snowy River, The. A. B. Paterson. NeLNL; PoAu-1; WePo
Man from the Crowd, The. Sam Walter Foss. PoLF

Man from the Top of the Mind, The. David Wagoner. NePoEA-2
Man Goin' Round [*or* Roun'], *with music.* *Unknown.* ABF; AS
Man had died on the cross, The. The Sepulcher. Annie Johnson Flint. STF
Man had something in the look of him, The. Karshish and Lazarus. Robert Browning. *Fr.* An Epistle Containing the Strange Medical Experience of Karshish, the Arab Physician. GoBC
Man has a soul of vast defines. Putney Hymn. *Unknown.* TrAS
Man has been standing, A. The Tunnel. Mark Strand. TDP; TwCP
Man Has No Smokestack. *Unknown.* STF
Man has, to pay his ransom here. The Ransom. Baudelaire. LO
Man He Killed, The. Thomas Hardy. BrPo; CBV; CMoP; CoBE; CoBMV; EnL; FaFP; GTBS-W; ILP; InP; LiTB; LiTM; MoAB; MoBrPo; NP; OQP; OTD; PoIE; PoPl; PoPo; TreF; UnPo; VP; WaaP; WHA
Man he was to all the country dear, A. The Parson. Goldsmith. *Fr.* The Deserted Village. WePo
Man, hef in mind and mend thy mis. Remember the Last Things. *Unknown.* MeEL
Man Hunt, The. Madison Cawein. AnAmPo; MAP
Man-Hunt, The. Carl Sandburg. *Fr.* The Four Brothers. OQP
Man I had a love for, The. An Old Woman's Lamentations. Villon, *pr. tr. by* J. M. Synge. MoBrPo; OBMV
Man I know has made an altar, A. Consecration. Edgar Tramp. SoP
Man I Met, The. Joseph Payne Brennan. FiSC
Man, I suck me tooth when I hear. Parang. Derek Walcott. ToPo
Man I Thought You Was Talking Another Language That Day. Victor Hernandez Cruz. BOLo
Man in a Room. William Carlos Williams. NP
Man in Blue, A. James Schuyler. ANYP
Man in Harmony with Nature. Jones Very. AP
Man in Nature. William Roscoe Thayer. AA
Man in righteousness arrayed, The. To Sally. John Quincy Adams, *after* Horace. AA; ALV; AWP; JAWP; LHV; WBP
Man in That Airplane, The. Oscar Williams. WaP
Man in the Bowler Hat, The. A. S. J. Tessimond. HaMV; POTE
Man in the corner, The. Fatigue. Peggy Bacon. OCS
Man in the Dress Suit, The. Robert L. Wolf. HBMV
Man in the Manmade Moon, The. X. J. Kennedy. StP
Man in the Mirror, The. Mark Strand. NYBP; YAP
Man in the Moon, The. "Hugh MacDiarmid." NeBP
Man in the Moon, The. James Whitcomb Riley. BOHV; HBV; HBVY; InMe; NA; OTPC; YT
Man in the Moon, The ("The Man in the Moon as he sails the sky"). *Unknown.* GaP; GFA; OTPC (1946 ed.); SoPo
Man in the Moon, The ("Mon in the mone stond and strit.") *Unknown.* MeEL
Man in the moon, The/ Came tumbling down [*or* down too soon]. Plum-Pudding [*or* Plum Porridge]. Mother Goose. BoChLi; OTPC; OxBoLi; OxNR; PPL; SAS; SiTL
Man in the Moon Drinks Claret, The ("Bacchus, the father of drunken Nowls"). *Unknown.* CoMu
Man in the moon drinks claret, The/ But he is a dull jack-a-dandy. *Unknown.* OXNR
Man in the moon looked down on the field, The. Jack o'Lantern. Anna Chandler Ayre. SoPo
Man in the moon looked out of the moon, The. The Children's Bedtime. Mother Goose. PCH
Man in the moon was caught in a trap, The. *Unknown.* OxNR
Man in the mune, The/ is making shune. *Unknown.* OxNR
Man in the Ocelot Suit, The. Christopher Brookhouse. CAD
Man in the Street. William Brown. QAH
Man in the Street Is Fed, The. Carl Sandburg. *Fr.* The People, Yes. AmPP (4th ed.); OxBA
Man in the Tree, The. Mark Strand. YAP
Man in the wilderness asked of [*or* said to] me, The [*or* A]. Mother Goose. BOHV; BoTP; FaBoCh; LiTG; LoGBV; NA; OTPC; OxNR; PPL; SiTL
Man in the yellow sweater who will, The. Rink. Dick Lourie. ThO
Man, in those early days. Corruption. Henry Vaughan. CAW; OBS
Man, introverted man, having crossed. Science. Robinson Jeffers. AmPP; CoBA; OxBA
Man Is a Fool. Joseph Capp. FaFP; SiTL
(Generalization.) TreFT, *diff. vers.*
Man is a fool and a bag of wind! Hakluyt Unpurchased. Franklin McDuffee. EtS
Man is a little world and bears the face. De Microcosmo. Thomas Bastard. SiCE
"Man Is a Lumpe Where All Beasts Kneaded Be." C. S. Lewis. BoPe
Man is a lumpe, where all beasts kneaded be. To Sir Edward Herbert, at Julyers. John Donne. MaMe; SCEP-1; SeCV-1
Man is a sacred city, built of marvellous earth. The Chief Centurions. John Masefield. *Fr.* The Tragedy of Pompey the Great. POTE; WGRP
Man is a shadow's dream! Cadgwith. Lionel Johnson. CoBE; PoVP
Man Is a Snow. Earle Birney. PeCV
Man is a torch borne in the wind; a dream. The Pilot. George Chapman. *Fr.* Bussy d'Ambois. EtS
Man Is a Weaver. Moses ibn Ezra, *tr. fr. Hebrew by* Emma Lazarus. TrJP
Man is blest that hath not gone, The. Beatus Vir. Psalm I, Bible, *O.T.*, *tr. by* Thomas Sternhold. ReIE; SiCE
Man is blind because of sin. Pis-Aller. Matthew Arnold. EPN; PoVP
Man is born, a man dies, A. Tir-Nan-Og. J. F. Hendry. NeBP
Man Is but a Castaway. Clarence Day. ImOP
Man Is for the Woman Made. Peter Anthony Motteaux. MeWo; UnTE
(A Rondelay.) BOHV
Man Is God's Nature. Richard Eberhart. EaLo; MoRP
Man Is His Own Star. John Fletcher. *Fr.* Upon an Honest Man's Fortune. OQP
Man Is in Pain. Philip Lamantia. NeAP
Man is in the fields, let us look with his eyes, A. Enigma. R. S. Thomas. ChMP
Man is most anxious not to stir. That Corner. Blanaid Salkeld. OnYI; OxBI
Man is permitted much. The Elements [*or* Chorus of the Elements]. Cardinal Newman. GoBC; OBRV; OBVV; PoVP; VA
Man is prone to hope and pray. A World without Pain. Emily May Young. SoP
Man is the world, and death th'ocean. Elegie on the Lady Marckham. John Donne. MaMe
Man knocked strongly at the door, The. The Man from Porlock. Helen Bevington. EvOK
Man knows not love—such love as women feel. Woman's Love. *Unknown.* WBLP
Man, like others, formed by God, A. The Saxons of Flint. Lewys Glyn Cothi. PrWP
Man looking into the sea. A Grave [or A Graveyard]. Marianne Moore. AnAmPo; CABA; CMoP; CrMA; ExPo; FaBoEn; ForPo; LiTA; MoPo; MoVE; NP; PoFS; PoIE; SeCeV; UnPo (3d ed.)
Man loved, heart and soul, his favorite cat, A. The Cat Changed into a Woman. La Fontaine. CIV
Man-made laws and doctrines pass. The Day Breaks. Thomas Curtis Clark. ChIP
Man-made World, A. Stephen Spender. MoRP
Man-making. Edwin Markham. MaRV; OQP; PGD
Man, Man, Man. *Unknown.* ALV; ErPo; FaFP; LiTL; SiTL
Man, matron, maiden. Robert Baden-Powell. CenHV
Man may be martyred in bondage. The Mainspring. Martha Eugenie Perry. CaP
Man may escape from rope and gun. John Gay. *Fr.* The Beggar's Opera, II, ii. CEP
Man May Live Thrice Nestor's Life, A. Thomas Norton. *See* Against Women either Good or Bad.
Man Meeting Himself. Howard Sergeant. *Fr.* The Leaves of Europe. ToPo
Man more kindly, in his careless way, A. A Portrait. Caroline Duer. AA
Man morose and dull and sad, A. Metaphysics. Franklin P. Adams. LHV
Man-Moth, The. Elizabeth Bishop. LiTA; LiTM (1970 ed.); MiAP; MoAB; MoAmPo (1950 ed.); PoCh
"Man Must Live, A." Charlotte Perkins Gilman. MaRV; OQP
Man Named Hods, A. *Unknown.* CoSo
Man Named Legion, The. Sara Henderson Hay. PoFr

Man named Peter stumbled bad, A. The God of One More Chance. *Unknown.* SoP
Man never knows precisely what is right. Essay on Man. *Unknown.* PoToHe (new ed.)
Man New Made. Shakespeare. *Fr.* Measure for Measure, II, ii. GoBC
Man, Not His Arms. Selden Rodman. WaP
Man o' Airlie, The, *sel.* Sarah Doudney.
Lesson of the Water Mill, The. HBV; PoToHe, *abr.*; TreFS
(Water Mill, The.) BLPA; WGRP
Man o'War Bird. Derek Walcott. TTY
Man of Calvary, The. "Sin Killer" Griffin. OuSiCo
Man of Crete. J. R. Hervey. AnNZ
Man of Culture, A. A. S. J. Tessimond. HaMV
Man of Experience, A. Laoiseach Mac an Bhaird, *tr. fr. Irish by* Frank O'Connor. KiLC
Man of Galilee. Mary Louise Deissler. BePJ
Man of Galilee, The. Hildegarde Hoyt Swift. ChIP
Man of Grass, The, *sel.* Roy Macnab.
"India became his jasmined youth, Goa." BoSA
Man of Kerioth, The, *sel.* Robert Norwood.
"But, this I found," *fr.* Act V. CaP
Man of kind and noble mind, A. How the Babes in the Wood Showed They Couldn't Be Beaten. Guy Wetmore Carryl. RIS
Man of Law's Prologue, Introduction to the. Chaucer. *Fr.* The Canterbury Tales. FiP
Man of life upright, The. Thomas Campion. BoPe; CoBE; EIL; EnRePo; MaRV; OAEP; OBSC; PAn; PoRA; PoSa; ReEn; SiCE; TOP; TuPP; ViBoPo
(Integer Vitae.) CBEP; GTSL; HBV; OBEV; PG (1945 ed.)
(Life Upright, The.) HBVY
Man of marble holds the throne, A. The Roman Stage. Lionel Johnson. BrPo
Man of Men, A. Leonard Charles Van Noppen. PGD
Man of Mode, The; or, Sir Fopling Flutter, *sels.* Sir George Etherege.
As Amoret with Phyllis Sat, *by* Sir Carr Scrope. SeCL
Song: "Pleasures of love, and the joys of good wine, The," *fr.* IV, i. CEP
Man of My Time. Salvatore Quasimodo, *tr. fr. Italian by* Allen Mandelbaum. PoPl
Man of Peace, The. Bliss Carman. DD; HH, *diff.*; OHIP
Man of Prayer, The. Christopher Smart. *See* Strong Is the Horse upon His Speed.
Man of Ross, The. Pope. *Fr.* Moral Essays, Epistle III. CoBE
Man of Science Speaks, The. Harriet Monroe. MaRV
Man of Sense, A. Richard Eberhart. MiAP
Man of song and man of science. The Priest. James Oppenheim. *Fr.* Night. MaRV
Man of Sorrows, The. *Unknown.* ChIP; MaRV; OQP; PGD
Man of the House. Katharine Tynan. CAW; ChrBoLe; JKPC; WHL
Man of the North Countrie, The. Thomas D'Arcy McGee. OnYI
Man of the Open West, The. Arthur W. Monroe. PoOW
Man of the rugged frame and calm, worn face. The Lincoln Memorial. Alma Adams Wiley. PEDC
Man of the World. Michael Hamburger. NePoEA-2
Man of Thessaly, A. *Unknown.* CBEP; LiTG; SiTL
("There was a man of Thessaly.") OxNR
Man of Valour to His Fair Lady, The. William Dunbar. MeEL
Man of Words, A. *Unknown.* BOHV; CBEP; FaFP; SiTL; TreFS
(Man of Words and Not of Deeds, A.) FaBoCh; LoGBV; OxBoLi
(Proverbs.) HBV
(Some Proverbs in Verse.) FaBoBe
Man on the Flying Trapeze, The. George Leybourne. ABF, *with music*; BeLS; BLPA, *with music*; FaBoBe; FaFP; LiTG; LoGBV; NeHB; OxBoLi; SiTL; YaD
(Flying Trapeze, The, *sl. diff. vers.* TreF
Man on the Hill, The. Maurice Hewlett. *Fr.* The Song of the Plow. POTE
Man prayed his way up from the beast. Reply. Janet Norris Bangs. OQP
Man prepared against all ills to come, A. The Christian Militant. Robert Herrick. HoPM
Man Proposes. Thomas á Kempis. *Fr.* Imitation of Christ, I, 19. TreF
Man proposes, God in His time disposes. On a Dead Child. Richard Middleton. OBVV
Man rejects imprisonment. Fall To. Howard Jones. NBP
Man puts your hand on the small, A. The Plains of Abraham. Michael Brownstein. YAP
Man rives the granite from its ledge. Dream across the Dark. Clifford J. Laube. JKCP (1955 ed.)
Man said, The. An Historic Moment. William J. Harris. BOLo
Man Said to the Universe, A. Stephen Crane. *Fr.* War Is Kind XXI. AmePo; AmPP; AP; CoBA; ImOP; InP; LiTM (1970 ed.); NCEP; TreFT
(Four Poems [III).) CrMA
(Man, The.) BOHV
(Man to the Universe, A.) TreFT
(War Is Kind [IV].) AnAmPo
Man said unto his angel, A. The Kings. Louise Imogen Guiney. GoBC; HBV; MAP; MoAmPo (1942 ed.)
Man sat in the felon's tank, alone, A. In the Tank. Thom Gunn. CBV
Man sat in the gallery, The. Words without Music. *Unknown.* WhC
Man sat on a rock and sought, A. Prehistoric Smith. David Law Proudfit. BOHV
Man Saw a Ball of Gold in the Sky, A. Stephen Crane. The Black Riders, XXXV. AmP; EvOK; LiTA; NePA; OTD; PoPl; PoPo
Man Saw a Ball of Gold, A. Ron Padgett. ANYP
Man shall come into this land, A. Bard's Chant. James Shirley. *Fr.* Saint Patrick for Ireland. ACP
Man should live in a garret aloof, A. Flight of the Goddess. Thomas Bailey Aldrich. HBV
Man so various, that he seemed to be, A. George Villiers, Duke of Buckingham. Dryden. *Fr.* Absalom and Achitophel. PoSa
Man stands, A. Aram Saroyan. ANYP
Man surprising himself, A. The Truckdriver. Coleman Barks. QAH
Man, take your gun: and put to shame. Take Your Gun. Jacob Bronowski. POTE
Man-Test. Edwin Markham. *See* The Testing.
Man that had six mortal wounds, a man, A. Cuchulain Comforted. W. B. Yeats. CMoP; LiTG; LiTM (rev. ed.)
Man that hails you Tom or Jack, The. William Cowper. *Fr.* On Friendship. TreFT
Man that I know likes the bare tree best, A. Full Moon. Clifford Bax. POTE
Man that was born of a woman. Job, Bible, *O.T.* AWP; ChTr; JAWP; OuHeWo; TrGrPo WBP; WGRP
Man that joins in life's career, The. The Parting Glass. Philip Freneau. AA; AmP; LHV
Man that mates wi' proverty, The. Comfort in Puirtith. Helen B. Cruickshank. OxBS
Man that never will declare his thought, The. On the Deception of Appearances. Sadi. *Fr.* The Gulistan. AWP; LiTW
Man that was old came a-courtin' one day, A. Old Shoes and Leggin's. *Unknown.* OuSiCo
Man, that with me trod, The. Tennyson. *Fr.* In Memoriam A. H. H., Epilogue. TRV
Man That Wouldn't Hoe Corn, The. *Unknown.* IHA
Man, the egregious egoist. Cold-blooded Creatures. Elinor Wylie. ImOP
Man the Enemy of Man. Sir Walter Scott. *See* Hunting Tribes of Air and Earth, The.
Man there is of fire and straw, A. William Wilson. Malcolm Cowley. AnAmPo; MoVE
Man to Gods image: Eve, to mans was made. To the Countesse of Huntingdon. John Donne. MaMe
Man to Jove his suit preferr'd, The. The Father and Jupiter. John Gay. *Fr.* Fables. EiCL
Man to Man. John McClure. HBMV
Man to the Angel, The. "Æ." OBVV; VA
Man to the plough. Farmers. *Unknown.* OtMeF
Man to the Universe, A. Stephen Crane. *See* Man Said to the Universe, A.
Man to whom illness was chronic, A. Limerick [*or* Beer]. *Unknown.* LiBL; SiTL

Man, twisted so with loves and hates. Man. Harold Lewis Cook. NP
Man unto His Fellow Man. Norman Corwin. *Fr.* On a Note of Triumph. TrJP
Man upon mold, whatsoever thou be. Money Is What Matters. *Unknown.* MeEL
Man Walking and Singing, A. Wendell Berry. AP
Man Walks in the Wind, A. Maurice Lesemann. AnAmPo; LiTL
"Man wants but little here below." The Wants of Man. John Quincy Adams. PoLF
Man was all shot through that came to-day, The. Connolly. Liam MacGowan. OnYI
Man was called Methuselah, The, I remember. Methuselah. Rosemary Dobson. The Devil and the Angel, VI. BoAV; PoAu-2
Man Was Drawing Near to Me, A. Thomas Hardy. InPo
Man Was Made to Mourn; a Dirge. Burns. CEP; PoIE
Man's Inhumanity to Man, *sel.* BLPA; FaFP; MaRV; NeHB
Man was sitting underneath a tree, A. Seumas Beg. James Stephens. EvOK; FaPON; GaP; RoGo; TSW
Man Watching. Alan Brownjohn. NYTB
Man went a-hunting at Reigate [*or* Rygate], A. *Unknown.* BoTP; RIS
Man went before a strange God, A. The Black Riders, LI. Stephen Crane. AP
Man went down to Panama, A. Percy MacKaye. *Fr.* Goethals, the Prophet-Engineer. OTD; PoRL; StVeCh
Man went forth one day at eve, A. Tragedy. "Æ." MoBrPo
Man went forth with gifts, A. Martin Luther King Jr. Gwendolyn Brooks. BOLo
Man Who Broke the Bank at Monte Carlo, The. Fred Gilbert. TreF
Man who cloaked his bitterness within, The. Thomas Hood. E. A. Robinson. HBMV; ML
Man Who Dreamed of Faeryland, The. W. B. Yeats. CMoP; OAEP (2d ed.); ViPo (1962 ed.)
Man who drew his strength from all, A. The Lincoln Statue. W. F. Collins. OHIP; PGD
Man who feels not, more or less, somewhat, The. Sonnet: Of Love in Men and Devils [*or* Love in Men and Devils]. Cecco Angiolieri da Siena. AWP; OnPM
Man who fiercest charged in fight, The. Stonewall Jackson. Herman Melville. AmePo
Man Who Finds That His Son Has Become a Thief, The. Raymond Souster. OBCV
Man who follow English ways. Civil Irish and Wild Irish. Laoiseach Mac an Bhaird. AnIL
Man Who Frets at Worldly Strife, The. Fitz-Greene Halleck *and* Joseph Rodman Drake. *Fr.* The Croaker Papers. AA
Man who goes for Christian resignation, The. Epigram. J. V. Cunningham. NePoAm; PV
Man Who Had Fallen among Thieves, A. E. E. Cummings. AP; CoBMV; LiTM; MoVE; OxBA; PIA; PoAn
Man Who Has Won, The, *sel.* Lyman Abbott.
"I want to walk by the side of the man." OTD
Man Who Hid His Own Front Door, The. Elizabeth MacKinstry. FaPON; GaP; TiPo
Man who in his life trusts in this world, A. Epitaph. *Unknown.* TrJP
Man who invented the women's waists that button down behind, The. Nemesis. James William Foley. BOHV
Man Who Married Magdalene, The. Louis Simpson. NePoEA
Man Who Married Magdalene, The: Variation on a Theme by Louis Simpson. Anthony Hecht. CoPo
Man who met a phalanx with their spears, The. The Good Hour. Louise Driscoll. HBMV
Man who misses all the fun, The. It Can Be Done. *Unknown* PoToHe (new ed.)
Man who never saw our land, The. He Ought to Know! John A. Stone. SGR
Man Who Rode to Conemaugh, The. John Eliot Bowen. PAH
Man who saw the light hanging on the tall end, The. The Borrower of Salt. Oscar Williams. *Fr* Variations on a Theme. LiTA; NePA
Man who seeks one thing in life, and but one, The. One Thing. "Owen Meredith." OQP; WBLP
Man who sold his lawn to standard oil, The. The War Against the Trees. Stanley Kunitz. PPON
Man Who Thinks He Can, The. Walter D. Wintle. *See* Thinking.
Man Who Thought He Was a Horse, The. Thomas Hornsby Ferril. NePoAm-2
Man Who Wanted to Be a Seagull, The. J. R. Hervey. AnNZ
Man who was about to hang himself, A. Circumstance. *Unknown, tr. by* Shelley. CBEP; MBW-2
Man, who with undaunted toils, The. The Elephant and the Bookseller. John Gay. *Fr.* Fables. EiCP; LoBV
Man Whom Men Deplore, A. Alfred Kreymborg. HBMV
Man Whom the Sea Kept Awake, The. Robert Bly. NePoEA
Man whose height his fear improved he, The. Medgar Evers. Gwendolyn Brooks. NoP
Man whose name was Johnny Sands, A. Johnny Sands. John Sinclair. CoMu; ViBoFo
Man Whose Thoughts, The. Sir Edward Dyer. TuPP
Man will need, A/ before his death. Winter Breath. Edward Weismiller. PoMa
Man with a Bull-Tongue Plow, *sel.* Jesse Stuart.
"There is shrill music in high winds at night," *st.* 293. PoMa
Man with a Furnace in His Hand. Lance Jeffers. BF
Man with a Hammer, The. Anna Wickham. MeWo
Man with a Little Pleated Piano, A. Winifred Welles. FaPON; GaP
Man with a marvelous mug, A. A Ballad in "G." Eugene Fitch Ware. PoLF
Man with a scythe: the torrent of his swing. Gardens No Emblems. Donald Davie. LiTM (1970 ed.); NePoEA-2
Man with his burning soul. Truth. John Masefield. WGRP
Man with his lion under the shed of wars, The. The Song of the Borderguard. Robert Duncan. NeAP
Man with nothing to do (to prove or verify), A. A Summer Fable, from Montaigne. Helen Bevington. NYTB
Man with One Small Hand. P. K. Page. MoCV; OBCV
Man with the blood in his sight, The. To Strike for Night. Lebert Bethune. NBP
Man with the Blue Guitar, The. Wallace Stevens. LiTA
Sels.
"I cannot bring a world quite round." CMoP
"Man bent over his guitar, The." CMoP; TPM; UnS
"Tom-tom, c'est moi. The blue guitar." CMoP
"Tune beyond us as we are, A." CMoP
Man with the Broken Fingers, The. Carl Sandburg. PoFr
Man With the Hoe, The. Edwin Markham. AA; AmePo; AmLP; AnAmPo; AnFE; APA; BLPA; CoAnAm; DD; EaLo; FaFP; FaPL; GTBS-W; HBV; LiTA; LiTM; MAP; MaRV; MCCG; MoAmPo; NAMP; NeHB; NeMA; OHFP; OQP; OTD; PEDC; PFY; PoFr; PoMa; PoPo; PPON; SoP; TreF; TrGrPo; TRV; WBLP; WGRP; WoL
"Bowed by the weight of centuries he leans," *sel.* WOW
Man with the Hoe, The; a Reply. John Vance Cheney. AA; DD, *abr.*
(Man with the Hoe, The.) HBV
Man with the Hollow Breast, The. Tania van Zyl. PeSA
Man with the Rake, The. Christopher Morley. *Fr.* Translations from the Chinese. EvOK
Man with Three Friends, The. Dora Greenwell. OBVV
Man Within, The. Annemarie Ewing. NePoAm-2
Man without a Road, The, X. Erik Lindegren, *tr. fr. Swedish by* Richard B. Vowles. LiTW
Man without Faith, The. Richard Church. MoRP; POTE; WePo
Man without Sense of Direction. John Crowe Ransom. LiTM (rev. ed.); NoP; OxBA
Man Writes to a Part of Himself, A. Robert Bly. PoIE (1970 ed.)
Man you know, assured and kind, The. Almost Human. C. Day Lewis. CMoP
"Man, you too, aren't you, one of these rough followers of the criminal?" In the Servants' Quarters. Thomas Hardy. MoAB; MoBrPo; MoRP
Man Young and Old, A, *sel.* W. B. Yeats.
Friends of His Youth, The. AtBAP
Man, your whole history. Brother Harlem Bedford Watts Tells Mr. Charlie Where Its At. Bobb Hamilton. BF
Mana Aboda. T. E. Hulme. FaBoMo
Management Area of Cherokee, The. The Trout Map. Allen Tate. FaBoMo
Managers, The. W. H. Auden. EnLit
Manager's desk revolves in business circles, The. The Daily Round. Ronald McCuaig. BoAV

Manahatta. . ./ A lovely name, he thought, and a lovely island. Early Dutch. Jennie M. Palen. GoYe
Mañanitas de Jalisco. *Unknown.* *See* Early Mornings.
Manassas. Catherine Anne Warfield. MC; PAH
Manchouli. William Empson. CoBMV
Manciple's Tale, The, *sel.* Chaucer. *Fr.* The Canterbury Tales.
Take Any Bird. OA
(Lat Take a Cat, *6ll.*) ChTr
Mandalay. Kipling. ATP; BEL; BoLiVe; BrPo; EnLi-2; EnLit; FaBV; HBV; LiTB; LiTM (rev. ed.); MoBrPo; PoVP; ShBV-2; SiTL; StaSt; TOP; TreF; TrGrPo; YT
Mandarin on the Air. Christopher Morley. PoMa
Mandevil's river of dry jewels grows. Part of Mandevil's Travels. William Empson. AtBAP
Mandoline, The. Jean Kenward. MuSP
Mandoline. Paul Verlaine, *tr. fr. French by* Arthur Symons. AWP; JAWP; OBMV; WBP
Mandrake Hert, The. Sidney Goodsir Smith. AtBAP; OxBS
Mandrake's Song. Thomas Lovell Beddoes. *Fr.* Death's Jest Book. NBM; PeER
Mandylion. Phyllis Harris. ThO
Mandy's Lay. Louis Untermeyer. StaSt
Mandy's Religion. Alice Corbin. *Fr.* Echoes of Childhood. PoNe
Manerathiak's Song. *Unknown, tr. fr. Eskimo by* Raymond De Coccola *and* Paul King. WHW
Manere of the Crying of ane Playe, The. William Dunbar. AtBAP
Manet: The Execution of Emperor Maximilian. W. D. Snodgrass. AmPC
Manfred. George Meredith. EPN
Manfred; a Dramatic Poem. Byron. BEL; EnLi-2 (1939 ed.); EnRP; EPN; MBW-2; MERP
Sels.
Coliseum, The, *fr.* III, iv. MCCG
Incantation, An, I, i. OBRV
Mangoes, The. Duraciné Vaval, *tr. fr. French by* Donald Devenish Walsh. PoNe
Mangers. W. H. Davies. MoRP
Mangrove in Crome. Clark Coolidge. ANYP
Mangy and gaunt I walk the tiles tonight. An Alley Cat. Nancy Byrd Turner. CIV
Manhattan. Morris Abel Beer. AmFN
Manhattan. Margaret Elward Lawless. PoMa
Manhattan. Charles Hanson Towne. SoP
Manhattan! All your symmetry of steel. Manhattan. Margaret Elward Lawless. PoMa
Manhattan Epitaphs: Lawyer. Alfred Kreymborg. OCS
Manhattan Lullaby. Rachel Field. AmFN; BiCB; OCS
Manhattan Menagerie. Joseph Cherwinski. GoYe
Manhole Covers. Karl Shapiro. AmFN; GoJo
Manhood. Oliver Wendell Holmes. *Fr.* Wind-Clouds and Star-Drifts. AP
Manhood. Sir Thomas More. EnRePo; TuPP
Manhood. Henry David Thoreau. MWA-1
Manhood End. Anthony Thwaite. NMP
Maniac, The. Thomas Russell. OBEC
Manifesto. Paris Leary. CoPo
Manifesto of the Soldier Who Went Back to War. Angel Miguel Queremel, *tr. fr. Spanish by* Donald Devenish Walsh. PoFr; WaaP
Manikin and Minikin. Alfred Kreymborg. MAPA
Manila. Eugene Fitch Ware. BOHV; FiBHP; InMe; PV; YaD
Manila Bay. Arthur Hale. PAH
Mankend I cale. Christ Calls Man Home. *Unknown.* MeEL
Mankind. Piet Hein. TIHL
Mankind Is Sick. Thomas Traherne. *Fr.* Christian Ethics. OxBoCh
Manlet, The. "Lewis Carroll." Par
Manliness. John Donne. CLwM
Manly Heart, The. George Wither. *See* Shall I, Wasting in Despair.
Manly Man, The. *Unknown.* BLPA; WBLP
Manna. Margaret E. Sangster. SoP
Mannahatta ("I was asking for something specific"). Walt Whitman. AA; HBV; MAP; MoAmPo; OuHeWo
Manner of a Poet's Germination, The. José Garcia Villa. PP
Manner of her death was thus, The. *Unknown.* WhC
Mannerly Margery Milk and Ale. John Skelton. NoP; ReEn
Manners. Mariana Griswold Van Rensselaer. FaPON; HBMV; HBVY; MPB
Manners in the dining-room. *Unknown.* OxNR
Mano; a Poetical History, *sels.* Richard Watson Dixon. VA
Of a Vision of Hell, Which a Monk Had.
Of Temperance in Fortune.
Skylark, The.
Manoeuvre, The. William Carlos Williams. LOW
Manor Farm, The. Edward Thomas. ExPo; HaMV; NP; SeCeV
Manor Lord, The. George Houghton. AA
Man's a Bubble. Robert Dodsley. CBEP
"Man's a dreamer, The!" Good! That places him. God's Dream. William Norris Burr. OQP
Man's a Man for A' That, A. Burns. BBV (1923 ed.); BEL; BoLiVe; CoBE; EnLi-2; EnPE; GTBS-W; InPo; LoBV; MaRV; MasP; OuHeWo; OxBS; PoMa; PoPo; TOP; TrGrPo; ViBoPo; WoL
(For A' That and A' That.) AnFE; CABA; CEP; EiPP; EnLit; FaBoBe; FaFP; HBV; HBVY; ILP; LiTB; LiTG; MCCG; NeHB; OAEP; OHFP; OQP; OTPC; WBLP
(Is There for Honest Poverty?) EiCP; EnL; EnRP; OBEC; PoFr; TreF
Man's a poor deluded bubble. Song. Robert Dodsley. CEP
Man's a strange animal, and makes strange use. Byron. PeER *Fr.* Don Juan, I.
Man's Amazement. *Unknown.* CoMu
Man's Anxious, but Ineffectual Guard against Death. Thomas Lovell Beddoes. ChER
Man's Bread, A. Josephine Preston Peabody. YeAr
Man's Civil War. Robert Southwell. SiCE
Man's Days. Eden Phillpotts. HBV; OBEV (new ed.); OBVV
Man's Destiny. Robert Browning. *Fr.* Paracelsus, V. MaRV
(Awakening of Man, The.) WGRP
("Progress is/The law of life.") OQP
Mans Fall, and Recovery. Henry Vaughan. AnAnS-1; MeP
Man's flitting life findes surest stay. John Thorn. SiCE
Man's Going Hence. Samuel Rogers. *Fr.* Human Life. OBNC
Man's Hand—and God's. Mae Traller. SoP
Man's ingress into the world is naked and bare. A Brief Sermon. *Unknown.* TreFS
Man's Inhumanity to Man. Burns. *Fr.* Man Was Made to Mourn; a Dirge. BLPA; FaFP; MaRV; NeHB
Man's inhumanity to man is hard. Inverse Ratio. *Unknown.* WhC
Man's Life. Henry W. Frost. SoP
Man's Life. William Hammond. OBS
Man's Life, after Posidonius or Crates. *At. to* Poseidippus, *tr. fr. Greek by* Nicholas Grimald. ReIE; SiCE; TuPP
Man's life is but vain, for 'tis subject to pain. The Angler's Song. *Unknown.* SeCL
Man's life is death. Yet Christ endured to live. Wednesday in Holy Week. Christina Rossetti. ChIP; PGD
Man's life is laid in the loom of time. The Loom of Time. *Unknown.* BLPA; MaRV; NeHB
Man's life is like a sparrow, mighty King! Persuasion. Wordsworth. Ecclesiastical Sonnets, XVI. MaRV; OQP
Man's life is well compared to a feast. A Comparison of the Life of Man. Richard Barnfield. OBSC; SiCE
Man's Life Likened to a Stage Play. Thomas Howell. SiCE
Man's life was once a span; now one of those. Man's Life. William Hammond. OBS
Man's life's a tragedy. His mother's womb. De Morte. *Unknown, at. to* Sir Henry Wotton. OBS
Man's Littleness in Presence of the Stars. Henry Kirke White. WBLP
Man's Love, A. Tove Ditlevsen, *tr. fr. Danish by* Martin S. Allwood. LiTW
Man's love is of man's life a thing apart. Byron. TreF *Fr.* Don Juan, I.
Mans Medley. George Herbert. MaMe; ViBoPo
Man's mind is larger than his brow of tears. To the Victor. William Ellery Leonard. MAP; MoAmPo (1942 ed.); PoFr
Man's Mortality. *At. to* Simon Wastell. *See also* Hos Ego Versiculos, *sl. diff. vers. by* Francis Quarles, *fr.* Argalus and Parthenia. *Fr.* Microbiblion. FaBoCh; HBV; LoGBV; SeCL; WBLP.
(Verses of Man's Mortality [*or* Mortalitie].) OBS; SeEP

Man's Natural Element. Abu-l-Ala al-Maarri, *tr. fr. Arabic by* R. A. Nicholson. LiTW
Man's Need. David Ross. PG (1945 ed.)
Man's no bigger than the way he treats his fellow man, The. Measuring a Man. *Unknown.* STF
Man's Pillow. Irving Browne. AA
Man's Place in Nature. *Unknown.* BOHV
Man's Plea. Francis Quarles. SoP
Man's Prayer, The. R. A. Daly. TrPWD
Man's Prime Desire. Jami, *tr. fr. Persian by* F. Hadland Davis. OnPM
Mans restlesse soule hath restlesse eyes and ears. Roger Williams. SCAP
Man's Roots, *sel.* R. N. Currey.
"Man's roots are not in earth; while trees and flowers." BoSA
Man's Service. Fulke Greville. *Fr.* Of Humane Learning. PoFr
("Chiefe use then in man of that he knowes, The.") OBS; SiCE
Man's spirit with spread wings. Limits. Sister Rita Agnes. JKCP (1955 ed.)
Man's Testament. Adam Lindsay Gordon. *See* Question Not.
Man's Way. L. A. G. Strong. HBMV
Man's Woman, A. Mary Carolyn Davies. PoLF
Manshape, that shone. Of a Death in Winter, I. Gerard Manley Hopkins. *Fr.* That Nature Is a Heraclitean Fire and of the Comfort of the Resurrection. BoW
Mansion, string of cottages, a farm, A. The Inherited Estate. Thom Gunn. ToPo
Mantelpiece of Shells, A. Ruthven Todd. NYBP
Mantis. Terence Heywood. BoSA
Mantis Friend, The. Vincent McHugh. NePoAm-2
Mantle of Mary, The. Patrick O'Connor. ISi
Manual System. Carl Sandburg. TiPo (1952 ed.)
Manuelzinho. Elizabeth Bishop. NYBP
Manufactured Gods. Carl Sandburg. WGRP
Manuscripts of God, The. Longfellow. *Fr.* The Fiftieth Birthday of Agassiz. MaRV; SoP; TRV
Many, The. Swinburne. *Fr.* Sonnets on English Dramatic Poets (1590-1650). PoVP
Many a fairer face than yours. To a Lady. Franklin P. Adams. FiBHP
Many a flower have I seen blossom. Gibberish. Mary Elizabeth Coleridge. MoVE
Many a green-fezz pilgrim falters. The Pilgrims. Anthony Delius. BoSA
Many a green isle needs must be. Written in the Euganean Hills, North Italy. Shelley. EnRP; GTBS; GTBS-D; GTBS-P; GTBS-W; GTSE; GTSL; PoEL-4
Many a hearth upon our dark globe sighs after many a vanished face. Vastness. Tennyson. PoVP; VA
Many a lip is gaping for drink. Eliza Cook. FiBHP *Fr.* Song of the Seaweed.
Many a long, long year ago. The Alarmed Skipper [*or* The Nantucket Skipper]. James T. Fields. AmSS; BOHV; EtS; GoTP; HBV; LHV; YaD
Many a man can sleep as he desires. Rooming-House Melancholy. Eric Kästner. LiTW
Many a Mickle. Walter de la Mare. FaBV; GTSE
Many a phrase has the English language. Emily Dickinson. DiPo
Many a starry night had they known. The Dogs of Bethlehem. Katharine Lee Bates. ChrBoLe
Many a stormcloud gathering o'er us. It Never Comes. *Unknown.* SoP
Many a summer is dead and buried, A. Spirits Everywhere. Ludwig Uhland. AWP
Many a time your arms 'round me would cling. The Teasing Lovers. Horace. Odes, III, 9. UnTE
Many a tree is found in the wood. A Salute to Trees. Henry van Dyke. StVeCh
Many and sharp the numerous ills. Man's Inhumanity to Man. Burns. *Fr.* Man Was Made to Mourn. BLPA; FaFP; MaRV; NeHB
Many Are Called. E. A. Robinson. InP; MAmP; MoVE; OxBA
Many are poets who have never penn'd. Byron. *Fr.* The Prophecy of Dante. ERoP-2
Many are praised, and some are fair. In Spain; Drinking Song. Emily Lawless. AnIV
Many are the doors of the spirit that lead. Doors of the Temple. Aldous Huxley. HBMV
Many are the joys. Intimations of Sublimity. Wordsworth. *Fr.* The Prelude. OBNC
Many are the sayings of the wise. The Ways of God to Man. Milton. *Fr.* Samson Agonistes. OBS; SeCeV
Many are the wand-bearers. Evoe. Edith M. Thomas. HBV
Many Birds. Blake. *Fr.* Auguries of Innocence. ThGo
Many Birds. Anne Welsh. PeSA
Many by valor have deserved renown. Horace, *tr. fr. Latin by* Sir Walter Ralegh. FCP
Many-colored fires of fall, The. Even in These Dying Leaves. Lon Woodrum. SoP
Many desire, but few or none deserve. The Advice. Sir Walter Ralegh. FCP; NCEP; SiPS
Many Happy Returns. Ted Berrigan. ANYP
Many have painted her. But there was one. Rainer Maria Rilke. *Fr.* The Book of Hours. CAW
Many have planted. Landscape. R. N. Currey. BoSA
Many have sung the summer's songs. Winter Song. V. Sackville-West. *Fr.* The Land. MoBrPo (1942 ed.)
Many hundred years ago. Noah's Carpenter. *Unknown.* SoP; STF
Many in aftertimes will say of you. Monna Innominata, XI. Christina Rossetti. OBNC; PoVP; ViBoPo; ViPo; VP
Many Indeed Must Perish in the Keel. Hugo von Hofmannsthal, *tr. fr. German by* Jethro Bithell. AWP; JAWP; TrJP; WBP
Many ingenious lovely things are gone. Nineteen Hundred and Nineteen. W. B. Yeats. LiTB; MasP; MoAB; MoPo; OnHM
Many Inventions, *sel.* Kipling.
Song of the Galley-Slaves. ChTr; GTBS-P; PoEL-5; PoFr
Many liberals don't just. Respectabilities. Jon Silkin. NePoEA-2
Many love music but for music's sake. On Music. Walter Savage Landor. GoJo; HBV; MuSP; VA
Many loved truth, and lavished life's best oil. James Russell Lowell. *Fr.* Ode Recited at the Harvard Commemoration, July 21, 1865. PFY; PoFr
Many-maned scud-thumper, tub. Winter Ocean. John Updike. ELU
Many, many welcomes. Snowdrop. Tennyson. OTPC (1946 ed.); PCH; PoRL
Many men of many minds. *Unknown.* WhC
Many now had left him, melting fast, The. The Lonely Christ. Edward Shillito. ChIP
Many people seem to think. Nonsense Quatrains. Gelett Burgess. CenHV
Many poems may be composed upon the same theme. Praising the Poets of That Country. Howard Nemerov. PP; TwAmPo
Many red devils ran from my heart. The Black Riders, XLVI. Stephen Crane. AP
Many shapes of wings. Environs. Larry Eigner. NeAP
Many sit at Jesus' table. Few Wholly Faithful. *Unknown.* BePJ
Many there be excelling in this kind. Michael Drayton. *Fr.* England's Heroical Epistles. SiCE; TuPP
Many Things. Oliver Wendell Holmes. PoToHe (new ed.)
Many Things Thou Hast Given Me, Dear Heart. Alice Wellington Rollins. AA
Many T'ousand Go, *with music.* *Unknown.* ABF
Many trees can stand unshaded. Trees and Cattle. James Dickey. NePoEA-2
Many weary .weeks divide me. The Ship's Cook, a Captive Sings. Hugo von Hofmannsthal. TrJP
Many winds, flowing edge to edge. The Winds. William Carlos Williams. AnAmPo
Many Wings. Isabel Fiske Conant. HBMV
Many with ears/ That hear not yet, shall have ears given them. Out of Wisdom Has Come Love. E. A. Robinson. *Fr.* The Three Taverns. MoRP
Many without Elegy. W. S. Graham. OxBS
Many Workmen. Stephen Crane. The Black Riders, XXXI. LiTA; NePA; PoPo
Manyo Shu, *sels.* *Tr. fr. Japanese by* Arthur Waley.
"Because he is young." Okura. AWP; JAWP; LiTW; WBP
"By way of pretext." Yakamochi. AWP; JAWP; LiTW; WBP

Manyo (continued)
(Pretext.) WoL
Come to Me. *Unknown, tr. by* Ishii *and* Obata. OnPM
"Dress that my brother has put on is thin, The." "The Lady of Sakanoye." AWP; JAWP; WBP
Elegy, An: "Though I see the white azaleas on the shore." *Unknown, tr. by* Ishii *and* Obata. OnPM
Endless, The. *Unknown.* OnPM
"For my sister's sake." Hitomaro. AWP; LiTW
Foreboding. *Unknown, tr. by* Ishil *and* Obata. OnPM
"How will you manage." Princess Daihaku. AWP; JAWP; WBP
(Crossing the Mountain Alone.) WoL
"I wish I could lend a coat." Akahito. AWP
"May the men who are born." Hitamaro. AWP
("May those who are born after me," *tr. by* Kenneth Rexroth.) LiTW
"Men of valor, The." Akahito. AWP, *tr. wr. at. to* Curtis Hidden Page
(Tanka.) InP
"My heart thinking." "The Lady of Sakanoye." AWP; JAWP; LiTW; WBP
"O boy cutting grass." Hitomaro. AWP
"O pine-tree standing." Hakutsu. AWP; JAWP; WBP
"On the moor of Kasuga." Hitomaro. AWP
"On the shore of Nawa." Hioki no Ko-okima. AWP
"Plum-blossom, The." Akahito. AWP
Referring to Flowers. *Unknown, tr. by* Ishil *and* Obata. OnPM
River of Heaven, The. *Unknown, tr. by* Lafcadio Hearn. AWP; LiTW
"Shall we make love." *Unknown.* AWP; LiTW
(Bright Night, A.) WoL
Tragic Memory. *Unknown, tr. by* Ishii *and* Obata. OnPM
"Unknown love." "The Lady of Sakanoye." AWP; JAWP; WBP
"What am I to do with my sister?" Prince Yuhara. AWP; JAWP; WBP
"When evening comes." Yakamochi. AWP; JAWP; LiTW; WBP
Manzanita, The. Yvor Winters. NYTB
Maori Girl's Song, A. Alfred Domett. OBVV
Map, The. Elizabeth Bishop. LoGBV; ReMP; RePo
Map, The. G. C. Oden. AmNP; NNP; PoNe (1970 ed.)
Map, The. Mark Strand. NYBP
Map of Mock-Begger Hall, The. *Unknown.* CoMu
Map of My Country. John Holmes. AmFN; MiAP
Map of Places, The. Laura Riding. FaBoMo; LiTA
Map of the Western Part of the Country of Essex in England, A. Denise Levertov. CoAP; ToPo
Map of the world is on the wall, A: its lying. Y.M.C.A. Writing Room. Roy Fuller. ToPo
Map of Verona, A. Henry Reed. ChMP
Map Reference T994724. John Pudney. WaP
Map shows me where it is you are, The. A Private Letter to Brazil. G. C. Oden. AmNP; Kal; NNP; PoNe (1970 ed.)
Maple and Sumach. C. Day Lewis. CoBMV; FaBoMo; Sonn
Maple buds are red, are red, The. A Song of Walking. Katherine Lee Bates. DD; OHIP
Maple Feast. Frances Frost. RePo; SiSoSe
Maple Hangs Its Green Bee Flowers, The. John Clare. AtBAP
Maple is a dainty maid, The. Autumn Fancies. *Unknown.* FaPON; MPB; StVeCh
Maple Leaf Forever, The. Alexander Muir. PTK
Maple Leaves. Thomas Bailey Aldrich. AnNE; GN; TOP
(October.) GoTP
Maple Leaves. Shiko, tr. fr. Japanese by H. G. Henderson. OnPM; SoPo
Maple owned that she was tired, The/ of always wearing green. Autumn Fashions. Edith M. Thomas. DD; YeAr
Maple's bloom is red, The. Of Red in Spring. David McCord. MAP; MoAmPo (1942 ed.)
Maples flare among the spruces, The. Harvest Home. Arthur Guiterman. YeAr
Maples have turned, The. Fire snaps on my tongue. On a Recent Protest against Social Conditions. David Posner. NYBP
Mappemounde. Earle Birney. OBCV; PeCV
Maps. Dorothy Brown Thompson. BrR; TiPo
Mar Quong, Chinese Laundryman. Christopher Morley. MPB
Marathon Runner, The. Fenton Johnson. CDC
Marble is veined as leaves and fruit. Braque. M. K. Joseph. AnNZ
Marble mausoleum solemnly holds the rich, A. Quatrains. Salah Jahin. TTY
Marble Statuette Harpist. Sara Van Alstyne Allen. GoYe
Marble-Top. E. B. White. FiBHP; WhC
Marble, weep, for thou dost cover. On Margaret Ratcliffe. Ben Jonson. ReIE; SeCP
Marcel Proust. William Jay Smith. NYTB
Marcellus. Vergil, *tr. fr. Latin by* Dryden. *Fr.* The Aeneid, VI. OBS
Marcellus, if you mark how he doth go. In Marcellum. Thomas Freeman. SiCE
March. Bryant. DD; GN; OTPC
March. John Clare. OA
March. Elizabeth J. Coatsworth. PDV; YeAr
March. Hart Crane. BoNaP
March. Emily Dickinson. *See* Dear March, come in!
March. William Everson. ErPo
March. Arthur Guiterman. YeAr
March. Eleanor Hammond. GFA
March. Nora Hopper. HBV
March. A. E. Housman. A Shropshire Lad, X. FaBoCh; LoGBV; PoVP
March. Lucy Larcom. OTPC (1946 ed.); PCH
March. Robert Loveman. AA
March. William Morris. *Fr.* The Earthly Paradise. HBV; OtMeF, *abr.*
March. Spenser. *Fr.* The Shepheardes Calendar. PIA
March, The. J. C. Squire. HBMV; OHIP; PoSC
March. Celia Thaxter. GoTP
March. Thomas Tusser. ReIE
March. Charles Henry Webb. AA
March. Wordsworth. *See* Written in March.
March brings the lamb. *Unknown.* RIS
March Dreams. Rose Henderson. MoSiPe
March Eclogue. Spenser. *Fr.* The Shepheardes Calendar. FosPo
March Evening. L. A. G. Strong. MoBrPo
March 1st. Kathleen Spivack. NYBP
March for Youth, A. K. G. Ossian-Nilsson, *tr. fr. Swedish by* Charles W. Stork. PoFr
March 4th Anno 1698/9; a Charracteristicall Satyre. John Saffin. *See* Satyretericall Charracter of a Proud Upstart.
March Hares. Andrew Young. HaMV; MoVE; POTE
March in the Ranks Hard-prest, and the Road Unknown, A. Walt Whitman. AmPP (4th ed.); OxBA
March into Virginia, The. Herman Melville. AmP; AP; LiTA; LiTG; MWA-1; NoP; PoIE; TrGrPo; UnPo (3d ed.); ViBoPo; WaaP
March is a worker, busy and merry. March. Eleanor Hammond. GFA
March is returning to that wonder-shore. A Cry. Francesco Bianco. CLwM
March, March [Ettrick and Teviotdale]. Sir Walter Scott. *See* Border Ballad.
March, march, head erect. *Unknown.* OxNR
March! March! March! from sunrise till it's dark. Marching Song of Stark's Men. Edward Everett Hale. MC; PAH
March! March! March! They are coming. March. Lucy Larcom. OTPC (1946 ed.); PCH
March, 1941. Paul Goodman. LiTA
March of Humanity, The. J. Corson Miller. HBMV
March of the Men of Harlech. *Unknown. See* Men of Harlech.
March of the Three Kings, The. *Unknown, tr. fr. Old French.* ChrBoLe; OHIP
March shakes the pussy willows out. Spring Families. Frances Frost. RePo
March Thoughts from England. Margaret L. Woods. OBVV
March to Moscow, The. Robert Southey. BOHV; FOL; SiTL
March Twilight. Louise Bogan. NePoAm-2
March Weather. Jon Swan. NYBP
March Wind, The. E. H. Henderson. BoTP
March Wind, The. *Unknown.* GFA
March Wind. Maud E. Uschold. YeAr
March Wind. Helen Wing. GFA
March-wind sang in a frosty wood, A. The Friendly Blight. Aubrey Thomas De Vere. IrPN

March Winds, The. George Washington Wright Houghton. YeAr
March Winds. Cecil Francis Lloyd. CaP
March Winds. Mother Goose. SoPo
March winds and April showers. Weather Wisdom [*or* Weather Signs]. *Unknown.* FaBoBe; GoTP; HBV; HBVV; OTPC; OxNR; PPL; RIS; StaST; TreF
March with his wind hath struck a cedar tall. On Queen Anne's Death. *Unknown.* ElL
Marché aux Oiseaux. Richard Wilbur. FiMAP
Märchen, The. Randall Jarrell. CMoP; FiMAP
Marching. Isaac Rosenberg. BrPo
Marching. Charles Simic. YAP
Marching Along. Robert Browning. Cavalier Tunes, I. ATP (1935 ed.); BEL; EnLi-2; EnLit; EPN; HBV; MCCG; OAEP; PoVP; ShBV-1; TOP; VA
Marching Song. Dana Burnet. MC; PAH
Marching Song. Robert Louis Stevenson. BoTP; FaPON; OTPC; TiPo
Marching Song. Ernst Toller, *tr. fr. German.* MaRV
Marching Song of Stark's Man, The. Edward Everett Hale. MC; PAH
Marching Song of the California Gold Rush, The. *Unknown. See* I Come From Salem City.
Marching through Georgia. Henry Clay Work. OTPC; PaA; PAH
Marcia and I went over the curve. Millions of Strawberries. Genevieve Taggard. FaPON; GoTP; MoShBr; MPB; TiPo
Marco Bozzaris. Fitz-Greene Halleck. AA; BeLS; FOL; GN; HBV; HoPM; PFY; TreF; WBLP
Marco Polo. Clarence Day. BOHV
Marcus Antoninus Cui Cognomen Erat Aurelius. Burns Singer. OxBS
Marcus Argentarius. Kenneth Rexroth. CrMA
Marcus Curtius. Oliver St. John Gogarty. OBMV
Marcus, the sluggard, dreamed he ran a race. The Sluggard. Lucilius. SD
Marcus, thou maker of idols, inspector of portents. Epigram on Marcus the Gnostic. St. Pothinus. CAW
Marcus Tullius Cicero's Death. Theodore Beza, *tr. fr. Latin by* Nicholas Grimald. ReIE
"Now have I lived, O Rome, enough for me," *sel.* TuPP
Mardi, *sel.* Herman Melville.
We Fish. GoTP
Mare, A. Kate Barnes. NYBP
Mare Liberum. Henry van Dyke. PaA; PAH
Mare Mediterraneum. John Nichol. VA
Mare Nostrum. Joel Oppenheimer. NeAP
Mare roamed soft about the slope, The. Orchard. Ruth Stone. TwAmPo
Mares of the Camargue, The. Frédéric Mistral, *tr. fr. Provençal by* George Meredith. *Fr.* Mirèio. AWP; PoPl
Margaret. Charles Cotton. *See* Resolution in Four Sonnets...Concerning Four Rural Sisters.
Margaret. Walter Savage Landor. *See* Mother, I Cannot Mind My Wheel.
Margaret. Craig Sterry. QAH
Margaret and Dora. Thomas Campbell. HBV
Margaret, are you grieving? Spring and Fall. Gerard Manley Hopkins. AnFE; BrPo; BWP; CaFP; CBV; ChTr; CMoP; DiPo; ELP; EnL; ExPo; FosPo; GoJo; GTBS-P; GTBS-W; ILP; LiTB; LiTM; MaPo (1969 ed.); MoAB; MoPo; MoVE; NoP; OAEP; PAn; PeVV; PIA; PoAn; PoE; PoEL-5; PoeP; PoFS; PoIE; PoPl; PoRA; PPON; PoSa; ReMP; SeCeV; SoP; TDP; ThWaDe; ViPo (1962 ed.); ViPP
Margaret Fuller. Amos Bronson Alcott. AA
Margaret Grady—I fear she will burn. The Witch. Katharine Tynan. OnYI
Margaret Love Peacock [for Her Tombstone, 1826]. Thomas Love Peacock. OBNC; OBRV; VA
Margaret mentioned Indians. Indians. John Fandel. AmFN; NYBP; RePo
Margaret my sweetest, Margaret I must go. The Souldiers Farewel to His Love. *Unknown.* CoMu
Margaret; or, The Ruined Cottage. Wordsworth. *Fr.* The Excursion, I. EnRP
(Ruined Cottage, The.) MBW-2
(Tale of Margaret, The.) ERoP-1
Margaret to Dolcino. Charles Kingsley. HBV
Margaret's beauteous—Grecian arts. Margaret and Dora. Thomas Campbell. HBV
Margaret's Song. Lascelles Abercrombie. *Fr* The New God; a Miracle. GTBS
Margarita first possest. The Chronicle; a Ballad. Abraham Cowley. BOHV; CEP; GoTL; SeCV-1; ViBoPo
Margaritae Sorori [*or* Sororis]. W. E. Henley. Echoes, XXXV. BoPe; CBEP; GBV; GTSL; InP; MCCG; MoBrPo; NeHB; NeMA; OBEV; OBNC; OBVV; OuHeWo; PoFS; PoPo; TrGrPo; UnPo (1st ed.); WGRP; WHA
(I. M. Margaritae Sorori [*or* Sororis]. BEL; EnLi-2 (1949 ed.); OQP; PoSa; PoVP; TDP; TOP
(In Memoriam Margaritae Sorori.) TreFT
(Late Lark, A.) PoRA
(Late Lark Twitters [from the Quiet Skies], A.) HBV
(So Be My Passing.) HBVY; MaRV
(Some Late Lark Singing.) TRV
Margarite of America, A, *sel.* Thomas Lodge.
Sonnet: "O shady vales, O fair enriched meads." ElL; OBSC
Margate, 1940. John Betjeman. NoP
Margery Mutton-pie. *Unknown.* OxNR
Marginalia. Richard Wilbur. CMoP; NMP
Marginalia for Pentecost. Leo L. Ward. JKCP (1955 ed.)
Margrave. Robinson Jeffers. CMoP
Marg'ret of humbler stature by the head. *See* Margaret of humbler stature. . .
Mari Magno, *sel.* Arthur Hugh Clough.
Currente Calamo. LoBV
Maria. G. A. Stevens. UnTE
Maria Aegyptiaca. John Heath-Stubbs. FaBoMo
Maria Bright. Walther von der Vogelweide, *tr. fr. Medieval German by* Ian G. Colvin. ISi
Maria Immaculata. Condé Benoist Pallen. JKCP
Maria intended a letter to write. How to Write a Letter. Elizabeth Turner. MoShBr; OTPC (1923 ed.)
Maria Jane. Alfred Scott-Gatty. BBGG
Maria Wentworth. Thomas Carew. AnAnS-2; ATP; MeLP; MePo; SeCV-1; SeEP
(Epitaph on Maria, Lady Wentworth.) EP
(Epitaph on Maria Wentworth.) PoEL-3
Inscription on the Tomb[e] of the Lady Mary Wentworth, The.) OBS
Maria, when you were only one. For Maria at Four. John Becker. BiCB
Mariale, *sel.* Bernard of Cluny, *tr. fr. Latin.*
"Every day/ To Mary pay." CAW
Mariam, *sel.* Lady Elizabeth Carew.
Chorus: "'Tis not enough for one that is a wife." LiTL
Marian. Thomas Ashe. VA
Marian. George Meredith. HBV
Marian at Tassajara Springs. William Witherup. QAH
Marian at the Pentecostal Meeting. Alden A. Knowlan. ELU
Marian Drury. Bliss Carman. HBV; VA
Marian I cannot begrudge. Marian at the Pentecostal Meeting. Alden A. Knowlan. ELU
Mariana. Tennyson. AWP; CABA; CBEP; CBV; CH; ChER; GTSL; HBV; InPo; JAWP; LiTL; MaPo; MaVP; MBW-2; MyFE; OAEP; OBEV; OBNC; OBRV; OBVV; OnPP; PeVV; Po; PoE; PoEL-5; PoFS; PoVP; ShBV-4; TOP; TrGrPo; UnPo (3d ed.); VaPo; ViBoPo; ViPo; ViPP; VP; WBP; WiR
"Her tears fell with the dews at even," *sel.* LO
Mariana in the South. Tennyson. MaVP; PoVP
Marianne, Madeline, Alys. Three Little Girls. Richard Aldington. BrPo
Marie. Lola Ridge. MAP; MoAmPo (1942 ed.)
Marie de Meranie, *sel.* John Westland Marston.
Parting of King Philip and Marie, The. VA
Marie Hamilton. *Unknown. See* Mary Hamilton.
Marie Magdalene. George Herbert. AnAnS-1; MaMe; MeP
Marie Magdalens Complaint at Christs Death. Robert Southwell. AnAnS-1; MeP; MePo
Marien Lee. Mary Howitt. OTPC (1923 ed.)
Marie's face is a weathered sign. Marie. Lola Ridge. MAP; MoAmPo (1942 ed.)
Marigold, The. Blake. *Fr.* Visions of the Daughters of Albion. AtBAP
Marigold, The ("The God above, for man's delight"). William Forrest. *See* New Ballade of the Marigolde, A.
Marigold, The ("To Mary our Queen"). William Forrest. ACP; CAW

Marigold. Richard Garnett. CIV
Marigold. Louise Townsend Nicholl. RePo
Marigold, The. Allen Upward. *Fr.* Scented Leaves from a Chinese Jar. NP
Marigold, The. George Wither. CBEP; OBS; SeCL; SeEP
Marigold So Likes the Lovely Sun[ne], The. Thomas Watson. AtBAP; LO
Marigolds. Louise Driscoll. BoTP
Marigolds. Robert Graves. BrPo
Marin. Philip Booth. NYBP
Marin-An. Gary Snyder. FRC
Marina. T. S. Eliot. AmP; BWP; ChMP; CMoP; EnLit; FaBoMo; GTBS-D; GTBS-P; InPo; LiTA; MBW-2; NoP; NP; PoE; PoFS; PoIE; TwAmPo
Marina. Gregory Orr. QAH
Marina's gone, and now sit I. Memory [*or* So Shuts the Marigold Her Leaves *or* Celadyne's Song]. William Browne. *Fr.* Britannia's Pastorals. ChTr; HBV; OBS
Marine Aquarium, The. Louis Dudek. *Fr.* Atlantis. MoCV
Marine Cemetery, The. Paul Valéry. *See* Cemetery by the Sea, The.
Marinell's former wound is healed. Thames Doth the Medway Wed. Spenser. *Fr.* The Faerie Queene, IV, xi. HW
Mariner, The. Allan Cunningham. EtS
Mariner, in the green spire. Land-Fall. George M. Brady. NeIP
Mariner sat on the shrouds one night, A. The Drowned Mariner. Elizabeth Oakes Smith. AA
Mariner, what of the deep? Deep Sea Soundings. Sarah Williams. EtS; WGRP
Mariners. David Morton. EtS; PoMa
Mariners, The. Margaret L. Woods. OBVV
Mariner's Bride, The. James Clarence Mangan, *after the Spanish.* IrPN
Mariners' Carol. W. S. Merwin. EaLo; PoDB
Mariner's Dream, The. William Dimond. BeLS; HBV
Mariners sleep by the sea, The. The Mariners. Margaret L. Woods. OBVV
Mariners' Song. Thomas Lovell Beddoes. *See* To Sea, to Sea.
Mariner's Song, The. Sir John Davies. OBSC
Mariner's Wife, The. William Julius Mickle, *See* Sailor's Wife, The. *also at. to* Jean Adam.
Marines' Hymn, The. *Unknown, at. to* L. Z. Phillips. PoRL; TreF; YaD
(Marines' Song, The.) PAL
Marionette, The. Irving Feldman. NYTB
Marionettes, The. Walter de la Mare. AtBAP; MMA
Mariposa Lily, The. Ina Donna Coolbrith. AA
Maris Stella. Mother Francis Raphael. JKCP
Maritae Suae. William Philpot. OBEV; OBVV
Marital Tragedy. Keith Preston. WhC
Mariushka's Wedding Song. *Unknown. tr. fr. Russian by* Michael Daly. HW
Marjorie's Almanac. Thomas Bailey Aldrich. FaPON; GFA; MPB; PRWS
Mark. Bible, *N.T.* *See* St. Mark.
Mark, The. Louise Bogan. MoPo; MoVE; NP
Mark. Ernest McGaffey. AA
Mark Anderson. W. W. Gibson. MMA
Mark Antony [*or* Anthony]. John Cleveland. ALV; AnAnS-2; InvP; SeCL; SeCP; SeEP; ViBoPo
(Whenas the Nightingale.) UnTE
("Whenas the nightingale chanted [*or* chaunted] her vespers.") EG; LiTL
"Mystical grammar of amorous glances," *sel.* DiPo
Mark Antony's Lament. Shakespeare. *See* Antony's Oration.
Mark but the semblance of Fucata's face. Sic Ars Diluditur Arte. Henry Parrot. SiCE
Mark [*or* Marke] but this flea, and mark[e] in this. The Flea. John Donne. AnAnS-1; ATP; CABA; CBEP; ForPo; HoPM; LiTB; LiTG; LiTL; MaMe; MePo; PAn; Po; PoAn; ReEn; ReIE; SCEP-1; SeCP; SeCV-1; SiTL; TDP; TrGrPo; TuPP
Mark Hopkins sat on one end of a log. Education. Arthur Guiterman. MaRV
Mark How the Bashful Morn [in Vain]. Thomas Carew. *See* Boldness in Love.
Mark how the lark and linnet sing. On the Death of Mr. Purcell. Dryden. UnS
Mark Lee was born a month before M. L. Black Boy. Carl Carmer. AnAmPo
Mark me how still I am! The sound of feet. The Statue of Lorenzo de' Medici. J. E. Nesmith. AA
Mark this song, for it is true. The Innocents. *Unknown.* OBB
Mark Twain; a Pipe Dream. Oliver Herford. BOHV
Mark well my doleful tale. A Carol for Twelfth Day. *Unknown.* OHIP
Mark when she smiles with amiable cheer. Amoretti, XL. Spenser. OBSC
Mark where the pressing wind shoots javelin-like. Modern Love, XLIII. George Meredith. AnFE; BEL; EnLi-2; EnLoPo; FaBoEn; FaPL; FosPo; GTBS-D; HBV; ILP; InPo; NBM; OAEP; OBEV; OBNC; PoEL-5; SeCV; ViPo; VP
Mark you the floor[e]? that square and speckled [*or* spekled] stone. The Church Floor [*or* The Church-Floore]. George Herbert. AnAnS-1; ATP; ExPo; MaMe; MeLP; MeP; OBS; PoE; SeCePo; SeCeV
Marke but this flea, and marke in this. *See* Mark but this flea, and mark in this.
Marke how the bashfull morne, in vaine. *See* Mark How the Bashful Morn.
Marke how yond eddy steales away. To My Mistris Sitting by a Rivers Side. Thomas Carew. AnAnS-2
Marke well this stone, it hydes a precious tresure. *Unknown.* SeCSL
Marke, when the evenings cooler wings. To Amoret. Henry Vaughan. SeCP
Marked for His Own. Pauline Prosser-Thompson. SoP
Market, The. Gary Snyder. *Fr.* Mts. & Rivers. CoPo
"Seventy-five feet hoed rows equals," *sel.* NaP
Market Day. Abigail Cresson. HBMV
Market Day. Mary Webb. CH
Market-Girl, The. Thomas Hardy. At Casterbridge Fair, IV. BEL; EnLi-2 (1949 ed.); EnLit; PoVP
Market Place, The. Walter de la Mare. Sonn
Market Square. A. A. Milne. TiPo (1959 ed.)
Market Town, The. Francis Carlin. HBMV
Marketing. E. J. Falconer. BoTP
Marlborough, *sel.* Charles Hamilton Sorley.
"So, there, when sunset made the downs look new." WGRP
Marlborough Poems, The, *sel.* Joseph Cardarelli.
"Rose do you know." QAH
Marlburyes Fate. Benjamin Tompson. SCAP
Marlow Madrigal, A. Joseph Ashby-Sterry. VA
Marlowe. Arthur Bayldon. PoAu-1
Marmion, *sels.* Sir Walter Scott.
Abbess, The, *fr.* II. GoBC
Challenge, *fr.* V. OtMeF
Christmas in the Olden Time, *fr. Introd. to* VI. GoBC; OTPC; PCH, 3 *ll.*
(Christmas: "The damsel donned her kirtle sheen," *abr.*) PCH
(Christmas in England, *abr.*) GN
(Christmas in Olden Time.) PoRL
("Heap on more wood!—the wind is chill," 3 *ll.*) TiPo
(Old Christmastide.) ChBR, 3 *ll.*; DD; MPB
Flodden, *fr.* VI. FOL; PoFr
(Battle, The.) EnRP; PoEL-4
("But as they left the dark'ning heath.") ELP
Leaders, Old Style, *fr.* III. OtMeF
Lochinvar, *fr.* V. ATP; BBV; BEL; BeLS; BoChLi; BoTP; CoBE; EnLi-2 (1949 ed.); EnLit; EnRP; EvOK; FaBoBe; FaBV; FaFP; FaPON; GN; GoTP; GoTS; GSP; HBV; InP; LoEn; MaC; MCCG; MemP; NeHB; OAEP; OBNC; OBRV; OnSP; OtMeF; OTPC; OxBS; PaPo; PCD; PoE; PoPo; PoRA; RoGo; ShBV-1; StPo; StVeCh; TIHL; TOP; TreF; WHA; YAT
(Young Lochinvar.) HBVY; RG
Marmion and Douglas, *fr.* VI. OHFP, *abr.; OtMeF; WHA, abr.*
(Battle, The.) EnRP
Nelson and Pitt, *fr. Introd. to* I. FOL
(Nelson, Pitt, Fox.) OBEV
("November's sky is chill and drear.") OBRV
O, Woman! *fr.* I. TreFS
Shepherd in Winter, The, *fr. Introd. to* IV. OTPC (1923 ed.)
Song: "Where shall the lover rest," *fr.* III. NBM
To William Erskine, Esq., *Introd. to* III.
("Like April morning clouds.") OBRV
("Thus while I ape the measure wild.") OBRV

"When dark December glooms the day," *fr. Introd. to* V. OBRV
Where Shall the Lover Rest, *fr.* III. CH, *abr.*; EnRP; GTBS; GTBS-D; GTBS-P; GTBS-W; GTSE, 4 *sts.*; GTSL
(Song: "Where shall. . .") OBRV; PoEL-4; ViBoPo
Maroon Girl, The. Walter Adolphe Roberts. PoNe
Marooned. Rachel Field. RePo
Marquette on the Shores of the Mississippi. John Jerome Rooney. CAW; JKCP
Marquis of Carabas, The. Robert Barnabas Brough. HBV
"Look at this skin—at fourscore years," *sel.* FiBHP
Marrakech. R. N. Currey. PeSA
Marrakech. Richard Eberhart. LiTM (1970 ed.)
Marrakech. William M. Hoffman. ThO
Marriage. Blake. OxBoLi
(When a Man Has Married a Wife.) ErPo; SiTL
("When a man has married a wife he finds out whether.") EiCL; PeER
Marriage. Austin Clarke. GTBS-P; OxBI
Marriage. Gregory Corso. CABA; CoAP; LiTM (1970 ed.); NeAP; PIA
Marriage, A. Robert Creeley. LiTM (1970 ed.); NeAP
Marriage. W. W. Gibson. HBV; MaRV
"I dreamt not that love's way," *sel.* LO
Marriage. Donald Hall. NePoEA
(Marriage: To K.) MoLP
Marriage, The. Mark Strand. YAP
Marriage. Mark Van Doren. MoLP
Marriage, The. Yvor Winters. HW; MoVE; QFR
Marriage à la Mode, *sels.* Dryden.
Prologue: "Lord, how reformed and quiet are we grown." MBW-1
Why Should a Foolish Marriage Vow? *fr.* I, i. CBEP; InPo; LiTL; ViBoPo
(Song: "Why should a foolish marriage vow.") AWP; CEP; EiPP; HW; ILP; MBW-1; PeRV; SeCV-2
(Songs From the Plays.) OAEP
Whilst Alexis Lay Prest, *fr.* IV, ii. ErPo; UnTE
(Song. A: "Whil'st Alexis lay prest.") CavP
Marriage and the Care o't. Robert Lochore. HBV
Marriage Charm. A. Nora Hopper. HBV
Marriage-Hater Match'd, The. *sel.* Thomas D'Urfey.
Hunting Song, *fr.* II, i. SeCL
(Brother Solon's Hunting Song.) CavP
(Solon's Song.) CEP; SeEP
Marriage is but a beast, some say. Samuel Butler. *Fr.* Hudibras. PeRV
Marriage of a Virgin, The. Dylan Thomas. ErPo; LiTM; PoE
(On the Marriage of a Virgin.) EnLoPo; HW; NoP
Marriage of Earth and Heaven, The. Jay Macpherson. OBCV
Marriage of Heaven and Earth, The. Howard Nemerov. NYBP
Marriage of Heaven and Hell, The. Blake. CEP; EiCL; EiPP; EnRP; ERoP-1; FosPo
Sels.
Proverbs of Hell. AtBAP; EnLi-2
"Rintrah roars and shakes his fires in the burden'd air." LoBV
Marriage of Pocahontas, The. Mrs. M. M. Webster. MC; PAH
Marriage of Sir Gawain, The. *Unknown.* BaBo; ESPB; OBB
Marriage of the Frog and the Mouse, The. *Unknown.* OA
Marriage of True Minds. Shakespeare. *See* Sonnets, CXVI.
Marriage of Two. C. Day Lewis. ChMP
Marriage of Wit and Science, The, *sel.* *Unknown.*
"Come, come, lie down, and thou shalt see." TuPP
Marriage Ring, The. Blake. HW
Marriage Ring, A. George Crabbe. LO; OBEV
(Hir Mother's Wedding Ring.) OBNC
(His Wife's Wedding Ring.) CBEP; OBRV
("Ring, so worn as you behold, The.") EnLoPo
Marriage Secret. *Unknown,* *tr. fr. Spanish by* Havelock Ellis. OnPM
Marriage Song. Judah Halevi, *tr. fr. Hebrew by* Alice Lucas. TrJP
Marriage Song. William Thomas Walsh. JKCP (1955 ed.)
Marriage: To K. Donald Hall. *See* Marriage.
Marriage Vow. *Unknown,* *tr. fr. Chinese by* David Rafael Wang. HW
Marri'd. Mary Gilmore. BoAu
Marrie dear. When in Rome. Mari E. Evans. AmNP
Married in white, you have chosen all right. Wedding Signs. *Unknown.* TreFT
Married Lover, The. Coventry Patmore. The Angel in the House, II, xii, 1. EPN; FaPL; GoBC; GTBS; HBV; LiTL; MeWo; OBEV; PoVP; TreFT; TrGrPo; VA
(Why, having won her, do I woo?") EG
Married Man Gonna Keep Your Secret, *with music.* *Unknown.* OuSiCo
Married man I was asking, A. Marriage Secret. *Unknown.* OnPM
Married Me a Wife, *with music.* *Unknown.* OuSiCo
Married twice now, I've had two. Mothers-in-Law. Robert Sward. CoPo
Marrow, The. Theodore Roethke. NYBP
Marrowbine Itch, The, *with music.* *Unknown.* OuSiCo
Marry, and love thy Flavia, for, shee. The Anagram. John Donne. Elegies, II. MaMe
Marry, I lent my gossip my mare, to fetch home coals. A Carman's Account of a Law-Suit. Sir David Lindsay. BOHV
Marry, if you would put me to verses or to dance. Shakespeare. King Henry V, *fr.* V, ii. LO
Marry Monday, marry for wealth. Old Superstitions. *Unknown.* HBV; HBVY; TreF
Marrying left your maiden name disused. Maiden Name. Philip Larkin. GTBS-P; ToPo
Mars and Venus. Robert Greene. *Fr.* Tullie's Love. OBSC
(Sonnet or Dittie: "Mars in a fury . . .") LoBV
Mars is braw in crammasy. The Bonnie Broukit Bairn. "Hugh MacDiarmid." FaBoCh; GoTS
Mars, most-strong, gold-helm'd, making chariots crack. To Mars. *Unknown.* *Fr.* Homeric Hymns. LoBV
Marseillaise, The [*or* La]. Claude Joseph Rouget de Lisle, *tr. fr. French by* Charles H. Kerr. HBV; PoFr; PTK; TreFS; WBLP
Marsh, The. W. D. Snodgrass. BoNaP; NePoEA; OTD; ToPo; WIRo
Marsh bank, lotus rank. Confucius. *Fr.* Songs of Ch'en. CTC
Marsh Song—At Sunset. Sidney Lanier. AmePo; CoBA; TOP
Marshal Lyautey. R. N. Currey. BoSA
Marshes of Glynn, The. Sidney Lanier. AA; AmePo; AmPP; AnFE; AP; ATP; CoAnAm; CoBA; HBV; LiTA; LiTG; MAmP; MCCG; NeMA; NePA; OxBA; PoIE; PoMa; TOP; WGRP; WHA
Sels.
"As the marsh-hen secretly builds on the watery sod." FaChP; MaRV; OQP
"Beautiful glooms, soft dusks in the noonday fire." PFY
"Glooms of the live-oaks, beautiful-braided and woven." TreFT
"Inward and outward to northward and southward." MAP; MoAmPo (1942 ed.)
"Oh, what is abroad in the marsh and the terminal sea?" EtS
"To the edge of the wood I am drawn, I am drawn." BBV (1951 ed.)
"Ye marshes, how candid and simple and nothing-withholding and free." PG; TRV
Marsiliun at Saragossa, Charles at the siege. Charles at the Siege. George Hetherington. AnIV
Marston ("Marston, dropping it in the grate, broke his pipe"). Stephen Spender. FaBoTw
Marston, thy muse enharbors Horace' vein. Ad Jo. [*or* Io.] Marston et Ben. Jonson [*or* Ionson]. John Weever. ReIE; SiCE; TuPP
Marsyas. Sir Charles G. D. Roberts. PeCV; VA
Marta of Milrone. Herman Scheffauer. SCC
Martha. Walter de la Mare. GBV; MoBrPo; OTPC (1946 ed.); TreFS
Martha has daughters. Children of Martha. Gilean Douglas. TwCaPo
Martha with joy received her blessed Lord. Mary and Martha. Francis Quarles. StJW
Marthy Had a Baby, *with music.* *Unknown.* OuSiCo
Marthy Virginia's Hand. George Parsons Lathrop. MC; PAH
Martial. Thomas Heyrick. CavP
Martial Cadenza. Wallace Stevens. NePA; OxBA
Martial in London. Mortimer Collins. ALV; BOHV; InMe
Martial, in sooth none should presume to write. De Poeta Martiali. Thomas Bastard. SiCE
Martial Mouse, A. Samuel Butler. OA
Martial Rage. Horace, *tr. fr. Latin by* William Boscawen. OnPM

Martial, the Things for to Attain. Martial. *See* Means to Attain Happy Life, The.
Martial, thou gav'st farre nobler epigrammes. To the Ghost of Martial. Ben Jonson. OAEP
Martiall Mayd stayd not him to lament, The. Spenser. *Fr.* The Faerie Queen, III. MBW-1
Martial's Quiet Life. Martial. *See* Means to Attain Happy Life, The.
Martian Maid, The. Brian Lazarus. SiTL
Martin. Joyce Kilmer. MAP; NeMA; OnPP; PFY
Martin Buber in the Pub. Max Harris. BoAV; PoAu-2
Martin Luther at Potsdam. Barry Pain. ALV; BOHV; NA
Martin Luther King Jr. Gwendolyn Brooks. BOLo
Martin said to his man. Martin to His Man [*or* Who's the Fool Now?]. *Unknown.* NA; SiTL
Martin sat young upon his bed. St. Martin and the Beggar. Thom Gunn. MoBS; ShBV-3
Martin to His Man. *Unknown.* NA
(Who's the Fool Now?) SiTL
Martyr, The. Natalie Flohr. ChIP; PGD
Martyr, The. Herman Melville. AmePo; LiPo; PoEL-5; PoIE; TrGrPo
"Good Friday was the day," *sel.* PoFr
Martyr Chief, The ("Nature, they say, doth dote"), *abr.* James Russell Lowell. *Fr.* Ode Recited at the Harvard Commemoration, July 21, 1865, VI. OQP
(Commemoration Ode, The.) PGD
(Lincoln.) DD
Martyr worthiest of the bleeding name, The. The True Martyr. Thomas Wade. EPN; OBVV
Martyrdom. "Rufus Learsi." TrJP
Martyrdom of Bishop Farrar, The. Ted Hughes. PoDB
Martyrdom of Brébeuf and Lalemant, 16 March 1649, The. E. J. Pratt. *Fr.* Brébeuf and His Brethren. OBCV
Martyrdom of Father Campion, The. Henry Walpole. ACP; GoBC
Martyrdom of Mary, Queen of Scots, The. Robert Southwell. *Fr.* At Fotheringay. ACP
Martyrdom of Two Pagans. Philip Whalen. NeAP
Martyred Saint, he lies upon his bier, A. Lincoln. Corinne Roosevelt Robinson. MaRV; OHIP
Martyred Soldier, The, *sel.* Henry Shirley.
"What are earthly honors." TuPP
Martyrs, The. Jay Macpherson. MoCV
Martyr's Death, A. Menahem ben Jacob, *tr. fr. Hebrew.* TrJP
Martyr's Hymn, The, *ad.* Francis H. Rose. MaRV
Martyr's Mass, A. Alfred Barrett. GoBC; JKCP (1955 ed.)
Martyr's Memorial. Louise Imogen Guiney. AA
Martyrs of the *Maine*, The. Rupert Hughes. PAH
Marvel No More. Sir Thomas Wyatt. CBEP; FCP; OBSC; PoE; ReIE; SiPS
Marvel of Marvels. Christina Rossetti. OBEV (1st ed.); OxBoCh
Marveling he stands on the cathedral's. Adam. Rainer Maria Rilke. MoRP
Marvell, still your fragrant rhyme. The Poet of Gardens. Daniel Henderson. HBMV
Marvellous Bear Shepherd, The. *Unknown.* FIW
Marvellous music laps me round. Materia Musica. Paul Jennings. MuSP
Marvell's Garden. Phyllis Webb. OBCV
Mary. "W. B." ChIP
Mary. Fray Angelico Chavez. ISi
Mary. John Clare. EnLoPo; FaBoEn; PeER
(To Mary: It Is the Evening Hour.) ChTr
Mary. Thomas Curtis Clark. ChIP
Mary. Eleanor Downing. JKCP
Mary. Robert Farren. ISi
Mary. Nellie Knight. ChIP
Mary. Margaret E. Sangster. DD
Mary. Rose Trumbull. MaRV
Mary Ambree. *Unknown.* OBB, *sl. abr.*; OTPC (1923 ed.), *abr.*
(Valorous Acts Performed at Gaunt by the Brave Bonny Lass, Mary Ambree, The.) TuPP
Mary Ames. *Unknown.* NA
Mary an' Martha Jes' Gone 'Long, *with music.* *Unknown.* BoAN-2
Mary and Elizabeth. St. Luke I: 39-45, Bible, *N.T.* (*Douay vers.*). ISi
Mary and Gabriel. St. Luke I: 26-38, Bible, *N.T.* (*Douay vers.*). ISi
Mary and Gabriel. Rupert Brooke. ISi
Mary and Her Child. *Unknown.* OxBoCh
Mary and Her Lamb. Sarah Josepha Hale. *See* Mary Had a Little Lamb.
Mary and Martha. Annie Johnson Flint. STF
Mary and Martha. Francis Quarles. StJW
Mary and Simeon. St. Luke II: 34-35, Bible, *N.T.* (*Douay vers.*). ISi
Mary and the Bramble. Lascelles Abercrombie. OBMV
Mary and the Lamb. Frank Dempster Sherman. InMe
Mary Ann. Joseph Tabrar. BoLP; PV
Mary Ann. *Unknown.* LiTG
Mary Ann/ Bought a box. Present. Miriam Clark Potter. BiCB
Mary Anne Lowder. *Unknown.* WhC
Mary Arden. Eric Mackay. VA
Mary at Nazareth. Cale Young Rice. StJW
Mary at the Cross. Clyde McGee. MaRV; PGD
Mary Beaton's Song ("Between the sunset and the sea."). Swinburne. *Fr.* Chastelard. HBV
(Between the Sunset and the Sea.) PoVP
Mary, beautiful and bright. Maris Stella. Mother Francis Raphael. JKCP
Mary Booth. Thomas William Parsons. AA
Mary Complains to Other Mothers. *Unknown.* MeEL
Mary, daughter of Saint Anne. Slumber-Song of the Blessed Mother. *Unknown.* ChrBoLe
Mary Desti's Ass. Frank O'Hara. ANYP
Mary, for the love of thee. Carol: The Five Joys of the Virgin. *Unknown.* ACP; ISi
Mary Gloster, The. Kipling. BeLS; OtMeF
Mary gould of golden hew, The. *Unknown.* SeCSL
Mary Had a Baby, Yes, Lord, *with music.* *Unknown.* BoAN-2
Mary had a little bird. The Canary. Elizabeth Turner. OTPC (1923 ed.)
Mary Had a Little Lamb. Sarah Josepha Hale. OxNR; SiTL, 4 *ll.*
(Mary and Her Lamb.) OnSP; SAS; TreFS
(Mary's Lamb.) FaBoBe; FaFP; FaPON; GFA; GoTP; HBV; HBVY; OTPC; RIS; SoPo; TiPo (1959 ed.)
Mary had a little lamb/ She set it on the shelf. *Unknown.* SiTL
Mary had a little lamb. An Old Song by New Singers. A. C. Wilkie. BOHV
Mary had a little llama. Happy Ending. Harry Silleck Grannatt. StaSt
Mary had a pretty bird. Mother Goose. PPL
Mary Had a William Goat, *with music.* *Unknown.* AS
Mary [*or* Marie] Hamilton. *Unknown.* BaBo; CBEP; ESPB (A *and* B *vers.*); NoP; OAEP; OuHeWo; OxBB; PoFS; ViBoFo, *with music*
(Queen's Marie, The.) OBB; OBEV
("Word's gane to the kitchen.") LO
Mary Hamilton's Last Goodnight. *See* Four Marys, The
Mary has a thingamajig clamped on her ears. Manual System. Carl Sandburg. TiPo (1952 ed.)
Mary Hynes. Padraic Fallon, *after the Irish of* Anthony Raftery. AnIV; OxBI
Mary Hynes. Frank O'Connor, *after the Irish of* Anthony Raftery. KiLC
Mary, I believ'd you quick. Fragment. Thomas Hood. NBM
Mary! I want a lyre with other strings. To Mary Unwin [*or* Sonnet to Mrs. Unwin]. William Cowper. BEL; CoBE; GTBS; GTBS-D; GTBS-P; GTBS-W; GTSE; GTSL; HBV; OAEP; OBEC; OBEV; TrGrPo
Mary Immaculate. Eleanor C. Donnelly. CAW; JKCP
Mary, in a dream of love. Dialogue between Mary and Gabriel. W. H. Auden. *Fr.* For the Time Being—A Christmas Oratorio. ISi
Mary, in the house of John. The Mother of Judas. Amelia Josephine Burr. WHL
Mary is a gentle name. Gentle Name. Selma Robinson. BiCB; MoShBr; MoSiPe
Mary is a lady bright. Nunc Gaudet Maria. *Unknown.* ISi
Mary Is with Child. *Unknown.* MeEL
Mary Jane. *Unknown.* NA
Mary Jane, the Milkmaid, *with music.* *Unknown.* BFSS

"Mary!" just one word. Known of Him. Barbara Cornet Ryberg. SoP
Mary Knew. Ida Norton Munson. ChIP
Mary laid her Child among. Carol. Norman Nicholson. NeBP; StJW
Mary Le More. George Nugent Reynolds. OnYI
Mary, long by Boss's Kisses bored. Don't Look Now but Mary Is Everybody. Peter Viereck. LiTA; LiTM (rev. ed.); ReMP
Mary McGuire's our cook, you know. This and That. Florence Boyce Davis. FaPON; GaP; TiPo (1952 ed.)
Mary Magdalene. Richard Burton. ChIP
Mary Magdalene. Dante Gabriel Rossetti. *See* Mary Magdalene at the Door of Simon the Pharisee.
Mary Magdalene. Leonora Speyer. HBMV; NP
Mary Magdalene and the Other Mary. Christina Rossetti. StJW
Mary Magdalene at the Door of Simon the Pharisee. Dante Gabriel Rossetti. GoBC; MaVP; PoVP; VA
Mary Magdalene, that easy woman. Lent. W. R. Rodgers. AnIL; DTC; NeBP; OxBI
Mary, maiden, mild and free. A Little Song. Robert Grosseteste. ISi
Mary, Mary [*or* Mistress Mary], quite contrary. Mother Goose. BoChLi; BrR; FaBoBe; FaFP; HBV; HBVY; OTPC; OxNR; PCH; PPL; RIS; SAS; SiTL; SoPo; StVeCh; TiPo
Mary Middling. Rose Fyleman. SUS
Mary Modyr, Cum and See. *Unknown.* OxBoCh
Mary Morison. Burns. AnFE; BEL; BoLiVe; CEP; CoBE; EnLi-2; EnLit; EnRP; GTBS; GTBS-D; GTBS-P; GTBS-W; GTSE; HBV; InPo; MCCG; OAEP; OBEC; OBEV; OuHeWo; OxBS; PoAn; TreFT; TrGrPo; WHA
("O Mary, at thy window be.") EG
(Song: Mary Morison.) AWP; JAWP; TOP; WBP
Mary, most serenely fair. To the Sistine Madonna. Cornelia Otis Skinner. ISi
Mary Mother, Heart Sublime. Mother's Petition, in Wartime. Helen M. Burgess. ChIP
Mary, Mother of our Maker. The Annunciation. St. Nerses. ISi
Mary O'Brian. J. Redwood Anderson. OnPP
Mary of Bethlehem. Mary King. ISi
Mary of Nazareth, *sel.* Abby Maria Hemenway.
Annunciation Night. ISi
Mary of the Wild Moor (*diff. versions*). *Unknown.* BaBo; BFSS, *with music*
(When Poor Mary Came Wandering Home, *frag., with music.*) AS
Mary on Her Way to the Temple. Ruth Schaumann, *tr. fr. German by* Edwin Buers. ISi
Mary on the Silvery Tide. *Unknown.* ShS
Mary Passes. *Unknown, tr. fr. German.* ISi
Mary Pondered All These Things. Edwin McNeill Poteat. ChIP
Mary, Queen of Heaven. *Unknown.* MeEL
Mary, Queen of Scots. Henry Glassford Bell. BeLS; BLPA; FaBoBe
Mary Queen of Scots. Burns. FOL
Mary Queen of Scots. Charles Tennyson Turner. HBV
Mary Ross, The. Blanche Edith Baughan. BoAu
Mary Salome, Widow. Anne Ryan. JKCP (1926 ed.)
Mary sat in the corner dreaming. In the Carpenter's Shop. Sara Teasdale. HBMV; StJW
Mary sat musing on the lamp-flame at the table. The Death of the Hired Man. Robert Frost. AmPP; AnNE; ATP; CMoP; CoBA; HoPM; MaC; MAP; MoAB; MoAmPo; NeMA; OxBA; SeCeV; TOP; TrGrPo; UnPo (1st ed.)
Mary Shakespeare. Ada Jackson. PoMa
Mary Shepherdess. Marjorie Pickthall. ISi; WHL
Mary Sings. Norah M. Holland. ChrBoLe
Mary Star of the sea! Lionel Johnson. *Fr.* Cadgwith. ISi
Mary Suffers with Her Son. *Unknown.* MeEL
Mary, the Blessed Virgins name. Profit and Loss: An Elegy upon the Decease of Mrs. Mary Gerrish. John Danforth. SCAP
Mary, the Christ long slain, passed silently. Motherhood. Agnes Lee. BLPA; HBMV; NP
Mary the Cook-Maid's Letter to Dr. Sheridan. Swift. LoBV; OnYI; OxBoLi
Mary, the maiden, walked out in the country. After the Annunciation. Eileen Duggan. ISi
Mary the mother and Jesu the child. Christmas Night. Alice Isabel Hazeltine. ChrBoLe
Mary the Mother of Jesus. The Spinner. Charles L. O'Donnell. GoBC; ISi
Mary the Mother sang to her Son. A Carol. Lizette Woodworth Reese. HBMV
Mary, the mother, sits on the hill. Carol [*or* Song]. Langdon Elwyn Mitchell. ChrBoLe; OHIP
Mary Tired. Marjorie Pickthall. ACV; PeCV (1967 ed.)
"Mary, uplifted to our sight." On the Feast of the Assumption. Eleanor Downing. JKCP
Mary, Virgin and Mother. Elizabeth Seton. JKCP
Mary walked in the daisies. Gabriel. Willard Wattles. HBMV
Mary Was a Red Bird, *with music. Unknown.* OuSiCo
Mary was busy and hurried. Mary and Martha. Annie Johnson Flint. STF
Mary Was Watching. *Unknown, tr. fr. Czech by* Mary Cochrane Vojacek. ISi
Mary, we hail thee, Mother and Queen compassionate. Salve Regina. *At. to* Hermanus Contractus. ISi
Mary Weeps for Her Child. *Unknown.* OxBoLi
Mary went through the thorn-wood wild. Mary Passes. *Unknown, tr. fr. German.* ISi
Mary,—what melodies mingle. Mary and the Lamb. Frank Dempster Sherman. InMe
Mary, when that little child. Mary. Rose Trumbull. MaRV
Mary Winslow. Robert Lowell. AnNE; ILP; MiAP; MoVE
Mary wore her red dress. Mary Was a Red Bird. *Unknown.* OuSiCo
Mary Wore Three Links of Chain, *with music. Unknown.* AS
Marye, maide, milde and fre. A Song to Mary. William of Shoreham. MeEL
Maryland Battalion, The. John Williamson Palmer. AA; HBV; MC; PaA; PAH
Maryland! My Maryland! James Ryder Randall. *See* My Maryland.
Maryland Resolves. *Unknown.* PAH
Maryland Virginia Caroline. Emblems. Allen Tate. AmPP (3d ed.); AWP; InPo
Maryland Yellow-Throat, The. Henry van Dyke. HBV
Mary's a Grand Old Name. George M. Cohan. TreFT
Mary's Assumption. Alfred J. Barrett. ISi
Mary's Baby. Shaemas O'Sheel. CAW; HBV; HBVY; JKCP
Mary's Easter. Marie Mason. DD
Mary's eyes are blue as azure. Shel Silverstein. BoLP
Mary's Ghost. Thomas Hood. FiBHP
Mary's Girlhood. Dante Gabriel Rossetti. CAW; GBV; GoBC; ISi; MaVP; PoVP; VP; WGRP
Mary's gone a-milking. Milking Pails. *Unknown.* CH
Mary's Lamb. Sarah Josepha Hale. *See* Mary Had a Little Lamb.
Mary's Lullaby. Elizabeth J. Coatsworth. ChrBoLe
Mary's Lullaby. Ivy O. Eastwick. ChBR
Mary's Son. Lucia Trent. ChIP; PGD
Mary's Song. Marion Angus. LO
Mary's Song. Eleanor Farjeon. ThGo
Mary's Vision. *Unknown, tr. fr. Irish by* Eleanor Hull. ISi
Ma's Tools. *Unknown.* PEDC
Masar. Walter Savage Landor. *Fr.* Gebir, V. LoBV
("Once a fair city, courted then by kings.") OBRV
Mask, The. Elizabeth Barrett Browning. CBEP; OBNC; OBVV
Mask. Elizabeth Cox. GoYe
Mask, The. Clarissa Scott Delany. CDC; PoNe
Mask, A. Milton. *See* Star That Bids the Shepherd Fold, The.
Mask. Stephen Spender. MoAB; MoBrPo; NeMA
Mask, The. W. B. Yeats. CLwM
Mask [*or* Masque] of Anarchy, The. Shelley. CABL; EnRP
Sels.
"As I lay asleep in Italy." FOL; PeER
"I met Murder on the way." PoG
"Last came Anarchy," *much abr.* PoFr
"Stand ye calm and resolute," *sts.* 79-91. LoBV
"What is Freedom?—ye can tell." PoG
Mask of Cupid, The. Spenser. *See* Masque of Cupid, The.
Mask of Love. Thomas Kinsella. NMP
Mask of Mutability, The. Spenser. *Fr.* The Faerie Queene, VII, 7. OBSC
(Seasons, *abr.*) GN
Mask Presented at Ludlow-Castle, A. Milton. *See* Comus.

Maske for Lydia, A. Thomas Randolph. AnAnS-2
Masked Ball, The. Wilson MacDonald. MaRV
Masked Shrew, The. Isabella Gardner. ImOP
Masks. Thomas Bailey Aldrich. AA
Mason, The. Robert Farren. JKCP (1955 ed.); OnYI; OxBI
Masque. Jewel C. Latimore. WSL
Masque of Anarchy, The. Shelley. *See* Mask of Anarchy, The.
Masque of Augurs, The, *sel.* Ben Jonson.
Apollo's Song. LoBV
Masque of Balliol, The, *sels.* Henry Charles Beeching, *and others.* CenHV
"First come I. My name is Jowett." Henry Charles Beeching.
"I am a most superior person." Henry Charles Beeching.
"I am Andrew Cecil Bradley." Cecil Arthur Spring-Rice.
"I am featly-tripping Lee." Henry Charles Beeching.
"I am Huxley, blond and merry." John Bowyer Buchanan Nichols.
"I am the Dean of Christ Church, Sir." Cecil Arthur Spring-Rice.
"Old tips come out as good as new." John Williams MacKail.
"Roughly, so to say, you know." John William MacKail.
"Upright and shrewd, more woo'd of fame." Henry Charles Beeching.
Masque of Beauty, The, *sel.* Ben Jonson.
Song: "When love at first did move." GoBC
Masque of Christmas, The. Ben Jonson. OxBoLi
Masque of Cupid, *sel.* Ben Jonson.
Up, Youths and Virgins, Up, and Praise. HW
Masque of Cupid, The. Spenser. *Fr.* The Faerie Queene, III, 11 *and* 12. PoEL-1 (*fr.* 12)
(Mask of Cupid, The, *fr.* 12.) OBSC
Masque of Hymen, *sel.* Ben Jonson.
Glad Time Is at His Point Arrived. HW
Masque of Life and Death, A. Witter Bynner. AnAmPo
Masque of Pandora, The, *sel.* Longfellow.
All-seeing Gods, The. OQP
Masque of Queen Bersabe, The, *sel.* Swinburne.
"I am the queen Herodias." AtBAP
Masque of Queens, The, *sel.* Ben Jonson.
Witches' Charmes, The, I-III. EIL; PoMS, *sl. shorter*; ThWaDe
Witches' Charm, III: "Owl is abroad, The." FaBoCh; LoBV; LoGBV; ReEn
Masque of Reason, A, *sels.* Robert Frost.
God's Speech to Job. OnHM
God's Thanks to Job. MoRP
Masque of the Inner-Temple and Gray's Inne, The, *sels.* Francis Beaumont.
"More pleasing were these sweet delights," III. OBS
"On blessed youths, for Love doth pause," II. OBS
"Peace and silence be the guide," V. OBS
(Three Songs, 3.) GoBC
Shake Off Your Heavy Trance, I. CBEP; ELU; OBS; OnPM; TrGrPo; ViBoPo
(Fit Only for Apollo.) ChTr
(Song for a Dance.) EIL; FaBoCh; LoGBV
(Three Songs, 1.) GoBC
(Superlative Dance and Song.) UnS
"Ye [*or* We] should stay longer if we durst," IV. OBS; TrGrPo; ViBoPo
(Three Songs, 2.) GoBC
Masque of the Middle Temple and Lincoln's Inn, The, *sels.* George Chapman.
Descend, Fair Sun! EIL; TuPP
Now, sleep, Bind Fast. TuPP
(Bridal Song.) EIL LO
Masque of the Twelve Months, The, *sel.* *Unknown, at. to* George Chapman.
Shine Out, Fair Sun, With All Your Heat. ChTr; ELP; FIW
(Song.) EIL
Masque Presented at Ludlow Castle, A. Milton. *See* Comus.
Masquerader, The. Aline Kilmer. HBMV
Mass at Dawn. Roy Campbell. PeSA
Mass of Love. *Unknown, tr. fr. Spanish by* Anna Pursche. LiTW; PoPl
Mass of the Grove, The. Dafydd ap Gwilym. BoPe
Mass was sung, and prayers were said, The. Dies Irae. *Par. fr. Latin by* Sir Walter Scott. *Fr.* The Lay of the Last Minstrel, VI. GoBC
Massa bin an' sol' yeh. O! Link o' Day. *Unknown.* TrAS
Massa ob de Sheepfol', De. Sarah Pratt McLean Greene. *See* Sheepfol', De.
Massachusetts Song of Liberty. Mercy Warren. PAH
Massachusetts to Virginia. Whittier. AmPP; AnNE; CoBA; WoL
Massacre of the Innocents, The. William Jay Smith. EaLo
Massacre of the Macpherson, The. William Edmondstoune Aytoun. CenHV; ChTr; OtMeF; VA
Massa's in de Cold, Cold Ground. Stephen Collins Foster. AA; IHA; TreF
Massasauga, The. Hamlin Garland. AA
Massenet/ Never wrote a Mass in A. Antony Butts. FiBHP
Massive gates of circumstance, The. Trifles. *Unknown.* HBV
Master, The. Thomas Curtis Clark. *See* Abraham Lincoln, the Master.
Master, The. "C. G. L." ImOP
Master, The. W. S. Merwin. NePoEA
Master, The. S. D. Robbins. BePJ
Master, The. E. A. Robinson. AmP; GTBS-W; HBV; HH; InP; LiPo; LiTA; LiTG; LiTM (rev. ed.); MAP; MoAB; MoAmPo; NeMA; NP; OHIP; OTPC (1946 ed.); PaA; PFY; PoRL
Master and Man. Sir Henry Newbolt. WhC
Master and the Leaves, The. Thomas Hardy. PoIE
Master and the slave go hand in hand, The. Sonnet. E. A. Robinson. PP
Master Artisan, make me over. "Tell Ye the Faint of Heart." Francis J. Rock. JKCP (1955 ed.)
Master Blacksmith, The. Arnold Andrews. OQP
Master Brunetto, this my little maid. Sonnet: To Brunnetto Latini. Dante. AWP
Master Builder, The. Myra Brooks Welch. SoP
Master Canterel at Locas Solus. David Shapiro. ANYP
Master-Chord, The. William Caldwell Roscoe. VA
Master City, The. Rose J. Orente. GoYe
Master, destined to be. A Small Thought Speaks for the Flesh. Carleton Drewry. MoRP
Master Edwards' May. Richard Edwards. *See* M. Edwards' May.
Master-Foe, The. William Baylebridge. *Fr.* Sextains. BoAV
Master Francesco, I have come to thee. Petrarch. Giosuè Carducci. AWP
Master Francis Beaumont's Letter to Ben Jonson. Francis Beaumont. BEL
(Francis Beaumont's Letter from the Country to Jonson.) SeCP
(Letter to Ben Jonson, A.) LoBV
(M. Francis Beaumont's Letter to Ben Jonson.) SeEP
(Mr. Francis Beaumont's Letter. . . *abr.*) OBS; ViBoPo
"What things have we seen, *sel.*" EnLit
"Master has come over Jordan, The." Christ and the Little Ones. Julia Gill. BLPA
Master He was hungry, The. The Blessing. Mary Colborne-Veel. BoAu
Master Hugues of Saxe-Gotha. Robert Browning. MuSP
Master I have, and I am his man. Master and Man. Mother Goose. NA; OxNR; TiPo
Master-Knot, The. Omar Khayyám, *tr. fr. Persian by* Edward Fitzgerald. *Fr.* The Rubáiyát. OnPM
Master Mariner, The. George Sterling. HBV; MAP; MoAmPo (1942 ed.)
Master Musician. Margaret Evelyn Singleton. ChIP
Master, no offering. My Offering. Edwin P. Parker. SoP
Master of discords John. The Harper. *Unknown.* AnIL; KiLC
Master of human destinies am I. Opportunity. John James Ingalls. AA; FaFP; HBV; HBVY; MaRV; OHFP; OQP; PoLF; TreF; WBLP; YaD
Master of Laborers, The. George Edward Day. PGD
Master of metaphor, at three. David. Walker Gibson. CrMA; NePoAm
Master of My Boat, The. Joseph Addison Richards, *wr. at. to* George Macdonald. OQP
(Boat, The.) MaRV
Master of spirits!/ hear me: King of Souls. The Darkness. Lionel Johnson. BrPo
Master of the Golden Glow, The. James Schuyler. ANYP

Master of Time, The. Jan van Nijlen, *tr. fr. Dutch by* A. J. Barnouw. LiTW
Master-Player, The. Paul Laurence Dunbar. MaRV; SoP; TRV
Master Singers, The. Rhys Carpenter. WGRP
Master Sky-Lark, *sels.* John Bennett.
Sky-Lark's Song, The. AA
Song of the Hunt, The. AA
Master-songs are ended, and the man, The. Walt Whitman. E. A. Robinson. AmePo; AmP; NePA; OxBA
Master Spirit, The. George Chapman. *Fr.* The Conspiracy of Charles, Duke of Byron, III, i. EtS
("Give me a spirit that on this life's rough sea.") MyFE; ViBoPo
Master stood in His garden, The. For the Master's Use [*or The Watered Lilies*]. *Unknown.* BLPA; BLRP; SoP
Master stood upon the mount, and taught, The. Progress. Matthew Arnold. ChIP; EPN; MaRV; StJW
Master Surgeon. Lucia Trent. ChIP
Master, the Swabber, The. Shakespeare. *Fr.* The Tempest, II, ii. InPo; ViBoPo
(None of Us Cared for Kate.) OnPM
(Stephano's Song.) WhC
Master, this very hour. This Very Hour. Lizette Woodworth Reese. AnAmPo; HBMV
Master, to do great work for Thee my hand. Life-Mosaic. Frances Ridley Havergal. TrPWD
Master Weaver, The. *Unknown.* STF
Master-Welder, The. Sarah Wingate Taylor. JKCP (1955 ed.)
Master, where abidest Thou? Rabbi, Where Dwellest Thou? Come and See. *Unknown.* BeJP
Master, whose fire kindled our glad surprise. The Master. "C. G. L." ImOP
Masterful Man, The. Henry Tyrrell. *See* Lincoln.
Masterindex: 23. Gil Orlovitz. ToPo
Masterpiece, The. Walter Conrad Arensberg. AnAmPo
Masterpiece, The. Walter Malone. PGD
Masterpiece of the taxidermist's art, A. Phar Lap in the Melbourne Museum. Peter Porter. PoAu-2
Masters. Kingsley Amis. NePoEA; PoPl
Masters, The. "Laurence Hope." HBV
Masters, The. Margaret Widdemer. HBMV
Master's Call, The. Henry Alford. *See* Bride, The.
Master's Call, The. Oswald J. Smith. SoP; STF
Master's in the Garden Again. John Crowe Ransom. AP
Masters, in This Hall. William Morris. ChTr
Master's Invitation, The. Anson Davies Fitz Randolph. AA
Master's Man, The. William G. Tarrant. MaRV; OQP
Masters of the Heart Touched the Unknown, The. Delmore Schwartz. FiMAP
Master's Touch, The. Horatius Bonar. BePJ; FaChP; HBV; MaRV; TrPWD; VA
(Touch of His Hand, The.) SoP
Master's Touch, The. *Unknown.* SoP
Mastery. Sara Teasdale. Interlude: Songs Out of Sorrow, II. HBV; WGRP
Matador. Richard Eberhart. NoP
Match, The. Andrew Marvell. MaMe
Match, A. Swinburne. ALV; BEL; ELP; EnLi-2; EnLit; GTBS-D; GTBS-W; *abr.*; GTSL; HBV; LiTL; OBVV; PG (1945 ed.); PoVP; TOP; VA
Match, The. Henry Vaughan. AnAnS-1; MeP
Match at Football, A, *sel.* Matthew Concanen.
Heaps on Heaps. SD
Match-bark of the younger dog sets fire to, The. Table-Birds. Kenneth Mackenzie. PoAu-2
Match with the Moon, A. Dante Gabriel Rossetti. NCEP
"Mater á Dios, preserve us." With Cortez in Mexico. Wilfred Campbell. PAH
Mater Amabilis. Aubrey Thomas De Vere. ISi
Mater Amabilis. Emma Lazarus. OHIP
Mater Christi. Aubrey Thomas de Vere. *Fr.* May Carols. PoVP
Mater Dei. Katharine Tynan. ISi
Mater Desiderata. Winthrop Mackworth Praed. OBVV
Mater Dolorosa. William Barnes. CH; HBV; MaRV; OBEV
(Mother's Dream, The) MemP; PoVP
Mater Dolorosa. John Fitzpatrick. JKCP
Mater Dolorosa. Elliott Napier. BoAu
Mater Dolorosa. John Banister Tabb. AnAmPo; StJW
Mater Incognita. Sister Mary Benvenuta. ISi
Mater Misericordiae. Sister St. Miriam of the Temple. JKCP (1955 ed.)
Materia Musica. Paul Jennings. MuSP
Materia Nupcial. "Pablo Neruda," *tr. fr. Spanish by* Clayton Eshleman. ErPo
Maternal Earth stirs redly from beneath. The Flaming Terrapin, I. Roy Campbell. MoBrPo
Maternal Lady with the Virgin Grace. Mary Lamb. ISi
(Aspiration.) CAW
Maternity. Jean Ingelow. *See* Seven Times Seven.
Maternity. Alice Meynell. NP; POTE
(Mother.) MawrV
(One Wept Whose Only Child Was Dead.) AnFE; TreFT
Mathematical. Jessica Nelson North. NP
Mathematics. Joel Oppenheimer. CoPo
Mathematics. Lionel Wiggam. PoMa
Mathematics of Encounter. Isabella Gardner. ErPo
Mathematics of Love. Michael Hamburger. NePoEA-2
Mathematics or the Gift of Tongues. Anna Hempstead Branch. ImOP
Mathmid, The. Hayyim Nahman Bialik, *tr. fr. Hebrew by* Maurice Samuel. AWP; PoFr, *abr.*
Matilda. Hilaire Belloc. CenHV; FaBoCh; LoGBV; OnMSP; StPo; YT
Matilda. F. Gwynne Evans. BBGG
Matilda, come hither, I pray. The Crocus. Mary Elliott. OTPC (1923 ed.)
Matilda got her stockings wet. Matilda. F. Gwynne Evans. BBGG
Matilda Jane, you never look. Doll's Song. "Lewis Carroll." OTPC (1946 ed.); SoPo
Matilda, Matriarch. Mazie V. Caruthers. CIV
Matilda Maud Mackenzie frankly hadn't any chin. How a Girl Was Too Reckless of Grammar by Far. Guy Wetmre Carryl. BOHV; FiBHP
Matilda, now go take thy bed. Requiem. Robert Davenport. *Fr.* King John and Matilda. SeCL; TuPP
Matilda postures on the window-sill. Fish-Day. Mazie V. Caruthers. CIV
Matilda told such dreadful lies. Matilda. Hilaire Belloc. CenHV; FaBoCh; LoGBV; OnMSP; StPo; YT
Matilda's busy mothering these days. Mothering. Mazie V. Caruthers. CIV
Matilda's grown grandmotherly these days. Matilda, Matriarch. Mazie V. Caruthers. CIV
Matilda's Manners. Mazie V. Caruthers. CIV
Matin Pandemoniums, The. Richard Eberhart. NYBP
Matin Song. Nathaniel Field. *See* Rise, Lady Mistresse, Rise!
Matin Song. Thomas Heywood. *See* Pack, Clouds, Away.
Matin-Song. *Unknown, tr. fr. German by* Jethro Bithell. WoL
Matins. Denise Levertov. AmPP (5th ed.); CoPo; PIA; ToPo
Matins. Henry van Dyke. MaRV
Matlock Bath. John Betjeman. NYBP
Matriarch of your chain and consort of the clouds. That Far Lone Mountain. Sister Mary Stephanie. JKCP (1955 ed.)
Matrix, *sel.* Dorothy Wellesley.
"Spiritual, the carnal, are one, The." OBMV
Matron-Cat's Song, The. Ruth Pitter. MemP
Matt Casey formed a social club that beat the town for style. The Band Played On. John F. Palmer. TreF
Mattens. George Herbert. AnAnS-1; MaMe; MeP; TrPWD
Matter. Louis Untermeyer. YT
Matter is indestructible. Smoke Stack. A. M. Sullivan. WaKn
Matter of Life and Death, A. Richard Aldridge. NePoAm
Matter of Life and Death, A. *sel.* Anne Ridler.
"I did not see the iris move." MoLP
Matter of Taste. *Unknown, tr. fr. Greek by* Louis Untermeyer. UnTE
Matter whose movement moves us all. Entropy. Theodore Spencer. ImOP
Matthew. Bible, *N.T.* *See* St. Matthew.
Matthew. Clive Sansom. HaMV
Matthew. Sister Margaret Teresa. JKCP (1955 ed.)
Matthew. Wordsworth. MBW-2; MERP
Matthew and Mark and Luke and holy John. Epi-strauss-ium. Arthur Hugh Clough. ViPP
Matthew and Mark, and Luke and John. The New Testament. Thomas Russell. TreFS
Matthew Arnold. W. H. Auden. MaPo (1969 ed.)

Matthew left his place of toil. Discipleship. C. O. Bales. STF
Matthew, Mark, Luke and John. *Unknown.* FaBoCh; GoTP; LoGBV; OTPC; OxNR; RIS; SiTL
(Bed Charm.) HBVY; PCH
(Before Sleeping.) CAW; CH; TreF
(Four Corners to My Bed.) ThGo
(Prayer.) OxBoLi
(Prayer before Sleeping.) WHL
(White Paternoster, The.) CBEP
Matthew, Mark, Luke, and John,/ Hold my horse till I leap on. *Unknown.* OxNR
Matthew met Richard; when or where. Matthew Prior. *Fr.* Alma; or, The Progress of the Mind. EiCP
Matthew X. 28. Roger Wolcott. SCAP
Matthew, whose skilful hand and well-worn spade. Sonnet. Thomas Edwards. EiCL
Maturity. J. Elgar Owen. WaP
Mauberley. Ezra Pound. *See* Hugh Selwyn Mauberley.
Maud. Henry S. Leigh. BOHV
Maud. Tennyson. MBW-2; OAEP; PoVP; ViPo; ViPP; VP
Sels.
"Birds in the high Hall-garden," *Pt.* I, xii. OTPC (1923 ed.); PeVV
"But the broad light glares and beats," Pt. II, xiii. SyP
"Cold and clear-cut face, why come you so cruelly meek," Pt. I, iii. SyP
Come into the Garden, Maud, Pt. I, xxii. BEL; BoLP; CBEP; EnLit; EPN; ExPo; FaBV; FiP; GTBS; GTSE; GTSL; HBV; LiTG; LiTL; MaVP; MCCG; OBVV; PaPo; PoIE; TreF; UnPo (1st ed.); VA
(Lyric from "Maud.") EnLi-2
(Maud.) GTBS-W; OBEV
(Song [from "Maud"].) AWP; InPo; JAWP; TOP; WBP
Dead, Long Dead, Pt. V, i. AtBAP; SyP
England, Pt. III, v.
"Go not, happy day," Pt. I, xvii. LiTL; OBVV; TOP
(Song: "Go not, happy day.") ATP
I Have Led Her Home, Pt. I, xviii. BEL; ChER; ELP; FiP; GTBS-D; PoEL-5
I Shall Have Had My Day. MeWo
"Is that enchanted moan only the swell," Pt. I, viii. SyP
"Long have I sigh'd for a calm: God grant I may find it at last!" Pt. I, ii. SyP
"Million emeralds break from the ruby-budded lime, A," Pt. I, iv. SyP
"My life has crept so long on a broken wing," Pt. III, vi. SyP
"O, let the solid ground," Pt. I, xi.
(I Shall Have Had My Day.) MeWo
(Song: "O, let the solid ground.") HBV
O That 'Twere Possible, Pt. II, iv. AtBAP; CBEP; EG; HBV; HoPM; OBEV, *sts.* 1 *and* 3; OBVV, *sts.* 1 *and* 3; OQP, *sts.* 1 *and* 3; PoFS
"See what a lovely shell," Pt. II, ii. BoNaP; PoEL-5
(Shell, The.) BoTP; GN; VA
Sleeping House, The, Pt. XIV, iv. FaBoEn; OBNC
There Is None like Her, Pt. XVIII, iii. FaBoEn; OBNC
Voice by the Cedar Tree, A, Pt. I, v. AtBAP; HBV
"What is she now? My dreams are bad," Pt. I, xix. SyP
Maud Muller. Whittier. AA; AmePo; AnEnPo; AnNE; BeLS; CoBA; FaBoBe; FaPL; HBV; OHFP; OnSP; PoLF; TIHL; TreF; WBLP
Saddest Words, The, 2 *ll.* NePA; SiTL
Maud Muller all that summer day. Mrs. Judge Jenkins, *parody.* Bret Harte. CABA; FiBHP; HBV; InP; WhC
Maud Muller Mutatur. Franklin P. Adams. HBMV
Maude Clare. Christina Rossetti. BeLS
Maudle—in Ballad, A. *Unknown.* BOHV
Maul, The. Mary E. Nealy. MC
Maumee Ruth. Sterling A. Brown. CDC
Maunder's Praise of his Strowling Mort, The. *Unknown.* OxBoLi
Maunding Soldier, The; or The Fruits of Warre Is Beggery. Martin Parker. CoMu; WaaP
Maureen. John Todhunter. HBV; OBEV (1st ed.); OBVV
Maurice de Guerin. Maurice Francis Egan. AA; JKCP
Mavrone. Arthur Guiterman. BOHV; FiBHP; InMe
Mawgan of Melhuach. Robert Stephen Hawker. EPN; VA
Max Schling, Max Schling, Lend Me Your Green Thumb. Ogden Nash. PV
Max Schmitt in a Single Scull. Richmond Lattimore. NePoAm-2
Maxim: "If he play, being young and unskilful." Kipling. *Fr.* Certain Maxims of Hafiz. OtMeF
Maxim Revised, A. *Unknown.* BLPA; NeHB; WBLP
Maximian Elegy V. Kenneth Rexroth. CrMA
Maxims (Cotton MS). *Unknown, tr. fr. Anglo-Saxon by* Charles W. Kennedy. AnOE
(Gnomic Verse from Cotton Manuscript.) YAT, *tr. by* Richard L. Hoffman
Maxims (Exeter Book). *Unknown, tr. fr. Anglo-Saxon by* Charles W. Kennedy. AnOE
(Gnomic Lines.) LiTW
Maximus, from Dogtown, I. Charles Olson. CoPo
Maximus, to Gloucester, Letter 19. Charles Olson. NMP
Maximus, to Himself. Charles Olson. NeAP; NMP; OPoP
Maxwel[l]ton braes [*or* banks] are bonnie. Annie Laurie. William Douglas, FaBoBe; FaBV; FaFP; GN; GTBS-W; HBV; InP; LiTG; LiTL; MCCG; OTPC; PTK; SiTL; TreF; WBLP *revised by* Lady John Scott.
May. William Barnes. GTBS-D; PoSC
"Mother o' blossoms, and ov all," 4 *ll.* ChTr
May. Stephan Moylan Bird. HBMV
May. Henry Sylvester Cornwell. HBV
May. Thomas Dekker. *See* O, the Month of May.
May. Richard Edwards. *See* M. Edwards' May.
May. Edward Hovell-Thurlow. HBV; OBEV; OBRV
May. George Macdonald. OTPC (1946 ed.)
May. John Shaw Neilson. NeLNL; PoAu-1
May, *sel.* John Francis O'Donnell.
"Open, sweet flowers, your eyes." IrPN
May. J. G. Percival. BoTP
May. Christina Rossetti. VP
("I cannot tell you how it was.") EG
May. Frank Dempster Sherman. PRWS
May. Spenser. *Fr.* The Faerie Queene, VII. GN; PoRL
May ("May's the merriest time of all"). *Unknown, tr. fr. Old Irish by* Frank O'Connor. AnIL; KiLC
May afternoon with birds in every bush. Poem in May. John Hewitt. NeIP
May all that dread the cruel feind of night. Warning to Travailers Seeking Accomodations at Mr. Devills Inn. Sarah Kemble Knight. SCAP
May and Death. Robert Browning. MBW-2
May, and the wall was warm again. W. R. Rodgers. Winter's Cold. EnLoPo
May Basket, The. Dora Read Goodale. PCH
May Basket, A. Lilian Bayne West. GFA
May, be thou never graced with birds that sing. Epitaph [*or* In Obitum M. S., X Maii, 1614]. William Browne. ElL; OBEV; OBS; PCD; SeCeV; SeEP
"May be true what I had heard." Berrying. Emerson. AtBAP
May Burden, A. Francis Thompson. HBV
May Carols, *sels.* Aubrey Thomas De Vere.
Divine Presence, The, I, 3. GoBC; MaRV
Fest. Puritatis, II, 1. PoVP
Festum Nativitatis, I, 12. IrPN
Implicit Faith, II, 64. GoBC
"In vain thy altars do they heap," III, 4.
(May Carol.) CAW
Mater Christi, I, 30. PoVP
"Night through yonder cloudy cleft, The," II, 20. IrPN
Turris Eburnia, II, 5. PoVP
"Who feels not, when the Spring once more," I, 1. IrPN
May Collin. Lady Isabel and the Elf-Knight (H *vers.*). *Unknown.* ESPB
May Colvin [*or* Colven]. *Unknown.* BuBa; MaC; OBB; OxBB; StPo; TrGrPo
May come up with bird-din. Nuts in May. Louis MacNeice. MoAB; MoBrPo (1950 ed.)
May-Day, *sels.* Emerson.
April and May. GN; OHIP
I Know the Trusty Almanac. BiS
Why Chidest Thou the Tardy Spring? BiS
May-Day. Aaron Hill. WaPE
May Day. Sara Teasdale. BoNaP; MemP; OTD; PoSC
May Day ("Good morning lords and ladies"). *Unknown.* RIS
May Day, A. Sir Henry Wotton. *See* On a Bank as I Sat a-Fishing.

May-Day at Sea. John F. Finerty. EtS
May Day Carol, A. *Unknown.* PoSC
(Greetings, 6 *ll.*) ThGo
(May-Day Song, *diff. vers.*) GoTP
May Day Dancing, The. Howard Nemerov. NYBP
May-Day! delightful day!/ Bright colours play the vale along. In Praise of May. *Unknown,* *tr. by* T. W. Rolleston. AnIV; BiS
May-day, delightful time! How beautiful the color! The Song of Finn. *Unknown,* *tr. by* John O'Donovan. OnYI
May Day Demonstrators. Maurice Lindsay. ACV
May Day Garland, The. Edmund Blunden. HBMV
Mayday on Holderness. Ted Hughes. ToPo
May-Day on Magdalen Tower. Thomas Herbert Warren. OBVV
May-Day Song. *Unknown.* *See* May Day Carol, A.
May de Lord—He will be glad of me. Bright Sparkles in the Churchyard. *Unknown.* AA
May, 1840. Hartley Coleridge. OBVV
May Evening. Eileen Brennan. NeIP
May every soul that touches mine. Making Life Worth While. "George Eliot." OQP
May 15th. Raymond Souster. MoCV
May Garden. John Drinkwater. HBMV
May God be praised for woman. On Woman. W. B. Yeats. CMoP
May God be praised! I have an equal skill. The Duel. Theodore Maynard. CAW
May God Give Strength. Peter Van Wynen. BLRP
May has come from out the showers. The Jewish May. Morris Rosenfeld. TrJP
May he fall in with beasts that scatter fire. Ballad against the Enemies of France. Villon, *tr. by* Swinburne. AWP; PoFr
May he have new life like the fall. John Coltrane—an Impartial Review. Alfred B. Spellman. NNP
May His counsels sweet uphold you. God Be with You. *Unknown.* PoToHe (new ed.)
May I borrow your handpainted cravat? Neckwear. Michael Silverton. PV
May I Feel Said He. E. E. Cummings. ErPo; LiTA; UnTE
May I find a woman fair. True Beauty. Francis Beaumont. ElL; HBV
May I for my own self song's truth reckon. The Seafarer. *Unknown,* *tr. by* Ezra Pound. AmP; AnAmPo; AP; CTC; EnL; ExPo; FaBoTw; LiTA; LiTW; OxBA; PoE; SeCeV (1967 ed.); StP
May I forever a Muse/ um. Vow. John Updike. NYBP
May I Woo the Lassie? *with music.* *Unknown,* *tr. fr. German by* Janet E. Tobitt. SaSa
May in the Green-Wood. *Unknown.* *See* In Summer.
May Is Building Her House. Richard Le Gallienne. HBVY; OHIP; YeAr; YT
May is Mary's month, and I. The May Magnificat. Gerard Manley Hopkins. AtBAP; ISi; PoLi; VP
May is the moneth maist amene. Of May. Alexander Scott. OxBS
May is the month when "the white throat builds." The Merry Month. "Miss X *and* Miss Y." InMe
May It Be. Boris Pasternak, *tr. fr. Russian by* C. M. Bowra. TrJP
May Jesus' grace and blessing. Morning Prayer for Day's Work. John Matthesius. SoP
May-June, 1940. Robinson Jeffers. AmPP (3d ed.); LiTA; LiTM (rev. ed.); MoAB; MoAmPo; NePA; StP; WaP
(Battle.) AmPP (4th ed.)
May Magnificat, The. Gerard Manley Hopkins. AtBAP; ISi; PoLi; VP
May Margaret. Theophile Marzials. HBV; VA
May Margaret [*or* Margret] sits [*or* stood] in her bower [*or* bouer] door. Hind [*or* Hynd] Etin. *Unknown.* BuBa; ESPB (B *vers.*); OBB
May Moon. Olive Driver. RePo
May moon rises bright and clear, The. Tom Pringle. Louis Simpson. NePoAm-2
May Morning. Marjorie Barrows. GFA
May Morning. Chaucer. *Fr.* The Book of the Duchesse. WHA
May Morning. Milton. *See* Song on May Morning.
May Morning. Celia Thaxter. AA
May Mornings. Ivy O. Eastwick. BrR; SiSoSe
May-Music. Rachel Annand Taylor. HBV
May my heart always be open to little. E. E. Cummings. AmPP; MoRP
May No Man Sleep. *Unknown.* NCEP
May nothing evil cross this door. Prayer for This [*or* a New] House. Louis Untermeyer. FaPON; MaRV; OTD; PoLF; PoToHe; TrPWD; TSW
May one kind grave unite each hapless name. Eloisa's Prayer For Abelard. Pope. *Fr.* Eloïsa to Abelard. GoBC
May others fear, fly, and traduce thy name. To the Learned Critic. Ben Jonson. PP
May our home be. Prayer For a New House. Martha Snell Nicholson. FaChP
May our home be a haven. Our Home. Phyllis C. Michael. SoP
May Poem: "Be glaid, al ye that luvaris bene." *Unknown.* OxBS
May Poem: "Now in this mirthfull tyme of May." *Unknown.* OxBS
May Poem: "O lusty May with Flora quene." *Unknown.* *See* Lusty May.
May Poem: "Quhen Flora had ourfret the firth." *Unknown.* *See* When Flora Had O'erfret the Firth.
May Queen, The. Tennyson. OTPC (1923 ed.); PoRL
Sels.
Conclusion to the May Queen and New Year's Eve. OTPC (1923 ed.)
"He taught me all the mercy, for he show'd me all the sin," 2 *ll.* ChIP
New Year's Eve. OTPC (1923 ed.)
"You must wake and call me early, call me early, mother dear," *first pt.* DD, 3 *sts.*; MPB; OTPC
May! queen of blossoms. May. Edward Hovell-Thurlow. HBV; OBEV; OBRV
May shall make the world anew. May. Frank Dempster Sherman. PRWS
May she be granted beauty and yet not. For My Daughter. W. B. Yeats. *Fr.* Prayer for My Daughter. MoRP
May Song. Wendell Berry. AP
May Song, A. "Violet Fane." OBVV; VA
May Song ("Spring is coming."). *Unknown.* HH
(Oxfordshire Children's May Song.) OTPC
("Spring is coming, spring is coming.") BoTP
May Sun Sheds an Amber Light, The. Bryant. AA
May Sunday, A. Thomas Caulfield Irwin. IrPN
May 10th. Maxine W. Kumin. BoNaP; NYBP
May the Ambitious Ever Find. *At. to* the Earl of Rochester *and to* Charles Sackville. SeCL; UnTE
May the Babylonish curse. A Farewell to Tobacco. Charles Lamb. BOHV; NBM; OBRV; OxBoLi
May the blessing of light be on you. An Old Irish Blessing. *Unknown.* TRV
May the bridesmaids. Night Singers. Sappho. HW
May the Cross and courteous Christ aid this beginning. Piers the Plowman's Creed. *Unknown.* MeEV
May the foemen's wives, the foemen's children. Europa. William Johnson Cory. NBM
May the glad dawn. My [*or* An] Easter Wish. *Unknown.* OQP; SoP
May the grace of Christ our Saviour. In Sweet Communion. John Newton. SoP; TRV
May the men who are born. Hitomaro. *Fr.* Manyo Shu. AWP
May the road rise to meet you. An Irish Wish. *Unknown.* TreFT
May the Sweet Name of Jseus. *Unknown,* *tr. fr. Irish by* Eleanor Hull. JKCP (1926 ed.)
(Communion Hymn of the Ancient Irish Church.) CAW
May the will come from Thee. Annul Wars. Nahman of Bratzlav. TrJP
May the will of God be done by us. A Night Prayer. *Unknown.* JKCP (1926 ed.)
May the wrath of the heart of my god be pacified! Penitential Psalm to the Goddess Anunit. *Unknown.* WGRP
May these delights be yours in the new year. New Year Wishes. May Sarton. MoRP
May they come, may they come. Song of the Highest Tower. Arthur Rimbaud. AWP; JAWP; WBP
May they wander [or stumble] stage by stage. The Traveller's Curse after Misdirection. Robert Graves. BrPo; CMoP; DTC; ExPo; FiBHP; HoPM; LiTM; MoAB; MoBrPo; NeMA; SiTL

May Thirtieth. *Unknown.* PoSC
May 30, 1893. John Kendrick Bangs. AA
May those who are born after me. Kakinomoto no Hitomaro. *Fr.* Manyo Shu. LiTW
May Time. *See* Maytime.
May Tree, The. William Barnes. LiTB; LoBV; POTE
May was a wonderful country. Wonderful Country. Miriam Waddington. PeCV
May we and all who bear thy name. By Gentle Love. *Unknown.* TRV
May we be a happy family. We. Phyllis C. Michael. SoP
May we have leave to ask, illustrious Mother. Purification of the Blessed Virgin. Joseph Beaumont. ISi
May winds gently lift the willow leaves, The. Bathing. John Keble. OTPC (1923 ed.)
May you drinke beare, or that adult'rate wine. To a Friend, Inviting Him to a Meeting upon Promise. Williams Habington. AnAnS-2
May you walk a little surer. My Easter Prayer. *Unknown.* SoP
Maybe Alone on My Bike. William Stafford. NYBP
Maybe it is true we have to return. Obsessions. Denise Levertov. LiTM (1970 ed.); NePoEA-2
Maybe that's mirabells ringing there. Epos. Julian Tuwim. LiTW
Maybe the men on little northern farms. Lonely Lover. Robert P. Tristram Coffin. MoLP
Maybe you ranted in the Grove. Ezry. Archibald MacLeish. MoVE
Maybe we knew each other better. Coda. Louis MacNeice. TDP
Maybrick trial is over now, The. Penal Servitude for Mrs. Maybrick. *Unknown.* OxBoLi; SiTL
Mayde's [*or* Maid's] Metamorphosis, The, *sels.* *Unknown, at. to* John Lyly *and to* Thomas Ravenscroft.
  By the Moon We Sport and Play. OTPC; TuPP
    (By the Moon.) CH
    (Fairy Dances, 1.) ElL
    (Fairy Frolic, The.) PCH, *longer sel.*
    (Urchins' Dance, The.) BoTP
  Elves' Dance, The. CH; FaPON; HH; MPB; PoRh
    (Fairy Dances, 2). ElL
    ("Round about in a fair ring-a.") BoTP
Mayflower, The. Erastus Wolcott Ellsworth. AA; FaBoBe; HH; MC; PAH
Mayflower. John Boyle O'Reilly. AA; PAH
Mayor of Scuttleton, The. Mary Mapes Dodge. GaP; NA
Mayors, The. Blake. *See* Good English Hospitality.
Maypole, A. Swift. CBEP; NCEP
May-Pole Dance. *Unknown.* *See* The Rural Dance about the Maypole.
May's the merriest time of all. May. *Unknown.* AnIL; KiLC
Mayster Sackvilles Induction. Thomas Sackville. *See* Mirror for Magistrates, A.
Maytime. Thomas Dekker. *See* O, the Month of May.
May-Time. Margaret Gant. PCH
May-Time. Christina Rossetti. BoTP
  ("There is but one May in the year.") TiPo
Maytime. *Unknown, tr. fr. Chinese by* L. Cranmer-Byng. *Fr.* Shi King. AWP
May Time. Sir Thomas Wyatt. *See* Sonnet: "You that in love find luck. . ."
Maze. Richard Eberhart. AnAmPo; NoP
Mazeppa. Byron. EnRP; MERP
  Sels.
  "Away, away, my steed and I." FOL
  "Up rose the sun; the mists were curl'd," OBRV
Mazeppa. Roy Campbell. AnFE
Mazilla and Mazura. *Unknown.* ChTr
Mazing around my mind like moths at a shaded candle. Ghosts. Robert Bridges. FaBoTw
Me. Walter de la Mare. BiCB; FaPON; ThGo; TiPo (1959 ed.)
Me. Hughes Mearns. *Fr.* Later Antigonishes. InMe
Me Alone. Lula Lowe Weeden. CDC
Me an' My Doney-Gal (*diff. vers. of* Doney Gal). *Unknown.* CoSo
Me an' my pardner an' my pardner's frien'. Long Summer Day. *Unknown.* OuSiCo
Me and My Dog. *Unknown.* PoAu-1
Me and my wife live all alone. Little Brown Jug. *Unknown.* ABF
Me and Prunes. Rupe Sherwood. PoOW
Me and the Mule. Langston Hughes. IDB
Me and Tuko go down to the Jew. Cuttin Down to Size. Henry Dumas. BF
Me clairvoyant. Variations on an Air: After Walt Whitman. G. K. Chesterton. InP; Par
Me, Colored. Peter Abrahams. *Fr.* Tell Freedom. PBA
Me Cupid made a happy slave. Song. Sir Richard Steele. OBEC
Me father was the keeper of the Eddystone Light. The Eddystone Light. *Unknown.* StPo
Me, go to Florida! This Is Pioneer Weather. William Carlos Williams. NePoAm-2
Me happy, night, night full of brightness. Ezra Pound. *Fr.* Homage to Sextus Propertius. ErPo; InvP
Me have ye gaoled and chained and burned. Song of the Old Man in Chains. Anatoli Vasilyevich Lunacharsky. *Fr.* Faust and the City. PoFr
Me Heart. G. K. Chesterton. OtMeF
Me, Hermes, near this breezy garden see! Spring for Travelers. *Unknown.* OnPM
Me I will throw away. The Self-Slaved. Patrick Kavanagh. MoBrPo (1962 ed.)
Me, I'm the man that dug the Murray for Sturt to sail down. They'll Tell You about Me. Ian Mudie. PoAu-2
Me Imperturbe. Walt Whitman. CoBA
Me Johnny Mitchell Man, *with music.* *Unknown.* TrAS
Me let the world disparage and despise. Honour. Ada Cambridge. BoAu
Me list no more to sing. Sir Thomas Wyatt. FCP; SiPS
Me Lord? can'st Thou mispend. Phineas Fletcher. *Fr.* The Divine Wooer. TrPWD
"Me loving subjects," sez she. Percy French. *Fr.* The Queen's Afterdinner Speech. OxBI
Me, Me, and None but Me. *Unknown.* ReIE
Me needeth not to boast; I am Eternity. Eternity. Sir Thomas More. EnRePo
Me prove it now—whoever doubt. Emily Dickinson. MWA-2
Me Quoque Vatem. Thomas Freeman. SiCE; TuPP
Me so oft my fancy drew. The Choice. George Wither. OBEV
Me that 'ave been what I've been. Chant-Pagan. Kipling. OAEP (2d ed.)
Me the gods turned to stone, but turned in vain. Niobe in Living Stone. *Unknown.* OnPM
Me-thinks already, from this chymick flame. The Rebirth of London. Dryden. *Fr.* Annus Mirabilis. PeRV
Me to You. Alex Raybin. ThO
Me to You. Alastair Reid. NYBP
Me Up at Does. E. E. Cummings. NYBP
Mea Culpa. "Ethna Carbery." CAW; JKCP; TrPWD
Meadow, The. John Wieners. CoPo
Meadow Brook Runs Over, The. Howard McKinley Corning. MAP; MoAmPo (1942 ed.)
Meadow-Field, The. Charles Sangster. *Fr.* Pleasant Memories. OBCV
Meadow for the little lambs, A. The Sweetest Place. Mary Frances Butts. PPL
Meadow Lark, The. Hamlin Garland. AA
Meadow Lark. Marion Mitchell Walker. GFA
Meadow larks rejoice, The, as the bright sun. The Prairie Schooner. Edwin Ford Piper. StVeCh (1940 ed.)
Meadow Mouse, The. Theodore Roethke. NaP; NoP; OA; PoeP; PoIE (1970 ed.); SeCeV (1967 ed.)
Meadow Talk. Nora Archibald Smith. PPL
Meadows, The. Ann *or* Jane Taylor. BoTP
Meadows in Spring, The. Edward Fitzgerald. *See* Old Song.
Meadows with yellow cowslips all aglow. The Wood-Dove's Note. Emily Huntington Miller. HBV
Meadowsweet. William Allingham. OBNC
Meandering Wye. Robert Bloomfield. *Fr.* The Banks of Wye. OBNC
Meaner than a brothel. Butcher Shop. Jorge Luis Borges. OnPM
Meaning, The. Ralph Gustafson. OBCV
Meaning of a Letter, The. *Unknown.* PoToHe (new ed.)
Meaning of Africa, The. Abioseh Nicol. PBA
  (Continent That Lies within Us, The.) ACV

Meaning of Prayer, The. Frances McKinnon Morton. *See* Breath of Prayer, A.
Meaning of the Look, The. Elizabeth Barrett Browning. ChIP; MaRV; SoP; TRV
Meaning of Violence, The. John Williams. NePoAm-2
Means and Ends. Humfrey Gifford. SoP
Means to Attain [a] Happy Life, The. Martial, ElL; EnLi-1 (1949 ed.) EnLit; EnRePo; HBV; OBEV; SiCE; ViBoPo; WoL, *tr. by* Sir Richard Fanshawe *tr. fr. Latin by* the Earl of Surrey.
(Epigram: "Things that make the happier life, are these, The," *tr. by* Ben Jonson.) EP
(Happy Life, The.) OnPM; SiPS
(Martial, the Things for to Attain.) FCP; PoIE; ReEn
(Martial's Quiet Life.) OBSC
(My Friend, the Things That Do Attain.) CABA; ForPo; NoP
(Things That Cause a Quiet Life, The.) TrGrPo; TuPP
(What Makes a Happy Life, *tr. by* Goldwin Smith.) AWP; JAWP; WBP
Meantime the sunlight melted from the shore. The Battle of Salamis. Aeschylus. *Fr.* The Persians. PoFr
Meanwhile Achilles, plung'd. Homer. *Fr.* The Iliad, I. PoPl
Meanwhile back at the wrenched back. Poison Meat. Tom Veitch. ANYP
Meanwhile, like an ermine. Igor's Escape. *Unknown, tr. fr. Russian by* Vladimir Nabokov. *Fr.* The Song of Igor's Campaign. FOL
Meanwhile the choleric Captain strode wrathful away to the council. The War-Token. Longfellow. *Fr.* The Courtship of Miles Standish. PAH
Meanwhile the Queen with many piteous drops. Titania. Thomas Hood. *Fr.* The Plea of the Midsummer Fairies. OBRV
Meanwhile the Son/ On his great expedition now appear'd. The Creation of the World. Milton. *Fr.* Paradise Lost, VII. MaPo
Meanwhile the Tuscan army. The Fight at the Bridge. Macaulay. *Fr.* Lays of Ancient Rome: Horatius. MaC; OtMeF
Meanwhile the woman, from her strawberry lips. Metamorphoses of the Vampire. Baudelaire. ErPo
Meare's milk and deer's milk. A Witch's Spell. *Unknown.* ChTr
Measure for Measure, *sels.* Shakespeare.
"Ay, but to die, and go we know not where," *fr.* III, i. TrEV
(Fear of Death, The.) TreFT
(Life and Death.) UnPo (1st ed.)
(On Death.) FiP
But Man, Proud Man, *fr.* II, ii. WHA
Doubts ("Our doubts are traitors"), *fr.* I, iv. MaRV
Isabella Condemns Tyranny, *fr.* II, ii. TreFT
Man New Made, *fr.* II, ii. GoBC
Not Thine Own, *fr.* I, i. MaRV
Take, O Take Those Lips Away, *fr*, IV, i (*also given, with add. st., in* The Bloody Brother, *by* John Fletcher, *and others*). AnFE; AtBAP; BEL; CBEP; DiPo; ElL; ELP; EnLi-1; EnLit; EnLoPo, 2 *sts9.; EnRePo; ExPo; FaBV; HBV, 2 sts.*; ILP; InPo; LiTB; LiTG; LiTL; LO; OAEP; OBEV; OnPM; OuHeWo; PoeP; PoIE; SeCeV; SiCE; TOP; ViBoPo; WHA
(Boy's Song to Mariana.) BoLiVe
(Frustra.) GTSL
(Love Forsworn.) MCCG
(Madrigal.) GTBS; GTBS-D; GTBS-P; GTBS-W; GTSE
(Sealed in Vain.) WoL
(Seals of Love.) MeWo; TrGrPo
(Song: "Take, O take those lips away.") FiP; ForPo; MemP; PoEL-2 (2 *sts.*); UnPo (1st ed.)
(Song at the Moated Grange, A.) OBSC
(Song for Mariana.) EG
(Songs from the Plays.) AWP; JAWP; WBP
"Well; come to me to-morrow," *fr.* II, ii. LO
Measure of a Man, The. *Unknown.* PoLF; STF
Measure of Memory, The. LeRoi Jones. FRC
Measure of Success. *Unknown.* STF
Measure thy life by loss instead of gain. Love's Strength. Harriet Eleanor Hamilton King. MaRV; OQP
Measured blood beats out the year's delay, The. Simple Autumnal. Louise Bogan. MAP; MoAB; MoAmPo; QFR; Sonn
Measurement. A. M. Sullivan. RePo; WaKn
Measurements can never tell it. Hiking Poem/ High Sierra. Lew Welch. FRC
Measuring a Man. *Unknown.* STF
Measuring out my life in flagons. Familiar Daemon. Roy Campbell. JKCP (1955 ed.)
Measuring worm with a hump on his back, A. Pedagogical Principles. Harry Amoss. CaP
Meat bubble when in. Ghost. Clark Coolidge. ANYP
Mechanic, The. Robert Creeley. NaP
Mechanical/ Oracles dot the sky. Gods in Vietnam. Eugene Redmond. NBP
Mechanical Optimist, The. Wallace Stevens. NAMP
Mecklenburg Declaration, The. William C. Elam. PAH
Medal, The; a Satire against Sedition. Dryden. CEP; EiPP
"Almighty crowd, thou shorten'st all dispute." PeRV
(Vox Populi.) OBS
Medallion. Sylvia Plath. NoP
Medallion. Ezra Pound. *Fr.* Hugh Selwyn Mauberley. NoP; SeCeV (1967 ed.)
Meddlesome Matty. Ann Taylor. HBV; HBVY; OnMSP; OTPC (1946 ed.)
Meddow Verse, The; or, Aniversary to Mistris Bridget Lowman. Robert Herrick. SeCV-1
Medea, *sel.* Lord De Tabley.
Chorus: "Sweet are the ways of death to weary feet." NBM; OBEV (new ed.); OBVV
Medea, *sels.* Euripides, *tr. fr. Greek.*
Chorus: "Upward and back to their fountains the sacred rivers are stealing," *tr. by* Arthur S. Way. PoFr
Chorus: "When love has passed its limits," *tr. by* Frederic Prokosch. LiTW
Medea, *sel.* Seneca, *tr. fr. Latin.*
Epithalamium for Murder, *tr. by* Ella Isabel Harris. HW
Medelwold and Sidselille. *Unknown. See* Leesome Brand.
Medgar Evers. Gwendolyn Brooks. NoP
Media Vita. Notker Balbulus, *tr. fr. Latin by* Frederick Rowland Marvin. CAW
Mediator, The. Elizabeth Barrett Browning. TrPWD
Mediatrix of Grace, The. Francis Burke. ISi
Medical Aid. Walter Hard. WhC
Medical Corps, The. Beatrice Barry. PEDC
Medici Tombs, The. W. W. E. Ross. NYTB
Medieval Appreciations. William M. T. Gamble. CAW
Medieval Christ Speaks on a Spanish Sculpture of Himself. Rochelle Owens. CoPo
Medieval Mirth. *Unknown. Fr.* The Squire of Low Degree. ACP
Medieval Norman Songs. *Unknown, tr. fr. French by* John Addington Symonds. AWP; JAWP; WBP
Mediocracy. Caryll Houselander. JKCP (1955 ed.)
Mediocrity [*or* Mediocritie] in Love Rejected. Thomas Carew. ALV; AnAnS-2; ATP; EnLit; EP; HBV; MeLP; MePo; NoP; SCEP-2; SeCL; SeCV-1; SeEP; VaPo
(Give Me More Love.) UnTE
(More Love or More Disdain.) MeWo; TrGrPo
(Song: "Give me more love or more disdain.") ForPo; LiTL; ViBoPo
Meditating in silence after the last note. J. C. Beaglehole. *Fr.* Considerations on Certain Music of J. S. Bach. AnNZ
Meditating on the glory of illustrious lineage. The Bitter Purple Willows. Allen Upward. *Fr.* Scented Leaves from a Chinese Jar. NP
Meditatio. Ezra Pound. FaBoCh; LoGBV; LOW
(Meditation.) WePo
Meditation. Donald Cox. MaRV
Meditation, A. Richard Eberhart. FiMAP; LiTA
Meditation. Roy Fuller. FaBoMo
Meditation. Paul Géraldy, *tr. fr. French by* Joseph T. Shipley. ALV
Meditation. Antoinette Goetschius. MaRV
Meditation. Toyohiko Kagawa. MaRV; SoP; TRV
Meditation, The. John Norris. PeRV
Meditation. Ezra Pound. *See* Meditatio.
Meditation. Blanaid Salkeld. OnYI
Meditation at Kew. Anna Wickham. AnEnPo; FaBoTw; MeWo; MoBrPo
Meditation at Oyster River. Theodore Roethke. MoAmPo (1962 ed.); NaP; NYBP
Meditation by Mascoma Lake. Donald C. Babcock. NePoAm-2

Meditation 8. Philip Pain. QFR
Meditation for Christmas, A. Selwyn Image. OBEV (new ed.)
Meditation for His Mistresse, A. Robert Herrick. OBEV; OBS; SeCP
Meditation in a Grove. Isaac Watts. *See* Sweet Muse.
Meditation in St. Mary's. Gertrude du Bois. ChIP
Meditation in Winter. William Dunbar. NCEP
(Meditatioun in Wyntir.) OxBS; SeCePo
Meditation in Winter. Leonard Mann. BoAV
Meditation of a Patriot. G. S. Fraser. LiTM (rev. ed.)
Meditation on a March Wind. Sister Mary Gilbert. JKCP (1955 ed.)
Meditation on a Memoir. J. V. Cunningham. QFR
Meditation on Communion with God. Judah Halevi, *tr. fr. Hebrew by* Solomon Solis-Cohen. TrJP
Meditation on Identity. David Wright. OPoP
Meditation on John Constable, A. Charles Tomlinson. NePoEA-2
Meditation on Saviours. Robinson Jeffers. CMoP
Meditation on Statistical Method. J. V. Cunningham. CoAP; ForPo; PIA; QFR
Meditation on the BMT. Paul Blackburn. CoPo
Meditation on Time. Sister Mary Athanasius. JKCP (1955 ed.)
Meditation under Stars. George Meredith. OAEP; VP
Meditation upon the Toothache, A. Laurence Lerner. NePoEA-2
Meditation, A: What Is a Stocking in Eternity? Lewis Mac Adams. ANYP; YAP
Meditations. Solomon ibn Gabirol, *tr. fr. Hebrew by* Emma Lazarus. TrJP
Meditations. Edward Taylor. *See* Preparatory Meditations.
Meditations for August 1, 1666. Philip Pain. SCAP
Meditations for July 19, 1666. Philip Pain. SCAP
Meditations for July 25, 1666, Philip Pain. SCAP
Meditations for July 26, 1666. Philip Pain. SCAP
Meditations in a Museum Cloister. Sister Maryanna. JKCP (1955 ed.)
Meditations in Time of Civil War. W. B. Yeats. CABL; PIA
Ancestral Houses, I. ChMP; LiTB; MoVE
I See Phantoms of Hatred and of the Heart's Fullness and of the Coming Emptiness, VII. LiTB
My Descendants, IV. LiTB
My House, II. LiTB
My Table, III. LiTB
Road at My Door, The, V. LiTB
Stare's Nest by My Window, The, VI. GTBS-P; LiTB
Meditations of a Gull. Sir John Davies. SICE
Meditations of a Hindu Prince. Sir Alfred Comyn Lyall. VA; WGRP
Meditations of a Tortoise Dozing under a Rosetree near a Beehive at Noon While a Dog Scampers About and a Cuckoo Calls from a Distant Wood. E. V. Rieu. FiBHP
Meditations of an Old Woman. Theodore Roethke. NaP
Sels.
First Meditation. AP
("On love's worst ugly day.") PoDB
I'm Here, II. CoAP; NYBP
Meditatioun in Wyntir. William Dunbar. *See* Meditation in Winter.
Mediterranean, The. Allen Tate. AmP; AP; ExPo; FaBoMo; InPo; LiTA; LiTG; LiTM; MAP; MoAB; MoAmPo; MoVE; NePA; PoCh; PoFS; ReMP; SeCeV; TwAmPo; VaPo
Medusa. Louise Bogan. HoPM; InPo; MAP; MoAB; MoAmPo; MoPo; MoVE
Medusa. Robert Kelley Weeks. AA
Meek and the Proud, The. Abraham ibn Chasdai, *tr. fr. Hebrew by* Joseph Chotzner. TrJP
Meek dew shone, the grass lay prostrate, The. The Tree. Ilya Ehrenburg. TrJP
Meek dwellers mid yon terror-stricken cliffs! The Alpine Flowers. Lydia Huntley Sigourney. AnAmPo
Meek-ey'd Morn appears, Mother of Dews, The. Summer Morning. James Thomson. *Fr.* The Seasons: Summer. OBEC
Meekly the sea. The Even Sea. May Swenson. WIRo
Mee-ow, mee-ow,/ Here's a little pussy-cat. Pussy-Cat and Puppy-Dog. Lilian McCrea. BoTP
Meet Me in St. Louis. Andrew B. Sterling. TreFT
Meet Me in the Green Glen. John Clare. GTBS-D; PeER
(Love, Meet Me in the Green Glen.) ELP
Meet Me in the Primrose Lane. John Clare. AtBAP
Meet me my love, meet me my love. The Juniper Tree. Wilfred Watson. BoLP; PeCV; WHW
Meet me tonight as usual at nine. Love Poem—1940. Miriam Hershenson. GoYe
Meet me to-night, lover, meet me. Moonlight. *Unknown.* AS
Meet-on-the-Road. *Unknown.* PoMS
Meet We No Angels, Pansie? Thomas Ashe. HBV; OBEV (1st ed.); OBVV
Meet women with tender bearing. The Voice of Experience. Goethe. ErPo; PV
Meet your Saviour in the morning. Keeping Victory. Walter E. Isenhour. SoP; STF
Meeting. Matthew Arnold. Switzerland, I. ELP; MBW-2; OAEP; ViPP
(Lake, The.) CBEP
Meeting, The. Louise Bogan. NePoAm-2; NYBP
Meeting. George Crabbe. HBV; OBEV
"My Damon was the first to wake," *sel.* LO
Meeting, A. C. Day Lewis. NYBP
Meeting. Charles Eglington. BoSA
Meeting. Arthur Davison Ficke. NP
Meeting. Sam Harrison. NeIP
Meeting, A. Heine, *tr. fr. German by* Louis Untermeyer. PoMS
Meeting, A. Daniel Hoffman. CoPo
Meeting. Josephine Miles. FiMAP
Meeting, The. Howard Moss. NYBP
Meeting ("If we shall live, we live"). Christina Rossetti. LO
Meeting ("They made the chamber sweet"). Christina Rossetti. *See* Pause, A.
Meeting, The. Muriel Rukeyser. MoAmPo; TrJP
Meeting. William Saphier. AnAmPo
Meeting, The. Katharine Tynan. BoPe
Meeting, The. Whittier. AmPP (3d ed.)
"And so I find it well to come," *sel.* FaChP
Meeting a monster of mourning wherever I go. Epistle to Dylan Thomas [*or* Epistle I]. George Barker. LiTM; PoIE
Meeting after Long Absence. Lilla Cabot Perry. AA
Meeting and Passing. Robert Frost. MaPo; OxBA
Meeting at Night. Robert Browning. AWP; BEL; BoLiVe; BoLP; CBEP; CBV; DiPo; ELP; EnL; EnLi-2; EnLit; EPN; FaBoEn; FaBV; FiP; GBV (1952 ed.); GTBS-D; GTBS-W; GTSL; HBV; InPo; InvP; JAWP; LiTL; MaVP; MBW-2; MCCG; MeWo; OAEP; OBEV; OBNC; PAn; PCD; PeVV; PG (1955 ed.); PoAn; PoPl; PoFS; PoPo; PoRA; PoVP; SeCePo; ShBV-3; TOP; TreFT; TrGrPo; UnPo (3d ed.); VA; ViBoPo; ViPo; ViPP; WBP; WePo
(Meeting at Night—Parting at Morning.) CaFP
Meeting by the Gjulika Meadow. Geoffrey Grigson. WaP
Meeting his mother makes him lose ten years. Between the Porch and the Altar. Robert Lowell. FiMAP; MiAP; NePoEA
Meeting-House Hill. Amy Lowell. AmPP (3d ed.); LoGBV; MAP; MoAmPo; NeMA; NP; OxBA; PFY; PoRA (rev. ed.)
Meeting in Winter. William Morris. EnLi-2 (1949 ed.)
Meeting Mary. Eleanor Farjeon. BiCB
Meeting Myself. Edward Lucie-Smith. NePoEA-2
Meeting of a Poetry Society. Henry Rago. AnAmPo
Meeting of Orion and Artemis. Richard Henry Horne. *Fr.* Orion. VA
Meeting of Sighs, The. Blanche Edith Baughan. BoAu
Meeting of the Clabberhuses, The. Sam Walter Foss. BOHV
Meeting of the Ships, The. Thomas Moore. EtS
Meeting of the Waters, The. Thomas Moore. AnIL; NBM; OxBoLi; PoEL-4
Meeting Point. Louis MacNeice. ChMP; MemP; POTE; WePo
Meeting the Easter Bunny. Rowena Bastin Bennett. GFA; SiSoSe; SoPo; SUS; TiPo; UTS
Meeting the first time for many years. A Meeting. C. Day Lewis. NYBP
Meeting Together of Poles & Latitudes; in Prospect. Margaret Avison. OBCV; PeCV
Meeting when all the world was in the bud. Loves of the Puppets. Richard Wilbur. CoPo
Meeting with Time, "Slack thing," said I. Time. George Herbert. EP; MaMe; SeCL
Meeting's in order, The. What's coming? What's to come? Town Meeting. John Hay. NePoAm

Meg Merrilies [*or* Merrilees] Keats. BoLiVe; BoTP; CBEP; ELP; FaBoCh; FaPON; FiP; GaP; GBV (1952 ed.); LoGBV; OnPP; OTPC; PCH; PoPo; PoRL; PRWS; RG; RIS; StVeCh; TiPo
(Old Meg.) PoeP; ThWaDe
Megalometropolitan Carnival, *sel.* David Gascoyne.
"When Night has been announced as theme, will it not cause surprise." ACV
Mehitabel Sings a Song. Don Marquis. *Fr.* Archy and Mehitabel. InMe
Mehitabel Tries Marriage. Don Marquis. *Fr.* Archys Life of Mehitabel. WePo
Mein Herz, mein Herz ist traurig. Heine, *tr. fr. German by* James Thomson. AWP
(My Heart, My Heart Is Mournful.) PoPl
Mein Kind, wir waren Kinder. Heine, *tr. fr. German by* Elizabeth Barrett Browning. AWP; JAWP; TrJP; WBP
Mein Liebchen, wir sassen zusammen. Heine, *tr. fr. German by* James Thomson. AWP; JAWP; WBP
(Forlornly.) OnPM
Melampus. George Meredith. BoC; EnLi-2; OBVV; PoEL-5
Melampus, when will love be void of fears? Song of Coridon and Melampus [*or* Coridon and Melampus' Song]. George Peele. *Fr.* The Hunting of Cupid. OBSC; TuPP
Melancholetta, *sel.* "Lewis Carroll."
"My dismal sister! Couldst thou know." FiBHP
Melancholia. Robert Bridges. CMoP
Melancholia. James Thomson. The City of Dreadful Night, XXI. AnEnPo; VA
("Anear the centre of that northern crest.") FaBoEn; GTBS-P; OAEP
Melancholia. *Unknown.* NA
Melancholy. John Fletcher *and* (*at.*) Thomas Middleton. *Fr.* The Nice Valour. EnLit; GTBS; GTBS-D; GTBS-P; GTBS-W; GTSE; GTSL; HBV; OBEV
(Hence All You Vain Delights.) AtBAP; OAEP; SeCL; TuPP; ViBoPo
(O Sweetest Melancholy.) TrGrPo
(Passionate Man's Song, The.) OBS; SiCE
(Song: "Hence all you vain delights.") PoEL-2
(Sweetest Melancholy.) BEL
Melancholy. William Habington. *Fr.* Castara, II. LoBV
Melancholy. Thomas Lodge. *See* Earth, Late Choked with Showers, The.
Melancholy. August Straum, *tr. fr. German by* Glauco Cambon. OnPM
Melancholy. Edward Thomas. MoVE; NoP
Melancholy Cowboy, The. *Unknown.* CoSo
Melancholy days are come, the saddest of the year, The. The Death of the Flowers. Bryant. AA; AnAmPo; AnNE; BoNaP; CoBA; DD; GN; HBV; OTPC; PoLF; TreF; WBLP
Melancholy desire of ancient things, A. On an Air of Rameau. Arthur Symons. MuSP; OBNC
Melancholy face Charles Carville had, A. Charles Carville's Eyes. E. A. Robinson. MaPo; NePA; OxBA
Melancholy, hence! go get. James Shirley. *Fr.* Changes; or, Love in a Maze. TuPP
Melancholy Knight, The, *sels.* Samuel Rowlands.
Poetaster, The. ElL
Sir Eglamour. ElL; FaBoCh; InvP; LoGBV; WaKn
Melancholy Lay, A. Marjory Fleming. FaBoCh; FiBHP; LoGBV; SiTL
(Six-Year-Old Marjory Fleming Pens a Poem.) TreFT
(Three Turkeys.) ThWaDe
Melancholy lieth dolorously ill. Arabs. Alfred Kreymborg. MAPA; TwAmPo
Melancholy little man was seated on the ground, A. Home. *Unknown.* HBV
Melancholy Pig, The. "Lewis Carroll." *Fr.* Sylvie and Bruno, *ch.* 10. FaPON; OTPC (1946 ed.); PPL
(Pig-Tale, The.) OA; WiR
Melancholy slackening that ensued, The. Cambridge and the Alps. Wordsworth. *Fr.* The Prelude. PoEL-4
Melancholy Year, The. Trumbull Stickney. NCEP
Melancthon. Marianne Moore. AtBAP; CrMA
Melbourne and Memory, *sel.* Frank Wilmot.
Towers at Evening, The. NeLNL
Melbourne Ode, A; the Agricultural Show, Flemington, Victoria. Frank Wilmot. BoAu
Melchior, Gaspar, and Balthazar. The Legend of the Saintfoin. Pamela Tennant. GBV (1922 ed.)
Melchior, Gaspar, Balthazar. The Ballad of the Cross. Theodosia Garrison. HBMV; HBVY
Melchior Vulpius. Marianne Moore. AP
Meleager. Ovid, *tr. fr. Latin by* Arthur Golding. *Fr.* Metamorphoses, VIII. CTC
Melfort Dalton, I knew you well. To an Old Tenor. Oliver St. John Gogarty. WhC
Melhill Feast. William Barnes. CBEP; OBNC
Melicertus' Description of His Mistress. Robert Greene. *Fr.* Menaphon. ReIE
(Of His Mistress.) ElL
Melilot. Muna Lee. NP
Melincourt, *sels.* Thomas Love Peacock.
Glee—the Ghosts. ViBoPo
Quintetto upon the Christmas Pie.
"My share of pie to win, I will dash through thick and thin." MyFE
Sun-Dial, The. ERoP-1; OBNC; OBRV
Melinda, who had never been. The Coquette. Aphra Behn. TrGrPo; ViBoPo
Melisea, Her Song in Scorn of Her Shepherd Narcissus. Jorge de Montemayor, *tr. fr. Spanish by* Bartholomew Young. *Fr.* Diana. TuPP
Melissa. *Unknown, tr. fr. Greek by* Louis Untermeyer. UnTE
Melita, Rhodopis, and young Rhodocleia. Embarrassed Judge. *Unknown.* UnTE
Melité, your eyes are Hera's. To Melité. Rufinus Domesticus. LiTW
Mellifluous as bees, these brittle men. On First Looking in on Blodgett's Keats's "Chapman's Homer." George Starbuck. PP
Mellow the moonlight to shine is beginning. The Spinning Wheel [*or* The Spinning-Wheel Song]. John Francis Waller. AnIV; BoLP; ChTr; StPo; VA
Mellow touch of musick most doth wound, The. Soft Musick. Robert Herrick. SeEP
Mellow year is hasting to its close, The. November. Hartley Coleridge. Sonnets on the Seasons, XII. LoBV; OBNC; OBRV; PeER; PoRL
Melodie Grotesque. Persis Greely Anderson. WhC
Melodies of Time, The. Thomas Hood. *Fr.* The Plea of the Midsummer Fairies. OBNC
Melons. Mary Mapes Dodge. GaP; TiPo
Melpomene among her livid people. The Two Masks. George Meredith. VA
Melpomene (at whose mischeifous tove). Carmen Elegiacum. Thomas Morton. SCAP
Melpomene, the Muse of tragic songs. Oenone's Complaint. George Peele. *Fr.* The Arraignment of Paris. ElL; OBSC
Melrose Abbey. Sir Walter Scott. *Fr.* The Lay of the Last Minstrel, II. SeCePo
("If thou wouldst view fair Melrose aright.") OBRV
(Sir William of Deloraine at the Wizard's Tomb.) OBNC
Melting of the Earl's Plate. George Walter Thornbury. VA
Melting Pot. Michael Echeruo. TTY
Melting Pot, The. Dudley Randall. BALP
Melton Mowbray Pork Pie, A. Richard Le Gallienne. BOHV; Par
Melville and Coghill. Andrew Lang. VA
Members, Don't Git Weary, *with music. Unknown.* BoAN-2
Memento. Federico García Lorca, *tr. fr. Spanish by* Eleanor L. Turnbull. OnPM
Memento. Winfield Townley Scott. FiMAP
Memento. Stephen Spender. AtBAP
Memento for Mortality [*or* Mortalitie], A. *At. to* Francis Beaumont *and to* William Basse. *See* On the Tombs in Westminster Abbey.
Mementos, I ("Sorting out letters and piles of my old"). W. D. Snodgrass. MeWo; MoAmPo (1962 ed.); NePoEA-2; PoIE (1970 ed.)
Mementos, II ("I found them there today"). W. D. Snodgrass. AmPC; NePoEA-2
Memling's Virgin with Apple. Adèle Naudé. BoSA
Memnon. Leslie Holdsworth Allen. BoAu
Memnon. Clinton Scollard. AA
Memo. Kenneth Fearing. CMoP
Memo. Hildegarde Flanner. NYBP
Memo from the Desk of X. Donald Justice. TwCP
Memoir. R. G. Howarth. PV

Memorabilia. Robert Browning. ACV; BEL; BoLiVe; CABA; CBEP; CLwM; EnLi-2; EnLit; EPN; FaBoEn; FiP; GTBS-W; HBV; ILP; LoBV; MBW-2; ML; NoP; OAEP; OBNC; PoVP; PP; SeCePo; TOP; TreFT; VA; ViPo; ViPP; WHA
Memorabilia. E. E. Cummings. OnHM
Memorandum. Rudy Bee Graham. PoNe (1970 ed.)
Memorandum. William Stafford. NYBP
Memorandum for Minos. Richard Kell. ELU
Memorandum on My Martinique, *sel.* Aimé Césaire, *tr. fr. French by* Lionel Able *and* Yvan Goll.
"Neither the teacher of the class nor the priest." PoNe
Memorial. Mae Winkler Goodman. PGD
Memorial. Clark Ashton Smith. FiSC
Memorial Day. William E. Brooks. HH; MaRV; OQP; PAL; PEDC; PGD; PoRL
Memorial Day. Emerette H. Dunning. OQP
Memorial Day. Theodosia Garrison. DD; MPB; OHIP; PEDC; PoSC
Memorial Day. Richard Watson Gilder. OHIP
Memorial Day. Louise Imogen Guiney. DD
Memorial Day. Joyce Kilmer. MaRV
Memorial Day. Samuel Ellsworth Kiser. *See* Memorial Day, 1889.
Memorial Day. Emma A. Lent. OQP; WBLP
Memorial Day. Clinton Scollard. *See* For Our Dead.
Memorial Day. Samuel F. Smith. *Fr.* Our Honored Heroes. OQP
Memorial Day. Cy Warman. DD; HH
Memorial Day. Alma Adams Wiley. PEDC
Memorial Day. McLandburgh Wilson. DD; MaRV
Memorial Day. Annette Wynne. MaRV; OHIP
Memorial Day, 1889. Samuel Ellsworth Kiser. DD; HH; PEDC
Memorial (For Two Young Seamen Lost Overboard in a Storm in Mid-Pacific, January, 1940). George Barker. LiTG; LiTM
Memorial for a Young Seaman, I. ReMP
(Three Memorial Sonnets.) MasP
Memorial of Africa, A, *sel.* George Macdonald.
This Infant World. EPN
(Sonnet: "This infant world.") OBVV
(World and Soul.) VA
Memorial Rain. Archibald MacLeish. AmPP (5th ed.); AnFE; BoLiVe; CMoP; CoAnAm; CoBA; LiTA; MAP; MoAB; MoAmPo; TwAmPo
Memorial Service for the Invasion Beach. Alan Dugan. NMP; TwCP
Memorial Sonnet. Marjorie Meeker. AnAmPo
Memorial Thresholds. Dante Gabriel Rossetti. The House of Life, LXXXI. MaVP; PoVP; ViPo
Memorial to D. C., *sels.* Edna St. Vincent Millay.
Chorus: "Give away her gowns," III. NP
Elegy: "Let them bury your big eyes," V. AmLP; AnNE; CMoP; HBMV; InP; MAP; MoAB; MoAmPo; NeMA; NePA; OxBA; PoRA
Epitaph: "Heap not on this mound," I. NP
Prayer to Persephone, II. NP
"O, loveliest throat of all sweet throats." OxBA
Memorial to the Great Big Beautiful Self-sacrificing Advertisers. Frederick Ebright. ThLM; WaP
Memorial Trees. Juvenal, *tr. fr. Latin by* George Lamb. OnPM
Memorial Verses. Matthew Arnold. BWP; CaBA; EPN; FiP; HBV; MaPo (1969 ed.); MBW-2; OAEP; PoVP; PP; VA; ViPo; ViPP
Memorial Wreath. Dudley Randall. IDB; NNP; PoNe (1970 ed.)
Memorials on the Slain at Chickamauga. Herman Melville. AA
Memories. Thomas Bailey Aldrich. AA
Memories. Alexander Hay Japp. VA
Memories. George Denison Prentice. AA
Memories. Arthur Stringer. HBV
Memories. Charles Hanson Towne. OQP
Memories. Whittier. AP; CoBA; OBVV
Memories of a Lost War. Louis Simpson. NePoAm
Memories of Childhood. Wu Tsung Ai, *tr. fr. Chinese by* Henry H. Hart. OnPM
Memories of President Lincoln. Walt Whitman. *See* When Lilacs Last in the Dooryard Bloom'd *and* O Captain! My Captain! *and* Hush'd Be the Camps Today *and* This Dust Was Once the Man.
Memories of West Street and Lepke. Robert Lowell. AmPP (5th ed.); NaP; PoeP; ToPo
Memories of Whitman and Lincoln. James Oppenheim. LiPo
Memory. Thomas Bailey Aldrich. AA; AmLP; AnFE; AnNE; APA; BoNaP; CoAnAm; MAP; MCCG; NeHB; OQP; PoLF; PoMa; PTK; TreFS
Memory, A. William Allingham. *See* Four Ducks on a Pond.
Memory, A. Rupert Brooke. BrPo
Memory ("Marina's gone, and now sit I"). William Browne. *Fr.* Britannia's Pastorals, III, Song 1. HBV
(Celadyne's Song.) OBS
(So Shuts the Marigold Her Leaves, *shorter sel.*) ChTr
Memory ("So shuts the marigold her leaves"). William Browne. *Fr.* Britannia's Pastorals, III, Song 1. OBEV
(Since She Is Gone.) LiTL
("So shuts the marigold her leaves.") EG; ViBoPo
Memory, The. Lord Dunsany. OxBI
Memory. Francis Erskine, Earl of Rosslyn. VA
Memory. Oliver Goldsmith. *Fr.* The Captivity, I. OBEC, *sl. diff. vers.*; OBEV
(Song: "O memory, thou fond deceiver.") ViBoPo
Memory. Helen Hoyt. NP; PoLF
Memory, A. Frederic Lawrence Knowles. HBV
Memory. Walter Savage Landor. ERoP-1; VA
Memory. Abraham Lincoln. BLPA; FaBoBe; NeHB; WBLP
Memory. Arthur Rimbaud, *tr. fr. French.* LiTW *tr. by* Norman Cameron; ReMP, *tr. by* Wallace Fowlie
Memory. Dante Gabriel Rossetti. CBEP
Memory ("I have a room whereinto no one enters"). Christina Rossetti. OBNC
Memory ("I nursed it in my bosom while it lived"). Christina Rossetti. OBNC
Memory. Shakespeare. *See* Sonnets, XXX.
Memory. Shelley. *See* Music, When Soft Voices Die.
Memory. Erik Johan Stagnelius, *tr. fr. Swedish by* Sir Edmund Gosse. AWP
Memory, A. L. A. G. Strong. PoPl; SiTL; WhC
Memory, A. Katharine Tynan. OxBI
Memory as Memorial in the Last. Edward Marshall. CoPo
Memory cannot linger long. So Wags the World. Ellen M. H. Cortissoz. AA
Memory carries my fancy back. The Little Golden Ring. *Unknown.* ShS
Memory Green. Archibald MacLeish. Po
Memory,hither come. Song. Blake. EG; EiPP; EnLit; PoEL-4
Memory: I can take my head and strike it on a wall on Cumberland Island. The Shark's Parlor. James Dickey. NYBP
Memory is a watery flower, when watered. In the Garden. Richard Eberhart. NePoAm-2
Memory of Boxer Benny (Kid) Paret, The. Frank Lima. PoNe (1970 ed.)
Memory of Brother Michael. Patrick Kavanagh. MoAB; OnYI; OxBI
Memory of Earth, The. "Æ." OBVV; PoVP
Memory of Kent, The. Edmund Blunden. HBMV
Memory of Kreisler once, A. The Musician. R. S. Thomas. MuSP
Memory of Lake Superior. George Dillon. MAP; MoAmPo (1942 ed.)
Memory of summer is winter's consciousness. Early Winter. Weldon Kees. NaP
Memory of the Dead, The. John Kells Ingram. AnIV; HBV; OnYI; OxBI; VA
Memory of the Players in a Mirror at Midnight, A. James Joyce. InvP; ViBoPo
Memory of time is here imprisoned, The. In a Strange House. Stanley J. Kunitz. NP
Memory, out of the mist, in a long slow ripple. Seagulls on the Serpentine. Alfred Noyes. EtS
Memphis Blues. Sterling A. Brown. BANP
Men. Archibald MacLeish. AmFN; MoAB; NP; YaD
Men. Dorothy Parker. BoLP
Men. Dorothy E. Reid. NeMA; StaSt
Men and brothers, who after us shall be. Ballade of the Hanged Men. Villon. LiTW
Men and Man. George Meredith. EPN
Men and women round thee, what are they, The. Companionship. Mary Elizabeth Coleridge. NBM

Men Are Children of this World. Moses ibn Ezra, *tr. fr. Hebrew by* Solomon Solis-Cohen. TrJP
Men Are Coming Back, The. Barry Cole. HYE
Men Are Made Human by the Mighty Fall. John Masefield. *Fr.* Sonnets ("Long, long ago"). EPN
Men Are the Devil. Mary Carolyn Davies. HBMV; YaD
Men are what they are, and what they do. Intimate Parnassus. Patrick Kavanagh. MoBrPo (1962 ed.)
Men at the Council Tables. Master Surgeon. Lucia Trent. ChIP
Men behind the Guns, The. John Jerome Rooney. AA; BLPA; EtS; FaBoBe; HBV; JKCP; MC; PaA; PAH; YaD
Men, brother men, that after us yet live. The Epitaph in Form of a Ballad. Villon, *tr. by* Swinburne. CTC; EnLi-2; OuHeWo
Men call you fair [*or* fayre], and you do[e] credit it. Amoretti, LXXIX. Spenser. ATP; AWP; BEL; EnLi-1; FaBoBe; HBV; JAWP; LiTL; NoP; PoAn; PoFS; ReIE; SiCE; Sonn; TOP; WBP
Men cannot guess the things they do. The Little Things. Elizabeth Isler. PoToHe (new ed.)
Men do not long endure the light. Fleur de Lys. Rayner Heppenstall. WaP
Men don't believe in a devil now. The Devil. *Unknown.* StF
Men, dying, make their wills; but wives. Woman's Will [or Wills]. John Godfrey Saxe. BOHV; FaFP; HBV; InP; ShM; SiTL; TreFT
Men Fade like Rocks. W. J. Turner. OBMV; POTE
Men Follow Simon. Raymond Kresensky. ChIP; OQP
Men found you subtle, master, blending skeins. Newman. George N. Shuster. JKCP (1926 ed.)
Men go to their garden for pleasure. In the Garden. *Unknown.* MaRV
Men grew sae cauld, maids sae unkind. The Blind Boy's Pranks. William Thom. OBEV
Men halt in the littered spot before the bank. Saturday in the County Seat. Elijah L. Jacobs. AmFN
Men Have Forged. Jay G. Sigmund. OQP
Men have left God not for other gods, they say. T. S. Eliot. *Fr.* The Rock. SoP; TRV
Men have made them gods of love. Pain. "Æ." MoBrPo
Men have their alien sons and love them. Son. Josephine Miles. FiMAP
Men heard this roar of parleying starlings, saw. February Afternoon. Edward Thomas. MoPW
Men, if you love us, play no more. In the Person of Womankind. Ben Jonson. SCEP-2; SeCP; SeCV-1
Men Improve with the Years. W. B. Yeats. BWP; MBW-2
Men in Green. David Campbell. BoAV; MoAuPo; NeLNL; PoAu-2
Men lied to them and so they went to die. Thermopylae [*or* Thermopylae and Golgotha]. Robert Hillyer. AnAmPo; MaRV
Men, like leaves, are winnowed in a train. Resurrection. William Henry Fanning. NYTB
Men long have fought for their flying flags. The Flag of Peace. Charlotte Perkins Gilman. NeHB; OQP
Men Loved Wholly beyond Wisdom. Louise Bogan. AnAmPo; HBMV; InPo; LiTA; LiTL; LiTM; NePA; PG (1955 ed.)
Men Made Out of Words. Wallace Stevens. MoAB; PoeP
Men make a camp; a swarm of bees a comb. What Makes a Home. Arthur Guiterman. SoP
Men march to war and come back on their shields. One Immortality. Norbert Engels. CAW
Men Marry What They Need. I Marry You. John Ciardi. MoLP
Men meet and part. Words Made of Water. Burns Singer. NePoEA-2
Men moving in a trench, in the clear noon. These Men. Leon Gellert. BoAV; MoAuPo; PoAu-1
Men, my brothers, men the workers, ever reaping something new. The Federation of the World. Tennyson. *Fr.* Locksley Hall. MaRV
Men never know. The Radical. Waring Cuney. CDC
Men never speak a good word. The Women Speak out in Defense of Themselves. Aristophanes. *Fr.* The Thesmophoriazusae. TreFT
Men of America, Answering the Call. Hal Borland. PoFr
Men of careful turns, haters of forks in the road. Gwendolyn Brooks. *Fr.* The Womanhood. BALP
Men of England. Thomas Campbell. PoFr
Men of England, wherefore plough. Song to the Men of England. Shelley. AnFE; EnL; EnLi-2 (1949 ed.); EnRP; ExPo; FiP; ILP; PAn; PeER; PoFr; PoPo; SeCeV; TrGrPo; ViBoPo; WoL
Men of "Forty-eight," The. Gerald Massey. PoFr
Men of Good Works. Michael Wigglesworth. *Fr.* The Day of Doom. AmPP
Men of Gotham, The. Thomas Love Peacock. *See* Three Men of Gotham.
Men of Harlech. *Unknown, tr. fr. Welsh by* John Oxenford. PoFr
(March of the Men of Harlech, *tr. by* William Duthie.) PTK
Men of learning say she must, The. Given Over. Thomas Woolner. VA
Men of Old, The. Richard Monckton Milnes. GTBS; GTSL; OBEV (new ed.); OBVV
Men of sin prevail, The. The Covenanter's Lament for Bothwell Brigg. Winthrop Mackworth Praed. OBRV
Men of the Alamo, The. James Jeffrey Roche. PAH; ThLM
Men of the earth, The, said, "We must war." Why. Robert Freeman. PGD
Men of the High North. Robert Service. ACV
Men of the *Maine*, The. Clinton Scollard. MC; PAH
Men of the *Merrimac*, The. Clinton Scollard. PAH
Men of the North. John Neal. AA
Men of the North and West. Richard Henry Stoddard. PAH
Men of the Rocks, *sel.* Joseph Gordon Macleod. OxBS
"Below the dancing larches freckled."
"Fire the heather."
"Our pastures are bitten and bare."
Men of thought! be up and stirring. Song. Charles Mackay. PoFr
Men of valor, The. Tanka. Akahito. *Fr.* Manyo Shu. AWP; InP; LiTW
Men once were surnamed for their shape and estate. Surnames. James Smith. BOHV
Men Only Pretend. *Unknown.* MeEL
Men proffer presents here to my people. Wulf and Eadwacer. *Unknown.* TrGrPo
Men, remember the marches and the halts. Apoem I. Henri Pichette. LiTW
Men rent me on rode. Jesus Bids Man Remember. *Unknown.* MeEL
Men said at vespers: "All is well!" Chicago. Whittier. MC; PAH; PoRL
Men, said the Devil. Mankind. Piet Hein. TIHL
Men saw no portents on that [winter] night. Young Lincoln. Edwin Markham. DD; LiPo; OHIP; OQP; PEDC
Men say, Columbia, we shall hear thy guns. America. Sydney Dobell. EPN; OBVV
Men say it was there where Exmoor ends in air. A Winter Legend. Geoffrey Johnson. FiSC
Men say the sullen instrument. In the Twilight. James Russell Lowell. AA; HBV
Men Say They Know Many Things. Henry David Thoreau. AnNE; ImOP; PoPl
Men seem as alike as the leaves on the trees. The Man from the Crowd. Sam Walter Foss. PoLF
Men seldom make passes. News Item [*or* Some Beautiful Letters]. Dorothy Parker. InMe; SiTL; TreF; YaD
Men share perceptions. The Switch Blade; or, John's Other Wife. Jonathan Williams. NeAP
Men talk of those the fields that till. Ballad of Poor Chimney Sweeps. Villon. WoL
Men that are men again; who goes home? G. K. Chesterton. *Fr.* Who Goes Home? OtMeF
Men that are safe, and sure, in all they doe. An Epistle Answering to One That Asked to Be Sealed of the Tribe of Ben. Ben Jonson. AnAnS-2; OAEP; SCEP-2; SeCV-1; TuPP
Men that delight to multiply desire. Caelica, XCIV [XCV]. Fulke Greville. OBS; SiCE
Men That Don't Fit In. Robert W. Service. BLPA
Men that worked for England, The. Elegy in a Country Churchyard. G. K. Chesterton. CBV; EvOK; HBMV; MMA; MoBrPo; NeMA; TreFT; TrGrPo; ViBoPo; WhC
Men the Angels eyed. Men and Man. George Meredith. EPN

Men Told Me, Lord! David Starr Jordan. MaRV; OQP; WGRP
Men Walked To and Fro. Blanaid Salkeld. NeIP
Men were connected with animals. The Shock. Larry Eigner. CoPo
Men who have loved the ships they took to sea. Mariners. David Morton. EtS; PoMa
Men Who March Away ("We be the King's men"). Thomas Hardy. *Fr.* The Dynasts, Pt. I, Act I, sc. i. CH
Men Who March Away ("What of the faith and fire within us"). Thomas Hardy. BEL; MMA; PoFr
Men Who Turn from God. T. S. Eliot. *Fr.* The Rock. MaRV
Men! whose boast it is that ye. Stanzas on Freedom. James Russell Lowell. CoBA; GN; MaRV; MC; OHIP; PGD; PoFr; PoNe
Men wrap themselves in smug cocoons. Conventionality. Eloise Hackett. MaRV
Menacing machine turns on and off, The. Terror Conduction. Philip Lamantia. NeAP
Menagerie, The. Harold Bond. YAP
Menagerie, The. William Vaughn Moody. AmPP (3d ed.); AP; PFY; TOP; YaD
Menaion, *sel.* St. Cosmas, *tr. fr. Greek.*
Purification, The. ISi
Menalcas and Enoisa. Philip Wharton. WaPE
Menaphon, *sels.* Robert Greene.
Doron's Jig [*or* Jigge]. AtBAP; PoEL-2; TuPP
(Jig, A.) EIL
Melicertus' Description of His Mistress. ReIE
(Of His Mistress.) EIL
Menaphon's Ditty ("Fair fields"). OBSC
Menaphon's Some ("Song say love"). LoBV; OBSC; ReIE
Samela. EIL; HBV; OBEV; OBSC; ViBoPo
(Doron's Description of Samela.) AtBAP; LoBV; PoEL-2; ReIE; SiCE; TuPP
Sephestia's Song to Her Child. AtBAP; CoBE; ELP; EnLi-1 (1949 ed.); EnLit; EnRePo; GTSL; LoBV; OBSC; PoEL-2; PoIE; ReEn; ReIE; SiCE; TrGrPo; TuPP
(Sephestia's Lullaby) HBV; OBEV
(Weep Not My Wanton.) CBEP; EIL; SeCePo; ViBoPo
Mend my broken mood. Prayer for Song. Fay Lewis Noble. TrPWD
Mendacity. A. E. Coppard. GTBS-W; LiTL; LiTM; OBMV
Mendax. Gotthold Ephraim Lessing, *tr. fr. German.* BOHV; PV
Mendelian Theory. *Unknown.* LiTM; SiTL
(Limerick: "There was a young lady called Starky.") CenHV
Mendicants, The. Bliss Carman. HBV; VA
Mending Sump. Kenneth Koch. NeAP; PV
Mending the Bridge. Douglas Stewart. AnNZ
Mending Wall. Robert Frost. AmFN; AmP; AmPP; AnNE; AP; CaFP; CMoP; CoBA; CoBMV; DiPo; ExPo; FaBV; FaFP; GTBS-W; HBV; ILP; InP; InPo; LaNeLa; LiTA; LiTM; MAP; MCCG; MoAB; MoAmPo; MoPW; MoVE; NeMA; NePA; NoP; NP; OHFP; OtMeF; OxBA; PAn; PFY; PoAn; PoE; PoeP; PoMa; PoPo; PoSa; PTK; RePo; SeCeV; TDP; TOP; ViBoPo; WHA
"Something there is that doesn't love a wall," *sel.* MaRV
"Mene, Mene, Tekel, Upharsin." Madison Cawein. PAH
Menelaus. Clarence Day. BOHV
Menelaus and Helen. Rupert Brooke. SeCePo
Menodotis ("Menodotis's portrait here is kept"). Leonidas of Alexandria, *tr. fr. Greek by* Richard Garnett. AWP; JAWP; LiTW; WBP
Mens Creatrix. Stanley J. Kunitz. NP
Men's hearts love gold and jade. Lodging with the Old Man of the Stream. Po Chü-i. AWP; JAWP; WBP
Men's Room in the College Chapel, The. W. D. Snodgrass. MoAmPo (1962 ed.)
Mental Cases. Wilfred Owen. BrPo; CMoP; FaBoMo; LiTM (rev. ed.); MMA; WaP
Mental Traveller, The. Blake. DiPo; EnRP; ERoP-1; MasP; PeER; PoEL-4
Mentis Trist. Robert Hillyer. HBMV
Mentors. Gwendolyn Brooks. Kal; PoNe
"Mentreché il Vento, Come Fa, Si Tace." Delmore Schwartz. The Repetitive Heart, II. AnFE; CoAnAm; TwAmPo
(Will You Perhaps.) FiMAP
Menu, The. Thomas Bailey Aldrich. HBV
Mercedes. Elizabeth Stoddard. AA
Merchandise. Seán Jennett. NeIP
Merchandise. Amy Lowell. LaNeLa; MAPA
Merchant and the Fidler's Wife, The. *Unknown.* CoMu; OxBB
Merchant, as crafty a man is he, The. Do You Plan to Speak Bantu? or, Abbreviation Is the Thief of Sanity. Ogden Nash. FiBHP
Merchant of Venice, The, *sels.* Shakespeare.
All That Glisters Is Not Gold, *fr.* II, vii. CTC
Fire Seven Times Tried This, The, *fr.* II, ix. CTC
"How sweet the moonlight sleeps upon this bank," *fr.* V, i. BoC; MemP; PoG; TreFS; TrGrPo
(In Tune with the Infinite.) MaRV
(Moonlight.) OHFP
(Sweet Harmony.) MuSP
In Such a Night, *fr.* V, i. ChTr; FiP; WHA
(Divine Harmony.) GoBC
(Duet.) CLwM
"Moon shines bright, The.—In such a night as this.") MemP
Let Me Play the Fool, *fr.* I, i. TrGrPo
Power of Music, The, *fr.* V, i. GN
Quality of Mercy [Is Not Strain'd], The, *fr.* IV, i. FaFP; LiTB; PTK; TRV
(Mercy.) BBV; MaRV; OHFP; OQP; OTPC; TrGrPo; WBLP
(Portia's Plea for Mercy.) TreF
Shylock's Defense, *fr.* III, i. TreFS
"Tell me where is fancy bred," *fr.* III, ii. AnFE; AtBAP; BEL; CH; DiPo; EG; EIL; ELP; EnLi-1; EnLit; EnRePo; ILP; InPo; LiTB; LiTG; LO; NoP; OAEP; PoEL-2; SeCeV; SiCE; TOP; ViBoPo; WHA
(Casket Song, A.) OBSC
(Fancy.) FaPON; TreFS; TrGrPo
(Love.) OBEV
(Madrigal.) GTBS; GTBS-D; GTBS-P; GTBS-W; GTSE
(Song, A.) BoLiVe; CTC; MemP; YAT
(Where Is Fancy Bred?) WePo
"There's not the smallest orb which thou behold'st," *fr.* V, i. LO
Merchant, that dost endeavor all thy days. Miserable Merchant. Samuel Rowlands. SiCE
Merchant, to Secure His Treasure, The. Matthew Prior. *See* Ode, An: "Merchant, to secure. . ."
Merchant will not credit you, The. Couldn't Stand the Press. Mart Taylor. SGR
Merchantman, The. John Davidson. OBVV
(Eclogue: The Merchantman.) PoVP
Merchants from Cathay. William Rose Benét. HBMV; MAP; MoAmPo; NeMA
Merchants have multiplied more than the stars of heaven. The Executive's Death. Robert Bly. CoAP; FRC; NaP
Merchants. Of the sea and of finance. Move Over. Charles Olson. FRC
Merchant's Tale, The, *abr.* Chaucer, *mod. vers. by* Frank Ernest Hill. *Fr.* The Canterbury Tales. UnTE
Mercies and Blessings. *Unknown.* STF
Mercies of the Year, The. John Danforth. SCAP
Merciful God, who readst my inmost mind. Prayer. Willem Bilderdijk. LiTW
Merciles[s] Beaute [*or* Beauty]. Chaucer. CBEP; CLwM; CTC; EnLi-1 (1949 ed.); EnLoPo; NoP; OBEV (1st ed.); PAn; StP
(Three Roundels of Love Unreturned.) MeEL
Merciles Beaute, I. AtBAP
(Merciless Beauty, I, *mod. vers.*) ACP
(Rondel of Merciless Beauty, *mod. vers. by* Louis Untermeyer.) MeWo; TrGrPo, *orig. vers. also*
(Roundel: "Your eyen two will slay me suddenly," *mod. vers.*) OnPM
Mercurius Gallo-Belgicus. John Donne. MaMe
Mercury. Josephine Miles. FiMAP
Mercury Bay Eclogue, *sel.* M. K. Joseph. AnNZ
"Child's castle crumbles, The; hot air shimmers."
Mercury shew'd Apollo, Bartas book. Nathaniel Ward. SCAP
Mercury's Song to Phaedra. Dryden. *See* Song: "Fair Iris I Love."
Mercutio Describes Queen Mab. Shakespeare. *See* Queen Mab.
Mercutio's Queen Mab Speech. Shakespeare. *See* Queen Mab.
Mercy ("The quality of mercy is not strained"). Shakespeare. *See* Quality of Mercy, The.

Mercy abundantly given. The Blessings of God. Mary D. Hughes. SoP
Mercy and Love. Robert Herrick. PoPo; SeCV-1
Mercy Is Most in My Mind. *Unknown.* CoBE
Mercy Killing. Kenneth Burke. TwAmPo
Mercy-Seat, The. Hugh Stowell. SoP
Mere dark is not so night-like as it seems. The Day's No Rounder than Its Angles Are. Peter Viereck. AmP
Mère Michel. *Unknown, tr. fr. French.* CIV
Merely the landscape of a vanished whim. Versailles. Adrienne Cecile Rich. NePoEA
Merely to say: "The hill is green." Poetry. William Soutar. HaMV
Merideth. *Unknown.* WhC
(On a Man Named Merideth.) GoTP
Meridians are a net. Objects. Richard Wilbur. NoP
Merie Sungen the Muneches. *Unknown. See* Monks of Ely, The.
Merit of True Passion, The. Sir Walter Ralegh. *See* Silent Lover, The.
Merits of Laughter and Lust. Eli Mandel. PeCV (1967 ed.)
Merlin. Emerson. AmePo; AmP; AmPP (4th ed.); AnNE; AP; MAmP; OxBA
Sels.
Merlin, I. AA; OxBA
Merlin, II. PoEL-4
Poet, The. BoLiVe
Merlin. Edwin Muir. CBEP; FaBoTw; FIW; MoPW; OxBS
Merlin and the Gleam. Tennyson. BEL; MaVP; OAEP; PoVP; VP
Follow the Gleam, IX. BBV; MaRV; OTPC (1946 ed.); PoRL; TreFT
Merlin and Vivien. Tennyson. *See* Idylls of the King.
Merlin Enthralled. Richard Wilbur. CMoP; NePoEA; NYBP
Merlin in the Cave; He Speculates Without a Book. Thom Gunn. NePoEA
Merlin, they say, an English prophet borne. Caelica, XXIII. Fulke Greville. NCEP
Merlin's Apple-Trees. Thomas Love Peacock. *Fr.* The Misfortunes of Elphin. OBRV
Merlin's Prophecy. Blake. ERoP-1
Mermaid, The. A. J. M. Smith. TwCaPo
Mermaid, The. Tennyson. FaPON; GN; GoTP; MPB; OTPC (1946 ed.); PCH; PoMS TSW
"Who would be/ A mermaid fair," *sel.* BoTP
Mermaid, The ("One [*or 'Twas a] Friday morn"*). *Unknown.* BaBo, *sl. diff. vers.*; ESPB (A *and* B *vers.*); LiTG; OuSiCo, *sl. diff. vers., with music*; SiTL; TreF; ViBoFo (A *vers.*; B *vers., with music*)
(One Friday Morn.) CH; OnMSP; OnSP; OTPC (1946 ed.)
Mermaid, The ("To yon fause stream"). *Unknown.* CH
Mermaid, The. Allen Upward. *Fr.* Scented Leaves from a Chinese Jar. NP
Mermaid at Zennor, The. John Heath-Stubbs. FaBoMo
Mermaid Tavern, The. Keats. *See* Lines on the Mermaid Tavern.
Mermaiden, A. Thomas Hennell. FaBoTw
Mermaidens, The. Heine. *See* Mond ist aufgegangen, Der.
Mermaidens, The. Laura E. Richards. BrR; StVeCh (1955 ed.)
Mermaidens' Vesper-Hymn, The. George Darley. Syren Songs, VI. FaBoEn; LoBV; OBNC; OBRV; PeER; PoEL-4
(Siren Chorus.) OxBI; ViBoPo
(Song of the Mermaids.) ChTr
Mermaids, The. Walter de la Mare. BrPo
(Hidden Mermaids, The.) OTPC
Mermaids. Kenneth Slessor. *Fr.* The Atlas. NeLNL; PoAu-2
Mermaids, The. Spenser. *Fr.* The Faerie Queene, II. ChTr
Mermaids and Mermen. Sir Walter Scott. *Fr.* The Pirate, *ch.* 16. EtS
Mermaid's not a human thing, A. Lost and Given Over. E. J. Brady. BoAu; PoAu-1
Merman, The. Tennyson. FaPON; GN; GoTP; OTPC (1946 ed.); PCD; PCH; PoMS
"Who would be/ A merman bold," *sel.* BoTP
Mer-Man and Marstig's Daughter, The. *Unknown, tr. fr. Danish by* Robert Jamieson. AWP; JAWP; WBP
Merops. Emerson. AmePo; AnFE; APA; CoAnAm; FaBoEn; MWA-1; OxBA
Merrie world did on a day, The. *See* Merry world did on a day, The.
Merrill's Brook. Winfield Townley Scott. FiMAP
Merrily, merrily,/ All the spring. Merry Birds. Rodney Bennett. BoTP
Merrily swim we, the moon shines bright. Song of the White Lady of Avenel. Sir Walter Scott. *Fr.* The Monastery. NBM
Merrily swinging on briar and weed. Robert of Lincoln. Bryant. AmePo; AnNE; BoChLi; DD; FaBoBe; FaPON; GFA; HBV; HBVY; HH; MPB; OTPC (1946 ed.); PCH; PRWS; PTK; WBLP
Merrimac Side, and Agiochook. Edward Everett Hale. From Potomac to Merrimac, III. PAH
Merritt Parkway. Denise Levertov. AmPP (5th ed.); NeAP; ToPo
Merry Are the Bells. *Unknown.* HBV; HBVY; MoShBr; OTPC; PPL, *abr.*; TiPo (1959 ed.)
Merry Autumn Days. Charles Dickens. PCH
Merry Bagpipes, The. *Unknown.* CoMu
Merry Ballad of Vintners, A. John Payne. ALV
Merry Bee, A. Joseph Skipsey. OBVV
Merry Beggars, The, *sel.* Richard Brome.
Come, Come Away! BiS
Merry Birds. Rodney Bennett. BoTP
Merry Boys of the Times. *Unknown. See* Courtier's Health, The.
Merry Christmas ("Merry Christmas to you, the young and the gay.") Phyllis C. Michael. SoP
Merry Country Lad, The. Nicholas Breton. *Fr.* The Passionate Shepherd. EIL; LoBV; OA
(Country Lad, The.) CBEP
(Happy Countryman, *shorter sel.*) CH
(Pastoral: "Who can live in heart so glad.") ELP; ReEn; TuPP
(Shepherd and Shepherdess.) OBSC
("Who can live in heart so glad.") PoE; SiCE; ViBoPo
Merry Couple Madly Met, A. *Unknown. See* Roaring Lad and the Ranting Lass, The.
Merry Cuckold, The. *Unknown.* CoMu
Merry cuckoo [*or* cuckow], messenger of spring, The. Amoretti, XIX. Spenser. ILP; MaPo (1969 ed.); OBSC; ReEn; ReIE; Sonn
Merry-go-round. Dorothy Walter Baruch. BrR; MPB (1956 ed.); SoPo; StVeCh; SUS; TiPo
Merry-go-round. Rachel Field. UTS
Merry-go-round. Langston Hughes. PoNe
Merry-go-round. Oliver Jenkins. GoYe
Merry-go-round, The. Roden Noel. VA
Merry-go-round, The. June. Mary Carolyn Davies. SiSoSe; TiPo (1959 ed.)
Merry-Go-Round, The. Rainer Maria Rilke, *tr. fr. German by* C. F. MacIntyre. CAD
Merry Green Fields of England, *with music. Unknown.* FTB
Merry Guide, The. A. E. Housman. A Shropshire Lad, XLII. OAEP (2d ed.); PoVP; ViPo
Merry Hae I Been Teethin a Heckle. Burns. NoP
Merry have we met. A Party Song. *Unknown.* BoTP
Merry Hay-Makers, The; or, Pleasant Pastime between the Young-Men and Maids, in the Pleasant Meadows. *Unknown.* CoMu; ErPo
Merry Heart, A. Proverbs, Bible *O.T. See* Lips of the Wise, The.
Merry Heart, The. Shakespeare. *See* Jog On, Jog On.
Merry Hoastess, The. *Unknown.* CoMu
Merry it is in May morning. By a Chapel as I Came. *Unknown.* ChTr
Merry it is in the good greenwood. Alice Brand. Sir Walter Scott. *Fr.* The Lady of the Lake. BeLS; HBV; HBVY; OnMSP; OTPC (1946 ed.)
Merry it is on a summer's day. A Swinging Song. Mary Howitt. OTPC (1923 ed.)
Merry it was in the grene [*or* green] forest. Adam Bel[l], Clym of the Clough, and William of Cloudesley. *Unknown.* BuBa; ESPB; OBB; OxBB
Merry Little Maid and Wicked Little Monk, The. *Unknown.* ErPo
Merry Little Men. Kathleen M. Chaplin. BoTP
Merry Man of Paris, The. Stella Mead. SUS
Merry March wind is a boisterous fellow, The. The March Wind. E. H. Henderson. BoTP
Merry [*or* Mirry] Margaret,/ As midsummer flower. To Mistress Margaret Hussey [*or* Merry Margaret]. John Skelton. *Fr.* The Garlande of Laurell. ACP; AnFE; AtBAP; CBEP; DiPo;

Merry (continued)
EnLoPo; FaBoCh; GN; GoBC; GoJo; GoTP; HBV; HoPM; InPo; LiTL; LoBV; LoGBV; NoP; OAEP; OBEV; OBSC; OTPC (1923 ed.); PG (1955 ed.); PoEL-1; PoIE; PoRA; PoSa; ReEn; RIS; SeCeV; SiCE; ThWaDe; TreFT; TrGrPo; TuPP; ViBoPo
Merry may the maid be. The Miller. Sir John Clerk of Penicuik. ChTr
Merry, merry, merry, cheery, cheery, cheery! Harvest. Thomas Nashe. *Fr.* Summer's Last Will and Testament. OBSC
Merry, merry sparrow! The Blossom. Blake. *Fr.* Songs of Innocence. CBEP; EiCL; FosPo; GoJo; OTPC (1923 ed.); ThWaDe
Merry Miner, The. Constance Rourke. RePo
Merry Miner, The. *Unknown.* IHA; StVeCh
Merry Month, The. "Miss X *and* Miss Y." InMe
Merry Month of March, The. Wordsworth. *See* Written in March.
Merry Note, A. Shakespeare. *See* When Icicles Hang by the Wall.
Merry Old Souls. Morris Bishop. WhC
Merry, rollicking, frolicking May. May. George Macdonald. OTPC (1946 ed.)
Merry sang the monks who in Ely fare. The Monks of Ely. *Unknown.* ACP; CAW
Merry Shanty Boys, The. *Unknown.* IHA
Merry Shepherdess, The. *Unknown.* *See* Amintas and Claudia.
Merry Sherwood, *sel.* John O'Keeffe.
Friar of Orders Gray, The. BOHV; OnYI; OxBI
Merry Sunshine. *Unknown.* MPB
Merry the green, the green hill shall be merry. Tune for a Lonesome Fife [*or* Another Song]. Donald Justice. NePoEA-2; NYBP
Merry voices chatterin'. Two-an'-six. Claude McKay. BANP; GoSl
Merry waves dance up and down, and play, The. Sport. Abraham Cowley. *Fr.* Love's Riddle. SeCL
Merry wind danced over the hill, A. Such a Blustery Day! Elizabeth Gould. BoTP
Merry Wives of Windsor, The, *sels.* Shakespeare.
Fie on Sinful Fantasy, *fr.* V, v. ViBoPo
"What, have I 'scaped love-letters," *fr.* II, ii. LO
Merry [*or* Merrie] World did on a day, The. The Quip. George Herbert. AnFE; ATP; BEL; CBEP; EnLit; ILP; LiTB; MaMe; MaPo; OAEP; OBS; OxBoCh; SCEP-1; SeCP; SeCV-1; SeEP; YAT
Merrythought's Song ("For Jillian of Berry"). Beaumont *and* Fletcher. *See* Jillian of Berry.
Merrythought's Song ("I would not be a servingman"). Beaumont *and* Fletcher. *Fr.* The Knight of the Burning Pestle. OBS
Mersa. Keith Douglas. FaBoMo
Merthymawr. George Woodcock. NeBP
Merthyr. Glyn Jones. PrWP
Mery hyt ys in May mornyng. *Unknown.* EnPo
Mesdames, never dare to deem those lovers yours. The Man Within. Annemarie Ewing. NePoAm-2
Meseemeth I heard cry and groan. The Complaint of the Fair Armoress [*or* Armouress]. Villon, *tr. by* Swinburne. AWP; CTC; UnTE; WoL
Meshed in a glow of nickel, glass. Ballad of the Drinker in His Pub. N. P. van Wyk Louw. PeSA
Mesnevi. Sadi, *tr. fr. Persian by* L. Cranmer-Byng. *Fr.* The Gulistan. AWP; JAWP; LiTW; WPB
Mesopotamia. Kipling. MMA
Mess Deck Casualty. Alan Ross. WaP
Mess is all asleep, my candle burns, The. A Wry Smile. Roy Fuller. WaaP; WaP
Mess-tent is full, and the glasses are set, The. The Battle Eve of the Irish Brigade. Thomas Osborne Davis. AnIV; OnYI
Message, The. John Donne. ATP (1935 ed.); EIL; EnLit; GTBS-W; HBV; LiTG; MaMe; MBW-1; MeLP; OBS; PoeP; SCEP-1; TuPP; ViBoPo; WHA; YAT
Message. Allen Ginsberg. NeAP
Message, The. Heine, *tr. fr. German by* Kate Freilgrath Kroeker. AWP; JAWP; WBP
Message, The. *At. to* Thomas Heywood. *See* Ye Little Birds That Sit And Sing.
Message, The. Meleager, *tr. fr. Greek by* Dudley Fitts. LiTW
Message, A. Anna Nelson Reed. OQP
Message, A. Elizabeth Stuart Phelps Ward. PAH
Message for the Nations of the World, A. Bertrand Russell. SiTL
Message from her set his brain aflame, A. Modern Love, V. George Meredith. ViPo; VP
Message from Home. Kathleen Raine. ImOP
Message Hidden in an Empty Wine Bottle. James Wright. AmPC
Message of Peace, The. Julia Ward Howe. PGD
Message of Peace, A. Longfellow. *See* When War Shall Be No More.
Message of Peace, A. John Boyle O'Reilly. OnYI
Message of the Bells, The. Thomas Curtis Clark. PGD
Message of the March Wind, The. William Morris. OBNC; OBVV; WiR
"Fair now is the springtide, now earth lies beholding," *sel.* GTBS-D
Message of the New Year, The. *Unknown.* *See* God's Will.
Message to General Montgomery. H. F. Ellis. WhC
Message to Siberia. Pushkin, *tr. fr. Russian by* Max Eastman. AWP; JAWP; PoFr; TTY; WBP; WoL
Message to the Bard. William Livingston, *tr. fr. Gaelic.* GoTS
Messages. Sophia Castro-Leon. QAH
Messages, The. W. W. Gibson. InP; MCCG; OHIP
Messages. Alfred Noyes. *Fr.* The Last Voyage. GoBC
Messages. Francis Thompson. CH; OtMeF
Messe of Nonsense, A. *Unknown.* OBS
Messed Damozel, The. Charles Hanson Towne. BOHV
Messenger, The. Alfred Noyes. GoBC
Messenger dispatch'd, again she view'd, The. Ave atque Vale. Dryden. *Fr.* Sigismonda and Guiscardo. OBS
Messenger of Sympathy and Love. The Meaning of a Letter. *Unknown.* PoToHe (new ed.)
Messenger Song, The. *At. to* John Calhoun. ShS
Messengers. Charles Hanson Towne. CAW
Messiah, The. Isaiah, VII: 14-25, Bible, *O. T.* AWP
Messiah, The. David Frishman, *tr. fr. Hebrew by* Maurice Samuel. LiTW
Messiah, The. Milton. *Fr.* Paradise Regained, I. OBS
Messiah. Pope. EiCL; OxBoCh
Rise, Crowned with Light [Imperial Salem, Rise], *sel., sl. diff.* GoBC; WGRP
(Hymn: "Rise, crowned with light. . .") NeHB
Messiah, The. Vergil, *tr. fr. Latin by* Dryden. Eclogues, IV. AWP; JAWP; OuHeWo; WBP
Sibylline Prophecy, The, *sel., tr. by* Roderick Gill. CAW
Messias. Thomas Merton. JKCP (1955 ed.)
Messidor. Swinburne. ViPo
Messmates. Sir Henry Newbolt. CH; HBV; MCCG; PeVV; ShBV-2
Metagnomy. N. H. Pritchard. NBP
Metal Checks, The. Louise Driscoll. NP
Metal Hoe Hill. *Unknown, tr. fr. Japanese by* Donald L. Philippi. *Fr.* Kojiki. HW
Metamorpho I. Joe Rosenblatt. MoCV
Metamorphoses, The. Randall Jarrell. FiMAP; TPM
Metamorphoses, *sels.* Ovid, *tr. fr. Latin.*
Acteon, *fr.* III, *tr. by* Arthur Golding. CTC
"At length my chariot wheel about the mark hath found the way," *introductory poem tr. by* Arthur Golding. ReIE
Baucis and Philemon, *fr.* VIII, *tr. by* Dryden. AWP; JAWP; MBW-1; WBP; WoL
(Philemon and Baucis, *tr. by* Arthur Golding.) CTC; OBSC
Conclusion: "Now have I brought a woork too end which neither Joves fierce wrath," *fr.* XV. CTC
Cyclops, *fr.* XIII. CTC
Daedalus, *fr.* VIII. CTC
Flood, The, *fr.* I, *tr. by* Dryden. ChTr
I Heard the Ruffian-Shepherd Rudely Blow, *fr.* XIII, *tr. by* Dryden. AtBAP
King Midas, *fr.* XI. CTC
Meleager, *fr.* VIII. CTC
Phoenix Self-born, The, *fr.* XV, *tr. by* Dryden. ChTr
Pyramus and Thisbe, *fr.* IV. LiTW, *tr. by* Arthur Golding; OuHeWo, *tr. by* Laurence Eusden
Sixth Booke, The, *tr. by* George Sandys. AnAnS-2
"Upon the hilles of Phrygie neere a Teyle there stands a tree, *fr.* VIII, *tr. by* Arthur Golding. EnPo
"Within the town (of whose huge walls so monstrous high and

thick)," *fr.* IV, *tr. by.* Arthur Golding. ReIE
Metamorphoses of M. John Peale Bishop. ErPo
Metamorphoses of the [*or* a] Vampire. Baudelaire, *tr. fr. French.* ErPo, *tr. by* Jackson Mathews; ReMP, *tr. by* Donald Justice
Metamorphosis. Eli Mandel. ACV
Metaphor. Clark Ashton Smith. FiSC
Metaphor for My Son. John Holmes. MiAP
Metaphysic Sphynx that preys on us, The. Epigram. John Swanwick Drennan. IrPN
Metaphysical Amorist, The. J. V. Cunningham. TwAmPo
Metaphysical Paintings, The. John Perreault. ANYP
Metaphysical Poem. Maxwell Bodenheim. AnAmPo
Metaphysical Sectarian, The. Samuel Butler. *See* Presbyterian Knight.
Metaphysics. Franklin P. Adams. LHV
Metaphysics. Oliver Herford. NA
Metempsychosis. Louella C. Poole. CIV
Metempsychosis. Kenneth Slessor. ViBoPo (1958 ed.)
Meteor's arc of quiet, The; a voiceless rain. Faint Music. Walter de la Mare. FaBoCh; LoGBV
Methinks all things have travelled since you shined. On the Sun Coming Out in the Afternoon. Henry David Thoreau. PoEL-4
Methinks already, from this Chymick flame. The New London [*or* London]. Dryden. *Fr.* Annus Mirabilis. FaBoCh; OBS SeCePo
Methinks amid my heart I hear. Psalm XXXVI. *Paraphrased by* Sir Philip Sidney. FCP
Methinks death like one laughing lyes. Epitaph. Caecil. Boulstr. Lord Herbert of Cherbury. AnAnS-2; SeCP
Methinks heroick poesie till now. To Sir William Davenant upon His Two First Books of Gondibert. Abraham Cowley. AnAnS-2; CEP; SeCV-1
Methinks how dainty sweet it were, reclined. Charles Lamb. Sonn
Methinks I am a prophet new inspir'd. John of Gaunt's Dying Speech. Shakespeare. King Richard II, *fr.* II, i. FiP
Methinks I draw but sickly breath. The Farewell. *Unknown.* OxBoCh
Methinks I see great Diocletian walk. Great Diocletian. Abraham Cowley. *Fr.* The Garden. ChTr
Methinks, I see how the blest swain was lay'd. To Amasia, Tickling a Gentleman. John Hopkins. PeRV
Methinks I see some crooked mimic jeer. Idea, XXXI. Michael Drayton. LoBV; SiCE; Sonn; TuPP
Me thinks, I see, with what a busy haste. On Zacheus. Francis Quarles. LoBV; MePo; OBS
Methinks I spy Almighty holding in. Meditation 68A. Edward Taylor. *Fr.* Preparatory Meditations, Second Series. AP
Methinks in Him there dwells alway. Risus Dei. Thomas Edward Brown. PoVP
Methinks my tenderness the grass must be. Unknown. Yoshiki. OnPM
Methinks some curious reader, I hear say. Ad Curiosum Lectorem. Thomas Bastard. SiCE
Methinks the Measure. Percy Adams Hutchison. AA
Methinks the poor town has been troubled too long. Song [*or* Bonny Black Bess] Charles Sackville, Earl of Dorset. CavP; CEP; PeRV; SeCL; SeCV-2
Methinks the soul within the body held. Birth and Death. Thomas Wade. VA
Me thinkes this draught such vertue does infuse. The Office of Poetry. Nathaniel Whiting. *Fr.* Il Insonio Insonnado. OBS
Methinks this world is oddly made. The Atheist and the Acorn. Countess of Winchilsea. EiCL
Methinks 'Tis pretty Sport [to Hear a Child]. Thomas Bastard. ElL; InvP
(On a Child Beginning to Talk.) CBEP
Methinks your looks are sad, your cheer appall'd. Shakespeare. *Fr.* King Henry VI, Pt. I, I, ii. FOL
Method, The. George Herbert. MaMe
Methought, as I beheld the rookery pass. The Rookery. Charles Tennyson Turner. VA
Methought I heard a butterfly. The Butterfly and the Bee. William Lisle Bowles. HBV; HBVY
Methought I heard a voice cry, "Sleep no more!" Sleep [*or* Conscience]. Shakespeare. *Fr.* Macbeth, II, ii. MaRV; MemP; TreFS
Methought I lived in icy times forlorn. Great Britain Through the Ice. Charles Tennyson Turner. Sonn
Methought I met a Lady yester even. William Alexander. *Fr.* A Vision of Oxford. OBVV
Methought I Saw. Milton. NoP
Methought I saw/ Life swiftly treading. The Sea of Death. Thomas Hood. ERoP-2; FaBoEn; LiTB; LoBV; OBNC; PeER; PoEL-4
Methought I Saw a Thousand Fearful Wrecks. Shakespeare. King Richard III, *fr.* I, iv. EtS
Methought I saw, as I did dream in bed. The Vision [*or* The Second Vision]. Robert Herrick. CBEP; UnTE
Methought I saw how wealthy men. Popular Song. *Unknown.* PoFr
Methought I Saw My Late Espoused Saint. Milton. *See* On His Deceased Wife.
Methought I Saw the Footsteps of a Throne. Wordsworth. SyP
Methought I Saw the Grave Where Laura Lay. Sir Walter Ralegh. *See* Vision upon This Conceit of the Faerie Queen.
Methought I stood where trees of every clime. A Dream. Keats. *Fr.* The Fall of Hyperion, I. OBNC; OBRV
Methought in fancy I did hear complain. The Lament of "La Belle Heaulmière." Villon. LiTW
Methought that in a solemn church I stood. The Sweeper of the Floor. George Macdonald. MaRV
Methought the stars were blinking bright. Sailing beyond Seas. Jean Ingelow. VA
Methoughte thus:—that hit was May. The Dream. Chaucer. *Fr.* The Book of the Duchesse. FiP
Methuselah. Rosemary Dobson. Devil and the Angel, VI. PoAu-2
("Man was called Methuselah, The, I remember.") BoAV
Methuselah ("Methuselah ate what he found on his plate"). *Unknown.* BLPA; FaBoBe; NeHB; TreFS
Methuselah! Song of a Thousand Years. Don Marquis. WePo
Meticulous, past midnight in clear rime. Voyages, V. Hart Crane. MoPo; MoVE
μητις... οὐ τις W. D. Snodgrass. Sonn
Metre Columbian, The. *Unknown.* Par
Metric Figure. William Carlos Williams. MAP; MoAB; MoAmPo; NeMA; NP
Metrical Feet. Samuel Taylor Coleridge. HBV
(Lessons for a Boy.) PCD
("Trochee trips from long to short.") ExPo
Metrodorus' Mind to the Contrary. Metrodorus, *tr. fr. Greek by* Nicholas Grimald. SiCE; TuPP
Metropolitan Nightmare. Stephen Vincent Benét. ImOP; NYBP
Metrum V. Henry Vaughan. PPON
Metrum Parhemiacum Tragicum. Eugenius Vulgarius, *tr. fr. Latin by* Helen Waddell. WaaP
Meuse and Marne have little waves, The. A Girl's Song. Katharine Tynan. OnYI
Mews Flat Mona. William Plomer. FaBoTw
Mexican Jo and Mexican Jane. Raking Walnuts in the Rain. Monica Shannon. BrR; SiSoSe
Mexican Market Woman. Langston Hughes. GaP; TiPo (1952 ed.)
Mexican Quarter. John Gould Fletcher. Arizona Poems, II. NP
Mexican Serenade. Arthur Guiterman. BOHV; BoLP; FiBHP
Mexico City Blues, *sels.* Jack Kerouac. NeAP
Chorus: "Big Engines, The," 146.
Chorus: "Essence of Existence, The," 182.
Chorus: "Glenn Miller and I were heroes," 179.
Chorus: "Got up and dressed up," 113.
Chorus: "Love's multitudinous boneyard," 230.
Chorus: "Nobody knows the other side," 127.
Chorus: "Old Man Mose," 221.
Chorus: "Only awake to Universal Mind," 183.
Chorus: "Praised be man, he is existing in milk," 228.
Chorus: "Saints, I give myself up to thee," 219.
Chorus: "Void that's highly embraceable, The," 225.
Chorus: "Wheel of the quivering meat, The," 211.
Mexico Is a Foreign Country, *sels.* Robert Penn Warren. FiMAP
Small Soldiers with Drum in Large Landscape, IV.
World Comes Galloping, The; a True Story, III.
Mexico Trail, The, *with music.* *Unknown.* BFSS

Mezzo Cammin. Longfellow. AmePo; AmPP (3d ed.); CBEP; CoBA; ILP; NoP
Mia Carlotta. T. A. Daly. InMe; MAP; MoAmPo (1942 ed.); NeMA; ShBV-3; TreFS; WePo; WhC
Micah, *sels.* Bible, *O.T.*
And They Shall Beat Their Swords into Plowshares. IV: 1-5. TreF
(Neither Shall They Learn War Any More.) TRV
Prince of Peace, The, V: 2. ChrBoLe
What Doth the Lord Require? VI: 6-8. MaRV
Wherewith Shall I Come before the Lord? VI: 6-8. TRV
Woe Is Me! VII: 1-6. TrJP
Mice. Rose Fyleman. BoTP; EvOK; FaPON; MoSiPe; MPB; PDV; SoPo; StVeCh; SUS; TiPo
Mice at the Door, The. Vincent McHugh. NePoAm-2
Mice Masticate from crumb to tooth. Repast. Gertrude Tiemer-Wille. GoYe
Mice That Ate Iron, The. *Unknown, tr. fr. Sanskrit by* Arthur W. Ryder. *Fr.* The Panchatantra. OuHeWo
Michael. Val Vallis. NeLNL
Michael. Wordsworth. BEL; DiPo; EnL; EnLi-2; EnLit; EnRP; EPN; ERoP-1; GoTL; MBW-2; MERP; NoP; OAEP; PAn; PoE; ShBV-3; TOP; UnPo (1st ed.); WHA
Michael Angelo: a Fragment, *sel.* Longfellow.
Dedication: "Nothing that is shall perish utterly." MAmP; MWA-1
Michael, as much good hap unto thy state. To Master Michael Drayton. Thomas Lodge. ReIE
Michael Hayd'n and Patrick Buggy one night got very druggy. The Scow on Cowden Shore, *vers.* III. Larry Gorman. ShS
Michael Met a White Duck. J. Dupuy. BoTP
Michael Robartes Bids His Beloved Be at Peace. W. B. Yeats. BrPo
(He Bids His Beloved Be at Peace.) Po
(Shadowy Horses, The.) SyP
Michael Robartes Remembers Forgotten Beauty. W. B. Yeats. BrPo; ViPo (1962 ed.)
(He Remembers Forgotten Beauty.) CTC; PoVP
Michael the Archangel. Katharine Tynan. JKCP
Michael the Archangel. Michael Williams. JKCP (1955 ed.)
Michael Walked in the Wood. Robert Greacen. NeIP
Michaelmas. Norman Nicholson. FaBoTw; MoBrPo (1950 ed.); POTi
Michael's Song. W. W. Gibson. BoTP
Michelangelo's Kiss. Dante Gabriel Rossetti. The House of Life, XCIV. MaVP; PoVP; ViPo
Michié Préval, *with music. Unknown, pr. tr. fr. French.* ABF
Michigan, My Michigan! Mrs. Henry F. Lyster. PoRL
Mickey Free's Song. Charles James Lever. *See* It's Little for Glory I Care.
Mickleham Way. Ivy O. Eastwick. BrR
Micky Thumps. *Unknown.* WePo
Microbe, The. Hilaire Belloc. BOHV; StaSt
Microbiblion, *sel.* Simon Wastell.
Man's Mortality. FaBoCh; HBV; LoGBV; SeCL; WBLP. *See also* Hos Ego Versiculos, *sl. diff. vers. by* Francis Quarles, *fr.* Argalus and Parthenia.
(Like as the Damask Rose.) LoBV
(Verses of Man's Mortality.) OBS; SeEP
Microcosm. Bertram Dobell. OBVV
Microcosmos, *abr.* Nigel Heseltine. NeBP
Microcosmus, *sel.* Thomas Nabbes.
Love Sets Order in the Elements. UnS
Micromutations. James Wright. NYBP
Microphone, The. Gertrude Van Winkle. GFA
Microscopic Trout and the Machiavellian Fisherman, The. Guy Wetmore Carryl. WhC
'Mid all the ceaseless rush of life. Refuge. Mabel E. McCartney. BLRP
'Mid all the traffic of the ways. A Prayer. John Oxenham. *Fr.* The Vision Splendid. MaRV; SoP
Mid April seemed like some November day. San Terenzo. Andrew Lang. VA
'Mid lava rock and glaring sand. The Bandit's Grave. Charles Pitt. SCC
'Mid pleasures and palaces though we may roam. Home, Sweet Home, with Variations, I. H. C. Bunner. BOHV; InMe
Mid pleasures and palaces though we may roam. Home, Sweet Home. John Howard Payne. AA; BLPA; FaBoBe; FaFP; FaPL; HBV; MaRV; NeHB; OTPC; PaPo; TreF; WBLP *Fr.* Clari, the Maid of Milan.
Mid-Rapture. Dante Gabriel Rossetti. The House of Life, XXVI. VP
'Mid roaring brooks and dark moss-vales. On the Death of a Recluse. George Darley. CBEP; OBVV
'Mid sunshine, cloud or stormy days. In Every Thing Give Thanks. *Unknown.* STF
'Mid the darkest scenes of life. God Is Near. Oswald J. Smith. SoP
Mid the flower-wreathed tombs I stand. Decoration. Thomas Wentworth Higginson. AA; OHIP
'Mid the mountains Euganean. Shelley. *Fr.* Lines Written among the Euganean Hills. ViBoPo
Mid the squander'd colour. Cheddar Pinks. Robert Bridges. ChMP; MoVE; POTE; SeCePo
Mid the white spouses of the Sacred Heart. To St. Mary Magdalen. Benjamin Dionysius Hill. AA
Midas, *sels.* John Lyly.
Daphne. EIL
(Apollo's Song.) HBV
("My Daphne's hair is twisted gold.") SiCE
(Song of Daphne to the Lute, A.) OBSC
Pan's Song. AtBAP; OBSC
(Pan's Syrinx.) ELP
(Pan's Syrinx Was a Girl.) ViBoPo
("Pan's Syrinx was a girl indeed.") SiCE
(Syrinx.) EIL; LoBV; SeCePo; WHA
Song to Apollo. AtBAP; OBSC
Midas, they say, possessed the art of old. Epigram. John Wolcott. ELU
Midas watched the golden crust. The Ungrateful Garden. Carolyn Kizer. NePoEA-2
Mid-August. Louise Driscoll. YeAr
Mid-August at Sourdough Mountain Lookout. Gary Snyder. NaP
Mid-Century. Mary Elizabeth Osborn. NePoAm
Midcentury Love Letter. Phyllis McGinley. MoLP; ViBoPo (1958 ed.)
Mid-country Blow. Theodore Roethke. BoNaP
Mid-Day. Hilda Doolittle ("H. D."). ViBoPo (1941 ed.)
Midday half-moon slopes in heaven, A. Gold. Glyn Jones. NeBP
Midden of rotting bodies of men, A. Corpses in the Wood. Ernst Toller. TrJP
Middle-Age. E. B. C. Jones. HBMV
Middle Age. Rudolph Chambers Lehmann. HBV
Middle Age. Robert Lowell. FRC; PoeP
Middle-aged, The. Adrienne Rich. NePoEA-2
Middle-aged Child. Inez Hogan. BiCB
Middle-aged life is merry, and I love to lead it. Peekaboo, I Almost See You. Ogden Nash. PoLF
Middle-aged Quixote. Louise Crenshaw Ray. JKCP (1955 ed.)
Middle Ages, The; Two Views. Leah Bodine Drake. NePoAm-2
Middle Ages sleep in alabaster, The. The Last Abbot of Gloucester. Wilfred Rowland Childe. CAW
Middle Kingdom, The. Allen Upward. *Fr.* Scented Leaves from a Chinese Jar. NP
Middle Passage. Robert Hayden. AmNP; IDB
Middle-Time, The. Lona M. Fowler. FaChP; TRV
Middle-Man. William H. Matchett. TPM
Middleness of the Road, The. Robert Frost. CrMA; LiTA
Mid-Forest Fear. Roderic Quinn. BoAu
Midges Dance aboon the Burn, The. Robert Tannahill. BoNaP; HBV
Midget, The. Philip Levine. NaP
Midnight. Dryden. ACP
Midnight. Archibald Lampman. OBCV; PeCV
Midnight. John Masefield. BrPo
Midnight. Thomas Middleton. *Fr.* Blurt, Master Constable. EIL; SeCePo
Midnight. Michael Roberts. OBMV; POTE
Midnight. Thomas Sackville. *See* Midnight Was Come.
Midnight. Margaret E. Sangster. SoP
Midnight ("The locks between her chamber"). Shakespeare. *Fr.* The Rape of Lucrece. OBSC
("Locks between her chamber and his will, The.") SiCE
Midnight. James Stephens. DTC
Midnight. Henry Vaughan. AnAnS-1; MeP; OAEP
Midnight at Mestre. Alfonso Gatto, *tr. fr. Italian by* Glauco Cambon. OnPM

Midnight black with clouds is in the sky, A. Earth. Bryant. AmePo; AP
Midnight came slowly sweeping on. Belshazzar. Heine. SoP
Midnight Court, The. Brian Merriman, *tr. fr. Modern Irish by* Frank O'Connor. AnIL; KiLC; OnYI, *tr. by* Arland Ussher
Maiden's Complaint, The, *sel., tr. by* Arland Ussher. LiTW
Midnight cry appalls the gloom, A. Johnny Appleseed. William Henry Venable. PaA; PAH
Midnight, December Thirty-first. Song for December Thirty-first. Frances Frost. YeAr
Midnight has come, and the great Christ Church Bell. All Souls' Night. W. B. Yeats. *Fr.* A Vision. MoVE; ReMP
Midnight Interior, A. Siegfried Sassoon. MoRP
Midnight is no time for/ Poetry. No Time for Poetry. Julia Fields. AmNP
Midnight Lamentation. Harold Monro. BrPo; ChMP; LO; ViBoPo
Midnight Mass. Sister Mary Madeleva. Christmas in Provence, II. WHL
Midnight Mass for the Dying Year. Longfellow. GoBC; PoRL
Midnight Moscow Airport. Moscow in the Wilderness, Segovia in the Snow. Lawrence Ferlinghetti. FRC
Midnight on March 27th. Gail Dusenbery. ThO
Midnight on the Great Western. Thomas Hardy. BWP; CH; CoBMV; PoG
Midnight past! not a sound of aught. The Portrait. "Owen Meredith." *Fr.* The Wanderer. HBV
Midnight Patrol. Eric Irvin. BoAV
Midnight Performance, A. Helen Wing. GFA
Midnight plane with its riding lights, The. Night Plane. Frances Frost. FaPON; PDV; TiPo (1959 ed.)
Midnight Prayer. Hayyim Nahman Bialik, *tr. fr. Hebrew by* Helena Frank. TrJP
Midnight Raffle. Langston Hughes. OCS
Midnight Ride of Paul Revere, The. Longfellow. *See* Paul Revere's Ride.
Midnight—September 19, 1881. John Boyle O'Reilly. PAH
Midnight Show. Karl Shapiro. OxBA
Midnight Skaters, The. Edmund Blunden. ExPo; FaBoTw; GoJo; GTBS-D; GTBS-P; MoBrPo; POTE; WePo
Midnight Special, The ("If you evah go to Houston). *Unknown.* ABF, *with music*; AS
Midnight Special ("Yonder come Roberta!"), *with music. Unknown.* AS; BFSS, *diff. vers.*
Midnight streets as I walk back, The. Letter I. Randall Swingler. WaP
Midnight the years last day the last. New Year's Eve, 1938. John Frederick Nims. MiAP
Midnight Train, The, *with music. Unknown.* AS
Midnight Was Come. Thomas Sackville. *Fr.* The Mirror for Magistrates. OA
(Midnight.) CH
Midnight's bell goes ting, ting, ting, ting, ting. Midnight. Thomas Middleton. *Fr* Blurt, Master Constable. EIL; SeCePo
Midocean like a pale blue morning-glory. Calm Morning at Sea. Sara Teasdale. EtS
Midpoint is past, The. The Bed. Giambattista Marino. HW
Mid-Rapture. Dante Gabriel Rossetti. The House of Life, XXVI. BEL; FaBoBe; HBV; MaVP; OAEP; PoE; PoVP; TOP; ViPo
Midst all the darke and knotty snares. Neither Durst Any Man from that Day Aske Him Any More Questions. Richard Crashaw. MaMe
Midst the Free Green Fields. Aristophanes, *tr. fr. Greek by* Ann Stanford. *Fr.* The Peace. HW
Midstream. Mao Tse-tung, *tr. fr. Chinese by* Earle Birney. MoCV
Midstream they met. Challenger and champion. The Swans. Clifford Dyment. MoVE; POTi
Midsummer. William Allingham. IrPN
Midsummer. Sybil Horatia Calverley. BiS
Midsummer. Hermann Hesse, *tr. fr. German by* Herman Salinger. LiTW
Midsummer. Sydney King Russell. BLPA; FaBoBe; NeHB
Midsummer. James Scully. NYBP; TwCP
Midsummer. Stephen Spender. AtBAP
Midsummer. John Townsend Trowbridge. AA; DD; HBV; HBVY
Midsummer. Ella Wheeler Wilcox. HBV
Midsummer Courtship. James Thomson. Richard Forest's Midsummer Night, VIII. OBVV
Midsummer Eve, a year ago, my mother she commanded. Midsummer Magic. Ivy O. Eastwick. BrR; TiPo
Midsummer Fantasy. Newman Levy. *See* Hottentot Tot, The.
Midsummer Frost. Isaac Rosenberg. MoBrPo (1950 ed.); MoPo
Midsummer Holiday, A, *sels.* Swinburne.
In the Water, II. PoVP
On a Country Road, I. PoVP; TOP
On the Verge, III. PoVP
Midsummer Jingle. Newman Levy. BoNaP; WhC
Midsummer Madness. *Unknown.* BOHV
Midsummer Magic. Ivy O. Eastwick. BrR; TiPo
Midsummer Melancholy. Margaret Fishback. PV
Midsummer Midnight Skies. W. E. Henley. PoVP
Midsummer Moon. "E. M. G. R." BoTP
Midsummer Morn. Frank Marshall Davis. GoSl
Midsummer Night. Marion Edey. YeAr
Midsummer Night. Elizabeth Gould. BoTP
Midsummer Night's Dream, A, *sels.* Shakespeare.
Asleep, My Love? *fr.* V, i. CTC; LBN
Bottom's Song, *fr.* III, i. CTC
(Ousel Cock, The.) ViBoPo
Course of True Love, The, *fr.* I, i. TreFS; WHA
Flower of This Purple Dye, *fr.* III, ii. CTC
Helen and Hermia, *fr.* III, ii. GN
"If we shadows have offended," *fr.* V, ii. OBSC
Love-in-Idleness, *fr.* II, i. TrGrPo
Lunatic, the Lover, and the Poet, The, *fr.* V, i. DiPo; FiP; InP; MasP
(Imagination.) GTBS-W; LiTB; LiTG
("Lovers and madmen have such seething brains," *sl. longer sel.*) PP
(Tricks of Imagination, The.) TreFS
Now the Hungry Lion Roars, *fr.* V, ii. AnFE; AtBAP; CH; ChTr; CTC; EG; EIL; EnRePo; FIW; LiTB; LiTG; OBSC; PAn; PIA; SeCeV; ViBoPo
(Epilogue.) LoBV
(Fairy Blessing, The.) OxBoLi
(Fairy Songs: "Now the hungry lion roars.") TrGrPo
(Lion of Winter, The.) WiR
(Puck Speaks.) ThWaDe
(Puck's Song.) BoLiVe; MoShBr; SiCE
(Song of Robin Goodfellow, A.) BoW
"Now, until the break of day," *fr.* V, ii.
(Fairy Songs.) TrGrPo
Oberon and Titania to the Fairy Train, *fr.* V, ii. GN
(Blessings on the Bride-Bed.) HW
(Through the House.) CTC
("Through the house give glimmering light.") SiCE
Over Hill, over Dale, *fr.* II, i. AnFE; BEL; EG; EIL; InvP; OBSC; PoRh; SiCE; ThWaDe; ViBoPo
(Fairy Land.) GBV; OBEV
(Fairy Queen, The.) OTPC (1946 ed.)
(Fairy Song, A.) BoTP
(Fairy Songs: "Over hill, over dale.") HBV; HBVY; PCD; TrGrPo
(Fairy's Song.) BoLiVe
(Fairy's Wander-Song.) FaPON; RIS
("How now spirit, whether wander you?") AtBAP
(Puck and the Fairy.) GN
(Song of the Fairy.) PCH
(Song: "Over hill, over dale.") EnLi-1
Seasons Alter, The, *fr.* II, i. BoW
Sunrise on the Sea, *fr.* III, ii. ChTr
"That very time I saw, —but thou couldst not," *fr.* II, i. MemP
Through the Forest Have I Gone, *fr.* II, ii. CTC
Up and Down, *fr.* III, ii. CTC
Violet Bank, A, *fr.* II, i. FaPON; OTPC (1946 ed.); PRWS; RePo
("I know a bank whereon the wild thyme blows.") BoNaP
(Titania's Bower.) PCH
(Where the Wild Thyme Blows.) PTK; TrGrPo
Yet but Three? *fr.* III, ii. CTC
You Spotted Snakes [with Double Tongue], *fr.* II, ii. AnFE; BoTP; EG; InvP; LiTB; LiTG; OBSC; OTPC (1923 ed.); PoeP; PoRA; ShBV-1; SiCE; ViBoPo
(Fairies' Lullaby, The.) EIL; WHA

Midsummer (continued)
(Fairies' Song, The.) LoBV
(Fairy Land, 2.) OBEV
(Fairy Lullaby.) FaPON; GoTP; RIS
(Fairy Songs: "You spotted snakes with double tongue.") HBV; TrGrPo
(Lullaby for Titania.) GN; RG
(Song: "You spotted snakes with double tongue.") FiP; MemP
(Song of the Fairies.) BoLiVe
Midsummer Night's Dream. Byron Vazakas. NePA
Midsummer['s] Noon in the Australian Forest, A. Charles Harpur. BoAu; BoAV; NeLNL; PoAu-1; VA
Midsummer Pause. Fred Lape. PoSC
Midsummer Song, A. Richard Watson Gilder. BoNaP; HBV; LHV; OTPC (1946 ed.); PRWS
Midsummer's Noon in the Australian Forest, A. Charles Harpur. *See* Midsummer Noon in the Australian Forest, A.
Midtown Poem. Robert Hershon. ThO
Midway. Naomi Long Madgett. NNP; PoNe (1970 ed.)
Midway the Journey. Dante, *tr. fr. Italian by* Laurence Binyon. *Fr.* Divina Commedia: Inferno, I. ExPo
Midways of a walled garden. Golden Wings [*or* An Ancient Castle]. William Morris. ChTr; OBNC; SeCePo; WHA
Midwest. John Frederick Nims. MoVE; PoPl
Midwest Town. Ruth Delong Peterson. AmFN
Midwife Cat. Mark Van Doren. OA
Midwife laid her hand on his thick skull, The. Thomas Shadwell the Poet. Dryden. *Fr.* Absalom and Achitophel, Pt. II. ChTr
Midwinter. Margaret E. Bruner. PoToHe
Midwinter. John Townsend Trowbridge. AA; AnAmPo; AnFE; APA; CoAnAm; GN; HBV; OTPC
Midwinter. Oscar Wilde. *Fr.* Humanitad. PCH
Midwinter spring is its own season. Little Gidding. T. S. Eliot. *Fr.* Four Quartets. ExPo; FaBoEn; GTBS-P; OAEP (2d ed.); PoIE; SeCeV (1967 ed.)
Midwinter Thaw. Lenore Pratt. CaP
Mid-Winter Waking. Robert Graves. BoPe; MoAB
Might and Right ("Might and right are always fighting"). Clarence Day. InMe
Might as well bury her. Maumee Ruth. Sterling A. Brown. CDC
Might I, if you can find it, be given. Saint Nicholas. Marianne Moore. NYBP; PoAn
"Might Is Right." Israel Zangwill. TrJP
Might these be thrushes climbing through almost. E. E. Cummings. CrMA
Mightier Church, A. Henry B. Carpenter. OQP
Mightiest, like some universal cataclysm. Griefs for Dead Soldiers. Ted Hughes. BoPe; POTi
Mighty bell is six o'clock, A. Six to Six. *Unknown.* PBA
Mighty change it is, and ominous, A. The Winter Shore. Thomas Wade. ERoP-2; NBM
Mighty, changeless God above! Prayer to Jesus. Mossén Tallante. OnPM
Mighty creature is the germ, A. The Germ. Ogden Nash. CenHV; MoShBr
Mighty drums echoing the voices. S, C, M. Ted Wilson. BF
Mighty Fortress, A. Psalms, XVI, Bible, *O.T.* *See* God Our Refuge.
Mighty Fortress Is Our God, A. Martin Luther, *tr. fr. German by* Frederic H. Hedge. AWP; EaLo; FaChP; HBV; MaRV; PoFr; TreFS
(Feste Burg ist unser Gott, Ein, *tr. by* M. Woolsey Stryker.) CTC
(Hymn: "Mighty fortress is our God, A.") WGRP
(Luther's Hymn.) SoP, *tr. by* Hedge; Sop, *tr. by* Thomas Carlyle
(Paraphrase of Luther's Hymn.) AA
Mighty hand from an exhaustless urn, A. The Flood of Years. Bryant. AA
Mighty Heart, The. Emerson. *Fr.* Woodnotes, II. AA
Mighty Hunter, The. Mrs. J. B. Worley. PoLF
Mighty Lord Is Money, A. Francisco de Quevedo, *tr. fr. Spanish by* William M. Davis. AnSP
Mighty Love. John Fletcher. *See* Hear, Ye Ladies.
Mighty mother, and her son, who brings, The. Pope. *Fr.* The Dunciad, I. AtBAP; EiPP; FosPo
Mighty Mountain Plains, The. Aubrey Thomas De Vere. IrPN
Mighty Must, The. W. S. Gilbert. *Fr.* Princess Ida. BOHV
Mighty, praised beyond compare. Rock of My Salvation. Mordecai ben Isaac. TrJP
Mighty river flows as when thine eyes, The. Out of Egypt Have I Called My Son. Caroline Hazard. StJW
Mighty Runner, A. E. A. Robinson, *after the Greek of* Nicarchus. SD
Mighty Sea! Cameleon-like Thou Changest. Thomas Campbell. EtS
Mighty soul that is ambition's mate, The. Disenchantment. Charles Leonard Moore. AA
Mighty Thoughts of an Old World, The. Thomas Lovell Beddoes. *Fr.* The Ivory Gate. EG; GoJo
(Song: "Mighty thoughts of an old world, The.") SiSw
(Song of Thanatos, The.) ERoP-2; NBM
(Stanzas: "Mighty thought of an old world, The.") TrGrPo
(Stanzas from "The Ivory Gate.") EnRP
Mighty waste of moaning waters lay, The. The Deep Dark Night. Tennyson. *Fr.* The Devil and the Lady. SeCePo
Mignon. Goethe, *tr. fr. German.* *Fr.* Wilhelm Meister's Apprenticeship, *Bk.* III, *ch.* 1. LiTW, *tr. by* Anthony Hecht; PoPl, *tr. by* Edgar A. Bowring
(Mignon's Song, *tr. by* James Elroy Flecker.) AWP; JAWP; WBP
Migod, a picture window. The One-Night Stand: An Approach to the Bridge. Paul Blackburn. ErPo
Migrant, The. Donald C. Babcock. NePoAm
Migrant Workers. Rochelle Ratner. QAH
Migrants. Ethel Anderson. BoAV
Mihailovich. Roy McFadden. NeIP
Mihi Adhaerere Deo Bonum Est. *Unknown.* *See* God Be in My Head.
Mikado, The, *sels.* W. S. Gilbert.
Humane Mikado, The. ALV; SiTL
(Let the Punishment Fit the Crime.) PoVP
(Mikado's Song, The.) LiTB
(My Object All Sublime.) TreFT
Ko-Ko's Song ("As some day it may happen"). LiTB; SiTL
(They'll None of 'em Be Missed.) EnLi-2 (1949 ed.); PoVP
Ko-Ko's Song ("There is beauty in the bellow of the blast"), 8 *ll.* PCD
Suicide's Grave, The. ALV; LiTG; LiTL; TreF; WhC
(Ko-Ko's Song.) FaFP
(Ko-Ko's Winning Song.) LiTB
(Titwillow.) SiTL
(Willow, Titwillow.) PoVP
Three Little Maids from School. PoVP; TreFT
To Sit in Solemn Silence. FiBHP; SiTL; WhC
Wand'ring Minstrel, A. TreFS
Mike. *Unknown.* ABF
Mike O'Day. *Unknown.* LiTG; LiTM (rev. ed.); SiTL; TreFT; WhC
Mild and slow and young. Girl Help. Janet Lewis. QFR
Mild Is the Parting Year. Walter Savage Landor. CBEP; NoP
(Autumn.) BoLiVe; OBEV (1st ed.)
(Ianthe.) TrGrPo
("Mild is the parting year, and sweet.") EiCP; EnLoPo; OBRV; PG
Mild, melancholy, and sedate he stands. The Hottentot. Thomas Pringle. OBRV
Mild offspring of a dark and sullen sire! To an Early Primrose [*or* The Early Primrose]. Henry Kirke White. HBV; OBNC; OBRV; OTPC (1923 ed.)
Mild yoke of Christ, most harsh to me not bearing. Paradox. Vassar Miller. NePoEA
Mile an' a Bittock, A. Robert Louis Stevenson. OxBS; SeCePo
Mile and mile and mile; but no one would gather. The Sea. Francis Webb. PoAu-2
Mile behind is Gloucester town, A. Gloucester Moors. William Vaughn Moody. AmPP; AP; ATP; FaPL; HBV; HT; MAP; MoAmPo (1942 ed.); OxBA; PFY; TOP; TreFT; WHA
Mile from Eden, A. Anne Ridler. MoPo
Mile out in the marshes, under a sky, A. The Town Dump. Howard Nemerov. CMoP
Mile with Me, A. Henry van Dyke. BLPA
Miles and miles of quiet houses, every house a harbour. The Suburbs. Enid Derham. BoAu
Miles Davis. Miles' Delight. Ted Joans. PoNe (1970 ed.)
Miles Keogh's Horse. John Hay. PAH; PoOW

Miles of pram in the wind and Pam in the gorse track. Pot-pourri from a Surrey Garden. John Betjeman. CenHV; DTC; FiBHP; PoCh
Miles Standish ban having a courtship. The Courtship of Miles Standish. William F. Kirk. PoMa
Miles thick with torpor nauseate the gardens. Three Variations, II. Boris Pasternak. TrJP
Military Harpist, The. Ruth Pitter. FaBoTw; MoVE; MuSP
Milk. James Schuyler. ANYP
Milk at the Bottom of the Sea. Oscar Williams. GTBS-W; LiTA; MoPo
Milk Below. *Unknown.* PCH
Milk-Cart Pony, The. Eleanor Farjeon. SUS; UTS
Milk for the Cat. Harold Monro. BoPe; BoTP; FaBoBe; FaFP; GoTP; HBVY; MemP; MoBrPo; OBMV; ShBV-1; SiTL; ThWaDe
Milk-glass bowl hanging by three chains, A. The Corpse-Plant. Adrienne Rich. CoPo
Milk Jug, The. Oliver Herford. HBMV; HBVY; PCH; TSW; UTS
Milk used to come in tall glass. Milk. James Schuyler. ANYP
Milk White Doe, The. *Unknown,* *tr. fr. French by* Andrew Lang. AWP
Milk-White Dove, The. *Unknown.* ChTr
Milk-white Hind, immortal and unchanged, A. The Churches of Rome and of England. Dryden. *Fr.* The Hind and the Panther. ACP; CEP; CoBE; EiPP; SeCV-2; SeEP
Milk-white Moon, Put the Cows to Sleep. Carl Sandburg. FaPON; StVeCh
Milker, The. Eileen Duggan. CoBE
Milking before Dawn. Ruth Dallas. ACV; AnNZ
Milking Kraal. F. C. Slater. BoSA; TDP
Milking-Maid, The. Christina Rossetti. BeLS
Milking Pails ("Mary's gone a-milking"). *Unknown.* CH
Milking Time. Elizabeth Madox Roberts. BoChLi; FaPON; GoJo; OTPC (1946 ed.); RIS; SUS; UTS
Milking Time. Christina Rossetti. *See* When the Cows Come Home.
Milkmaid, The. William Allingham. IrPN
Milkmaid, The. Austin Dobson. HBV
Milkmaid, The. Thomas Hardy. SiTL
Milkmaid. Laurie Lee. ChMP; FaBoTw
Milkmaid, The. Jefferys Taylor. OTPC (1923 ed.)
Milkmaid singing leaves her bed, The. John Clare. *Fr.* The Shepherd's Calendar: February. OBRV
Milkmaid's Life, The. Martin Parker. TuPP
Milkmaid's Song. Tennyson. *Fr.* Queen Mary. EPN
(Song of the Milkmaid.) HBV
Milkman, The. Leonard Feeney. MoSiPe
Milkman, The. Isabella Gardner. NePA
Milkman, The. Jane W. Krows. SoPo
Milkman, The. Christopher Morley. GaP; MPB
Milkman, The. "Seumas O'Sullivan." GaP; SUS
Milkman, The. *Unknown.* BoTP
Milkman's Horse, The. *Unknown.* SoPo
Milkweed. James Wright. NaP
"Milkweed, and a buttercup, and cow-slip, A." Her Dairy. Peter Newell. NA; PCH
Milk-Wort and Bog Cotton. "Hugh MacDiarmid." NeBP
Milky Way, The. Allen Upward. *Fr.* Scented Leaves from a Chinese Jar. NP
Mill, A [*or* The]. William Allingham. ChTr; IrPN; NBM; SeCePo
Mill, The. E. A. Robinson. AmP; CMoP; ForPo; MaPo; MoVE; NePA; NoP; PoIE; PoSa
Mill, The. Emile Verhaeren, *tr. fr. French by* Ludwig Lewisohn. WoL
Mill Girl. James K. Baxter. AnNZ
Mill goes toiling slowly around, The. Nightfall in Dordrecht. Eugene Field. AA; PRWS
Mill-Pond, The. Edward Thomas. POTE
Milla the glorie of whose bewteous rayes. *Unknown.* SeCSL
Millenium. James Kenneth Stephen. *See* To R. K.
Miller, A. Chaucer. *Fr.* The Canterbury Tales: Prologue. GoTP, *mod. vers. by* Louis Untermeyer; WePo, *mod. vers. by* Nevill Coghill
Miller, The. Sir John Clerk of Penicuik. ChTr
Miller, The. John Cunningham. CEP; OBEC
Miller. Stuart Peterfreund. QAH
Miller, Miller. Ivy O. Eastwick. BoTP
Miller of the Dee, The. Charles Mackay. HBV; OTPC
Miller, stout and sturdy as the stones, The. A Miller. Chaucer, *mod. by* Louis Untermeyer. *Fr.* The Canterbury Tales: Prologue. GoTP
Miller That Made His Will, The, *with music.* *Unknown.* BFSS
Miller was a chap of sixteen stone, The. Chaucer, *mod. by* Nevill Coghill. *Fr.* The Canterbury Tales: Prologue. WePo
Miller was a stout carl, for the nones, The. Seven Pilgrims. Chaucer. *Fr.* The Canterbury Tales: Prologue. TrGrPo
Miller's Daughter, The. Tennyson. CBEP; UnTE
"It is the miller's daughter," *sel.* EG; GTBS; GTBS-W; LiTG; LiTL; OBEV; OBVV; TrGrPo
(Song: "It is the miller's daughter.") GTSL; HBV
Miller's daughter, The/ Combs her hair. Spinning Song. Edith Sitwell. MoAB; MoBrPo
Miller's mill-dog lay at the mill-door, The. Bingo [*or* Bobby Bingo]. *Unknown.* CH; OTPC (1946 ed.); RIS
Miller's Tale, The. Chaucer. *Fr.* The Canterbury Tales. MBW-1; OxBoLi
Sels.
Carpenter's Young Wife, The. ExPo
Young Woman. BoW
Miller's wife had waited long, The. The Mill. E. A. Robinson. AmP; CMoP; ForPo; MaPo; MoVE; NePA; NoP; PoIE; PoSa
Millery, millery, dustipole. *Unknown.* OxNR
Million brown, The. The Shoemaker's Booth. Robert Hershon. ThO
Million butterflies rose up from South America, A. Annual Legend. Winfield Townley Scott. CoAP; GTBS-W; LiTA; LiTM; WaP
Million emeralds break from the ruby-budded lime. A. Tennyson. *Fr.* Maud. SyP
Million Little Diamonds, A. Mary Frances Butts. AA; TVC
(Water Jewels.) OTPC (1946 ed.)
Million million spermatozoa, A. Fifth Philosopher's Song. Aldous Huxley. MoBrPo (1942 ed.); SiTL
Million years of death some star, A. Micromutations. James Wright. NYBP
Millionaires, presidents—even kings. Everyday Things. Jean Ayer. BoTP
Millions Are Learning How. James Agee. NAMP; PoPl
Millions of cradles up in the trees. Waking Up. *Unknown.* TVC
Millions of Strawberries. Genevieve Taggard. FaPON; GoTP; MoShBr; MPB; TiPo
Millions who pass you see. To a Blue Hippopotamus. Ellen de Young Kay. ForPo; NePoEA
Millman Song, The, *with music.* *Unknown.* ShS
Millom Old Quarry. Norman Nicholson. ChMP; HaMV
Mills of Lancashire grind very small, The. Sir Leo Money. *Fr.* King Cotton. MaRV; OQP
Mills of the Gods, The. *Unknown.* BLPA
Milton, *sels.* Blake.
And Did Those Feet in Ancient Time, *fr.* Preface. AtBAP; ATP; AWP; BEL; CABA; CaFP; CBEP; EG; EiPP; EnRP; ERoP-1; FaBoCh; FaBV; FOL; InPo; LoBV; LoGBV; MaRV; NoP; OAEP; OBRV; PAn; PG (1945 ed.); PoAn; PoE; PoEL-4; PoFS; PoRA; PoSa; SeCeV; StJW; TOP; UnPo (1st ed.); ViBoPo; WBP; WGRP
(Chariot of Fire.) OnPM
(Jerusalem.) BBV (1951 ed.); BoTP; EaLo; EvOK; GTBS-W; MemP; OBEV (new ed.); OtMeF; PPON; ShBV-2; WaaP
(New Jerusalem, The.) BoLiVe; FaBoEn; LiTB; LiTG; TrGrPo
(Preface to "Milton.") AnFE; CEP; EiCL; ILP; NeHB; PoeP; PoIE
(Prelude:) OBNC
(Song: "And did those feet in ancient time.") WoL
(Stanzas from "Milton.") EnLi-2; EnLit
(Till We Have Built Jerusalem.) OQP
"Los is by mortals nam'd Time," *fr.* I. OBRV
Nightingale and Flowers, *fr.* II. LoBV
(Birdsong.) FaBoEn
(Choir of Day, The.) EnRP
(Lark's Song, The, *shorter sel.*) WiR
(Vision of the Lamentation of Beulah, A.) ERoP-1; OBNC
Reason and Imagination, *fr.* II. EnRP
Wild Thyme, The, *fr.* II. WiR
Wine-Press of Los, The, *fr.* I. EnRP
Milton. Longfellow. AA; AmePo; AmLP; AmP; AmPP; AP;

Milton (continued)
AWP; InPo; MAmP; MWA-1; NePA; NoP; TOP; TrGrPo
Milton. Lloyd Mifflin. AA
Milton. Tennyson. EnLi-2; EnLit; EPN; InP; NoP; OAEP; PoFS; PoVP; SP; TOP
Milton. Wordsworth. *See* London, 1802.
Milton Abbas Rhyme, The. *Unknown.* SiTL
Milton! I think thy spirit hath passed away. Milton. Oscar Wilde. BrPo
Milton: On the Busts of Milton, in Youth and Age ("Milton, our noblest poet"). William Lisle Bowles. Sonn
Milton! Thou Shouldst Be Living at This Hour. Wordsworth. *See* London, 1802.
Milton, you did them wrong the hour you sang. The Lord of All. Edwin Markham. CAW
Milton's Prayer of [*or* for] Patience. Elizabeth Lloyd Howell. AA; MaRV; SoP; TRV
Mima. Walter de la Mare. BiCB; BrPo
Mimi, do you remember. Biftek aux Champignons. Henry Augustin Beers. AA; AmLP; HBV
Mimma Bella, *sels.* Eugene Lee-Hamilton.
"Have dark Egyptians stolen thee away," I. HBV; Sonn
"Oh, bless the law that veils the future's face," VI. HBV; Sonn
"Oh, rosy as the lining of a shell," IV. HBV
"One day, I mind me, now that she is dead," VIII. HBV
"Two springs she saw—two radiant Tuscan springs," II. HBV
"What essences from Idumean palm," XX. HBV
Mimnermus in Church. William Johnson Cory. EPN; GTBS; GTSE; HBV; LO; OBEV; TreFT; VA
Mimnermus Incert. Walter Savage Landor. PoEL-4
Mimshi Maiden, The. Hugh McCrae. MoAuPo; NeLNL
Minaret Bells, The. Thackeray. RIS
Minarets wave on the plains of Stamboul, The. Eastern Serenade. William E. Aytoun *and* Sir Theodore Martin. InMe
Mincemeat. Elizabeth Gould. BoTP
Mind. Richard Wilbur. CMoP; ForPo; NePA; NePoEA; PoIE; PoSa; TwAmPo
Mind and Matter. *Unknown.* *See* Limerick: "There was a faith-healer of Deal."
Mind burn its wafers, The. The Firing Squad. Harry Mathews. ANYP
Mind Content, A. Robert Greene. *See* Sweet Are the Thoughts That Savor of Content.
Mind Diseased, A. Shakespeare. *See* Remorse.
Mind drowned in the sun may dream of birds, The. A Balcony with Birds. Howard Moss. NePoEA
Mind from nature, divorced by love, The. Around the Fish; after Paul Klee. Howard Moss. MoPo
Mind has shown itself at times, The. For the Marriage of Faustus and Helen. Hart Crane. AP; NePA
Mind in the purest play is like some bat. Mind. Richard Wilbur. CMoP; ForPo; NePA; NePoEA; PoIE; PoSa; TwAmPo
Mind, Intractable Thing, The. Marianne Moore. LiTM (1970 ed.); NYBP
Mind Is an Enchanting Thing, The. Marianne Moore. AP; CMoP; CoBMV; CrMA; InvP; MoAB; MoAmPo (1950 ed.); MoPo; OxBA; PIA; Po; ReMP; TwAmPo
Mind is its own place, and in itself, The. Myself Am Hell. Milton. *Fr.* Paradise Lost, I. MaRV
Mind is not, The. The Perishing Bird. D. G. Jones. MoCV
Mind of man is this world's true dimension, The. A Treatie of Human Learning. Fulke Greville. FCP
Mind of the people is like mud, The. Talking with Soldiers. W. J. Turner. ChMP; FaBoTw; GTBS-D; MoBrPo
Mind, with its own eyes and ears, The. The Mind's Liberty. W. H. Davies. MoBrPo
Minding Our Own Business. William Brown. QAH
Minds awake in bodies that were asleep. Pandora and the Moon. Merrill Moore. MAP; MoAmPo
Mind's eye sees as the heart mirrors, The. To Sleep. Robert Graves. MoVE
Mind's Liberty, The. W. H. Davies. MoBrPo
Mine. Emily Dickinson. *See* Mine by the right of the white election!
Mine. Frank Polite. NYBP
Mine are the night and morning. Song of Nature. Emerson. AnNE; HBV
Mine are the tactics. Wondering How. William Brown. QAH
Mine Argosy from Alexandria. Christopher Marlowe. *Fr.* The Jew of Malta, I, i. ChTr
("Give me the merchants of the Indian mines.") LO
Mine be a cot beside a hill. A Wish. Samuel Rogers. BoTP; EPN; GTBS; GTBS-D; GTBS-P; GTBS-W; GTSE; GTSL; HBV; MCCG; OBEC; OBEV (new ed.); OBVV; OTPC (1923 ed.); RIS; TreFS
Mine by the right of the white election! Emily Dickinson. FaPL; MAmP; MeWo; NoP
Mine ears have heard your distant moan. Lines. J. C. Squire. WhC
Mine eye bewrays. Love Cannot Live. *Unknown.* EIL
Mine eye, mine ear, my will, my wit, my heart. Gulling Sonnets, V. Sir John Davies. Sonn
Mine eye with all the deadly sins is fraught. Henry Constable. *Fr.* Diana. SiCE; TuPP
Mine eyes are ope, yet perceive I nought. A Morning Meditation: I. William Alabaster. EP
Mine Eyes Beheld the Blessed Pity. Dante, *tr. fr. Italian by* Dante Gabriel Rossetti. La Vita Nuova, XXIII. LiTW
("Mine eyes beheld the blessed pity spring.") AWP
(Sonnet.) PoPl
Mine eyes have seen the glory of hard/ work at least. George Starbuck. *Fr.* Poem Issued by Me to Congressmen. WOW
Mine eyes have seen the glory of the coming of the Lord. Battle Hymn of the [American] Republic. Julia Ward Howe. AA; AmLP; AnAmPo; AnFE; APA; BBV (1923 ed.); BLPA; CH; CoAnAm; CoBA; DD; EaLo; FaBoBe; FaFP; FaPL; FaPON; GN; GoTP; HBV; HBVY; InP; LiTG; MaRV; MC; NeHB; NePA; OBVV; OHIP; OQP; OtMeF; OTPC PaA; PAH; PAL; PAP; PoFr; PTK; RG; SoP; ThLM; TIHL; TOP; TrAS; TreF; TRV; WBLP; WGRP; YaD
Mine Host of the "The Golden Apple." Thomas Westwood. DD; GN; OHIP; OTPC
Mine No. 6. Malcolm Cowley. *Fr.* Blue Juniata, I. InP; MAP; MoAmPo (1942 ed.)
Mine old dear enemy, my froward master. Petrarch, *tr. fr. Italian by* Sir Thomas Wyatt. FCP; SiPS
Mine own John Poynz [*or* Poins], since ye delight to know. Of the Courtier's Life. Sir Thomas Wyatt. Satires, I. CoBE; FCP; FosPo; GoTL; NoP; OBSC; PoEL-1; ReEn; ReIE; SiCE; SiPS; TuPP
Mine own zweet Jone, let me not moan. Jack Shows His Qualities and Great Good Will to Jone. Thomas Howell. ReIE; TuPP
Mine Sweepers. Kipling. ShBV-4
Mine to the core of the heart, my beauty! Plighted. Dinah Maria Mulock Craik. HBV
Mine was a Midwest home—you can keep your world. One Home. William Stafford. AmFN; CoAP; NePA
Mine Were the Streets of Nazareth. Nettie Rooker. SoP
Mine will last though others fall to dust. The Enigma. Richard Eberhart. NYBP; PoIE (1970 ed.)
Mine, yet no longer mine. Nativity. Ruth Gilbert. *Fr.* The Blossom of the Branches. ACV
Miner, The. Maxwell Bodenheim. NP
Miner, The. Alfred Castner King. PoOW
Mineral Collection. Abbie Huston Evans. NP
Miners. Wilfred Owen. BrPo; GTBS-D; MoAB; MoBrPo; NoP
Miner's Dream, The, *with music.* John A. Stone. SGR
Miner's Farewell, The, *with music.* Mart Taylor. SGR
Miner's Lament, The, II ("I've just come down from the mines"). David G. Robinson. SGR
Miner's Lament, The, I ("When the gold fever raged, I was doing very well"), *with music.* John A. Stone. SGR
Miner's Lament, The, II ("Vainly I strive to make a 'live' at mining"). *Unknown.* SGR
Miners' Meeting, A, *with music.* John A. Stone. SGR
Miner's Protégée, The. *Unknown.* IHA
Miner's Song, The. Charles E. Winter. IHA
Miners' Wives. Joe Corrie. OxBS
Mingled/ breath and smell. Subway Rush Hour. Langston Hughes. OCS
Mingled aye with fragrant yearnings. Blue Moonshine. Francis G. Stokes. NA
Mingling my prayer. Saigyo Hoshi, *tr. fr. Japanese by* Arthur Waley. AWP
Minguillo's Kiss. *Unknown,* *tr. fr. Spanish by* Sir John Bowring. BOHV

Minion Wife, A. Nicholas Udall. *Fr.* Ralph Roister Doister. ElL
Miniskirtminiskirt. A Concrete Poem. Anthony Mundy. PV
Minister, The. Fenton Johnson. AnAmPo; Kal
Minister, New Style, A. Timothy Dwight. *Fr.* The Triumph of Infidelity. AmPP (3d ed.)
Minister of birds, islands, and pools. Cortege for Colette. Jean Garrigue. NYBP
Minister of Wine, The. Omar Khayyám, *tr. fr. Persian by* Edward Fitzgerald. *Fr.* The Rubáiyát. OnPM
Minister said it wad dee, The. Last Lauch. Douglas Young. OxBS; SeCePo
Minister, why do you direct your artilliery against my nets? A Fisher's Apology. Arthur Johnstone. GoTS
Minister's Wife, The. *Unknown.* SoP
Miniver Cheevy. E. A. Robinson. AmPP; AnNE; AP; AWP; BÖHV; CaFP; CBEP; CBV; ChTr; CLwM; CMoP; CoBA; CoBMV; FaBoCh; FaBV; FaFP; ForPo; HBV; InMe; InPo; JAWP; LHV; LiTA; LiTM; LoGBV MaC; MAP; MaPo; MCCG; MoAB; MoAmPo; NAMP; NeMA; NePA; NoP; NP; OnPP; OxBA; PAn; PFY; Po; PoEL-5; PoLF; PoPl; PoPo; PoRA; PoSa; PTK; SeCeV; ShBV-4; StP; TDP; TOP; TreF; TrGrPo; VaPo; WBP; WHA; WhC; YaD
Miniver Cheevy, Jr., *parody.* David Fisher Parry. InMe; WhC
Minna. Maxwell Bodenheim. MAPA
Minnesota, hail to thee! Hail! Minnesota! Truman E. Rickard *and* Arthur Upson. PoRL
Minnie. Eleanor Farjeon. GoTP
Minnie. Thomas Caulfield Irwin. IrPN
Minnie and Mattie. Christina Rossetti. *Fr.* Sing-Song. BoTP; GaP; GoJo; InvP; SUS; TiPo
(Minnie, Mattie and May.) TSW
Minnie and Mrs. Hoyne. Kenneth Fearing. AnEnPo; PoRA
Minnie and Winnie. Tennyson. HBV; HBVY; NA; OTPC; PPL
Minnie can't make her mind up. Minnie. Eleanor Farjeon. GoTP
Minnie, Mattie and May. Christina Rossetti. *See* Minnie and Mattie.
Minnows. Keats. *Fr.* I Stood Tiptoe upon a Little Hill. BoPe; FaPON; GN; GoTP; RIS
(I Stood Tiptoe.) MyFE
Minor Bird, A. Robert Frost. CMoP; LOW
Minor Poet, A. Alexander Smith. *Fr.* A Life-Drama. VA
Minor Prophet, A, *sels.* "George Eliot."
Life's Purpose. MaRV
Tide of Faith, The. TRV
Minotaur, The. Eldon Grier. PeCV
Minotaur Poems, *sels.* E. W. Mandel.
"It has been hours in these rooms" I. OBCV
"My father was always out in the garage," II. MoCV; OBCV
Orpheus, VI. OBCV
Minot's Ledge. Fitz-James O'Brien. OnYI
Minott, Lee, Willard, Hosmer, Meriam, Flint. Hamatreya. Emerson. AnNE; FaBoEn. *See also* Bulkeley, Hunt, Willard, Hosmer. . .
Minstrel, The, *sels.* James Beattie.
"Ah! who can tell how hard it is to climb," I. CEP; EiPP; EnPE, *abr.*
But Who the Melodies of Morn Can Tell, 2 *sts., fr.* I. ViBoPo
(Nature and the Poets.) OBEC, 5 *sts.*; SeCePo, 3 *sts.*
Nature's Charms, *fr.* I. OBEC
Minstrel, The. Goethe, *tr. fr. German by* James Clarence Mangan. AWP
Minstrel and genius, to whose songs or sighs. Autumnal Ode. Aubrey Thomas De Vere. OBNC
Minstrel Boy, The. Thomas Moore. ACP; AnIL; BBV (1923 ed.); CoBE; FaBoBe; FaFP; GN; GoBC; GoTP; HBV; MemP; OAEP; OnYI; OTPC; PoFr; RG; RoGo; StaSt; TreF
Minstrel Responds to Flattery, The. Sir Walter Scott. *Fr.* The Lay of the Last Minstrel. OBNC
Minstrels and Maids. William Morris. *See* Outlanders, Whence Come Ye Last?
Minstrel's Song. Thomas Chatterton. *Fr.* Aella. DiPo; HBV; LoBV; PeER; TrGrPo, *sl. abr.*; WHA
(My Love Is Dead.) WiR
(Mynstrelles Songe.) AnFE; BEL; CEP; EiCL; EiPP; EnLi-2; EnLoPo; OBEC
(O, Sing unto My Roundelay.) CH, *abr.*; GTBS-W; LiTB
(Song: "O sing unto my roundelay.") ATP (1935 ed.), *sl. abr.*; LiTL; LO, *abr.*
(Song from "Aella.") LiTG; OBEV; TOP
Mint by Night. Alfred Barrett. JKCP (1955 ed.)
Mint Julep, The. Charles Fenno Hoffman. AA; AmePo
Minuet, The. Mary Mapes Dodge. OHFP
Minuet on Reaching the Age of Fifty, A. George Santayana. FaFP; HBMV; LiTM; NePA
Minute, The. Karl Shapiro. ATP (1953 ed.); MiAP; MoVE; UnPo (3d ed.)
Minute, A. *Unknown. See* Minutes of Gold.
Minute made visible and heard. The Earth. Leonard Mann. BoAV; MoAuPo; NeLNL
Minute-Men of North Boro', The. Wallace Rice. PAH
Minutes are numbered by the fall of sands. John Ford. *Fr.* The Lover's Melancholy. PoEL-2
Minutes of Gold. *Unknown.* PoToHe
(Minute, A.) SoP
Mir träumte von einem Königskind. Heine, *tr. fr. German by* Richard Garnett. AWP
Mir träumte wieder der alte Traum. Heine, *tr. fr. German by* James Thomson. AWP; JAWP; WBP
(Superfluous Bite.) OnPM
Miracle. Liberty Hyde Bailey. OHIP; OQP; YeAr
Miracle. Edith Daley. MaRV
Miracle, The. Walter de la Mare. CoBE; LiTB; UnPo (3d ed.)
Miracle, The. Allan Dowling. ErPo
Miracle, The. Elsie Melchert Fowler. BiCB
Miracle, A. "George Klingle." OQP
Miracle. Edith Mirick. ChIP
Miracle. Lizette Woodworth Reese. MAP; MoAmPo
Miracle, The. Caelius Sedulius, *tr. fr. Latin by* H. T. Henry. *Fr.* Carmen Paschale. CAW
Miracle for Breakfast, A. Elizabeth Bishop. AmP; FiMAP; LiTA; MiAP; StP
Miracle Indeed, A. Purohit. OBMV
Miracle, A? Is it more strange than nature's common way? A Miracle. "George Klingle." OQP
Miracle of Spring, The. Piet Hein. TIHL
Miracle of the Dawn, The. Madison Cawein. HBV
Miracle of the world, I never will deny. To His Mistress. Henry Constable. *Fr.* Diana. OBSC; ReEn; TuPP
Miracle traced on a plate in, The. Alden Van Buskirk. *Fr.* Nightletter. YAP
Miracles. Conrad Aiken. HBMV; MAP; MoAmPo; NeMA
Miracles. Arna Bontemps. GoSl; PoNe
Miracles. Roy Helton. MaRV
Miracles ("I believe a leaf of grass"). Walt Whitman. Song of Myself, XXXi. MaRV
(Leaf of Grass, A.) OQP
(Leaves of Grass.) YT
(Poem XXXI.) SeCeV
(Song of Myself, XXXI.) AmPP; AnFE; BoLiVe; CoAnAm; CoBA; LiTA; MAP; MoAmPo; NeMA OxBA; PG (1955 ed.); TrGrPo
Miracles ("Why, who makes much of a miracle?"). Walt Whitman. AmePo; BBV (1951 ed.), *abr.*; CoBA; FlW; GoTP; HBVY; LeNeLa; MoRP; NeMA; OQP; OTD; PoMa; RePo; StVeCh; WaKn; YT
Miracles of Our Lady, The, *sel.* Gonzalo de Berceo, *tr. fr. Spanish by* Longfellow.
San Miguel de la Tumba. CAW
Miraculously, through prayer to Saint Anthony. Robert Fitzgerald. *Fr.* Adulescentia. SD
Mirage. R. P. Blackmur. *Fr.* Sea Island Miscellany. GTBS-W; LiTM; MoVE
Mirage. Christina Rossetti. EnLi-2; PoRA
(Hope I Dreamed of, The.) MeWo
Mirage, The. Oscar Williams. CrMA; LiTL; LiTM; NePA
Mirage at Mickleham. Francis Meynell. MemP
Miramichi Lightning. Alfred G. Bailey. OBCV; TwCaPo
Miranda's Song. W. H. Auden. *Fr.* The Sea and the Mirror. FaBoMo
Mirèio, The, *sels.* Frédéric Mistral, *tr. fr. French.*
Cocooning, The, *tr. by* Harriet Waters Preston. AWP; JAWP; PoPl; WBP; WoL
Mares of the Camargue, The, *tr. by* George Meredith. AWP; PoPl
Miriam, *sel.* Whittier.
Bible, The. MaRV; NeHB; OQP; SoP; TreFT
(Book Our Mothers Read, The.) BLRP; TRV

Miriam (continued)
(Knowledge.) PoToHe (new ed.)
("We search the world for truth; we cull.") FaChP
Miriam, Mary, Maria, Marie. Mary. Fray Angelico Chavez. ISi
Miriam, strike your cymbal. Jerusalem Delivered. Louis Untermeyer. MAP
Miriam Tazewell. John Crowe Ransom. TDP
Miriamne—Miriamne—yes, and Mio. In All These Turning Lights I Find No Clue. Maxwell Anderson. *Fr.* Winterset. TreFT
Miriam's Song. Thomas Moore. *See* Sound the Loud Timbrel.
Mirie it is, while sumer ilast. How Long This Night Is. *Unknown.* MeEL; SeCePo
Mirror, The. Edgar Bowers. QFR
Mirror, The. W. H. Davies. MoSiPe
Mirror, The. Judah Halevi, *tr. fr. Hebrew by* Emma Lazarus. TrJP
Mirror, The. M. Whitcomb Hess. JKCP (1955 ed.)
Mirror, The. Blanche Mary Kelly. GoBC; TrPWD
Mirror. James Merrill. CoAP; NePoEA-2; TwAmPo
Mirror. Sylvia Plath. NYBP
Mirror, The. Dante Gabriel Rossetti. SyP
Mirror. John Updike. WaKn
Mirror for Magistrates, A [*or* The], *sels.* William Baldwin, *and others.*
How Jacke Cade Traiterously Rebelling agaynst His Kyng, Was for His Treasons and Cruell Doinges Wurthely Punyshed. *At. to* William Baldwin. SiCE
How Shore's Wife, Edward the Fourth's Concubine, Was by King Richard Despoiled of All Her Goods and Forced to Do Open Penance. Thomas Churchyard. ReIE
How Thomas Wolsey Did Arise unto Great Authority and Government, His Maner of Life, Pompe, and Dignity, and How Hee Fell Downe into Great Disgrace, and Was Arested of High Treason. Thomas Churchyard. SiCE
Induction to "The Mirror [*or* A Myrrour] for Magistrates." Thomas Sackville, Earl of Dorset. BEL; OBSC; Po, *abr.*; ReEn; ReIE; TuPP
(Complaint of Henrie Duke of Buckingham, The.) PoEL-1
(Mayster Sackvilles Induction.) SiCE
Sels.
"Hydeous hole al vaste, withouten shape, An." EnPo
Midnight Was Come. OA, 2 *sts.*
(Midnight.) CH
Sleep ("By him lay heavy Sleep..."). WHA
Troy ("But Troy, alas..."). SeCePo
Vision of Sorrow ("But how can I describe..."). LoBV
Vision of War, A ("Lastlie stode warre..."). FaBoEn
Winter. EIL; SeCePo
Mirror for Poets, A. Thom Gunn. LiTM (1970 ed.); ML; NePoEA
Mirror in February. Thomas Kinsella. GTBS-P; PIA
Mirror, let us through the glass. The Flight into Egypt. W. H. Auden. *Fr.* For the Time Being. OAEP (2d ed.); OxBA
Mirror, Mirror. Robert Graves. HBMV
"Mirror, mirror, on the wall." Five Epigrams, 5. Donald Hall. NePoAm-2
Mirror, mirror, tell me. *Unknown.* GoTP
Mirror of Knighthood, The, *sels.* *At. to* Robert Parry.
Except I Love, *fr.* II. EIL
Song: "Fond affection, hence, and leave me!" *fr.* III. EIL
Mirror of men's eyes delights me less, The. Laus Virginitatis. Arthur Symons. EnLoPo
Mirror of Mortality, A. Thomas Proctor. ReIE
Mirror of poet! mirror of our age! Upon Ben Jonson. Edmund Waller. SCEP-2; SeCV-1
Mirror Perilous, The. Alan Dugan. LiTM (1970 ed.); TwCP
Mirror tastes him, The. Morning. Jim Harrison. WIRo
Mirrors. Elizabeth Jennings. NePoEA
Mirrors: never yet has anyone described. Four Sonnets to Orpheus. Rainer Maria Rilke. *Fr.* Sonnets to Orpheus. LiTW
Mirry Margaret,/ As midsomer flowre. *See* Merry Margaret.
Mirth ("'Tis mirth that fills the veins with blood"). Beaumont *and* Fletcher. *Fr.* The Knight of the Burning Pestle. EIL; SiCE
(Laugh and Sing.) TrGrPo
Mirth. Robert Herrick. LiTB
Mirth. Christopher Smart. *Fr.* Hymns for the Amusement of Children. EiCP
Mirth. *Unknown.* SeCL
Mirth and Music. William Barnes. MuSP
Mirth, with Thee I Mean to Live. Milton. *Fr.* L'Allegro. FaBV
Mirthful Lunacy. Thomas Stoddart. *Fr.* The Death-Wake; or, Lunacy. OBNC
Mis' Smith. Albert Bigelow Paine. BOHV; PoLF
Misacmos, of Himself, Who Loves to Be Worst in the Company. Sir John Harington. SiCE
Misadventures at Margate. "Thomas Ingoldsby." *Fr.* The Ingoldsby Legends. BOHV; HBV
Miscegeneous Zebra, The. Roland Young. *See* Zebra, The.
Miscellaneous Thoughts, *sel.* Samuel Butler.
Inventions. CBV; PV
Misconceptions. Robert Browning. AtBAP; CBEP; EnLi-2 (1949 ed.); EPN; GTBS; OBEV; OBVV; PoVP; TOP; VA
Misdeeming eye! that stoopest to the lure. Lewd Love Is Loss. Robert Southwell. ACP
Misdirection. Eleanor Slater. MoSiPe
Mise en Scène. Robert Fitzgerald. NYBP
Miser, The. Laura Bell Everett. OQP
Miser. Gordon LeClaire. CaP
Miser. Harold Vinal. MCCG
Miser till his last quick breath, A. To One Who Worshipped Gods of Gold. John Richard Moreland. MaRV
Miser with an eager face, A. The World's Miser. Theodore Maynard. CAW; JKCP; MoBrPo (1942 ed.)
Miserable Merchant. Samuel Rowlands. SiCE
Miseremini mei, ye that be my friends! On the Death of the Noble Prince King Edward the Fourth. John Skelton. ReIE
Miserere. David Gascoyne. FaBoMo; NeBP
Sels.
Ecce Homo. ChMP; FaBoTw; LiTM (rev. ed.); OnHM
Ex Nihilo. GTBS-P
Lachrymae. AtBAP; BoW; POTE
Pieta. POTE
Miserere. Gaspar Núñez de Arce, *tr. fr. Spanish by* Thomas Walsh. CAW
Miserere my maker. *Unknown.* SeCSL
Miserie. George Herbert. MaMe; PoEL-2
Miserly Patron, A. *Unknown, tr. fr. Old Irish by* Myles Dillon. AnIL
Miser's mind thou hast, A. Of a Rich Miser. George Turberville. EnRePo
Misery. John Holmes. NYBP
Misery. Shao Ch'ang Heng, *tr. fr. Chinese by* Henry H. Hart. OnPM
"Misery," he said, "to have no chin." Soles Occidere et Redire Possunt, VIII. Aldous Huxley. ViBoPo (1941 ed.)
Misery is a good thing if misery is spread. Misery. John Holmes. NYBP
Misery is greater, as I live, The. Modern Love, XXIV. George Meredith. ViPo; VP
Misery of Jerusalem, The. Lamentations, I, Bible, *O.T.* AWP
(Lamentation for the Fall of Jerusalem.) LiTW
Misery of Man, The. Alexander Craig. SeCL
Misery of the Beggars at the Gate of Zenkoji, The. Issa, *tr. fr. Japanese by* Max Bickerton. PoFr
Misfit, The—1939-1945. C. Day Lewis. BoC
Misfortune to have lived not knowing thee! Emerson. Amos Bronson Alcott. AA
Misfortunes Never Come Singly. Harry Graham. FaFP; NA; SiTL; TreFT
(Nurse.) MaC
Misfortunes of Elphin, The, *sels.* Thomas Love Peacock.
Merlin's Apple-Trees. OBRV
Not Drunk Is He, 4 *ll.* ViBoPo
(Who Is Drunk? 4 *ll.*) OnPM
Song of Gwyntho. OBRV
Song of the Four Winds, The. ERoP-1; OBRV; WiR
War-Song of Dinas Vawr, The, *fr. ch.* 11. ALV; AWP; CABA; EnRP; ERoP-1; EvOK; ExPo; FaBoCh; GTBS; InvP; JAWP; LiTG; LoBV; MyFE; NBM; OBRV; OnMSP; PTK; ShBV-2; StPo; TOP; ViBoPo, 4 *ll.*; WaaP; WBP; WhC; WiR
Misgivings. Herman Melville. AmePo; AmP; AP; CBEP; GTBS-D; MAmP; MWA-1; NePA; OxBA
Mishka. John Gray. SyP
Miskatonic river. Universes. Adrian Henri. HYE

Misogonus, *sel.* *Unknown.*
"Sing care away with sport and play." ReEn
(Song to the Tune of Heart's Ease, A.) TuPP
Misplaced? *Unknown,* *tr. fr. Spanish by* Havelock Ellis. OnPM
Miss April's come and I have found. Golden Tacks. Mildred D. Shacklett. GFA
Miss Bailey's Ghost. George Colman, the Younger. *See* Unfortunate Miss Bailey.
Miss Biddy Fudge to Miss Dorothy. Thomas Moore. *Fr.* The Fudge Family in Paris. NBM
Miss Brown, before these walls unquote. Notation in Haste. Elias Lieberman. GoYe
Miss Buss and Miss Beale. *Unknown.* CenHV
Miss Caroline Cricket. Caroline Cricket. C. Lindsay McCoy. GFA
Miss Danae, when fair and young. An English Padlock. Matthew Prior. CEP; EiPP; FaBoEn; OBEC
Miss Ella she is twenty-nine. California Bloomer. John A. Stone. SGR
Miss Esther Williams. Penny Wise and Found Poolish. W. W. Watt. PoPo
Miss Euphemia. John Crowe Ransom. CMoP
Miss Flora McFlimsey, of Madison Square. Nothing to Wear. William Allen Butler. PoLF
Miss Foggerty's Cake. *Unknown.* BLPA
Miss Helen Slingsby was my maiden aunt. Aunt Helen. T. S. Eliot. PoSa
Miss Hen. Booth Lowrey. IHA
Miss J. Hunter Dunn, Miss J. Hunter Dunn. A Subaltern's Love Song. John Betjeman. ChMP; EvOK; MeWo; ShBV-4; TwCP
Miss James. A.A. Milne. MoShBr; MPB
("Diana Fitzpatrick Mauleverer James.") TiPo
Miss Kilmansegg and Her Precious Leg, *sels.* Thomas Hood.
Gold. OQP; WBLP
(Her Moral.) VA
Her Death. VA
Miss Kilmansegg's Birth. OxBoLi
Miss Kilmansegg's Honeymoon. NBM
Miss Loo. Walter de la Mare. CMoP
(Miss Low.) HBV
Miss Lucy she is handsome. Take Yo' Time, Miss Lucy. *Unknown.* GoSl
Miss Lucy she is slender, Miss Lucy she is stout. I Am Fur from My Sweetheart. *Unknown.* CoSo
Miss Lydia Banks, though very young. The Good Girl. Elizabeth Turner. Mrs. Turner's Object-Lessons, VIII. OTPC (1923 ed.)
Miss M.'s a nightingale. 'Tis well. On a Poetess. Gerard Manley Hopkins. PP
Miss Mary was sitting one fine summer day. The Journeyman Tailor. *Unknown.* BFSS
Miss Melerlee. John Wesley Holloway. BANP; PoNe
Miss Minnie McFinney of Butte. Limerick. *At. to* Carolyn Wells. LiBL; WhC
Miss Multitude at the Trombone. J. B. Morton. MuSP
Miss Nancy Ellicott. Cousin Nancy. T. S. Eliot. MWA-2; PoSa
Miss Nancy's Gown. Zitella Cocke. AA
Miss One, Two, and Three. *Unknown.* OxNR
Miss Rafferty wore taffeta. The Private Dining Room. Ogden Nash. CaFP; ExPo; NYBP; PoCh; VaPo
Miss Ravenel's Conversion, *sel.* John William DeForest.
National Hymn, A. PAL
Miss Rosie. Lucille Clifton. TwCP
Miss Snooks, Poetess. Stevie Smith. PV
Miss Sophia. Elizabeth Turner. OTPC (1923 eed.)
Miss T. Walter de la Mare. CenHV; FaBoBe; GFA; GoJo; MoShBr; MPB (1956 ed.); PDV; PoRh; SoPo; SUS; TiPo; TSW
Miss Thompson Goes Shopping. Martin Armstrong. ShBV-2; WePo
Miss Tristam's poulet ended thus: "Nota bene." Mr. Placid's Flirtation. Frederick Locker-Lampson. PeVV
"Miss Ulalume, there are questions that linger here". Abbreviated Interviews with a Few Disgruntled Literary Celebrities. Reed Whittemore. FiBHP
Miss Wagnalls, when I brought you here. The Girl I Took to the Cocktail Party. Trevor Williams. FiBHP
Miss You. David Cory. BLPA; FaBoBe; NeHB; TreFS
Miss You. *Unknown.* PoToHe (new ed.)
Missa Papae Marcelli. J. P. McAuley. BoAV
Missa Vocis. R. P. Blackmur. ReMP
Missal, The. Rosemary Dobson. BoAV; MoAuPo
Missal, The. Ruth Pitter. CAW
Missed Again. John T. Durward. JKCP (1926 ed.)
Missed Train, The. Thomas Hardy. MaPo
Missel-Thrush, The. Andrew Young. BiS
Misses Poar Drive to Church, The. Josephine Pinckney. AnAmPo; InP
Misshapen, black, unlovely to the sight. A Bulb. Richard Kendall Munkittrick. AA
Missing. A. A. Milne. MoShBr; PDV
Missing. John Pudney. HaMV; WePo
Missing. John Banister Tabb. TrPWD
Missing all, prevented me, The. Emily Dickinson. AP
Missing Dates. William Empson. CBV; ChMP; CMoP; CoBMV; FaBoEn; FaBoMo; ForPo; LiTB; LiTM; MoAB; MoBrPo (1962 ed.); MoPo; PoIE; ViBoPo (1958 ed.)
Missing Link, The. Oliver Herford. CenHV
Missing My Daughter. Stephen Spender. AtBAP; BoC; GTBS-P
Missing Person, The. Donald Justice. NYBP; TPM
Missionaries, The. Robert McIntyre. FaChP
Missionaries. *Unknown.* SoP
Missionary, The. Sister Mary Eleanore. WHL
Missionary, The. Henry W. Frost. SoP
Missionary. D. M. Thomas. HYE
Missionary Cry, A. A. B. Simpson. SoP
Missionary from the Mau told me, A. A Magus. John Ciardi. HYE
Missionary Prayer, A. Martin Luther, *tr. fr. German.* SoP
Missions. Laura S. Copenhaver. SoP
Missions. *Unknown.* STF
Mississippi Concerto. Rolland Snellings. BF
Mississippi Girls. *Unknown.* *See* Kansas Boys.
Missive, The. Sir Edmund Gosse. HBV
Missouri Maiden's Farewell to Alabama, A. "Mark Twain." *Fr.* The Adventures of Tom Sawyer, *ch.* 21. InMe
Missouri Rhapsody. James Daugherty. RePo
Missouri she's a mighty river. Shenandoah. *Unknown.* ABF
Missouri Traveller Writes Home, A; 1830. Robert Bly. NePoEA
"Missy Sick." *Unknown.* CoMu
Mist, The. Nellie Burget Miller. GFA
Mist. Henry David Thoreau. *Fr.* A Week on the Concord and Merrimack Rivers. AA; AmePo; AmLP; AmPP (4th ed.); AWP; HBMV; InPo; JAWP; MWA-1; OxBA; WBP
(Low-anchored Cloud.) InOP; NoP; ViBoPo
Mist, The. *Unknown,* *formerly at. to* Dafydd ap Gwilym, *tr. fr. Welsh by* George Borrow. PrWP
Mist. Andrew Young. FlW
Mist and All, The. Dixie Willson. BrR; FaPON; MPB; SoPo; YeAr
Mist and cold descend from the hills of Wales. Evening in Camp. Patricia Ledward. WaP
Mist clogs the sunshine. Consolation. Matthew Arnold. ViPo
Mist condenses, The. A Warm Winter Day. Julian Cooper. BoNaP
Mist Forms. Carl Sandburg. CMoP
Mist is a soft white pussy-cat, The. The Mist. Nellia Burget Miller. GFA
Mist lay still on Heartbreak Hill, The. Ipswich Bar. Esther Willard Bates *and* Brainard L. Bates. HBMV
Mist was driving down the British Channel, A. The Warden of the Cinque Ports. Longfellow. AA; AmPP (3d ed.); HBV; WHA
Mistake, The. Theodore Roethke. NePoAm-2; UnTE
Mistake, The. *Unknown.* PaPo
Mistaken fair, lay Sherlock by. Verses Written in a Lady's Sherlock "Upon Death." Earl of Chesterfield. CBEP; CEP; OBEC
Mistaken Resolve, The. Martial. *See* To Julius.
Mistakes. George W. Swarberg. STF
Mistakes. Ella Wheeler Wilcox. PoToHe
Mistakes are dredged up again. Unalterables. Arthur Gregor. NYBP
Mistaking brains praise Norgus' wit for great. In Norgum. *Unknown.* TuPP
Mr. A. E. Housman on the Olympic Games, *parody.* E. V. Knox. WhC

Mr. and Mrs. Discobbolos. Edward Lear. SiTL
Mr. and Mrs. Spikky Sparrow. Edward Lear. SAS
Mister Angleworm. ——Manchester. GFA
Mr. Apollinax. T. S. Eliot. OnHM
Mr. Attila. Carl Sandburg. ImOP; TPM
Mr. Barney Maguire's Account of the Coronation. "Thomas Ingoldsby." *Fr.* The Ingoldsby Legends. VA
Mister Beers. Hugh Lofting. FaPON; GaP; RePo
Mr. Beetle. Emily Hover. BoTP
Mr. Bernard Shaw. E. C. Bentley. *Fr.* Clerihews. CenHV
Mr. Blake was a regular out-and-out hardened sinner. The Lost Mr. Blake. W. S. Gilbert. EnLi-2 (1949 ed.); InMe
Mr. Bleaney. Philip Larkin. NePoEA-2; PoIE
Mr. Bourne and His Wife, *with music.* *Unknown.* FTB
Mr. Brown. Rodney Bennett. BoTP
Mister Carrot. Dorothy Aldis. GFA
Mister chairman and ladies and gentleman. The Eyes Have It. William Stephens. NAMP
Mr. Coggs. E. V. Lucas. BoTP; GaP; GFA; HBV; HBVY
(Mr. Coggs, Watchmaker.) FaPON; MPB
Mr. Cromek. Blake. ChTr
Mr. Cypress's Song. Thomas Love Peacock. *See* There Is a Fever of the Spirit.
Mr. East gave a feast. Mother Goose. OTPC; OxNR; SiTL
Mr. Edwards and the Spider. Robert Lowell. AmP; AP; CABA; CBV; CMoP; CoAP; ILP; LiTM (1970 ed.); MaPo (1969 ed.); MoAB; MoPo; MoVE; NePoEA; PoeP; ReMP; SeCeV; ToPo; TwCP
Mr. Eliot Pastor of the Church of Christ at Roxbury. Edward Johnson. SCAP
Mr. Eliot's Day. Robert Francis. NYBP
Mr. Eliot's Sunday Morning Service. T. S. Eliot. MaPo; PoFS
Mr. Finney's Turnip. *Unknown.* BOHV; GFA; HBV; HBVY; NA
Mr. Flood's Party. E. A. Robinson. AmP; AmPP; AnAmPo; AnEnPo; AnNE; AP; AWP; BoLiVe; CABA; CaFP; CBV; CMoP; CoBMV; CrMA; EvOK; FaFP; FaPL; HoPM; ILP; InP; InPo; JAWP; LiTA; LiTM (rev. ed.); MAP; MaPo; MoAB; MoAmPo; NePA; NP; OxBA; PAn; PoE; PoPl; PoPo; PoRA; PoSa; ReMP; SeCeV; TDP; TreFT; TrGrPo; UnPo (3d ed.); ViBoPo; WBP
Mister Fly. Thomas Miller. OTPC 1923 ed.)
Mr. Francis Beaumont's Letter to Ben Jonson. Francis Beaumont. *See* Master Francis Beaumont's Letter to Ben Jonson.
Mister Frog Went a-Courting. *Unknown.* *See* Frog Went a-Courting.
Mr. Grumble. *Unknown.* *See* Father Grumble.
Mr. Frost Goes South to Boston. Firman Houghton. Par
Mr. Heath-Stubbs as you must understand. Epitaph. John Heath-Stubbs. NePoEA
Mr. Hecatomb Styrax, the owner of a large estate and of large muscles. Moeurs Contemporaines. Ezra Pound. OnHM
Mr. Hilaire Belloc. E. C. Bentley. *Fr.* Clerihews. CenHV
Mister Horse. Ron Padgett. YAP
Mr. Hosea Biglow Speaks. James Russell Lowell. *See* Letter from Mr. Ezekiel Biglow of Jaalam to the Hon. Joseph T. Buckingham, A.
Mr. Hosea Biglow to the Editor of the Atlantic Monthly. James Russell Lowell. *Fr.* The Biglow Papers, 2d Series, No. X. AA, *abr.*; PoEL-5
(Hosea Biglow's Lament, *abr.*) PFY
Mr. Ibister, and Betsy his sister. *Unknown.* OxNR
Mr. J. M. S——e Catechized on His One Epistle to Mr. Pope. Samuel Wesley. *See* Epigram on Miltonicks.
Mr Johnson's Policy of Reconstruction. Charles Graham Halpine. PAH
Mr. Jones. Harry Graham. Some Ruthless Rhymes, VIII. CenHV; FaFP; LiTG; MaC; SiTL
(Common Sense.) FiBHP; OtMeF
Mr. Le Strange His Verses in the Prison at Linn. Sir Roger L'Estrange. *See* Loyalty Confin'd.
Mr. Leach made a speech. Forensic Jocularities. *Unknown.* OxBoLi
Mr. Lear. Edward Lear. *See* How Pleasant to Know Mr. Lear.
Mr. Lear, I'm the Akond of Swat. A Reply from the Akond of Swat. Ethel Talbot Scheffauer. FiBHP
Mr. Lerner. Joseph Joel Keith. FiSC
Mr. Macklin's Jack o'Lantern ("Mr. Macklin takes his knife"). David McCord. FaPON
Mr. Mandragon, the Millionaire, he wouldn't have wine or wife. The Good Rich Man. G. K. Chesterton. DTC
Mr. Meant-To. *Unknown.* WBLP
Mr. Merry's Lament for "Long Tom." John Gardiner Calkins Brainard. AA
Mr. Minnitt. Rose Fyleman. GaP; HBVY; PCH
Mr. Molony's Account of the Ball. Thackeray. HBV
Mr. Molony's Account of the Crystal Palace. Thackeray. *See* Crystal Palace, The.
Mr. Moon. Bliss Carman. FaPON; GaP; RePo; SUS
Mr. Murple's got a dog that's long. Noctambule. George Johnston. MoCV
Mr. Nixon. Ezra Pound. *Fr.* Hugh Selwyn Mauberley. CMoP; MoAmPo (1962 ed.)
Mr. Nobody. *Unknown.* BoTP; FaPON; GaP; HBVY; MPB (1956 ed.); OTPC; PoMS; StVeCh
Mr. Ody met a body. Edith Nesbit. CenHV
Mr. Pennycomequick. P. M. Stone. BoTP
Mr. Placid's Flirtation. Frederick Locker-Lampson. PeVV
Mr. Pollington Remembers a Poet. Hyam Plutzik. FiMAP
Mr. Pope. Allen Tate. AP; CABA; MAP; ML; MoAB; MoAmPo; TwCP
Mr. Pope's Welcome from Greece. John Gay. OBEC, *abr.*; OxBoLi, *abr.*; PoEL-3
Mr. Pyme. Harry Behn. PDV; TiPo
Mr. Rand and Mr. NcNally. I Wonder What Became of Rand, McNally. Newman Levy. InMe; WhC
Mr. Ripley Parodies Mr. Nash—or Vice Versa. Julian Brown. FiSC
Mister Robin and his wife have started south once more. Traveling Light. Minnie Leona Upton. PCH
Mr. Scarecrow. Sheila Braine. BoTP
Mr. Sludge, "The Medium," *br. sel.* Robert Browning.
Religion. MaRV; SoP
Mr. Smith. William Jay Smith. FiBHP
Misters Socrates Snooks, a lord of creation. Socrates Snooks. Fitz Hugh Ludlow. BLPA
Mr. Speeds will clean his auto. Some Who Do Not Go to Church. *Unknown.* WBLP
Mr. Squirrel. V. M. Julian. BoTP
Mr. Symons at Richmond, Mr. Pope at Twickenham. Julian Symons. WaP
Mr. T/ bareheaded. The Artist. William Carlos Williams. HoPM; NYBP; PIA
Mister Thomas Jones. Bringing Him Up. Lord Dunsany BBGG; PV
Mr. Thomas Shepheard. Edward Johnson. SCAP
Mr. U Will Not Be Missed. E. E. Cummings. SiTL; TDP
Mr. Vanessa took the phone. Parallax. Maxwell Anderson. NYBP
Mr. Walter de la Mare Makes the Little Ones Dizzy. Samuel Hoffenstein. Par; SiTL
Mr. Ward of Anagrams Thus. Nathaniel Ward. SCAP
Mr. Wells. Elizabeth Madox Roberts. FaPON; GaP; HBMV; HBVY; TSW
Mr. Whittier. Winfield Townley Scott. CrMA; OnHM
Mr. Wild wore. Paratrooper. John Giorno. ANYP
Mister William. W. S. Gilbert. TOP
Mr. Wright went out to fish. The Right Way to Fish. *Unknown.* WhC
Mr. Z. M. Carl Holman. Kal
Mistletoe Bough, The. Thomas Haynes Bayly. BLPA; HBV; NeHB; PaPo; TreFS
Mistletoe Sprites. Solveig Paulson Russell. ChBR
Mistral. Barbara Howes. NYBP
Mistress, The, *sels.* Abraham Cowley.
Against Hope. GTBS-W; LiTB; LiTG; LoBV; MeLP; MePo; OBS; SeCV-1
All-over Love. LiTL; SeCL
Change, The. AnAnS-2; BEL; CoBE; FaBoEn; LO; MeLP; MePo; OBS; ReEn; SCEP-2; SeCP; SeCV-1
Clad All in White. SeCV-1
Hope. SCEP-1
Love and Life. SeEP
My Diet. LiTL; LO; SeCL; SeEP
Platonic[k] Love. SCEP-2; SeCV-1; SeEP
Spring, The. BWP; CLwM; LO; MeLP; OBS; ReEn; SeEP
(Love's Absence in the Spring.) LiTL
Thief, The. BEL; EnLi-1; EnLit; OAEP; SeCL; WHA

Thraldome, The. SCEP-2; SeCV-1
Welcome, The. SeCV-1
Wish, The. BEL; BoC; CavP; CoBE; EnLi-1; EnLit; FaPL; GTBS-W; HBV; LiTB; LiTG; NoP; OAEP; OBEV; OBS; SeCL; SeCV-1; SeEP; TOP; TrGrPo; ViBoPo; WHA
Written in Juice of Lemmon. AnAnS-2; SeCP; SeCV-1
Mistress, The: A Song. Earl of Rochester. CavP; MePo; OBS; PeRV
(His Mistress.) OnPM
"Age in her embraces past, An," *sel.* AtBAP; ViBoPo
Mrs. Alfred Uruguay. Wallace Stevens. AP; MoPo; NePA; TwCP
Mrs. Ambrose watched the iridescence. Water-Images. Mary Elizabeth Osborn. NePoAm-2
Mistress Anne. To Mistress Anne. John Skelton. EnRePo
Mrs. Arbuthnot. Stevie Smith. NYTB
Mrs. Barks. Rose Fyleman. BrR
Mistress, behold in this true-speaking glass. Barnabe Barnes. Parthenophil and Parthenophe, I. Sonn; TuPP
Mrs. Brown. Rose Fyleman. BoTP; GaP; TiPo
Mrs. Brown and the Famous Author. Stoddard King. ATP
Mrs. Bubb was gay and free, fair, fat, and forty-three. The One Horse Chay. *Unknown.* OxBoLi
Mrs. C. (Or Any Other Too Practical Person). Rowena Bastin Bennett. GaP
Mrs. Caribou. William Jay Smith. PoMS
Mistress Comfort. Elizabeth Gould. BoTP
Mrs. Crudeman. Sir Osbert Sitwell. HaMV
Mrs. Frances Harris's Petition. Swift. *See* To Their Excellencies the Lords Justices of Ireland, the Humble Petition of Frances Harris.
Mrs. Golightly. Gertrude Hall. AA
Mistress Hale of Beverly. Lucy Larcom. PAH
Mrs. Hobart-Constantine awakens. Two Ladies Bidding Us "Good Morning." James P. Vaughn. NNP
Mrs. Huff is up a miff tree. Let Your Pastor Know. *Unknown.* STF
Mrs. Indiarubber Duck. D. Carter. BoTP
Mrs. Jenny Wren. Rodney Bennett. BoTP
Mrs. Judge Jenkins, *parody.* Bret Harte. CABA; FiBHP; HBV; InP; WhC
Mrs. Loewinsohn &c. Ron Loewinsohn. NeAP
Mrs. Lombardi's month-old son is dead. Italian Extravaganza. Gregory Corso. CoPo; OCS
Mrs. McGrath. *Unknown.* OnYI
Mrs. MacQueen. Walter de la Mare. BoTP
Mrs. Malone. Eleanor Farjeon. PoMS
Mrs. Malooly. Agnes Lee. NP
Mistress Margaret Hussey. John Skelton. *See* To Mistress Margaret Hussey.
Mrs. Marmaduke Moore, at the age of ten. The Seven Spiritual Ages of Mrs. Marmaduke Moore. Ogden Nash. MoAmPo (1950 ed.)
Mrs. Mary Blaize. Goldsmith. *See* Elegy on That Glory of Her Sex, Mrs. Mary Blaize, An.
Mistress Mary, quite contrary. *See* Mary, Mary, quite contrary.
Mrs. Mason bought a basin. *Unknown.* OxNR
Mrs. Mother Has a Nose. James Broughton. SiTL
Mrs. Ocean takes in washing. Washday. Elizabeth F. Upson. GFA
Mistress of all my senses can invite. Caelia. Richard Duke. PeRV
"Mistress of gods and men! I have been thine." Pygmalion. William Bell Scott. EPN; VA
Mistress of the manse, The, *sel.* Josiah Gilbert Holland.
Lullaby: "Rockaby, lullaby, bees in the clover." AA; HBV
(Rockaby, Lullaby.) PRWS, *abr.*
Mistress of the Matchless Mine. Clyde Robertson. PoOW
Mistress of the roses, The. Unguarded. Ada Foster Murray. HBV
Mistress of Vision, The. Francis Thompson. BrPo; CH, *abr.*; OBVV
Mrs. Peck-Pigeon. Eleanor Farjeon. PDV; SoPo; StVeCh (1955 ed.); SUS; TiPo; UTS
Mrs. Reece Laughs. Martin Armstrong. POTE
Mrs. Santa Claus' Christmas Present. Alice S. Morris. PoSC
Mrs. Severin. Winfield Townley Scott. FiMAP; NePoAm
Mrs. Seymour Fentolin. Oliver Herford. HBMV
Mrs. Smith. Frederick Locker-Lampson. BOHV; HBV
Mrs. Snipkin and Mrs. Wobblechin. Laura E. Richards. PoRh; SoPo; StVeCh (1955 ed.); TiPo
Mrs. Southern's Enemy. Sir Osbert Sitwell. AtBAP; ViBoPo
Mrs. Spider. Myra Cohn Liningston. PDV
Mrs. Squirrel/ In a tree. Squirrel. James S. Tippett. RePo
Mrs. Swartz. Don Marquis. ThLM
Mrs. Throckmorton's bull-finch sang a song. Homage to William Cowper. Donald Davie. NePoEA
Mrs. Turner's Object-Lessons, *sels.* Elizabeth Turner.
Godd Girl, The, VIII. OTPC (1923 ed.)
Letter, The, IX. OTPC (1923 ed.)
Mrs. Williams. Edgar Lee Masters. *Fr.* Spoon River Anthology. NAMP
Mrs. Winkelsteiner. Dorothy E. Reid. NeMA; StaSt
Mistress without Compare, A. *at. to* Charles d'Orleans. MeEL
Mistresses. *Unknown, tr. fr. Irish by* Frank O'Connor. KiLC
Mistrust To-Morrow. Horace. *See* To Leuconöe.
Mistrustful minds be moved. Sir Thomas Wyatt. FCP; SiPS
Mists and Rain. Baudelaire, *tr. fr. French by* Arthur Symons. OnPM; SyP
Mists Are Rising Now, The. Hasye Cooperman. GoYe
Mists of Daybreak. Buson, *tr. fr. Japanese by* William N. Porter. MPB
Mists rise over, The/ The still pools at Asuka. Three Poems from the Japanese, II. Yamabe no Akahito, *tr. fr. Japanese by* Kenneth Rexroth. HoPM; LiTW
Misty-moisty was the morn. How Do You Do? *Unknown.* ChTr
Misty mornin' doon the shore wi a hushed and caller air, A. The Smoky Smirr o' Rain. George Campbell Hay. ACV
Misunderstanding. Henry W. Frost. SoP
Misunderstanding. Irving Layton. PV
Mitherless Bairn, The. William Thom. HBV; VA
Mither's Lament, The. Sydney Goodsir Smith. ACV; OxBS
Mithraic Emblems, *sel.* Roy Campbell.
To the Sun. EaLo; FaBoTw
Mithras, God of the Morning, our trumpets waken the wall! A Song to Mithras. Kipling. FOL
Mithridates. Emerson. AP
Mitten Song, The. Marie Louise Allen. BrR; SoPo; SUS; TiPo
Mix a Pancake. Christina Rossetti. GFA; OTPC (1946 ed.); PoRh; SoPo; SUS; TiPo (1952 ed.)
(Pancake, The.) BoTP; HBVY; PCH
Mixed Beasts. Kenyon Cox. RIS
Sels.
Bumblebeaver, The. TiPo
Kangarooster, The. TiPo
Octopussycat, The. FaPON; SoPo; TiPo
Mixed flower fragrance hung about. Kitten and Firefly. Marie Grimes. CIV
Mixer, The. Louis MacNeice. FaBoTw
Mixture of chloroform and oil of cloves. The Place of Pain in the Universe. Anthony Hecht. CrMA
Mixtures of this garden, The. In the Garden; Villa Cleobolus. Lawrence Durrell. ChMP
Miyoko San. Mary NcNeil Fenollosa. AA
Mizpah. Julia A. Baker. BLPA; FaBoBe; NeHB; OQP
Mmmm/ I get up and am seized by the present. Mister Horse. Ron Padgett. YAP
Mnemosyne. Trumbull Stickney. AmePo; AnFE; CoAnAm; CrMA; LiTA; NCEP; OxBA; TDP; TwAmPo; ViBoPo (1958 ed.)
Mnemosyne Lay in Dust, *sels.* Austin Clarke. OPoP
"One night he heard heart-breaking sound," VI.
"Past the house where he was got," I.
"Rememorised, Maurice Devane," XVIII.
"Straight-jacketing sprang to every lock," II.
Mo Craoibhin Cno. Edward Walsh. IrPN
Moan in the Form of a Ballade. Maurice Baring. WhC
Moan, Moan, Ye Dying Gales. Henry Neele. HBV
Moanin', *with music.* *Unknown.* ABF
Moanish Lady! *with music.* *Unknown.* AS
Mob within the heart, The. Emily Dickinson. MWA-2
Mobile Bay, *with music.* *Unknown.* SoAmSa
Mobile, immaculate and austere. A Pastoral. Geoffrey Hill. NePoEA-2
Möbius. Phillip Hey. YAP
Moby Dick, *sel.* Herman Melville.
Father Mapple's Hymn, *fr. ch.* 9. AmePo; EtS
(Ribs and Terrors, The.) EaLo; ViBoPo
(Whale, The.) PoPl; TrGrPo

Mock-bird in a village, A. The Mocking Bird and the Donkey. José Rosas. PCD
Mock Caliph, The. *Unknown, tr. fr. Arabic by* Richard F. Burton. *Fr.* The Thousand and One Nights. EnLi-1
Mock Medicine. *Unknown.* MeEL
Mock On, Mock On, Voltaire, Rousseau. Blake. AtBAP; CABA; EiCL; EiPP; EnRP; ERoP-1; ILP; NoP; OAEP; OBNC; OBRV; OxBoCh; PoEL-4; PoeP; PoFS; PoIE
(Mockery, 2 *sts.*) TrGrPo
(Scoffers, The.) LiTB; OnPM; SeCeV; UnPo
Mock Pop Forsooth: A Tale of Life and Death. James W. Thompson. WSL
Mock Song, A. Alexander Brome. SeCL
Mock Turtle's Song, The. "Lewis Carroll." *See* Lobster Quadrille, The.
Mockery. Blake. *See* Mock On, Mock On, Voltaire, Rousseau.
Mockery. Katherine Dixon Riggs. BrR; MPB; SP
Mockery murders love, they say, and she. Foolish Proverb. *Unknown.* MeWo; UnTE
Mocking-Bird, The. Ednah Proctor Clarke. AA
Mocking-Bird, The. Paul Hamilton Hayne. AmPP (3d ed.)
Mocking Bird, The. Richard Hovey. TSW
Mockingbird, The. Randall Jarrell. NYBP; OA
Mocking Bird, The. Sidney Lanier. AA; AmPP (3d ed.)
Mocking-Bird, The. Frank Lebby Stanton. AA
Mocking-Bird, The. Henry Jerome Stockard. AA
Mocking Bird and the Donkey, The. José Rosas, *tr. fr. Spanish by* Bryant. PCD
Mockingbird leans, A. Letter to a Poet. Robert Hass. YAP
Mocking Fairy, The. Walter de la Mare. GBV; MoBrPo; MoShBr
Mocking the water with their wings. To One Older. Marian Margaret Boyd. HBMV
Mocking your slow sepulchral horns. Song for a Proud Relation. Patrick MacDonogh. OnYI
Mode of the person becomes the mode of the world, The. Conversation with Three Women of New England. Wallace Stevens. NePA
Model, A. Dollie Radford. VA
Model and the Statue, The. Michelangelo, *tr. fr. Italian by* John Addington Symonds. OnPM
Model for the Laureate, A. W. B. Yeats. CMoP
Moderate tasks and moderate leisure. The Second Best. Matthew Arnold. EPN
Moderation. Horace, *tr. fr. Latin by* William Cowper. *Fr.* Odes. PoToHe (new ed.)
Modern Baby, The. William Croswell Doane. BLPA; YaD
Modern Ballad, A; the Ups and Downs of the Elevator Car. Caroline D. Emerson. BrR
Modern Beauty. Arthur Symons. EnLit; HBV; MoBrPo; PoVP
Modern Columbus, A. Eleanor Robbins Wilson. PoMa
Modern Declaration. Edna St. Vincent Millay. MoLP
Modern Dragon, A. Rowena Bastin Bennett. GFA; PDV; SoPo; TiPo; UTS
Modern Hiawatha, The, *parody.* George A. Strong. *Fr.* The Song of Milkanwatha. BBV (1951 ed.); BOHV; FaFP; FaPON; FiBHP; HBV; InMe; LiTG; MoShBr; NA; Par; SiTL; TreFS; WhC; YaD
(Hiawatha's Mittens.) ShBV-1
Modern house, with great glass eye, The. Anecdote of the Sparrow. Robert Pack. NePA
Modern Jonas, The. *Unknown.* PAH
Modern Language Association, The. A Salute to the Modern Language Association, Convening in the Hotel Pennsylvania, December 28th-30th. Morris Bishop. WhC
Modern Love. Keats. CBEP; OBNC
Modern Love. George Meredith. PoVP; ViPo; ViPP; VP
Sels.
"All other joys of life he strove to warm," IV. GTBS-D; OAEP; VA
(Kinship with the Stars, 6 *ll.*) GTBS-W
"Am I failing? For no longer can I cast," XXIX. CABA; FaPL; OAEP
"At dinner, she is hostess, I am host," XVII. EnLit; ILP; OAEP; Sonn
(Hiding the Skeleton.) VA
"At last we parley: we so strangely dumb," XLVI. EnLit; OAEP
"But where began the change; and what's my crime?" X. EnLit; NBM; PoEL-5
"By this he knew she wept with waking eyes," I. AnEnPo; BEL; EnLi-2; EnLit; EnLoPo; HBV; ILP; NBM; OAEP; Po; PoAn; PoEL-5; Sonn; StP
(End of Love, The.) HoPM
"He found her by the ocean's moaning verge," XLIX. BEL; EnLi-2; HBV; OAEP; PoE
"Here Jack and Tom are paired with Moll and Meg," XXVIII. InvP; NBM; PoEL-5; ViPo
"How many a thing which we cast to the ground," XLI. EnLit; HBV
"I am not of those miserable males," XX. EnLit
"I am to follow her. There is much grace," XLII. ViBoPo
"I play for seasons, not eternities!" XIII. EPN; FaBoEn; OBNC; PoIE; Sonn
"In our old shipwrecked days there was an hour," XVI. BEL; EnLi-2; GTBS; GTBS-D; HBV; LO; PoFS; WHA
(Love Dies.) SeCePo
"It chanced his lips did meet her forehead cool," VI. ViBoPo
"It ended, and the morrow brought the task," II. BEL; EnLi-2; HBV; OAEP
"It is the season of the sweet wild rose," XLV. NBM; PoEL-5
"Love ere he bleeds, an eagle in high skies," XXVI. HBV
"Mark where the pressing wind shoots javelin-like," XLIII. AnFE; BEL; EnLi-2; EnLoPo; FaBoEn; FaPL; FosPo; GTBS-D; HBV; ILP; InPo; NBM; OAEP; OBNC; PoEL-5; SeCeV; ViPo
(Love's Grave.) OBEV
"Not solely that the future she destroys," XII. EnLit; EnLi-2; OAEP ViBoPo
"Their sense is with their senses all mixed in." BEL
"They say that Pity in Love's service dwells," XLIV.
(Coin of Pity, The.) VA
"This was the woman; what now of the man?" III. HBV; Sonn
"Thus piteously Love closed what he begat," L. AnFE; BEL; CaFP; EnLi-2; EnLit; EnLoPo; FaBoEn; FaPL; GTBS-D; GTBS-P; GTSL; HBV; ILP; InPo; LoBV; NBM; OAEP; OBNC; PoAn; PoE; PoEL-5; PoIE; SeCeV; Sonn; TreFT; TrGrPo; UnPo (1st ed.; ViBoPo; WHA
(Dusty Answer, A.) SeCePo
"We saw the swallows gathering in the sky," XLVII. AnFE; BEL; BoLiVe; ELP; EnLi-2; EnLoPo; FaBoEn; GTBS-D; GTBS-P; GTSL; MemP; OBNC; PoAn; SeCeV; ViBoPo; WHA
(One Twilight Hour.) VA
"We three are on the cedar-shadowed lawn," XXI. OAEP
"What are we first? First, animals; and next," XXX. AnEnPo; NBM; OAEP; PoEL-5; Sonn; ViBoPo
"What soul would bargain for a cure that brings," XIV. HBV
"Yet it was plain she struggled, and that salt," VIII. EnLit; GTBS-D; OAEP; Sonn
Modern Love Songs. Faraah Nuur, *tr. fr. Somali by* B. W. Andrzjewski *and* I. M. Lewis. TTY
Modern Major-General, The. W. S. Gilbert. *Fr.* The Pirates of Penzance. InMe; PCD, *abr.*
(Major-General, The.) OnPP
(Major-General's Song.) CoBE; NBM
Modern malady of love is nerves, The. Nerves. Arthur Symons. BrPo; FaBoTw; MoBrPo; SyP
Modern Miracle. William Atherton. SoP
Modern Ode to the Modern School. John Erskine. YaD
Modern Orchard, A. David O'Neil. AnAmPo
Modern Poet, The. Alice Meynell. *See* Song of Derivations, A.
Modern Romance, A. Paul Engle. PoPl
Modern Romans, The. Charles Frederick Johnson. AA; LHV
Modern Saint, The. Richard Burton. OQP
Modern Woman to Her Lover, The. Margaret Widdemer. HBMV
Modernist married a fundamentalist wife, A. Marital Tragedy. Keith Preston. WhC
Modernists, The. Tom MacInnes. CaP
Modernity. F. L. Lucas. LO
Modes of the court so common are grown, The. John Gay. *Fr.* The Beggar's Opera. NoP
Modest and needy is my destiny in thy world, O God! Kibbutz Sabbath. Levi Ben Amittai. EaLo
Modest front of this small floore, The. An Epitaph Upon Mr.

Ashton a Conformable Citizen. Richard Crashaw. MaMe; OBS
Modest Love, A. Sir Edward Dyer. *See* Lowest Trees Have Tops, The.
Modest Wit, A. Selleck Osborn. BLPA; BOHV; HBV
Modestly we violets cower. Violets. P. A. Ropes. BoTP
Modo and Alciphron. Sylvia Townsend Warner. MoBrPo
Modred was in Cornwall, and summoned many knights. Arthur's Last Fight. Layamon. *Fr.* The Brut. MeEV
Modyr Whyt as Lyly Flowr, *abr.* *Unknown.* AtBAP
Moebius Strip, The. Charles Olson. OPoP
Moeurs Contemporaines. Ezra Pound. OnHM
Mofaddaliyat. *See* Mufaddaliyat.
Mog the Brunette. *Unknown.* CoMu
Moggy and Me. James Hogg. HBV
Mohammed and Seid. Harrison Smith Morris. AA
Mohini Chatterjee. W. B. Yeats. MoRP
Moist Moon People. Carl Sandburg. MAP; MoAmPo
Moist with one drop of thy blood, my dry soul. Resurrection. John Donne. Sonn
Moistened osier of the hoary willow, The. The Coracle. Lucan. ChTr
Mokie's Madrigal. Ronald McCuaig. NeLNL
Molded to the owl is what the owl spits out. Natural Architecture. John Hay. NePoAm
Mole, The. John Clare. SeCeV
Mole, The. Roy Daniells. WHW
Mole, The. Edith King. GFA
Mole, The. William H. Matchett. WIRo
Mole, The. E. L. Mayo. WaKn
Mole. William Jay Smith. RePo
Mole, The. *Unknown.* EiCL
Mole Catcher. Edmund Blunden. OBMV
Molecatcher. Albert D. Mackie. GoTS
Mole, The (it may have been vole: I can't distinguish). The Mole. Roy Daniells. WHW
Mole Talk. Leo Kennedy. PeCV
Moles. William Stafford. NYBP
Moll-in-the-wad and I fell out. *Unknown.* OxNR
Mollesse. Josephine Jacobsen. NePoAm-2
Mollie [*or* Ollie] McGee. Edgar Lee Masters. *Fr.* Spoon River Anthology. NP
Mollis Abuti. Swift. ChTr
Mollusk, The. James J. Montague. PoMa
Molly Asthore. *Unknown,* *tr. fr. Irish by* Sir Samuel Ferguson. IrPN
Molly Bawn. *Unknown.* BaBo; ViBoFo
(Molly Bond, *with music.*) BFSS
(Shooting of His Dear.) OxBoLi
Molly Bawn and Brian Oge. *Unknown.* OnYI
Molly Maguire at Monmouth. William Collins. OTPC; PaA; PAP
Molly Malone. *Unknown.* *See* Cockles and Mussels.
Molly Means. Margaret Walker. AmNP; Kal; PoNe; StPo
Molly Mog; or, The Fair Maid of the Inn. John Gay. CEP; CoMu
Molly Pitcher. Laura E. Richards. MC; PAH; ThLM; YaD
Molly Pitcher. Kate Brownlee Sherwood. GA; GoTP; MC; OTPC (1946 ed.); PAH; PAL
Moly. Edith M. Thomas. HBV
Mom I'm All Screwed Up. Frank Lima. ANYP
Moment, A. Stopford Brooke. IrPN
Moment, A. Mary Elizabeth Coleridge. PoVP
Moment. Howard Nemerov. PoDB
Moment, The. Kathleen Raine. CMoP; MoPW
Moment, The. Theodore Roethke. NYBP
Moment, The. David Rowbotham. BoAV
Moment, The. Kendrick Smithyman. AnNZ
Moment, A. L. A. G. Strong. NeMA
Moment after the moment of love, The. King's X. Hollis Summers. StP
Moment before Conception, The. Eve Merriam. UnTE
Moment by Moment. Daniel W. Whittle. BLRP
Moment Eternal, The. Robert Browning. *See* Now.
Moment I glanced at the mirk-windowed mansion, The. The Spectre. Walter de la Mare. WhC
Moment in Ostia. Sister Mary Thérèse. JKCP (1955 ed.)
Moment in the Morning, A. *Unknown, at. to* Arthur Lewis Tubbs. SoP
(To Begin the Day.) BLRP
Moment more and I may be, A. "In a Moment." *Unknown.* SoP
Moment Musicale. Bliss Carman. HBMV
Moment Musicale. Wallace Gould. AnAmPo
Moment of silence first, then there it is, A. The Dial Tone. Howard Nemerov. NYBP; ToPo
Moment of the Rose, The. Dunstan Thompson. LiTA
Moment of Vision, The. Richard Eberhart. MoRP
Moment Please, A. Samuel Allen. AmNP; IDB; Kal
Moment the wild swallows like a flight, A. A Thunderstorm. Archibald Lampman. CaP
Momentous to himself as I to me. Epigram. Sir William Watson. AnEnPo
Moments. Hervey Allen. HBMV
Moments. Marcel Schwob, *tr. fr. French by* William Brown Meloney. TrJP
Moments/ when I care about nothing. Apologies. Marge Piercy. ThO
Moment's halt, A—a momentary taste. Omar Khayyám, *tr. by* Edward Fitzgerald. *Fr.* The Rubáiyát. PoFr
Moments He Remembers, The. Mark van Doren. NYBP
Moment's Interlude, A. Richard Aldington. POTE
Moment's patience, gentle Mistress Anne, A. William Shakespeare to Mrs. Anne, Regular Servant to the Rev. Mr. Precentor of York. Thomas Gray. CEP; ILP
Moments there are when heart and brain ring clear. Moments. Hervey Allen. HBMV
Momist. Amy Groesbeck. GoYe
Momotara. Rose Fyleman. TiPo
Momus. E. A. Robinson. ViBoPo
Mon in the mone stond and strit. The Man in the Moon. *Unknown.* MeEL
Mona Lisa. *See Also* Monna Lisa.
Mona Lisa. John Kendrick Bangs. BOHV
Mona Lisa. Edward Dowden. OnYI
(Leonardo's "Monna Lisa.") VA
Mona Lisa, A. Angelina Weld Grimké. CDC
Mona Lisa. Walter Pater. OBMV
Monadnock through the Trees. E. A. Robinson. InP; TOP
Monaghan. Shane Leslie. OnYI
Monangamba. Antonio Jacinto, *tr. fr. Portuguese by* Alan Ryder. TTY
Monarch, The. William Cowper. *See* Verses Supposed to Be Written by Alexander Selkirk . . .
Monarch oak, the patriarch of the trees, The. The Oak. Dryden. OHIP
Monarch of Gods and Daemons, and all Spirits. Prometheus Unbound. Shelley. BEL; CoBE; EnLi-2; EnRP; EPN; ERoP-2; FiP; MBW-2; MERP
Monarch who wears a shrieking crown, The. George Barker. Holy Poems, III. MoPo
Monarche, The, *sel.* Sir David Lindsay.
After the Flood. OxBS
Monaro, The. David Campbell. BoAV
Monasteries. Charles David Webb. NePoAm-2
Monastery, The, *sels.* Sir Walter Scott.
Book of Books, The ("Within this ample volume lies"), *fr. ch.* 12. MaRV; NeHB; OQP; SoP; TreFT
(Bible, The.) BLRP; TRV
(Sir Walter Scott's Tribute.) WBLP
Border Ballad, *fr. ch.* 25. EnLit; EPN; GN; HBV; PCD
(Blue Bonnets over the Border.) OxBS
(Border March.) EnRP
(March, March.) ViBoPo
"Indifferent, but indifferent—pshaw! he doth it not," *fr. ch.* 21. NBM
Song of the White Lady of Avenel, *fr. ch.* 5. NBM
Mond ist aufgegangen, Der. Heine, *tr. fr. German by* James Thomson. AWP; OuHeWo
(Mermaidens, The.) OnPM
Monday. William Stafford. NYBP
Monday for wealth. Days of the Week. *Unknown.* TreFT
Monday I was 'rested, Tuesday I was fined. Lookin' for the Bully of the Town. *Unknown.* BaBo
Monday is a good day. The Days of the Week. John Farrar. GFA
Monday Morning. Helen Wing. GFA
Monday morning back to school. David McCord. TiPo (1959 ed.)
Monday's child is fair of [*or* in] face. Mother Goose. BiCB; BLPA; BoChLi; BoTP; CBEP; FaBoBe; FaBoCh; GoTP; HBV;

Monday's (continued)
HBVY; LiTG; LoGBV; MoShBr; NeHB; OTPC; OxNR; PPL; SiTL; SoPo; StaSt; StVeCh; TreF
Mone, Member, Mone. *Unknown.* ABF
Monet: "Les Nymphéas." W. D. Snodgrass. CoAP
Money. Richard Armour. FaFP; PoPl; PoPo; TreFS; WaKn; WhC
Money. Victor Contoski. ThO
Money. W. H. Davies. OBEV (new ed.); OBMV; OBVV
Money. Jehan du Pontalais, *tr. fr. French by* Henry Carrington. BOHV
Money, *with music.* *Unknown.* AS
Money abides not in the palm. The Sieve. Sadi. LiTW
Money and a Friend. *Unknown.* BLPA; NeHB
Money Is What Matters. *Unknown.* MeEL
Money, thou bane of bliss and source of woe. Avarice. George Herbert. GTBS-W; LiTB; MaMe
Money was once well known, like a townhall or the sky. Behaviour of Money. Bernard Spencer. LiTB
Moneyless Man, The. Henry Thompson Stanton. BLPA
Mongolian Horse, The. Tu Fu, *tr. fr. Chinese by* Chi Hwang Chu *and* Edna Worthley Underwood. OnPM
Mongolian Idiot. Karl Shapiro. FiMAP
Mon-goos, The. Oliver Herford. *Fr.* Child's Natural History. AA; AmePo; HBV
Mongrel bred of every strain. Epitaph for Tristan-Joachim-Edouard Corbière, Philosopher, Stray, Stillborn. Tristan Corbière. LiTW
Mongrel Pup, A. Nancy Byrd Turner. PoMa
Mongst all the palaces in Hells command. Richard Crashaw. *Fr.* Sospetto d'Herode. SeCV-1
'Mongst illustrious men in the Bible there be. An Aristocratic Trio. Judson France. PV
'Mongst the world's wonders, there doth yet remain. Female Glory. Richard Lovelace. MyFE
'Mongst those long rowes of crownes that guild your race. To the Queen's Maiesty. Richard Crashaw. MaMe
Mongst whom, some there were bards, that in their sacred rage. The Fourth Song. Michael Drayton. *Fr.* Polyolbion. PrWP
Monk, The. Blake. *See* I Saw a Monk of Charlemain.
Monk and His Pet Cat, The. *Unknown, tr. fr. Old Irish.* CH, *tr. by* Kuno Meyer; OnYI, *tr. by* Whitley Stokes, John Strachan, *and* Kuno Meyer, *arr. by* Kathleen Hoagland
(Monk and His Cat, The, *tr. by* Robin Flower.) OA
(Pangur Ban, *tr. by* Robin Flower.) AnIL; FaBoCh; LoGBV; OnYI; OxBI
(Scholar and the Cat, The, *tr. by* Frank O'Connor.) KiLC
(White Cat and the Student, The, *tr. by* Robin Flower.) RIS
Monk and the Peasant, The. Margaret E. Bruner. PoToHe
Monk Arnulphus uncorked his ink, The. The Court Historian. George Walter Thornbury. HBV; OBVV; PeVV
Monk Begging, Kyoto. Edith Shiffert. NYTB
Monk in the Kitchen, The. Anna Hempstead Branch. AnFE; APA; CoAnAm; MAP; MAPA; MoAmPo
"There is no small work unto God," *sel.* MaRV
Monk of Casal-Maggiore, The. Longfellow. *Fr.* Tales of a Wayside Inn: The Sicilian's Tale, Pt. III. AmPP (4th ed.); OxBA
(Sicilian's Tale, The.) AP
Monk of Great Renown, The. *Unknown.* CoMu
Monk sat in his den, The. The Weak Monk. Stevie Smith. FaBoTw
Monk there was, a monk mastery, A. Seven Pilgrims. Chaucer. *Fr.* The Canterbury Tales: Prologue. TrGrPo
Monk was preaching, The: strong his earnest word. A Legend. Adelaide Anne Procter. GoBC; JKCP
Monk, A, when his rites sacerdotal were o'er. The Philosopher's Scales. Jane Taylor. HBV
Monkey, The. Nancy Campbell. NP
Monkey, The. Mary Howitt. GN
Monkey, The. Vladislav Khodasevich, *tr. fr. Russian by* Babette Deutsch. PoPo
Monkey. Josephine Miles. FiMAP; LiTM (1970 ed.)
Monkey. William Jay Smith. TiPo (1959 ed.)
Monkey and the Cat, The. La Fontaine, *tr. fr. French.* CIV
Monkey and the organ man, The. The Organ-Grinder. Jimmy Garthwaite. BrR
Monkey, little merry fellow. The Monkey. Mary Howitt. GN
Monkey married the baboon's sister, The. The Monkey's Wedding. *Unknown.* AS; BLPA; NA
Monkey, monkey, bottle of beer. *Unknown.* RIS
Monkey Monkey Moo! So Many Monkeys. Marion Edey. SoPo; TiPo
Monkey was a-settin' on a railroad track. *Unknown.* GoTP
Monkeys. Padraic Colum. AnFE
Monkeys. Joaquin Miller. *Fr.* With Walker in Nicaragua. OA; PCH
Monkeys, The. Marianne Moore. CMoP; LiTA; NAMP; OxBA; SeCeV; TwAmPo
(My Apish Cousins.) AnFE; APA; CoAnAm
Monkeys, The. Edith Osborne Thompson. TiPo; UTS
Monkeys and the Crocodile, The. Laura E. Richards. BoChLi; FaPON; ShM; SoPo; SUS; TiPo; UTS
Monkey's Glue, The. Goldwin Goldsmith. NA
Monkeys in a forest. Where. Walter de la Mare. NYBP
Monkey's Raincoat, The. Basho, *tr. fr. Japanese by* Harold G. Henderson. SoPo
Monkey's Wedding, The. *Unknown.* AS, *with music*; BLPA; NA
Monkeys winked [*or* Winked] too much and were afraid of snakes, The. The Monkeys [*or* My Apish Cousin]. Marianne Moore. AnFE; APA; CoAnAm; LiTA; NAMP; OxBA; SeCeV; TwAmPo
Monks. Cardinal Newman. GoBC
Monks ask/ Ancient masters. 3 Meditations. Gene Fowler. ThO
Monks at Ards, The. Patrick Maybin. NeIP
Monks of Bangor's March, The. Sir Walter Scott. CAW
Monks of Ely, The. *Unknown.* ACP; CAW
(Merie Sungen the Muneches.) AtBAP
Monk's Tale, The, *sels.* Chaucer. *Fr.* The Canterbury Tales.
Croesus. MyFE
Tale of Hugelin, Count of Pisa, The. MyFE
Monna Innominata. Christina Rossetti. ViPo; VP
Sels.
Abnegation ("If there be any one can take my place"), XII. VA
"I wish I could remember that first day," II. Sonn
(First Day, The.) EnLi-2; FaBoBe; HBV; LO; MeWo
"'Love me, for I love you'—and answer me," VII. Sonn
"Many in aftertimes will say of you," XI. OBNC; PoVP; ViBoPo
Trust ("If I could trust mine own self with your fate"), XIII. VA
"Youth gone, and beauty gone if ever there," XIV. OBNC; Sonn; ViBoPo
Monna Lisa. *See also* Mona Lisa.
Monna Lisa. James Russell Lowell. AmLP
Monochord, The. Dante Gabriel Rossetti. The House of Life, LXXIX. MaVP; PoVP; ViPo
Monochrome. Louise Imogen Guiney. AnAmPo
Monody. Herman Melville. AnFE; AP; CoAnAm; GTBS-W; LiTA; MAmP; MWA-1; NCEP; PoEL-5; PoIE
Monody on a Century. Earle Birney. CaP
Monody on the Demolition of Devonshire House. Siegfried Sassoon. FaBoTw
Monody to the Memory of a Young Lady, *sel.* Cuthbert Shaw.
Time's Balm, *abr.* OBEC
Monogramania. Eve Merriam. UnTE
Monologue. Alicia L. Johnson. WSL
Monologue of a Deaf Man. David Wright. POTE (1959 ed.)
Monotone. Alfred Kreymborg. WOW
Monotonous evil clock, The. A Round Number. Keith Douglas. NeBP
Monseigneur Plays. Theodosia Garrison. HBMV
Monserrat. William Edwin Collin. CaP
Monsieur Gaston. A. M. Klein. MoCV
Monsieur Pipereau. James Whaler. MAP; MoAmPo (1942 ed.)
Monsieur the Curé down the street. The Curé's Progress. Austin Dobson. HBV; PoVP; VA
Monsignore,/ Right Reverend Bishop Valentinus. A Blue Valentine. Joyce Kilmer. ISi; JKCP; LHV
Monsoon. Kenneth Slade Alling. NePoAm
Monsoon. David Wevill. NYBP
Monster, The. Dorothy Quick. FiSC
Monster, The. Henry Rago. SiTL
Monster is loose, The. Television-Movie. Kirby Congdon. WOW

Monster taught, A/ To come to hand. Song of a Train. John Davidson. BrPo
Monsters. Quillevic, *tr. fr. French by* Patricia Terry. OnPM
Monstrous Marriage, The. William Carlos Williams. MoPo
Monstrous, uncouth, their vast leaves amply spread. Palm House, Botanic Gardens. George Hetherington. NeIP
Mont Blanc. Shelley. EnRP; ERoP-2; MaPo; MBW-2; MERP; PIA; PP
Montana. Charles C. Cohan. PoRL
Montana Eclogue. William Stafford. NYBP
Montana, Nothing like Boston. James Welch. YAP
Montana Pastoral. J. V. Cunningham. MoAmPo (1962 ed.); PoIE
Montana Visit. Craig Sterry. QAH
Montana Wives. Gwendolen Haste. AmFN; OTD
Montanus' Sonnet. Thomas Lodge. *Fr.* Rosalynde; or, Euphues' Golden Legacy. AtBAP; PoEL-2; TuPP
("Phoebe sat/ Sweet she sat.") SiCE
Monte Pellegrino, mauve, bald and granite skull. Nelson at Palermo. Alan Ross. POTi
Montefiore. Ambrose Bierce. AA; AnAmPo; PFY
Montenegro. Tennyson. PoVP
Monterey. Charles Fenno Hoffman. AA; FaBoBe; HBV; MC; OTPC (1923 ed.); PaA; PAH; PAP; PTK; ThLM
Montezuma. Witter Bynner. *Fr.* Chapala Poems. NP
Montgomery. J. C. Hall. ChMP
Montgomery at Quebec. Clinton Scollard. PAH
Month after month the gathered rains descend. To the Nile. Shelley. OBRV; Sonn
Month can never forget the year, The. Carol. John McClure. HBMV
Month is amber, The. October. John Updike. PDV
Month of Falling Stars, The. Ella Higginson. YeAr
Month of gold, A: gold flowers, gold sun. The Golden Month. Marion Doyle. YeAr
Month of January—smoky is the vale. Aneirin. *Fr.* Odes of the Month. FlW
Month of leaves,/ Month of roses. June. Irene F. Pawsey. BoTP
Month of May, The. Beaumont *and* Fletcher. *Fr.* The Knight of the Burning Pestle. ChTr
Month of the drowned dog, The. After long rain the land. November. Ted Hughes. GTBS-P; NePoEA-2; NMP; NoP; OPoP; POTi
Month of the Thunder Moon, The. Marion Doyle. YeAr
Month, sweet little-ones, is past, A. The Mother's Return. Dorothy Wordsworth. OTPC (1923 ed.)
Month was June, the day was hot, The. The Orange. Charles *and* Mary Lamb. OTPC (1923 ed.)
Months, The. Sara Coleridge. *See* Garden Year, The.
Months, The ("January cold"). Christina Rossetti. *Fr.* Sing-Song. FaPON; RIS
Months, The; a Pageant, *sel.* Christina Rossetti.
October: "I've brought you nuts and hops." BoTP
Months, The. Sheridan. PCH
Months, The. *Unknown.* ChTr
Months of the Tribe, The. Howard McCord. YAP
Montmartre. Langston Hughes. Kal
Montoro's Song against Count Alvaro de Luna, High Constable of Castile. Eduardo Marquina, *tr. fr. Spanish by* Dorothea Mackellar. MoAuPo
Montreal. A. M. Klein. CaP; MoCV; OBCV
Montreal. William Douw Lighthall. VA
Montrose to His Mistress. James Graham, Marquess of Montrose. *See* My Dear and Only Love.
Montross. Charles Cotton. SeCL
Monument, The. Elizabeth Bishop. LiTA; MoPo; PoIE; PP
Monument, A. Charles Madge. FaBoMo
Monument. A. M. Sullivan. GoYe
Monument for the Soldiers, A. James Whitcomb Riley. DD; PoRL
Monument Mountain. Bryant. BeLS
Monument of Cleita, The. Edward Cracroft Lefroy. *Fr.* Echoes from Theocritus. AWP; JAWP; WBP
Monument outlasting bronze, The. The Ancient and Modern Muses. Francis Turner Palgrave. VA
Monument to Resignation, The. Jon Anderson. YAP
Monument which thou beholdest here, The. Epitaph for Himself. Lord Herbert of Cherbury. AnAnS-2
Monumental Memorial of Marine Mercy, A. Richard Steere. SCAP
Mony ane talks [*or* speaks] o' the grass, the grass. Willie and Earl Richard's Daughter (B *and* C *vers.*). *Unknown.* ESPB
Moo! Robert Hillyer. WhC
Moo cow is a mammal not, The. The Pleasant Cow. Grace Taber Hallock. RePo
Moo-Cow-Moo, The. Edmund Vance Cooke. FaFP; MoShBr; PTK
Mood, A. Winifred Howells. AA
Mood, A. Amélie Rives. AA
Mood from 3000 B.C. Genevieve Taggard. OTPC (1946 ed.)
Mood passes/ spring comes. Spel VI. Robert Kelly. *Fr.* Thor's Thrush. YAP
Moods, The. Fannie Stearns Davis. HBV
Moods. Leib Kwitko, *tr. fr. Yiddish by* Joseph Leftwich. TrJP
Moods, The. W. B. Yeats. CTC
Moods have laid their hands across my hair, The. The Moods. Fannie Stearns Davis. HBV
Moods of Rain. Vernon Scannell. BoNaP
Moon, The. Azumamaro, *tr. fr. Japanese by* Asataro Miyamori. OnPM
Moon, The. Charles Best. *See* Sonnet of the Moon, A.
Moon, The. Bhasa, *tr. fr. Sanskrit by* A. Berriedale Keith. LiTW
Moon, The. Elizabeth J. Coatsworth. *See* Field Are Spread, The.
Moon, The. W. H. Davies. BrPo; MoBrPo; MoVE; NeMA; POTE; StaSt
Moon, The. Emily Dickinson. *See* Moon was but a chin of gold, The.
Moon, The. Eliza Lee Follen. HBV; HBVY; MPB; RIS
(Oh, Look at the Moon.) BoTP; OTPC; SAS
Moon, The. Louise Ayres Garnett. SiSoSe
Moon, The. Robert Beverly Hale. SiTL
Moon, The. Oliver Herford. GFA
Moon. Langston Hughes. *Fr.* A House in Taos. CDC
Moon, The. Kotomichi, *tr. fr. Japanese by* Asataro Miyamori. OnPM
Moon. Henry Rowe. OBEV
Moon, The. Ryuho, *tr. fr. Japanese.* SoPo
Moon, The ("And like a dying lady"). Shelley. BoLiVe; FaBoCh; LoGBV; OBEV; TDP
(Waning Moon, The.) AnFE; CH; ChER; PoG; TrGrPo
Moon, The ("Art thou pale for weariness"). Shelley. BoLiVe; OBEV
(Fragment: To the Moon.) EnRP
(To the Moon.) AnFE; BoNaP; ChER; EPN; ERoP-2; GTBS; GTBS-D; GTBS-W; GTSE; GTSL; LoBV; MBW-2; MCCG; OnPM; RePo; TrGrPo; ViBoPo
Moon, The. Sir Philip Sidney. *See* Astrophel and Stella: Sonnets, XXXI.
Moon. William Jay Smith. PDV
Moon, The. Edith Södergran, *tr. fr. Finnish by* Erik Wahlgren *and* Martin S. Allwood. LiTW
Moon, The. *Unknown.* PCH
("I see the moon.") GoTP; OxNR; TiPo
Moon, The/ Casts the shadow of the plum. Memories of Childhood. Wu Tsung Ai. OnPM
Moon, a sweeping scimitar, dipped in the stormy straits, The. Winged Man. Stephen Vincent Beneét. MAP; MoAmPo
Moon above the milky field, The. Night-Piece. Léonie Adams. MAP; MoAB; MoAmPo
Moon and Fog. August Derleth. FiSC
Moon and seven Pleiades have set, The. Alone. Sappho, *tr. by* William Ellery Leonard. AWP
Moon and the Night and the Men, The. John Berryman. CoAP; WaP
Moon and the Nightingale, The. Milton. *See* Evening in Paradise.
Moon and the Yew Tree, The. Sylvia Plath. CoAP; NaP; NYBP
Moon at the Fortified Pass, The. Li Po, *tr. fr. Chinese by* Witter Bynner *and* Kiang Kang-hu. LiTW; WaaP
Moon at the full. Europe has burst its banks. The Inundation. Howard Sergeant. *Fr.* The Leaves of Europe. ToPo
Moon behind High Tranquil Leaves, The. Robert Nichols. OBMV
Moon Cars, that race of ghosts, but once "the world's." Lines Based on a 1924 Advertisement. Geoffrey Lehmann. NYTB
Moon-Child, The. "Fiona Macleod". CH; EtS
Moon-Children. Michael Lewis. TSW

Moon Closes, The. Robert Kelly. YAP
Moon-Come-Out. Eleanor Farjeon. TiPo
Moon comes every night to peep, The. The White Window. James Stephens. StVeCh; SUS; TiPo
Moon Compasses. Robert Frost. DiPo; MoVE
Moon controls her horses, The. Tides. Josephine Williams. PCD
Moon-cradle's rocking and rocking, The. The Ballad of Downal Baun. Padraic Colum. SUS
Moon Door. Mary Kennedy. BoLP
Moon drops one or two feathers into the field, The. Beginning. James Wright. FRC
Moon Festival. Tu Fu, *tr. fr. Chinese by* Kenneth Rexroth. NaP
Moon fills up its hollow bowl of milk, The. The Postures of Love, V. Alex Comfort. NeBP
Moon Fishing. Lisel Mueller. CoAP
Moon, Flowers, Man. Su Tung P'o, *tr. fr. Chinese by* Kenneth Rexroth. NaP
Moon Folly. Fannie Stearns Davis. *Fr.* Songs of Conn the Fool. RG; SP
Moon had long since sunk behind the mists, The. Dawn. "P. S. M." MCCG
Moon has gone to her rest, The. A Nocturne. Wilfrid Scawen Blunt. OBMV
Moon has left the sky, The. Night in Lesbos. George Horton. AA
Moon his mare, all silver-bright, The. The Chase. W. H. Davies. BrPo
Moon in heaven's garden, among the clouds that wander. Spinning in April. Josephine Preston Peabody. HBV
Moon, in her pride, once glanced aside, The. The Moon Sings [*or* The Moon's Love]. *Unknown.* OxBoLi; SeCL
Moon in September, The. Kashiprosad Ghose. ACV
Moon in the Water, The. Ryota, *tr. fr. Japanese.* SoPo
Moon in Your Hands, The. Hilda Doolittle ("H. D."). NYBP
Moon is a sow, The. Song for Ishtar. Denise Levertov. NaP; PoIE (1970 ed.)
Moon is able to command the valley tonight, The. Moist Moon People. Carl Sandburg. MAP; MoAmPo
Moon is as complacent as a frog, The. Autumn Night. Evelyn Scott. AnAmPo
Moon is bright, and the winds are laid, and the river is roaring by, The. In the Moonlight. David McKee Wright. AnNZ; BoAu
Moon is dead, I saw her die, The. The Moon's Funeral. Hilaire Belloc. MoSiPe
Moon is distant from the sea, The. Emily Dickinson. DiPo
Moon is fully risen, The. Der Mond ist aufgegangen [*or* The Mermaidens]. Heine. AWP; OnPM; OuHeWo
Moon Is Hiding In, The. E. E. Cummings. AtBAP
Moon is like a big round cheese, The. The Moon. Oliver Herford. GFA
Moon is like a lamp, The. The Weathercock. Rose Fyleman. BoTP
Moon is round as a jack-o'-lantern, The. Hallowe'en. Frances Frost. TiPo (1959 ed.)
Moon is setting in the west, The. Song of the Hesitations. Paul Blackburn. NMP
Moon is soft arising, The. Nightfall. Antonio de Trueba. CAW
Moon Is the Number 18, The. Charles Olson. NMP
Moon Is to Blood. Richard Duerden. NeAP
Moon Is Up, The. Alfred Noyes. ShBV-1
Moon Is Up, The. *Unknown.* NA
Moon is up, and yet it is not night, The. Byron. *Fr.* Childe Harold's Pilgrimage. AnFE
Moon is weaving in the street, The. The Weaving. Harold Lewis Cook. MoSiPe
Moon, The? It is a griffin's egg. Yet Gentle Will the Griffin Be. Vachel Lindsay. MAPA; PDV; SP; StVeCh; TSW; TwAmPo
Moon It Shines, The. *Unknown, tr. fr. German.* SAS
Moon, like a round device, The. Snow. Madison Cawein. MAP; PFY
Moon looked down on its double, The. Reflected Glory. Fannie Brown. SoP
Moon-Madness. Victor Starbuck. HBMV
Moon Magic. Viscountess Grey of Fallodon. PCH
Moon Magic. Leigh Hanes. StaSt
Moon, moon,/ Mak' me a pair o' shoon. *Unknown.* OxNR
Moon Now Rises [to Her Absolute Rule], The. Henry David Thoreau. FaBoEn; PoEL-4
Moon of Brooklyn, The. Nathalia Crane. AnAmPo
Moon of her brow, it is beaming, The. Two Songs in Praise of Steingerd, 1. Cormac Ogmundarson. LiTW
Moon on the one hand, the dawn on the other, The. The Early Morning [*or* Early Dawn]. Hilaire Belloc. BoNaP; BoTP; GTBS-D; HBMV; HBVY; JKCP; POTE; RIS; ThGo; WaKn
Moon Rainbow, A. Robert Browning. BoC
Moon resumed all heaven now, The. The Arctic Moon. Joaquin Miller. *Fr.* The Yukon. MAP; MoAmPo (1942 ed.)
Moon, The, revolves outside; possibly, black air. Study in a Late Subway. Muriel Rukeyser. OnHM
Moon Rider. William Rose Benét. YT
Moon rises, The. The red cubs rolling. The Breath of Night. Randall Jarrell. CrMA
Moon seems like a docile sheep, The. The Moon-Sheep. Christopher Morley. UTS
Moon Shadow. George Bowering. MoCV
Moon Shadows. Adelaide Crapsey. AnAmPo; LA; NeMA
Moon shall be a darkness, The. Love's Constancy [*or* Valentine Promise]. *Unknown.* LO; MeWo; PoSC
Moon, The: she shakes off her cloaks. Promontory Moon. Galway Kinnell. TwAmPo
Moon-Sheep, The. Christopher Morley. UTS
Moon shines bright, The. *Unknown.* OxNR
Moon shines bright, The: in such a night as this. In Such a Night [*or* The Divine Harmony *or* Duet]. Shakespeare. *Fr.* The Merchant of Venice, V, i. ChTr; CLwM; FiP; GoBC; MemP; WHA
Moon shines bright, The; the stars give a light. May-Day Carol [*or* Song *or* Greeting]. *Unknown.* GoTP; PoSC; ThGo
Moon shines clear as silver, The. Sun and Moon. Charlotte Druitt Cole. BoTP
Moon shines down on Flanders Fields, The. Crosses. Mabel Hicks. PEDC
Moon shines in my body, but my blind eyes cannot see it, The. Songs of Kabir [*or* Two Songs]. Kabir. LiTW; WGRP
Moon shines on the Isle of Inishtrahull, The. Dawn in Inishtrahull. D. J. O'Sullivan. OnYI
Moon Ship, The. *Unknown. tr. fr. Japanese.* GFA
Moon silent mike breasts. Clark Coolidge. ANYP
Moon silvers the bay, she waxes, she wanes, The. The Eternal Kinship. Maurice E. Peloubet. GoYe
Moon Sings, The. *Unknown.* OxBoLi
(Moon's Love, The.) SeCL
Moon So Round and Yellow. Matthias Barr. GFA; HBV; HBVY; OTPC
Moon Song. Chuba Nweke. PBA
Moon Song. Hilda Conkling. SP; TiPo
Moon Song. Claude McKay. *See* Song of the Moon, A.
Moon that now and then last night, The. Snow Harvest. Andrew Young. BoNaP
Moon, The—the moon, so silver and cold. Miss Kilmansegg's Honeymoon. Thomas Hood. *Fr.* Miss Kilmansegg and Her Precious Leg. NBM
Moon...the moon...the moon...the moon, The. The Old Coon-Dog Dreams. Kenneth Porter. GoTP
Moon, they say, called Mantis, The. How Death Came. *Unknown.* PeSA; TTY
Moon upon her fluent route, The. Emily Dickinson. QFR
Moon was but a chin of gold, The. Emily Dickinson. BoChLi; BoTP
Moon was like a boat one night, The. Three Hours. Vachel Lindsay. ATP
Moon was round, The. The Whisperer. James Stephens. WGRP
Moon was shady, and soft airs, The. The Dog and the Water-Lily. William Cowper. OAEP
Moon was shining silver bright, The. Old Dan Tucker. *Unknown.* TrAS
Moon was up, the lake was shining clear, The. Wordsworth. *Fr.* The Prelude. FaBoEn
Moon-Watching by Lake Chapala. Al Young. WSL
Moon wedded the Sun, The. Sun, Moon and Thunder. *Unknown.* OnPM
Moon-white waters wash and leap, The. The Coves of Crail. "Fiona Macleod." VA

Moon with dewy lustre bright, The. Lament for Tinoretta. William Collins. Three Fragements, 3. WaPE
Moon Worshippers, The. Eric Robertson Dodds. POTE
Moonbeam. Hilda Conkling. BrR
Moonbeam floateth from the skies, A. Orkney Lullaby. Eugene Field. GoTP
Moonbeams kelter i the lift, The. The Man in the Moon. "Hugh MacDiarmid." NeBP
Moonbeams over Arno's vale in silvery flood were pouring, The. The Veery. Henry van Dyke. AA
Moone-Calfe, The, *sel.* Michael Drayton.
"It was not long e're he perceiv'd the skies." PoEL-2
Mooni. Henry Clarence Kendall. BoAu; OBEV; OBVV
Moonless Darkness Stands Between. Gerard Manley Hopkins. WePo
Moonless night—a friendly one, A. Running the Batteries. Herman Melville. PaA; PAH; ThLM
Moonlight. Walter de la Mare. EnLoPo
Moonlight, The. Ann Hawkshaw. BoTP
Moonlight. Edward Moxon. OBRV
Moonlight. Berta Hart Nance. AmFN
Moonlight. Shakespeare. *See* How Sweet the Moonlight Sleeps upon This Bank.
Moonlight. Jacques Tahureau, *tr. fr. French by* Andrew Lang. AWP
Moonlight. Maud E. Uschold. StVeCh (1955 ed.)
Moonlight, *with music.* *Unknown.* AS
Moonlight. Paul Verlaine. *See* Clair de lune.
Moonlight and music and the sound of waves. The Sleepers. Louis Untermeyer. MoLP
Moonlight bends over black silence. Minna. Maxwell Bodenheim. MAPA
Moonlight breaks upon the city's domes [*or* city towers], The. A Song of the Moon [*or* Moon Song]. Claude McKay. PoNe; TSW
Moonlight filled them both with sundry glamors, The. Et Sa Pauvre Chair. Alec Brock Stevenson. HBMV
Moonlight in Autumn. James Thomson. *Fr.* The Seasons: Autumn. OBEC
Moonlight in Italy. Elizabeth Clementine Kinney. AA
Moonlight in such places alters faces. Moon and Fog. August Derleth. FiSC
Moonlight is a gentle thing, The. The Moonlight. Ann Hawkshaw. BoTP
Moonlight is shining, The. Mother Moon. Amelia Josephine Burr. TVC; WHL
Moonlight Night on the Port. Sidney Keyes. DTC
Moonlight on Lake Sydenham. Wilson MacDonald. CaP
Moonlight . . . Scattered Clouds. Robert Bloomfield. *Fr.* The Framer's Boy. OBNC
Moonlight silvers the shaken tops of trees. Nocturne of Remembered Spring. Conrad Aiken. HBMV
Moonlight Song of the Mocking-Bird. William Hamilton Hayne, AA
Moonlight touched the sombre waters white, The. The Abandoned. Arthur Symons. SyP
Moonlight washes the west side of the house. Winter Verse for My Sister. William Meredith. NYBP
Moonlit Apples. John Drinkwater. BoNaP; BoPe; BoTP; OBMV; PoRA
Moonlit Doorway, The. Kenneth Mackenzie. MoAuPo
Moonmoth and grasshopper that flee our page. A Name for All. Hart Crane. PP
Moonpoison, mullock of sacrifice. Joseph Gordon Macleod. *Fr.* The Ecliptic: Cancer, or, The Crab. NeBP
Moonrise. Hilda Doolittle ("H. D."). NP
Moonrise. Abbie Huston Evans. NP
Moonrise. Gerard Manley Hopkins. MoAB; MoBrPo; SeCePo
Moonrise. D. H. Lawrence. GTBS-W; LiTM; NP
Moonrise. Frank Dempster Sherman. AA
Moonrise in City Park. Josephine Miles. FiMAP
Moonrise in the Rockies. Ella Higginson. AA
Moons. John Haines. ThO
Moon's a devil jester, A. The Traveler. Vachel Lindsay. MoAmPo; NeMA
Moon's a holy owl-queen, The. What Grandpa Mouse Said. Vachel Lindsay. UTS
Moon's a little arch, The. A Classic Case. Gilbert Sorrentino. NeAP
Moon's a little prairie-dog. What the Rattlesnake Said. Vachel Lindsay. TSW
Moon's a peck of corn, The. The Old Horse in the City. Vachel Lindsay. UTS
Moon's a steaming chalice, The. What Semiramis Said. Vachel Lindsay. MAPA; TwAmPo
Moon's Funeral, The. Hilaire Belloc. MoSiPe
Moon's glow by seven fold multiplied, turned red. After Reading St. John the Divine. Gene Derwood. LiTM; NePA; Sonn
Moon's greygolden [*or* soft golden] meshes make, The. Alone. James Joyce. InvP; NP
Moon's little skullcap, The. Front Street. Howard Moss. NYBP
Moon's Love, The. *Unknown.* *See* Moon Sings, The.
Moon's my constant mistress, The. Tom o' Bedlam ['s Song]. *Unknown.* CH; FaBoCh; LO; LoGBV; PoRA (rev. ed.); ShBV-4; WaKn
Moon's on the lake, and the mist's on the brae, The. MacGregor's Gathering. Sir Walter Scott. AnFE; OxBS; PoFr
Moon's Orchestra, The. John Gould Fletcher. *Fr.* Down the Mississippi. HT; LaNeLa; LiTA; NP
Moon's Ship, The. Hitomaro, *tr. fr. Japanese by* Ishii *and* Obata. OnPM
Moon's soft golden meshes make, The. *See* Moon's greygolden meshes make, The.
Moon's the North Wind's Cooky, The. Vachel Lindsay. BoChLi; BrR; EvOK; FaFP; FaPON; GoTP; PDV; PoRh; SoPo; SP; StVeCh; SUS; TSW
Moonshine. Walter de la Mare. FiBHP
Moonstar, The. Dante Gabriel Rossetti. The House of Life, XXIX. MaVP; PoVP; ViPo; VP
Moonsweet the summer evening locks. Sheepbells. Edmund Blunden. BrPo
Moontan. Mark Strand. NYBP
Moor, The. Ralph Hodgson. MoBrPo
Moor, The. R. S. Thomas. BoPe
Moorland Night. Charlotte Mew. ChMP; ViBoPo
Moorland waste lay hushed in the dusk of the second day, The. Le Mauvais Larron. Rosamund Marriott Watson. VA
Moorlands of the Not. *Unknown.* NA
Moors, Angels, Civil Wars. Keith Sinclair. AnNZ
Moosehead Lake, *with music.* *Unknown.* OuSiCo
Mopoke. Louis Lavater. NeLNL; PoAu-1
Moppsikon Floppsikon Bear, The. Edward Lear. *See* Limerick: "There was on old person of Ware."
Moral Alphabet, A, *sel.* Hilaire Belloc.
B Stands for Bear. ShM
Moral Bully, The. Oliver Wendell Holmes. AmePo; AnAmPo; AnNE
Moral Essays, *sels.* Pope.
"As hags hold sabbaths, not for joy but spite," *fr.* Epistle II. ExPo
As the Twig Is Bent, 2 *ll.*, *fr.* Epistle I. TreF
Characters of Women; Flavia, Atossa, and Cloe, *fr.* Epistle II. OBEC
Chloe, *fr.* Epistle II. AWP; JAWP; WBP
(Characters from the Satires: Chloe.) InPo
("Yet Cloe sure was form'd without a spot.") ErPo
Coxcomb Bird, The, *fr.* Epistle I. LiTB; SiTL
Death of Buckingham, The, *fr.* Epistle III. FiP
(Death of the Duke of Buckingham, The.) ExPo
(Duke of Buckingham, The.) OBEC
Gem and the Flower, The, *fr.* Epistle I. OBEC
Heaven's Last Best Work, *fr.* Epistle II. OBEC
Man of Ross, The, *fr.* Epistle III. CoBE
Of the Use of Riches ("'Tis strange, the miser..."), *fr.* Epistle IV. CABL; EiCL; EiPP; PoEL-3; MBW-1
(To Richard Boyle, Earl of Burlington.) BWP
Of the Use of Riches ("Who shall decide, when doctors disagree"), *fr.* Epistle III. MBW-1
To a Lady; of the Characters of Women, *fr.* Epistle II. BWP; MaPo (1969 ed.); MBW-1; NoP; OxBoLi; SiTL
("Nothing so true as what you once let fall," *sel.*) FaBoEn
(Of the Characters of Women,) EiCL; PoFS
Ruling Passion, The, *fr.* Epistle I. BOHV, *br. sel.*
("Search then the Ruling Passion.") ViBoPo
Sir Balaam, *fr.* Epistle III. MaPo
Timon's Villa, *fr.* Epistle IV. MaPo; OBEC
(At Timon's Villa.) ExPo
(Satire on Riches.) PoLi

Moral (continued)
Wharton, *fr.* Epistle I. AWP; JAWP; WBP
(Characters from the Satires: Wharton.) InPo
Woman's Ruling Passions, *fr.* Epistle II. OBEC
"Yes, you despise the man to books confin'd," Epistle I. CEP
Moral in Sèvres, A. Mildred Howells. AA; HBV
Moral massacre, the murder, the rape of religion, The. The Child. Reginald Massey. ACV
Moral Song. John Farrar. RePo
Moral Story II. David Wright. ChMP; PeSA
Moral Taxi Ride, The. Erich Kästner, *tr. fr. German by* Jerome Rothenberg. ErPo
Moral Tetrastich, A. Sir William Jones. *See* Baby, The.
Moral Warfare, The. Whittier. AnNE; PAL; PoFr; TreFT, *sts.* 3-4
New Challenge, The, *sel.* MaRV
Morality. Matthew Arnold. EPN; GTBS; GTSL; HBV; PoVP; SoP; TOP; ViPo; ViPP
"We cannot kindle when we will." MaRV, *sts.* 1-2; OQP, *st.* 1
Morality. Jean Garrigue. ELU
Morality of Poetry, The. James Wright. PP
Morals. James Thurber. *Fr.* Further Fables for Our Times. FaBV
Morando, the Tritameron of Love, *sel.* Robert Greene.
Fickle Seat Whereon Proud Fortune Sits, The. ReIE
Mordent for a Melody. Margaret Avison. ACV
More about People. Ogden Nash. Po
More Ancient Mariner, A. Bliss Carman. VA
More Animals. Oliver Herford.
Cow, The. NA
Hen, The. LBN; NA
More ballads! here's a spick and span new supplication. A Free Parliament Litany. *Unknown.* OxBoLi
More beautiful and soft than any moth. The Landscape near an Aerodrome. Stephen Spender. AnEnPo; AnFE; CoBMV; EnLit; LiTM; MoAB; MoBrPo; MoVE; OAEP (2d ed.); PoAn; ReMP; ShBV-4; StP; WoL
More beautiful than any gift you gave. The Token. F. T. Prince. FaBoTw
More beautiful than the remarkable moon and her noble light. Ingeborg Bachmann. BoNaP
More brightly must my sprit shine. The Spirit's Grace. Janie Screven Heyward. HBMV
More discontents I never had. Discontents in Devon. Robert Herrick. AnAnS-2; OAEP; PoeP; ReEn; SCEP-2; SeCV-1; SeEP
More Dissemblers besides Women, *sel.* Thomas Middleton.
"Come, my dainty doxies," *fr.* IV, i. TuPP
More famed than Rome, as splendid as old Greece. My America. Thomas Curtis Clark. OQP; PEDC
More Foreign Cities. Charles Tomlinson. NePoEA-2
More Hair. Samuel Hoffenstein. SiTL
More haughty than the rest, the wolfish race. The Presbyterians. Dryden. *Fr.* The Hind and the Panther, I. OBS
More Holiness. Philip Paul Bliss. SoP
More humane Mikado never, A. The Humane Mikado [*or* The Mikado's Song *or* My Object All Sublime]. W. S. Gilbert. *Fr.* The Mikado. ALV; LiTB; PoVP; SiTL; TreFT
More ill at ease was never man than Walbach, that Lord's day. The Legend of Walbach Tower. George Houghton. PAH
More Letters Found near a Suicide. Frank Horne. *See* Letters Found near a Suicide.
"More Light! More Light!" Anthony Hecht. CoAP; NePoEA-2; TwCP
More Light Shall Break from Out Thy Word. Allen Eastman Cross. MaRV
More Love or More Disdain. Thomas Carew. *See* Mediocrity in Love Rejected.
More Love or More Disdain. Charles Webbe. *See* Against Indifference.
More Love to Christ. Elizabeth Payson Prentiss. SoP
More Lovely Grows the Earth. Helena Coleman. CaP
More lovely than the rose. Christmas Night. Marion Lochhead. MaRV
More luck to honest poverty. For A' That and A' That, *parody.* Shirley Brooks. Par
More marvels have occurred in Britain than in any other country that I know of. Sir Gawain and the Green Knight. *Unknown.* EnL
More my own poor wishes would commend me, The. Sonnet. Petrarch. Sonnets to Laura: To Laura in Life, CVIII. PoFr
More Nudes for Florence. Harold Witt. ErPo
More of Thee. Horatius Bonar. BLRP
More on a mission. American Patrol. William Brown. QAH
More out of dearest duty now than joy. Breviary on the Subway. Leonard McCarthy. JKCP (1955 ed.)
More paper blackened with more signatures. The Night There Was Dancing in the Streets. Elder Olson. NePA
More pleasing were these sweet delights. Francis Beaumont. *Fr.* The Masque of the Inner-Temple and Gray's Inne. OBS
More Power to Cromwell. Egan O'Rahilly, *tr. fr. Modern Irish by* P. S. Dinneen *and* T. O'Donoghue. OnYI
More Prayer. *Unknown.* STF
More precious than Aladdin's jewels. Treasure. Elizabeth-Ellen Long. BiCB
More rain has fallen this winter. Weather. Mary Ursula Bethell. AnNZ
More rapid than hail. Akiko Yosano, *tr. fr. Japanese by* Kenneth Rexroth. LiTW
More secure is no one ever. Security. Lina Sandell. SoP; STF
"More ships!" some cry; "more guns!" More Prayer. *Unknown.* STF
More shower than shine. Valentines to My Mother, 1880. Christina Rossetti. DD
More shy than the sky violet. Quaker Ladies. Ellen Mackay Hutchinson Cortissoz. AA
More soft than press of baby lips. Pussy-Willows. Arthur Guiterman. OTPC (1946 ed.)
More Sonnets at Christmas. Allen Tate. LiTA; LiTM; NePA; WaP
More Strong than Time. Victor Hugo, *tr. fr. French by* Andrew Lang. AWP; JAWP; WBP
More Than. Fay Inchfawn. SoP
More than Flowers We Have Brought. Nancy Byrd Turner. SiSoSe
More than half beaten, but fearless. Battle Cry. John G. Neihardt. HBMV
More than Most Fair. Fulke Greville. Caelica, III. ElL; SiCE
(To His Lady.) OBSC
More than most fair[e], full of the living fire. Amoretti, VIII. Spenser. BoLiVe; CABA; HBV; MeWo; NoP; OAEP; Sonn; TrGrPo
More Than Most People. Eldon Grier. MoCV
"More than my brothers are to me." In Memoriam A. H. H., LXXIX. Tennyson. EnLi-2; EPN; OAEP; ViPo; VP
More than Quit. Martial. *See* Epigram: "To John I owed great obligation."
More than the ash stays you from nothingness! The Phoenix. J. V. Cunningham. QFR
More than the Moment. Sister Claude of Jesus. JKCP (1955 ed.)
"More Than They All." L. M. Warner. SoP
More than those. Rosa Nascosa. Maurice Hewlett. OBVV
More than two crosses stand on either side. Ave Crux, Spes Unica! Edward Shillito. ChIP; MaRV; OQP
More than We Ask. Faith Wells. BLRP
More things are wrought by prayer. Prayer. Tennyson. *Fr.* Idylls of the King *and* Morte d'Arthur. BLRP; OQP; TreF; WGRP
More Truth and Light. John Robinson. TRV
More Walks. "Thomas Ingoldsby." BOHV
More we live, more brief appear, The. The River of Life [*or* A Thought Suggested by the New Year]. Thomas Campbell. FaFP; GTBS; GTBS-D; GTBS-P; GTBS-W; GTSE; GTSL; HBV; LiTB; LiTG; OBNC
More white than whitest lilies far. To Electra. Robert Herrick. ExPo; UnTE
More whyght thou art then primrose leaf my Lady Galatee. Cyclops. Ovid. *Fr.* Metamorphoses. CTC
More years ago than I can state. My Last Illusion. John Kendall. FiBHP; WhC
Morels. William Jay Smith. BoNaP; NYBP; TDP
Moreso. Alfred Starr Hamilton. QAH
Moreton Miles, *sel.* William Baylebridge.
"Wherever I go, I do no wrong," LIV. BoAV
Morgan. Edward Harrington. PoAu-1
Morgan. Edmund Clarence Stedman. AA; AmePo; HBV

Morgan Stanwood. Hiram Rich. PAH
Morgana. Gabriele D'Annunzio, *tr. fr. Italian by* L. R. Lind. LiTW
Morgan's Country. Francis Webb. BoAV
Morgante maggiore, Il, *sels.* Luigi Pulci, *tr. fr. Italian.*
Appeal for Illumination, *fr.* 1 *tr. by* Byron. ISi
Prophecy. PAH
Morgenlied. John Addington Symonds. Sonn
Morisco, A. Jasper Fisher. *Fr.* Fuimus Troes. SeCL; TuPP
(Song; a Morisko.) SeEP
Moritura. Margaret Gilman Davidson. AA
Morituri Salutamus. Longfellow. CoBA; MAmP; MWA-1
Sels.
"For age is opportunity no less." PoToHe (new ed.)
It Is Too Late! PoLF
(Too Late?) WBLP
Old Age. SoP
Moriturus. Edna St. Vincent Millay. AnAmPo; GTBS-W; LiTA; NAMP
Mormon Bishop's Lament, The. *Unknown.* CoSo
Mormon Immigrant Song, A. *At. to* George A. Hicks. CoSo
Morn. Helen Hunt Jackson. AA
Morn comes freshly from the east, The. John Francis O'Donnell. *Fr.* Adare. IrPN
Morn is cold, The. A whiteness newly-brought. Frost-Morning. William Alexander. IrPN
Morn of the year, of day and May the prime! May-Day on Magdalen Tower. Thomas Herbert Warren. OBVV
Morn was cloudy and dark and gray, The. The Battle of Morris Island. *Unknown.* PAH
Morn when first it thunders in March, The. Old Pictures in Florence. Robert Browning. PoVP
Morna's Hill, *sel.* James Stuart.
Distant Prospect of the City of Armagh, A. IrPN
Morning. Blake. BoLiVe; EG; ERoP-1; FaBoCh; LoBV; LoGBV; OBRV; PeER
Morning. Charles Stuart Calverley. FiBHP; NBM
Morning. Hilda Conkling. NP
Morning. Sir William Davenant. *See* Lark Now Leaves His Wat'ry Nest, The.
Morning. Emily Dickinson. *See* Will there really be a morning?
Morning. Ivy O. Eastwick. BoTP
Morning. Dorothy Hamilton Gallagher. SiSoSe
Morning. Bernette Golden. TNV
Morning. Jim Harrison. WIRo
Morning, The. John Gay. *See* Of Walking the Streets by Day.
Morning. Keats. *Fr.* Imitation of Spenser. GN
Morning. John Keble. OBRV
Morning. Hugh McCrae. BoAV
Morning. Henry Reed. MoVE; NeBP
Morning. Philip Henry Savage. AA
Morning. Shelley. *Fr.* Prometheus Unbound. ShBV-3
Morning. Jane Taylor. HBV
Morning. Sara Teasdale. NP
Morning. Jones Very. AnNE
Morning. Samuel Waddington. OBVV
Morning,/ the door opening, changing. Checking the Traps. Denis Johnson. QAH
Morning After, The. Heine, *tr. fr. German by* Louis Untermeyer. ErPo; UnTE
Morning After, The. Dorothy Wellesley. OBMV
Morning after Death, The. Emily Dickinson. *See* Bustle in the house, The.
Morning again, nothing has to be done. Second Poem. Peter Orlovsky. NeAP
Morning and evening. Goblin Market. Christina Rossetti. AnFE; AtBAP; BoTP; DTo; GoTL; OAEP; OnSP; PAn; PoVP; ViPo; VP
Morning and Evening. Antoni Slonimski, *tr. fr. Polish by* Watson Kirkconnell. TrJP
Morning and evening, sleep she drove away. The Spinning Woman. Leonidas of Tarentum. AWP; JAWP; WBP
Morning and Evening Star. Plato, *tr. fr. Greek by* Shelley. AWP; JAWP; WBP
(Aster.) LiTW
(Star.) OnPM; WoL
(To Stella.) EnLoPo; InPo; MBW-2; ViBoPo
Morning, and streaks of heavenly blue. London Spring. Antoni Slonimski. TrJP
Morning answers, The. Square in Savannah. Jason Miller. ThO
Morning at Arnheim. William Jay Smith. NePoEA
Morning at the Beach. John Farrar. RIS
Morning at the Temple of Kobai. Edith Shiffert. NYTB
Morning at the Window. T. S. Eliot. AmPP; AnEnPo; CABA; CAD; CoBA; InPo; JAWP; MAP; MoAmPo (1942 ed.); NeMA; NePA; OnPM; WBP; WePo
Morning Bell of Fang T'a, The. Hsi P'ei Lan, *tr. fr. Chinese by* Henry H. Hart. OnPM; WoL
Morning: blue, cold and still. January. Weldon Kees. CoAP
Morning Breaks, The. John Oxenham. OQP
(Coming Day, The.) MaRV
Morning breaks like a pomegranate, The. Wedding Morn. D. H. Lawrence. MoAB; MoBrPo
Morning Bus. John Coulter. CaP
Morning by morning waken me, my Father. Teach Me. Freda Hanbury Allen. SoP
Morning came at me like a flung snowball. Puerto Rican Side-Street. Louis Dudek. TwCaPo
Morning came up as other mornings came. Grubber's Day. Jay G. Sigmund. AnAmPo
Morning Challenge. Charles E. Bayley. SoP
Morning Clouds. Nellie Burget Miller. GFA
Morning comes, and thickening clouds prevail, The. The Clouded Morning. Jones Very. AP
Morning comes, The; not slow, with reddening gold. Frederick Goddard Tuckerman. *Fr.* Sonnets. AmePo; AP
Morning comes, the night decays, the watchmen leave their stations, The. Empire Is No More. Blake. *Fr.* America: A Prophecy. EnRP
Morning comes to consciousness, The. Preludes, II. T. S. Eliot. AnAmPo; BoLiVe (1945 ed.); CoBA; InP; LiTA; LiTM; NoP; OBMV; PoPo; ReMP; UnPo
Morning Cometh, The. Anne Catherine White. SoP
Morning Concert—Nantucket. Isabel Harriss Barr. JKCP (1955 ed.)
Morning Drum-Call, The. Robert Louis Stevenson. EPN
Morning, evening, noon, and night. The Boy and the Angel. Robert Browning. OTPC; PoVP
Morning Express. Siegfried Sassoon. HaMV; ShBV-3; WePo
Morning Fancy. Mary McNeil Fenollosa. AA
Morning-Glories. Basho, *tr. fr. Japanese by* H. G. Henderson. OnPM
Morning-Glory, The. Florence Earle Coates. HBV
Morning-Glory, The. Maria White Lowell. AA; HBV
Morning Glory, The. *Unknown, tr. fr. Chinese by* Helen Waddell. *Fr.* Shi King. AWP; JAWP; WBP
Morning-glory, climbing the morning long, The. Indiana. Hart Crane. *Fr.* The Bridge: Powhatan's Daughter. AnFE; CoAnAm; LiTA; TwAmPo
Morning glory climbs above my head, The. The Morning Glory. *Unknown. Fr.* Shi King. AWP; JAWP; WBP
Morning Hair. *Unknown, tr. fr. Japanese by* Ishii *and* Obata. OnPM
Morning has broken. A Morning Song. Eleanor Farjeon. WePo
Morning haze. Haze. Buson. RePo
Morning Hours, The. *Unknown, tr. fr. Arabic by* Mohammed Marmaduke Pickthall. PoPl
Morning Hymn, *abr.* Cecil Frances Alexander. OTPC
Morning Hymn. Joseph Beaumont. OxBoCh; TrPWD
Morning Hymn. St. Gregory the Great, *tr. fr. Latin by* Edward Caswall. CAW; WGRP
Morning Hymn. Thomas Ken. FaFP; MaRV; OBS, *abr.*; OTPC; TreFS
(Awake, My Soul.) OxBoCh
Morning Hymn, A. Charles Wesley. CEP; OBEC; PoEL-3; TrPWD
(Christ, Whose Glory Fills the Skies.) ELP; OxBoCh
(True Light, The.) SoP
Morning Hymn of Adam and Eve. Milton. *See* Adam's Morning Hymn.
Morning, if this late withered light can claim. The Zonnebeke Road. Edmund Blunden. MMA
Morning in Camp. Herbert Bashford. AA
Morning in Spring. Louis Ginsberg. GoYe
Morning in the North-West. Arthur Stringer. CaP
Morning in the Park. John Ciardi. MiAP
Morning, in the Pastures Near Suisun. Philip Dow. QAH

Morning is a little lass. Small Song. Frances Frost. RePo
Morning is a state of mind. Morning. Bernette Golden. TNV
Morning is bright and sunlit, and the west wind running smoothly, The. Message to the Bard. William Livingston. GoTS
Morning is cheery, my boys, arouse, The! Reveille. Michael O'Connor. AA; HBV
Morning is clean and blue, and the wind blows up the clouds, The. Irradiations, XXII. John Gould Fletcher. MAP; NePA; NP
Morning is the gate of day, The. The Sentinel. Annie Johnson Flint. BLRP; MaRV; OQP
Morning Light. Mary Effie Lee Newsome. AmNP; CDC; PoNe
Morning Light, The. *Unknown.* SoP
Morning Light for One with Too Much Luck, The. Delmore Schwartz. FiMAP
Morning Light Is Breaking, The. Samuel F. Smith. WGRP
(Daybreak.) BLRP
(Success of the Gospel.) SoP
Morning Light Song. Philip Lamantia. NeAP
Morning Meditation, A: I. William Alabaster. EP
Morning Mist, The. Robert Southey. OTPC
Morning mists still haunt the stony street, The. Enter Patient, I. W. E. Henley. *Fr.* In Hospital. BrPo; PoVP
Morning Moon. Victor Contoski. ThO
'Morning, Morning. Ray Mathew. PoAu-2
Morning, Noon, and . . . Hawley Truax. NYBP
Morning of a cold month, The. The International Brigade Arrives at Madrid. "Pablo Neruda." WaaP
Morning of May, A. *Unknown. See* In Summer.
Morning of the winter's, The. Leaping Falls. Galway Kinnell. NePoAm-2
Morning, on a beach. A man & woman sitting by fire. Moon Is to Blood. Richard Duerden. NeAP
Morning on the Lièvre. Archibald Lampman. SD
Morning on the misty highlands. Sandpipers. Helen Merrill Egerton. CaP
Morning on the St. John's. Jane Cooper. NYBP
Morning Overture; Chorus of Dogs. Pearl Strachan. GoTP
Morning Porches, The. Donald Hall. NePoAm-2
Morning Prayer. Nissim Ezekiel. ACV
Morning Prayer, A. Betty Perpetuo. SoP; STF
Morning Prayer ("Now that the daylight fills the sky"). *Unknown.* FaChP
Morning Prayer ("When little things would irk me"). *Unknown.* PoToHe
Morning Prayer. *At. to* Rebecca J. Weston. *See* Prayer, A: "Father, we thank Thee for the night."
Morning Prayer, A. Ella Wheeler Wilcox. MaRV; OQP; PoToHe
Morning Prayer for Day's Work. John Matthesius. SoP
Morning Purples All the Sky, The. Roman Breviary, *tr. fr. Latin.* BePJ
Morning Quatrains, The. Charles Cotton. PeRV
Morning Serenade. Madison Cawein. HBV
Morning Shall Awaken, The. Bernard of Cluny, *tr. fr. Latin by* John Mason Neale. SoP
Morning sits outside afraid, The. Night and Morning. Dorothy Aldis. PoSC; YeAr
Morning Song. Karle Wilson Baker. HBMV; PCD
Morning-Song. George Darley. *Fr.* Sylvia; or, The May Queen. VA
(Serenade: "Awake thee, my lady-love.") HBV
Morning Song. Sir William Davenant. *See* Lark Now Leaves His Wat'ry Nest, The.
Morning Song. Alan Dugan. CAD; CBV; ELU
Morning Song, A. Eleanor Farjeon. WePo
Morning Song. Afanasi Afanasievich Fet, *tr. fr. Russian by* Max Eastman. AWP
Morning Song. Solomon ibn Gabirol, *tr. fr. Hebrew by* Nina Davis Salaman. TrJP
Morning Song. Sylvia Plath. CBV
Morning Song, A. Shakespeare. *See* Hark! Hark! the Lark.
Morning Song. Kurt M. Stein. FiBHP
Morning Song for a Lover. Howard Sergeant. ToPo
Morning Song for Imogen, A. Shakespeare. *See* Hark! Hark! the Lark.
Morning Song of Senlin. Conrad Aiken. *Fr.* Senlin; a Biography, Pt. II, ii. AmP; CMoP; HBMV; LiTA; LiTM; OxBA; ReMP
(Morning Song.) InP; MAP; MoAB; MoAmPo; NeMA; NP; TrGrPo; WoL
(Selin; a Biography.) PoMa
Morning Star, The. Emily Brontë. ChTr
Morning Star. James J. Galvin. ISi
Morning Star, The. John Hall. SeCL
Morning star is not a star, The. Logging, I. Gary Snyder. *Fr.* Myths & Texts. OPoP
Morning Sun. Louis MacNeice. MoAB; MoBrPo; NeMA; TwCP
Morning sun shines from the east, The. Ode on Science. Jezaniah Sumner. TrAS
Morning Thanksgiving. John Drinkwater. BoTP
Morning that he drowned the white ship came, The. At the Discharge of Cannon Rise the Drowned. Hubert Witheford. AnNZ
Morning that the world began, The. Why Nobody Pets the Lion at the Zoo. John Ciardi. RePo
Morning Track, The. Edward Parone. NYBP
Morning! Wake up! Awaken! All the boughs. Week-End, VI. Harold Monro. YT
Morning was never here, nor more dark ever. Blue Cockerel. W. S. Merwin. TwAmPo
Morning-Watch, The. Henry Vaughan. AnAnS-1; BoC; EP; LiTB; LoBV; MaPo; MeP; MePo; NoP; OBS; OxBoCh; ReEn; SeCePo; ViBoPo
Morning Work. D. H. Lawrence. MoAB; MoBrPo (1950 ed.)
Morning Workout. Babette Deutsch. NePoAm-2; SD
Morning Worship. Mark Van Doren. NePoAm-2; TwAmPo
Morning's fair, the lusty sun, The. The Country Walk. John Dyer. PrWP
Morning's moist and fog-veiled, The. Elegies, V. Philippe Thoby-Marcelin. PoNe
Morning's work went quickly done, The. That Familiar Stranger. Felix Stefanile. FiSC
Mornings you trudge these beaches with misgivings. A Book of Shells. Randy Blasing. YAP
Mornin's Mornin', The. Gerald Brennan. BLPA
Morns are meeker than they were, The. Emily Dickinson. AA; AnNE; BoNaP; FaPON; HBV; LHV; MPB; PCH; PoPl; TiPo; ToP; TreFT; TSW; YeAr
Morocco. R. N. Currey. BoSA
Moron, The. *Unknown.* MemP; TreFT; YaD
("See the happy moron.") CenHV
Morpheus, *sel.* Hilda Doolittle ("H. D."). FaBoMo
Choros: "Give me your poppies."
Morpheus, the lively son of deadly sleep. Astrophel and Stella, XXXII. Sir Philip Sidney. FCP; ReEn; SiPS
Morphine combined with scopolamine is called. Gerald Butler. *Fr.* This Side of Orion. QAH
Morris Dance, The. *Unknown.* MuSP
Morrissey and the Russian Sailor, *with music. Unknown.* AS
Morrow's Message, The. Dante Gabriel Rossetti. The House of Life, XXXVIII. GTSE; MaVP; PoVP; ViPo; VP
Mors Benefica. Edmund Clarence Stedman. AA
Mors et Vita. Richard Henry Stoddard. AA
Mors et Vita. Samuel Waddington. HBV
Mors Iabrochii. *Unknown.* NA
Mors, Morituri Te Salutamus. Francis Burdett Money-Coutts. OBVV
Mortal and Immortal. Robert Cassie Waterston. SoP
Mortal Combat. Alice Fay di Castagnola. GoYe
Mortal Combat. Mary Elizabeth Coleridge. OBVV
Mortal Grief. Francisco de Figueroa, *tr. fr. Spanish by* Sir John Bowring. OnPM
Mortal Love. Basil Dowling. AnNZ
Mortal my mate, bearing my rock-a-heart. To His Watch. Gerard Manley Hopkins. MoAB; MoBrPo
Mortal, Sneer Not at the Devil. Heine, *tr. fr. German by* Emma Lazarus. *Fr.* Homeward Bound. TrJP
Mortality. James Devaney. BoAV; PoAu-1
Mortality. Gerald Gould. MoBrPo (1942 ed.)
Mortality. William Knox. *See* Oh! Why Should the Spirit of Mortal Be Proud?
Mortality. Naomi Long Madgett. NNP; PoNe (1970 ed.)
Mortality. *Unknown. See* Inscription, An: "Grass of levity."
Mortality, behold and fear. On [*or* Lines on] the Tombs in Westminster Abbey [*or* A Memento for Mortality]. *Unknown, at. to* Francis Beaumont, *also to* William Basse. ACP; BEL; CH; EIL; FaBoCh; GoBC; GTBS; GTBS-D; GTBS-P; GTBS-W;

GTSE; HBV; InP; LoBV; LoGBV; MaRV; OBEV; OBS; SeEP; ShBV-3; TOP; TrGrPo; ViBoPo; WePo
Mortally. James Kirkup. NeBP
Mortals, that behold a Woman. Assumpta Maria. Francis Thompson. ISi
Morte Arthur (*Alliterative*), *sels.* *Unknown,* *tr. fr. Middle English.*
"Arthur turns into Tuscany when the time is favorable," *mod.* MeEV
Sir Gawain Encounters Sir Priamus. PoEL-1
Morte d'Arthur. Tennyson. *Incorporated in* Idylls of the King, *with changes, as* The Passing of Arthur. AnEnPo; ATP; BBV; BEL; BoLiVe; DTo; EnL; EnLi-2; FaBoBe; FiP; HBV; ILP; MBW-2; NoP; OAEP; OnSP; PoAn; PoE; PoEL-5; PoVP; SeCeV; ShBV-3; TOP; UnPo (1st ed.); ViPo; ViPP; VP; WHA
Sels.
"And slowly answered Arthur from the barge." FaBoEn; GTSL
(Prayer.) BoPe
"Old order changeth, yielding place to new, The." SoP; TRV
(Prayer.) MaRV
(Prayer for the Dead.) GoBC
Prayer ("More things are wrought by prayer"). BLRP; OQP; TreF; WGRP
"Then saw they how there hove a dusky barge." VA
Mortem, Quae Violat Suavia, Pellit Amor. William Johnson Cory. NBM
Mortification. George Herbert. AnAnS-1; MaMe; MeP; MePo; OAEP; PoFS; SeCP; ViBoPo
Mortifying Mistake, A. Anna Maria Pratt. AA; HBV; HBVY; RePo
(Little Mistake, A.) RIS
Mortimeriados, *sels.* Michael Drayton. ReIE
Death of Edward, The.
"Low'ring heaven had mask'd her in a cloud, The."
To the Excellent and Most Accomplish'd Lady, Lucy, Countess of Bedford.
Mortmain. Robert Penn Warren. PoCh
Morvin. John Fuller. NePoEA-2
Morwennae Statio. Robert Stephen Hawker. GoBC
Mos' Done Toilin' Here, *with music.* *Unknown.* BoAN-2
Mosaic Harlem. Henry Dumas. BF
Mosaic Worker, The. Arthur Wallace Peach. BLRP
Mosby at Hamilton. Madison Cawein. PAH
Moschatel. Daniel James O'Sullivan. NeIP
Moscow in the Wilderness, Segovia in the Snow. Lawrence Ferlinghetti. FRC
Mose ("Mose is black and evil"). Sterling A. Brown. Kal
Moses. Sydney Tremayne. OxBS
Moses; a Play, *sel.* Isaac Rosenberg.
"Yesterday as I lay nigh dead with toil." FaBoMo
Moses and Jesus. Israel Zangwill. TrJP
Moses, from whose loins I sprung. The Jew. Isaac Rosenberg. MoBrPo; PoFr
Moses Miles. Bob Maxey. WSL
Moses—No Man Knoweth His Sepulchre. Bryant. SoP
Moses supposes his toeses are roses. *Unknown.* OxNR
Mosquito, The. D. H. Lawrence. SiTL
Mosquito. John Updike. FIW
Mosquito Knows, The. D. H. Lawrence. CBV; OA
Moss-gathering. Theodore Roethke. CoBMV; FiMAP; ILP
Moss of His Skin, The. Anne Sexton. CoAP
Moss-Rose, The. Sir Henry Newbold. HBV
Moss Supplicateth for the Poet, The. Richard Henry Dana. AA
Most Acceptable Gift, The. Matthias Claudius, *tr. fr. German by* J. M. Campbell. BLRP
Most Blessed Lady, comfort to such as call. Dedication of the Chronicles of England and France. Robert Fabyan. ISi
Most chivalrous fish of the ocean. The Rhyme of the Chivalrous Shark. Wallace Irwin. ShM
Most every meal, when he's at home, my father says. Her Great Secret. Strickland Gillilan. PEDC
Most Excellent Song Which Was Salomon's, The. Michael Drayton. *Fr.* The Harmony of the Church. ReIE
Most fair and lovely maid, look from the shore. To Delia, XLI. Samuel Daniel. Sonn; TuPP
Most fragile of all is the cherry-bloom. Ki no Tsurayuki, *tr. fr. Japanese by* I. W. Furukami. LiTW
Most glorious Lord of life [*or* lyfe], that on this day. Amoretti, LXVIII [*or* Easter *or* Easter Morning]. Spenser. ATP; BoC; CABA; CAW; DD; ElL; EnRePo; FaChP; HBV; LiTB; MaPo (1969 ed.); MaRV; NoP; OBEV; OHIP; OxBoCh; PoE; ReEn; ReIE; SeCeV; SiCE; Sonn; StJW; TrPWD; TRV
Most glorious of all the Undying, many-named, girt round with awe! Hymn to Zeus. Cleanthes, *tr. by* Edward Hayes Plumptre. WGRP
Most high Lord. Cantico del Sole. St. Francis of Assisi, *tr. by* Ezra Pound. CTC
Most high, omnipotent Good Lord. The Canticle of the Sun. St. Francis of Assisi. WHL
Most holy Night, that still dost keep. The Night. Hilaire Belloc. HBV; OBEV (new ed.); OBVV
Most holy Satyr. Holy Satyr. Hilda Doolittle ("H. D."). MAP; MoAmPo
Most Honored Guest. Walter Shea. ChIP
Most like an Arch This Marriage. John Ciardi. MoLP; PoPl
Most like some agèd king it seemed to me. Recollections of Burgos. Richard Chenevix Trench. OBRV
Most Lovely Shade. Edith Sitwell. AtBAP; FaBoTw; GTBS-P; POTE
Most Men Know Love But as a Part of Life. Henry Timrod. *See* Quatorzain.
Most modern wits, such monstrous fools have shown. Sir Fopling Flutter. Dryden. DiPo
Most near, most dear, most loved and most far. Sonnet to My Mother [*or* To My Mother]. George Barker. BoC; DTC; FaBoMo; FaFP; FIW; GTBS-D; GTBS-W; LiTB; LiTM; MemP; MoAB; MoPW; PG (1955 ed.); SeCePo; Sonn; TwCP; VaPo; ViBoPo (1958 ed.); WaP
Most needy aren oure neighebores, The. The Poor. William Langland. *Fr.* The Vision of Piers Plowman. PoEL-1
Most of It, The. Robert Frost. CABA; CaFP; CrMA; FosPo; MaPo; MoPo; NePA; PIA; PoIE; PoSa
Most of my days are passed away, yet my heart is still impure. The Worthless Heart. Immanuel di Roma. TrJP
Most pines that fight their way to upper light. Dance of Death. Kimball Flaccus. AnAmPo
Most Pithy and Pleasant History of Glaucus and Scylla, The. Thomas Lodge. *Fr.* Scylla's Metamorphosis. ReIE
Most poets to a muse that is stone-deaf cry. On the Oxford Book of Victorian Verse. "Hugh MacDiarmid." MoBrPo
Most present of all the watchers where we camped, The. When We Looked Back. William Stafford. NYBP
Most Quietly at Times. Cäsar Flaischlen, *tr. fr. German by* Jethro Bithell. AWP; JAWP; WBP
Most respected/ comrades heirs and descendants. At the Top of My Voice. Vladimir Mayakovsky. OnHM
Most royal/ affluent/ advertisement. Wig. Kirk Hall. BF
Most-Sacred Mountain, The. Eunice Tietjens. HBM; HT; MoRP
Most she touched me by her muteness. Emily Dickinson. BiS
Most souls, 'tis true, but peep out once an age. Pope. *Fr.* Elegy to the Memory of an Unfortunate Lady. CH; ELU
Most Sovereign Lady. *Unknown.* MeEL
Most stupendous show they ever gave, The. In Memory of the Circus Ship *Euzkera.* Walker Gibson. FiBHP; NePoAm
Most Sweet It Is [with Unuplifted Eyes]. Wordsworth. *See* Inner Vision, The.
Most that I know but one. Care. Josephine Miles. NYBP
Most unlikely rebel, he, A. The Unlikely Rebel. Franklin D. Elmer, Jr. ChIP
Most Unloving One, The. Samuel Daniel. *See* To Delia: "My spotless love. . ."
Most Vital Thing in Life, The. Grenville Kleiser. OTD; PoToHe (new ed.)
Most weeds, whilst young. Francis Daniel Pastorius. SCAP
Most worthy of praise were the virtuous ways. Little Red Riding Hood. Guy Wetmore Carryl. FiBHP; HBV; YaD
Most worthye she is in towne, The. In Praise of Ivy. *Unknown.* MeEL
Most wounds can Time repair. At Ease. Walter de la Mare. ChMP; GTBS-P
Most wretched heart, most miserable. Sir Thomas Wyatt. FCP; SiPS
Mostly Are We Mostless. José Garcia Villa. TwAmPo
Mot eran dous miei cossir. Arnaut Daniel, *tr. fr. French by* Harriet Waters Preston. AWP
Motect, A. *Unknown.* SeEP
Moth, The. Walter de la Mare. BrPo; FaBoEn; MoVE; NoP; ShBV-3
Moth and the Flame, The. George Taggert. TreF
Moth ate a word, A. The [*or* A] Book-Worm [*or* Book-

Moth (continued)
Moth]. *Unknown.* *Fr.* Riddles. AnOE; CoBE; EnLi-1; EnLit; OA; YAT
Moth belated, sun and zephyr-kist, A. To a Moth That Drinketh of the Ripe October. Emily Pfeiffer. VA
Moth-eyed/ by the neon sign. Mom I'm All Screwed Up. Frank Lima. ANYP
Moth Miller. Aileen Fisher. UTS
Moth-Song. Ellen Mackay Hutchinson Cortissoz. AA
Moth-Terror. Benjamin De Casseres. TrJP
Mother, The. Sarah Louise Arnold. PEDC
Mother. Thomas Curtis Clark. PGD
Mother, The. Sara Coleridge. OBVV
Mother. George Cooper. *See* Our Mother.
Mother. Mary Mapes Dodge. OTPC (1946 ed.)
(Birdies with Broken Wings.) PRWS
Mother. Max Ehrmann. PoToHe
Mother. Sister M. Eulalia. WHL
Mother. Thomas W. Fessenden. *See* To Mother.
Mother. Rose Fyleman. DD; HH; MPB; SiSoSe
Mother, The. S. S. Gardons. NePoEA-2
Mother. Hermann Hagedorn. *See* Mother in the House, The.
Mother. Theresa Helburn. FaPON; HBV; OHIP; TSW
Mother. Daniel Lawrence Kelleher. NeIP
Mother, The. George Newell Lovejoy. DD
(Gift, The.) PGD
Mother, The. Catulle Mendès, *tr. fr. French by* W. J. Robertson. TrJP
Mother. Alice Meynell. *See* Maternity.
Mother. Kathleen Norris. PoToHe
Mother, The. Nettie Palmer. BoAu; PoAu-1
Mother, The. Padraic Pearse. OnYI
Mother, The. Kathryn White Ryan. CAW
Mother. Keith Sinclair. AnNZ
Mother, The. Raymond Souster. PeCV
Mother. Emily Taylor. PGD
Mother ("Each day to her a miracle"). *Unknown.* PGD
Mother, The ("From out the south the genial breezes sigh"). *Unknown, tr. fr. Chinese by* George Barrow. OHIP
Mother, A ("God sought to give the sweetest thing"). *Unknown.* SoP
Mother ("If I could take the beauty of the orchid"). *Unknown.* SoP
Mother ("Whenever I look in her kind eyes"). *Unknown.* DD
Mother. Percy Waxman. PEDC
Mother. Whittier. *Fr.* Snow-bound. AA; OHIP; PFY
Mother. Margaret Widdemer. *See* Watcher, The.
Mother—a Portrait. Ethel Romig Fuller. PGD
Mother and Child. Ivy O. Eastwick. SiSoSe
Mother and Child, The. Vernon Watkins. NeBP
Mother and her Child, A. Redemption. Mary Winter Ware. SoP
Mother and Her Son on the Cross, The. *Unknown.* MeEL
Mother and maid and soldier, bearing best. A Portrait. Brian Hooker. HBV
Mother and Poet. Elizabeth Barrett Browning. HBV; VA
Mother and Son. Allen Tate. LiTA; MAP; MoAB; MoAmPo; MoVE
Mother and son. Bedtime Tales. Joseph Joel Keith. FiSC
Mother, at that word your eloquent body spoke. The Poet Prays Her. Daniel Berrigan. JKCP (1955 ed.)
Mother, at the portal a little child is standing. The Christmas Child. *Unknown.* PCH
Mother before a Soldier's Monument, A. Winnie Lynch Rockett. PGD
Mother Bombie, *sel.* John Lyly.
O Cupid! Monarch over Kings. ElL; SiCE
(Fools in Love's College.) TrGrPo
(Song of Accius and Silena.) OBSC
Mother came when stars were paling, A. The Fairy Boy. Samuel Lover. OTPC (1923 ed.)
Mother Carey. John Masefield. FaBoTw
Mother Carey's Chicken. Theodore Watts-Dunton. OBVV
(Ode to Mother Carey's Chicken, *sl. diff.*) VA
Mother Country, The. Benjamin Franklin. PAH
Mother Country. Christina Rossetti. OxBoCh
Mother Crab and Her Family, The. L. T. Manyase, *tr. fr. Xhosa by* Jack Cope *and* C. M. Maanyangwa. PeSA
Mother Dark. Francesca Yetunde Pereira. PBA
Mother Duck. Ann Hawkshaw. *See* Dame Duck's First Lecture on Education.
Mother Earth. Harriet Monroe. NP
Mother Earth, are the heroes dead? Heroes. Edna Dean Proctor. HBV
Mother England. Edith M. Thomas. AA; HBV
Mother fragrant in her dust and grace, The. Celestine. Robert Fitzgerald. MoVE
Mother Goose. *Rhymes indexed by first lines.*
Mother Goose. *Unknown.* SoPo
Mother Goose (circa 2054). Irene Sekula. ShM; SiTL
Mother Goose for Grown Folks, *sel.* Adeline D. T. Whitney.
Humpty Dumpty. HBV
Mother Goose Rhyme. Kenneth Rexroth. ErPo
Mother Goose Sonnets, *sels.* Harriet S. Morgridge. AA
Jack and Jill
Simple Simon.
Mother Goose Up-to-Date, *parodies.* Louis Untermeyer. MoAmPo
Edgar A. Guest Syndicates [*or* Considers] "The Old Woman Who Lived in a Shoe." MoAmPo; WhC
(Just Home.) StaSt
Mother-heart doth yearn at eventide, The. When Even Cometh On. Lucy Evangeline Tilley. AA
Mother, here there are shadowy salmon. Letter from Oregon. William Stafford. NaP
Mother, Home, Heaven. William Goldsmith Brown. DD; FaBoBe; HBV
Mother Hubberd's Tale. Spenser. *See* Prosopoia; or, Mother Hubberd's Tale.
Mother, I Cannot Mind My Wheel. Walter Savage Landor, *first st. par. fr. the Greek of* Sappho. AWP, *st.* 1; BoLiVe; CABA; EG; EnLi-1, *st.* 1; EnRP; HBV; JAWP, *st.* 1; LiTL; MeWo; OAEP; OBEV; OBRV; PG; StP; TOP; TrGrPo; WBP
(Margaret.) VA
Mother I longs to get married. Whistle Daughter Whistle. *Unknown.* ErPo
Mother, I went to China this morning. Who Can Say. Alastair Reid. NePoEA
Mother in Egypt, A. Marjorie Pickthall. CaP; HBV
Mother in gladness, Mother in sorrow. W. Dayton Wedgefarth. PoToHe
Mother in her office holds the key, The. Queen of the World. *Unknown.* PGD
Mother in the House, The. Hermann Hagedorn. DD; HBMV; OHIP; PoRL
(Mother.) PoToHe
Mother in the Snow-Storm, The. Seba Smith. PaPo
Mother Is a Sun, A. Peggy Bennett. PoSC
Mother is gone. Bird songs wouldn't let her breathe. Requiem. William Stafford. NaP
Mother, is this the darkness of the end. For "Our Lady of the Rocks." Dante Gabriel Rossetti. MaVP; OxBoCh
Mother land/ Long lain asleep. Mother Dark. Francesca Yetunde Pereira. PBA
Mother likes the frocks and hats. Shop Windows. Rose Fyleman. SoPo; TiPo; UTS
Mother Love. Janie Alford. PGD
Mother Love. Kipling. *See* Mother o' Mine.
Mother Love. *Unknown.* SoP
Mother Marie Therese. Robert Lowell. CoPo; FiMAP
Mother Mary, thee I see. Communion. Caroline Giltinan. CAW; JKCP
Mother Mary's mind. Mary Pondered All These Things. Edwin McNeill Poteat. ChIP
Mother Maudlin the Witch. Ben Jonson. *Fr.* The Sad Shepherd. ChTr
Mother, may I go out [*or* in] to [*or* and] swim? *Unknown.* FaPON; OTPC; OxNR; RIS; SAS; SiTL
Mother mine. Valentine to My Mother. Christina Rossetti. BoChLi
Mother mine, Mother mine, what do you see? Ballad. Annemarie Ewing. NePoAm
Mother Moon. Amelia Josephine Burr. TVC; WHL
Mother Most Powerful. Giovanni Dominici, *tr. fr. Italian by* Thomas Walsh. CAW
Mother, mother. The One Who Struggles. Ernst Toller. TrJP
Mother, Mother, Make My Bed. *Unknown.* ELP
"Mother, mother, what is that." *Unknown.* ExPo

Mother, my Mary Gray. The Division of Parts. Anne Sexton. NePoEA-2
Mother Nature had a wash day. Nature's Wash Day. Marguerite Gode. GFA
Mother needs Thee, Lord, A. A Mother's Prayer. Jeanette Saxton Coon. STF
Mother o' blossoms, and ov all. William Barnes. *Fr.* May. ChTr
Mother o' Mine. Kipling. The Light That Failed: Dedication. FaFP; MaRV; NeHB; OQP; TRV; WBLP
(Mother Love.) SoP
"Mother, O mother, go riddle my sport." The Brown Girl. *Unknown.* BaBo
Mother of a Daughter. Louis Johnson. AnNZ
Mother of Christ, hear Thou Thy people's cry. Alma Redemptoris. *Unknown.* WHL
Mother of Christ long slain, forth glided she. Motherhood. Agnes Lee. BLPA; HBMV; NP
Mother, The, of Christ the Priest and of His/ royal and priestly people. The Mediatrix of Grace. Francis Burke. ISi
Mother of England, and sweet nurse of all. Ad Reginam Elizabetham. Thomas Bastard. SiCE
Mother of God, The. *Unknown, tr. fr. Greek by* G. R. Woodward. *Fr.* Horologium. ISi
Mother of God, The. W. B. Yeats. EnLP
Mother of God, mother of man reborn. Invocation. Arthur J. Little. *Fr.* Christ Unconquered. ISi
Mother of God! no lady thou. Our Lady. Mary Elizabeth Coleridge. CAW; OBEV (new ed.); OBMV; OBVV; TOP
Mother of God that's Lady of the Heavens. Two Translations from Villon [*or* A Translation from Villon]. *Pr. tr. by* J. M. Synge. MoBrPo; NeMA
Mother of God, whose burly love. On the Eve of the Feast of the Immaculate Conception, 1942. Robert Lowell. WaaP
"Mother of heaven, regina of the clouds." Le Monocle de Mon Oncle. Wallace Stevens. AnAmPo; AnFE; AP; APA; CoAnAm; CoBMV; LiTM; MAPA; MoAB; NP; TwAmPo
Mother of Hermes! and still youthful Maia! Fragment of an Ode to Maia, Written on May Day, 1818, Keats. EnRP; EPN; ERoP-2; MBW-2; OAEP; OBEV; OBRV; PeER; PoEL-4
Mother of Judas, The. Amelia Josephine Burr. WHL
Mother of life indulges all our wandering, The. Return to Ritual. Mark Van Doren. MoVE
Mother of light! how fairly dost thou go. Ode to the Moon. Thomas Hood. OBVV
Mother of memories, mistress of mistresses. The Balcony. Baudelaire, *tr. by* F. P. Strum. PIA
Mother of memories! O mistress-queen! Le Balcon. Baudelaire, *tr. by* Lord Alfred Douglas. AWP
Mother of Men. Brian Hooker. HBMV
Mother of Men. Stephen Southwold. HBMV
Mother of Men, grown strong in giving. Mother of Men. Brian Hooker. HBMV
Mother of musings, Contemplation sage. The Pleasures of Melancholy. Thomas Warton, the Younger. CEP; EiPP; EnRP
Mother of nations, of them eldest we. America to England. George Edward Woodberry. AA
Mother of revolutions, stern and sweet. To France. Ralph Chaplin. HBMV
Mother of the Fair Delight. Ave. Dante Gabriel Rossetti. GoBC; ISi; OxBoCh; ViPo
Mother of the House, The. Proverbs, XXXI: 25-29, Bible, *O.T.* GoTP; PGD; OQP
("Strength and honour are her clothing.") PoSC
Mother of the Muses, we are taught, The. Memory. Walter Savage Landor. ERoP-1; VA
Mother of the Rose, The. James M. Hayes. JKCP
Mother of Us All, The, *sel.* Gertrude Stein.
"We cannot retrace our steps." CrMA
Mother plays a march. Away We Go. Aileen Fisher. TiPo (1959 ed.)
Mother-Prayer. Margaret Widdemer. HBMV
Mother said to call her if the H bomb exploded. Belief. Josephine Miles. CBV; FiMAP
Mother Sarah's Lullaby. Itzig Manger, *tr. fr. Yiddish by* Jacob Sonntag. TrJP
Mother says. Counting Sheep. Eileen Fisher. SoPo
Mother says I'm six. Hard Lines. Tom Robinson. BiCB
Mother sent me on the holy quest, The. The Living Chalice. Susan Mitchell. HBMV
Mother shake the cherry-tree. Let's Be Merry. Christina Rossetti. *Fr.* Sing-Song. FaPON; PoVP; TiPo
Mother Shipton's Prophecies. *At to* Charles Hindley. BLPA
Mother Sings, A. Lois Duffield. SoP
Mother sings a song of youth and May, The. A Very Happy Family. Joseph G. Francis. CIV
Mother-Song. Alfred Austin. *Fr.* Prince Lucifer. HBV; VA
Mother Superior. George MacBeth. HYE; NMP
Mother Tabbyskins. Elizabeth Anna Hart. CenHV; CIV
(Old Mother Tabbyskins, *with music.*) FTB
"Mother, the poplars cross the moon." Refugees. Grace Hazard Conkling. NP
Mother Thought, A. Edgar A. Guest. PEDC
Mother to Her Infant, The. Thomas Miller. OTPC (1923 ed.)
Mother to her son did say, The. The Maiden Hind. *Unknown.* LiTW
Mother to Son. Langston Hughes. AmNP; BiCB; BoChLi (1950 ed.); CDC; GoSl; IHA; OCS; OTD; PoNe; StVeCh; TTY
Mother took/ Some milk and flour. The Miracle. Elsie Melchert Fowler. BiCB
Mother Understands, A. G. A. Studdert-Kennedy. OQP
Mother was a wolf; snarled her long. Recollection. Donald D. Govan. NBP
Mother Wept. Joseph Skipsey. HBV; OBVV; VA
Mother wept, A: where were You, God. Calvary. Libby Stopple. GoYe
Mother Who Died Too, The. Edith M. Thomas. AA
Mother, who knew/ what hardship shakes. Our Lady of the Refugees. Sister Mary Maura. ISi
Mother who owns Christ as Lord, The. God's Ideal Mother. Cora M. Pinkham. STF
Mother! whose virgin bosom was uncrossed. The Virgin [*or* Sonnet to the Virgin]. Wordsworth. CAW; CoBE; GoBC; ISi
Mother will not turn, who thinks she hears, The. Broken Music. Dante Gabriel Rossetti. The House of Life, XLVII. MaVP; PoVP; VA; ViPo; VP
Mother with Young Kittens, A. Richard Hart. CIV
Motherhood. Josephine Dodge Daskam Bacon. HBV
Motherhood. Karl M. Chworowsky. PGD
Motherhood. Agnes Lee. BLPA; HBMV; NP
Motherhood. William L. Stidger. PGD
Motherhood. May Swenson. CoAP
Mothering. Mazie V. Caruthers. CIV
"Mother-in-law" they say, and yet. To "His" Mother. Minnie Price. SoP
Motherless. Elizabeth Barrett Browning. *Fr.* Aurora Leigh, I. VA
Motherless Soft Lambkin. Christina Rossetti. *Fr.* Sing-Song. RIS
Mothers. Edwin L. Sabin. PEDC
Mothers. *Unknown.* PGD
Mothers,/ That hope of yours, your joyful burden. To the Mothers. Ernst Toller. TrJP
Mothers and Children. Orrick Johns. AnAmPo; HBMV
Mothers and fathers of sons, what will you be saying. It Is Not Too Late. Lucia Trent. PGD
Mothers—and Others. Amos R. Wells. SoP; WBLP
Mothers are the queerest things! Mothers. Edwin L. Sabin. PEDC
Mothers are waiting in the yard, The. For a Junior School Poetry Book. Christopher Middleton. FIW
Mother's Birthday, A. Henry van Dyke. MaRV; OHIP
Mother's Choice, The. *Unknown.* OxBoLi
Mothers, Daughters. Shirley Kaufman. QAH
Mother's Day. Edna Tucker Muth. PEDC
Mother's Dream, The. William Barnes. *See* Mater Dolorosa.
Mother's gone a-visitin' to spend a month er two. Lonesome. Paul Laurence Dunbar. MPB; PoRL
Mother's Hands. W. Dayton Wedgefarth. PoToHe
Mother's Hymn, The. Bryant. DD; MaRV; OHIP
Mother's Idol Broken The, *sel.* Gerald Massey.
Our Wee White Rose. HBV
Mothers' Lament at the Slaughter of the Innocents, The. *Unknown, tr. fr. Middle Irish by* Kuno Meyer. OnYI
Mother's Lament for the Death of Her Son, A. Burns. HoPM
Mother's Love. Thomas Burbidge. VA
Mother's Love. Ross B. Clapp. WBLP

Mother's Love. James Montgomery. PGD, *st.* 1
Mother's Love ("Her love is like an island"). *Unknown.* OQP; SoP
(My Mother's Love.) STF
Mother's love, A—how sweet the name! A Mother's Love. James Montgomery. PGD
Mother's Malison, The; or, Clyde's Waters. *Unknown.* BaBo; ESPB (A *and* B *vers.*)
(Clyde Water, *longer, diff. vers.*) OBB
(Clyde's Waters.) OxBB
Mother's Name, A. *Unknown.* PGD
Mothers of America. Ave Maria. Frank O'Hara. ANYP
Mothers of Men. Amelia Josephine Burr. OQP
Mothers of Men, The. Joaquin Miller. PGD
(Bravest Battle, The.) WBLP, *sl. abr.*
Mothers of our Forest-Land, The. The Mothers of the West. William D. Gallagher. MC; PAH
Mothers of the Earth, The. Grace Noll Crowell. PEDC
Mothers of the West, The. William D. Gallagher. MC; PAH
Mother's Party. Aileen Fisher. BiCB
Mother's Petition, in Wartime. Helen M. Burgess. ChIP
Mother's Picture, A. Edmund Clarence Stedman. OHIP
Mother's Prayer, A. Jeanette Saxton Coon. STF
Mother's Prayer, A. Margaret E. Sangster. MaRV; SoP; TrPWD
(Father Speaks, A.) STF
Mother's Prayer, The. Dora Sigerson Shorter. HBV
Mother's Return, The. Dorothy Wordsworth. OTPC (1923 ed.)
Mother's Reward, A. Ona Freeman Lathrop. MaRV
Mother's Sacrifice, The. Lydia Huntley Sigourney. PaPo
Mother's Soliloquy, A. Hetty Wright. WaPE
Mother's Song, The. Virginia Woodward Cloud. AA
Mother's Song, A. Francis Ledwidge. EtS
Mother's Song, A. Christina Rossetti. *See* Love Me—I Love You.
Mother's Song ("My heart is like a fountain true"). *Unknown.* GN; HBV
Mother's Tale, The. Eleanor Farjeon. BiCB
Mothers who have seen him die—your first child, your only one. Fourth Station. Paul Claudel. ISi
Mother who raise/ A child by the book. Double Duty. W. E. Farbstein. PoPl; WhC
Mothers-in-Law. Robert Sward. CoPo
Moths, The. Julian Bell. POTE
Moths. Julia Fields. PoNe (1970 ed.)
Moths, The. William H. Matchett. WIRo
Moths, The. W. S. Merwin. FRC
Moth's Kiss, First, The. Robert Browning. *Fr.* In a Gondola. AtBAP; GTSL; MeWo; OBEV; OBVV; UnTE
(Song: "Moth's kiss, first, The!") BoLiVe; HBV; TrGrPo
Motif for Mary's Dolors. Sister Mary Madeleva. ISi
Motif from the Second Shepherd's Play. Sister Mary Maura. JKCP (1955 ed.)
Motion, The. Theodore Roethke. SeCeV (1967 ed.)
Motion of gathering loops of water, The. The Glass Bubbles. Samuel Greenberg. LiTA; NePA
Motion of the Earth, The. Norman Nicholson. ImOP
Motionless, gentle as it always was. And Then Her Burial. Merrill Moore. MAP; MoAmPo (1942 ed.)
Motionless sat the shadow at the helm. Thomas Westwood. *Fr.* The Quest of the Sancgreall. PeVV
Motive for Metaphor, The. Wallace Stevens. AP; MoAB; MoAmPo (1950 ed.)
Motive of All of It, The. Muriel Rukeyser. MiAP
Motives of Rhythm, The. Robert Conquest. PP
Motley. Walter de la Mare. MMA
Motley's the Only Wear. Shakespeare. *Fr.* As You Like It, II, vii. TrGrPo
(Worthy Fool, A.) TreFT
Motor Bus, The. A. D. Godley. OtMeF
Motor Cars. Rowena Bastin Bennett. FaPON; GFA; PoMa; SoPo; TiPo
Motorcycle. Benjamin Sturgis Pray. GoYe
Motto, The. Abraham Cowley. AnAnS-2; CLwM; SCEP-2; SeCP
Motto. Langston Hughes. PoNe (1970 ed.)
Motto. *Unknown, ad. fr. German by* Louis Untermeyer. *Fr.* Proverbs. RIS; TiPo
Motto for a Tree-planting. Richard Watson Gilder. PoRL
Motto to the Songs of Innocence & of Experience. Blake. ERoP-1
Mould, The. Gladys Cromwell. AnAmPo; MAP; NP
Mould of clouds inflamed the skin of the sky, A. Illusion. Ján Rak. LiTW
Mounsier Mingo. *Unknown.* CBEP
Mount, The. Léonie Adams. MAP; MoAB; MoAmPo; MoVE; NP
Mount Badon. Charles Williams. FaBoTw
Mt. [*or* Mount] Lykaion. Trumbull Stickney. *Fr.* Sonnets from Greece. AmLP; AnAmPo; AnFE; APA; CoAnAm; MoVE; NePA; OxBA; Sonn; TrGrPo
(Alone on Lykaion.) MAP; MoAmPo (1942 ed.)
Mount, mount for the chase! let your lassoes be strong. The White Steed of the Prairies. *Unknown.* CoSo
Mount of Blessing, The. William M. Runyan. FaChP
Mount of Olives ("Sweet sacred hill! on whose fair brow"). Henry Vaughan. Po
Mount of Olives ("When first I saw true beauty, and thy Joys"). Henry Vaughan. AnAnS-1; MeP
Mount Parnassus. Austin Clarke. NYTB
Mount Rainier. Herbert Bashford. AA
Mount Vernon, the Home of Washington. William Day. OHIP; PoRL
(Mount Vernon.) DD
Mountain, The, *sel.* William Ellery Channing.
"In this sweet solitude." PFY
Mountain, The. Emily Dickinson. *See* Mountain sat upon the plain, The.
Mountain, The. Geoffrey Dutton. MoAuPo
Mountain, The. Robert Finch. CaP
Mountain, The. Robert Frost. AmPP (3d ed.); CoBA; FaBV; HT; PoeP
Mountain, The. Mikhail Yurevich Lermontov, *tr. fr. Russian by* Max Eastman. AWP; JAWP; WBP
Mountain Air. John Galsworthy. OQP
Mountain and the Squirrel, The. Emerson. *See* Fable: "Mountain and the squirrel, The."
Mountain Cemetery, The. Edgar Bowers. NePoEA
Mountain Climber, The. Antonia Pozzi, *tr. fr. Italian by* Glauco Cambon. OnPM
Mountain Convent. Laura Benét. GoYe
Mountain Cottage, The, *with music.* John A. Stone. SGR
Mountain Creed. Medora Addison Nutter. GoYE
Mountain Dawn. Gene Boardman Hoover. StaSt
Mountain Evenings. Jamie Sexton Holme. PoOW
Mountain gorses, ever-golden. Lessons from the Gorse. Elizabeth Barrett Browning. HBV
Mountain Hamlet. Lew Sarett. PoMa
Mountain he flew over did not want him, The. The Mountain. Geoffrey Dutton. MoAuPo
Mountain Heart's-Ease, The. Bret Harte. HBV
Mountain held the town as in a shadow, The. The Mountain. Robert Frost. AmPP (3d ed.); CoBA; FaBV; HT; PoeP
Mountain in Labor, The. Aesop, *rhymed tr. fr. Greek by* William Ellery Leonard. AWP
Mountain in the Sky, The. Howard McKinley Corning. NP
Mountain Lake, The. Richard Church. AtBAP; POTE
Mountain Liars. Ann Woodbury Hafen. PoOW
Mountain Liberty. Ernest Rhys. *Fr.* The Ballads of the Last Prince. PoFr
Mountain like a beast, A. Dunedin Revisited. Denis Glover. AnNZ
Mountain Lion. D. H. Lawrence. AtBAP; HaMV; ShBV-2
Mountain Meadows. Martha Keller. BoNaP
Mountain Medicine. Elizabeth-Ellen Long. AmFN
Mountain over Aberdare, The. Alun Lewis. ACV
Mountain peaks put on their hoods, The. Twilight Song. John Hunter-Duvar. *Fr.* De Roberval; a Drama. VA; WHW
Mountain pine is a man at arms, The. The Elm. Odell Shepard. HBMV
Mountain Road, The. Enid Derham. BoAu
Mountain roads ends here, The. Lyell's Hypothesis Again. Kenneth Rexroth. MoVE; OnHM
Mountain sat upon the plain, The. Emily Dickinson. FaBV; NeMA; OnPM; PoeP; YT
Mountain sheep are sweeter, The. The War-Song of Dinas Vawr. Thomas Love Peacock. *Fr.* The Misfortunes of Elphin. ALV; AWP; CABA; EnRP; ERoP-1; EvOK; ExPo; FaBoCh; GTBS; InvP; JAWP; LiTG; LoBV; MyFE; NBM; OBRV; OnMSP; OtMeF; PTK; ShBV-2; StP; StPo; TOP; ViBoPo; WaaP; WBP; WhC; WiR

Mountain Song. Harriet Monroe. HBV; NP
Mountain Sprite, The. Thomas Moore. OTPC (1923 ed.)
Mountain summits sleep, The: glens, cliffs, and caves. Sleep upon the World [*or* Fragment]. Alcman. AWP; ChTr; JAWP; WBP
Mountain teeth, tips of anemious rippled stone. On the Subject of Waves. Eldon Grier. MoCV; PeCV (1967 ed.)
Mountain to the Pine, The. Clarence Hawkes. AA
Mountain Top. *Unknown. See* Liza Jane.
Mountain Tree, The. Hugh Connell. NeIP
Mountain was in great distress and loud, A. The Mountain in Labor. Aesop. AWP
Mountain Whippoorwill, The. Stephen Vincent Benét. IHA; StPo; TrGrPo; YaD; YT
Mountain Wind, A. "Æ." AWP; JAWP; WBP
Mountain Woman, The. Dubose Heyward. AnAmPo; NP; OnPP
Mountain Wreath, The, *sel.* Petar Petrovic Njegos. *tr. fr. Serbian by* James William Wiles.
Speech of Abbot Stephen. PoFr
Mountaineers, The. Dannie Abse. PP
Mountaineer, The. Robert Nathan. TrJP
Mountaineer is working with his Bible, The. Quatrina. Joseph Bennett. LiTA
Mountains. Ann Nolan Clark. StVeCh (1955 ed.)
Mountains, The. Walter de la Mare. BrPo
Mountains, The. Louis Dudek. CaP
Mountains, The. Walker Gibson. SD
Mountains. Lucy Larcom. WBLP
Mountains and Man ("Mountains and ocean waves"). *Unknown, tr. fr. Japanese by* Basil Hall Chamberlain. OnPM
Mountains and plains. Winter. Joso. OnPM; WoL
Mts and Rivers, *sels.* Gary Snyder.
Market, The. CoPo
"Seventy-five feet hoed rows equals." NaP
Mountains, The, and the lonely death at last. To a Traveler. Lionel Johnson. AnEnPo; MoBrPo; NBM
Mountains Are a Lonely Folk, The. Hamlin Garland. PoMa; RePo; TreFT
Mountains are moving, rivers. The Redwoods. Louis Simpson. AmFN; CoAP; FIW; PP
Mountains are the high places. Mountains. Ann Nolan Clark. StVeCh (1955 ed.)
Mountain's giddy height I sought, A. The Lay of the Trilobite. May Kendall. CenHV
Mountains grow unnoticed, The. Emily Dickinson. MoAB; MoAmPo; TrGrPo
Mountains in the Desert, The ("The mountains blue now"). Robert Creeley. CoPo
Mountains loom upon the path we take. Song to the Mountains. *Unknown.* AWP; JAWP; WBP
Mountains, The? Rising from some wet ravine. The Mountains. Walker Gibson. SD
Mountains they are [*or* Mountains are a] silent folk, The. The Mountains Are a Lonely Folk. Hamlin Garland. PoMa; RePo; TreFT
Mountains waver through my tears, The. Lullaby for a Man-Child. Jean Starr Untermeyer. YT
Mountainy Childer, The. Elizabeth Shane. HBMV
Mountebanks, The. Charles Henry Luders. AA
Mountebank's Mask, The, *sel.* Thomas Campion.
Hours of Sleepy Night, The. ElL
(Dismissal.) OBSC
Mounted on Kyrat strong and fleet. The Leap of Roushan Beg. Longfellow. StVeCh
Mourn, hapless Caledonia, mourn. The Tears of Scotland. Tobias Smollett. CEP; OBEC
Mourn her in the valleys, you young lovers, and throughout your gloom. W. H. Oliver. *Fr.* Death and the Maiden. AnNZ
Mourn No More. John Fletcher, *and others. See* Weep No More.
Mourn not for man, speeding to lay waste. Of Mourners. Dorothy Livesay. PeCV
Mourn Not the Dead. Ralph Chaplin. HBMV; MaRV; OQP; PoFr; ViBoPo
Mourne no more faire widdow. The Widow's Solace. Thomas Deloney. SiCE
Mourner, The. W. H. Davies. POTE
Mourner à la Mode, The. John Godfrey Saxe. LHV
Mourner's Bench, The. Edgar Lee Masters. CMoP
Mourners Came at Break of Day, The. Sarah Flower Adams. HBV
Mourners slowly bring Him through the gloom, The. He Is Buried. William A. Donaghy. *Fr.* The Stations of the Cross. JKCP (1955 ed.)
Mournful Madonnas with pathetic smiles. Meditations in a Museum Cloister. Sister Maryanna. JKCP (1955 ed.)
Mournful majesty of human greatness, The. Diaduminius. Pierre Benoît. CAW
Mournful muse of two despairing swains, The. The Eighth Pastoral of Virgil. Vergil. *Fr.* Eclogues. EiCP
Mournful Numbers. Morris Bishop. WhC
Mournful Nut-Tree, The. Antipater of Sidon, *tr. fr. Greek by* Lord Neaves. OnPM
Mournfully answer my groan, dark vales and Dorian water. Epitaph of Bion. Moschus. WoL
Mourning. Andrew Marvell. CABA; MaMe; SeCP
Mourning. Josephine Van Fossan. STF
Mourning Bride, The, *sels.* William Congreve.
"Heaven hath no rage like love to hatred turned," *fr.* III, viii. TreF
"Music has charms to sooth a savage breast," *fr.* I, i. ViBoPo
Mourning Conquest, The. *Unknown.* CoMu
Mourning Dove. Clinch Calkins. MeWo
Mourning-dove, that sang all evening, The. Dismal Observations. John Hall Wheelock. ML
Mourning Garment, The. Robert Greene. *See* Greene's Mourning Garment.
Mourning Picture. Adrienne Rich. CoAP
Mourning Poem for the Queen of Sunday. Robert Hayden. NoP
Mouse, The. Elizabeth J. Coatsworth. BoTP; FaPON; MoShBr; MoSiPe; OTPC (1946 ed.); PCD; RIS; SoPo; SUS; TiPo; UTS
Mouse. Hilda Conkling. SoPo; StVeCh; TiPo
Mouse, The. Jean Garrigue. TwCP
Mouse, The. Hugh McCrae. PoAu-1
Mouse, The. *Unknown, tr. fr. Chinese by* Isaac Taylor Headland. PCH
Mouse, The. Thirza Wakley. BoTP
Mouse, a Cat, and an Irish Bull, A. John Banister Tabb. CIV
Mouse and the Cake, The. Eliza Cook. OTPC (1923 ed.)
Mouse in the Wainscot, The. Ian Serraillier. PDV
Mouse That Gnawed the Oak-Tree Down, The. Vachel Lindsay. ILP; LOW; StaSt
Mouse, the Frog and the Little Red Hen, The. *Unknown.* BoTP
Mouse the trap had slapped on, but not caught, A. Ballad of the Mouse. Robert Wallace. NYBP
Mouse, whose martial value has so long, A. A Martial Mouse. Samuel Butler. OA
Mouse Whose Name Is Time, The. Robert Francis. LOW
Mousemeal. Howard Nemerov. TwCP
Mouse's Lullaby, The. Palmer Cox. PCH
Mouse's Nest. John Clare. CBV; ChTr; ExPo; LiTB; LoBV; SeCeV
Mousetrap, The. Christian Morgenstern, *tr. fr. German by* W. D. Snodgrass. OA
Mousie, mousie,/ Where is your little wee housie? Conversation. Rose Fyleman. BoTP
Mouth and Eyes. *Unknown, tr. fr. Spanish by* Havelock Ellis. OnPM
Mouth and the Ears, The. Shem-Tob ben Joseph Palquera, *tr. fr. Hebrew by* Joseph Chotzner. TrJP
Mouth down in the timothy. Grass. John Holmes. MiAP
Mouth like old silk soft with use, A. A Leaving. William Plomer. OBMV
Mouth of the Hudson, The. Robert Lowell. AmFN; CAD; CoPo; FRC; NaP; OCS; TDP; TPM
Mouth to mouth joined we lie, her naked breasts. Tantalus [*or* Tantalos]. Paulus Silentiarius. ErPo; LiTW
Mouths. Louis Dudek. PeCV
Move Continuing, The. Al Young. WSL
Move Eastward, Happy Earth. Tennyson. ViPP
Move him into the sun. Futility. Wilfred Owen. AtBAP; CBEP; ChMP; CMoP; CoBMV; FaBoMo; GTBS-D; GTBS-P; LiTM; LO; MMA; MoAB; MoBrPo; MoPW; NeMA; NoP; OAEP (2d ed.); PoE; SeCePo; TrGrPo
Move into the clear. In the Open. Ruth Pitter. BoPe
Move me that jasmine further from the bed. The Deaths of Myron and Klydone. Augusta Davies Webster. *Fr.* In a Day. VA

Move on with a will, nor dream thou back. At Dawn of the Year. "George Klingle." PGD
Move Over. Charles Olson. FRC
Move over, Ali Baba! Now there comes. Autosonic Door. Dorothy Brown Thompson. GoYe
Move to California, The, *sel.* William Stafford.
Written on the Stub of the First Paycheck. PoAn
Move to the Fore. *Unknown.* SoP
Moved by Her Music. Richard Gillman. NePoAm-2
Moved by the miracles of saints. The Raising of the Dead. Rosemary Dobson. PoAu-2
Movement of Fish, The. James Dickey. FRC; NYBP
Moves in me now the tongues, the gongs. To the Ladies. Arnold Kenseth. PPON
Movie-Going. John Hollander. CoAP
Movie Queen. James P. Vaughn. NNP
Movies. Clark Coolidge. ANYP
Movies, The. Florence Kiper Frank. NP
Movies for the Home. Howard Moss. NePoEA-2; NYBP
Movies in the Fire. Mildred D. Shacklett. GFA
Movies, Left to Right. Robert Sward. NYBP
Moving. Eunice Tietjens. GaP; TiPo
Moving Along. William Hunt. YAP
Moving Day. Helen M. Hartman. PoRL
Moving Finger, The. Omar Khayyám, *tr. fr. Persian by* Edward Fitzgerald. *fr.* the Rubáiyát. OnPM
("Moving Finger writes, and having writ, The.") EG; GTBS-W
Moving form or rigid mass, A. Song of the Screw. *Unknown.* NA
Moving from Cheer to Joy, from Joy to All. Next Day. Randall Jarrell. NYBP
Moving from the left to left, the light. View of the Capitol from the Library of Congress. Elizabeth Bishop. AmFN; FiMAP
Moving is all over, The. Moving Day. Helen M. Hartman. PoRL
Moving moon went up the sky, The. Samuel Taylor Coleridge. *Fr.* The Rime of the Ancient Mariner. LO
Moving sun-shapes on the spray, The. Going and Staying. Thomas Hardy. CMoP
Moving through the Silent Crowd. Stephen Spender. EnLi-2 (1949 ed.)
Moving with her. Feather River Valley, 1956. Coleman Barks. QAH
Moving with you. Poet to Dancer. Bernice Kavinoky. UnS
Mow the grass in the cemetery, darkies. Two at Norfolk. Wallace Stevens. FaBoMo
Mower, The. *Unknown.* CoMu
Mower Against Gardens, The. Andrew Marvell. AnAnS-1; BWP; ILP; LiTB; MaMe; MaPo (1969 ed.); OAEP; PoEL-2; PP; ReEn; SCEP-2; SeCV-1; SeEP; UTS
Mower in Ohio, The. John James Piatt. AA
Mower to [*or* of] the Glow-Worms [*or* Glow worms], The. Andrew Marvell. ALV; AtBAP; AWP; BoC; BWP; CBEP; EG; ELP; FosPo; InPo; InvP; MemP; OnPM; OxBoLi; SeCL; SeCP; TrGrPo
(Mower to Glow-Worms, The.) ReEn
(Mower to the Glo-Worms, The.) AnAnS-1; EnLoPo; MaMe; MePo; OBS; PoEL-2; SCEP-2
(To Glow-Worms.) RIS
Mowers, The. William Allingham. IrPN
Mowers, The. Myron B. Benton. YeAr
Mowers begin, The. Watchers. W. S. Merwin. NaP
Mower's scythe had passed o'er summer fields, The. God's Aftermath. Frances Brook. SoP
Mower's Song, The. Andrew Marvell. AnAnS-1; BWP; CavP; CBV; EnL; LiTL; LoBV; MaMe; NoP; PAn; PoEL-2; ReEn; SCEP-2; SeCL; SeCP; SeCV-1
Mowers, weary and brown and blithe. Scythe Song. Andrew Lang. GN; HBV; PCD; PoVP; VA
Mowing. Robert Frost. AmPP; AnFE; AnNE; APA; BWP; CMoP; CoAnAm; DiPo; ExPo; HBMV; HoPM; LiTA; MAmP; NeMA; NP; OxBA; ShBV-3; TwAmPo; UnPo (3d ed.); YT
Mowing, The. Sir Charles G. D. Roberts. ExPo; OBCV
Moxford Book of English Verse, The, *sels.* Archibald Stodart-Walker. CenHV
Counsel to Girls.
Early Bacon.
Inflictis.
Moy Castle. *Unknown.* GoTP; OnSP
Moyst with one drop of thy blood, my dry soule. Resurrection. John Donne. AnAnS-1; MaMe; MeP; OBS
Moytura, *sel.* William Larminie.
Sword of Tethra, The. OnYI
Mozart. Maurice Baring. MuSP
Mozart. Charles Higham. MuSP
Mozart. Jane Mayhall. NYTB
Mozart at Zell-am-See. Vernon Watkins. MuSP
Mozart, Goethe, and the Duke of Wellington. The Augsburg Adoration. Randall Jarrell. NYBP
Mozart, 1935. Wallace Stevens. AmP; UnS
Mozart Perhaps. John Hall Wheelock. UnS
Mozart's Grave. Paul Scott Mowrer. GoYe
Mozart's "Linz" Symphony. Margaret Stanley-Wrench. MuSP
Msitu mpunga: kibanda kina vitatu vyumba mwezi utatosha. Mswaki. James Brodey. ANYP
Mu'allaqát, The, *sels.* *Tr. fr. Arabic.*
Abla. Antar, *tr. by* E. Powys Mathers. AWP; JAWP; LiTW; WBP
"Have the poets left a single spot for a patch to be sewn?" Antar, *tr. by* A. J. Arberry. TTY
Ode: "Weep, ah weep love's losing." Imr el Kais, *tr. by* Lady Anne Blount. AWP
(Weep Love's Losing.) LiTW
Pour Us Wine. Ibn Kolthúm, *tr. by* E. Powys Mathers. AWP
Much Ado about Nothing, *sels.* Shakespeare.
Beauty Is a Witch, *fr.* II, i. TrGrPo
Epitaph: "Done to death by slanderous tongues," *fr.* V, iii. CTC
("Done to death by slanderous tongues.") OBSC
Pardon, Goddess of the Night, *fr.* V, iii. OBSC; SiCE; ViBoPo
(Song: "Pardon, goddess of the night,") CTC
Sigh No More, Ladies [Sigh No More], *fr.* II, iii. AnFE; AWP; BoLP; CBEP; CTC; DiPo; EG; EIL; ELP; EnLi-1 (1949 ed.); EnLit; ExPo; HBV; InMe; InPo; JAWP; LiTB; LiTG; LiTL; MCCG; MeWo; OAEP; PAn; PoEL-2; SeCeV; SiCE; SiTL; TOP; TreFS; TrGrPo; ViBoPo; WBP
(Balthasar's Song.) ALV; BoLiVe; OBSC
(Song: "Sigh no more, ladies, sigh no more.") FiP
Much as he left it when he went from us. Why He Was There. E. A. Robinson. CMoP
Much as I own I owe. Closed for Good. Robert Frost. MoAmPo (1950 ed.)
Much, beauty, is, less, than, the, face, of. José Garcia Villa. Divine Poems, 102. POTE (1959 ed.)
Much cry and little wool. Back. Weldon Kees. NaP; TwAmPo
Much did I rage when young. Youth and Age. W. B. Yeats. ELU
Much-discerning Public hold, A. La Nuit Blanche. Kipling. MoBrPo
Much for Little. *Unknown.* SoP
Much had passed/ Since last we parted. Byron Recollected at Bologna. Samuel Rogers. *Fr.* Italy. OBNC
Much Has Been Said . . . *Unknown.* CoMu
Much have I labored, much read o'er. Alas for Youth. Firdausi. AWP; JAWP; LiTW; WBP
Much have I roved by Sandy River. By Sandy Waters. Jesse Stuart. AmFN
Much have I spoken of the faded leaf. November. Elizabeth Stoddard. AA
Much have I travail'd in the realms of gold. On First Looking into the Dark Future. Roger Lancelyn Green. CenHV
Much have I travell'd [*or* travelled *or* traveled] in the realms of gold. On First Looking into Chapman's Homer. Keats. AnFE; ATP; BEL; BoLiVe; BWP; CABA; CaFP; CBEP; CBV; CH; ChER; ChTr; CLwM; CoBE; DD; DiPo; EG; EnL; EnLi-2; EnLit; EnRP; EPN; ERoP-2; ExPo; FaBoBe; FaBoCh; FaBoEn; FaBV; FaFP; FaPL; FiP; ForPo; FosPo; GN; GTBS; GTBS-D; GTBS-P; GTBS-W; GTSE; GTSL; HBV; HBVY; HoPM; ILP; InP; InPo; LiTB; LiTG; LoBV; LoGBV; MaPo; MBW-2; MCCG; MERP; ML; NeHB; NoP; OAEP; OBEV; OBNC; OBRV; OTPC; OuHeWo; PAn; PoAn; PoEL-4; PoeP; PoFS; PoIE; PTK; RoGo; SeCeV; ShBV-3; Sonn; StP; TIHL; TOP; TreF; TrGrPo; UnPo (1st ed.); ViBoPo; WHA; YAT
Much have we heard the peevish world complain. On Friend-

ship. William Whitehead. OBEC
Much honoured were my humble home. Challenge. Sir Walter Scott. *Fr.* Marmion. OtMeF
Much-hugged rag-doll is oozing cotton from her ruined figure, The. September. Robert Lowell, *ad. fr. Russian of* Boris Pasternak. NaP
Much I remember of the death of men. The Tomb of Michael Collins. Denis Devlin. OPoP; OxBI
Much Knowledge, Little Reason. Sir John Davies. *Fr.* Nosce Teipsum. ChTr
(Knowledge and Reason.) OBSC
Much Love. *Unknown, tr. fr. Bohemian folk song.* PCH
Much madness is divinest sense. Emily Dickinson. AmePo; AmPP; AP; CBEP; CMoP; CoBA; DiPo; ELU; ILP; LiTA; LiTM (rev. ed.); NoP; OnPM; OxBA; PFY; PoFr
Much of transfiguration that we hear. The Interlude. Karl Shapiro. MoVE
Mucilla dyes her locks, 'tis said. *See* Mycilla dyes her locks, 'tis said.
Muck Farmer, The. R. S. Thomas. POTi
Muckish Mountain (The Pig's Back.) Shane Leslie. AnIV
Muckle-mou'd Meg. James Ballantine. HBV; VA
Muckle-Mouth Meg. Robert Browning. HBV; MeWo; OtMeF; PoVP; VA
Mud. Polly Chase Boyden. FaBV; MPB; SoPo; TiPo
Mud. Richard Church. MoBrPo (1942 ed.)
Mud Cakes. Mildred D. Shacklett. GFA
Mud in a river flown in a bill to your eaves, The. The History of Communications and a Running Account. Pien Chih-lin. LiTW
Mud is very nice to feel. Mud. Polly Chase Boyden. FaBV; MPB; SoPo; TiPo
Mud put. The House. Robert Creeley. CoPo
Mud through my toes I'm from this land. Testimony to an Inquisitor. William Stafford. NePoAm-2
Mud Turtle, The. Howard Nemerov. NYBP; OPoP
Mud Turtles. Grace Taber Hallock. RePo
Muddled Metaphors. Tom Hood. NA
Muddling up the wooden stairs one night, in my socks. Spiders. David Wevill. MoCV
Muddy meek river, oh, it was splendid sport. Big Dam. W. R. Moses. AmFN
Muddy Rat, The. Horiguchi Daigaku, *tr. fr. Japanese by* Kenneth Rexroth. LiTW
Mudville team was desperate in that big championship game, The. Casey—Twenty Years After. *At. to* S. P. McDonald. GSP
Mufaddaliyat, The, *sels.* *Tr. fr. Arabic by* Sir Charles Lyall.
Gone Is Youth. Salamah, Son of Jandal. AWP
His Camel. Alqamah. AWP; JAWP; WBP
Old Age. Al-Aswad, Son of Ya'fur. AWP
Muffin Man, The. Anne Croasdell. BoTP
Muffin-Man, The. Madeleine Nightingale. GaP
Muffin man walked down our street, The. The Muffin Man. Anne Croasdell. BoTP
Muffin-Man's Bell, The. Ann Hawkshaw. BoTP; OTPC
Muffle the wind. Orders. A. M. Klein. WHW
Muffled. Edmund Blunden. Sonn
Muffled drum's sad roll has beat, The. The Bivouac of the Dead. Theodore O'Hara. AA; AnAmPo; BLPA; DD; FaPL; HBV; HH; MC; NeHB; PaA; PAH; PAL; PAP; PoRL; TreF
Mugford's Victory. John White Chadwick. PAH
Muhammedan Call to Prayer. Bilal, *tr. fr. Arabic by* Raoul Abdul. TTY
Muiopotmos, *sel.* Spenser.
Butterfly, The. BoC
Muirland Meg. Burns. ErPo
(She'll Do It.) UnTE
Mulata—to Skinny. Frank Lima. ANYP
Mulberry Garden, The, *sel.* Sir Charles Sedley.
Child and Maiden, *fr.* III, ii. GTBS; GTBS-D; GTBS-P; GTBS-W; GTSE; GTSL; LiTL; TOP
("Ah Cloris! that I now could sit.") CavP; OAEP; OBS
(Song: " Ah Cloris! that I now could sit." SeCV-2; ViBoPo
(To Chloris.) HBV; OBEV; SeCL
Mulberry is a double tree, The. Banjo Boomer. Wallace Stevens. WaKn
Mule in the Mines, The. *Unknown.* ChTr
(Campfire and Bunkhouse.) CoSo
Mule Skinner's Song, The, *with music.* *Unknown.* AS
Mules. Ted Walker. NYBP
Mules, I think, will not be here this hour, The. Empedocles on Etna. Matthew Arnold. MaVP; ViPP
Mulford. Whittier. AA
Mulier Amicta Sole. Fray Angelico Chavez. ISi
Mullabinda. David Rowbotham. PoAu-2
Mullion. A. P. Herbert. SD
Multi-colored hosts drift down the sky, The. Two Leaves. Jesse Stuart. FiSC
Multiplication. Joyce Kilmer. WHL
Multiplication is vexation. Mother Goose. BrR; GoTP; OTPC; RIS; TreFS
Multitude of the skies, gold riddle of millions of stars. Dain do Eimhir, XVII. Sorley Maclean. NeBP
Multiversity, The. Robert Duncan. FRC
"Multum Dilexit." Hartley Coleridge. EnRP; HBV; VA
Mumbo, Jumbo. Food for Thought. Michael Lewis. RIS
Mumford. Ina M. Porter. PAH
Mummia. Rupert Brooke. BrPo
Mummies and skeletons, out of your stones. Song by the Deaths. Thomas Lovell Beddoes. PeER
Mummy, The. Vernon Watkins. MoPo; NeBP
Mummy, A/ crumbling/ in the bar. Primavera. Frank Lima. ANYP
Mummy Slept Late and Daddy Fixed Breakfast. John Ciardi. PDV
Mumps. Elizabeth Madox Roberts. FaPON; GaP; MPB; SoPo; TSW
Munching a plum on. To a Poor Old Woman. William Carlos Williams. TDP
Munch's Scream. Donald Hall. NePoEA
Mundus et Infans. W. H. Auden. LiTB; LiTM; MoAB; MoBrPo (1950 ed.)
Mundus Morosus. Frederick William Faber. ACP; CAW; NBM
(World Morose, The.) OBVV
Munestruck. "Hugh MacDiarmid." NeBP
Munich Elegy No. 1. George Barker. LiTG; LiTM; SeCePo; WaP
Munich Mannequins, The. Sylvia Plath. NaP
Municipal. Kipling. BrPo; WhC
Municipal Gallery Revisited, The. W. B. Yeats. GTBS-P; LiTB
Munitions Expert. W. H. Auden. *Fr.* On This Island, XVIII. MaRV
Muppim and Huppim! Strike blows on your drums! The Dance of Despair. Hayyim Nahman Bialik. TrJP
Mural of Borodino. Lucile Adler. NYTB
Murder House. Elizabeth J. Coatsworth. FiSC
Murder in the Cathedral, *sels.* T. S. Eliot.
Forgive Us, O Lord. EaLo
Last Temptation, The. TreFT
Murder Mystery. David Wagoner. TwAmPo
Murder of Maria Marten, The. W. Corder. CoMu
Murder of Moses, The. Karl Shapiro. EaLo
Murder of Saint Thomas of Kent, The. *Unknown.* ACP
Murder of the Tsarevich Dimitri by Boris Godunov, The. *Unknown, tr. fr. Russian by* N. Kershaw Chadwick. LiTW
Murder of William Remington, The. Howard Nemerov. CMoP; CoAP
Murder Pact, The. Shakespeare. *See* Vaulting Ambition.
Murder Trial, The. Perseus Adams. PeSA
Murder Will Out. Chaucer. *Fr.* The Canterbury Tales: The Nun's Priest's Tale. MyFE
Murdered Girl Is Found on a Bridge, The. Jane Hayman. NYBP
Murdered, I went, risen. The Life. James Wright. NaP
Murdered Little Bird. *Unknown.* FiBHP
Murdered Traveller, The. Bryant. CoBA
Murderer, The. Paul Petrie. NYBP
Murderers, The. Shakespeare. *See* Sleep ("Methought I heard a voice").
Murderers/ of Emmet Till. Salute. Oliver Pitcher. Kal
Murdering Beauty. Thomas Carew. OAEP
Murky waves / Covered over the children of evil. Cædmon (?) *Fr.* Genesis. YAT
Murmur from the Stable, The. Rubén Darío, *tr. fr. Spanish by* Agnes Blake Poor. CAW
Murmur of a bee, The. Emily Dickinson. AnFE; APA; CoAnAm; MAP; MoAmPo; NeMA; OnPM; TRV

Murmur of the mourning ghost, The. The Ballad of Keith of Ravelston [*or* Keith of Ravelston]. Sydney Thompson Dobell. *Fr.* The Nuptial Eve. CH; GTBS; HBV; OBEV; OBVV; TOP
Murmuring in empty shells, A. The Relic. Robert Hillyer. GoYe; UnS
Murmuring of Pine Trees, The. Ryokwan, *tr. fr. Japanese by* Asataro Miyamori. OnPM
Murphy in Manchester. John Montague. NMP
Murrough Defeats the Danes, 994. *Unknown. See* On the Defeat of Ragnall . . .
Musa of the sea-blue eyes. On a Singing Girl. Elinor Wylie. TOP
Muscles flex, contract, The. Spring Poem. Julian Symons. NeBP
Musco, that always kept with policy. Henry Parrot. SiCE
Muscovy Drake, The. E. A. S. Lesoro, *tr. fr. Sotho by* Dan Kunene *and* Jack Cope. PeSA
Muse, The. Anna Akhmatova, *tr. fr. Russian by* Stanley Kunitz. ML
Muse, The. Abraham Cowley. BEL; Po
Muse, The. W. H. Davies. BrPo
Muse, The/ in her dark habit. The Well. Denise Levertov. AP
Muse and Poet. Robert Bridges. OBMV
Muse at daybreak stuttering, informs my bed, The. Daybreak. Tony Towle. ANYP
Muse, bid the morne awake. To His Valentine. Michael Drayton. AtBAP; PoEL-2
Muse, disgusted at an age and clime, The. On the Prospect of Planting Arts and Learning in America [*or* Verses on . . .]. George Berkeley. CEP; CoBE; EiCL; EiPP; FaFP; HBV; OBEC; OnYI; Po; PoE; PP; SeCePo; SeCeV; TreF; TrGrPo; ViBoPo
Muse-haunted. Hugh McCrae. PoAu-1
Muse in Late November. Jonathan Henderson Brooks. PoNe
Muse in the New World, The. Walt Whitman. Song of the Exposition, II, III, *abr.* MAP; MoAmPo
("Come, Muse migrate from Greece and Ionia.") PP
Muse not that by thy mind thy body is led. To Mr. R. W. John Donne. MaMe
Muse of Fire, A. Shakespeare. *Fr.* King Henry V, Prologue to Act I. ChTr
("O for a Muse of fire, that would ascend.") MemP
Muse of my native land! loftiest Muse! Keats. Endymion, IV. EnRP
Muse of the many-twinkling feet! whose charms. The Waltz. Byron. PAn
Muse on Death. Palladas, *tr. fr. Greek by* Robert Guthrie MacGregor. OnPM
Muse Reviving, The. Sir John Davies. SiPS
Muse should be sprightly, The. A Skeltoniad. Michael Drayton. PoEL-2; PP
Muse to an Unknown Poet, The. Paul Potts. FaBoTw
Muse with the hero's brave deeds being fired, The. Captain Death. *Unknown.* CoMu
Musée des Beaux Arts. W. H. Auden. BWP; CABA; CaFP; CBV; ChMP; CMoP; CoBMV; DiPo; EnL; ExPo; FaFP; ForPo; FosPo; GTBS-P; LiTB; LiTG; LiTM; MaPo; MoAB; MoPo; NePA; NoP; OAEP (2d ed.); PG (1955 ed.); PIA; PoAn; PoFS; PoIE; PoRA; PoSa; SeCePo; SeCeV; StP; TreFT; TrGrPo (rev. ed.); TwCP
Muses, The. Edith M Thomas. HBV
Muses/ Muses of Sicily. The Fourth Eclogue. Vergil. *Fr.* Eclogues. LiTW
Muses' Elysium, The, *sels.* Michael Drayton.
  Cloris and Mertilla. LoBV
  Description of Elysium, The. AnAnS-2; TuPP
  Fine Day, A. BoTP; GN; OTPC; PCH
  (Lines: "Clear had the day been from the dawn.") LoBV
  (Sixt Nimphall, The.) OBS
  (Sixth Nymphal, The.) TuPP
  Nymphs' Song, The. SeCL
  Poet's Paradise, The. WiR
  Prothalamion: "This day must Tita married be." HW
  Second Nimphall, The. AnAnS-2
    "With full-leav'd lillies I will stick." AtBAP
  Seventh Nimphall, The. AnAnS-2
  Tenth Nimphall, The. AnAnS-2
Muse's fairest light in no dark time, The. On Ben Jonson. Sidney Godolphin. CBEP
Muses, I oft invoked your holy aid. Astrophel and Stella, LV. Sir Philip Sidney. FCP; SiPS; TuPP
Muses Love Me, The. Horace, *tr. fr. Latin by* John Conington. OnPM
Muses of Australia, The. Victor Daley. BoAu
Muses of Sicily, loftier be our song! The Sibylline Prophecy. Vergil. *Fr.* The Fourth Eclogue. CAW; ISi
Muses that Fame's loose feathers beautify. A Coronet for His Mistress Philosophy, X. George Chapman. ReIE; Sonn
Muses that sing love's sensual empery [*or* emperie]. Sonnet [*or* Love and Philosophy]. George Chapman. A Coronet for His Mistress Philosophy, I. CoBE; EIL; LoBV; OBSC; PoE; SeCePo; Sonn; TuPP
Muses wrapped in mysteries of light, The. The Whirlwind Road. Edwin Markham. AA
Museum, The. William Abrahams. WaP
Museum of Modern Art on West Fifty-third Street, The. Tulips and Addresses. Edward Field. NYBP
Museum-Piece. Audrey Alexandra Brown. CaP
Museum Piece. Lawrence P. Spingarn. GoYe
Museum Piece. Richard Wilbur. CMoP; MiAP; NePA; PoIE; PoPl; TDP
Museums. Louis MacNeice. CMoP; MoBrPo; NAMP
Museums and stockmarkets protect me, The. Four Stanzas Written in Anxiety. George Jonas. MoCV
Museums offer us, running from among the buses. Museums. Louis MacNeice. CMoP; MoBrPo; NAMP
Mushroom Gatherers, The. Donald Davie. NePoEA-2
Mushroom is the elf of plants, The. Emily Dickinson. DiPo; MWA-2; NePA
Mushrooms. Mike Evans. HYE
Mushrooms. Sylvia Plath. BoNaP; NePoEA-2
Mushrooms grew/ overnight. Mushrooms. Mike Evans. HYE
Mushrooms pert and pink. Sunday Morning. Isidor Schneider. AnAmPo
Music. Conrad Aiken. *See* Calyx of the Oboe Breaks, The.
Music, The. Baudelaire, *tr. fr. French by* Arthur Symons. SyP
Music. Ecclesiasticus, XXXII: 5-6, Bible, Apocrypha. TrJP
Music. Thomas Carlyle. WBLP
Music. G. K. Chesterton. JKCP (1955 ed.)
Music. Hilda Conkling. HH; MPB
Music. Alice Corbin. NP
Music. Walter de la Mare. HH; MuSP; PoRL
Music. George Du Maurier, *after the French of* Sully-Prudhomme. CBEP; OBEV (new ed.); OBVV
Music. Emerson. AnNE; FaBV; GoTP; MaRV; WGRP (Fragments.) OQP
Music. Eleanor Farjeon. TiPo (1959 ed.)
Music. *At. to* John Fletcher, *also to* Shakespeare. *See* Orpheus With His Lute.
Music. Amy Lowell. AnAmPo; YaD
Music. Wilfred Owen. MuSP
Music. Charles Phillips. CAW; JKCP
Music. Anne Ryan. CAW
Music ("If music be the food of love"). Shakespeare. *See* If Music Be the Food of Love.
Music ("Orpheus with his lute"). *At. to* Shakespeare, *also to* John Fletcher. *See* Orpheus with His Lute.
Music ("Music, when soft voices die"). Shelley. *See* Music, When Soft Voices Die.
Music ("Silver key of the fountain of tears."). Shelley. *See* Fragment, A: To Music.
Music. Edith M. Thomas. HBV
Music. Tony Towle. ANYP
Music. W. J. Turner. MuSP
Music. *Unknown.* MaRV
Music and Drum. Archibald MacLeish. MoRP
Music and Memory. John Albee. AA
Music and Tartar voices; horses; the kiss. The Emperor's Double. Robert Gittings. NYTB
Music and Words. Elizabeth Jennings. UnS
Music at the Bower of Bliss, The. Spenser. *Fr.* The Faerie Queene, II, 12. MyFE
Music at Twilight. George Sterling. HBV
Music Box, A. Abbie Farwell Brown. PPL
Music can not stay. Pediment: Ballet. Louise Townsend Nicholl. UnS

Music Comes. John Freeman. MuSP
Music creates two grenadiers, scarlet and tall. Haydn—Military Symphony. Keith Douglas. MuSP
Music, dear solace to my thoughts neglected. Solace to my Thoughts. *Unknown.* MuSP
Music Divine. *Unknown.* MuSP
Music first and foremost of all! Art poétique [*or* The Art of Poetry]. Paul Verlaine, *tr. by* Arthur Symons. AWP; SyP
"Music for a while." Song at Night. Norman Nicholson. FaBoTw
Music God. Mark Van Doren. UnS
Music Grinders, The. Oliver Wendell Holmes. WhC
Music had the heat of blood, The. During Music. Arthur Symons. MoBrPo; VA
Music-Hall, The. Theodore Wratislaw. VA
Music has charms to soothe a savage breast. Congreve. *Fr.* The Mourning Bride, I. ViBoPo
Music I Heard [with You]. Conrad Aiken. Discordants, I. AWP; CMoP; FaFP; GTBS-W; HBV; LiTA; LiTL; LiTM; OTD; OxBA; PG; PoMa; PoPo; PoRA; TreFT
(Bread and Music.) MAP; MoAB; MoAmPo; NeMA; YT
("Music I heard with you was more than music.") BoLP
Music in a Spanish Town (Cordoba 1936). Laurie Lee. MuSP
Music in Camp. John R. Thompson. AA; BLPA; HBV; PaA; PAP
Music in the Air. Fanny Crosby. OTD
Music in the Air. George Johnston. PeCV (1967 ed.)
Music in the Air. Ronald McCuaig. ErPo
Music in the Night. Harriet Prescott Spofford. AA
Music in the Rec Hut. Hubert Creekmore. WaP
Music in Venice. Louis Simpson. NYBP
Music is well said to be the speech of angels. Music. Thomas Carlyle. WBLP
Music Lesson, A. Alexander Hay Japp. VA
Music lifting and falling. Aria. Rolfe Humphries. NYBP
Music Magic. Edmund Leamy. JKCP
Music-Makers, The. Arthur O'Shaughnessy. *See* Ode: "We are the music-makers."
Music met Leviathan returning, A. Peter Quennell. *Fr.* Leviathan. MoBrPo
Music, murmur me to slumber. Evensong. Ruth Schaumann. CAW
Music, music hath its sway. The Flight of Malzah. Charles Heavysege. *Fr.* Saul. VA
Music of a Friend, The. Louis V. Ledoux. OQP
Music of a Tree, The. W. J. Turner. MoBrPo
Music of Colours: The Blossom Scattered. Vernon Watkins. ACV; LiTB
Music of Colours—White Blossom. Vernon Watkins. FaBoMo; LiTM; WaP
Music of Hungary. Anne Reeve Aldrich. AA
Music of the autumn winds sings low, The. Autumn. Edwin Curran. HBMV; TSW
Music of the Dawn. Virginia Bioren Harrison. HBV
Music of the dignity of souls, The. Crass Times Redeemed by Dignity of Souls. Peter Viereck. MiAP
Music of the Future, The. Oliver Herford. CenHV; MuSP; PoMa
Music of the Night. John Neal. AA; AmePo
Music of the Other World. Ted Wilson. BF
Music on the Water. George Johnston. MoCV
Music, The! the/ music! as when Casals struck. William Carlos Williams. *Fr.* The Desert Music. UnS
Music [*or* Musick] to hear, why hear'st thou music sadly? Sonnets, VIII. Shakespeare. MuSP; PoEL-2; ViBoPo
Music, When Soft Voices Die. Shelley. BoLiVe; CBV; FaBV; ForPo; GTBS; GTBS-D; GTBS-P; GTBS-W; GTSE; GTSL; LiTB; LiTG; LiTL; MCCG; MeWo; OBEV; OBRV; OTPC (1946 ed.); PCD; PoSa; PTK; TreFT; TrGrPo; WHA
(Memory.) MaRV
(Music.) CH
(To——.) AtBAP; ATP; AWP; BEL; EnL; EnLi-2 (1949 ed.); EnLit; EnRP; EPN; ExPo; FiP; ILP; InPo; JAWP; LoBV; MERP; NoP; OAEP; OBNC; PoE; PoEL-4; PoPo; SeCePo; TOP; ViBoPo; WBP; YAT
Musica No. 3. Richard Duerden. NeAP
Musical Ass, The. Tomás de Iriarte, *tr. fr. Spanish.* BOHV
Musical Box. Jean Kenward. MuSP
Musical Critic Anticipates Eternity, A. Siegfried Sassoon. UnS
Musical Evening, A. Joseph G. Francis. CIV
Musical Instrument, A. Elizabeth Barrett Browning. BEL; EnLi-2; FaBoBe; FaPON; FosPo; GBV; GoTP; GTBS; GTSL; HBV; HBVY; MCCG; MemP; MuSP; OAEP; OBEV; OBVV; OnMSP; OTPC (1946 ed.); PoRL; PoVP; ShBV-3; TOP; VA; ViPo; YT
(Great God Pan, The.) WiR
Musical Love. Michael Drayton. *Fr.* Idea MuSP
Musical Vietnams. Boo Allen. WOW
Musicall Strife, The; in a Pastorall Dialogue. Ben Jonson. SCEP-2
Musician. Louise Bogan. GoJo; NYBP; UnS
Musician, The. R. P. Lister. UnS
Musician, The. R. S. Thomas. MuSP
Musician to His Love, The. Percy French. MuSP
Musicians wrestle everywhere. Emily Dickinson. UnS
Musick Commended, and Scraping Ridiculed, etc. Thomas D'Urfey. MuSP
Musick in time. *Unknown.* SeCSL
Musick, thou Queen of Heaven, care-charming-spel. To Musick. Robert Herrick. UnS
Musick to heare, why hear'st thou musick sadly. *See* Music to hear. . .
Musicks Duell. Richard Crashaw. *See* Music's Duel.
Musicks Empire. Andrew Marvell. *See* Music's Empire.
Music's Duel. Richard Crashaw. CLwM; CoBE; GoTL; SeEP
(Musicks Duell.) MaMe; OBS; SCEP-1; SeCP; SeCV-1
Music's Empire. Andrew Marvell. MuSP
(Musicks Empire.) MaMe; SCEP-2
Music's Silver Sound. Shakespeare. *Fr.* Romeo and Juliet, IV, v. GN; HH
Music's Tragedy. W. H. Davies. MuSP
Musing, between the sunset and the dark. Kindred. George Sterling. NP
Musing by a River. Moses Browne. WaPE
Musing, I sit on my cushioned settle. Firelight. Heine. CIV
Musing Maiden, The. Thomas Hardy. BEL
Musing on Venice and the thought of thee. John Addington Symonds. Sonn
Musing upon the restles bisinesse. Prologue. Thomas Hoccleve. *Fr.* De Regimine Principum. PoEL-1
Musings. William Barnes. OBNC
Musings of an Insomniac. Edith Ogutsch. FiSC
Musk-ox smells, The. The Long River. Donald Hall. NePoEA-2
Musketaquid. Emerson. AP; CoBA
Musmee, The. Sir Edwin Arnold. VA
Musophilus, or Defence of All Learning, *abr.* Samuel Daniel. ReEn
Sels.
English Poetry. OBSC
(Poetry of England, The.) CoBE
"Fond man, Musophilus, that thus dost spend." ReIE; SiCE; TuPP
(Poet and Critic.) OBSC
"How many thousands never heard the name." PP
To the Right Worthy and Judicious Favorer of Virtue, Master Fulke Greville. ReIE; SiCE
Mussel Hunter at Rock Harbor. Sylvia Plath. NYBP
Musselburgh Field. *Unknown.* ESPB
Mussolini's pet Marshal, Graziani. Limerick. T. R. Ybarra. LiBL
Must/ All this aching. Alun Lewis. ELU
Must ever the morning return? Hymns to the Night, II. "Novalis." LiTW
Must hapless man, in ignorance sedate. Celestial Wisdom. Juvenal. Satires, X. AWP; JAWP; WBP
Must have begun through Friday. The Trip for Hell and Self. Joseph Cardarelli. QAH
Must I in my most hopefull yeares. *Unknown.* SeCSL
Must I shoot the. Watts. Conrad Kent Rivers. BOLo
"Must I submissive bow to earth my head?" Faith. Theodore Maynard. OQP
Must I tell again. The Daemon. Louise Bogan. NYBP
Must I then see, alas! eternal night. Elegy Over a Tomb. Lord Herbert of Cherbury. AnAnS-2; AtBAP; EIL; EP; FaBoEn; ForPo; MeLP; MePo; OBEV (new ed.); OBS; PoEL-2; QFR; SeEP; ViBoPo
Must it be always so whenever rain. Revenants. Joseph Auslander. NP
Must noble Hastings immaturely die. Upon the Death of the Lord

Must (continued)
Hastings. Dryden. CEP; ReEn; SeCV-2
Must we be devyded now. *Unknown.* SeCSL
Must we part, Von Hügel, though much alike, for we. W. B. Yeats. *Fr.* Vacillation. OBMV
Mustache. William M. Hoffman. ThO
Mustang Gray, The, *with music. Unknown.* ABF; BFSS; CoSo
Mustapha, *sels.* Fulke Greville.
Chorus Primus: Wise Counsellors. OBS
Chorus Quintus: Tartarorum. OBS
Chorus Sacerdotum. ATP; FaBoEn; InvP; MePo; OBS; PoEL-1; SeCePo; SiCE; TuPP
(Chorus: "Oh wearisome condition of humanity!") PoIE (1970 ed.); ViBoPo
(O Wearisome Condition of Humanity.) CBEP; CBV; EG; LiTB; SeCeV
Chorus Tertius: Of Time; Eternitie. OBS
Mustard and Cress. Norman Gale. TVC
Muster Out the Rangers. *Unknown.* CoSo
Musterer, The. Eileen Duggan. CoBE
Mutabilitie. Spenser. *See* Mutability.
Mutability. Rupert Brooke. BrPo
Mutability. Shelley. BEL; BoLiVe; CBEP; CoBE; EnLi-2; EnLit; EnRP; EPN; ERoP-2; FaBoEn; HBV; MERP; NoP; OBNC; PoPo; TOP; ViBoPo; YAT
Mutability [*or* Mutabilitie]. Spenser. *Fr.* The Faerie Queene, VII, 7 *and* 8. FaBoEn; OxBoCh; PoEL-1
("When I bethinke me on that speech whyleare," *fr.* 8.) MBW-1; ReEn
Mutability. Wordsworth. Ecclesiastical Sonnets, Pt. III, Sonnet XXXIV. BWP; CABA; EnLi-2; EnRP; EPN; ERoP-1; ExPo; LiTB; MBW-2; NoP; OBRV; OQP; PeER; PoE; PoEL-4; SeCeV; Sonn; StP
("From low to high doth dissolution climb.") EG
Mutans Nomen Evae. Eric Gill. CAW
Mutation. Bryant. AmPP (3d ed.)
Mutations of the Phoenix, *sel.* Herbert Read.
"Phoenix, bird of terrible pride." FaBoTw
Mute bird sidles through soft valleys of air, A. Afternoon in Anglo-Ireland. Bruce Williamson. NeIP
Mute figures with bowed heads. The Refugees. Sir Herbert Read. BrPo; MoBrPo (1942 ed.)
Mute he sat in the saddle—mute 'midst our full acclaim. A Christopher of the Shenandoah. Edith M. Thomas. PAH
Mute is the final hour, and all that lives. Dies Irae. Inger Hagerup. LiTW
Mute Opinion. Thomas Hardy. CMoP; ViPo
Mute, sightless visitant. Helen Keller. Edmund Clarence Stedman. AA
Mutes, The. Denise Levertov. NaP
Mutilated choir boys, The. The Choir Boys. Heine. *Fr.* Die Heimkehr. AWP; LiTW
Mutter, Die, sagt, "Nau Lieschen listen here." Mama's Advice. Kurt M. Stein. InMe
Muttering at the crowd, indifferent. The Death of an Old Man. Michael Hamburger. NePoEA
Mutterings over the Crib of a Deaf Child. James Wright. PoPl; StP
Mutton and Leather. *Unknown.* CoMu
Mutual forgiveness of each vice. The Gates of Paradise. Blake. LiTB; PoEL-4
Mutual Kindness. Bryant. SoP
Muvver was barfin' 'er biby one night, A. "Biby's" Epitaph. *Unknown.* FiBHP
Muzzy with drink, I let my humor recline. The Ghost of an Education. James Michie. NYBP
My absent daughter—gentle, gentle, maid. A Living Memory. William Augustus Croffut. AA
My Absent God. Cecil Hemley. PoDB
My Ace of Spades. Ted Joans. BOLo
My Africa. Michael Dei-Anang. PBA
My age fallen away like white swaddling. Age. Philip Larkin. CMoP
My aged friend, Miss Wilkinson. The Bards. Walter de la Mare. DTC; PV
My Aim. George Linnaeus Banks. *See* What I Live For.
My Ain Countree. Mary Augusta Demarest. HBV; TRV; WGRP
My Ain Fireside. Elizabeth Hamilton. FaBoBe; HBV
My Ain Kind Dearie, O. Burns. GoTS
My Ain Wife. Alexander Laing. HBV; VA
My Airedale Dog. W. L. Mason. GFA; SoPo; UTS
My All. Horatius Bonar. SoP
My Altar. John H. Styles, Jr. MaRV
(At My Mother's Knee.) STF
My ambition is to live to be eighty. Crossing the Bar. Gavin Ewart. CBV
My America. Thomas Curtis Clark. OQP; PEDC
My America. Oliver La Grone. NNP
My American host in Madras in his moist air-conditioned apartment. Americans Are Afraid of Lizards. Karl Shapiro. AmFN
My ancestor was called on to go out. The Wind at Your Door. Robert D. Fitzgerald. PoAu-2
My ancestors were fine, long men. Square-Toed Princes. Robert P. Tristram Coffin. AmFN
My Angel. Jonathan Henderson Brooks. PoNe
My Angeline. Harry B. Smith. *Fr.* The Wizard of the Nile. BOHV; InMe
My anguish, my anguish! I writhe in pain! The End of the World. Jeremiah, Bible, *O.T.* PPON
My Anna! though thine earthly steps are done. Frederick Goddard Tuckerman. *Fr.* Sonnets. AP
My Anna! When for her my head was bowed. Frederick Goddard Tuckerman. *Fr.* Sonnets. AP
My annals have it so. Emus. Mary Fullerton. PoAu-1
My anxious soul tonight is stirred. The Gain of Losses. Sadie Louise Miller. SoP
My Apish Cousins. Marianne Moore. *See* Monkeys, The.
My April Lady. Henry van Dyke. HBV
My ardors [*or* ardours] for emprize nigh lost. On an Invitation to the United States. Thomas Hardy. AWP; InPo; JAWP; WBP
My arm full of needles my. Me to You. Alex Raybin. ThO
My arms are round you, and I lean. To the Oaks of Glencree. J. M. Synge. ELU; MoBrPo; OxBI
My arms are warm. Aram Saroyan. ANYP
My arms were always quiet. Gesture. Winifred Welles. HBMV; MaRV
My aspens dear, whose airy cages quelled. Binsey Poplars [Felled 1879]. Gerard Manley Hopkins. BoNaP; BrPo; CoBMV; EG; ELP; FlW; MoVE; NoP; PIA; PoPo; UnPo (3d ed.); VP
My attire is noiseless when I tread the earth. Wild Swan. *Unknown. Fr.* Riddles. AnOE
My Aunt. Oliver Wendell Holmes. AmePo; AmP; AmPP; AnNE; CoBA; HBV; MCCG; TreFS
My aunt she died a month ago. Death of My Aunt. *Unknown.* OxBoLi; SiTL
My Aunt's Spectre. Mortimer Collins. BOHV
"My author and disposer, what thou biddest." Thus Eve to Adam. Milton. *Fr.* Paradise Lost. FaBV
My Autumn Walk. Bryant. AA
My Babes in the Wood. Sarah Morgan Bryan Piatt. AA
My baby, wouldst thou treasure hoard? The Treasure. Dorothy Frances McCrae. BoAu
My ball is in a bunch of fern. Mullion. A. P. Herbert. SD
My bands of silk and miniver. Full Moon. Elinor Wylie. CrMA; MAP; MoAB; MoAmPo
My banks they are furnish'd with bees. Hope [*or* The Shepherd's Home]. William Shenstone. *Fr.* A Pastoral Ballad. BoNaP; GN; OBEC
My Barbaric Yawp. Walt Whitman. *Fr.* Song of Myself. NePA
("Spotted hawk swoops by and accuses me, The.") CoBA; PP; TrGrPo
My bark is wafted to the strand. My Pilot. Washington Gladden. OQP
My Barrow. Elizabeth Fleming. GFA
My Bath. John Stuart Blackie. VA
My beak is bent downward, I burrow below. Plow. *Unknown. Fr.* Riddles. AnOE
My beasts, go feed upon the plain. Egloga Secunda. Barnabe Googe. ReIE
"My beautiful dog, my dear dog." Prose Poem: The Dog and the Flask. Baudelaire. OnPM
My Beautiful Lady. Thomas Woolner. OBVV; VA
My beautiful! my beautiful! that standest meekly by. The Arab to His Favorite Steed [*or* Arab's Farewell to His Horse]. Caroline E. S. Norton. BeLS; BLPA; PaPo; PTK; TreFS

My beauty is not wine to me. The Song of the Narcissus. *Unknown. Fr.* The Thousand and One Nights. AWP
My Bed. Lucy Sprague Mitchell. SoPo
My Bed Is a Boat. Robert Louis Stevenson. GFA; HBV; HBVY; OTPC; PCH; PeVV; StVeCh; TreFS
My bed is so empty that I keep [on] waking up. Winter Night. Emperor Ch'ien Wen-ti. AtBAP; BoW; OnPM; WePo
My bed rocks me gently. Aubade. Dilys Laing. NMP
My bed will fold up where I fold. Convalescence, III. David McCord. WhC
My Beige Mom. Edward S. Spriggs. BF
My beloved brother, my heart burneth for thy love. The Lovely Delightful Song of Thy Sister. *Unknown.* LiTW
My Beloved Is Mine, and I Am His. John Quarles. SoP
(Long Did I Toil.) MaRV
My Beloved Is Mine, and I Am His; He Feedeth among the Lilies. Francis Quarles. *Fr.* Emblems. MePo; OBS; TrGrPo, *abr.*
(Canticle.) FaBoEn
(Divine Rapture, A, 3 *sts.*) HBV; LO; OBEV; TDP
(Even [*or* Ev'n] like Two Little Bank-dividing Brooks.) MeLP
(He Is Mine, 3 *sts.*) LiTL
(Mystical Ecstasy, A, 3 *sts.*) GTSL
My beloved spake, and said unto me. For, Lo, the Winter Is Past. The Song of Solomon, Bible, *O.T.* LO; TreF
My Best. Annabelle Jones. SoP
My best belovit brother of the band. To R. Hudson. Alexander Montgomery. OxBS
My best Christmases. The Day before Christmas. Raymond Souster. PeCV (1967 ed.)
My Betsey-Jane, it would not do. To Betsey-Jane, on Her Desiring to Go Incontinently to Heaven. Helen Parry Eden. HBMV
My Bible. Edgar A. Guest. *Fr.* My Books and I. MaRV
My Bible and I. M. H. Knobloch. SoP
My Bible and I. Charles Sandford. FaChP; SoP, *abr.*
My Bible and I. *Unknown.* STF
My Bird. "Fanny Forester." AA
My Bird-wrung Youth. Patrick Anderson. PeCV
My Birth. Minot Judson Savage. AA; WGRP
My Birthday. Thomas Moore. HBV
"'My birthday!' What a different sound," 4 *ll.* PoRL
My birthday is coming and I will be six. The Birthday Bus. Mary Ann Hoberman. BiCB
My birthday is coming tomorrow. Growing Up. *Unknown.* BiCB
"My birthday, Nelly, and your wedding day!" Washington's Last Birthday. Alfred Noyes. PoMa
"My birthday"—what a different sound. My Birthday. Thomas Moore. HBV; PoRL
My Birthday's in Winter. Zhenya Gay. BiCB
My Bishop's Eyes. *Unknown.* WhC
(Praying and Preaching.) GoTP
My black hills have never seen the sun rising. Shancoduff. Patrick Kavanagh. OxBI
My Blackness Is the Beauty of This Land. Lance Jeffers. BF; NBP
My blessed Lord, art thou a lilly flower? Meditation. Edward Taylor. *Fr.* Preparatory Meditations, First Series. MeP
My Blessed Lord, how doth thy beautious spouse. Edward Taylor. *Fr.* Preparatory Meditations, Second Series. SCAP
My blessed mother dozing in her chair. A Valentine to My Mother, 1882. Christina Rossetti. OHIP
My Blessing Be on Waterford. Winifred M. Letts. HBMV
My blood so red. The Call. *Unknown.* OBEV
My bloodstream chokes on gall and spleen. Quatrain. Barend Toerien. PeSA
My Boat. Joseph Addison Richards. SoP
My Boat Is on the Shore. Byron. *See* To Thomas Moore.
My boat sails downstream. Love Song. *Unknown.* TTY
My Boat Swings Out and Back. Laurence Binyon. WePo
My body answers you, my blood. Music of Hungary. Anne Reeve Aldrich. AA
My body being dead, my limbs [*or* lims] unknown. The Preparative. Thomas Traherne. AnAnS-1; MeP; OxBoCh; PoEL-2
My body, eh? Friend Death, how now? Habeas Corpus. Helen Hunt Jackson. AA; AnAmPo; WGRP
My Body in the Walls Captived. Sir Walter Ralegh. CBEP; FCP; FlW; ReIE; SeCePo; SiPS
My body is a poem. Anatomy Lesson. Ilo Orleans. RIS
My body is weary to death of my mischievous brain. Nebuchadnezzar. Elinor Wylie. MAP; MoAmPo; NeMA
My body sleeps: my heart awakes. Indian Love-Song. "Owen Meredith." VA
My Bohemia. Arthur Rimbaud, *tr. fr. French by* R. G. Stern. ReMP
My Bonie Mary. Burns. *See* My Bonnie Mary.
My bonnie blithe fisher-maiden. Du schönes Fischer-Mädchen. Heine. OuHeWo
My Bonnie Highland Laddie. Burns. UnTE
My Bonnie [*or* Bonie] Mary. Burns. HBV; OBEV; ViBoPo
(Farewell, A: "Go fetch to me a pint o' wine.") GTBS; GTBS-D; GTBS-P; GTBS-W; GTSE; GTSL
(Go Fetch to Me a Pint o' Wine.) BEL; EiPP; EnRP; PoE
(Silver Tassie, The.) OBEC
My Bonny Black Bess. *Unknown.* CoMu; ViBoFo
(Bonnie Black Bess, *with music.*) BFSS; CoSo
My Bonny Lass, Thine Eye. Thomas Lodge. ReIE
(Love's Witchery.) ElL
My Book Holds Many Stories. Annette Wynne. HH
My Book of Life. Frances Humphrey. STF
My Books. Longfellow. AA
My Books and I, *sel.* Edgar A. Guest.
My Bible. MaRV
My Books I'd Fain Cast Off, I Cannot Read. Henry David Thoreau. *See* Summer Rain, The.
My Boy and His Saviour. William C. Fisher. SoP
My boy, be cool, do things by rule. Nimble Dick. Adelaide O'Keeffe. OTPC (1923 ed.)
My Boy Jack. Kipling. OtMeF
My boy Kree? Kree. A. C. Gordon. AA
My Boy Tammy. Hector MacNeill. CH
("Whar hae ye been a'day—my boy Tammy?") LO
My boy was scarcely ten years auld. Leesome Brand. *Unknown.* BaBo (A *vers.*); ESPB
My boyhood went: it went where went the trace. Lost Years. Eugene Lee-Hamilton. OBVV
My boys, they lied to you. To a Commencement of Scoundrels. Samuel Hazo. WOW
My brain is like the ravaged shores—the sand. At Night. Frances Cornford. MoBrPo
My brethren all attend. The Zealous Puritan. *Unknown.* OBS; SeEP
"My brethren . . ." And a bland, elastic smile. The Evangelist. Donald Davie. NePoEA
"My bride is not coming, alas!" says the groom. At the Altar-Rail. Thomas Hardy. *Fr.* Satires of Circumstance. MoAB; MoBrPo; PoVP
My brides are ravished away, are ravished away. Verdi at Eighty. Martin Bell. MuSP
My Brigantine. James Fenimore Cooper. *Fr.* The Water Witch, *ch.* 15. AA; EtS
My Brother. Dorothy Aldis. SoPo; TiPo
My Brother. James Danner. BF
My Brother and Me. Clarence Reed. BF
My Brother Bert. Ted Hughes. BBGG
My brother Cain, the wounded, liked to sit. Abel. Demetrios Capetanakis. AtBAP; GTBS-P; WaaP
My brother has a little flute. The Fairy Flute. Rose Fyleman. BoTP
My brother is inside the sheet. My Brother. Dorothy Aldis. SoPo; TiPo
My brother is skull and skeleton now. Epitaph. William Montgomerie. OxBS
My brother Jack was nine in May. The Baby's Debut. Horace Smith *and* James Smith. ALV; BOHV; OBRV; Par
My Brother's Death. Howard McCord. YAP
My brow with pain is often coryougated. Take Nothing For Granite. Nate Salsbury. InMe
My brudder sittin' on de tree of life. Roll, Jordan, Roll. *Unknown.* AA
My Burial Place. Robinson Jeffers. AP
My business is words. Words are like labels. Said the Poet to the Analyst. Anne Sexton. TwAmPo
My Butterfly. Robert Frost. AmePo
My button gloves are very white. Easter Parade. Marchette Chute. BrR; SiSoSe
My Cabinets Are Oyster-Shells. Margaret Cavendish, Duchess of

My (continued)
Newcastle. *See* Sea-Goddess, The.
My calm and herculean dad. Gaiety of Descendants. Douglas Newton. NeBP
My Camping Ground. Morris Rosenfeld, *tr. fr. Yiddish by* Aaron Kramer. TrJP
My Candidate. Norman H. Crowell. YaD
My Candle Burns at Both Ends. Edna St. Vincent Millay. *See* First Fig.
My Captain. Dorothea Day. BePJ; BLPA
(Captain, The.) MaRV
My cares on mine everlasting night. To Delia, XXX. Samuel Daniel. AtBAP; OBSC; PoIE
My cartridge belt is empty. The Huntsman. John Wheelwright. CrMA
My case is this: I love Zepheria bright. Gulling Sonnets, VIII. Sir John Davies. Sonn; TuPP
My Cat. Baudelaire, *tr. fr. French.* CIV
My Cat and I. Edna Gearhart. CIV
My cat is quiet. Cat. Dorothy Baruch. SoPo; SUS; TiPo; UTS
My Cat Jeoffry [*or* Jeoffrey]. Christopher Smart. *Fr.* Jubilate Agno. ChTr; FaBoCh; GoTP; LiTB; PoSa; SeCePo; SiTL; WiR
(Cat, The.) BoW, *abr.*
(For I Will Consider My Cat Jeoffry.) AtBAP; CTC; EiCL; EiCP; EiPP; NoP; PeER; PIA; PoEL-3; SeCeV
My cat, Matilda, sits upon the floor. Matilda's Manners. Mazie V. Caruthers. CIV
My cat Timothy who has such lovely eyes. Timothy. Rose Fyleman. UTS
My cat, washing her tail's tip, is a whorl. Cat on Couch. Barbara Howes. PoSa
My Catbird. William Henry Venable. AA; HBV; PFY
My ceiling shows not brave. Vanity of Riches. Horace. Odes, II, 18. WoL
My chant must enclose hell. The Tusks of Blood. Samuel Greenberg. MoPo
My Charge. Leslie Pinckeny Hill. MaRV
My cheap toy lamp. Child's Song. Robert Lowell. NMP
My cherrystones! I prize them. Precious Stones. Charles Stuart Calverley. InMe
My Child. John Pierpont. AA; HBV
My Child Came Home. Stefan George. *tr. fr. German by* Carol North Valhope *and* Ernst Morwitz. LiTW
My child came to me with the equinox. The Storm-Child. May Byron. HBV
My child, ob-serve the use-ful Ant. The Ant. Oliver Herford. LBN
My child, the Duck-billed Plat-y-pus. The Platypus. Oliver Herford. FiBHP; NA
My child, we were two children. Mein Kind, wir waren Kinder. Heine. AWP; JAWP; WBP
My child, what painful vistas are before you! To a Very Young Gentleman. Christopher Morley. PoMa
My childhood all a myth. The Myth. Edwin Muri. CMoP
My childhood is a sphere. Childhood [*or* The Review]. Thomas Traherne. CBEP; TrGrPo
My childhood's home I see again. Memory. Abraham Lincoln. BLPA; FaBoBe; NeHB; WBLP
My children, my little dears. The Mother Crab and Her Family. L. T. Manyase. PeSA
My children! speak not ill of one another. To Poets. Walter Savage Landor. ViBoPo
My chile? Lord, no she's none o' mine. The Borrowed Child. Howard Weeden. AA
My Chinese uncle, gouty, deaf, half-blinded. Grotesques Robert Graves. CMoP
My Choice. Grace B. Renfrow. BePJ
My choice, a slim, fair comely girl. Ode to a Chosen Girl. Hywel ab Owain Gwynedd, *tr. by* Gwyn Williams. PrWP
My Christ. Virginia Auler. SoP
My Christ is the sweep of the lofty elm. "What Think Ye of Christ?" Geraldine Farrar. StJW
My Christ was a Jew. My Christ. Virginia Auler. SoP
My Christmas gifts were few: to one. To a Lady. Thomas William Parsons. AA
My Chum. *Unknown.* SoP
My chums will burn their Indian weeds. Smith of Maudlin. Walter Thornbury. PeVV
My Church ("My church has but one temple"). "E. O. G." BLPA
My Church ("On me nor Priest nor Presbyter nor Pope"). *Unknown.* MaRV; OQP
My City. James Weldon Johnson. BANP; CDC; PoNe; TIHL
My city, my beloved, my white. N. Y. Ezra Pound. NP
My city slept. The Beginning of a Long Poem on Why I Burned the City. Lawrence Benford. NBP; TTY
My Clarion Call. Alberto Ghiraldo, *tr. fr. Spanish.* PoFR
My clear-cut heart, my tender soul. Jules Laforgue. *Fr.* Asides from the Clowns. PoPl
My Cleo's blush is tender, slow. Tender, Slow. *Unknown.* ErPo
My closest and dearest! Dirge on the Death of Art O'Leary. *Tr. by* Eleanor Hull. AnIV
My clothing was once of the linsey wolsey fine. Poor Old Horse. *Unknown.* CH
My clumsiest dear, whose hands shipwreck vases. Love Poem. John Frederick Nims. CBV; HoPM; MiAP
My clumsy poem on the inn-wall none cared to see. The Poem on the Wall. Po Chü-i. ML
My coachman, in the moonlight there. Without and Within. James Russell Lowell. BOHV; HBV; TOP
My comforts drop and melt away like snow. The Answer. George Herbert. MaMe
My Companion. Joyce Ramage. BePJ; SoP
My Companion. Charles Wesley. STF
My Company. Sir Herbert Read. BrPo; FaBoMo; MMA
My Comrade. Edwin Markham. AA
My Comrade. James Jeffrey Roche. AA
My conscience hath a thousand several tongues. Shakespeare. *Fr.* King Richard III, V, iii. MemP
My couch lay in a ruined hall. A Dream. Emily Brontë. NBM
My counterpane is soft as silk. A Child's Song of Christmas. Marjorie Pickthall. BoTP; HBV; HBVY; YeAr
My Country. Mikhail Yurevich Lermontov, *tr. fr. Russian by* Frances Cornford *and* E. P. Salaman. LiTW
My Country. Dorothea Mackellar. BoAu; PoAu-1
My Country. Robert Whitaker. OQP
My Country, *sels.* George Edward Woodberry.
"For thou art founded in the eternal fact." PoFr
"O destined Land." AA
O Land Beloved. PAH
My Country Is the World. *Unknown, at. to* Robert Whitaker. PGD
(World-Brotherhood.) MaRV
My country is the world; I count/ No son of man my foe. My Country. Robert Whitaker. OQP
My country need not change her gown. Emily Dickinson. AmFN
My country, O my land, my friends. Purgatorio. Hart Crane. NAMP
My Country, Right! Thomas Curtis Clark. PGD
"My country, 'tis of thee." Assembly; Harlem School. Eugene T. Maleska. GoYe
My country, 'tis of thee. America. Samuel Francis Smith. AA; DD; FaBoBe; FaFP; FaPON; GFA; HBV; HBVY; HH; MaRV; MC; OTPC; PaA; PAL; PEDC; PoFr; PoLF; PoRL; PTK; SoP; TreF; WBLP; YaD
My country, 'tis of thee/ Land where things used to be. New National Anthem. *Unknown.* CoSo
My country 'tis of thee./ Sweet land of felony. Ambrose Bierce. YaD
My country, 'tis to thee and all thy ways. Star-spangled Ode. Phyllis McGinley. ThLM
My countryman, the poet, wears a Stetson. David Wright. *Fr.* Seven South African Poems. PeSA
My countrymen have now become too base. April 1962. Paul Goodman. NMP
My countrymen, though we are young as yet. The Circling Hearths. Roderic Quinn. BoAu
My Country's Flag. Juniata Stafford. HH
My coursers are fed with the lightning. The Charioteer. Shelley. *Fr.* Prometheus Unbound. OBRV; ShBV-3
My Cousin German came from France. *Unknown.* FaBoCh; LoGBV
My cousins, lean hunters. Love Lifted Me. Paris Leary. CoPo
My cousin's wife, the diabetic. Upon Differences of Opinion. Hy Sobiloff. SiTL
My Creed. Alice Cary. WGRP
My Creed. Henry W. Frost. SoP

My Creed. Jeannette L. Gilder. WGRP
My Creed. Edgar A. Guest. MaRV
My Creed. S. E. Kiser. PoToHe
My Creed. Howard Arnold Walter. FaFP; OQP; PoLF; SoP; WBLP
(I Would Be True.) MaRV; PoToHe (new ed.); TRV
My Cross. Zitella Cocke. HBV
My crown desired, my true love and joy. A Love Letter to Elizabeth Thatcher. Thomas Thatcher. SCAP
My crown is in my heart, not on my head. Content. Shakespeare. King Henry VI, Pt. III, *fr.* III, i. MaRV; PoToHe (new ed.)
My curse be on the day when first I saw. Sonnet: To the Lady Pietra degli Scrovigni. Dante. AWP
My curse upon your venom'd stang. Address to the Toothache. Burns. BOHV
My dad was a soldier and fought in the wars. The Hero. Leroy F. Jackson. SiSoSe
My daddie is a cankert carle. Low Doun in the Broom. *Unknown.* GoTS
My Daddy has paid the rent. Good Times. Lucille Clifton. TwCP
My daddy is an engineer. Wanderin'. *Unknown.* AS
My daddy smells like tobacco and books. Smells (Junior). Christopher Morley. BoChLi; GFA; MPB; TiPo
My daddy went a-huntin'. The Grey Goose. *Unknown.* WaKn
My Dad's Dinner Pail. Edward Harrigan. BLPA
My Daily Creed. *Unknown.* FaChP; MaRV; SoP; TRV
(Creed, A.) STF
My Daily Melon. G. Bishop-Dubjinsky. ThO
My Daily Prayer. Eva Gray. STF
My Daily Prayer. Grenville Kleiser. BLRP; MaRV; SoP
My dame hath a lame tame crane. *Unknown.* OxNR
My Damon was the first to wake. Meeting. George Crabbe. HBV; LO; OBEV
My Dancing Day. *Unknown.* *See* To-Morrow Shall Be My Dancing Day.
My Daphne's hair is twisted gold. Daphne [*or* Apollo's Song]. John Lyly. *Fr.* Midas. EIL; HBV; OBSC; SiCE
My dark-headed Käthchen, my spit-kitten darling. Song. John Manifold. BoLP; DTC
My darkling child the stars have obeyed. George Barker. *Fr.* To My Son. TwCP
My darling boy, so early snatched away. Of Such Is the Kingdom. Francis Greenwood Peabody. MaRV
My Darling Dear, My Daisy Flower. John Skelton. *See* Lullay, Lullay.
My darling little fishing rods. A Song of Satisfaction on Completing an Overhauling of Fishing Tackle. Leslie P. Thompson. WhC
My darling, now the slumber of the night. Sonnet. George Henry Boker. *Fr.* Sonnets: a Sequence on Profane Love. AmePo
My darling, thou art flowerlike. A Prayer. Heine. OnPM
My darling, we sat together. Mein Liebchen, wir sassen zusammen [*or* Forlornly]. Heine. AWP; JAWP; OnPM; WBP
My daughter, at eleven. Little Girl, My Stringbean, My Lovely Woman. Anne Sexton. NYBP
My daughter cries, and I. Child Crying. Anthony Thwaite. NePoEA-2
My Daughter Louise. Homer Greene. HBV
My day was filled with many things. Crowded Out. Florence White Willett. STF
My Days among the Dead Are Past [*or* Passed]. Robert Southey. EnRP; HBV; MaRV; OBRV; TOP; TreFT
(His Books.) OBEV
(Scholar, The.) GTBS; GTBS-D; GTBS-P; GTBS-W; GTSE; GTSL
My days are full of pleasant memories. Phantoms. Thomas Ashe. VA
My days are in the yellow leaf. Remorse. Byron. *Fr.* On This Day I Complete My Thirty-sixth Year. MaRV; TRV
My days' delights, my springtime joys fordone. A Poem Entreating of Sorrow. Sir Walter Ralegh. FCP; SiPS
My Days Have Been So Wondrous Free, *with music.* Thomas Parnell. TrAS
(Song: "My days have been so wond'rous free.") CEP; EiPP
My Days of Love Are Over. Byron. *Fr.* Don Juan. FaBoEn; OBNC
("No more—no more—Oh! never more, my heart.") PeER
My Dead. Frederick Lucian Hosmer. WGRP
(Friends Beyond.) MaRV
My dead father speaks to me. Death Mask of a Fisherman. George Bruce. ACV
My dead [*or* dear] love came to me, and said. The Apparition [*or* A Dream]. Stephen Phillips. MaRV; OBEV (new ed.); OBVV
My dear—:/ I do thank you. Letter for Melville 1951. Charles Olson. CoPo
"My dear, adieu! my sweet love, farewell!" *sel.* *Unknown.*
"Wilt thou forsake me? and wilt thou leave me." LO
My Dear and Only Love. James Graham, Marquess of Montrose. CavP; OBS; SeCL
(I'll Never Love Thee More.) CBEP; HBV; OBEV
(Montrose to His Mistress.) LoBV; OxBS, 2 *sts.*; ViBoPo
(Proper New Ballad, A.) LO
(Touch, The, 4 *ll.*) OtMeF
My dear brother Ned. The *South Carolina.* *Unknown.* PAH
My dear Castara, t'other day. Pastoral Dialogue, Castara and Parthenia. Thomas Flatman. CEP
My dear companion, and my faithful friend! An Address to His Elbow-Chair, New Cloath'd. William Somervile. CEP; OBEC
My dear daddie bought a mansion. The Little Bird. Walter de la Mare. BiCB; BrR
My dear, darkened in sleep, turned from the moon. To Judith Asleep. John Ciardi. LiTL; LiTM (1970 ed.); MiAP; MoLP; ToPo
My dear, do you [*or* you must] know. The Babes in the Wood. *Unknown.* OTPC (1946 ed.); PPL; RIS
My dear, dumb friend, low lying there. To My Dog "Blanco." Josiah Gilbert Holland. PoLF
My dear friend Davies, some against us partial. To Mr. [*or* Master] John Davies. Sir John Harington. SiCE; TuPP
My dear, I do fear that this fiery love. Englynion to His Love. David Jones. PrWP
My Dear Lady. *Unknown.* *Fr.* The Trial of Treasure. EIL
("Am not I in blessed case.") TuPP
My dear little crane. A Pet Crane. *Unknown.* AnIL
My dear love came to me, and said. *See* My dead love came to me.
My Dear Mistress. Earl of Rochester. *See* Song: "My dear mistress has a heart."
My dear, naïve, ingenuous child. Don't Say You Like Tchaikowsky. Paul Rosner. FiBHP
My dear, observe the rose! though she desire it. Elegy IX. William Bell. NePoEA
My Dear One is mine as mirrors are lonely. Miranda's Song. W. H. Auden. *Fr.* The Sea and the Mirror. FaBoMo
My dear son John's deceas'd ah! gone from hence. A Brief Elegie on My Dear Son John. John Saffin. SCAP
My dear, the time has come to say. A Song of Parting. Compton Mackenzie. HBV; OBVV
My Dear was a mason. The Man with a Hammer. Anna Wickham. MeWo
My dear, when I was very young. To a Lady on Her Marriage. William Bell. NePoEA
My dear, when you. For Vicki at Seven. Sydney King Russell. BiCB
My dear you must know that a long time ago. *See* My dear, do you know.
My dear young friend, whose shining wit. Comic Miseries. John Godfrey Saxe. BOHV
My deare, deare, Lord I do thee Saviour call. Meditation. Edward Taylor. *Fr.* Preparatory Meditations, First Series. MeP
My deare deare Lord, I know not what to say. Meditation CXLVI [*or* Return, Oh Shulamite, Return Return]. Edward Taylor. *Fr.* Preparatory Meditations, Second Series. MAmP; MWA-1
My dearely loved friend how oft have we. To My Most Dearely-Loved Friend Henery Reynolds Esquire, of Poets and Poesie. Michael Drayton. AnAnS-2
My Dearest Baby, Go to Sleep. Thomas Miller. OTPC
My dearest Betty, my more lovèd heart. Elisa, or an Elegy upon the Unripe Decease of Sir Antony Irby. Phineas Fletcher. ViBoPo

My dearest dear, my honey love. Winter-Night Song. Ford Madox Ford. NP
My dearest dear, the time draws near. The Lover's Lament. *Unknown.* AS
My dearest dust, could not thy hasty day. Epitaph on the Monument of Sir William Dyer at Colmworth, 1641. Lady Catherine Dyer. EnLoPo
My dearest love! when thou and I must part. The Legacy. Henry King. AnAnS-2
My Dearest Mistress. *Unknown.* EnRePo
My dearest Rival, least our love. Sir John Suckling. MeLP
"My Dearling." Elizabeth Akers Allen. AA
My dearly loved friend, how oft have we. To My Most Dearly-loved [Friend] Henry Reynolds. Michael Drayton. OAEP; OBS; ReEn; SeEP; TuPP
My dears, 'tis said in days of old. The Bee, the Ant, and the Sparrow. Charles Cotton. RIS
My Death. A. J. M. Smith. OBCV
My Death. Carl Zuckmayer, *tr. fr. German by* E. B. Ashton. TrJP
My death must come; but when, I do not know. Waiting for Death. Michelangelo. OnPM
My death was arranged by special plans in Heaven. A New England Bachelor. Richard Eberhart. MoAmPo (1962 ed.)
My debt to you, Belovèd. Debts. Jessie B. Rittenhouse. HBMV
My Delight. Gamaliel Bradford. HBMV
My Delight and Thy Delight. Robert Bridges. AnFE; CMoP; GTSL; HBV; LiTL; NBM; OAEP; OBEV; OTD; PoEL-5; PoVP; TOP
My Descendants. W. B. Yeats. Meditations in Time of Civil War, IV. CABL; LiTB; PIA
My Desire. Charles Wesley. SoP
My Desk. Humbert Wolfe. YT
"My deth I love, my lif ich hate." A Cleric Courts His Lady. *Unknown.* MeEL
My Didyma is dark, but I aspire. Didyma. *Unknown.* UnTE
My Diet. Abraham Cowley. *Fr.* The Mistress. LiTL; LO; SeCL; SeEP
My dishes went unwashed today. Labor Not in Vain. *Unknown.* STF
My dismal sister! Couldst thou know. "Lewis Carroll." *Fr.* Melancholetta. FiBHP
My Dog. John Kendrick Bangs. BLPA; FaBoBe; MPB; OTD; OTPC (1946 ed.); StVeCh; UTS
My Dog. Marchette Chute. FaPON; MoSiPe; PDV; SoPo; TiPo
My Dog. Tom Robinson. SoPo
My dog, half whippet, lives to run. Roo. Mary Oliver. NYTB
My Dog I was ever well pleased to see. My Dog Tray. John Byrom. SeCePo
My dog lay dead five days without a grave. The Pardon. Richard Wilbur. CBV; NePoEA; NoP; ToPo
My dog listens when I talk. My Dog. Tom Robinson. SoPo
My Dog, Spot. Rodney Bennett. BoTP
My Dog Tray. John Byrom. SeCePo
My Dog Tray. Thomas Campbell. *See* Harper, The.
My Doggie. C. Nurton. BoTP
My dog's so furry I've not seen. The Hairy Dog. Herbert Asquith. BoChLi; FaPON; PDV; SoPo; StVeCh; SUS; TiPo; UTS
My dolly hung her stocking up. *Unknown.* GFA
My dolour is ane cup. Ressaif My Saul. R. Crombie Saunders. OxBS
My Donkey. Rose Fyleman. TiPo
My donkey has a bridle. The Donkey. Rose Fyleman. BoTP
My donkey, my dear. My Donkey. Rose Fyleman. TiPo
My Dove Is One the Onely One of Her Mother. Edward Taylor. *See* Preparatory Meditations: "What shall I say. . ."
My dove, my beautiful one. James Joyce. *Fr.* Chamber Music, XIV. HW
My Doves. Elizabeth Barrett Browning. OTPC
My Dream. *Unknown.* BOHV; NA; SiTL
("I dreamed a dream next Tuesday week.") GoTP
My Dreams Are of a Field Afar. A. E. Housman. PeVV
My Dreams, My Works, Must Wait Till after Hell. Gwendolyn Brooks. NoP
My dreams wear thinner as the years go by. The Years. John Hall Wheelock. CrMA
My dreams were doleful and drear. Song. Thomas Caulfield Irwin. IrPN
My Drinking Song. Richard Dehmel, *tr. fr. German by* Ludwig Lewisohn. AWP
My driver came this morning on the run. A Battle-Plane in France. O. C. A. Child. PaA
My duchess was the werst she laffed she bitte. Sonnet. Ernest Walsh. ErPo
My dugout canoe goes. Paddling Song. *Unknown.* PBA
My Early Home. John Clare. BoTP; HBV; OTPC (1923 ed.); PoLF
My Easter Prayer. *Unknown.* SoP
My Easter Wish. *Unknown.* SoP
(Easter Wish, An.) OQP
My Education. James Kenneth Stephen. WhC
My eighth spring in England I walk among. This Landscape, These People. Zulfikar Ghose. ACV
My embarrassment at his nakedness. The Pool. Robert Creeley. CoAP
My enemies came to get me. A Form of Adaptation. Robert Creeley. AmPC
My Enemy. Alice Williams Brotherton. AA
My Enemy. Edwin L. Sabin. OQP
My enemy came nigh. Hate. James Stephens. MoAB; MoBrPo; NP; OBVV; TSW
My enemy had bidden me as guest. The Compassionate Fool. Norman Cameron. CBEP; GTBS-P
My Epitaph. David Gray. MaRV; OBVV; VA
My epitaph write on your heart. Love's Epitaph. William Cavendish, Duke of Newcastle. CBEP
My Estate. John Drinkwater. HBMV
My Evening Prayer. *At. to* C. Maud Battersby, *also to* Charles H. Gabriel. BLPA; FaBoBe; NeHB
(Evening Prayer.) OQP
(Help Me to Live!) SoP
My every waking hour. To J. S. Robert J. Misch. ALV
My existence in the world has been. The Wake. Tsurayuki. WoL
My eye cannot turn toward you. The First of May. Barbara Guest. AmPC
My eye descending from the hill surveys. The Thames from Cooper's Hill. Sir John Denham. *Fr.* Cooper's Hill. OBS; ReEn; SeCePo; ViBoPo
My eye is not on Calvary, nor on Bethlehem the Blessed. Sorley Maclean. *Fr.* Dain Eile. NeBP
My eyelids red and heavy are. A Poor Scholar of the 'Forties. Padraic Colum. AnIL; OxBI
My eyes are filmed, my beard is grey. The Time of the Barmecides. James Clarence Mangan. EnRP; RoGo
My eyes are turned aside from this vile race. From out the Glow the Wrath of Heaven Spoke. Stefan George. OnPM
My eyes are white stones. River God's Song. Anne Ridler. NYBP
My eyes catch ruddy necks. Marching. Isaac Rosenberg. BrPo
My eyes dyed by the green of the leaves. The Bored Mirror. Syuichi Nagayasu. LiTW
My Eyes That Hurry to See. Bilhana, *formerly at. to* Chauras, *tr. fr. Sanskirt by* E. Powys Mathers. *Fr.* Black Marigolds. OnPM
My eyes were all too wary. The Kerry Lads. Theodosia Garrison. HBMV
My Face. Anthony Euwer. *See* Limerick: "As a beauty I'm not a great star."
My face is [*or* is wet] against the grass—the moorland grass is wet. Moorland Night. Charlotte Mew. ChMP; ViBoPo
My face is wet with rain. Walking at Night. Amory Hare. PoLF
My Face Looks Out. Edwin Honig. NYTB
My faint spirit was sitting in the light. Shelley. *See* From the Arabic.
My Fair Lady. *Unknown.* *See* Who Shall Have My Fair Lady?
My fair, look from those turrets of thine eyes. Michael Drayton. Idea's Mirrour, XXXIV. OBSC; SiCE
My Fair, no beauty of thine will last. Song. Alice Meynell. VA
My fair says, she no spouse but me. Inconsistency of Women's

Love [*or* On the Inconstancy of Women]. Catullus. OnPM; PV
My fairest child, I have no song to give you. A Farewell. Charles Kingsley. BLPA; BoTP; DD; GN; HBV; HBVY; NeHB; OTPC; PoVP; TreF; VA
My Faith. Ananda Acharya. WGRP
My Faith. Frederic Lawrence Knowles. *See* Tenant, The.
My faith is all a doubtful thing. Symbol. David Morton. HBMV; MaRV; OQP; StJW
My Faith Looks Up to Thee. Ray Palmer. WGRP
(Faith.) AA; HBV
(Looking to Jesus.) SoP
My faithful friend, if you can see. Impossibilities to His Friend. Robert Herrick. SiSw
My Familiar. John Godfrey Saxe. AnNE; HBV; TreFS
My family married me to the other end of the world. Song of Grief. Liu Hsi-Chun. HW
My Far-off Home. Li Po. *See* On a Quiet Night.
My Father. Rae Dalven. GoYe
My Father above, beholding the meekness. The Child Jesus to Mary the Rose. John Lydgate. CAW; GoBC; ISi
My father and mother were Irish. The Ninepenny Fidil. Joseph Campbell. HBMV
My father and mother were Irish. Irish. Edward J. O'Brien. MoSiPe; SiSoSe
My father and my mother died and left me young and poor. The Orphan. *Unknown.* KiLC
My Father, and Your Father, to My God, and Your God. Edward Taylor. *See* Preparatory Meditations: "My shattred phancy. . ."
My father bequeathed me no wide estates. Heirloom. A. M. Klein. OBCV; PeCV; TrJP
My father bought an undershirt. Song of the All-Wool Shirt. Eugene Field. StPo
My father bound me to a trade in Waterford's fair town. The *Flying Cloud.* *Unknown.* AmSS
My father brought the emigrant bundle. Europe and America. David Ignatow. AmFN
My father came in the darkness. Hyena. *Unknown.* TTY
My Father Cares. Mabel E. Brown. SoP
My Father Cares. Margaret Spencer Johnson. SoP
My father carries a pearl-handled knife. A Wonderful Man. Aileen Fisher. SiSoSe
My Father Christmas passed away. The Skeptic. Robert Service. PV
My father could go down a mountain faster than I. That Dark Other Mountain. Robert Francis. SD
My father could hear a little animal step. Listening. William Stafford. PIA
My father dear, so far from here. My Father Gave Me a Lump of Gold. *Unknown.* OuSiCo
My father died a month ago. *Unknown.* OxNR; SiTL
My father, gasping, in his white calked shoes. The Course. Robert Huff. CoAP
My Father Gave Me a Lump of Gold, *with music.* *Unknown.* OuSiCo
My father got me strong and straight and slim. The End. Marguerite Wilkinson. *Fr.* Songs of an Empty House. HBMV
My father has a pair of shoes. Shoes. Tom Robinson. SoPo; TiPo
My father hated moonlight. Moonlight. Berta Hart Nance. AmFN
My father he died, but I never knew how [*or* can't tell you how]. The Swapping Song. *Unknown.* OxNR; RIS
My father, he gave me a bantam man. Le Petit Mari. *Unknown.* OuSiCo
My father he left me three acres of land. Mad Farmer's Song [*or* Sing Ivy]. *Unknown.* BoTP; BrR; NA; OxNR; RIS
My father, he was a mountaineer. The Ballad of William Sycamore. Stephen Vincent Benét. AnAmPo; BoLiVe; HBMV; MAP; MoAmPo; MPB; OnSP; PFY; PoRA; TreFT
My father he's at the kiln away. The Charcoal-Burner's Son. Erik Gustaf Geijer. WoL
My Father in the Night Commanding No. Louis Simpson. CoAP; NePoEA-2; NYBP; TwCP
My father is a quiet man. Fruit of the Flower. Countee Cullen. PoLF; PoNe
My father is happy or we should be poor. From the Day-Book of a Forgotten Prince. Jean Starr Untermeyer. HBMV; TSW
My father is a strange man. No One Can Be Trusted, Something Tells Me. Craig Sterry. QAH
My father is dead. Song of the Bush-Shrike. *Unknown.* PeSA
My father is the nightingale. *Unknown.* LO
My Father, it is surely a blue place. Hunchback Girl: She Thinks of Heaven. Gwendolyn Brooks. Kal
My Father Knows. Wilbur Fisk Tillett. BLRP
My Father leads me day by day. My Father Cares. Margaret Spencer Johnson. SoP
My father left me three acres of land. *See* My father he left me. . .
My father lies black and hushed. The Worker. Richard W. Thomas. BF; PoNe (1970 ed.)
My Father Loved the Jumping-off Place. Robert P. Tristram Coffin. RePo
My father made a synagogue of a boat. Two Fishermen. Stanley Moss. CoAP
My Father Moved through Dooms of Love. E. E. Cummings. AmP; AnFE; AP; AtBAP; CaFP; CMoP; CoAnAm; CoBMV; CrMA; FaBoMo; LiTA; MoAB; MoPo; MoVE; NoP; OxBA; PoCh; PoIE; TwAmPo; UnPo (3d ed.); VaPo
My Father, My Son. John Malcolm Brinnin. NYBP
My Father: October 1942. William Stafford. NaP
My father owns the butcher shop. *Unknown.* FaFP; SiTL
My father played the melodion. Patrick Kavanagh. *Fr.* A Christmas Childhood. DTC
My father puzzles me. The Farm Boy. Katharine Atherton Grimes. PoMa
My father smiled this morning when. Keep Smiling. *Unknown.* WBLP
My father thought that fact was dull. Garland for a Storyteller. Jessie Farnham. GoYe
My father tore out his native roots. My Father. Rae Dalven. GoYe
My father used to say. Silence. Marianne Moore. CMoP; FaBoEn; FaBoMo; FIW; LiTA; PG (1955 ed.); PoIE; PoPo; PoSa; ViBoPo
My father was a Frenchman. *Unknown.* OxNR
My father was a gambler, he learnt me how to play. The Gambler. *Unknown.* ViBoFo
My father was a mountaineer. *See* My father, he was a mountaineer.
My father was a pioneer. My Father Loved the Jumping-off Place. Robert P. Tristram Coffin. RePo
My father was a sailor. Sailors [*or* Folk Songs]. *Unknown.* AWP; LiTW; OnPM
My Father was a scholar and knew Greek. Development. Robert Browning. MaVP; PoVP
My father was a soldier young, the finest you might see. The Soldier Boy. Johan Ludvig Runeberg. WoL
My father was always out in the garage. Minotaur Poem II. Eli Mandel. MoCV; OBCV
My father was born with a spade in his hand and traded it. Elegy. John Ciardi. ToPo
My father who owned the wagon-shop. Percy Bysshe Shelley. Edgar Lee Masters. *Fr.* Spoon River Anthology. ML
My Fatherland. William Cranston Lawton. AA
My Father's at the Helm. *Unknown.* BePJ
My Fathers Came from Kentucky. Vachel Lindsay. *Fr.* Alexander Campbell. AmFN; HBMV
My Father's Child. "Stuart Sterne." AA
My Father's Close. *Unknown,* *tr. fr. Old French by* Dante Gabriel Rossetti. AWP; PoVP
My father's face is brown with sun. Father. Frances Frost. FaPON; SiSoSe; StVeCh (1955 ed.); TiPo (1959 ed.)
My father's father's father and he who fathered him. Family History. John Maher Murphy. JKCP (1955 ed.)
My father's friend came once to tea. A Recollection. Frances Cornford. ELU; TSW
My Father's Voice in Prayer. May Hastings Nottage. BLRP
My Father's Watch. John Ciardi. ImOP
My Father's way may twist and turn. He Maketh No Mistake. A. M. Overton. SoP; STF
My Father's World. Maltbie D. Babcock. *See* This Is My Father's World.
My fathers wrote their names in sweat. Signatures. Candace Thurber Stevenson. AmFN
My favorite dress. Her Favorites. Mattie Lee Hausgen. PCH; PoPl
My Favorite Tree. Margarete Münsterberg. GFA
My Feet. Gelett Burgess. BOHV; NA; PCH
(Nonsense Verses.) HBV

My (continued)
(Queer Quatrains.) RIS
My feet/ are rooted in a/ poison lake. Pearl Cleage. WSL
My feet strike an apex of the apices of the stairs. Infinity. Walt Whitman. *Fr.* Song of Myself, XLIV-XLV. AA
My feet toe in, as Indians' do. By One, Unsure. Melville Cane. NYTB
My feet took a walk in heavenly grass. Heavenly Grass. Tennessee Williams. PoPl
My, Fellowship, with, God. José Garcia Villa. EaLo
My female friends, whose tender hearts. Swift. *Fr.* Verses on the Death of Dr. Swift. SeCePo; ViBoPo
My fifthe housbonde, god his soule blesse! Chaucer. *Fr.* Canterbury Tales: The Wife of Bath's Prologue. FiP
My fingers are but stragglers at the rear. Stragglers. Pietro Aretino. ErPo
My fingers feed in the fields of wood. Picture Framing. Bert Meyers. ELU
My First Love. Harry Graham. FiBHP
My first love sighed for brooches. Prices. Louis Ginsberg. TrJP
My first small book was nourished in the dark. Karl Shapiro. Recapitulations, V. FiMAP
My first thought was, he lied in every word. Childe Roland to the Dark Tower Came. Robert Browning. AnFE; ATP; BEL; DTo; EnL; FosPo; MaVP; MBW-2; OAEP; OtMeF; PeVV; Po; PoVP; SeCeV; TOP; VA; ViPo; ViPP; VP
My flattering fortune, look thou never so fair. To Fortune. Sir Thomas More. ACP
My flesh is out of fashion for eternity. A Synonym for God. John Fandel. JKCP (1955 ed.)
My flesh is sad, alas, and I have read the books. Sea Breeze. Stéphane Mallarmé. ReMP
My flocks feed [*or* flock feeds] not, my ewes breed [*or* breeds] not. The Unknown Shepherd's Complaint [*or* A Shepherd's Complaint]. Richard Barnfield. EIL; OBSC; TuPP
My flower, my honor, my honey, my joy. Englynion. *Unknown.* PrWP
My flowery and green age was passing away. He Understands the Great Cruelty of Death. Petrarch, *pr. tr. by* J. M. Synge. Sonnets to Laura: To Laura in Death, XLVII. OBMV
My Foe. *Unknown.* BOHV
My foe was dark, and stern, and grim. My Enemy. Alice Williams Brotherton. AA
My folk, now answere me. Jesus Reproaches His People. *Unknown.* MeEL
My food is but spare. The Cottager's Hymn. Patrick Brontë. MaRV
My food was pallid till I heard it ring. King Midas. Howard Moss. CoAP
My foot in the stirrup, my pony won't stan'. Good-by, Old Paint. *Unknown.* ABF; CoSo
My footsteps press where, centuries ago. The Red Men. Charles Sangster. CaP
My Former Hopes Are Fled. William Cowper. OxBoCh
My fortitude is all awry. She Sees Another Door Opening. Firman Houghton. Par
My fortune and my choice this custome break. Omnibus. John Donne. MaMe
My foster-children were not slack. Lament for Corc and Niall of the Nine Hostages. *At. to* Torna. OnYI
My Frail and Earthly Bark, by Reason's Guide. Thomas Lodge. ReIE
My Friend. Marjorie Lorene Buster. STF
My Friend. Paul Gerhardt, *tr. fr. German by* Catherine Winkworth. SoP
My Friend ("The Christian, like his Lord of old"). *Unknown.* SoP
My Friend ("I've found a friend whose equal"). *Unknown.* SoP
My friend and I have built a wall. Wall. Elizabeth Morrow. MaRV
My friend awaited truth. It made me proud. A Commemoration for the Physicist X. Paul Oppenheimer. NYTB
My friend conceived the soul hereafter dwells. Aspiration. Edward William Thomson. OBVV
My friend from Asia has powers and magic. Credo. Robinson Jeffers. AnEnPo; MAP; MoAB; MoAmPo; PoPl
My friend, have you heard of the town of Nogood. The Town of Nogood. William Edward Penney. BLPA
My friend, he wed a suffragette. Gee, But There's Class to a Man Like That. Charles A. Jones. OTD
My friend, if you wilt credit me in aught. Who Minds to Bring His Ship to Happy Shore. Jasper Heywood. SiCE
My friend is lodging high in the eastern range. To Tan Ch'i-u. Li Po. AWP
My Friend Maloney. Charles Causley. POTi
My friend, my bonny friend, when we are old. The Word. John Masefield. MaRV
My friend, speak always once, but listen twice. The Mouth and the Ears. Shem-Tob ben Joseph Palquera. TrJP
My Friend, the Cat. Carrie W. Stryker. CIV
My Friend the Caterpillar. David Russell. NYTB
My friend, the talks I have with you. Conversation with a Friend. George Abbe. NYTB
My Friend, the Things That Do Attain. Martial, *tr. by* the Earl of Surrey. *See* Means to Attain Happy Life, The.
My friend thy beauty seemeth good. The Penurious Quaker; or, The High Priz'd Harlot. *Unknown.* CoMu
My Friends. W. S. Merwin. NoP
My friends are borne to one another. Martin Buber in the Pub. Max Harris. BoAV; PoAu-2
My Friends Are Little Lamps to Me. Elizabeth Whittemore. PoToHe (new ed.)
My friend who married the girl I. Watts. Shirley Kaufman. QAH
My friends, the leaves, who used to entertain me. In Coventry. James J. Daly. CAW
My friends without shields walk on the target. My Friends. W. S. Merwin. NoP
My freshmen/ settle in. Achilles. Freshmen. Barry Spacks. NYBP
My funeral-shaft, and marble shapes that dwell. Baucis. Erinna. AWP
My Funny Umbrella. Alice Wilkins. GFA
My gal don' wear button-up shoes. Georgia Land. *Unknown.* OuSiCo
My Gal Sal. Paul Dresser. TreFT
My Galilees. Belle Chapman Morrill. MaRV
My galleon of adventure. San Francisco. Walter Adolphe Roberts. PoNe
My Galley Charged with Forgetfulness. Sir Thomas Wyatt. *See* Lover Compareth His State to a Ship, The.
My garage is a structure of excessive plainness. Detail. Mary Ursula Bethell. AnNZ
My Garden. Thomas Edward Brown. DD; EnLit; FaBV; GBV; GTSL; HBV; HBVY; MaRV; NeHB; OBEV; OBVV; OQP; OTPC (1946 ed.); PoFS; PoLF; PoVP; SoP; TOP; TRV; TreF; WBLP; WGRP; YT
(Garden, A.) GoTP
My Garden. W. H. Davies. BoNaP
My Garden, *sel.* Emerson.
Words of the Gods. OQP
My Garden. Norah Hussey. BoTP
My Garden. Janice Appleby Succorsa. HoPM
My Garden. Frederic E. Weatherly. OTPC (1946 ed.)
My garden bears testimony to divinity. Testimony. Eva Moad Turner. OQP
My garden blazes brightly with the rose-bush and the peach. In Springtime. Kipling. BrPo
My garden-ground of grief, where self-will's seeds are sown. A Strange Description of a Rare Garden-Plot. Nicholas Breton. ReIE
My Garden Is a Pleasant Place. Louise Driscoll. BLPA; FaBoBe; NeHB
My gentle child, behold this horse. The Racing-Man. A. P. Herbert. FiBHP; WhC
My ghost pets are like shadows on the wall. Ghost Pet. Horatio Colony. GoYe
My Ghostly Father. Charles d'Orléans. CBEP; NoP
(Confession.) ChTr
(Confession of a Stolen Kiss.) MeEL
(Kiss, The.) ACP
(My Gostly Fader, I Me Confess.) EG; EnLoPo
(Roundel.) EnPo
My Gift. Christina Rossetti. *Fr.* A Christmas Carol: "In the bleak mid-winter." BrR; ChBR; FaPON; MaRV; OTPC (1946 ed.); SiSoSe
(Birthday Gift, A.) PRWS

("What can I give Him?") BiCB; FaChP
My girl hath violet eyes and yellow hair. The Little Milliner. Robert Buchanan. BeLS
My girl I say be on your guard. Death and the Maiden. *Unknown.* KiLC
My girl is dark, but she is my desire. *Unknown, ad. fr. Greek by* Louis Untermeyer. MeWo
My girl is thin, yet that is why. True Love. *Unknown.* UnTE
My girl, thou gazest much. The Lover to His Lady. George Turberville. CTC; OBSC; SiCE; TuPP
My girl's tall with hard long eyes. E. E. Cummings. *Fr.* Sonnets—Realities. UnTE
My Glass Is Half Unspent. Francis Quarles. OxBoCh
My glass shall not persuade me I am old. Sonnets, XXII. Shakespeare. EG; OBSC; Sonn
My glittering sky, high, clear, profound. The Lovers. Marya Zaturenska. MoAmPo
My glorious Lord thy work upon my hand. Meditation CLIII. Edward Taylor. *Fr.* Preparatory Meditations, Second Series. MAmP
My glory, honor, all depend. The Gentleman. Menahem ben Judah Lonzano. TrJP
My gloves and cravat! Chaplin's Sad Speech. Rafael Alberti. LiTW
My Glumdalclitch, come here and sit with me. A Tryst in Brobdingnag. Adrienne Cecile Rich. NYBP
My God. Solomon ibn Gabirol, *tr. fr. Hebrew by* Alice Lucas. *Fr.* Fr. The Royal Crown. TrJP
My God, a verse is not a crown. The Quidditie. George Herbert. MaMe; PoEL-2; SCEP-1
My God and King! to thee. Anguish. Henry Vaughan. MemP; SoP
My God Has Spoken. Paul Verlaine. *See* God Has Spoken.
My God, how endless is thy love. The Love of God. Isaac Watts. SoP
My God, how gracious art thou! I had slipt. The Relapse. Henry Vaughan. AnAnS-1; MeP
My God, How Wonderful Thou Art. Frederick William Faber. GoBC; TrPWD
My God, I heard this day. Man. George Herbert. AnAnS-1; BoLiVe; CABA; InPo; MaMe; MaPo; MeP; MePo; NoP; OAEP; PAn; PoEL-2; SCEP-1; SeCP; SeCV-1; TrGrPo; TrPWD
My God, I know that those who plead. My God. Solomon ibn Gabirol. *Fr.* The Royal Crown. TrJP
My God, I Love Thee. St. Francis Xavier, *tr. fr. Latin by* Edward Caswall. CAW; MaRV
(Hymn: "My God, I love thee, not because.") SoP; WGRP
My God, I read this day. Affliction. George Herbert. MaMe
My God, I thank Thee who hast made. Thankfulness. Adelaide Anne Procter. MaRV; SoP; TrPWD
My God, if writings may. Obedience. George Herbert. AnAnS-1; MaMe; MeP
My God! is any hour so sweet. The Hour of Prayer. Charlotte Elliott. SoP; STF
My God Is Love. Love. Toyohiko Kagawa. SoP; TRV
My God Is Near. Carlton Buck. SoP
My God is not a chiselled stone. True Knowledge. Panatattu. WGRP
My God! looke on me with thine eye. His Ejaculation to God. Robert Herrick. SeCV-1
My God, my Father, while I stray. Thy Will Be Done! Charlotte Elliott. SoP
My God, my God, let me for once look on thee. Robert Browning. *Fr.* Pauline. TrPWD
My God, my God, what queer corner am I in. In the Deep Museum. Anne Sexton. MoAmPo (1962 ed.); ToPo
My God, my God, why hast thou forsaken me? A Cry in Distress. Psalm XXII, Bible, *O.T.* TrGrPo
My God (oh, let me call Thee mine). A Prayer. Anne Bronë. TrPWD; VA
My God said: "Love me, son! Dost thou not see." Mystical Dialogue. Paul Verlaine. LO
My God, the bitter-tasting mouth was me. Homage (Diptych, 2). R. J. Schoeck. GoYe
My God, the poore expressions of my love. Perseverance. George Herbert. MaMe
My God, thou that didst dye for me. The Dedication. Henry Vaughan. AnAnS-1; MeP
My God, when I walk[e] in those groves. Religion. Henry Vaughan. AnAnS-1; MeP; OBS; OxBoCh
My God, where is that ancient heat towards thee. To His Mother [*or* Sonnet]. George Herbert. AnAnS-1; MaMe; MeP; PoFS; SeEP; Sonn
My God, whose law I believe in, and have signed to serve in my best. Prayer on the Night before Easter. John Holmes. MoRP
My golden locks Time hath to silver turn'd. A Farewell to Arms. George Peele. *See also* His Golden Locks . . . *Fr.* Polyhymnia. MemP.
My good blade carves the casques of men. Sir Galahad. Tennyson. BEL; EPN; GTBS; HBV; LiTG; MaRV; OBVV; OnPP; OTPC; PoVP; TreF; VA; ViPo; ViPP
My Good Old Man, *with music. Unknown.* BFSS
My goodness, my goodness,/ It's Christmas again. Christmas. Marchette Chute. BrR; ChBR; SiSoSe
My Gostly Fader, I Me Confess. Charles d'Orléans. *See* My Ghostly Father.
"My Grace Is Sufficient for Thee." *Unknown.* BePJ; BLRP; SoP
My gracious friend, whose arts are all refining. Confessed. Josephine Miles. FiMAP
My Gracious Lord, I would thee glory doe. Edward Taylor. *Fr.* Preparatory Meditations, Second Series. SCAP
My granddad, viewing earth's worn cogs. Going to the Dogs. *Unknown.* TreFS
My grandfather found. Dunbarton. Robert Lowell. NoP
My grandfather had two very fine hens. Merry Green Fields of England. *Unknown.* FTB
My grandfather was an elegant gentleman. David Wright. *Fr.* Seven South African Poems. PeSA
My grandfather's beard. On the Photograph of a Man I Never Saw. Hyam Plutzik. FiMAP
My grandfather's clock was too large for the shelf. Grandfather's Clock. Henry Clay Work. FaFP; NeHB; TreF
My Grandfather's Funeral. James Applewhite. YAP
My grandfather's hands were wise and hard. Rivets. N. S. Olds. EtS
My Grandmother. Perseus Adams. PeSA
My Grandmother said, "Now isn't it queer." Wonders of Nature. *Unknown.* ThGo
My grandmother sent me a new-fashioned three-cornered cambric country-cut handkerchief. *Unknown.* OxNR
My grandmother, she, at the age of eight-three. Grandmother's Old Armchair. *Unknown.* BLPA
My Grandmother's Funeral. Jascha Kessler. AmPC
My Grandmother's Love Letters. Hart Crane. CMoP; FaBoBe; MoAB; PG (1945 ed.)
My grandmothers were strong. Lineage. Margaret Walker. BOLo; Kal
My Grandser was a fearsome man! Grandser. Abbie Farwell Brown. HBMV
My grandsire sailed three years from home. The Master Mariner. George Sterling. HBV; MAP; MoAmPo (1942 ed.)
My granny saw the devil walk at twilight. Top Hat and Tales. Lorna Beers. FiSC
My Grave. Thomas Osborne Davis. ACV; OnYI
My Greaty-great Grannie is terribly small. Greaty-great Grannie. Lysbeth Boyd Borie. GaP
My grey-barked trees wave me in. I Stroll. Peter Redgrove. NePoEA-2
My grief, my grief, maid without sin. The Body's Speech. Donal MacCarthy, First Earl Clancarty. KiLC
My Grief on Fál's Proud Plain, *sel.* Geoffrey Keating, *tr. fr. Late Middle Irish by* Padraic Pearse.
"From my grief on Fál's proud plain I sleep." OnYI
My Grief on the Sea. *Unknown, tr. fr. Modern Irish by* Douglas Hyde. AnIL; LiTW; OBEV; OBVV; OnYI; OxBI
My grief! that they have laid you in the town. Synge's Grave. Winifred M. Letts. AnIV
My gudame wes a gay wif, bot scho wes ryght [*or* rycht] gend. The Ballad of Kynd Kittok. William Dunbar. GoTS; OxBoLi
My guest! I have not led you thro'. Interlude. Walter Savage Landor. GTBS-P
My Guide. Robert Jones Burdette. MaRV
Christ, *sel.* BePJ
My Guide. George Francis Savage-Armstrong. VA
My hair is gray [*or* grey], but not with years. The Prisoner of Chillon. Byron. BeL; CaBL; DTo; EnLi-2; EnLit; EnRP;

My (continued)
EPN; HBV; MaC; MBW-2; MERP; OnSP; PoLF
My Hairt Is Heich Aboif. *Unknown.* OxBS
My hand cannot reach heaven's height. The Poet Meets Venus and Her Priest. John Gower. *Fr.* Confessio Amantis. MeEV
My hand cannot smooth your sigh. Microcosmos, III. Nigel Heseltine. NeBP
My Hand in His. *Unknown.* SoP
My hand is dirty. The Dirty Hand. Mark Strand. YAP
My hand is lonely for your clasping, dear. You and I. Henry Alford. BLPA; FaBoBe; NeHB
My hand is weary with writing. Columcille the Scribe. *At. to* St. Columcille. AnIL; OnYI
My hand waving from the window. Platform Goodbye. H. B. Mallalieu. WaP
My hands are gnarled and my hair is gray. Fourscore Years. *Unknown.* SoP
My hands that guide a needle. Instruction. Hazel Hall. NP
My Handsome Gilderoy. *Unknown.* AtBAP; CH
My happier state. Of Middle Life. *Unknown.* SeCL
My happiness depends on an electric appliance. The Telephone. Edward Field. CAD
My happy days are past. The Unhappy Miner. *Unknown.* SGR
My Happy Life. Mildmay Fane, Earl of Westmorland. CavP
My hart is fled from mee yet live I doe. *Unknown.* SeCSL
My Hate. Marvin Bell. YAP
My hat's off—my jersey's torn. Robin Hood. Patience Adrian Ross. PCH
My head is bald, my breath is bad. Late-Flowering Lust. John Betjeman. CMoP; ErPo; NMP
My head is like lead, and my temples they bulge. Hangover. Philip H. Rhinelander. WhC
My head, my heart, mine eyes, my life—nay more. A Letter to Her Husband, Absent upon Public Employment. Anne Bradstreet. MAmP; SCAP
My Head on My Shoulders. Jeremy Ingalls. GoYe
My Heart. Elizabeth Madox Roberts. NP
My heart,/ The sun hath set. All's Well. William A. Quayle. MaRV
My heart aches, and a drowsy numbness pains. Ode to a Nightingale [*or* To a Nightingale]. Keats. AnEnPo; AnFE; AtBAP; ATP; AWP; BEL; BoLiVe; BWP; CABA; CaFP; CBV; ChER; ChTr; CoBE; DiPo; EnL; EnLi-2; EnLit; EnRP; EPN; ERoP-2; ExPo; FaBoBe; FaBoEn; FaFP; FaPL; FiP; ForPo; FosPo; GBV; GTBS; GTBS-D; GTBS-P; GTBS-W; GTSE; GTSL; HBV; HBVY; ILP; InP; InPo; JAWP; LiTB; LiTG; LoBV; MaPo; MasP; MBW-2; MCCG; MemP; MERP; NoP; OAEP; OBEV; OBNC; OBRV; OnP; OtMeF; OuHeWo; PAn; PeER; PIA; Po; PoAn; PoE; PoEL-4; PoeP; PoFS; PoIE; PoPo; PoRA; PTK; SeCeV; ShBV-3; StP; TOP; TreF; TrGrPo; UnPo; VaPo; ViBoPo; WBP; WHA; WoL
My Heart and I. Elizabeth Barrett Browning. HBV; VA
My heart and I were not so very well acquent. Upon Discovering One's Own Intolerance. Sara Henderson Hay. MaRV
My Heart at Rest. Sir Charles Sedley. *See* To Celia.
My hearts beats to the feet of the first faithful. An Interlude. Robert Duncan. NoP
My heart, being hungry, feeds on food. The Hungry Heart. Edna St. Vincent Millay. TSW
My heart, complaining like a bird. Burning Bush. Karle Wilson Baker. HBMV
My heart cried like a beaten child. Song Making. Sara Teasdale. WGRP
My heart did heave, and there came forth, O God! Affliction. George Herbert. MaMe
My heart dissolved to see Thee bleed. At the Cross. *Unknown.* STF
My heart felt need to die. The Scourge. Stanley Kunitz. CrMA
My heart fills up with beauty, as I stand. Gay Head. Neilson Abeel. HT
My heart has fed today. Completion. Eunice Tietjens. HBMV; NP
My heart has grown rich with the passing of years. The Solitary. Sara Teasdale. MAP; MoAmPo; NeMA; WHA
My heart has thank'd thee, Bowles! for those soft strains. To the Reverend [*or* Rev.] W. L. Bowles. Samuel Taylor Coleridge. EnRP; Sonn
My heart, I cannot still it. Auspex. James Russell Lowell. AmLP; AmPP (3d ed.); AnFE; AnNE; AP; APA; CoAnAm; GTBS-W; HBV; NePA; OBVV; PoEL-5
My heart I gave thee not to do it pain. The Lover Forsaketh His Unkind Love. Sir Thomas Wyatt. FCP; Sonn
My heart in pieces like the bits. Poem. Tom Clark. ANYP
My heart, imprisoned in a hopeless isle. Michael Drayton. Idea's Mirrour, XXII. OBSC; SiCE
My Heart Is a Lute. *At. to* Lady Anne Lindsay, *also to* Lady Blanche Elizabeth Lindsay. HBV; VA
My heart is a-breaking, dear tittie. Tam Glen. Burns. ALV; AWP; BEL; CEP; InPo; JAWP; OAEP; OBEC; OxBS; TOP; WBP
My heart is a dark forest where no voice is heard. Solitudes. John Hall Wheelock. MoLP
My heart is bare to God who knows no wrong. Ode—Imitated from the Psalms. Nicolas Joseph Laurent Gilbert. CAW
My heart is beating up and down. My Heart. Elizabeth Madox Roberts. NP
My heart is chilled and my pulse is slow. Lost Light. Elizabeth Akers Allen. HBV
My heart is cold and weather-worn. Nameless Song. Elinor Wylie. CoBA
My heart is empty. All the fountains that should run. Aridity. C. S. Lewis. BoC
My heart is far from Liffey's tide. Mo Craoibhin Cno. Edward Walsh. IrPN
My Heart Is Fixed. James A. Sanaker. SoP
My Heart Is Heavy. Sara Teasdale. NP
My Heart Is High [*or* Heich] Above. *Unknown.* ErPo; GoTS; LO; OBEV
My Heart Is in the East. Judah Halevi, *tr. fr. Hebrew.* TrJP
My heart is in woe. The Downfall of the Gael. Fearflatha O'Gnive, *tr. by* Sir Samuel Ferguson. AnIV; AWP; JAWP; OnYI; WBP
My heart is lighter than the poll. The New-slain Knight. *Unknown.* ESPB
My heart is like a fountain true. Mother's Song. *Unknown.* GN; HBV
My heart is like a ship on Neptune's back. Emaricdulfe, XXIX. "E. C." Sonn; TuPP
My heart is like a singing bird. A Birthday. Christina Rossetti. AWP; BoLiVe; BoLP; CH; CoBE; EG; EnLi-2; FaFP; FaPL; GTBS; GTSE; GTSL; InvP; JAWP; LiTB; LiTG; LiTL; LoBV; MeWo; OAEP; OBEV; OBVV; OuHeWo; PCD; PeVV; PoE; PoVP; ShBV-4; ThWaDe; TOP; TreFS; TrGrPo; TSW; ViBoPo; ViPo; VP; WBP; WHA; WiR; YT
My heart is parched by unbelief. Drought. Betty Bruechert. SoP
My heart is sair [*or* sore]—I dare na [*or* not] tell. For the Sake o' [*or* of] Somebody. Burns. AtBAP; WePo
My heart is set him down, twixt hope and fears. Thomas Watson. *Fr.* Hecatompathia. ReIE
My heart is sore—I dare not tell. *See* My heart is sair . . .
My heart is withered and my health is gone. The Wave of Cliona. James Stephens, *after* Egan O'Rahilly. CMoP
My heart is young—the breath of blowing trees. Certainties. Helen Frazee-Bower. *Fr.* Two Married. HBMV
My Heart Leaps Up [When I Behold]. Wordsworth. AtBAP; ATP; BEL; BiCB; BoLiVe; CABA; CaFP; CoBE; DiPo; EG; EnLi-2; EnLit; EnRP; EPN; ERoP-1; ExPo; FaBoEn; FaBV; FaFP; GTBS; GTBS-D; GTBS-P; GTBS-W; GTSE; GTSL; ILP; InPo; LoBV; MaPo (1969 ed.); MBW-2; MCCG; MERP; NoP; OAEP; OBNC; OBRV; OTD; OTPC; OuHeWo; PCD; PoAn; PoeP; PoPl; PoPo; PoSa; SoP; SoPo; TiPo; TOP; TreF; TrGrPo; TRV; ViBoPo; YAT; YT
(Rainbow, The.) BLPA; CBEP; DD; HBV; HBVY; LiTB; LiTG; NeHB; OBEV; RoGo
(Rainbow in the sky.) RIS
My heart leaps up when I behold. Song to Be Sung by the Father of Infant Female Children. Ogden Nash. MoAmPo
My heart lies light in my own breast. The Wind Bloweth Where It Listeth. Susan L. Mitchell. AnIV
My heart, like a bird, veered up in joyous flight. A Voyage to

Cythera, Baudelaire, *tr. by.* Hubert Creekmore. LiTW

My heart loves as heavy as the horse that climbs the hill. *Unknown, tr. fr. Welsh by* Menna Gallie. ELU

My Heart, My Heart Is Mournful. Heine. *See* Mein Herz, mein Herz ist traurig.

My heart of gold as true as steel. A Nonsense Carol. *Unknown.* OxBoLi

My heart overfloweth with a good matter. Psalm XLV, Bible, *O.T.* HW

My heart rebels against my generation. Odes, II. George Santayana. AmePo; AnFE; ATP; CoAnAm; PoFr; TwAmPo; ViBoPo

My heart rejoices in God's will. Grace to Do Without. *Unknown.* SoP

My heart rejoiceth in the Lord, mine horn is exalted. The Song of Hannah [*or* Hannah's Song of Thanksgiving]. First Samuel, Bible, *O.T.* AWP; LiTW

My heart rose when I looked on Sampford. Walking Sampford Way. Paul L. Grano. BoAu

My Heart Shall Be Thy Garden. Alice Meynell. HBV

My heart that was so passionless. Rencontre. Jessie Fauset. CDC

My heart the anvil where my thoughts do beat. Idea, XL (*also given as XLIV in Idea's Mirrour*). Michael Drayton. HBV; ReIE

My heart—the wretched thing—is today. With Its Quiet Tongue. Kamala Das. NP

My heart, thinking. "Lady of Sakanoye." *Fr.* Manyo Shu. AWP; JAWP; LiTW; WBP

My heart was fired, as from his sight it turned. The Dream of Dakiki. Firdausi. WGRP

My heart was heavy, for its trust had been. Forgiveness. Whittier. AmPP (3d ed.); MaRV

My Heart Was Wandering [in the Sands]. Christopher Brennan. *Fr.* The Twilight of Disquietude. BoAu; BoAV; PoAu-1

My heart will break—I'm sure it will. False Love and True Logic. Laman Blanchard. BOHV

My hearties, row your boat. Woman Takes Life with Her Own Hand. John Morgan. *Fr.* Variations on *The Aeneid.* YAP

My heart's an old spinet with strings. The Spinet. Andrew Lang. MuSP

My heart's best! Uncourtly Love. Walther von der Vogelweide. LiTW

My Heart's Desire. *Unknown.* STF

My heart's despair. Isabel. Sydney Dobell. OBVV

My Heart's in the Highlands. Burns. AnEnPo; AWP; BBV (1923 ed.); BEL; CEP; CoBE; EnRP; FaBoBe; FaFP; FaPON; GN; HBV; HT; InPo; JAWP; LiTG; LiTL; NeHB; OTD; OTPC; PoPl; RIS; SD; ShBV-2; StaSt; TOP; TreFT; WaKn; WBP

My heart's so heavy with a hundred things. Sonnet: In Absence from Becchina. Cecco Angiolieri da Siena. AWP; JAWP; WBP

My help, my hope, my strength shall be. The Law. Abraham ibn Ezra. TrJP

My Hereafter. Juanita de Long. WGRP

My hero is na deck'd wi' gowd. The Hero. Robert Nicoll. HBV; VA

My Hero: to Robert Gould Shaw. Benjamin Brawley. BANP; PoNe

My Hiding Place. Kathryn T. Bowsher. STF

My highway is unfeatured air. Hymn of the Earth. William Ellery Channing. AA; AnNE

My history extends/ Where moved my tourist hands. Abroad Thoughts from Home. Donald Hall. NePoEA

My Home. *Unknown.* NA

My home is a house/ Near a wood. The Country Child. Irene Thompson. BoTP

My home is on the rolling deep. My Home. *Unknown.* NA

My home's in Montana, I wear a bandanna. Cowboy's Lament (C vers.). *Unknown.* CoSo

My Honey, My Love. Joel Chandler Harris. *Fr.* Uncle Remus and His Friends. AA; FaBoBe

My Honeyed Languor. "Eduard Bagritzky," *tr. fr. Russian by* Babette Deutsch. TrJP

My honoured lord, forgive the unruly tongue. Elinor Wylie. *Fr.* One Person. NP

My hope, alas, hath me abused. Sir Thomas Wyatt. FCP; SiPS

My hope and heart is with thee—thou wilt be. To J. M. K. Tennyson. PoVP; ViPo

My hopes retire; my wishes as before. Persistence. Walter Savage Landor. *Fr.* Ianthe. OBNC; VA

My Horses. Jean Jaszi. SoPo

My horse's feet beside the lake. A Farewell. Matthew Arnold. *Fr.* Switzerland. MBW-2; OAEP; ViPP; VP

My House. George Bruce. OxBS

My House. Jane W. Krows. SoPo

My House. Claude McKay. CDC

My House. Robert Pack. PoDB

My House. Robert Louis Stevenson. ILP

My House. W. B. Yeats. Meditations in Time of Civil War, II. CABL; LiTB; PIA

My house/ is granite. My House. George Bruce. OxBS

My house has crickets. Crickets and Mice. Joseph Joel Keith. StVeCh (1955 ed.)

My House Has Windows. Anna Blake Mezquida. OQP

My house is little, but warm enough. My Little House. May Byron. OQP

My house is made of graham bread. Queer Quatrains. Gelett Burgess. RIS

My house is not quiet, I am not loud. Fish in River. *Unknown. Fr.* Riddles. AnOE

My house is red—a little house. A Happy Child. Kate Greenaway. BoTP; PPL; OTPC

My house, my fairy/ palace. Jeronimo's House. Elizabeth Bishop. MiAP

My house stands high. The Harp of the Wind. Frances Shaw. NP

My hovering thoughts would fly to heaven, and quiet nestle in the sky. Man's Civil War. Robert Southwell. SiCE

My humble Muse sad, and in lonely state. To His Excellency Joseph Dudley. John Saffin. SCAP

My hungry eyes through greedy covetize. Amoretti, XXXV. Spenser. BWP

My Husband ("My husband's a jockey"). *Unknown.* CoMu

My husband is far, far away. The Wife. *Unknown. Fr.* Shi King. OnPM; WoL

My husband's a jockey, a jockey, a jockey. My Husband. *Unknown.* CoMu

My husband's a saucy foretopman. Eight Bells. *Unknown.* SaSa

My Hut. E. Mathias. BoTP

My hut, in spring! Spring in My Hut. Sodo. OnPM; RePo

My Influence. *Unknown.* STF

My Inmost Hope. Sarah Copia Sullam, *tr. fr. Italian.* TrJP

My Inside-Self. Rachel Field. FaPON

My Invention. Shel Silverstein. PV

My Jack. John Francis O'Donnell. IrPN

My Jean. Burns. *See* Of A' the Airts.

My Jesus, as Thou Wilt. Benjamin Schmolke [*or* Schmolck], *tr. fr. German.* (Consecration.) BLRP, *abr.*; SoP

My Joy, My Jockey, My Gabriel. George Barker. First Cycle of Love Poems, V. ErPo; MoAB; MoBrPo (1950 ed.); MoPo; MoPW

(Love Poem.) NeBP

My joy, my life, my crown! A True Hymn. George Herbert. InVP; MaMe; OxBoCh

My Kate. Elizabeth Barrett Browning. OBVV; OHFP; WBLP

My Kingdom. Louisa May Alcott. MaRV

My Kite. Beatrice Brown. GFA

My kite grabbed on a gusty gale. Kite Tales. Rose Waldo. GFA

My kitten slept in a cushioned chair. Change. Lalia Mitchell Thornton. CIV

My kitten walks on velvet feet. Night. Lois Weakley McKay. SiSoSe

My kitty has a little song. Song for a Child. Helen B. Davis. SoPo

My Laddie. Amélie Rives. HBV

My Laddie's Hounds. Marguerite Elizabeth Easter. AA

My Lady. Philip James Bailey. *Fr.* Festus. OBVV ("I loved her for that she was beautiful.") LO

My Lady Carries Love. Dante, *tr. fr. Italian by* Dante Gabriel Rossetti. La Vita Nuova, XII. AWP; JAWP; OnPM; WBP (Within Her Eyes.) LiTW

My Lady Esther, beautiful. Esther. Fray Angelico Chavez. GoBC
My Lady Has the Grace of Death. Joseph Plunkett. OxBI
My Lady Is a Pretty One. *Unknown.* OxBoLi
My lady looks so gentle and so pure. Sonnet. Dante. *Fr.* La Vita Nuova. AWP; JAWP; WBP
My lady mine, I send. Canzonetta: Of His Lady and of His Making Her Likeness. Jacopo da Lentino. AWP
My Lady Nature and Her Daughters. Cardinal Newman. GoBC
My lady pleases me and I please her. The Growth of Love, XXX. Robert Bridges. Sonn
My lady seems of ivory. Praise of My Lady. William Morris. HBV; PoVP; ViPo
My Lady Spring. *Unknown.* BoTP
My Lady Takes the Sunlight for Her Gown. Thomas Cole. NePoAm
My Lady unto Madam makes her bow. Modern Love, XXXVI. George Meredith. ViPo; VP
My lady walks her morning round. The Henchman. Whittier. CLwM; HBV; OBEV (new ed.); OBVV
My lady was found mutilated. Ballad. Leonard Cohen. OBCV
My Lady Wind. *Unknown.* HBV; HBVY; OTPC (1923 ed.); PCH
("My Lady Wind, my Lady Wind.") PPL
My lady woke upon a morning fair. On His Lady's Waking. Pierre de Ronsard. AWP
My lady, you are of all beauty shrine. To Rosemound; a Balade. Chaucer. PoLi
My Lady's birthday crowns the growing year. In February. Henry Simpson. HBV
My Lady's face it is they worship there. Sonetto XXXV: To Guido Orlando. Guido Calvalcanti. CTC
My Lady's Grave. Emily Brontë. *See* Song: "Linnet in the rocky dells, The."
My lady's presence makes the roses red. Sonnet. Henry Constable. *Fr.* Diana. CoBE; EIL; HBV; OBSC; ReIE; SiCE
My lady's senses are so pure and fine. Sonnet. George Henry Boker. *Fr.* Sonnets: a Sequence on Profane Love. AmePo
My Lady's Slipper. *Unknown.* *See* Lass of Lochroyan, The.
My Lady's Tears. *Unknown.* *See* I Saw My Lady Weep.
My lamp, full charged with its sweet oil, still burns. Hero Entombed, I. Peter Quennell. FaBoMo; LiTB
My Land. Thomas Osborne Davis. DD; HBV; MPB (1956 ed.); PAL; OTPC
(This Native Land.) BoTP
My Land Is Fair for Any Eyes to See. Jesse Stuart. FaPON; TiPo (1959 ed.)
My Language. Heinz Politzer, *tr. fr. German by* Heinz Politzer. LiTW
My lank limp lily, my long lithe lily. A Maudle-in Ballad. *Unknown.* BOHV
My Last Afternoon with Uncle Devereux Winslow. Robert Lowell. ForPo
My last defense. Old Mary. Gwendolyn Brooks. TDP
My Last Duchess. Robert Browning. ATP; AWP; BEL; BeLS; BoLiVe; CABA; CaFP; CBEP; CBV; CoBE; DiPo; EnL; EnLi-2; EnLit; EPN; ExPo; FaBoEn; FaFP; FiP; ForPo; FosPo; GTBS-P; HBV; HoPM; ILP; InP; InPo; JAWP; LiTB; MasP; MaVP; MBW-2; MCCG; NoP; OAEP; OBNC; OnPP; OtMeF; OuHeWo; PAn; PeVV; PIA; PoAn; PoE; PoEL-5; PoFS; PoIE; PoLF; PoPo; PoSa; PoVP; SeCeV; ShBV-4; StP; TOP; TreFS; TrGrPo; UnPo (1st ed.); VA; VaPo; ViPo; ViPP; VP; WBP; WHA; YAT
My Last Illusion. John Kendall. FiBHP; WhC
My Last Terrier. John Halsham. HBV
My Last Thought. José Rizal, *tr. fr. Spanish by* Murat Halstead. PoFr
My latest sun is sinking fast. Christian's Victory—Triumph. J. Haskell. SoP
My least height flowers late with buds. Where Unimaginably Bright. Oliver Hale. GoYe
My lefe is faren in a lond. The One I Love Is Gone Away. *Unknown.* MeEL
My leg? It's off at the knee. Fleurette. Robert W. Service. TIHL
My Legacy. Helen Hunt Jackson. HBV
My Legs Are So Weary. Gelett Burgess. LBN
My Lesbia, I will not deny. Upon Lesbia—Arguing. Alfred Cochrane. HBV
My Lesbia, let us live and love. Courtship. Alexander Brome. CavP
My Lessons in the Jail. Miriam Waddington. MoCV
My Letter. Grace Denio Litchfield. AA
My letters all dead paper, mute and white! Sonnets from the Portugese, XXVIII. Elizabeth Barrett Browning. CoBE; EnLi-2; EnLit; HBV; ViBoPo; ViPo
My Liege, I Did Deny No Prisoners. Shakespeare. King Henry IV, Pt. I, *fr.* I, iii. WaaP
(Staff Officer, The: "But I remember. . .") OtMeF
My Life. J. Gordon Howard. SoP
My Life. Henrietta C. Parks. TNV
My life closed twice before its close. Emily Dickinson. AA; AmPP (4th ed.); AnAmPo; AnFe; AnNE; AP; APA; AtBAP; BoLiVe; CBEP; CoAnAm; DiPo; EG; FaBoEn; GTBS-D; GTBS-W; ILP; LiTA; LiTL; LiTM; LO; MAP; MAPA; MemP; MeWo; MoAB; MoAmPo; MoVE; MWA-2; NePA; OBEV (new ed.); OBVV; OxBA; PFY; PoeP; PoPl; TIHL; TreFT; TrGrPo; TwAmPo; ViBoPo; WHA
My life could have ended then, crouched over the pool. The Rock Pool. Philip Hobsbaum. NYTB
My life ebbs from me—I must die. First or Last. Margaret Veley. VA
My life flows on in endless song. How Can I Keep from Singing? *Unknown.* FaChP
My life had stood—a loaded gun. Emily Dickinson AmPP (5th ed.); AP; PoE
My life has been tedious. Release. Peter Schjeldahl. ANYP
My Life Has Been the Poem. Henry David Thoreau. AmePo; ML
My life has crept so long on a broken wing. Tennyson. Maud, Pt. III, vi. SyP
My life hath been one love—no blot it out. John Clare. *Fr.* Child Harold. PeER
My Life Is a Bowl. May Riley Smith. BLPA
My life is a wearisome journey. The Toils of the Road [*or* The End of the Way]. Harriet Cole. BLRP; SoP
My life is but a weaving. The Weaver. *Unknown.* SoP
My life is but an instant, a fleeting hour above me. My Song of Today. St. Thérèse of Lisieux. CAW
My life is cast. Sifting. Victor E. Beck. GoYe
My life is done, yet all remains. Robert the Bruce. Edwin Muir. OxBS
My Life is Full of Weary Days. Tennyson. PoVP
My life is legends of the yellow haired. Nor Mars His Sword. Dunstan Thompson. NePA
My life is like a dream. From Disciple to Master. Monk Gibbon. AnIV
My life is like a music-hall. Prologue. Arthur Symons. BrPo
My life is like a stroll upon the beach. The Fisher's Boy. Henry David Thoreau. AA; AnAmPo; AnNE; ChTr
My Life Is like the Summer Rose. Richard Henry Wilde. FaPL; HBV; TreFT
(Stanzas.) AA
My life is measur'd by this glasse, this glasse. On an Hour[e]-Glasse. John Hall. MeLP; MePo
My life is now a burthen growne. *Unknown.* SeCSL
My life more civil is and free. Independence. Henry David Thoreau. AmPP (3d ed.); AnNE; CoBA; PoFr; TreFS
My life must touch a million lives in some way ere I go. My Prayer. *Unknown.* BLRP
My life shall touch a dozen lives before this day is done. As I Go on My Way. Strickland Gillilan. MaRV
My life touched yours for a very brief space. The Beauty of Jesus in Me. Alice Hansche Mortenson. SoP
My life was never so precious. Inscription for the Tank. James Wright. TwCP
My life's a shade, my days. Hope in Death. Samuel Crossman. SoP
My Life's Delight. Thomas Campion. *See* Come, Oh, Come, My Life's Delight.
My Light and My Salvation. Psalms, XXVII, Bible, *O.T.* (*Moulton, Modern Reader's Bible*). MaRV
(Deliverance of Jehovah, The, *Moulton, Modern Reader's Bible.*) WGRP

(Serentiy of Faith, The, 7-14, *tr. by* J. E. McFayden.) BLRP
My Light! My Way! Graf von Zinzendorf, *tr. fr. German by* John Wesley. MaRV
(Plea, A.) SoP
My Light Thou Art. Earl of Rochester. *Fr.* To His Mistress. MeWo; PG
(To His Mistress.) BoLP; LiTL
My Light with Yours. Edgar Lee Masters. NP
My Li'l John Henry, *with music. Unknown.* ABF
My limbs are wasted with a flame. La Bella Donna della Mia Mente. Oscar Wilde. UnTE
My limbs I will fling. Song. William Strode. *Fr.* The Floating Island. CBEP; SeCL
My limbs were weary, and my head oppressed. The Nightingale. *Unknown.* StP
My lips from this day forgot how to smile. Auguste Lacaussade. *Fr.* Les Salaziennes. TTY
My Lips Would Sing. Edmund Leamy. JKCP
My little bed is wide enough. The White Dream. May Doney. HBMV
My Little Bird. Bunyan. *See* Of the Child with the Bird at the Bush.
My Little Birds. *Unknown, tr. fr. Arabic by* Henrietta Siksek-Su'ad. FaPON
My little boy at Christmas-tide. The Toy Cross. Roden Noel. VA
My little boy was not yet four years old. The Journey. Walter de la Mare. InP
My little boy, with pale, round cheeks. The Shadows. George Macdonald. ' TRV
My little breath, under the willows by the water-side we used to sit. A Lover's Lament. *Unknown.* AWP; JAWP; WBP
My Little Brother. Mary Lundie Duncan. OTPC (1923 ed.)
My Little Dear. Dollie Radford. VA
My little dears, who learn to read, pray early learn to shun. Cautionary Verses [to Youth of Both Sexes]. Theodore Hook. BOHV; HBV
My Little Dog. Pearl Forbes MacEwen. BoTP
My little doves have left a nest. My Doves. Elizabeth Barrett Browning. OTPC
My Little Dreams. Georgia Douglas Johnson. BANP; CDC; GoSl; PoNe
My Little Fool. *Unknown.* TuPP
My Little Girl. Samuel Mintern Peck. AA
My Little House. May Byron. OQP
My Little House. J. M. Westrup. BoTP
My little lady I may not leave behind. To My Lady Mirriel Howard. John Skelton. *Fr.* The Garlande of Laurell. LoBV
My Little Lodge. *Unknown, tr. fr. Old Irish by* Fred Norris Robinson. OnYI
My little lord, methinks 'tis strange. A Prognostication on Will Laud, Late Archbishop of Canterbury. *Unknown.* OxBoLi
My Little Love. Charles B. Hawley. HBV
My little love, do you remember. The Chess-Board. "Owen Meredith." HBV; OBVV; VA
My Little Lover. Cécile Sauvage, *tr. fr. French by* Alan Conder. LO
My little Mädchen found one day. A Chrysalis. Mary Emily Bradley. AA; HBV
My little maiden two years old, just able. The Eternal Search. Sir William Watson. PoVP
My little milliner has slipp'd. A Machine Hand. Thomas Ashe. OBVV
My Little Neighbor. Mary Augusta Mason. AA; GFA
My little old man and I fell out. *Unknown.* OxNR
My Little One. Edgar Fawcett. SoP
My little one begins his feet to try. The First Step. Andrew Bice Saxton. AA
My little one, sleep softly. Lullaby. Harriet Monroe. NP
My Little Pony. *Unknown.* SAS
My Little Pretty One, *in mod. Eng. Unknown.* LO, *st.* 1
My Little Sister. *Unknown.* OTPC (1923 ed.)
My little sisters, the birds, much bounden are ye unto God. Sermon to the Birds. St. Francis of Assisi. TreF
My little son, who look'd from thoughtful eyes. The Toys. Coventry Patmore. ACP; AnFE; BeLS; BoC; CAW; CBEP; EnLit; EPN; FaFP; FaPL; GoBC; GTBS; GTBS-W; GTSL; HBV; JKCP; MaRV; MemP; OBEV; OBVV; PG; PoToHe (new ed.); PoVP; SoP; TIHL; TreFS; TrGrPo; TrPWD; TRV; VA; ViBoPo; YT
My little soul I never saw. Little Gray Songs from St. Joseph's, XLVII. Grace Fallow Norton. HBV
My little stone. Letters [*or* Notes] Found near a Suicide. Frank Horne. AmNP; CDC; PoNe
My little white kitten's asleep on my knee. The White Kitten. "Marian Douglas." SAS
My Load. Mary Butterfield. SoP
My load's a little lighter now. Because You Passed My Way. Eleanor Taylor Rhodes. SoP
My locker, green steel. Game Resumed. Richmond Lattimore. NYBP
My Lode-Star. Robert Browning. *Fr.* Pauline. MaRV
My Lodge at Wang-ch'uan after a Long Rain. Wang Wei, *tr. fr. Chinese by* Witter Bynner. LiTW
My lodging it is on the cold ground. Song. Sir William Davenant. *Fr.* The Rivals. PeRV; SeCL
My Log Cabin Home, *with music.* John A. Stone. SGR
My long two-pointed ladder's sticking through a tree. After Apple-picking. Robert Frost. AMP; AmPP (5th ed.); AnAmPo; AnNE; AP; BWP; CaFP; CMoP; CoBMV; DiPo; ForPo; LiTA; MAP; MaPo (1969 ed.); MoAB; MoAmPo; MoPo; MoVE; MWA-2; NP; OxBA; PoAn; ReMP; RoGo; StP; TDP; UnPo; ViBoPo; WoL
My Lord. Martha Snell Nicholson. BePJ; SoP
My Lord All-Pride. Earl of Rochester. PeRV
My Lord and King. Tennyson. *See* In Memoriam A. H. H.: "Love is and was my lord and king."
My Lord came to me once a King. A Ballad of Wonder. Eleanor Slater. MaRV
My Lord Hides Himself. Kabir, *tr. fr. Hindi.* MaRV
My Lord, how full of sweet content. Since God Is There. Mme Guyon, *tr. by* William Cowper. MaRV
My Lord I fain would praise thee well but finde. Meditation. Edward Taylor. *Fr.* Preparatory Meditations, First Series. MeP
My Lord, I have no clothes to come to thee. I Need Thee. George Macdonald. FaChP; MaRV
My Lord, I was accustomed to swill about the sky. The Dove Apologizes to His God for Being Caught by a Cat. Anthony Eaton. PeSA
My lord is all a-glow. Wedding Song. *Unknown. Fr.* Shi King. LiTW
My Lord Knows Best for Me. Eva Gray. SoP
My Lord, my Life, can Envy ever bee. Meditation Thirty-three. Edward Taylor. *Fr.* Preparatory Meditations, First Series. AtBAP; MeP; PoEL-3
My lord said to my lady. Lamkin (K *vers.*). *Unknown.* ESPB
My Lord Says He's Gwineter Rain Down Fire, *with music. Unknown.* BoAN-2
My Lord Tomnoddy. Robert Barnabas Brough. FiBHP; VA
My Lord Tomnoddy got up one day. Hon. Mr. Sucklethumbkin's Story. "Thomas Ingoldsby." *Fr.* The Ingoldsby Legends. OBRV
My Lord Tomnoddy's the son of an Earl. My Lord Tomnoddy. Robert Barnabas Brough. FiBHP; VA
My Lord, What a Mornin', *with music. Unknown.* BoAN-1
My Lord, What a Morning. Waring Cuney. TTY
My Lord, when he went back. Legacy. Ruth Winant Wheeler. ChIP
My lord will soon be here! Home from the Wars. Hsüeh T'ao. OnPM
My Lord would make a cross for me. My Cross. Zitella Cocke. HBV
My Lord's a-Writin' All de Time, *with music. Unknown.* BoAN-1
My Lord's Motoring. Vincent Starrett. CIV
My Lords, my Lord of Warwick. Joan of Arc to the Tribunal. Anthony Frisch. CaP
My Lords, we heard you speak: you told us all. The Third of Februray, 1852. Tennyson. PoFr
My lords, with your leave. A New War Song by Sir Peter Parker. *Unknown.* PAH
My lord's young daughter in the earth finds rest. The Step Mother. Helen Adam. FiSC
My Lost Youth. Longfellow. AA; AmePo; AmPP; AnFE; AnNE; AP; APA; AWP; CLwM; CoAnAm; CoBA; EtS; ExPo; FaBoBe; FaBV; FaFP; GoJo; GTBS-D; GTBS-W; GTSE; HBV; HT; InPo; JAWP; LaNeLa, *abr.*; LiTA; MAmP; MCCG; MWA-1; NePA; OBEV; OTPC; OxBA; PCD; PFY; Po; PoEL-5; PoLF; PoRA; RG; RoGo; SeCeV; StP; TOP; TreF; ViBoPo; WBP

My (continued)
Sea Memories, *sel.* FaPON; MPB
My loud machine for making hay. An Old Field Mowed. William Meredith. NYBP
My Love. E. E. Cummings. ErPo; LiTL; LiTM
My Love. Bartholomew Griffin. *See* Sonnet: "Fair is my love that feeds among the lilies."
My Love. James Russell Lowell. FaBoBe; FaPL; HBV
My love/ Good, the earth gathered us into one garland. Twin Epitaph. Menke Katz. NYTB
My love/ Is like the grasses. Ono no Yoshiki. *Fr.* Kokin Shu. AWP; LiTW
My love and I among the mountains strayed. A Pastoral. J. B. B. Nichols. VA
My love and I for kisses play'd. Kisses. William Strode. NeHB
My love and I, the other day. The Snake. Thomas Moore. HBV
My love and my delight. The Lament for Art O'Leary. Eileen O'Leary. AnIL; KiLC
My Love and My Heart. Henry S. Leigh. BOHV; CIV
My Love behind Walls. Heather Spears. OBCV
My Love Bound Me. *At. to* Thomas Campion. *See* Kisses.
My love came back to me. All Souls' Night. Frances Cornford. Two Poems, II. EnLoPo
My love came up from Barnegat. The [*or* A] Puritan's Ballad. Elinor Wylie. BoLP; HBMV; LiTL; PFY; PoRA; TSW
My love comes down from the mountain. Love on the Mountain. Thomas Boyd. AnIV; BoLP; HBV; OxBI
My love could walk in richer hues. W. H. Davies. LO
My love dwelt in a northern land. Romance. Andrew Lang. HBV; PCD; PTK; VA
My Love Eats an Apple. Ralph Gustafson. MoCV
My love for him shall be. Medieval Norman Songs, XII. *Unknown, tr. by* John Addington Symonds. AWP; JAWP; WBP
My Love for Thee. Richard Watson Gilder. HBV
"My love for you has faded"—thus the Bad. Versions of Love. Roy Fuller. LiTM (1970 ed.); ToPo
My love gave me a king's robe. Wardrobe. Sister Mary Madeleva. GoBC
My love gave me a passion-flower. The Passion-Flower. Margaret Witter Fuller. HBV
My love has built a bonny ship, and set her on the sea. *See* My love he built.
My love has left me has gone from me. Souvenirs. Dudley Randall. Kal
My love has sicklied unto loath. Select Passages from a Coming Poet. "F. Anstey." BOHV
My love has talk'd with rocks and trees. In Memoriam A. H. H., XCVII. Tennyson. EPN; ViPo; VP
My love Hath Vowed He Will Forsake Me. Thomas Campion. EP
(Maid's Complaint, A.) UnTE
My love he [has] built a bonny ship, and set her on the sea. The Lowlands [*or* Lawlands] o' [*or* of] Holland. *Unknown.* CH; OBB
My love, he built me a bonnie [*or* bonny] bower. Lament of the [*or* a] Border Widow [*or* Bonnie Bower]. *Unknown.* BFSS; CH; HBV; LO; OBB; OTPC (1923 ed.); OxBB
My love he was as fine a fellow. The Gallows Tree. *Unknown.* BaBo
My love he went to Burdon Fair. Memories. Alexander Hay Japp. VA
My Love, I Cannot Thy Rare Beauties Place. William Smith. *Fr.* Chloris. InvP
(Sonnet.) EIL
My love I give to you a threefold thing. Branwell's Sestina. James Reaney. *Fr.* A Suit of Nettles. MoCV
My Love in Her Attire. *Unknown.* LiTB; NoP; SiTL
(Beauty's Self.) MeWo; TrGrPo; UnTE
(Madrigal: "My love in her attire doth show her wit.") CLwM; EIL; HBV; LiTG; LiTL; OBEV; OBSC; PG; ReEn; TuPP
("My Love in her attire doth show her wit.") EG; GTBS-P; GTSE; GTSL; ViBoPo
(Poetry of Dress, The, 3.) GTBS; GTBS-D; GTBS-W
My love is a lotus blossom. Love Song. *Unknown.* TTY
My love is a rider and [*or* wild] broncos he breaks. Bucking Bronco. *Unknown.* ABF; CoSo
My Love Is a Tower. C. Day Lewis. AtBAP
My love is as a fever, longing still. Sonnets, CXLVII. Shakespeare. CBEP; DiPo; HoPM; LO; NoP; PoEL-2; ReEn; ReIE
My Love Is Dead. Thomas Chatterton. *See* Minstrel's Song.
My Love Is in a Light Attire. James Joyce. Chamber Music, VII. HW; LOW; StP
My Love Is like a Myrtle. Moses ibn Ezra, *tr. fr. Hebrew by* Solomon Solis-Choen. TrJP
My Love Is like a Red Red Rose. Burns. *See* Red, Red Rose, A.
My Love Is like the Sun. *Unknown.* AnIV
My love is like [*or* lyke] to ice [*or* yse], and I to fire [*or* fyre]. Amoretti, XXX. Spenser. ATP; BoLiVe; CBV; ErPo; LiTB; LiTG; LiTL; PG (1955 ed.); TrGrPo
My love is like unto th' eternal fire. Sir Thomas Wyatt. FCP
My love is male and proper-man. The Contemplative Quarry. Anna Wickham. HBMV; NP
My Love Is neither Young nor Old. *Unknown.* EnRePo; OBSC
My love is o' comely height an' straight. White an' Blue. William Barnes. GTBS-P
My love is of a birth as rare. The Definition of Love. Andrew Marvell. AnAnS-1; AnFE; BoLiVe; BWP; CBEP; DiPo; EP; FaBoEn; ForPo; FosPo; GTBS-W; LiTB; LiTG; LiTL; LoBV; MaMe; MaPo; MeLP; MePo; NoP; OAEP; OBEV (new ed.); PIA; Po; PoE; PoEL-2; PoFS; PoIE; ReEn; SCEP-2; SeCePo; SeCeV; SeCL; SeCP; SeCV-1; SeEP; StP; TreFT; TrGrPo; UnPo; VaPo; WHA
My Love Is Past ("Resolved to dust, entombed here lieth Love"). Thomas Watson. *Fr.* Hecatompathia. TuPP
(Here Lieth Love.) EIL
(Love's Grave.) OBSC
My Love Is Past ("Ye captive souls of blindfold Cyprian's boat"). Thomas Watson. *Fr.* Hecatompathia. ReIE
My Love Is Sleeping. Kenneth Leslie. OBCV
My love is strengthen'd though more weak in seeming. Sonnets, CII. Shakespeare. AWP; CLwM; EIL; LiTG; LiTL; OAEP; OBEV; OBSC; SiCE; TOP; ViBoPo
My love is the flaming Sword. Sunday up the River, XVI. James Thomson. OBVV
My Love is the voice of a song. David McKee Wright. *Fr.* Dark Rosaleen. PoAu-1
My love leads the white bulls to sacrifice. Processional. Alice Archer James. AA
My love lies in the gates of foam. The Churchyard on the Sands. Lord De Tabley. CH; GTBS-D; HBV; LoBV; OBNC
My love lies underground. Hymn to Priapus. D. H. Lawrence. CMoP; CoBMV; MoAB; OBMV
My love looks like a girl to-night. The Bride. D. H. Lawrence. BoPe
My love, my love, thus spoke my love to me. Thus Spoke My Love. Pieter Corneliszoon Hooft. LiTW
My Love o'er the water bends dreaming. Sunday up the River, XII [*or* Reflection]. James Thomson. EnLit; OBEV (1st ed.)
My Love, Oh, She Is My Love. *Tr. fr. Irish by* Douglas Hyde. AnIV
My love on Wednesday letting fall her body. In a Time of Crisis. Lawrence Durrell. LiTM
My love sent me a chicken without e'er a bone. *Unknown.* OxNR
My love she is a gentlewoman. Auld Matrons. *Unknown.* BaBo; ESPB
My Love, She's But a Lassie Yet. Burns. ViBoPo
My Love She's But a Lassie Yet. James Hogg. HBV
(She's But a Lassie Yet.) LiTL
My love sometimes makes her shrill. Our Garden. Philip Dow. QAH
My Love-Song. Else Lasker-Schüler, *tr. fr. German by* Jethro Bithell. TrJP
My love stood by me at the dawn of day. Union of Love. Jami. OnPM
My Love Sways, Dancing. Moses ibn Ezra, *tr. fr. Hebrew by* Emma Lazarus. LiTW
My love, this is the bitterest, that thou. Any Wife to Any Husband. Robert Browning. FaBoEn; OBNC; OtMeF; PoVP
My love to fight the Saxon goes. A Spinning Song. John Francis O'Donnell. IrPN

My love to shew her cold desire. *Unknown.* SeCSL
My Love too Stately is to be but fair. Electra. Francis Howard Williams. AA
My love took scorn my service to retain. Sir Thomas Wyatt. FCP; SiPS
My love was mask'd and armed with a fan. Licia, XXIII. Giles Fletcher. ReIE
My love within a forest walked alone. Love in Moonlight. Bhartrihari. LiTW
"My love, you are timely come, let me lie by your heart." The Door and the Window. Henry Reed. NeBP
My love, you know that I have never used. Unfinished Portrait. Elinor Wylie. CoBA
My loved [*or* lov'd], my honored [*or* honor'd], much-respected friend. The Cotter's Saturday Night. Burns. BEL; BeLS; CEP; EiCL; EiCP; EiPP; EnL; EnLi-2; EnLit; EnRP; FaBoBe; HBV; MCCG; OAEP; OBEC; TOP
My loved one is unique, without a peer. Love Song. *Unknown.* TTY
My lover he is a cowboy. The Jolly Cowboy. *Unknown.* CoSo
My lover is a fool more wise. Riddles. Sister Mary Madeleva. JKCP (1955 ed.)
My lover is but a small man. Fruit. *Unknown.* OnPM
My Loves. John Stuart Blackie. OBVV
My loves as vertuous as yours is when you sware affection. *Unknown.* SeCSL
My Love's Guardian Angel. William Barnes. AtBAP; NBM; PoEL-4
My love's manners in bed. The Way. Robert Creeley. AP; LiTM (1970 ed.); NeAP
My Lucy was charming and fair. The Shepherd's Despair. Thomas Dermody. OnYI
My Lulu. *Unknown. See* Lulu.
My Lute and I. Sir Thomas Wyatt. MeEL
My lute, awake and praise the Lord. A Song of the Lute in the Praise of God and Dispraise of Idolatry. John Hall. ReIE
My lute, awake! perform the last. The Lover Complaineth the Unkindness of His Love [*or* To His Lute]. Sir Thomas Wyatt. AtBAP; BoW; CABA; CaFP; CBEP; CoBE; EG; ElL; ELP; EnL; EnLit; EnPo; EnRePo; FaBoEn; FCP; ILP; MaPo; NoP; OAEP; OBEV; OBSC; PG; PoAn; PoE; PoEL-1; PoFS; QFR; ReEn; ReIE, 2 *vers.*; SiCE; SiPS; StP; TrGrPo; TuPP; ViBoPo
My lute, be as thou wast [*or* wert] when thou didst grow. Sonnet [*or* To His Lute]. William Drummond of Hawthornden. EG; ElL; GTBS; GTBS-D; GTBS-P; GTBS-W; GTSE; GTSL; LoBV; OBS; Sonn; UnS; ViBoPo
My Luve Is Like a Red, Red Rose. *See* Red Red Rose, A.
"My luve she lives in Lincolnshire." Alison and Willie. *Unknown.* BaBo; ESPB
My Luve's in Germany. *Unknown.* CH
My Luve's like a Red, Red Rose. Burns. *See* Red, Red Rose, A.
My Madeline. Walter Parke. BOHV
My Madonna. Robert W. Service. BLPA
My maid Mary,/ She minds her [*or* the] dairy. Mother Goose. OxNR; PCH; PPL; RIS
My maisters all attend you. Turners Dish of Lentten Stuffe; or, A Galymaufery. William Turner. CoMu
My Maker shunneth me. Spiritual Isolation. Isaac Rosenberg. TrJP
My Mall, I mark that when you mean to prove me. The Author to His Wife, of a Woman's Eloquence. Sir John Harington. ErPo
My Mammy Was a Wall-eyed Goat. *Unknown.* ChTr
My mammy's in the cold, cold ground. Po' Boy. *Unknown.* AS
My man is a bone ringèd with weed. First Woman's Lament [*or* Lament]. Brenda Chamberlain. NeBP; NeIP
My Man John, *with music. Unknown.* SaSa
My man Thomas. John Fletcher. EnLoPo
My Man Was Here Today. Ruby C. Saunders. WSL
My Many-Coated Man. Laurie Lee. NYBP; POTi
My Mary. William Cowper. *See* To Mary.
My Maryland. James Ryder Randall. AA; AnAmPo; APA; CoBA; FaBoBe; FaFP; HBV; JKCP; MC; PaA; PAH; PoFr; TreF
(Maryland, My Maryland.) PoRL
My Master. Harry Lee. *See* My Master Was So Very Poor.
My Master and I. *Unknown.* CoMu
My master bade me watch the flock by night. The Shepherd Who Stayed. Theodosia Garrison. OHIP
My master Bukton, when of Christ our king. Counsel upon Marriage. Chaucer. PoLi
My Master Hath a Garden. *Unknown.* AtBAP; CH; GBV (1952 ed.)
My Master was a man who knew. The Outdoor Son of God. William L. Stidger. ChIP
My Master was a worker. The Master's Man. William G. Tarrant. MaRV; OQP
My Master Was So Very Poor. Harry Lee. TRV
(My Master.) ChIP; MaRV
My Master's Face. William Hurd Hillyer. ChIP; MaRV; SoP
My masters, I thank you, it's time to pack home. Thomas Deloney. *Fr.* Jack of Newbury. ReIE
My masters twain made me a bed. The Canoe. Isabella Valancy Crawford. OBCV; OnYI; VA
My Mate Bill. G. H. Gibson. PoAu-1
My meaning is to work what woundes love hath wrought. Of the Mighty Power of Love. Edward de Vere, Earl of Oxford. TuPP
My memory of Heaven awakes. Coventry Patmore. *Fr.* The Angel in the House. EG
My Midnight Meditation. *At. to* Henry King, *also to* John King. MePo; OBS; SeCL
My milk-white doo', said the young man. The Young Man and the Young Nun. A. D. Mackie. OxBS
My mill grinds pepper and spice. *Unknown.* OxNR
My Mind and I. Hilda Conkling. NP
My mind has thunderstorms. Thunderstorms. W. H. Davies. HBV; POTE; TSW
My mind i th' mines of rich philosophy. On My Lord Bacon. John Danforth. SCAP
My mind is like a clamorous market place. The Market Place. Walter de la Mare. Sonn
My mind is sad and weary thinking how. Odell. James Stephens. MoAB; MoBrPo
My Mind Keeps Out the Host of Sin. Edmund Elys. NCEP
My mind lets go a thousand things. Memory. Thomas Bailey Aldrich. AA; AmLP; AnFE; AnNE; APA; BoNaP; CoAnAm; MAP; MCCG; NeHB; OQP; PoLF; PoMa; PTK; TreFS
My mind slips back to lesser men. After the Record Is Broken. James A. Emanuel. NYTB
My Mind to Me a Kingdom Is. Sir Edward Dyer. BEL; CoBE; ElL; EnLi-1; EnLit; EnRePo; FaBoBe; HBV; LiTB; LiTG; MaRV, 3 *sts.*; MCCG; NeHB; OuHeWo; PG, *sl. abr.*; PoE; PoFS; PoIE; PoSa; ReEn; SiCE; TreFS; TrGrPo; TuPP; ViBoPo; WGRP
(Contentment, *abr.*) OTPC
(Kingdom.) LoBV; OBSC
(My Mynde to Me a Kyngdome Is.) AtBAP; PoEL-1
My mind was once the true survey. The Mower's Song. Andrew Marvell. AnAnS-1; BWP; CavP; CBV; EnL; LiTL; LoBV; MaMe; NoP; PAn; PoEL-2; ReEn; SCEP-2; SeCL; SeCP; SeCV-1
My Mirror. Aline Kilmer. AnAmPo; NP
My Mistress. Richard Brathwaite. *Fr.* The English Gentlewoman. SeCL
My Mistress. Thomas Lodge. *See* My Mistress When She Goes.
My Mistress. William Warner. ElL
My mistress' eyes are nothing like the sun. Sonnets, CXXX. Shakespeare. ATP; AWP; BEL; BoLP; CABA; CaFP; CBEP; CBV; DiPo; EnL; EnLi-1 (1949 ed.); EnLit; ExPo; HBV; HoPM; ILP; InvP; JAWP; LiTB; LiTL; MaPo (1969 ed.); NoP; OAEP; OtMeF; PAn; PIA; PoAn; PoE; PoeP; PoIE; PP; ReEn; ReIE; SeCeV; SiCE; Sonn; StP; TOP; WBP
My mistress frowns when she should play. Fa La La [*or* Madrigal]. *At. to* John Hilton. CH; OxBoLi; SiTL
My mistress is a paragon. My Mistress. William Warner. ElL
My mistress is as fair as fine. Madrigals, 6. *At. to* Thomas Ravenscroft. CH; OxBoLi; SiTL
My mistress is in music passing skillful. My Mistress Makes Music. *Unknown.* UnTE
My mistress loves noe woodcokes. *Unknown.* SeCSL
My mistress lowers and saith I do not love. Sir Philip Sidney. FCP

My Mistress Makes Music. *Unknown.* UnTE
My mistress When She Goes. Thomas Lodge. *Fr.* The Life and Death of William Longbeard. EG; SiCE; TuPP
(Her Rambling.) LoBV; OBSC
(My Mistress.) TrGrPo
My Mistress's Boots. Frederick Locker-Lampson. BOHV; HBV; InP; TOP
My misunderstandings: for years I thought "muso bello" meant "Bell Muse." Taking a Walk with You. Kenneth Koch. AmPC; ANYP
My mither's ay glowran o'er me. Katy's Answer. Allan Ramsay. CEP; EiPP
My moods are as a sailboat coming through. To Mary, of Sailing. Richard Snyder. NYTB
My Moon. Gordon Bottomley. *Fr.* Night and Morning Songs. NP
My Morning Song. George Macdonald. TRV
My mortal love's a rabbit skin. Apology. Vassar Miller. NePoEA
My Most. My Most. O My Lost! José Garcia Villa. Divine Poems, 57. BoW; POTE (1959 ed.)
My Mother. Amelia Josephine Burr. DD; HBMV
My Mother. Josephine Rice Creelman. DD; OHIP
My Mother. J. F. Cuthriell. SoP
My Mother. Francis Ledwidge. HBMV; OHIP
My Mother. Claude McKay. AnEnPo
My Mother. Robert Mezey. NaP
My Mother. Bertha Nolan. PGD
My Mother. William Bell Scott. VA
My Mother. Ann Taylor. BLPA, *abr.*; DD, *much abr.*; MaRV, *abr.*; OHIP; PaPo; PEDC; TreF, *sl. abr.*
My Mother ("She carried me under her heart"). *Unknown.* SoP
My Mother ("They say the most of mothers"). *Unknown.* STF
My Mother. Samuel N. Wilson. PEDC
My mother and. Eulogy. Carolyn M. Rodgers. WSL
My mother and your mother. *Unknown.* OxNR; SAS
My Mother Bids Me Bind My Hair. Anne Hunter. CBEP; HBV; OBEC
My mother bore me. Foolish Child. *Unknown.* PBA
My mother bore me in an island town. Sea Born. Harold Vinal. HBMV
My mother bore me in the southern wild. The Little Black Boy. Blake. *Fr.* Songs of Innocence. AnFE; AtBAP; AWP; BEL; BoC; CABA; CaFP; CBEP; CBV; CEP; TreFS; DiPo; EiPP; EnL; EnLi-2; EnLit; EnPE; EnRP; ERoP-1; ForPo; HBV; ILP; InPo; LoGBV; MyFE; NoP; OAEP; OBEC; OBEV; OBNC; OxBoCh; PAn; PoEL-4; PoeP; PoFr; PoIE; PoNe; SeCeV; TDP; TOP; TreFS; TrGrPo
My mother called me to her deathbed side, these words she said to me. Coon Can. *Unknown.* AS
My mother groaned! my father wept. Infant Sorrow. Blake. *Fr.* Songs of Experience. BoLiVe; BWP; CBEP; DiPo; EiCL; EiPP; EnL; FaBoEn; MaPo (1969 ed.); OBNC; PeER; PoEL-4; PoeP; PoFS
My mother has the prettiest tricks. Song for My Mother: Her Words. Anna Hempstead Branch. *Fr.* Songs for My Mother. BoChLi; FaPON; HH; OHIP; OnPP; SiSoSe; TiPo (1959 ed); YeAr; YT
My mother is looking down on my small brother. Dusk. Leonard E. Nathan. NYTB
My mother, living by the sea. First Aid. Peter Hopegood. NeLNL
My mother made me a cambric shirt. The Cambric Shirt (B *vers.*). *Unknown.* BFSS
My Mother Once Told Me. Yehuda Amichai, *tr. fr. Hebrew by* Assia Gutmann. NYBP
My mother plays an Oud. Poem: a Piece. James T. Stewart. BF
My mother—preferring the strange to the tame. The Intruder. Carolyn Kizer. FRC; NePoEA-2
My mother said that I never should. Gypsies in the Wood. *Unknown.* BoTP; DTC; FaBoCh; LoGBV; OxBoLi; OxNR; SiTL
My mother said to me. Admonitions. Margaret Bell Houston. MoSiPe
My mother says I must not pass. The Witch in the Glass. Sarah Morgan Bryan Piatt. AA
My mother sends our neighbors things. Neighborly. Violet Alleyn Storey. GaP; TiPo
My mother she's so good to me. A Boy's Mother. James Whitcomb Riley. DD; HBVY; HH; OHIP; OTPC; PoRL; PPL
My mother taught me. The Milky Way. Allen Upward. *Fr.* Scented Leaves from a Chinese Jar. NP
My mother taught me purple. Taught Me Purple. Evelyn Tooley Hunt. OCS
My mother taught me to be good. Poem for Mother's Day. Margaret Fishback. InMe
My mother twines me roses wet with dew. The Child's Quest. Frances Shaw. NP
My Mother Was a Lady; or, If Jack Were Only Here. Edward B. Marks. TreF; YaD
My mother was a singing wind I never knew. The Christmas Tree. Mary E. Wilkins Freeman. PEDC
"My mother was an ill woman." The Laird of Wariston (B *vers.*) [*or* The Death of Lord Warriston]. *Unknown.* BaBo; OxBB
My mother, when young, scrubbed laundry in a tub. In an Iridescent Time. Ruth Stone. MoAmPo (1962 ed.); PoPl; TwAmPo
My mother whistled softly. The Little Whistler. Frances Frost. PDV; SoPo; StVeCh (1955 ed.); TiPo
My mother, who has a hide. The Hide of My Mother. Edward Dorn. NeAP
My Mother Would Be a Falconress. Robert Duncan. NoP
My mother writes from Trenton. My Mother. Robert Mezey. NaP
My Mother's Bible. George Pope Morris. AA; BLRP; PaPo; SoP; WBLP
My mother's form was spare and keen. Generations. Robert Clark. PoAu-2
My Mother's Garden. Alice E. Allen. BLPA; FaBoBe; NeHB
My Mother's Hands. Anna Hempstead Branch. *See* Her Hands.
My Mother's Hands. *Unknown.* TreFS
My mother's hands are cool and fair. Songs [*or* A Song] for My Mother: Her Hands. Anna Hempstead Branch. DD; HH; MPB; OHIP; OnPP; PoRL; RG; YT
My Mother's House. Eunice Tietjens. HBMV; NP
My mother's lamp once out. Scenes of Childhood. James Merrill. CoAP
My Mother's Love. *Unknown.* *See* Mother's Love.
My mother's maids when they do sew and spin. Of the Mean and Sure Estate. Sir Thomas Wyatt. Satires, II. BEL; FCP; OA; ReIE; SiCE; SiPS; TuPP
My mother's name was Mary, she was so good and true. Mary's a Grand Old Name. George M. Cohan. TreFT
My Mother's Prayer. T. C. O'Kane. BLPA; FaBoBe
My Mother's Table. Hy Sobiloff. NePA; TwAmPo
My mouth doth water, and my breast doth swell. Astrophel and Stella, XXXVII. Sir Philip Sidney. FCP; ReEn; ReIE; SiPS; Sonn; TuPP
My Mouth Is Very Quiet. José Garcia Villa. AnFE; CoAnAm; TwAmPo
My muscles unravel. Why I Will Not Get Out of Bed. James Tate. YAP
My Muse. Stevie Smith. ML
My Muse and I, Ere Yough and Spirits Fled. George Colman, the Younger. ELU
My muse, by thee restor'd to life. An Altar and Sacrifice to Disdain for Freeing Him from Love. *Unknown.* ReIE; SiCE
My muse may well grudge at my heavenly joy. Astrophel and Stella, LXX. Sir Philip Sidney. FCP; ReEn; SiPS
My Muse sits forlorn. My Muse. Stevie Smith. ML
My muse, though airy, glides softly along. The Song of the Pen. Judah Al-Harizi. TrJP
My Muse will now by chymistry draw forth. To the Learned and Reverend Mr Cotton Mather, on His Excellent Magnalia. Grindall Rawson. SCAP
My music-loving self this afternoon. Sheldonian Soliloquy. Siegfried Sassoon. UnS
My Mynde to Me a Kingdome Is. Sir Edward Dyer. *See* My Mind to Me a Kingdom Is.
My Naked Aunt. Archibald MacLeish. NePA
My naked simple life was I. My Spirit. Thomas Traherne. SCEP-1; SeCV-2
My Name and I. Robert Graves. NYBP
My name engraved herein. A Valediction: Of My Name in the Window. John Donne. EnRePo; MaMe; MBW-1; QFR; SCEP-1

My Name in Mother's Prayer. *Unknown.* SoP
My name is Bill. Bill. J. S. Salzburg. BiCB
My name is Colin Clout. The Prelates. John Skelton. *Fr.* Colyn Cloute. TrGrPo
My name is Darino, the poet. You have heard? The Hell-Gate of Soissons. Herbert Kaufman. GSP
My name is Ebenezer Brown. Epigram. J. V. Cunningham. PIA
My name is Edgar Poe and I was born. On the Edge. Philip Levine. CoAP
My name is Edward Hollander [*or* Gilbert Howelding *or* Henry Hollinder], as you may understand. The *Flying Cloud.* *Unknown.* ABF; BaBo; IHA; ShS (*vers.* II); SoAmSa; ViBoFo
My name is Frank Bolar, lone [*or* 'nole] bachelor [*or* bach'lor] I am. The Lane County Bachelor [*or* Starving to Death on a Government Claim]. *Unknown.* AS; IHA
My name is Jack Shepherd; I come from Nashville town. The State of Arkansas. *Unknown.* BFSS
My name is James A. Wright, and I was born. At the Executed Murderer's Grave. James Wright. AmPC
My name is Jew. The Permanent Delegate. Yuri Suhl. PPON; WOW
My name is Joe Bowers. *See* My name it is Joe Bowers.
My Name Is John Wellington Wells. W. S. Gilbert. *Fr.* The Sorcerer. PoMS
My name is Juan Murray, and sad for my fate. Juan Murray. *Unknown.* CoSo
My name is Larry Gorman, to you I mean no harm. The Scow on Cowden Shore, *vers.* I. Larry Gorman. ShS
My Name Is Legion. Edward Sandford Martin. MaRV (Which Is Me?) OQP
My name is Mr. Worth. Crinolines and Bloomers. *Unknown.* ThLM
My name is Nell, right candid I tell. *See* My name it is Nell . . .
My name is O'Kelly, I've heard the Revelly. Shillin' a Day. Kipling. OAEP (2d ed.); ViBoPo
My name is old Jack Palmer. The Old Keg of Rum. *Unknown.* PoAu-1
My name is Parrot, a bird of paradise. Parrot's Soliloquy [*or* The Parrot]. John Skelton. *Fr.* Speak, Parrot. ACP; OxBoLi; PoEL-1
My name is Peter Emberly [*or* Embley]. Peter Emberley (*diff. versions*). John Calhoun. ShS
My name is Sam, an' I don't give a damn. A Cowboy Dance Song. *Unknown.* CoSo
My name is Stanford Barnes. The State of Arkansas. *Unknown.* CoSo; TrAS
My name is William Edwards, I live down Cove Creek way. The T.V.A. *Unknown.* TrAS
My name it is Bill Stafford; I was born in Buffalo town. The Arkansaw Traveler. *Unknown.* ViBoFo
My name it is Donald Macdonald. Donald Macdonald. James Hogg. PoFr
My name it is [*or* is] Joe Bowers. Joe Bowers. *Unknown.* ABF; ATP; BaBo; BFSS; CoSo; SGR; TrAS; TreFS; ViBoFo
My name it is [*or* is] Nell, right [*or* quite] candid I tell. Nell Flaherty's Drake. *Unknown.* AnIV; OA; OnYI
My name, my country—what are they to thee? No Matter. Paulus Silentiarius. AWP; EnLi-1; JAWP; OuHeWo; WBP
My name was Amaryllis. I. On Amaryllis, a Tortoyse. Marjorie Pickthall. PeCV (1967 ed.)
My Name Was Legion. Hildegarde Hoyt Swift. AmFN
My name was William Kidd, when I sailed, when I sailed. The Ballad of Captain Kidd. *Unknown.* AmSS
My name's Mister Benjamin Bunny. Limerick. Frederic Edward Weatherly. CenHV
My namesake, Little Boots, Caligula. Caligula. Robert Lowell. CoPo
My Nanie, O. Burns. EnLi-2 (1949 ed.)
(Song: My Nanie, O.) EnLi-2 (1939 ed.)
My Nannie's Awa'. Burns. GN; HBV; OTPC (1923 ed.)
My native country then, which so brave spirits hast bred. The Forest of Arden. Michael Drayton. *Fr.* Polyolbion: The Thirteenth Song. SeEP
My Native Land. Sir Walter Scott. *See* Breathes There the Man.
My Native Land, thy Puritanic stock. The Rejected "National Hymns," II. "Orpheus C. Kerr." BOHV; InMe
My Nebraska. Theodore C. Diers. PoRL
My Need. Grace E. Troy. SoP
My Need. *Unknown.* STF
My Needle Says. Hazel Hall. NP
My Neighbor. E. A. Repass. SoP
My neighbor Hunk's house and mine. Near Neighbors. Swift, *after* Martial. AWP
My neighbor lives on the hill. Differences. Paul Laurence Dunbar. TreFS
My neighbor moves less and less, attempts less. Dark Women. Ted Hughes. ToPo
My neighbor, who is he? My Neighbor. E. A. Repass. SoP
My neighbor's books sit primly in a row. Books. Florence Van Cleve. HH
My Neighbor's Reply. *Unknown.* PoToHe
My Neighbor's Roses. Abraham L. Gruber. BLPA; NeHB; OQP; PoToHe
My neighbor's willow sways its frail. The Willow. Tu Fu. NaP
My net/ Is heavy with weed. The Disappointed Shrimper. P. A. Ropes. BoTP
My New-cut Ashlar. Kipling. *See* Dedication, A: "My new-cut ashlar. . ."
My New Rabbit. Elizabeth Gould. BoTP
My New Umbrella. M. M. Hutchinson. BoTP
My New World. Irving Browne. AA
My New Year Prayer. *Unknown.* STF
My noble, lovely, little Peggy. A Letter to the Honorable Lady Miss Margaret-Cavendish-Holles-Harley [*or* To a Child of Noble Birth]. Matthew Prior. CEP; EiCP; LoBV; OBEC; OBEV; OTPC (1923 ed.); PRWS; SeCePo
My November Guest. Robert Frost. AnFE; APA; BoLiVe; CLwM; CoAnAm; HBMV; MoVE; NP; OxBA; PoLF; TwAmPo; ViBoPo
My Object All Sublime. W. S. Gilbert. *See* Humane Mikado, The.
My occupation is river man, as you may well know. Jack Haggerty. Dan McGinnis. ShS
My ocean-soul was free, without mistrust. The Last Boats. Endre Ady. LiTW
My Offering. Edwin P. Parker. SoP
My Old Beaver Cap, *with music.* *Unknown.* BFSS
My Old Bible. *Unknown.* BLRP; SoP; STF
My Old Black Billy. Edward Harrington. PoAu-1
My old companion! and my friend. To My Worthy Friend Mr. James Bayley. Nicholas Noyes. SCAP
My Old Counselor. Gertrude Hall. AA
My Old Hammah, *with music.* *Unknown.* AS
(Rocks in de Mountens, *diff. vers., with music.*) SoAmSa
My Old Kentucky Home. Stephen Collins Foster. AnAmPo; AnFE; APA; CoAnAm; FaBoBe; FaBV; FaFP; FaPL; HBV; OTPC; PoLF; PoRL; StaSt; TrAS, *with music;* TreF; TrGrPo
(My Old Kentucky Home, Good-Night.) AA
My old love for the water has come back again. Sea Call. Margaret Widdemer. TSW
My old man's a white old man. Cross. Langston Hughes. AmNP; AnAmPo; BANP; IDB; LiTM (1970 ed.); PoLF; PoNe
My old mule. Me and the Mule. Langston Hughes. IDB
My Old True Love, *with music.* *Unknown.* OuSiCo
My oldest friend, mine from the hour. Guardian Angel. Cardinal Newman. GoBC
My ole massa promised me. Shine On. Luke Schoolcraft. TrAS
My once dear love; hapless that I no more. The Surrender. Henry King. AnAnS-2; LO; MePo; TrGrPo
My onely Lord, when with no muddy sight. Let Him Kiss Me with the Kisses of His Mouth. Edward Taylor. *Fr.* Preparatory Meditations, Second Series. MWA-1
My only love is always near. Unrealized Ideal. Frederick Locker-Lampson. TSW
My only need—you ask me, and I tell you. Sonnet XXXIII. Mark Van Doren. MoLP
My Only Plea. Walter J. Kuhn. SoP
My only son, more God's than mine. Jesus and His Mother. Thom Gunn. CaFP; EaLo
My Only Star. Francis Davison. ElL
My Opinion. Charles Sackville. PeRV
My Orders. Ethelwyn Wetherald. MaRV
My Other Chinee Cook. Brunton Stephens. PoAu-1
My Other Me. Grace Denio Litchfield. AA; HBV
My Owen. Ellen Mary Patrick Downing. HBV

My own! The Jester and His Daughter. Tom Taylor. *Fr.* The Fool's Revenge. VA
My Own Cáilin Donn. George Sigerson. FaBoBe; HBV
My own dear love, he is strong and bold. Love Song. Dorothy Parker. InMe; NeMA
My own dim life should teach me this. In Memoriam A. H. H., XXXIV. Tennyson. CoBE; EnL; EPN; FosPo; MaPo; MaRV; OQP; SeCePo; ViPo; VP
My Own Epitaph. John Gay. CBV; EiCL; SeCePo; SeCeV; TOP; TreFT
(Epigram: "Life is a jest. . .") ALV; HBV
(Epitaph: "Life is a jest . . .") InP
(His Epitaph.) OnPM
(His Own Epitaph.) ViBoPo
My Own Heart Let Me More Have Pity On. Gerard Manley Hopkins. BoC; BrPo; CoBMV; FaBoMo; LiTM; MoAB; MoBrPo (1950 ed.); NoP; PoDB; Sonn; ViPP; VP
My Own Hereafter. Eugene Lee-Hamilton. WGRP
My own in a foreign land. The Jewish Conscript. Florence Kiper Frank. TrJP
My Own, My Native Land. Sir Walter Scott. *See* Breathes There the Man.
My Own Shall Come to Me. John Burroughs. *See* Waiting.
My Own Simplified Spelling. E. V. Knox. SiTL
My Pa held me up to the moo-cow-moo. The Moo-Cow-Moo. Edmund Vance Cooke. FaFP; MoShBr; PTK
My Pa says that he used to be. Forgetful Pa. Edgar A. Guest. IHA; PoRL
My Papa's Waltz. Theodore Roethke. AmP; CaFP; CBV; CrMA; FlW; HoPM; ILP; LiTM (1970 ed.); MiAP; MoAB; NoP; PoeP; PoIE; PoSa; TDP
My Parents Kept Me from Children Who Were Rough. Stephen Spender. FlW; MoPW; OAEP (2d ed.); OTD
My parents raised me tenderly; they had no child but me. The Maid I Left Behind. *Unknown.* ShS
"My parents taught me well, as I sailed, as I sailed." Captain Kidd. *Unknown.* IHA
My parents think they can separate me. The Parted Lovers. *Unknown.* WOW
My Paris is a land where twilight days. Paris. Arthur Symons. SyP
My part is not to choose the way. My Lord Knows Best for Me. Eva Gray. SoP
My Party. Queenie Scott-Hopper. BoTP
My passion is as mustard strong. A New Song of New Similes. John Gay. BOHV; InMe; SiTL
My Past Has Gone to Bed. Siegfried Sassoon. AtBAP
My "Patch of Blue." Mary Newland Carson. BLPA; NeHB
My path lay towards the Mourne again. The Saw-Mill. James Clarence Mangan. PeER
My path lies in obscurity. The Guide. Dawn Finlay. SoP
My pathway lies through worse than death. Conquest. Georgia Douglas Johnson. AmNP
My patron saint, St. Valentine. Valentine Verses. Thomas Nelson Page. DD
My Peace I Give unto You. St. John, XIV: 1-31, Bible, *N.T.* WoL
(Peace of Christ, The, XIV: 1-27.) TreFS
My Peace I Give unto You. G. A. Studdert-Kennedy. MaRV
(Blessed Are the Eyes That See.) SoP
My peace is broken, my white gentle sleep. The April Earth. Max Eastman. AnEnPo
"My Peace," the peace of the Lord Most High. Peace. Margaret E. Sangster. TRV
My Peggy [Is a Young Thing]. Allan Ramsay. *Fr.* The Gentle Shepherd. CoBE; EiCL; GN, *abr.*; HBV; OTPC (1923 ed.), *abr.*; OxBS
(Peggy.) OBEV; ViBoPo
(Sang: "My Peggy is a young thing.") CEP; EiPP; LoBV; OBEC
My pen, obey my will a while. A Ditty of the Pen Inveighing against Usury and False Dealing. John Hall. ReIE
My Pen, Take Pain [a Little Space]. Sir Thomas Wyatt. CBEP; EP; FCP; PP; SiPS
(To His Pen.) OBSC
My Penguin Playmate. Donald E. Cooke. MPB (1956 ed.)
My pensioners who daily. Pensioners. Winifred M. Letts. BoTP
My pensive Sara! thy soft cheek reclined. The Eolian Harp. Samuel Taylor Coleridge. EnRP; ERoP-1; MBW-2; MERP; NoP
My People. Doug Palmer. ThO
My people, hearken, 'tis the drum. Dare to Be Free. Georg Herwegh. PoFr
My people, what have I done to thee? The Reproaches. *Unknown.* WHL
My people? Who are they? Who Are My People? Rosa Zagnoni Marinoni. BLPA; PoToHe
My period had come for prayer. Emily Dickinson. EaLo; PoIE
My Phyllis [*or* Phillis] hath the morning sun. Phyllis, XV. Thomas Lodge. ACP; EIL; LoBV; OBEV; OBSC; SiCE; TuPP; ViBoPo
My Picture Left in Scotland. Ben Jonson. AnAnS-2; EnRePo; ForPo; LiTL; MePo; PIA; PoEL-2; QFR; SeCP; SeCV-1
My pictures blacken in their frames. Death of the Day. Walter Savage Landor. NoP
My pig-faced kingdom with tongues of wrong. Secular Elegies. George Barker. ToPo
My Pilgrimage. Sir Walter Ralegh. *See* Passionate Man's Pilgrimage, The.
My Pilot. Washington Gladden. OQP
My Pipe. Christopher Morley. LHV
My pipe is lit, my grog is mixed. The Bachelor's Dream. Thomas Hood. BOHV
My pipe is old. My Pipe. Christopher Morley. LHV
My plaid awa [*or* away], my plaid awa. The Elfin Knight. *Unknown.* BaBo (A *vers.*); BuBa; CH; ViBoFo (A *vers.*)
My Plan. Marchette Chute. BiCB; BrR; FaPON
My Playmate. Mary I. Osborn. BoTP
My Playmate. Whittier. AnFE; AP; APA; CoAnAm; CoBA; HBV; OBVV; PCD; PG (1945 ed.)
My Poem. Nikki Giovanni. BOLo; TNV
My Poet, thou canst touch on all the notes. Sonnets from the Portuguese, XVII. Elizabeth Barrett Browning. HBV; WHA
My Poetry. Kotaro Takamura, *tr. fr. Japanese by* Takamichi Ninomiya *and* D. J. Enright. PoLJ
My Policeman. Rose Fyleman. BoChLi; SoPo; TiPo
My Political Faith. George Frederick Cameron. PeCV
My Pompous Friend. Lawrence Emerson Nelson. PoMa
My Pony. "A." GFA; PRWS
My poor old bones—I've only two. The Lonely Scarecrow. James Kirkup. PDV
My poplars are like ladies trim. The Poplars. Theodosia Garrison. HBMV; OHIP; PoRL; StVeCh
My Portrait. Moishe-Leib Halpern, *tr. fr. Yiddish by* Joseph Leftwich. TrJP
My potter's busy wheel is where. In Any Office. Amy Carmichael. FaChP
My Prairies. Hamlin Garland. FaPON
My Prayer. Horatius Bonar. BLRP
My Prayer. Loraine Burdick. SoP
My Prayer. Lucy Carruth. SoP
My Prayer. Annie Johnson Flint. SoP
My Prayer. John Newton. *See* Prayer Answered by Crosses.
My Prayer. Mark Guy Pearse. OQP; SoP
My Prayer. Flora Emily Smith. SoP
My Prayer. Henry David Thoreau. DD; HBV; HBVY; OQP; PoPl
(Great God, I Ask Thee for No Meaner Pelf.) AP; MAmP; TrPWD
(Prayer: "Great God, I ask thee for no meaner pelf.") AmePo; AnNE; MaRV, *abr.*
My Prayer ("Lord Jesus, make Thyself to me"). *Unknown.* BePJ; BLRP; SoP
My Prayer ("My life must touch a million lives"). *Unknown.* BLRP
My precious life I spent considering. Take the Crust. Sadi. *Fr.* The Gulistan. AWP
My presence shall go with thee. Unafraid. E. Margaret Clarkson. SoP
My Presence Shall Go with Thee. H. Isabel Graham. SoP
My pretty cat to my heart I hold. My Cat. Baudelaire. CIV
My Pretty Little Miss, *with music.* *Unknown.* BFSS
My Pretty Little Pink, *with music.* *Unknown.* AS
My Pretty Rose Tree. Blake. *Fr.* Songs of Experience. PoeP
My pride should effect your escape. Pride. Josephine Miles. FiMAP
My prime of youth is but a frost of cares. Elegy [*or* On the Eve

of His Execution *or* Written on the Eve of Execution]. Chidiock Tichborne. ACP; AnFE; CBEP; ChTr; CoBE; EG; ElL; ForPo; FosPo; GoBC; GTBS-W; HBV; LiTB; LiTG; LoBV; NoP; OBSC; PG (1955 ed.); PoIE; PoSa; PoFS; ReEn; TreFT; TrGrPo; TuPP; ViBoPo
My process had regressed, in the last couple of. Be Natural, Baby. Ruby C. Saunders. WSL
My prow is tending toward the west. My New World. Irving Browne. AA
My puppy likes. Puppy. Aileen Fisher. SoPo
My Puritan Grandmother! — I see her now. Sea Lavender. Louise Morey Bowman. CaP
My Queen. *Unknown.* HBV
My Queen. William Winter. AA
My quiet kin, must I affront you. Preliminary to Classroom Lecture. Josephine Miles. FiMAP
My quietness has a man in it, he is transparent. In Memory of My Feelings. Frank O'Hara. NeAP
My quill is charged with fire. Song of Hate. Jacob ben David Frances. TrJP
My Radcliffe, when thy reckless youth offends. *See* My Ratclif, when thy reckless. . .
My Radio. Gertrude Van Winkle. GFA
My Ramboling Son. *Unknown. See* Lord Randal.
My Ratclif [*or* Ratcliffe *or* Radcliffe], when thy reckless youth offends. Exhortation to Learn by Others' Trouble. Earl of Surrey. FCP; SiCE; SiPS; TuPP
My ravist spreit in that desart terribill. Nightmare. Gawin Douglas. *Fr.* The Palace of Honor. PoEL-1
My Recollectest Thoughts. Charles Edward Carryl. *Fr.* Davy and the Goblin, *ch.* 7. HBV; HBVY; NA
My Record ends: But hark! e'en now I hear. George Crabbe. *Fr.* The Parish Register. OBRV
My red engine goes chuff-chuff-choo! chuff-chuff-choo! My Toys. Lilian McCrea. BoTP
My red horse has his stable. My Horses. Jean Jaszi. SoPo
My Redeemer and my Lord. A Prayer. Longfellow. SoP
My Rendezvous with God. Anne M. Waite. SoP
My Risen Lord. *Unknown.* OQP; SoP
My Rival. Kipling. OnPP
My Road. Oliver Opdyke. HBV
My road is fenced with the bleached, white bones. Drought. Will H. Ogilvie. BoAu
My roads stretch out. Marshal Lyautey. R. N. Currey. BoSA
My robe is noiseless when I roam the earth. A Swan. *Unknown.* OuHeWo
My roof is hardly picturesque. An Autumn Flitting. George Cotterell. VA
My Room. Gelett Burgess. *See* I Wish That My Room Had a Floor.
My room as usual a disorder of books. Crisis. G. S. Fraser. NeBP
My room in Florence was the color of air. Above the Arno. May Swenson. NYBP
My room's a square and candle-lighted boat. The Country Bedroom. Frances Cornford. MemP; MoBrPo
My Rose. Hildegarde Hawthorne. AA
My rug is red. My couch, whereon I deal. The Map. G. C. Oden. AmNP; NNP; PoNe (1970 ed.)
My Sabine Farm. Eugene Field. InMe
My sacrament of wine and broken bread. On a Cold Day. W. H. Davies. BoPe
My sad bad rain that falls. Rain Song. Jean Garrigue. NYTB
My Sad Captains. Thom Gunn. LiTM (1970 ed.); NePoEA-2; PoCh; ToPo
My sad great Piers that met a small field flower. The Plowman. Max Harris. BoAV
My Sailor of Seven. Gerald Brenan. BiCB
My salamander in a world of flame. Cherry Tree. Sacheverell Sitwell. AtBAP
My sange es in sihting. A Song of Love for Jesus. Richard Rolle of Hampole. MeEL
My saull and lyfe, stand up and see. Ane Sang of the Birth of Christ. John Wedderburn, *after* Martin Luther. ChTr
My Saviour. Dora Greenwell. SoP
My Saviour. Mary Hallet. ChIP
My Saviour's Face. *Unknown.* SoP
My Saviour's Love for Me. William C. Fisher. SoP
My Saxon shrine! the only ground. Morwennae Statio. Robert Stephen Hawker. GoBC
My Secret. John Banister Tabb. WaKn
My secrets cry aloud. Open House. Theodore Roethke. AP; CoBMV; NoP; PoeP
My Sense of Sight. Oliver Herford. HBMV; HBVY
My seven sons came back from Indonesia. Peter Viereck. CoAP
My sexual feats. Fred Apollus at Fava's. Nicholas Moore. ErPo; NeBP
My Shadow. Robert Louis Stevenson. FaBoBe; FaBV; FaPON; GFA; HBV; HBVY; LiTG; MPB; NeHB; OTD; OTPC; PCH; PDV; PoVP; RIS; SoPo; StVeCh; TiPo; TreF
My shag-hair Cyclops, come let's ply. The Song in Making of the Arrows [*or* Vulcan's Song]. John Lyly. *Fr.* Sapho and Phao. ElL; LoBV; OBSC; TuPP
My share of pie to win, I will dash through thick and thin. Quintetto upon the Christmas Pie. Thomas Love Peacock. *Fr.* Melincourt. MyFE
My Share of the World. Alice Furlong. HBV; OBVV
My shattred Phancy stole away from mee. Meditation XXIX [*or* My Father, and Your Father, to My God, and Your God.] Edward Taylor. *Fr.* Preparatory Meditations, First Series. AP; MWA-1; SCAP
My Sheep Are Thoughts. Sir Philip Sidney. *Fr.* Arcadia. SiCE; SiPS
(Dorus His Comparisons.) ReIE
My Sheep I Neglected. Sir Gilbert Elliot. *See* Amynta.
My shepherd's unkind; alas, what shall I do? The Lamentation of Chloris. *Unknown.* CoMu
My Ship. Edmund Leamy. JKCP; SUS
My Ship and I. Robert Louis Stevenson. BoChLi; PPL
My ship is an old ship and her sails are grey are torn. My Ship. Edmund Leamy. JKCP; SUS
My Ship Is on de Ocean, *with music. Unknown.* BoAN-2
My Ships. Ella Wheeler Wilcox. PoLF
(Love Ship.) SoP
My Shoes. Charles Simic. CoAP
My shoes are almost dead. Caesar. W. S. Merwin. FRC; NaP
My shoes fall on the house top that is so far beneath me. Climb. Winifred Welles. BiCB; TSW
My short and happy day is done. The Stirrup-Cup. John Hay. AA; HBV
My shoulders ache beneath my pack. Prayer of a Soldier in France. Joyce Kilmer. CAW; GoBC
My Silks and Fine Array. Blake. *See* Song: "My silks and fine array."
My silver stag is fallen—on the grass. The Silver Stag. Kathleen Raine. FaBoMo
My simple heart, bred in provincial tenderness. Sonnet. G. S. Fraser. NeBP
My sin! my sin, My God, these cursed dregs. Meditation. Edward Taylor. *Fr.* Preparatory Meditations, First Series. MeP; SCAP
My Singing Aunt. James Reeves. ShM
My sinnes are like the haires upon my head. The Authour's Dreame. Francis Quarles. *Fr.* Argalus and Parthenia. OBS
My sins, my sins, my Savior! In the Garden. John S. B. Monsell. OQP
My Sister. Hyam Plutzik. FiMAP
My sister and I. Plans. Helen Morgan Brooks. NNP; PoNe (1970 ed.)
My sister and I when we were close together. Sisters. Dorothy Roberts. CaP
My Sister Helen. Drummond Allison. FaBoTw
My Sister Jane. Ted Hughes. FIW
My sister! my sweet sister! if a name. Epistle to Augusta [*or* To Augusta]. Byron. AnEnPo; EnRP; EPN
My Sister She Works in a Laundry, *with music. Unknown.* AS
(How The Money Rolls In.) TreFT
My sisters played beyond the doorway. Detail from an Annunciation by Crivelli. Rosemary Dobson. NeLNL; PoAu-2
My Sister's Sleep. Dante Gabriel Rossetti. EnL; EPN; ExPo; LoBV; MaVP; MyFE; OAEP; PoVP; SeCeV; ViPo; ViPP
My Six Toothbrushes. Phyllis McGinley. GoYe
My slain! Oh silver-hoof! Oh clover breath! Unbridled Now. Laura Lourene LeGear. GoYe
My sleep falters and the good dreams. Lost. Alfred Alvarez. NMP
My sleep was like a prenatal death. The Awakening. K. William Kgositsile. BF

My smallest and last child smashed the shell. Broken Shell. Winfield Townley Scott. NYTB
My softness heaves its spiral canopy. Snail. Elisabeth Eybers. PeSA
My Son. James D. Hughes. BLPA
My Son. Douglas Malloch. MaRV
My son Augustus, in the street, one day. Quiet Fun. Harry Graham. ShM
My Son, Come Tell It to Me, *with music. Unknown.* BFSS
My son, despise not the chastening of the Lord. Happy Is the Man That Findeth Wisdom. Proverbs, Bible, *O.T.* TreF
My son, forsake your art. A Mhic, ná Meabhraigh Eigse. *Unknown, tr. by* Máire MacEntee. OxBI
My son has birds in his head. Daedalus. Alastair Reid. NYBP
My son, if thou come to serve the Lord, prepare thy soul for temptation. Ecclesiasticus, Bible, Apocrypha. BoC
My son invites me to witness with him. Mousemeal. Howard Nemerov. TwCP
My son, keep my words. Proverbs, Bible, *O.T.* LO
My son knelt down beside his bed. There Shall Be Wars. Anna Williams. SoP
My Son, My Executioner. Donald Hall. NePoEA
My son, these maxims make a rule. Address to the Unco Guid, or the Rigidly Righteous. Burns. AnFE; BoLiVe; EiCL; FosPo; HBV; LoBV; OAEP; TreFS. *See also* O ye wha are sae guid yoursel.
My son, thou wast my heart's delight. On the Death of My Son Charles. Daniel Webster. AA
My son was killed while laughing at some jest. A Son. Kipling. *Fr.* Epitaphs of the War. ChMP; PoVP
"My son!" What simple, beautiful words! To My Unborn Son. Cyril Morton Horne. BLPA
My Song. Hazel Hall. HBMV
My Song. Rabindranath Tagore. OHIP
My song, I fear that thou wilt find but few. Epipsychidion. Shelley. EnRP; EPN; ERoP-2
My song is love unknown. Love Unknown. Samuel Crossman. BoC
My Song of Today. St. Thérèse of Lisieux, *tr. fr. French by* Prioress Augustine of the Mother of God. CAW
My song that was a sword is still. My Song. Hazel Hall. HBMV
My song, thus now in thy conclusions. The Visions of Petrarch. Petrarch, *tr. by* Spenser. EnLi-1
My Song to the Jewish People. Leib Olitski, *tr. fr. Yiddish by* Jacob Sonntag. TrJP
My Songs Are Poisoned! Heine, *tr. fr. German by* Louis Untermeyer. AWP; JAWP; WBP
My songs have been the songs of the daylight. Songs in the Night. J. Lyall. SoP
My songs, they say, are poisoned. My Songs Are Poisoned. Heine. AWP; JAWP; WBP
My songs to sell, good sir! Vendor's Song. Adelaide Crapsey. AnFE; APA; CoAnAm; HBV; MAP; MoAmPo (1942 ed.)
My Sons. Ron Loewinsohn. NeAP
My sons, and ye the children of my sons. Jacob. Arthur Hugh Clough. ViPP
My sons, behold what portion I do give. The Contents of the Scedule Which Sir John of Bordeaux Gave to His Sons. Thomas Lodge. *Fr.* Rosalynde. ReIE; SiCE
My Sore Thumb. Burges Johnson. HBVY
My Sorrow. "Seumas O'Sullivan." *See* Starling Lake, The.
My sorrow diligent would sweep. The Confessional. Helen Parry Eden. JKCP
My sorrow is so wide. Kings River Canyon. Kenneth Rexroth. NaP
My sorrow that I am not by the little dún. The Starling Lake [*or* My Sorrow]. "Seumas O'Sullivan." AnIV; AWP; HBV; JAWP; NP; WBP
My sorrow, when she's here with me. My November Guest. Robert Frost. AnFE; APA; BoLiVe; CLwM; CoAnAm; HBMV; MoVE; NP; OxBA; PoLF; TwAmPo; ViBoPo
My Sort o' Man. Paul Laurence Dunbar. AmNP
My soul/ cried out to you. Tears and a Dream. Marsha Ann Jackson. TNV
My Soul and I. Charles Buxton Going. MaRV
My soul, asleep between its body-throes. The Soul Stithy. James Chapman Woods. VA
My soul, be not disturbed. Address to My Soul. Elinor Wylie. AmLP; AnFE; APA; AWP; CoAnAm; LiTM; MoRP; OxBA; PoFr
My soul before Thee prostrate lies. Hope Springing Up. John Wesley. BePJ
My soul, calm sister, towards thy brow doth mount. A Sigh. Stéphane Mallarmé, *tr. by* Alan Condor. OnPM
My soul, calm sister, towards thy brow, whereon scarce grieve. Sigh. Stéphane Mallarmé, *tr. by* Arthur Symons. AWP; JAWP; SyP; WBP
"My Soul Doth Magnify the Lord." Amos R. Wells. FaChP
My soul doth magnify the Lord. The Magnificat [*or* Hymn of the Blessed Virgin]. St. Luke, Bible, *N.T.* CAW; MaRV; WGRP; WHL
My Soul Doth Pant towards Thee. Jeremy Taylor. *See* Prayer, The: "My soul doth pant towards thee."
My soul goes clad in gorgeous things. Souls. Fannie Stearns Davis. HBMV
My soul has solitudes. Loneliness. Father Edwin Essex. JKCP (1926 ed.); TrPWD
My soul in reverence now prays. Mother's Day. Edna Tucker Muth. PEDC
My Soul in the Bundle of Life. *Unknown, tr. fr. French by* E. Margaret Rowley. *Fr.* The Dead Sea Scrolls. TrJP
My soul is a witness for my Lord. Who'll Be a Witness for My Lord? *Unknown.* BoAN-1
My soul is like the oar that momently. Struggle. Sidney Lanier. CBEP; LiTA; OxBA
My soul is like this cloudy, flaming opal ring. Opals. Arthur Symons. PoVP
My Soul Is Robbed. Isaac Rosenberg. MoPo
My soul is sad and much dismayed. The Valley of the Shadow of Death. William Cowper. EiCP
My soul is sailing through the sea. Barnacles. Sidney Lanier. OQP; SoP
My Soul Is Weary of My Life. Job, X: 1-22, Bible, *O.T.* EaLo
My soul leans toward Him; stretches out its arms. George Macdonald. *Fr.* Within and Without. WGRP
My soul lives in my body's house. Doubt. Sara Teasdale. LO
My soul looked down from a vague height with Death. The Show. Wilfred Owen. LiTB; LiTG; LiTM (rev. ed.); MoAB; MoBrPo (1950 ed.); NAMP; WaaP; WaP
My soul, praise thou the Lord always! Lauda Anima Mea. Psalm CXLVI, Bible, *O.T., tr. by* John Hopkins. ReIE
My soul shall be a telescope. "My Soul Doth Magnify the Lord." Amos R. Wells. FaChP
My Soul Shall Cling to Thee. Charlotte Elliott. BePJ
My soul, sit thou a patient looker-on. Epigram: Respice Finem [*or* The Human Touch]. Francis Quarles. MaRV; OBEV; PoToHe; TreFT
My soul stands at the window of my room. Nostalgia. Karl Shapiro. AnFE; AP; CMoP; CoAnAm; CoAP; CoBMV; LiTM; NePA; TrJP; TwAmPo; TwCP; WaaP
My soul surcharged with grief now loud complains. Sonnet. Rachel Morpurgo. TrJP
My soul, there is a country [*or* countrie]. Peace. Henry Vaughan. AnAnS-1; AnFE; AWP; BEL; BoC; BWP; CBEP; CBV; ChTr; EaLo; EG; ELP; EnLit; FaBoCh; GN; HBV; HT; InPo; LoGBV; MeP; MePo; OAEP; OBEV; OBS; Po; PoFS; ReEn; SCEP-1; SeCL; SeCV-1; SeEP; SoP; UnPo (1st ed.); WePo; WGRP; WHA; YAT
My Soul Thirsteth for God. Psalms, XLII, Bible, *O.T.* TrGrPo (Psalm XLII.) AWP; JAWP; WoL
(Search, The, *Moulton, Modern Reader's Bible.*) WGRP
My soul thy sacrifice! I choose thee out. Poems of the Arabic. *Unknown. Fr.* The Thousand and One Nights. ErPo
My soul to-day. Drifting. Thomas Buchanan Read. AA; GN; HBV; HT
My soul was an old horse. Pegasus [*or* A Glut on the Market]. Patrick Kavanagh. FaBoTw; MoAB; OnYI; OxBI
My soul within the bed of heaven doth grow. William Alabaster. Sonn
My soule a world is by contraccion. Sonnet. William Alabaster. AnAnS-1; MeP
My soule is like a bird; my flesh, the cage. Francis Quarles. *Fr.* Emblems. MeP
My soule, Lord, quailes to thinke that I should bee. Meditation. Edward Taylor. *Fr.* Preparatory Meditations, First Series. MeP

My soul's a new-fledged bird: it tries to fly. Even as the Bird. E. Merrill Root. ChIP

My Soul's Been Anchored in de Lord, *with music.* *Unknown.* BoAN-2

My South. Don West. PoNe

My Specialty Is Living Said. E. E. Cummings. MoVE

My Species. D. M. Black. HYE

My Spectre around Me [Night and Day]. Blake. CBEP; ERoP-1; NCEP; OxBoCh; PeER

My sperm is lyre in your blood your. Poem. William Knott. YAP

My Spirit. Thomas Traherne. SCEP-1; SeCV-2

My spirit has pass'd in compassion and determination around the whole earth. Walt Whitman. *Fr.* Salut au Monde. AtBAP

My spirit is a pestilential city. Desolate. Claude McKay. CDC

My spirit is too weak—mortality. On Seeing the Elgin Marbles. Keats. BEL; BoLiVe; CABA; CoBE; DiPo; EnLi-2; EnLit; EnRP; ERoP-2; GTBS-W; LiTB; MaPo (1969 ed.); MBW-2; PAn; Po; PoeP; PoIE; SeCeV; TrGrPo; WHA

My spirit like a shepherd boy. Song. V. Sackville-West. HBMV

My Spirit Longeth for Thee. John Byrom. *See* Desponding Soul's Wish, The.

My ·spirit to yours, dear brother. To Him That Was Crucified. Walt Whitman. AnEnPo; MaRV; MoRP; StJW

My Spirit Will Grow Up. Ruth Evelyn Henderson. OQP

My Spirit Will Not Haunt the Mound. Thomas Hardy. MoBrPo; OBNC; QFR; TOP

My spotless love hovers with purest wings. Beauty, Time and Love [*or* The Most Unloving One *or* Sonnets to Delia]. Samuel Daniel. To Delia, XII. HBV; OBEV; OBSC; SeCePo; SiCE

My Springs. Sidney Lanier. UnPo

My Star. Robert Browning. BEL; BoLiVe; EPN; EvOK; FaPON; HBV; MBW-2; OAEP; OTPC (1946 ed.); OuHeWo; PoVP; StaSt; TOP; TrGrPo; UnPo (1st ed.); ViPo; ViPP

My Star. Plato, *tr. fr. Greek by* Alexander Lothian. EnLi-1; OuHeWo

My Step-Grandfather. Harold Lenoir Davis. NP

My stock lies dead, and no increase. Grace. George Herbert. MaMe; SeCV-1

My Study. Paul Hamilton Hayne. AmPP (3d ed.)

My study's ornament, thou shell of death. Cyril Tourneur. *Fr.* The Revenger's Tragedy. ViBoPo

My Subtle and Proclamant Song. Seán Jennett. NeIP

My suffering public, take it not amiss. The Problem of the Poles. John Kendall. WhC

My suit is just, just Lord, to my suit hark. Psalm XVII. Sir Philip Sidney. FCP

My sun has set, I dwell. Despised and Rejected. Christina Rossetti. MaRV; StJW

My Sun-killed Tree. Marguerite Harris. GoYe

My Sun Sets to Rise Again. Robert Browning. *Fr.* At the Mermaid. MaRV

My sweet did sweetly sleep. Stolen Pleasure. William Drummond of Hawthornden. EnLoPo

My Sweet Gazelle! Immanuel di Roma, *tr. fr. Italian.* TrJP

My sweet love is faire to see. *Unknown.* SeCSL

My Sweet Old Etcetera. E. E. Cummings. *Fr.* Is 5. AmPP (5th ed.); AnMPo; CABA; NAMP; NePA; OxBA; PoPl; WaaP; WaP

My Sweet Sweeting. *Unknown.* CH, *sl. abr.* ("Ah, my sweet sweeting.") LO

My Sweetest Lesbia [Let Us Live and Love]. Thomas Campion, *after the Latin of* Catullus. AnEnPo; AtBAP; AWP; CABA; CBEP; CBV; EIL; EnL; EnLi-1; EnRePo; JAWP; LoBV; NoP; OBSC; PAn; PoAn; PoFS; PoRA; ReEn; ReIE; SiCE; TrGrPo; TuPP; UnTE; WBP (Let Us Live and Love.) MeWo (To Lesbia.) HBV (Vivamus Mea Lesbia atque Amemus.) EG; SeCeV; StP

My sweetheart's a mule in the mines. *See* My sweetheart's the mule in the mines.

My sweetheart's a sailor. Sailor. Eleanor Farjeon. BrR; PoRh

My sweetheart's Dainty Lips. Judah Halevi, *tr. fr. Hebrew by* Emma Lazarus. TrJP

My sweetheart's the [*or* a] mule in the mines. The Mule in the Mines [*or* Campfire and Bunkhouse]. *Unknown.* ChTr; CoSo

My swing is my airship. The Swing Ship. Mildred D. Shacklett. GFA

My Swinging Shadow. Grace Wilson Coplen. GFA

My sword I shook. The Sword. Abu Bakr. TTY

My Table. W. B. Yeats. Meditations in Time of Civil War, III. CABL; LiTB; PIA

My table shows the tracks of tiny feet. Souvenirs. Margaret E. Bruner. CIV

My tall sunflowers love the sun. Sunflowers. Clinton Scollard. HBMV; MPB

My tameless will doth recklessly pursue. Of His Foolish Passion for Laura. Petrarch. Sonnets to Laura: To Laura in Life, VI. EnLi-1; OuHeWo

My Task. Maude Louise Ray. FaChP; MaRV

My Task. Robert Louis Stevenson. MaRV

My Taxicab. James S. Tippett. GFA; MPB

My tea is nearly ready and the sun has left the sky. The Lamplighter. Robert Louis Stevenson. FaFP; GaP; MPB; OTD; OTPC; PCH; PoVP; TreF; TVC

My tears are true, though others be divine. Henry Constable. *Fr.* Diana. OBSC

My tears were Orion's splendor with sextuple suns and the million. Tears. Edith Sitwell. CMoP; MoPo

My Temper. *Unknown.* STF

My temples throb, my pulses boil. To Minerva [*or* Fewer Books, More Salad]. Thomas Hood. BOHV; ChTr; FiBHP; HBV; InMe; OnPM; OxBoLi; SiTL; TOP; WhC

My tender parents brought me up, providing me full well. The Lexington Murder. *Unknown.* BaBo; OuSiCo

My tent stands in a garden. An Autumn Garden. Bliss Carman. HBV

My terminus near,/ The clouds already closing in upon me. Walt Whitman. *Fr.* Prayer of Columbus. MaRV

My thanks for all Thou gavest through the years. Gratitude. Mikhail Lermontov. LiTW; OnPM

My thanks, friends of the County Scientific Association. Perry Zoll. Edgar Lee Masters. *Fr.* Spoon River Anthology. CrMA; NP

My Thing Is My Own. *Unknown.* CoMu

My thirsty soul desires her drought. A Prisoner's Song of Jerusalem. *Unknown.* ACP

My Thirty Years. Juan Fransico Manzano, *tr. fr. Spanish by* Oliver Cobarn *and* Ursula Lehrburger. TTY

My thought awaked me with Thy Name. Meditation on Communion with God. Judah Halevi. TrJP

My thought is caught in the eyes of love. Entanglement. Francis Sparshott. MoCV

My Thought Was on a Maid So Bright. *Unknown.* ISi

My thought was thus—that it was May. May Morning. Chaucer. *Fr.* The Book of the Duchess. WHA

My thoughts are all in yonder town. The Friend's Burial. Whittier. OBVV

My thoughts are as a garden-plot, that knows. Thy Garden. Mu'tamid, King of Seville. AWP

My thoughts are fixed in contemplation. John Marston. *Fr.* Antonio and Mellida. ViBoPo

My Thoughts Are Not Your Thoughts. Isaiah, LV: 8-13, Bible, *O.T.* TrJP

My Thoughts Are Winged with Hopes. George Clifford. EIL (To Cynthia.) OBSC

My thoughts by night are often filled. Castles in the Air. Thomas Love Peacock. HBV

My Thoughts Do Harbour. Shakespeare. *Fr.* The Two Gentlemen of Verona, III, i. CTC

My Thoughts Hold Mortal Strife. William Drummond of Hawthornden. *See* Madrigal: "My thoughts. . ."

My thoughts impelled me to the resting-place. Elegy. Moses ibn Ezra. TrJP

My thoughts, like sailors becalmed in Cape Town harbor. Sailor's Harbor. Henry Reed. MoAB; MoBrPo (1962 ed.)

My thoughts, my grief! are without strength. A Poem Written in Time of Trouble by an Irish Priest. *Unknown, tr. by* Lady Gregory. OBMV

My thoughts turn south. A White City. James Schuyler. ANYP

My Thread. David Hofstein, *tr. fr. Yiddish by* Joseph Leftwich. TrJP

My throat is of gold, with a pretty black crescent. Meadow Lark. Marion Mitchell Walker. GFA

My Thrush. Mortimer Collins. HBV; OTPC (1923 ed.)
My tidings for you: the stag bells. Summer Is Gone. *Unknown.* FaBoCh; LoGBV; OnYI
My time is nearly up. At Sea. Vera E. Guerard. TNV
My time, O ye Muses, was happily spent. A Pastoral. John Byrom. OBEC
My times are drawing in. The Musterer. Eileen Duggan. CoBE
My Times Are in Thy Hand. Christopher Newman Hall. VA
My Tommy's gone, what shall I do? Tommy's Gone to Hilo. *Unknown.* ShS
My tongue-tied Muse in manners holds her still. Sonnets, LXXXV. Shakespeare. Sonn
My top is blue and silver, with a belt of emerald green. Hidden. ffrida Wolfe. TVC
My towers at last! These rovings end. L'Envoi: The Return of the Sire de Nesle. Herman Melville. AnFE; APA; CoAnAm; ViBoPo
My townspeople, beyond in the great world. Gulls. William Carlos Williams. FaBoEn; NoP; OxBA; TwAmPo
My Toys. Lilian McCrea. BoTP
My Treasures. Robert Louis Stevenson. SAS
My Trewest Tresowre. Richard Rolle of Hampole. *See* Song of the Passion, A.
My tricycle's a camel. The Race. Aileen Fisher. UTS
My Triumph. Whittier. AnNE
My truimph lasted till the drums. Emily Dickinson. NoP; WaaP
My True Love. Ivy O. Eastwick. SiSoSe
My True Love. Sir Philip Sidney. *See* My True Love Hath My Heart.
My true love has gone to France. Shoo, Shoo, Shoo-Lye. *Unknown.* ABF
My true love has my heart and I would be. Formal Lyric. W. J. Turner. FaBoTw
My True Love Hath My Heart [and I Have His]. Sir Philip Sidney. *Fr.* Arcadia. AtBAP; BoLiVe; CBEP; CH; CoBE; DiPo; EG; EP; FaBoBc; FCP; HBV; ILP; LiTG; LiTL; MaPo; MeWo; OAEP; OnPM; PoE; PoEL-1; PTK; ReEn; SeCeV; SiCE; TrGrPo; ViBoPo; WePo
(Arcadian Duologue.) SiPS
(Bargain, The.) OBEV; OtMeF; PG; TreFS
(Ditty, A.) AWP; GTBS; GTBS-D; GTBS-P; GTBS-W; GTSE; GTSL; InPo; JAWP; PoRL; TOP
(Ditty: Heart Exchange.) EnLit
(Heart Exchange.) LiTB; LoBV
(Just Exchange.) FaBoEn
(Song: "My true love hath my heart.") EnLi-1
(Sonnet: "My true love hath my heart.") EIL; WHA
(True Love.) ALV; BoPe; ChTr; MemP; OBSC
My True Sailor Boy, *with music.* *Unknown.* BFSS
My Trundle Bed. J. G. Baker. BLPA; FaBoBe
My Trust. Samuel Rodigast. SoP
My Trust. *Unknown.* SoP
My Trust, *sel.* Whittier.
"Picture memory brings to me, A," *first 3 sts.* OHIP; PGD; PoRL
My Two Daughters. Victor Hugo, *tr. fr. French by* Alan Conder. LO
My two white rabbits. Rabbits. Dorothy W. Baruch. SoPo; SUS; TiPo; UTS
My Uncle Ben, who's been. Kiph. Walter de la Mare. TiPo (1959 ed.)
My uncle Jack is a preacher. Pansies. Tom Robinson. BoChLi (1950 ed.)
My Uncle Jasper in Siam. Ponjoo. Walter de la Mare. ShM
My Uninvited Guest. May Riley Smith. AA; WGRP
My Valentine. Mary Catherine Parsons. SoPo; TiPo (1952 ed.)
My Valentine. Robert Louis Stevenson. *See* Romance.
My verse is satire; Dorset, lend your ear. Satire I. Edward Young. *Fr.* Love and Fame, the Universal Passion. EiCL
My verse will reach you. Vladimir Mayakovsky. *Fr.* At the Top of My Voice. LiTW
My verses dream-rich and tender you've read. Poet of Farewell. Christian Werleigh. PoNe
My very strict Aunt Matilda can't. Aunt Matilda. Barbara Euphan Todd. BoC
My vision is emptying. Olive Grove. Lewis MacAdams. ANYP
My Voice. Oscar Wilde. BrPo
My voice is still for war. Addison. *Fr.* Cato. PoFr
My Wage. Jessie Belle Rittenhouse. BLPA; NeHB; PoMa; PoToHe (new ed.)
My walls outside must have some flowers. Truly Great. W. H. Davies. HBV; OBMV; OBVV
My wand strikes me no joy till loosened weeping. Third Madrigal. Gene Derwood. NePA
My wandringe thoughts have travelde rounde. *Unknown.* SeCSL
My Way Is Not Thy Way. D. H. Lawrence. CMoP
My Way's Cloudy, *with music.* *Unknown.* BoAN-1
My Wealth. Frank St. Way. SoP
My week-days pile in me like dirty clothes. Days. Edgar Paiewonsky. QAH
My weeping and the starlight. Nocturne. Juan Ramón Jiménez. OnPM
My Wellington boots go/ Thump-thump, thump-thump. Boots and Shoes. Lilian McCrea. BoTP
My What-is-it. Robert Frost. RIS
My whiskey is/ a tough way of life. Drink. William Carlos Williams. OxBA
My whistle is senseless. Gycerin. Frank Lima. ANYP
My white tiger bounding in the west! Welcome My World. Denis Devlin. AnIV
My whole tho' broken heart, O Lord. Wholly the Lord's. Richard Baxter. SoP
My Wife. Robert Louis Stevenson. WePo
(Husband to a Wife, A.) BoC
(To My Wife.) MaRV; TRV
(Trusty, Dusky, Vivid, True.) HBV
My wife and I live [*or* lived] all alone. Little Brown Jug. *Unknown.* FaFP; TrAS; TreF; YaD
My wife and I lived all alone. Ballad of the Despairing Husband. Robert Creeley. AmPC; NeAP; ToPo
My wife asleep, her soft face turned from me. Sonnet: The Window. Carl Bode. ToPo
My wife broke a dollar tube of perfume. The Problem. Paul Blackburn. NeAP
My wife bursts into the room. The Loneliness of the Long Distance Runner. Alden Nowlan. PV
My wife has tattoos on her neck. I'm Married. Eric Torgersen. QAH
My wife is left-handed. For Hettie. LeRoi Jones. CBV; NeAP
My Wife's a Wanton Wee Thing. *Unknown.* CoMu
My Wife's a Winsome Wee Thing. Burns. HBV; LiTL
My wife's new pink slippers. The Thinker. William Carlos Williams. MoLP
My Wild Irish Rose. Chauncey Olcott. TreFT
My wild will was captured, yet under the yoke. My Will. *Unknown.* SoP
My Will. *Unknown.* SoP
My will lies there, my hope, and all my life. Thomas Lovell Beddoes. *Fr.* Death's Jest Book. LO
My William was a soldier, and he says to me, says he. An Eastern Question. H. M. Paull. BOHV
My Wind Is Turned to Bitter North. Arthur Hugh Clough. OAEP
My window is the open sky. Immortality. Arthur Sherburne Hardy. AA
My window looks upon a world grown gray. Midwinter. Margaret E. Bruner. PoToHe
My window opens out into the trees. Solace. Clarissa Scott Delany. AmNP; CDC; PoNe
My window shows the travelling clouds. The Alchemist in the City. Gerard Manley Hopkins. NoP
My windows now are giant drops of dew. The Rat. W. H. Davies. BoPe
My windows open to the autumn night. Cadgwith. Lionel Johnson. CoBE; GTBS; JKCP; OBVV; PoVP
My Winsome Dear. Robert Fergusson. *Fr.* Leith Races. SeCePo
My Wish. Patience Strong. RePo
My Wishes. Patrick Healy, *tr. fr. Modern Irish by* John D'Alton. OnYI
My Woe Must Ever Last. Sir Walter Ralegh. EIL
My Woman. Catullus, *tr. fr. Latin by* Gilbert Highet. PoPl
My women surround me. The Downtown Swan Thing. Thomas Hanna. QAH
My Woodcock. Patrick Reginald Chalmers. CenHV
My woods, obscurely dim, will shelter. Abstract Painter in Spring. Rosamond Haas. NYTB

My words and thoughts do both expresse this notion. Our Life is Hid with Christ in God. George Herbert. MaMe
My Words are sad notes best tosses aside. Poem for Joyce. Johnie Scott. WSL
My words for you. The Words of Finn. *Unknown.* ChTr
My words I know do well set forth my mind. Astrophel and Stella, LXIV. Sir Philip Sidney. FCP; SiPS
My words were delicately breathed. To Claudia Homonoea. Elinor Wylie. TOP
My Work. *Unknown.* MaRV
My work is done. Angel. Cardinal Newman. *Fr.* The Dream of Gerontius. GoBC
My work is finished; I am strong. Longfellow. *Fr.* Christus. ChIP
My Work with Snow. William Hunt. YAP
My World. Chauncey R. Piety. MaRV; OQP
My world is a painted fresco, where coloured shapes. Dreams Old and Nascent. D. H. Lawrence. WGRP
My world was night. The Blind Youth. Clive Sansom. MemP
My Worthy Lord, I Pray You. George Gascoigne. PoEL-1
(Gascoigne's Woodmanship.) EnRePo; QFR
My Yallow Gal, *with music.* *Unknown.* ABF
My Yoke Is Easy. St. Matthew, Bible, *N.T.* *See* Come Unto Me.
My Yoke Is Easy. Gladys Latchaw. ChIP; MaRV
My young love said to me, "My brothers won't mind." She Moved Through the Fair. Padraic Colum. GTBS-D; InvP
My young Mary do's mind the dairy. The Happy Husbandman; or, Country Innocence. *Unknown.* CoMu
My younger years I did employ. A Reflection on the Course of Human Life. William Lloyd. PrWP
My Youth It Was Free. *Unknown.* SeCL
My youth was nothing but a storm, tenebrous, savage. The Enemy. Baudelaire, *tr. by* Arthur Symons. OnPM
My Zipper Suit. Marie Louise Allen. BrR; SUS; TiPo
Myall in Prison, The. Mary Gilmore. BoAV; PoAu-1
Mycenae. Alphaeus, *tr. fr. Greek by* Anne Hyde Greet. OnPM
Mycerinus. Matthew Arnold. MaVP; PoVP; ViPo
Mycilla [*or* Mucilla] dyes her locks, 'tis said. On an Old Woman. Lucillius. AWP; LiTW; OnPM
Mydas. John Lyly. *See* Midas.
Myne owne John Poynz. . . *See* Mine own John Poynz . . .
Mynstrelles Songe: "Angelles bee wrogte to bee of neidher kynde." Thomas Chatterton. *Fr.* Aella. EnLoPo
Mynstrelles Songe: "Boddynge flourettes bloshes atte the lyghte, The." Thomas Chatterton. *See* Song of the Three Minstrels.
Mynstrelles Songe: "O! synge untoe mie roundelaie." Thomas Chatterton. *See* Minstrel's Song.
Myra. Fulke Greville. *See* I, with Whose Colors Myra Dressed Her Head.
Myriad singers pour their treasures. The Songs We Need. Bernard Freeman Trotter. MaRV
Myriads and myriads plumed their glittering wings. Leaves. Katharine Tynan. BoTP
Myriads of motley molecules through space. Soul and Sense. Hannah Parker Kimball. AA
Myrtilla, tonight. A Corsage Bouquet. Charles Henry Luders. HBV
Myrtis, *sel.* Walter Savage Landor. *Fr.* Pericles and Aspasia.
"Friends, whom she lookt at blandly from her couch." OBRV; VA
Myrtle, and eglantine. The Flower-Seller. William Young. *Fr.* Wishmakers' Town. AA
Myrtle and the Vine, The, *sel.* George Colman. Gluggity Glug. HBV
Myrtle, as I lie here, wrapped in. Reflections in a Hospital. Emanuel Eisenberg. ALV
Myrtle bush grew shady, The. Jealousy. Mary Elizabeth Coleridge. CH; EnLoPo; NBM; OBNC; PoVP
"Myrtle loves Harry"—It is sometimes hard. Aphrodite Metropolis. Kenneth Fearing. CAD
Myself. Edgar A. Guest. BLPA; MaRV; NeHB; OQP
Myself. Edwin C. Swanson. SoP
Myself. *Unknown.* OQP
Myself. Walt Whitman. Song of Myself, I. AA; FaBoBe
(I Celebrate Myself.) NePA
("I celebrate myself, and sing myself.") PoFS (I-XLVIII, *much abr.*)
Myself Am Hell. Milton. *Fr.* Paradise Lost, I *and* IV. MaRV
Myself grown old do fearfully frequent. Case History. Arthur W. Bell. WhC
Myself, I rather like the bat. The Bat. Ogden Nash. PV
Myself unto myself will give. The Holy Office. James Joyce. FaBoTw; SiTL
Myself When Young Did Eagerly Frequent. Omar Khayyám. *See* Worldly Wisdom.
Myselves/ The grievers. Ceremony after a Fire Raid. Dylan Thomas. CMoP; CoBMV; ExPo; MoPo; PoDB; WaP
Mysteries. Emily Dickinson. *See* Murmur of a bee, The.
Mysteries, The. L. A. G. Strong. HaMV
Mysteries: if a nymph naked and golden. Microcosmos, XX. Nigel Heseltine. NeBP
Mysterious Biography. Carl Sandburg. SiSoSe
Mysterious Cat, The. Vachel Lindsay. ChTr; FaPON; GoJo; MPB; PoRh; SoPo; SP; StVeCh; TiPo; UTS
Mysterious Landscape. Hans Carossa, *tr. fr. German by* R. F. C. Hull. LiTW
Mysterious Music of Ocean, The. *Unknown.* EtS
Mysterious Night. Joseph Blanco White. *See* To Night.
Mysterious night! Spread wide thy silvery plume. Night. John Addington Symonds. HBV
Mysterious Night, when our first parent knew. To Night [*or* Night *or* Night and Death]. Joseph Blanco White. AnFE; AnIV; BoC; CBEP; EG; EPN; GoBC; GTBS-W; HBV; JKCP (1926 ed.); MaRV; OBEV (new ed.); OBRV; RoGo; Sonn; TreFS; ViBoPo; WGRP
Mysterious Nothing! how shall I define. Nothing. Richard Porson. BOHV
Mysterious Power! Gentle Friend! Prayer to the Dynamo. Henry Adams. AmePo
Mysterious Way, The. William Cowper. *See* Light Shining Out of Darkness.
Mystery, The. *At. to* Amergin, *tr. fr. Old Irish by* Douglas Hyde. OnYI
Mystery. Jerome B. Bell. MaRV
Mystery. Elizabeth Barrett Browning. OBVV; UnPo
Mystery, The. Ralph Hodgson. BoLiVe; CAW; CH; HBV; MaRV; MoAB; MoBrPo; NeMA; NP; OQP; SoP; WGRP
Mystery. Claire McAllister. TwAmPo
Mystery, The. George Francis Savage-Armstrong. VA
Mystery, A. "Gabriel Setoun." PPL
Mystery, The. Sara Teasdale. HBMV
Mystery, The. *Unknown, tr. fr. Irish by* Douglas Hyde. OxBI
Mystery, The. Lilian Whiting. AA
Mystery. "Yehoash," *tr. fr. Yiddish by* Marie Syrkin. TrJP
Mystery: Catherine the bride of Christ. For a Marriage of St. Catherine. Dante Gabriel Rossetti. SiSw
Mystery: lo! betwixt the sun and moon. Astarte Syriaca. Dante Gabriel Rossetti. PoVP
Mystery of Cro-a-tàn, The. Margaret Junkin Preston. PAH
Mystery of Dawn, ere yet the glory streams. Laurence Binyon. The Sirens, III, 3. GoTL (1949 ed.)
Mystery of Death, The. First Corinthians, XV: 51-58, Bible, *N.T.* BBV (1951 ed.)
Mystery of Pain. Emily Dickinson. *See* Pain has an element of blank.
Mystery of Life in Christ, The. Elizabeth Payson Prentiss. SoP
Mystery of the Innocent Saints, The, *sel.* Charles Péguy, *tr. fr. French by* Joseph T. Shipley.
"I have often played with man, saith the Lord." CAW
Mystic, The. Witter Bynner. HBV
Mystic. Sylvia Plath. NYBP
Mystic, The. Cale Young Rice. MaRV; WGRP
Mystic, The. Tennyson. OAEP
Mystic and Cavalier. Lionel Johnson. MoBrPo; SeCePo; ViPP
Mystic as Soldier, A. Siegfried Sassoon. NP; WGRP
(I Lived My Days Apart.) PTK
Mystic Borderland, The. Helen Field Fischer. OQP; WBLP
(There Is a Mystic Borderland.) PoToHe
Mystic Drum, The. Gabriel Okara. TTY
Mystic finishes in Time, The. Insomniacs, The. Adrienne Cecile Rich. NYBP
Mystic Magi, The. Robert Stephen Hawker. ChTr
(Southern Cross, The.) OxBoCh

Mystic River. John Ciardi. AmP; NYBP
Mystic Song, A. *Unknown. See* Chanson mystique.
Mystic Union, The. *Unknown, tr. fr. Punjabi by* Puran Singh. OnPM
Mystical Dialogue. Paul Verlaine, *tr. fr. French by* Alan Conder. LO
Mystical Ecstacy, A. Francis Quarles. *See* My Beloved Is Mine, and I Am His; He Feedeth among the Lilies.
Mystical grammar of amorous glances. John Cleveland. *Fr.* Mark Antony. DiPo
Mystical Poets. Amado Nervo, *tr. fr. Spanish by* Thomas Walsh. CAW
Mystical, sorrowful, stiff and still. The Discoverer. Nathalia Crane. PoMa; YT
Mystical strains unheard. A Clymène. Paul Verlaine. AWP; JAWP; WBP
"Mysticism Has Not the Patience to Wait for God's Revelation." Richard Eberhart. MoPo
Mystic's Prayer, The. "Fiona Macleod." HBV; MaRV; TrPWD; WGRP
Mystic's Prayer. *Unknown.* MaRV
Myth, A. Charles Kingsley. *See* Night Bird, The.
Myth, The. Edwin Muir. CMoP
Myth. Ned O'Gorman. TwAmPo
Myth of Arthur, The. G. K. Chesterton. HBMV
Mythical centaur, The. Centaur in the Groundlevel Apartment. Eric Pfeiffer. NYTB
Mythical Journey, The. Edwin Muir. ILP; OxBS
(Journey, The.) MoVE
Mythmaking. Kathleen Spivack. YAP
Mythological Episode. Robert H. Barlow. FiSC
Mythological Sonnets, *sels.* Roy Fuller.
"How startling to find the portraits of the gods," XVI. ErPo; Sonn
"Suns in a skein, the uncut stones of night," VIII. GTBS-P
"That the dread happenings of myths reveal," XII. Sonn
"There actually stood the fabled riders," II. Sonn
"Well now, the virgin and the unicorn," VII. Sonn
Mythology. Lawrence Durrell. DTC
Mythos. Ralph Gustafson. PeCV
Myths. Guy Butler. BoSA; PeSA
Myths & Texts, *sels.* Gary Snyder.
Burning, *abr.* NeAP
Amitabha's Vow, X. NaP
John Muir on Mt. Ritter, VIII. FlW
Maitreya the Future Buddna, IV. NaP
"Night here, a covert," IX. NaP
"Spikes of new smell driven up nostrils," XIII. NaP
"Stone-flake and salmon," XV. NaP
Text, The, XVII. NaP
Hunting.
"All beaded with dew," VII. NaP
"How rare to be born a human being," XVI. NaP
"Out the Greywolf valley," XII. NaP
"Swallow-shell that eases birth, The," IV. NaP
This Poem Is for Bear, VI. NaP
This Poem Is for Birds, III. NaP
This Poem Is for Deer, VIII. NaP
Logging.
"Again the ancient, meaningless," V. NaP
"Each dawn is clear," VIII. NaP; NMP; OPoP
"Groves are down, The," XIV. NaP
"Lodgepole/ cone/ seed waits for fire," XV. NaP
"Morning star is not a star, The," I. OPoP
"Pines, under pines," IV. OPoP
"Stood straight/ holding the choker high," III. NaP; NMP
Mythos of Samuel Huntsman, The. Hyam Plutzik. LiTM (1970 ed.)
Myxomatosis. Philip Larkin. CMoP; ELU

N

N. B., Symmetrians. Gene Derwood. LiTA; NePA
N. Y. Ezra Pound. NP
Naaman's Song. Kipling. OtMeF
Nabara, The. C. Day Lewis. HaMV
Nae heathen name shall I prefix. To Miss Ferrier. Burns. CBEP
Nae man wha loves the lawland tongue. The Makar. William Soutar. OxBS
Nae shoon to hide her tiny taes. The Babie. Jeremiah Eames Rankin. AA; HBV
Nahant. Emerson. AmPP (5th ed.); MWA-1
(Waves.) AA
Naiad for Grecian Waters! Queen Guennivar's Round. Robert Stephen Hawker. CoBE
Naiad, hid beneath the bank. Anteros [*or* A Dirge]. William Johnson Cory. OBNC; OBVV
Naiads, and ye pastures cold. Telling the Bees. Andrew Lang. VA
Nail-torn God, The. Edwin Markham. MaRV
Nails. Leonard Feeney. WHL
Nails, The. Charles Wharton Stork. StJW
Naked and breast to breast we lie. Tormenting Virgin. *Unknown.* UnTE
Naked and hungry come we into this world. *Unknown.* ThGo
Naked and knowing my heart my love had left on. The Jewels. Baudelaire. ErPo
Naked and the Nude, The. Robert Graves. NYBP; SiTL
Naked angels sing lustful songs. Dream. Alex Raybin. ThO
Naked apples, woolly-coated peaches. Poem for Psychoanalysts and/or Theologians. C. S. Lewis. BoPe
Naked before the glass she said. Young Woman. Howard Nemerov. CBV; ErPo; FiMAP
Naked earth is warm with Spring, The. Into Battle. Julian Grenfell. HBV; LoBV; MMA; OBEV (new ed.); OBMV; OtMeF; POTE; ShBV-3; WaaP
Naked, he sags across her cumbered knees. C. Day Lewis. *Fr.* Pieta. BoPe
Naked house, a naked moor, A. The House Beautiful. Robert Louis Stevenson. PoVP
Naked I lie in the green forest of summer. A Summer Day. Li Po. OnPM
Naked I saw thee. Ideal. Padraic Pearse. AnIV; AWP; CAW; JAWP; JKCP; LiTW; NP; OnYI; WBP
Naked in Borneo. May Swenson. NYBP
Naked is the earth. Poems, 3. Antonio Machado. AWP; LiTW
Naked Love did to thine eye. Ice and Fire. Sir Edward Sherburne. CavP
Naked she lay, clasped in my longing arms. The Imperfect Enjoyment. Earl of Rochester. ErPo; UnTE
Naked sun, A—a yellow sun. Omen. Birago Diop. FlW
Naked to earth was I brought—naked to earth I descend. Vanity of Vanities. Palladas. AWP; JAWP; TRV; WBP
Naked woman and a dead dwarf, A. Three Poems, 3. Stephen Crane. AP
Naked woman, black woman. Black Woman. Léopold Sédar Senghor. TTY
Naked World, The. Sully-Prudhomme, *tr. fr. French by* William Dock. ImOP
Nam Semen Est Verbum Dei. Louis Imogen Guiney. CAW
Namaqualand after Rain. William Plomer. ACV; BoSA
Namby-Pamby. Henry Carey. Par
Name, The. Robert Creeley. CoPo; ToPo
Name, The. Eileen Duggan. ISi
Name, The. Henry W. Frost. SoP
Name, The. Don Marquis. HBV
Name. Ron Padgett. YAP
Name, The/ in remedies in. Improved 4-Way. Tom Veitch. ANYP
Name for All, A. Hart Crane. PP
Name in block letters. *None that signified.* A Form of Epitaph. Laurence Whistler. GTBS-P
Name in the Sand, A. Hannah Flagg Gould. AA; SoP
Name is immortal but only the name, for the rest, The. Jew. Karl Shapiro. ToPo
Name like a River, The. W. S. Graham. FaBoTw
Name of Christ is Wonderful, for wonderful is He, The. The Glorious Name. Amos R. Wells. BePJ
Name of commonwealth is past and gone, The. Byron. *Fr.* Ode on Venice. PoFr
Name—of it—is "Autumn," The. Emily Dickinson. PoeP
Name of Jesus, The. Annie Johnson Flint. BePJ
Name of Jesus, The. John Newton. MaRV; OBEC; SoP; STF
(How Sweet the Name of Jesus Sounds.) OxBoCh
(Precious Name, The.) BePJ
"Jesus! my Shepherd, Husband, Friend," *sel.* TrPWD

Name of Mary. John Boyle O'Reilly. JKCP
Name of Mother, The. George Griffith Fetter. PGD
Name of Old Glory, The. James Whitcomb Riley. DD, *abr.*; GN
Name of Osmund Toulmin, the Gentleman-Jockey, The. Osmund Toulmin. Sir Osbert Sitwell. AtBAP
Name of the beast is, The. Small Comment. Sonia Sanchez. NBP
Name of Washington, The. Arthur Gordon Field. PAL; PGD
Name of Washington, The. George Parsons Lathrop. DD; HH
Name the leaves on all the trees. My Loves. John Stuart Blackie. OBVV
Name thou wearest does thee grievous wrong, The. The Mocking-Bird. Henry Jerome Stockard. AA
Nameless Doon [*or* Dun], The. William Larminie. AnIL; IrPN; NBM; OxBI
(Nameless Ruin, The.) OnYI
Nameless Grave, A. Longfellow. PoIE (1970 ed.)
Nameless, he crept from the hutch of creation. Love for a Hare. Melvin Walker La Follette. NePoEA-2
Nameless Maiden, The. *Unknown.* ErPo
Nameless One, The. James Clarence Mangan. ACP; EnRP; EPN; GoBC; GTBS; GTSE; HBV; IrPN; NBM; OBEV; OnYI; OxBI
Nameless Ones, The. Conrad Aiken. NePA; OxBA
Nameless Ruin, The. William Larminie. *See* Nameless Doon, The.
Nameless Saints, The. Edward Everett Hale. MaRV; OQP; WGRP
Nameless Song. Elinor Wylie. CoBA
Nameless, the village. The People. Dorothy Livesay. *Fr.* The Colour of God's Face. PeCV (1967 ed.)
Names. Dorothy Aldis. BoChLi; SUS
Names. Jorge Guillén, *tr. fr. Spanish by* Eleanor L. Turnbull. LiTW
Names, The. Charles Lamb. OTPC (1923 ed.)
Names. Lisel Mueller. TPM
Names and Order of the Books of the Old Testament. Thomas Russell. *See* Old Testament, The.
Names (for Mother). Elwyn Chauncey West. DD
Names from the War. Bruce Catton. AmFN
Naming of Cats, The. T. S. Eliot. RePo
Naming of Parts. Henry Reed. Lessons of the War, I. CaFP; CBV; DTC; GoJo; HoPM; ILP; LiTB; LiTM (rev. ed.); MoAB; MoBrPo (1962 ed.); MoVE; PoPl; PoRA (rev. ed.); SeCePo; SeCeV (1967 ed.); ShBV-3; SiTL; StP; ViBoPo (1958 ed.); WaP; WePo
("Today we have naming of parts.") TrGrPo (rev. ed.)
Naming the Baby. May Richstone. BiCB
Namkwin Pul. Bernard Gutteridge. WaP
Nana Kru ("Nana, Nana Kru"). *Unknown, tr. fr. Kru by* R. Van Richards. PBA
Nanak and the Sikhs, *sel. Unknown, tr. fr. Hindustani.*
"How shall I address thee?" WGRP
Nancy Dawson. Herbert P. Horne. HBV; VA
Nancy Hanks. Rosemary Benét *and* Stephen Vincent Benét. FaBV; FaPON; GBV (1952 ed.); LaNeLa; LiPo; NeMa; PoPl; RePo; SiSoSe; StVeCh (1955 ed.); TiPo
Nancy Hanks. Harriet Monroe. LiPo
Nancy Hanks dreams by the fire. Fire-Logs. Carl Sandburg. NP
Nancy Hanks, Mother of Abraham Lincoln. Vachel Lindsay. ATP (1935 ed.); CMoP; LiPo; MAP; MoAmPo; ThLM
Nancy Lee. Frederic E. Weatherly. AmSS, *with music*; VA
Nanny. Francis Davis. HBV
Nanny's Sailor Lad. William Allingham. IrPN
Nano's Song. Ben Jonson. *Fr.* Volpone; or, The Fox, I, ii. BoLiVe; LoBV; TrGrPo
(Fools.) ElL; TuPP
("Fools, they are the only nation.") InvP
(Song: "Fooles, they are the onely nation.") AnAnS-2
Nantucket. William Carlos Williams. OxBA; TDP
Nantucket Skipper, The. James Thomas Fields. *See* Alarmed Skipper, The.
Nantucket Whalers. Daniel Henderson. EtS
Naomi and Ruth. Ruth, I: 8-17, Bible, *O.T.* TrJP
Naomi looks for her child. Song. William Knott. YAP
Naomi (Omie) Wise. *Unknown.* BaBo (A *and* B *vers.*); ViBoFo, *with music*
Nap. Mark Van Doren. TwAmPo
Naphtha. Frank O'Hara. ANYP
Napkin and Stone. Vernon Watkins. NYBP
Naples Again. Arthur Freeman. NYBP
Napoleon. Byron. *Fr.* Childe Harold's Pilgrimage, III. OBRV
Napoleon. Walter de la Mare. CBV; FaBoCh; FaBoTw; LoGBV; MoVE; OtMeF
Napoleon and the British Sailor. Thomas Campbell. BeLS
Napoleon writes me. The Departed Friend. Salvador Novo. WoL
Narcissist's eye is blue, fringed with white and covered, The. The Eye. Michael Benedikt. YAP
Narcissus. Alistair Campbell. AnNZ
Narcissus. William Cowper. OTPC
Narcissus. Thomas M. Disch. HYE
Narcissus. Charles Gullans. NePoEA
Narcissus. Donald Petersen. NePoEA-2
Narcissus. John Press. UnTE
Narcissus. Paul Valéry, *tr. fr. French by* Joseph T. Shipley. AWP
Narcissus and Some Tadpoles. Victor J. Daley. PoAu-1
Narcissus, Come Kiss Us! *Unknown.* ErPo
Narcissus in a Cocktail Glass. Frances Minturn Howard. GoYe
Narrative. Louis Dudek. CaP
Narrative. Elisabeth Eybers, *tr. fr. Afrikaans by* Elisabeth Eybers. PeSA
Narrative, A. Theodore Spencer. NeMA; WaKn; WhC
Narrative of the Black Magicians, The. Larry Neal. BF
Narrow Doors, The. Fannie Stearns Davis. HBMV
Narrow fellow in the grass, A. Emily Dickinson. AmePo; AmLP; AmPP (4th ed.); AP; AtBAP; ATP (1953 ed.); BoLiVe; CABA; CBEP; CMoP; CoBA; DiPo; ExPo; FaFP; FlW; GoJo; GoTP; GTBS-D; HoPM; ILP; LiTA; LiTM (rev. ed.); MAmP; MAPA; MCCG; MoAB; MoPW; MWA-2; NoP; OA; OxBA; PoAn; PoE; PoEL-5; PoeP; PoIE; PoLF; PoPo; SeCeV; TDP; TwAmPo; YT
Narrow glade unfolded, such as Spring, A. An Interview near Florence. Samuel Rogers. *Fr.* Italy. OBNC
Narrow paths beside the flower-beds run, The. The Moths. Julian Bell. POTE
Narrow River is salty blue. Marooned. Rachel Field. RePo
Narrow, thorny path he trod, The. The Ascetic. Victor J. Daley. PoAu-1
Narrow Window, A. Florence Earle Coates. OQP; SoP
Narrowing of knowledge to one window to a door, A. Elegy for William Soutar. William Montgomerie. NeBP; OxBS
Nasal whine of power whips a new universe, The. Power. Hart Crane. *Fr.* The Bridge: Cape Hatteras. MAP; MoAB; MoAmPo; WoL
Naseby; Late Autumn. Basil Dowling. AnNZ
Nashe's old queens who bartered young and fair. Lament. Richard Wilbur. FiMAP
Naso, you are many men's man; and yet. To Naso. Catullus. ErPo
Nasturtiums, The. *Unknown.* GFA
Natchul-born Easman. *Unknown. See* Casey Jones.
Nathan. Herman Melville. *Fr.* Clarel. MAmP
Nathan Hale. Francis Miles Finch. DD; MC; PAH; PAL; PAP; PoFr, *abr.*; ThLM
Nathan Hale. William Ordway Partridge. PAL
Nathan Hale. *Unknown.* PAH
Nathan, no thought today. The Bratzlav Rabbi to His Scribe. Jacob Glatstein. TrJP
Nathan Suffrin. Edgar Lee Masters. *Fr.* The New Spoon River. CMoP
Nation of hayricks spotting the green solace, A. The Airman Who Flew over Shakespeare's England. Hyam Plutzik. PoPl
Nation of trees, drab green and desolate grey, A. Australia. A. D. Hope. ACV; BoAV; MoAuPo; OnHM
"Nation Shall Speak Peace . . ." William Soutar. POTE
Nation spoke to a nation, A. Our Lady of the Snows. Kipling. ACV
National Athem [Finnish], *abr.* Johan Ludvig Runeberg, *tr. fr. Swedish by* Elias Gordon. PoFr
National Hymn, A. John William DeForest. *Fr.* Miss Ravenel's Conversion. PAL
National Hymn: "God of our fathers, whose almighty hand." Daniel C. Roberts. PaA; PAL
National Hymn: "My Country, 'tis of thee." Samuel Francis Smith. *See* America.

National Hymns, The. "Orpheus C. Kerr." *See* Rejected "National Hymns," The.
National Miner, The, *with music.* John A. Stone. SGR
National Ode, Read at the Celebration in Independence Hall, Philadelphia, July 4, 1876. Bayard Taylor. PAH
America, *sel., fr.* III. AA; PAL; PoFr
National Paintings, The. Fitz-Greene Halleck *and* Joseph Rodman Drake. *Fr.* The Croaker Papers. AA
National Presage. John Kells Ingram. OnYI
National Song: "America, my own!" William Henry Venable. DD *abr.*; MC; PAH
National Song: "Rise, Magyar." Alexander Petofi, *tr. fr. Hungarian by* William N. Loew. PoFr
National Winter Garden. Hart Crane. *Fr.* The Bridge: Three Songs. AmP; ErPo; LiTA; LiTM (rev. ed.); OxBA; TDP
Nationalism. Dan Simmons. WSL
Nationality. Mary Gilmore. BoAV; NeLNL; PoAu-1
Nationality in Drinks, *sel.* Robert Browning.
"Here's to Nelson's memory," III. ViPo
Nations. Michael Brownstein. ANYP
Nation's Birthday, The. Mary E. Vandyne. DD; HH
Nation's Shrine, The. Alma Adams Wiley. PEDC
Nation's Strength, A. *Unknown, wr. at. to* Emerson. MaRV; PAL; PGD; SoP; TRV
"Not gold, but only man can make," *sel.* AmFN; FaPON; OTD
Nation's Wealth, A. John Dyer. *Fr.* The Fleece, III. OBEC
Native, The. W. S. Merwin. NePoEA-2; PoRA (rev ed.)
Native-born. Eve Langley. BoAV; NeLNL; PoAu-2
Native Companions Dancing. John Shaw Neilson. NeLNL
Native Inhabitant. Douglas Stewart. NeLNL
Native Irishman, The. *Unknown.* OnYI
Native Land. Gina Ballantyne. BoAu
Native Land. Sir Walter Scott. *See* Breathes There the Man.
Native Moments. Walt Whitman. NePA; OxBA
Native Son. Gertrude Callaghan. JKCP (1955 ed.)
Native Working on the Aerodrome. Roy Fuller. NeBP
Nativitie [*or* Nativity]. John Donne. AnAnS-1; MaMe; MeP; OBS; Sonn
Nativitie, The. William Drummond of Hawthornden. *See* Angels, The.
Nativitie of Christ, The. Robert Southwell. MeP
Nativity, The. Richard Crashaw. *See* In the Holy Nativity of Our Lord God.
Nativity. John Donne. *See* Nativitie.
Nativity, The. Henry W. Frost. SoP
Nativity. Ruth Gilbert. *Fr.* The Blossom of the Branches. ACV
Nativity. Gladys May Casely Hayford (Aquah Laluah). CDC; PBA; PoNe; TTY
Nativity, The. Milton. *See* On the Morning of Christ's Nativity.
Nativity. James Montgomery. *See* Angels, from the Realms of Glory.
Nativity. W. R. Rodgers. NeBP
Nativity, The. E. Merrill Root. ChIP
Nativity. May Sarton. NePoAm-2
Nativity, The. *Unknown.* MeEL
Nativity, The. Henry van Dyke. *Fr.* To the Child Jesus. MaRV
("Could every time-worn heart but see Thee once again.") TrPWD
Nativity, The. Charles Wesley. *See* Hark! the Herald Angels Sing.
Nativity Chant, The. Sir Walter Scott. *Fr.* Guy Mannering. ChTr; FaBoCh; LoGBV
Nativity Ode. St. Cosmas, *tr. fr. Greek by* John Mason Neale. CAW
Nativity of Christ, The. Luis de Góngora, *tr. fr. Spanish by* Longfellow. CAW
Nativity of Our Lord, The. Christopher Smart. *Fr.* Hymns and Spiritual Songs. EiCP; LoBV; PoEL-3
(Christmas Day, *sts.* 6-9.) ChTr
Nativity Song. Jacopone da Todi, *ad. fr. Latin by* Sophie Jewett. OHIP
Natura Benigna. Theodore Watts-Dunton. Sonn
Natura in Urbe. E. B. White. WaKn
Natura Naturans. Kathleen Raine. NYBP
Natura Naturata. Sir John Denham. CEP; NCEP; PeRV
Natural Architecture. John Hay. NePoAm
Natural Causes. Winfield Townley Scott. LiTL
Natural History, The, *sel.* Harold Monro.
"Vixen woman, The." OBMV
Natural History of Pliny, The. Vincent McHugh. NePoAm-2
Natural History of Selborne, The, *sel.* Gilbert White.
"While deepening shades obscure the face of day." LO
Natural Law. Babette Deutsch. MoLP
Natural Magic. "Æ." BEL
Natural Magic. Robert Browning. PoVP
Natural mop. Reality. Herbert Lee Pitts. WSL
Natural Selection. David Brock. TwCaPo
Natural silence of a tree, The. Fortune. Charles Madge. MoPW
Natural Tears. Thomas Hood. *See* Epigram: "After such years of dissension and strife."
Naturally it is night. Air. W. S. Merwin. AmPC; CoPo; NaP
Nature. Mark Akenside. *Fr.* The Pleasures of Imagination, IV. LoBV
Nature. Byron. *See* Ocean, The.
Nature. H. D. Carberry. PoNe
Nature. John Clare. CBEP
Nature ("The rounded world is fair to see"). Emerson. ILP; MWA-1
Nature ("A subtle chain of countless rings"). Emerson. AmePo; AmLP; AmPP; AWP; ILP; InPo
Nature ("Winters know"). Emerson. GBV (1952 ed.)
Nature. George Herbert. MaMe; OAEP
Nature. Longfellow. AA; AmePo; AmPP (3d ed.); AnNE; AP; BoNaP; CoBA; FaBoBe; HBV; InP; MaRV; PoLF; PoMa; SoP; TOP; TreFT; TrGrPo; TRV; WHA
Nature. Walter Stone. NYBP
Nature. Henry David Thoreau. FaBoBe; HBV; OTD; OTPC
Nature. Jones Very. AnAmPo; AP; HBV
Nature. Alfred de Vigny, *tr. fr. French by* Margaret Jourdain. AWP; JAWP; WBP
Nature, a jealous mistress, laid him low. Epigram on the Death of Edward Forbes. Sydney Dobell. VA
Nature and Art. Pope. *Fr.* Essay on Criticism, I. TreFT
Nature and God. William Cowper. *Fr.* The Task. CoBE
Nature and God—I neither knew. Emily Dickinson. MWA-2
Nature and he went ever hand in hand. A Priest. Norman Gale. VA
Nature and Life. George Meredith. Po; PoIE; VP
Nature and nature's laws lay hid by night. Epitaph Intended for Sir Isaac Newton. Pope. BWP; CBV; CEP; EiCL; ExPo; FaBoEn; FiP; ImOP; InP; MaRV; OAEP; SeCeV; TOP; ViBoPo
Nature and Religion. Sam Walter Foss. *Fr.* The Higher Catechism. OQP
Nature and the Child. John Lancaster Spalding. *Fr.* God and the Soul. AA
Nature and the Poet. Wordsworth. *See* Elegiac Stanzas Suggested by a Picture of Peele Castle, in a Storm.
Nature and the Poets. James Beattie. *See* But Who the Melodies of Morn Can Tell?
Nature at Three. Bettye Breeser. BiCB
Nature Be Damned. Anne Wilkinson. OBCV
"I took my watch beside the rose," *sel.* PeCV (1967 ed.)
Nature, creations law, is judg'd by sense. Upon Love Fondly Refus'd for Conscience Sake. Thomas Randolph. AnAnS-2
Nature doth have her dawn each day. Stanzas. Henry David Thoreau. AmLP
Nature! great parent! whose unceasing hand. Winter Winds. James Thomson. *Fr.* The Seasons: Winter. UnPo (1st ed.)
Nature had long a treasure made. The Match. Andrew Marvell. MaMe
Nature had made them hide in crevices. New Hampshire, February. Richard Eberhart. FiMAP; LiTM (1970 ed.); PoAn; TwCP
Nature has perpetual tears. Sir Herbert Read. *Fr.* The Analysis of Love. MoBrPo (1942 ed.)
Nature in Her Working. Richard Stanyhurst. NCEP
Nature, in thy largess, grant. To Mother Nature. Frederic Lawrence Knowles. HBV
Nature in War-Time. Herbert Palmer. HaMV
Nature is a temple from whose living pillars. Correspondences. Baudelaire, *tr. by* R. G. Stern. ReMP
Nature is a temple where we live ironically. Correspond-

ences. Baudelaire, *tr. by* Arthur Symons. SyP
"Nature is blind." Overheard in a Barbershop. Irving Layton. NMP
"Nature" is what we see. Emily Dickinson. MAmP
Nature Lover. John Frederick Nims. CBV
Nature, Man, Eternity. Henry Vaughan. *See* Bird, The, *and* Man *and* World, The.
Nature Morte. Louis MacNeice. CMoP
Nature most calm is often a crisis. Chesapeake. Gerta Kennedy. NYBP
Nature needs five; custom takes seven. Hours of Sleep. *Unknown.* GoTP
Nature No Self-Acting Instrument. Elizabeth Rundle Charles. SoP
Nature Note. Arthur Guiterman. SUS
Nature nothing shows more rare. Shells. T. Sturge Moore. SeCePo
Nature of an Action, The. Thom Gunn. ACV; NePoEA
Nature of Love, The. James Kirkup. EaLo
Nature of Love, The. Lucretius. *See* Concerning the Nature of Love.
Nature of the Cat, The, *sel.* E. V. Lucas.
Cat's Conscience, The. CIV; PoLF
Nature one hour appears a thing unsexed. Francis Thompson. *Fr.* Contemplation. OBNC
Nature Poem. Ruth Herschberger. OnHM
Nature reads not our labels, "great" and "small." The Man with the Hoe; a Reply. John Vance Cheney. AA; DD; HBV
Nature selects the longest way. A Northern Suburb. John Davidson. NBM; OBNC
Nature Study, After Dufy. Helen Bevington. NYBP
Nature That Framed [*or* Fram'd] Us of Four Elements. Christopher Marlowe. *Fr.* Tamburlaine the Great, Pt, I, Act II, sc. vii. MyFE; PoEL-2; TrGrPo
(Perfect Bliss and Sole Felicity.) SeCePo
Nature, That Gave the Bee. Sir Thomas Wyatt. CBEP
("Nature, that gave the bee so feat a grace.") FCP
Nature, That Washed Her Hands [in Milk]. Sir Walter Ralegh. CABA; EnRePo; FCP; NoP; ReEn; ReIE; TuPP
(Love and Time.) SiPS
Nature, the Artist. Frederic Lawrence Knowles. AA
Nature the False Goddess. James Jeffrey Roche. JKCP
Nature, they say, doth dote. The Martyr Chief [*or* Lincoln]. James Russell Lowell. *Fr.* Ode Recited at the Harvard Commemoration. DD; OQP; PGD
Nature! thou may'st fume and fret. To Miss Arundell. Walter Savage Landor. OBVV
Nature withheld Cassandra in the skies. Fragment of a Sonnet. Pierre de Ronsard. AWP; JAWP; OuHeWo; WBP
Nature's Charms. James Beattie. *Fr.* The Minstrel, I. OBEC
Nautre's confectioner the bee. Fuscara or the Bee Errant. John Cleveland. AnAnS-2
Nature's Creed. *Unknown.* MaRV; OHIP
(Handiwork of God, The.) TRV
Nature's decorations glisten. Christmas Day. Christopher Smart. Hymns and Spiritual Songs, Hymn XXXII. ChTr
Nature's Easter Music. Lucy Larcom. OHIP
Nature's Embassy, *sel.* Richard Brathwaite.
Nightingale, The. EIL
Nature's Enchantment. Keats. *See* To One Who Has Been Long in City Pent.
Nature's first green is gold. Nothing Gold Can Stay. Robert Frost. AmPP (5th ed.); BoLiVe; ILP; MAP; MaPo (1969 ed.); MoAB; MoAmPo; NeMA; PoPo; StP; WHA
Nature's Friend. W. H. Davies. PoRL; RG; TSW
Nature's Healing. Wordsworth. *Fr.* The Prelude, XII. EPN
Nature's Influence on Man. Mark Akenside. *Fr.* The Pleasures of Imagination, III. OBEC
(Created Universe, The.) LoBV
("Oh! blest of heav'n whom not the languid songs.") CEP
Nature's Key-Notes. Thomas Caulfield Irwin. IrPN
Nature's lay idiot [*or* Ideot], I taught thee to love. Elegy VII. John Donne. *Fr.* Elegies. MaMe; PoeP; SeCP
Nature's Lineaments. Robert Graves. FaBoTw
Natures Naked Jem. George Chapman. *See* Corinna Bathes.
Nature's Questioning. Thomas Hardy. BEL; CoBMV; EPN; InPo; MoPo; NoP; PoDB; PoFS; PoIE
Nature's Sorrow Cure. Catherine Cate Coblentz. OQP
Nature's Travail. *Unknown, tr. fr. Greek by* Goldwin Smith. AWP
Nature's Wash Day. Marguerite Gode. GFA
Naughty Blackbird, The. Kate Greenaway. *See* Child's Song.
Naughty Boy. Robert Creeley. AmPC
Naughty Boy, The. Keats. *See* Song about Myself, A.
Naughty Darkey Boy, The. *Unknown.* *See* Cruel Naughty Boy, The.
Naughty Lord & the Gay Young Lady, The. *Unknown.* CoMu
Naughty Preposition, The. Morris Bishop. FiBHP; NYBP; PV
Nausea. Catherine Davis. NePoEA
Nausea. E. L. Mayo. MiAP
Nausicaa ("Now when they came to the bright running river"). Homer, *tr. fr. Greek by* Sir William Marris. *Fr.* The Odyssey, VI. LiTW
Nausicaa ("The servants then"). Homer, *tr. fr. Greek by* George Chapman. *Fr.* The Odyssey, VI. OBS
Nausicäa. Irving Layton. ErPo
Nautical Ballad, A. Charles Edward Carryl. *Fr.* Davy and the Goblin, *ch.* 8. FaPON; GFA; HBV; MPB; OTPC (1946 ed.); RePo; StVeCh
(Walloping Window-Blind, The.) GoTP; InMe; LBN; MoShBr; TreFS; WhC
Nautical Extravaganza, A. Wallace Irwin. GSP; StPo
(Nautical Extravagance, A.) StVeCh
Nautilus, The. Charlotte Smith. OTPC (1923 ed.)
Nautilus Island's hermit. Skunk Hour. Robert Lowell. AmPP (5th ed.); AP; CMoP; CoAP; FRC; MaPo (1969 ed.); MoAmPo (1962 ed.); NMP; PoAn; PoeP; PoIE; TDP
Nauty Pauty Jack-a-Dandy. *Unknown.* OxNR
Navaho [*or* Navajo] Prayer. *Unknown.* *See* Prayer to the Mountain Spirit.
Navajo, The. Elizabeth Coatsworth. AmFN
Navajo Children, Canyon de Chelly, Arizona. Christopher Middleton. FlW
Naval Engagement. Tom Veitch. ANYP
Navel. Coleman Barks. *Fr.* Body Poems. QAH
Navies nor armies can exalt the state. Richard Watson Gilder. InP
Navigators, The. W. J. Turner. OBMV
Nay, be you pardoner or cheat. Villon's Ballade. Andrew Lang, *after* Villon. HBV
Nay but you, who do not love her. Song. Robert Browning. AnFE; BoLiVe; BoLP; EPN; GTBS-W; HBV; LiTL; MaPo; MeWo; OBEV (1st ed.); PoVP; TrGrPo; ViBoPo
Nay, come and visit me, sweet friend. Invitation to a Mistress. *Unknown.* UnTE
Nay, Death, thou art a shadow! Even as light. Lux Est Umbra Dei. John Addington Symonds. VA
Nay, do not grieve tho' life be full of sadness. Transience. Sarojini Naidu. MCCG
Nay, do not wrong Him by Thy heavy thoughts. Take Him. Horatius Bonar. FaChP
Nay, I cannot come into the garden just now. Maud. Henry S. Leigh. BOHV
Nay, I have loved thee! Theseus and Ariadne. Lloyd Mifflin. AA
Nay, Ivy, Nay. *Unknown.* CBEP; CH
(Holly and Ivy.) MeEL
Nay, Lord, not thus! white lilies in the spring. Sonnet on Hearing the *Dies Irae* Sung in the Sistine Chapel. Oscar Wilde. TrPWD
Nay! nay! Ivy. Holly against Ivy. *Unknown.* MeEL
Nay, nay, sweet England, do not grieve! "How Sleep the Brave." Walter de la Mare. TOP
Nay, pish; nay, phew! faith and will you? fie! A Maiden's Denial [*or* The Reluctant Lady]. *Unknown.* ErPo; UnTE
Nay, prethee dear, draw nigher. A Loose Saraband. Richard Lovelace. CavP; PoEL-3
Nay, prithee do, be coy and slight me. The Contrary. Alexander Brome. CavP
Nay prithee tell me, Love, when I behold. The Transfiguration of Beauty. Michelangelo. AWP
Nay, smile not at my sullen brow. To Inez. Byron. *Fr.* Childe Harold's Pilgrimage. MBW-2
Nay, soft and fair, good world; post not too fast. Epigram. Francis Quarles. *Fr.* Emblems. EP
Nay, tell me now in what strange air. Ballade of Dead Ladies. Villon, *tr. by* Andrew Lang. HBV

Nay, tempt me not, my Corydon; I tell you once again. Football and Rowing—an Eclogue. Alfred Denis Godley. CenHV
Nay, tempt me not to love again. Thomas Moore. *Fr.* Odes to Nea. OBNC
Nay then, farewell, if this be so. To Avisa. *At. to* Henry Willoby. *Fr.* Willobie His Avisa. ElL
"Nay then," quoth Adon, "you will fall again." Venus Abandoned. Shakespeare. *Fr.* Venus and Adonis. LO; OBSC
Nay, traveler! rest. This lonely yew tree stands. Lines Left upon a Seat in a Yew Tree. Wordsworth. EPN; MBW-2; MCCG
Nay, why should I fear Death. Laus Mortis. Frederic Lawrence Knowles. HBV
"Nay, with my goodwill." The Hell-Ride of Brynhild. *Unknown. Fr.* The Elder Edda. OuHeWo
Nay, Xanthias, feel unashamed. Ad Xanthiam Phoceum. Franklin P. Adams, *after* Horace. AWP; JAWP; WBP
Nay, you shall see mine orchard. Shakespeare. King Henry IV, Pt. II, Act V, sc. iii. MyFE
Nay, you wrong her, my friend, she's not fickle; her love she has simply outgrown. Outgrown. Julia C. R. Dorr. HBV
Nazareth. Thomas Curtis Clark. ChIP
Nazareth Shop, The. Robert McIntyre. StJW
(In the Carpenter Shop, *shorter vers.*) ChIP; GoTP; OQP; SoP
Ne Plus Ultra. Samuel Taylor Coleridge. ERoP-1
Neaera's Kisses. Johannes Secundus, *tr. fr. Latin by* John Nott. *Fr.* Basia. UnTE
Neap-Tide. Swinburne. PoVP; ViPo
Near a field overflowing. Roy Kloof Went Riding. Sydney Clouts. BoSA
Near a shady wall a rose once grew. The Rose Still Grows beyond the Wall. A. L. Frink. BLPA
Near an Old Prison. Frances Cornford. OBMV
Near Anio's Stream I Spied a Gentle Dove. Wordsworth. PeER
Near Avalon. William Morris. CBEP; PoVP
Near Barbizon. Galway Kinnell. NePoAm-2
Near Dover, September, 1802. Wordsworth. EnRP; MBW-2; TOP
(September, 1802; Near Dover.) MaPo; MERP; OAEP
(Sonnet: September, 1802.) ChER
Near Dusk. Joseph Auslander. FaPON; OTPC (1946 ed.)
Near Helikon. Trumbull Stickney. *Fr.* Sonnets from Greece. AnFE; CoAnAm; LiTA; NCEP; TwAmPo
Near him she stole, rank after rank. The Woman Who Came behind Him in the Crowd. George Macdonald. StJW
Near Lanivet, 1872. Thomas Hardy. AWP; CMoP; LoBV
Near Midnight. Norman MacCaig. OPoP
Near Mons. Neil Myers. NYTB
Near Neighbors. Swift. *after the Latin of* Martial. AWP
Near Périgord. Ezra Pound. CABL; FaBoMo; LiTA; LiTM (rev. ed.)
"I loved a woman," III. NP
Near Seven Springs, where the Churn rises, is Calmsden. Capturing a Spring. Rosemary Joseph. NYTB
Near strange, weird temples, where the Ganges' tide. The Bayadere. Francis Saltus Saltus. AA
Near the Base Line. Samuel L. Albert. NePoAm-2
Near the Cross. *At. to* Jacopone da Todi. *See* Stabat Mater Dolorosa.
Near the dawn Mary went. Dawn. Miriam Lefevre Crouse. ChIP
Near the dry river's water-mark we found. A Note Left in Jimmy Leonard's Shack. James Wright. TPM
Neat the edge, as on a shelf. Cat on the Porch at Dusk. Dorothy Harriman. GoYe
Near the great pyramid, unshadowed, white. Oblivion. W. W. Gibson. NP
Near the Lake. George Pope Morris. AA
Near the mountain's summit, when the bells. The Fox. R. Williams Parry. PrWP
Near the river with white waves, we probed. Apology of the Young Scientists. Celia Dimmette. GoYe
Near the road brim. Pittsburgh. Hy Sobiloff. NePA
Near the top a bad turn some dare. Well. Whether There Is Sorrow in the Demons. John Berryman. LiTM (1970 ed.)
Near this spot. Epitaph to a [Newfoundland] Dog. Byron. BLPA; TreFS
Near to a bank with roses set about. The Shepherd's Anthem. Michael Drayton. ReIE
Near [*or* Neare] to the silver Trent. Sirena [*or* Song to Sirena *or* The Jovial Shepheard's Song]. Michael Drayton. *Fr.* The Shepherd's Sirena. AtBAP; CBEP; PoEL-2; OBEV; SeCL; SeEP; TuPP
Near where I live there is a lake. Fringed Gentians. Amy Lowell. BrR; FaPON; MPB; OTD; SP
Near where the riotous Atlantic surge. Fragment. William Allingham. IrPN
Near where yonder evening star. Cockayne Country. Agnes Mary F. Robinson. OBVV; VA
Near Wilton sweet, huge heaps of stone are found. The Seven Wonders of England. Sir Philip Sidney. FCP
Near yonder copse, where once the garden smiled. The Village Preacher [*or* The Country Parson]. Goldsmith. *Fr.* The Deserted Village. MaRV; OBEC; OTPC (1923 ed.); TRV; WGRP
Nearer. Robert Nichols. NP
Nearer Home. Phoebe Cary. AA; AmePo; AnAmPo; BLRP; HBV; NeHB; OQP; SoP; TreF; WBLP; WGRP
Nearer, My God, to Thee. Sarah Flower Adams. BLRP; FaBoBe; FaFP; FaPL; MaRV; NeHB; TreF; WBLP; WGRP
(Nearer to Thee.) HBV; PoLF; SoP; VA
Nearest Friend, The. Frederick W. Faber. TreFS
Nearest the Dearest. Coventry Patmore. The Angel in the House, II, i, 4. HBV
Nearest Way to God, The. "Angelus Silesius," *tr. fr. German by* Paul Carus. OnPM
Nearing Again the Legendary Isle. C. Day Lewis. *Fr.* The Magnetic Mountain. CoBMV; FaBoTw; GTBS-W; LiTB; MoAB; MoBrPo; MoPW; NeMA; ReMP
Nearing La Guaira. Derek Walcott. TTY
Nearing Winter. Ernest Sandeen. NYBP
Nearly any child will share. Generosity. Virginia Brasier. StVeCh (1955 ed.)
Nearly Ready. Mary Mapes Dodge. PRWS
Nearly right, The. To the Tune of the Coventry Carol. Stevie Smith. FaBoTw
Neat little book, full of pictures, was bought, A. The New Book. Elizabeth Turner. OTPC (1923 ed.)
Neat little packet from Hobart set sail, A. The *Waterwitch. Unknown.* PoAu-1
Neat young lady at work in the garden, A. A Sweetheart in the Army (B *vers.*). *Unknown.* BaBo
'Neath Blue-Bell or Streamer. Poe. *See* Song: "Neath blue-bell or streamer."
'Neath leafy hawthorn in a garden gay. Troubadour Alba. *Unknown.* EnLi-1
'Neath northern skies thou hid'st thy punctual nest. The Loon. Theodore Harding Rand. CaP
'Neath the spiring of spruces. God's Acre. Blanche Edith Baughan. BoAu
Neatness in Apparel. Charles *and* Mary Lamb. OTPC (1923 ed.)
Neatness, madam, has. The Truth Is Quite Messy. William J. Harris. BOLo
Nebraska. Jon Swan. PoPo; WIRo
Nebuchadnezzar. Irwin Russell. HBV; IHA
Nebuchadnezzar. *Unknown.* SiTL
Nebuchadnezzar. Elinor Wylie. MAP; MoAmPo; NeMA
Necessary Miracle, A. Eda Lou Walton. NYBP
Necessity. Harry Graham. WePo
("Late last night I slew my wife.") ShM
Necessity of Religion, The. Walt Whitman. *Fr.* Starting from Paumanok. MaRV
Neckan, The. Matthew Arnold. GBV (1952 ed.)
Necks. Rowena Bennett. RePo
Neckwear. Michael Silverton. PV
Necromancers, The. John Frederick Nims. PoCh
Necropolis. Karl Shapiro. MoAB
Ned Braddock. John Williamson Palmer. MC; PAH
Ned Bratts. Robert Browning. CABL
Nedjé. Roussan Camille, *tr. fr. French by* Mercer Cook. PoNe
Need. Babette Deutsch. MoLP
Need, The. Siegfried Sassoon. TrPWD
Need of an Angel. Raymond Souster. CaP
Need of Being Versed in Country Things, The. Robert Frost. FaBoEn; OxBA; PoeP; PoSa
Need of Loving. Strickland Gillilan. *See* Folks Need a Lot of Loving.
Need of the Hour, The. Edwin Markham. PaA; PAL
Needle, The. Grace Cornell Tall. GoYe

Needle, The. Samuel Woodworth. GN; HBV
Needle, needle open up. The Lace Maker. Barbara Howes. NYTB
Needle Travel. Margaret French Patton. HBMV
Needles and pins, needles and pins. Mother Goose. BoChLi; FaBoBe; GoTP; HBV; OTPC; SiTL
Needless to catalogue heroes. No Man Knows War. Edwin Rolfe. TrJP; WaP
Needless Worry. Emerson. *See* Borrowing.
Needs. Elizabeth Rendall. HBMV
Needs Must I Leave, and Yet Needs Must I Love. Henry Constable. *Fr.* Diana. InvP; OBSC; SiCE
Needy are our neighbours, if we note rightly, The. The Sufferings of the Poor. William Langland. *Fr.* The Vision of Piers Plowman. PoFr; PoLi
"Needy Knife-grinder! whither are you going?" The Friend of Humanity and the Knife-Grinder [*or* The Knife-Grinder *or* Sapphics]. George Canning *and* John Hookham Frere. BOHV; CEP; EiCL; FOL; HBV; InMe; OBEC; Par; TOP
Ne'er trouble thyself at the times or their turnings. A Catch. *Unknown.* SeCL
Ne'er was the sky so deep a hue. The Inn by the Road. C. E. Warner. OQP
Nefarious War, The. Li Po, *tr. fr. Chinese by* Shigeyoshi Obata. WoL
Negation is the spectre, the reasoning power in man, The. Reason and Imagination. Blake. *Fr.* Milton. EnRP
Negative Love. John Donne. MaMe; ReEn; SCEP-1
Negatives, The. Philip Levine. NePoEA-2
Neglected long had been my useless lyre. On the Defeat at Ticonderoga or Carilong. *Unknown.* PAH
Neglectful Edward. Robert Graves. BrPo; MoBrPo; NeMA
Negro, The. James A. Emanuel. Kal
Negro/ in the cane fields. Cane. Nicolás Guillén. PoNe
Negro, The/ With the trumpet at his lips. Trumpet Player. Langston Hughes. TPM; TTY
Negro Hero. Gwendolyn Brooks. Kal
Negro holds firmly the reins of his four horses, The. The Drayman. Walt Whitman. *Fr.* Song of Myself, XIII. PoNe
Negro Judge, A. Frederick Seidel. CoPo
Negro Love Song, A. Paul Laurence Dunbar. BANP; PoNe
Negro Peddler's Song, A. Fenton Johnson. AmNP
Negro Poets. Charles Bertram Johnson. BANP
Negro Reel, *with music.* *Unknown.* AS
Negro Serenade. James Edwin Campbell. BANP
Negro Sermon, A; Simon Legree. Vachel Lindsay. *See* Simon Legree — a Negro Sermon.
Negro Singer, The. James David Corrothers. BANP
Negro Sings, A. Normil Sylvain, *tr. fr. French by* Edna Worthley Underwood. PoNe
Negro Soldiers, The. Roscoe Conkling Jamison. BANP
Negro Speaks of Rivers, The. Langston Hughes. AmFN; AmNP; BANP; CDC; GoSl; IDB; NoP; PoNe; TTY
Negro Spiritual ("Sable is my throat"). Perient Trott. PoNe
Negro Spiritual: "Swing low, sweet chariot." *Unknown.* *See* Swing Low, Sweet Chariot.
Negro Spirituals. Rosemary Benét *and* Stephen Vincent Benét. AmFN; FaPON
Negro Woman. Lewis Alexander. CDC
Negro Woman, A. William Carlos Williams. BWP; PoIE
Negroes. Maxwell Bodenheim. PoNe
Negroes, labouring, The. Guadalupe, W. I. Nicolás Guillén. TTY
Neighbour. J. R. Hervey. AnNZ
Neighbor. Edgar Paiewonsky. QAH
Neighbor, The. Rainer Maria Rilke, *tr. fr. German by* Jessie Lemont. OnPM
Neighbour mine not long ago there was, A. A Tale for Husbands. Sir Philip Sidney. *Fr.* Arcadia. SiPS
Neighbor sits in his window and plays the flute, The. Music. Amy Lowell. AnAmPo; YaD
Neighbor thought that they, A. The Planetary Arc-Light. August Derleth. GoYe
Neighboring. Christina Rossetti. *Fr.* Sing-Song. GaP; PCH
Neighborly. Violet Alleyn Storey. GaP; TiPo
Neighbors. Marilyn Francis. GoYe
Neighbors, The. Theodosia Garrison. HBMV
Neighbors. Arthur Guiterman. OTD
Neighbors. "Lennox." InMe
Neighbors. Anne Blackwell Payne. GFA
Neighbors. Anne Spencer. CDC
Neighbors. Helen Wing. GFA
Neighbors Help Him Build His House, The. *Unknown, tr. fr. Japanese by* Witter Bynner. LiTW
Neighbors of Bethlehem, The. *Unknown, tr. fr. French.* OHIP
Neighbors of the Christ Night. Nora Archibald Smith. ChrBoLe; PRWS
Neighing North, The. Annie Charlotte Dalton. CaP
Neither Durst Any Man from That Day Aske Him Any More Questions. Richard Crashaw. MaMe
Neither Here nor There. W. R. Rodgers. FaBoMo; GTBS-W; LiTB; LiTM; MoAB; MoBrPo (1950 ed.); NeBP; ViBoPo (1958 ed.)
Neither Hook nor Line. Bunyan. SD
Neither lighter nor heavier. Kite. Hollis Summers. NYTB
Neither love, the subtlety of refinement. The Presence. William Everson. ErPo
Neither malt nor Milton can. In Humbleness. Daniel G. Hoffman. NePA
Neither of them was better than the other. From Plane to Plane. Robert Frost. MoAmPo (1950 ed.)
Neither on horseback nor seated. Walt Whitman at Bear Mountain. Louis Simpson. CBV; LiTM (1970 ed.); ML; NePoEA-2; PoCh; PP
Neither Out Far nor in Deep. Robert Frost. AmP; AmPP (5th ed.); AP; CABA; CBV; ChTr; CoBMV; CrMA; DiPo; LiTA; MoAB; MWA-2; NoP; PAn; PoeP; TiPo (1952 ed.)
Neither Poverty nor Riches. Proverbs XXX: 7-9, Bible, *O.T.* TrJP
Neither Shall They Learn War Any More. Micah, Bible, *O.T.* *See* And They Shall Beat Their Swords into Plowshares.
Neither sighs, nor tears, nor mourning. Song. *Unknown.* SeCL
Neither Spirit nor Bird. *Tr. fr. Shoshone Indian by* Mary Austin. AWP; JAWP; PG; WBP
Neither the teacher of the class nor the priest with his catechism. Aimé Césaire. *Fr.* Memorandum on My Martinique. PoNe
Neither tribal nor trivial he shouts. Newsboy. Irving Layton. CaP
Neither war, nor cyclones, nor earthquakes. Antipater of Thessalonica. Kenneth Rexroth. CrMA
Neither will I put myself forward as others may do. Eternal Masculine. William Rose Benét. AWP; InPo; MAP; MoAmPo
Nekros. John Banister Tabb. AmP
Nell. Raymond Knister. *Fr.* A Row of Stalls. OBCV
Nell Flaherty's Drake. *Unknown.* AnIV; OA; OnYI
Nell Gwynne's Looking-Glass. Laman Blanchard. HBV; VA
Nell scolded in so loud a din. A Quiet Life and a Good Name. Swift. CBEP
Nellie Rakerfield. Nell. Raymond Knister. *Fr.* A Row of Stalls. OBCV
Nelly Trim. Sylvia Townsend Warner. ErPo; MoAB; MoBrPo
Nelson. Archibald T. Strong. *Fr.* Sonnets of the Empire. BoAu
Nelson and Pitt. Sir Walter Scott. *Fr.* Marmion, *Introd. to* I. FOL
(Nelson, Pitt, Fox.) OBEV
("November's sky is chill and drear.") OBRV
Nelson at Palermo. Alan Ross. POTi
Nelson, Pitt, Fox. Sir Walter Scott. *See* Nelson and Pitt.
Nelson Street. "Seumas O'Sullivan. OxBI
Nelson's on a column. Trafalgar Square. Rose Fyleman. UTS
Nemea. Lawrence Durrell. ChMP; FaBoTw; GTBS-P
Nemean Odes. Pindar. *See* Odes.
Nemesis. Emerson. AtBAP; PoIE
Nemesis. James William Foley. BOHV
Nemo Nascitur Artifex. Henry Parrot. SiCE
Neo-classical Poem. William Jay Smith. WaP
Neo-Classical Urn, The. Robert Lowell. NoP
Neon Diaspora. David Henderson. BF
Neon glitter of night. Beale Street, Memphis. Thurmond Snyder. NNP
Neoplatonic Soliloquy. Donald C. Babcock. NePoAm
Nepenthe, *sels.* George Darley.
"As from the moist and gelid sleep." OnYI
Hoopoe. OBNC
Hurry Me Nymphs. NBM
(Lines: "Hurry me Nymphs! O, hurry me.") HoPM

Nepenthe (continued)
"List no more the ominous din." OBRV
"Lo! in the mute, mid wilderness." OBRV
(Unicorn, The.) ChTr; ERoP-2; FaBoEn; NBM; OBNC; PoEL-4
O Blest Unfabled Incense Tree. AnIV; ChER; EG; FaBoCh; GTBS-D; OBRV; PeER
(Hundred-sunned Phenix.) OBNC
(Phoenix, The.) CBEP; ChTr; ERoP-2; LoBV; OBVV; WiR
"O fast her amber blood doth flow." OBRV
(Phoenix, The.) OBEV (new ed.)
Onward to Far Ida. OBNC
"Over a bloomy land, untrod." OBRV
(In Dreamy Swoon.) OBNC
"Solitary wayfarer!" OBRV
"Thou whose thrilling hand in mine." OBRV
Nephelidia. Swinburne. *Fr.* The Heptalogia. ALV; BoHV; EnLi-2 (1949 ed.); HBV; InMe; NA; OAEP; Par; PeVV; PoFS; PoVP; ViPo; VP
"From the depth of the dreamy decline of the dawn," *sel.* HoPM
Nephews and nieces,—love your leaden statues. Paul and Virginia. John Wheelwright. CrMA
Nephon's Song. George Darley. *Fr.* Sylvia; or, The May Queen. VA
(Elfin Pedlar, The.) BoTP
Neptune. Thomas Campion. *See* Hymn in Praise of Neptune.
Neptune and Mars in council sate. Louisburg. *Unknown.* PAH; ThLM
Neptune, the mighty Marine God, I sing. Homeric Hymn to Neptune. George Chapman. EtS
Neptune's Triumph, *sel.* Ben Jonson.
Chorus: "Spring all the Graces of the age," *also in* The Fortunate Isles and Their Union. OBS; SeCL
Nereid, Grand Turk, Good Intent. Waterfront. Oliver Jenkins. EtS
Nereides; or, Sea-Eclogues, *sels.* William Diaper.
Eclogue: "Lycon begin—begin the mournful tale." SeCePo
Sea Eclogue: "Otys, begin." LoBV
Nereids, The. Charles Kingsley. *Fr.* Andromeda. NBM
Nerves. Elizabeth Jennings. NYTB
Nerves. Arthur Symons. BrPo; FaBoTw; MoBrPo; SyP
Nervous smile as gaze meets, A. Face to Face. Denise Levertov. FRC; TPM
Nervy with neons, the main drag. At Barstow. Charles Tomlinson. TwCP
Nescit Vox Missa Reverti. J. V. Cunningham. ELU
Nest, The. Mary Elliott. OTPC (1923 ed.)
Nest is built, the song hath ceas'd, The. The Silenced Singer. William James Linton. VA
Nested. Habberton Lulham. HBV
Nesting Ground, The. David Wagoner. PoCh
Nesting-Time. Christina Rossetti. *See* Wrens and Robins . . .
Nesting Time. Douglas Stewart. PoAu-2
Nestor's Speech to Achilles and Agamemnon. Homer, *tr. fr. Greek by* George Chapman. *Fr.* The Iliad, I. ReEn
Nests are in the hedgerows, The. To a Child of Fancy. Lewis Morris. HBV
Nests well hidden. Secret Places. Irene Thompson. BoTP
Nestus Gurley. Randall Jarrell. NoP; TwCP
Net, The. W. R. Rodgers. AnIL; ErPo; NMP; OxBI
Net-Braiders, The. Thomas Wade. VA
Net eases, swaying into the sea, The. Dolphin. John Unterecker. ThO
Net Menders, The. Brian Vrepont. BoAV; PoAu-2
Net of Law, The. James Jeffrey Roche. HBV; PV
Net-of-smoke, A. For Mack. A. X. Nicholas. WSL
Net to Snare the Moonlight, A. Vachel Lindsay. CMoP; PoLF
Netley Abbey. William Lisle Bowles. Sonn
Nets are real, The—heroin (sniffed) clears them. For Artaud. Michael McClure. NeAP
Nets to Catch the Wind. John Webster. *See* All the Flowers of the Spring.
Netted Strawberries. Gordon Bottomley. AtBAP
Nettle, the Flower, The. Morton Dauwen Zabel. NP
Network, The. Robert Finch. CaP
Neurotic, The. C. Day Lewis. ACV
Neutral island facing the Atlantic, The. Neutrality. Louis MacNeice. CoBMV
Neutral Tones. Thomas Hardy. BrPo; BWP; CABA; CMoP; CoBMV; FosPo; ILP; LiTL; MaPo; MeWo; MoBrPo; PAn; PoeP; PoFS; PoVP; SyP; ViPo (1962 ed.); ViPP; VP
Neutrality. Sidney Keyes. MoAB; MoBrPo (1962 ed.)
Neutrality. Louis MacNeice. CoBMV
Neutrality Loathsome. Robert Herrick. LiTB
("Ye Cannot Serve God and Mammon.") PoFr
Nevada. Lawrence Gurney. GoYe
Nevada Cowpuncher to His Beloved, A. *Unknown.* SCC
Nevadaville upon a hill/ The home of Cousin Jack and Jill. The Fight at Nevadaville. *Unknown.* PoOW
Never a beak has my white bird. Thistle-Down. Clara Doty Bates. AA
Never a careworn wife but shows. Wives in the Sere. Thomas Hardy. BrPo
Never a mouse. Geometry. Alfred Kreymborg. AnAmPo
Never a trial that is not there. Moment by Moment. Daniel W. Whittle. BLRP
Never Admit the Pain. Mary Gilmore. NeLNL; PoAu-1
Never Again. Hugh McCrae. BoAu
Never again, beneath some fern or flower. To a Dead Cricket. Mnasalcas. RIS
Never again rejoicing in the surges that I sunder. The Dolphin's Tomb. Anyte. OA
Never again shall we beat out to sea. Fiddler's Green. Theodore Goodridge Roberts. CaP
Never again Would Birds' Song Be the Same. Robert Frost. CrMA; ForPo; NoP; Sonn
Never and never, my girl riding far and near. In Country Sleep. Dylan Thomas. LiTB; LiTM (rev. ed.)
Never Another. Mark Van Doren. MoRP
Never any more,/ While I live. In a Year. Robert Browning. AtBAP; EPN
Never any more shall the golden sun. The Fallen Poplar. Mary Webb. InP
Never Ask Me Why. Silvia Margolis. GoYe
Never ask of money spent. The Hardship of Accounting. Robert Frost. FaBoCh; FaFP; LoGBV; SiTL; WhC
Never be disenchanted of. Through Nightmare. Robert Graves. BoPe; Po
Never Being, But Always at the Edge. Stephen Spender. CMoP
Never, being damned, see Paradise. Those Not Elect. Léonie Adams. MoVE; PoDB
Never believe me, if I love. The Careless Lover. Sir John Suckling. CavP
"Never burn witchwood," my old Granny said. Witchwood. May Justus. SiSoSe
Never can I forget my woe. The Crusade. Rinaldo d'Aquino. CAW
Never, even in a dream. The Wanderer: Abroad. William Carlos Williams. TwAmPo
Never fear the phantom bird. Mentis Trist. Robert Hillyer. HBMV
Never for common signs dispraise or praise. To Young Imaginaries in Knowledge. Petrarch. *Fr.* Seven Penitential Psalms. ReEn
Never forget this when the talk is clever. The Sacred Order. May Sarton. ImOP
Never forget who brings the rain. Turn of the Moon. Robert Graves. BoC
Never Get a Lickin' till I Go Down to Bimini, *with music.* *Unknown.* OuSiCo
Never Get Out! John Galsworthy. OtMeF
Never Give All the Heart. W. B. Yeats. CMoP; EnL; EnLit; GTSL; HBV; MoLP
Never had child a more adventurous life. Iulus. Eleanor Glenn Wallis. NePoAm-2
Never has ship sailed on that sea. The Stone-Age Sea. Helen Hoyt. NP
Never have I been in the south. Mount Parnassus. Austin Clarke. NYTB
Never have I found a place, or a season, without beauty. The Desert. C. E. S. Wood. *Fr.* The Poet in the Desert. AnEnPo
Never heard happier laughter. Long View. Genevieve Taggard. MoAmPo
Never in a costly palace did I rest on golden bed. Henry van Dyke. *Fr.* The Toiling of Felix. ChIP
Never lived a Yankee yet. In the Catacombs. Harlan Hoge Ballard. BOHV
Never Love [Unless You Can]. Thomas Campion. EG; ElL; LoBV; NoP; ReEn; SiCE; TrGrPo; TuPP; ViBoPo; YAT

(Advice to a Girl). CoBe; EnLit; GTSL; HBV; LiTL; MeWo
Never love with all your heart. Song in Spite of Myself. Countee Cullen. BALP
Never May the Fruit Be Plucked. Edna St. Vincent Millay. CrMA; MoLP
Never mind avarice; the hills. Thinking of Hölderlin. Christopher Middleton. NePoEA-2
Never mind how the pedagogue proses. To Fanny. Thomas Moore. HBV
Never mind the clouds which gather. I Have Always Found It So. Birdie Bell. BLRP
Never mind the day we left, or the way the women clung to us. The Klondike. E. A. Robinson. PaA; PAH; ThLM
Never More. *See* Nevermore.
Never, never again. The Moment. Kathleen Raine. CMoP
Never, Never Can Nothingness Come. Norma Keating. GoYe
Never, never may the fruit be plucked from the bough. Never May the Fruit Be Plucked. Edna St. Vincent Millay. CrMA; MoLP
Never Night Again. Lilian Cox. ChIP; MaRV
Never No More. James K. Baxter. AnNZ
Never on this side of the grave again. A Life's Parallels. Christina Rossetti. NBM; PoEL-5
Never once—since the world began. God's Sunshine. John Oxenham. WBLP
Never pain to tell thy love. Blake. ERoP-1
Never pass a nun. How to Walk in a Crowd. Robert Hershon. ThO
Never presume that in this marble stable. The Brass Horse. Drummond Allison. FaBoTw
Never Said a Mumbalin' Word, *with music. Unknown.* ABF; TrAS
Never saw him. The Negro. James A. Emanuel. Kal
Never say die. Well-packed Wisdom. Benjamin Franklin. *Fr.* Poor Richard's Almanac. StaSt
Never Seek to Tell Thy Love. Blake. *See* Love's Secret.
"Never shall a young man." For Anne Gregory. W. B. Yeats. CMoP; DiPo; DTC; ExPo; FaBoMo; FaFP; ForPo; GTBS-W; InPo; LiTL; LiTM; LoBV; PoSa; SeCeV; SiTL; TDP
Never sings a city-robin on the gray-stone window-ledges. Returning. Ruth Guthrie Harding. HBV
Never stoops the soaring vulture. The Ghosts. Longfellow. *Fr.* The Song of Hiawatha. LoBV
Never Such Love. Robert Graves. FaBoEn
Never talk to me of waltzing it. Waltzing It. William Thomas Moncrieff. UnS
Never the nightingale. Dirge. Adelaide Crapsey. HBV; NP
Never the Spirit Was Born. *Unknown, tr. fr. Sanskrit by* Sir Edwin Arnold. *Fr.* Bhagavad Gita. MaRV; TreFT
Never the Time and the Place. Robert Browning. CaFP; EnLoPo; EPN; HBV; MaPo (1969 ed.); MBW-2; PoVP; ViPo; VP
Never the tramp of foot or horse. Farewell to Anactoria. Sappho. AWP; LiTW
Never think she loves him wholly. Appraisal. Sara Teasdale. MAP; MoAmPo
Never, though sky from sky divide by night. What Is Unwoven. Arthur Freeman. NYTB
Never to be lonely like that. Face to Face. Adrienne Rich. LiTM (1970 ed.); NoP; TPM
Never to see a nation born. The Great Virginian. James Russell Lowell. *Fr.* Under the Old Elm. PGD
Never to see ghosts? Then to be. Ghosts. Alastair Reid. FiSC; NYBP
Never to Visit You. Don Shea. QAH
Never Too Late, *sels.* Robert Greene.
Infida's Song. AtBAP; OBSC
(Sweet Adon.) NoP
("Sweet Adon', dar'st not glance thine eye?") LO
Palmer's Ode, The. CTC; EnRePo; OBSC; SiCE; TuPP
Never twice that river. By the River Eden. Kathleen Raine. NYBP
Never until the mankind making. A Refusal to Mourn the Death, by Fire, of a Child in London. Dylan Thomas. AtBAP; CABA; ChMP; CMoP; CoBMV; DiPo; FaBoEn; FaFP; FosPo; GTBS-P; GTBS-W; InPo; LiTB; LiTG; LiTM; MaPo; MasP; MoAB; MoBrPo (1962 ed.); MoPo; MoVE; NeBP; OAEP (2d ed.); PAn; PIA; Po; PoAn; PoDB; PoIE; PoPl; SeCePo; StP; TDP; ToPo; TwCP; UnPo (3d ed.); VaPo; WaaP
Never was I less alone than being alone. To His Posterity. Henry Parker, Baron Morley. TuPP
Never was there a man much uglier. Vain Gratuities. E. A. Robinson. MaPo; NePA
Never was there path our childhood used to roam. New Horizons. Sidney Royse Lysaght. HBMV
Never we needed Thee so sore. In Time of Need. Katharine Tynan. TrPWD
Never Weather-beaten Sail. Thomas Campion. BoC; CBEP; ChTr; EG; EIL; GoBC; OBSC; OxBoCh; PoEL-2; SiCE; TuPP
(O Come Quickly!) GTSE; MaRV; OBEV; TreFT
Never Will You Hold Me. Charles Divine. HBMV
Never yet was a springtime. Awakening. Margaret E. Sangster. AA
Nevermore/ Shall the shepherds of Arcady follow. The God-Maker, Man. Don Marquis. HBV; WGRP
Nevermore Alone. Elizabeth Barrett Browning. *See* Go from Me.
Never More, Sailor. Walter de la Mare. EtS
Never more will I protest. The Indifferent. Francis Beaumont. EIL; EnLit; HBV
Never More Will the Wind. Hilda Doolittle ("H. D."). *Fr.* Hymen. CTC; SiSw; TrGrPo
(Hymen.) ViBoPo
Nevertheless. Gustav Davidson. GoYe
Nevertheless. Marianne Moore. BWP; CMoP; ForPo; MoAB; OxBA; SeCeV
New Adam, The. Frank Belknap Long. FiSC
New Age, The. Frederic Lawrence Knowles. MaRV
(Victory Which Is Peace, The.) OQP
New Approach Needed. Kingsley Amis. PPON
New Arrival, The. George Washington Cable. AA; HBV
New Baby Calf, The. Edith Newlin Chase. SoPo; TiPo
New Ballad, A. Mary Leapor. WaPE
New Ballad, A. *Unknown.* PAH
New Ballade of the Marigolde, A. William Forrest. CoMu
(Margiold, The.) PoLi
New Balow, The. *Unknown.* CoMu
New Banner, The. Katrina Trask. PEDC
New Bath Guide, The, *sels.* Christopher Anstey.
Letter Containing a Panegyric on Bath, VI, *abr.* OBEC
Taste and Spirit, X. CEP; EiCL
New beauties push her from the stage. The Aging Coquette. John Trumbull. *Fr.* The Progress of Dulness. AnNE
New Being, The. Kenneth Patchen. ToPo
New Birth, The. Jones Very. AP; FaChP; MAmP
New Book, The. Elizabeth Turner. OTPC (1923 ed.)
New-born. *See* Newborn.
New Brooms. Robert Wilson. *Fr.* The Three Ladies of London. EIL
(Conscience's Song.) OBSC
New Bundling Song, A. *Unknown.* ErPo
New Canaans Genius; Epilogus. Thomas Morton. SCAP
New Castalia, The. William Hayes Ward. AA
New Cecilia, The. Thomas Lovell Beddoes. ERoP-2; PeER
New Challenge, The. Whittier. *Fr.* The Moral Warfare. MaRV
New Charon, The. Robert Herrick. ReEn
New Chitons for Old Gods, *sel.* David McCord.
Euterpe; a Symmetric. UnS
New Church Organ, The. Will M. Carleton. BOHV; PoLF
New City, The. Marguerite Wilkinson. MaRV, *abr.*; OQP; PEDC
New Colossus, The. Emma Lazarus. AmePo; AmFN; FaBV; FaFP; FaPL; FaPON; MaRV; OTD; PAL; PGD; PoLF; PoPl; TIHL; TreFS; TRV
"Give me your tired, your poor," *sel.* PoFr
(Inscription on the Statue of Liberty.) PaA; PoRL
New-come. *See* Newcome.
"New commandment, A," said the smiling Muse. Adakrue Nemontai Aiona. Emerson. MWA-1
New Construction; Bath Iron Works. G. Stanley Koehler. NePoAm-2
New couple is being united in the hall, The. Wedding Celebration. Tenrai Kono. HW
New Courtly Sonnet of the Lady Greensleeves, A. *Unknown. See* Greensleeves.
New Crucifixion. Earl Bigelow Brown. ChIP
New Crucifxion. Thomas Curtis Clark. ChIP
New Crusade, The. Katharine Lee Bates. MC

New Dance, A. S. E. Anderson. NBP
New-dated from the terms that reappear. To Oxford. Gerard Manley Hopkins. BrPo
New Day, The, *sels.* Richard Watson Gilder.
After-Song. AA
Prelude: "Night was dark, though sometimes a faint star, The." HBV; PoLF
Song: "Not from the whole wide world I chose thee," Pt. IV, Song IV. AA
Song: "Years have flown since I knew thee first," Pt. IV, Song VII. AA
New Day, The. Fenton Johnson. BANP
New desire to understand, A. R. G. E. Richard Eberhart. NYTB
New doth the sun appear. Change Should Breed Change. William Drummond of Hawthornden. *Fr.* Flowers of Sion. OBEV; OxBoCh
New Dreams for Old. Thomas Curtis Clark. OQP
New Dreams for Old. Cale Young Rice. HBV
New Duckling, The. Alfred Noyes. *Fr.* Touchstone on a Bus. BoTP; FaPON; MPB
New Dummy, The. Geoffrey Grigson. LiTM (rev. ed.)
New Dunciad, The, *sel.* Pope.
"Yet, yet a moment, one dim ray of light," IV. EiCL
New Dynamo. Gerald Raftery. PoMa
New Earth, A. John Oxenham. MaRV
New England. James Gates Percival. AA
New England. George Denison Prentice. AA
New England. E. A. Robinson. AmP; CABA; CBV; FaBoEn; ForPo; InPo; MAP; MoAB; MoAmPo; MoVE; OxBA; NoP; VaPo; WhC
New England. William Carlos Williams. PoeP
New England Bachelor, A. Richard Eberhart. MoAmPo (1962 ed.)
New England Church, A. Wilton Agnew Barrett. SoP; WGRP
New England Fog. Gertrude Callaghan. JKCP (1955 ed.)
New England Is New England Is New England. Brenda Heloise Green. GoYe
New England Landscape. DuBose Heyward. HT
New England Suite. Charles Philbrick. TwAmPo
New England was tall clippers. Citizens in the Round. Robert P. Tristram Coffin. RePo
New Englanders Are Maples. Robert P. Tristram Coffin. AnNE
New England's Annoyances. *Unknown.* AnAmPo, *abr.*; PAH
(Forefathers' Song.) AnNE
(Old Song, Wrote by One of Our First New-England Planters, An.) SCAP
New England's Chevy Chase, April 19, 1775. Edward Everett Hale. HBV; HBVY; PAH; PAL; PoRL; YaD
New-England's Crisis. Benjamin Tompson. SCAP
"Not ink, but bloud and tears," *sel.* AnAmPo
New England's Dead. Isaac McLellan, Jr. AA; PEDC
New England's Growth. William Bradford. PAH
New England's poet, rich in love as years. To Whittier. James Russell Lowell. CoBA
New English Canaan, *sels.* Thomas Morton.
Prologue. SCAP
Songe, The: "Drinke and be merry, merry, merry boyes." AmPP
New Every Morning. "Susan Coolidge." STF
New every morning is thy love. Hymn. John Keble. NBM
New every morning now the clerk docks off. Summer Holidays. W. R. Rodgers. LiTB
New Excavations. Leonora Speyer. InP
New Ezekiel, The. Emma Lazarus. AA; AnAmPo
New Faces, The. W. B. Yeats. GTBS-P; MoVE
New Farm Tractor. Carl Sandburg. FaPON
New feet within my garden go. Emily Dickinson. DiPo
New Fern, A. "A." PRWS
"New Flower, A—Pure and Untorn." Sister Mary Norbert Körte. ThO
New Forms. Peter Redgrove. NMP
New Freedom, The. Olive Tilford Dargan. HBMV
New friends are no friends; how can that be true? Of Friendship. Sir John Harington. SiCE
New Frontier by candelight, The. Dinner at Eight. Katie Louchheim. NYTB
New Garden, The. Reginald Arkell. RePo
New Gethsemane. Hazel M. Kerr. ChIP
New Ghost, The. Fredegond Shove. BoPe; ChMP; HBMV; MoVE; OxBoCh
New God, The. Witter Bynner. *Fr.* The New World. WGRP
New God, The. James Oppenheim. WGRP
New God, The; a Miracle, *sel.* Lascelles Abercrombie.
Margaret's Song. GTBS
New Guinea. J. P. McAuley. PoAu-2
New Guinea Lament. J. P. McAuley. BoAV
New Hampshire. T. S. Eliot. Landscapes, I. FaBoCh; GTBS-P; LoBV; LoGBV; LOW; NoP; PoSa; ThWaDe
New Hampshire. Robert Frost. AmPP (4th ed.)
New Hampshire. Donald Hall. NePoEA-2
New Hampshire Boy, A. Morris Bishop. HBMV
New Hampshire Farm Woman. Rachel Graham. GoYe
New Hampshire, February. Richard Eberhart. FiMAP; LiTM (1970 ed.); PoAn; TwCP
New Heart, The. *Unknown, tr. fr. Chinese.* WGRP
New Heaven, A. John Gould Fletcher. MAP; MoAmPo
New Heaven and Earth. D. H. Lawrence. CMoP
New Heaven, New War [*or* Warre]. Robert Southwell. AnAnS-1; LoBV; MeP; MePo; NoP; OBSC
(Come to Your Heaven, You Heavenly Choirs [*or* Quiries]!) EG; OxBoCh; PoLi
New Hellas, The. Irwin Edman. InMe
New Holland is a barren place, in it there grows no grain. The Lowlands of Holland. *Unknown.* OxBB
New Horizons. Sidney Royse Lysaght. HBMV
New House, The. Joseph Easton McDougall. CaP
New House, The. Edward Thomas. HBMV; MoAB; MoBrPo; OBEV (new ed.); POTE; PrWP
New Household, A. Longfellow. *Fr.* The Hanging of the Crane, Pt. I. GN
New Houses. Grace Noll Crowell. PEDC
New Hunting Song, A. *Unknown.* CoMu
New Hymns for Solitude, *sel.* Edward Dowden.
"I found Thee in my heart, O Lord." TrPWD
New Icarus, The. Vassar Miller. ToPo
New Idol, A. Laurence Binyon. PoFr
New Inn, The, *sels.* Ben Jonson.
"It was a beauty that I saw," *fr.* IV, iv. AnAnS-2; OBS; ReEn; SeCL; SeEP
(Lovel's Song.) TrGrPo
"What else/ Is love, but the most noble, pure affection," *fr.* III, ii. LO
New Integrationist, The. Don L. Lee. BOLo
New Interlude of Vice, Containing the History of Horestes, A. John Pickering. *See* Horestes.
New Jersey city where I did dwell. The Butcher Boy. *Unknown.* BaBo
New Jerusalem, The. Revelation, XXI, Bible, *N.T.* TrGrPo (1-6, 10-12, 21, 23-25)
New Jerusalem, A [*or* The]. Blake. *See* And Did Those Feet in Ancient Time.
New Jerusalem, The. *Unknown, at. to* "F. B. P.," *after the Latin* Urbs Beata Hierusalem. BoPe; HBV; OBEV; OxBoCh; ViBoPo, *longer vers.*
(Heavenly City, The.) GoBC
(Hierusalem.) CTC; OBSC
(Hierusalem, My Happie Home.) AtBAP; PoEL-2
(Jerusalem.) FaBoCh; LoGBV
(Jerusalem, My Happy Home.) CBEP; EIL, *longer vers.*; MaRV, *shorter vers.*; NoP; SiCE, *longer vers.*; WGRP
(O Mother Dear, Jerusalem.) WGRP
(Song Made by F. B. P., A.) CoMu
New Jewish Hospital at Hamburg, The. Heine, *tr. fr. German by* Charles Godfrey Leland. TrJP
New joy, new joy unto our king. Psalm XXI. *Paraphrased by* Sir Philip Sidney. FCP
"New King Arrives in His Capital by Air . . ."—Daily Newspaper. John Betjeman. OxBoLi; WhC
New Law, The. Blake. *Fr.* The Everlasting Gospel. StJW
("Jesus was sitting in Moses' Chair.") OxBoCh
New Leaf, The [*or* A]. Kathleen Wheeler, *wr. at. to* Helen Field Fischer. BLRP; MaRV; OQP; PGD; PoToHe; SoP; STF; WBLP
New Leaves. Juan Ramón Jiménez, *tr. fr. Spanish by* H. R. Hays. PoPl
New Legends. Robert Graves. AtBAP
New Life. Amelia Josephine Burr. HBV
New Life, The. Dante. *See* Vita Nuova, La.

New Life. Joseph E. Kariuki. TTY
New Light, A. William Hawkins. MoCV
New Limericks. *Unknown.* StaSt
New London, The. Dryden. *Fr.* Annus Mirabilis. FaBoCh; OBS
(London.) SeCePo
(Rebirth of London, The.) PeRV
New Love and the Old, The. Arthur O'Shaughnessy. *See* Song: "I made another garden, yea."
New Love, New Life. Amy Levy. OBVV
New Man, The. Jones Very. AP
New Married Couple, The; or, A Friendly Debate between the Country Farmer and His Buxome Wife. *Unknown.9* CoMu
New Mars, The. Florence Earle Coates. PGD
New Memorial Day, The. Albert Bigelow Paine. DD; HH; OQP; PEDC
New mercies, new blessings. New Things. Frances Ridley Havergal. BLRP; SoP
New Mexico. Polly Chase Boyden. TiPo
New Mexico and Arizona. George Canterbury. PoOW
New Miles Poem. Alden Van Buskirk. YAP
New Mistress, The. A. E. Housman. A Shropshire Lad, XXXIV. MoBrPo (1950 ed.); PoVP
New Moon. Edmund Blunden. BrPo
New Moon, The. Bryant. OTPC
New Moon, The. Eliza Lee Follen. BoChLi; PPL; TVC
New Moon. D H. Lawrence. BoNaP
New moon hangs like an ivory bugle, The. The Penny Whistle. Edward Thomas. MoAB; MoBrPo; MuSP
New moon hung in the sky, The. Prescience. Thomas Bailey Aldrich. AA; OBVV
New Moon in January. Ted Hughes. ToPo
New Moon in November. W. S. Merwin. PoIE (1970 ed.)
New moon in the sky. Haiku. Basho. Po
New moon, of no importance, The. New Moon. D. H. Lawrence. BoNaP
New Morality. George Canning, John Hookham Frere, *and others* . CEP
New Moses, The. M. K. Joseph. AnNZ
New-mown hay smell and wind of the plain. Population Drifts. Carl Sandburg. OxBA
New Name, The. *Unknown.* SoP
New National Anthem. *Unknown.* CoSo
New National Hymn, A. F. Marion Crawford. HH; PAH
New Negro, The. James Edward McCall. CDC; OTD
New Negro strides upon the continent, The. Melvin Tolson. *Fr.* Rendezvous with America. WOW
New Neighbor, The. Rose Fyleman. GaP; SoPo; TiPo
New neighbors came to the corner house. Clean Curtains. Carl Sandburg. WoL
New Occasions Teach New Duties. James Russell Lowell. *Fr.* The Present Crisis. TreFT
New Order, The. Phyllis McGinley. AmFN
New Order of Chivalry, A. Thomas Love Peacock. CenHV
New Orleans. Hayden Carruth. AmFN
New Orleans. Lola Ridge. MAP; MoAmPo (1942 ed.)
New Orleans Balcony, A. Dorothy Haight. CAW
New Orleans jail, no jail at all. Po' Boy. *Unknown.* ABF
New Pastoral, The, *sel.* Thomas Buchanan Read.
Blennerhassett's Island. PAH; ThLM
New Patriotism, A. Chauncey R. Piety. PGD
New Philosophy, The. John Donne. *Fr.* An Anatomy of the World: The First Anniversary. ExPo
New Physician, The. Stephen Chalmers. HBMV
New Poet, A. William Canton. HBV; VA
New Prince, New Pompe. Robert Southwell. AnAnS-1; ELP; EP; GN; MaRV; MeP; OBSC; OHIP; ReIE; SiCE; StJW; ThWaDe; TuPP
("Behold, a silly tender babe.") EG
(Humble Pomp.) GoTP
(In Freezing Winter Night.) FIW
New Prison. Charles Cotton. PeRV
New Ring, The. Karl Shapiro. MoLP
New Roof, The. Francis Hopkinson. PAH
New season brought sure the visible good. Restoration. Woodridge Spears. GoYe
New Shakespeare, A. Andrew Lang. CenHV
New Sheriff, The. LeRoi Jones. NoP
"New Shirt, A!" Why? Paul Grano. PoAu-2
New Shoes. Marjorie Seymour Watts. PCH; SoPo
New Shoes. Alice Wilkins. GFA; SUS; TiPo
New shoes, new shoes. Choosing Shoes. ffrida Wolfe. BrR; SoPo; SUS; TiPo
New Sights. *Unknown.* BoTP
New-silver-crescented the moon forth came. The New Moon. Edmund Blunden. BrPo
New Sinai, The. Arthur Hugh Clough. PoVP; ViPo
New-slain Knight, The. *Unknown.* ESPB
New Snow. Catharine Bryant Rowles. YeAr
New Song, The. Arthur Gordon Field. PGD
New Song, A. John Gay. BOHV; InMe
(New Song of New Similes, A.) SiTL
New Song, A. Joseph Stansbury. PAH
New Song, A ("As near beauteous Boston lying"). *Unknown.* PAH
New Song Called the Curling of the Hair, A. *Unknown.* CoMu
New Song Called the Gaspee, A. *Unknown.* PAH
New Song Composed on the Death of Lord Nelson, A. *Unknown. See* Death of Nelson, The.
New Song Entitled the Warming Pan, A. *Unknown.* CoMu
New Song of an Orange, A. *Unknown.* CoMu
New Song of Mary, A. *Unknown.* MeEL
New Song of New Similes, A. John Gay. *See* New Song, A.
New Song of Wood's Halfpence, A. Swift. OxBoLi
New Song on the Birth of the Prince of Wales, A. *Unknown.* CoMu
New Song, A; or Lilliburlero. Thomas, Lord Wharton. *See* Lilli Burlero.
New Song to an Old Tune, A. *Unknown.* PAH
New Song to Sing about Jonathan Bing, A. Beatrice Curtis Brown. SoPo
New Sound, The. Roger Aplon. YAP
New Spoon River, The, *sels.* Edgar Lee Masters.
Chandler Nicholas. NAMP
Euripides Alexopoulos. CMoP
Howard Lamson. NAMP; ViBoPo
Jay Hawkins. CMoP
Nathan Suffrin. CMoP
"Urge of the seed, The." OQP
New Spring, A. A. D. Mackie. OxBS
New Start, A. *Unknown.* OQP
New Strain. George Starbuck. TwCP
New Sun, The. John Wain. NePoEA-2
New Technique. Richard Armour. PoPo
New Temples. Lexie Dean Robertson. OQP
New Tenants, The. E. A. Robinson. NP
New Testament, The. Thomas Russell. TreFS
New Testament, Revised Edition. Sister Mary Catherine. ISi
New Things. Frances Ridley Havergal. SoP
New Things and Old. Sister Mary Madeleva. GoBC
New ties, fifteen each, ten. Ties. Raymond Souster. MoCV; OBCV
New Time. *Unknown.* BLRP
New Trinity, The. Edwin Markham. PGD
New Version, The. William James Lampton. BOHV
New Vestments, The. Edward Lear. BOHV; OnPP
New Victory, The. Margaret Widdemer. WGRP
New View, The. John Holmes. MiAP
New Vintage, The. Douglas Le Pan. OBCV
New War Song by Sir Peter Parker, A. *Unknown.* PAH
New-washed moon drew up from the sea's dark rim, The. Atlantic Moonrise. Vivian L. Virtue. PoNe
New Wife and the Old, The. Whittier.
New Wine, Old Bottles. Colin Newbury. AnNZ
New Wings for Icarus, *sel.* Henry Beissel.
"In the one-two domestic goose one-two one-two step," II. MoCV
New Words for an Old Song. Babette Deutsch. NePoAm
"New words, new metres, new emotions—all." Modernity. F. L. Lucas. LO
New Words to the Tune of "O'Donnel Abu." Jim Connell. OnYI
New World, The, *sel.* Louis James Block.
Final Struggle, The. PAH
New World, The, *sels.* Witter Bynner.
Grieve Not for Beauty. NP
New God, The. WGRP
"Somebody called Walt Whitman." InP
New World, The. Paul Engle. AmFN
New World. Brewster Ghiselin. MoVE
New World, The, *sel.* Edgar Lee Masters.
"This America is an ancient land." AmFN

New World, A. Shelley. *See* Chorus: "World's great age begins anew, The."
New World, The. Jones Very. AA; AnNE; AP
New World of Will. David Shapiro. ANYP
New Worlds. Milton. *Fr.* Paradise Lost, III. OBS (Panorama, The, *shorter sel.*) WHA
New World's sweetest singer, The! Time may lay. Longfellow. Craven Langstroth Betts. DD
New Year, The. Augustus Henry Baldwin. *Fr.* On the Threshold. DD
New Year, The. Donald E. Cooke. MPB (1956 ed.)
New Year, The. George Cooper. DD; PEDC
New Year, The. Charles Cotton. CEP; GoTL; OBS
New Year, The. Dinah Maria Mulock Craik. BrR; DD; HH; MPB; OTPC (1946 ed.); PCH; YeAr
New Year, A. Mary Carolyn Davies. OQP; YeAr
New Year, The. Lillian Gilchrist Gard. OQP
New Year, The. Homera Homer-Dixon. BLRP; SoP
New Year, The. Omar Khayyám, *tr. fr. Persian by* Edward Fitzgerald. *Fr.* The Rubáiyát. OnPM
New Year. John J. Moment. MaRV
New Year, The. Raymond Orner. SoP
New Year, The. Horatio Nelson Powers. OQP; PoRL; PoToHe
New Year, A. Margaret E. Sangster. DD, *abr.*; PEDC
New Year, A. Dora Sigerson Shorter. YeAr
New Year. Stephen Spender. AWP
New Year, The. J. D. Templeton. OQP; PGD
New Year, The. Tennyson. *See* In Memoriam A. H. H., CVI: "Ring out, wild bells. . ."
New Year. Thomas Wearing. MaRV
New Year ("Dear Master, for this coming year"). *Unknown.* SoP
New Year, The ("God gives to you another year"). *Unknown.* STF
New Year, The ("I am the little New Year, ho, ho!"). *Unknown.* BoTP
New Year, The ("Oh! I'm the New Year"). *Unknown.* BoTP
New Year ("Over the threshold a gallant newcomer"). *Unknown.* HH
New Year, The ("With gladness hail the dawning year"). *Unknown.* PEDC
New Year Carol, A: "Here we bring new water." *Unknown.* AtBAP; BoTP; CH; FIW; OxBoLi; PoSC; ThWaDe
New Year Ditty. Christina Rossetti. PoRL
New Year Idyl, A, *sel.* Eugene Field.
"Upon this happy New Year night." PoSC
New yeare forth looking out of Ianus gate. Amoretti, IV. Spenser. ReEn
New year hath come in sight, The. The Eighteenth Song. Hadewijch. LiTW
New Year Is a Banner, The. Margaret E. Sangster. PEDC
New Year is an open door, The. The New Year. Raymond Orner. SoP
New Year Letter, *sel.* W. H. Auden.
"O Unicorn among the cedars." FaBoEn
New Year met me somewhat sad. New Year Ditty. Christina Rossetti. PoRL
New Year Prayer. Edgar Daniel Kramer. PEDC
New Year Song. Emily Huntington Miller. DD; HH; PoRL
New Year Thoughts. "N. M. B." SoP
New Year Wish, A. Frances Ridley Havergal. BLRP
New Year Wish, A. Mary J. Lewis. SoP
New Year Wish, A. *Unknown.* BLRP
New Year Wishes. May Sarton. MoRP
New yeares, expect new gifts: Sister, your harpe. Ben Jonson. SeCP
New-Yeares Gift, A. Thomas Carew. SCEP-2
New-Yeares-Gift Sung to King Charles, 1635, A. Ben Jonson. SeCP
New Year's. Gail Dusenbery. ThO
New Years and Old. Maud Frazer Jackson. PGD
New Year's Burden, A. Dante Gabriel Rossetti. AtBAP
New Year's Day. Richard Crashaw. MaMe; SeEP
New Year's Day. Rachel Field. SoPo; TiPo
New Year's Day. Robert Lowell. AmPP (5th ed.); CABA; LiTM (1970 ed.); NePoEA
New Year's Day. *Unknown.* PEDC
New Year's Days. Celia Standish. BoTP
New Year's Eve. F. A. Bartleson. PAP
New Year's Eve. John Berryman. LiTM (1970 ed.); NMP
New Year's Eve, *sel.* John Davidson.
Imagination. MoBrPo
New Year's Eve. Thomas Hardy. MoBrPo
New Year's Eve. D. H. Lawrence. ErPo
New Year's Eve. H. B. Mallalieu. WaP
New Year's Eve ("If you're waking, call me early"). Tennyson. *Fr.* The May Queen. OTPC (1923 ed.)
New Year's Eve ("Ring out, wild bells"). Tennyson. *See* In Memoriam A. H. H., CVI: "Ring out, wild bells, to the wild sky."
New Year's Eve in Solitude. Robert Mezey. NaP
New Year's Eve in Troy. Adrienne Rich. NePoEA-2
New Year's Eve—Midnight. Frederika Richardson Macdonald. VA
New Year's Eve, 1938. John Frederick Nims. MiAP
New Year's Gift to Brian Lord Bishop of Sarum, A. William Cartwright. MePo
New Year's Gift to Phyllis, The. Matthew Prior. CBEP
New Year's Hymn. Robert Browning. *See* All Service Ranks the Same with God.
New Year's Message, A. Martha Snell Nicholson. SoP
New Year's near, glass autumn long gone. Edwin Denby. ANYP
New Year's Poem. Margaret Avison. LiTM (1970 ed.); OBCV
New Year's Promise, A. *Unknown.* BLRP
New Year's Thoughts. Lillian Gray. OQP
New Year's Wish, A. "J. H. S." BLRP
New Year's Wishes. Frances Ridley Havergal. BLRP; STF
New-Yeeres Gift, The, or Circumcisions Song, Sung to the King in the Presence at White Hall. Robert Herrick. SeCV-1
New York. "Æ." OBMV
New York. Arthur Guiterman. PaA
New York. Tony Towle. ANYP
New York-Albany. Lawrence Ferlinghetti. PoCh
New York! At first I was confused by your beauty. To New York. Léopold Sédar-Senghor. PBA
New York City. George Abbe. GoYe
New York City. Maxwell Bodenheim. HBMV
New York—December, 1931. Babette Deutsch. ImOP
New York in August. Donald Davie. NMP
New York in the Spring. David Budbill. CAD
New York, it would be easy to revile. New York City. Maxwell Bodenheim. HBMV
New York Skyscraper, A, *sel.* James Oppenheim.
"O sprawling city! worlds in a world!" MaRV
New York's lovely weather hurts my forehead. For You. Ted Berrigan. ANYP
New Zealand, *sel.* Hubert Church.
"Ye wandering winds that from your threshing floor." AnNZ
New Zealand. William Pember Reeves. BoAu
New Zealand Comforts. John Barr of Craigielee. AnNZ
New Zealand Regret, A. Eleanor Elizabeth Montgomery. VA
Newark Abbey. Thomas Love Peacock. OBNC
Newark, for Now (68). Carolyn M. Rodgers. WSL
New-born, The. Helen Hoyt. NP
Newborn Death. Dante Gabriel Rossetti. The House of Life, XCIX-C. MaVP; PoVP; ViPo
New-come Chief. James Russell Lowell. *Fr.* Under the Old Elm, III. MC
Newcomer's Wife, The. Thomas Hardy. PoFS; VP
Newer Vainglory, The. Alice Meynell. JKCP; MaRV; MoRP; OQP
Newes from Virginia. Richard Rich. PAH
Newest moon is not so far, The. Neighbors. Anne Blackwell Payne. GFA
Newfoundland. E. J. Pratt. TwCaPo
Newly Discovered "Homeric" Hymn, A. Charles Olson. NeAP
Newly-wedded, The. Winthrop Mackworth Praed. HBV; MaRV; VA
Newlyweds, The. Cloyd Mann Criswell. PoLF
Newlyweds, The. John Updike. PV
Newlyweds' Accident, The. David Hilton. QAH
Newlyweds' Cuisine, The. Wang Chien, *tr. fr. Chinese by* David Rafael Wang. HW
Newlyweds' Separation, The. Tu Fu, *tr. fr. Chinese by* David Rafael Wang. HW
Newman. George N. Shuster. JKCP (1926 ed.)
Newport North-Window View. Philip Whalen. FRC
Newport Street, E. Douglas Goldring. HBMV
News. Louis Dudek. *Fr.* Provincetown. MoCV

News. Frank Lima. ANYP
News. Vern Rutsala. WOW
News, The. "Sec." TRV
News, The. Charles Sprague. *Fr.* Curiosity. AA
News. Thomas Traherne. *Fr.* The Third Century. GTBS-W; MePo; OBEV; SCEP-1; SeCV-2; SeEP
(On News.) AnAnS-1; FaBoEn; MeP; QFR
News for the Delphic Oracle. W. B. Yeats. CMoP; CoBMV; LiTB; LiTM; MoPo; OAEP (2d ed.)
News from a foreign [*or* forein *or* forrein] country came. News [*or* On News]. Thomas Traherne. *Fr.* The Third Century. AnAnS-1; FaBoEn; GTBS-W; MeP; MePo; OBEV; QFR; SCEP-1; SeCV-2; SeEP
News from Colchester. Sir John Denham. PeRV
News from Mount Amiata. Robert Lowell, *ad. fr. the Italian of* Eugenio Montale. NaP
News from Norwood. Christopher Middleton. NePoEA-2
News from Plymouth, *sel.* Sir William Davenant.
O Thou That Sleep'st, *fr.* III, i. CBEP; EG; InvP
(Song.) SeEP
News from the Cabin. May Swenson. NMP; NYBP
News from the Court. David Wagoner. NePoAm-2; NePoEA-2
News from the heavens! All wars are at an end. Rare News. Nicholas Breton. *Fr.* Bower of Delights. ReIE
News from the House. Michael Dennis Browne. NYBP
News from Yorktown. Lewis Worthington Smith. MC; PAH
News is yellowing in the rain, The. The Paper in the Meadow. Oscar Williams. PG (1955 ed.)
News Item. Dorothy Parker. SiTL; TreF; YaD
(Some Beautiful Letters: News Item.) InMe
News lapped at us out of all, The. The Sirens. Donald Finkel. NePoEA
News! News! Eleanor Farjeon. SiSoSe
News of a Baby. Elizabeth Riddell. BoAV
News of My Friends. Grant Code. FiSC
News of the dead is heard through words of the living. The Speech of the Dead. Anne Ridler. ChMP
News of the Phoenix. A. J. M. Smith. ELU; MoCV; PeCV (1967 ed.)
News of the World. Anne Ridler. MoLP
News of the World I ("Cold shuttered loveless star, skulker in clouds"). George Barker. FaBoMo; LiTB
News of the World II ("In the first year of the last disgrace"). George Barker. DTC; FaBoTw; LiTB
News of the World III ("Let her lie naked here, my hand resting"). George Barker. AtBAP; FaBoTw; LiTB; LiTM (rev. ed.)
News, The! our morning, noon, and evening cry. The News. Charles Sprague. *Fr.* Curiosity. AA
News Reel. *See* Newsreel.
News Report. David Ignatow. ErPo, TwCP
News Stand, The. Daniel Berrigan. CAD
News to the King. Augusta Webster. VA
Newsboy. Irving Layton. CaP
Newspaper, The, *sel.* George Crabbe.
"I sing of news, and all those vapid sheets." PPON
Newspaper. Aileen Fisher. SoPo
Newspaper is a Collection of Half-Injustices, A. Stephen Crane. *Fr.* War Is Kind, XII. AmePo; AmPP (5th ed.); AP; CoBA; NCEP; ViBoPo
(Newspaper, A.) AmP
Newsreel. C. Day Lewis. ILP; MoAB; MoBrPo (1950 ed.); NeMA
News Reel. David Ross. GoYe
Newstead Abbey. Byron. ChER
Newsvendor with his hut and crutch, The. The Imprisoned. Robert Fitzgerald. TwCP
Newt, The. David McCord. TiPo (1959 ed.)
Newton. Wordsworth. *Fr.* The Prelude, III. ImOP
Newton to Einstein. Jeannette Chappell. GoYe
Next at our altar stood a luckless pair. George Crabbe. *Fr.* The Parish Register, II. OBRV
Next came Covetousness; I cannot describe him. Avarice. William Langland. *Fr.* The Vision of Piers Plowman. PoLi
Next comes the dull disciple of thy school. Byron. *Fr.* English Bards and Scotch Reviewers. OBRV; PP
Next Day. Rachel Field. *Fr.* A Circus Garland. SoPo; StVeCh
Next Day. Randall Jarrell. NYBP
Next died the lady, who yon hall possess'd. The Lady of the Manor. George Crabbe. *Fr.* The Parish Register, III. OBNC
Next died the Widow Goe, an active dame. George Crabbe. *Fr.* The Parish Register, III. EnPE
Next Door. Richard Wilbur. NoP
Next, for October, to some sheltered coign. Sonnets of the Months: October. Folgore da San Geminiano. AWP
Next his chamber, beside his study. The Bishop's Harp. Robert Mannyng. ACP
Next I come to the manna, the heavenly gift of honey. Vergil. *Fr.* Georgics. FIW
Next Marlowe, bathed in the Thespian springs. Christopher Marlowe. Michael Drayton. *Fr.* To Henry Reynolds, of Poets and Poesy. ChTr
Next Next Shortest Poem in the World, The. Martha Salemme. SiTL
Next of Kin. H. B. Mallalieu. WaP
Next of Kin. Christina Rossetti. HBV
Next, Please. Philip Larkin. EiCP; MoBrPo (1962 ed.); NePoEA; PoIE
Next Shortest Poem in the World, The. *Unknown.* SiTL
Next these, a troop of buisy spirits press. Dryden. *Fr.* Absalom and Achitophel, Pt. II. CEP; SeCV-2
Next Time. Laura Simmons. PGD
Next, to a lady I must bid adieu. The Dean's Lady. George Crabbe. LoBV
Next to of Course God America I. E. E. Cummings. AmFN; AmP; AmPP (5th ed.); AnNE; AP; CABA; CBV; ExPo; FosPo; InPo; LiTM; NePA; NoP; OxBA; PoIE; PoPo; SiTL; ThLM; WaaP; YaD
(147.) PoFr
Next unto Him Was Neptune Pictured. Spenser. *Fr.* The Faerie Queene, III, 11. EtS
Next Voice You Hear, The. Thomas P. McDonnell. JKCP (1955 ed.)
Next War, The. Robert Graves. BrPo
Next War, The. Wilfred Owen. AnEnPo; Sonn; WaP
Next War, The. Sir Osbert Sitwell. MMA
Next week they're goin' to lay me off because I'm gettin' old. The Old Quartermaster. Gordon Grant. EtS
Next week will be publish'd (as "Lives" are the rage). "The Living Dog" and "The Dead Lion." Thomas Moore. OBRV
Next whose fortune 't was a tale to tell, The. Fitz Adam's Story. James Russell Lowell. AmePo; AmPP (5th ed.); MWA-1
Next Year. Nora Perry. PoToHe
Next year the grave grass will cover us. Street Corner College. Kenneth Patchen. MoAmPo
Ngoni Burial Song. *Unknown, tr. fr. Zulu.* PeSA
Niagara. Adelaide Crapsey. MAP; MoAmPo (1942 ed.)
Niagara. Edward F. Garesché. JKCP
Niagara. Lydia Huntley Sigourney. AmLP
Nibble, nibble, little sheep. Sheep. Samuel Hoffenstein. AnAmPo; TrJP
Nibelungenlied. *Unknown.* *See* Song of the Nibelungs, The.
Nice Correspondent, A. Frederick Locker-Lampson. HBV
Nice Day for a Lynching. Kenneth Patchen. PoNe
Nice Girls Don't Chase the Boys, *with music.* *Unknown, tr. fr. French by* Janet E. Tobitt. SaSa
Nice Mister Carrot. Mister Carrot. Dorothy Aldis. GFA
Nice Mrs. Eberle early had been told. La Donna È Perpetuum Mobile. Irwin Edman. NYBP
Nice old lady named Tweedle, A. Limerick. *Unknown.* LiBL
Nice Part of Town, A. Alfred Hayes. NYBP
Nice to be God. The Convent. Jeanne D'Orge. AnAmPo
Nice Valour, The, *sel.* John Fletcher *and (at.)* Thomas Middleton.
Melancholy, *fr.* III, iii. GTBS; GTBS-D; GTBS-P; GTBS-W; GTSE; GTSL; HBV; OBEV
(Hence All You Vain Delights.) AtBAP; OAEP; SeCL; TuPP; ViBoPo
(O Sweetest Melancholy.) TrGrPo
(Passionate Man's Song, The.) OBS; SiCE
(Song: "Hence all you vain delights.") PoEL-2
(Sweetest Melancholy.) BEL
Nice young man about the town, A. I've Got the Giggles Today. A. P. Herbert. FiBHP
Nice young ma-wa-wan [*or* ma-wan-wan], A. The Rattlesnake Song. *Unknown.* ABF; BFSS; CoSo; IHA; RePo

Nicest child I ever knew, The. Charles Augustus Fortescue. Hilaire Belloc. OnPP
Nicest Story, The. Abbie Farwell Brown. HH
Nicholas Ned. Laura E. Richards. *Fr.* Nonsense Verses. RIS
Nicholas Nye. Walter de la Mare. BoChLi; BoTP; HBMV; OA
Nicht Is Neir Gone, The. Alexander Montgomerie. *See* Night Is Near Gone, The.
Nick and the Candlestick. Sylvia Plath. CoAP
Nickajack Cave. Coleman Barks. QAH
Nickle Bet, A. Etheridge Knight. CAD
Nicky, the word has come to the West Coast. Smoke. Charles Wright. NYBP
Nicodemus. Harry Kemp. OQP
Nicodemus, *sel.* Andrew Young.
Conversion. MaRV
Nicolas Gatineau. Arthur S. Bourinot. CaP
Nicorn's Dower, The. Peter Hopegood. MoAuPo
Nievie nievie nick nack. *Unknown.* OxNR
Nigga Section, The. Welton Smith. BF
Nigger. Frank Horne. BANP; CDC
Nigger. Karl Shapiro. OxBA
Nigger mighty happy w'en he layin' by co'n. The Plough-Hands' Song. Joel Chandler Harris. *Fr.* Uncle Remus, His Songs and His Sayings. AA; LHV
Niggers and spics and assorted what nots. Everything. Janice Marie Gadsden. WSL
Nigh one year ago. Lucifer and Elissa. Philip James Bailey. *Fr.* Festus. VA
Nigh to a grave that was newly made. The Old Sexton. Park Benjamin. AA; HBV
Night. Sabine Baring-Gould. *See* Now the Day Is Over.
Night, The. Hilaire Belloc. HBV; OBEV (new ed.); OBVV
Night. William Rose Benét. MAP; MoAmPo; NeMA
Night. Hayyim Nahman Bialik, *tr. fr. Hebrew by* Maurice Samuel. AWP; LiTW
Night ("Still the Faint harps"). Blake. *Fr.* The Four Zoas. BoW
Night ("The sun descending in the west"). Blake. *Fr.* Songs of Innocence. AnFE; AtBAP; BoNaP; BoTP; CBEP; CEP; CH; CoBE; EnRP; FaBoBe; FaPON; GoTP; GTBS-D; HBV; HBVY; MaPo; MyFE; OBEC; OBEV; OTPC (1923 ed.); OxBoCh; PoE; PoLF; RIS; SAS; ShBV-3; StaSt, 2 *sts.*; TreFT; WiR
(Guardian Angels of the Creatures.) BoC
Night. Robert Bly. NaP
Night. John Brown. OBEC
Night. Christine Wood Bullwinkle. OTPC (1946 ed.); PCH
Night. Mary Frances Butts. OTPC (1946 ed.); PRWS
Night. Witter Bynner. *Fr.* To Celia. NP
Night ("It is the hush of night"). Byron. *See* It Is the Hush of Night.
Night. George Chapman. *Fr.* The Shadow of Night. OBSC
Night. Charles Churchill. *See* Night; an Epistle to Robert Lloyd.
Night. Hartley Coleridge. NCEP
Night, *sel.* Victor J. Daley.
"Suns, planets, stars, in glorious array." PoAu-1
Night, The. Lawrence Durrell. *Fr.* Eight Aspects of Melissa. NeBP
Night. Donald Jeffrey Hayes. CDC
Night. Charles Heavysege. OBCV
Night. Hermann Hesse, *tr. fr. German by* Ludwig Lewisohn. AWP; JAWP; WBP
Night. Patricia Hubbell. PDV
Night. Solomon ibn Gabirol, *tr. fr. Hebrew by* Emma Lazarus. TrJP
Night. Jami, *tr. fr. Persian by* Samuel Robinson. LiTW
Night. Robinson Jeffers. AmPP (3d ed.); AP; AWP; CoBMV; InPo; JAWP; LiTA; MAP; MoAmPo; MoPo; NoP; NP; OxBA; WBP; WHA
Night. Glyn Jones. NeBP
Night, The. Helen Leuty. BoTP
Night, The. Myra Cohn Livingston. PDV
Night. Lois Weakley McKay. SiSoSe
Night. "Gabriela Mistral," *tr. fr. Spanish by* Alice Jane McVan. LiTW
Night. James Montgomery. HBV
Night, *sels.* James Oppenheim.
"Machinery is enough for a scientist." TRV
Priest, The. MaRV
Night, *sel.* Charles Péguy, *tr. fr. French by* Anne Green *and* Julian Green.
"Nights follow each other and are linked." LiTW
Night. Petrarch, *tr. by* Earl of Surrey. *See* Complaint by Night of the Lover Not Beloved, A.
Night. Henri de Régnier, *tr. fr. French by* "Seumas O'Sullivan." AWP; JAWP; WBP
Night. Thomas William Rolleston. HBV
Night. Carl Sandburg. *Fr.* The Windy City. OCS
Night. Shelley. *See* To Night.
Night. Sir Philip Sidney. *Fr.* Arcadia. SiPS
Night. Robert Southey. *Fr.* Thalaba the Destroyer. GN
(Night in The Desert.) OTPC
Night, The. James Stephens. *See* Check.
Night. S. D. R. Sutu, *tr. fr. Sotho by* Dan Kunene *and* Jack Cope. PeSA; TTY, *abr.*
Night. John Addington Symonds. HBV
Night. Arthur Symons. MoBrPo; PoVP
Night. Sara Teasdale. BrR; FaPON; MoSiPe; SoPo; SUS; TiPo
(It Is Not Far.) StVeCh
Night. *Unknown.* BoTP
Night, The ("Dear night, this world's defeat"). Henry Vaughan. *See* Dear Night, This World's Defeat.
Night, The ("Through that pure virgin-shrine"). Henry Vaughan. AnAnS-1; BWP; LiTB; MeLP; MeP; MePo; NoP; OBEV (new ed.); OBS; OxBoCh; PoEL-2; PoFS; ReEn; SCEP-1; SeCeV; SeCL; SeCV-1; SeEP; UnPo (1st ed.); VaPo
Night. Joseph Blanco White. *See* To Night.
Night ("Tired Nature's sweet restorer"). Edward Young. *Fr.* Night Thoughts, I. CEP; EiPP; OBEC, *shorter sel.*; SeCePo, *br. sel.*
("Tired Nature's sweet restorer, balmy sleep!") EnPE; EnRP, abr.
Night, A,/ a night all full of murmurs. Nocturne III. José Asunción Silva. LiTW
Night/ And death rides fast on foul breath. Night Slivers. Darwin T. Turner. NBP
Night:/ And the taut. Night Music. Chester Kallman. PoPl
Night,/ And the yellow pleasure of candlelight. Song of the Rain. Hugh McCrae. BoAV; MoAuPo; PoAu-1
Night, The/ Blackbright with shadows that caress. To Our First Born. Ebon Dooley. BP
Night, The/ creeps in. The Night. Myra Cohn Livingston. PDV
Night, a grey sky, a ghostly sea. At Dieppe: On the Beach. Arthur Symons. PoVP; SyP
Night a spongy dimness fill'd with moonshine, The. Three Fragments, II. William Allingham. IrPN
Night after Night. "Stuart Sterne." AA
Night after night forever the dolls lay stiff. The Dolls. John Ciardi. ToPo
Night after night I always come to you. Reunion. John Gould Fletcher. MoLP
Night after night I lie like this listening. Archibald MacLeish. *Fr.* The Hamlet of A. MacLeish. AnAmPo
Night air brings strange whisperings, vague scents, The. Columbus [*or* Great Master Dreamer]. Charles Buxton Going. HH; PEDC (1931 ed.)
Night Airs. Walter Savage Landor. BoNaP
(Night Airs and Moonshine.) ChTr
Night Alert. Alison Boodson. NeBP
Night; an Epistle to Robert Lloyd. Charles Churchill. NCEP
What Is't to Us? *sel.* SeCePo
Night, and a bitter sky, and strange birds crying. The Pathfinders. Vance Palmer. BoAu
Night and Day. Mary Mapes Dodge. PRWS
Night and Day. Michael Drayton. *See* Idea: "Dear, why should you . . ."
Night and Day. Sidney Lanier. AA; AnAmPo; MAP; MoAmPo (1942 ed.)
Night and Death. Joseph Blanco White. *See* To Night.
Night, and its muffled creakings, as the wheels. The Shako. Robert Lowell, *after* Rilke. OnHM; Sonn
Night and Love. Sir Edward Bulwer-Lytton. *See* When Stars Are in the Quiet Skies.
Night and Morning. Dorothy Aldis. PoSC; YeAr
Night and Morning. Robert Browning. *See* Meeting At Night *and* Parting at Morning.
Night and Morning. Austin Clarke. AnIL; MoAB; NeIP

Night and Morning Songs, *sels.* Gordon Bottomley.
Dawn. BiS; BoTP; MoBrPo; NP
Elegiac Mood. NP
My Moon. NP
Night, and on all sides only the folding quiet. Night. S. D. R. Sutu. PeSA; TTY
Night; and once again. Waiting. Masaoka Shiki. OnPM
Night and one single ridge of narrow path. Water and Air. Robert Browning. *Fr.* Pauline. OBRV
Night and Storm in the Alps. Byron. *See* Lake Leman ("Clear, placid Leman!").
Night and the Child. Judith Wright. SeCePo
Night and the distant rumbling; for the train. Last Evening. Rainer Maria Rilke. OnPM; WaaP
Night, and the down by the sea. At Dieppe: Rain on the Down. Arthur Symons. BrPo; OBNC; OBVV; SyP
Night, and the heavens beam serene with peace. Night. Solomon ibn Gabirol. TrJP
Night and the Pines. Duncan Campbell Scott. OBCV
Night and we heard heavy and cadenced hoofbeats. The Return. John Peale Bishop. LiTA; LiTM; MoPo; MoVE; OxBA; TwAmPo; UnPo (3d ed.); WaP
Night and Wind. Arthur Symons. BrPo
Night appeared to authorise it, The. Jason and Medea. Alun Lewis. CBEP
Night arches England, and the winds are still. Peace. Walter de la Mare. MoAB; MoBrPo; NeMA
Night as Well as Brightest Day. Thomas Campion. *Fr.* A Relation of the Late Royal Entertainment Given by the Lord Knowles. TuPP
Night at Gettysburg. Don C. Seitz. OHIP
Night Attack. Donald M. Woodruff. TwCaPo
Night attendant, a B. U. sophomore. Waking in the Blue. Robert Lowell. CoAP; MoAmPo (1962 ed.)
Night Before America, The. Norma Farber. FOL
Night before Christmas, The. Clement Clarke Moore. *See* Visit from St. Nicholas, A.
Night before Christmas, The. Christmas Snow. John Moore. StaSt
Night before Larry Was Stretched, The. *Unknown.* AnIV; IrPN; OnYI; OxBoLi
Night before the Battle of Waterloo, The. Byron. *See* Waterloo ("There was a sound . . .").
Night before Waterloo. Byron. *See* Waterloo ("There was a sound . . .").
Night Bird, The. Charles Kingsley. OTPC (1946 ed.)
(Myth, A.) GN; VA
Night Blessing. *Unknown.* HBVY; PCH
(Good Night.) SAS
Night-blooming Cereus, The. Harriet Monroe. AA
Night Boat. Audrey Alexandra Brown. CaP
Night by the Sea, A. Heine, *tr. fr. German by* Howard Mumford Jones. *Fr.* The North Sea. AWP
(Night on the Shore, *tr. by* Emma Lazarus.) LiTW
Night came, but without darkness or repose. The Fire of London. Dryden. *Fr.* Annus Mirabilis. FaBoEn; FlW
Night Clouds. Amy Lowell. MAP; MoAmPo; MoSiPe; NeMA; NP; PoPl; PoPo; RePo; WHA
Night comes again to bring us rest. Prayer at Eventide. R. B. Y. Scott. MaRV
Night comes, an angel stands. Nocturne. Kathleen Raine. ChMP
Night Comes Apace. Evan V. Shute. CaP
Night comes to the man who can pray. New Year's Eve in Solitude. Robert Mezey. NaP
Night Coming Out of a Garden. Lord Alfred Douglas. MoBrPo (1942 ed.)
Night Concert. Virginia Earle. JKCP (1955 ed.)
Night Court, The. Ruth Comfort Mitchell. HBV
Night creeps in, The. Twilight. Ch'en Yün. LiTW
Night creeps over the city. Dawn Patrol; Chicago. Richard V. Durham. GoSl
Night Crow. Theodore Roethke. AmP; BiS; ELU; MoVE
Night Dancers. Thomas Kennedy. MoSiPe
Night Don Juan came to pay his fees, The. Don Juan in Hell. Baudelaire. AWP; SyP
Night drops/ within black America. Nocturnal. Herman L. McMillan. TNV
Night Encampment outside Troy. Homer, *tr. fr. Greek by* Tennyson. *Fr.* The Iliad, VIII. RoGo
Night Enchantment. Eleanor Muth. SiSoSe
Night enters the skin's pores. First Note. Jason Miller. ThO
Night Express. MacKnight Black. NP
Night Express, The. Cosmo Monkhouse. OBVV
Night Falls on China. W. H. Auden. CoBMV
Night Falls on Eden. Milton. *See* Evening in Paradise.
Night Feeding. Muriel Rukeyser. MiAP
Night Flight. George Whalley. CaP
Night for Adventures. Victor Starbuck. HBV
Night Full of Nothing, A. Keith Sinclair. AnNZ
Night gathers itself into a ball of dark yarn. Night. Carl Sandburg. *Fr.* The Windy City. OCS
Night goes, the fog lifts, there. Foreign Summer. W. S. Merwin. AmPC
Night grows dark, and weird, and cold, The; and thick drops patter on the pane. The Rain Comes Sobbing to the Door. Henry Kendall. ACV
Night grows no flower children. Ascendancy. Herbert A. Simmons. NBP
Night Had Gone, The. Annie Porter Johnson. SoP
Night had pitched her tar-dark tent, The. Southwestern Night. Angelico Chavez. JKCP (1955 ed.)
Night Has a Thousand Eyes, The. Francis William Bourdillon. FaFP; GTSL; HBV; LiTG; LiTL; MCCG; MeWo; OBEV (new ed.); OBVV; OHFP; OQP; OTD; OTPC; PoPo; PoToHe (new ed.) TreF; WBLP; WePo; VA
(Light.) BLPA; FaBoBe; NeHB; TSW
(Light and Love.) MaRV
Night has come truly now. The Oracle. A. E. Coppard. FaBoTw
Night has secreted us. Amen. Richard W. Thomas. BF
Night he died, earth's images all came, The. Poet. Peter Viereck. HoPM; MiAP; MoAmPo (1950 ed.); PP
Night her blackest sables wore, The. A Song. Thomas D'Urfey. CavP
Night Herding Song. Harry Stephens. CoSo, *with music*; RePo; TrAS, *with music.*
(Cowboy Songs: "Oh, slow up, dogies, quit your roving round.") OuSiCo
Night here, a covert. Burning, IX. Gary Snyder. *Fr.* Myths & Texts. NaP
Night herons cry. By the Fire. Elizabeth J. Coatsworth. RePo
Night hides our thefts; all faults then pardoned be. In the Dark None Dainty. Robert Herrick. CBEP; ELU
Night huddled our town. In Dear Detail, by Ideal Light. William Stafford. NaP
Night Hunt, The. Thomas MacDonagh. OxBI; RoGo
Night Hymns on Lake Nipigon. Duncan Campbell Scott. CoBE; OBCV
Night I brought the cows home, The. The Herd Boy. Haniel Long. HBMV
Night in a Village, A. Ivan Savich Nikitin, *tr. fr. Russian by* P. E. Matheson. AWP; JAWP; WBP
Night in Boston. Jim Harrison. ThO
Night in Camp. Herbert Bashford. AA
Night in Italy, A, *sel.* "Owen Meredith."
"Sweet are the rosy memories." OBEV (1st ed.)
Night in June, A. Duncan Campbell Scott. OBCV
Night in June, A. Wordsworth. *Fr.* The Sun Has Long Been Set. BoTP
Night in Lesbos, A. George Horton. AA
Night in Martindale. Kathleen Raine. NeBP
Night in November. David McCord. NYTB
Night in the bloodstained snow: the wind is chill. Hialmar Speaks to the Raven. Leconte de Lisle. AWP
Night in the Desert. Robert Southey. *See* Night.
Night in the east, like to a shrouded nun. The Coming of Night. Thomas Wade. ERoP-2
Night in the far Judean land. A Christmas Carol. Mary A. O'Reilly. JKCP
Night in the House by the River. Tu Fu, *tr. fr. Chinese by* Kenneth Rexroth. NaP
Night in the Wood, A. Nancy M. Hayes. *See* At Night in the Wood.
Night Interpreted. Everett Hoagland. NBP
Night is a cavalier dauntless and bold. Night. Christine Wood Bullwinkle. OTPC (1946 ed.); PCH
Night is a purple pumpkin. Night. Patricia Hubbell. PDV
Night is an ancient sorceress, The. Song. Simeon S. Frug. LiTW

Night is beautiful, The. Poem. Langston Hughes. CDC
Night is calm, the cygnet's down, The. On a Calm Summer's Night. John Nicholson. EnLoPo
Night is come. Finis [*or* Day's End]. Sir Henry Newbolt. GaP; RIS; TiPo
Night is come, but not too soon, The. The Light of Stars [*or* The Little Moon]. Longfellow. BoTP; OTPC
Night is come like to the day, The. Evening Hymn [*or* A Colloquy with God]. Sir Thomas Browne. *Fr.* Religio Medici. MaRV; OBS; OxBoCh; SeCL
Night is dark, The. And Yet. Errol B. Sloan. BLRP
Night is dark, the wind has dashed, The. Midnight Prayer. Hayyim Nahman Bialik. TrJP
Night is darkening round me, The. Emily Brontë. EnLi-2 (1949 ed.); OBNC; PoEL-5
(Song.) NBM
Night is dull and dark. James Macpherson. *Fr.* The Six Bards. PeER
Night Is Fallen. Mary Elizabeth Coleridge. POTE
Night Is Falling, The. James Clarence Mangan. IrPN
Night Is Freezing Fast, The. A. E. Housman. AtBAP; CBV; CMoP; EG; GTBS-D; LiTM; LoBV; MoPo; NoP; POTE
Night is full of stars, full of magnificence, The. Bagley Wood. Lionel Johnson. AnFE
Night is full of the crying, The. Triolet. Alexander K. Laing. YT
Night is late, the house is still, The. For Charlie's Sake. John Williamson Palmer. HBV
Night is light and chill, The. Night and Wind. Arthur Symons. BrPo
Night is like an old cat, The. Darkness. Peggy Bacon. BrR
Night is long, the moor is bare, the hill is brown, The. Wisdom in Winter. *Unknown.* *Fr.* The Black Book of Carmarthen. PrWP
Night is made for cooling shade, The. At Sea. John Townsend Trowbridge. AmePo
Night is measureless, The, no voice, no cry. The Letter. John Hall Wheelock. AnEnPo; LiTL
Night Is Near Gone, The. Alexander Montgomerie. GoTS; OBEV
(Hey! Now the Day Dawns, *orig. and mod. vers.*) CH
(Nicht Is Neir Gone, The.) AtBAP; OxBS
Night Is Nearing. James Clarence Mangan, *after the Persian.* IrPN
Night is not darkness. Avowal. A. M. Sullivan. JKCP (1926 ed.)
Night is o'er England, and the winds are still. Peace. Walter de la Mare. MMA
Night is on the downland, on the lonely moorland. Night on the Downland. John Masefield. Lollingdon. Downs, XVIII. GoYe; GTBS-W; LiTM; MoBrPo; MoPo
Night is soft with summer; yon faint arch, The. John Plummer Derwent Llwyd. *Fr.* The Vestal Virgin. CaP
Night is something watching. Song to Night. Elizabeth J. Coatsworth. WaKn
Night is soundless but its tide has turned, The. Knowing What Time It Is at Night. Louise Townsend Nicholl. PG (1955 ed.)
Night is the time for rest. Night. James Montgomery. HBV
Night is the true democracy. Night's Mardi Gras. Edward J. Wheeler. HBV
Night is thick with storm and driving cloud, The. Australia, 1914. Archibald T. Strong. *Fr.* Sonnets of the Empire. BoAu
Night is white, The. Birch Trees. John Richard Moreland. DD; HBMV; HBVY; OHIP
Night it was a holy night, The. Godly Girzie. Burns. CoMu; ErPo; UnTE
Night it was, sweet as the morning of life, A. Night. Jami. LiTW
Night John Henry is born an ax, The. Melvin B. Tolson. *Fr.* Harlem Gallery. TTY
Night Journey, The. Rupert Brooke. BrPo
Night Journey. Theodore Roethke. AmFN; NYBP; TPM
Night knows nothing of the chants of night, The. Restatement of Romance. Wallace Stevens. LiTL; MoLP
Night-Labour. Quentin Stevenson. POTE (1959 ed.)
Night Landing. John Gould Fletcher. Down the Mississippi, VI. HT; LiTA; NP
Night Laundry. James Merrill. CBV
Nightletter, *sel.* Alden Van Buskirk.
"Miracle traced on a plate in, The." YAP
Night Letter. Tyner White. YAP
Night like a silver peacock in the sky. Poetry and Science. W. J. Turner. SeCePo
Night like purple flakes of snow. Night. Donald Jeffrey Hayes. CDC
Night Long, The. Imr el Kais, *tr. fr. Arabic by* Lady Anne Blunt *and* Wilfrid Scawen Blunt. LiTW
Night Loves Us, The. Louis Adeane. NeBP
Night Magic. Amelia Josephine Burr. MPB; SP
Night Mail, The. W. H. Auden. ChTr; PoSa; ShBV-3; WePo
Night-March, The. Herman Melville. AnFE; CoAnAm; LiTA
Night Mirror, The. John Hollander. NYBP
Night Mists. William Hamilton Hayne. AA
Night Moths, The. Edwin Markham. HBMV
Night Music. Chester Kallman. PoPl
Night Musick for Thérèse. Dachine Rainer. NePoAm-2
Night my father got me, The. The Culprit. A. E. Housman. PG (1955 ed.); VP
Night, A: mysterious, tender, quiet, deep. A Common Inference. Charlotte Perkins Gilman. AA; AmePo; AnAmPo; WGRP
Night Note. James Oppenheim. MAP; MoAmPo (1942 ed.)
Night Nurse Goes Her Round, The. John Gray. LoBV; OBNC
Night of Forebeing, The. Francis Thompson. *See* From the Night of Forebeing.
Night of Gods, The. George Sterling. MAP; MoAmPo (1942 ed.); PFY; WHA
Night of Marvels, The. Sister Violante do Ceo, *tr. fr. Portuguese by* Sir John Bowring. CAW
Night of nights drew to its tardy close, The. Love's Mortality. Richard Middleton. WHA
Night of Rain. Bernice Kenyon. HBMV
Night of Sine. Léopold Sédar-Senghor, *tr. fr. French by* Ulli Beier. PBA
Night of Sorrow, The. Li Po, *tr. fr. Chinese by* Shigeyoshi Obata. WoL
Night of Spring. Thomas Westwood. BoTP; CBEP; OBVV; TOP
Night of the Dance, The. Thomas Hardy. BrPo
Night of the Full Moon, The. Lloyd Frankenberg. BoLP
Night of the Immaculate Conception. Juan Maragall, *tr. fr. Spanish by* Thomas Walsh. CAW
Night of Trafalgar, The. Thomas Hardy. *Fr.* The Dynasts, Pt. I, Act V, sc. vii. ChTr; FaBoCh; MoBrPo; OBMV; OTD; PoVP; ShBV-1
(Boatman's Song, The.) WaaP
(Trafalgar.) CH
Night of utter silences, A. Shadows. "Yehoash." TrJP
Night of Wind. Frances Frost. FaPON; TiPo
Night on Clinton. Robert Mezey. NaP
Night on earth and sky. A Terrible Thought. Eliezer Steinberg. TrJP
Night on the bloodstained snow: the wind is chill. Hialmar Speaks to the Raven. Leconte de Lisle. AWP; SyP
Night on the Downland. John Masefield. Lollingdon Downs, XVIII. GTBS-W; LiTM; MoBrPo; MoPo
("Night is on the downland, on the lonely moorland.") GoYe
Night on the Prairie. Rufus B. Sage. PoOW
Night on the Prairies. Walt Whitman. MoRP
Night on the Shore. Heine. *See* Night by the Sea, A.
Night-owl shrieked: a gibbous moon peered pallid o'er the yew, The. The Conscience-Curst. "F. Anstey." CenHV
Night Out. R. A. Simpson. PoAu-2
Night passed, & Enitharmon, e'er the dawn, return'd in bliss. Song of Enitharmon. Blake. *Fr.* Vala; or, The Four Zoas. ERoP-1
Night Patrol. Alan Ross. POTi
Night Peril. Sydney King Russell. FiSC
Night-Piece. Léonie Adams. MAP; MoAB; MoAmPo
Night Piece. A. E. Coppard. POTE
Night-Piece, The. Robert Herrick. *See* Night Piece, to Julia.
Night Piece. Robert Hillyer. MAP; MoAmPo
Nightpiece. James Joyce. SyP
Night Piece. John Manifold. MoBrPo (1950 ed.)
(Nightpiece.) LiTM; WaP
Night-Piece. Raymond Richard Patterson. CAD
Night Piece, A. Edward Shanks. HBMV
Night Piece. Edith Sitwell. NP

Night-Piece, A. *Unknown.* *See* O Night, O Jealous Night.
Night-Piece. John Hall Wheelock. CBV
Night-Piece, A. Wordsworth. EnRP
Night-Piece on Death, A. Thomas Parnell. CEP; EiPP; OBEC; SeCePo
"Death speaks:/ When men my scythe and darts supply," *sel.* OnYI
Night-Piece, A; or, Modern Philosophy. Christopher Smart. VaPo
Night Piece to Another Julia. Paul Fearon. CIV
Night-Piece, to Julia. Robert Herrick. AnAnS-2; AnFE; AtBAP; ATP; BEL; CBV; CoBE; EG; ELP; EnLi-1 (1949 ed.); EnLit; FaPL; FosPo; HBV; ILP; InvP; LiTB; LiTL; LoBV; MaPo; MeWo; NeHB; NoP; OAEP; OBEV; OBS; PCD; PoEL-3; PoeP; PoFS; PoIE; PoRA; ReEn; SCEP-2; SeCeV; SeCL; SeCP; SeCV-1; SeEP; ShBV-2; TOP; TreFT; VaPo; WHA
(Night-Piece, The.) OTPC; UnTE
On a Dark Road, *sel.* BoTP
Night-piercing, whitely illuminant. Keraunograph. Hayden Carruth. NMP
Night Plane. Frances Frost. FaPON; PDV; TiPo (1959 ed.)
Night Prayer, A. *Unknown,* *tr. fr. Irish by* Eleanor Hull. JKCP (1926 ed.)
Night Quarters. Henry Howard Brownell. GN
Night Sky, The. Sir Charles G. D. Roberts. VA
Night Refuses a Dreamer, The. Grant Code. FiSC
Night Ride. Sir Herbert Read. BoLP; WePo
Night-Ride, The. Kenneth Slessor. NeLNL
Night sank upon the dusky beach, and on the purple sea. Macaulay. *Fr.* The Armada. OBNC; PeVV
Night saw the crew like pedlers with their packs. Lunar Stanzas. Henry Coggswell Knight. BOHV; NA
Night, say all, was made for rest, The. Upon Visiting His Lady by Moonlight. "A. W." CTC; OBSC; ReIE; TuPP
Night School. Elias Lieberman. NYTB
Night Serene, The. Luis de León, *tr. fr. Spanish by* Thomas Walsh. CAW; TrJP; WoL
Night Shore. Barry O. Higgs. PeSA
Night Shower. Brock Milton. PoMa
Night Singers. Sappho, *tr. fr. Greek by* Virginia Tufte. HW
Night Sky, A. Robert Creeley. FRC
Night Sky, The. *Unknown.* BoTP
Night sleeps, but the chill, The. The Harp of David. Jacob Cohen. TrJP
Night slides down the mountain side. Bahnhofstrasse. Clifford Dyment. POTi
Night Slivers. Darwin T. Turner. NBP
Night throbs on, The; O, let me pray, dear Lord! Motherhood. Josephine Dodge Daskam Bacon. HBV
Nightsong. Philip Booth. MoLP
Night Song. A. R. D. Fairburn. AnNZ
Night Song. Wallace Gould. AnAmPo
Night Song at Amalfi. Sara Teasdale. MAP; MeWo; MoAmPo
(Night Song of Amalfi.) NeMA
Night Song for a Child! Charles Williams. OBEV (new ed.)
Night Song for Two Mystics. Paul Blackburn. NeAP
Night Song of the Fish. Christian Morgenstern. FIW
Night Songs. Thomas Kinsella. ACV
Night Sowing. David Campbell. BoAV; PoAu-2
Night, Stars, Glow-Worms. H. Leivick, *tr. fr. Yiddish by* Jacob Sloan. LiTW
Night stilled the field, and every golden stook. Cornfield. Leo Cox. CaP
Night stirs but wakens not, her breathings climb. Animula Vagula. A. Y. Campbell. HBMV
Night stirs the trees. By Achmelvich Bridge. Norman MacCaig. OxBS
Night Storm. William Gilmore Simms. EtS
Night Stuff. Carl Sandburg. NP; TSW
Night that has no star lit up by God, The. The New World. Jones Very. AA; AnNE; AP
Night that Paddy Murphy died, The. Paddy Murphy. *Unknown.* PV
Night that smells of sailor's tar, A. Lounge Bar. James K. Baxter. Cressida, XII. AnNZ
Night the green moth came for me, The. Green Moth. Winifred Welles. BoChLi (1950 ed.); FaPON; StVeCh; TiPo; UTS
Night, the starlesse night of passion, The. Sonnet. William Alabaster. AnAnS-1; MeP; Sonn
Night There Was Dancing in the Streets, The. Elder Olson. NePA
Night Things Are Soft and Loud. Zhenya Gay. RePo
Night Thought. Gerald Jonas. NYBP
Night Thought of a Tortoise Suffering from Insomnia on a Lawn. E. V. Rieu. FiBHP
Night-Thoughts. Solomon ibn Gabirol, *tr. fr. Hebrew by* Emma Lazarus. TrJP
Night Thoughts, *sels.* Edward Young.
Happiness an Art, *fr.* Night VIII. OBEC
"Live ever here, Lorenzo?—shocking thought!" *fr.* Night III. EnRP
Man ("How poor, how rich, how abject"), *fr.* Night I. MaRV
"On nature's Alps I stand," *fr.* Night IX. MaRV
Procrastination ("Be wise today; 'tis madness to defer"), *fr.* Night I. AnEnPo; OBEC, *abr.*
Night I ("Tired Nature's sweet restorer"). CEP; EiPP; EnPE; EnRP, *abr.*; OBEC; SeCePo, *br. sel.*
Night Thoughts in Age. John Hall Wheelock. MoVE; NYBP; PoDB
Night Thoughts over a Sick Child. Philip Levine. NePoEA-2
Night Thoughts While Travelling. Tu Fu, *tr. fr. Chinese by* Kenneth Rexroth. NaP
Night through yonder cloudy cleft, The. Aubrey Thomas De Vere. *Fr.* May Carols. IrPN
Night tinkles like ice in glasses, The. November Night, Edinburgh. Norman MacCaig. NMP
Night, too long illumined, comes a stranger, The. In the Proscenium [*or* War's Clown in the Proscenium]. Gene Derwood. GTBS-W; LiTA; LiTM (rev. ed.); NePA
Night too quickly passes, The. The Roaring Days. Henry Lawson. BoAV; NeLNL
Night Train. Robert Francis. LOW
Night Train. Adrien Stoutenburg. PDV
Night Vigil in the Left Court of the Palace, A. Tu Fu, *tr. fr. Chinese by* Witter Bynner. LiTW
Night Walk. Sylvia Plath. NYBP
Night walked down the sky, The. A Memory. Frederic Lawrence Knowles. HBV
Night-Walker, The; or, The Little Thief, *sel.* John Fletcher.
"I've walked through all the lodgings," *fr.* II, i. MyFE
Night Walkers, The. Kendrick Smithyman. AnNZ
Night was coming very fast, The. The Hens. Elizabeth Madox Roberts. FaPON; GoJo; GoTP; HBMV; MPB; PDV; PoRh; SoPo; SP; StVeCh; SUS; TiPo; TSW; UTS
Night Was Creeping. James Stephens. *See* Check.
Night was dark and fearful, The. The Watcher. Sarah Josepha Hale. AA
Night was dark, though sometimes a faint star, The. Prelude. Richard Watson Gilder. *Fr.* The New Day. HBV; PoLF
Night was done; we rose and after. This Summer's Love. Mikhail Alekseyevich Kuzmin. OnPM
Night was faint and sheer, The. An October Nocturne. Ivor Winters. CBV
Night was growing old, The. In the Night. *Unknown.* NA
Night was made for cooling shade, The. At Sea. John T. Trowbridge. EtS
Night was made for rest and sleep. Interim. Clarissa Scott Delany. CDC; PoNe
Night was thick and hazy, The. Robinson Crusoe's Story. Charles Edward Carryl. *Fr.* Davy and the Goblin. AA; BeLS; BoChLi; BOHV; FiBHP; HBV; HBVY; InMe; LHV; MCCG; MPB; OnPP; OTPC (1946 ed.); PCD; PoRA; PoRh; TreFT; TSW
Night was time, the. The Three Stars of Prophecy. David Gascoyne. POTE
Night was winter in his roughest mood, The. William Cowper. *Fr.* The Task, VI. EnRP; OBEC
Night Watch, A. *Unknown.* The Passionate Pilgrim, XIV. OBSC
Night Watch, The. William Winter. AA
Night-Watch Prayer. Henry van Dyke. SoP
Night Watchmen. Jimmy Garthwaite. BrR
Night-watchmen think of dawn and things auroral. Blindman's Buff. Peter Viereck. LiTM (1970 ed.); MiAP; MoAmPo (1950 ed.)
Night when last I saw my land, The. Forgettin'. "Moira O'-Neill." HBV
Night Will Never Stay, The. Eleanor Farjeon. BoTP; CH; FaPON; HBMV; PoRh; SiSoSe; SoPo; StVeCh; TSW

Night Wind, The. Emily Brontë. ChER; ChTr; NCEP; OAEP; PoSa; RoGo
Night Wind, The. Eugene Field. FaPON
Night-Wind. Beatrix Demarest David. AA
Night Wind. Feodor Tyutchev, *tr. fr. Russian by* C. M. Bowra. LiTW
Nightwind sings and rustles through the reeds, The. Nocturne in G Minor. Karl Gustav Vollmoeller. AWP; LiTW
Night, Window, Wind. Jack Anderson. ThO
Night Winds. Adelaide Crapsey. QFR
Night with a Holy-Water Clerk, A. *Unknown.* MeEL
Night with a Wolf, A. Bayard Taylor. *See* Story for a Child, A.
Night! with all thine eyes look down! A Bridal Song. Shelley. HW
Night without of wind and rain, A. After the Storm. Annie Howe Thomson. SoP
Night you got away, I dreamed you rose, The. To a Fugitive. James Wright. TPM
Nightfall. Kalidasa, *tr. fr. Sanskrit by* Arthur W. Ryder. LiTW
Nightfall. Una Marson. PoNe
Nightfall. Charles Hanson Towne. *See* At Nightfall.
Nightfall. Antonio de Trueba, *tr. fr. Spanish by* Thomas Walsh. CAW
Nightfall. Feodor Tyutchev, *tr. fr. Russian by* Valadimir Nabokov. LiTW
Nightfall in Dordrecht. Eugene Field. AA; PRWS
Nightfall in Inishtrahull. Daniel James O'Sullivan. NeIP
Nightfall, that saw the morning-glories float. On the Skeleton of a Hound. James Wright. LiTM (1970 ed.); NePoEA; TwAmPo
Nightfishing, The, *sel.* W. S. Graham.
"We are at the hauling then hoping for it." FIW
Nightflight and Sunrise. Geoffrey Dutton. BoAV
Nightgown, Wife's Gown. Robert Sward. ELU
Nightingale, The. Mark Akenside. *See* Ode to the Evening Star.
Nightingale, The. Richard Barnfield. *Fr.* The Passionate Pilgrim. AWP; GTBS; GTBS-D; GTBS-P; GTBS-W; GTSE; JAWP; OTPC (1923 ed.); TOP; WBP
(As It Fell upon a Day.) EG; ReEn; ViBoPo
(Ode, An: "As it fell upon a day.") ElL; LoBV; OBSC; ReIE; SiCE; TuPP
(Philomel.) CH; GTSL; HBV; OBEV
(To the Nightingale.) LiTG
Nightingale, The. Elizabeth Belloc. JKCP (1955 ed.)
Nightingale, The. Richard Brathwaite. *Fr.* Nature's Embassy. ElL
Nightingale, The. Samuel Taylor Coleridge. EnRP; ERoP-1; MERP; NoP; PeER
("'Tis the merry nightingale.") OBRV
Nightingales, *sel.* ChTr
Nightingale, The. Gerald Griffin. CAW; JKCP
(To the Blessed Virgin Mary.) OnYI
Nightingale, The. W. E. Henley. *See* To A. D.
Nightingale, The. Keats. *See* Ode to a Nightingale.
Nightingale, The. Edward Moxon. OBRV
Nightingale, The. Petrarch, *tr. fr. Italian by* Thomas LeMesurier. Sonnets to Laura: To Laura in Death, XLIII. LiTW; PoPl
Nightingale, The. Sir Philip Sidney. AtBAP; ElL; EnLi-1; GTBS-W; LiTB; LoBV; NoP; OBSC; PAn; SiPS; TuPP; UnPo (1st ed.); WHA
(Nightingale, as Soon as April Bringeth, The.) EnRePo; FCP; GTSL; LiTG; MaPo; ReEn; SiCE; StP
(Philomela.) HBV; OBEV
Nightingale, The. John Addington Symonds. VA
Nightingale, The. Katharine Tynan. BoTP
Nightingale, The ("Both old and young, I pray lend an ear"), *with music. Unknown.* ShS
Nightingale, The ("The little pretty nightingale"). *Unknown.* TrGrPo
("Little pretty nightingale, The.") EG; LO
("Lytyll prety nyghtyngale, The.") OAEP
Nightingale, The ("My limbs were weary, and my head oppressed"). *Unknown.* StP
Nightingale, The ("One morning, one morning, one morning in May"). *Unknown. See* One Morning in May.
Nightingale, The. Sir John Vanbrugh. *Fr.* Aesop. SeCL
Nightingale, The. Wordsworth. DD
(O Nightingale.) AtBAP
(O Nightingale! Thou Surely Art.) HBV
Nightingale and Flowers. Blake. *Fr.* Milton, II. LoBV
(Birdsong.) FaBoEn
(Choir of Day, The.) EnRP
(Lark's Song, The, *shorter sel.*) WiR
("Thou hearest the nightingale.") OBRV
(Vision of the Lamentation of Beulah [over Ololon], A.) ERoP-1; OBNC
Nightingale and [the] Glow-Worm, The. William Cowper. BoChLi; BoPe; EiCL; GoTP; HBV; NeHB; OnMSP; OTPC; PRWS; RIS
Nightingale and the Lark, The. Ernest Whitney. ATP (1935 ed.)
Nightingale, as soon as April bringeth, The. Sir Philip Sidney. *See* Nightingale, The.
Nightingale has a lyre of gold, The. To A. D. [*or* The Blackbird *or* The Nightingale]. W. E. Henley. Echoes, XVIII. AnFE; BEL; HBV; HoPM; MeWo; MoBrPo; NeMA; OuHeWo; PoVP; TOP; TrGrPo; TSW; ViBoPo
Nightingale I never heard. My Catbird. William Henry Venable. AA; HBV; PFY
Nightingale made a mistake, A. The Singing Lesson. Jean Ingelow. DD; HBV; OTPC (1946 ed.)
Nightingale near the House, The. Harold Monro. HBMV; MoBrPo
Nightingale on the flowering plum, The. Peasant and Geisha Songs. *Unknown.* LiTW
Nightingale, A, once lost his voice from too much love. Youth and Age. Ridgely Torrence. *Fr.* The House of a Hundred Lights. AA
Nightingale, that all day long, A. The Nightingale and [the] Glow-Worm. William Cowper. BoChLi; BoPe; EiCL; GoTP; HBV; NeHB; OnMSP; OTPC; PRWS; RIS
Nightingale Weather. Andrew Lang. ACV
Nightingales. Robert Bridges. AtBAP; BrPo; BWP; CMoP; CoBMV; EnLi-2 (1949 ed.); ExPo; FaBoEn; ForPo; GTBS; HBMV; LiTB; LiTM; MoAB; MoBrPo; MoPo; OA; OBEV; OBMV; OBNC; OBVV; Po; PoPl; PoVP; SeCeV; SiSw; TrGrPo; UnPo
Nightingales. Samuel Taylor Coleridge. *Fr.* The Nightingale. ChTr
Nightingales. Grace Hazard Conkling. HBMV
Nightingale's Nest, The. John Clare. PeER
Nightingales of Surrey, The. Jessie B. Rittenhouse. MaRV
Nightingales warble about it. The Secret. George Edward Woodberry. *Fr.* Wild Eden. AA; HBV
Nightingales warbled without. In the Garden at Swainston [*or* Valedictory]. Tennyson. GoBC; OBEV (new ed.); OBNC; OBVV; PoVP; ViPo
Nightly Deed, A. Charles Madge. NeBP
Nightly I mark and praise, or great or small. Retractions, XV. James Branch Cabell. HBMV
Nightly tormented by returning doubt. The Struggle. Sully-Prudhomme. AWP; PoPl
Nightmare. Joseph Payne Brennan. FiSC
Nightmare. Gawin Douglas. *Fr.* The Palace of Honor. PoEL-1
Nightmare. Isabella Gardner. CoAP
Nightmare. W. S. Gilbert. *See* Lord Chancellor's Song.
Nightmare. R. H. Grenville. FiSC
Nightmare, The. Jascha Kessler. AmPC
Nightmare, The. Sorley Maclean. NeBP
Nightmare. Anne Marx. FiSC
Nightmare Abbey, *sels.* Thomas Love Peacock.
There Is a Fever of the Spirit, *fr. ch.* 11. EPN; GTSE
(Mr. Cypress's Song.) LO
(Song by Mr. Cypress.) ERoP-1; OBNC; OBRV; Par
Three Men of Gotham, *fr. ch.* 11. FaBoCh; GTBS; GTBS-D; GTSL; LiTG; MyFE, *st.* 1; OBEV SiTL; TOP
(Catch, A: "Seamen three!") ViBoPo
(Men of Gotham, The.) CH; OTPC (1946 ed.)
(Seaman Three.) OBRV; PeER; WiR
("Seamen three, what men be ye?") EG
(Wise Men of Gotham, The.) LoBV
Nightmare at Noon. Stephen Vincent Benét. OxBA
Nightmare in Morganza. Joseph Joel Keith. FiSC
Nightmare leaves fatigue. Louis MacNeice. *Fr.* Autumn Journal. AnIL
Nightmare Number Four. Robert Bloch. FiSC

Nightmare Number Three. Stephen Vincent Benét. MaC; MoAmPo (1950 ed.)
Nightmare of a Cook. Chester Kallman. CrMA
Nightpiece. John Manifold. *See* Night Piece.
Night's Ancient Cloud. Thomas Keohler. AnIV
Nights are cold, the nights are long, The. The Cottager to Her Infant [*or* The Cottager's Lullaby]. Dorothy Wordsworth. CH; HBV; OTPC (1923 ed.); PRWS
Nights are warm again, The. St. Kilda. Barrie Reid. BoAV
Night's come—I've lost my path. A Warrior at Nightfall. *Unknown.* GaP
Night's diadem around thy head. Fairest of Freedom's Daughters. Jeremiah Eames Rankin. PAH
Night's Fall Unlocks the Dirge of the Sea. W. S. Graham. FaBoMo
(Night's Fall.) NeBP
Night's first sweet silence fell, and on my bed. The Malady of Love Is Nerves. Petronius Arbiter. AWP
Nights follow each other and are linked. Charles Péguy. *Fr.* Night. LiTW
Night's held breath, The. Night. Arthur Symons. MoBrPo; PoVP
Nights in the desert, he always dreamed of voyage. The Exile. Margaret Benaya. NYTB
Night's Mardi Gras. Edward J. Wheeler. HBV
Nights on the Indian Ocean. Cale Young Rice. EtS
Nights put day in motion once again. This Suite. David Mus. YAP
Nights Remember, The. Harold Vinal. HBMV
Night's Song. *At. to* Sir William Davenant. *Fr.* Luminalia. SeCL
Nights, the railway-arches, the bad sky, The. Rimbaud. W. H. Auden. SyP
Night's wing is on the east—the clouds repose. Approach of Evening. George Croly. IrPN
Nightsea and violet wave. A Storm of Love. Hilary Corke. NYBP
Nihil Humani Alienum. Titus Munson Coan. AA
Nihon Shoki, *sel.* *Unknown, tr. fr. Japanese by* Donald L. Philippi.
Dawn Song. HW
Nijinsky. Doris Ferne. CaP
Nijinsky's ashes here in peace repose. For Nijinsky's Tomb. Frances Cornford. UnS
Nikki-Roasa. Nikki Giovanni. BP; CAD; NBP
Nikolina. Celia Thaxter. GN; HBV; OTPC (1946 ed.)
Nil Admirari. Congreve. OBEC
Nil Perdunt Mendici. Henry Parrot. SiCE
Nile, The. Elizabeth J. Coatsworth. HT
Nile, The. Leigh Hunt. EnRP; OBNC; OBRV; ViBoPo
(Thought of the Nile, A.) ERoP-1; NBM
Nilotic Elegy. G. S. Fraser. WaP
Nima, The. Jorge Isaacs, *tr. fr. Spanish by* Alice Jane McVan. TrJP
Nimble as dolphins to. Gimboling. Isabella Gardner. ErPo
Nimble cat and lazy maid, A. On Maids and Cats. Henricus Selyns. SCAP
Nimble Dick. Adelaide O'Keeffe. OTPC (1923 ed.)
Nimble sigh, on thy warm wings. To Amoret. Henry Vaughan. EnLoPo
Nimble Stag, The. Edmund G. V. Knox. HBMV
Nimbus. Douglas Le Pan. MoCV; OBCV; PeCV
Niminy, piminy. Food for Thought. Michael Lewis. RIS
Niminy piminy/ Gilbert and Sullivan. Geeandess. William Cole. PV
Nimium Fortunatus. Robert Bridges. *See* Fortunatus Nimium.
Nimmo. E. A. Robinson. HBMV
Nimphidia. Michael Drayton. *See* Nymphidia.
Nimrud and the Gnat. *Unknown, tr. fr. Arabic by* Sir Edwin Arnold. OnPM
Nina loved compromising. Three Women. Alan Dienstag. ErPo
Nina's cross: her alphabet. Cubes. Mary Fullerton. PoAu-1
Nine adulteries, 12 liaisons, 64 fornications and something approaching a rape. The Temperaments. Ezra Pound. ErPo
Nine grenadiers, with bayonets in their guns. The Dream of a Little Boy Who Lived at Nine-Elms. William Brighty Rands. GaP; PPL; RIS
Nine Inch Will Please a Lady. Burns. ErPo
Nine months I waited in the dark beneath. Pro Sua Vita. Robert Penn Warren. MAP; MoAmPo
Nine Nectarines and Other Porcelain. Marianne Moore. OxBA
Nine o'Clock. Louis Simpson. PoNe
Nine-o'clock bell! School-Bell. Eleanor Farjeon. BrR; FaPON; SiSoSe
Nine times the space that measures day and night. Fallen Angels. Milton. *Fr.* Paradise Lost. DiPo
Nine white chickens come. A Black November Turkey. Richard Wilbur. AmLP; FiMAP; MoAB
Nine years ago I was diggin' up the land. The True Paddy's Song. *Unknown.* OuSiCo
Ninepenny Fidil, The. Joseph Campbell. HBMV
1918-1941. Robert D. Fitzgerald. BoAV
1956. Daniel G. Hoffman. PoCh
1945. Sheila Cussons, *tr. fr. Afrikaans by* Jack Cope *and* Uys Krige. PeSA
1944—on the Invasion Coast. Jack Beeching. WaP
1914. Rupert Brooke. HBV; NP
Sels.
Dead, The ("Blow out, you bugles"), III. BEL; FaPL; MCCG; OQP; PoFr; TreF; WGRP
Dead, The ("These hearts were woven"), IV. AnFE; ATP; BrPo; CH; EnLit; GTBS-W; GTSL; LiTB; LiTG; MCCG; MMA; OtMeF; PoRL; POTE; SeCeV; ShBV-4; Sonn; TOP; YT
Peace, I. EPN; MaRV; MMA; POTE; TreFT; WGRP
Safety, II. BrPo; EnLoPo; PoFr
Soldier, The, V. AnFE; BBV; BEL; BoLiVe; BrPo; EnLit; EPN; ExPo; FaBoEn; FaBV; FaFP; FaPL; GTBS; GTBS-W; GTSL; InP; LiTB; LiTM; MaC; MaRV; MCCG; MoBrPo; MoVE; NeHB; NeMA; OBEV (new ed.); OTPC (1946 ed.); PoLF; PoMa; PoPl; PoPo; PoRA; POTE; ShBV-3; Sonn; TOP; TreF; TrGrPo; ViBoPo; WaP; WHA; YT
(Soldier, The, 1914-1918.) BoC
MCMXIV. Philip Larkin. PoeP
1914. Frank Wilmot. BoAu; MoAuPo
1914—and After, *sel.* James Oppenheim.
Create Great Peace, 17 *ll.* MaRV
1914 Autumn and Winter. Maurice Hewlett. *Fr.* The Song of the Plow. PoFr
Nineteen Hundred and Nineteen. W. B. Yeats. LiTB; MasP; MoAB; MoPo; OnHM
Nineteen! of years a pleasant number. Aetate XIX. Herman Charles Merivale. OBVV; VA
1917-1919. Henry Martyn Hoyt. HBMV
1916 Seen from 1921. Edmund Blunden. MMA
1967. Thomas Hardy. PG (1945 ed.); VP
1938. Ruth Pitter. LO
1935. Stephen Vincent Benét. MAP; MoAmPo; NeMA
1934. Richard Eberhart. TwAmPo
1934. Donald Hall. PoPl
Nineteen Thirty-nine, *sel.* Charles Brasch.
Poland, October. AnNZ
1926. Weldon Kees. CoAP; NaP
Nineteen Twenty-six. Wilson MacDonald. MaRV
Nineteen years now. Anniversary. R. S. Thomas. ToPo
Nineteenth Century and After, The. W. B. Yeats. MBW-2
Nineteenth of April (1861), The. Lucy Larcom. MC; PAH
Nineteenth Psalm, The. Bible, *O.T.* *See* Heavens Declare the Glory of God, The.
Ninetieth Psalm. Isaac Watts. *See* O God Our Help in Ages Past.
Ninety and Nine, The. Elizabeth Cecilia Clephane. *See* There Were Ninety and Nine.
Ninety-nine. Carolyn Hancock. RIS
Ninety-nine in the Shade. Rossiter Johnson. BOHV
90 North. Randall Jarrell. AP; CoAP; CoBMV; FiMAP; ILP; MoAB; MoPo; MoVE
Nineveh. Robert Eyres Landor. *Fr.* The Impious Feast. OBRV
Nineveh, Tyre. Memphis Blues. Sterling A. Brown. BANP
Nino, the Wonder Dog. Roy Fuller. CBV
Ninth Ecologue, The ("Gorbo, as thou camest this way"). Michael Drayton. *See* Gorbo and Batte.
Ninth Eclogue. Vergil. *See* Lycidas and Moeris.
Ninth Eglog, The ("What time the weatherbeaten flocks"). Michael Drayton. *Fr.* The Shepherd's Garland. ReIE
Ninth Elegy, *sel.* Muriel Rukeyser.
Antagonists, The. FiMAP
Ninth Hour, The. Caroline Hazard. ChIP; OQP

Ninth Moon. Li Ho, *tr. fr. Chinese by* Ho Chih-yuan. LiTW
Ninth of April, The. Otto Gelsted, *tr. fr. Danish by* Joy Davidman. PoFr
Ninth of July, The. John Hollander. CoAP
Ninth Philosopher's Song. Aldous Huxley. ViBoPo
Niobe. John Donne. MaMe
Niobe, *sel.* Frederick Tennyson.
"I too remember, in the after years." VA
Niobe in Living Stone. *Unknown, tr. fr. Greek by* Lord Neaves. OnPM
Niobe on Phrygian sands. The Wish. Thomas Stanley. AWP; JAWP; WBP
Niplets. *Unknown, tr. fr. Greek by* Wallace Rice. ErPo
Nipper and the Nanny-Goat. Off to Yakima. Leroy F. Jackson. GaP
Nirvana. Sir Edwin Arnold. *Fr.* The Light of Asia, VIII. VA
Nirvana. *Unknown.* BOHV
(Clam, A.) StaSt
Nirvana. John Hall Wheelock. HBMV; MAP; MoAmPo; NP; TSW
Nisus writes epigrams and so do I. Thomas Bastard. SiCE
'Nita, Juanita. Elegy for Helen Trent. Paris Leary. CoPo
Nittygritty. Joseph Bevans Bush. WSL
No! Eliza Cook. PoToHe (new ed.)
No! Thomas Hood. BOHV; ChTr; FiBHP; GoTP; HBV; NBM.
(November.) BBV; GN; OTPC (1946 ed.); RIS
(November in England.) PTK
No!!/ Anywhere my father goes. War. William Alfred McLean, Jr. BOLo
No abbey's gloom, nor dark cathedral stoops. Sleepy Hollow. William Ellery Channing. SoP
No and Yes. Thomas Ashe. HBV
No Angel Led. James Jeffrey Roche. *Fr.* Washington. DD
No Answer. Laurence Whistler. MoVE
No answer, yet I called her name. The Trick. W. H. Davies. ChMP
No Armistice in Love's War. Ralph Cheyney. PGD
No Baby in the House. Clara Dolliver. HBV
No bars are set too close, no mesh too fine. Political Reflection. Howard Nemerov. ELU
No beauty spot should ladies wear. Upon a Patch Face. Thomas, Lord Fairfax. SeCL
No Beauty We Could Desire. C. S. Lewis. BoPe
No bees, no honey. Well-packed Wisdom. Benjamin Franklin. *Fr.* Poor Richard's Almanac. StaSt
No beggar she in the mighty hall where her bay-crowned sisters wait. Arizona. Sharlot Mabridth Hall. PAH
No berserk thirst of blood had they. Lexington. Whittier. MC; PAH
No bird has ever uttered note. Originality. Thomas Bailey Aldrich. AnNE
No bitterness: our ancestors did it. Ave Caesar. Robinson Jeffers. MoVE; OxBA
No blacker than others in winter, but. Burning Mountain. W. S. Merwin. NYBP
No blustering winter storm could fell the peach tree. Peach Tree in the Garden of an Empty House. John Press. NYTB
No boy chooses war. Sailors on Leave. Owen Dodson. AmNP
No Bread for the Poor. *Unknown. See* Orphan Girl, The ("No home, no home").
No butler, no second maid, no blood upon the stair. Crime Club. Weldon Kees. NaP
No Buyers; a Street Scene. Thomas Hardy. LiTB; NoP
No cannibal, come. Everybody's Homesick Soldier Boy. Jonathan Williams. HYE
No ceaseless vigil with hard toil we keep. Compensation. Thomas Stevens Collier. AA
No changes of support—only. Last Month. John Ashbery. ANYP; CoAP
No Cherub's heart or hand for us might ache. Good Friday Evening. Christina Rossetti. PGD
No Child. Padraic Colum. AnFE; OBMV; POTE
No, children, my trips are over. The Engineer's Story. *Unknown.* BeLS
No Chuck, you were wrong. To Chuck—Concerning a Rendezvous in Siam. Jack Charles. WaKn
No city primness train'd my feet. Rustic Childhood. William Barnes. OBNC
No city shall I call my own. R. Ellsworth Larsson. *Fr.* O City, Cities! AnAmPo
No Clock with Numbered Eyes. Christopher Hassall. POTE
No cloud can hide the glow of living faith. The Light of Faith. Edgar Dupree. BLRP
No cloud, no relique of the sunken day. The Nightingale. Samuel Taylor Coleridge. EnRP; ERoP-1; MERP; NoP; PeER
No clouds are in the morning sky. Autumn Song [*or* Going a-Nutting]. Edmund Clarence Stedman. BBV (1923 ed.); DD; GN
No Cock Crows at Morning. Horace Gregory. CMoP
No Coming to God without Christ. Robert Herrick. OxBoCh; TRV
No Communication. Mark Van Doren. BiS
No Country You Remember. Robert Mezey. AmPC; PIA; ToPo
No courtier this, and naught to courts he owed. Thomas Hood. Sir William Watson. PoVP
No Coward Soul Is Mine. Emily Brontë. *See* Last Lines.
No Credit. Kenneth Fearing. CMoP
No Curtain. F. R. Scott. NYTB
No Death. Philip Bourke Marston. VA
No decent man will cross a field. Evelyn Ray. Amy Lowell. MAP; MoAmPo
No dip and dart of swallows wakes the black. The Canal. Aldous Huxley. HBMV
No Distant Lord. Maltbie D. Babcock. MaRV
(Companionship.) SoP; STF
No Doctors Today, Thank You. Ogden Nash. ShBV-4
No Doubt. Helen Baker Adams. STF
No doubt a sonnet, even in modern style. There Is a Time. Frederic J. Osborn. MemP
No doubt left. Enough deceiving. James Agee. *Fr.* Lyrics. MAP; MoAmPo; PoPl
No doubt on the hills of Nazareth. Hilltops. Leslie Savage Clark. ChIP
No doubt this active will. The Mould. Gladys Cromwell. AnAmPo; MAP; NP
No dragon's blood breaking in crimson flowers. Landscape with figures. A. R. D. Fairburn. AnNZ
No dream of mortal joy. Love and Lust. Isaac Rosenberg. ChMP; TrJP
No dust have I to cover me. An Inscription by the Sea [*or* Variations of Greek Themes, XI]. E. A. Robinson, *after* Glaucus. AWP; ChTr; ELU; InP; JAWP; TOP; WBP
No early buds of laughing spring. Valentine. "C. W. T." RePo; YeAr
No East or West. John Oxenham. FaChP; MaRV; SoP; TRV
(All One in Christ.) BLRP
(Brothers of the Faith.) ChIP; OQP
(In Christ.) STP
No, editors don't care a button. Thoughts on Editors. Thomas Moore. WhC
No egg on Friday Alph will eat. Of Alphus. John Parkhurst, *tr. by* Timothe Kendall. TuPP
No Empty Hands. Michael Brownstein. ANYP
No Enemies. Charles Mackay. GoTP; MaRV
No Envy, John Carter. Merrill Moore. NeMA
No Escape. Harriet L. Delafield. GoYe
No Escape. Lilith Lorraine. FiSC
No Faith. Mark Van Doren. AnFE; CoAnAm
No "fan is in his hand" for these. The Threshing Machine. Alice Meynell. SeCePo
No Fault in Women. Robert Herrick. BOHV; HBV
No fawn-tinged hospital pajamas could cheat him of his austerity. The Old Jew. Maxwell Bodenheim. NP
No feathered bird can weave. Skywriting. Mary Maxtone. BrR
No fence will keep a growing boy outside. Father of the Man. Elizabeth Mabel Bryan. GoYe
No flattring pellow pon my beed. *Unknown.* SeCSL
No flocks that roam the valleys free. The Pitying Heart. Goldsmith. PCH
No flowers now to wear at/ Sunset. The Waning of the Harvest Moon. John Wieners. CoPo
No, for I'll save it! Seven years since. Apparent Failure. Robert Browning. PoVP
No form of human framing. One in Christ. Henry van Dkye. SoP; TRV
No freeman, saith the wise, thinks much on death. The End. Wallace Rice. AA

No Friend like Music. Daniel Whitehead Hicky. PoToHe

No Funeral Gloom. William Allingham, *wr. at. to* Ellen Terry. BLPA; MaRV; NeHB

No Furlough. Stephen Stepanchev. WaP

No further, fathering logos, withering son. The Worm in the Whirling Cross. John Malcolm Brinnin. MoPo

"No gables are burning." The Attack on Finnsburg. *Unknown.* BEL

No Generation Gap, *sel.* Art Berger. "When I was a young man/ coming up." WOW

No girl among the much-loved few. Under a Spell. Catullus. OnPM

No Goddess is thy parent, nor th'art of Dardanus offspring. Dido to Aeneas. Vergil, *tr. by* Richard Stanyhurst. *Fr.* The Aeneid, IV. AnIV

No Great, No Small. Emerson. *See* Informing Spirit, The.

No Greater Love. *Unknown.* STF

No grim last judge recording on a slate. Last Judgment. Stanton A. Coblentz. MaRV

No Gull's Wings. Paul Engle. PoMa

No hand has been allowed to touch. Inscription on a Chemise. *Unknown. Fr.* The Thousand and One Nights. ErPo

No Harm to Lovers. Albius Tibullus, *tr. fr. Latin by* Hubert Creekmore. LiTW

No haste but good, where wisdom makes the way. Seven Sonnets in Sequence, VII. George Gascoigne. Sonn

No heavier lies the everlasting snow. Truth. Cecil Francis Lloyd. CaP

No Hint of Stain. William Vaughn Moody. *Fr.* An Ode in Time of Hesitation. AA

No hint upon the hilltop shows. Inspiration. John Banister Tabb. WGRP

No, his exit by the gate. Exit. Sandy Starr and Willie Gee, III. William Stanley Braithwaite. BANP

No holy pointer, no unchanging Light. In Our Time. Huw Menai. MaRV

"No home, no home," cried an orphan girl. The Orphan Girl. *Unknown.* AS

No hope have I to live a deathless name. Poietes Apoietes. Hartley Coleridge. OBNC

No house of stone. The Elements. W. H. Davies. MoBrPo; OBVV; RePo; WaKn; YT

No human figure stirr'd, to go or come. Thomas Hood. *Fr.* The Haunted House. MyFE

No human singing can. Music and Words. Elizabeth Jennings. UnS

No hungry hawke poore patridge to devoure. Mr. Thomas Shepheard. Edward Johnson. SCAP

No, I Am Not as Others Are. Villon, *tr. fr. French by* Arthur Symons. AWP; JAWP; WBP

No, I am not death wishes of sacred rapists, singing. I, Too, Know What I Am Not. Bob Kaufman. NBP

No, I am through and you can call in vain. Admonition. Philip Stack. BLPA

No! I don't begrudge en his life. The Bachelor. William Barnes. PeVV

No, I had set no prohibiting sign. Trespass. Robert Frost. FaBV

No, I have never found. Places, Loved Ones. Philip Larkin. CMoP; NePoEA

"No, I have tempered haste." The Mount. Léonie Adams. MAP; MoAB; MoAmPo; NP

No! I shan't envy him, who'er he be. The Choice. John Norris. CavP

No, I would not like to meet Bob Dylan. Citizen. Peter Schjeldahl. ANYP

No—I'll endure ten thousand deaths. Chaste Florimel. Matthew Prior. ErPo

No. I'll have no bawds. Ben Jonson. *Fr.* The Alchemist. ViBoPo

No, I'm not afraid of death. Soliloquy I. Richard Aldington. BrPo

No. I'm not an Englishman with a partisan religion. Tragic Guilt. Keidrych Rhys. WaP

No image carved with cunning hand, no cloth of purple dye. To His Familar Friend. Nicholas Grimald. TuPP

No Images. Waring Cuney. AmNP; BANP; CDC; GoSl; PoNe; TTY

No! Indeed. Sir Thomas Wyatt. MeEL

No Jewel so Worthy. Jacopo da Lentino, *tr. fr. Italian by* Dante Gabriel Rossetti. OnPM

"No land," said Noah. Noah and the Rabbit. Hugh Chesterman. MemP; OA

No Laws. Brian Allwood. WaP

No leaf is left unmoistened by the dew. Prayer by Moonlight. Roberta Teale Swartz. TrPWD

No letters to the frontier come. Homeward. Li Pin. OuHeWo

No-life drags on in the shuttered heart. Old Woman Sitting in the Sun. Mary L. Inman. NYTB

No life in earth, or air, or sky. Crotalus. Bret Harte. AA; PFY

No lifeless thing of iron and stone. Brooklyn Bridge. Sir Charles G. D. Roberts. PAH

No light except the stars, but from the cliff. The Sea Birds. Van K. Brock. NYBP

No, little worm, you need not slip. The Worm. Ann Taylor. PCH; PPL; SAS

No Loathsomnesse in Love. Robert Herrick. AnAnS-2; PoeP

No longer am I what I was. Of Himself. Clément Marot. OnPM

No longer ask me, gentle friends. Luckless Collins. William Collins. Three Fragments, 1. WaPE

No longer, borne down insensible rivers. The Drunken Boat. Arthur Rimbaud. ReMP

No longer by the oak, O blackbird, sing. A Blackbird. Marcus Argentarius. LiTW

No longer casual hand to lip. Blind, I Speak to the Cigarette. Joanne de Longchamps. GoYe

No longer heed we war and strife. Thus Speak the Slain. Carl Holliday. PGD

No longer homes are flame against. Litany for Peace. Leslie Savage Clark. PGD

No longer, Lord, thy sons shall sow. Pax Nobiscum. Earl Marlatt. MoRP

No longer mourn for me, when I am dead. Sonnets, LXXI. Shakespeare. AWP; BEL; BoLiVe; CBEP; CoBE; EiL; EnL; EnLi-1; EnLit; EnRePo; EP; GTBS; GTBS-D; GTBS-P; GTBS-W; GTSE; GTSL; HBV; ILP; InPo; JAWP; LiTB; LO; NoP; OAEP; OBSC; OuHeWo; PIA; PoE; PoIE; PoRA; PTK; ReEn; ReIE; SeCeV; SiCE; Sonn; TOP; TreFT; TrGrPo; ViBoPo; WBP; WHA

No longer now do perfumed swains and merry wanton youths. The Passing of Lydia. Horace. Odes, I, 25. UnTE

No longer, O scholars, shall Plautus. Future of the Classics. *Unknown.* BOHV

No longer of Him be it said. Citizen of the World. Joyce Kilmer. OQP; StJW

No longer soiled with stain of earth, what seemed his mantle shone. Simile. Sir Samuel Ferguson. *Fr.* Congal. IrPN

No longer the wife of the hero. The Vamp Passes. James J. Montague. HBMV

No longer throne of a goddess to whom we pray. Full Moon. Robert Hayden. Kal

No longer to lie reading *Tess of the d'Urbervilles.* The Lesson. Robert Lowell. NMP; NoP

No longer torn by what she knows. The Poor Relation. E. A. Robinson. AnAmPo; MAPA; PoIE

No Love, to Love of Man and Wife. Richard Eedes. InvP (Of Man and Wife.) EiL

No lovelier hills than thine have laid. England. Walter de la Mare. HT

No lover saith, I love, nor any other. The Paradox. John Donne. MaMe; OAEP; SCEP-1

No luck, there's no room here. A Word for the Innkeeper. Paul Grano. MoAuPo

No lullaby is older than the rain. Small Rain. Alice Lawry Gould. MoSiPe

No McTavish. Genealogical Reflection. Ogden Nash. ALV

No man can bid a fool or sage. The Power of Thought. Süsskind von Trimberg. TrJP

No man can choose what coming hours may bring. What Man May Choose. Priscilla Leonard. MaRV

No man e'er found a happy life by chance. Happiness an Art. Edward Young. *Fr.* Night Thoughts, VIII. OBEC

No Man, If Men Are Gods. E. E. Cummings. InvP; MoPo; NePA

No man is born into the world whose work. Labor [*or* Work]. James Russell Lowell. *Fr.* A Glance behind the Curtain. MaRV; PEDC; PoSC

No man knew whence the strange bird came. The Bird. Jorge de Lima. LiTW

No man knows his father till he sees. The Way to Know a Father. Robert P. Tristram Coffin. PoRL
No Man Knows War. Edwin Rolfe. TrJP; WaP
"No man may him hyde." Sun! Marianne Moore. NP
No man outlives the grief of war. The Permanence of the Young Men. William Soutar. NeBP; OxBS
No man should stand before the moon. A Sense of Humour. Vachel Lindsay. MAPA; TwAmPo
No Man's Land. James H. Knight-Adkin. MCCG
No map shows my Jerusalem. The Burning-Glass. Walter de la Mare. StJW
No Marvel Is It. Bernard de Ventadour, *tr. fr. Provençal by* Harriet Waters Preston. AWP; LiTW; OuHeWo
No Master. W. H. Davies. PoFr
No Master. William Morris. PoFr; PoVP
No Matter. Paulus Silentiarius, *tr. fr. Greek by* William Cowper. AWP; EnLi-1; JAWP; OuHeWo; WBP
No matter how grouchy you're feeling. Limerick [*or* The Smile]. Anthony Euwer. *Fr.* The Limeratomy. HBMV; LiBL; WhC
No matter how the chances are. Jerry an' Me. Hiram Rich. HBV
No matter how you love me. Guadalupe. Grace Hazard Conkling. NP
No matter where they lived the same dream came. The Castaways. Marya Zaturenska. TrGrPo (1942 ed.)
No matter why, nor whence, nor when she came. The Story of the Ashes and the Flame. E. A. Robinson. MaPo (1969 ed.)
No Miracle. Daniel Corkery. AnIV
No monuments or landmarks guide the stranger. A Country Without a Mythology. Douglas Le Pan. MoCV
No Moon, No Star. Babette Deutsch. NYBP; WIRo
No more be grieved at that which thou hast done. Sonnets, XXXV. Shakespeare. CABA; CBEP; NoP; UnPo
No More Booze. *Unknown.* TrAS, *with music*; TreF (Fireman, Save My Child.) AS, *with music*
Nor more, Clarinda, shall thy charms. To Clarinda. *Unknown.* SeCL
No More Dams I'll Make. Shakespeare. *Fr.* The Tempest, II, ii. ViBoPo
No More Destructive Flame. Francis X. Connolly. ISi
No more for them shall Evening's rose unclose. Epicedium. J. Corson Miller. DD; HBMV; PAH
No more from out the sunset. Onus Probandi [*or* Sandy Star]. William Stanley Braithwaite. Sandy Star and Willie Gee, V. BANP; HBMV
No More Hiroshimas. James Kirkup. POTi
No more in any house can I be at peace. A Dream. Charles Williams. OBEV (new ed.)
No more in dreams as once it draws me there. A House of the Eighties. Edmund Wilson. AnFE; CoAnAm
No more lewd lays of lighter loves I sing. Barnabe Barnes. *Fr.* A Divine Century of Spiritual Sonnets. Sonn; TuPP
No more marble let him have. Epitaph Inscribed on a Small Piece of Marble. James Shirley. CavP
No more, my dear, no more these counsels try. Astrophel and Stella, LXIV. Sir Philip Sidney. BEL; CoBE; FaPL; FCP; HBV; OBSC; ReEn; SiCE; SiPS; Sonn; TOP; TuPP
No more, my Stella, to the sighing shades. To Stella. Hester Chapone. OBEC
No more my visionary soul shall dwell. Pantisocracy. Samuel Taylor Coleridge. EnRP
No more, no more. The Riddle. Alexander Brome. OBS
No more—no more in Cashel town. The Roving Worker. *Unknown.* OnYI
No more—no more—Oh! never more on me. My Days of Love Are Over. Byron. *Fr.* Don Juan, I. FaBoEn; OBNC; PeER
No More, O Maidens. Alcman, *tr. fr. Greek by* Olga Marx *and* Ernst Morwitz. LiTW
No More, O My Spirit. Euripides, *tr. fr. Greek by* Hilda Doolittle ("H. D."). AWP
No more of talk where God or angel guest. Paradise Lost, IX. Milton. FosPo; MBW-1; NoP; OBS; SeEP
No more of your titled acquaintances boast. Epigram. Burns. ALV
No more peck of corn for me, no more, no more. Many T'ousand Go. *Unknown.* ABF
"No more shall I see." Frithiof's Farewell. Esaias Tegnér. *Fr.* Frithiof's Saga. AWP; JAWP; WBP
No more shall I, since I am driven hence. To Larr. Robert Herrick. BoW; SeCV-1
No more shall I work in the factory. The Factory Girl. *Unknown.* ABF
No more shall meads be deckt [*or* decked] with flowers. The Protestation. Thomas Carew. CavP; OuHeWo
No more shall walls, no more shall walls confine. Hosanna. Thomas Traherne. PoEL-2; SCEP-1; SeCV-2
No more the battle or the chase. Indian Summer. John Banister Tabb. AA; DD
No more the English girls may go. High Germany. Edward Shanks. OBMV
No more the jousts and tourneys. Toledo. José Zorrilla. CAW
No more the morn, with tepid rays. Winter: An Ode. Samuel Johnson. CLwM
No More the Slow Stream. Floris Clark McLaren. OBCV
No more the smoke-wisp signal climbs; no more. Rex Ingamells. *Fr.* Forgotten People. BoAu
No more the swanboat on the artificial lake. Blind Date. Conrad Aiken. MoVE; ViBoPo (1958 ed.)
No More the Thunder of Cannon. Julia C. R. Dorr. OHIP
No more the wide Mawnkato pearled with the ice under blue January sky. Charley III. Stephen Sandy. NYTB
No more these simple flowers belong. Burns. Whittier. CoBA
No more upon my bosom rest thee. Woman's Song. Edward Shanks. LO
No more wine? then we'll push back chairs and talk. Bishop Blougram's Apology. Robert Browning. OBNC; OtMeF; PoEL-5; ViPo; ViPP
No more with candied words infect mine ears. Tell Me No More. William Drummond of Hawthornden. TrGrPo
No more with overflowing light. For a Dead Lady. E. A. Robinson. AmLP; AmPP (4th ed.); AnFE; AnNE; AP; APA; BWP; CMoP; CoAnAm; CoBMV; FaBoEn; ForPo; GTBS-D; GTBS-W; InP; InvP; LiTA; LiTM; MAmP; MAP; MAPA; MaPo (1969 ed.); MoAB; MoAmPo; OxBA; PoEL-5; PoRA; ReMP; TreFT; TwAmPo; VaPo; ViBoPo; WHA
No More Words. Franklin Lushington. PAH
No more work and no more play. Good Night. Ruth Ainsworth. BoTP
No more, ye warblers of the wood, no more. Sonnet on the Death of Robert Riddell of Glenriddell. Burns. Sonn
No mortal thing enthralled these longing eyes. Celestial Love. Michelangelo, *tr. by* John Addington Symonds. AWP; JAWP; WBP
No music He heard, and no angels He saw. The Welcome. Leonard Feeney. WHL
No Music, thou art not the "food of Love." Fragment to Music. Shelley. MuSP
No! my desires are limited; nor expand. The Wish. John Dancer. SeCL
No myrtle can obliterate a name. Your Glory, Lincoln. Mae Winkler Goodman. PGD
No Names. *Unknown, tr. fr. Irish by* Frank O'Connor. KiLC
No Nation Liveth unto Itself. *Unknown.* MaRV
No nearer home than Nassau Bay. Rondeau in Wartime. James Bertram. AnNZ
No need to hush the children for her sake. Out of Hearing. Jane Barlow. HBV
No! never such a draught was poured. A Ballad of the Boston Tea-Party. Oliver Wendell Holmes. MC; PaA; PAH; PAL; PoFr; ThLM
No, Never Think. Pushkin, *tr. fr. Russian by* Babette Deutsch. ErPo
No new poems his brush will trace. On Hearing Someone Sing a Poem by Yüan Chen. Po Chü-i. ML
No night could be darker than this night. Twelfth Night. Laurie Lee. BoC
No night is there! Heaven. Clarence A. Vincent. OQP
No! No! Bird in the darkness singing. The Tsigane's Canzonet. Edward King. AA
No, no, fair heretic[k], it needs must be. Song. Sir John Suckling. *Fr.* Aglaura. AnAnS-2; AtBAP; CABA; CBEP; LiTL; LoBV; OBS; PoIE; ReEn; SeEP
"No, no; for my virginity." A True Maid. Matthew Prior. ALV; CBV; EiCL; ErPo; LiTG; MeWo; PV
No, no; Go from me. I have left her lately. A Virginal. Ezra Pound. AmPP; AP; APA; CMoP; CoAnAm; CoBMV;

ILP; MAP; MeWo; MoAB; MoAmPo; NeMA; NePA; OxBA; PoAn; Sonn; TwAmPo
No, no, go not to Lethe, neither twist. Ode on Melancholy [*or* On Melancholy]. Keats. AnFE; AtBAP; ATP; BEL; BoLiVe; BWP; CABA; CaFP; CBEP; CBV; CoBE; DiPo; EG; EnL; EnLi-2; EnLit; EnRP; EPN; ERoP-2; ExPo; FaBoEn; FiP; ForPo; GTBS-W; HBV; ILP; LiTB; LO; MaPo; MBW-2; MERP; NoP; OAEP; OBEV; OBNC; PAn; PeER; PoE; PoEL-4; PoFS; PoIE; PoRA; SeCeV; StP; TOP; TreFS; TrGrPo; VaPo; ViBoPo
No, no I did not bargain for so much. Too Much. Edwin Muir. LiTB
No, No! I Ne'er Shall Love Thee Less. Henry Cromwell. SeCL
No, no. I well remember—proofs, you said. The Demon-Lover. James Abraham Hillhouse. *Fr.* Hadad. AA
No, No, It Is Not Dying. César Malan. SoP
No, No, Nigella. *Unknown.* EnRePo
No, no, no, no! Come, let's away to prison. Shakespeare. *Fr.* King Lear, V, iii. MemP
No, no, no, no, I cannot hate my foe. Song. Sir Philip Sidney. FCP; SiPS
No, no, no, no, resistance is but vain. Song. Anthony Henly. SeCL
No no no no, they were too far apart. The Goat Milkers. John Stevens Wade. ThO
No, No, Poor Suffering [*or* Suff'ring] Heart. Dryden. *Fr.* Cleomenes, II, ii. AtBAP; GTBS-W; LiTB; LiTG; LiTL; LoBV; QFR; ViBoPo
(One Happy Moment.) OBEV (new ed.)
(Song: "No, no, poor suff'ring heart, no change endeavour.") CEP; NoP; SeCV-2
No, no, the falling blossom is no sign. Song. George Meredith. EnLit
No, no, the utmost share. Robert Herrick. *Fr.* To Electra. LO
No, no, this bitterness is no new thing. Northwind. Gene Baro. NePoEA-2
No, no—'tis not love—You may talk till dooms day. No True Love Between Man and Woman. *Unknown.* PeRV
No, not cold beneath the grasses. In My Father's House. Robert Freeman. OQP
No, Not Despairingly. Horatius Bonar. SoP
No! not for those of women born. From a Hint in the Minor Poets. Samuel Wesley. CBEP; OBEC
No, not in the halls of the noble and proud. The Quakeress Bride. Elizabeth Clementine Kinney. AA
No, Not the Owl. T. I. Moore. MoAuPo
No not this old whalehall can whelm us. Mappemounde. Earle Birney. OBCV; PeCV
No, nothing is asleep in this demesne. The Sleeping Beauty. Robert Layzer. NePoEA
No notice in the papers. Tombstone with Cherubim. Horace Gregory. NAMP
No one/ ran up. In-Group. Lionel Kearns. PeCV (1967 ed.)
Noone and a Star Stand, Am to Am. E. E. Cummings. NePoAm-2
"Noone" autumnal this great lady's gaze. E. E. Cummings. CrMA
No One Can Be Trusted, Something Tells Me. Craig Sterry. QAH
No one can communicate to you. Face of Poverty. Lucy Smith NNP; PoNe (1970 ed.)
No one can tell you why. Heart's Needle, IV. W. D. Snodgrass. NePoEA; PIA
No One Cares Less Than I. Edward Thomas. MoVE
No one could have a blacker tail. Othello Jones Dresses for Dinner. Ed Roberson. PoNe (1970 ed.)
No one could tell me where my soul might be. The Search. Ernest Crosby. AA; OQP
No one dies cleanly now. Eclogue. Frederic Prokosch. ViBoPo
No one ever plucked. Robert Browning. *Fr.* The Ring and the Book. ChIP
No one goes there now. The Tune of Seven Towers. William Morris. PoVP; ViPP
No One in Particular. John Perreault. ANYP; YAP
No one in the garden. Laughter. Olive Enoch. BoTP
No one need feel alone looking up at leaves. Looking Up at Leaves. Barbara Howes. BoNaP
No one sees me. The All-seeing God. Longfellow. *Fr.* The Masque of Pandora. OQP
No One So Much as You. Edward Thomas. ChMP
No one spoke. Haiku. Ryota. LiTW
No one was in the fields. Tom's Angel. Walter de la Mare. BoC; POTE
No one was with me there. Estranged. Walter de la Mare. FaBoEn
"No one will milk a cow within." Forbidden Drink. Robert Lovett. WhC
No one will remember. Child of the Long Grass. Roy Macnab. BoSA
No one would notice that gap between two fields. A Road in the Weald. Richard Church. HaMV
No one's going to read. A Dance for Militant Dilettantes. Al Young. WSL
No Other Choice. *Unknown. See* Fain Would I Change That Note.
No Pains Comparable to His Attempt ("Like as the doleful dove delights alone to be"). William Hunnis. ReIE
No Pain[e]s Comparable to His Attempt ("What watch, what woe, what want, what wrack."). William Hunnis. EnPo; TuPP
(Shipmen, The.) OBSC
No painter's brush, nor poet's pen. A Mother's Name. *Unknown.* PGD
No paraphrase does. English A. John Ciardi. ToPo
No passenger was known to flee. Emily Dickinson. MoVE
No path at all goes somewhere. Woodlore. Kim Kurt. NePoAm-2
No Peace. *Unknown, tr. fr. Sanskrit by* Joseph Nadin Rawson. *Fr.* The Upanishads. OnPM
No people on the golf-links, not a crack. North Coast Recollections. John Betjeman. CMoP
No permanent possession of the sky. To the Greatest City in the World. Rolfe Humphries. PoMa
No pictured likeness of my Lord have I. My Master's Face. William Hurd Hillyer. ChIP; MaRV; SoP
No place is safe, no temple yields defence. The Times. Marcus Manilius. LiTW
No Platonic Love. William Cartwright. CABA; ErPo; FosPo; ILP; InvP; LiTB; SiTL
(No Platonique Love.) PoEL-2
No Pleasure without Some Pain. Thomas, Lord Vaux. EIL; EnRePo; SiCE; TuPP
(Death in Life.) OBSC
No poet, sure, can be so stupid. An Explanatory Epistle. John Banks. WaPE
No Possum, No Sop, No Taters. Wallace Stevens. AmP; MoVE; OxBA; PoeP; PoFS
No price is set on the lavish summer. What Is So Rare as a Day in June? James Russell Lowell. *Fr.* The Vision of Sir Launfal: Prelude to Pt. I. NePA; TIHL
No pride hath he who sings of escape from love. James Stephens. *Fr.* Theme with Variations. POTE
No prisoner can tell his honest thought. Prison Song. Richard Coeur de Lion, *tr. by* Henry Adams. LiTW
No Prisoner of Time. William H. Hudnut, Jr. ChIP
No purple mars the chalice; not a bird. The Exquisite Sonnet. J. C. Squire. HBMV
No quarrel ever stirred. Of Quarrels. Arthur Guiterman. OTD; TiPo
No Question. George Dillon. AmLP
No quirt—right?—nor spur. To My Mouse-colored Mare. Tristan Corbière. ErPo
No rack can torture me. Emily Dickinson. MAmP; MaPo; MoAB; MoPo; MWA-2
No Reason Why. Thomas Brown. *See* I Do Not Love Thee, Doctor Fell.
No Regrets. *Unknown.* SoP
No Return. Vassar Miller. CoPo; ToPo
No Road. Philip Larkin. MoBrPo (1962 ed.); OPoP
No rock along the road but knows. Poet. Donald Jeffrey Hayes. AmNP; PoNe
No roofes of gold o're riotous tables shining. Description of a Religious House and Condition of Life. Richard Crashaw. MaMe
No Room. Dorothy Conant Stroud. STF
No Room. Robert Whitaker. ChIP
No room for mourning: he's gone out. William Wordsworth. Sidney Keyes. ChMP; GTBS-D; POTE; SeCePo

No runner clears the final fence. The Unfinished Race. Norman Cameron. OxBS
"No," said Patience patiently, and pulled from his wallet. Providence. William Langland. *Fr.* The Vision of Piers Plowman. PoLi
No season. Outlook Uncertain. Alastair Reid. NePoEA-2
No Season for Our Season. Willard Maas. AnAmPo
No second love shall e'er my heart surprise. Elegy: to Delia. James Hammond. Love Elegies, XII. CEP
No Second Troy. W. B. Yeats. BrPo; BWP; CBV; CMoP; EnLoPo; GTBS-P; MaPo; MBW-2; NP; PoE; PoEL-5; PoeP; PoIE; PoSa; SeCePo
No Sects [*or* Sect] in Heaven. Elizabeth H. Jocelyn Cleaveland. BLPA; TreFS
No secular sound—this is the house of prayer. Woodland. Sister Margaret Teresa. JKCP (1926 ed.)
No sheep in the folds. Christmas. Betty Scott Stam. BePJ
No shepherds now, in smooth alternate verse. George Crabbe. *Fr.* The Village. PP
No shop does the bird use. Elizabeth J. Coatsworth. ThGo
No show of bolts and bars. Love. Henry David Thoreau. CBEP; OBVV; OQP
No sign is made while empires pass. Continuity. "Æ." MoBrPo; NBM; NeMA; PoVP
No single hour can stand for naught. John Clare. OBNC
No Single Thing Abides. Lucretius, *tr. fr. Latin by* W. H. Mallock. *Fr.* De Rerum Natura. AWP; ImOP, *abr.*; JAWP; PG (1945 ed.); WBP
No Sky at All. Hashin. *See* Loneliness.
No Slave beneath the Flag. George Lansing Taylor. DD, *abr.*
No sleep! I rise and burn the night away. The Protagonist. Peter Hopegood. MoAuPo; PoAu-2
No sleep. The sultriness pervades the air. The House-Top. Herman Melville. AP; LiTA; MAmP; MWA-1; NCEP; NoP; TDP
No sleep like hers, no rest. White Roses. Ernest Rhys. VA
No sleep tonight. Summary. Sonia Sanchez. BF
No slightest golden rhyme he wrote. A Hint from Herrick. Thomas Bailey Aldrich. HBV
No sly usurping dream defeats the will. The Settled Men. George M. Brady. NeIP
No Snake in Springtime. Elizabeth J. Coatsworth. AnAmPo
No Socrates to teach her a last love. For the Antigone. Andras Hamori. NYTB
No song of a soldier riding down. The Ride of Colin Graves. John Boyle O'Reilly. PAH
No sooner come, but gone, and fal'n asleep. On My Dear Grand-Child Simon Bradstreet. Anne Bradstreet. SCAP
No sooner had th' Almighty ceas't, but all. Heaven. Milton. *Fr.* Paradise Lost, III. OBS
No sound of any storm that shakes. Hillcrest. E. A. Robinson. AP; CoBMV; FaBoEn; MAmP; MoAB; OxBA; PIA; PoIE
No sound—yet my room fills up with thunder. The Peeper. Peter Davison. ErPo
No Spare Time. Ishikawa Kimiko, *tr. fr. Japanese by* Ishii *and* Obata. OnPM
No spring nor summer beauty hath such grace. The Autumnal [1]. John Donne. Elegies, IX. AtBAP; DiPo; EnL; MaMe; NoP; OAEP; PoEL-2; ReEn; SCEP-1; SeCV-1; SeEP; TuPP; ViBoPo
No Star Is Ever Lost. Adelaide Anne Procter. *Fr.* A Legend of Provence. MaRV
No stars her eyes, to clear the wandering night. Phyllis, VIII. Thomas Lodge. Sonn; TuPP
No state is enviable. To the luck alone. Modern Love, XIX. George Meredith. ViPo; VP
No stately column marks the hallowed place. Alamance. Seymour W. Whiting. PAH
No stir in the air, no stir in the sea. The Inchcape Rock. Robert Southey. BeLS; ChTr; FaBoBe; GN; GoTP; HBV; HBVV; OBRV; OnSP; OTPC; PaPo; TreFS
No storehouse nor barn have we. The Birds of the Air. Hollis Freeman. STF
No stranger pilgrims wear the shepherd's way. To Mary at Christmas. John Gilland Brunini. ISi
No Sudden Thing of Glory. Alice Meynell. StJW
(Advent Meditation.) MoRP
No Sufferer for Her Love. *Unknown, tr. fr. Late Middle Irish by* Robin Flower. AnIL
No sun—no moon! No! [*or* November *or* November in England]. Thomas Hood. BBV; BOHV; ChTr; FiBHP; GN; GoTP; HBV; NBM; OTPC (1946 ed.); PTK; RIS
No sunny ray, no silver night. Threnody. Thomas Lovell Beddoes. EnRP
No Swan So Fine. Marianne Moore. AmLP; AP; CoBMV; NoP; OxBA
No Sweeter Thing. Adelaide Love. PGD
No syrup or perfume. Nox. Salvador Díaz Mirón. HW
No taller than the grass. A Child Drowns in the Sea of Its Own Imagining. Kathleen Fraser. YAP
No teacher I of boys or smaller fry. Allen Beville Ramsay. CenHV; PV
No tears, no sorrowing farewells. When I Go Home. Milton Lee. OQP
No, they are come; their horn is lifted up. Gerard Manley Hopkins. *Fr.* Six Epigrams. SeCePo
No, they cannot touch me for coyning. I am the king himselfe. Shakespeare. *Fr.* King Lear, IV, vi. AtBAP
No Thoroughfare. Ruth Holmes. BoTP
No! those days are gone away. Robin Hood. Keats. AWP; BEL; EnLi-2; EnLit; EnRP; EPN; InPo; OTPC (1946 ed.); PCD; PoeP
No Thyng Ys to Man So Dere. Robert Mannyng. *See* Praise of Women.
No Time. Terence Tiller. NeBP
No Time. *Unknown.* SoP
No Time for God. Norman L. Trott. BLRP; STF
No Time for God. *Unknown.* SoP
No Time for My Lord? Beth Coombe Harris. SoP
No Time for Poetry. Julia Fields. AmNP
No time, no time for study. First Things First. "M. E. H." SoP
No, Time, thou shalt not boast that I do change. Sonnets, CXXIII. Shakespeare. BoLiVe; OAEP; OBSC; SiCE; Sonn; TrGrPo
No Time to Hate. Emily Dickinson. *See* I had no time to hate, because.
No time to read, no time to pray. Stop a Minute! *Unknown.* STF
No, 'tis in vain to seek for bliss. Felicity. Isaac Watts. OxBoCh
No tongue can tell, no pen describe. Stanzas. Philip Freneau. CoBA
No tranquil ordered day of ours. In Memoriam. Ada Jackson. PGD
No True Love between Man and Woman. *Unknown.* PeRV
No Truer Word. Walter Savage Landor. *See* Epigram: "No truer word, save God's. . ."
No Trust in Men. *Unknown, tr. fr. Spanish by* Havelock Ellis. OnPM
No Trust in Time. William Drummond of Hawthornden. LoBV
(Sonnet: "Look how the flower which ling'ringly doth fade.") SeCL
(Thy Sun Posts Westward.) SeCePo
No Trust in Women. *Unknown, tr. fr. Spanish by* Havelock Ellis. OnPM
No trust to metals nor to marbles, when. Epitaph on the Tomb of Sir Edward Giles and His Wife. Robert Herrick. QFR
No, 'twasn't here dat tree firs' grew. The Woman's Tongue Tree. Arthur Guiterman. PoMS
No two eyes gaze alike. Janus. Madeline Mason. GoYe
No Uneasy Refuge. Blanaid Salkeld. AnIV
No use, no use, now, begging Recognize! Amnesiac. Sylvia Plath. NYBP
No use to speak, no good to tell you that. Communication. Elizabeth Jennings. NePoEA
No usual words can bear the woe I feel. For I Am Sad. Don Marquis. BOHV
No vainer thing there can be found amid this vale of strife. The Uncertainty of Life. Barnabe Googe. SiCE
No vision and you perish. Some Faith at Any Cost. Harriet Du Autermont. MaRV
No walls confine! Can nothing hold my mind? Insatiableness. Thomas Traherne. OxBoCh
No wandering any more where the feet stumble. Marriage. Mark Van Doren. MoLP
No warm, downy pillow His sweet head pressed. The Heavenly

Stranger. Ada Blenkhorn. BLRP
No water is still, on top. The Movement of Fish. James Dickey. FRC; NYBP
"No water so still as the/ dead fountains of Versailles." No Swan So Fine. Marianne Moore. AmLP; AP; CoBMV; NoP; OxBA
No Way Is Good. Poseidippus, *tr. fr. Greek by* William Hay. OnPM
No way too long—no path too steep. Stefan George. *Fr.* Das Jahr der Seele. AWP
No weather can unbrother brothers. Tour in Rain. Raymond Roseliep. FiSC
No wind of life may strike within. Dutch Seacoast. Kenneth Slessor. *Fr.* The Atlas. PoAu-2
No wind-wakeness hers. A cricket's creed. Sunday in the Country. May Swenson. NePoAm-2
No Woman Born. Robert Farren. OxBI
No wonder that Oxford and Cambridge profound. Epigram. *Unknown.* WaPE
No wonder the birds make whittlings of sound, that the hemlock. Sun-up in March. Abbie Huston Evans. NePoAm
No wonder you so oft have wept. Francis Burdett Money-Coutts. *Fr.* A Little Sequence. OBVV
No word, no lie, can cross a carven lip. Silence. T. Sturge Moore. QFR; SyP
No word that is not flesh, he said. A Reason for Writing. Theodore Spencer. TwAmPo
No Words Are Lost. Margaret Widdemer. PoMa
No world but this for your eye. Requiem for an Abstract Artist. Jascha Kessler. AmPC
No, worlding, no, 'tis not thy gold. The Second Rapture. Thomas Carew. UnTE
No Worst, There Is None. Gerard Manley Hopkins. BrPo; BWP; CABA; CBEP; CMoP; DiPo; EnL; EnLi-2 (1949 ed.); FaBoMo; ForPo; GTBS-P; LiTB; LiTM; LoBV; MaPo; MoAB; MoBrPo (1950 ed.); NoP; PeVV; PoEL-5; PoeP; PoIE; PPON; ReMP; StP; ViPo (1962 ed.); ViPP; VP
(Life Death Does End.) SeCePo
(Sonnet: "No worst, there is none.") FaBoEn; MoVE; OBNC
(Terrible Sonnets, The, II.) MoPo
Noah. Roy Campbell. *Fr.* The Flaming Terrapin. BoSA
Noah. Roy Daniells. PeCV (1967 ed.); WHW
Noah. Hermann Hagedorn. MoRP
Noah an' Jonah an' Cap'n John Smith. Don Marquis. LHV; LoGBV; PoLF
Noah and the Flood. Genesis, VI: 5-VIII: 22, Bible, *O.T.* OuHeWo
Noah and the Rabbit. Hugh Chesterman. MemP; OA
Noah and the Waters, *sel.* C. Day Lewis.
Chorus: "Since you have come thus far." OAEP (2d ed.)
Noah's Ark. Marguerite Young. MoPo
Noah's Carpenters. *Unknown.* SoP; STF
Noah's Flood. *Unknown, tr. fr. Anglo-Saxon. Fr.* Genesis. AnOE, *tr. by* Charles W. Kennedy; BEL
Noah's Floud, *sel.* Michael Drayton.
"Eternall and all-working God, which wast." PoEL-2
Noah's Raven. W. S. Merwin. AmPC; NoP
Noah's Song. Evan Jones. PoAu-2
Nobility. Alice Cary. OHFP; OQP; WBLP
(Noble Life, The.) MaRV
Nobility. Tennyson. *Fr.* Lady Clara Vere de Vere. OTPC (1946 ed.)
Noble, The. Wordsworth. *Fr.* The Prelude, IX. ChTr
Noble Balm. Ben Jonson. *See* Ode, An: "High-spirited friend."
Noble Fisherman, The, or Robin Hood's Preferment. *Unknown.* ESPB; OBB
Noble Friar, that worthy beggar, The. The Friar's Tale. Chaucer, *mod. by* Edwin M. Everett. *Fr.* The Canterbury Tales. EnLi-1 (1949 ed.)
Noble heart [*or* hart], that harbours virtuous [*or* vertuous] thought, The. The Fight of the Red Cross Knight and the Heathen Sansjoy. Spenser. *Fr.* The Faerie Queene, I, 5. FiP; ViBoPo
Noble hedge of ancient yew, A. Open to Visitors. E. V. Milner. ELU
Noble horse with courage in his eye, The. Aristocrats. Keith Douglas. NePoEA
Noble Kinsmen, The. Fletcher *and* Shakespeare. *See* Two Noble Kinsmen, The.
Noble Life, The. Alice Cary. *See* Nobility.
Noble Love. Richard Flecknoe. ACP
Noble mayd, still standing, all this vewd, The. The Masque of Cupid. Spenser. *Fr.* The Faerie Queene, III. PoEL-1
Noble, nasty course he ran, A. Epitaph on the Late King of the Sandwich Isles. Winthrop Mackworth Praed. FiBHP
Noble Nature, The. Ben Jonson. *See* It Is Not Growing like a Tree.
Noble range it was, of many a rood, A. Places of Nestling Green. Leigh Hunt. *Fr.* The Story of Rimini. EnRP; OBRV
Noble Ritter Hugo, Der. Ballad of the Mermaid [*or* Ballad by Hans Breitmann]. Charles Godfrey Leland. BOHV; CenHV; FiBHP; PaPo
Noble Sisters. Christina Rossetti. CoBE
Noble Soldier, The, *sel.* Thomas Dekker, Samuel Rowley, *and* John Day.
O Sorrow, Sorrow. SeCL
Noble-Tuck Man, The. Jean Ingelow. NA
Noble Voyage, The. Earl of Surrey. PoLi
Nobleman's Wedding, The. William Allingham. IrPN
Nobleman's Wedding, The. *Unknown.* AnIV
Nobles and heralds, by your leave. Epitaph on Himself [*or* Prior's Epitaph]. Matthew Prior. HBV; TreFS; TrGrPo
Noblesse Oblige. Jessie Fauset. CDC
Noblest bodies are but gilded clay. Of Death. Samuel Harding. *Fr.* Sicily and Naples. CBEP; SeCL
Noblest Charis, you that are. His Discourse with Cupid. Ben Jonson. *Fr.* A Celebration of Charis. AnAnS-2; SeCP
Noblest Roman, The. Shakespeare. *See* Portrait of Brutus.
Noblest thoughts my soul can claim, The. The Name of Mother. George Griffith Fetter. PGD
Nobly, nobly Cape Saint Vincent to the North-west died away. Home-Thoughts, from the Sea. Robert Browning. AWP; BEL; CaFP; CBEP; EnLi-2 (1949 ed.); FaBoCh; FiP; GTBS; GTSL; ILP; InP; InPo; JAWP; MaVP; MBW-2; OAEP; OBEV; OBVV; OTPC; PoVP; ShBV-2; TOP; ViPo; ViPP; WBP
Nobody. Burns. LiTL
Nobody, A. Emily Dickinson. *See* I'm nobody! Who are you?
Nobody. Robert Graves. POTE; TPM
"Nobody." John Stevens Wade. ThO
Nobody believes in Fate any more, nobody listens to the Norns. Waiting and Peeking. V. R. Lang. NePA
Nobody Comes. Thomas Hardy. MoVE; PoFS; ViPP
Nobody comes to the graveyard on the hill. The Hill above the Mine. Malcolm Cowley. NAMP; PoPl
Nobody ever galloped on this road. The Dead Ride Fast. R. P. Blackmur. MoPo
Nobody heard him, the dead man. Not Waving, but Drowning. Stevie Smith. GTBS-P
Nobody I know would like to be buried. Thanksgiving for a Habitat. W. H. Auden. NYBP
Nobody in the lane, and nothing, nothing but blackberries. Blackberrying. Sylvia Plath. NYBP
Nobody Knows. Helen Coale Crew. GFA
Nobody knows. The Need. Siegfried Sassoon. TrPWD
Nobody Knows but Mother. Mary Morrison. BLPA
Nobody Knows—but Mother. *Unknown.* PEDC
Nobody Knows de Trouble I See [*or* I've Seen]. *Unknown.* BoAN-1, *rare vers., with music;* BoAN-2, *familiar vers., with music*
Nobody knows me. Number 5—December. David Henderson. BOLo
Nobody knows of the work it makes. Nobody Knows—but Mother. *Unknown.* PEDC
Nobody knows the other side. Chorus. Jack Kerouac. *Fr.* Mexico City Blues. NeAP
Nobody knows what is in the black house. The Sea House. William Goodreau. NYTB
Nobody knows what's growing in Bridget. The Bulge. George Johnston. MoCV; PV
Nobody knows who planted those pink roses. The Ramblers. Virginia Linton. NYTB
Nobody lives in the cottage now. Fairy Feet. Phyllis L. Garlick. BoTP
Nobody Loses All the Time. E. E. Cummings. AnNE; CMoP; FIW; LiTM; TwCP
Nobody noogers the shaff of a sloo. On a Flimmering Floom You Shall Ride. Carl Sandburg. GoYe
Nobody painted Mrs. Aherne's store. Dakota: Five Times Six. Joseph Hansen. NYBP

Nobody planted roses, he recalls. "Summertime and the Living." Robert Hayden. Kal; PoIE (1970 ed.); TwCP
Nobody stays here long. Not in the Guide-Books. Elizabeth Jennings. LiTM (1970 ed.); NePoEA
Nobody stuffs the world in at your eyes. Show. Margaret Avison. PeCV
Nobody took any notice of her as she stood on the causey curb [*or* kerb]. The Market-Girl. Thomas Hardy. At Casterbridge Fair, IV. BEL; EnLi-2 (1949 ed.); EnLit; PoVP
Nobody wanted this infant born. Burial. Mark Van Doren. MoBS
Nobody wants to stay on the beach now. The Fisherman. Douglas Stewart. ACV
Nobody's Child. Phila H. Case. TreF
Nocht o' Mortal Sicht. Bessie J. B. Macarthur. OxBS
Noctambule. George Johnston. MoCV
Noctiflora. Maurice Lesemann. NP
Nocturn. Francis Thompson. POTE
Nocturnal. Herman L. McMillan. TNV
Nocturnal. Os Marron. NeBP
Nocturnal Reverie, A. Countess of Winchilsea. BWP; CEP; EiCL; EiPP; FaBoEn; GoTL; LoBV; OBEC; PoEL-3; SeCePo
Nocturnal Sketch, A. Thomas Hood. BOHV; FiBHP; NBM; SiTL
Nocturnal upon Saint Lucy's Day [Being the Shortest Day], A. John Donne. CBEP; EnRePo; EP; GTBS-W; LiTB; LiTG; MaPo; MBW-1; NoP; PIA; PoE; ReIE
(Nocturnal[l] upon S. Lucies Day.) AnAnS-1; AtBAP; BoW; FaBoEn; MaMe; MeLP; MeP; MePo; OBS; PoEL-2; SCEP-1; SeCP; SeCV-1; SeEP
Nocturne: "All the earth a hush of white." Amelia Josephine Burr. HBV
Nocturne: "Be thou at peace this night." Edward Davison. CH
Nocturne: "Blue water. . . a clear moon." Li Po, *tr. fr. Chinese by* Shigeyoshi Obata. OnPM
Nocturne: "I walked beside the deep, one night of stars." Victor Hugo, *tr. fr. French.* CAW
Nocturne: "Keen winds of cloud and vaporous drift." Richard Garnett. OBVV
Nocturne, A: "Moon has gone to her rest, The." Wilfrid Scawen Blunt. OBMV
Nocturne: "My weeping and the starlight." Juan Ramón Jiménez, *tr. fr. Spanish by* Thomas Walsh. OnPM
Nocturne III: "Night, A,/ a night all full of murmurs." José Asunción Silva, *tr. fr. Spanish by* Lloyd Watson. LiTW
(Nocturne: "One night," *tr. by* Thomas Walsh.) WoL
Nocturne: "Night comes, an angel stands." Kathleen Raine. ChMP
Nocturne: "'Nothin' or everythin' it's got to be." John V. A. Weaver. AnAmPo; HBMV; NP
Nocturne: "One night." José Asunción Silva. *See* Nocturne III: "Night, A."
Nocturne: "Over New England now, the snow." Frances Frost. BoNaP
Nocturne: "Red flame flowers bloom and die, The." Crosbie Garstin. CH
(On the Back Veld.) ACV
Nocturne: "See how dark the night settles on my face." Naomi Long Madgett. BALP
Nocturne: "See how the dying west puts forth her song." Richard Church. ChMP
Nocturne: "Sleep that like the couched dove." Gerald Griffin. VA
(Sleep That like the Couchèd Dove.) OnYI
Nocturne: "Softly blow lightly." Donald Jeffrey Hayes. CDC
Nocturne: "This cool night is strange." Gwendolyn Bennett. BANP
Nocturne: "Up to her chamber window." Thomas Bailey Aldrich. HBV
Nocturne, The: "Why the hell do you use all that black." Carl Bode. ToPo
Nocturne: "Wildness of haggard flights." Roussan Camille, *tr. fr. French by* Seth L. Wolitz. TTY
Nocturne: "Wind is blowing from the hill, The." H. A. Vaughan. PoNe
Nocturne at Bethesda. Arna Bontemps. AmNP; BALP; BANP; CDC; PoNe
Nocturne: Georgia Coast. Daniel Whitehead Hicky. AmFN
Nocturne in a Deserted Brickyard. Carl Sandburg. AmPP; CoBA; MAP; MoAmPo; NP
Nocturne in G Minor. Karl Gustav Vollmoeller, *tr. fr. German by* Ludwig Lewisohn. AWP; LiTW
Nocturne of Remembered Spring. Conrad Aiken. HBMV
Nocturne of the Wharves. Arna Bontemps. BANP; PoNe (1970 ed.)
Nocturne Varial. Lewis Alexander. PoNe
Nod. Walter de la Mare. AtBAP; BoTP; EnLit; GoTP; HBMV; MoAB; ThWaDe; TSW
Nodding, its great head rattling like a gourd. Original Sin; a Short Story. Robert Penn Warren. AmP; CrMA; FiMAP; GTBS-W; LiTA; LiTM; MoVE; ReMP
Nodding oxeye bends before the wind, The. The Fear of Flowers. John Clare. AnFE; EG; NBM; OBRV; SeCeV
Nodes. Alice Corbin. NP; WGRP
Noe falce, noe faithles Lindamor. *Unknown.* SeCSL
Noe longer torture mee, in dreams. Anti-Platonicke. George Daniel. CavP
Noe more of teares I have not left in store. *Unknown.* SeCSL
Noe more unto my thoughts appeare. Song [*or* Quatrains]. Sidney Godolphin. MeLP; MePo; OBS
Noe, noe I never was in love. *Unknown.* SeCSL
Noe, she ne're lov'de, 'twas the excess. *Unknown.* SeCSL
Noe, twas her eyes. *Unknown.* SeCSL
Noel. Hilaire Belloc. HBMV; JKCP; TSW
Noel. Gail Brook Burket. PGD
Noël. Richard Watson Gilder. AA
Noel; Christmas Eve, 1913. Robert Bridges. CAW; LiTB; MoVE
Noël de Thevet. *Unknown, tr. fr. French by* Edward Bliss Reed. ChrBoLe
Noel! Noel! Laura Simmons. PGD
Noël Tragique. Ramon Guthrie. ErPo
Noise, business, and failures. Letter to Duncan. Gail Dusenbery. ThO
Noise Grimaced. Larry Eigner. NeAP
Noise of hammers once I heard. The Hammers. Ralph Hodgson. GoJo; MoBrPo; PoIE; PoMa; POTE
Noise of trampling, the wind of trumpets, The. Blake. *Fr.* The French Revolution. ChER
Noise of water teased his literal ears, The. Persistent Explorer. John Crowe Ransom. NoP; OxBA
Noise of Waters, The. James Joyce. *See* All Day I Hear.
Noise That Time Makes, The. Merrill Moore. MoAmPo (1962 ed.); NP; Sonn; TrGrPo (rev. ed.) YaD
Noiseless Patient Spider, A. Walt Whitman. AmePo; AmPP; AnFE; AP; APA; ATP (1935 ed.); AWP; BWP; CABA; CBV; CoAnAm; DiPo; EvOK; ExPo; GTBS-W; InPo; JAWP; LiTA; LiTG; MAP; MaRV; MoAmPo; MoRP; MWA-1; NeMA; NePA; NoP; OnPM; OxBA; PAn; PoIE; PoSa; PP; TDP; TrGrPo; TRV; WBP
(Spider, The.) WiR
Noises coming down the stairs. Rest Hour. George Johnston. WHW
Noises in the Night. Lilian McCrea. BoTP
Noises new to sea and land. The Big Tent under the Roof. Ogden Nash. RePo
Noises of the street come up subdued, The. An Upper Room. Daniel Lawrence Kelleher. NeIP
Noises that strive to tear. The Inner Silence. Harriet Monroe. HBMV; NP
Noisette on my garden path, A. The Shadow Rose. Robert Cameron Rogers. AA
Noisy cricket, The. Watanabe Suiha, *tr. fr. Japanese by* Geoffrey Bownas *and* Anthony Thwaite. FIW
Noisy now are the sparring sparrows, but noisier. All Over the World. Geoffrey Johnson. HaMV
Noisy pearls noisy pearl coat. Gertrude Stein. *Fr.* Sacred Emily. AtBAP
Noisy sparrows in our clematis, The. George Levison. William Allingham. IrPN
Noli Aemulari. Arthur Hugh Clough. *See* In Controversial Foul Impureness.
Noli Me Tangere. Robert Lowell. *See* Death of the Sheriff, The.
Nomad Exquisite. Wallace Stevens. AtBAP
Non Amo Te. Thomas Brown. *See* I Do Not Love Thee, Doctor Fell.
Non Dolet. Oliver St. John Gogarty. JKCP (1926 ed.); OBMV; OnYI; OxBI
(Our Friends Go with Us.) POTE
Non Dolet. Swinburne. PoVP; ViPP

"Non ego hoc ferrem calida juventa." At Thirty Years. Byron. *Fr.* Don Juan, I. FiP
Non Nobis. Henry Cust. OBEV; OBVV
Non Poem about Vietnam, A. Carolyn M. Rodgers. WSL
Non Sum Qualis Eram Bonae sub Regno Cynarae. Ernest Dowson. AnFE; AWP; BLPA; BoLP; BrPo; BWP; CABA; EnLi-2; EnLit; EnLoPo; FaBoBe; FaPL; GTBS-D; GTBS-P; GTBS-W; HBV; InPo; LiTG; LiTL; LiTM (rev. ed.); LO; MoBrPo; NeHB; NoP; OBEV (new ed.); OBMV; OBNC; OBVV; PeVV; PG; PoFS; PoPl; PoVP; TreF; TrGrPo; ViBoPo; ViPP
(Cynara.) AnEnPo; BeLS; CLwM; FaFP; LiTB; OtMeF; PoRA; UnPo; UnTE
(Faithful in My Fashion.) MeWo
(To Cynara.) NeMA
Non Sum Qualis Eram in Bona Urbe Nordica Illa. John Hollander. ErPo
Nona Domenica Garnaro sits in the sun. John Ciardi. *Fr.* Fragments from Italy. ToPo
Nona poured oil on the water and saw the eye. The Evil Eye. John Ciardi. AtBAP; MoBS
Non-being then existed not nor being. Hymn of Creation. *Unknown.* *Fr.* The Rigveda. LiTW
None but a Muse in love, can tell. On Fruition. Sir Charles Sedley. ErPo
None but a Tuscan hand could fix ye here. On the Picture of the Three Fates in the Palazzo Pitti, at Florence. Arthur Henry Hallam. OBRV
None but He. Christina Rossetti. *See* None Other Lamb.
None but one can harm you. The Foe Within. Longfellow. MaRV
None but Thyself. *Unknown.* FaChP
None call thee flower! . . . I will not so malign. To the Milkweed. Lloyd Mifflin. AA
None can experience stint. Emily Dickinson. MAmP
"None can usurp this height," return'd that shade. Ars Gratia Artis. Keats. *Fr.* The Fall of Hyperion. OBRV
None could ever say that she. True or False [*or* Love's Madness]. Catullus. AWP; JAWP; OuHeWo; WBP
None ever climbed to mountain height of song. A Woman's Hand. Sir Gilbert Parker. *Fr.* A Lover's Diary. VA
None Is Happy. Hartmann von Aue, *tr. fr. German by* Jethro Bithell. AWP
None like Him, of the sons of men. The Fairest He. Horatius Bonar. BePJ
None of Self and All of Thee. Theodore Monod. BLRP; FaChP
(Christ Alone.) STF
None of the brass hatters had seen. Lt. Cmdr. T. E. Sanderson. James Scully. TPM
None of Us Cared for Kate. Shakespeare. *See* Master, the Swabber, The.
None of us understood the secret dark of the blackboards. The Collegiate Angels. Rafael Alberti. FIW
None other fame mine unambitious muse. To Delia, XIVIII [LV]. Samuel Daniel. ReEn; SiCE; Sonn; TuPP
None Other Lamb [None Other Name]. Christina Rossetti. OxBoCh; TrPWD; TRV
(None but He.) SoP
None shall know it but the wise. Trance and Transformation. Goethe. LiTW
None spake when Wilson stood before. Catherine Kinrade. Thomas Edward Brown. OBVV
None walked behind that shoddy rain-swept hearse. Mozart's Grave. Paul Scott Mowrer. GoYe
Nonentity. D. H. Lawrence. BoPe
Nones. W. H. Auden. CoBMV
Nonetheless Ali Baba had no richer cave. Quebec Liquor Commission Store. A. M. Klein. ACV; OBCV
Non-Euclidean Elegy. John Frederick Nims. MoVE
Nongtongpaw. Charles Dibdin. BOHV; HBV
Nonne Preestes Tale, The. Chaucer. *See* Nun's Priest's Tale, The.
Nonpareil. Matthew Prior. EnLoPo
Nonpareil's Grave, The. M. J. McMahon. *See* Jack Dempsey's Grave.
Non-seasonal/ temperature control. Weather Forecast. David Kilburn. HYE
Nonsense. Thomas Moore. *See* If You Have Seen.
Nonsense. Robert Haven Schauffler. HBMV
Nonsense. *Unknown.* *See* Odd but True.
Nonsense Alphabet ("A was an ape"). Edward Lear. SAS
Nonsense Alphabet, A ("A was once an apple-pie"). Edward Lear. SoPo; SUS
(A. Apple Pie.) PPL
("A was once an apple-pie.") TiPo
Nonsense Carol, A. *Unknown.* OxBoLi
Nonsense Limericks. Edward Lear. *See* Nonsense Verses.
Nonsense Pictures in Rhyme. Edward Lear. MPB
Nonsense Quatrains: "Ah, yes! I wrote the 'Purple Cow'." Gelett Burgess. *See* Cinq Ans Après.
Nonsense Quatrains: "I never saw a Purple Cow." Gelett Burgess. *See* Purple Cow, The.
Nonsense Quatrains: "I sent my Collie to the wash." Gelett Burgess. CenHV
Nonsense Quatrains: "Many people seem to think." Gelett Burgess. CenHV
Nonsense Quatrains: "Proper way to leave a room, The." Gelett Burgess. CenHV
Nonsense Rhymes. Gelett Burgess. *See* Nonsense Verses.
Nonsense Song. *Unknown, ad. fr. German by* Michael Lewis. RIS
Nonsense Verses. Gelett Burgess. HBV
(Nonsense Rhymes.) TSW
Nonsense Verses. Charles Lamb. BOHV; NA
Nonsense Verses. Edward Lear. HBV; OTPC; StVeCh
(Lear's Limericks.) OTPC; OxBoLi; RIS
(Limericks.) BoChLi; BOHV; LBN; NA; StaSt
(Nonsense Limericks.) TSW
Nonsense Verses. Laura E. Richards. RIS
Nonsun Blob A. E. E. Cummings. PoE
Nooked underneath steep, sterile hills that rise. An Old Seaport. *Unknown.* EtS
Nooksack Valley. Gary Snyder. NaP
Noon. John Clare. OBRV; SeCePo
Noon. Robinson Jeffers. MAP; MoAmPo
Noon: and the gentle air. A swallow's wing. The Dead. John Williams. NePoAm-2
Noon—and the north-west sweeps the empty road. February. William Morris. *Fr.* The Earthly Paradise. ViPo
Noon in the park. . .A tropic sun. Brothers. Elias Lieberman. PoMa
Noon is hot, The. When we have crossed the stream. Matthew Arnold. *Fr.* Empedocles on Etna, I, ii. PoVP
Noon Is on the Cattle-Track, The. Rex Ingamells. BoAu
Noon on Alameda Street. Hildegarde Flanner. LiTM
Noon Quatrains. Charles Cotton. LoBV
Noon sun beats down the leaf; the noon. Grapes Making. Léonie Adams. MoVE; NePA; UnPo (3d ed.)
Noon was shady, and soft airs, The. The Dog and the Water-Lily. William Cowper. OAEP
Noonday April Sun, The. George Love. IDB; NNP
Noonday Sun. Kathryn Jackson *and* Byron Jackson. FaPON; TiPo
Noonlight is sudden full of the spirits. The Storm. Robert Wallace. NYBP
Noontide. John Keble. OTPC (1923 ed.)
Nooses of double meanings swing. Conversation Piece. Arthur Freeman. ErPo
Noosing of the Sun-God, The. Jessie Mackay. ACV
Nor cold, nor stern, my soul! yet I detest. Lines Composed in a Concert-Room. Samuel Taylor Coleridge. MuSP
Nor do I fear the satire's venim'd bite. De Se. John Weever. ReIE
Nor dread nor hope attend. Death. W. B. Yeats. ChMP; GTBS-D; MemP; POTE; ShBV-4
Nor exults he nor complains he; silent bears whate'er befalls him. Ever Watchful. Ta' Abbata Sharra. AWP; JAWP; WBP
Nor Eye Has Seen. Isaac Watts. SoP
Nor force nor fraud shall sunder us! America, II. Sydney Dobell. EPN; HBV; OBVV; PaA; PAL
Nor had great Hector and his friends the rampire overrun. Homer. *Fr.* The Iliad, XII. AtBAP
Nor happiness, nor majesty, nor fame. Political Greatness. Shelley. EnRP; EPN
Nor hath He given these blessings for a day. That the Soul Is Immortal, and Cannot Die. Sir John Davies. *Fr.* Nosce Teipsum. TuPP
Nor House nor Heart. Elinor Lennen. PGD
Nor ice nor fire shall harm you now. Admonition. John L. Bonn. JKCP (1955 ed.)
Nor idle all, though naught he sees in thine. Frederick Goddard Tuckerman. *Fr.* Sonnets. MAmP

Nor Is It Written. Laura Riding. Three Sermons to the Dead, III. FaBoMo; LiTA
Nor lady's wanton love, nor wandering knight. Satire I. Joseph Hall. *Fr.* Virgidemiarum. SiCE; TuPP
Nor less meant Promus when that vow he made. Perdat Qui Caveat Emptor. Henry Parrot. SiCE
Nor less when spring had warmed the cultured vale. The Raven's Nest. Wordsworth. *Fr.* The Prelude. ShBV-3
Nor looks that backward life so bare to me. Frederick Goddard Tuckerman. *Fr.* Sonnets. PoIE
Nor Mars His Sword. Dunstan Thompson. NePA
Nor may his flesh-house, when the spirit leaves it. The Hour of Death. *Unknown. Fr.* The Seafarer. PoLi
Nor mine own fears, nor the prophetic soul. *See* Not mine own . . .
Nor skin nor hide nor fleece. Lethe. Hilda Doolittle ("H. D."). AmLP; CMoP; LiTM (1970 ed.); MAP; MoAmPo; NeMA; PG (1945 ed.); PoRA; TrGrPo; ViBoPo
Nor sleep, nor journey, nor affray. A Child's Game. Karle Wilson Baker. PCD
Nor step, nor speech of human thing is near. The Capse. Thomas Wade. ERoP-2
Nor when the youthful pair more closely join. Concerning the Nature of Love. Lucretius. *Fr.* De Rerum Natura. ErPo
Nor will the search be hard or long. Alexander Geddes. *Fr.* Epistle to the President of the Scottish Society of Antiquaries: On Being Chosen a Correspondent Member. OxBS
Nor Will These Tears Be the Last. Goethe, *tr. fr. German by* Stephen Spender. LiTW
Nora. Dora Sigerson Shorter. HBMV
Norah. Zoë Akins. AV; HBV
Nora's Vow. Sir Walter Scott. BOHV
Nor'easter. Bianca Bradbury. EtS
Norembega. Whittier. PAH
Norfolk. John Betjeman. ChMP
Norfolk Girls, The, *with music. Unknown.* AmSS
Norfolk Memorials. Coman Leavenworth. LiTA
Norfolk sprang [*or* spring *or* sprung] thee, Lambeth holds thee dead. An Epitaph on Thomas Clere. Earl of Surrey. CBEP; FCP; NCEP; SiPS
Norman Abbey. Byron. *Fr.* Don Juan, XIII. OBRV
Normandy markets, The. In Normandy. E. V. Lucas. GaP
Norns Watering Yggdrasill, The. William Bell Scott. VA
Norris Dam. Selden Rodman. PoNe
Norse am I when the first snow falls. The Song of the Ski. Wilson MacDonald. CaP
Norse Lullaby. Eugene Field. BoTP; MPB; SUS
Norse Sailor's Joy. Wilfrid Thorley. EtS
Norsemen, The. Whittier. PAH
North. Philip Booth. NePoEA; PoPl
North, The. Stephen Spender. *See* Polar Exploration.
North and South. Claude McKay. AmPP (5th ed.); GoSl
North and South. Florida Watts Smyth. StaSt
North and the South, The. Elizabeth Barrett Browning. OBVV
North Coast Recollections. John Betjeman. CMoP
North Country, The. Robert Browning. *Fr.* The Flight of the Duchess. PCH
North Country, The. D. H. Lawrence. OAEP (2d ed.)
North-country maid up to London had stray'd, A. The Oak and the Ash. *Unknown.* FaBoCh; LoGBV
North Dakota Hymn. James W. Foley. PoRL
North-east. *See* Northeast.
North, East, South, and West. *Unknown.* BOHV
North French air may make any flat land clear and beautiful. Ypres. Ivor Guerney. FOL
North Infinity Street. Conrad Aiken. AP
North is weather, Winter, and change. North. Philip Booth. NePoEA; PoPl
North Labrador. Hart Crane. CMoP; FaBoMo
North London. Alan Ross. POTi
North of Wales, The. Herbert Morris. NePoAm-2
North Philadelphia, Trenton, and New York. Richmond Lattimore. NYBP
North Pickenham. Caman Leavenworth. *Fr.* Norfolk Memorials. LiTA
North Sea, The, *sels.* Heine, *tr. fr. German.*
Epilog, *tr. by* Louis Untermeyer. AWP; JAWP; WBP
(Epilogue, *tr. by* Emma Lazarus.) TrJP
Evening Twilight, *tr. by* John Todhunter. AWP; JAWP; WBP
Night by the Sea, A, *tr. by* Howard Mumford Jones. AWP
(Night on the Shore, *tr. by* Emma Lazarus.) LiTW
North Sea Undertaker's Complaint, The. Robert Lowell. NePoEA; NoP; PIA; PoeP
North Ship, The. Philip Larkin. FlW
North Shore. Peter Davison. CoPo
North, south, east, west, the settlers scatter wide. Alex Wilmot. *Fr.* The Landing of the British Settlers of 1820. ACV
North Star West. Earle Birney. TwCaPo
North-west. *See* Northwest.
Northwind. Gene Baro. NePoEA-2
North Wind, The. Dorothy Gradon. BoTP
North Wind, The. Lindoln Reis. PCH
North Wind and the Child, The. *Unknown, tr. fr. Greek.* PCH
North Wind Came Up Yesternight, The. Robert Bridges. SeCeV
North wind came whistling through the wood. Friends. L. G. Warner. OTPC (1946 ed.)
North wind clanged on the sharp hill-side, The. The Dirge of Kildare. Aubrey Thomas De Vere. IrPN
North wind doth blow, The. Mother Goose. BoTP; GFA; HBV; OTPC; OxNR; PCH; PPL; RIS; SAS; SoPo; StVeCh
North wind fall'n, in the new-starrèd night, The. The Hesperides. Tennyson. MBW-2; PAn; SyP; ViPP
North wind is a beggar, The. Winds a-Blowing. May Justus. BrR
"North Wind, North Wind—oh, whither so fast?" *Unknown.* GFA
North wind rolls the white grasses and breaks them, The. A Song of White Snow. Ts'en Ts'an, *tr. by* Witter Bynner. LiTW
North wind shakes the shivering moon, The. The North Wind. Lincoln Reis. PCH
North winds send hail, south winds bring rain. A Description of the Properties of Winds All the [*or* at All) Times of the Year. Thomas Tusser. ReIE; SiCE; TuPP; WiR
Northboun'. Ariel Williams Holloway. BANP; CDC; GoSl; PoNe
Northbound. Larry Rubin. NYTB
North-east Wind, The. Charles Kingsley. *See* Ode to the North-east Wind.
Northeast wind was the wind off the lake, The. Cook County [*or* Weather]. Archibald MacLeish. CrMA; MAP; MoAmPo
Northern Boulevard. Edwin Denby. CrMA
Northern Farmer; New Style. Tennyson. BOHV; BoLiVe; EPN; MBW-2; PeVV; PoVP; ShBV-4; ViPo
Northern Farmer: Old Style. Tennyson. BEL; EPN; MBW-2; OAEP; PoVP; VA; ViPo
Northern Lass, The, *sels.* Richard Brome.
"Bonny, bonny bird I had, A." TuPP
Song: "Peace, wayward barne! O cease thy moan!" SeCL
Northern Legion, A. Sir Herbert Read. FaBoMo; SeCePo
Northern Light. L. A. G. Strong. POTE
Northern Lights are flashing, The. Canadian Hunter's Song. Susanna Strickland Moodie. VA
Northern Seas. William Howitt. GN; OTPC (1923 ed.)
Northern Soldier, The. Philip Freneau. AmPP (3d ed.)
Northern Spring, A. Gene Baro. NePoEA-2
Northern Star, The. *Unknown.* HBV
Northern Suburb, A. John Davidson. NBM; OBNC
Northern View. Harriet Plimpton. NYTB
Northern Vigil, A. Bliss Carman. OBEV (new ed.); OBVV; PeCV
Northern Water Thrush. D. G. Jones. PeCV (1967 ed.)
Northern wind/ sweeping down from the Sahara. Exile in Nigeria. Ezekiel Mphahlele. PBA
Northumberland Betrayd by Dowglas. *Unknown.* ESPB; OBB; OxBB
Northumbrian Sequence, *sels.* Kathleen Raine.
"Let in the wind." CMoP
"Pure I was before the world began." CMoP
Northward in Thy Sir Skammel dwelt. Ebbé Skammelson. *Unknown.* BaBo
Nor'-West Courier, The. John E. Logan. VA
Nosce Teipsum. Sir John Davies. SiPS
Sels.
Acclamation, An. OxBoCh; TuPP
Affliction. OBSC
Dedication: "Strongest and the noblest argument, The," II. SiPS
Dedication: "To that clear majesty which in the north," I. OBSC; SiPS
(To My Most Gracious Dread Sovereign.) ReIE; SiCE

Immortality of the Soul, The ("For why should we the busy soul believe"). ViBoPo
In What Manner the Soul[e], Is United to the Body. LiTB; PoEL-2
(Soul and the Body, The.) CTC; OBSC
Knowledge and Reason. OBSC
(Much Knowledge, Little Reason.) ChTr
Man, 3 *sts.* EIL; OBEV, 2 *sts.*
(I Know Myself a Man.) ChTr
(Vanity of Human Learning, The, 2 *sts.*) MaRV
(Which Is a Proud, and Yet a Wretched Thing.) WHA
Of Human Knowledge. ReIE; SiCE; TuPP
Of the Soul of Man and the Immortality Thereof. ReIE
That the Soul Is Immortal, and Cannot Die. TuPP
"We seek to know the moving of each sphere." MyFE
Nose and the Eyes, The. William Cowper. MPB
(Dispute between Nose and Eyes.) OTPC
(Report of an Adjudged Case; Not to Be Found in Any of the Books.) BOHV
Nose, nose, jolly red nose. Mother Goose. (*also appears in* Beaumont *and* Fletcher's "The Knight of the Burning Pestle," I, iii. BrR; FaBoCh; LoGBV; OxNR
Nosegay, A. John Reynolds. OBEV
(Garden's Queen, The.) SeCL
Nosegay Always Sweet, A, for Lovers to Send for Tokens of Love at New Year's Tide, or for Fairings. *At. to* William Hunnis. EIL; ReIE
Nosegay for Laura, A. Francis Fawkes. WaPE
Nosegay, lacking flowers fresh, A. A Nosegay Always Sweet, for Lovers to Send for Tokens of Love at New Year's Tide, or for Fairings. *At. to* William Hunnis. EIL; ReIE
Nostalgia. Walter de la Mare. CoBMV; LiTM (1970 ed.)
Nostalgia. D. H. Lawrence. NP
Nostalgia. Louis MacNeice. GTBS-D; OnYI
Nostalgia. Karl Shapiro. AnFE; AP; CMoP; CoAnAm; CoAP; CoBMV; LiTM; NePA; TrJP; TwAmPo; TwCP; WaaP
Nostalgie d'Automne. Leslie Daiken. NeIP
Not a bark was heard, not a warning note. The Lay of the Vigilantes. *Unknown.* PoOW
Not a cabin in the Glen shuts its door to-night. Christmas Eve in Ireland. Katharine Tynan. ChrBoLe
Not a care hath Marien Lee. Marien Lee. Mary Howitt. OTPC (1923 ed.)
Not a Cloud in the Sky. Richard Armour. WhC
Not a drum was heard, not a funeral note. The Burial of Sir John Moore after [*or* at] Corunna. Charles Wolfe. AnIV; BBV; BEL; CBEP; ChTr; EnRP; EPN; FaFP; FaPL; FOL; GN; GTBS; GTBS-D; GTBS-P; GTBS-W; GTSE; GTSL; HBV; HBVY; InP; LiTG; MaC; MCCG; MemP; NeHB; OBEV; OBRV; OnSP; OnYI; OTPC; OxBI; PaPo; PCD; PoRA; RoGo; TOP; TreF; WaaP; WBLP; WHA
Not a man is stirring. Riding at Daybreak. Sun Yün Fêng. FIW
Not a melon can I eat. Recollections of My Children. *Unknown.* OnPM
Not a sign of life we rouse. Battery Moving Up to a New Position from Rest Camp: Dawn. Robert Nichols. MMA
Not a Sou Had He Got. "Thomas Ingoldsby." *Fr.* The Ingoldsby Legends: The Cynotaph. HBV
Not a sound disturbs the air. A Midsummer Noon in the Australian Forest. Charles Harpur. BoAu; BoAV; NeLNL; PoAu-1; VA
Not a thing on the river McCluskey did fear. The Little Brown Bulls. *Unknown.* BaBo; OuSiCo
Not a Tree. Thomas Blackburn. NYTB
Not after but within this poem I stalk my lovers. Alden Van Buskirk. *Fr.* Tales. YAP
Not After nor Before. "Angelus Silesius," *tr. fr. German by* Paul Carus. OnPM
Not Aladdin magian. Staffa. Keats. SiSw
Not All Immaculate. Laura Riding. *Fr.* Three Sermons to the Dead. LiTA
Not all of them must suffer. Saints. George Garrett. EaLo
Not All Sweet Nightingales. Luis de Góngora, *tr. fr. Spanish by* Sir John Bowring. CAW
Not All the Crosses. Lucile Kendrick. ChIP
Not Alone. Princess Ki, *tr. fr. Japanese by* Ishii *and* Obata. OnPM
Not Alone for Mighty Empire. William Pierson Merrill. TrPWD
(People's Thanksgiving, The.) MaRV
Not alone in Palestine those blessed feet have trod. Where the Blessed Feet Have Trod. "Michael Field." OxBoCh; StJW
Not alone those camps of white, old comrades of the wars. Camps of Green. Walt Whitman. PoE
Not always as the whirlwind's rush. The Call of the Christian. Whittier. SoP
Not always to the swift the race. The Law of Averages. "Troubadour." FiBHP; InMe
Not an epic, being not loosely architectured. King John's Castle. Thomas Kinsella. OxBI
Not another bite, not another cigarette. Search. Raymond Souster. ELU; OBCV
Not Any More. Dorothy Aldis. BoChLi
Not any more to be lacked. Emily Dickinson. MAmP
Not any sunny tone. Emily Dickinson. AnFE; APA; CoAnAm; MAPA; TwAmPo
Not as all other women are. My Love. James Russell Lowell. FaBoBe; FaPL; HBV
Not as Black Douglas, bannered, trumpeted. Two Wise Generals. Ted Hughes. MoBS
Not as I am, nor as I wish to be. The Strange Pangs of a Poor Passionate Lover. *Unknown.* TuPP
Not As I Will. Helen Hunt Jackson. OQP
Not as in time past, mountainy spaces. Looking Down on Mesopotamia. Mary Ursula Bethell. AnNZ
Not as the songs of other lands. An Australian Symphony. George Essex Evans. ACV; BoAu
Not as the white nations know thee. The Black Madonna. Albert Rice. CDC
Not As These. Dante Gabriel Rossetti. The House of Life, LXXV. MaVP; PoVP; ViPo
Not as they planned it or will plan again. The Day. Witter Bynner. PGD; PoFr
Not as when some great Captain falls. Abraham Lincoln. Richard Henry Stoddard. AA; FaBoBe; LiPo; PAH
Not as with Sundering of the Earth. Swinburne. *Fr.* Atalanta in Calydon. PoVP
Not as you had dreamed was the battle's issue. To a Young Leader of the First World War. Stefan George. WaaP
Not Ashamed of Christ. Joseph Grigg. *See* Ashamed of Jesus.
Not at midnight, not at morning, O sweet city. Caryatid. Léonie Adams. LiTM (1970 ed.); MoVE
Not at the first sight, not with a dribbed shot. Astrophel and Stella, II. Sir Philip Sidney. FCP; MaPo; PIA; ReEn; ReIE; SiCE; SiPS; TuPP
Not Baal, but Christus-Jingo! Heir. The Image in the Forum. Robert Buchanan. ChIP
Not baser than his own homekeeping kind. The Journeyman. Ralph Hodgson. AtBAP
Not because of their beauty—though they are slender. The Twins. Judith Wright. PoAu-2
Not because of victories. Te Deum. Charles Reznikoff. TrJP
Not-Being was not, Being was not then. Brahma, the World Idea. *Unknown. Fr.* Rig-Veda. WGRP
Not born to the forest are we. Song of the Camels [*or* Twelfth Night]. Elizabeth J. Coatsworth. ChBR; FaPON; RIS
Not by Bread Alone. *Unknown, tr. fr. Greek by* James Terry White. OQP; PoLF; TreFT
Not by instruction may this Self be gained. The Self. *Unknown. Fr.* The Upanishads. OnPM
Not by lost killers stranded. The Biggest Killing. Edward Dorn. CoPo
Not by one measure mayst thou mete our love. Equal Troth. Dante Gabriel Rossetti. The House of Life, XXXII. MaVP; PoVP; ViPo; VP
Not by the ball or brand. Vanquished. Francis Fisher Browne. AA; DD; HBV
Not by the city bells that chime the hours. A Summer Day. Florence Harrison. BoTP
"Not by the justice that my father spurn'd." Mycerinus. Matthew Arnold. MaVP; PoVP; ViPo
Not by the poets. Discovery of This Time. Archibald MacLeish. LiTA; WaP
Not Caesar's birth made Caesar to survive. Virtue the Best Monument. Sir Walter Ralegh. FCP

Not caring to observe the Wind. Of Loving at First Sight. Edmund Waller. SeCP
Not Celia That I Juster Am. Sir Charles Sedley. *See* To Celia.
Not Changed, but Glorified. *Unknown.* STF
Not clipping your beards, why clip you your nails? Of Clipping and Cleaning. John Heywood. CBV
Not "common speech." Denise Levertov. *Fr.* Common Ground. PP
Not costly domes, nor marble towers. Memorial Day. Samuel F. Smith. *Fr.* Our Honored Heroes. OQP
Not Dead. Robert Graves. HBMV
Not drowsihood and dreams and mere idleness. In Sleep. Richard Burton. AA
Not Drunk Is He. Thomas Love Peacock. *Fr.* The Misfortunes of Elphin. ViBoPo
(Who Is Drunk? 4 *ll.*) OnPM
Not entirely enviable, however envied. The Master. W. S. Merwin. NePoEA
Not even dried-up leaves. Thesis, Antithesis, and Nostalgia. Alan Dugan. CAD
Not even if with a wizard force I might. Caput Mortuum. E. A. Robinson. NP
Not even when the early birds. The Rabbit. W. H. Davies. GFA
Not Every Day Fit for Verse. Robert Herrick. PoRA; SeEP
Not every ghost has died before it haunts. Perfumes. Terence Tiller. FaBoMo
Not every man has gentians in his house. Bavarian Gentians. D. H. Lawrence. AtBAP; CMoP; DiPo; FaBoCh; FaBoMo; GoJo; GTBS-P; LiTB; LoGBV; NoP; OAEP (2d ed.); PoE; PoIE; PoSa; SeCeV; UnPo (3d ed.); ViBoPo
Not far above me in the boughs he sat, a solemn thing. The Whistling Jack. John Shaw Neilson. NeLNL
Not far advanced [*or* advanc'd] was morning day. Marmion and Douglas [*or* The Battle]. Sir Walter Scott. *Fr.* Marmion, VI. EnRP; OHFP; WHA
Not far from Cambridge, close to Trumpington. The Reeve's Tale. Chaucer. *Fr.* The Canterbury Tales. UnTE
Not far from old Kinvara, in the merry month of May. The Ould Plaid Shawl. Francis A. Fahy. HBV; JKCP (1926 ed.)
Not far from Paris, in fair Fontaine-bleau. The Angelus. Florence Earle Coates. HBV
Nor far from that most famous theatre. Sir Samuel Garth. *Fr.* The Dispensary. CEP
Not far from these Phoenician Dido stood. Dido among the Shades. Vergil, *tr. by* Dryden. *Fr.* The Aeneid, VI. OBS
Not fifty summers yet have passed thy clime. Oliver Goldsmith, the Younger. *Fr.* The Rising Village. OBCV
Not Flesh of Brass. Job, VI: 1-13, Bible, *O.T.* TrJP
Not for its Own Sake. Hazel Littlefield. GoYe
Not for me a giantess. Requirements. Nicarchus. ErPo
Not for one hour; so much the daily task. "Could Ye Not Watch One Hour?" Godfrey Fox Bradby. MaRV
Not for one single day. The Day—The Way. John Oxenham. FaChP; TRV
Not for our lands, our wide-flung prairie wealth. We Thank Thee. Thomas Curtis Clark. OQP; PEDC; PGD; PoToHe (1941 ed.)
Not for That City. Charlotte Mew. MoBrPo
Not for the broken bodies. Broken Bodies. Louis Golding. HBMV
Not for the fishermen's sake. Backwater Pond: The Canoeists. W. S. Merwin. PoPl
Not for the joys that I have known. A Prayer of Thanksgiving. Margaret E. Sangster. SoP
Not for you/ Is mourning. To The Living. Ernst Toller. PoFr
Not forgetting Ko-jen, that. More Foreign Cities. Charles Tomlinson. NePoEA-2
Not from a vain or shallow thought. Monumental Human Expressions. Emerson. *Fr.* The Problem. OQP
Not from my reverent sires hath come. Poet's Prayer. Adelaide Love. TrPWD
Not from successful love alone. Halcyon Days. Walt Whitman. NePA; OxBA
Not from the earth, or skies. Health of Body Dependent on Soul. Jones Very. WGRP
Not from the glory of the cloud's pile and rift. Elegy on the Eve. George Barker. WaaP
Not from the stars do I my judgement pluck. Sonnets, XIV. Shakespeare. MasP; SiCE; Sonn
Not from the whole wide world I chose thee. Song. Richard Watson Gilder. *Fr.* The New Day. AA
Not from This Anger. Dylan Thomas. LiTB
Not from two who supped with You. Reality. Amelia Josephine Burr. ChIP
Not furred nor wet, the pointing words yet make. Beaver Pond. Anne Marriott. ACV
Not gold, but only man can make. *Unknown.* *Fr.* A Nation's Strength. AmFN; FaPON; OTD
Not Gone Yet. John Swanwick Drennan. IrPN
Not greatly moved with awe am I. The Two Deserts. Coventry Patmore. The Unknown Eros, I, xviii. BoNaP; PoVP; VA
Not Grieved for Israel. Jesse F. Webb. SoP
Not Growing Old. *Unknown.* SoP
Not guns, not thunder, but a flutter of clouded drums. Fireworks. Babette Deutsch. NYBP
Not half the storms that threaten me. A Christian's Testimony. *Unknown.* SoP
Not He That Knows. Thomas May. *Fr.* The Tragedy of Cleopatra. SeCL
("Not he that knows how to acquire.") TuPP
(Song, A.) SeEP
Not Heat Flames Up and Consumes. Walt Whitman. NePA
Not Heaving from My Ribb'd Breast Only. Walt Whitman. NePA
Not here! the white North has thy bones; and thou. Sir John Franklin; On the Cenotaph in Westminster Abbey. Tennyson. InP
Not Honey. Hilda Doolittle ("H. D."). AnFE; APA; CoAnAm; MAPA; MoPo; TwAmPo
(Fragment 113.) LiTA
Not-"How did he die?" But—"How did he live?" The Measure of a Man. *Unknown.* PoLF; STF
Not hurled precipitous from steep to steep. The River Duddon, XXXII. Wordsworth. Sonn
Not I. Robert Louis Stevenson. NA; WePo
Not I. *Unknown.* BLRP
(Christ Honored, Loved, Exalted.) SoP
Not I, but God. Annie Johnson Flint. STF
Not I myself know all my love for thee. The Dark Glass. Dante Gabriel Rossetti. The House of Life, XXXIV. EPN; HBV; MaVP; PoVP; TOP; VA; ViPo; VP
Not I, not I, but the wind that blows through me! Song of a Man Who Has Come Through. D. H. Lawrence. BoPe ChMP; CMoP; CoBMV; FaBoMo; GTBS-P; LiTM; MoPo; PoIE; SeCeV; ViBoPo
Not Ideas about the Thing but the Thing Itself. Wallace Stevens. ViBoPo (1958 ed.)
Not if men's tongues and angels' all in one. William Shakespeare. Swinburne. *Fr.* Sonnets on English Dramatic Poets. PoVP; TrGrPo
Not, I'll not, carrion comfort, Despair, not feast on thee. Carrion Comfort [*or* Sonnet]. Gerard Manley Hopkins. AnFE; AtBAP; BoC; BWP; CABA; CMoP; CoBE; EnLi-2; FaBoEn; LiTB; LiTG; MaPo; MoPo; MoVE; NoP; OAEP; OBNC; OxBoCh; PoDB; PoEL-5; PoeP; PoIE; PoLi; PoVP; Sonn; VaPo; ViPo; ViPP; VP
Not in a Silver Casket Cool with Pearls. Edna St. Vincent Millay. AnEnPo; CMoP; MemP
Not in a valley ivoried with grain. Winter Apples. Winifred Welles. AnAmPo
Not in Dumb Resignation. John Hay. MaRV; WGRP
(Thy Will Be Done.) WBLP
Not in Narrow Seas, *sels.* Allan Curnow. AnNZ
Bishop Boundary-rides His Diocese, The.
Water Is Burred with Rain, The.
Not in rich furniture, or fine aray. The H. Communion. George Herbert. AnAnS-1; MaMe; MeP
Not in sleep I saw it, but in daylight. Kindly Vision. Otto Julius Bierbaum. AWP; JAWP; WBP
Not in Solitude. F. W. H. Myers. *Fr.* St. Paul. OQP
Not in the ancient abbey. Threnody for a Poet. Bliss Carman. CaP
Not in the cosmic vast alone. Life of Our Life. Henry Burke Robins. MaRV
Not in the crises of events. The Spirit's Epochs. Coventry Patmore. *Fr.* The Angel in the House. EG; GoBC
Not in the dire, ensanguined front of War. The Men of the

Maine. Clinton Scollard. MC; PAH
Not in the field of vision stands His form. Inner Vision. *Unknown.* *Fr.* The Upanishads. OnPM
Not in the Guide-Books. Elizabeth Jennings. LiTM (1970 ed.); NePoEA
Not in the Lucid Intervals of Life. Wordsworth. EPN
Not in the morning vigor, Lord, am I. Strength in Weakness. Richard Burton. MaRV
Not in the rustle of water, the air's noise. Night in Martindale. Kathleen Raine. NeBP
Not in the sepulchre Thou art. Passiontide Communion. Katharine Tynan. TrPWD
Not in the silence only. My Prayer. Horatius Bonar. BLRP
Not in the sky. The Lost Pleiad. William Gilmore Simms. AA
Not in the solitude. Hymn of the City. Bryant. AmePo
Not in the time of pleasure. The Rainbow. John Vance Cheney. OQP
Not in the wind-hushed isles and gardens Elysian. The City of God. Anna Louise Strong. MaRV
Not in the world of light alone. The Living Temple. Oliver Wendell Holmes. *Fr.* The Autocrat of the Breakfast-Table. AA; AmePo; AmPP (3d ed.); AP
Not in those climes where I have late been straying. To Ianthe. Byron. *Fr.* Childe Harold's Pilgrimage. FaBoEn; OBNC
Not in thy body is thy life at all. Life-in-Love. Dante Gabriel Rossetti. The House of Life, XXXVI. MaVP; PoVP; ViPo; VP
Not in Vain. Emily Dickinson. *See* If I can stop one heart from breaking.
Not in Vain. *Unknown.* BLRP
Not in works or vain endeavors. The God in Whom We Trust. *Unknown.* STF
Not ink, but bloud and tears now serve the turn. Benjamin Tompson. *Fr.* England's Crisis. AnAmPo
Not Iris in Her Pride. George Peele. *Fr.* The Arraignment of Paris. ViBoPo
Not Jerusalem—lowly Bethlehem. Lowly Bethlehem. Count Zinzendorf. TrAS
Not just folklore, or. Fast Ball. Jonathan Williams. NeAP
Not Just for the Ride. *Unknown.* *See* Limerick: "There was a young lady of Niger."
Not Knowing. Mary Gardiner Brainard. AA
Faith and Sight, *sel.* FaChP; MaRV
"I know not what shall befall me: God hangs a mist o'er my eyes." TRV
Not knowing where he was or how he got there. A Bewilderment at the Entrance of the Fat Boy into Eden. Daryl Hine. OBCV
Not Late Enough. Hazel Townson. PV
Not least, 'tis ever my delight. Morning. Philip Henry Savage. AA
Not less because in purple I descended. Tea at the Palaz of Hoon. Wallace Stevens. CBEP; FaBoMo; NP
Not light of love, lady! The Lover Exhorteth His Lady to Be Constant. *Unknown.* OBSC; TuPP
Not like the brazen giant of Greek fame. The New Colossus. Emma Lazarus. AmePo; AmFN; FaBV; FaFP; FaPL; FaPON; MaRV; OTD; PAL; PGD; PoLF; PoPl; TIHL; TreFS; TRV
Not lips of mine have ever said. In Youth. Evaleen Stein. AA
Not long ago from hence I went. The Lusty Fryer of Flanders. *Unknown.* CoMu
Not long ago it was a bird. A Volunteer's Grave. William Alexander Percy. HBMV
Not long ago, the writer of these lines. To——. Poe. MWA-1
Not Lost, but Gone Before. Caroline Elizabeth Sarah Norton. BLRP; PaPo; WBLP
Not lost or won but above all endeavour. Fidelity. Trumbull Stickney. AnFE; CoAnAm; LiTA; TwAmPo
Not Lotte. Katherine Hoskins. ErPo
Not Love, Not War. Wordsworth. CLwM
Not Made with Hands. Lilith Lorraine. ChIP
Not magnitude, not lavishness. Greek Architecture. Herman Melville. MWA-1; NoP
"Not Marble nor the Gilded Monuments." Archibald MacLeish. AmPP (3d ed.); AP; CMoP; CoBMV; ILP; LiTL; MeWo; MoAB; PoRA; TwCP; ViBoPo
Not marble, nor the gilded monuments. Sonnets, LV. Shakespeare. AnEnPo; AnFE; ATP; AWP; BEL; BWP; CABA; CBEP; CLwM; CoBE; CTC; DiPo; EG; EnL; EnLi-1; EnLit; EnRePo; EP; ExPo; FaBoEn; FaFP; ForPo; GTBS-W; ILP; InPo; JAWP; LiTB; LiTG; LiTL; LoBV; MaPo (1969 ed.); MasP; NoP; OAEP; OBSC; OuHeWo; PAn; PoE; PoEL-2; PoeP; PoPo; PoRA; PoSa; PP; ReEn; ReIE; SeCeV; SiCE; Sonn; TDP; TOP; TrGrPo; VaPo; ViBoPo; WBP
Not marching now in fields of Thrasimene [*or* Thrasymene]. The Tragical History of Doctor Faustus. Christopher Marlowe. CoBE; EnLi-1; EnLit
Not men but heads of the hydra. The Multiversity. Robert Duncan. FRC
Not merely for our pleasure, but to purge. "Ej Blot til Lyst." William Morton Payne. AA
Not merely in matters material, but in things of the spirit. America First! G. Ashton Oldham. PGD
Not met and marred with the year's whole turn of grief. James Agee. *Fr.* Lyrics. MAP; MoAmPo; PoPl
Not 'mid the thunder of the battle guns. The Birth of Australia. Percy Russell. VA
Not midst the lightning of the stormy fight. Stonewall Jackson. Henry Lynden Flash. AA; DD; PAH
Not Mine. Julia C. R. Dorr. SoP
Not mine, not mine the choice. My All. Horatius Bonar. SoP
Not [*or* Nor] mine own fears, not the prophetic soul. Sonnets, CVII [*or* I'll Live in This Poor Rime]. Shakespeare. AWP; CABA; CBEP; CTC; DiPo; EG; EnLi-1; FiP; InPo; JAWP; LiTB; LiTG; LoBV; MaPo; MasP; NoP; OAEP; OBSC; OuHeWo; PoFr; PoIE; ReEn; ReIE; SeCeV; SiCE; TOP; WBP
Not mine to draw the cloth-yard shaft. The Satirist. Harry Lyman Koopman. AA
Not more of light I ask, O God. A Prayer. Florence Holbrook. SoP
Not more of light I ask, O God. Understanding. *Unknown.* PoToHe (new ed.)
Not my hands but green across you now. The Lady in Kicking Horse Reservoir. Richard Hugo. CoAP
Not noisily, but solemnly and pale. Irradiations, XXI. John Gould Fletcher. NP
Not now, but in the coming years. Some Time We'll Understand. *At. to* Maxwell N. Cornelius *and to* James McGranahan. BLRP; SoP; WBLP
Not now expecting to live forever. Dublin Bay. Ewart Milne. NeIP
Not of all my eyes wandering on the world. Ash-Boughs. Gerard Manley Hopkins. BoPe
Not of Itself but Thee. *Unknown, tr. fr. Greek by* Richard Garnett. AWP
Not of ladies, love, or graces. La Araucana. Alonso de Ercilla y Zúñiga. OuHeWo
Not of the princes and prelates with periwigged charioteers. A Consecration. John Masefield. BEL; EnLit; HBMV; InP; MCCG; MoAB; MoBrPo; NeMA; OtMeF; PoFr; WHA
Not of the sunlight. Follow the Gleam. Tennyson. Merlin and the Gleam, IX. BBV; MaRV; OTPC (1946 ed.); PoRL; TreFT
Not of This World. Bartolomé Leonardo de Argensola, *tr. fr. Spanish by* Sir John Bowring. OnPM
Not oft such marvel the years reveal. The People's King. Lyman Whitney Allen. PGD
Not often, when the carnal dance is mad. The Final Faith. George Sterling. CAW
Not on a prayerless bed, not on a prayerless bed. Exhortation to Prayer. Margaret Mercer. AA
Not on an altar shall mine eyes behold thee. Real Presence. Ivan Adair. OQP; WGRP
Not on our golden fortunes builded high. The Forgotten Man. Edwin Markham. PoLF
Not on Sunday Night. *Unknown.* STF
Not on the neck of prince or hound. The Splendid Spur. Sir Arthur Quiller-Couch. HBV; HBVY; VA
Not One Is Turned Away from God. Dorothy Conant Stroud. STF
Not Only around Our Infancy. James Russell Lowell. *Fr.* The Vision of Sir Launfal. FaFP; GTBS-W; NePA
Not only how far away, but the way that you say it. Judging Distances. Henry Reed. Lessons of the War, II. ChMP; FaBoMo; GTBS-P; LiTB; MoAB
Not Only in the Christmas-Tide. Mary Mapes Dodge. ChBR

Not (continued)
Not only on Judean hills. The Christ of Today. Thomas Curtis Clark. SoP
Not only once, and long ago. Christ Is Crucified Anew. John Richard Moreland. ChIP; MaRV; PGD
Not only sands and gravels. One Step Backward Taken. Robert Frost. MWA-2; OnHM
Not only that thy puissant arm could bind. Wellington. Benjamin Disraeli. EPN; FOL; OBVV; VA
Not only the soot from the city air. The Floor Is Dirty. Edward Field. NeAP
Not only there where jewelled vestments blaze. The Poor Man's Daily Bread. Denis A. McCarthy. JKCP
Not only we, the latest seed of time. Godiva. Tennyson. BeLS
"Not ours," say some, "the thought of death to dread." The Great Misgiving. Sir William Watson. HBV; OBEV (1st ed.); OBVV
Not Ours the Vows. Bernard Barton. HBV; MaRV
Not out of the East but the West. The Star of Sangamon. Lyman Whitney Allen. PGD
Not Overlooked. James Oppenheim. NP
Not Palaces [an Era's Crown]. Stephen Spender. BoLiVe (1939 ed.); CMoP; EnLi-2 (1949 ed.); LiTB; LiTM; MoAB; MoBrPo; NeMA; NoP; PoAn; WaP
Not picnics or pageants or the improbable. Terror. Robert Penn Warren. MoPo; NePA; WaP
Not Poppy, nor Mandragora. Shakespeare. *Fr.* Othello, III, iii. WHA
Not probable—the barest chance. Emily Dickinson. MWA-2
Not proud of station, nor in worldly pelf. Frederick Goddard Tuckerman. *Fr.* Sonnets. AmePo
Not Quite Fair. H. S. Leigh. InMe
Not quite sixteen. Nedjé. Roussan Camille. PoNe
Not Ragged-and-tough. *Unknown.* ChTr
Not roses, joyn'd with lillies, make. Pure Platonicke. George Daniel. CavP
Not Self-denial. Elise Gibbs. NYTB
Not serried ranks with flags unfurled. What Makes a Nation Great? Alexander Blackburn. OQP; WBLP
Not she for whom proud Troy did fall and burn. The Lover in the Praise of His Beloved and Comparison of Her Beauty. *Unknown.* ReIE; TuPP
Not she. Not freedom. Of Old Sat Freedom on the Heights. Hildegarde Flanner. PoFr
Not she with traitorous kiss her Saviour stung. Woman. Eaton Stannard Barrett. HBV; OnYI; OxBI; SoP
Not so, for living yet are those. A Dead Past. *At. to* C. C. Munson. BLRP; WBLP
Not So Impossible. *Unknown. See* I Saw a Peacock.
Not So in Haste, My Heart. *Unknown, at. to* Bayard Taylor *and to* Bradford Torrey. MaRV
(Be Still, My Heart.) STF
(Rest.) SoP
Not solely that the future she destroys. George Meredith. Modern Love, XII. EnLit; ViBoPo; ViPo; VP
Not solitarily in fields we find. Earth's Secret. George Meredith. EPN; PoVP
Not songs of loyalty alone are these. Walt Whitman. *Fr.* To a Foil'd European Revolutionaire. PoFr
Not soon shall I forget. Farewell. Katharine Tynan. CH
Not Spring's/ Thou art. Arbutus. Adelaide Crapsey. MoAmPo (1942 ed.)
Not Such Your Burden. Agathias Scholasticus, *tr. fr. Greek by* William M. Hardinge. AWP; JAWP; WBP
Not that by this disdain. The Repulse. Thomas Stanley. AnAnS-2; LO; MeLP; MePo; OBS
Not that her blooms are marked with beauty's hue. To Mr. Gray. Thomas Warton, the Younger. Sonnets, VI. Sonn
Not that I have cause for celebration. New Year's Eve. H. B. Mallalieu. WaP
Not that I love thy children, whose dull eyes. Sonnet to Liberty. Oscar Wilde. PoFr
Not That, If You Had Known. Trumbull Stickney. NCEP
Not that in colour it was like thy haire. The Bracelet. John Donne. Elegies, XI. MaMe
Not That It Matters. Edna St. Vincent Millay. CMoP
Not that the earth is changing, O my God! On Refusal of Aid between Nations. Dante Gabriel Rossetti. CoBE; EPN; LoBV; PoVP; TOP
Not that the pines were darker there. The Long Voyage. Malcolm Cowley. AnFE; CoAnAm; GBV (1952 ed.); NePA; TwAmPo; WaKn
Not that thy hand is soft, is sweet, is white. Henry Constable. *Fr.* Diana. OBSC
Not that we are weary. In the Trenches. Richard Aldington. MMA
Not the angelic host of Moors were the foe. Moors, Angels, Civil Wars. Keith Sinclair. AnNZ
Not the calm—the clarity. Antecedents. Charles Tomlinson. CMoP
Not the Circean wine. The Dread of Height. Francis Thompson. JKCP
Not the cougar leaping to myth. Man Is a Snow. Earle Birney. PeCV
Not the last struggles of the sun. On the Death of Southey. Walter Savage Landor. OBVV
Not the round natural world, not the deep mind. Frederick Goddard Tuckerman. *Fr.* Sonnets. AmePo; NoP
Not the setting of the Pleiades so fearful is to me. The Terrifying Tell-Tale. Antipater. OnPM
Not theirs the vain, tumultuous bliss. Husband and Wife. Edward Harry William Meyerstein. LO
Not There. *Unknown.* STF
Not there, my dear, not there. Bargain Basement. F. T. Macartney. MoAuPo
Not these appal. Faith's Difficulty. Theodore Maynard. TrPWD
Not Thine Own. Shakespeare. *Fr.* Measure for Measure, I, i. MaRV
Not this dark stand of pines that house/ Quick deer. World, Defined. Edward Weismiller. AnAmPo
Not this spring shall return again. Aftermath. Margaret McCulloch. PGD
Not those elate upon the mountain height. Test. Helen Pursell Roads. OQP
Not those patient men who knocked and were unheeded. 1918-1941. Robert D. Fitzgerald. BoAV
Not Thou but I. Philip Bourke Marston. BLPA
Not Thou from Us! Richard Chenevix Trench. ChIP
Not though I know she, fondly, lies. Song: The Hopeless Comfort. Robert Gould. CEP
Not Three—but One. Esther Lilian Duff. HBMV
Not through the rational mind. The Recapitulation. Richard Eberhart. MoRP
Not to arrive since faring forth there is no road. Cancelled Itinerary. Frederick Mortimer Clapp. LiTM (rev. ed.)
Not to be believed, this blunt savage wind. Paper Mill. Joseph Kalar. AnAmPo
Not to be born at all. Sophocles. *Fr.* Oedipus at Colonus. PoG
Not to Be Ministered To. Maltbie D. Babcock. SoP; TrPWD
(Today, O Lord.) OQP
"Not to be tuneless in old age!" Henry Wadsworth Longfellow. Austin Dobson. DD; HBV
Not to dance with her. A Triviality. Waring Cuney. CDC
Not to Die. Simonides, *tr. fr. Greek by* Lord Neaves. OnPM
Not to Forget Miss Dickinson. Marshall Schacht. LiTM
Not to Keep. Robert Frost. AmPP; AnAmPo; CMoP; OxBA
Not to know vice at all, and keepe true state. Epode. Ben Jonson. SeCP; SeCV-1
Not to lose the feel of the mountains. The Double-Headed Snake. John Newlove. MoCV
Not to Love. Robert Herrick. OAEP
Not to scatter bread and gold. Love's Nobility. Emerson. *Fr.* Celestial Love. TreF
Not to the hills where cedars move. The Wish. Thomas Flatman. SeCL
Not to the swift, the race. Reliance. Henry van Dyke. FaFP
Not to the twelve alone. Communion. Phoebe Smith Bachelder. ChIP
Not to the weak alone. The Call to the Strong. William Pierson Merrill. BLRP
Not to You I Sighed. Stephen Spender. WePo
Not Tonight, Josephine. Colin Curzon. ErPo
Not too chary, not too fast. Requirements. Rufinus. ErPo
Not Too Deeply in Love. Cecco Angiolieri da Siena. *See* Sonnet: He Will Not Be Too Deeply in Love.
Not too lean, and not too fat. Requirements. Rufinus. ErPo

Not-too-near slip softly by, The. Convalescence, I. David McCord. WhC
Not too old, and not too young. Requirements. Honestus. ErPo
Not too pallid, as if bleach't. Requirements. Xenos Palaestes. ErPo
Not trust you, dear? Nay, tis not true. One Way of Trusting. Hannah Parker Kimball. AA
Not twice a twelve-month you appear in print. Epilogue to the Satires [*or* One Thousand Seven Hundred and Thirty Eight]. Pope. CEP; EiCL; NoP
Not Understood. Thomas Bracken. BLPA; NeHB
Not unto the Forest. Margaret Widdemer. HBMV
Not unto us, not unto us. America Prays. Arthur Gordon Field. PGD
Not unto us, O Lord. Non Nobis. Henry Cust. OBEV; OBVV
Not upon earth, as you suppose. "Tu Non Se' in Terra, Si Come Tu Credi. . ." Kathleen Raine. NeBP
Not Waving but Drowning. Stevie Smith. GTBS-P
Not weaned yet, without comprehension loving. Love's Immaturity. E. J. Scovell. LiTB
Not Weighing. . .But Pardoning. Amy Carmichael. FaChP
Not what, but Whom, I do believe. Credo. John Oxenham. BLRP; ChIP; MaRV; OQP; StJW
Not what I am, O Lord, but what Thou art. More of Thee. Horatius Bonar. BLRP
Not what men see. Beauty of the World. Frank Wilmot. MoAuPo
Not what we did shall be the test. Emily Dickinson. CoBA
Not what we have, but what we use. Things That Count. *Unknown.* SoP
Not what you get, but what you give. Of Giving. Arthur Guiterman. TiPo
Not when, with self dissatisfied. With Self Dissatisfied. Frederick L. Hosmer. TrPWD
Not where the battle red. On the Death of Jackson. *Unknown.* PAH
Not while they walked, though he seemed strangely sure. Emmaus. Rainer Maria Rilke. BoPe
Not white and shining like an ardent flame. The Ten Lepers. Katharine Tynan. MaRV; StJW
Not Wholly Lost. Raymond Souster. OBCV
Not with a clamor of golden deeds. Gandhi. Angela Morgan. OTD
Not with a club, the heart is broken. Emily Dickinson. AmePo; AP; LiTA; WHA
Not with an outcry to Allah nor any complaining. The Captive. Kipling. BoPe
Not with Libations. Edna St. Vincent Millay. *See* Sonnet: "Not with libations. . ."
Not with more glories, in th' etherial plain. Pope. *Fr.* The Rape of the Lock. FaBoEn; ViBoPo; WHA
Not with my hands. Benediction. Donald Jeffrey Hayes. AmNP; PoNe
Not with our mortal eyes. Whom Having Not Seen We Love. Isaac Watts. SoP
Not with slow, funereal sound. An Ode: On the Unveiling of the Shaw Memorial of Boston Common, May 31, 1897. Thomas Bailey Aldrich. AA; HBV; PAH
Not with the cheer of battle in the throat. Sir Henry Yule. *Fr.* The Birkenhead. OtMeF
Not with the high-voiced fife. Peace. Clinton Scollard. OQP; PoRL
Not with vain tears, when we're beyond the sun. Sonnet. Rupert Brooke. BrPo
Not without Beauty. John A. B. McLeish. CaP
Not without heavy grief of heart did he. Epitaphs, VIII. Gabriello Chiabrera. AWP; JAWP; WBP
Not woman-faced and sweet, as look. Michael the Archangel. Katharine Tynan. JKCP
Not writ in water nor in mist. For John Keats, Apostle of Beauty. Countee Cullen. Four Epitaphs, 2. AmNP; CDC; Kal
Not Writing. Joseph Cardarelli. QAH
Not Wrongly Moved. William Empson. *See* Sonnet: "Not wrongly moved by this dismaying scene."
"Not ye who have stoned, not ye who have smitten us," cry. Arraignment. Helen Gray Cone. AA
Not yesterday, not yet a day. The Annunication. Margaret Devereaux Conway. ISi
Not yet, dear love, not yet: the sun is high. The Parting Hour. Olive Custance. HBV; VA
Not yet! Do not yet touch. The Turning of the Leaves. Vernon Watkins. FaBoMo; NeBP
Not yet five, and the light. After Hours. Robert Mezey. AmPC; NaP; ToPo
Not yet had Nessus crossed the narrow ford. Inferno. Dante. *Fr.* Divina Commedia. EnLi-1
Not yet, not yet; it's hardly four. One More Quadrille. Winthrop Mackworth Praed. OBRV
"Not yet, not yet; steady, steady!" Bunker Hill. George Henry Calvert. BeLS; DD; FaBoBe; MC
Not yet trodden under wholly. Enthusiasm. James Clarence Mangan. IrPN
Not yet will those measureless fields be green again. The Cenotaph. Charlotte Mew. MMA
Not young, I think. The Cap That Fits. Austin Dobson. TSW
Not Yours but You. Christina Rossetti. ChIP; MaRV
Nota: man is the intelligence of his soil. The Comedian as the Letter C. Wallace Stevens. NePA; OXBA; TwAmPo
Notable Description of the World, A. *At. to* William Smith. ReIE
Notably fond of music, I dote on a sweeter tone. The Clink of the Ice. Eugene Field. InMe
Notation in Haste. Elias Lieberman. GoYe
Note. Frank Lima. ANYP
Note Bene, A. Karl Mikael Bellman, *tr. fr. Swedish by* Charles W. Stork. OnPM
Note-Book of a European Tramp, The, *sel.* Michael Hamburger.
"Townsman on his yielding bed, The," XI. NePoEA
Note from an Intimate Diary. Emanuel Litvinov. NeBP
Note from the Pipes, A. Leonora Speyer. HBMV
Note from Thoreau, N.M. John Morgan. YAP
Note in Lieu of a Suicide. Donald Finkel. CoPo
Note Left in Jimmy Leonard's Shack, A. James Wright. TPM
Note of Humility, A. Arna Bontemps. PoNe
Note on Bone. Howard McCord. YAP
Note on Intellectuals. W. H. Auden. FiBHP; PoPl; SiTL
Note on Local Flora. William Empson. AtBAP; FaBoMo; MoVE; ToPo
Note on the Latin Gerunds, A. Richard Porson. *See* Dido.
Note to Gongyla. Sappho, *tr. fr. Greek by* D. L. Feldstone. LiTW
Note to Wang Wei. John Berryman. ML; NYBP
Notes after Blacking Out. Gregory Corso. NeAP
Notes for a Bestiary. Terence Heywood. LiTM
Notes for a Movie Script. M. Carl Holman. AmNP; Kal; PoNe
Notes for a Speech. LeRoi Jones. CoPo
Notes for My Son. Alex Comfort. LiTM (1970 ed.); MoBrPo (1950 ed.); NeBP; SeCePo
Notes for the Chart in 306. Ogden Nash. NYBP
Notes Found near a Suicide. Frank Horne. *See* Letters Found near a Suicide.
Notes from a Slave Ship. Edward Field. PP
Notes from an Ohio Tavern. Sandford Lyne. QAH
Notes Made in the Piazza San Marco. May Swenson. CoAP
Notes of an Interview. William Johnson Cory. NBM
Notes on a Certain Terribly Critical Piece. Reed Whittemore. PP
Notes on a Child's Coloring Book. Robert Patrick Dana. PoPl
Notes on a Girl. Peter Kane Dufault. ErPo
Notes on a Life to Be Lived. Robert Penn Warren. NYBP
Notes on a Track Meet. David McCord. SD
Notes to the Life of Ovid. Andras Hamori. NYTB
Notes toward a Supreme Fiction, *sels.* Wallace Stevens.
"Bethou me, said sparrow, to the crackled blade." LiTM (rev. ed.); MoPo; NePA
(Bethou Me, Said Sparrow.) CrMA
"It feels good as it is without the giant." MoPo; NePA
"It is the celestial ennui of apartments." MoPo; NePA
"Lion roars at the enraging desert, The." MoPo; NePA
"President ordains the bee to be, The." AtBAP; LiTA
Soldier, There Is a War [between the Mind]. LiTM (rev. ed.) NePA
We Reason of These Things. CrMA
Nothin' Done. Sam S. Stinson. LHV

"Nothin' or everythin' it's got to be." Nocturne. John V. A. Weaver. AnAmPo; HBMV; NP
Nothin very bad happen to me lately. Henry's Confession. John Berryman. The Dream Songs, LXXVI. NaP; TwCP
Nothing. Richard Porson. BOHV
Nothing. Barrie Reid. BoAV
Nothing. Burns Singer. OxBS
Nothing and the Soul. Bhartrihari, *tr. fr. Sanskrit by* Paul Elmer More. OnPM
Nothing before, nothing behind. Faith. Whittier. TRV
Nothing Better. *Unknown.* STF
Nothing Between. C. A. Tindley. BePJ
Nothing but No and I, and I and No. Idea, V. Michael Drayton. PoEL-2
Nothing can turn them from the ends that call. The Parachutes. Charles Gullans. NYTB
Nothing could have brought him to the door. The Cat and the Miser. Mark Van Doren. TPM
Nothing could make me sooner to confesse. Of the Progres of the Soule; The Second Anniversarie. John Donne. AnAnS-1; MeP; ReEn; SCEP-1; SeCP; SeEP
Nothing, either great or small. What Must I Do to Be Saved? *Unknown.* STF
Nothing Fair on Earth I See. "Angelus Silesius," *tr. fr. German by* Catherine Winkworth. BePJ
Nothing for a dirty man. All That Is Lovely in Men. Robert Creeley. NaP
Nothing Gold Can Stay. Robert Frost. AmPP (5th ed.); BoLiVe; ILP; MAP; MaPo (1969 ed.); MoAB; MoAmPo; NeMA; PoPo; StP; WHA
Nothing happens only once. Circle One. Owen Dodson. Kal
Nothing has been quite the same. After Reading the Review of "Finnegans Wake." Melville Cane. WhC
Nothing here is bitter. Wisdom. Phyllis Hanson. GoYe
Nothing I have is worth a tear. Song. E. N. da Costa Andrade. POTE
Nothing if not utterly in death. So? James P. Vaughn. AmNP
Nothing in Heaven Functions as it Ought. X. J. Kennedy. Sonn
Nothing in the voice of the cicada. Basho, *tr. fr. Japanese by* R. H. Blyth. FIW
Nothing in this bright region melts or shifts. From the Highest Camp. Thom Gunn. Sonn; TwCP
Nothing Is. Sun-Ra. BF
Nothing is better, I well think. The Leper. Swinburne. LO
Nothing is easy! Pity then. James Stephens. LO
Nothing Is Enough. Laurence Binyon. MoBrPo; POTE
Nothing Is Given: We Must Find Our Law. W. H. Auden. Po
Nothing is plumb, level or square. Love Song: I and Thou. Alan Dugan. AP
Nothing is quite so quiet and clean. Snow in Town. Rickman Mark. BoTP; TVC
Nothing is real. The world has lost its edges. Scarcely Spring. Louis Untermeyer. GoTP; MAP; MoAmPo (1942 ed.)
Nothing is so beautiful as spring. Spring. Gerard Manley Hopkins. ACV; BoLiVe; BoNaP; BrPo; CaFP; DiPo; EG; FaBoEn; FaBV; ForPo; ILP; InvP; JKCP; LiTM; LO; MaPo; MoAB; MoBrPo; MoVE; OAEP (2d ed.); OBMV; OBNC; OnHM; OxBoCh; PoDB; PoLi; SoP; StP; ViPP; VP
Nothing Lovely as a Tree. Frederick J. Bryant, Jr. BF
"Nothing much here!" they say. With careless glance. Auction Sale—Household Furnishings. Adele de Leeuw. PoToHe (new ed.)
Nothing now to mark the spot. Next Day. Rachel Field. *Fr.* A Circus Garland. SoPo; StVeCh
Nothing older than stone but the soil and the sea and the sky. The Mason. Robert Farren. JKCP (1955 ed.); OnYI; OxBI
Nothing out there that I didn't already see. A dump, an overpopulated. Children of the Cosmos. Kuwasi Balagon. BF
Nothing remained: Nothing, the wanton name. The Annihilation of Nothing. Thom Gunn. NePoEA-2
Nothing sacred here: no hysterical woman chewing. Verse. Richmond Lattimore. PP
Nothing sings from these orange trees. On Watching the Construction of a Skyscraper. Burton Raffel. OCS
Nothing so difficult as a beginning. The Author's Purpose [*or* Romantic to Burlesque]. Byron. *Fr.* Don Juan, IV. BEL; CoBE; EnRP; EPN; FiP; PoFS
Nothing so sharply reminds a man he is mortal. Departure in the Dark. C. Day Lewis. ChMP; CoBMV; MoPo; TwCP
Nothing so true as what you once let fall. Of the Characters of Women [*or* To a Lady]. Pope. *Fr.* Moral Essays, II. BWP; EiCL; FaBoEn; MaPo (1969 ed.); MBW-1; NoP; OxBoLi; PoFS; SiTL
Nothing stays so long that it. The Broken Kaleidoscope. Walter de la Mare. NYTB
Nothing that is shall perish utterly. Dedication. Longfellow. *Fr.* Michael Angelo: A Fragment. MAmP
Nothing the Blood Cannot Cover. F. E. Robinson. SoP
Nothing! thou elder brother ev'n to shade. Upon Nothing. Earl of Rochester. AtBAP; EiCL; FosPo; MePo; OBS; PeRV; Po; PoEL-3; SeEP; TrGrPo; ViBoPo
Nothing to Do? Shelley Silverstein. BBGG
Nothing to do but work. The Pessimist. Ben King. ALV; BLPA; BOHV; CTC; FaFP; InMe; LiTG; NA; NeHB; TreFT; WaKn; WePo
Nothing to do, Nellie Darling. School Days. Will D. Cobb. TreFT
Nothing to drink in the. Quickly Aging Here. Denis Johnson. QAH
Nothing to Fear. Kingsley Amis. ErPo
Nothing to Say, You Say? Conrad Aiken. Preludes for Memnon, IX. LiTA; TwAmPo
Nothing to Wear. William Allen Butler. BOHV; HBV; PoLF
Nothing to Wish or to Fear. John Newton. BePJ
Nothing was left of me. A Dream of Burial. James Wright. NaP
Nothing wild. Inertia. Audrey McGaffin. NePoAm
Nothing will ever change beside this river. Changeless Shore. Sarah Leeds Ash. GoYe
Nothing will give delight. Nausea. Catherine Davis. NePoEA
Nothing would sleep in that cellar, dank as a ditch. Root Cellar. Theodore Roethke. AmPP (5th ed.); BoNaP; CBV; FiMAP; NoP; PoeP
Nothinge one earth remaines to show so right. *Unknown.* SeCSL
Nothing's wholly mine on earth. Poet-Hearts. Count Joseph von Eichendorff. CAW
Notice. David McCord. SoPo
Notice the convulsed orange inch of moon. Sonnets—Actualities. E. E. Cummings. AnAmPo
Notice with what careful nonchalance. Portrait. Hyam Plutzik. FiMAP
Noting in slow sequence by waterclock of rain. The Walk in the Garden. Conrad Aiken. PoCh
Notions of freedom are tied up with drink. The Drunkards. Malcolm Lowry. NYBP
Notre Dames des Champs. J. M. Synge. SyP
Notre Dame des Petits. Louis Mercier, *tr. fr. French by* Liam Brophy. ISi
Nottamun Town. *Unknown.* NCEP; OxBoLi; SiTL
Nou goth sonne under wod. Now Goeth Sun under Wood [*or* Pity for Mary *or* Sunset on Calvary]. *Unknown.* AtBAP; MeEL; NCEP; NoP
Nought have I to bring. November. Christina Rossetti. YeAr
Nought is there under heav'ns wide hollownesse. Spenser. *Fr.* The Faerie Queene, I. MBW-1
Nought loves another as itself. A Little Boy Lost. Blake. *Fr.* Songs of Experience. CBEP; CEP; EnLi-2; EnLit; EnRP; OAEP; PeER; PoIE; ViBoPo
Nought of the bridal will I tell. Hymn for the Dead. Sir Walter Scott. *Fr.* The Lay of the Last Minstrel, VI. OBRV
Noureddin, the Son of the Shah. Clinton Scollard. BOHV
Nova. Robinson Jeffers. CMoP
Novel. Robert Lax. ThO
Novel, The. Denise Levertov. AP
Novel, The. Wallace Stevens. ReMP
November. Laurence Binyon. SyP
November. Robert Bridges. NBM; PoEL-5; OBNC
November. William Cullen Bryant. Sonn
November. John Clare. GoTP; PoG
"Landscape sleeps in mist from morn till noon, The," *sel.* FIW
November. C. L. Cleaveland. DD; HBV

November. Elizabeth J. Coatsworth. YeAr
November. Hartley Coleridge. Sonnets on the Seasons, XII. LoBV; OBRV; PeER; PoRL
(Sonnet: November.) OBNC
November. Elizabeth Daryush. QFR
November, *sel.* John Davidson.
Epping Forest. GTSL
November. Richard Watson Dixon. *See* Song: "Feathers of the willow, The."
November. Aileen Fisher. SiSoSe; TiPo (1959 ed.)
November. Mahlon Leonard Fisher. HBV; PFY
November. Thomas Hood. *See* No!
November. Ted Hughes. GTBS-P; NePoEA-2; NMP; NoP; OPoP; PoTi
November. John Keble. OBEV (new ed.); OBVV
(Forest Leaves in Autumn.) OBNC
(Red o'er the Forest.) OxBoCh
November. Douglas Malloch. OTD
November. Hilda Morris. *See* November Wears a Paisley Shawl.
November. William Morris. *Fr.* The Earthly Paradise. EPN; GTSL; ViPo; ViPP
November. James Reaney. *Fr.* A Suit of Nettles. OBCV; PIA
November. Margaret Rose. BoTP
November. Christina Rossetti. YeAr
November. Spenser. *Fr.* The Shepheardes Calender. MaPo; PoEL-1
"Up then Melpomene thou mournefulst Muse of nyne," *sel.* AtBAP
(Dido My Dear, Alas, Is Dead.) ChTr
November. Elizabeth Stoddard. AA
November. Emile Verhaeren, *tr. fr. French by* Ludwig Lewisohn. WoL
November Afternoons. Sister Mary Madeleva. GoBC
November Blue. Alice Meynell. MoBrPo; YT
November—but the town. Gambol. Dennis Trudell. QAH
November chill blaws loud wi' angry sugh. November Evening. Burns. *Fr.* The Cotter's Saturday Night. OBEC; UnPo (1st ed.)
November comes. November. Elizabeth J. Coatsworth. YeAr
November Cotton Flower. Jean Toomer. CDC
November, 1806 ("Another year!"). Wordsworth. OBRV; PoFr
November Eleventh. Katherine Burton. PoRL
November Evening. Burns. *Fr.* The Cotter's Saturday Night. UnPo (1st ed.)
November Eves (November evenings! Damp and still). James Elroy Flecker. MoVE; SyP
November 1 ("How clear, how keen"). Wordsworth. EPN
November Fugitive. Henry Morton Robinson. *See* December Fugitive.
November Garden. Louise Driscoll. YeAr
November in England. Thomas Hood. *See* No!
November is a spinner. November. Margaret Rose. BoTP
November Light, Short Days Dark Fiery Sunsets. William Knott. YAP
November Morning. Edmund Blunden. WePo
November Morning. Evaleen Stein. YeAr
November Night. Adelaide Crapsey. AnAmPo; FaPON; MAP; MoAmPo (1942 ed.); MPB; NeMA; NP; PFY; WePo
November Night, Edinburgh. Norman MacCaig. NMP
November, 1941. Roy Fuller. MoPo
November Poppies. Hilary Corke. NYBP
November Rain. Maud E. Uschold. YeAr
November rain's down-pouring all night long. The Gone. Jesse Stuart. FiSC
November 7th. "Pablo Neruda," *tr. fr. Spanish by* Lloyd Mallan. PoFr
November should be cold and grey. Weather Vanes. Frances Frost. SiSoSe
November Sunday Morning. Alvin Feinman. CoAP; FosPo
November Surf. Robinson Jeffers. CrMA; MoPo; NoP; OxBA
November through a Giant Copper Beech. Edwin Honig. NYBP
November Twenty-sixth Nineteen Hundred and Sixty-three. Wendell Berry. AP; LiTM (1970 ed.)
November 2 A.M. Conspiracy. Sara Bard Field. AnEnPo
November Wears a Paisley Shawl. Hilda Morris. YeAr
(November.) PCH
November woods are bare and still. Down to Sleep. Helen Hunt Jackson. GN
November's Come. Joseph C. Lincoln. RePo
November's sky is chill and drear. Sir Walter Scott. Marmion, *Introd. to* I. OBRV
Novice, The. Edward Davison. ErPo
Novice when I came beneath thy gaze, A. Stanzas concerning Love. Stefan George. AWP; JAWP; WBP
Novices, The. Denise Levertov. NaP
Now. G. Bishop-Dubjinsky. ThO
Now. Donald E. Bogle. TNV
Now. Robert Browning. CBEP; EnLi-2 (1949 ed.); MeWo; PoVP
(Moment Eternal, The.) UnTE
Now. Mary Barker Dodge. AA
Now. Thomas Ken. OxBoCh
Now. Harriet Monroe. HBV
Now!/ Not now!/ Give me them again. In a Balcony. Robert Browning. EnLi-2 (1949 ed.); PoVP; ViPP
Now/ poem and month. William Harmon. *Fr.* Treasury Holiday. QAH
Now a knightlier sort you'll never find. Medieval Appreciations. William M. T. Gamble. CAW
Now after David had lived seventy years. The Death of David. Hayyim Nahman Bialik. TrJP
Now again the world is shaken. Foundations. Henry van Dyke. TRV
Now al is done; bring home the bride againe. Spenser. *Fr.* Epithalamion. FiP
Now All at Once It Is Colder. Marge Piercy. ThO
Now all day long the man who is not dead. Mother and Son. Allen Tate. LiTA; MAP; MoAB; MoAmPo; MoVE
Now all good fellows, fill the bowl, fill the bowl. Drinking Song for Present-Day Gatherings. Morris Bishop. ALV
Now all my teachers are dead except silence. A Scale in May. W. S. Merwin. FRC
Now all of change. Sir Thomas Wyatt. FCP; SiPS
Now all the cloudy shapes that float and lie. "Such Stuff as Dreams Are Made Of." Thomas Wentworth Higginson. AA
Now all the flowers that ornament the grass. Unreturning. Elizabeth Stoddard. AA
Now all the hosts are marching to the grave. Resurrection. D. H. Lawrence. NP
Now all the peacefull regents of the night. *See* Now all ye peacefull. . .
Now all the truth is out. To a Friend Whose Work Has Come to Nothing. W. B. Yeats. AnFE; AWP; BoC; DiPo; ForPo; GTBS-W; InPo; JAWP; LiTG; LiTM (rev. ed.); MBW-2; MoAB; MoBrPo; NP; OBMV; WBP
Now all the ways are open. The New Freedom. Olive Tilford Dargan. HBMV
Now all things melt and shift. Archibald Fleming MacLiesh. *Fr.* The Destroyers. NAMP
Now all ye [*or* the] peacefull regents of the night. George Chapman. *Fr.* Bussy d'Ambois, II, ii. LO; PoEL-2
Now along the solemn heights. Recessional. Sir Charles G. D. Roberts. HBV
Now am I a tin whistle. A Fresh Morning. J. C. Squire. WhC
Now among good harvests. Harvests. Marie de L. Welch. PoFr
Now and Afterwards. Dinah Maria Mulock Craik. PoLF; WGRP
Now and again I like to see. The Complete Hen. Elizabeth J. Coatsworth. GoTP
Now and, I fear, again. Table Talk. Donald Mattam. FiBHP
Now and Then. Margaret E. Sangster. TRV
Now and Then. Jane Taylor. OTPC (1923 ed.)
Now apprehension, with terrible dragon-eyes. The Annual Solution. Edwin Meade Robinson. InMe
Now are our prayers divided, now. At the "Ye That Do Truly." Charles Williams. OxBoCh
Now are the bells unlimbered from their spires. Pilgrimage. Eileen Duggan. AnNZ
Now are the forests dark and the ways full. Southern Summer. Francis Stuart. NeIP
Now are the Tritons heard, to Loving-land to call. Song. Michael Drayton. *Fr.* Polyolbion. AtBAP
Now are the winds about us in their glee. Song in March. William Gilmore Simms. AA; DD; HBV

Now are those peaks unscalable sierras. On Having Grown Old. E. G. Moll. BoAV
Now are you a marsupial? Are You a Marsupial? John Becker. RePo
Now, aren't men asses. Second News Item. *Unknown.* SiTL
Now Arethusa from her snow couches arises. Shelley's *Arethusa* Set to New Measures. Robert Duncan. OPoP
Now, around the world, the mills. New Crucifixion. Earl Bigelow Brown. ChIP
Now, a-roving, a-roving. A-Roving, *vers.* II. *Unknown.* ShS
Now as at all times I can see in the mind's eye. The Magi. W. B. Yeats. BoPe; BrPo; BWP; CaFP; CMoP; CoBMV; ELU; MaPo; MBW-2; NoP; NP; PoAn; PoDB; PoIE; StP
Now as before do you not hear their voices. Holderlin. Delmore Schwartz. MoRP
Now as even's warning bell. Solitude. John Clare. EnRP
Now as I go between sands red and yellow as poppies. Journey from New Zealand. "Robin Hyde." AnNZ
Now as I was young and easy under the apple boughs. Fern Hill [*or* Under the Apple Boughs]. Dylan Thomas. AtBAP; BoC; CABA; ChMP; CMoP; CoBMV; DiPo; EnL; EvOK; FaBoEn; FaBV; FosPo; GoJo; GTBS-D; GTBS-P; LiTB; LiTM; LoGBV; MaPo; MasP; MoAB; MoBrPo (1950 ed.); MoPo; MoPW; MoVE; NeMA; NoP; OAEP (2d ed.); PAn; PIA; Po; PoAn; PoLF; PoPl; PoRA; PrWP; RoGo; ShBV-4; ThWaDe; ToPo; TrGrPo (rev. ed.); TwCP; ViBoPo (1958 ed.); WaKn; WePo
Now, as in Tullias tombe, one lampe burnt cleare. The Good-Night. John Donne. MaMe
Now as the night treads softly on its way. Midnight Patrol. Eric Irvin. BoAV
Now as the river fills with ice. Crew Cut. David McCord. SD
Now as the train bears west. Night Journey. Theodore Roethke. AmFN; NYBP; TPM
Now as Then. Anne Ridler. WaP
Now as these slaughtered seven hundreds hear. On the *Struma* Massacre. Ralph Gustafson. OBCV
Now as we fall back from below the ridge. Retreat. J. K. Clark. NYTB
Now austere lips are laid. The Hard Lovers. George Dillon. AnAmPo
Now Autumn comes, the wise fool of the year. Autumn. Frances Winwar. GoYe
Now, before I sleep. Night Songs. Thomas Kinsella. ACV
Now before the feast of the passover. The Last Supper. St. John, Bible, *N.T.* OuHeWo
Now begin wailing notes; the flesh is thrilled. Paolo and Francesca. Dante. *Fr.* Divina Commedia: Inferno, V. ExPo
Now beginneth Glutton for to go to shrift. The Glutton. William Langland. *Fr.* The Vision of Piers Plowman. ACP
Now bid thy soul man's busy scenes exclude. Books. George Crabbe. *Fr.* The Library. OBEC
Now blest be the Briton, his beef and his beer. Bacon and Eggs. A. P. Herbert. WhC
Now blows the white rose round our garden pales. The Spring. John Francis O'Donnell. IrPN
Now bold Robin Hood to the north would go. Robin Hood and the Scotchman. *Unknown.* ESPB
Now, boys, if you will listen, I will sing to you a song. The Lumber Camp Song. *Unknown.* ShS
Now boys, we're on the steamer *Natchez.* Roustabout Holler. *Unknown.* OuSiCo
Now Brigham Young is a Mormon bold. Brigham Young (B *vers.*). *Unknown.* CoSo
Now burst above the city's cold twilight. Six o'Clock. Trumbull Stickney. NCEP; OxBA
"Now, by Columba!" Con exclaimed. Denis Florence MacCarthy. *Fr.* The Foray of Con O'Donnell A.D. 1495. OnYI
Now, by her troth, she hath been, Phaedra says. In Phaedram. Thomas Freeman. TuPP
Now, by my love, the greatest oath that is. My Diet. Abraham Cowley. *Fr.* The Mistress. LiTL; LO; SeCL; SeEP
Now by the path I climbed, I journey back. Edna St. Vincent Millay. CMoP
Now by the verdure on thy thousand hills. Adequacy. Elizabeth Barrett Browning. SoP
Now by this lake, this fallen thunderstorm. Four Poems for April. Louis Adeane. NeBP
Now came jolly Summer, being dight. Summer. Spenser. *Fr.* The Faerie Queene, VII. GN
Now Came Still Evening On. Milton. *See* Evening in Paradise.
Now Camilla's fair fingers are plucking in rapture the pulsating strings. Camilla. Charles Augustus Keeler. AA
Now can you see the monument? It is of wood. The Monument. Elizabeth Bishop. LiTA; MoPo; PoIE; PP
Now Cana sees a wonder new. The Miracle. Caelius Sedulius. *Fr.* Carmen Paschale. CAW
Now Cease, My Wandering Eyes. *Unknown.* ReIE; TuPP
Now Charito is sixty. But her hair. Ageless. *Unknown.* UnTE
Now, Charles Gustavus Anderson is my right and proper name. Charles Gustavus Anderson, *vers.* I. *Unknown.* ShS
Now cheer our hearts this eventide. At Eventide. *Unknown, tr. by* Robert Bridges. MaRV
Now Christendom bids her cathedrals call. Elegy X. William Bell. NePoEA
Now Clear the Triple Region of the Air. Christopher Marlowe. *Fr.* Tamburlaine the Great, Pt. I, Act IV, sc. ii. TrGrPo
Now Close the Windows. Robert Frost. LOW; WePo
Now coil up your nonsense 'bout England's great Navy. Charge the Can Cheerily. *Unknown.* AmSS
Now, come all you young sailors and listen to me, sure I'll tell you a story. As I Went a-Walking down Ratcliffe Highway, *vers.* I. *Unknown.* ShS
Now, come all you young sailors and listen to me, with your way, hay, blow the man down. Blow the Man Down, *vers.* I. *Unknown.* ShS
Now come, my boon companions. Thomas Randolph. EG
Now come the rosy dogwoods. In October. Bliss Carman. YeAr
Now come, ye Naiads, to the fountains lead. The Home of the Naiads. John Armstrong. *Fr.* The Art of Preserving Health. OBEC
Now come, young men, and list to me. Macaffie's Confession. *Unknown.* BeLS; CoSo
Now comes my lover tripping like the roe. George Peele. *Fr.* David and Bethsabe. ViBoPo
Now Comes the Blast of Winter. *Unknown.* SeCePo
Now comes the graybeard of the north. Winter Days. Henry Abbey. AA
Now comes the Paschal Victim bringing. Victimae Paschali Laudes. Wipo. CAW
Now cometh the fearful hour of the Passion. A Sequence, with Strophes in Paraphrase Thereof. Francis Burke. CAW
Now concerning spiritual gifts, brethren. Spiritual Gifts. First Corinthians, Bible, *N.T.* WoL
Now condescend, Almighty King. An Evening Hymn for a little Family. Ann *or* Jane Taylor. OTPC (1946 ed.)
Now cracking grass encrusts the yard. For My Students, Returning to College. John Williams. NePoAm-2
Now crouch, ye kings of greatest Asia. Emperor of the Threefold World [*or* The Bloody Conquests of Mighty Tamburlaine]. Christopher Marlowe. *Fr.* Tamburlaine the Great, Pt. II, Act IV, iii. ChTr; TrGrPo
Now dandelions in the short, new grass. Dandelions. John Albee. AA
Now, dearest, lend a heedful ear. Autumn. Kalidasa. *Fr.* The Seasons. AWP; JAWP; WBP
Now death has sealed my warthog's eyes. Epitaph on a Warthog. J. B. Morton. PV
Now Delia breathes in woods the fragrant air. Elegy: On Delia's Being in the Country. James Hammond. *Fr.* Love Elegies. CEP
"Now did you mark a falcon." Noble Sisters. Christina Rossetti. CoBE
Now dis-band all the bands of kin. Family Poem. John Holloway. NMP
Now do our eyes behold. Lament for the Two Brothers Slain by Each Other's Hand. Aeschylus. *Fr.* The Seven against Thebes. AWP; JAWP; WBP
Now do the birds in their warbling words. Song. Patrick Hannay. SeCL
Now Does Our World Descend. E. E. Cummings. AP; NYBP
Now does Spains fleet her spatious wings unfold. On the Victory Obtained by Blake over the Spaniards. Andrew Marvell. MaMe

Now, don't you want to know something concernin'. The Ballad of Davy Crockett. *Unknown.* ABF
Now dost Thou dismiss Thy servant, O Lord. Nunc Dimittis. St Luke, Bible, *N.T.* WGRP; WHL
Now Dreary Dawns the Eastern Light. A. E. Housman. CMoP
Now Dry Thy Eyes. Mikhail Alekseyevich Kuzmin, *tr. fr. Russian by* Babette Deutsch. OnPM
Now dumb is he who waked the world to speak. On Hearing the News from Venice. George Meredith. PoVP
Now each creature joys the other. An Ode. Samuel Daniel. *Fr.* To Delia. ElL; LoBV; OBSC; SiCE; TuPP
Now early sink away the starry Twins. Midsummer. William Allingham. IrPN
Now England lessens on my sight. To England. Charles Leonard Moore. AA
Now English eyes the cancerous sun behold! Charles Madge. *Fr.* The Hours of the Planets. BoSA
Now Entertain Conjecture of a Time. Shakespeare. King Henry V, Prologue to IV. WaaP
(Eve of Agincourt, The.) ShBV-3
Now Europe's balanced, neither side prevails. The Balance of Europe. Pope. CBV; SeCeV; TOP
Now, even now, I yield, I yield. Now Is the Accepted Time. Charles Wesley. BePJ
Now evermore, lest some one hope might ease. The Portents. Lucan, *tr. by* Christopher Marlowe. *Fr.* Pharsalia. OBSC
Now Every Child. Eleanor Farjeon. BiCB; SUS
(Our Brother Is Born.) ChrBoLe
Now, every day, the runner sun applies. October. Willard Trask. CLwM
Now every leaf, though colorless, burns bright. Sonnet to the Moon. Yvor Winters. TwAmPo
Now everything that shadowy thought. In Festubert. Edmund Blunden. OBMV
Now, except that he had two heads, Mr. Dooley was in most ways a perfectly normal human being. Mr. Ripley Parodies Mr. Nash—or Vice Versa. Julian Brown. FiSC
Now fades the last long streak of snow. In Memoriam A. H. H., CXV [*or* Spring]. Tennyson. BEL; BoC; CoBE; DD; EPN; FaBoEn; GTBS-D; GTBS-P; HBV; MaPo; OAEP; OBEV (1st ed.); OBNC; PoE; PoSa; SeCeV; ShBV-4; TreFT; ViBoPo; ViPo; VP; YT
Now faith is the substance of things hoped for. The Evidence. Hebrews, Bible, *N.T.* TRV
Now far and near on field and hill. So This Is Autumn. W. W. Watt. OTD; PoPl
Now fare-you-well! my bonny ship. Nanny's Sailor Lad. William Allingham. IrPN
Now, fathers, now our meeting's over. Now Our Meeting's Over. *Unknown.* ABF
Now fayre, fayrest of every fayre. To the Princess Margaret Tudor. William Dunbar. SiSw
Now ferkes to the firthe thees fresche men of armes. Sir Gawain Encounters Sir Priamus. *Unknown.* *Fr.* Morte Arthure. PoEL-1
Now fie on foolish love, it not befits. Fie on Love. Francis Beaumont. AnEnPo
Now fie upon that everlasting life, I dye. Valiant Love. Richard Lovelace. SCEP-2; SeCP
Now fields are striped in green and brown. The Busy Body. Rachel Field. InMe
Now find I true that hath been often told. He Declares That Albeit He Were Imprisoned in Russia, Yet His Mind Was at Liberty and Did Daily Repair to His Friend. George Turberville. TuPP
Now first, as I shut the door. The New House. Edward Thomas. HBMV; MoAB; MoBrPo; OBEV (new ed.); POTE; PrWP
Now, flaming up the heavens, the potent sun. Summer. James Thomson. *Fr.* The Seasons. StP
Now folded back across the changing earth. Lines to the Unborn. Patrick D. Waddington. TwCaPo
"Now for a brisk and cheerful fight!" The Fight at [the] San Jacinto. John Williamson Palmer. AA; DD; PaA
Now for one day, from sun to sun. The Star of Bethlehem. Alice Corbin Henderson. ChrBoLe
Now for the broken bodies. Broken Bodies. Louis Golding. MaRV
Now for the crown and throne of Israel. George Peele. *Fr.* David and Bethsabe. ViBoPo
Now friends if you'll listen to a horrible tale. The Dreary Black Hills. *Unknown.* IHA
Now from the dark, a deeper dark. Calling In the Cat. Elizabeth J. Coatsworth. AnAmPo; NeMA; OA
Now from the darkness of myself. Escape and Return. Elizabeth Jennings. NePoEA
Now from the World the Light of God Is Gone. Robert Nathan. MaRV
Now from their slumber waking. Comrades. Henry R. Dorr. MC; PAH
Now from your easts you issue forth, and wee. Going to the Chappell. John Donne. MaMe
Now, gentle friend, if thou be kind. The Author's Life. Thomas Tusser. ReIE
Now gentle sleep hath closed up those eyes. A Stolen Kiss [*or* Sonnet upon a Stolen Kiss *or* The Theft). George Wither. *Fr.* Fair Virtue, the Mistress of Philarete. HBV; LiTL; MeWo; PoIE (1970 ed.); SeCL; UnTE
Now get thee back, retreat, depart, O Serpent. He Overcometh the Serpent of Evil in the Name of Ra. *Unknown.* *Fr.* Book of the Dead. AWP
Now, Gibbon has told the story of old. Fighting McGuire. William Percy French. CenHV
Now, Gilbert, you know you're our man. To G. K. Chesterton. Joseph Mary Plunkett. OnYI
Now ginnes [*or* gins] this goodly frame of Temperaunce [*or* Temperance]. The Legend of Sir Guyon [*or* The Bower of Bliss]. Spenser. *Fr.* The Faerie Queene, II. PoEL-1; WHA
"Now, give us a wrap." Baby Lapp's Ride. *Unknown.* SAS
"Now give us lands where the olives grow." The North and the South. Elizabeth Barrett Browning. OBVV
Now glory to the Lord of Hosts, from whom all glories are! Ivry [*or* The Battle of Ivry]. Macaulay. FaBV; FoL; GN; HBV; HBVY; OBRV; OTPC; RG; VA; WBLP
Now glowing Venus wakes. New Guinea Lament. J. P. McAuley. BoAV
Now God alone that made all things. The Leather Bottel. John Wade. PeRV; SeCL
Now God be praised that I have known. Free Men. Struthers Burt. PoFr
Now, God be thanked Who has matched us with His hour. Peace. Rupert Brooke. 1914, I. EPN; HBV; MaRV; MMA; NP; POTE; TreFT; WGRP
Now God preserve, as you well do deserve. The Masque of Christmas. Ben Jonson. OxBoLi
Now Goeth [*or* Go'th] Sun under Wood. *Unknown.* CBEP; NCEP; NoP
(Pity for Mary.) MeEL
(Sunset on Calvary.) AtBAP
Now good night. Good Night! Eleanor Farjeon. ThGo
Now gowans sprout and lavrocks sing. An Ode to Mr. F——. Allan Ramsay. CEP
Now gracious plenty rules the board. Thanksgiving. Florence Earle Coates. PEDC; TrPWD
Now grapes are plush upon the vines. Contrary Theses, I. Wallace Stevens. OxBA
Now green, now burning, I make a way for peace. Tenth Elegy: Elegy in Joy. Muriel Rukeyser. MiAP
Now grimy April comes again. For City Spring. Stephen Vincent Benét. PoPl
Now had night measured with her shadowy cone. Then When I Am Thy Captive, Talk of Chains. Milton. *Fr.* Paradise Lost, IV. WHA
Now had the Almight Father from above. The Scheme of Redemption. Milton. *Fr.* Paradise Lost, III. StJW
"Now half a hundred years had I been born." His Statement of the Case. James Herbert Morse. AA
Now Hamlet, where's Polonius? Shakespeare. *Fr.* Hamlet, IV, iii. AtBAP
Now hand in hand, you little maidens, walk. Spring. André Spire. AWP; BoLP
Now hands to seed-sheet, boys! Sower's Song. Thomas Carlyle. OBVV; VA
Now hardly here and there an hackney-coach. A Description of the Morning. Swift. BWP; CABA; CaFP; CBV; CEP; EiCL; EiCP; EiPP ExPo; FaBoEn; FosPo; ILP; PoFS; PoIE; SeCeV; StP; ViBoPo
Now has ended the battle of Saul. Saul. Nathan Alterman. TrJP

Now has the blue-eyed spring. A Catch for Spring. Robert Nichols. GBV
Now has the lingering month at last gone by. Atalanta's Defeat. William Morris. *Fr.* The Earthly Paradise. VA
Now hath my life across a stormy sea. On the Brink of Death [*or* His Great Love on High]. Michelangelo. AWP; JAWP; OnPM; WBP
Now hath the summer reached her golden close. September. Archibald Lampman. PeCV
Now haud your tongue, baith wife and carle. Harlaw. Sir Walter Scott. *Fr.* The Antiquary, *ch.* 40. EnLi-2; OxBB
Now have I brought a woork too end which neither Joves fierce wrath. Conclusion. Ovid. *Fr.* Metamorphoses. CTC
Now have I lived, O Rome, enough for me. Theodore Beza, *tr. by* Nicholas Grimald. *Fr.* Marcus Tullius Cicero's Death. TuPP
Now Having Proved Thy Fond Delays. Edward Howard. SeCL
Now he begins: his fingers feel. The Surgeon. W. J. Funk. PoMa
"Now, he belongs to the ages." The Soul of Lincoln. Chauncey R. Piety. PGD
Now he has seen the girl Hsiang-Hsiang. Chinese Ballad. Li Chi, *ad. by* William Empson. NoP; ToPo
Now He is Dead. Alistair Campbell. AnNZ
Now he is gone and we had not understood one another. The Year's Ending. St. J. Page Yako. PeSA
Now he was coming voluntary home. Return of the Prodigal. A. E. Johnson. JKCP (1955 ed.)
Now, he who knows old Christmas. Old Christmas. Mary Howitt. GN; OTPC
Now heap the branchy barriers up. The Keepers of the Pass. Sir Charles G. D. Roberts. VA
Now heaven be thanked, I am out of love again. Freedom. "Jan Struther." POTE
Now heed and hearken, gentle folk. Bethlehem. Arthur Ketchum. ChrBoLe
Now here I think needful a pause for to make. A Digression from Husbandry to a Point or Two of Huswifery. Thomas Tusser. ReIE
Now here, now there, lightheaded, crazed with grief. A Psalm of the Early Buddhist Sisters. *Unknown.* WGRP
Now hid from sight are great Mount Fusi's fires. Hidden Fires. *Unknown.* OnPM
Now high and low, where leaves renew. Canzo of Bird-Songs and Love [or Autet e bas]. Arnaut Daniel. CTC; LiTW
Now his nose's bridge is broken, one eye. On Hurricane Jackson. Alan Dugan. CoAP; SD
Now Hollow Fires Burn Out to Black. A. E. Housman. A Shropshire Lad, LX. PoVP
Now how I came to get this hat 'tis very strange and funny. Where Did You Get That Hat? Joseph J. Sullivan. TreF
Now I am six and going on seven. Growing Up. Arthur Guiterman. BiCB
Now I am slow and placid, fond of sun. With Child. Genevieve Taggard. AnAmPo; AnEnPo; MAP; MoAmPo
Now I am thankful this unbroken flesh. Fisherman's Son. Charles Bruce. CaP
Now I am tired of being Japanese. Picture of a Castle. William Meredith. NePoEA
Now I am young and credulous. Wisdom Cometh with the Years. Countee Cullen. Kal
Now I believe tradition, which doth call. Upon the Author; by a Known Friend. Benjamin Woodbridge. SCAP
Now I can be sure of my sleep. On the Hill below the Lighthouse. James Dickey. NePoEA-2
Now I can see what Helen was. A Lovely Woman. W. H. Davies. FaBoTw
Now, I confess, I am in Love. A Rhapsody. *Unknown.* SeCL
Now I find my arms. Sassafras Memories. Edward S. Spriggs. BF
Now I find [*or* see] thy looks were feigned. An Ode [*or* Song]. Thomas Lodge. *Fr.* Phyllis. EIL; EnRePo; LoBV; OBSC; SiCE; TuPP
Now I go down here and bring up a moon. Auctioneer. Carl Sandburg. PDV
Now I Have Come to Reason. C. Day Lewis. CMoP
Now I Have Found a Friend. Henry Hope. BePJ; SoP
Now I have found the reasons why. *Unknown.* SeCSL
Now I have found thee, I will ever more. Upon the Crucifix [*or* Sonnet.] William Alabaster. AnAnS-1; MeP; PoEL-2
Now I have lost you, I must scatter. Farewell, Sweet Dust. Elinor Wylie. AnAmPo; LiTA
Now I have tempered haste. The Mount. Léonie Adams. MoVE
Now I have touched you near the grated bone. Postscript. Mary Mills. NePoAm
Now I have touched your soil I will go back. Frank Wilmot. *Fr.* The Gully. NeLNL
Now I know why I dream. Spring. Allen Van Newkirk. YAP
Now I Lay Me. *Unknown.* *See* Now I Lay Me Down to Sleep.
Now I lay me down to dreams. Nursery Rhymes for Surrealists. Grant Code. FiSC
"Now I Lay Me Down to Sleep." Eugene Henry Pullen. AA; FaBoBe
"Now I lay me down to sleep. . .." A Foxhole for the Night. John Quinn. BoAV
Now I Lay Me Down to [Take My] Sleep, *diff. versions.* *Unknown.* FaFP; OxNR; SiTL; TreF
(Children's Prayers.) BLRP
(Evening Prayer, An.) MaRV
(Now I Lay Me.) SoPo
Now I must betray myself. Prothalamion. Delmore Schwartz. OxBA
Now I pray the man who may love this lay. Cynewulf. *Fr.* Fates of the Apostles. AnOE
Now I put on the thimble of dream. The Red Bird Tapestry. May Swenson. TwAmPo
Now I See. Frances Ridley Havergal. SoP
Now I see the leaves tilting. Variations on a Still Morning. Thomas Cole. NePoAm
Now I see thy looks were feigned. *See* Now I find thy looks. . .
Now I shall reach over. With Lilacs in My Eye. Lucile Coleman. GoYe
Now I tell what my mother told me to-day as we sat at dinner together. The Indian Woman. Walt Whitman. *Fr.* The Sleepers. PCD; PCH
Now I wake and see the light. Children's Prayers. *At. to* Eugene Henry Pullen. BLRP
Now I want/ Spirits to endorce, art to enchant. Shakespeare. *Fr.* The Tempest: Epilogue. MyFE
Now I was born on the Rio Grande. Rio Grande, *vers.* II. *Unknown.* ShS
Now I Went Down to the Ringside and Little Henry Armstrong Was There. Kenneth Patchen. ToPo
Now I will do nothing but listen. Song of Myself, XXVI. Walt Whitman. HoPM; MaPo
Now I will fashion the tale of a fish. The Whale. *Unknown.* *Fr.* Physiologus. AnOE; OA
Now if Euterpe held me not in scorn. Euterpe. Thomas Bailey Aldrich. Sonn
Now if ever it is time to cleanse Helicon. Homage to Sextus Propertius, V. Ezra Pound. CrMA
Now, if ever, let poets sing. Let Dreamers Wake. Lilith Lorraine. PGD
Now if the dull and thankless heart declare. Malediction upon Myself. Elinor Wylie. AnAmPo
"Now, if the fish will only bite, we'll have some royal fun." Timid Hortense. Peter Newell. NA
Now, If You Will Look in My Brain. José Garcia Villa. AnFE; CoAnAm; TwAmPo
Now I'll tell you of my history since eighteen forty seven. Poker Jim. *Unknown.* SGR
Now, I'm a good Rebel, now that's just what I am. I'm a Good Old Rebel. Innes Randolph. ABF
Now, I'm leaving old England, the land that I love. The First of the Emigrants. *Unknown.* ShS
Now I'm Resolved to Love No More. Alexander Brome. ALV
Now in her green mantle blythe Nature arrays. My Nannie's Awa. Burns. GN; HBV; OTPC (1923 ed.)
Now, in his joy. The Wind. John Banister Tabb. AnAmPo
Now in midsummer come and all fools slaughtered. Credences of Summer. Wallace Stevens. AP; CoBMV
Now in the/ black. Timothy L. Porter. WSL
Now in the Bloom. Florence Kiper Frank. GoYe
Now in the circulating torrent of the stars. In Conjunction. Charles Madge. FaBoMo; NeBP
Now, in the evenings, when the light. The Generations. George M. Brady. OnYI

"Now—in the hour that melts with homesick yearning." Dante's Angels. Dante. *Fr.* Divina Commedia: Purgatorio. BoC
Now in the Mayday twilight. Evening in May. Gabriele d'Annunzio. WoL
Now in the night where the nameless crickets make. Letter to the Night. Lloyd Frankenberg. AnAmPo
Now in the Palace Gardens. Trumbull Stickney. Eride, V. AnFE; CoAnAm; LiTA; NCEP; TwAmPo
Now in the sad declenshion of thy tyme. *Unknown.* SeCSL
Now in the suburbs and the falling light. Father and Son. Stanley Kunitz. PoAn; TwCP
Now in the summer of life, sweetheart. Will You Love Me in December as You Do in May? James J. Walker. TreFT
Now in the third voice. W. S. Graham. *Fr.* The Dark Dialogues. OxBS
Now in the Time of This Mortal Life. Norman Nicholson. NeBP
Now in this mirthfull tyme of May. May Poem. *Unknown.* OxBS
Now in this while gan Daedalus a wearinesse to take. Daedalus. Ovid. *Fr.* Metamorphoses. CTC
Now, innocent, within the deep. M., Singing. Louise Bogan. CrMA; GoJo; LiTA; NePA
Now into the saddle, and over the grass. The Pony Express. Dorothy Brown Thompson. AmFN
Now is a great and shining company. Resurgam. Struthers Burt. HBMV
Now is Christ risen from the dead. Death's Conqueror. First Corinthians, Bible, *N.T.* MaRV
Now is come Midsummer Night. Song for Midsummer Night. Elizabeth J. Coatsworth. YeAr
Now is earth visibly gone over to spirit. Jones's Pasture. Abbie Huston Evans. NP
Now Is Farewell. Blanaid Salkeld. NeIP
Now is it most like as if on ocean. The Voyage of Life. Cynewulf. *Fr.* Christ 2. AnOE
Now is it pleasant in the summer-eve. Amusements. George Crabbe. *Fr.* The Borough. OBRV
Now is Light, sweet mother, down the west. Evening Songs, III. John Vance Cheney. AA
Now is mon hol and soint. When Death Comes. *Unknown.* MeEL
Now is my Chloris fresh as May. *Unknown.* OBSC
Now is my way clear, now is the meaning plain. The Last Temptation. T. S. Eliot. *Fr.* Murder in the Cathedral. TreFT
Now is Past. John Clare. PeER
Now Is the Accepted Time. Charles Wesley. BePJ
Now Is the Air Made of Chiming Balls. Richard Eberhart. ToPo
Now is the autumn of the Tree of Life. Progress of Unbelief. Cardinal Newman. GoBC
Now is the bright morning star, Day's harbinger. Song on a May Morning. Milton. PoRL
Now Is the Cherry in Blossom. Mary E. Wilkins Freeman. AA
Now is the earth a place of desolation. A Wreath for One Lost. Harold Vinal. FiSC
Now is the focus of all hopes. A Violin Concerto. James Reeves. MuSP
Now Is the High-Tide of the Year. James Russell Lowell. *Fr.* The Vision of Sir Launfal: Prelude to Part First. TreFS
Now is the hour of the bell, now am I caught. John Donne's Defiance. J. R. Hervey. AnNZ
Now is the hour when, swinging in the breeze. Harmonie du Soir. Baudelaire. AWP; JAWP; WBP
Now is the month of maying. Song. *Unknown.* EG; OBSC
Now is the night, foreshadowed of our fears. Edwin Booth. Alice Brown. HBV
Now is the ox-eyed daisy out. James Reaney. WHW
Now is the pause between asleep and awake. The Spring Equinox. Anne Ridler. NeBP
Now is the sailing time. Soft blows the breeze. Spring Sailing. Leonidas. OnPM
Now is the time for all good men. Testing, Testing. Dan Dillon. PV
Now is the time for mirth. To Live Merrily, and to Trust to Good Verses. Robert Herrick. AnAnS-2; AWP; BEL; InPo; InVP; LoBV; MaPo (1969 ed.); MyFE; OBS; PP; ReEn; SCEP-2; SeCP; SeCV-1; SeEP
Now is the time for burning of the leaves. The Burning of the Leaves. Laurence Binyon. ChMP; DTC; GTBS-D; GTBS-P; MoVE; POTE
Now is the Time of Christmas. *Unknown.* MeEL
Now is the time that hills put on. Spring Signs. Rachel Field. InMe
Now is the time, when all the lights wax dim. To Anthea. Robert Herrick. OAEP; OBS; PoEL-3; SeEP
Now is the time when cheery crickets. Autumn! Nancy Byrd Turner. YeAr
Now is the winter of our discontent. Evil Designs [*or* Hate the Idle Pleasures]. Shakespeare. King Richard III, *fr.* I, i. TreF; TrGrPo
Now Isabel the young afflicted queen. Richard II as Captive. Samuel Daniel. *Fr.* The Civil Wars. SiCE
Now Israel loved Joseph more than all his children. Joseph and His Brethren. Genesis, Bible, *O.T.* OuHeWo
Now it begins. Now the subaqueous evening. A Is for Alpha; Alpha Is for A. Conrad Aiken. NePA
Now it came to pass in the days when the judges ruled. Ruth, Bible, O.T. EnLi-1; OuHeWo; WoL
Now it grows dark. Hymn to Night. Melville Cane. MAP; MoAmPo
Now it is April, then the great bull of May. For Irma During April. Tony Towle. YAP
Now it is autumn and the falling fruit. The Ship of Death. D. H. Lawrence. CMoP; FaBoTw; GTBS-P; LiTB; LoBV; MasP; NoP; OAEP (2d ed.)
Now it is fifteen years you have lain in the meadow. Lines for an Interment. Archibald MacLeish. CMoP; InP; MaRV
Now it is night, now in the brilliant room. De Anima. Howard Nemerov. ToPo
Now it is only hours before you wake. Letter to My Daughter. Donald Finkel. CoAP
Now it is seven years since you were the Queen. The Decay of Vanity. Ted Hughes. POTE (1959 ed.)
Now, it takes all 'ands to man the capstan. Rolling Home, *vers.* II. *Unknown.* ShS
Now it was Spring. Grant at Appomattox. Gertrude Claytor. GoYe
Now, it's blow, you winds, 'ow I long to hear you. Blow, Boys, Blow, *vers.* III. *Unknown.* ShS
Now, it's one cold and dreary morning in December. Mainsail Haul, *vers.* I. *Unknown.* ShS
Now, I've got no use for the women. Bury Me Out on the Prairie. *Unknown.* CoSo
Now Ixion's wheel is stilled. Missa Papae Marcelli. J. P. McAuley. BoAV
Now Jesus knew that they were desirous to ask him. Be of Good Cheer; I Have Overcome the World. St. John Bible, *N.T.* TreFS
Now, Jesus, Mary's Son, be unto Thee. A Wish. *Unknown.* CAW
Now Jones had left his new-wed bride to keep his house in order. A Code of Morals. Kipling. OnSP
Now, Joy is born of parents poor. Joy and Pleasure. W. H. Davies. OBMV
Now joy, the flower of heaven. The Splendid Flower. Etta May Van Tassel. JKCP (1955 ed.)
Now keep that long revolver at your side. Sonnet. George Hetherington. NeIP
Now Kindness. Peter Viereck. LiTA
Now, ladies, if you'll listen, a story I'll relate. Pearl Bryan. *Unknown.* BaBo
Now, lamb, no longer naughty be. The Lamb. Kate Greenaway. OTPC (1923 ed.); PPL; SAS
Now, landsmen, list! There is no sight more fair. Norse Sailor's Joy. Wilfrid Thorley. EtS
Now lay up thy barley land, dry as ye can. October's Husbandry. Thomas Tusser. CoBE
Now leave the check-reins slack. To the Man after the Harrow. Patrick Kavanagh. GTBS-P
Now Lent is come, let us refrain. Stanzas for Lent. James Howell. PrWP
Now let me alone, though I know you won't. Barney O'Hea. Samuel Lover. OnYI
Now let music, light as an enchanter's hands. A Charm for the Ear-Ache. James Kirkup. BoPe; POTi
Now let no charitable hope. Let No Charitable Hope. Elinor Wylie. AnAmPo; HBMV; LiTA; LiTM; MAP; MoAB; MoAmPo; NePA; OxBA; TrGrPo; WOW

Now let the drums roll muffled; let the bells'. Charles Heavysege. *Fr.* Count Filippo. PeCV
Now let us honor with violin and flute. Song. May Sarton. MoRP
Now let us praise the Keeper of the Heavenly Kingdom. Hymn. Cædmon. YAT
Now Liddisdale has lain long in. Dick o the Cow. *Unknown.* BaBo; ESPB; OBB; OxBB
Now Liddesdale has ridden a raid. Jock o' the Side. *Unknown.* ESPB (B *vers.*); OBB; OxBB
Now lies the Lord in a most quiet bed. Now Sleeps the Lord. Margaret L. Woods. StJW
Now light the candles; one; two; there's a moth. Repression of War Experience. Siegfried Sassoon. BrPo; MMA
Now lighted windows climb the dark. Manhattan Lullaby. Rachel Field. AmFN; BiCB; OCS
Now, like a magpie, he collects the bright. "Trade" Rat. Eleanor Glenn Wallis. NePoAm
Now list and lithe you gentleman. Northumberland Betrayed by Douglas. *Unknown.* ESPB; OBB; OxBB
Now list you, lithe you, gentlemen. Robin Hood and Queen Katherine. *Unknown.* ESPB
Now listen to boasting which leaves the heart dazed. Al-Samau'al ibn Adiya. *Fr.* Are We Not the People. TrJP
Now listen you landsmen unto me, to tell you the truth I'm bound. The Crocodile. *Unknown.* CBEP
Now lived the youth in freedom, but debarred. Peter Grimes. George Crabbe. *Fr.* The Borough. WePo
Now, Lord, or never they'll believe on Thee. On the Miracle of Loaves. Richard Crashaw. ACP; MaMe
Now, Lord, send them summer, some manner of joy. Prayer for Rich and Poor. William Langland. *Fr.* The Vision of Piers Plowman. BoC
Now, Lord, upon Thy Sea of Air. Mary Louisa Anderson. MaRV
Now Love Dies. John Ford. *See* Song: "Oh, no more, no more, too late."
Now lufferis cummis with larges lowd. The Petition of the Gray Horse, Auld Dunbar. William Dunbar. OxBS
Now many are the stately ships that northward steam away. The Lover Thinks of His Lady in the North. Shaemas O'Sheel. HBV
Now May He Who from the Dead. John Newton. SoP
Now may I see the time hath beene in vaine. *Unknown.* SeCSL
Now may we turn aside and dry our tears. Inis Fal. *Tr. by* James Stephens. OBMV
Now Memory, false, spendthrift Memory. Lough Bray. Standish James O'Grady. IrPN
Now milkmaids' pails are deckt with flowers. Stool Ball. *Unknown.* CH
Now miners, if you'll listen, I'll tell you quite a tale. Coming around the Horn. John A. Stone. ABF; SGR
Now mirk December's dowie face. The Daft Days. Robert Fergusson. CEP
"Now, Miss Clara point your toe." The Dancing Lesson. Eliza Grove. OTPC (1923 ed.)
Now Mrs. Eberle early had been told. La Donna E Perpetuum Mobile. Irwin Edman. FiBHP
Now Morning from her orient chamber came. Imitation of Spenser. Keats. ATP; EnRP; GN; MBW-2
Now must all satisfaction. Certain Mercies. Robert Graves. CoBMV; GTBS-P
Now must I learn to live at rest. Sir Thomas Wyatt. FCP; SiPS
Now must I wait. The Blank Book Letter. Samuel Greenberg. LiTA
Now must we hymn the Maker of heaven. The Hymn of the World's Creator. Cædmon. CAW
Now must we praise heaven's Keeper. The Creation. *CA* Edmon PoLi
Now my boys if you will listen, I'll sing you a little song. The Cruise of the *Bigler.* *Unknown.* SoAmSa
Now my charms are all o'erthrown. Epilogue. Shakespeare. *Fr.* The Tempest. CTC
Now, my co-mates and brothers in exile. The Uses of Adversity [*or* The Banished Duke Speaks to His Retainers]. Shakespeare. *Fr.* As You Like It, II, i. LiTB; LiTG; TreFS; TrGrPo
Now, my fair'st friend. Some Flowers o' the Spring. Shakespeare. *Fr.* The Winter's Tale, IV, iii. ChTr
Now my legs begin to talk. Thaw in the City. Lou Lipsitz. YAP
Now, my name is Samuel Hall, Sam Hall. Sam Hall. *Unknown.* ViBoFo
Now, my son, is life for you. Wishes for My Son. Thomas MacDonagh. AnIV; GoBC; HBMV; JKCP; TSW
Now my thick years bend your back. The Turn of the Road. Fannie Stearns Davis. HBMV
Now nature hangs her mantle green. Mary Queen of Scots. Burns. FOL
Now, night; and once again. Avalon. Audrey McGaffin. NePoAm
Now night walks down the garden path. Ghosts. Winifred Adams Burr. FiSC
Now not a window small or big. For Christmas. Rachel Field. ChBR; GaP
Now, now the fight's done, and the great god of war. Song. Nathaniel Lee. *Fr.* Theodosius; or, The Force of Love. PeRV
Now, now the sun is fled. Drinking Song. William Cartwright. *Fr.* The Royal Slave. SeCL
Now, now, the world. Love: Two Vignettes, II. Robert Penn Warren. MeWo
Now, now's the time so oft by truth. An Epithalamie to Sir Thomas Southwell and His Lady. Robert Herrick. HW
Now, O Lord, please lend me thine ear. The Cowman's Prayer. *Unknown.* CoSo
Now o'er the topmost pine. Morning. Samuel Waddington. OBVV
Now, of all the trees by the king's highway. Aunt Mary. Robert Stephen Hawker. JKCP; OHIP
Now of my life each gay and greener year. The Jealous Enemy. Petrarch. Sonnets to Laura: to Laura in Death, XLVII. LiTW
Now of that long pursuit. Our God Finds Us. Francis Thompson. *Fr.* The Hound of Heaven. BoC; FaChP
Now of that vision I, bereaven. Grace of the Way. Francis Thompson. MoAB; MoBrPo
Now of the conqueror this isle had Brutain unto name. William Warner. *Fr.* Albion's England. ReIE
Now, on a sudden, I know it, the secret, the secret of life. Revealed. Harry Lyman Koopman. AA
Now on the shining/ back breaking water. Icarus. Kendrick Smithyman. AnNZ
Now on the verge of spring the icy silver leaf. Return to Spring. Florence Ripley Mastin. GoYe
Now once again the Christ keeps watch beside. New Gethsemane. Hazel M. Kerr. ChIP
Now once again the gloomy scene explore. The Pauper's Funeral. George Crabbe. *Fr.* The Village. FaBoEn; OBNC
Now once there was a wooden fence. The Wooden Fence. Christian Morgenstern. LiTW
Now once upon a time the King of Astrakhan, at that. The Lacquer Liquor Locker. David McCord. FiBHP; InMe
Now one and all, you roses. A Wood Song. Ralph Hodgson. GoJo; HBV
Now orange blossoms filigree. Ain't Nature Commonplace! Arthur Guiterman. FiBHP; InMe
Now Our Meetings Over, *with music.* *Unknown.* ABF
Now over the path. The Odyssey of a Snail. Federico García Lorca. FIW
Now Philippa Is Gone. Anne Ridler. FaBoTw
Now ponder well, you parents dear. The Babes [*or* Children] in the Wood[s]. *Unknown.* EnSB; HBV; HBVY; OBB; OnSP; OTPC (1923 ed.)
Now, poor Rufus he has come to town. Rufus's Mare. George Calhoun. ShS
Now poor Tom Dunstan's cold. Tom Dunstan: or, The Politician. Robert Buchanan. HBV; PoFr
"Now, pray, where are you going, child?" said Meet-on-the-Road. Meet-on-the-Road. *Unknown.* PoMS
Now put aside the flute; sing no sweet air. Consummation. *Unknown.* UnTE
Now quenched each midnight window is. Now unimpeded. The Single Woman. Frances Cornford. ELU
Now rede me, dear mither, a sonsy rede. The Mer-Man and Marstig's Daughter. *Unknown.* AWP; JAWP; WBP
Now rest for evermore, my weary heart! A sè stesso. Giacomo Leopardi. AWP; JAWP; WBP
Now Robin Hood, Will Scadlock and Little John. Robin Hood and the Prince of Aragon. *Unknown.* ESPB
Now, rocking horse! rocking horse! where shall we go? Through

Nurseryland. *Unknown.* BoTP
Now St. Joseph's cottage stood. A Legend of Cherries. Charles Dalmon. HBMV; TSW
"Now say," he said, "were it not worse indeed." Dante. *Fr.* Divina Commedia: Paradiso. PoFr
Now science is a dandy thing—explaining, as it can. Folks, I Give You Science! Al Graham. WhC
Now secretness dies of the open. For the Nightly Ascent of the Hunter Orion over a Forest Clearing. James Dickey. TwCP
Now see the shaper breath and blow. The Glassblower. Geoffrey Johnson. NYTB
Now Serena be not coy. To His Love When He Had Obtained Her. Sir Walter Ralegh. FCP
Now seven days from land the gulls still wheel. Transport. William Meredith. WaP
Now shall I walk. The Best Friend. W. H. Davies. OBMV
Now shall the body. The Cloud of Unknowing. Philip Murray. NePoAm-2
Now shall we see, that nature hath no end. George Chapman. *Fr.* Bussy d'Ambois, V, ii. PoEL-2
Now she burnes as well as I. Song: To Her Againe, She Burning in a Feaver. Thomas Carew. AnAnS-2; SeCP
Now She Is Like the White Tree-Rose. C. Day Lewis. *Fr.* From Feathers to Iron. CMoP; FaBoTw; MoBrPo
Now she will lean away to fold. A Girl in a Window. James Wright. ErPo
Now shout into my dream. These trumpets snored. Farewell in a Dream. Stephen Spender. MoAB; MoBrPo
Now show thy joy, frolic in angels' sight. Leviathan. Jay Macpherson. MoCV
Now Silent Falls. Walter de la Mare. SiSw
"Now since mine even is come at last." The Ride to the Lady. Helen Gray Cone. AA
Now sit thee down, Melpomene. A Sonnet upon the Pitiful Burning of the Globe Playhouse in London. *Unknown.* TuPP
Now, sitting by her side, worn out with weeping. The Dream of the World without Death. Robert Buchanan. *Fr.* The Book of Orm. VA
Now skrinketh rose and lilye-flour. The Penitent Hopes in Mary. *Unknown.* MeEL
Now, skulls, rise from the hills, your hour is come. The Last Day. Daniel Sargent. CAW
Now Sleep and Take Thy Rest. Fernando de Rojas, *tr. fr. Spanish by* James Mabbe. *Fr.* Celestina. SeCL
Now, Sleep, Bind Fast. George Chapman. *Fr.* The Masque of the Middle Temple and Lincoln's Inn. TuPP
(Bridal Song.) ElL
("Now sleep, bind fast the flood of air.") LO
Now sleep the mountain-summits, sleep the glens. Vesper. Alcman. OA
Now Sleeps the Crimson Petal [Now the White]. Tennyson. *Fr.* The Princess, Pt. VII. AnFE; AtBAP; BoLiVe; BWP; CABA; CaFP; CBEP; CBV; ChER; ChTr; DiPo; ELP; EnL; EnLi-2; EPN; FiP; GTBS-D; GTBS-P; ILP; MaPo; MBW-2; MeWo; NoP; OBNC; OBVV; PAn; PoAn; PoE; PoEL-5; PoIE; PoFS; PoVP; ShBV-3; StP; TreFT; TrGrPo; UnTE; ViBoPo; ViPo; ViPP
(Song: "Now sleeps the crimson petal.") ExPo; FaBoBe; LoBV; NeHB
(Songs from "The Princess.") OAEP; SeCeV
(Summer Night.) OBEV; SeCePo; UnPo (1st ed.); WePo
Now Sleeps the Gorge. Alistair Campbell. AnNZ
Now Sleeps the Lord. Margaret L. Woods. StJW
Now so high,/ Now so low. The Swing. Mary I. Osborn. BoTP
Now, solitary, and in pensive guise. James Thomson. *Fr.* The Seasons: Winter. FaBoEn
Now some may drink old vintage wine. Early Morning Meadow Song. Charles Dalmon. ALV; CH; HBMV
Now, sometimes in my sorrow shut. In Memoriam A. H. H., XXIII. Tennyson. EnLi-2; EPN; OBEV (1st ed.); TOP; ViPo; VP
Now south and south and south the mallard heads. The North Sea Undertaker's Complaint. Robert Lowell. NePoEA; NoP; PIA; PoeP
Now speech is very curious. Words. Nancy Byrd Turner. TSW
Now Spring brings back the tepid breeze. Spring. Catullus. PoPl
Now Springs the Spray. *Unknown.* MeEV, *mod. vers. by* Mabel Van Duzee
(Now Sprinkes the Spray, *Middle English vers.*) AtBAP; PoEL-1
(Singing Maid, The.) MeEL
Now stamp the Lord's Prayer on a grain of rice. Altarwise by Owl-Light, VII. Dylan Thomas. CoBMV; GTBS-W; LiTM; MaSP; Sonn
Now stands our love on that still verge of day. Sonnets, XX. James Agee. MAP; MoAmPo
Now, starflake frozen on the windowpane. Moment. Howard Nemerov. PoDB
Now stood Eliza on the wood-crown'd height. Eliza. Erasmus Darwin. PaPo
Now stoops the sun, and dies day's cheerful light. The Gauls Sacrifice Their Prisoners. C. M. Doughty. *Fr.* The Dawn in Britain. FaBoTw
Now stop your noses, readers, all and some. Og and Doeg. Dryden. *Fr.* Absalom and Achitophel, Pt. II. FiP; PeRV
Now Strike Your Sailes Ye Jolly Mariners! Spenser. *Fr.* The Faerie Queene, I, 12, *and* II, 6. EtS
Now, suddenly, the table rocks, a bell. Séance. William Abrahams. NYBP
Now summer finds her perfect prime. Heaven, O Lord, I Cannot Lose. Edna Dean Proctor. AA
Now sunk the sun, now twilight sunk, and night. Night. John Brown. OBEC
Now sure, within this twelve-month past. Love and Life. Abraham Cowley. *Fr.* The Mistress. SeEP
Now swarthy Summer, by rude health embrowned. Summer Images. John Clare. OBNC
Now, Sym was a Glug; and 'tis mentioned so. The Growth of Sym. C. J. Dennis. ACV
Now take your fill of love and glee. A Double Ballad of Good Counsel. Villon. AWP
Now tell us what 'twas all about. Robert Southey. *Fr.* The Battle of Blenheim. OQP
Now Thank We All Our God. Martin Rinkart, *tr. fr. German by* Catherine Winkworth. FaChP; TreFS
Now that a letter gives me ground at last. The Beach Head. Thom Gunn. ToPo
Now That Can Never Be Done. Sister Maris Stella. GoBC
Now that compelling silver throat. Haydn: The Horn. Daniel Berrigan. TwAmPo
Now that day doth end. At Day's End. *Unknown.* TreFT
Now that Fate is dead and gone. Song. Edith Sitwell. MoAB; MoBrPo (1950 ed.); NeMA
Now That Fierce Few. E. E. Cummings. NoP
Now That I Am Clean Again. Stephen Vincent Benét. MemP
Now that I am dressed I'll go. Peadar Og Goes Courting. James Stephens. BoLP; WhC
Now that I have cooled to you. Postlude. William Carlos Williams. AnAmPo; NP
Now that I have decided I must go. The Missionary. Sister Mary Eleanore. WHL
Now that I have your face by heart, I look. Song for the Last Act. Louise Bogan. AmLP; NePoAm; NYBP
Now that I know how passion. Knowledge. Louise Bogan. HBMV
Now that I, tying thy glass mask tightly. The Laboratory; Ancien Régime. Robert Browning. ATP; BoLiVe; OBEV (new ed.); OBVV; PoFS; PoVP; ShBV-3; ViPo; ViPP; YT
Now that I'm old. Winter. Issa. OnPM
Now that I'm old I do not venture far. An Old Cat Meditates. Margaret E. Bruner. CIV
Now that it doesn't matter so much any longer. This Way Out. Margaret Fishback. ALV
Now that it is moonlight, I must be mournful. Trinket. Winifred Welles. NP
Now that my seagoing self-possession wavers. Autobiography. Charles Causley. LiTM (1970 ed.); Sonn
Now that no shrill hunting horn. An Old Dog. Celia Duffin. PCD
Now that of absence the most irksome night. Astrophel and Stella, LXXXIX. Sir Philip Sidney. FCP; SiPS
Now that our hero has come back to us. On Seeing Larry Rivers' "Washington Crossing the Delaware" at the Museum of Modern Art. Frank O'Hara. FRC
Now that our love has drifted. Finis. Waring Cuney. AmNP; BANP; PoNe

Now that summer's ripen'd bloom. A Landscape. John Cunningham. CEP
Now that the April of your youth adorns. Ditty in Imitation of the Spanish. Lord Herbert of Cherbury. AnAnS-2; EIL; OBS; SeEP
Now that the ashen rain of gummy April. A Hyacinth for Edith. A. J. M. Smith. TwCaPo
Now that the barbarians have got as far as Picra. Translation. Roy Fuller. ChMP
Now that the chestnut candles burn. Elegy for a Mis-spent Youth. Jon Stallworthy. MeWo
Now that the daylight fills the sky. Morning Prayer. *Unknown.* FaChP
Now that the evening gathers up the day. These Images Remain. May Sarton. MoLP
Now That the Flowers. Cullen Jones. GoYe
Now that the flush of summer is gone. The Kernel. Frank Kendon. MoBrPo (1942 ed.)
Now that the hearth is crowned with smiling fire. Another Birthday. Ben Jonson. WiR
Now that the hills are all a-glow. Detour—Gypsy Trail Closed. Sara Henderson Hay *and* Raymond Holden. StaSt
Now that the hunger born of spring. Second Blossoming. Ruth Lechlitner. NYTB
Now that the midd day heate doth scorch my shame. Sonnet. William Alabaster. AnAnS-1; MeP
Now that the others are gone, all of them, forever. Tomorrow. Kenneth Fearing. CMoP
Now that the red glare of thy fall is blown. Francis Thompson. *Fr.* Ode to the Setting Sun. OBNC
Now that the spring hath filled our veins. A Round. William Browne. ViBoPo
Now that the tower is standing. The Tower. Agnes Lee. NP
Now that the Truth Is Tried. Thomas Whythorne. EIL
Now that the Village-Reverence doth lye hid. A New-Years-Gift to Brian Lord Bishop of Sarum. William Cartwright. MePo
Now That the Winter's Gone. Thomas Carew. BoTP; EG; OTPC; PoSC
(Spring, The.) AnAnS-2; CavP; FaBoEn; GN; PoE; PoEL-3; PoFS; PoIE; PoSa; RIS; SCEP-2; SeCV-1; TrGrPo; WiR
Now that the world is all in a maze [*or* amaze]. The Unconcerned. Thomas Flatman. CEP; FaBoCh; PeRV
Now that the world of snow. In Early Spring. Richard Aldridge. NYTB
Now that the young buds are tipped with a falling sun. Early Spring. Sidney Keyes. FaBoMo; MoBrPo (1962 ed.)
Now that these wings to speed my wish ascend. The Philosophic Flight [*or* Spurning the Earth]. Giordano Bruno. AWP; OnPM; PoFr
Now that they've got it settled whose I be. The Pauper Witch of Grafton. Robert Frost. *Fr.* Two Witches. CMoP; CrMA; MWA-2
Now that we're almost settled in our house. In Memory of Major Robert Gregory. W. B. Yeats. AnIL; DiPo; OAEP (2d ed.); PAn; PoFS
Now that we've done our best and worst, and parted. The Busy Heart. Rupert Brooke. HBV; MemP; MoBrPo
Now That You Are Gone. J. Patrick Walsh. JKCP (1955 ed.)
Now that you have freely given me leave to love. To a Lady That Desired I Would Love Her. Thomas Carew. CavP
Now that you lie. Before Sleep. Anne Ridler. NeBP
Now that you would leave me. Love-Faith. Harry Kemp. HBMV
Now the ambassadors have gone, refusing. Meditation. Roy Fuller. FaBoMo
Now the beautiful business of summer is over. Birthday. Jean Starr Untermeyer. MAP; MoAmPo (1942 ed.)
Now, the boys and the girls went out huckleberry hunting. Huckleberry Hunting. *Unknown.* ShS
Now the bright crocus flames, and now. In the Spring. Meleager, *tr. by* Andrew Lang. AWP; JAWP; WBP
Now the bright morning-star, day's harbinger. Song on May Morning [*or* On May Morning]. Milton. BoLiVe; BoNaP; CH; DD; ExPo; GN; HBV; HBVY; NoP; OTD; OTPC; PoPl; PoRL; RG; TrGrPo; YeAr
Now the *Chesapeake* so bold. The *Shannon* and the *Chesapeake.* *Unknown.* AmSS
Now the cool twilight, glowing. Evening. Harold Monro. FaBoTw
Now the cormorants are coming in to roost. Shag Rookery. William Hart-Smith. AnNZ
Now the Day Is Over. Sabine Baring-Gould. MaRV; OTPC; PCH, 5 *sts.*
(Child's Evening Hymn.) SoP; VA; WGRP
(For Evening.) TreFT
(Hymn: "Now the day is over.") NBM
(Night.) ThGo
Now the dead past seems vividly alive. Heritage. Claude McKay. PoNe
Now the descending triumph stops its flight. The Day of Judgement. David Young. OxBoCh
Now the dreary night is done. Morning Hymn. Cecil Frances Alexander. OTPC
Now the dreary winter's over. Spring Song. Nahum. TrJP
Now the drowsy sunshine. Evening. Harry Behn. TiPo (1959 ed.)
Now the ears, so I always had thunk. The Ears. Anthony Euwer. *Fr.* The Limeratomy. HBMV
Now the Earth, the Skies, the Air. *Unknown.* EIL
Now the first silly bastard he got in an aeroplane. Ops in a Wimpey. *Unknown.* CoMu
Now the Four-way Lodge is opened, now the Hunting Winds are loose. The Feet of the Young Men. Kipling. GBV; OtMeF; PoRL
Now the frog, all lean and weak. The Sweet o' the Year. George Meredith. BoNaP
Now the frontiers are all closed. Ultimatum. Peggy Pond Church. TRV
Now the frosty stars are gone. Ariel in the Cloven Pine. Bayard Taylor. AA
Now the full-throated daffodils. From Feathers to Iron. C. Day Lewis. ViBoPo
Now the furnaces are out. Piper, Play. John Davidson. TOP
Now the golden fields of sunset rose on rose to me-ward fall. Day and Dark. George Cabot Lodge. AnAmPo; AnFE; APA; CoAnAm
Now the golden morn aloft. Ode on the Pleasure Arising from Vicissitude. Thomas Gray. CEP; EiCP; GTBS; GTBS-D; GTBS-P; GTBS-W; GTSE; GTSL; OBEC; PeER
Now the good man's away from home. Sally Sweetbread. Henry Carey. CoMu
Now the great flower of the world. Prothalamium. Edith Sitwell. HW
Now the heart sings with all its thousand voices. The Gateway. A. D. Hope. ErPo; UnTE
Now the Hungry Lion Roars. Shakespeare. *Fr.* A Midsummer Night's Dream, V, ii. AnFE; AtBAP; CH; ChTr; CTC; EG; EIL; EnRePo; FIW; LiTB; LiTG; OBSC; PAn; PIA; SeCeV; ViBoPo
(Epilogue.) LoBV
(Fairy Blessing, The.) OxBoLi
(Fairy Songs.) TrGrPo
(Lion of Winter, The.) WiR
(Puck Speaks.) ThWaDe
(Puck's Song.) BoLiVe; MoShBr; SiCE
(Song of Robin Goodfellow, A.) BoW
Now the ice lays its smooth claws on the sill. Scotland's Winter. Edwin Muir. OxBS
Now the joys of the road are chiefly these. The Joys of the Road. Bliss Carman. HBV; HBVY; OBVV; TSW
Now the Laborer's Task Is O'er. John Lodge Ellerton. BLPA; HBV; MaRV, *abr.*; TreFS; WGRP
Now the last day of many days. The Recollection [*or* To Jane]. Shelley. ChER; EPN; GTBS; GTBS-D; GTBS-P; GTBS-W; GTSE; GTSL; MBW-2; NoP; OBNC; OBRV
Now the last drop, both sweet and fierce. Middle-Age. Emily B. C. Jones. HBMV
Now the last light of amber day is dying. Adoration. David Morton. MaRV
Now the late fruits are in. For a Wine Festival. Vernon Watkins. NYTB
Now the Leaves Are Falling Fast. W. H. Auden. CMoP; CoBMV; StP
Now the light o' the west is a-turn'd to gloom. Evenen in the Village. William Barnes. GTSE
Now the little rivers go. Winter Streams. Bliss Carman. YeAr
Now the long blade of the sun, lying. Thebes of the Seven Gates. Sophocles. *Fr.* Antigone. WaaP

Now, the Lord made the bee and the bee did make the honey. Swansea Town. *Unknown.* ShS
Now the Lusty Spring. John Fletcher. *See* Love's Emblems.
Now the man has a child. *Unknown, tr. fr. Japanese by* Geoffrey Bownas *and* Anthony Thwaite. FIW
Now the meadow drinks. Spel V. Robert Kelly. *Fr.* Thor's Thrush. YAP
Now the midwinter grind. Middle Age. Robert Lowell. FRC; PoeP
Now the moisty wood discloses. Spring Morning. Frances Cornford. BoTP
Now the Most High Is Born. James Ryman. MeEL
Now the New Year reviving old desires. The New Year. Omar Khayyám, *tr. by* Edward Fitzgerald. *Fr.* The Rubáiyát. OnPM
Now the Noisy Winds are Still. Mary Mapes Dodge. OTD; PRWS; YeAr
Now the North wind ceases. Tardy Spring. George Meredith. OBEV (1st ed.)
Now the old barns limber. Autumn Morning. Frances Frost. RePo
Now the plains come to adore the mountain wall. Colorado. Robert Fitzgerald. MoPo
Now the quietude of earth. The Hermit. "Æ." BEL; PoVP
Now the rich cherry whose sleek wood. Country Summer. Léonie Adams. AnEnPo; ATP (1953 ed.); BoLiVe (1939 ed.); GoJo; LiTM; MAP; MoAB; MoAmPo; MoPo; MoVE; TrGrPo; TwAmPo; ViBoPo (1958 ed.)
Now the rite is duly done. The Newly-wedded. Winthrop Mackworth Praed. HBV; MaRV; VA
Now the shiades o' the elems da stratch muore an muore. Evening, and Maidens. William Barnes. OBEV (new ed.); OBVV
Now the small birds come to feast. Winter Feast. Frances Frost. YeAr
Now the sneeze is a joy-vent, I s'pose. The Sneeze. Anthony Euwer. *Fr.* The Limeratomy. HBMV
Now the snow is vanished clean. Québec May. Earle Birney. WHW
Now the stock have started dying, for the Lord has sent a drought. Song of the Artesian Water. A. B. Paterson. ACV
Now the stone house on the lake front is finished. A Fence. Carl Sandburg. AmP; InP
Now the storm begins to lower. The Fatal Sisters. Thomas Gray. BEL; CEP; CoBE; EiCP; EiPP; EnPE; EnRP; NoP; OAEP; PeER
Now the sudden shower's done. Thunder Pools. Robert P. Tristram Coffin. LOW
Now the sun again, like a bloody convict. The Rising Sun. Lawrence Durrell. *Fr.* Eight Aspects of Melissa. NeBP
Now the sun's gane out o' sight. Up in the Air. Allan Ramsay. CEP
Now the swift rot of the flesh is over. My Sister. Hyam Plutzik. FiMAP
Now the thing the Negro has got to do. View from the Corner. Samuel Allen. BP
Now the time comes when you are bored with Antiquity. Zone. Guillaume Apollinaire. OnHM
Now, the times are hard and the wages low. Time for Us to Leave Her. *Unknown.* ShS
Now the trouble with setting down a: written calypso. Calypsomania. Anthony Brode. FiBHP
Now the white-buskined lamb. At Bungendore. James McAuley. PoAu-2
Now the Widow McGee and Larrie O'Dee. Larrie O'Dee. William W. Fink. BOHV; HBV; OTPC (1946 ed.)
Now the wild bees that hive in the rocks. The Brown Bear. Mary Austin. FaPON; MBP; OTPC (1946 ed.); PoSC; UTS; WaKn
Now the winds are all composure. Spring. Christopher Smart. *Fr.* St. Philip and St. James. LoBV; OBEC
Now the Winter's Come to Stay. *Unknown.* IHA
Now the wood, in sun and leisure. The Bargain. Neidhart von Reuental. LiTW
Now, the wry Rosenbloom is dead. Cortège for Rosenbloom. Wallace Stevens. TwAmPo
Now Thebes stood in good estate, now Cadmus might thou say. Acteon. Ovid. *Fr.* Metamorphoses. CTC
Now then, shipmates, come gather and join in my ditty. The *Cumberland's* Crew. *Unknown.* ShS
Now there is frost upon the hill. Where It Is Winter. George O'Neil. HBMV
Now there is none of the living who can remember. Epitaph for a Concord Boy. Stanley Young. WaKn
Now There Is Nothing Left. L. A. MacKay. CaP; PeCV
Now there shall be a new song and a new star. To Mother—in Heaven. Bennett Weaver. OQP
Now they are gone with all their songs and sins. Sonnet. John Masefield. *Fr.* Sonnets ("Like bones"). InP
Now they are resting. Fine Work with Pitch and Copper. William Carlos Williams. NoP; OxBA
Now they call me Hanging Johnny. Hanging Johnny. *Unknown.* ShS
Now they have come, those afternoons in November. November Afternoons. Sister Mary Madeleva. GoBC
Now they have two cars to clean. Do It Yrself. Larry Eigner. NeAP
Now think on't, Nell the glover fair. Ballade of the Fair Helm-Maker. Villon. UnTE
Now this is my first counsel. Counsels of Sigrdrifa. *Unknown.* *Fr.* The Elder Edda. AWP
Now this is new: that I (habitué). First Day of Teaching. Bonaro W. Overstreet. TrPWD
Now this is the Law of the Jungle—as old and as true as the sky. The Law of the Jungle. Kipling. *Fr.* The Second Jungle Book. BoChLi; LiTB; OA; PoEL-5; PoVP; ShBV-1; VA
Now this Ophelia was a wiser woman. Spouse. Witter Bynner. AnFE; CoAnAm
Now those that are low spirited I hope won't think it wrong. A New Hunting Song. *Unknown.* CoMu
Now thou hast loved [*or* lov'd] me one whole day. Woman's Constancy. John Donne. AnAnS-1; EnLit; LiTL; MaMe; MBW-1; NoP; PoE; PoeP; PoFS; ReIE; SCEP-1; SeCV-1; SeEP; TuPP
Now thought seeks shelter, lest the heart melt. Recovery. F. R. Scott. CaP
Now Thrice Welcome Christmas. *Unknown.* OHIP
Now Through Night's Caressing Grip. W. H. Auden. PoRA
Now, through the dusk. The World of Dream. Walter de la Mare. GaP
Now Time's Andromeda on this rock rude. Andromeda. Gerard Manley Hopkins. FaBoMo; LiTB
Now to attune my dull soul, if I can. Bleue Maison. Edmund Blunden. BrPo
Now to be clean he must abandon himself. The Swan Bathing. Ruth Pitter. MoBrPo
Now to great Britain we must make our way. Of England, and of Its Marvels. Fazio degli Uberti. AWP; JAWP; WBP
Now to th'ascent of that steep savage hill. Satan Journeys to the Garden of Eden. Milton. *Fr.* Paradise Lost, IV. ChTr
Now Tomlinson gave up the ghost in his house in Berkeley Square. Tomlinson. Kipling. BeLS; OtMeF; PoVP
Now too nigh/ Th' archangel stood. Milton. *Fr.* Paradise Lost, XII. PoIE
Now touch the air softly. A Pavane for the Nursery. William Jay Smith. BoLP; GoJo; MoAmPo (1962 ed.); NePoAm-2; PoSC
Now tow'rd the *Hunter's* gloomy sides we came. The Hospital Prison Ship. Philip Freneau. The British Prison Ship, III. AmPP (5th ed.)
Now trees are weedy mazes, upright, still. Larch Hill. Leslie Daiken. OnYI
Now trouble comes between the forest's selves. Russian New Year. Bill Berkson. ANYP
Now turne again my theme, thou jolly swayne. The Tale of Calidore. Spenser. *Fr.* The Faerie Queene. StP
Now Turnus rolls aloof o'er empty plains. The Death of Turnus. Vergil. *Fr.* The Aeneid, XII. WoL
Now, 'twas twenty-five or thirty years since Jack first saw the light. Jack Was Every Inch a Sailor. *Unknown.* WHW
Now twenty springs had cloath'd the park with green. The Toilette; a Town Eclogue. John Gay. CEP
Now two have met, now two have met. The Great Grey Water. E. J. Brady. BoAu
Now, until the break of day. Fairy Songs. Shakespeare. *Fr.* A Midsummer Night's Dream, V, ii. TrGrPo
Now unto Him who brought His people forth. Benediction. Stephen Phillips. *Fr.* Herod. MaRV
Now, upon Syria's land of roses. A Syrian Evening. Thomas Moore. *Fr.* Lalla Rookh. PeER

Now upon this piteous year. The Stranger. Jean Garrigue. LiTA; LiTM; TwCP
Now Venus is an evening star. Waiting. Hilary Corke. ErPo
Now very quietly, and rather mournfully. A House. J. C. Squire. NV
Now wait till I put on my gospel shoes. If I Got My Ticket, Can I Ride? *Unknown.* OuSiCo
Now wanderer in hostile forests, exile. Flower of Exile. Max Dunn. BoAV
Now War Is All the World About. Sir Richard Fanshawe. *Fr.* Il Pastor Fido. LoBV
(Ode, An, upon Occasion of His Majesties [*or* Majesty's] Proclamation in the Year 1630.) BoPe; MePo; OBS
Now warm with ministerial ire. The Liberty Pole. John Trumbull. *Fr.* M'Fingal, III. AmPP (3d ed.)
Now wat ye wha I met yestreen. The Young Laird and Edinburgh Katy. Allan Ramsay. CEP; EiPP
Now we are back to normal, now the mind is. Louis MacNeice. *Fr.* Autumn Journal. CMoP
Now we are civilized, the old men die. Old Men's Ward. Elma Dean. GoYe
Now we are left out. Funeral Song. *Unknown.* PeSA
Now We Are Sick. J. B. Morton. PV
Now we begin another day together. Prayer at Dawn. Edwin McNeill Poteat. TrPWD
Now we enter a strange world, where the Hessian Christmas. After the Industrial Revolution. Robert Bly. CoAP
Now we have always with us men—these men! Memo. Hildegarde Flanner. NYBP
Now we remember all: the wild pear-tree. Pictures by Vuillard. Adrienne Rich. TwAmPo
Now weave the winds to music of June's lyre. June. Theodore Harding Rand. CaP
Now Welcome Summer. Chaucer. *See* Roundel, A: "Now welcom, somer. . ."
Now welcome, welcome, baby-boy, unto a mother's fears. The Irish Mother in the Penal Days. John Banim. AnIV
Now wend we to the Palmalle. Domine, Quo Vadis? *Unknown.* ACP; CAW
Now we're afloat upon the tropic sea. Tropical Weather. Epes Sargent. EtS
Now we're warping her into the docks. Galloping Randy Dandy O! *Unknown.* SoAmSa
Now westward Sol had spent the richest beams. Music's Duel. Richard Crashaw. CLwM; CoBE; GoTL; MaMe; OBS; SCEP-1; SeCP; SeCV-1; SeEP
Now what do you think. *Unknown.* OxNR; SiTL
Now what in the world shall we dioux. The Sioux. Eugene Field. FiBHP; GoJo
Now What Is Love. Sir Walter Ralegh. *See* Description of Love, A.
Now what is love I will thee tell. Thomas Heywood. *Fr.* The Rape of Lucrece. LO
Now, what news on the Rialto? Shylock's Defense. Shakespeare. *Fr.* The Merchant of Venice, III, i. TreFS
Now what you all know about this? Stagolee (A *vers.*). *Unknown.* ViBoFo
Now when drowning imagination clutches. Word over All. C. Day Lewis. OAEP (2d ed.)
Now when I could not find the road. The Shepherd's Hut. Andrew Young. ThWaDe
Now when I have thrust my body. To Forget Me. Theodore Weiss. CoAP
Now when I sleep the thrush breaks through my dreams. A Dream in Early Spring. Fredegond Shove. MoVE
Now when I stand upon the stair alone. The Child upon the Stair. Carolyn Hall. TSW
Now when Jesus was born in Bethlehem of Judea. The Visit of the Wise Men. St. Matthew, Bible, *N.T.* ChrBoLe
Now, when my roses are half buds, half flowers. The Dragonfly. W. H. Davies. BoPe
Now When So Much Has Passed. George Seferis, *tr. fr. Modern Greek by* Bernard Spencer *and* Nanos Valaoritis. LiTW
Now when the blackboard has explained. The Child's Power of Wonder. P. K. Saha. ACV
Now, when the cheerless empire of the sky. James Thomson. *Fr.* The Seasons: Winter. OxBS
Now when the lumber camp is done. Send Her On Along. *Unknown.* IHA
Now when the rosy fingered morning faire. Spenser. *Fr.* The Faerie Queene, I. BoLiVe
Now, when the smoking ruins smoulder low. To J. S. Bach. Michael Thwaites. MoRP
Now when they came to the bright running river. Nausicaa. Homer. *Fr.* The Odyssey, VI. LiTW
Now where are all the gay raftsmen? The Raftsmen. *Unknown.* IHA
"Now where are ye goin,'" ses I, "wid the shawl." The Road. Patrick R. Chalmers. HBV
"Now, where are you going this beautiful day?" The Baby in the Basket. Emily Carter. SAS
Now whether folks are Methodists. That Radio Religion. William Ludlum. WBLP
Now, whether it were by peculiar grace. Wordsworth. *Fr.* Resolution and Independence. Par
Now, while amid those dainty downs and dales. To His Pandora, from England. Alexander Craig. Sonn; TuPP
Now, while our money is piping hot. The Merchantman [*or* Eclogue: The Merchantman]. John Davidson. OBVV; PoVP
Now while Rogero learns the arms and name. Angelica and the Ork. Ariosto. *Fr.* Orlando Furioso, X. OBSC
"Now, while she's changing," said the Dean. The Wedding Sermon. Coventry Patmore. *Fr.* The Angel in the House. PoVP
Now while the night her sable veil hath spread. William Drummond of Hawthornden. EG
Now while the solemn evening shadows sail. Swans. Wordsworth. *Fr.* An Evening Walk. OBEC
Now while the sunset offers. Santa Barbara Beach. Ridgely Torrence. HBMV
Now while the wind is up, I hear. Ghostly Reaper. Harold Vinal. FiSC
Now, while thou hast the wondrous power of word. The Gift of Speech. Sadi. *Fr.* The Gulistan. AWP; LiTW
"Now whither go ye?" Would that we did know. Our Poets' Breed. Luis Montoto y Rautenstrauch. CAW
Now who is he on earth that lives. Medieval Norman Songs, X. *Unknown, tr. by* John Addington Symonds. AWP
Now who will rise. A Question. P. T. Forsyth. OQP
Now why should I, who sneer and frown. He Visits a Hospital. Rolfe Humphries. AnAmPo
Now will I a lover be. The Combat. Thomas Stanley. AWP
Now will I tell you no more of their serving. *Unknown.* *Fr.* Sir Gawain and the Green Knight. YAT
Now will you stand for me, in this cool light. Love in the Museum. Adrienne Cecile Rich. NePoEA; NYBP
Now wilt me take for Jesus Sake. A Prayer. Katharine Tynan. OBVV
Now winds of winter glue. Upon New Year's Eve. Sir Arthur Quiller-Couch. OBVV
Now winter downs the dying of the year. At Year's-End [*or* Year's-End]. Richard Wilbur. CoAP; FiMAP; LiTM (rev. ed.); MiAP; NePA; NePoEA; NYBP; PoAn; PoIE
Now Winter melts beneath. Solvitur Acris Hiems. Francis Sylvester Mahony. IrPN
Now Winter Nights Enlarge. Thomas Campion. AnFE; AtBAP; BEL; ElL; ELP; EnLi-1 (1949 ed.); EnRePo; FlW; LoBV; NoP; OBSC; PG (1955 ed.); PoRA; QFR; SeCePo; SiCE; TuPP; ViBoPo; WoL
(Winter.) CLwM
(Winter Nights.) CBEP; OBEV
Now, winter's dolorous days are o'er, and through. Sonnet. Thomas Caulfield Irwin. IrPN
Now winter's winds are banished from the sky. Spring. Meleager. AWP; JAWP
Now wintry blasts have come again. Love Laughs at Winter. *Unknown.* UnTE
Now with a clean thread. The Spider. David McCord. MAP
Now with a general peace the world was blest. Dryden. *Fr.* Astraea. CEP
Now with a sigh November comes to the brooding land. Autumn in Carmel. George Sterling. HT
Now with drums. Light. Hermann Hagedorn. MoRP
Now with earth riven and a bloodied sun. We Shall Say. Miriam Allen deFord. GoYe
Now with gray hair begins defeat. Farewell to Town. Laurence Housman. HBMV

Now with the bells through the apple bloom. Wantage Bells. John Betjeman. WePo
Now with the coming in of the spring the days will stretch a bit. The County Mayo. Anthony Raftery, *tr. by* James Stephens. AnIL
Now with the slow revolving year. Two Old Lenten Rhymes, II. *Unknown.* WHL
Now with the springtime the days will grow longer. County Mayo. Anthony Raftery, *tr. by* Frank O'Connor. KiLC
Now with your head thrown back. I Tell of Another Young Death. Cesar Tiempo. TrJP
Now wolde I faine sum merthes make. Song for My Lady [*or* A Song in His Lady's Absence]. A. Godwhen. CH; EG; LO; MeEL; OxBoLi
Now would I tread my darkness down. When I Am Dead. Owen Dodson. Kal
Now would I weave her portrait out of all dim splendour. Portrait. Ezra Pound. OBVV
Now would to God swift ships had ne'er been made! Sopolis. Callimachus. AWP
Now Wu Tao-tzu, continuing his stroll. A Flight of Wild Geese. Harold Stewart. MoAuPo
"Now, yield thee, or by Him who made." Sir Walter Scott. *Fr.* The Lady of the Lake. OxBS
Now you are holding my skull in your hand. A Meditation. Richard Eberhart. FiMAP; LiTA
Now You Are in Your Country. Frank Kendon. POTE
Now you are nearer than my heart. Morning Song for a Lover. Howard Sergeant. ToPo
Now you are nodding in every well-bred garden. Daffodils. Gina Ballantyne. BoAu
Now you are one with us, you know our tears. To America, on Her First Sons Fallen in the Great War. E. M. Walker. PAH
Now you come again. Happiness of 6 A.M. Harvey Shapiro. NYBP
Now, you great stanza, you heroic mould. Single Sonnet. Louise Bogan. AnEnPo; Sonn
Now you have freely given me leave to love. To a Lady That Desired I Would Love Her. Thomas Carew. AnAnS-2; BWP; EP; LiTL; LoBV; MeLP; MePo; OBS; SCEP-2; SeCL; SeCV-1; SeEP
Now you have made a perfect new. Polemic. Anthony Ostroff. NYTB
Now you may have Him, Mary, they are done. Thirteenth Station. William A. Donaghy. *Fr.* The Stations of the Cross. ISi
Now You're Content. André Spire, *tr. fr. French by* Stanley Burnshaw. TrJP
Now you're married you must obey. *Unknown.* GoTP; RIS
Nowadays the mess is everywhere. The Survivors. Daryl Hine. TwCP
Nowe welcome, somor, with sonne softe. Welcome, Summer. Chaucer. *Fr.* The Parlement of Foules. MeEL
Nowel! nowel! nowel!/ Nowel! nowel! nowel! Man Exalted. *Unknown.* MeEL
Nowel! nowel! nowel!/ Sing we with mirth. Mary Is with Child. *Unknown.* MeEL
Nowell, Nowell. Robert Finch. TwCaPo
Nowell, nowell, nowell, nowell,/ Tydynges gode I thynke to telle. The Borys Hede That We Bryng Here [*or* A Christmas Carol]. *Unknown.* EnLit; YAT
Nowell sing we now all and some. Nowell Sing We. *Unknown.* ChTr
Nowhere. Floyce Alexander. QAH
Nowhere are we safe. Hymn Written after Jeremiah Preached to Me in a Dream. Owen Dodson. AmNP; Kal
Nowhere is one alone. Wood and Hill. Andrew Young. HaMV
Now's the time for mirth and play. For Saturday [*or* Hymn for Saturday *or* A Lark's Nest]. Christopher Smart. *Fr.* Hymns for the Amusement of Children. CBEP; EiCP; FaBoCh; LoGBV
Nox. Salvador Diaz Miron, *tr. fr. Spanish by* Samuel Beckett. HW
Nox Benigna. William Pember Reeves. AnNZ
Nox Est Perpetua. Marion Lochhead. LO
Nox Ignatiana. James J. Daly. CAW; JKCP
Nox Nocti Indicat Scientiam. William Habington. *Fr.* Castara, III. ACP; AnAnS-2; CAW; GoBC; GTSL; HBV; LoBV; MeLP; MePo; OBEV; OBS; PoFr; PoLi; SeCL
(When I Survey the Bright.) OxBoCh
Nox was lit by lux of Luna, The. Carmen Possum. *Unknown.* BLPA
Nuances of a Theme by Williams. Wallace Stevens. CMoP; LiTA
Nubia. Bayard Taylor. HBV
Nuclear wind, when wilt thou blow. Paul Dehn. *Fr.* A Leaden Treasury of English Verse. FiBHP
Nude. Harold Witt. ErPo
Nude Descending a Staircase. X. J. Kennedy. CoAP; NePoEA-2; PIA
Nude in a Fountain. Norman MacCaig. OxBS
Nude Kneeling in Sand. John Logan. ErPo
Nude Republic, The. John Perreault. ANYP
Nudging and thrusting to the light. Gideon at the Well. Geoffrey Hill. NePoEA
Nudities. André Spire, *tr. fr. French by* Jethro Bithell. AWP; ErPo; TrJP, *tr. by* Stanley Burnshaw
Nugatory. E. B. White. BOHV
Nugly Little Man, The. Marion St. John Webb. TVC
Nuit Blanche. Katherine Hoskins. NMP
Nuit Blanche; North End. Conrad Aiken. OxBA
Nulla Fides. Patrick Carey. SeEP
Nullum Stimulum Ignavis. Henry Parrot. SiCE
Numb, stiff, broken by no sleep. Night Thoughts over a Sick Child. Philip Levine. NePoEA-2
Number 5—December. David Henderson. BOLo
Numberless are the world's wonders, but none. Choral Ode. Sophocles. *Fr.* Antigone. LiTW
Numbers, *sels.* Bible, *O.T.*
Balaam's Blessing, XXIV: 5-9. TrGrPo
Benediction, VI: 24-26. TrGrPo
(Blessing, A,) ThGo
(Blessing of the Priests.) TrJP
Song of the Well, XXI: 17-18. TrJP
Numbers. Agnes Lee. NP
Numbers, The. Joel Oppenheimer. CoPo
Numbers, *sels.* Constantino Suasnavar, *tr. fr. Spanish by* Muna Lee.
"I have lost my shoes," XXVI. FaPON
"I look up hotels," XXX. OnPM
Numbers and Faces, *sel.* W. H. Auden.
"Kingdom of Number is all boundaries, The." ImOP
Numerella Shore, The. "Cockatoo Jack." PoAu-1
Numerous host of dreaming saints succeed, A. The Duke of Buckingham. Dryden. *Fr.* Absalom and Achitophel, Pt. I. FaBoEn
Nun, The. Leigh Hunt. ALV; BOHV; HBV; InMe; OBRV; OBVV
(If You Be a Nun.) PG (1945 ed.)
Nun, The. Edward Moore. WaPE
Nun, The. Arthur Symons. BrPo
Nun Snow. Alfred Kreymborg. AnFE; APA; CoAnAm; MAPA; TwAmPo
Nun Speaks to Mary, A. Sister Mary Madeleva. ISi
Nun Takes the Veil, A. Gerard Manley Hopkins. *See* Heaven-Haven.
Nun to Mary, Virgin, A. Sister Mary St. Virginia. ISi
Nunaptigne . . .In our land—ahe, ahe, ee, ee, iee. The Wind Has Wings. *Unknown.* WHW
Nunc Dimittis, The. St. Luke, II: 29-32, Bible, *N.T.* WGRP; WHL
Nunc Gaudet Maria. *Unknown.* ISi
Nunc Scio, Quid Sit Amor. L. A. MacKay. OBCV
Nuns at Eve. John Malcolm Brinnin. MoAB; TwCP
Nuns Fret Not at Their Convent's Narrow Room. Wordsworth. BEL; CABA; CoBE; EnL; EnRP; EPN; ILP; MBW-2; NoP; OAEP; PoPo; PP; Sonn; TOP
(Prefatory Sonnet.) OBRV
(Sonnet: "Nuns fret not at their convent's narrow room.") OBEV; ViBoPo
Nuns, his nieces, bring the priest in the next. A Far Cry after a Close Call. Richard Howard. NYBP
Nuns in the Wind. Muriel Rukeyser. FiMAP
Nuns of the Perpetual Adoration. Ernest Dowson. PoVP; TOP; ViPP
Nun's Priest's Tale, The. Chaucer. *Fr.* The Canterbury Tales. AnFE; AtBAP; BEL; CABL; CoBE; EnL, *mod. by* Theodore Morrison; EnLi-1; MaPo; MBW-1; NoP; OAEP; OuHeWo, *mod. by* J. U. Nicolson; PoEL-1; SeCeV; StP;

Nun's (continued)
TOP, *abr.*; TrGrPo, *orig., with mod. vers. by* Frank Ernest Hill
Sels.
Murder Will Out. MyFE
Poor Widow's Cock, The, 6 *ll.* MyFE
"There lived, as authors tell, in days of yore," *mod. by* Dryden. MBW-1
"This Chauntecleer stood hye up-on his toos." FiP
Nu-numma-kwiten formerly sang. The Song of Nu-Numma-Kwiten. *Unknown.* PeSA
Nuptiae post Nummos. Henry Parrot. SiCE; TuPP
Nuptial. Mary Fabyan Windeatt. JKCP (1955 ed.)
Nuptial Eve, A. Sydney Dobell. OBNC; VA
Ballad of Keith of Ravelston, The, *sel.* HBV; OBEV; OBVV; TOP
(Keith of Ravelston.) CH; GTBS
("Ravelston, Ravelston," 3 *sts.*) LO
Nuptial Hymn. Henry Peacham. *Fr.* The Period of Mourning. EIL
Nuptial Sleep. Dante Gabriel Rossetti. The House of Life, VI (A). LoBV; MaVP; ViPo; ViPP; VP
Nuptial Song. Lord De Tabley. GTBS-P; OBVV; PeVV
Nuptial Song. Henricus Selyns. SCAP
Nuptial Verse to Mistress Elizabeth Lee Now Lady Tracy, A. Robert Herrick. HW
Nuptiall Song, or Epithalamie, on Sir Clipseby Crew and His Lady, A. Robert Herrick. AtBAP; HW; PoEL-3; SCEP-2; SeCP; SeCV-1
Nuptials of Attila, The, *abr.* George Meredith. PeVV
Nuremberg. Longfellow. AmPP; CoBA; HBV; MWA-1
Nuremburg, U.S.A. William Knott. YAP
Nurse. Harry Graham. *See* Misfortunes Never Come Singly.
Nurse-Life Wheat, Within His Green Husk Growing, The. Caelica, XL. Fulke Greville. EnRePo; EP; NCEP
(Youth and Maturity.) OBSC
Nurse looks round my clinic screen, The. Convalescence, IV. David McCord. WhC
Nurse No Long Grief. Mary Gilmore. PoAu-1
Nursery, The. Conrad Aiken. *Fr.* The Coming Forth by Day of Osiris Jones. LOW
Nursery, The. Mrs. Motherly. SAS
Nursery boast, The. On Seeing My Birthplace from a Jet Aircraft. John Pudney. NYBP
Nursery Legend, A. Henry S. Leigh. BOHV
Nursery Rhyme. W. H. Auden. SiSw
Nursery Rhyme of Innocence and Experience. Charles Causley. GoJo; POTi; WePo
Nursery Rhymes à la Mode. *Unknown.* BOHV
Nursery Rhymes for Surrealists. Grant Code. FiSC
Epitaph for a Wooden Soldier.
Nos Moraturi Te Salutamus.
Prayer in Blackout.
Nursery Rhymes for the Tender-hearted, *sels.* Christopher Morley.
"I knew a black beetle, who lived down a drain," IV. HBMV; YaD
"Scuttle, scuttle, little roach," I. FaFP; HBMV; SiTL; YaD
Nursery Song, A. Ann A. G. Carter. OTPC (1923 ed.); PPL; SAS
Nursery Song, A. Laura E. Richards. BoChLi; HBV; HBVY; TVC
Nursery Song in Pidgin English. *Unknown.* BOHV; WhC
Nurse's Prayer, A. Ruth Winant Wheeler. FaChP
Nurse's Song ("When the voices of children are heard on the green/ And laughing"). Blake. *Fr.* Songs of Innocence. AWP; BoChLi; CBEP; CEP; CH; EiCL; EiPP; EnRP; FaBoBe; GaP; GoTP; HBV; HBVY; InPo; MPB; OBEC; OnPM; OTPC (1923 ed.); RG; ThWaDe; TiPo (1952 ed.); WoL
(Play Time.) FaPON
Nurse's Song ("When the voices of children are heard on the green/ And whisp'rings"). Blake. *Fr.* Songs of Experience. CEP; EnLi-2 (1949 ed.); PoFS; TOP
Nurse's Song. *Unknown, tr. fr. German.* ThWaDe
Nut-brown Ale, The. *At. to* John Marston. EIL
Nut-brown Maid, The. *Unknown.* LiTL; MeEV; OBB; OBEV; OBSC
Nutcrackers and the Sugar-Tongs, The. Edward Lear. ALV; PoLF
Nut-gathering Lass, The. Burns. UnTE
Nuts an' May. *Unknown.* EvOK
Nuts in May. Louis MacNeice. MoAB; MoBrPo (1950 ed.)
Nutting. Wordsworth. CBEP; EnRP; ERoP-1
Nutting Time. Emilie Poulsson. BrR
Nyarlathotep. H. P. Lovecraft. HYE
Nydia's Song. Sir Edward Bulwer-Lytton. *Fr.* The Last Days of Pompeii, III, *ch.* 2. OBVV
Nymph and a Swain, A. Congreve. *Fr.* Love for Love. ALV; SeCL; UnTE
(Song; Set by Mr. John Eccles.) SeEP
Nymph Complaining for the Death of Her Faun, The. Andrew Marvell. AnAnS-1; AtBAP; CBEP; CH; GoTL; HBV; LoBV; MaMe; MePo; NoP; OBS; PAn; PoEL-2; ReEn; SCEP-2; SeCP; SeCV-1
"With sweetest milk and sugar first," *sel.* OA
(Girl and Her Fawn, The.) BoTP; OTPC (1923 ed.)
(Girl Describes Her Fawn, The.) GTSL
(Nymph and Her Fawn, The.) FaBoCh; LoGBV
Nymph Diana's Song, The. Jorge de Montemayor, *tr. fr. Spanish by* Bartholomew Young. ReIE
Nymph Fanaret, the gentlest maid. The Penance. Nahum Tate. CavP
Nymph I come once more awooing. Ay or Nay? Ralph Schomberg. *Fr.* The Judgment of Paris. TrJP
Nymph, nymph, what are your beads? Overheard on a Saltmarsh. Harold Monro. BoTP; CH; FaPON; GoJo; MoShBr; PCD; PCH; PoMS; SP; ThWaDe; TiPo
Nymph of the downward smile and sidelong glance. To G. A. W. Keats. Sonn
Nymph of the Garden Where All Beauties Be. Sir Philip Sidney. Astrophel and Stella, LXXXII. FCP; InvP; SiPS
Nymph Selvagia, The, Her Song. Jorge de Montemayor, *tr. fr. Spanish by* Bartholomew Young. *Fr.* Diana. TuPP
("Shepherd, who can pass such wrong.") SiCE
(Song.) EIL
Nymph that undoes me is fair and unkind, The. Silvia. Sir George Etherege. CavP; SeCL
Nymph there was in Arcadie, A. Alpheus and Arethusa. Eugene Howell Daly. AA
Nymphidia; or, The Court of Fairy. Michael Drayton. OAEP; ReEn; TuPP
(Nimphidia, the Court of Fayrie.) SeEP
Sels.
Adventures of Oberon, King of the Fairies, While Searching for Queen Mab, The. OA
Arming of Pigwiggen, The. GN; OTPC
(Pigwiggen.) BoTP
(Pigwiggen Arms Himself.) MoShBr
Queen Mab's Chariot. OTPC
("Pigwiggen was this fairy knight.") ViBoPo
(Queen Mab's Journey to Pigwiggen.) PCH
(Queen's Chariot.) OBS
Nymphs, The, *sel.* Leigh Hunt.
"There are the fair-limbed nymphs o' the woods." OBNC; OBRV
Nymphs and Satyrs. Gavin Ewart. PV
Nymphs and shepherds, dance no more. Song [*or* Third Song]. Milton. *Fr.* Arcades. AtBAP; CBEP; ELP; FiP; SeCL; ViBoPo
Nymph's Disdain of Love, A. *Unknown.* EIL; SiCE; TuPP
Nymphs of sea and land, away. Nuptial Hymn. Henry Peacham. *Fr.* The Period of Mourning. EIL
Nymph's Passion, A. Ben Jonson. CLwM; EnLit
(Nymph's Secret, A.) OBEV (new ed.)
Nymph's Reply to the Shepherd, The. Sir Walter Ralegh. ATP; BWP; CABA; CaFP; CBV; CLwM; CoBE; CTC; DiPo; EIL; EnL; EnLi-1; ExPo; FCP; FosPo; GTBS-W; HBV; HoPM; ILP; LiTB; LiTG; LiTL; LoBV; NoP; OAEP; OuHeWo; PAn; PG (1945 ed.); Po; PoE; PoFS; PoPo; PoSa; ReEn; ReIE; SeCePo; SeCeV; SiCE; SiPS; SiTL; StP; TOP; TreFS; TrGrPo; TuPP; WHA
(Answer to Marlowe.) OBSC; UnPo (1st ed.)
(Her Reply.) CBEP; OBEV
(Reply.) ViBoPo
Nymph's Secret, A. Ben Jonson. *See* Nymph's Passion, A.
Nymphs' Song, The. Michael Drayton. *Fr.* The Muses' Elysium. SeCL
Nymph's Song to Hylas, The. William Morris. *See* I Know a Little Garden Close.
Nyum-nyum, The. *Unknown.* NA

O

O. Richard Wilbur. LiTA; MoPo; StP
O/ Out of a bed of love. Holy Spring. Dylan Thomas. WaP
Oh/ well/ (she/ con-/ soled/ her-/ self). Novel. Robert Lax. ThO
Oh, a capital ship for an ocean trip. The Walloping Window Blind. Charles Edward Carryl. *Fr.* Davy and the Goblin. MoShBr. *See also* Capital ship for an ocean trip, A.
Oh, a dainty plant is the ivy green. The Ivy Green. Charles Dickens. *Fr.* Pickwick Papers, *ch.* 6. BoNaP; HBV; HBVY; OTPC (1946 ed.); RIS; VA
O, a gallant set were they. A Huguenot. Mary Elizabeth Coleridge. OBVV; PoVP
Oh, a grand old time has the earth. Mother Earth. Harriet Monroe. SP
Oh, a leper must be a terrible thing to see. The Vocation of St. Francis. Sister Mary Eleanore. CAW; WHL
Oh, a little Dutch soldier from over the Rhine. Snapoo. *Unknown.* SoAmSa
O, a little talk wid Jesus, makes it right. A Little Talk wid Jesus Makes It Right. *Unknown.* BoAN-2
Oh, a long, long time and a very long time. A Long Time Ago, *vers.* IV. *Unknown.* ShS
Oh, a lush green English meadow—it's there that I would lie. The Poplars. Bernard Freeman Trotter. CaP
Oh, a man there lives on the western plains. The Cowboy. *Unknown.* CoSo
Oh, a pearl is a thing of much value. A Student's Kiss. *Unknown.* OnPM
Oh! a private buffoon is a light-hearted loon. The Family Fool. W. S. Gilbert. *Fr.* The Yeomen of the Guard. ALV; InMe; SiTL
Oh, a raftsman's life is a wearisome one. The Pinery Boy. *Unknown.* IHA
Oh, a sailor's life is the life for me. The Warrior's Lament. Sir Owen Seaman. FiBHP
Oh, a shantyman's life is a wearisome life [*or* drearisome one]. A Shantyman's Life. *Unknown.* AS; ShS (*vers.* I); TrAS
Oh, a wonderful horse is the Fly-away Horse. The Fly-away Horse. Eugene Field. GoTP; PTK
O, a wonderful stream is the river [of] Time. The Isle of [the] Long Ago [*or* The Long Ago]. Benjamin Franklin Taylor. BLPA; FaFP; HBV; NeHB; PTK; TreFS; WBLP
Oh, a Yankee ship came down the river. Blow, Boys, Blow, *vers.* II. *Unknown.* ShS
"O, Aaron Burr, what have you done?" Aaron Burr. Stephen Vincent Benét. InMe
O Abishag, my little serving-maid. Abishag. André Spire. TrJP
O absent presence! Stella is not here. Astrophel and Stella, CVI. Sir Philip Sidney. FCP; SiPS
Oh, aged Time! how far, and long. The Roman Legions. John Mitford. VA
O African mother, so full of fear. To Whom Shall They Go? *Unknown.* STF
O ah drove three mules foh Gawge McVane. The Mule Skinner's Song. *Unknown.* AS
O Alison [*or* Allison] Gross, that lives in yon towr [*or* tower]. Alison [*or* Allison] Gross. *Unknown.* BaBo; BuBa; CH; ESPB; FaBoCh; OBB; OxBB
O all-happy, successful, O too great for words! Take My Wings and Dance with Me. Aristophanes. *Fr.* The Birds. HW
Oh, all the ladies of the world. Broom. John Farrar. GFA
Oh all ye, who passe by, whose eyes and minde. The Sacrifice. George Herbert. AtBAP; MaMe; PoEL-2; ReEn; SCEP-1
O all you little blackey tops. Scaring Crows. *Unknown.* BoTP; OxNR
O Amber Day, amid the Autumn Gloom. William Talbot Allison. CaP
O Amiable Lovely Death. Shakespeare. *Fr.* King John, III, iv. TreFT
Oh, ancient sin, oh, bathtub gin. Bathtub Gin. Philip H. Rhinelander. WhC
O angel bird, O winged word whom I. The Burden of Everyday. Buddhadeva Bose. LiTW
Oh! Angells, stand agastard at my song. I Have Eate My Hony Comb with My Hony. Edward Taylor. *Fr.* Preparatory Meditations, Second Series. MWA-1
O, answer me a question, Love, I pray. The Sweetest Story Ever Told. R. M. Stults. TreFS
O Apple Betty fiend, attend. Lines to a Man Who Thinks That Apple Betty with Hard Sauce Is Food for a Human Being. George S. Kaufman. InMe
O apple blossoms. Japanese Hokku. Lewis Alexander. CDC
O! Are Ye Sleepin[g] Maggie? Robert Tannahill. OBRV; OxBS
Oh, as I walked down the Landing Stage. We're All Bound to Go. *Unknown.* AmSS
Oh, as I went a-walkin' down Ratcliffe 'Ighway,/ I stepped into Paddy West's house. Paddy West. *Unknown.* ShS
Oh, as I went a-walking down Ratcliffe 'Ighway,/ I spied a flash packet. As I Went a-Walking down Ratcliffe Highway, *vers.* II. *Unknown.* ShS
Oh, ask in faith! Against the ill thou dreadest. Heart-Hushings. *Unknown.* SoP
O Autumn, laden with fruit, and stained. To Autumn. Blake. BoNaP; CLwM; ERoP-1; WiR
O babbling spring, than glass more clear. The Fountain of Bandusia [*or* O Fons Bandusiae]. Horace, *tr. by* Austin Dobson. OuHeWo; VA
O baby, where you been so long? Lord, Lord, Lord, Lord! Levee Moan. *Unknown.* AS
Oh, back in the fall of nineteen-two. "Haec Olim Meminisse Iuvabit." Deems Taylor. InMe
Oh, bad the march, the weary march. Fontenoy, 1745. Emily Lawless. AnIV; PoFr
Oh, band in the pine-wood, cease! The Band in the Pines. John Esten Cooke. AA
O-Bar Cowboy. *At. to* Bill Wagon. CoSo
O barber, spare those hairs. Barber, Spare Those Hairs. John Love, Jr. YaD
Oh, be not ether-borne, poet of earth. Poet of Earth. Stephen Henry Thayer. AA
O be swift. The Helmsman. Hilda Doolittle ("H. D."). AnAmPo; CMoP; OxBA
Oh be thou blest with all that Heav'n can send. To Mrs. M. B. on Her Birthday. Pope. CEP; EnLoPo; FaBoEn; OBEC
Oh Beach Love Blossom. Judson Crews. UnTE
O beams of steel are slim and black. Song of the Builders. Jessie Wilmore Murton. AmFN
O bear him where the rain can fall. Elegy on William Cobbett. Ebenezer Elliott. VA
O bear me to the paths of fair Pell Mell. The Pell Mell Celebrated. John Gay. *Fr.* Trivia; or, The Art of Walking the Streets of London, II. EnLi-1 (1949 ed.)
Oh, beautiful are the flowers of your garden. The Lover Sings of a Garden. Helen Hoyt. NP
O beautiful beneath the magic moon. In the Piazza at Night. Arthur Hugh Clough. *Fr.* At Venice. ViPo
O beautiful for spacious skies. America the Beautiful. Katharine Lee Bates. BLPA; DD; EaLo; FaBoBe; FaBV; FaFP; FaPL; FaPON; HBMV; HBVY; MaRV; MC; MCCG; MPB; NeHB; OQP; OTD; OTPC (1946 ed.); PaA; PAL; PCD; PEDC; PoRL; PTK; TIHL; TreF; WBLP; WGRP; YaD
O beautiful forever! I Saw Eternity. Louise Bogan. LiTA; StP
O Beautiful, My Country. Frederick L. Hosmer. MaRV; MC; PGD
Oh, beautiful rose, please tell me. The Rose Leaf. Flora L. Osgood. SoP
O beautiful young dead! Soldier-Dead. Gilbert Emery. PEDC
O Beauty (beams, nay, flame). A Description of Beauty. Giambattista Marini. OBSC
O beech, unbind your yellow leaf, for deep. Ghostly Tree. Léonie Adams. MAP; MoAB; MoAmPo
O Bella Età de l'Oro. Tasso. *See* Pastoral, A: "Oh happy golden age."
O Bells in the Steeple. May Riley Smith. PCH
O Bessie Bell and Mary Gray. Bessie [*or* Bessy] Bell and Mary Gray. *Unknown.* ESPB; LO; OBB; OxBB; ViBoFo. *For Mother Goose vers., see* Bessy Bell and Mary Gray.
"O Billie, billie, bonny billie." Bothwell Bridge [*or* The Battle of Bothwell Bridge]. *Unknown.* BaBo; ESPB; OxBB
O Billows Bounding Far. A. E. Housman. BoNaP
O Billy Riley, *with music.* *Unknown.* SoAmSa

O Bird at night, who, hearing, could forget. Bird at Night. Marion Ethel Hamilton. GoYe
O Bird, So Lovely. Louis Golding. TrJP
O bird, thou dartest to the sun. Song. Maria White Lowell. AA
Oh, Bisham Banks are fresh and fair. A Marlow Madrigal. Joseph Ashby-Sterry. VA
O bitter moon, O cold and bitter moon. Eagle Sonnets, IX. Clement Wood. HBMV
O Bitter Sea. William Morris. *Fr.* The Life and Death of Jason, IV. PoVP
(Song of the Argonauts.) EtS
O bitter wind toward the sunset blowing. The Only Son. Sir Henry Newbolt. HBV
O bitterness never spoken, the death mask etched in silver. Salvos for Randolph Bourne. Horace Gregory. CMoP; NAMP
O Black and Unknown Bards. James Weldon Johnson. AmNP; BANP; NoP; PoNe; StJW; TTY; UnS
O, blackbird! sing me something well. The Blackbird. Tennyson. OTPC
O Blackbird, what a boy you are! Vesper[s]. T. E. Brown. BoC; BoTP; EnLit; MemP; YT
Oh, blackbird with the shining yellow beak. Secrets. Luisa Hewitt. PCH
O black-maned, horse-haired, unworthy one. To the Noble Woman of Llanarth Hall. Evan Thomas. PV
Oh Blame Not the Bard. Thomas Moore. OnYI
Oh, Blank Confusion. Wordsworth. *Fr.* The Prelude, VII. AtBAP
Oh, bless the law that veils the Future's face. Mimma Bella, VI. Eugene Lee-Hamilton. HBV; Sonn
Oh! bless'd of Heaven, whom not the languid songs. *See* Oh! blest of heav'n. . .
O blessed bodie! Whither art thou thrown? Sepulchre. George Herbert. AnAnS-1; MaMe; MeP; SCEP-1
O blessed Dead! beyond all earthly pains. A Threnody: In Memory of Albert Darasz. William James Linton. VA
O blessed freedom of the press! Gentle Reminders. Goethe. PoFr
O Blessèd House, That Cheerfully Receiveth. Karl Johann Philipp Spitta, *tr. fr. German by* Charles William Schaeffer. TrPWD
O blessed man, that in th'advice. Psalm I, Bible, *O.T.* SCAP
O Blessed Moment. Avis B. Christiansen. SoP
O Blessed Word. *Unknown.* SoP
O blest of all the scattered spots that lie. Home to Sermio. Catullus. OnPM
Oh! blest [*or* bless'd] of heav'n [*or* heaven], whom not the languid songs. Nature's Influence on Man [*or* The Created Universe]. Mark Akenside. *Fr.* The Pleasures of Imagination. CEP; LoBV; OBEC
O Blest Unfabled Incense Tree. George Darley. *See* Phoenix, The.
O Blisful Light. Chaucer. *See* Wooing of Criseide, The.
Oh, blithe and bonny is fair Scotland, where the bluebells gently grow. The Paisley Officer, *vers.* I. *Unknown.* ShS
O blithe new-comer! I have heard. To the Cuckoo. Wordsworth. BEL; BoLiVe; BoTP; CBEP; CoBE; ELP; EnLit; EnRP; EPN; ERoP-1; FaFP; FiP; GoTP; GTBS; GTBS-D; GTBS-P; GTBS-W; GTSE; GTSL; LiTG; LoBV; MBW-2; MCCG; MERP; OBRV; OTPC; OuHeWo; PeER; PoeP; PoLF; PTK; ShBV-2; TOP; TreFT; TrGrPo
Oh blithely [*or* blythely] shines the bonny [*or* bonnie] sun. We'll Go to Sea No More. *Unknown.* ChTr; EtS
Oh, blow away, I long to hear you. Blow, Boys, Blow, *vers.* I. *Unknown.* ShS
Oh, blow the man down, boys [*or* bullies], blow the man down. Blow the Man Down. *Unknown.* AmSS; SoAmSa; TrAS
Oh, blow the man down, Johnny, blow him right down. Blow the Man Down, *vers.* III. *Unknown.* ShS
O Blue Jay up in the maple tree. The Blue Jay. Susan Hartley Swett. PRWS
O blush not so! O blush not so! Sharing Eve's Apple. Keats. ChER; ErPo
Oh blythely shines the bonnie sun. *See* Oh blithely shines the bonny sun.
Oh, Boney was a warrior. Boney, *vers.* II. *Unknown.* ShS
Oh Boney's on the sea. The Shan Van Vocht. *Unknown.* OxBoLi
O bonnie bird, that in the brake, exultant, dost prepare thee. The Waking of the Lark. Eric Mackay. VA
O bonny Baby Livingston. Bonny Baby Livingston. *Unknown.* BaBo; ESPB
O bonny, bonny sang the bird. The Unquiet Grave. *Unknown.* EnSB
Oh book! infinite sweetnesse! let my heart. The H. Scriptures. George Herbert. AnAnS-1; MaMe; MeP; SCEP-1
O, born in luckless hour, with every Muse. To the Editor of Mr. Pope's Works. Thomas Edwards. Sonn
O Boston, though thou now art grown. Of Boston in New England. William Bradford. SCAP
Oh, Boston's a fine town, with ships in the bay. Home, Dearie, Home. *Unknown.* AmSS; SoAmSa
Oh, both my shoes are shiny new. Autobiography. Dorothy Parker. WhC
O Bottomless Depths of God's Infinite Love. Graf von Zinzendorf, *tr. fr. German by* John Gambold. SoP
Oh, bow your head, Tom Dooley. Tom Dooley. *Unknown.* ViBoFo
O bowl that held the hot imprisoned fire. The Skull. Mary E. Fullerton. BoAu
O boy cutting grass. Hitomaro. *Fr.* Manyo Shu. AWP
O Boy God, Muse of Poets. Ode to Fidel Castro. Edward Field. CoPo
O Boys! O Boys! Oliver St. John Gogarty. DTC; OBMV
O boys, we're goin' for to fight. Way Down in Mexico. *Unknown.* CoSo
O brant, brant, One is waiting for you. Eskimo String-Figure Chant. E. Hope Kerr, *tr. fr. Eskimo song.* TwCaPo
O Brazil, the Isle of the Blest. Gerald Griffin. ACP
(Hy-Brasail, the Isle of the Blest.) BLPA
Oh Breathe Not His Name. Thomas Moore. AnIL; BEL; CoBE; EnLi-2; EnRP; FaPL; HBV; TreFS
Oh! breathe upon this hapless world. Ode to Peace. *Unknown.* PAH
"O brent's your brow, my Lady Elspat." Lady Elspat. *Unknown.* ESPB; OBB
O bretheren, my way. My Way's Cloudy. *Unknown.* BoAN-1
O briar-scents, on yon wet wing. George Meredith. EG
Oh Bright Oh Black Singbeast Lovebeast Catkin Sleek. Michael McClure. CoPo
O brightness of my bright eyes, how art thou? On the Death of His Child. Faydi. LiTW
O, Brignall banks are wild and fair. Brignall Banks [*or* The Outlaw *or* Edmund's Song *or* Song]. Sir Walter Scott. *Fr.* Rokeby, III. BEL; EnLi-2; EnRP; EPN; GTBS; GTBS-D; GTBS-P; GTBS-W; GTSE; GTSL; HBV; OAEP; OBEV; OBRV; OtMeF; PoRA; TOP
O broad-breasted Queen among nations! Boston. John Boyle O'Reilly. PAH
O brooding Spirit of Wisdom and of Love. Prayer. Sir William Rowan Hamilton. IrPN
Oh, Brother Christ, come play with me. The Christ-Child [*or* The Christ Child's Christmas]. Laura Spencer Portor. PEDC; StJW
Oh, Brother Green, do come to me. Brother Green. *Unknown.* BFSS
O brother in the restless rest of God! Zora Cross. *Fr.* Elegy on an Australian Schoolboy. PoAu-1
O brother, lift a cry, a long world cry. Peace. Edwin Markham. PGD; WBLP
O Brother Man. Whittier. MaRV; SoP; TRV
O Brother Planets, unto whom I cry. Isolation. Josephine Preston Peabody. AA; AnAmPo
O Brother Tree. Max Michelson. NP; TrJP
O brother, what is there to say. Ernest Dowson. John Hall Wheelock. HBMV
O brothers mine, take care! Take care! The White Witch. James Weldon Johnson. BANP; CDC
O brothers mine, today we stand. Fifty Years, 1863-1913. James Weldon Johnson. BANP; PoFr; PoNe
O brothers, who must ache and stoop. To My Brothers. Norman Gale. VA
O Bruadair. James Stephens, *after the Irish of* David O'-Bruidair. OxBI
O Bury Me beneath the Willow, *with music.* *Unknown.* AS
Oh, bury me beside my knife and six-shooter. Dodge City, the End of the Trail. *Unknown.* CoSo
"Oh, bury me not in the deep, deep sea." The Ocean Burial. Edwin H. Chapin. ShS; ViBoFo

"Oh, bury me not on the Chickamauga!" Bury Me Not on the Chickamauga. *Unknown.* BFSS
O Bury Me Not on the Lone Prairie. *Unknown. See* Dying Cowboy, The ("Oh, bury me not. . .").
O, but how white is white, white from shadows come. Music of Colours: The Blossom Scattered. Vernon Watkins. ACV; LiTB
Oh, but it is dirty! Filling Station. Elizabeth Bishop. NYBP
Oh, but life went gayly, gayly. In the House of Idiedaily. Bliss Carman. OBVV; PFY
Oh, but my husband, Matthew. Splendid Isolation. Katharine Lee Bates. LHV
Oh! but my mind is weary! The Summer's Revel. Pierre de Ronsard. Odes, II, 18. WoL
Oh but, says one, tradition set aside. Tradition. Dryden. *Fr.* Religio Laici. OBS; PoLi
Oh, but she was dark and shrill. Nursery Rhymes à la Mode. *Unknown.* BOHV
O but we talked at large before. Sixteen Dead Men. W. B. Yeats. PIA
O, by an' by, by an' by. By an' By. *Unknown.* BoAN-1
O By the By. E. E. Cummings. OxBA
Oh, by Thy cross and passion, by Thy pain. Litany. Marie LeNart. ChIP
"O Çaesar, we who are about to die." Morituri Salutamus. Longfellow. CoBA; MAmP; MWA-1
O! California, *with music.* Isaac W. Baker. SGR
Oh, California, *with music. Unknown, at. to* John Nichols. *See* I Come From Salem City.
Oh, California, land of gold. California over the Left. "Jack the Grumbler." SGR
Oh, call my brother back to me. The [Child's] First Grief. Felicia Dorothea Hemans. BLPA; CH; NeHB
O call not me to justify the wrong. Sonnets, CXXXIX. Shakespeare. RelE
O calm, yellow-haired girl, all gold is the burden on thy head. A Reproach to Morvyth. Dafydd ap Gwilym. LiTW
O cam ye in by the House o Rodes. John Thomson and the Turk (B *vers.*). *Unknown.* ESPB
O camel in the zoo. Camel. Mary Britton Miller. TiPo (1959 ed.); UTS
O camp of flowers, with poplars girded round. Memory. Erik Johan Stagnelius. AWP
O, can ye sew cushions? Can Ye Sew Cushions? *Unknown.* FaBoCh; LoGBV
O Canada. Basile Routhier, *tr. fr. French by* Robert Stanley Weir. PTK
Oh, Cape Cod girls are very fine girls. Cape Cod Girls. *Unknown.* TrAS
Oh, Cape Cod girls they have no combs. Cape Cod Girls. *Unknown.* AmSS
O Captain! My Captain! Walt Whitman. *Fr.* Memories of President Lincoln. AA; AmePo; AmPP (3d ed.); AnFE; AP; APA; BBV (1923 ed.); BoLiVe; BWP; CoAnAm; CoBA; DD; FaBoBe; FaBoCh; FaBV; FaFP; FaPON; GN; GTBS; GTBS-W; HBV; HBVY; HH; InP; LaNeLa; LiPo; LiTA; LiTG; LoGBV; MAP; MaRV; MC; MoAmPo; MPB; NeHB; NeMA; NePA; OBEV; OHFP; OHIP; OQP; OTD; OTPC; OuHeWo; PaA; PAH; PAL; PAP; PCD; PEDC; PG (1945 ed.); Po; PoFr; PoLF; PoPl; PoRL; RG; RoGo; StaSt; StVeCh; ThLM; TOP; TreF; TrGrPo; TSW; YT
O Captain of the wars, whence won Ye so great scars? The Veteran of Heaven. Francis Thompson. ChIP; HBV; MaRV; PoLi
Oh, Captain of wide western seas. San Gloria. "Tom Redcam." PoNe
O Carib Isle! Hart Crane. AP; MoPo; NePA; OnHM
O Carpenter of Nazareth. Upon This Rock. Robert Whitaker. ChIP
O Cat of Carlish [*or* Churlish] Kind. John Skelton. *See* Cursing of the Cat, The.
O Catch Miss Daisy Pinks. Alistair Campbell. AnNZ
Oh, cease, my wandering soul. Fulfillment. William A. Muhlenberg. WGRP
O Cedar-tree, Cedar, my mother. Song of Basket-Weaving. Constance Lindsay Skinner. AnAmPo
O, celestial beings. Marriage Vow. *Unknown.* HW
O Celius! think, or Lesbia, once your pride. Lesbia's Disgrace. Catullus. OnPM
O chansons foregoing. Epilogue. Ezra Pound. OxBA
Oh, Charley, he's a nice [*or* fine] young man. Weevily Wheat. *Unknown.* ABF; AS
O Charmian,/Where think'st thou he is now? Shakespeare. *Fr.* Antony and Cleopatra, I, v. MemP
O Chatterton! how very sad thy fate! Sonnet to Chatterton. Keats. ERoP-2
O child, had I thy lease of time! such unimagined things. A Child of To-Day. James Buckham. AA
O Child of Beauty Rare. Goethe, *tr. fr. German by* William E. Aytoun. ISi
O child of nations, giant-limbed. Canada. Sir Charles G. D. Roberts. PeCV; PoFr; VA
O children of men, O sons and daughters of sorrow. Song for Tomorrow. Lucia Trent. PGD
O chillen, run, de Conjuh man. De Conjuh Man. James Edwin Campbell. BANP
O Chloe, why wish you that your years. To Chloe. William Cartwright. OBEV
O Christ, great Lover of all souls. Thy Kingdom Come! Thomas Curtis Clark. ChIP
O Christ, in Thee my soul hath found. Found in Thee. *Unknown.* SoP
O Christ my Lord and King. Thy Kingdom Come. A. B. Simpson. BePJ
O Christ, my Lord, which for my sins didst hang upon a tree. Though Here in Flesh I Be [*or* Through Thy Cross and Passion]. Philip Howard. CoBE; PoLi
O Christ of Calvary, This Lent. Alice Mortenson. BePJ
O Christ of God! whose life and death. Vesta. Whittier. OBEV (1st ed.); TrPWD; WHA
O Christ of Olivet, you hushed the wars. Edwin Markham. *Fr.* The Christ of the Andes. TrPWD
O Christ, the glorious Crown. Hymn. Philip Howard. ACP; CAW
O Christ, the Way. George L. Squier. MaRV
O Christ, they took Your living words. Walls. Myriam Page. ChIP
O Christ Thou Art within Me like a Sea. Edith Lovejoy Pierce. MaRV; TrPWD
O Christ, Who Died. John Calvin Slemp. ChIP; TrPWD
O Christ who holds the open gate. The Ploughman. John Masefield. *Fr.* The Everlasting Mercy. AtBAP; SoP; TreFS; TRV
O Christ, who mountest up the sky. Ascension Hymn. Jean Batiste de Santeuil. CAW
Oh, Christmas is a jolly time. A Christmas Song. Florence Evelyn Dratt. MaRV
O Christmas, merry Christmas. Bells Across the Snow. Frances Ridley Havergal. SoP
O Christmas night! day's light transcending. Nuptial Song. Henricus Selyns. SCAP
Oh Christmas, that your Gift of Gifts might be. Noel! Noel! Laura Simmons. PGD
Oh! Christmas time is coming again. Emily Jane. Laura E. Richards. RIS
O Church of God. Rolland W. Schloerb. MaRV
O Church of God triumphant, above the world's dark fears. Church Triumphant. S. Ralph Harlow. MaRV
O cities of Euphrates! Ages. Friedrich Hölderlin. OnPM
O City, Cities! *sel.* R. Ellsworth Larsson.
"No city shall I call my own." AnAmPo
O City, Look the Eastward Way. Enid Derham. BoAu
O city metropole, isle riverain! Montreal. A. M. Klein. CaP; MoCV; OBCV
O city of the world, with sacred splendor blest. Longing for Jerusalem. Judah Halevi. TrJP
O clipper ships! where are, where are ye now? Clipper Ships. John Anderson. EtS
O clock, your long and solemn tones. The Horologe. Clark Ashton Smith. FiSC
O cloud, the parching spirit stirs thy pity. Kalidasa. *Fr.* The Cloud-Messenger. LiTW
O Columbia, the gem of the ocean. Columbia, the Gem of the Ocean [*or* Red, White and Blue]. David T. Shaw. FaBoBe; PAL; WBLP
O come, all my young lovers. The Unconstant Lover. *Unknown.* TrAS
O Come, All Ye Faithful. *Unknown, at. to* St. Bonaventure, *tr. fr. Latin by* Frederick Oakeley. FaFP; TreFS; YaCaBo (Adeste Fideles.) CAW; MaRV; PTK; WGRP; WHL, 2 *sts.*
Oh, come all ye true bold raftsmen, and friends both far and

Oh (continued)
near. Whalen's Fate. *Unknown.* ShS
"O come and be my mate!" said the eagle to the hen. Wedded Bliss. Charlotte Perkins Gilman. HBV
Oh, come and go, you almost child, entrancing. Rainer Maria Rilke. *Fr.* Sonnets to Orpheus. UnS
O come and take thou me/ Beneath thy wing. Beneath Thy Wing. Hayyim Nahman Bialik. TrJP
Oh, come, cowboys, and listen to my song! The U-S-U Range. *At. to* G. W. Barr. CoSo
O come, let us sing unto the Lord. Psalm XCV, Bible, *O.T.* AWP; BLRP; BoChLi (1950 ed.); JAWP; OHIP; OnPM; OuHeWo
Oh, come let us welcome sweet Sabbath the Queen! Welcome, Queen Sabbath. Zalman Schneour. TrJP
O, come, list awhile, and you soon shall hear. The Female Smuggler. *Unknown.* AmSS
Oh Come, Little Children. Phyllis McGinley. FaBV
Oh, come my joy, my soldier boy. Ballad. Henry Treece. WaP
O, come, my lad, or go, my lad. The Betrothal. Edna St. Vincent Millay. NP; PG
O Come, O Come, Emmanuel, *with music.* *Unknown.* YaCaBo
O come, our Lord and Saviour. *Unknown.* BLRP
O Come Out of the Lily. Ruth Pitter. AnFE
O Come Quickley! Thomas Campion. *See* Never Weather-beaten Sail.
O come, soft rest of cares! come, Night! Bridal Song [*or* Song *or* Come, Night]. George Chapman. *Fr.* Hero and Leander. EG; OBEV; OnPM; ViBoPo
O come sweet death, sang Bach. Horn. James Hayford. NePoAm-2
Oh, Come to Me When Daylight Sets. Thomas Moore. EnRP
O come to the garden, dear brother, and see. Snow. Jane Taylor. OTPC (1923 ed.); PCH; PPL
O! Come to the Greenwood Shade. Alexander McLachlan. PeCV
Oh, come where the cyanides silently flow. The Chemist to His Love. *Unknown.* BOHV
Oh, come with me in my little canoe. Ossian's Serenade [*or* The Burman Lover]. Calder Campbell. BLPA; NeHB; TrAS
O come with me into this moonlight world. The Night of the Full Moon. Lloyd Frankenberg. BoLP
O come you pious youth! adore. Jupiter Hammon. *Fr.* An Address to Miss Phillis Wheatley. AmPP (5th ed.)
O comrades. Poem for the Living. Harold Andrew. TwCaPo
Oh, concerning of some gentlemen who lived down below. Hog Rogues on the Harricane. *Unknown.* OuSiCo
O Contemporaries. Louis Dudek. TwCaPo
O cool in the summer is salad. Salad. Mortimer Collins. ALV; BOHV; Par
O cool is the valley now. James Joyce. Chamber Music, XVI. HW
Oh! could I acquire my fullest desire. My Wishes. Patrick Healy. OnYI
O could I tell ye surely would believe it! Experience [*or* St. Paul Speaks]. Frederic W. H. Myers. *Fr.* Saint Paul. BoC; MaRV
Oh, could we keep the Christmas thrill. The Whole Year Christmas. Angela Morgan. SoP; TRV
Oh, could we weep. Nurse No Long Grief. Mary Gilmore. PoAu-1
Oh country, fair and grand. The Patriot Hymn. Nathan Haskell Dole. PaA
O Country People. John Hewitt. ACV
O courteous Christ—kind guest, most gracious host. To a Crucifix. Anna Wickham. MoBrPo
O cricket, from your cheery cry. Basho, *tr. fr. Japanese by* Curtis Hidden Page. AWP; JAWP; LiTW; PoPo; WBP
"O crikey, Bill!" she ses to me, she ses. Culture in the Slums. W. E. Henley. BoHV; CenHV; HBV; InMe
O Cross on which my Saviour died. Calvary. Henry W. Frost. SoP
O crucified Son of God, I pray. An Easter Prayer. Chester M. Davis. SoP
O Crudelis Amor. Thomas Campion. *See* When Thou Must Home.
O cruel cloudless space. Nativity. May Sarton. NePoAm-2
"O cruel Death, give three things back." Three Things. W. B. Yeats. AtBAP; DTC; FaBoEn; OBMV
O cruel Love! on thee I lay. Sapho's Song. John Lyly. *Fr.* Sapho and Phao. OBSC
O cruel manger, how bleak, how bleak! The Babe of Bethlehem. Condé Benoist Pallen. JKCP
O Cruel Still. Horace, *tr. fr. Latin by* Philip Francis. OnPM
Oh! cruel were my parents as tore my love from me. *Unknown.* LO
O crystal Well. Minnie. Thomas Caulfield Irwin. IrPN
O cuckoo. *Unknown.* *Fr.* Kokin Shu. AWP
O Cuckoo! shall I call thee bird. To the Cuckoo. F. H. Townsend. ChTr
O Cupid! Monarch over Kings. John Lyly. *Fr.* Mother Bombie. ElL; SiCE
(Fools in Love's College.) TrGrPo
(Song of Accius and Silena.) OBSC
O curfew of the setting sun! O Bells of Lynn! The Bells of Lynn. Longfellow. AA
Oh, cut me reeds to blow upon. Tampico. Grace Hazard Conkling. HBMV
O D V. *Unknown.* BOHV
O Daedalus, Fly away Home. Robert Hayden. IDB; NoP; PoNe
O daffodils, come out, I pray. Daffodils. *Unknown.* SUS
O dainty gland, whose lobulated grace. To the Parotid Gland. —— Schlesinger. WhC
Oh Danaan brethren. At My Whisper. Lyle Donaghy. AnIV
O Dandelion. *Unknown.* *See* Dandelion, The ("O dandelion").
O dandelion, rich and haughty. The Dandelion. Vachel Lindsay. BrR
"O dandelion, yellow as gold." The [*or* O] Dandelion. *Unknown.* BoTP; PCH
O dappled throat of white! Shy, hidden bird! The Lonely Bird. Harrison Smith Morris. AA
O Dark, Dark, Dark, *abr.* Milton. *Fr.* Samson Agonistes. WHA
("O wherefore was my birth from heaven foretold.") AnFE
O dark-haired girl, let us now. From an Irish-Latin Macaronic. Geoffrey Taylor. NeIP
O darlin', you can't love but one. Darlin'. *Unknown.* ABF
O David, highest in the list. Christopher Smart. *Fr.* A Song to David. OxBoCh
O David, if I had/ Your power. That Harp You Play so Well. Marianne Moore. HBMV; MAP; MoAB; MoAmPo; NP
O dawn upon me slowly, Paradise! Come Slowly, Paradise. James Benjamin Kenyon. AA
O day most calm, most bright. Sunday. George Herbert. MaMe; OBSC; SeCV-1; SeEP
O Day of Rest and Gladness. Christopher Wordsworth. MaRV; WGRP
(Lord's Day, A.) SoP
O day of roses and regret. Memorial Day. Louise Imogen Guiney. DD
O days and hours, your work is this. In Memoriam A. H. H., CXVII. Tennyson. BEL; EnLi-2; EPN; HBV; MaPo; OAEP; ViPo; VP
Oh, days of beauty standing veiled apart. Prevision. Ada Foster Murray. HBV
Oh, de band o' Gideon. De Band o' Gideon. *Unknown.* BoAN-1
O, de birds ar' sweetly singin'. 'Weh down Souf. Daniel Webster Davis. BANP
O de black cat cotch ole Sambo Lee. De Black Cat Crossed His Luck. James D. Corrothers. CIV
O, de blin' man stood on de road an' cried. De Blin' Man Stood on de Road an' Cried. *Unknown.* BoAN-1
Oh, de boll weevil am a li'l [*or* little] black bug. Ballet [*or* Ballad] of de Boll Weevil [*or* Boll Weevil Song]. Unknown. AS; TrAS
O de Glory Road! O de Glory Road! De Glory Road. Clement Wood. HBMV; IHA; PFY; YaD
Oh, de good ole chariot swing so low. Swing Low, Sweet Chariot. *Unknown.* AA
Oh, de grubbin' hoe's a-rustin' in de conah. The Deserted Plantation. Paul Laurence Dunbar. IHA
Oh, de hearse keep a-rollin'. I Feel Like My Time Ain't Long. *Unknown.* OuSiCo
O, de light-bugs glimmer down de lane. Negro Serenade. James Edwin Campbell. BANP

O, de ol' ark's a-moverin. De Ol' Ark's a-Moverin' an' I'm Goin' Home. *Unknown.* BoAN-2
Oh, de ol' sheep done know de road. De Ol' Sheep Done Know de Road. *Unknown.* BoAN-2
Oh, de weathah it is balmy an' de breeze is sighin' low. Li'l' Gal. Paul Laurence Dunbar. GoSl
Oh, de white gal ride in a automobile. De Black Gal. *Unknown.* ABF
O' de wurl' ain't flat. Northboun'. Ariel Williams Holloway. BANP; CDC; GoSl; PoNe
Oh! Dear! *Unknown. See* Oh! Dear! What Can the Matter Be?
O dear and loving God. Prayer for Living and Dying. Christopher La Farge. TrPWD
O Dear Dark Head, bowed low in death-black sorrow. Dear Dark Head. William Rooney. JKCP (1926 ed.)
O dear life, when shall it be. Astrophel and Stella: Tenth Song. Sir Phillip Sidney. EnRePo; FCP; SiPS
O Dear Me! Walter de la Mare. TiPo
O Dear O. *Unknown.* ErPo
Oh! Dear! What Can the Matter Be? *Unknown.* LiTL; LO; OTPC; OxNR
("Dear, dear! what can the matter be?") PPL
(Oh! Dear!) CH; PCD
O dearest, canst thou tell me why. Warum sind denn die Rosen so blass. Heine. AWP; JAWP; WBP
O Dearest Dread, most glorious King. A Prayer unto Christ the Judge of the World. Michael Wigglesworth. SCAP
O dearly-bought revenge, yet glorious! Heroic Vengeance. Milton. *Fr.* Samson Agonistes. OBS
O Death. Ecclesiasticus, XLI: 1-4, Bible, Apocrypha (*Moulton, Modern Reader's Bible).* TrJP
(On Death—a Sonnet.) MaRV
O Death. *with music. Unknown.* TrAS
O Death,/ How bitter is the remembrance of thee. O Death [*or* On Death—a Sonnet]. Ecclesiasticus, Bible, Apocrypha (*Moulton, Modern Reader's Bible.*) MaRV; TrJP
O Death, Rock Me Asleep. *At. to* George Boleyn, *also to* Anne Boleyn. CBEP; EG; ElL; TrGrPo; TuPP
(Death.) OBSC
("O death, O death, rocke mee asleepe.") EnPo
(O Death, Rock Me on Sleep.) ChTr
O Death, That Maketh Life So Sweet. William Morris. *Fr.* The Life and Death of Jason, XII. PoVP; ViPo
O Death, when thou shalt come to me. Strong as Death. H. C. Bunner. HBV
Oh! Death Will Find Me. Rupert Brooke. *See* Sonnet: "Oh, Death will find me, long before I tire."
Oh, deem not they are blest alone. Blessed Are They That Mourn. Bryant. SoP
O deep and clear as is the sky. To Silence. T. Sturge Moore. BrPo
O deep, creating Light. Eagle Song. Gordon Bottomley. *Fr.* Suilven and the Eagle. MoBrPo
O Deep of Heaven, 'tis thou alone art boundless. The Night Sky. Sir Charles G. D. Roberts. VA
Oh! Dem Golden Slippers. James A. Bland. GoSl
O depth of wealth, and knowledge in God! To Him Be Glory. Romans, Bible, *N.T.* TRV
O depth sufficient to desire. Adam's Song to Heaven. Edgar Bowers. QFR
O Desolate Eves [along the Way, How Oft]. Christopher Brennan. *Fr.* The Wanderer. BoAV; CoBE; PoAu-1
O destined Land, unto thy citadel. George Edward Woodberry. *Fr.* My Country. AA
O Deus, Ego Amo Te. *Unknown, at. to* St. Francis Xavier, *tr. fr. Latin by* Gerard Manley Hopkins. PoLi; TrPWD
Oh, dewy was the morning, upon the first of May. Manila. Eugene Fitch Ware. BOHV; FiBHP; InMe; PV; YaD
Oh, dey whupped him up de hill. Never Said a Mumbalin' Word. *Unknown.* ABF; TrAS
O did you ever hear o' [*or* of the] brave Earl Brand. Earl Brand. *Unknown.* OBB; OxBB
Oh did you go to see the show. The Orange Lily O. *Unknown.* IrPN
Oh Did You Hear? Shelley Silverstein. PoSC
Oh! did you ne'er hear of Kate Kearney? Kate Kearney. Lady Morgan. BLPA; FaBoBe; NeHB
Oh, did you once see Shelley plain. Memorabilia. Robert Browning. CBEP
O did you see a troop go by. The Camp within the West. Roderic Quinn. BoAu; PoAu-1
Oh, did you see him riding down. Riding Down. Nora Perry. AA; HBV
O differing human heart. Personality. Archibald Lampman. PeCV (1967 ed.)
O dim delicious heaven of dreams. John Francis O'Donnell. *Fr.* Reminiscences of a Day. IrPN
Oh, dis is de day we pick on de banjo. Gimme de Banjo. *Unknown.* ShS
O distant Christ, the crowded, darkening years. Doubt. Margaret Deland. MaRV; TrPWD
O divinest star of heaven! Prayer to Venus. John Fletcher. *Fr.* The Mad Lover. SeCL
Oh, do, my Johnny Boker. Johnny Boker. *Unknown.* AmSS
Oh do [*or* doe] not die, for I shall hate. A Fever [*or* Feaver]. John Donne. DiPo; MaMe; SCEP-1
O Do Not Go. Henry Vaughan. *Fr.* Rules and Lessons. MemP; SoP
O do not grieve, Dear Heart, nor shed a tear. Margaret Cavendish, Duchess of Newcastle. EnLoPo
O Do Not Prize Thy Beauty. *Unknown. See* Do Not, Oh, Do Not Prize.
O do not use me/ After my sinnes. Sighs and Grones. George Herbert. AtBAP; MaMe; PoEL-2
Oh do [*or* doe] not wanton with those eyes. A Song. Ben Jonson. AnAnS-2; HBV; NoP; OBS; ReEn; SCEP-2; SeCP
Oh, do you remember Sweet Betsy from Pike. *See* Oh, don't you remember. . .
"Oh Doctor, oh Doctor, I have come, come, come." The Dumb Maid. *Unknown.* BFSS
O doe not goe from us and bring. *Unknown.* SeCSL
O doe not melt thyselfe in vaine. *Unknown.* SeCSL
Oh doe not wanton with those eyes. *See* Oh do not wanton with those eyes.
O Domine Deus! Speravi in te. Prayer before Execution. Mary, Queen of Scots. CAW; WGRP
O Donall Oge, if you go across the sea. Donall Oge; Grief of a Girl's Heart. *Unknown.* OnYI; OxBI
O don't be sorrowful, darling! Don't Be Sorrowful, Darling. Rembrandt Peale. HBV
Oh don't you remember Bill Walker, the great. The Sonora Filibusters. John A. Stone. SGR
Oh! don't you remember black Alice, Sam Holt. A Ballad of Queensland (Sam Holt). G. H. Gibson. PoAu-1
Oh, don't you [*or* do you] remember sweet Betsy from Pike. Betsy [*or* Sweet Betsy] from Pike. *Unknown, at. to* John A. Stone. AmPP (4th ed); AS; BaBo; BFSS; OxBoLi; SGR; TrAS; TreFT; ViBoFo
Oh, don't you remember the shady old camp. The Shady Old Camp. John A. Stone. SGR
Oh! don't you see the turtle-dove. The Turtle Dove. *Unknown.* LO; OxBoLi
O Dowland, Old John Dowland. Hal Summers. MuSP
O down in the orchard. Apple Harvest. Helen Leuty. BoTP
O dreadfull justice, what a fright and terrour. Justice. George Herbert. MaMe
O Dreams, O Destinations. C. Day Lewis. MoPo
Sels.
Sonnet: "To travel like a bird, lightly to view." ChMP
"Symbols of gross experience!—our grief." Sonn
"To travel like a bird, lightly to view." GTBS-P; Sonn
O dreamy, gloomy, friendly trees. The Trees. Herbert Trench. POTE
"O dreary life," we cry, "O dreary life!" Patience Taught by Nature. Elizabeth Barrett Browning. OxBoCh
O Duty,/ Why hast thou not the visage of a sweetie or a cutie? Kind of an Ode to Duty. Ogden Nash. TrGrPo; UnPo (3d ed.); WhC
O d'you hear the seas complainin', and complainin', while it's rainin'? The Doom-Bar. Alice E. Gillington. VA
"O Earl Rothes, an thou wert mine." Earl Rothes. *Unknown.* BaBo; ESPB
Oh, Earlier Shall the Rosebuds Blow. William Johnson Cory. HBV
O early one morning I walked out like Agag. The Streets of Laredo. Louis MacNeice. ChTr; MoBS
O Earth! Richard Realf. *See* Word, The.
O earth-and-autumn of the setting sun. Indian Summer. William Ellery Leonard. *Fr.* Two Lives, Pt. III. AnAmPo; HBMV; NP; PG (1945 ed.)

O Earth! Art Thou Not Weary? Julia C. R. Dorr. AA
O Earth, How Like to Heav'n. Milton. *Fr.* Paradise Lost, IX. MaPo
O earth, I count the praises. Praise of Earth. Elizabeth Barrett Browning. OBVV
O Earth, I will have none of thee. The Heart's Low Door. Susan Mitchell. HBMV
O earth, lie heavily upon her eyes. Rest. Christina Rossetti. EnLi-2; EPN; GTBS; HBV; OBEV; OBNC; OBVV; TOP; TrGrPo; VP
O Earth Mother, who consents to everything, who forgives. You (V). Tom Clark. ANYP
O Earth, O dewy mother, breathe on us. A Prayer. Archibald Lampman. TrPWD
O Earth, Sufficing All Our Needs. Sir Charles G. D. Roberts. CaP
O Earth! thou hast not any wind that blows. The Word [*or* O Earth *or* The World]. Richard Realf. *Fr.* Symbolisms. AA; AmLP; AnEnPo; MaRV; TRV; WGRP
O Earth! throughout thy borders. Easter Carol. George Newell Lovejoy. ChIP; DD; OHIP; OQP; PGD
O Earth, Turn! George Johnston. MoCV
O Earth, unhappy planet born to die. Epitaph for the Race of Man, IV. Edna St. Vincent Millay. AmP
O Earth, who daily kissed His feet. Holy Saturday. John Banister Tabb. MaRV; StJW
Oh Ease Oh Body-Strain Oh Love Oh Ease Me Not! Michael McClure. Wound-Bore. CoPo
Oh, East is East, and West is West, and never the twain shall meet. The Ballad of East and West. Kipling. AnFE; BBV (1951 ed.); BEL; BeLS; BrPo; FaBoBe; FaBV; HBV; MaC; MaRV; PoPo; PoVP; TRV; TSW; VA
Oh, Eleazar Wheelock was a very pious man. Eleazar Wheelock. Richard Hovey. WHC
O embittered joy. Fiend's Weather. Louise Bogan. MoVE
O Empress high, celestial Queen most rare. Ballad of Our Lady. William Dunbar. ISi
O empty cross, portentous against the sky. In Him Ye Are Made Full. William H. Hudnut, Sr. ChIP
Oh, England./ Sick in head and sick in heart. England. *Unknown.* CBEP; ELU; SeCL
O England, Country of My Heart's Desire. E. V. Lucas. BoTP
Oh, England is a pleasant place for them that's rich and high. The Last [*or* Old] Buccaneer. Charles Kingsley. BeLS; EtS; EvOK; FaBoBe; GoTP; HBV; MCCG; MoShBr; PeVV; PoVP; ShBV-1; VA
O English mother, in the ruddy glow. In Snow. William Allingham. IrPN
O Englishwoman on the Pincian. Thomas Edward Brown. *Fr.* Roman Women. OBNC
O Eros, all-subduing. To Eros. Anacreon, *tr. by* John Ounsted. LiTW
O erth! on erth it is a wonders case. The Epitaph of Graunde Amour. Stephen Hawes. *Fr.* The Pastime of Pleasure. OBSC
O Eternal, in thy majesty ride. Jewish Arabic Liturgies. *Unknown.* TrJP
"Oh, Eve, where is Adam?" Adam in the Garden Pinnin' Leaves. *Unknown.* OuSiCo
O ever beauteous, ever friendly, tell. Elegy to the Memory of an Unfortunate Lady. Pope. ACP; HBV; OBEC; OBEV
Oh, ever skill'd to wear the form we love! To Hope. Helen Maria Williams. *Fr.* Julia, a Novel. OBEC
Oh, ever thus from childhood's hour, I've seen my fondest hopes recede. Muddled Metaphors. Tom Hood. NA
O everlasting kingdom of the scepter. He Maketh Himself One with the Only God Whose Limbs Are the Many Gods. *Unknown.* *Fr.* Book of the Dead. AWP; JAWP; WBP
O Everlasting Light! Christ Is All. Horatius Bonar. BePJ
Oh, every fall the chestnut men. Chestnut Stands. Rachel Field. SiSoSe
Oh, every year hath its winter. Every Year. *Unknown.* SoP
Oh, everything is far. Lament. Rainer Maria Rilke. PoPl; TrJP
O eyes which do the spheres of beauty move. Astrophel and Stella, XLII. Sir Philip Sidney. FCP; SiPS; Sonn
Oh, face to face with trouble. Margaret E. Sangster. *Fr.* Face to Face with Trouble. PoToHe
O, fain would I, before I die. *Unknown.* LO
O faint, delicious, spring-time violet! The Violet. William Wetmore Story. HBV
O fair Acoka-tree, with love's own red. The Sign. Bhartrihari. LiTW
O fair and stately maid, whose eyes. To Eva. Emerson. GTBS
Oh Fair Enough Are Sky and Plain. A. E. Housman. A Shropshire Lad, XX. MCCG; PoVP; YT
Oh, fair immaculate rose of the world, rose of my dream, my Rose! The Rose of Flame. "Fiona Macleod." PoVP
O, Fair New Mexico. Elizabeth Garrett. PoRL
O fair [*or* faire] sweet face, O eyes celestial[l] bright. Song. John Fletcher. *Fr.* Women Pleas'd. OBS; PoEL-2
Oh, Fair to See. Christina Rossetti. *Fr.* Sing-Song. DD; FaPON; MPB; OHIP; OTPC (1946 ed.); TiPo; YeAr
O faire content where do'st thou dwell. *Unknown.* SeCSL
O Faire! O Sweete! Sir Philip Sidney. *See* Song: "O fair! O sweet!"
O Fairest of the Rural Maids. Bryant. AA; AmLP; AmPP; AnAmPo; AnFE; AnNE; AP; APA; CoAnAm; CoBA; FaPL; LaNeLa; MWA-1; ViBoPo
"O fairest rose, with rosebud mouth," I sighed. God behind the Veil. Jami. OnPM
Oh, fairies love a holly tree. Holly Fairies. Aileen Fisher. ChBR
O faithless world, and thy more faithless part. A Poem Written by Sir Henry Wotton, in His Youth. Sir Henry Wotton. AnAnS-2
O Fall of the leaf, I am tired. Leaf. John Hewitt. NeIP
O, Falmouth is a fine town with ships in the bay. Home [*or* Falmouth]. W. E. Henley. GN; HBV; MoBrPo; PoLF
O false and treacherous probability. Caelica, CIII [CIV]. Fulke Greville. OBS; OxBoCh
O far away, and far away. The Happy Islands. Isabel Maud Peacocke. BoAu
O far-off darling in the South. Coeur de Lion to Berengaria. Theodore Tilton. AA
O far-off rose of long ago. A Far-off Rose. Josephine Preston Peabody. AA
O far withdrawn into the lonely West. To K. H. Thomas Edward Brown. OBNC
Oh, fare you well, I wish you well [*or* we're homeward bound]. Good-bye, Fare You Well. *Unknown.* AmSS; SoAmSa
Oh farmer have you a daughter fair, parlay-voo. Hinky Dinky. *Unknown.* TrAS
O fast her amber blood doth flow. The Phoenix. George Darley. *Fr.* Nepenthe. OBEV (new ed.); OBRV
O, fastidious mind, gorging on absolutes, remember. Promises. Ruth Forbes Sherry. GoYe
O fate, O fault, O curse, child of my bliss! Astrophel and Stella, XCIII. Sir Philip Sidney. FCP; SiPS
Oh father, answer me. Dialogue. Howard Nemerov. NYBP; PoPl
O Father, bless me good or bad. *Unknown.* ThGo
O Father give me grace and sense. *Unknown.* ThGo
Oh Father—if Thou wouldst indeed. Father. Arthur Davison Ficke. TrPWD
O Father, keep me through this day. My Daily Prayer. Eva Gray. STF
"Oh, Father! oh, Father! go build me a boat." My True Sailor Boy. *Unknown.* BFSS
O Father of Mercy. Richard Langhorn. *Fr.* The Affections of My Soul. PeRV
O Father, Thou Who Givest All. John Haynes Holmes. MaRV
O Father, we approach Thy throne. Adam's Hymn in Paradise [*or* The Hymn of Adam]. Joost van den Vondel. CAW; WGRP
O, father's gone to market town, he was up before the day. A Midsummer Song. Richard Watson Gilder. BoNaP; HBV; LHV; OTPC (1946 ed.); PRWS
O Faustus/ Now hast thou but one bare hour to live. Faustus Faces His Doom. Christopher Marlowe. TreFT
O fayre Astrea, whyther, whyther art thou gone. *Unknown.* SeCSL
O Fearfull, Frowning Nemesis. Samuel Daniel. *Fr.* Cleopatra. PoEL-2
"O Felix Culpa!" *Unknown.* *See* Adam Lay Ibounden.
O fellow-citizens of storm-tossed lands. The New Banner. Katrina Trask. PEDC
O fickle as the heart of May. Gorse. Helen Foley. POTE

"Oh, fill me flagons full and fair." Ballad of a Bridal. Edith Nesbit. VA
O fire of light divine. To the Virgin. Rodríguez del Padrón. OnPM
O first created and creating source. Ode to the Sea. Howard Baker. OxBA; UnPo (1st ed.)
Oh, flame and pain that sweeps me once again! Cassandra's Lament. Aeschylus. *Fr.* Agamemnon. LiTW
O Flame of Living Love. St. John of the Cross. *See* Living Flame of Love, The.
O flavorless white hour. Winter among the Days. Raymond Holden. MAP; MoAmPo (1942 ed.)
O flesh and blood, comrade to tragic pain. The Growth of Love, XXI. Robert Bridges. Sonn
O flower of all that springs from gentle blood. Epitaphs, VII. Gabriello Chiabrera. AWP
O Flower of flowers, our Lady of the May! Our Lady of the May. Lionel Johnson. ISi
O flower of passion, rocked by balmy gales. Gold-of-Ophir Roses. Grace Atherton Dennen. AA
O Fly My Soul. James Shirley. *Fr.* The Imposture; II, ii. AtBAP; EG; OBS; OxBoCh
(Hymn, A: "O fly, my soul!") GoBC; OBEV (1st ed.)
(Song of Nuns, A.) ACP; CAW
Oh fly not, pleasure, pleasant-hearted pleasure. Song. Wilfrid Scawen Blunt. JKCP; OBEV (1st ed.); OBVV; ViBoPo
O Fons Bandusiae. Horace. *See* To the Fountain of Bandusia.
O foolish builders!/ Not as the Architect Eternal planned. Danger. Theodora L. Paine. PGD
O Foolishnes of Men. Milton. *Fr.* Comus. AtBAP
(Comus's Praise of Nature.) poEL-3
("O foolishness of men! that lend their ears.") ViBoPo
O for a Booke [*or* Book]. *Unknown.* CH; PCH; PoSC; SiSoSe
(Open Sesame.) BoTP
Oh, for a Bowl of Fat Canary. John Lyly. *See* Serving Men's Song, A.
Oh! for a Closer Walk with God. William Cowper. *See* Walking with God.
O for a Faith That Will Not Shrink. William Hiley Bathurst. *See* Unshrinking Faith.
O for a ferryman to steer my yearning. Home-Sickness. Hedwig Lachmann. TrJP
O for a heart of calm repose. Peace. *Unknown.* STF
Oh for a heart that weeps o'er souls. A Heart That Weeps. Oswald J. Smith. SoP; STF
O for a heart to praise my God. Upon My Heart. Charles Wesley. FaChP
O for a lodge in a garden of cucumbers! Ninety-nine in the Shade. Rossiter Johnson. BOHV
Oh for a lodge in some vast wilderness. Slavery. William Cowper. *Fr.* The Task. CoBE; EnRP; OAEP
Oh, for a man to take me out. Wanted: One Cave Man with Club. Margaret Fishback. WhC
O for a Moon to Light Me Home. Walter de la Mare. OTPC
O for a Muse of fire, that would ascend. A Muse of Fire. Shakespeare. *Fr.* King Henry V, Prologue to Act I. ChTr; MemP
Oh, for a Pentecost ("Oh, for a passionate passion for souls"). *Unknown.* BLRP
(Intercession.) SoP
Oh for a Poet—for a Beacon Bright. E. A. Robinson. NePA; OxBA; Sonn
(Sonnet.) AmePo; ILP; PP
O for a sculptor's hand. Balaam. John Keble. OBNC
Oh! for a Steed. Thomas Osborne Davis. IrPN
O, for a thousand tongues to sing. Triumph of His Grace. Charles Wesley. BePJ; SoP
Oh, for an hour when the day is breaking. Nanny. Francis Davis. HBV
O for Doors to Be Open and an Invite with Gilded Edges. W. H. Auden. OAEP (2d ed.); ViBoPo
(O for Doors to Be Open.) AtBAP; CoBMV
Oh, for 'is heart is like the sea. They All Love Jack. *Unknown.* ShS
Oh, for me a horse and saddle. Just a-Ridin'! Badger Clark. SCC
O for my sake do you with Fortune chide. Sonnets, CXI. Shakespeare. SiCE; TOP
O for one hour of youthful joy! The Old Man Dreams. Oliver Wendell Holmes. HBV
O for one minute hark what we are saying! A Prayer. Frederic W. H. Myers. TrPWD
O for our upland meads. Shepherd and Shepherdess. Thomas Hennell. FaBoTw
O for Some Honest Lover's Ghost. Sir John Suckling. *See* Doubt of Martydom, A.
O, for some sunny spell. To Dream of Thee. Keats. *Fr.* Lines to Fanny. MeWo
Oh, for that sweet untroubled rest. The Sleep of Spring. John Clare. ERoP-2
O for that warning voice, which he who saw. Milton. *Fr.* Paradise Lost, IV. MBW-1; PoEL-3
Oh, for the day when Polish armies sweeping. Waiting for Sunrise. Zygmunt Krasinski. PoFr
Oh for the face and footstep!—Woods and shores! Frederick Goddard Tuckerman. *Fr.* Sonnets. AP
Oh for the good old times! When all was new. The Della Cruscans. William Gifford. *Fr.* The Baviad. OBEC
O for the mighty wakening that aroused. The Half-asleep. Thomas Wade. OBEV (1st ed.)
O for the perfumes that arise. Non Sum Qualis Eram in Bona Urbe Nordica Illa. John Hollander. ErPo
Oh, for the Time When I Shall Sleep. Emily Brontë. *Fr.* The Philosopher. ATP
O for the times which were (if any). Tempora Acta. "Owen Meredith." OBVV; VA
Oh, for the veils of my far away youth. Lost Illusions. Georgia Douglas Johnson. BANP
O for the Wings of a Dove. Euripides, *tr. fr. Greek by* Gilbert Murray. *Fr.* Hippolytus. AWP; JAWP; WBP
(Chorus: "Could I take me to some cavern for mine hiding.") BoPe; ShBV-4
(Longing.) PCD
O fortunate man! who tilled the stubborn soil. Elegy. Arthur Davison Ficke. NYTB
O fortunate, O happy day. A New Household. Longfellow. *Fr.* The Hanging of the Crane, I. GN
O Fortune, thou'rt not worth my least exclaim. John Donne. *Fr.* Elegies, XII: His Parting from Her. CoBE
O fountain-mouth, O giving, O mouth that speaks. Four Sonnets to Orpheus. Rainer Maria Rilke. *Fr.* Sonnets to Orpheus. LiTW
O fountain of Bandusia! To the Fountain of Bandusia. Horace, *tr. by* Eugene Field. AA; AWP; JAWP; WBP
O frail Adam. Epitaph for Mr. Moses Levy. *Unknown.* TrJP
Oh frame some little word for me. The Clue. Charlotte Fiske Bates. AA
O France When Thou Art Prone and Bound. Victor Hugo, *tr. fr. French by* Wilfrid Thorley. PoFr
O France, with what a shamed and sorry smile. An American to France. Alice Duer Miller. HBMV
Oh Freedom! thou art not, as poets dream. Bryant. *Fr.* Antiquity of Freedom. PoFr
O Friend, hope in Him while thou livest. Hope in Him While Thou Livest. Kabir. MaRV
O Friend, I know not which way I must look. Written in London, September, 1802 [*or* England, 1802 *or* In London, September, 1802 *or* London, 1802]. Wordsworth. BoLiVe; ChER; EnLi-2; EnRP; EPN; GTBS; GTBS-D; GTBS-P; GTBS-W; GTSL; HBV; MaRV; MBW-2; MERP; OBEV; PAn; PoPo; PPON; TrGrPo
O friend, like some cold wind to-day. To a Desolate Friend. William James Dawson. VA
O Friend of souls! how blest the time. Friend of Souls. *Unknown.* BePJ
O Friend—see the lighting there! The Storm. Imr el Kais. LiTW
Oh friend, whom glad or grave we seek. A Lover of Music to his Pianoforte. Leigh Hunt. MuSP
O friends! with whom my feet have trod. The Eternal Goodness. Whittier. AA; AmePo; AmPP (3d ed.); AnAmPo; AnFE; AnNE; APA; CoAnAm; CoBA; MaRV; OHFP; WGRP
O frivolous mind of man. Fragment of Chorus of a "Dejaneira." Matthew Arnold. MBW-2; ViPP
Oh frog went a-courtin' and he did ride, uh-huh, uh-huh. Frog Went a-Courtin'. *Unknown.* TrAS
Oh, full and soft, upon the orange trees. Tropic Sunset. Walter Adolphe Roberts. *Fr.* Boyhood Etchings. PoNe
O! Full of Scorpions. Shakespeare. *Fr.* Macbeth, III, ii. FiP

O furrowed plaintive face. The Hurrier. Harold Monro. MoBrPo
Oh, futile search of earth which ends in sorrow. In Christ Alone. Connie Calenberg. SoP
Oh Future! thou secreted peace. Emily Dickinson. MWA-2
Oh! fye upon care. The Ranting Wanton's Resolution; 1672. *Unknown.* CoMu
Oh, gaily sings the bird! and the wattle-boughs are stirred. Whisperings in Wattle-Boughs. Adam Lindsay Gordon. BoAu; OBVV
O gain that lurk'st ungainèd in all gain! Desiderium Indesideratum. Francis Thompson. PoIE (1970 ed.); StJW
O gallant brothers of the generous South. Henry Peterson. *Fr.* Ode for Decoration Day. AA; FaBoBe
Oh gallant was our galley from her carven steering-wheel. The Galley-Slave. Kipling. BEL; BrPo; PeVV
Oh, gallantly they fared forth in khaki and in blue. America's Welcome Home. Henry van Dyke. MC
Oh, Galuppi, Baldassaro, this is very sad to find! A Toccata of Galuppi's. Robert Browning. AnFE; ATP (1935 ed.); CBEP; EnLi-2 (1949 ed.); GTBS-P; HBV; LiTB; LoBV; MaVP; MBW-2; NCEP; NoP; OAEP; OtMeF; PoAn; PoE; PoFS; PoVP; ViPo; ViPP; VP; WHA
O, Gambler, Git Up off o' Yo' Knees, *with music.* *Unknown.* BoAN-1
O Gather Me the Rose. W. E. Henley. Echoes, III. BEL; MoBrPo
(Collige Rosas.) OBVV; PG
Oh gather the thoughts of your early years. Early Thoughts. William Edward Hartpole Lecky. OnYI
Oh! gay pretty valentines gladly we send. The Valentine's Message. Mildred J. Hill. GFA
O generation of the thoroughly smug and thoroughly uncomfortable. Salutation. Ezra Pound. LoGBV; MoAB; MoAmPo (1950 ed.); MoPW; OxBA
O Genevieve, I'd give this world. Sweet Genevieve. George Cooper. TreFS
O gentle, gentle land. Night Sowing. David Campbell. BoAV; PoAu-2
O gentle, gentle summer rain. Invocation to Rain in Summer [*or* Summer Invocation]. William C. Bennett. GN; HBV; OTPC
O Gentle Love. George Peele. *Fr.* The Arraignment of Paris. ElL
(Colin, the Enamored Shepherd, Singeth This Passion of Love.) ReIE
(Colin's Passion of Love.) OBSC
O gentle queen of the afternoon. Poem. W. S. Graham. NeBP
O Gentle Ships. Meleager, *tr. fr. Greek by* Andrew Lang. AWP
O gentle sleep, come, wave thine opiate wing. On Dreams. Sir Samuel Egerton Brydges. Sonn
O gentle Sleep! do they belong to thee. To Sleep. Wordsworth. Sonn
O gentle sleep, that teachest man to die. To Sleep. Jan Kochanowski. LiTW
Oh gentlemen gentlemen don't worry. John Gill. *Fr.* Spring Malediction. WOW
Oh, gentlemen, listen, I pray. The Rover's Apology. W. S. Gilbert. *Fr.* Trial by Jury. ALV
O gie the lass her fairin', lad. Gie the Lass Her Fairin'. Burns. CoMu; ErPo
O, gimme yo' han'. Gimme Yo' Han'. *Unknown.* BoAN-2
Oh, Gingilee, my aching heart. Gingilee. Moishe-Leib Halpern. TrJP
Oh, git around, Jinny, git around. Jinny Git Around. *Unknown.* OuSiCo
Oh, Give Me a Home Where the Buffalo Roam. *Unknown.* *See* Home on the Range, A.
O give me back my rigorous English Sunday. The Fresh Start. Anna Wickham. ViBoPo
Oh, give me, Lord, Thy love for souls. The Soul Winner's Prayer. Eugene M. Harrison. STF
O give thanks unto the Lord, for He is good. O Give Thanks. Psalm CXVIII, Bible, *O.T.* TrJP
O give thanks unto [*or* to] the Lord; for he is good [*or* gracious]. Thanksgiving. Psalm CXXXVI, Bible, *O.T.* AWP; BoChLi (1950 ed.); OHIP
Oh, give us pleasure in the flowers to-day. A Prayer in Spring. Robert Frost. MaRV; MoRP; OTPC (1946 ed.); TrPWD; WePo; YeAr; YT
O give yee thanks unto the Lord. Psalm CVII, Bible, *O.T.* SCAP
O glad New Year! O glad New Year! New Year's Day. *Unknown.* PEDC
O Glorious Childbearer. Joseph Campbell. OnYI
O Glorious Christ of God; I live. Cotton Mather. SCAP
O Glorious Immensity. Deus Immensa Trinitas. *Unknown.* CAW
O glorious Lady of the Light. Death-Bed Hymn of Saint Anthony of Padua. St. Anthony of Padua. CAW
Oh glorious mystery of Love. Glorious Mystery. Avis B. Christiansen. SoP
Oh glorious spirits, who after all your bands. To All Angels and Saints. George Herbert. MaMe; SeCV-1
O glory of the lighted mind. The Everlasting Mercy. John Masefield. StJW
O Glory of Virgins. Fortunatus, *tr. fr. Latin by* Sister Maura. ISi
"O go again," said the King. King Arthur's Death. *Unknown.* ACP
O God,/ forever I turn in this hard crystal. The Prayer of the Goldfish. Carmen Bernos de Gasztold. PDV
O God,/ I am little and very black. The Prayer of the Cricket. Carmen Bernos de Gasztold. TIHL
O god above, relent. Here Followeth the Songe of the Death of Mr. Thewlis. *Unknown.* CoMu
O God, beloved God, in pity send. John Masefield. BoPe
O God, beneath Thy guiding hand. The Pilgrim Fathers. Leonard Bacon. MaRV; WGRP
O God creator, in whose hand. The Airmen's Hymn. Harry Webb Farrington. MaRV
O God, early in the morning do I cry unto Thee. Dietrich Bonhoeffer, Awaiting Execution in a Concentration Camp, Prays for His Fellow Prisoners. Dietrich Bonhoeffer. BoC
O God, grant us the serenity to accept. Prayer for Serenity. Reinhold Niebuhr. TreFT
O God! Have Mercy, in This Dreadful Hour. Robert Southey. TrPWD
O God, Hear Thou the Nation's Prayer. Irving Maurer. MaRV
O God, How Many Years Ago. Frederic William Henry Myers. HBMV
O God, I love thee, I love thee. O Deus, Ego Amo Te. *Unknown, tr. by* Gerard Manley Hopkins. PoLi; TrPWD
O God, I love Thee in the stars at night. Prayer. Nadejda de Bragança. MaRV
O God, I Need Thee! *Unknown* SoP
Oh God, I offer Thee my heart. Consecration. *Unknown.* TRV
Oh God! if this indeed be all. If This Be All. Anne Brontë. TrPWD
O God, in the dream the terrible horse began. The Dream. Louise Bogan. LiTA; LiTM; MoAB; MoAmPo (1950 ed.)
O God, in whom my deepest being dwells. A Psalm. Edmund Blunden. TrPWD
O God, inasmuch as without Thee. Limerick. *Unknown.* LiBL
O God, keep not Thou silence. Keep Not Thou Silence. Psalm LXXXIII, Bible, *O.T.* TrJP
Oh, God, let me be beautiful in death. Last Plea. Jean Starr Untermeyer. TrPWD
Oh god, let's go. Please. Robert Creeley. ML
O God, make it rain! Prayer for Rain. Herbert E. Palmer. HaMV; POTE; WePo
O God! methinks it were a happy life. King Henry VI Yearns for a Simple Life. Shakespeare. King Henry VI, Pt. III, *fr.* II, v. TreFS
O God most glorious, called by many a name. The Hymn of Cleanthes. Cleanthes, *tr. by* James Adam. MaRV
O God! my God! have mercy now. Supposed Confessions of a Second-rate Sensitive Mind. Tennyson. ViPP
O God, my master God, look down and see. The Artisan. Alice Brown. TrPWD
O God, no more Thy miracle withhold. Prayer for Miracle. Anna Wickham. GoTP; OQP; YT
O God, not like a stagnant pool. My Life. J. Gordon Howard. SoP
O God! O Montreal! Samuel Butler. DTC; NBM; OxBoLi
(Psalm of Montreal, A.) CBEP
O God, O Venus, O Mercury, patron of thieves. The Lake Isle.

Ezra Pound. CABA; CrMA; SiTL
O God of Battles, who art still. On the Eve of War. Danske Dandridge. PAH
O God of Calvary and Bethlehem. The Hem of His Garment. Ann Elizabeth Hamilton. TrPWD
Oh, God of dust and rainbows, help us see. Two Somewhat Different Epigrams, I. Langston Hughes. Kal; NePoAm-2
O God of Earth and Altar. G. K. Chesterton. *See* Hymn, A: "O God of earth and altar."
O God of ev'ry kind of earth. Rule On. Phyllis C. Michael. SoP
O God of Field and City. John Haynes Holmes. MaRV
O God of Goodness, Forwardness, and Fulness. Prayer. Doris Hedges. GoYe
O God of grace, Thou God of free salvation. Prayer for Missionaries, A. Henry W. Frost. SoP
O God of Light. R. B. Y. Scott. MaRV
O God of love, O King of peace. Christ the Consoler. Henry W. Baker. BePJ
O God of Love, to Thee We Bow. William Vaughan Jenkins. MaRV
O God of love unbounded! Lord supreme! Prayer to God. "Placido." CAW; TTY
O God of strength, fabled Omnipotence. Cry for a Dead Soldier. Mary L. Inman. NYTB
O God of the Impossible. "J. H. S." SoP
O God, our Father if we had but truth! A Prayer. Edward Rowland Sill. AA
O God, Our Help in Ages Past. Isaac Watts. EaLo; HBV; MaRV; NeHB; OxBoCh; Po; SoP; TOP; WGRP
(Man Frail and God Eternal.) CBEP; EiCL; EiPP; OBEC; PoE; PoEL-3
(Ninetieth Psalm.) BLRP
(Recessional.) TreF
O God that art the sole hope of the world. The Venerable Bede, *tr. fr. Latin by* Helen Waddell. BoC
O God, the cleanest offering. Father Damien. John Banister Tabb. ACP; AmP; JKCP
O God, the heathen are come into Thine inheritance. The Heathen Are Come into Thine Inheritance. Psalm LXXIX, Bible, *O.T.* TrJP
O God, the Rock of Ages. Edward H. Bickersteth. BLPA
O God, thou art my right wiseness. Cum Invocarem. Psalm IV, Bible, *O.T.*, *tr. by* Thomas Sternhold. SiCE
O God, Thou art the object of my love. Hymn of Love. St. Francis Xavier. WHL
O God, Thy heavens, in the hush of night. The City of God. Henry B. Robins. MaRV
O God, thy moon is on the hills. Kelpius's Hymn. Arthur Peterson. AA
O God, thy ways are dark. Edward Bliss Reed. *Fr.* Prayer: "She cannot tell my name." MaRV
O God to Thee I Yield. Thomas Edward Brown. PoVP
O God, unknown, invisible, secure. John Addington Symonds. *Fr.* An Invocation. MaRV; TrPWD; TRV
O God, we thank Thee for everything. The One Thousandth Psalm. Edward Everett Hale. SoP; TRV
O God, when You send for me, let it be. Prayer to Go to Paradise with the Asses. Francis Jammes. AWP; BoPe; JAWP; WBP
O God, where do they tend—these struggling aims? Robert Browning. *Fr.* Pauline. WGRP
O God, Who guid'st the fate of nations. Hymn. Gunnar Wennerberg. PoFr
O God, who has three eyes. Song of the Young Girls. *Unknown.* OnPM
O God, whose daylight leadeth down. George Macdonald. *Fr.* Evening Hymn. TrPWD
O God Whose Love Is over All. John Haynes Holmes. MaRV
O God, Whose Smile Is in the Sky. John Haynes Holmes. MaRV
O God, whose will is life and peace. Prayer for Peace. Rolland W. Schloerb. MaRV
O God, within whose sight. Prayer for the Churches. John Oxenham. OQP
O goddess! give me back the ready laughter. To the Frivolous Muse. George Meason Whicher. InMe
O Goddess! hear these tuneless numbers, wrung. Ode to Psyche. Keats. CABA; CaFP; CBEP; ChER; DiPo; EnRP; EPN; ERoP-2; GTBS-W; HBV; LiTB; LoBV; MaPo; MBW-2; MERP; NoP; OAEP; OBEV; OBNC; OBRV; PeER; PIA; PoEL-4; PP; StP; ViBoPo; WHA
O Goddess of the gloomy scene. Ode to Horror. *Unknown.* WaPE
O Godhead hid, devoutly I adore Thee. Adoro Te Devote. St. Thomas Aquinas. CAW
O gold Hyperion, love-lorn Porphyro. Keats. William Wilberforce Lord. *Fr.* Ode to England. AA
O Golden Fleece. George Barker. *Fr.* Secular Elegies. LiTM; MoAB; MoBrPo (1950 ed.)
(Love Poem.) LiTL
("O Golden Fleece she is where she lies tonight.") ErPo; NeBP
Oh, golden-lilied Queen—immortal France! France. Elliott Napier. BoAu
O golden lyre, who art Phoebus' treasure. The First Pythian Ode of Pindar. Pindar. Pythian Odes, I. WoL
O golden-red and tall chrysanthemums. Chrysanthemums. F. S. Flint. MoBrPo (1942 ed.)
Oh! Golden rose! Oh. Glittering lilly white. Edward Taylor. *Fr.* Preparatory Meditations, Second Series. SCAP
O golden-tongued Romance, with serene lute! On Sitting Down to Read "King Lear" Once Again. Keats. ATP; DiPo; EnRP; ERoP-2; MaPo (1969 ed.); MBW-2; NoP
Oh, good gigantic smile o' the brown old earth. Robert Browning. *Fr.* James Lee's Wife. BoLiVe; EPN; OBVV; YT
"O good Lord Judge, and sweet Lord Judge." The Maid Freed from the Gallows. *Unknown.* AnFE; BaBo (A *vers.*); ESPB; InPo; TOP; ViBoFo (A *vers.*)
O good New Year! we clasp. Address to the New Year. Dinah Maria Mulock Craik. PEDC
O good painter, tell me true. An Order for a Picture. Alice Cary. BLPA
O good Sun/ Look thou down upon us. Song for Fine Weather. *Tr. by* Constance Lindsay Skinner. AWP; JAWP; WBP
O Goodly Hand. Sir Thomas Wyatt. FCP; InvP; SiPS
(His Lady's Hand.) OBSC
O Goody, it's coming, the circus parade. The Circus Parade. Olive Beaupré Miller. TiPo
O gracious city well-beloved. The Laud of Saint Catherine. Swinburne. *Fr.* Siena. CAW
O gracious God, O Saviour sweet. O That I Had Wings like a Dove. *Unknown.* OxBoCh
O Gracious Shepherd. Henry Constable. OxBoCh
O grammar-rules, O now your virtues show. Astrophel and Stella, LXIII. Sir Philip Sidney. FCP; SiPS; TuPP
O grandest of the Angels, and most wise. Litany to Satan. Baudelaire. AWP; SyP
O grasses wet with dew, yellow fallen leaves. A Glimpse. Frances Cornford. OBMV
O gratious Lord, how shall I know. The H. Communion. George Herbert. MaMe
O graveyard. Lay Dis Body Down. *Unknown.* ABF
O Great Mary. The Gaelic Litany to Our Lady. *Unknown.* CAW; ISi
O great, rebellious and ferocious sea! Against the Hope of Reconstruction. F. T. Marinetti. OnHM
O Great Spirit! Voyager's Prayer. *Unknown.* TRV; WGRP
O great sun of heaven, harm not my love. An Incantation. Marguerite Wilkinson. NP
Oh, green grow the lilacs and so does the rue. Green Grow the Lilacs. *Unknown.* TreFT
Oh! greenly and fair in the land of the sun. The Pumpkin. Whittier. DD; OHIP
O Grief! *Unknown.* EIL
Oh, grieve not, ladies, if at night. Grieve Not, Ladies. Anna Hempstead Branch. AnAmPo; FaFP; HBV
Oh, grim and gloomy. Grim and Gloomy. James Reeves. RePo
O guns, fall silent till the dead men hear. The Anxious Dead. John McCrae. OHIP
Oh, had it been mine, that upper room. The Upper Room. Belle F. Owens. ChIP
O had she not been fair and thus unkind. To Delia, VII. Samuel Daniel. ReIE
O had truth power, the guiltless could not fall. His Petition to Queen Anne of Denmark (1618) [*or* Petition to the Queen]. Sir Walter Ralegh. FCP; SiPS
Oh! had you eyes, but eyes that move. Formosae Puellae. Herbert P. Horne. VA

O [*or* Ah,] had you seen the Coolun. The Coolun. Maurice O'Dugan. AnIV; OnYI; OxBI
O Hallelujah!—now I see. Second Benefit! Mary Ferguson. SoP
"Oh Hangman, oh Hangman, oh Hangman hold your rope.' The Hangman Tree. *Unknown.* BFSS
Oh, hapless sire, distraught with cares. The Yoke. Kalonymos ben Kalonymos. *Fr.* The Touchstone. TrJP
O happiest village! how I turned to you. Old Homes. Edmund Blunden. MoVE
Oh, happiness! he said, and took his life. Five Epigrams, 2. Donald Hall. NePoAm-2
Oh Happiness! our being's end and aim! Pope. *Fr.* An Essay on Man, Epistle IV. ATP
O happy age of gold; happy hours. O Bella Età de l'Oro. Tasso, *tr. by* Henry Reynolds. *Fr.* Aminta. FosPo
O happy are they that have forgiveness got. Psalm XXXII. *Paraphrased by* Sir Thomas Wyatt. FCP
O happy dames, that may embrace. Complaint of the Absence of Her Lover Being upon the Sea [*or* A Lady Complains *or* The Seafarer]. Earl of Surrey. EIL; ELP; EnPo; FCP; OBEV; OBSC; ReEn; SiCE; SiPS
Oh, happy day, that fixed my choice. Happy Day. Philip Doddridge. SoP
Oh, happy folk, contented folk, and ye that go with gold. The Red Cross Christmas Seal. Theodosia Garrison. PEDC
O happy golden Age. A Pastoral[l]. Tasso, *tr. by* Samuel Daniel. *Fr.* Aminta. OBSC; PoEL-2; ReEn; ReIE
Oh, happy, happy maid. A Nuptial Eve. Sydney Dobell. OBNC; VA
O Happy Home. Karl J. P. Spitta, *tr. fr. German.* FaChP, 2 *sts.*; MaRV
(O Happy House, *tr. by* Sarah Findlater.) SoP
O happy life, whose love is found! Queen and Slave. Mortimer Collins. OBVV
O happy seafarers are ye. William Morris. *Fr.* The Life and Death of Jason. ViBoPo
Oh, happy shades to me unblest! The Shrubbery. William Cowper. BWP; CBEP; CEP; FaBoEn; GTSL; NCEP; OBEC; PoIE; StP
O happy Sleep! thou bear'st upon thy breast. Sleep. Ada Louise Martin. HBV
O Happy Soul. Washington Gladden. FaChP; MaRV
O happy Thames that didst my Stella bear. Astrophel and Stella, CIII. Sir Philip Sidney. FCP; HBV; ReEn; SiPS
O happy the huntsman returns to his native wood. Ode. Frederic Prokosch. ViBoPo (1941 ed.)
O happy Tithon! if thou know'st thy hap. Earl of Stirling. *Fr.* Aurora, Song IX. OBEV
O happy trees that we plant today. Tree Planting. *Unknown.* OHIP
Oh, happy wind, how sweet. Happy Wind. W. H. Davies. OTPC (1946 ed.); PCH; RIS; StaSt; TSW
O happy world to-day if we could know. Thought for Easter. Mary E. McCullough. MaRV
O hard endeavor, to blend in with these. Elegy in Six Sonnets. Frederick Goddard Tuckerman. *Fr.* Sonnets. QFR
Oh hard is the bed they have made him. Illic Jacet. A. E. Housman. VP
Oh, hark the dogs are barking, love. The Banks of the Condamine. *Unknown.* PoAu-1
Oh, hark the pulses of the night. The Reason. James Oppenheim. HBV
O hark! 'tis the note of the Schmaltztenor! Schmaltztenor. M. W. Branch. FiBHP
Oh, hark to the brown thrush! hear how he sings! Joy-Month. David Atwood Wasson. HBV
O Hark to the Herald. Eleazar ben Kalir, *tr. fr. Hebrew by* Israel Zangwill. TrJP
O harmless feast. Song. Barten Holyday. *Fr.* Technogamia. EIL
O, hate me not for my grey hair. To His Mistress, Who Said She Hated Him for His Grey Hairs [*or* A Song: In the Name of a Lover]. William Wycherley. SeCL; SeCV-2
O hateful harm! condicion of poverte! Prologue to the Man of Law's Tale. Chaucer. *Fr.* The Canterbury Tales. FiP
Oh, haul away the bowline, the packet ship's a-rollin'! Haul Away, Joe, *vers.* II. *Unknown.* ShS
Oh, haul pulley, yoe! Cheer'ly, O! *Unknown.* AmSS
Oh, Haunting Spirit of the Ever True. Allan Knight Chalmers. MaRV
O, have ye been in love, me boys. I Met Her in the Garden Where the Praties Grow. *Unknown.* AS
O have ye na heard o' the fause Sakelde? Kinmont Willie. *Unknown.* BaBo; BEL; ESPB; OBB; OxBB
O, have you been in Gudbrand's dale, where Laagen's mighty flood. Thoralf and Synnöv. Hjalmar Hjorth Boyesen. AA
Oh, have you heard the news, my Johnny? One More Day. *Unknown.* SoAmSa
O have you seen my fairy steed? "She Wandered after Strange Gods." Laura Benét. HBMV
O, have you seen the leper healed. The Healing of the Leper. Vernon Watkins. FaBoTw
O have you seen the Stratton flood. Stratton Water. Dante Gabriel Rossetti. OxBB
Oh, He who walked with fishermen. A Fisherman Speaks. Scharmel Iris. ChIP
Oh, Hear Me Prayin', *with music.* *Unknown.* BoAN-2
O hear ye that foul and fiendish laughter. War. J. Gilchrist Lawson. WBLP
O heard ye not of [*or* na o'] the silly blind Harper. The Lochmabyn Harper. *Unknown.* BuBa; OBB; OxBB
O heard ye of a bloody knight. Lady Isabel and the Elf-Knight (B *vers.*). *Unknown.* BaBo
O heard ye of Sir James the Rose. Sir James the Rose. *Unknown.* ESPB
O heard ye yon pibroch sound sad in the gale. Glenara. Thomas Campbell. HBV
O hearken, all ye little weeds. Candlemas. Alice Brown. AA; PoRL
O hearken and hear, and I will you tell. The Friar in the Well (B *vers.*). *Unknown.* ESPB
O hearken and hear the while I will tell. The Friar and the Fair Maid. *Unknown.* UnTE
Oh, hearken to my story, hearken gentles all. The Prodigal Son. *Unknown.* SaSa
O Heart. Maurice Rowntree. OQP
O heart, be at peace, because. Against Unworthy Praise. W. B. Yeats. AnFE
O heart, be lifted up; O heart be gay. Good Friday. *Unknown.* BoC
O heart, hold thee secure. Walter de la Mare. BoPe
O Heart of hearts, the chalice of love's fire. Cor Cordium. Swinburne. ATP (1935 ed.); EPN; MaVP; PoVP; TOP; ViPo; VP
O heart of mine, we shouldn't worry so. Just Be Glad. James Whitcomb Riley. WBLP
O Heart of Spring! Shaw Neilson. BoAu
Oh heart rejoice! For I Have Done a Good and Kindly Deed. Franz Werfel. TrJP
O Heart, Small Urn. Hilda Doolittle ("H. D."). AtBAP
O heart submissive in this martyrdom. The Assumption. John Gilland Brunini. ISi
O Heart, that beats with every human heart. O Heart. Maurice Rowntree. OQP
O heart, the equal poise of love's both parts. Richard Crashaw. *Fr.* The Flaming Heart. EG; ReEn; TrGrPo
O heart, why dost thou sigh, and wilt not break? When He Thought Himself Contemned. Thomas Howell. EIL; ReIE; TuPP
O hearts are bruised and dead. Our Work. William W. How. SoP
O heavenly colour [*or* color], London town. November Blue. Alice Meynell. MoBrPo; YT
O heavenly fool! thy most kiss-worthy face. Anna Wickham. LO
O Heavy Step of Slow Monotony. Ernst Toller, *tr. fr. German by* Ashley Dukes. TrJP
Oh heere's my mother: I ha strange newes for you. John Webster. *Fr.* The Devil's Law-Case, III, iii. AtBAP
O height dispersed and head. Happiness in the Trees. Joseph Ceravolo. ANYP
O Heitsi-Eibib. Hunter's Prayer. *Unknown.* PeSA
O helpless few in my country. The Rest. Ezra Pound. AmP; AmPP; MAP; MoAB; MoAmPo; OxBA; PP; WOW
Oh, here's a jolly lark. The Old Marquis and His Blooming Wife. *Unknown.* CoMu
O Hero, Hero, thus he cry'de full oft. Christopher Marlowe. *Fr.* Hero and Leander. AtBAP
Oh, hero of our younger race! Washington. Harriet Monroe. *Fr.* Commemoration Ode. AA; OQP; PoRL

O Hesperus! thou bringest all good things. Evening [*or* Hesperus *or* Hesperus the Bringer]. Byron. *Fr.* Don Juan, III. AWP; BoLiVe; JAWP; OnPM; OTPC; OuHeWo; TOP; TrGrPo; WBP
O hideous little bat, the size of snot. The Fly. Karl Shapiro. CoBA; LiTM; MiAP; MoVE; NePA; TwAmPo
Oh ho! oh ho! Pray, who can I be? Guessing Song. Henry Johnstone. OTPC (1946 ed.); PRWS
"Oh, hold your hand, butcher!" this fair one she cried. The Silk Merchant's Daughter, *vers.* I. *Unknown.* ShS
"Oh, Hollow! Hollow! Hollow!" W. S. Gilbert. *Fr.* Patience. PoVP
O holy Aether, and swift-winged Winds. The Wail of Prometheus Bound. Aeschylus. *Fr.* Prometheus Bound. WGRP
O Holy, blessed, glorious Trinitie. To the Holy Trinitie. Ben Jonson. SCEP-2
Oh, holy cause. Sung on a Sunny Morning. Jean Starr Untermeyer. TrPWD
O Holy City seen of John. The Holy City. W. Russell Bowie. MaRV
O Holy God, undone by guilt depressing. Worship. Henry W. Frost. SoP
O holy Jerusalem, Vision of peace. Advent Lyrics, III. *Unknown.* *Fr.* Christ I. AnOE
O holy Love, religious saint! Ditty. Sir Robert Chester. *Fr.* Love's Martyr. EIL
O Holy Mother, thou who still dost send. At the Tomb of Rachel. "Yehoash." TrJP
O holy Saviour! Friend unseen! My Soul Shall Cling to Thee. Charlotte Elliott. BePJ
O holy virgin! clad in purest white. To Morning. Blake. EnRP; ERoP-1
O Holy Water. Margot Ruddock. OBMV
"O hone a rie'! O hone a rie'!" Glenfinlas. Sir Walter Scott. GoTL
O honest face, which all men knew. Richard Henry Stoddard. *Fr.* Abraham Lincoln. PAH
Oh, honey, li'l honey, come and lay yo' wooly head. Lullaby. Edmund S. Leamy. GBV (1922 ed.)
O! Honour! Honour! Honour! Oh! the Gain! God's Selecting Love in the Decree. Edward Taylor. *Fr.* God's Determinations. PoEL-3
O hotspur torrent, crested high in air. A Freshet. Antiphilus of Byzantium. LiTW
O hour of all hours, the most blest upon the earth. The Dinner Hour. "Owen Meredith." *Fr.* Lucile. VA
O hour of incest! Cyril Tourneur. *Fr.* The Revenger's Tragedy, I, iii. AtBAP
O how came I that loved stars, moon, and flame. The Image of Delight. William Ellery Leonard. AnFE; APA; CoAnAm; HBMV; MAP; MoAmPo (1942 ed.)
O how can they look up to heaven. Lesson of Love. Simon Browne. SoP
O how canst thou renounce the boundless store. Nature's Charms. James Beattie. *Fr.* The Minstrel, I. OBEV
O, how comely it is, and how reviving. The Deliverer [*or* Out of Adversity]. Milton. *Fr.* Samson Agonistes. LH; OBEV; OBS; SeCeV
O' How deep is thy love says/ the Hymnal. Sept. 1957. Edward Marshall. CoPo
O how feeble is man's power. John Donne. *Fr.* Song: "Sweetest love, I do not go." LO
Oh, how hard it is to find. Song. Thomas Campbell. CLwM
O how I faint when I of you do write. Sonnets, LXXX. Shakespeare. ReEn; SiCE
O! how I long to be at rest! Aspiration. William Drennan. IrPN
Oh, how I love Humanity. The World State. G. K. Chesterton. CoBE; PoPo
O How I Love Thy Law. Isaac Watts. STF
Oh, how I love to skip alone. Skipping Along Alone. Winifred Welles. SoPo; TiPo
Oh I wish the sun was bright in the sky. The Terrible Robber Men. Padraic Colum. LOW
O, how may I/ Call this a lightning? With a Kiss I Die. Shakespeare. *Fr.* Romeo and Juliet, V, iii. LiTL
O, how much more doth beauty beauteous seem. Sonnets, LIV. Shakespeare. AWP; EIL; EnLi-1 (1949 ed.); JAWP; LiTG; OBEV; OBSC; PoeP; ReEn; ReIE; SiCE; TOP; ViBoPo; WBP
O how my mind/ Is gravell'd. Confusion. Christopher Hervey. Par
Oh, how my pulse pipes to go riding, go riding. Riding. Harry Amoss. CaP
O! how my thoughts do beat me. *Unknown.* OBSC
Oh how oft I wake and find. To My God. George Macdonald. FaChP; TrPWD; TRV
O how oft shalt thou complain. Richard Crashaw. *Fr.* A Hymn to the Name and Honor of the Admirable Saint Teresa. PoLi
O how one ugly trick has spoiled. Meddlesome Matty. Ann Taylor. HBV; HBVY
Oh! how shall I get it, how shall I get it? The Egg. Laura E. Richards. MPB; TiPo (1952 ed.)
O How Sweet Are Thy Words! Anne Steele. BLRP
Oh, how the nights are short. Midsummer Courtship. James Thomson. *Fr.* Richard Forest's Midsummer Night. OBVV
O how the pleasant airs of true love be. Astrophel and Stella, LXXVIII. Sir Philip Sidney. FCP; SiPS
O, how this spring of love resembleth. This Spring of Love. Shakespeare. *Fr.* The Two Gentlemen of Verona, I, iii. ChTr
Oh, how with brightness hath Love filled my way. Ideal Passion XXX. George Edward Woodberry. HBMV
O human hearts,/ Beating through fear, through jealousy. Prepare. Witter Bynner. PGD
Oh humming all and. Detach, Invading. Ron Padgett. ANYP
Oh, Huntsman, when will the hunting stop. To Charlotte Corday. Sir Osbert Sitwell. ChMP
O hurry where by water among trees. The Ragged Wood. W. B. Yeats. BoC; LO; PoPo
Oh, hush, my heart, and take thine ease. April Weather. Lizette Woodworth Reese. DD; HBMV
Oh, hush thee, here in the hollow. Mary's Lullaby. Elizabeth J. Coatsworth. ChrBoLe
Oh hush thee, little Dear-my-Soul. Christmas Eve. Eugene Field. OHIP
O, hush thee, my babie [*or* baby], thy sire was a knight. Lullaby of an Infant Chief. Sir Walter Scott. EnRP; FaPON; GoTP; HBV; MPB; OTPC; PCH; PoRH; PRWS; RIS; TVC
Oh! hush thee, my baby, the night is behind us. Seal Lullaby. Kipling. *Fr.* The Jungle Book: The White Seal. FaPON; PoRA; PRWS; TiPo (1959 ed.)
O! hush thee, my darling, sleep soundly my son. Lullaby. *Unknown.* TrJP
Oh! hush Thee, Oh! hush Thee, my Baby so small. Cradle Song at Bethlehem. E. J. Falconer. BoTP
O hushed October morning mild. October. Robert Frost. GoJo; MAmP; MaPo; MWA-2
O Hymen, Long Their Coupled Joys Maintain! Sir Philip Sidney. *See* Epithalamium: "Let Mother Earth now deck herself in flowers."
O Hymen! O Hymenee! Walt Whitman. ErPo
Oh I am a bachelor, I live all alone. The Foggy Foggy Dew. *Unknown.* PoG
Oh, I am a brave desperado. A Song of the Movie Mexican. Edwin Meade Robinson. LHV
Oh, I am a rusty cowboy. The Drifter. Dave Hughes. CoSo
Oh, I am a Texas cowboy, far away from home. The Texas Cowboy. *Unknown.* CoSo
O I am sick, I am sick to death, tis soe. *At. to* Henry Hughes. SeCSL
Oh I am the King of Siam, I am! Dynastic Tiff. Geoffrey Hellman. ALV
Oh, I am weary of a heart that brings. Helios. Joel Elias Springarn. AA
Oh, I be vun of the useful troibe. A Rustic Song. Anthony C. Deane. FiBHP; InMe
O I C. *Unknown.* SiTL; WhC
Oh, I can hear you, God, above the cry. Wind in the Pine. Lew Sarett. MaRV; OTPC (1946 ed.); TrPWD; TRV
Oh, I come from the world below. Rise Me Up from Down Below. *Unknown.* ShS
O I do love thee, meek Simplicity. To Simplicity. Samuel Taylor Coleridge. Sonn
O I Do Love, Then Kiss Me. Robert Jones. *See* Madrigal: "O I do love, then kiss me."
Oh, I don't want to be a gambler. I Don't Want to Be a Gambler. *Unknown.* AS
O I feel like the kinks in the paws of the Sphinx. Hotel Continental. William Jay Smith. WaP

"O I forbid you maidens a' [*or* all]." Tam Lin [*or* Tamlane]. *Unknown.* BaBo; BuBa; CABL; ESPB; OBB; OBEV; OxBB; OxBS; ViBoFo
Oh, I had a horse and his name was Bill. The Horse Named Bill. *Unknown.* AS
O I hae come from far away. The Witch's Ballad. William Bell Scott. AnFe; CH; EvOK; NBM; OBEV; OBVV; PeVV
O, I ha'nt got no home, nor nothing else, I s'pose. Life in California. David G. Robinson. SGR
Oh! I have been North, and I have been South, and the East hath seen me pass. North, East, South, and West. *Unknown.* BOHV
Oh I have grown so shrivelled and sere. Body of John. R. A. K. Mason. AnNZ
Oh! I haved loved thee fondly, ever. Stanzas to Pale Ale. *Unknown.* BOHV
Oh, I have slipped the surly bonds of earth. High Flight. John Gillespie Magee, Jr. BBV (1951 ed.); FaFP; FaPON; MaC; MaRV; OTD; PGD; POTE; SoP; TreFS; TRV; WaKn
Oh, I have sown my love so wide. After Parting. Sara Teasdale. TOP
Oh, I have walked in Kansas. Kansas. Vachel Lindsay. HT; TOP
Oh, I know a certain woman who is reckoned with the good. A Pin. Ella Wheeler Wilcox. BOHV
O, I know de Lord. I Know de Lord's Laid His Hands on Me. *Unknown.* BoAN-2
Oh! I know why the alder trees. I Know. Elsa Barker. HBMV
Oh! I love to travel far and near throughout my native land. Wizard Oil. *Unknown.* AS
O I say my Mammy Dinah,/ What is the matter? Sing Sally O! *Unknown.* SoAmSa
O I see flashing that this America is only you and me. Walt Whitman. *Fr.* By Blue Ontario's Shore. PoIE
O, I shall run mad! John Webster. *Fr.* The Devil's Law Case. LO
Oh, I should like to ride the seas. Song of Perfect Propriety. Dorothy Parker. InMe
Oh, I should love to be like one of those. The Youth Dreams. Rainer Maria Rilke. AWP; JAWP; TrJP; WBP
Oh, I used to sing a song. The Endless Song. Ruth McEnery Stuart. BOHV
O, I wad like to ken—to the beggar-wife says I. The Spaewife. Robert Louis Stevenson. BrPo; OxBS; PoVP; VA
Oh, I want to win me hame. Lament of the Scotch-Irish Exile. James Jeffrey Roche. BOHV
Oh! I was harsh to say that I could part. The Recantation. Albius Tibullus. LiTW
Oh, I was honest in the womb. Scarabs for the Living VI. R. P. Blackmur. TwAmPo
Oh, I was hungry from head to foot. Old Bill. *Unknown.* ABF
Oh, I went down South for to see my Sal. Polly Wolly Doodle. *Unknown.* TreF; YaD
Oh, I went down to Framingham. Spooks. Nathalia Crane. ShM; StaSt
O I went into the stable. Our Goodman. *Unknown.* ESPB
Oh, I will go with carefree laugh. Inexperience. June Breining. PoMa
"Oh, I will put my ship in order." The Drowsy Sleeper (B *vers.*). *Unknown.* BaBo
O I will sing to you a sang. The Clerk's Twa Sons o Owsenford. *Unknown.* BaBo; ESPB
Oh! I wish I were a tiny brown bird from out the south. Valentine's Day. Charles Kingsley. BoTP
O! I wish the sun was bright in the sky. The Terrible Robber Men. Padraic Colum. HBMV; RG
Oh, I wonder they break not in blossom. Stones and Blossoms. *Unknown.* OnPM
O I Won't Lead a Homely Life. Thomas Hardy. UnS
Oh, I woud I wee a cose, cose fiend. Sim Ines. Jane Stubbs. FiBHP
Oh, I would be a channel, Lord. I Would Be a Channel. Myra Brooks Welch. SoP
Oh, I would be a cowboy and with the cowboys stand. Up the Trail. *Unknown.* CoSo
Oh, I would like to be a ghoul. Desire. Nathalia Crane. MAP; MoAmPo (1942 ed.)
Oh, if ever I get married, it will be in june. The Banks of the Roses. *Unknown.* ShS
Oh, if I could only make you see. Her Mother. Alice Cary. OHIP
O if love were had for asking. The Sailor's Sweetheart. Duncan Campbell Scott. PeCV
Oh, if my love offended me. Pet's Punishment. Joseph Ashby-Sterry. BOHV
O, if the world I make. The Dream. Arthur Symons. SyP
Oh, if the world were mine, Love. If. James Jeffrey Roche. HBV
Oh if They Only Knew! Edith L. Mapes. BLRP; WBLP
Oh, if thou knew'st how thou thyself dost harm. To Aurora. Earl of Stirling. Aurora, XXXIII. ElL; FaFP; GTBS; GTBS-D; GTBS-P; GTBS-W; GTSE; GTSL; Sonn
Oh, if you love her. Advice to a Lover. S. Charles Jellicoe. HBV
Oh, if you were a little boy. Wishes. Kate Greenaway. BoChLi (1950 ed.)
Oh! ignorant boy, it is the secret hour. Phraxanor to Joseph. Charles Jeremiah Wells. *Fr.* Joseph and His Brethren. VA
O ignorant poor man, what dost thou bear. An Acclamation. Sir John Davies. *Fr.* Nosce Teipseum. OxBoCh; TuPP
Oh, I'm a good old rebel, that's what I am. The Rebel [*or* Good Old Rebel]. Innes Randolph. ABF; OxBoLi; ThLM
Oh, I'm a gwinter sing, gwinter sing. Gwinter Sing All along de Way. *Unknown.* BoAN-1
Oh, I'm a little Tuchman. The Little Dutchman. Mary Mapes Dodge. GaP
Oh, I'm a-gwine to leave you, Shallo. Shallo Brown. *Unknown.* SoAmSa
Oh I'm in love with the janitor's boy. The Janitor's Boy. Nathalia Crane. GoTP; NeMA; PoLF; StaSt
Oh, I'm mad for Don Juan. How to Tell Juan Don from Another. Gardner E. Lewis. FiBHP
Oh! I'm the New Year. The New Year. *Unknown.* BoTP
Oh, in Byrontown of high renown. Byrontown. Larry Gorman. ShS
Oh, in eighteen hundred and forty-one [*or* sixty-one]. Paddy Works on the Railway [*or* Poor Paddy. . .]. *Unknown.* AmSS; AS; SoAmSa
Oh, in South Australia where I was born. South Australia. *Unknown.* ShS
Oh in whose grove have we wakened, the bees. Two Horses. W. S. Merwin. NePA; TwAmPo
O, Inexpressible as Sweet. George Edward Woodberry. Wild Eden, VII. AA; HBV; PFY
(Song: "O, inexpressible as sweet.") InMe
Oh! is it bale-fire in thy brazen hand. To the Goddess of Liberty. George Sterling. PoFr
Oh Is It the Jar of Nations. A. E. Housman. MaPo
(Jar of Nations, The.) LiTB
Oh, is it, then, Utopian. De Profundis. Dorothy Parker. ErPo
O, is not this a holy spot? On Laying the Cornerstone of the Bunker Hill Monument. John Pierpont. AnNE; PAH
Oh, isn't it fun—when the rain comes down? My Funny Umbrella. Alice Wilkins. GFA
O it fell out upon a day. The Laird o Drum. *Unknown.* ESPB
O, it is excellent. Isabella Condemns Tyranny. Shakespeare. *Fr.* Measure for Measure, II, ii. TreFT
O, it is great for our country to die, where ranks are contending. Elegiac. James Gates Percival. AA; HBV
O it is hard to work for God. Right Must Win. Frederick William Faber. JKCP; MaRV; VA
Oh, it *is* life! to see a proud. Gallantly within the Ring. John Hamilton Reynolds. SD
Oh, it is up in the Highlands. Bonnie James Campbell. *Unknown.* BFSS
Oh, it was not a pheasant cock. The Drowned Lady. *Unknown.* ChTr
O, it was out by Donnycarney. It Was Out by Donnycarney. James Joyce. Chamber Music, XXXI. MeWo; MoBrPo; OBVV; WePo
O Italy, I see the lonely towers. To Italy. Giacomo Leopardi. AWP; WoL
Oh, it's a southerly wind and a cloudy sky. Southerly Wind. *Unknown.* ShS
Oh, it's H-A-P-P-Y I am, and it's F-R-double-E. The Bells. *Unknown.* BOHV; FiBHP
Oh, it's hell to sit in a side car when the trucks are crashing by. Ode to a Side Car. "J. P. H." PaA

O it's hippity hop to bed! Hippity Hop to Bed. Leroy F. Jackson. GFA; TiPo
"Oh, it's Hynde Horn fair, and it's Hynde Horn free." Hynde Horn. *Unknown.* GN
O it's I that am the captain of a tidy little ship. My Ship and I. Robert Louis Stevenson. BoChLi; PPL
Oh, it's move along, you dogies, don't be driftin' by th' way. Cowboy's Salvation Song. Robert V. Carr. PoOW
Oh, it's now I'm on the Lone Star Trail until I get too old. The Lone Star Trail. *Unknown.* BFSS
Oh, it's Sindbad the sailor and Robinson Crusoe. Sindbad. *Unknown.* SoAmSa
Oh, it's treat the cook with a pleasant look. Campfire and Bunkhouse. *Unknown.* CoSo
Oh, it's twenty gallant gentlemen. The Last Hunt. William Roscoe Thayer. AA; FaBoBe; HBV
O it's up in the Highlands. Bonnie James Campbell. *Unknown.* BaBo (A *vers.*); ESPB
"Oh! I've got a plum-cake, and a fine feast I'll make." The Plum-Cake [*or* Another Plum-Cake]. Ann Taylor. HBVY; OTPC (1923 ed.)
"Oh, I've had ten men before you." Ballad of Mistress Death. Denis Devlin. NMP
Oh, I've ridden plenty of horses. Noonday Sun. Kathryn Jackson *and* Byron Jackson. FaPON; TiPo
Oh, Jack St. James can always cut a dash. Anthony Delius. *Fr.* The Great Divide. BoSA
Oh, Jack's come home from sea today. Our Jack's Come Home Today. *Unknown.* ShS
O Jan Vermeer of Delft, descend, come near. She Lives with the Furies of Hope and Despair. Delmore Schwartz. FiMAP
"Oh, Jane, do be careful!" Jane, Do Be Careful. Irene Page. BBGG
Oh, Jane was a neighbor for six months or more. Jane Was a Neighbor. *Unknown.* BaBo
O Jealous Night. *Unknown.* *See* O Night, O Jealous Night.
O Jean Baptiste, pourquoi. Pourquoi You Greased. *Unknown.* ChTr
O Jean, my Jean, when the bell ca's the congregation. Tam i' the Kirk. Violet Jacob. GoTS; HBMV; POTE
O Jellon Grame sat in Silver Wood. Jellon Grame. *Unknown.* BaBo; ESPB; OBB; OxBB
Oh! Jesse was the man, he traveled through the land. Jesse James (C *vers.*). *Unknown.* CoSo
O Jesu. Jean Jacques Olier. WHL
O Jesu Parvule. *Unknown, at. to* John Brackley. ISi
O Jesus! at Thy feet we wait. Come, Lord Jesus. Charles Wesley. BePJ
O Jesus Christ! I'm hit, he said; and died. The Last Laugh. Wilfred Owen. CBV
O Jesus, do Thou lead me. Following. Henry W. Frost. SoP
O Jesus, hidden God, I cry to thee. Veni, Domme Jesu. Henry Augustus Rawes. WHL
O Jesus, I Have Promised. John E. Bode. *See* To the End.
O Jesus! Jesus! dearest Lord! Jesus, My God and My All. Frederick William Faber. BePJ
O Jesus, keep my candle burning bright. *Unknown.* ThGo
O Jesus, King most wonderful. The Conqueror Renowned. St. Bernard of Clairvaux. BePJ
O Jesus, little King. Gifts. Sister Mary of the Visitation. WHL
O Jesus, living in Mary. O Jesu. Jean Jacques Olier. WHL
O Jesus! Sweet the Tears I Shed. Ray Palmer. BePJ
O Jesus, Thou the beauty art. The King in His Beauty. St. Bernard of Clairvaux. BePJ
O Jesus! When I Think of Thee. George W. Bethune. BePJ
O Job, Job (uh-huh). Job. *Unknown.* OuSiCo
Oh, John Clare. Vain Dream for John Clare. Joan Hutton. NYTB
O Johney was as brave a knight. Johnie Scot. *Unknown.* BaBo (A *vers.*); ESPB
Oh, Johnny came over the other day. The Rio Grande. *Unknown.* ABF
Oh, Johnny Fife and Johnny's wife. Johnny Fife and Johnny's Wife. Mildred Plew Meigs. GaP; SoPo; TiPo
Oh, Johnny O Dutchman rode out in the frost. Johnny O Dutchman. *Unknown.* BFSS
O Jonathan Bing, O Bingathon Jon. A New Song to Sing about Jonathan Bing. Beatrice Curtis Brown. SoPo
O Joseph, of the holy family least. The Father. Dorothy Scott Ballard. ChIP
O joy of creation. What the Bullet Sang. Bret Harte. AA; CBEP; MAP; MoAmPo (1942 ed.); OBEV; OBVV; PFY
O joy! that in our embers. Wordsworth. *Fr.* Ode: Intimations of Immortality. OQP
O joy, too high for my low style to show! Astrophel and Stella, LXIX. Sir Philip Sidney. BoLiVe; FCP; MaPo; PoFS; ReEn; SiCE; SiPS; TrGrPo; TuPP
Oh joyous cantor! Ode to the Smiths. Charles Thomas. WSL
O joys [*or* joyes]! Infinite sweetness! with what flowers [*or* flowres]. The Morning Watch. Henry Vaughan. AnAnS-1; BoC; EP; LiTB; LoBV; MaPo; MeP; MePo; NoP; OBS; OxBoCh; ReEn; SeCePo; ViBoPo
O joys of love and joys of fame. The Last Hour. Ethel Clifford. HBV
Oh, Juley, you're a lady. Juley. *Unknown.* SoAmSa
O Julie Ann Johnson. Julie Ann Johnson. *Unknown.* ABF
O June has her diamonds, her diamonds of sheen. October in New Zealand. Jessie Mackay. BoAu
O June, O June, that we desired so. June. William Morris. *Fr.* The Earthly Paradise. PoVP; ViBoPo; ViPo
O kangaroo, O kangaroo. The Kangaroo. Ogden Nash. WhC
Oh, keep your kisses, young provoking girl! The Kiss. *Unknown.* OnYI; OxBI
O keeper of the Sacred Key. Forceythe Willson. AA
O ken ye Wullie Broon, Jeanie. Bonnie Jeanie. J. B. Morton. ShBV-4
O Kia-Kunae, praise! The Chief's Prayer after the Salmon Catch. Constance Lindsay Skinner. NP
Oh, kind folks, listen to my song. Abraham's Daughter. Septimus Winner. TrAS
O kindly house, where time my soul endows. The Old House. George Edward Woodberry. HBMV
"O King Amasis, hail!" Amasis. Laurence Binyon. OBVV
O King, enthroned on high. Make Us Thine. *Unknown.* FaChP
Oh King of grief! (a title strange, yet true). The Thanksgiving. George Herbert. AnAnS-1; MaMe; MeP; SCEP-1
Oh King of Saints, how great's thy work, say we. Edward Johnson. SCAP
Oh King of stars! Hospitality in Ancient Ireland. *Unknown.* OnYI
O king of Terrors! whose unbounded sway. To Death. Countess of Winchilsea. HBV
O King of the starry sky. Starry Sky. *Unknown.* AnIL
Oh! King who hast the key. Exspecto Resurrectionem. Charlotte Mew. LO
O kiss, which dost those ruddy gems impart. Astrophel and Stella, LXXXI. Sir Philip Sidney. FCP; SiPS; Sonn
Oh, kneel to that God force of love. Prayer. Lucia Trent. ChIP
O knit me, that am crumbled dust! the heape. Distraction. Henry Vaughan. NCEP; SeCP
Oh, la, Willie, I'll tell your mamma. Going to Boston. *Unknown.* ABF
Oh! ladies and gentlemen, please to draw near; I'll sing of a man who lived in Hartfordshire. Down, Down Derry Down. *Unknown.* AS
O lady amorous. Canzonetta: A Bitter Song to His Lady. Pier Moronelli di Fiorenza. AWP; JAWP; WBP
O Lady leal and lovesomest. To Our Lady. Robert Henryson. ACP; CAW
O lady, leave thy silken thread. Song. Thomas Hood. HoPM
O Lady Moon. Christina Rossetti. *Fr.* Sing-Song. PRWS (Lady Moon.) PCH
Oh lady, oh lady, oh lady of Flower. Lady Flower. *Unknown.* BFSS
O Lady of the Passion, dost thou weep? Our Lady of the Passion. John Mauropus. ISi
O Lady, rock never your young son young. Young Hunting. *Unknown.* BaBo (A *vers.*); ESPB; OBB; OxBB; ViBoFo
O Lady, together with the Child you take. Cry from the Battlefield. Robert Menth. ISi
Oh, lady, wake! the azure moon. Ballad of Bedlam. *Unknown.* NA
O lady, when the tipped cup of the moon blessed you. Song. Ted Hughes. BoPe; POTi
O lake of sylvan shore! when gentle Spring. A Forest Lake.

O (continued)
Charles Tennyson-Turner. PeER
O Lamb Give Me My Salt. *Unknown, tr. fr. Ibo by* Dennis C. Osadebay. PBA
O Lamb of God, O little infant lying. Agnus Dei. Victor Kinon. CAW
Oh, Lamkin was a mason. Lamkin (C *vers.*). *Unknown.* BaBo
O Land Beloved. George Edward Woodberry. *Fr.* My Country. PAH
Oh, land of Castile, you do raise me up. Castile. Miguel de Unamuno. PoPl
O Land, of every land the best. Peace. Phoebe Cary. PAH
O land of gold, I sing to thee. Alaska. *Unknown.* PoRL
O, land of mud and mist, where man is wet and shivers. Such Is Holland! Petrus Augustus de Genestet. FlW
Oh, landlord, have you a daughter fair, parley-voo? Hinky Dinky, Parley Voo? *Unknown.* ABF
O Lapwing. Blake. BiS; ChTr
("O lapwing thou fliest around the heath.") ERoP-1
Oh, larch tree with scarlet berries. Larch Tree. Laurie Lee. NeBP
Oh lark, lark of my silence. Longings. José Moreno Villa. OnPM
O lark! sweet lark. The Singer. Edmund Clarence Stedman. PRWS
Oh! Larry M'Hale he had little to fear. Larry M'Hale. Charles James Lever. *Fr* Charles O'Malley, the Irish Dragoon. OnYI
Oh last and best of Scots! who dids't maintain. Upon the Death of the Viscount [*or* Earl] of Dundee [*or* Epitaph on John Graham of Claverhouse]. Dryden. ACP; MBW-1; OBS; PoFr
O laud the Lord, the God of hosts commend. Psalm CL. Countess of Pembroke. EP
O Lawd, Black Betty, Bambalam. Black Betty. *Unknown.* ABF
Oh, Lawd, How Long? *with music. Unknown.* ABF
Oh Lawd I Went Up on the Mountain, *with music. Unknown.* OuSiCo
Oh, Lawd. Shot my pistol in de heart o' town. Shot My Pistol in de Heart of Town. *Unknown.* ABF
Oh, lay my ashes on the wind. The Curse. Edna St. Vincent Millay. NP
O, Lay Thy Hand in Mine, Dear. Gerald Massey. HBV
Oh, lead me to a quiet cell. Portrait of the Artist. Dorothy Parker. WhC
Oh leaden heeld. Lord, give, forgive I pray. Edward Taylor. *Fr.* Preparatory Meditations First Series. SCAP
O leafy yellowness you create for me. October. Patrick Kavanagh. GTBS-P
O League of Kindness, woven in all lands. The League of Love in Action. Edwin Markham. PEDC
O learned man who never learned to learn. The Myth of Arthur. G. K. Chesterton. HBMV
Oh leave his body broken on the rocks. On a Dying Boy. William Bell. NePoEA
Oh! leave the past to bury its own dead. To One Who Would Make Confession. Wilfrid Scawen Blunt. The Love Sonnets of Proteus, LXII. HBV; ViBoPo
O leave them, Muse! O leave them to their woes. Keats. *Fr.* Hyperion. ViBoPo
O leave this barren spot to me! The Beech Tree's Petition. Thomas Campbell. GTSL; HBV
O lend to me, sweet nightingale. The Daughter of Mendoza. Mirabeau Bonaparte Lamar. AA; HBV
O, lest your true love may seem false in this. Shakespeare. *Fr.* Sonnets, LXXII. LO
Oh, let a father's curse be on thy soul. To the Lord Chancellor. Shelley. ViBoPo
O let me be in loving nice. Punctilio. Mary Elizabeth Coleridge. OBEV (new ed.); OBVV; TOP
O let me die a-singing! Morning Fancy. Mary McNeil Fenellosa. AA
O, Let Me Kiss. Karl Gjellerup, *tr. fr. Danish by* Charles Wharton Stork. PoPl
Oh, let me know. For Easter [*or* Easter Prayer]. Frances Ridley Havergal. OQP; SoP
O let me, Lady, silence calumny. Protestation. Bertrans de Born. LiTW
Oh, let me lay my head tonight upon your breast. I Am Your Wife. *Unknown.* PoToHe (new ed.)
O let me leave the plains behind. Shakespeare. Sir William Watson. HBV
O Let Me Love unto Myself Alone. Arthur Hugh Clough. *Fr.* Dipsychus. OAEP, *abr.;* ViPP, *sl.diff.*
O, let me reverently kiss thine eye. O, Let Me Kiss. Karl Gjellerup. PoPl
Oh, let me run and hide. Spring Ecstasy. Lizette Woodworth Reese. MAP; MoAmPo
Oh, let mee not serve so, as those men serve. Elegie VI. John Donne. *Fr.* Elegies. MaMe
O let mee still and silente lye. *Unknown.* SeCSL
O let sweete slumber dreames. *Unknown.* SeCSL
Oh let the magpie blow. Heart of Light. David Campbell. BoAV
O let the solid ground. Song [*or* I Shall Have Had My Day]. Tennyson. *Fr.* Maud. HBV; MeWo
O, let the soul her slumbers break. Ode on the Death of His Father. Jorge Manrique. WoL
Oh, Let Thy Teachings. Immanuel di Roma, *tr. fr. Hebrew by* Joseph Chotzner. TrJP
Oh, Let Us Howl Some Heavy Note. John Webster. *Fr.* The Duchess of Malfi, IV, ii. InvP; SiCE
(Hark, Now Everything Is Still.) HW
(Madman's Song, The.) ElL
O, let us pay the time but needful woe. Shakespeare. *Fr.* King John, V, vii. PoFr
Oh let your shining orb grow dim. To the Sun. Roy Campbell. *Fr.* Mithraic Emblems. EaLo; FaBoTw
Oh let-n me ride, oh let-n me ride. Low Down Chariot. *Unknown.* OuSiCo
Oh, let's fix us a julep and kick us a houn'. Boogie-woogie Ballads. St. Clair McKelway. PoNe
Oh, let's go up the hill and scare ourselves. The Bonfire. Robert Frost. InvP
O Liberty, thou goddess heavenly bright. Addison. *Fr.* A Letter from Italy. PoFr
Oh, life is a glorious cycle of song. Some Beautiful Letters: Comment. Dorothy Parker. ALV; InMe
O Life! that mystery that no man knows. Life. Lizzie M. Little. VA
Oh Life, thou Nothing's younger brother! Life and Fame. Abraham Cowley. AnEnPo; LiTG
O life, what lets thee from a quick decease? I Die Alive. Robert Southwell. ReIE; SiCE
O Life with the sad seared face. To Life. Thomas Hardy. TOP
O, Lift One Thought. Samuel Taylor Coleridge. *See* Epitaph: "Stop, Christian passerby."
O lifted face of mute appeal! Come Love or Death. Will Henry Thompson. AA
O Light Invisible, We Praise Thee. T. S. Eliot. *Fr.* The Rock. MoRP; OxBoCh; TrPWD
O Light serene! present in one [*or* him] who breathes. Ideal Beauty. Fernando de Herrera. CAW
Oh Light Was My Head. C. Day Lewis. *Fr.* Two Songs (Written to Irish Airs). OAEP (2d ed.)
O, like a queen's her happy tread. Song. Sir William Watson. HBV
Oh, like a tree. The Tree. John Freeman. BoTP
O l'il' lamb out in de col'. Hymn. Paul Laurence Dunbar. AA
O-o-o-oh, lil' man. Chahcoal Man. *Unknown.* AS
O lilac. Lilac. F. S. Flint. HBMV
O Lily of the King, low lies thy silver wing. Lilium Regis. Francis Thompson. HBMV; JKCP; WGRP
O limerick, Learest of lyrics. Lessons in Limericks, III. David McCord. InMe
Oh, limpid stream of Tyrus, now I hear. A Classic Ode. Charles Battell Loomis. NA
O Lionel has the itch to etch. The Itch to Etch. Harold A. Larrabee. WhC
Oh! list to the lay of a poor Irish harper. Bold Phelim Brady, the Bard of Armagh. *Unknown.* OnYI
O, listen for a moment lads, and hear me tell my tale. Jim Jones. *Unknown.* PoAu-1
O listen, gude peopell, to my tale. The Laird o Logie (B *vers.*). *Unknown.* ESPB
Oh listen, listen, ladies gay! Rosabelle [*or* Harold's Song]. Sir Walter Scott. *Fr.* The Lay of the Last Minstrel, VI. BeLS; EnLi-2; EnRP; GTBS; GTBS-D; GTBS-P; GTBS-W; GTSE; GTSL; HBV; OTPC
Oh! listen, little children, to a proper little song. A Nursery Legend. Henry S. Leigh. BOHV

Oh! listen, man! Immortality. Richard Henry Dana. AA; WGRP
Oh, listen to the tale of Mister William, if you please. Mister William. W. S. Gilbert. TOP
O little bird, I'd be. To a Songster. John Banister Tabb. InP
O little bird, you sing. The Secret. Arthur Wallace Peach. HBMV
Oh, little body, do not die. A Child Ill. John Betjeman. DTC
O little buds, break not so fast. Budding-Time Too Brief. Evaleen Stein. AA
Oh, little cat beside my stool. Cinderella's Song. Elizabeth Madox Roberts. PoRh
O Little Child of Bethlehem. The Silent Stars Go By. Harriet Hartridge Tompkins. MaRV
Oh, little Christ, why do you sigh. Christmas Eve in France. Jessie Redmond Fauset. BANP
O little city-gals, don't never go it. Spring. James Russell Lowell. *Fr.* The Biglow Papers, 2d Series, No. VI. MCCG
Oh, little Dame Crump with her little hair broom. Little Dame Crump. *Unknown.* FTB
Oh, little did the wolf-child care. Romulus and Remus. Kipling. FOL
O little fleet! that on thy quest divine. Columbus and the *Mayflower.* Richard Monckton Milnes. MC; PAH
O little flower, you love me so. A Child's Fancy. "A." PRWS
O little friend, I wait on you with praise. The Resurrection and the Life. Robert Norwood. MaRV
O little friend, your nose is ready: you sniff. Dog[s]. Harold Monro. GoTP; MoBrPo
O little frozen peach blossoms. April Fools. Katherine Brégy. JKCP (1955 ed.)
Oh! Little Girl! A Negro Sings. Normil Sylvain. PoNe
O little head of gold! O candle of my house! Lullaby of a [*or* the] Woman of the Mountain. Padraic Pearse. NP; OnYI
O little hearts, beat home, beat home. Swallow Song. Marjorie Pickthall. CaP
O little lambs! the month is cold. Lambs in the Meadow. Laurence Alma-Tadema. PRWS
O little land of lapping seas. The Promised Land. Jessie E. Sampter. TrJP
O little lark, you need not fly. In the Heart. Anna Bunston de Bary. MaRV
Oh, little loveliest lady mine! A Valentine. Laura E. Richards. AA; DD; HH; MPB; YeAr
O little mouse, so frightened of each sound. O Pity Our Small Size. Benjamin Rosenbaum. TrJP
O little self, within whose smallness lies. Sonnet. John Masefield. *Fr.* Sonnets ("Long long ago"). HBV; POTE; SoP; WGRP
O little soldier with the golden helmet. Dandelion. Hilda Conkling. BoChLi; FaPON; GFA; MPB; PDV; PoRh; TiPo; TSW; TVC
"O little Son, upon your brow." Young Jesus. Leslie Savage Clark. ChIP
O little town, O little town. Bethlehem. Clinton Scollard. MaRV
O Little Town of Bethlehem. Phillips Brooks. AA; AmePo; BLRP; FaFP; FaPON; GN; HBV; HH; MaRV; NeHB; OHIP; OTPC; PCH; PTK; TreF; WBLP; WGRP; YaCaBo
Oh little town of Bethlehem, how still we see thee lie. Carol with Variations. Phyllis McGinley. PoPo
O lively, O most charming pug. *See* O lovely O most charming pug.
Oh! lives there, Heaven! beneath thy dread expanse. The Pilgrim of a Day. Thomas Campbell. OBRV
O living flame of love. The Living Flame of Love. St. John of the Cross. LiTW
O living image of eternal youth! Trilby. Alice Brown. AA
O living pictures of the dead. The War Films. Sir Henry Newbolt. MaRV
O living will that shalt endure. In Memoriam A. H. H., CXXXI [*or* Prayer *or* The Truths That Never Can Be Proved]. Tennyson. BEL; BoLiVe; CoBE; DiPo; EnL; EnLi-2; EnLit; EPN; FaBoBe; ForPo; HBV; MaRV; OAEP; TOP; ViPo; VP; WGRP
Oh! Loard remember me! Black Sunrise. Art Wilson. WSL
O loathsome place, where I. Earl of Surrey. FCP; SiPS
O London is a dainty place. London Is a Fine Town. *Unknown.* CoMu
Oh! London town, you are grim and grey. London. T. P. Cameron Wilson. HBMV
Oh London Town's a fine town, and London sights are rare. London Town. John Masefield. OtMeF; YAT
O lonely bay of Trinity. The Cable Hymn. Whittier. PAH; ThLM
O Lonely Heart. Oswald J. Smith. SoP
Oh! lonely is our old green fort. Old Fort Meigs. *Unknown.* MC; PAH
O lonely trumpeter, coasting down the sky. To a Wild Goose over Decoys. Lew Sarett. MAP; NP
O lonely workman, standing there. In the Moonlight. Thomas Hardy. NP
O lonesome sea-gull, floating far. Sea-Birds. Elizabeth Akers Allen. AA; FaBoBe; HBV
O long ago, when Faery-land. Riquet's Song. Stopford Brooke. *Fr.* Riquet of the Tuft. VA
Oh, long long. The Grass on the Mountain. Mary Austin. AmFN; AWP; FaPON; JAWP; WBP
Oh! Look at the Moon. Eliza Lee Follen. *See* Moon, The.
O look how the loops and balloons of bloom. Stormy Day. W. R. Rodgers. LiTB
Oh, look up and down that long, lonesome road. Long, Lonesome Road. *Unknown.* OuSiCo
Oh, loosen the snood that you wear, Janette. Janette's Hair. Charles Graham Halpine. HBV
Oh! Lord. Antoinette T. Payne. TNV
O Lord!/ Thou hast given me a body. Thanksgiving for the Body. Thomas Traherne. ImOP
O Lord, as I Thee have both prayed and pray. Psalm XXXVIII. *Paraphrased by* Sir Thomas Wyatt. FCP
O Lord, as you lay so soft and white. A Christmas Song. Teresa Brayton. JKCP
O Lord, at Joseph's humble bench. The Carpenter. George Macdonald. TrPWD; TRV
O Lord, fulfill Thy will. Thy Will. Christina Rossetti. *Fr.* Christ Our All in All. SoP
Oh Lord, give me a plane. Queen of Horizons. Joseph Dever. ISi; JKCP (1955 ed.)
O Lord, How Excellent Is Thy Name. Psalms, VIII, Bible, *O.T.* TreFS
O Lord, How Long Shall I Cry? Habakkuk, I: 2-II: 20, Bible, *O.T.* LiTW
O Lord, how many do increase. Domine Quid Multiplicati Sunt. Psalm III, Bible, *O.T., tr. by* Thomas Sternhold. SiCE
Oh, Lord, I cannot teach another. My Prayer. Loraine Burdick. SoP
O Lord, I Come Pleading. James Gilchrist Lawson. BLRP
"O Lord," I cried, "the shadows are deep." By Candlelight. Lorie C. Gooding. SoP
O Lord, I pray. Not to Be Ministered to [*or* Today, O Lord]. Maltbie D. Babcock. OQP; SoP; TrPWD
O Lord, I pray: that for each happiness. Petition. John Drinkwater. TrPWD
Oh, Lord, I present myself to Thee. A Dedication. *Unknown.* SoP
O Lord, I wonder at thy lov. Thomas Traherne. *Fr.* The Approach. TrPWD
O Lord, I would be great. I Would Be Great. Hattie B. McCracken. OQP
O Lord, in me there lieth nought. Psalm CXXXIX. Countess of Pembroke. OBSC; OxBoCh
O Lord, it is not hard to love. Prayer for Neighborhood Evangelism. Annette Jansen. STF
O Lord, it was all night. Sun. James Dickey. TPM
Oh, Lord, I've never lived where churches grow. A Cowboy's Prayer. Badger Clark. SoP
O Lord Jesus, let me know myself, let me know Thee. Petitions of Saint Augustine. *Unknown.* WHL
Oh Lord! methought, what pain it was to drown! A Dream of Wrecks. Shakespeare. King Richard III, *fr.* I, iv. ChTr
O Lord, My Best Desire Fulfil. William Cowper. OxBoCh
O Lord My God, Let Flesh and Blood. *Unknown.* ReIE
O Lord, my God, Thou art my trustful stay. Psalm VII. *Paraphrased by* Sir Philip Sidney. FCP
O Lord! My Hiding Place. Thomas Raffles. BePJ
O Lord my sinne doth over-charge thy brest. Sinnes Heavie Loade. Robert Southwell. AnAnS-1; MeP
O Lord! O Lord! how are the seas of thought. In the Depths of Night. Manuel Gutiérrez Nájera. CAW

Oh, Lord, Oh, my Lord! Keep Me f'om Sinkin' Down. *Unknown.* BoAN-1
O Lord of all compassionate control. The Portrait. Dante Gabriel Rossetti. The House of Life, X. MaVP; OAEP; PoVP; ViPo; VP
O Lord of heaven, and earth, and sea! Giver of All [*or* Giving to God] Christopher Wordsworth. MaRV; SoP; VA
O Lord of Hosts! Almighty King! Army Hymn. Oliver Wendell Holmes. SoP
O Lord of Life and God of Love. The Teacher's Prayer. Nancy Byrd Turner. SoP
O Lord of Life, Thy Kingdom Is at Hand. Marion Franklin Ham. MaRV
O Lord of Life, Thy quickening voice awakes my morning song. My Morning Song. George Macdonald. TRV
O Lord, our God, Thy mighty hand. Peace Hymn of the Republic. Henry Van Dyke. SoP; TRV
O Lord, our Lord, how excellent is thy name. Psalm VIII, Bible, *O.T.* AWP; EnLi-1; JAWP; MaRV; OnPM; OTPC (1946 ed.); OuHeWo; PG (1955 ed.); TreFS; TrGrPo; TrJP
O Lord, our Lord! how wondrously (quoth she). The Prioress' Tale. Chaucer, *mod. by* Wordsworth. *Fr.* The Canterbury Tales. GoBC
O Lord, our Lord, thy name how merveillous. The Prioress's Prologue [*or* The Prioress's Tale *or* Prologe of the Prioresses Tale]. Chaucer. *Fr.* The Canterbury Tales. AtBAP; MBW-1; OAEP; OxBoCh
O Lord, permit us here to raise our voice. The Holy Angels. *Unknown.* *Fr.* The Little Office of the Holy Angels. WHL
O Lord, Save We Beseech Thee. *Unknown.* TrJP
O Lord, seek us, O Lord, find us. Lord, Save Us, We Perish. Christina Rossetti. TrPWD
O Lord, since in my mouth, Thy mighty name. Psalm VI. *Paraphrased by* Sir Thomas Wyatt. FCP
O Lord, So Sweet. *Unknown.* NCEP
O Lord, support us all the day long of this troublous life. Until the Shadows Lengthen. Cardinal Newman. SoP; TRV
O Lord that rul'st our mortal line. Psalm VIII. *Paraphrased by* Sir Philip Sidney. FCP
O Lord, the Giver of my days. A Heathen Hymn. Sir Lewis Morris. MaRV
O Lord, the hard-won miles. A Prayer. Paul Laurence Dunbar. TrPWD
O Lord, the sun is low. Evening. Robert J. Craig. SoP
O Lord, the whistling sword is beauty. Headsong. Joseph Bennett. LiTM (rev. ed.); NePA
O Lord, Thou Hast Enticed Me. Jeremiah, XX: 7-10, Bible, *O.T.* TrJP
O Lord, Thou hast exalted me. Psalm XXX. *Paraphrased by* Sir Philip Sidney. FCP
Oh Lord! thou hast known me, and searched me out. An Hymn on the Omnipresence. John Byrom. CEP; TrPWD
O Lord, thou hast searched me, and known me. The Searcher of Hearts Is Thy Maker. Psalm CXXXIX, Bible, *O.T.* BoC; WGRP
O Lord, thou hast to Poland lent thy might. Polish National Hymn. Aloizy Felsinki. PoFr
O Lord, Thy Wing Outspread. William John Blew. VA
Oh Lord, upon whose will dependeth my welfare. Psalm LXXXVIII. *Paraphrased by* the Earl of Surrey. FCP
O Lord, we come this morning. Listen, Lord. James Weldon Johnson. BANP
Oh Lord, when all our bones are thrust. Supplication. Edgar Lee Masters. TrPWD
O Lord, who knowest every need of mine. A Woman's Prayer. *Unknown.* SoP
O Lord! who seest from yon starry height. The Image of God. Francisco Aldana. CAW; WGRP
O Lord whose mercy never fails. Pro Libra Mea. Joseph I. C. Clarke. TrPWD
"O Lord, why grievest Thou?" By the Earth's Corpse. Thomas Hardy. PoDB; ViPo
O Lord, why must thy poets peak and pine. Priest or Poet. Shane Leslie. CAW; WGRP
O Lord, wilt thou not look upon our sore afflictions. Blake. *Fr.* Vala; or, The Four Zoas. ViBoPo
O Lord, you know my inmost hope and thought. My Inmost Hope. Sarah Copia Sullam. TrJP
O Lords! O rulers of the nation! The People's Petition. Wathen Mark Wilks Call. OBVV; PoFr; VA
O Lordy, jes' give me a long white robe! Choose You a Seat 'n Set Down. *Unknown.* OuSiCo
Oh! lose the winter from thine heart, the darkness from thine eyes. May-Music. Rachel Annand Taylor. HBV
O loss of sight, of thee I most complain! The Blindness of Samson. Milton. *Fr.* Samson Agonistes. LiTB; UnPo
Oh, Love and Death go ever hand in hand. Love and Life. Winfred Ernest Garrison. OQP
O Love, Answer. Anne Ridler. SeCePo
O love, are all those arrowes gone. *Unknown.* SeCSL
"O love, art thou a silver fish?" Isabella Valancy Crawford. *Fr.* The Canoe. ACV
O Love, be fed with apples while you may. Sick Love [*or* O Love in Me]. Robert Graves. CMoP; FaBoMo; GTBS-P; POTE
Oh, Love builds on the azure sea. Love's Land. Isabella Valancy Crawford. CaP
O Love Divine. John S. B. Monsell. SoP
O love divine, that stooped to share. Hymn of Trust. Oliver Wendell Holmes. *Fr.* The Professor at the Breakfast Table. AA; MaRV; NeHB; SoP; TrPWD
O Love, give me a passionate heart. A Prayer. Irene Rutherford McLeod. TrPWD
O Love! how cold and slow to take my part. Love, as a Warrior Lord. Ovid. LiTW
O Love, How Strangely Sweet. John Marston. *Fr.* The Dutch Courtesan. AtBAP; TuPP
(Song.) ElL; LO
O Love, how thou art [*or* Love, how thou'rt] tired out with rhyme! Margaret Cavendish, Duchess of Newcastle. EnLoPo; LO
O love, how utterly am I bereaved. Sonnets from "One Person." Elinor Wylie. NP
O Love, I never, never thought. Cancion. Juan II of Castile. AWP; JAWP; WBP
O Love, if you were here. If You Were Here. Philip Bourke Marston. HBV; VA
O Love in Me. Robert Graves. *See* Sick Love.
"Oh love is fair, and love is rare;" my dear one she said. There's Wisdom in Women. Rupert Brooke. BoLP; HBV
O, Love Is Not a Summer Mood. Richard Watson Gilder. HBV
O Love, Love, Love! O withering might! Fatima. Tennyson. LO; SeCePo; UnTE
O Love, my love, and perfect bliss. Medieval Norman Songs, VIII. *Unknown,* *tr. by* John Addington Symonds. AWP; JAWP; WBP
Oh Love! no habitant of earth thou art. The Fatal Spell. Byron. *Fr.* Childe Harold's Pilgrimage, IV. OBNC; ViBoPo
Oh, Love—no, Love! All the noise below, Love. Epilogue. Robert Browning. *Fr.* Ferishtah's Fancies. ViPP
O Love! O Glory! what are ye who fly. The Siege of Ismail. Byron. *Fr.* Don Juan, VII *and* VIII. WoL
O Love, O thou that, for my fealty. Sonnet: To Love, in Great Bitterness [*or* In Great Bitterness]. Cino da Pistoia. AWP; OnPM
O Love of God. Horatius Bonar. SoP
O love of God, God's love, love that alone. For All Sorts and Conditions. Norman Nicholson. EaLo
O love of God, how strong and true. O Love of God. Horatius Bonar. SoP
O Love of God incarnate. Incarnate Love. Wilbur Fisk Tillett. BLRP
O Love of God Most Full. Oscar Clute. SoP
O love, so sweet at first. Disarmed. Laura Catherine Redden Searing. AA
O Love, That Dost with Goodness Crown. John W. Chadwick. TrPWD
O Love! that stronger art than wine. Song [*or* Of Love]. *At. to* Aphra Behn *and to* —— Ousley. *Fr.* The Lucky Chance (*by* Aphra Behn). LO; SeCL
O Love That Triumphs over Loss. Walter Russell Bowie. MaRV
O Love That Wilt Not Let Me Go. George Matheson. MaRV; SoP; TreFS; TrPWD; TRV; WGRP
O Love, the interest itself in thoughtless heaven. W. H. Auden. FaBoMo; MoPo; NAMP; NePA; OAEP (2d ed.); ReMP
"Oh! Love," they said [*or* cried], "is King of Kings." Song. Rupert Brooke. HBV; TSW
Oh, love this house, and make of it a home. For a New Home. Rosa Zagnoni Marinoni. PoToHe
O love, this morn when the sweet nightingale. William

Morris. *Fr.* The Earthly Paradise. EG
O love, thou Judas of the martyred soul! Amor Aeternalis. Clark Ashton Smith. FiSC
O Love, thou knowest well how that this lady. Canzone: To the Lady Pietra, of Sienna. Dante. LiTW
O Love! thou makest all things even. Love. Sarah Flower Adams. VA
O Love, Thy Hair! Kamal ud-Din of Isfahan, *tr. fr. Persian by* Ethel Watts Mumford *and* Louis H. Gray. LiTW
O Love triumphant over guilt and sin. L'Envoi [*or* Life]. Frederic Lawrence Knowles. ChIP; FaChP; MaRV; OQP; TrPWD; TRV
O love, turn from the unchanging sea, and gaze. October. William Morris. *Fr.* The Earthly Paradise. EPN; FaBoEn; OBNC; ViPP
O love, what hours were thine and mine. The Daisy. Tennyson. EnLoPo; OBNC; OBVV; PoEL-5; VA
O Love! what shall be said of thee? Fragoletta. Swinburne. UnTE
O Love, when in my day of doom. The Gardener. Laurence Housman. TrPWD
O Love, who all this while hast urged me on. Canzone: To Love and to His Lady. Guido delle Colonne. AWP
O Love, whose patient pilgrim feet. The Golden Wedding. David Gray. FaBoBe; HBV
O, loveliest throat of all sweet throats. Edna St. Vincent Millay. *Fr.* Memorial to D. C. OxBA
O lovely age of gold! The Golden Age. Tasso. *Fr.* Aminta. AWP; WoL
Oh, Lovely Appearance of Death, *with music.* George Whitefield. OuSiCo
O lovely April, rich and bright. Song. Gustave Kahn. TrJP
Oh Lovely Fishermaiden. Heine, *tr. fr. German by* Louis Untermeyer. AWP; JAWP; WBP
(Du schönes Fischer-Mädchen, *tr. by* Sir Theodore Martin.) OuHeWo
(Fisher-Maiden, The, *tr. by* James Thomson.) OnPM
O lovely Galatea, sweeter than. The Love Song of Polyphemus. Luis de Góngora. *Fr.* Polyphemus and Galatea. LiTW
O lovely maiden, thou hast drawn my heart. The Unhappy Lover. Judah Al-Harizi. TrJP
Oh, lovely Mary Donnelly, my joy, my only best. Lovely Mary Donnelly. William Allingham. AnIV; GTSE; HBV; IrPN; VA
O lovely [*or* lively] O most charming pug. A Sonnet on a Monkey [*or* To a Monkey]. Marjory Fleming. ALV; FaFP; FiBHP; GoTP; LiTG; MemP; SiTL
Oh, Lovely Rock. Robinson Jeffers. Po
O lovely thing. Psalm XCII. *Paraphrased by the* Countess of Pembroke. EP
Oh! lovely voices of the sky. Hymn for Christmas. Felicia Dorothea Hemans. GN; OTPC
Oh, lovers' eyes are sharp to see. The Maid of Neidpath. Sir Walter Scott. BeLS; EnRP; GTBS; GTBS-D; GTBS-P; GTBS-W; GTSE; GTSL
O lovers, this song I give to you. Song. A. R. D. Fairburn. *Fr.* To Daphnis and Chloe in the Park. AnNZ
O loyal to the royal in thyself. To the Queen. Tennyson. *Fr.* Idylls of the King. PoVP
Oh Lucky Jim! *Unknown.* ChTr
O lucky prison, blithe captivity. The Lover's Prison. Ariosto. OnPM
O ludicrous and pensive trinity. Romeo and Juliet. H. Phelps Putnam. ErPo
O luely, luely, cam she in. The Tryst. William Soutar. ErPo; GoTS; GTBS-D; NeBP; OxBS
O Lusty May with Flora quene. Lusty May [*or* May Poem]. *Unknown.* OBEV; OxBS
Oh Lydia, when I hear you rave. To the Polyandrous Lydia. Franklin P. Adams. HBMV
O Lynx, wake Silenus and Casey. Ezra Pound. *Fr.* Canto LXXIX. AtBAP; POTE (1959 ed.)
O lyre of gold, Apollo's. The Power of Music. Pindar. *Fr.* Pythian Odes, I. UnS
O Lyric Love. Robert Browning. *Fr.* The Ring and the Book, I. EPN; FiP; OAEP
(Dedication: "O Lyric Love. . .") CoBE
(Lyric Love.) OBVV; TOP
("O lyric Love, half angel and half bird.") PoVP
O. M. B. Ford Madox Brown. VA
O Mad Spring, One Waits. Merrill Moore. AnAmPo
O magic sleep! O comfortable bird. Life Again. Keats. *Fr.* Endymion. SeCePo
O magical word, may it never die from the lips that love to speak it. Our Mothers. *Unknown.* OQP
O Magnet-South. Walt Whitman. LaNeLa
O Mahsr! let dis gath'rin fin' a blessin' in yo' sight! Blessing the Dance. Irwin Russell. *Fr.* Christmas Night in the Quarters. AnAmPo
O Maistres Myn. *Unknown.* *See* O Mistress Mine.
O Maker of the Mighty Deep. Voyagers [*or* Thy Sea Is Great, Our Boats Are Small]. Henry van Dyke. MaRV; OQP; TRV
O Maker of the starry world. O Stelliferi Conditor Orbis. Boethius. BoPe
O Mally's Meek, Mally's Sweet. Burns. GN; HBV; OTPC
"O man of little wit." The Pine to the Mariner. George Turberville. EtS
O Man of my own people, I alone. The Jew to Jesus. Florence Kiper Frank. ChIP; HBMV; MaRV; NP; StJW; TRV; WGRP
O man that for Fergus of the feasts dost kindle fire. Song of the Forest Trees. *Unknown.* OnYI
Oh man, the twistings and enclaves. Ode to the Negative Universe. Michael McClure. FRC
O Man, who walked by Galilee. Man of Galilee. Mary Louise Deissler. BePJ
O! Mankind. *Unknown.* NoP
(See! Here, My Heart.) MeEL
Oh, man's capacity / For spiritual sorrow. The Crucifixion. Alice Meynell. OxBoCh; PoLi
Oh, many a day have I made good ale in the glen. The Outlaw of Loch Lene. *Unknown, tr. by* Jeremiah Joseph Callanan. AnIV; CH; IrPN; OBEV; OBRV; OnYI; OxBI
Oh, many a leaf will fall to-night. The Dear Old Toiling One. David Gray. VA
Oh, many have told of the monkeys of old. A Darwinian Ballad. *Unknown.* BOHV
O many the tents that gave their riches to me of old! The Assignation. Imr el Kais. LiTW
O Marduk, lord of countries, terrible one. *Unknown.* *Fr.* Hymn to Marduk. WGRP
O Mariners! Archibald Rutledge. EtS
O mark yon rose-tree! When the west. Love's Likeness. George Darley. OBVV
O Martyred Spirit. George Santayana. TrPWD
O Mary, at thy window be. Mary Morison [*or* Song]. Burns. AnFE; AWP; BEL; BoLiVe; CEP; CoBE; EG; EnLi-2; EnLit; EnRP; GTBS; GTBS-D; GTBS-P; GTBS-W; GTSE; HBV; InPo; JAWP; MCCG; OAEP; OBEC; OBEV; OuHeWo; OxBS; PoAn; TOP; TreFT; TrGrPo; WBP; WHA
Oh, Mary, dear, oh, Mary, fair. Molly Asthore. *Unknown.* IrPN
"O Mary, go and call the cattle home." The Sands of Dee. Charles Kingsley. *Fr.* Alton Locke. BBV (1923 ed.); BeLS; BoChLi; CH; FaPON; GBV (1952 ed.); GN; GTBS; GTBS-D; GTSE; HBV; MCCG; MPB; NeHB; OBEV (1st ed.); OnSP; OTPC; PoMS; PoVP; PTK; RG; ShBV-2; TreF; TSW; VA; WBLP
Oh, Mary had a little lamb, regarding whose cuticular. The Original Lamb. *Unknown.* BOHV; InMe
O Mary Hamilton to the kirk is gane. Mary Hamilton. *Unknown.* OxBB
O Mary Pierced with Sorrow. Kipling. *Fr.* Song before Action. ISi
Oh, Mary's lovelier than anything that grows. Prisoner's Song. Horace Gregory. NP
O Master, Let Me Walk with Thee. Washington Gladden. MaRV; SoP; WGRP
(Service.) BLRP; TRV
O Master Masons. Ernst Toller, *tr. fr. German by* Ashley Dukes. TrJP
"O master of fortunes and of poverties." Antonio Machado. *Fr.* Iberian God. PoFr
O Master of the common weal. The Master of Laborers. George Edward Day. PGD
O Master of the Galilean Way. A Prayer for Christian Unity. Molly Anderson Haley. ChIP; OQP
O Master of the heart, whose magic skill. To the Author of *Clarissa.* Thomas Edwards. Sonn
O Master of the Loving Heart. Calvin W. Laufer. SoP
O Master of the modern day. A Hymn for the New Age. William Steward Gordon. MaRV; OQP

O Master of the waking world. The Waking World. Frank Mason North. MaRV
O Master Workman of the Race. Jay T. Stocking. MaRV; TRV
Oh, Masters, you who rule the world. The Masters. "Laurence Hope." HBV
Oh May, bonnie May is to the yowe buchts gane. The Laird o' Ochiltree Wa's. *Unknown.* OxBB
O May I Join the Choir Invisible. "George Eliot." EPN; GTBS; GTBS-W; GTSL; HBV; MaRV; OBNC; SoP; TOP; TreFS; TRV; VA; WGRP
(Choir Invisible, The.) NeHB; OBVV; OHFP; OQP; WBLP
O may I with myself agree. John Dyer. *Fr.* Grongar Hill. TrGrPo
Oh, may my constant feet not fail. Chorus. Sophocles. *Fr.* Oedipus Rex. WGRP
O May she comes and May she goes. The Bonny Hind [*or* Heyn]. *Unknown.* ESPB; OxBB; ViBoFo
Oh, Mayflower, made of filigree gold. Virginia. Vachel Lindsay. ATP (1935 ed.)
O me! what eyes hath love put in my head. Sonnets, CXLVIII [*or* Blind Love]. Shakespeare. GTBS; GTBS-D; GTBS-P; GTBS-W; GTSE; GTSL
O! Meary, when the zun went down. Woone Smile Mwore. William Barnes. VA
O meeting is a pleasure, but parting is grief. The Cuckoo. *Unknown.* CBEP
O melancholy bird, a winter's day. The Heron. Edward Hovell-Thurlow. HBV
O Melancholy, linger here awhile! Keats. *Fr.* Isabella or the Pot of Basil. ViBoPo
"O 'Mella, my dear, this does everything crown!" The Ruined Maid. Thomas Hardy. BrPo; CABA; CMoP; ErPo; FiBHP; LiTB; MaPo; NoP; PeVV; PoeP; PoG; SeCeV; SiTL; ViPo (1962 ed.)
O Memory! celestial maid! Ode to Memory. William Shenstone. Po
O memory, thou fond deceiver. Memory [*or* Song]. Goldsmith. *Fr.* The Captivity. OBEC; OBEV; ViBoPo
O men from the fields! A Cradle Song. Padraic Colum. AS; GoBC; ISi; OnYI; OxBI; StJW; WHL
O men, walk on the hills. Poem. Maxwell Bodenheim. TrJP
O Men, with sisters dear! Sweated Labor. Thomas Hood. *Fr.* The Song of the Shirt. MaRV
Oh Menelaus,/ Oh my poor friend. On Hearing the First Cuckoo. Richard Church. MoBrPo (1942 ed.); OBMV
O merciful Father, my hope is in thee! Prayer before Execution. Mary Queen of Scots. CAW; MaRV; TRV; WGRP
O Merlin in your crystal cave. Merlin. Edwin Muir. CBEP; FaBoTw; FIW; MoPW; OxBS
O Meropé!/ And where art thou. Distraught for Meropé. Richard Henry Horne. *Fr.* Orion. VA
O merry hae I been teethin a heckle. Merry Hae I Been Teethin a Heckle. Burns. NoP
O Merry May the Maid Be. Sir John Clerk. HBV
O! mestress, why. Distant as the Duchess of Savoy. *Unknown.* EnPo; MeEL
O Metaphysical Tobacco. *Unknown.* TuPP
Oh, Mexico, my Mexico. Santy Anna, *vers.* II. *Unknown.* ShS
O mice! if here you come for food, you'd better go elsewhere. A Poor Scholar to Mice *Unknown.* OnPM
O Michael, you are at once the enemy. Garden-Lion. "Evelyn Hayes." ChTr
O mickle yeuks the keckle doup. Justice to Scotland. *Unknown.* BOHV; InMe
O might those sighes and teares returne againe. Holy Sonnets, III. John Donne. AnAnS-1; AnEnPo; MaMe; MasP; MeP; OBS; SCEP-1; SeEP; Sonn
O mighty Caesar! dost thou lie so low? Mark Antony's Lament. Shakespeare. *Fr.* Julius Caesar, III, i. TreFS
O mighty God, Which for us men. A Prayer. Humphrey Gifford. OxBoCh
O Mighty, Melancholy Wind. John Todhunter. *See* Song: "Bring from the craggy haunts of birch and pine."
O mighty-mouthed inventor of harmonies. Milton. Tennyson. EnLi-2; EnLit; EPN; InP; NoP; OAEP; PoFS; PoVP; TOP
O mighty Nothing! unto thee. And He Answered Them Nothing. Richard Crashaw. EP; MaMe; MePo
O mighty, powerful, strong one of Ashur. *Unknown.* *Fr.* Hymn to Marduk. WGRP
O mighty river! strong, eternal will. The Great River. Henry van Dyke. TrPWD
O Mind of God, Broad as the Sky. Oliver Huckel. TrPWD
O mine own sweet heart. Simon and Susan. *Unknown.* OxBoLi
O Miserable sorrow withouten cure. Sir Thomas Wyatt. FCP; SiPS
O missionaries of the Blood! Ambassadors of God! The Missionaries. Robert McIntyre. FaChP
Oh Mr. Froude, how wise and good. Killarney. Charles Kingsley. WhC
"Oh Mrs. McGrath!" the sergeant said. Mrs. McGrath. *Unknown.* OnYI
O Mistress Mine ("O Mistress mine, till you I me commend"). *Unknown.* GoTS; MeEL
(O Maistres Myn.) OxBS
O Mistress Mine Where Are You Roaming? Shakespeare. *Fr.* Twelfth Night, II, iii. AnFe; BEL; BoLP; CBEP; CLwM; CTC; DiPo; EG; EIL; ELP; EnL; EnLi-1; EnLit; EnRePo; ExPo; FaBV; FaFP; InMe; InPo; LiTB; LoBV; MaPo (1969 ed.); MCCG; MemP; MeWo; NoP; OAEP; OBSC; OtMeF; OuHeWo; PAn; PoE; PoeP; PoFS; PoPo; PoRA; SeCeV; ShBV-2; SiCE; TOP; TreFT; TrGrPo; ViBoPo; WePo; WHA
(Carpe Diem.) GTBS; GTBS-D; GTBS-P; GTBS-W; GTSE; GTSL
(Clown's Song.) FaBoEn
(Feste's Song[s].) ALV
(Song: "O mistress mine, where are you roaming?") FiP; GoJo; HBV; PG (1945 ed.)
(Songs from the Plays.) AWP; JAWP; WBP
(Sweet-and-twenty.) LiTG; LiTL; OBEV
(Two of Feste's Songs.) BoLiVe
O mitsch mein inkum stinkum buckerroom. Ja, Ja, Ja! *Unknown.* ShS
O Mollie, O Mollie, 'tis for your sake alone. Jack o' Diamonds. *Unknown.* CoSo
"Oh Molly, pretty Molly, come go with me." Pretty Molly. *Unknown.* BFSS
O money is the meat in the cocoanut. Money. *Unknown.* AS
O mongrel land! My America. Oliver La Grone. NNP
"O monstrous, dead, unprofitable world." Written in Emerson's Essays. Matthew Arnold. ILP; Sonn; VA
O Monument of shame to this out time! Rousseau. Schiller. PoFr
O Mooder Mayde. Chaucer. *See* Invocation: "O mother-maid! O maiden-mother free!"
O Moon, Mr. Moon. Mr. Moon. Bliss Carman. FaPON; GaP; RePo; SUS
O moon, O hide thy golden light. O World, Be Not So Fair. Maria Jäger. HBV
O Moon! the oldest shades 'mong oldest trees. Keats. *Fr.* Endymion, III. EnRP
Oh Moon! when I look on thy beautiful face. Poetic Thought. *Unknown.* FiBHP; SiTL
O Morning-Maker, deign that ray. Plea for Hope. Francis Carlin. TrPWD
O Mors Aeterna. Horace Gregory. CMoP
O Mors! Quam Amara Est Memoria Tua Homini Pacem Habenti in Substantiis Suis. Ernest Dowson. BrPo; GTSL; OBMV; PG; ViPP
O mortal boy we cannot stop. To the Powers of Desolation. Genevieve Taggard. WOW
O mortal folk, you may behold and see. An Epitaph [*or* His Epitaph]. Stephen Hawes. *Fr.* The Pastime of Pleasure. ACP; BoPe; CBEP; ChTr; GoBC; MyFE; OBEV; OBSC; OtMeF; SeCeV; TrGrPo; ViBoPo
O mortal man how longe wilte thow remaine. *Unknown.* SeCSL
O mortal man, that lives by bread. Sally Birkett's Ale. *Unknown.* ChTr
O mortal man, who livest here by toil. James Thomson. The Castle of Indolence. BEL; CEP; EiCP; EiPP; EnLi-2 (1949 ed.)
O [*or Oh*], *most high, almighty, good Lord God.* *Canticle of the Sun [or* The Song of the Creatures]. St. Francis of Assisi, *tr. by* Matthew Arnold. BoC; CAW; GoBC; LiTW; MaRV; OuHeWo; TreFS
O Most High, Omnipotent, Good Lord. Canticle of the Sun. St. Francis of Assisi, *tr. by* Eleanor Turnbull. WoL

O most just Vizier, send away. The Sick King in Bokhara. Matthew Arnold. PoVP
O most unconscious daisy! To a School-Girl. John Shaw Neilson. PoAu-1
O Mother dear, didst thou but hear. Dialogue of the Cross. Frederick Spee. CAW
O Mother Dear, Jerusalem. *Unknown.* *See* New Jerusalem, The.
O Mother Eve, I do believe that after all you're glad you ate. Ode to Eve. Edwin Meade Robinson. InMe
Oh Mother, holiest Mother, Mother Night! To Night, the Mother of Sleep and Death. John Addington Symonds. Sonn
Oh, mother, I shall be married to Mr. Punchinello. *Unknown.* OxNR
O mother, lay your hand on my brow! The Sick Child. Robert Louis Stevenson. CH; PoSC
O mother-maid! O maiden-mother free! Invocation [*or* Prayer to the Blessed Virgin]. Chaucer. *Fr.* The Canterbury Tales: Prologue of the Prioress's Tale. ACP; CAW; ISi
O Mother Mary, Flower of all womankind. Ballade to Our Lady. Sebastian Brant, *tr. by* Alexander Barclay. *Fr.* The Ship of Fools. ISi
O mother, mother, I swept the hearth, I set his chair and the white board spread. All Souls' Night. Dora Sigerson Shorter. VA
O mother, mother! I'm so cold! Chickens in Trouble. *Unknown. tr. by* Emilie Poulsson. PPL
O mother-my-love, if you'll give me your hand. Child and Mother. Eugene Field. HH; MPB
Oh mother my mouth is full of stars. Song of the Dying Gunner A.A.1. Charles Causley. POTi
"Oh, Mother, oh, Mother, come listen to me." Lord Thomas and the Brown Girl. *Unknown.* BFSS
Oh Mother of a Mighty Race. Bryant. AP; CoBA; DD, *sl. abr.*; FaBoBe; HBV; HBVY, *sl. abr.*; MC; PaA; PAH, *sl. abr.*; PAL; PoFr, *abr.*
(America.) AA
O Mother of Fair Love, it was not alone. Cause of Our Joy. Sister Maris Stella. ISi
O Mother Race! to thee I bring. Ode to Ethiopia. Paul Laurence Dunbar. BALP
O Mothers of the Human Race. Robert Whitaker. PGD
Oh, mountains loom the grandest in Montana. In Montana. Washington Jay McCormick. SiTL; WhC
Oh mourn, oh mourn, ye Lowlands. The Bonny Earl of Murray (B *vers.*). *Unknown.* BaBo
O Muse! by thee conducted down, I dare. The Court of Neptune. John Hughes. EtS
O Muse! relate (for you can tell alone). The Triumph of Dulness. Pope. *Fr.* The Dunciad. OBEC
O muse that swayest the sad Northern Song. To the Muse of the North. William Morris. PoVP
O my aged Uncle Arly! Incidents in the Life of My Uncle Arly. Edward Lear. MoShBr; NA; NBM; OxBoLi; SiTL; TrGrPo; WhC
Oh my Beauty of Night!—close, close quick your robe. Belle-de-nuit. Ignace Nau. PoNe
Oh, my beloved, have you thought of this. Edna St. Vincent Millay. HBMV
Oh my blacke soule! now thou art summoned. Holy Sonnets, IV. John Donne. AnAnS-1; MaMe; MasP; MeP; MePo; MyFE; OBS; SCEP-1; Sonn
O my body! I dare not desert the likes of you in other men and women. Walt Whitman. *Fr.* I Sing the Body Electric. ErPo
Oh my boy: Jesus. The Confession Stone. Owen Dodson. TTY
O my brothers of the wilderness. Charm for Going a-Hunting. Mary Austin. RePo
O my chief good! The Passion [*or* Good Friday]. Henry Vaughan. AnAnS-1; MaMe; MeP; SCEP-1
Oh! my daddy was a fool about a yallow gal. My Yallow Gal. *Unknown.* ABF
O my dark Rosaleen. Dark Rosaleen. *Unknown, at. to* Hugh O'Donnell, *tr. by* James Clarence Mangan. ACP; AnFE; AnIL; AnIV; AWP; CH; CoBE; EnRP; GTSL; HBV; IrPN; JAWP; JKCP; LiTW; LO; OBEV; OBVV; OnYI; OxBI; PoFr; PTK; VA; ViBoPo; WBP
Oh, My Darling Clementine. Percy Montross. FaBoBe; FaFP; SGR, *with music*; TreF
O my deerest I shall grieve thee. The Complement. Thomas Carew. CavP
O my deir hert, young Jesus sweit. Balulalow [*or* Cradle Song.] James, John, *and* Robert Wedderburn. EaLo; LoBV; OBEV; OxBoCh
O my earliest love, who, ere I number'd. First Love. Charles Stuart Calverley. BoHV; FiBHP; InMe
Oh, my fair Pastheen is my heart's delight. Pastheen Finn [*or* Páistin Fionn]. *Unknown.* IrPN; OxBI
O my fine, my honeycolored Duke of Marmalade! Elegy of the Duke of Marmalade. Luis Palés Matos. LiTW
Oh, My Geraldine. F. C. Burnand. BOHV; NA
O my God, my God. By Solitary Fires. Elizabeth Barrett Browning. *Fr.* Aurora Leigh, V. VA
O my God, Thou hast wounded me with love. A Confession. Paul Verlaine. CAW; WGRP
Oh, my golden slippers am laid away. Oh, Dem Golden Slippers. James A. Bland. GoSl
Oh, My Good Lord, Show Me de Way, *with music.* *Unknown.* BoAN-2
Oh, my hammer. The Hammer Song. *Unknown.* ABF
O My Harte Is Wo. *Unknown.* AtBAP
Oh, my heart is in the highlan's. The Highlands. Henry W. Frost. SoP
O my heart is the unlucky heir of the ages. Personal History; for My Son. Ruthven Todd. NeBP
O my heart's heart, and you who are to me. Monna Innominata, V. Christina Rossetti. CoBe; ViPo; VP
O my Heart, my Mother, my Heart, my Mother. He Approacheth the Hall of Judgment. *Unknown.* *Fr.* Book of the Dead. AWP; JAWP; WBP
O My Honey, Take Me Back, *with music.* *Unknown.* AS
Oh, my laddie, my laddie. My Laddie. Amélie Rives. HBV
Oh, my laddie! Oh, my laddie! A Mother Thought. Edgar A. Guest. PEDC
O my land! O my love! Lament for Banba. Egan O'Rahilly, *tr. by* James Clarence Mangan. AnIV; AWP; JAWP; WBP
O my little almost island, little island Sirmio. Return to Sirmio. Catullus. LiTW
Oh, My Liver and My Lungs, *with music.* *Unknown.* OuSiCo
Oh, my Lord. My Lord, What a Morning. Waring Cuney. TTY
O my Lord, how Thy compassion. On a Sick Bed. Martha Snell Nicholson. FaChP
O my love! my wife! Everlasting Rest. Shakespeare. *Fr.* Romeo and Juliet, V, iii. WHA
O my lover, blind me. The Tired Woman. Anna Wickham. MeWo; MoBrPo
O my Lucasia, let us speak our love. To My Lucasia, in Defence of Declared Friendship. Katherine Philips. MeLP
O My Luve's like a Red, Red Rose. Burns. *See* Red, Red Rose, A.
Oh, my mother's moaning by the river. The Lonely Mother. Fenton Johnson. GoSl; NP; PoNe
Oh, my name is Bob the Swagman, before you all I stand. The Old Bark Hut. *Unknown.* PoAu-1
Oh! my name is John Wellington Wells. My Name Is John Wellington Wells. W. S. Gilbert. *Fr.* The Sorcerer. PoMS
Oh, my name is Larry Gorman, to you I mean no harm. The Scow on Cowden Shore, *vers.* II. Larry Gorman. ShS
Oh, my name is Peter Emberley. Peter Emberley, *vers.* I. John Calhoun. ShS
Oh, my name it is Sam Hall [*or* is Samuel Hall]. Sam [*or* Samuel] Hall. *Unknown.* ABF; ChTr; CoSo
Oh, my name was Robert Kidd, as I sailed, as I sailed. Captain Kidd. *Unknown.* BBV (1923 ed.); MoShBr; TrAS; ViBoFo
O My Poor Darling. Wilfred Watson. EnLoPo
O my pretty cock and my pretty crowing cock. Mother Goose. PCH
O My Saviour and Redeemer. Alice Mortenson. BePJ
O my soul, do thou keep silence. Communion Hymn. Henry W. Frost. SoP
O My Swallows! Ernst Toller, *tr. fr. German by* Ashley Dukes. TrJP
Oh, my sweet mother, 'tis in vain. On My Sweet Mother. Sappho. PoPl
O my sweet nightingales, why are you dumb again? For Autumn. Eleanor Farjeon. ThGo

O my thoughts' sweet food, my only owner. Sir Philip Sidney. FCP
O my trade it is the rarest one. The Stranger's Song. Thomas Hardy. BrPo
O my true love's a smuggler and sails upon the sea. The Smuggler. *Unknown.* WhC
O my worshipful lord, an't please your grace. Shakespeare. King Henry IV, Pt. II, *fr.* II, i. LO
Oh! Mystery of Man. Wordsworth. *Fr.* The Prelude, XII. FiP
O Mystic Rose, in God's fair garden growing. Rosa Mystica. Denis A. McCarthy. JKCP
Oh, Nancy Dawson, hio! Cheer'ly, Man. *Unknown.* AmSS
O Nancy, Wilt Thou Go with Me? Thomas Percy. HBV
(Song: "O Nancy, wilt thou go with me?") CEP
O nature! I do not aspire. Nature. Henry David Thoreau. FaBoBe; HBV; OTD; OTPC
O Navis. Austin Dobson. VA
O nectar! O delicious stream! Love. Thomas Traherne. SCEP-1; SeCV-2
Oh never call it waste of wishing. Aspiration. Eileen Duggan. JKCP (1955 ed.)
Oh never in this hard world was such an absurd. Nesting Time. Douglas Stewart. PoAu-2
Oh never marry Ishmael! Song for Unbound Hair. Genevieve Taggard. PG; PoRA
Oh, never, never more will I go to Cashel. The Journeyman. *Unknown.* KiLC
Oh! never say at I was false of heart. Sonnets, CIX [*or* The Unchangeable]. Shakespeare. BEL; CLwM; EIL; GTBS-D; GTBS-P; GTBS-W; GTSE; GTSL; HBV; LiTG; LiTL; LO; OBEV; OBSC; SiCE; WoL
Oh, never say that you have reached the very end. We Survive! Hirsch Glick. TrJP
O Never Star Was Lost. Robert Browning. TreFT
(Faith.) OQP
Oh never talk again to me. The Girl of Cadiz. Byron. BWP
O New England, thou canst not boast. A Word to New England. William Bradford. SCAP
O Night here stay! I want no morning light. The Mock Caliph. *Unknown.* *Fr.* The Thousand and One Nights. EnLi-1
O night, O eyes of love! Drinking Song. *Unknown.* *Fr.* The Thousand and One Nights. LiTW
O Night, O Jealous Night [Repugnant to My Pleasures]. *Unknown.* EG; LO; ReIE; TuPP
(Night-Piece, A.) EIL
(O Jealous Night.) UnTE
(To Night.) OBSC
O night, O sweet though sombre span of time! The Defence of Night. Michelangelo. CAW; OnPM
O Night O Trembling Night. Stephen Spender. ErPo; NeBP
O Night, the ease of care, the pledge of pleasure. Night. Sir Philip Sidney. *Fr.* Arcadia. SiPS
O Nightingale. Milton. *See* To the Nightingale.
O nightingale. Nakatsukasa, *tr. fr. Japanese by* Arthur Waley. LiTW
O Nightingale. Wordsworth. *See* Nightingale. The.
O nightingale of woodland gay. Medieval Norman Songs, XVI. *Unknown, tr. by* John Addington Symonds. AWP
O Nightingale That on Yon Bloomy Spray. Milton. *See* To the Nightingale.
O nightingale, the poet's bird. A Song about Singing. Anne Reeve Aldrich. AA
O Nightingale! Thou Surely Art. Wordsworth. *See* Nightingale, The.
Oh! ninna and anninia! Sardinian Lullaby [*or* Sleep, Baby Boy]. *Unknown.* FaPON; RiS
Oh No. Robert Creeley. AmPC; NaP
Oh, No! Mary Mapes Dodge. BBGG
O no, beloved, I am most sure. An Ode upon a Question Moved, Whether Love Should Continue for Ever? Lord Herbert of Cherbury. LiTL; OBS; ViBoPo
Oh, No Cross That I May Carry! Alice Mortenson. BePJ
O No, John! *Unknown.* *See* One Answer, The.
Oh No More, No More, Too Late. John Ford. *See* Song: "Oh, no more, no more, too late."
Oh, No! We Never Mention Her. Thomas Haynes Bayly. PaPo
O noble brow, so wise in thought! Washington [*or* When Shall We See Thy Like Again?]. Mary Wingate. HH; OHIP; PGD
O Noble England. A Joyfull New Ballad. Thomas Deloney. CoMu; ViBoPo
O noble, gracious English tongue. A Grub Street Recessional. Christopher Morley. InMe
O noble Oisin, son of the king. Oisin in the Land of Youth. Michael Comyn. AnIL
O Noble Virgin. Prudentius, *tr. fr. Latin by* Raymond F. Roseliep. *Fr.* Cathemerinon. ISi
Oh, north and east from Conran. Southerly. E. J. Brady. NeLNL
O North, with all thy vales of green! Thou Hast Put All Things Under His Feet. Bryant. SoP
Oh, Northern men—true hearts and bold. Cast Down, but Not Destroyed. *Unknown.* PAH
O not by Phidias' art alone. The Mirror. M. Whitcomb Hess. JKCP (1955 ed.)
Oh, not for more or longer days, dear Lord. A Prayer. B. Y. Williams. MaRV; SoP
O! Nothing earthly save the ray. Al Aaraaf. Poe. AmP; AP
O nothing, in this corporal earth of man. The Heart [*or* All's Vast *or* Correlated Greatness]. Francis Thompson. AnFE; BoLiVe; GTBS-P; MemP; MoAB; MoBrPo; OBMV; Sonn
O, now for ever/ Farewell the tranquil mind! Othello's Farewell to His Career [*or* Farewell Content]. Shakespeare. *Fr.* Othello, III, iii. TreFT; TrGrPo
O now I know: a smile. Rest O Sun I Cannot. Joseph Tusiani. GoYe
Oh, now that it's vacation time. Vacation Time. Rowena Bennett. SiSoSe
O Now the Drenched Land Wakes. Kenneth Patchen. ToPo
Oh now, the white fury of the spring. The White Fury of the Spring. Lizette Woodworth Reese. SiSw
O nuclear wind, when wilt thou blow. Paul Dehn. PV
O Nymph, compar'd with whose young bloom. To Lady Anne Fitzpatrick, when about Five Years Old, with a Present of Shells. Horace Walpole. CEP; OBEC
O nymph with the nicest of noses. Foam and Fangs. Walter Parke. BOHV
Oh, oh, how the wild winds blow! Wild Winds. Mary Frances Butts. OTPC; PRWS
Oh, Oh, where shall I lament. *Unknown.* SeCSL
O of our every fortune, thou, the fateful symbol! Funeral Toast. Stéphane Mallarmé. LiTW
O often have I prayed, and thought. Oblique. Archibald Rutledge. TRV
O ole Zip Coon he is a larned skoler [*or* skolar]. Zip Coon [*or* Old Zip Coon]. *Unknown, at. to* Bob Farrell. TrAS; YaD
Oh, on an early morning I think I shall live forever! Poem in Three Parts. Robert Bly. NaP
Oh, once I had a fair true lover. The Lover Freed from the Gallows. *Unknown.* BFSS
Oh! once I was a "right smart" lad. The Pike County Miner. Mart Taylor. SGR
O once I was happy but now I'm forlorn. The Flying Trapeze. George Lebourne. TreF
O only Source of all our light and life. Qui Laborat, Orat. Arthur Hugh Clough. BEL; EnLi-2; EPN; PoVP; TrPWD; ViPo; ViPP
O, Open the Door to Me, O! Burns. FaBoCh; LoGBV
(Oh, Open the Door, Some Pity to Shew.) EiCL
(Open the Door to Me, O.) AtBAP; PoEL-4
O, Opportunity, thy guilt is great. Opportunity. Shakespeare. *Fr.* The Rape of Lucrece. LiTB; OBSC; PoEL-2
Oh, our manhood's prime vigor! No spirit feels waste. David's Song. Robert Browning. *Fr.* Saul. BoLiVe; OtMeF
Oh, out in the West where the riders are ready. Roll a Rock Down. Henry Herbert Knibbs. AnAmPo; PFY
O Paddy dear, an' did ye hear the news that's goin' round? The Wearin' o' [*or* Wearing of] the Green. *Unknown.* AnIL; AnIV; AWP; DD; FaFP; FOL; HBV; HH; JAWP; OnYI; OxBoLi; PoFr; PoSC; SiTL; TreF; WBP
O pale! O vivid! dear! Conquered. Zoë Akins. HBMV
"O paleys, whylom croune of houses alle." The Complaint of Troilus. Chaucer. *Fr.* Troilus and Criseyde. DiPo; OBEV (new ed.)
Oh, paltry miracles. Miracle. Edith Mirick. ChIP
O pansy-eye, O polished face. Debutantrum. William Rose Benét. InMe; LHV

O Paradise! O Paradise! Frederick William Faber. *See* Paradise.
O Parcy Reed has Crozer ta'en. Parcy Reed. *Unknown.* OxBB
O, pardon me, thou bleeding piece of earth. Shakespeare. *Fr.* Julius Caesar, III, i. MemP; TreFS
O Parent of each lovely Muse. Ode to Fancy. Joseph Warton. CEP; EiPP; EnPE; WaPE
Oh, pass around your bottle, we'll all take a drink. Pass Around Your Bottle. *Unknown.* OuSiCo
Oh, Passage town is of great renown. The Town of Passage. *Unknown.* OxBoLi
O pastoral heart of England! like a psalm. Upon Eckington Bridge, River Avon. Sir Arthur Quiller-Couch. OBVV; POTE
O patience, that dost wait eternally! Sonnet. Pedro Malon de Chaide. CAW
O patron saints of all my friends! Friends. Lionel Johnson. GoBC
O pensive, tender maid, downcast and shy. Song: To Psyche. William Morris. *Fr.* The Earthly Paradise: May. VA
O peony, O pink inverted bell. A Peony for Apollo. Charles Edward Eaton. GoYe
O people-chosen! are ye not. To the Thirty-ninth Congress. Whittier. PAH
O perfect [*or* perfite] light, which [*or* quhilk] shaid away. A Summer Day [*or* Of the Day Estivall]. Alexander Hume. LoBV; OBEV (1st ed.); OxBS
O Perfect Love. Dorothy F. Gurney. MaRV
Oh, Peter, go ring dem bells. Peter, Go Ring Dem Bells. *Unknown.* BoAN-1
"O Peter, O Apostle, hast thou seen my bright love?" The Keening of Mary. *Unknown.* ISi
Oh, Peterkin Pout and Gregory Grout. A Nursery Song. Laura E. Richards. BoChLi; HBV; HBVY; TVC
O Petrarch, head and prince of poets all. A Praise of Petrarch and of Laura, His Lady. *Unknown.* ReIE
O petty blood-nobility of ours! Dante. *Fr.* Divina Commedia: Paradiso. PoFr
O Phoebus embattling the high wall of Ilium. Chorus: The Kings of Troy. Euripides. *Fr.* Andromache. WaaP
"Oh, Piggy, what was in you trough." The Greedy Piggy That Ate Too Fast. Eliza Grove. OTPC (1923 ed.)
O pine-tree standing. Hakutsu. *Fr.* Manyo Shu. AWP; JAWP; WBP
O piteous race! Judaism. Cardinal Newman. ACP
O Pittie. Thomas Dekker. *See* Priest's Song, A.
O Pity Our Small Size. Benjamin Rosenbaum. TrJP
Oh pity poor Reuben Ranzo. Reuben Ranzo. *Unknown.* SoAmSa
O pitying angel, pause, and say. In Paradise. Arlo Bates. AA
Oh pleasant eventide! Twilight Calm. Christina Rossetti. BoNaP; GTSE; OBNC
O pleasant exercise of hope and joy. The French Revolution [*or* Residence in France, Continued]. Wordsworth. *Fr.* The Prelude, XI. EnLi-2; FiP; FOL; MBW-2; OBRV; PoEL-4; TOP
Oh, Please Don't Get Up! Ogden Nash. NePA; SiTL
O Please Read Backwards. Tyner White. YAP
O pleasing thoughts, apprentices of love. Phyllis, I. Thomas Lodge. SiCE; Sonn; TuPP
O plovers flying over the evening waves. The Plovers. Hitomaro. OnPM
Oh-h-h-h, po' roustabout don't have no home. Roustabout Holler. *Unknown.* OuSiCo
O, po' sinner, O, now is yo' time. What Yo' Gwine to Do When Yo' Lamp Burn Down? *Unknown.* BoAn-1
O poet of the future! The Future. George Frederick Cameron. OBCV
O poet rare and old! Astraea. Whittier. AA
O Poet, then, forbear. Austin Dobson, *after* Théophile Gautier. *Fr.* Ars Victrix. InP
O poet, what do you do? I praise. Praise. Rainer Maria Rilke. ChTr
O Polish mother, if the radiant eyes. To a Polish Mother. Adam Mickiewicz, *tr. by* Jewell Parish *and* George R. Noyes. CAW
O Polish mother, if the radiant light. To a Polish Mother. Adam Mickiewicz, *tr. by* Watson Kirkconnell. LiTW
O Polly, love, O Polly, the rout has just begun. High Germany. *Unknown.* CBEP; FOL; WaaP
"O Polly, you might have toy'd and kist." John Gay. *Fr.* The Beggar's Opera. EnLoPo
Oh, poor old Reuben Ranzo. Reuben Ranzo. *Unknown.* AmSS; ShS, *vers.* I *and* II
"Oh, poor Reuben Ranzo." Poor Reuben Ranzo. Arthur H. Clarke. IHA
"O poppy Death!—sweet poisoner of sleep!" Scylla's Lament. Thomas Hood. *Fr.* Hero and Leander. EnRP
O Possible and Probable. Adventure. Grace Fallow Norton. HBMV
O potent Earth, and Heaven god-built. Earth and Sky. Euripides. EaLo
O, pour upon my soul again. Rosalie. Washington Allston. AA
Oh! poverty is a weary thing, 'tis full of grief and pain. The Sale of the Pet Lamb. Mary Howitt. CH
O Poverty! thou source of human art. A Hymn to Poverty. Edward Moore. WaPE
O power of Love, O wonderous mystery! Love. Katrina Trask. AA
O Power to whom this earthly clime. Peccavi, Domine. Archibald Lampman. MaRV
O Powers Celestial, with what sophistry. Barnabe Barnes. *Fr.* Parthenophil and Parthenophe. EnLoPo
O prairie mother, I am one of your boys. Carl Sandburg. *Fr.* Prairie. NP
O, praise an' tanks! De Lord he come. Song of the Negro Boatman. Whittier. *Fr.* At Port Royal. GN
O praise God in his holiness: praise him in the firmament of his power. Laudate Dominum. Psalm CL, Bible, *O.T.* ChTr
O praying one, who long has prayed. Ask and Ye Shall Receive. Mrs. Havens. BLRP
O precious codex, volume, tome. To a Thesaurus. Franklin P. Adams. BOHV; PoPl; SiTL; WhC
O precious Father, as we bow. Thanksgiving. *Unknown.* SoP
O Prince of Life, Thy life hath tuned. The Prince of Life. John Oxenham. TrPWD
O Prince of Peace, who came to bless. Forgive. Lalia Mitchell Thornton. BePJ
Oh Promise Me. Clement Scott. FaFP; TreF
O Prophets and Redeemers! Stanton A. Coblentz. ChIP
O Proserpina!/ For the flowers now. Perdita's Garden. Shakespeare. *Fr.* The Winter's Tale, IV, iii. WHA
Oh, Prue she has a patient man. She Is Overheard Singing. Edna St. Vincent Millay. InMe
O pulsing heart with voice attuned. Giotto's Campanile. Thomas O'Hagan. JKCP
O Purblind Race. Tennyson. *Fr.* Idylls of the King: Geraint and Enid. OQP
O pure of soul, and fond and deep of heart. To His Wife. Daniel Henry Deniehy. BoAV
O pure reformers! not in vain. The Reformers. Whittier. MaRV
Oh, put no trust in women! No Trust in Women. *Unknown.* OnPM
Oh, put not your trust in men, dear! No Trust in Men. *Unknown.* OnPM
O Queen, awake to thy renown. Honor and Desert. Coventry Patmore. *Fr.* The Angel in the House. FaPL; HBV
O queen of heaven, be joyful, alleluia. Regina Coeli. *Unknown, tr. by* Winfred Douglas. ISi
O queen of heaven, rejoice. *Unknown.* WHL
O quick quick quick, quick hear the song-sparrow. Cape Ann. T. S. Eliot. *Fr.* Landscapes. EvOK; GoJo; LoGBV; ThWaDe
Oh, quiet peoples sleeping bed by bed. A Solis Ortus Cardine. Ford Madox Ford. ViBoPo
Oh, rabbit, rabbit, rabbit, a-hash. Rabbit Hash. *Unknown.* ABF
O radiant luminary of light interminable. A Prayer to the Father of Heaven. John Skelton. PoIE; SiCE; TrPWD; TuPP
O raging seas, and mighty Neptune's reign! Coming Homeward Out of Spain. Barnabe Googe. ElL; EnPo; EnRePo; ReIE; SiCE; TuPP
O rain at seven. Virginia. Hart Crane. *Fr.* The Bridge: Three Songs. LiTA
O rain, depart with blessings. Song of the Dew. *Unknown.* TrJP

O! raise the woeful Pillalu. An Irish Lamentation. Goethe. AWP
Oh, rare Harry Parry. *Unknown.* OxNR; SiTL
O Reader! hast thou ever stood to see. The Holly Tree. Robert Southey. EnRP; HBV
Oh, religion is a fortune, I really do believe. Religion Is a Fortune I Really Do Believe. *Unknown.* BoAn-2
O reverend Chaucere, rose of rethoris all. William Dunbar. *Fr.* The Goldyn Targe. PP
O reverend sir, I do declare. Widow Bedott to Elder Sniffles. Frances Miriam Whitcher. BOHV
O rich young lord, thou ridest by. Compensation. James Edwin Campbell. BANP
O Ring the Bells. Kate Greenaway. SAS
"O, rise up, Willy Reilly [*or* Willie Riley], and come along with me." Willy Reilly [or Willie Riley). *Unknown.* BaBo (A *vers.*); HBV; OnYI; OuSiCo
O Risen Saviour, when the daylight wanes. When the Daylight Wanes. Thomas Tiplady. MaRV
O river, green and still. Boy in Ice. Laurie Lee. NYBP
O river winding to the sea! Haverhill, 1640-1890. Whittier. MAmP
Oh, rock-a-by, baby mouse, rock-a-by, so! The Mouse's Lullaby. Palmer Cox. PCH
O, Rocks Don't Fall on Me, *with music.* *Unknown.* BoAN-1
Oh, Roll on Babe, *with music.* *Unknown.* OuSiCo
Oh, roll the cotton, roll me, boys. Roll the Cotton Down, *vers.* I. *Unknown.* ShS
Oh Rome! my country! City of the soul! Rome [*or* Rome and Freedom]. Byron. *Fr.* Childe Harold's Pilgrimage, IV. BEL; EPN; InP; MaPo; ShBV-3
O Romeo, Romeo! wherefore art thou Romeo? Shakespeare. *Fr.* Romeo and Juliet, II, ii. WHA
O Rose, O Rainbow. Nicholas Moore. NeBP
O Rose the Red and White Lilly. Rose the Red and White Lilly. *Unknown.* ESPB; OBB; OxBB
O rose, thou art sick! The Sick Rose. Blake. *Fr.* Songs of Experience. AtBAP; AWP; BEL; BoLiVe; BoW; BWP; CABA; CaFP; CBEP; CBV; ChER; ChTr; DiPo; EG; EiCL; EiPP; ELP; EnL; EnLoPo; ERoP-1; ExPo; FaBoEn; ForPo; FosPo; GTBS-D; ILP; InPo; JAWP; LoBV; MaPo; NoP; OAEP; OBNC; OnPM; PeER; PIA; PoAn; PoEL-4; PoeP; PoFS; PoG; PoIE; PoSA; SeCeV; ShBV-4; StP; TOP; TrGrPo; ViBoPo; WBP
O Rose with Two Hearts. Sacheverell Sitwell. Rosario d'Arabeschi; Poems and Rose Portraits, II. POTE (1959 ed.)
Oh roses for the flush of youth. Christina Rossetti. ELP; GTBS; GTBS-P; LoBV; ViBoPo; ViPo; VP
O Ross, thou wale of hearty cocks. To Mr. Alexander Ross. James Beattie. OxBS
Oh, rosy as the lining of a shell. Mimma Bella, IV. Eugene Lee-Hamilton. HBV
Oh, round the corner we will go. Round the Corner. *Unknown.* SoAmSa
Oh, rouse you, rouse you, men at arms. Great Swamp Fight. Caroline Hazard. PAH
O roving muse, recall that wondrous year. The Great Frost. John Gay. *Fr.* Trivia; or, The Art of Walking the Streets of London. OBEC; SeCePo
O rowan tree, O rowan tree! thou'lt aye be dear to me! The Rowan Tree. Lady Nairne. HBV
O Ruddier than the Cherry. John Gay. *Fr.* Acis and Galatea. ELP; LiTL; ViBoPo
(Air: "O ruddier than the cherry.") EiCL
(Song: "O ruddier than the cherry.") EiPP; HBV; OBEC; OBEV (1st ed.)
O ruddy Lover. The Clover. Margaret Deland. AA
O ruined father dead, long sweetly rotten. For the Word Is Flesh. Stanley J. Kunitz. AnAmPo; NP
O ruinous morning, unjustifiable. Crash at Leithfield. Allen Curnow. AnNZ
O Sabbath rest by Galilee! Calm. Whittier. SoP
O sacred friendship, Heaven's delight. Friendship. Cervantes. OnPM
O Sacred Head, Now Wounded. *Unknown, at. to* St. Bernard of Clairvaux *and to* Arnulf von Loewen, *tr. fr. Latin into German by* Paul Gerhardt, *tr. fr. German by* James W. Alexander. BePJ; MaRV, *abr.*
(Passion Hymn, *tr. by* Henry Williams Baker.) SoP
O sacred lance that heals the wound it makes. The Damascus Road. Daniel Hughes. ChIP
O sacred poesie, thou spirit of artes. Ben Jonson. *Fr.* The Poetaster. PoEL-2
O Sacred Providence, who from end to end. Providence. George Herbert. MaMe
Oh, sacred union with the Perfect Mind. The Inward Life. *Unknown.* SoP
O sad, O sad my spirit was. Exile. Paul Verlaine. LO
O sad, sad world, O world that knows not love. Dirge. Edith Lovejoy Pierce. MaRV
O Sailor, Come Ashore. Christina Rossetti. *Fr.* Sing-Song. BoTP; BrR; GaP
(Coral.) GFA
O sailor sailor tell me why. Scarabs for the Living, I. R. P. Blackmur. AnFE; CoAnAm; TwAmPo
"O sailor, tell me, tell me true." Elihu. Alice Cary. PaPo
Oh! St. Patrick was a gentleman. St. Patrick Was a Gentleman. Henry Bennett. DD; PoRL; SiSoSe
O sairly may I rue the day. The Women Folk. James Hogg. HBV
Oh, Sally Brown, of New York City. Sally Brown. *Unknown.* AmSS
Oh, Sally Racket, hi-oh! Cheerly, Man. *Unknown.* SoAmSa
O Salutaris Hostia. St. Thomas Aquinas, *tr. fr. Latin.* WHL
Oh, Santa [*or* Santy] Anna fought for fame [*or* gained the day]. Santa [*or* Santy] Anna. *Unknown.* AmSS; SoAmSa
O saving Victim opening wide. O Salutaris Hostia. St. Thomas Aquinas. WHL
O Saviour, welcome to my heart. Welcome to My Heart. *Unknown.* BePJ; SoP
O Saviour, when we have no work. Hymn of the Unemployed. Thomas Tiplady. MaRV
O Saw Ye Bonnie Lesley. Burns. *See* Bonnie Lesley.
"O saw ye my father? or saw ye my mother?" The Grey Cock. *Unknown.* BaBo (B *vers.*); ESPB
O saw ye not fair Ines? Fair Ines. Thomas Hood. EnRP; HBV; OBEV; OBRV; OBVV; PG (1945 ed.); TOP; UnPo (1st ed.); VA
O, Saw Ye the Lass. Richard Ryan. FaBoBe; HBV
Oh, say, can you see, by the dawn's early light. The Star-Spangled Banner [*or* Defence of Fort M'Henry]. Francis Scott Key. AA; AmePo; BBV; BLPA; DD; FaBoBe; FaFP; FaPL; FaPON; HBV; HBVY; HH; InP; MaRV; MC; NeHB; NePA; OTD; OTPC; PaA; PAH; PAL; PAP; PEDC; PoFr; PoRL; PTK; ThLM; TreF; WBLP; YaD
O say, dear life, when shall these twinborn berries. *Unknown.* EG
O say, have you seen at the Willows so green. The Ballad of the Emeu. Bret Harte. BOHV
O Say, My Brown Drimin. *Unknown, tr. fr. Modern Irish by* James Joseph Callanan. OnYI
O say, my flattering heart. Loves She like Me? Samuel Woodworth. AA
Oh! say not woman's love [*or* heart] is bought. Song. Isaac Pocock, *wr. at to* Thomas Love Peacock. *Fr.* The Heir of Vironi. HBV
O say were [*or* was] you ever in Rio Grande. Rio Grande. *Unknown.* LO; SoAmSa; TrAS
O say what is that thing call'd Light. The Blind Boy. Colley Cibber. CEP; GTBS; GTBS-D; GTBS-P; GTBS-W; GTSE; GTSL; HBV; NeHB; OBEC; PRWS; RoGo; TreFS
Oh, say, what is this fearful, wild. The Hippopotamus. Oliver Herford. NA
Oh! say you so, bold sailor. The Herald Crane. Hamlin Garland. HBV
Oh, says the linnet, if I sing. Birds' Lament. John Clare. PoEL-4
Oh science, I love the touch of velvet. Mad Sonnet 5. Michael McClure. FRC
O Scotia! my dear, my native soil! Prayer for My Native Land. Burns. *Fr.* The Cotter's Saturday Night. MaRV
O sea born and obscene. An Invocation to the Goddess. David Wright. NMP
O Sea, take all, since thou hast taken him. Henry I to the Sea. Eugene Lee-Hamilton. PeVV
O Sea! . . . 'Tis I, risen from death once more. To Helen. Delmore Schwartz. NYTB
O search the heart and belly you may find. Forebears. Elizabeth Riddell. BoAV

O season of repetition and return. Spring 1940. W. H. Auden. OAEP (2d ed.)
O Season supposed of all free flowers. Song of the Springtide. *Unknown.* BOHV
O see how narrow are our days. Prayer of the Maidens to Mary. Rainer Maria Rilke. AWP
O See How Thick the Goldcup Flowers. A. E. Housman. A Shropshire Lad, V. BoLP; CLwM; EnLi-2; FaBV; MeWo; MoBrPo; PoVP
(Good-by, Young Man, Good-by.) EnLit
O seeded grass, you army of little men. Irradiations, IX [XV]. John Gould Fletcher. AnAmPo; MAP; MAPA; MoAmPo; NeMA; NePA; PoPo; TwAmPo
Oh, seek me not within a tomb. Envoi. John G. Neihardt. *See also* Seek not for me . . . HBV; NP; OQP; WGRP.
O seeker of the Greater Light. The Circle. Carol Coates. CaP
O! sely anker, that in thy celle. Ballade [*or* Go Sad Complaint]. Charles duc d'Orléans. EnPo; MeEL
Oh send to me apple that hasn't any kernel. *Unknown, tr. fr. Welsh by* Gwyn Williams. FaBoCh; LoGBV
O servant of God's holiest charge. Christopher Smart. *Fr.* A Song to David. ViBoPo; WoL
Oh, setting sun, had you no aureole? February 12, 1809. Gail Brook Burket. PGD
O sextant of the meetin house, which sweeps. To the "Sextant" [*or* A Appeal for Are]. Arabella M. Willson. BOHV
O Shadow. Shadow Dance. Ivy O. Eastwick. SoPo; TiPo
O shady vales! O fair enrichèd meads! Thomas Lodge. ElL; OBSC
O! shairly ye hae seen my love. Ballad. William Soutar. NeBP; WePo
Oh shall I never never be home again? Brumana. James Elroy Flecker. BrPo; HT
O shame to men! Devil with devil damned. Satan on War. Milton. *Fr.* Paradise Lost, II. MaRV
O Shannadore, I love your daughter. The Wide Mizzoura. *Unknown.* AS
O She Is as Lovely-Often. Kenneth Patchen. ToPo
Oh, she is fair: fair as the eastern morn. Seeing a Lady. John Tatham. *Fr.* Ostella. LO; SeCL
Oh! she is good, the little rain! and well she knows our need. The Little Rain. Tu Fu. FaPON
O she looked out of the window. The Two Magicians. *Unknown.* ChTr; OxBoLi
Oh, she walked unaware of her own increasing beauty. She Walked Unaware. Patrick MacDonogh. BoLP; ErPo; FaBoTw; NeIP; OnYI; OxBI
Oh, she was a lady all alive! Eighteenth Century Lady. Rose O'Neill. NYTB
O she was playing with her cat. Femme et Chatte. Paul Verlaine, *tr. by* Ashmore Wingate. CIV
Oh, Shenandoah, I long to hear you. Shenandoah. *Unknown.* AmFN; SoAmSa; TrAS; TreFT
Oh, Shenandoah, I love your daughter. Shenandoah. *Unknown.* AmSS
O Shepherd with the bleeding feet. The Good Shepherd. Christina Rossetti. ChIP
O shepherds! take my crook from me. Adieu. Eleanor Elizabeth Montgomery. VA
O shield me from his rage, celestial Powers! Esther Johnson. LO
O ship incoming from the sea. Off Rivière du Loup. Duncan Campbell Scott. EtS; HBV; MCCG; OBCV; PTK
O Ship! new billows sweep thee out. The Ship of State. Horace. Odes, I, 14. AWP; JAWP; WBP
O Ship of State. Longfellow. *See* Ship of State, The.
O Ship, Ship, Ship. Arthur Hugh Clough. Songs in Absence, XIV. PoVP
"Oh Shit a Riot!" Jacques Wakefield. BF
O Sicily, O Tuscany, where I. Easter Sunday, 1945. G. A. Borgese. NePoAm
"Oh, sick I am to see you, will you never let me be?" The New Mistress. A. E. Housman. A Shropshire Lad, XXXIV. MoBrPo (1950 ed.); PoVP
Oh! sigh no more, no longer paint the air. Sonnet. George Henry Boker. *Fr.* Sonnets. AmLP
O sigh of the sea, O soft lone-wandering sound. The Calling. George Sigerson. JKCP (1926 ed.)
O sight of pity, shame and dole! The Singer in the Prison. Walt Whitman. BeLS
Oh, sight too dearly bought! Sleeping Beauty. William Drummond of Hawthornden. LiTL
O Silent God, Thou whose voice afar. A Litany at [*or* of] Atlanta. W. E. B. DuBois. BANP; CDC; PoNe
O silver-throated swan. The Dying Swan. T. Sturge Moore. GTBS-D; OBMV; SeCePo; SyP
Oh, silver tree. Jazzonia. Langston Hughes. AmNP; BANP; Kal
Oh silvery streamlet of the fields. The Stream of Life. Bryant. AnNE
O simple as the rhymes that tell. Lincoln—the Boy. James Whitcomb Riley. LiPo
O simple Nature, how I do delight. Nature. John Clare. CBEP
O sing a song of Bethlehem. Songs of Jesus. Louis F. Benson. MaRV
Oh, sing a song of phosphates. Boston Nursery Rhymes. Joseph Cook. BOHV
O sing the glories of our Lord. A Psalm for Sunday Night. Thomas Pestel. OxBoCh
Oh sing unto Jehovah a new song. *See* O sing unto the Lord a new song.
O, Sing unto My Roundelay. Thomas Chatterton. *See* Minstrel's Song.
O sing unto the Lord [*or* Jehovah] a new song. The Floods Clap Their Hands. Psalm XCVIII, Bible, *O.T.* BLRP; EaLo; StaSt; TrGrPo; TrJP
O singer of Persephone! Theocritus. Oscar Wilde. HBV; OxBI; ShBV; StP
O singer of the field and fold. For a Copy of Theocritus. Austin Dobson. HBV; VA
O singing wind. The Fir-Tree. Edith M. Thomas. OHIP
O, sinner, sinner, you better pray. Death's Gwineter Lay His Cold Icy Hands on Me. *Unknown.* BoAN-2
"Oh, sister, these are midnight dreams." The Braes o' Yarrow (A *and* B *vers.*). *Unknown.* BFSS
O! sisters too. The Coventry Carol. *Unknown.* MeEL
Oh Sky, you look so drear! Earth and Sky. Eleanor Farjeon. BoChLi; PoSC; SUS
O skylark! I see thee and call thee joy! To a Skylark. George Meredith. EnLit
O Slavery! thou frost of the world's prime. Chorus. Shelley. *Fr.* Hellas. PoFr
O Sleep. Grace Fallow Norton. HBV
Oh, Sleep, Fond Fancy. *Unknown.* ElL
Oh, Sleep Forever in the Latmian Cave. Edna St. Vincent Millay. CMoP; ExPo; LiTM; MAP; MoAmPo; MoVE; SeCeV; ViBoPo
(Endymion.) AnEnPo
Oh! sleep in peace where poppies grow. Reply to "In Flanders Fields." John Mitchell. BLPA; PAL
O sleep, my babe, hear not the rippling wave. Sara Coleridge. *Fr.* Phantasmion. OBEV (1st ed.); OBNC; OBRV;
O Sleep, O tranquil son of noiseless Night. To Sleep. Giovanni della Casa. AWP; JAWP; WBP
Oh, slow to smite and swift to spare. Abraham Lincoln [*or* The Death of Lincoln]. Bryant. AmePo; AmP; AP; CoBA; DD; ForPo; HH; InP; LiPo; MC; OHIP; PaA; PAH; PoPo
Oh, slow up, dogies, quit your roving round. Night-herding Song [*or* Cowboy Songs]. Harry Stephens. CoSo; OuSiCo; RePo; TrAS
O smitten mouth! O forehead crowned with thorn! For Our Sakes. Oscar Wilde. PGD
O smoother me to death. *Unknown.* SeCSL
Oh! Snatch'd Away in Beauty's Bloom. Byron. EnRP; FiP; HBV; InP; LoBV; OBRV; TOP
(Elegy: "Oh! snatch'd away.") GTBS; GTBS-D; GTBS-P; GTBS-W; GTSE; GTSL
Oh, so cool. Moral Song. John Farrar. RePo
O soft embalmer of the still midnight. To Sleep [*or* Sonnet to Sleep]. Keats. AtBAP; BoC; BoLiVe; BWP; ChTr; EnLi-2; EnRP; EPN; ERoP-2; FlW; GTBS-W; LoBV; MBW-2; OAEP; OBEV; OBRV; PAn; PIA; PoE; PoEL-4; PoeP; Sonn; TDP; ViBoPo; WHA
Oh soft flowing rivers. My South. Don West. PoNe
O Softly Singing Lute. Francis Pilkington. OAEP
O Solitary of the Austere Sky. Sir Charles G. D. Roberts. CaP
O solitary pine, how many. Solitary Pine. Prince Ichihara. OnPM

O Solitude! If I Must with Thee Dwell. Keats. *See* To Solitude.
O solitude, romantic maid! Solitude [*or* Ode to Solitude]. James Grainger. CEP; OBEC; ViBoPo
Oh, solitude! thou wonder-working fay. The Imaginative Crisis. *Unknown.* BOHV
Oh some are fond of red wine, and some are fond of white. Captain Stratton's Fancy. John Masefield. MoBrPo; OBEV (new ed.); OnPP
Oh some have killed in angry love. A Rope for Harry Fat. James K. Baxter. MoBS
Oh something just now must be happening there! Home Thoughts. Claude McKay. GoSl
O sometimes in the street, or in the Paris Metro. Remembrance. Antoni Slonimski. TrJP
O somewhere, somewhere, God unknown. A Last Appeal. Frederic W. H. Myers. MaRV; VA
Oh, somewhere there are people who. Midsummer Melancholy. Margaret Fishback. PV
O Son of God, Afflicted. *Unknown, tr. fr. Greek by* John Brownles. STF
O Son of God and Son of Man. A Vision. Henry W. Frost. SoP
O son of God! Thy children we. Light of the World. Sylvester Judd. BePJ
O Son of Man. Frank Fletcher. MaRV
O son of man, by lying tongues adored. On the Russian Persecution of the Jews. Swinburne. Sonn
O Son of Man, Thou Madest Known. Milton S. Littlefield. TrPWD
O son of man, when thou findest wine. Five Arabic Verses in Praise of Wine, V. *Unknown.* TrJP
O Son of Man, who walked each day. The Fellowship of Prayer. Nancy Byrd Turner. BePJ
O Son of mine, when dusk shall find thee bending. From Generation to Generation. Sir Henry Newbolt. FaBoTw
O son of Virginia, thy mem'ry divine. Our Washington. Eliza W. Durbin. HH; PEDC
O song as yet unsung! A Song as Yet Unsung. "Yehoash." TrJP
O Sons of Earth. Pope. *Fr.* An Essay on Man, Epistle IV. TreFT
O sons of men, that toil, and love with tears! The Fair Maid and the Sun. Arthur O'Shaughnessy. BeLS; VA
Oh, sons of sorrow, listen to me. James Bird. *Unknown.* BFSS
O! sop of sorrow, sonkin into cair. Cresseid's Complaint against Fortune. Robert Henryson. *Fr.* The Testament of Cresseid. MeEL
O Sorrow! Keats. *See* Song of the Indian Maid.
O Sorrow, cruel fellowship. In Memoriam A. H. H., III. Tennyson. EnL; EnLi-2; EPN; MaPo; OAEP; TOP; ViPo; VP
O sorrow! He is one who jumps. Springbok. *Unknown.* PeSA
O Sorrow, Sorrow. Thomas Dekker, Samuel Rowley, *and* John Day. *Fr.* The Noble Soldier. SeCL
O Sorrow, wilt thou live with me. In Memoriam A. H. H., LIX. Tennyson. EPN; GTSL; ViPo; VP
O sorrowful and ancient days. Metrum Parhemiacum Tragicum. Eugenius Vulgarius. WaaP
O Soul, canst thou not understand. Aridity. "Michael Field." BoC; FaChP; OBMV; OxBoCh; TRV
O soul, O God, O glory of liberty. Swinburne. *Fr.* The Eve of Revolution. PoFr
O soul of mine, awake,awake. Easter. Henry W. Frost. SoP
O Soul, with Storms Beset. Solomon ibn Gabirol, *tr. fr. Hebrew by* Alice Lucas. TrJP
O sound the grand symphony down through the years! The Symphony. Charlotte Grant MacIntyre. FaChP
O sovereign power of love! O grief! O balm! Keats. *Fr.* Endymion, II. EnRP; OBNC; ViBoPo
O Sower of Sorrow. Joseph Plunkett. CAW
Oh, Spanish composers may seem quite *castizo.* Iberia. Leo Kirschenbaum. UnS
O spirit of the summertime! Song. William Allingham. IrPN
O Spirit, that dost prefer. A Poet-Preacher's Prayer. Milton. *Fr.* Paradise Lost, I. MaRV
O spitefull bitter thought! Assurance. George Herbert. MaMe; OxBoCh
O sprawling city! worlds in a world! James Oppenheim. *Fr.* A New York Skyscraper. MaRV
O spread agen [*or* ageän] your leaves an' flow'rs. The Woodlands. William Barnes. BoNaP; GTBS-D; OBVV; PoVP
O Spring, Come Prettily In. Adolf Strodtmann. CAW
O spring has set off her green fuses. The Seasons in North Cornwall. Charles Causley. ACV; POTi
O Spring, I know thee! Seek for sweet surprise. In Early Spring. Alice Meynell. AnFE; HBV
Oh spring that hides the wrinkled earth in green. Sonnet. George Henry Boker. *Fr.* Sonnets. AmLP
O Spring, thou youthful beauty of the year. Spring. Giovanni Battista Guarini. AWP; JAWP; OnPM; WBP
Oh! spring was in his shining eyes. True and False. Isabelle Valancy Crawford. PeCV (1967 ed.)
O Spring's a pleasant time. Aye Waukin' O! *Unknown.* GoTS
O sprinting of the wind over land. Invocation to the Wind. Joseph Kalar. AnEnPo
O stagnant east-wind, palsied mare. A Room on a Garden. Wallace Stevens. NoP
O Star of France. Walt Whitman. PoFr
O Star of Galilee. Savonarola, *tr. fr. Latin by* R. R. Maden. ISi
O star of morning and of liberty! Divina Commedia, VI. Longfellow. AmePo; AmP; AmPP; AnAmPo; AnFE; AnNE; AP; APA; CoAnAm; CoBA; GoBC; ILP; NePA; NoP; OxBA; TOP
O Star that led the Wise Men from the East. Star of Bethlehem. Florence Van Cleve. OQP
O Star (the fairest one in sight). Choose Something like a Star. Robert Frost. AnNE; MoAB; MoAmPo (1950 ed.); NeMA; PoCh
O Starry Temple of Unvalted Space. William Alabaster. AnAnS-1
(Sonnet.) MeP
Oh, stately though we walk. The Wall. Isidor Schneider. PG (1933 ed.)
O statue, stand still! Hans Christian Andersen in Central Park. Hy Sobiloff. PoPl
O Stay, Sweet Love. *Unknown.* EG; MeWo; TrGrPo
O steadfast trees that know. Man and Nature. Robert Kelley Weeks. AA
O Stelliferi Conditor Orbis. Boethius, *tr. fr. Latin by* Alfred, King of England. BoPe
O stiffly shapen houses that change not. Suburbs on a Hazy Day. D. H. Lawrence. OBMV
O still, white face of perfect peace. Ripe Grain. Dora Read Goodale. HBV
O stoodent A has gone and spent. Ballad with an Ancient Refrain. *Unknown.* NA
Oh, Stop Being Thankful All over the Place. Ogden Nash. NePA; SiTL
Oh stormy, stormy world. Happiness Makes Up in Height for What It Lacks in Length. Robert Frost. MoAB; MoAmPo; MoPo
Oh, Stormy's gone, that good old man. Stormalong. *Unknown.* AmSS
O strange awakening to a world of gloom. Wagner. Maurice Baring. MuSP
O strange devices that alone divide. Eyes. Walter de la Mare. BrPo
O Strassburg. *Unknown, tr. fr. German by* C. F. MacIntyre. WaaP
O, strew the way with rosy flowers. Song. James Clarence Mangan. IrPN
Oh, strong and faithful and enduring. The Return. Martha Ostenso. CaP
Oh strong ridged and deeply hollowed. Smell. William Carlos Williams. MoAB; MoAmPo
O strong sun of heaven, harm not my love. An Incantation. Marguerite Wilkinson. NP
O Strong to Bless. Elizabeth Daryush. QFR
O strong was the wood in the ashen oar. Lament for Seán. D. J. O'Sullivan. NeIP
O, Struck beneath the Laurel. George Edward Woodberry. Wild Eden, XXXIII. AA; PFY
Oh stupid miracle of my own devising. Eastertide. Carl Bode. *Fr.* The Sacred Seasons. ToPo
O such a commotion under the ground. Flower Chrous. *Unknown, wr. at. to* Emerson. BoTP; PCH
Oh! such a funny thing I found. A Discovery. Arthur A. Knipe. GFA

Oh such a tiny colony. Helmet Orchid. Douglas Stewart. BoAV
O sug'red talk wherewith my thoughts do live. Licia, LII. Giles Fletcher. ReIE
O suitably-attired-in-leather-boots. Fragment of a Greek Tragedy. A. E. Housman. CenHV; Par
O sun and skies and clouds of June. *See* O suns and skies and clouds of June.
O sun! Instigator of cocks! Salute. Archibald MacLeish. CMoP
Oh sun, oh good comrade, good friend. Riding Song. Isidor Schneider. PG (1933 ed.)
O Sun of Life. Thomas Curtis Clark. ChIP
O Sun, when I stand in my green leaves. To the Sun from a Flower. Guido Gezelle. FaPON; LiTW
Oh Sunne,/ Burne the great sphere thou mov'st in. Shakespeare. *Fr.* Antony and Cleopatra, IV, xv. AtBAP
O suns [*or* sun] and skies and clouds of June. October's Bright Blue Weather. Helen Hunt Jackson. AmePo; BBV (1923 ed.); BLPA; BoChLi; DD; FaBoBe; GN; HBVY; NeHB; OTD; OTPC (1946 ed.); PoSC; TreFT
O sunstruck spray, where change and changeless meet. Some Refrains at the Charles River. Peter Viereck. PoCh
O supreme Light, who dost thy glory assert. The Vision of God. Dante. *Fr.* Divina Commedia: Paradiso, XXXIII. ExPo
O surely, surely life is fair. Fiorentina. Ernest Myers. OBVV
Oh, Susan Blue. Susan Blue. Kate Greenaway. MPB; OTPC (1946 ed.); TiPo
Oh, Susan Van Dusan. Susan Van Dusan. *Unknown.* ABF
Oh! Susanna. Stephen Collins Foster. FaFP; PaA; RIS; StaSt; TrAS, *with music*; TreF
O Swallow, Swallow, Flying, Flying South. Tennyson. *Fr.* The Princess, Pt. IV. AtBAP; GTBS; GTSL; HBV; PoVP
(Songs from "The Princess.") ViPo
O swan of slenderness. The Little Red Lark. Alfred Perceval Graves. HBV
Oh swearing and telling. Cockcrow. Eithne Wilkins. NeBP
O, sweep of stars over Harlem Streets. Stars. Langston Hughes. OCS
O sweet and luminous Bird. Celestial Bird. Jessica Powers. JKCP (1955 ed.)
O Sweet Anne Page. William Shenstone. SeCePo
(Slender's Ghost.) EiPP
O sweet are tropic lands for waking dreams! North and South. Claude McKay. AmPP; GoSl
Oh, Sweet Content. W. H. Davies. CH
O Sweet Content. Thomas Dekker. *See* Happy Heart, The.
O Sweet Delight. Thomas Campion. GTSE
("O sweet delight, O more than human bliss.") EG
(Song: "O sweet delight...") HBV
O sweet everlasting Voices, be still. The Everlasting Voices. W. B. Yeats. AWP; JAWP; WBP
O sweet incendiary! show here thy art. Richard Crashaw. *Fr.* The Flaming Heart. PoFS; SeEP
O sweet is love, and sweet is lack! Francis Thompson. EG
O sweet Queen-city of the golden South. Patrick Moloney. Sonnets—Ad Innuptam, VII. BoAu
O sweet September! thy first breezes bring. Sweet September. George Arnold. GN
O Sweet Spontaneous. E. E. Cummings. AnNE; AP; BoLiVe (1945 ed.); CBV; NoP
(La Guerre.) MAP; MoAB; MoAmPo
(O Sweet Spontaneous Earth.) OxBA; TrGrPo
O sweet the time, when neither folly might. Truth's Complaint over England. Thomas Lodge. ACP (1952 ed.)
O sweet to-morrow! Song of Hope. Thomas Hardy. VP
Oh, sweet Virginia hills! George Washington. Francesca Falk Miller. PEDC
O sweet wild April. Sweet Wild April. William Force Stead. HBV; HBVY
O Sweet Woods (*three sonnets*). Sir Philip Sidney. *Fr.* Arcadia. AtBAP; CoBE, *first sonnet*; PoEL-1; TuPP
(Delight of Solitariness, The.) LiTB
(Dorus's Song.) LoBV
("O sweet woods, the delight of solitariness!") FCP; SiCE
(Solitariness.) OBSC; SiPS
O sweete and bitter monuments of paine. Upon the Ensignes of Christes Crucifyinge [*or* Sonnet]. William Alabaster. AnAnS-1; MeP; MePo
O sweeter than the marriage-feast. He Prayeth Best. Samuel Taylor Coleridge. *Fr.* The Rime of the Ancient Mariner, VII. MaRV
Oh, sweetest invitation this sin-worn earth hath known. Christ's Invitation. *Unknown.* SoP
O Sweetest Melancholy. John Fletcher *and at.,* Thomas Middleton. *See* Melancholy.
O Sweetheart, Hear You. James Joyce. Chamber Music, XVIII. HBMV; MeWo; MoBrPo
O swift forerunners, rosy with the race. Sunrise on Mansfield Mountain. Alice Brown. HBV
O swinging sword of Carroll hail! Carroll's Sword. *At. to* Dallan MacMore. KiLC
O sylvan prophet, whose eternal fame. Hymn for St. John's Eve. *Unknown.* AWP
O! synge untoe mie roundelaie. Mynstrelles Songe. Thomas Chatterton. *Fr.* Aella. AnFE; BEL; CEP; EiCL; EiPP; EnLi-2; EnLoPo; EnRP; OBEC. *See also* Minstrel's Song.
O, Tabby of the yellow eyes. To a Cat. Fanny Elizabeth Perkins. CIV
Talk Not to Me. Byron. *See* Stanzas Written on the Road between Florence and Pisa.
Oh, tamp 'em up solid. Tie-tamping Chant. *Unknown.* ABF
O Tan-faced Prairie-Boy. Walt Whitman. FaPON; LO; OxBA
O tardy plane-tree. Plane-Tree. F. S. Flint. MoBrPo (1942 ed.)
Oh, teach me, thou forest, to testify glad. Aspirations. Adam G. Oehlenschlaeger. SoP
O tears, no tears, but rain from Beauty's skies. Astrophel and Stella, C. Sir Philip Sidney. FCP; ReIE; SiPS; Sonn
Oh, tell me, children who have seen. Christmas. Mary Mapes Dodge. BiCB
O tell me, drayman, who quietly descend. The Drayman. Giovanni Pascoli. OnPM
Oh! tell me have you ever seen a red, long-leg'd flamingo? The Flamingo. Lewis Gaylord Clark. BOHV; NA
O Tell Me How to Woo Thee. Robert Graham. *See* If Doughty Deeds.
Oh, tell me, little children, have you seen her. Nikolina. Celia Thaxter. GN; HBV; OTPC (1946 ed.)
"Oh tell me, sailor, tell me true." The Gray Swan. Alice Cary. BeLS; BLPA; GN
Oh, tell me what you see. Nonesense Song. *Ad. by* Michael Lewis. RIS
O tell me whence that joy doth spring. The Queer. Henry Vaughan. MaPo; PoEL-2
O Tempora! O Mores! Thomas Freeman. SiCE
O tender dove, sweet circling in the blue. Vale! Roden Noel. OBVV
O tender shade! To a Photograph. John Banister Tabb. AmP
O tender time that love thinks long to see. A Vision of Spring in Winter. Swinburne. PoVP
O Tender under Her Right Breast. George Barker. *Fr.* Second Cycle of Love Poems. MoAB; MoBrPo (1950 ed.); NeMA
(Love Poem.) NeBP
O tenderly the haughty day. Ode [Sung in the Town Hall, Concord, July 4, 1857]. Emerson. AA; AnNE; DD; GN; MPB; PaA; PAL; PoRL
O Thalassa! Thalassa! Where, where. The Singers. George Bruce. OxBS
O than the fairest day, thrice fairer night. For the Nativity of Our Lord. William Drummond. StJW
O thank you for giving me the chance. Thank You. Kenneth Koch. NeAP
Oh! thank you, good Dobbin, you've been a long track. Good Dobbin. Ann *or* Jane Taylor. SAS
Oh, thanks for all since the days long past. Synnöve's Song. Björnstjerne Björnson. LiTW; PoPl
Oh that bright impossible beast of the mind. Virgin and Unicorn. John Heath-Stubbs. NeBP
Oh, that day there was a great demand for sailors. Mainsail Haul, *vers.* II. *Unknown.* ShS
O that frog or flower that stealthily. Mythological Episode. Robert H. Barlow. FiSC
Oh that horse I see so high. A Gift of Great Value. Robert Creeley. NaP
Oh! that I always breath'd in such an aire. The Experience.

Oh (continued)
Edward Taylor. *Fr.* Preparatory Meditations, First Series. AmPP (4th ed.)
O that I could a sinne once see! Sinne. George Herbert. MaMe
O that I could my Lord receive. The Conquering Love of Jesus. Charles Wesley. BePJ
Oh that I could suavely pass. Otherwhere. Frances Angevine Gray. FiSC
O That I Had Wings like a Dove. *Unknown.* OxBoCh
Oh that I had wings like a dove! Wings. *Fr.* Psalm LV, Bible, *O.T.* AWP; FaPON; PCD; PCH
Oh that I knew how all thy lights combine. The H. Scriptures. George Herbert. SCEP-1
Oh That I Knew Where I Might Find Him. Job, XXIII: 3, 8-10, Bible, *O.T.* MaRV
O that I knew whether Sulayma is dwelling in the valley of the demesne. Remembrance. Ibnul'l-Farid. LiTW
O that I might believe that time. Device. Sir Herbert Read. MoBrPo (1942 ed.)
Oh, that I were a lovely flower. The Flower. *At. to* Samuel Speed. OxBoCh; SeCL
Oh! that I were a poet now in grain! An Elegie upon that Reverend . . . Mr. Thomas Shepard. Urian Oakes. SCAP
Oh that I were an orange-tree. Employment. George Herbert. OBS
"O that I were as sure to live, immortal, and sustain." Homer. *Fr.* The Iliad, VIII. AtBAP
Oh That I Were in the Wilderness. Jeremiah, IX: 1-10, Bible, *O.T.* TrJP
O that I were lying under the olives. March Thoughts from England. Margaret L. Woods. OBVV
Oh that I were where I would be. *Unknown.* OxNR; SiTL
Oh, That Joy So Soon Should Waste. Ben Jonson. *See* Song: "Oh, that joy . . ."
Oh! that last day in Lucknow fort. The Relief of Lucknow. Robert T. S. Lowell. HBV; StPo
O that mine eyes might closèd be. A Prayer. Thomas Ellwood. WGRP
Oh! that my life were a lasting dream! *See* Oh! that my young life were a lasting dream.
Oh, that my load of sin were gone. The Light Yoke and Easy Burden. Charles Wesley. BePJ
Oh that my lungs could bleat like butter'd peas [*or* buttered pease]. Odd but True [*or* Nonsense]. *Unknown.* NA; SiTL
Oh that my soul a marrow-bone might seize! Sonnet Found in a Deserted Madhouse. *Unknown.* BOHV; InvP; NA; SiTL
Oh! that my young life were a lasting dream. Dreams. Poe. AmPP (4th ed.); CBEP; OxBA
O that our dreamings all, of sleep or wake. Keats. *Fr.* Epistle to John Hamilton Reynolds. EPN; ERoP-2
O that the chemist's magic art. On a Tear. Samuel Rogers. HBV
Oh! that the desert were my dwelling-place. The Ocean [*or* By the Deep Sea]. Byron. *Fr.* Childe Harold's Pilgrimage, IV. BEL; ILP; OBNC; PoEL-4
O that the pines which crown yon steep. Evening Melody. Aubrey Thomas De Vere. GoBC; HBV
O that this last farewell. *Unknown.* LO; SeCSL
"O that this too [too] solid flesh would melt." On a Young Lady's Going into a Shower Bath. Francis Scott Key. UnTE; YaD
O! that this too too solid flesh would melt. Frailty, Thy Name Is Woman. Shakespeare. *Fr.* Hamlet, I, ii. TreFS; TrGrPo
Oh that those lips had language! Life has passed. On the Receipt of My [*or* Lines on Receiving His] Mother's Picture Out of Norfolk. William Cowper. BEL; CEP; CH; CoBE; EiPP; EnLi-2 (1949 ed.); EnLit; EnPE; EnRP; FiP; HBV; MemP; NoP; OAEP; OBEC; OHIP; PoE; PoIE; TOP
O That 'Twere Possible. Tennyson. *Fr.* Maud, Pt. II, iv. AtBAP; CBEP; EG; HBV; HoPM; OBEV; OBVV; OQP; PoFS
Oh! that we two were maying. Song. Charles Kingsley. *Fr.* The Saint's Tragedy. HBV; VA
O that you were yourself! but, love, you are. Sonnets, XIII. Shakespeare. OAEP; SiCE
Oh, the agony of having too much power! The Interne. Maxwell Bodenheim. NP
Oh, the anchor's aweigh, the anchor's aweigh. The Anchor's Aweigh. *Unknown.* ShS
Oh, the anguish of Mary! Not There. *Unknown.* STF
Oh, the auld house, the auld house. The Auld House. Lady Nairne. HBV; OTPC (1923 ed.)
Oh, the banks of May are fair. To a Carmelite Postulant. Michael Earls. CAW; JKCP
O the barberry bright, the barberry bright. Song against Children. Aline Kilmer. SP; TSW
Oh, the beautiful maiden has gone away. A Garland of Recital Programs. Franklin P. Adams. InMe
Oh, the beauty of the Christ Child. Offertory. Mary Mapes Dodge. HH; PRWS
Oh, the bitter shame and sorrow. None of Self and All of Thee [*or* Christ Alone]. Theodore Monod. BLRP; FaChP; STF
Oh, the blue blue bloom. Pansy. Mary Effie Lee Newsome. CDC
O the bonny Christ Church Bells. Christ Church Bells. *At. to* Henry Aldrich. CBEP; SeCL
Oh, the boys and the girls went a-huckleberry hunting. Huckleberry Hunting. *Unknown.* SoAmSa
Oh, the brave old Duke of York. *Unknown.* OxNR
Oh, the broom, the bonny, bonny broom. The Bonny Broom. *Unknown.* BFSS
O the broom, the yellow broom. The Broom Flower. Mary Howitt. HBV
O, the captain went below. The Captain Went Below. *Unknown.* AmSS
Oh, the comfort—the inexpressible comfort of feeling safe with a person. Friendship. Dinah Maria Mulcok Craik. BLPA; NeHB; PoToHe (new ed.)
Oh, the cow-puncher loves the whistle of the rope. From the Chuck Wagon. *Unknown.* ABF
O the crossbones of Galway. Galway. Louis MacNeice. OxBI
Oh, the Cuckoo, he is royal bird. Cuckoo's Palace. William Brighty Rands. BiS
Oh the dance of our Sister! The Dance of the Rain. Eugene Marais. PeSA
Oh! the days are gone, when beauty bright. Love's Young Dream. Thomas Moore. HBV; WBLP
Oh, the days gone by! Oh, the days gone by! The Days Gone By. James Whitcomb Riley. TreF
Oh, the days of the Kerry dancing! The Kerry Dance. James Lyman Molloy. OnYI
O the days of the Messiah are at hand, are at hand! Ballad of the Days of the Messiah. A. M. Klein. TrJP
Oh, the days were ever shiny. My Love and My Heart. Henry S. Leigh. BOHV; CIV
Oh, the Devil in hell they say he was chained. Hell in Texas. *Unknown.* ABF; BLPA; CoSo
Oh! the dew-wet grass of the meadow in North Carolina. John Wasson. Edgar Lee Masters. *Fr.* Spoon River Anthology. LaNeLa
O the evening's for the fair, bonny lassie O! Bonny Lassie O! John Clare. CH
Oh the falling snow! For Snow. Eleanor Farjeon. CH; TiPo
Oh, the fisherman is a happy wight! The Fisherman's Chant. F. C. Burnand. BOHV
Oh! the French are on the sea [*or* say]. The Shan Van Vocht. *Unknown.* AnIL; AnIV; OnYI; PoFr
O the gallant fisher's life. The Angler. John Chalkhill. HBV
Oh, the gen'ral raised the devil with the kernel, so 'tis said. Bugs. Will Stokes. BBV (1923 ed.); MoShBr
Oh, the girl that I loved she was handsome. The Man on the Flying Trapeze. George Leybourne. ABF; FaFP; LiTG; LoGBV; OxBoLi; SiTL
O the girl with the eyes. True Romance. Edwin Honig. SiTL
Oh the glowing beauty. A Yellow Daffodil. Alice Hansche Mortenson. SoP
Oh, the gold hills of Ireland. They Who Wait. Charles Buxton Going. HBMV
Oh, the good ole chariot swing so low. Swing Low, Sweet Chariot. *Unknown.* AA
O the green glimmer of apples in the orchard. Ballad of Another Ophelia. D. H. Lawrence. ChTr; CoBMV; MoVE
O the green things growing, the green things growing. Green

Things Growing. Dinah Maria Mulock Craik. DD; FaFP; GN; HBV; HBVY; OHIP; OTPC
O the grey, grey company. The Grey Company. Jessie Mackay. BoAu
Oh, the hearts of men, they are rovers, all! Ulysses Returns, IV. Roselle Mercier Montgomery. HBMV
Oh the hills of dear New Castle. Our Delaware. George B. Hynson. PoRL
Oh, the hog-eye man is the man for me [*or* men are all the go]. The Hog-Eye Man. *Unknown.* AS; SoAmSa
Oh the Inconstant. N. P. van Wyk Louw, *tr. fr. Afrikaans by* Jack Cope *and* Uys Krige. PeSA
Oh, the joy of looking forward. He Is Coming. Gladys M. Gearhart. STF
Oh! The king's gane gyte. Cophetua. "Hugh MacDiarmid." OxBS
Oh, the last steer has been branded. A Cowboy's Love Song. *Unknown.* SCC
Oh, the little birds are singing in the budding willow trees. The Gardener. Lucy Fitch Perkins. PCH
Oh, the little birds sang east, and the little birds sang west. Round Our Restlessness. Elizabeth Barrett Bowning. *Fr.* Rhyme of the Duchess May. MaRV; TRV
Oh, the little brown bull came down from the mountain. Tearin' Out-a Wilderness. *Unknown.* ABF
Oh, the little flax flower! The Flax Flower. Mary Howitt. PRWS
O the little rusty dusty miller. *Unknown.* OxNR
Oh, the littles that remain! After. Lizette Woodworth Reese. HBV
Oh, the lives of men, lives of men. Bindlestiff. Edwin Ford Piper. HBMV; MAP
O, the lovely rivers and lakes of Maine! The Lovely Rivers and Lakes of Maine. George B. Wallis. BLPA
O the Man in the Moon has a crick in his back. The Man in the Moon. James Whitcomb Riley. BOHV; HBV; HBVY; NA; OTPC; YT
Oh the many joys of a harlot's wedding. Hail Wedded Love! Jay Macpherson. MoCV
O, the Marriage! Thomas Osborne Davis. OBVV
Oh, the men who laughed the American laughter. American Laughter. Kenneth Allan Robinson. AmFN; PaA; TreFS
Oh the miller, the dusty, musty miller. A Ballad of All the Trades. *Unknown.* CoMu; ErPo; UnTE
Oh, the Month of May! Thomas Dekker. *Fr.* The Shoemaker's Holiday, III, v. EIL; ViBoPo
(May.) OBSC
(Maytime.) TrGrPo
Oh, the moon shines bright, and we sail to-night. Bound for Sourabaya! Charles Henry Souter. BoAu
Oh! the night that I struck New York. The Bowery. Charles Hale Hoyt. TreF; YaD
Oh the North Countree is a hard countree. The Ballad of Yukon Jake. Edward E. Paramore, Jr. BeLS; BLPA; NeHB
Oh, the old gray mare, she ain't what she used to be. Old Gray Mare. *Unknown.* AS
Oh! the old swimmin'-hole! whare the crick so still and deep. The Old Swimmin'-Hole. James Whitcomb Riley. BeLS; FaFP; HBV
O the opal and the sapphire of that wandering western sea. Beeny Cliff. Thomas Hardy. OBNC; PoVP
O the Ploughboy was a-ploughing. The Simple Ploughboy. *Unknown.* FaBoCh; LoGBV; OBB
Oh, the prairie dogs are screaming. A Cow Camp on the Range. *Unknown.* CoSo
Oh! the pride of Portsmouth water. The Lost War-Sloop. Edna Dean Proctor. PAH
O the quietest home in earth had I. The Bald-headed Tyrant. Mary E. Vandyne.
O the Raggedy Man! He works fer Pa. The Raggedy Man. James Whitcomb Riley. BoChLi; FaPON; GoTP; HBV; HBVY; MPB; OTD; OTPC; StVeCh; TiPo; TreFS
O, the rain, the weary, dreary rain. Twenty Golden Years Ago. James Clarence Mangan. IrPN; NBM, *abr.*; OnYI; PeER
Oh, the Roman was a rogue. Lay of Ancient Rome. Thomas R. Ybarra. BOHV; HBV; InMe; LHV; WhC
Oh, the roses we plucked for the blue. The New Memorial Day. Albert Bigelow Paine. DD; HH; OQP; PEDC
Oh, the sad day! The Sad Day [*or* Death *or* Song]. Thomas Flatman. OBEV; PeRV; SeCL
Oh, the sea is deep. Song for a Suicide. Langston Hughes. PoNe (1970 ed.)
Oh, the shambling sea is a sexton old. The Gravedigger. Bliss Carman. BoNaP; MAP; MoAmPo (1942 ed.)
Oh! the shearing is all over. The Old Bullock Dray. *Unknown.* PoAu-1
Oh the sheer joy of it! Sheer Joy. Ralph Spaulding Cushman. SoP; TRV
O the shepherds in Judea. The Shepherds in Judea. Mary Austin. ChrBoLe; DD
Oh, the ships will come and the ships will go. Get up, Jack! John, Sit Down! *Unknown.* ABF
Oh, the sky is so blue. Child's Evensong. Ethel Robb. GFA
Oh, the smartest clipper you can find. Clear the Track. *Unknown.* SoAmSa
Oh! the snow, the beautiful snow. The Beautiful Snow. John Whittaker Watson. BLPA; TreF; WBLP
O the spring will come. The Spring Will Come. H. D. Lowry. BoNaP
Oh the summer's afloat on spindrift beaches. Never No More. James K. Baxter. AnNZ
Oh, the sun sets red, the moon shines white. The *Armstrong* at Fayal. Wallace Rice. PAH
Oh, the sweet contentment. Coridon's Song. John Chalkhill. HBV; ViBoPo
Oh, the swift plunge into the cool, green dark. Louis Untermeyer. *Fr.* Swimmers. PFY
Oh, the tidal waves of our suffering. The Law. Albert Haynes. NBP
Oh, the times are hard and the wages low. Across the Western Ocean. *Unknown.* AmSS; AS; SoAmSa
Oh, the times are hard and the wages low. Leave Her Johnny [*or* Leave Her, Bullies, Leave Her]. *Unknown.* AS; SoAmSa (B *vers.*)
Oh! the tragedy. A Mordern Orchard. David O'Neil. AnAmPo
O the vines were golden, the birds were loud. Fable. Frederic Prokosch. LiTM; WaP
O the way sometimes is low. The Tryst. Lauchlan MacLean Watt. MaRV
Oh, the West Virginia hills! The West Virginia Hills. Ellen King *and* H. E. Engle. PoRL
Oh, the white-sea-gull, the wild sea-gull. The Sea-Gull. Mary Howitt. BoTP
Oh, the wide world's ways! The Way of the World. Ryota. OnPM
Oh, the Wild Joy of Living. Robert Browning. *See* David's Song.
O the wild trees of my home. The Wild Trees. Laurie Lee. BoPe; GTBS-D
Oh, the wind blow east. The Wind Blow East. *Unknown.* OuSiCo
Oh, the wind from the desert blew in!—Khamsin. Khamsin. Clinton Scollard. AA; PFY
Oh, the wind is brisk and biting. Christmas Shoppers. Aileen Fisher. ChBR
Oh, the work was hard and the wages low. Time to Leave Her. *Unknown.* AmSS
Oh, the world is all too rude for thee, with much ado and care. A World for Love. John Clare. PG
Oh, them days on Red Hoss Mountain, when the skies was fair 'nd blue. Casey's Table d'Hote. Eugene Field. PoOW
O! then, I see, Queen[e] Mab hath been[e] with you. Queen Mab [*or* Mercutio's Queen Mab Speech]. Shakespeare. *Fr.* Romeo and Juliet, I, iv. BoC; BoW; FaPON; FiP; FIW; LiTB; MPB; OTPC; TreF
"Oh, then tell me, Shawn O'Ferrall." The Rising of the Moon. John Keegan Casey. AnIV; IrPN; OnYI
O Theophilus. Margaret Allonby. BoSA
O there are heavenly heights to reach. Trust. C. A. Fox. SoP
Oh! there are spirits of the air. To Coleridge. Shelley. CBEP; ERoP-2
Oh, there are those, a sordid clan. The Child's Heritage. John G. Neihardt. HBV
O, there are times/ When all this fret. Daily Trials. Oliver Wendell Holmes. PoEL-5
Oh, there be many candles bright. The Gift. Laura Spencer Portor. PEDC
O, there be many things. Many Things. Oliver Wendell Holmes. PoToHe (new ed.)

O there is a little artist. The Fairy Artist. Nellie M. Garabrant. PCH; PoPl
Oh there is blessing in this gentle breeze. The Prelude: Introduction—Childhood and School-Time. Wordsworth. BEL; EnLit; ERoP-1; FosPo; MBW-2; TreFT
Oh! there is never sorrow of heart. Wordsworth. *Fr.* The Force of Prayer. MaRV
Oh, there once was a lady, and so I've been told. Fable. Dorothy Parker. ALV
O, there once was a puffin. There Once Was a Puffin. Florence Page Jaques. SoPo; TiPo
Oh! there once was a swagman camped in a Billabong. Waltzing Matilda. A. B. Paterson. WhC
Oh! there was a moanish lady. Moanish Lady. *Unknown.* AS
O there was a woman, and she was a widow. Flowers in the Valley. *Unknown.* AtBAP; OnMSP; OxBoLi; SiSw
Oh! there was an old soldier. There Was an Old Soldier. *Unknown.* AS; TrAS
Oh, there were fifteen men in green. Men in Green. David Campbell. BoAV; MoAuPo; NeLNL; PoAu-2
O there were lights and laughter. Voices. Witter Bynner. MAP; MoAmPo (1942 ed.); PCH; TSW
O there were three jolly hunters. The Three Jolly Hunters. James Whitcomb Riley. WaKn
Oh, there's mony a gate eawt ov eawr teawn-end. Th' Sweetheart Gate. Edwin Waught. VA
Oh, these spring days! Spring Days. Basho. OnPM
O these wakefull wounds of thine! On the Wounds of Our Crucified Lord. Richard Crashaw. MaMe; SeEP
Oh, they call me Hanging Johnny. Hanging Johnny. *Unknown.* SoAmSa
Oh, think how hard it is to die when young! Charles Heavysege. *Fr.* Jephthah's Daughter. CaP
Oh, Think Not I Am Faithful to a Vow. Edna St. Vincent Millay. CMoP; FaBV
(Sonnet.) MasP; NP
Oh! think to step ashore. Stepping Ashore. Robert E. Selle. SoP
O, this is a sin-tryin' world. This Is a Sin-tryin' World. *Unknown.* TrAS
O this is the beast that does not have being! Rainer Maria Rilke. Sonnets to Orpheus, Pt. II, IV. ReMP
O thorn-crowned brow. Behold the Man! *Unknown.* STF
O thorn-crowned sorrow, pitiless and stern. Sorrow. Katrina Trask. AA
Oh those were happy days, heaped up with wineskins. Silenus in Proteus. Thomas Lovell Beddoes. EnRP
O Thou/ God of all long desirous roaming. Rupert Brooke. *Fr.* The Song of the Pilgrims. TrPWD
O thou afflicted, drunken not with wine! Dirge for the Ninth of Ab. *Unknown.* TrJP
O thou all-eloquent, whose mighty mind. Man's Going Hence. Samuel Rogers. *Fr.* Human Life. OBNC
O Thou almighty will. Strength, Love, Light. Robert II, King of France. WGRP
Oh, thou alphabetic row. A. B. C. Eliza Cook. OTPC (1923 ed.)
O thou art such, that I could be. Henry Vaughan. LO
O Thou, as represented here to me. Our Known Unknown [*or* From the Pope's Speech]. Robert Browning. *Fr.* The Ring and the Book, X. OQP
O Thou best gift from heaven. Send Me. *Unknown.* MaRV
O thou by Nature taught. Ode to Simplicity. William Collins. BEL; CEP; EiCP; EiPP; EnLi-2 (1949 ed.); EnRP; GTSL; NoP; OBEC; OBEV; PoFS; UnPo (1st ed.)
O Thou Eternal One! Gavril Romanovich Derzhavin, *tr. fr. Russian by* Sir John Bowring. WGRP
O Thou Eternal Source of Life. Rolland W. Schloerb. TrPWD
O thou fair silver Thames, O clearest crystal flood! Song to Beta. Michael Drayton. *Fr.* The Shepherd's Garland: Third Eclogue. OBSC
O Thou, from whom all goodness flows. Remember Me! Thomas Haweis. BePJ
O Thou great author of the world. A Prayer. Sister Albertus Magnus. WHL
O Thou Great Being! what Thou art. Prayer under the Pressure of Violent Anguish. Burns. TrPWD
O thou great Friend to all the sons of men. The Way, the Truth, and the Life. Theodore Parker. ChIP; TrPWD
O thou great movement of the universe. Bryant. *Fr.* An Evening Revery. AA
O Thou great mystery. Indian Prayer. Chief Joseph Strongwolf. TRV
O thou great Power, in whom I move. A Hymn to My God in a Night of My Late Sicknesse [*or* It Is Finished]. Sir Henry Wotton. AnAnS-2; BePJ; MeLP; MePo; OBS
O thou great wrong, that, through the slow-paced years. The Death of Slavery. Bryant. AA; DD; PoFr
O Thou Immortal Deity. Shelley. TrPWD
O thou in heaven and earth the only peace. The Plan of Salvation. Milton. *Fr.* Paradise Lost, III. WGRP
Oh, thou! in Hellas deemed of heavenly birth. Byron. *Fr.* Childe Harold's Pilgrimage, I. MBW-2
O Thou, in whom we live and move. A Poet's Grace. Burns. TrPWD
O thou Moor of Morería. Abenamar, Abenamar. *Unknown.* AWP; OuHeWo
Oh! thou, my Lord, thou king of saints, here mak'st. Meditation LXII [*or* While the King Sitteth at His Table]. Edward Taylor. *Fr.* Preparatory Meditations, Second Series. MAmP; MWA-1
O thou, my lovely boy, who in thy power. Sonnets, CXXVI. Shakespeare. MyFE; ReIE; Sonn
O Thou my monster, Thou my guide. Prayer in Mid-Passage. Louis MacNeice. EaLo
O Thou my soule, Jehovah blesse. Psalm CIII, Bible, *O.T.* SCAP
O thou newcomer who seek'st Rome in Rome. Rome. Joachim du Bellay. AWP; JAWP; WBP
O Thou not made with hands. The City of God. Francis Turner Palgrave. MaRV; WGRP
O thou of angels the most wise and fair. The Litanies of Satan. Baudelaire. EnLi-2
O thou of little faith. Hitherto Hath the Lord Helped. *Unknown.* BLRP; SoP
O Thou of soul and sense and breath. In Memory of Abraham Lincoln. Oliver Wendell Holmes. LiPo
O Thou, our Saviour, brother, friend. For the Peace of Jerusalem. Charles Wesley. BePJ
O thou pale form. Robert Browning. *Fr.* Pauline. ChIP
O Thou pure fountain of pure love, my Lord! To Our Lord. Francisco Galvam. CAW
O thou so fair in summers gone. Freedom. Tennyson. PoVP
O thou soft naturall death, thou art joint-twin. John Webster. *Fr.* The White Devil, V, iii. AtBAP
O thou that achest, pulse o' the unwed vast. Adam to Lilith. Christopher Brennan. *Fr.* Lilith. PoAu-1
O thou that after toil and storm. In Memoriam A. H. H., XXXIII. Tennyson. EPN; TOP; ViPo; VP
O thou that cleavest heaven. Bird's Song at Morning. William James Dawson. VA
Oh thou, that dear and happy isle. Andrew Marvell. *Fr.* Upon Appleton House. OxBoLi
O Thou, that dost cover the heavens. Song of the Wind and the Rain. Solomon ibn Gabirol. TrJP
O thou that from the green vales of the west. To Spring [On the Banks of the Cam]. William Stanley Roscoe. OBVV; UnPo (1st ed.)
O thou that from thy mansion. For My Funeral. A. E. Housman. BoPe; CMoP; TrPWD; ViBoPo
O thou that held'st the blessed Veda dry. Hymn to Vishnu. Jayadeva. *Fr.* Gita Govinda. AWP
O Thou, that in the heavens dost dwell. *See* O Thou, wha in the heavens. . .
O thou that lovest a pure, and whitend soul! Dressing. Henry Vaughan. AnAnS-1; MeP
O thou that often hast within thine eyes. Sonnet: He Speaks of a Third Love. Guido Cavalcanti. AWP
O thou that rollest above, round as the shield. Ossian's Address to the Sun. James Macpherson. *Fr.* Carthon. BEL
O thou, that sendest out the man. England and America in 1782. Tennyson. EPN; MC; OTPC (1946 ed.); PaA; PAH; PAL; PoFr; PoVP
O Thou, that sitt'st [*or* sit'st] upon a throne. A Song to David. Christopher Smart. AtBAP; CEP; ChTr; EiCL; EiCP; EiPP; EnPE; GoTL; LaA; LoBV; MasP; OBEC; OBEV; PeER; PoEL-3; TrGrPo; UnS
O Thou That Sleep'st like Pig in Straw. Sir William Davenant. *See* Song: "O thou that sleep'st. . ."

Oh thou that swing'st upon the waving hair [*or* haire *or* eare]. The [*or* To the] Grasshopper [*or* Ode]. Richard Lovelace. AnAnS-2; AtBAP; BWP; CBV; FaBoEn; LoBV; MeLP; MePo; NoP; OBEV; OBS; Po; ReEn; SCEP-2; SeCePo; SeCL; SeCV-1; SeEP
O thou that with surpassing glory crowned. Satan's Soliloquy. Milton. *Fr.* Paradise Lost, IV. LiTB; OBS
O Thou! the first fruits of the dead. Buriall. Henry Vaughan. SeCV-1
O thou, the friend of man, [*or* assign'd]. Ode to Pity. William Collins. CEP; EiCP; EiPP; EnPE
O thou the span of whose omnipotence. Out of Grotius His Tragedy of Christes Sufferinges. Richard Crashaw. MaMe
O thou to whom, athwart the perished days. Mary Arden. Eric Mackay. VA
O Thou to Whom the Musical White Spring. E. E. Cummings. InPo
(Sonnet: "O thou to whom. . .") NP
O Thou to whom, without reserve. Thy Will Be Done in Me. Fanny Crosby. MaRV
O Thou, to whose all-searching sight. My Light! My Way! [*or* A Plea]. Graf von Zinzendorf. MaRV; SoP
O Thou transcendent! Passage to More than India. Walt Whitman. *Fr.* Passage to India. MoRP
O thou undaunted daughter of desires! Upon the Book and Picture of the Seraphical Saint Teresa. Richard Crashaw. *Fr.* The Flaming Heart. CoBE; OBEV; WHA
O Thou unknown, Almighty Cause. A Prayer in the Prospect of Death. Burns. HBV; MaRV; TrPWD; WGRP
O Thou, wha [*or* that] in the heavens [*or* heav'ns] does dwell. Holy Willie's Prayer. Burns. BEL; BOHV; CEP; EiCL; EiPP; EnL; EnPE; EnRP; FosPo; GoTS; NoP; OxBoLi; OxBS; PeER; PoE; PoEL-4; TOP; VaPo; ViBoPo
O thou! whatever title suit thee. Address to the Deil. Burns. CEP; EiCP; EiPP; EnPE; EnRP; GoTS; OAEP; OxBS; PoE; PoEL-4; UnPo (1st ed.)
O Thou which to search out the secret parts. To Mr. S. B. John Donne. MaMe
O Thou who all-things hast of nothing made. Deo Opt. Max. George Sandys. *Fr.* Paraphrase on the Psalms. OBS
O thou who art of all that is. Through Unknown Paths. Frederick L. Hosmer. TrPWD
O Thou Who Art Our Author and Our End. Sir John Beaumont. TreFT
O thou who at Love's hour ecstatically. Love's Testament. Dante Gabriel Rossetti. The House of Life, III. MaVP; PoVP; ViPo; VP
O Thou who bidst the torrent flow. Whittier. *Fr.* Hymn from the French of Lamartine. TrPWD
O Thou Who Camest from Above. Charles Wesley. *See* Hymn: "O Thou who camest from above."
O thou, who dist furnish. Hymn to Moloch. Ralph Hodgson. HBMV
Oh Thou, who didst with pitfall and with gin. There Is No Sin. Omar Khayyám, *tr. by* Edward Fitzgerald. *Fr.* The Rubáiyát. OnPM
Oh, Thou! Who Dry'st the Mourner's Tear. Thomas Moore. TrPWD
O thou who giving helm and sword. The Dreamer. Walter de la Mare. CMoP; OTPC (1923 ed.)
O Thou, who kindly dost provide. A Poet's Grace. Burns. TrPWD
O Thou, who love in mercy hast created. Thomas Tiplady. *Fr.* A Wedding Hymn. MaRV
O Thou who lovest not alone. The Aim. Sir Charles G. D. Roberts. MaRV; PeCV
Oh thou, who man of baser earth didst make. Equity with God. Omar Khayyám. *Fr.* The Rubáiyát. EaLo; OnPM; SeCeV
O thou who movest onward with a mind. Epitaphs, III. Gabriello Chiabrera. AWP; JAWP; WBP
O thou, who passest thro' our vallies [*or* through our valleys] in. To Summer. Blake. CEP; ERoP-1; WiR
O thou, who plumed with strong desire. The Two Spirits. Shelley. CH; EPN; ERoP-2; WiR
O Thou who seest all my grief. A Prayer in the Night. Oswald J. Smith. SoP
O thou who sitt'st a smiling bride. Ode to Mercy. William Collins. EiCP
O Thou who speedest time's advancing wing. He Asketh Absolution of God. *Unknown.* *Fr.* Book of the Dead. AWP
O Thou, whose bounty fills my cup. Gratitude. Jane Crewdson. FaChP
O thou whose cheeks are the Pleiades and whose lips are coral. To a Young Lover. Amur Mu'izzi. LiTW
O Thou Whose Compassionate Care. W. H. Bathurst. SoP
O Thou whose equal purpose runs. Invocation. Wendell Phillips Stafford. MaRV; TrPWD
O thou whose face hath felt the Winter's Wind. What the Thrush Said. Keats. DiPo; MBW-2; PeER
O thou! whose fancies from afar are brought. To H. C. Wordsworth. ChER; EnRP; ERoP-1; HBV; MBW-2; OBRV; PoEL-4
O Thou Whose Feet Have Climbed Life's Hill. Louis F. Benson. MaRV
O Thou, whose glorious orbs on high. Hymn of [*or* to] the West. Edmund Clarence Stedman. HBV; PaA; PAH; TrPWD
O Thou Whose Gracious Presence Blest. Louis F. Benson. *See* Dedication: "O thou. . ."
O Thou Whose Image. Arthur Hugh Clough. *See* Hymnos Ahymnos.
O thou, whose mighty palace roof doth hang. Hymn to Pan. Keats. *Fr.* Endymion. AtBAP; ChER; EPN; ERoP-2; OBRV; PeER; PoEL-4
O Thou Whose Pow'r. Boethius, *tr. fr. Latin by* Samuel Johnson. TrPWD
O thou whose wisdom is the rule of kings. Man's Prime Desire. Jami. OnPM
O thou with dewy locks, who lookest down. To Spring. Blake. ATP; BoC; BoNaP; BoTP; CBEP; CEP; EG; EnRP; ERoP-1; HBV; OBEC; OBEV; PoEL-4; PoLF; UnPo; WiR
O Thought! Süsskind von Trimberg, *tr. fr. Middle High German.* TrJP
O thought, fly to her when the end of day. Old Memory. W. B. Yeats. Po
O Thought, free gift to humankind! O Thought! Süsskind von Trimberg. TrJP
O thoughtful herte, plunged in distresse. John Lydgate. *Fr.* The Life of Our Lady. EnPo
Oh, threats of Hell and Hopes of Paradies! This Life Flies. Omar Khayyám, *tr. by* Edward Fitzgerald. *Fr.* The Rubáiyát. OnPM
O thy bright eyes must answer now. Plead for Me [*or* God of Visions *or* To Imagination]. Emily Brontë. EnLi-2 (1949 ed.); NBM; PoEL-5; TrGrPo
O tide-enwreathed and time-tormented Man. The Gatineaus. James Wreford Watson. CaP
"O time, whence comes the mother's moody look amid her labours." The Lacking Sense. Thomas Hardy. CMoP; PoEL-5
O Time! who know'st a lenient hand to lay. Time and Grief [*or* Sonnet]. William Lisle Bowles. ATP; CEP; EnRP; FaBoEn; HBV; LO; OBEC; OBEV
Oh, Timely Happy, Timely Wise, *sel.* John Keble.
As We Pray, *last st.* MaRV
Oh, 'tis little Mary Cassidy's the cause of all my misery. Little Mary Cassidy. Francis A. Fahy. HBV
Oh! 'tis of a bold major a tale I'll relate. A Longford Legend. *Unknown.* OnYI; StPo
"Oh 'tis time I should talk to your mother." Ask and Have [*or* How to Ask and Have]. Samuel Lover. BOHV; HBV; TreFS
O to Be a Dragon. Marianne Moore. CTC; GoYe; PoPl
Oh to be at Crowdieknow. Crowdieknowe. "Hugh MacDiarmid." OxBS
O to be blind! The Blind Man at the Fair. Joseph Campbell. AnIV; AWP; JAWP; WBP
Oh, to be in England. Home-Thoughts from Abroad. Robert Browning. AnEnPo; AnFE; AWP; BBV; BEL; BoLiVe; BoNaP; BoTP; CBEP; CBV; CoBE; DiPo; EG; EnLi-2 (1949 ed.); EnLit; EPN; FaBoBe; FaBoEn; FaBV; FaFP; FaPON; FiP; GBV (1922 ed.); GN; GTBS; GTBS-W; GTSL; HBV; HBVY; HT; ILP; InPo; JAWP; LiTB; LiTG; MaVP; MBW-2; MCCG; MemP; NeHB; NoP; OAEP; OBEV; OBNC; OBVV; OtMeF; OTPC; PCH; PoFS; PoIE; PoLF; PoPo; PoRA; PoVP; SeCeV; ShBV-2; TOP; TreF; TrGrPo; VA; ViPo; ViPP; VP; WBP; WHA; YAT; YT
"Oh! to be in England." Home Truths from Abroad, *parody.* *Unknown.* Par

Oh, To Be in England Now the Weather's There! *Unknown.* SiTL
Oh, to be "kept for Jesus!" Kept for Jesus. Edith E. Cherry. BePJ
Oh, to be there to-night! Ada Cambridge. *Fr.* On Australian Hills. PoAu-1
O to Be Up and Doing. Robert Louis Stevenson. *Fr.* Our Lady of the Snows. SoP; TreFT, *diff. vers.*; TRV
Oh to be used of Jesus. A Yielded Instrument. Avis B. Christiansen. SoP
Oh! to be wafted away. Quatrain. *Unknown.* NA
Oh, to come home once more, when the dusk is falling. A Song of Twilight. *Unknown.* HBV
Oh, to feel the fresh breeze blowing. The Song of the Forest Ranger. Herbert Bashford. HBV; OHIP
Oh, to feel the tremble of a ship beneath my feet again. Sea Urge. *Unknown.* PoMa
Oh! to Have a Birthday. Lois Lenski. BiCB
O, to have a little house! An [*or* The] Old Woman of the Roads. Padraic Colum. BoC; BoTP; CAW; CH; FaBoBe; FaPON; GaP; GBV (1952 ed.); GoBC; GTSL; HBMV; JKCP; MoBrPo; MPB; NP; OBEV (new ed.); OnPP; OTPC (1946 ed.); PG; PoRA; RePo; SP; StVeCh; TreFS; YT
Oh, to have died that day at Langemarck! For Justice. Bernard Freeman Trotter. PTK
Oh, to part now, and, parting now. After Love. Arthur Symons. NeHB
O to scuttle from the battle and to settle on an atoll far from brutal mortal neath a wattle portal! Titles [*or* What'll Be the Title?] Justin Richardson. FiBHP; ShBV-3
Oh, to vex me, contraries [*or* contraryes] meet in one. Inconstancy [*or* Devout Fits]. John Donne. Holy Sonnets, XIX. AnAnS-1; EP; MaMe; MaRV; MasP; MBW-1; MeP; NoP; PoEL-2; SCEP-1; SeCePo; Sonn
Oh to what height will love of greatnesse drive. Upon Mr. Thomas Coryats Crudities. John Donne. *Fr.* Satires. MaMe
Oh, Tommy's gone, what shall I do? Tommy's [*or* Tom's] Gone to Hilo. *Unknown.* AmSS; SoAmSa
O touch me not unless thy soul. Unless. Ella Maria Dietz Glynes. AA
"O Trade! O Trade! would thou wert dead!" The Symphony. Sidney Lanier. AmPP; AP; ATP (1935 ed.); CoBA; LiTA; PoPo
O tragic hours when lovers leave each other. Partings. Charles Guérin. AWP
O transient voyager of heaven! To a Wreath of Snow. Emily Brontë. PeER
Oh tree nursed by freedom! Song of the Mound. Wincenty Pol. PoFr
O trees, to whom the darkness is a child. Advice to a Forest. Maxwell Bodenheim. TrJP
O tremble! O tremble, O tremble. Six Sunday. Hart Leroi Bibbs. NBP
O Trivia Goddess, leave these low abodes. Of Walking the Streets by Night. John Gay. *Fr.* Trivia, or, The Art of Walking the Streets of London, III. EiCP; EnLi-1 (1949 ed.)
"O Troy Muir, my lily-flower." The Queen of Scotland. *Unknown.* ESPB
O truant Muse, what shall be thy amends. Sonnets, CI. Shakespeare. Sonn
O true and tried, so well and long. In Memoriam A. H. H., Epilogue. Tennyson. EPN; HW; ViPo; VP
Oh! true was his heart while he breathèd. The King of Thule. Goethe. *Fr.* Faust. AWP; JAWP; WBP
O, Tuomy! you boast yourself handy. Andrew Magrath's Reply to John O'Tuomy. Andrew Magrath. OnYI
Oh turn away those cruel eyes. The Relapse. Thomas Stanley. AnAnS-2; OBEV; SeCL
O Turn Once More. Duncan Campbell Scott. CoBE
Oh 'twas a poor country, in Autumn it was bare. The Poor, Poor Country. John Shaw Neilson. NeLNL
Oh, 'twas bitter cold/ As our steamboat rolled. The Red-Breast of Aquitania. Francis S. Mahony. OnYI
Oh! 'twas Dermot O'Nowlan McFigg. The Humours of Donnybrook Fair [*or* The Donnybrook Jig]. Charles O'Flaherty, *wr. at. to* Viscount Dillon. BOHV; OnYI
O 'twas on a bright mornin' in summer. Who's the Pretty Girl Milkin' the Cow? *Unknown.* AS
O Tweed! a stranger, that with wandering feet. The Tweed Visited. William Lisle Bowles. Sonn
O twilight, twilight! evermore to hear. Music at Twilight. George Sterling. HBV
"O tyrant, armed with insolence and pride!" Homer. *Fr.* The Iliad, I PoFr
O Ubi? Nusquam. R. W. Dixon. LO
O Unas, watch out for pitfalls. Inscription on the Pyramid of Unas. *Unknown.* LiTW
O undistinguished Dead! Rank and File. Austin Dobson. PoVP
O unhatch'd bird, so high preferr'd. Ode; To the Roc. William John Courthope. *Fr.* The Paradise of Birds. VA
O unicorn among the cedars. W. H. Auden. *Fr.* New Year Letter. FaBoEn
O universal Mother, who dost keep. Hymn to Earth the Mother of All. *Unknown.* *Fr.* Homeric Hymns. AWP; JAWP; OuHeWo; WBP
Oh, up aloft this yard must go. So Handy. *Unknown.* SoAmSa
"O Urizen! Creator of men! mistaken Demon of heaven!" Take Thy Bliss, O Man. Blake. *Fr.* Visions of the Daughters of Albion. EnRP
O valiant Hearts, who to your glory came. The Supreme Sacrifice. John Stanhope Arkwright. WGRP
O vast earth-apple, waiting to be fried. To a Sinister Potato. Peter Viereck. OnHM
Oh Venice! Venice! when thy marble walls. Ode on Venice. Byron. CABL
O, very gloomy is the House of Woe. The Haunted House. Thomas Hood. SeCePo; WePo
O vile ingrateful me. (Biothanatos). Joseph Beaumont. OBS
Oh, Virgin Joy of all the world art thou. Mary, Virgin and Mother. Elizabeth Seton. JKCP
O virgin mother, daughter of thy Son. Saint Bernard's Prayer to Our Lady. Dante. *Fr.* Divina Commedia: Paradiso. ISi
Oh virgin queen of mountain-side and woodland. The Pine Tree for Diana. Horace. AWP
O Virtuous Light. Elinor Wylie. AnAmPo; LiTG; MAP; MoAB; MoAmPo; MoPo; NePA
O Voice That Calls to Me. R. B. Y. Scott. MaRV
O votary of earthly idol's fane. One Heart, One Love. Jami. OnPM
O wad some power the giftie gie us. As Others See Us. Burns. *Fr.* To a Louse. MaRV
O wad this braw hie-heapit toun. The Prows o' Reekie. Lewis Spence. OxBS
O Wahkonda (Master of Life) pity me! A Dance Chant. *Tr. by* D. G. Brinton. WGRP
"Oh, wait a minute! I see my father coming." The Raspel Pole. *Unknown.* BFSS
Oh, wake her, oh, shake her. Johnny Walk Along to Hilo. *Unknown.* ShS
O Wall-flower! or ever thy bright leaves fade. The Wall-Flower. Henrik Wergeland. AWP; JAWP; WBP
"O waly, waly, my gay goss-hawk." The Gay Goshawk. *Unknown.* ESPB
O waly, waly up the bank. Waly, Waly [*or* Forsaken *or* Jamie Douglas]. *Unknown.* BaBo; EG; ELP; EnLoPo; EnSB; GoTS; GTBS; GTBS-D; GTBS-P; GTBS-W; GTSE; GTSL; HBV; LO; OBB; OBEV; OBS; OxBS; ViBoFo; ViBoPo; WHA
O wanderer in the southern weather. An Indian Song. W. B. Yeats. VA
O wanderer, lost on the mountain bare. Wayfarer's Song. Henry W. Frost. SoP
Oh, Wasn't Dat a Wide River? *with music.* *Unknown.* BoAN-1
"Oh, wasn't he hard on poor sinners this mornin'?" The Fret of Father Carty. Joseph I. C. Clarke. JKCP (1926 ed.)
Oh, wast thou with me, dearest, then. In Memoriam A. H. H., CXXII. Tennyson. EPN; TOP; ViPo; VP
O water, voice of my heart, crying in the sand. The Crying of Water. Arthur Symons. AnEnPo; MoBrPo
Oh, we come on the sloop *John B.* The *John B.* Sails. *Unknown.* AS
Oh, we don't get no justice here in Atlanta. We Don't Get No Justice Here in Atlanta. *Unknown.* OuSiCo
Oh, we had an old hen and she had a wooden leg. Another Little Drink. *Unknown.* TrAS, *with* Old Zip Coon
Oh, we started down from Roto when the sheds had all cut out. On the Road to Gundagai. *Unknown.* PoAu-1
O we were sisters seven, Maisry. Fair Mary of Wallington [*or*

The Bonny Earl of Livingston]. *Unknown.* ESPB; OxBB
O we were sisters, sisters seven. Earl Crawford. *Unknown.* BaBo; ESPB
O weariness of men who turn from God. Men Who Turn from God. T. S. Eliot. *Fr.* The Rock. MaRV
O Wearisome Condition [of Humanity]. Fulke Greville. *See* Chorus Sacerdotum.
O weary fa' the east wind. The Winds. Swinburne. TOP
Oh! Weary Mother. Barry Pain. *Fr.* The Poets at Tea. NA
O Weary Pilgrims, Chanting of Your Woe. Robert Bridges. The Growth of Love, XXIII. CMoP; MoAB; MoBrPo; PoVP
Oh, weep for Mr and Mrs Bryan! The Lion. Ogden Nash. CenHV; MemP; ShM
Oh! Weep for Those. Byron. AnEnPo
Oh well done Lord E[ldo]n! and better done R[yde]r! An Ode to the Framers of the Frame Bill. Byron. CoMu
O well for him whose will is strong! Will. Tennyson. EPN
O well I love the spring. A Wife's Song. William Cox Bennett. HBV
"O well is me, my gay [*or* jolly] goshawk." The Gay Goshawk. *Unknown.* BuBa; GN; HBV; RG
Oh, Wellington! (or "Villainton") for Fame. Wellington [*or* On Wellington]. Byron. *Fr.* Don Juan, IX. FiP; OBRV; OxBoLi; PeER
"O well's me o my gay goss-hawk." The Gay Goshawk [*or* Goss-Hawk]. *Unknown.* BaBo; CABL; EnLit; ESPB; OBB; OxBB; TOP
O, Were My Love. Burns. HBV; OBEV
(O Were My Love Yon Lilac Fair.) ChTr
Oh, we're up in the morning ere breaking of day. The Railroad Corral. *Unknown.* CoSo
O, were you on the mountain, or saw you my love? Were You on the Mountain? *Unknown.* BoLP; PV
Oh Wert Thou in the Cauld Blast. Burns. BEL; BoLiVe; EiCL; EiPP; ELP; EnL; EnLi-2; EnLit; EnPE; EnRP; GBV; MeWo; NoP; OAEP; OBEC; OuHeWo; OxBS; PeER; TOP; TrGrPo; UnPo (3d ed.); WHA
(Address to a Lady.) CEP
O Western Wind. *Unknown.* *See* Western Wind, When Wilt Thou Blow?
Oh wha are sae happy as me an' my Moggy? Moggy and Me. James Hogg. HBV
"Oh wha [*or* what] hae ye brought us hame now, my brave lord." Muckle-mou'd Meg. James Ballantine. HBV; VA
O wha my babie-clouts will buy. The Rantin' Dog the Daddie O't. Burns. EiCL; OxBoLi
"O wha will bake my bridal bread." Fair Annie (E *vers.*). *Unknown.* ESPB
"O wha will lace my shoes sae small?" The Lass of Roch Royal (A *vers.*). *Unknown.* ViBoFo
"O wha [*or* who] will shoe my bonnie [*or* bonny] foot?" The Lass of Lochroyan. *Unknown.* BuBa; HBV; OBB; OBEV (1st ed.)
O wha woud wish the win to blaw. Brown Adam. *Unknown.* ESPB; OBB, OxBB
Oh, whar shill [*or* shall] we go w'en de great day comes. Revival Hymn. Joel Chandler Harris. *Fr.* Uncle Remus; His Songs and His Sayings. HBV; MCCG
"O whare are ye gaun [*or* are you going]?" The False Knight [*or* Fause Knicht] upon [*or* on] the Road [*or* The False Knight and the Wee Boy]. *Unknown.* AtBAP; BuBa; CBEP; CH; EnSB; ESPB; FaBoCh; OxBoLi; OxBS
"O whare hae ye been a' day, Lord Donald, my son?" Lord Randal (B *vers.*). *Unknown.* BaBo; ESPB
"O whare hae ye been a' day, my bonnie wee croodlin dow?" Lord Randal. *Unknown.* BaBo (C *vers.*); ESPB (J *vers.*); ViBoFo (C *vers.*)
O whare hae ye been, my dearest dear. James Harris (D *vers.*) [*or* The Carpenter's Wife]. *Unknown.* ESPB; OxBB
"O whare hae ye been, Peggy?" Young Peggy. *Unknown.* BaBo; ESPB
O Wha's Been Here afore Me, Lass. "Hugh MacDiarmid." AtBAP; FaBoTw; NeBP; OBMV, *abr.*
O Wha's the Bride? "Hugh MacDiarmid." ErPo; GTBS-P; LiTM (1970 ed.); OxBS; PoIE
"Oh, what a ball it will be!" they said. Grand Finale. Sara King Carleton. FiSC
O what a cunning guest. Confession. George Herbert. AnAnS-1; MaMe; MeP; ReEn
Oh, what a fund of joy jocund lies hid in harmless hoaxes! The Practical Joker. W. S. Gilbert. *Fr.* His Excellency. BOHV
O what a happy soul am I! Blind But Happy. Fanny Crosby. FaChP; MaRV; OTD; SoP; TRV
O what a loud and fearful shriek was there. Kosciusko. Samuel Taylor Coleridge. EnRP; Sonn
Oh, what a night for a soul to go! Iter Supremum. Arthur Sherburne Hardy. AA
O, what a noble mind is here o'erthrown! A Shakespeare Gallery: Hamlet. Shakespeare. *Fr.* Hamlet, III, i. MaC
Oh! what a plague [*or* pain] is love. Phillada [*or* Phyllida] Flouts Me [*or* The Disdainful Shepherdess]. *Unknown.* CoMu; ElL; HBV; InvP; OBEV; OBSC; ReEn; TrGrPo; ViBoPo
O, what a rogue and peasant slave am I! Shakespeare. *Fr.* Hamlet, II, ii. MemP; TreFT
Oh, what a set of vagabundos. Morgan. Edmund Clarence Stedman. AA; HBV
O what a tangled web we weave. A Word of Encouragement. J. R. Pope. ELU; FiBHP; PV; SiTL
O! what a thing is love? who can define. Meditation. Edward Taylor. *Fr.* Preparatory Meditations, Second Series. MeP
Oh, what a thing is man! how farre from power. Giddinesse. George Herbert. MaMe
Oh! What a thing is man? Lord, who am I? Meditation Thirty-eight. Edward Taylor. *Fr.* Preparatory Meditations, First Series. AnNE; AP; MAmP; MWA-1; OxBA
O! What a thing is might right mannag'd? Meditation [*or* The Almighty]. Edward Taylor. *Fr.* Preparatory Meditations, Second Series. MeP; MWA-1
O, what a war of looks was then between them! Shakespeare. *Fr.* Venus and Adonis. UnTE
Oh, what a world of flummery—there's nothing but deceit in it. The Ragged Coat. John Woodward. SGR
Oh, what a you say, seekers. Die in de Fiel'. *Unknown.* BoAN-1
Oh, what amiss may I forgive in Thee. Sidney Lanier. *Fr.* The Crystal. TRV
O what an eve was that which ushered in. Sonnets—Ad Innuptam, VI. Patrick Moloney. BoAu
O what are heroes, prophets, men. Pan. Emerson. ILP
Oh, what are you waiting for here, young man? The Bridge. James Thomson. Sunday Up the River, II. OBVV; PoVP; TOP
O what avails the sceptred race. Rose Aylmer. Walter Savage Landor. FaBoEn
O [*or* Ah,] what can ail thee, knight-at-arms [*or* wretched wight]. La Belle Dame sans Merci. Keats. AnFE; AtBAP; ATP; AWP; BBV; BEL; BeLS; BoLiVe; CABA; CBEP; CBV; CH; ChTr; CLwM; CoBE; DiPo; DTo; ELP; EnL; EnLi-2; EnLit; EnRP; ERoP-2; ExPo; FaBoBe; FaBoCh; FaFP; FiP; ForPo; FosPo; GBV; GoJo; GoTP; GTBS; GTBS-D; GTBS-P; GTBS-W; GTSE; GTSL; HBV; HoPM; ILP; InP; InPo; InvP; JAWP; LiTB; LiTG; LO; LoBV; LoEN; LoGBV; MaC; MasP; MBW-2; MCCG; MemP; MERP; MyFE; NoP; OAEP; OBEV; OBMV; OBNC; OBRV; OnSP; OtMeF; OTPC (1923 ed.); PAn; PeER; PG; PIA; PoAn; PoE; PoEL-4; PoeP; PoFS; PoIE; PoPo; PoRA; PoSa; RG; SeCeV; ShBV-3; SiSw; StP; StPo; TOP; TreFT; TrGrPo; UnPo; VaPo; ViBoPo; WaKn; WePo; WHA; WoL
O what can you give me? Gwalia Deserta, XV. Idris Davies. DTC
O what could be more nice? Light Listened. Theodore Roethke. ToPo; UnTE
Oh, what delirious fun this is. Ego's Dream. Alfred Kreymborg. MAPA
Oh, what do the sea shells murmur. Sea Shells. Clinton Scollard. BrR
"Oh, what hae ye brought us hame now, my brave lord." *See* "Oh, wha hae ye brought us hame now, my brave lord."
O what harper could worthily harp it. The Schoolmaster Abroad with His Son. Charles Stuart Calverley. BOHV; MemP
Oh, what have you got for dinner, Mrs. Bond? *Unknown.* OxNR
O What If the Fowler? Charles Dalmon. BiS; CH
Oh, what is abroad in the marsh and the terminal sea? Sidney

Oh (continued)
Lanier. *Fr.* The Marshes of Glynn. EtS
"Oh, what is longer than the way?" *Unknown.* LO
"Oh! what is that comes gliding in." Sally Simpkin's Lament. Thomas Hood. BOHV; EnRP; ShM
Oh what is that country. Mother Country. Christina Rossetti. OxBoCh
O What Is That Sound [Which so Thrills the Ear]. W. H. Auden. AnFE; ExPo; FlW; HaMV; LiTB; PoE; SiSw
(Ballad.) MaC; MoAB; MoBrPo; PoFr; PoPo; ViBoPo (1958 ed.); WaP
(Quarry, The.) CMoP
Oh, what know they of harbors. Plymouth Harbor. Ernest Radford, *wr. at. to* Dollie Maitland Radford. HBV
O what must it have cost the angels. Birth of Mary. Rainer Maria Rilke. MoRP
O What Pleasure 'Tis to Find. Aphra Behn. *Fr.* Lycidus. UnTE
Oh, what precious peace I find. The Hour of Prayer. Georgia B. Adams. STF
Oh, what shall be the burden of our rhyme. Cadences: Major. John Payne. VA
"Oh! what shall I do?" sobbed a tiny mole. Who'll Help a Fairy? *Unknown.* BoTP
Oh, what shall my blue eyes go see. To Baby. Kate Greenaway. MPB
Oh, what shall we do with a drunken sailor. The Drunken Sailor; or, Early in the Morning. *Unknown.* ShS
O what to me the little room. The Heart of the Woman. W. B. Yeats. GTSL; POTE
Oh, what was your name in the States? What Was Your Name in the States? *Unknown.* AS
O, what would people say if you. Lizard. Agnes Maxwell-Hall. PoNe
Oh, what's de use of workin' so hard. In de Mornin! *Unknown.* SoAmSa
O what's the blood 'at's [*or* thats] on your sword. Son David. *Unknown.* OxBB; OxBS
Oh! what's the matter? what's the matter? Goody Blake and Harry Gill. Wordsworth. BEL; MERP; Par
Oh, what's the matter wi' you, my lass. Jimmy's Enlisted, or, The Recruited Collier. *Unknown.* CoMu
Oh, what's the way to Arcady. The Way to Arcady. H. C. Bunner. AA; BOHV; InMe; PFY
O what's the weather in a beard? Dinky. Theodore Roethke. PoeP
Oh, when I am safe in my sylvan home. In the Woods. Emerson. *Fr.* Good-bye. OQP
Oh, when I come to die. Give Me Jesus. *Unknown.* BoAN-1
Oh, when I go down to Bimini. Never Get a Lickin' Till I Go Down to Bimini. *Unknown.* OuSiCo
O, when I hear at sea. Wind and Wave. Charles Warren Stoddard. AA
O When I Take My Love Out Walking. Kenneth Patchen. ToPo
Oh when I think of my long-suffering race. Enslaved. Claude McKay. BALP
Oh, when I was a great big lad. My Old Beaver Cap. *Unknown.* BFSS
Oh, When I Was in Love with You. A. E. Housman. A Shropshire Lad, XVIII. BoLiVe; FaBV; InP; LiTB; LiTL; MeWo; MoBrPo; NBM; NeMA; OAEP; PoVP; ViPo; WePo
(Then and Now.) YT
O when in San Francisco do. Scenic. John Updike. CAD
Oh! when my friend and I. Friendship. Robert Blair. *Fr.* The Grave. OBEC
O when our clergie, at the dreadfull day. On Those That Deserve It. Francis Quarles. MePo; OBS
Oh when the early morning at the seaside. East Anglian Bathe. John Betjeman. GTBS-D; SD
O when the half-light weaves. The Sad Mother. Katharine Tynan. VA
Oh, when the ripe acorns. Acorns. Edith King. GFA
O when the saints go marchin' in. When the Saints Go Marchin' In. *Unknown.* EaLo
Oh! when thy fingers touch the notes, I think. To Sheila Playing Haydn. Sylvia Lynd. LO
O when will they let them love. 1938. Ruth Pitter. LO
Oh, when you see them flying. The Little Flags. John Clair Minot. DD; HH; PEDC
Oh, whenever I went away, the story I'd like to tell. The *Campañero. Unknown.* ShS
Oh Where and Oh Where Is My Little Wee Dog? *Unknown.* OTPC
Oh where! and oh where is your Highland laddie gone? The Bluebells of Scotland. *Unknown.* HBV; OTPC (1946 ed.); TreFS
O Where Are Kings and Empires Now. Arthur Cleveland Coxe. MaRV
(House Not Made with Hands, A.) SoP, *abr.*
O Where Are You Going? W. H. Auden. *Fr.* The Orators. CBV; CMoP; LiTB; MoVE; Po; PoIE; UnPo (3d ed.); VaPo
(Epilogue: "'O where are you going?' said reader to rider.") EnLit; FaBoCh; LoGBV; ShBV-3; SiTL
(Five Songs, *sel.*) LiTM (1970 ed.)
(Song.) EnL
(Three Companions, The.) TDP
"O Where are you going?" *See* "O, whare are ye gaun?"
O, where are you going, "Goodspeed" and "Discovery"? Southern Ships and Settlers. Stephen Vincent Benét. AmFN
"Oh, where are you going, my dear kind husband." The Best Old Feller in the World. *Unknown.* BFSS
"O where are you going?" said reader to rider. O Where Are You Going? [*or* Epilogue *or* Song]. W. H. Auden. *Fr.* The Orators. CBV; CMoP; EnL; EnLit; FaBoCh; LiTB; LiTM (1970 ed.); LoGBV; MoVE; Po; PoIE; ShBV-3; SiTL; TDP; UnPo (3d ed.); VaPo
O where are you going? says Milder to Malder. The Cutty Wren. *Unknown.* CBEP; GTBS-W; LiTG; NCEP; OxBoLi; SiTL; WiR
O where are you going so early? he said. The Milkmaid. William Allingham. IrPN
"Oh where are you going to, all you Big Steamers." Big Steamers. Kipling. Par
O where are you going to, my pretty little dear. Dabbling in the Dew. *Unknown.* CH
"Oh, where are you going with your lovelocks flowing." Amor Mundi. Christina Rossetti. NBM; PoEL-5; PoVP; ViPo
Oh! Where Do Fairies Hide Their Heads. Thomas Haynes Bayly. HBV; HBVY; OTPC; VA
O where do you go, and what's your will. London Feast. Ernest Rhys. VA
"O where hae [*or* ha *or* have] ye [*or* you] been, Lord Randal, my son?" Lord Randal. *Unknown.* AtBAP; ATP; AWP; BaBo (A *vers.*); BEL; BoLiVe; CABA; CBEP; CoBE; DiPo; EnL; EnRP; EnSB; ESPB; ForPo; FosPo; GBV (1952 ed.); HBV; HoPM; ILP; InP; InPo; JAWP; LiTB; LiTG; LiTL; LoBV; MeWo; NoP; OBB; OnSP; OuHeWo; OxBB; OxBS; PoIE; PoPo; SeCeV; ShBV-1; StP; TOP; TreF; TrGrPo; UnPo; ViBoFo; (A *and* B *vers.*); WBP
Oh, where has my honey gone? The Lost Love. Fenton Johnson. NP
Oh where have you been all the day. In the Woods. Dorothy Baker. BoTP
"Oh, where have you been, Billy boy, Billy boy." Billy Boy. *Unknown.* BLPA; IHA
"O where have you been, Lord Randal, my son?" *See* "O where hae ye been, Lord Randal, my son?"
"O where have you been, my long, long [*or* long-lost] love." The Demon [*or* Daemon] Lover. *Unknown.* BaBo (C *vers.*); BuBa; CABA; CBEP; EnL; EnLi-1; EnLit; EnSB; ESPB; FlW; LiTB; OBB; PoAn; PoMS; PoPo; TOP; UnPo; ViBoFo (A *vers.*)
Oh where have you been to, Lord Rendel my son? Lord Rendal. *Unknown.* PoG
"Oh, where have you been to-day, Terence, my son?" Lord Randal (D *vers.*). *Unknown.* BaBo
Oh, where is the boy dressed in jacket of gray. Lost—Three Little Robins. *Unknown.* DD; PEDC
"Oh, where is the sea?" the fishes cried. Where Is God? Minot J. Savage. OQP
O where is tiny Hewe? The Goblin's Song. James Telfer. ChTr
Oh, where, Kincora! is Brian the Great? Kincora [*or* Lamentation of Mac Liag for Kincora]. *Unknown.* AnIL; AnIV; OnYI; OxBI
Oh where, oh where has my little dog gone? *Unknown.* OxNR
Oh, where the white quince blossom swings. Japanesque. Oliver Herford. FiBHP
"Oh, where was I last Christmas night." Oh, Who Will Shoe Your Bonney Feet? *Unknown.* BFSS

"O where were ye, my milk-white steed." The Broomfield Hill. *Unknown.* CH
Oh, where will be the birds that sing. A Hundred Years to Come. Hiram Ladd Spencer, *wr. at. to* William Goldsmith Brown. HBV
"O where will ye gang to, and where will ye sleep." The Witch-Mother. Swinburne. TOP
"Oh, where'd you git yo' learnin'? Please tell it to me." My Li'l John Henry. *Unknown.* ABF
Oh! wherefore come ye forth, in triumph from the North. The Battle of Naseby. Macaulay. FOL; GTBS; HBV; OBRV; ShBV-3; VA
O wherefore was my birth from Heaven foretold. O Dark, Dark, Dark. Milton. *Fr.* Samson Agonistes. AnFE; WHA
Oh, where's that girl that will go with me. Campfire and Bunkhouse. *Unknown.* CoSo
"O, whet your saws and shine your knives." Crawford Long and William Morton. Rosemary Benét *and* Stephen Vincent Benét. OTD; PoMa
"O which is the last rose?" The Last Rose. John Davidson. OBEV (1st ed.)
Oh, whiffaree an' a-whiffo-rye. Honey, Take a Whiff on Me. *Unknown.* LiTM; OxBoLi; SiTL
O while within a Jewish breast. Hatikvah—a Song of Hope. Naphtali Herz Imber. TrJP
Oh, whiskey is the life of man. Whiskey! Johnny [*or* Whiskey for My Johnny]. *Unknown.* AmSS; ShS (*vers.* II)
O whisper, O my soul! The afternoon. The Tired Worker. Claude McKay. BANP
O Whistle an' I'll Come to Ye [*or* You], My Lad. Burns. *See* Whistle an' I'll Come to Ye, My Lad.
O white and midnight sky! O starry bath! The Celestial Passion. Richard Watson Gilder. AA; AnAmPo
O white clay, O fine clay of the earth cold. Fine Clay. Winifred Shaw. MoAuPo; PoAu-1
O White Mistress. Don Johnson. NNP
O white priest of eternity. Kinchinjunga. Cale Young Rice. AnAmPo; HBV
O white, white, light moon, that sailst in the sky. Donald. Henry Abbey. AA
O White Wind. Christopher Brennan. MoAuPo; OnPM
(O White Wind, Numbing the World.) BoAu
Oh, whither am I rapt beyond myself? Thomas Dekker. *Fr.* Old Fortunatus. ViBoPo
O whither goest thou, pale student. Ye Laye of Ye Woodpeckore. Henry A. Beers. NA
Oh whither, oh why, and oh wherefore. Goosey Goosey Gander—by Various Authors (Swinburne's Version). William Percy French. CenHV
O, whither sail you, Sir John Franklin? A Ballad of Sir John Franklin. George Henry Boker. AA; HBV; OnMSP
O Whither Shall I Fly? Francis Quarles. OxBoCh
O who are thou with that queenly brow. Roisin Dubh. Aubrey Thomas De Vere. AnIV
Oh, who can sleep/ On a Summer night. Night Enchantment. Eleanor Muth. SiSoCe
Oh who can speak, what numbers can reveal. Pompey and Cornelia. Lucan. *Fr.* Pharsalia. OBEC
O, who dat a-comin' ovah yondah. Who Dat a-Comin' ovah Yondah? *Unknown.* BoAN-1
Oh, who has not heard of the Northmen of yore. America. Arthur Cleveland Coxe. *Fr.* England and America. MC; PAH
Oh who is/ so cosy with. The End of the Day. Robert Creeley. AmPC
Oh, who is so merry, so merry, heigh ho! The Light-hearted Fairy [*or* The Fairy]. *Unknown.* BoChLi; BoTP; FaPON; GaP; MPB (1956 ed.); OTPC; PCH; PPL; SUS; TiPo (1952 ed.)
Oh! who is that poor foreigner that lately came to town. Irish Molly O. *Unknown.* HBV
Oh Who Is That Young Sinner. A. E. Housman. AtBAP; CBEP; ChMP; FaBoTw
"O, who is this that seeks at night." A Legend of Gethsemane. Teresa Hooley. StJW
Oh! who on the mountain, the plain, or the wave. The Song of the Micmac. Joseph Howe. CaP
Oh, Who Regards. *Unknown.* EIL
Oh! who rides by night thro' the woodland so wild? The Erl-King. Goethe, *tr. by* Sir Walter Scott. AWP; JAWP; OTPC (1946 ed.); WBP
O who shall, from this dungeon, raise. A Dialogue between the Soul and Body. Andrew Marvell. AnAnS-1; EP; MaMe; MeLP; MeP; MePo; OBS; OxBoCh; PAn; PIA; PoEL-2; PoFS; ReEn; SCEP-2; SeCP; SeCV-1; SeEP
Oh who that ever lived and loved. Our Friend the Egg. Clarence Day. BOHV
O, who will drive the chariot when she comes? She'll Be Comin' round the Mountain. *Unknown.* AS
Oh, who will follow old Ben Milam into San Antonio? The Valor of Ben Milam. Clinton Scollard. HBV; MC; PAH
O who will give me tears? Come all ye springs. Grief. George Herbert. MaMe
"O who will shoe my bonny foot?" *See* "O wha will shoe my bonnie foot?"
"O who will shoe my fair foot." Fair Annie of Lochyran. *Unknown.* AS
"Oh, who will shoe your foot, my dear?" The Lass of Roch Royal (B *vers.*). *Unknown.* ViBoFo
O who will shoe your pretty little foot. Who Will Shoe Your Pretty Little Foot. *Unknown.* AS
O who will show me those delights on high? Heaven. George Herbert. AnAnS-1; BoLiVe; MaMe; MeP; SeCP; TrGrPo
"O, who will speak from a womb or cloud," and cloud. To George Barker. Gene Derwood. NePA
O who will walk a mile with me. A Mile with Me. Henry van Dyke. BLPA
Oh! who would keep a little bird confined? The Bird in a Cage. William Lisle Bowles. TVC
Oh, who would stay indoor, indoor. Huting Song. Richard Hovey. *Fr.* King Arthur. HBV
O who would wish the wind to blow. Brown Adam. *Unknown.* BuBa
O, why?—/ Only a dove can venture that reply. Elm Angel. Harold Monro. FaBoMo
Oh, why can't things stay as they were? The Old Man. Beatrice Herford. PEDC
Oh, why did e'er my thoughts aspire. Song. Charles Sackville. SeCL
O why do you walk through the fields in gloves. To a Fat Lady Seen from the Train. Frances Cornford. BLPA; ELU; GoJo; LiTM; MoBrPo; NeMA; OBMV; OnPP; SiTL; WePo; YT
Oh, why does New York go to France for its fun. Come to Britain; a Humble Contribution to the Movement. A. P. Herbert. WhC
Oh, why does the white man follow my path. The Indian Hunter. Eliza Cook. BLPA
Oh, why don't you [*or* I] work like other men do? Hallelujah, I'm a Bum [*or* Hallelujah, Bum Again]. *Unknown.* ABF; AS; TrAS
Oh why is heaven built so far. De Profundis. Christina Rossetti. CoBE; OuHeWo; PoVP; VP
O why left I my hame? The Exile's Song. Robert Gilfillan. HBV; VA
Oh, why, my brother-mariners, so near the boisterous wave. Too Near the Waves. Poseidippus. OnPM
Oh! Why Should the Spirit of Mortal Be Proud? William Knox. BLPA; FaFP; HBV; NeHB; OQP; TreF; WBLP; WGRP
(Mortality.) MaRV
O wide and shining, miles on miles. Far Distances. Henry W. Clark. OQP
O wild West Wind, thou breath of autumn's being. Ode to the West Wind. Shelley. AnEnPo; AnFe; ATP; AWP; BEL; BoLiVe; BoNaP; BWP; CABA; CaFP; CBEP; CBV; CH; CoBE; DiPo; EnL; EnLi-2; EnLit; EnRP; EPN; ERoP-2; ExPo; FaBoBe; FaBoEn; FaBV; FaFP; FaPL; FiP; ForPo; FosPo; GTBS; GTBS-D; GTBS-P; GTBS-W; GTSE; GTSL; HBV; ILP; InP; InPo; JAWP; LiTB; LiTG; LoBV; MaPo; MBW-2; MCCG; MemP; MERP; NoP; OAEP; OBEV; OBNC; OBRV; OHFP; OTPC (1946 ed.); OuHeWo; PAn; PeER; PIA; PoAn; PoE; PoEL-4; PoFS; PoIE; PoLF; PoMa; PoPo; PoRA; PoSa; SeCeV; ShBV-4; StP; TOP; TreFS; TrGrPo; UnPo; VaPo; ViBoPo; WBP; WHA; YAT
O will ye choose to hear the news? Mr. Molony's Account of the Ball. Thackeray. HBV
O, Willie Brew'd a Peck o' Maut. Burns. *See* Willie Brew'd a Peck o' Maut.
"O Willie my son, what makes you sae sad?" Willie's Lyke-Wake. *Unknown.* BaBo

Oh, Willie was a plowboy. The Banks of Dundee. *Unknown.* BaBo
O Willie's gane to Melville Castle. Willie's Gane to Melville Castle. *Unknown.* SaSa
O Willie's large o' [*or* of] limb and lith [*or* bone]. The Birth of Robin Hood [*or* Willie and Earl Richard's Daughter]. *Unknown.* BuBa; ESPB; OBB; OxBB
O Willy was as brave a lord. Willie o' Douglas Dale. *Unknown.* BaBo; ESPB
Oh, wilt thou have my hand, Dear, to lie along in thine? Inclusions. Elizabeth Barrett Browning. HBV; OBVV; TOP; UnTE
O wind from the sea! O wind from the sea! Sea-Song. Irene Rutherford McLeod. YT
O Wind of the Mountain! Thomas Westwood. VA
O wind, rend open the heat. Heat. Hilda Doolittle ("H. D."). *Fr.* The Garden. AP; CMoP; MAP; MoAmPo; NeMA; OxBA; PoIE; PoPo; TSW; UnPo; WHA
O wind, thou hast thy kingdom in the trees. Wind of Summer. "Michael Field." VA
O Wind, Where Have You Been? Christina Rossetti. *Fr.* Sing-Song. BoTP
O wind, why do you never rest. Christina Rossetti. *Fr.* Sing-Song. TiPo
Oh, winds blow cool! Oh, young leaves, sift! Ruth Goes By. Edna Tucker Muth. PEDC
O Winds of heaven, pray. Poppies. *Unknown.* MPB
O winds that blow across the sea. The Wind's Song. "Gabriel Setoun." HBV; HBVY; OTPC; PPL
Oh, Wing Tee Wee. Wing Tee Wee. J. P. Denison. BOHV
O winter! bar thine adamantine doors. To Winter. Blake. AnEnPo; ERoP-1; WiR
Oh Winter! ruler of th' inverted year. Winter. William Cowper. *Fr.* The Task, IV. OBEC
O winter wind, lat grievin be. Villanelle. Margaret Winefride Simpson. OxBS
O Winter's a beautiful time of the year. Winter. Enid Blyton. BoTP
O wise little birds, how do you know. What the Birds Do. Harriet McEwen Kimball. FaChP
O, Woman! ("O, Woman! in our hours of ease). Sir Walter Scott. *Fr.* Marmion. TreFS
O Woman Full fo Wile. *At. to* Geoffrey Keating, *tr. fr. Late Middle Irish by* Padraic Pearse. OnYI
O woman, let thy heart not cleave. Forepledged. John Lancaster Spalding. AA
O woman of my love, I am walking with you on the sand. Love Song. Arthur Symons. PoVP
O woman of the piercing wail. A Lament for the Princes of Tyrone and Tyrconnel. *Tr. by* James Clarence Mangan. AnIV
O Woman of Three Cows, agra! The Woman of Three Cows. *Unknown, tr. by* James Clarence Mangan. AnIL; EnRP; IrPN; OnYI; OxBI
O woman, shapely as the swan. "I Shall Not Die for Thee." Padraic Colum. CTC
O, wonder!/ How many goodly creatures are there here! Brave New World. Shakespeare. *Fr.* The Tempest, V, i. TrGrPo
O wonderful nonsense of lotions of Lucky Tiger. Haircut. Karl Shapiro. FiMAP; MoPo; MoVE; TwCP
Oh, wonderful story of deathless love. He Cares. "Susan Coolidge." MaRV
Oh, wonderful, wonderful Word of the Lord! The Wonderful Word. John Newton. SoP
O wondrous night of star and song. Prayer on Christmas Eve. Nancy Byrd Turner. MaRV
O wondrous scene is Meeker. Lines on Mountain Villages. "Sunset Joe." PoOW
O Word of God Incarnate. William Walsham How. MaRV; SoP; TRV
"O words are lightly spoken." The Rose Tree. W. B. Yeats. CMoP; DiPo; ELP; GTBS-D; OBMV; PoFr
O words, o words, and shall you rule. Words. Stella Benson. MoBrPo (1942 ed.)
O words, which fall like summer dew on me! Rural Poesy. Sir Philip Sidney. *Fr.* Arcadia. EIL; MaPo
O World. Alice Corbin. NP
O World. George Santayana. Sonnets, III. HBMV; MaRV; PoLF; TrGrPo; TRV
(Faith.) OQP; WGRP
(O World, Thou Choosest Not the Better Part.) ATP; MAP; MoAmPo; TIHL; TreFS
(Sonnet: O World.) AmLP
O World, Be Nobler. Laurence Binyon. GTSL; HBV; MoBrPo; OBEV; TOP
O World, Be Not So Fair. Maria Jager, *tr. fr. German by* Grace Fallow Norton. HBV
"Oh, World-God, give me wealth!" the Egyptian cried. Gifts. Emma Lazarus. TrJP; WGRP
O World, I cannot hold thee close enough! God's World. Edna St. Vincent Millay. CMoP; CoBA; FaBoBe; FaBV; GoTP; HBV; MAP; MCCG; MoAmPo; MoRP; NP; PoPl; PoSC; RePo; TSW; YT
O world, in very truth thou art too young. Written at Florence. Wilfrid Scawen Blunt. OBEV (1st ed.); OBVV
O world invisible, we view thee. In No Strange Land [*or* The Kingdom of God]. Francis Thompson. AnFE; AtBAP; BoLiVe; BoPe; BrPo; CaFP; ChIP; CoBE; EaLo; GoBC; GTBS; GTBS-P; HBMV; LiTB; LiTG; MaRV; MemP; MoAB; OBEV (new ed.); OQP; OxBoCh; Po; PoIE; PoLi; POTE; PoVP; SeCeV; ShBV-4; TreFT; TrGrPo; TRV; WGRP; WoL
O world! O life! O time! A Lament. Shelley. AtBAP; BoLiVe; ChER; ChTr; EG; EnLi-2 (1949 ed.); EnLit; EnRP; EPN; GTBS; GTBS-D; GTBS-P; GTBS-W; GTSE; GTSL; LoBV; MemP; OAEP; OBRV; PoPo; PoRA; TOP; TreFT; TrGrPo; WHA
O world of love and beauty. Hymn. George Edward Hoffman. MaRV
O world that changes under my hand. O World. Alice Corbin. NP
O world that turneth as a vane that veers! Heliodore. John Daniel Logan. CaP
O World, Thou Choosest Not the Better Part. George Santayana. *See* O World.
O world watched over by the cold moon and the mindless stars. Invocation. Carleton Drewry. MoRP
Oh, worship the King all glorious above. The Majesty and Mercy of God. Sir Robert Grant. OHIP; SoP; WGRP
Oh would I could subdue the flesh. Senex. John Betjeman. CBV; DTC
Oh would I were a politician. Yes and No. Ogden Nash. MaRV
O would I were where I would be! Suspiria. *Unknown.* OBEV (new ed.)
Oh, Would That I Knew. Al-Samau'al Ibn Adiya, *tr. fr. Arabic.* TrJP
O would that in the world there were no night. On His Love. Dakiki. LiTW
Oh, would that working I might shun. Ode to Work in Springtime. Thomas R. Ybarra. BOHV; HBMV
Oh would you know why Henry sleeps. Inhuman Henry; or, Cruelty to Fabulous Animals. A. E. Housman. BBGG; FiBHP
O, woven in one wide loom thro' the throbbing weft of the whole. Alfred Noyes. *Fr.* The Loom of Years. MaRV
O write it up above your hearth. A Dublin Ballad; 1916. "Dermot O'Byrne." AnIV; OxBI
O, write my name. De Angels in Heab'n Gwineter Write My Name. *Unknown.* BoAN-2
Oh, Yankee Doodle beats the world. City Council. David G. Robinson. SGR
"O ye, all ye that walk in Willowwood." Willowwood, 3. Dante Gabriel Rossetti. The House of Life, LI. MaVP; OAEP; PoVP; ViPo; ViPP; VP
Oh, Ye Censurers. Al-Samau'al Ibn Adiya, *tr. fr. Arabic by* Hartwig Hirschfeld. TrJP
O ye dales. Nature. Mark Akenside. *Fr.* The Pleasures of Imagination, IV. LoBV; PeER
O ye Northumbrian shades, which overlook. Early Influences. Mark Akenside. *Fr.* The Pleasures of Imagination, IV. OBEC
O Ye Sweet Heavens! Thomas William Parsons. AA
O ye that look on Ecstasy. Ecstasy. Rachel Annand Taylor. GoTS; SiSw
O you chorus of indolent reviewers. Tennyson. PV
O ye that put your trust and confidence. A Rueful Lamentation on the Death of Queen Elizabeth. Sir Thomas More. LiTB; LiTG; OBSC
O Ye That Would Swallow the Needy. Amos, VIII: 4-10, Bible, *O.T.* TrJP
O [*or* A] ye wha are sae guid yoursel. Address to the Unco Guid, or the Rigidly Righteous. Burns. AnFE; BEL; BoLiVe;

CEP; CoBE; EiCL; EiPP; EnLit; EnPE; EnRP; FosPo; HBV; LoBV; OAEP; OBEC; OxBS; PoFr; SeCeV; TOP; TreFS; TrGrPo; ViBoPo
O ye who see with other eyes than ours. Life and Death. Lilla Cabot Perry. AA
Oh ye! who so lately were blithesome and gay. The Butterfly's Funeral. *Unknown.* OTPC (1923 ed.)
Oh, ye who taste that love is sweet. Ye who Taste That Love Is Sweet. William Michael Rossetti. OQP
Oh ye! who teach the ingenuous youth of nations. Don Juan, II. Byron. EnRP
Oh ye who tread the Narrow Way. The Buddha at Kamakura. Kipling. LoBV
O ye, whose cheek the tear of pity stains. Epitaph on My Father. Burns. MaRV
Oh, ye whose hearts are resonant, and ring to war's romance. Jean Desprez. Robert W. Service. GSP
Oh, ye wild waves, shoreward dashing. The Song of the Wild Storm-Waves. Percy F. Sinnett. VA
O year, grow slowly. Exquisite, holy. Slow Spring. Katharine Tynan. BoTP; MemP
O year that is going, take with you. A Prayer for the New Year. Laura F. Armitage. OQP
O years, and age, farewell! Eternity. Robert Herrick. SeCL; WHA
O Years Unborn. John Richard Moreland. PGD
O yellow bird, yellow bird. The Yellow Bird. *Unknown.* BiS
O yellow flowers that Herrick sung! To Daffodils. Austin Dobson. InP
"O, yellow jack's here." Walter Reed. Rosemary Benét and Stephen Vincent Benét. OTD
Oh, yes, I'm gwine up, gwine up. Gwine Up. *Unknown.* BoAN-1
Oh, yes, my lads, we'll roll alee. Come Down, You Bunch of Roses, Come Down. *Unknown.* ShS
O yes, O yes! if any maid. Cupid's Indictment [*or* A Song of Diana's Nymphs]. John Lyly. *Fr.* Galathea. EIL; OBSC
Oh, Yes! Oh, Yes! Wait 'til I Git on My Robe, *with music.* *Unknown.* BoAN-2
Oh yes, we are so thankful. The Black Army. S. E. K. Mqhayi. PeSA
Oh, yes, we've be'n fixin' up some sence we sold that piece o' groun'. Sary "Fixes Up" Things. Albert Bigelow Paine. BOHV
Oh yesterday the cutting edge drank thirstily and deep. Tomorrow. John Masefield. MoBrPo; NeMA; OtMeF; POTE; StaSt; TrGrPo; YT
Oh! yet a few short years of useful life. Wordsworth. *Fr.* The Prelude, XIV. OBRV
Oh yet we trust that somehow good. In Memoriam A. H. H., LIV [*or* The Larger Hope]. Tennyson. AnFE; AtBAP; BEL; BoLiVe; DiPo; EaLo; EnL; EnLi-2; EnLit; EPN; ExPo; FaPL; GTBS-W; GTSL; HBV; LiTB; LiTG; LoBV; MaPo; MaRV; OAEP; OBNC; OQP; OuHeWo; PoE; PoFS; PoIE; SeCeV; TOP; TreFS; TrGrPo; TRV; UnPo; ViPo; VP; WGRP; YAT
Oh Yield, Fair Lids. Sheridan. OnYI
O yonge fresshe folkes, he or she. *See* O younge freshe folkes, he and she.
O you. Carrefour. Amy Lowell. MoLP
O you are a rajah in your rage. Courage for the Pusillanimous. Paul Roche. GoYe
O you dear trees, you have learned so much of beauty. This Way Only. Lesbia Harford. PoAu-1
Oh, you know Joe Silovatsky. Me Johnny Mitchell Man. *Unknown.* TrAS
O you liar tell me this. The Liar. *Unknown.* KiLC
Oh, you may drive a horse to water. *Unknown.* SiTL
Oh, you may sing your gypsy songs. The Little Gods. Abigail Cresson. PoMa
Oh, you may take a highway. Highways and Byways. John Vanderbilt. PCD
O you not only worshipful but dear. Credo. Zona Gale. TrPWD
O, you plant the pain in my heart with your wistful eyes. Maureen. John Todhunter. HBV; OBEV; OBVV
O you so long dead. To My Brother. Louise Bogan. NYBP
O you that from some southern land. Ode to the Nightingale. John Kendall. InMe
O you that hear[e] this voice. Astrophel and Stella: Sixth Song. Sir Philip Sidney. FCP; OBSC; SiPS
Oh, you who live on the Heliconian mountain. Hymn to Marriage, for Manlius and Junia. Catullus. HW
Oh, you who love me not, tell me some way. Tell Me Some Way. Lizette Woodworth Reese. PG
Oh, You Wholly Rectangular. E. R. Cole. GoYe
O you whom God hath called and set apart. The Ideal City. Washington Gladden. OQP
O you would house me in silken frocks. The Wild Goat. Claude McKay. CDC
O You Young Eagles! Edgar Lee Masters. PoFr
O Young and Fearless Prophet. S. Ralph Harlow. MaRV; TrPWD; TRV
Oh! young Lochinvar has [*or* is] come out of the West. Young Lochinvar, *parody.* *Unknown.* *at. to* J. J. Fay. BOHV; FiBHP; InMe
Oh, young Lochinvar is come out of the west. Lochinvar. Sir Walter Scott. *Fr.* Marmion, V. ATP; BBV; BEL; BeLS; BoChLi; BoTP; CoBE; EnLi-2 (1949 ed.); EnLit; EnRP; EPN; EvOK; FaBoBe; FaBV; FaFP; FaPON; GN; GoTP; GoTS; GSP; HBV; HBVY; InP; LoEn; MaC; MCCG; MemP; NeHB; OAEP; OBNC; OBRV; OnSP; OtMeF; OTPC; OxBS; PaPo; PCD; PoE; PoPo; PoRA; RG; RoGo; ShBV-1; StPo; StVeCh; TIHL; TOP; TreF; WHA; YAT
O young Mariner. Merlin and the Gleam. Tennyson. BEL; MaVP; OAEP; PoVP; VP
Oh Young Men Oh Young Comrades. Stephen Spender. NAMP
O younge freshe [*or* yonge fresshe] folkes, he or [*or* and] she. Exhortation to Youth [*or* The Love Unfeigned]. Chaucer. *Fr.* Troilus and Criseyde. CAW; ExPo; LO; OBEV; PoLi
O youngest, best-loved daughter of Hsieh. An Elegy. Yüan Chen. LiTW
Oh, your sweetness, softness, smoothness! Lassitude. Paul Verlaine. ErPo
Oh, your thighs. Love Poem. Judson Crews. UnTE
O, you're braw wi' your pearls and your diamonds. Lassie, What Mair Wad You Hae? Heine. GoTS; OxBS
"Oh, you're welcome home again," said the young man to his love. The Grey Cock (A *vers.*). *Unknown.* BaBo
Oh youth, beware! that laurel-rose. Larissa. Thomas Love Peacock. *Fr.* Rhododaphne. OBRV
O Youth Whose Hope Is High. Robert Bridges. VA
O Youth with Blossoms Laden. Arthur Wallace Peach. HBMV
O Zeus our king and Night our friend. Chorus. Aeschylus. *Fr.* Agamemnon. LiTW
O zummer clote! when the brook's a-sliden [*or* a-glidèn]. The Clote (Water Lilly). William Barnes. ELP; GTBS-D; PoEL-4
O' zummer night, as day did gleam. The Lost Little Sister. William Barnes. PoEL-4
Oak. Philip Child. CaP
Oak, The. Dryden. OHIP
Oak, The. Mary Elliott. OTPC (1923 ed.)
Oak, The. George Hiil. HH
Oak, The. George Pope Morris. AmePo
Oak, The. Tennyson. EPN; FaPON; MPB; PoPl; PoVP; YT
Oak and Lily. Ben Jonson. *See* It Is Not Growing like a Tree.
Oak and Olive. James Elroy Flecker. HBMV
Oak and the Ash, The. *Unknown.* FaBoCh; LoGBV
Oak and the Beech, The. Thomas Love Peacock. *See* Song: "For the tender beech and the sapling oak."
Oak and the Brere, The. Spenser. *Fr.* The Shepheardes Calender: February. OBSC
Oak and the Reed, The. La Fontaine, *tr. fr. French by* Elizur Wright. OuHeWo
Oak, fern, ivy and pine. Little Epithalamium. Chester Kallman. CrMA
Oak is called the king of trees, The. Trees. Sara Coleridge. BoTP; DD; MPB; OHIP; PCH; TVC
Oak Leaves. Elizabeth J. Coatsworth. StVeCh
Oak leaves are big as the mouse's ear. Every One to His Own Way. John Vance Cheney. AA
Oak leaves holding on. Period. George Amabile. YAP
Oak oak! like like. Drunken Winter. Joseph Ceravolo. ANYP
Oak of Guernica, The. Wordsworth. FOL

Oak one day addressed the reed, The. The Oak and the Reed. La Fontaine. OuHeWo
Oak Tree, The. William Barnes. *See* Girt Woak Tree That's in the Dell, The.
Oak-Tree, The. *Unknown.* CBEP
Oaktree cannot be mistaken, An. Not a Tree. Thomas Blackburn. NYTB
Oakeley, whenas the bass you beat. To E. M. O. Thomas Edward Brown. WhC
Oaks, how subtle and marine, The. Bearded Oaks. Robert Penn Warren. AmP; AnFE; CoAnAm; FiMAP; LiTM; MoAmPo (1950 ed.); MoVE; OnHM; ReMP; TDP; TwCP; VaPo
Oars fell from our hands, The. The Island. George Woodcock. MoCV; NeBP
Oarsmen, The, *sel.* Rabindranath Tagore.
"We have know sins and evils every day." MaRV
Oasis. Edward Dowden. OxBI
Oath, The. Allen Tate. LiTM; OxBA
Oatmeal was in their blood and in their names. The Gathering. E. J. Pratt. *Fr.* Towards the Last Spike. MoCV; OBCV
Oats, peas, beans and barley grow. *Unknown.* RIS
Obedience. Phoebe Cary. PCH
Obedience. George Herbert. AnAnS-1; MaMe; MeP
Obedience. Robert Herrick. PoFr
Obedience. George Macdonald. BePJ; BLRP; FaChP; MaRV; TreFT; TRV; WGRP
(Decision.) SoP
(What Christ Said.) ChIP; HBV; OQP; OTPC
Obedience. *Unknown.* SoP
Oberammergau. Leonora Speyer. AnAmPo; HBMV
Obermann Once More. Matthew Arnold. EPN; PoEL-5; PoVP
East, The, *sel.* OtMeF
Oberon and Titania to the Fairy Train. Shakespeare. *Fr.* A Midsummer Night's Dream, V, ii. GN
(Through the House.) CTC
(Through the house give glimmering light.") SiCE
Oberon, the Fairy Prince, *sel.* Ben Jonson.
Buz, Quoth the Blue Fly. NA; TuPP
("Buzz, quoth the blue fly," *sl. diff.*) OxNR
(Catch, A.) EIL
Oberon's Feast. Robert Herrick. BoLiVe; OAEP; OTPC (1923 ed.); PoeP; SeCV-1; TrGrPo
"Little mushroom table spread, A," *sel.* ViBoPo
Obit on Parnassus. F. Scott Fitzgerald. InMe; NYBP; WhC
Obituary. "Max Adeler." DTC
Obituary. Anthony Brode. FiBHP
Obituary. Thomas William Parsons. AA; HBV; HBVY
Obituary. Louis Untermeyer. MAP
Obituary columns of our paper, The. Synchronized. Larry Rubin. FiSC
Object among dreams, you sit here with your shoes off, An. A Girl in a Library. Randall Jarrell. FiMAP
Objects. W. H. Auden. NePoAm-2
Objects. Richard Wilbur. NoP
Objects are disposed: the sky is suitable, The. November, 1941. Roy Fuller. MoPo
Objects of the Summer Scene, The. Thomas Caulfield Irwin. IrPN; NBM
Objet d'Art. Lucien Stryk. NYTB
Oblation. A. Newberry Choyce. HBMV
Oblation, The. Swinburne. BoLP; EnLit; HBV; PoVP
Obligations. Jane Cooper. AmPC; NePoEA-2
Obliged by frequent visits of this man. Fleckno, an English Priest at Rome. Andrew Marvell. MaMe; SeEP
Oblique. Archibald Rutledge. TRV
Obliterate/ mythology as you unwind. The Cavern. Charles Tomlinson. NMP
Oblivion. Jessie Redmond Fauset, *fr. the French of* Massillon Coicou. BANP; PoNe
Oblivion. W. W. Gibson. NP
Oblivion. Ellis Ayitey Komey. PBA
Oboes on the terrace held a chord, The. Professor Drinking Wine. Alasdair Clayre. PV
O'Bruidar. James Stephens, *after the Irish of* David O'Bruaidar. *See* O Bruadair.
Obscure and Dark Is All the Gloomy Air. Robert Greene. *Fr.* Perimedes the Blacksmith. RelE
Obscure Night of the Soul, The. St. John of the Cross, *tr. fr. Spanish by* Arthur Symons. AWP; BoC; CAW; OBMV; OuHeWo
(Dark Night of the Soul, The, *tr. by* E. Allison Peers.) ErPo; LiTW
(Upon a Gloomy Night, *tr. by* Roy Campbell.) AtBAP; PeSA
Obscure Writer, An. John Donne. MaMe; RelE
Obscurely yet most surely called to praise. Praise in Summer. Richard Wilbur. NoP PP
Obscurest night involved the sky. The Castaway. William Cowper. AtBAP; BEL; BWP; CABA; CBEP; CBV; CEP; CoBE; EiCL; EiCP; EiPP; ELP; EnLi-2; EnLit; EnPE; EnRP; FaBoEn; FiP; GTSL; InPo; NoP; OAEP; OBEC; PeER; PoE; PoEL-3; PoFS; PoSa; TDP; TOP
Obscurity ("Obscurity becomes the final peace"). Jessica Powers. JKCP (1955 ed.)
Obsequies of Stuart. John Reuben Thompson. PAH
Obsequies of [*or* to] the Lord Harrington. John Donne. MaMe
"Thou seest me here at midnight, now all rest," *sel.* MyFE
Obsequies to the Lady Anne Hay. Thomas Carew. AnAnS-2
Observation. Samuel Hoffenstein. PoMa
Observation. Dorothy Parker. FiBHP
(Some Beautiful Letters.) InMe
Observation of Facts. Charles Tomlinson. NePoEA-2
Observe, dear George, this nut so small. The Oak. Mary Elliott. OTPC (1923 ed.)
Observe, from his trunk upwards. The Geranium Man. Zulfikar Ghose. NYTB
Observe God in His works: here fountains flow. Henry Vaughan. *Fr.* Rules and Lessons. TRV
Observe how he negotiates his way. Swimmer. Robert Francis. CrMA; NePoAm
Observe. I myself will proceed/ To put him in his place. Cyrano de Bergerac Discusses His Nose. Edmond Rostand. *Fr.* Cyrano de Bergerac. TreFS
Observe. Ridged, raised, tactile, the horror. Munch's Scream. Donald Hall. NePoEA
Observe the Cat upon this page. The Cat. Oliver Herford. FaBV
Observe the Hellespont a while. *Unknown.* SeCSL
Observe the Roman Forum: turn away. Morality. Jean Garrigue. ELU
Observe the weary birds ere night be done. Orinda to Lucasia. Katherine Philips. LO; SeCL
Observe the Whole of It. Thomas Wolfe. TreFT
Observe the Whooping Crane. The Whooping Crane. Vassar Miller. ToPo
Observe this man, he is an engineer. Revelation. Nancy Keesing. PoAu-2
Observing point by point mere instances. On a Baltimore Bus. Charles G. Bell. NePoAm
Obsessions. Denise Levertov. LiTM (1970 ed.); NePoEA-2
Obsessions governing an art, The. Aids to Composition. Robert Conquest. PP
Obsidian lasher, partly pip oversmokes. Movies. Clark Coolidge. ANYP
Obviously, in a plutocracy. Childe Harold to the Round Tower Came. William Carlos Williams. PoeP
Occasional mornings when an early fog. Housewife. Josephine Miles. FiMAP
Occasional Yarrow, The. Stevie Smith. PoG
Occasioned by General Washington's Arrival in Philadelphia, on His Way to His Residence in Virginia. Philip Freneau. PAH
Occasions drew me early to this city. Milton. *Fr.* Samson Agonistes. FIW; FOL
Occupation: Housewife. Phyllis McGinley. Sonn
Ocean, The. Psalms, CVII: 23-32, Bible, *OT.* *See* They That Go Down to the Sea in Ships.
Ocean, The ("Roll on thou deep and dark blue ocean, rol"). Byron. *Fr.* Childe Harold's Pilgrimage, IV, *sts.* 179-183. BoLiVe; PTK; TrGrPo; UnPo (1st ed.)
(Address to the Ocean.) TreFS
(Apostrophe to the Ocean.) EtS; OHFP; WBLP
(Roll On, Thou Dark Blue Ocean.) FaPON
(Roll On, Thou Deep and Dark Blue Ocean.) AtBAP
(To the Ocean.) GN; WGRP
"There is a pleasure in the pathless woods," *sts.* 178-183. EPN; InP; MaPo; MaRV, 9 *ll.*; MCCG; OBRV; PoIE; ShBV-3; ViBoPo
(And I Have Loved Thee, Ocean!) WHA
(By the Deep Sea.) OBNC
(Deep and Dark Blue Ocean.) ChTr
(Nature.) BEL

(Oh, that the desert were my dwelling-place.") ILP; PoEL-4
(Ocean, The, 4 *sts.*) FaBV
(Roll On, Thou Deep and Dark Blue Ocean.) FiP
(Sea, The.) FaBoBe; HBV; LiTB; LiTG
(There Is Pleasure in the Pathless Woods, 9 *ll.*) TreF
Ocean, The. Louis Dudek. *Fr.* Provincetown. MoCV
Ocean. Robinson Jeffers. AP; CoBMV
Ocean. Louis Lavater. BoAu
Ocean, The. Moschus, *tr. fr. Greek by* Shelley. AWP; JAWP; WBP
Ocean. Robert Pollok. *Fr.* The Course of Time. EtS
Ocean, The. George D. Prentice. EtS
Ocean, The. John Augustus Shea. EtS
Ocean. Adrien Stoutenburg. WIRo
Ocean Burial, The. Edwin H. Chapin. ShS, *with music*; ViBoFo
Ocean does not shrink or vaster grow, The. The Hidden Truth. Jami. LiTW; OnPM
Ocean-Fight, The. *Unknown.* PAH
Ocean has not been so quiet for a long while, The. Evening Ebb. Robinson Jeffers. AmPP (3d ed.); OTPC (1946 ed.)
Ocean Lullaby, An. Charles Keeler. EtS
Ocean of Life, The. Longfellow. *See* Ships That Pass in the Night.
Ocean said to me once, The. Stephen Crane. The Black Riders, XXXVII. MWA-2
Ocean Spills, The. Samuel Hoffenstein. ALV
Ocean stood like crystal, The. The soft air. The Birth of Venus. *Unknown.* EtS
Ocean thunders in the caverned sky, The. Homecoming in Storm. Bernice L. Kenyon. EtS
Ocean to Cynthia, The. Sir Walter Ralegh. OBSC, *sl. abr.*; ReIE
(Eleventh and Last Book of the Ocean to Cynthia, The.) NCEP
(Ocean's Love to Cynthia, The.) SiPS
Sels.
"But stay, my thoughts, make end, give fortune way." TuPP
"Sufficeth it to you, my joys interred." FCP
"To seeke new worlds, for golde, for prayse, for glory." FaBoEn
"With youth, is deade the hopes of loves returne." FaBoEn
Ocean too has winter-views serene, The. Winter Views Serene. George Crabbe. *Fr.* The Borough. OBNC
Ocean twanging away there, The. The Parting. Adrienne Rich. WIRo
Ocean Wanderer, The. *Unknown.* BOHV; NA
Ocean, with a calm sardonic titter, The. Anthony Delius. *Fr.* The Great Divide. BoSA
Ocean Wood, The. Lord De Tabley. CBEP
Ocean's Love to Cynthia, The. Sir Walter Ralegh. *See* Ocean to Cynthia, The.
Och hey! for the splendour of tartans! The Return. Pittendrigh Macgillivray. GoTS; OxBS
Och hon for somebody! Somebody. *Unknown.* OxBS
Och, hush ye then, och hush ye. Hush Song. Elizabeth Shane. MoSiPe
Och! the Coronation! what celebration. Mr. Barney Maguire's Account of the Coronation. "Thomas Ingoldsby." VA
Och, when we lived in ould Glenann. A Song of Glenann. "Moira O'Neill." HBV
Ock Gurney and old Pete were there. The Countrymen. John Masefield. *Fr.* Reynard the Fox. CMoP
Octaves, *sels.* E. A. Robinson. ILP
"Here by the windy docks I stand alone," XXIII.
"Like a white wall whereon forever breaks," XVIII.
"Prophet of dead words defeats himself, The," XX.
October. Thomas Bailey Aldrich. *See* Maple Leaves.
October. John Bayliss. NeBP
October. Bill Berkson. ANYP
October. Nancy Birckhead. StaSt
October. T. A. Daly. JKCP
October. Robert Frost. GoJo; MAmP; MaPo; MWA-2
October. Rose Fyleman. RePo; SiSoSe; TiPo (1959 ed.)
October. John Murray Gibbon. PTK
October. Patrick Kavanagh. GTBS-P
October. Denise Levertov. NoP
October. Helen McMahan. PoRL
October. William Morris. *Fr.* The Earthly Paradise. EPN; OBNC; ViPP
"O love, turn from the unchanging sea, and gaze," *sel.* FaBoEn
October. Dollie Radford. VA
October. Christina Rossetti. *Fr.* The Months; a Pageant. BoTP
October. Spenser. *Fr.* The Shepheardes Calender. EnPo; ReEn; ReIE; SiCE
(Contempt of Poetry, The.) OBSC
(October Eclogue.) PP
"But, ah! Maecenas is yclad in clay," *sel.* MyFE
October. Dylan Thomas. *Fr.* Poem in October. YeAr
October. Edward Thomas. ChMP; MoVE; POTE
October. Willard Trask. CLwM
October. John Updike. PDV
October. Jones Very. AnNE
October. S. W. Whitman. BoTP
October, and a rain-blurred face. At the Fishing Settlement. Alistair Campbell. AnNZ
October,—and the skies are cool and grey. Late Autumn. William Allingham. IrPN
October at last has come! The thicket has shaken. Autumn. Pushkin. AnEnPo; AWP
October Birthday. Sister Mary Madeleva. JKCP (1955 ed.)
October! Can I stand it one more year? The Game. Walker Gibson. NePoAm-2
October Eclogue. Spenser. *See* October.
October 1803 ("When, looking on the present face of things"). Wordsworth. EnRP
October 1. Karl Shapiro. FiMAP; MoAB; MoAmPo (1950 ed.)
October Flies. Jascha Kessler. AmPC
October 14, 1644. Lord Herbert of Cherbury. AnAnS-2
October gave a party. October's Party. George Cooper. BoChLi; BoTP; HBV; HBVY; OTPC; PoLF; RePo; RIS; SiSoSe
October in New England. Home Thoughts. Odell Shepard. HBMV
October in New Zealand. Jessie Mackay. BoAu
October in Tennessee. Walter Malone. AA
October is a breakfast food. A Bowl of October. Helen Bevington. RePo
October is a piper. Autumn Song. Margaret Rose. BoTP
October Journey. Margaret Walker. AmNP; IDB; PoNe
October Magic. Myra Cohn Livingston. PDV
October Maples, Portland. Richard Wilbur. CoPo
October Morning. John James Piatt. YeAr
October Night. Agnes Louise Dean. YeAr
October, 1942. Roy Fuller. WaP
October Nocturne, An. Ivor Winters. CBV
October of the Angels. James J. Daly. WHL
October Redbreast, The. Alice Meynell. MoBrPo
October 16: The Raid. Langston Hughes. BOLo
October turned my maple's leaves to gold. Maple Leaves [*or* October]. Thomas Bailey Aldrich. AnNE; GN; GoTP; TOP
October XXIX, 1795 (Keats' Birthday). William Stanley Braithwaite. CDC
October Winds. Virginia D. Randall. YeAr
October's bellowing anger breaks and cleaves. Autumn. Siegfried Sassoon. NP
October's Bright Blue Weather. Helen Hunt Jackson. AmePo; BBV (1923 ed.); BLPA; BoChLi; DD; FaBoBe; GN; HBVY; NeHB; OTD; OTPC (1946 ed.); PoSC; TreFT
October's Husbandry. Thomas Tusser. CoBE
October's lap holds patches. October. Helen McMahan. PoRL
October's Party. George Cooper. BoChLi; BoTP; BrR; HBV; HBVY; OTPC; PoLF; RePo; RIS; SiSoSe
October's Song. Eleanor Farjeon. PoSC
Octopus. Arthur Clement Hilton. CenHV; Par
Octopus, The. James Merrill. CoAP; TwAmPo
Octopus, The. Ogden Nash. NePA; SoPo; TiPo; WePo
Octopussycat, The. Kenyon Cox. *Fr.* Mixed Beasts. FaPON; RIS; SoPo; TiPo
Oculi Augent Dolorem. Barnabe Googe. *See* Out of Sight, Out of Mind.
Oculist prescribes me spectacles, The. On Oculists. J. C. Squire. WhC
Odcomb's Complaint, *sel.* John Taylor.
Sonnet: Mackado, Fustian and Motley. CBEP
(Sonnet: "Sweet semi-circled Cynthia played at maw.") EIL
Odd but True. *Unknown.* SiTL
(Nonsense.) NA
Odd Conceit, An. Nicholas Breton. EIL; OBSC; SiCE; TuPP

Odd (continued)
(Song: "Lovely kind, and kindly loving.") LO
Odd Ones, The. Ruth Suckow. MCCG
Odd silence/ Falls as we enter, An. Dreams of Water. Donald Justice. NYBP
Odd to a Krokis. *Unknown.* NA
Oddities composed the sum of the news. For the Lost Generation. Galway Kinnell. NePoAm; PPON
Oddity Land, *sels.* Edward Anthony. TiPo (1959 ed.)
"I know a barber."
"I know seven mice."
Ode, *sel.* Alessandro Manzoni, Fifth of May, The—Napoleon. *tr. fr. Italian by* William Dean Howells. CAW
Ode: "Absence, hear thou my protestation." John Hoskins. *See* Absence.
Ode: Allusion to Horace. Mark Akenside. CEP
Ode, An: "As it fell upon a day." Richard Barnfield. *See* Nightingale, The.
Ode: "As late I sought the spangled bowers." Anacreon, *tr. fr. Greek by* Thomas Moore. OuHeWo
Ode: "At her fair hands." Walter Davison. *See* How Can the Heart Forget Her.
Ode: Autumn. Thomas Hood. *See* Autumn ("I saw old Autumn").
Ode, An: "Awake fair Muse for I intend." William Browne. OBS; SeEP
Ode: "Bards of Passion and of Mirth." Keats. BEL; ChER; EnRP; EPN; GTBS; GTSE; GTSL; MERP; OAEP; OBRV; TOP
(Bards of Passion and of Mirth.) EnLi-2; EnLit; OBEV
(Ode on the Poets.) ATP (1935 ed.); GTBS-D; GTBS-P; GTBS-W
(To the Poets.) HBV; ViBoPo
Ode: "Come leave the loathed stage." Ben Jonson. *See* Ode to Himself ("Come leave . . .").
Ode: "Come, let us drink away the time." Charles Cotton. CavP
Ode II: Dialogue between Him and His Heart, A. Walter Davison. *See* How Can the Heart Forget Her.
Ode: Dying Christian to His Soul, The. Pope. *See* Dying Christian to His Soul, The.
Ode: "Gathering the echoes of forgotten wisdom." George Santayana. Odes, III. AmePo; AnAmPo; AnFE; APA; CoAnAm; TwAmPo
Ode: "Give me the harp of epic song." Anacreon, *tr. fr. Greek by* Thomas Moore. OuHeWo
Ode: "God save the Rights of Man!" Philip Freneau. AmPP (3d ed.); AP; CoBA; PoFr
Ode: "Good night, my Love." Charles Cotton. ViBoPo
Ode: Grasshopper, The. Richard Lovelace. *See* Grasshopper, The.
Ode, An: "High-spirited friend." Ben Jonson. BWP
(Noble Balm.) OBEV
Ode V: His Farewell to His Unkind and Unconstant Mistress. Francis Davison. ReIE
Ode: "How are thy servants blest, O Lord!" Addison. *See* How Are Thy Servants Blest.
Ode: "How sleep the brave, who sink to rest." William Collins. *See* How Sleep the Brave.
Ode: "I am the spirit of the morning sea." Richard Watson Gilder. AA
Ode: "I care not for the idle state." Anacreon. *tr. fr. Greek by* Thomas Moore. OuHeWo
Ode: "I hate that drum's discordant sound." John Scott of Amwell. *See* Drum, The.
Ode: "I saw old Autumn in the misty morn." Thomas Hood. *See* Autumn ("I saw old Autumn").
Ode: "I saw the smiling bard of pleasure." Anacreon, *tr. fr. Greek by* Thomas Moore. OuHeWo
Ode: "Idea of justice may be precious, An." Frank O'Hara. NeAP
Ode, An: "I'm going to write a novel, hey." John Updike. FiBHP
Ode: Intimations of Immortality from Recollections of Early Childhood. Wordsworth. AnFE; AWP; BEL; BoLiVe; CABA; CaFP; ChER; CoBE; DiPo; EnL; EnLi-2; EnLit; EnRP; EPN; ERoP-1; ExPo; FiP; ForPo; FosPo; ILP; InP; InPo; InvP; JAWP; LiTB; LiTG; LoBV; MaPo; MasP; MBW-2; MCCG; MERP; NoP; OAEP; OBEV; OBNC; OBRV; OuHeWo; PAn; PeER; PlA; Po; PoAn; PoEL-4; PoeP; PoFS; PoIE; SeCeV; StP; TOP; TrGrPo; ViBoPo; WBP

(Intimations of Immortality from Recollections of Early Childhood.) ATP; WoL
(Ode on Intimations of Immortality from Recollections of Early Childhood.) FaFP; GTBS; GTBS-D; GTBS-P; GTBS-W; GTSE; GTSL; MaRV, *abr.*; OHFP; ShBV-4; TreF, *abr.*; VaPo; WHA
"There was a time when meadow, grove, and stream." BoC
(Ode on the Intimations of Immortality from Recollections of Early Childhood.) AtBAP; HBV
Sels.
"O joy that in our embers."
(Ode on Intimations of Immortality, *st.* 9.) OQP
"Our birth is but a sleep and a forgetting." BiCB; EaLo; FaBV; MemP; PoG; PoSa; TRV; WGRP
(Intimations of Immortality.) ChTr, *sts.* 5 *and* 6; FaBoEn, *st.* 5; OQP, *st.* 5
(Ode on Intimations of Immortality, *sts.* 1-2.) OQP
Ode: "Listen to the Muse's lyre." Anacreon, *tr. fr. Greek by* Thomas Moore. OuHeWo
Ode: "Love thy country, wish it well." George Bubb Dodington. CEP; OBEC
(Love Thy Country.) CBEP
(Shorten Sail.) OBEV (1st ed.)
Ode, An: "Merchant, to secure his treasure, The." Matthew Prior. AWP; CABA; CBEP; CEP; EiCL; EiCP; EiPP; EnLoPo; InPo; JAWP; NoP; PoE; PoRA; SeCL; ViBoPo; WBP
(Merchant to Secure His Treasure, The.) GTBS; GTBS-D; GTBS-P; GTBS-W; GTSE; GTSL; OnPM
(Song: Dissembler, The.) MeWo
(Song: "Merchant to secure his treasure, The.") AnFE; HBV; LiTL; OBEV; TrGrPo
Ode: "My heart rebels against my generation." George Santayana. Odes, II. AmePo; AnFE; APA; ATP; CoAnAm; PoFr; TwAmPo; ViBoPo
Ode, An: "Now each creature joys the other." Samuel Daniel. EIL; LoBV; OBSC; SiCE; TuPP
Ode: "Now I find thy looks were feigned." Thomas Lodge. Fr. Phyllis. EIL; EnRePo; OBSC; SiCE; TuPP
(Song: "Now I see thy looks were feigned.") LoBV
Ode: "O happy the huntsman . . .,"V. Frederic Prokosch. ViBoPo (1941 ed.)
Ode: "O tenderly the haughty day." Emerson. AA; DD, *abr.*; MPB; PaA; PAL
(Ode Sung in the Town Hall, Concord, July 4, 1857.) AnNE; GN; PoRL
Ode: Of Cynthia. *Unknown.* SiCE
(Of Cynthia.) OBSC
Ode: "Of thee the Northman by his beachèd [*or* bleachèd] galley." George Santayana. Odes, V. AmePo; AnAmPo; AnFE; APA; CoAnAm; TwAmPo
(Ode to the Mediterranean.) EtS
Ode: Of Wit. Abraham Cowley. AnAnS-2; CEP; MeLP; MePo; OAEP; SCEP-2; SeCP; SeCV-1; SeEP
(Of Wit.) OBS; ReEn
Ode: On Intimations of Immortality from Recollections of Early Childhood. Wordsworth. *See* Ode: Intimations of Immortality. . .
Ode: On the Death of William Butler Yeats. A. J. M. Smith. OBCV; PeCV
Ode, An: On the Unveiling of the Shaw Memorial on Boston Common. Thomas Bailey Aldrich. AA; HBV; PAH
Ode: "Once more the country calls." Allen Tate. *See* Ode to Our Young Pro-Consuls of the Air.
Ode: "Peer of gods he seemeth to me, the blissful." Sappho. *See* To a Bride.
Ode: Rose, The. Richard Lovelace. *See* Rose, The.
Ode: Salute to the French Negro Poets. Frank O'Hara. NeAP; PoNe (1970 ed.)
Ode: "Sculptor, wouldst thou glad my soul." Anacreon, *tr. fr. Greek by* Thomas Moore. OuHeWo
Ode, An: Secundum Artem. William Cowper. FosPo; PP
Ode, An: "Sire of the rising day." Lord De Tabley. OBVV; PoVP
Ode: "Sleep sweetly in your humble graves." Henry Timrod. AmePo; AmPP; HBV; MAmP; OxBA; StP
(At Magnolia Cemetery.) AA; AmP; AnAmPo
(Decoration Day at Charleston.) DD
(Magnolia Cemetery.) PaA
(Ode Sung on the Occasion of Decorating the Graves of the Confederate Dead.) AP; MC
(Ode to the Confederate Dead.) PAL; TreFT

Ode: "Slowly the black earth gains the yellow." George Santayana. Odes, IV. AmePo; AnFE; APA; CoAnAm; TwAmPo
Ode: Solitude, at an Inn. Thomas Warton, the Younger. CEP
Ode: "Spacious firmament on high, The." Addison. *See* Spacious Firmament on High, The.
Ode: Spirit Wooed, The. Richard Watson Dixon. OBNC
Ode: Sung in the Town Hall, Concord, July 4, 1857. Emerson. *See* Ode: "O tenderly the haughty day."
Ode: "Tell me, thou soul of her I love." James Thomson. OBEC
Ode VIII: That All Other Creatures Have Their Abiding in Heaven, Hell, Earth, Air, Water, or Fire; but He in All of Them. Francis Davison. RelE
Ode: "They journeyed." Ibn al-Arabi, *tr. fr. Arabic by* R. A. Nicholson. AWP; LiTW
Ode, An: To Himself ("Come leave the loathed stage"). Ben Jonson. *See* Ode to Himself ("Come leave . . .").
Ode, An: To Himself ("Where do'st thou careless lie"). Ben Jonson. *See* Ode to Himself, An ("Where do'st thou . . .").
Ode: To My Pupils. W. H. Auden. *See* Which Side Am I Supposed to Be On?
Ode: To the Cuckoo. Michael Bruce, *revised by* John Logan. *See* To the Cuckoo.
Ode: To the Roc. William J. Courthope. *Fr.* The Paradise of Birds. VA
Ode: "Tonight is so coarse with chocolate." Louis MacNeice. CMoP
Ode: "Until thine hands clasp girdlewise." Sadi, *tr. fr. Persian by* R. A. Nicholson. AWP
Ode: "Vulcan! hear your glorious task." Anacreon, *tr. fr. Greek by* Thomas Moore. OuHeWo
Ode: "Was ever man of nature's framing." Charles Cotton. CavP; PeRV
Ode: "We are the music-makers," 3 *sts.* Arthur O'Shaughnessy. EnLi-2; EnLit; GBV (1952 ed.); GTBS; GTBS-D; GTSE; GTSL; HBV, 9 *sts.*; InP; LiTG; MaRV; MoBrPo (1942 ed.); NeHB; NeMA; OBEV; OBVV; OnYI; OxBI, 2 *sts.*; PoFr; PoFS; PoRL 6 *sts.*; PoVP, 9 *sts.*; TIHL; TOP; TreF; TrGrPo; TSW; ViBoPo; WHA
(Dreamers of Dreams, The.) PTK
(Music Makers, The.) FaBV; OtMeF
(Poets, The.) YT
(We Are the Music-Makers.) GTBS-W; OQP
Ode: "Weep, ah weep love's losing." Imr el Kais. *See* Weep Love's Losing.
Ode: "What god will choose me from this labouring nation." George Santayana. Odes, I. AmePo; AnFE; APA; CoAnAm; TwAmPo
Ode: "When I walk forth into the woods." Barnabe Barnes. *Fr.* Parthenophil and Parthenophe. TuPP
Ode: "Where do'st thou careless lie." Ben Jonson. *See* Ode to Himself, An ("Where do'st thou . . .").
Ode, An: "While blooming youth, and gay delight." Matthew Prior. EiCL
Ode: "Who can Support the anguish of Love?" Ibn al-Arabi, *tr. fr. Arabic by* R. A. Nicholson. AWP; LiTW
Ode, An: "Why doth heaven bear a sun." Barnabe Barnes. *Fr.* Parthenophil and Parthenophe. EIL; OBSC
Ode: "Why will they never sleep." John Peale Bishop. LiTA; LiTM; MoPo; MoVE; NePA; TwAmPo
Ode: "Without the evening dew and showers," 6 *sts.* Charles Cotton. ViBoPo
Ode: "Women tell me every day, The." Anacreon, *tr. fr. Greek by* Thomas Moore. LoBV; OuHeWo
Ode: Written during the Battle of Dunkirk, May, 1940. Sir Herbert Read. *See* Ode Written during the Battle of Dunkirk . . .
Ode: Written in the Beginning of the Year 1746. William Collins. *See* How Sleep the Brave.
Ode for a Master Mariner Ashore. Louise Imogen Guiney. AA; GoBC; JKCP
Ode for a Social Meeting. Oliver Wendell Holmes. BOHV
Ode for Ben Jonson, An. Robert Herrick. AWP; BEL; CoBE; DiPo; EG; EnLi-1; EnLit; InPo; InvP; JAWP; LoBV; PoE; PoFS; PoSa; SeCP; SeEP; TOP; TrGrPo; UnPo; WBP
(Ode for Him, An.) AnAnS-2; NoP; OAEP; OBS; SCEP-2; SeCV-1
(Ode for Him [Ben Jonson], An.) MaPo
Ode for Decoration Day. Henry Peterson. OHIP
"O gallant brothers of the generous South," *sel.* AA; FaBoBe
Ode for Decoration Day. Henry Timrod. PoRL
Ode for Him, An. Robert Herrick. *See* Ode for Ben Jonson, An.
Ode for Music on St. Cecilia's Day. Pope. CEP
Descend, Ye Nine, *sel.* GN
Ode for Soft Voice. Michael McClure. NeAP
Ode for the American Dead in Korea. Thomas McGrath. NePoEA; PoPl
Ode for the Burial of a Citizen. John Ciardi. LiTM (1970 ed.); MiAP
Ode for the Fourth of July, 1876, An. James Russell Lowell. CoBA
Flawless His Heart, *sel.* MC; PAH
Ode for the New Year, An. *At. to* John Gay. OxBoLi
Ode for Washington's Birthday. Oliver Wendell Holmes. DD
(Washington's Birthday.) PEDC
Ode—Imitated from the Psalms. Nicolas Joseph Laurent Gilbert, *tr. fr. French by* Thomas Walsh. CAW
Ode in a Night of Overhanging Weather. Vincent McHugh. WaKn
Ode in Honor of St. Cecilia's Day, An. Dryden. *See* Alexander's Feast.
Ode in Imitation of Alcaeus, An. Sir William Jones. *See* What Constitutes a State?
Ode in Imitation of Horace, An. Congreve. PeRV
Ode, in Imitation of Pastor Fido. George Lyttelton. CEP
Ode in May. Sir William Watson. MoBrPo (1942 ed.); OBEV; OBVV; PoVP; WGRP
Ode in Memory of the American Volunteers Fallen for France. Alan Seeger. PAH
Ode in the Praise of Sack, An. *Unknown.* OBS
Ode in Time of Hesitation, An. William Vaughn Moody. AmePo; AmPP; AnFE; AP; APA; ATP; CoAnAm; HBV; OxBA; PaA; PAH; TOP
Sels.
No Hint of Stain, *st.* 9. AA
Robert Gould Shaw, *sts.* 5 *and* 6. AA
Ode Inscribed to the Earl of Sunderland at Windsor, An. Thomas Tickell. OBEC
Ode Inscribed to W. H. Channing. Emerson. AmePo; AmP; AmPP; AnNE; AP; CoBA; ILP; MAmP; MWA-1; NoP; OxBA; PPON, *abr.*; TOP; WoL
"God who made New Hampshire, The," *sel.* ViBoPo
Ode Occasion'd by the Death of Mr. Thomson. William Collins. *See* Ode on the Death of Mr. Thomson.
Ode of Lament. Randolph Jeck. WhC
Ode on a Distant Prospect of Clapham Academy. Thomas Hood. CBEP
Ode on a Distant Prospect of Eton College. Thomas Gray. ATP (1935 ed.); BEL; CABA; CEP; CoBE; EiCL; EiCP; EiPP; EnLi-2 (1949 ed.); EnLit; EnPE; ExPo; FosPo; GTBS; GTBS-D; GTBS-P; GTBS-W; GTSE; GTSL; LiTB; LiTG; NoP; OAEP; OBEC; OuHeWo; PAn; PoE; PoEL-3; SeCeV; StP; TOP; ViBoPo
(On a Distant Prospect of Eton College.) HBV
Where Ignorance Is Bliss, *sel.* TreF
Ode on a Grecian Urn. Keats. AnEnPo; AnFE; AtBAP; ATP; AWP; BEL; BoC; BoLiVe; BWP; CABA; CaFP; CBEP; CBV; ChER; CoBE; DiPo; EnL; EnLi-2; EnLit; EnRP; EPN; ERoP-2; ExPo; FaBoBe; FaBoEn; FaFP; FaPL; FiP; ForPo; FosPo; GTBS-W; GTSL; HBV; HBVY; HoPM; ILP; InP; InPo; JAWP; LiTB; LiTG; LoBV; MaPo; MaSP; MBW-2; MCCG; MemP; MERP; NoP; OAEP; OBEV; OBNC; OBRV; OHFP; OuHeWo; PAn; PeER; PIA; Po; PoAn; PoE; PoEL-4; PoeP; PoFS; PoIE; PoMa; PoPo; PoSa; PTK; SeCeV; ShBV-4; StP; TOP; TreF; TrGrPo; UnPo; WBP; WHA
(On a Grecian Urn.) ViBoPo
Ode on a Sermon Against Glory. Mark Akenside. CEP; EiCL
Ode on a Storm. *Unknown.* EiCL
Ode on Advancing Age. Richard Watson Dixon. NBM
Ode on Conflicting Claims. Richard Watson Dixon. VA
Ode on Contemplating Clapham Junction. Christopher Middleton. *Fr.* Herman Moon's Hourbook. NePoEA-2
Ode on Indolence. Keats. EnRP; ERoP-2; GTBS-W; LiTB; MERP; OBNC

Ode on Intimations of Immortallty from Recollections of Early Childhood. Wordsworth. *See* Ode: Intimations of Immortality . . .
Ode on Leaving the Great Town. Thomas Randolph. *See* Ode to Mr. Anthony Stafford to Hasten Him into the Country, An.
Ode on Lyric Poetry. Sir James Marriott. Po
Ode on Melancholy. Keats. AnFE; AtBAP; ATP; BEL; BoLiVe; BWP; CABA; CaFP; CBEP; CBV; CoBE; DiPo; EnL; EnLi-2; EnLit; EnRP; EPN; ERoP-2; ExPo; FaBoEn; FiP; ForPo; GTBS-W; ILP; LiTB; LO; MaPo; MBW-2; MERP; NoP; OAEP; OBEV; OBNC; PAn; PeER; PoE; PoEL-4; PoFS; PoIE; PoRA; SeCeV; StP; TOP; TreFS; TrGrPo; VaPo
(“No, no, go not to Lethe, neither twist.”) EG
(On Melancholy.) HBV; ViBoPo
Cancelled [First] Stanza of the Ode on Melancholy, *sel.* ERoP-2; SyP
Ode on Miss Harriet Hanbury at Six Years Old, An. Sir Charles Hanbury Williams. OBEC
Ode on Science, *with music.* Jezaniah Sumner. TrAS
Ode on Solitude. Pope. ATP; AWP; BoPe; CEP; DiPo; EiCL; ExPo; FiP; FIW; GoBC; HBV; HBVY; InPo; JAWP; MBW-1; NoP; OAEP; OBEC; OnPP; OTPC (1923 ed.); PoE; PoFS; PoIE; PoPl; PoRA; SeCeV; SeCL; TreFS; ViBoPo; WBP
(Contented Man, The.) InMe
(Happy the Man.) MaRV
(“Happy the man whose wish and care.”) EG
(Ode to Solitude.) InvP
(Quiet Life, The.) ALV; GTBS; GTBS-D; GTBS-P; GTBS-W; PoPo; PoToHe
(Solitude.) BoLiVe; CBEP; FaFP; GTSE; GTSL; MCCG; NeHB; PG (1955 ed.); TrGrPo
Ode on Superstition, *sel.* Vincenzo Monti, *tr. fr. Italian by* William Dean Howells.
“Tyrant has fallen, The.” PoFr
Ode on the Birth of Our Saviour, An. Robert Herrick. GN, *sts.* 1-3; OTPC (1923 ed.)
Instead of Neat Inclosures, *sel.* ChTr
Ode on the Celebration of the Battle of Bunker Hill, June 17, 1825, *sel.* Grenville Mellen.
Lonely Bugle Grieves, The. AA
Ode on the Death of a Favorite [*or* Favourite] Cat, Drowned in a Tub [*or* Bowl] of Goldfishes. Thomas Gray. ATP; BEL; CBEP; CEP; EiCL; EiCP; EnLi-2 (1949 ed.); EnLit; FaBoBe; HoPM; NeHB; NoP; OAEP; OBEC; OTPC (1923 ed.); PAn; PoE; PoEL-3; TOP; VaPo; YAT
(Cat and the Fish, The.) WiR
(On a Favorite [*or* Favourite] Cat, Drowned in a Tub of Goldfishes.) BeLS; GBV (1952 ed.); GN; GTBS; GTBS-D; GTBS-P; GTBS-W; GTSE; GTSL; InvP; LiTB; LiTG; MCCG; OBEV; OnSP; ShBV-2
(On the Death of a Favourite [*or* Favorite] Cat, Drowned in a Tub of Goldfishes.) BOHV; CIV; ExPo; HBV; InMe; PoLF; PoRA; SeCeV; TDP
Ode on the Death of His Father. Jorge Manrique, *tr. fr. Spanish by* Longfellow. WoL, *abr.*
(Coplas on the Death of His Father, the Grandmaster of Santiago, *tr. by* Thomas Walsh.) CAW
Ode on the Death of Mr. Thomson. William Collins. EiCP; EiPP; OBEC
(Ode Occasion'd by the Death of Mr. Thomson.) EiCL
(Ode on the Death of Thomson.) CBEP; PeER; SeCePo
Ode on the Death of the Duke of Wellington. Tennyson. BEL; HBV; OBVV; PCD; PoVP; TOP; UnPo (1st ed.; VA; ViPo; ViPP
Sels.
“People's voice, A! we are a people yet.” ACV
Strength—Human. SoP
“Thank him who isled us here, and roughly set.” PoFr
What Know We Greater than the Soul? *br. sel.* MaRV
Ode on the Death of Thomson. William Collins. *See* Ode on the Death of Mr. Thomson.
Ode on the Despoilers of Learning in an American University (1947), An. Yvor Winters. ExPo; StP
Ode on the Intimations of Immortality from Recollections of Early Childhood. Wordsworth.
See Ode: Intimations of Immortality . . .
Ode on the Morning of Christ's Nativity. Milton. *See* On the Morning of Christ's Nativity.
Ode on the Pleasure Arising from Vicissitude. Thomas Gray. CEP, *abr.*; EiCP; GTBS; GTBS-D; GTBS-P; GTBS-W; GTSE; GTSL; OBEC; PeER
Ode on the Poetical Character. William Collins. CEP; EiCL; EiCP; EiPP; EnPE; EnRP; ERoP-1; OAEP; PeER; PoEL-3; PoFS; StP
Ode on the Poets. Keats. *See* Ode: “Bards of Passion and of Mirth.”
Ode, An, on the Popular Superstitions of the Highlands of Scotland [Considered as the Subject of Poetry]. William Collins. CEP; EiCL; EiCP; EiPP; EnPE; EnRP; OAEP; OBEC
St. Kilda, *sel.* FaBoEn
Ode on the Spring. Thomas Gray. CEP; EiCP; GTBS; GTBS-D; GTBS-P; GTBS-W; GTSE; GTSL; HBV
Peopled Air, The, *sel.* OA
Ode on Venice. Byron. CABL
“Name of Commonwealth is past and gone, The,” *fr.* IV. PoFr
Ode pour l'Election de Son Sepulchre. Ezra Pound. *See* E. P. Ode pour l'Election de Son Sepulchre.
Ode Recited at the Harvard Commemoration, July 21, 1865. James Russell Lowell. AA; AmPP; AP; CoBA; HBV; MAmP; PaA; PAH; TOP
(Commemoration Ode, The.) AnAmPo
Sels.
Abraham Lincoln, VI. PAP
(Lincoln.) AnNE
(Our Martyr-Chief.) OHIP; PEDC, *abr.*
(“Such was he, our Martyr-Chief.”) InP
Bow Down, Dear Land, XI, *abr., and* XII. DD
“I, with uncovered head,” *fr.* VIII *and* XII. OHIP
“Life may be given in many ways,” *fr.* V *and* VI. LiPo
“Many loved Truth, and lavished life's best oil,” III, VIII, *and* XII. PoFr
(Harvard Commemoration Ode, III *and* IV.) PFY
Martyr Chief, The, *abr., fr.* VI. OQP
(Commemoration Ode, The.) PGD
(Lincoln.) DD
Ode Sung in the Town Hall, Concord, July 4, 1857. Emerson. *See* Ode: “O tenderly the haughty day.”
Ode Sung on the Occasion of Decorating the Graves of the Confederate Dead. Henry Timrod. *See* Ode: “Sleep sweetly in your humble graves.”
Ode to a Bobtailed Cat. *Unknown.* BOHV; CIV
Ode to a Butterfly. Thomas Wentworth Higginson. AA; FaBoBe; HBV
Ode to a Chosen Girl. Hywel ab Owain Gwynedd, *tr. fr. Welsh by* Gwyn Williams. PrWP
Ode to a Dental Hygienist. Earnest A. Hooton. FiBHP; WhC
Ode to a Friend. William Mason. OBEC
Ode to a Lady Whose Lover Was Killed by a Ball. Byron. ERoP-2
Ode to a Model. Vladimir Nabokov. PoPl
Ode to a Nightingale. Keats. AnEnPo; AnFE; AtBAP; ATP; AWP; BEL; BoLiVe; BWP; CABA; CaFP; CBV; ChER; CoBE; DiPo; EnL; EnLi-2; EnLit; EnRP; EPN; ERoP-2; ExPo; FaBoBe; FaBoEn; FaFP; FaPL; FiP; ForPo; FosPo; GBV; GTBS; GTBS-D; GTBS-P; GTBS-W; GTSE; GTSL; HBV; HBVY; ILP; InP; InPo; JAWP; LiTB; LiTG; LoBV; MaPo; MasP; MBW-2; MCCG; MemP; MERP; NoP; OAEP; OBEV; OBNC; OBRV; OtMeF; OuHeWo; PAn; PeER; PIA; Po; PoAn; PoE; PoEL-4; PoeP; PoFS; PoIE; PoPo; PoRA; PTK; SeCeV; ShBV-3; StP; TOP; TreF; TrGrPo; UnPo; VaPo; WBP; WoL
(Ode to the Nightingale.) WHA
(To a Nightingale.) ChTr; ViBoPo
Sels.
Magic Casements. FaBV
Nightingale, The, *st.* 7. DD
Ode to a Side Car. “J. P. H.” PaA
Ode to a Water Nymph. William Mason. Po
Ode to a Young Lady, Somewhat Too Sollicitous about Her Manner of Expression. William Shenstone. CEP
Ode to an Æolus's Harp. William Mason. WaPE
Ode to Anactoria. Sappho. *See* To a Bride.
Ode to Aphrodite. Sappho, *tr. fr. Greek.* AWP, *tr. by* William Ellery Leonard; EnLi-1, *tr. by* Sir Edwin Arnold;

OuHeWo. *tr. by* Sir Edwin Arnold, *wr. at. to* John Addington Symonds
(Immortal Aphrodite. *tr. by* Lindley W. Hubbell.) LiTW
Ode to Apollo. Keats. ERoP-2
Ode to Arnold Schoenberg. Charles Tomlinson. NePoEA-2
Ode to Autumn. Thomas Hood. *See* Autumn ("I saw old Autumn").
Ode to Autumn. Keats. *See* To Autumn.
Ode to Beauty. Emerson. AmPP (5th ed.); AP; ForPo; MWA-1; PoEL-4
Ode to Chloris. Charles Cotton. CavP
Ode to Cupid. Charles Cotton. CavP
Ode to Duty. Wordsworth. AWP; BEL; EnLit; EnRP; EPN; ERoP-1; GTBS; GTBS-D; GTBS-P; GTBS-W; GTSE; GTSL; HBV; InPo; JAWP; MaRV; MBW-2; MERP; NoP; OBEV; OBRV; PoFS; TOP; TreFS; TRV; WBP; WGRP
Stern Daughter of the Voice of God, *sel.* HBVY
Ode to England, *sels.* William Wilberforce Lord. AA
Keats.
Wordsworth.
Ode to Ethiopia. Paul Laurence Dunbar. BALP
Ode to Eve. Edwin Meade Robinson. InMe
Ode to Evening. William Collins. AnEnPo; AnFE; ATP; AWP; BEL; BWP; CABA; CaFP; CBEP; CBV; CEP; CoBE; EiCL; EiCP; EiPP; EnL; EnLi-2; EnPE; EnRP; ExPo; FaBoBe; FaBoEn; FosPo; GTSL; HBV; InP; InPo; JAWP; LiTB; LiTG; LoBV; MasP; NoP; OAEP; OBEC; OBEV; OuHeWo; PeER; PIA; Po; PoE; PoEL-3; PoFS; SeCePo; SeCeV; StP; TOP; TreFT; TrGrPo; UnPo (1st ed.); ViBoPo; WBP; WHA
("If aught of oaten stop, or pastoral song.") EG
(To Evening.) AtBAP; GTBS; GTBS-D; GTBS-P; GTBS-W; GTSE; ShBV-4
Ode to Evening. Joseph Warton, *wr. at. to* Thomas Warton, the Younger. ATP; UnPo (1st ed.); WaPE
Ode to Fancy. Joseph Warton. CEP; EiPP; EnPE; WaPE
Invocation to Fancy, *sel.* OBEC
Ode to Fanny, *sel.* Keats.
"Ah! dearest love, sweet home of all my fears." ChER
Ode to Fear. William Collins. CEP; EiCL; EiCP; EiPP; EnPE; OAEP; Po; TrGrPo, *abr.*
Ode to Fidel Castro. Edward Field. CoPo
Ode to Fortune. Fitz-Greene Halleck *and* Joseph Rodman Drake. *Fr.* The Croaker Papers. AA
Ode to Freedom. Thomas of Strengnaes, *tr. fr. Swedish by* Elias Gordon. PoFr
Ode to Hengist and Horsa. Robinson Jeffers. SiSw
Ode to Himself ("Come leave the loathed stage"). Ben Jonson. AnAnS-2; SeCP; SeEP
(Ode, An: To Himself.) OBS; ReEn; AnAnS-2; SeCP; SeEP
(To Himself.) SeCL
Ode to Himself, An ("Where do'st thou careless lie"). Ben Jonson. AnAnS-2; AtBAP; EnRePo; ExPo; FaBoEn; LiTB; NoP; OAEP; OBS; PoEL-2; PoFr; QFR; SCEP-2; SeCePo; SeCeV; SeCP; SeCV-1; SeEP; TuPP
(To Himself.) SeCL
Ode to Himself. Sir Walter Raleigh. WhC
Ode to Horror. *Unknown.* WaPE
Ode to Independence, *sel.* Tobias Smollett.
Independence. OBEC
("Thy spirit, Independence, let me share!") PoFr
Ode to Jamestown. James Kirke Paulding. PAH
Ode to Joy. Frank O'Hara. NeAP
Ode to Joy. Schiller, *tr. fr. German by* Norman Macleod. LiTW
Ode to Leven Water. Tobias Smollett. CEP; OBEV
Ode to Liberty. Thomas Chatterton. *See* Freedom's War Song.
Ode to Liberty. Shelley. BEL; MBW-2
"Thou huntress swifter than the moon," *sel.* PoFr
Ode to Life. Anna Letitia Barbauld. SoP
Ode to Machines. Louis Ginsberg. PoMa
Ode to Memory. William Shenstone. Po
Ode to Mercy. William Collins. EiCP
Ode to Michael Goldberg's Birth and Other Births. Frank O'Hara. NeAP
Ode to Mirth. Tobias George Smollett. WaPE
Ode to Mr. [*or* Master] Anthony Stafford to Hasten Him into the Country, An. Thomas Randolph. AnAnS-2; FaBoEn; HBV; OBEV; OBS; SeCL; SeEP; ViBoPo
("Come, spur away.") EG
(Ode on Leaving the Great Town.) GoTL
Ode to Mr. F ——, An. Allan Ramsay. CEP
Ode to Morning. William Mason. WaPE
Ode to Mother Carey's Chicken. Theodore Watts-Dunton. *See* Mother Carey's Chicken.
Ode to Myself, An. Thomas Dermody. OnYI
Ode to Naples. Shelley. ATP (1935 ed.)
"I stood within the City disinterred," *sel.* EPN
Ode to Napoleon Buonaparte, *sel.* Byron.
Washington. DD; MC; OHIP; PaA; PAH; PAL
(Cincinnatus of the West, The.) PoRL
Ode to New Jersey. Elias F. Carr. PoRL
Ode to Our Young Pro-Consuls of the Air. Allen Tate. AmPP (3d ed.)
(Ode: "Once more the country calls.") WaP
Ode to Peace. *Unknown.* PAH
Ode to Pity. William Collins. CEP; EiCP; EiPP; EnPE
Ode to Psyche. Keats. CABA; CaFP; CBEP; ChER; DiPo; EnRP; EPN; ERoP-2; GTBS-W; HBV; LiTB; LoBV; MaPo; MBW-2; MERP; NoP; OAEP; OBEV; OBNC, OBRV; PeER; PIA; PoEL-4; PP; StP; WHA
(To Psyche.) ViBoPo
"Surely I dreamt to-day, or did I see," *sel.* LO
Ode to Quinbus Flestrin. Pope. OAEP
Ode to Rain. *Unknown, tr. fr. Russian.* PCH
Ode to Rhys ap Maredudd of Tywyn. Dafydd Nanmor, *tr. fr. Welsh by* Sir Idris Bell. PrWP
Ode to Simplicity. William Collins. BEL; CEP; EiCP; EiPP; EnLi-2 (1949 ed.); EnRP; GTSL; NoP; OBEC; OBEV; PoFS; UnPo (1st ed.)
Ode to Slavdom, *sel.* Petar Preradovic, *tr. fr. Croatian by* Paul Selver.
"But so long as/ This prison-planet." PoFr
Ode to Sleep. Tobias George Smollett. WaPE
Ode to Solitude. James Grainger. *See* Solitude.
Ode to Solitude. Pope. *See* Ode on Solitude.
Ode to Spain—after the Revolution of March, *sel.* Manuel José Quintana, *tr. fr. Spanish by* Thomas Walsh.
"Swear, 'Rather death than tyrants in the land!'" PoFr
Ode to Spring in the Metropolis, An. Sir Owen Seaman. FiBHP; WhC
Ode to Stephen Dowling Bots, Dec'd. "Mark Twain." *Fr.* The Adventures of Huckleberry Finn. FiBHP
Ode to Thaliarchus. Horace. *See* To Thaliarchus.
Ode to the Cambro-Britains and Their Harp, His Ballad of Agincourt. Michael Drayton. *See* Agincourt.
Ode to the Chinese Paper Snake. Richard Eberhart. CrMA
Ode to the Confederate Dead. Allen Tate. AnFE; AP; ATP (1953 ed.); CABA; CoAnAm; FaBoMo; InPo; LiTA; LiTM; MAP; MoAB; MoAmPo; MoPo; MoVE; NoP; NP; OxBA; PIA; PoIE; ReMP; SeCeV; TwAmPo; UnPo; ViBoPo (1958 ed.)
Ode to the Confederate Dead. Henry Timrod. *See* Ode: "Sleep sweetly in your humble graves."
Ode to the Country Gentlemen of England, An, *sel.* Mark Akenside.
England Unprepared for War. OBEC
Ode to the Cuckoo. Michael Bruce. EiPP
Ode to the Departing Year. Samuel Taylor Coleridge. EnRP; MERP
Ode to the Earl of Northumberland, *sel.* Christopher Smart.
On a Bed of Guernsey Lilies. BWP; OBEC
Ode to the Evening Star. Mark Akenside. CEP; OBEC
(Nightingale, The.) HBV, *sl. abr.*; OBEV, *sl. abr.*
(To the Evening Star.) PoEL-3
Ode to the Fatherland, *sel.* Manuel María Flores, *tr. fr. Spanish by* Alice Stone Blackwell.
"We lift our standard to the mountain top." PoFr
Ode to the Flag. Charles C. Crellin. PEDC
Ode to the Fourth of July, *with music.* Daniel George. TrAS
Ode to the Framers of the Frame Bill, An. Byron. CoMu
Ode to the Germans. Thomas Campbell. PoFr
Ode to the Hayden Planetarium. Arthur Guiterman. ImOP
Ode to the Hon. Miss Carteret. Ambrose Philips. WaPE
Ode to the Human Heart. Laman Blanchard. BOHV; InMe; NA
Ode to the Idiots. Arthur Pfister. WSL
Ode to the Inhabitants of Pennsylvania. *Unknown.* PAH
Ode to the Maguire. *At. to* Eochadh O'Hussey. *See* O'Hussey's Ode to the Maguire.

Ode to the Mediterranean. George Santayana. *See* Ode: "Of thee the Northman . . ."
Ode to the Moon. Thomas Hood. OBVV
Ode to the Negative Universe. Michael McClure. FRC
Ode to the Nightingale. Keats. *See* Ode to a Nightingale.
Ode to the Nightingale, *parody.* John Kendall. InMe
Ode to the North-east Wind. Charles Kingsley. GN; GTBS
(North-east Wind, The, *much abr.*) OTPC
Ode to the Pious Memory of the Accomplished Young Lady, Mrs. Anne Killigrew. Dryden. *See* To the Pious Memory of the Accomplished Young Lady, Mrs. Anne Killigrew.
Ode to the Present Century. Thomas Merton. JKCP (1955 ed.)
Ode to the Sea. Howard Baker. OxBA; UnPo (1st ed.)
Ode to the Setting Sun. Francis Thompson. GoBC
Sels.
"If with exultant tread." OHIP
"Now that the red glare of thy fall is blown." OBNC
Sun, The. MoAB; MoBrPo
Ode to the Sky of the New Atlantis. Emilio Oribe, *tr. fr. Spanish by* Muna Lee. PoFr
Ode to the Smiths. Charles Thomas. WSL
Ode to the Spirit of Earth in Autumn, *sel.* George Meredith.
"Great Mother Nature! teach me, like thee." EPN
Ode to the Virgin. Petrarch. *See* To the Virgin Mary.
Ode to the Virginian Voyage. Michael Drayton. *See* To the Virginian Voyage.
Ode to the West Wind. Shelley. AnEnPo; AnFE; ATP; AWP; BEL; BoLiVe; BoNaP; BWP; CABA; CaFP; CBEP; CBV; CH; CoBE; DiPo; EnL; EnLi-2; EnLit; EnRP; EPN; ERoP-2; ExPo; FaBoBe; FaBoEn; FaBV; FaFP; FaPL; FiP; ForPo; FosPo; GTBS; GTBS-D; GTBS-P; GTBS-W; GTSE; GTSL; HBV; ILP; InP; InPo; JAWP; LiTB; LiTG; LoBV; MaPo; MBW-2; MCCG; OAEP; OBEV; OBRV; OHFP; MemP; MERP; NoP; OBNC; OTPC (1946 ed.); OuHeWo; PAn; PeER; PIA; PoAn; PoE; PoEL-4; PoFS; PoIE; PoLF; PoMa; PoPo; PoRA; PoSa; SeCeV; ShBV-4; StP; TOP; TreFS; TrGrPo; UnPo; VaPo; ViBoPo; WBP; WHA; YAT
Sels.
"Make me thy lyre, even as the forest is." MaRV
West Wind, The, 2 *ll.* PCH
Ode to Tobacco. Charles Stuart Calverley. ALV; BOHV; FiBHP; HBV; InMe; TOP; WhC
Ode to Winter. Thomas Campbell. GTBS; GTBS-D; GTBS-P; GTBS-W; GTSE; GTSL
Ode to Wisdom. Elizabeth Carter. OBEC
Ode to Work in Springtime. Thomas R. Ybarra. BOHV; HBMV
Ode to Zion. Judah Halevi, *tr. fr. Hebrew by* Nina Davis Salaman. TrJP
Ode, An, Upon a Question Moved, Whether Love Should Continue for Ever? Lord Herbert of Cherbury. AnAnS-2; LiTL; MeLP; MePo; OBS; SeCP; SeEP
Sels.
"Long, their fixed eyes to heaven bent." LO
"O no, beloved, I am most sure." ViBoPo
Ode upon Doctor Harvey. Abraham Cowley. PoEL-2
"Coy Nature (which remain'd, though aged grown)," *sel.* Par
Ode upon Liberty, *sel.* Abraham Cowley.
"'Tis morning; well; I fain would yet sleep on." PoFr
Ode, An, upon Occasion of His Majesties Proclamation in the Year 1630. Sir Richard Fanshawe. *See* Now War is All The World About.
Ode Which Was Prefixed to a Prayer Booke Given to a Young Gentlewoman, An. Richard Crashaw. *See* Prayer: "Lo here a little volume. . ."
Ode Written at Vale-Royal Abbey in Cheshire. Thomas Warton, the Younger. CoBE
Ode Written during the Battle of Dunkirk, May, 1940, *sel.* Sir Herbert Read.
"Happy are those who can relieve/ suffering with prayer," V. MaRV
Ode Written during the War with America, 1814, *sel.* Robert Southey.
Bower of Peace, The. MC; PAH
Ode Written in the Beginning of the Year [*or* Ode Written in] 1746. William Collins. *See* How Sleep The Brave.
Ode Written in the Peak[e], An. Michael Drayton. OBS; ReIE
Odell. James Stephens. MoAB; MoBrPo
Odes, *sels.* Anacreon, *tr. fr. Greek by* Thomas Moore.
"As late I sought the spangled bowers." OuHeWo
"Give me the harp of epic song." OuHeWo
"I care not for the idle state." OuHeWo
"I saw the smiling bard of pleasure." OuHeWo
"Listen to the Muse's lyre." OuHeWo
"Sculptor, wouldst thou glad my soul." OuHeWo; UnTE
"Vulcan! hear your glorious task." OuHeWo
"Why so coy, my lovely maid," *tr. by* Ambrose Philips. EiCL
"Women tell me every day, The." LoBV; OuHeWo
Odes, *sels.* Hafiz, *tr. fr. Persian.*
"Comrades, the morning breaks," II, *tr. by* Richard Le Gallienne. AWP
"Days, The, of spring are here! the eglantine," X, *tr. by* Gertrude Lowthian Bell. AWP; JAWP; WBP
"Grievous folly shames my sixtieth year, A," IV, *tr. by* Richard Le Gallienne. AWP
"I cease not from desire," IX, *tr. by* Gertrude Lowthian Bell. AWP; WoL
"I have borne the anguish of love," XI, *tr. by* John Hindley. AWP; JAWP; OuHeWo; WBP
"I said to heaven that glowed above," XII, *tr. by* Emerson. AWP; OuHeWo
"Jewel of the secret treasury, The," VI, *tr. by* Gertrude Lowthian Bell. AWP; JAWP; LiTW; WBP
"Lady that hast my heart within thy hand," VIII, *tr. by* Gertrude Lowthian Bell. AWP; LiTW
"Oft have I said, I say it once more," XIII, *tr. by* Emerson. AWP; OuHeWo
"Rose is not the rose unless thou see, The," III, *tr. by* Richard Le Gallienne. AWP; LiTW
"Saki, for God's love, come and fill my glass," I, *tr. by* Richard Le Gallienne. AWP
"Where is my ruined life, and where the fame," V, *tr. by* Gertrude Lowthian Bell. AWP
"Wind from the east, oh, lapwing of the day," VII, *tr. by* Gertrude Lowthian Bell. AWP
Odes, *sels.* Horace, *tr. fr. Latin.*
I, 3. To the Ship in Which Virgil Sailed to Athens ("Sic te diva potens Cypri"), *tr. by* Dryden. AWP
I, 4. To Lucius Sestius ("Solvitur acris hiems"), *tr. by* Sir Theodore Martin. OuHeWo
(Winter to Spring, *tr. by* Louis MacNeice.) LiTW
I, 5. To Pyrrha ("Quis multa gracilis"), *tr. by* Milton. AWP; CLwM; JAWP; WBP
(Another to the Same, *tr. by* William Browne.) WiR
(Fifth Ode of Horace, *tr. by* Milton.) EnLoPo; MaPo (1961 ed.); PoEL-3
(For Whom, Pyrrha? *tr. by* Milton.) LiTW
(Horace to Pyrrha, *tr. by* Eugene Field.) LHV
(To a Girl, *tr. by* Milton.) WiR
(To Pyrrha, *tr. by* Goldwin Smith.) EnLi-1; OuHeWo
I, 9. To Thaliarchus ("Vides ut alta"), *tr. by* Dryden. AWP; CavP; JAWP; MBW-1; PeRV; WBP
(Ode to Thaliarchus.) LiTW
I, 11. To Leuconöe ("Tu ne quaesieris"). AA, *tr. by* Roswell Martin Field, *and by* Eugene Field; ALV, *tr. by* Eugene Field; LoBV, *tr. by* Charles Start Calverley
(Ad Leuconoen, *par. by* Franklin P. Adams.) AWP; JAWP; WBP
(Ask Not Ungainly, *tr. by* Ezra Pound.) CTC
(Mistrust To-Morrow, *tr. by* Charles Stuart Calverley.) OnPM
I, 13. Tell Me, Lydia ("Cum tu, Lydia"), *tr. by* William Boscawen. OnPM
(To the Polyandrous Lydia, *par. by* Franklin P. Adams.) HBMV
I, 14. The Ship of State ("O navis, referent"), *tr. by* William Ewart Gladstone. AWP; JAWP; WBP; OuHeWo, *tr. by* Sir Stephen E. De Vere
(Seek a Haven, *tr. by* Charles Stuart Calverley.) OnPM
I, 21. Invocation: "Maidens young and virgins tender" ("Dianam tenerae dicite virgines"), *tr. by* Louis Untemeyer. AWP; JAWP; WBP
I, 22. Integer Vitae, *tr. by* Sir Theodore Martin. EnLi-1
(To Aristius Fuscus.) OuHeWo
I, 23. To Chloe ("Vitas hinnuleo"), *tr. by* Austin Dobson. AWP; JAWP; WBP; LiTW, *tr. by* Patrick Branwell Brontë; OuHeWo, *tr. by* Goldwin Smith

(Time to Choose a Lover, *tr. by* Patrick Branwell Brontë.) OnPM; UnTE

I, 25. Young Men Come Less Often, The—Isn't It So? ("Parcius iunctas quatiunt fenestras"), *tr. by* Robert Fitzgerald. ErPo

(Passing of Lydia, The, *tr. by* Louis Untermeyer.) UnTE

I, 31. By the Flat Cup ("Quid dedicatum"), *tr. by* Ezra Pound. CTC

I, 33. Albi, Ne Doleas ("Albi, ne doleas"), *tr. by* Austin Dobson. AWP

(It Always Happens, *tr. by* Thomas Charles Baring.) UnTE

I, 37. The Death of Cleopatra ("Nunc est bibendum"), *tr. by* Sir Stephen E. De Vere. EnLi-1; OuHeWo

I, 38. Persian Fopperies ("Persicos odi"), *tr. by* William Cowper. AWP; JAWP; WBP; WoL

(Frippery, *tr. by* L. R. Lind.) LiTW

(I Hate Their Empty Shows, *tr. by* William Cowper). OnPM

(Persian Pomp, *tr. by* William Cowper.) EnLi-1

(Persicos Odi, *par. by* Franklin P Adams.) HBMV

(To His Cup-Bearer, *tr. by* Sir Theodore Martin.) OuHeWo

(To His Servant, *tr. by* Christopher Smart.) EiCL

II, 3. To Quintus Dellius ("Aequam memento"), *tr. by* Herman Merivale. OuHeWo

II, 4. Ad Xanthium Phoceum ("Ne sit ancillae"), *par. by* Franklin P. Adams. AWP; JAWP; WBP

II, 5. Too Young for Love ("Nondum subacta"), *tr. by* Louis Untermeyer. UnTE

II, 7. "Pompeius, best of all my comrades, you and I" ("O saepe mecum"), *tr. by* John Wight. WaaP

(Returned Warrior, *tr. by* John Wight.) LiTW

II, 8. Barine, the Incorrigible ("Ulla si iuris"), *tr. by* Louis Untermeyer. UnTE

("Did any punishment attend," *tr. by* Sir Charles Sedley.) PeRV

II, 10. To Licinius ("Rectius vives"), *tr. by* william Cowper. AWP; JAWP; WBP

(Golden Mean, The.) HBV, *tr. by* William Cowper

(To Licinius Murena, *tr. by* William Cowper.) EnLi-1; OuHeWo

(Translated out of Horace, which begins Rectius vives, *tr. by* Sir Philip Sidney.) FCP; ReIE

Moderation, *br. sel., tr. by* William Cowper. PoToHe (new ed.)

II, 11. To an Ambitious Friend ("Quid bellicosus"), *tr. by* Matthew Arnold. AWP

II, 14. To Postumus ("Eheu fugaces"), *tr. by* Sir Stephen Edward De Vere. LiTW; OuHeWo

II, 18. Vanity of Riches ("Non ebur neque aureum"), *tr. by* T. Rutherford Clark. WoL

III, 1. The Profane ("Odi profanum vulgus"), *par. by* Abraham Cowley. AWP

III, 2. "Let the youth hardened by a sharp soldier's life" ("Angustam amice"), *tr. by* Gardner Taplin *and* Richard Eberhart. WaaP

III. 9 The Reconciliation ("Donec gratus eram"). MeWo. *tr. by* Louis Untermeyer; OuHeWo, *tr. by* Sir Theodore Martin

(February 14, 22 B.C., *par. by* Franklin P. Adams.) InMe

(Teasing Lovers, The, *tr. by* Louis Untermeyer.) UnTE

III, 10. Extremum Tanain, *tr. by* Austin Dobson. AWP; JAWP; WBP

III, 13. To the Fountain of Bandusia ("O fons Bandusiae"), *tr. by* Eugene Field. AA; AWP; JAWP; WBP

(Bandusia, Stainless Mirror, *tr. by* Charles Stuart Calverley.) OnPM

(Fountain of Bandusia, The, *tr. by* Austin Dobson.) OuHeWo

(O Fons Bandusia, *tr. by* Austin Dobson.) VA

III, 18. To Faunus ("Faune, Nympharum"), *tr. by* Alfred Noyes. LiTW

III, 22. The Pine Tree for Diana ("Montium custos nemorumque"), *tr. by* Louis Untermeyer. AWP

III, 23. To Phidyle ("Caelo supinas si tuleris"), *tr. by* Austin Dobson. AWP

III, 28. Holiday ("Festo quid potius die"), *tr. by* Louis Untermeyer. AWP; JAWP; WBP

III, 29. To Maecenas ("Tyrrhena regum progenies"), *par. by* Dryden. AWP; JAWP; PoFr, *sel.*; WBP

(Happiness, 4*ll.*) TreF

(Happy the Man, *br. sel.*) MaRV

("Happy the man, and happy he alone.") OTD; PeRV

(Horat. Ode 29. Book 3.) CEP; SeCV-2

(Twenty-ninth Ode of the Third Book.) MBW-1

III, 30. This Monument Will Outlast ("Exegi monumentum aere perennius"), *tr. by* Ezra Pound. CTC

IV, 1. To Venus ("Intermissa, Venus"), *tr. by* Ben Jonson. AWP

("Again? New tumults in my breast?" *tr. by* Pope.) SiSw

IV, 3. Gift of Song, The ("Quem tu, Melpomene semel"), *tr. by* Christopher Smart. LiTW

IV, 7. "Snow dissolv'd no more is seen" ("Diffugere nives"), *tr. by* Samuel Johnson. CLwM; EiCL

(Diffugere Nives, *tr. by* A. E. Housman.) MaPo (1969 ed.); NoP

IV, 10. To Ligurinus ("O crudelis adhuc"), *par. by* Sir Edward Sherburne. CavP

IV, 11. To Phyllis ("Est mihi nonum"), *tr. by* Eugene Field. InMe

IV, 13. Revenge ("Audivere, Lyce"), *tr. by* Louis Untermeyer. AWP; WoL

Odes, *sels.* Pindar, *tr. fr. Greek.*

First Pythian Ode· *tr. by* Arthus S. Way. WoL

(Power of Music, The, *tr. by* H. T. Wade-Gery *and* C. M. Bowra, *sel.*) UnS

I Bless This Man, *fr.* Nemean Ode XI, *tr. by* Richmond Lattimore. SD

Island of the Blest, The, *fr.* Olympian Ode II, *tr. by* Gilbert West. OBEC

Nemean Ode, VI, *tr. by* Richmond Lattimore. LiTW

Olympian Ode, VI, *tr. by* Richmond Lattimore. LiTW

To Hiero the Syracusan, Olympian Ode I, *tr. by* Abraham Moore. EnLi-2; OuHeWo

(First Olympionique to Hiero of Syracuse, Victorious in the Horse-Race, The, *tr. by* Ambrose Philips.) ATP

Odes, *sel.* Pierre de Ronsard, *tr. fr. French by* Curtis Hidden Page.

Summer's Revel, The, II, 18. WoL

Odes, I-V. George Santayana.

"Gathering the echoes of forgotten wisdom," III. AmePo; AnAmPo; AnFE; APA; CoAnAm; TwAmPo

"My heart rebels against my generation," II. AmePo; AnFE; APA; ATP; CoAnAm; PoFr; TwAmPo; ViBoPo

"Of thee the Northman by his beachèd [*or* bleachèd] galley," V. AmePo; AnAmPo; AnFE; APA; CoAnAm; TwAmPo

(Ode to the Mediterranean.) EtS

"Slowly the black earth gains the yellow," IV. AmePo; AnFE; APA; CoAnAm; TwAmPo

"What god will choose me from this labouring nation," I. AmePo; AnFE; APA; CoAnAm

Odes of the Months, *sel.* Aneirin, *tr. fr. Welsh by* W. Probert.

"Month of January—smoky is the vale." FlW

Odes to Nea, *sels.* Thomas Moore.

"I pray you, let us roam no more." OBNC; OBRV

"Nay, tempt me not to love again." OBNC

Odi et Amo. Catullus, *tr. fr. Latin by* Ezra Pound. CTC

(Love and Hate, *tr. by* Thomas Moore.) OnPM

(To Lesbia, *tr. by* Abraham Cowley.) PoPl

O'Donnell Aboo. Michael Joseph McCann. OnYI

Odour, The. George Herbert. AnAnS-1; MaMe; MeP; OBS

Odor of a rose, The: light of a star. Shelley. Alexander Hay Japp. VA

Odor of Blood, The. Thomas McGrath. NePoEA

Odorous air, morn's messenger, now spread, The. The Crusaders Behold Jerusalem. Tasso. *Fr.* Jerusalem Delivered, III. CAW

Odorous shade lingers the fair day's ghost, An. Night. Henri de Régnier. AWP; JAWP; WBP

O'Driscoll drove with a song. The Host [*or* Folk] of the Air. W. B. Yeats. BrPo; CH; LoEn; OnYI; PoVP; SeCeV; VA; ViPo (1962 ed.)

O'Duffy's Ironsides. "Tom Moore, Jr." OnYI

Odysseus Dying. Sheila Wingfield. OxBI

Odysseus has come home, to the gully farm. The Homecoming. James K. Baxter. AnNZ

Odysseus heard the sirens; they were singing. The Sirens. John Manifold. LiTB; LiTM; MoBrPo (1962 ed.); Sonn; VaPo; WaP

Odysseus' Song to Calypso. Peter Kane Dufault. ErPo

Odyssey, The, *sels.* Homer, *tr. fr. Greek.*

Odyssey (continued)
Boar Hunt, The, *fr.* XIX, *tr. by* Robert Fitzgerald. FlW
"But Minerva fetch'd/ The winds from sea," *fr.* V, *tr. by* George Chapman. EnLi-1
"Downe to the king's most bright-kept baths they went," *fr.* IV, *tr. by* George Chapman. CTC
End of the Suitors, The, *fr.* XXII, *tr. by* George Chapman. OBS
Escape from Cyclop, The, *fr.* IX, *tr. by* George Chapman. LiTW
"For my part, I'le not meddle with the cause," *fr.* XIV, *tr. by* George Chapman. CTC
"From her bed's high and odoriferous roome," *fr.* IV, *tr. by* George Chapman. CTC
"In mean time flew our ships, and straight we fetched," *fr.* XII, *tr. by* George Chapman. TuPP
Nausicaa ("Now when they came to the bright running river"), *fr.* VI, *tr. by* Sir William Marris. LiTW
Nausicaa ("The servants then"), *fr.* VI, *tr. by* George Chapman. OBS
"Now this was the reply Odysseus made," *fr.* IX, *tr. by* Robert Fitzgerald. ML
"Our ship now pass'd the streights of th' ocean flood," *fr.* XII, *tr. by* George Chapman. RelE
Return of Ulysses, The, *abr., fr.* XXI, *tr. by* Bryant. BBV (1923 ed.)
Sacrifice, The, *fr.* III, *tr. by* George Chapman. OBS
Scylla and Charybdis, *fr.* XII, *tr. by* George Chapman. OBS
Sirens, The: Scylla and Charybdis, *fr.* XII, *tr. by* Pope. LiTW
(Ulysses and the Sirens, *shorter sel., tr. by* George Chapman.) ReEn
"Twelve herds of oxen, no lesse flockes of sheepe," *fr.* XIV, *tr. by* George Chapman. CTC
Ulysses and His Dog, *fr.* XVII, *tr. by* Pope. FiP; OBEC
("And a dog, lying there, lifted its head," *pr. tr. by* Martin Johnson.) LO
Ulysses Hears the Prophecies of Tiresias, *fr.* XI, *tr. by* George Chapman. LoBV
Ulysses in the Waves, *fr.* V, *tr. by* George Chapman. OBS
"Where neither king nor shepheard want comes near, *fr.* IV, *tr. by* George Chapman. CTC
Odyssey, The. Andrew Lang. GTBS-D; HBV; InP; LoBV; OBEV; OBNC; OBVV; OtMeF; PoLF; PoRA; PoVP; TOP; VA; ViBoPo; WHA; YT
Odyssey of a Snail, The. Federico García Lorca, *tr. fr. Spanish by* Roy Campbell. FlW
Odyssey of Big Boy. Sterling A. Brown. BANP; CDC
Oedipus. Thomas Blackburn. FaBoTw
Oedipus, *sels.* Dryden.
Incantation to Oedipus, *fr.* III, i. SiSw
Spell, A, *fr.* III, i. WiR
Oedipus. Edwin Muir. CMoP
Oedipus at Colonus, *sels.* Sophocles, *tr. fr. Greek.*
Choral Poem: "Land beloved of horsemen, fair, The," *tr. by* Robert Fitzgerald. LiTW
(Chorus: "Land of running horses, fair, The.") SiSw
Grove of Colonus, The, *tr. by* Walter Headlam. WoL
"Not to be born at all." PoG
Old Age, *tr. by* A. E. Housman. LiTW
(Chorus: "What man is he that yearneth," *tr. by* A. E. Housman.) AWP; JAWP; WBP
("Endure what life God gives and ask no longer span," *tr. by* W. B. Yeats.) DTC; OBMV
Oedipus at San Francisco. Donald Finkel. CoPo
Oedipus Rex [*or* Oedipus Tyrannus], *sels.* Sophocles, *tr. fr. Greek.*
Chorus: "Oh, may my constant feet not fail, *tr. by* Robert Whitelaw. WGRP
Chorus from "King Oedipus" ("For this one thing above all I would be praised a man"), *tr. by* W. B. Yeats. LiTW
Creon, *tr. by* F. Storr. PoFr
Oedipus to the Oracle. Wesley Trimpi. NePoEA
Oenone. Tennyson. BEL; EnLi-2; EnLit; EPN; MaVP; MBW-2; OAEP; OBRV; PoVP; ViBoPo; ViPo; ViPP; VP
Way to Power, The, *br. sel.* MaRV; OQP
Oenone's Complaint. George Peele. *Fr.* The Arraignment of Paris. EIL; OBSC
O'er a low couch the setting sun. The Baron's Last Banquet. Albert Gorton Greene. AA; BeLS
O'er all my songs the image of a face. The Negro Singer. James David Corrothers. BANP
O'er all the hill-tops. Wanderer's Night-Songs, II. Goethe, *tr. by* Longfellow. AWP; InP; JAWP; OnPM; PoPl; WBP; WoL
O'er better waves to speed her rapid course. Purgatory. Dante, *tr. by* Henry F. Cary. *Fr.* Divina Commedia. OuHeWo
O'er books the mind inactive lies. Conversation. Hannah More. *Fr.* Bas Bleu. OBEC
O'er Cambridge set the yeoman's mark. Lexington. Sidney Lanier. *Fr.* The Psalm of the West. PaA; PAH; PAL
O'er desert plains, and rushy meers. Song. William Shenstone. FaBoEn
O'er faded heath-flowers spun or thorny furze. The Gossamer. Charlotte Smith. ViBoPo
O'er golden sands my waters flow. The Enchanted Spring. George Darley. BoNaP; NBM
O'er Huron's wave the sun was low. The Battle of Bridgewater. *Unknown.* PAH
O'er many a sea, through many a tribe and nation. World without End. Catullus. LiTW
O'er sunbaked plains he winds his way. The Rattlesnake. Robert V. Carr. PoOW
O'er the glad waters of the dark-blue sea. The Corsair's Life [*or* Song of the Corsairs]. Byron. *Fr.* The Corsair, I. EtS
O'er the high and o'er the lowly. Our National Banner. Dexter Smith. PAH
O'er the level plains, where mountains greet me as I go. Time's Song. Winthrop Mackworth Praed. EnRP; NBM
O'er the men of Ethiopia she would pour her cornucopia. Husband and Heathen. Sam Walter Foss. BOHV
O'er the rough main with flowing sheet. The *Bonhomme Richard* and *Serapis* [*or* On the Memorable Victory by Captain Paul Jones]. Philip Freneau. PAH
O'er the rugged mountain's brow. Some Ruthless Rhymes, VI. Harry Graham. CenHV
O'er the Smooth Enamelled Green. Milton. *See* Song: "O'er the smooth. . ."
O'er the snow, through the air, to the mountain. Alpine Spirit's Song. Thomas Lovell Beddoes. OBNC
O'er the warrior gauntlet grim. Parricide. Julia Ward Howe. PAH
O'er the waste of waters cruising. Song: On Captain Barney's Victory over the Ship *General Monk.* Philip Freneau. PAH
O'er the Water to Charlie. Burns. FaBoCh
O'er the wet sands an insect crept. An Autograph. James Russell Lowell. AA
O'er the wide-spreading plains rolled the emigrant trains. The Dust of the Overland Trail. James Barton Adams. PoOW
O'er the Wild Gannet's Bath. George Darley. *Fr.* Ethelstan. ChTr; PoEL-4
(Runilda's Chant.) OnYI
O'er the yellow crocus on the lawn. A Russian Fantasy. Nathan Haskell Dole. AA
O'er town and cottage, vale and height. Valley Forge. Thomas Buchanan Read. *Fr.* The Wagoner of the Alleghanies. MC; PAH
Of a Cat's Look. John Heywood. SiCE; TuPP
Of a Certain Green-Eyed Monster. Esther Lilian Duff. HBMV
Of a Certain [*or* Certaine] Man. Sir John Harington. BOHV; SiCE
Of a Child That Had Fever. Christopher Morley. PFY
Of a Contented Mind. Thomas, Lord Vaux. CoBE; EIL; EnRePo; GoBC; MaRV; RelE; SiCE; TuPP
(Content.) OBSC; QFR
(On a Contented Mind.) HBV
Of a Cozener. John Hoskins. TuPP
Of a Dead Poet. Lord Alfred Douglas. JKCP (1926 ed.)
Of a Death in Winter ("Manshape, that shone"). Gerard Manley Hopkins. *Fr.* That Nature Is a Heraclitean Fire and of the Comfort of the Resurrection. BoW
Of a Death in Winter ("The ravenous earth that now wooes her"). John Donne. *Fr.* Elegie: Death. BoW
Of a Fair Lady Playing with a Snake. Edmund Waller. *See* To a Fair Lady Playing with a Snake.
Of a Fair Shrew. Sir John Harington. *See* Fair, Rich, and Young.
Of a Flatterer. John Davies of Hereford. SiCE
Of a great heroine [*or* heroin] I mean to tell. A Panegyric on Nelly. *Unknown, at. to* the Earl of Rochester. PeRV; UnTE, *abr.*

Of a Gull. Sir John Davies, *after the Latin of* Martial. SiCE; TuPP
Of a Husband Hang'd. John Heywood. ReIE
Of a little take a little. *Unknown.* OxNR
Of a Mistress. Sir Aston Cokayne. CavP; SeCL
Of a New-married Student. *Unknown.* CBV; SiCE; TuPP
Of a pendulum's mildness, with her feet up. A Timepiece. James Merrill. NePoEA-2
Of a Poet Patriot. Thomas MacDonagh. CAW; HBMV; OnYI; OxBI; PoFr
(On a Poet Patriot.) AnIV; TSW
Of a Precise Tailor. Sir John Harington. BOHV
Of a Rich Miser. George Turberville. EnRePo
Of a Rose, a Lovely Rose. *Unknown.* AtBAP; BoW; OBEV; OxBoCh
Of a Sheep's Eye. John Heywood. SiCE; TuPP
Of a Spider. Wilfrid Thorley. BrR; FaPON; PDV
Of a steady winking beat between. Paraphrase. Hart Crane. MoVE; TwAmPo
Of A' the Airts [the Wind Can Blow]. Burns. AWP; BEL; CoBE; EiCP; EiPP; EnLi-2; EnRP; FaPL; GoTS; InPo; JAWP; LoBV; NoP; OAEP; OBEC; OxBS; TOP; ViBoPo
(I Love My Jean.) CEP; EnLit; GN; HBV, *with* 2 *add. sts. by* John Hamilton; ILP; OTPC (1923 ed.)
(Jean.) GTBS; GTBS-D; GTBS-P; GTBS-W; GTSE; GTSL; MCCG; OBEV; PoMa; TreFS; TrGPo; WePo
(My Jean!) CBV; OuHeWo
Of a' the festivals we hear. Hallowe'en. John Mayne. HBV
Of a' the maids o fair Scotland. Young Benjie. *Unknown.* BaBo; ESPB; OBB; OxBB
Of a Vision of Hell, Which a Monk Had. Richard Watson Dixon. *Fr.* Mano; a Poetical History. VA
Of Adam's first wife, Lilith, it is told. Body's Beauty. Dante Gabriel Rossetti. The House of Life, LXXVIII. ATP (1953 ed.); EnL; HBV; ILP; MaVP; PAn; PoEL-5; PoVP; Sonn; TrGrPo; ViPo; ViPP
Of Albion's glorious ile the wonders whilst I write. The First Song. Michael Drayton. *Fr.* Polyolbion. ReIE
Of Alice in Wonderland. "Lewis Carroll." Alice's Adventures in Wonderland, *introd.* VA
Of all beasts he learned the language. Hiawatha's Brothers. Longfellow. *Fr.* The Song of Hiawatha, III. PCH
Of all chaste birds the phoenix doth excel. Of Rosalind [*or* Rosalynd]. Thomas Lodge. *Fr.* Rosalynde. GoBC; PoLi; ReIE; SiCE
Of all creatures women be best. What Women Are Not. *Unknown.* MeEL
Of all dear days is Christmas Day. Christmas Day. Margaret E. Sangster. PEDC
Of all great Nature's tones that sweep. Implicit Faith. Aubrey Thomas De Vere. *Fr.* May Carols. GoBC; MaRV
Of All He Would Do. Cecco Angiolieri da Siena. *See* Sonnet: Of All He Would Do.
Of all life's plagues I recommend to no man. On a Deaf Housekeeper. *Unknown.* BOHV
Of all mad creatures, if the learn'd are right. Why Did I Write? Pope. *Fr.* Epistle to Dr. Arbuthnot. OBEC
Of all my epigrams, reader, read not one. Ad Lectorem. John Weever. ReIE
Of all of the gruesome attempts at a towsome. Owen Seaman. Louis Untermeyer. *See also* Of all the mismated pairs ever created. ALV.
Of all our antic [*or* antick] sights and pageantry. The Medal; a Satire against Sedition. Dryden. CEP; EiPP
Of all sad words of tongue or pen. The Saddest Words. Whittier. *Fr.* Maud Muller. NePA; SiTL
Of all the animals on earth. Christmas Song. Elizabeth-Ellen Long. ChBR; SiSoSe
Of all the barbarous middle ages, that. Byron. Don Juan, XII. MERP
Of all the beasts that live, we must. Cats and Humans—All the Same. Anthony Euwer. CIV
Of all the beasts which we for our veneriall name. Michael Drayton. *Fr.* Polyolbion. OBS
Of all the birds from East to West. Chanticleer. Katharine Tynan. HBV; HBVY; MPB; OTPC; TiPo; TSW
Of all the birds that ever I see. *Unknown.* SeCSL
Of All the Birds That I Do Know. George Gascoigne. *See* Praise of Philip Sparrow, The.
Of all the birds that rove and sing. Jenny Wren. Walter de la Mare. BiS
Of all the birds upon the wing. The Blackbird. William Barnes. GTSE; HBV
Of all the burthens man must bear. Plutus, Cupid and Time. John Gay. *Fr.* Fables. EiCP
Of all the causes which conspire to blind. Pope. An Essay on Criticism Pt. II. CoBE; EnL; FaBoEn; ILP; PoIE; TreFT
Of all the cities in Romanian lands. Theodore and Honoria. Dryden. SeEP
Of all the floures in the mede. The Daisy. Chaucer. *Fr.* The Legend of Good Women: Prologue. LO
Of all the flowers rising now. Maritae Suae. William Philpot. OBEV; OBVV
Of all the fonts from which man's heart has drawn. The Guerdon of the Sun. George Sterling. HBMV
Of all the gay places the world can afford. Letter Containing a Panegyric on Bath. Christopher Anstey. *Fr.* The New Bath Guide. OBEC
Of all the gentle tenants of the place. Sons of Indolence. James Thomson. *Fr.* The Castle of Indolence, I. OBEC
Of all the girls that are so smart. Sally in Our Alley. Henry Carey. AWP; BOHV; CBEP; CEP; CoMu; EiCL; EiPP; FaBoBe; FaFP; FaPL; GTBS; GTBS-D; GTBS-P; GTBS-W; GTSE; GTSL; HBV; InMe; JAWP; LiTG; LiTL; LO; MemP; NeHB; OBEC; OBEV; PG (1945 ed.); PoE; PoSC; PTK; RIS; SiTL; TiPo (1952 ed.); TOP; TreF; ViBoPo; WBP
Of all the girls that e'er were seen. Ballad. John Gay. CoMu; ErPo
Of all the grain our nation yields. A Panegyrick upon Oates. *At. to* Richard Duke. PeRV
Of all the gruesome attempts at a twosome. *See* Of All of the gruesome. . .
Of all the heavenly gifts that mortal men commend. Of Friendship. Nicholas Grimald. SiCE
Of All the Idiots That Abound. Samuel Hoffenstein. RePo
Of all the kings that ever here did reign. Astrophel and Stella, LXXV. Sir Philip Sidney. FCP; SiPS
Of all the Lombards, by their trophies knowne. Sir William Davenant. *Fr.* Gondibert. SeCV-1
Of all the many trees there are. My Favorite Tree. Margarete Münsterberg. GFA
Of all the meals you can buy for money. A Song of Bread and Honey. Richard Le Gallienne. PCH
Of All the Men. Thomas Moore. BOHV; FiBHP
Of all the mismated pairs ever created. Owen Seaman. Louis Untermeyer. BOHV. *See also* Of all of the gruesome attempts at a twosome.
Of all the places on the map. In Philistia. Bliss Carman. ALV
Of all the pleasant ways. Driving in the Park. *Unknown.* OxBoLi
Of all the prizes/ That earth can give. True Riches. *Unknown.* MaRV
Of all the race of silver-wingèd flies. The Butterfly. Spenser. *Fr.* Muiopotmos BoC
Of all the rides since the birth of time. Skipper Ireson's Ride. Whittier. AmePo; AmP; AmPP; AnNE; AP; BeLS; BOHV; CoBA; GBV; HBV; InMe; InP; OnSP; OTPC; OxBA; PAH; PFY; PoLF; PoPo; StPo; StVeCh (1940 ed.); ThLM; TreFS; YaD; YT
Of all the sayings in this world. *Unknown.* OxNR
Of all the seasons in the year. The Bonny Harvest Moon. John Barr of Craigielee. AnNZ
Of all the shafts to Cupid's bow. The Three Arrows. Edward Fitzgerald. OBVV
Of all the ships upon the blue. Captain Reece. W. S. Gilbert. CenHV; EvOK; FiBHP; GN; HBV; MaC; OTPC
Of all the souls that stand create. Emily Dickinson. AA; AmePo; AmPP (5th ed.); AnFE; AnNE; AP; APA; CoAnAm; DiPo; FaPL; GTBS-D; MAmP; MaPo; MeWo; MWA-2; NePA; TOP; TrGrPo
Of all the sounds despatched abroad. Emily Dickinson. AnFE; CoAnAm; MAPA; TwAmPo
Of all the stars that bathe the heavens in glory. La Donna e Mobile. "A. K." FiBHP; InMe
Of all the theocratic beasts. Ubasti. Gelett Burgess. CIV
Of all the thoughts of God that are. The Sleep. Elizabeth Barrett Browning. HBV; MaRV; SoP; TRV; VA; WGRP
Of all the toasts that Britain boasts. Polly Peachum. Henry Carey. WaPE
Of all the torments, all the cares. Rivals [*or* The Rival *or* Song]. *At. to* Sir George Etherege *and to* William Walsh. CavP;

Of (continued)
HBV; LiTL; OBEC; OBEV; ViBoPo
Of all the trees in England. Trees. Walter de la Mare. GTBS; OHIP
Of all the tyrannies of human kind. Dryden. *Fr.* The Hind and the Panther, I. PoFr
Of all the various lots around the ball. The Poet; a Rhapsody. Mark Akenside. PP
Of all the wild deeds upon murder's black list. Verses on Daniel Good. *Unknown.* CoMu; OxBB
Of all the wimming doubly blest. A Grain of Salt. Wallace Irwin. BOHV; HBV; WhC
Of all the wives as e'er you know. Nancy Lee. Frederic E. Weatherly. AmSS; VA
Of all the words that have been borne. Know That I Am God. Lon Woodrum. SoP
Of all the world's enjoyments. The Fisherman's Song. Thomas D'Urfey. ALV
Of all thes kene conquerours to carpe it were kynde. The Tournament of Tottenham. *Unknown.* OxBoLi
Of all things beautiful and good. Brotherhood. Edwin Markham. OQP
Of all things human which are strange and wild. James Thomson. *Fr.* The City of Dreadful Night. LoBV; ViBoPo
Of all trades agoing, begging it is my delight. The Happy Beggarman. *Unknown.* OnYI
Of all we meet on life's great stream. One Here and There. *Unknown.* SoP
Of all wemen that ever were borne. Mary Complains to Other Mothers. *Unknown.* MeEL
Of Alphus. John Parkhurst, *tr. fr. Latin by* Timothe Kendall. TuPP
Of Ameinias nothing more is known for sure. Ameinias. John Simon. ELU
Of an Ancient Spaniel in Her Fifteenth Year. Christopher Morley. WaKn
Of an Heroical Answer of a Great Roman Lady to Her Husband. Sir John Harington. ErPo
Of an old King in a story. Variations on an Air: After W. B. Yeats. G. K. Chesterton. InP; Par
Of an Old Song. William E. H. Lecky. WGRP
Of an old Souldier of the Queens. An Old Souldier of the Queens. *Unknown.* OBS
Of an Orchard. Katharine Tynan. GoBC; HBV; OBVV; WGRP
Of asphodel, that greeny flower. William Carlos Williams. *Fr.* Asphodel, That Greeny Flower. PP
Of Astraea. Sir John Davies. *Fr.* Hymns of Astraea. SiCE; TrGrPo; TuPP
Of Baiting the Lion. Sir Owen Seaman. BOHV; NA
Of Ballad-Singers. John Gay. *Fr.* Trivia; or The Art of Walking the Streets of London, III: Of Walking the Streets by Night. EnLi-1 (1949 ed.)
(Ballad Singers.) MuSP
Of beasts am I, of men was he most brave. The Lion over the Tomb of Leonidas. *Unknown.* AWP; JAWP; WBP
Of Beauty. Sir Richard Fanshawe. *See* Of Time.
Of Beauty, *sel.* John Hall.
"What do I here! what's beauty? 'las." LO
Of Birds and Birders. John Heywood. SiCE
Of Blue China. Andrew Lang. *See* Ballade of Blue China.
Of Books. John Florio. EIL
Of Boston in New England. William Bradford. SCAP
Of bronze and blaze. Emily Dickinson. AP; MAmP; MAPA; MoPo; NoP; TwAmPo
Of caterpillars Fabre tells how day after day. Caterpillars. John Freeman. ChMP
Of Caution. Francesco da Barberino, *tr. fr. Italian by* Dante Gabriel Rossetti. AWP; JAWP; OnPM; WBP
Of Ceaseless Thoughts My Mind Hath Fram'd His Wings. Thomas Lodge. ReIE
Of Certain Irish Fairies. Arthur Guiterman. PoLF
Of Cinna's Election. Sir John Harington. SiCE
Of Clementina. Walter Savage Landor. HBV; OBEV
(In Clementina's Artless Mien.) OBRV; ViBoPo
Of Clergymen and Their Livings. Sir John Harington. TuPP
Of Clipping and Cleaning. John Heywood. CBV
Of Commerce and Society. Geoffrey Hill. NePoEA-2
Of Common Meddlers. John Heywood. SiCE
Of Constance holy legends tell. The Nun. Edward Moore. WaPE
Of cool sweet dew and radiance mild. Simples. James Joyce. HBMV; NP; PoPl
Of Corinna's Singing. Thomas Campion. *See* When to Her Lute Corinna Sings.
Of Cornelius. Everard Guilpin. *Fr.* Skialetheia. SiCE; TuPP
Of course I prayed. Emily Dickinson. AP; MAP; MoAmPo
Of course, I thought I'd never let him stay. Silhouette. Violet Alleyn Storey. CIV
Of course I tried to tell him. Poets Hitchhiking on the Highway. Gregory Corso. NeAP
Of course, the entire effort is to put myself. Thoughts during an Air Raid. Stephen Spender. MoBrPo (1950 ed.); NeMA; ViBoPo
Of course you have read of the wicked ways. The Ballad of Chicken Bill. F. E. Vaughn. PoOW
Of Courtesy. Arthur Guiterman. OTD; TiPo
Of courtesy, it is much less. Courtesy. Hilaire Belloc. ACP (1952 ed.); BoC; HBMV; JKCP; OtMeF
Of Crossing the Street. John Gay. *Fr.* Trivia; or, The Art of Walking the Streets of London, III: Of Walking the Streets by Night. EnLi-1 (1949 ed.)
Of Cupid. Henry Chettle. *See* Wily Cupid.
Of Cynthia. *Unknown.* *See* Ode: Of Cynthia.
Of daily soilure laving. Night Landry. James Merrill. CBV
Of dames, of knights, of arms, of love's delight. Ariosto. *Fr.* Orlando Furioso, I. ReIE
Of Death. Robert Garnier. *See* Chorus: "Alas, with what tormenting fire."
Of Death. Samuel Harding. *Fr.* Sicily and Naples. CBEP; SeCL
Of Death. Samuel Sheppard. SeCL
Of Death. James Shirley. *See* Glories of Our Blood and State.
Of deepest blue of summer skies. Alice. Herbert Bashford. HBV
Of DeWitt Williams on His Way to Lincoln Cemetery. Gwendolyn Brooks. PoNe
Of Difference between Wise Men and Fools. John Heywood. ReIE
Of Disdainful Daphne. M. H. Nowell. EIL
Of Dissembling Words. Sir Thomas Wyatt. *See* Honesty.
Of Don Pedro and His Poetry. Sir John Harington, *after the Latin of* Martial. SiCE
Of Drinking. Abraham Cowley. *See* Drinking.
Of Drunkenness. George Turberville. TuPP
Of Eden lost, in ancient days. Rondeau, Humbly Inscribed to the Right Hon. William Eden. *At. to* George Ellis. OBEC
Of Edenhall, the youthful Lord. The Luck of Edenhall. Ludwig Uhland, *tr. by* Longfellow. AWP; StPo
Of Edwards of the Chapel. Barnabe Googe. ReIE
Of Enclosing a Common. Sir John Harington. SiCE
Of England and of Its Marvels. Fazio degli Uberti, *tr. fr. Italian by* Dante Gabriel Rossetti. AWP; JAWP; WBP
Of English Verse. Edmund Waller. AnAnS-2; CavP; EiCL; OBS; PP; SCEP-2; SeCP
Of Enough and a Feast. John Heywood. SiCE; TuPP
Of every step I took in pain. The Recompense. Anna Wickham. NP
Of everykune tre. The Hawthorn. *Unknown.* ChTr
Of famed Megistias here behold the tomb. Prophetic Death. Simonides. OnPM
Of Faustus, a Stealer of Verses. Sir John Harington. SiCE; TuPP
Of few words, Sir, you seem to be. *Unknown.* SiPS
Of Fiammetta Singing. Boccaccio, *tr. fr. Italian by* Dante Gabriel Rossetti. *Fr.* Sonnets. AWP
(Fiammetta.) GoBC
Of fields with dead bestrewed around. Upon the Feast of St. Simon and St. Jude. Samuel Johnson. EiCP
Of fire, fire, fire I sing. London Mourning in Ashes. *Unknown.* FOL; PeRV
Of Florence and of Beatrice. Dante at Verona. Dante Gabriel Rossetti. MaVP
Of Fortune, *abr.* Thomas Kyd. *Fr.* Cornelia. EIL
Of Fortune. Sir Thomas More. CoBE
Of Fortune's Power. Richard Edwards. ReIE
Of fret, of dark, of thorn, of chill. Opposition. Sidney Lanier. AmPP (3d ed.); AnFE; APA; CoAnAm; LiTA
Of Friendship. Nicholas Grimald. SiCE
Of Friendship. Sir John Harington, *after the Latin of* Martial. SiCE

Of funerals, the saddest. Funeral. Vyacheslav Ivanov. OnPM
Of Galla's Goodly Periwig. Sir John Harington. SiCE
Of Giving. Arthur Guiterman. TiPo
Of gladde things there be four, ay four. Gladde Things. *Unknown.* TiPo (1952 ed.)
Of God to thy doings, a time there is sent. A Description of Time, and the Year. Thomas Tusser. SiCE
Of God we ask one favor. Emily Dickinson. EaLo
Of God's Great power in the Leviathan. Job, Bible, *O.T.* *See* Leviathan.
Of Good Sauce. Sir John Harington. SiCE
Of Greatness in Teaching. Leslie Pinckney Hill. MaRV
Of green and hexagonal glass. The Bottle. Walter de la Mare. MoPo; POTE
Of Heaven Considered as a Tomb. Wallace Stevens. AnFE; AnNE; APA; CoAnAm; QFR
Of Heaven or Hell I have no power to sing. An Apology [*or* Prologue]. William Morris. *Fr.* The Earthly Paradise. AWP; BEL; BLPA; CoBE; EnLi-2; EnLit; EPN; FaBoEn; GTBS-W; GTSL; HBV; InP; LiTB; LoBV; NoP; OAEP; OBNC; OtMeF; PoIE; PoVP; TOP; VA; ViBoPo; ViPo; ViPP
Of heavenly stature, but most human smile. Written in the Visitors' Book at the Birthplace of Robert Burns. George Washington Cable. AA
Of Her Breath. Robert Herrick. EG
Of heroes and statesmen I'll just mention four. Paul Jones—a New Song. *Unknown.* PAH
Of Heywood. John Heywood. ReIE; SiCE; TuPP
(Art Thou Heywood.) NCEP
Of high Honour should be her hood. The Garment of Good Ladies. Robert Henryson. ACP
Of highway dust the Buddha made his throne. Gautama. Thomas S. Jones, Jr. AnAmPo
Of Him who did salvation bring. His Salvation. Bernard of Clairvaux. SoP
Of Himself. Clément Marot, *tr. fr. French by* Alan Conder. OnPM
Of Himself. Meleager, *tr. fr. Greek by* Richard Garnett. AWP
Of His Choice of a Sepulchre. Andrew Lang. *See* Ballade of His Choice of a Sepulchre.
Of His Cynthia. Fulke Greville. Caelica, LII. ElL; ELP; NoP
(Another, of His Cynthia.) TuPP
(Away with These Self-loving Lads.) AtBAP; EnRePo; SiCE
(Cynthia.) OBSC
(Song to His Cynthia.) ViBoPo
(Sonnet.) ReIE
Of His Dear Son, Gervase. Sir John Beaumont. *Fr.* Of My Dear Son Gervase Beaumont. OBEV
("Dear Lord, receive my son, whose winning love.") GoBC
Of His Death. Meleager, *tr. fr. Greek by* Andrew Lang. AWP
Of His Divine Poems. Edmund Waller. *See* Of the Last Verses in the Book.
Of His Foolish Passion for Laura. Petrarch, *tr. fr. Italian by* Susan Wollaston. Sonnets to Laura: To Laura in Life, VI. EnLi-1; OuHeWo
Of His Lady. Chaucer. *See* Balade: "Hyd, Absolon, thy gilte tresses clere."
Of His Lady. *Unknown.* ElL
Of His Lady's Face. Jacopo da Lentino, *tr. fr. Italian by* Dante Gabriel Rossetti. OnPM
(Sonnet: Of His Lady's Face.) AWP
Of His Lady's Old Age. Pierre de Ronsard, *tr. fr. French by* Andrew Lang. *Fr.* Sonnets pour Hélène. AWP; CTC; JAWP; WBP
(To Helen.) OuHeWo
Of His Last Sight of Fiammetta. Boccaccio, *tr. fr. Italian by* Dante Gabriel Rossetti. *Fr.* Sonnets. AWP; JAWP; OnPM; WBP
(Fiammetta.) GoBC
Of His Love Called Anna. Sir Thomas Wyatt. ReIE; TuPP
Of His Love That Pricked Her Finger with a Needle. Sir Thomas Wyatt. ReIE
("She sat and sewed that hath done me the wrong.") FCP
Of His Majesties Receiving the News of the Duke of Buckingham's Death. Edmund Waller. SeCV-1
Of His Mistress. Robert Greene. *See* Melicertus' Description of His Mistress.
Of His Mistress. Peter Hausted. *Fr.* The Rival Friends. EG; SeCL
Of His Mistress Grown Old. William Hicks. SeCL
Of His Muse. Sir John Harington. SiCE
Of His Return[e] from Spain[e]. Sir Thomas Wyatt. FaBoEn; ReIE; TuPP
(In Spain.) OBSC; SeCePo
(Tagus, Farewell.) CBEP; EnRePo; QFR
("Tagus, farewell, that westward with thy streams.") EnPo; FCP; ReEn; SiCE
Of History More Like Myth. Jean Garrigue. NYBP
Of Holding of a Nose. John Heywood. ReIE
Of Homer's Odyssey. Sir John Davies. *Fr.* Orchestra. EG
Of Honest Theft. To My Good Friend Master Samuel Daniel. Sir John Harington. SiCE
Of Howard's stem a glorious branch is dead. Elegy for Margaret Howard, Lady Buckhurst. Robert Southwell. CoBE
Of Human Knowledge. Sir John Davies. *Fr.* Nosce Teipsum. ReIE; SiCE; SiPS; TuPP
Of Human Life. Henry King. *See* Sic Vita.
Of Human Progress. Lucretius, *tr. fr. Latin by* William Ellery Leonard. *Fr.* Of the Nature of Things (De Rerum Natura). WoL
Of Humane Learning, *sel.* Fulke Greville. *See* Treatie of Human Learning.
Of Impatience Which Brings All Our Gains to Nothing. Jacopone da Todi, *tr. fr. Italian by* Mrs. Theodore Beck. CAW
Of Improving the Present Time, *sel.* Congreve.
Nil Admirari. OBEC
Of Joan's Youth. Louise Imogen Guiney. AA; HBV
Of John Bunyans Life. John James. SCAP
Of Jolly Good Ale and Old. *At. to* William Stevenson. *See* Back and Side Go Bare, Go Bare.
Of Jonathan Chapman/ Two things are known. Johnny Appleseed. Rosemary Benét *and* Stephen Vincent Benét. BoChLi (1950 ed.); MPB; OTD; OTPC (1946 ed.); TrAS
Of Kings and Things. Lillian Morrison. CAD
Of Labienus. John Owen, *tr. fr. Latin by* Thomas Harvey. *Fr.* Four Epigrams. PrWP
Of late/ Since I parted from Liadin. Liadin and Curither. *Unknown.* OnYI
Of late a noble steamer, the *Cedar Grove* by name. The Loss of the *Cedar Grove.* *Unknown.* ShS
Of Late and Never. John Heywood. TuPP
Of late, in one of those most weary hours. The Garden of Boccaccio. Samuel Taylor Coleridge. EPN
Of Leinster, famed for maidens fair. Colin and Lucy [*or* Lucy and Colin]. Thomas Tickell. CEP; EiPP; OBEC; OTPC (1923 ed.)
Of Liberty; an Essay, *sel.* Abraham Cowley.
Portrait of a Freeman. PoFr
Of Liberty and Charity, *sel.* Richard Realf.
Holy Nation, A. PoFr
Of Liddisdale the common thievis. Aganis the Thievis of Liddisdale. Sir Richard Maitland. GoTS
Of Life. Andrew Lang. VA
Of Life and Death. Ben Jonson. ReIE
Of Little Faith. Harold Trowbridge Pulsifer. EtS
Of little use the man you may suppose. The Poet's Use. Pope. *Fr.* The First Epistle of the Second Book of Horace. OBEC
Of living creatures most I prize. Butterfly. William Jay Smith. GoJo; RePo; TiPo (1959 ed.)
Of London Bridge, and the Stupendous Sight, and Structure Thereof. James Howell. ChTr
Of Love. *At. to* Aphra Behn. *See* Song: "Oh Love! that stronger art than wine."
Of Love. Kahlil Gibran. *Fr.* The Prophet. PoLF
Of Love. James Sandford. ElL
Of Love ("Long annoys and short contentings"). *Unknown.* SeCL
Of Love. Sir Thomas Wyatt. FCP
Of Love and Time. John Henderson. BoAV
Of love he sang, full hearted one. A Forced Music. Robert Graves. MoBrPo
Of Love of Silence and of Solitude. Thomas à Kempis. *Fr.* Imitation of Christ. TreF
Of loves and ladies, knights and arms, I sing. Orlando Furioso, I. Ariosto. EnLi-1

Of love's designed joys. Stay, O Stay. A. E. Coppard. MoBrPo (1942 ed.)
Of Loving a Dog. John Heywood. SiCE; TuPP
Of Loving at First Sight. Edmund Waller. SeCP
Of Lynus, Borrowing. Sir John Harington. SiCE
Of Maids' Inconstancy. Richard Brathwaite. *Fr.* A Strappado for the Devil. ElL
Of Man and Nature. Horace Mungin. BOLo
Of Man and Wife. Richard Eedes. *See* No Love, to Love of Man and Wife.
Of manners gentle, of affections mild. On Mr. Gay; in Westminster Abbey, 1732 [*or* Epitaph XI]. Pope. CEP; FiP
Of Man's first disobedience, and the fruit. Invocation to the Heavenly Muse [*or* The Fallen Angels]. Milton. Paradise Lost, I. ATP; BEL; BoLiVe; CoBE; DiPo; EnL; EnLi-1; EnLit; FaBoEn; FiP; FosPo; MBW-1; OAEP; OuHeWo; PoEL-3; PoFS; SeEP; TOP; TreFS; WoL
Of many marvels in my time. A Description of a Strange (and Miraculous) Fish. Martin Parker. CoMu
Of many things adulterate. Epitaph; for Himself. Tristan Corbière. AWP
Of Margaret. John Crowe Ransom. NoP
Of Mary. A New Song of Mary. *Unknown.* MeEL
Of May. Alexander Scott. OxBS
Of men, nay beasts; worse, monsters; worst of all. Phineas Fletcher. The Locusts, or Apollyonists, I. SeCV-1; SeEP
Of Mere Being. Wallace Stevens. PoIE (1970 ed.)
Of Middle Life. *Unknown.* SeCL
Of mine acquaintance a certain young man. John Heywood. *Fr.* A Dialogue Containing the Number of the Effectual Proverbs in the English Tongue. ReIE
Of Misery. Thomas Howell. ElL; TuPP
Of Mistress D. S. Barnabe Googe. EnRePo
Of Modern Poetry. Wallace Stevens. AmP; AmPP (4th ed.); InvP; MaPo (1969 ed.); NePA; OxBA; PP
Of Money. Barnaby Googe. CBV; ElL; EnRePo; EP; ForPo; NoP
Of mortal blessings here the first is health. The Four Blessings. *Unknown.* OnPM
Of mortal parents is the hero born. Hoffer. Wordsworth. FOL
Of Mourners. Dorothy Livesay. PeCV
Of My Dear Son [*or* Sonne], Gervase Beaumont. Sir John Beaumont. OBS; SeCL; SeEP; ViBoPo, *abr.*
"Dear Lord, receive my son, whose winning love," *sel.* GoBC
(Of His Dear Son, Gervase.) OBEV
Of my deep hunger. S. Funaroff. *Fr.* Dusk of the Gods. NAMP
Of My Lady Isabella Playing on the Lute. Edmund Waller. MePo
Of my lady, wel me rejoise I may. Hoccleve's Humorous Praise of His Lady [*or* A Description of His Ugly Lady]. Thomas Hoccleve. MeEL; OAEP
Of my ould loves, of their ould ways. Memories. Arthur Stringer. HBV
Of Myself. Abraham Cowley. *Fr.* A Vote. OAEP; OBS; SeCL
("This Only Grant Me.") SeEP; TreFT
Of myself I can tell a true song-tale. Afar on the Floodways. *Unknown.* The Seafarer, Pt. I. PoLi
Of myself, my dear joy, if you wish to be told. An Irishman's Christening. *Unknown.* OnYI
Of Narrow Streets. John Gay. *Fr.* Trivia; or, The Art of Walking the Streets of London, II: Of Walking the Streets by Day. EnLi-1 (1949 ed.)
Of Natural Forces. Elizabeth Chesley. NYTB
Of Nature broad and free. Arbor Day Song. Mary A. Heermans. HH
Of Nelson and the North. The Battle of the Baltic. Thomas Campbell. CBEP; CoBE; EnRP; FOL; GN; GTBS; GTBS-D; GTBS-P; GTBS-W; GTSE; GTSL; HBV; NBM; OBEV; OTPC (1923 ed.); RoGo
Of Neptune's empire let us sing. In Praise of Neptune. Thomas Campion. BoNaP; CBEP; EtS; GTSL; OBEV; OBSC; WiR
Of Nicolette. E. E. Cummings. HBMV
Of Nothing and Althing. John Heywood. SiCE
Of old, a man who died. Immortal Flowers. Wallace Rice. AA
Of old, all invitations ended. Thoughts on Being Invited to Dinner. Christopher Morley. HBMV
Of old our fathers' God was real. Exit God. Gamaliel Bradford. HBMV; InMe; MaRV
Of Old Sat Freedom on the Heights. Hildegarde Flanner. PoFr
Of Old Sat Freedom on the Heights. Tennyson. BEL; HBV; OAEP; PoFr; PoVP; ViPo
(Freedom.) MaRV
Of old the Muses sat on high. The Muses. Edith M. Thomas. HBV
Of old when folk lay sick and sorely tired. On Hygiene. Hilaire Belloc. MoBrPo
Of old, when Scarron his companions invited. Retaliation. Goldsmith. CEP; EiPP; LaA; OAEP; OxBoLi; TOP
Of On That Is So Fayr and Bright. *Unknown.* *See* Hymn to the Virgin.
Of One Blood Hath God Created. Henry B. Robins. MaRV
Of One Dead. Leo Kennedy. PeCV
Of One Dead. Tennyson. In Memoriam A. H. H., XIV. LiTB; LiTG
Of One Hanged. John Heywood. ReIE
Of One Self-slain. Charles Hanson Towne. WGRP
Of One That Is So Fair and Bright. *Unknown.* *See* Hymn to the Virgin, A.
Of one who grew up at Gallipoli. War Story. Jon Stallworthy. ELU
Of One Who neither Sees nor Hears. Richard Watson Gilder. AA
Of One Who Seemed to Have Failed. S. Weir Mitchell. AA
Of Order in Our Lord Christ. *At. to* St. Francis of Assisi. *See* Cantica: Our Lord Christ.
Of Our Lord's Passion, *sel.* St. Bernard of Clairvaux, *tr. fr. Latin.*
"In Thine hour of holy sadness." ChIP
Of Pansa. Everard Guilpin. *Fr.* Skialetheia. ReIE
Of Perfect Friendship. *At. to* Henry Cheke. *See* Plain Description of Perfect Friendship, A.
Of Phyllis. William Drummond of Hawthornden. *See* Phyllis.
Of Pick-Pockets. John Gay. *Fr.* Trivia; or The Art of Walking the Streets of London, III: Of Walking the Streets by Night. EnLi-1 (1949 ed.)
Of Preachers. William Cowper. *Fr.* The Task, II. SoP
Of priests we can offer a charmin' variety. Father O'Flynn. Alfred Perceval Graves. BOHV; HBV; OnYI
Of Prometheus, how undaunted. Prometheus. Longfellow. MWA-1
Of purpose love chose first for to be blind. Sir Thomas Wyatt. FCP
Of Quarrels. Arthur Guiterman. OTD; TiPo
Of quiet things, of things at rest. Beside Lilia Dead. Sister Mary Catherine. JKCP (1955 ed.)
Of Rama. Herman Melville. AnFE; CoAnAm; LiTA
Of Rebellion. John Heywood. ReIE
Of Red in Spring. David McCord. MAP; MoAmPo (1942 ed.)
Of Rome. Herman Melville. *Fr.* Clarel. OxBA
Of Rosalind. Thomas Lodge. *Fr.* Rosalynde. GoBC
(Of Rosalynd.) PoLi
(Sonetto: "Of all chaste birds the phoenix doth excel.") ReIE; SiCE
Of Scolding Wives and the Third Day Ague. Henricus Selyns. SCAP
Of Seals and Arms. John Taylor. CBEP
Of Silk Is Her Fishing-Line. *Unknown, tr. fr. Chinese by* Arthur Waley. *Fr.* The Book of Songs. HW
Of Sir Philip Sidney. Sir John Beaumont. GoBC
Of Snow. Norman Brick. WaP
Of Solitude. Abraham Cowley. OBS; SeCL; SeEP
Essay on Solitude ("Hail, old patrician trees, so great and good"), *sel.* ViBoPo
Of Sorrow, 'tis as Saints have said. Sorrow. Helen Parry Eden. JKCP
Of speckled eggs the birdie sings. Singing. Robert Louis Stevenson. GaP; GFA; PCH; SUS
Of Spenser's Faerie Queene [*or* Fairy Queen]. Thomas Freeman. SiCE; TuPP
Of Spenser's Faery Queen. Sir Walter Ralegh. *See* Vision upon This Conceit of the Faerie Queene, A.
Of Such as Had Forsaken Him. Sir Thomas Wyatt. TuPP
(Epigram: "Lux, my fair falcon, and your fellows all.") SiPS
(Lux, my fair falcon.) NoP; SiCE

Of Such Is the Kingdom. Francis Greenwood Peabody. MaRV
"Of Such Is the Kingdom of God." Jemima Luke. *See* I Think When I Read. . .
Of Summum Bonum. Sir John Harington. SiCE
Of sundry sorts that were, as the musician likes. English Musical Instruments. Michael Drayton. *Fr.* Polyolbion. MuSP
Of Swimming in Lakes and Rivers. Bertolt Brecht, *tr. fr. German by* H. R. Hays. SD
Of Tabacco. Sir John Davies. ReIE
Of Tact. Arthur Guiterman. MoShBr
(How Are You?) WhC
Of Taking Things Wrong. John Heywood. ReIE
Of Temperance in Fortune. Richard Watson Dixon. *Fr.* Mano; a Poetical History. VA
Of that short roll of friends writ in my heart. To Mr. I. L. John Donne. MaMe
Of that wherein thou art a questioner. Sonnet: To Dante Alighieri (He Interprets Dante Alighieri's Dream). Dante da Maiano. AWP
Of that world's conquest and the fortunate wars. The Argument. Archibald MacLeish. *Fr.* Conquistador. AtBAP
Of the beast. . .an angel. The Everlasting Contenders. Kenneth Patchen. CrMA; NaP
Of the beauty of kindness I speak. Kindness. T. Sturge Moore. OBMV
Of the birds that fly in the farthest sea. The Flying Fish. John Gray. ChTr; LoBV; OBNC
Of the Birth and Bringing Up of Desire. Edward de Vere, Earl of Oxford. OBSC; ReIE; SiCE; TuPP
Of the Blessèd Sacrament of the Altar. Robert Southwell. GoBC; OBEV (new ed.)
Of the Book-Hunter. Andrew Lang. VA
Of the Characters of Women, Pope. Moral Essays, Epistle II. EiCL; PoFS
Sels.
To a Lady. BWP; MaPo (1969 ed.); MBW-1; NoP; OxBoLi; SiTL
("Nothing so true as what you once let fall," *longer sel.*) FaBoEn
"Yet Cloe sure was form'd without a spot." ErPo
Of the Child with the Bird at the Bush. Bunyan. CBEP; SeCL; SeEP
(My Little Bird.) OBS
Of the Clock and the Cock. George Turberville. EnRePo
Of the Cosmic-Blueprints. Sun-Ra. BF
Of the Courtier's Life. Sir Thomas Wyatt. Satires, I. CoBE; GoTL; OBSC; ReIE; SiCE; TuPP
(Epistle to John Poins.) FosPo
(Mine Own John Poins.) NoP
(Satire I: "Mine own John Poynz.") PoEL-1; ReEn; SiPS
(To John Poynz.) FCP
Of the dark past. Ecce Puer. James Joyce. PoIE; PoPl; StP
Of the Day Estivall. Alexander Hume. *See* Summer Day.
Of the Death of Kings. Shakespeare. King Richard II, *fr.* III, ii. ChTr
("For heaven's [*or* God's] sake, let us sit upon the ground.") HoPM; PoFr
Of the Death of Sir Thomas Wyatt [the Elder]. Earl of Surrey. *See* On the Death of Sir Thomas Wyatt.
Of the divine and human thought. A Spinozaism. John Swanwick Drennan. IrPN
Of the erl Hugelyn of Pyse the langour. The Tale of Hugelin, Count of Pisa. Chaucer. *Fr.* The Canterbury Tales: The Monk's Tale. MyFE
Of the Father's Love Begotten. Prudentius, *tr. fr. Latin.* BePJ
Of the filth and order of the world. A Series 5.8. John Wieners. CoPo
Of the first Paradice there's nothing found. On St. James's Park, as Lately Improved by His Majesty. Edmund Waller. AnAnS-2; CEP
Of the French Kings Nativity. Benjamin Harris. SCAP
Of the Gentle Heart. Guido Guinicelli. *See* Canzone: Of the Gentle Heart.
Of the Going Down of the Sun. Bunyan. CH
Of the Golden World. Thomas Howell. SiCE; TuPP
Of the Great and Famous [Ever-to-Be-Honored Knight, Sir Francis Drake]. Robert Hayman. CH; FaBoCh; NoP
Of the Great Marriage between Grand Amour and La Belle Pucelle. Stephen Hawes. The Pastime of Pleasure, XXXIX. ReIE
Of the Holy Eucharist. *Unknown.* ACP (1952 ed.)
Of the Implements for Walking the Streets, and Signs of the Weather. John Gay. *Fr.* Trivia. CEP; EiCP
Of the Incomparable Treasure of the Scripture. *Unknown.* TRV
Of the Last Verses in the Book. Edmund Waller. AnAnS-2; BEL; CEP; CoBE; FaBoEn; HBV; MePo; NoP; OAEP; OBS; PeRV; PoE; PoFS; SCEP-2; SeCL; SeCP; SeCV-1; SeEP; ViBoPo
(Of His Divine Poems.) LoBV
Sels.
Old Age ("The seas are quiet"). BoC; MaRV; OBEV; TreFT
(Last Verses.) OxBoCh
Soul's Dark Cottage, The. ChTr
Of the light of the dawn let none be silent. On a Papyrus of Oxyrhynchus. *Unknown.* CAW
Of the Lost Ship. Eugene Richard White. AA
Of the Manner of Addressing Clouds. Wallace Stevens. AnFE; APA; CoAnAm
Of the Mathematician. Alice Clear Matthews. GoYe
Of the Mean and Sure Estate. Seneca, *tr. fr. Latin by* Sir Thomas Wyatt. *See* Stond Who So List upon the Slipper Toppe.
Of the Mean and Sure Estate [Written to John Poins]. Sir Thomas Wyatt. Satires, II. BEL; OA; ReIE; SiCE; TuPP
("My mother's maids, when they did sew and spin.") SiPS
(To John Poynz.) FCP
Of the Mean Estate. Thomas, Lord Vaux. SiCE
Of the Mighty Power of Love. Edward de Vere, Earl of Oxford. TuPP
Of the million or two, more or less. Instans Tyrannus. Robert Browning. PoFr
Of the Months. Folgore da San Geminiano. *See* Sonnets of the Months.
Of the Moon. Charles Best. *See* Sonnet of the Moon, A.
Of the myriad afflictions that beset Hellas. The Breed of Athletes. Euripides. SD
Of the Nativity of the Lady Rich's Daughter. Henry Constable. OBSC
Of the Nature of Things. Lucretius. *See* De Rerum Natura.
Of the New Prosody. Brewster Ghiselin. MoVE
Of the Night, Let the Bridegroom Sing. Statius, *tr. fr. Latin by* D. A. Slater *and* Virginia Tufte. *Fr.* Epithalamium for Stella and Violentilla. HW
Of the old heroes when the warlike shades. The Loyall Scot. Andrew Marvell. MaMe
Of the old house, only a few crumbled. The House That Was. Laurence Binyon. MoBrPo
Of the onset, fear-inspiring, and the firing and the pillage. The Sack of Deerfield. Thomas Dunn English. PAH
Of the Passing Away of Brynhild. William Morris. *Fr.* The Story of Sigurd the Volsung. PoVP; VA
Of the Pillars of the Church. Sir John Harington. SiCE
Of the primeval priest's assum'd power. The Book of Urizen. Blake. ERoP-1
Of the Progress[e] of the Soul[e]; the Second Anniversary. John Donne. AnAnS-1; MaMe; SCEP-1; SeCP; SeEP
(Second Anniversarie, The: Of the Progres of the Soule.) MeP
Sels.
Contemplation of Our State in Our Deathbed. OBS
("Think then, my soul, that death is but a groom.") OxBoCh, *longer sel.*
"Forget this rotten world; and unto thee." FaBoEn
"Nothing could make me sooner to confesse." ReEn, *longer sel.*
Our Companie in the Next World. OBS
"She of whose soul, if we may say 'twas gold." TuPP
Soules Ignorance in This Life and Knowledge in the Next, The. OBS
Of the pursuit of beauty and the husk that remains. Sir Walter Raleigh. William Carlos Williams. *Fr.* In the American Grain. OnHM
Of the Realme of Scotland. Sir David Lindsay. *Fr.* The Dreme. OxBS
Of the Resurrection of Christ. William Dunbar. OxBoCh; PoLi
(Hymn of the Resurrection, A.) MeEL
(On the Resurrection of Christ.) OxBS; PoEL-1
Of the Sad Lot of the Humanists in Paris. George Buchanan, *pr. tr. fr. Latin.* GoTS
Of the Senses. John Heywood. ReIE

Of the Small Respect Had of Learned Men in General. John Davies of Hereford. SiCE
Of the Soul of Man and the Immortality Thereof. Sir John Davies. *Fr.* Nosce Teipsum. ReIE
Of the Stalking of the Stag. Sir Owen Seaman. CenHV
Of the Surface of Things. Wallace Stevens. ELU; NP
Of the Terrible Doubt of Appearances. Walt Whitman. NePA
Of the Unscathing Fire. Anne Ridler. *See* Phoenix Answered, The.
Of the Use of Riches ("'Tis strange, the miser. . ."). Pope. Moral Essays, Epistle IV. CABL; EiCL; EiPP; MBW-1; PoEL-3
(To Richard Boyle, Earl of Burlington.) BWP
Of the Use of Riches ("Who shall decide, when doctors disagree"). Pope. *Fr.* Moral Essays, Epistle III. MBW-1
Of the Vanity of Man's Life. *Unknown.* SiCE; TuPP
(On the Vanity of Man's Life.) OBSC
("Vain is the fleeting wealth.") EG
Of Thee, Kind Boy. Sir John Suckling. *See* Sonnet: "Of thee (kind boy) I ask no red and white."
Of thee the Northman by his beachèd [*or* bleachèd] galley. Odes, V [*or* Ode to the Mediterranean]. George Santayana. AmePo; AnAmPo; AnFE; APA; CoAnAm; EtS; TwAmPo
Of their lament white-armed Andromache. The Lamentations. Homer. *Fr.* The Iliad, XXIV. LiTW
Of thes four letters purpose I. A New Song of Mary. *Unknown.* MeEL
Of thes Frer Minours me thenkes moch wonder. Friars' Enormities. *Unknown.* MeEL
Of these houses. San Martino del Carso. Giuseppe Ungaretti. OnPM
Of these the false Achitophel was first. Achitophel [*or* The False Achitophel *or* Shaftesbury]. Dryden. *Fr.* Absalom and Achitophel, Pt. I. AtBAP; AWP, *br. sel.*; FiP InPo; JAWP; OBS; PeRV; PoEL-3; SeCePo; ViBoPo; WBP; WHA, *br. sel.*
Of these two spitefull Rocks, the one doth shove. Scylla and Charybdis. Homer. *Fr.* The Odyssey, XII. OBS
Of thick and thin, light, heavy, dark, and clear. A Notable Description of the World. *At. to* William Smith. ReIE
Of Things Not Seen. Leslie Savage Clark. ChIP
Of this bad world the loveliest and the best. On a Dead Hostess. Hilaire Belloc. MoBrPo; MoVE
Of this fair volume which we world do name. The Book of the World [*or* The Lessons of Nature]. William Drummond of Hawthornden. CH; GTBS; GTBS-D; GTBS-P; GTBS-W; GTSE; GTSL; HBV; MCCG; PCD; SeCePo; SeCL; TOP
Of this high grace with bliss conjoined. Jorge de Montemayor, *tr. by* Sir Philip Sidney. *Fr.* Diana. FCP
Of this worlds theatre in which we stay. Amoretti, LIV. Spenser. NoP; ReEn; ReIE
Of Thomas Traherne and the Pebble Outside. Sydney Clouts. BoSA
Of those at famed Thermopylae who lie. Thermopylae. Simonides, *tr. by* Lord Neaves. OnPM
Of Those Who Walk Alone. Richard Burton. HBV
Of those whom I have known, the few and fatal friends. Largo. Dunstan Thompson. LiTA; LiTM; MoPo; WaP
Of Three Damsels in a Meadow. John Payne. OBVV
Of three eyes, I would still give two for one. The Third Eye. Jay Macpherson. MoCV
Of Three Girls and [of] Their Talk. Boccaccio, *tr. fr. Italian by* Dante Gabriel Rossetti. *Fr.* Sonnets. AWP; JAWP; OnPM; WBP
Of thy life [*or* lyfe], Thomas, this compass well mark. The Golden Mean. Earl of Surrey. EnPo; FCP; SiPS
Of Time. Sir Richard Fanshawe. *Fr.* Il Pastor Fido. SeCL
(Of Beauty.) InMe
Of Titus. Everard Guilpin. *Fr.* Skialetheia. ReIE; SiCE; TuPP
Of Treason. Sir John Harington. ALV; CBV; ExPo; OxBoLi; SiCE; TuPP
(Epigram: "Treason doth never prosper.") HBV; OtMeF
(On Treason.) ELU; FiBHP
(Treason.) CBEP; LiTG; SiTL
("Treason doth never prosper; what's the reason?") DiPo
(Treason Never Prospers, *sl. diff., at. to* James Harrington.) InvP
Of True Liberty. Sir John Beaumont. OBS; PoFr
Of two fair virgins, modest, though admired. On a Nun [*or* Sonnet]. Jacopo Vittorelli. AWP; CAW; JAWP; LiTW; WBP
Of Two Religions. Sir John Harington. SiCE
Of votive lights there were only seven. Ash Wednesday. Rosa Zagnoni Marinoni. PoRL; WHL
Of W. W. (Americanus). James Kenneth Stephen. *See* Sincere Flattery.
Of Walking the Streets by Day. John Gay. *Fr.* Trivia; or, The Art of Walking the Streets of London. EiPP
Sels.
Dangers of Football, The. EnLi-1 (1949 ed.)
Morning, The. EnLi-1 (1949 ed.)
(On Walking the Streets by Day.) TOP
Of Narrow Streets. EnLi-1 (1949 ed.)
Pell Mell Celebrated, The. EnLi-1 (1949 ed.)
Pleasure of Walking through an Alley, The. EnLi-1 (1949 ed.)
"Thus far the muse has traced in useful lays." CEP; EnLi-1 (1949 ed.)
Of Walking the Streets by Night. John Gay. *Fr.* Trivia; or, The Art of Walking the Streets of London, III. EiCP
Sels.
"Consider, reader, what fatigues I've known." EnLi-1 (1949 ed.)
Evening, The. EnLi-1 (1949 ed.)
"O Trivia, Goddess, leave these low abodes." EnLi-1 (1949 ed.)
Of Ballad-Singers. EnLi-1 (1949 ed.)
Of Crossing the Street. EnLi-1 (1949 ed.)
Of Pick-Pockets. EnLi-1 (1949 ed.)
Of Watchmen. EnLi-1 (1949 ed.)
Of wealthy lustre was the banquet-room. The Banquet. Keats. *Fr.* Lamia. SeCePo
Of what an easie quick accesse. Prayer. George Herbert. AtBAP; MaMe
"Of what are you afraid, my child?" inquired the kindly teacher. Wild Flowers. Peter Newell. NA
Of what are you weaving your life today. The Threads You Use. Alice Hansche Mortenson. SoP
Of What Are Your Clothes Made? Ann *or* Jane Taylor. OTPC (1923 ed.)
Of what avail are any words to tell. Communion. T. Turner. LO
Of what avail these willing finite minds. Descent of the Holy Ghost. John Gilland Brunini. JKCP (1955 ed.)
Of what good can Paradise be. Paradise. Immanuel di Roma. TrJP
Of white and tawny, black as ink. Variation on a Sentence. Louise Bogan. ImOP
Of who we and all they are. The Grapevine. John Ashbery. ANYP
Of Wit. Abraham Cowley. *See* Ode: Of Wit.
Of woman and wine, of woods and spring. Inexhaustible. Israel Zangwill. TrJP
Of Women. Richard Edwards. EIL
Of Women. *Unknown, tr. fr. Arabic by* E. Powys Mathers. *Fr.* The Thousand and One Nights. ErPo; PV
Of Women No More Evil. *Unknown, tr. fr. Late Middle Irish by* Robin Flower. AnIL
Of Wonder. Mary Gilmore. BoAV; NeLNL
Of worthy Captain Lovewell, I purpose now to sing. Lovewell's Fight. *Unknown.* BaBo; HBV; PAH
Of Wounds. Sister Mary Madeleva. ISi
Of wounds and sore defeat. Pandora's Song. William Vaughn Moody. *Fr.* The Fire-Bringer. BBV; GBV; HBV; PFY; PTK
Of your trouble, Ben, to ease me. Her Man Described by Her Own[e] Dictamen. Ben Jonson. *Fr.* A Celebration of Charis. AnAnS-2; AtBAP; SeCP
Of Youth He Singeth. R. Wever. *See* In Youth Is Pleasure.
Of Zeno. Everard Guilpin. *Fr.* Skialetheia. SiCE
Off a Puritane. *Unknown.* *See* Two Puritans.
Off all the lords in faire Scotland. The Heir of Linne. *Unknown.* ESPB
Off an ancient story I'll tell you anon. King John and the Bishop. *Unknown.* BaBo; ESPB
Off Banks Peninsula. Denis Glover. AnNZ
Off Broadway, where they sell those photographs. Manhattan Menagerie. Joseph Cherwinski. GoYe
Off Februar the fyiftene nycht. The Dance of the Sevin Deidly Synnis. William Dunbar. GoTS; OxBS
Off from Boston. *Unknown.* MC; PAH

Off from the shore at last he took his way. The Discoverer. Arthur Gordon Field. PGD
Off Highway 106. Cherrylog Road. James Dickey. CoAP; NYBP; TPM; TwCP
Off in the twilight hung the low full moon. Full Moon. Sappho. AWP; JAWP; WBP
Off Manilly. Edmund Vance Cooke. PAH
Off Portland: wind east, visibility eight. Hydrographic Report. Frances Frost. EtS
Off Rivière du Loup. Duncan Campbell Scott. EtS; HBV; MCCG; OBCV; PTK
Off Saguenay. A. G. Bailey. ACV
Off-shore, by islands hidden in the blood. I, Maximus of Gloucester, to You. Charles Olson. LiTM (1970 ed.)
Off Spectacle Island. Richard Eberhart. ToPo
Off the coast of Ireland. Seascape. Langston Hughes. BrR
Off the Ground. Walter de la Mare. RG; StaSt; StPo; YT
Off to Sea Once More, 2 *vers., with music.* *Unknown.* ShS
(Jack Wrack, *with music.*) ABF
Off to the Fishing Ground. L. M. Montgomery. CaP
Off to Yakima. Leroy F. Jackson. GaP
Off Viareggio. Kenneth Pitchford. CoPo
Off we go into the wild blue yonder. The U. S. Air Force. Robert Crawford. PoRL
Off We Go to Market. Gwen A. Smith. BoTP
Off with sleep, love, up from bed. Love in May. Jean Passerat. AWP
Off with the ruffle! Washington. Robert Haven Schauffler. PaA
Off with your hat! along the street. The Marquis of Carabas. Robert Brough. HBV
Off with your hat as the flag goes by! The Old Flag. Henry Cuyler Bunner. PAL; PGD
Off Womanheid Ane Flour Delice. *Unknown.* OxBS
Offender, The. Denise Levertov. NePoEA-2
Offensive, The. Keith Douglas. NeBP
Offer, An. Arthur Guiterman. TrJP
Offering. Leslie Savage Clark. ChIP
Offering, An. George Herbert. MaMe
Offering, The. Olive Cecilia Jacks. MaRV
Offering. Thomas MacDonagh. ACV
Offerings. Rodrigo De Reinosa. CLwM
Offertory. Mary Mapes Dodge. HH
Office building treads the marble dark, The. The Minute. Karl Shapiro. ATP (1953 ed.); MiAP; MoVE; UnPo (3d ed.)
Office feels like a sealed glass case today, The. What Grandma Knew. Edward Field. CoPo; FRC
Office of Poetry, The. Nathaniel Whiting. *Fr.* Il Insonio Insonnado. OBS
Office of the Holy Cross[e], The. Richard Crashaw. MaMe
"Third hour's deafen'd with the cry, The." *Sel.* PoG
Officer Brady. Robert W. Chambers. BOHV; InMe
Officers get all the steak[s], The. World War I. *Unknown.* FaFP; SiTL; TreFT
Officers' Mess (1916). Harold Monro. BrPo
Officers' Prison Camp Seen from a Troop-Train, An. Randall Jarrell. WaP
Off'rings of the Eastern[e] kings of old, The. Royal[l] Presents. Nathaniel Wanley. MaRV; OBS; OxBoCh
Offshore. Philip Booth. SD
Oft am I by the women told. Age. Abraham Cowley. AWP; CavP; JAWP; OnPM; WBP
Oft, as we run the weary way. Courage. Stopford Brooke. WGRP
Oft did I hear our eyes the passage were. Sir John Davies. *Fr.* Sonnets to Philomel. SiPS
Oft had I heard of Lucy Gray. *See* Oft I had heard of Lucy Gray.
Oft happening on some halting paraphrase. Of a Dead Poet. Lord Alfred Douglas. JKCP (1926 ed.)
Oft has it been my lot to mark. The Chameleon. James Merrick. HBV
Oft has our poet wisht, this happy seat. Epilogue Spoken at Oxford by Mrs. Marshall [*or* Epilogue Spoken by Mrs. Boutell]. Dryden. ATP; CEP; FaBoEn; MBW-1; SeCV-2
Oft have I heard my lief[e] Corydon report on a love-day. Hexametra Alexis in Laudem Rosamundi [*or* In Praise of Rosamund]. Robert Greene. *Fr.* Greene's Mourning Garment. AtBAP; ElL; PoEL-2; TuPP
Oft have I heard of Lucy Gray. *See* Oft I had heard of Lucy Gray.
Oft have I mused, but now at length I find. A Farewell. Sir Philip Sidney. ElL; EnLi-1; EnRePo; FCP; OBSC; ReIE; SiCE; SiPS
Oft have I mused the cause to find. Ladies' Eyes Serve Cupid Both for Darts and Fire. "A. W." OBSC
Oft have I said, I say it once more. Odes. Hafiz, *tr. by* Emerson. AWP; OuHeWo
Oft have I searcht both court and towne. *Unknown.* SeCSL
Oft Have I Seen at Some Cathedral Door. Longfellow. Divina Commedia, I. TreF
(Dante.) OBEV (new ed.)
(Divina Commedia, I.) AmePo; AmP; AmPP; AnAmPo; AnFE; AnNE; AP; APA; ATP; CoAnAm; CoBA; GoBC; HBV; ILP; MWA-1; NePA; NoP; OQP; OxBA; PoE; Sonn; ViBoPo
(On Dante's "Divine Comedy.") AnEnPo
(On Translating the "Divina Commedia.") OuHeWo
(Peace through Prayer.) MaRV
(Three Sonnets on the Divina Commedia, I.) SeCeV
Oft have I seen, when that renewing breath. Resurrection and Immortality. Henry Vaughan. AnAnS-1; MeP
Oft have I sigh'd for him that heares me not. Thomas Campion. FaBoEn
Oft Have I Stood by Thee. Robert Browning. *Fr.* Pauline. MaRV
Oft have I stood upon the foaming strand. Darkness. James Naumburg Rosenberg. AA
Oft have I wakened ere the spring of day. Will It Be So? Edith M. Thomas. *Fr.* The Inverted Torch. AA
Oft have I walked these [*or* the] woodland paths. Under the Leaves. Albert Laighton. HBV; OHIP
Oft have you seen a swan superbly frowning. To Charles Cowden Clarke. Keats. EnRP
Oft I had heard of Lucy Gray. Lucy Gray; or, Solitude. Wordsworth. BEL; BeLS; CH; EnRP; EPN; ERoP-1; FiP; GTSL; HBV; MBW-2; MERP; OAEP; OBRV; OnSP; OTPC; PoFS; PRWS; SeCeV; TOP; TreFS; UnPo (1st ed.)
Oft I must strive with wind and wave. Anchor. *Unknown.* *Fr.* Riddles. AnOE
Oft in my laughing rhymes I name a gull. Of a Gull. Sir John Davies. SiCE; TuPP
Oft in My Thought. Charles d'Orleans. NoP
Oft in the after days, when thou and I. Ad Matrem. Julian Fane. HBV
Oft in the Silent Night. Otto Julius Bierbaum, *tr. fr. German by* Ludwig Lewisohn. AWP; JAWP; WBP
Oft in the Stilly Night. Thomas Moore. AnFE; BEL; CBEP; CoBE; EnLit; EnRP; EPN; FaBoBe; GoBC; LiTB; LiTG; LoBV; MCCG; NeHB; OAEP; OBNC; OBRV; OTPC; OxBI; PoEL-4; WHA
(Light of Other Days, The.) FaFP; GTBS; GTBS-D; GTBS-P; GTBS-W; GTSE; GTSL; HBV; MaRV; OBEV; TreF; WePo
(Scotch Air.) PoE
Oft it befalls by the grace of God. Fates of Men. *Unknown.* AnOE
Oft I've implored the Gods in vain. A Prayer for Indifference. Fanny Greville. LoBV; OBEC
Oft o'er my brain does that strange fancy roll. Sonnet: Oft o'er My Brain [*or* Composed on a Journey Homeward]. Samuel Taylor Coleridge. ChER; Sonn
Oft-repeated Dream, The. Robert Frost. *Fr.* The Hill Wife. NP; PG (1945 ed.)
Oft shall the soldier think of thee. Ben Milam. William H. Wharton. PAH
Oft since thine earthly eyes have closed on mine. Sarah Helen Whitman. Sonnets from the Series Relating to Edgar Allan Poe, III. AA
Oft Thou Hast [with Greedy Ear]. *Unknown.* EnRePo; TuPP
Oft times I get to thinkin' of the changes times has wrought. A Veteran Cowboy's Ruminations. John M. Kuykendall. PoOW
Oft times I kneel among the hilltop pine trees. God's Gardener. Phyllis C. Michael. SoP
Oft times it seems my load of care. Take Thou My Hand. Phyllis C. Michael. SoP
Oft to the Wanderer, weary of exile. The Wanderer. *Unknown.* AnOE; EnL; LiTW
Oft-told Tale, An. *Unknown.* SGR
Oft upon the twilight plain. Ode, Solitude, at an Inn. Thomas Warton, the Younger. CEP

Oft when my spirit doth spre[a]d her bolder wing[e]s. Amoretti, LXXII. Spenser. EG: EnLi-1; OAEP; OBSC; SiCE; Sonn
Oft when the fires of sunset were sinking and dying. The Wood-Gatherers. F. C. Slater. BoSA
Oft with true sighs, oft with uncallèd tears. Astrophel and Stella, LXI. Sir Philip Sidney. FCP; SiPS
Often,/ Stepping so delicately through the shrubbery of learning. Salt. Monk Gibbon. OxBI
Often beneath the wave, wide from this ledge. At Melville's Tomb. Hart Crane. AmLP; AP; ATP (1953 ed.); CBV; CoBMV; FosPo; InPo; MoAmPo (1962 ed.); NePA; NoP; Po; PoIE; ReMP; SeCeV (1967 ed.); UnPo
Often darkness fills the pathway of the pilgrim's onward track. The One Who Plans. *Unknown.* SoP
Often, for pastime, mariners will ensnare. The Albatross. Baudelaire. SyP
Often had I found her fair. Chorale. A. D. Hope. ErPo; UnTE
Often, half-way to sleep. In Procession. Robert Graves. TwCP
Often I Am Permitted to Return to a Meadow. Robert Duncan. NMP
Often I have heard it said. Her Lips [*or* Song]. Walter Savage Landor. HBV; NeHB
Often I saw, as on my balcony. Christ Church Meadows, Oxford. Donald Hall. NYBP
Often I talk to men, on this or that. Talk. Philip A. Stalker. FiBHP
Often I think of the beautiful town. My Lost Youth [*or* Sea Memories]. Longfellow. AA; AmePo; AmPP; AnFE; AnNE; AP; APA; AWP; CLwM; CoAnAm; CoBA; EtS; ExPo; FaBoBe; FaBV; FaFP; FaPON; GoJo; GTBS-D; GTBS-W; GTSE; HBV; HT; InPo; JAWP; LaNeLa; LiTA; MAmP; MCCG; MPB; MWA-1; NePA; OBEV; OTPC; OxBA; PCD; PFY; Po; PoEL-5; PoLF; PoRA; RG; RoGo; SeCeV; StP; TOP; TreF; ViBoPo; WBP
Often I try/ To analyse the quality. In Church. R. S. Thomas. BoPe
Often I watch the walkers on the street. On the Street. Hazel Hall. NP
Often in summer on a tarred bridge plank standing. Wild Bees. James K. Baxter. AnNZ
Often in the morning the fog is thick over Jersey. A View of Jersey. Edward Field. NeAP
Often Rebuked, Yet Always Back Returning. *At. to* Emily Brontë. *See* Stanzas: "Often rebuked, yet always back returning."
Often the lone man waits for mercy. The Lone Man. *Unknown.* *Fr.* Widsith. PoLi
Often the lonely one longs for honors. The Wanderer. *Unknown.* EnLi-1 (1949 ed.)
Often the pain of living have I met. The Pain of Living. Eugenio Montale. OnPM
Often the road-menders gather. Fever. "Klabund." OnPM
Often the western wind has sung to me. A Prayer. Lord Alfred Douglas. CAW; JKCP (1926 ed.); TrPWD
Often the woodman scares them as he comes. Wood-Pigeons. John Masefield. ChMP
Often this thought wakens me unawares. Night. Hermann Hesse. AWP; JAWP; WBP
Often waking/ before the sun decreed the kind of day. The Author of *Christine.* Richard Howard. CoAP
Often we spent an intimate night. The Room and the Windows. Feng Chih. LiTW
Often, when o'er tree and turret. Hic Vir, Hic Est. Charles Stuart Calverley. NBM; OxBoLi
Often with heavy burdens freighted. The Coach of Time. Pushkin. LiTW
Oftener Seen, the More I Lust, The. Barnabe Googe. *See* Out of Sight, Out of Mind
Ofttimes for sport the mariners will take. The Albatross. Baudelaire, *tr. by* Frances Winwar. EnLi-2
Ofttimes have I heard you speak of one who commits a wrong. Crime and Punishment. Kahlil Gibran. *Fr.* The Prophet. PoToHe (new ed.)
Ofttimes I get to thinking of the changes time has wrought. The Old-Time Cowboy. *Unknown.* CoSo
Oft-times it has been told. *Constitution* and *Guerrière.* *Unknown.* ABF
Og and Doeg. Dryden. *Fr.* Absalom and Achitophel, Pt. II. AWP; FiP, *shorter sel.*; JAWP; WBP
("And hasten Og and Doeg to rehearse.") MBW-1
(Characters from the Satires: Og and Doeg.) InPo
("Doeg though without knowing.") PoEL-3
"Now stop your noses readers, all and some," *sel.* PeRV
Ogden Nash Gets All the Cash. David McCord. ML
Ogier the Dane. William Morris. *See* Song from "Ogier the Dane."
O'Grady's Goat ("O'Grady lived in Shanty row"). Will S. Hays. PoLF
Ogres and Pygmies. Robert Graves. CABA; CBV; CMoP; FaBoMo; LiTB; LiTM; SeCePo; SeCeV
Ohnawa. John Hunter-Duvar. *Fr.* De Roberval. VA
Oho for the woods where I used to grow. The Song of the Christmas Tree. Blanche Elizabeth Wade. OHIP
Oho! have you seen the Frost-King. The Frost-King. Mary Mapes Dodge. DD
O'Hussey's Ode to the Maguire. *At. to* Eochadh O'Hussey, *tr. fr. Late Middle Irish by* James Clarence Mangan. AnIV; IrPN; SeCePo
(Hugh Maguire, *tr. by* Frank O'Connor.) AnIL; KiLC
(Ode to the Maguire, *tr. by* James Clarence Mangan.) OnYI; OxBI
Oil Painting of the Artist as the Artist. Archibald MacLeish. Frescoes for Mr. Rockefeller's City, IV. NAMP; OnHM; UnPo
Oisin. *Unknown,* *tr. fr. Irish by* Frank O'Connor. KiLC
Oisin in the Land of Youth. Michael Comyn, *tr. fr. Modern Irish by* Tomás O'Flannghaile. AnIL
Oisin, tell me the famous story. The Wanderings of Oisin. W. B. Yeats. BrPo
Ojibwa War Songs. *Unknown,* *tr. fr. Ojibwa Indian by* H. R. Schoolcraft. AWP; JAWP; WBP
O.K. ("O.K./ you scat taking.") Victor Hernandez Cruz. BF
OK, it's imperishable or a world as Will. The Same Old Jazz. Philip Whalen. NeAP
Okay a nightingale. Robin Blaser. *Fr.* The Faerie Queene. CoPo
Okefenokee Swamp. Daniel Whitehead Hicky. AmFN
Oklahoma. Harriet Parker Camden. PoRL
Oklahoma Plates. Randy Blasing. YAP
Ol' Ark's a-Moverin' an' I'm Goin' Home, De, *with music.* *Unknown.* BoAN-2
Ol' Clothes. *Unknown.* PoToHe (new ed.)
Ol' Cow Hawse, The. Earl Alonzo Brininstool. SCC
Ol' Dan Tucker clomb a tree. Old Dan Tucker. *Unknown.* ABF
Ol' Doc' Hyar. James Edwin Campbell. BANP
Ol' Hag, You See Mammy? *with music.* *Unknown.* OuSiCo
Ol' Jinny Mine, The. Daisy L. Detrick. PoOW
Ol' John Brown. *Unknown.* ABF
Ol' Man, De. Alonzo W. Combs. IHA
Ol' Mother Hare, *with music.* *Unknown.* ABF
Ol' Rattler, *with music.* *Unknown.* ABF
Ol' Sheep Done Know de Road, De, *with music.* *Unknown.* BoAN-2
Old. Ralph Hoyt. AA
Old, The. Roden Noel. OBEV (1st ed.); OBVV; YT
(Dying.) VA
Old, The/ Old winds that blew. Night Winds. Adelaide Crapsey. QFR
Old Abe Lincoln [Came Out of the Wilderness], *with music.* *Unknown.* AS; TrAS
Old Abram Brown. *Unknown.* RIS
("Old Abram Brown is dead and gone.") OxNR
Old Adam. Thomas Lovell Beddoes. *Fr.* Death's Jest Book. ELP
Old Adam, The. William Rose Benét. YaD
Old Adam, The. Denise Levertov. NaP
Old Adam, *with music.* *Unknown.* AS
Old Adam, the Carrion Crow. Thomas Lovell Beddoes. *See* Song: "Old Adam, the carrion crow."
Old Age. Al-Aswad, Son of Ya'fur, *tr. fr. Arabic by* Sir Charles Lyall. *Fr.* The Mufaddaliyat. AWP
Old Age. Maxwell Bodenheim. MAP; MoAmPo (1942 ed.)
Old Age. Longfellow. *Fr.* Morituri Salutamus. SoP
Old Age. Sir Philip Sidney. *Fr.* Arcadia. SiPS
Old Age. Sophocles, *tr. fr. Greek by* A. E. Housman. *Fr.* Oedipus at Colonus. LiTW
(Chorus: "What man is he that yearneth," *tr. by* A. E. Housman.) AWP; JAWP; WBP

("Endure what life God gives and ask no longer span," *tr. by* W. B. Yeats.) OBMV
Old Age. Edmund Waller. *Fr.* Of the Last Verses in the Book. BoC; MaRV; OBEV; OxBoCh; TreFT
Old Age am I, with lockes thin and hoar. Age. Sir Thomas More. EnRePo; TuPP
Old Age Home, The. Theodore Holmes. CoPo
Old age is. To Waken an Old Lady. William Carlos Williams. InPo; NoP; PoeP; PoIE; QFR
Old Age of Michelangelo, The. F. Templeton Prince. PeSA
Old Age, on tiptoe, lays her jewelled hand. A Minuet on Reaching the Age of Fifty. George Santayana. FaFP; HBMV; LiTM; NePA
Old Age Pensioner, The. Joseph Campbell. AnIL
Old Air, An. F. R. Higgins. AnIL
Old I Am ("Old am I in years and wisdom and."). Herman Charles Bosman. PeSA
Old Amusement Park. Marianne Moore. NYBP
Old Anchor Chanty. Herbert Trench. AnFE
Old, and abandon'd by each venal friend. Impromptu [*or* On Lord Holland's Seat Near Margate, Kent]. Thomas Gray. CABA; EiCP; HoPM; MyFE; NCEP; PeER; SeCePo; SeCeV
Old and alone sit we. The Old Men. Walter de la Mare. MoAB; MoBrPo
Old and crippled veteran to the War Department came, An. Scott and the Veteran. Bayard Taylor. PaA; PAP
Old and New ("Farewell, Old Year!"). *Unknown.* BLRP
Old and New ("She went up the mountain"). *Unknown, tr. fr. Chinese by* Arthur Waley. AWP; LiTW
Old and New Art. Dante Gabriel Rossetti. The House of Life, LXXIV-LXXVI.
Husbandman, The, III. MaVP; PoVP; ViPo
Not As These, II. MaVP; PoVP; ViPo
St. Luke the Painter, I. GoBC; MaVP; PoVP; ViPo
Old and New Year Ditties, *sel.* Christina Rossetti.
Passing Away [Saith the World], III. EPN; GoBC; GTBS-W; OBEV (1st ed.); OBNC; OBVV; TOP; ViPo
Old and quiet house set down, An. Possessions. Lizette Woodworth Reese. HBMV
Old and sick, you turn away from mirrors, whether. Late Reflections. Babette Deutsch. NYBP
Old and the New, The. "Q. B. M." SoPo
Old and Young. Francis William Bourdillon. VA
Old and Young Courtier, The. *Unknown. at. to* Thomas Dekker. CLwM; ViBoPo
(Old and the New Courtier, The.) CoMu
Old Angler, The. Walter de la Mare. GoTL (1949 ed.); OAEP (2d ed.)
Old Apis, old sacred bull. A Song for Old Apis. James Schevill. FiMAP
Old Are Sleepy, The. Harold Lenoir Davis. NP
Old Arm-Chair, The. Eliza Cook. ATP; OTPC (1923 ed.); PaPo; WBLP
Old as I am, for ladies' love unfit. Apology for Love. Boccaccio. LiTW
Old Astronomer to His Pupil, The. Sarah Williams. BLPA
"Though my soul may set in darkness," 2 *ll.*; MaRV; TRV
Old Atheist Pauses by the Sea, An. Thomas Kinsella. ELU
Old Bachelor, The, *sel.* Congreve.
"Thus grief still treads upon the heels of pleasure," 2 *ll. fr.* V, iii. TreF
Old Bachelor, An. Tudor Jenks. BOHV; LHV
Old Bachelor, The ("I am a stern old bachelor"), *with music. Unknown.* ABF
Old Balaam. *Unknown.* PoOW
Old Bangum. *Unknown.* *See* Sir Lionel.
Old Barbarossa. Sleeping Heroes. Edward Shanks. OBMV
Old Bard Speaks, The. Joseph R. N. Maxwell. JKCP (1955 ed.)
Old Bark Hut, The. *Unknown.* PoAu-1
Old Baron, The. Thomas Miller. VA
Old Battle-Field, An. Frank L. Stanton. OQP
Old battle field, fresh with spring flowers again. All That Is Left. Basho. AWP; LiTW; PoPo; WaaP
Old Bayou, The. Madison Cawein. PFY
Old Beard a-Shakin', *with music. Unknown.* BFSS
Old bellwether, The. Lamb. Humbert Wolfe. MoBrPo
Old Ben Franklin was a merry old soul. Merry Old Souls. Morris Bishop. WhC
Old Bill (2 *vers.*), *with music. Unknown.* ABF
(Dis Mornin', Dis Evenin', So Soon, *sl. diff.*) AS
Old Bill Barnacle sticks to his ship. The Barnacle. A. P. Herbert. RIS
Old Bill the Whaler said to me. Bill the Whaler. Will Lawson. PoAu-1
Old Bill's Memory Book. William Rose Benét. InMe
Old Birch, who taught the village school. The Retort. George Pope Morris. BOHV; HBV
Old Black Billy an' Me, The. Louis Esson. BoAu; NeLNL
Old Black Joe. Stephen Collins Foster. FaFP; IHA; TreFS
Old Black Men. Georgia Douglas Johnson. CDC; PoNe
Old Blue. Robert P. Tristram Coffin. OA
Old Blue. *Unknown.* OuSiCo, *with music*; SD *diff. vers.*
Old Blue was tough. Old Blue. Robert P. Tristram Coffin. OA
Old Boards. Robert Bly. NaP
Old Boat, The. Lenore Pratt. CaP
Old Boniface he loved good cheer. *Unknown.* OxNR
Old Books Are Best. Beverly Chew. HBV
Old Botany Bay. Mary Gilmore. PoAu-1
Old boys, the cracked boards spread before. Bread. James Dickey. NoP
Old Brass Wagon, *with music. Unknown.* AS
Old Bridge, The. Hilda Conkling. MPB; PoPo; SP
Old Bridge at Florence, The. Longfellow. HT
Old bridge has a wrinkled face, The. The Old Bridge. Hilda Conkling. MPB; SP
Old Brother Ass stands mumchance in the sun. Brother Ass. Eric Irvin. BoAV
Old brown hen and the old blue sky, The. Continual Conversation with a Silent Man. Wallace Stevens. LiTM (rev. ed.); NePA
Old Brown Horse, The. W. K. Holmes. BoTP
Old Brown Schoolhouse, The. *Unknown.* TreF
Old brown thorn-trees break in two high over Cummen Strand, The. Red Hanrahan's Song about Ireland. W. B. Yeats. *Fr.* Hanrahan and Cathleen the Daughter of Hoolihan. ACV; CMoP; FaBoCh; FaBoMo; LoGBV; OnYI; OxBI
Old Buccaneer, The. Charles Kingsley. *See* Last Buccaneer, The.
Old Buck's Ghost. Frank Benton. PoOW
Old Buffer, An. Frederick Locker-Lampson. CenHV
Old Bullock Dray, The. *Unknown.* PoAu-1
Old Burying-Ground, The. Whittier. AP
Old Cabin, The. Paul Laurence Dunbar. PoLF
Old castle towers o'er the billow, An. Fineen the Rover. Robert Dwyer Joyce. JKCP (1926 ed.)
Old castles on the cliff arise. John Dyer. *Fr.* Grongar Hill. ViBoPo
Old Cat and the Young Mouse, The. La Fontaine, *tr. fr. French.* CIV
Old Cat Care. Richard Hughes. OBMV; ShBV-1; ThWaDe
Old Cat Meditates, An. Margaret E. Bruner. CIV
Old Cavalier, The. Sir Francis Hastings Doyle. VA
Old Chang, the Crab. *Unknown, tr. fr. Chinese by* Isaac Taylor Headland. PCH
Old charcoal-seller, An. The Charcoal-Seller. Po Chü-i. WoL
Old Chartist, The. George Meredith. FOL; NBM
"Whate'er I be, old England is my dam!" *sts.* 1-5. PoFr
Old Chaucer doth of Thopas [*or* Topas] tell. Nymphidia; or, The Court of Fairy. Michael Drayton. OAEP; ReEn; SeEP; TuPP
Old Chaucer, like the morning star. On Mr. Abraham Cowley, His Death and Burial amongst the Ancient Poets. Sir John Denham. AnAnS-2; OBS; SeCV-1
Old Chief, feeling now well-nigh his end, The. A Chippewa Legend. James Russell Lowell. MPB
Old Chisholm Trail, The. *Unknown.* BeLS; BFSS, *with music*; CoSo, *add. sts., with music*; FaBoBe; TreFT
(Chisholm Trail, The, *diff. vers., with music.*) TrAS
(Old Chizzum Trail, The, *diff. vers., with music.*) ABF
Old Christmas. Roy Helton. *See* Old Christmas Morning.
Old Christmas. Mary Howitt. GN; OTPC
Old Christmas. Sir Walter Scott. PTK
Old Christmas Carol, An ("Joseph was an old man"). *Unknown.* *See* Cherry Tree Carol, The.
Old Christmas Greeting, An. *Unknown.* *See* Christmas Greeting ("Sing hey! Sing hey!").
Old Christmas Morning. Roy Helton. MAP; MoAmPo; NeMA
(Old Christmas.) MaC; PoMS
Old Christmas Returned. *Unknown.* GN; OHIP

Old Christmastide. Sir Walter Scott. *See* Christmas in the Olden Time.
Old Churchyard of Bonchurch, The. Philip Bourke Marston. HBV; NBM; OBNC; OBVV; VA
Old City, The. Ruth Manning Sanders. CH
Old Cloak, The. *Unknown.* BuBa; OBB; OBEV; OBSC; TrGrPo
(Tak Your Auld Cloak about Ye, *sl. diff.*) OxBS
(This Winter's Weather It Waxeth Cold.) InvP
Old Clock on the Stairs, The. Longfellow. CoBA; HBV; OTPC, *sl. abr.*; WBLP
Old Coach Road, The. Rachel Field. GFA
Old College Song with Variant Lines to Suit. *Unknown.* TreFT
Old Conservative, The. L. Frank Tooker. EtS
Old Continentals, The. Guy Humphreys McMaster. *See* Carmen Bellicosum.
Old Convict, The. H. A. Vaughan. PoNe
Old Coon-Dog Dreams, The. Kenneth Porter. GoTP
Old Cornish Litany, An. *Unknown. See* Litany for Halloween.
Old Cottagers, The. John Clare. OBRV
Old Countryside. Louise Bogan. AmLP; LiTA; NePA; NP; TwAmPo
Old Couple, The, *sel.* Thomas May.
"Dear, do not your fair beauty wrong," III, i. EG; TuPP; ViBoPo
(Love's Prime.) SeCL
Old Cove, The. Henry Howard Brownell. PAH
Old Cowboy, The. *Unknown.* CoSo
Old Cowboy's Lament, The. Robert V. Carr. PoOW
Old Cowman, The. Badger Clark. SCC
Old Cowman, The/ cross-legged, sat before the fire. Eighteen-ninety. E. Richard Shipp. PoOW
Old Crabbed Men. James Reeves. ChMP; ErPo
Old cradle of an infant world. Ode to Jamestown. James Kirke Paulding. PAH
Old creeping time, with silent tread. On the Birthday of a Young Lady. William Whitehead. OTPC (1923 ed.)
Old Crow, The, *with music. Unknown.* FTB
Old Crow, upon the tall tree-top. The Crow. Mrs. Alexander. BoTP; OTPC (1946 ed.); PCH
Old Crumbly Crust, *with music. Unknown.* BFSS
Old Crummles, *with music. Unknown.* FTB
Old Cumberland Beggar, The. Wordsworth. CABL; EnRP; ERoP-1; LaA; MBW-2; MERP; PoE
Old Cyniras to the Nymphs this net: no more. Old Fisherman. Julian. OnPM
Old Dad Morton has got us in jail, 'tis hard. The Cryderville Jail. *Unknown.* ABF
Old Daddy Darkness. James Ferguson, *ad. fr. Scotch.* RIS
Old Daddy Witch. *Unknown.* ExPo
Old Dame Cricket. *Unknown.* GFA
Old Damon's Pastoral. Thomas Lodge. OBSC; SiCE
Old Dan Tucker. Daniel Decatur Emmett. ABF; TrAS, *with music*
Old Dan Tucker, *with music. Unknown.* ABF; TrAS
Old Dan'l. L. A. G. Strong. ELU; MoBrPo; NeMA; PoSC; WhC
Old Deep Sing-Song. Carl Sandburg. FIW
Old Diamond Joe was a rich old jay. Diamond Joe. *Unknown.* CoSo; OuSiCo
Old Dick Johnson, gentleman adventurer. The Dick Johnson Reel. "Jake Falstaff." EvOK; WhC
Old Doctor Foster. *Unknown.* OxNR
Old Dog, An. Celia Duffin. PCD
Old Dog, The. Robert Frost. *See* Span of Life, The.
Old Dog. Leonard Twynham. StaSt
Old dog barks backward without getting up, The. The Span of Life [*or* The Old Dog]. Robert Frost. DiPo; FIW; HoPM; LiTM; RIS; SiTL
Old Dog lay in the summer sun. Sunning. James S. Tippett. SiSoSe; SUS; TiPo
Old Doll, The. Wilhelmina Seegmiller. MPB
Old draught-ox, worn in the furrowed field, The. The Draught-Ox. Addoeus. OnPM
Old dream comes again to me, The. Mir träumte wieder der alte Traum [*or* Superfluous Bite]. Heine. AWP; JAWP; OnPM; WBP
Old Dubuque. Dave Etter. AmFN
Old Earthworks. Thomas Sweeney. OQP
Old Eben Flood, climbing alone one night. Mr. Flood's Party. E. A. Robinson. AmP; AmPP; AnAmPo; AnEnPo; AnNE; AP; AWP; BoLiVe; CABA; CaFP; CBV; CMoP; CoBMV; CrMA; EvOK; FaFP; FaPL; HoPM; ILP; InP; InPo; JAWP; LiTA; LiTM (rev. ed.); MAP; MaPo; MoAB; MoAmPo; NePA; NP; OxBA; PAn; PoE; PoPl; PoPo; PoRA; PoSa; ReMP; SeCeV; TreFT; TrGrPo; TDP; UnPo (3d ed.); ViBoPo; WBP
Old Egyptians hid their wit. On Mr. Nash's Picture. Jane Brereton. WaPE
Old Ellen Sullivan. Winifred Welles. FaPON; GaP; MPB; TiPo
Old elm trees flock round the tiled farmstead, The. Childhood. Sir Herbert Read. BrPo
Old Emily. Hyacinthe Hill. GoYe
Old Enemy, The. Sara Teasdale. MaRV
Old England is eaten by knaves. Song. Alexander McLachlan. *Fr.* The Emigrant. OBCV
Old England's sons are English yet. Ready, Ay, Ready. Herman Charles Merivale. HBV; OTPC; PTK; VA
Old English Carol: "All you that in this house be here." *Unknown.* OHIP
Old English Charm Song. *Unknown.* CAW
Old English Prayer. *Unknown.* TreFT
Old Essex Door. Agnes MacCarthy Hickey. GoYe
Old Euclid drew a circle. Euclid. Vachel Lindsay. ImOP; MAPA; NAMP; PoPo; TSW; TwAmPo; YaD
Old Face, An. Francesca Falk Miller. PEDC
Old face of the mother of many children, The. The Justified Mother of Men. Walt Whitman. *Fr.* Faces. OHIP
Old Falcon, The. Eleanor Baldwin. NYTB
Old Familiar Faces, The. Charles Lamb. AWP; BLPA; CBEP; EnLit; EnRP; EPN; FaBoBe; FaFP; GTBS; GTBS-D; GTBS-P; GTBS-W; GTSE; GTSL, *sl. abr.*; HBV; JAWP; LiTG; NBM; NeHB; OBEV; OBRV; PCD; PG; PoPl; PoSa; TOP; TreF; ViBoPo; WBP; YAT
("I have had playmates, I have had companions.") EG
Old Farmer Alone. Robert P. Tristram Coffin. MoLP
Old Farmer Giles. *Unknown.* OxNR
Old Farmer Oats and his son Ned. Song. John Jay Chapman. PoEL-5
Old Fashioned Fun. Thackeray. BOHV; InMe
Old-fashioned Garden, The. John Russell Hayes. AA
Old-fashioned Love. *Unknown.* MaC
(Original Love-Story, An.) BoLP
Old-fashioned Poet, An. Ada Foster Murray. HBV
Old Father Annum. Leroy F. Jackson. GaP; SiSoSe
Old Father Greybeard. *Unknown.* OxNR
Old Father Grimes, that good old man. Roll, Johnny Booger. *Unknown.* BFSS
Old Father Ocean calls my Tyde. A Song of the River Thames. Dryden. *Fr.* Albion and Albanius. FaBoEn
Old Fellow. Ernest Walsh. ErPo
Old Feminist, The. Phyllis McGinley. ThLM
Old Fence Post. Leigh Hanes. GoYe
Old Field Mowed, An. William Meredith. NYBP
Old Figurehead Carver, The. H. A. Cody. EtS
Old fish fiddle with their fins and glide, The. Aquarium. George T. Wright. NYBP
Old Fisherman. Julianus, *tr. fr. Greek by* Lord Neaves. OnPM
Old Fisherman, The. *Unknown, tr. fr. Chinese by* C. W. Luh. OnPM
Old Fitz, who from your suburb grange. To Edward Fitzgerald. Tennyson. LoBV; PoEL-5
Old Flag, The. H. C. Bunner. PAL; PGD
Old Flag. Hubbard Parker. DD; HH; OTPC (1946 ed.); PoRL
Old Flag Forever, The. Frank L. Stanton. DD; HH
(Our Flag Forever.) PGD
Old Flagman, The. Carl Sandburg. YaD
Old Flemish Lace. Amelia Walstien Carpenter. AA
Old Flood Ireson, all too long. A Plea for Flood Ireson. Charles Timothy Brooks. PAH
Old Folks at Home. Stephen Collins Foster. AA; FaBoBe; FaFP; HBV; InP, *with music*; TreF; WBLP
(Swanee River.) PoRL
Old forgetting, An. After Pain. Marjorie Meeker. NP
Old Fort Meigs. *Unknown.* MC; PAH
Old Fortunatus, *sels.* Thomas Dekker.
"Behold you not this globe, this golden bowl." ViBoPo
Fortune and Virtue. GoTL

(Fortune.) OBSC
(Fortune Smiles.) AtBAP
O Pittie. AtBAP
"Oh, whither am I rapt beyond myself?" ViBoPo
Song: "Virtue's branches wither, virtue pines." ElL
(Priest's Song, A.) OBSC
("Virtue's branches wither, virtue pines.") SiCE
"Stay, Fortunatus, once more hear me speak." ViBoPo
Old Forty-nine. Mart Taylor. SGR
Old friend, dear friend. A. R. D. Fairburn. *Fr.* To a Friend in the Wilderness. AnNZ
Old friend, I greet you! you are still the same. To One Who Denies the Possibility of a Permanent Peace. Lady Margaret Sackville. HBMV; MaRV
Old friend, your place is empty now. No more. To Scott. Winifred Letts. PoLF
Old friends/ when I was young. Song. Louis Zukofsky. NYTB
Old Friendship. Eunice Tietjens. NP
Old Fritz, on this rotating bed. A Flat One. W. D. Snodgrass. AmPC; AP; LiTM (1970 ed.); NePoEA-2; PoCh
Old Furniture. Thomas Hardy. MoVE
Old Gaelic Lullaby, An. *Unknown. See* Gaelic Lullaby.
Old Garden, The. Joseph von Eichendorff, *tr. fr. German by* Werner Heider. LiTW
Old Gardener Time. Rachel Field. GBV (1952 ed.)
Old Gardens. Arthur Upson. HBV
Old General, The. Sir Charles Hanbury Williams. *Fr.* Isabella. OBEC
Old German Mottos. *Unknown, ad. by* Louis Untermeyer. StaSt
Old Ghost, The. Thomas Lovell Beddoes. WiR
Old gilt vane and spire receive, The. The Late, Last Rook. Ralph Hodgson. MoBrPo
Old Glory! say who. The Name of Old Glory. James Whitcomb Riley. GN
Old Gods, The. Edwin Muir. EaLo; FaBoMo; POTE
Old gods, avaunt! The rosy East is waking. Courage, All. Edwin Markham. HBMV
Old Grahame he is to Carlisle gone. Bewick and Graham. *Unknown.* BaBo; ESPB
Old Gramophone Records. James Kirkup. MuSP; NYBP
Old Gray [*or* Grey] Goose, The. *Unknown.* ABF, *with music;* ChTr; FTB, *with music*
("Go tell old Nancy.") LaNeLa
Old gray hoss come tearin' out-a wilderness, De. Tearin' Out-a Wilderness. *Unknown.* ABF
Old Gray Mare, *with music. Unknown.* AS
Old Gray Squirrel. Alfred Noyes. PoMa
Old Grenadier's Story, The. George Walter Thornbury. VA
Old Grey Goose, The. *Unknown. See* Old Gray Goose, The.
Old Grey Hearse goes rolling by, The. The Hearse Song. *Unknown.* ABF; AS; DTC; OxBoLi
Old grey shade of the mountain, The. In the Selkirks. Duncan Campbell Scott. CaP
Old Grey Wall, The. Bliss Carman. CaP
Old Grimes. Albert Gorton Greene. AnAmPo; BeLS; BOHV; HBV; HBVY; InMe; OnPP; OTPC; StaSt; TreFS
Old Gumbie Cat, The. T. S. Eliot. GoTP
Old guy put down his beer, The. Do the Dead Know What Time It Is? Kenneth Patchen. MoAmPo
Old Habitant, An. Frank Oliver Call. *Fr.* A Sonnet Series of French Canada. CaP
Old Hen and the Cock, The. John Gay. *Fr.* Fables. EiCP
Old Hercynian Forest sent, The. The Village Stork. Bayard Taylor. PFY
Old Heywood, have with thee, in his odd vein. To Old John Heywood the Epigrammatist, Wheresoever. John Davies of Hereford. SiCE
Old Hokum Buncombe, The. Robert E. Sherwood. InMe
Old Home, The. Madison Cawein. HBV
Old Homes. Edmund Blunden. MoVE
Old Horace on a summer afternoon. Classical Criticism. George Lynde Richardson. AA
Old Horn to All Atlantic said. Frankie's Trade. Kipling. EtS
Old horse dies slow, The. When Structure Fails Rhyme Attempts to Come to the Rescue. William Carlos Williams. PP
Old Horse in the City, The. Vachel Lindsay. UTS
Old Horse in the Field, The. Viola Meynell. MemP
Old horse, old horse, what brought [*or* how came] you here? The Sailor's Grace [*or* Blow the Man Down, *vers.* V]. *Unknown.* ShS; SoAmSa
Old Hound. Florence Ripley Mastin. PoMa
Old House, The. William Barnes. OBVV
Old House, The. George Edward Woodberry. HBMV
Old house leans upon a tree, The. Deserted. Madison Cawein. MAP; MCCG
Old House waits for no one, The. The House on Maple Hill. Stanley McNail. FiSC
Old Houses. Homer D'Lettuso. PoToHe (new ed.)
Old Houses. Jennie Romano. PoToHe (new ed.)
Old Houses of Flanders, The. Ford Madox Ford. CTC; HT
Old Hundred. Mark Van Doren. UnS
Old Hundredth. Thomas Ken. UnS
Old Hundredth. William Kethe. *See* Hundredth Psalm, The.
Old Hymns, The. Frank L. Stanton. BLRP
Old I Am. Herman Charles Bosman. PeSA
Old I Am. Thomas Stanley, *after the Greek of* Anacreon. AWP; OnPM
Old, indeed, as his people go—three score years and ten. The Councillor. Cullen Gouldsbury. BoSA
Old Inmate, An. Kenneth Mackenzie. PoAu-2
Old Inn on the Eastern Shore. William H. Matchett. NePoEA
Old Inn-Sign, The. Wilfrid Thorley. BrR
Old inventive poets, had they seen, The. The River Duddon, XX. Wordsworth. EnLi-2
Old Irish Blessing, An. *Unknown.* TRV
Old Iron. Douglas Stewart. BoAV
Old Ironsides. Oliver Wendell Holmes. AA; AmePo; AmLP; AmPP (3d ed.); AP; BBV; BLPA; CoBA; DD; EtS; FaBoBe; FaFP; FaPL; FaPON; GN; HBV; HBVY; MaC; MC; MCCG; NeHB; OTD; OTPC; OuHeWo; PaA; PAH; PAL; PAP; PoPL; PoRL; PTK; ThLM; TreF; YaD
Old Ironsides at anchor lay. The Main-Truck; or, A Leap for Life. George Pope Morris, *also at. to* Walter Colton. PaPo; PoLF
Old Jack-o'-lantern lay on the ground, An. Judging by Appearances. Emilie Poulsson. MPB
Old January. Spenser. *Fr.* The Faerie Queene, VII, 7. YeAr
Old Jew, The. Maxwell Bodenheim. NP
Old Jim Finley had a little pig. Jim Finley's Pig. *Unknown.* FTB
Old Joan. Kathleen Conyngham Greene. PCH
Old Jockey, The. F. R. Higgins. AnIV; GTBS-D; OBMV; OxBI
Old Joe. *Unknown.* OxBoLi
Old Joe Brown, he had a wife. *Unknown.* GoTP
Old Joe Clark[e], *with music. Unknown.* ABF; TrAS, *diff. vers.*
Old Joe Digger, Sam and Dave. Groun' Hog. *Unknown.* ABF
Old Joe is dead, and gone to hell. Old Joe. *Unknown.* OxBoLi
Old John Bax. Charles H. Souter. PoAu-1
Old John Henry. James Whitcomb Riley. OnPP
Old Joyce. Seán Jennett. NeIP
Old Jumpety-Bumpety-Hop-and-Go-One. The Kangaroo. *Unknown.* SoPo
Old Keg of Rum, The. *Unknown.* PoAu-1
Old King, The. John Heath-Stubbs. NePoEA
Old King Cole. E. A. Robinson. HBV
Old King Cole was a merry old soul. Mother Goose. BoChLi; ExPo; FaBoBe; FaFP; GaP; HBV; HBVY; OTPC; OuSiCo; OxNR; PPL; RIS; SiTL; SoPo; StVeCh (1940 ed.)
Old King Cole was a merry old soul. Variations on an Air. G. K. Chesterton. InP
Old King James made a vow. King William and King James. *Unknown.* BFSS
Old Kitchen Clock, The. Ann Hawkshaw. BoTP; OTPC (1923 ed.)
Old Knight, The. George Peele. *See* His Golden Locks. . .
Old Lady, The. Humbert Wolfe. InP; OnPP; TSW
Old lady, when last year I sipped your tea. To An Old Lady Dead. Siegfried Sassoon. MemP
Old Lady Who Swallowed a Fly, The. *Unknown.* ShM
Old lady writes me in a spidery style, An. A Letter from Brooklyn. Derek Walcott. ToPo
Old Lambro pass'd unseen a private gate. Byron. *Fr.* Don Juan, III. EnRP
Old lame Bridget doesn't hear. The Shadow People. Francis Ledwidge. GaP; MCCG; MPB; PCH; SP; TSW
Old Lamp, The. *Unknown.* SoP
Old lane, an old gate, an old house by a tree, An. The Old

Old (continued)
Home. Madison Cawein. HBV
Old Leadville was booming in eighty-eight. The Little Johnny Mine. Daisy L. Detrick. PoOW
Old Lecher, The. Louis O. Coxe. TwAmPo
Old Lem. Sterling A. Brown. IDB; PoNe; TTY
Old Lesson. *Unknown.* TreFT
Old Liberals, The. John Betjeman. ChMP
Old Line Fence, The. A. W. Bellaw. BOHV
Old Lines; a Fragment. Dino Campana, *tr. fr Italian by* Glauco Cambon. OnPM
Old lions/ be with us now. Ode in a Night of Overhanging Weather. Vincent McHugh. WaKn
Old Lizette on Sleep. Agnes Lee. HBMV
Old Log House. James S. Tippett. BrR; FaPON; RePo
Old London's time-encrusted walls. London, 1940. A. A. Milne. MaRV
Old-long-syne. *Unknown.* OBS
Old looking glass grows darker, it is true. Color Alone Can Speak. Louise Townsend Nicholl. NePoAm
Old Looney of Rhyme, An. *Unknown.* SiTL
Old Love. William Morris. GTBS; ViPo; ViPP
Old Love, The. Katharine Tynan. HBMV
Old Love. Keith Wilson. ThO
Old Lover to a Young Gentlewoman, An. *Unknown.* TuPP
Old Loves. Henry Murger, *tr. fr. French by* Andrew Lang. AWP
Old Mackenzie Trail, The. John A. Lomax. SCC
Old, mad, blind, despised, and dying king, An. England in 1819 [*or* Sonnet: England in 1819]. Shelley. BWP; CABA; CBEP; EnL; EnLi-2 (1949 ed.); EnRP; EPN; ERoP-2; FiP; MaPo (1969 ed.); NoP; OAEP; OBRV; PoFS; SeCePo; SeCeV; Sonn; StP; TrGrPo
Old Maid, The. George Barlow. VA
Old Maid. J. U. Nicholson. HBMV
Old maid, an old maid, An. *Unknown.* OxNR
Old Man, The. Beatrice Herford. PEDC
Old Man. Elizabeth Jennings. NePoEA-2
Old Man. Edward Thomas. ChMP; LiTM (1970 ed.); MoVE; SeCeV
Old Man, An. Wordsworth. FaBoCh; LoGBV
(Animal Tranquility and Decay.) ERoP-1
(Sketch, A.) BoPe
Old Man and Jim, The. James Whitcomb Riley. AA; BOHV; LHV; StPo
Old Man and the Ass, The. La Fontaine, *tr. fr. French by* Elizur Wright. OnPM
Old Man and Young Wife, The. *Unknown.* CoMu
Old man asked the girl what she wanted for supper, The. An Old Man's Courtship. *Unknown.* BFSS
Old Man at a Cricket Match. Norman Nicholson. HaMV; POTi
Old Man at the Crossing, The. L. A. G. Strong. OBMV
Old man bending I come among new faces, An. The Wound-Dresser. Walt Whitman. AmePo; AmPP (5th ed.); AP; CoBA; MWA-1; ViBoPo
Old man called for Johnny, The. Johnny and the Highwayman. *Unknown.* BFSS
Old man dozed, The. The hospital quietened. Burns Singer. *Fr.* Sonnets for a Dying Man. NePoEA-2
Old Man Dreams, The. Oliver Wendell Holmes. HBV; PoLF
Old Man from Peru, An. *Unknown.* *See* Limerick: "There was an old man from Peru."
Old man, going [*or* traveling] a lone highway, An. The Bridge Builder [*or* Building the Bridge for Him]. Will Allen Dromgoole. FaChP; MaRV; NeHB; OQP; PoToHe; SoP; STF; TreFS; TRV
Old man had been listless, but he perked, The. End of Steel. Thomas Saunders. CaP
Old man had his box and wheel, The. The Scissors-Grinder. Vachel Lindsay. MAPA; TwAmPo
Old man in a lodge within a park, An. Chaucer. Longfellow. AA; AmePo; AmLP; AmP; AmPP; AP; ATP (1935 ed.); AWP; CBEP; CBV; CLwM; DiPo; InPo; InvP; JAWP; MAmP; ML; MWA-1; NePA; NoP; OBEV (new ed.); OBVV; OnPP; OxBA; PoIE (1970 ed.); PoRA; PP; PTK; Sonn; TOP; TrGrPo; WBP
Old Man in the Moon, The. *Unknown.* PCH
Old Man in the Park. Mary Elizabeth Osborn. NePoAm-2
Old man leaning on a gate, An. From My Window. Mary Elizabeth Coleridge. OBNC
Old Man Long Ago. Nancy Byrd Turner. GaP
Old Man Mose. Chorus. Jack Kerouac. *Fr.* Mexico City Blues. NeAP
Old Man Mountain. Alfred Noyes. GoBC
Old man never had much to say. The Old Man and Jim. James Whitcomb Riley. AA; BOHV; LHV; StPo
Old Man of Boulogne, An. *Unknown.* *See* Limerick: "There was an old man of Boulogne."
Old Man of St. Bees. W. S. Gilbert. *See* Limerick: "There was a young man of St. Bees."
Old Man of Tennessee. John Hay. NePoAm-2
Old man of the sea, briny bell. Now Is Farewell. Blanaid Salkeld. NeIP
Old Man of Verona, The. Claudian, *tr. fr. Latin by* Abraham Cowley. AWP; JAWP; WBP; WoL
Old Man, or Lad's-Love—in the name there's nothing. Old Man. Edward Thomas. ChMP; LiTM (1970 ed.); MoVE; SeCeV
Old Man Playing with Children. John Crowe Ransom. MoPW
Old Man Pondered. John Crowe Ransom. MAP; MoAmPo
Old Man Pot. Lyon Sharman. CaP
Old Man Rain. Madison Cawein. GaP; PoSC
Old man, riding on his ass, An. The Old Man and the Ass. La Fontaine. OnPM
Old Man Said, An. Padraic Colum. *See* Deer of Ireland, The.
Old man sits in wrinkled reverie, An. An Evasion. Douglas Livingstone. PeSA
Old man stood at eventide, An. It Might Have Been. Walter E. Isenhour. SoP
Old Man to His Scythe, The. Denis Wrafter. NeIP
Old man, traveling a lone highway, An. *See* Old man going a lone highway, An.
Old man walks to me, The. Lawrence McGaugh. *Fr.* Glimpses, xii. BOLo
Old man went to meetin', for the day was bright and fair, The. The Preacher's Vacation. *Unknown.* BLPA
Old Man Who Lived in a Wood, The. *Unknown.* MoShBr; MPB
("There was an old man who lived in a wood.") StVeCh
Old man whose black face, An. The Rainwalkers. Denise Levertov. CAD; NePoEA-2
Old man, whose flannel undershirt, An. The Beekeeper. Jack Matthews. NYTB
Old Man with a Beard. Edward Lear. *See* Limerick: "There was an old man with a beard,/ Who said, 'It is just as I feared!' "
Old Man with a Mowing Machine. May Carleton Lord. GoYe
Old Mandarin, The/ Always perplexes his friend the Adjuster. Unearned Increment. Christopher Morley. SiTL; WhC
Old Mandarin was always pleased, The. Psychoanalysts. Christopher Morley. WhC
Old Man's Carousal, The. James Kirke Paulding. AA
Old Man's Comforts [and How He Gained Them], The. Robert Southey. HBV; HoPM; PaPo; Par; YAT
(Father William.) OTPC
Old Man's Complaint, The: by Mr Wells. *Unknown.* PeRV
Old Man's Courtship, An. *Unknown.* BFSS
Old man's fair-haired consort, whose dewy axle-tree, The. Slowly, Slowly [*or* Lente, Lente]. Ovid. AWP; LiTW; WoL
Old man's flamingo-coloured kite, An. Earthquake. James Kirkup. POTi
Old Man's Idyl, An. Richard Realf. AA; HBV
Old Man's Song, An. Richard Le Gallienne. HBV; VA
Old Man's Toes, The. Eleanor Farjeon. PoRh
Old Man's Winter Night, An. Robert Frost. AmPP; AnAmPo; AnEnPo; AnNE; AWP; BoLiVe; CoBA; HBMV; JAWP; MAP; MoAB; MoAmPo; MoVE; MWA-2; NP; OnPP; OxBA; PoMa; WBP
Old Man's Wish, The. Walter Pope. BoPe; CoMu, *longer vers.;* OBS; SeEP
(Wish, The.) SeCL
Old man's words, The (something has skittered the cattle). The Panther Possible. William D. Barney. FiSC
Old Mansion. John Crowe Ransom. OxBA
Old Manuscript. Alfred Kreymborg. MAP; NeMA; NP
Old Maps. Eunice Tietjens. BrR
Old Mare, The. Elizabeth J. Coatsworth. MAP; MoAmPo
Old Marlborough Road, The. Henry David Thoreau. PoEL-4

Old Marquis and His Blooming Wife, The. *Unknown.* CoMu
Old Marrieds, The. Gwendolyn Brooks. AmNP; PoNe
Old Marse John. *Unknown.* TTY
Old Mary. Gwendolyn Brooks. TDP
Old Masters, The. Emile Verhaeren, *tr. fr. French by* Jethro Bithell. AnEnPo
Old May Song. *Unknown.* AtBAP; BoTP; CH; HH
Old Mayor climbed the belfry tower, The. The High-Tide on the Coast of Lincolnshire (1571). Jean Ingelow. BeLS; GBV; GN; GTBS; GTBS-D; GTSL; HBV; NBM; OBVV; OnMSP; OtMeF; PaPo; ShBV-3; TOP; VA
Old Meg ("Old Meg she was a gipsy"). Keats. *See* Meg Merrilies.
Old Meg of Kitrann. Joseph Joel Keith. FiSC
Old memories waken old desires. Lovers Parted. Lesbia Harford. BoAu
Old Memory. W. B. Yeats. Po
Old Men, The. Walter de la Mare. MoAB; MoBrPo
Old Men, The. Irving Feldman. TwCP
Old Men, The. Alexander Javitz. TrJP
Old Men. Nancy Keesing. BoAV
Old Men. Ogden Nash. EvOK
Old Men, The. Ernest Rhys. POTE
Old Men Admiring Themselves in the Water, The. W. B. Yeats. CMoP; FaBoCh; GoJo; LoGBV; ViPo (1962 ed.)
Old Men and Old Women Going Home on the Street Car. Merrill Moore. MAP; MoAmPo
Old Men and Young Men. John Holmes. WaKn
Old Men Are Facts. Vivian Smith. NeLNL
Old men are full of zest and information. Old Men and Young Men. John Holmes. WaKn
Old Men on the Blue. Thomas Hornsby Ferril. PoOW
Old men sat with hats pull'd down, The. The White Rose over the Water. George Walter Thornbury. VA
Old men sit by the chimney piece and drink the good red wine, The. The Green Estaminet. A. P. Herbert. HBMV
Old men, white-haired, beside the ancestral graves. Basho. AWP; JAWP; PoPo; WBP
Old Menalcas on a day. The Palmer's Ode. Robert Greene. *Fr.* Never Too Late. CTC; EnRePo; OBSC; SiCE; TuPP
Old Men's Ward. Elma Dean. GoYe
Old Michael. George M. Brady. NeIP
Old Mike Clancy went out for a stroll. Two Days. T. A. Daly. LHV
Old Mill, The. Thomas Dunn English. AA
Old Mr. Chang, I've oft heard it said. Old Chang, the Crab. *Unknown, tr. by* Isaac Taylor Headland. PCH
Old Mr. Tatterlock. Irene Cheyne. MoAuPo
Old Mrs. Caribou lives by a lake. Mrs. Caribou. William Jay Smith. PoMS
Old Mrs. Jarvis. Elizabeth Fleming. BoTP
Old Mrs. Kawabata. Yase: September. Gary Snyder. FRC
Old Mrs. Tressider. The Scarf. Ivy O. Eastwick. BoTP
Old Molly Means was a hag and a witch. Molly Means. Margaret Walker. AmNP; Kal; PoNe; StPo
Old Montague. M. K. Joseph. *Fr.* The Lovers and the City. AnNZ
Old moon is tarnished, The. Sea Lullaby. Elinor Wylie. BoNaP; NeMA
Old moon my eyes are new moon with human footprint. Poem Rocket. Allen Ginsberg. CoPo
Old Morgan. G. D. Roberts. BoTP
Old Mortality, *sels.* Sir Walter Scott.
And What Though Winter Will Pinch Severe, *fr. ch.* 19. EnRP
Sound, Sound the Clarion, *fr. ch.* 34. Thomas O. Mordaunt, *formerly at. to* Scott. AnFE; InP; OAEP; OQP; TOP
(Answer.) OBEV (1st ed.)
(Call, The.) GTBS-W; OBEV (new ed.)
(Clarion.) BEL
(One Crowded Hour.) MaRV; TrGrPo
(Sound the Clarion.) TreFS
Old Mother, The. *Unknown.* PoToHe
Old Mother Duck has hatched a brood. Dame Duck's First Lecture on Education [*or* Mother Duck]. Ann Hawkshaw. BoTP; OTPC (1923 ed.); SAS
Old Mother Earth woke up from her sleep. A Spring Song. *Unknown.* PoLF
Old Mother Goose when/ She wanted to wander. Mother Goose. BoTP; OTPC (1923 ed.); OxNR; PPL; RIS; SoPo
Old Mother Hubbard. Sarah Catherine Martin. BoChLi; BoTP; GoTP; FaBoBe; HBV; HBVY; OnMSP; OTPC; OxNR; RIS; SAS; SiTL; SoPo; StVeCh; TiPo (1959 ed.)
Old Mother Niddity Nod. *Unknown.* OxNR
Old Mother Shuttle. *Unknown.* EvOK; OxNR
Old Mother Tabbyskins. Elizabeth Anna Hart. *See* Mother Tabbyskins.
Old Mother Twitchett has [*or* had] but one eye. Mother Goose. HBV; HBVY; OTPC; OxNR; RIS; SiTL; SoPo; TiPo
Old Mother Wind. *Unknown, tr. fr. Chinese by* Isaac Taylor Headland. PCH
Old Mother Witch. *Unknown.* RIS
Old Mothers. Charles S. Ross. *See* Dear Old Mothers.
Old Music Box, The. Rachel Field. BoChLi
Old Navy, The. Frederick Marryat. *See* Captain Stood on the Carronade, The.
Old New Hampshire. John F. Holmes. PoRL
Old Nick in Sorel ("Old Nick took a fancy, as many men tell"). Standish O'Grady. *fr.* The Emigrant. OBCV; TDP
Old Nick, who taught the village school. The Retort. George Pope Morris. BOHV; HBV
Old Noah he had an ostrich farm and fowls on the largest scale. Wine and Water. G. K. Chesterton. *Fr.* The Flying Inn. ACP (1952 ed.); CenHV; FiBHP; GoBC; HBMV; InMe; LiTM; MoBrPo; ShBV-4; ViBoPo
Old Noah once he built the Ark. One More River. *Unknown.* TreFS
Old North State, The. William Gaston. PoRL, *abr.*
Old Nuns. James M. Hayes. JKCP
Old Nurse, The. Frances Cornford. MemP
Old Nurse Winter. Jean Starr Untermeyer. TSW
Old Nurse's Song, The. Edith Sitwell. NeMA; TSW
Old Oak Tree, The, *with music.* *Unknown.* ShS
Old Oaken Bucket, The, *parody.* *Unknown.* BLPA; FaFP; WBLP
Old Oaken Bucket, The. Samuel Woodworth. BLPA; FaBoBe; FaFP; NeHB; OTPC (1946 ed.); PaPo; PTK; TreF; WBLP
(Bucket, The.) AA; AmePo; HBV
"How dear to this heart are the scenes of my childhood,", *sel.* FaPON
Old ocean was/ Infinity of ages ere we breathed. The Beatific Sea. Thomas Campbell. EtS
Old October. Thomas Constable. HBV
Old, Old Bible, The. Marianne Farmingham. SoP
Old, old lady, The. The Old Lady. Humbert Wolfe. InP; OnPP; TSW
Old, Old Song, The. Charles Kingsley. *See* Young and Old.
Old One, lie down. Up the Hill, down the Hill. Eleanor Farjeon. PoSC
Old Orange Flute, The. *Unknown.* MuSP
(Ould Orange Flute, The.) OxBoLi
"Old order changeth, yielding place to new, The." Prayer [*or* Prayer for the Dead]. Tennyson. *Fr.* Morte d'Arthur. GoBC; MaRV; SoP; TRV
Old Paint. *Unknown.* *See* Good-by, Old Paint.
Old Paintings on Italian Walls. Kathleen Raine. NYBP
Old Parish Church, Whitby, The. Hardwicke Drummond Rawnsley. OBVV
Old Parson Beanes hunts six dayes of the week. Upon Parson Beanes. Robert Herrick. AnAnS-2
Old Pastor, The. John Banister Tabb. AmP
Old Peasant in the Billiard Saloon, The. Huw Menai. ACV
Old Peasant Woman at the Monastery of Zagorsk, The. James Schevill. NMP
Old Peter Grimes made fishing his employ. Peter Grimes. George Crabbe. The Borough, Letter XXII. EiCL; EnPE; EnRP; NoP; PoEL-4
Old Peter led a wretched life. The Perils of Invisibility. W. S. Gilbert. StPo
Old Peter Prairie-Dog. Prairie-Dog Town. Mary Austin. FaPON; StVeCh (1955 ed.); TiPo
Old Pictures in Florence. Robert Browning. PoVP
Old Pilot Tunnels under the English Channel, The. James Schevill. FiMAP
Old Pilot's Death, The. Donald Hall. TPM
Old pine, you whisper like the waves. The Whispering Pine Tree. Mariana Griswold Van Rensselaer. PCH
Old Place, The (New Zealand). Blanche Edith Baughan. AnNZ; BoAu
Old Pluvius, month of rains, in peevish mood. Spleen. Baudelaire. PIA

Old Poem: "Cold, cold the year draws to its end." *Unknown, tr. fr. Chinese by* Arthur Waley. AWP
Old poets fostered under friendlier skies. Poets and Their Bibliographies. Tennyson. PP
Old Pond, The. Basho. *See* Haiku: "Ancient pond, The."
Old Pope Is Comforted by the Thought of the Young Pompilia, The. Robert Browning. *Fr.* The Ring and the Book, X. BoC
Old priest Peter Gilligan, The. The Ballad of Father Gilligan [*or* Father Gilligan.] W. B. Yeats. AnIV; EaLo; EnLit; HBV; InP; InPo; MoBrPo; NeMA; OnYI; PoPo; PoRA; TSW; WaKn; WePo; WHL
Old Prison, The. Judith Wright. NeLNL; PoAu-2
Old professor of zoology, The. The Parrot. James Elroy Flecker. FaBoTw
Old Python Nose with the wind-rolling ears. To a Dead Elephant. Douglas Livingstone. PeSA
Old Quartermaster, The. Gordon Grant. EtS
Old Quin Queeribus. Nancy Byrd Turner. EvOK; GaP; SoPo; TiPo
Old Rat's Tale, An. *Unknown.* GFA
(What Became of Them?) BOTP
Old Red Hoss Mountain. Cy Warman. PoOW
Old Repair Man, The. Fenton Johnson. AmNP
Old Rhyme ("Here comes a lusty wooer"). *Unknown. See* Here Comes a Lusty Wooer.
Old Rhyme, An ("I went to market and bought me a cat"). *Unknown.* BoTP
Old ridiculous partner is back again, The. The She Wolf. Muriel Spark. NYBP
Old River Road. Blanche Whiting Keysner. GoYe
Old Road, The. Jones Very. AA
Old Road to Paradise, The. Margaret Widdemer. HBMV
Old Robin of Portingale. *Unknown.* ESPB, *abr.* OBB
Old Rodilard, a certain cat. The Council Held by the Rats. La Fontaine. CIV; OuHeWo
Old Roger. *Unknown.* OxBoLi
Old Room, The. W. S. Merwin. NYBP
Old Rosin, the Beau. *Unknown.* CoSo
Old Ross, Cockburn, and Cochrane too. The Battle of Baltimore. *Unknown.* PAH
Old rude church, with bare, bald tower, is here, The. Wordsworth's Grave. Sir William Watson. EnLit; GoTL; HBV; OBNC; PoVP
Old Ruralities. Charles Tennyson Turner. Sonn
Old rutted roads have been turned to macadams, The. John Adams. Rosemary Benét *and* Stephen Vincent Benét. PAL
Old Sailor, The. Glenn Ward Dresbach. EtS
Old Sailor, The. A. A. Milne. CenHV
Old Sailor, The. Elizabeth Riddell. MoAuPo
Old Sailor's Song. *Unknown.* SoAmSa
Old Saint, The. Muriel Stuart. HBMV
Old Sam Smith. The Shepherd. Mary Gilmore. ACV; PoAu-1
Old Sam was black and long of limb. Ancestry. William A. Donaghy. JKCP (1955 ed.)
Old Sam's Wife. *Unknown.* ChTr
(On the Wife of a Parish Clerk.) ShM
Old sandpiper contemplates his age, The. Summer's Early End at Hudson Bay. Hayden Carruth. NYBP
Old Santa Claus puts on his cap. Santa Claus. *Unknown.* GFA
Old Santa Fé Trail, The. Richard Burton. PAH
Old Santa Is an Active Man. Lois Lenski. ChBR
Old Saul. Lizette Woodworth Reese. MAP; MoAmPo
Old Scent of the Plum Tree. Fujiwara Ietaka, *tr. fr. Japanese by* E. Powys Mathers. AWP
Old School List, The. James Kenneth Stephen. CenHV
Old School Tie-up, The. Laurence McKinney. WhC
Old Scottish Cavalier, The. William Edmondstoune Aytoun. GN; HBV; PoVP
Old Scout's Lament, The. William F. Drannan. CoSo; PoOW
Old scythe in the hedge. The Old Man to His Scythe. Denis Wrafter. NeIP
Old sea captains, when their work, The. Between Brielle and Manasquan. Oliver St. John Gogarty. OnYI
Old sea-dog on a sailor's log, An. The Powerful Eyes o' Jeremy Tait. Wallace Irwin. FiBHP; StPo
Old Seaport, An. *Unknown.* EtS
Old Seawoman. Gordon LeClaire. CaP
Old Sergeant, The, *sel.* Forceythe Willson.
"Come a little nearer, doctor." AA; BeLS; PaA
Old Shellover. Walter de la Mare. AtBAP; BoTP; UTS
Old Shepherd's Prayer. Charlotte Mew. EaLo; MoAB; MoBrPo
Old Ship Riggers. H. A. Cody. EtS
Old Ships, The. James Elroy Flecker. AnFE; BoPe; BrPo; CH; CLwM; EnLit; EtS; EvOK; FOL; GTBS-D; GTSL; HT; MoBrPo; MoVE; OBMV; OtMeF; PoRA; POTE; RoGo; ShBV-3; WHA
Old Ships. Louis Ginsberg. HBMV
Old Ships. David Morton. BBV; EtS; StVeCh; TSW
Old Sexton, The. Park Benjamin. AA; HBV
Old, shade-baked dog bolted, The. The Dog. Sandford Lyne. QAH
Old shoe, an old pot, an old skin, An. Autumn Sequence. Adrienne Rich. NoP
Old Shoes and Leggin's, *with music. Unknown.* OuSiCo
Old shuddering Wordsworth, I'm in your country. Wordsworth and the Woman. Reed Whittemore. CBV
Old Silver church in a forest, An. Poet to His Love. Maxwell Bodenheim. BoLP; MAP; MoAmPo (1942 ed.); PoPl
Old Singer, The. Eden Phillpotts. MuSP
Old Sir Simon the king. *Unknown.* OxNR
Old sisters at our Maris Stella House. Mother Marie Therese. Robert Lowell. CoPo; FiMAP
Old Skinflint. W. W. Gibson. OBMV
Old Smoky. *Unknown. See* Wagoner's Lad, The.
Old Snapshot. Ronald Everson. MoCV
Old snow gets up and moves taking its, The. December among the Vanished. W. S. Merwin. NaP
Old Socrates, whose wisdom did excel. To Master Edward Cobham. Barnabe Googe. EnRePo
Old Sodos no longer makes saddles. Lola Ridge. *Fr.* The Ghetto. MAP; MoAmPo (1942 ed.)
Old Soldier. Padraic Colum. OBMV; POTE
Old Soldier Dead. Annette Kohn. HH
Old Song, The. G. K. Chesterton. FaBoTw
Old Song. Louis Dudek. ACV
Old Song. Edward Fitzgerald. GN, *abr.*; OBEV; OBVV
(Meadows in Spring.) HBV
Old Song, The. Charles Kingsley. *See* Young and Old.
Old Song. F. R. Scott. PeCV
Old Song ("Haste thee, Winter, haste away!"). *Unknown.* PCH
Old Song, An. "Yehoash," *tr. fr. Yiddish by* Marie Syrkin. AWP; JAWP; LiTW; WBP
Old Song by New Singers An. A. C. Wilkie. BOHV
Old Song Ended, An. Dante Gabriel Rossetti. *See* Friar of Orders Grey, The.
Old song made by an agéd old [*or* old aged] pate, An. The Old and Young [*or* the New] Courtier. *Unknown.* CLwM; CoMu; ViBoPo
Old Song of Fairies, An. *Unknown. See* Fairy Queen, The.
Old Song Resung, An. Charles Larcom Graves. CenHV
Old Song Re-sung, An. John Masefield. EvOK; ExPo; LiTB
Old Song Resung, An. W. B. Yeats. *See* Down by the Salley Gardens.
Old Song Reversed, An. Richard Henry Stoddard. AA
Old Song Written during Washington's Life. *Unknown.* OHIP
Old Song, Wrote by One of Our First New-England Planters, An. *Unknown. See* New England's Annoyances.
Old Songs, The. Sir Owen Seaman. InMe
Old Songs Die, The. Music. Alice Corbin. NP
Old Sorrow I shall meet again. Childhood. John Banister Tabb. HBV
Old Souldier of the Queens, An. *Unknown.* OBS
Old Souls. Thomas Gordon Hake. VA
Old South Boston Aquarium stands, The. For the Union Dead. Robert Lowell. AmPP (5th ed.); CoAP; FRC; LiTM (1970 ed.); MaPo (1969 ed.); NaP; NMP; NoP; PoAn; PoeP; SeCeV (1967 ed.); TDP; TwCP
Old Squaw, The. Indian Sky. Alfred Kreymborg. NP
Old Squire, The. Wilfrid Scawen Blunt. HBV; OBEV (new ed.); OBVV; SD; VA
Old Stoic, The. Emily Brontë. CBV; EnLi-2; EnLit; FaPL; OAEP; OBEV (new ed.); OBNC; OBVV; OxBI; PoFr; PoLF; PoPl; PoPo; PoVP; TreFT; TrGrPo; VA; ViBoPo; YT
Old Stormy [*or* Stormalong] was a fine [*or* gay] old man. Stormalong. *Unknown.* ShS; SoAmSa

Old Story, The ("Like many a one"). E. A. Robinson, *par. fr. the Greek of* Marcus Argentarius. AWP; JAWP; LiTW; WBP
Old Story, An ("Strange that I did not know him then"). E. A. Robinson. AnNE; HBMV; MAP; MaRV; MoAmPo; NeMA; TreFS
Old Story Over Again, The. James Kenney. OnYI
Old story went that the cajoling hag, The. The Hag. Ted Hughes. CBV
Old Street, An. Virginia Woodward Cloud. AA
Old Stuff. Bert Leston Taylor. BOHV; HBMV; LHV
Old Summerhouse, The. Walter de la Mare. CMoP; GTBS-P; MoPo
Old sun, the gold sun, The. Sun and Wind. Eleanor Farjeon. OTPC (1946 ed.)
Old *Supurb*, The. Sir Henry Newbolt. BBV (1923 ed.)
Old Susan. Walter de la Mare. CMoP; InP; MoBrPo; NeMA; OnPP; PoRL; TreFS
Old Sweet Dove of Wiveton, The. Stevie Smith. OA; PoG
Old Sweetheart of Mine, An. James Whitcomb Riley. BeLS; BLPA; NeHB
"As one who cons at evening o'er an album all alone," *sel.* TreFS
Old Swimmer, The. Christopher Morley. SD
Old Swimmin'-Hole, The. James Whitcomb Riley. BeLS; FaFP; HBV
Old Tale, An. Marya Zaturenska. NP
Old tales were told of Sigemund's daring. The Tale of Sigemund. *Unknown.* *Fr.* Beowulf. AnOE
Old Talk. Winfield Townley Scott. FiMAP
Old Temple in Mountains. Chang Chi, *tr. fr. Chinese by* Arthur Christy. OnPM
Old Tennis Player. Gwendolyn Brooks. SD
Old Testament, The. Thomas Russell. TreFS
(Names and Order of the Books of the Old Testament.) BLPA
Old Testament Contents. *Unknown.* BLPA
Old Thad Stevens. Kenneth Porter. NePoAm-2
Old, the mad, the blind have fairest daughters, The. The Beauty of Job's Daughters. Jay Macpherson. ACV; MoCV; PoCh
Old Things Need Not Be Therefore True. Arthur Hugh Clough. *See* Ah! Yet Consider It Again.
Old thorn tree in a stony place, An. Ode: On the Death of William Butler Yeats. A. J. M. Smith. OBCV; PeCV
Old Thought, An, *abr.* Maurice Hewlett. *Fr.* The Song of the Plow. PoFr
Old Thought, An. Charles Henry Luders. AA
Old Tillie Turveycombe. Tillie. Walter de la Mare. PoMS; TiPo
Old-Time Circus Clown, The. Frank L. Staunton. OTD
Old-Time Cowboy, The ("Ofttimes I get to thinking"). *Unknown.* CoSo
Old Time is lame and halt. Wie langsam kriechet sie dahin. Heine. AWP
Old-Time Sea-Fight, An. Walt Whitman. *Fr.* Song of Myself, XXXV. MaC; OnMSP
(Battle of the *Bonhomme Richard* and the *Serapis.*) UnPo (3d ed.)
(John Paul Jones.) PAL
("Would you hear of an old-time sea-fight?") CoBA; SeCeV; TrGrPo
Old-Time Service. Thomas Churchyard. *Fr.* A Fayned Fancye betweene the Spider and the Gowte. OBSC
Old Timers. Carl Sandburg. AnAmPo; NP; YaD
Old Times Were the Best, The. James Whitcomb Riley. FaFP
Old Tippecanoe. *Unknown.* PAH; ThLM
Old tips come out as good as new. John William Mackail. *Fr.* The Masque of Balliol. CenHV
Old Tithon must forsake his dear. *Unknown.* *Fr.* Wily Beguiled. TuPP
Old Tityrus to Eugenia, *sel.* Charles Cotton.
"Eugenia, young and fair and sweet." ViBoPo
Old Toast. *Unknown.* WePo
Old town lies afar, An. There Is an Old City. Karl Bulcke. AWP; JAWP; WBP
Old Tree, The. Andrew Young. GoJo
Old Tubal Cain was a man of might. Tubal Cain. Charles Mackay. GTBS; MPB; WBLP
Old Tune, An. Gérard de Nerval, *tr. fr. French by* Andrew Lang. AWP; HBV; JAWP; WBP
(Fantasy.) LiTW, *tr. by* Anthony Bower; SiSw, *tr. by* Geoffrey Wagner
Old Uncle Jim was as blind as a mole. Uncle Jim. Alice Corbin. *Fr.* Echoes of Childhood. PoNe
Old Venice grappled with the Turk. Captain Loredan. Edward King. PFY
Old Vicarage, Grantchester, The. Rupert Brooke. BrPo; FaBV; GoTL (1949 ed.); MoBrPo; MoVE; PoRA; ShBV-3; TOP; WePo
"Ah, God! to see the branches stir," *sel.* HT
Old Violin, The. Dorothy M. Barter-Snow. SoP
Old Violin, The. Maurice Francis Egan. AA; JKCP
Old Virginny. James A. Bland. FaBV
Old Voyager. Walter Blackstock. GoYe
Old waggon drudges through the miry lane, The. The Waggoner. Edmund Blunden. AnFE
Old Walt Whitman. Old Walt. Langston Hughes. ML
Old warder of these buried bones. In Memoriam A. H. H., XXXIX. Tennyson. EPN; OAEP; PoEL-5; ViPo; VP
Old watch, The: their. Vapor Trail Reflected in the Frog Pond. Galway Kinnell. OPoP
Old Waterford Woman, An. Mary Devenport O'Neill. NeIP
Old West, the old time, The. Spanish Johnny. Willa Cather. ABF; FaPON; HBMV; MPB; NP; OTD; PFY; RePo; WaKn
Old Wharves, The. Rachel Field. SoPo
Old wheel ruts deep still mark the trace. Wheel Ruts. James Daugherty. RePo
Old Whom God Loves, The. Robert Browning. *Fr.* A Death in the Desert. BoC
Old Wichet. *Unknown.* StPo
Old Wife and the Ghost, The. James Reeves. PDV; PoMS; ShM
Old Wife in High Spirits. "Hugh MacDiarmid." NMP; OPoP
Old Wife's Song. Eleanor Farjeon. RePo
Old Wife's Tale, The. George Peele. *See* Old Wives' Tale, The.
Old Willie Gray will sit and stare. The Monaro. David Campbell. BoAV
Old wind stirs the hawthorn tree, The. The Road of Remembrance. Lizette Woodworth Reese. HBV
Old wine filled him, and he saw, with eyes, The. Maurice de Guérin. Maurice Francis Egan. AA; JKCP
Old wine to drink! A Winter Wish [*or* Give Me the Old]. Robert Hinckley Messinger. AA; HBV; ViBoPo
Old Winter. Thomas Noel. DD, *abr.*; GN; HBV; OTPC (1923 ed.); PoSC
Old Winter is a sturdy one. Winter. *Unknown.* DD
Old Winter sad, [is] in snow yclad. Old Winter. Thomas Noel. DD; GN; HBV; OTPC (1923 ed.)
Old Wives Prayer, The. Robert Herrick. SeCV-1
Old Wives' [*or* Wife's] Tale, The, *sels.* George Peele.
Harvester's Song ("All ye that lovely lovers be"). TrGrPo
"Lo! here we come a-reaping, a-reaping," *4ll.* OBSC
Song at the Well, The. AtBAP; ExPo; SeCeV
(Celanta at the Well of Life.) LoBV; ThWaDe
(Fair Maiden.) PoEL-2
(Gently Dip.) ELP
(Voice from the Well [of Life Speaks to the Maiden], The.) CBEP; ChTr; FaBoEn
(Voice Speaks from the Well, A.) FaBoCh; LoGBV; OBSC; OxBoLi; SiTL
Spell, A. ChTr
"Whenas [*or* When as] the rye reach to the chin." EnLoPo; FaBoCh; InvP; LO; LoGBV; NoP; OBSC; SiTL; TuPP; ViBoPo
(Song.) ALV; AtBAP; ElL; FaBoEn; LoBV; OxBoLi; PoEL-2
(Summer Song, A.) OBEV (new ed.)
(When as the Rye.) SeCePo
(Whenas the Rye.) CBEP; ELP
Old Woman, The. John Bunker. CAW
Old Woman, The. Joseph Campbell. ACV; AWP; GoBC; HBMV; JAWP; MCCG; MoBrPo; NeHB; NeMA; NP; OnYI; OxBI; POTE; PoToHe (new ed.); TreFT; ViBoPo; WBP; YT
Old Woman, The. Beatrix Potter. GoJo; PDV
Old Woman, The. Marjorie Allen Seiffert. AnAmPo; NP
Old Woman, An. Edith Sitwell. CoBMV; MoPo
Old Woman. Iain Crichton Smith. NePoEA-2
Old woman—/ I can see you. Retrospect. Pearl Cleage. WSL

Old woman across the way, The. The Whipping. Robert Hayden. BP; IDB
Old Woman All Skin and Bone, *with music.* *Unknown.* TrAS
Old woman has forgotten her face, The. Evasion. Blanaid Salkeld. NeIP
Old Woman in a Cage. Christopher Hampton. NYTB
Old woman is cutting carnations, An. Driving through Belgium. Michael Brownstein. ANYP
Old Woman Laments in Springtime, An. Edith Sitwell. LO; ViBoPo
Old woman must stand, The. *Unknown.* OxNR
Old Woman of Beare [Regrets Lost Youth], The. *Unknown. See* Woman of Beare, The.
Old Woman of Berkeley, The. Robert Southey. OBRV
Old Woman of the Roads, An [*or* The]. Padraic Colum. BoC; BoTP; CAW; CH; FaBoBe; FaPON; GaP; GBV (1952 ed.); GoBC; GTSL; HBMV; JKCP; MoBrPo; MPB; NP; OBEV (new ed.); OnPP; OTPC (1946 ed.); PG; PoRA; RePo; SP; StVeCh; TreFS; WHA; YT
Old woman, old and bent and worn. Morning Bus. John Coulter. CaP
Old woman, old woman, are you fond of smoking? The Deaf Woman's Courtship. *Unknown.* SaSa
"Old woman, old woman, shall we go a-shearing?" Mother Goose. BoChLi; OTPC; OxNR; RIS; TiPo (1952 ed.)
"Old woman, old woman, will you go a-shearing?" The Deaf Woman's Courtship. *Unknown.* BFSS
Old Woman, outside the Abbey Theater, An. L. A. G. Strong. FiBHP; MoBrPo
Old Woman Remembers, The. Lady Gregory. OnYI
Old woman sits on a bench before the door and quarrels, The. Fawn's Foster-Mother. Robinson Jeffers. AmPP (3d ed.)
Old Woman Sitting in the Sun. Mary L. Inman. NYTB
Old Woman Speaks of the Moon, An. Ruth Pitter. BoC
Old woman went to market and bought a pig, An. *Unknown.* OxNR
Old Woman Who Bought a Pig, The, *with music.* *Unknown.* BFSS
Old Woman Who Lived in a Shoe, The. *Unknown.* LiTG; OxBoLi. *For* Mother Goose *vers., see* There was an old woman who lived in a shoe.
Old Woman Who Lives in the Town, The. Pringle Barret. PCH
Old Woman Who Went to Market, The, *with music.* *Unknown.* BFSS
Old Woman with Flowers, An. Agnes Lee. NP
Old Woman's Answer to a Letter from Her Girlhood, An. Susan L. Emory. CAW
Old Woman's Lamentations, An. Villon. *See* Complaint of the Fair Armouress, The.
Old Woman's Song. Thomas Cole. NePoAm-2
Old Women, The. George Mackay Brown. NePoEA-2; OxBS
Old Women. Babette Deutsch. HBMV
Old Women, The. Arthur Symons. PoVP
Old women do not know this piercing song. Desdemona. Sister Mary Jeremy. JKCP (1955 ed.)
Old Women Remember. Rosalie Boyle. NYTB
Old women say that children asleep are saints, The. The Sleeping Saint. Melvin Walker La Follette. CoPo
Old women say that men don't know. Becoming a Dad. Edgar A. Guest. PoLF
Old women sit at Willowsleigh and spin, The. Spinners at Willowsleigh. Marya Zaturensky. HBMV
Old women sit, stiffly, mosaics of pain. Old Women. Babette Deutsch. HBMV
Old-World Effect, An. Siegfried Sassoon. CMoP
Old world staggers, The, but a young, triumphant world is born. Toward a True Peace. Lucia Trent *and* Ralph Cheyney. *Fr.* Ten Years After. PGD
Old, worn harp that had been played, An. The Master-Player. Paul Laurence Dunbar. MaRV; SoP; TRV
Old Year, The. John Clare. PG
Old Year, The. Clarence Urmy. OQP; PGD; PoToHe
Old Year and the New, The. Annie Johnson Flint. BLRP
Old Year, going, take with you. Farewell and Hail! Thomas Curtis Clark. PGD
Old Year is a diary where is set, The. Ethel Romig Fuller. *Fr.* Diary. PGD
Old Year's Prayer, The. Minna Irving. PGD
Old yellow stucco, The. Winter Nightfall. J. C. Squire. ShBV-3
Old Yew, which graspest at the stones. In Memoriam A. H. H., II. Tennyson. BWP; ELP; EnLi-2; EPN; FaBoEn; GTBS-D; GTBS-P; MaPo; OAEP; OBNC; PIA; PoEL-5; SeCeV; UnPo (3d ed.); ViPo; VP
Old Zip Coon. *Unknown, at. to* Bob Farrell. *See* Zip Coon.
Olde Menalcas on a day. The Palmer's Ode. Robert Greene. *Fr.* Never Too Late. OBSC
Olden Days, The. Joseph Hall. *Fr.* Virgidemiarum. OBSC ("Time was, and that was termed the time of gold.") SiCE
Olden Love-making. Nicholas Breton. DiPo; OBSC
Older Grown. Kate Greenaway. BiCB
Older I grow, The. Triolet on a Downhill Road. Margaret Fishback. WhC
Older than Eden's planting, older than elves. The Word of Willow. Leah Bodine Drake. FiSC
Oldest Cemetery. Mark Van Doren. FiSC
Oldest of friends, the trees! Trees. Thomas Curtis Clark. OQP; PGD
Oldest Soldier, The. Robert Graves. DTC
Olduvai. Leroy Smith, Jr. NYTB
Ole Billy William ("Ole Mistah Billy William Goat"). Booth Lowery. IHA
Ole Tam on Bord-a Plouffe. William H. Drummond. PTK
O'Leary, from Chicago, and a first-class fightin' man. Yanks. James W. Foley. PaA
Olger the Dane and Desiderio. Charlemagne. Longfellow. *Fr.* Tales of a Wayside Inn. AnAmPo; FaFP; MWA-1
Olim Haec Meminisse Juvabit. Henry Parrot. SiCE
Olim Meminisse Juvabit. Aline Kilmer. JKCP
O'Lincoln Family, The. Wilson Flagg. HBVY; OTPC (O'Lincon Family, The.) HBV
Olive, *sel.* Joachim du Bellay, *tr. fr. French.*
Sonnet to Heavenly Beauty, A, CXIII, *tr. by* Andrew Lang. AWP; CTC; JAWP; WBP
(Sonnet: "If life on earth be less than is a day," *tr. by* Armel O'Conner.) CAW
(Sonnet: "If of our life the span be not a day," *tr. by* Eleanor L. Turnbull.) WoL
Olive, The. A. E. Housman. MaPo
Olive. Swinburne. GTBS
Olive Branch, The. Robert Herrick. OnPM
Olive Garden, The. Rainer Maria Rilke, *tr. fr. German by* J. B. Leishman. BoPe
Olive Grove. Lewis MacAdams. ANYP
Olive Grove. James Merrill. NePoAm
Olive in its orchard, The. The Olive. A. E. Housman. MaPo
Olive Tree, The. Sabine Baring-Gould. GN; OTPC (1946 ed.); SoP
Olive Trees. Padraic Colum. NePoAm
Olive Trees. Bernard Spencer. FaBoMo
Oliver Wendell Holmes. William Hamilton Hayne. DD
Oliver Wiggins. "Stanley Vestal." IHA
Olivia. Elijah Fenton. WaPE
Olivia. Edward Pollock. AA
Olivia. Tennyson. *Fr.* The Talking Oak. GN
Olivia's lewd, but looks devout. Olivia. Elijah Fenton. WaPE
Olivier Metra's Waltz of Roses. La Mélinite: Moulin-Rouge. Arthur Symons. PeVV; SyP
Ollie, Answer Me. Stephen Berg. NaP
Ollie [*or* Mollie] McGee. Edgar Lee Masters. *Fr.* Spoon River Anthology. NP
Olrig Grange, *sel.* Walter C. Smith.
Daughters of Philistia. VA
Olympia, *sl. abr.* Boccaccio, *tr. fr. Latin by* Sir Israel Gollancz. WoL
Olympian Odes. Pindar. *See* Odes.
Olympian sunlight is the Poet's sphere. The Crystal. Titus Munson Coan. AA
Olympias' matchless son, whenas he knew. To Samuel Daniel, Prince of English Poets. Francis Davison. ReIE
Olympic Girl, The. John Betjeman. SD
Olympicus, don't look into a mirror. The Boxer's Face. Lucilius. SD
Om. "Æ." VA
Omar and Death, *abr.* Omar Khayyám, *tr. fr. Persian by* Edward Fitzgerald. *Fr.* The Rubáiyát. GTSE
("Ah, with the Grape my fading life provide," *abr.*)

GTBS-P; GTBS-W; OBEV; OBVV
(Ritual of the Grape.) OnPM
Omar and the Persian. Sarah Williams. VA
Omar for Ladies, An. Josephine Dodge Daskam Bacon. HBV
Ombre and basset laid aside. The South Sea Bubble. Countess of Winchilsea. CBEP
Ombre at Hampton Court. Pope. *Fr.* The Rape of the Lock, III. OBEC
("Close by those meads, for ever crowned with flowers.") FiP; OxBoLi; WHA
Ombre Chinoise. Amy Lowell. NP
Ombres Chinoises. Babette Deutsch. TPM
Omelet of A. MacLeish, The. Edmund Wilson. NYBP; Par
Omen. Birago Diop, *tr. fr. French by* Moore and Beier. FlW
Omens. James H. Cousins. OnYI
Omens. Michael Hamburger. NMP
Ominous length uncoiling and thin, An. Rattlesnake, The. Alfred Purdy. WHW
Omit, omit, my simple friend. To an Ambitious Friend. Horace. AWP
Omnia Exeunt in Mysterium. George Sterling. AnAmPo; WGRP
Omnia Somnia. Joshua Sylvester. OBS
(Go, Silly Worm.) ElL
Omnia Somnia. Rosamund Marriott Watson. HBV
Omnia Vanitas. Dugald Buchanan, *tr. fr. Gaelic.* GoTS
Omnia Vincit. Alfred Cochrane. HBV
Omnia Vincit. *Unknown. See* Fain Would I Change That Note.
Omnibus. John Donne. MaMe
Omnibus across the bridge, An. Symphony in Yellow. Oscar Wilde. MoBrPo; OTPC (1946 ed.); PCH; SyP
Omnipotence. Mabel Brown Denison. SoP
"Omnipotence Divine," I pray in awe. I Turn the Key. Winifred Corrigan. JKCP (1955 ed.)
Omnipotent and steadfast God. John Brown's Prayer. Stephen Vincent Benét. *Fr.* John Brown's Body. AtBAP; NP; PoNe
Omnipotent confederate of all good. Prayer. Amos N. Wilder. TrPWD
Omnipresence. Stanton A. Coblentz. MaRV
Omnipresence. Edward Everett Hale. SoP; TRV; WGRP
Omnipresent. Frank G. Weaver. SoP
Omnipresent Self. *Unknown, tr. fr. Sanskrit by* Joseph Nadin Rawson. *Fr.* The Upanishads. OnPM
Omniscience. Blanche Mary Kelly. TrPWD
Omnium Exeunt in Mysterium. George Sterling. *See* Omnia Exeunt in Mysterium.
Omphalos; the Well. Seán Jennett. NeIP
On a Bad Singer. Samuel Taylor Coleridge. BOHV; TreF
(Desired Swan-Song, The.) UnS; WhC
(Swan Song.) GoTP
(Swans Song.) EvOK; MemP
On a Baltimore Bus. Charles G. Bell. NePoAm
On a Bank [*or* the Banck] as I Sat [*or* Sate] a-Fishing. Sir Henry Wotton. AnAnS-2; LoBV; MyFE; OBS; SeCP
(Description of the Spring, A.) SeCL
(May Day, A.) CH
On a bank, beside a willow. The Tears of Amynta, for the Death of Damon. Dryden. MaPo
On a bank of flowers, in a summer-day. Blooming Nelly. Burns. UnTE
On a bare branch. Basho, *tr. fr. Japanese by* Geoffrey Bownas *and* Anthony Thwaite. FlW
On a Bas-Relief. Wesley Trimpi. NePoEA
On a battle-trumpet's blast. Shelley. *Fr.* Prometheus Unbound. OBRV
On a Beautiful Landscape. William Bowles. PoPo
On a Beautiful Youth Struck Blind with Lightning. Goldsmith, *after the Spanish.* OAEP
On a Bed of Guernsey Lilies. Christopher Smart. *Fr.* Ode to the Earl of Northumberland. BWP; OBEC
On a Birthday. J. M. Synge. ChTr; OBMV
On a Blind Girl. Baha Ad-din Zuhayr, *tr. fr. Arabic by* E. H. Palmer. AWP
On a Bookseller. Goldsmith. PV
On a Bougainvillaea Vine in Haiti [*or* at the Summer Palace]. Barbara Howes. MoAmPo (1962 ed.); NYBP
On a Boy's First Reading of "King Henry V." S. Weir Mitchell. AA; PFY
On a brown isle of Lough Corrib. Celibacy. Austin Clarke. JKCP (1926 ed.)
On a bull's hollow horn. Reaping the Barley. Jorge Carrera Andrade. WoL
On a Bust of Dante. Thomas William Parsons. AA; AnAmPo; HBV
On a Bust of Lincoln. Clinton Scollard. PEDC
On a Calm Summer's Night. John Nicholson. EnLoPo
On a Cast from an Antique. George Pellew. AA
On a center staff and on two cross bars. The Mother. Kathryn White Ryan. CAW
On a Certain Engagement South of Seoul. Hayden Carruth. AmFN; NMP; OPoP
On a Certain Lady at Court. Pope. ALV; BoLiVe; CBEP; CEP; CoBe; EiCL; EnLit; HBV; OAEP; OBEC; OBEV; TrGrPo
On a Certain Lord Giving Some Thousand Pounds for a House. David Garrick. PV
On a Certain Scholar. W. Craddle. SiTL; WhC
On a Child. Walter Savage Landor. *See* Child of a Day.
On a Child Beginning to Talk. Thomas Bastard. *See* Methinks 'Tis Pretty Sport.
On a Child Who Lived One Minute. X. J. Kennedy. NYBP
On a Child with a Wooden Leg. Bertram Warr. OBCV
On a cleere morne as Phoebus run his race. *Unknown.* SeCSL
On a Clergyman's Horse [Biting Him]. *Unknown.* GoTP; LiTG; OxBoLi; SiTL; TreFT; WhC
On a Cock at Rochester. Sir Charles Sedley. PeRV
On a Cock Which Was Stolen from a Good Priest. Egan O'Rahilly, *tr. fr. Modern Irish by* P. S. Dinneen *and* T. O'Donoghue. OnYI
On a Cold Day. W. H. Davies. BoPe
On a Cold Night. J. V. Cunningham. PoIE; QFR
On a cold winter day the snow came down. Proud Little Spruce Fir. Jeannie Kirby. BoTP
On a Contented Mind. Thomas, Lord Vaux. *See* Of a Contented Mind.
On a Country Road. Swinburne. *Fr.* A Midsummer Holiday. PoVP; TOP
On a Damaske Rose Sticking upon a Ladies Breast. Thomas Carew. AnAnS-2
On a dark and stormy night, as the train rattled on. In the Baggage Coach Ahead. Gussie L. Davis. TreFS
On a Dark Road. Robert Herrick. *Fr.* Night-Piece to Julia. BoTP
On a dark stormy mornin' when the snow was a-fallin'. The Wreck on the Somerset Road. *Unknown.* OuSiCo
On a dark, stormy night. The Wreck of Number Nine. *Unknown.* BFSS
On a Day—Alack the Day! Shakespeare. *Fr.* Love's Labour's Lost, IV, iii. ElL; ViBoPo
(Blossom, The.) OBEV; TDP
(Dumain's Rhymes.) OBSC
(Love's Perjuries.) GTBS; GTBS-D; GTBS-P; GTBS-W; GTSE; GTSL; HBV
(Passionate Shepherd's Song, The.) ReIE
On a day when the breath of roses. The Unwanted. C. Day Lewis. PoPl
On a Day's Stint. Sir Walter Scott. NBM
On a Dead Child. Robert Bridges. BrPo; CBV; CMoP; EnLi-2 (1949 ed.); GTSL; LiTB; LiTG; LiTM (rev. ed.); OAEP; OBEV (1st ed.); OBMV; OBNC; ViBoPo
On a Dead Child. Richard Middleton. OBVV
On a Dead Hostess. Hilaire Belloc. MoBrPo; MoVE
On a Dead Lady. Alfred De Musset, *tr. fr. French by* Germaine Loir. EnLi-2 (1949 ed.)
On a Dead Poet. Frances Sargent Osgood. AA
On a Dead Scholar, *sel.* St. Columcille, *tr. fr. Old Irish by* Robin Flower.
"Lon's away/ Cill Garad is sad today." AnIL
On a Dead Teacher. Gerald Raftery. JKCP (1926 ed.)
On a Deaf Housekeeper. *Unknown.* BOHV
On a Dentist. *Unknown. See* Epitaph on a Dentist.
On a Discovery Made Too Late. Samuel Taylor Coleridge. EnRP; Sonn
On a Distant Prospect of Eton College. Thomas Gray. *See* Ode on a Distant Prospect of Eton College.
On a Doctor Named Isaac Letsome. John Coakley Lettsom. *See* On Dr. Isaac Letsome.
On a Dream. Keats. CBEP; EnRP; ERoP-2; MBW-2

On (continued)
(Dream, after Reading Dante's Episode of Paolo and Francesca, A.) DiPo
On a Drop of Dew. Andrew Marvell. AnAnS-1; BWP; EnLi-1; FosPo; GoBC; GTBS-W; ILP; LiTB; LiTG; MaMe; MaPo (1969 ed.); MeLP; MeP; MePo; OBS; OuHeWo; OxBoCh; PoAn; PoFS; ReEn; SCEP-2; SeCP; SeCV-1; SeEP; UnPo (1st ed.)
(Drop of Dew, A.) WoL
On a Dying Boy. William Bell. NePoEA
On a Fair Beggar. Philip Ayres. EnLoPo; LO; OBS; SeCL; SeEP
On a Fair Morning. *Unknown.* ViBoPo
On a fair summer's morning of soft recreation. The Blackbird. *Unknown.* OnYI
On a Fair Woman. Francis Burdett Money-Coutts. OBVV
On a Family Picture. Thomas Edwards. Sonn
On a Fan That Belonged to the Marquise de Pompadour. Austin Dobson. ALV; OBVV; PoVP; ViBoPo
(On a Fan.) HBV; VA
On a Favorite Cat, Drowned in a Tub of Goldfishes. Thomas Gray. *See* Ode on the Death of a Favorite Cat, Drowned in a Tub of Goldfishes.
On a Ferry Boat. Richard Burton. AA
On a Fifteenth-Century Flemish Angel. David Ray. NePoEA-2
On a fine Sunday morning I mounted my steed. Sabbath-Day Chace. Philip Freneau. WoL
On a flat road runs the well-train'd runner. The Runner. Walt Whitman. PCH; SD; TSW
On a Flimmering Floom You Shall Ride. Carl Sandburg. GoYe
On a Fly Drinking Out of [*or* from] His Cup. William Oldys. EG; FaFP; GoTP; GTBS-W; LiTG; OBEV; TDP; TrGrPo; ViBoPo
(Anacreontick, An.) EiCL
(Fly, The.) CBEP; OBEC
(To a Fly.) OTPC (1923 ed.)
On a Flyleaf of Burns's Songs. Frederic Lawrence Knowles. HBV; PoMa
On a Fly-Leaf of Longfellow's Poems, *sel.* Whittier.
Undying Soul, The. MaRV
On a Fly-Leaf of Schopenhauer's "Immortality." Ruth Guthrie Harding. MaRV
On a Foolish Person. *Unknown.* CBV
On a Fortification at Boston Begun by Women. Benjamin Tompson. PAH; SCAP
On a Foule Morning, Being Then to Take a Journey. Richard Crashaw. MaMe
On a Fowler. Isidorus, *tr. fr. Greek by* William Cowper. AWP
On a Full-Length Portrait of Beau Marsh, *wr.* [Nash]. Earl of Chesterfield. *See* Immortal Newton Never Spoke.
On a General Election. Hilaire Belloc. *See* On a Great Election.
On a Gentleman in a Late Engagement against the Turks, Was Slain and Thrown Overboard, and She Since Mad. *Unknown.* SeCL
On a Gentlewoman Walking in the Snow[e]. William Strode. *See* On Chloris Walking in the Snow.
On a German Tour. Richard Porson. *See* Epigram on an Academic Visit to the Continent.
On a Girdle. Edmund Waller. ALV; AnAnS-2; AWP; BEL; CABA; CavP; CEP; EnLi-1; EnLit; GTBS; GTBS-D; GTBS-P; GTBS-W; GTSE; GTSL; HBV; InMe; InPo; JAWP; LiTB; LiTG; LiTL; LoBV; MeWo; NoP; OAEP; OBEV; OBS; PG (1945 ed.); PoAn; PoFS; PoIE; PoRA; SCEP-2; SeCePo; SeCL; SeCV-1; SeEP; StP; TOP; TreFS; TrGrPo; UnTE; ViBoPo; WBP; WHA
("That which her slender waist confined.") EG
On a Gloomy Easter. Alice Freeman Palmer. MaRV; OHIP
On a grassy pillow. Happy Myrtillo. Henry Carey. SeCePo
On a Grave at Grindelwald. Frederic William Henry Myers. VA
On a Grave in Christ-Church, Hants. Oscar Fay Adams. AA
On a Gravestone. *Unknown.* PCD
On a Great Election. Hilaire Belloc. OxBoLi; WhC
(On a General Election.) MoVE
On a Great Man Whose Mind Is Clouding. Edmund Clarence Stedman. AA
On a Grecian Urn. Keats. *See* Ode on a Grecian Urn.
On a Greek Vase. Frank Dempster Sherman. AA
On a green island in the Main Street traffic. Pro Patria. Constance Carrier. NePoAm; NYBP
On a green slope, most fragrant with the spring. My Rose. Hildegarde Hawthorne. AA
On a Halfpenny which a Young Lady Gave a Beggar, and which the Author Redeemed for Half-a-Crown. Henry Fielding. CBEP
On a Hand. Hilaire Belloc. BoLP; ELU
On a Hare. William Cowper. BoPe
On a hill that grac'd the plain. Thyrsis' Praise of His Mistress. William Browne. ReIE
On a hill there blooms a palm. Hayyim Nahman Bialik. *Fr.* Songs of the People. AWP; JAWP; WBP
On a hill there grows a flower. A Pastoral of Phillis and Corydon [*or* Phyllida and Corydon *or* Ipsa Quae]. Nicholas Breton. CoBE; ElL; LO; OBSC; SiCE; TrGrPo; TuPP
On a hillside in Italy. On an Italian Hillside. Richard Weber. NMP
On a holy day when sails were blowing southward. The Straying Student. Austin Clarke. AnIL; MoAB; NeIP; OxBI
On a Honey Bee [Drinking from a Glass of Wine and Drowned Therein]. Philip Freneau. AmPP; AP; CoBA; TDP
(To a Honey Bee.) AA; YaD
On a Horse and a Goat. R. P. Lister. PV
On a hot summer Sunday. The Cemetery at Academy, California. Philip Levine. NaP
On a Journey. Basho, *tr. fr. Japanese by* H. G. Henderson. OnPM
On a Lady Singing. Isaac Rosenberg. FaBoTw
On a Lady Singing Lawes's Music to Milton's Ode on the Nativity. J. C. Squire. MuSP
On a Lady Sleeping. *Unknown.* SeCL
On a Lady Throwing Snowballs at Her Lover. Christopher Smart. VaPo
On a Lady Who Beat Her Husband. *Unknown.* FiBHP
On a Lady with Foul Breath. Thomas Parnell. PoE
On a Little Bird. Martin Armstrong. *See* Bird's Epitaph, A.
On a little green knoll. Old Log House. James S. Tippett. BrR; FaPON; RePo
On a little piece of wood. Mr. and Mrs. Spikky Sparrow. Edward Lear. SAS
On a lonely road quite long ago. The Arkansas Traveler. *At. to* Sanford C. Faulkner. PoRL
On a Lonely Spray. James Stephens. AnFE; OnYI
On a Lord. Samuel Taylor Coleridge. FiBHP; PV
On a Lute Found in a Sarcophagus. Sir Edmund Gosse. GTSL; VA
On a Magazine Sonnet. Russell Hilliard Loines. AA; BOHV; InP; SiTL
On a Maid [*or* Maide] of Honour Seen by a Scholar in Somerset Garden. Thomas Randolph. EP; MePo
On a Man Named Merideth. *Unknown.* *See* Merideth.
On a May Morning. Milton. *See* Song on May Morning.
On a Memory of Beauty. G. S. Fraser. FaBoMo; NeBP
On a Midsummer['s] Eve. Thomas Hardy. FaBoTw; GTSL
On a midsummer night, on a night that was eerie with stars. August Night. Sara Teasdale. MAP; MoAmPo
On a Miniature. Henry Augustin Beers. AA
On a Miscellany of Poems [to Bernard Lintott]. John Gay. CEP; EiCL; EiPP
On a Mistress of Whose Affections He Was Doubtful. Thomas Nabbes. *Fr.* The Spring's Glory. SeCL
On a Monday morning it began to rain. Jay Gould's Daughter. *Unknown.* AS
On a Monument in France Which Marks the Last Resting Place of an Army Mule. *Unknown.* ShM
On a Monument to Marti. Walter Adolphe Roberts. PoNe; TTY
On a mountain of sugar-candy. Phantasus, I—8. Arno Holz. LiTW
On a Nankin Plate. Austin Dobson. PoVP
On a Newcastle Architect. *Unknown.* WhC
On a night of mist and rain. Phyllis. Sydney King Russell. ErPo
On a Night of Snow. Elizabeth J. Coatsworth. CIV; GoTP; MAP; MoAmPo; MoShBr
On a night the sun and the earth and the weather. The Pepper Tree. Sister Mary Madeleva. RIS

On a Nightingale in April. "Fiona Macleod." HBV; OBVV; PoVP
On a Note of Triumph, *sel.* Norman Corwin.
Man unto His Fellow Man. TrJP
On a Nun. Jacopo Vittorelli, *tr. fr. Italian by* Byron. AWP; CAW; JAWP; WBP
(Sonnet: Addressed by a Father Mourning His Recently Deceased Married Daughter to the Father Whose Daughter Had Entered a Convent.) LiTW
On a Painted Lady. William Pattison. WaPE
On a Painted Woman. Shelley. SiTL
On a Painting by Patient B of the Independence State Hospital for the Insane. Donald Justice. CoAP; NePoEA-2
On a Pair of Garters. Sir John Davies. CBEP; EG; SiPS
On a Pair of Shoes Presented to Him, *sel.* Egan O'Rahilly, *tr. fr. Modern Irish by* P. S. Dinneen *and* T. O'Donoghue.
"I have received jewels of conspicuous beauty." OnYI
On a Papyrus of Oxyrhynchus. *Unknown.* CAW
On a Parisian Boulevard. James Kenneth Stephen. England and America, II. InMe
On a Photo of Sgt. Ciardi a Year Later. John Ciardi. MiAP
On a Picture by Pippin, Called "The Den." Selden Rodman. PoNe
On a Picture by Poussin Representing Shepherds in Arcadia. John Addington Symonds. FaBoBe; HBV
On a Picture of a Black Centaur by Edmund Dulac. W. B. Yeats. SyP
On a Picture of Leander. Keats. TOP
(On an Engraved Gem of Leander.) CBEP
(Sonnet: On a Picture of Leander.) EnRP
On a Picture of Lincoln. John Vance Cheney. PGD
On a Piece of Music. Gerard Manley Hopkins. UnS
On a Piece of Tapestry. George Santayana. AA
On a Poet Patriot. Thomas MacDonagh. *See* Of a Poet Patriot.
On a Poetess. Gerard Manley Hopkins. PP
On a Poet's Lips I Slept. Shelley. *See* Poet's Dream, The.
On a Political Prisoner. W. B. Yeats. BWP; NoP; OBMV; PoE
On a Politician. Hilaire Belloc. *See* Epitaph on the Politician.
On a Portrait of Columbus. George Edward Woodberry. AA
On a Portrait of Mme Rimsky-Korsakov. Kingsley Amis. MuSP; NePoEA-2
On a Prayer Booke Sent to Mrs. M. R. Richard Crashaw. *See* Prayer: "Lo here a little volume. . .
On a Pretty Madwoman. Matthew Prior. CEP; EiCL
On a Prohibitionist Poem. G. K. Chesterton. ViBoPo
On a Proud Fellow. *Unknown.* PV
On a Puppy. Feng Chih, *tr. fr. Chinese by* Chu K'an. LiTW
On a Puritanicall Lock-Smith. William Camden. ShM; WhC
(On a Thieving Locksmith, *sl. diff. vers.*) GoTP
On a Quiet Conscience. Charles I, King of England. CH; PCD
On a Quiet Night. Li Po, *tr. fr. Chinese by* Shigeyoshi Obata. WoL
(My Far-off Home.) OnPM
On a rainy day, a sky. View from an American Window. Peter Fellowes. QAH
On a Recent Protest against Social Conditions. David Posner. NYBP
On a Replica of the Parthenon. Donald Davidson. MoVE
On a Return from Egypt. Keith Douglas. NeBP; NePoEA
On a Rhine Steamer. James Kenneth Stephen. England and America, I. InMe; NBM
On a rock, whose haughty brow. Thomas Gray. *Fr.* The Bard. SeCePo
On a Rope Maker Hanged. William Browne. CavP
On a Rosebud Sent to Her Lover. *Unknown.* AtBAP; SeCL
("Tender bud within herself doth close, The.") LO
On a Row of Nuns in a Cemetery. R. G. Howarth. ELU
On a Royal Demise. Thomas Hood. FiBHP; PV
On a Ruined House in a Romantic Country. Samuel Taylor Coleridge. Par; Sonn
(House That Jack Built, The.) BOHV
On a rusty iron throne. The Fulness of Time. James Stephens. MemP
On a Schoolmaster. *Unknown, tr. fr. Greek by* Lord Neaves. OnPM
On a Scooter. D. A. Greig. PeSA
On a Sculptured Head of the Christ. Mahlon Leonard Fisher. HBV
On a Sea-Storm nigh the Coast. Richard Steere. SCAP
On a Seal. Plato, *tr. fr. Greek by* Thomas Stanley. AWP; JAWP; WBP; WoL
On a Sense of Humor. Frederick Locker-Lampson. BOHV; InP
On a sepia ground. New England Landscape. DuBose Heyward. HT
On a shining silver morning long ago. David McKee Wright. *Fr.* Dark Rosaleen. PoAu-1
On a showery night and still. The Dandelions. Helen Gray Cone. DD; GFA; HBV; PRWS
On a Sick Bed. Martha Snell Nicholson. FaChP
On a Singing Girl. Elinor Wylie. TOP
On a Sleeping Friend. Hilaire Belloc. POTE
On a small six-acre farm dwelt John Grist the miller. Under the Drooping Willow Tree. *Unknown.* CBEP; OxBoLi
On a Snowy Day. Dorothy Aldis. *See* Snow.
On a snug evening I shall watch her fingers. Piano after War. Gwendolyn Brooks. AmNP; Kal; PoNe
On a Soldier Fallen in the Philippines. William Vaughn Moody. AmPP (3d ed.); AP; HBV; MAP; MC; MoAmPo (1942 ed.); PaA; PAH; ThLM
On a Spaniel, Called Beau, Killing a Young Bird. William Cowper. EiCL; FaBoCh; PRWS; OA
On a Spark of Fire Fixing on a Gentlewoman's Breast. Thomas Philipott. SeCL
On a Spider. Edward Littleton. WaPE
On a Spring Board. Edward Cracroft Lefroy. OBVV
On a Squirrel Crossing the Road in Autumn, in New England. Richard Eberhart. LiTM (1970 ed.); NePA; PoCh
On a starred night Prince Lucifer uprose. Lucifer in Starlight. George Meredith. AnEnPo; AnFE; ATP; BEL; BoLiVe; CABA; CaFP; CBEP; CBV; CH; CoBE; EnL; EnLi-2; EnLit; EPN; ExPo; ForPo; HBV; HoPM; ILP; InP; InPo; LiTB; LiTG; LoBV; MemP; OAEP; OBEV; OBNC; OBVV; PG (1955 ed.); PoEL-5; PoFS; PoIE; PoPo; PoSa; PoVP; SeCeV; ShBV-4; Sonn; TOP; TreFT; TrGrPo; UnPo; VA; ViBoPo; ViPo; ViPP; VP
On a Steamer. Dorothy W. Baruch. FaPON
On a Steamship. Upton Sinclair. MaRV
On a straw-colored day. Dream. Solomon Edwards. NNP; PoNe (1970 ed.)
On a street in Knoxville. Street Scene—1946. Kenneth Porter. PoNe
On a Subway Express. Chester Firkins. PFY; YaD
On a summer's day when the sea was rippled. The Ship That Never Returned. Henry Clay Work. BLPA
On a summer's day while the waves were rippling, with a quiet and a gentle breeze. The Ship That Never Returned. *Unknown.* AS
On a Sunbeam. Thomas Heyrick. MePo
On a Sunday morn sat a maid forlorn. Wait till the Sun Shines, Nellie. Andrew B. Sterling. TreFS
On a Sunday mornin' it begins to rain. Casey Jones. *Unknown.* ABF; ViBoFo (C *vers.*)
On a Sundial. Hilaire Belloc. MoVE; PV
On a Tear. Samuel Rogers. HBV
On a Thieving Locksmith. William Camden. *See* On a Puritanicall Lock-Smith.
On a throne of new gold the Son of the Sky is sitting among his Mandarins. The Emperor. Tu Fu. AWP
On a Thrush Singing in Autumn. Sir Lewis Morris. OBVV; VA
On a Time the Amorous Silvy. *Unknown.* LO; SeEP; TuPP; ViBoPo
(Amorous Silvy, The.) UnTE
(Awakening, The.) CLwM
(Silvy.) SeCL
(Wakening, The.) OBEV
On a Tired Housewife. *Unknown.* EvOK; WePo
(Epitaph: "Here lies a poor woman who was always tired.") TreF
On a train in Texas German prisoners eat. Defeat. Witter Bynner. PoNe
On a Travelling Speculator. Philip Freneau. AA
On a Treatise of Charity. Richard Crashaw. MaMe
On a tree by a river a little tom-tit. The Suicide's Grave [*or* Tit-Willow]. W. S. Gilbert. *Fr.* The Mikado. ALV; FaFP; LiTB; LiTG; LiTL; PoVP; SiTL; TreF; WhC
On a Tree Fallen across the Road. Robert Frost. MWA-2; PoeP
On a Valetudinarian. Ibn al-Rumi, *tr. fr. Arabic by* J. D. Carlyle. LiTW

On a Very Young, Very Dead Soldier. Richard Gillman. NePoAm
On a View of Pasadena from the Hills. Yvor Winters. QFR
On a Violet in Her Breast. Thomas Stanley. OBS
On a Virtuous Young Gentlewoman That Died Suddenly. William Cartwright. CBEP; OBEV
On a Wag in Mauchline. Robert Burns. ELU; FiBHP
(Epitaph for James Smith.) ALV
On a Waiter. David McCord. *See* Epitaph on a Waiter.
On a Watchman Asleep at Midnight. James Thomas Fields. CenHV
On a Wet Day. Franco Sacchetti. *See* Catch: On a Wet Day.
On a wet night, laden with books for luggage. The Poet on the Island. Richard Murphy. NMP
On a wet pavement the white sky recedes. The Bitter World of Spring. William Carlos Williams. PoeP
On a white field. The Sower. R. Olivares Figueroa. FaPON; OnPM
On a wide-open, windless Autumn morning. The Plough-Horse. Rhoda Coghill. OnYI
On a Wife. Francis Burdett Money-Coutts. OBVV
On a Windy Day. Zhenya Gay. RePo
On a winter evening, by a winter fire. A Hymn to No One Body. James Palmer Wade. NAMP
On a winter night/ When the moon is low. Christmas Eve. Marion Edey. YeAr
On a winter's night. The Two Foxes. *Unknown.* FTB
On a winter's night long time ago. Noël. Hilaire Belloc. HBMV; JKCP; TSW
On a withered bough. A Crow. Basho. OnPM
On a Woman's Inconstancy. Sir Robert Ayton. *See* I Loved Thee Once.
On a World War Battlefield. Thomas Curtis Clark. PGD
On a Young Lady's Going into a Shower Bath. Francis Scott Key. UnTE; YaD
On a Young Married Couple. Richard Crashaw. *See* Epitaph upon Husband and Wife Which Died and Were Buried Together, An.
On a Young Poetess's Grave. Robert Buchanan. VA
On Aesthetics, More or Less. Peter Kane Dufault. NYBP
On Again Meeting a Lady. Otomo Miyori, *tr. fr. Japanese by* Asataro Miyamori. OnPM
On Alexis. Plato, *tr. fr. Greek by* Thomas Stanley. AWP
On Algernon Sidney. *Unknown.* PeRV
On alien ground, breathing an alien air. Where a Roman Villa Stood, above Freiburg. Mary Elizabeth Coleridge. OBNC; PoMa
On all that the Lord laboured He lavished His love. The Vision of the Holy Church [*or* Love]. William Langland. *Fr.* The Vision of Piers Plowman. BoC; BoPe
On Amaryllis, a Tortoyse. Marjorie Pickthall. PeCV (1967 ed.)
On an Air of Rameau. Arthur Symons. MuSP; OBNC
On an American Soldier of Fortune Slain in France. Clinton Scollard. MC
On an Anniversary. J. M. Synge. OBMV
On an early Sunday in April, a feeble day. An Extract from Addresses to the Academy of Fine Ideas. Wallace Stevens. GTBS-W; LiTA; LiTM (rev. ed.)
On an East Wind from the Wars. Alan Dugan. AP
On an Engraved Gem of Leander. Keats. *See* On a Picture of Leander.
On an Hour-Glass [*or* Houre-Glasse]. John Hall. MeLP; MePo
"This gapes for marriage, yet his fickle head," *br. sel.* LO
On an Ill-managed House. Swift. AnIV
On an Imaginary Journey to the Continent. Richard Porson. *See* Epigram on an Academic Visit to the Continent.
On an Indian Tomineios, The Least of Birds. Thomas Heyrick. PeRV
On an Infant Dying as Soon as Born. Charles Lamb. GTBS; GTBS-D; GTBS-P; GTBS-W; GTSE; GTSL; OBEV; OBRV
On an Infant Eight Months Old. *Unknown.* SiTL; WhC
On an Insignificant Fellow. Lord Curzon. PV
On an Intaglio Head of Minerva. Thomas Bailey Aldrich. HBV; InMe
On an Invitation to the United States. Thomas Hardy. AWP; InPo; JAWP; WBP
On an Island. J. M. Synge. MoBrPo; OBVV; PeVV
On an Italian Hillside. Richard Weber. NMP
On an Old Horn. Wallace Stevens. LiTA
On an Old Muff. Frederick Locker-Lampson. CenHV; VA
On an Old Song. William Edward Hartpole Lecky. HBV
On an Old Sun Dial. *Unknown.* TreFT
(Love over All.) OQP
On an Old Toper Buried in Durham Churchyard, England. *Unknown.* ShM
On an Old Woman. Lucillius, *tr. fr. Greek by* William Cowper. AWP; LiTW; OnPM
On an olive-crested steep. Virgil's Tomb. Robert Cameron Rogers. AA
On an Unpleasant Woman. Catullus, *tr. fr. Latin by* George Lamb. OnPM
On an Unsuccessful Attempt to Draw Lord Boyle's Picture. Elizabeth Rowe. WaPE
On an Upright Judge. Swift. *See* On The Upright Judge, Who Condemned the "Drapier's" Printer.
On an Urn. Richard Garnett. VA
On and on,/ O white brother! The Sea Bird to the Wave. Padraic Colum. EtS; RePo; SUS
On Andrew Turner. Burns. PV
On Angels. W. W. E. Ross. MoCV
On Another's Sorrow. Blake. *Fr.* Songs of Innocence. AWP; CBEP; CEP; EiCL; EnRP; FaBV; LiTG; MaRV; OTPC (1923 ed.); PeER; PoEL-4; SoP; ViBoPo
On Apples. David Ross. NYBP
On Archaeanassa. Plato, *tr. fr. Greek by* Thomas Stanley. AWP
On Aristophanes. Plato, *tr. fr. Greek by* Lord Neaves. OnPM
On Ascending a Hill Leading to a Convent. Francisco Manuel de Mello, *tr. fr. Spanish by* Felicia Dorothea Hemans. CAW
On Australian Hills, *sel.* Ada Cambridge.
"Oh, to be there to-night!". PoAu-1
On Bala Hill. Samuel Taylor Coleridge. Sonn
On Beau Nash's Picture, Which Once Stood between the Busts of Newton and Pope. Jane Brereton. InP
On Beauty; a Riddle. Matthew Prior. CEP
On Becoming Man. R. P. Lister. PV
On Behalf of Some Irishmen Not Followers of Tradition. "*A* E." AnIL; PoFr
On Being a Woman. Dorothy Parker. BOHV; PoLF
On Being Arrived at the Age of Twenty-Three. Milton. *See* On His Having Arrived at the Age of Twenty-Three.
On Being Asked for a War Poem. W. B. Yeats. MoVE; PP
On Being Brought from Africa to America. Phillis Wheatley. BALP; Kal; TTY
On Being Chosen Poet of Vermont. Robert Frost. ML
On Being Invited to a Testimonial Dinner. William Stafford. NePoAm-2
On Being Sixty. Po Chü-i, *tr. fr. Chinese by* Arthur Waley. AWP
On Being Told That One's Ideas Are Victorian. Sara Henderson Hay. InMe
On Bell-Ringers. Voltaire, *tr. fr. French.* ShM
On Bellosguardo, when the year was young. To Vernon Lee. Amy Levy. VA
On Ben Jonson. *At. to* John Cleveland, *See* Elegy on Ben Jonson, An. *also at. to* James Cleyton.
On Ben Jonson. Sidney Godolphin. CBEP
On Blenheim. Swift, *after the Latin of* Martial. OnPM
(Verses on Blenheim.) AWP
On Blenheim House. Abel Evans. CBEP; OBEC
On blessed youths, for Jove doth pause. Francis Beaumont. *Fr.* The Masque of the Inner-Temple and Gray's Inne. OBS
On Blindness. Joseph Cardarelli. QAH
On blood, smoke, rain and the dead. Who Knows Where. Detlev von Liliencron. AWP
On bluish inlets bristling. The Painter. Robert Fitzgerald. MoVE
On Board the *Cumberland* (March 7, 1862). George Henry Boker. PAH
On Board the Steamer, *with music.* *Unknown.* SGR
On Breton heaths the village craftsmen's hands. The Calvaries. Peter Williamson. NYTB
On brick and stone and trees all stark and bare. To the City in the Snow. Agnes O'Gara Ruggeri. MoSiPe
On broad plains of bright sound. The White Peacock. Mary Mills. NePoAm
On Broadway. George Sylvester Viereck. OQP
On Butler's Monument. Samuel Wesley. *See* On the Setting Up of Mr. Butler's Monument . . .
On Calais Sands. Andrew Lang. PoVP; VA

On Calvary's Lonely Hill. Herbert Clark Johnson. PoNe
On Calvert's plains new faction reigns. Maryland Resolves. *Unknown.* PAH
On Catania and Syracuse Swallowed Up by an Earthquake. Anna Seward, *after the Italian of* Vincenzo da Filicaja. Sonn
On Catching a Dog-Daisy in the Mower. Peter Redgrove. NePoEA-2
On Catullus. Walter Savage Landor. OBEV; TOP; ViBoPo
On Censure. Swift. CBEP
On Charles II. Earl of Rochester. *See* Epitaph on Charles II.
On charts they fall like lace. Delos. Lawrence Durrell. NeBP
On Children. Kahlil Gibran. *Fr.* The Prophet. PoPl; PoToHe (new ed.)
On China Blue. Sir Stephen Gaselee. WhC
On Chloris Walking in the Snow. William Strode. ELP; HBV (8th ed.); NoP; SeCL
(Chloris in the Snow.) GTBS-W; HBV (6th ed.); OBEV
("I saw fair Chloris walk alone.") EG
(On a Gentlewoman Walking in the Snow[e].) BoC; OBS; SeEP
On Christians, Mercy Will Fall. *Unknown, tr. fr. Welsh by* D. M. Lloyd. *Fr.* The Black Book of Carmarthen. PrWP
On Christmas Day. Clement Paman. OxBoCh; SeCL
(On Christmas Day to My Heart.) OBS
On Christmas-Day. Thomas Traherne. OBS; PoEL-2
"Shake off thy sloth, my drowsy soul, awake," *sel. 8 sts.* OxBoCh
On Christmas Day I weep. Christmas Mourning. Vassar Miller. CoPo; MoAmPo (1962 ed.)
On Christmas day in seventy-six. Battle of Trenton. *Unknown.* MC; PAH; PAP
On Christmas Day to My Heart. Clement Paman. *See* On Christmas Day.
On Christmas Eve. Edith Lovejoy Pierce. MoRP
On Christmas Eve I lay abed. Christmas Eve. John Drinkwater. HBMV
On Christmas Eve I turned the spit. *Unknown.* OxNR
On Christmas Eve my mother read. Christmas Eve. Edna Kingsley Wallace. BoTP
On Christmas Eve the little stars. Christmas Eve. Charlotte Druitt Cole. BoTP
On Christmas eve they filled the house, some fifty guests all told. Christmas at Babbitt's. Henry Hallam Tweedy. MaRV; TRV
On Christmas Eve while hamlets sleep. Legends of Christmas. Aileen Fisher. ChBR
On Christmas Eve, would you believe, the forest gave a party. A Christmas Party. Carolyn Sherwin Bailey. PCH
On Christmas Morn. *Unknown.* *See* Words from an Old Spanish Carol.
On City Streets. Margaret E. Bruner. PoToHe
On Clarastella Singing. Robert Heath. OBS
On Clarastella Walking in Her Garden. Robert Heath. CavP; OBS; SeCL
On Clergymen Preaching Politics. John Byrom. SeCePo
On cliffs against the sky. Ship's Bell. Glenn Ward Dresbach. BoC
On Common Ground. R. P. Blackmur. Scarabs for the Living, III. CrMA
On Commonwealth, on Marlborough. Technologies. George Starbuck. NYBP
On Court-Worme. Ben Jonson. SeCP
On Critics. Matthew Prior. *See* In Imitation of Anacreon.
On crystal rims, they wheel in space. Snowflakes. Alice Behrend. GoYe
On Cupid's bow how are my heart-strings bent. Astrophel and Stella, XIX. Sir Philip Sidney. FCP; SiPS
On Dante Alighieri. Michelangelo. *See* Soul of Dante, The.
On Dante's "Divine Comedy." Longfellow. *See* Oft Have I Seen . . .
On days like these. Washing. Randall Jarrell. TDP
On Dean Inge. Humbert Wolfe. ChTr
On Death. Keats. SyP
On Death. Walter Savage Landor. *See* Death Stands above Me.
On Death. Shakespeare. *Fr.* Measure for Measure, III, i. FiP
On Death, *sel.* Angelos Sikelianos, *tr. fr. Modern Greek by* Kimon Friar.
"Listen to the roar of your liberation!" LiTW
On Death—a Sonnet. Ecclesiasticus, Bible, Apocrypha. *See* O Death.
On December, the sixth. Trenton and Princeton. *Unknown.* PAH
On Degree. Shakespeare. *Fr.* Troilus and Cressida, I, iii. ExPo
("Heavens themselves, the planets and this center, The.") ImOP
On Digital Extremities. Gelett Burgess. *See* I'd Rather Have Fingers than Toes.
On Dirphys' wrinkled slope we fell. The Athenian Dead. Simonides. WoL
On Disbanding the Army. David Humphreys. PAH
On Discovering a Butterfly. Vladimir Nabokov. NYBP
On Dives. Richard Crashaw. *See* Dives Asking a Drop.
On Dr. Crank's Victory over the Gout. Sneyd Davies. WaPE
On Dr. Isaac Letsome. *Unknown, at. to* John Coakley Lettsom. LiTG
(Candid Physician, The.) TreFT
(On a Doctor Named Isaac Letsome.) GoTP
(On Dr. Lettsom, by Himself.) PV
(Self-composed Epitaph on a Doctor by the Name of I. Letsome.) WhC
On Dr. Woodford's Paraphrase on the Canticles. Thomas Flatman. PeRV
On Don Juan del Norte, Not Don Juan Tenorio del Sur. Alan Dugan. ErPo
On Donne's Poetry. Samuel Taylor Coleridge. CABA; CaFP; CBEP; ERoP-1; InvP; NoP; OAEP; PP; SeCePo
On Douglas Bridge I met a man. Ballad of Douglas Bridge. Francis Carlin. AnIV; HBMV; OxBI
On Dow Crag. Patric Dickinson. POTi
On Dreams. Sir Samuel Egerton Brydges. Sonn
On Drinking. Abraham Cowley. *See* Drinking.
On Dulcina. *At. to* Sir Walter Ralegh. *See* Dulcina.
On Durer's "Melencolia." Sir William Watson. VA
On dusty benches in the park. Reflections in a Little Park. Babette Deutsch. ELU; NePoAm
On Dwelling. Robert Graves. CBEP; CMoP; MoPW; MoVE
On ear and ear two noises too old to end. The Sea and the Skylark. Gerard Manley Hopkins. LiTB; NoP; OBMV; PoeP; PoVP
On Easter Day. Celia Thaxter. FaPON; YeAr
On Easter morn,/ On Easter morn. Easter. Elizabeth J. Coatsworth. YeAr
On Easter morn/ Up the faint cloudy sky. Easter. Hilda Conkling. HH; TiPo (1952 ed.)
On Easter morn at early dawn. Meeting the Easter Bunny. Rowena Bennett. GFA; SiSoSe; SoPo; SUS; TiPo; UTS
On Easter Morning. Eben E. Rexford. BLRP
On Easter morning two egrets. Two Egrets. John Ciardi. CaFP
On Eastnor Knoll. John Masefield. CH; FlW; MCCG; ShBV-3
On Editing Scott Fitzgerald's Papers. Edmund Wilson. CrMA; NYBP
On Edward Seymour, Duke of Somerset. *Unknown.* *See* Poor Estate to Be Holden for Best, The.
On either side the river lie. The Lady of Shalott. Tennyson. AnFE; ATP; BEL; BeLS; BoLiVe; CABL; DiPo; EnL; EnLi-2; EnLit; EPN; FaFP; FiP; FosPo; GBV; GN; GTSL; HBV; InP; LiTG; MaC; MaVP; MBW-2; MCCG; OAEP; OBEV; OBRV; OBVV; OnSP; OTPC; PAn; PoE; PoVP; RG; SeCeV; ShBV-1; TOP; TreF; ViPo; ViPP; VP; WePo; WHA; WiR
On Eleanor Freeman, Who Died 1650, Aged 21. *Unknown.* OBEV (new ed.)
On Elizabeth L. H. Ben Jonson. *See* Epitaph on Elizabeth, L. H.
On English Monsieur. Ben Jonson. NoP
On Entering a Chapel. John Davidson. MaRV; OQP
On Entering a Forest. Elinor Lennen. PGD
On Euripides. *Unknown, tr. fr. Greek by* Lord Neaves. OnPM
On Even Keel. Matthew Green. *Fr.* The Spleen. OBEC
On every schoolhouse, ship, and staff. Half-Mast. Lloyd Mifflin. PAH
On every wind there comes the dolorous cry. Ballade of the Unchanging Beauty. Richard Le Gallienne. InP

On eves of cold, when slow coal fires. Town Owl. Laurie Lee. POTi; ToPo
On Exodus III, 14, I Am That I Am. Matthew Prior. CEP
On Falling Asleep by Firelight. William Meredith. NYBP
On Falling Asleep to Birdsong. William Meredith. PoCh
On Fame. John Banks. WaPE
On Fame ("Fame, like a wayward girl, will still be coy"). Keats. *See* Two Sonnets on Fame.
On Fame ("How fever'd is that man"). Keats. *See* Two Sonnets on Fame.
On Fanny Godwin. Shelley. ChER; FaBoEn; OBNC
On far hills. Takahama Kyoshi, *tr. fr. Japanese by* Geoffrey Bownas *and* Anthony Thwaite. FIW
On Fell. Gotthold Lessing, *tr. fr. German.* ShM
On File. John Kendrick Bangs. PoToHe (new ed.); WBLP
On First Entering Westminster Abbey. Louise Imogen Guiney. AA
On First Hearing Beethoven. George Barker. UnS
On First Looking in on Blodgett's Keats's "Chapman's Homer." George Starbuck. PP
On First Looking into Chapman's Homer. Keats. AnFE; ATP; BEL; BoLiVe; BWP; CABA; CaFP; CBEP; CBV; CH; ChTr; CLwM; CoBE; DD; DiPo; EnL; EnLi-2; EnLit; EnRP; EPN; ERoP-2; ExPo; FaBoBe; FaBoCh; FaBoEn; FaBV; FaFP; FaPL; FiP; ForPo; FosPo; GN; GTBS; GTBS-D; GTBS-P; GTBS-W; GTSE; GTSL; HBV; HBVY; HoPM; ILP; InP; InPo; LiTB; LiTG; LoBV; LoGBV; MaPo; MBW-2; MCCG; MERP; ML; NeHB; NoP; OAEP; OBEV; OBNC; OBRV; OTPC; OuHeWo; PAn; PoAn; PoEL-4; PoeP; PoFS; PoIE; PTK; RoGo; SeCeV; ShBV-3; Sonn; StP; TIHL; TOP; TreF; TrGrPo; UnPo (1st ed.); ViBoPo; WHA; YAT
(On Looking into Chapman's Homer.) EG
(Sonnet: On First Looking into Chapman's Homer.) ChER
On First Looking into Loeb's Horace. Lawrence Durrell. LiTM (1970 ed.); ToPo
On First Looking into the Dark Future. Roger Lancelyn Green. CenHV
On Fleas. Augustus De Morgan. *See* Great Fleas.
On Fleas. Swift. TreFS
On Fleet. Shepheard's Takeing away a Child's Bread and Butter. Matthew Prior. PeRV
On fog days, early mornings wet at the mirror. The Old Pilot Tunnels under the English Channel. James Schevill. FiMAP
On Forney's Slough the million gather. A Gryphon Sighted in an Iowa Flyway. N. G. Westerfield. NYTB
On Fort Sumter. *Unknown, ad. fr.* Where There's a Will There's a Way *by* John Godfrey Saxe. MC; PAH
On Freedom. James Russell Lowell. *See* Slaves.
On Friday morning as we set sail. *See* One Friday morn when we set sail.
On Friendship, *sel.* William Cowper.
"Man that hails you Tom or Jack, The." TreFT
On Friendship. William Whitehead. OBEC
On Fruition. Sir Charles Sedley. ErPo
On Galveston Beach. Barbara Howes. MoAmPo (1962 ed.)
On Garland Sunday, the weaver told me. Garland Sunday. Padraic Colum. GoYe
On Gaulstown House. Swift. CBEP
On Gay Wallpaper. William Carlos Williams. MAP; MoAB; MoAmPo
On Giving. Kahlil Gibran. *Fr.* The Prophet. MaRV; PoPl
On Glaister's Hill, *sel.* William Jeffrey. OxBS
Carlyle on Burns.
On Going Home. Marjorie L. Agnew. GoYe
On Going to a Tavern. Wang Chi, *tr. fr. Chinese by* Arthur Waley. OnPM
On Going to Bed. John Donne. *See* Going to Bed.
On Going to the Wars. Earle Birney. WaP
On golden seas of drink, so the Greek poet said. Alcohol. Louis MacNeice. LiTM
On gossamer nights when the moon is low. The Fairy Thrall. May Byron. HBV; HBVY; VA
On Growing Old. John Masefield. BEL; CMoP; CoBE; FaFP; HBMV; LiTB; LiTM; MoAB; MoBrPo; MoRP; PG; PoLF; PoRA; TreFS; ViBoPo; WHA
"Be with me, Beauty, for the fire is dying," *sel.* InP
On Growing Old. Srinavas Rayaprol. ACV
On Gut. Ben Jonson. AnAnS-2; EP; NoP
On Halloween. Shelley Silverstein. PoSC
On Hampstead Heath. W. W. Gibson. EPN; HBV; NP
On hand is 27. Macrobius Mingling with Nature. Rochelle Owens. CoPo
On, happy shades—to me unblessed! The Shrubbery. William Cowper. EiPP
On Having Grown Old. E. G. Moll. BoAV
On he goes, the little one. Tortoise Family Connections. D. H. Lawrence. BrPo; ChMP; HaMV
On Hearing a Broadcast of Ceremonies in Connection with Conferring of Cardinals' Hats. Denis Wrafter. NeIP
On Hearing a Flute at Night from the Wall of Shou-hsiang. Li Yi, *tr. fr. Chinese by* Witter Bynner. UnS
On Hearing a Lady Praise a Certain Rev. Doctor's Eyes. George Outram. BOHV; TreFT
On Hearing a Symphony of Beethoven. Edna St. Vincent Millay. GTBS-W; InP; LiTA; LiTM; MAP; MasP; MoAB; MoAmPo; NeMA; NePA; NP; TrGrPo; TwAmPo; UnS
On Hearing Jazz. Alice Phelps-Rider. PoMa
On Hearing Mrs. Woodhouse Play the Harpsichord. W. H. Davies. BrPo; MuSP
On Hearing Someone Sing a Poem by Yüan Chen. Po Chü-i, *tr. fr. Chinese by* Arthur Waley. ML
On Hearing That the Students of Our New University Have Joined the Agitation against Immoral Literature. W. B. Yeats. FaBoTw
On Hearing That Torture Was Suppressed Throughout the Austrian Dominions. John Bampfylde. Sonn
On Hearing the First Cuckoo. Richard Church. MoBrPo (1942 ed.); OBMV
On Hearing the News from Venice. George Meredith. PoVP
On Heaven. Ford Madox Ford. CTC
"And my dear one sat in the shadows," *sel.* ViBoPo
On Helen's heart the day were night! The First Kiss. Norman Gale. VA
On Hellespont, guilty of true love's blood. Hero and Leander. Christopher Marlowe. AnFE; AtBAP; CABA; LoBV; NoP; OAEP; OBSC; PoEL-2; ReEn; ReIE; SeCePo; SiCE; TuPP
On Her Absence. Thomas Rymer. SeCL
On Her Child's Death. Kaga no Chiyo, *tr. fr. Japanese by* Curtis Hidden Page. LiTW
(Haiku: "I wonder in what fields today.") CaFP
On Her Coming to London. Edmund Waller. HBV
On Her Entering Her Room. Richardson Pack. WaPE
On her great venture, man. Earth and Man. George Meredith. EPN; ViPo
On Her Laugh. Clément Marot. *See* Madam d'Albert's Laugh.
On Her Pleading Want of Time. George Lyttelton. WaPE
On her side, reclining on her elbow. So-and-So Reclining on Her Couch. Wallace Stevens. AmPP (5th ed.); LiTM; PoeP; SiTL
On her still lake the city sits. At Venice. Arthur Hugh Clough. ViPo
On Her Twenty-fifth Birthday. Louis Hasley. JKCP (1955 ed.)
On her white breast a sparkling cross she wore. Pope. *Fr.* The Rape of the Lock. ACP
On hill and plain, in the islands of the sea. Englyn. *Unknown. Fr.* The Black Book of Carmarthen. PrWP
On him the unpetitioned heavens descend. A Counsel of Moderation. Francis Thompson. MoBrPo
On Himself. Charles Churchill. *Fr.* The Prophecy of Famine. OBEC
On Himself. Walter Savage Landor. *See* On His Seventy-fifth Birthday.
On Himself. James Russell Lowell. *See* Lowell.
On Himself. Swift. AnIV
On Himself, upon Hearing What Was His Sentence. James Graham, Marquess of Montrose. *See* Verses Composed on the Eve of His Execution.
On Himself ("Born I was to meet with age"). Robert Herrick. ChTr
(On Himselfe.) SeCV-1
On Himself ("Worke is done, The: young men, and maidens set"). Robert Herrick. SeCP
On Himself ("Young I was who now am old"). Robert Herrick. UnTE
On his arms he wears. Tattooed. William Plomer. ChMP
On His Baptismal Birthday. Samuel Taylor Coleridge. MaRV
On His Being Arrived at the Age of Twenty-three. Milton. *See*

On His Having Arrived at the Age of Twenty-three.
On His Blindness. Milton. ATP; AWP; BEL; BoC; BoLiVe; BWP; CBEP; ChTr; CoBE; DiPo; EnLi-1; EnLit; FaBoEn; FaBV; FaFP; FaPL; FiP; FlW; FosPo; GBV (1952 ed.); GN; GTBS; GTBS-D; GTBS-P; GTBS-W; GTSE; GTSL; HBV; HBVY; InPo; JAWP; LiTB; MaRV; MCCG; MemP; OBEV; OuHeWo; OxBoCh; PCD; PG (1945 ed.); PoEL-3; PoFS; PoIE; PoLF; PoMa; PoPl; PoPo; PoRA; ShBV-4; SoP; TIHL; TOP; TreF; TrGrPo; TRV; UnPo; WBP; WHA
(Sonnet: "When I consider how my light is spent.") AnFE; LoBV; MBW-1; MeP; OBS; Po; SeCL; SeEP; VaPo
(Sonnet on His Blindness.) BBV; FaBoBe; NeHB; OHFP; OQP; OTPC (1946 ed.); WGRP
(When I Consider How My Light Is Spent.) CABA; CaFP; CBV; EnL; ExPo; ILP; InP; LiTG; MaPo; NoP; OAEP; SeCeV; Sonn; ViBoPo; YAT
On His Books. Hilaire Belloc. ACP (1952 ed.); MoBrPo; OxBoLi; PoPl; SiTL; TreFT; WhC
(Epigram: "When I am dead I hope it may be said.") OtMeF
On his death-bed poor Lubin lies. A Reasonable Affliction. Matthew Prior. ALV; EiCL; HBV; MeWo; ShM; TreFT; TrGrPo; WhC
On His Deceased Wife. Milton. ATP; BEL; BWP; CBEP; DiPo; EnLi-1; ExPo; FaFP; GTBS-W; InPo; LiTB; LiTG; LiTL; OBEV; PoFS; SeCeV; StP; TOP; TreFS
(Katherine Milton: Died MDCLVIII.) FaBoEn
(Methought I Saw My Late Espoused Saint.) CABA; ForPo; ILP; MaPo; NoP; PAn; PoAn
("Methought I saw my late espoused Saint.") EnLoPo; PIA; Sonn
(On His Late Wife.) PoEL-3
(Sonnet: "Methought I saw my late espousèd saint.") MBW-1; OBS; SeCL; SeEP; VaPo
(Sonnet on His Deceased Wife.) LoBV
On His Dog. John Gay. ALV
On His 86th Birthday. Thomas Hardy. ACV
On His Exile to Iona. St. Columcille, *tr. fr. Old Irish by* Douglas Hyde. CAW; LiTW
On His First Sonne. Ben Jonson. *See* On My First Son.
On His Friend, Joseph Rodman Drake. Fitz-Greene Halleck. *See* On the Death of Joseph Rodman Drake.
On His Garden Book. Francis Daniel Pastorius. SCAP
On His Having Arrived at the Age of Twenty-three. Milton. ATP; AWP; BEL; BWP; CoBE; DiPo; EnLi-1; JAWP; MCCG; OuHeWo; TOP; TrGrPo; WBP
(How Soon Hath Time, the Subtle Thief of Youth.) CABA; CBV; EG; EnL; ExPo; ForPo; GTBS-W; InPo; LiTB; NoP; OAEP; SeCePo; SeCeV; Sonn; YAT
(On Being Arrived at the Age of Twenty-three.) PoIE
(On His Being Arrived at His twenty-third Year.) EnLit
(On His Being Arrived to the Age of Twenty-three.) MaRV
(On His 24th Birthday.) FaBoEn
(On His Twenty-third Birthday.) FiP
(Sonnet: "How soon hath Time, the subtle thief of youth.") LiTG; LoBV; MBW-1; MeP; OBS; SeCL; SeEP; TRV; ViBoPo
(Sonnet: On His Being Arrived at the Age of Twenty-three.) HBV
On His Lady's Waking. Pierre de Ronsard. *tr. fr. French by* Andrew Lang. AWP
On His Late Espoused Saint. Sir Kenelm Digby. ACP
On His Late Wife. Milton. *See* On His Deceased Wife.
On His Love. Dakiki, *tr. fr. Persian by* R. A. Nicholson. LiTW
On His Mistress [*or* Mistris]. John Donne. Elegies, XVI. AnAnS-1; CABL; CBV; CLwM; LiTB; LiTG; MaMe; MeLP; MyFE; PoEL-2; ReEn; SCEP-1; SeCeV; SeCP; TuPP; ViBoPo
(Elegie: On His Mistris.) MePo; SeCV-1
(Elegy on His Mistress.) LoBV; SeEP
On His Mistress. *Unknown, at. to* Henry Noel *and to* William Strode. *See* Beauty Extoll'd.
On His Mistress Crossing the Sea. Thomas Cary. SeCL
(On His Mistresse Going to Sea.) OBS
On His Mistress Drowned. Thomas Sprat. ATP; EnLoPo; SeCL
On His Mistress' Garden of Herbs. *Unknown.* SeCL
On His Mistress Going from Home. *Unknown.* OBS
On His Mistress [*or* Mistris], the Queen of Bohemia. Sir Henry Wotton. AnAnS-2; EnLoPo; LoBV; MeLP; MePo; MyFE; OBS; ReEn; SeCP; SeEP; TrGrPo; ViBoPo
(Elizabeth of Bohemia.) CBEP; FaBoCh; GTBS; GTBS-D; GTBS-P; GTBS-W; GTSE; GTSL; HBV; OBEV; OtMeF, 5 *ll.*; TOP
(To His Mistress, Elizabeth, Queen of Bohemia.) ELP
("You meaner beauties of the night.") EG
On His Mistresse Going to Sea. Thomas Cary. *See* On His Mistress Crossing the Sea.
On His Mistris. John Donne. *See* On His Mistress.
On His Mistris That Lov'd Hunting. *Unknown.* OBS
On His Mistris, the Queen of Bohemia. Sir Henry Wotton. *See* On His Mistress. . .
On His Ninth Decade. Walter Savage Landor. *See* To My Ninth Decade.
On His Own Agamemnon and Iphigeneia. Walter Savage Landor. OBRV
On His Own Death. Walter Savage Landor. *See* Death Stands above Me.
On His Seventy-fifth Birthday. Walter Savage Landor. *Fr.* The Last Fruit off an Old Tree. AnEnPo; AnFE; BEL; BoLiVe; EPN; InP; InPo; LiTB; MaRV; OAEP; PoE; SeCeV; TIHL; TOP; TreF; TrGrPo; WHA
(Dying Speech of an Old Philosopher.) FaPL; GTBS-P; NoP; ViBoPo; YAT
(End, The.) SeCePo
(Envoi.) FaBoEn
(Finis.) GTBS-W; OBEV; OBVV; OnPP
(I Strove with None.) ChTr; EG; EnRP; GTBS; GTSL; HBV; MCCG; MemP; OBNC; PoIE; PoPo; PoSa
(Introduction: "I strove with none, for none was worth my strife.") EnLi-2
(On Himself.) VA
On His "Sonnets of the Wingless Hours." Eugene Lee-Hamilton. VA
On His Twenty-third Birthday. Milton. *See* On His Having Arrived at the Age of Twenty-three.
On His Wife's Death. Henry King. *See* Exequy, The.
On hoary Conway's battlemented height. With a Rose from Conway Castle. Julia C. R. Dorr. AA
On Homer's Birthplace. Thomas Heywood. ML
On Hope, by Way of Question and Answer, betweene A. Cowley, and R. Crashaw. Abraham Cowley *and* Richard Crashaw. MaMe; MePo. *See also* Against Hope *and* For Hope.
On Horror. Robert Hershon. ThO
On horseback, and. There He Was. Alan Dugan. CBV
On How the Cobler. *Unknown.* SCAP
On Hurricane Jackson. Alan Dugan. CoAP; SD
On Hygiene. Hilaire Belloc. MoBrPo
On Imagination. Phillis Wheatley. AmPP (5th ed.); PoNe
On Inclosures. *Unknown.* OxBoLi
On Independence. Jonathan Mitchell Sewall. PAH
On Installing an American Kitchen in Lower Austria. W. H. Auden. NYBP
On Ithaca Standing. Lawrence Durrell. FaBoTw
On Izumo Cliff. Basho, *tr. fr. Japanese by* H. G. Henderson. OnPM
On J. W. Ward. Samuel Rogers. ALV
On Jean Fréron. Voltaire, *tr. fr. French by* Alan Conder. OnPM
On Joe. P. Dodd. *See* Epigram: "Joe hates a sycophant. It shows."
On John Adams, of Southwell. Byron. PV
On John Bun. *Unknown.* GoTP
(John Bun.) ShM; WhC
On John Donne's Book of Poems. John Marriott. CH
On John Grubb. *Unknown.* WhC
On Jordan's Bank. Byron. ChER
On Jordan's bank the Baptist's cry. Glad Tidings from the King of Kings. Charles Coffin. BePJ
On Jordan's banks the Arab's camels stray. On Jordan's Bank. Byron. ChER
On Jordan's stormy banks I stand. The Promised Land. Samuel Stennett. SoP; TrAS
On July 5 the Associated Press gave the news to the world. Harangue on the Death of Hayyim Nahman Bialik. César Tiempo. TrJP
On June 15, 1215, King John met the barons. Magna Charta. *Unknown.* OHFP; WBLP
On K. W. 3d. *Unknown.* PeRV
On Keats. Shelley. ML

On Kiley's Run. Andrew Barton Paterson. BoAu
On King Arthur's Round Table, at Winchester. Thomas Warton, the Younger. *See* Sonnet: On King Arthur's Round Table at Winchester.
On Kingston Bridge. Ellen M. H. Cortissoz. AA
On Knighthood. Folgore da San Geminiano, *tr. fr. Italian by* John Addington Symonds. AWP; JAWP; WBP
On Knowing Nothing. A. J. M. Smith. PeCV (1967 ed.)
On Knowing When to Stop. L. J. Bridgman. BOHV
On Lady Poltagrue, a Public Peril. Hilaire Belloc. ALV; MoBrPo; PV; TreFT; WhC
On Lake Pend Oreille. Richard Shelton. NYBP
On land and sea I strove with anxious care. Bombed in London. Kipling. *Fr.* Epitaphs of the War. PoVP
On Lavater's Song of a Christian to Christ. Goethe, *tr. fr. German by* Walter Kaufmann. ELU
On Laying the Cornerstone of the Bunker Hill Monument. John Pierpont. AnNE; PAH
On Laying Up Treasure. Lois Smith Hiers. GoYe
On Leaping over the Moon. Thomas Traherne. AtBAP; LiTB; LoBV; SCEP-1; SeCV-2
On Leaving Bruges. Dante Gabriel Rossetti. CBEP
On Leaving Mrs. Brown's Lodgings. Sir Walter Scott. NBM
On Leaving My Native Land. William Lloyd Garrison. SoP
On Leaving Some Friends at an Early Hour. Keats. MERP
On Leaving Ullswater. Kathleen Raine. NeBP
On Lebanon. David Gray. AA
On Lending a Punch-Bowl. Oliver Wendell Holmes. AA; CoBA
On Leslie Moore. *Unknown.* GoTP
On Leven's banks, while free to rove. Ode to Leven Water. Tobias Smollett. CEP; OBEV
On Liberty and Slavery. George Moses Horton. Kal; PoNe
On Life's Way. Charles F. Deems. OQP
(Worry.) MaRV
On Lighting the Fire. May Swenson. NYTB
On Limited Warfare. *Unknown.* SiTL
On Lincoln's Birthday. John Kendrick Bangs. HH
On Linden, when the sun was low. Hohenlinden [*or* The Battle of Hohenlinden]. Thomas Campbell. BeLS; CBEP; CH; ChTr; EnRP; FaBoCh; FOL; GN; GTBS; GTBS-D; GTBS-P; GTBS-W; GTSE; GTSL; HBV; OBNC; OBRV; OnMSP; OTPC (1923 ed.); PaPo; RoGo; TreF; WaaP; WBLP; WePo; WHA
On Lisa's Golden Hair. Francisco de Quevedo y Villegas, *tr. fr. Spanish by* Roy Campbell. AtBAP
On Living Too Long. Walter Savage Landor. *See* On Timely Death.
On long, serene midsummer days. Wild Roses. Edgar Fawcett. HBV
On longer evenings. Coming. Philip Larkin. MoBrPo (1962 ed.)
On Looking at a Copy of Alice Meynell's Poems, Given Me, Years Ago, by a Friend. Amy Lowell. NP
On Looking at Stubbs's Anatomy of the Horse. Edward Lucie-Smith. NePoEA-2
On Looking Backward. Ernestine Mercer. MaRV
On Looking into Chapman's Homer. Keats. *See* On First Looking into Chapman's Homer.
On Looking into E. V. Rieu's Homer. Patrick Kavanagh. ML
On Looking into Henry Moore. Dorothy Livesay. OBCV
On Looking into Robert Frost in Kanji. William Meredith. ML
On Looking up by Chance at the Constellations. Robert Frost. CMoP; NePA; NP
On Lord Holland's Seat near Margate, Kent. Thomas Gray. *See* Impromptu.
On Love. Countess of Winchilsea. SeCL
(Song, A: "Love, thou art best of human joys.") SeEP
On love's worst ugly day. Theodore Roethke. Meditations of an Old Woman. AP; NaP; PoDB
On Luck. Mark Goldman. NYTB
On Lucretia Borgia's Hair. Walter Savage Landor. AnFE; EnRP; TOP; UnPo (1st ed.); VA
(On Seeing a Hair of Lucretia Borgia.) CABA; OAEP
On Lucy, Countess[e] of Bedford. Ben Jonson. AnAnS-2; BWP; EnRePo; OAEP; OBS; SCEP-2; SeCP; SeCV-1; SeEP; TuPP
On Lutestrings Cat-eaten. Thomas Master. CLwM; MuSP
On Lydia Distracted. Philip Ayres. EnLoPo; SiSw; Sonn
On Maids and Cats. Henricus Selyns. SCAP
On Main one night when they sounded the chimes. In Medias Res. William Stafford. StP
On Mammon. Herman Melville. *Fr.* Clarel. OxBA
On Man. Walter Savage Landor. NBM; OBNC; OBRV
(Man.) VA
On Man, on Nature, and on Human Life. Wordsworth. *Fr.* The Recluse. EnRP; EPN; ERoP-1; NoP; OBRV
On many a lazy river, in many a sparkling bay. The Little Boats of Britain. Sara E. Carsley. CaP
On many and many a soft, still summer's night. Towards the North Star. John Gould Fletcher. LaNeLa
On Marcus the Physician. Nicarchos, *tr. fr. Greek by* Dudley Fitts. LiTW
On Margaret Ratcliffe. Ben Jonson. ReIE; SeCP
On market days we always call. Mrs. Barks. Rose Fyleman. BrR
On Marriage. Richard Crashaw. HW; MaMe; ReEn
On Marriage. Thomas Flatman. ELU; FiBHP; WhC
(Bachelor's Song, The.) EnLoPo
On Martha Snell. *Unknown.* GoTP
("Poor Martha Snell, she's gone away.") WhC
On Mary, Duchess of Richmond. Richard Flecknoe. SeCL
On Maurus the Rhetor. Palladas of Alexandria, *tr. fr. Greek by* Dudley Fitts. LiTW
On Mayday we dance. *Unknown.* BoTP
On May-day, when the lark began to ryse. *Unknown.* LO
On May Morning. Milton. *See* Song on May Morning.
On me and on my children! Cromwell and Henrietta Maria. William Gorman Wills. *Fr.* Charles the First. VA
On me he shall ne'er put a ring. Feminine Arithmetic. Charles Graham Halpine. BOHV
On me nor Priest nor Presbyter nor Pope. My Church. *Unknown.* MaRV; OQP
On me to rest, my bird, my bird. Rest. "Æ." POTE
On Meesh-e-gan, *with music.* *Unknown.* ABF; TrAS
On Meeting a Stranger in a Bookshop. Oscar Williams. NePA
On Meeting Li Kuei-nien down the River. Tu Fu, *tr. fr. Chinese by* Witter Bynner. LiTW
On Melancholy. Keats. *See* Ode on Melancholy.
On Melting down the Plate; or, The Piss-Pot's Farewel, 1697. *Unknown.* PeRV
On Mercenary and Unjust Bailiffs. Henricus Selyns. SCAP
On Middleton Edge. Andrew Young. ELU; POTE; SD
On Milton's "Paradise Lost." Andrew Marvell. *See* On Mr. Milton's "Paradise Lost."
On Minding One's Own Business. James Wright. PoPl
On Mr. Abraham Cowley, His Death and Burial amongst the Ancient Poets. Sir John Denham. AnAnS-2
(On Mr. Abraham Cowley.) SeCV-1
"Old Chaucer, like the morning star," *sel.* OBS
On Mr. Edward Howard upon His British Princes. Charles Sackville. PeRV
On Mr. Francis Beaumont (Then Newly Dead). Richard Corbet. OBS
On Mr. G. Herberts Booke Intituled the Temple. Richard Crashaw. MaMe; OxBoCh; SCEP-1; SeCV-1
(On Mr. George Herberts Booke Intituled the Temple.) AnAnS-1; MeP
On Mr. Gay; in Westminster Abbey, 1732. Pope. FiP
(Epitaph: "Of manners gentle.") CEP
On Mr. Hobbs, and His Writings. John Sheffield, Duke of Buckingham and Normanby. PoEL-3
On Mr. Milton's Paradise lost. Andrew Marvell. MaMe
(On Milton's "Paradise Lost.") OAEP
(On Paradise Lost.) PeRV; SeEP
"Well mightst thou scorn thy readers to allure," *sel.* PP
On Mr. Nash's Picture. Jane Brereton. WaPE
On Mr. Paine's "Rights of Man." Philip Freneau. PoFr
On Mr. Partridge. *Unknown.* WhC
On Mr. Wm. Shakespeare. William Basse. *See* Elegy on Shakespeare.
On Mrs. Biddy Floyd. Swift. CEP
On Mistress Nicely, a Pattern for Housekeepers. Thomas Hood. OBRV
On Mrs. W——. Nicolas Bentley. FiBHP
On Mites. Stephen Duck. EiCL
On Monday man gave God. Adam and God. Anne Wilkinson. MoCV
On Monday, Monday. My True Love. Ivy O. Eastwick. SiSoSe

On Monsieur Coué. Charles Inge. FaFP; SiTL
On moonlight bushes. Nightingales. Samuel Taylor Coleridge. *Fr.* The Nightingale. ChTr
On moonlit heath and lonesome bank. A. E. Housman. A Shropshire Lad, IX. BrPo; CMoP; OAEP; PoVP
On moony nights the dogs bark shrill. At Night. Frances Cornford. StaSt; TSW
On Morpheus. *Unknown.* SeCL
On Mt. Iron. Charles Brasch. AnNZ
On Mount Tsukuba. Mushimaro, *tr. fr. Japanese by* Basil Hall Chamberlain. OnPM
On Moving into a Skylight Room. Sister Rita Agnes. JKCP (1926 ed.)
On Mundane Acquaintances. Hilaire Belloc. ELU; FiBHP; MoVE
On Music. Walter Savage Landor. GoJo; HBV; MuSP; VA
On Music. Thomas Moore. MuSP
On My Bed I Sought Him. The Song of Solomon, III: 1-5, Bible, *O.T.* TrJP
On My Birthday July 21. Matthew Prior. OBEV
On My Dear Grand-Child Simon Bradstreet. Anne Bradstreet. SCAP
On My First Daughter. Ben Jonson. AnAnS-2; EnRePo; EP; LoBV; NoP; OBS; PoFS; ReIE; SeCP; SeCV-1; SeEP
On My First Son [*or* Sonne]. Ben Jonson. AnAnS-2; AtBAP; AWP; BWP; CABA; CaFP; CoBE; DiPo; EIL; EnL; EnRePo; ExPo; FaBoEn; ForPo; FosPo; InPo; LiTB; LoBV; MaPo; NoP; OAEP; OnPM; PIA; PoE; PoEL-2; PoFS; PoIE; QFR; ReEn; ReIE; SCEP-2; SeCP; SeCV-1; SeEP; StP; TuPP; UnPo (3d ed.); WoL
(On His First Sonne.) OBS
On my flute, tipped with jade, I sang a song to mortals. Prose Poem: Sages' Dance. Judith Gautier. OnPM
On My Joyful Departure from the City of Cologne. Samuel Taylor Coleridge. InvP
(On My Joyful Departure from the Same [City].) WhC
On My Lady Isabella Playing on the Lute. Edmund Waller. SeCP
On my little guitar. On My Old Ramkiekie. C. Louis Leipoldt. PeSA
On my little magic whistle I will play to you all day. The Magic Whistle. Margaret Rose. BoTP
On My Lord Bacon. John Danforth. SCAP
On my perambulator. Perambulator Poems, I. David McCord. WhC
On My Old Ramkiekie. C. Louis Leipoldt, *tr. fr. Afrikaans by* Anthony Delius. PeSA
On My Short-Sightedness. Prem Chaya. FIW
On My Sorrowful Life. Moses ibn Ezra, *tr. fr. Hebrew by* Solomon Solis-Cohen. TrJP
On My Sweet Mother. Sappho, *tr. fr. Greek by* Thomas Moore. PoPl
On My Thirty-third Birthday. Byron. MBW-2; OBRV
On my wedding night. The Toilette. Chu Ching-Yü. HW
On Myself. Countess of Winchilsea. TrGrPo
On Nanus Mounted Upon an Ant. Richard Crashaw. MaMe
On National Vanity. J. E. Clare McFarlane. PoNe
On nature's Alps I stand. Edward Young. *Fr.* Night Thoughts. MaRV
On Nature's invitation do I come. Wordsworth. *Fr.* The Recluse. ERoP-1
On New Year's Day, as I heard say. Dicky of Ballyman. *Unknown.* OTPC (1946 ed.)
On New-Year's Day, 1640. To the King. Sir John Suckling. SCEP-2; SeCV-1
On News. Thomas Traherne. *See* News.
On No Work of Words Now. Dylan Thomas. FaBoTw; LiTB
On Noman, a Guest. Hilaire Belloc. PV
On Not Hearing the Birds Sing in Ireland. Padraic Colum. NePoAm
On ochre walls in ice-formed caves shaggy Neanderthals. To My Son Parker, Asleep in the Next Room. Bob Kaufman. Kal; TwCP
On Oculists. J. C. Squire. WhC
On old Cold Crendon's windy tops. The Fox Awakes. John Masefield. *Fr.* Reynard the Fox. MoVE; OA
On. On compassion shall never enter heere, tis tyme. *Unknown.* SeCSL
On, On, Forever. Harriet Martineau. VA
On one fixed point all nature moves. On the Uniformity and Perfection of Nature. Philip Freneau. AmePo; AmPP; CoBA
On one of those days with the Legion. A Day with the Foreign Legion. Reed Whittemore. CoAP; LiTM (1970 ed.); NePoEA
On One Peter and His Wife. Walter Savage Landor. CBV
On one Saturday evenin'. Harvey Logan. *Unknown.* OuSiCo
On One Who Died Discovering Her Kindness. John Sheffield, Duke of Buckingham and Normanby. LO; OBEV
On One Who Died in May. Clarence Chatham Cook. AA
On One Who Made Long Epitaphs. Pope. ALV
On Opening a New Book. Abbie Farwell Brown. YeAr
On other cloudy afternoons. The Double. Irving Feldman. NYBP
On other fields and other scenes the morn. Burnt Lands. Sir Charles G. D. Roberts. VA
On Our Crucified Lord, Naked and Bloody. Richard Crashaw. *See* Upon the Body of Our Blessed Lord, Naked and Bloody.
On Our Farm. Esther Antin. RIS
On Our Lady of Blachernae. *Unknown, Tr. fr. Greek by* Shane Leslie. ISI
On our last night together. The Sluggard. A. E. Coppard. MoBrPo (1942 ed.)
On our lone pathway bloomed no earthly hopes. Sonnet to Edgar Allan Poe. Sarah Helen Whitman. Sonnets from the Series Relating to Edgar Allan Poe, V. AA; AnAmPo
On our Pharsalian Plaines, comprizing space. Seaconk Plain Engagement. Benjamin Tompson. SCAP
On Our Thirty-ninth Wedding Day. Jonathan Odell. CaP
On Oxford. Keats. Par
On Palladio's rural theme, a farmhouse. Air Tunnel, Monticello. Bink Noll. ToPo
On Paradise Lost. Andrew Marvell. *See* On Mr. Milton's "Paradise Lost."
On Parent Knees. Sir William Jones. *See* Baby, The.
On Parting with Moses ibn Ezra. Judah Halevi, *tr. fr. Hebrew by* Solomon Solis-Cohen. TrJP
On Passing a Friend's House. Wang Wei, *tr. fr. Chinese by* Arthur Christy. OnPM
On Passing the New Menin Gate. Siegfried Sassoon. AnEnPo; OBMV; Sonn
On Passing through the Haymarket. Nikolai Nekrasov, *tr. fr. Russian by* Babette Deutsch. OnPM
On Passing Two Negroes on a Dark Country Road Somewhere in Georgia. Conrad Kent Rivers. IDB; NNP
On Peace. *At. to* Samuel Speed. *See* Peace.
On Peter Robertson. John Gibson Lockhart. SiTL
On Peter Robinson. Francis Jeffrey. OxBoLi; WhC
On Philiphaugh a fray began. The Battle of Philiphaugh. *Unknown.* ESPB
On Philosophy. Barbara Marshall. TNV
On Playwright. Ben Jonson. NoP
On Poet-Ape. Ben Jonson. Sonn
On Poetry; a Rhapsody. Swift. EiCL
Sels.
"All Human Race wou'd fain be Wits." PoEL-3
"Hobbes clearly proves that every creature." PP
(Critics.) OBEC; SeCePo
On poetry and geometric truth. Wordsworth. *Fr.* The Prelude, V. SyP
On Portents. Robert Graves. FaBoMo
On Presenting to a Lady a White Rose and a Red, on the Tenth of June. William Somervile. *See* Presenting to a Lady a White Rose. . .
On primal rocks she wrote her name. Our Country. Julia Ward Howe. DD; MC; PaA; PAH; PAL
On Primrose Hill in the early spring. Primrose Hill. Rose Fyleman. BoTP
On Prince Frederick. *Unknown.* GoTP; OxBoLi; TreFS; WhC
On Professor Drennan's Verse. Roy Campbell. GTBS-P; WhC
On quarry walls the spleenwort spreads. Rockferns. Norman Nicholson. MoBrPo (1950 ed.); NeMA
On Queen Anne's Death. *Unknown.* EIL
On rainy days alone I dine. On Himself. Swift. AnIV
On Reading. Thomas Bailey Aldrich. AA
On Reading a Poet's First Book. H. C. Bunner. AA
On Reading a Soviet Novel. Roy Fuller. ToPo
On Reading Gene Derwood's "The Innocent." Willard Maas. NePA

On Reading the *Metamorphoses*. George Garrett. NePoAm-2
On Reading the War Diary of a Defunct Ambassador. Siegfried Sassoon. CMoP
"World will find no pity in your pages, The," *sel.* PoFr
On Receiving a Copy of Mr. Austin Dobson's "Old World Idylls." James Russell Lowell. AP
On Receiving a Crown of Ivy from the Same (Keats). Leigh Hunt. Sonn
On Receiving News of the War. Isaac Rosenberg. MMA; MoBrPo
On Recrossing the Rocky Mountains after Many Years. John Charles Frémont. PoOW
On Reformed Gamester. Ben Jonson. ReIE
On Refusal of Aid between Nations. Dante Gabriel Rossetti. CoBE; EPN; LoBV; PoVP; TOP
On Re-Reading the Complete Works of an Elder Poet. Winfield Townley Scott. ML
On Returning to Teach. Marvin Bell. . YAP
On Revisiting Cintra after the Death of Catarina. Luís de Camoes, *tr. fr. Spanish by* Richard Garnett. AWP
On Richard Dent, Lordland. *Unknown.* GoTP
On Richmond Hill there lives a lass. The Lass of Richmond Hill. James Upton. HBV
On Riots. Cy Leslie. NBP
On Roman feet my stumbling Muse declines. An Elegiack Verse, on . . . Mr. Elijah Corlet. Nehemiah Walter. SCAP
On Rome in the Pontificate of Julius II. Michelangelo, *tr. fr. Italian by* John Addington Symonds. PoFr
On Rome's Pardons. *At. to* the Earl of Rochester. PeRV
"On royal crowns and purples, I." Long John. Padraic Fallon. NeIP
On Rutt the Judge. Charles Cotton. PeRV
On St. James's Park, as Lately Improved by His Majesty. Edmund Waller. AnAnS-2; CEP
On St. Martin's evening green. Nuns at Eve. John Malcolm Brinnin. MoAB; TwCP
On St. Peter Casting Away His Nets at Our Saviours Call. Richard Crashaw. MaMe
On St. Peter Cutting of Malchus His Eare. Richard Crashaw. *See* Malchus' Ear.
On Samuel Pease. *Unknown.* ShM
On Saturday morning there was a great battle. The Battle of Argoed Llwyfain. Taliesin. PrWP
On Saturday night. Mother Goose. OTPC (1923 ed.); OxNR
On Saturday sailed from Bremen. Gerard Manley Hopkins. *Fr.* The Wreck of the *Deutschland.* SeCePo
On Scafell Pike. Ted Walker. NYBP
On scent of game from town to town he flew. On a Travelling Speculator. Philip Freneau. AA
On Scotland. John Cleveland. BOHV; PV
On Scott's [Poem] "The Field of Waterloo." Thomas, Lord Erskine. FiBHP; WhC
On Scratchbury Camp. Siegfried Sassoon. HaMV
On Seein an Aik-Tree Sprent wi Galls. Robert Garioch. OxBS
On Seeing a Dead Man. Prince Shotoku, *tr. fr. Japanese by* Ishii *and* Obata. OnPM
On Seeing a Hair of Lucretia Borgia. Walter Savage Landor. *See* On Lucretia Borgia's Hair.
On Seeing a Lady's Garter. *Unknown.* ErPo
On Seeing a Lock of Milton's Hair. Keats. PP
On Seeing a Piece of Our Artillery Brought into Action. Wilfred Owen. LiTM (1946 ed.)
On Seeing a Poet of the First World War on the Station at Abbeville. Charles Causley. ChMP; LiTM (1970 ed.); NMP
On Seeing a Pompous Funeral for a Bad Husband. *Unknown.* ShM
On Seeing Larry Rivers' "Washington Crossing the Delaware" at the Museum of Modern Art. Frank O'Hara. FRC
On Seeing My Birthplace from a Jet Aircraft. John Pudney. NYBP
On Seeing Swift in Laracor. Brinsley MacNamara. AnIV; OxBI
On Seeing the Elgin Marbles [for the First Time]. Keats. BEL; BoLiVe; CABA; CoBE; DiPo; EnLi-2; EnLit; EnRP; ERoP-2; GTBS-W; LiTB; MaPo (1969 ed.); MBW-2; PAn; Po; PoeP; PoIE; SeCeV; TrGrPo; WHA
On Seeing Two Brown Boys in a Catholic Church. Frank Horne. BANP; CDC; PoNe; TTY
On Seeing Weather-beaten Trees. Adelaide Crapsey. InP; MAP; MCCG; MoAmPo (1942 ed.); NeMA
On Seeming to Presume. Lawrence Durrell. LiTM (rev. ed.)
On Setting Out. William Dickey. CBV
On Shakespeare. Milton. BEL; BoLiVe; CoBE; DiPo; EnLit; GTBS-W; InvP; LoBV; MeLP; MePo; NoP; OAEP; PG (1945 ed. *and* 1955 ed.); PoRA; SeCePo; SeCL; SeEP; TOP; TrGrPo; WHA
(Epitaph on the Admirable Dramatic Poet, William [*or* W.] Shakespeare, An.) CLwM; HBV; ViBoPo
On shallow straw, in shadeless glass. Take One Home for the Kiddies. Philip Larkin. ELU
On Shooting Particles beyond the World. Richard Eberhart. GTBS-W; LiTA; LiTM (rev. ed.)
On shores of Sicily a shape of Greece! A Shepherd Maiden. Edward Cracroft Lefroy. *Fr.* Echoes from Theocritus. VA
On Sight of a Gentlewomans Face in the Water. Thomas Carew. SeCV-1
On Sir Francis Drake. *Unknown. See* Epigram: On Sir Francis Drake.
On Sir Henry Clinton's Recall. *Unknown.* PAH
On Sir Henry Ferrett, M.P. J. B. Morton. PV
On Sir John Vanbrugh. Abel Evans. *See* Epitaph on Sir John Vanbrugh.
On Sir Philip Sidney. Henry Constable. *See* On the Death of Sir Philip Sidney.
On Sir Philip Sidney. Matthew Royden. *Fr.* An Elegy, or Friend's Passion for His Astrophil. EIL
On Sir Voluptuous Beast. Ben Jonson. EP
On Sitting Down to Read "King Lear" Once Again. Keats. ATP; DiPo; EnRP; ERoP-2; MaPo (1969 ed.); MBW-2; NoP
On Sivori's Violin. Frances Sargent Osgood. AA
On Skugg. Benjamin Franklin. *See* Here Skugg Lies Snug.
On Snow-Flakes Melting on His Lady's Breast. William Martin Johnson. AA; AmLP
On softest pillows my dim eyes unclose. Vita Benefica. Alice Wellington Rollins. AA
On Some Buttercups. Frank Dempster Sherman. AA
On Some Shells Found Inland. Trumbull Stickney. AnFE; APA; CoAnAm; LiTA; LiTG; NCEP; NePA; Sonn; TwAmPo
On Some South African Novelists. Roy Campbell. AnFE; BoSA; ChMP; CoBE; GTBS-P; MoBrPo; MoPW; MoVE; PoPl; SiTL; WhC
On Some Trees Needlessly Slain. Stanton A. Coblentz. TRV
On Something That Walk[e]s Somewhere. Ben Jonson. CoBE; SeCP; SeCV-1; TuPP
On Southey's Death. Walter Savage Landor. TOP
On Spies. Ben Jonson. NoP
On Springfield Mountain there did dwell. Springfield Mountain. *Unknown.* BaBo; Po; TrAS; ViBoFo (A, B, C, *and* D *vers.*)
On starry heights. The Conflict of Convictions. Herman Melville. AP; MAmP; MWA-1
On Stella's Birthday. Swift. *See* Stella's Birthday, Written in the Year 1718.
On stifling summer days. Old Inn on the Eastern Shore. William H. Matchett. NePoEA
On still black waters where the stars lie sleeping. Ophelia. Arthur Rimbaud. ChTr
On stormy days. Brooms. Dorothy Aldis. GFA; SoPo
On stormy seas we six years sailed. Sept ans sur mer. *Unknown.* OuSiCo
On Stubborn Michael Shay. *Unknown.* GoTP
On Sturminster Foot-Bridge. Thomas Hardy. OAEP
On Such a Day. Mary Elizabeth Coleridge. GTBS-D; LO; MoVE
On such a day as this I think. An April Day. Joseph S. Cotter, Jr. CDC
On such a day St. Francis walked. Return. Mary S. Hawling. PoMa
On Such a Wet and Blustery Night. Ralph Gustafson. PeCV
On summer afternoons I sit. La Vie C'est la Vie. Jessie Redmond Fauset. BANP; CDC; PoNe
On summer days a rustling tree. Alike. Dorothy Aldis. RePo
On summer evenings blue, pricked by the heat. Sensation. Arthur Rimbaud, *tr. by* Jethro Bithell. AWP; JAWP; WBP
On summer evenings blue, where ears of wheat. Sensation. Arthur Rimbaud, *tr. by* T. Sturge Moore. SyP
On summer eves with wild delight. Bat. John Clare. *Fr.* Childhood. OA
On summer mornings when it's hot. The Milkman's Horse. *Unknown.* SoPo

On summer nights when moonbeams flow. The Worked-out Mine. Edward Dyson. BoAu; WoL
On Sunday in the Sunlight. William Rose Benét. HBMV
On Sunday morning, then he comes. Mr. Wells. Elizabeth Madox Roberts. FaPON; GaP; HBMV; HBVY; TSW
On Sunday Morning Well I Knew. *Unknown, tr. fr. Italian by* John Addington Symonds. OnPM
(Popular Songs of Tuscany.) AWP
On sunny slope and beechen swell. Burial of the Minnisink. Longfellow. LaNeLa
On Susan Pattison. *Unknown.* CBEP
On Syrian Hills. Richard Burton. ChIP
On Taine. Alfred Ainger. ALV
On Taking a Bachelor's Degree. Christopher Smart. VaPo
On Taking a wife. Thomas Moore. BOHV; TreF
("Come, Come," Said Tom's Father.) WHC
(Epigram: "'Come, come,' said Tom's father, 'at your time of life.'") ALV; HBV
(Joke Versified, A.) LiTG; SiTL
On Taking up One's Cross. St. Luke, IX: 23-26, Bible, *N.T.* TreFT
On taut air—bells; lifted, adoring eyes. Immolation. Robert Farren. OnYI
On Ternissa's Death. Walter Savage Landor. *See* Ternissa! You Are Fled!
On Thame's bank, a gentle youth. On Her Pleading Want of Time. George Lyttelton. WaPE
On that big estate there is no rain. Monangamba. Antonio Jacinto. TTY
On that first day so singular. The Secret. John Richard Moreland. OQP
On that gray night of mournful drone. A Man Was Drawing Near to Me. Thomas Hardy. InPo
On that last night before we went. In Memoriam A. H. H., CIII. Tennyson. EnLi-2; EPN; OAEP; PoEL-5; ViPo; VP
On that wild verge in the late light he stood. Preludes to Definition, II. Conrad Aiken. TwAmPo
On the Acequia Madre. Alice Corbin. NP
On the Adequacy of Landscape. Wallace Stevens. PoeP
On the Anniversary of the Death of Frank O'Hara. Sotère Torregian. YAP
On the Anniversary of the Storming of the Bastille, at Paris, July 14th, 1789. Philip Freneau. AmPP (3d ed.); CoBA
On the Annunciation. *Unknown, tr. fr. Greek by* Shane Leslie. ISi
On the Annunciation of Fra Angelico. Manuel Machado, *tr. fr. Spanish by* Thomas Walsh. CAW
On the Antiquity of Microbes. Strickland Gillilan. WhC
(Lines on the Antiquity of Microbes.) InP
(Lines Written on the Antiquity of Microbes.) TreFT
On the Appeal from the Race of Sheba: II. Leopold Sedar Senghor, *tr. fr. French by* John Reed *and* Clive Wake. TTY
On the Approach of Summer, *sel.* Thomas Warton, the Younger.
Sunshine after a Shower. OTPC
On the Aristocracy of Harvard ("Here's to good old Boston"). John Collins Bossidy. *See* Boston Toast, A.
On the Aristocracy of Harvard ("I come from good olde Boston"). *At. to* Samuel C. Bushnell. BOHV. *See also* Boston Toast, A.
On the Army of Spartans, Who Died at Thermopylae. Simonides. *See* Thermopylae.
On the Assumption [of the Virgin Mary]. Richard Crashaw. *See* On the Glorious Assumption of Our Blessed Lady.
On the Asylum Road. Charlotte Mew. MoBrPo (1950 ed.)
On the Atchafalaya. Longfellow. *Fr.* Evangeline, Pt. II. AA
On the Athenian Dead at Ecbatana. Plato, *tr. fr. Greek by* Ralph Gladstone. PoPl
On the Attic cost. The First Day. Neil Weiss. NYTB
On the Author. Burns. *See* Lines on the Author's Death.
On the Back Veld. Crosbie Garstin. *See* Nocturne: "Red flame flowers and die, The."
On the Bad Government of Toledo. Gómez Manrique, *tr. fr. Spanish by* Thomas Walsh. WoL
On the Balcony. D. H. Lawrence. BrPo
On the Banishment of Cicero. Philip Wharton. WaPE
On the Banisters. Margaret E. Gibbs. BoTP
On the Bank as I Sat a-Fishing. Sir Henry Wotton. *See* On a Bank as I Sat a-Fishing.
On the bank the maiden sat. Trouble Not the Maiden's Soul. Johan Ludvig Runeberg. LiTW
On the banks of Allan Water. Allan Water. Matthew Gregory Lewis. HBV; OTPC (1923 ed.)
On the Banks of the Wabash, Far Away. Paul Dresser. PoRL; TreFT
On the banks of the Xenil, the dark Spanish maiden. The Pumpkin. Whittier. DD; OHIP
On the Baptized Ethiopian [*or* Aethiopian]. Richard Crashaw. MaMe; NoP; SeCV-1; SeEP
On the bare mountain. Distant View. Uys Krige. PeSA
On the Beach. Charles Stuart Calverley. ALV; FiBHP
On the Beach. Emilie Blackmore Stapp. GFA
On the Beach. Arthur Symons. *Fr.* At Dieppe. PoVP; SyP
On the Beach at Calais. Wordsworth. *See* It Is a Beauteous Evening, Calm and Free.
On the Beach at Fontana. James Joyce. AnEnPo; LO; MoBrPo; NP; OBMV
On the Beach at Night. Walt Whitman. AmPP (4th ed.); AWP; BoLiVe; ChTr; InPo; MAP; MoAmPo; NeMA; NePA; NoP; OBVV; OxBA
On the Big Horn. Whittier. PAH
On the Birth of a Child. Louis Untermeyer. NeMA
On the Birth of His Son. Su T'ung-po, *tr. fr. Chinese by* Arthur Waley. AWP; JAWP; LiTW; OnPM; TRV; WBP; WoL
("Families, when a child is born.") PV
On the Birthday of a Young Lady. William Whitehead. OTPC (1923 ed.)
On the black tarmac playground dark. Deaf-and-Dumb School. Anthony Delius. PeSA
On the Bleeding Wounds of Our Crucified Lord. Richard Crashaw. MaMe; SeCV-1
(Upon The Bleeding Crucifix, *later vers.*) MaMe; SeCP
"Jesu, no more! It is full tide," *sel.* TrGrPo
On the Blessed Virgin's Bashfulness. Richard Crashaw. EnLi-1; ILP; ISi; MaMe; OAEP
On the Block: Another Night Search. Jay Wright. ThO
On the bloody field of Monmouth. Molly Maguire at Monmouth. William Collins. OTPC; PaA; PAL
On the blue plains in wintry days. Native Companions Dancing. John Shaw Neilson. NeLNL
On the bluff of the Little Big Horn. Miles Keogh's Horse. John Hay. PAH; PoOW
On the Breaking-up of a School. Tadhg O'g O'Huiginn, *tr. fr. Late Middle Irish by* Osborn Bergin. AnIL
On the Bridge. Kate Greenaway. MCCG; MPB; SAS
On the Bridge. Arthur Reed Ropes. VA
On the Bridge of Athlone; a Prophecy. Donagh MacDonagh. OxBI
On the Brink. Charles Stuart Calverley. VA
On the Brink of Death. Michelangelo, *tr. fr. Italian by* John Addington Symonds. AWP; JAWP; WBP
(His Great Love on High.) OnPM
On the British Invasion. Philip Freneau. PAH
On the British King's Speech. Philip Freneau. PAH
On the Building of Springfield. Vachel Lindsay. AmPP (3d ed.); InP; MoRP; NAMP; OHFP; PaA; SoP; TOP; WHA
On the Burial of His Brother. Catullus, *tr. fr. Latin by* Aubrey Beardsley. AWP; EnLi-1; JAWP; OuHeWo; WBP
On the Calculus. J. V. Cunningham. PoIE; QFR
On the Campagna. Elizabeth Stoddard. AA
On the Cantos of Spenser's *Faerie Queene,* Lost in the Passage from Ireland. Thomas Edwards. Sonn
On the Capture of the *Guerrière.* Philip Freneau. PAH
On the Cards and Dice. Sir Walter Ralegh. EnRePo; FCP
(Prognostication upon Cards and Dice, A.) SiPS
On the Castle of Chillon. Byron. *See* Sonnet on Chillon.
On the Charlie So Long, *with music. Unknown.* AS
On the Cliff. Hal Summers. ChMP
On the Cliffs, *sel.* Swinburne.
Sappho. VA
On the Coast near Sausalito. Robert Hass. YAP
On the Coast of Coromandel. The Courtship of the Yonghy-Bonghy-Bo [*or* The Yonghy-Bonghy Bo]. Edward Lear. BOHV; EnLoPo; EvOK; GoTP; HBV; LBN; NA; OnMSP; OTPC; WiR
On the Coast of Coromandel. Sir Osbert Sitwell. MoBrPo; SeCePo
On the Coincidence of the Feasts of the Annunciation and the Resurrection in 1627. Sir John Beaumont. ACP (1926 ed.)

On the Collar of a Dog [Presented by Mr. Pope to the Prince of Wales]. Pope. *See* Epigram: "I am his Highness' dog at Kew."
On the Collar of a Dog. Swift. StP
On the Coming of Age of a Rich, Extravagant Young Man. Samuel Johnson. *See* Short Song of Congratulation, A.
On the Completion of the Pacific Telegraph. Jones Very. AP
On the corner—116th and Lenox. Harlem Freeze Frame. Lebert Bethune. BF
On the Couch. Oscar Williams. WaP
On the Countess Dowager of Pembroke. William Browne, *wr. at. to* Ben Jonson. BEL, *abr.*; CABA; CavP; EG, *abr.*; EnLi-1; InvP; PoEL-2; PoRA (rev. ed.); SeCeV; SeEP; UnPo (1st ed.)
(Epitaph: "Underneath this sable hearse," *abr.*) OBEV
(Epitaph on the Countess Dowager of Pembroke.) CBEP; HBV; LoBV, *abr.*; OBS, *abr.*
(Epitaph on the Countess of Pembroke.) MyFE, *abr.*
(On the Countess of Pembroke.) AWP; JAWP; TOP; TreFS, *abr.*; WBP; WoL
(On the Death of Marie, Countess of Pembroke.) OnPP; ReEn; SeCL; WHA
(On the Dowager Countess of Pembroke.) ViBoPo
("Underneath this sable hearse.") InP
On the Countess of Dorchester. Charles Sackville. CavP
On the craggy mountain-top the mist. Majuba Hill. Roy Macnab. BoSA; PeSA
On the Creation and Ontogony. *Unknown, tr. fr. Lenape Indian by* C. S. Rafinesque. *Fr.* Wallam Olum. LiTA
On the crooked arm of Columbus, on his cloak. Pigeons. Alastair Reid. NePoEA; NYBP; SiTL; TwCP
On the Crucifix. Michelangelo, *tr. fr. Italian by* Longfellow. CAW
On the Crucifixion. Giles Fletcher. *Fr.* Christ's Victory and Triumph. OxBoCh
On the Curve-Edge. Abbie Huston Evans. NYBP
On the Danger of War. George Meredith. CoBE; EPN; PPON
On the Danube. Robert Conquest. NMP
On the dark hill's western side. Evening Hymn. Cecil Frances Alexander. OTPC (1923 ed.)
On the day that Christ ascended. The Anger of Christ. Richard Watson Gilder. StJW
On the day when the lotus bloomed. Rabindranath Tagore. Gitanjali, XX. NP
On the Dead. Walter Savage Landor. NBM
On the Death of a Cat, a Friend of Mine Aged Ten Years and a Half. Christina Rossetti. CIV
On the Death of a Child. Edward Silvera. PoNe
On the Death of a Favorite Cat. *Unknown.* CIV
On the Death of a Favorite Cat, Drowned in a Tub of Goldfishes. Thomas Gray. *See* Ode on the Death of a Favorite Cat . . .
On the Death of a Friend's Child, *sel.* James Russell Lowell.
"'Tis sorrow builds the shining ladder up." MaRV
On the Death of a Journalist. Roy Campbell. CoBE
On the Death of a Lady's Dog. Earl of Roscommon. CavP
On the Death of a Lady's Owl. Moses Mendes. TrJP
On the Death of a Metaphysician. George Santayana. AA; AmLP; AnFE; APA; CoAnAm; MAP; MoAmPo; ViBoPo
On the Death of a Monkey. Thomas Heyrick. MePo
On the Death of a New Born Child. Mei Yao Ch'en, *tr. fr. Chinese by* Kenneth Rexroth. NaP
On the Death of a Nightingale. Thomas Randolph. AnAnS-2
On the Death of a Particular Friend. James Thomson. *See* Verses Occasioned by the Death of Dr. Aikman.
On the Death of a Pious Lady. Olof Wexionius, *tr. fr. Swedish by* Sir Edmund Gosse. AWP; JAWP; WBP
On the Death of a Recluse. George Darley. CBEP; OBVV; OxBI
On the Death of a Young and Favorite Slave. Martial, *tr. fr. Latin by* Goldwin Smith. AWP; JAWP; LiTW; WBP
On the Death of an Acquaintance. Oscar Williams. Variations on a Theme, I. LiTA; NePA
On the Death of an Aged Friend. Roselle Mercier Montgomery. MaRV
On the Death of an Emperor Penguin in Regent's Park, London. David Wright. NYBP
On the Death of an Epicure. Richard Graves. CBEP
On the Death of Anne Brontë. Charlotte Brontë. ViBoPo
On the Death of Benjamin Franklin. Philip Freneau. DD; PAH; ThLM
On the Death of Captain Nicholas Biddle. Philip Freneau. PAH
On the Death of Catarina de Attayda. Luís de Camoes, *tr. fr. Portuguese by* R. F. Burton. AWP; JAWP; WBP
On the Death of Charles I. James Graham, Marquess of Montrose. *See* Epitaph on King Charles I.
On the Death of Commodore Oliver H. Perry. John Gardiner Calkins Brainard. PAH
On the Death of Crashaw. Abraham Cowley. *See* On the Death of Mr. Crashaw.
On the Death of Dr. Robert Levet. Samuel Johnson. *See* On the Death of Mr. Robert Levet.
On the Death of Dr. Swift. Swift. *See* Verses on the Death of Dr. Swift.
On the Death of Francis Thompson. Alfred Noyes. OBVV
On the Death of Frank O'Hara. Sotère Torregian. YAP
On the Death of Friends in Childhood. Donald Justice. CBV
On the Death of His Child. Faydi, *tr. fr. Persian by* Edward G. Browne. LiTW
On the Death of His Son. Lewis Glyn Cothi, *tr. fr. Welsh by* Gwyn Williams. PoPl
On the Death of Jackson. *Unknown.* PAH
On the Death of Joseph Rodman Drake. Fitz-Greene Halleck. AA; AmePo; AmLP; AnAmPo; DD; HBV; MaRV; PAH; PoEL-4; TreFS
(Joseph Rodman Drake.) BLPA; FaPL
(On His Friend, Joseph Rodman Drake, *st.* 1.) OBVV
On the Death of King Charles I. James Graham, Marquess of Montrose. *See* Epitaph on King Charles I.
On the Death of Little Mahala Ashcraft. James Whitcomb Riley. AA
On the Death of M. d'Ossoli and His Wife, Margaret Fuller. Walter Savage Landor. PAH; VA
On the Death of Marie, Countess of Pembroke. William Browne. *See* On the Countess Dowager of Pembroke.
On the Death of Mary. Rainer Maria Rilke, *tr. fr. German by* M. D. Herter Norton. ISi
On the Death of Mr. Crashaw. Abraham Cowley. AnAnS-2; MeLP; MePo; NoP; OBS; SCEP-2; SeCP; SeCV-1; SeEP; ViBoPo
(On the Death of Crashaw.) GoBC
On the Death of Mr. Purcell. Dryden. UnS
On the Death of Mr. Richard West. Thomas Gray. *See* Sonnet on the Death of Richard West.
On the Death of Mr. Robert Levet, a Practiser in Physic. Samuel Johnson. BWP; CBEP; CEP; EiPP; HBV; OBEC; OBEV; PoE; PoFS
(Lines on the Death of Mr. Levett.) FaBoEn
(On the Death of Dr. Robert Levet.) EiCL; EiCP; NoP; PoEL-3; VaPo
"In Misery's darkest cavern known," *sel.* ViBoPo
On the Death of Mr. William Aikman the Painter, *sel.* James Thomson.
Verses Occasioned by the Death of Dr. Aikman. OBEC
(On the Death of a Particular Friend.) OBEV
On the Death of Mr. William Hervey. Abraham Cowley. AnAnS-2; CBEP; GTSL; OBEV, *abr.*; OBS, *abr.*; SeCP; SeCV-1; SeEP
"It was a dismal and a fearful night," *sel.* ViBoPo
On the Death of Mrs. Browning. Sydney Dobell. VA
On the Death of Mrs. (now Lady) Throckmorton's Bullfinch. William Cowper. HBV
On the Death of My Son Charles. Daniel Webster. AA
On the Death of Phillips. *Unknown.* OBSC
On the Death of President Garfield. Oliver Wendell Holmes. PAH
On the Death of Pushkin. Mikhail Yurevich Lermontov, *tr. fr. Russian by* Martha Dickinson Bianchi. PoFr
On the Death of Pym. William Drummond of Hawthornden. ALV
On the Death of Robert Browning. Swinburne. A Sequence of Sonnets on the Death of Robert Browning, VII. EnLit; EPN; PoVP
On the Death of Roger Casement. Padraic Colum. PoFr
On the Death of Sir Albert Morton's Wife. Sir Henry Wotton. *See* Upon the Death . . .
On the Death of Sir Philip Sidney. Henry Constable. GoBC; OBEV
(On Sir Philip Sidney.) OBSC
(To Sir Philip Sidney's Soul.) EIL; SeCePo
On the Death of Sir Thomas Wyatt [the Elder]. Earl of Surrey. BEL; CBEP; EnLi-1 (1949 ed.); FosPo; GoTL

(Of the Death of Sir Thomas Wyatt [the Elder].) FaBoEn; RelE; SiCE; TuPP
(Tribute to Wyatt, A.) EnLit; SiPS
("Wyatt resteth here, that quick could never rest.") EnPo; FCP; NCEP; NoP; ReEn
On the Death of Southey ("Not the last struggles of the Sun"). Walter Savage Landor. OBVV
On the Death of the Noble Prince King Edward the Fourth. John Skelton. RelE
On the Death of Theodore Roethke. William Witherup. QAH
On the Deaths of Thomas Carlyle and George Eliot. Swinburne. BEL; HBV; PoVP; TOP; VA
On the Death of William Edward Burghardt Du Bois. Conrad Kent Rivers. NBP
On the Decease of the Religious and Honourable Jno Haynes Esqr. John James. SCAP
On the Deception of Appearances. Sadi, *tr. fr. Persian by* L. Cranmer-Byng. *Fr.* The Gulistan. AWP; LiTW
On the deck of Patrick Lynch's boat I sat in woeful plight. The County of Mayo. *At. to* Thomas Flavell [*or* Lavelle], *tr. by* George Fox. AnIV; IrPN; OBEV; OnYI; OxBI
On the Defeat at Ticonderoga or Carilong. *Unknown.* PAH
On the Defeat of Henry Clay. William Wilberforce Lord. PAH
(On the Defeat of a Great Man.) AA
On the Defeat of Ragnall by Murrough King of Leinster A. D. 994. *Unknown, tr. fr. Middle Irish by* Kuno Meyer. OnYI
(Murrough Defeats the Danes, 994, *tr. by* Frank O'Connor.) KiLC
On the Democracy of Yale. Frederick Scheetz Jones. BOHV; HBV; WhC; YaD
(To New Haven.) TreFS
On the Departure of Sir Walter Scott from Abbotsford, for Naples. Wordsworth. EnRP
On the Departure of the British from Charleston. Philip Freneau. PAH
On the Departure Platform. Thomas Hardy. BWP; LO; OBNC
On the Desert ("On the desert/ A silence"). Stephen Crane. War Is Kind, XI. AP; LiTM (1970 ed.)
On the desert, between pale mountains, our cries. Two Songs of Advent. Yvor Winters. NP
On the Detraction Which Followed upon My Writing Certain Treatises ("A Book was writ of late called *Tetrachordon*"). Milton. SeCeV; Sonn
On the Detraction Which Followed upon My Writing Certain Treatises ("I did but prompt the age"). Milton. ATP; ExPo; MaPo; PAn; Sonn; TOP
("I Did But Prompt the Age.") NoP
(On the Same.) SeCeV; Sonn
(Second Sonnet on "Tetrachordon.") PoFr
(Sonnet.) MBW-1
On the Discoveries of Captain Lewis. Joel Barlow. AmPP(5th ed.): MC; PAH
On the Doorstep. Thomas Hardy. MoVE
On the Dowager Countess of Pembroke. William Browne. *See* On the Countess Dowager of Pembroke.
On the Downtown Side of an Uptown Street. William Johnston. BOHV
On the Dunes. Sara Teasdale. NP
On the dusty earth-drum. Rain Music. Joseph S. Cotter, Jr. BANP; BrR; CDC; PCH
On the Dutchess of Portsmouth's Picture. *At. to* Dryden. PeRV
On the Earl of Strafford's Trial and Death. John Denham. LoBV
On the Eclipse of the Moon of October 1865. Charles Tennyson Turner. OBNC
On the Edge. Philip Levine. CoAP
On the edge of a lawn where weeds. The Death of a Dove. James Schevill. FiMAP
On the Edge of the Copper Pit. Pauline Henson. GoYe
On the Edge of the Pacific. Theodore Maynard. CAW
On the Edition of Mr. Pope's Works with a Commentary and Notes. Thomas Edwards. Sonn
On the 18th of April in '28. Happy Lifetime to You. Franklin P. Adams. InMe
On the eighteenth of September in eighteen seventy three. The Winter of '73. Larry Gorman. ShS
On the eighth day God died: his bearded mouth. The Worms of History. Robert Graves. MoPo
On the eighth day of March it was, some people say. The Birth of Saint Patrick. Samuel Lover. BOHV; DD; HBV; OTD; PoRL; PoSC
On the eighth day, the rain stopped before dusk. The Loon's Egg. Peter Dale Scott. MoCV
On the Embankment. W. W. Gibson. PoFr
On the Emigration to America. Philip Freneau. AmPP (3d ed.); PAH
On the Eta, the Untouchables. Issa, *tr. fr. Japanese by* Max Bickerton. PoFr
On the Eve of Bunker Hill. Clinton Scollard. *See* Eve of Bunker Hill, The.
On the Eve of His Execution. Chidiock Tichborne. *See* Elegy: "My prime of youth is but a frost of cares."
On the Eve of New Wars. Louis Untermeyer. MAP
On the Eve of the Feast of the Immaculate Conception, 1942. Robert Lowell. WaaP
On the Eve of War. Danske Dandridge. PAH
On the Expressway. Robert Dana. OCS
On the Extinction of the Venetian Republic. Wordsworth. BEL; BoLiVe; CLwM; EnL; EnLi-2; EnLit; EnRP; EPN; FOL; GTBS; GTBS-D; GTBS-P; GTBS-W; GTSE; GTSL; HBV; HT; LoBV; MBW-2; MCCG; MERP; NoP; OAEP; OBEV; OBNC; OBRV; OuHeWo; PoFr; Sonn; TOP; TrGrPo; ViBoPo
On the fair green hills of Rio. The Burglar of Babylon. Elizabeth Bishop. NYBP
On the Fair Weather just at the Coronation. Katherine Philips. PeRV
On the far reef the breakers. The Tide Will Win. Priscilla Leonard. MaRV; TRV
On the Farm. R. S. Thomas. POTi
On the farm it never mattered. The Assistance. Paul Blackburn. NeAP
On the Feast of the Assumption. Eleanor Downing. JKCP
On the fine wire of her whine she walked. Mosquito. John Updike. FIW
On the first day good enough father and son. Target Practice. Donald Finkel. NePoEA-2
On the first day of Christmas my true love sent to me a partridge in a pear tree. The Twelve Days of Christmas. *Unknown.* RePo
On the first day of snow, my train. Letter VIII. Randall Swingler. WaP
On the first day of the week cometh Mary Magdalene. St. John, Bible, *N.T.* LO
On the first day, the lifted siege at last. A Death in Hospital. John Lehmann. AtBAP; ChMP
On the first Easter, ere the harbinger. Mary. Nellie Knight. ChIP
On the first hour of my first day. The Beginner. Kipling. *Fr.* Epitaphs of the War. FaBoTw
On the first of March. The Crows. *Unknown.* OxNR; RIS
On the first of the feast of feasts. Epilogue. Robert Browning. ViPo
On the first summer day I lay in the valley. On the Third Day. Stephen Spender. NeBP
On the Fitness of Seasons. Enzo, King of Sardinia, *tr. fr. Italian by* Dante Gabriel Rossetti. OnPM
On the Flightiness of Thought. *Unknown, tr. fr. Middle Irish by* Kuno Meyer. OnYI
On the floor of the low, white-clouded seas. Glints of the Year—from a Window. Thomas Caulfield Irwin. IrPN
On the Fly-Leaf of a Book of Old Plays. Walter Learned. HBV
On the Fly-Leaf of Manon Lescaut. Walter Learned. AA
On the Following Work and Its Author. Jonathan Mitchell. SCAP
On the forgotten si/ ding. Tank Town. John Atherton. NYBP
On the fourteenth of April we sailed from England. The Fair *Princess Royal. Unknown.* SoAmSa
On the fourteenth of April we sailed from the strand. The Bold *Princess Royal, vers.* I. *Unknown.* ShS
On the Frontispiece of Isaacsons Chronologie Explained. Richard Crashaw. MaMe
On the Frozen Lake. Wordsworth. *Fr.* The Prelude, I. FaBoCh; LoGBV
("And in the frosty season, when the sun.") InP; MyFE; PoMa
(Skating.) CH; GN; GoTP; SD; ShBV-3
On the Future of Poetry. Austin Dobson. PoVP

On the Gentlemen in *The Dunciad*. *Unknown*. EiCL
On the Glorious Assumption of Our Blessed Lady. Richard Crashaw. ISi; OBS; PoLi
(In the Glorious Assumption of Our Blessed Lady.) LoBV; MaMe
(On the Assumption.) AnAnS-1; MaMe; MeP
On the Gold Mines. B. W. Vilakazi, *tr. fr. Zulu.* PeSA
(In the Gold Mines, *abr.*) TTY
On the Grand Canal. David Gascoyne. SeCePo
On the Grasshopper and Cricket. Leigh Hunt. *See* To the Grasshopper and the Cricket.
On the Grasshopper and Cricket. Keats. BoC; BoLiVe; BWP; CBEP; DiPo; EnL; EnLi-2; EnLit; EnRP; EPN; ERoP-2; ExPo; FaBoBe; GN; GoTP; HBV; ILP; InP; InPo; LiTB; MaPo (1969 ed.); MBW-2; MERP; OA; OuHeWo; PoeP; PoIE; SeCeV; Sonn; TrGrPo
(Grasshopper and the Cricket, The.) BoTP; OTPC
(Poetry of Earth [Is Never Dead], The.) GTBS-W; LiTG; PoPo; WiR
On the Grassy Banks. Christina Rossetti. *Fr.* Sing-Song. UTS
(Lambs at Play.) BoTP
(Woolly Lambkins.) StVeCh
On the Grave of a Young Cavalry Officer Killed in the Valley of Virginia. Herman Melville. AP
On the Great Plateau. Edith Franklin Wyatt. HBMV; NP
On the great streams the ships may go. Robert Louis Stevenson. *Fr.* The Canoe Speaks. SD
On the green banks of Shannon when Sheelah was nigh. The Harper [*or* Poor Dog Tray *or* The Irish Harper and His Dog]. Thomas Campbell. CBEP; CH; GoTP; MPB; NCEP; PTK
On the green sheep-track, up the heathy hill. Samuel Taylor Coleridge. *Fr.* Fears in Solitude. OBNC
On the grey sand beside the shallow stream. Ego Dominus Tuus. W. B. Yeats. CMoP; NP
On the Hall at Stowey. Charles Tomlinson. CMoP
On the Head of a Stag. Edmund Waller. Po
On the headland's grassed and sheltered side. Storm. Judith Wright. PoAu-2
On the Heart's Beginning to Cloud the Mind. Robert Frost. CMoP
On the Height. Eunice Tietjens. HBMV; NP
On the Heights. Basho, *tr. fr. Japanese by* H. G. Henderson. OnPM
On the Heights. Lucius Harwood Foote. AA
On the heights of great endeavor. Attainment. Madison Cawein. WGRP
On the Hellenics. Walter Savage Landor. *Fr.* The Hellenics. BEL; EnRP; EPN
(Proem to Hellenics.) ViBoPo
On the High Cost of Dairy Products. James McIntyre. FiBHP
On the high hill pastures. Wild Thyme. Joyce Sambrook. BoTP
On the highway. Está Muy Caliente. George Bowering. MoCV
On the Hill below the Lighthouse. James Dickey. NePoEA-2
On the hill of weeping. The Two Mothers. Shane Leslie. ISi
On the hill's top we stood. Distances. Jeremy Kingston. NYBP
On the Hon. Simon Harcourt. Pope. OnPM; WoL
On the hottest day of the year I rode the mail. The Insult. Robert Layzer. NePoEA
On the Hurry of This Time. Austin Dobson. HBV; PoVP
On the Idle Hill of Summer. A. E. Housman. A Shropshire Lad, XXXV. MoBrPo; NeMA; OAEP (2d ed.); OBNC; OuHeWo; PoVP; TDP
On the Imprint of the First English Edition of the Works of Max Beerbohm. Max Beerbohm. PV
On the Inconstancy of Women. Catullus. *See* Inconsistency of Women's Love.
On the Infancy of Our Saviour. Francis Quarles. OBS; OxBoCh; SeCePo; SeCL
(Child Jesus, The.) StJW
On the Instability of Youth. Thomas, Lord Vaux. EnRePo
On the Island. L. E. Sissman. NYBP
On the Island, finding you naked and pearled. That Summer's Shore. John Ciardi. ErPo
On the island of Skip-scoop-anellie. Skip-Scoop-Anellie. Tom Prideaux. FiBHP
On the isle of Pago Pago, land of palm trees, rice and sago. Rain. Newman Levy. BOHV
On the itching back. Teemothy Hatch. Wilson MacDonald. WhC
On the jetty, our fingers shading. In the Beginning. Daniel G. Hoffman. PP
On the Just and the Unjust. Blanche Edith Baughan. BoAu
On the Lacedaemonian Dead at Plataea. Simonides. WaaP
On the Ladies' Head-Dresses. James Greenwood. WaPE
On the Lake. V. Sackville-West. ChMP; MoVE; OBMV
On the large highway of the awful air that flows. The Fish-Hawk. John Hall Wheelock. AnAmPo; EtS; HBMV
On the Late Massacre in Piedmont [*or* Piemont]. Milton. ATP; AWP; BEL; BWP; CABA; CBEP; CBV; DiPo; EnL; EnLi-1; EnLit; ExPo; GTBS; GTBS-D; GTBS-P; GTBS-W; GTSE; GTSL; HBV; ILP; InP; InPo; JAWP; LiTB; LoBV; MaPo; MBW-1; NoP; OAEP; OnPM; OuHeWo; PAn; PIA; Po; PoAn; PoFS; PoIE; SeCeV; ShBV-3; Sonn; StP; TOP; UnPo; ViBoPo; WaaP; WBP; WoL
(On the Late Massacher in Piemont.) PoEL-3
(On the Massacre in Piedmont.) FOL; WHA
(Sonnet: On the Late Massacre in Piedmont.) OBS; SeCL; SeEP
On the Late S. T. Coleridge. Washington Allston. AA
On the Late Successful Expedition against Louisbourg. Francis Hopkinson. PAH
On the Lawn. Cametas, *tr. fr. Greek by* Anne Hyde Greet. OnPM
On the Lawn at the Villa. Louis Simpson. CoAP
On the Lido. Arthur Hugh Clough. *Fr.* At Venice. ViPo
On the Life-Mask of Abraham Lincoln. Richard Watson Gilder. AA; HBV; PoRL
On the Life of Man. Henry King. *See* Sic Vita.
On the Life of Man. Sir Walter Ralegh. FCP; OAEP; QFR
(All the World's a Stage.) OBSC
(What Is Our Life?) CBV; EnRePo; EP; ForPo; ILP; MePo; PoIE
("What is our life? A play of passion.") EG; ReEn; SiPS
On the London Fire's Monument. George Villiers, Duke of Buckingham. PeRV
On the long dusty ribbon of the long city street. "All Ye That Pass By." John Masefield. CMoP
On the long shore, lit by the moon. The Goose Fish. Howard Nemerov. CaFP; CMoP; FiMAP; LiTM (1970 ed.); NePoEA; NMP; NoP
On the Lord General Fairfax at the Siege of Colchester. Milton. MBW-1; NoP; OBS; Sonn
(Fairfax, Whose Name in Arms through Europe Rings.) MaPo
On the Lord Mayor and Court of Aldermen, Presenting the Late King and Duke of York Each with a Copy of Their Freedoms, Anno Dom. 1674. Andrew Marvell. CoMu
On the Loss of the *Royal George*. William Cowper. AnFE; BEL; BWP; EtS; FiP; GN; HBV; InPo; MyFE; OAEP; OBEC; RoGo; TrGrPo
(Loss of the *Royal George*, The.) CBEP; GTBS; GTBS-D; GTBS-P; GTBS-W; GTSE; GTSL; WHA
On the low table by the bed. Mark Anderson. W. W. Gibson. MMA
On the lowlands where the angular shadows. The New Adam. Frank Belknap Long. FiSC
On the Manner of Addressing Clouds. Wallace Stevens. QFR
On the March. Richard Aldington. BrPo
On the marches of Pamplona—out to sun and wind and star. La Preciosa. Thomas Walsh. ISi
On the Margin Wrought. William Drummond of Hawthornden. *See* Book of the World, The.
On the Marginal Way. Richard Wilbur. CoAP
On the Marriage of a Beauteous Young Gentlewoman with an Ancient Man. Francis Beaumont. LiTL; ViBoPo
On the Marriage of a Virgin. Dylan Thomas. *See* Marriage of a Virgin, The.
On the Massacre in Piedmont. Milton. *See* On the Late Massacre in Piedmont.
On the Memorial building's. Under Cancer. John Hollander. CoAP
On the Memory of Mr. Edward King [Drown'd in the Irish Seas]. John Cleveland. AnAnS-2; OBS; SeCP; SeEP
On the Miracle of Loaves. Richard Crashaw. ACP; MaMe
On the Miracle of Multiplyed Loaves. Richard Crashaw. MaMe

On the Monument Erected to Mazzini at Genoa. Swinburne. VA
On the Moor. Cale Young Rice. HBV
On the moor of Kasuga. Hitomaro. *Fr.* Manyo Shu. AWP
On the Morning of Christ's Nativity. Milton. AnFE; AtBAP; BEL; CoBE; ExPo; GoTL; HBV; MasP; MBW-1; MeLP; MeP; NoP; OBS; OxBoCh; PAn; PoE; PoEL-3; SeCeV; SeEP; TOP; UnPo (1st ed.); WGRP
(Nativity, The, *without hymn.*) SoP
(Ode on the Morning of Christ's Nativity.) GBV, *without hymn*; GTBS; GTBS-D; GTBS-P; GTBS-W; GTSE; GTSL; LiTB; LiTG; MaRV, *abr.*; PoFS
Sels.
Hymn on the Morning of Christ's Nativity. OBEV; OtMeF, *abr.*; StJW
(On the Morning of Christ's Nativity.) FiP
Hymn: "It was the winter wild," *sts.* 1-23. WHA
"But peaceful was the night," *sts.* 5-13. FaBoCh; LoGBV
(Peaceful Night, The, *sts.* 5-7.) ChrBoLe
Magi, The, 2 *ll.* ChTr
"Shepherds on the lawn, The." BoC
On the morning of noise. Poem at Thirty. John Woods. CoPo
On the Mountain. M. K. Joseph. AnNZ
On the Mountain. Neidhart von Reuental, *tr. fr. German by* Jethro Bithell. AWP; JAWP; LiTW; WBP
On the mountain peak, called "Going-To-The-Sun." The Apple-Barrel of Johnny Appleseed. Vachel Lindsay. AmFN; CMoP; MAP; MoAmPo; NeMA; OxBA
On the mountain peak, called "Going-to-the-Sun." The Comet of Going-to-the-Sun. Vachel Lindsay. CMoP
On the Mountains. Alcman, *tr. fr. Greek by* C. M. Bowra. LiTW
On the mountains of Judea. The Expectation. Frederick William Faber. *Fr.* Our Lady's Expectation. ACP
On the mountains of the prairie. The Peace-Pipe. Longfellow. *Fr.* The Song of Hiawatha. AnNE
On the Move. Thom Gunn. ForPo; LiTM (1970 ed.); NePoEA-2; NMP; NoP; OPoP; ShBV-4; ToPo; TwCP; UnPo (3d ed.)
On the Murder of Martin Luther King. Stan Rice. QAH
On the Name of Jesus. Richard Crashaw. *See* To the Name above Every Name, the Name of Jesus.
On the Nativity of Christ. William Dunbar. OBEV; OxBoCh
On the Nativity of Christ Our Lord. Joseph Bennett. NePA
On the Nature of Love. Wilfrid Scawen Blunt. The Love Sonnets of Proteus, XXII. ViBoPo
On the Nature of Things. Lucretius. *See* De Rerum Natura.
On the navel of the Boer's domain. Lesotho. B. Makalo Khaketla. PeSA
On the Needle of a Sundial. Francis Quarles. OBS; TrGrPo
(Compass Needle, A.) CBEP
On the New Forcers of Conscience under the Long Parliament. Milton. CABA; PoFr; Sonn; StP
On the New York Central from Chicago to South Bend. Vendor. Raymond Roseliep. FiSC
On the night of the Belgian surrender the moon rose. The Moon and the Night and the Men. John Berryman. CoAP; WaP
On the night of the execution. The Execution. Alden Nowlan. PeCV (1967 ed.)
On the north and south of the house—spring tide. An Unexpected Visit. Tu Fu. OnPM
On the North Shore a reptile lay asleep. The Precambrian Shield. E. J. Pratt. *Fr.* Towards the Last Spike. MoCV; OBCV
On the ocean that hollows the rocks where ye dwell. O Brazil [*or* Hy-Brasail], the Isle of the Blest. Gerald Griffin. ACP; BLPA
On the outer Barcoo where the churches are few. A Bush Christening. A. B. Paterson. PoAu-1
On the outermost far-flung ridge of ice and snow. Inspiration. W. W. Gibson. WGRP
On the outside grows the furside. The Sleeping-Bag. Herbert George Ponting. CenHV
On the overgrown road. Autumn. Victor Contoski. ThO
On the Oxford Book of Victorian Verse. "Hugh MacDiarmid." MoBrPo
On the Oxford Carrier ("Here lieth one who did most truly prove"). Milton. BOHV; NA
(Another on the University Carrier.) CABA
On the Parapet of Notre Dame. Charles J. Quirk. *Fr.* Quatrains. CAW
On the Park Bench. Kenneth Slade Alling. NePoAm
On the pavements the sexless toys run down. Fête Champêtre. Kenneth Allott. POTE
On the Photograph of a Corps Commander. Herman Melville. MWA-1
On the Photograph of a Lynching. Wendell Phillips Stafford. PoFr
On the Photograph of a Man I Never Saw. Hyam Plutzik. FiMAP
On the Phrase, "To Kill Time." Voltaire, *tr. fr. French.* ALV; MemP; PV
On the Picture of a "Child Tired of Play." Nathaniel Parker Willis. HBV
On the Picture of the Three Fates in the Palazzo Pitti, at Florence. Arthur Henry Hallam. OBRV
On the Pilots Who Destroyed Germany in the Spring of 1945. Stephen Spender. NeBP; Po
On the Plains. Francis Brooks. *Fr.* Intaglios. AA
On the Plough-Man. Francis Quarles. OBS
On the Poet O'Shaughnessy. Dante Gabriel Rossetti. *See* Limerick: "There's an Irishman, Arthur O'Shaughnessy."
On the Poet's Leer. David Ray. NePoEA-2
On the poplars and oaks. The Bard's Song. Sir Robert Stapylton. SeCePo
On the Porch. Harriet Monroe. NP
On the porch of the three-storied flat. The Next Voice You Hear. Thomas P. McDonnell. JKCP (1955 ed.)
On the Portrait of a Woman about to Be Hanged. Thomas Hardy. CMoP
On the Portrait of Shakespeare Prefixed to the First Folio Edition, 1623. Ben Jonson. HBV; OTPC (1923 ed.)
(To the Reader.) EnRePo
On the Praise of Poetry. Abraham Cowley. CLwM
On the President's State Visit to Mexico. Jack Marshall. YAP
On the Princess Mary. John Heywood. *See* Praise of His Lady, A.
On the Prodigall. Richard Crashaw. MaMe
On the Proposal to Erect a Monument in England to Lord Byron. Emma Lazarus. AA
On the Prospect of Planting Arts and Learning in America. George Berkeley. EiCL; FaFP; OnYI; PP; SeCeV; TreF; TrGrPo
(Verses on the Prospect of Planting Arts and Learning in America.) CEP; CoBE; EiPP; OBEC; Po; PoE; SeCePo; ViBoPo
On the proud bankes of great Euphrates flood. Psalme 137, *par. by* George Herbert. Bible, *O.T.* Mame
On the Quay. John Joy Bell. HBV
On the Queen's Return from the Low Countries. William Cartwright. MePo; OBEV
On the Receipt of My Mother's Picture Out of Norfolk. William Cowper. BEL; CEP; CoBE; EiPP; EnLi-2 (1949 ed.); EnLit; EnPE; EnRP; FiP; HBV; NoP; OAEP; OBEC; PoE; PoIE; TOP
(Lines on Receiving His Mother's Picture, *abr.*) CH; MemP; OHIP
"Could Time, his flight reversed, restore the hours," *sel.* WHA
On the Reed of Our Lord's Passion. William Alabaster. PoEL-2
On the Relative Merit of Friend and Foe, Being Dead. Donald Thompson. WaP
On the Religion of Nature. Philip Freneau. AmePo; AmPP; CoBA; MAmP; Po
On the Religious Memory of Mrs. Catharine Thomason. Milton. Sonn
(Sonnet XIV: On the Religious Memorie of Mrs. Catherine Thomason My Christian Friend Deceas'd December, 1646.) OBS
On the Reported New Outbreak of Christianity. James H. McCabe. JKCP (1955 ed.)
On the Resurrection of Christ. William Dunbar. *See* Of the Resurrection of Christ.
On the Reverend Jonathan Doe. *Unknown.* ChTr
On the Rhine. Matthew Arnold. LO; VP
On the Rising Generation. Howard Dietz. ALV
On the Road. Paul Laurence Dunbar. AA
On the Road. Tudor Jenks. NA
On the Road. John Oxenham. StJW
On the Road. Charles G. D. Roberts. PTK

On the road over head. An Old Waterford Woman. Mary Devenport O'Neill. NeIP
On the road, the lonely road. The Stab. Will Wallace Harney. AA
On the road through the hills I thought I heard it. Half-heard. Christopher Koch. PoAu-2
On the Road to Anster Fair. William Tennant. *Fr.* Anster Fair. OBRV
On the Road to Arden. T. A. Daly. LHV
On the Road to Chorrera. Arlo Bates. AA
On the Road to Emmaus. St. Luke, XXIV: 13-36, Bible, *N.T.* TreFS
On the Road to Gundagai. *Unknown.* PoAu-1
On the road to Raffydiddle. The Road to Raffydiddle. Mildred Plew Meigs. TiPo (1952 ed.)
On the Road to Vicenza. Ralph Gustafson. CaP
On the Road to Woodlawn. Theodore Roethke. FiMAP
On the roads at night I saw the glitter of eyes. Eyes of Night-Time. Muriel Rukeyser. MiAP; NePA
On the rock the turtles get. Mud Turtles. Grace Taber Hallock. RePo
On the Ruins of a Country Inn. Philip Freneau. *See* Stanzas Occasioned by the Ruins of a Country Inn . . .
On the Russian Persecution of the Jews. Swinburne. Sonn
On the Sabbath-day. Barbara. Alexander Smith. GoTS; GTBS; HBV; OBEV (1st ed.); OBVV
On the Sacrament. Elizabeth Rowe. Three Hymns, 2. WaPE
On the Safe Side. Lord Dunsany. OxBI
On the Sale by Auction of Keats' Love Letters. Oscar Wilde. AnEnPo
On the salt water streets. Venice Recalled. Bruce Boyd. NeAP
On the Same. Roy Campbell. BoSA
On the Same. Milton. *See* On the Detraction Which Followed upon My Writing Certain Treatises ("I did but prompt").
On the Same [Helen]. Matthew Prior. *See* Helen Was Just Slipped into Bed.
On the school platform, draping the folding seats. Political Meeting. A. M. Klein. MoCV; OBCV
On the Sea. Keats. ATP (1935 ed.); BoLiVe; BWP; CABA; CoBE; DiPo; EnL; EnRP; EPN; ERoP-2; ExPo; GTBS-W; HBV; LiTB; MaPo; MBW-2; MCCG; NoP; PoeP; SeCeV; Sonn; TrGrPo; YAT
(Sonnet on the Sea.) EtS; PeER; SeCePo; ViBoPo
On the sea and at the Hogue, sixteen hundred ninety-two. Hervé Riel. Robert Browning. BEL; BeLS; FaBoBe; GN; HBV; MCCG; OnMSP; OtMeF; OTPC (1946 ed.); PoVP; TOP
On the sea or in the air. God Is with Me. Oswald J. Smith. STF
On the Sea Wall. C. Day Lewis. SeCePo
On the Sea-Shore near Calais. Wordsworth. *See* It Is a Beauteous Evening, Calm and Free.
On the second of October, a Monday at noon. Walter Lesly. *Unknown.* BaBo; ESPB
On the secret map the assassins. Rivers and Mountains. John Ashbery. ANYP; CoAP; FRC
On the Setting Sun. Sir Walter Scott. MaRV
On the Setting Up of Mr. Butler's Monument in Westminster Abbey. Samuel Wesley. ALV; CBEP; InvP; OBEC; PPON; WhC
(On Butler's Monument.) BOHV
On the Seventh Anniversary of the Death of My Father. Robert Pack. NePoEA
On the seventh day the storm lay dead. The Dyke-Builder. Henry Treece. LiTB; LiTM; WaP
On the sheep-cropped summit, under hot sun. Cat and Mouse. Ted Hughes. EaLo
On the shore of Nawa. Hioki no Ko-Okima. *Fr.* Manyo Shu. AWP
On the shores of Lake Michigan. These Children of the Wind. Carl Sandburg. *Fr.* The People, Yes. BiS; StVeCh; WePo
On the sightless seas of ether. Mikhail Lermontov. *Fr.* The Demon. AWP
On the Site of a Mulberry-Tree. Dante Gabriel Rossetti. CBEP; NCEP
On the Skeleton of a Hound. James Wright. LiTM (1970 ed.); NePoEA; TwAmPo
On the skim of the wharf where the planks split. Bucket of Sea-Serpents. Howard Ant. GoYe
On the Slain Collegians. Herman Melville. MAmP; MWA-1
On the Slope of the Desolate River. Rabindranath Tagore. Gitanjali, LXIV. OBMV
On the small marble-paved platform. Margrave. Robinson Jeffers. CMoP
On the Smooth Brow and Clustering Hair. Walter Savage Landor. EPN
On the smooth steep escalator, four storeys'/ Rise. The City Considered as a Tulip Tree. Carl Bode. *Fr.* London Sonnets. ToPo
On the Snake. *Unknown.* PAH
On the Snuff of a Candle. Sir Walter Ralegh. FCP; SiPS
On the Sonnet. Keats. CABA; ERoP-2; MBW-2; NoP; PAn
(If by Dull Rhymes Our English Must Be Chained.) PP
(Sonnet on The Sonnet.) PeER
On the Soul. Emperor Hadrian. *See* To His Soul.
On the South Downs. Sara Teasdale. MAP; MoAmPo; YT
(On the Sussex Downs.) NP
On the southern mountain: a cassia tree. Ancient Quatrain. *Unknown.* HW
On the Speech of Robert Emmet. Robert Southey. PoFr
On the spool pedestal. Work Room. Kenward Elmslie. ANYP
On the Staircase. Eleanor Farjeon. SiSoSe
On the Staircase. Wade Wellman. FiSC
On the stiff twig up there. Black Rook in Rainy Weather. Sylvia Plath. LiTM (1970 ed.); NePoEA-2; NoP; PoDB; PP
On the Still Surviving Markes of Our Saviours Wounds. Richard Crashaw. MaMe
On the stone terrace, underneath the shade. The Summer Landscape; or, The Dragon's Teeth. Rolfe Humphries. NYBP
On the Street. Hazel Hall. NP
On the street where we used to go to school. Is It for This I Live? Sotère Torregian. YAP
On the *Struma* Massacre. Ralph Gustafson. OBCV
On the Subject of Poetry. W. S. Merwin. PP
On the Subject of Waves. Eldon Grier. MoCV; PeCV (1967 ed.)
On the Subjugation of Switzerland. Wordsworth. *See* Thought of a Briton on the Subjugation of Switzerland.
On the suburban street, guarded by patient trees. I Did Not Know the Truth of Growing Trees. Delmore Schwartz. LiTM (1970 ed.)
On the Suicide of a Friend. Reed Whittemore. NMP
On the Sultan Mahmúd. Firdausi, *tr. fr. Persian by* R. A. Nicholson. LiTW
On the summer road that ran by our front porch. Lizards and Snakes. Anthony Hecht. CoPo; TPM; TwCP
On the Summit. Margaret E. Sangster. SoP
On the Sun Coming Out in the Afternoon. Henry David Thoreau. PoEL-4
On the sunblasted and sterile island of Vil. Vil for the Layman. Marge Piercy. ThO
On the Sunday morning, just at the hour of ten. The *Bigler.* *Unknown.* AmSS
On the sunny hillside sleeping. Beneath the Flag. *Unknown.* HH
On the Sussex Downs. Sara Teasdale. *See* On the South Downs.
On the Swag. R. A. K. Mason. AnNZ
On the Swiss. Wordsworth. *See* Swiss Peasant, The.
On the tallest day in time, the dead came back. V-J Day. John Ciardi. MiAP; OTD; PoPl
On the taut shore, the bald skull. Resurrection. Robert Pack. NePoEA-2
On the Telescopic Moon. John Swanwick Drennan. IrPN
On the temple bell. Spring Scene. Taniguchi Buson. PoPl
On the tenth day of December. Musselburgh Field. *Unknown.* ESPB
On the Third Day. Stephen Spender. NeBP
On the third day from this (Saint Brendan said). The Burial of Saint Brendan. Padraic Colum. OxBI
On the third day of May. The Boy and the Mantle. *Unknown.* UnTE
On the third day rose Arp. Resurrection of Arp. A. J. M. Smith. MoCV
On the Threshold. Augustus Henry Baldwin. HH; PEDC
New Year, The, *sel.* DD

On the Threshold. Karl Kraus, *tr. fr. German by* Albert Bloch. TrJP
On the Threshold. *Unknown.* BLPA
On the threshold of heaven, the figures in the street. To an Old Philosopher in Rome. Wallace Stevens. AP
On the Toilet Table of Queen Marie-Antoinette. J. B. B. Nichols. MemP
On the Tomb of Bliss Carman. Bliss Carman. *See* Envoy: "Have little care that life is brief."
On the Tomb of Sophocles. Simmias, *tr. fr. Greek.* OnPM
(Wind, Gentle Evergreen.) CBEP
On the Tombs in Westminster Abbey. *At. to* Francis Beaumont, *also to* William Basse. ACP; BEL; CH; GTBS; GTBS-D; GTBS-P; GTBS-W; GTSE; InP; LoBV; OBEV; ShBV-3; TOP; TrGrPo; ViBoPo
(Lines on the Tombs in Westminster.) GoBC; MaRV
(Memento for Mortality [*or* Mortalitie], A, *diff. vers., longer.*) ElL; FaBoCh; LoGBV; OBS; SeEP
(On the Tombs in Westminster.) HBV
(Tombs in Westminster, The.) WePo
On the top of old Smoky all covered in snow. Old Smoky. *Unknown.* BaBo
On the top of the Crumpetty Tree. The Quangle Wangle's Hat. Edward Lear. BoChLi; GFA; PeVV; PoRh; RIS; SAS; StaSt
On the top of the mount. The Bald Old Woman. *Tr. by* I. T. Headland. GaP
On the tower of Little Saling. Little Saling. Olaf Baker. HBMV
On the Trail to Idaho. *Unknown.* CoSo; PoRL
On the twelfth day of July. Orange Lilies. James Reaney. WHW
On the Twenty-fifth of July. David Cornel DeJong. NYBP
On the twenty-second of June. *At. to* Ben Jonson. WhC
On the Twenty-third Psalm. *Unknown.* *See* He Leadeth Me.
On the unbreathing sides of hills. Squatter's Children. Elizabeth Bishop. NePoAm-2
On the Uniformity and Perfection of Nature. Philip Freneau. AmePo; AmPP; CoBA
On the Universality and Other Attributes of the God of Nature. Philip Freneau. AmePo; AmP; AP; ForPo
On the University Carrier ("Here lieth one who did most truly prove"). Milton. *See* On the Oxford Carrier.
On the University Carrier (Who Sickn'd in the Time of His Vacancy) ("Here lies old Hobson"). Milton. FaBoCh; LoGBV; MePo
On the Unusual Cold and Rainie Weather in the Summer, 1648. Robert Heath. OBS
On the up-platform at Morpeth station. The Complaint of the Morpethshire Farmer. Basil Bunting. CTC
On the Upright Judge, Who Condemned the "Drapier's" Printer. Swift. SiTL
(On an Upright Judge.) ALV
On the Use of New and Old Words in Poetry. Anna Seward. Sonn
On the Vanity of Earthly Greatness. Arthur Guiterman. HoPM; NAMP; PoPl; PoPo; PV; TrJP; WhC
On the Vanity of Man's Life. *Unknown.* *See* Of the Vanity of Man's Life.
On the vast aerial ocean. Mikhail Lermontov. *Fr.* The Demon. OnPM
On the Verge. Swinburne. A Midsummer Holiday, III. PoVP
On the Verge. William Winter. AA
On the Victory Obtained by Blake over the Spaniards. Andrew Marvell. MaMe
On the Victory of Poland and Her Allies over the Sultan Osman, 1621. Casimir Sarbiewski, *tr. fr. Latin by* Francis Sylvester Mahony. CAW
On the "Vita Nuova" of Dante. Dante Gabriel Rossetti. MaVP; PoVP
On the volcanic hill. Precarious Ground. Leah Bodine Drake. GoYe
On the Wall. Immanuel di Roma, *tr. fr. Hebrew by* Solomon Solis-Cohen. TrJP
On the wall beside the kitchen door. Growing. Frances Frost. BiCB
On the wan sea-strand. Evening Twilight. Heine. *Fr.* The North Sea. AWP; JAWP; WBP
On the warm night. The Black Boundary. Lewis Warsh. YAP
On the Water of Our Lords Baptisme. Richard Crashaw. MaMe; SeEP
On the water the first wind. Spring. W. S. Merwin. NaP
On the Way. Georg Trakl, *tr. fr. German by* Ernst Sigler. LiTW
On the way to Kew. W. E. Henley. Echoes, XXXVIII. OBNC; OBVV; PoVP; ViBoPo
On the way to my daily occupation. Life. Franklin P. Adams. InMe
On the Way to the Island. David Ferry. NePoAm-2
On the Way to the Mission. Duncan Campbell Scott. CaP
On the way up from Steep I met some children. To Edward Thomas. Alun Lewis. WaP
On the Welsh Marches. Walter Stone. NYBP
On the white throat of the useless passion. Ad Finem. Ella Wheeler Wilcox. BLPA
On the Wide Heath. Edna St. Vincent Millay. CMoP
On the wide level of a mountain's head. Time, Real and Imaginary. Samuel Taylor Coleridge. EnRP; ERoP-1; MERP; OBEV; OBRV
On the wide veranda white. A Corn-Song. Paul Laurence Dunbar. AA
On the Wife of a Parish Clerk. *Unknown.* *See* Old Sam's Wife.
On the wind of January. A Year's Windfalls. Christina Rossetti. BoTP; OTPC (1923 ed.); PRWS; YeAr
On the Wing. Christina Rossetti. StP; VP
On the World. Swift. *See* Day of Judgement, The.
On the Wounds of Our Crucified Lord. Richard Crashaw. MaMe; SeEP
On the yard shines white the autumnal moon. The Rats. Georg Trakl. LiTW
On these ancient disks, smooth-backed, severe. Old Gramophone Records. James Kirkup. MuSP; NYBP
On these electric branches. Miracles. Roy Helton. MaRV
On these occasions, the feelings surprise. Father and Son. Delmore Schwartz. LiTA
On these white cliffs, that calm above the flood. Dover Cliffs [*or* At Dover Cliffs]. William Lisle Bowles. CEP; EnRP; HBV; OBEC; Sonn; ViBoPo
On things asleep, no balm. The Longing. Theodore Roethke. NaP
On This Day I Complete My Thirty-sixth Year. Byron. AnFE; BEL; CABA; CoBE; EnL; EnLi-2; EnLit; EnRP; EPN; ERoP-2; FiP; HBV; ILP; MaPo; MBW-2; MCCG; MERP; NoP; OAEP; OnPP; PAn; PeER; TreFT; ViBoPo; YAT
Remorse, *sel.* MaRV
("My days are in the yellow leaf.") TRV
On this day man's disgust is known. On Shooting Particles beyond the World. Richard Eberhart. GTBS-W; LiTA; LiTM (rev. ed.)
On this feast day, O cursèd day and hour. Christopher Marlowe. *Fr.* Hero and Leander, First Sestiad. ViBoPo
On this great day a child of time and fate. Inauguration Day. Richard Watson Gilder. PoRL
On this great plain the eye. Canterbury. Basil Dowling. AnNZ
On this hill crossed. The Poem. Galway Kinnell. NaP
On this hotel their rumpled royalties. West Forties, The: Morning, Noon, and Night. L. E. Sissman. CoAP; NYBP
On This Island. W. H. Auden. CBV; FlW
(Look, Stranger, on This Island Now.) PAn
On this lone isle, whose rugged rocks affright. Sonnet: Suppos'd to be Written at Lemnos [*or* Philoctetes]. Thomas Russell. CEP; FaBoEn; LoBV; OBEC
On This Most Voluptuous Night of the Year. William Carlos Williams. CBV
On This My Sick-Bed Beats the World. Jiri Wolker, *tr. fr. Czech by* Karl W. Deutsch. WaaP
On this night that is cold. Otomo no Yakamochi, *tr. fr. Japanese by* Arthur Waley. LiTW
On this resemblance—where we find. Elizabeth Tollet. LO
On this road. Haiku. Basho. LiTW
On This Sea-Floor. Ralph Gustafson. PeCV (1967 ed.)
On this shattered sky, on these panes of sweet water. Death Is Dead. Paul Eluard. OnPM
On this sweet bank your head thrice sweet and dear. Youth's Spring-Tribute. Dante Gabriel Rossetti. The House of Life, XIV. MaVP; PoVP; ViPo; VP
On this tree thrown up. Spindrift. Galway Kinnell. NaP; NYBP

On this wondrous sea. Emily Dickinson. AA
On Thomas Carew. *Unknown.* CBEP
On Thomas Hood. Walter Savage Landor. PV
On Thomas Moore's Poems. *Unknown.* FiBHP; SiTL
On Thomas Woodcock. *Unknown.* WhC
On those great waters now I am. When We Are upon the Seas. George Wither. *Fr.* Hallelujah. BEL
On Those That Deserve It. Francis Quarles. MePo; OBS
On Those Who Fell. Simonides, *the younger, tr. fr. Greek by* John Herman Merivale. OnPM
On Those Who Fell at Thermopylae. Simonides. *See* Thermopylae Ode, The.
On thrones from China to Peru. A Model for the Laureate. W. B. Yeats. CMoP
On through the Libyan sand. Gordon. Ernest Myers. VA
On, through the lovely archipelago. Charles Sangster. *Fr.* The St. Lawrence and the Saguenay. PeCV
On thy fair bosom, silver lake. To Seneca Lake [*or* Seneca Lake]. James Gates Percival. AnNE; BoTP
On thy wild and windy upland, Tornamona. Shane O'Neill. Seumas MacManus. OnYI
On thy wild banks, by frequent torrents worn. To the River Arun. Charlotte Smith. Sonn
On tilted toes he tries to reach. Nature at Three. Bettye Breeser. BiCB
On Time. Richard Hughes. MoBrPo
On Time. Milton. BoC; BWP; CABA; DiPo; GTBS-W; LiTB; LiTG; LoBV; MaPo; MeP; MePo; OBEV; OBS; OxBoCh; PoE; PoPo; SeCeV; StP; TRV
On Time with God. C. D. Nutter. STF
On Timely Death. Walter Savage Landor. TOP
(On Living Too Long.) VA
On tip-toe comes the gentle dark. Good Night. Dorothy Mason Pierce. BrR; SiSoSe; TiPo (1952 ed.)
On to Richmond. John R. Thompson. PAH
On to the Morgue, *with music. Unknown.* AS
On Tobacco. Thomas Pestel. ElL
On Top of Old Smoky. *Unknown.* FaFP; SiTL; TreFT
On top of that if you know me I pronounce you an ignu. Ignu. Allen Ginsberg. NaP
On Top of Troubled Waters. Dorothy J. Langford. BePJ
On Translating the "Divina Commedia." Longfellow. Divina Commedia, I, II, III, V. OuHeWo
On Treason. Sir John Harington. *See* Of Treason.
On Troy. Oliver St. John Gogarty. WhC
On True Worth. Sadi, *tr. fr. Persian by* L. S. Costello. LiTW
On Tsukuda-Isle in July. Munetake, *tr. fr. Japanese by* Asataro Miyamori. OnPM
On Tuesday morn at half-past six o'clock. James Rigg. James Hogg. Par
On Two Brothers. Simonides, *tr. fr. Greek by* W. H. D. Rouse. AWP
On Two Lovers Struck Dead by Lightning. Pope. PoAn
On Two Ministers of State. Hilaire Belloc. PV
On Viewing a Florist's Whimsy at Fifty-ninth and Madison. Margaret Fishback. WhC
On Visiting the Graves of Hawthorne and Thoreau. Jones Very. AP
On Visiting the Tomb of Burns. Keats. BWP
On Waking. Joseph Campbell. AnIV; NP
On Waking. Alida Carey Gulick. GoYe
On Waking from a Dreamless Sleep. Annie Fields. AA
On Walking the Streets by Day. John Gay. *See* Of Walking the Streets by Day.
On wan dark night on Lac St. Pierre. The Wreck of the *Julie Plante* [*or* The *Julie Plante*]. William Henry Drummond. BeLS; BLPA; BOHV; CaP; FaBoBe; FaPON; HBV; IHA; InMe; NA; OBCV; PeCV; StaSt; TreFS; WhC
On War. Crystal Kilgore. TPM
On Watching the Construction of a Skyscraper. Burton Raffel. OCS
On Waterloo's ensanguined plain. On Scott's [Poem] "The Field of Waterloo." Thomas, Lord Erskine. FiBHP; WhC
On Wearing Ears. William J. Harris. BOLo
On Wellington. Byron. *See* Wellington.
On Wenlock Edge [the Wood's in Trouble]. A. E. Housman. A Shropshire Lad, XXXI.
BoLiVe; BrPo; CABA; CLwM; CoBMV; GTBS-P; HBV; ILP; LiTB; MaPo; MasP; MemP; MoAB; MoBrPo; NBM; NoP; OAEP (2d ed.); OBNC; OuHeWo; PAn; PoE; PoEL-5; PoIE; PoRA; PoVP; ShBV-4; ViPo; VP
(Wenlock Edge.) OBEV
On Westwall Downes. William Strode. FaBoEn; PoEL-2
(On Westwell Down[e]s) CBEP; SeCL; SeEP
On what a brave and curious whim. Clocks. Louis Ginsberg. TrJP
On what divine adventure has he gone? Pilot and Prophet [*or* Roosevelt—Pilot and Prophet!]. Charles Hanson Towne. DD; PEDC
On what foundation stands the warrior's pride? Charles XII [of Sweden]. Samuel Johnson. *Fr.* The Vanity of Human Wishes. FOL; OBEC; ViBoPo
On what long tides. Fires of Driftwood. Isabel Ecclestone Mackay. CaP
On what silent feet it comes. The Third Day. Edith Lovejoy Pierce. MoRP
On "Who Wrote Icon Basilike" by Dr. Christopher Wordsworth, Master of Trinity. Benjamin Hall Kennedy. PV
On Will Smith. *Unknown.* SiTL
On Willy's birthday, as you see. A Party. Laura E. Richards. BiCB; SiSoSe; SoPo
On windy days the mill. The Unfortunate Miller. A. E. Coppard. FaBoTw; POTE
On winter nights the fiddling wind see-saws. "Soft Sell." Lorna Beers. FiSC
On with another new love. Two Songs, 2. Abraham Reisen. LiTW
On with the hosts that toil, and on with the young and strong. A March for Youth. K. G. Ossian-Nilsson. PoFr
On with the Message! [On, On, and On]! Wesley Duewel. SoP; STF
On with thine embassy! To Gabriel of the Annunciation. Peter Abelard. CAW
On Wodin's day, sixth of December, thirty-nine. *In re* Solomon Warshawer. A. M. Klein. MoCV
On Wordsworth. Hartley Coleridge. FiBHP
(He Lived amidst th' Untrodden Ways.) Par; SiTL
(Imitation of Wordsworth, An.) CBEP
On Woman. W. B. Yeats. CMoP
On woodlands ruddy with autumn. My Autumn Walk. Bryant. AA
On Work. Kahlil Gibran. *Fr.* The Prophet. PoToHe (new ed.)
On Worship. George Herbert. *Fr.* The Church Porch. MaRV
On yellow days in summer when the early heat. The Cicadas. Judith Wright. FlW
On Yes Tor. Sir Edmund Gosse. CH
On yon hill's top which this sweet plain commands. Invites His Nymph to His Cottage. Philip Ayres. EnLoPo
On yonder hill there is a red deer. Riddle. *Unknown.* ChTr
On yonder hill there sits a noble knight. The Cambric Shirt (C *vers.*). *Unknown.* BFSS
On yonder hill there stands a creature. The One Answer [*or* O No, John]! *Unknown.* ErPo; GoTP; MeWo; PDV; UnTE
On yonder hill there stands a tree. Tree on the Hill. *Unknown.* OTPC; PPL
On your bald, dirty head you wear. To an Old Fraud. Martial. LiTW
On your bare rocks, O barren moors. The Barren Moors. William Ellery Channing. AA
On your midnight pallet lying. A. E. Housman. A Shropshire Lad, XI. PoVP
On your verdant throne elate. The Cicada. *Unknown.* OuHeWo
On Zacheus. Francis Quarles. LoBV; MePo; OBS
Onan. Paris Leary. CoPo
Once. Eric N. Batterham. CH
Once. Walter de la Mare. BoPe
Once. *Unknown.* CH
Once/ I went for an ocean trip. On a Steamer. Dorothy W. Baruch. FaPON
Once a Big Molicepan. *Unknown.* FaPON
Once a boy beheld a bright. The Rose. Goethe. AWP; JAWP; WBP
Once a boy espied a rose. Briar-Rose. *Unknown.* RIS
Once a Child. Emily Dickinson. *See* It troubled me as once I was.
Once a dream did weave a shade. A Dream. Blake. *Fr.* Songs of Innocence. CBEP; CH; EnRP; MPB; OA; PoRh; TVC
Once a fair city, courted then by kings. Masar. Walter Sav-

age Landor. *Fr.* Gebir. LoBV; OBRV
Once a Frenchman who'd promptly said "Oui". *Unknown.* SiTL
Once a gay wit, subsequently a wretched instructor. The Father. Richmond Lattimore. NePoAm-2
Once a jolly swagman camped by a billabong. Waltzing Matilda. Andrew Barton Paterson. ChTr; PoAu-1; StPo; WaKn; WhC
Once a Kansas zephyr strayed. Zephyr. Eugene Fitch Ware. PoLF
Once a little baby lay. The First Christmas. Emilie Poulsson. OHIP; PCH
Once a little baby, on a sunny day. The Story of Baby's Blanket. Emilie Poulsson. PPL
Once a little boy, Jack, was, oh! ever so good. The Sad Story of a Little Boy That Cried. *Unknown.* BBGG
Once a little satellite. Little Satellite. Jane W. Krows. SoPo
Once a little sugar ant made up his mind to roam. The Ant Explorer. C. J. Dennis. NeLNL
Once a mouse, a frog, and a little red hen. The Mouse, the Frog and the Little Red Hen. *Unknown.* BoTP
Once a pallid vestal. The Vestal. Nathalia Crane. AnAmPo; MAP; MoAmPo (1942 ed.); TrJP
Once a poor widow, aging year by year. The Nun's Priest's Tale. Chaucer. *Fr.* The Canterbury Tales. EnL
Once a rover of the sea, captain of a barkentine. The Captain of St. Kitts. Beulah May. EtS
Once a wife in Bethlehem. A Prayer for a Sleeping Child. Mary Carolyn Davies. OHIP
Once again our glad thanksgivings. Thanksgiving. A. B. Simpson. STF
Once again the scurry of feet—those myriads. The Face of the Waters. Robert D. Fitzgerald. BoAV; MoAuPo; PoAu-2
Once again thou flamest heavenward, once again we see thee rise. Hymn. Tennyson. *Fr.* Akbar's Dream. PoVP
Once Alien Here. John Hewitt. NeIP
Once, and but once found in thy company. The Perfume. John Donne. Elegies, IV. AnAnS-1; MaMe; SeCP
Once and Upon. Madeline Gleason. NeAP
Once around a daisy counting. Counting on Flowers. John Ciardi. PP
Once as a child I loved to hop. Adam's Footprint. Vassar Miller. NePoEA; ToPo
Once, as a lad, alone in bed. And Left Me Stranded on a Hush. Doyle Hennessy. JKCP (1955 ed.)
Once as I travelled through a quiet evening. Egrets. Judith Wright. GoJo
Once, as methought, fortune me kiss'd [*or* kist]. The Lover Rejoiceth the Enjoying of His Love [*or* A Promise]. Sir Thomas Wyatt. FaBoEn; FCP; OBSC; ReIE; SiPS
Once, as old Lord Gorbals motored. Lord Gorbals. Harry Graham. ShBV-2
Once as we were sitting by. Spring 1942. Roy Fuller. LiTM; NeBP; WaaP
Once at a simple turning of the way. William Vaughn Moody. *Fr.* Jetsam. MAP; MoAmPo (1942 ed.)
Once Before. Mary Mapes Dodge. AA
Once between us the Atlantic. Sundered. Israel Zangwill. TrJP
Once—but no matter when. A Chronicle. *Unknown.* NA; SiTL
Once by mishap two poets fell a-squaring. Comparison of the Sonnet and the Epigram. Sir John Harington. SiCE; TuPP
Once by the Pacific. Robert Frost. AmLP; AmPP; AnFE; BWP; CBV; CMoP; CoAnAm; CoBMV; GTBS-W; HT; ILP; InPo; LiTA; LiTM; MAP; MaPo (1969 ed.); MoAB; MoAmPo; NePA; NP; PoAn; PoDB; PoFS; PoPo; Sonn
Once came an exile, longing to be free. Blennerhassett's Island. Thomas Buchanan Read. *Fr.* The New Pastoral. PAH; ThLM
Once children in Scotland contracted the throbbing foot. Four Stories. David Shapiro. ANYP
Once Daedalus in distant Crete. Mythos. Ralph Gustafson. PeCV
Once did I love and yet I live. *Unknown.* LO; OBSC; SiCE
Once did my Philomel reflect on me. Sir John Davies. *Fr.* Sonnets to Philomel. SiPS
Once Did My Thoughts. *Unknown.* ELP; TuPP
("Once did my thoughts both ebb and flow.") LO
Once did she hold the gorgeous east in fee. On the Extinction of the Venetian Republic. Wordsworth. BEL; BoLiVe; CLwM; EnL; EnLi-2; EnLit; EnRP; EPN; FOL; GTBS; GTBS-D; GTBS-P; GTBS-W; GTSE; GTSL; HBV; HT; LoBV; MBW-2; MCCG; MERP; NoP; OAEP; OBEV; OBNC; OBRV; OuHeWo; PoFr; Sonn; TOP; TrGrPo; ViBoPo
Once, dreaming of eternal fire. On a Horse and a Goat. R. P. Lister. PV
Once, ere God was crucified. The Abdication of Fergus Mac Roy. Sir Samuel Ferguson. AnIL
Once for candy cook had stolen. W. H. Auden. PV
Once for our consolation it seemed, O Lord. No More Destructive Flame. Francis X. Connolly. ISi
Once, from the parapet of gems and glow. A Flight from Glory. Eugene Lee-Hamilton. VA
Once git a smell o' musk into a draw. Sunthin' in the Pastoral Line. James Russell Lowell. *Fr.* The Biglow Papers. AmPP (3d ed); AP; CoBA; MCCG; MWA-1; PFY
Once gold and vermilion on white plaster. Mural of Borodino. Lucile Adler. NYTB
Once, grave Laodicean profiteer. Lourenço Marques. Charles Eglington. PeSA
Once hairy scenter did transgress. *Unknown.* *Fr.* Riddles. CoBE
Once he will miss, twice he will miss. Death. *Unknown.* *Fr.* The Thousand and One Nights. AWP; JAWP; WBP
Once her brother's child, for fun. The Careless Niece. Carolyn Wells. ShM
Once hid in a fiery twist. The Scratch. James Dickey. AP
Once hoary winter chanced—alas! Why Ye Blossome Cometh before Ye Leafe. Oliver Herford. AA
Once hooked ever after lives in lack, The. Nescit Vox Missa Reverti. J. V. Cunningham. ELU
Once I am sure there's nothing going on. Church Going. Philip Larkin. CMoP; ForPo; GTBS-P; HaMV; ILP; LiTM (1970 ed.); MoBrPo (1962 ed.); NePoEA; NoP; PIA; PoDB; PoeP; PoIE; ToPo; TwCP; UnPo (3d ed.)
Once I could ignore. The Giving In. Marvin Bell. YAP
Once I courted a beauty, beauty bright. The Fair Young Miss. *Unknown.* BFSS
Once I cried for new songs to sing. I Sing No New Songs. Frank Marshall Davis. PoNe
Once I delighted in a single tree. The Exulting. Theodore Roethke. *Fr.* The Dying Man. PoDB
Once I dressed up. Juan Chi. *Fr.* Fifteen Poems of My Heart. FIW
Once I followed horses. Thistledown. Denis Glover. AnNZ
Once I fought a shadow. The Duel. Harold Trowbridge Pulsifer. HBMV
Once I found riches here. The Discovery. Stanley Snaith. LO; POTE
Once I had a green door. Joan's Door. Eleanor Farjeon. BiCB
Once I had passed the shortened autumn day. The Suire. Thomas Caulfield Irwin. IrPN
Once I heard a hobo, singing by the tie-trail. The Long Road West. H. H. Knibbs. IHA
Once I heard a prima donna sing. Man's Hand—and God's. Mae Traller. SoP
Once I heard a song of sweetness. Against a Thorn. *Unknown.* SoP
Once I knew a brisk young farmer. William Hall. *Unknown.* BFSS
Once I knew a fine song. 'Scaped. Stephen Crane. The Black Riders, LXV. AA
Once I knew a little girl, and I loved her as my life. Do Come Back Again. *Unknown.* OuSiCo
Once I knew for every rain. The Stranger. Richard Sullivan. JKCP (1955 ed.)
Once I knowed old lady. The Rich Old Lady. *Unknown.* OuSiCo
Once I learnt in wilful hour. On a Wife. Francis Burdett Money-Coutts. OBVV
Once I lived with my brothers, images. The Centaur Overheard. Edgar Bowers. NYTB
Once I lost my temper. My Temper. *Unknown.* STF
Once I Nearly Touched a Bird. Mary Jane Carr. RePo
Once I Pass'd through a Populous City. Walt Whitman. AmPP (4th ed.); NePA; OxBA; TDP

Once I prayed to the Lord of Battles. Repentance. Thomas Curtis Clark. ChIP
Once, I remember well the day. The Enthusiast; an Ode. William Whitehead. OBEC
Once I saw a little bird going hop, hop, hop. Mother Goose. BoTP; GFA; OxNR; SAS; StVeCh
Once I saw Death go sporting through a plain. Death's Apology. Francisco Manuel de Mello. CAW
Once I saw it with uncaring eyes. This Hill. Otomo Yakamochi. OnPM
Once I saw large waves. At Sea. Jean Toomer. BALP
Once I saw mountains angry. Ancestry. Stephen Crane. The Black Riders, XXII. AA
Once I Thought to Die for Love. *Unknown.* EIL
Once I was a boy and I sat in a meadow with flowers in it. Time Passes. R. P. Lister. NYBP
Once I was a brakeman on the E-r-i-e Canal. The Erie Canal Ballad. *Unknown.* ABF
Once I was a monarch's daughter. Once. *Unknown.* CH
Once I was a serving maid who worked in Drury Lane. Bell-bottomed Trousers. *Unknown.* UnTE
Once I was a tiny tad. Innocence. George S. Chappell. YaD
Once I was Achaemenides's field. The Good Earth. *Unknown.* OnPM
Once I was at a nobleman's wedding. The Nobleman's Wedding. *Unknown.* AnIV
Once I was good like the Virgin Mary and the minister's wife. The Scarlet Woman. Fenton Johnson. BANP; PoNe
Once I was happy, but now I'm forlorn. The Man on the Flying Trapeze. George Leybourne. BeLS; BLPA; FaBoBe; NeHB; YaD
Once I was jealous of lovers. Now I am. The Valley. Stanley Moss. NYBP
Once I was part of the music I heard. Youth in Age. George Meredith. PoVP
Once I went to Fairyland—but it's years and years ago. When You Go to Fairyland. *Unknown.* PCD
Once I wished I might rehearse. Freedom. Emerson. PoFr
Once in a dream (for once I dreamed of you). On the Wing. Christina Rossetti. StP; VP
Once in a dream I saw the flowers. Paradise; in a Dream. Christina Rossetti. HBV; OxBoCh; PoVP; ViPo; WGRP
Once, in a finesse of fiddles found I ecstasy. *See* Once, in finesse of fiddles found I ecstasy.
Once in a golden hour. The Flower. Tennyson. EPN; HBV; InP; PoVP
Once in a hundred years the lemmings come. The Lemmings. John Masefield. CMoP
Once in a lifetime the white fawn run. Old Wife's Song. Eleanor Farjeon. RePo
Once in a lifetime, we may see the veil. Midnight—September 19, 1881. John Boyle O'Reilly. PAH
Once in a Lonely Hour. John Hall Wheelock. NP
Once, in a night as black as ink. How Samson Bore Away the Gates of Gaza. Vachel Lindsay. MoRP; NP
Once in a Saintly Passion. James Thomson. BBV (1951 ed.); PoVP; TreFS
(Vanity.) PV
Once in a simple quest. Through a Fog of Stars. John Nixon, Jr. MaRV
Once in a while/ we'd find a patch. The Children. William Carlos Williams. NePoAm-2
Once in a while a curious weed unknown to me. William Jones. Edgar Lee Masters. *Fr.* Spoon River Anthology. ImOP
Once in a wood at winter's end. Winter's End. Howard Moss. NePoEA
Once in an arbor was my mistress sleeping. Madrigal. Barnabe Barnes. *Fr.* Parthenophil and Parthenophe. TuPP
Once in an Eastern palace wide. I Tell the King. *Unknown.* SoP
Once, in [a] finesse of fiddles found I ecstasy. The Embankment [*or* Fantasia of a Fallen Gentleman]. T. E. Hulme. ELU; FaBoMo; GTBS-P; MoBrPo (1942 ed.); SeCePo
Once in his shop a workman wrought. The Camel's Nose. Lydia Huntley Sigourney. OTPC (1923 ed.); PRWS
Once, in my darkest hour, in some dim place. Lux in Tenebris. *Unknown.* GoBC
Once in my garret—you being far away. Rupert Brooke, II. W. W. Gibson. HBMV
Once in our lives. A Farewell to Wives. *Unknown.* SeCL
Once in Persia reigned [*or ruled*] a king. Even This Shall Pass Away [*or* The King's Ring]. Theodore Tilton. BLPA; HBV; MaRV; NeHB; PTK; TreFS; WGRP
Once in Royal David's City. Cecil Frances Alexander. MaRV; OTPC; PTK; YaCaBo, *with music*
(Christmas Hymn, A.) OHIP
(Good Tidings of Great Joy!) ThGo
Once, in the city of Kalamazoo. Kalamazoo. Vachel Lindsay. HT
Once in the dear dead days beyond recall. Love's Old Sweet Song. G. Clifton Bingham. FaBoBe; TreF
Once, in the gathering twilight. Recompense. Loring Williams. FiSC
Once in the wind of morning. The Merry Guide. A. E. Housman. A Shropshire Lad, XLII. OAEP (2d ed.); PoVP; ViPo
Once in the winter. The Forsaken. Duncan Campbell Scott. CaP; TwCaPo; WHW
Once in winter shone the ground and full sped. On the Nativity of Christ Our Lord. Joseph Bennett. NePA
Once it smiled a silent dell. The Valley of Unrest. Poe. AP; MWA-1; PoEL-4; TDP; ViBoPo
Once it was difficult to keep to roads. Roads. Ruth Dallas. AnNZ
Once it was enough simply. Reaching the Horizon. Robert Mezey. NaP
Once it was the blessing. Jesus Only. A. B. Simpson. BePJ
Once, long ago, a friend gave me a book. The Gift. Margaret E. Bruner. PoToHe
Once, long ago, an aged seer. The Seer. Lewis Turco. FiSC
Once, long ago, set close beside a wood. The Nun's Priest's Tale. Chaucer. *Fr.* The Canterbury Tales. TrGrPo
Once, Man entirely free, alone and wild. The Swiss Peasant [*or* On the Swiss]. Wordsworth. OBEC; PoFr
Once, measuring his height, he stood. The Boy Jesus. John Banister Tabb. StJW
Once mermaids mocked your ships. Mermaids. Kenneth Slessor. NeLNL; PoAu-2
Once more are we met for a season of pleasure. Cattle Round-up. H. D. C. McLachlan. SCC
Once more around should do it, the man confided. Flight of the Roller-Coaster. Raymond Souster. ACV; PeCV; WHW
Once more fictitious joy is spread. Nowell, Nowell. Robert Finch. TwCaPo
Once More Fields and Gardens. Tao Yuan-ming. *See* Returning to the Fields.
Once more following blue grief of evening. In Hellbrunn. Georg Trakl. LiTW
Once more I move among you, dear familiar places. Amagansett Beach Revisited. John Hall Wheelock. NYBP
Once more I saw him. In the lofty room. Robert Louis Stevenson. BrPo
Once more in misted April. An April Morning. Bliss Carman. DD; GBV; HBMV; HBVY
Once More into the Breach. Shakespeare. *See* Once More unto the Breach. . .
Once more, listening to the wind and rain. The Return. Arna Bontemps. CDC; PoNe
Once more on the morrow-morning fair shineth the glorious sun. Of the Passing Away of Brynhild. William Morris. *Fr.* The Story of Sigurd the Volsung. PoVP; VA
Once more, once more, my Mary dear. Memories. George Denison Prentice. AA
Once more Orion and the sister Seven. A Welcome to Dr. Benjamin Apthorp Gould. Oliver Wendell Holmes. ImOP
Once more! our God, vouchsafe to shine. Wednesday, January 1, 1701. Samuel Sewall. SCAP
Once more the ancient [*or* northbound] wonder. Easter, 1923 [*or* Easter]. John G. Neihardt. AnAmPo; HBMV; OHIP
Once more the changed year's turning wheel returns. Barren Spring. Dante Gabriel Rossetti. *Fr.* The House of Life, LXXXIII. FaBoEn; MaVP; NoP; OBNC; PoEL-5; PoVP; Sonn; VaPo; ViPo
Once more the country calls. Ode to Our Young Pro-Consuls of the Air. Allen Tate. AmPP (3d ed.); WaP
Once more the cuckoo's call I hear. Spring. Aubrey Thomas De Vere. *Fr.* The Year of Sorrow. OBNC
Once more the Heavenly Power/ Makes all things new. Early Spring. Tennyson. DD; HBV; HBVY

Once more the liberal year laughs out. Harvest Hymn. Whittier. *Fr.* For an Autumnal Festival. OHIP; PGD; PoRL
Once more the lumbering earth heaves its chill flank. Intempestiva. Henry Longan Stuart. JKCP (1926 ed.)
Once more the northbound wonder. *See* Once more the ancient wonder.
Once more the stars of love cross. Excerpts from a "Gothic Notebook." Mario Luzi. *Fr.* Gothic Notebook. LiTW
Once more the storm is howling, and half hid. A Prayer for My Daughter. W. B. Yeats. BWP; CABA; CMoP; CoBMV; EnL; GTBS-W; LiTB; LiTG; LiTM (rev. ed.); LoBV; MasP; MoAB; PAn; PoLF; PoPo; PoRA (rev. ed.); VaPo
Once more this Autumn-earth is ripe. The Australian. Arthur Adams. BoAu; PoAu-1
Once more, through God's high will and grace. Spring. Aubrey Thomas De Vere. *Fr.* The Year of Sorrow: Ireland—1849. IrPN
Once more to distant ages of the world. Wordsworth. *Fr.* The Excursion. InP
Once More unto the Breach [Dear Friends, Once More]. Shakespeare. King Henry V, *fr.* III, i. FaBV; PoSa; WaaP
(Blast of War, The.) TrGrPo
(Henry V at Harfleur.) TreF
(Henry V before Harfleur.) ShBV-2
(Henry V to His Soldiers.) PoFS
(Henry Fifth's Address to His Soldiers.) WHA
Once more we sail with a favoring gale. Rolling Down to Old Maui. *Unknown.* SoAmSa
Once, morn by morn, when snowy mountains flamed. Picture of a Bull. Joaquin Miller. AmPP (3d ed.)
Once Musing as I Sat. Barnabe Googe. LO; TuPP
(Fly, The.) CH
("Once musing as I sat, and candle burning by." SiCE
Once my feet trod Nineveh. The Babe. Monk Gibbon. OxBI
Once my hands were always trying. Resting. A. B. Simpson. SoP
Once my heart was a summer rose. Song. Edith Sitwell. ChMP; GTBS-D
Once, on a cliff, I saw perfection happen. The Heart of Light. Winifred Welles. NP
Once on a silver and green day, rich to remember. Brindabella. Douglas Stewart. PoAu-2
Once on a Time. Kendall Banning. HBV
Once on a Time. Margaret Benson. HBV
Once on a time a knight of high degree. The Merchant's Tale. Chaucer. *Fr.* The Canterbury Tales. UnTE
Once on a time, a monarch, tir'd with whooping. Apple Dumplings and a King. "Peter Pindar." OBEC
Once on a time, a nightingale. The Nightingale. Sir John Vanbrugh. *Fr.* Aesop. SeCL
Once on a time a young giraffe. Oliver Herford. *Fr.* The Untutored Giraffe. ShM
Once on a time, all in a town. A New Ballad. Mary Leapor. WaPE
Once, on a time and in a place. The Arrogant Frog and the Superior Bull. Guy Wetmore Carryl. StPo
Once on a time, as old stories rehearse. A Ballad to the Tune of "The Cut-Purse." Swift. PP
Once on a time did Eucritus and I. Harvest-Home. Theocritus. *Fr.* Idylls. AWP
Once on a time I used to be. Harlot's Catch. Robert Nichols. ErPo; FaBoTw
Once on a time, I used to dream. Once on a Time. Margaret Benson. HBV
Once on a time, in rainy weather. The Dog and the Cat and the Duck and the Rat. Eliza Lee Follen. CIV
Once on a time it came to pass. The Piece of Glass and the Piece of Ice. John Hookham Frere. OTPC (1923 ed.)
Once on a time old Johnny Bull flew in a raging fury. Yankee Doodle. George Pope Morris. PaA
Once on a time, once on a time. Once on a Time. Kendall Banning. HBV
Once on a time, some centuries ago. The Monk of Casal-Maggiore [*or* The Sicilian's Tale]. Longfellow. *Fr.* Tales of a Wayside Inn. AmPP (4th ed.); AP; OxBA
Once on a time there lived a man. Peter Gray. *Unknown.* OuSiCo
Once on a time—'twas long ago. The Youth and the Northwind. John Godfrey Saxe. StPo
Once on Saipan at the end of the rains. An Island Galaxy. John Ciardi. ToPo
Once, once, in Washington. Patriotic Tour and Postulate of Joy. Robert Penn Warren. NYBP
"Once. . .once upon a time. . ." Martha. Walter de la Mare. GBV; MoBrPo; OTPC (1946 ed.); TreFS
Once Only. Ato Tobira, *tr. fr. Japanese by* Ishii *and* Obata. OnPM
Once-over, The. Paul Blackburn. ErPo; NeAP
Once over summer streams the ice-crusts harden. No Return. Vassar Miller. CoPo; ToPo
Once Paumanok. Two Guests from Alabama. Walt Whitman. *Fr.* Out of the Cradle Endlessly Rocking. OA
Once quiet meant discord and pain. Witnesses. Cecil Hemley. PoDB
Once ran my prayer as runs the brook. Be Merciful. John T. McFarland. OQP
Once riding in Old Baltimore. Incident. Countee Cullen. BoChLi (1950 ed.); CDC; GoSl; IDB; MoSiPe; OQP; PoNe; WOW
Once Switzerland was free! With what a pride. Switzerland. James Sheridan Knowles. *Fr.* William Tell. PoFr
Once the Days. Denis Glover. AnNZ
Once the Emperor Charles of Spain. The Emperor's Bird's-Nest. Longfellow. BiS; MPB
Once the head is gray. A Catch. Richård Henry Stoddard. AA
Once the land had no great names and no history. Names from the War. Bruce Catton. AmFN
Once the orioles sang in chorus. Ballade of Big Plans. Dorothy Parker. InMe
Once the Wind. Mark Van Doren. TwAmPo
Once there came a man. Four Poems, II. Stephen Crane. CrMA; MWA-2
Once there lived a little man. The Little Disaster. *Unknown.* BoTP; SAS
Once there lived side by side two little maids. I Don't Want to Play in Your Yard. Philip Wingate. TreFT
Once there was a boy who never. Father's Day (—So He Says). *Unknown.* SoP
Once there was a fence there. Former Barn Lot. Mark Van Doren. FaBV; LOW; MAP; MoAmPo; PDV; PoPl
Once there was a little boy. The Perfect Child. Monica Shannon. BoChLi
Once there was a little boy, whose name was Robert Reece. An Overworked Elocutionist. Carolyn Wells. BLPA
Once there was a little Kitty. Long Time Ago [*or* Kitty *or* Little Kitty]. Elizabeth Prentiss. BoTP; CIV; GFA; MoShBr; MPB; SAS; TVC
Once there was a snowman. *Unknown.* GFA
Once there was a spaniel. Bed-Time Story. Melville Cane. GoTP
Once there was an elephant. Eletelephony. Laura E. Richards. BoChLi; FaPON; GoJo; MPB; PDV; SoPo; TiPo; YaD
Once there was dwelling in my district. The Friar's Tale. Chaucer. *Fr.* The Canterbury Tales. PoAn, *mod.*
Once there was neither heaven nor earth. The Two Pigeons. *Unknown.* OnPM
Once they minted Our Lady in multiple golden medallions. Ox-Bone Madonna. James J. Galvin. ISi
Once this soft turf, this rivulet's sands. The Battle-field. Bryant. AA; AmePo; CoBA; PAL; PoLF
Once to Every Man and Nation. James Russell Lowell. *Fr.* The Present Crisis. PAL; TRV
(Truth and Falsehood.) SoP
Once to his master a disciple cried. The Ways of Love. Jami. OnPM
Once to life I said, yes! To Life I Said Yes. Chaim Grade. TrJP
Once to the verge of yon steep barrier came. The Recluse. Wordsworth. BEL
Once, Twice, Thrice. *Unknown.* ErPo; PV
Once, twice, thrice/ I give thee warning. *Unknown.* OxNR
Once upon a Great Holiday. Anne Wilkinson. WHW
Once upon a midnight dreary, while I pondered, weak and weary. The Raven. Poe. AA; AmePo; AmP; AmPP; AnFE; AP; APA; BBV (1923 ed.); BeLS; BLPA; CH; CoAnAm; CoBA; FaBoBe; FaBoCh; FaBV; FaFP; FaPL; GN; GoJo; HBV; LiTA; LiTG; LoGBV; MCCG; MWA-1; NeHB; NePA; OHFP; OnSP; OTPC; OxBA; PaPo; PCD; PFY; PG (1945 ed.); PoPo;

Once (continued)
PoRA; PTK; RoGo; TDP; TOP; TreF; ViBoPo; WBLP; WHA
Once upon a Time. Gabriel Okara. PBA
Once upon a Time. D'Arcy W. Thompson. GaP
(Funny Old Man and His Wife.) SUS
Once upon a time. Catch a Little Rhyme. Eve Merriam. PDV
Once upon a time. Mr. Pyme. Harry Behn. PDV; TiPo
Once upon a time, in a little wee house. Once upon a Time [*or* Funny Old Man and His Wife]. D'Arcy W. Thompson. GaP; SoPo; SUS
Once upon a time, in truth, not very long ago. Making It, or Black Corruption. Donald Green. WSL
Once upon a time, son. Once Upon a Time. Gabriel Okara. PBA
Once upon a time there were three little foxes. The Three Foxes. A. A. Milne. GoJo; MoShBr; StVeCh (1955 ed.)
Once upon a time, was a place. Boys Will Be Princes. William Heyen. NYTB
Once upon Iceland's solitary strand. The Broken Oar. Longfellow. AmePo
Once upon the earth at the midnight hour. The Wooing Lady. William Jay Smith. NePoEA
Once, walking home, I passed beneath a tree. The Music of a Tree. W. J. Turner. MoBrPo
Once was a fiddler. Play could he. A Fiddler. Walter de la Mare. LOW; UnS
Once was every woman the witch. Witches. Ted Hughes. GoYe
Once we were strong. Charles Mair. *Fr.* Tecumseh. PeCV
Once we were wayfarers, then seafarers, then airfarers. Post Early for Space. Peter J. Henniker-Heaton. AmFN
Once when I looked at willows, I would say. Actual Willow. Winifred Welles. MAP
Once, when I was little, as the summer night was falling. The Wastrel. Reginald Wright Kauffman. HBV
Once when my heart was passion-free. Communion. John Banister Tabb. MaRV; WGRP
Once when she was very small. Biography. Mavor Moore. TwCaPo
Once when the snow of the year was beginning to fall. The Runaway. Robert Frost. AnNE; AWP; BBV (1951 ed.); BoChLi; CH; FaBoCh; FaPON; GoJo; GoTP; GTBS-D; HaMV; InPo; JAWP; LoGBV; MAP; MCCG; MoAB; MoAmPo; MPB; NeMA; PDV; PoRL; RePo; ShBV-3; StVeCh; TiPo; TSW; TwCP; WBP
Once when the wind was on the roof. Beyond. Hannah Parker Kimball. AA
Once when they gathered long ago. No Room. Robert Whitaker. ChIP
Once When You Were Walking. Annette Wynne. SUS
Once, with a whirl of thought oppressed. The Day of Judgment. Swift. EiPP
Once would the early sun steal in through my eastern window. Once. Walter de la Mare. BoPe
Once You Git the Habit. *At. to* Berton Braley. *See* Habit, The.
Once you have let the first blade. The Salt Marsh. James Dickey. FRC
Once you said joking slyly, "If I'm killed." The Faithful. Jane Cooper. AmPC; NePoEA-2
Oncet in the museum. Two Ways. John V. A. Weaver. HBMV; NP
One, The. Everard Jack Appleton. MaRV
One! E. E. Cummings. CAD
One, The. Patrick Kavanagh. MoBrPo (1962 ed.)
One a valley among the peaks of humanity. Malcolm X. Vernoy E. Hite. TNV
One Almost Might. A. S. J. Tessimond. ChMP
One alone, a sister without her peer. A Love Song. *Unknown.* LiTW
One after one they left us. Lost Beliefs. William Dean Howells. AmePo
One afternoon, finding nothing to do. Getting On. Stephen Sandy. CAD
One A.M. X. J. Kennedy. ELU; NYTB
One and His Mistress a-Dying. *Unknown.* SeCL
One and One. C. Day Lewis. OAEP (2d ed.); UnS
One and One. Mary Mapes Dodge. HBV; HBVY; PPL
One and one—Are one. Emily Dickinson. PoIE
One and one only is the splendid Lover. The Splendid Lover. John Richard Moreland. ChIP; PGD
One-and-twenty. Samuel Johnson. *See* Short Song of Congratulation, A.
One Answer, The. *Unknown.* GoTP; PDV
(O No, John!) ErPo; MeWo; UnTE
One April Day. John Richard Moreland. ChIP
One asked a sign from God; and day by day. The Seekers. Victor Starbuck. MaRV; WGRP
One ask'd me where the roses grew? The Rosarie. Robert Herrick. InMe
One asked of regret. Regret. Richard Le Gallienne. VA
One autumn night, in Sudbury town. The Wayside Inn. Longfellow. *Fr.* Tales of a Wayside Inn. CoBA
One bails out into space. Flight. Barbara Howes. NYBP
One Beauty Still. George Dillon. MAP; MoAmPo (1942 ed.)
One before the Last, The. Rupert Brooke. OBVV
One black brother with good intentions. The Almost Revolutionist. Tena L. Lockett. WSL
One black horse standing by the gate. The Farmyard. A. A. Attwood. BoTP
One Blackbird. Harold Monro. *Fr.* Strange Meetings. BoTP; RIS; StaSt
One bland elipse in cornflower blue. Rigor Viris. Margaret Avison. CaP
One blessing had I, than the rest. Emily Dickinson. LiTA; MWA-2
One bliss for which. Taboo to Boot. Ogden Nash. FiBHP
One block away from my house is an office building. Tie Your Tongue, Sir? Robert Paul Smith. CAD
One boxing glove. Appendix. Coleman Barks. *Fr.* Body Poems. QAH
One Bright Morning. *Unknown.* EvOK
One brought me the news of your death, O Herakleitos my friend. Elegy on Herakleitos. Callimachus. LiTW
One by his father kept long time to school. Of Two Religions. Sir John Harington. SiCE
One by One. Hazel Hall. NP
One by One. Adelaide Anne Procter. GN; HBV
One by one, as harvesters, all heavy laden. Sacheverell Sitwell. *Fr.* Agamemnon's Tomb. MoBrPo
One by one, like leaves from a tree. Leaves. Sara Teasdale. HBV; NP; PoPl
One by one, one by one. One by One. Hazel Hall. NP
One by one the pale stars die before the day now. Sailing at Dawn. Sir Henry Newbolt. EtS
One by one the sands are flowing. One by One. Adelaide Anne Procter. GN; HBV
One by one they appear in. My Sad Captains. Thom Gunn. LiTM (1970 ed.); NePoEA-2; PoCh; ToPo
One calm and cloudless winter night. Medusa. Robert Kelley Weeks. AA
One came in. Night Peril. Sydney King Russell. FiSC
One candidate has been nominated. The Election. Robert Pack. CoPo
One cannot have enough. Soliloquy of a Tortoise on Revisiting the Lettuce Beds after an Interval of One Hour While Supposed to Be Sleeping in a Clump of Blue Hollyhocks. E. V. Rieu. FiBHP
One Careless Look. John Clare. LiTL
("One gloomy eve I roam'd about.") AnFE; EG
One Centred System. Joel Barlow. *See* League of Nations, A.
One Certainty, The. Christina Rossetti. OBNC
One chance, The. Scar. Coleman Barks. *Fr.* Body Poems. QAH
One chestnut, only one. Baby's Hands. Gomei. MPB
One Christmas eve, when Santa Claus. Santa Claus and the Mouse. Emilie Poulsson. ChBR; GFA; UTS
One Christmas night in the long ago. God's Unspeakable Gift. Mrs. Macey P. Sealey. BePJ
"One ciarog knows another ciarog." The Tinkers. Joseph Campbell. OnYI
One City Only. Alice Corbin. NP
One cloud, one day. Anything Remembered. Alfred Starr Hamilton. QAH
One could not want a clearer season, when things age but do not grow. October Flies. Jascha Kessler. AmPC
One Country. Frank Lebby Stanton. AA; PaA; PAL

One Crowded Hour. Thomas O. Mordaunt. *See* Sound, Sound the Clarion.
One crown not any seek. Emily Dickinson. MaRV
One crucifixion is recorded only. Emily Dickinson. AnNE
One cup for my self-hood. The Poets at Tea, 10. Barry Pain. Par
One dark December day, the text-books teach. The Phoenix Liberty. Helen Parry Eden. PoFr
One Day. Rupert Brooke. MoLP
One day a statistician great. Doomed. *Unknown.* CIV
One day as I sat and suffered. The Heretic. Bliss Carman. WGRP
One day as I unwarily did gaze. Amoretti, XVI. Spenser. ReEn
One Day at a Time. Annie Johnson Flint. SoP
One Day at Rouen. Sister Mary Bernetta. JKCP (1955 ed.)
One day between the Lip and the Heart. The Lip and the Heart. John Quincy Adams. AA; AmLP; LHV; OTD
One day, by appointment, Maria I met. Maria. G. A. Stevens. UnTE
One day, from beyond the foliage. Prose Poem: Mysterious Flute. Judith Gautier. OnPM
One day, Good-bye met How-d'-y'-do. How-d'-y'-do and Good-bye. William Robert Spencer. OTPC (1923 ed.)
One day I could not read or play. Clouds. Norman Ault. HBVY
One day I looked at myself. Reflection. *Unknown.* STF
One day I made a taxicab. My Taxicab. James S. Tippett. GFA; MPB
One day, I mind me, now that she is dead. Mimma Bella, VIII. Eugene Lee-Hamilton. HBV
One day I observed a grey hair in my head. The Grey Hair. Judah Halevi. TrJP
One day I saw a downy duck. Good Morning. Muriel Sipe. SoPo; SUS; TiPo
One day I saw a ship upon the sands. Sea Irony. John Langdon Heaton. AA
One day I thought I'd have some fun. The Horse Wrangler. D. J. O'Malley. CoSo
One day I thought I'd have some fun. The Tenderfoot. *Unknown.* AS
One day I was walking out on the mountain. The Cowboy's Lament (B *vers.*). *Unknown.* ViBoFo
One day I wrote her name upon the strand. Amoretti, LXXV. Spenser. AnFE; ATP; AWP; BEL; BoLiVe; BWP; CABA; CBEP; CoBE; EIL; EnLi-1; EnLit; EP; FiP; ForPo; HBV; ILP; JAWP; LiTB; LiTG; LiTL; MaPo (1969 ed.); NoP; OAEP; PAn; PG (1955 ed.); PIA; PoE; PoFS; ReEn; ReIE; SeCePo; SeCeV; SiCE; Sonn; StP; TOP; ViBoPo; WBP
One day in a dream as I lay at the edge of a cliff. Dream. William Jay Smith. MoVE
One day in a lonesome grove. The Lonesome Grove. *Unknown.* TrAS
One day in the blue month of September. In Memory of Marie A. Bertolt Brecht. LiTW
One day, it thundered and lightened. Adam, Lilith, and Eve. Robert Browning. HBV; MeWo; PoVP; ViPP
One day, mamma said: "Conrad dear." The Story of Little Suck-a-Thumb. Heinrich Hoffman. EvOK; HBV; HBVY
One Day More, *with music.* *Unknown.* AmSS
One day more / These muttering shoalbrains leave the helm to me. James Russell Lowell. *Fr.* Columbus. PGD
One day my life will end. Biography. "Jan Struther." InMe
One day, nigh weary of the irksome way. Spenser. *Fr.* The Faerie Queene, I. BoLiVe
One day, not here, you will find a hand. Again. Charlotte Mew. MoAB; MoBrPo; NeMA
One Day of Rain. Joseph Payne Brennan. FiSC
One day on our village in the month of July. Death of an Aircraft. Charles Causley. MoBS; POTi
One day one young Creole Candio. Criole Candjo. *Unknown.* ABF
One day, or no, one night. The Salt and Pepper Dance. Jimmy Garthwaite. GFA
One day people will touch and talk perhaps easily. Daydream. A. S. J. Tessimond. SeCePo
One day that black and shining angel who. Black Angel. Lewis Thompson. AtBAP
"One day that we mustered on Sliabh Truim." *Unknown.* *Fr.* The Hunt of Sliabh Truim. OnYI
One day the amorous Lysander. The Disappointment. Earl of Rochester. UnTE
One day the dreary old King of Death. Death's Ramble. Thomas Hood. BOHV
One day the god of fond desire. Song. James Thomson. EnLoPo
One day the letters went to school. The Letters at School. *Unknown.* OTPC (1923 ed.)
One day the Nouns were clustered in the street. Permanently. Kenneth Koch. CoAP; NoP
One day, the vine. The Rebellious Vine. Harold Monro. BoPe; BrPo; WaKn
One day there came with glowing soul. The Story of Macha. *Unknown.* *Fr.* Dinnshenchas. OnYI
One day there entered at my chamber door. My Uninvited Guest. May Riley Smith. AA; WGRP
One day there reached me from the street. The Goatherd. Grace Hazard Conkling. GaP; TiPo
One day thou didst desert me—then I learned. To Imagination. Edith M. Thomas. AA
One day through the primeval wood. The Calf-Path. Sam Walter Foss. HBV; HBVY; PoLF
One day we built a snowman. Snowman. *Unknown.* GFA
One day we took a journey. Pop-Corn Land. Elsie F. Kartack. GFA
One day, when childhood tumbled the spongy tufts. Crane. Joseph Langland. NYBP
One day when Father and I had been. Moon Magic. Viscountess Grey of Fallodon. PCH
One day when I was studying with Stan Musial. Baseball. Tom Clark. ANYP
One day when I went visiting. I Held a Lamb. Kim Worthington. SoPo; TiPo (1959 ed.)
One day when walking down the street. My Load. Mary Butterfield. SoP
One Day When We Went Walking. Valine Hobbs. BrR; SoPo
One died upon a lonely Cross. The Atonement. Gerald Gould. POTE
One dignity delays for all. Emily Dickinson. AnAmPo; NoP
One does such work as one will not. In the Matter of Two Men. James David Corrothers. BANP
One dove has its head turned. Girl with Doves. Stephen Gray. PeSA
One Down. Richard Armour. SD; WhC
One dreamed and saw a gland write Hamlet, drink. A Dream of Surreal Science. Sri Aurobindo Ghose. ACV
One Driveth Out Another. John Heywood. ReIE
One duck stood on my toes. Feeding Ducks. Norman MacCaig. OxBS
One dwelt in darkness and sang within his dwelling. The Banquet. Louise Driscoll. MaRV
One effort more, my altar this bleak sand. Walt Whitman. *Fr.* The Prayer of Columbus. OQP; PGD; PoRL
One elf, I trow, is diving now. Song of the Elfin Steersman. George Hill. AA
One-erum, two-erum. *Unknown.* OxNR
One-ery, ore-ery [*or* two-ery], ickery, Ann. *Unknown.* FaPON; OxNR; RIS; SiTL
One-ery, Two-ery, Trickery, Seven. *Unknown.* OxNR
One eve. when St. Columba strode. The Cross of the Dumb. "Fiona Macleod." ChrBoLe
One Evening. W. H. Auden. PoAn
One evening as a maid did walk. The Trooper and Maid. *Unknown.* BaBo
One evening as I chanced to stray along the banks of Clyde. The *Lady of the Lake.* *Unknown.* ShS
One evening as the sun went down [*or* when the sun was low]. The Big Rock Candy Mountains. *Unknown.* ChTr; TreFT; WePo
One evening fair when Venus bright her radiant beams displayed. The Irish Girl's Lament. *Unknown.* ShS
One evening last June as I rambled. The Little Eau Pleine. *Unknown.* IHA
One evening late I chanced to stray. MacKenna's Dream. *Unknown.* OnYI
One evening (surely I was led by her). Wordsworth. *Fr.* The Prelude, I. OBRV
One evening walking out, I o'ertook a modest colleen. Among the Heather. William Allingham. IrPN

One evening when the sun was low. *See* One Evening as the sun went down.
One evening while reclining. Accepted and Will Appear. "Parmenas Mix." BOHV
One evening, while the cooler shade she sought. Dryden. *Fr.* The Hind and the Panther, I. PoEL-3
One ever hangs where shelled roads part. At a Calvary near the Ancre. Wilfred Owen. MoRP
One evil action every day. Vade Mecum. Rolfe Humphries. CBV
One eye? a thousand rather, and a thousand more. It is Better to Go into Heaven with One Eye. Richard Crashaw. MaMe
One Face Alone. Sara Coleridge. *Fr.* Phantasmion. VA
One face looks out from all his canvases. In an Artist's Studio. Christina Rossetti. EnLi-2; NoP; OAEP
One fantee wave. Edith Sitwell. *Fr.* Gold Coast Customs. OBMV
One feather is a bird. The Voice. Theodore Roethke. AmLP
One Fight More. Theodosia Garrison. PC
One fine day in the middle of the night. *Unknown.* CenHV
One flame-winged brought a white-winged harp-player. Passion and Worship. Dante Gabriel Rossetti. The House of Life, IX. MaVP; PoVP; ViPo; VP
One Foot in Eden. Edwin Muir. CMoP; FosPo; GTBS-P
One-foot waterfall, A. Contentment in Poverty. Issa. RePo
One for her Club and her own Latch-key fights. An Omar for Ladies. Josephine Dodge Daskam Bacon. HBV
One for [the] money. Mother Goose. OxNR; StVeCh (1955 ed.)
One for sorrow, two for joy. *Unknown.* OxNR
One Forgotten, The. Dora Sigerson Shorter. PoRL
One Friday morn when [*or* On Friday morning as] we set sail. The Mermaid [*or* One Friday Morn]. *Unknown.* CH; ESPB; OnMSP; OnSP; OTPC (1946 ed.); ViBoPo (A *vers.*)
One general song of praise arise. Lorenzo de Medici. *Fr.* Orazione. SoP
One Gift I Ask. Virginia Bioren Harrison. HBV
One Girl. Sappho, *tr. fr. Greek by* Dante Gabriel Rossetti. AWP; EnLi-1; JAWP; OuHeWo; WBP
(Beauty.) ViBoPo
(Young Bride, A.) LiTW
One gloomy eve I roam'd about. One Careless Look. John Clare. AnFE; EG; LiTL
One God, The. *Unknown, tr. fr. Egyptian by* E. A. Wallis Budge. MaRV
One Good Turn Deserves Another. *Unknown.* ShM
One granite ridge. Piute Creek. Gary Snyder. CoAP; NaP
One great truth in life I've found. Those We Love the Best. Ella Wheeler Wilcox. PoToHe
One grey and foaming day. R. P. Blackmur. Sea Island Miscellany, V. MoVE
One had grown almost affluent: one had. Elegy for an Estrangement. John Holloway. NePoEA
One half of me was up and dressed. The Gentle Check. Joseph Beaumont. SeCL
One hand is smaller than the other. Man with One Small Hand. P. K. Page. MoCV; OBCV
One Happy Moment. Dryden. *See* No, No, Poor Suffering Heart.
One hears and sees. Black Orpheus. Frederick J. Bryant, Jr. BF
One Heart, One Love. Jami, *tr. fr. Persian by* F. Hadland Davis. OnPM
One heifer and one fleecy sheep. Aristeides. Antipater of Sidon. AWP
One Here and There. *Unknown.* SoP
One hero dies,—a thousand new ones rise. Nathan Hale. William Ordway Partridge. PAL
One holy Church of God appears. The Church Universal. Samuel Longfellow. MaRV; SoP; WGRP
One Home. William Stafford. AmFN; CoAP; NePA
One honest John Tomkins, a hedger and ditcher. Contented John. Jane Taylor. HBV; HBVY
One Hope, The. Dante Gabriel Rossetti. The House of Life, CI. BEL; EnLi-2; EnLit; EPN; HBV; MaVP; PoVP; ViPo; ViPP
One Horse Chay. *Unknown.* OxBoLi
"One-Hoss Shay" The; or, The Deacon's Masterpiece. Oliver Wendell Holmes. *See* Deacon's Masterpiece, The.
One Hour to Madness and Joy. Walt Whitman. AnAmPo
One hue of our flag is taken. The Rejected "National Hymns," VI. "Orpheus C. Kerr." BOHV; InMe
111. E. E. Cummings. AnEnPo
One hundred feet from off the ground. Long-Suffering of God. Christopher Smart. *Fr.* Hymns for the Amusement of Children. EiCP
One Hundred Fifty-first Psalm, A. Henry B. Robins. MaRV
151st Psalm, The. Karl Shapiro. EaLo
147. E. E. Cummings. *See* Next to of Course God.
104 Boulevard Saint-Germain. Kenneth Pitchford. NYBP
121st Chorus. Jack Kerouac. TPM
One I love. *Unknown.* OxNR
One I Love Is Gone Away, The. *Unknown.* MeEL
One imagines the lives of the Prince. Winter In Etienburgh. Stephen Parker. NYBP
One Immortality. Norbert Engels. CAW
One in a Thousand of Years of the Night. Delmore Schwartz. FiMAP
One in Christ. Henry van Dyke. SoP; TRV
One in herself not rent by schism, but sound. The Catholic Church. Dryden. *Fr.* The Hind and the Panther, II. OBS; SeEP
One in the boat cried out. The Door. L. A. G. Strong. MoBrPo
One in the Infinite. George Francis Savage-Armstrong. PC; VA
One in thy thousand statues we salute thee. The Black Virgin. G. K. Chesterton. ISi
One is not hale until one inhales. On Apples. David Ross. NYBP
"One is reminded of a certain person." Kite Poem. James Merrill. NoP; TwCP
One keeps a secret for me. The Secret. Mary Morison Webster. PeSA
One Kind of Humility. Jean Starr Untermeyer. MAP; MoAmPo (1942 ed.)
One Kingfisher and One Yellow Rose. Eileen Brennan. BiS; NeIP
One king's daughter said to anither. Sheath and Knife. *Unknown.* CH; ESPB; LO
One-l lama, The. The Lama. Ogden Nash. FaBoCh; FaPON; FiBHP; LoGBV; PV; RePo; SiTL
One last look at your hills, Lysander. Learning Destiny. Herman Charles Bosman. PeSA
One lesson, Nature, let me learn of [*or* from] thee. Quiet Work. Matthew Arnold. EnL; EnLit; EPN; FaBoBe; HBV; MaVP; MCCG; NeHB; OAEP; OQP; PoIE; PoPo; PoRL; PoVP; TrGrPo; ViPP; YAT; YT
One little dicky-bird/ Hopped on my shoe. Ten Little Dicky-Birds. A. W. I. Baldwin. BoTP
One little Indian boy making a canoe. Ten Little Indian Boys. M. M. Hutchinson. BoTP; SoPo
One little minute more, Maud. Darling, Tell Me Yes. John Godfrey Saxe. HBV
One little noise of life remained—I heard. On the Eclipse of the Moon of October 1865. Charles Tennyson Turner. OBNC
One Little Rose. *Unknown.* SoP
(Kindness during Life.) STF
One looks from the train. The Orient Express. Randall Jarrell. AmP; AP; CMoP; CoAP; CoBMV; FiMAP
One Lost, The. Isaac Rosenberg. MoBrPo
One Love. Edward Shillito. *See* I Am the Last.
One Lowly Path. "G. T. S." SoP
"One lump or two? It's comforting to think." Conversation. Berenice C. Dewey. InMe
One man craves a scarf or glove. Civilization. Stanton A. Coblentz. OQP
One man in a house. To Landrum Guy, Beginning to Write at Sixty. James Dickey. PP
One Man Walking a Deserted Platform. Philip Larkin. ToPo
One Man's Goose; or, Poetry Redefined. George Starbuck. PP
One man's shoulder, another man's thigh. The Unknown Soldier. Charles A. Wagner. AnAmPo
One March Day. *Unknown.* PCH
One memory I have from childhood. Paradigm of a Hero. Jack Mathews. TPM
One midnight, deep in starlight still. Bankrupt. Cortlandt W. Sayers. PoLF; PoToHe (new ed.)

One might speak to great length. The Three Corners of Reality. Marvin Bell. YAP
One misty moisty morning. Mother Goose. BoTP; FaBoBe; HBV; HBVY; OTPC; OxNR; PDV; PPL; RIS; SAS; StVeCh (1955 ed.); TiPo
One moment take thy rest. Alas. Walter de la Mare. CLwM
One moment the boy, as he wander'd by night. The Sea-Maids' Music. Ernest Myers. VA
One More Day, *with music. Unknown.* SoAmSa
One more little spirit to Heaven has flown. Little Libbie. Julia A. Moore. ATP
One More New Botched Beginning. Stephen Spender. NYBP
One More Quadrille. Winthrop Mackworth Praed. OBRV
One More River. *Unknown.* SiTL; TreFS
One more Unfortunate. The Bridge of Sighs. Thomas Hood. BEL; BeLS; EnLi-2; EnLit; EnRP; GTBS; GTBS-D; GTBS-P; GTBS-W; GTSE; GTSL; HBV; HoPM; LiTG; OBEV; OBVV; PG; TreF; VA; WBLP; WHA
One morn before me were three figures seen. Ode on Indolence. Keats. EnRP; ERoP-2; GTBS-W; LiTB; MERP; OBNC
One morn I rose and looked upon the world. The Dawn. *Unknown.* PoToHe (new ed.)
One morning a weasel came swimming. The Weasel. *Unknown.* ChTr
One morning, as we travelled in the fields. The Riders Held Back. Louis Simpson. PIA
One morning before Titan thought of stirring his feet. Reverie at Dawn [*or* The Reverie]. Egan O'Rahilly. AnIL; KiLC
One morning I got up. The Little Bird. *Unknown.* PBA
One Morning in May. *Unknown.* AS, *with music*; BaBo; BFSS, *with music*
(Nightingale, The.) UnTE
One morning in spring/ We marched from Devizes. Fife Tune. John Manifold. BoAV; ExPo; FaFP; GoJo; GTBS-W; LiTB; LiTL; LiTM; LoGBV; ShBV-3; SiTL; WaaP WaP
One morning in the month of June. The Royal Fisherman. *Unknown.* ChTr
One Morning, Oh! So Early. Jean Ingelow. HBV
One morning, one morning, one morning in May. One Morning in May [*or* The Nightingale]. *Unknown.* AS; BaBo; BFSS; UnTE
One morning, one morning, one morning in May. The Rebel Soldier. *Unknown.* LoBGV; OxBoLi
One morning, one morning, the weather being fine. I Must and I Will Get Married. *Unknown.* TrAS
One Morning the World Woke up. Oscar Williams. FaFP; WaaP; WaP
One morning when I went downtown. Morning in Spring. Louis Ginsberg. GoYe
One morning, when Spring was in her teens. Two Fishers. *Unknown.* BOHV
One Morning When the Rain-Birds Call. Lloyd Roberts. CaP
One motionless, yet swift as thought. The All. *Unknown. Fr.* The Upanishads. OnPM
One must have a mind of winter. The Snow Man. Wallace Stevens. AnEnPo; AP; BWP; CoBMV; CrMA; ForPo; GoJo; NoP; NP; Po; PoFS; PoIE; QFR; RemP; TDP
One nail driveth out another with strokes so stout. One Driveth Out Another. John Heywood. ReIE
One nears with Harvard-man expression. Crossing Boston Common. Louise Dyer Harris. WhC
One need not be a chamber—to be haunted. Emily Dickinson. AmePo; DiPo; SyP
One Night. Marchette Chute. ChBR
One Night. W. W. Gibson. POTE
One night,/ One night all full of murmurs. Nocturne. José Asunción Silva. WoL
One night a score of Erris men. Danny. J. M. Synge. AnEnPo; PeVV
One night, all tired with the weary day. The Gnat. Joseph Beaumont. CBEP; LoBV; OBS
One night as Dick lay fast asleep. Full Moon. Walter de la Mare. AtBAP; BoNaP; TiPo
One night, as dreaming on my bed I lay. There Was No Place Found. Mary Elizabeth Coleridge. OxBoCh
One night came on a hurricane. The Sailor's Consolation. William Pitt [*wr. at. to* Charles Dibdin]. BBV; BeLS; EtS; HBV; LBN; MemP; OTPC (1946 ed.); StVeCh (1955 ed.); TreFS
One night came Winter noiselessly and leaned. The Frosted Pane. Sir Charles G. D. Roberts. HBV
One night he heard heart-breaking sound. Austin Clarke. *Fr.* Mnemosyne Lay in Dust. OPoP
One night he lay on my breast. One Night. W. W. Gibson. POTE
One night I dreamed I was locked in my Father's watch. My Father's Watch. John Ciardi. ImOP
One night I held all Europe in my arms. The Enemy. John Waller. NeBP
One night I lay asleep in Africa. Bookra. Charles Dudley Warner. AA; HBV
One night I met when stepping out. Frustrated Male. Hughes Mearns. *Fr.* Later Antigonishes. InMe; SiTL
One night I reached a cave: I slept, my head. Incident on a Journey. Thom Gunn. NePoEA
One night i' th' year[e], my dearest Beauties, come. To His Lovely Mistresses. Robert Herrick. CTC; OAEP; SeCP
One night I wandered alone from my comrades' huts. A Moment's Interlude. Richard Aldington. POTE
One night in late October. Judged by the Company One Keeps [*or* The Company One Keeps]. *Unknown, at. to* Aimor R. Dickson. BLPA; NeHB; TreFT; YaD
One night of the two bad years. The Nightmare. Sorley Maclean. NeBP
One night on the fall beef round-up. The Cowboy's Fate. Wallace D. Coburn. PoOW
One night Polly Oliver lay musing in bed. Polly Oliver's Rambles. *Unknown.* ViBoFo
One night poor Jim had not a sou. Facts. W. H. Davies. BrPo
One night quite bang up to the mark. Johnny Raw and Polly Clark. *Unknown.* CoMu
One Night Stand. LeRoi Jones. NeAP
One-Night Stand, The: An Approach to the Bridge. Paul Blackburn. ErPo
One night the wind it blew cold. Mary of the Wild Moor. *Unknown.* BaBo
One night upon the southern sea. The Silence of God. Sir Osbert Sitwell. WaKn
One night when I got frisky. I'll Never Get Drunk Any More. *Unknown.* OnYI
One night when I went down. The Heap of Rags. W. H. Davies. BrPo
One night you did not arrive. Someone I Lost. Jon Silkin. OPoP
One No. 7. John Frederick Frank. GoYe
One observes them, one expects them. Turkeys Observed. Seamus Heaney. FIW
One o'clock in the letter-box. The Meeting. Muriel Rukeyser. MoAmPo; TrJP
One of her hands, one of her cheeks lay under. A Supplement of an Imperfect Copy of Verses of Mr. Wil. Shakeseare. Sir John Suckling. SeEP
One of my foes deprived me of life. *Unknown. Fr.* Riddles. EnLit
One of the crowd went up. The Unknown God. Alice Meynell. BoPe
One of the days when one's a martyr. Sad September Sentiments. Edwin Meade Robinson. YT
One of the Jews (50 A.D.). C. P. Cavafy, *tr. fr. Modern Greek by* Rae Dalven. TrJP
One of the Kings of Scanderoon. The Jester Condemned to Death. Horace Smith. BOHV
"One of the Least of These." Lois Duffield. SoP
One of the more intelligent members. For the Fly-Leaf of a School-Book. Norman Cameron. OxBS
One of the Pharisees desired [Jesus] that he would eat with him. St. Luke, Bible, *N.T.* LO
One of the Regiment. Douglas Le Pan. CaP
One of the Sidhe. Mary Kennedy. FiSC
One of the Sweet Old Chapters. *Unknown.* SoP
One of the two according to your choice. Haidee. Byron. *Fr.* Don Juan. SeCePo
One of These Days. *Unknown.* SoP
One of those queer, artistic dives. The Women of the Better Class. Oliver Herford. HBMV
One of us in the compartment stares. Two Travelers. C. Day Lewis. EnLit
One of Us Two. Ella Wheeler Wilcox. PoToHe
One of Wally's Yarns. John Masefield. BrPo
One Old Ox ("One old ox opening oysters"). *Unknown.* ChTr

One (continued)
(One Old Oxford Ox.) OTPC (1923 ed.)
One only rose our village maiden wore. Flos Florum. Arthur Joseph Munby. VA
One other bitter drop to drink. The Rubicon. William Winter. HBV
One ought not to have to care. Loneliness. Robert Frost. *Fr.* The Hill Wife. CMoP; FaBoEn; NoP; NP
One Paddy Doyle lived near Killarney. Doran's Ass. *Unknown.* OnYI
One pale goldfish patrols the globe on teacher's desk. After School: Room Three. William Stafford. NYTB
One pale November day. Affaire d'Amour. Margaret Deland. HBV
One Perfect Rose. Dorothy Parker. ALV; FiBHP
One Person, *sels.* Elinor Wylie.
"I hereby swear that to uphold your house." NePA; Sonn
(House Sonnet.) LiTL
(Sonnet from "One Person.") LiTA; MAP; MoAB; MoAmPo
(Sonnets from "One Person.") NP; OxBA
"Let us leave talking of angelic hosts."
(Sonnets from "One Person.") OxBA
"Little beauty that I was allowed, The." Sonn
"My honored lord, forgive the unruly tongue."
(Sonnets from "One Person.") NP
"O love, how utterly I am bereaved."
(Sonnets from "One Person.") NP
"Upon your heart, which is the heart of all."
(Sonnets from "One Person.") NP
"When I perceive the sable of your hair."
(Sonnets from "One Person.") NP
One petal of a blood-red tulip pressed. Hallucination, I. Arthur Symons. SyP
One phrase of these plain country people. Getting Through. Robert P. Tristram Coffin. AnNE
One Piecee Thing. *Unknown, quoted by* "Lewis Carroll" *in* A Tangled Tale, VI. WhC
One place have I in heaven above. One Lowly Path. "G. T. S." SoP
One pleasant summer evening, 'twas in the month of May. The Mountain Cottage. John A. Stone. SGR
One pleasant summer morning it came a storm of snow. The Crooked Gun. *Unknown.* OuSiCo
One Poet Visits Another. W. H. Davies. DTC; FaBoTw
One potato, two potato. Counting-out Rhymes. *Unknown.* FaPON
One Presenting a Rare Book to Madame Hull. John Saffin. SCAP
One Race, One Flag. A. R. D. Fairburn. AnNZ
One rat across the floor and quick to floor's a breeze. Lucifer Alone. Josephine Miles. CBV
One remains, the many change and pass, The. Lumen de Lumine. Shelley. *Fr.* Adonais. GoBC; InP
One righteous word for Law—the common will. The Pilgrim Fathers. John Boyle O'Reilly. PEDC
One road leads to London. Roadways. John Masefield. BEL; BoTP; GTSL; HT; MCCG; PoPo; RePo
One, round the candytuft. I Spy. N. E. Hussey. BoTP
One sat within a hung and lighted room. Love and Poverty. Elisabeth Cavazza Pullen. AA
One Saturday. "Marian Douglas." AA
One scene as I bow to pour her coffee. Vacation. William Stafford. AmFN
One shadow glides from the dumb shore. Gloucester Harbor. Elizabeth Stuart Phelps Ward. AA
One Shall Be Taken and the Other Left. Aline Kilmer. NP
One she floats as Venice might. The Lost Cities. Lawrence Durrell. ToPo
One Ship Drives East. Ella Wheeler Wilcox. *See* Winds of Fate, The.
One ship drives east and another drives west. The Winds of Fate. Ella Wheeler Wilcox. SoP; TRV
One shoulder up, the other down. The Scarecrow. H. L. Doak. OnYI
One side of the coin has a vicious monarch's face. Render unto Caesar. Rolfe Humphries. CrMA
One side of the potato-pits was white with frost. A Christmas Childhood. Patrick Kavanagh. AnIL; OxBI
One silent night of late. The Cheat of Cupid; or, The Ungentle Guest. Robert Herrick. AWP; PG (1945 ed.); SeCeV
One simple and effective rhyme. Woodpigeons at Raheny. Donald Davie. PP
One small life in God's great plan. God's Plan. "Susan Coolidge." *Fr.* Commonplace. MaRV
One soft June night Nettie Blaine rode in. The Coquette. Muriel Earley Sheppard. IHA
One solitary bird melodiously. Evening. Charles Sangster. ACV; CaP
One son was a jewel to me. On the Death of His Son. Lewis Glyn Gothi. PoPl
One Sort of Poet. A. J. M. Smith. NYTB
One Spring, the Old Philosopher, feeling his bones. The Story of Two Gentlemen and the Gardener. Christopher Logue. CABL
One standing on the empty beach. Ballykinlar; May, 1940. Patrick Maybin. NeIP
One star/ Is better far. Thomas Traherne. *Fr.* The Apostasy. CoBE
One Star Fell and Another. Conrad Aiken. Preludes for Memnon, LVII. BoLP; MAP; MoAmPo; PoPo
One star is Minnesota. The Flag. Shelley Silverstein. PoSC
One steed I have of common clay. Comrades. Henry Ames Blood. AA
One Step at a Time. *Unknown.* WBLP
One Step Backward Taken. Robert Frost. MWA-2; OnHM
One step twix't me and death, (twas Davids speech). Roger Williams. SCAP
One still dark night, I sat alone and wrote. Frederick Goddard Tuckerman. *Fr.* Sonnets. AmePo; AP
One stitch dropped as the weaver drove. A Single Stitch. Susan Coolidge. SoP
One stormy day in winter. The Splinter. James Kenneth Stephen. CenHV
One stormy morn I chanced to meet. A Kiss in the Rain. Samuel Minturn Peck. BOHV
One Stormy Night. *Unknown.* *See* Two Little Kittens.
One stormy night, when winds blew wild. And Thus He Spoke. John A. Stone. SGR
One summer evening (led by her) I found. Wordsworth. *Fr.* The Prelude, I. FiP; FlW; MyFE; PIA; ShBV-3; ViBoPo
One summer, high in Wyoming. Before the Storm. Kenneth O. Hanson. CoAP
One summer I stayed/ On a farm, and I saw. The Two Families. Joyce L. Brisley. BoTP
One summer morning a daring band. The Ballad of Ishmael Day. *Unknown.* PAH
One summer's day a fox was passing through. The Fox and the Grapes. Joseph Lauren. GoTP; RIS
One summer's day in the month of May. The Big Rock Candy Mountain. *Unknown.* MaC
One Sunday after dark I went to take the air. Youpe! Youpe! River Along. *Unknown.* IHA
One Sunday morning, into Youghall walking. Youghall Harbor. *Unknown.* OnYI
One Sunday morning soft and fine. Brigadier. *Unknown.* MoCV; NMP
One sweet of hands, one starred for grace. A Woman of Words. Amanda B. Hall. HBMV
One sweetly solemn thought. Nearer Home. Phoebe Cary. AA; AmePo; AnAmPo; BLRP; FaFP; HBV; NeHB; OQP; SoP; TreF; WBLP; WGRP
One tawny paw is all it takes to squash. Some Lines in Three Parts. Peter Viereck. MiAP; MoAmPo (1950 ed.)
One that I cherished. Falstaff's Lament over Prince Hal Become Henry V. Herman Melville. ViBoPo
One that is ever kind said yesterday. The Folly of Being Comforted. W. B. Yeats. AnIL; AnIV; BoPe; BrPo; BWP; GTBS; GTSL; MBW-2; NoP; Po; PoE; ViPo (1962 ed.)
One there is above all others. A Friend That Sticketh Closer Than A Brother. John Newton. SoP
One there lived on the east side of the city. Meeting. Josephine Miles. FiMAP
One There Was. Stella Fisher Burgess. ChIP; StJW
One they hunt by night, The. I Am Ham Melanite. William Millett. GoYe
One Thing. "Owen Meredith." OQP; WBLP
One Thing at a Time. M. A. Stodart. PoToHe (new ed.)
One thing at a time. *Unknown.* OxNR
One thing comes and another thing goes. Fair Annet's Song. Elinor Wylie. AmLP

One thing has a shelving bank. A Drumlin Woodchuck. Robert Frost. GoYe; WaKn
One Thing Have I Desired. Amy Carmichael. FaChP
One Thing I of the Lord Desire. *Unknown.* STF
One thing in all things have I seen. The Secret [*or* Unity]. "Æ." MBP; MoBrPo; MoRP; PoVP
One thing is sure. The Pulse. Mark Van Doren. MAP; MoAmPo; PoPl
One Thing Needful, The. Vassar Miller. PoCh
One Thing Needful, The. Max Isaac Reich. BLRP
One thing that is bow-legged. Rainbow. D. H. Lawrence. CBV
One thing that literature would be greatly the better for. Very like a Whale. Ogden Nash. DTC; PoLF; ShBV-3; TrGrPo
One thing to sing the beloved, another, alas! The Third Duino Elegy. Rainer Maria Rilke. LiTW
One thing you left with us, Jack Johnson. Strange Legacies. Sterling A. Brown. Kal; TTY
One Thought for My Lady. Bloke Modisane. PBA
One thought into one word. One Thought for My Lady. Bloke Modisane. PBA
One Thousand Fearful Words for Fidel Castro. Lawrence Ferlinghetti. CoPo
One thousand saxophones infiltrate the city. Battle Report. Bob Kaufman. CAD; TTY
One Thousand Seven Hundred and Thirty-eight. Pope. *See* Epilogue to the Satires.
One Thousandth Psalm, The. Edward Everett Hale. SoP; TRV
One Time. Douglas Livingstone. PeSA
One time, as they walk'd forth e're break of day. The Wolf and the Dog. John Oldham. *Fr.* A Satyr Address'd to a Friend, That Is About to Leave the University, and Come Abroad in the World. PeRV
One Time Henry Dreamed the Number. Doughtry Long. BP
One time, in Alexandria, in wicked Alexandria. Thais. Newman Levy. BOHV; FiBHP; InMe
One tiny golden upward-pointing flame. Candle and Book. Nina Willis Walter. TRV
One to All Men. Plato, *tr. fr. Greek by* Lord Neaves. OnPM
One to destroy is murder by the law. The Criminality of War. Edward Young. PGD
One to make ready. A Line-up. *Unknown.* OxNR; PCH
One to make ready. The Start. *Unknown.* SD
One Token. W. H. Davies. BrPo
One Twilight Hour. George Meredith. *See* Modern Love: "We saw the swallows. . ."
One, two,/ Buckle my shoe. Mother Goose. BoChLi; BoTP; GoTP; HBV; HBVY; OTPC; OxNR; PCH; PPL; RIS; SAS; SiTL; SoPo; StVeCh; TiPo
One, Two, Buckle My Shoe. Ogden Nash. BiCB
One-two, is one to you. Ball. Kate Greenaway. PCH
One, Two, Three. Samuel L. Albert. NePoAm-2
One, Two, Three! H. C. Bunner. FaPON; HBV; InP; MPB; OTPC; PCH; PoLF; PRWS; TSW; TVC
One, Two, Three. "Robin Christopher." RIS
One, two, three,/ Caroline, what is the matter with you, my dear? Un, Deux, Trois. *Unknown.* ABF
One, two, three,/ I love coffee. *Unknown.* OxNR
One! two! three!/ Outside the school. Sing-Song Rhyme. *Unknown.* BoTP; SiSoSe
One, Two, three,/ The bumble-bee. *Unknown.* RIS
One, two, three, four,/ Mary at the cottage door. Mother Goose. OxNR; PCH
1, 2, 3, 4, 5!/ I caught a hare alive. Mother Goose. TiPo
One, two, three, four, five,/ Once I caught a fish alive. *Unknown.* OxNR
One, two, three, four, five, six, seven,/ All good children go to heaven. *Unknown.* RIS
1-2-3 was the number he played but today the number came 3-2-1. Dirge. Kenneth Fearing. AmP; CaFP; HoPM; LiTM; NAMP; PoIE; PoRA; PoSa; ThLM; TrJP
One, two, whatever you do. *Unknown.* OxNR
One ugly trick has often spoiled. Meddlesome Matty. Ann Taylor. HBV; HBVY; OnMSP; OTPC (1946 ed.)
One unkind word in the early morn. The Boomerang. Carrie May Nichols. PoToHe
One wading a Fall meadow finds on all sides. The Beautiful Changes. Richard Wilbur. CMoP; CoAP; FiMAP; ILP; SeCeV (1967 ed.)
One was fire and fickleness, a child, The. Voltaire and Gibbon. Byron. *Fr.* Childe Harold's Pilgrimage, III. OBRV
One was kicked in the stomach. Gangrene. Philip Levine. AmPC
One Way. Tommy Witaker. TNV
One Way of Love. Robert Browning. HBV; OtMeF; PoVP; TOP; VA
One Way of Trusting. Hannah Parker Kimball. AA
One-Way Song, *sels.* Wyndham Lewis.
"I would set all things whatsoever front to back." CTC
"In any medium except that of verse," XXIV. PP; SiTL
One weapon I would keep. Preparedness. Jean Grigsby Paxton. PGD
One Week. Carolyn Wells. LBN
One Wept Whose Only Child Was Dead. Alice Meynell. *See* Maternity.
One White Hair, The. Walter Savage Landor. HBV; VA
One Who Dared to Die. Thomas Curtis Clark. ChIP
One who has loved the hills and died, a man. Pony Rock. Archibald MacLeish. CMoP
One, who is not, we see: but one, whom we see not, is The Higher Pantheism in a Nutshell. Swinburne. *Fr.* The Heptalogia. ALV; BOHV; HBV; NA; Par; PeVV; PoVP; SiTL; ViPo; ViPP; VP
One who lets down Cassiopeia's hair, The. Constellation. Merrill Moore. TrGrPo (1942 ed.)
One Who Plans, The. *Unknown.* SoP
One Who Struggles, The. Ernst Toller, *tr. fr. German by* E. Ellis Roberts. TrJP
One Who Watches. Siegfried Sassoon. TrJP
One whom I knew, a student and a poet. Epitaph [*or* Poem]. Alex Comfort. MoBrPo (1950 ed.); SeCePo
One Wife for One Man. Frank Aig-Imoukhuede. PBA
One will be close beside you as you stare. At Palomar. Sister Mary Edwardine. JKCP (1955 ed.)
One with eyes the fairest. Chorus: Love Song. Euripides. *Fr.* Cyclops. AWP; JAWP; WBP
One with Nature. Shelley. *Fr.* Adonais. MaRV
One without looks in tonight. The Fallow Deer at the Lonely House. Thomas Hardy. AWP; BWP; CH; CMoP; InPo; MoVE
One woman may robe herself in a tunic of white wool. Bilitis. Pierre Louys. *Fr.* The Songs of Bilitis. UnTE
One word beyond all rules. Love. Gordon LeClaire. CaP
One Word Is Too Often Profaned. Shelley. CBEP; GTBS; GTBS-D; GTBS-P; GTBS-W; GTSE; LiTB; LiTG; LiTL; MCCG; NeHB; TreFT; WHA
(Desire of the Moth, The.) BoLiVe
(Love.) FiP
(To——: "One word is too often profaned.") ATP; BEL; ELP; EnL; EnLi-2; EnRP; EPN; ExPo; FaBoEn; FaBV; GTSL; HBV; ILP; LoBV; OAEP; OBEV; OBNC; OBRV; PG; PoE; PoLF; ShBV-4; TOP; TrGrPo; ViBoPo
Worship, *sel.* MaRV
One Word More. Robert Browning. FiP; HBV; OtMeF; PoEL-5; PoVP; VA; ViBoPo, *abr.*; ViPP
Phases of the Moon, *sel.* ChTr
One word of well directed wit. David and Goliath. John Banister Tabb. PoMa
"One World." Brent Dow Allinson. MaRV
One World. Dante. *Fr.* Divina Commedia. MaRV
One would be in less danger. Family Court. Ogden Nash. FiBHP
One would like to be able to write something for them. For the Unknown Seamen of the 1939-45 War Buried in Iona Churchyard. Iain Crichton Smith. BoPe
One would never assume, from the toy bulldogs taking the air. A Nice Part of Town. Alfred Hayes. NYBP
One would not hope to meet. Thoughts at the Museum. Eileen Brennan. OnYI
One Writeing against His Prick. *Unknown.* PeRV
One writes, that "other friends remain." In Memoriam A. H. H., VI. Tennyson. BEL; EnLi-2; EPN; MaPo (1969 ed.); OAEP; PoEL-5; ViPo; VP
One writes when. Two Poems. Edward Marshall. CoPo
One X. E. E. Cummings. FaBoMo
One Year Ago ("One year ago my path was green.") Walter Savage Landor. EnLi-2
One Year to Live. Mary Davis Reed. PoToHe (new ed.)

One (continued)
(If but One Year.) STF
(If I Had but One Year to Live.) SoP
O'Neill's War Song. Michael Hogan. OnYI
Onely a little more. *See* Only a little more.
Onely Joy, now here you are. *See* Only Joy, now here you are.
Onely the Reverend Grave and Godly Mr. Buckly Remaines. Edward Johnson. SCAP
Oneness with Him. George Macdonald. MaRV
One's grand flights, one's Sunday baths. The Sense of the Sleight-of-Hand Man. Wallace Stevens. AP; BWP; CABA; CoBMV; LiTM (rev. ed.); MoAB; MoAmPo (1950 ed.); MoPo; TwCP
One's none. *Unknown.* OxNR
One's-Self I Sing. Walt Whitman. AmePo; AmPP (4th ed.); AnAmPo; CoBA; DiPo; OxBA; PoPo
Onion, The. C. C. Ward. PCH
Onion Bucket. Lorenzo Thomas. BF
Onion Skin, The. Kenneth Pitchford. *Fr.* Good for Nothing Man. CoPo
Onion Skin in Barn. Kenneth Slade Alling. NePoAm
Onions. Swift. *Fr.* Verses for Fruitwomen. AnIV; OnYI
Only. Harriet Prescott Spofford. HBV
Only/ a little/ yellow/ school bus. Snow Country. Dave Etter. AmFN
Only a baby, fair and small. George Washington. *At. to* Eliza Cook. MPB; OHIP; PEDC
Only a Baby Small. Matthias Barr. HBV; HBVY; OTPC (1923 ed.); PaPo
Only a Beauty, Only a Power. John Masefield. MoRP
Only a bit of color. Our Flag. Frances Crosby Hamlet. PGD
Only a Cowboy. *Unknown.* CoSo
Only a Dad. *Unknown.* SoP
Only a few it touched at first. The Lie. Howard Nemerov. NYTB
Only a Flower. Toyohiko Kagawa. MaRV
Only a fool would eat his heart out so. Ballad of the Bushman. Eileen Duggan. CoBE
Only a Gambler Loves Peace. Eunice de Chazeau. OnPM
"Only a housemaid!" She looked from the kitchen. Unsatisfied. Oliver Wendell Holmes. AnNE
Only [*or* Onely] a little more. His Poetry [*or* Poetrie] His Pillar. Robert Herrick. AnAnS-2; EG; EnL; EnLit; FaBoEn; LoBV; MyFE; OBS; QFR; SCEP-2; SeCL; SeCP; SeEP
Only a Little Thing. Mrs. M. P. Handy. PoToHe
Only a Little Time. *Unknown.* SoP
Only a little while since we first met. Song. Brian Hooker. HBMV
Only a man harrowing clods. In Time of "The Breaking of Nations." Thomas Hardy. AnEnPo; CaFP; CMoP; CoBMV; EnLi-2 (1949 ed.); EnLit; ExPo; ForPo; GTBS-W; GTSL; ILP; InP; LiTB; LiTM; LoBV; MaPo (1969 ed.); MMA; MoAB; MoBrPo; MoRP; NeMA; NoP; NP; OAEP (2d ed.); OBEV (new ed.); PoAn; PoPo; PoSa; POTE; PoVP; QFR; SeCeV; ShBV-3; TDP; TreF; VP
Only a manger, cold and bare. The Christmas Symbol. *Unknown.* OQP
Only a Smile. *Unknown.* STF
Only a tender little thing. A Snowdrop. Harriet Prescott Spofford. GN
Only a touch, and nothing more. Kate Temple's Song. Mortimer Collins. HBV; VA
Only a Word. Lois Elizabeth Ridenour. SoP
Only an exile, a Japanese. Fabre, the Bughunter. James Schevill. FiMAP
Only awake to Universal Mind. Chorus. Jack Kerouac. *Fr.* Mexico City Blues. NeAP
Only Be Willing to Search for Poetry. Yuan Mei. PDV
Only because she said. Sosei Hoshi, *tr. fr. Japanese by* I. W. Furukami. LiTW
Only begotten Son, seest thou what rage. Free Will and God's Foreknowledge. Milton. *Fr.* Paradise Lost, III. ExPo
Only believe! How sweet that tender message. Faith. Avis B. Christiansen. SoP
Only blossoms of the plains are black, The. The Plains. Roy Fuller. BoSA; MoPo
Only by sorrows' ladder shall we rise. Sorrows' Ladder. Gertrude Callaghan. CAW
Only cows can loll at ease. Pastorale. Mildred Weston. PoMa
Only for these I pray. Two Prayers. Charlotte Perkins Gilman. OQP; WGRP
Only from chaos/ Is creation. Song for These Days. Patrick F. Kirby. GoBC
Only from day to day. To-Day John Boyle O'Reilly. OnYI
Only ghost I ever saw, The. Emily Dickinson. MWA-2; NePA
Only Heaven Is Given Away. Rose Darrough. MaRV
Only in my deep heart I love you, sweetest heart. A Farewell. "Æ." OBVV
Only Jealousy of Emer, The, *sel.* W. B. Yeats.
Song: "Woman's beauty, A, is like a white/ frail bird." MoAB
Only Jesus Will I Know. Charles Wesley. BePJ
Only [*or* Onely] joy, now here you are. Astrophel and Stella: Fourth Song. Sir Philip Sidney. AtBAP; ElL; EnRePo; FaPl; FCP; InvP; OBSC; ReEn; ReIE; SiCE; TuPP; SiPS; UnTE
Only kid, An! an only kid. Had Gadya—A Kid, a Kid. *Unknown.* TrJP
Only last week, walking the hushed fields. Father and Son. F. R. Higgins. ACV; BoC; LiTM; OBMV; OxBI; PG (1955 ed.); POTE
Only leaf upon its tree of blood, The. The Red Heart. James Reaney. CaP
Only legal swindle which the people cannot sever, The. The Steam Navigation Thieves. John A. Stone. SGR
Only less sure of all I never knew. Fiftieth Birthday. Peter Viereck. NYTB
Only loneliness is the wind's, The. Submergence. Hazel Hall. NP
Only look at this nosegay of pretty wild flowers. The Wild Wreath. *Unknown.* OTPC (1923 ed.)
Only man that e'er I knew. Blake. PV
Only mother he could afford was a skinny old man, The. Because They Were Very Poor That Winter. Kenneth Patchen. NaP
Only My Opinion. Monica Shannon. FaPON; MPB; SoPo; StVeCh (1955 ed.); TiPo
Only Name Given under Heaven, The. Anne Steele. BePJ
Only news I know, The. Emily Dickinson. BoLiVe
Only, O Lord, in Thy dear love. As We Pray [*or* Help Us to Live]. John Keble. MaRV; SoP; TRV
Only of You [*or* Thee] and Me. Louis Untermeyer. HBV; MemP
Only once more and not again—the larches. In Ampezzo. Trumbull Stickney. AnFE; APA; CoAnAm; CrMA; NCEP; TwAmPo
Only One. George Cooper. *See* Our Mother.
Only One, The. Jo Gardner. BePJ
Only One King. John Richard Moreland. ChIP; PGD
Only One Life. Gladys M. Bowman. STF
Only one more day, my Johnny. One Day More. *Unknown.* AmSS
Only One Mother. George Cooper. *See* Our Mother.
Only one who has lifted the lyre. Four Sonnets to Orpheus. Rainer Maria Rilke. *Fr.* Sonnets to Orpheus. LiTW
Only our love hath no decay. John Donne. *Fr.* The Anniversary. LO
Only passages of a poetry, no more! Structure of Rime XXIII. Robert Duncan. FRC
Only Pretty Ringtime, The. A. V. Bowen. POTE
Only quiet death. Threnody. Waring Cuney. AmNP; BANP
Only real airship, The. The Dirigible. Ralph Bergengren. FaPON; SoPo
Only response, The. Poem. William Knott. YAP
Only Rose, The. Juan Ramón Jiménez, *tr. fr. Spanish by* John Crow. OnPM
Only Seven. Henry S. Leigh. BOHV; HBV
Only Silence. Arthur S. Bourinot. CaP
Only Son, The. Sir Henry Newbolt. HBV
Only stand high a long enough time your lightning will come. The Summit Redwood. Robinson Jeffers. AmPP (3d ed.)
Only, sweet Love, afford me but thy heart. For Her Heart Only. *Unknown.* ElL; LO
Only teaching on Tuesdays, book-worming. Memories of West Street and Lepke. Robert Lowell. AmPP (5th ed.); NaP; PoeP; ToPo
Only Tell Her That I Love. Lord Cutts. *See* Song: "Only tell her that I love."
Only that which made us, meant us to be mightier by and by. That

Which Made Us. Tennyson. *Fr.* Locksley Hall Sixty Years After. OQP
Only the Arab stallion will I. To a Man on His Horse. F. T. Prince. MoPW
Only the Beards Are Different. Bruce Dawe. PoAu-2
Only the creaking murmur of the wheel. Twelve o'Clock Boat. J. A. R. McKellar. BoAV; MoAuPo
Only the Dead. Reed Whittemore. NYBP
Only the diamond and the diamond's dust. Epitaph for the Race of Man, II. Edna St. Vincent Millay. MoPo
Only the Dream Is Real. Anderson M. Scruggs. OQP
Only the hands are living; to the wheel attracted. Casino. W. H. Auden. MoPo
Only the Heart. Marjorie Freeman Campbell. CaP
Only the island which we sow. Sir Richard Fanshawe. *Fr.* An Ode, upon Occasion of His Majesty's Proclamation in the Year 1630. BoPe
Only the lamps are live. Coming of the Fog. Clifford Dyment. POTi
Only the Lion and the Cock. After Galen. Oliver St. John Gogarty. OBMV; PoRA
Only the Moonlight. Paul Engle. TDP
Only the nicorn knows. The Nicorn's Dower. Peter Hopegood. MoAuPo
Only the prism's obstruction shows aright. Deaf and Dumb. Robert Browning. MaRV
Only the sand, only the sand. El Alamein Revisited. Roy Macnab. PeSA
Only the short, broad, splayed feet. Young Shepherd Bathing His Feet. Peter Clarke. PBA
Only thing I have of Jane MacNaughton, The. The Leap. James Dickey. FRC
Only the wholesomest foods you eat. Poems in Praise of Practically Nothing, II. Samuel Hoffenstein. BOHV; InMe; SiTL; TrJP
Only the Wind Says Spring. Helen Janet Miller. GoTP
Only thing to cheer me, The. Nature's Sorrow Cure. Catherine Cate Coblentz. OQP
Only this evening I saw again low in the sky. Martial Cadenza. Wallace Stevens. NePA; OxBA
Only thorns for the Master. Crowns. Louise Upham Brooks. ChIP
Only those coral insects live. The Builders. Judith Wright. SeCePo
"Only through Me!" . . .The clear, high call comes pealing. Dies Irae—Dies Pacis. John Oxenham. MaRV
Only Thy Dust. Don Marquis. PoLF
Only to find Forever, blest. Heaven. Martha Dickinson Bianchi. AA; HBV
Only to those who have climbed the dusky hill. The Swans. Randall Swingler. POTE
Only Tourist in Havana Turns His Thoughts Homeward, The. Leonard Cohen. MoCV
Only track now visible was one, The. Crossing the Alps. Wordsworth. *Fr.* The Prelude, VI. CoBE
Only true God, betwixt whom and me, The. Ad Deum. George Chapman. ReIE
Only twice is womankind. Praise of Women. Palladas of Alexandria. LiTW
Only two patient eyes to stare. Faded Pictures. William Vaughn Moody. AP
Only Waiting. Frances Laughton Mace. BLPA
Only walls. No grass, nor glass. Factory Street in Daylight. Paul Zech. WoL
Only Way to Have a Friend, The. *Unknown.* PoToHe (new ed.)
Only Way to Win, The. *Unknown.* WBLP
Only what is heroic and courageious moves our blood. Michael McClure. The Flowers of Politics, II. NeAP
Only when he was old enough, and silent. His Trees. Mark Van Doren. AnFE; CoAnAm
Only when heaven is unaffronted can we make friends with stars. Heaven and Earth. Frederic Thompson. CAW
Onondaga Madonna, The. Duncan Campbell Scott. PeCV
Ons in your grace I knowe I was. What Once I Was. Sir Thomas Wyatt. EnPo; MeEL
Onset, The. Patric Dickinson. POTi
Onset, The. Robert Frost. AmP; AnNe; AP; CMoP; CoBMV; MoAB; MoAmPo; NeMA; OxBA
Onward! Sabine Baring-Gould. *See* Onward, Christian Soldiers.
Onward. Jared Bell Waterbury. SoP
Onward and Upward. John Charles Earle. MaRV
Onward, Christian Soldiers. Sabine Baring-Gould. FaBoBe; FaPL; HBV; MaRV; NeHB; OTPC; PCH; TreF; WGRP (Onward!) SoP
Onward flies the rushing train. The Engine Driver. "G. S. O" BoTP
Onward led the road again. Hell Gate. A.E. Housman. UnPo
Onward! Onward! —'neath curse and blow. The Way of the Cross. Joseph I. C. Clarke. CAW
Onward they came in their joy. The Nereids. Charles Kingsley. *Fr.* Andromeda. NBM
Onward to Far Ida. George Darley. *Fr.* Nepenthe. OBNC
Onwardness. Doris Hedges. CaP
Oocuck, The. Justin Richardson. FiBHP
Oom-pah. Hugh Lofting. GaP
Oon of the greatest authors that men rede. Murder Will Out. Chaucer. *Fr.* The Canterbury Tales: The Nun's Priest's Tale. MyFE
Oor best-lo'ed makar has but late grown cauld. Carlyle on Burns. William Jeffrey. *Fr.* On Glaister's Hill. OxBS
Opal. Josephine Miles. FiMAP
Opal heart of afternoon, The. The Bracelet of Grass. William Vaughn Moody. AP
Opal ring and a holly tree, An. Sailor's Woman. Annette Patton Cornell. GoYe
Opals. Arthur Symons. PoVP
Ope your doors and take me in. The House of the Trees. Ethelwyn Wetherald. CaP; OQP; VA
Open. Larry Eigner. NeAP
Open a window on the world. The Puppet Dreams. Conrad Aiken. *Fr.* Punch; the Immortal Liar. MAP
Open Air Performance of "As You Like It", An. E. J. Scovell. ChMP
Open Door, The. Grace Coolidge. MaRV; TRV
Open Door, The. Ida Norton Munson. ChIP
Open Door, The. *Unknown, tr. fr. Irish by* Frank O'Connor. KiLC
Open door says, "Come in," The. Doors. Carl Sandburg. LOW
Open foe may prove a curse, An. Poor Richard's Wisdom. Benjamin Franklin. GoTP
Open House. Theodore Roethke. AP; CoBMV; NoP; PoeP
Open Letter. Owen Dodson. BALP
Open Letter to John Doe. Edward Doro. TwAmPo
Open mouthed statues built with. Eclipse. Albert E. Haynes, Jr. BF
Open My Eyes. Betty Scott Stam. STF
Open Question, An. Thomas Hood. NBM
Open Range. Kathryn Jackson *and* Byron Jackson. FaPON; TiPo
Open Road, The. Walt Whitman. *See* Song of the Open Road.
Open road and a wide road, An. Road Song. Margaret E. Sangster. PoMa
Open Sea, The. Dorothea Mackellar. BoAu
Open Sea, The. William Meredith. CoAP; NePoEA; UnPo (3d ed.)
Open Secret, An. Caroline Atherton Mason. AA
Open Secret, An. *Unknown.* BoChLi
Open Sesame. *Unknown. See* O for a Booke.
Open, sweet flowers, your eyes. John Francis O'Donnell. *Fr.* May. IrPN
Open the breast. The Signature of Pain. Alan Porter. POTE
Open the Door. Marion Edey. SiSoSe; TiPo
Open the Door ("Open the door, let in the air") *Unknown.* SoP
Open the Door ("Open the door! Who's there within?") *Unknown.* ElL; LO
Open the door and who'll come in? Open the Door. Marion Edey. SiSoSe; TiPo
"Open the door, some pity to show!" The Palmer. Sir Walter Scott. OTPC (1923)
Open the Door to Me, O. Burns. *See* O, Open the Door to Me, O!
Open the Gates. *Unknown, tr. fr. Hebrew by* Israel Zangwill. TrJP
Open the gates. The Bonny Earl of Murray. *Unknown.* ESPB
Open the old cigar-box, give me a Cuba stout. The Betrothed. Kipling. HBV

"Open the window, and let me in." The Rain. *Unknown.* GFA
Open the window on the high. Earth Tremor in Lugano. James Kirkup. NYBP
Open Thy Doors, O Lebanon. Zechariah, XI: 1-14, Bible, *O.T.* AWP
Open to Me! He Commandeth a Fair Wind. *Unknown. Fr.* Book of the Dead. AWP
Open to Visitors. E. V. Milner. ELU
Open wound which has been healed anew, An. Sonnet. Richard Chenevix Trench. TrPWD
"Open, ye everlasting gates!" The Great Creator from His Work Returned. Milton. *Fr.* Paradise Lost, Bk. VII, *ll.* 565-601. TreFT
Open Your Eyes. Emma Boge Whisenand. PoToHe (new ed.)
Open your gates for him. Harold at Two Years Old. Frederic W. H. Myers. HBMV
Open your windows. In a Girl's Album. Cedric Dover. WePo
Opened like a big new colored-picture book. Indian Summer—Buffalo Summer. Winfield Townley Scott. FiMAP
Opening Door. Winifred Adams Burr. FiSC
Opening of the Tomb of Charlemagne, The. Sir Aubrey de Vere. HBV
Opening our windows toward Jerusalem. Toward Jerusalem. Amy Carmichael. MaRV
Opening Prayer, An. *Unknown.* SoP
Opening Session of Congress Rock and Roll, The. Gail Dusenbery. ThO
Opening up a mud duck. The Ems Dispatch. Ron Padgett. ANYP
Opening Year, The. *Unknown, tr. fr. Latin by* F. Pott. BLRP
Openly, yes,/ with the naturalness. Melancthon. Marianne Moore. AtBAP; CrMA
Opera in English? Benjamin M. Steigman. WhC
Opera singer softly sang, The. Essence. Samuel Greenberg. MoPo; NePA
Opera star named Maria, An. *Unknown.* GoTP
Operatic Note. Melville Cane. UnS
Operation. Alfred Alvarez. NMP; OPoP
Operation, The. Robert Creeley. NaP; ToPo
Operation. W. E. Henley. *Fr.* In Hospital. PoVP
Operation, The. W. D. Snodgrass. CBV; StP; ToPo
Operation—Souls. *Unknown.* STF
Operative No. 174 Resigns. Kenneth Fearing. NYBP
Ophelia. Arthur Rimbaud, *tr. fr. French by* Brian Hill. ChTr
Ophelia. Vernon Watkins. MoVE
Ophelia's Death. Shakespeare. *Fr.* Hamlet, V, i. ChTr
Ophelia's Songs. Shakespeare. *Fr.* Hamlet, V, v.
And Will He [or A'] Not Come Again? EG; InPo; PoEL-2; ViBoPo
(Ophelia's Songs, 2.) AnFE; TrGrPo
He Is Dead and Gone, Lady. LO
How Should I Your True Love Know. ChTr; EG; EnLoPo; InPo; LiTB; LiTG; LiTL; PoRA; QFR; ViBoPo
(Friar of Orders Grey, The.) GoBC
(Ophelia's Song.) OBSC
(Ophelia's Songs, 1.) AnFE; TrGrPo
(Song.) CH
Tomorrow Is [*or* Good Morrow 'Tis] Saint Valentine's Day. EnLoPo; InPo; PV; ViBoPo
(Ophelia's Song.) UnTE
(Saint Valentine's Day.) LiTB; LiTG
(Song.) FaPON; HH; MPB; SiSoSe
Ophra. Judah Halevi, *tr. fr. Hebrew by* Nina Salaman. LiTW; TrJP
Opifex. Thomas Edward Brown. OBVV; PoVP
Opinion, let me alone: I am not thine. Remonstrance. Sidney Lanier. AmePo
Opinions of the New Chinese Student. Regino Pedroso, *tr. fr. Spanish by* Langston Hughes. PoNe
(Opinions of the New Student.) TTY
Opium Clippers. Daniel Henderson. EtS
Opium Fantasy, An. Maria White Lowell. AnFE; APA; CoAnAm
Opossum. William Jay Smith. GoTP; TiPo (1959 ed.)
Opponent Charm Sustained, The. Samuel Greenberg. MoPo
Opportune Overthrow of Humpty Dumpty, The. Guy Wetmore Carryl. BBGG
Opportunity. Berton Braley. WBLP
Opportunity. Madison Cawein. AA
Opportunity. W. Audrey P. Good. SoP
Opportunity. Harry Graham. DTC
Opportunity. John James Ingalls. AA; FaFP; HBV; HBVY; MaRV; OHFP; OQP; PoLF; TreF; WBLP; YaD
Opportunity. Machiavelli, *tr. fr. Italian by* James Elroy Flecker. AWP; JAWP; WBP
Opportunity. Walter Malone. BLPA; FaBoBe; HBV; MaRV; NeHB; OQP; WBLP; YaD
Opportunity. Edwin Markham. OQP
Opportunity. Shakespeare. *Fr.* The Rape of Lucrece. LiTB; OBSC
("Opportunity thy guilt is great.") PoEL-2
Opportunity. Edward Rowland Sill. AnNE; BBV; BLPA; GN; GoTP; HBV; HBVY; MAP; MaRV; MCCG; MoAmPo (1942 ed.); NeHB; NeMA; OHFP; PCD; PoMa; StP; TreFS; TSW; WGRP; YaD
(Broken Sword, The.) PoToHe
Opposites. José Moreno Villa, *tr. fr. Spanish by* Eleanor L. Turnbull. OnPM
Opposition, The. Samuel Hazo. NYTB
Opposition. Sidney Lanier. AmPP (3d ed.); AnFE; APA; CoAnAm; LiTA
Oppressed and few, but freemen yet. The Mecklenburg Declaration. William C. Elam. PAH
Oppressed with grief, in heavy strains I mourn. Elegy by Green for Byles's Cat. Joseph Green. CIV
Ops in a Wimpey. *Unknown.* CoMu
Optimism. Newton Mackintosh. BOHV
Optimism. Blanaid Salkeld. NeIP
Optimism. Ella Wheeler Wilcox. *See* Talk Happiness.
Optimist, The. D. H. Lawrence. MoPW
Optimist, The ("The optimist fell ten stories"). *Unknown.* BLPA; GoTP; NeHB; TreFT; YaD
Optimist, The ("When the world is all against you"). *Unknown.* PV
Optimist and Pessimist. *Unknown, at. to* McLandburgh Wilson. *See* Difference, The.
Optimist builds himself safe inside a cell, The. The Optimist. D. H. Lawrence. MoPW
Optimist fell ten stories, The. The Optimist. *Unknown.* BLPA; GoTP; NeHB; TreFT; YaD
Options. "O. Henry." FiBHP
Opus rises to fortissimo, The. Lengthy Symphony. Persis Greely Anderson. WhC
Opusculum paedagogum. Study of Two Pears. Wallace Stevens. AmPP (4th ed.); AP; MaPo (1969 ed); OxBA; PoeP; TDP
Or else I sat on in my chamber green. Reading. Elizabeth Barrett Browning. *Fr.* Aurora Leigh. GN; HH
Or else, in an afternoon of minor reflection. Time in the Rock, XCIII. Conrad Aiken. MoVE
Or ever a lick of Art was done. Bygones. Bert Leston Taylor. BOHV; HBMV
Or Ever the Earth Was. Charles Leonard Moore. AA
Or ever the knightly years were gone. To W. A. [*or* When I Was a King in Babylon]. W. E. Henley. Echoes, XXXVII. BLPA; EnLi-2; HBV; OuHeWo; PaPo; PoVP; TreF
"Or from what spring doth your opinion rise." Sir John Davies. *Fr.* Orchestra. UnS
Or His Bestowals There. Alice Meynell. *See* Christ in the Universe.
Or I shall live your epitaph to make. Sonnets, LXXXI. Shakespeare. OAEP; OBSC
Or is it all illusion? Do the years. David P. Berenberg. *Fr.* Two Sonnets. HBMV
Or lookt I back unto the times hence flown. To Master Denham, on His Prospective Poem. Robert Herrick. AnAnS-2
Or love me less [*or* mee lesse] or love me [*or* mee] more. Song. Sidney Godolphin. CavP; MePo; OBS; SeCL; SeEP
Or, Pyrrha, tell me who's the guy. Horace the Wise. Morrie Ryskind. HBMV
Or rushing thence, in one diffusive band. The Sheep-washing. James Thomson. *Fr.* The Seasons: Summer. EnLi-2
Or Scorne, or pittie on me take. The Dreame. Ben Jonson. PoEL-2

Or shall I say, Vain word, false thought. Alteram Partem. Arthur Hugh Clough. PoVP
Or so our cleaning woman tells us. Black Is Beautiful. Townsend T. Brewster. TNV
Or the black centaurs, statuesquely still. Ambuscade. Hugh McCrae. BoAV; PoAu-1
Or to the beach descending, with joined hands. Alfred Domett. *Fr.* Ranolf and Amohia. AnNZ
Or what is closer to the truth. When I Buy Pictures. Marianne Moore. OxBA
Or you, or I, Nature did wronge! *Unknown.* SeCSL
Oracle, The. Coleman Barks. QAH
Oracle, The. A. E. Coppard. FaBoTw
Oracle, The. Arthur Davison Ficke. HBV
Oracle. E. L. Mayo. MiAP
Oracle at Delphi. Robert Bagg. NePoAm-2
Oracle of Delphi, The. Adèle Naudé. BoSA
Oracles, The. A. E. Housman. AnFE; NoP; PoFr; RoGo
Oracular Portcullis, The. James Reaney. ErPo; PeCV
Oral Messages, *sel.* Lawrence Ferlinghetti.
"Dog trots freely in the street, The." ToPo
(Dog.) NoP
Orange, The. Charles *and* Mary Lamb. OTPC (1923 ed.)
Orange air grows fetid with smoke, The. Mess Deck Casualty. Alan Ross. WaP
Orange Bears, The. Kenneth Patchen. NaP
Orange County Plague: Scenes. Laurence Lieberman. CoPo
Orange in the middle of a table. Against Still Life. Margaret Atwood. MoCV
Orange Lilies. James Reaney. WHW
Orange Lily O, The. *Unknown.* IrPN
Orange Tree, The. John Shaw Neilson. BoAV; MoAuPo; NeLNL; PoAu-1
Orange Tree by Day. Sacheverell Sitwell. *Fr.* The Red-gold Rain. AtBAP
(Red-gold Rain, The.) MoBrPo
Orange Tree by Night. Sacheverell Sitwell. *Fr.* The Red-gold Rain. AtBAP
Oranges, The. Abu Dharr, *tr. fr. Arabic by* A. J. Arberry. TTY
Oranges and lemons whirl around. St. Dexter's Fire. Dave Etter. ThO
Oranges at Jaffa gate, The. Gates. Sister Mary Madeleva. GoBC
Oranges in a wooden bowl. Still-Life. Ronald Perry. NePoEA-2
Orara. Henry C. Kendall. BoAu; PoAu-1
Oration, An, *sel.* Kenneth Porter. *Fr.* To the Younger Old-Americans.
"Too long we have cheated our bellies with crumbs of tradition." PoFr
Oration, An, Entitled "Old, Old, Old, Old Andrew Jackson," *abr.* Vachel Lindsay. ATP (1935 ed.) YaD
Orator. Emerson. *Fr.* Quatrains. AnNE; OxBA
Orator, The. Roy McFadden. OnYI
Orator from rhetorick gardens picks, The. Meditation XLIV. Edward Taylor. *Fr.* Preparatory Meditations, Second Series. MAmP
Orators, The, *sel.* W. H. Auden.
O Where Are You Going? LiTB; MoVE; Po; PoIE; UnPo (3d ed.); VaPo
(Epilogue: "'O where are you going?' said reader to rider.") EnLit; FaBoCh; LoGBV; ShBV-3; SiTL
(Five Songs, *sel.*) LiTM (1970 ed.)
(Song.) EnL
Orazione, *sel.* Lorenzo de Medici, *tr. fr. Italian by* William Roscoe.
"One general song of praise arise." SoP
Orb I like is not the one, The. The Quiet Eye. Eliza Cook. VA
Orb Weaver, The. Robert Francis. OA; PPON
Orbits. Richard Le Gallienne. VA
Orchard. Hilda Doolittle ("H. D."). AnFE; APA; AtBAP; CMoP; CoAnAm; CoBA; ExPo; LiTA; LiTM (1970 ed.); MAP; MoAmPo; OxBA
Orchard. Ruth Stone. TwAmPo
Orchard and the Heath, The. George Meredith. OBNC
Orchard at Avignon, An. Agnes Mary Frances Robinson. HBV
Orchard by the Shore, The; a Pastoral. Elinor Sweetman. OBVV
Orchard-Pit, The. Dante Gabriel Rossetti. EnLoPo; NBM; NCEP; PeVV; PoEL-5; SyP
Orchard Song. Sappho, *tr. fr. Greek by* Edwin M. Cox. LiTW
"Orchards," said Johnny Appleseed. Johnny Appleseed. Arthur S. Bourinot. CaP
Orchards, we linger here because. For [*or* Upon] a Second Marriage. James Merrill. HW; NePoEA
Orchestra; or, A Poem of [*or* on] Dancing. Sir John Davies. OBSC; ReIE, *abr.*; SiPS; TuPP
Sels.
Dance of Love, The. ElL; SeCePo
Dancing Sea, The. ChTr
(Sea Danceth, The.) EtS
"Dauncing (bright Lady) then began to bee." AtBAP; FaBoEn; PoEL-2
Dedications, I: To His Very Friend, Master Richard Martin. SiPS
Dedications, II: To the Prince. SiPS
Of Homer's Odyssey. EG
"Or from what spring doth your opinion rise." UnS
"Yet, once again, Antinous did reply." LO
Orchids. Theodore Roethke. NMP; OPoP
Ordeal by Fire, The, *sel.* Edmund Clarence Stedman.
"Thou who dost feel Life's vessel strand." WGRP
Order. *At. to* St. Francis of Assisi. *See* Cantica: Our Lord Christ.
Order and Disorder. Richard Eberhart. PoDB
Order for a Picture, An. Alice Cary. BLPA
Order, The, goes; what if we rush ahead. Next Time. Laura Simmons. PGD
Order is a lovely thing. The Monk in the Kitchen. Anna Hempstead Branch. AnFE; APA; CoAnAm; MAP; MAPA; MoAmPo
Order to View. Louis MacNeice. TDP
Orders. A. M. Klein. WHW
Ordinary, The, *sel.* William Cartwright.
Good Eating Song, A. SeCL
Ordinary Dog, The. Nancy Byrd Turner. TiPo
Ordinary Evening in Cleveland, An. Lewis Turco. NYBP
Ordinary Evening in New Haven, An, *sel.* Wallace Stevens.
"Inescapable romance, inescapable choice." ReMP
Ordinary people are peculiar too. Conversation. Louis MacNeice. FaBoMo
Ordinary People on Sunday. Tom Veitch. ANYP
Ordinary valour only works, The. "F. Anstey." CenHV
Ordinary Women, The. Wallace Stevens. OxBA
Ordination. Sister Mary Immaculate. GoBC
Ore in the crucible is pungent, smelling like acrid wine, The. Iron Wine. Lola Ridge. NP
O're the desert, cross the meadows. Song a-la-Mode. Sir Charles Sedley. PeRV
O're the Smooth Enameld Green. Milton. *See* Song: "O'er the smooth. . ."
Oread. Hilda Doolittle ("H. D."). AP; AWP; CMoP; ExPo; GoJo; InP; JAWP; MAP; MoAmPo; MoVE; NeMA; OxBA; RePo; TSW; WBP
Oregon Message, An. William Stafford. CoAP
Oregon State Song. J. A. Buchanan. PoRL
Oregon Trail, The. William Rose Benét. PaA
Oregon Trail, The. Arthur Guiterman. FaPON; MPB
Oregon Trail, 1851. James Marshall. IHA; PaA; StVeCh
Oregon Winter. Jeanne McGahey. AmFN
O'Reilly's Reply. Richard Weber. NMP
Orestes pointed out what was despotic. Elegy to Sports. David Shapiro. ANYP
Orestes Pursued. Charles David Webb. NePoAm-2
Organ-Grinder, The. Jimmy Garthwaite. BrR
Organ Grinders' Garden, The. Mildred Plew Meigs. GaP; SoPo
Organist, The. George W. Stevens. BLPA
Organist, The. *Unknown.* BLPA
Organist in Heaven, The. Thomas Edward Brown. LoBV (1949 ed.); MuSP; OBVV
(Wesley in Heaven.) OBNC
Orgasm completely, The. Sonnet. Tom Clark. ANYP; CoAP; YAP
Orient Express, The. Randall Jarrell. AmP; AP; CMoP; CoAP; CoBMV; FiMAP
Orient Ode. Francis Thompson. CoBE
Orient Wheat. Adrienne Cecile Rich. NePoEA
Oriental Apologue, An. James Russell Lowell. PoEL-5
Orientale. E. E. Cummings. NP; PG

Oriflamme. Jessie Fauset. BANP
(I Think I See Her.) GoSl
Origin, far side of a lake, The. The Alchemist. Robert Kelly. CoPo
Origin of Baseball, The. Kenneth Patchen. Po
Origin of Centaurs, The. Anthony Hecht. NePoEA
Origin of Didactic Poetry, The. James Russell Lowell. PoEL-5
Origin of Ireland, The. *Unknown.* BOHV
Original./ Ragged-round. Malcolm X. Gwendolyn Brooks. BALP; BP; TTY
Original Cuss, An. Keith Preston. ALV; WhC
Original Lamb, The, *parody.* *Unknown.* BOHV; InMe
Original Love-Story, An. *Unknown.* *See* Old Fashioned Love.
Original Sin. Robinson Jeffers. MoAB; MoAmPo (1950 ed.); MoVE
Original Sin. Alexander Laing. NYBP
Original Sin; a Short Story. Robert Penn Warren. AmP; CrMA; FiMAP; GTBS-W; LiTA; LiTM; MoVE; ReMP
Original something, fair maid, you would win me, An. To a Young Lady, Who Asked Me to Write Something Original for Her Album. Thomas Campbell. StP
Originality. Thomas Bailey Aldrich. AnNE
Origins and Savage Period of Mankind. Lucretius, *tr. fr. Latin by* William Ellery Leonard. *Fr.* Of the Nature of Things (De Rerum Natura). OuHeWo
Origins of Vegetable and Animal Life. Lucretius, *tr. fr. Latin by* William Ellery Leonard. *Fr.* Of the Nature of Things (De Rerum Natura). OuHeWo
(Origins of Life, The.) LiTW
Oriki Erinle. *Unknown,* *tr. fr. Yoruba by* Ulli Beier. PBA; TTY
Orinda to Lucasia. Katherine Philips. LO; SeCL
Orinda to Lucasia Parting, October, 1661, at London. Katherine Philips. OBS
Oriole. Edgar Fawcett. *See* To an Oriole.
Oriole. Marion Mitchell Walker. GFA
Oriole with joy was sweetly singing, The. In the Shade of the Old Apple Tree. Harry H. Williams. TreFT
Orioles ("Orioles shine in blue air") Joseph Langland. WIRo
Orion. Paul Engle. AnAmPo
Orion. Adrienne Rich. NoP
Orion. Charles Tennyson Turner. VA
Orion; an Epic Poem, *sels.* Richard Henry Horne. VA
Akinetos.
Distraught for Meropé.
Eos.
In Forest Depths.
Meeting of Orion and Artemis.
Orion Seeks the Goddess Diana. Sacheverell Sitwell. *Fr.* Landscape with the Giant Orion. MoVE
Orion, tonight forsake your distant walking. Orion. Paul Engle. AnAmPo
Orishas. Larry Neal. NBP
Orisons. Edwin McNeill Poteat. OQP
Orkney Interior. Ian Hamilton Finlay. NMP; OPoP
Orkney Lullaby. Eugene Field. GoTP
Orlando Furioso, *sels.* Ariosto, *tr. fr. Italian.*
Angelica and the Ork, *fr.* X, *tr. by* Sir John Harington. OBSC
Lunar Valley of Lost Things, The, *fr.* XXXIV, *tr. by* Sir John Harington. LiTW
"Of loves and ladies, knights and arms, I sing," *fr.* I, *tr. by* William Stewart Rose. EnLi-1
("Of dames, of knights, of arms, of love's delight," *tr. by* Sir John Harington.) ReIE
"Soone after he a christall streame espying," *fr.* XXXIV, *tr. by* Sir John Harington. SiCE
"Though an ill mind appear in simulation," *fr.* IV, *tr. by* William Stewart Rose. EnLi-1
Orlando's Rhymes. Shakespeare. *Fr.* As You Like It, III, ii. OBSC
(Why Should This a Desert Be.) CTC
Orlo's Valediction. Jon Manchip White. NePoEA
Ornamental Water. Louise Townsend Nicholl. NePoAm
Ornithology in Florida. Arthur Guiterman. InMe
Oro Stage, The. H. H. Knibbs. IHA
Oro, the islandmen. The Waistcoat. Padraic Fallon. OxBI
O'Rourk's Frolic. Hugh MacGowran. *See* Description of an Irish Feast, The.
Orphan, The, *sel.* Thomas Otway.
Come All Ye Youths. OAEP
Orphan, The. *Unknown,* *tr. fr. Irish by* Frank O'Connor. KiLC
Orphan Born. Robert J. Burdette. BOHV
Orphan Boy's Tale, The. Amelia Opie. PaPo
Orphan Girl, The ("No home, no home"). *Unknown.* AS
(Coal Miner's Child, The, *diff. vers., with music.*) OuSiCo
(Mag's Song, *diff. vers., with music.*) AS
"Orphan Hours, the Year is dead." Dirge for the Year. Shelley. DD; GN; HBV; HBVY
Orphans. Randy Rhody. WOW
Orphan's Song, The. Sydney Dobell. CH; ELP; GTBS-D; OBNC; OTPC; PPL
Orpheus. *At. to* John Fletcher, *See* Orpheus with His Lute. *also to* Shakespeare.
Orpheus. J. F. Hendry. NeBP
Orpheus. E. W. Mandel. Minotaur Poems, VI. OBCV
Orpheus. Elizabeth Madox Roberts. MAP; MoAmPo
Orpheus. W. D. Snodgrass. CABA; ToPo
Orpheus. Yvor Winters. MoVE
Orpheus and Eurydice. Robert Browning. *See* Eurydice to Orpheus.
Orpheus and Eurydice. Geoffrey Hill. NePoEA-2; PoIE
Orpheus calling. The grass parts, the seas. Wedding Song. Nancy Willard. ThO
Orpheus' Dream. Edwin Muir. SiSw
Orpheus in Greenwich Village. Jack Gilbert. PP
Orpheus in the Underworld. David Gascoyne. FaBoTw
Orpheus, O Orpheus, gently touch thy Lesbyan lyre. *Unknown.* SeCSL
Orpheus was a sadist. Spring. Allen Van Newkirk. YAP
Orpheus with His Lute. *At. to* John Fletcher, *also to* Shakespeare. King Henry VIII, *fr.* III, i. CBEP; EnRePo; GN; OAEP; TrGrPo; ViBoPo
(Music.) FaBoCh; LoGBV
(Orpheus.) ElL; OBEV; OTPC; PoRL; UnS
("Orpheus with his lute made trees.") AtBAP; ChTr; SiCE; TuPP
(Song: "Orpheus with his lute made trees.") OBS; PoEL-2
Orphic Interior. Leonardo Sinisgalli, *tr. fr. Italian by* Creighton Gilbert. LiTW
Orra, *sel.* Joanna Baillie.
Outlaw's Song, The, *fr.* III. OBEV; OTPC (1923 ed.); PoFr
(Song of the Outlaws.) OBRV
Orsames' Song. Sir John Suckling. *See* Why So Pale and Wan?
Orson of the Muse, An. George Meredith. EPN
Orthodox. Mark Guy Pearse. MaRV
Orthodox, orthodox, wha believe in John Knox. The Kirk's Alarm. Burns. OxBoLi
Ortiz. Hezekiah Butterworth. PAH
Ortus. Ezra Pound. LiTA; NePA; NP
Ortus Novus Urbe Britannus. Henry Parrot. TuPP
Ortygia. Jessie Mackay. BoAu
O'Ryan was a man of might. Irish Astronomy. Charles G. Halpine. HBV
Oscar. Bill Berkson. ANYP
Oscar was a radish. Vegetable Fantasies. Helen Hoyt. RIS
Oscar Wilde. *At. to* Swinburne. PeVV; SiTL
Osculation. Henry Sydnor Harrison. InMe
Osmund Toulmin. Sir Osbert Sitwell. AtBAP
Osorio. Samuel Taylor Coleridge. *See* Remorse.
Osprey sails about the sound, The. The Fisherman's Hymn. Alexander Wilson. AA; EtS
Ossawatomie. Carl Sandburg. CMoP; OxBA; PFY
Ossian. Joseph Payne Brennan. FiSC
Ossian, *sel.* John Francis O'Donnell.
"Spoke my heart in the dearth of the night." IrPN
Ossian's Address to the Sun. James MacPherson. *Fr.* Carthon. BEL
Ossian's Serenade. Calder Campbell. BLPA; NeHB
(Burman Lover, The, *with music.*) TrAS
Ostella, *sel.* John Tatham.
Seeing a Lady. SeCL
("Oh, she is fair: fair as the eastern morn.") LO
Ostia Antica. Anthony Hecht. NePA
Ostler, The. Hyam Plutzik. Horatio, II. FiMAP
'Ostler Joe. George R. Sims. BeLS; BLPA; HBV; TreF
Ostracized as we are with God. Apology of Genius. Mina Loy. QFR
Ostrava. Petr Bezruc, *tr. fr. Czech by* David Daiches. LiTW

Ostrich Is a Silly Bird, The. Mary E. Wilkins Freeman. FaPON; LBN; OTPC (1946 ed.); SoPo; TiPo (1959 ed.); WaKn
Ostriches & Grandmothers! LeRoi Jones. NeAP
Oterborne, *sel.* *Unknown.*
Yt fell abowght the Lamasse tyde. OxBS
Othello, *sels.* Shakespeare.
"And let the canakin clink, [clink]," *fr.* II, iii. LiBL
Death of Othello, V, ii. FiP
("I pray you, in your letters,") InP.
(Othello's Farewell.) TreFS
Desdemona's Song, *fr.* IV, iii. LoBV
"Dost thou in conscience think—tell me, Emilia," *fr.* IV, iii. MyFE
Good Name, A, *fr.* III, iii. FaFP; OTPC (1946 ed.); TreFS
("Good name in man and woman, dear my lord.") OTD; YAT
"I have laied these sheetes you bad me on the bed. *fr.* IV.iii. AtBAP
"It is the cause, it is the cause, my soule, *fr.* V,ii. AtBAP; MemP
(Othello and Desdemona.) BoC; FiP
"It is the very error of the moon," *fr.* V, ii. MyFE
Not Poppy, nor Mandragora, *fr.* III, iii. WHA
Othello's Defense, *fr.* I, iii. TreF
Othello's Farewell to his Career, *fr.* III, iii. TreFT
(Farewell Content.) TrGrPo
"Perdition catch my soul," *br. sel. fr.* III, iii. LO
"What did thy song boad Lady?" *fr.* V, ii. AtBAP
Othello Jones Dresses for Dinner. Ed Roberson. PoNe (1970 ed.)
Othello: Tomcat. Laura Simmons. CIV
Other. *See also* T'other.
Other, An ("The purest soule that e're was sent"). Thomas Carew. AnAnS-2; SeCV-1; SeEP
Other, An ("This little vault, this narrow room"). Thomas Carew. *See* Epitaph, An: "This little vault, this narrow room."
Other beauties others move. The Effect of Love. Thomas Campion. MeWo
Other Children. Helen Wing. GFA; OTPC (1946 ed.)
Other day a partridge, The. The Talk of the Town. Ed Fisher. FiBHP
Other day I went upstairs, The. Elizabeth Ann Peabody. Ivy O. Eastwick. BrR
Other day to my surprise, The. The Beetle. Edith King. GFA
Other day, when I looked at a tree, The. Roots. Louis Ginsberg. TrJP
Other Fellow's Job, The. Strickland W. Gillilan. WBLP
Other Garden, The. John Gill. ThO
Other Journey, The. Katherine Garrison Chapin. MoVE
Other Little Boats, The. Edward Shanks. FOL
Other loves may sink and settle. The Strange Music. G. K. Chesterton. OtMeF
Other Man, The, *sel.* Kipling.
"When the earth was sick and the skies were grey." PoG
Other Mother, The. F. M. Roger. SoP
Other One, The. Harry Thurston Peck. AA
Other night before the storm, The. The Storm. Richard *and* Louis Untermeyer. RIS
Other Person's Place, The. Donald H. Hover. STF
Other ranchers came this morning, The. Day of the Wolf. Keith Wilson. WIRo
Other Sheep I Have, Which Are Not of This Fold. Bryant. TrPWD
(Prayer to Make Your Own, A.) SoP, 4 *sts*
Other Shore, The, *with music.* *Unknown.* ABF
Other Side of a Mirror, The. Mary Elizabeth Coleridge. CBEP
Other Side of the Sky, The. W. Graham Robertson. PPL
Other slow arts entirely keep the brain. Love's Harmony. Shakespeare. *Fr.* Love's Labour's Lost, IV, iii. CLwM
Other World, The. Harriet Beecher Stowe. AA; HBV; WGRP
Other World, The. *Unknown.* *tr. fr. Egyptian by* Robert Hillyer. *Fr.* Book of the Dead. AWP; JAWP; WBP
Othere, the old sea-captain. The Discoverer of the North Cape. Longfellow. AnNE; AtBAP; ShBV-1; StVeCh (1940 ed.)
Others. Harry Behn. SoPo; TiPo (1959 ed.)
Others. Charles D. Meigs. MaRV; OQP; SoP; WBLP
Others, The. "Seumas O'Sullivan." AnIV; GBV; HBMV; NP; OxBI
Others. *Unknown.* STF
Others abide our question. Thou art free. Shakespeare. Matthew Arnold. AnFE; ATP; BEL; BoLiVe; BoPe; CABA; CaFP; CBEP; CLwM; CoBE; EnLi-2; EnLit; EPN; FiP; GTBS; GTSE; GTSL; HBV; InP; InvP; MaVP; MBW-2; NoP; OAEP; OBEV; OBVV; OnPP; OTPC (1923 ed.); OuHeWo; PoIE; PoPo; PoRL; PoVP; Sonn; TOP; TrGrPo; ViBoPo; ViPo; ViPP; VP; WHA
Others always skip over the word. In Praise of BIC Pens. David Hilton. QAH
Others because you did not keep. A Deep-Sworn Vow. W. B. Yeats. CMoP; ELU; PoPo; ReMP; UnPo
Others endure man's rule: he therefore deems. The Unconquered Air. Florence Earle Coates. PoMa
Others have seen men die. On Knowing Nothing. A. J. M. Smith. PeCV (1967 ed.)
Others, I Am Not the First. A. E. Housman. A Shropshire Lad, XXX. CMoP; LiTB; MoBrPo; NAMP; PoVP
Others make verses of grace. Ardor. Gamaliel Bradford. HBMV
Others may need new life in Heaven. Speculative. Robert Browning. EPN; PoVP
Others May Praise What They Like. Walt Whitman. Par
. . .Others more mild,/ Retreated in a silent valley, sing. Milton. *Fr.* Paradise Lost, II. MyFE
Others taunt me with having knelt at well-curbs. For Once, Then, Something. Robert Frost. AnFE; AP; BWP; CoAnAm; ForPo; PoFS
Others weary of the noise. Mothers—and Others. Amos R. Wells. SoP; WBLP
Otherwhere. Frances Angevine Gray. FiSC
Otherwise. Aileen Fisher. SoPo; SUS
Ottawa. Duncan Campbell Scott. VA
Otter, An. Ted Hughes. BoC; NePoEA-2; NMP; OPoP
Otters. Padraic Colum. *See* River-Mates.
Otto. Gwendolyn Brooks. PDV
Otto. Theodore Roethke. PoeP; ToPo
O'Tuomy's Drinking Song. John O'Tuomy, *tr. fr. Modern Irish by* John O'Daly, *vers. by* James Clarence Mangan. OnYI
Otys, begin. Sea Eclogue. William Diaper. *Fr.* Nereides; or, Sea-Eclogues. LoBV
Ou Phrontis. Charles Causley. AtBAP; NePoEA
Ou Som Sourroucou, *with music.* *Unknown.* *tr. fr. French.* ABF
Oubit, The. Charles Kingsley. BOHV; PoVP
O-u-g-h. Charles B. Loomis. BOHV
Oui, oui, Monsieur, Timagami. Pierre of Timagami in New York. Wilson Macdonald. WhC
Oul' Grey Mare, The. *Unknown.* AnIV
Ould Doctor Mack. Alfred Perceval Graves. BOHV
Ould Orange Flute, The. *Unknown.* *See* Old Orange Flute, The.
Ould Plaid Shawl, The. Francis A. Fahy. HBV; JKCP (1926 ed.)
Ounce code orange. Clark Coolidge. ANYP
Ouphe and goblin! imp and sprite! Elfin Song. Joseph Rodman Drake. *Fr.* The Culprit Fay. AA; PoMS
Our admiral gave orders on the same day. Kelly the Pirate (C *vers.*). *Unknown.* BSNS
Our age bereft of nobility. A Poem for Painters. John Wieners. NeAP
Our anchors drag and our cables surge. The Cheer of the *Trenton.* Walter Mitchell. EtS
Our Andy's gone with cattle now. Andy's Gone with Cattle. Henry Lawson. PoAu-1
Our author by experience finds it true. Prologue to "Aureng-Zebe." Dryden. ATP; BWP; CBEP; CEP; EiCL; EiPP; FiP; MBW-1; OBS; OxBoLi; PP; SeCeV; SeCV-2; SeEP; SiTL
Our Baby's Rabbits. *Unknown.* SAS
Our backyards touched somewhere upon the hill. Neighbors. Marilyn Francis. GoYe
Our Ball. Winthrop Mackworth Praed. *Fr.* Letters from Teignmouth. EnRP
Our balloon man has balloons. The Balloon Man. Dorothy Aldis. TiPo
Our band is few but true and tried. Song of Marion's Men.

Our (continued)
Bryant. AmePo; AnNE; CoBA; DD; HBV; HBVY; MC; PAH; PAP; ThLM; TreF
Our bark is on the waters: wide around. "Pater Vester Pascit Illa." Robert Stephen Hawker. CAW; CoBE; VA
Our bark was [out] far, far from [the] land. The Sailor's Grave. *Unknown, at. to* Eliza Cook. BLPA; ShS; SoAmSa
Our barn roof has three lovely holes. Three Lovely Holes. Winifred Welles. StVeCh
Our Beautiful West Coast Thing. Richard Brautigan. FRC
Our Bias. W. H. Auden. AtBAP; CMoP; NoP
Our Birth Is but a Sleep and a Forgetting. Wordsworth. *Fr.* Ode: Intimations of Immortality from Recollections of Early Childhood. BiCB; ChTr; EaLo; FaBoEn; FaBV; MemP; OQP; PoG; PoSa; TRV; WGRP
Our Birthday. Marion Edey. BiCB; SiSoSe
Our Blessed Lady's Lullaby. Richard Verstegan. *See* Lullaby: "Upon my lap. . ."
Our blest Redeemer, ere He breathed. The Holy Spirit. Harriet Auber. MaRV
Our Blood and State. James Shirley. *See* Glories of Our Blood and State.
Our Bodies. Denise Levertov. NaP
Our bodies were sunlit spattered. The Serpent of God. Cerise Farallon. UnTE
Our Bonny-boots Could Toot It, Yea and Foot It. *Unknown.* NCEP
Our brains ache, in the merciless iced east winds that knive us. Exposure. Wilfrid Owen. BoPe; FaBoMo; LiTM (rev. ed.); MMA; MoVE; OnHM; WaP
Our Brother Christ. Ozora Stearns Davis. *See* We Bear the Strain of Earthly Care.
Our brother Clarence goes to school. Big Brother. Elizabeth Madox Roberts. FaPON; GaP; MPB
Our Brother Is Born. Eleanor Farjeon. *See* Now Every Child.
Our brother says that Will was born. Dick and Will. Elizabeth Madox Roberts. BiCB
Our brows are wreathed with spindrift and the weed is on our knees. The Coastwise Lights. Kipling. EtS
Our bugles sang truce—for the night-cloud had lowered. The Soldier's Dream. Thomas Campbell. BeLS; EnRP; FaPL; GTBS; GTBS-D; GTBS-P; GTBS-W; GTSE; GTSL; HBV; MCCG; RoGo; TreFS
Our Burden Bearer. Phillips Brooks. FaChP; MaRV; SoP; TRV
(Helper, The.) SoP
(Unfalling One, The.) BLRP
Our Calvary. Constance Holm. OQP
Our campfires shone bright on the mountains. Sherman's March to the Sea [*or* Song of Sherman's. . .]. Samuel H. M. Byers. BFSS; DD; HBV; MC; OTPC; PAH; PAP
Our Canoe Idles in the Idling Current. Kenneth Rexroth. ErPo
Our Casuarina Tree. Toru Dutt. ACV; VA
Our Cat. Janet Vaughn. PCD
Our Cause. William James Linton. VA
Our caves do not go Boom! and make one nervy. Sterkfontein. Ruth Miller. PeSA
Our Children's Children Will Marvel. Ilya Ehrenburg, *tr. fr. Russian by* Jeannette Eyre. WaaP
Our Christ. Harry Webb Farrington. BePJ; MaRV; OQP; SoP; STF; TRV
Our Christ. Lucy Larcom. MaRV; OQP; StJW
Our Christmas pudding was made in November. Pudding Charms. Charlotte Druitt Cole. BoTP
Our Circus. Laura Lee Randall. GFA; TiPo (1952 ed.); UTS
Our city's sons and daughters. School Days in New Amsterdam. Arthur Guiterman. FaPON
Our Clock. Florence Eakman. SiSoSe
Our Colonel. Arthur Guiterman. DD; HH; PoRL
Our Companie in the Next World. John Donne. *Fr.* Of the Progresse of the Soule. OBS
Our Country. Julia Ward Howe. DD; MC; PaA; PAH; PAL
Our Country. Siegfried A. Mahlman. *See* God Bless Our Native Land.
Our Country. Anna Louise Strong. MaRV; OQP
Our Country hath a gospel of her own. America's Gospel. James Russell Lowell. MaRV; PGD
Our Country's Call. Bryant. AnNE; MC; PaA; PAH
Our Country's Emblem. *Unknown.* WBLP
Our courage is an old legend. The Defeated; for Wales. Alun Lewis. PrWP
Our crosses are hewn from different trees. Golgotha. Frederic L. Knowles. OQP
Our Daily Bread. Maltbie D. Babcock. *See* "Give Us This Day Our Daily Bread."
Our Daily Bread. Adelaide Anne Procter. JKCP
Our darkness stays, the only dark we know. Degrees of Shade. H. A. Pinkerton. NePoAm
Our Dead. Edwin Markham. OQP
(Epitaph, An: "Let us not think of our departed dead.") MaRV
Our Dead. Robert Nichols. WGRP
Our Dead Heroes. Rose Terry Cooke. HH
Our Dead, Overseas. Edwin Markham. DD; MC
Our death implicit in our birth. The Paradox. Ruth Pitter. MaRV
Our Delaware. George B. Hynson. PoRL
Our Dim Eyes Seek a Beacon. *Unknown.* OQP
Our Dinah is a Persian cat. Dinah. Norman Gale. OTPC (1946 ed.)
Our doctor had called in another. In the Children's Hospital. Tennyson. HBV; PoVP
Our Dog. Janet Vaughn. PCD
Our doom is in our being. We began. Sonnets, II. James Agee. MAP; MoAmPo
Our door was shut to the noon-day heat. Cézanne. Alfred Kreymborg. NP
Our doubts are traitors. Doubts. Shakespeare. *Fr.* Measure for Measure, I, iv. MaRV
Our earthly homes are simple things. Home. Martha Snell Nicholson. STF
Our Echoes Roll from Soul to Soul. Tennyson. *See* Bugle Song, The.
Our Enemies Have Fallen. Tennyson. *Fr.* The Princess, Pt. VI. PoVP
Our England's heart is sound as oak. Heart and Will. William James Linton. VA
Our English critics their dull wits keep straining. On Taine. Alfred Ainger. ALV
Our English gamesters scorne to stake. Roger Williams. SCAP
Our epoch takes a voluptuous satisfaction. Hypocrite Auteur. Archibald Macleish. AmPP (5th ed.); MoVE; NePA
Our Ever-present Guide. *Unknown.* BePJ
Our eyeless bark sails free. The Earth. Emerson. AA
Our eyes are holden that we do not see. Faith and Sight. Anna M. King. BLRP
Our eyes have viewed the burnished vineyards. Letter to a Friend. Robert Penn Warren. MAP; MoAmPo
Our fairest garland, made of Beauty's flowers. Contention between Four Maids Concerning That Which Addeth Most Perfection to That Sex. Sir John Davies. SiPS
Our faith is in the Christ who walks. Thomas Curtis Clark. *Fr.* The Faith of Christ's Freemen. ChIP
Our faith is not in dead saints' bones. The Faith of Christ's Freemen. Thomas Curtis Clark. OQP
Our families in Thine Arms enfold. In Thine Arms. Oliver Wendell Holmes. TRV
Our Father. Ray Mathew. FIW
Our Father. Roberta Teale Swartz. MoRP
Our father/ married for good. For My Sister, Contemplating Divorce. Marvin Bell. TDP
Our Father, grant us to lie down in peace. Evening Prayer. *Unknown.* TrJP
Our Father in heaven hallowed be Thy name. The Poem of the Our Father. St. Matthew, Bible, *N.T.* CAW
Our Father Land! and wouldst thou know. Father Land and Mother Tongue. Samuel Lover. HBV
Our Father our all-wielding is. The "Pater Noster." *Unknown.* ACP; CAW
Our Father, Our King. *Unknown.* *tr. fr. Hebrew.* TrJP
Our Father which [*or* who] art in heaven. The Lord's Prayer. St. Matthew, Bible. *N.T.* EaLo;MaRV;PoLF;TrGrPo;TRV
Our Father, whose creative Will. W. H. Auden. *Fr.* For the Time Being. TrPWD
Our Fathers. Ecclesiasticus, Bible, Apocrypha. *See* Let Us Now Praise Famous Men.
Our fathers all were poor. The Fathers. Edwin Muir. **OxBS**

Our fathers came to search for gold. Australia's on the Wallaby. *Unknown.* PoAu-1
Our fathers did but use the world before. Thomas Bastard. SiCE
Our Father's Door. Oliver Wendell Holmes. *Fr.* The Professor at the Breakfast Table. OQP
Our fathers fought for Liberty. Fourth of July Ode. James Russell Lowell. HH; PAL, 4 sts.; PoRL; TSW
Our father's God! from out whose hand. Centennial Hymn. Whittier. AA; MC; PaA; PAH; PAL; TOP
Our Father's Hand. Anne Johnson Flint. BLRP
Our fathers in their books and speech. Orient Wheat. Adrienne Cecile Rich. NePoEA
Our fathers to creed and tradition were tied. Commercial Candour. G. K. Chesterton. ALV; WhC
Our fathers to their graves have gone. The New Challenge. Whittier. *Fr.* The Moral Warfare. MaRV; TreFT
Our fathers were fellows of substance and weight. Commissary Report. Stoddard King. ALV; ShM
Our Father's World. Margaret E. Sangster. MaRV
Our fathers wrung their bread from stocks and stones. Children of Light. Robert Lowell. AP; CBV; CMoP; FiMAP; MoAB; OxBA; PoAn; PoPl; ToPo
Our feet have wandered from Thy path. Wanderers. Thomas Curtis Clark. ChIP; OQP; TrPWD
Our first ancestor (Abram) alone received his religion from Heaven. Therefore We Preserve Life. Shen Ch'üan. TrJP
Our First Century. George Woodberry. AmePo; PAH
Our Flag. Frances Crosby Hamlet. PGD
Our Flag. Mary H. Howliston. GFA
Our Flag. Margaret E. Sangster. PEDC
Our Flag Forever. Frank L. Stanton. *See* Old Flag Forever, The.
Our flesh was a battle-ground. The Litany of the Dark [*or* Black] People. Countee Cullen. EaLo; MaRV; MoRP; StJW; TrPWD
Our floods' queen Thames for ships and swans is crowned. Idea, XXXII. Michael Drayton. NoP; SiCE; TuPP
Our forty-gun frigate from Baltimore came. Paul Jones. *Unknown.* BaBo
Our Friend the Egg. Clarence Day. BOHV
Our Friends Go with Us. Oliver St. John Gogarty. *See* Non Dolet.
Our friendship, Robert, firm through twenty years. A Letter to Robert Frost. Robert Hillyer. MoAmPo
Our gaieties, our luxuries. Arthur Hugh Clough. *Fr.* Dipsychus, Pt. II, so. ii. EPN
Our Garden. Philip Dow. QAH
Our garden's very near the trains. Trains. Hope Shepherd. BoTP
Our God and Father surely knows. The Father Knows. "F. L. H." BLRP
Our God and God of our fathers. Prayer for Dew. Eleazar ben Kalir. TrJP
Our God Finds Us. Francis Thompson. *Fr.* The Hound of Heaven. BoC
("Now of that long pursuit.") FaChP
Our God, Our help in Ages Past. Isaac Watts. *See* O God, Our Help in Ages Past.
Our good King Charles within his youthful prime. The Royal Love Scene. Ernest Dowson. UnTE
Our Goodman. *Unknown.* BaBo; EnLi-1; ESPB (A *and* B *vers.*); ViBoFo (A *and* B *vers.*); UnTE
(Three Nights Drunk, *diff. vers., with music.*) OuSiCo
Our Guiding Light. S. F. Logsdon. SoP
Our happiest earthly comradeships hold a foretaste. Robert Bridges. *Fr.* The Testament of Beauty, IV. MaRV
Our Happy Home. *Unknown* ThGo
Our Hasty Life. *Unknown.* TuPP
Our hearth has been lighted! First Grandchild. M. Whitcomb Hess. JKCP (1955 ed.)
Our hearths are gone out, and our hearts are broken. The Raven Days. Sidney Lanier. AmePo; CBEP; NePA; OxBA
Our hearts beat quicker, we lift our voices. The Dawn. Robert Buchanan. GTSE
Our hearts go by green-cliffed Kinsale. The Island. Christopher Morley. HT
Our Heavenly Father, *sel.* Frederick William Faber.
"My God! how wonderful Thou art." GoBC; TrPWD
Our Help. Psalms, CXXIV; 8, Bible, *O.T.* TRV
Our Heritage. Joseph Mary Plunkett. *See* This Heritage to the Race of Kings.
Our Heritage. Jesse Stuart. AmFN
Our Heroes. Phoebe Cary. BLPA
Our Heroic Times, *sel.* George Henry Boker.
Lincoln. DD; GA; MC; OHIP
Our Hired Girl. James Whitcomb Riley. HBV; HBVY; OTPC
Our Hired Man (and His Daughter, Too). Monica Shannon. FaPON
Our History. Catherine Cate Coblentz. BrR; FaPON
Our history is grave noble and tragic. Men. Archibald Macleish. AmFN; MoAB; NP; YaD
Our history sings of centuries. Our History. Catherine Cate Coblentz. BrR; FaPON
Our Home. Phyllis C. Michael. SoP
Our homes are eaten out by time. The Town Betrayed. Edwin Muir. CMoP
Our Honored Heroes, *sel.* Samuel F. Smith.
Memorial Day. OQP
Our horse fell down the well around behind the stable. Good-by Liza Jane. *Unknown.* AS
Our Hoste sey wel that the brighte sonne. Introduction to the Man of Law's Prologue. Chaucer. *Fr.* The Canterbury Tales. FiP
Our House. Nellie Burget Miller. GFA
Our House. Dorothy Brown Thompson. BrR
Our house had wings for children, chandeliers. The Exile. Larry Rubin. GoYe
Our Hunting Fathers Told the Story. W. H. Auden. PoE
Our Hymn. Oliver Wendell Holmes. BOHV
Our images withdraw, the rose returns. Beyond Possession. Elizabeth Jennings. BoC; NePoEA
Our indolence was despair. We were still at times struck. An Interlude. John Peale Bishop. LiTA
Our Insufficiency to Praise God Suitably for His Mercy. Edward Taylor. *Fr.* God's Determinations. LiTA
Our Jack's Come Home Today, *with music.* *Unknown.* ShS
Our journey had advanced. Emily Dickinson. AtBAP; LiTA; LiTM (rev. ed.); MoAB; PoEL-5; QFR
Our Joyful Feast. George Wither. *See* Christmas Carol, A: "So now is come our joyful'st feast."
Our keels are furred with tropic weed that clogs the crawling tides. The Captive Ships at Manila. Dorothy Paul. PAH
Our king has wrote a lang letter. Lord Derwentwater. *Unknown.* BaBo; ESPB
Our king he has a secret to tell. The Bonny Lass of Anglesey. *Unknown.* ESPB
Our king he kept a false steward. Sir Aldingar. *Unknown.* BaBo (A *vers.*); ESPB; OBB; OxBB
Our king lay at Westminster. Hugh Spencer's Feats in France. *Unknown.* ESPB
Our King went up upon a hill high. Henry before Agincourt: October 25,1415. John Lydgate. CH
Our kites seem. The Two Kites. James Reaney. TwCaPo
Our Known Unknown. Robert Browning. *Fr.* The Ring and the Book. OQP
Our Lady. Robert Bridges. ISi
Our Lady. Mary Elizabeth Coleridge. CAW; OBEV (new ed.); OBMV; OBVV; TOP
Our Lady, Help of Christians. Paul Claudel, *tr. fr. French by* Sister Mary David. ISi
Our Lady in the Middle Ages. Frederick William Faber. ACP; CAW; ISi
Our Lady is my fear. Family Portrait. Leonard Feeney. ISi
Our Lady of France. Lionel Johnson. ISi
Our Lady of Good Voyage. Lucy A. K. Adee. ISi
Our Lady of Mercy. Sister Mary Bertrand. ISi
Our Lady of the Apocalypse. Sister Mary Bertrand. JKCP (1955 ed.)
Our Lady of the Libraries. Sister Mary Ignatius. ISi
Our Lady of the May. Lionel Johnson. ISi
Our Lady of the Passion. John Mauropus, *tr. fr. Greek by* Elizabeth Barrett Browning. ISi
Our Lady of the Refugees. Sister Mary Maura. ISi
Our Lady of the Rocks. Dante Gabriel Rossetti. *See* For "Our Lady of the Rocks."
Our Lady of the Rosary. Francis A. Gaffney. JKCP
Our Lady of the Sea. Alfred Noyes. OBVV

Our Lady of the Skies. James M. Hayes. ISi
Our Lady of the Snows. Lionel Johnson. JKCP
Our Lady of the Snows. Kipling. ACV
Our Lady of the Snows, *sel.* Robert Louis Stevenson.
O to Be Up and Doing. SoP; TreFT, *diff. vers.*; TRV
Our Lady of the Waves. George Mackay Brown. NePoEA-2
Our Lady on Calvary. Sister Michael Marie. ISi
Our Lady Peace. Mark Van Doren. WaP
Our Lady smiles on youthful nuns. Old Nuns. James M. Hayes. JKCP
Our Lady walks the desolated lands. Mater Misericordiae. Sister St. Miriam of the Temple. JKCP (1955 ed.)
Our Lady walks the parapets of heaven. Our Lady of Mercy. Sister Mary Bertrand. ISi
Our Lady went forth pondering. The Annunciation. *Unknown, tr. fr. German.* ISi
Our Lady went into a strange country. Regina Angelorum. G. K. Chesterton. ISi
Our Lady with Two Angels. Wilfred Rowland Childe. ISi
Our Lady's Assumption. Sister Agnes. JKCP (1955 ed.)
Our Lady's Death. Benjamin Dionysius Hill. JKCP
Our Lady's Expectation, *sel.* Frederick William Faber.
Expectation, The. ACP
Our Lady's Labor. John Duffy. ISi
Our Lady's Lullaby. Richard Verstegan. *See* Lullaby: "Upon my lap. . ."
Our Lady's Salutation. Robert Southwell. *See* Virgins Salutation, The.
Our Lady's Song. *Unknown.* OBEV (new ed.)
(Cradle Song of the Virgin.) ISi
(Jesu, Swetë Sonë Derë.) EnL
(Virgin's Song, The.) AtBAP
Our Largest and Smallest Cities. Nettie Rhodes. OCS
Our Left. Francis Orrery Ticknor. MC; PAH
Our life is but a summer's day. A Churchyard in Wales. *Unknown.* SiTL; WhC
Our Life is Hid with Christ in God. George Herbert. MaMe
Our life is likest a long sea-voyage. The Christ. Cynewulf. EnLi-1
Our life is twofold: sleep hath its own world. The Dream. Byron. BeLS; CABL; ChER; ERoP-2
Our Light Afflictions. *Unknown.* BLRP
Our Lips and Ears. *Unknown.* BLPA; NeHB; TreF; WBLP
(Rhymes to Remember.) StaSt
"Our little babe," each said, "shall be." The Wonder Child. Richard Le Gallienne. VA
Our little bird in his full day of health. The Vacant Cage. Charles Tennyson Turner. VA
Our Little Calf. Dorothy Aldis. TiPo (1959 ed.)
Our Little Cowgirl. *Unknown.* SCC
Our little kinsmen after rain. Emily Dickinson. FaPON; ImOP
Our Little Life. Shakespeare. *See* Our Revels Now Are Ended.
Our little systems have their day. Tennyson. *Fr.* In Memoriam A. H. H., Proem. TRV
Our lives are not renewable, yet we seek extinctions. High Summer. Jascha Kessler. AmPC
Our lives are Swiss. Emily Dickinson. AP; MWA-2
Our lives float on quiet waters. Quiet Waters. Blanche Shoemaker Wagstaff. BLPA
Our Lombard country-girls along the coast. A Last Confession. Dante Gabriel Rossetti. NCEP; ViPP
Our Lord and Our Lady. Hilaire Belloc. GoBC; HBMV; ISi; JKCP; WHL
Our Lord in His Circumcision to His Father. Richard Crashaw. MaMe
Our lords are to the mountains gane. Hughie Graham. *Unknown.* OxBB
Our Love Shall Be the Brightness. James Wreford Watson. CaP
Our Love Was a Grim Citadel. R. A. K. Mason. AnNZ
Our love was conceived in silence and must live silently. At the Dark Hour. Paul Dehn. WaP
Our love was like most other loves. The Belle of the Ball-Roon. Winthrop Mackworth Praed. ViBoPo
Our Madonna at Home. Rafael Pombo. CAW
Our many years are made of clay and cloud. Destiny. Harrison Smith Morris. AA
Our March. Vladimir Mayakovsky. *tr. fr. Russian by* Babette Deutsch *and* Avrahm Yarmolinsky. AWP; PoFr
Our Martyr-Chief. James Russell Lowell. *See* Abraham Lincoln.
Our Master. Whittier. BLRP; StJW; TRV; WBLP
Sels.
"Immortal Love, forever full," *sts.* 1-16, *abr.* MaRV; SoP; WGRP
"We may not climb the heavenly steeps," *sts.* 5-16, *abr.* BePJ; ChIP; OQP
Our Master lies asleep and is at rest. Mary Magdalene and the Other Mary. Christina Rossetti. StJW
Our Master toiled a carpenter. Song of Christian Workingmen. Thomas Curtis Clark. OQP
Our masters of satire are vigorous gents. Wasted Ammunition. Stoddard King. InMe
Our millions rose in arms, one fateful day. Armistice Day Vow. Dorothy Gould. PGD
Our Missionaries. Margaret E. Sangster. MaRV
Our Mr. Toad. David McCord. TiPo (1959 ed.)
Our Modest Doughboys. Charlton Andrews. PAH
Our Mother. George Cooper. BoTP; HH; OHIP; OTPC; PPL
(Mother.) PCH
(Only One.) AA
(Only One Mother.) FaPON; MPB; OTD; SiSoSe
Our Mother. *Unknown.* PEDC
Our Mother, loved of all thy sons. Sea and Shore. Harry Lyman Koopman. AA
Our mother sang tunes. Our Mother's Tunes. Eleanor Farjeon. MPB
Our mother, the pride of us all. Mugford's Victory. John White Chadwick. PAH
Our Mother Tongue. Richard Monckton Milnes. GN; OTPC
(Envoy to an American Lady, An.) VA
Our mother, while she turned her wheel. Mother. Whittier. *Fr.* Snow-bound. AA; OHIP; PFY
Our Mothers. *Unknown.* OQP
Our Mother's Tunes. Eleanor Farjeon. MPB
Our motors pierce the clouds. They penetrate. These Times. Gertrude Ryder Bennett. MaRV; OQP
Our moulting days are in their twilight stage. Garnishing the Aviary. Margaret Danner. Far from Africa: Four Poems, 1. AmNP; BP; NNP
Our Movement. Paul Eluard, *tr. fr. French by* Stephen Spender *and* Frances Cornford. LiTW
Our Nation Forever. Wallace Bruce. OHIP; PEDC
Our National Banner. Dexter Smith. PAH
Our Nation's birth gave history your name. Washington. John A. Prentice. OHIP
Our nation's movies, foolish, false, erotic. Essay in Defense of the Movies. Walker Gibson. NePoAm
Our Native Birds. Nathan Haskell Dole. BOHV
Our native cactus closes. Good Night. Bernard Isaac Durward. JKCP (1926 ed.)
Our Native Land. Kalakaua, King of the Hawaiian Islands, *tr. fr. Hawaiian by* Henry L. Sheldon. PoRL
Our Native Land. Siegfried A. Mahlmann *and* William E. Hickson. *See* God Bless Our Native Land!
Our neighbor, Mrs. Waters' only son. Casualty. Edwin McNeill Poteat. MaRV
Our neighbor's dog ate. The Man in the Ocelot Suit. Christopher Brookhouse. CAD
Our night repast was ended: quietness. Youth and Age. William Bell Scott. VA
Our nuns come out to shop in the afternoon. Intercessors. Austin Clarke. NMP
Our Orders. Julia Ward Howe. AA
Our Own. Margaret E. Sangster. BLPA; NeHB; PoToHe
Our passions are most like to floods and streams. To the Queen. Sir Walter Ralegh. *See also* Passions are liken'd best to floods and steams. CBEP; EIL; FCP; OAEP; OBSC; SiPS; TuPP.
Our pastures are bitten and bare. Joseph Gordon Macleod. *Fr.* Men of the Rocks. OxBS
Our paths began at distant points in space. Juncture. Rea Lubar Duncan. PoNe (1970 ed.)
Our People. William Stafford. NoP
Our Pets. Esther Antin. *Fr.* On Our Farm. RIS
Our Photographs. Frederick Locker Lampson. ALV
Our Polite Parents. Carolyn Wells. BBGG
Our Prayer. George Herbert. MaRV; PGD; SoP
(Gratefulness.) MaMe

(Heart to Praise Thee, A.) SoP; TRV
Our Prayer of Thanks. Carl Sandburg. NP
"For the gladness here where the sun is shining at evening," *sel.* TRV
Our Presidents. *Unknown.* BLPA
Our quin's seek, an very seek. Queen Eleanor's Confession. *Unknown.* ESPB
Our Refuge. Psalms, XLVI, Bible, *O.T.* (*Moulton, Modern Reader's Bible).* MaRV
(Psalm XLVI: "God is our refuge . . .") AWP; OnPM
(Refuge, The, *Moulton, Modern Reader's Bible.*) WGRP
(Though the Earth Be Removed.) TrGrPo
Our Revels Now Are Ended. Shakespeare. *Fr.* The Tempest, IV, i. DiPo; GTBS-W; LiTB; LiTG; MaRV; PG; ShBV-3; WHA
(Clouds.) BoC
(Our Little Life.) OQP
(Prospero.) FiP
(Prospero Ends the Revels.) TreF
(Stuff of Dreams, The.) FaBV; TrGrPo
Our river is wide; our river is deep. The River Bridge. James S. Tippett. GFA
Our Rock. Francis Scott Key. BePJ; SoP; STF
Our Ruins. Reed Whittemore. NoP
Our rural ancestors, with little blest. The Ideals of Satire. Pope. *Fr.* First Epistle of the Second Book of Horace. FiP
"Our saints are poets, Milton and Blake." Encounter. Denis Devlin. OnYI
Our sardine fishermen work at night in the dark of the moon. The Purse-Seine. Robinson Jeffers. CMoP; NoP; OxBA
Our Saviour/ (Paterne of true holinesse). Ensamples of Our Saviour. Robert Southwell. PoEL-2
Our Saviour's cross, begilt with guiltless blood. The Cross. Thomas Bancroft. StJW
Our second Eve puts on her mortall shroude. The Virgine Maries Conception. Robert Southwell. MeP; ReIE
Our Share in Calvary. Horatius Bonar. SoP
Our share of night to bear. Emily Dickinson. OQP
(Life.) AA
Our shepherds all as pilgrims have departed. Boots and Saddles. Nicolas Saboly. OHIP
Our ship is a cradle on ocean's blue billow. An Ocean Lullaby. Charles Keeler. EtS
Our ship now pass'd the streights of th' ocean flood. Homer. *Fr.* The Odyssey, XII. ReIE
Our shops and farms wide open lie. The Invader. Norman Cameron. POTE
Our Silly Little Sister. Dorothy Aldis. EvOK; FaPON
Our Singing Strength. Robert Frost. AnAmPo; AtBAP; CoBA; InP
Our single purpose was to walk through snow. Polar Exploration. [*or* The North]. Stephen Spender. ChMP; FaBoMo; MoAB; MoPo
Our Sister. Horatio Nelson Powers. HBV
Our skipping ropes lie silent. Ten O'Clock. Patricia Hubbell. OCS
Our songs are dead, and dead in vain. The Flower. Lee Wilson Dodd. HBMV
Our sorrow sends its shadow round the earth. J. A. G. Julia Ward Howe. PAH
Our steeds remounted and the summons given. Wordsworth. *Fr.* The Prelude, II. SyP
Our steps are scattered far. In the Wilderness. Edith Lovejoy Pierce. TrPWD
Our storm[e] is past, and that storm's tyrannous rage. The Calm. John Donne. CABL; LoBV; MaMe; MePo; ReEn; ReIE; SeEP; StP; TuPP
Our Story. Thomas MacDonagh. MemP
Our Sweetest Songs. Shelley. *Fr.* To a Skylark. MaRV
Our tears have fallen for this world of stone. My Subtle and Proclamant Song. Seán Jennett. NeIP
Our Times Are in His Hands. Mary D. Freeze. STF
Our Times Are in Thy Hand. William F. Lloyd. SoP
Our times are much degenerate from those. To His Noble Friend, Mr. Richard Lovelace, upon His Poems. Andrew Marvell. MaMe
Our top-sails reef'd and filled away. The Norfolk Girls. *Unknown.* AmSS
Our Traveller. Henry Cholmondeley-Pennell. BOHV; InMe
Our tree breaks in this earth, a fallow life. Korea. Vincent Buckley. BoAV
Our True Beginnings. Wrey Gardiner. NeBP
Our trust is now in thee. Beauregard. Catherine Anne Warfield. MC; PaA; PAH
Our twelve months go round and round. January 1. Marnie Pomeroy. PoSC
Our Two Opinions. Eugene Field. AA; IHA; MAP; MoAmPo (1942 ed.); PFY
Our uncle called us on the phone. Surprise. Harry Behn. BiCB; TiPo (1959 ed.)
Our uncle, innocent of books. The Uncle. Whittier. *Fr.* Snow-bound. GoTP
Our vales are sweet with fern and rose. The Old Burying-Ground. Whittier. AP
Our vicar still preaches that Peter and Poule. Soldier's Song. Sir Walter Scott. *Fr.* The Lady of the Lake. NBM; ViBoPo
Our Village—by a Villager. Thomas Hood. CBEP; InMe; PoEL-4
Our walk was far among the ancient trees. To M. H. Wordworth. EiCP
Our Wars Are Wars of Life. Robert Browning. *Fr.* Before. StJW
("Our wars are wars of life, and wounds of love.") ChIP
Our Washington. Eliza W. Durbin. HH; PEDC
Our Wee White Rose. Gerald Massey. *Fr.* The Mother's Idol Broken. HBV
Our window is a magic frame. The Magic Window. Eleanor Hammond. MPB
Our window is stained. Alfred Kreymborg. *Fr.* Berceuse Ariettes. PG (1955 ed.)
Our words are no steadier than our journeys. For Kayak Magazine. Lou Lipsitz. YAP
Our Work. William W. How. SoP
Our world is. Jacques Wakefield. WSL
Our youth began with tears and sighs. Ballade of Middle Age. Andrew Lang. HBV
Our youth is like a rustic at the play. The Rustic at the Play. George Santayana. HBV; MAP; MoAmPo; OBVV
Oure hoste gan to swere as he were wood. The Pardoner's Prologue and Tale. Chaucer. *Fr.* The Canterbury Tales. NoP
Oure kinge went forth to Normandy. A Carol of Agincourt. *Unknown.* MeEL
Ours all are marble halls. Song of the Kings of Gold. Ebenezer Jones. VA
Ours, and All Men's. James Russell Lowell. *See* Washington ("Soldier and statesman . . .").
Ours is a dark Eastertide, and a scarlet spring. The Old Road to Paradise. Margaret Widdemer. HBMV
Ours is a great, wild country. The North Country. Robert Browning. *Fr.* The Flight of the Duchess. PCH
Ours is no venal pomp to-day—we seek no vain parade. Scotland's Tribute To Wallace. James MacFarlan. PoFr
Ours not to sleep in shady bowers. The Northern Soldier. Philip Freneau. AmPP (3d ed.)
Ours was a happy lot. Chorus of Batavian Women. Joost van den Vondel. WoL
Ousel Cock, The. Shakespeare. *See* Bottom's Song.
Out. Nathaniel Burt. MoLP
Out. Howard McCord. YAP
Out, alas!/ You'd be so lean. Flowers. Shakespeare. *Fr.* The Winter's Tale, IV, iii. UnPo (1st ed.)
Out and Fight. Charles Godfrey Leland. PAH
Out beyond the sunset, could I but find the way. The Golden City of St. Mary. John Masefield. HT
Out by the front walk—have you seen? St. Patrick's Day. Eleanor Hammond. GFA
Out came the captain of the gallant ship. The Ship a-Raging. *Unknown.* BFSS
Out come the leaves. The Neighbors Help Him Build His House. *Unknown.* LiTW
Out comes the bee. Leaving the House of a Friend. Basho. RePo
Out-dated Poem. Dick Gallup. ANYP
Out Fishin'. Edgar A. Guest. PoLF
Out for a walk, after a week in bed. Urban Convalescence, An. James Merrill. CoAP
Out for a walk the other day. Chanson Mystique [*or* Mystic Song.] *Unknown.* CAW; WGRP

Out for my evening stroll. The Power-House. Christopher Morley. MaRV
Out from Gloucester. Harlan Trott. EtS
Out from his bed the breaking seas. A Dream Observed. Anne Ridler. NeBP
Out from the City's dust and roar. The Forgotten Grave. Austin Dobson. VA
Out from the harbor of Amsterdam. Henry Hudson's Quest. Burton Egbert Stevenson. HBV; MC; PAH; PAL
"Out from the horror of infernal deeps." The Complaint of Rosamund. Samuel Daniel. OBSC; ReEn; ReIE; SiCE; TuPP
Out from the realm of the glory-light. Commissioned. Henry W. Frost. SoP
Out from the tall plantation gate. The Misses Poar Drive to Church. Josephine Pinckney. AnAmPo; InP
Out from this fluted shell the muffled roar. Sea Shell. Elizabeth Stanton Hardy. MaRV
Out goes the rat. Counting-out Rhymes. *Unknown.* FaPON
Out I came from the dancing-place. Ashore. "Laurence Hope." HBV
Out in a dark, lost kingdom of their own. Nor'easter. Bianca Bradbury. EtS
Out in a world of death, far to the northward lying. The Winter Lakes. Wilfred Campbell. BoNaP; OBCV
Out in the Cold. George Starbuck. NYBP
Out in the Dark. Edward Thomas. BrPo; CH; FaBoEn; GTBS-P; LiTM; MoAB; MoBrPo; MoVE; ShBV-3
Out in the dark beyond my gates. New Year's Eve in Troy. Adrienne Rich. NePoEA-2
Out in the dark it throbs and glows. On the Verge. William Winter. AA
Out in the dark night long. Counter-sign. Arthur Ketchum. *Fr.* Legends for Trees. HBMV
Out in the dark over the snow. Out in the Dark. Edward Thomas. BrPo; CH; FaBoEn; GTBS-P; LiTM; MoAB; MoBrPo; MoVE; ShBV-3
Out in the dark something complains. Cradle Song. F. R. Higgins. POTE
Out in the desert spaces, edged by a hazy blue. The Valley That God Forgot. Henry Herbert Knibbs. PCD
Out in the Fields. *Unknown. See* Out in the Fields with God.
Out in the fields which were green last May. A Child's Thought of Harvest. "Susan Coolidge." BoChLi (1939 ed.); DD; OHIP; OPTC (1946 ed.); PoSC
Out in the Fields with God. *Unknown, at. to* Louise Imogen Guiney *and to* Elizabeth Barrett Browning. BLRP; DD; GoTP; HBV; HBVY; MaRV; MPB; OQP; OTPC (1946 ed.); SoP; TRV; WBLP; WGRP
(Out in the Fields.) NeHB; TreFS
(Song from "Sylvan," A.) BLPA
Out in the garden,/ Up in a tree. The Blackbird. Phyllis Drayson. BoTP
Out in the garden/ When school was done. Bubbles. L. Nicholson. BoTP
Out in the garden,/ Out in the sun. The Pigeons. Rodney Bennett. BoTP
Out in the garden, sunny and still. Freedom. Joan Agnew. BoTP
Out in the late amber afternoon. In Shadow. Hart Crane. TwAmPo
Out in the misty moonlight. Ghosts. R. K. Munkittrick. AA; YT
Out in the night thou art the sun. Star of Ethiopia. Lucian B. Watkins. BANP
Out in the sky the great dark clouds are massing. Ships That Pass in the Night. Paul Laurence Dunbar. BANP; CDC
Out in the south, when the day is done. The Song of the Spanish Main. John Bennett. HBV
Out in the sunshine fair and free. Written on the Road. Mary Mapes Dodge. BiCB
Out in the waving meadow grass. Fairy Umbrellas. Lucy Diamond. GFA
Out in the Wood. Clinton Scollard. MoSiPe
Out in the Woods with Father. David McCord. ThGo
Out in the yellow meadows, where the bee. Modern Love, XI. George Meredith. ViPo; VP
Out into rain, out into slow streets, out into my name. Aubade. Eric Torgersen. QAH
Out it spake Lizee Linzee. Lizie Lindsay. *Unknown.* ESPB
Out of a cavern on Parnassus' side. The New Castalia. William Hayes Ward. AA
Out of a fired ship, which, by no way. Epigram: A Burnt Ship. John Donne. DiPo; MaMe; WaaP
Out of a Northern city's bay. The Cruise of the Monitor. George Henry Boker. MC; PAH; ThLM
Out of an empty sky, the dust of hours. Towers of Song. Malcolm Cowley. NP
Out of an Old Poet. Barnabe Googe. EP
Out of autumn like a blade. Autumn Journey. Denise Levertov. NeBP
Out of Barclay's Euphormion. Richard Crashaw. MaMe
Out of Bounds. Jon Stallworthy. TPM
Out of Bounds. John Banister Tabb. JKCP; MaRV; TRV
Out of brightness, a brightness out of brightness. The Waltz. Hilary Corke. NYBP
Out of Catullus. Catullus. *See* Counting Kisses.
Out of Catullus ("Unto nobody my woman saith she had rather a wife be"). Catullus, *tr. fr. Latin by* Sir Philip Sidney. FCP
Out of childhood into manhood. Hiawatha and Mudjekeewis. Longfellow. *Fr.* The Song of Hiawatha. AnNE
Out of Darkness. Sister Maris Stella. JKCP (1955 ed.)
Out of Doors. Walter Conrad Arensberg. AnAmPo
Out of Doors. E. North. BoTP
Out-of-Doors. Robert Whitaker. TrPWD
Out of Egypt Have I Called My Son. Caroline Hazard. StJW
Out of French. Sir Charles Sedley. PeRV
Out of green and stony dales, where, like enormous dice. A City of the North. James Kirkup. POTi
Out of Grotius His Tragedy of Christes Sufferinges. Richard Crashaw. MaMe
Out of Hearing. Jane Barlow. HBV
Out of her house she crept. Miss Euphemia. John Crowe Ransom. CMoP
Out of his body grows revolving steel. The Significance of John Brown. Stephen Vincent Benét. *Fr.* John Brown's Body. PaA
Out of his cottage to the sun. Old Dan'l. L. A. G. Strong. ELU; MoBrPo; NeMA; PoSC; WhC
Out of Horace. Richard Crashaw. MaMe
Out of it steps the future of the poor. The Door. W. H. Auden. Sonn
Out of John Brown's Strong Sinews. Stephen Vincent Benét. *Fr.* John Brown's Body. WHA
Out of Luck. Abraham ibn Ezra, *tr. fr. Hebrew by* Solomon Solis-Cohen. TrJP
Out of Martiall. Richard Crashaw. MaMe
Out of me unworthy and unknown. Anne [*or* Ann] Rutledge. Edgar Lee Masters. *Fr.* Spoon River Anthology. AmFN; AmLP; AmP; CMoP; FaFP; ILP; InPo; LiPo; LiTA; LiTM (rev. ed.); MAP; MoAmPo; MoVE; NeHB; NeMA; NePA; NP; OHFP; OxBA; PaA; PG (1945 ed.); PoPl; PoSa; PoSC; PTK; ThLM; TrGrPo
Out of midnight smile on me. Barrier. John Frederick Nims. JKCP (1955 ed.)
Out of my [*or* one's] birth. Horoscope. J. V. Cunningham. NePoAm; PoIE
Out of my door I step into. The Old Love. Katharine Tynan. HBMV
Out of my longing. dusk-aware. Candle Song. Anna Elizabeth Bennett. GoYe
Out of my need you come to me, O Father. Recognition. Margaret E. Sangster. MaRV
Out of my own great woe. Proem. Heine. AWP
Out of my sorrow. Duet. Leonora Speyer. HBMV
Out of My Soul's Depth. Thomas Campion. OxBoCh
Out of My Study Window. Reed Whittemore. PoPl
Out of my window late at night I gape. In the Night. Elizabeth Jennings. NePoEA; NYBP
Out of November; Speaking for One. David McCord. MAP
Out of one golden breath. Love-Song. Else Lasker-Schuler. TrJP
Out of Our Shame. Norman Rosten. TrJP
Out of Petronius. Richard Crashaw. MaMe
Out of Sight, Out of Mind. Barnabe Googe. BOHV; EIL; EnRePo; EP; PoIE; ReEN; TuPP
(Oculi Augent Dolorem.) SiCE
(Oftener Seen. the More I Lust, The.) InvP
Out of sleep. Allen Curnow. AnNZ
Out of Sorts. W.S. Gilbert. *Fr.* The Grand Duke. ALV
Out of Soundings. Padraic Fallon. NeIP

Out of Superstition. Boris Pasternak, *tr. fr. Russian by* Babette Deutsch. LiTW
Out of That Sea. David Ferry. NePoAm-2
Out of the air a time of quiet came. The Clipper Loitered South. John Masefield. *Fr.* Dauber. EtS
Out of the Ark's Grim Hold. Roy Campbell. *Fr.* The Flaming Terrapin. OA
Out of the base, insensate clod. The Luminous Hands of God. Eleanor Kenly Bacon. OQP
Out of the blackthorn edges. The Love Song. Ivor Gurney. EnLoPo
Out of the bosom of the air. Snow-Flakes [*or* Snow]. Longfellow. AmLP; AnNE; AP; BBV (1951 ed.); BoTP; ChTr; MAmP; NoP; PCH; PoEL-5; WiR
Out of the church she follow'd them. Maude Clare. Christina Rossetti. BeLS
Out of the cleansing night of stars and tides. Brooklyn Bridge at Dawn. Richard Le Gallienne. HBMV
Out of the clothes that cover me. Inspect Us. Edith Daniell. BOHV
Out of the cloud my Lord the Sun. Easter Hymn. Michael Thwaites. MoRP
Out of the clover and blue-eyed grass. Driving Home the Cows. Kate P. Osgood. AA; AmePo; BeLS; HBV; PAH; TreFS
Out of the complicated house, come I. The Hills. Frances Cornford. MoBrPo
Out of the conquered past. After a Dolmetsch Concert. Arthur Upson. PFY
Out of the Cradle Endlessly Rocking. Walt Whitman. AA; AmePo; AmPP; AnAmPo; AnFE; AP; APA; ATP (1935 ed.), *orig.*; AWP; BWP; CABA; CaFP; CoAnAm; CoBA; DiPo; ExPo; FaPL; ForPo; ILP; InPo; MAmP; MAP, *abr.*; MoAmPo; MWA-1; NePA; NoP; OxBA; PFY, *abr.*; PoEL-5; SeCeV; StP; TOP; TreFS; ViBoPo, *abr.*; WBP; WHA
(Brown Bird, The.) OBVV
Two Guests from Alabama, *sel.* OA
Out of the damp black night. The End of a Leave. Roy Fuller. NeBP
Out of the dark. Tracks in the Snow. Elizabeth J. Coatsworth. BoChLi (1950 ed.)
Out of the dark a shadow. *See* Out of the dusk a shadow.
Out of the dark raw earth. Alabama. Julia Fields. PoNe (1970 ed.)
Out of the darkness of time and the stress of an impulse unending. The Wave. John Curtis Underwood. EtS
Out of the deep and the dark. The Poet. Yone Noguchi. NP; WGRP
Out of the Deep Have I Called unto Thee, O Lord. Christina Rossetti. VP
Out of the deep, my child, out of the deep. De Profundis, I. Tennyson. ILP
Out of the deeps I cry to thee, O God! A Prayer. Richard Le Gallienne. TrPWD
Out of the delicate dream of the distance. Madeira from the Sea. Sara Teasdale. HT
Out of the Depths. Frederic Lawrence Knowles. TrPWD
Out of the depths, from cleft to cleft. Vinco. Elliot Field. ChIP
Out of the depths [*or* deep] have I cried [*or* called] unto thee, O Lord. De Profundis. Psalm CXXX, Bible, *O.T.* BLRP; BoC; EnLi-1; LiTW; MaRV; OnPM; TreF; TrGrPo; TrJP; WGRP; WHL
Out of the dusk a shadow. Evolution. John Banister Tabb. AA; AmP; AmePo; InP; OQP; PFY; PoPl; TreF
Out of the dusk into whose gloom you went. Sonnets of a Portrait Painter, L. Arthur Davison Ficke. AnAmPo
Out of the Earth. Mary Carolyn Davies. HBMV
Out of the earth beneath the water. The Mud Turtle. Howard Nemerov. NYBP; OPoP
Out of the earth come good things. One, Two, Three. "Robin Christopher." RIS
Out of the earth, out of the air, out of the water. Rapparees. Richard Murphy. *Fr.* The Battle of Aughrim. OPoP
Out of the Earth, this love. For Our Women. Larry Neal. BF
Out of the earth to rest or range. The Passing Strange. John Masefield. AnFE; BoLiVe; LiTB; MoAB; MoBrPo; MoPo; NP; OBEV (new ed.)
Out of the east the hero came. The Hero. George Woodcock. TwCaPo
Out of the East the plane spun; over rolling. Selden Rodman. *Fr.* Lawrence; the Last Crusade. NAMP
Out of the East we have followed a star. The Carol of Three Kinds. Nora Hopper Chesson. ChrBoLe
Out of the factory chimney, tall. Smoke Animals. Rowena Bastin Bennett. PDV; RePo
Out of the fat lands. Man Child. Michael Breathnach. JKCP (1926 ed.)
Out of the fire. Pool. Carl Sandburg. AP
Out of the focal and foremost fire. Little Giffen. Francis Orrery Ticknor. AA; AmePo; CoBA; DD; FaPL; HBV; MaC; MC; PaA; PAH; PCD; PTK; TreFS
Out of the fog and the gloom. The True Story of Skipper Ireson. Charles Buxton Going. YT
Out of the frozen earth below. The Crocus. Harriet Eleanor Hamilton King. VA
Out of the garden in the gathering gloom. Shrine in Nazareth. Sister Mary St. Virginia. ISi
Out of the ghetto streets where a Jewboy. Autobiographical. A. M. Klein. MoCV
Out of the golden [remote] wild west where the sea without shore is. Hesperia. Swinburne. OBNC; OBVV; VA
Out of the Greeke, Cupid's Cryer. Richard Crashaw. MaMe
Out of the grey [*or* gray] air grew snow and more snow. Snow. W. R. Rodgers. LiTG; LiTM (rev. ed.)
Out of the heart there flew a little singing bird. Youth. Virginia Woodward Cloud. AA
Out of the Heat. Amy Carmichael. FaChP
Out of the highest agonies of pain. The Poet. Grace Noll Crowell. InP
Out of the hills of Habersham. Song of the Chattahoochee. Sidney Lanier. AA; AmePo; AmFN; AmP; AmPP; AnAmPo; AnEnPo; AP; BBV (1923 ed.); BoNaP; CoBA; DiPo; FaBoBe; FaBV; HBV; InP; LaNeLa; LiTA; MAP; MCCG; MoAmPo (1942 ed.); NePA; OHFP; OTPC (1946 ed.); PCD; RG; TreF; YaD; YT
Out of the Hitherwhere. James Whitcomb Riley. BLPA
Out of the horror of the deepe. *Unknown.* SeCSL
Out of the house and power of her parents. Wedding Song. Conrad Ferdinand Meyer. HW
Out of the Hurly-Burly. "Max Adeler." CenHV
Out of the icy storms the white hare came. Ecclesiastes. Joseph Langland. NePoEA; PoPl
Out of the Italian ("Love now no fire hath left him"). Richard Crashaw. MaMe
Out of the Italian ("To thy lover"). Richard Crashaw. MaMe; SeCV-1
Out of the Italian ("Would any one the true cause find"). Richard Crashaw. MaMe
Out of the Land of Heaven. Leonard Cohen. MoCV
(Poem for Marc Chagall.) OBCV
Out of the land of the burning sun. Song of Hannibal; Rome. Marcus B. Christian. GoSl
Out of the light that dazzles me. My [*or* The] Captain. Dorothea Day. BePJ; BLPA; MaRV
Out of the living word. The Book of Kells. Howard Nemerov. EaLo
Out of the matrix of the sky and sea. Father Point in August. Leo Cox. TwCaPo
Out of the midnight sky a great dawn broke. The Shepherd Speaks. John Erskine. ChIP; MaRV; OQP
Out of the mid-wood's twilight. In the Forest. Oscar Wilde. SyP
Out of the mighty Yule log came. The Yule Log. William Hamilton Hayne. AA
Out of the mud two strangers came. Two Tramps in Mud Time. Robert Frost. AmPP; AnNE; AP; BoLiVe; CMoP; CoBA; CoBMV; LiTA; LiTM; MAP; MasP; MoAB; MoAmPo; NAMP; NePA; PoFS; TrGrPo; UnPo (3d ed.)
Out of the mud which covers me. Inflictis. Archibald Stodart-Walker. *Fr.* The Moxford Book of English Verse. CenHV
Out of the Night. W. E. Henley. *See* Invictus.
Out of the night and the north. The Train Dogs. E. Pauline Johnson. TwCaPo; WHW
Out of the night of the sea. At Carbis Bay. Arthur Symons. PoVP
Out of the Night That Covers Me. W. E. Henley. *See* Invictus.

Out of the night to my leafy porch they came. The Night Moths. Edwin Markham. HBMV
Out of the north on a Christmas tree. The Coming of Mary Louise. Gertrude Boughton Urquhart. PCH
Out of the North the wild news came. The Rising. Thomas Buchanan Read. *Fr.* The Wagoner of the Alleghanies. PAH; TreFS
Out of the northeast/ galloped a white charger. The White Horse. Tu Fu. ChTr
Out of the Old House, Nancy. Will Carleton. AA; IHA
Out of the Poisonous East. W. E. Henley. London Voluntaries, IV. SyP
(Largo e Mesto.) BrPo
Out of the rocked cradle. Out of the Cradle Endlessly Rocking. Walt Whitman. ATP (1935 ed.)
Out of the Rolling Ocean the Crowd. Walt Whitman. ViBoPo
Out of the scabbard of the night. Dawn. Frank Dempster Sherman. MAP; TRV
Out of the Sea. Witter Bynner. MoLP
Out of the showering snow itself to build. The Winter House. Norman Cameron. CBEP
Out of the sighs and breath of each small citizen. The City: Midnight.. Bruce Dawe. PoAu-2
Out of the silence, the wind. Requiem. William Thomas Walsh. JKCP (1955 ed.)
Out of the sparkling sea. Battle: Hit. W. W. Gibson. MCCG; NP; PoPo
Out of the storm that muffles shining night. Garden under Lightning. Leonora Speyer. PFY
Out of the strain of the doing. Harvest Home. W. M. L. Fay. FaChP
Out of the table endlessly rocking. Just Friends. Robert Creeley. NeAP
Out of the tense awed darkness, my Frangepani comes. Rainy Season Love Song. Gladys May Casely Hayford. CDC
Out of the terra cotta still a voice. Etruscan Warrior's Head. Helen Rowe Henze. GoYe
Out of the tomb we bring Badroulbadour. The Worms at Heaven's Gate. Wallace Stevens. NP
Out of the utmost pitch of wilderment. De Profundis. Amos N. Wilder. TrPWD
Out of the uttermost ridge of dusk, where the dark and the day are mingled. The Tryst of the Night. May C. G Byron. VA
Out of the Vast. Augustus Wright Bamberger. MaRV; OQP; TRV
(Each a Part of All.) WBLP
Out of the vastness that is God. A Litany for Latter-Day Mystics. Cale Young Rice. WGRP
Out of the Whirlwind. Job, Bible, *O.T.* *See* Voice Out of the Whirlwind, The.
Out of the wild sweet grape, I have trampled a wine. On Laying Up Treasure. Lois Smith Hiers. GoYe
Out of the Wilderness. Ulrich Troubetzkoy. GoYe
Out of the wind and the wind's image. To My Wife. John Bayliss. POTE
Out of the window the trees in the Square. Red May. Agnes Mary Frances Robinson. HBMV
Out of the winds' and the waves' riot. Ebb Tide. Marjorie Pickthall. CaP
Out of the wine-pot cried the fly. The Fly. Philip Ayres. CavP
Out of the wood of thoughts that grows by night. Cock Crow. Edward Thomas. GTBS-P; MoAB; MoBrPo; NeMA
Out of their slumber Europeans spun. Snow in Europe. David Gascoyne. MoPW
Out of these depths. De Profundis. David Gascoyne. *Fr.* Miserere. NeBP
Out of these thin, thin cups I drink pale tea. Bone China. R. P. Lister. NYBP
Out of this anteroom whose light is broken. The Anteroom. Denise Levertov. NeBP
Out of This Life. *Unknown.* SoP; STF
Out of this town there riseth a high hill. Of a Vision of Hell, Which a Monk Had. Richard Watson Dixon. *Fr.* Mano; a Poetical History. VA
Out of this ugliness may come. Glasgow Street. William Montgomerie. OxBS
Out of this wilderness, this stony time. What Sanguine Beast? LeRoy Smith, Jr. NePoAm
Out [*or* Owt] of thise blake wawes for to saile [*or* saylle]. Chaucer. *Fr.* Troilus and Criseyde. EnLi-1; ILP; PP
Out of Tune. W. E. Henley. Echoes, XL. MoBrPo
Out of us all. Words. Edward Thomas. NoP; WePo
Out of Virgil, In the Praise of the Spring. Richard Crashaw. MaMe
Out of what calms and pools the cool shell grows. The Atoll in the Mind. Alex Comfort. FaBoMo; GTBS-W; LiTB; LiTM; POTE; SeCePo
Out of what dark, what light? From a country no man knows. The Quickening. Ruth Gilbert. *Fr.* The Blossom of the Branches. ACV
Out of Wisdom Has Come Love. E. A. Robinson. *Fr.* The Three Taverns. MoRP
Out of Your Hands. Theodore Weiss. CoPo
Out of Your Sleep Arise and Wake. *Unknown.* NoP
(Man Exalted.) MeEL
Out of your whole life give but a moment! Now [*or* The Moment Eternal]. Robert Browning. CBEP; EnLi-2 (1949 ed.); MeWo; PoVP; UnTE
Out on a limb and frantically sawing. Martyrdom of Two Pagans. Philip Whalen. NeAP
Out on a ranch way out West. Sun of a Gun. *Unknown.* CoSo
Out on the bare grey roads, I pass. Touch It. Robert Mezey. NaP
Out on the board the old shearer stands. Click Go the Shears, Boys. *Unknown.* PoAu-1
Out on the breeze. Flag Song [*or* A Song for Flag Day]. Lydia Avery Coonley Ward. HH; MPB; OTPC (1946 ed.); PEDC; PoRL; YeAr
Out on the endless purple hills, deep in the clasp of somber night. The Little Gray Lamb. Archibald Beresford Sullivan. ChrBoLe
Out on the furthest tether let it run. The Undiscovered Planet. Norman Nicholson. ChMP; FaBoMo; POTi
Out on the margin of moonshine land. The Lugubrious Whing-Whang. James Whitcomb Riley. BOHV; NA; YaD
Out on the roads of sky the moon stands poised. Elegy. Roy McFadden. NeIP
Out on the wastes of the Never Never. Where the Dead Men Lie. Barcroft Henry Boake. BoAu; BoAV; NeLNL; PoAu-1
Out on the water was the same display. E. J. Pratt. *Fr.* The *Titanic.* PeCV
Out, Out. Robert Frost. AmPP (4th ed.); CABA; CBV; ILP; InP; OxBA; PoeP; PoIE; PoPo; TDP; UnPo
Out, Out, Brief Candle! Shakespeare. *See* Tomorrow and Tomorrow and Tomorrow.
Out, out, harrow! Into bale am I brought. Satan and Pilate's Wife. *Unknown.* ACP
Out rode from his wild, dark castle. The Legend of Heinz von Stein. Charles Godfrey Leland. BOHV; HBV
Out shopping, little Julia spied. The Coconut. "Ande." FiBHP
Out the Greywolf valley. Hunting, XII. Gary Snyder. *Fr.* Myths & Texts. NaP
Out There. Bill Berkson. ANYP; YAP
Out there in the fighting. What the Old Women Say. Archibald MacLeish. TPM
Out There Somewhere. H. H. Knibbs. BLPA
Out there, we've walked quite friendly up to Death. The Next War. Wilfred Owen. AnEnPo; Sonn; WaP
Out there, with little else to do. Robben Island. Robert Dederick. PeSA
Out they came from Liberty, out across the plains. Oregon Trail, 1851. James Marshall. IHA; PaA; StVeCh
Out through the fields and the woods. Reluctance. Robert Frost. AmPP; CMoP; ExPo; GTBS-D; MAP; MoAB; MoAmPo; OxBA; Po; PoFS
Out to Old Aunt Mary's. James Whitcomb Riley. FaFP; OHFP
Out to the world's dim boundary line. "Gone West." G. A. Studdert-Kennedy. OQP
Out, traitor Absence, darest thou counsel me. Astrophel and Stella, LXXXVIII. Sir Philip Sidney. FCP; SiPS
Out upon It! I Have Loved. Sir John Suckling. *See* Constant Lover, The.
Out upon the round-up boys, tell you what you get. Campfire and Bunkhouse. *Unknown.* CoSo
Out walking in the frozen swamp one gray day. The Wood-Pile. Robert Frost. AmP; CABA; CoBMV; FosPo;

LiTA; MAmP; MAPA; NoP; SeCeV; TwAmPo; VaPo; YT
Out walking ties left over from a track. Cross Ties. X. J. Kennedy. CoPo
Out went the taper as she hurried in. Keats. *Fr.* The Eve of St. Agnes. ViBoPo
Out West is windy. New Mexico. Polly Chase Boyden. TiPo
Out West, they say, a man's a man. Etude Géographique. Stoddard King. AmFN; IHA; WhC
Out West, where the stars are brightest. The Great Grey Plain. Henry Lawson. BoAu
Out where the handclasp's a little stronger. Out Where the West Begins. Arthur Chapman. BLPA; FaBoBe; FaFP; HBV; NeHB; PaA; PoOW; SCC; TreF
Out where the line of battle cleaves. The Red Cross Nurses. Thomas L. Masson. PEDC
Out where the sky and the sky-blue sea. Flying Fish. Mary McNeill Fenollosa. AA
Out Where the West Begins. Arthur Chapman. BLPA; FaBoBe; FaFP; HBV; NeHB; PaA; PoOW; SCC; TreF
Out where the white waves whisper. Out from Gloucester. Harlan Trott. EtS
Out with the tide, beneath the morning sun. The Lightship. Josephine Winslow Johnson. MoSiPe
Outbound, your bark awaits you. Were I one. Godspeed. Whittier. Sonn
Outcast, The. "Æ." LO; OxBI; POTE
Outcast, The. John Davidson. MoBrPo (1942 ed.)
Outcast. Claude McKay. AmNP; BALP; BP; MoBrPo
Outcast, a horror to his kind. On the Just and the Unjust. Blanche Edith Baughan. BoAu
Outcast bones from a thousand biers. Ballade. Don Marquis. *Fr.* Archy and Mehitabel. WhC
Outcrop stone is miserly. Still-Life. Ted Hughes. NYBP
Outdoor Christmas Tree, The. Aileen Fisher. SiSoSe
Outdoor Litany, An. Louise Imogen Guiney. TrPWD
Outdoor Son of God, The. William L. Stidger. ChIP
Outer and Inner. George Meredith. PrWP
Outer and the Inner Man, The. Shakespeare. *See* Sonnets, CXLVI.
Outer, The—from the inner. Emily Dickinson. MAmP
Outgoing Sabbath. *Unknown, tr. fr. Yiddish by* Joseph Leftwich. TrJP
Outgrown. Julia C. R. Dorr. HBV
Outlanders, The. Andrew Glaze. NYBP
Outlanders, Whence Come Ye Last? William Morris. *Fr.* The Earthly Paradise. OxBoCh; StJW
(Minstrels and Maids.) GN
Outlandish Knight, The. *Unknown.* GoTP; RIS; ShM; StaSt
Outlaw, The. Badger Clark. SCC
Outlaw. John Giorno. ANYP
Outlaw, The. Sir Walter Scott. *See* Brignall Banks.
Outlaw Murray, The. *Unknown.* ESPB; OBB, *sl. diff.*; OxBB
Outlaw of Loch Lene, The. *Unknown, tr. fr. Modern Irish by* Jeremiah Joseph Callanan. AnIV; CH; IrPN; OBEV; OBRV; OnYI; OxBI
Outlaws. Robert Graves. WIRo
Outlaw's Song, The. Joanna Baillie. *Fr.* Orra, III. OBEV; OTPC (1923 ed.); PoFr
(Song of the Outlaws.) OBRV
Outlined in fire against primeval night. Zarathustra. Thomas S. Jones, Jr. AnAmPo
Outlook Uncertain. Alastair Reid. NePoEA-2
Outlook wasn't brilliant for the Mudville nine that day, The. Casey at the Bat. Ernest L. Thayer. AmePo; BLPA; BOHV; FaPON; HBV; LHV; OTD; PaPo; PoPl; PTK; SD
Outlook wasn't brilliant for the Mudvillettes, it seems, The. Casey's Daughter at the Bat. Al Graham. InMe
Outrageous hourly with his wife is Peter. On One Peter and His Wife. Walter Savage Landor. CBV
Outside. Hugh Chesterman. BoTP
Outside. Phyllis Harris. ThO
Outside. William Stafford. NePoAm-2
Outside Bristol Rovers Football Ground. The Ballad of Billy Rose. Leslie Norris. MoBS
Outside Dunsandle. Sacheverell Sitwell. ChMP
Outside hove Shasta, snowy height on height. Train-Mates. Witter Bynner. MAP; MoAmPo (1942 ed.); PFY
Outside Kimberley. N. H. Brettell. BoSA
Outside my blind a bird lit in a tree. A Play of Opposites. Gray Burr. CoPo
Outside that bulbous Babylon. English Beach Memory: Mr. Thuddock. Sir Osbert Sitwell. NYBP
Outside the barracks now the bugle called, and woke. Dawn. Baudelaire. WoL
Outside the Bureau all the trams and trains. Laid Off. Francis Webb. BoAV
Outside the Chancel Door. *Unknown.* ShM
Outside the city gate willows rise like smoke. The Honeymooners. Yu Ch'ien. HW
Outside the courtroom. Sharpeville Inquiry. Anne Welsh. PeSA
Outside, the cubist fells are drawn again. Cockley Moore, Dockray, Penrith. Norman Nicholson. NeBP
Outside the Door. Annette Wynne. SoPo; SUS
Outside the great cathedral door. Knight Olaf. Heine. HW
Outside the house an ash-tree hung its terrible whips. Discord in Childhood. D. H. Lawrence. CBEP; ELU; MoPW
Outside the lilacs blurred. Keep Darkness. Leslie Nelson Jennings. FiSC
Outside the village, by the public road. The Dried-up Fountain. Robert Leighton. VA
Outside the world crackles like a daily. A Room I Once Knew. Henry Birnbaum. GoYe
Outside—wind heavy and wet. Elegies, I. Philippe Thoby-Marcelin. PoNe
Outspoken buttocks in pink beads. National Winter Garden. Hart Crane. *Fr.* The Bridge: Three Songs. AmP; ErPo; LiTA; LiTM (rev. ed.); OxBA; TDP
Outspread world to span, The. Empedocles' Song. Matthew Arnold. *Fr.* Empedodes on Etna, I, ii. TOP
Outstretched at ease his furry form. My Friend, the Cat. Carrie W. Stryker. CIV
Outward. John G. Neihardt. HBV
Outward. Louis Simpson. NYBP
Outward Bound. Thomas Bailey Aldrich. AA; EtS
Outward Bound. Edward Sydney Tylee. PAH
Outward from the planets are blown the fumes of thought. The Awakening. Don Marquis. HBMV
Outward Man Accused, The. Edward Taylor. *Fr.* God's Determinations. LiTA
Outwardly splendid as of old. The Church Today. Sir William Watson. MaRV; WGRP
Outweighing all, heavy out of the souvenir bundle. Three American Women and a German Bayonet. Winfield Townley Scott. FiMAP; NMP; OnHM
Outwit me, Lord, if ever hence. Security. Charles L. O'Donnell. TrPWD
Outwitted. Edwin Markham. AnAmPo; BLPA; ELU; MAP; MaRV; MCCG; MoAmPo; NeMA; OQP; PoPo; PoToHe; TreFT; TRV
Out-worn heart, in a time out-worn. Into the Twilight. W. B. Yeats. BEL; EPN; HBV; PoPo; PoVP; ViPo (1962 ed.)
Ov all the birds upon the wing. The Blackbird. William Barnes. GTSE; HBV
Oven Bird, The. Robert Frost. AmPP (4th ed.); AP; AWP; BWP; CoBMV; CrMA; ForPo; FosPo; InPo; JAWP; MAPA; MaPo; NoP; OxBA; Po; Sonn; TwAmPo; UnS; VaPo
Over a bloomy land untrod. In Dreamy Swoon. George Darley. *Fr.* Nepenthe. OBNC; OBRV
Over a ground of slate and light gravel. The Sanctuary. Howard Nemerov. NePoEA
Over a lost orchard I have strayed. Edgar Lee Masters. *Fr.* The Lost Orchard. LaNeLa
Over a pipe the Angel of Conversation. Inter Sodales. W. E. Henley. HBV
Over a scarred and war-town world. The Bethlehem Star Shines On! Alice Mortenson. BePJ
Over a wild and stormy sea. Mother Shipton's Prophecies. *At. to* Charles Hindley. BLPA
Over against the treasury. His Gift and Mine. Edith B. Gurley. BLRP
Over against the triumph and the close. A Sunset. Aldous Huxley. MoBrPo (1942 ed.)
Over All the Face of Earth Main Ocean Flowed. Milton. *Fr.* Paradise Lost, VII. EtS
Over and back. At Ithaca. Hilda Doolittle ("H. D."). AnAmPo
Over and over again to people. The Limits of Submission. Faarah Nuur. TTY
Over and over, when the wayside dust has grayed us. To Be Said at the Seder. Karl Wolfskehl. TrJP
Over and Under. William Jay Smith. TiPo (1959 ed.)

Over and under/ The shaking sky. Iron-Wind Dances. Lew Sarett. Thunderdrums, V. MAP
Over back where they speak of life as staying. The Investment. Robert Frost. BWP; CMoP; OxBA
Over Bright Summer Seas. Robert Hillyer. NYBP
Over crimson clover-seas. The Quest. Clinton Scollard. BrR
Over dead craters, hushed with snows. *See* After volcanoes husht.
Over deep drifts of snow. The Ox. Sara Maynard. ChrBoLe
Over Guiana, Clouds, *sel.* A. J. Seymour. PoNe
"Over Guiana, clouds./ Little curled feathers."
Over-Heart, The. Whittier. OQP, *abr.; WGRP*
"World sits at the feet of Christ, The,"*sel.* ChIP; MaRV; TRV
Over here in England I'm helpin' wi' the hay. Corrymeela. "Moira O'Neill." AnIV; AWP; HBV; JAWP; WBP
Over Hill, Over Dale. Shakespeare. *Fr.* A Midsummer Night's Dream, II, i. AnFE; BEL; EG; EIL; InvP; OBSC; PoRh; SiCE; ThWaDe; ViBoPo
(Fairy Land.) GBV; OBEV
(Fairy Queen, The.) OTPC (1946 ed.)
(Fairy Song, A.) BoTP
(Fairy Songs: "Over hill, over dale.") HBV; HBVY; PCD; TrGrPo
(Fairy's Song.) BoLiVe
(Fairy's Wander-Song.) FaPON; RIS
("How now spirit, whether wander you?") AtBAP
(Puck and the Fairy.) GN
(Song: "Over hill, over dale.") EnLi-1
(Song of the Fairy.) PCH
Over hill, over dale, we have hit the dusty trail. The Caisson Song. Edmund L. Gruber. PAL; TreF
Over hills and high mountains. The Wandering Maiden; or, True Love at Length United. *Unknown.* CoMu
Over his face his gray hair drifting hides his labor-glory in smoke. Pittsburgh. James Oppenheim. StaSt
Over his keys the musing organist. The Vision of Sir Launfal. James Russell Lowell. AmePo; AnNE; HBV; LiTA; LiTG; MCCG; OnMSP; PoLF; PoRL
Over his millions, Death has lawful power. On the Death of M. d'Ossoli and His Wife, Margaret Fuller. Walter Savage Landor. PAH; VA
Over in the Meadow. "Olive A. Wadsworth." GFA; MoShBr; OTPC (1946 ed.); PoRh; SAS; SoPo
(Wonderful Meadows, The.) UTS
Over Jordan. *Unknown. See* Poor Wayfaring Stranger.
Over kings and priests and scholars. Letrilla; the Lord of Dollars. Francisco de Quevedo y Villegas. WoL
Over marsh and swamp and pond. Peepers. Melville Cane. RePo
Over mountains, pride. The Praise of Ben Dorain. Duncan Ban MacIntyre. GoTS
Over my garden. Indifference. Louise Driscoll. PoMa
Over my head, I see the bronze butterfly. Lying in a Hammock at William Duffy's Farm. James Wright. FRC; NaP; PIA
Over my shaded doorway. A Bird's Nest. Elizabeth Akers Allen. PEDC (1931 ed.)
Over New England now, the snow. Nocturne. Frances Frost. BoNaP
Over old roofs and past decaying spires. Harbour Whistles. H. P. Lovecraft. HYE
Over our head the branches made. The Mountebanks. Charles Henry Luders. AA
Over rock and wrinkled ground. Beagles. W. R. Rodgers. FaBoTw; OnYI; SD
Over Salève. George Herbert Clarke. CaP
Over Sir John's Hill. Dylan Thomas. CABL; DiPo; LiTB; LiTM (rev. ed.); MoAB; VaPo
Over that breathing waste of friends and foes. Sonnet: The Army Surgeon. Sydney Thompson Dobell. NCEP
Over the/ seaworthy. A Tapestry for Bayeux. George Starbuck. TDP
Over the ball of it. Pisgah-Sights. Robert Browning. PoVP
Over the black mountain, acorss the black bay, into the black night and beyond. Encounter. Uys Krige. PeSA
Over the bleak and barren snow. Tony O! Colin Francis. CH; PV
Over the books of bricks. Landscape near a Steel Mill. Herschel Horn. PPON
Over the borders, a sin without pardon. Keepsake Mill. Robert Louis Stevenson. TSW
Over the Bridge. Li Kwang-t'ien, *tr. fr. Chinese by* Harold Acton *and* Ch'en Shih-hsiang. LiTW
Over the briny wave I go. The Kayak. *Unknown.* FaPON; GFA; OTPC (1946 ed.); PCH; RePo
Over the Carnage Rose Prophetic a Voice. Walt Whitman. AmPP (3d ed.)
Over the chimney the night wind sang. What the Chimney Sang. Bret Harte. OTD
Over the City. The First Zeppelin. James S. Tippett. GFA
Over the climbing meadows. Dandelions. Frances M. Frost. TiPo
Over the cradle the mother hung. Where Shall the Baby's Dimple Be? Josiah Gilbert Holland. BLPA
Over the dark water. A Kayak Song. Lucy Diamond. BoTP
Over the dim blue hills. Maire My Girl. John Keegan Casey. AnIV; IrPN; JKCP (1926 ed.); OnYI
Over the dim confessional cried. A Priest's Prayer. Martha Dickinson Bianchi. AA
Over the Door at the Entrance into the Apollo. Ben Jonson. *See* Verses Placed over the Door. . .
Over the downs there were birds flying. On the South [*or* Sussex] Downs. Sara Teasdale. MAP; MoAmPo; NP; YT
Over the eye behind the moon's cloud. Raison d'Etre. Oliver Pitcher. AmNP;Kal; NNP
Over the far-flung purple moor. Lines from an Elegy on the Death of His Wife. Kakinomoto no Asomi Hitomaro. LiTW
Over the Fields. Adeline White. BoTP
Over the fields to Shottery, fresh with a wet-green scent. The Path to Shottery. Cornelia Otis Skinner. MoSiPe
Over the fields where the cornflowers grow. Over the Fields. Adeline White. BoTP
Over, the four long years! And now there rings. Oxford. Lionel Johnson. OBNC;OBVV
Over the Garden Wall. Eleanor Farjeon. StVeCh
Over the gate the willow. Spring Scene at River Town. *Unknown.* OnPM
Over the Great City. Edward Carpenter. WGRP
Over the great windy waters, and over the clear-crested summits. En Route. Arthur Hugh Clough. *Fr.* Amours de Voyage, I. EPN; ViPP
Over the green and yellow rice fields. Rabindranath Tagore. *Fr.* The Gardener. NP
Over the gulf and soaring of the city. Diretro al Sol. Charles G. Bell. NePoAm
Over the half-finished houses. The Roofwalker. Adrienne Rich. CoAP
Over the heady wine. Verse, Violence, and the Vine. James Vincent Cunningham. NYTB
Over the Heather [the Wet Wind Blows]. W. H. Auden. EnLi-2 (1949 ed.); PoRA
(Roman Soldier on the Wall, A.) WePo
(Roman Wall Blues.) DTC
Over the Hill. George Macdonald. GaP
Over the hill and over the dale. Dawlish Fair. Keats. PeER
Over the hill came horsemen, horsemen whistling. A Stared Story. William Stafford. TPM
Over the hill the clouds race by. Clouds. Helen Wing. GFA
Over the hill the farm-boy goes. Evening at [*or* on] the Farm. John Townsend Trowbridge. BBV (1923 ed.); FaPON; GN; MPB; MoShBr; RIS; StVeCh (1940 ed.)
Over the hill to feed my sheep. Weevily Wheat (B *vers.*). *Unknown.* ABF
Over the Hill to the Poor-House. Will Carleton. ATP (1935 ed.); BeLS; BLPA; FaFP; PaPo; TreF
Over the hills/ Where the edge of the light. The Witches' Ride. Karla Kuskin. PDV
Over the Hills and Far Away. John Gay. *See* Song: "Were I laid on Greenland's coast."
Over the Hills and Far Away. W. E. Henley. HBVY; TreF; TSW
(Stanzas: "Where forlorn sunsets flare and fade.") HBV
(Where Forlorn Sunsets Flare and Fade.) PoVP
Over the Hills and Far Away. *Unknown.* GaP; RIS
("Tom he was a piper's son.") OxNR; TiPo (1952 ed.)

(Tom, He Was the Piper's Son.) OTPC; PPL
(Tom, the Piper's Son.) PCH
Over the Hills with Nancy, *abr.* Gelett Burgess. WhC
Over the ice she flies. Skating. Kipling. SD
Over the land freckled with snow half-thawed. Thaw. Edward Thomas. BiS; ELU; FaBoTw; FlW; GTBS-P; HaMV; MoAB; MoBrPo; NeMA
Over the lids of thine eyes. Images. Richard Schaukal. AWP
Over the lonesome hollows. A Paris Nocturne. "Fiona Macleod." SyP
Over the long-shut house. Greek Excavations. Bernard Spencer. ChMP
Over the lotus leaves. Lotus Leaves. Mitsukuni. OnPM
Over the low, barnacled, elephant-colored rocks. Meditation at Oyster River. Theodore Roethke. MoAmPo (1962 ed.); NaP; NYBP
Over the mists of a century they come, and their tramping feet. Independence Day To-Day. Margaret E. Sangster. PEDC
Over the monstrous shambling sea. Marsh Song—At Sunset. Sidney Lanier. AmePo; CoBA; TOP
Over the mountains/ And under the waves. Love Will Find Out the Way [*or* The Great Adventurer]. *Unknown.* CBEP; FaBoCh; FaFP; GN; GTBS; GTBS-D; GTBS-P; GTBS-W; GTSE; GTSL; HBV; LiTG; LiTL; LO; LoGBV; MeWo; OBEV; OTPC (1923 ed.); PCD; SeCL; SeEP; TreFS; TuPP; WiR
Over the mountains,/ Over the plains. Trains. James S. Tippett. FaPON; GFA; OTPC (1946 ed); SoPo; SUS; TiPo
Over the multiple terrors of Mars. T. Inglis Moore. *Fr.* Kookaburra. NeLNL
Over the plain two dark. The Triumph of Chastity. Barbara Howes. NePoAm-2
Over the plains where Persian hosts. The Cyclamen. Arlo Bates. AA; HBV
Over the Rim of Glory. After Reading Twenty Years of Grantland Rice. Don Skene. InMe
Over the River. Nancy Woodbury Priest. HBV
Over the river. Ferry-Boats. James S. Tippett. SoPo
Over the river and through the wood. Thanksgiving Day. Lydia Maria Child. DD; FaPON; GFA; GoTP; HH; MPB; OHIP; OTD; OTPC; PCH; PEDC; PRWS; PTK; SAS; SiSoSe; StVeCh; TreFS
Over the river on the hill. The Two Villages. Rose Terry Cooke. HBV
Over the river, over the bay. Ferry-Boats. James S. Tippett. GFA; SUS; TiPo
Over the river they beckon to me. Over the River. Nancy Woodbury Priest. HBV
Over the roof-tops race the shadows of clouds. Irradiations, III [V]. John Gould Fletcher. AnAmPo; AnFE; APA; LaNeLa; MAP; MAPA; MoAmPo; NeMA; NePA; NP; PFY; TwAmPo
Over the Roofs. Sara Teasdale. NP
Over the Sea Our Galleys Went. Robert Browning. *See* Song: "Over the sea. . ."
Over the sea the stork flies. St. Gregory's Day. *Unknown, tr. fr. Czech.* PCH
Over the Sea to Skye. Robert Louis Stevenson. *See* Sing Me a Song.
Over the seagulls and the gull white roofs the music lies like heat. Tabernacles. Gerrit Lansing. CoPo
Over the seas tonight, love. Sea Lyric. William Stanley Braithwaite. GoSl
Over the shining pavement of the sea. The Ship. Louise A. Doran. EtS
Over the shoulders and slopes of the dune. The Daisies. Bliss Carman. BoNaP
Over the snow at night. The Winter Lightning for Paul. Howard Nemerov. FiMAP; MoVE
Over the threshold a gallant new-comer. New Year. *Unknown.* PECD (1931 ed.)
Over the turret, shut in his ironclad tower. Craven. Sir Henry Newbolt. BBV (1923 ed.); HBV; HBVY; PAH
Over the village, on the hill. The Two Villages. Rose Terry Cooke. HBV
Over the warts on the bumpy. Sadie's Playhouse. Margaret Danner. Kal
Over the water an old ghost strode. The Old Ghost. Thomas Lovell Beddoes. WiR
Over the water and over the sea [*or* lea]. Mother Goose. OTPC (1923 ed.); OxNR; RIS
Over the waters but a single bough. Robert Hillyer. Sonnets, XXIII. HBMV
Over the wave-patterned sea-floor. Greeting. Ella Young. AnIV
Over the Way. Mary Mapes Dodge. BOHV
Over the west side of this mountain. Lyrebirds. Judith Wright. GoJo
Over the wilds of Sugano. The Tempest. Mabuchi. OnPM
Over the wintry. Soseki. PDV
Over the Wintry Threshold. Bliss Carman. HBV
Over their edge of earth. The Little Clan. F. R. Higgins. OBMV
Over Their Graves. Henry Jerome Stockard. AA; OHIP
Over them all, we sit aloft and sing. Shadows of Sails. John Anderson. EtS
Over these blunted, these tormented hills. Kanheri Caves. Dom Moraes. TDP
Over this battered track. Express Train. Karl Kraus. TrJP
Over this hearth—my father's seat. The Returned Volunteer to His Rifle. Herman Melville. ThLM
Over 2000 Illustrations and a Complete Concordance. Elizabeth Bishop. FiMAP; PoDB
Over us stands the broad electric face. Terminal. Karl Shapiro. AmLP
Over Yonder's a Park ("He bare him up, he bare him down"). *Unknown.* *See* Falcon, The.
Over Yonder's a Park ("Over yonder's a park which is newly begun") (B *vers.*). *Unknown.* BaBo
Over you falls the sea-light, festive yet pale. Ireland. Francis Stuart. NeIP
Over your dead heart I'll lift. I'll Be Your Epitaph. Leonora Speyer. HBMV
Overanxious. *Unknown.* SoP
Over-Confident Man, The. *Unknown.* SoP
Overdose of beautiful words, An. 12th Raga: For John Wieners. David Meltzer. NeAP
Overflow. John Banister Tabb. CAW; HBV; PTK
Overgrown Back Yard, The. John Holmes. CrMA; NePoAm
Overhead at sunset all heard the choir. The Singers in a Cloud. Ridgely Torrence. AnAmPo; HBMV; UnS
Overhead on a wing under heaven, treading. To Father Gerard Manley Hopkins, S.J. George Barker. Sonn
Overheard at a Sculpture Show at a Museum. *Unknown.* SiTL
Overheard in a Barbershop. Irving Layton. NMP
Overheard in an Orchard. Elizabeth Cheney. BLRP; FaChP; MaRV; SoP; TRV
(Feathered Faith.) STF
Overheard in the Louvre. X. J. Kennedy. ELU
Overheard on a Saltmarsh. Harold Monro. BoTP; CH; FaPON; GoJo; MoShBr; PCD; PCH; PoMS; SP; ThWaDe; TiPo
Overlander, The. *Unknown.* PoAu-1
Overloaded, undermanned. The Coasters. Thomas Fleming Day. AA; PFY
Over-logical fell for the witch, The. The Useful. W. H. Auden. CMoP
Overlord. Bliss Carman. CaP
(Veni Creator: "Lord of the grass and hill.") MoRP; WGRP
Overnight, a Rose. Caroline Giltinan. HBMV; SoP
Overnight in the Apartment by the River. Tu Fu, *tr. fr. Chinese.* ChTr
Overnight my garden is Yoknapatawpha. Starlings. Ted Olson. PV
Overnight, very/ Whitely, discreetly. Mushrooms. Sylvia Plath. BoNaP; NePoEA-2
Overripe Fruit. Kasmuneh, *tr. fr. Arabic.* TrJP
Overseer of the Poor. James Hayford. NePoAm-2
Oversoul. "Æ." MaRV; PoVP
(Krishna.) VA
Overtakelessness of those, The. Emily Dickinson. MoRP
Overthrow of Lucifer, The. Phineas Fletcher. *Fr.* The Purple Island, XII. OBS
Overtones. William Alexander Percy. DD; HBMV; HBVY; MaRV
Overture. Emmett Jarrett. *Fr.* Design for the City of Man. ThO
Overture. Walter Savage Landor. *Fr.* Thrasymedes and Eunoë. VA
Overture to Strangers. Phyllis Haring. PeSA
Overtures to Death. C. Day Lewis. CMoP
Overworked Elocutionist, An. Carolyn Wells. BLPA
Overworked Horse, The. Gerald Gould. MoBrPo (1942 ed.)

Overworld, The. Thomas Hardy. The Dynasts, Pt. III, After Scene. WoL
Ovibos, The. Robert Hale. FiBHP
Ovid is the surest guide. Written in an Ovid. Matthew Prior. EiCL
Ovid on the Dacian Coast. Dunstan Thompson. NYBP
Ovid's Banquet of Sense, *sels.* George Chapman.
Corinna Bathes. OBSC
(Natures Naked Jem.) FaBoEn
"Earth from heavenly light conceived heat, The." RelE
Ovid's Fifth Elegy. Ovid. *See* In Summer's Heat.
Oviparous Tailor, The. Thomas Lovell Beddoes. NBM
(Tailor, The.) WiR
Owd Pinder. Edwin Waugh. VA
Owed to Dickens, 1956. Jan Burroway. NePoAm-2
Owed to New York. Byron Rufus Newton. BLPA; NeHB; TreFS
Owen, not to use flattery (as they). In Owenni Epigrammata. Thomas Freeman. SiCE
Owen Seaman. Louis Untermeyer. ALV; BOHV
Owen's praise demands my song. The Triumphs of Owen. Thomas Gray, *after* Meilir ap Gwalchamai. CEP; EnRP; LiTW; PoEL-3; PrWP
Owl. Edward Brathwaite. NYTB
Owl. Gregory Corso. CBV
Owl. Peter Kane Dufault. NYBP
Owl, The. William Jay Smith. PDV
Owl, The. Tennyson. BoTP; CBEP; DD; FaBoCh; GBV (1952 ed.); GoTP; LoGBV; MoShBr; MyFE; OTPC; PCH; PRWS; RIS; StaSt; UTS
(Song: Owl, The.) FaPON; GoJo; HBV; HBVY; MPB; OBRV; SUS; ThWaDe
(When Cats Run Home.) CH; EG
Owl, The. Edward Thomas. BiS; ChTr; DTC; FaBoTw; GTBS-P; LiTB; MemP; NoP; PoIE; PoSa; UnPo (3d ed.)
Owl, The. *Unknown, tr. fr. German.* SAS
Owl, The. Robert Penn Warren. MAP; MoAmPo
Owl, The. Roland Young. BOHV
Owl against Robin, *abr.* Sidney Lanier. LaNeLa
Owl and the Eel and the Warming-Pan, The. Laura E. Richards. EvOK; HBV; HBVY; PPL
Owl and the Fox, The. *Unknown.* BLPA
(Tragic Tale of Hooty the Owl, The, *sl. diff.*) FTB
Owl and the Nightingale, The, *abr. Unknown, at. to* Nicholas de Guildford, *tr. fr. Middle English.* MeEV
Owl and the Pussy-Cat, The. Edward Lear. BeLS; BoChLi; BOHV; BoTP; CBEP; CIV; EnLi-2 (1949 ed.); FaBoBe; FaBoCh; FaFP; FaPON; GFA; GoJo; GoTP; GSP; GTBS-P; HBV; HBVY; LBN; LiTG; LoGBV; MemP; MoShBr; MPB; NA; NeHB; OnSP; OtMeF; OTPC; OxBoLi; PCD; PCH; PDV; PoLF; PoPl; PoRA; PoRh; PoSa; PoVP; PRWS; RIS; SAS; ShBV-1; SiTL; SoPo; StVeCh; SUS; TiPo; TreFS; TrGrPo; TSW; TVC; UTS; WePo; WhC
Owl-Critic, The. James Thomas Fields. BLPA; BOHV; CenHV; EvOK; GoTP; GSP; HBV; RIS; StPo; TreFS; WBLP; YaD
Owl expires, The! Death gave the dreadful word. On the Death of a Lady's Owl. Moses Mendes. TrJP
Owl has come, The. Eyes. W. H. Davies. BrPo
Owl, horned wizard of the night, An. Three Nocturns. Sir Osbert Sitwell. POTE
Owl is abroad, the bat and the toad, The. Witches' Charm [*or* Charm.] Ben Jonson. *Fr.* The Masque of Queens. FaBoCh; LoBV; LoGBV; ReEn
Owl Is an Only Bird of Poetry, An. Robert Duncan. NeAP
Owl is hooting in the grove, An. Winter Night. Roy Fuller. NeBP
Owl is very very wise, The. The Owl. Roland Young. BOHV
Owl King, The. James Dickey. CoPo
(Call, The.) NePoEA-2
Owl that lives in the old oak tree, The. The Owl. William Jay Smith. PDV
Owl, the Eel and the Warming-Pan, The. Laura E. Richards. *See* Owl and the Eel. . .
Owl to her mate is calling, The. The Fate of the Oak. "Barry Cornwall." OHIP; OTPC
Owls have feathers lined with down, The. The Hedgehog and His Coat. Elizabeth Fleming. BoTP
Owls roost like gray lamps up here, The. Brobdingnag. Adrien Stoutenberg. NYBP
Owls—they whinny down the night. Outlaws. Robert Graves. WIRo
Ownership. Lizette Woodworth Reese. MAP; MoAmPo
Owning. Wilmot B. Lane. CaP
Owre the Muir amang the Heather. Jean Glover. HBV
Owt of thise blake wawes for to saylle. *See* Out of thise blake wawes. . .
Ox, The. Giosuè Carducci, *tr. fr. Italian.* OnPM, *tr. by* Glauco Cambon; WoL, *tr. by* Lorna de' Lucchi
Ox, The. John Gray. GBV (1952 ed.)
Ox, The. Sara Maynard. ChrBoLe
Ox, The. Mary Morison Webster. PeSA
Ox and Donkey's Carol. Sister Maris Stella. PoRL
Ox and the Ass, The. Five Carols for Christmastide, V. Louise Imogen Guiney. ISi
Ox-Bone Madonna. John Duffy. ISi
Ox-Bone Madonna. James J. Galvin. ISi
Ox-driving Song, *with music. Unknown.* OuSiCo
Ox he openeth wide the doore, The. Tryste Noël [*or* Five Carols for Christmastide, I]. Louise Imogen Guiney. HBV; ISi; JKCP; OBVV
Ox-Tamer, The. Walt Whitman. CBEP
Ox with horned head, The. Pan Jezisku. *Unknown.* ChrBoLe
Oxen, The. Thomas Hardy. BoLiVe; BoPe; BoTP; BWP; CaFP; ChrBoLe; CLwM; CMoP; CoBMV; EnL; FosPo; GTBS-W; GTSL; HBMV; LiTM; MaPo; MaRV; MoAB; MoBrPo; MoRP; NoP; OAEP; OTPC (1946 ed.); PAn; PIA; Po; PoAn; PoDB; PoeP; PoIE; PoSa; PoVP; ShBV-2; SoP; StJW; TSW; ViPP; VP
Oxford. Richard Aldridge. NYTB
Oxford. Keith Douglas. NePoEA
Oxford. Lionel Johnson. OBNC; OBVV
Oxford. Archibald T. Strong. *Fr.* Sonnets of the Empire. BoAu
Oxford & Cambridge. Sir William Browne. WhC
(Epigram: "King to Oxford sent a troop of horse, The.") ALV
Oxford Bells. Sister Maris Stella. GoBC
Oxford Idyll, An. Thomas Edward Brown. PoVP
Oxford Is a Stage. Edward Nolan. CenHV
Oxford Nights. Lionel Johnson. BrPo; EnLit
Oxford, since late I left thy peaceful shore. Sonnet: To Oxford. Thomas Russell. ATP; CEP; OBEC; Sonn
Oxford to London, 1884. In a Railway Compartment. John Fuller. NePoEA-2
Oxfordshire Children's May Song. *Unknown. See* May Song ("Spring is coming.")
Oxus. Matthew Arnold. *Fr.* Sohrab and Rustum. VA
Oxygen. Joan Swift. NYBP
Oye, oyeye. Battle Songs of the King Tshaka. *Unknown.* PeSA
Oyster, The. Ogden Nash. ALV; PV
Oyster, The. Sir Walter Scott. *See* Herring, The.
Oyster and the Litigants, The. La Fontaine, *tr. fr. French by* Elizur Wright. WoL
Oyster shuts his gates to form the pearl, The. The Precious Pearl. Pat Wilson. AnNZ; TDP
Oysters. Swift. ErPo
Oyster's a confusing suitor, The. The Oyster. Ogden Nash. ALV; PV
Ozymandias. Shelley. ATP; AWP; BEL; BoLiVe; CABA; CaFP; CBEP; CBV; CLwM; CoBE; DiPo; EnL; EnLi-2; EnLit; EnRP; EPN; ERoP-2; ExPo; FaBoBe; FaBoCh; FaBoEn; FaFP; FiP; ForPo; GoTP; HoPM; HT; ILP; InP; InPo; JAWP; LoBV; LoGBV; MaPo; MaRV; MBW-2; MCCG; MERP; MyFE; NeHB; NoP; OAEP; OBNC; OTD; OuHeWo; PAn; PG (1955 ed.); Po; PoAn; PoE; PoFS; PoIE; PoLF; PoPo; PoRA; PoSa; PTK; RoGo; SeCeV; ShBV-3; Sonn; StP; SyP; TDP; TIHL; TrGrPo; UnPo (1st ed.); WaKn; WBP; WHA; YAT
(Ozymandias of Egypt.) BeLS; CH; GTBS; GTBS-D; GTBS-P; GTBS-W; GTSE; GTSL; HBV; HBVY; OTPC (1946 ed.); PoG; TreF
Ozymandias Revisited. Morris Bishop. ALV

P

P Is for Paleontology. Milton Bracker. FiBHP; InMe; WhC
P.S. Jascha Kessler. AmPC
P. Shut, shut the door, good John! fatigu'd, I said. *See* Shut, shut the door, good John! fatigued, I said.
Pa followed the pair to Pawtucket. *See* But he followed the pair. . .
Pa lays around 'n' loafs all day. Options. "O. Henry." FiBHP
Pablo. Grace Hazard Conkling. GaP
Pace, pace, go the ladies, oh! *Unknown.* SAS
Paces. Sophia Castro-Leon. QAH
Pacific Door. Earle Birney. PeCV; TwCaPo
Pacific Engagement, The. *Unknown. Fr.* Bungiana. WhC
Pacific Railway, The. C. R. Ballard. OTD; PAH
Pacific Sonnets, *sel.* George Barker.
"And now there is nothing left to celebrate," XII. LiTM (rev. ed.); NeBP; Sonn
Pacific Winter. Hildegarde Flanner. NP
Pacifist, The. Hilaire Belloc. MoVE
Pack, Clouds, Away. Thomas Heywood. *Fr.* The Rape of Lucrece, IV, vi. BiS; BoTP; ElL; GTBS; GTSE; OTPC; ThWaDe; ViBoPo; WHA
(Good-Morrow.) ALV; CH; TOP
(Matin Song.) GTSL; HBV; MemP; OBEV; ShBV-1
("Pack, clouds, away, and welcome day.") EG; GTBS-D; GTBS-P; GTBS-W
(To Give My Love Good-Morrow.) MeWo
(Waking Song.) RIS
Package, The. Aileen Fisher. SoPo
Packed in my mind lie all the clothes. The Inward Morning. Henry David Thoreau. AmP; AmPP (3d ed); AP; CLwM; MAmP; MWA-1; NoP
Packed with woodpeckers, my head knocks. Raking Leaves. Robert Pack. CoPo; NYBP
Packet of Letters. Louise Bogan. LiTL
Packing a Photograph from Firenze. William H. Matchett. NePoEA
Pact. Kenneth Fearing. CMoP
Pact, The. Alfred Noyes. MaRV
Pact, A. Ezra Pound. AmPP (5th ed.); CBEP; CBV; ELU; LiTA; ML; MoPW; NePA; OxBA; Po; PoPl
Pad, Pad. Stevie Smith. ELU
Paddle Your Own Canoe. Sarah K. Bolton. FaFP
Paddling Pool, The. E. M. Adams. BoTP
Paddling Song. *Unknown, tr. fr. Bantu by* Max Exner. PBA
Paddy Doyle, *with music. Unknown.* AmSS; ShS; SoAmSa
Paddy Get Back, *with music. Unknown.* AmSS; ShS; SoAmSa
Paddy, in want of a dinner one day. Paddy O'Rafther. Samuel Lover. BOHV; HBV; StPo
Paddy McCabe was dying one day. Father Molloy. Samuel Lover. BOHV; HBV
Paddy Murphy. *Unknown.* PV
Paddy O'Rafther. Samuel Lover. BOHV; HBV; StPo
Paddy the Beaver. Thornton Burgess. RePo
Paddy West, *with music. Unknown.* ShS
Paddy Works on the Railway, *with music. Unknown.* AmSS; SoAmSa
(Paddy Works on the Erie, *with music.*) ABF
(Pat Works on the Railway.) TrAS
(Poor Paddy Works on the Railway, *with music.*) AS
Paddy's Metamorphosis. Thomas Moore. OnYI
Padraic O'Conaire, Gaelic Storyteller. F. R. Higgins. OBMV; OnYI; OxBI
Padstow Night Song, The. *Unknown.* ChTr
Paean. Jonathan Henderson Brooks. CDC
Pagan Epitaph. Richard Middleton. OBVV; TOP
Pagan gods of force reclaim their altars, The. Today. Thomas Curtis Clark. ChIP
Pagan Prayer. Alice Brown. WGRP
Pagan Reinvokes the Twenty-third Psalm, A. Robert L. Wolf. HBMV; TrPWD
Paganini. Christopher Middleton. MuSP
Pagan's Baptism, A. A. S. Cripps. BoSA
Pagans wild confesse the bonds, The. Roger Williams. SCAP
Page IX. Gertrude Stein. WaKn
Page of Illustrations, The. Peter Schjeldahl. ANYP
Page of Lancelot, The. May Kendall. VA
Pageant, The. Whittier. AmLP
Pageant of Man, The, *sel.* Stanton A. Coblentz.
Patient Is Time. MaRV
Pageant of Seamen, The. May Byron. HBV
Page's Road Song, A. William Alexander Percy. TrPWD; YeAr
Pages' Song, The. Shakespeare. *See* It Was a Lover and His Lass.
Pagett, M.P. Kipling. BrPo
Pagget, a school-boy, got a sword, and then. Upon Pagget. Robert Herrick. FaBoCh; LoGBV
Paid on Both Sides, *sel.* W. H. Auden.
Chorus: "To throw away the key and walk away." MoBrPo
(Walking Tour.) CMoP
Pain. "Æ." MoBrPo
Pain. Maltbie D. Babcock. FaChP
Pain. St. John Lucas. HBV
Pain. Harriet Monroe. NP
Pain. Coventry Patmore. PoLi
Pain. Elsie Robinson. PoToHe (new ed.)
Pain. Leonora Speyer. HBMV
Pain. *Unknown. See* Lord, Take Away Pain.
Pain gnaws at my heart like a rat that gnaws at a beam. The Rat. Arthur Symons. SyP
Pain has an element of blank. Emily Dickinson. AP; CBEP; DiPo; LiTA; LiTM (rev. ed.); MoAB; MoAmPo (1950 ed.); OnPM
Pain is a beckoning hand. Pain. Leonora Speyer. HBMV
Pain is a blacksmith. Blacksmith Pain. Otto-Julius Bierbaum. AWP; JAWP; WBP
Pain is my familiar, now. To My New Mistress. Beverly Bowie. PoPl
Pain of Living, The. Eugenio Montale, *tr. fr. Italian by* Glauco Cambon. OnPM
Pain of loving you, The. A Young Wife. D. H. Lawrence. BrPo; ChMP; ELP; MoBrPo; StP
Pain of too poignant beauty fills the heart. The World's Desire. William Rose Benét. TrPWD
Painful and brief the act. Eve on the barren shore. Eve in Reflection. Jay Macpherson. OBCV
Painful Question, The. Warner B. Wims. TNV
Painfully writhed the few last weeds upon those houseless uplands. An Infantryman. Edmund Blunden. ViBoPo
Painless at last, his being escaped from the terrible. The Harrowing of Hell. Rainer Maria Rilke. BoPe
Pains and Gains. Edward de Vere, Earl of Oxford. ElL
Pains of Education, The. Charles Churchill. SiTL
Pains of insecurity surround me. Back Again, Home. Don L. Lee. BALP
Pains of Sleep, The. Samuel Taylor Coleridge. CBEP; EnRP; EPN; ERoP-1; MERP; NCEP; OAEP; OBNC; OBRV; SeCePo; SyP
(Child's Evening Prayer, A.) OTPC (1923 ed.); TrPWD
Pains, reading, study, are their just pretence. Verbal Critics. Pope. *Fr.* Epistle to Dr. Arbuthnot. OBEC; PP
Pains the sharp sentence the heart in whose wrath it was uttered. Pardon. Julia Ward Howe. PAH
Paint-flaken, it is paint-flaken. March, Upstate. William Bronk. NYBP
Paint last the King, and a dead shade of Night. Andrew Marvell. *Fr.* Last Instructions to a Painter. OBS
Paint triggers the serene. The Clock Works. Lewis MacAdams. ANYP; YAP
Painted Fan, A. Louise Chandler Moulton. AA
Painted Head. John Crowe Ransom. AP; CoBMV; CrMA; LiTA; LiTG; LiTM (rev. ed.); MoPo; MoVE; OxBA; PoIE; ReMP
(Painting; a Head.) MAP; MoAB; MoAmPo
Painted Hills of Arizona, The. Edwin Curran. HBMV; HT; PFY
Painted Indian rides no more, The. *Unknown.* WhC
Painter, The. Robert Fitzgerald. MoVE
Painter and poet, runner and disk-thrower. One of the Jews. C. P. Cavafy. TrJP
Painter, my unmatch'd desert. The Picture. Thomas Stanley. AWP; JAWP; UnTE; WBP
Painter in New England, A. Charles Wharton Stork. HBMV
Painter once more thy pencell reassume. Further Advice to a Painter. Andrew Marvell. MaMe

Painter Who Pleased Nobody and Everybody, The. John Gay. BeLS; CEP
Painter, you're come, but may be gone. The Picture of Her Mind. Ben Jonson. GoBC
Painter's Mistress, The. James Elroy Flecker. BrPo
Painting; a Head. John Crowe Ransom. *See* Painted Head.
Painting by Chimes. Bernadette Mayer. ANYP
Painting of a Lobster by Picasso. Hy Sobiloff. NePA; TwAmPo
Paintings of Roses. Robert Hershon. ThO
Paintings with stiff. Primitives. Dudley Randall. BALP
Pair, A. Karl Gjellerup, *tr. fr. Danish by* Charles Wharton Stork. OnPM; PoPl
Pair of Lovers, A. Jeanne Robert Foster. HBMV
Pair of Lovers in the Street, A. Arthur Adams. BoAu
Pair of steady Rooks, A. The Death of Master Tommy Rook. Eliza Cook. OTPC (1923 ed.)
Pair of Wings, A. Stephen Hawes. MeEL
Pairing-Time Anticipated. William Cowper. BOHV
Paisley Officer, The, 2 *vers., with music. Unknown.* ShS
Páistín Fionn. *Unknown. See* Pastheen Finn.
Palabras Cariñosas. Thomas Bailey Aldrich. AA; HBV; InP
Palabras Grandiosas. Bayard Taylor. *Fr.* The Echo Club. BOHV
Palace. Dorothy Vena Johnson. GoSl
Palace of Art, The. Tennyson. BEL; EnLi-2; MaVP; MBW-2; OAEP; PoVP; UnPo (1st ed.); ViPo; ViPP; VP
To——: With the Following Poem, *introd.* MBW-2; ViPo; ViPP; VP
Palace of Honor, The, *sel.* Gawin Douglas.
Nightmare. PoEL-1
Palace of the Fairies, The. Michael Drayton. OTPC
Palace of the Gnomes. Maria Gowen Brooks. *Fr.* Zophiel; or, The Bride of Seven. AA
Palace of Truth, The. William Langland. *Fr.* The Vision of Piers Plowman. ACP
Palace Poem, A. Hsüeh Feng, *tr. fr. Chinese by* Witter Bynner. LiTW
Palaces are sombre cliffs by night, The. On the Grand Canal. David Gascoyne. SeCePo
Palanquin Bearers. Sarojini Naidu. MoSiPe
Palatine, The. Willa Cather. HBMV; InP; NP
Palatine, The. Whittier. EtS
Palaver's No Prayer. John Ciardi. ToPo
Pale amber sunlight falls across. Autumnal. Ernest Dowson. OBNC
Pale and by the hand and like two friends. Autumn Twilight. Henri de Régnier. LiTW
Pale and soul-sick woman with wan eyes, A. The Age. Herbert Edwin Clarke. VA
Pale beech and pine so [*or* pine-tree] blue. In a Wood. Thomas Hardy. *Fr.* The Woodlanders. InP; OAEP; OBNC; PoPl; ViPo (1962 ed.)
Pale beryl sky, with clouds. A Winter Twilight. Arlo Bates. AA
Pale, beyond porch and portal. Proserpine. Swinburne. *Fr.* The Garden of Proserpine. ChTr; FaBoEn
Pale Blue Casket, The. Oliver Pitcher. NNP; TTY
Pale, brown Moses went down to Egypt land. Benediction. Bob Kaufman. PoNe (1970 ed.); WOW
Pale brows, still hands and dim hair. The Lover Mourns for the Loss of Love. W. B. Yeats. Po
Pale, climbing disk, who dost lone vigil keep. To the Moonflower. Craven Langstroth Betts. AA
Pale Cold Moon, The. William Renton. WePo
Pale darts still quivering, crocuses. Poem at Equinox. Hilary Corke. NYBP
Pale dressed evening star, The. Twinkling Gown. Dorothy Vena Johnson. GoSl
Pale Ebenezer thought it wrong to fight. The Pacifist. Hilaire Belloc. MoVE
Pale from the watery west, with the pallor of winter a-cold. In Winter. Arthur Symons. BrPo
Pale genius roves alone. Emerson. *Fr.* Fragments on the Poet and the Poetic Gift. TOP
Pale green of the *English Hymnal!* Yattendon hymns. The Old Liberals. John Betjeman. ChMP
Pale hands I loved beside the Shalimar. Kashmiri Song. "Laurence Hope." BLPA; FaBoBe; FaFP; NeHB; TreF
Pale Heinrich he came sauntering by. The Window-Glance. Heine. AWP
Pale inke, thou art not black enough of hew. *Unknown.* SeCSL
Pale Is Death. Joachim du Bellay, *tr. fr. French by* Hubert Creekmore. LiTW
Pale is the February sky. The Twenty-second of February. Bryant. DD; HH; MPB; OTPC (1946 ed.); PoRL
Pale Italian peasant, A. At the Shrine. Richard Kendall Munkittrick. AA
Pale light tatters the stones beyond the hemlock. Sudden Frost. David Wagoner. PoPl
Pale moon was rising above the green mountain, The. The Rose of Tralee. William Pembroke Mulchinock, *also at. to* C. Mordaunt Spencer. OnYI; TreFT
Pale New Lights Cling. Don Shea. QAH
Pale road winds faintly upward into the dark skies, The. The Glow-Worm. Edward Shanks. WHA
Pale rose is a smell that has no fountain, A. Gertrude Stein. *Fr.* Scenes. AtBAP
Pale sand edges England's Old/ Dominion. Virginia Britannia. Marianne Moore. MoVE
Pale stars are gone, The! Shelley. Prometheus Unbound, IV. EnLi-2 (1949 ed.)
Pale Sun, The ("Pale sunbeams gleam"). John Clare. PeER
Pale Woman, The. Arthur Symons. FaBoTw
Palely intent, he urged his keel. At the Cannon's Mouth. Herman Melville. PAH
Palermo. Harriet Eleanor Hamilton King. *Fr.* The Disciples. VA
Palermo, Mother's Day, 1943. William Belvin. PoPl
Palestine. Whittier. WBLP
Palimpsest. Hyman Edelstein. CaP
Palinode, A. Edmund Bolton. ElL; InvP; OBSC; PoEL-2; SiCE; TuPP
Palinode. Oliver St. John Gogarty. OBMV; PG (1955 ed.)
Palinode, A. Robert Greene. *Fr.* Greene's Groatsworth of Wit. OBSC
("Deceiving world, that with alluring toys.") SiCE
Palinode. James Russell Lowell. AA
Palladium. Matthew Arnold. EPN; FaBoEn; GTBS-P; MaVP; NoP; OAEP; OBNC; PoVP; ViPP; VP
Pallas an old-wife. Haughtie thoughts o're-throw. The Sixth Booke. Ovid. *Fr.* Metamorphosis. AnAnS-2
Pallas saw Venus arm'd, and streight she cry'd. Upon the Same. Richard Crashaw. MaMe
Pallid Cuckoo. David Campbell. PoAu-2
Pallid cuckoo, The. Late Winter. J. P. McAuley. NeLNL; PoAu-2
Pallid, mis-shapen he stands. The world's grimed thumb. In the Dock. Walter de la Mare. ChMP; LiTM (1970 ed.); Sonn
Pallid rout stepping like phantoms, A. Tourists in a Sacred Place. Sir Herbert Read. MoBrPo (1942 ed.)
Pallid taper its long prayer recites, A. Sursum. Guillermo Valencia. CAW
Pallid with too much longing. Laus Veneris. Louise Chandler Moulton. AA; HBV
Pallidly sleeping, the Ocean's mysterious daughter. Elegy on a Dead Mermaid Washed Ashore at Plymouth Rock. Robert Hillyer. EtS
Palm, The. Roy Campbell. MoBrPo
Palm at the end of the mind, The. Of Mere Being. Wallace Stevens. PoIE (1970 ed.)
Palm House, Botanic Gardens. George Hetherington. NeIP
Palm Leaves of Childhood. G. Adali-Mortti. PBA
Palm of the Hand. Rainer Maria Rilke, *tr. fr. German by* Jessie Lemont. OnPM
Palm, Palm, Palm Sunday. Palm Sunday. *Unknown.* PCH
Palm Sunday. Francis Jammes, *tr. fr. French by* Theodore Yung. CAW
Palm Sunday. John J. Moment. MaRV
Palm Sunday. *Unknown, tr. fr. Greek.* PCH
Palm-Sunday. Henry Vaughan. AtBAP
Triumphant Entry, The, *sel.* MaRV; StJW
Palm Sunday and Monday. Edwin McNeill Poteat. ChIP; MaRV
Palm-Sunday Hymn, A. William Herebert. MeEL
Palm Sunday Hymn. George Klingle. ChIP
Palm Sunday: Naples. Arthur Symons. BrPo; PeVV
Palm-Tree, The. Adb-ar-Rahman I, *tr. fr. Arabic by* J. B. Trend. AWP; JAWP; WBP
Palm-Tree, The. Henry Vaughan. AnAnS-1; MeP
Palm-Tree and the Pine, The. Richard Monckton Milnes. HBV
Palm Tree Mates with Palm. Claudian, *tr. fr. Latin by* Mau-

rice Platnauer *and* Virginia Tufte. *Fr.* Epithalamium for Honorius and Maria. HW
Palmer, The. John Heywood. *Fr.* The Four P's. ACP; CAW
Palmer, The. William Langland. *Fr.* The Vision of Piers Plowman. ACP; CAW
Palmer, The. Sir Walter Scott. OTPC
Palmer's Ode, The. Robert Greene. *Fr.* Never Too Late. CTC; EnRePo; OBSC; SiCE; TuPP
Palms, The. David Knight. MoCV
Palms and Myrtles. Eleazar ben Kalir, *tr. fr. Hewbrew by* Alice Lucas. TrJP
Palms of Mammon have ordained, The. The Revealer. E. A. Robinson. DD
Palmström hasn't a crumb in the house. The Mousetrap. Christian Morgenstern. OA
Palos, Spain, 1492. Annette Wynne. HH
Paltry Nude Starts on a Spring Voyage, The. Wallace Stevens. NP
Pamela in Town. Ellen Mackay Hutchinson Cortissoz. AA; HBV
Pamela was too gentle to deceive. The Tree in Pamela's Garden. E. A. Robinson. MoLP
Pamphlet. Luis Muñoz Marín, *tr. fr. Spanish by* Muna Lee. PoFr; WoL
Pan. Emerson. ILP
Pan and Syrinx. W. R. Rodgers. NMP
Pan and the Cherries. Paul Fort, *tr. fr. French by* Jethro Bithell. AWP; PoMS
Pan, blow your pipes and I will be. A Note from the Pipes. Leonora Speyer. HBMV
Pan came out of the woods one day. Pan with Us. Robert Frost. GBV (1952 ed.); OxBA
Pan—did you say he was dead, that he'd gone, and for good. Pan-Pipes. Patrick Chalmers. HBMV
Pan-imbued/ Tempe wood. Pastoral. Francis Thompson. PoLi
Pan in Pandemonium. Berton Braley. LHV
Pan in Vermont. Kipling. WhC
Pan in Wall Street. Edmund Clarence Stedman. AA; AmePo; AnAmPo; HBV; PFY
Pan is not dead, but sleeping in the brake. Villanelle of the Living Pan. Walter Adolphe Roberts. PoNe
Pan Jezisku. *Unknown, tr. fr. Slovakian by* Leclaire Alger. ChrBoLe
Pan Learns Music. Henry van Dyke. PCH
Pan leave piping, and gods have done feasting. The Green-Gown. *Unknown.* CoMu
Pan loved his neighbour, Echo. Love's Lesson. Moschus. AWP
Pan on a tram! in a crooked horn blowing. Spring. Hugh McCrae. ACV
Pan-Pipes. Patrick Chalmers. HBMV
Pan, stay awhile. On the Lawn. Cametas. OnPM
Pan-thrilled saplings swayed in sportive bliss, The. May. Stephen Moylan. HBMV
Pan went dancing up and down the city. Pan in Pandemonium. Berton Braley. LHV
Pan with Us. Robert Frost. GBV (1952 ed.); OxBA
Panama. Amanda Theodosia Jones. PAH
Panama. James Jeffrey Roche. MC; PAH; PoRL
Pancake, The. Christina Rossetti. *See* Mix a Pancake.
Panchatantra, The, *sels.* *Unknown, tr. fr. Sanskrit by* Arthur W. Ryder.
  Fool and False. AWP; JAWP; WBP
  Heron That Liked Crab-meat, The. OuHeWo
  How the Crow-Hen Killed the Black Snake. OuHeWo
  "In houses where no snakes are found." LiTW
  "In sensuous coil." LiTW
   (Kings.) AWP; PoFr
  Leap and Creep. OuHeWo
  Mice That Ate Iron, The. OuHeWo
  Penalty of Virtue, The. AWP; PoFr
  Poverty. AWP; PoFr
  "Some eat the countries; these are kings." LiTW
  "Some things a man should tell his wife." LiTW
  "'Tis hard to find in life." LiTW
   (True Friendship.) AWP; JAWP; WBP
  "'Tis only saints in youth." LiTW
Panda, The. William Jay Smith. RePo
Pandemonium and Its Architect. Milton. *Fr.* Paradise Lost, I. PoFS; TreFS
Pandora and the Moon. Merrill Moore. MAP; MoAmPo
Pandora's Songs. William Vaughn Moody. *Fr.* The Fire-Bringer.
  "Along the earth and up the sky." GBV
  "I stood within the heart of God." AnFE; APA; CoAnAm; GBV; MAP; MoAmPo (1942 ed.); OQP; WGRP
  "Of wounds and sore defeat." BBV; GBV; HBV; PFY; PTK
Pandosto, *sel.* Robert Greene.
  Fawnia. HBV; OBEV; OBSC
   ("Ah, were she pitiful as she is fair.") EG; TrGrPo, *abr.*; ViBoPo
   (In Praise of His Loving and Best-beloved Fawnia.) AtBAP; PoEL-2
Panegyric [on Nelly], A. *Unknown, at. to* the Earl of Rochester. PeRV; UnTE, *abr.*
Panegyric on Geese, A. Francis Sylvester Mahony. OnYI
Panegyric on the Ladies. *Unknown.* BOHV
Panegyrick to My Lord Protector, A [*or* Panegyrick upon O. Cromwell]. Edmund Waller. OBS; SCEP-2
  "While with a strong and yet a gentle hand," *sel.* SeCV-1
Panegyrick upon Oates, A. *At. to* Richard Duke. PeRV
Paneled in Pine. Marguerite George. FiSC
Pang of the long century of rains, The. The Lament of Edward Blastock. Edith Sitwell. OBMV
Pange Lingua Gloriosa. St. Thomas Aquinas. *See* Hymn: "Sing, my tongue, the Saviour's Glory."
Pangloss' Song. Richard Wilbur. NePoAm-2
  (Pangloss's Song; a Comic-Opera Lyric.) AP
Pangolin, The. Marianne Moore. AP; CoBMV; CrMA
Pangs That Guard the Gates of Joy, The. Christopher J. Brennan. BoAu
Pangur Ban. *Unknown. See* Monk and His Pet Cat, The.
Panhandle Cob. *At. to* H. D. Maclachlan. CoSo
Panic, *sels.* Archibald MacLeish. MAP; MoAmPo
  Final Chorus.
  Panic ("Slowly the thing comes").
Pannyra of the Golden Heel. Albert Samain. AWP
Panope. Edith Sitwell. MoAB; MoBrPo; NP
Panorama, The. Milton. *See* New Worlds.
Pans Anniversarie; or, The Shepherds Holy-Day. Ben Jonson. AnAnS-2
  Thus, Thus Begin, *sel.* TuPP
   ("Thus, thus begin the yearly rites.") OBS
Pan's Song. John Lyly. *Fr.* Midas, IV, i. AtBAP; OBSC
   (Pan's Syrinx.) ELP
   (Pan's Syrinx Was a Girl.) ViBoPo
   ("Pan's Syrinx was a girl indeed.") SiCE
   (Syrinx.) ElL; LoBV; SeCePo; WHA
Pansies. Tom Robinson. BoChLi (1950 ed.)
Pansies, lilies, kingcups, daisies. To the Small Celandine. Wordsworth. EnRP; HBV; MERP; NoP; OBRV; OTPC
Pansy. Mary Effie Lee Newsome. CDC
Pansy and the Prayer-Book, The. Matilda Barbara Betham-Edwards. OBVV
Pansy-face and raspberry-paws. To a Cat Purring. Florence Small Edsall. CIV
Pantheist's Song of Immortality, The. Constance Caroline Woodhill Naden. VA
Panther, The. Ogden Nash. FaPON; MoShBr; SoPo; TiPo (1959 ed.)
Panther,The. Rainer Maria Rieke. *Tr. fr. German.*
—— *Tr. by* Donald Heiney. PIA
—— *Tr. by* J. B. Leishman. FlW
—— *Tr. by* Jessie Lemont. OA; OnPM
—— *Tr. by* C. F. MacIntyre. LiTW
Panther, The. *Unknown.* NA
  (Kindly Advice.) BOHV
Panther and Peacock. Gwen Harwood. PoAu-2
Panther is like a leopard, The. The Panther. Ogden Nash. FaPON; MoShBr; SoPo; TiPo (1959 ed.)
Panther, knowing that his spotted hide, The. Amoretti, LIII. Spenser. EnRePo
Panther lies next to Wharncliffe. Appalachian Front. Robert Lewis Weeks. AmFN; NYBP
Panther Possible, The. William D. Barney. FiSC
Panther sure the noblest, next the Hind, The. The Church of England. Dryden. *Fr.* The Hind and the Panther, I. OBS
Pantisocracy. Samuel Taylor Coleridge. EnRP
Pantomime. Paul Verlaine, *tr. fr. French by* Arthur Symons. AWP; JAWP; SyP; WBP
Paolo and Francesca. Dante, *tr. fr. Italian. Fr.* Divina

Paolo (continued)
Commedia: Inferno, V. ExPo, *tr. by* Laurence Binyon; TreFT, *tr. by* Byron
Papa above! Emily Dickinson. AmPP (5th ed.)
Papa John. Jorge de Lima, *tr. fr. Portuguese by* John Nist. TTY
Papageno. W. D. Snodgrass. NoP
Paper. Benjamin Franklin. LHV
Paper Boats. Rabindranath Tagore. FaPON; MCCG; PCH; SP
"Day by day I float my paper boats," *sel.* FlW
Paper in the Meadow, The. Oscar Williams. PG (1955 ed.)
Paper, little sticks and a cord. The Kite. José Moreno Villa. OnPM
Paper Mill. Joseph Kalar. AnAmPo
Paper Nautilus, The. Marianne Moore. CBV; FaBoMo
Paper of Pins, A, *with music. Unknown.* ABF; BFSS
(Keys of Heaven, The, *sl. diff., with music.*) FTB
Papermill Graveyard. Ben Belitt. NYBP
Papers say he died in a swimming pool, The. On the Death of Theodore Roethke. William Witherup. QAH
Paphos. Lawrence Durrell. NYBP
Pap's got the pattent-right, and rich as all creation. Back to Griggsby's Station. James Whitcomb Riley. BLPA
Papuan Shepherd, A. Francis Webb. *Fr.* A Drum for Ben Boyd. PoAu-2
Parable. Peggy Bennett. ELU
Parable, A. George L. Kress. STF
Parable, A. James Russell Lowell. ChIP; MaRV, *sl. abr.*; PGD, *abr.*
Parable. Robert Pack. NePoEA-2
Parable. William Soutar. HaMV
Parable for Poetasters, A. Oliver St. John Gogarty. WhC
Parable from Liebig, A. Charles Kingsley. SoP
Parable of the Mustard Weed, The. Dora Hagemeyer. StaSt
Parable of the Old Man and the Young. Wilfred Owen. BoPe; FlW; MemP
Parable of the Spirit, A. John Arthur Goodchild. VA
Parable of the Talents, The. St. Matthew, XXV: 14-30, Bible, *N.T.* EnLi-1
Parabola, The. Hooper Reynolds Goodwin. PoMa
Parabolas of grief, the hills are never. In Africa. Roy Fuller. BoSA
Paracelsus, *sels.* Robert Browning.
Awakening of Man, The, *fr. V.* WGRP
Development of Man, *fr.* V. EPN
Faith, *fr.* V. TreFT
Heap Cassia, Sandal-Buds, and Stripes. GTSL; MyFE; OBRV; PoVP
(Song: "Heap cassia, sandal-buds and stripes." AnFE; OBEV; WHA
In His Good Time, *br. sel.* OQP
(I Go to Prove My Soul.) MaRV
"Progress is the law of life," *fr.* V. OQP
(Man's Destiny.) MaRV
Scene in a Garden, *fr.* I. PCH
Song: "Over the sea our galleys went," *fr.* IV. OBRV; VA
(Over the Sea Our Galleys Went.) PoVP
(Wanderers, The.) OBEV; OBVV
Song: "Thus the Mayne glideth," *fr.* V. OBRV
(Thus the Mayne Glideth.) PoVP
Truth Is Within, *fr.* I. MaRV
Parachute. Stanley Snaith. HaMV
Parachute Descent. David Bourne. WaP
Parachutes, The. Charles Gullans. NYTB
Parachutes, My Love, Could Carry Us Higher. Barbara Guest. NeAP
Parachutist, The. Jon Anderson. NYBP
Paraclete. Jorge de Lima, *tr. fr. Portuguese by* Dudley Poore. PoFr
Parade, The. Mary Esther Badley. PEDC
Parade. Rachel Field. *Fr.* A Circus Garland. SoPo; StVeCh; UTS
Parade, The. Ashton Greene. NePoAm
Parade, A. Mary Catherine Rose. SoPo
Parade, The. Marjorie Seymour Watts. PCH
Paradice on earth is found, A. *See* Paradise on earth is found, A.
Paradigm. Babette Deutsch. TrJP
Paradigm of a Hero. Jack Mathews. TPM
Parading near Saint Peter's flood. The Battle of Lake Champlain. Philip Freneau. PAH
Paradise. George Birdseye. BOHV
(Paradise; a Hindoo Legend.) HBV
Paradise. Charles G. Blanden. OQP
Paradise. Dante. *See* Paradiso.
Paradise. Frederick William Faber. HBV; VA
(O Paradise! O Paradise!) WGRP
Paradise. George Herbert. BoLiVe; MaMe; SeCP; TrGrPo
Paradise. Omar Khayyám. *See* Rubáiyát of Omar Khayyám of Naishápúr.
Paradise. John Milton. *Fr.* Paradise Lost, IV. OBS
Paradise. Immanuel di Roma, *tr. fr. Hebrew by* Joseph Chotzner. TrJP
Paradise. Christina Rossetti. HBV; OxBoCh; PoVP; WGRP
(Paradise; in a Dream.) ViPo
Paradise. E. N. Sargent. NYBP
Paradise; a Hindoo Legend. George Birdseye. *See* Paradise.
Paradise; in a Dream. Christina Rossetti. *See* Paradise.
Paradise Lost, *sels.* Milton.
Adam and Eve ("Birds their choir apply; airs, vernal airs, The"), *Bk.* IV, *ll.* 264-656 *abr.* CLwM
(Eternal Spring, The.) GN
Adam and Eve ("So passed they naked on"), *Bk.* IV, *ll.* 319-355. SeCePo
Adam, First Man of Men, *Bk.* VIII, *ll.* 250-299. MaPo
"All these and more came flocking; but with looks," *Bk.* I, *ll.* 522-571. MyFE
And God Created the Great Whales, *Bk.* VII, *ll.* 391-416. EtS
"And in a moment will create," *Bk.* VII, *ll.* 154-634, *abr.* YAT
Ark, The, *Bk.* XI, *ll.* 719-753. EtS
"As when a vulture on Imaus bred," *Bk.* III, *ll.* 431-443. HoPM
Atonement, The, *Bk.* III, *ll.* 227-265. OBS
Beelzebub Rises to Speak, *Bk.* II, *ll.* 284-309. UnPo (1st ed.)
Council of Satan, The, *Bk.* I, *ll.* 271-669. PoEL-3
Creation of Man, The, *Bk.* VII, *ll.* 505-534. PeRV
Creation of Woman, The, *Bk.* VIII, *ll.* 452-489. PeRV
"Descend from Heaven, Urania, by that name," *Bk.* VII, *ll.* 1-39. MBW-1
(Invocation to Urania.) FiP; OBS
Description of Chaos, *Bk.* II, *ll.* 890-950. PeRV
Eden, *Bk.* IV, *ll.* 246-268. DiPo
Eve, *Bk.* IX, *ll.* 417-466. OBS
Eve Penitent, *Bk.* X, *ll.* 914-946. OBS
Eve to Adam, *Bk.* IV, *ll.* 639-656. FaBoEn; TreFS; TrGrPo, *ll.* 639-658
(Eve Speaks to Adam.) ChTr
Eve's Speech to Adam, *Bk.* IV, *ll.* 449-477. DiPo
Eve's Temptation and Fall, *Bk.* IX, *ll.* 494-792. DiPo
Exit from Eden, *Bk.* XII, *ll.* 561-649. DiPo
Fall, The, *Bk.* IX, *ll.* 385-1189. PoEL-3
Fallen Angels, *Bk.* I, *ll.* 50-67. DiPo
First Day of Creation, The, *Bk.* VII, *ll.* 192-260. OxBoCh
(Creation of the World, The, *ll.* 192-242.) MaPo
Flight of Satan, The, *Bk.* II, *ll.* 629-635, 1011-1055.
Free Will and God's Foreknowledge, *Bk.* III, *ll.* 80-134. ExPo
Gabriel Meets Satan, *Bk.* IV, *ll.* 823-1015. LoBV
Garden, The, *Bk.* IV, *ll.* 205-304. MaPo (1969 ed.)
"God made thee perfet, not immutable," *Bk.* V, *ll.* 524-540. PoFr
Great Creator from His Work Returned, The. *Bk.* VIII, *ll.* 565-601. TreFT
"Hail, holy light, offspring of Heaven first-born!" *Bk.* III, *ll.* 1-55. AtBAP; ATP, *ll.* 1-137; ExPo; FiP; FosPo; GTBS-W; InP; LoBV; MBW-1; OAEP; PoIE; SeEP; ShBV-4; ViBoPo; WHA
(Hymn to Light,*ll.* 1-50.) FaBoEn
(Invocation to Light.) MaPo (1969 ed.)
(Light.) LiTB; OBEV; OBS
Hail Wedded Love, *Bk.* IV, *ll.* 319-775, *abr.* HW
"He, above the rest/ In shape and gesture proudly eminent," *Bk.* I, *ll.* 589-604. InP
"He ended, and they both descend the hill," *Bk.* XII, *ll.* 606-649. ATP; SeEP
(Banishment, The, *ll.* 624-649.) OBS
(Banishment from Paradise, *ll.* 607-649.) TreFS

(Expulsion from Paradise, The.) BEL, *ll.* 606-649; ChTr, *ll.* 633-649
(Leave Taking, *ll.* 610-649.) FaBoEn
(Their Banishment, *ll.* 625-649.) SeCePo
"He ended; and thus Adam last replied," *Bk.* XII, *ll.* 552-649. CoBE; MyFE
(Retreat from Paradise, The.) PoEL-3
Heaven, *Bk.* III, *ll.* 344-371. OBS
Hell, *Bk.* II, *ll.* 475-628. OBS
"High on a throne of royal state, which far," *Bk.* II, *complete.* AtBAP, *ll.* 1-505, 506-628; CoBE, *ll.* 1-505; EnL, *ll.* 1-889, *abr.*; EnLi-1; EnLit; FosPo; MBW-1; OAEP; SeEP, *ll.* 1-505; TOP
"Him the Almighty Power/ Hurld headlong flaming," *fr. Bk.* I. AnFE, *ll.* 44-109, 283-330; MyFE, *ll.* *44-191*
(Fallen Angels, The, ll, 44-74.) FaBoEn
(Satan Defiant, *ll.* 44-109.) WHA
Inner Light, *Bk.* III, *ll.* 40-55. MaRV
Invocation: "Of man's first disobedience, and the fruit," *Bk.* I, *ll.* 1-26. DiPo
"Is this the region, this the soil, the clime," *Bk.* I, *ll.* 242-270. MyFE
(Fall of the Angels, The, *ll.* 242-363.) FiP
(Satan Ponders His Fallen State, *ll.* 242-263.) TreFS
Lucifer, *Bk.* I, *ll.* 594-615. UnPo (1st ed.)
Mammon, *Bk.* I, *ll.* 679-684. MaRV
Myself Am Hell ("The mind is its own place"), *Bk.* I, *ll.* 254-255, *Bk.* IV, *ll.* 73-80. MaRV
New Worlds, *Bk.* III, *ll.* 543-571. OBS
(Panorama, The, *ll.* 540-565.) WHA
"No more of talk where God or angel guest," *Bk.* IX, *complete.* FosPo; MBW-1; NoP; SeEP, *ll.* 1-47
(Subject of Heroic Song, The, *ll.* 1-47.) OBS
"Now came still evening on and twilight gray," *fr. Bk.* IV. PoG, *ll.* 598-609; PoIE, *ll.* 598-609, 639-658; SeEP, *ll.* 598-775
(Evening in Paradise.) FaBoEn, *ll.* 598-609; GN, *ll.* 598-609; LoBV, *ll.* 598-688
(Moon and the Nightingale, The, *ll.* 598-609.) ChTr
(Night Falls on Eden, *ll.* 598-609.) PoFS; TreFS
"Now too nigh/ Th' archangel stood," *Bk.* XII, *ll.* 624-649. PoIE
O Earth, How Like to Heav'n, *Bk.* IX, *ll.* 99-178. MaPo
"O for that warning voice, which he who saw," *Bk.* IV, *ll.* 1-755. MBW-1
"Of Man's first disobedience, and the fruit," *Bk.* I, *complete.* ATP; BEL; BoLiVe; CoBE; EnL; EnLi-1; EnLit; FiP, *ll.* 1-26; FosPo, *abr.*; MBW-1; OAEP; OuHeWo; SeEP, *ll.* 1-26; TOP
(Fallen Angels, The, *ll.* 1-363.) WoL
(Invocation.) FaBoEn, *ll.* 1-26; PoEL-3, *ll.* 1-26; PoFS, *ll.* 1-49
(Invocation to the Heavenly Muse, *ll.* 1-26.) TreFS
"Others more mild,/ Retreated in a silent valley, sing," *Bk.* II, *ll.* 546-627. MyFE
Over All the Face of Earth Main Ocean Flowed, *Bk.* VII, *ll.* 278-308. EtS
Pandemonium and Its Architect, *fr. Bk.* I. PoFS, *ll.* 710-751; TreFS, *ll.* 710-746
Paradise, *Bk.* IV, *ll.* 257-294. OBS
Place of the Damned, The, *Bk.* II, *ll.* 582-603. FaBoEn
Plan of Salvation, The, *Bk.* III, *ll.* 274-343. WGRP
Poet-Preacher's Prayer, A, *Bk.* I, *ll.* 17-19, 22-26. MaRV
Prospect of Eden, The, *Bk.* IV, *ll.* 1-775. PoEL-3
Satan, *fr. Bk.* I. TreFT, *ll.* 36-75; TrGrPo, *ll.* 36-543, *abr.*; SeCePo, *Bk.* I, *ll.* 283-313, *and Bk.* II, *ll.* 1010-1055
Satan and His Host, *Bk.* I, *ll.* 527-669. OBS
Satan and the Fallen Angels, *Bk.* I, *ll.* 283-313. LiTB; OBS
(Superior Fiend, The, *ll.* 283-330.) MaPo
Satan Beholds Eve, *Bk.* IX, *ll.* 445-472. PoFS
Satan Discovers Eden, *Bk.* IV, *ll.* 131-196, *abr.* ExPo
Satan Journeys to the Garden of Eden, *Bk.* IV, *ll.* 172-201. ChTr
Satan Looks upon Adam and Eve in Paradise, *Bk.* IV, *ll.* 288-324. TreFS
Satan on War, *Bk.* II, *ll.* 496-505. MaRV
Satan Views the World, *Bk.* II, *ll.* 1010-1055. WHA
Satan's Adjuration, *Bk.* I, *ll.* 105-124. FaBoEn
Satan's Metamorphosis, *Bk.* X, *ll.* 504-547. StP
Satan's Pride ("Is there no place"), *Bk.* IV, *ll.* 79-110. MaRV
Satan's Soliloquy, *Bk.* IV, *ll.* 32-113. LiTB; OBS
Satan's Speech, *Bk.* I, *ll.* 249-263. DiPo
Scene in Paradise, A, *Bk.* IV, *ll.* 23-55, *abr.* GN
Scheme of Redemption, The, *Bk.* III, *ll.* 56-343. StJW
"She, as a veil down to the slender waist," *Bk.* IV, *ll.* 304-311. ErPo
"Silent, and in face/ Confounded, long they sat, as stricken mute," *Bk.* IX, *ll.* 1064-1189. EnL
"So spake the archangel Michael; then paused," *fr. Bk.* XII. EnL, *ll.* 466-649; MBW-1, *ll.* 476-649
"So talked the spirited sly snake; and Eve," *Bk.* IX, *ll.* 613-833. EnL
"Southward through Eden went a river large," *Bk.* IV, *ll.* 223-311. ViBoPo
Standing on Earth, *Bk.* VII, *ll.* 23-39. ChTr
Sum of Wisdom, The, *Bk.* XII, *ll.* 557-587. MaPo
Summons, The, *Bk.* I, *ll.* 299-587, *abr.* WHA
Sweet Is the Breath of Morn, *Bk.* IV, *ll.* 641-656.
(World Beautiful, The, *ll.* 641-649.) GN
Then, When I Am Thy Captive, Talk of Chains, *Bk.* IV, *ll.* 970-1015. WHA
These Are Thy Glorious Works, *Bk.* V, *ll.* 153-159. MaRV
(Adam's Morning Hymn, *ll.* 153-210.) WGRP
(Morning Hymn of Adam, *ll.* 153-165, 195-208.) TrPWD
(Morning Hymn of Adam and Eve, *ll.* 153-208.) OxBoCh
Thus Eve to Adam, *Bk.* IV, *ll.* 635-658. FaBV
(With Thee Conversing, *ll.* 639-656.) WiR
"Thus was this place/ A happy rural seat of various view," *Bk.* IV, *ll.* 246-268, 285-527. ATP
(Eden, *ll.* 246-268.) FaBoEn
"To him she hasted; in her face excuse," *Bk.* IX, *ll.* 853-1033. EnL
"To whom the wingèd Hierarch replied," *Bk.* V, *ll.* 468-710. MBW-1
"To whom thus also th' angel last replied," *Bk.* XII, *ll.* 574-649. FiP
War in Heaven, *Bk.* VI, *ll.* 801-892. DiPo
War in Heaven (The First Battle), *Bk.* VI, *ll.* 44-405, *abr.* ExPo
"We may no longer stay: go, waken Eve," *Bk.* XII, *ll.* 594-649. FosPo
Wedded Love, *fr. Bk.* IV. OBS, *ll.* 750-755; PoFS, *ll.* 736-775
(Epithalamion: "Haile wedded love," *ll.* 750-775.) MaPo (1969 ed.)
(Their Wedded Love, *ll.* 750-775.) SeCePo
What Though the Field Be Lost? *Bk.* I, *ll.* 105-124. EaLo
"With grave/ Aspect he rose," *Bk.* II, *ll.* 300-389, 629-648, 879-1055. ATP
Paradise of Birds, The, *sels.* William John Courthope.
Birdcatcher's Song. VA
Dodoism, *br. sel.* OtMeF
In Praise of Gilbert White. VA
Ode: To the Roc. VA
Paradise [*or* Paradice] on earth is found, A. The Description of Elysium [*or* The Poets' Paradise]. Michael Drayton. *Fr.* The Muses' Elysium. AnAnS-2; TuPP; WiR
Paradise Regained. Milton. CABL
Sels.
Athens, *Bk.* IV, *ll.* 236-364. OBS
("Look once more e're we leave this specular Mount," *ll.* 236-284.) SeEP; ViBoPo
(Vision of Athens, *ll.* 237-284.) TOP
But to His Mother Mary, *Bk.* II, *ll.* 60-108. ISi
First Temptation, The, *Bk.* I, *ll.* 303-502. OxBoCh
Messiah, The, *Bk.* I, *ll.* 182-293. OBS
Parthians, The, *Bk.* III, *ll.* 310-343. OBS
Rome, *Bk.* IV, *ll.* 44-108. OBS
Satan's Guile, *Bk.* I, *ll.* 357-405. LiTB; OBS
Table Richly Spread, A, *Bk.* II, *ll.* 340-365. FaBoCh; LoGBV
"They err who count it glorious to subdue," *Bk.* III, *ll.* 71-107. PoFr
True and False Glory, *Bk.* III, *ll.* 43-107. LiTB; OBS
"With that (such power was given him then), he took," *Bk.* III, *ll.* 250-443, *Bk.* IV, *ll.* 449-639. StJW
Paradisi Gloria. Thomas William Parsons. AA; OQP
Paradiso, *sels.* Dante, *tr. fr. Italian. Fr.* Divina Commedia.
Being Underived, *fr.* I, *tr. by* Longfellow. CAW
"Into the justice of eternity," *fr.* XIX, *tr. by* Jefferson Butler Fletcher. PoFr

Paradiso (continued)
"Now say,' he said, 'were it not worse indeed,' " *fr.* VIII, *tr. by* Jefferson Butler Fletcher. PoFr
"O petty blood-nobility of ours!" *fr.* XVI, *tr. by* Jefferson Butler Fletcher. PoFr
One World, 4 *ll.* MaRV
Paradise, *abr., tr. by* Henry F. Cary. OuHeWo
Paradise: Cacciaguida's Prophecy to Dante, *fr.* XVII, *tr. by* Frances Winwar. EnLi-1
Primal Cause, The, *fr.* XXVIII, *tr. by* Longfellow. CAW
Saint Bernard's Prayer to Our Lady, *fr.* XXXIII, *tr. by* Louis How. ISi
("Thou Virgin Mother, daughter of thy Son," *tr. by* Longfellow.) CAW
Saints in Glory, The, *fr.* XXXI, *tr. by* Henry F. Cary. WGRP
Paradox. E. Margaret Clarkson. SoP
Paradox, The. John Donne. MaMe; OAEP; SCEP-1
Paradox. Paul Laurence Dunbar. Kal
Paradox. Angelina Weld Grimké. CDC
Paradox, A. Richard Lovelace. Po
Paradox. Huw Menai. MaRV
Paradox. Vassar Miller. NePoEA
Paradox, A. Earl of Pembroke. ElL
Paradox, The. Francesca Yetunde Pereira. PBA
Paradox, The. Ruth Pitter. MaRV
Paradox, A. Aurelian Townsend. AnAnS-2; EP; SeCP
Paradox, A. *Unknown.* ShM
Paradox of Time, The. Austin Dobson, *after the French of* Pierre de Ronsard. AWP; HBV; JAWP; PG (1945 ed.); WBP
Paradox: That Fruition Destroys Love, *sel.* Henry King.
"Since lovers' joys then leave so sick a taste." ErPo; LO
Paradox: the Birds. Karl Shapiro. CrMA
Paradoxes. Christina Rossetti. *Fr.* Sing-Song. OTPC (1946 ed.)
(Pin Has a Head, A.) RIS
Paragon of Animals, The. Pope. *See* Know Then Thyself.
Parallax. Maxwell Anderson. NYBP
Parallel Texts. Robert Kelly. CoPo
Parang. Derek Walcott. ToPo
Paranoia in Crete. Gregory Corso. NeAP
Paraphrase. Hart Crane. MoVE; TwAmPo
Paraphrase from the French, A. Matthew Prior. OxBoLi
Paraphrase on the Psalms of David, A, *sels.* George Sandys. OBS
Deo Opt. Max., Psalm CIV.
Psalme CXXXVII.
Paraphrase on Thomas à Kempis, A. Pope. GoBC; OBEC
"Speak, Gracious Lord, oh speak; thy Servant hears," *sel.* TrPWD
Parasite. Alfred Kreymborg. NP
Parasite lichen. Lichen. Mary Fullerton. PoAu-1
Paratrooper. John Giorno. ANYP
Parcy Reed. *Unknown.* OxBB
Pardners. Berton Braley. SCC
Pardon. Julia Ward Howe. PAH
Pardon, The. Richard Wilbur. CBV; NePoEA; NoP; ToPo
Pardon, goddess of the night. Song. Shakespeare. *Fr.* Much Ado about Nothing, V, iii. CTC; OBSC; SiCE; ViBoPo
Pardon, great enemy. Her Friends Bring Her a Christmas Tree. W. B. Yeats. Upon a Dying Lady, VII. LiTB
Pardon, Lord, the lips that dare. Whittier. *Fr.* Andrew Rykman's Prayer. TrPWD
Pardon me, lady, but I wanta ast you. Drug Store. John V. A. Weaver. HBMV; NP; ThLM; YaD
Pardon mine ears, both I and they do pray. Astrophel and Stella, LI. Sir Philip Sidney. FCP; SiPS
Pardon my Lord, I humbly beg the same. Meditation CXXXII. Edward Taylor. *Fr.* Preparatory Meditations, Second Series. MAmP
Pardon, Old Fathers. W. B. Yeats. *Fr.* Responsibilities. OAEP (2d ed.)
("Pardon, old fathers, if you still remain.") PoEL-5
Pardon our visit to this place. The Framework Knitters Petition. C. Briggs. CoMu
Pardon the faults in me. Wife to Husband. Christina Rossetti. VA; ViPo
Pardoner's Tale, The. Chaucer. *Fr.* The Canterbury Tales. BEL; CABL; CoBE; EnL, *mod. by* Theodore Morrison; EnLi-1; EnLit; FiP, *abr.*; FosPo; MBW-1; NoP; OAEP; PoEL-1; PoIE
Sels.
Introduction: "'Thou beel amy, thou Pardoner,' he sayde," 11 *ll.* FosPo
"Thise ryotoures three, of which I tell." MyFE
("These rioters, of whom I make my rime.") WHA
Parent of all, omnipotent. The American Patriot's Prayer. *Unknown.* PAH
Parent of blooming flowers and gay desires. Ode: In Imitation of Pastor Fido. George Lyttelton. CEP
Parent of joy! heart-easing mirth. Ode to Mirth. Tobias George Smollett. WaPE
Parentage. Alice Meynell. PeVV
Parental Ode to My Son, [Aged Three Years and Five Months,] A. Thomas Hood. BOHV; HBV; PoLF; PTK
(To My Son.) RIS
(To My Son, Aged Three Years and Five Months.) FaPON
"Thou happy, happy elf!" *sel.* FiBHP
Parental Recollections. Mary Lamb. OBRV
(Child, A.) OBEV
(In Memoriam.) GTSL
Parenthood. John Farrar. MPB; OHIP
Parents are sinful now, for they must whisper. Marriage. Austin Clarke. GTBS-P; OxBI
Parents, The; People Like Our Marriage. Gwendolyn Brooks. TPM
Parfum exotique. Baudelaire. *See* Exotic Perfume.
Paring the Apple. Charles Tomlinson. CMoP; NePoEA-2; NMP; PoIE
Paris. E. E. Cummings. *See* Paris: This April Sunset Completely Utters.
Paris. Arthur Symons. SyP
Paris at Night. Tristan Corbière, *tr. fr. French by* Kenneth Koch and Georges Guy. SyP
Paris in 1815, *sel.* George Croly.
A Fauxbourg, Pt. I, xx. OBRV
Paris in the Snow. Léopold Sédar-Senghor, *tr. fr. French by* Ulli Beier. PBA
Paris lay hushed beneath the midday sun. On the Parapet of Notre Dame. Charles J. Quirk. CAW
Paris Nocturne, A. "Fiona Macleod." SyP
Paris; the Seine at Night. Charles Divine. HBMV
Paris: This April Sunset Completely Utters. E. E. Cummings. NAMP
(Paris.) CLwM
Parish Church, The. Julio Herrera y Reissig, *tr. fr. Spanish by* Thomas Walsh. CAW
Parish Poor-House, The. George Crabbe. *Fr.* The Village. OBEC
Parish Priest, The. Chaucer. *See* Good Parson, The.
Parish priest, The/ Of Austerity. The Preacher's Mistake. Brewer Mattocks, *sometimes at. to* William Croswell Doane. BLPA; MaRV; PoToHe; StaSt
Parish Register, The, *sels.* George Crabbe.
Baptisms, Pt. I.
"Behold the cot!" OBRV
Marriages, Pt. II.
"Next at our altar." OBRV
Burials, Pt. III. EiCL
Ancient Virgin, An. OBNC
Lady of the Manor, The. OBNC
"My record ends" OBRV
"Next died the Widow Goe, an active dame." EnPE
"There was, 'tis said, and I believe, a time." EiPP
Parisian Idyl, A, *sel.* George Moore.
"This is the twilight of the summer dead." SyP
Park, The. Robin Blaser. CoPo
Park, The. James S. Tippett. BrR; SUS; TiPo
Park Avenue Cat. Frances M. Frost. CIV
Park-bench strategists have called a truce, The. Washington Square. Francesco Bianco. CLwM
Park Concert. James Michie. MuSP
Park in Milan, The. William Jay Smith. CAD; CoAP
Park is filled with night and fog, The. Spring Night. Sara Teasdale. BoLP; FaBoBe; HBMV; LiTA; LiTL; LiTM (1946 ed.); MAP; MoAmPo; NeMA; PG (1945 ed.)
Park is green and quiet, The. Charles Reznikoff. OCS
Park Pigeons. Melville Cane. CAD
Park Poem. Paul Blackburn. CoPo

Parked among benches of oak, in the nooks of the church. The Poor in Church. Arthur Rimbaud. LiTW
Parking Lot World of Sergeant Pepper, The. Charles Johnson. WSL
Parkinson and the Octopus ["Parkinson broached the octopus"). Norma Farber. FiSC
Parklands, The. Stevie Smith. MoBS
Parks and Ponds. Emerson. PoEL-4
Park's trees have been growing all week, The. Travel. Marvin Bell. TDP
Parlement of Foules, The, *sels.* Chaucer.
Proem: "Lyf so short, the craft so long to lerne, The." FiP; MyFE
(Parliament of Fowls, The.) ViBoPo
Roundel: "Now welcom somer, with thy sonnë softe." ATP; CTC
(Foules Rondel, *orig., with mod. vers.* [The Birds' Rondel] *by* Louis Untermeyer.) TrGrPo
(Now Welcome Somer.) SeCePo
(Now Welcome Summer.) CBEP; PoLi
(Qui Bien Aime à Tard Oublie.) EnLoPo
(Welcome, Summer.) MeEL
Parley of Beasts. "Hugh MacDiarmid." LO; MoBrPo; OA; OBMV
Parley with His Empty Purse, A. Thomas Randolph. OBS
Parliament Hill. Henry Howarth Bashford. BrR; MPB; SP
Parliament Hill Fields. John Betjeman. FaBoTw; HaMV
Parliament of Bees, The, *sels.* John Day. ViBoPo
"High steward of thy vines."
"I will have one built/ Like Pompey's theatre."
"This baseness follows your profession."
Parliament of Cats. D. J. Enright. NMP
Parliament of England, Ye, *with music.* *Unknown.* SoAmSa
Parliament of Fowls, The. Chaucer. *See* Parlement of Foules, The.
Parlor Car. Dorothy Brown Thompson. PoMa
Parlor Cat, A. Louella C. Poole. CIV
Parnell. W. B. Yeats. CMoP
Parnell's Memory. Thomas Michael Kettle. ACP; JKCP (1926 ed.)
(Parnell.) AnIV
Parochial Theme. Wallace Stevens. LiTA
Parodie, A: "Souls joy, when thou art gone." George Herbert. AnAnS-1; MaMe; MeP; OBS; SCEP-1
Parody, A: "Farewell! A long farewell to all our school days!" Edith Putnam Painton. PEDC
Parody on "A Psalm of Life." *Unknown, sometimes at. to* Oliver Wendell Holmes. BLPA
Parody on Thomas Hood's "The Bridge of Sighs." *Unknown.* FiBHP
Parrhasius. Nathaniel Parker Willis. AA
Parricide. Julia Ward Howe. PAH
Parrot, The. Thomas Campbell. OTPC
Parrot, The. James Elroy Flecker. FaBoTw
Parrot, The ("Long since I'd ceased to care"). W. W. Gibson. OBMV
Parrot, The. John Skelton. *See* Parrot's Soliloquy.
Parrot. William Jay Smith. RePo
Parrot and the carrot we may easily confound, The. Robert W. Wood. PV
Parrot Cry, The. "Hugh MacDiarmid." OxBS
Parrot Fish, The. James Merrill. NYTB
"Parrot, if I had your wings." The Boy and the Parrot. John Hookham Frere. OTPC (1923 ed.)
Parrots, The ("Somewhere, somewhen I've seen") W. W. Gibson. CH; RoGo
Parrot's Soliloquy. John Skelton. *Fr.* Speak, Parrot. PoEL-1
(Parrot, The.) ACP
(Speke, Parrot.) OxBoLi
Parrot's voice snaps out, The. "Psittacus Eois Imitatrix Ales ab Indis." Sacheverell Sitwell. AtBAP; MoBrPo
Parry, of all my friends the best. The Invitation. Goronwy Owen. LiTW; PrWP
Parsifal. Robert Duncan. NoP
Parsifal. Paul Verlaine, *tr. fr. French by* John Gray. *Fr.* Amour. SyP
Parsifal has put off the boys and girls. Parsifal. Robert Duncan. NoP
Parsley, parsley, everywhere. Sprig Fever. Margaret Fishback. BOHV
Parsnip, The. Ogden Nash. NePA; WePo
Parson, The. Goldsmith. *Fr.* The Deserted Village. WePo
Parson Allen's Ride. Wallace Bruce. MC; PAH
Parson Gray. Goldsmith. BOHV; NA
Parson Grocer, The. *Unknown.* CoMu
Parson having a tithe pig or two, A. John Heath. SiCE
Parson, The, him answered, "Bendicite!" The Shipman. Chaucer. *Fr.* The Canterbury Tales: Prologue. ACP
Parson of a country town was he, The. The Good Parson. Chaucer. *Fr.* The Canterbury Tales: Prologue. ACP; BoPe; CAW; MaRV; TRV; WGRP
Parson's Looks, The. Burns. OxBoLi
Parson's Pleasure. Barry O. Higgs. PeSA
Parson's Prayer, The. Ralph Spaulding Cushman. MaRV
(Preacher's Prayer, A.) STF
Part of a Letter. Richard Wilbur. CMoP
Part of a Novel, Part of a Poem, Part of a Play, *sels.* Marianne Moore.
Hero, The. CMoP; OnHM; OxBA; TwAmPo
Steeple-Jack, The. AmLP; AmPP; AP; CoBMV; CMoP; CrMA; ExPo; FaBoMo; ILP; MoPo; NoP; OnHM; OxBA; TwAmPo
Part of an Ode of Horace Paraphras'd by the Duke of Buckingham, 1680. George Villiers, Duke of Buckingham. PeRV
Part of Mandevil's Travels. William Empson. AtBAP
Part of Plenty. Bernard Spencer. ErPo; LiTB; LiTL; LiTM; MoLP
Part-Time Tenant. Edna Meudt. FiSC
Partaking of the miraculous. Apparition of Splendor. Marianne Moore. NePoAm
Parted. Alice Meynell. PeVV
Parted Love. Dante Gabriel Rossetti. The House of Life, XLVI. MaVP; PoVP; ViPo; VP
Parted Lovers. Judah Halevi, *tr. fr. Hebrew by* Nina Salaman. LiTW
Parted Lovers, The. *Unknown, tr. fr. Amerindian by* John Reade. WOW
Parted Souls. Lord Herbert of Cherbury. AnAnS-2; SeCP
Parterre, The. E. H. Palmer. BOHV; NA
Parthenophil and Parthenophe, *sels.* Barnabe Barnes.
"Ah, sweet content, where is thy mild abode?" LXVI. ReEn; Sonn; TuPP
(Content.) OBSC
(Sonnet: "Ah, sweet Content, where is thy mild abode?") ElL
"Burn on, sweet fire, for I live by that fuel," LXXXVII. TuPP
"Dark night! Black image of my foul despair," LXXXIII. Sonn
"I burn, yet am I cold; I am a-cold, yet burn," XXXI. PoIE
"I wish no rich-refined Arabian gold," XLVIII.
(Parthenope.) CBEP
"Jove for Europa's love took shape of bull," LXIII. ReEn
Madrigal I: "O Powers Celestial, with what sophistry." EnLoPo
Madrigal: "Once in an arbor was my mistress sleeping." TuPP
Madrigal XIII: "Soft, lovely, rose-like lips, conjoined with mine." EnLoPo
"Mistress, behold, in this true-speaking glass," I. Sonn; TuPP
Ode: "When I walk forth into the woods." TuPP
Ode, An: "Why doth heaven bear a sun." ElL; OBSC
"This careful head, with divers thoughts distressed," XCIX. TuPP
"Write! write! help! help, sweet Muse! and never cease," XVIII. Sonn
Parthians, The. Milton. *Fr.* Paradise Regained, III. OBS
Partial Muse has, from my earliest hours, The. Charlotte Smith. Sonn
Partial Resemblance. Denise Levertov. CoAP; NaP
Parting. "Æ." PoVP
Parting. Matthew Arnold. Switzerland, II. ViPP; VP
Parting, The. James K. Baxter. Cressida, VI. AnNZ
Parting. Emily Dickinson. *See* My life closed twice before its close.
Parting, The. Michael Drayton. *See* Idea: "Since there's no help. . ."
Parting. Judah Halevl, *tr. fr. Hebrew by* Nina Salaman. AWP; TrJP
Parting, The. Elizabeth Jennings. NePoEA-2
Parting. Gerald Massey. HBV
Parting. Thomas Middleton. *Fr.* A Chaste Maid in Cheapside. ElL
("Weep eyes, break heart!") TuPP
Parting, The. John Oldham. PeRV

Parting. Coventry Patmore. PoToHe
Parting. Kathleen Raine. LiTL
Parting, The. Adrienne Rich. WIRo
Parting. William Caldwell Roscoe. OBVV
(For Ever.) HBV
Parting, The. Sappho, *tr. fr. Greek by* Olga Marx *and* Ernst Morwitz. LiTW
Parting, A. Wang Wei, LiTW,*tr. by* Witter Bynner; OnPM, *tr. by* W. J. B. Fletcher.
Parting. W. B. Yeats. FaBoTw
Parting after a Quarrel. Eunice Tietjens. BoLP; HBMV; NP
Parting as Descent. John Berryman. LiTA; MoAmPo (1950 ed.)
Parting at Dawn. John Crowe Ransom. AnAmPo
Parting at Morning. Robert Browning. AWP; BEL; CBEP; CBV; DiPo; EnL; EnLi-2; EnLit; EPN; FaBoEn; FaBV; FiP; GBV (1952 ed.); GTSL; HBV; JAWP; MaVP; MBW-2; MCCG; MemP; OAEP; OBEV; OBNC; OBVV; PAn; PCD; PoAn; PoVP; ShBV-3; TOP; TreFT; UnPo (3d ed.); VA; ViPo; ViPP; WBP; WiR
Parting at Morning. Dietmar von Aist, *tr. fr. German by* F. C. Nicholson. AWP
Parting Friends, *with music. Unknown.* ABF
Parting friends put me the query. Anglo-Eire Vignette. Patric Stevenson. NeIP
Parting Gift. Elinor Wylie. LOW; OxBa
Parting Glass, The. Philip Freneau. AA; AmP; LHV
Parting golden haze, A. L'Oiseau Bleu. Gordon Bottomley. BrPo
Parting Guest, A. James Whitcomb Riley. HBV; MAP; MoAmPo (1942 ed.); NeMA; PoMa; TreFT; VA
Parting Hour, The. Olive Custance. HBV; VA
Parting of Hector and Andromache, The. Homer, *tr. fr. Greek. Fr.* The Iliad, VI. SeEP, *tr. by* George Chapman; TreFS, *tr. by* William B. Smith *and* Walter Miller
(Hector and Andromache, *shorter sel, tr. by* Pope.) OBEC
(Hektor and Andromache, *tr. by* Maurice Hewlett.) LiTW
(Hektor [*or* Hector] to Andromache, *shorter sel.*) ReEn, *tr. by* George Chapman; WaaP, *tr. by* Richmond Lattimore
("I myself will now go home and see," *tr. by* George Chapman.) ReIE
(Last Parting of Hector and Andromache, The, *tr. by* Dryden.) SeEP
("She with his sight made breathless haste to meet him," *shorter sel., tr. by* George Chapman.) ViBoPo
Parting of King Philip and Marie, The. John Westland Marston. *Fr.* Marie de Meranie. VA
Parting of the Red Sea, The. *Unknown, tr. fr. Anglo-Saxon by* Charles W. Kennedy. *Fr.* Exodus. AnOE
Parting of the Ways, The. Joseph B. Gilder, *wr. at. to* Jeannette L. Gilder. AA; HBV; PAH
"Be thou guardian of the weak," *sel.* MaRV
(Will to Serve, The.) OQP
Parting of Venus and Old Age, The. John Gower. *Fr.* Confessio Amantis, VIII. PoEL-1
Parting Verse, the Feast There Ended, The. Robert Herrick. SeCV-1
Parting, without a Sequel. John Crowe Ransom. DTC; LiTL; MAP; MoAB; MoAmPo; MoVE; NP; OxBA
Partings. Charles Guerin, *tr. fr. French by* Jethro Bithell. AWP
Partner, The. Theodore Roethke. Four for Sir John Davies, II. NePA; NePoAm
Partner, leave that grub. War in Camp. John A. Stone. SGR
Partner, remember the hills? The Hills. Berton Braley. MCCG
Partners. Jaime Castiello. WaKn
Partridge berry, bittersweet. Counting-out Rhyme for March. Frances Frost. YeAr
Parts of trees, The. Rain. Ross Parmenter. NYTB
Party. Constance Carrier. NePoAm-2
Party, The. Paul Laurence Dunbar. AmNP
Party, A. Laura E. Richards. BiCB; SiSoSe; SoPo
Party, The. Reed Whittemore. CAD; CoAP
Party Bid. Aletha Humphreys. FiSC
Party finished early, 'twas on the stroke of nine, The. The Keyhole in the Door. *Unknown.* CoMu
Party Knee. John Updike. FiBHP
Party Line. Joseph Joel Keith. FiSC
Party Song, A ("Merry have we met"). *Unknown.* BoTP
Parvenant. Arthur Hugh Clough. Spectator ab Extra, III. OxBoLi; PeVV
Parvuli Ejus. Aubrey Thomas De Vere. IrPN
Parzival, *sel.* Eithne Wilkins.
Dreamers and the Sea, The. NeBP
Pa's Chickens. Homer Roberts. IHA
Pasa Thalassa Thalassa. E. A. Robinson. EtS; LaNeLa, *abr.*
Pascal's abyss went with him at his side. The Abyss. Baudelaire. SyP
Paschal Poem, *sel.* Lynn Strongin.
"Run, run, run with the rising moon." ThO
Pass Around Your Bottle, *with music. Unknown.* OuSiCo
Pass forth, my wonted cries. Sir Thomas Wyatt. FCP; SiPS
Pass It On. Henry Burton. BLRP; MaRV; SoP
Pass It On ("Love demands the loving deed"). *Unknown.* SoP
Pass It On! ("When the Savior has given you a blessing."). *Unknown.* STF
Pass not too near these outcast sons of men. The Way. Laura Simmons. ChIP
Pass of Kirkstone, The. Wordsworth. HBV
Pass Office Song. *Unknown, tr. fr. Afrikaans by* Peggy Rutherford. PBA; TTY
Pass On. Theodorides, *tr. fr. Greek by* W. H. D. Rouse. WoL
Pass On the Torch. Allen Eastman Cross. OQP
Pass, thou wild light. Leavetaking. Sir William Watson. HBV; PoVP
Pass we the ills, which each man feels or dreads. Power. Matthew Prior. *Fr.* Solomon. LoBV; PoEL-3
Pass within/ A maze of corridors contrived for sin. A Vault inside the Castle at Goito. Robert Browning. *Fr.* Sordello. MyFE
Passage. Hart Crane. CMoP; ExPo; MoVE
Passage Charles Dallery. Ron Padgett. YAP
Passage, immediate passage! The blood burns in my veins! The Sea of Faith. Walt Whitman. *Fr.* Passage to India. OQP
Passage of a Year, The. *Unknown. Fr.* Sir Gawain and the Green Knight. PoEL-1
Passage of an August. Eithne Wilkins. NeBP
Passage to India, *abr.* Lus de Camoes, *tr. fr. Portuguese by* J. J. Aubertin. *Fr.* The Lusiads. WoL
Passage to India. Walt Whitman. AmePo; AmPP (4th ed.); CoBA; DiPo; MWA-1; Po; PoEL-5
Sels.
"Ah, more than any priest," *fr.* XI-XIII. WGRP
"Bathe me O God in thee, mounting to thee," *fr.* XI. TrPWD
Passage to More than India, *fr.* XIII. MoRP
(Sea of Faith, The.) OQP
"Sail forth—steer for the deep waters only." TRV
Passages. Larry Eigner. NeAP
Passamquoddy's Apple Toddy. James W. Foley. LHV
Passed the end of a day in the provinces. The End of a Day in the Provinces. Jules Laforgue. SyP
Passenger Train. Edith Newlin Chase. SoPo
Passenger train stood in the shed. Ol' John Brown. *unknown.* ABF
Passenger who e're thou art. His Epitaph. Richard Crashaw. MaMe
Passengers, The. David Antin. NYBP
Passenjare, The. Isaac H. Bromley. FiBHP
Passer, The. George Abbe. SD
Passer Mortuus Est. Edna St. Vincent Millay. CMoP; MAP; MoAmPo; OxBA
Passer-by, A. Robert Bridges. BoC; BrPo; CaFP; CMoP; CoBMV; EnLit; EtS; ForPo; GTBS-W; GTSE; GTSL; HBV; LiTB; LiTM; MoAB; MoBrPo; NBM; OAEP; OBNC; OBVV; PoVP; SeCeV; ShBV-3; VA; WiR
Passerby being fair about sacrifice, A. Chickens the Weasel Killed. William Stafford. NaP
Passer-by might just as well be blind, A. Walls. Robert Francis. CrMA
Passetyme, The. Stephen Hawes. *See* Epitaph: "O mortal folk. . ."
Passetyme of Pleasure, The. Stephen Hawes. *See* Pastime of Pleasure, The.
Passing a dull red college-block. A Walk in Würzburg. William Plomer. NYBP
Passing across the billowy sea. Popular Songs of Tuscany [*or* Giving a Heart]. *Unknown.* AWP; JAWP; OnPM; WBP
Passing and Glassing. Christina Rossetti. FaBoEn; OBNC; VA
Passing Away. Lucian, *tr. fr. Greek by* Walter Leaf. WoL

Passing Away [Saith the World]. Christina Rossetti. Old and New Year Ditties, III. EPN; GoBC; GTBS-W; OBEV (1st ed); OBNC; OBVV; TOP; ViPo
Passing Bell, The. Thomas Heywood. *Fr.* The Rape of Lucrece. SeCL
Passing Bell, The. James Shirley. ACP
Passing-Bell, The. *Unknown.* SeCL; SeEP
Passing Bell at Stratford, The. William Winter. AA
Passing between the stumbling generations. The Wandering Jew Comes to the Wall. Edmond Fleg. *Fr.* The Wall of Weeping. TrJP
Passing By. *Unknown.* *See* There Is a Lady Sweet and Kind.
Passing Christ, The. Richard Watson Gilder. *See* Passing of Christ, The.
Passing feet pause as they pass. Marian. Thomas Ashe. VA
Passing Flower, The. Harry Kemp. HBMV
Passing glance, a lightning long the skies, A. Sonnet. William Drummond of Hawthornden. ViBoPo
Passing Glimpse, A. Robert Frost. InP; NeMA
Passing I saw her as she stood beside. The Gypsy Girl. Henry Alford. HBV; OTPC (1923 ed.)
Passing into the wilderness of twisted trees. The Souvenir. Robert Creeley. FRC
Passing motorist glanced back, A. The Shack. Nellie Burget Miller. PoOW
Passing of Arthur, The. Tennyson. *See also* Morte d'Arthur. *Fr.* Idylls of the King. CoBE; EPN; OBNC.
Passing of Christ, The, *sel.* Richard Watson Gilder.
Real Christ, The. OQP
("Behold Him now as He comes!") ChIP; MaRV
Passing of Lydia, The. Horace, *tr. fr. Latin by* Louis Untermeyer. Odes, I, 25. UnTE
Passing of March, The. Robert Burns Wilson. HBV
Passing of the Buffalo, The. Hamlin Garland. StVeCh
Passing of the Forest, The. William Pember Reeves. AnNZ
Passing of the Shee, The. J. M. Synge. OnYI
Passing of the Unknown Soldier, The. Vilda Sauvage Owens. DD; MC
Passing one day beside Niagara's stream. Quietness. Henry W. Frost. SoP
Passing Out. Philip Levine. AmPC
Passing out of a great city. Initial. Arthur Boyars. NePoEA-2
Passing out of the shadow. Just Passing. *Unknown.* BLRP
Passing policeman found a little child, A. The Little Lost Child. Edward B. Marks. TreFS
Passing Strange, The. John Masefield. AnFE; BoLiVe; LiTB; MoAB; MoBrPo; MoPo; NP; OBEV (new ed.)
Passing the Cape. Otomo Tabito, *tr. fr. Japanese by* Ishii *and* Obata. OnPM
Passing the Graveyard. Andrew Young. DTC
Passing Through. Annie Johnson Flint. BLRP; SoP
Passing through huddled and ugly walls. The Harbor. Carl Sandburg. CBV; CoBA; NP; PoPl
Passing today by a cottage, I shed tears. C. S. Lewis. LO
Passing Visit to Helen. D. H. Lawrence. CMoP
Passing Years, The. James McGinlay. SoP
Passion, A. Earl of Essex. *See* Happy Were He.
Passion. Galway Kinnell. NePoAm
Passion, A. James McMichael. PIA
Passion, The. Milton. MeP
Passion, The. Henry Vaughan. AnAnS-1; MeP
(Good Friday.) MaMe; SCEP-1
Passion and Worship. Dante Gabriel Rossetti. The House of Life, IX. MaVP; PoVP; ViPo; VP
Passion came to me in the form of order, A. Order and Disorder. Richard Eberhart. PoDB
Passion Hymn. Saint Bernard of Clairvaux. *See* O Sacred Head, Now Wounded.
"Passion o' me!" cried Sir Richard Tyrone. The Sally from Coventry. George Walter Thornbury. HBV
Passion of a Lover, The. George Gascoigne. EnRePo
(Gascoigne's Passion.) NCEP
Passion of Jesus, The. *Unknown.* MeEL
Passion of M'Phail, The, *sels.* Horace Gregory.
"Do I have to prove I can sell anything?" I. CMoP
They Were All like Geniuses, IV. NYBP
"Lunchroom bus boy, The, who looked like Orson Welles. TwAmPo
This Is the Place to Wait, V. MoAmPo
("When you are caught breathless in an empty station." V.) CMoP
Passion of Our Lady, The, *sel.* Charles Peguy, *tr. fr. French by* Julian Green.
"For the past three days she had been wandering, and following." ISi
Passion the fathomless spring, and words the precipitate waters. The Lyrical Poem. Richard Garnett. VA
Passionate are palms that clasp in double fist. In the Wind's Eye. R. P. Blackmur. Scarabs for the Living, II. CrMA
Passionate Clerk to His Love, The. Ronald McCuaig. MoAuPo
Passionate Encyclopedia Britannica Reader to His Love. "Maggie." InMe
Passionate Man's Pilgrimage, The. Sir Walter Ralegh. AnFE; AtBAP; BoPe; CABA; CBEP; ChTr; ElL; EnRePo; EP; FaPL; FCP; ILP; LiTB; LoBV; MePo; NoP; OAEP; OBSC; OxBoCh; PoAn; PoE; PoEL-2; PoIE; ReEn; SeCePo; SiCE; TrGrPo; TuPP; YAT, *abr.*
("Give me my scallop-shell of quiet.") AnFE; EG; PoRA; TRV, 3 *sts.*
(His Pilgrimage.) BEL; CoBE; DTC; EnLit; HBV; OBEV; PoFS; TOP; WePo
(My Pilgrimage.) WGRP
(Pilgrimage, The.) BBV (1951 ed.); CAW; SiPS; TreFS; ViBoPo, *abr.*
Passionate Man's Song, The. John Fletcher. *See* Melancholy.
Passionate Pilgrim, The, *sels.* Shakespeare, *and others.*
Beauty ("Beauty is but a vain and doubtful good"), XIII. *Unknown.* OBSC
Crabbed Age and Youth, XII. Shakespeare. CBV; HBV; LiTB; OBEV; ReEn; TreFS; UnTE; ViBoPo
(Age and Youth.) ElL; FaBoEn
("Crabbed age and youth cannot live together.") SiCE; YAT
(Madrigal, A: "Crabbed age and youth.") GBV (1952 ed.); GTBS; GTBS-D; GTBS-P; GTBS-W; GTSE; GTSL
(Youth and Age.) OBSC
Fair Is My Love, VII. *At. to* Shakespeare. ElL; NoP
If Music and Sweet Poetry, VIII. Richard Barnfield. ViBoPo
(To His Friend Master R. L., in Praise of Music and Poetry.) ElL
It Was a Lording's Daughter. *Unknown, at. to* Shakespeare. ElL
Contenions. HBV
Night Watch, A ("Good night, good rest, Ah! neither be my share"), XIV. *Unknown.* OBSC
Nightingale, The. Richard Barnfield. AWP; GTBS; GTBS-D; GTBS-P; GTBS-W; GTSE; JAWP; OTPC (1923 ed.); TOP; WBP
(As It Fell upon a Day.) EG; ReEn; ViBoPo
(Ode, An: "As it fell upon a day.") ElL; LoBV; OBSC; ReIE; SiCE; TuPP
(Philomel.) CH; GTSL; HBV; OBEV
(To the Nightingale.) LiTG
Sweet Rose, Fair Flower, X. *At. to* Shakespeare. ElL
Venus, with Young Adonis Sitting By Her, XI. Bartholomew Griffin. ViBoPo
Passionate Reader to His Poet, The. Richard Le Gallienne. HBV; VA
Passionate Shepherd, The, *sels.* Nicholas Breton.
Aglaia. OBSC
Merry Country Lad, The. ElL; LoBV; OA
(Country Lad, The.) CBEP
(Happy Countryman, *shorter sel.*) CH
(Pastoral II [III]: "Who can live in heart so glad.") ELP; ReEn; TuPP
(Shepherd and Shepherdess.) OBSC
("Who can live in heart so glad.") SiCE; ViBoPo
Pastoral I: "Flora hath been all about." TuPP
Pretty Twinkling Starry Eyes. ElL
Passionate Shepherd to His Love, The, 6 *sts.* Christopher Marlowe. AnEnPo; ATP; AWP; BEL; BoLiVe; BoLP; BWP; CABA; CaFP; CBEP; CBV; CLwM; CoBE; CTC; DiPo; ElL; ELP; EnL; EnLi-1; EnLit; EP; ExPo; FaBoBe; FaBoEn; FaFP; FCP; FosPo; GBV (1952 ed.); GTBS, 7 *sts.*; GTBS-D, 7 *sts.*; GTBS-P, 7 *sts.*; GTBS-W, 7 *sts.*; GTSE, 7 *sts.*; GTSL, 7 *sts.*; HBV; HoPM; ILP; InPo; JAWP; LiTB; LiTG; LiTL, 5 *sts.*; LoBV; MemP, 7 *sts.*; MeWo; NeHB; NoP; OAEP; OBEV; OBSC; OTD; OuHeWo;

Passionate (continued)
PAn; PG (1945 ed.); Po; PoE; PoFS; PoIE; PoLF; PoPo; PoRA, 7 *sts.*; PoSa; ReEn; ReIE; SeCePo; SeCeV; SiCE; SiTL; StP; ThWaDe; TOP; TreF; TrGrPo; TuPP; UnPo (1st ed.); UnTE; ViBoPo, 7 *sts.*; WBP; WePo; WHA; YAT
("Come live with me and be my love," 7 *sts.*) EG
(Shepherd to His Love, The.) GN, 7 *sts.*; OTPC (1923 ed.), 7 *sts.*; RG, 7 *sts.*
(Shepherd's Plea, The.) SiPS
Passionate Shepherd's Song, The. Shakespeare. *See* On a Day—Alack the Day!
Passionate Sword, The. Jean Starr Untermeyer. HBMV; MaRV; TrJP; TrPWD
Passionately fierce the voice of God is pleading. The Christian Soldier. G. A. Studdert-Kennedy. *Fr.* The Suffering God. MaRV
Passion Flower, The. Charles G. Blanden. ChIP; OQP
Passion-Flower, The. Margaret Witter Fuller. HBV
Passions, The; an Ode to [*or* for] Music. William Collins. BEL; CEP; CoBE; EiCL; EiCP; EiPP; EnLi-2 (1949 ed.); GoTL; GTBS; GTBS-D; GTBS-P; GTBS-W; GtSE; GTSL; HBV; LoBV; OBEC
Passions are liken'd [*or* likened] best to floods and streams. The Silent Lover. Sir Walter Ralegh. LiTB; OBEV; PG; ViBoPo. *See also* Our passions are most like to floods and streams.
Passion's Hounds. Thomas Lodge, *after the French of* Pierre de Ronsard. Phyllis, XXXI. OnPM
("Devoid of reason, thrall to foolish ire.") ReEn; SiCE
Passions That We Fought With, The. Trumbull Stickney. NCEP
Passiontide Communion. Katharine Tynan. TrPWD
Passive I lie, looking up through leaves. Seventh Day. Kathleen Raine. ChMP
Passive within the heart. The Meaning of Violence. John Williams. NePoAm-2
Passivity. Mary Fullerton. BoAV
Passover. John Beauchamp Thompson. ChIP
Passover Eve. Fania Kruger. GoYe
Passover in the Holy Family, The. Dante Gabriel Rossetti. GoBC; MaVP
Passport beyond Tyranny. David Ross. PG (1945 ed.)
Passus II: Lady Meed. William Langland, *mod. by* Albert C. Baugh. *Fr.* The Vision of Piers Plowman. EnLit
Password, The. Reginald C. Eva. ChIP
Past, The. Bryant. AA; TOP
Past, The. Emerson. AmePo; AmP; FaBoCh; LiTA; LoGBV; PoEL-4
Past. John Galsworthy. HBV
Past. Winifred Howells. AA
Past, The/ Is but the cinders. The Search. Kwesi Brew. PBA
Past ages did the ancient poets grace. The Honor Done to Poets of Old and Modern Poets. Thomas Heywood. CLwM
Past all calculation and belief it came so huge. William Harmon. *Fr.* Treasury Holiday. QAH
Past and Present. Thomas Hood. *See* I Remember, I Remember.
Past can be no more, The. Now. Thomas Ken. OxBoCh
Past eighty, but never in eighty years. Dick Straightup. Ted Hughes. POTi; ToPo
Past Help. Cecco Angiolieri da Siena, *tr. fr. Italian by* Dante Gabriel Rossetti. OnPM
(Sonnet: He Is Past All Help.) AWP
Past is fresh, dust is fresh, The. Ebb. John Lyle Donaghy. NeIP
Past is past, and if one. Salute. James Schuyler. ANYP; NeAP
Past Is the Present, The. Marianne Moore. PP
Past love, past sorrow, lies this darkness. Requiem. Kathleen Raine. NeBP
Past my window runs a tree. The Changing Wind. Julian Orde. NeBP
Past ploughed and fallow, at the top. Glenarm. John Lyle Donaghy. NeIP
Past Ruin'd Ilion Helen Lives. Walter Savage Landor. AnFE; AWP; BoLiVe; CBEP; CLwM; CTC; ELP; EnLoPo; EnRP; EPN; ExPo; FaBoEn; GTBS-D; InPo; JAWP; LiTL; LO; LoBV; NoP; OAEP; OBNC; OBRV; OQP; Po; PoAn; PoE; PoEL-4; PoIE; PoRA (rev. ed.); PoSa; TOP; TreFT; TrGrPo; UnPo (1st ed.); ViBoPo; WBP
Fr. Ianthe.
(Ianthe.) LiTB
(To Ianthe.) CBV
(Verse: "Past ruined Ilion Helen lives.") HBV; OBEV
Past the closed portals of earthly Kings. The Bethlehem Road. Ida Norton Munson. ChIP
Past the gibbet-stock all stuck with nails. John Masefield. *Fr.* Reynard the Fox. ViBoPo
Past the house where he was got. Austin Clarke. *Fr.* Mnemosyne Lay in Dust. OPoP
Past them he strode. The Hinds of Kerry. William S. Wabnitz. GoYe
"Past two o'clock and Cornwallis is taken." News from Yorktown. Lewis Worthington Smith. MC; PAH
Past walks here, noiseless, unasked, alone, The. An Old Street. Virginia Woodward Cloud. AA
Pastel. Francis Saltus Saltus. AA
Pastel. Arthur Symons. SyP
Pastel, A. Paul Verlaine. *See* Clair de lune.
Pastheen Finn. *Unknown, tr. fr. Irish by* Sir Samuel Ferguson. IrPN
(Páistín Fionn.) OxBI
Pastime. Henry VIII, King of England. *See* Pastime with Good Company.
Pastime [*or* Passetyme] of Pleasure, The, *sels.* Stephen Hawes.
"And as Dame Fame was in laudation," *fr. ch.* 44. ReIE
"And forasmuch that he made Nature," *fr. ch.* 23. ReIE
"And in meanewhyle the gentyll porteres," *fr. ch.* 38. EnPo
Dame Musike, *fr. ch.* 16. MuSP; PoEL-1
Epitaph: "O mortal folk, you may behold and see," *fr. ch.* 42. ACP; BoPe; CBEP; OBEV; OtMeF; TrGrPo
(Epitaph of Graunde Amoure.) ChTr; OBSC; SeCeV
(His Epitaph.) GoBC
("O mortal folk, you may behold and see.") MyFE
(Passetyme, The.) ViBoPo
Excusation of the Auctor, The, *fr. ch.* 46. ReIE
Here Begynneth the Passe Tyme of Pleasure. SiCE
How Grand Amour Walked in a Meadow and Met with Fame Environed with Tongues of Fire, *fr. ch.* 1. ReIE
Of the Great Marriage between Grand Amour and La Belle Pucelle, *fr. ch.* 39. ReIE
Seven Deadly Sins, The, *fr. ch.* 42. PoEL-1
"Than forth I went into a meadow green," *fr. ch.* 22. ReIE
Time and Eternity, *fr. ch.* 44. PoEL-1
True Knight, The, *fr. ch.* 27. ACP; AnEnPo; OBEV
(True Knighthood.) TrGrPo
Pastime with Good Company. Henry VIII, King of England. PrWP; TuPP
(Good Company.) TrGrPo
(Pastime.) CTC; OBSC
Pastor, The. William C. Summers. STF
Pastor M'Gadi's startling blackness. Halo. R. N. Currey. PeSA
Pastoral: "Afternoon wears on, The." David Wright. NYBP
Pastoral, A: "Along the lane beside the mead." Norman Gale. HBV
Pastoral, A: "By the side of a green stagnate pool." G. A. Stevens. CoMu; ErPo
Pastoral: "Death./ The death of a million." Ron Loewinsohn. NeAP
Pastoral: "Dove walks with sticky feet, The." Kenneth Patchen. AtBAP; NaP
Pastoral: "Enquiring fields, courtesies, The." Allen Tate. AP
Pastoral: "Farmer turns for home, The; his team's glad tread." Muriel Lewis. MoAuPo
Pastoral: "Farmhouse skyline, draped with trees, The." Alan Creighton. CaP
Pastoral I: "Flora hath been all about." Nicholas Breton. *Fr.* The Passionate Shepherd. TuPP
Pastoral, A: "Flower of the medlar." Theophile Marzials. HBV; VA
Pastoral, A: "From thence into the open fields he fled." Spenser. *Fr.* The Faerie Queene, VI, 9. OBSC
Pastoral X: "Grapes are ripe, the frost is near, The." Robert Hillyer. LOW
Pastoral: "Hill was flowing with sheep, The." Marion Strobel. NP

Pastoral: "I, who have ridden the world." Willard Trask. CLwM
Pastoral: "If it were only still!" Edna St. Vincent Millay. RePo
Pastoral, A: "In the merry month of May." Nicholas Breton. *See* Phyllida and Corydon ("In the merry month of May").
Pastoral: "In the old days the white gates swung." Clifford Dyment. MoVE
Pastoral: "It's the Spring." W. E. Henley. In Hospital, XXII. Po
Pastoral: "Little sparrows, The." William Carlos Williams. TwCP
Pastoral, A: "Mobile, immaculate and austere." Geoffrey Hill. NePoEA-2
Pastoral, A: "My love and I among the mountains strayed." J. B. B. Nichols. VA
Pastoral, A: "My time, O ye Muses, was happily spent." John Byrom. OBEC
Pastoral [*or* Pastorall], A: "Oh happy golden age." Tasso, *tr. fr. Italian by* Samuel Daniel. *Fr.* Aminta. PoEL-2; ReEn; ReIE
(Golden Age, The, *tr. by* Leigh Hunt.) AWP; WoL
(O Bella Età de l'Oro, *tr. by* Henry Reynolds.) FosPo
(Pastoral of Tasso, A, *tr. by* Samuel Daniel.) OBSC
Pastoral, A: "On a hill there grows a flower." Nicholas Breton. *See* Pastoral of Phillis and Corydon, A.
Pastoral: "Pan-imbued/ Tempe wood." Francis Thompson. PoLi
Pastoral: "So soft in the hemlock wood." Robert Hillyer. MAP; MoAmPo
Pastoral, A: "Sweet birds, that sit and sing amid the shady valleys." Nicholas Breton. EIL; ReIE; SiCE
(Phyllis.) OBSC; TrGrPo
("Sweet birds! that sit and sing amid the shady valleys.") EG
Pastoral, A: "There went out in the dawning light." *Unknown, tr. fr. Latin by* John Addington Symonds. AWP; UnTE
(Pastoral Dialogue.) OnPM
Pastoral: "When I was younger." William Carlos Williams. AmPP (5th ed.); OxBA
Pastoral: "Who can live in heart so glad." Nicholas Breton. *See* Merry Country Lad, The.
Pastoral, A: "Wise old apple tree in spring, The." Robert Hillyer. BoNaP; OTD
Pastoral Ballad, A. William Shenstone. CEP
Sels.
Absence, Pt. I. OBEC
Hope, Pt. II. BoNaP; OBEC
(Shepherd's Home, The.) GN
I Have Found Out a Gift For My Fair, Pt. II. BiS
Pastoral Courtship, A, *sel.* Thomas Randolph.
"Being set, let's sport a while." ViBoPo
Pastoral Courtship, A. Earl of Rochester. UnTE
Pastoral Dialogue. *Unknown, See* Pastoral, A: "There went out in the dawning light."
Pastoral Dialogue, Castara and Parthenia. Thomas Flatman. CEP
Pastoral Elegy, A. Albius Tibullus, *tr. fr. Latin by* Sir Charles Abraham Elton. AWP
(Elegy: "Let others pile their yellow ingots high.") LiTW
Pastoral Hymn. Addison. OBEC
Pastoral[l] Hymn[e], A: "Happy choristers of air." John Hall. EG; MeLP; OBS; OxBoCh; SeCL; TrPWD
Pastoral Landscape. Ambrose Philips. *See* Sixth Pastoral, The.
Pastoral of Phillis and Corydon, A. Nicholas Breton. CoBE; SiCE; TuPP
(Ipsa Quae.) OBSC
("On a hill there grows a flower.") LO
(Pastoral, A: "On a hill there grows a flower.") EIL
(Phyllida and Corydon: "On a hill there grows a flower.") TrGrPo
Pastoral of Tasso, A. Tasso. *See* Pastoral, A: "Oh happy golden age."
Pastoral on the King's Death, The. Written in 1648. Alexander Brome. OBS
Pastoral Poem, *sel.* Edward Richard, *tr. fr. Welsh by* Evan Evans.
Poet's Welcome, The. PrWP
Pastoral Poesy. John Clare. ACV; ERoP-2
Pastoral Song for the Nuptials of Charles, Duke of Lorraine, *sel.* Pierre de Ronsard, *tr. fr. French by* Cécile Schreiber *and* Virginia Tufte.
Wager, The. HW
Pastoral Verses on Two Lovers. *Unknown.* CLwM
Pastorale: "Only cows can loll at ease." Mildred Weston. PoMa
Pastorale: "Willow tree leans, A." Robert A. Davis. GoSl
Pastorall, A: "O happy golden age." Tasso. *See* Pastoral, A: "O happy golden age."
Pastorall Dialogue, A ("As Celia rested in the shade"). Thomas Carew. AnAnS-2; CavP
Pastorall Dialogue, A ("This Mossie Bank They Prest"). Thomas Carew. AnAnS-2; SeCP
Pastorall Hymne, A. John Hall. *See* Pastoral Hymn: "Happy choristers of air."
Pastorals, *sels.* Ambrose Philips.
First Pastoral, The ("If we, O Dorset"). EiCL
Sixth Pastoral, The ("How still the sea!"). CEP
(Pastoral Landscape, *abr.*) OBEC
Pastorals, *sels.* Pope.
Summer. CEP
Winter. EiCL
Pastorella. *At. to* Sir Henry Sheers. SeCL
Pastor's Friend, The. *Unknown.* STF
Pastourelle. Donald Jeffrey Hayes. AmNP
Partourelle. *Unknown.* OBSC
("'Hey, troly, loly lo, maid, whither go you?'") LO
Pasts. Alfred Kreymborg. NP
Pasture, The. Robert Frost. AmLP; AmPP; AnNE; BoC; CMoP; DiPo; FaPON; GoJo; LaNeLa; MAP; MaPo (1969 ed.); MemP; MoAB; MoAmPo; MoShBr; MWA-2; NeMA; OTD; OxBA; PDV; Po; PoPl; PoRh; SoPo; SP; StVeCh; SUS; TiPo; TSW; UTS; ViBoPo; WePo
Pasture, A. Frederic Lawrence Knowles. AA
Pasture, stone wall, and steeple. Question in a Field. Louise Bogan. NYBP
Pat-a-cake, pat-a-cake, baker's man. Mother Goose. OTPC; OxNR; PCH; PPL; RIS; SAS; StVeCh
"Pat-a-cake, pat-a-cake, in the bright sun." Sand Cooking. *Unknown.* PCH
Pat it, kiss it. When Baby Hurts Her Hand. *Unknown.* PPL; SAS
Pat pat! a little cake. *Unknown, tr. fr. German.* SAS
Pat Works on the Railway, *with music. Unknown. See* Paddy Works on the Railway.
Pat Young. Kenneth Mackenzie. PoAu-2
Patapan. Bernard de la Monnoye. *See* Burgundian Carol.
Patch of Old Snow, A. Robert Frost. CMoP; OCS; PoFS
Patch-Shaneen. J. M. Synge. LoBV
Patchwork. Clinton Scollard. OQP
Patchwork Quilt, The. Elizabeth Fleming. BoTP
Patchwork Quilt, The. Dora Sigerson Shorter. HBMV
Pater Filio. Robert Bridges. CMoP; OBEV; OBVV; PoVP; ViBoPo
"Pater Noster," The. *Unknown.* ACP; CAW
"Pater Vester Pascit Illa." Robert Stephen Hawker. CAW; CoBE; VA
Paterson, *sels.* William Carlos Williams.
"Before the grass is out the people are out." ReMP
"Better than Flowers." MoLP
Episode 17. OxBA
Library, The. AtBAP
Preface: "To make a start," I. AP; CMoP; CoBMV
"Signs Everywhere of Birds Nesting, While." MoVE
Sunday in the Park. CrMA
"Without invention nothing is well spaced." PP
"Your lovely hands." MoLP
Path, The. Sybil Leonard Armes. FaChP
Path, The, *sel.* William Cullen Bryant.
"Path we planned beneath Octobers' sky, The." MAmP
Path, The. Edward Thomas. BrPo; MoVE
Path by which we twain did go, The. Tennyson. In Memoriam A. H. H., XXII. EnLi-2; EPN; TOP; ViPo; VP
Path Flower. Olive Tilford Dargan. HBMV
Path in the Sky, The. Amos R. Wells. SoP
Path of the Old Spells, The. Donald Sinclair, *Tr. fr. Gaelic.* GoTS
Path of the Padres, The. Edith D. Osborne. AmFN
Path of the Stars, The. Thomas S. Jones, Jr. ChIP; MoRP; WGRP

Path of Wisdom, The. Baruch, III: 9-IV: 4, Bible, Apocrypha. TrJP
Path That Leads to Nowhere, The. Corinne Roosevelt Robinson. BLPA; HBMV; NeHB
Path that runs to Paradise climbs up a stone-heaped hill, The. Fiddlers' Green. Margaret Widdemer. YT
Path through which that lovely twain, The. Shelley. *Fr.* Prometheus Unbound, II, ii. AtBAP; ViBoPo
Path to Shottery, The. Cornelia Otis Skinner. MoSiPe
Path was steep and snowy—the way was hard and cold. On the Summit. Margaret E. Sangster. SoP
Path we planned beneath October's sky, The. William Cullen Bryant. *Fr.* The Path. MAmP
Pathfinder—and Path-clincher! John Charles Frémont. Charles F. Lummis. PAH
Pathfinders, The. Vance Palmer. BoAu
Paths of my disquiet, The. John Landless beside the Road. Iwan Goll. OnPM
Pathway to Paradise, The. Ozora Stearns Davis. OQP
Patience, *sels.* W. S. Gilbert.
Bunthorne's Song. FiBHP; LiTB; NBM; SiTL; VaPo
(Aesthete, The.) ALV; EnLi-2
(Song: Bunthorne.) PoVP
Fable of the Magnet and the Churn, The. FaPON; MPB; OnMSP; OTD; RePo
"Oh, Hollow! Hollow! Hollow!" PoVP
Recitation and Song: "Am I alone." WoL
(Bunthorne's Recitative and Song.) CoBE
(Recitative and Song: Bunthorne.) PoVP
Song: Colonel. PoVP
Patience. Harry Graham. FiBHP; MoShBr; WhC
Patience. Gerard Manley Hopkins. *See* Sonnet: "Patience, hard thing! the hard thing but to pray."
Patience. William James Linton. VA
Patience. E. E. Nott-Bower. WhC
Patience. G. A. Studdert-Kennedy. OQP; TrPWD
Patience, *sel.* *Unknown.*
Jonah. ACP
Patience. Sir Thomas Wyatt. OBSC; SiPS; TrGrPo
(Patience, Though I Have Not.) FCP; MaPo; NoP; SiCE
Patience, for I have wrong. Sir Thomas Wyatt. FCP; SiPS
Patience for my device. Sir Thomas Wyatt. FCP; SiPS
Patience, Hard Thing! Gerard Manley Hopkins. *See* Sonnet: "Patience, hard thing! the hard thing but to pray."
Patience is a virtue. *Unknown.* OxNR
Patience, my lord! why, 'tis the soul of peace. Thomas Dekker. *Fr.* The Honest Whore, I. ViBoPo
Patience of all my smart. Sir Thomas Wyatt. FCP; SiPS
Patience of Job is a story old, The. Will God's Patience Hold Out for You? Edythe Johnson. STF
Patience on a Monument. Shakespeare. *See* She Never Told Her Love.
Patience Taught by Nature. Elizabeth Barrett Browning. OxBoCh
Patience, Though I Have Not. Sir Thomas Wyatt. *See* Patience.
Patience with the Living. Margaret Elizabeth Sangster. PoToHe
Patient above his tinted tiles he bent. The Mosaic Worker. Arthur Wallace Peach. BLRP
Patient and Meek Grissill. John Phillip. *See* Comedy of Patient and Meek Grissell.
Patient Church, The. Cardinal Newman. GoBC
Patient Griselda. Chaucer, *mod. by* Edward Hodnett. *Fr.* The Canterbury Tales: The Clerk's Tale. PoRA
Patient Grissill. Thomas Dekker. *See* Pleasant Comedy of Patient Grissill, The.
Patient Is Rallying, The. Weldon Kees. NaP
Patient Is Time. Stanton A. Coblentz. *Fr.* The Pageant of Man. MaRV
Patient Potter, The. *Unknown.* SoP
Patient Scientists, The. Bertha Gerneaux Woods. MaRV; OQP
Patient she is—long suffering, our Land. America. Florence Earle Coates. PEDC
Patient, we pray and wait and weep and pray. The Sit-in. Darwin T. Turner. BALP
Patmos. Edith M. Thomas. HBV
Patriarch, The. Burns. CoMu
Patriarchal Home, The. Charles Jeremiah Wells. *Fr.* Joseph and His Brethren. VA
Patrick Goes to School. Alicia Aspinwall. MPB
Patrick Sarsfield, Lord Lucan. *Unknown.* *See* Farewell, O Patrick Sarsfield.
Patrick you chatter too loud. The Praise of Fionn. *Unknown.* KiLC
Patrick's Breastplate. *At. to* St. Patrick. *See* Deer's Cry, The.
Patrico's Song. Ben Jonson. *See* Gipsy Song.
Patriot, The. Robert Browning. EPN; GTBS-D; MemP; PoRA; PoVP; TrGrPo; ViPP
Patriot, The. Thomas Godfrey, *paraphrased from* Psalm I, Bible, *O.T.* PoFr
Patriot, The. Sir Walter Scott. *See* Breathes There the Man.
Patriot Hymn, The. Nathan Haskell Dole. PaA
Patriotic Song ["I'll wreathe my sword in myrtle bough"). Callistratus, *tr. fr. Greek by* Henry Wellesley. PoFr
Patriotic Tour and Postulate of Joy. Robert Penn Warren. NYBP
Patriotism. "Susan Coolidge." OQP
Patriotism. Sir Walter Scott. *See* Breathes There the Man.
Patriotism at Squawville. *Unknown.* PAP
Patriots of Mankind. Christopher Smart. PoFr
Patriot's Pass-Word, The. James Montgomery. *See* Arnold von Winkelried.
Patroclus' Body Saved. Homer, *tr. fr. Greek by* E. R. Dodds. *Fr.* The Iliad, XVII. WaaP
Patrol, The. J. H. Knight-Adkin. MCCG
Patrol. Ralph Pomeroy. CoPo
Patrol; Buonamary. Bernard Gutteridge. WaP
Patrol[l]ing Barnegat. Walt Whitman. CBEP; GTSE; LoBV; NePA; NoP
Patroness. Gerald William Barrax. Kal
Patter of the Shingle, The. *Unknown.* BLPA
Pattering rush like the rattle of hail, The. A Cowboy Race. J. C. Davis. SCC
Pattern, The. Robert Creeley. FRC
Pattern of Saint Brendan. Francis MacManus. AnIV; OxBI
Patterne often drawne in minde, The. *Unknown.* SeCSL
Patterns. Amy Lowell. AmPP; AnFE; AnNE; APA; ATP; AWP; BoLiVe; BoLP; CoAnAm; CoBA; FaFP; FosPo; HBV; JAWP; LiTA; MAP; MoAmPo; NeMA; NePA; NP; OnMSP; OxBA; PoFr; TOP; TreFS; TrGrPo; UnPo (1st ed.); WBP
Patterns of old green-gold trees. Autumn. D. R. Beeton. PeSA
Pattonio, the Pride of the Plain. *Unknown.* CoSo
Patty-cake, patty-cake/ Marcus Antonius. Tact. Paul Pascal. PV
Patty-Poem. Nick Kenny. PoToHe
Pau-Puk-Keewis. Longfellow. *Fr.* The Song of Hiawatha. CoBA
Pauca Mea, *sel.* Christopher Brennan.
I Said, This Misery Must End. PoAu-1
Paudeen. W. B. Yeats. MaPo; PoEL-5
Paul. Earl Marlatt. OQP
Paul. John Oxenham. TRV
Paul. James Wright. NePoEA; PoPl
Paul and Silas, bound in jail. All Night Long. *Unknown.* AS
Paul and Virginia. John Wheelwright. CrMA
Paul Bunyan. Arthur S. Bourinot. TwCaPo
(Legend of Paul Bunyan, A.) AmFN
"He came,/ striding," *sel.* FaPON
Paul Faber, Surgeon, *sel.* George Macdonald.
That Holy Thing, *fr. ch.* 49. ChIP; FaChP; HBV; MaRV; OBEV; OBVV; OQP; StJW; TrPWD; TRV; WGRP
Paul Jones ("An American [*or* A forty-gun *or* Our forty-gun] frigate from Baltimore came"). *Unknown.* BaBo; OTD; PAH; PAL; ViBoFo
(Paul Jones' Victory, *with music.*) TrAS
Paul Jones ("A song unto Liberty's brave buccaneer"). *Unknown.* PAH
Paul Jones—a New Song. *Unknown.* PAH
Paul Klee. John Haines. ThO
Paul Laurence Dunbar. James David Corrothers. BANP; PoNe
Paul, let thy faces from the canvas look. Paul Veronese: Three Sonnets, I. Sir Samuel Ferguson. IrPN
Paul on the Road to Damascus. The Acts, IX: 3-6, Bible, *N.T.* TreF
Paul Revere's Ride. Longfellow. *Fr.* Tales of a Wayside Inn: The Landlord's Tale, Pt. I. AmePo; AmPP (4th ed.); AnNE; BBV; BeLS; BLPA; CaFP; CoBA; DD; FaBoBe; FaBV; FaFP;

FaPON; GoTP; HBV; HBVY; LoGBV; MC; NeHB; OHFP; OnSP; OTD; PaA; PAH; PAL; PAP; PEDC; PoFr; PoRL; PTK; RePo; RIS; StPo; StVeCh; ThLM; TiPo (1952 ed.); TreF; TrGrPo; WBLP; YaD
(Midnight Ride of Paul Revere, The.) PaPo
Paul said and Peter said. Blondie Goes to Heaven. *Unknown.* MemP; OtMeF
Paul Veronese: Three Sonnets. Sir Samuel Ferguson. IrPN
Pauline, *sels.* Robert Browning.
Andromeda. OBRV
"My God, my God, let me for once look on thee." TrPWD
My Lode-Star. MaRV
"O God, where do they tend—these struggling aims?" WGRP
"O thou pale form." ChIP
Oft Have I Stood by Thee. MaRV
Shelley. OBRV
"Stay we here/ With the wild hawks?" MyFE
Water and Air. OBRV
Pauline ("Pauline, Pauline/ I don' love nobody but you"), *with music. Unknown.* OuSiCo
Paul's midnight voice prevail'd; his music's thunder. Epigram. Francis Quarles. *Fr.* Emblems. LoBV
Paul's Wife. Robert Frost. AnAmPo; CABL
Paulus a pamphlet doth in prose present. Henry Parrot. TuPP
Pauper, A. Allen Tate. LiTM
Pauper Witch of Grafton, The. Robert Frost. *Fr.* Two Witches. CMoP; CrMA; MWA-2
Pauper's Drive, The. Thomas Noel. PaPo
Pauper's Funeral, The. George Crabbe. *Fr.* The Village. FaBoEn; OBNC
Pause. Mary Ursula Bethell. AnNZ
Pause. Ann Hamilton. HBMV
Pause. Rosa Zagnoni Marinoni. FiSC
Pause, A. Christina Rossetti. GTBS-D
(Meeting.) HBV
Pause came in the fighting and England held her breath, A. The Other Little Boats. Edward Shanks. FOL
Pause, courteous spirit!—Balbi supplicates. Epitaphs, IX. Gabriello Chiabrera. AWP
Pause en Route. Thomas Kinsella. OxBI
Pause for Breath, A. Ted Hughes. NYBP
Pause not with lingering foot, O pilgrim, here. On Ascending a Hill Leading to a Convent. Francisco Manuel de Mello. CAW
Pause of Thought, A. Christina Rossetti. FaBoEn; OBNC
Pause, Traveller! whosoe'er thou be. Inscribed upon a Rock. Wordsworth. SyP
Pauses, II. Jose Gorostiza, *tr. fr. Spanish by* H. R. Hays. OnPM
Pavane for the Nursery, A. William Jay Smith. BoLP; GoJo; MoAmPo (1962 ed.); NePoAm-2; PoSC
Pave the sky with stars for Punch. Conrad Aiken. *Fr.* Punch; the Immortal Liar. NP
Pavement Artist, The. James Kirkup. HaMV
Pavilion on the Pier, The. Byron Vazakas. NePA
Pawky auld carle came o'er the lea, The. The Gaberlunzie Man. *Unknown, at. to* James IV, King of Scotand. EnSB; GoTS; OxBB; OxBS
Pawky Duke, The. David Rorie. GoTS
Pawnbroker, The. Maxine Kumin. TDP
Pawnbrokers. Marguerite Wilkinson. HBMV
Pawning the Coffers of Sand. *Unknown, tr. fr. Spanish by* R. Selden Rose *and* Leonard Bacon. *Fr.* The Cid. LiTW
Pawns, The. Frank Betts. HBMV
Pawns, The. William Young. *Fr.* Wishmakers' Town. AA
(Losers, The.) HBMV
Pawn-shop man knows hunger, The. Street Window. Carl Sandburg. OCS
Pawnshop Window. R. H. Grenville. GoYe
Pax. D. H. Lawrence. MaRV
Pax Nobiscum. Earl Marlatt. MoRP
Pax Paganica. Louise Imogen Guiney. AA
Pay Day at Coal Creek, *with music. Unknown.* OuSiCo
Paying a Debt. Chevalier de Boufflers, *tr. fr. French by* Leigh Hunt. OnPM
Pay-Off. Kenneth Fearing. CMoP
Paysage Choisi. Francis Sparshott. MoCV
Paysage Moralisé. W. H. Auden. *See* Hearing of Harvests Rotting in the Valleys.
Paysage Moralisé. John Hollander. ErPo; NePoEA
Pcheek pcheek pcheek pcheek pcheek. The Avenue Bearing the Initial of Christ into the New World. Galway Kinnell. CAD; CoPo; LiTM (1970 ed.); NePoEA-2; PoDB
Pea-Fields, The. Sir Charles G. D. Roberts. OBCV; PeCV
Peace, The, *sel.* Aristophanes, *tr. fr. Greek by* Ann Stanford.
Midst the Free Green Fields. HW
Peace. Bhartrihari, *tr. fr. Sanskrit by* Paul Elmer More. AWP
Peace. Rupert Brooke. 1914, I. EPN; MaRV; MMA; POTE; TreFT; WGRP
(1914, I.) HBV; NP
Peace. Charles Stuart Calverley. NBM; WhC
Peace. Phoebe Cary. PAH
Peace. Avis B. Christiansen. SoP
Peace. John Clare. BoPe
Peace. Walter de la Mare. MMA; MoAB; MoBrPo; NeMA
Peace. Irwin Edman. TrJP
Peace. Henry W. Frost. SoP
Peace. Jessie Rose Gates. SoP
(Peace after Sorrow, *abr.*) MaRV
Peace. Samuel Greenberg. CrMA
Peace. Frances Ridley Havergal. SoP
Peace. George Herbert. AnAnS-1; AWP; ChTr; ELP; ExPo; InPo; JAWP; MaMe; MeP; OxBoCh; ReEn; SCEP-1; SeCeV; SeEP; WBP
(Resurrection.) BoPe
Peace, The. Ralph Hodgson. CBV
Peace. Gerard Manley Hopkins. AtBAP; BoC; ELP; GTBS-D; GTBS-P; OAEP (2d ed.)
Peace. Barbara Drake Johnston. SoP
Peace. Longfellow. *See* When War Shall Be No More.
Peace, The. Henry Luttrell. *Fr.* Advice to Julia. OBRV
Peace. Edwin Markham. PGD; WBLP
Peace. Harold Trowbridge Pulsifer. MC; PEDC
Peace. Margaret E. Sangster. TRV
Peace. Clinton Scollard. OQP; PoRL
Peace. *At. to* Samuel Speed. BoPe; OxBoCh; SeCL
(On Peace.) SeEP
Peace. Harriet Beecher Stowe. *See* Hymn: "When winds are raging o'er the Upper ocean."
Peace ("O for a heart of calm repose"). *Unknown.* STF
Peace ("Pees maketh plente"). *Unknown.* MeEL
Peace. Henry van Dyke. MaRV
Peace. Henry Vaughan. AnAnS-1; AnFE; AWP; BEL; BWP; CBEP; CBV; ChTr; EaLo; ELP; EnLit; FaBoCh; GN; HBV; HT; InPo; LoGBV; MeP; MePo; OAEP; OBEV; OBS; Po; PoFS; ReEn; SCEP-1; SeCL; SeCV-1; SeEP; SoP; UnPo (1st ed.); WePo; WGRP; WHA; YAT
("My soul, there is a country.") EG
(Peace of Heaven, The.) BoC
Peace. Brian Vrepont. BoAu
Peace. G. O. Warren. HH; PEDC
Peace. Adeline D. T. Whitney. PAH
Peace after a Storm. William Cowper. SoP
Peace after Sorrow. Jessie Rose Gates. *See* Peace.
Peace and Joy. Shelley Silverstein. PoSC
Peace and Joy. G. A. Studdert-Kennedy. *See* Suffering God, The.
Peace and Joy in Jesus Christ. Johann Franck. BePJ
Peace and Mercy and Jonathan. First Thanksgiving of All. Nancy Byrd Turner. FaPON; PAL; RePo; SiSoSe
Peace and Rest. W. H. Davies. BoPe
Peace and Silence. Georg Trakl. *See* Rest and Silence.
Peace and silence be the guide. Francis Beaumont. *Fr.* The Masque of the Inner-Temple and Gray's Inne. GoBC; OBS
Peace! and There Is No Peace. Jeremiah, VIII: 1-22, Bible, *O.T.* WoL
Peace, battle-worn and starved. Peace. G. O. Warren. HH; PEDC
Peace Be around Thee. Thomas Moore. OTPC (1923 ed.)
Peace, be at peace, O thou my heaviness. Sois sage o ma douleur. Baudelaire. AWP; JAWP; WBP
Peace, Be Still! George Matheson. SoP
Peace, Be Still. Maude Steenburg. SoP
Peace! Be Still. *Unknown.* OQP
Peace be unto you. Shalom Aleichem. *Unknown.* TrJP
Peace be with you, gentle scrivener. Sholom Aleichem. Elias Lieberman. TrJP
Peace beldam Eve, surcease thy suit. A Young Man to an Old

Peace (continued)
Woman Courting Him. John Cleveland. AnAnS-2
Peace by Night. Sister Mary Madeleva. GoBC
Peace Call, The. Edgar Lloyd Hampton. PEDC
Peace, childish Cupid, peace: thy fingered eye. Epigram. Francis Quarles. *Fr.* Emblems. EP
Peace, come away: the song of woe. In Memoriam A. H. H., LVII. Tennyson. EPN; OAEP; TOP; ViPo; VP
Peace, deep and rich. Prayer to Peace. Euripides. *Fr.* Cresophontes. PoPl
Peace Delegate. Douglas Livingstone. PeSA
Peace does not mean the end of all our striving. Peace and Joy [*or* The Christian Soldier]. G. A. Studdert-Kennedy. *Fr.* The Suffering God. MaRV; OQP; TRV
Peace-Giver, The. Swinburne. *See* Christmas Antiphon, A.
Peace Hymn for England and America. George Huntington. PaA
Peace Hymn of the Republic. Henry van Dyke. SoP; TRV
Peace in her chamber, wheresoe'er. First Love Remembered. Dante Gabriel Rossetti. PoVP
Peace in the sober house of Jonas dwelt. Jonas Kindred's Household. George Crabbe. *Fr.* The Frank Courtship. OBNC
Peace in the Welsh Hills. Vernon Watkins. ChMP; GTBS-P
Peace in the World. John Galsworthy. MaRV; PoLF
Peace in thy hands. The Ghost. Walter de la Mare. OAEP (2d ed.); POTE
Peace is declared, and I return. The Return. Kipling. MoBrPo; NeMA
Peace is not an elusive thing. Peace. Barbara Drake Johnson. SoP
"Peace Is the Tranquillity of Order." Robert Wilberforce. GoBC; JKCP (1955 ed.)
Peace lies profound on these forgotten acres. Meditation by Mascoma Lake. Donald C. Babcock. NePoAm-2
Peace, like a Lamb. Leonard Clark. WePo
Peace Message, The. Burton Egbert Stevenson. PAH
Peace Must Come As a Troubadour. Marie Drennan. OQP
Peace mutt'ring thoughts, and do not grudge to keep. Content. George Herbert. MaMe
Peace now and ever on this gravestone be. At My Father's Grave. Matthias Claudius. WoL
Peace of a Good Mind, The. Sir Thomas More. *Fr.* The Twelve Weapons of Spiritual Battle. EnRePo
Peace of Christ, The. St. John, Bible, *N.T.*. *See* My Peace I Give unto You.
Peace of Christ, The. John Antes La Trobe. BePJ
Peace of great doors be for you, The. For You. Carl Sandburg. MAP; MoAmPo; MoRP; WaKn
Peace of Heaven, The. Henry Vaughan. *See* Peace.
Peace of joys, The. Three Blessings. *Unknown.* BoPe
Peace of the Roses, The. Thomas Philipps. ACP
Peace of Wild Things, The. Wendell Berry. NYTB
Peace on Earth. Anatolius, *tr. fr. Greek.* BePJ
Peace on Earth. Bacchylides, *tr. fr. Greek by* John Addington Symonds. AWP; JAWP; WBP
Peace on Earth. Helen Wieand Cole. ChIP; OQP
Peace on Earth. Sanuel Longfellow. PGD
Peace on Earth. Edmund H. Sears. *See* It Came upon the Midnight Clear.
Peace on Earth. William Carlos Williams. LiTA; LOW; MAP; NP; PFY; ViBoPo
Peace on New England, on the shingled white houses, on golden. Jehu. Louis MacNeice. LiTG; LiTM (rev. ed.); MoAB; WaP
Peace on the earth,/ Joyfully sang the angels long ago. Through the Ages. Margaret Hope. PGD
Peace! peace! A mighty Power, which is as darkness. Shelley. *Fr.* Prometheus Unbound. OAEP
Peace, peace be unto all the world. War and Peace. Alexander Petofi. PoFr
Peace, peace! he is not dead, he doth not sleep. He Is Not Dead [*or* Against Oblivion *or* An Elegy on the Death of John Keats.] Shelley. *Fr.* Adonais. FaBoEn; LO; MaRV; OBNC; TreFS
Peace, peace! I know 'twas brave. Content. Henry Vaughan. SCEP-1
Peace, peace, my friend; these subjects fly. George Crabbe. *Fr.* Sir Eustace Grey. PoEL-4
Peace, peace, my hony, do not cry. Christs Reply. Edward Taylor. *Fr.* God's Determinations. MAmP; MWA-1; PoEL-3
Peace, peace on earth! the heart of man forever. Peace on Earth. Samuel Longfellow. PGD
Peace, peace, peace, make no noise. A Ditty. John Day. *Fr.* Humour Out of Breath. ElL
Peace, Perfect Peace. Edward H. Bickersteth. BePJ; BLRP; FaChP; SoP; WGRP
Peace-Pipe, The. Longfellow. *Fr.* The Song of Hiawatha. AnNE
Peace pratler, do not lowre [*or* lour]. Conscience. George Herbert. AnAnS-1; EP; MaMe; MeP
Peace, Shepherd, peace! What boots it singing on? Genius Loci. Margaret L. Woods. HBV; OBEV; OBVV
Peace, the one-time radiant goddess. The Child of Peace. Selma Lagerlof. PoPl
Peace! The perfect word is sounding, like a universal hymn. In the Dawn. Odell Shepard. WGRP
Peace, the wild valley streaked with torrents. The Straw. Robert Graves. MoVE
Peace, there is peace in this awaking. Waking. Patrick MacDonogh. NeIP
Peace through Prayer. Longfellow. *See* Oft Have I Seen. .
Peace to all such! but were there one whose fires. Atticus [*or* Characters from the Satires: Atticus *or* Portrait of Atticus]. Pope. *Fr.* Epistle to Dr. Arbuthnot. AWP; InPo; JAWP; MaPo; OBEC; PoFS; PoSa; SeCePo; ShBV-4; UnPo (1st ed.); ViBoPo; WBP; WHA
Peace to the quiet dead. The Elegy of the Kremlin Bells. Marya Zaturenska. *Fr.* Elegies over John Reed. NP
Peace to the Slumberers! Thomas Moore. HBV; OnYI
Peace to the Statue. *Unknown, tr. fr. Greek by* Lord Neaves. OnPM
Peace to these little broken leaves. Leaves. W. H. Davies. MoBrPo
Peace to-night, heroic spirit! Requiem for a Young Soldier. Florence Earle Coates. OHIP
Peace Triumphant. Cale Young Rice. PEDC
Peace Universal. Anna H. Thorne. PEDC; PoRL
"Peace upon earth!" was said. We sing it. Christmas: 1924. Thomas Hardy. PV
Peace, war, religion. This Tokyo. Gary Snyder. NeAP
Peace Was My Earliest Love. Edna St. Vincent Millay. NYTB
Peace, wayward barne! O cease thy moan! Song. Richard Brome. *Fr.* The Northern Lass. SeCL
Peace! What Do Tears Avail? "Barry Cornwall." VA
Peace you were always there. Prayer. James Kirkup. BoPe
Peaceable Kingdom, The. Isaiah, XI: 6-9, Bible, *O.T.* FaPON (XI: 6); LiTW
Peaceable Kingdom, The. Marge Piercy. TwCP; WOW
Peaceable Race, The. T. A. Daly. HBV
Peaceful, archangelic sun, A. The Ruined Farm. William Plomer. BoSA
Peaceful bite of hamburger and your mind is blown into space, A. New York. Tony Towle. ANYP
Peaceful Death. Walt Whitman. OQP
Peaceful life;—just toil and rest, A. Lincoln. James Whitcomb Riley. DD; LiPo; OHIP
Peaceful Night, The. Milton. *Fr.* On the Morning of Christ's Nativity. ChrBoLe
("But peaceful was the night.") FaBoCh; LoGBV
Peaceful Shepherd, The. Robert Frost. *Fr.* A Sky Pair. MAP; MoAB; MoAmPo; MoRP
Peaceful spot is Piper's Flat, A. The folk that live around. How McDougal Topped the Score. Thomas E. Spencer. PoAu-1
Peaceful Western Wind, The. Thomas Campion. EnRePo; LoBV
Peacefulness. Henry W. Frost. SoP
Peacemaker, The. W. H. Davies. BoPe
Peacemaker, The. Joyce Kilmer. CAW; MaRV; PoFr
Peach, The. Abbie Farwell Brown. GFA
Peach, The. Charles *and* Mary Lamb. OTPC (1923 ed.)
Peachblossoms flutter like pink butterflies, The. Prose Poem: Indifference. Judith Gautier. OnPM
Peach Tree, The. Edith Sitwell. NP
Peach Tree in the Garden of an Empty House. John Press. NYTB
Peach Tree with Fruit. Padraic Colum. BoNaP
Peaches, The. Joel Oppenheimer. CoPo

Peacock and Nightingale. Robert Finch. OBCV
Peacock-eye of the half-moon long since up, The. The Moonlit Doorway. Kenneth Mackenzie. MoAuPo
Peacock in Leucadia loved a maid, A. From Burton the Anatomist. Maurice James Craig. NeIP
Peacock moulted; soon a jay was seen, A. The Jay in the Feathers of the Peacock. La Fontaine. OnPM
Peacock of Java, The. William Jay Smith. RePo
Peacocks. Walter Adolphe Roberts. PoNe
Peacocks scream and the pear trees quiver. And the Pear Trees Shiver. Jocelyn Macy Sloan. FiSC
Peadar Og Goes Courting. James Stephens. BoLP; WhC
Peaks, The. Stephen Crane. War Is Kind, XVIII. AA; AmP; HBV; WGRP
(In the Night.) AmePo; AP; MWA-2
Peaks, and the starlit skies, the deeps of the fathomless seas, The. God Within Yet Above. Sir Lewis Morris. MaRV
Peaks in a sea of light! Not moaningly. Main Range. James Picot. BoAu
Peanuts. *Unknown.* FaFP; SiTL
("Boy stood on the burning deck, The.") GoTP
Pear, The. Ruth Stone. TwAmPo
Pear Tree. Hilda Doolittle ("H. D."). AP; CMoP; HBMV; MAP; MoAmPo; NeMA; UnPo
Pear-Tree, The. Mary Gilmore. PoAu-1
Pear-Tree, The. Iwan Goll, *tr. fr. German by* Babette Deutsch *and* Avram Yarmolinsky. TrJP
Pear Tree, The. E. Elizabeth Longwell. BrR
Pear Tree, The. Edna St. Vincent Millay. MAP; MoAmPo
Pear Tree, The. *Unknown, tr. fr. Chinese by* Allen Upward. AWP; JAWP; WBP
Pearl, The. Hans Christian Andersen, *tr. fr. Danish by* Charles Wharton Stork. LiTW
Pearl, The. George Herbert. AnAnS-1; EP; FaBoEn; MaMe; MeP; MePo; OxBoCh; PoEL-2; ReEn; SCEP-1; SeCP; SeCV-1
Pearl, The. *Unknown.* MeEV, *mod. vers. by* Sophie Jewett
Queen of Courtesy, The, *sel.* ACP; CAW, *mod. vers.*; ISi, *mod. vers. by* Stanley Perkins Chase
Pearl, a Girl, A. Robert Browning. CBEP; PoVP
Pearl Avenue runs past the high-school lot. Ex-Basketball Player. John Updike. NYBP; TPM
Pearl Bryan. *Unknown.* BaBo; ViBoFo
Pearl Diver. William Rose Benét. AnAmPo
Pearl Harbor. John C. Frolicher. OTD
Pearl of Great Price, The. William Chatterton Dix. SoP
Pearl of the White Breast. *Tr. fr. Modern Irish by* George Petrie. AnIV; OnYI
Pearl that the Prince full well might prize. The Pearl. *Unknown.* MeEV
Pearls of a day hung in the topmost height, The. The Yorkshire Moors. Hal Summers. HaMV
Pearls of the Faith, *sel.* Sir Edwin Arnold.
After Death in Arabia, *abr.* HBV; VA; WGRP
"Farewell, friends! Yet not farewell." MaRV
Pearls Seen through Amber. *Unknown, tr. fr. Arabic by* E. Powys Mathers. *Fr.* The Thousand and One Nights. LiTW
Pearly Everlasting, The. Ernest Fewster. CaP
Peas. *Unknown. See* I eat my peas with honey.
Peasant. Alfred Kreymborg. MAP
Peasant. W. S. Merwin. NYBP
Peasant, A. R. S. Thomas. ToPo
Peasant, The. Leonard Wolf. NYBP
Peasant and Geisha Songs. *Unknown, tr. fr. Japanese by* Kenneth Rexroth. LiTW
"Cicada cries out, The."
"First time I saw you, The."
"In the open sea."
"In the summer, by the river."
"Nightingale on the flowering plum, The."
Peasant and the Sheep, The. Ivan Andreyevich Krylov, *tr. fr. Russian by* C. Fillingham Coxwell. AWP; JAWP; WBP
Peasant Declares His Love, The. Emile Roumer, *tr. fr. French by* John Peale Bishop. ErPo; LiTW; PoNe; TTY
Peasant haled a sheep to court, A. The Peasant and the Sheep. Ivan Andreyevich Krylov. AWP; JAWP; WBP
Peasant once unthinkingly, A. The Monk and the Peasant. Margaret E. Bruner. PoToHe
Peasant Poet, The. John Clare. ERoP-2; OBNC; WGRP
Peasant stood before a king and said, A. Ahab Mohammed. James Matthew Legaré. AA
Peasant sun went crushing grapes, The. Laurence Dakin. *Fr.* Tancred, I, i. CaP
Peasant to his lord paid yearly court, A. The Cottager and His Landlord. Milton. OTPC (1923 ed.)
Peasantry. Eileen Duggan. CoBE
Peasants, The. Alun Lewis. FaBoMo; LiTM (1970 ed.)
Peasants my forebears were. Forebears. Monk Gibbon. NeIP
Pease-porridge [*or*-pudding] hot. Mother Goose. BoChLi; FaFP; HBV; HBVY; OTPC; OxNR; PCH; PPL; RIS; SiTL; SoPo; StVeCh (1940 ed.); TiPo
Peat-Cutters. Geoffrey Johnson. HaMV
Peau de Chagrin of State Street, The. Oliver Wendell Holmes. AP
Pebble, The. Elinor Wylie. MAP; MoAmPo; MoRP
Pebbles. Edith King. BoTP; GFA
Pebbles. Herman Melville. AP; MAmP
Peblis to the Play. *Unknown.* GoTS
Peccavi, Domine. Archibald Lampman. MaRV
Peck of Gold, A. Robert Frost. LaNeLa; PDV; PoG
Pecos Puncher, The. *Unknown.* CoSo
Peculiar ghost! great and immortal ghost! Epitaph for the Poet V., XVII. Arthur Davison Ficke. HBMV
Pedagogical Principles. Harry Amoss. CaP
Pedant dove, the poet who admires him, The. Literary Landscape with Dove and Poet. Phyllis McGinley. NePoAm-2
Pedantic Literalist. Marianne Moore. APA; CoAnAm
Peddler's Caravan, The. William Brighty Rands. *See* Pedlar's Caravan, The.
Pedestrian's Plaint, The. E. V. Lucas. CenHV
Pedigree. Emily Dickinson. *See* Pedigree of honey, The.
Pedigree, The. Thomas Hardy. CoBMV
Pedigree. Mary Mills. NePoAm
Pedigree of honey, The. Emily Dickinson. FaBV; GoTP; NeMA; TSW; YaD
Pediment: Ballet. Louise Townsend Nicholl. UnS
Pediment of Appearance, The. Wallace Stevens. Po
Pedlar. Confucius, *tr. fr. Chinese by* Ezra Pound. *Fr.* Wei Wind. CTC
Pedlar, The. Shakespeare. *See* Lawn as White as Driven Snow.
Pedlar, A. *Unknown. See* Fine Knacks for Ladies.
Pedlar Jim. Florence Hoare. BoTP
Pedlar's [*or* Peddler's] Caravan, The. William Brighty Rands. BoChLi; BoTP; GaP; GFA; HBV; HBVY; MPB; OTPC; PCH; PRWS; RIS; SoPo; StVeCh (1940 ed.);TVC
Pedlar's Song, The ("Lawn as white. . ."). Shakespeare. *See* Lawn as White as Driven Snow.
Pedlar's Song, The ("When daffodils. . ."). Shakespeare. *See* When Daffodils Begin to Peer.
Pedler, The. Charlotte Mew. HBMV
Pedra. John William Burgon. BLPA
(Petra.) NeHB
Pedro. Phoebe W. Hoffman. GoYe
Peedy, Peedy; Pally, Ludy; Lady Whistle. To Be Said to Baby's Fingers. *Unknown.* SAS
Peekaboo, I Almost See You. Ogden Nash. PoLF
Peeler and the Goat, The. *Unknown.* AnIL
Peeler, hast thou found my treasure. I've Lost My——. Harry Cholmondeley-Pennell. CenHV
Peeler's Lament, The. *Unknown.* CoSo
Peeper, The. Peter Davison. ErPo
Peepers. Melville Cane. RePo
Peepin' through the knothole. Go Get the Axe. *Unknown.* AS; TrAS
Peeping Tom. Francis Hope. ErPo
Peer Gynt. Charles Hamilton Sorley. HBMV
Peer of gods he seemeth to me, the blissful. Peer of the Gods [*or* Ode]. Sappho, *tr. by* John Addington Symonds. EnLi-1; LiTW
Peer of the golden gods is he to Sappho. Ode to Anactoria. Sappho, *tr. by* William Ellery Leonard. AWP
Peerless yet hapless maid of Q! Dirge. *Unknown.* BOHV
Peers of heav'n kept a parliament, The. Ad Michaelem Drayton. John Weever. ReIE
Pees maketh plente. Peace. *Unknown.* MeEL
Peeter a Whi[t]feild he hath slaine. Jock o' the Side. *Unknown.* ESPB; ViBoFo
Peewee, The. John Townsend Trowbridge. *See* Pewee, The.

Peewits on the Hills. Alice V. Stuart. ACV
Peg-Leg's Fiddle. Bill Adams. BBV; ETS; RePo
Pegasos are steaming, The. Winter Rains: Cataluña. Philip Levine. NaP
Pegasus. C. Day Lewis. AtBAP
Pegasus. Patrick Kavanagh. FaBoTw; MoAB; OxBI
(Glut on the Market, A.) OnYI
Pegasus Lost. Elinor Wylie. MAP; MoAmPo; NeMA
Peggy. Allan Ramsay. *See* My Peggy.
Peggy. Blanaid Salkeld. OnYI
Peggy Considers Her Grandmothers. Josephine Pinckney. NP
Peggy Said Good Morning. John Clare. ELP
Peggy's Wedding. Thomas Edward Brown. EnLit
Pelican, The. Philippe de Thaun, *tr. fr. French by* Richard Wilbur. WaKn
Pelican, The. *Unknown.* TreFS
Pelicans. Robinson Jeffers. MAP; MoAmPo
Pelicans My Father Sees, The. Sister Maris Stella. GoBC
Pell Mell Celebrated, The. John Gay. *Fr.* Trivia; or, The Art of Walking the Streets of London, II: Of Walking the Streets by Day. EnLi-1 (1949 ed.)
Pelleas and Ettarre. Tennyson. *See* Idylls of the King.
Pellicanus is the word. The Pelican. Philippe de Thaun. WaKn
Pelops and Hippodamia, *sel.* Matthew Grove.
In Praise of His Lady. ElL
Pelters of Pyramids. Richard Henry Horne. VA
Pemmy Was a Pretty Girl. *Unknown.* OTPC
Pen and the Album, The. Thackeray. VA
Pen of a ready writer, Lord, The. Penman's Prayer. Charles E. Bayley. SoP
Pen stops in a phrase of a letter home, The. Music in the Rec Hut. Hubert Creekmore. WaP
Penal Law. Austin Clarke. ELU; GTBS-P
Penal Servitude for Mrs. Maybrick. *Unknown.* OxBoLi; SiTL
Penalties of Baldness, The. Sir Owen Seaman. FiBHP
Penalty of Virtue, The. *Unknown, tr. fr. Sanskrit by* Arthur W. Ryder. *Fr.* The Panchatantra. AWP; PoFr
Penance, The. Nahum Tate. CavP
Pencil and Paint. Eleanor Farjeon. PDV
Pendennis, *sel.* Thackeray.
At the Church Gate, *fr. ch.* 32. EPN; HBV; VA
Pendulous mouth, you flap in a wind. Mouths. Louis Dudek. PeCV
Pendulum Rhyme. Selma Robinson. InMe
Penelope. Judy Thurman. NYTB
Penelope for her Ulysses' [*or* Ulisses] sake. Amoretti, XXIII. Spenser. BWP; CoBE; ReEn; ReIE
Penelope, That Longed for the Sight. *Unknown.* EnRePo
Penguin, A. Oliver Herford. FiBHP; PV
Penguin on the Beach. Ruth Miller. PeSA
Pen-guin sits upon the shore, The. A Penguin. Oliver Herford. FiBHP; PV
Penicillin. Frank Lima. ANYP
Penitence. William Cowper. *See* Walking with God.
Penitence. Thomas Moore. *See* Were Not the Sinful Mary's Tears.
Penitence. Pedro Soto de Rojas, *tr. fr. Spanish by* Sir John Bowring. OnPM
Penitent, The. Edna St. Vincent Millay. ALV; BOHV; YaD
Penitent, The. Jeremy Taylor. OBS; OxBoCh
Penitent Hopes in Mary, The. *Unknown.* MeEL
Penitent Nun, The. John Lockman. ErPo; UnTE
Penitent Palmer's Ode, The. Robert Greene. *Fr.* Francesco's Fortunes. LoBV; OBSC
Penitential Psalm ("I, thy servant, full of sighs, cry unto thee"). *Unknown, tr. fr. Babylonian.* WGRP
Penitential Psalm to the Goddess Anunit ("May the wrath of my god be pacified"). *Unknown, tr. fr. Babylonian.* WGRP
Penitential Psalms. Sir Thomas Wyatt. *See* Psalms, Bible, *O.T.*
Penman's Prayer. Charles E. Bayley. SoP
Penmanship. Tom Clark. ANYP
Pennies. Joyce Kilmer. CAW
Penniless. Toyohiko Kagawa. MaRV
Pennines in April. Ted Hughes. WePo
Pennsylvania. Helen Hall Bucher. PoRL
Pennsylvania Dutch mouse. Lancaster County Tragedy. W. Lowrie Kay. ShM
Pennsylvania Station. Langston Hughes. AmNP; Kal
Penny, The. Laura Benét. PCH
Penny and penny. *Unknown.* OxNR
Penny for a ball [*or* spool] of thread, A. Pop Goes the Weasel. *Unknown.* RIS; SoPo; TreFT
Penny is heavier that the shrew, A. The Masked Shrew. Isabella Gardner. ImOP
Penny lost in the lak, The. *Unknown.* *Fr.* Colkelbie Sow. OxBS
Penny Problem. John Farrar. GaP
Penny Trumpet. Raphael Rudnik. NYBP
Penny Whistle, The. Edward Thomas. MoAB; MoBrPo; MuSP
Penny Whistle Blues. E. H. L. Island. InMe
Penny Wise and Found Poolish. W. W. Watt. PoPo
Penny Wish, A. Irene Thompson. BoTP
Pennycandystore Beyond the El, The. Lawrence Ferlinghetti. CAD; NoP
Pensées de Noël. A. D. Godley. BOHV; InMe
Pensioners. Winifred M. Letts. BoTP
Pensive at eve on the hard world I mused. Sonnets Attempted in the Manner of Contemporary Writers. Samuel Taylor Coleridge. Sonn
Pensive photograph, A. To a Portrait. Arthur Symons. VA
Pensy Ant, right trig and clean, A. The Caterpillar and the Ant. Allan Ramsay. SeCePo
Pentagon Exorcism. Allen Ginsberg. WOW
Pentagonia. G. E. Bates. NYBP
Pentecost. Adelbert Sumpter Coats. TrPWD
Pentecost. James Kirkup. BoPe
Pentecost. Laura Simmons. ChIP
Pentucket. Whittier. MC; PAH
Penumbra. Dante Gabriel Rossetti. PoVP
Penurious Quaker, The; or, The High Priz'd Harlot. *Unknown.* CoMu
Peonies of the temple. The Temple That Charged Admission. Issa. PoFr
Peony for Apollo, A. Charles Edward Eaton. GoYe
People, The. Tommaso Campanella, *tr. fr. Italian by* John Addington Symonds. AWP; JAWP; OnPM; WBP; WoL
People, The, *sels.* "Robin Hyde." AnNZ
"After we'd left off loving, long after that," I.
"But letting go. . . hands, eyes, teeth, body, all ways," IV.
"How she grew old happened in fine-darned places," II.
People. D. H. Lawrence. BrPo
People. Lois Lenski. FaPON; OCS; SoPo
People, The. Dorothy Livesay. *Fr.* The Colour of God's Face. PeCV (1967 ed.)
People, The. Elizabeth Madox Roberts. GoJo; SoPo; TiPo
People, The. W. B. Yeats. CMoP
People all over at this time of year. Resolutions?—New and Old. Harvey E. Rolfe. STF
People along the sand, The. Neither Out Far nor in Deep. Robert Frost. AmP; AmPP (5th ed.); AP; CABA; CBV; ChTr; CoBMV; CrMA; DiPo; LiTA; MoAB; MWA-2; NoP; PAn; PoeP; TiPo (1952 ed.)
People always say to me. The Question. Karla Kuskin. PDV
People and a Heron. Robinson Jeffers. ReMP
People—and a lot/ I don't care for. Perambulator Poems, IV. David McCord. WhC
People are of two kinds, and he. Tribute on the Passing of a Very Real Person. *Unknown.* PoToHe (new ed.)
People are putting up storm windows now. Storm Windows. Howard Nemerov. PoIE
People arrive to worship in their church. The Church. Jules Romain. WGRP
People as Flowers. Francis Maguire. JKCP (1955 ed.)
People at the Party, The. Lisel Mueller. NePoAm-2
People buy a Lot of Things. Annette Wynne. PDV; SoPo; UTS
People buying and selling, consuming pleasures, The. Reference to a Passage in Plutarch's Life of Sulla. Robinson Jeffers. CrMA
People chained to aurora, A. Civilization and Its Discontents. John Ashbery. TwCP
People expect old men to die. Old Men. Ogden Nash. EvOK
People Going By. Elizabeth Madox Roberts. GaP
People Has No Obituary, The. Eunice Clark. NAMP
People have teased and vexed me. Two Songs. Heine. WoL
People Hide Their Love. Emperor Wu Ti, *tr. fr. Chinese by* Arthur Waley. LiTW

People in the Park, The. Léonie Adams. MoVE
People is a beast of muddy brain, The. The People. Tommaso Campanella. AWP; JAWP; OnPM; WBP; WoL
People, Look East, *with music.* Eleanor Farjeon. YaCaBo
People made a ring, The. The Hemorrhage. Stanley Kunitz. WaP
People of Ireland—I am an old woman; I am near my end. A Leitrim Woman. John Lyle Donaghy. OnYI; OxBI
People of Spain think Cervantes, The. Cervantes. E. C. Bentley. *Fr.* Clerihews. CenHV; EvOK; FiBHP
People of Tao-chou, The. Po Chü-i, *tr. fr. Chinese by* Arthur Waley. ChTr
People of the Phoenix do not say "the Phoenix," The. Conventicle. Gerrit Lansing. CoPo
People on Sunday. Edwin Denby. ANYP
People say they have a hard time. For de Lawd. Lucille Clifton. TwCP
People simper and drawl. Gnat. Rosalie Moore. GoTP
People that I meet and pass. Faces. Sara Teasdale. OCS
People, The, that walked in darkness have seen a great light. The Prince of Peace. Isaiah, Bible, *O.T.* ChrBoLe
People Trying to Love. Stephen Berg. NaP
People vs. the People, The. Kenneth Fearing. MoAmPo (1950 ed.)
People waddle on the boat, The. Dolphins. Molly Michaels. RIS
People walk upon their heads, The. Topsy-turvy Land. H. E. Wilkinson. BoTP; SoPo
People were bathing, and posturing themselves on the beach. The Gods! The Gods! D. H. Lawrence. CMoP
People who have what they want are very fond of telling people. The Terrible People. Ogden Nash. NePA; SiTL
People Who Must. Carl Sandburg. OCS; PDV; SAS
People Will Live On, The. Carl Sandburg. *Fr.* The People, Yes. AmPP; BoLiVe (1945 ed.); MoAmPo; NAMP; OxBA; TrGrPo
People Will Talk. Samuel Dodge. TreFS, *sl. diff.*; WBLP, *sl. abr.*
People with Proud Chins. Carl Sandburg. PFY
People wondered what Dan Wholebrook found. Star-Pudding. Robert P. Tristram Coffin. PoPo
People, Yes, The, *sels.* Carl Sandburg.
  Best, The, *fr.* Sec. 51. MaRV
  Copperfaces, The, *fr.* Sec. 51. RePo
  "From the four corners of the earth," Sec. 1. CMoP
  Hope Is a Tattered Flag, Sec. 16. NAMP
  "Lincoln?/ He was a mystery in smoke and flags," Sec. 57. LiPo
  Man in the Street Is Fed, The, Sec. 99. AmPP (4th ed.); OxBA
  People Will Live On, The, Sec. 107. AmPP; BoLiVe (1945 ed.); MoAB; MoAmPo; MoPo; NAMP; NePA; TrGrPo
  "People, yes, the people, The," Sec. 86. BBV (1951 ed.); NAMP; PoFr
  Sleep Is a Suspension, Sec. 106. NAMP
  They Have Yarns, Sec. 45. AmFN; LiTA; MoAmPo; RePo
    (American Yarns.) StVeCh (1955 ed.)
    (Yarns.) GoTP
    (Yarns of the People.) NeMA
  These Children of the Wind, *fr.* Sec. 13. BiS
    (Children of the Wind.) StVeCh; WePo
  "Who can make a poem of the depths of weariness," Sec. 83. MaRV; NAMP
Peopled Air, The. Thomas Gray. *Fr.* Ode on the Spring. OA
People's Anthem, The. Ebenezer Elliott. *See* When Wilt Thou Save the People?
People's Attorney, servant of the right! Wendell Phillips. Amos Bronson Alcott. AA; PoFr
People's King, The. Lyman Whitney Allen. PGD
People's Petition, The. Wathen Mark Wilks Call. OBVV; PoFr; VA
People's Prayer, The. Amos R. Wells. SoP
People's Thanksgiving, The. William Pierson Merrill. *See* Not Alone for Mighty Empire.
People's voice, A! we are a people yet. Tennyson. *Fr.* Ode on the Death of the Duke of Wellington. ACV
"Pep." Grace G. Bostwick. WBLP
Pepper Tree, The. Sister Mary Madeleva. RiS
Peppertrees, the peppertrees, The! Scenes from the Life of the Peppertrees. Denise Levertov. LiTM (1970 ed.); NeAP
Peppery Man, The. Arthur Macy. FaPON; GaP
Per Amica Silentia Lunae. Ronald de Carvalho, *tr. fr. Portuguese by* Harold Morland. LiTW
Per Ardua ad Astra. John Oxenham. TrPWD
Per Aspera. Florence Earle Coates. FaChP; HBMV
Per Contra. Mahlon Leonard Fisher. ChIP; MaRV
Per Diem et per Noctem. Mary Stanley. AnNZ
Per Iter Tenebricosum. Oliver St. John Gogarty. AnIL; OBMV; OxBI
Per Pacem ad Lucem. Adelaide Anne Procter. MaRV; SoP; TrPWD; VA
Perambulator Poems (I-VII). David McCord. WhC
"Perceived and taken things right thou hast long." Of Taking Things Wrong. John Heywood. ReIE
Perception of an object costs. Emily Dickinson. MAmP
Perchance in days to come. Strange Love. Moses ibn Ezra. TrJP
Perchance it was her eyes of blue. A Vague Story. Walter Parke. BOHV
Perchance it was the peace that stirless breasts. The Presence of the Spirit. Giulio Salvadori. CAW
Perchance that I might learn what pity is. Thou Alone Art Good [*or* A Prayer for Purification]. Michelangelo. AWP; OnPM
Perch'd on a lofty oak. The Raven and the Fox. La Fontaine. OnPM
"Perchè Pensa? Pensando S'Invecchia." Arthur Hugh Clough. PoVP
  (To Spend Uncounted Years of Pain.) OBNC; ViPP
Perched in a tower of this ancestral Wall. At the Greal Wall of China. Edmund Blunden. GTBS-P; HaMV
Perched on a great fall of air. Landscape with Figures. Keith Douglas. NePoEA
Perched on its yellow peak beneath a sky. Toledo. Antonio Gomez Restrepo. CAW
Perched on my city office-stool. The Ice-Cart. W. W. Gibson. ShBV-2
Percival Wilberforce Henderson Crane. The Scandalous Tale of Percival and Genevieve. Newman Levy. WhC
Percussion, Salt and Honey. Stuart Peterfreund. QAH
Percussive, furious, this wind. Mistral. Barbara Howes. NYBP
Percy Bysshe Shelley. Edgar Lee Masters. *Fr.* Spoon River Anthology. ML
Percy Bysshe Shelley. Dante Gabriel Rossetti. Five English Poets, 5. PoVP
Percy is my name; my accent is good. A Maine Roustabout. Richard Eberhart. TPM
Percy [*or* Persè] out of Northumberland, The. Chevy Chase [*or* The Ancient Ballad of Chevy Chase *or* The Hunting of the Cheviot]. *Unknown.* BaBo (A *vers.*); BEL; BuBa; EnRP; ESPB; OBB; OxBB; ViBoPo; WHA
Percy Shelley. John Peale Bishop. ErPo
Percy/ 68. Glenn Myles. NBP
Perdat Qui Caveat Emptor. Henry Parrot. SiCE
Perdie, I said it not. *See* Perdye I Saide Yt Not.
Perdita. Florence Earle Coates. AA
Perdita. John Swanwick Drennan. IrPN
Perdita. James Hebblethwaite. BoAu
Perdita's Garden. Shakespeare. *Fr.* The Winter's Tale, IV, iii. WHA
Perdition catch my soul. Shakespeare. *Fr.* Othello, III, iii. LO
Perdy, [*or* Perdie] I Said It Not. Sir Thomas Wyatt. FCP; PoEL-1
  (Constancy.) OBSC
  (Perdie, I Said It Not.) EnRePo; SiPS
Père Lalemant. Marjorie Pickthall. CaP; OBCV; PeCV; TwCaPo
Père Sévère, Le. *Unknown, tr. fr. French by* Andrew Lang. AWP; JAWP; WBP
Peregrine. Elinor Wylie. HBMV
Peregrine White and Virginia Dare. Rosemary Benét *and* Stephen Vincent Benét. PoRh
Peregrine's Sunday Song. Elinor Wylie. NYBP
Perennial fluctuation,/ Interior lift of the sea. Cuvier Light. Pat Wilson. AnNZ
Perennial Mourner. Sydney King Russell. FiSC
Perfect. Glyn Jones, *arr. by* "Hugh MacDiarmid." FIW; NeBP
Perfect and endles circls are. *Unknown.* SeCSL
Perfect Bliss and Sole Felicity. Christopher Marlowe. *See* Nature That Framed Us of Four Elements.
Perfect Child, The. Molly Michaels. RIS
Perfect Child, The. Monica Shannon. BoChLi

Perfect Day, A. Carrie Jacobs Bond. TreF; WBLP
Perfect Gift, The. Julia Benson Parker. BePJ
Perfect Greyhound, The. *Unknown.* PCH
Perfect, Heaven-made marriage, A. Holy Matrimony. Maybell Whiting Leal. SoP
Perfect Life, The. Jorge Carrera Andrade, *tr. fr. Spanish by* Dudley Fitts. LiTW; WoL
Perfect Life, The. Charles Francis Richardson. BePJ
Perfect little body, without fault or stain on thee. On a Dead Child. Robert Bridges. BrPo; CBV; CMoP; EnLi-2 (1949 ed.); GTSL; LiTB; LiTG; LiTM (rev. ed.); OAEP; OBEV (1st ed.); OBMV; OBNC; ViBoPo
Perfect Love ("Perfect love the Father giveth"). *Unknown.* STF
Perfect Peace. Isaiah, XXVI: 3, Bible, *O.T.* TRV
Perfect Peace. Frances Ridley Havergal. SoP
Perfect Reactionary, The. Hughes Mearns. SiTL; WhC
Perfect shield bedecks some Thracian now, A. The Poet's Shield. Archilochus. LiTW
Perfect Tribute, The. Shakespeare. *Fr.* Julius Caesar, V, v. MaRV
Perfect Woman. Wordsworth. *See* She Was a Phantom of Delight.
Perfection. Francis Carlin. FaFP; HBMV
Perfection. Ruth Scofield Fargo. OQP
Perfection-bright figure, daily with me sojourning. Hymn to the Guardian Angel. J. Corson Miller. JKCP (1926 ed.)
Perfection, if't hath ever been attayned. In the Due Honor of the Author Master Robert Norton. John Smith. SCAP
Perfection is terrible, it cannot have children. The Munich Mannequins. Sylvia Plath. NaP
Perfection, of a kind, was what he was after. Epitaph on a Tyrant. W. H. Auden. ELU
Perfection of Dentistry, The. Marvin Bell. CoAP; YAP
Perfectly happy now, he looked at his estate. Voltaire at Ferney. W. H. Auden. GTBS-W; LiTM; NePA; PoE
Perfervid Roc, sitting on candle light, The. The Roc. Richard Eberhart. CMoP
Perforated Spirit, The. Morris Bishop. FiBHP; PoPo
Performance, The. James Dickey. CoAP; LiTM (1970 ed.); NePoEA-2; TDP
Performance of "Boris Godunov," A. Robert Conquest. MuSP
Performances, assortments, résumés. The Tunnel. Hart Crane. *Fr.* The Bridge. AmP; AP; CMoP; LiTA; LiTG; MAP; MoAB; MoAmPo; MoVE; NePA; OxBA; PoFS
Performing Seal, The. Rachel Field. *Fr.* A Circus Garland. SoPo; StVeCh; TiPo (1959 ed.); UTS
Perfume, The. John Donne. Elegies, IV. AnAnS-1; MaMe
Perfume. *Unknown, tr. fr. Greek by* Louis Untermeyer. UnTE
Perfume is the same, the same the hue, The. The Avenue of Trees. Tsurayuki. OnPM
Perfume of the iris, sweet citron, The. The Words, the Words, the Words. William Carlos Williams. PoeP
Perfume of your body dulls my sense, The. Flower of Love. Claude McKay. BALP
Perfumes. Terence Tiller. FaBoMo
Pergamon city of the Phrygians. The Aftermath. Euripides. *Fr.* Iphigenia in Aulis. WaaP
Perhaps. W. H. Auden. MoPo; NePA; OAEP (2d ed.); ReMP
(Prologue: "O love, the interest itself in thoughtless Heaven.") FaBoMo; NAMP
Perhaps. Pringle Barret. PCH
Perhaps. Bob Kaufman. Kal
Perhaps/ You will remember. October 16: The Raid. Langston Hughes. BOLo
Perhaps a dream; yet surely truth has beamed. Frederick Goddard Tuckerman. *Fr.* Sonnets. AP; MAmP
Perhaps a Prayer. James Schevill. FiMAP
Perhaps he plays with cherubs now. A Phantasy of Heaven. Harry Kemp. HBMV; TSW
Perhaps he will come at the dawning. When Will He Come? *Unknown.* SoP; STF
"Perhaps I may allow the dean." Swift. *Fr.* Verses on the Death of Dr. Swift. FaBoEn; OnYI
Perhaps, if you/ Are very good. Hob the Elf. Norman M. Johnson. BoTP
Perhaps it is no matter that you died. To Hasekawa. Walter Conrad Arensberg. HBV
Perhaps it is well now. We Who Are Left. George Whalley. CaP
Perhaps it was being inside of something. The History of the World as Pictures. Nancy Sullivan. CoPo
Perhaps it was never the flowers. Turkish Garden. C. A. Trypanis. NYTB
Perhaps, long hence, when I have pass'd away. She, to Him. Thomas Hardy. OBEV (new ed.)
Perhaps on such a day as this—but. Picasso's "Portrait de Femme." Irving Feldman. NYTB
Perhaps she hears the breath of kneelers here. Requiem. Nathalia Crane. *Fr.* The Death of Poetry. MoAmPo (1942 ed.)
Perhaps she watches where a silver bay. La Madonna di Lorenzetti. John Williams Andrews. HBMV
Perhaps some needful service of the state. Epitaphs, II. Gabriello Chiabrera. AWP
Perhaps the accident of a bird. An Instance. Alastair Reid. PP
Perhaps the Best Time. William Meredith. NePoEA
Perhaps the day would not have seemed so long. "If I Had Prayed." M. Joyce Roder. SoP
Perhaps there is no magic in this dull old world of ours. Music Magic. Edmund Leamy. JKCP
Perhaps Today. J. Danson Smith. SoP
Perhaps Today. *Unknown.* STF
Perhaps Where He Is Only Loving Rockets Can Land. Brian Patten. HYE
Perhaps you expected a face that was free from tears. Narcissus. Paul Valéry. AWP
Perhaps you find the angel most improbable? Poem for a Christmas Broadcast. Anne Ridler. NeBP
Perhaps you may a-noticed I been soht o' solemn lately. I Didn't Like Him. Harry B. Smith. BOHV
Peri Poietikes. Louis Zukofsky. CoPo
Pericles, *sel.* Shakespeare.
"Sinful father, The/ Seem'd not to strike," *fr.* I, ii. PoFr
Pericles and Aspasia, *sels.* Walter Savage Landor.
Behold, O Aspasia! I Send You Verses, *fr.* CXC. LoBV; OBNC ("Beauty! thou art a wanderer on the Earth.") ViBoPo
Copy of Verses sent by Cleone to Aspasia, A, *fr.* CXXI. LoBV
Corinna, from Athens, to Tanagra, *fr.* XLIV. OBEV (new ed.); OBVV
(Corinna to Tanagra.) OBNC; OBRV; ViBoPo, *abr.*
(Corinna to Tanagra from Athens.) TOP
Death of Artemidora, The, *fr.* LXXXV. BEL; EnRP; EPN; InP; OBNC; SeCeV; VA
("Artemidora! Gods invisible.") ViBoPo
Dirce, *fr.* CCXXX. AnFE; AWP; BoLiVe; CBEP; CBV; CTC; EnRP; ExPo; FaBoEn; InPo; JAWP; LiTB; LoBV; MemP; NoP; OAEP; OBEV; OBNC; OBRV; PoEL-4; PoRA; SeCeV; StP; TOP; TreFT; TrGrPo; VA; ViBoPo; WBP; WHA; WhC
(Stand Close Around.) ChTr
("Stand close around, ye Stygian set.") EG; GTBS-D
Little Aglae, *fr.* CXIII. VA
Myrtis, *fr.* LIII. OBRV; VA
Pericles, Prince of Tyre. Shakespeare. *See* Pericles.
Perigoo's Horse. *At. to* George Calhoun *and to* John Calhoun. ShS
Perigot's and Cuddy's Roundelay. Spenser. *Fr.* The Sheperdes Calendar: August. EP
(It Fell upon a Holy Eve.) InvP; PoE
(Perigot and Willye.) LoBV
(Roundelay, A: "It fell upon a holy eve." EIL
Perilla! to thy fates resign'd. A Copy of Verses sent by Cleone to Aspasia. Walter Savage Landor. *Fr.* Pericles and Aspasia. LoBV
Perilous Life, A ("A perilous life, and hard"). *Unknown.* EtS
Perils of Darkness. Shakespeare. *Fr.* King Richard II, III, ii. TreFT
Perils of Invisibility, The. W. S. Gilbert. StPo
Perils of Obesity, The. Harry Graham. FiBHP
Perimedes, *sels.* Robert Greene.
Coridon and Phillis. OBSC
(Phillis and Corydon.) HBV
Fair Is My Love for April is [*or* April's in] Her Face. HBV; ReIE; ViBoPo
(Fair Is My Love.) EIL
Obscure and Dark Is All the Gloomy Air. ReIE
Period. George Amabile. YAP
Period of Mourning, The, *sel.* Henry Peacham.

Nuptial Hymn. ElL
Peri's Lament for Hinda, The. Thomas Moore. *Fr.* Lalla Rookh. OBNC
Perishing Bird, The. D. G. Jones. MoCV
Permanence. Francis Meynell. HBV; MoBrPo (1942 ed.)
Permanence of the Young Men, The. William Soutar. NeBP; OxBS
Permanent Delegate, The. Yuri Suhl, *tr. fr. Yiddish by* Max Rosenfeld *and* Walter Lowenfels. PPON; WOW
Permanent Tourists, The. P. K. Page. LiTM (1970 ed.)
Permanently. Kenneth Koch. CoAP; NoP
Permit me here a simple brief aside. To Calliope. Robert Graves. CMoP; NYTB
Permit Me Voyage. James Agee. MAP; MoAmPo
Permitted to assist you, let me see. St. Valentine. Marianne Moore. NYBP
Pernicious Weed. William Cowper. InMe; WhC
Perpetual Christmas. Arthur Gordon Field. PGD
Perpetual night and endless sleep. Nox Est Perpetua. Marion Lochhead. LO
Perpetuum Mobile. Edith Sitwell. HBMV
Perplext in faith, but pure in deeds. A Stronger Faith. Tennyson. *Fr.* In Memoriam A. H. H., XCVI. MaRV; TRV
Perplext no more with Human or Divine. The Minister of Wine. Omar Khayyám, *tr. by* Edward Fitzgerald. *Fr.* The Rubáiyát. OnPM
Perrie, Merrie, Dixi, Domini, *with music. Unknown.* BFSS
Perry Zoll. Edgar Lee Masters. *Fr.* Spoon River Anthology. CrMA; NP
Perry's Victory. *Unknown.* PAH
Perry's Victory—a Song. *Unknown.* PAH
Perry's Victory on Lake Erie. James Gates Percival. PaA; PAP
Persè owt of Northombarlande, The. *See* Percy out of Northumberland, The.
Persepolis. Christopher Marlowe. *Fr.* Tamburlaine the Great, Pt. I, Act II, sc. v. CLwM
(And Ride in Triumph.) WHA
Perseus. Louis MacNeice. CoBMV; GTBS-W; LiTM; ReMP; StP
Perseverance. George Herbert. MaMe
Perseverance. *Unknown. See* Always Finish.
Perseverance. *Unknown.* SoP
Perseverance; or, Half a Coronet, *sel.* A. P. Herbert.
Finale. InMe
Pershing at the Tomb of Lafayette. Amelia Josephine Burr. PAH
Persian Eclogues, *sel.* William Collins.
Eclogue the Second. CEP
Persian fable, A, says; One day. Influence. *Unknown.* MaRV
Persian Fopperies ("Persicos odi"). Horace, *tr. fr. Latin by* William Cowper. Odes, I, 38. AWP; JAWP; WBP; WoL
(Frippery, *tr. by* L. R. Lind.) LiTW
(I Hate Their Empty Shows, *tr. by* William Cowper.) OnPM
(Persian Pomp, *tr. by* William Cowper.) EnLi-1
(Persicos Odi, *par. by* Franklin P. Adams.) HBMV
(To His Cup-Bearer, *tr. by* Sir Theodore Martin.) OuHeWo
(To His Servant, *tr. by* Christopher Smart.) EiCL
Persian galleys plumed with warriors, The. Before Salamis. William Bedell Stanford. NeIP
Persian Miniature. William Jay Smith. CoAP; MoVE
Persian penman named Aziz, A. The Careful Penman. *Unknown.* BOHV
Persian Pomp. Horace. *See* Persian Fopperies.
Persian Song, A. Hafiz, *tr. fr. Persian by* Sir William Jones. AWP; OBEC; OuHeWo
(Persian Song of Hafiz, A.) PrWP
Persian Version, The. Robert Graves. CMoP; LiTB; LiTM (rev. ed.); SiTL
Persians, *sel.* Aeschylus, *tr. fr. Greek by* G. M. Cookson.
Salamis, *tr. by* G. M. Cookson. WaaP, *shorter sel.*
(Battle of Salamis, The, *tr. by* Gilbert Murray.) PoFr
Persia's Crew, The, *with music. Unknown.* SoAmSa
Persia's pomp, my boy, I hate. To His Cup-Bearer. Horace, *tr. by* Sir Theodore Martin. OuHeWo
Persicos Odi. Franklin P. Adams, *after* Horace. *See* Persian Fopperies.
Persicos Odi. Charles Edmund Merrill, Jr. AA
Persicos Odi. Thackeray. *See* Ad Ministram.
Persimmon, lo, The! To Her Husband, at the Wedding. Kaga no Chiyo. LiTW
Persistence. William Savage Landor. *Fr.* Ianthe. VA
("My hopes retire; my wishes as before.")
Persistency of Poetry. Matthew Arnold. MBW-2
Persistent Explorer. John Crowe Ransom. NoP; OxBA
Person from Porlock, The. Robert Graves. BoC; ML
Person from Porlock, A. R. S. Thomas. BoC
Person had become a master in the art of wrestling, A. The Wrestler. Sadi. *Fr.* The Gulistan. OuHeWo
Person is always self-conscious about his head, A. Thoughts on One's Head. William Meredith. SiTL
Person, or a Hymn on and to the Holy Ghost. Margaret Avison. PeCV (1967 ed.)
Person who can do, The. Poem. Alan Dugan. ErPo
Personal. Langston Hughes. AmNP; PoNe
Personal. Samuel Yellen. NYBP
Personal History; for My Son. Ruthven Todd. NeBP
Personal Jihad. Gaston Neal. BF
Personal Letter to the Ephesians. Carl Bode. ToPo
Personal Poem. Kendrick Smithyman. AnNZ
Personal Poem #8. Ted Berrigan. ANYP
Personal Poem #7. Ted Berrigan. ANYP
Personal Talk. Wordsworth. BEL; CABA; DiPo; EnRP; EPN; InPo
"I am not one who much or oft delight," I. MyFE
Personality. Archibald Lampman. PeCV (1967 ed.)
Personality. Carl Sandburg. CrMA
Personally, I don't care whether a detective-story writer was educated in night school or day school. Don't Guess, Let Me Tell You. Ogden Nash. SiTL
Personified Sentimental, The. Bret Harte. NA
Perspective. Margaret Avison. OBCV; PeCV
Perspective. Victor Contoski. ThO
Perspective never withers from their eyes. Quaker Hill. Hart Crane. *Fr.* The Bridge. LiTA; LiTM (rev. ed.)
Perspective of Co-ordination. Arthur Davison Ficke. NP
Perspectives. Dudley Randall. AmNP
Perspectives Are Precipices. John Peale Bishop. LiTA; LiTM; MoVE; NePA
Persuasion. Wordsworth. Ecclesiastical Sonnets, XVI. MaRV; OQP
Persuasions to Enjoy; a Song. Thomas Carew. EnLi-1; FosPo; OBEV
(Persuasions to Enjoy.) HBV; SeCL
(Perswasions to Enjoy.) AnAnS-2; MePo; SCEP-2; SeCP; SeCV-1
Persuasions to Love. Thomas Carew. LiTL
"For that lovely face will fail," *sel.* ViBoPo
Pert paradox, whose green and summer claws. Praying Mantis. Felix Stefanile. FiSC
Perturbation at Dawn. Ibn Maatuk, *tr. fr. Arabic by* E. Powys Mathers. LiTW
Perturbations of Uranus, The. Roy Fuller. ErPo
Perugia. Amelia Josephine Burr. HBV
Perverse habit of cat-goddesses, A. Cat-Goddesses. Robert Graves. MoVE; NYBP
Peruse my leaves thro' ev'ry part. Verses Wrote in a Lady's Ivory Table-Book. Swift. EiCL; NCEP
Pesach Has Come to the Ghetto Again. Binem Heller, *tr. fr. Yiddish by* Max Rosenfeld. TrJP
Persistency of Poetry. Matthew Arnold. PoVP
Peschiera. Arthur Hugh Clough. HBV; PoVP; VA; ViPo
Pesci Misti. L. Aaronson. FaBoTw
Pessimism. Newton Mackintosh. BOHV
Pessimist, The. Ben King. ALV; BLPA; BOHV; FaFP; InMe; LiTG; NA; NeHB; TreFT; WaKn; WePo
(Sum of Life, The, *abr.*) CTC
Pessimist, The. *Unknown.* PoToHe (new ed.)
Pessimist and Optimist. Thomas Bailey Aldrich. AnNE; TOP
Pessimist's a cheerless man, The. The Pessimist. *Unknown.* PoToHe (new ed.)
Pet Crane, A. *Unknown, tr. fr. Old Irish by* Myles Dillon. AnIL
Pet Lamb, The. Wordsworth. OTPC; PRWS; SAS
Pet Name, The. Elizabeth Barrett Browning. HBV
Pet Shop. Robert Sward. ELU
Pet was never mourned as you. Last Words to a Dumb Friend. Thomas Hardy. PoFS; OAEP (2d ed.)
Petals fall in the fountain, The. Ts'ai Chi'h. Ezra Pound. NoP

Petals (continued)
Pete at the Zoo. Gwendolyn Brooks. LOW; PDV
Pete Rousecastle the sailor's son. Rousecastle. David Wright. MoBS
Pete the Parrot and Shakespeare. Don Marquis. ML
Peter. Laura Benét. HBMV
Peter. Michael Dennis Browne. NYBP
Peter. Earl Marlatt. MoRP
Peter. Marianne Moore. AnAmPo; CMoP; NoP; OxBA
Peter. John Oxenham. SoP
Peter and James and John. Good Friday. Lizette Woodworth Reese. OQP
Peter and John. Elinor Wylie. HBMV; MaC; MAP; MoAB; MoAmPo; MoBS; MoRP; StJW
Peter and Linda in my car gone to Easthampton. Red River. Lewis Mac Adams. YAP
Peter and Michael were two little menikin. *Unknown.* BoTP
Peter and Polly. Esther Antin. *Fr.* On Our Farm. RIS
Peter at Fourteen. Constance Carrier. NePoAm
Peter at some immortal cloth, it seemed. The Death of Peter Esson. George Mackay Brown. NePoEA-2
Peter Bell, *sels.* Wordsworth.
  Among the Stars. GoTP
  Crescent Boat, The. ThWaDe
Peter Bell [a Lyrical Ballad]. John Hamilton Reynolds. OBNC; OBRV
  "It is the thirty-first of March," *sel.* Par
Peter Bell the Third, *sel.* Shelley.
  "Among the guests who often stayed," Part the Fifth. ChER
Peter Cooper. Joaquin Miller. AA
Peter denied, but Jesus did not scold. The Focus of That Face. Edwin McNeill Poteat. ChIP
Peter Emberley, 3 *vers, with music.* John Calhoun. ShS
Peter, Go Ring Dem Bells, *with music.* *Unknown.* BoAN-1
Peter Gray, *with music.* *Unknown.* OuSiCo
Peter Grimes. George Crabbe. The Borough, Letter XXII. EiCL; EnPE; EnRP; NoP; PoEL-4
  Sels.
  "Alas, for Peter not a helping hand," *br. sel.* OBRV
  "I am escaped," he said, when none pursued. MeMP
  "Now live the youth in freedom, but debarred." WePo
  "Thus by himself compell'd to live each day." FaBoEn; OBNC; SeCePo
Peter had experienced the tight, nauseous desire. The Wickedness of Peter Shannon. Alden Nowlan. MoCV
Peter hath lost his purse, but will conceal it. Henry Parrot. TuPP
Peter is a funny cat. Peter and Polly. Esther Antin. *Fr.* On Our Farm. RIS
Peter meanwhile perceived the time draw nigh. The Bandit Peter Mancino's Death. *Unknown.* CAW
Peter of the brothers three. Peter. Laura Benét. HBMV
Peter, outworn. Peter. John Oxenham. SoP
Peter Parasol. Wallace Stevens. NP
Peter, Peter, along the ground. Four Sides to a House. Amy Lowell. NP; PoRA
Peter, Peter, pumpkin-eater. Mother Goose. BoChLi; FaBoBe; FaFP; HBV; HBVY; OTPC; OxNR; PCH; PPL; RIS; SiTL; SoPo; TiPo (1959 ed.)
Peter Piper picked a peck of pickled [*or* pickling] pepper[s]. Mother Goose. BoChLi; FaBoBe; FaFP; FaPON; HBV; HBVY; OTPC; OxNR; RIS; SiTL; StVeCh; TiPo (1959 ed.); TreFS
Peter Quince at the Clavier. Wallace Stevens. AmPP (4th ed.); AnFE; AnNE; AP; APA; ATP (1953 ed.); CABA; CBV; CLwM; CMoP; CoAnAm; CoBMV; ExPo; ForPo; HBMV; ILP; InPo; LiTM; MAP; MAPA; MaPo (1969 ed.); MoAB; MoAmPo; NAMP; NP; OxBA; PAn; PoAn; ReMP; TDP; TrGrPo; TwAmPo; TwCP; UnPo (3d ed.); VaPo; ViBoPo; WoL
Peter Simson's Farm. Edward Dyson. BoAu
Peter sleep-walks. Peter. Michael Dennis Browne. NYBP
Peter Stuyvesant. Rosemary Benét *and* Stephen Vincent Benét. OTD
Peter Stuyvesant's New Year's Call. Edmund Clarence Stedman. PaA; PAH
Peter White will never [*or* ne'er] go right. Mother Goose. OTPC; OxBoLi; OxNR; PPL; RIS
Peterhead in May. Burns Singer. OxBS
Peterhof. Edmund Wilson. GoJo
Peter's Tears. Thomas Hood. TreFT
Petit Mari, Le, *with music.* *Unknown.* OuSiCo
Petit Testament, Le. Villon, *tr. fr. French.*
  (Lesser Testament, The, *abr., tr. by* John Payne.) WoL
  (Little Testament, The, *tr. by* John Heron Lepper.) OuHeWo
Petit, the Poet. Edgar Lee Masters. *Fr.* Spoon River Anthology. AnFE; APA; CMoP; CoAnAm; ILP; InPo; LaNeLa; LoGBV; MAP; MoAmPo; MoVE; NeMA; OxBA; PoSa; PPON
Petition, A. Thomas Bailey Aldrich. AA
Petition. W. H. Auden. *See* Sir, No Man's Enemy.
Petition. John Drinkwater. TrPWD
Petition. Clinton Scollard. MaRV
Petition. Eleanor Slater. TrPWD
Petition, A. Robert Ernest Vernède. InP
Petition for a Miracle. David Morton. *Fr.* Boke of Two Ladies. ISi
Petition for an Absolute Retreat, The. Countess of Winchilsea. OBEC, *abr.*; PoEL-3
  "Give me, O indulgent fate!" *sel.* TrGrPo
Petition of the Gray Horse, Auld Dunbar, The. William Dunbar. OxBS
Petition of Tom Dermody to the Three Fates in Council Sitting, The. Thomas Dermody. AnIV
Petition of Youth before Battle. John Bunker. CAW
Petition to Have Her Leave to Die. "A. W." OBSC
  (Give Me Leave.) TrGrPo
  ("When will the fountain of my tears be dry.") EG
Petition to the Queen. Sir Walter Ralegh. FCP
Petition to Time, A. "Barry Cornwall." VA
Petitions of Saint Augustine. *Unknown.* WHL
Petra. John William Burgon. *See* Pedra.
Petrarch. Giosuè Carducci, *tr. fr. Italian by* William Dudley Foulke. AWP
Petrarch for Laura. Claire McAllistair. SiSw
Petrified Fern, The. Mary Lydia Bolles Branch. AA
Petrillo, *parody.* "Gilbertulus." WhC
Petron, the Desert Father. Lawrence Durrell. *Fr.* Eight Aspects of Melissa. NeBP
Petruchio Is Undaunted by Katharina. Shakespeare. *Fr.* The Taming of the Shrew, I, ii. TreFT
Pets, The. Robert Farren. CoBE; OA; OxBI
Pets are the hobby of my brother Bert. My Brother Bert. Ted Hughes. BBGG
Pet's Punishment. Joseph Ashby-Sterry. BOHV
Pettichap's Nest, The. John Clare. BoPe
Pettitoes are little feet, The. *Unknown.* OxNR
Petty Officers' Mess, The. Roy Fuller. ChMP
Petty sneaking knave I knew, A. Cromek. Blake. FiBHP; PV
'Petually/ constrained am I. To His Wife. John Skelton. CBEP
Petunias in mass formation. Giardino Pubblico. Sir Osbert Sitwell. ChMP
Peveril of the Peak, *sel.* Sir Walter Scott.
  "'Speak not of niceness when there's chance of wreck,'" *fr. ch.* 38. NBM
Pew, pew. The Milk-white Dove. *Unknown.* ChTr
Pewee [*or* Peewee], The. John Townsend Trowbridge. HBV; OTPC
Peyote Poem, *sel.* Michael McClure.
  "Clear—the senses bright—sitting in the black chair—Rocker —," I. NeAP
Phaeton. Eli Mandel. PeCV (1967 ed.)
Phaleuciacs I: "Time nor place did I want; what held me tonguetide?" *Unknown.* SiCE
Phaleuciacs II: "Wisdom warns me to shun that once I sought for." *Unknown.* SiCE
Phallic Symbol, The. Nicholas Moore. NeBP
Phallus going around a corner, A. Banana. Adrian Mitchell. PV
Phantasmion, *sels.* Sara Coleridge.
  He Came Unlook'd For. OBRV; VA
  (Song: "He came unlook'd for, undesir'd.") CBEP; OBVV
  I Was a Brook. OBRV
  "O sleep, my babe, hear not the rippling wave." OBEV (1st ed.); OBNC; OBRV
  One Face Alone. VA
Phantasus ("Its roof among the stars projected"). Arno Holz, *tr. fr. German by* Ludwig Lewisohn. AWP; JAWP; WBP
Phantasus, I-8 ("On a mountain of sugar-candy"). Arno

Holz, *tr. fr. German by* Babette Deutsch *and* Avrahm Yarmolinsky. LiTW
Phantasus, VI-14 ("I wish you were real!"). Arno Holz, *tr. fr. German by* Babette Deutsch *and* Avrahm Yarmolinsky. LiTW
Phantasy ("All is phantom that we mid fare"). *Unknown.* ACP
Phantasy of Heaven, A. Harry Kemp. HBMV; TSW
Phantom. Samuel Taylor Coleridge. ERoP-1; LO; PoEL-4; SiSw
Phantom Bark, The. Hart Crane. CMoP
Phantom Horsewoman, The. Thomas Hardy. CaFP; CMoP; LO; PoEL-5; SiSw
Phantom Light of the Baie des Chaleurs, The. Arthur Wentworth Hamilton Eaton. CaP; PoMS
Phantom-Lover, The. Thomas Lovell Beddoes. *See* Phantom-Wooer, The.
Phantom Mail Coach, The. L. O. Welcome. PoMS
Phantom or Fact. Samuel Taylor Coleridge. EnRP; ERoP-1
Phantom Ship, The. J. W. De Forest. EtS
Phantom Ship, The. Longfellow. EtS
Phantom-Wooer, The. Thomas Lovell Beddoes. CBV; EnRP; ERoP-2; OBRV; PeER; TrGrPo; ViBoPo; WiR
(Phantom-Lover, The.) LO
Phantoms. Thomas Ashe. VA
Phantoms. Harry McGuire. CAW
Phantoms All. Harriet Prescott Spofford. AA; PFY
Phar Lap in the Melbourne Museum. Peter Porter. PoAu-2
Pharaoh Cheops lived to die, The. Cheops. James Schevill. FiMAP
Pharaoh of the Exodus is eight feet fall, The. After Reading Translations of Ancient Texts on Stone and Clay. Charles Reznikoff. SiSw
Pharaoh's Army Got Drownded, *with music.* *Unknown.* AS
Pharisee and Publican. Richard Crashaw. *See* Two Went Up to the Temple to Pray.
Pharisee and the Publican, The. St. Luke, XVIII: 9-14, Bible, *N.T.* TreFT
Pharisee murmurs when the woman weeps, conscious of guilt, The. Sequaire. Godeschalk. CTC
Pharsalia, *sels.* Lucan, *tr. fr. Latin.*
Cato's Address to His Troops in Lybia, *fr.* IX, *tr. by* Nicholas Rowe. OBEC
Pompey and Cornelia, *fr.* V, *tr. by* Nicholas Rowe. OBEC
Portents, The, *fr.* I, *tr. by* Christopher Marlowe. OBSC
"Wars worse then civil on Thessalian plains," *fr.* I, *tr. by* Christopher Marlowe. RelE
Phases of the Moon. Robert Browning. *Fr.* One Word More. ChTr
Phases of the Moon. John Dos Passos. OTD
Phases of the Moon, The. Christina Rossetti. *Fr.* Sing-Song. MemP
Pheasant ("Pheasant sat by a bush"). Zullikar Ghose. ACV
Pheasant, The. Robert P. Tristram Coffin. TiPo
Pheasant. Sidney Keyes. HaMV
Pheasant, The. Pope. *Fr.* Windsor Forest. GoTP
("See! from the brake the whirring pheasant springs.") FaBoEn; PoEL-3
Phèdre, *sels.* Racine, *tr. fr. French.*
Conquest of Love, The, *tr. by* Lacy Lockert. LiTW
Pheidippides. Robert Browning. PoVP
Phenix, The. George Darley. *See* Phoenix, The.
Phenomena. Robinson Jeffers. OxBA
Phenomenon, The. Karl Shapiro. CMoP; NMP; NYBP
Philadelphia sky,/ Seen by Jane. Alfred-Seeable Philadelphia Sky. Eli Siegel. CAD
Philander. Donald Hall. ELU; ErPo
Philanderer, The. Moses Mendes. *Fr.* The Chaplet. TrJP
Philaret on Willy cals. The Fourth Eglogue. George Wither. *Fr.* The Shepherd's Hunting. SeCV-1
Philarete Praises Poetry. George Wither. *Fr.* The Shepherd's Hunting. OBS
Philatelic Lessons: The German Collection. Lawrence P. Spingarn. NYBP
Philemon and Baucis. Ovid. *See* Baucis and Philemon.
Philip, foozling with his cleek. Some Ruthless Rhymes, VII. Harry Graham. CenHV
Philip My King. Dinah Maria Mulock Craik. HBV; VA
Philip Sparrow. John Skelton. *See* Phyllyp Sparowe.
Philip van Artevelde, *sels.* Sir Henry Taylor.
Elena's Song. OBEV; OBRV; OBVV
(Song: "Quoth tongue of neither maid nor wife.") VA
John of Launoy. VA
Philip van Artevelde. VA
Revolutions. PoFr; VA
Song: "Down lay in a nook my lady's brach." VA
Philippians, *sel.* Bible, *N.T.*
Think on These Things, IV: 8. TreFT
("Whatsoever things are true.") TiPo (1952 ed.)
Philippine Madonna. Louise Crenshaw Ray. ISi
Philippines were drenched in sun, The. Portrait Philippines. Alfred A. Duckett. PoNe
Philips, whose touch harmonious could remove. An Epitaph on [*or* upon the Celebrated] Claudy Philips, a Musician [Who Died Very Poor]. Samuel Johnson. CBEP; EiCL; OBEC; UnS
Philira. Sir John Vanbrugh. *Fr.* The Provoked Wife. SeCL
(Song: "Fly, fly, you happy shepherds, fly.") SeEP
Philistines are forming fours, The. The War with the Weeds. Keith Sinclair. AnNZ
Phillada Flouts Me. *Unknown.* OBEV; TrGrPo; ViBoPo
(Disdainful Shepherdess, The.) OBSC
(Oh, What a Plague Is Love!) InvP
(Phillida Flouts Me.) CoMu; HBV; ReEn
(Phyllida Flouts Me.) ElL
Phillida and Coridon. Nicholas Breton. *See* Phyllida and Corydon ("In the merry month of May").
Phillida Flouts Me. *Unknown.* *See* Phillada Flouts Me.
Phillida [*or* Phyllida] was a fair [*or* fayer] maid. Harpalus' Complaint [of Phillida's Love]. *Unknown.* OBSC; TuPP; ViBoPo
Phillida's Love-Call to Her Corydon, and His Replying. *Unknown.* *See* Phyllida's Love-Call to Her Corydon. . .
Phillips! whose touch harmonious could remove. *See* Philips! whose touch. . .
Phillis. Thomas Lodge. *See* Phyllis.
Phillis. *Unknown.* UnTE
Phillis and Amintas. *Unknown.* *See* Coy Shepherdess, The.
Phillis and Corydon. Arthur Colton. HBV
Phillis and Corydon. Robert Greene. *See* Coridon and Phillis.
Phillis at first seemed much afraid. Phillis. *Unknown.* UnTE
Phillis, be gentler, I advise. Song. Earl of Rochester. CavP; EiCL; PeRV
Phillis for Shame Let Us Improve. Charles Sackville. *See* Song: "Phyllis, for shame, let us improve.
Phillis Is My Only Joy. Sir Charles Sedley. *See* Song: "Phyllis is my only joy."
Phillis kept sheep along the western plains. Coridon and Phillis [*or* Phillis and Corydon]. Robert Greene. *Fr.* Perimedes. HBV; OBSC
Phillis Knotting. Sir Charles Sedley. *See* Hears Not My Phyllis.
Phillis, let's shun the common fate. Song. Sir Charles Sedley. LO; PeRV; SeCV-2
Phillis, men say that all my vows. Song. Sir Charles Sedley. PeRV
Phillis on the new made hay. The Coy Shepherdess; or, Phillis and Amintas. *Unknown.* CoMu
Phillis; or, The Progress of Love. Swift. ExPo; PoEL-3
(Phyllis.) EiCP
(Phyllis, or the Progress of Love.) CLwM
Phillis, though your all-powerful charms. To His Mistress. George Villiers, Duke of Buckingham. CavP
Phillis took a red rose from the tangles of her hair. Phillis and Corydon. Arthur Colton. HBV
Phillis, why shou'd we delay. *See* Phyllis, why should we delay.
Phillis's Age. Matthew Prior. *See* Phyllis's Age.
Philo is richly 'rayed, and beareth high. In Philonem. Thomas Bastard. SiCE
Philo, with twelve yeares study, hath been griev'd. An Obscure Writer. John Donne. MaMe; RelE
Philocles. Leonidas of Tarentum, *tr. fr. Greek by* F. A. Wright. AWP
Philoctetes, *sels.* Lord De Tabley.
Chorus: "In wonder and time-mists." PoVP
Chorus: "Throned are the gods, and in." NBM
Philoctetes. Thomas Russell. *See* Sonnet: Suppos'd to Be Written at Lemnos.
Philological. John Updike. ELU
Philomel. Richard Barnfield. *See* Nightingale, The.
Philomel to Corydon. William Young. AA

Philomela. Matthew Arnold. AtBAP; BEL; BoLiVe; BWP; EnL; EnLi-2; EnLit; GTBS; GTBS-D; GTSE; GTSL; HBV; ILP; InP; MaPo; MaVP; MBW-2; MCCG; OAEP; OBEV; PIA; PoFS; PoIE; PoVP; SeCeV; TOP; UnPo (1st ed); VA; ViPo; ViPP; VP; WHA
Philomela. John Crowe Ransom. AmP; ChTr; CMoP; FosPo; MoVE; OxBA; PoFS
Philomela. Sir Philip Sidney. *See* Nightingale, The.
Philomela, the Lady Fitzwater's Nightingale, *sels.* Robert Greene.
Philomela's Ode That She Sung in Her Arbor. ReIE; SiCE; TuPP
(Philomela's Ode [in Her Arbour].) OBSC
(Sitting by a River's Side.) LO; NoP
Philomela's Second Ode. OBSC; SiCE
Philon the Shepherd. *Unknown.* *See* Faithless Shepherdess, The.
Philosopher, A. John Kendrick Bangs. HBV
Philosopher, The, *sel.* Emily Brontë.
"'Oh, for the time when I shall sleep.'" ATP
Philosopher, A. Sam Walter Foss. BOHV
Philosopher, The. Edna St. Vincent Millay. CMoP; TOP
Philosopher, The. Sara Teasdale. PoToHe
Philosopher and comrade, not for thee. A Cat. Jules Lemaitre. CIV
Philosopher and Her Father, The. Shirley Brooks. CenHV
Philosopher and the Lover, The; to a Mistress Dying. Sir William Davenant. *See* To a Mistress Dying.
Philosopher to His Mistress, The. Robert Bridges. CMoP; LiTM (rev. ed.); OAEP; PoEL-5
Philosopher, whom dost thou most affect. Epigram. Richard Garnett. HBV
Philosophers, The. Po Chü-i. *See* Lao-tzu.
Philosophers devoid of reason find. The Great Idealist. Jami. LiTW; OnPM
Philosopher's Devotion, The. Henry More. SeCL
Philosopher's Disquisition Directed to the Dying Christian, The, *sel.* Sir William Davenant.
"Tell me, why Heav'n at first did suffer sin?" PeRV
Philosopher's Garden. John Oxenham. PoMa
Philosophers Have Measured Mountains. George Herbert. *See* Agonie, The.
Philosopher's Scales, The. Jane Taylor. HBV
Philosophic Apology, The. Samuel Greenberg. MoPo; NePA
Philosophic Flight, The. *At. to* Giordano Bruno. AWP; PoFr
(Spurning the Earth.) OnPM
Philosophical Poem on Cats, A. Fillmore Hyde. CIV
Philosophy. John Kendrick Bangs. PoToHe (new ed.)
Philosophy. Heine, *tr. fr. German by* James Thomson. OnPM
(Zu fragmentarisch ist Welt und Leben, *tr. by* Charles G. Leland.) AWP
Philosophy. Dorothy Parker. InMe
Philosophy shows us 'twixt monkey and man. "Caudal" Lecture. William Sawyer. BOHV
Philosophy the great and only heir. To the Royal Society. Abraham Cowley. AnAnS-2; CEP; SCEP-2
Philotas. Samuel Daniel. *See* Tragedie of Philotas, The.
Phineas Pratt. Gloria Macarthur. GoYe
Phizzog. Carl Sandburg. RePo; TiPo (1952 ed.)
Phoebe Dawson. George Crabbe. GoTL
Phoebe on Latmus. Michael Drayton. *Fr.* Endimion and Phoebe. OBSC
("In Ionia whence sprang old poet's fame.") ReIE
Phoebe runs in from the warm rain. Sonnet. Lewis Mac Adams. YAP
Phoebe sate,/ Sweet she sate. Montanus' Sonnet. Thomas Lodge. *Fr.* Rosalynde. AtBAP; PoEL-2; SiCE; TuPP
Phoebe's getting old they say. Anniversary in September. Beatrice Curtis Brown. BiCB
Phoebe's Sonnet. Thomas Lodge. ViBoPo
Phoebus and Pan. Thomas Campion. MuSP
Phoebus, Arise! William Drummond of Hawthorndon. EIL; GoTS
(Invocation: "Phoebus, arise!") OBEV
(Song: "Phoebus arise/ And paint the sable skies.") HBV; LoBV; OBS; SeEP; ViBoPo
(Summons to Love.) GTBS; GTBS-D; GTBS-P; GTBS-W; GTSE; GTSL
Phoebus, art thou a god, and canst not give. Funeral Elegy on the Death of His Very Good Friend, Mr. Michael Drayton. Sir Aston Cokayne. OBS
Phoebus, farewell! A sweeter saint I serve. A Sweeter Saint I Serve. Sir Philip Sidney. *Fr.* Arcadia. SiPS
Phoebus, lie still, and take thy rest. To Phoebus Seeing a Lady before Sunrise. Edmund Prestwich. SeCL
Phoebus, make haste, the day's too long, be gone. A Letter to Her Husband. Anne Bradstreet. AmP; AmPP; AnFE; APA; CoAnAm; LiTA
Phoebus, the car. He Inspects His Armory. Hyam Plutzik. FiMAP
Phoebus was judge between Jove, Mars, and Love. Astrophel and Stella, XIII. Sir Philip Sidney. FCP; SiPS
Phoebus with Admetus. George Meredith. EnLi-2; OBEV; OBVV
Phoenix, The. A. C. Benson. OBEV; OBVV; ShBV-4
Phoenix, The. J. V. Cunningham. QFR
Phoenix, The ("O blest unfabled incense tree"). George Darley. *Fr.* Nepenthe. CBEP; ChTr; ERoP-2; LoBV; OBVV; WiR
(Hundred-sunned Phenix.) OBNC
(O Blest Unfabled Incense Tree.) AnIV; AtBAP; ChER; EG; FaBoCh; GTBS-D; LoGBV; OBRV; PeER
Phoenix, The ("O fast her amber blood doth flow"). George Darley. *Fr.* Nepenthe. OBEV (new ed.)
("O fast her amber blood doth flow.") OBRV
Phoenix, The. Ogden Nash. CenHV; NePA
Phoenix, The. Howard Nemerov. LiTM (1970 ed.); NePA
Phoenix, The. W. H. Oliver. AnNZ
Phoenix, The. Siegfried Sassoon. ChTr
Phoenix, The. Richard Selig. MemP
Phoenix, The. Theodore Spencer. CrMA
Phoenix, The, *sels.* *Unknown, tr. fr. Anglo-Saxon.*
"Lo! I have learned of the loveliest of lands," *tr. by* Charles W. Kennedy. AnOE
"'Tis a region calm of sunny groves," *shorter sel., tr. by* J. D. Spaeth. LiTW
Phoenix and the Turtle, The. Shakespeare. CABA; CBEP; CBV; EnRePo; EP; FaBoEn; GTBS-W; LiTB; LiTG; LiTL; LoBV; MaPo; MasP; MePo; MyFE; NoP; OBEV; OBSC; PoEL-2; PoeP; SeCePo; SeCeV; SiCE; StP; TDP
Phoenix Answered, The. Anne Ridler. ChMP; POTE
(Of the Unscathing Fire.) LiTL; MoLP
Phoenix, bird of terrible pride. Sir Herbert Read. *Fr.* Mutations of the Phoenix. FaBoTw
Phoenix comes of flame and dust. The Phoenix. Howard Nemerov. LiTM (1970 ed.); NePA
Phoenix Liberty, The. Helen Parry Eden. PoFr
Phoenix, phoenix in the blood. Appeal to the Phoenix. Louis Untermeyer. UnTE
Phoenix Self-born, The. Ovid, *tr. fr. Latin by* Dryden. *Fr.* Metamorphoses, XV. ChTr
Phono, at the Boar's Head. Henri Coulette. *Fr.* The War of the Secret Agents. NePoEA-2
Phosphorescence. Melville Cane. RePo
Photo of someone else's childhood, A. The Old Adam. Denise Levertov. NaP
Photograph. James J. Galvin. JKCP (1955 ed.)
Photograph: Mother and Father: 1930. Bert Lee. WOW
Photograph of Isadora Duncan, A. Robert E. Hayden. PoNe
Phrases, *sel.* Arthur Rimbaud, *tr. fr. French by* Oliver Bernard.
"I have stretched ropes from belfry to belfry." FIW
Phraxanor to Joseph. Charles Jeremiah Wells. *Fr.* Joseph and His Brethern. VA
Phryne. John Donne. MaMe; TuPP
Phyllida and Corydon ("In the merry month of May"). Nicholas Breton. *Fr.* The Honourable Entertainment Given to the Queen's Majesty in Progress at Elvetham, 1591. EIL; OAEP; OBSC; ReIE; SeCePo
(In the Merry Month of May.) MeWo; PoSa
("In the merry month of May.") EG
(Pastoral, A.) PTK; TrGrPo
(Phillida and Corydon [*or* Coridon].) HBV; OBEV; ReEn; TuPP; UnTE; ViBoPo
(Ploughman's [*or* Plowman's] Song, The.) FaBoEn; LiTL; OBSC; SiCE
Phyllida and Corydon ("On a hill there grows a flower"). Nicholas Breton. *See* Pastoral of Phillis and Coridon, A.
Phyllida Flouts Me. *Unknown.* *See* Phillada Flouts Me.
Phyllida was a fair maid. *See* Phillida was a fair maid.
Phyllida's Love-Call [to Her Corydon, and His Replying]. *Unknown.* AnFE; EIL; OBSC

(Corydon, Arise, My Corydon!) InvP
(Phillida's Love-Call [to Her Corydon, and His Replying]). OBEV; TuPP
Phyllidula. Ezra Pound. FaBoTw
Phyllip Sparrow. John Skelton. *See* Phyllyp Sparowe.
Phyllis. Nicholas Breton. *See* Pastoral, A: "Sweet birde, that sit and sing. . ."
Phyllis. William Drummond of Hawthornden. GN; OTPC
(Of Phyllis.) ElL; HBV; LiTL
Phyllis. Dryden. *See* Wherever I Am, and Whatever I Do.
Phyllis, *sels.* Thomas Lodge.
"Devoid of reason, thrall to foolish ire," *after the French of* Pierre de Ronsard, XXXI. ReEN; SiCE
(Passion's Hounds.) OnPM
"Dewy,-roseate morn had with her hairs, The," IX. SiCE
"I hope and fear, I pray and hold my peace," XXXV. Sonn
"I would in rich and golden-colored rain," XXXIV. ReEn
"I'll teach thee, lovely Phillis, what love is," XXVI. TuPP
"Love guards [*or* guides] the roses of thy lips," XIII. EG; ElL; ReEn; SiCE; Sonn; TuPP
(Fidelity.) OBSC
(To Phyllis.) ViBoPo
(Phillis, 2.) OBEV
"My Phyllis [*or* Phillis] hath the morning sun," XV. ElL; SiCE; TuPP
(Phillis.) LoBV; OBEV, 12 *ll.*; OBSC
(Phyllis.) ACP
(To Phyllis, the Fair Shepherdess.) ViBoPo
"No stars her eyes, to clear the wandering night," VIII. Sonn; TuPP
"O pleasing thoughts, apprentices of love," I. SiCE; Sonn; TuPP
Ode, An: "Now I find thy looks were feigned." ElL; EnRePo; SiCE; TuPP
(Song: "Now I see thy looks were feigned," *sl. diff.*) LoBV
"Some praise the looks, and others praise the locks," XX. Sonn
Phyllis. Sydney King Russell. ErPo
Phyllis. Sir Charles Sedley. *See* Song: "Phyllis Is My Only Joy."
Phyllis. Swift. *See* Phillis, or the Progress of Love.
Phyllis. *Unknown.* SeCL
Phyllis. *Unknown, tr. fr. Latin by* John Addington Symonds. UnTE
Phyllis and the Philosopher. Josephine Pinckney. NP
Phyllis [*or* Phillis], for shame, let us improve. Song [*or* The Advice]. Charles Sackville. CavP; CEP; OBS; SeCL; SeCV-2
Phyllis, I pray. To Phyllis. *Unknown.* SeCL
Phyllis Inamorata. Francis Andrewes. SeCL
Phyllis Lee. Oliver Herford. BOHV
Phyllis, or the Progress of Love. Swift. *See* Phillis . . .
Phyllis, though your all powerful charms. To His Mistress. George Villiers, Duke of Buckingham. SeCL
Phyllis [*or* Phillis], why should we delay. To Phyllis [*or* Phillis]. Edmund Waller. AnAnS-2; CavP; CEP; MeWo; NoP; OAEP; SCEP-2; SeCP; TrGrPo; UnTE
Phyllis you boast of perfect health in vain. The Incurable, an Epigram. Matthew Prior. EiCL
Phyllis's Age. Matthew Prior. CEP; EiCL
(Phillis's Age.) BOHV; EnLoPo
Phyllyp Sparowe. John Skelton.
(Philip Sparrow.) PoEL-1; ReIE, *abr.*
Sels.
Commendations of Mistress Jane Scrope, The. OBSC
("Howe [*or* How] shall I report," *abr.*) EG; ViBoPo
Cursing of the Cat, The. OA
(Curse on the Cat, A, *shorter sel.*) EvOK
(O Cat of Carlish Kind.) ChTr
("That vengeance I ask and cry.") SiCE
(Vengence on Cats.) PoSa
Funeral of Philip Sparrow, The, *abr.* ACP
"Pla ce bo./ Who is there, who?" CoBE, *abr.*; EnPo; OxBoLi, *abr.*; PoEL-1; ReEn; ReIE; TuPP
(Placebo.) AtBAP
(Sparrow's Dirge, The.) OBSC
"When I remember again." SeCePo
(Sparrow's Dirge, The.) FaBoCh; LoGBV
Physical Geography. Louise Townsend Nicholl. ImOP
Physiologus, *sel.* *Unknown, tr. fr. Anglo-Saxon by* Charles W. Kennedy.
Whale, The. AnOE; OA
Piano. D. H. Lawrence. BWP; CBEP; CBV; CMoP; GTBS-P; InvP; LiTB; MoAB; MoBrPo; MuSP; NeMA; NoP; OAEP (2d ed.); PoE; PoIE; UnPo (3d ed.); VaPo
Piano, The. Paul Verlaine, *tr. fr. French by* Sir Edward Marsh. LiTW
Piano after War. Gwendolyn Brooks. AmNP; Kal; PoNe
Piano and Drums. Gabriel Okara. PBA; TTY
Piano Practice. Howard Moss. NYBP
Piano Practice. Ian Serraillier. BBGG
Piano Recital. Babette Deutsch. NePoAm
Piano Tuner, Untune Me That Tune. Ogden Nash. UnS
Piazza di Spagna. Willard M. Grimes. GoYe
Piazza Piece. John Crowe Ransom. AP; BWP; CBEP; CBV; CoBMV; ErPo; FosPo; InPo; MAP; MoAB; MoAmPo; MoPW; MoVE; NeMA; OxBA; PG (1955 ed.); Po; PoIE (1970 ed.); PoSa; SiSw; Sonn; TreFT; TrGrPo
Piazza Tragedy, A. Eugene Field. FiBHP
Piazzas. Barbara Guest. NeAP
Pibroch. Ted Hughes. NePoEA-2; PoCh; PoDB
Pibroch of Donuil [*or* Donald] Dhu. Sir Walter Scott. EnLi-2; EnRP; EPN; FaBoCh; FOL; HBV; InPo; NBM; OxBS; PeER; PoEL-4; ShBV-1
(Gathering Song of Donald Dhu [*or* Donuil Dhu], The.) GN; RG
(Gathering Song of Donald the Black.) GTBS; GTBS-D; GTBS-P; GTBS-W; GTSE; GTSL
Picador Bit, The. Bink Noll. ToPo
Picasso and Matisse. Robert Francis. NePoAm
Picasso, who knows everything, will tell you. Cocteau's *Opium*: 2. Donald Finkel. CoPo
Picasso's "Portrait de Femme." Irving Feldman. NYTB
Piccadilly. Thomas Burke. HBMV
Picciola. "Orpheus C. Kerr." AA
Piccolomini, The, *sel.* Schiller, *tr. fr. German by* Samuel Taylor Coleridge.
Thekla's Song, *fr.* II, vi. AWP; JAWP; WBP
Pick a Bale o' Cotton, *with music. Unknown.* ABF
Pick a quarrel, go to war. W. H. Auden. PV
Pick Me Up. William Jay Smith. RePo
Pick upon Pick. Alex Comfort. NeBP
Pickaxes, pickaxes swinging today. Bam, Bam, Bam. Eve Merriam. PDV
Picking Up Sticks. Eleanor Farjeon. PCH
Pick-up, The. J. V. Cunningham. UnTE
Pickup in Tony's Hashhouse. Kenneth Pitchford. *Fr.* Good for Nothing Man. CoPo; ErPo
Picket-Guard, The. Ethel Lynn Beers, *sometimes at. to* Lamar Fontaine. HBV; MC; PaA; PAH; PAP
(All Quiet along [*or* on] the Potomac.) AA; BeIS; FaBoBe; FaFP; PaPo; TrAS, *with music*; TreFS
Pickety fence, The. David McCord. TiPo (1959 ed.)
Pickwick Papers, *sel.* Charles Dickens.
Ivy Green, The, *fr. ch.* 6. BoNaP; HBV; HBVY; OTPC (1946 ed.); RIS; VA
Picnic, The. Dorothy Aldis. TiPo (1952 ed.)
Picnic, A. Aileen Fisher. SoPo
Picnic. Hugh Lofting. GoJo; SUS
Picnic, The. John Logan. BoLP; NePoEA-2
Picnic. Ray Mathew. BoAV
Picnic, The. Elizabeth Madox Roberts. RIS
Picnic Boat, The. Carl Sandburg. WoL
Picnic Day. Rachel Field. SiSoSe; SoPo; TiPo
Picnic; the Liberated. M. Carl Holman. PoNe (1970 ed.)
Picnics. *Unknown.* BoTP
Pict Song, A. Kipling. FOL
Pictor Ignotus. Robert Browning. CTC; PoVP; ViPo; ViPP
Picture, The. Heine, *tr. fr. German by* James Thomson. OnPM
Picture, The, *sel.* Philip Massinger.
Song: "Blushing rose and the purple flower, The." LiTL; ViBoPo
(Song of Pleasure, A.) SeCL; UnTE
Picture, The. Thomas Stanley, *after the Greek of* Anacreon. AWP; JAWP; UnTE; WBP
Picture, A. *Unknown.* *See* Sweet Love, If Thou Wilt Gain a Monarch's Glory.
Picture and book remain. An Acre of Grass. W. B. Yeats. CMoP; GTBS-D; MBW-2; POTE
Picture Framing. Bert Meyers. ELU

Picture memory brings to me, A. Whittier. *Fr.* My Trust. OHIP; PGD; PoRL
Picture of a Bull. Joaquin Miller. AmPP (3d ed.)
Picture of a Castle. William Meredith. NePoEA
Picture of Her Mind, The. Ben Jonson. GoBC
Picture of J. T. in a Prospect of Stone, The. Charles Tomlinson. PoCh
Picture of Little T. C. in a Prospect of Flowers, The. Andrew Marvell. AnAnS-1; BWP; CBEP; ExPo; GTSL; HBV; LiTB; MaMe; MeLP; MemP; MeP; MePo; NoP; OBEV; OBS; PoE; SCEP-2; SeCeV; SeCP; SeCV-1
Picture of Seneca Dying in a Bath. Matthew Prior. CEP
Picture People. Rowena Bennett. MPB (1956 ed.); YeAr
Picture Postcard of a Zoo. Oscar Williams. Sonn
Picture-Show. Siegfried Sassoon. CMoP
Picture That Is Turned toward the Wall, The. Charles Graham. TreF
Pictures. F. Ann Elliott. BoTP
Pictures. Cicely Fox Smith. EtS
Pictures at an Exhibition. Nathan Rosenbaum. GoYe
Pictures by Vuillard. Adrienne Rich. TwAmPo
Pictures in the Fire. Patience Strong. RePo
Pictures of the Gone World, *sels.* Lawrence Ferlinghetti.
Away above a Harborful, Sec.1. NMP
"Dada would have liked a day like this," Sec. 23. NeAP
Fortune, Sec.7. CAD; OCS
"Just as I used to say," Sec. 2. TDP; ToPo
"Sarolla's women in their picture hats," Sec.8. NeAP
Piece by piece I seem. 33. Adrienne Rich. CoPo
Piece of Black Bread, A. "Eduard Bagritsky," *tr. fr. Russian by* C. M. Bowra. TrJP
Piece of Clay, A. *Unknown.* OQP
(Sculptor, The.) PoToHe (new ed.)
(Sculpture.) MaRV; PoLF
Piece of Glass, and the Piece of Ice, The. John Hookham Frere. OTPC (1923 ed.)
Piecemeal the summer dies. Exeunt. Richard Wilbur. BoNaP; ELU; FiMAP; PoLF; TwAmPo; WIRo
Pieces of animals, pieces of all my friends. The Antagonists. Muriel Rukeyser. *Fr.* Ninth Elegy. FiMAP
Pied Beauty. Gerard Manley Hopkins. AnEnPo; AnFe; ATP (1953 ed.); AWP; BoLiVe; BrPo; BWP; CABA; CaFP; CBV; CLwM; CMoP; CoBE; CoBMV; DiPo; EaLo; EnL; EnLi-2 (1949 ed.); EnLit; FaBoEn; FaBoMo; FaFP; FlW; GoJo; GoTP; GTBS; GTBS-D; GTBS-P; GTBS-W; ILP; InPo; InvP; LiTB; LiTG; LiTM; MaPo; MaRV; MemP; MoAB; MoBrPo; MoRP; MoVE; NAMP; NeMA; NoP; OAEP (2d ed.); OBEV (new ed.); OBMV; OBNC; PAn; PG (1955 ed.); PoAn; PoDB; PoeP; PoPl; PoPo; PoRA; PoVP; ReMP; ShBV-3; SoP; StP; ThWaDe; TIHL; TreFS; TrGrPo; TRV; ViBoPo; ViPo; ViPP; VP; WaKn; WePo
("Glory be to God for dappled things.") EG
Pied Piper of Hamelin, The. Robert Browning. BBV; BeLS; BoChLi; BOHV; FaBoBe; FaBoCh; FaFP; GN; GoTP; GSP; HBV; HBVY; LoGBV; MBW-2; OnSP; OtMeF; OTPC; PoE; PoVP; RG; RIS; ShBV-1; StVeCh; TiPo (1952 ed.)
"Into the street the Piper stept," *sel.* BoTP
Pied quarts of Chevrolets trim blent Sir her eyes on, The. Ron Padgett. *Fr.* Some Bombs. ANYP
Pier. James Scully. WIRo
Pier delle Vigne. Dante, *tr. fr. Italian by* John Ciardi. *Fr.* Divina Commedia: Inferno. HoPM
Pier-Glass, The. Robert Graves. CMoP; CoBMV; MoAB
Pier in Berkeley, The. Stan Rice. QAH
Pierced are Thy feet, O Lord, pierced are Thy hands. The Divine Passion. Hortensio Félix Paravicino y Arteaga. CAW
Piere Vidal Old. Ezra Pound. MoAB
Piero della Francesca. Anne Ridler. FaBoMo
Pierre Falcon. Le Tombeau de Pierre Falcon. James Reaney. MoCV
Pierre of Timagami in New York. Wilson MacDonald. WhC
Pierre put the gold in the morning into the ring-machine. The Ring. Harry Mathews. ANYP
Pierrette in Memory. William Griffith. *Fr.* Loves and Losses of Pierrot. HBV
Pierrot. Sara Teasdale. BoLP; PoPo
Pierrot, no sentimental swain. Pantomime. Paul Verlaine. AWP; JAWP; SyP; WBP
Pierrot stands in the garden. Pierrot. Sara Teasdale. BoLP; PoPo
Piers are pummelled by the waves, The. The Fall of Rome. W. H. Auden. CBV
Piers Plainness' Seven Years' Prenticeship, *sel.* Henry Chettle.
Wily Cupid. EG
(Aeliana's Ditty.) ALV; OBSC
(Of Cupid.) EIL
Piers Plowman. William Langland. *See* Vision of Piers Plowman, The.
Piers the Plowman's Creed, *sl. abr.* *Unknown,* *tr. fr. Middle English.* MeEV
Pieta. Guy Butler. BoSA
Pieta, *sel.* C. Day Lewis.
"Naked, he sags across her cumbered knees." BoPe
Pieta. David Gascoyne. *Fr.* Miserere. NeBP; POTE
Pietà. James McAuley. PoAu-2
Pig, The. Ogden Nash. SiTL
Pig, The. Robert Southey. BOHV; PeER
Pig, if I am not mistaken, The. The Pig. Ogden Nash. SiTL
Pig lay on a barrow dead, The. View of a Pig. Ted Hughes. CBV; FlW; LiTM (1970 ed.); POTi; TwCP
Pig mask upon the wall, The. Bloodtotem. Keith Wilson. ThO
Pig-Tale, The. "Lewis Carroll." *See* Melancholy Pig, The.
Pig Tale, A. James Reeves. SoPo
Pigalle:/ A neon rose. Montmartre. Langston Hughes. Kal
Pigeon, The. Richard Church. WePo
Pigeon English. Sara Henderson Hay. BiS
Pigeon-Feeders in Battery Park, The. Julia Cooley Altrocchi. GoYe
Pigeons, The. Rodney Bennett. BoTP
Pigeons, The. Maud Burnham. PCH; PPL
Pigeons. Alastair Reid. NePoEA; NYBP; SiTL; TwCP
Pigeons are cooing along the eaves. Notre Dames des Champs. J. M. Synge. SyP
Pigeons Just Awake. Hilda Conkling. YT
Pigeons on the grass alas. Gertrude Stein. *Fr.* Four Saints in Three Acts. CrMA
Pigeon's Story, The. Jeannie Kirby. BoTP
Pigeons that peck at the grass in Trinity Church-yard, The. Trinity Place. Phyllis McGinley. MoAmPo (1962 ed.); OCS
Piggy-Wig found he had four little feet. What Piggy-Wig Found. Enid Blyton. BoTP
Pig's Tail, The. Norman Ault. BoTP
Pigwiggen. Michael Drayton. *See* Arming of Pigwiggen, The.
Pigwiggen was this fairy knight. Michael Drayton. *Fr.* Nymphidia. ViBoPo
Pike, The. Edmund Blunden. AnFE; LiTM (1970 ed.); MoVE; ShBV-3
"And nigh this toppling reed, still as the dead," *sel.* OA
Pike, The. John Bruce. SD
Pike. Ted Hughes. LiTM (1970 ed.); NePoEA-2; NMP; OPoP; POTi
Pike County Miner, The, *with music.* Mart Taylor. SGR
Pike, three inches long, perfect. Pike. Ted Hughes. LiTM (1970 ed.); NePoEA-2; NMP; OPoP; POTi
Pikes Peak. *Unknown.* PoOW
Pike's Peakers, The. Lawrence N. Greenleaf. PoOW
Pike's Peakers! All! From whatsoever climes. Grand Opening of the People's Theatre. O. J. Goldrick. PoOW
Pilaster, The. Elizabeth Madox Roberts. NP
Pilate and Caiaphas. The Black Christ. Arthur Shearly Cripps. BoSA
Pilate made report to Rome. Death of Christ. Arthur R. Macdougall, Jr. ChIP
Pilate, Pilate, wash your hands. Again the Story Is Told. Ada Jackson. MaRV
Pilate Remembers. Thomas Durley Landels. *Fr.* Pontius Pilate. MaRV
Pile high the hickory and the light. Winter Night. Edna St. Vincent Millay. PoRL
Pile on the soil; thrust on the soil. Song of the Fairies. *Unknown.* OnYI
Pile the bodies high at Austerlitz and Waterloo. Grass. Carl Sandburg. AmPP; AWP; BBV (1951 ed.); BoLiVe; FaBV; JAWP; MAP; MaRV; MCCG; MoAB; MoAmPo; MoVE; NeMA; NoP; NP; OHFP; OxBA; PoLF; PoMa; PoPl; PoPo; TrGrPo; WaaP; WBP; WHA

Piled deep below the screening apple-branch. The Orchard-Pit. Dante Gabriel Rossetti. EnLoPo; NBM; NCEP; PeVV; PoEL-5; SyP
Pilgrim, The. Bunyan. *Fr.* The Pilgrim's Progress. BoTP; EvOK; GN; HBV; MaRV; OtMeF; OTPC; PCH; RG; TiPo (1952 ed.)
(Pilgrim['s] Song, The.) CBEP; CoMu; ELP; OBS; SoP, *ad.*; WaKn; WiR
("Who would true valor see.") MemP; PeRV
Pilgrim, The. Eleanor Downing. JKCP
Pilgrim, The. "E. Foxton." AA
Pilgrim, The. Edwin Markham. MaRV
Pilgrim. A. M. Sullivan. JKCP (1955 ed.)
Pilgrim, The. Richard Wightman. WGRP
Pilgrim, The. W. B. Yeats. PoSa
Pilgrim am I, on my way, A. The Pilgrim. "E. Foxton." AA
Pilgrim and a stranger, A. Song of the Sojourner. Paul Gerhardt. SoP
Pilgrim and the Herdboy, The. Robert Buchanan. OBVV
Little Herd-Boy's Song, The, *sel.* BoTP
Pilgrim at Rome, The. *Unknown, tr. fr. Old Irish by* Kuno Meyer. AnIL
(Word of Warning, A, *tr. by* Frank O'Connor.) KiLC
Pilgrim Fathers, The. Leonard Bacon. MaRV; WGRP
Pilgrim Fathers, The. Felicia Dorothea Hemans. *See* Landing of the Pilgrim Fathers, The.
Pilgrim Fathers, The. John Boyle O'Reilly. PEDC
Pilgrim Fathers, The. John Pierpont. AA; DD; HBV; HH; MC; PAH
Pilgrim Fathers, The. Wordsworth. PAH; PoRL
Pilgrim Fathers, The—where are they? The Pilgrim Fathers. John Pierpont. AA; DD; HBV; HH; MC; PAH
Pilgrim from the East, The. Gustave Kahn, *tr. fr. French by* Jethro Bithell. TrJP
Pilgrim hearts that sought a holy shrine, The. Land of Destiny. Catherine Parmenter. PEDC
Pilgrim of a Day, The. Thomas Campbell. OBRV
Pilgrim of the night, The. In the Azure Night. Bartolomé Galindez. CAW
Pilgrim Song, The. Bunyan. *See* Pilgrim, The.
Pilgrim Song. Florence Earle Coates. OHIP
Pilgrim Way, The. John Oxenham. OQP
Pilgrimage, The. Albrecht von Johannsdorf, *tr. fr. German by* F. C. Nicholson. LiTW
Pilgrimage. Austin Clarke. OxBI
Pilgrimage. Eileen Duggan. AnNZ
Pilgrimage. Henry W. Frost. SoP
Pilgrimage, The. George Herbert. AnAnS-1; ChTr; MaMe; MeP
Pilgrimage. Elinor Lennen. PGD
Pilgrimage. Catherine Parmenter. PEDC
Pilgrimage, The. Sir Walter Ralegh. *See* Passionate Man's Pilgrimage, The.
Pilgrimage, The. Ed Sanders. ANYP
Pilgrimage, The. Henry Vaughan. AnAnS-1; MeP; NCEP
Pilgrimage. Blanche Shoemaker Wagstaff. MaRV
Pilgrimage towards Loves Holy Land, A. Thomas Campion. *See* Love's Pilgrims.
Pilgrims, The. Anthony Delius. BoSA
Pilgrims, The. Adelaide Anne Procter. UnPo
Pilgrims, The. Swinburne. PoVP
Pilgrims and the Peas, The. "Peter Pindar." BOHV
Pilgrims Came, The. Annette Wynne. GFA; MPB; OHIP
Pilgrims landed, worthy men, The. The Pilgrims' Thanksgiving Feast. Arthur Guiterman. WhC
Pilgrims of the trackless deep. Pilgrim Song. Florence Earle Coates. OHIP
Pilgrims of Thibet, The. Cale Young Rice. PFY
Pilgrim's Progress, The, *sels.* Bunyan.
Pilgrim, The. BoTP; EvOK; GN; HBV; MaRV; OtMeF; OTPC; PCH; RG; TiPo (1952 ed.)
(Pilgrim['s] Song, The.) CBEP; CoMu; ELP; OBS; SoP, *ad.*; WaKn; WiR
("Who would true valour see.") MemP; PeRV
Shepherd Boy's Song, The. BoTP; MaRV; OTPC (1923 ed.); PCH, *st.* 1; SoP; ThGo; TRV
(Enough.) BLRP
(He That Is Down.) CBEP
("He that is down, needs fear no fall.") SeEP
(Shepherd Boy Sings [in the Valley of Humiliation], The.) EaLo; EG; GBV; GN; HBV; HBVY; OBEV; OQP; OTD; WGRP
(Shepherd's Boy's Song, The.) PeRV
(Shepherd's Song, The.) BoC; OxBoCh
(Song of Low Degree, A.) STF
(Song of the Shepherd in the Valley of Humiliation.) CavP; OBS
"What danger is the pilgrim in?" PeRV
Pilgrim's Song. Psalms, CXXI, Bible, *O.T.* *See* I Will Lift Up Mine Eyes unto the Hills.
Pilgrim's Song. Bunyan. *See* Pilgrim, The.
Pilgrim's Song. Bernhard S. Ingemann, *tr. fr. Danish by* Sabine Baring-Gould. WGRP
Pilgrims' Thanksgiving Feast, The. Arthur Guiterman. WhC
Pilk lauds the verse of Jobble to the skies. Perpetuum Mobile. Edith Sitwell. HBMV
Pillar-Box, The. Jiri Wolker. *tr. fr. Czech by* Paul Selver. LiTW
Pillar of Fame, The. Robert Herrick. AnAnS-2; SCEP-2; SeCP
Pillar of fire by night, A. The Song of Sherman's Army. Charles Graham Halpine. MC; PAH; PAP
Pillar of fire went before them by night, A. The New Moses. M. K. Joseph. AnNZ
Pillar of the Cloud, The. Cardinal Newman. ACP; AnEnPo; AWP; BEL; EnLi-2; EPN; FaFP; GoBC; HBV; JAWP; JKCP; MaRV; NBM; OBNC; Po; PoEL-5; PoVP; SoP; TIHL; TOP; TrPWD; TRV; VA; WBP; WGRP
(Lead, Kindly Light.) FaBoBe; FaPL; InP; MyFE; NeHB; TreF; UnPo (3d ed.)
(Light in the Darkness.) OBRV
Pillar perished is whereto I leant, The. Sir Thomas Wyatt. FCP
Pillars of death! carved syrens! tearful urn! Erinna to Her Friend. Erinna. OnPM
Pillow Cases. Richard Armour. WhC
Pills to Purge Melancholy, *sel.* Thomas d'Urfey.
Maid's Longing, The. SiTL
Pilot, The. George Chapman. *Fr.* Bussy d'Ambois, I, i. EtS
Pilot, The. *Unknown.* STF
Pilot and Prophet. Charles Hanson Towne. DD
(Roosevelt—Pilot and Prophet.) PEDC
Pilot Cove. C. J. Dennis. WhC
Pilot from the Carrier, A. Randall Jarrell. MoPo; TPM
Pilot in the Jungle, The. John Ciardi. MiAP
Pilots, Man Your Planes. Randall Jarrell. MoAB; MoAmPo (1950 ed.)
Pimpernel. Charlotte Druitt Cole. BoTP
Pin, The. Ann Taylor. HBV; HBVY
Pin, A. Ella Wheeler Wilcox. BOHV
Pin Has a Head, A. Christina Rossetti. *See* Paradoxes.
Pin-swin or spine-swine, The. His Shield. Marianne Moore. DTC; LiTM; NePA; TwAmPo
Pin-up Girl. Louis O. Coxe. WaP
Pin wheels whirling round. Fourth of July Night. Dorothy Aldis. SiSoSe; TiPo
Pinafore. W. S. Gilbert. *See* H.M.S. Pinafore.
Pinch him, pinch him, black and blue. Song by Fairies. John Lyly. *Fr.* Endymion. OAEP; OBSC; ReEn; TuPP
Pinch of Salt, A. Robert Graves. BoPe; HBMV; MoBrPo
Pindar. Antipater of Sidon, *tr. fr. Greek by* John Addington Symonds. AWP
Pindar is imitable by none. The Praise of Pindar. Abraham Cowley. SCEP-2
Pindar Peel, of Passamquoddy. Passamquoddy's Apple Toddy. James W. Foley. LHV
Pindaric Ode, A: To the Immortal Memory and Friendship of That Noble Pair, Sir Lucius Cary and Sir Henry Morison. Ben Jonson. *See* To the Immortal Memory. . .
Pindarick ("Let ancients boast no more"). *At. to* the Earl of Rochester. PeRV
Pine, The. Augusta Davies Webster. DD; HBV; OHIP
Pine at Timber-Line, The. Harriet Monroe. NP
Pine Bough, The. Richard Aldridge. NePoAm; PoSC
Pine-crowned hills against the sky. Christmas Eve. Catherine Parmenter. PEDC; PGD
Pine Gum. W. W. E. Ross. OBCV
Pine Music. Kate Louise Brown. BoTP
Pine needle carpets and crisp brown leaves. Fairy Carpets. Anne Blackwell Payne. GFA

Pine Needles, *sel.* William H. Hayne.
"If Mother Nature patches." PCH
(Sewing.) GFA; OTPC (1946 ed.)
Pine needles cover the silent ground. Woodlands. Sir Herbert Read. BrPo
Pine to the Mariner, The. George Turberville. EtS
Pine-trail [*or* Pinetrail]; and all the hours are white, are long. A Walk on Snow. Peter Viereck. MiAP; OnHM
Pine Tree, The. Heine. *See* Fichtenbaum steht einsam, Ein.
Pine-Tree Buoy, A. Harrison Smith Morris. AA
Pine Tree for Diana, The ("Montium custos nemorumque"). Horace, *tr. fr. Latin by* Louis Untermeyer. Odes, III, 22. AWP
Pine tree standeth lonely, A. Ein Fichtenbaum steht einsam. Heine, *tr. by* James Thomson. AWP; JAWP; OuHeWo; WBP
Pine Trees and the Sky; Evening. Rupert Brooke. MCCG
Pine trees explode, The. Haiku. "Luke." QAH
Pine Woods, The. John, Lord Hanmer. VA
Pinery Boy, The. *Unknown.* IHA
Pines, The. Julie Mathilde Lippmann. AA
Pines. Anderson M. Scruggs. PoMa
Pines, The. Harriet Prescott Spofford. AA
Pines, and a blur of lithe young grasses. From a Car-Window. Ruth Guthrie Harding. HBMV
Pines and the Sea, The. Christopher Pearse Cranch. AA; AmLP; AnAmPo; HBV; ILP
Pines are white-powdered, The. New Snow. Catharine Bryant Rowles. YeAr
Pines, under pines. Logging, IV. Gary Snyder. *Fr.* Myths & Texts. OPoP
Pines were dark on Ramoth hill, The. My Playmate. Whittier. AnFE; AP; APA; CoAnAm; CoBA; HBV; OBVV; PCD; PG (1945 ed.)
Pinetrail; and all the hours are white, are long. *See* Pine-trail...
Piney Woods. Malcolm Cowley. NYBP
Pining for Love. Francis Beaumont. BoLP
Pink Almond. Katharine Tynan. BoTP
Pink and black of silk and lace, The. Impression. Arthur Symons. SyP
Pink confused with white. The Pot of Flowers. William Carlos Williams. QFR
Pink Dominoes. Kipling. CenHV
Pink Locust, The. William Carlos Williams. PP
Pink, small and punctual. Emily Dickinson. FaBV
Pinkletinks. Grace Elisabeth Allen. GoYe
Pinta, the Nina and the Santa Maria, The. John Tagliabue. AmFN
Pinto. *Unknown.* CoSo
Pinwheel. Dilys Laing. NYTB
Pinwheel's Song, The. John Ciardi. PDV
Pioneer, The. Eugene Field. PoOW
Pioneer, The. Arthur Guiterman. MPB; TiPo
Pioneer, The. Edna St. Vincent Millay. PoFr
Pioneer Mother, The. Ethel Romig Fuller. PGD
Pioneer of Monaro, A. Francis Webb. MoAuPo
Pioneer state built a College to share, A. Here We Have Idaho. Harry A. Powell. PoRL
Pioneer Woman. Vesta Pierce Crawford. PoOW
Pioneer Woman, The—In the North Country. Eunice Tietjens. AmFN
Pioneers. Badger Clark. FaBoBe
Pioneers. Hamlin Garland. AA
Pioneers. Arthur W. Jose. BoAu
Pioneers. Frederick William Ophel. BoAu
Pioneers ("For the first man to climb the hill"). *Unknown.* MaRV
Pioneers! O Pioneers! Walt Whitman. AmePo; AmPP; ATP; CoBA; FaBoBe; MPB; PaA; TOP; UnPo (1st ed.); WHA
Pioneers, The; or, Twenty Years After. William Plomer. BoSA
Pioneers, the cat men, and the wolves, The. The Frontier. Donald Hall. CBV
Pious Celinda. Congreve. *See* Pious Selinda.
Pious Editor's Creed, The. James Russell Lowell. The Biglow Papers, 1st Series, No. VI. AmePo; AnNE; TOP
(Candidate's Creed, The, *abr.*) BOHV; YaD
Pious Selinda. Congreve. HBV; UnTE
(Pious Celinda.) ALV; ELP; ErPo
(Song: "Pious Selinda goes to prayers.") CBV; InMe
Pious words are but a bubble. Poem on a Slippery Sidewalk. Kenneth Porter. WhC
Pip! pop! flippety flop! The Song of the Cornpopper. Laura E. Richards. BoChLi
Pipe, The. Sir John Squire. PoPl
Pipe and Can ("The Indian weed"). *At. to* Robert Wisdome. *See* Religious Use of Taking Tobacco, A.
Pipe and Can ("Whenas the chill sirocco blows"). *Unknown. See* In Praise of Ale.
Pipe of Peace, The. F. L. Lucas. HaMV
Pipe of Tobacco, A, *sels.* Isaac Hawkins Browne.
"Blest Leaf! whose aromatic gales dispense." Par
(In imitation of Pope.) OBEC
"Boy! bring an ounce of Freeman's best." Par
In imitation of Young. OBEC
Pipe of Tobacco, The. *At. to* John Usher. HBV
Pipe-Player, The. Sir Edmund Gosse. VA
Pipe thee high and pipe thee low. Pipings. J. Paget-Fredericks. BrR
Pipe, with solemn interposing puff, The. Pernicious Weed. William Cowper. InMe; WhC
Piped a tiny voice hard by. The Chickadee. Emerson. *Fr.* The Titmouse. FaPON; GFA; OTPC (1946 ed.)
Piped the blackbird on the beechwood spray. Little Bell. Thomas Westwood. GN; HBV; OTPC (1946 ed.); TVC
Piper, The. Blake. *See* Piping down the Valleys Wild.
Piper, The. Rachel Field. PoRh
Piper, A [*or* The]. "Seumas O'Sullivan." BoTP; CH; FaPON; GaP; MoShBr; MPB; OxBI; PDV; PoRh; TiPo
Piper o' Dundee, The. *Unknown.* OxBS
Piper of Arll, The. Duncan Campbell Scott. PeCV
Piper on the Hill, The. Dora Sigerson Shorter. HBV; HBVY; OnYI; OTPC (1923 ed.)
Piper, Play. John Davidson. TOP
"Piper, sit thee down and write." Blake. *Fr.* Songs of Innocence: Piping down the Valleys Wild. YT
Piper's music fills the street, The. To the Poet T. J. Mathias. Walter Savage Landor. PV
Piper's Progress, The. Francis Sylvester Mahony. FiBHP
Pipes, The. Lou Lipsitz. YAP
Pipes and Drums. Lilian Holmes. GFA
Pipes at Lucknow, The. Whittier. FOL; GN; HBVY
Pipes in the Sty. John Kendall. WhC
Pipes o' Gordon's Men, The. J. Scott Glasgow. HBV
Pipes of the misty moorlands. The Pipes at Lucknow. Whittier. FOL; GN; HBVY
Piping down the Valleys Wild (*Introd. to* Songs of Innocence). Blake. CBEP; FaBoCh; FaBV; GBV; InvP; LoGBV; OBEC; PAn; PoRh; PRWS; TreFS; UnS
(Happy Songs.) GoTP; RIS
(Introduction: "Piping down the valleys wild.") AnFE; BEL; BWP; CEP; DiPo; EiCL; EiPP; EnLit; EnPE; EnRP; ERoP-1; FosPo; GoJo; ILP; OAEP; OBNC; PeER; PoAn; PoE; PoEL-4; PoeP; PoIE; SeCeV; ThWaDe; TrGrPo; YAT
(Introduction to "Songs of Innocence.") CoBE; EnLi-2; ExPo; FaBoBe; NeHB; OuHeWo; PG (1945 ed.); Po; TiPo; ViBoPo; WHA
(Piper, The.) AWP; BoChLi; BoTP; GaP; InPo; JAWP; MPB; OTPC; PDV; RoGo; TOP; WBP
(Reeds of Innocence.) GTBS-W; HBV; HBVY; LiTB; LiTG; OBEV
(Songs of Innocence: Introduction.) EiPP; LoBV
"Piper, sit thee down and write," *last 2 sts.* YT
Piping hot, smoking hot. *Unknown.* OxNR
Piping Peace. James Shirley. *Fr.* The Imposture. I, ii. ACP; LoBV; OBEV (new ed.)
(Io.) OBS; SeCL; SeEP
(Song: "You virgins that did late despair.") PoEL-2
(You Virgins.) ViBoPo
Piping sharp as a reed. The Nesting Ground. David Wagoner. PoCh
Pipings. J. Paget-Fredericks. BrR
Pipling. Theodore Roethke. NePA; SiTL
Pippa Passes. Robert Browning. PoVP; ViPP
Sels.
All Service Ranks the Same with God, *fr.* Introduction. BEL; MaRV; OQP; TreFT
(God's View of Service.) SoP
(Service.) TrGrPo; TSW
(Song: "All service ranks the same with God.") LoBV
"Day!/ Faster and more fast," *fr.* Introduction. GTSL
(Sunrise.) OQP

"Give her but a least excuse to love me," *fr.* sc. ii. EPN; GTBS; GTSL; ViBoPo
Year's at the Spring, The, *fr.* sc. i. BEL; BLPA; BoChLi; DD; EPN; FaBoBe; FaBV; GTBS; GTSL; InP; NeHB; PoRL; PoToHe (new ed.); StVeCh; TSW; YeAr
(Good Morning.) PRWS
(Pippa's Song.) BBV (1923 ed.); BoTP; BrR; CBEP; EnLi-2; FaFP; FaPON; GoJo; GTBS-W; LiTB; LiTG; OBEV; OBVV; OHIP; OQP; OTPC; PCH; PDV; PoPo; ShBV-1; SiTL; SoP; TreF; TRV; UnPo (3d ed.)
(Song: "Year's at the spring, The.") EnLit; HBV; HBVY; MaRV; MCCG; PoPl; PTK; RG; TOP; TrGrPo; VA; WGRP; YAT
(Song from "Pippa Passes.") ATP; GBV
(Spring Song.) GoTP
You'll Love Me Yet! *fr.* sc. iii. EPN; HoPM; MeWo; OBEV (1st ed.)
(Song: "You'll love me yet! and I can tarry.") HBV
Pirate, The, *sels.* Sir Walter Scott.
Claud Halcro's Invocation, *fr. ch.* 23. NBM
Mermaids and Mermen, *fr. ch.* 16. EtS
Song of the Reim-Kennar, The, *fr. ch.* 6. OAEP; OBNC
(Song of the Tempest, The.) PeER
Pirate Don Durk of Dowdee. Mildred Plew Meigs. BoChLi; GaP; PCD; PDV; PoRh; SoPo; TiPo
Pirate of High Barbary, The. *Unknown. See* Salcombe Seaman's Flaunt to the Proud Pirate, The.
Pirate Story. Robert Louis Stevenson. BeLS; FaPON; GFA; GoTP; OTPC (1946 ed.); PoVP; TiPo; VA
Pirate Treasure. Abbie Farwell Brown. EtS
Pirate Wind. Mary Jane Carr. BrR; SiSoSe
Pirates. Elizabeth J. Coatsworth. EtS
Pirates. Alfred Noyes. MCCG
Pirates, after all, were usually. Pirates. Elizabeth J. Coatsworth. EtS
Pirates' Fight, The. Joseph Schull. *Fr.* The Legend of Ghost Lagoon. CaP
Pirates of Penzance, The, *sels.* W. S. Gilbert.
Modern Major-General, The. InMe; PCD, *much abr.*
(Major-General, The.) OnPP
(Major-General's Song.) CoBE; NBM
Policeman's Lot, The. ALV; NeHB; PoVP; TreFT; TrGrPo
Pirates' Tea-Party, The. Dorothy Una Ratcliffe. BoTP
Pirithous being over hault of mynde and such a one. Philemon and Baucis. Ovid. *Fr.* Metamorphoses. CTC
Pirouette. Audre Lorde. NNP
Pis-Aller. Matthew Arnold. PoVP
Pisan Cantos, The. Ezra Pound. *See under* Canto.
Piscatorie Eclogues, *sels.* Phineas Fletcher.
Chromis, IV. LoBV
"Fisher-lad, A (no higher dares he look)," III. SeCV-1
Pisces. R. S. Thomas. POTi
Pisgah. Willard Wattles. WGRP
Pisgah-Sights. Robert Browning. PoVP
Pish! 'tis an idle fond excuse. Forbidden Fruit. Charles Cotton. PeRV
Piss/ aint never smelled sweet. A Portrait of Johnny Doller. D. L. Graham. BF
Pissarro's One Pure Note. G. Bishop-Dubjinsky. ThO
Pistons, valves and wheels and gears. Engineers. Jimmy Garthwaite. SoPo
Pit, A—but Heaven over it. Emily Dickinson. AP; MWA-2
Pit of Bliss, The. James Stephens. AnFE
Pit, pat, well-a-day. *Unknown.* OxNR
Pit Viper. George Starbuck. NYBP; TDP
Pitch here the tent, while the old horse grazes. Juggling Jerry [*or* The Last Words of Juggling Jerry]. George Meredith. BEL; BeLS; BoLiVe; EnLit; EPN; HBV; OAEP; OnPP; SeCePo; TOP; VA; ViPo; VP
Pitcher. Robert Francis. CaFP; NePoAm; PP; SD
Pitcher, The. Yüan Chen, *tr. fr. Chinese by* Arthur Waley. AWP; JAWP; WBP
Pitcher of Mignonette, A. H. C. Bunner. AA; HBV; InP; PFY
Pitcher plant makes a living by, The. The Resident Worm. James Hayford. NePoAm-2
Pitcher the gunner is brisk and young. Molly Pitcher. Laura E. Richards. MC; PAH
Pith of faith is gone, The. And as there lie. Child of Loneliness. Norman Gale. WGRP
Pitiful mouth, saith he, that living gavest. Henry's Lament. Samuel Daniel. *Fr.* The Complaint of Rosamond. OBSC
Pitiful the playing of the flood with dire destruction! Egan O'Rahilly. *Fr.* The Storm. OnYI
Pitiful these crying swans to-night. The Icebound Swans. *Unknown.* OA
Pitiless heat from heaven pours. Summer. Kalidasa. *Fr.* The Seasons. AWP
Pitted and pock-marked by a roving gun. Crucifix. Edith Lovejoy Pierce. ChIP
"Pitter patter!" Falls the rain. The Umbrella Brigade. Laura E. Richards. SoPo; SUS; TiPo
Pitter-patter, hear it raining? Rain. Lilian McCrea. BoTP
Pittsburgh. Witter Bynner. AmFN
Pittsburgh. James Oppenheim. StaSt
Pittsburgh. Hy Sobiloff. NePA
Pitty Patty Polt! *Unknown.* BoTP
Pity. Babette Deutsch. WHA
Pity and Love. *Unknown.* ALV; SeCL
Pity beyond all telling, A. The Pity of Love. W. B. Yeats. AnIV; CMoP
Pity for Mary. *Unknown. See* Now Goeth Sun under Wood.
Pity Me Not. Edna St. Vincent Millay. AnNE; MAP; MoAB; MoAmPo; NeMA; NePA; TrGrPo
(Pity Me Not because the Light of Day.) CMoP; OxBA
Pity me on my pilgrimage to Loch Derg! At Saint Patrick's Purgatory. *At. to* Donnchadh mor O'Dala. AnIL; LiTW; OnYI
Pity me, Stranger! shed one passing tear. Four Years Only. *Unknown.* OnPM
Pity! mourn in plaintive tone. The Death of Lesbia's Bird [*or* The Dead Starling]. Catullus. AWP; OnPM
Pity Not. William Haskell Simpson. *Fr.* In Arizona. HBMV; NP
Pity not! The Army gave. Ex-Clerk. Kipling. *Fr.* Epitaphs of the War. PoVP
Pity now poor Mary Ames. Mary Ames. *Unknown.* NA
Pity of beauty in distress. Pity and Love. *Unknown.* ALV; SeCL
Pity of It, The. Thomas Hardy. CMoP; InP; LiTM (rev. ed.); WaP
Pity of Love, The. W. B. Yeats. AnIV; CMoP
Pity of the Leaves, The. E. A. Robinson. AA; MoAmPo (1950 ed.)
Pity, oh pity! death had power. Thomas Freeman. SiCE; TuPP
Pity, pity, pity. A True Love Ditty. Thomas Middleton. *Fr.* Blurt, Master Constable. ElL
Pity poor lovers who may not do what they please. The Envy of Poor Lovers. Austin Clarke. NMP
Pity reminds my tears. Fallen Flyer Aged 19. David Ross. PG (1955 ed.)
Pity, repulsion, love and anger. Poem. Roy Fuller. NeBP
Pity the nameless, and the unknown, where. The Nameless Ones. Conrad Aiken. NePA; OxBA
Pity the nightly tiger: fierce and wise. The Fear of Beasts. William Meredith. TPM
Pity This Busy Monster, Manunkind. E. E. Cummings. AmP; AmPP (5th ed.); AP; CoBA; CoBMV; CrMA; ILP; LiTA; LiTM; MoVE; NePA; OxBA; PoAn; StP; WOW
Pity this girl. The Stranger. Brother Antoninus. CBV; ToPo
Pity this man who, slave to an affliction. The Ailing Parent. Lora Dunetz. NePoAm-2
Pity those men who from the start. A Song about Great Men. Michael Hamburger. NePoEA
Pity us not/ Because we tried to battle and to go. From Beyond. Lucia Trent. PGD
Pity would be no more. The Human Abstract. Blake. *Fr.* Songs of Experience. DiPo; EiPP; EnRP; ERoP-1; MaPo; PoEL-4
Pity you Phelim Quinn of the bogs and the fidgety finger. Swan Curse. A. W. Sullivan. NYTB
Pitying Heart, The. Goldsmith. PCH
Pius, the springtime rolls like a wave upon our land. To Blessed Pius X at Easter. John Hazard Wildman. JKCP (1955 ed.)
Piute Creek. Gary Snyder. CoAP; NaP
Pixie, kobold, elf, and sprite. Hallowe'en. Joel Benton. DD; OTPC (1946 ed.); PoRL
Pixies, slipping, dipping, stealing. Cornish Magic. Ann Durell. FaPON
Pla ce bo. *Indexed as* Placebo.
Place a custard stand in a garden. The Invention of New Jersey. Jack Anderson. ThO
Place and the Person, The, *sel.* Henry Reed.

Place (continued)
"From the far horizon, and breaking in triumph towards him." GTBS-D
Place-Ghost. August Derleth. FiSC
Place in Thy Memory, A. Gerald Griffin. HBV; VA
(Song: "Place in thy memory, Dearest, A.") BLPA; NeHB
Place is called the Golden Cock, The. Lunch at the Coq D'or. Peter Davison. TwCP
Place is growing difficult, The. Flails of bramble. The Secret Garden. Thomas Kinsella. TwCP
Place is palpable me, for here I was born, The. Nostalgia. D. H. Lawrence. NP
Place is the focus. What is the language? In Defense of Metaphysics. Charles Tomlinson. MoBrPo (1962 ed.)
Place Me in the Breach. Yehuda Karni, *tr. fr. Hebrew by* Sholom J. Kahn. TrJP
Place of Cupid's Fire, The. Thomas Campion. *See* Beauty, Since You So Much Desire.
Place of Pain in the Universe, The. Anthony Hecht. CrMA
Place of Peace, The. Edwin Markham. FaChP; MaRV; OQP; SoP; TreFT; TRV
Place of Prayer, The. Carlton Buck. SoP
Place of Prayer, The. William Cowper. SoP
Place of prayer is not confined, The. The Place of Prayer. Carlton Buck. SoP
Place of Repair. *Unknown.* SoP
Place of Rest, The. "Æ." WGRP
Place of the Damned, The. Milton. *Fr.* Paradise Lost, II. FaBoEn
Place of the Solitaires, The. Wallace Stevens. NP; SyP
Place where our two gardens meet, The. The Wall. Henry Reed. LiTB
Pla ce bo./ Who is there, who? Phyllyp Sparowe [*or* Philip Sparrow *or* The Sparrow's Dirge]. John Skelton. AtBAP; CoBE; EnPo; OBSC; OxBoLi; PoEL-1; ReEn; ReIE; TuPP
Placed in a country on a desert verging. Delusions VIII. Charles Madge. BoSA
Places. Carl Sandburg. NP
Places. Sara Teasdale. HT
Places among the stars. The Black Riders, XXIII. Stephen Crane. AP
Places I love come back to me like music. Places. Sara Teasdale. HT
Places, Loved Ones. Philip Larkin. CMoP; NePoEA
Places of Nestling Green. Leigh Hunt. *Fr.* The Story of Rimini. OBRV
("Noble range it was, of many a rood, A.") EnRP
Placid Man's Epitaph, A. Thomas Hardy. MoBrPo
Placid, rotted harbour has no voice, The. Arrival and Departure. Charles Eglington. BoSA; PeSA
Placido's Farewell to His Mother. "Placido." *See* Farewell to My Mother.
Plague Charm. *Unknown.* FOL
("Ring-a-ring o' roses.") OxNR
Plague is love, a plague! but yet, A. The Little Love God. Meleager. AWP
Plague of Dead Sharks. Alan Dugan. AP; LiTM (1970 ed.)
Plague take all your pedants, say I! Sibrandus Schafnaburgensis. Robert Browning. *Fr.* Garden Fancies, II. CTC; EnLi-2 (1949 ed.)
Plaidie, The. Charles Sibley. BOHV; HBV
Plain be the phrase, yet apt the verse. A Utilitarian View of the *Monitor's* Fight. Herman Melville. AmePo; AmPP (5th ed.); AP; MWA-1
Plain-Chant for America. Katherine Garrison Chapin. PAL; PoFr
Plain Chant of the Hill Country. Sister Mary David. JKCP (1955 ed.)
Plain Dealing. Alexander Brome. OBS
Plain Dealing's Downfall. Earl of Rochester. BWP; PeRV
Plain Description of Perfect Friendship, A. *At. to* Henry Cheke. TuPP
(Of Perfect Friendship.) EIL
Plain Direction, A. Thomas Hood. OTPC (1946 ed.)
Plain Fare (Night Thoughts on Crossing the Continent by Bus). Daryl Hine. CBV; CoAP
Plain Golden Band, The, 2 *versions, with music.* *At. to* Joe Scott. ShS
Plain his garb;/ Such as might suit a rustic Sire. The Tale of Margaret. Wordsworth. *Fr.* The Excursion, I. ERoP-1
Plain Language from Truthful James. Bret Harte. AmePo; AmPP; BeLS; BLPA; BOHV; CoBA; CTC; DD; FaBoBe; HBV; InMe; LHV; MAP; MoAmPo (1942 ed.); OnSP; PFY; PoE; TreF; WhC; YaD
(Heathen Chinee, The.) CenHV
(Plain Talk from Truthful James.) AnAmPo
Plain Man's Dream, A. Frederick Keppel. AA
Plain Sense of Things, The. Wallace Stevens. PIA
Plain-Song. Jean Cocteau, *tr. fr. French by* W. J. Strachan. LiTW
"I have sung, to deceive the evil-sounding clock of time," *sel., tr. by* Wallace Fowlie. PoPl
Plain Tales from the Hills, *sels.* Kipling.
By the Hoof of the Wild Goat. OBNC
(Predestination.) LoBV
"He drank strong waters and his speech was coarse." PV
Plain Talk. William Jay Smith. FiBHP; MoAmPo (1962 ed.)
Plain Talk from Truthful James. Bret Harte. *See* Plain Language from Truthful James.
Plain tilt-bonnet on her head, A. In the Days of Crinoline. Thomas Hardy. WhC
Plain truth would never serve. Take It from Me. Kenneth O. Hanson. CoAP
Plain was grassy, wild and bare, The. The Dying Swan. Tennyson. GTSE; OTPC; PeER; WiR
Plainest lodge room in the land was over Simpkins' store, The. The Lodge Room over Simpkins' Store. Lawrence N. Greenleaf. PoOW
Plainness. Jorge Luis Borges. *tr. fr. Spanish by* Norman Thomas Di Giovanni. NYBP
Plains. W. H. Auden. NePA
Plains, The. Roy Fuller. BoSA; MoPo
Plains of Abraham, The. Michael Brownstein. YAP
Plaint. Ebenezer Elliott. OBEV; OBVV
(Land Which No One Knows, The.) HBV
Plaint. Charles Henri Ford. AtBAP; MoVE; PPON
Plaint of the Camel, The. Charles Edward Carryl. *Fr.* The Admiral's Caravan. AnAmPo; BoTP; EvOK; FaPON; HBV; HBVY; OTPC (1946 ed.); PoRh; SoPo; SP; StVeCh; UTS
(Camel's Complaint, The.) AmePo
(Camel's Lament, The.) GoTP
Plaint of the Wife, The. *Unknown,* *tr. fr. Russian by* W. R. S. Ralston. AWP; JAWP; WBP
Plainte Eternelle. Lord Alfred Douglas. PoVP
Plaintive sonnet flow'd from Milton's pen, A. Sonnet: Anniversary, February 23, 1795. William Mason. OBEC
Plan, A. John Alden Carpenter. RIS
Plan for a Novel. Frederic Thompson. JKCP (1955 ed.)
Plan of Salvation, The. Milton. *Fr.* Paradise Lost, III. WGRP
Plane Geometer. David McCord. NYBP
Plane Geometry. Emma Rounds. ImOP
Plane leaves, The. Autumn Rain. D. H. Lawrence. BrPo
Plane, released, its twin blades waving, The. The Aviator. Aleksandr Blok. OnHM
Plane-Tree. F. S. Flint. MoBrPo (1942 ed.)
Plane-Tree, The. Amy Levy. *See* London Plane-Tree, A.
Planet, The. Carl Bode. ToPo
"Planet, A, doesn't explode of itself," said drily. Earth. John Hall Wheelock. LiTM (1970 ed.); PV
Planet Moon, *sel.* Will Dyson. MoAuPo
"Planet moon and dancing star."
Planet on the Table, The. Wallace Stevens. ML; PoeP
Planetary Arc-Light, The. August Derleth. GoYe
Planh for the Young English King. Bertrans de Born, *tr. fr. Provençal by* Ezra Pound. LiTW
Plankton. Ruth Miller. PeSA
Plans. Helen Morgan Brooks. NNP; PoNe (1970 ed.)
Plans. Luisa Hewitt. PCH
Plans. Dorothy Brown Thompson. BiCB
Planster's Vision, The. John Betjeman. PoPl
Plant a Tree. Lucy Larcom. DD; HBVY; OHFP; PGD; WBLP
Plant cut down to the root, The. Elizabeth J. Coatsworth. TiPo (1952 ed.)
Plant of noble stemme, forward and faire, A. Upon the Death of Mr. Herrys. Richard Crashaw. MaMe
Plant Poems. Edward Field. FRC
Plantation Ditty, A. Frank Lebby Stanton. AA; HBV; LHV
Plantation Play-Song. Joel Chandler Harris. *Fr.* Uncle Remus, His Songs and His Sayings. MCCG

Planted by the Master's hand. Wait. John Banister Tabb. FaChP
Planted Skull, The. Peter Viereck. PP
Planter's Charm. Fay Yauger. InP
Planter's Daughter, The. Austin Clarke. OxBI
Planticru, The. Robert Rendall. OxBS
Planting a Tree. Nancy Byrd Turner. RePo; YeAr
Planting Beans. T'ao Ch'ien, *tr. fr. Chinese by* C. W. Luh. OnPM
Planting Bulbs. Katharine Tynan. JKCP
Planting Flowers on the Eastern Embankment. Po Chü-i, *tr. fr. Chinese by* Arthur Waley. BoNaP
(Gardener, The.) BoPe
Planting of the Apple Tree, The. Bryant. AA; AnNE; DD, *much abr.*; GN; HBV; HBVY; LaNeLa; MPB (1956 ed.); OHIP; StVeCh
"Come, let us plant the apple tree," *sel.* PoSC
Planting Trees. V. H. Friedlaender. BoNaP
Plants and trees made poor and old, The. Albinovanus, *tr. fr. Latin by* Sir Walter Ralegh. FCP
Plants Stand Silent Round Me, The. Johannes Jorgensen, *tr. fr. Danish by* Robert S. Hillyer. OnPM
Plaque. Bruce Ruddick. CaP
Plastic Glass, The. Josephine Miles. FiMAP
Platform Goodbye. H. B. Mallalieu. WaP
Plato, a Musician. Leontius, *tr. fr. Greek by* A. J. Butler. UnS
Plato and Pythagoras. How the Consolations of Philosophy Worked Out in Actual Practice. Anthony Haden-Guest. HYE
Plato, despair! Meditation on Statistical Method. J. V. Cunningham. CoAP; ForPo; PIA; QFR
Plato to Theon. Philip Freneau. AA
Plato Told [Him]. E. E. Cummings. AmFN; AmPP (5th ed.); CrMA; CTC; MoVE; OxBA; PIA; SeCeV (1967 ed.); ThLM
Platonic Lady, The. Earl of Rochester. UnTE
Platonic Love. Philip Ayres. Sonn
Platonick Love. Abraham Cowley. *Fr.* The Mistress. SCEP-2; SeCV-1
(Platonic Love.) SeEP
Platonick Love. Lord Herbert of Cherbury. AnAnS-2; OBS
(Platonic Love.) SeEP
Plato's Tomb. *Unknown. See* Spirit of Plato.
Plattsburg Bay! Plattsburg Bay! The Battle of Plattsburg Bay. Clinton Scollard. MC; PAH
Platypus, The. Oliver Herford. FiBHP; NA
Play. Charles Stuart Calverley. PCD
Play, The. C. J. Dennis. *Fr.* The Sentimental Bloke. PoAu-1
Play, The. James B. Kenyon. HBV
Play About, Do. Ransetsu, *wr. at. to* Basko, *tr. fr. Japanese by* Harold G. Henderson. SoPo
Play-acting. Frances Barber. GoYe
Play, Beggars, Play! "A. W." *See* In Praise of a Beggar's Life.
Play is done; the curtain drops, The. The End of the Play. Thackeray. *Fr.* Dr. Birch and His Young Friends. FaFP; GN; TreF; VA
Play it once. Saturday Night. Langston Hughes. MAP; MoAmPo
Play me a march, low toned and slow—a march for a silent tread. A Dead March. Cosmo Monkhouse. HBV; OBVV; VA
Play of "King Lear," The. Sir William Watson. VA
Play of Opposites, A. Gray Burr. CoPo
Play of the Four P's. John Heywood. *See* Four P's, The.
Play of the Weather, The, *sels.* John Heywood.
English Schoolboy, The. ACP
"Sir, I pray you, be you not master god?" CoBE
Play on the seashore. Shore. Mary Britton Miller. SUS; TiPo (1952 ed.)
Play on Words, A. Eugene Field. WhC
Play, play, while yet it is day. Play. Charles Stuart Calverley. PCD
Play seems out for an almost infinite run, The. It Bids Pretty Fair. Robert Frost. CaFP
Play Song. Peter Clarke. PBA
Play-Song. *Unknown, tr. fr. Greek by* J. M. Edmonds. LiTW
Play that thing. Jazz Band in a Parisian Cabaret. Langston Hughes. BANP; MAP; MoAmPo
Play the Game. Sir Henry Newbolt. *See* Vitai Lampada.
Play the St. Louis Blues. Request for Requiems. Langston Hughes. ShM
Play the tune again; but this time. To a Child at the Piano. Alastair Reid. MuSP
Play their offensive and defensive parts. Good Christians. Robert Herrick. LiTB
Play Time. Blake. *See* Nurse's Song ("When the voices of children are heard on the green/ And laughing").
Play was done, The. An Epilogue at Wallack's. John Elton Wayland. AA
Play was each, pleasure each. Cuchullain's Lament over Fardiad [*or* Cuchulain's Lament for Ferdiad]. *Tr. by* George Sigerson. AnIL; AnIV
Playboy of the dawn. Gone Boy. Langston Hughes. NePoAm-2
Playboy of the Demi-World, The, 1938. William Plomer. FaBoTw
Played-out Humorist, The. W. S. Gilbert. *Fr.* His Excellency. BOHV
Players. George Crabbe. *Fr.* The Borough, Letter XII. EiCL
Players Ask for a Blessing on the Psalteries and on Themselves, The. W. B. Yeats. PoDB; UnS
Playful Crickets, The. *Unknown. See* Game of Tag, A.
Playful monkey frisks with grand, A. Retinue. Paul Verlaine. ErPo
Playground of the Pixie. Grant Code. FiSC
Playgrounds. Laurence Alma-Tadema. BoTP; HBV; HBVY; OTPC; PCH; PPL
Playhouse Key, The. Rachel Field. BoTP; FaPON; MPB
Playing a phonograph record of a windy morning. From the Duck-Pond to the Carousel. Muriel Rukeyser. FiMAP
Playing Cards, The. Pope. *Fr.* The Rape of the Lock, III. ChTr
Playing on the virginals. Jean Ingelow. GTBS
Playing one day with Rhodope at dice. A Game of Dice. *Unknown.* UnTE
Playing, she puts her instrument to sleep. Improvising. Louise Townsend Nicholl. NePoAm-2
Playing upon the hill three centaurs were! The Centaurs. James Stephens. AnEnPo
Playmates. Lillian Everts. GoYe
Playmates, The. Sir William Watson. PoVP
Plays. Walter Savage Landor. HBV; NoP; OnPM; OxBoLi; PoPo; PV; VA
(Alas, How Soon [the Hours Are Over].) EnRP; EPN; TOP
(Epigram.) ALV
Playthings. William Cowper. WaaP
Playwright. John Woods. CoPo
Playwright, convict of public wrongs to men. On Playwright. Ben Jonson. NoP
Plea, The. John Drinkwater. MoRP
Plea. Eileen Duggan. JKCP (1955 ed.)
Plea, A. Graf von Zinzendorf. *See* My Light, My Way.
Plea Based on a Sentence from a Letter Received by the Indiana State Welfare Department. James Tate. YAP
Plea for a Captive. W. S. Merwin. NePoEA-2; NYBP
Plea for a Cat. Jewell Bothwell Tull. CIV
Plea for a Plural, A. Rudolf Chambers Lehmann. CenHV
Plea for Alias, A. James Schevill. FiMAP
Plea for Flood Ireson, A. Charles Timothy Brooks. PAH
Plea for Haste, A. Petronius, *tr. fr. Latin by* Louis Untermeyer. UnTE
Plea for Hope. Francis Carlin. TrPWD
Plea for Mercy, A. Kwesi Brew. PBA
Plea for Postponement, A. Petronius, *tr. fr. Latin by* Louis Untermeyer. UnTE
Plea for Promiscuity, A. Edmund Waller. *See* To Phyllis.
Plea for Tolerance. Margaret E. Bruner. PoToHe (new ed.)
Plea for Trigamy, A. Sir Owen Seaman. BOHV
Plea of the Midsummer Fairies, The, *sels.* Thomas Hood.
Fairy's Reply to Saturn, The. OBNC
Green Dryad's Plea, The. OBNC
Melodies of Time, The. OBNC
Shakespeare. OBRV
Shakespeare: The Fairies Advocate. OBNC
Tender Babes. OBRV
Titania. OBRV
Plea to Boys and Girls, A. Robert Graves. GTBS-P
Plea to Eros. *Unknown, tr. fr. Greek by* Louis Untermeyer. UnTE

Plead for Me. Emily Brontë. EnLi-2 (1949 ed.); PoEL-5
(God of Visions.) TrGrPo
(To Imagination.) NBM
Pleaders, The. Peter Davison. NYBP
Pleasant Comedie of Old Fortunatus, The. Thomas Dekker. *See* Old Fortunatus.
Pleasant Comedy of Patient Grissell [*or* Grissill], *sels.* Thomas Dekker *and others.*
Bridal Song: "Beauty, arise, show forth thy glorious shining, *fr.* V, ii. OBSC; TrGrPo
(Beauty, Arise!) EIL
("Beauty arise, show forth thy glorious shining.") TuPP
Golden Slumbers [Kiss Your Eyes], *fr.* IV, ii. CH; ELP; HBV; OTPC; PoE; ReEn; ShBV-4; SiCE; TuPP; ViBoPo
(Cradle Song.) OBSC; TrGrPo
(Lullaby.) EIL; LoBV
Happy Heart, The, *fr.* I, i. GTBS; GTBS-D; GTBS-P; GTBS-W; GTSE; GTSL; HBV; MemP; WoL
(Art Thou Poor?) CBEP
("Art thou poor, yet hast thou golden slumbers?") EG; OAEP; SiCE; TOP; TuPP; ViBoPo
(Basket-Maker's Song, The.) OBSC; ThWaDe; TrGrPo
(Content.) BBV (1923 ed.); EnLi-1
(O Sweet Content.) AtBAP; BEL; ShBV-2
(Song of the Basket Maker.) PTK
(Sweet Content.) CH; EIL; EnLit; LoBV; OBEV; OtMeF; PG; TreFT; WHA
Pleasant Cow, The. Grace Taber Hallock. RePo
Pleasant Historie of Albino and Bellama, The. Nathaniel Whiting. *See* Le Hore di Recreatione.
Pleasant is the theme that falls to my care. The Enchanted Fawn. *Unknown.* *Fr.* Dinnshenchas. OnYI
Pleasant isle of Rügen looks the Baltic water o'er, The. The Brown Dwarf of Rügen. Whittier. PoMS
Pleasant journey, little book. To the Lady with a Book. *Unknown.* KiLC
Pleasant little villages that grace the Irish glynns, The. Song of the Little Villages. James B. Dollard. CAW; JKCP
Pleasant Memories, *sel.* Charles Sangster.
Meadow-Field, The. OBCV
Pleasant New Ballad of Two Lovers, A. *Unknown.* CoMu
Pleasant New Court Song, A. *Unknown.* CoMu
Pleasant Pastime between the Young-Men and Maids, in the Pleasant Meadows. *Unknown.* *See* Merry Hay-Makers, The.
Pleasant place I was at today, A. The Woodland Mass. Dafydd ap Gwilym. PrWP
Pleasant Sounds. John Clare. BoPe; CBEP
Pleasant Things. Byron. *See* 'Tis Sweet.
Please. Robert Creeley. ML
Please. Rose Fyleman. MPB
Please, everybody, look at me! Five Years Old. Marie Louise Allen. BiCB
Please excuse this letter. The Letter. Beatrice M. Murphy. PoNe
Please Excuse Typing. J. B. Boothroyd. FiBHP; SiTL
Please God, take care of little things. A Prayer for Little Things. Eleanor Farjeon. ThGo
Please Lord, take care of my child. Oh! Lord. Antoinette T. Payne. TNV
"Please, may I hold your hand, dear Lord?" River of Life. Elayne Tedder. SoP
Please Tell Me Just the Fabuli. Shel Silverstein. ELU
Please to remember. Guy Fawkes Day. *Unknown.* FOL; OTPC (1923 ed.); OxNR
Please to Ring the Belle. Thomas Hood. HBV
Please your grace, from out your store. The Beggar, to Mab the Fairy Queen. Robert Herrick. OTPC (1923 ed.)
Pleasent Delusion of a Sumpteous Citty. Sarah Kemble Knight. SCAP
Pleased Intimacy, The. Bilhana, *formerly at. to* Chauras, *tr. fr. Sanskrit by* E. Powys Mathers. *Fr.* Black Marigolds. OnPM
Pleasing Constraint, The. Aristaenetus, *tr. fr. Greek by* Richard Brinsley Sheridan *and* Nathaniel Brassey Halhed. ALV; ErPo
Pleasure ("Pleasure could be carried to"). *Unknown,* *tr. fr. German by* Louis Untermeyer. UnTE
Pleasure and Sorrow. Robert Browning Hamilton. *See* Along the Road.
Pleasure Is Too Surely Found. Herbert A. Kenny. JKCP (1955 ed.)
Pleasure It Is. William Cornish. CBEP; CH; MeEL; TuPP
(Gratitude.) CTC; OBSC
(Spring.) BoNaP; ChTr
Pleasure me not, for love's pleasure drained me. In the Interstices. Ruth Stone. ErPo
Pleasure of Hope, The. Pope. *See* Hope.
Pleasure of Walking through an Alley, The. John Gay. *Fr.* Trivia; or, The Art of Walking the Streets of London, II. EnLi-1 (1949 ed.)
Pleasure Reconciled to Virtue [*or* Vertue]. Ben Jonson. AnAnS-2
Hymn to Comus, *sel.* EIP; OAEP
(Hymn to the Belly.) SeCePo; SiTL
(Song: To Comus.) SeEP
Pleasures. Denise Levertov. AP; NeAP
Pleasures, Beauty, Youth Attend Ye. John Ford. *Fr.* The Lady's Trial. LiTL; ViBoPo
Pleasures lie thickest where no pleasures seem. Hidden Joys. Laman Blanchard. VA
Pleasures newly found are sweet. To the Same Flower. Wordsworth. EnRP
Pleasures of a poultry yard, The. The Swan and the Cook. La Fontaine. BoChLi
Pleasures of Hope, The, *sel.* Thomas Campbell.
"At summer eve, when Heaven's ethereal bow." EnRP
Pleasures of Imagination, The, *sels.* Mark Akenside.
Early Influences, *fr.* IV. OBEC
Invocation to the Genius of Greece, *fr.* I. OBEC
Nature, *fr.* IV. LoBV
("O ye dales," *shorter sel.*) PeER
Nature's Influence on Man, *fr.* III. OBEC
(Created Universe, The.) LoBV
("Oh! blest of heav'n, whom not the languid songs.") CEP
Poets, *fr.* IV. OBEC
That Delightful Time. SeCePo
"With what attractive charms this goodly frame," *fr.* I. EiPP; EnPE; EnRP
Pleasures of Love, The. Wilfrid Scawen Blunt. HBV
Pleasures of love, and the joys of good wine, The. Song. Sir George Etherege. *Fr.* The Man of Mode. CEP
Pleasures of Melancholy, The. Thomas Warton, the Younger. CEP; EiPP
Sels.
"Mother of musings, Contemplation sage." EnRP
Solemn Noon of Night, The. OBEC; SeCePo
Pleasures of Memory, The, *sel.* Samuel Rogers.
Inscription on a Grot. OBEC
Pleasures of Merely Circulating, The. Wallace Stevens. LiTA; LOW; OnHM
Pleasures that I most enviously sense. The Cat. Walter Adolphe Roberts. CIV
Pledge, The. Adelaide Crapsey. NP; TOP
Pleiades, The. Arthur Adams. BoAu
Pleiades, The. Mary Barnard. NYBP
Pleiades, The. Elizabeth J. Coatsworth. ImOP
Pleiads, The. John Banister Tabb. UTS
Plenitude. A. M. Sullivan. JKCP (1926 ed.)
Plenteous place is Ireland for hospitable cheer, A. The Fair Hills of Ireland. *Unknown,* *tr. by* Sir Samuel Ferguson. AnIV; IrPN; OBEV; OBVV; OnYI
Plentiful snow deepens the path to the woods. Snow. Ruth Stone. NYBP
Plighted. Dinah Maria Mulock Craik. HBV
Plodder Seam, The. *Unknown.* ELP
Plot against Proteus, The. A. J. M. Smith. OBCV; PeCV
Plot against the Giant, The. Wallace Stevens. CaFP; CMoP; OxBA
Plot Improbable, Character Unsympathetic. Elder Olson. NePA
Plot to Assassinate the Chase Manhattan Bank, The. Carl Larsen. PPON
Plough, The. Richard Henry Horne. OBEV; OBVV; VA
(Plow, The.) HBV
Plough-Hands' Song, The. Joel Chandler Harris. *Fr.* Uncle Remus, His Songs and His Sayings. AA; LHV
Plough-Horse, The. Rhoda Coghill. OnYI
Ploughboy, The. John Clare. PoEL-4
Plougher, The. Padraic Colum. AnFE; GoBC; GTSL; HBMV; OnYI
(Plower, The.) MoBrPo; NeMA

Ploughing on Sunday. Wallace Stevens. AmLP; FaPON; GoJo; PoPl; ThWaDe
Ploughland has gone to bent, The. Gin the Goodwife Stint. Basil Bunting. CTC
Ploughman, The. Karle Wilson Baker. WGRP
Ploughman, The. Gordon Bottomley. POTE
Ploughman, The. John Masefield. *Fr.* The Everlasting Mercy. AtBAP
("O Christ who holds the open gate.") TreFS
Ploughman, The. Gilbert Thomas. HBMV
Ploughman, The. *Unknown.* CoMu
Ploughman at the Plough. Louis Golding. HBMV; OHIP
Ploughman he's a bonnie lad, The. The Ploughman. *Unknown.* CoMu
Ploughman Singing. John Clare. BoPe
Ploughman, whose gnarly hand yet kindly wheeled. The Waving of the Corn. Sidney Lanier. AP
Ploughman's Song, The. Nicholas Breton. *See* Phyllida and Corydon ("In the merry month of May").
Plovers, The. Hitomaro, *tr. fr. Japanese by* Ishii *and* Obata. OnPM
("Plovers cry, The," *tr. by* Kenneth Rexroth.) LiTW
Plow, The. Richard Henry Horne. *See* Plough, The.
Plow. *Unknown, tr. fr. Anglo-Saxon by* Charles W. Kennedy. *Fr.* Riddles. AnOE
Plower, The. Padraic Colum. *See* Plougher, The.
Plowing; a Memory. Hamlin Garland. StVeCh
Plowman, The. Burns. UnTE
Plowman, The. Max Harris. BoAV
Plowman. Sidney Keyes. MoAB; PoRA
Plowman, The. Raymond Knister. OBCV; PeCV; TwCaPo
Plowman of Today, The. Hamlin Garland. StVeCh
Plowman's Song, The. Nicholas Breton. *See* Phyllida and Corydon.
Plowman's Song. Raymond Knister. CaP
Pluck me ten berries from the juniper. Recipe, *parody.* A. P. Herbert. *Fr.* Two Gentlemen of Soho. WhC
Pluck the Fruit and Taste the Pleasure. Thomas Lodge. *Fr.* Robert, Second Duke of Normandy. EIL
(Carpe Diem.) OBSC
(Song.) CLwM; EnRePo
Plucking the Rushes. *Unknown, tr. fr. Chinese by* Arthur Waley. OnPM; ShBV-4; WoL
Plum-blossom, The. Akahito. *Fr.* Manyo Shu. AWP
Plum Blossoms ("Far across hill and dale"). Basho, *tr. fr. Japanese.* SUS
Plum Blossoms ("So sweet the plum trees smell"). Ranko. *See* Plum Trees.
Plum-Cake, The. Ann Taylor. HBVY
(Another Plum-Cake.) OTPC (1923 ed.)
Plum Tree, The. James Reaney. CaP
Plum Tree by the House, The. Oliver St. John Gogarty. OBEV (new ed.); PoRA
Plum Trees. Ranko, *tr. fr. Japanese.* FaPON; MPB
(Plum Blossoms: "So sweet the plum trees smell!") SoPo; SUS
Plump Mr. Pl'f is washing his hands of America, The. Oil Painting of the Artist as the Artist. Archibald MacLeish. Frescoes for Mr. Rockefeller's City, IV. NAMP; OnHM; UnPo
Plump, the pompous bosomed bird, The. Pigeon English. Sara Henderson Hay. BiS
Plumpuppets, The. Christopher Morley. FaPON; GaP; MPB; TiPo
Plums are like blue pendulums, The. The Plum Tree. James Reaney. CaP
Plums in the sun. The Backyard on Fulton Street. Gail Dusenbery. ThO
Plunged in night, I sit alone. Samson. Frederick George Scott. VA
Plunger. Carl Sandburg. BoLiVe; NeMA
Plunging and labouring on in a tide of visions. In Front of the Landscape. Thomas Hardy. OBNC
Plunging limbers over the shattered track, The. Dead Man's Dump. Isaac Rosenberg. BrPo; CABL; FaBoMo; GTBS-P; LiTM; MMA; MoPo; TrJP; WaP
Plunging rocks, whose ravenous throats, The. Mortem, Quae Violat Suavia, Pellit Amor. William Johnson Cory. NBM
Plutarch. Agathias Scholasticus, *tr. fr. Greek by* Dryden. AWP; JAWP; WBP
(Epigram on Plutarch.) MBW-1
Pluto and Venus. *Unknown, tr. fr. Greek by* William Hay. OnPM
Pluto's Council. Tasso, *tr. fr. Italian by* Edward Fairfax. *Fr.* Godfrey of Bulloigne. OBSC
Plutus, Cupid, and Time. John Gay. *Fr.* Fables. EiCP
Pluviose. Julian Bell. ChMP
Plymouth Harbor. Ernest Radford. HBV
Plymouth Harvest, The. William Bradford. PCH
Plymouth Rock. Olive Driver. RePo
Po' Boy, *with music. Unknown.* AS; TrAS, *diff. vers.*
(As I Set Down to Play Tin-Can, *with music, diff. vers.*) OuSiCo
Po' Boy (*diff. ballad*). *Unknown. See* Cryderville Jail, The.
Po' Boy Blues. Langston Hughes. BANP
Po Chu-i, balding old politician. As I Step Over a Puddle at the End of Winter. James Wright. FRC; NaP
Po' Farmer, *with music. Unknown.* OuSiCo
Po' Laz'us *with music. Unknown.* ABF; OuSiCo, *diff. vers.*
Po' lil' brack sheep dat strayed away. De Sheepfol' [*or* The Little Black Sheep]. *At. to* Paul Laurence Dunbar, *also to* Sarah Pratt McLean Greene. MaRV; WBLP
Po' Mourner's Got a Home at Las', *with music. Unknown.* BoAN-2
Poacher, The. R. S. Thomas. POTi
Poacher, The. *Unknown. See* Lincolnshire Poacher, The.
Pobble Who Has No Toes, The. Edward Lear. BOHV; FaBoCh; GaP; GoTP; HBV; HBVY; InP; LBN; LiTG; LoGBV; MaC; MoShBr; MPB; NA; OnSP; OTPC; WhC; YT
Pocahontas. George Pope Morris. MC; PAH
Pocahontas. Thackeray. AmFN; DD; FaPON; GN; GoTP; MC; MPB; OnMSP; OTPC; PAH; PAL; ThLM
Pocket and Steeple. M. A. De Wolfe Howe. WhC
Pocket Guide for Servicemen. Hubert Creekmore. WaP
Pocket Handkerchief to Hem, A. Christina Rossetti. *Fr.* Sing-Song. RIS; SAS
(Stitching.) OTPC (1946 ed.); PPL
Pockets. Rowena Bennett. RePo
Pockets. Susan Adger Williams. BrR
Pod of the Milkweed. Robert Frost. LiTM (1970 ed.)
Poe, a very sick man in Baltimore. The Poets of Hell. Karl Shapiro. NYBP
Poe and Longfellow. James Russell Lowell. *Fr.* A Fable for Critics. AmPP (5th ed.); AnNE; AP; OxBA
("There comes Poe, with his raven, like Barnaby Rudge.") CoBA
Poe-'em of Passion, A. Charles Fletcher Lummis. BOHV; ShM
Poem: a Piece. James T. Stewart. BF
Poem: "After your death." William Knott. YAP
Poem: "Ah I know what happiness is!" Blanche Taylor Dickinson. CDC
Poem: "Alright if I have to be famous let it be for this great." William Knott. YAP
Poem: "Always prudent but unprepared." Alan Dugan. CBV
Poem: "And this digester, this digester of food." Conrad Aiken. *Fr.* Time in the Rock. VaPo
Poem: "And when I pay death's duty." Robin Blaser. NeAP
Poem: "As rock to sun or storm." Niall Sheridan. OnYI
Poem: "As the cat." William Carlos Williams. CABA; FaPON; InvP; LOW; NoP; PDV; PoAn; ThWaDe
Poem: "Back at San Francisco Greyhound, leaning." James Brodey. ANYP
Poem: "Beach holds and sifts us through her dreaming fingers, The." William Knott. YAP
Poem: "Black Revolution is passing you bye, The." Nikki Giovanni. WSL
Poem: "By the road to the contagious hospital." William Carlos William. *See* Spring and All.
Poem: "Child—in all the flying sky." Josephine Strongin. AnAmPo
Poem, The: "Coming late, as always." W. S. Merwin. PP
Poem: "Death walks through the mind's dark woods." Henry Treece. NeBP
Poem, A: Dedication of the Pittsfield Cemetery, September 9, 1850, *sel.* Oliver Wendell Holmes.
"Father of all! in Death's relentless claim." TrPWD
Poem: "Distinction is in fire and division, The." José Garcia Villa. POTE (1959 ed.)
Poem: "Engineer pushes a button in the mountains, An." Tony Towle. ANYP
Poem: "Especially when the October wind." Dylan Thomas.

Poem (continued)
See Especially When the October Wind.
Poem: "Everyone who is anyone is moving away." Sotère Torregian. YAP
Poem: "For years I've heard." Robin Blaser. NeAP
Poem: "Force that through the green fuse drives the flower, The." Dylan Thomas. *See* Force That Through the Green Fuse, The.
Poem: "Geranium, houseleek, laid in oblong beds." John Gray. SyP
Poem: "Grecian tulip and the gothic rose, The." Terence Tiller. POTE
Poem: "Guest came from faraway, A." *Unknown, tr. fr. Chinese by* David Rafael Wang. HW
Poem: "Hate is only one of many responses." Frank O'Hara. NeAP
Poem: "He lying spilt like water from a bowl." Alison Boodson. ErPo; NeBP
Poem: "Heart of the heartless world." John Cornford. *See* Huesca.
Poem: "High on a ridge of tiles." Maurice James Craig. NeIP
Poem: "Hold my breath as there's a sound on the stairs." Joel Sloman. ThO
Poem: "How about an oak leaf." James Schuyler. ANYP
Poem: "I am beginning to alter." Bernadette Mayer. ANYP
Poem: "I am one man, worshipping silk knees." William Knott. YAP
Poem: "I burn for England with a living flame." Gervase Stewart. *See* I Burn for England . . .
Poem: "I cannot tell, not I, why she." Walter Savage Landor. ERoP-1
Poem: "I do not want to be your weeping woman." Alison Boodson. NeBP
Poem: "I heard of a man." Leonard Cohen. ELU
Poem: "I knew a woman, lovely in her bones." Theodore Roethke. *See* I Knew a Woman.
Poem: "I met a sad girl in our town." Keith Sinclair. ACV
Poem, The: "I sing th'adventures of mine worthy wights." Thomas Morton. SCAP
Poem: "I take four devils with me when I ride." Gervase Stewart. WaP
Poem: "If the drink that satisfied." R. A. K. Mason. ACV
Poem: "I'll tell you how the sun rose." Emily Dickinson. *See* I'll tell you how the sun rose.
Poem: "In its going down, the moon." Robert Hogg. MoCV
Poem: "In the dark caverns of the night." Henry Treece. NeBP
Poem: "Is to love, this—to nurse a name." Rhoda Coghill. NeIP
Poem: "It must be true." William Knott. YAP
Poem, The: "It's all in." William Carlos Williams. PoeP
Poem: "Krushchev is coming the right day!" Frank O'Hara. NeAP
Poem: "Lana Turner has collapsed!" Frank O'Hara. FRC
Poem: "Like a deaf man meshed in his endless silence." John Wain. PoCh
Poem: "Like musical instruments." Tom Clark. ANYP
Poem, A: "Like to an Hermit poore in place obscure." *At. to* Sir Walter Ralegh. *See* Like to a Hermit.
Poem: "Little brown boy." Helene Johnson. AmNP; BANP; CDC
(Little Brown Boy.) GoSl
Poem: "Maggie and Milly and Molly and May." E. E. Cummings. *See* Maggie and Milly and Molly and May.
Poem: "My heart in pieces like the bits." Tom Clark. ANYP
Poem: "My sperm is lyre in your blood your." William Knott. YAP
Poem: "Night is beautiful, The." Langston Hughes. CDC
Poem: "O gentle queen of the afternoon." W. S. Graham. NeBP
Poem: "O men, walk on the hills." Maxwell Bodenheim. TrJP
Poem: "One whom I knew, a student and a poet." Alex Comfort. *See* Epitaph: "One whom I knew, a student and a poet."
Poem: "Only response, The." William Knott. YAP
Poem, A: "Out upon it! I have loved." Sir John Suckling. *See* Constant Lover, The.
Poem: "Person who can do, The." Alan Dugan. ErPo
Poem: "Pity, repulsion, love and anger." Roy Fuller. NeBP
Poem: "Process in the weather of the heart, A." Dylan Thomas. *See* Process in the Weather of the Heart, A.
Poem: "Ran jet self into starscum 0067 hrs." Jeff Nuttall. HYE
Poem, The: "Rise Oedipeus, and if thou canst unfould." Thomas Morton. SCAP
Poem: "Sky is cut into sections and put on a frame, The." Tony Towle. ANYP
Poem: "So they begin. With two years gone." Boris Pasternak, *tr. fr. Russian by* C. M. Bowra. TrJP
Poem: "Some are too much at home in the role of wanderer." Denise Levertov. NeBP
Poem: "Something, so great a sweetness, came." Jean Garrigue. NYTB
Poem: "There is lightning on the edge of the water." Lewis Mac Adams. YAP
Poem: "These grasses, ancient enemies." Keith Douglas. NeBP
Poem: "This room is very old and very wise." Sam Harrison. NeIP
Poem: "Through the dark aisles of the wood." Henry Treece. NeBP
Poem: "To go, to leave the classics and the buildings." Gavin Ewart. NeBP
Poem: "Two/ Gorillas." Frank Lima. ANYP
Poem: "Upended, it crouches on broken limbs." Charles Tomlinson. CMoP
Poem: "Upstood upstaffed passing sinuously away." Russell Atkins. PoNe
(Christophe.) PoNe (1970 ed.)
Poem: "We are such stuff as dreams are made of, and these." Hugo von Hofmannsthal, *tr. fr. German by* Jethro Bithell. LiTW
Poem: "We drank Thunderbird all night." James T. Stewart. BF
Poem: "We used to float the paper boats in spring." Donald D. Olsen. PoPl
Poem, The: "What ailes Pigmalion? Is it lunacy." Thomas Morton. SCAP
Poem: "What of radishes lettuce peas." John Gill. ThO
Poem: "When our hands are alone." William Knott. YAP
Poem: "Wisdom has no end and folly no ornament." Nathan Alterman, *tr. fr. Hebrew by* Herbert Howarth. LiTW
Poem. "Woke this A.M." James Brodey. ANYP
Poem: "You, who in April laughed, a green god in the sun." Brenda Chamberlain. NeBP
Poem, The. Galway Kinnell. NaP
Poem/ is/ word/ list. William Harmon. *Fr.* Treasury Holiday. QAH
Poem About Baseballs, A. Denis Johnson. QAH
Poem about Love, A. G. S. Fraser. NeBP
Poem About Morning. William Meredith. NYBP
Poem about Waking. David Ferry. NePoAm-2
Poem against the Rich. Robert Bly. NMP
Poem at Equinox. Hilary Corke. NYBP
Poem at Thirty. Sonia Sanchez. BF
Poem at Thirty. John Woods. CoPo
Poem Beginning "The." Louis Zukofsky. CoPo
Poem Beginning with a Line by Pindar, A. Robert Duncan. NeAP
"The light foot hears you and the brightness begins," *sel.* NMP
Poem by a Perfectly Furious Academician. *Unknown.* FiBHP
Poem by Stages, *sels.* Charles Madge. BoSA
"Adventures of my separate bark The," XIX.
"Among all the myths and masks and make-believes," XXXII.
"First, erected ironworks in a spiry hollow," XXIV.
"Flesh is sad but there are books unread, The," XXXI.
"To us, goddess, who are in barbary," I.
Poem by the Charles River. Robin Blaser. NeAP
Poem by the Clock Tower, Sumner. James K. Baxter. ACV
Poem Containing Some Remarks on the Present War, A. *Unknown.* PAH
Poem Entreating of Sorrow, A. Sir Walter Ralegh. SiPS
("My days' delight, my springtime joys fordone.") FCP
Poem for a Christmas Broadcast. Anne Ridler. NeBP
Poem for a Dead Aunt. Barbara L. Greenberg. QAH
Poem for a Painter. Floyce Alexander. QAH
Poem for a Selfpitying Friend/ for Lost Loves. Sandford Lyne. QAH
Poem for Black Hearts, A. LeRoi Jones. BP; IDB
Poem for Christmas, A. C. A. Snodgrass. PoToHe (new ed.)
Poem for Combatants. Alan White. MaRV
Poem for Easter. Laurie Lee. BoC

Poem for Ed's Birthday. Eugene Lesser. FRC
Poem for 8th Graders. Sonia Sanchez. WOW
Poem for Epiphany. Norman Nicholson. PoPl; StJW
Poem for Everybody, A. Eugene Lesser. FRC
Poem for Fathers, A. Keith Wilson. ThO
Poem for Gerard. E. L. Mayo. ML
Poem for Good Friday. D. G. Jones. PeCV (1967 ed.)
Poem for Joyce. Johnie Scott. WSL
Poem for Marc Chagall. Leonard Cohen. *See* Out of the Land of Heaven.
Poem for Martha. Alex Raybin. ThO
Poem for Max Nordau, A. E. A. Robinson. AmePo
Poem for Mother's Day. Margaret Fishback. InMe
Poem for Museum Goers, A. John Wieners. NeAP
Poem for My Thirty-second Birthday. John Ciardi. MiAP
Poem for Painters, A. John Wieners. NeAP
Poem for Psychoanalysts and/ or Theologians. C. S. Lewis. BoPe
Poem for the Atomic Age. Emanuel Litvinov. NeBP
Poem for the Disappearing Bear. Dan Gillespie. QAH
Poem for the Insane, A. John Wieners. NeAP
Poem for the Living. Harold Andrew. TwCaPo
Poem for the Meeting of the American Medical Association, A. Oliver Wendell Holmes. PoEL-5
Poem for the Old Man, A. John Wieners. NeAP
Poem for Thel—the Very Tops of Trees. Joseph Major. NBP
Poem for Trapped Things, A. John Wieners. NeAP
Poem for You. Robert Pack. NePoEA
Poem from Deal. David Shapiro. ANYP
Poem from Llanybri. Lynette Roberts. NeBP
Poem from London, 1941. George Woodcock. NeBP
Poem I Should Like to Write, The. Margaret A. Windes. MaRV; OQP
Poem, A, in Defence of the Decent Ornaments of Christ-Church, Oxon, Occasioned by a Banbury Brother, Who Called Them Idolatries, *sels.* *Unknown.* OBS
  Beauty in Worship.
  Chruch-Windows, The, *abr.*
Poem in June. Milton Acorn. WHW
Poem in Karori. Louis Johnson. AnNZ
Poem in May. John Hewitt. NeIP
Poem in October ("It was my thirtieth year to heaven"). Dylan Thomas. BoC; CaFP; CoBMV; DiPo; EnL; GTBS-W; LiTB; LiTM (rev. ed.); MaPo; MoVE; NeBP; NoP; OAEP (2d ed.); PAn; PIA; PoIE; PoPl; PoRA; SeCePo; StP; TDP; ToPo; WePo
  October ("A springful of larks in a rolling"), *br. sel.* YeAr
Poem in Prose. Archibald MacLeish. LiTL; MoLP; PoPl
Poem in the Matukituki Valley. James K. Baxter. AnNZ
Poem in the rock and, The. Epitaph. R. S. Thomas. WePo
Poem in Three Parts. Robert Bly. NaP
Poem in Time of War. William Abrahams. WaP
Poem in Which My Legs Are Accepted. Kathleen Fraser. YAP
Poem Intended to Incite the Utmost Depression, A. Samuel Hoffenstein. BOHV; SiTL
Poem Issued by Me to Congressmen, *sel.* George Starbuck.
  "Mine eyes have seen the glory of hard/ work at least." WOW
Poem Looking for a Reader, A. Don L. Lee. BP
Poem makes truth a little more disturbing, The. Hands. Donald Finkel. CoAP
Poem must not charm us like a play, The. Against the False Magicians. Thomas McGrath. NePoEA; PP
Poem must resist the intelligence, The. Man Carrying Thing. Wallace Stevens. PoIE; SyP
Poem, neither Hilláryous Norgay. Gardner E. Lewis. FiBHP
Poem (No Name No. 2). Nikki Giovanni. BOLo
Poem of Bunker Hill, The, *sel.* Harry Brown.
  "Then once more men's ears were full of 'Yankee Doodle,'" *abr., fr.* Conclusion. PoFr
Poem of Circumstance. Jean Cocteau, *tr. fr. French by* Joseph T. Shipley. CAW
Poem of Holy Madness, *sel.* Ray Bremser.
  "Let me lay it to you gently, Mr. Gone!" NeAP
Poem of Love, A. Kay Boyle. WOW
Poem of Margery Kempe, A. Howard Nemerov. FiMAP
Poem of Privacy, A. *Unknown,* *tr. by* John Addington Symonds. ALV
Poem of Ten "Ones," The. Hô P'ei Yü, *tr. fr. Chinese by* Henry H. Hart. FLW
Poem of the Conscripted Warrior. "Rui Nogar," *tr. fr. Portuguese by* Dorothy Guedes *and* Philippa Rumsey. TTY
Poem of the Future Citizen. José Craveirinha, *tr. fr. Portuguese by* Dorothy Guedes *and* Philippa Rumsey. TTY
Poem of the mind in the act of finding, The. Of Modern Poetry. Wallace Stevens. AmP; AmPP (4th ed.); InvP; MaPo (1969 ed.); NePA; OxBA; PP
Poem of the Our Father, The. St. Matthew, Bible, *N.T.* *See* Lord's Prayer, The.
Poem of the Son. "Gabriela Mistral," *tr. fr. Spanish by* Langston Hughes. PoPl
Poem of the Universe, The. Charles Weldon. VA
Poem on a Slippery Sidewalk. Kenneth Porter. WhC
Poem on Canada, *sels.* Patrick Anderson.
  Cold Colloquy, V. CaP; PeCV
  "What are you . . .? they ask," *shorter sel.* TwCaPo
  Coming of the White Man, The, II. CaP; MoCV
Poem on Elijahs Translation, A. Benjamin Colman. SCAP
Poem on Hampstead Heath. Louis Adeane. NeBP
Poem on His Birthday. Dylan Thomas. DiPo; SeCeV (1967 ed.)
Poem on Spring, The. Arthur Guiterman. LHV
Poem on the Wall, The. Po Chü-i, *tr. fr. Chinese by* Arthur Waley. ML
Poem, or Beauty Hurts Mr. Vinal. E. E. Cummings. AmP; MoAB; MoAmPo; MoVE; OxBA; PoIE
Poem Put into My Lady Laiton's Pocket, A. Sir Walter Ralegh. FCP; SiPS
Poem Read at Joan Mitchell's. Frank O'Hara. ANYP
Poem Rocket. Allen Ginsberg. CoPo
Poem Sacred to the Memory of Sir Isaac Newton, A. James Thomson. CEP; EiPP
Poem should be, as our best ever are, A. The Whole Duty of a Poem. Arthur Guiterman. PoToHe (new ed.)
Poem should be palpable and mute, A. Ars Poetica. Archibald MacLeish. AmP; AmPP; AP; AWP; CaFP; CBV; CMoP; CoBMV; DiPo; ExPo; HoPM; InP; InPo; LiTA; LiTM; MAP; MoAB; MoAmPo; NAMP; NeMA; NP; OxBA; PoAn; PoPl; PoPo; PoRA (rev. ed.); PP; ReMP; SeCeV; TwAmPo; VaPo
Poem That Took the Place of a Mountain, The. Wallace Stevens. ML
Poem That Tries to Be a Tree, The. Phillip Hey. YAP
Poem to a Nigger Cop. Bobb Hamilton. BF TTY
Poem To Be Cast into the Sea in a Bottle. James Kirkup. BoPe
Poem to Be Said on Hearing the Birds Sing, A. *Unknown,* *tr. fr. Irish by* Douglas Hyde. AnIV; AWP; JAWP; WBP
Poem to Delight My Friends Who Laugh at Science-Fiction, A. Edwin Rolfe. NePA; NePoAm; PPON; ThLM
Poem to Explain Everything About a Certain Day in Vermont, A. Genevieve Taggard. NYBP
Poem, to Jane Wilson on Television. James Brodey. ANYP
Poem to Lou. Guillaume Apollinaire, *tr. fr. French by* Hubert Creekmore. LiTW
Poem to Negro and Whites. Maxwell Bodenheim. PoNe
Poem to Poetry. William Knott. YAP
Poem to the Man on My Fire Escape. Diane Wakoski. CoPo
Poem upon the Caelestial Embassy, A. Richard Steere. SCAP
Poem upon the Death of Oliver Cromwell, A. Andrew Marvell. MaMe
  "I saw him dead, a leaden slumber lies," *sel.* OBS; PeRV; ViBoPo
  (Cromwell Dead.) ChTr
Poem upon the page is as massive as, The. Ted Berrigan. ANYP
Poem upon the Triumphant Translation of . . . Mrs. Anne Eliot, A. John Danforth. SCAP
Poem with the Answer, A. Sir John Suckling. *See* Constant Lover, The ("Out upon it").
Poem without a Main Verb. John Wain. NePoEA-2; NMP
Poem Written by Sir Henry Wotton, in His Youth, A. Sir Henry Wotton. AnAnS-2
Poem Written During Sleep. Sotère Torregian. YAP
Poem Written in Time of Trouble by an Irish Priest, A. *Unknown,* *tr. fr. Irish by* Lady Gregory. OBMV
Poem, Written on the Eve of Execution. Chidiock Tichborne. *See* Elegy: "My prime of youth is but a frost of cares."
Poema Morale. Charles Gullans. NePoEA
Poems. Hilda Conkling. ExPo; NP
Poems. Léon Damas, *tr. fr. French by* Langston Hughes. PoNe
Poems. Julius Lester. Kal

Poems. Antonio Machado, *tr. fr. Spanish by* John Dos Passos.
"Figures in the fields against the sky." AWP; JAWP; WBP
(Four Poems, 2.) LiTW
"Frail sound of a tunic trailing, A." AWP; JAWP; WBP
(Four Poems, 1.) LiTW
"Naked is the earth." AWP
(Four Poems, 3.) LiTW
"We think to create festivals." AWP
(Four Poems, 4.) LiTW
Poems. Philip O'Connor. LiTM
Poems about the Moon. Vachel Lindsay. MAPA; TwAmPo
Poems are bullshit unless they are. Black Art. LeRoi Jones. BF; BP
Poems are made by fools like me. Atheist. E. Y. Harburg. PV
Poems are written by poets for the people. Find a Role, Define a Role. Raymond Turner. WSL
Poems by the Roadside. St. Luke, XII: 32-37; St. Matthew, V: 14-16, XVI: 17-19, Bible, *N.T.* CAW
Poems Come Easier, The. Ray Mathew. BoAV
Poems for My Brother Kenneth. Owen Dodson. IDB; PoNe
(For My Brother.) BALP
Poems for My Daughter. Horace Gregory.
(Stanzas for My Daughter.) MoVE
"Tell her I love she will remember me," *sel.* MAP; MoAmPo
Poems from a First Year in Boston. George Starbuck. NePoEA-2; TwAmPo
"Becalmed in old Back Bay's dead water sulk,"IV. PoDB
Poems from MSS. Blake. *Poems indexed separately by titles and first lines.*
Poems from the Coalfields. Ian Healy. PoAu-2
Advice from a Nightwatchman.
Air Shaft.
Poems in Praise of Practically Nothing, *sels.* Samuel Hoffenstein.
"Only the wholesomest foods you eat." BOHV; InMe; SiTL; TrJP
"You buy some flowers for your table." BOHV; FiBHP; InMe; SiTL; TrJP
"You buy yourself a new suit of clothes." BOHV; InMe; SiTL
"You get a girl; and you say you love her." BOHV; InMe; SiTL
"You hire a cook, but she can't cook yet." InMe; WhC
"You leap out of bed; you start to get ready." BOHV; InMe; SiTL
"You meet a girl and you surrender." InMe
"You practise every possible virtue." BOHV; InMe
"You take a bath, and sit there bathing." EvOK; InMe
"You work and work and keep on working." WhC
"You're a good girl; you're gray with virtue." InMe
"You're kind to women, children, worms." InMe
Poems of My Lambretta. Paul Goodman. NMP; OPoP
Poems of Night. Galway Kinnell. NaP
Poems of Our Climate, The. Wallace Stevens. AmP; MoPo; OxBA; PP; TrGrPo (rev. ed.); TwCP
Poems of Passion, Carefully Restrained So as to Offend Nobody. Samuel Hoffenstein. InMe
Poems of Solitary Delights, *sel.* Tachibana Akemi, *tr. fr. Japanese by* Geoffrey Bownas *and* Anthony Thwaite.
"What a delight it is." FIW
Poems of the Arabic, *sel.* *Unknown, tr. fr. Arabic by* Sir Richard Francis Burton. *Fr.* The Thousand and One Nights.
"My soul thy sacrifice! I choose thee out." ErPo
Poems to a Brown Cricket. James Wright. NaP; NYBP
Poe's Cottage at Fordham. John Henry Boner. AA
Poesy to Prove Affection Is Not Love, A. Sir Walter Ralegh. *See* Conceit Begotten by the Eyes.
Poet, The. Philip James Bailey. *Fr.* Festus. VA
Poet, The. Joel Benton. WGRP
Poet, The. H. C. Bosman. BoSa
Poet, The. Elizabeth Barrett Browning. WGRP
Poet, The. Bryant. AA; AmPP (3d ed.); AP; CoBA; InP; MAmP; PP
Poet, The. Witter Bynner. *See* Poet Lived in Galilee, A.
Poet, The. Grace Noll Crowell. InP
Poet, The. T. A. Daly. JKCP
Poet, The. W. H. Davies. DTC
Poet, The. C. Day Lewis. OxBI
Poet, The. Paul Laurence Dunbar. Kal
Poet, The, *sel.* Emerson.
"Right upward on the road of fame." PP
Poet, The ("Thy trivial harp"). Emerson. *Fr.* Merlin. BoLiVe
Poet ("To clothe the fiery thought"). Emerson. *Fr.* Quatrains. AnNE; OnPM; OxBA
Poet, The. Padraic Fiacc. NeIP
Poet, The. Anita Grannis. HBMV
Poet, A. Thomas Hardy. VP
Poet. Donald Jeffrey Hayes. AmNP; PoNe
Poet, The ("At Morn, at Noon, at Eve, and Middle Night"). Keats. ERoP-2
Poet, The ("Where's the Poet? show him! show him"). Keats. *See* Where's the Poet?
Poet, The. James Kirkup. PP
Poet, The. Mary Sinton Leitch. HBMV; PoMa
Poet, The. Haniel Long. HBMV
Poet, The. Amy Lowell. WGRP
Poet, The. Edwin Markham. WGRP
Poet, The. Cornelius Mathews. AA
Poet, The. Angela Morgan. SoP; WGRP
"Why hast thou breathed, O God, upon my thoughts," *sel.* TrPWD
Poet, The. Yone Noguchi. NP; WGRP
Poet, The. Seumas O'Brien. JKCP (1926 ed.)
Poet, The. Bernard O'Dowd. BoAu
Poet, The. Pope. *See* Immortality of Verse, The.
Poet, The. Rainer Maria Rilke, *tr. fr. German by* Selden Rodman. *Fr.* Sonnets to Orpheus. OnHM
Poet, The. William Rooney. JKCP (1926 ed.)
Poet. Karl Shapiro. AnFE; CMoP; CoAnAm; LiTM (1970 ed.); MoAB; MoAmPo (1950 ed.); ToPo; TwAmPo
"Poet." William Jay Smith. RePo
Poet, The. Tennyson. EnL; EnLit; MBW-2; OAEP; PoVP; PP; ViPo; ViPP
"And Freedom rear'd in that august sunrise," *sel.* PoFr
Poet. Peter Viereck. HoPM; MiAP; MoAmPo (1950 ed.)
Poet, The. Sir William Watson. TrGrPo
(Four Epigrams.) MoBrPo (1942 ed.)
Poet, The. Walt Whitman. By Blue Ontario's Shore, IX-XVII. MoAmPo (1950 ed.)
Poet, The; a Rhapsody. Mark Akenside. PP
Poet and Critic. Samuel Daniel. *Fr.* Musophilus; or, Defence of All Learning. OBSC
("Fond man, Musophilus, that thou dost spend.") ReIE; SiCE; TuPP
Poet and gangster reach in the dark. The Escapade. David Ignatow. PP
Poet and Goldsmith. Vernon Watkins. PoCh
Poet and His Book, The. Edna St. Vincent Millay. AmLP; MAP; MoAmPo; NePA
Poet, and His Patron, The. Edward Moore. Fables for the Female Sex, V. CEP; EiCL
(Fable: The Poet and His Patron.) WaPE
Poet and His Song, The. Paul Laurence Dunbar. PoRL
Poet and Lark. "Madeline Bridges." AA; HBV
Poet and Peasant. R. H. Long. PoAu-1
Poet and saint! to thee alone are given. On the Death of [Mr.] Crashaw. Abraham Cowley. AnAnS-2; GoBC; MeLP; MePo; NoP; OBS; SCEP-2; SeCP; SeCV-1; SeEP; ViBoPo
Poet and the Child, The. Winifred Howells. AA
Poet and the Dun, The. William Shenstone. PP
Poet and the French Revolution, The. Wordsworth. *Fr.* The Prelude, XI. EPN
Poet and the Rose, The. John Gay. *Fr.* Fables. EiCP
Poet and the Wood-Louse, The. Helen Parry Eden. HBV
Poet and the World, The. Byron. *Fr.* Childe Harold's Pilgrimage, III. SeCePo
("I have not loved the world, nor the world me.") OBRV
Poet at Fifty, The. Laurence Lerner. PeSA
Poet at Night-Fall, The. Glenway Wescott. LiTM (1946 ed.); NP
Poet at Seven, The. Donald Justice. TwAmPo
Poet at Seven, The. Robert Lowell, *ad. fr. the French of* Arthur Rimbaud. NaP
Poet at the Breakfast Table, The, *sel.* Oliver Wendell Holmes.
Epilogue to the Breakfast-Table Series. AA
Poet, be seated at the piano. Mozart, 1935. Wallace Stevens. AmP; UnS

Poet by poet launched upon that sea. Genesis. Elizabeth Sewell. ML
Poet, The, Byron/ Was made of iron. Important People. Louis Untermeyer, *and others.* StaSt
Poet, cast your careful eye. On Seeing a Poet of the First World War on the Station at Abbeville. Charles Causley. ChMP; LiTM (1970 ed.); NMP
Poet Confides, The. Herbert T. J. Coleman. CaP
Poet Considers Perfection, The. Elizabeth Virginia Raplee. MaRV
Poet Describes His Love, The. Robert Nathan. HBMV
Poet gathers fruit from every tree, The. The Poet. Sir William Watson. MoBrPo (1942 ed.); TrGrPo
Poet, gentle creature as he is, The. Wordsworth. *Fr.* The Prelude, I. PP
Poet had a cat, A. How a Cat Was Annoyed and a Poet Was Booted. Guy Wetmore Carryl. CIV; MAP; MoAmPo (1942 ed.)
Poet hath the child's sight in his breast, The. The Poet. Elizabeth Barrett Browning. WGRP
Poet, having taken the bridle off his tongue, A. The Intoxicated Poet. Allen Upward. *Fr.* Scented Leaves from a Chinese Jar. NP
Poet, A!—He Hath Put His Heart to School. Wordsworth. EnRP
Poet heard a skylark sing, A. The Super-Lark. R. H. Long. BoAu
Poet-Hearts. Joseph von Eichendorff, *tr. fr. German by* George N. Shuster. CAW
Poet honed, The. Lyric Barber. Liboria E. Romano. GoYe
Poet! I come to touch thy lance with mine. Wapentake. Longfellow. AA
Poet in a golden clime was born, The. The Poet. Tennyson. EnL; EnLit; MBW-2; OAEP; PoVP; PP; ViPo; ViPP
Poet in his lone yet genial hour, The. Apologia pro Vita Sua. Samuel Taylor Coleridge. EnRP; ERoP-1; PP
Poet in His Poverty, The. Nizami, *tr. fr. Persian by* Samuel Robinson. LiTW
Poet in Life and Death, The. *Unknown, tr. fr. Greek by* Lord Neaves. OnPM
Poet in the City, The. Catherine C. Liddell. VA
Poet in the Desert, The, *sels.* Charles E. S. Wood.
  Desert, The ("Never have I found a place"). AnEnPo
  Desert, The ("She is a nun"), *abr.* AnAmPo; MAP
  "Desert murmurs to the sun a strange murmur, The." PoFr
  "I have come into the desert," *abr.* NP
  "Suddenly night flung wide the sapphire gate." PoFr
  Sunrise ("The lean coyote, prowler of the night"). GoTP; MAP; PFY
  "This is the pedigree of degradation." PoFr
Poet in Winter. Edward Lucie-Smith. TwCP
Poet is a lazy man, The. Achievement. Morris Abel Beer. PoMa
Poet is hunchbacked, The. The Life of the Poet. Philip Dow. QAH
Poet is, or ought to be, a hater of the city, The. Rural Bliss. Anthony C. Deane. InMe
Poet is priest. Death to Van Gogh's Ear! Allen Ginsberg. NaP
Poet, Jesus, speak to me. The Poet of Palestine. William L. Stidger. ChIP
Poet, let passion sleep. Art, II. Alfred Noyes. OBEV (new ed.)
Poet Lived in Galilee, A. Witter Bynner. OQP
  (Poet, The.) WGRP
Poet Loosed a Wingèd Song, The. Joseph Campbell. OnYI
Poet Loves a Mistress[e], But Not to Marry, The. Robert Herrick. ALV; CavP; ErPo
Poet Meets Venus and Her Priest, The. John Gower, *tr. fr. Middle English by* Muriel Bowden. *Fr.* Confessio Amantis, I. MeEV
Poet of Bray, The. John Heath-Stubbs. ML
Poet of Earth. Stephen Henry Thayer. AA
Poet of Farewell. Christian Werleigh, *tr. fr. French by* Edna Worthley Underwood. PoNe
Poet of Gardens, The. Daniel Henderson. HBMV
Poet of nature, thou hast wept to know. To Wordsworth. Shelley. EnRP; EPN; ERoP-2; FiP; MCCG; NoP; PoPo; PoRL; Sonn
Poet of One Mood, A. Alice Meynell. HBMV
Poet of Palestine, The. William L. Stidger. ChIP
Poet of the pulpit, whose full-chorded lyre. Bartol. Amos Bronson Alcott. AA
Poet of urban affairs, The. The City Enscriber. Bob Maxey. WSL
Poet on Sol III, The. Far Out. Robert Conquest. HYE
Poet on the Island, The. Richard Murphy. NMP
Poet Prays, The. Grace Noll Crowell. TrPWD
Poet Prays Her, The. Daniel Berrigan. JKCP (1955 ed.)
Poet Prays to the Cross, The. *Unknown. Fr.* The Dream of the Rood. PoLi
Poet-Preacher's Prayer, A. Milton. *Fr.* Paradise Lost, I. MaRV
Poet seldom finds the way, A. Form 1040A. Phyllis Eleanor Armstrong. SiTL
Poet Shadwell, The. Dryden. *See* Shadwell.
Poet Songs (I-III). Karle Wilson Baker. HBMV
  "Dropped feathers from the wings of God," III.
  "I cast my nets in many streams," II.
  "I shall not get my poem done," I.
Poet Speaks, The. Georgia Douglas Johnson. AmNP
Poet Speaks from the Visitors' Gallery, A. Archibald MacLeish. NYBP
Poet stood in the sombre town, The. The Poet in the City. Catherine C. Liddell. VA
Poet, take up your lyre. The New Song. Arthur Gordon Field. PGD
Poet Tells about Nature, The. Merrill Moore. NP
Poet Thinks, A. Lui Chi, *tr. fr. Chinese by* E. Powys Mathers. AWP; JAWP; LiTW; PG (1945 ed.); WBP
Poet to a Painter, A. Aubrey Thomas De Vere. Sonn
Poet to Dancer. Bernice Kavinoky. UnS
Poet to His Beloved, A. W. B. Yeats. BrPo; MoLP
Poet to His Love. Maxwell Bodenheim. BoLP; MAP; MoAmPo (1942 ed.); PoPl
Poet to the Birds, The. Alice Meynell. NP
Poet Tries to Turn in His Jock, The. David Hilton. QAH
Poet *vs.* Parson. Ebenezer Elliott. Sonn
Poet was busted by a topless judge, A. Sermonette. Ishmael Reed. WOW
Poet who sleepest by this wandering wave! Sir William Watson. Wordsworth's Grave, II. GoTL; HBV
Poet with Sea Horse. Alastair Reid. ML
Poet writ a song of May, A. The First Song. Richard Burton. AA
Poeta Fit, Non Nascitur. "Lewis Carroll." NBM
Poeta Nascitur. Thomas Ashe. VA
Poetaster, The, *sels.* Ben Jonson.
  "If I freely may discover," *fr.* II, ii. EG; ReEn; TuPP
  (Hermogenes's Song.) PoIE
  (Song: "If I freely may discover.") AnAnS-2; EIL
  "O sacred poesie, thou spirit of artes," *fr.* I, ii. PoEL-2
  Swell Me a Bowl, *fr.* III, i. TuPP
  "There is no bountie to be shew'd to such," *fr.* III, vi. PoEL-2
Poetaster, The. Samuel Rowlands. *Fr.* The Melancholy Knight. EIL
Poetic Land, The. William Caldwell Roscoe. OBVV
Poetic Pains. William Cowper. *Fr.* The Task, II. FiP
  (Poetry: Satire and Pulpit.) CoBE
Poetic Thought. *Unknown.* FiBHP; SiTL
Poetical Commandments. Byron. *Fr.* Don Juan, I. FiP; OBRV
  ("If ever I should condescend to prose.") OxBoLi
  (Poet's Credo.) SeCePo
Poetical Economy. Harry Graham. CenHV; SiTL; TreFS
Poetical Numbers. Pope. *Fr.* An Essay on Criticism. OBEC; SeCePo
  ("But most by numbers judge a poet's song.") AnFE; InP; PP
Poetical Philander only thought to love. Philander. Donald Hall. ELU; ErPo
Poetics. Robert Browning. PoVP
Poetics against the Angel of Death. Phyllis Webb. MoCV
Poetry. Lucius Harwood Foote. AA
Poetry. Ella Heath. HBV; WGRP
Poetry. Edwin Markham. AA
Poetry. Marianne Moore. AmP; AmPP (5th ed.); AnFE; AP; APA; ATP (1953 ed.); CABA; CBV; CMoP; CoAnAm; CoBMV; ExPo; ILP; InPo; LiTA; LiTM; ML; MoAB; MoAmPo (1950 ed.); NePA; NP; OxBA; PoAn; PoIE; PoPo; PoSa; PP; ReMP; SeCeV; StP; TreFT; TwAmPo; ViBoPo (1958 ed.)

Poetry (continued)
"I too dislike it," *sel.* NAMP
Poetry. Eric Priestley. WSL
Poetry. William Soutar. HaMV
Poetry,/ you are an electric. Poem to Poetry. William Knott. YAP
Poetry, almost blind like a camera. Imaginary Elegies, I-IV. Jack Spicer. NeAP
Poetry and Learning. George Chapman. *Fr.* The Epistle Dedicatory to Chapman's Translation of the Iliad. OBS
("Princes statue, A, or in marble carv'd.") AtBAP
Poetry and Philosophy. Thomas Randolph. *Fr.* An Eclogue to Mr. Johnson. OBS
Poetry and Science. W. J. Turner. SeCePo
Poetry and Thoughts on Same. Franklin P. Adams. HBMV
Poetry Defined. John Holmes. PP
Poetry drives its lines into her forehead. A Young Highland Girl Studying Poetry. Iain Crichton Smith. NePoEA-2; PP
Poetry, Emily. Brief History. Olga Hampel Briggs. GoYe
Poetry for Supper. R. S. Thomas. POTi; ToPo
Poetry Is a Destructive Force. Wallace Stevens. OxBA
Poetry is a projection across silence. Ten Definitions of Poetry. Carl Sandburg. MAP; MoAmPo
Poetry Is Death Cast Out. Sydney Clouts. PeSA
Poetry Is Happiness. Wrey Gardiner. NeBP
Poetry is no uneasy refuge, stilly centred. No Uneasy Refuge. Blanaid Salkeld. AnIV
Poetry is the supreme fiction, madame. A High-toned Old Christian Woman. Wallace Stevens. AP; CBV, CMoP; CoBMV; MoVE; PoeP; PoFS
Poetry of a Root Crop, The. Charles Kingsley. LoBV
Poetry of Departures. Philip Larkin. CMoP; NePoEA; NMP; PoeP; ToPo; TwCP
Poetry of Dress, The. Robert Herrick. *See* Delight in Disorder *and* Upon Julia's Clothes.
Poetry of Dress, The. *Unknown.* *See* My Love in Her Attire.
Poetry of Earth Is Never Dead, The. Keats. *See* On the Grasshopper and Cricket.
Poetry of England, The. Samuel Daniel. *See* English Poetry.
Poetry of tragedy is never dead, The. Am I My Neighbor's Keeper? Richard Eberhart. PoAn; ToPo
Poetry; Satire and Pulpit. William Cowper. *See* Poetic Pains.
Poetry's a gift wherein but few excell. Nathaniel Ward. SCAP
Poets. Mark Akenside. *Fr.* The Pleasures of Imagination, IV. OBEC
Poets, The. Elizabeth Barrett Browning. *Fr.* Aurora Leigh, I. VA
Poets. Hortense Flexner. HBMV
Poets, The. Robert Graves. MoPW
Poets, The. Leigh Hunt. *See* Dearest Poets, The.
Poets. Joyce Kilmer. AnAmPo; NP; WGRP
Poets, The. Scudder Middleton. HBMV
Poets, The. Arthur O'Shaughnessy. *See* Ode: "We are the music-makers."
Poets, The. David Wevill. PP
"Poet's age is sad, The; for why?" Prologue to "Asolando." Robert Browning. PoVP; ViPo; ViPP
Poets Agree to Be Quiet by the Swamp, The. David Wagoner. CoAP
Poets and Linnets. Tom Hood. CenHV; HBV
Poets and Their Bibliographies. Tennyson. PP
Poets are singing the whole world over. Rus in Urbe. Clement Scott. HBV; VA
Poets at Tea, The. Barry Pain. BOHV; HBV; Par
(Macaulay at Tea.) CenHV
Oh! Weary Mother, *sel.* NA
Poet's Bread. Sister Mary Philip. GoBC
Poet's Call, The. Thomas Curtis Clark. WGRP
Poet's cat, sedate and grave, A. The Retired Cat. William Cowper. BOHV; CIV; OTPC (1923 ed.) *sl. abr.*
Poet's Credo. Byron. *See* Poetical Commandments.
Poet's daily chore, The. Lens. Anne Wilkinson. MoCV; OBCV; PeCV
Poet's Dream, The. William Dunbar. *Fr.* The Golden Targe. PoEL-1
Poet's Dream, The. Shelley. *Fr.* Prometheus Unbound, I. GTBS; GTBS-D; GTBS-P; GTBS-W; GTSE; GTSL
("On a poet's lips I slept.") AnFE; AtBAP; ChER; ELP; FiP; PoG; ShBV-3; ViBoPo
Poets Easily Consoled. Christopher Morley. LHV
Poet's Epitaph, A. Ebenezer Elliott. VA
Poet's Epitaph, A. Wordsworth. EnRP; MBW-2; OBRV; PeER; UnPo (1st ed.)
Poet's eye obscenely seeing, The. Lawrence Ferlinghetti. *Fr.* A Coney Island of the Mind. LiTM (1970 ed.)
Poet's Eye-View, A. Anne Wilkinson. TwCaPo
Poet's Fate, The. Thomas Hood. ELU; FiBHP; PV
Poet's faults, A: some are his own. The Motives of Rhythm. Robert Conquest. PP
Poet's Grace, A. Burns. TrPWD
Poet's Guilt, The. Arthur Pfister. WSL
Poet's Harvesting, The. Charles J. O'Malley. CAW
Poets have muddied all the little fountains, The. Abla. Antara. *Fr.* The Mu'allaqát. AWP; JAWP; LiTW; WBP
Poets henceforth for pensions need not care. A Comfort for Poor Poets. Sir John Harington. SiCE
Poets Hitchhiking on the Highway. Gregory Corso. NeAP
Poet's Hope, A. William Ellery Channing. AmePo
"Lady, there is a hope that all men have," *sel.* AA; AnAmPo
Poet's imageries are noble ways, The. Courts, The. Alice Meynell. BoPe; MemP
Poets in Africa. Roy Campbell. ACV
Poets in Time of War. Bertram Warr. CaP
Poet's Journal, The, *sel.* Bayard Taylor.
"God, to whom we look up blindly." TrPWD
Poets light but lamps, The. Emily Dickinson. AmePo; ML; PP
Poets, like disputants, when reasons fail. Epilogue. Dryden. *Fr.* All for Love. DiPo
Poets like shepherds on green hills. The Shepherds. Beren Van Slyke. GoYe
Poets loiter all their leisure. The Hour Glass. Edward Quillinan. OBRV
Poets Lose Half the Praise. Edmund Waller. PP
Poet's Lot, The. Oliver Wendell Holmes. PoEL-5
Poets Love Nature. John Clare. CBEP; ERoP-2
Poets make pets of pretty, docile words. Pretty Words. Elinor Wylie. HBMV; RePo; YaD; YT
Poets may boast (as safely-vain). Of English Verse. Edmund Waller. AnAnS-2; CavP; EiCL; OBS; PP; SCEP-2; SeCP
Poets may sing of their Helicon streams. The Federal Constitution. William Milns. PAH
Poet's Mind, The. Tennyson. ViPP
"Vex not thou the poet's mind," *sel.* PoG
Poets of Hell, The. Karl Shapiro. NYBP
Poets of Peace and Gladness, The. Sister Mary Norbert Körte. ThO
Poets' Paradise, The. Michael Drayton. *See* Description of Elysium, The.
Poet's Prayer. Adelaide Love. TrPWD
Poet's Prayer, The. Stephen Phillips. WGRP
Poet's Progress, A. Michael Hamburger. NePoEA; PP
Poet's Protest. Doris Hedges. CaP
Poet's Proverb, A. Arthur Guiterman. MaRV
Poet's Reflection, The. Tony Connor. CBV
Poet's Resurrection. Dryden. *Fr.* Ode to the Pious Memory of . . . Mrs. Anne Killigrew. WHA
Poet's Secret, The. Elizabeth Stoddard. AA
Poet's Shield, The. Archilochus, *tr. fr. Greek by* Sir William Marris. LiTW
Poet's Simple Faith, The. Victor Hugo, *tr. fr. French by* Edward Dowden. OQP; TRV; WGRP
(Where Goest Thou?) MaRV
Poet's Song, The. Tennyson. ELP; FiP; GBV (1952 ed.); PoVP; TOP
Poet's Song to His Wife, The. "Barry Cornwall." HBV; VA
Poet's soul has sung its way to God, A. The Dead Singer. Mary Ashley Townsend. AA
Poets survive in fame. Lector Aere Perennior. J. V. Cunningham. QFR
Poet's Thought, A. "Barry Cornwall." VA
Poet's thoughts are of the skies, The. Poet and Peasant. R. H. Long. PoAu-1
Poets to Come. Walt Whitman. AmePo; AnAmPo; CoBA; LiTA; PoPo; TrGrPo; YaD
Poet's Use, The. Pope. *Fr.* The First Epistle of the Second Book of Horace. OBEC
Poet's Voice, The. Blake. *See* Hear the Voice of the Bard.

Poet's Vow, The, *sel.* Elizabeth Barrett Browning.
Rosalind's Scroll. HBV; OBEV (1st ed.)
Poet's Welcome, The. Edward Richard, *tr. fr. Welsh by* Evan Evans. *Fr.* Pastoral Poem. PrWP
Poet's Welcome to His Love-begotten Daughter, A. Burns. LiTB; OxBoLi; PoEL-4; SiTL; ViBoPo
(Poet's Welcome to His Illegitimate Child, The.) BoC
Poets, who in time of war. Poets in Time of War. Bertram Warr. CaP
Poet's Wish, The; an Ode. Allan Ramsay. CEP; EiPP; OBEC
Poet's words are winged with fire, The. The Poet. Joel Benton. WGRP
Poets yeggs and thirsties. E. E. Cummings. *Fr.* Is 5. AnAmPo
Poets, your subjects, have their parts assigned. Prologue to the University of Oxford, 1674. Dryden. BWP
Poietes Apoietes. Hartley Coleridge. OBNC
Poinsettia petal drops, A. The rain pastes twisted flowing drapery. Family Reunion. Hollis Summers. GoYe
Point beheld I, that was raying out, A. The Primal Cause. Dante. *Fr.* Divina Commedia: Paradiso. CAW
Point is turned, The; the twilight shadow fills. Between the Rapids. Archibald Lampman. VA
Point of No Return. Mari Evans. NNP
Point of Noon, The. Christopher Brennan. MoAuPo
Point of one white star is quivering still, The. Morning. Shelley. *Fr.* Prometheus Unbound. ShBV-3
Point Shirley. Sylvia Plath. NoP
Point, the Line, the Surface and Sphere, The. Claude Bragdon. *Fr.* The Beautiful Necessity. ImOP
Point where beauty and intelligence meet, The. Sonnet. Gavin Ewart. WaP
Pointed Boots. Christopher Middleton. *Fr.* Herman Moon's Hourbook. NePoEA-2
Pointed houses lean so you would swear, The. Amsterdam. Francis Jammes. AWP; FaPON; JAWP; WBP
Pointed People, The. Rachel Field. FaPON
Pointillism. Joseph Bennett. SiTL
Pointless Pride of Man, The. *Unknown.* MeEL
Points of View. Amy Lowell. LOW
Poised between going on and back, pulled. The Base Stealer. Robert Francis. GoJo; SD
Poised, relaxed, as a cat that waits. Boxer. Joseph P. Clancy. SD
Poised to plunge beneath the waves of sleep. Plain-Song. Jean Cocteau. LiTW
Poison Ivy! Katharine Gallagher. SiSoSe
Poison Meat. Tom Veitch. ANYP
Poison of insult and the bile of torment, The. Freedom. Georgi Efimovich Nechayev. PoFr
Poison Tree, A. Blake. *Fr.* Songs of Experience. AnFE; AWP; BoLiVe; BWP; CABA; CaFP; CBEP; CBV; DiPo; EiCL; EnL; EnLi-2; EnLit; EnRP; ERoP-1; FaFP; HoPM; InPo; JAWP; LiTB; LiTG; MaPo; NoP; OAEP; OtMeF; PoAn; PoEL-4; PoeP; PoFS; PoMS; SiSw; TOP; TreFS; TrGrPo; VaPo; WBP
("I was angry with my friend.") EG; GTBS-W
Poisoned, by our own lips! That exchange of eloquences. The Technique of Power. Jascha Kessler. AmPC
Poisoned Lands. John Montague. NMP
Poisoned Man, The. James Dickey. ToPo
Poker Jim, *with music. Unknown.* SGR
Poland, France, Judea ran in her veins. An Electric Sign Goes Dark. Carl Sandburg. HBMV
Poland, October. Charles Brasch. *Fr.* Nineteen Thirty-nine. AnNZ
Polar DEW has just warned that, The. Your Attention Please. Peter Porter. HYE
Polar Exploration. Stephen Spender. ChMP; MoAB; MoPo
(North, The.) FaBoMo
Polar Quest, The. Richard Burton. AA
Pole Star for This Year. Archibald MacLeish. AmPP; NAMP; NePA; OxBA
(Pole Star.) AP; CoBMV
Pole, the Bear, and Cassiopeia, The. Night Piece. A. E. Coppard. POTE
Pole Vault. Shiro Murano, *tr. fr. Japanese by* Satoru Sato *and* Constance Urdang. SD
Polemic. Anthony Ostroff. NYTB
'Poleon Dore. William Henry Drummond. BBV (1923 ed.)
Poles are flying where the two eyes set, The. Discoveries. Vernon Watkins. LiTM; PoIE; WaP
Poles rode out from Warsaw against the German, The. The Abnormal Is Not Courage. Jack Gilbert. CoAP
Policeman, The. Marjorie Seymour Watts. PCH; TiPo
Policeman buys shoes slow and careful, The. Psalm of Those Who Go Forth before Daylight. Carl Sandburg. AnAmPo; FIW; MoShBr; OxBA; StVeCh
Policeman, policeman, don't take me. I Stole Brass. *Unknown.* ChTr
Policeman walks with heavy tread, The. Action Rhyme. E. M. Adams. BoTP
Policeman's Lot, The. W. S. Gilbert. *Fr.* The Pirates of Penzance. ALV; NeHB; PoVP; TreFT; TrGrPo
Policy. Carolyn Wells. WhC
Polifemo y Galatea. Luis de Góngora. *See* Polyphemus and Galatea.
Polish National Hymn, *abr.* Aloizy Felsinki, *tr. fr. Polish by* Paul Soboleski. PoFr
Polish Rider, The. Derek Walcott. ToPo
Polish superintendent snores behind the wall, The. Neighbor. Edgar Paiewonsky. QAH
Polite Song. Theodore Spencer. CLwM
Politeness. A. A. Milne. PoPl
Politeness. Elizabeth Turner. HBV; HBVY
Politeness. *Unknown. See* Hearts, like Doors.
Politest musician that ever was seen, The. The Music of the Future. Oliver Herford. CenHV; MuSP; PoMa
Politic Peter meets his friend ashore. Samuel Rowlands. SiCE
Political Chaos in Italy. Dante, *tr. fr. Italian by* Longfellow. *Fr.* Divina Commedia: Purgatorio, VI. WoL
Political Greatness. Shelley. EnRP; EPN
Political Meeting. A. M. Klein. MoCV; OBCV
Political Poem. LeRoi Jones. CoAP
Political Reflection. Howard Nemerov. ELU
Politician, A. E. E. Cummings. LiTM
(Politician Is an Arse Upon, A.) SiTL
Politics. Emerson. AmePo; MWA-1
Politics. Tennyson. CoBE; PoRL
Politics. W. B. Yeats. CMoP; PoPo; POTE; StP
Politics of Rich Painters, The. LeRoi Jones. CoPo
Polka Lyric, A. Gilbert Abbott à Beckett. *See* Holiday Task, A.
Poll Tax (1378). Maurice Hewlett. *Fr.* The Song of the Plow. PoFr
Polly, *sel.* John Gay.
"Sleep, O sleep," Air XXIII. ViBoPo
(Song.) FaBoEn
Polly. William Brighty Rands. GoTP; OTPC (1923 ed.); PRWS; VA
Polly, Dolly, Kate and Molly. *Unknown.* BBGG
Polly, from me, though now a love-sick youth. To a Young Lady. Richard Savage. CBEP; OBEC
Polly Oliver's Rambles, *with music. Unknown.* ViBoFo
Polly Pansy. William Brighty Rands. SAS
Polly Peachum. Henry Carey. WaPE
Polly, Peg, and Poppety. Kate Greenaway. SAS
Polly Perkins. *Unknown.* BoLP; DTC; ELP; OxBoLi
Polly Picklenose ("Polly, Polly, goodness gracious"). Leroy F. Jackson. BBGG
Polly, put the kettle on. Mother Goose. BrR; OTPC; OxNR; PCH; SAS; StVeCh (1940 ed.)
Polly Williams, *with music. Unknown.* ABF
Polly Wolly Doodle. *Unknown.* TreF; YaD
Polly's Peg's and Poppety's. Polly, Peg, and Poppety. Kate Greenaway. SAS
Polo Grounds. Rolfe Humphries. HoPM; SD
Polo Match. Sunday, 2 P.M. Josephine Miles. FiMAP
Polo Player. Daniel Whitehead Hicky. MoSiPe
Polonius. Walter de la Mare. AtBAP
Polonius' Advice to Laertes. Shakespeare. *Fr.* Hamlet, I, iii. BBV; OQP; PoPl
("And these few precepts in thy memory.") MasP
(Be True, 3 *ll.*) PCD; PCH
(Polonius' Advice to His Son.) MaRV; TreF
(Polonius to Laertes.) GN
("There, my blessing with you!") OTD
(This above All.) TrGrPo
("This above all: to thine own self be true.") TRV
(To Thine Own Self Be True.) FaFP; LiTB; LiTG
Polonius and the Ballad-Singers. Padraic Colum. NP
Polonius to Laertes. Shakespeare. *See* Polonius' Advice to Laertes.

Polwart on the Green. Allan Ramsay. CEP; EiCL
Polycrates, whose passing hap caus'd him to lose his fate. Of Fortune's Power. Richard Edwards. ReIE
Polyhymnia, *sel.* George Peele.
His Golden Locks Time Hath to Silver Turned. AtBAP; EIL; EnRePo; LoBV; NoP; PoE; PoIE; PoSa; ReEn; ReIE; TuPP; ViBoPo; WHA
(Farewell to Arms, A.) AnFE; BoC; CoBE; EG; EnLi-1; HBV; MemP; OBEV; PoRA
(Old Knight, The.) CBEP; ChTr; OBSC; TrGrPo
(Sonnet, A: "His golden locks time hath to silver turn'd.") ELP; FaBoEn; PoEL-2; SiCE
Polyolbion, *sels.* Michael Drayton.
"Away yee barb'rous woods," *fr.* Third Song. OBS
Birds in the Fens, *fr.* Five and Twentieth Song. ChTr
"Earle Bouglasse for this day," *fr.* Two and Twentieth Song. OBS
English Musical Instruments, *fr.* Fourth Song. MuSP
Fools Gaze at Painted Courts, *fr.* Eighteenth Song. ChTr
Hawking, *fr.* Twentieth Song. SD
"Mongst whom, some there were bards, that in their sacred rage," *fr.* Fourth Song. PrWP
"Now are the Tritons heard, to loving-land to call," *fr.* Twentieth Song. AtBAP
"Of Albion's glorious ile the wonders whilst I write," *fr.* First Song. ReIE
Thirteenth Song, The, *abr.* ReEn
Sels.
Forest of Arden, The ("My native Country then, which so brave spirits hast bred"). SeEP
"Forest so much fallen from what she was before, The." SeCePo
"Of all the beasts." OBS
"Upon the midlands now th' industrious muse doth fall." ReIE; TuPP
"When Phoebus lifts his head." OBS
"To these, the gentle South," *fr.* Second Song. OBS
"World of mightie kings, A," *fr.* Twentieth Song. OBS
Wrestlers, *fr.* First Song. SD
Polyphemus and Galatea, *sel.* Luis de Góngora, *tr. fr. Spanish by* Frances Fletcher.
Love Song of Polyphemus, The. LiTW
Polyphiloprogenitive. Mr. Eliot's Sunday Morning Service. T. S. Eliot. MaPo; PoFS
Polyphonic symphony of napalm bombs, A. Musical Vietnams. Bob Allen. WOW
Pome. For Weird. Hearts. & All You Mothers. Ahmed Legraham Alhamisi. BF
Pomegranate, The. Louis Dudek. OBCV; PeCV
Pomegranate Circus, The. Richard Brautigan. FRC
Pomegranates. Roy Campbell. AtBAP
Pomegrantes. Paul Valéry, *tr. fr. French by* Herman Salinger. LiTW
Pomegranates come from red hot pearls. Fruits of Experience. James Broughton. SiTL
Pomona. William Morris. WiR
Pomp of the Persian I hold in aversion, The. Persicos Odi. Franklin P. Adams. HBMV
Pompadour, The. George Walter Thornbury. BeLS
Pompeius, best of all my comrades, you and I. Returned Warrior. Horace. *Fr.* Odes. LiTW; WaaP
Pompey and Cornelia. Lucan, *tr. fr. Latin by* Nicholas Rowe. *Fr.* Pharsalia, V. OBEC
Pompilia. Robert Browning. The Ring and the Book, VII. MaVP; MBW-2; OAEP; PoVP; ViPo; ViPP
Ponce de Leon. Edith M. Thomas. OTD; PAH
Pond, The. W. H. Davies. ChMP
Pond, The. Howard Nemerov. FiMAP
Pond, The. Jane Taylor. OTPC (1923 ed.)
Pond, The. Anthony Thwaite. NYBP
Pond, The. James Whaler. *Fr.* Runaway. MAP; MoAmPo (1942 ed.)
Ponder, Darling, These Busted Statues. E. E. Cummings. CMoP; SeCeV (1967 ed.); SiTL
Ponder the words, O Lord, that I do say. Psalm V. *Paraphrased by* Sir Philip Sidney. FCP
Ponder thy cares, and sum them all in one. Sonnet. Sir David Murray. *Fr.* Caelia. EIL
Ponder, ye Just, the scoffs that frequent go. Prophets Who Cannot Sing. Coventry Patmore. CoBE; PoVP
Pondy Woods. Robert Penn Warren. MAP; MoAmPo
Ponies, The. W. W. Gibson. WaKn
Ponjoo. Walter de la Mare. ShM
Ponsonby Perks. Laura E. Richards. Nonsense Verses, II. RIS
Pont du Carrousel. Rainer Maria Rilke, *tr. fr. German by* Jessie Lemont. OnPM
Pontius Pilate, *sel.* Thomas Durley Landels.
Pilate Remembers. MaRV
Pontoon Bridge Miracle, The. Vachel Lindsay. *Fr.* Every Soul Is a Circus, IV. LiTM (rev. ed.); LoBV; NePA
Pontoosuce. Herman Melville. MAmP
Pony, The. Rachel MacAndrew. BoTP
Pony Express, The. Dorothy Brown Thompson. AmFN
Pony Rock. Archibald MacLeish. CMoP
Pooh! Walter de la Mare. FiBHP
Pooh—men! Baby. Florence Kiper Frank. HBMV
Pool, The. Fritz S. Burnell. BoAu
Pool, The. Alice Corbin. NP
Pool, The. Robert Creeley. CoAP
Pool, The. Hilda Doolittle ("H. D"). CMoP; ExPo; NP
Pool, The. Leah Bodine Drake. FiSC
Pool, The. E. L. Mayo. MiAP
Pool. Carl Sandburg. AP
Pool, A. Thomas Whitbread. NYBP
Pool in a garden green, A. The Other Side of the Sky. W. Graham Robertson. PPL
Pool Players, Seven at the Golden Shovel. Gwendolyn Brooks. *See* We Real Cool.
Poor, The. William Langland. *See* Sufferings of the Poor, The.
Poor, The. Carl Sandburg. NP
Poor, The. Speer Strahan. CAW; JKCP
Poor, The. Emile Verhaeren, *tr. fr. French by* Ludwig Lewisohn. AWP; JAWP; WBP; WoL
Poor, The. William Carlos Williams. MoAB; MoAmPo; NeMA; NoP
Poor, and the dazed, and the idiots, The. Hurrying Away from the Earth. Robert Bly. NaP; WOW
Poor and Wealthy Children. Edward L. Crane. SoP
Poor Balzac, relegated to a back room. Balzac. Darcy Gottlieb. NYTB
Poor benighted Hindoo, The. Limerick. Cosmo Monkhouse. HBV; PCD; TWS
Poor Bird. Walter de la Mare. FlW
Poor bird! I do not envy thee. The Robin. George Daniel. UnPo (1st ed.)
Poor Boy. *Unknown.* *See* Coon Can.
Poor Brother. *Unknown.* NA
Poor but Honest. *Unknown.* LiTG; OtMeF; OxBoLi
(It's the Same the Whole World Over.) UnTE
(She Was Poor but She Was Honest.) ErPo; FiBHP; SiTL
Poor Can Feed the Birds, The. John Shaw Neilson. PoAu-1
Poor Celia once was very fair. The Advice. Thomas Flatman. CavP
Poor Children. Victor Hugo, *tr. fr. French by* Swinburne. AWP; JAWP; WBP
(Children of the Poor, The.) LiTW
Poor Creature! nay, I'll not say poor. To a Moth. Charles Edward Thomas. AA
Poor Dad he got five years or more as everybody knows. *Unknown.* FOL
Poor Dear Grandpapa. D'Arcy W. Thompson. BOHV; NA
Poor degenerate from the ape, A. The First Philosopher's Song. Aldous Huxley. AWP; HBMV; InPo; JAWP; WPB
Poor Dick! though first thy airs provoke. Dick Hairbrain Learns the Social Graces. John Trumbull. *Fr.* The Progress of Dulness. AmPP (5th ed.)
Poor Diggings. Mart Taylor. SGR
Poor Doctor Blow went out of church. Queen Anne's Musicians. Thomas Hennell. FaBoTw
Poor Dog Bright. *Unknown.* SAS
Poor Ed Sanders: no sooner had he gotten in good. William Harmon. *Fr.* Treasury Holiday. QAH
Poor Estate, The. Robert Greene. *See* Sweet Are the Thoughts That Savor of Content.
Poor Estate to Be Holden for Best, The. *Unknown, at. to* Edward Seymour, Duke of Somerset. SiCE; TuPP
(On Edward Seymour, Duke of Somerset.) OBSC
Poor Fool. Evan V. Shute. CaP
Poor for Our Sakes. Mary Brainerd Smith. BLRP

Poor French Sailor's Scottish Sweetheart, A. William Johnson Cory. VA
Poor Fritz, poor Fritzchen, Frédéric Chopin. Chopin in London. Philip Hobsbaum. *Fr.* Study in a Minor Key. MuSP
Poor Girl. Stephen Spender. FaBoMo
("Poor girl, inhabitant of a strange land.") GTBS-D
Poor Girl's Meditation, The. *Unknown, tr. fr. Irish by* Padraic Colum. OBMV
Poor Grandpa. R. C. O'Brien. ShM
Poor have childher and to spare, The. Quantity and Quality. Winifred M. Letts. HBMV
Poor have little, The. Enough Not One. Benjamin Franklin. TRV
Poor heart, lament. The Method. George Herbert. MaMe
Poor Henry. Walter de la Mare. HBMV
Poor human race that must. So to Fatness Come. Stevie Smith. PoG
Poor humble roach. To a Humble Bug. Linda Lyon Van Voorhis. GoYe
Poor I saw at the cloister gate, The. The Poor. Speer Strahan. CAW; JKCP
Poor in Church, The. Arthur Rimbaud, *tr. fr. French by* Gerard Previn Meyer. LiTW
Poor in my youth, and in life's later scenes. Riches. *Unknown.* AWP
Poor in wit or judgment, like all poor, The. The Envious Critick. William Wycherley. PeRV; PV
Poor Is the Life That Misses. *Unknown.* EIL; UnTE
Poor Jack. Charles Dibdin. BeLS; HBV
Poor Jane Higgins. A Pig Tale. James Reeves. SoPo
Poor Johnny was bended well-nigh double. Apple-Seed John. Lydia Maria Child. DD; OHIP; OTPC
Poor Kid. William Cole. PV
Poor Kings. W. H. Davies. HBV
Poor Kit hath lost her key. Kit Hath Lost Her Key. *Unknown.* UnTE
Poor Kitty Popcorn, *with music.* *Unknown.* AS
Poor lad once and a lad so trim, A. Jean Richepin's Song. Herbert Trench. LiTG; LiTM (rev. ed.); OBMV; OxBI; POTE
Poor Lady Dumpling. *Unknown.* FTB
Poor Lil' Brack Sheep. Ethel M. C. Brazelton. BLPA
Poor little bee, The. Ke-ni-ga Song. *Tr. by* Natalie Barnes. MPB
Poor little daws, hungry little daws. Daw's Dinner. Joyce Kilmer. CAW
Poor little foal of an oppressèd race! To a Young Ass. Samuel Taylor Coleridge. EnRP; MBW-2; OBEC
Poor little Lucy. The Lost Shoe. Walter de la Mare. BoChLi (1939 ed.); BrR; TSW
Poor little Nellie is weeping tonight. Why Did They Dig Ma's Grave So Deep? George Cooper. TreFS
Poor little, pretty, fluttering thing. To His Soul [*or* Adriani Morientis ad Animam Suam]. Emperor Hadrian, *tr. by* Matthew Prior. CEP; InP; SeCL
Poor little Willie. Little Willie. Gerald Massey. PaPo
Poor lone Hannah. Hannah Binding Shoes. Lucy Larcom. GN; HBV
Poor lonely willow tree. The Brook and the Willow Tree. *Unknown.* GFA
Poor Lonesome Cowboy. *Unknown.* ABF; AS; CoSo, *with music*; TiPo
Poor Lucy Lake was overgrown. Lucy Lake. Newton Mackintosh. BOHV; HBV
Poor mad Poll, pretty Poll. Mad Poll. J. Corson Miller. JKCP (1955 ed.)
Poor man went to hang himself, A. One Good Turn Deserves Another. *Unknown.* ShM
Poor man went to the rich man's doors, The. Precedent. Paul Laurence Dunbar. AmePo
Poor Man's Daily Bread, The. Denis A. McCarthy. JKCP
Poor Man's Pig, The. Edmund Blunden. MoBrPo
Poor man's sins are glaring, The. Rich and Poor; or, Saint and Sinner. Thomas Love Peacock. SiTL
Poor Martha Snell, she's gone away. On Martha Snell. *Unknown.* GoTP; WhC
Poor Matthias. Matthew Arnold. PoEL-5
("Poor Matthias! Wouldst thou have.") CIV
Poor Me. *Unknown, tr. fr. French by* Richard Beaumont. ErPo
Poor men's God that gives them sleep, The. Overseer of the Poor. James Hayford. NePoAm-2
Poor Mortals. Sir Robert Howard *and* John Dryden. *Fr.* The Indian Queen. PoIE
(Song of Aerial Spirits.) AtBAP
Poor Naked Wretches. Shakespeare. *See* Take Physic Pomp.
Poor of the Borough, The: Peter Grimes. George Crabbe. *See* Peter Grimes.
Poor of the Borough, The; the Parish-Clerk. George Crabbe. *Fr.* The Borough, Letter XIX. EiCL
Poor Old Cannon, The. Elinor Wylie. LHV
Poor Old Horse. David Holbrook. NePoEA-2
Poor Old Horse. *Unknown.* CH
Poor old Jonathan Bing. Jonathan Bing. Beatrice Curtis Brown. FaPON; GaP; OnMSP; PCD; PDV; RIS; SoPo; TiPo
Poor old king with sorrow for my crown, A. Lear. Thomas Hood. VA
Poor Old Lady. *Unknown.* GoTP; SoPo
Poor old lady, set her aside. The Old Mother. *Unknown.* PoToHe
Poor old lady, she swallowed a fly. Poor Old Lady. *Unknown.* GoTP; SoPo
Poor Old Man, The. J. C. Squire. HBMV
(How They Do It.) InMe
Poor Old Man, *with music.* *Unknown.* ShS; SoAmSa
Poor Old Pilgrim Misery. Thomas Lovell Beddoes. *Fr.* The Bride's Tragedy. EnRP
(Hesperus Sings.) VA
Poor old Robinson Crusoe! Mother Goose. BoTP; OTPC; OxNR; RIS
Poor old widow in her weeds, A. A Widow's Weeds. Walter de la Mare. AtBAP; FaBV
Poor old woman, A/ Four score and a day. Mickleham Way. Ivy O. Eastwick. BrR
Poor Omie Wise. *Unknown.* *See* Naomi Wise.
Poor Paddy Works on the Railway. *Unknown.* *See* Paddy Works on the Railway.
Poor painters oft with silly poets join. Cupid. Sir Philip Sidney. *Fr.* Arcadia. SiPS
Poor Parson, The. Chaucer. *See* Good Parson, The.
Poor Poet-Ape, that would be thought our chief. On Poet-Ape. Ben Jonson. Sonn
Poor Poll. Robert Bridges. MoPo; OxBoLi
Poor, Poor Country, The. John Shaw Neilson. NeLNL
Poor pussy-cat mew. Mother Goose. *See* Pussy-cat Mew. . .
Poor Relation, A. Audrey McGaffin. NePoAm-2
Poor Relation, The. E. A. Robinson. AnAmPo; MAPA; PoIE
Poor Reuben Ranzo. Arthur H. Clark. IHA
Poor Richard's Almanac, *sels.* Benjamin Franklin.
Poor Richard's Wisdom. GoTP
Well-packed Wisdom. StaSt
Poor Scholar, The. Abraham ibn Chasdai, *tr. fr. Hebrew by* Joseph Chotzner. TrJP
Poor Scholar of the 'Forties, A. Padraic Colum. AnIL; OxBI
Poor Scholar to Mice, A. *Unknown, tr. fr. Greek by* Lord Neaves. OnPM
Poor slaves, how terrible this Death is to them! George Chapman. *Fr.* Caesar and Pompey. ViBoPo
Poor Snail, The. J. M. Westrup. BoTP
Poor Son of Mary, The. Spanish Lullaby. *Unknown, ad. by* Louis Untermeyer. RIS
Poor Soul. Shakespeare. *See* Sonnets, CXLVI.
Poor soul! God's goodness hath been great to thee. Gratitude. Shakespeare. King Henry VI, Pt. II, *fr.* II, i. MaRV
Poor soul sat sighing by a sycamore tree, The. Desdemona's Song. Shakespeare. *Fr.* Othello, IV, iii. LoBV
Poor [*or* Poore] soul sat sighing by a sycamore tree, The: Sing [*or* O] willow, willow, willow. The Complaint of a Lover Forsaken of His Love [*or* The Green Willow]. *Unknown.* CoMu; OBSC
Poor soul, the centre [*or* center] of my sinful earth. Sonnets, CXLVI [*or* Soul and Body *or* The Death of Death]. Shakespeare. AtBAP; ATP; AWP; BEL; BoLiVe; BWP; CABA; CaFP; CAW; CBEP; CBV; CoBE; DiPo; EaLo; EIL; EnL; EnLi-1; EnRePo; ExPo; FaBoEn; ForPo; GoBC; GTBS; GTBS-D; GTBS-P; GTBS-W; GTSE; GTSL; HBV; InPo; JAWP; LiTB; LiTG; LO; MaPo; MaRV; MasP; MemP; MyFE; NoP; OBEV; OBSC; OxBoCh; PAn; PIA; PoAn; PoEL-2; PoeP; PoIE; ReEn; ReIE; SeCeV; SiCE; Sonn; StP; TOP;

Poor (continued)
TreFS; TrGrPo; UnPo (1st ed.); ViBoPo; WBP; WHA
Poor South! Her books get fewer and fewer. J. Gordon Coogler. FiBHP
Poor tired Tim! It's sad for him. Tired Tim. Walter de la Mare. ALV; BoTP; FaPON; GaP; MoShBr; MPB; OnPP; SoPo; TiPo; TSW
Poor Tom, or the Sailor's Epitaph. Charles Dibdin. *See* Tom Bowling.
Poor Uncle Joe. Sartorial Solecism. R. E. C. Stringer. FiBHP
Poor vaunting earth, gloss'd with uncertain pride. George Alsop. SCAP
Poor Voter on Election Day, The. Whittier. OTD; PAL; PoRL
"Poor wanderer," said the leaden sky. The Subalterns. Thomas Hardy. CMoP; MaPo; MoAB; MoBrPo; TDP
Poor Wat. Shakespeare. *Fr.* Venus and Adonis. OBSC; UnPo (1st ed.)
Poor wayfaring man of grief, A. The Stranger and His Friend. James Montgomery. SoP
Poor Wayfaring Stranger, *with music.* *Unknown.* BFSS; TrAS
(Over Jordan, *with Music.*) OuSiCo
Poor wayworn creature! Oh, sorely harried deer. Feud. Lew Sarett. AnAmPo; MAP
Poor who begs with bated breath, The. The Price of Begging. Emmanuel ben David Frances. TrJP
Poor Widow's Cock, The. Chaucer. *Fr.* The Canterbury Tales: The Nun's Priest's Tale. MyFE
Poor Withered Rose. Robert Bridges. VA
Poor Working Girl, The, *with music.* *Unknown.* AS
Poore bird! I doe not envie thee. The Robin. George Daniel. OBS
Poore Man Payes for All, The. *Unknown.* CoMu
Poore nation, whose sweet sap and juice. The Jews. George Herbert. MaMe
Poore pensive I o're chargde with woe. *At. to* Thomas Carew. SeCSL
Poore silly soul, whose hope and head lies low. Vanitie. George Herbert. MaMe
Poore soule, in this thy flesh what dost thou know? The Soules Ignorance in This Life and Knowledge in the Next. John Donne. *Fr.* Of the Progresse of the Soule. OBS
Poore soule sate sighing by a sicamore tree, A. *See* Poor soul sat sighing by a sycamore tree, The.
Poore things be those vowes we boast on. *Unknown.* SeCSL
Poore wench was sighing, and weeping amaine, A. The Bard. James Shirley. ErPo
Poore widwe somdeel stape in age, A. Nun's Priest's Tale, The. Chaucer. *Fr.* The Canterbury Tales. NoP
Pop bottles pop-bottles. Song of the Pop-Bottlers. Morris Bishop. FaPON; FiBHP
Pop Goes the Weasel, *diff. versions.* *Unknown.* RIS; SoPo; TreFT
Pop Goes the Weasel ("Up and down the City Road"). *Unknown.* *See* Up and down the City Road.
Popcorn. Phillip Hey. YAP
Pop-Corn Land. Elsie F. Kartack. GFA
Popcorn Man, The. Edith D. Osborne. GFA
Popcorn man, The,/ At the park. The Popcorn-Popper. Dorothy Walter Baruch. BrR
Popcorn Party, The. "E. R. B." GFA
Popcorn peanuts clams and gum. Bar-Room Matins. Louis MacNeice. EaLo; NYBP
Popcorn-Popper, The. Dorothy Walter Baruch. BrR
Pop Corn Song, A. Nancy Byrd Turner. FaPON; GFA; MPB
Pope, The. Robert Browning. The Ring and the Book, X. MBW-2; ViPo; ViPP
Pope, The. Charles Lever. *Fr.* Harry Lorrequer. BOHV
(Pope He Leads a Happy Life, The.) HBV
Pope and the Net, The. Robert Browning. BOHV
Pope at Twickenham. Charles Kent. VA
Pope He Leads a Happy Life, The. Charles Lever. *See* Pope, The.
Pope he is a happy man, The. Commanders of the Faithful. Thackeray. ALV
Popish Plot, The. Dryden. *Fr.* Absalom and Achitophel, Pt. I. ACP
Poplar, The. Richard Aldington. HBMV; NP
Poplar. Gottfried Benn, *tr. fr. German by* Christopher Middleton. PoPl
Poplar drops beside the way, The. In April. Elizabeth Akers Allen. OTPC (1946 ed.); PRWS
Poplar-Field, The. William Cowper. BWP; CBEP; CH; ChTr; EiPP; ELP; FiP; FlW; ForPo; GTBS; GTBS-D; GTBS-P; GTBS-W; GTSE; GTSL; HBV; ILP; InPo; OBEC; Po; PoEL-3; PoSa; RoGo; SeCeV; ShBV-1; TrGrPo; UnPo (3d ed.); WiR
Poplar is a lonely tree, The. Poplars. Edward Bliss Reed. DD; HBMV; HBVY; OHIP; PEDC
Poplar Tree. Padraic Colum. NePoAm
Poplars. Hilda Conkling. NP
Poplars, The. Theodosia Garrison. HBMV; OHIP; PoRL; StVeCh
Poplars. Helen Leuty. BoTP
Poplars. Edward Bliss Reed. DD; HBMV; HBVY; OHIP; PEDC
Poplars, The. Bernard Freeman Trotter. CaP
Poplars and the ancient elms, The. Theocritus. Sir Edmund Gosse. VA
Poplars are fell'd [*or* felled], farewell to the shade, The. The Poplar-Field. William Cowper. BWP; CBEP; CH; ChTr; EiPP; ELP; FiP; FlW; ForPo; GTBS; GTBS-D; GTBS-P; GTBS-W; GTSE; GTSL; HBV; ILP; InPo; OBEC; Po; PoEL-3; PoSa; RoGo; SeCeV; ShBV-1; TrGrPo; UnPo (3d ed.); WiR
Poplars are standing there still as death. Southern Mansions. Arna Bontemps. AmFN; AmNP; BALP; BANP; IDB; Kal; LiTM (1970 ed.); PoNe; TTY
Poplars bow forward and back, The. Poplars. Hilda Conkling. NP
Poplars in the fields of France, The. In France. Frances Cornford. HBMV
Poplar's Shadow, The. May Swenson. NYBP
Poppies. P. A. Ropes. BoTP
Poppies. *Unknown,* *tr. fr. Japanese by* William N. Porter. MPB
Poppies. Charles Weekes. OnYI
Poppies in July. Sylvia Plath. NaP
Poppies in the Garden, The. ffrida Wolfe. BoTP
(Poppies.) PCH
Poppies in the Wheat. Helen Hunt Jackson. AA; PFY
Poppies paramour the girls. Song. Haniel Long. HBMV
Poppy, The. Jane Taylor. OTPC; TVC
Poppy, The. Francis Thompson. MoBrPo; OBEV (1st ed.); PoVP
Poppy Grows upon the Shore, A. Robert Bridges. PoVP
Popular Ballad: "Never Forget Your Parents." Franklin P. Adams. BOHV
Popular heart is a cannon first, The. Emily Dickinson. MWA-2
Popular Rhymes. Blake. ThGo
Popular Song: "Methought I saw how wealthy men." *Unknown.* PoFr
Popular Songs of Tuscany. *Unknown,* *tr. fr. Italian by* John Addington Symonds.
"I see the dawn e'en now begin to peer." AWP
"I would I were a bird so free." AWP
"It was the morning of the first of May." AWP; JAWP; WBP
"On Sunday morning well I knew." AWP; OnPM
"Passing across the billowy sea." AWP; JAWP; WBP
(Giving a Heart.) OnPM
"Sleeping or waking, thou sweet face." AWP; JAWP; WBP
"Strew me with blossoms when I die." AWP; JAWP; WBP
"What time I see you passing by." AWP
Popularity. Robert Browning. PoVP; PP
Population Drifts. Carl Sandburg. OxBA
Porch, The. Philip Pain. SCAP
Porchlight coming on again, The. 1926. Weldon Kees. CoAP; NaP
Porcupine, The. Ogden Nash. MemP
Porcupine, The. Galway Kinnell. NaP
Porcus, that foul unsociable hog. In Porcum. John Heath. SiCE; TuPP
Porgy, Maria, and Bess. DuBose Heyward. PoNe
Poring on Caesar's death with earnest eye. Julius Caesar and the Honey-Bee. Charles Tennyson Turner. NBM; OA
Pornographic Poem. John Giorno. ANYP
Porous. William Carlos Williams. NYBP
Porphyria's Lover. Robert Browning. AtBAP; AWP; BeLS;

BoLiVe; CABA; GTBS; GTSE; GTSL; HBV; ILP; InPo; JAWP; MaPo; MaVP; MBW-2; MeWo; OAEP; OBEV; OuHeWo; PAn; PoVP; ShBV-4; TOP; TreFT; TrGrPo; ViPo; ViPP; VP; WBP
Porpoise. Guillaume Apollinaire, *tr. fr. French by* Lillian White Spencer. OnPM
Porpoise, The. Ogden Nash. RePo
Port, The. Bernadette Mayer. ANYP
Port after Stormie Seas. Spenser. *See* What if Some Little Paine the Passage Have.
Port Authority Terminal: 9 A.M. Monday. Chad Walsh. PPON
Port Bou. Stephen Spender. MoPo; TwCP
Port o' Heart's Desire, The. John S. McGroarty. HBV
Port of Embarkation. Randall Jarrell. MiAP
Port of Holy Peter. John Masefield. AtBAP; OBMV; POTE; ShBV-2
Port of Many Ships. John Masefield. OBMV
Portent. Richard Church. MoBrPo (1942 ed.)
Portent, The. Herman Melville. AmePo; AmPP; AP; CaFP; CBEP; ExPo; MAmP; MWA-1; NoP; OxBA; PoEL-5; PoFS; TDP; WiR
Portents, The. Lucan, *tr. fr. Latin by* Christopher Marlowe. *Fr.* Pharsalia, I. OBSC
Portents and Prodigies are [*or* have] grown so frequent. Wild Weather. Dryden. *Fr.* All for Love. AtBAP; BoW
Porter shouted, "Syracuse," The. Reveille. Hughes Mearns. *Fr.* Later Antigonishes. InMe; SiTL
Porter to th' infernall gate is Sin, The. Sin, Despair, and Lucifer. Phineas Fletcher. *Fr.* The Locusts, or Apollyonists. OBS
Portia. Oscar Wilde. BrPo
Portia's Plea for Mercy. Shakespeare. *See* Quality of Mercy, The.
Portico. Rubén Darío, *tr. fr. Spanish by* Thomas Walsh. CAW
Portion of this yew. Transformations. Thomas Hardy. PIA; PoIE
Portland County Jail, *with music.* *Unknown.* AS
"Portland" Going Out, The. W. S. Merwin. NYBP
Portly Roman Senator was sipping his Rock and Rye, A. A War Bird's Burlesque. *Unknown.* AS
Portly wood-louse, full of cares, A. The Poet and the Wood-Louse. Helen Parry Eden. HBV
Portrait. George Leonard Allen. CDC
Portrait, A. Joseph Ashby-Sterry. HBV; VA
Portrait. Louise Bogan. HBMV
Portrait, A. Elizabeth Barrett Browning. GN; HBV; OTPC
Portrait ("Buffalo Bill's.") E. E. Cummings. *See* Buffalo Bill's.
Portrait ("Here is little Effie's head"). E. E. Cummings. AnAmPo
Portrait. Jeanne D'Orge. AnAmPo
Portrait, A. Caroline Duer. AA
Portrait. Alan Dugan. TPM
Portrait. Kenneth Fearing. MoAmPo
Portrait, The. Robert Graves. CABA; CMoP
Portrait, A. Brian Hooker. HBV
Portrait, A. Keats. *See* Spenserian Stanzas on Charles Armitage Brown.
Portrait, The. "Owen Meredith." *Fr.* The Wanderer. HBV
Portrait. Adèle Naudé. PeSA
Portrait. Hyam Plutzik. FiMAP
Portrait. Ezra Pound. OBVV
Portrait. Pushkin, *tr. fr. Russian by* Babette Deutsch. OnPM
Portrait, The ("O Lord of all compassionate control"). Dante Gabriel Rossetti. The House of Life, X. MaVP; OAEP; PoVP; ViPo; VP
Portrait, The ("This is her picture as she was"). Dante Gabriel Rossetti. GTSE; MaVP; OAEP; PoVP; VA; ViPo; VP
Portrait. Sydney King Russell. PoMa
Portrait, A. Robert Louis Stevenson. SeCePo
Portrait, The. Countess of Winchilsea. *Fr.* The Birthday of Catharine Tufton. OBEV
Portrait at Wentworth. Ebenezer Elliott. Sonn
Portrait by a Neighbor. Edna St. Vincent Millay. FaPON; GaP; LOW; MoShBr; MPB; PDV; SP; TiPo; TSW
Portrait d'une Femme. Ezra Pound. AnAmPo; AP; APA; CABA; CLwM; CMoP; CoAnAm; ForPo; HBMV; MAP; MoAB; MoAmPo; MoVE; NoP; PoAn; PoFS; TwAmPo; TwCP
Portrait in Stone. Charles Tomlinson. NYTB
Portrait in the Guards, A. Laurence Whistler. GTBS-P
Portrait in Winter. Katherine Garrison Chapin. GoYe
Portrait of a Boy. Stephen Vincent Benét. HBMV; MCCG; NeMA; PoMa
Portrait of a Certain Gentleman. Sara Henderson Hay. NYTB
Portrait of a Child. Louis Untermeyer. HBMV
Portrait of a Cree. "Katherine Hale." CaP
Portrait of a Florentine Lady, The. Lizette Woodworth Reese. HBMV
Portrait of a Freeman. Abraham Cowley. *Fr.* Of Liberty; an Essay. PoFr
Portrait of a Girl. Conrad Aiken. *See* This Is the Shape of the Leaf.
Portrait of a Girl with Comic Book. Phyllis McGinley. CrMA
Portrait of a Lady. T. S. Eliot. AnAmPo; CoAnAm; ForPo; HBMV; LiTG; MAP; MAPA; MoAmPo (1942 ed.); NP; TwAmPo; TwCP
Portrait of a Lady. William Carlos Williams. AmPP (5th ed.); CMoP; NoP; OxBA; PoIE; TwAmPo
Portrait of a Lady in the Exhibition of the Royal Academy. Winthrop Mackworth Praed. *Fr.* Every-Day Characters. CLwM; NBM; PoEL-4
Portrait of a Machine. Louis Untermeyer. MoAmPo (1962 ed.); ShBV-3
Portrait of a Physician. Sir Samuel Garth. *Fr.* The Dispensary. PeRV
Portrait of a Poet. Edgar Lee Masters. *Fr.* Jack Kelso. ATP
Portrait of a Very Old Man. Sara E. Carsley. CaP
Portrait of an Indian. R. E. Rashley. CaP
Portrait of an Old Woman. Arthur Davison Ficke. MAP; NP
Portrait of Atticus. Pope. *See* Atticus.
Portrait of Brutus. Shakespeare. *Fr.* Julius Caesar, V, v. TrGrPo
(Brutus.) GoTP
(Noblest Roman, The.) FaFP; PTK; TreFS
(Shakespeare Gallery, A: Brutus.) MaC
Portrait of Caesar. Shakespeare. *Fr.* Julius Caesar, I, ii. TrGrPo
(Shakespeare Gallery, A: Caesar.) MaC
Portrait of Cressida. Shakespeare. *Fr.* Troilus and Cressida, IV, v. TrGrPo
Portrait of Helen. Shakespeare. *Fr.* Troilus and Cressida, II, ii, *and* IV, i. TrGrPo
Portrait of Henry VIII, The. Earl of Surrey. *See* Sardanapalus.
Portrait of Hudibras. Samuel Butler. *See* Presbyterian Knight.
Portrait of Johnny Doller, A. D. L. Graham. BF
Portrait of Milton, The. Dryden. *See* Lines Printed under the Engraved Portrait of Milton.
Portrait of One Dead. Conrad Aiken. *Fr.* The House of Dust, Pt. III, vi. HBMV; NP; WHA
Portrait of Sidrophel. Samuel Butler. *Fr.* Hudibras, Pt. II, Canto III. PoEL-3
(Character of Sydrophel, The.) PeRV
(Sir Sidrophel, the Conjuror.) FaBoEn
Portrait of the Artist. Dorothy Parker. WhC
Portrait of the Artist as a Prematurely Old Man. Ogden Nash. CrMA; FaFP; LiTA; LiTM; NePA; SiTL
Portrait of the Boy as Artist. Barbara Howes. MoAmPo (1962 ed.)
Portrait of the Prioress, The. Chaucer. *Fr.* The Canterbury Tales: Prologue. MaPo (1969 ed.)
(Seven Pilgrims, *mod. by* Louis Untermeyer.) TrGrPo
(Three Canterbury Pilgrims, *mod. by* Louis Untermeyer.) MaC
Portrait Philippines. Alfred A. Duckett. PoNe
Portrait with Background. Oliver St. John Gogarty. OBMV
Portraits. Robert Fitzgerald. OnHM
Ports of death are sins, The; of life, good deeds. Of Life and Death. Ben Jonson. ReIE
Portugal's ships in vain. Avarice. Luis de León. WoL
Posie, The. George Herbert. MaMe
Posies for Thine Own Bedchamber. Thomas Tusser. SiCE
Positivists, The. Mortimer Collins. BOHV
Possession. Richard Aldington. MoBrPo
Possession. Lynne Lawner. ErPo
Possession. Wade Robinson. SoP

Possession ("Heaven above is softer blue"). *Unknown.* BLRP; FaChP; TRV
Possessions. Lizette Woodworth Reese. HBMV
Possessive Lover, The. Ovid, *tr. fr. Latin by* Christopher Marlowe. *Fr.* Amores. UnTE
Possibilities. Peter Kane Dufault. NYBP
Possibles we dare, The. Love's Progress. Theodore Roethke. FiMAP; PoeP
Possum and the Moon, The. David Campbell. MoAuPo; NeLNL
Possum lies curled, The. Daydreamers. Norma L. Davis. PoAu-2
Possum up de gum tree. Little Gal at Our House. *Unknown.* ABF
Post-Boy, The. William Cowper. *See* Winter Evening, The ("Hark! 'tis the twanging horn").
Post-boy drove with fierce career, The. Alice Fell. Wordsworth. BEL; BeLS; OTPC
Post Captain, The. Charles Edward Carryl. BOHV; PCD
Post Early for Space. Peter J. Henniker-Heaton. AmFN
Post-Impressionism. Bert Leston Taylor. BOHV; HBMV; InMe
Post-Meridian. Wendell Phillips Garrison. AA
  Afternoon.
  Evening.
Post Mortem. Verna Loveday Harden. CaP
Post Mortem. Robinson Jeffers. MAP; MoAmPo; MoPo; TrGrPo
Post-Mortem. Fanny Parnell. *See* After Death.
Post Mortem. Shakespeare. *See* Sonnets, XXXII.
Post-Obits and the Poets. Martial, *tr. fr. Latin by* Byron. AWP; JAWP; OuHeWo; WBP
Post-Rail Song, *with music.* *Unknown.* AS
Post-Roads. Kenneth Slessor. *Fr.* The Atlas. PoAu-2
Post That Fitted, The. Kipling. CenHV; HBV; OnMSP
Post-War. Eileen Duggan. AnNZ
Postage Stamp Lesson, The. *Unknown.* STF
Postcard, A. Edwin Denby. ANYP
Postcard from the Volcano, A. Wallace Stevens. AmPP; AP; LiTA; PoeP
Postcard: Two Figures from an Oriental Print. Ethel Livingston. ThO
Posted. John Masefield. Sonn
Poster Girl, The, *parody.* Carolyn Wells. HBV; InMe
Poster with my picture on it, The. Unwanted. Edward Field. CoPo; PPON
Postern Gate, The, *sel.* Walter Rauschenbusch.
  Little Gate to God, The. MaRV
  ("In the castle of my soul.") TRV
Posters show my country blonde and green, The. Meditation of a Patriot. G. S. Fraser. LiTM (rev. ed.)
Posthumous. Henry Augustin Beers. AA
Posthumous Coquetry. Théophile Gautier, *tr. fr. French by* Arthur Symons. AWP; PeVV
Posthumous Tales, *sels.* George Crabbe.
  Ancient Mansion, The, X. ChTr
  Young Paris, XIX. OBRV
Posthumus, not the last of many more. Suum Cuique Pulchrum. Henry Parrot. TuPP
Postlude. William Carlos Williams. AnAmPo; NP
Postlude: for Goya. Ramon Guthrie. NMP
Postman, The. William Cowper. *See* Winter Evening, The ("Hark! 'tis the twanging horn").
Postman, The. Laura E. Richards. SoPo; TiPo
Postman, The. Christina Rossetti. *Fr.* Sing-Song. GaP; GFA; PCH
  ("Eight o'clock.") RIS; SAS
Postman, The. Clive Sansom. BoTP
Postman, The. Alice Todd. BoTP
Postman, The. *Unknown.* FaPON
Postman comes when I am still in bed, The. A Sick Child. Randall Jarrell. InvP; TDP
Postman's Bell Is Answered Everywhere, The. Horace Gregory. MoAmPo; MoVE; NYBP
Postman's Knock. Rodney Bennett. BoTP
Postponement. Thomas Hardy. PoVP; ViPo (1962 ed.)
Postscript. W. H. Auden. FIW
Postscript. Mary Mills. NePoAm
Postscript. Raymond Souster. PeCV
Postscript for Gweno. Alun Lewis. GTBS-P; WePo
Postscript to "Retaliation," A. Austin Dobson. PoVP
Posture of the tree, The. Lovers in Winter. Robert Graves. NYBP; Po
Postures of Love, The. Alex Comfort. NeBP
  "There is a white mare that my love keeps," *sel.* FaBoMo
  (Love Poem.) ErPo
Posturing. C. S. Lewis. BoPe
Posy Ring, The. Clement Marot, *tr. fr. French by* Ford Madox Ford. AWP; JAWP; WBP
Pot and Kettle. Robert Graves. HBMV
Pot Geranium, The. Norman Nicholson. POTi
Pot of Flowers, The. William Carlos Williams. QFR
Pot of wine among flowers, A. Drinking Alone in the Moonlight. Li Po. AWP
Potato. Richard Wilbur. CrMA; LiTA; MoAB; TrGrPo (rev. ed.); TwAmPo
Potato Digger. Frances Frost. NYTB
Potato Harvest, The. Sir Charles G. D. Roberts. CaP
Potatoes. E. V. Lucas. *Fr.* Counsel to Those That Eat. GaP
Potatoes' Dance, The. Vachel Lindsay. BoChLi; FaPON; MPB; SP; SUS
Potatoes on the table. Potatoes. E. V. Lucas. GaP
Potion, The. Winnie Lynch Rockett. ChIP
Potiphar Gubbins, C. E. Study of an Elevation, in Indian Ink. Kipling. BOHV; InMe
Potomac, The. Karl Shapiro. AP; CoBMV; ToPo
Potomac Side. Edward Everett Hale. *Fr.* From Potomac to Merrimac. PAH
Potomac Town in February. Carl Sandburg. EvOK; WaKn
Potpourri from a Surrey Garden. John Betjeman. CenHV; DTC; FiBHP; PoCh
Potpourri in Rhyme. *Unknown.* SiTL
Potter, The ("Down there a poor woman"). *Unknown, tr. fr. Geez by* Halim El-Dabh. TTY
Potter, The ("The potter worked at his task"). *Unknown.* SoP
Potter and the Clay, The. Jeremiah, XVIII: 1-11, Bible, *O.T.* WoL
Potter stood at his daily work, The. The Patient Potter. *Unknown.* SoP
Potter worked at his task, The. The Potter. *Unknown.* SoP
Potter's Face, The. Hazel H. Simon. SoP
Potter's Hand, The. M. F. Clarkson. SoP
Potter's Song, The. Longfellow. *See* Kéramos.
Poultries, The. Ogden Nash. CenHV
Pounded spise both tast & sent doth please, The. At Fotheringay [*or* Decease, Release: Dum Morior Orior]. Robert Southwell. NCEP; PoEL-2; SiCE
Pounds and Ounces. Michael Brownstein. ANYP
Pour Down. John Holmes. NePoAm
Pour l'Election de Son Sepulchre. Ezra Pound. *See* E. P. Ode pour l'Election de Son Sepulchre.
Pour O pour that parting soul in song. Song of the Son. Jean Toomer. AmNP; BP; CDC; Kal; MAP; PoNe
Pour, O Rain! Ode to Rain. *Unknown, tr. fr. Russian.* PCH
Pour the unhappiness out. Another Weeping Woman. Wallace Stevens. MoVE; NP
Pour Us Wine. Ibn Kolthum, *tr. fr. Arabic by* E. Powys Mathers. *Fr.* The Mu'allaqát. AWP
Pour, varlet, pour the water. The Poets at Tea [*or* Macaulay at Tea]. Barry Pain. BOHV; CenHV; HBV; Par
Pour wine, and cry, again, again, again. Heliodore. Meleager, *tr. by* Andrew Lang. OBVV
Poure Persoun, The. Chaucer. *See* Good Parson, The.
Poure widwe [*or* wydwe], somdel stape in age, A. *See* Povre widwe, somdel stape in age, A.
Pouring music, soft and strong, The. A Song. Frederic William Henry. VA
Pourquoi You Greased. *Unknown.* ChTr
Poussie, poussie, baudrons. *Unknown.* OxNR
Poverty. Charles Simic. YAP
Poverty. Theognis, *tr. fr. Greek by* John Hookham Frere. AWP; JAWP; OnPM; WBP
Poverty. Thomas Traherne. OxBoCh
Poverty ("A beggar to the graveyard hied"). *Unknown, tr. fr. Sanskrit by* Arthur W. Ryder. *Fr.* The Panchatantra. AWP; PoFr
Poverty and Poetry. Thomas Tickell. WaPE
Poverty in London. Samuel Johnson. *Fr.* London. ChTr; OBEC

("By numbers here from shame or censure free.") EnLi-1 (1949 ed.); ViBoPo
Poverty Not All Loss. William Langland, *mod. by* Henry W. Wells. *Fr.* The Vision of Piers Plowman. PoLi
Povre Ame Amoureuse. Louise Labé, *tr. fr. French by* Robert Bridges. AWP
Povre widwe, somdel stape in age, A. The Nun's Priest's Tale. Chaucer. *Fr.* The Canterbury Tales. AnFE; AtBAP; BEL; CABL; CoBE; EnLi-1; MaPo; MBW-1; OAEP; PoEL-1; SeCeV; StP; TOP; TrGrPo
Powder and scent and silence. The young dwarf. Clair de Lune. Anthony Hecht. NYBP
Power. Thomas Stephens Collier. AA
Power. Hart Crane. *Fr.* The Bridge: Cape Hatteras. MAP; MoAmPo
(Cape Hatteras, *longer sel.*) WoL
("Nasal whine of power whips a new universe, The.") MoAB
Power. Grace Noll Crowell. PoMa
Power, *sel.* Matthew Prior. *Fr.* Solomon.
"Pass we the ills, which each man feels." LoBV
Power, The. Stan Rice. QAH
Power. Duncan Campbell Scott. TwCaPo
Power above powers, O heavenly Eloquence. English Poetry [*or* Poetry of England]. Samuel Daniel. *Fr.* Musophilus. CoBE; OBSC
Power and the Glory, The. Siegfried Sassoon. OBMV
Power Failure. Joel Sloman. ThO
Power from God. Isaiah, Bible, *O.T.* *See* They That Wait upon the Lord.
Power from the unknown God, A. Shelley. *Fr.* Hellas. StJW
Power-House, The. Christopher Morley. MaRV
Power-house, A. Classic Scene. William Carlos Williams. AmP; OxBA; WoL
Power lies in my hand. The Sibyl. Joan LaBombard. GoYe
Power of Fancy, The. Philip Freneau. AmPP; AP; CoBA
Power of Littles, The. *Unknown.* TreFT
Power of Love, The. Dryden. *Fr.* Cymon and Iphigenia. OBS
Power of Love, The. John Fletcher. *See* Hear, Ye Ladies.
Power of Love, The. *Unknown, tr. fr. Arabic by* E. Powys Mathers. *Fr.* The Thousand and One Nights. LiTW
Power of Malt, The. A. E. Housman. *Fr.* A Shropshire Lad, LXII. HBV
Power of Music, The. Dryden. *See* Alexander's Feast.
Power of Music, The. Pindar. *See* First Pythian Ode.
Power of Music, The. Shakespeare. *Fr.* The Merchant of Venice, V, i. GN
Power of Numbers, The. Abraham Cowley. *Fr.* Davideis, I. OBS
Power of Poets, The. Ben Jonson. *Fr.* Epistle To Elizabeth, Countess of Rutland. WHA
Power of Prayer, The. Richard Chenevix Trench. *See* Prayer: "Lord, what a change. . ."
Power of princes rests in the consent, The. Obedience. Robert Herrick. PoFr
Power of raven be thine. Good Wish. *Unknown.* FaBoCh; LoGBV
Power of Silence, The. W. H. Davies. BrPo
Power of the Dog, The. Kipling. BLPA
Power of Thought, The. Süsskind von Trimberg, *tr. fr. Middle High German.* TrJP
Power of Time, The. Swift. CBEP; PV
(Shall I Repine.) NCEP
Power Station. T. W. Ramsey. HaMV
Power, that gives with liberal hand, The. On the Religion of Nature. Philip Freneau. AmePo; AmPP; CoBA; MAmP; Po
Power to thine elbow, thou newest of sciences. Darwinity. Herman C. Merivale. BoHV; InMe; NA
Power was given at birth to me, The. One Token. W. H. Davies. BrPo
Powerful Eyes o' Jeremy Tait, The. Wallace Irwin. FiBHP; StPo
Powers and Times Are Not Gods. W. H. Auden. *Fr.* For the Time Being; a Christmas Oratorio. MoRP
Powers of Love, The. George Moses Horton. BALP
Powhatan's Daughter. Hart Crane. *See* Bridge, The.
Powwow. W. D. Snodgrass. NYBP
Pox of this fooling, and plotting of late, A. The Careless Good Fellow. John Oldham. CEP; PeRV; SeCV-2
Pox on pelfe why should we love it. *Unknown.* SeCSL
Practical Answer, A. Shirley Brooks. SiTL
Practical hand at catching fish is necessitous, A. Sea Scape with Parable. Richard Eberhart. PoDB
Practical Joker, The. W. S. Gilbert. *Fr.* His Excellency. BOHV
Practical People. Robinson Jeffers. NAMP
Practical Program for Monks, A. Thomas Merton. CoPo
"Practically all you newspaper people." The Clown. Donald Hall. NYBP
Practices/ silence, the way of wind. As a Possible Lover. LeRoi Jones. AmNP
Practising the Virginals. William Browne. MuSP
Praesto. Thomas Edward Brown. ChIP
Praeterita ex Instantibus. William Douw Lighthall. VA
Praetorium Scene: Good Friday. Elinor Lennen. PGD
Prairie. Herbert Bates. AA
Prairie. K. N. Llewellyn. YeAr
Prairie. Carl Sandburg. LaNeLa
Sels.
Look at Six Eggs. FaPON
"O prairie mother." NP
Prairie Birth. Grace Stone Coates. PaA
Prairie child. Nancy Hanks. Harriet Monroe. LiPo; OHIP
Prairie-Dog Town. Mary Austin. FaPON; StVeCh (1955 ed.); TiPo
Prairie goes to the mountain. Open Range. Kathryn Jackson *and* Byron Jackson. FaPON; TiPo
Prairie-Grass Dividing, The. Walt Whitman. Po
Prairie Graveyard. Anne Marriott. CaP; OBCV; PeCV
Prairie Ride, A. William Vaughn Moody. AnEnPo
Prairie Schooner, The. Edwin Ford Piper. StVeCh (1940 ed.)
Prairie Spring. Edwina Fallis. SUS
Prairie Summer. Dave Etter. ThO
Prairie Sunset, A. Walt Whitman. CoBA
Prairie Water Colour, A. Duncan Campbell Scott. OBCV
Prairie Wind. Duncan Campbell Scott. ACV
Prairie Wolves. Robert V. Carr. PoOW
Prairies, The. Bryant. AmePo; AMP; AmPP (3d ed.); AnAmPo; AP; CoBA; MAmP; OxBA; Po; PoE; PoEL-4
"These are the gardens of the Desert, these," *sel.* InP
Praise. Mary Anderson. BoTP
Praise. Edith Daley. SoP; TRV
Praise. Henry W. Frost. SoP
Praise. R. H. Grenville. PoToHe (new ed.)
Praise. Guido Guinicelli. *See* Sonnet: He Will Praise His Lady.
Praise ("King of Glorie, King of Peace"). George Herbert. AnAnS-1; MaMe; MeP
Praise ("Lord, I will mean and speak thy praise"). George Herbert. MaMe
Praise ("To write a verse or two is all the praise"). George Herbert. MaMe
Praise. "Seumas O'Sullivan." HBV
Praise. Rainer Maria Rilke, *tr. fr. German.* ChTr
Praise ("I hear ten thousand voices singing"). *Unknown.* SoP
Praise ("Then lift up the head with a song"). *Unknown.* PCH
Praise. Henry Vaughan. AnAnS-1; MeP
Praise and Love. William Brighty Rands. OBVV
Praise and Prayer. Sir William Davenant. *Fr.* Gondibert. GoBC; OBEV
Praise at Midnight. Carrie Judd Montgomery. SoP
Praise be to God, the Designer, Builder of Earth and of Heaven! Allah, the Artificer. *Unknown.* OnPM
Praise Blindness, Eyes. *Unknown.* ReIE
Praise Doubt. Mark Van Doren. EaLo; MoRP
Praise for an Urn. Hart Crane. AmP; AnFE; AP; ATP (1953 ed.); AWP; CMoP; CoAnAm; CoBMV; InPo; LiTG; LiTM (rev. ed.); MAP; MoAB; MoAmPo; MoVE; NoP; OxBA; PoE; ReMP; UnPo (3d ed.)
Praise for Sick Women. Gary Snyder. NeAP
Praise for the Fountain Opened. William Cowper. EiPP
(Fountain Opened, The.) SoP
(Olney Hymns.) CEP
Praise God. *Unknown.* PPL
Praise God from whom all blessings flow. Old Hundredth. Thomas Ken. UnS
Praise God, who wrought for you and me. Magnificat. Arthur Symons. UnTE

Praise God, ye peoples of the earth. Doxology for Peace. R. B. Y. Scott. MaRV
Praise, hard as that is in a world where fires. Sent Ahead. John Hay. NePoAm
Praise Him, all ye heights of heaven. Laudate for Christmas. Prudentius. CAW
Praise Him who makes us happy. Never Another. Mark Van Doren. MoRP
Praise in Summer. Richard Wilbur. NoP; PP
Praise is a quiet and a gracious thing. Praise. R. H. Grenville. PoToHe (new ed.)
Praise is devotion fit for mighty minds. Praise and Prayer. Sir William Davenant. *Fr.* Gondibert. GoBC; OBEV
Praise, O my heart, with praise from depth and height. Adam's Song of the Visible World. Ridgely Torrence. TrPWD
Praise of Amen Ra! Hymn to Amen Ra, the Sun God. *Unknown.* WGRP
Praise of Ben Dorain, The. Duncan Ban MacIntyre, *tr. fr. Gaelic by* "Hugh MacDiarmid." GoTS
Praise of Ceres. Thomas Heywood. *See* Song: "With fair Ceres, Queen of grain."
Praise of Created Things. St. Francis of Assisi. FaPON; GBV (1952 ed.)
Praise of Derry, The. St. Columcille, *tr. fr. Gaelic by* D. P. Conygnham. CAW
Praise of Dust, The. G. K. Chesterton. MemP; MoBrPo; OtMeF; POTE
Praise of Earth. Elizabeth Barrett Browning. OBVV
Praise of Engineers. James J. Donohue. JKCP (1955 ed.)
Praise of Famous Men. Ecclesiasticus, Bible, Apocrypha. *See* Let Us Now Praise Famous Men.
Praise of Fionn, The. *Unknown, tr. fr. Irish by* Frank O'-Connor. KiLC
Praise of His Lady, A. John Heywood, *wr. at. to* Thomas Heywood. ElL; HBV; OBEV; SiCE; TuPP; ViBoPo
(Description of a Most Noble Lady, A.) CoBE
(On The Princess Mary.) OBSC
Praise of His Love, A. Earl of Surrey, *wr. at. to* Thomas Heywood. CenL; ElL; TuPP; WHA
(Give Place, Ye Lovers.) CoBe; EnRePo; FCP; ReEn; SiPS
(His Incomparable Lady.) OBSC
(In Praise of His Love.) CLwM
Praise of Homer. George Chapman. *Fr.* The Dedication *to tr. of* The Odyssey. OBS
Praise of Husbandry, The. Thomas Tusser. TuPP
(As True as Thy Faith, This Riddle Thus Saith.) SiCE
Praise of Industry, The. James Thomson. *Fr.* The Castle of Indolence, II. OBEC
Praise of Little Women. Juan Ruiz, Archpriest of Hita, *tr. fr. Spanish by* Longfellow. *Fr.* The Book of Good Love. AWP
Praise of Mary. *Unknown, tr. fr. Old French by* Henry Sorg. ISi
Praise of meaner wits this work like profit brings, The. Sir Walter Ralegh. FCP; SiPS
Praise of My Lady. William Morris. HBV; PoVP; ViPo
Praise of New England. Thomas Caldecot Chubb. GoYe
Praise of New Netherland, The. Jacob Steendam. PAH
Praise of Our Soldiers, The. Thomas Churchyard. TuPP
Praise of Petrarch and of Laura, His Lady, A. *Unknown.* ReIE
Praise of Philip Sparrow, The. George Gascoigne. OA; ViBoPo
(Of All the Birds That I Do Know, *abr.*) CH; NCEP
Praise of Pindar, The. Abraham Cowley. CEP; SCEP-2
Praise of Poets. William Browne. *Fr.* Britannia's Pastorals, II, Songs 1 *and* 2. OBS
Praise of the Pudding. Joel Barlow. *Fr.* The Hasty Pudding, I. AnNE
Praise of Women. Robert Mannyng. OBEV
(No Thyng Ys to Man So Dere.) BoC; LO
Praise of Women. Palladas of Alexandria, *tr. fr. Greek by* Dudley Fitts. LiTW
Praise the good angel doubt. Praise Doubt. Mark Van Doren. EaLo; MoRP
Praise the Lord. Milton. *See* Let Us with a Gladsome Mind.
Praise the Lord and Pass the Ammunition. Frank Loesser. YaD
Praise the Lord for all the seasons. Praise. Mary Anderson. BoTP
Praise the Lord, O My Soul! Psalms, CIV, Bible, *O.T.* ThGo
Praise, then, to Uriel, who in unlikely places. William Force Stead. *Fr.* Uriel, Pt. IV. OxBoCh
Praise Thou Sion, praise Thy Saviour. Lauda Sion. St. Thomas Aquinas. WHL
Praise to God, immortal praise. Love to God. Anna Letitia Barbauld. SoP
Praise to Jesus! William Ball. BePJ
Praise to Jesus. Martin Luther, *tr. fr. German by* Richard Massie. SoP
Praise to Light. Thomas Cole. NePoAm-2
Praise to the blocked word. Praise to the Stutterer. Menke Katz. NYTB
Praise to the End! Theodore Roethke. ToPo
Praise to the Holiest in the Height. Cardinal Newman. *Fr.* The Dream of Gerontius. PoEL-5
(Chorus of Angels.) NBM
(Fifth Choir of Angelicals.) GoBC
Praise to the Stutterer. Menke Katz. NYTB
Praise to Thee. *Unknown, tr. fr. Irish.* FaChP
Praise ye the Lord!/ For it is good to sing praises unto our God. Who Maketh the Grass to Grow. Psalm CXLVII, Bible, *O.T.* FaPON; TiPo (1952 ed.)
Praise ye the Lord./ Praise ye the Lord. A Song of Praise. Psalm CXLVIII, Bible, *O.T.* TrGrPo; TrJP
Praise ye the Lord for the avenging of Israel. The Song of Deborah [and Barak]. Judges, Bible, *O.T.* AWP; LiTW
Praise ye the Lord. Praise God in His sanctuary. Psalm CL, Bible, *O.T.* OnPM; TiPo (1952 ed.); TRV; UnS
Praise ye the Lord. Praise, O ye servants of the Lord. Psalm CXIII, Bible, *O.T.* OnPM
"Praise ye the Lord!" The psalm to-day. Thanksgiving in Boston Harbor. Hezekiah Butterworth. AA; DD; MC; OHIP; PAH
Praise youth's hot blood, if you will. Age in Prospect. Robinson Jeffers. BoLiVe; MAP; MoAB; MoAmPo; NeMA
Praised and exalted. Alabado. *Unknown.* TrAS
Praised Be Diana's Fair and Harmless Light. Sir Walter Ralegh. FCP; PAn; SiCE; TuPP
(Diana.) OBSC
(Homage to Diana.) WiR
(Shepherd's Praise of Diana, The.) SiPS
Praised be man, he is existing in milk. Chorus. Jack Kerouac. *Fr.* Mexico City Blues. NeAP
Praised be our Lord for our brother the sun. Thanksgiving for the Earth. Elizabeth Goudge. YeAr
Praised be the God of love. Antiphon. George Herbert. MaMe
Praised be the name of the Lord, who created the wine. Five Arabic Verses in Praise of Wine, III. *Unknown.* TrJP
Praised Be the Psalmist. David Ross. PG (1955 ed.)
Praise-God Barebones. Ellen Hutchinson Cortissoz. AA
Praisers of women in their proud and beautiful poems, The. "Not Marble nor the Gilded Monuments." Archibald MacLeish. AmPP (3d ed.); AP; CMoP; CoBMV; ILP; LiTL; MeWo; MoAB; PoRA; TwCP; ViBoPo
Praises of a Countrie Life, The. Ben Jonson. SeCP
Praises of God, The. *Unknown, tr. fr. Middle Irish by* Kenneth Jackson. AnIL
Praises of King George VI. A. Z. Ngani, *tr. fr. Xhosa by* Jack Cope. PeSA
Praises of Laura Transcend His Poetic Power, The ("Ashamed at times that I am silent"). Petrarch, *tr. fr. Italian by* Robert Guthrie MacGregor [Susan Wollaston, *wr.*]. Sonnets to Laura: To Laura in Life, XVIII. EnLi-1; OuHeWo
Praises of the King Dingana (Vesi). *Unknown, tr. fr. Zulu.* PeSA
Praises of the King Tshaka. *Unknown, tr. fr. Zulu.* PeSA
Praises of the Train. Demetrius Segooa, *tr. fr. Sotho.* PeSA
Praises to those who can wait. Zealots of Yearning. David Rokeah. TrJP
Praiseworthy are the Thracians, who lament. Best Not to Be Born. Archias. OnPM
Praising the Poets of That Country. Howard Nemerov. PP; TwAmPo
Prancing mounts and twinkling wheels, The. The King of Kings. Lon Woodrum. BePJ
Pranks that Padus play'd, The. The Second Egloge Entituled Fortunatus. Mantuan, *tr. by* George Turberville. *Fr.* The Eglogs of the Poet B. Mantuan Carmelitan. ReIE

Prattle. John Ciardi. BiCB
Prattling Swallows. Nicostratus, *tr. fr. Greek by* Thomas Moore. OnPM
Praxiteles and Phryne. William Wetmore Story. AA; BeLS
Pray! Irene Arnold. BLRP; STF
Pray! Amos R. Wells. STF
Pray but one prayer for me 'twixt thy closed lips. Summer Dawn. William Morris. AtBAP; CBEP; FaBoEn; GTBS; GTBS-D; GTSL; LoBV; OBEV; OBNC; OBVV; ViBoPo; ViPo
Pray, Christian, Pray! *Unknown.* STF
Pray, do not mock me. Shakespeare. *Fr.* King Lear, IV, vii. MemP
Pray don't find fault with the man who limps. Don't Find Fault. *Unknown.* SoP
Pray! for earth has many a need. Pray! Amos R. Wells. STF
Pray for the Dead. Arthur Wentworth Hamilton Eaton. AA; PoRL
Pray—Give—Go. Annie Johnson Flint. BLRP; STF
(Threefold Work, The.) SoP
Pray in the early morning. Pray! Irene Arnold. BLRP; STF
Pray list to me a modest while. Advice to Worriers. George S. Kaufman. ALV
Pray On! *Unknown.* STF
Pray Pity for Bill Smith. Paul L. Grano. BoAu
Pray steal me not, I'm Mrs. Dingley's. On the Collar of a Dog. Swift. StP
Pray thee, take care, that tak'st my book in hand. To the Reader. Ben Jonson. MaPo; NoP; OAEP; ReIE; SCEP-2; SeCV-1; TuPP
Pray, where are the little bluebells gone. About the Fairies. Jean Ingelow. BoTP
Pray where would lamb and lion be. Nature Be Damned. Anne Wilkinson. OBCV
Pray why are you so bare, so bare. The Haunted Oak. Paul Laurence Dunbar. BANP
Pray with Faith. Joseph Hart. SoP
Pray without Ceasing. Ophelia Guyon Browning. *See* Sometime, Somewhere.
Prayer: "And slowly answer'd Arthur from the barge." Tennyson. *Fr.* Morte d'Arthur. BoPe
("And slowly answer'd Arthur from the barge.") FaBoEn; GTSL
Prayer, A: "Angels, where you soar." Alfred Noyes. PoPl
Prayer, A: "As I lie in bed." Joseph Seamon Cotter, Jr. BANP
Prayer: "As I walk through the streets." F. S. Flint. TrPWD
Prayer: "Be not afraid to pray—to pray is right." Hartley Coleridge. MaRV; OQP; Sonn; TreFT; VA
Prayer, A: "Be Thou my vision, O Lord of my heart." *Unknown, tr. fr. Old Irish by* Eleanor Hull. OnYI
Prayer: "Bear with me, Master, when I turn from Thee." Edith Lovejoy Pierce. ChIP; TrPWD
Prayer: "Bless Thou this year, O Lord!" Andrew Stuart Currie Clarke. PGD
(Prayer for a Happy New Year, A.) BLRP
Prayer, A: "Clother of the lily, Feeder of the sparrow." Christina Rossetti. OBVV
(They Toil Not neither Do They Spin.) TrPWD
Prayer: "Dear God, the light is come, our outgrown creeds." *Unknown.* OQP
Prayer, A: "Dear, let me dream of love." Selwyn Image. VA
Prayer: "Dear Lord and Father of mankind." Whittier. *Fr.* The Brewing of Soma. TreFT
Prayer, A: "Dear Lord, for all in pain." Amy Carmichael. SoP
Prayer: "Dear Refuge of my weary soul." Anne Steele. SoP
Prayer, A: "Each day I walk with wonder." Clinton Scollard. TrPWD
Prayer, A: "Eternal God, our life is but." "Yehoash," *tr. fr. Yiddish by* Isidore Goldstick. TrJP
Prayer: "Father, I scarcely dare to pray." Helen Hunt Jackson. *See* Last Prayer, A.
Prayer, A: "Father in Heaven! from whom the simplest flower." Felicia Dorothea Hemans. TrPWD
Prayer, A: "Father, we thank Thee for the night." *At. to* Rebecca J. Weston. SoPo; TVC
(Child's Prayer, A.) BoTP
(Father, We Thank Thee.) MaRV; OTPC (1946 ed.)
(Morning Prayer.) PCH
Prayer: "For the few hours of life allotted me." *Unknown, tr. fr. Latin by* Abraham Cowley. PoFr
Prayer, A: "From falsehood and error." Digby Mackworth Dolben. GoBC
Prayer, A: "Give me [*or* us] a good digestion, Lord." Thomas Harry Basil Webb, *after* A Prayer Found in Chester Cathedral. PoMa; STF
(Ancient Prayer, An.) BBV (1951 ed.); BLPA; FaBoBe; NeHB; SoP
(Prayer Found in Chester Cathedral, A.) PoToHe (new ed.); TreFS
Prayer, A: "Give me the faith that asks not 'Why?' " *Unknown.* SoP
Prayer, A: "Give me work to do." *Unknown.* PGD
Prayer, A: "Give us a good Digestion, Lord." *Unknown. See* Prayer, A: "Give me a good digestion. . ."
Prayer: "God, although this life is but a wraith." Louis Untermeyer. *See* Prayer: "God, though this life. . ."
Prayer, A: "God, give me sympathy and sense." Margaret Bailey. SoP; TRV
Prayer, A: "God, is it sinful if I feel." Mary Dixon Thayer. HBMV; TrPWD
Prayer: "God, listen through my words to the beating of my heart." Marguerritte Harmon Bro. TrPWD
Prayer: "God of light and blossom." James P. Mousley. GoYe
Prayer, A: "God of the Granite and the Rose!" Elizabeth Doten. *Fr.* Reconciliation. OQP
("God of the Granite and the Rose.") TrPWD
Prayer: "God, though [*or* although] this life is but a wraith." Louis Untermeyer. GoTP; MAP; MaRV; MoAmPo; NeMA; OQP; PoFr; PoMa; StaSt; TOP; TrJP; WGRP; YT
Prayer: "God who created me." Henry Charles Beeching. *See* Prayers.
Prayer: "Great God, I ask Thee for no meaner pelf." Henry David Thoreau. *See* My Prayer.
Prayer: "Have pity on us, Power just and severe." John Hall Wheelock, *after* St. Theresa of Avila. EaLo; NePoAm; NYTB
Prayer: "How prone we are." Connie Calenberg. SoP
Prayer: "I ask good things that I detest." Robert Louis Stevenson. TrPWD
Prayer: "I ask you this." Langston Hughes. CDC; EaLo
Prayer: "I asked for bread; God gave a stone instead." *Unknown.* OQP; SoP
Prayer: "I do not ask a truce." Peter Gething. OQP
Prayer: "I had thought of putting an/ altar." Isabella M. Brown. NNP; PoNe (1970 ed.)
Prayer, A: "I kneel not now to pray that Thou." Harry Kemp. HBV; MaRV, *abr.*; WGRP
Prayer: "I know not by what methods rare." Eliza M. Hickok. *See* This I Know.
Prayer: "I often say my prayers." John Burton. MaRV
Prayer, A: "I pray for you, and yet I do not frame." Mary Dixon Thayer. MaRV
Prayer, A: "I pray not for the joy that knows." Marion Franklin Ham. TrPWD
Prayer, A: "I pray Thee O Lord." Juljan Tuwim, *tr. fr. Polish by* Wanda Dynowska. TrJP
Prayer, A: "I would, dear Jesus, I could break." John D. Long. OQP
Prayer, A: "If I dare pray for one." Vernon Watkins. MoRP; PoPl
Prayer: "If I must of my senses lose." Theodore Roethke. TwCP
Prayer: "If, when I kneel to pray." Charles Francis Richardson. AA; SoP
Prayer: " In the bright bay of your morning, O God." Claire Goll, *tr. fr. German by* Babette Deutsch *and* Avrahm Yarmolinsky. TrJP
Prayer: "In this hour of worship." *Unknown.* SoP
Prayer, A: "It is my joy in life to find." Frank Dempster Sherman. TreFS
Prayer, A: "Jesus, Thy life is mine!" *Unknown. See* Jesus, Thy Life Is Mine!
Prayer: "Keep me from fretting, Lord, today." May Carleton Lord. PGD
Prayer: "Last night I crept across the snow." John Farrar. ChrBoLe; OTPC (1946 ed.); PoRL
Prayer, A: "Let me do my work each day." Max Ehrmann. BLPA; FaBoBe; MaRV; NeHB; PoToHe
Prayer: "Let me not know how sins and sorrows glide." James Elroy Flecker. TrPWD

Prayer, A: "Let me work and be glad." Theodosia Garrison. TrPWD
Prayer: "Let us not look upon." Witter Bynner. EaLo
Prayer: "Lo here a little volume, but great book!" Richard Crashaw. HBV; MaMe; SCEP-1
(Ode Which Was Prefixed to a Prayer Booke Given to a Young Gentlewoman, An.) AnAnS-1; MeP
(On a Prayer Booke Sent to Mrs. M. R.) MaMe
(Prayer; an Ode.) SeEP
"Dear soul be strong, *sel.*" ErPo
Prayer: "Lord, as thou wilt, bestow." Eduard Mörike, *tr. fr. German by* John Drinkwater. TrPWD
Prayer, A: "Lord, for the erring thought." William Dean Howells. *See* Undiscovered Country, The.
Prayer: "Lord, forgive." Pauline Schroy. OQP
Prayer: "Lord God of the oak and the elm." George Villiers. TrPWD
Prayer: "Lord, grant us eyes to see, and ears to hear." Christina Rossetti. ChIP
(Thou Thyself.) FaChP
Prayer, A: "Lord, I come, and simply resting." *Unknown.* SoP
Prayer, A: "Lord, in mercy pardon me." Frances Ridley Havergal. SoP
Prayer, A: "Lord, let me live like a regular man." Berton Braley. BLPA
Prayer, A: "Lord, let not my religion be." Clarence M. Burkholder. OQP
Prayer: "Lord, make me an instrument of Thy Peace." St. Francis of Assisi. *See* Lord, Make Me an Instrument of Your Peace.
Prayer: "Lord, make me sensitive to the sight." Barbara Marr. TrPWD
Prayer, A: "Lord, make my childish soul stand straight." "William Laird." HBMV
Prayer, A: "Lord, not for light in darkness do we pray." John Drinkwater. HB√; MaRV; OBVV; TrPWD; WGRP
Prayer: "Lord, the newness of this day." Henry van Dyke. SoP; TRV
Prayer: "Lord, what a change within us one short hour." Richard Chenevix Trench. MaRV; TRV; WBLP; WGRP
(Hour with Thee, An.) BePJ; SoP
(In Thy Presence.) OQP
(Power of Prayer, The.) PoToHe
(Prevailing Prayer.) BLRP; FaChP
(Sonnet: "Lord, what a change within us one short hour.") TrPWD
Prayer, A: "Lord, when on my bed I lie." John Oxenham. SoP
(Whirring Wheels.) TRV
Prayer: "Make me feverish, sleepless, and breathless." "Anna Akhmatova," *tr. fr. Russian by* Babette Deutsch. OnPM
Prayer: "Matthew, Mark, Luke, and John." *Unknown. See* Matthew, Mark, Luke, and John.
Prayer: "Merciful God, who readst my inmost mind." Willem Bilderdijk, *tr. fr. Dutch by* A. J. Barnouw. LiTW
Prayer, A: "'Mid all the traffic of the ways." John Oxenham. *Fr.* The Vision Splendid. SoP
("'Mid all the traffic of the ways.") MaRV
Prayer: "More things are wrought by prayer." Tennyson. *See* Morte d'Arthur.
Prayer, A: "My darling, thou art flowerlike." Heine, *tr. fr. German by* James Thomson. OnPM
Prayer, A: "My God (oh, let me call Thee mine)." Anne Brontë. TrPWD; VA
Prayer, A: "My Redeemer and my Lord." Longfellow. SoP
Prayer, The: "My soul doth pant towards thee." Jeremy Taylor. SeCL
(My Soul Doth Pant towards Thee.) TrPWD
Prayer, A: "Not more of light I ask, O God." Florence Holbrook. SoP
Prayer, A: "Now wilt me take for Jesus' sake." Katharine Tynan. OBVV
Prayer, A: "O brooding Spirit of Wisdom and of Love." Sir William Rowan Hamilton. IrPN
Prayer, A: "O Earth, O dewy mother, breathe on us." Archibald Lampman. TrPWD
Prayer, A: "O for one minute hark what we are saying!" Frederic W. H. Myers. TrPWD
Prayer: "O God, I love Thee in the stars at Night." Nadejda de Bragança. MaRV
Prayer: "O God of earth and altar." G. K. Chesterton. *See* Hymn, A: "O God of earth and altar."
Prayer: "O God of Goodness, Forwardness, and Fulness." Doris Hedges. GoYe
Prayer, A: "O God, our Father, if we had but truth." Edward Rowland Sill. AA
Prayer: "Oh, kneel to that God force of love." Lucia Trent. ChIP
Prayer, The: "O living will that shalt endure." Tennyson. *See* In Memoriam A. H. H.: "O living will."
Prayer, A: "O Lord, the hard-won miles." Paul Laurence Dunbar. TrPWD
Prayer, A: "O Love, give me a passionate heart." Irene Rutherford McLeod. TrPWD
Prayer, A: "O mighty God, Which for us men." Humphrey Gifford. OxBoCh
Prayer, A: "Oh, not for more or longer days, dear Lord." B. Y. Williams. MaRV; SoP
Prayer, A: "O, that mine eyes might closèd be." Thomas Ellwood. WGRP
Prayer, A: "O Thou great Author of the World." Sister Albertus Magnus. WHL
Prayer: "Of what an easie quick accesse." George Herbert. AtBAP; MaMe
Prayer, A: "Often the western wind has sung to me." Lord Alfred Douglas. CAW; JKCP (1926 ed.); TrPWD
Prayer: "Old order changeth, yielding place to new, The." Tennyson. *See* Morte d'Arthur.
Prayer: "Omnipotent confederate of all good." Amos N. Wilder. TrPWD
Prayer, A: "Out of the deeps I cry to thee, O God!" Richard Le Gallienne. TrPWD
Prayer: "Peace, you were always there." James Kirkup. BoPe
Prayer: "Prayer is the mightiest force that men can wield." *Unknown.* SoP
Prayer: "Prayer must be grounded on the Word." *Unknown.* STF
Prayer: "Prayer the churches [*or* church's] banquet, angels age. George Herbert. AnAnS-1; BoC; CABA; DTC; ELP; FaChP; MaMe; MaPo; MeP; MePo; NoP; OBS; OxBoCh; Po; PoEL-2; SCEP-1; SeCV-1; SeEP; Sonn; TRV
Prayer: "Prayer—the fragrance of a flower." Robert Maguire. SoP
Prayer, A: "Purge me, O God." Wilbur Humphrey Fowler. MaRV
Prayer: "She cannot tell my name." Edward Bliss Reed. HBMV
"O God, thy ways are dark," *sel.* MaRV
Prayer: "Spirit of Christ my sanctification." *Unknown, tr. fr. Spanish by* Thomas Walsh. CAW
Prayer: "Take from the earth its tragic hunger, Lord." Hazel J. Fowler. TrPWD
Prayer, A: "Teach me, Father, how to go." Edwin Markham. BoTP; DD; HBMV; HBVY; MaRV; OTPC (1946 ed.); PGD; PoRL; RG; SoP; StVeCh; TrPWD; TRV; TSW; WGRP
Prayer, A: "Tend me my birds, and bring again." Norman Gale. TrPWD
Prayer: "These are the gifts I ask of thee." Henry van Dyke. WGRP
Prayer: "This evening, our Father." *Unknown.* OuSiCo
Prayer, A: "Those who love Thee may they find." George F. Chawner. BLRP
Prayer: "Thou who didst multiply, by Galilee." Frances Crosby Hamlet. ChIP
Prayer, A: "Through every minute of this day." John Oxenham. BLRP; TRV
(Be with Me, Lord!) TRV
(Golden Cord, The.) FaChP
Prayer: "Thy blessing on the boys—for time has come." Haim Guri, *tr. fr. Hebrew by* Ruth H. Lask. TrJP
Prayer, A: "To Thy continual Presence, in me wrought." William Ellery Channing. TrPWD
Prayer: "To worship Him who is my Father-God." Henry W. Frost. SoP
Prayer, A: "Until I lose my soul and lie." Sara Teasdale. HBMV; TrPWD
Prayer, A: "We know the paths wherein our feet should press." John Drinkwater. *See* Purpose.
Prayer: "What a commanding power." Thomas Washbourne. WGRP

Prayer, A: "What weight of ancient witness can prevail." Dryden. *See* Private Judgment Condemned.
Prayer, A: "When I look back upon my life nigh spent." George Macdonald. TrPWD
Prayer: "When the last sea is sailed." John Masefield. GTSL
(D'Avalos' Prayer.) TrPWD
Prayer: "Where then shall Hope and Fear their objects find?" Samuel Johnson. *Fr.* The Vanity of Human Wishes. OBEC
("Where then shall Hope. . .") EnLi-1 (1949 ed.)
Prayer: "White Captain of my soul, lead on." Robert Freeman. ChIP; MaRV; OQP
(Soldier's Prayer, A.) TrPWD
Prayer, The: "Wilt thou not visit me?" Jones Very. MaRV; OxBA; TrPWD
Prayer after Illness, A. Violet Alleyn Storey. TrPWD
Prayer against Indifference. Joy Davidman. AnAmPo; AnEnPo; TrPWD
Prayer against Love. Catullus, *tr. fr. Latin by* Jack Lindsay. LiTW
Prayer; an Ode. Richard Crashaw. *See* Prayer: "Lo here a little volume. . ."
Prayer and Promises. William Olney. SoP
Prayer—Answer. Ednah D. Cheney. *See* Larger Prayer, The.
Prayer Answered. *Unknown. See* Prayer of an Unknown Confederate Soldier.
Prayer Answered by Crosses. John Newton. FaChP
(My Prayer.) STF
Prayer at a Nursery Window. Frances Stoakley Lankford. FaChP
Prayer at a Wedding. Charles Carroll Albertson. SoP
Prayer at Dawn. Diarmuid O'Shea, *tr. fr. Irish by* Frank O'Connor. KiLC
Prayer at Dawn. Edwin McNeill Poteat. TrPWD
Prayer at Eventide. R. B. Y. Scott. MaRV
Prayer at Eventide. *Unknown.* SoP
Prayer before Birth. Louis MacNeice. AnMoPo; GTBS-P; LiTB; OAEP (2d ed.); TwCP
Prayer before [Her] Execution. Mary Queen of Scots, *tr. fr. Latin by* John Fawcett. CAW; MaRV; TRV; WGRP
Prayer before Going to Sleep. *Unknown, tr. by* Eleanor Hull. JKCP (1926 ed.)
Prayer before Meat. Una W. Harsen. ChIP; TrPWD
Prayer before Sleep. Alice Lucas. TrJP
Prayer before Sleeping. *Unknown. See* Matthew, Mark, Luke, and John.
Prayer before Study. Theodore Roethke. TrPWD
Prayer Brings Rain, A. Tasso, *tr. fr. Italian by* Edward Fairfax. *Fr.* Godfrey of Bulloigne. OBSC
Prayer by Moonlight. Roberta Teale Swartz. TrPWD
Prayer by the Open Book. E. Margaret Clarkson. SoP
Prayer during Battle. Hermann Hagedorn. TrPWD
Prayer for a Bride's House. Christie Lund. SoP
Prayer for a Day's Walk. Grace Noll Crowell. PoToHe
Prayer for a Happy New Year, A. Andrew Stuart Currie Clarke. *See* Prayer: "Bless Thou this year, O Lord!"
Prayer for a Little Home, A. Florence Bone. BLPA; FaBoBe; FaFP; MaRV; NeHB; OQP; PCH; SoP
(Prayer for a Little House.) TreFT
Prayer for a Marriage, A. Mary Carolyn Davies. TrPWD
Prayer for a New House. Martha Snell Nicholson. FaChP
Prayer for a New House. Louis Untermeyer. *See* Prayer for This House.
Prayer for a Pilot. Cecil Roberts. BBV; FaPON; OTPC (1946 ed.)
(Prayer for the Pilot.) TrPWD
Prayer for a Play House. Elinor Lennen. TrPWD
Prayer for a Preacher, A. Edward Shillito. TrPWD
Prayer for a Priest. *Unknown.* WHL
Prayer for a Sleeping Child, A. Mary Carolyn Davies. OHIP
Prayer for a Very New Angel. Violet Alleyn Storey. BLPA; TreFS
Prayer for All Poets at This Time. Irwin Edman. TrPWD
Prayer for Aviators, A. Norman E. Richardson. MaRV
Prayer for Broken Little Families, A. Violet Alleyn Storey. PoToHe
Prayer for Brotherhood, A. John S. Hoyland. MaRV
Prayer for Brotherhood. Viney Wilder. OTD
Prayer for Charity, A. Edwin O. Kennedy. TrPWD
Prayer for Christian Unity, A. Molly Anderson Haley. ChIP; OQP
Prayer for Contentment. Edwin McNeill Poteat. TrPWD
Prayer for Courage. Rabindranath Tagore. MaRV
Prayer for Courage. Louis Untermeyer. OQP
Prayer for Dew. Eleazar ben Kalir, *tr. fr. Hebrew by* Israel Zangwill. TrJP
Prayer for Dreadful Morning. E. Merrill Root. TrPWD
Prayer for Every Day, A. Mary Carolyn Davies. BLPA; FaBoBe; NeHB; PoToHe
Prayer for Every Day. *Unknown, tr. fr. Fanti by* Kweku Martin. PBA
Prayer for Faith, A. Michelangelo, *tr. fr. Italian by* John Addington Symonds. OnPM
Prayer for Faith, A. Alfred Norris. BLRP
Prayer for Faith, A. Margaret E. Sangster. PoToHe
Prayer for Family Love, A. John S. Hoyland. MaRV
Prayer for Forbearance. *Unknown.* LoBV
Prayer for Forgiveness, A. Charles Wesley. *See* Break My Heart of Stone.
Prayer for Gentleness to All Creatures. John Galsworthy. BoTP
Prayer for Gentlewomen and Others to Use, A. Nicholas Breton. SiCE
Prayer for Guidance. Henry W. Frost. SoP
Prayer for Help, A. *Unknown.* SoP
Prayer for His Lady, A. Oliver St. J. Gogarty. NYTB
Prayer for His Lady's Life. Propertius, *tr. fr. Latin by* Ezra Pound. *Fr.* Elegies, II, 28. NoP
Prayer for Humility. Henry Francis Lyte. SoP
Prayer for Indifference. Fanny Greville. LoBV; OBEC
"I ask no kind return of love," 3 *sts.* LO; OBEV
Prayer for Inspiration, A. Michelangelo. *See* For Inspiration.
Prayer for Light. Stanton A. Coblentz. TrPWD
Prayer for Little Things, A. Eleanor Farjeon. ThGo
Prayer for Living and Dying. Christopher La Farge. TrPWD
Prayer for Love, A. Elsa Barker. OQP
Prayer for Messiah. Leonard Cohen. OBCV
Prayer for Miracle. Anna Wickham. GoTP; OQP; YT
Prayer for Missionaries, A. Henry W. Frost. SoP
Prayer for Mother, A. *Unknown.* SoP
Prayer for My Daughter, A. W. B. Yeats. BWP; CABA; CMoP; CoBMV; EnL; GTBS-W; LiTB; LiTG; LiTM (rev. ed.); LoBV; MasP; MoAB; PAn; PoLF; PoPo; PoRA (rev. ed.); VaPo
Sels.
For My Daughter. MoRP
"I have walked and prayed for this young child an hour." ViBoPo; WoL
Prayer for My Native Land. Burns. *Fr.* The Cotter's Saturday Night. MaRV
Prayer for My Son, A. Yvor Winters. CrMA; TrPWD
Prayer for Neighborhood Evangelism. Annette Jansen. STF
Prayer for One Dead. Julia C. R. Dorr. OQP
Prayer for Our Home. John S. Hoyland. MaRV
Prayer for Pain. John G. Neihardt. HBV; NP; PFY; TrPWD; WGRP
Prayer for Peace, A. William Adams Brown. MaRV
Prayer for Peace, A. John Oxenham. SoP
Prayer for Peace. Johnstone G. Patrick. TrPWD
Prayer for Peace. Rolland W. Schloerb. MaRV
Prayer for Peace: II. Léopold Sédar Senghor, *tr. fr. French by* John Reed *and* Clive Wake. TTY
Prayer for Peace, A. Edward Rowland Sill. TrPWD
Prayer for Pentecost, A. Catherine Bernard Brown. BLRP
Prayer for Purification, A. Michelangelo. *See* Thou Alone Art Good.
Prayer for Purity. Jemima Luke. SoP
Prayer for Rain. Herbert E. Palmer. HaMV; POTE; WePo
Prayer for Rain. *Unknown, tr. fr. Finnish. Fr.* Kalevala. WGRP
Prayer for Recollection, A. *Unknown, tr. fr. Irish by* Frank O'Connor. KiLC
Prayer for Redemption. *Unknown.* TrJP
Prayer for Reptiles. Patricia Hubbell. PDV
Prayer for Rich and Poor. William Langland, *mod. by* Nevill Coghill. *Fr.* The Vision of Piers Plowman. BoC
Prayer for St. Innocent's Day, A. Helen Parry Eden. CAW
Prayer for Serenity. Reinhold Niebuhr. TreFT
Prayer for Shut-Ins. Ruth Winant Wheeler. PoToHe (new ed.)
Prayer for Song. Fay Lewis Noble. TrPWD
Prayer for Sophistication. Mark Turbyfill. NP
Prayer for Strength. Margaret E. Bruner. MaRV; PoToHe
Prayer for Strength. Samuel Johnson. MaRV; SoP; TRV

Prayer for Strength, A. Michelangelo, *tr. fr. Italian by* John Addington Symonds. OnPM
Prayer for Strength. Rabindranath Tagore. Gitanjali, XXXVI. MaRV
(For Strength.) MoRP
Prayer for Teachers, A. Marguerite Emilio. OQP
Prayer for Thanksgiving, A. Joseph Auslander. TrPWD
Prayer for the Age. Myron H. Broomell. TrPWD
Prayer for the Churches. John Oxenham. OQP
Prayer for the Day, A. *Unknown.* SoP
Prayer for the Dead. Tennyson. *See* Morte d'Arthur.
Prayer for the Healing of the Wounds of Christ, A. Laurence Housman. MaRV
Prayer for the Home, *sel.* Edgar A. Guest.
"Lord, this humble house we'd keep." MaRV; TRV
Prayer for the Household, A. Robert Louis Stevenson. SoP; TRV
Prayer for the New Year, A. A. B. Simpson. SoP
Prayer for the New Year, A. Violet Alleyn Storey. TrPWD
Prayer for the New Year, A. *Unknown.* BLRP
Prayer for the Old Courage, A. Charles Hanson Towne. TrPWD
Prayer for the Pilot. Cecil Roberts. *See* Prayer for a Pilot.
Prayer for the Poor. William Langland, *mod. by* Henry W. Wells. *Fr.* The Vision of Piers Plowman. PoLi
Prayer for the Presence of Christ, A. Thomas Tiplady. *See* Grace.
Prayer for the Royal Marriage. John Masefield. HW
Prayer for the Speedy End of Three Great Misfortunes. *Unknown, tr. fr. Irish* by Frank O'Connor. DTC; OBMV
Prayer for the Useless Days. Edith Lovejoy Pierce. TrPWD
Prayer for This Day. Hildegarde Flanner. TrPWD
Prayer for This House. Louis Untermeyer. FaPON; MaRV; OTD; PoLF; PoToHe; TSW
(Prayer for a New House.) TrPWD
Prayer for Today, A. Charles Nelson Pace. MaRV; OQP
Prayer for Wings. Dmitry Merezhkovsky, *tr. fr. Russian by* Babette Deutsch. OnPM
Prayer Found in Chester Cathedral, A. T. H. B. Webb. *See* Prayer: "Give me a good digestion, Lord."
Prayer from 1936, A. Siegfried Sassoon. TrPWD
Prayer Hymn. "M. K. H." ChIP; OQP
Prayer in a Country Church. Ruth B. Van Dusen. TrPWD
Prayer in a June Garden. *Unknown.* FaChP
Prayer in Affliction. Violet Alleyn Storey. MaRV; TrPWD
Prayer in April. Sara Henderson Hay. MaRV; OQP; TrPWD
Prayer in Darkness, A. G. K. Chesterton. BoC; MoBrPo; PoLF; TrGrPo
Prayer in Late Autumn, A. Violet Alleyn Storey. TrPWD
Prayer in Mid-Passage. Louis MacNeice. EaLo
Prayer in Sorrow. Frederick L. Hosmer. *See* Father, to Thee.
Prayer in Spring, A. Robert Frost. MaRV; MoRP; OTPC (1946 ed.); TrPWD; WePo; YeAr; YT
Prayer in the Night, A. Oswald J. Smith. SoP
Prayer in the Prospect of Death, A. Burns. HBV; MaRV; TrPWD; WGRP
Prayer in the Spirit. George Croly. *See* Spirit of God, Descend Upon My Heart.
Prayer in Time of Blindness, A. Clement Wood. TrPWD
Prayer in Time of War. Henry Treece. WaP
Prayer Is a Power. Phyllis C. Michael. SoP
Prayer is appointed to convey. Pray with Faith. Joseph Hart. SoP
Prayer is the breath of God in man. The Worth of Prayer. Benjamin Beddome. SoP
Prayer is the little implement. Emily Dickinson. NoP
Prayer is the mightiest force that men can wield. Prayer. *Unknown.* SoP
Prayer is the soul's sincere desire. What Is Prayer? James Montgomery. BLRP; FaChP; MaRV; SoP; STF; TRV; WGRP
Prayer, Living and Dying, A. Augustus Montague Toplady. *See* Rock of Ages.
Prayer Moves the Hand That Moves the World. John A. Wallace. *See* God the Omniscient.
Prayer must be grounded on the Word. Prayer. *Unknown.* STF
Prayer of a Beginning Teacher. Ouida Smith Dunnam. TrPWD
Prayer of a Modern Thomas. Edward Shillito. ChIP; MaRV; PGD
Prayer of a Patriot. Henry J. von Schlichten. BePJ; SoP
Prayer of a Soldier in France. Joyce Kilmer. CAW; GoBC
Prayer of a Teacher. Dorothy Littlewort. TrPWD
Prayer of an Unbeliever. Lizette Woodworth Reese. TrPWD
Prayer of an Unemployed Man. W. C. Ackerly. MaRV; PoToHe
Prayer of an Unknown Confederate Soldier. *Unknown.* TreFT
(Prayer Answered.) STF
Prayer of Any Husband. Mazie V. Caruthers. MaRV; PoToHe
Prayer of Beaten Men, The. William Hervey Woods. *Fr.* The House of Broken Swords. HBV
Prayer of Busy Hands, A. B. Y. Williams. MaRV
Prayer of Calcas, The. *Unknown, tr. fr. Welsh by* Gwyn Williams. *Fr.* Troelus a Chresyd. PrWP
Prayer of Columbus. Walt Whitman. AmPP (4th ed.)
Sels.
"All my emprises have been fill'd with Thee." TRV
"My terminus near,/ The clouds already closing in upon me." MaRV
"One effort more, my altar this bleak sand." OQP; PGD; PoRL
"Thou knowest my years entire, my life." TrPWD
Prayer of Cyrus Brown, The. Sam Walter Foss. BOHV; LHV; StaSt
(Cyrus Brown's Prayer.) SoP
Prayer of Praise to Mary, A. *Unknown.* WHL
Prayer of St. Francis Xavier. Pope. TrPWD
Prayer of Steel. Carl Sandburg. *See* Prayers of Steel.
Prayer of Thanksgiving, A. Margaret E. Sangster. SoP
Prayer of the Cat, The. Carmen Bernos de Gasztold, *tr. fr. French by* Rumer Godden. PDV
Prayer of the Cock, The. Carmen Bernos de Gasztold, *tr. fr. French by* Rumer Godden. TIHL
Prayer of the Cricket, The. Carmen Bernos de Gasztold, *tr. fr. French by* Rumer Godden. TIHL
Prayer of the Dog, The. Carmen Bernos de Gasztold, *tr. fr. French by* Rumer Godden. TIHL
Prayer of the Five Wounds, A, *sel.* *Unknown.*
"Jhesu Cryst, myn leman swete." AtBAP
Prayer of the Goldfish, The. Carmen Bernos de Gasztold, *tr. fr. French by* Rumer Godden. PDV
Prayer of the Little Ducks [Who Went into the Ark], The. Carmen Bernos de Gasztold, *tr. fr. French by* Rumer Godden. PDV; ThGo
Prayer of the Maidens to Mary. Rainer Maria Rilke, *tr. fr. German by* Jethro Bithell. AWP
Prayer of the Mouse, The. Carmen Bernos de Gasztold, *tr. fr. French by* Rumer Godden. PDV
Prayer of the Night Chant, A. *Unknown, tr. fr. Navajo Indian by* Washington Matthews. ExPo
Prayer of the Old Horse, The. Carmen Bernos de Gasztold, *tr. fr. French by* Rumer Godden. PDV
Prayer of the Peoples, A. Percy MacKaye. TrPWD, 3 *sts.*; WGRP
Prayer of the Quest, The. Eleanor B. Stock. MaRV
Prayer of the Unemployed. Raymond Kresensky. OQP
Prayer of the Unemployed. *Unknown.* MaRV
Prayer of the Young Stoic. Stephen P. Dunn. TrPWD
Prayer on Christmas Eve. Nancy Byrd Turner. MaRV
Prayer on Entering Church. *Unknown.* SoP
Prayer on Fourth of July. Nancy Byrd Turner. OTD; YeAr
Prayer on the Night before Easter. John Holmes. MoRP
Prayer Perfect, The. James Whitcomb Riley. MaRV; OQP
(Love's Prayer.) AA
Prayer-Poem, A. Mary S. Edgar. *See* God, Who Touchest Earth. . .
Prayer Rug, The. Sara Beaumont Kennedy. HBMV
Prayer That an Infant May Not Die. Francis Jammes, *tr. fr. French by* Joseph T. Shipley. CAW
Prayer the churches [*or* church's] banquet, angels age. Prayer. George Herbert. AnAnS-1; BoC; CABA; DTC; ELP; FaChP; MaMe; MeP; MePo; NoP; OBS; OxBoCh; Po; PoEL-2; SCEP-1; SeEP; Sonn; TRV
Prayer—the fragrance of a flower. Prayer. Robert Maguire. SoP
Prayer Time. Ruby Weyburn Tobias. SoP
Prayer to Christ Our Lord, *mod.* Cynewulf. PoLi
Prayer to Escape from the Market Place, A. James Wright. NaP
Prayer to Go to Paradise with the Asses. Francis Jammes, *tr. fr. French by* Jethro Bithell. AWP; BoPe; JAWP; WBP
(Prayer to Go to Paradise with the Donkeys, A, *tr. by* Richard Wilbur.) EaLo; MoRP; OA; LiTW, *tr. by* Vernon Watkins

("When You elect to call me, God, O call," *tr. by* Alan Conder.) LO
Prayer to God. "Plácido," *tr. fr. Spanish by* Raoul Abdul. CAW; TTY
Prayer to Jesus. Mossén Tallante, *tr. fr. Spanish by* Sir John Bowring. OnPM
Prayer to Make Your Own, A. Bryant. *See* Other Sheep I Have Which Are Not of This Fold.
Prayer to Peace. Euripides, *tr. fr. Greek by* Moses Hadas. *Fr.* Cresophontes. PoPl
Prayer to Persephone. Edna St. Vincent Millay. Memorial to D. C., II. NP
Prayer to St. Lucy. John Heath-Stubbs. BoPe
Prayer to St. Patrick. Ninine, *tr. fr. Old Irish by* Whitley Stokes *and* John Strachan. OnYI
Prayer to Santa Maria del Vade. Juan Ruiz, Archpriest of Hita. CAW
Prayer to the Blessed Virgin, A. Chaucer. *See* Invocation: "O mother-maid!"
Prayer to the Blessed Virgin. Rodríguez del Padrón, *tr. fr. Spanish by* Sir John Bowring. CAW
Prayer to the Crucifix. Mossén Juan Tallante, *tr. fr. Spanish by* Thomas Walsh. CAW
Prayer to the Dynamo. Henry Adams. AmePo
Prayer to the Father of [*or* in] Heaven, A. John Skelton. PoIE; SiCE; TrPWD; TuPP
Prayer to the Giver. Charles Hanson Towne. OQP
Prayer to the God Thot. *Unknown, tr. fr. Egyptian by* Ulli Beier. TTY
Prayer to the Holy Spirit. E. Margaret Clarkson. SoP
Prayer to the Holy Trinity, A. Richard Stanyhurst. *See* Prayer to the Trinity, A.
Prayer to the Hunting Star, Canopus. *Unknown, tr. fr. Bushman by* W. H. I. Bleek *and* Jack Cope. PeSA
Prayer to the Mountain Spirit. *Tr. fr. Navaho Indian by* Mary Austin, *tr. wr. at. to* G. W. Cronyn *and to* Edward S. Yeomans. WGRP
(Navaho [*or* Navajo] Prayer.) PoRL; StVeCh
Prayer to the Sacrament of the Altar, A. *Unknown.* MeEL
Prayer to the Trinity. James Edmeston. HBV; VA
(Hymn: "Lead us, heavenly Father, lead us.") NeHB
Prayer to the Trinity, A. Richard Stanyhurst. CoBE; EIL; TuPP
(Prayer to the Holy Trinity, A.) PoEL-2
(To the Trinity.) OxBoCh
Prayer to the Trinity, A. *Unknown.* MeEL
Prayer to the Virgin. *Unknown. See* Hymn to the Virgin.
Prayer to the Virgin. *Unknown, tr. fr. Middle Irish by* John Strachan *and* Kuno Meyer. OnYI
Prayer to the Virgin of Chartres. Henry Adams. AmePo; CAW; GoBC; ISi; MWA-2
Prayer to the White Man's God. Charles Anderson. BF
Prayer to the Wind, A. Thomas Carew. AnAnS-2; SCEP-2
Prayer to the Young Moon. *Unknown, tr. fr. Bushman by* W. H. I. Bleek *and* Jack Cope. PeSA
Prayer to Time, A. Siegfried Sassoon. MemP
Prayer to Venus. Chaucer, *mod. vers. by* John Hall Wheelock. *Fr.* The Canterbury Tales: The Knight's Tale. LiTL
Prayer to Venus. John Fletcher. *Fr.* The Mad Lover. SeCL
Prayer to Venus. Lucretius, *See* Address to Venus. *tr. by* Spenser.
Prayer under the Pressure of Violent Anguish. Burns. TrPWD
Prayer unsaid, and mass unsung. The Sea Ritual [*or* Deadman's Dirge]. George Darley. Syren Songs, V. CH; ERoP-2; OBNC; OBRV; OnYI; OxBI; PoG; SiSw; WiR
Prayer unto Christ the Judge of the World, A. Michael Wigglesworth. SCAP
Prayers. Henry Charles Beeching. BoTP; MaRV; OBVV; VA
(Boy's Prayer, A.) GN; OTPC (1946 ed.), *st.* 1; PoRL, *st.* 1
(Prayer.) SD
Prayers. Flora Hastings. OTPC (1923 ed.)
Prayers I make will then be sweet indeed, The. For Inspiration [*or* A Prayer for Inspiration *or* To the Supreme Being]. Michelangelo. AWP; CAW; GoBC; JAWP; LiTW; OQP; SoP; TrPWD; TRV; WBP; WGRP
Prayers in the whitewashed sitting-room. Afrikaans Homestead. Peter Jackson. BoSA
Prayers Must Have Poise. Robert Herrick. LiTB
Prayers of a Christian Bridegroom. Pierre Poupo, *tr. fr. French by* Cécile Schreiber *and* Virginia Tufte. HW
Prayers of Steel. Carl Sandburg. AnAmPo; AP; CBV; CMoP; FaPON; MAP; MoAmPo; MPB; NeMA; NP; OCS; PDV; PFY; PoMa; TrPWD; YaD
(Prayer of Steel.) OQP
Prayerwheel 2. David Meltzer. NeAP
Praying and Preaching. *Unknown. See* My Bishop's Eyes.
Praying-Mantis, The. Annie Charlotte Dalton. TwCaPo
Praying Mantis, The. Ogden Nash. PV
Praying Mantis. Felix Stefanile. FiSC
Praying Mantis Visits a Penthouse, The. Oscar Williams. FaFP; LiTM; NePA
Pre Domina. Jean Lipkin. PeSA
Preach about the old sins, Preacher! Charlotte Perkins Gilman. *Fr.* To the Preacher. MaRV
Preach wisdom unto him who understands! Che Sara Sara. Victor Plarr. HBV
Preacher, The. Al-Mahdi, *tr. fr. Arabic by* A. J. Arberry. TTY
Preacher and the Slave, The. *Unknown, at. to* Joe Hill. AS, *with music*; PPON; TrAS, *with music*
Preacher does better, The. Stand By. *Unknown.* STF
Preacher Sought to Find Out Acceptable Words, The. Richard Eberhart. WaP
Preacher was a strange and lonely man, The. Legend of the Hills. Lilith Lorraine. FiSC
Preacher works from morn till night, The. Soft Job. William C. Summers. STF
Preachers, The. Norman Nicholson. NeBP
Preacher's Mistake, The. Brewer Mattocks, *sometimes at. to* William Croswell Doane. BLPA; MaRV; PoToHe; StaSt
Preacher's Prayer, A. Ralph Spaulding Cushman. *See* Parson's Prayer, The.
Preacher's Prayer, The. George Macdonald. MaRV; SoP; TRV
Preachers; the True vs. the Insincere. William Cowper. *Fr.* The Task, II. MaRV
Preacher's Urgency, A. Richard Baxter. *Fr.* Love Breathing Thanks and Praise. MaRV
("I preached as never sure to preach again.") TRV
Preacher's Vacation, The. *Unknown.* BLPA
Preacher's Wife, The. *Unknown.* SoP; STF
Preaching and Not Doing. William Langland, *mod. by* Henry W. Wells. *Fr.* The Vision of Piers Plowman. PoLi
Preachment for Preachers. Sebastian Brant, *tr. fr. German by* Alexander Barclay. *Fr.* The Ship of Fools. ACP; CAW
Preamble to N[icholas] B[reton] His Garden-Plot, The. Nicholas Breton. ReIE
Precambrian Shield, The. E. J. Pratt. *Fr.* Towards the Last Spike. MoCV; OBCV
Precarious Ground. Leah Bodine Drake. GoYe
Precaution. Heine. *See* Fürchte Nichts, geliebte Seele.
Precede me into this elusive country. The Caravan. Gwendolyn MacEwen. MoCV
Precedent. Paul Laurence Dunbar. AmePo
Precedents. Israel Newman. NYTB
Precept of Silence, The. Lionel Johnson. ACP (1926 ed.); CAW; HBV; MemP; MoBrPo; PoToHe (1941 ed.); PoVP; SoP; ViBoPo; ViPP
Precepts He Gave His Folk. Elijah ben Menahem Hazaken of Le Mans, *tr. fr. Hebrew by* Israel Zangwill. TrJP
Precious Blood, The. *Unknown.* STF
Precious Friend, The. *Unknown, tr. fr. French.* SoP
"Precious in the sight of the Lord". *Unknown.* BLRP
Precious Moments. Carl Sandburg. MAP; MoAmPo
Precious—mouldering pleasure—'tis, A. Emily Dickinson. DiPo
Precious Name, The. John Newton. *See* Name of Jesus, The.
Precious, oh how precious is that blessed sleep. "Precious in the Sight of the Lord." *Unknown.* BLRP
Precious Pearl, The. Pat Wilson. AnNZ; TDP
Precious Stones. Charles Stuart Calverley. InMe
Precious Stones. Christina Rossetti. *See* Emerald Is as Green as Grass, An.
Precious Things. *Unknown.* GoSl; TTY
Precious thought, my Father knoweth. God Knoweth Best [*or* Your Father Knoweth]. *Unknown.* BLRP; WBLP
Precious Words. Emily Dickinson. *See* He ate and drank the precious words.
Precipice, The. John Banister Tabb. AmP

Precision. Peter Collenette. FlW
Predator. Peter Fellowes. QAH
Predestination. Kipling. *See* By the Hoof of the Wild Goat.
Predestination. Omar Khayyám, *tr. fr. Persian by* Edward Fitzgerald. *Fr.* The Rubáiyát. OnPM
Pre-Existence. Frances Cornford. HBMV; POTE; WaKn
Pre-Existence. Paul Hamilton Hayne. HBV
Preface. W. H. Auden. *Fr.* The Sea and the Mirror. LiTA; SeCeV
Preface. Theodore Weiss. NMP
Preface: "And did those feet in ancient time." Blake. *See* And Did Those Feet in Ancient Time.
Preface, The: "Infinity, when all things it beheld." Edward Taylor. *Fr.* Gods Determinations. AmLP; AmPP; AP; ILP; MAmP; MWA-1; OxBA; SCAP
Preface: "To make a start." William Carlos Williams. *Fr.* Paterson, I. AP; CMoP; CoBMV
Preface to a Musician. Richard Church. MuSP
Preface to a Twenty Volume Suicide Note. LeRoi Jones. AmNP; Kal; NNP; PoNe (1970 ed.); TTY
Preface to "Milton." Blake. *See* And Did Those Feet in Ancient Time.
Preface to the Book of Housewifery, The. Thomas Tusser. SiCE
Preface to the Buyer of This Book, A. Thomas Tusser. SiCE; TuPP
Prefatory Poem, on. . .*Magnalia Christi Americana,* A. Nicholas Noyes. SCAP
Prefatory Poem to the Little Book, Entituled, *Christianus per Ignem,* A. Nicholas Noyes. SCAP
Prefatory Sonnet. Henry Kendall. BoAV
Prefatory Sonnet. Wordsworth. *See* Nuns Fret Not at Their Convent's Narrow Room.
Prefer the Cash. Omar Khayyám, *tr. fr. Persian by* Edward Fitzgerald. *Fr.* the Rubáiyát. OnPM
("Some for the glories of this world; and some.") PoPl
Prefer the cherry when the fruit hangs thick. Under the Boughs. Gene Baro. BoNaP
Preference, A. John Farrar. GFA
Preference. Daniel Sargent. ISi
Preferring "resemblance to beauty." An Esthetic of Imitation. Donald Finkel. NePoEA
Pregnant again with th'old twins Hope, and Feare. To Mr. T. W. John Donne. MaMe
Pregnant Woman. Ingrid Jonker, *tr. fr. Afrikaans by* Jack Cope *and* Uys Krige. PeSA
Prehistoric Burials. Siegfried Sassoon. MoBrPo
Prehistoric Camp, A. Andrew Young. CBEP; MoPW
Prehistoric Huntsman, The. Donald Wandrei. FiSC
Prehistoric Smith. David Law Proudfit. BOHV
Preiching of the Swallow, The. Robert Henryson. OxBS
Prejudice. Georgia Douglas Johnson. AmNP
Prejudice against the Past, The. Wallace Stevens. LiTM (rev. ed.)
Prelates, The. John Skelton. *Fr.* Colyn Cloute. TrGrPo
Preliminary to Classroom Lecture. Josephine Miles. FiMAP
Prelude, The [or, Growth of a Poet's Mind], *much abr.* Wordsworth. EnRP; OAEP
Sels.
"Among that band of Officers was one," *fr.* IX; *Oxford ed., incl.* Vaudracour and Julia. ChER
"To a lodge that stood, *fr.* Vaudracour and Julia. EvOK
"And in the frosty season, when the sun," *fr.* I. InP; MyFE; PoMa
(On the Frozen Lake.) FaBoCh; LoGBV
(Skating.) CH, *shorter sel.;* GN; GoTP; SD, *shorter sel.;* ShBV-3
As If Awakened, Summoned, *fr.* III. AtBAP
Band of Military Officers, A, *fr.* IX. EnLi-2
"Beside the pleasant Mill of Trompington," *fr.* III. OBRV
Blest the Infant Babe, *fr.* II. AtBAP
Books, V. MBW-2
Stone and the Shell, The. ERoP-1
"Whereupon I told,/ That once in the stillness of a summer's noon." PoEL-4
Cambridge and the Alps, VI. ERoP-1
Imagination. FiP
"When the third summer freed us from restraint." MBW-2
Childhood ("When he had left the mountains"), *fr.* I. CoBE
Communion with Nature, *fr.* II. TOP
("For I would walk alone," *sl. diff.*) OBRV
Conclusion: "It was a Summer's night, a close warm night," *fr.* XIV. FaBoEn; OBNC
("It was a close, warm, breezeless summer night," *longer sel.*) MBW-2; PoEL-4
Consummate Happiness, *fr.* IV. OBNC
Crossing the Alps ("The only track now visible was one"), *fr.* VI. CoBE
Dedicated Spirit, A, *fr.* IV. SeCePo
Enough of Humble Arguments, *fr.* VIII. AtBAP
"Fair seed-time had my soul, and I grew up," *fr.* I. EnL; EnLi-2; ExPo; NoP; OBRV *shorter sel., sl. diff.*; PoEL-4
(Childhood and School-Time.) FaBoEn; OBNC
(Fair Seed-Time Had My Soul.) AtBAP; MaPo
(Presences of Nature in Boyhood.) EPN
"Favorite pleasure hath it been with me, A," *fr.* IV, *Oxford ed.* OBRV
Fishing, *fr.* I. SD
France, XI, ERoP-1
"O pleasant exercise of hope and joy!" EnLi-2; MBW-2; OBRV
(French Revolution, The.) FiP; FOL; TOP
(Residence in France, Continued.) PoEL-4
"Gracious spirit o'er this earth presides, A," *fr.* V. OBRV
"He was of stature tall," *fr.* IV. SyP
Imagination and Taste, How Impaired and Restored. ERoP-1, XII; MERP, XII *and* XIII
"There are in our existence spots of time," *fr.* XII *and* XIII. FosPo; LO; MBW-2; PoEL-4
"Ye motions of delight, that through the fields," *fr.* XII *and* XIII. OBNC
"Immeasurable height, The," *fr.* VI. PeER
"In a throng, a festal company," *fr.* IV. OBRV
In One of Those Excursions, *fr.* XIV. MaPo
(Ascent of Mount Snowdon.) ERoP-1
(Conclusion: "In one of those excursions, may they ne'er.") FosPo
Influence of Natural Objects, *fr.* I. AWP; InPo; JAWP; LoBV; MCCG; OBRV; WBP
(Boyhood, *sl. longer sel.*) WHA
(Wisdom and Spirit of the Universe.) AtBAP; PeER
Intimations of Sublimity, *fr.* II. OBNC
Introduction—Childhood and School-Time, I. BEL; EnLit; ERoP-1; FosPo; MBW-2
"Oh there is blessing in this gentle breeze." TreFT
"Moon was up, the lake was shining clear, The," *fr.* I. FaBoEn
Nature's Healing, *fr.* XII. EPN
Newton, *fr.* III. ImOP
Noble, The, 3 *ll., fr.* IX. ChTr
Oh, Blank Confusion, *fr.* VII. AtBAP
Oh! Mystery of Man, *fr.* XII. FiP
"Oh! yet a few short years of useful life," *fr.* XIV. OBRV
"On poetry and geometric truth," *fr.* V. SyP
"One summer evening (led by her) I found," *fr.* I. FiP; FlW; MyFE; PIA; ViBoPo
("One evening—surely I was led by her," *Oxford ed.*) OBRV
(Stolen Boat, The.) ShBV-3
"Out steeds remounted and the summons given," *fr.* II. SyP
Poet and the French Revolution, The, *fr.* XI. EPN
"Poet, gentle creature as he is, The," *fr.* I. PP
Raven's Nest, The, *fr.* I. ShBV-3
Residence at Cambridge, III. MBW-2
Residence in France.
"Cheered with this hope," *fr.* X. BEL; PoEL-4
"France lured me forth," *fr.* IX *and* X. BEL; MBW-2
"It was a beautiful and silent day," X. ERoP-1
Residence in London, *fr.* VII.
"As the black storm upon the mountain-top." PoEL-4
(Blind Beggar, The.) ERoP-1
"Rise up, thou monstrous anthill on the plain." MBW-2
Retrospect—Love of Nature Leading to Love of Man, *fr.* VIII. MBW-2
School-Time, II. BEL; ERoP-1; MBW-2
Shepherd, The, *fr.* VIII.
"Yet, hail to you/ Moors, mountains, headlands, and ye hollow vales." ERoP-1
"There 'tis the Shepherd's task the winter long," *shorter sel.* OBNC

Simplon Pass, The, *fr.* VI. InPo; PoeP; PoFS; SyP
(Alpine Descent.) WHA
("Brook and road, The.") OBRV
(Down the Simplon Pass.) EPN
("Melancholy slackening that ensued, The.") PoEL-4
"Single tree there was, A," *fr.* VI, *Oxford ed.* OBRV
"Strong shock, A." *fr.* XI. MaPo (1969 ed.)
Summer Vacation, *fr.* IV.
"Bright was the summer's noon when quickening steps." MBW-2
"When first I made/ Once more the circuit of our little lake." OBRV, *shorter sel.*
"Yet in spite/ Of pleasure won, and knowledge not withheld." PoEL-4
(Rededication to Nature, The.) ERoP-1
There Was a Boy, *fr.* V. BoLiVe; BWP; ChER; FaBoCh; FaBoEn; LoGBV; MaPo; MCCG; MyFE; OBNC; OBRV; PoEL-4; PoeP
(Boy of Winander, The.) ERoP-1
(Echoes.) BoPe
(Winander Lake.) FiP
"Thought is with me sometimes, and I say, A," *fr.* V. PeER
"'Tis told by one whom stormy waters threw," *fr.* VI. ImOP
To Coleridge in Sicily, *fr.* XI. OBNC
'Twere Long to Tell, *fr.* II. AtBAP
"Twilight was coming on, yet through the gloom," *fr.* V. SyP
Universal Heart of Man, The, *fr.* XIII. TOP
Prelude: "Along the roadside, like the flowers of gold." Whittier. *Fr.* Among the Hills. AmePo; AP; CoBA; OxBA; PoEL-4; TOP
Prelude: "And did those feet in ancient time." Blake. *See* And Did Those Feet in Ancient Time.
Prelude: "As one, at midnight, wakened by the call." W. W. Gibson. MoBrPo
Prelude: "Dim, gradual thinning of the shapeless gloom." Siegfried Sassoon. *See* Troops, The.
Prelude: "England! awake! awake! awake!" Blake. *See* England! Awake! Awake! Awake!
Prelude: "Fields from Islington to Marybone, The." Blake. *See* Fields from Islington. . .
Prelude: "How could I love you more?" Richard Aldington. BrPo
Prelude: "Hush'd is each busy shout." A. C. Benson. OBVV
Prelude: "I saw the constellated matin choir." Edmund Clarence Stedman. AA
Prelude: "Night was dark, though sometimes a faint star, The." Richard Watson Gilder. *Fr.* The New Day. HBV; PoLF
Prelude: "Over his keys." James Russell Lowell. *Fr.* The Vision of Sir Launfal. LiTA; LiTG; PoLF
Prelude: "Rimbaud and Verlaine, precious pair of poets." Conrad Aiken. *See* Rimbaud and Verlaine. . .
Prelude, A: "Spirit that moves the sap in spring." Maurice Thompson. AmePo; HBV
Prelude: "Still south I went and west and south again." J. M. Synge. AWP; BoNaP; ChTr; HBMV; JAWP; MoBrPo; NeMA; OBMV; PoFr; TSW; WBP
Prelude: "Stood, at the closed door, and remembered." Conrad Aiken. Preludes for Memnon, LII. LiTM
Prelude: "This is not you?" Conrad Aiken. Preludes for Memnon, VI. MAP; MoAB; MoAmPo
Prelude: "This is the forest primeval. The murmuring pines and the hemlocks." Longfellow. *See* Prologue to "Evangeline."
Prelude: "This short straight sword." R. A. K. Mason. AnNZ
Prelude: Tristram and Iseult. Swinburne. *See* Tristram and Iseult.
Prelude: Troops, The. Siegfried Sassoon. *See* Troops, The.
Prelude XXIII: "We are those same children who amazed." Stefan George, *tr. fr. German by* C. F. MacIntyre. WaaP
Prelude: "What makes a plenteous harvest." Vergil, *tr. fr. Latin by* Dryden. *Fr.* Georgics. AWP
Prelude: "What shall we do—what shall we think—what shall we say?" Conrad Aiken. Preludes for Memnon, XXIX. FaBoMo
Prelude: "Whatever ripened in these lines." Clemens Brentano, *tr. fr. German by* Werner Heider. LiTW
Prelude: "Winter evening settles down, The." T. S. Eliot. Preludes, I. AmPP; ExPo; GBV (1952 ed.); MAP; MoAmPo (1942 ed.); MoShBr; NeMA; OCS; ShBV-3; TiPo (1952 ed.)
(Preludes.) AnAmPo; BoLiVe (1945 ed.); CoBA; DiPo; GTBS-W; InP; LiTA; LiTM; OBMV; PoFS; PoPl; PoPo; ReMP; UnPo; WePo
Prelude: "Winter for a moment takes the mind." Conrad Aiken. Preludes for Memnon, I. LiTM; NP; OxBA
(Preludes to Attitude, IV.) LiTA; TwAmPo
Prelude: "Woman, woman, let us say these things to each other." Conrad Aiken. NYBP
Prelude: "Words, words, ye are like birds." Josephine Preston Peabody. AA
Prelude: "You went to the verge, you say, and come back safely." Conrad Aiken. Preludes for Memnon, XIV. TwCP
(Preludes to Attitude, III.) LiTA; LiTG; TwAmPo
Prelude for Spring. Dorothy Livesay. PeCV
Prelude from "The Vision of Sir Launfal." James Russell Lowell. *See* Prelude: "Over his Keys."
Prelude of the New Testament ("Hail Mary full of grace!"). St. Luke, I: 28, 38, 42, II: 10-11, 14, Bible, *N.T.* (*Douay vers.*). CAW
Prelude sounded in a honky-tonk cafe, A. Out-dated Poem. Dick Gallup. ANYP
Prelude to Akwasidae. *Unknown, tr. fr. Twi by* Halim El-Dabh. TTY
Prelude to an Evening. John Crowe Ransom. AP; CoBMV; ILP; MAP; MoAB; MoAmPo; MoPo; MoVE; NePA; OxBA; PoCh
Prelude to Commencement. Marie de L. Welch. NYBP
Prelude to Cricket. Thomas Moult. *Fr.* Summer Days. POTE
("Before we came the moon-soaked dews were here.") MemP
Prelude to Songs before Sunrise. Swinburne. MaVP; PoVP; ViPo
Prelude to Space. C. S. Lewis. HW
Prelude to this smooth scene—mark well, The. After Jena. Thomas Hardy. *Fr.* The Dynasts. WaaP
Preludes (I-IV). T. S. Eliot. AmP; AnAmPo; BoLiVe (1945 ed.); CoBA; DiPo; GTBS-W; InP; LiTA; LiTM; MoVE; NoP; OBMV; PoFS; PoPl; ReMP; SeCePo; TDP; TwCP; UnPo; WePo
Sels.
"Morning comes to consciousness, The," II. PoPo
"Winter evening settles down, The," I. MoShBr; OCS; PoPo; TiPo (1952 ed.)
(Prelude.) AmPP; ExPo; GBV (1952 ed.); MAP; MoAmPo (1942 ed.); NeMA; ShBV-3
Preludes. Coventry Patmore. *See* Attainment, The, *and* Unthrift.
Preludes for Memnon; or, Preludes to Attitude, *sels.* Conrad Aiken.
"Beloved, let us once more praise the rain," VII. LiTA; TwAmPo
"Come let us take another's words and change the meaning," XXXVII. NoP
"Despair, that seeking for the *Ding-an-sich,*" V. PoDB
"First note, simple, The," XXI. LiTA; TwAmPo
"Keep in the heart the journal nature keeps," XLII. CMoP; NePA; OxBA
"Nothing to say, you say?" LIII. LiTA; TwAmPo
"One star fell and another as we walked," LVII. BoLP; MaP; MoAmPo; PoPo
"Rimbaud and Verlaine, precious pair of poets," LVI. FaBoMo; LiTA; LiTM (rev. ed.); MoPo; NAMP; NePA; TwAmPo; TwCP
"Sleep; and between the closed eyelids," III. LiTA; LiTG; PoDB; TwAmPo
"So, in the evening, to the simple cloister," XX. LiTA; TwAmPo
(Cloister.) MAP; MoAB; MoAmPo;
"Stood, at the closed door," LII. LiTM
"Then came I to the shoreless shore of silence," XXXIII. LiTA; NePa; OxBA; TwAmPo
"This is not you?" VI. MAP; MoAB; MoAmPo
"Time has come, the clock says time has come, The," XXVIII. NePA; OxBA
"Two coffees in the Espanol," II. LiTA; LiTG; TwAmPo
"Watch long enough, and you will see the leaf," XIX. CMoP; NePA; OxBA
"What shall we do—what shall we think—what shall we say?" XXIX. FaBoMo
"Winter for a moment takes the mind," I. LiTA; LiTM; MoPo; MoVE; NP; OxBA; StP; TwAmPo
"World is intricate, and we are nothing, The," L. NoP

Preludes (continued)
"You went to the verge, you say," XIV. LiTA; LiTG; TwAmPo; TwCP
Preludes to Attitude. Conrad Aiken. *See* Preludes for Memnon.
Preludes to Definition. Conrad Aiken. *See* Time in the Rock.
Prelusive. Herman Melville. *Fr.* Clarel. AmPP (5th ed.)
Premonition. Edith Ogutsch. FiSC
Premonition. Laura Goodman Salverson. CaP
Prenatal Fantasy. Walter H. Kerr. FiSC
Preparation. Thomas Edward Brown. OBEV (new ed.); OBVV; TOP
Preparation of the Pyre for Patroclus. Homer. *See* Pyre of Patroclus, The.
Preparations. *Unknown.* *See* Yet If His Majesty, Our Sovereign Lord.
Preparative, The. Thomas Traherne. AnAnS-1; MeP; OxBoCh; PoEL-2
Preparatory Meditations, *sels.* Edward Taylor.
First Series.
"Am I thy gold? Or purse, Lord, for thy wealth," VI. AmLP; AmPP (4th ed.); AP; AtBAP; LiTA; MeP; NePA; NoP; OxBA
"Begracde with glory, gloried with grace," XXXI. MeP
"Daintiest draught thy pensill over drew, The," XXX. MWA-1
"I kenning through astronomy divine," VIII. AmP; AmPP; AP; AtBAP; LiTA; MAmP; NoP; OxBA; PoEL-3; SCAP; StP
"Leafe gold, Lord of thy golden wedge o'relaid," XVI. MAmP
"Lord, art thou at the table head above," IV. AmPP; AP; AtBAP; MWA-1; NePA; OxBA
"Lord, do away my motes: and mountains great," XLIX. EP
"My blessed Lord, art thou a lilly flower," V. MeP
"My deare deare, Lord, I do thee Saviour call," II. MeP
"My Lord I fain would praise thee well but finde," XXXIV. MeP
"My Lord, my life, can envy ever bee," XXXIII. AtBAP; MeP; PoEL-3
"My shattred Phancy stole away from mee," XXIX. AP; MWA-1; SCAP
"My sin! my sin! My God, these cursed dregs," XXXIX. MeP; SCAP
"My soule, Lord, quailes to thinke that I should bee," XXXVII. MeP
"Oh! that I always breath'd in such an aire," III. AmPP (4th ed.)
"Oh! What a thing is man? Lord, who am I," XXXVIII. AnNE; AP; MAmP; MWA-1; OxBA
"Still I complain: I am complaining still," XL. AP; MAmP; MeP; MWA-1; OxBA; PoEL-3
"Stupendious love! All saints astonishment," X. OxBA
"Thy grace, dear Lord's my golden wrack," XXXII. EP; MAmP; MeP; MWA-1; NoP; SCAP
"Thy human[e] frame, my glorious Lord, I spy," VII. LiTA; VaPo
"View, all ye eyes above, this sight which flings," XX. AP
"What glory's this, my Lord? Should one small point," XXI. MAmP
"What love is this of thine, that cannot bee," I. AmPP (4th ed.); AnNE; AP; ForPo; MeP; PoEL-3; SCAP
"When thy Bright Beams, my Lord, do strike mine Eye," XXII. MAmP
"Would God I in that Golden City were," XXIII. MAmP
Second Series.
"All dull, my Lord, my spirits flat, and dead," VII. MAmP; MWA-1
"Angells sung a carole at thy birth, The," CX. MWA-1
"Callst thou me friend? What rhetorick is this," CLVI. MeP
"Dull, dull, my Lord, my fancy dull I finde," CXXXI. MAmP
"Eternal Life! What life is this, I pray," XC. MWA-1
"Head, my Lord, an honourable piece, An," XXXVI. MeP
"Help, oh! my Lord, anoint mine eyes to see," CXIII. MAmP; MWA-1
"It grieves mee, Lord, my fancy's rusty: rub," XCII. MAmP
"Like to the marigold, I blushing close," III. AnNE; SCAP
"Methinks I spy Almighty holding in," LXVIII. AP
"My Blessed Lord, how doth thy beautious spouse," CL. SCAP
"My deare deare Lord, I know not what to say," CXLVI. MAmP; MWA-1
"My glorious Lord thy work upon my hand," CLIII. MAmP
"My gracious Lord, I would thee glory doe," IV. SCAP
"My onely Lord, when with no muddy sight," XCVII. MWA-1
"Oh! Angells, stand agastard at my song," LXXXV. MWA-1
"Oh! Golden rose! Oh. Glittering lilly white," II. SCAP
"Oh leaden heeld. Lord, give, forgive I pray," I. SCAP
"Oh! thou, my Lord, thou king of saints, here mak'st," LXII. MAmP; MWA-1
"O! what a thing is love? who can define," LXVI. MeP
"O! What a thing is might right mannag'd," XLVIII. MeP; MWA-1
"Orator from rhetorick gardens picks, The," XLIV. MAmP
"Pardon my Lord, I humbly beg the same," CXXXII. MAmP
"Should I with silver tooles delve through the hill," LVI. MAmP; OxBA; SCAP
"Star, bright morning star, the shining Sun, A," CXIV. MAmP; MWA-1
"Vine, my Lord, a noble vine indeed, A," XCVIII. MeP
"Vines of Lebanon that briskly grew, The," LXV. MeP
"What shall I say, my deare deare Lord," CXLII. MWA-1
"Wonders amazed! Am I espoused to thee," CXLIII. MWA-1
"Ye angells bright, pluck from your wings a quill," LX. PoEL-3
Prepare. Witter Bynner. PGD
Prepare for songs; he's come, he's come. The New Yeeres Gift, or Circumcisions Song, Sung to the King in the Presence at White Hall. Robert Herrick. SeCV-1
Prepare, prepare the iron helm of war. A War Song to Englishmen. Blake. *Fr.* King Edward the Third. CH; OHIP; WaaP
"Prepare to meet the King of Terrors," cried. Epigram. Ebenezer Elliott. PeER
Prepared for a Soldiers' and Sailors' Monument in Boston. James Russell Lowell. TOP
("To those who died for her on land and sea.") InP
Preparedness. Edwin Markham. FaFP; MAP; MoAmPo; NeMA; OQP; YT
Preparedness. Jean Grigsby Paxton. PGD
Preparing for the Wedding. Claudian, *tr. fr. Latin by* Maurice Platnauer *and* Virginia Tufte. *Fr.* Epithalamium for Honorius and Maria. HW
Pre-Raphaelite, A/ Had to have things right. Christopher Morley. WhC
Presage and caveat not only seem. The Window Sill. Robert Graves. AtBAP; EnLoPo
Presage of Storme. George Chapman. *Fr.* Eugenia. FaBoEn
Presaging. Rainer Maria Rilke, *tr. fr. German by* Jessie Lemont. AWP; JAWP; WBP
Presbyterian Church Government. Samuel Butler. *Fr.* Hudibras, I, 3. OBS
Presbyterian Knight and Independent Squire, *abr.* Samuel Butler. *Fr.* Hudibras, I, 1. OBS
(Hudibras, the Presbyterian Knight, *abr.*) OxBoLi; SiTL
(Metaphysical Sectarian, The.) MeLP
(Portrait of Hudibras.) AtBAP; PoEL-3
Presbyterian Wedding, The. *Unknown.* CoMu; ErPo
Presbyterians, The. Dryden. *Fr.* The Hind and the Panther, I. OBS
Prescience. Thomas Bailey Aldrich. AA; OBVV
Prescience. Donald Jeffrey Hayes. PoNe
Prescience. Margaret Widdemer. HBMV
Prescott, press my Ascot waistcoat. Sportif [*or* Ascot Waistcoat]. David McCord. FiBHP; NYBP
Prescription. A. L. Guerard. SoP
Prescription of Painful Ends. Robinson Jeffers. LiTA; MoAB; MoAmPo; OxBA
Presence, The. William Everson. ErPo
Presence, The. Robert Graves. ChMP
Presence, The. Denise Levertov. NaP; NePoEA-2
Presence. Mary E. McCullough. MaRV
Presence. John Moffit. MoRP
Presence, The. Jones Very. PoIE
Presence of an External Master of Knowledge. Wallace Stevens. NePA

Presence of good, The. The Measure of Memory. LeRoi Jones. FRC
Presence of Mind. Harry Graham. WhC
Presence of Snow. Melville Cane. GoYe
Presence of the Spirit, The. Giulio Salvadori, *tr. fr. Spanish by* Thomas Walsh. CAW
Presences of Nature in Boyhood. Wordsworth. *See* Fair Seed-Time Had My Soul.
Presences Perfected. Siegfried Sassoon. MoBrPo
Present. Miriam Clark Potter. BiCB
Present, The. Adelaide Anne Procter. WGRP
Present Age, The. Arthur Cleveland Coxe. BLPA; MaRV
(We are Living, We Are Dwelling.) TRV
Present Crisis, The. James Russell Lowell. AmePo; CoBA; MaRV; OHFP; OQP, *abr.*
Sels.
"Careless seems the great Avenger; history's pages but record." TreFT; TRV
"Count me o'er earth's chosen heroes." WGRP
New Occasions Teach New Duties. TreFT
Once to Every Man and Nation. PAL; TRV
(Truth and Falsehood.) SoP
Present in Absence. John Hoskins. *See* Absence.
Present to a Lady, A. *Unknown.* ErPo
Presentation, The. Robert Southwell. MeP
Presentiment. Ambrose Bierce. AA
Presentiment—is that long shadow—on the lawn. Emily Dickinson. AmePo; AmPP; AP; CABA; CBEP; CBV; ELU; FaBoEn; InPo; OxBA; PoeP
Presenting to a Lady a White Rose and a Red, on the Tenth of June. William Somervile. CEP
(On Presenting to a Lady a White Rose and a Red on the Tenth of June.) OBEC
Presently at our touch the teacup stirred. Voices from the Other World. James Merrill. TwCP
Presents. Marchette Chute. BrR; ChBR; EvOK; SiSoSe; StVeCh
Presents of money, furs and pearls. The Right Time. *Unknown.* UnTE
Preserve a respectful demeanor. To a Baked Fish. Carolyn Wells. FiBHP
Preserve that old kettle, so blackened and worn. My Dad's Dinner Pail. Edward Harrigan. BLPA
Preserve thy sighs, unthrifty girle! Song: The Souldier going to the Field. Sir William Davenant. CavP; MePo
Preserve us, Lord, by thy dear Word. Turk and Pope. Robert Wisdom. ReIE
President Garfield. Longfellow. PAH
President Johnson to. Said. George Starbuck. PV
President Lincoln's Grave. Caroline Atherton Briggs Mason. DD; OHIP
President Ordains the Bee to Be, The. Wallace Stevens. *Fr.* Notes toward a Supreme Fiction. AtBAP; LiTA
Presidential Address to a Party of Exiles Leaving for the Moon. Howard Nemerov. ML
Press, The. *Unknown.* PaPo
Press Close Bare-Bosom'd Night. Walt Whitman. *Fr.* Song of Myself. MeWo
Press-Gang, The. *Unknown.* ChTr
Press [*or* Presse] me not to take more pleasure. The Rose. George Herbert. AtBAP; LiTB; MaMe; PoEL-2; PoIE
Press of the Spoon River *Clarion* was wrecked, The. Carl Hamblin. Edgar Lee Masters. *Fr.* Spoon River Anthology. AmP; CMoP; ILP; LiTA; LiTM (rev. ed.)
Press often for, (nor, than at this time more). Vox Oppressi, To the Lady Phipps. Richard Henchman. SCAP
Press Onward. *Unknown.* FaFP
Press—the Press—the glorious Press, The. The Press. *Unknown.* PaPo
Presse me not to take more pleasure. *See* Press me not. . .
Pressed Gentian, The. Whittier. AnAmPo
Pressure ("Pressed out of measure and pressed to all length"). *Unknown.* SoP
Pressures, The. LeRoi Jones. CBV
Prest by the load of life, the weary mind. Prologue. Samuel Johnson. *Fr.* The Good-natur'd Man (*by* Goldsmith). LoBV
Prester John had apes of gold. Polite Song. Theodore Spencer. CLwM
Presto Furioso. Sir Owen Seaman. BOHV
Presto, pronto! Two boys, two horses. Boy Riding Forward Backward. Robert Francis. NePoAm-2
Presumption. Eileen Duggan. CAW
Presumptuous, The. W. H. Auden. CMoP
Pretences. Ibn Rashiq, *tr. fr. Arabic by* A. J. Arberry. TTY
Pretending. Myra Cohn Livingston. BiCB
Pretense. Helen Welshimer. PoMa
Pretext. Yakamochi, *tr. fr. Japanese by* Arthur Waley. *Fr.* Manyo Shu. WoL
("By way of pretext.") AWP; JAWP; LiTW; WBP
Prethee Cloe, not so fast. To Cloe. John Oldmixon. PeRV
Prettiest girl that ever I saw, The. Sucking Cider through a Straw. *Unknown.* AS
Prettiest lady that ever I've seen, The. Pretty Lady. Rose Fyleman. BoTP
Prettiest Things, The. Camilla Doyle. YT
Pretty a Day, A. E. E. Cummings. CMoP
Pretty Beads. Dick Gallup. ANYP
Pretty brook was running at play, A. *Unknown.* GFA
Pretty Cow. Ann *or* Jane Taylor. *See* Cow, The.
Pretty Fair Maid, A. *Unknown.* *See* Sweetheart in the Army, A.
Pretty fair miss all in the garden, A. The Love Token. *Unknown.* BaBo
Pretty flowers, tell me why. The Flowers. *Unknown.* OTPC (1923 ed.)
Pretty Futility. Elizabeth J. Coatsworth. MAP
Pretty game, my girl, A. The Flirt. W. H. Davies. EnLoPo
Pretty Girl of Loch Dan, The. Sir Samuel Ferguson. HBV
Pretty girls of the fall, The. The Falls. F. D. Reeve. NYBP
Pretty good firm is "Watch & Waite," A. The Best Firm. Walter G. Doty. HBV; HBVY; RIS
Pretty John Watts. *Unknown.* OxNR
Pretty Lady. Rose Fyleman. BoTP
Pretty little boy and a pretty little girl, A. Courtesy. Mary Mapes Dodge. BrR
Pretty little crocus, in your cosy bed. Waking Up. *Unknown.* BoTP
Pretty Maid, The. Paul Fort. *See* Ballade: "Pretty maid, she died, she died. . ., The."
Pretty Maid. *Unknown.* OTPC; OxNR
Pretty maid both kind and fair, A. The Very Pretty Maid of This Town, and the Amorous 'Squire Not One Hundred Miles from the Place. *Unknown.* CoMu
Pretty Maid Marion. Ivy O. Eastwick. BoTP
Pretty maid, pretty maid, where have you been? Pretty Maid. *Unknown.* OTPC; OxNR
Pretty maid she died, she died, in love-bed as she lay, The. Ballade [*or* The Pretty Maid]. Paul Fort. AWP; JAWP; OBMV; WBP
Pretty Maids Beware! *Unknown.* CoMu
Pretty Mary, *with music.* *Unknown.* BFSS
Pretty Miss Apathy. Pooh! Walter de la Mare. FiBHP
Pretty Molly ("Jump up behind me and away we will ride"), *with music.* *Unknown.* BFSS
Pretty Molly ("Oh Molly, pretty Molly, come go with me"), *with music.* *Unknown.* BFSS
"Pretty Moo-cow, will you tell." The Cow. Mrs. Motherly. PPL; SAS
Pretty Polly. Byron Herbert Reece. BoLP
Pretty Polly. E. Merrill Root. MAP
Pretty Polly ("Get up, get up, pretty Polly, he says"). *Unknown.* UnTE
Pretty Polly ("Go get me some of your father's gold"), *with music.* *Unknown.* AS
Pretty Polly ("He followed her up, he followed her down"). *Unknown.* *See* Lady Isabel and the Elf-knight.
Pretty Polly ("I courted pretty Polly the livelong night"), *with music.* *Unknown.* OuSiCo
Pretty Polly ("Pretty Polly lay rolling one night on her bed"), *with music.* *Unknown.* BFSS
"Pretty Polly goes dressed in red." Pretty Polly. Byron Herbert Reece. BoLP
Pretty Polly Pansy. Polly Pansy. William Brighty Rands. SAS
"Pretty Polly, pretty Polly, come go 'long with me." The Gosport Tragedy (B *vers.*). *Unknown.* BaBo
Pretty rabbits are so tame, The. Our Baby's Rabbits. *Unknown.* SAS

Pretty red Squirrel lives up in a tree, The. The Squirrel. Mary Howitt. BoTP
Pretty sneaking knave I knew, A. Mr. Cromek. Blake. ChTr
Pretty task, A; and so I told the Fool. Epilogue. Dryden. *Fr.* Aureng-Zebe. SeEP
Pretty task, Miss S——, to ask, A. I'm Not a Single Man [*or* Lines in a Young Lady's Album]. Thomas Hood. ALV; HBV
Pretty Thing, A. *Unknown.* UnTE
Pretty Twinkling Starry Eyes. Nicholas Breton. *Fr.* The Passionate Shepherd. ElL
Pretty Wantons. *Unknown.* ElL
Pretty Words. Elinor Wylie. HBMV; RePo; YaD; YT
Pretty young actress, a stammerer, A. Limerick. Eille Norwood. CenHV
Pretzel Man, The. Rachel Field. SoPo
Prevailing Prayer. Richard Chenevix Trench. *See* Prayer: "Lord, what a change. . ."
Prevalent Poetry. Charles Follen Adams. CenHV
Prevention of Stacy Miller, The. Peter Miller. MoCV
Prevision. Ada Foster Murray. HBV
Prey for us the Prince of Pees. A Song to John, Christ's Friend. *Unknown.* MeEL
Priam. Dudley Fitts. OnHM
Priam and Achilles. Homer, *tr. fr. Greek.* *Fr.* The Iliad, XXIV. OBEC, *tr. by* Pope; OBS, *tr. by* George Chapman
Priapus and the Pool, *sels.* Conrad Aiken.
  And Already the Minutes, V [VI]. InPo
  "Fade, then,—die, depart, and come no more," XVII. AmLP
  Portrait of a Girl, IV. GoJo
  See, as the Carver Carves a Rose, XVI [XIX]. AnAmPo; PFY
    (Carver, The.) HBMV
  "There is nothing moving there." IX. CMoP
  "There was an island in the sea," XV. CMoP
    (Atlantis.) SiSw
  This Is the Shape of the Leaf, IV [V]. AnAmPo; AtBAP; CMoP; HBMV; MAPA; NePA; OxBA; TrGrPo; WHA
    (Portrait of a Girl.) MAP; MoAmPo; TSW
  When Trout Swim down Great Ormond Street, III [IV]. AmLP; AnAmPo; CaFP; InPo; MAPA; PFY
    (Whim.) TSW
Priapus, with his god's virility. Design for a List of Pictures. Arthur Symons. FaBoTw
Price He Paid, The. Ella Wheeler Wilcox. WBLP
Price of, The/ milk has. The Sacrifice. Norman Jordan. BF
Price of a Drink. Josephine Pollard. PaPo
Price of Begging, The. Emmanuel ben David Frances, *tr. fr. Hebrew by* A. B. Rhine. TrJP
Price of Experience, The. Blake. *See* Song of Enion.
Price of Wisdom, The. Job, XXVIII: 1-28, Bible, *O.T.* TrGrPo
Price seemed reasonable, The. Telephone Conversation. Wole Soyinka. FlW; TTY
Prices. Louis Ginsberg. TrJP
Pride. Violet Jacob. OxBS
Pride. Josephine Miles. FiMAP
Pride, The. John Newlove. MoCV
Pride and ambition, and peevishness too. Song. *Unknown.* SeCL
Pride and Hesitation. Cerise Farallon. UnTE
Pride and Prejudice. Linwood D. Smith. TNV
Pride held my will. The Help-Givers. Laurence Housman. MaRV
Pride Is Out. *Unknown.* CBEP
Pride Is the Canker. *Unknown.* *See* Do Not, Oh, Do Not Prize.
Pride of a Jew, The. Judah Halevi, *tr. fr. Hebrew by* Israel Cohen. TrJP
Pride of every grove I chose, The. The Garland. Matthew Prior. SeCL
Pride of the height, the clear firmament, the beauty of heaven, The. Sun, Moon and Stars. Ecclesiasticus, Bible, Apocrypha. BoC
Pride of wrights, the joy of smiths abide, The. The Junk Shop. Henri Coulette. NYBP
Pride of Youth. Dante Gabriel Rossetti. The House of Life, XXIV. FaBoEn; MaVP; OBNC; PoVP; ViPo; ViPP; VP
Pride of Youth, The. Sir Walter Scott. *See* Proud Maisie.
Pride, the Never-Failing Vice of Fools. Pope. *Fr.* Essay on Criticism, *Pt.* II. TreFT
  ("Of all the causes which conspire to blind.) CoBE; EnL; FaBoEn; ILP; PoIE
Pride, where wit fails, steps in to our defence. Pope. *Fr.* An Essay on Criticism. YAT
Priest, A. Norman Gale. VA
Priest, The. James Oppenheim. *Fr.* Night. MaRV
Priest and Pagan. Albert Durrant Watson. CaP
Priest and the Mulberry-Tree, The. Thomas Love Peacock. *Fr.* Crotchet Castle. BoTP; GN; OnMSP; OTPC; RIS; StPo
Priest-mannerly the mind. Missa Vocis. R. P. Blackmur. ReMP
Priest of Christ, The. Thomas Ken. SoP; TRV
Priest of Coloony, The. W. B. Yeats. OnYI
Priest of God, unto thee I come. Absolution. Edward Willard Watson. AA
Priest or Poet. Shane Leslie. CAW; WGRP
Priest Rediscovers His Psalm-Book, The. *Unknown, tr. fr. Irish by* Frank O'Connor. KiLC
Priestcraft and Private Judgement. Dryden. *Fr.* Religio Laici. OBS
Priesthood, The. George Herbert. AnAnS-1; MaMe; MeP
Priesthood, The. Yvor Winters. NP
Priest's Chant, The. John Fletcher. *See* Evening Song.
Priest's Lament, The. Robert Hugh Benson. ACP
Priests of Apollo, sacred be the Roome. The Sacrifice to Apollo. Michael Drayton. OBS; SeEP
Priest's Prayer, A. Martha Dickinson Bianchi. AA
Priest's Song, A. Thomas Dekker. *Fr.* Old Fortunatus. OBSC
  (O Pittie.) AtBAP
  (Song: "Virtue's branches wither, virtue pines.") ElL; SiCE
Priests told me they were my enemies. Dirty Thoughts. Victor Contoski. ThO
Prim old room where memories stir, A. In an Old Nursery. Patrick R. Chalmers. HBMV
Primacy of Dullness, The. Dryden. *See* Shadwell.
Primal Cause, The. Dante, *tr. fr. Italian by* Longfellow. *Fr.* Divina Commedia: Paradiso, XXVIII. CAW
Primaleon of Greece, *sel.* Anthony Munday.
  Beauty Sat Bathing [by a Spring]. CBEP; ElL; UnTE
    (Beauty Bathing.) OBEV; PG (1955 ed.)
    (Colin.) GTBS; GTBS-D; GTBS-P; GTBS-W; GTSE; GTSL
    (To Colin Clout.) OAEP; OBSC; TuPP; ViBoPo
Primavera. Frank Lima. ANYP
Prime. W. H. Auden. *Fr.* Horae Canonicae. CMoP; MaPo (1969 ed.); PoDB
Prime cantante! My Catbird. William Henry Venable. AA; HBV; PFY
Prime of Life, The. Walter Learned. HBV
Primer. Samuel Hoffenstein. BOHV
Primer Lesson. Carl Sandburg. FaPON; MAP; MoAmPo; MoShBr; PoPl; RePo; StVeCh; TSW
Primer of Consequences. Virginia Brasier. ShM
Primer of Plato. Jean Garrigue. MoVE
Primer of the Daily Round, A. Howard Nemerov. NYBP
Primeval Forest. Longfellow. *See* Prologue to "Evangeline."
Primeval night had repossessed. Festum Nativitatis. Aubrey Thomas De Vere. IrPN
Primitives. Dudley Randall. BALP
Primo Vere. Giosue Carducci, *tr. fr. Italian by* John Bailey. AWP; JAWP; WBP
Primrose, The [Being at Montgomery Castle]. John Donne. MaMe; MeP; SCEP-1
Primrose, The. Robert Herrick. HBV; OBEV; ViBoPo
Primrose by the Wayside, A. Anna Bunston de Bary. MaRV
Primrose Dame, A. Gleeson White. HBV; VA
Primrose Hill. Olive Custance. JKCP
Primrose Hill. Rose Fyleman. BoTP
Primrose in the green forest, The. Song. Thomas Deloney. *Fr.* The Gentle Craft. TiPo (1959 ed.); ViBoPo
Primrose in the sheade do blow, The. *See* Primrwose in the sheade do blow, The.
Primroses. Alfred Austin. OBVV
Primrwose [*or* Primrose] in the sheade do blow, The. Blackmwore Maidens. William Barnes. GTBS; HBV; PoVP; ShBV-3; VA
Prince Absalom and Sir Rotherham Redde. Evening. Edith Sitwell. MoBS
Prince and bishop and knight and dame. The Losers [*or* The

Pawns]. William Young. *Fr.* Wishmakers' Town. AA; HBMV
Prince Arthur, *sel.* Sir Richard Blackmore.
Description of Chaos. PeRV
Prince Arthur. Spenser. *Fr.* The Faerie Queene, I, 7. OBSC
Prince Finikin. Kate Greenaway. SAS
Prince Heathen (A *and* B *vers.*). *Unknown.* ESPB
Prince Henry the Navigator. Sydney Clouts. PeSA
Prince Lucifer, *sels.* Alfred Austin.
Grave-Digger's Song. VA
Mother-Song. VA
(Mother-Song from "Prince Lucifer.") HBV
Prince of Life, The. John Oxenham. TrPWD
Prince of Peace. Isaiah, IX: 6, Bible, *O.T.* BoPe
Prince of Peace, The. Micah, V: 2, Isaiah, IX: 2, 6-7, Bible, *O.T.* ChrBoLe
Prince of Peace, The. Edward Henry Bickersteth. BePJ
Prince of Peace, The. Philip Doddridge. MaRV; SoP
(Savior Comes, The.) SoP
Prince of Peace, The. Harry Emerson Fosdick. MaRV; TrPWD
Prince of Wales' Marriage. *Unknown.* CoMu
Prince Peter. Nancy Byrd Turner. GaP; RIS
Prince Riquet's Song. Stopford Augustus Brooke. *Fr.* Riquet of the Tuft. VA
Prince Robert. *Unknown.* ESPB (A *and* B *vers.*); LoEn; OBB, *sl. abr.*; OxBB
Prince Rupert's drop, paper muslin ghost. Pedantic Literalist. Marianne Moore. APA; CoAnAm
Prince Tatters. Laura E. Richards. GaP; HBV; HBVY; MPB
Prince William, of the Brunswick race. The Royal Adventurer. Philip Freneau. PAH
Princely Ditty in Praise of the English Rose, A. Thomas Deloney. BoTP
Princely eagle, and the soaring hawke, The. William Wood. SCAP
"Princes!—and you, most valorous." The Prodigals. Austin Dobson. InP
Prince's Progress, The, *sel.* Christina Rossetti.
"Too late for love, too late for joy," *sel.* ViBoPo
(Bride Song.) OBEV; OBVV; TOP
(Too Late For Love.) PoVP
Princes statue, A, or in marble carv'd. George Chapman. *Fr.* The Epistle Dedicatory to Chapman's Translation of the Iliad. AtBAP; OBS
Princess, The, *sels.* Tennyson.
"As thro' [*or* through] the land at eve we went," *fr.* Pt. I. AnFE; AtBAP; GTBS; GTBS-W; LiTB; LiTG; LiTL; MaRV; OBVV; PoVP; TreFS; VA
(Reconciliation, The.) HBV
(Songs from "The Princess.") OAEP; ViPo
(We Kiss'd Again with Tears.) PoToHe
"Ask me no more: the moon may draw the sea," *fr.* Pt. VI. AnFE; AtBAP; BoLiVe; EnLi-2; EnLit; GTBS-W; HBV; LiTB; MaPo; MeWo; OBNC; PoEL-5; PoVP; TreFT; TrGrPo; VA; UnTE; ViPP
(Songs from "The Princess.") OAEP; ViPo
Bugle Song, *fr.* Pt. III. ATP; BEL; BoChLi; EnLit; FaPON; GN; HBV; MCCG; MPB; PCD; PG (1945 ed.); RG; StVeCh; TreF; VA
(Blow, Bugle, Blow.) ChTr; FaFP; GTBS-W; LiTB; LiTG; OBEV; TSW; UnS; WePo; WiR
(Bugle, The.) ShBV-2
(Horns of Elfland, The.) GBV
(Lyrics from "The Princess.") OuHeWo
(Our Echoes Roll from Soul to Soul.) MaRV
(Song: "Splendor [*or* Splendour] falls on castle walls, The.") ExPo; LoBV; MemP; NeHB; PoPl; ThWaDe; TOP
(Songs from "The Princess.") AWP; InPo; JAWP; OAEP; ViPo; WBP
(Splendor [*or* Splendour] Falls [on Castle Walls], The.) AnFE; AtBAP; BoLiVe; CBEP; CBV; CH; CoBE; ELP; EnL; EnLi-2; EPN; FaBoCh; FaBV; FiP; GoJo; GTBS; GTBS-D; GTBS-P; GTSL; ILP; InP; LoGBV; MaPo (1969 ed.); MBW-2; NoP; OBNC; OBVV; OQP; OTPC; PeVV; PoE; PoEL-5; PoIE; PoVP; RoGo; TrGrPo; ViBoPo; ViPP; VP
Come Down, O Maid [from Yonder Mountain Height], *fr.* Pt. VII. AnEnPo; AnFE; AtBAP; BoPe; CABA; CaFP; CBEP; DiPo; EG; EnL; FosPo; GTBS; GTBS-P; MaPo; OBEV; OBNC; OBVV; PoE; PoVP; TOP; TreFT; ViBoPo; ViPo; ViPP; WHA
(Idyl, An.) TrGrPo
(Shepherd's Song.) LoBV
(Song.) FaBoEn
(Songs from The Princess.") EnLi-2; OAEP; SeCeV
Home They Brought Her Warrior Dead, *fr.* Pt. V. BEL; BoLiVe; EnLi-2; HBV; MaRV; OTPC (1923 ed.); PoVP; TreFS; TrGrPo; ViPP
(Lyrics from "The Princess.") OuHeWo
(Songs from "The Princess.") OAEP; ViPo
"I loved her, one/ Not learned, save in gracious household ways," *fr.* Pt. VII. PGD
"Now sleeps the crimson petal, now the white," *fr.* Pt. VII. AnFE; AtBAP; BoLiVe; BWP; CABA; CaFP; CBEP; CBV; ChER; ChTr; DiPo; ELP; EnL; EnLi-2; EPN; FiP; GTBS-D; GTBS-P; ILP; MaPo; MBW-2; MeWo; NoP; OBNC; OBVV; PAn; PoAn; PoE; PoEL-5; PoFS; PoIE; PoVP; ShBV-3; StP; TreFT; TrGrPo; UnTE; ViBoPo; ViPP
(Song: "Now sleeps the crimson petal, now the white.") ExPo; FaBoBe; LoBV; NeHB
(Songs from "The Princess.") OAEP; SeCeV; ViPo
(Summer Night.) OBEV; SeCePo; UnPo (1st ed.); WePo
"O Swallow, Swallow, flying, flying south," *fr.* Pt. IV. AtBAP; GTBS; GTSL; HBV; PoVP
(Songs from "The Princess.") ViPo
"Our enemies have fallen, have fallen: the seed," *fr.* Pt. VI. PoVP
"Sweet and low, sweet and low," *fr.* Pt. II. BEL; BoChLi; BoTP; CoBE; EnLi-2; EnLit; EPN; EtS; FaBoBe; FaPON; GFA; GoTP; ILP; InP; MBW-2; MCCG; MPB; NeHB; OTPC; PG (1945 ed.); PoE; PoPl; PoVP; PRWS; ShBV-1; StVeCh; TreF; TrGrPo; TSW; VA; ViPP
(Lullaby: "Sweet and low, sweet and low.") GBV (1922 ed.); HBV; HBVY; PoLF; PoRh; TVC
(Lyrics from "The Princess.") OuHeWo
(Song: "Sweet and low.") ThWaDe; YAT
(Songs from "The Princess.") ViPo
"Tears, idle tears, I know not what they mean," *fr.* Pt. IV. AnFE; AtBAP; BEL; BoLiVe; BWP; CABA; CaFP; CBV; DiPo; EG; EnL; EnLi-2; EnLit; EPN; FiP; ForPo; FosPo; GTBS; GTBS-P; GTBS-W; GTSL; HBV; LiTB; LiTG; MaPo; MasP; MBW-2; MCCG; NeHB; NoP; OBNC; OBVV; PG (1945 ed.) PoAn; PoE; PoEL-5; PoFS; PoIE; PoPo; PoVP; ShBV-4; TreF; TrGrPo; UnPo; VA; ViBoPo; ViPP; WePo; WHA
(Lyrics from "The Princess.") OuHeWo
(Song: "Tears, idle tears, I know not what they mean.") FaBoEn; PoPl; TOP
(Songs from "The Princess.") AWP; InPo; JAWP; OAEP; SeCeV; ViPo; WBP
"This world was once a fluid haze of light," 4 *ll.* ImOP
"Thy voice is heard thro' rolling drums," *fr.* Interlude. OBVV; PoVP; TrGrPo; VA
(Songs from "The Princess.") ViPo
Woman and Man, *abr., fr.* Pt. VII. OQP
Princess, The. W. J. Turner. HBMV
Princess and the Gypsies, The. Frances Cornford. StPo
Princess Ida, *sels.* W. S. Gilbert.
Arac's Song. FiBHP; WhC
Disagreeable Man, The. ALV; FiBHP; MPB; PoVP
Mighty Must, The. BOHV
Princess is sad, The. What brings tears to her eyes? Sonatina. Rubén Darío. WoL
Princess of pretty pets. The Little Rebel. Joseph Ashby-Sterry. VA
Princess of Scotland, The. Rachel Annand Taylor. GoTS; SiSw
Princess Sabbath. Heine, *tr. fr. German by* Charles Godfrey Leland. TrJP
Principally. Tom Veitch. ANYP
Principes portas tollite. The Harrowing of Hell. *Unknown.* ACP; CAW
Principles of aerodynamics converging in the light. The Dynasties, the Sky Overhead. Randy Blasing. YAP
Print, with his hand, his eye, was more than print. Hiroshige. Mark M. Perlberg. NYBP
Printer, to Her Majesty, The. Leon Lichfield. HW
Printer to the Reader, The. *At. to* Richard Jones. ElL, ***abr.***; ReIE
Printer's Error. P. G. Wodehouse. FiBHP
Prior to Miss Belle's Appearance. James Whitcomb Riley. BOHV
Prioress's Tale, The. Chaucer. *Fr.* The Canterbury Tales. ACP, ***mod.***; BEL; GoBC, *mod. vers. by* Wordsworth; ISi, ***mod.***

Prioress's (continued)
vers. by Frank Ernest Hill; LoBV; MBW-1; OAEP; OxBoCh
Prologue of the Prioresses Tale. AtBAP; MBW-1; OAEP
Invocation: "O mother maid! O maiden-mother free," *sel., mod. by* Frank Ernest Hill. ISi
(O Mooder Mayde.) BoW
(Prayer to the Blessed Virgin, 7 *ll.; mod.*) CAW
(Two Invocations of the Virgin, 2 *ll.; mod.*) ACP
Prior's Epitaph. Matthew Prior. *See* Epitaph on Himself.
Priscilla and John Alden lie at rest. American History. Marguerite Janvrin Adams. PoRL
Prism, The. H. A. Pinkerton. NePoAm
Prison. *Unknown, tr. fr. Spanish by* Havelock Ellis. OnPM
Prison gets to be a friend, A. Emily Dickinson. MWA-2
Prison House, The. Alan Paton. PeSA
Prison Moan, *with music. Unknown.* OuSiCo
Prison Song. Richard Coeur de Lion, *tr. fr. Old French by* Henry Adams. LiTW
Prison Sonnet. Wilfrid Scawen Blunt. CAW
(Honour Dishonoured.) OBMV
Prisoned in Windsor, He Recounteth His Pleasure There Passed. Earl of Surrey. BEL; CoBE; FaBoEn; OAEP; PoE; ReIE; SiCE; TuPP
(In Windsor Castle.) OBSC; SeCePo
(So Cruel Prison.) EnRePo; EP; ILP; NoP
("So cruel [*or* crewell] prison how could betide, alas.") EnPo; FCP; ReEn; SiPS
Prisoner, A. "Æ." *See* Terence MacSwiney.
Prisoner, The. Marcos Ana, *tr. fr. Spanish by* Chloe Vulliamy *and* Stephen Sedley. BoPe
Prisoner, The. Emily Brontë. AnFE; EnLi-2 (1949 ed.)
(Prisoner, The; a Fragment.) OAEP
Sels.
"He comes with western winds, with evening's wandering airs." BoC; ELP; GTBS-D
"Still let my tyrants know, I am not doom'd to wear." ChER; EG; MemP; OBEV; OBNC; OBVV
Prisoner. Marguerite George. GoYe
Prisoner, The. William Plomer. ChMP; PeSA
Prisoner, The. Po Chü-i, *tr. fr. Chinese by* Arthur Waley. PoFr
Prisoner, The. Rainer Maria Rilke, *tr. fr. German by* J. B. Leishman. BoPe
Prisoner, The. Irwin Stark. NYTB
Prisoner, The; a Fragment. Emily Brontë. *See* Prisoner, The.
Prisoner for Life, A, *with music. Unknown.* BFSS; CoSo
Prisoner Freed, A. Geoffrey Dutton. BoAV
Prisoner of Chillon, The. Byron. BEL; BeLS; CABL; DTo; EnLi-2; EnLit; EnRP; EPN; HBV; MaC; MBW-2; MCCG; MERP; OnSP; PoLF
Sels.
"I made a footing in the wall." OBRV
"Lake Leman lies by Chillon's walls." OBRV
"Light broke in upon my brain, A." OBRV
Sonnet on Chillon. AnEnPo; ATP; BEL; BoLiVe; EnLi-2; EnLit; EnRP; EPN; ExPo; FiP; ILP; InP; LiTB; LoBV; MBW-2; OAEP; OBRV; PoFR; PoFS; PoPo; SeCeV; Sonn; TOP; TreFS; TrGrPo; YAT
("Eternal Spirit of the chainless Mind!") PoPl
(Freedom's Hero.) MaRV
(On the Castle of Chillon.) GTBS; GTBS-D; GTBS-P; GTBS-W; GTSE; GTSL
Prisoner of War. Gertrude May Lutz. GoYe
Prisoners. F. W. Harvey. MMA
Prisoners. Randall Jarrell. OxBA; WaP
Prisoners. Nancy Barr Mavity. HBMV
Prisoners, The. Stephen Spender. FaBoMo; GTBS-D; MoAB; MoBrPo
Prisoners. *Unknown. See* Dainty Fine Bird.
Prisoners in the dark of wood. Flames. E. Merrill Root. PoMa
Prisoner's Song. Horace Gregory. NP
Prisoner's Song, A. Mme Guyon. *See* Little Bird I Am, A.
Prisoner's Song of Jerusalem, A. *Unknown.* ACP
Prissie was a turnip. Vegetable Fantasies. Helen Hoyt. RIS
Prithee, Chloe, Not So Fast. John Oldmixon. SeCL
Prithee, honey-sweet husband, let me bring thee to Staines. Shakespeare. King Henry V, Act II, sc. iii. MyFE
Prithee (lest maids should censure thee) but say. Robert Herrick. *Fr.* His Parting with Mrs. Dorothy Kennedy. MyFE
Prithee now, fond fool, give o'er. A Dialogue between Strephon and Daphne. Earl of Rochester. CavP; SeCV-2
Prithee, say aye or no. The Resolute Courtier. Thomas Shipman. ErPo; LO; SeCL
Prithee tell me, Dimple-Chin. Toujours Amour. Edmund Clarence Stedman. HBV
Prithee tell me what a beau is. The Beau. *Unknown.* WaPE
Private, A. Edward Thomas. GTBS-P; MMA
Private Blair of the Regulars. Clinton Scollard. PAH
Private Devotion. Phoebe Hinsdale Brown. *See* I Love to Steal Awhile Away. AA
Private Dining Room, The. Ogden Nash. CaFP; ExPo; NYBP; PoCh; VaPo
Private Enterprise. Christopher Morley. MaRV
Private faces in public places. W. H. Auden. PV
Private Judgment Condemned. Dryden. *Fr.* The Hind and the Panther, I. OBS
(Prayer, A: "What weight of ancient witness can prevail.") FiP
Private Letter to Brazil, A. G. C. Oden. AmNP; Kal; NNP; PoNe (1970 ed.)
Private madness has prevailed, A. O Virtuous Light. Elinor Wylie. AnAmPo; LiTG; MAP; MoAB; MoAmPo; MoPo; NePA
Private Meeting Place, The. James Wright. NYBP
Private of the Buffs, The. Sir Francis Hastings Doyle. GTBS; HBV; InP; OBEV (new ed.); OBVV; PaPo; PoVP; VA
Private Worship. Mark Van Doren. LiTL; MoVE
Privately, your pencil makes. Snapshot of a Pedant. George Garrett. NePoAm-2
Prize Cat, The. E. J. Pratt. PeCV; TwCaPo
Prize of the Margaretta, The. Will Carleton. PAH
Prizegiving. Gwen Harwood. PoAu-2
Pro Libra Mea. Joseph I. C. Clarke. TrPWD
Pro Mortuis. Francis Turner Palgrave. VA
Pro Patria. Constance Carrier. NePoAm; NYBP
Pro Patria Mori. Thomas Moore. GTBS; GTBS-D; GTBS-P; GTBS-W; GTSE; GTSL
(When He, Who Adores Thee.) HoPM; OBRV
Pro Sua Vita. Robert Penn Warren. MAP; MoAmPo
Probe foramini a cat. Fabula. *Unknown.* CIV
Problem, The. Paul Blackburn. NeAP
Problem, The. Emerson. AA; AmePo; AmP; AmPP; AnAmPo; AnNE; AP; AWP; CoBA; HBV; JAWP; LiTA; MAmP; MaRV; MWA-1; NePA; NoP; OuHeWo; OxBA; TOP; WBP; WGRP
"Not from a vain or shallow thought," *sel.* OQP
Problem, A, hypothetical, in the form of a piercing dilemma. P.S. Jascha Kessler. AmPC
Problem in Logic. Phocylides, *tr. fr. Greek by* Lord Neaves. OnPM
Problem in Morals, A. Howard Moss. ErPo
Problem in Social Geometry—the Inverted Square! Ray Durem. NBP
Problem of the Poles, The. John Kendall. WhC
Problem that confronts me here, The. Auditors In. Patrick Kavanagh. OxBI
Problem, The: to remember. Report to the Blue Guard. Robert Hershon. ThO
Problems of a Journalist. Weldon Kees. NaP
Problems of a Writing Teacher, The. David Ray. NePoEA-2
Process, The. Robert Kelly. CoPo
Process. Charles L. O'Donnell. TrPWD
Process in the Weather of the Heart, A. Dylan Thomas. MoAB; NoP
(Poem.) NeBP
Process of time worketh such wonder. Sir Thomas Wyatt. FCP; SiPS
Procession, The. Margaret Widdemer. YeAr
Procession of the Flowers, The. Sydney Dobell. *See* Chanted Calendar, A.
Procession with the Standard of a Faction, The; a Cantata, *sel. Unknown.*
Liberty Pole, The. PAH
Processional. Alice Archer James. AA
Processional. William Jay Smith. NePoAm
Proclaimed Queene and mother of a God. The Visitation. Robert Southwell. MeP
Proclamation. Ær. fr. Isaiah, XLIX, Bible, *O.T.* StaSt
Proclamation, The. Longfellow. *Fr.* John Endicott. PAH
Proclamation, A. *Unknown.* PAH

Proclamation, The. Whittier. PAH; ThLM
Procne. Peter Quennell. ChMP; FaBoMo; GTBS-W; LiTB; LiTM; MoBrPo
Procne, Philomela, and Itylus. Philomela. John Crowe Ransom. AmP; ChTr; CMoP; FosPo; MoVE; OxBA; PoFS
Proconsul of Bithynia. To Petronius Arbiter. Oliver St. John Gogarty. OBMV
Procrastination. Martial, *tr. fr. Latin by* Abraham Cowley. AWP; JAWP; LiTW; OuHeWo; WBP
(To-Morrow.) OnPM
Procrastination ("Be wise to-day"). Edward Young. *Fr.* Night Thoughts: Night I. AnEnPo; OBEC, *abr.*
Prodigal, The. Elizabeth Bishop. CoAP; FiMAP; InvP; LiTM (1970 ed.); MoAB; NYBP; TwCP
Prodigal. Ellen Gilbert. GoBC; MaRV
Prodigal, The. Sara Henderson Hay. StaSt
Prodigal, The. Lon Woodrum. SoP
Prodigal of loves and barbecues. To the (Supposed) Patron. Geoffrey Hill. NePoEA-2
Prodigal Son, The. St. Luke, XV: 11-32, Bible, *N.T.* TreF
(Gospel According to Saint Luke, The: "And Jesus said. . .") LO
Prodigal Son, The. A. E. Coppard. MoBrPo (1942 ed.)
Prodigal Son, The. James Weldon Johnson. StJW
Prodigal Son, The. E. A. Robinson. MAP; MoAmPo
Prodigal Son, The. Arthur Symons. BrPo
Prodigal Son, The, *with music. Unknown, tr. fr. Flemish by* Alice M. G. White. SaSa
Prodigals, The. Austin Dobson. InP
Prodigals. Charles L. O'Donnell. HBMV
Prodiggus reptile! long and skaly kuss. Some Verses to Snaix. *Unknown.* NA
Prodigy, The. A. P. Herbert. EvOK
Prodjeckin' Son, De. Booth Lowrey. IHA
Proem: "I love the old melodious lays." Whittier. AA; AmPP; AnNe; AP; CoBA; HBV; NePA; NoP; OxBA
Proem: "If this little world to-night." Oliver Herford. *See* If This Little World To-night.
Proem: "Lo, thus, as prostrate, 'In the dust I write.'" James Thomson. *Fr.* The City of Dreadful Night. EnLit; GoTS; OAEP; OxBS; ViBoPo
Proem: "Out of my own great woe." Heine, *tr. fr. German by* Elizabeth Barrett Browning. AWP
Proem: "Snug in my easy chair." W. W. Gibson. *See* Snug in My Easy Chair.
Proem: "Strong Son of God, immortal Love." Tennyson. *See* In Memoriam A. H. H.: "Strong Son of God. . ."
Proem: "There is no rhyme that is half so sweet." Madison Cawein. AA; BoNaP
Proem: To Brooklyn Bridge. Hart Crane. *See* To Brooklyn Bridge.
Proem, A: "When in my walks I meet some ruddy lad." Samuel Ward. AA; AmLP
Proem to Hellenics. Walter Savage Landor. *See* On the Hellenics.
Proem to "The Kid." Conrad Aiken. *Fr.* The Kid. MoAB
Proem to "The Parlement of Foules." Chaucer. FiP; MyFE
(Parliament of Fowls, The.) ViBoPo
Proemium I: "As in the greatest of societies." Everard Guilpin. *Fr.* Skialetheia. ReIE
("As in the greatest of societies.") SiCE
Proemium in Librum Primum. John Marston. *Fr.* The Scourge of Villainy. ReIE
Profane, The. Abraham Cowley, *after the Latin of* Horace. AWP
Professor at the Breakfast Table, The, *sels.* Oliver Wendell Holmes.
Crooked Footpath, The, *fr. ch.* 4. HBV; TreF
Hymn of Trust, *fr. ch.* 11. AA; MaRV; NeHB
Our Father's Door, *fr. ch.* 4. OQP
Sun-Day Hymn, A, *fr. ch.* 12. AnNE; InP; MaRV; WGRP
Two Streams, The, *fr. ch.* 6. AP
Under the Violets, *fr. ch.* 10. AA
Professor Burke's symphony, "Colorado Vistas." Cultural Notes. Kenneth Fearing. CMoP
Professor Drinking Wine. Alasdair Clayre. PV
Professor Eisenbart, asked to attend. Prizegiving. Gwen Harwood. PoAu-2
Professor Eisenbart, with grim distaste. Panther and Peacock. Gwen Harwood. PoAu-2
Professor Nocturnal. Raymond Roseliep. FiSC
Professor of Medieval Balladry. Sister Mary Maura. JKCP (1955 ed.)
Professor Palamedes darts down Westow Street. News from Norwood. Christopher Middleton. NePoEA-2
Professor strolls at dusk in the college garden, The. Processional. William Jay Smith. NePoAm
Professor, you've convinced me a semester of astronomy. To Harold Jacoby. Irwin Edman. InMe
Professors. Harold A. Larrabee. InMe
Proffered Love Rejected. Sir John Suckling. CavP; ErPo; NCEP
(Rejected Offer, The.) UnTE
Proffered Rose, The. Wenceslas, King of Bohemia, *tr. fr. German by* Jethro Bithell. LiTW
Profile on the Pillow, The. Dudley Randall. BP
Profit and Loss ("Profit?—Loss?"). John Oxenham. OQP
Profit and Loss: An Elegy upon the Decease of Mrs. Mary Gerrish. John Danforth. SCAP
Profit or Loss. Grace E. Troy. SoP
Profound the radiance issuing. Eve. David Gascoyne. GTBS-P
Prognosis. Louis MacNeice. CMoP; OxBI
Prognostic. Samuel Yellen. NePoAm
Prognostication on Will Laud, Late Archbishop of Canterbury, A. *Unknown.* OxBoLi
Prognostication upon Cards and Dice, A. Sir Walter Ralegh. *See* On the Cards and Dice.
Program Note on Sibelius. Donald Babcock. UnS
Progress. Edith Agnew. AmFN
Progress. Matthew Arnold. EPN; MaRV; StJW
"Master stood upon the Mount, and taught, The," *sel.* ChIP
Progress. Sally Belfrage. PV
Progress. Samuel Hoffenstein. ThLM
Progress. David McCord. ImOP
Progress. Barbara C. Ryberg. SoP; STF
Progress. Ella Wheeler Wilcox. BLPA
Windows of the Soul, *sel.* OQP
Progress. Frank Wilmot. BoAu
Progress is/ The law of life, man is not Man as yet. Man's Destiny [*or* The Awakening of Man]. Robert Browning. *Fr.* Paracelsus, V. MaRV; OQP; WGRP
Progress of Beauty, The. Swift. BWP; CABA; EiCL; ForPo; FosPo; NCEP; PAn
Progress of Dulness, The, *sels.* John Trumbull.
Aging Coquette, The. AnNE
Amorous Temper, An. AmPP (4th ed.)
Dick Hairbrain Learns the Social Graces. AmPP (5th ed.)
Harriet Simper Has Her Day. AmPP (4th ed.)
Tom Brainless as Student and Preacher. AmPP (4th ed.)
Tom Brainless at College. AmPP (3d ed.); ATP (1935 ed.)
Tom Brainless Seeks a Wife. AmPP (3d ed.)
Progress of Evening. Walter Savage Landor. OBNC
Progress of Faust, The. Karl Shapiro. DiPo; MoAB; NYBP; OnHM
Progress of Man, The, *sels.* George Canning *and* John Hookham Frere *and* William Gifford.
Canto First, *by* Canning. EiCL
Canto Twenty-third, *abr., by* Canning *and* Frere. CEP
Progress of Marriage, The. Swift. EiCP
Progress of Photography, The. Byron Vazakas. MoPo
Progress of Poesy, The. Matthew Arnold. EnL; MBW-2; PoVP; PP
Progress of Poesy, The. Thomas Gray. ATP; AWP; BEL; CBEP; CEP; CoBE; EiCL; EiCP; EiPP; EnLi-2 (1949 ed.); EnLit; EnPE; EnRP; GTBS; GTBS-D; GTBS-W; GTSE; GTSL; HBV; NoP; OAEP; OBEC; OBEV; PoFS; PP; ViBoPo
(Progress of Poesie, The.) GTBS-P
Progress of Poetry, The. Swift. CABA; CBEP; EiCL; EiCP; InvP; OnYI
Progress of Sir Jack Brag, The. *Unknown.* PAH
Progress of the Soul, The ("I sing the progress of a deathless soul"), *sels.* John Donne.
"Great Destiny the commissary of God." OxBoCh
"It quickned next a toyfull ape." PoEL-2
Whale, The. ChTr; PoSa
Progress of the Soul, The ("Nothing could make me sooner to confess"). John Donne. *See* Of the Progress of the Soul; the Second Anniversary.
Progress of Unbelief. Cardinal Newman. GoBC
Progress of Wit, The; a Caveat. Aaron Hill. EiCL
Progression. Francis Scarfe. NeBP

Progression. Inez Clark Thorson. MaRV
Progression of the Species. Brian W. Aldiss. HYE
Prohibition, The. John Donne. ElL; MaMe; MBW-1; MeLP; OBS; SCEP-1; TuPP
"Take heed of loving me," *sel.* EG
Prohibition. Don Marquis. PoPl; WhC
Prohibition agents came, The. Mrs. Swartz. Don Marquis. ThLM
Prohibition makes you. Prohibition. Don Marquis. PoPl; WhC
Projected from the bilious Childe. Manfred. George Meredith. EPN
Projection, A. Reed Whittemore. NePoEA; WaKn
Proletaria. Bernard O'Dowd. BoAu
Proletarian Portrait. William Carlos Williams. OCS
Proletarian, unlikely bird, no monarch, A. On the Death of an Emperor Penguin in Regent's Park, London. David Wright. NYBP
Prolog: "Books composed before our day," The. John Gower, *tr. fr. Middle English by* Muriel Bowden. *Fr.* Confessio Amantis. MeEV
Prolog, The: "There was a priest in the land." Layamon, *tr. fr. Middle English. Fr.* The Brut. MeEV
Prologue: "All the animals in my poems go into the ark." Jon Silkin. PoDB
Prologue: "Ane doolie season to ane careful dyte." Robert Henryson. *Fr.* The Testament of Cresseid. GoTS
Prologue: "Delusions of the days that once have been." Longfellow. *Fr.* Giles Corey of the Salem Farms. PAH
Prologue, The: "Famous poets with the muses nine, The." Alexander Barclay. *Fr.* Certain Eclogues. ReIE
Prologue: "For who can longer hold? when every press." John Oldham. *Fr.* Satires upon the Jesuits. CEP; SeCV-2
Prologue: "Forget six counties overhung with smoke." William Morris. *Fr.* The Earthly Paradise. BEL; EPN, *abr.*
(Earthly Paradise, The: Introduction.) ViPo, *abr.*
(Introduction.) ViPP
Prologue: "He who writ this, not without pains and thought." Dryden. *Fr.* Secret Love; or, The Maiden Queen. MBW-1
Prologue: "I first adventure, with foolhardy might." Joseph Hall. *Fr.* Virgidemiarum. ReEn; ReIE; SiCE; ViBoPo
Prologue: "I heard an angel speak last night." Elizabeth Barrett Browning. *Fr.* A Curse for a Nation. PoVP
Prologue: "If yet there be a few that take delight." Dryden. *Fr.* The Loyal General (*by* Nahum Tate). CEP; SeCV-2
Prologue: "In a somer sesun [*or* summer season], when softe [*or* soft] was the sonne [*or* sun *or* when the sun was softest]." William Langland. *Fr.* The Vision of Piers Plowman. BEL; CoBE; EnLi-1, *mod. by* W. A. Neilson *and* K. G. T. Webster; EnLit, *mod. by* Albert C. Baugh
(Field Full of Folk, The, *mod. vers.*) MeEV
(Field of Folk, The.) PoEL-1
(Induction, The, *shorter sel., mod. by* Henry W. Wells.) PoLi
Prologue, The: "In the moneth of May when the new tender green." *Unknown.* ReIE
Prologue: "Lord, can a crumb of earth [*or* dust] the earth outweigh." Edward Taylor. AmLP; AP; MeP
Prologue: "Lord, how reformed and quiet are we grown." Dryden. *Fr.* Marriage à la Mode. MBW-1
Prologue: "'Lordynges,' quod he, 'in chirches whan I preche.'" Chaucer. *Fr.* The Canterbury Tales: The Pardoner's Tale. FosPo
Prologue: "Lose this day loitering, 'twill be the same story." Goethe. *See* Lose This Day Loitering.
Prologue: Moments in a Glade. Alan Stephens. QFR
Prologue: "Musing upon the restless bisinesse." Thomas Hoccleve. *Fr.* De Regimine Principum. PoEL-1
Prologue: "My life is like a music-hall." Arthur Symons. BrPo
Prologue: "O love, the interest itself in thoughtless Heaven." W. H. Auden. *See* Perhaps.
Prologue: "Of Heaven or Hell I have no power to sing." William Morris. *See* Apology, An: "Of Heaven or Hell. . ."
Prologue: "Our author, by experience, finds it true." Dryden. *See* Prologue to "Aureng-Zebe."
Prologue: "'Poet's age is sad, The: for why?'" Robert Browning. *See* Prologue to "Asolando."
Prologue: "Prest by the load of life, the weary mind." Samuel Johnson. *Fr.* The Good-natur'd Man (*by* Goldsmith). LoBV
Prologue: "Rawish dank of clumsy winter ramps, The." John Marston. *Fr.* Antonio's Revenge. LoBV; ViBoPo
Prologue: "See, my loved Britons, see your Shakespeare rise." Dryden. *Fr.* Troilus and Cressida. CEP; MBW-1; SeCV-2
Prologue: "So oft as I with state of present time." Spenser. *Fr.* The Faerie Queene, V. PoFS
Prologue: "Strong Son of God, immortal Love." Tennyson. *See* In Memoriam A. H. H.: "Strong Son of God. . ."
Prologue: "These alternate nights and days, these seasons." Archibald MacLeish. MAP; MoAmPo
Prologue: "This day winding down now." Dylan Thomas. GTBS-W
Prologue: "This worthy limitour, this noble frere." Chaucer. *Fr.* The Canterbury Tales: The Friar's Tale. EnLi-1 (1949 ed.)
Prologue, A: "Thou Speaker of all wisdom in a Word." Coventry Patmore. PoLi
Prologue, The: "To sing of wars, of captains, and of kings." Anne Bradstreet. AmPP (3d ed.); AP; OxBA; SCAP
Prologue: "Tonight we strive to read, as we may best." Longfellow. *Fr.* John Endicott. PAH
Prologue: "We who with songs beguile your pilgrimage." James Elroy Flecker. *See* Prologue to "The Golden Journey to Samarkand."
Prologue: "Whan that Aprill with his shoures soote." *See* Canterbury Tales, The: Prologue.
Prologue: "What flocks of critics hover here to-day." Dryden. *Fr.* All for Love. DiPo
Prologue: "When learning's triumph o'er her barb'rous foes." Samuel Johnson. EiCP
Prologue and Epilogue to "Tyrannick Love; or, The Royal Martyr." Dryden. OAEP
Prologue, Each to the Other, *sel.* Christopher La Farge.
"Here is no tragedy." AnAmPo
Prologue for a Bestiary. Ronald Perry. NePoEA-2
Prologue for a Magician. Arthur Guiterman. PoMS
Prologue in Heaven. Goethe, *tr. fr. German by* Shelley. *Fr.* Faust. AWP; JAWP; WBP
Prologue of the Prioress's Tale, The. Chaucer. *See* Prioress's Tale, The.
Prologue of the Pardoner's Tale, The. Chaucer. *Fr.* The Canterbury Tales. BEL; CABL; FosPo; MBW-1; NoP; OAEP
(Prologue to the Pardoner's Tale.) CoBE; EnL, *mod. by* Theodore Morrison
Prologue Spoken by Mr. Garrick at the Opening of the Theatre Royal [*or* in Drury-Lane], 1747. Samuel Johnson. CEP; EiCL; EiPP; MBW-1; NoP; OBEC; PoFS; SeCeV
Prologue to a Saga. Dorothy Parker. InMe
Prologue to "Antonio's Revenge." John Marston. *See* Prologue: "Rawish dank of clumsy winter ramps, The."
Prologue to "Asolando." Robert Browning. PoVP; ViPo
(Prologue: "'Poet's age is sad, The: for why?'") ViPP
Prologue to "Aureng-Zebe." Dryden. ATP; BWP; CEP; EiPP; FiP; OBS; OxBoLi; PP; SeCeV; SiTL
(Prologue: "Our author by experience finds it true.") CBEP; EiCL; MBW-1; SeCV-2; SeEP
Prologue to "Evangeline." Longfellow.
(In the Forest.) PCD
(Prelude.) MWA-1
(Primeval Forest, *abr.*) WBLP
("This is the forest primeval.") AmPP; CoBA InP; TreF
Prologue to "La Saisiaz." Robert Browning. PoVP
Prologue to "Love Triumphant." Dryden. OxBoLi; SiTL
Prologue to Mr. Addison's Tragedy of Cato. Pope. CEP; EiCL
Prologue to Morning. Hermann Hagedorn. MaRV
Prologue to "Rhymes and Rhythms." W. E. Henley. PoVP
Prologue to "Rhymes to Be Traded for Bread." Vachel Lindsay. LaNeLa
Prologue to "Secret Love; or, The Maiden-Queen." Dryden. MBW-1; SeCV-2; SeEP
(First Prologue to "Secret Love; or The Maiden Queen.") PeRV
Prologue to Sir Thopas. Chaucer. *Fr.* The Canterbury Tales. Par
Prologue to the Avowis of Alexander. John Barbour. *Fr.* The Buik of Alexander. OxBS
Prologue to "The Canterbury Tales." Chaucer. *See* Canterbury Tales, The.
Prologue to "The Earthly Paradise." William Morris. *See* Pro-

logue: "Forget six counties overhung with smoke."
Prologue to the First Satire ("I never did"). Persius, *tr. fr. Latin by* Dryden. *Fr.* Satires. AWP
Prologue to "The Golden Journey to Samarkand." James Elroy Flecker. BrPo
(Prologue: "We who with songs beguile your pilgrimage.") GoJo; GTBS; OBMV
Prologue to "The Good-natur'd Man." Samuel Johnson. *See* Prologue: "Prest by the load of life, the weary mind."
Prologue to the Man of Law's Tale. Chaucer. *Fr.* The Canterbury Tales. FiP
Prologue to the Prioress's Tale. Chaucer. *See* Prioress's Tale, The.
Prologue to the Pardoner's Tale. Chaucer. *See* Prologue of the Pardoner's Tale.
Prologue to "The Tempest." Dryden. EiPP; EnL; MBW-1; NoP; PoE;
Prologue to the University of Oxford, 1673. Dryden. OBS; PP
Prologue to the University of Oxford, 1674. Dryden. BWP
Prologue to the University of Oxford, 1676. Dryden. MBW-1
Prologue to the Wife of Bath's Tale, The. Chaucer. *See* Wife of Bath's Prologue, The.
Prologues are over, The. It is a question now. Asides on the Oboe. Wallace Stevens. AP; MoAB; MoAmPo
Prologues to the Aeneid, *sels.* Gawin Douglas.
Difficulties of Translation, The, *abr., fr.* Prologue to Bk. I. GoTS
"Frend, farly nocht; na caus is to complene," *fr.* Prologue to Bk. X. OxBoCh
Prologue to Book VII, The. OxBS
Winter. SeCePo
Prologue to Book XIII, The. OxBS
"Quhill schortly, with the blesand torch of day." AtBAP
Prologues to What Is Possible. Wallace Stevens. NePoAm
Prolonged Sonnet: When the Troops Were Returning from Milan. Niccolò degli Albizzi, *tr. fr. Italian by* Dante Gabriel Rossetti. AWP
(Troops Returning from Milan.) OnPM
(When the Troops Were Returning from Milan.) WaaP
Prolonged Sonnet. Simone dall' Antella, *tr. fr. Italian by* Dante Gabriel Rossetti. AWP
Promenade. Sam Cornish. BF
Promenade. David Ignatow. TrJP
Promenades and Interiors, *sel.* François Coppée, *tr. fr. French by* Joseph T. Shipley.
"I am writing near the lamp." CAW
Promenading their. The Return to Work. William Carlos Williams. NYBP
Prometheus. Byron. EnRP; EPN; ERoP-2; VaPo
Prometheus. W. W. Gibson. EPN
Prometheus. Goethe, *tr. fr. German by* John S. Dwight. AWP; JAWP; WBP; WoL
Prometheus. Longfellow. MWA-1
Prometheus Bound. Aeschylus, *tr. fr. Greek by* Elizabeth Barrett Browning. EnLi-2 (1939 ed.)
Sels.
Prometheus in the Earthquake, *tr. by* G. M. Cookson. LiTW
Prometheus the Teacher of Men, *tr. by* G. M. Cookson. LiTW
Wail of Prometheus Bound, The, *tr. by* Elizabeth Barrett Browning. WGRP
Prometheus Unbound. Sister Miriam. JKCP (1955 ed.)
Prometheus Unbound. Shelley. BEL; CoBE, *much abr.*; EnLi-2; EnRP; ERoP-2; MBW-2; MERP
Sels.
Asia ("My soul is an enchanted boat"), *fr.* II, v. PoFS; ViBoPo
(Asia's Song.) ATP (1935 ed.); UnPo (1st ed.)
Chorus of Spirits: "From unremembered ages we," *fr.* I. LoBV
Curse, The, *fr.* I. PoFr
Day of Liberty, The, *fr.* III, iv. EPN
Day of Love, The, *fr.* IV. EPN
End of Tyranny, The, *fr.* III, iv. ShBV-3
"I wandering went/ Among the haunts and dwellings of mankind," *fr.* III, iv. FiP
"Joy, the truimph, the delight, the madness, The!" *fr.* IV. AtBAP
Life of Life, *fr.* II, v. CH; FiP
(Chorus: "Life of Life! thy lips enkindle.") LoBV
(Hymn to the Spirit of Nature.) GTBS; GTBS-D; GTBS-W; GTSE
("Life of Life! thy lips enkindle.") AnFE; AtBAP; LO; OBRV; PoEL-4; ViBoPo
"Loud deep calls me home even now to feed it, The," *fr.* III, ii. ChER
"Monarch of Gods and Daemons, and all Spirits," I. EPN; FiP, *sel.*
Morning, *fr.* II, i. ShBV-3
"My coursers are fed with the lightning," *fr.* II, iv. OBRV
(Charioteer, The.) ShBV-3
"On a battle-trumpet's blast," *fr.* I. OBRV
"On a poet's lips I slept," *fr.* I. AnFE; AtBAP; ChER; ELP; FiP; PoG; ShBV-3; ViBoPo
(Poet's Dream, The.) GTBS; GTBS-D; GTBS-P; GTBS-W; GTSE; GTSL
"Pale stars are gone, The!" IV. EnLi-2 (1949 ed.)
"Path through which that lovely twain, The," *fr.* II, ii. AtBAP; ViBoPo
"Peace! Peace! A mighty power, which is as darkness," *fr.* IV. OAEP
Rainbow's Arch, A, *fr.* I. ShBV-3
"Soon as the sound had ceased whose thunder filled," *fr.* III, iv. ChER
"Sphere, which is as many thousand spheres, A," *fr.* IV. ImOP
"This is the day which down the void abysm," *fr.* IV. EnLit; OQP; PoIE; SeCeV
(Demogorgon's Song.) MaPo (1969 ed.)
(Demogorgon's Speech.) LoBV
(Final Victory, The.) ShBV-3
"Thou, Earth, calm empire of a happy soul," *fr.* IV. OBRV
Who Reigns? *fr.* II, iv. SeCePo
"Ye congregated powers of heaven, who share," *fr.* III. EnLit
Prometheus When First from Heaven. Sir Edward Dyer. PoIE (1970 ed.); TuPP
("Prometheus when first from heaven high.") FCP
Prometheus, with Wings. Michael Ondaatje. PeCV (1967 ed.)
Promiscuous lovers/ Pine to have. A Problem in Morals. Howard Moss. ErPo
Promiscuous tags and liberal lip I hate. Written in Flight from His Royal Patron. Al Mutanabbi. LiTW
Promise. "Æ." BoC; POTE
Promise. Paul Laurence Dunbar. NoP
Promise, The. Mary B. Fowler. STF
Promise. Florence Lacey. BoTP
Promise, A. Sir Thomas Wyatt. *See* Lover Rejoiceth the Enjoying of His Love, The.
Promise in Disturbance, The. George Meredith. *Fr.* Modern Love. VP
("How low when angels fall their black descent.") ViPo
Promise Lan', De. John Richard Moreland. IHA
Promise Made, A. *Unknown.* FaFP; SiTL
Promise Me a Rose. Bob Merrill. BoLP
Promise of a Constant Lover, The. *Unknown.* ElL; ReIE
Promise of our years was caught, The. Monody on a Century. Earle Birney. CaP
Promise of Peace. Robinson Jeffers. AP; BoLiVe; CoBMV; GTBS-W; LiTA; LiTM (rev. ed.); MAP; MoAB; MoAmPo; NePA
Promise of these fragrant flowers, The. With a Spray of Apple Blossoms. Walter Learned. AA
Promise was broken too freely, The. Galway Kinnell. *Fr.* The Avenue Bearing the Initial of Christ into the New World. NaP
Promise Your Hand. Henry Rago. NMP
Promised Country, The. Speer Strahan. JKCP
Promised Land, The. Jessie E. Sampter. TrJP
Promised Land, The. Samuel Stennett. SoP; TrAS, *with music*
Promises. Ruth Forbes Sherry. GoYe
Promises of mother, The. I Hear You. Shirley Kaufman. QAH
Promises of the World, The. Moses ibn Ezra, *tr. fr. Hebrew by* Solomon Solis-Cohen. *Fr.* The World's Illusion. TrJP
Promissory Note, The. Bayard Taylor. BOHV; HBV; Par
Promontory Moment, The. May Swenson. NYBP
Promontory Moon. Galway Kinnell. TwAmPo
Promotion. John Oxenham. MaRV

Promotion lately was bestow'd. *Unknown. Fr.* Riddles. CoBE
Prompted to seek my bliss abov the skies. Felicity. Thomas Traherne. SCEP-1
Prone couple still sleeps, A. First Light. Thomas Kinsella. OPoP
Prone in Gethsemane upon His face. Gethsemane. Annette von Droste-Hülshoff. CAW
Pronouns. Karle Wilson Baker. TreFT
Pronunciation of Erse, The. A. D. Hope. PV
Proof. Ethel Romig Fuller. FaChP; MaRV; MoSiPe; TRV
(God Hears Prayer.) OQP
Proof, The. Richard Wilbur. EaLo
Proof Positive. Deems Taylor, *tr. fr. French.* UnTE
Proofs of Buddha's Existence. *Unknown.* WGRP
Prope ripam fluvii solus. Malum Opus. James Appleton Morgan. NA
Proper Clay. Mark Van Doren. PoRA; TrGrPo
Proper Ditty, A. *Unknown.* RelE
Proper evaluation of words and letters. To the Peoples of Earth. Sun-Ra. BF
Proper fathers behind their ashen faces, The. Poem in Karori. Louis Johnson. AnNZ
Proper New Ballad, A. James Graham, Marquess of Montrose. *See* My Dear and Only Love.
Proper New Ballad, A, Intituled The Fairies' Farewell or God-a-Mercy Will. Richard Corbet. *See* Fairies' Farewell, The.
Proper New Song Made by a Student in Cambridge, A. Thomas Richardson. TuPP
Take Heed of Gazing Overmuch, *sel.* EIL
Proper scale would pat you on the head, The. The Scales. William Empson. CMoP; LiTM (rev. ed.)
Proper Song, A, Entitled: Fain Would I Have a Pretty Thing to Give unto My Lady. *Unknown. See* Fain Would I Have a Pretty Thing.
Proper Sonnet, A, How Time Consumeth All Earthly Things. *Unknown, at. to* Thomas Proctor. OBSC; SiCE; TuPP
(How Time Consumeth All Earthly Things.) ChTr; EIL
(Sic Transit.) TrGrPo
Proper Sonnet, A, Intituled: I Smile to See How You Devise. *Unknown.* RelE
Proper Study of Man [*or* Mankind], The. Pope. *See* Know Then Thyself.
Proper way for man to pray, The. The Prayer of Cyrus Brown [*or* Cyrus Brown's Prayer]. Sam Walter Foss. BOHV; LHV; SoP; StaSt
Proper way to leave a room, The. Nonsense Quatrains. Gelett Burgess. CenHV
Propertian. L. A. MacKay. *Fr.* Erotica Antiqua. PeCV
Propertius! nerve thy spirit for the fight. Cynthia, Cynthia. Propertius. LiTW
Prophecy, A. Walter Savage Landor. *See* Proud Word You Never Spoke.
Prophecy, A. *At. to* Arthur Lee. PAH
Prophecy, A. Christopher Levenson. ErPo
Prophecy. Marjorie Meeker. NP
Prophecy. Luigi Pulci, *tr. fr. Italian. Fr.* Il Morgante maggiore. PAH
Prophecy. Walter Shedlofsky. FiSC
Prophecy. Tennyson. *Fr.* Locksley Hall. GTBS-W; TreF; WBLP
(Federation of the World.) MaRV; PoRL
(For I Dipped into the Future.) PoLF
("For I dipped [or dipt] into the future, far as human eye could see.") PGD; TRV
Prophecy, A. Maurice Thompson. *Fr.* Lincoln's Grave. AA
Prophecy. Gulian Verplanck. MC
Prophecy, The. Lon Woodrum. MaRV
Prophecy. Elinor Wylie. AnAmPo
Prophecy in Flame. Frances Minturn Howard. AmFN
Prophecy of Dante, The, *sel.* Byron.
"Many are poets who have never penn'd." ERoP-2
Prophecy of Diana, The. Layamon, *tr. fr. Middle English. Fr.* The Brut. MeEV
Prophecy of Famine, The; a Scots Pastoral. Charles Churchill. EiPP
Prophecy of Samuel Sewall, The. Whittier. MAmP
Prophecy of Taliesin, The. Taliesin, *tr. fr. Welsh by* George Borrow. PoFr
Prophecy Sublime, The. Frederick Lucian Hosmer. *See* Thy Kingdom, Come, O Lord.
Prophet, The. Thomas Curtis Clark. HH; PEDC
Prophet, The. Abraham Cowley. TrGrPo
Prophet, The, *sels.* Kahlil Gibran.
Crime and Punishment. PoToHe (new ed.)
Of Love. PoLF
On Children. PoPl; PoToHe (new ed.)
On Giving. MaRV; PoPl
On Work, *abr.* PoToHe (new ed.)
Prophet, The. Pushkin, *tr. fr. Russian by* Babette Deutsch *and* Avrahm Yarmolinsky. AWP; EaLo; JAWP; LiTW; WBP; WGRP
Prophet, The. "Yehoash," *tr. fr. Yiddish by* Isidore Goldstick. TrJP
Prophet and Fool. Louis Golding. HBMV
Prophet Jeremiah and the Personification of Israel, The. *At. to* Eleazar Ben Kalir, *tr. fr. Hebrew by* Nina Davis Salaman. TrJP
Prophet Lost in the Hills at Evening, The. Hilaire Belloc. JKCP; OxBoCh
Prophet of dead words defeats himself, The. E. A. Robinson. Octaves, XX. ILP
Prophet of the body's roving. Walt Whitman. Edwin Honig. NePA
Prophet, scourged by his own hand, progressed, The. John the Baptist. Louis Simpson. NePoEA
Prophetess, The. Dorothy Livesay. MoCV
Prophetess. Whittier. *Fr.* Snow-bound. AA
Prophetess, The; or, The History of Dioclesian, *sel. At. to* Dryden *and to* Thomas Betterton.
What Shall I Do? SeCL
Prophetic Death. Simonides, *tr. fr. Greek by* Lord Neaves. OnPM
Prophetic Hour, The. Michael Thwaites. PoFr
Prophets, The. Richard Shelton. NYBP
Prophets, gazing toward the mountains. The Home Winner. Gene Lindberg. PoOW
Prophets, preaching in new stars. The Pontoon Bridge Miracle. Vachel Lindsay. *Fr.* Every Soul Is a Circus. LiTM (rev. ed.); LoBV; NePA
Prophet's vision leaves me cold, The. City of God. R. H. Long. BoAu
Prophets Who Cannot Sing. Coventry Patmore. *Fr.* The Unknown Eros, II, xvi. CoBE; PoVP
Propinquity Needed. Charles Battell Loomis. BOHV; InMe
Proportion. Ben Jonson. *See* It Is Not Growing like a Tree.
Proposal. Robert Sward. ELU
Proposal. *Unknown.* TreFS
Proposition, The. Paul Blackburn. ErPo
Proposition. Nicolás Guillén, *tr. fr. Spanish by* Langston Hughes. FaPON; PoNe; TTY
Propositions. Phyllis Webb. MoCV
Propped on the bar. Sam. Arthur St. John Adcock. WhC
Propriety. Marianne Moore. UnS
Props. John Oxenham. FaChP; TRV
Props assist the house, The. Emily Dickinson. MWA-2
Prosaic miles of streets stretch all round. Seder-Night. Israel Zangwill. TrJP
Prose and Poesy; a Rural Misadventure. Thomas R. Ybarra. WhC
Prosepoem. William Knott. YAP
Prose Poem: Angels, The. Théodore de Banville, *tr. fr. French by* Stuart Merrill. OnPM
Prose Poem: By the River. Judith Gautier, *tr. fr. French by* Stuart Merrill. OnPM
Prose Poem: Dog and the Flask, The. Baudelaire, *tr. fr. French by* Arthur Symons. OnPM
Prose Poem: Harlequin. Théodore de Banville, *tr. fr. French by* Stuart Merrill. OnPM
Prose Poem: House in the Heart. Judith Gautier, *tr. fr. French by* Stuart Merrill. OnPM
Prose Poem: Indifference. Judith Gautier, *tr. fr. French by* Stuart Merrill. OnPM
Prose Poem: Irremediable, The. Emile Hennequin, *tr. fr. French by* Stuart Merrill. OnPM
Prose Poem: Mysterious Flute. Judith Gautier, *tr. fr. French by* Stuart Merrill. OnPM
Prose Poem: Red Flower, The. Judith Gautier, *tr. fr. French by* Stuart Merrill. OnPM
Prose Poem: Sadness of the Husbandman. Judith Gautier, *tr. fr.*

French by Stuart Merrill. OnPM
Prose Poem: Sages' Dance. Judith Gautier, *tr. fr. French by* Stuart Merrill. OnPM
Prose Poem: Stranger, The. Baudelaire, *tr. fr. French by* Stuart Merrill. OnPM
Prose Poem: Window, The. Baudelaire, *tr. fr. French by* Stuart Merrill. OnPM
Prose Poem: Words. Emile Hennequin, *tr. fr. French by* Stuart Merrill. OnPM
Proserpina. Thomas Campion. *See* Hark, All You Ladies That Do Sleep! OAEP
Proserpine. Swinburne. *Fr.* The Garden of Proserpine. ChTr
("Pale, beyond porch and portal.") FaBoEn
Proserpine at Enna. Ronald Bottrall. SeCePo
Proserpine may pull her flowers. Song of the Stygian Naiades. Thomas Lovell Beddoes. EnRP; ERoP-2; PeER
Proserpine's Ragout. Mary Leapor. WaPE
Prosit Neujahr. George Santayana. InMe
Prosopopoia; or, Mother Hubberd's Tale, *abr.* Spenser. ReIE
At Court, *sel.* PoFr
Prospect. Thomas Curtis Clark. PoRL
Prospect, The. Thomas Hardy. NeMA
Prospect is bare and white, The. Winter Dusk. Richard Kendall Munkittrick. BOHV
Prospect of Children, A. Lawrence Durrell. *Fr.* Eight Aspects of Melissa. NeBP
Prospect of Death, A. Andrew Young. DTC
Prospect of Eden, The. Milton. *Fr.* Paradise Lost, IV. PoEL-3
Prospect of Heaven Makes Death Easy, A. Isaac Watts. *See* Heaven.
Prospect of the Future Glory of America. John Trumbull. AmPP (5th ed.)
Prospecting Dream, *with music.* John A. Stone. SGR
Prospectus. Wordsworth. *Fr.* The Recluse. NoP
("On Man, on Nature.") EnRP; EPN; ERoP-1; OBRV
Prosper, Archambault, Gilbert, and Cinema. The War of the Secret Agents. Henri Coulette. AmPC
Prospero [Ends the Revels]. Shakespeare. *See* Our Revels Now Are Ended.
Prospice. Robert Browning. AnFE; BEL; BoLiVe; CBEP; CBV; CoBE; DD; DiPo; EnL; EnLi-2; EnLit; EPN; FaBoEn; FaBV; FaPL; FiP; GTBS; GTBS-W; GTSL; HBV; HBVY; ILP; InP; LiTB; LiTL; MaRV; MBW-2; MCCG; NeHB; OAEP; OBEC; OBVV; OQP; OuHeWo; PoIE; PoLF; PoRA; PoVP; SeCeV; SoP; TIHL; TOP; TreFS; TrGrPo; TRV; UnPo (1st ed.); VA; ViPo; ViPP; WGRP; YT
Prostrate, self-scorning. Prayer for Wings. Dmitry Sergeyevich Merezhkovsky. OnPM
Protagonist. Edith Henrich. MoRP
Protagonist, The. Peter Hopegood. MoAuPo; PoAu-2
Protė, thou art not dead; but thou hast passed. Immortality. *Unknown.* OnPM
Protection of Jehovah, The. Psalms, XXIII, Bible, *O.T.* *See* Lord Is My Shepherd, The.
Protector, The, *sel.* George Wither.
"This glorious title hath in it exprest." PoFr
Protest, A. Arthur Hugh Clough. VA
Protest. Countee Cullen. CDC
Protest. Vassar Miller. ToPo
Protest, A. Sir Thomas Wyatt. OBSC; SiPS
("Heaven and earth and all that hear me plain.") FCP
Protest against the Ballot. Wordsworth. EPN
Protest in Passing. Leonora Speyer. HBMV
Protest in the Sixth Year of Ch'ien Fu, A (A.D. 879). Ts'ao Sung, *tr. fr. Chinese by* Arthur Waley. FaBV; LiTW; MoPW; OnPM; PoFr
Protest of the Illiterate, The, *sel.* Gelett Burgess.
"I seen a dunce of a poet once, a-writin' a little book." FiBHP
Protestation. Bertrans de Born, *tr. fr. Provençal by* John Peale Bishop. LiTW
Protestation, The. Thomas Carew. CavP; OuHeWo
Protestation, The. Selwyn Image. VA
Proteus; or, The Shapes of Conscience. Rolfe Humphries. LiTM (1946 ed.)
Protevangelium of James, The, *sel.* *Unknown.* Lament of Saint Ann, The. CAW
Prothalamion. Michael Drayton. *Fr.* The Muses Elizium. HW
Prothalamion, *sel.* Robert Hillyer.
Second Section: "The hills turn hugely in their sleep." MAP; MoAmPo
Prothalamion. Maxine W. Kumin. NYBP
Prothalamion. Delmore Schwartz. OxBA
Prothalamion. Spenser. AnFE; AtBAP; ATP; AWP; BEL; CABA; CaFP; ChTr; CoBE; ElL; EnL; EnLi-1; EnLit; EnRePo; FaBoEn; FosPo; GoTL; GTBS; GTBS-D; GTBS-P; GTBS-W; GTSE; GTSL; HBV; HW; InPo; LiTB; LiTG; LiTL; LoBV; MaPo; MCCG; NoP; OBEV; OBSC; OuHeWo; PAn; PIA; PoE; PoIE; ReEn; ReIE; SeCePo; ShBV-4; SiCE; StP; TOP; UnPo (1st ed.); VaPo; ViBoPo; WHA
"With that I saw two swannes of goodly hewe," *sel.* BoC
Prothalamion. Terence Tiller. NeBP
Prothalamion. Francis Brett Young. HBMV
Prothalamium. Donagh MacDonagh. NeIP
Prothalamium. May Sarton. HW; NePoAm
Prothalamium. Edith Sitwell. HW
Prothalamium. A. J. M. Smith. CaP
Prothalamium for Bobolink and His Louisa A Poem. Gertrude Stein. HW
Protogenes and Apelles. Matthew Prior. GoTL
Proton, neutron, electron. This Age, This Faust. George Reavey. SiTL
Protus. Robert Browning. FOL
Proud, The. Frances Frost. OQP
Proud Aegyptian queen, her Roman guest, The. *See* Proud Egyptian queen. . .
Proud and lowly, beggar and lord. London Bridge. Frederic Edward Weatherly. VA
Proud and rest-ive Chim-pan-zee, The. Having a Wonderful Time. D. B. Wyndham Lewis. FiBHP
Proud as Apollo on his forked hill. Bufo. Pope. *Fr.* Epistle to Dr. Arbuthnot. OBEC
Proud Chloe's Heart. Horace, *tr. fr. Latin by* William Boscawen. OnPM
Proud Egyptian [*or* Aegyptian] queen, her Roman guest, The. And She Washed His Feet with Her Tears, and Wiped Them with the Hairs of Her Head [*or* The Magdalen]. Sir Edward Sherburne. ACP; CBEP; ChTr; GoBC; MeLP; MemP; OBS; OxBoCh; SeCL; SeEP
Proud Florentines, The. Keats. *Fr.* Isabella; or, The Pot of Basil. PoFr
Proud fountains, wave your plumes. Fountains. Sir Osbert Sitwell. MoBrPo
Proud in thy love, how many have I cited. *Unknown.* *Fr.* Zepheria. ReIE; Sonn; TuPP
Proud inclination of the flesh. Villanelle. Dilys Laing. ErPo; NMP
Proud Lady Margaret. *Unknown.* BaBo; ESPB; OBB
(Proud Margret.) OxBB
Proud Little Spruce Fir. Jeannie Kirby. BoTP
Proud Maisie. Sir Walter Scott. *Fr.* The Heart of Midlothian, *ch.* 38. AtBAP; CBEP; ChTr; CoBE; EnLi-2; EnLit; EnRP; EPN; ERoP-1; GoTS; GTSL; HBV; ILP; InP; LoBV; NBM; OAEP; OBEV; OBRV; OTPC (1923 ed.); OxBS; PoE; PoEL-4; PoPo; SeCePo; SeCeV; ShBV-1; StP; TrGrPo; UnPo
(Madge Wildfire Sings.) OBNC
(Pride of Youth, The.) GTBS; GTBS-D; GTBS-P; GTBS-W
("Proud Maisie is in the wood.") EG; FaBoCh; LoGBV
Proud Margret. *Unknown.* *See* Proud Lady Margaret.
Proud men/ Eternally/ Go about. The Kallyope Yell. Vachel Lindsay. BoLiVe
Proud Motherhood. Frank Laurence Lucas. FOL
Proud New York. John Reed. HBMV; NP
Proud of my broken heart, since thou didst break it. Emily Dickinson. MWA-2; ViBoPo
Proud of my music, let me often make. Stéphane Mallarmé. *Fr.* L'Après-midi d'un faune. ErPo
Proud of my pride. A Tale Told by a Head. Lois Moyles. NYBP
Proud of you, fond of you, clinging so near to you. My Owen. Ellen Mary Patrick Downing. HBV
Proud Paulus, late my secrecies revealing. Of Honest Theft. To My Good Friend Master Samuel Daniel. Sir John Harington. SiCE
Proud Riders. Harold Lenoir Davis. AnAmPo; NP
Proud Song, A. Marguerite Wilkinson. HBMV
Proud Songsters. Thomas Hardy. FIW; PoSa
Proud Toad, The. Grace Taber Hallock. RePo
Proud Trees, The. Walter H. Kerr. NePoAm-2

Proud, Unhoped-for Light. Raymond Holden. MAP; MoAmPo (1942 ed.)
Proud Vegetables, The. Mary McNeil Fenollosa. GFA
Proud who never loved, The. Sublimation. Alex Comfort. ErPo; UnTE
Proud with success, richly pleased. Alexander Jannai. C. P. Cavafy. TrJP
Proud Word You Never Spoke [but You Will Speak]. Walter Savage Landor. *Fr.* Ianthe. EnLoPo; EPN; GTBS; GTSL; OBEV; TOP; ViBoPo
(Prophecy, A.) VA
Proudest now is but my peer, The. The Poor Voter on Election Day. Whittier. OTD; PAL; PoRL
Proudly the moon rides, cresting. Lines for a Night Driver. Peter Kane Dufault. WIRo
Proudly the note of the trumpet is sounding. O'Donnell Aboo. Michael Joseph McCann. OnYI
Prove the Doctrine. *Unknown.* SoP
Provençal Lovers; Aucassin and Nicolette. Edmund Clarence Stedman. HBV
Proverb, A. *Unknown, tr. fr. Turkish by* E. Powys Mathers. BoLP
Proverb reporteth, no man can deny, The. *Unknown. Fr.* Tom Tyler and His Wife. ElL; SiCE; TuPP
Proverbs, *sels.* Bible, *O.T.*
"Doth not wisdom cry? and understanding put forth her voice?" VIII: 1, 22-31, 34-36. BoC
("Lord possessed me in the beginning of his ways, The," VIII: 22-31, *Douay vers.*) ISi
(Voice of Wisdom, The. VIII: 22-31.) TreFT
Drunkard, The, XXIII: 29-35. TrJP
(Wine and Woe, *Moulton, Modern Reader's Bible.*) MaRV
Fear of the Lord, The, I: 7. TrJP
Foolish Woman, A, IX: 13-18. TrGrPo
Good Wife, The, XXXI: 10-31. TrGrPo
(Mother of the House, XXXI: 25-29.) GoTP; OQP; PGD
("Strength and honour are her clothing," XXXI: 25-29.) PoSC
(Virtuous Wife, The, XXXI: 10-31.) MaRV
(Virtuous Woman, The, XXXI: 10-31.) TrJP; TRV (10-12, 27-31)
Happy Is the Man That Findeth Wisdom, III: 11-18. TreF
(Happy Is the Man, III: 13-18.) TrJP
"He that is slow to anger is better than the mighty," XVI: 32. FaPON; TiPo (1952 ed.)
House of Wisdom, The, IX: 1-6. TrGrPo
Legacy, The, IV: 1-13. TrJP
Lips of the Wise, The, XV: 1-5, 7-8, 15-17. TrGrPo
(Merry Heart, A, XV: 1, 13, 15-17.) StVeCh
("Soft answer turneth away wrath, A, " XV: 1) TiPo (1952 ed.)
"My son, keep my words," VII: 1, 4-10, 12-27. LO
Neither Poverty nor Riches, XXX: 7-9. TrJP
Reproof, A, VI: 6-11. TrGrPo
(Go to the Ant.) FaPON (6-8); LiTW; TreFT; TrJP
(Sluggard, The—a Sonnet, *Moulton, Modern Reader's Bible.*) MaRV
Seven Evils, VI: 16-19. TrGrPo
(Sower of Discord, A, *Moulton, Modern Reader's Bible.*) MaRV
She of the Impudent Face, VII: 6-27. TrJP
"There be four things which are little upon the earth," XXX: 24-28. PoG
(Four Things.) FaPON; GoTP
"Withdraw thy foot from thy neighbor's house," XXV *and* XXX, *abr.* PoG
Word Fitly Spoken, A, XXV: 11. FaPON
Words of Agur, The, XXX: 4, 15-16, 18-19, 24-28. TrGrPo
(Too Wonderful, XXX: 18-19.) TrJP
Proverbs. Samuel ha-Nagid, *tr. fr. Hebrew by* Israel Abrahams. TrJP
Proverbs. *Unknown, ad. fr. German by* Louis Untermeyer. RIS
Sels.
Day-Dreamer. TiPo
Good Advice. TiPo (1952 ed.)
(Old German Mottos: Advice.) StaSt
Lesson from a Sun-Dial. TiPo
Motto. TiPo
Short Sermon. TiPo
Proverbs of Hell. Blake. *Fr.* The Marriage of Heaven and Hell. AtBAP; EnLi-2
Proverbs of King Alfred, *sels. At. to* Alfred, King of England, *tr. fr. Middle English. WaKn*
Provide, Provide. Robert Frost. AMP;AmPP (5th ed.);AtBAP; CABA;CBV;CMoP;MoAB;MWA-2; PoeP;TDP;TwCP
Providence. William Cowper. *See* Light Shining Out of Darkness.
Providence. Vincenzo da Filicaja, *tr. fr. Italian by* Leigh Hunt. CAW
Providence. Reginald Heber. GN; HBV; OHIP
(Lo, the Lilies of the Field.) OTPC (1923 ed.)
Providence. George Herbert. MaMe
Providence. William Langland. *mod. by* Henry W. Wells. *Fr.* The Vision of Piers Plowman. PoLi
Providence. Cale Young Rice. WGRP
Province I govern is humble and remote, The. To Li Chien. Po Chü-i. AWP
Provincetown, *sels.* Louis Dudek. MoCV
Avant Garde.
Fishing Village.
News.
Ocean, The.
Provincia Deserta. Ezra Pound. CrMA; OxBA
Proving. Georgia Douglas Johnson. CDC
Provoked Wife, The, *sel.* Sir John Vanbrugh.
Philira. SeCL
(Song: "Fly, fly, you happy shepherds, fly.") SeEP
Prowling wolf, whose shaggy skin, A. The Wolf and the Dog. La Fontaine. LiTW; PoFr
Prows o' Reekie, The. Lewis Spence. OxBS
Proximity to the sea is hereby abolished. Gulf of Mexico. Alfonso Reyes. OnHM
Prue, my dearest maid, is sick. Upon Prudence Baldwin Her Sickness. Robert Herrick. OAEP; PoeP; SeCV-1
Prune acrylic whose. Clark Coolidge. ANYP
Prune thou thy words, the thoughts control. Flowers without Fruit. Cardinal Newman. EPN
Pruned Tree, The. Howard Moss. NYBP
Pruners; Conca di Marini. Joseph Langland. NePoEA
Pruning Trees. Po Chü-i, *tr. fr. Chinese* by Arthur Waley. FIW
Pruning Vines. Howard McKinley Corning. MAP; MoAmPo (1942 ed.)
P's and Q's. Rupert Sargent Holland. OTPC
P's the Proud Policeman. Phyllis McGinley. *Fr.* All around the Town. SoPo; TiPo
Psalm LVIII: "And call ye this to utter what is just." Countess of Pembroke, *paraphrased fr.* Bible, *O.T.* EP
Psalm VI: "And on that day, upon the heavenly scarp." A. M. Klein. *Fr.* The Psalter of Avram Haktani. PeCV
Psalm LVI: "Fountain of pity now with pity flow." Countess of Pembroke, *paraphrased fr.* Bible, *O.T.* EP
Psalm CXXX: "From depth of sin and from a deep despair." Sir Thomas Wyatt, *paraphrased fr.* Bible, *O.T.* FCP
Psalm: "Happy is the man whom Thou hast set apart." "Yehoash," *tr. fr. Yiddish by* Isidore Goldstick. TrJP
Psalm CXLIII: "Hear my prayer, O Lord, hear my request." Sir Thomas Wyatt, *paraphrased fr.* Bible, *O.T.* FCP
Psalm LXXXIV: "How lovely are thy dwellings fair!" Milton, *paraphrased fr.* Bible, *O.T.* TrPWD
Psalm CXXXVII: "I love thy kingdom, Lord." Timothy Dwight. *See* I Love Thy Kingdom, Lord.
Psalm: "I proclaim Thee great and wonderful." Murilo Mendes, *tr. fr. Portuguese by* Dudley Poore. MoRP
Psalm XLIII: "Judge of all, judge me." Sir Philip Sidney, *paraphrased fr.* Bible, *O.T.* EP
Psalm CII: "Lord, hear my prayer, and let my cry pass." Sir Thomas Wyatt, *paraphrased fr.* Bible, *O.T.* FCP
Psalm XII: "Lord, help, it is high time for me to call." Sir Philip Sidney, *paraphrased fr.* Bible, *O.T.* EP
Psalm, A: "O God, in whom my deepest being dwells." Edmund Blunden. TrPWD
Psalm XXXII: "O happy are they that have forgiveness got." Sir Thomas Wyatt, *paraphrased fr.* Bible, *O.T.* FCP
Psalm CL: "O laud the Lord, the God of hosts commend." Countess of Pembroke, *paraphrased fr.* Bible, *O.T.* EP
Psalm XXXVIII: "O Lord, as I Thee have both prayed and pray." Sir Thomas Wyatt, *paraphrased fr.* Bible, *O.T.* FCP
Psalm CXXXIX: "O Lord, in me there lieth nought." Countess

of Pembroke, *paraphrased fr.* Bible, *O.T.* OBSC; OxBoCh
Psalm VIII: "O Lord, our Lord," *sel.* Christopher Smart, *paraphrased fr.* Bible, *O.T.*
"Lord what is man, that he should find." TrPWD
Psalm VI: "O Lord, since in my mouth, Thy mighty name." Sir Thomas Wyatt, *paraphrased fr.* Bible, *O.T.* FCP
Psalm LXXXVIII: "Oh Lord, upon whose will dependeth my welfare." Earl of Surrey, *paraphrased fr.* Bible, *O.T.* FCP
Psalm XCII: "O lovely thing." Countess of Pembroke, *paraphrased fr.* Bible, *O.T.* EP
Psalm LI: "Rue on me, Lord, for Thy goodness and grace." Sir Thomas Wyatt, *paraphrased fr.* Bible, *O.T.* FCP
Psalm XIX: "Spacious firmament on high, The." Addison. *See* Spacious Firmament on High, The.
Psalm XXXV: "Speak thou for me, against wrong speaking foes." Sir Philip Sidney, *paraphrased fr.* Bible, *O.T.* EP
Psalm LXXV: "Thee, God, O thee, we sing, we celebrate." Countess of Pembroke, *paraphrased fr.* Bible, *O.T.* EP
Psalm XII: "These were the ones who thanked their God." A. M. Klein. *Fr.* The Psalter of Avram Haktani. PeCV
Psalm: "They have burned to Thee many tapers." Jessie E. Sampter. OQP
Psalm LXXIII: "Though, Lord, to Israel thy graces plenteous be." Earl of Surrey, *paraphrased fr.* Bible, *O.T.* FCP
Psalm XXXVII: "Trust in the Lord." Charles Frederic Sheldon, *paraphrased fr.* Bible, *O.T.* BLRP
Psalm, The: "While Northward the hot sun was sinking o'er the trees." Robert Bridges. FaBoTw; LiTB
Psalm XLIX: "World-dwellers all give heed to what I say." Countess of Pembroke, *paraphrased fr.* Bible, *O.T.* EP
Psalm against the Darkness. A. M. Sullivan. MaRV
Psalm Concerning the Castle. Denise Levertov. TwCP
Psalm for Christmas Day. Thomas Pestel. OxBoCh
Psalm for Moderns, A. Thomas P. McDonnell. JKCP (1955 ed.)
Psalm for Sonny Rollins. Walt Delegall. BF
Psalm for Sunday Night, A. Thomas Pestel. OxBoCh
Psalm of Battle. *Unknown, tr. fr. Arabic by* E. Powys Mathers. *Fr.* The Thousand and One Nights. AWP; JAWP; WBP
Psalm of Confidence, A. Horace Westwood. MaRV
Psalm of David, A. Psalms, XXIII Bible, *O.T.* *See* Lord Is My Shepherd, The. CBV
Psalm of David, A. Psalms, VIII, Bible, *O.T.* *See* What Is Man?
Psalm of Life, A, *parody.* Andrew Lang. CenHV
Psalm of Life, A. Longfellow. AA; AmePo; AnNE; CoBA; DiPo; FaBoBe; FaPL; HBV; HBVY; MaRV; NeHB; OHFP; OTD; PaPo; PoLF; PoPl; SoP; TreF; UnPo; WBLP; YaD
Life, *sel.* GN
(Lives of Great Men All Remind Us, *shorter sel.*) DD
Psalm of Montreal, A. Samuel Butler. *See* O God! O Montreal!
Psalm of Praise. Psalms, C, Bible, *O.T.* *See* Thanksgiving.
Psalm of St. Priapus, The. James Broughton. ErPo
Psalm of Silence, The. Konstantin Dmitreyevich Balmont, *tr. fr. Russian by* Babette Deutsch and Avrahm Yarmolinsky. OnPM
Psalm of the Early Buddhist Sisters, A. *Unknown.* WGRP
Psalm of the Fruitful Field. A. M. Klein. WHW
Psalm of the Singing Grave. Alexander Janta, *tr. fr. Polish by* Gladys Anthony White *and* Alexander Janta. LiTW
Psalm of the West, The, *sels.* Sidney Lanier.
Land of the Wilful Gospel. PAH
Lexington. PaA; PAH; PAL
(Battle of Lexington, *shorter sel.*) PAP
Story of Vinland, The. PAH; ThLM
Triumph, The. PAH
Psalm of Those Who Go Forth before Daylight. Carl Sandburg. AnAmPo; FIW; MoShBr; OxBA; StVeCh
Psalm to My Belovèd. Eunice Tietjens. BoLP; ErPo
(Fulfillment.) PoToHe (new ed.)
Psalm to the Holy Spirit. A. M. Sullivan. TrPWD
Psalm to the Son, A. Marguerite Wilkinson. TrPWD
Psalme CXXXVII: "As on Euphrates shady banks we lay." George Sandys. *Fr.* A Paraphrase on the Psalms of David. OBS
Psalme Twenty-three ("Happy me! O happy sheepe!"). George Herbert, *paraphrased. fr.* Psalms, XXIII, Bible, *O.T.* MaMe
Psalms, *sels.* Bible, *O.T.*
Psalm I ("Blessed is the man. . ."). AWP; JAWP; WoL
(Beatus Vir, *tr. by* Thomas Sternhold.) ReIE; SiCE
(Blessed Is the Man.) EnLi-1
(Godly and the Ungodly, The.) TreF
(Happy Is the Man.) TrJP
("O blessed man, that in th'advice," Bay Psalm Book.) SCAP
(Patriot, The, *paraphrased by* Thomas Godfrey.) PoFr
(Psalm I: "He blessed is who neither loosely treads," *paraphrased by* Sir Philip Sidney.) FCP
(Tree and the Chaff, The, *Moulton, Modern Reader's Bible.*) WGRP
Psalm II ("Why do the heathen rage. . .").
(Psalm II: "What ails this heathenish rage?" *paraphrased by* Sir Philip Sidney.) FCP
Psalm III ("Lord, how are they increased that trouble me!").
(Domine Quid Multiplicati Sunt, *tr. by* Thomas Sternhold.) SiCE
(Psalm III: "Lord, how do they increase," *paraphrased by* Sir Philip Sidney.) FCP
Psalm IV ("Hear me when I call. . .").
(Cum Invocarem, *tr. by* Thomas Sternhold.) SiCE
(Psalm IV: "Hear me, O hear me when I call," *paraphrased by* Sir Philip Sidney.) FCP
Psalm V ("Give ear to my words. . .").
(Psalm V: "Ponder the words, O Lord, that I do say," *paraphrased by* Sir Philip Sidney.) FCP
Psalm VI ("O Lord rebuke me not. . .").
(Psalm VI: "Lord, let not me a worm by Thee be shent," *paraphrased by* Sir Philip Sidney.) FCP
(Psalm VI: "O Lord, since in my mouth, Thy mighty name," *paraphrased by* Sir Thomas Wyatt.) FCP
Psalm VII ("O Lord, my God. . .").
(Psalm VII: "O Lord, my God, Thou art my trustful stay," *paraphrased by* Sir Philip Sidney.) FCP
Psalm VIII ("O Lord, our Lord. . ."). AWP; JAWP; OnPM; OuHeWo; PG (1955 ed.);
(How Glorious Is Thy Name.) TrJP
(O Lord, How Excellent Is Thy Name.) TreFS
(Psalm VIII: "O Lord that rul'st our mortal line," *paraphrased by* Sir Philip Sidney.) FCP
(Psalm of David, A.) OTPC (1946 ed.)
(Song of Praise, A.) EnLi-1
(What Is Man?) MaRV; TrGrPo
"Lord what is man, that he should find," 4-9, *paraphrased by* Christopher Smart. TrPWD
When I Consider Thy Heavens, 3-8. FaPON; ImOP; InP
Psalm IX ("I will praise thee, O Lord. . .").
(Psalm IX: "With all my heart, O Lord, I will praise Thee," *paraphrased by* Sir Philip Sidney.) FCP
I Will Sing Thy Praise, 1-2. FaPON
Psalm X ("Why standest thou afar off. . .").
(Psalm X: "Why standest Thou so far," *paraphrased by* Sir Philip Sidney.) FCP
Psalm XI ("In the Lord put I my trust. . .").
(Psalm XI: "Since I do trust Jehova still," *paraphrased by* Sir Philip Sidney.) FCP
Psalm XII ("Help, Lord; for the godly man ceaseth. . .").
(Psalm XII: "Lord, help, it is high time for me to call," *paraphrased by* Sir Philip Sidney.) EP; FCP
Psalm XIII ("How long wilt Thou forget me. . .").
(Psalm XIII: "How long, O Lord, shall I forgotten be?" *paraphrased by* Sir Philip Sidney.) FCP
Psalm XIV ("The fool hath said in his heart, There is no God"). OnPM
(Fool Hath Said in His Heart, The.) TrJP
(Psalm XIV: "The foolish man, by flesh and fancy led," *paraphrased by* Sir Philip Sidney.) FCP
Psalm XV ("Lord, who shall abide. . ."). OuHeWo
(Psalm XV: "In tabernacle Thine, O Lord, who shall remain?" *paraphrased by* Sir Philip Sidney.) FCP
Psalm XVI ("Preserve me, O God. . .").
(Psalm XVI: "Save me, Lord, for why Thou art," *paraphrased by* Sir Philip Sidney.) FCP
I Have a Goodly Heritage, 5-9. TreFT
Psalm XVII ("Hear the right, O Lord. . .").
(Psalm XVII: "My suit is just, just Lord, to my suit hark," *paraphrased by* Sir Philip Sidney.) FCP

Psalms (continued)
Psalm XVIII ("I will love thee, O Lord. . .").
(Psalm XVIII: "Thee will I love, O Lord, with all my heart's delight," *paraphrased by* Sir Philip Sidney.) FCP
Psalm XIX ("The heavens declare. . ."). AWP; InP (1-4); JAWP; OuHeWo; PoG (1-6); TRV; WoL
(Glory of God The.) TrJP
(God's Glory.) TrGrPo
(Heavens Above and the Law Within, The, *Moulton, Modern Reader's Bible.*) WGRP
(Heavens Declare the Glory of God, The.) FaPON (1-4); MaRV (1-6); ShBV-1; TreF
("Heavens doe declare, The." *Bay Psalm Book.*) SCAP
(Nineteenth Psalm.) WBLP
(Psalm XIX: "The heavenly frame sets forth the fame," *paraphrased by* Sir Philip Sidney.) FCP
God's Precepts Perfect, 7-9. BLRP
Heavens, The, 1-6. ChTr
Law Within, The, 7-14, *Moulton, Modern Reader's Bible.* MaRV
Psalm XX ("The Lord hear thee. . .").
(Psalm XX: "Let God, the Lord, hear thee," *paraphrased by* Sir Philip Sidney.) FCP
Psalm XXI ("The king shall joy. . .").
(Psalm XXI: "New joy, new joy unto our king," *paraphrased by* Sir Philip Sidney.) FCP
Psalm XXII ("My God, my God. . .").
(Cry in Distress, A, 1-15.) TrGrPo
(Psalm XXII: "My God, my God, why hast Thou me forsaken?" *paraphrased by* Sir Philip Sidney.) FCP
Psalm XXIII ("The Lord is my shepherd. . ."). AWP; CBEP; CBV; EnLi-1; ExPo; JAWP; OHIP; OnPM; OuHeWo; PG (1955 ed.); PoPo; RelE; RePo; TiPo (1952 ed.); TRV; WBLP; WoL
("God of love my shepherd is, The," *paraphrased by* George Herbert.) CBV; MaMe
("Happy me! O happy sheepe!" *paraphrased by* George Herbert.) MaMe
(Lord Is My Shepherd, The.) FaPON; MaRV; PoLF; StVeCh; TreF; TrJP
(Lord's My Shepherd, The, *Scottish Psalter.*) FaChP; SoP; TRV
(Protection of Jehovah, The, *Moulton, Modern Reader's Bible.*) WGRP
(Psalm XXIII: "The Lord, the Lord my shepherd is," *paraphrased by* Sir Philip Sidney.) FCP
(Psalm of David.) SUS
(Shepherd's Psalm, The.) PCD; PCH
(Twenty-third Psalm, The.) FaBoBe; NeHB; OTPC (1946 ed.); PoPl; StaSt; TrGrPo
Psalm XXIV ("The Earth is the Lord's. . ."). AWP; EnLi-1; JAWP; OHIP; OnPM; OuHeWo; TiPo (1952 ed.); WoL
(Earth is the Lord's, The.) EaLo; FaPON (1-4); TreFT; TrJP
(Lift Up Your Heads [O Ye Gates].) PCD; PCH; TrGrPo
(Psalm XXIV: "The earth is God's, and what the globe of," *paraphrased* by Sir Philip Sidney.) FCP
Psalm XXV ("Unto thee, O Lord. . .").
(Psalm XXV: "To Thee, O Lord most just," *paraphrased by* Sir Philip Sidney.) FCP
"All the paths of the Lord are lovingkindness and truth," 10, 15-17; LI: 1-13, 9-12, 17; CIV: 1-4, 8-13. BoC
Psalm XXVI ("Judge me, O Lord. . .").
(Psalm XXVI: "Lord, judge me and my case," *paraphrased by* Sir Philip Sidney.) FCP
Psalm, XXVII ("The Lord is my light. . .").
(Deliverance of Jehovah, The, *Moulton, Modern Reader's Bible.*) WGRP
(Lord Is My Light and My Salvation, The, *abr.*) TreFT
(My Light and My Salvation, *Moulton, Modern Reader's Bible.*). MaRV
(Psalm XXVII: "The shining Lord He is my light," *paraphrased by* Sir Philip Sidney.) FCP
Serenity of Faith, The, 7-14, *tr. by* McFadyen. BLRP
Psalm XXVIII ("Unto thee will I cry. . .").
(Psalm XXVIII: "To Thee, Lord, my cry I send," *paraphrased by* Sir Philip Sidney.) FCP
Psalm XXIX ("Give unto the Lord. . ."). AWP; OnPM
(Psalm XXIX: "Ascribe unto the Lord of light," *paraphrased by* Sir Philip Sidney.) FCP
(Twenty-fourth Psalm, The [*wr.*].) PoPo
Psalm XXX ("I will extol thee. . .").
(Psalm XXX: "O Lord, Thou hast exalted me," paraphrased by Sir Philip Sidney.) FCP
Psalm XXXI ("In thee, O Lord. . .").
(Psalm XXXI: "All, all my trust, Lord, I have put in Thee," *paraphrased by* Sir Philip Sidney.) FCP
Psalm XXXII ("Blessed is he whose transgression. . .").
(Psalm XXXII: "Blessed is the man whose filthy stain," *paraphrased by* Sir Philip Sidney.) FCP
(Psalm XXXII: "O happy are they that have forgiveness got," *paraphrased by* Sir Thomas Wyatt.) FCP
Psalm XXXIII ("Rejoice in the Lord. . .").
(Psalm XXXIII: "Rejoice in God, O ye," *paraphrased by* Sir Philip Sidney.) FCP
Psalm XXXIV ("I will bless the Lord. . .").
(Psalm XXXIV: "I, even I, will always," *paraphrased by* Sir Philip Sidney. FCP
Psalm XXXV ("Plead my cause, O Lord. . .").
(Psalm XXXV: "Speak Thou for me, against wrong speaking foes," *paraphrased by* Sir Philip Sidney.) EP; FCP
Psalm XXXVI ("The transgression of the wicked. . .").
(Psalm XXXVI: "Methinks amid my heart I hear," *paraphrased by* Sir Philip Sidney.) FCP
Psalm XXXVII ("Fret not thyself. . ."). WoL
(Psalm XXXVII: "Fret not thyself, if thou do see," *paraphrased by* Sir Philip Sidney.) FCP
(Psalm XXXVII: "Trust in the Lord," *paraphrased by* Charles Frederic Sheldon.) BLRP; TreFT, 1-4, 7
Fret Not Thyself because of Evildoers. TiPo (1952 ed.), 1, 2, 35, 36, 37
Psalm XXXVIII ("O Lord, rebuke me not. . .").
(Psalm XXXVIII: "Lord, while that Thy rage doth bide," *paraphrased by* Sir Philip Sidney.) FCP
(Psalm XXXVIII: "O Lord, as I Thee have both prayed and pray," *paraphrased by* Sir Thomas Wyatt.) FCP
Psalm XXXIX ("I said: 'I will take heed to my ways' ").
(Lord, Make Me to Know Mine End.) TrJP
(Psalm XXXIX: "Thus did I think: I well will mark my way," *paraphrased by* Sir Philip Sidney.) FCP
Psalm XL ("I waited patiently. . .").
(Psalm XL: "While long I did with patient constancy," *paraphrased by* Sir Philip Sidney.) FCP
Psalm XLI ("Blessed is he. . .").
(Psalm XLI: "He blessed is who with wise temper can," *paraphrased by* Sir Philip Sidney.) FCP
Psalm XLII ("As the hart panteth. . ."). AWP; BoC; JAWP; TRV (1-5, 7-8); WoL
(As the Hart Panteth.) TrJP
(My Soul Thirsteth for God.) TrGrPo
(Psalm XLII: "As the chafed hart which brayeth," *paraphrased by* Sir Philip Sidney.) FCP
(Search, The, XLII *and* XLIII, *Moulton, Modern Reader's Bible.)* WGRP
(Where is Thy God? *paraphrased by* J. Lewis Milligan.) MaRV
Psalm XLIII ("Judge me, O God. . ."). OnPM
(Psalm XLIII: "Judge of all, judge me," *paraphrased by* Sir Philip Sidney.) EP; FCP
(Search, The, XLII *and* XLIII, *Moulton, Modern Reader's Bible.*) WGRP
Psalm XLV ("My heart is inditing. . .").
("My heart overfloweth with a good matter," *Book of Common Prayer.*) HW
"Queen stood on thy right hand, The," Psalm XLIV, *Douay vers.*, 10-16. ISi
Psalm XLVI ("God is our refuge. . ."). AWP; OnPM; TreFT; TRV
(From Psalm XLVI, *abr.*) PC
(God Is Our Refuge, *paraphrased by* George Sandys.) SoP
(Our Refuge, *Moulton, Modern Reader's Bible.*) MaRV
(Refuge, The, *Moulton, Modern Reader's Bible.*) WGRP
(Though the Earth Be Removed.) TrGrPo
Psalm XLIX ("Hear this, all ye people. . .").
(Psalm XLIX: "World-dwellers all give heed to what I say," *paraphrased by* the Countess of Pembroke.) EP
Psalm LI ("Have mercy upon me, O God. . .").
("Have mercy upon me, O God, after thy great goodness," *Book of Common Prayer*). LiTW
(Psalm LI: "Rue on me, Lord, for Thy goodness and grace," *paraphrased by* Sir Thomas Wyatt.) FCP
Psalm LV ("Give ear to my prayer. . ."). AWP

(Wings, 6-7.) FaPON; PCD; PCH
Psalm LVI ("Be merciful unto me, O God. . .").
(Psalm LVI: "Fountain of pity now with pity flow," *paraphrased by* the Countess of Pembroke.) EP
Psalm LVIII ("Do ye indeed speak righteousness. . .").
(Psalm LVIII: "And call ye this to utter what is just," *paraphrased by* the Countess of Pembroke.) EP
Psalm LXII ("Truly my soul waiteth. . .").
(Leave It All Quietly to God, 1-8, *tr. by* James Moffatt.) MaRV
Psalm LXV ("Praise waiteth for thee. . ."), *sel.*
"Thou visiteth the earth," 9-13. OHIP
Psalm LXVII ("God be merciful unto us, and bless us"). OnPM
Let the Nations Be Glad, 1-5. FaPON
Psalm LXX ("Make haste, O God, to deliver me"). OnPM
Psalm LXXIII ("Truly God is good. . .").
(Psalm LXXIII: "Though, Lord, to Israel thy graces plenteous be," *paraphrased by* the Earl of Surrey.) FCP
Psalm LXXV ("Unto thee, O God, do we give thanks").
(Psalm LXXV: "Thee, God, O thee, we sing, we celebrate," *paraphrased by* the Countess of Pembroke.) EP
Psalm LXXVII ("I cried unto God. . ."). AWP
Psalm LXXIX ("O God, the heathen are come into Thine inheritance").
(Heathen Are Come into Thine Inheritance, The.) TrJP
Psalm LXXXIII ("O God, keep not Thou silence").
(Keep Not Thou Silence.) TrJP
Psalm LXXXIV ("How amiable are thy tabernacles. . ."). TRV
(Psalm LXXXIV: "How lovely are thy dwellings fair!" *paraphrased by* Milton.) TrPWD
How Lovely Are Thy Tabernacles, 1-5. TrJP
Psalm LXXXVIII ("O Lord God of my salvation. . .").
(Psalm LXXXVIII: "Oh Lord, upon whose will dependeth my welfare," *paraphrased by* the Earl of Surrey.) FCP
Psalm XC ("Lord, thou hast been our dwelling place. . ."). AWP; EaLo
(God, Our Dwelling Place, *Moulton, Modern Reader's Bible.*) MaRV
Psalm XCI ("He that dwelleth. . ."). AWP; WoL
(Everlasting Arms, *Moulton, Modern Reader's Bible.*) WGRP
(God Our Refuge, *Moulton, Modern Reader's Bible.*) MaRV
(Mighty Fortress, A.) TrGrPo
Psalm XCII ("It is a good thing to give thanks unto the Lord. . .").
("It is good to sing Thy praises and to thank Thee, O Most High," *paraphrased.*) FaChP
(Psalm XCII: "O lovely thing," *paraphrased by* the Countess of Pembroke.) EP
Psalm XCIII ("The Lord reigneth. . .").
(Jehovah's Immovable Throne, *Moulton, Modern Reader's Bible.*) WGRP
Psalm XCV ("O come, let us sing. . .). AWP; BLRP, *abr.*; JAWP; OHIP, *abr.*; OnPM; OuHeWo
(Thanksgiving, 1-7.) BoChLi (1950 ed.)
Psalm XCVIII ("O sing unto the Lord. . .").
(Floods Clap Their Hands, The.) TrGrPo
(O Sing unto the Lord a New Song.) EaLo; TrJP
(Sing unto Jehovah.) BLRP
(Sing unto the Lord.) StaSt
Psalm C ("Make a joyful noise. . ."). MPB; OHIP; OnPM; PG (1955 ed.); RePo; TiPo (1952 ed.); TRV; UnS; YAT
("Be joyfull in the Lorde," *The Great Bible.*) YAT
(Be Thankful unto Him.) FaPON
(Exhortation to Praise God Cheerefully, An, *King James vers.*). YAT
(Hundredth Psalm, The, *metrical vers. by* William Kethe.) OtMeF
("Make ye jubilation to God al the earth," XCIX, *Douay vers.*) YAT
(Old Hundredth, *metrical vers. by* William Kethe.) MaRV
(Psalm of Praise, A.) SiSoSe; SUS
(Scotch Te Deum, *metrical vers. by* William Kethe.) WGRP
(Thanksgiving.) BoChLi (1950 ed.); StVeCh
Psalm CII ("Hear my prayer, O Lord. . .").
(Psalm CII: "Lord, hear my prayer, and let my cry pass," *paraphrased by* Sir Thomas Wyatt.) FCP
Psalm CIII ("Bless the Lord, O my soul. . ."). AWP; JAWP; TiPo (1952 ed.) (1-5)
(Hymn of the World Within, The, *Moulton, Modern Reader's Bible.*) WGRP
("O thou my soule, Jehovah blesse," *Bay Psalm Book.*) SCAP
Psalm CIV ("Bless the Lord, O my soul. . .") OHIP, *sel.*
(Bless the Lord, O My Soul.) TrJP
(Hymn of the World Without, 1-24, *Moulton, Modern Reader's Bible.*) WGRP
(Praise the Lord, O My Soul!) ThGo
Rich Earth, The. 16-24. GoTP
Psalm CVII ("O give thanks . . .").
("O give yee thanks unto the Lord," *Bay Psalm Book.*) SCAP
They That Go Down to the Sea in Ships, *sel.* BBV (1951 ed.) (23-31); ChTr (23-31); EtS (23-30); FaPON (23-24); GaP (23-24)
(Ocean, The, 23-32, *Moulton, Modern Reader's Bible.*) WGRP
Psalm CXIII ("Praise ye the Lord. . ."). OnPM
Psalm CXIV ("When Israel came forth out of Egypt").
(When Israel Came Forth out of Egypt.) TrJP
("When Israel came out of Egypt," *Book of Common Prayer.*) LiTW
Psalm CXVIII ("'O give thanks unto the Lord, for He is good' ").
(O Give Thanks.) TrJP
Psalm CXXI ("I will lift up mine eyes. . ."). AWP; BBV (1951 ed.); CBEP; EnLi-1; JAWP; OnPM; OuHeWo; PoG; TRV
(I Will Lift Up Mine Eyes [unto the Hills].) FaPON; TreF
(Pilgrim's Song, *Moulton, Modern Reader's Bible.*) WGRP
(Song of Safety, A.) PCH
(Song of Trust, A.) PCD; TrGrPo
(Unto the Hills, *paraphrased by* John Campbell.) MaRV
Psalm CXXII ("I was glad when they said unto me. . ."). TRV
Psalm CXXIV ("If it had not been the Lord. . ."). OnPM
Our Help, 8. TRV
Psalm CXXVI ("When the Lord turned again the captivity of Zion"). BoPe; OnPM
(Like unto Them That Dream.) TrJP
Psalm CXXVII ("Except the Lord build the house. . .). OnPM; TreFT; TRV
(Except the Lord Build the House.) TrJP
Psalm CXXVIII ("Blessed is every one that feareth the Lord"). TRV
(Beati Omnes, *tr. by* Thomas Sternhold.) ReIE; SiCE
Psalm CXXX ("Out of the depths. . ."). EnLi-1; LiTW (*Book of Common Prayer*); OnPM
(De Profundis.) BLRP; MaRV; TreF; WGRP; WHL
(In Darkness and Aridity.) BoC
(Out of the Depths.) TrJP
(Psalm CXXX: "From depth of sin and from a deep despair," *paraphrased by* Sir Thomas Wyatt.) FCP
(Song of Supplication, A.) TrGrPo
Psalm CXXXII ("Behold, how good and how pleasant it is").
(To Dwell Together in Unity.) TrJP
Psalm CXXXIII ("Behold, how good. . ."). AWP; JAWP; OnPM; TRV
(Unity of Mankind). TreFT
Psalm CXXXIV ("Behold, bless ye the Lord. . ."). TRV
Psalm CXXXVI ("O give thanks. . ."). AWP; OHIP
(Thanksgiving, 1-9, 26). BoChLi (1950 ed.)
"To him that smote Egypt in their firstborn," 10-24. PoFr
Psalm CXXXVII ("By the rivers of Babylon. . ."). AWP; CaFP; ExPo; JAWP; LiTW; OnPM; PG (1955 ed.); StaSt (1-6, *ad.*)
(By the Rivers of Babylon.) TrJP
("On the proud bankes of great Euphrates flood," *paraphrased by* George Herbert.) MaMe
(Psalm: "I love thy kingdom, Lord," *paraphrased by* Timothy Dwight.) AmePo
(Psalme CXXXVII: "As on Euphrates shady banks," *paraphrased by* George Sandys.) OBS
(Song of Exile, A.) TrGrPo
Thou Wilt Revive Me, 6-8. TreFT
Psalm CXXXIX ("O Lord, thou has searched me. . ."). BoC

Psalms (continued)
(Psalm CXXXIX: "O Lord, in me there lieth nought," *paraphrased by* the Countess of Pembroke.) OBSC; OxBoCh
(Searcher of Hearts Is Thy Maker, The, *Moulton Modern Reader's Bible.*) WGRP
Psalm CXLIII (Hear my prayer, O Lord. . .").
(Psalm CXLIII: "Hear my prayer, O Lord, hear my request," *paraphrased by* Sir Thomas Wyatt.) FCP
Psalm CXLV ("I will extol thee, my God. . ."), *sel.*
Lord Is Good to All, The, 9. TRV
Psalm CXLVI ("Hallelujah,/ Praise the Lord, O my soul").
(Hallelujah.) TrJP
(Lauda Anima Mea, *tr. by* John Hopkins.) RelE
Psalm CXLVII ("Praise ye the Lord"). TiPo (1952 ed.), *abr.*
(Foot, Fin or Feather.) OA
"Sing unto the Lord," *sel.* OHIP; PoRL; SoPo
Who Maketh the Grass to Grow, FaPON 1, 5, 8-9, 16-18, 20.
Psalm CXLVIII ("Praise ye the Lord. . .").
(Hallelujah Chorus, A, Smith-Goodspeed *tr.*) MaRV
(Praise Ye the Lord.) TrJP
(Song of Praise, A.) TrGrPo
Psalm CL ("Praise ye the Lord. . ."). OnPM; TiPo (1952 ed.); TRV; UnS
(Closing Doxology, The, Smith-Goodspeed *tr.*) MaRV
(Laudate Dominum.) ChTr
(Psalm CL: "O laud the Lord, the God of hosts commend," *paraphrased by* the Countess of Pembroke.) EP
Psalms of Love. Peter Baum, *tr. fr. German by* Jethro Bithell. AWP
Psalter of Avram Haktani, The, *sels.* A. M. Klein.
Psalm VI: "And on that day, upon the heavenly scarp." PeCV
Psalm XII: "These were the ones who thanked their God." PeCV
Psalter of the Blessed Virgin Mary, *sels.* St. Bonaventure, *tr. fr. Latin by* Sister Mary Emmanuel. ISi
"Psittacus Eois Imitatrix Ales ab Indis." Sacheverell Sitwell. AtBAP; MoBrPo
Psyche. Samuel Taylor Coleridge. ERoP-1
Psyche. Alfred Starr Hamilton. QAH
Psyche. Jones Very. AP
Psyche to Cupid: Her Ditty. James Broughton. ErPo
Psyche with the Candle. Archibald MacLeish. MoLP
Psychedelic Firemen. David Henderson. NBP
Psychoanalysis. Gavin Ewart. NYBP
Psychoanalysts. Christopher Morley. WhC
Psychological Prediction. Virginia Brasier. BBGG
Psychologists, psychiatrists. Basic. Ray Durem. PoNe (1970 ed.)
Psychology Class. Elizabeth K. Campbell. TwCaPo
Psycholophon. Gelett Burgess. CenHV; NA
Psychometrist. James Stephens. POTE
Ptolemy, poor Ptolemy. The Old Nurse's Song. Edith Sitwell. NeMA; TSW
Pub. Julian Symons. LiTB; LiTM; WaP
Public Aid for Niagara Falls. Morris Bishop. InMe
Public Garden, The. Robert Lowell. AP; NoP; PoeP; PoRA (rev. ed.)
Public haunt they found her in, A. A Girl of Pompeii. Edward Sandford Martin. AA; HBV
Public Holiday; Paris. Joyce Horner. GoYe
Public Library. Candace T. Stevenson. GoYe
Public Nuisance, A. Reginald Arkell. SD
Publication—is the auction. Emily Dickinson. AmePo; AmPP (5th ed.); CoBA
Puccini was Latin, and Wagner Teutonic. The Birds. Ogden Nash. *Fr.* The Carnival of Animals. UnS
Puck and the Fairy. Shakespeare. *See* Over Hill, over Dale.
Puck Goes to Court. Fenton Johnson. CDC; GoSl
Puck of Pook's Hill, *sels.* Kipling.
Cities and Thrones and Powers. CBV; FaBoEn; GoJo; GTBS-D; MemP; MoVE; OBNC; PoEL-5; POTE; PoVP; SeCeV; ShBV-4; ViPP
Harp Song of the Dane Women. AtBAP; FaBoEn; OAEP (2d ed.); OBNC; OtMeF; PoRA; POTE; SeCePo; ShBV-3
Land of Our Birth. BoTP; MaRV
(Children's Song, The.) PoVP
Puck's Song ("See you the ferny ride that steals"). FaBoCh; FaBV; LoGBV
Smuggler's Song, A. ShBV-1
Puck Speaks. Shakespeare. *See* Now the Hungry Lion Roars.
Puck's Song ("Now the hungry lion"). Shakespeare. *See* Now the Hungry Lion Roars.
Pudden Tame. *Unknown.* ChTr
("What's your name?") GoTP
Pudding and pie. Greedy Jane. *Unknown.* HBVY
Pudding Charms. Charlotte Druitt Cole. BoTP
Pudding Prepared and Eaten, The. Joel Barlow. *Fr.* The Hasty Pudding, III. AnNE
Puddle, The. Eden Phillpotts. HBMV
Pudgy. Frank Lima. ANYP
Puella Mea. E. E. Cummings. CLwM
Puella Parvula. Wallace Stevens. PoFS
Puer Aeternus. Kathleen Raine. NYBP
Puer ex Jersey. *Unknown.* NA
Puerto Rican Side-Street. Louis Dudek. TwCaPo
Puerto Rico Song. William Carlos Williams. NYBP
Puffed up with luring to her knees. The Flute. Joseph Russell Taylor. AA
Pug-Dog and Spitz. F. Hey. SAS
Puir Dash, thou'rt getting auld and frail. To My Auld Dog Dash. John Barr of Craigielee. AnNZ
Puk-Wudjies. Patrick R. Chalmers. BoTP; DD; HBVY
Pulkovo Meridian, The, *sel.* Vera Inber, *tr. fr. Russian by* Dorothea Prall Radin *and* Alexander Kaun.
Leningrad: 1943. WaaP
Pull down the shades baby neighbors don want to see what you do. Crawl Blues. Vincent McHugh. ErPo
Pull Down Thy Vanity. Ezra Pound. *See* Ant is a Centaur, The.
Pull me down, ladybug. Ladybug. Raymond Souster. MoCV
"Pull, men, for, lo, see there they blow!" Brand Fire New Whaling Song Right from the Pacific Ocean. *Unknown.* EtS
Pull my daisy. Song: Fie My Fum. Allen Ginsberg. ErPo
Pull up the bell-flow'rs of the spring. St. Mark. Christopher Smart. *Fr.* Hymns and Spiritual Songs. EiCP
Pulled from our ruts by the made-to-order gale. Trans Canada. Francis Reginald Scott. PeCV
Pulley, The. George Herbert. AnFE; AtBAP; ATP; AWP; BEL; BoLiVe; CBEP; CBV; CenL; CoBE; DiPo; EaLo; EnL; EnLi-1; ExPo; FaBoEn; HBV; ILP; InPo; LiTB; LiTG; MaMe; MaRV; MemP; MePo; NoP; OAEP; OBEV; OBS; OtMeF; OuHeWo; OxBoCh; PAn; PoAn; PoFS; PoIE; PoSa; ReEn; SCEP-1; SeCeV; SeCL; SeCP; SeCV-1; SeEP; StP; TIHL; TreFT; TrGrPo; UnPo (1st ed.); ViBoPo; WHA
(Gifts of God, The.) GTBS; GTBS-D; GTBS-P; GTBS-W; GTSE; GTSL; TRV
Pulling the dead sun's weight through County Meath. Cycling to Dublin. Robert Greacen. OnYI
Pulpit, therefore (and I name it filled), The. The True Preacher. William Cowper. *Fr.* The Task, II. MaRV
Pulse, The. Denise Levertov. FRC
Pulse, The. Mark Van Doren. MAP; MoAmPo; PoPl
Pulse of Darkness, The. John Fandel. JKCP (1955 ed.)
Pult'ney, methinks you blame my breach of word. Epistle III. John Gay. EiCP
Pumpkin, The. Robert Graves. PDV; PoMS
Pumpkin, The. Whittier. DD; OHIP; PoRL; PoSC
Pumpkin Speaks, A. Amanda Barris. PCH
Pumpkin tendrils creep, The. Late Summer. Kinoshita Yuji. FIW
Pumpkins. John Cotton. BoNaP
Punch and Judy. *Unknown.* OxNR
Punch, Brothers, Punch! *Unknown.* CBEP
Punch, the Immortal Liar, *sels.* Conrad Aiken.
"Build a house of gold for Punch," Third Voice. NP
"Like a tower of brass is Punch," Fourth Voice. NP
"Look, he comes! how tall he is," Second Voice. NP
"Pave the sky with stars for Punch!" First Voice. NP
Puppet Dreams, The.
"Open a window on the world." MAP; MoAmPo
"Sheba, now let down your hair." MAP; MoAmPo
"There is a fountain in a wood." MAP; MoAmPo; NeMA
"Solomon, Clown, put by your crown," Fifth Voice. NP
Punchinello. Hugh de Burgh. CAW
Punching Clock, The. Milos Macourek, *tr. fr. Czech by* Michael Flach. LiTW

Punctilio. Mary Elizabeth Coleridge. OBEV (new ed.); OBVV; TOP
Punctual as bad luck. The Family Goldschmitt. Henri Coulette. CoAP
Punctually at Christmas the soft plush. White Christmas. W. R. Rodgers. ChMP; GTBS-W; LiTM; MoAB; MoBrPo (1950 ed.); PPON; SeCePo
Puny child who knows he can have but little love, The. Our Lady, Help of Christians. Paul Claudel. ISi
Pup een da Snow, Da. T. A. Daly. TSW
Pupil to His Master, The. Fannie Stearns Davis. PFY
Puppet Dreams, The. Conrad Aiken. *Fr.* Punch; the Immortal Liar. MAP; MoAmPo
"There is a fountain in a wood," *sel.* NeMA
Puppet Play, The. Padraic Colum. RoGo
Puppet Player, The. Angelina Weld Grimké. CDC
Puppets. P. K. Page. MoCV
Puppets. Paul Verlaine. *See* Fantoches.
Puppy. Aileen Fisher. SoPo
Puppy and I. A. A. Milne. BoTP; FaPON; PDV; SoPo; TiPo
Puppy's Problem, A. Emilie Poulsson. PPL
Pure air trembles, O pitiless God. Noon. Robinson Jeffers. MAP; MoAmPo
"Pure as the snow," we say. Ah! never flake. Mary Immaculate. Eleanor C. Donnelly. CAW; JKCP
Pure blood domestic, guaranteed. The Prize Cat. E. J. Pratt. PeCV; TwCaPo
Pure Cinna makes no question he's elect. Of Cinna's Election. Sir John Harington. SiCE
Pure contralto sings in the organ loft, The. Song of Myself, XV. Walt Whitman. MaPo
Pure Death. Robert Graves. AWP; CoBMV; GTBS-P; InPo; MoAB; MoPo
Pure fasted faces draw unto this feast. Easter Communion. Gerard Manley Hopkins. BrPo
Pure Heart, The. Tennyson. *Fr.* Sir Galahad. MaRV; TreF
Pure Hypothesis, A. May Kendall. VA
Pure I was before the world began. Kathleen Raine. *Fr.* Northumbrian Sequence. CMoP
Pure is the body on the Earth. He Singeth in the Underworld. *Unknown.* *Fr.* Book of the Dead. AWP; JAWP; WBP
Pure Is the Dewy Gem. Jeremiah Joseph Callanan. IrPN
Pure Mathematician, A. Arthur Guiterman. PoMa
Pure Nails Brightly Flashing. Stéphane Mallarmé, *tr. fr. French by* Charles Glenn Wallis. LiTW
Pure of heart and therefore hungry. A Cicada. Li Shang-yin. OuHeWo
Pure Platonicke. George Daniel. CavP
Pure Poet, The. Roy Fuller. ToPo
Pure poetry, programme of the living heart. The Network. Robert Finch. CaP
Pure Products. Denise Levertov. NMP
Pure Products of America, The. William Carlos Williams. OnHM; OxBA
(Elsie.) AnAmPo
(To Elsie.) AP; CABA; CMoP; CoBMV; SeCeV (1967 ed.)
Pure Simple Love. Aurelian Townsend. AnAnS-2; SeCP
Pure Spirit of the always-faithful God. Hymn for Pentecost. James Clarence Mangan. CAW; JKCP
Pure Spirit! that within a form of clay. The Disembodied Spirit. Fernando de Herrera. OnPM
Pure stream, in whose transparent wave. To Leven Water. Tobias George Smollett. OBEV
Pure, the bright, the beautiful, The. Things That Never Die. Charles Dickens. MaRV; SoP
Pure? What does it mean? Fever 103 degrees. Sylvia Plath. NMP
Pure white the shields their arms upbear. The Fairy Host. *Tr. by* Alfred Perceval Graves. AnIV
Pure woman is to a man a crown. The Virtuous Wife. Süsskind von Trimberg. TrJP
Purer in Heart. *Unknown.* STF
Purest Soul[e] that e're was sent, The. An Other. Thomas Carew. AnAnS-2; SeCV-1; SeEP
Purgatorio. Hart Crane. NAMP
Purgatorio, *sels.* Dante. *Fr.* Divina Commedia.
Celestial Pilot, *fr.* II, *tr. by* Longfellow. WGRP
"How haughty was thy mien," *fr.* VI, *tr. by* Jefferson Butler Fletcher. PoFr
Political Chaos in Italy, *fr.* VI, *tr. by* Longfellow. WoL
Purgatory, I, II, XXX-XXXIII, *with summaries of other cantos, tr. by* Henry F. Cary. OuHeWo
Purgatory: Dante's Dream, *fr.* IX, *tr. by* Frances Winwar. EnLi-1
"'Twas now the hour that turneth back desire," *fr.* VIII, *tr. by* Longfellow. CAW
"Veracious people, The" *fr.* XXX, *tr. by* Longfellow. CAW
Purgatory. W. B. Yeats. CMoP
Purgatory May Be Paradise. Sadi, *pr. tr. fr. Persian by* Sir Edwin Arnold. *Fr.* The Gulistan. OuHeWo
Purge me, O God. A Prayer. Wilbur Humphrey Fowler. MaRV
Purification, The. Richard Church. MoBrPo (1942 ed.); POTE
Purification, The. St. Cosmas, *tr. fr. Greek.* *Fr.* Menaion. ISi
Purification, The, *sel.* John Keble.
Purity of Heart, *abr.* BLRP
Purification of the Blessed Virgin. Joseph Beaumont. ISi
Purist, The. Ogden Nash. FiBHP; GoJo; MoAmPo (1950 ed.); MoShBr; NeMA; PV; ShM; TreFT
Purist to Her Love, The. Margaret Fishback. WhC
Puritan, The. Karl Shapiro. MoAmPo (1950 ed.)
Puritan Lady, A. Lizette Woodworth Reese. AnAmPo; InP; MAP; MoAmPo; NP
Puritan on His Honeymoon, The. Robert Bly. NePoEA
Puritan Sonnet. Elinor Wylie. Wild Peaches, IV. MAP; MoAB; MoAmPo; NeMA; TrGrPo
(Wild Peaches, IV.) InP
Puritan Severus oft doth read, The. In Severum. Sir John Davies. ReIE
Puritan spring beauties stood freshly clad for church, The. The Spring Beauties. Helen Gray Cone. AA
Puritan's Ballad, The. Elinor Wylie. BoLP; HBMV; LiTL; PFY; PoRA; TSW
Purity of Heart. John Keble. *Fr.* Purification. BLRP
Purple and white the crocus flowers. Crocuses in the Grass. John Gray. CAW
Purple cloud hangs half-way down, A. Before Sunrise in Winter. Edward Rowland Sill. AA
Purple Clover. Emily Dickinson. *See* There is a flower that bees prefer.
Purple Cow, The. Gelett Burgess. AmePo; BOHV; FaFP; FaPON; FiBHP; HBV; HBVY; InP; LBN; LiTM; NA; NeHB; NePA; PDV; PoLF; PoPl; SiTL; SoPo; StaSt; TiPo; TreFS; YaD
(Nonsense Quatrains.) CenHV
(Nonsense Rhymes.) TSW
Purple cow's projected feast, The. The Purple Cow. Gelett Burgess. AmePo
Purple heather is the cloak, The. The Bog Lands. William A. Byrne. AnIV; JKCP (1926 ed.)
Purple horses with orange manes. Merry-Go-Round. Rachel Field. UTS
Purple Island, The, *sels.* Phineas Fletcher.
"But ah! let me under some Kentish hill," *fr.* I. ViBoPo
Desiderium, *fr.* I. OBS
Overthrow of Lucifer, The, *fr.* XII. OBS
Purple morning left her crimson bed, The. The Crusaders Reach Jerusalem. Tasso. *Fr.* Jerusalem Delivered. EnLi-1
Purple robed, with crownèd hair. The Pawns. Frank Betts. HBMV
Purple sky, the down's long spine, The. The Novice. Edward Davison. ErPo
Purple, yellow, red, and green. *Unknown.* OxNR
Purpose. John Drinkwater. OQP
(Prayer, A: "We know the paths wherein our feet should press.") SoP
Purpose. Langdon Elwyn Mitchell. *Fr.* To a Writer of the Day. AA
Purpose. John James Piatt. AA
Purpose of Amendment, A. Helen Parry Eden. JKCP
Purpose of Fable-writing, The. Phaedrus, *tr. fr. Latin by* Christopher Smart. AWP
Purpose of its sex is obvious, The. Skyscraper. Byron Vazakas. OnHM
Purpose of Prayer, The. Anna Temple Whitney. *See* Kneeling Camel, The.
Purse-Seine, The. Paul Blackburn. CoPo
Purse-Seine, The. Robinson Jeffers. CMoP; NoP; OxBA
Purse, who'll not know you have a Poet's been. A Parley with His Empty Purse. Thomas Randolph. OBS

Pursue no more (my thoughts!) that false unkind. The Retreat. Henry King. AnAnS-2
Pursuer, eluder. While the Bells Ring. Lora Dunetz. NePoAm
Pursuing beauty, men descry. Song [*or* A Song in the Second Act]. Thomas Southerne. *Fr.* Sir Antony Love. PeRV; SeCL; SeEP
Pursuit. Juljan Tuwim, *tr. fr. Polish by* Watson Kirkconnell. TrJP
Pursuit[e], The. Henry Vaughan. OAEP; SeCP; TrPWD
Pursuit. Robert Penn Warren. CrMA; FiMAP; LiTA; MoAmPo (1962 ed.); MoPo; NePA; PoFS; ReMP; TwAmPo; TwCP
Pursuit of Love. *Unknown. See* Art Thou Gone in Haste?
Pursuite, The. Henry Vaughan. *See* Pursuit, The.
Push about the brisk bowl, 'twill enliven the heart. The Ass. Moses Mendes. *Fr.* The Chaplet. TrJP
Push hard across the sand. A Song in Time of Order (1852). Swinburne. PoVP
Pushan, God of Pasture. *Unknown, tr. fr. Sanskrit* by Romesh Dutt. *Fr.* The Rig-Veda. AWP; JAWP; WBP
Pushcart Row. Rachel Field. BrR; SoPo
Puss and the Boots, The, *sel.* H. D. Traill.
"Put case I circumvent and kill him: good." Par
Puss came dancing out of a barn. *Unknown.* OxNR
Pussicat, Wussicat. *Unknown.* OTPC (1923 ed.)
("Pussicat, wussicat, with a white foot.") OxNR;PPL
Pussy. Jane Taylor. *See* I Like Little Pussy.
Pussy and the Mice. *Unknown.* MoShBr
Pussy can sit by the fire and sing. The First Friend. Kipling. *Fr.* Just-so Stories. MPB
Pussy-Cat. Ann Hawkshaw. OTPC (1923 ed.)
Pussy-Cat and Puppy-Dog. Lilian McCrea. BoTP
Pussy cat ate the dumplings. *Unknown.* OxNR
Pussy-cat Mew [*or* Mole] jumped over a coal. Mother Goose. GFA; OTPC; OxNR; PCH; SAS
Pussy-cat, pussy-cat, where have you been? Mother Goose. BoChLi; BoTP; FaBoBe; FaFP; HBV; HBVY; OTPC; OxNR; PCH; PoPl; PPL; RIS; SAS; SiTL; SoPo; StVeCh; TiPo
Pussycat, pussycat with a white foot. Pussicat Wussicat. *Unknown.* OTPC (1923 ed.); OxNR; PPL
Pussy-cat sits by the fire. *See* Pussy sits beside the fire.
Pussycat Sits on a Chair. Edward Newman Horn. ELU
Pussy-Cat Who Visited the Queen. Carolyn Wells. CIV
Pussy has a whiskered face. Four Pets. Christina Rossetti. *Fr.* Sing-Song. PPL; TiPo
Pussy in Bed. *Unknown. See* Why Is Pussy in Bed?
Pussy, Pussy, Do Not Mew. William Bourn Oliver Peabody. SAS
Pussy [*or* Pussy-cat] sits beside [*or* by] the fire. *Unknown.* OTPC; OxNR; PPL; RIS; SAS
Pussy that climbs to the top of the tree, The. The Cat. Helen Hay Whitney. GFA
Pussy Willow. Kate L. Brown. PCH; PPL
Pussy Willow had a secret. An Open Secret. *Unknown.* BoChLi
Pussy Willows. Rowena Bennett. GFA
Pussy-Willows. Aileen Fisher. RePo
Pussy-Willows. Arthur Guiterman. OTPC (1946 ed.)
Pussy Willows. Mary E. Plummer. GFA; MPB
Pussy Willows. *Unknown.* GFA
Pussywillow's buds are soft, The. Spring Is in the Making. Nona Keen Duffy. YeAr
"Pussy, you lift your paws so high." The Cat in the Snow. F. Hey. SAS
Put away the Christ Child. After-Christmas Poem. Elizabeth-Ellen Long. ChBR
Put away the flutes. Song for War. W. R. Rodgers. NeBP
Put by thy days like withered flowers. Unregarding. Walter de la Mare. CMoP
Put case I circumvent and kill him: good. H. D. Traill. *Fr.* The Puss and the Boots. Par
Put Down. Léon Damas, *tr. fr. French by* Seth L. Wolitz. TTY
Put 'em up solid, they won't come down! Post-Rail Song. *Unknown.* AS
Put every tiny robe away! In Vain. Rose Terry Cooke. AA
Put Forth, O God, Thy Spirit's Might. Howard Chandler Robbins. TrPWD
Put Forth Thy Leaf, Thou Lofty Plane. Arthur Hugh Clough. *See* In a London Square.
Put Grief Away. Robert K. Ekvall. *Fr.* Tibetan Comforter. MaRV
Put in the sickles and reap. Messidor. Swinburne. ViPo
Put It Through. Edward Everett Hale. MC; PAH
"Put off that mask of burning gold." The Mask. W. B. Yeats. CLwM
Put on that uniform, my son. This Is for Freedom, My Son. Charles Stewart. TNV
Put Out My Eyes, and I Can See You Still. Rainer Maria Rilke, *tr. fr. German by* Babette Deutsch. MaRV
(Extinguish My Eyes, *tr. by* Jessie Lemont.) OnPM
Put out the candle, close the biting rose. The End of the Story. Terence Tiller. ChMP; NeBP
Put out the light and let the embers die. *Unknown, ad. fr. Greek by* Louis Untermeyer. MeWo
Put out the lights now! The Christmas Tree. C. Day Lewis. GTBS-D
Put out the mourners from your heart. To One of Little Faith. Hildegarde Flanner. HBMV
Put out to sea, if wine thou wouldest make. Sent from Egypt with a Fair Robe of Tissue to a Sicilian Vinedresser. T. Sturge Moore. OBEV (new ed.); OBVV
Put the rubber mouse away. For a Dead Kitten. Sarah Henderson Hay. CIV; StaSt
Put them aside—I hate the sight of them! Relics. George Frederick Cameron. PeCV
Put them in print? Posthumous. Henry Augustin Beers. AA
Put Up Again Thy Sword into Its Place. Helen Parry Eden. MemP
"Put up the sword!" The voice of Christ once more. Disarmament. Whittier. PGD
"Put up thy sword." So Peter found. Put Up Again Thy Sword into Its Place. Helen Parry Eden. MemP
Put your finger in Foxy's hole. *Unknown.* OxNR; SiTL
Put your head, darling, darling, darling. Dear Dark Head [*or* Cean Dubh Deelish]. *Tr. by* Sir Samuel Ferguson. ACV; AnIV; BoLP; IrPN; OBEV (1st ed.); OnYI; OxBI; SeCePo; UnTE
Putney Hymn, *with music. Unknown.* TrAS
Putting God in the nation's life. God in the Nation's Life. *Unknown.* BLRP; WBLP
Putting in the Seed. Robert Frost. ErPo; FaBoEn; OxBA
Putting the World to Bed. Esther W. Buxton. TVC
Putting to Sea. Louise Bogan. LiTM
Puva. . .puva. . .puva. Lullaby. *Tr. by* Natalie Curtis. SUS
Puzzle. Sidney Cooksley. NYTB
Puzzled Census-Taker, The. John Godfrey Saxe. HBV
Puzzled Centipede, The. Mrs. Edward Craster. *See* Centipede Was Happy Quite, A.
Puzzled Game-Birds, The. Thomas Hardy. ViPo (1962 ed.); VP
Puzzles. John Drinkwater. WaKn
Puzzling Example, A. Virginia Sarah Benjamin. BiCB
Pwlldu—an eternal place! Ballad of the Equinox. Vernon Watkins. PrWP
Pygmalion. Hilda Doolittle ("H. D."). AnAmPo; WGRP, *abr.*
Pygmalion. Louis Johnson. AnNZ
Pygmalion. Albert G. Miller. InMe
Pygmalion. William Bell Scott. EPN; VA
Pygmalion and Galatea, *sel.* W. S. Gilbert.
"Thing is but a statue after all, The," *abr.* VA
Pygmalion thought that women were a great abomination. Pygmalion. Albert G. Miller. InMe
Pygmalion to Galatea. Robert Graves. PG
"Pygmies Are Pygmies Still, Though Percht on Alps." Gwendolyn Brooks. PoNe (1970 ed.)
(But Can See Better There, and Laughing There.) Kal
Pylons, The. Stephen Spender. AWP; CMoP; EnLi-2 (1949 ed.); EnLit
Pyms Anarchy, *abr. At. to* Thomas Jordan. OBS
Pyramids first, which in Egypt were laid, The. The Seven Wonders of the Ancient World. *Unknown.* TreFT
Pyramids of flesh sweat pyramids of stone. Homo Faber: the Shell Game. Marge Piercy. ThO
Pyramis; or, The House of Ascent. A. D. Hope. PoAu-2
Pyramus and Thisbe, *sel.* Laurence Dakin.
"How sweetly sings this stream," *fr.* III, iii. CaP
Pyramus and Thisbe. John Donne. MaMe; ReIE
Pyramus and Thisbe. Ovid, *tr. fr. Latin. Fr.* Metamorphoses, IV. LiTW, *tr. by* Arthur Golding; OuHeWo, *tr. by* Laurence Eusden

("Within the town, of whose huge walls so monstrous high and thick," *tr. by* Arthur Golding.) RelE
Pyramus and Thisbe. John Godfrey Saxe. HBV; OnMSP
Pyre of Patroclus, The. Homer, *tr. fr. Greek by* Pope. *Fr.* The Iliad, XXIII. OBEC
(Preparation of the Pyre for Patroclus, *shorter sel.*) UnPo (1st ed.)
Pythagoras. Thomas S. Jones, Jr. AnAmPo
Pythagoras planned it. Why did the people stare? The Statues. W. B. Yeats. AnIL
Pythagoras th'art right. *Unknown.* SeCSL
Pythian Odes. Pindar. *See* Odes.
Python, The. Hilaire Belloc. EvOK; HBVY; NA; ShM; StaSt
Python. Grace Hazard Conkling. NP
Python I should not advise, A. The Python. Hilaire Belloc. ShM
Pythoness, The. Kathleen Raine. FaBoMo; MoBrPo (1962 ed.); ViBoPo (1958 ed.)
Pyxidanthera, The. Augusta Cooper Bristol. AA

Q

Q Is for the Quietness. Phyllis McGinley. OCS
Qua Cursum Ventus. Arthur Hugh Clough. BEL; EnLi-2; EnLit; EPN; EtS; GTBS; HBV; OAEP; OBEV (new ed.); OBVV; PoIE; PoVP; TOP; TreFT; VA; ViPo; ViPP
Quack! Walter de la Mare. TiPo
"Quack! Quack!" Ducks at Dawn. James S. Tippett. SiSoSe; SoPo; TiPo; UTS
Quadrille, A. "Lewis Carroll." *See* Lobster Quadrille, The.
Quadroon mermaids, Afro angels, black saints. A Ballad of Remembrance. Robert Hayden. AmNP; IDB; PoNe
Quaerit Jesum Suum Maria. Richard Crashaw. ACP; CAW; MaMe
Quail. Bernard O'Dowd. BoAu
Quail and rabbit hunters with tawny hounds. Hunters in the Snow: Brueghel. Joseph Langland. LiTM (1970 ed.); NePoEA
Quaint old house with brilliant tiles. Holland. Barbara Jane Provost. PCH
Quaker Graveyard, The. Silas Weir Mitchell. AA
Quaker Graveyard in Nantucket, The. Robert Lowell. AmLP; AP; CABL; CMoP; CoBMV; FiMAP; HT; LiTM (1970 ed.); MiAP; MoAB; MoPo; MoVE; NePA; NMP; NoP; OxBA; PoeP; PoIE; ReMP; SeCeV (1967 ed.); ToPo; TwAmPo; UnPo (3d ed.); ViBoPo (1958 ed.)
Quaker Hill. Hart Crane. *Fr.* The Bridge. LiTA; LiTM (rev. ed.)
Quaker Ladies. Ellen Mackay Hutchinson Cortissoz. AA
Quaker Meeting-House. William Ellery Leonard. PFY
Quaker of the Olden Time, The. Whittier. AnNE
Quaker Widow, The. Bayard Taylor. AA
Quakeress Bride, The. Elizabeth Clementine Kinney. AA
Quaker's Meeting, The. Samuel Lover. BOHV; CenHV; OnYI
Quaker's Song, The. *Unknown.* CoMu
Quaker's wife got up to bake, The. *Unknown.* OxNR
Quaker's Wooing, The, *with music.* *Unknown.* AS; BFSS
Quality of Heaven, The. William Carlos Williams. PoeP
Quality of Mercy, The ("The quality of mercy is not strained."). Shakespeare. *Fr.* The Merchant of Venice, IV,i. FaFP; LiTB; LiTG; PTK
(Mercy.) BBV; MaRV; OHFP; OQP; OTPC; TrGrPo; WBLP
(Portia's Plea for Mercy.) TreF
("Quality of mercy is not strain'd, The.") TRV
Quality of night that you hate most is its black, The. Three Movements and a Coda. LeRoi Jones. BF
Quality of Pain, A. Barbara D. Holender. NYTB
Quality of these trees, green height, The; of the sky, shining, of water. Shine, Republic. Robinson Jeffers. AmFN; MoRP
Quan lo ruis de la fontana. Jaufré Rudel, *tr. fr. Provençal by* John Peale Bishop. LiTW
Quandary. Mrs. Edward Craster. *See* Centipede Was Happy Quite, A.
Quangle Wangle's Hat, The. Edward Lear. BoChLi; GFA; PeVV; PoRh; RIS; SAS; StaSt
Quantity and Quality. Winifred M. Letts. HBMV
Quantrell, *with music.* *Unknown.* ABF; CoSo (A *and* B *vers.*)
Quantum Est Quod Desit. Thomas Moore. *See* Did Not.
Quarrel, The. Conrad Aiken. LiTL; MAP; MoAB; MoAmPo; MoLP; PoPl
Quarrel, The. Eleanor Farjeon. FaPON
Quarrel, The. Homer, *tr. fr. Greek by* Sir William Marris. *Fr.* The Iliad, I. WoL
("Achilles' baneful wrath resound, O goddess that impos'd," *shorter sel., tr. by* George Chapman.) RelE
("O Goddess! sing the wrath of Peleus' son," *shorter sel., tr. by* Bryant.) EnLi-1
Quarrel. Jean McDougall. GoBC; JKCP (1955 ed.)
Quarrel of the sparrows in the eaves, The. The Sorrow of Love. W. B. Yeats. MoAB; MoBrPo; PoEL-5; ViPo (1962 ed.)
Quarrel with Fortune, A. Benjamin Colman. SCAP
Quarrel with Juventius. Catullus, *tr. fr. Latin by* George Lamb. OnPM
Quarrelling. Isaac Watts. *See* Let Dogs Delight.
Quarrelsome Trio, The. "L. G." WBLP
Quarried from snow, the dark walks lead to doors. Windows. Randall Jarrell. OPoP
Quarries in Syracuse. Louis Golding. TrJP
Quarry, The. W. H. Auden. *See* O What Is That Sound Which So Thrills the Ear.
Quarry, The. Juan Boscán, *tr. fr. Spanish by* Grace Hardendorff Burr. LiTW
Quarry, The. Vassar Miller. NePoEA-2
Quarry, The. William Vaughn Moody. AnAmPo
Quarry Pool, The. Denise Levertov. ToPo
Quarry whence thy form majestic sprung, The. Washington's Statue. Henry T. Tuckerman. AA
Quarter horse, A, no rider. Horse. Jim Harrison. WIRo
Quarter of pleasures where the rich are always waiting. The Capital. W. H. Auden. CMoP; MoPW
Quartette, The. Walter de la Mare. BoC; CBEP; MuSP
Quasi-stellar Radio Sources. Howard McCord. NYTB
Quatorzain. Henry Timrod. AA
(Most Men Know Love but as a Part of Life.) AmP; Sonn
(Sonnet: "Most men know love but as a part of life.") HBV
Love and Life, *sel.* OQP
Quatrain: "Christ bears a thousand crosses now." Charles G. Blanden. ChIP; PGD
Quatrain: "Golf links lie so near the mill, The." Sarah N. Cleghorn. *See* Golf Links, The.
Quatrain, A: "Hark at the lips of the pink whorl of shell." Frank Dempster Sherman. AA
Quatrain: "Here is the Truth in a little creed." Edwin Markham. MaRV; OQP
(Creed, A.) ChIP
Quatrain: "Jack eating rotten cheese, did say." Benjamin Franklin. *See* Jack and Roger.
Quatrain: "My bloodstream chokes on gall and spleen." Barend Toerien, *tr. fr. Afrikaans by* Barend Toerien. PeSA
Quatrain: "Oh! to be wafted away." *Unknown.* NA
Quatrain: "Sarmèd, whom they intoxicated from the cup of love." Sarmèd the Yuhud, *tr. fr. Persian by* David Shea. TrJP
Quatrain: "Squeak's heard in the orchestra, A." George T. Lanigan. WhC
Quatrain: "This existence has, without the azure sphere, no reality." Sarmèd the Yahud, *tr. fr. Persian by* David Shea. TrJP
Quatrain: "Though love repine." Emerson. *See* Sacrifice.
Quatrain: "Young Apollo, golden-haired, A." Frances Cornford. *See* Youth.
Quatrains. Gwendolyn B. Bennett. CDC
"Brushes and paints are all I have," I.
"How strange that grass should sing," II.
Quatrains, *sels.* Emerson.
Gardener. MWA-1; OxBA
Orator. AnNE; OxBA
Poet. AnNE; OnPM; OxBA
Sacrifice. HBV; HBVY; MaRV; TRV
(Faith.) OtMeF
(Quatrain: "Though love repine.") OQP
Quatrains. Sidney Godolphin. *See* Song: "Noe more unto my thoughts appeare."
Quatrains. Salah Jahin, *tr. fr. Arabic by* Samir M. Zoghby. TTY
Quatrains. Omar Khayyám. *See* Rubáiyát of Omar Khayyám.

Quatrains for a Bank Cashier. Samuel A. De Witt. PG (1955 ed.)
Quatrina. Joseph Bennett. LiTA
Qu'avec-vous, oui, belle blonde, *with music.* *Unknown.* OuSiCo
Quayside. Robert Graves. FaBoMo
Quebec. Eldon Grier. PeCV
Quebec Farmhouse. John Glassco. PeCV (1967 ed.)
Quebec Liquor Commission Store. A. M. Klein. ACV; OBCV
Québec May. Earle Birney. WHW
Quebec, the grey old city on the hill. At Quebec. Jean Blewett. CaP
Queen. Dom Moraes. NePoEA-2
Queen, The. Kenneth Pitchford. NYBP
Queen, The. William Winter. HBV
Queen,/ thou holdest in thine arms. To the Most Holy Mother of God. *Unknown.* ISi
Queen and Huntress. Ben Jonson. *See* Hymn to Diana.
Queen and Slave. Mortimer Collins. OBVV
Queen Anne. *Unknown.* ChTr
Queen Anne's Lace. Mary Leslie Newton. BrR; FaPON; GFA; MoShBr; MPB; SP
Queen Anne's Musicians. Thomas Hennell. FaBoTw
Queen-Ann's Lace. William Carlos Williams. AmPP (5th ed.); AP; MAP; MoAB; MoAmPo; NoP; TDP
Queen Bee, The. Mary K. Robinson. BoTP
Queen Bess was Harry's daughter. Stand forward partners all. The Looking-Glass. Kipling. EvOK; FaBoTw; GTSL; OBMV; OnPP
Queen Cleopatra. Conrad Aiken. Variations, X. HBMV
Queen Eleanor and Her Dwarf. George Darley. *Fr.* Thomas à Becket. PeER
Queen Eleanor's Confession. *Unknown.* BaBo; ESPB (A *and* B *vers.*)
Queen Elizabeth at Tilbury. Thomas Deloney. SiCE
Queen Elizabeth Tudor, as a Girl, on Trial for Heresy. *Unknown.* PoG
Queen, for whose house my fathers fought. Adieux à Marie Stuart. Swinburne. PoVP
Queen Guennivar's Round. Robert Stephen Hawker. CoBE
Queen Guinevere had fled the court. Guinevere. Tennyson. *Fr.* Idylls of the King. EnLit; EPN; MaVP
Queen in Parliament, 1941, The. A. P. Herbert. OnPP
Queen is gone a-hunting in the royal wood, The. A-Hunting. Jennie Dunbar. BoTP
Queen is taking a ride today, The. The Queen's Last Ride. Ella Wheeler Wilcox. BLPA
Queen Jane was in labour full six weeks and more. The Death of Queen Jane. *Unknown.* BaBo (A *vers.*); ESPB
Queen Jeanie, Queen Jeanie, travel'd six weeks and more. The Death of Queen Jane. *Unknown.* ESPB (B *vers.*); ViBoFo
Queen lived in the South, A. Dagonet's Canzonet. Ernest Rhys. HBV; SiSw
Queen Mab. Thomas Hood. DD; HBV; HBVY; OTPC, *abr.*; PCH; PPL; StVeCh; TVC
Dream Fairy, The, *sel.* BoTP
Queen Mab. Ben Jonson. *Fr.* The Satyr, sc. i. HBV; OTPC (1923 ed.)
(Mab the Mistress-Fairy.) EIL
("This is Mab the mistress-fairy.") SiCE
Queen Mab. Shakespeare. *Fr.* Romeo and Juliet, I, iv. BoC; FaPON; FiP; GoTP; MPB; OTPC, *abr.*; PoFS
(Mercutio Describes Queen Mab.) TrGrPo
(Mercutio's Queen Mab Speech.) LiTB; TreF
(Queene Mab.) BoW
(Shakespeare Gallery, A: Queen Mab.) MaC
Queen Mab, *sels.* Shelley.
Dedication: To Harriet—. EPN
Magic Car Moved On, The, *fr.* I. GN
War Is the Statesman's Game, *fr.* IV. PPON
Queen Mab's Chariot. Michael Drayton. *Fr.* Nymphidia. OTPC
("Pigwiggen was this Fairy Knight.") ViBoPo
(Queen Mab's Journey to Pigwiggen.) PCH
(Queen's Chariot, The.) OBS
Queen Mary, *sel.* Tennyson.
Milkmaid's Song. EPN
(Song of the Milkmaid.) HBV
Queen of all Queens, oh! Wonder of the loveliness of women. Hymn to the Virgin Mary. Conal O'Riordan. ISi
Queen of all streets, Fifth Avenue. Thompson Street. Samuel McCoy. HBMV
Queen of all streets, you stand alway. Piccadilly. Thomas Burke. HBMV
Queen of Aragon, The, *sel.* William Habington.
"Fine young folly, though you were," *fr.* IV, i. OBS
(Song.) FaBoEn; MePo
Queen of brave nations—Liberty! To Liberty. Casimir Sarbiewski. PoFr
Queen of Cheese. James McIntyre. FiBHP
Queen of Corinth, The, *sel.* John Fletcher, *and others.*
Weep No More, *fr.* III, ii, *at. to* Fletcher. AtBAP; BEL; CH; EIL; LiTG; OBEV; OnPM; TOP; ViBoPo
(Mourn No More.) TrGrPo
("Weep no more, nor sigh, nor groan.") TuPP
Queen of Courtesy, The. *Unknown, tr. fr. Middle English. Fr.* The Pearl. ACP; CAW; ISi, *mod. vers. by* Stanley Perkins Chase
Queen of Crete, The. John Grimes. HBMV
Queen of Egypt yawned and frowned, The. Events. George O'Neil. HBMV
Queen of Elfland's Nourice, The. *Unknown.* OBB
(Queen of Elfan's Nourice, The.) ESPB
"I heard a cow low, a bonnie cow low," *sel.* FaBoCh
Queen of Fairies, The. *Unknown. See* Fairy Queen, The.
Queen of fragrance, lovely rose. The Rose-Bud. William Broome. CEP; LoBV; OBEC; OBEV
Queen of Hearts, The. Christina Rossetti. PeVV
Queen of Hearts, The,/ She made some tarts. Mother Goose. BoChLi; FaBoBe; HBV; HBVY; OTPC; OxNR; PCH; PPL; RIS; SiTL
Queen of Heaven, of Hell eke Emperess. To the Virgin. John Lydgate. ACP; CAW; GoBC; PoLi
Queen of Horizons. Joseph Dever. ISi; JKCP (1955 ed.)
Queen of Paphos, Erycine, The. *Unknown.* EIL
Queen of Scotland, The. *Unknown.* ESPB
Queen of Seasons, The. Cardinal Newman. GoBC
Queen of the Angels, The. Boccaccio, *tr. fr. Italian by* Thomas Walsh. CAW; ISi
Queen of the heavens, we hail thee. Ave Regina Coelorum. *Unknown.* ISi
Queen of the silver bow!—by thy pale beam. To the Moon. Charlotte Smith. Sonn
Queen of the World. *Unknown.* PGD
Queen of the Year, The. Edna Dean Proctor. DD
Queen Sabbath. Hayyim Nahman Bialik, *tr. fr. Hebrew by* Jessie Sampter. TrJP
Queen sat in her balcony, The. Gil, the Toreador. Charles Henry Webb. AA
Queen she sent to look for me, The. Grenadier. A. E. Housman. EG; OBMV
Queen stood on thy right hand, The. Psalm XLIV, Bible, *O.T. (Douay vers.).* ISi
Queen Venus wander'd away with a cry. Our Lady of the Sea. Alfred Noyes. OBVV
Queen Victoria. *Unknown.* CoMu; FOL
Queen Victoria. Humbert Wolfe. MoBrPo
Queen Virtue's court, which some call Stella's face. Astrophel and Stella, IX. Sir Philip Sidney. FCP; SiPS
Queen was beloved by a jester, A. The Cap and Bells. W. B. Yeats. GTSL; MoAB; MoBrPo; OBVV
Queen was in her chamber, and she was middling old, The. The Looking Glass. Kipling. GTSL; OBMV
Queen was in the parlor, The. Contemporary Nursery Rhyme. *Unknown.* PV
Queen was sick for her hills, The. Mood from 3000 B.C. Genevieve Taggard. OTPC (1946 ed.)
Queen Wasp, A. Walter de la Mare. AtBAP
Queen went from me while I slept, The. Queen. Dom Moraes. NePoEA-2
Queen Yang-se-fu. Yang-se-fu. "Yehoash," *tr. fr. Yiddish by* Isidore Goldstick. TrJP
Queene and Huntresse. Ben Jonson. *See* Hymn to Diana.
Queene Mab. Shakespeare. *See* Queen Mab.
Queene of Corinth, The. John Fletcher, *and others. See* Queen of Corinth, The.
Queens, The. Robert Fitzgerald. NYBP
Queens. J. M. Synge. ChTr; MoBrPo; OBMV; OnYI; PeVV
Queen's Afterdinner Speech, The, *sel.* Percy French.
"'Me loving subjects,' sez she." OxBI

Queen's Chariot, The. Michael Drayton. *See* Queen Mab's Chariot.
Queen's Dream, The. *Unknown.* PeVV
Queen's Last Ride, The. Ella Wheeler Wilcox. BLPA
Queen's Marie, The. *Unknown. See* Mary Hamilton.
Queen's Men, The. Kipling. AtBAP
Queens of Hell had lissome necks to crane, The. The Tall Girl. John Crowe Ransom. Sonn; TDP
Queen's Song. Stopford Augustus Brooke. *Fr.* Riquet of the Tuft. VA
Queen's Song, The. James Elroy Flecker. BrPo; HBV
Queen's Vespers, The. Aubrey Thomas De Vere. VA
Queen's Wake, The, *sel.* James Hogg.
Kilmeny, *fr.* Night II. CABL; GBV (1922 ed.); HBV; OBEV; OBRV; OnSP; OtMeF
(Bonny Kilmeny Gaed up the Glen, *abr.*) GoTS
Queer, The. Henry Vaughan. MaPo; PoEL-2
Queer are the ways of a man I know. The Phantom Horsewoman. Thomas Hardy. CaFP; CMoP; LO; PoEL-5; SiSw
Queer Habits. Corneille McCarn. GFA
Queer Poem. Malcolm Lowry. NYTB
Queer Quatrains. Gelett Burgess. RIS
Queer Things. James Reeves. PoMS
Queerly walking by a slow and pagan clock. Warning to Snake-Killers. Robert H. Barlow. FiSC
Queer's Song. Richard Howard. *Fr.* Gaiety. ErPo
Quehn Merche wes with variiand windis past. William Dunbar. *Fr.* The Thrissil and the Rois. HW
Quellisma, Seven Variations. G. Bishop-Dubjinsky. ThO
Quentin Durward, *sel.* Sir Walter Scott.
County Guy, *fr. ch.* 4. BEL; EPN; OAEP; OBRV; TOP
(Serenade, A: "Ah! County Guy.") GTBS; GTBS-D; GTBS-P; GTBS-W; GTSE; GTSL
(Song.) CH
Query. Lucie McKee. NYTB
Query. Lucia Trent. ChIP
Quest, The. *sel.* W. H. Auden.
Useful, The. CMoP
Quest, The. Grace Goodhue Coolidge. OTD
Quest, The. Ellen Mackay Hutchinson Cortissoz. HBV
Quest, The. Gladys Cromwell. HBMV
Quest, The. Chester B. Emerson. OQP
Quest, The. Eva Gore-Booth. MaRV; OQP
Quest, The. Clinton Scollard. BrR
Quest, The. Eliza Scudder. MaRV; TrPWD
(Who by Searching Can Find Out God?) WGRP
Quest. Edmund Clarence Stedman. *Fr.* Corda Concordia. AA
Quest, The. Harold Vinal. GoYe
Quest, The. James Wright. NYBP
Quest Eternal, The. Alice M. Pullen. MaRV
Quest Eternal, The, *sel.* Brajendranath Seal.
"I was one with the woods; my body, the earth." ACV
Quest of Silence, The, *sel.* Christopher Brennan.
Fire in the Heavens, and Fire along the Hills. PoAu-1
Quest of the Orchis, The. Robert Frost. AmePo
Quest of the purple cow, The. Hilda Johnson. BOHV
Quest of the Sancgreall, The, *sel.* Thomas Westwood.
"Motionless sat the shadow at the helm." PeVV
Questing. Anne Spencer. CDC
Question. Howard McKinley Corning. ChIP
Question, The. Robert Duncan. NeAP
Question, A. P. T. Forsyth. OQP
Question, The. Norman Gale. ELU; FiBHP
Question, The. W. W. Gibson. BEL; MMA
Question, The. Karla Kuskin. PDV
Question, A. Edna Livingston. GoYe
Question, The. Edwin Muir. BoPe
Question, The. F. T. Prince. ChMP; GTBS-P; PeSA
Question, The ("I dreamed that, as I wandered by the way"). Shelley. CH; EnRP; EPN; FiP; HBV; MemP; MyFE; OBEV; OBRV; PeER
(Dream of the Unknown. A.) GTBS; GTBS-D; GTBS-P; GTBS-W; GTSE; GTSL
Question. May Swenson. LiTM (1970 ed.); NePoEA
Question, A. J. M. Synge. ELU; MoBrPo; OBMV; OBVV; OxBI
Question, The. Rachel Annand Taylor. ChIP; HBV; MaRV
Question, The. Frederick Goddard Tuckerman. AP
Question, A ("I ask thee, whence those ashes were"). *Unknown.* CBEP; SeCL
Question, A ("If I really, really trust him"). *Unknown.* BLRP
Question, The ("Were the whole world good as you"). *Unknown.* WBLP
Question and Answer. Samuel Hoffenstein. FiBHP; PV
Question and Answer. Kathleen Raine. MoBrPo (1962 ed.)
Question & Answer. Edward Hersey Richards. *See* Wise Old Owl, A.
Question and answer. Dialogue, without End. Isabel Harriss Barr. JKCP (1955 ed.)
Question Answer'd, The. Blake. *Fr.* Several Questions Answered. EiCL; ELU; ERoP-1; ErPo; ViBoPo
Question in a Field. Louise Bogan. NYBP
Question in the Cobweb, The. Alastair Reid. WaKn
Question is, The. The Painful Question. Warner B. Wims. TNV
Question Is Proof, The. Elizabeth Bartlett. NePoAm-2
Question, lords and ladies, is, The. Percy Shelley. John Peale Bishop. ErPo
Question Mark, The. Persis Greely Anderson. PoMa; WhC
Question Not. Adam Lindsay Gordon. *Fr.* Ye Wearie Wayfarer, Fytte VIII. PoToHe
(Man's Testament.) OtMeF
Question of Sacrifice, A. Sister M. Eulalia. WHL
Question to Life. Patrick Kavanagh. MoBrPo (1962 ed.)
Question to Lisetta, The. Matthew Prior. OBEV
Questioning. Grace Noll Crowell. DD
Questioning Faces. Robert Frost. ELU; TDP
Questioning Lydia ("Lydia, dic, per omnes"). Horace, *tr. fr. Latin by* Louis Untermeyer. Odes, I, 8. InP
Questioning Spirit, The. Arthur Hugh Clough. PoVP
Questionings. Frederic Henry Hedge. HBV
Questions. Lord Thomson of Cardington. OtMeF
Questions at Night. Louis Untermeyer. FaPON; GoTP; OTPC (1946 ed.); RIS
Questions for a Flying Squirrel to Answer. Rachel Field. RePo
Questions for the Candidate. John Holmes. PP
Questions of the Hour, *sel.* S. M. B. Piatt.
"How old is God? Has He grey hair?" MemP
Questions with Answers. *Unknown.* BOHV
Questo di Verde. Thomas Watson. TuPP
Quha Is Perfyte. Alexander Scott. *See* Wha Is Perfyte.
Quhen Alysandyr Our King Was Dede. *Unknown. See* When Alexander Our King Was Dead.
Quhen Flora had ourfret the firth. When Flora Had O'erfret the Firth [*or* May Poem]. *Unknown.* OBEV; OxBS
Quhen he wes yung, and cled in grene. Quhy Sowld Nocht Allane Honorit Be? *Unknown.* OxBS
Quhen Noye had maid his sacrifyce. After the Flood. Sir David Lindsay. *Fr.* The Monarche. OxBS
Quhen thai him fand, and gud Wallace him saw. *See* When they him fand. . .
Quhen that I had oversene this regioun. Of the Realme of Scotland. Sir David Lindsay. *Fr.* The Dreme. OxBS
Quhill schortly, with the blesand torch of day. Gawin Douglas. *Fr.* Prologues to the Aeneid. AtBAP
Quho is at my windou, quho? quho? *Unknown. See* Who Is at My Window.
"Quhy dois your brand sae drop wi' bluid." *See* "Why does your brand sae drap wi' bluid."
Quhy Sowld Nocht Allane Honorit Be? *Unknown.* OxBS
Quhy will ye, merchantis of renoun. To the Merchantis of Edinburgh. William Dunbar. OxBS
Qui Bien Aime a Tard Oublie. Chaucer. *See* Roundel, A: "Now welcom, somer. . ."
Qui Laborat, Orat. Arthur Hugh Clough. BEL; EnLi-2; EPN; PoVP; TrPWD; ViPo; ViPP
Qui nunc dancere vult modo. A Holiday Task [*or* A Polka Lyric]. Gilbert Abbott à Beckett, *also at. to* Barclay Philips. BOHV; NA
Qui Perdiderit Animam Suam. Richard Crashaw. ACP
Quia Amore Langueo ("In a tabernacle"). *Unknown.* ACP; CoBE, *sts.* 1-3; ISi, *tr. fr. Middle English by* E. M. Clerke; MeEL
Quia Amore Langueo ("In a valley [*or* vaile] of this restless mind [*or* restles mynd]"). *Unknown.* AtBAP; CBEP; EnLit; LiTG; LiTL; LO; OBEV; NoP; OxBoCh; PoEL-1; PoLi, *abr.*; WoL
"Quia Multum Amavi." Oscar Wilde. ACP (1926 ed.)
Quick, The. Sean Jennett. NeBP

Quick compunction cannot serve, The. The Selector's Wife. Mary Fullerton. MoAuPo
Quick-falling dew. Basho, *tr. fr. Japanese by* Curtis Hidden Page. AWP; JAWP; WBP
Quick, for the tide is sifting down the shore. Pause. Ann Hamilton. HBMV
Quick gleam, that ridest on the gossamer! To the Gossamer-Light. Charles Tennyson Turner. VA
Quick! Hoist the jib and cast us off, my son. Over Bright Summer Seas. Robert Hillyer. NYBP
Quick hoof-beats down a moonless country highway. Edmund Campion. Sister Mary St. Virginia. JKCP (1955 ed.)
Quick in spite I said unkind/ Words. Brazen Tongue. William Rose Benét. MAP; MoAmPo
Quick lunch! quick lunch! the neon cries, and I. Essay on Lunch. Walker Gibson. NYBP
Quick night. The World Is Full of Remarkable Things. LeRoi Jones. BF; BP
Quick now—loose it—here at the stable door. Here at the Stable Door. Sister Mary Paulinus. JKCP (1955 ed.)
Quick, painter, quick, the moment seize. Currente Calamo. Arthur Hugh Clough. *Fr.* Mari Magno. LoBV
Quick, quick you. On Lighting the Fire. May Swenson. NYTB
Quick return to me, come tonight, my budding. Note to Gongyla. Sappho. LiTW
Quick sea shone, The. Sunrise at Sea. Swinburne. *Fr.* Tristram of Lyonesse. EtS
Quick sparks on the gorse-bushes are leaping, The. The Wild Common. D. H. Lawrence. CoBMV
Quick, woman, in your net. The Net. W. R. Rodgers. AnIL; ErPo; NMP; OxBI
Quickening, The. Ruth Gilbert. *Fr.* The Blossom of the Branches. ACV
Quickening. Christopher Morley. HBMV
Quickening, The. Stella Weston Tuttle. GoYe
Quicker/ than that, can't. A Sight. Robert Creeley. NaP
Quickly Aging Here. Denis Johnson. QAH
Quickly and pleasantly the seasons blow. Sonnets, I. Robert Hillyer. HBMV
Quickness. Henry Vaughan. BoC; BWP; ELP; LoBV; MaPo; MeLP; MePo; OBS; OxBoCh; ReEn; SCEP-1; SeCePo; SeCP; SeCV-1
Quicksand Years. Walt Whitman. MaRV
Quid Non Speremus, Amantes? Ernest Dowson. HBV
Quid Petis, O Fily? *Unknown.* SeCeV
Quidditie, The. George Herbert. MaMe; PoEL-2; SCEP-1
Quién Sabe? Ruth Comfort Mitchell. PoMa
Quiet, The. W. W. Gibson. BEL
Quiet. Marjorie Pickthall. OBCV; PeCV; TwCaPo
Quiet. Ernest Radford. OBVV
Quiet. Giuseppe Ungaretti, *tr. fr. Italian by* Allen Mandelbaum. PoPl
Quiet. Yaha, *tr. fr. Japanese by* Harold Gould Henderson. WoL
Quiet as are the quiet skies. A Smiling Demon of Notre Dame. Sophie Jewett. AA
Quiet as conscience on the stock exchange. Common Terns. Patric Dickinson. POTi
Quiet Days. Mildred T. Mey. PoToHe (new ed.)
Quiet deepens, The. You will not persuade. Farewell to Van Gogh. Charles Tomlinson. CMoP; GTBS-P; NMP
Quiet Enemy, The. Walter de la Mare. BrPo; CMoP
Quiet Eye, The. Eliza Cook. VA
Quiet Flower, The. Josephine W. Johnson. MoRP
Quiet from Fear of Evil. "S. C. M'K." BLRP
Quiet Fun. Harry Graham. ShM
Quiet Glades of Eden, The. Robert Graves. ErPo
Quiet home had Parson Gray, A. Parson Gray. Goldsmith. BOHV; NA
Quiet Hour, The. Louise Hollingsworth Bowman. BLRP
Quiet Hour, The. Harvey E. Haver. SoP
Quiet is what we need. By telephone. Private Enterprise. Christopher Morley. MaRV
Quiet Kingdom, The. Carl Busse, *tr. fr. German by* Ludwig Lewisohn. AWP; JAWP; WBP
Quiet Life, The. *Unknown.* EIL; GoBC; HBV; OTPC
(Herdmen, The.) OBSC
(What Pleasure Have Great Princes.) ReIE; SiCE
Quiet Life and a Good Name, A. Swift. CBEP
Quiet Mind, The ("I have a treasure which I prize"). *Unknown.* SoP
Quiet Mind, The ("I joy not in no earthly bliss"). *Unknown.* OBSC
("I joy not in no earthly bliss.") SiCE
Quiet Night, The. Heine, *tr. fr. German by* Emma Lazarus. LiTW
Quiet Nights, The. Katharine Tynan. HBV
Quiet of the Dead, The. Mary Morison Webster. PeSA
Quiet Pilgrim, The. Edith M. Thomas. AA
Quiet Place, The. George A. McCauliff. JKCP (1955 ed.)
Quiet Singer, The. Charles Hanson Towne. HBV
Quiet, sleep! or I will make. A Charm. Thomas Randolph. *Fr.* The Jealous Lovers. SeCL
Quiet Soul, A. John Oldham. *Fr.* To the Memory of Mr. Charles Morwent. OBEV
Quiet Street, The. Nan McDonald. NeLNL
Quiet the self, and silence brims like spring. Scarabs for the Living, IX. R. P. Blackmur. TwAmPo
Quiet Things. Grace Noll Crowell. PoLF
Quiet Things. "I. W." OQP
Quiet Waters. Blanche Shoemaker Wagstaff. BLPA
Quiet Woman, The. Genevieve Taggard. AnEnPo; NP
Quiet woods in the hot Eastertide, The. Woods and Kestrel. Julian Bell. ChMP
Quiet Work. Matthew Arnold. EnL; EnLit; EPN; FaBoBe; HBV; MaVP; MCCG; NeHB; OAEP; OQP; PoIE; PoPo; PoRL; PoVP; TrGrPo; ViPP; YAT; YT
Quietly. Kenneth Rexroth. ErPo
Quietly and while at rest on the trim grass I have gazed. The Air of June Sings. Edward Dorn. NeAP
Quietly as rosebuds. Love's Coming. Shaw Neilson. BoAu; MoAuPo; PoAu-1
Quietly I enter the closet. Communion. P. M. Snider. PoToHe (new ed.)
Quietly sipping rain that sucks the rose, The. Pacific Winter. Hildegarde Flanner. NP
Quietly the children wait. The Children. Clifford Dyment. ChMP
Quietness. ——Doran. FaChP; SoP
Quietness. Henry W. Frost. SoP
Quietness clings to the air. The Snow Fall. Archibald MacLeish. LOW; PoPl
Quietude of a soft wind, The. The Creditor. Louis MacNeice. EaLo; ShBV-3
Quill of the goose is a very slight thing, The. Impromptu. Francis Atterbury. WaPE
Quilt, The. Mary Effie Lee Newsome. CDC
Quilt. John Updike. WaKn
Quilted/ patches, unlike the smooth slick loveliness. Making. Phyllis Webb. PoCh
Quinks, The. Don Marquis. YaD
Quinquireme of Nineveh from distant Ophir. Cargoes. John Masefield. AnEnPo; ATP; BEL; CMoP; DiPo; EnLi-2 (1949 ed.); EnLit; ExPo; FaBV; FaPON; FosPo; GTBS-D; GTSL; ILP; LiTM; MCCG; MoAB; MoBrPo; NP; OBEV (new ed.); OBMV; OBVV; OtMeF; PCH; PoPo; PoRA; PTK; RoGo; SeCeV; ShBV-1; SP; TiPo (1952 ed.); TOP; TreF; WePo; YT
Quintetto upon the Christmas Pie, *sel.* Thomas Love Peacock. *Fr.* Melincourt.
"My share of pie to win, I will dash through thick and thin." MyFE
Quintilia Dead. Catullus, *tr. fr. Latin by* George Lamb. OnPM
Quintius, if it's thy wish and will. To Quintius. Catullus. OnPM
Quip, The. George Herbert. AnFE; ATP; BEL; CBEP; EnLit; ILP; LiTB; MaMe; MaPo; OAEP; OBS; OxBoCh; SCEP-1; SeCP; SeCV-1; SeEP; YAT
Quip to the Reader. Timothe Kendall. *See* To the Reader.
Quire of bright Beauties in spring did appear, A. The Lady's Song. Dryden. LoBV
"Quis pro Domino?" Robert Browning. *Fr.* The Ring and the Book, X. OAEP
Quit yo' long-time talkin' 'bout yo' heavy hipted woman. The Heavy-hipted Woman. *Unknown.* ABF
Quit You like Men. William Herbert Hudnut. OQP
Quite by Chance. Frederick Langbridge. BOHV
Quite close to the abrupt city. Seal Rocks: San Francisco. Robert Conquest. PP
Quite Forsaken. D. H. Lawrence. BrPo

Quite is high. Styro. Clark Coolidge. ANYP; YAP
Quite often wishbones go to church. The Bones Go to Church. Florence Dolby Wolfe. SoP
Quite, quite./ Oh I agree. Restricted. Eve Merriam. TrJP
Quite rightly, we remained among the living. The Survivors. Adrienne Cecile Rich. NYBP
Quite spent with thoughts I left my cell, and lay. Vanity of Spirit. Henry Vaughan. AnAnS-1; MeP; ReEn
Quite Suddenly. J. W. H. Nichols. FaChP; SoP
Quite unexpectedly as Vasserot. The End of the World. Archibald MacLeish. AnEnPo; AP; CaFP; CBV; CMoP; CoBMV; HoPM; ILP; LiTM; MAP; MoAB; MoAmPo; NeMA; NePA; NP; OxBA; Po; PoIE; PoPo; PoSa; Sonn; StP; TrGrPo
Quits. Thomas Bailey Aldrich. AA
Quits. Matthew Prior. *See* Epigram: "To John I ow'd great obligation."
Quitter, The. *Unknown.* BLPA; WBLP
Quitting my horse, a cup with you I drank. "So Farewell." Wang Wei. OnPM
Quivering, unseen atoms of air, The. Love Passing By. Gustavo Adolfo Bécquer. Rimas, X. OnPM
Quivira. Arthur Guiterman. PAH; PFY
Quixotic is his enterprise and hopeless his adventure is. The Played-out Humorist. W. S. Gilbert. *Fr.* His Excellency. BOHV
Quo life, the warld is mine. The Flyting o' Life and Daith. Hamish Henderson. OxBS
Quo Ruis ab Demens? Londons Progress. Thomas Freeman. SiCE
Quo Vadis? Myles E. Connolly. JKCP(1926 ed.); MaRV; TRV
Quod Dunbar to Kennedy. William Dunbar. OxBoLi
Quod Tegit Omnia. Yvor Winters. MoVE; QFR
Quoits. Mary Effie Lee Newsome. CDC; GoSl
Quondam was I in my lady's gras. Sir Thomas Wyatt. EnPo
Quoniam Ego in Flagella Paratus Sum. William Habington. ACP
Quot Bipedes Aurum. Thomas Freeman. SiCE
Quoth John to Joan. *Unknown.* CH
(Clown's Courtship, The.) BOHV
Quoth Rab to Kate, My sonsy dear. Marriage and the Care o't. Robert Lochore. HBV
Quoth Satan to Arnold: "My worthy good fellow." Epigram. *Unknown.* PAH
Quoth tongue of neither maid nor wife. Elena's Song [*or* Song]. Sir Henry Taylor. *Fr.* Philip van Artevelde, II. OBEV; OBRV; OBVV; VA
Qwhen Alexander [*or* Quhen Alysandyr] our kynge was dede. When Alexander Our King Was Dead. *Unknown.* AtBAP; GoTS

R

R. Alcona to J. Brenzaida. Emily Brontë. *See* Remembrance.
R. G. E. Richard Eberhart. NYTB
R. I. P. "Jan Struther." InMe
R is for the Restaurant. Phyllis McGinley. *Fr.* All Around the Town. TiPo (1959 ed.)
R. L. S. A. E. Housman. NoP
Ra has purified the heavens. Inscription on the Pyramid of Pepi I. *Unknown.* LiTW
Rabbi Ben Ezra. Robert Browning. ATP (1935 ed.); BBV (1951 ed.), *abr.*; BEL; CoBE; EnLi-2; EnLit; EPN; FaFP; FiP; GTBS; GTBS-W; GTSL; HBV; LiTG; MaRV; MasP; MaVP; MBW-2; OAEP; OBNC; OBVV; OQP, *much abr.*; OuHeWo; PoFS; PoVP; TOP; UnPo (1st ed.); ViPo; ViPP; VP; WGRP; YT, *cond.*
"Grow old along with me!" *sel.* BiCB, 6 *ll.*; FaBV; MCCG, 6 *ll.*; OTD, 12 *ll.*; PoPl; PoToHe; SoP, 5 *sts.*; TreFT, 6 *ll.*; TRV, 6 *ll.*
Rabbi Ben Levi, on the Sabbath, read. The Legend of Rabbi Ben Levi. Longfellow. *Fr.* Tales of a Wayside Inn. AnNE; GBV (1952 ed.)
Rabbi Nathan twoscore years and ten, The. The Two Rabbins. Whittier. AmePo
Rabbi, Where Dwellest Thou? Come and See. *Unknown.* BePJ
Rabbi Yom-Tob of Mayence Petitions His God. A. M. Klein. TrJP
Rabbi Yussell Luksh of Chelm. Jacob Glatstein, *tr. fr. Yiddish by* Nathan Halper. TrJP
Rabbit, The. W. H. Davies. GFA
Rabbit, The. Camilla Doyle. StaSt
Rabbit, The. Georgia Roberts Durston. GFA; SoPo
Rabbit, The. Edith King. BoTP; GFA; HBMV; SoPo; StVeCh
Rabbit, The. John Lewisohn. PCD
Rabbit, The. Elizabeth Madox Roberts. BoChLi; GoTP; MPB; SoPo; TiPo; TSW; UTS
Rabbit. Tom Robinson. FaPON
Rabbit, The. *Unknown.* FiBHP; SiTL
Rabbit as King of the Ghosts, A. Wallace Stevens. OA; ThWaDe
Rabbit Cry. Edward Lucie-Smith. NePoEA-2
Rabbit has a charming face, The. The Rabbit. *Unknown.* FiBHP; SiTL
Rabbit has a habit, The. The Rabbit. Georgia Roberts Durston. GFA; SoPo
Rabbit Hash, *with music.* *Unknown.* ABF
Rabbit Leaves, The. Dennis Schmitz. YAP
Rabbit sits upon the green, The. Vice Versa. Christian Morgenstern. OA
Rabbit thieves in silver suit, The. Clothes. Frances Frost. RePo
Rabbit: timid brother! My teacher and philosopher! The Perfect Life. Jorge Carrera Andrade. LiTW; WoL
Rabbit works its ears, and tries, A. The Rabbit. W. H. Davies. GFA
Rabbits. Dorothy Baruch. SoPo; SUS; TiPo; UTS
Rabbits, The. *Unknown, tr. fr. German.* PCH; SAS
("Between the hill and the brook, ook, ook.") PPL
Rabbits and squirrels. The Reason. Dorothy Aldis. TiPo (1952 ed.)
Rabbits' Song outside the Tavern, The. Elizabeth J. Coatsworth. *See* Song of the Rabbits outside the Tavern.
Rabble hate, the gentry feare, The. The State of the Nation (1680). *Unknown.* PeRV
Rabble Soldier. *See* Jack o'Diamonds; or, The Rabble Soldier.
Rabboni! Master! Mother Loyola. WHL
Rabia. *Unknown, tr. fr. Arabic by* James Freeman Clarke. HBV
Raccoon an' a possum. Cotton Field Song. *Unknown.* ABF
Raccoon on the Road. Joseph Payne Brennan. GoYe
Raccoons. Aileen Fisher. PDV
Race, The. Aileen Fisher. UTS
Race of nobles may die out, A. Kossuth. James Russell Lowell. FOL
Race of the *Oregon,* The. John James Meehan. PAH
Race perhaps, A. You might have called it that. Pier. James Scully. WIRo
Race Prejudice. Alfred Kreymborg. ELU
Racer's Widow, The. Louise Glück. NYBP
Rachel. Ruth Gilbert. AnNZ
Rachel. Charles Jeremiah Wells. *Fr.* Joseph and His Brethren. VA
Racing Eight, A. James L. Cuthbertson. PoAu-1
Racing-Man, The. A. P. Herbert. FiBHP; WhC
Rack upon rack of leaves all elbowing. Spring. W. R. Rodgers. OnYI
Rackheath. Coman Leavenworth. *Fr.* Norfolk Memorials. LiTA
Racoon ("The racoon wears a black mask"). Kenneth Rexroth. *Fr.* A Bestiary. FiBHP
(Advices from Rexroth's Bestiary.) SiTL
Raderus. John Donne. MaMe
Radiance of that star that leans on me, The. Delay. Elizabeth Jennings. NePoEA
Radiant Ranks of Seraphim. Valery Bryusov, *tr. fr. Russian by* Babette Deutsch *and* Avrahm Yarmolinsky. AWP; JAWP; WBP
Radiant Sister of the Day. Shelley. *Fr.* To Jane: The Invitation. ThWaDe
Radiator knocked and hissed, The. The Madman Looks at His Fortune. Dick Lourie. ThO
Radiator Lions. Dorothy Aldis. GoBP; MPB; SoPo; UTS
Radical, The. Waring Cuney. CDC
Radical Song of 1786, A. St. John Honeywood. PAH
Radio, The. Edgar A. Guest. PEDC

Radio. A. S. J. Tessimond. HaMV
Radio that told me about the death of Billy the Kid, The. Billy the Kid. Jack Spicer. CoPo
Radio under the Bed, The. Reed Whittemore. NYBP
Radio waves coming over the air. Magic Waves. Gertrude Van Winkle. GFA
Radium. Agnes Lee. PoMa
Raftery's Dialogue with the Whiskey. Padraic Fallon. DTC
Raftsmen, The. *Unknown.* IHA
Rag Doll and Summer Birds. Owen Dodson. PoNe
Ragged-and-Tough. Not Ragged-and-Tough. *Unknown.* ChTr
Ragged brown carpet, vast and bare. To the Veld. Arthur Shearly Cripps. ACV
Ragged Coat, The. John Woodward. SGR
Ragged Robin. Elizabeth Godley. BoTP
Ragged Robin and Bouncing Bet. Alice Reid. DD
Ragged, unheeded, stooping, meanly shod. The Poor Can Feed the Birds. John Shaw Neilson. PoAu-1
Ragged Wood, The. W. B. Yeats. LO; PoPo; ViPo (1962 ed.)
("O hurry where by water among trees.") BoC
Raggedy Man, The. James Whitcomb Riley. BoChLi; FaPON; GoTP; HBV; HBVY; MPB; OTD; OTPC; StVeCh; TiPo; TreFS
Raggle Taggle Gypsies, The. *Unknown. See* Wraggle Taggle Gipsies, O!, The.
Raging and the ravenous, The. The Tigress. Ruth Pitter. FaBoTw; HaMV; NYTB
Raging Canawl, *with music.* Unknown. AS
(Ragin' Can-all, *diff. vers.*) IHA
(Raging Can-all, *diff. vers.*) ABF
Raglan. Sir Edwin Arnold. VA
Ragman, The. *Unknown.* FTB
Ragout Fin de Siècle. Erich Kästner, *tr. fr. German by* Walter Kaufmann. ErPo
Ragpicker, The. Frances Shaw. NP
Rags. Edmund Vance Cooke. BLPA
Rags and tatters,/ Tatters and rags. Ragged Robin. Elizabeth Godley. BoTP
Ragwort, The. John Clare. ChTr
Ráhat, The. John Jerome Rooney. AA
Raid, The. William Everson. OnHM
Raider, The. W. R. Rodgers. AnIL; MoBrPo (1950 ed.)
Raiders, The. Will H. Ogilvie. ShBV-2
Railroad, The. Henry David Thoreau. *See* What's the Railroad.
Railroad Bill, *with music.* *Unknown.* ABF; AS, *diff. vers.*
Railroad bridge's, De/ A sad song. Homesick Blues. Langston Hughes. CDC; MAP; MoAmPo; NeMA; PoPl
Railroad Cars Are Coming, The. *Unknown.* AmFN; AS, *with music;* BrR; FaPON; MPB
Railroad Corral, The, *with music.* *Unknown.* CoSo; TrAS
Rail-road crossing. *Unknown.* RIS
Railroad track is miles away, The. Travel. Edna St. Vincent Millay. FaPON; InMe; LaNeLa; MoShBr; MoSiPe; MPB; NP; PDV; PFY; RePo; StVeCh; TiPo
Railroad tracks; the flight/ of a rocket. The Old and the New. "Q. B. M." SoPo
Railroad Train, The. Emily Dickinson. *See* I like to see it lap the miles.
Railroad yard in San Jose. In Back of the Real. Allen Ginsberg. AmPP (5th ed.)
Railroaders and Hobos. *Unknown. See* I Don't Like No Railroad Man.
Railway Junction, The. Walter de la Mare. CBEP; ChMP
Railway Station. John Hay. WaP
Railway Stationery, The. Kenneth Koch. ANYP; NoP
Railway Train, The. Emily Dickinson. *See* I like to see it lap the miles.
Railway Tunnel, The. Queenie Scott-Hopper. TVC
Rain. Kenneth Slade Alling. HBMV
Rain. Einar Benediktsson, *tr. fr. Icelandic by* Watson Kirkconnell. LiTW
Rain, The. Lord Bowen. *See* Rain It Raineth, The.
Rain. "Robin Christopher." RIS; StaSt
Rain. Elizabeth J. Coatsworth. CIV
Rain. Louis Coxe. NYTB
Rain, The. Robert Creeley. CoAP
Rain, The. W. H. Davies. BoTP; EnLit; PCH; POTE; RIS; TiPo
Rain. Frank Marshall Davis. GoSl
Rain. Christopher Fry. *Fr.* The Boy with a Cart. BoC
Rain. Sam Harrison. NeIP
Rain. W. E. Henley. SyP
Rain, The. George Herbert. BoC
Rain. Langston Hughes. *Fr.* A House in Taos. CDC
Rain. Patrick F. Kirby. GoBC
Rain. Newman Levy. BOHV
Rain. Vachel Lindsay. CMoP
Rain. Lilian McCrea. BoTP
Rain. Howard Moss. ErPo
Rain. "Seumas O'Sullivan." OnYI
Rain. Ross Parmenter. NYTB
Rain. James Whitcomb Riley. BoNaP
Rain. Frances Shaw. HBMV
Rain, The. Robert Louis Stevenson. BoChLi; GFA; GoJo; MPB; NeHB; OTPC (1946 ed.); PCH; PPL; RIS; SoPo; StVeCh; SUS; TiPo
Rain. Adrien Stoutenburg. PDV
Rain. Bert Leston Taylor. RIS
Rain. Edward Thomas. POTE
Rain. Tu Fu, *tr. fr. Chinese by* Chi Hwang Chu *and* Edna Worthley Underwood. OnPM
Rain, The ("Open the window"). *Unknown.* GFA
Rain, The ("The rain came down"). *Unknown.* GFA
Rain, The ("Rain on the green grass"). *Unknown.* BoTP; TiPo
("Rain on the green grass.") OxNR
Rain. William Carlos Williams. AP; CoBMV
Rain. Helen Wing. GFA
Rain. James Wright. NaP
Rain. Ella Young. TiPo (1952 ed.)
Rain:/ Grey, rat-grey rain. Rain on Castle Island. Kitahara Hakushu. FIW
Rain advances like a king, The. Rains. Kalidasa. *Fr.* The Seasons. AWP
Rain after a Vaudeville Show. Stephen Vincent Benét. MAP; MoAmPo
Rain and the Rainbow, The. Leo Fredericks. ACV
Rain and the thought of rain. Out There. Bill Berkson. ANYP; YAP
Rain and wind, the rain and wind, raved endlessly, The. Melancholy. Edward Thomas. MoVE; NoP
Rain at Night. Helen Walker Homan. JKCP (1955 ed.)
Rain at Night. Helen Hoyt. LiTM; NP
Rain at Wildwood. May Swenson. NYBP
Rain before seven. Weather Signs [*or* Signs and Charms *or* Rhymes about the Weather]. *Unknown.* FaBoBe; GoTP; HBV; HBVY; OTPC; OxNR; StaSt; TreF
Rain begins, The. This is no summer rain. Oregon Winter. Jeanne McGahey. AmFN
Rain came down in torrents, The. The Rain. *Unknown.* GFA
Rain Clouds. Elizabeth-Ellen Long. BrR
Rain comes in various sizes. Rain Sizes. John Ciardi. SoPo
Rain Comes Sobbing to the Door, The. Henry Kendall. ACV
Rain-Crow, The. Madison Cawein. AA
Rain, do not fall. Mist. Andrew Young. FIW
Rain, do not hurt my flowers, but quickly spread. The Rain. George Herbert. BoC
Rain does down in torrents pour, The. McKinley Brook. George Calhoun. ShS
Rain drifts forever in this place. The Falls of Glomach. Andrew Young. OxBS
Rain falls briskly on my worn shelter-half. Inner Brother. Stephen Stepanchev. WaP
Rain falls down upon the grass, The. April Puddle. Rowena Bennett. TiPo (1959 ed.)
Rain Falls on Ioannina. Marge Piercy. ThO
Rain fell like grass growing, The. Rain at Wildwood. May Swenson. NYBP
Rain, frost or snow, or hot or cold. Milk Below. *Unknown.* PCH
Rain had fallen, the Poet arose, The. The Poet's Song. Tennyson. ELP; FiP; GBV (1952 ed.); PoVP; TOP
Rain has silver sandals, The. Footwear. May Justus. SoPo; YeAr
Rain has such fun in April. Rain in April. Eleanor Hammond. GFA
Rain hits over and over. Rain. Adrien Stoutenburg. PDV
Rain imprinted the step's wet shine, The. On the Doorstep. Thomas Hardy. MoVE
Rain in April. Eleanor Hammond. GFA

Rain in my ears: impatiently there raps. Essay on Memory. Robert D. Fitzgerald. BoAV; MoAuPo
Rain in Spring. "Gabriel Setoun." PPL
Rain in Summer, *sl. abr.* Longfellow. BBV (1923 ed.); GN; OTPC
"How beautiful is the rain!" *first* 15 *ll.* BoChLi; BoTP; PCH; PoG; RIS
Rain in the city. City Rain. Rachel Field. GFA; SoPo; TiPo
Rain in the Night. Amelia Josephine Burr. MPB; SP; TiPo
Rain in the Southwest. Reeve Spencer Kelley. AmFN
Rain in the Street. John Gould Fletcher. Arizona Poems, VI. NP
Rain Inters Maggiore. Alfred Kreymborg. AnAmPo
Rain is clinging to the round rose-cheek, The. After Rain. Eleanor Farjeon. BoChLi
Rain is due to fall, The. A Poet Thinks. Lui Chi. AWP; JAWP; LiTW; PG (1945 ed.); WBP
Rain is plashing on my sill, The. The Unknown Dead. Henry Timrod. AmP; AP; MAmP
Rain is raining all around, The. Rain. Robert Louis Stevenson. GFA; GoJo; MPB; NeHB; OTPC (1946 ed.); PCH; PPL; RIS; SoPo; StVeCh; SUS; TiPo
Rain is raining all around, The. Rain. Bert Leston Taylor. RIS
Rain It Raineth, The. Lord Bowen. FiBHP; PV
(Just and Unjust.) PoPl; WhC
(Rain, The.) FaFP; LiTG; SiTL
("Rain it raineth on the just, The.") CenHV
Rain It Raineth Every Day, The. Shakespeare. *See* When That I Was and a Little Tiny Boy.
Rain, It Streams on Stone, The. A. E. Housman. CMoP; VP
Rain, its tiny pressure, The. Romanze, or the Music Students. Frank O'Hara. FRC
Rain, midnight rain, nothing but the wild rain. Rain. Edward Thomas. POTE
Rain Music. Joseph S. Cotter, Jr. BANP; BrR; CDC; PCH
Rain, Night, and Wine. Asclepiades, *tr. fr. Greek by* Charles Glenn Wallis. LiTW
Rain of London pimples, The. London Rain. Louis MacNeice. NoP
Rain on a Cottage Roof. Freda Laughton. OnYI
Rain on a Grave. Thomas Hardy. CoBMV; HBV; OAEP
Rain on Castle Island. Kitahara Hakushu, *tr. fr. Japanese by* Geoffrey Bownas *and* Anthony Thwaite. FIW
Rain on Rahoon falls softly, softly falling. She Weeps over Rahoon. James Joyce. NP; ViBoPo
Rain on South-East England. Donald Davie. NYTB
Rain on the Down. Arthur Symons. *Fr.* At Dieppe. BrPo; OBVV
Rain on the face of the Sea. Commonplaces. Kipling. BOHV; HBV
Rain on the green grass. The Rain. *Unknown.* BoTP; OxNR; TiPo
Rain on the Roof. Coates Kinney. HBV
Rain on the windows, creaking doors. The Division. Thomas Hardy. PG (1945 ed.); PoeP; VP
Rain over a Continent. Galway Kinnell. TwAmPo
Rain patters on a sea that tilts and sighs. Absences. Philip Larkin. PoCh
Rain Portrait. John Unterecker. ThO
Rain, Rain. Zoë Akins. HBMV
Rain, Rain! *Unknown, tr. fr. Russian by* W. R. S. Ralston. OnPM
Rain, Rain,/ Are you there yet? Rain-Talk. Raelene Newell White. PCH
Rain, rain/ Beating against the pane! Why? *Unknown.* FaChP
Rain, rain—fall, fall. Rain, Rain. Zoë Akins. HBMV
Rain, rain, go away. Mother Goose. OxNR; RIS; SAS; SiTL; SoPo; TiPo
Rain, rain, go to Spain. *Unknown.* OxNR
Rain, rain on Tyburn tree. To the English Martyrs. Francis Thompson. JKCP
Rain rains sair on Duriesdyke, The. Duriesdyke. Swinburne. OxBB
Rain Riders. Clinton Scollard. GaP; SoPo; TiPo
Rain rins doun through Mirry-land toune, The. Sir Hugh; or, The Jew's Daughter (B *vers.*). *Unknown.* ESPB
Rain, said the first, as it falls in Venice. Song Tournement: New Style. Louis Untermeyer. CrMA
Rain set early in to-night, The. Porphyria's Lover. Robert Browning. AtBAP; AWP; BeLS; BoLiVe; CABA; GTBS; GTSE; GTSL; HBV; ILP; InPo; JAWP; MaPo; MaVP; MBW-2; MeWo; OAEP; OBEV; OuHeWo; PAn; PoVP; ShBV-4; TOP; TreFT; TrGrPo; ViPo; ViPP; VP; WBP
Rain Sizes. John Ciardi. SoPo
Rain Song. Jean Garrigue. NYTB
Rain Song. Robert Loveman. *See* April Rain.
Rain Song, The. Alex Rogers. BANP
Rain-sunken roof, grown green and thin. The Barn. Edmund Blunden. MoBrPo; SeCePo
Rain-Talk. Raelene Newell White. PCH
Rain thunderstorms over the Potomac, in Georgetown. Rainscapes, Hydrangeas, Roses, and Singing Birds. Richard Eberhart. MoAmPo (1962 ed.)
Rain to the wind said, The. Lodged. Robert Frost. RePo
Rain was full of the freshness, The. The Dark and Falling Summer. Delmore Schwartz. NYBP
Rain was over, and the brilliant air, The. Landscapes. Louis Untermeyer. HBV
Rain was raining cheerfully, The. The Vulture and the Husbandman. Arthur Clement Hilton. CenHV
Rain, with a silver flail. Whale. William Rose Benét. EtS; MAP; MoAmPo
Rainbow, The. Genesis, VIII: 13, Bible, *O.T.* BoC
Rainbow, The. John Vance Cheney. OQP
Rainbow, The. Vine Colby. HBMV
Rainbow, The. W. H. Davies. BrPo
Rainbow, The. Walter de la Mare. SoPo; TiPo
Rainbow. Robert Huff. NePoEA-2
Rainbow. D. H. Lawrence. CBV; FIW
Rainbow, The. David McCord. FaPON; RiS; SoPo
Rainbow, The. Coventry Patmore. The Angel in the House, II, iii, 2. GTBS-P
Rainbow, The. Christina Rossetti. *See* Boats Sail on the Rivers.
Rainbow, The. Wordsworth. *See* My Heart Leaps Up.
Rainbow, The—a Riddle. Schiller, *tr. fr. German.* OTPC (1946 ed.)
Rainbow arches in the sky, The. The Rainbow. David McCord. FaPON; RiS; SoPo
Rainbow at night. Weather Wisdom [*or* Rhymes about the Weather]. *Unknown.* FaBoBe; GoTP; HBV; HBVY; OTPC; PCH; PPL; RIS; TreF
Rainbow Fairies, The. Lizzie M. Hadley. BoTP; OTPC (1946 ed.); TVC
"Two little clouds one April day," *sel., sl. diff.* GFA
Rainbow in the morning. Country Proverbs. *Unknown.* StaSt
Rainbow in the Sky. Wordsworth. *See* My Heart Leaps Up.
Rainbow Lands. Howard McKinley Corning. NP
Rainbow o'er the sea of afternoon, The. Sonnet. Thomas Caulfield Irwin. IrPN
Rainbow on the ocean, The. So Slow to Die. George Edward Woodberry. *Fr.* Wild Eden. AA
Rainbow Willow, *with music. Unknown.* BFSS
Rainbows. Dixie Willson. GFA
Rainbows all lie crumpled on these hills, The. The Painted Hills of Arizona. Edwin Curran. HBMV; HT; PFY
Rainbow's Arch, A. Shelley. *Fr.* Prometheus Unbound. ShBV-3
Rainbows are lovely things. The Rainbow. W. H. Davies. BrPo
Raindrops. Isla Paschal Richardson. GFA
Raindrops. *Unknown.* PCH
Rainer,/ the man who was about to celebrate his 52nd birthday. The Death of Europe. Charles Olson. NeAP
Rainfall Follows the Plough, The. *Unknown.* SoP
Raining came with dawning. At Dawn. J. M. Synge. SyP
Raining on earth/ Means weeping in heaven. Rain. "Robin Christopher." RIS; StaSt
Raining, raining. Rain in the Night. Amelia Josephine Burr. MPB; SP; TiPo
Rains, The. Kalidasa, *tr. fr. Sanskrit by* Arthur W. Ryder. *Fr.* The Seasons. AWP
Rain's Already with Us, The. Salvatore Quasimodo, *tr. fr. Italian by* Allen Mandelbaum. PoPl
Rains are warm, The. Shaman Song 10. Gene Fowler. ThO
Rain's lovely gray daughter has lost her tall lover. Fog. Kenneth Patchen. NaP

Rains of Spring, The. Lady Ise, *arr. by* Olive Beaupré Miller. SUS; TiPo
Rainscapes, Hydrangeas, Roses, and Singing Birds. Richard Eberhart. MoAmPo (1962 ed.)
Rainwalkers, The. Denise Levertov. CAD; NePoEA-2
Rainy country this, that I am monarch of, A. The King of the Rainy Country. Baudelaire. WoL
Rainy Day, A. Joseph C. Lincoln. OTD; RePo
Rainy Day, The. Longfellow. AnNE; AWP; HBV; InPo; MaRV; NeHB; PoLF; PoPl; PTK; TreFT
Rainy Day, A. Emilie Blackmore Stapp. GFA
Rainy Day, The. Rabindranath Tagore. FlW
Rainy Day Song. Violet Alleyn Storey. YeAr
Rainy Morning. Jessica Nelson North. NP
Rainy Nights. Irene Thompson. BoTP
Rainy Season, The. William Meredith. NePoEA
Rainy Season Love Song. Gladys May Casely Hayford. CDC
Rainy Song. Max Eastman. FaBoBe; HBMV
Rainy Summer, The. Alice Meynell. GoJo; MemP; MoVE; SiSw
Rainy Summer. Ruth Pitter. MoVE; UnPo (3d ed.)
Raise a Rukus Tonight, *with music.* *Unknown.* ABF
Raise the Cromlech high! The Lament of Maẹv Leith-Dherg. *Unknown.* OnYI
Raise the light, my page! that I may see her. Iseult of Ireland. Matthew Arnold. Tristram and Iseult, II. PoVP
Raise up, boys, raise up, raise up. Shack Bully Holler. *Unknown.* ABF
Raised are the dripping oars. The Youth of Nature. Matthew Arnold. PoVP
Raised in a canebrake, and suckled by a lion. Cowboy Talks to a Pitching Horse. *Unknown.* CoSo
Raised on six-shooters till I get big enough to eat ground shotguns. The Boasting Drunk in Dodge. *Unknown.* CoSo
Raising of the Bride. John Donne. MaMe
Raising of the Dead, The. Rosemary Dobson. PoAu-2
Raising of the Flag, The. Condé Benoist Pallen. JKCP
"Lift up the banner of our love," *sel.*. OTD
Raison d'Etre. Oliver Pitcher. AmNP; Kal; NNP
"Rake" Windermere. Leonard Pounds. PaPo
Rakes of Mallow, The. *Unknown.* IrPN; OnYI
Raking Leaves. Robert Pack. CoPo; NYBP
Raking Walnuts in the Rain. Monica Shannon. BrR; SiSoSe
Rakob is dead, what is left of him travels. Funeral in Hungary. Kay Boyle. AnEnPo
Raleigh Was Right. William Carlos Williams. AmPP (5th ed.); CBV; PP
Râles of Easter . . . The sucking. Invitation to a Sabbath. Harry Mathews. ANYP
Rally round the flag, boys. The Stars and Stripes. James T. Fields. HH
Rallying Song. Callinus. *See* Call to Action, A.
Ralph Leech believes (and he can read and write). Ebenezer Elliott. *Fr.* The Year of Seeds. Sonn
Ralph Roister Doister, *sels.* Nicholas Udall. EIL
I Mun Be Married a Sunday.
Minion Wife, A.
Ralphius. John Donne. MaMe
Ram, The. Robert P. Tristram Coffin. AnAmPo
Ram, The. *Unknown.* *See* Derby Ram, The.
Ram, ass, and horse, my Kyrnos, we look over. Advice to Kyrnos. Theognis, *tr. by* T. F. Higham. LiTW
Ram in the sacred tree, The. The Other Garden. John Gill. ThO
Ram of Darby, The. *Unknown.* *See* Derby Ram, The.
Ramble, The. Alexander Radcliffe. PeRV
Ramble-eer, The. *Unknown.* PoAu-1
Ramblers, The. Virginia Linton. NYTB
Rambling along the marshes. Flight of the Wild Geese. William Ellery Channing. PFY
Rambling Cowboy, The, *with music.* *Unknown.* BFSS; CoSo
Rambling Gambler, *with music.* *Unknown.* CoSo
Rambling Lady, The. Thomas Southerne. *See* Sir Antony Love.
Rambling Sailor, The. Charlotte Mew. HBMV; PoRA
Rambunctious Brook. Frances Frost. BrR
Ramon. Bret Harte. BeLS
Ran jet self into starscum 0067 hrs. Poem. Jeff Nuttall. HYE
Ranchers. Maurice Lesemann. NP
Randal Groveling works where I work. Song from a Two-Desk Office. Byron Buck. NYBP
Random Reflections on a Cloudless Sunday. John Hall Wheelock. NePoAm
Random Reflections on a Summer Evening. John Hall Wheelock. NYBP
Rang'd on the Line Opposed, Antonius Brings. Vergil, *tr. fr. Latin by* Dryden. *Fr.* The Aeneid, VIII. WaaP
Range-finding. Robert Frost. AmLP; CABA; MaPo; TPM
Range Riders, The. *Unknown.* CoSo (A *and* B *vers.*)
Range Rider's Soliloquy, The. Earl Alonzo Brininstool. PoOW
Ranger, A. Badger Clark. SCC
Ranger, The. *Unknown.* *See* Yankee Man-of-War, The.
Range's filled up with farmers and there's fences ev'rywhere, The. The Old Cowboy's Lament. Robert V. Carr. PoOW
Rank and File. Austin Dobson. PoVP
Rank with the flesh of man and beast. The Lido. Edmund Wilson. ErPo
Rann I Made. Padraic Pearse. NP
Rann of the Three, The. *Unknown,* *tr. fr. Irish by* Thomas Walsh. CAW; WHL
(Sacred Trinity, The, *tr. by* Eleanor Hull.) JKCP (1926 ed.)
Rannoch by Glencoe. T. S. Eliot. Landscapes, IV. FaBoEn; LoGBV
Ranolf and Amohia, *sels.* Alfred Domett.
"About the heights, soft clouds, a few." AnNZ
"And near some river-mouth—shoal—marshy-wide." AnNZ
"And Tangi and his tribe thus much had gained." AnNZ
"But evening now." AnNZ
Captain Cook. FOL
"In deep blue sky the sun is bright." AnNZ
"It was a wondrous realm beguiled." ACV
"Or to the beach descending, with joined hands." AnNZ
"So Ranolf felt when over wood and wild." AnNZ
Ransom, The. Baudelaire, *tr. fr. French by* Alan Conder. LO
Rantin' Dog the Daddie o't, The. Burns. EiCL; OxBoLi
Rantin Laddie, The. *Unknown.* BaBo (A *and* B *vers.*); ESPB
Rantin, Rovin Robin. Robert Burns. OxBS
Ranting Wanton's Resolution, The; 1672. *Unknown.* CoMu
Rap! Rap.—The watchman in Po Ti Town! Day Comes. Tu Fu. OnPM
Rapacious Spain follow'd her hero's triumph o'er the main. The Lust of Gold. James Montgomery. *Fr.* The West Indies. PAH
Rape of Europa, The. R. P. Blackmur. CrMA
Rape of Lucrece, The, *sels.* Thomas Heywood.
"Now what is love I will thee tell." LO
Pack, Clouds, Away. BiS; BoTP; EG; EIL; GTBS; GTBS-D; GTBS-P; GTBS-W; GTSE; OTPC; ThWaDe; ViBoPo; WHA
(Good-Morrow.) ALV; CH; TOP
(Matin Song.) GTSL; HBV; MemP; OBEV; ShBV-1
(To Give My Love Good-Morrow.) MeWo
(Waking Song.) RIS
Passing Bell, The. SeCL
Valerius on Women. HBV
("She that denies me, I would have.") ErPo; LO; UnTE
Rape of Lucrece, The. Shakespeare. BeLS
Sels.
"For much imaginary work was there," 5 *ll.* MyFE
"Locks between her chamber and his will, The." SiCE
Midnight. OBSC
"O opportunity thy guilt is great." PoEL-2
(Opportunity.) LiTB; OBSC
Time's Glory. ChTr
Troy Depicted. OBSC
Rape of the Lock, The. Pope. AtBAP; ATP; BEL; BoLiVe, *abr.*; BWP; CABA; CABL; CEP; CoBE; DiPo; EiCL; EiPP; EnL; EnLi-1; EnLit; ForPo; FosPo; ILP; MaPo; MasP; MBW-1; NoP; OAEP; OuHeWo; PAn; PIA; Po; PoAn; PoE; PoEL-3; PoFS; SeCeV; StP; TOP; TrGrPo, *sl. abr.*; VaPo
Sels.
"Close by those meads, for ever crown'd with flowers," III. FiP; OxBoLi, *sl. abr.*; WHA, *abr.*
(Ombre at Hampton Court, *shorter sel.*) OBEC
"Not with more glories, in th' etherial plain," *fr.* II. FaBoEn; ViBoPo; WHA
"On her white breast a sparkling cross she wore," *fr.* II. ACP

Playing Cards, The, *fr.* III. ChTr
"She said: then, raging to Sir Plume repairs," *fr.* IV. MyFE
Toilet, The, *fr.* I. OBEC
(Belinda's Morning.) ExPo
Raphael, *sel.* Whittier.
Destiny ("We shape ourselves the joy or fear.") MaRV
Raphael's San Sisto Madonna. George Henry Miles. CAW
Rapid, The. Charles Sangster. CaP; WHW
Rapid Transit. James Agee. AnAmPo; MoAmPo; NAMP
Rapidly cruising or lying on the air there is a bird. The Frigate Pelican. Marianne Moore. InvP
Rapids at Night. Duncan Campbell Scott. CaP
Rapier, lie there! and there, my hat and feather! The Poetaster. Samuel Rowlands. *Fr.* The Melancholy Knight. ElL
Rapparees. Richard Murphy. *Fr.* The Battle of Aughrim. OPoP
Rapture, A. Thomas Carew. AnAnS-2; CavP; ErPo; SCEP-2; SeCP; ViBoPo
(I Will Enjoy Thee Now.) LiTL; UnTE, *abr.*
Rapture. Stefan George, *tr. fr. German by* Ludwig Lewisohn. AWP; JAWP; WBP
(Transport, *tr. by* Carol North Valhope *and* Ernst Morwitz.) LiTW
Rapture, The ("Sweet infancy!/ O Heavenly Fire!"). Thomas Traherne. NoP; OBS; SCEP-1
Rapture; an Ode. Richard Watson Dixon. OxBoCh
Rapunzel. William Morris. PoVP
Rapunzel Song. Gerard Previn Meyer. NYTB
Rarae Aves. Franklin P. Adams. WhC
Rare Moments. Charles Henry Phelps. AA
Rare News. Nicholas Breton. *Fr.* Bower of Delights. ReIE
Rare old bird is the Pelican, A. The Pelican. *Unknown.* TreFS
Rare Willy Drowned in Yarrow. *Unknown. See* Willy Drowned in Yarrow.
Rarely, Rarely, Comest Thou. Shelley. *See* Song: "Rarely, rarely, comest thou."
Rarest of ladies, all of all I have. To the Excellent and Most Accomplish'd Lady, Lucy, Countess of Bedford. Michael Drayton. *Fr.* Mortimeriados. ReIE
Rash author, 'tis a vain presumptuous crime. Nicolas Boileau-Despréaux, *tr. by* Sir William Soames *and* John Dryden. *Fr.* L'Art poétique. EnLi-1; PP
Rash virtue, whose ambitious wing. Hope. Sarah Wingate Taylor. JKCP (1955 ed.)
Raspel Pole, The, *with music. Unknown.* BFSS
Rastignac at 45. Thom Gunn. TDP; TPM
Rat, The. W. H. Davies. BoPe
Rat, The. Arthur Symons. SyP
Rat, The. Andrew Young. WePo
Rat-a-tat-tat. The Drummer. Anne Robinson. SUS
Rat-a-tat-tat, rat-a-tat-tat. The Postman. Clive Sansom. BoTP
Rat is the concisest tenant, The. Emily Dickinson. MAmP
Rat Riddles. Carl Sandburg. OCS
Rat too has a skin (to tan), A. Sans Equity and sans Poise. Confucius. *Fr.* Yung Wind. CTC
Rat too, rat too, tat too, rat tat too. A Call to the Guard by a Drum. Alexander Radcliffe. PeRV
Ratcatcher and Cats, The. John Gay. CIV
Ratcatcher's Daughter, The. *Unknown.* ChTr; OxBoLi
Rather arid delight. Emily Dickinson. MWA-2
"Rather dead than spotted"; and/ believe it. Then the Ermine. Marianne Moore. NePoAm
Rather had we been ground. Lament of Granite. David Ross. PG (1945 ed.)
Rather notice, mon cher. To a Solitary Disciple. William Carlos Williams. PP
Rather than your fine hotels. Sightseers in a Courtyard. Nicolás Guillén. TTY
Rathers. Mary Austin. FaPON
Ration Party. John Manifold. WaP
Rats, The. Georg Trakl, *tr. fr. German by* Ernst Sigler. LiTW
Rattat! Rattat!/ There's the postman at the door. Postman's Knock. Rodney Bennett. BoTP
Rattlesnake, The. Robert V. Carr. PoOW
Rattlesnake, The. Alfred Purdy. WHW
Rattlesnake, The [a Ranch Haying Song]. *Unknown.* CoSo, *with music:* IHA; RePo
(Rattle Snake, *with music.*) ABF
(Rattlesnake Song, The, *with music.*) BFSS
Rauf Coilyear, *sel. Unknown.*
"Coilyear, gudlie in feir, tuke him be the hand, The." OxBS
Rav, The/ Of Northern White Russia declined. Illustrious Ancestors. Denise Levertov. AmPP (5th ed.); ToPo
Ravaged Villa, The. Herman Melville. AP; CTC; GTBS-D; MAmP; MWA-1; PoEL-5
Ravelston, Ravelston. Sydney Dobell. *Fr.* The Ballad of Keith of Ravelston. LO
Raven, The. Samuel Taylor Coleridge. OTPC (1923 ed.); WiR
Raven, The. Clifford Dyment. POTi
Raven, The. Poe. AA; AmePo; AmP; AmPP; AnFE; AP; APA; BBV (1923 ed.); BeLS; BLPA; CH; CoAnAm; CoBA; FaBoBe; FaBoCh; FaBV; FaFP; FaPL; GN; GoJo; HBV; LiTA; LiTG; LoGBV; MCCG; MWA-1; NeHB; NePA; OHFP; OnSP; OTPC; OxBA; PaPo; PCD; PFY; PG (1945 ed.); PoPo; PoRA; PTK; RoGo; TDP; TOP; TreF; ViBoPo; WBLP; WHA
Raven, The. Adrienne Rich. NePoEA-2
Raven, The. E. A. Robinson. *after the Greek of* Nicarchus. AWP; JAWP; LiTW; UnS; WBP
Raven and the Fox, The. La Fontaine, *tr. fr. French by* Elizur Wright. OnPM
Raven croak'd as she sate at her meal, The. The Old Woman of Berkeley [*or* The Witch]. Robert Southey. OBRV; WiR
Raven crouched in a tree, A. The Raven. Clifford Dyment. POTi
Raven Days, The. Sidney Lanier. AmePo; CBEP; NePA; OxBA
Raven sat upon a tree, A. The Sycophantic Fox and the Gullible Raven. Guy Wetmore Carryl. AA; AnAmPo; BLPA; CenHV; FaFP; FiBHP; HBV; InMe; LHV; MAP; MoAmPo (1942 ed.); ShBV-3; TreFT
Ravenglass Railway Station, Cumberland. Norman Nicholson. NYBP
Ravenous earth that now wooes her to be, The. Of a Death in Winter, II. John Donne. *Fr.* Elegie: Death. BoW
Ravenous Time has flowers for his food. Time Eating. Keith Douglas. FaBoMo; NeBP
Raven's Nest, The. Wordsworth. *Fr.* The Prelude, I. ShBV-3
Ravens shall pick. *Unknown. Fr.* The Combat of Ferdiad and Cuchulain. OnYI
Ravings. Thomas Hood, the Younger. Par
Ravish me in thine answere; art thou rare. Cyril Tourneur. *Fr.* The Revenger's Tragedy, II, ii. AtBAP
Ravished by all that to the eyes is fair. Michelangelo. AWP; JAWP; WBP
Ravngard and Memering. *Unknown. See* Sir Aldingar.
Rawish dank of clumsy winter ramps, The. Prologue. John Marston. *Fr.* Antonio's Revenge. LoBV; ViBoPo
Raysing of the Bridegroome. John Donne. MaMe
Razor Seller, The. "Peter Pindar." BOHV; HBV; InMe
Razors pain you. Résumé [*or* Some Beautiful Letters]. Dorothy Parker. ALV; InMe; PoPl; PoPo; ShM; TrJP; WhC
Re. Vito Hannibal Acconci. YAP
Re: the question of poems. Memo from the Desk of X. Donald Justice. TwCP
Re-Act for Action ("Re-act to Animals"). Don L. Lee. NBP; WSL
Reach down, O Steady Hand enclose him fast. The Vision. Walter Greenough. DD
Reach forth Thy hand! William Force Stead. *Fr.* Uriel, Pt. V, i. OxBoCh
Reach me a blue pencil of the moon. Ur Burial. Richard Eberhart. NePoAm
Reach me down my Tycho Brahe. The Old Astronomer to His Pupil. Sarah Williams. BLPA
Reach, with your whiter hands, to me. To the Water Nymphs, Drinking at the Fountain. Robert Herrick. AnAnS-2; EG; PoFS; ViBoPo
Reaching Back. Saundra Sharp. WSL
Reaching down arm-deep into bright water. Shells. Kathleen Raine. ImOP
Reaching-Out Poem. Kathleen Fraser. YAP
Reaching the Horizon. Robert Mezey. NaP
Reactionary Critic. Martial, *tr. fr. Latin by* Thomas Fuller. OnPM
Read here,/ This is the story of Evarra—man. Evarra and His Gods. Kipling. MoBrPo
Read here (sweet maid) the story of my woe [*or* wo]. Idea's

Read (continued)
Mirrour, I. Michael Drayton. OBSC; ReIE
Read in my face a volume of despairs. To Delia, XXXIX. Samuel Daniel. EnRePo
Read me a lesson, Muse, and speak it loud. Written upon the Top of Ben Nevis. Keats. ERoP-2
Read me no moral, priest, upon my life. The Condemned. Edward Howland. AA
Read Me, Please! Robert Graves. NYBP
Read no more of cantos Pisan. To a Young Poet. Harry M. Meacham. GoYe
Read not this Book, in any case. Of the Incomparable Treasure of the Scriptures. *Unknown.* TRV
"Read out the names!" and Burke sat back. The Fighting Race. Joseph I. C. Clarke. AA; AmePo; BLPA; DD; HBV; LHV; MC; OnYI; PaA; PAH; PFY; YaD
Read the Bible Through. Amos R. Wells. STF
Read then, but first thyself prepare. Reading the Book. *Unknown.* FaChP
Reade in these roses, the sad story. Red, and White Roses. Thomas Carew. AnAnS-2
Readen ov a Head-Stwone. William Barnes. CH; HBV (Head-Stone, The.) OBVV
Reader, behold! this monster wild. Infant Innocence. A. E. Housman. EnLi-2 (1949 ed.); WhC
Reader beneath this marble stone. Upon Mr. Bennet, Procurer Extraordinary. Alexander Radcliffe. PeRV
Reader, could his limbs be found. Epitaph on a Bombing Victim. Roy Fuller. NeBP; ToPo
Reader! I am no poet: but I grieve! To the Reader. Urian Oakes. SCAP
Reader, if thou cast thine eye. Epitaph on Mistress Mary Draper. Charles Cotton. CavP
Reader, my book flies low, and comes not near. Ad Lectorem. Thomas Bastard. SiCE
Reader, pass on—don't waste your time. *Unknown.* WhC
Reader, preserve thy peace; those busy eyes. An Elegie upon the Death of the Lord Hastings. Sir John Denham. ReEn; SeCV-1
Reader, remember that I do forewarn thee. Lectori Quomodo Legat. Thomas Freeman. SiCE
Reader, stay/ And if I had no more to say. An Epitaph on Master Philip Gray. Ben Jonson. NoP
Reader, there is no biting in my verse. Ad Lectorem. Thomas Bastard. SiCE
Reader, we are getting ready to pull out. Epilogue: Author to Reader. Henri Coulette. *Fr.* The War of the Secret Agents. NePoEA-2
Reader, within this church Sir Philip Sidney lies. Epitaph on Sir Philip Sidney. Lord Herbert of Cherbury. SeEP
Reader Writes, The. Carl Crane. PoPl; WhC
Readers and the hearers like my books, The. Critics and Cooks [*or* Against Writers That Carp at Other Men's Books]. Sir John Harington, *after the Latin of* Martial. ALV; AWP; OnPM; TuPP
Readers of the *Boston Evening Transcript,* The. The *Boston Evening Transcript.* T. S. Eliot. BWP; MWA-2; NePA
Reading. Elizabeth Barrett Browning. *Fr.* Aurora Leigh, I. GN; HH
("Good from a Book.") PoRL
Reading a book of tales. The Emotion of Fiction. Roy Fuller. LiTM (1946 ed.)
Reading a Letter. D. H. Lawrence. NoP
Reading a Medal. Terence Tiller. GTBS-P
Reading Hesiod. Marcus Argentarius, *tr. fr. Greek by* Humbert Wolfe. WoL
Reading in Li Po. After the Last Dynasty. Stanley Kunitz. NMP
Reading in Ovid the sorrowful story of Itys. Thomas Trevelyan. Edgar Lee Masters. *Fr.* Spoon River Anthology. AnFE; APA; CoAnAm; MoPo
Reading in War Time. Edwin Muir. WaP
Reading Mother, The. Strickland Gillilan. BLPA
Reading Reverdy. Ron Padgett. YAP
Reading the Book. *Unknown.* FaChP
Reading the Brothers Grimm to Jenny. Lisel Mueller. NYBP
Reading the headlines in the revolutionary. The Second Man. Julian Symons. WaP
Reading them over and over. These Poems I Have So Loved. Leonora Speyer. PG (1955 ed.)
Reading Time: 1 Minute 26 Seconds. Muriel Rukeyser. MoPo; NePA
Reading Tolstoy. John Peter. BoSA
Reading Yeats I Do Not Think. Lawrence Ferlinghetti. ML
Readings, Forecasts, Personal Guidance. Kenneth Fearing. MoAmPo
Ready. Phoebe Cary. PAH; PAP
Ready, Ay, Ready. Herman Charles Merivale. HBV; OTPC; PTK; VA
Ready she sat with one hand to turn o'er. Leigh Hunt. *Fr.* The Story of Rimini. EvOK
Ready They Make Hauberks Sarrazinese. *Unknown, tr. fr. French by* C. K. Scott Moncrieff. *Fr.* The Song of Roland. WaaP
Ready to seek out death in my disgrace. Henry Constable. *Fr.* Diana. OBSC; SiCE
Ready with leaves and with buds stood the tree. The Tree. Björnstjerne Björnson. DD; HH; MPB; OHIP; PRWS
Readymade. John Perreault. ANYP
Real. Emily Dickinson. *See* I like a look of agony.
Real Christ, The. Richard Watson Gilder. *Fr.* The Passing of Christ. OQP
Real Estate. *Unknown.* SiTL
Real Happiness. Goldsmith. *Fr.* The Traveller. OBEC
Real original, I think, A. An Original Cuss. Keith Preston. ALV; WhC
Real Presence. Ivan Adair. OQP; WGRP
Real Property. Harold Monro. BoNaP; BoPe
Real Santa Claus, A. Frank Dempster Sherman. ChBR; GaP
Real was always something that came out of streets, The. The Epiphany. George Strong. GoYe
Real Woman, A. Keats. LiTL
Realism. Thomas Bailey Aldrich. AnNE
Realism. A. C. Benson. VA
Reality. Martha Dickinson Bianchi. AA
Reality. Amelia Josephine Burr. ChIP
Reality. Sir Aubrey De Vere. WGRP
Reality. Frances Ridley Havergal. BePJ; SoP; WGRP
Reality. Yvette Johnson. TNV
Reality. Angela Morgan. WGRP
Reality. Herbert Lee Pitts. WSL
Reality. Raymond Souster. CaP
Reality, reality,/ Lord Jesus Christ Thou art to me! Reality. Frances Ridley Havergal. BePJ; SoP; WGRP
Reality! Reality! What Is It? Richard Eberhart. FiMAP
Realization. Ananda Acharya. WGRP
Realization. Mahlon Leonard Fisher. AnAmPo
Really I know. Poems. Léon Damas. PoNe
Really, what a shocking scene! A Man of Experience. Laoiseach Mac an Bhaird. KiLC
Realm is here of masquing light, A. Light at Equinox. Léonie Adams. CrMA
Realm of Fancy, The. Keats. *See* Fancy.
Reaper, The. L. H. Allen. MoAuPo; NeLNL; PoAu-1
Reaper, The. Robert Duncan. CrMA
Reaper, The. John Banister Tabb. ACP
Reaper, The. Wordsworth. *See* Solitary Reaper, The.
Reaper and the Flowers, The. Longfellow. AnNE; HBV
Reapers. Jean Toomer. CDC; Kal
Reapers, The. Lauchlan MacLean Watt. PGD
Reapers that with whetted sickles stand, The. Poetry and Philosophy. Thomas Randolph. *Fr.* An Eclogue to Mr. Johnson. OBS
Reaping the Barley. Jorge Carrera Andrade, *tr. fr. Spanish by* Muna Lee. WoL
Reapings, The. Theodore Weiss. NMP
Rear Guard, The. Irene Fowler Brown. PAH
Rear-Guard, The. Siegfried Sassoon. ACV; BoLiVe; MCCG; MoBrPo; NeMA; WaP
Rear Porches of an Apartment Building. Maxwell Bodenheim. AnAmPo; NP
Rear Vision. William Jay Smith. NYBP
Rearmament. Robinson Jeffers. OxBA
Rearrange a wife's affection? Emily Dickinson. AnNE; PoEL-5
Reason, The. Dorothy Aldis. TiPo (1952 ed.)
Reason, The. Leonard Bacon. YaD
Reason, A. Robert Creeley. NaP
Reason. Ralph Hodgson. *See* Reason Has Moons.
Reason. Josephine Miles. FiMAP; PoCh
Reason, The. James Oppenheim. HBV

Reason. John Tatham. CavP
Reason. *Unknown.* TreF
Reason and I long time known friends. Reason. John Tatham. CavP
Reason and Imagination. Blake. *Fr.* Milton. EnRP
Reason and Revelation. Dryden. *Fr.* Religio Laici. OBS; PoLi
("Dim as the borrow'd beams of moon and stars.") OxBoCh; ViBoPo, *br. sel.*
(Finite Reason.) LoBV
(Reason and Religion.) FiP
Reason Fair to Fill My Glass, A. Charles Morris. HBV
Reason for Not Writing Orthodox Nature Poetry. John Wain. HaMV; PP; ToPo
Reason for Skylarks, The. Kenneth Patchen. NaP
Reason for the Pelican, The. John Ciardi. PDV; PoPl; SoPo
Reason for Writing, A. Theodore Spencer. TwAmPo
Reason Has Moons. Ralph Hodgson. MoVE, 9 *ll.*; ShBV-4
(Reason.) MoBrPo; PoIE
("Reason has moons, but moons not hers.") FaBoCh; LoGBV; SiTL
Reason I Stay on Job So Long, *with music.* *Unknown.* ABF
Reason, in faith thou art well serv'd, that still. Astrophel and Stella, X. Sir Philip Sidney. FCP; MaPo; ReEn; SiCE; SiPS
Reason is our soul's left hand, faith her right. To the Countess of Bedford. John Donne. ATP (1953 ed.); MaMe
Reason, tell me thy mind, if here be reason. Love and Reason. Sir Philip Sidney. *Fr.* Arcadia. SiPS
Reason, the Use of It in Divine Matters. Abraham Cowley. AnAnS-2
Reason thus with life. Life and Death. Shakespeare. *Fr.* Measure for Measure, III, i. UnPo (1st ed.)
Reason Why, The. Thomas Lovell Beddoes. OBRV
Reason why all colors look deeper, The. Gerald Butler. *Fr.* This Side of Orion. QAH
Reason why my brother's so severe, The. Mary Lamb. MuSP
Reason why our work is brittle, The. The Reason. Leonard Bacon. YaD
Reasonable Affliction, A ("Helen was just slipped into bed"). Matthew Prior. *See* Helen Was Just Slipped into Bed.
Reasonable Affliction, A ("On his death-bed poor Lubin lies"). Matthew Prior. ALV; HBV; MeWo; ShM; TreFT; TrGrPo; WhC
Reasons for and against Marrying Widows. Henricus Selyns. SCAP
Reasons for Attendance. Philip Larkin. CBV; OPoP; PoeP; ToPo
Reasons for Drinking. Henry Aldrich. BOHV; InMe; YaD
(Catch, A: "If all be true that I do think.") InvP; OBS; SeEP
(Five Reasons [for Drinking], The.) LiTG; SiTL; TreFT
(If All Be True That I Do Think.) SeCL
Reasons for Music. Archibald MacLeish. NePA
Rebecca. Hilaire Belloc. BoChLi (1939 ed.); RIS; StaSt
Rebecca and Rowena, *sel.* Thackeray.
Age of Wisdom, The. ALV; HBV; VA; WhC
(Love at Two Score.) PoVP
Rebecca's After-Thought. Elizabeth Turner. HBV HBVY
(I Almost Did—Very Nigh—Had Not God Stopped the Lie.) ThGo
Rebecca's Hymn. Sir Walter Scott. *Fr.* Ivanhoe, *ch.* 40. EnRP
("When Israel, of the Lord Beloved.") ViBoPo
Rebel, The. Hilaire Belloc. CoBE; PoFr
Rebel, The. Mari E. Evans. AmNP; IDB
Rebel, A. John Gould Fletcher. MAP; MoAmPo
Rebel. Irene Rutherford McLeod. HBMV
"Beyond the murk," *sel.* WGRP
Rebel, The. Padraic Pearse. OnYI; PoFr
Rebel, The. Innes Randolph. ThLM; OxBoLi
(Good Old Rebel, A *and* B *vers., with music.*) ABF
Rebel Scot, The, *sel.* John Cleveland.
"Come, keen iambics, with your badger's feet." OBS; ViBoPo
Rebel Soldier, The. *Unknown.* LoGBV; OxBoLi
(Rabble Soldier, *diff. vers., with music.*) AS
(Troubled Soldier, The, *diff. vers., with music.*) AS
Rebellion against death, the old rebellion. The Old Enemy. Sara Teasdale. MaRV
Rebellion shook an ancient dust. April Mortality. Léonie Adams. AnAmPo; MAP; MoAB; MoAmPo
Rebellious fools that scorn to bow. The Bracelet. Thomas Stanley. AnAnS-2
Rebellious, he studied. The Chiseler. Francis X. Maynard. JKCP (1955 ed.)
Rebellious heart, in the grip of fate. Soul Growth. Annerika Fries. OQP
Rebellious Vine, The. Harold Monro. BoPe; BrPo; WaKn
Rebels. Ernest Crosby. MC; PAH
Rebels from Fairy Tales. Hyacinthe Hill. WOW
Rebirth. Margaret E. Bruner. PoToHe
Rebirth. Paula Giddings. WSL
Rebirth. Kipling. GTSL; LoBV; OBNC
Rebirth. Stan Rice. QAH
Re-Birth. *Unknown, tr. fr. Bushman by* W. H. I. Bleek *and* Jack Cope. PeSA
Rebirth of London, The. Dryden. *See* New London, The.
Re-Birth of Venus, The. Geoffrey Hill. NePoEA
Rebuff. Samuel L. Albert. NePoAm-2
Rebuke me not! I have nor wish nor skill. John Addington Symonds. Sonn
Recall, The. Kipling. BoPe; NoP; POTE; PoVP
Recall, The. James Russell Lowell. AP
Recall. Reed Whittemore. NYBP
Recalling War. Robert Graves. CMoP; CoBMV; ForPo; LiTM (rev. ed.); MMA; WaP
Recantation, The. Albius Tibullus, *tr. fr. Latin by* James Cranstoun. LiTW
Recapitulation, The. Richard Eberhart. MoRP
Recapitulations, *sels.* Karl Shapiro.
"At one the Apocalypse had spoken," II. FiMAP
"I was born downtown on a wintry day," I. FiMAP
"My first small book was nourished in the dark," V. FiMAP
"We waged a war within a war," XI. PoNe
"When nuns were spitted and poets fell," XIII. FiMAP
Receipt to Restore Stella's Youth, A. Swift. Po
Receive, Beloved. Virginia Earle. JKCP (1955 ed.)
Receive, dear friend, the truths I teach. To Licinius [Murena]. Horace, *tr. by* William Cowper. AWP; EnLi-1; HBV; JAWP; OuHeWo; WBP
Receive my body, pretty bed. Going to Bed at Night. Adelaide O'Keeffe. OTPC (1923 ed.)
Receive these writs, my sweet and dearest friend. Coelia, XX. William Percy. ReIE
Receiving Communion. Vassar Miller. NePoEA-2
Recent Dialogue, A. Thomas Moore. NBM
Recently in the south of England. Ode to Hengist and Horsa. Robinson Jeffers. SiSW
Recessional. Georgia Douglas Johnson. CDC; PoNe
Recessional. Kipling. AWP; BBV; BEL; BLPA; BLRP; BoLiVe; BrPo; CABA; EnLi-2; EnLit; EPN; FaBV; FaFP; GN; GTBS; GTBS-W; GTSL; HBV; HBVY; InP; InPo; JAWP; LiTB; LiTM; MaRV; MCCG; MoBrPo; NeHB; NeMA; OAEP (2d ed.); OBEV; OBNC; OBVV; OHFP; OQP; PoE; PoMa; PoVP; PTK; SoP; TreF; TrGrPo; TRV; TSW; ViBoPo; ViPP; WBLP; WBP; WGRP; WHA; YAT
(Lest We Forget!) YT
Recessional, The. Sir Charles G. D. Roberts. HBV
Recessional. Isaac Watts. *See* O God, Our Help in Ages Past.
Recessional for the Class of 1959 of a School for Delinquent Negro Girls. Joseph R. Cowen. PoNe (1970 ed.)
Recipe. A. P. Herbert. *Fr.* Two Gentlemen of Soho. WhC
Recipe. *Unknown, tr. fr. German by* Louis Untermeyer. UnTE
Recipe for a Happy Life. Margaret of Navarre. PoMa
Recipe for a Marriage. Phyllis McGinley. TIHL
Recipe for an Evening Musicale. Phyllis McGinley. UnS; WhC
(Evening Musicale.) Sonn
Recipe for Living. Alfred Grant Walton. PoToHe (new ed.)
Reciprocity. John Drinkwater. NeMA; NP
Reciprocity. Vassar Miller. NePoEA
Recital, *sel.* Louise Townsend Nicholl.
"In the motionless haze of interior heat." UnS
Recitation and Song: "Am I alone." W. S. Gilbert. *Fr.* Patience. WoL
(Bunthorne's Recitative and Song.) CoBE
(Recitative and Song: Bunthorne.) PoVP
Recitative. Hart Crane. FaBoMo
Recitative. Ronald McCuaig. PoAu-2

Recitativo: "I rage, I melt, I burn." John Gay. *Fr.* Acis and Galatea. EiCL
Reckoning, The. Naomi Long Madgett. Kal
Recluse, A. Walter de la Mare. BoPe
Recluse, The. Wordsworth. *See also* Excursion, The. BEL. *Sels.*
"Bleak season was it, turbulent and wild." ERoP-1
"On Man, on Nature." EnRP; EPN; ERoP-1; OBRV (Prospectus.) NoP
"On Nature's invitation do I come." ERoP-1
Recluses, The. Stuart Z. Perkoff. NeAP
Recogitabo Tibi Omnes Annos Meos. William Habington. *See* Time! Where Didst Thou Those Years Inter.
Recognition. John White Chadwick. AA
Recognition. Margaret E. Sangster. MaRV
Recognition, The. William Sawyer. HBV
Recognition. John Banister Tabb. ChIP; JKCP; OQP
Recognition of Death. Joseph Payne Brennan. FiSC
Recognition of Eve, The. Karl Shapiro. *Fr.* Adam and Eve. MoAB; ToPo
Recollection. Anne Reeve Aldrich. AA
Recollection, A. John Peale Bishop. LiTA; Sonn; TwAmPo
Recollection. Amelia Walstien Carpenter. AA
Recollection, A. Frances Cornford. ELU; TSW
Recollection. Donald D. Govan. NBP
Recollection, The. Shelley. GTBS; GTBS-D; GTBS-P; GTBS-W; GTSE; GTSL; NoP
(To Jane; the Recollection.) ChER; EPN; MBW-2; OBNC; OBRV
"We wandered to the Pine Forest," *sel.* CH
Recollection in Autumn. Valentin Iremonger. OnYI (Elizabeth.) NeIP
(This Houre Her Vigill.) OxBI
Recollections of Burgos. Richard Chenevix Trench. OBRV
Recollections of Love. Samuel Taylor Coleridge. ChER
Recollections of My Children. *Unknown, tr. fr. Japanese by* Basil Hall Chamberlain. OnPM
Recollections of the Arabian Nights. Tennyson. PoVP
Recommendation, The. Richard Crashaw. MaMe; PoLi
Recompense. Grace Noll Crowell. PCD
Recompense. John Richard Moreland. OQP
Recompense. Nixon Waterman. HBV
Recompense, The. Anna Wickham. NP
Recompense. Loring Williams. FiSC
Reconcilement, The. John Sheffield. CEP; LiTL; LO; OBEV
Reconciliation. "Æ." MoRP; OBMV; OxBI; PoVP
Reconciliation. C. Day Lewis. TwCP
Reconciliation, *sel.* Elizabeth Doten.
"God of the Granite and the Rose!" TrPWD
(Prayer, A: "God of the Granite and the Rose!") OQP
Reconciliation, The ("Donec gratus eram"). Horace, *tr. fr. Latin.* Odes, III, 9. MeWo, *tr. by* Louis Untermeyer; OuHeWo, *tr. by* Sir Theodore Martin
(February 14, 22 B.C. *par. by* Franklin P. Adams.) InMe
(Teasing Lovers, The, *tr. by* Louis Untermeyer.) UnTE
Reconciliation. Charles Mackay. *See* Under the Holly Bough.
Reconciliation, The. Archibald MacLeish. MoAmPo
Reconcilation. Caroline Atherton Briggs Mason. AA
Reconciliation. J. U. Nicholson. HBMV
Reconciliation, The. Tennyson. *See* As Thro' the Land at Eve We Went.
Reconciliation. *Unknown, tr. fr. Late Middle Irish by* Kenneth Jackson. AnIL
Reconciliation. John Hall Wheelock. CrMA
Reconciliation. Walt Whitman. AmePo; AnAmPo; AnEnPo; BoLiVe; CoBA; FaBoEn; GTBS-D; MAP; MaRV; MoAmPo; MWA-1; NeMA; NoP; OxBA; PoE; TrGrPo; WaaP
Reconnaissance. Arna Bontemps. AmNP; Kal
Reconsecration. Dorothy Gould. PGD
Record Perpetual Loss. Mary Stanley. AnNZ
"Record Room—6-3-5-3-5—." Clerk in the Hospital Record Room in Summer. Merrill Moore. Sonn
Record Stride, A. Robert Frost. NePA
Recorder, tax collector, landlord, friends. Ode for the Burial of a Citizen. John Ciardi. LiTM (1970 ed.); MiAP
Recorders Ages Hence. Walt Whitman. MAP; MoAmPo; NePA
Recorders in Italy. Adrienne Cecile Rich. TwAmPo; UnS
Recovery, The. Edmund Blunden. CBEP; MoBrPo; MoPW
Recovery. F. R. Scott. CaP
Recovery, The. Thomas Traherne. AnAnS-1; MeP
Recovery from Mental Illness. H. C. Bosman. BoSA
Recreation. Eric Priestley. WSL
Recreation. Jane Taylor. NBM; OBRV; OxBoLi
Recrimination. Ella Wheeler Wilcox. AA
Recruit, The. Robert W. Chambers. AA; BOHV; HBV; PFY
Recruit, The. A. E. Housman. A Shropshire Lad, III. PoVP
Recruited Collier, The. *Unknown. See* Jimmy's Enlisted.
Recruiting Drive. Charles Causley. NePoEA; PPON; TPM
Recuerdo. Edna St. Vincent Millay. AmFN; BoLP; EvOK; FaFP; LiTA; LiTL; LiTM; NP; OxBA; PTK; ThLM
Recurrence, The. Edwin Muir. MoPo
Red. Countee Cullen. GoSl
Red and green neon lights, the jazz hysteria. Nuit Blanche; North End. Conrad Aiken. OxBA
Red and the Green, The. Anne Wilkinson. MoCV
Red, and White Roses. Thomas Carew. AnAnS-2
Red and yellow of the Autumn salt-grass, The. At Tide Water. Sir Charles G. D. Roberts. PeCV
Red are the hands of the reapers. The Reapers. Lauchlan MacLean Watt. PGD
Red armchair is empty, The. The Dance. John Haines. ThO
Red as the lips of Rahab. The Scarlet Thread. Daniel Henderson. HBMV
Red at night,/ Sailor's delight. Rules of the Road. *Unknown.* SoAmSa
Red Atlantis. John Haines. ThO
Red Bird Tapestry, The. May Swenson. TwAmPo
Red Book of Hergest, The, *sel. Unknown, tr. fr. Middle Welsh by* Ernest Rhys.
Lament for Urien, The. OBMV
Red brick monastery in, The. The Semblables. William Carlos Williams. AP
Red bricks in the suburbs, white horse on the wall. Ballad to a Traditional Refrain. Maurice James Craig. SeCePo
Red-Bud, the Kentucky Tree, The. Christmas at Freelands. James Stephens. ILP
Red candles. Smoky red lights. The Red Nude. Dave Etter. ThO
Red-cap sang in Bishop's wood, A. Path Flower. Olive Tilford Dargan. HBMV
Red Cockatoo, The. Po Chü-i, *tr. fr. Chinese by* Arthur Waley. ChTr; LiTW; MoPW; OA; OuHeWo
Red Cow Is Dead, The. E. B. White. NYBP
Red Cross, The. Edna Jacques. PoRL
Red Cross, The. Henry van Dyke. PEDC
Red Cross Christmas Seal, The. Theodosia Garrison. PEDC
Red Cross Knight. Spenser. The Faerie Queene, I, 1. GoBC (2 *sts.*)
("Gentle knight was pricking on the plaine, A.") ATP; BoLiVe, *abr.*; CoBE; ExPo; FosPo; MBW-1; YAT, 3 *sts.*
Red Cross Nurse, The. Edith M. Thomas. PEDC
Red Cross Nurses, The. Thomas L. Masson. PEDC
Red Cross Nurses. Gervase Stewart. WaP
Red Cross Spirit Speaks, The. John H. Finley. PEDC
Red dawn clouds coming up! the heavens proclaim you. Morning Light Song. Philip Lamantia. NeAP
Red deer loves the chaparral, The. The Rocky Mountain Sheep. Mary Austin. MPB
Red Eyes of rabbits, The. The Springtime. Denise Levertov. CoAP
Red firelight on the Sioux tepees. Cottonwood Leaves. Badger Clark. TiPo
Red flame-flowers, bloom and die, The. Nocturne [*or* On the Black Veld.] Crosbie Garstin. ACV; CH
Red fool, my laughing comrade. To a Comrade in Arms. Alun Lewis. FaBoTw; MoBrPo (1962 ed.)
Red for Santa's fur-lined cloak. All in Red. Eileen Mathias. BoTP
Red foxgloves against a yellow wall streaked with plum-colored shadows. Ombre Chinoise. Amy Lowell. NP
Red Geranium and Godly Mignonette. D. H. Lawrence. GTBS-P
Red Geraniums. Martha Haskell Clark. BLPA; NeHB
Red Ghosts Chant, The. Lilian White Spencer. PoOW
Red gold of pools. Harvest Sunset. Carl Sandburg. TSW
Red-Gold Rain, The, *sels.* Sacheverell Sitwell.
Orange Tree by Day. AtBAP; MoBrPo
Orange Tree by Night. AtBAP

Red granite and black diorite, with the blue. The Skeleton of the Future. "Hugh MacDiarmid." GoTS; MoBrPo; OBMV; ShBV-4
Red-haired Man's Wife, The. James Stephens. HBMV; MoBrPo; OBVV
Red Hanrahan's Song about Ireland. W. B. Yeats. *Fr.* Hanrahan and Cathleen the Daughter of Hoolihan. ACV; BEL; CMoP; FaBoCh; FaBoMo; LoGBV; OnYI; OxBI
Red Harlaw. Sir Walter Scott. *See* Harlaw.
Red-Headed Restaurant Cashier. Carl Sandburg. CMoP
Red Heart, The. James Reaney. CaP
Red Hugh. Thomas McGreevy. *See* Aodh Ruadh O'Domhnaill.
Red in Autumn. Elizabeth Gould. BoTP
Red Iron Ore. *Unknown.* ABF, *with music*; AS, *with music*; IHA, *with music*; TiPo (1952 ed.), *abr.*
Red Jack. Mary Durack. PoAu-1
Red Jacket. Fitz-Greene Halleck. AA
Red leaf. And beside it, a red leaf alive. Salamander. Muriel Rukeyser. WIRo
Red leaves fall upon the lake, The. Threnody. John Farrar. BrR; BoChLi; GFA; SUS
Red leaves flutter. Cover. Frances Frost. SUS
Red Light Saloon, The, *with music.* *Unknown.* ShS
Red lips are not so red. Greater Love. Wilfred Owen. ACV; AtBAP; BoLiVe; BrPo; CBV; CMoP; EnLi-2 (1949 ed.); EnLoPo; FaBoMo; FaFP; GTBS-P; GTBS-W; LiTB; LiTG; LiTM; LO; MasP; MoAB; MoBrPo; NAMP; OAEP (2d ed.); SeCeV; ViBoPo; WaaP; WaP
Red Man's Wife, The. *Unknown, tr. fr. Modern Irish by* Douglas Hyde. OnYI; OxBI; SeCePo
Red May. Agnes Mary Frances Robinson. HBMV
Red Men, The. Charles Sangster. CaP
Red mountain, red forest. The Situation. Sydney Clouts. BoSA
Red Nude, The. Dave Etter. ThO
Red o'er the Forest. John Keble. *See* November.
Red of the bushwood fire. Camp Fire. Beatrice Marion Bromley. ACV
Red paths that wander through the gray, and cells. With God Conversing. Gene Derwood. LiTA; LiTM; MoRP; NePA
Red Peony, The. Buson, *tr. fr. Japanese by* Harold G. Henderson. RePo
Red Poppies. "Fiona Macleod." *Fr.* Sospiri di Roma. VA
Red rain spatter under the redhaw, The. Redhaw Rain. Carl Sandburg. Po
Red, Red Rose, A. Burns. AtBAP; AWP; BEL; BoLP; CABA; CBEP; CBV; CEP; ChTr; CoBE; EiCL; EiCP; EiPP; EnL; EnLi-2; EnLit; FaBV; FaFP; ForPo; HBV; ILP; InPo; InvP; JAWP; MCCG; MemP; MeWo; OBEC; OBEV; OnPM; OtMeF; OuHeWo; OxBS; PCD; PG; PoAn; PoE; PoEL-4; PoIE; PoLF; PoMa; PoPo; PoRL; PoSa; PTK; SeCeV; TOP; ViBoPo; WBP; WePo; YAT
(My Love Is [*or* Luve's] like a Red Red Rose.) AnFE; EnRP; FaBoBe; LiTB; LiTG; NeHB; OAEP; OTD; PAn; PoSC; ShBV-4
(My Luve.) BoLiVe; HoPM; TrGrPo
(O My Luve's [*or* Luve Is *or* Love Is] like a Red, Red Rose.) DiPo; ELP; ExPo; FaBoCh; FosPo; GoTS; GTBS; GTBS-D; GTBS-P; GTBS-W; GTSE; GTSL; LiTL; LoGBV; TreF; WHA
(Song: "My luve is like a red, red rose.") LoBV
Red Riding Hood. Guy Wetmore Carryl. HBV; YaD
Red Right Returning. Louis O. Coxe. MoVE; WaP
Red River. Lewis Mac Adams. YAP
Red river, red river. Virginia. T. S. Eliot. Landscapes, II. NoP; PoSa
Red River Shore, *with music.* *Unknown.* ABF; CoSo
Red River Valley. *Unknown.* AS, *with music*; BFSS, *with music*; CoSo, *with music*; FaBoBe; FaFP; TrAS, *with music*; TreFS
Red Robin, The. John Clare. BiS
Red rock wilderness, The. The Wilderness. Sidney Keyes. LiTB; LiTM (rev. ed.); NeBP
Red Rooster, The. Hilda Conkling. TSW
Red Rose, proud Rose, sad Rose of all my days! To the Rose upon the Rood of Time. W. B. Yeats. OAEP (2d ed.); Po; ViPo (1962 ed.)
Red rose whispers of passion, The. A White Rose. John Boyle O'Reilly. AA; ACP; AnAmPo; HBV; OBEV; OBVV; OnYI; PoPl
Red Sea. James Agee. *Fr.* Two Songs on the Economy of Abundance. MAP; MoAmPo
Red Sea Place in Your Life, The. Annie Johnson Flint. *See* At the Place of the Sea.
Red Skins left their agency, the soldiers left their post, The. The Indian Ghost Dance and War. W. H. Prather. PoOW
Red Sky at Morning. Gilbert Thomas. LO; TreFS
Red sky at night. *Unknown.* OxNR
Red sky in the morning. Kobayashi Issa, *tr. fr. Japanese by* Geoffrey Bownas *and* Anthony Thwaite. FIW
Red Slippers. Amy Lowell. NP
Red stockings, blue stockings. *Unknown.* OxNR
Red sun, remember. On Mt. Iron. Charles Brasch. AnNZ
Red the dust and brown the rock. Native Inhabitant. Douglas Stewart. NeLNL
Red Thread of Honour, The. Sir Francis Hastings Doyle. BBV; OtMeF; PoVP
Red-tiled ships you see reflected, The. Five Vignettes. Jean Toomer. BALP
Red-tiled towers of the old Chateau, The. Chateau Papineau. S. Frances Harrison. CaP; VA
Red-Top and Timothy. Lucy Larcom. BoChLi (1939 ed.); UTS
Red towers lofty and glowing, The. Old Lines; a Fragment. Dino Campana. OnPM
Red veins in the Gravensteins, The. Hannah Dustin. Louis O. Coxe. TwAmPo
Red Wheelbarrow, The. William Carlos Williams. AmLP; CMoP; FIW; ForPo; FosPo; HoPM; LiTA; LiTM (1970 ed.); MoAB; MoAmPo; NoP; PoAn; PoeP; UnPo (3d ed.); VaPo (Spring and All.) EvOK; ThWaDe
Red, White, and Blue. David T. Shaw. *See* Columbia, the Gem of the Ocean.
Red Wig, The. *Unknown.* CoMu
Red Wind, The. Lionel Johnson. PoVP
Red Wine. Justin Richardson. PV
Redbreast Chasing a Butterfly, The. Wordsworth. OTPC
Redbreast, Early in the Morning. Emily Brontë. NCEP
Red-Breast of Aquitania, The. Francis S. Mahony. OnYI
Rededication. Emanuel Litvinoff. WaP
Rededication to Nature, The. Wordsworth. *See* Prelude, The: Summer Vacation
Redeemer, The. "Fiona Macleod." WGRP
Redeemer, The. Siegfried Sassoon. MMA; WGRP
Redemption. Thomas Curtis Clark. SoP
Redemption. George Herbert. AnAnS-1; BWP; CABA; EaLo; EP; ExPo; GTBS-W; LiTB; LiTG; MaMe; MaPo (1969 ed.); MeLP; MePo; NoP; OBS; PoSa; PoE; SCEP-1; SeCeV; SeCP; SeCV-1; SeEP; Sonn; StJW
Redemption. Mary Winter Ware. SoP
Redeployment. Howard Nemerov. LiTM (1970 ed.); NePA; ThLM; TrJP
Redesdale and Wise William. *Unknown.* ESPB
Redhaw Rain. Carl Sandburg. Po
Rediscovery. George Awoonor-Williams. TTY
Redondillas. Sister Juana Inéz de la Cruz, *tr. fr. Spanish by* Garrett Strange. CAW
Redoubted knights, and honorable Dames. Malbecco and Hellenore. Spenser. *Fr.* The Faerie Queene, III, 9 *and* 10. MaPo; NoP
Redshanks, The. Julian Bell. LO; OBMV
Redwing, The. Patric Dickinson. BoPe; HaMV; POTi
Redwoods, The. Louis Simpson. AmFN; CoAP; FIW; PP
Reed, A, *sel.* Elizabeth Barrett Browning.
Sympathy. SoP, 1 *st.*
Reed, The. Henry Bernard Carpenter. AA
Reed, The. Caryll Houselander. ISi
Reed, The. Mikhail Yurevich Lermontov, *tr. fr. Russian by* J. J. Robbins. AWP; JAWP; WBP
Reed-Player, The. Archibald MacLeish. HBMV; PTK
Reed-Player, The. Duncan Campbell Scott. VA
Reeds in the Loch Sayis, The. *Unknown.* GoTS
(Reid in the Loch Sayis, The.) OxBS
Reeds of Innocence. Blake. *See* Piping down the Valleys Wild.
Reeds of Runnymede, The. Kipling. FOL
Reef Wrack. Clement B. Christesen. BoAu
Reefing Topsails. Walter Mitchell. EtS
Reek and the Rambling Blade, The, *with music.* *Unknown.* OuSiCo

Reever ryves at the gullie, The. Wemen's Wather. T. S. Law. OxBS
Reeve's Tale, The. Chaucer, *mod. vers. by* Frank Ernest Hill. *Fr.* The Canterbury Tales. UnTE
"At Trumpyngtoun nat fer from Cantebrigge," *sel., orig. vers.* ViBoPo
Reference to a Passage in Plutarch's Life of Sulla. Robinson Jeffers. CrMA
Referring to Flowers. *Unknown, tr. fr. Japanese by* Ishii *and* Obata. *Fr.* Manyo Shu. OnPM
Refined Man, The. Kipling. *Fr.* Epitaphs of the War. FaBoTw; MMA
Refiner's Fire, The. *Unknown.* BLRP; SoP
Reflected Glory. Fannie Brown. SoP
Reflected in the penisioner's eye. Karoo Town. Robert Dederick. PeSA
Reflecting all. The Vial. David Galler. NYTB
Reflection. Margaret Allonby. BoSA
Reflection, A. Thomas Hood. NBM; PV
(Epigram: "When Eve upon the first of men," *wr. at. to* Thomas Moore.) HBV
Reflection. Lew Sarett. MoSiPe
Reflection. Kurt M. Stein. InMe
Reflection, The. Edward Taylor. *See* Preparatory Meditations: "Lord, art thou at the table. . ."
Reflection. James Thomson. Sunday up the River, XII. EnLit
("My Love o'er the water bends dreaming.") OBEV (1st ed.)
Reflection. W. J. Turner. OBMV
Reflection. *Unknown.* STF
Reflection by a Mailbox. Stanley Kunitz. TrJP; WaP
Reflection from Rochester. William Empson. ToPo
Reflection in Blue. David McCord. MoAmPo (1942 ed.)
Reflection of a car on a window across, The. Power Failure. Joel Sloman. ThO
Reflection on the Course of Human Life, A. William Lloyd, Bishop of St. Asaph. PrWP
Reflections. Cyrus E. Albertson. MaRV
Reflections. Edna Becker. MaRV; OQP; SoP; TRV
Reflections, *sel.* George Crabbe.
Late Wisdom. HBV, *abr.*; OBEV, *abr.*; TrGrPo
("We've trod the maze of error round.") OBRV
Reflections, *sel.* Philip Freneau.
Americans! PPON
Reflections. Carl Gardner. NNP
Reflections. Amy Lowell. *Fr.* Chinoiseries. AnAmPo; NP; PoRA (rev. ed.)
Reflections at Dawn. Phyllis McGinley. FiBHP
Reflections in a Hospital. Emanuel Eisenberg. ALV
Reflections in a Little Park. Babette Deutsch. ELU; NePoAm
Reflections in a Slum. "Hugh MacDiarmid." NMP; OPoP
Reflections in an Iron Works. "Hugh MacDiarmid." NAMP
Reflections in Bed. Julian Symons. LiTM; WaP
Reflections on an Ideal Existence. Sara Henderson Hay. CIV
Reflections on Cleopathera's Needle. Cormac O'Leary. BOHV
Reflections on Having Left a Place of Retirement. Samuel Taylor Coleridge. EnRP; MERP; OBEC
Reflections on Ice-breaking. Ogden Nash. FaFP; LiTM; NePA; ShBV-4; SiTL
Reflections on the Fall of France, June, 1940. Eiluned Lewis. POTE
Reflections on the River. Andrew Young. ACV
Reflections on Water. Kenneth Pitchford. CoPo
Reflections Outside of a Gymnasium. Phyllis McGinley. SD
Reflections upon a Recurrent Suggestion by Civil Defense Authorities That I Build a Bombshelter in My Backyard. Reed Whittemore. PoCh
Reflexion, The. Edward Taylor. *See* Preparatory Meditations: "Lord, art thou at the table . . ."
Reformation of Godfrey Gore, The. William Brighty Rands. *See* Godfrey Gordon Gustavus Gore.
Reformed Pirate, The. T. G. Roberts. WHW
Reformed Wife, The, *sel.* *At. to* Charles Burnaby *and to* William Burnaby.
Upon a Sickly Lady. SeCL
Reformers, The ("O pure reformers!"). Whittier. MaRV
Refracted Lights. Celia Parker Wooley. WGRP
Refrain. Joseph Cardarelli. QAH
Refrain: "Come and kiss me, Mistress Beauty." Douglas Brooke Wheelton Sladen. *Fr.* Charles II. VA
Refreshment. George Edward Hoffman. ChIP
Refrigerium. Cardinal Newman. *See* Rest.
Refrigerium. Frederick Goddard Tuckerman. AP
Refuge. "Æ." HBV; OnYI; POTE
Refuge. Hervey Allen. HBMV
Refuge, The. Psalms, XLVI, Bible, *O.T.* *See* Our Refuge.
Refuge. Archibald Lampman. PeCV (1967 ed.)
Refuge. Mabel E. McCartney. BLRP
Refuge. Lew Sarett. HBMV; MaRV
Refuge. John Thompson. BoAu
Refuge. William Winter. HBV
Refuge and Present Help, A. Isaac Watts. SoP
Refugee. Naomi Long Witherspoon. PoNe
Refugee Blues. W. H. Auden. InPo; LiTA; LiTM; WePo
(Song: "Say this city has ten million souls.") NYBP
Refugee in America. Langston Hughes. AmFN; WaKn
Refugees. Grace Hazard Conkling. NP
Refugees, The. Randall Jarrell. MoAB; MoAmPo (1950 ed.)
Refugees. Louis MacNeice. LiTB; WaP
Refugees, The. Sir Herbert Read. BrPo; MoBrPo (1942 ed.)
Refusal, A. Barnabe Googe. EnRePo; NoP
Refusal, A. Thomas Hardy. LiTB
Refusal. Raymond Kresensky. OQP
Refusal to Mourn the Death, by Fire, of a Child in London, A. Dylan Thomas. AtBAP; CABA; ChMP; CMoP; CoBMV; DiPo; FaBoEn; FaFP; FosPo; GTBS-P; GTBS-W; InPo; LiTB; LiTG; LiTM; MaPo; MasP; MoAB; MoBrPo (1962 ed.); MoPo; MoVE; NeBP; OAEP (2d ed.); PAn; PIA; Po; PoAn; PoDB; PoIE; PoPl; SeCePo; StP; TDP; ToPo; TwCP; UnPo (3d ed.); VaPo; WaaP
Refuses/ To refuse the racket. Old Tennis Player. Gwendolyn Brooks. SD
Refusing to fall in love with God, he gave. Didymus. Louis MacNeice. EaLo
Reg wished me to go with him to the field. My Mother. Claude McKay. AnEnPo
Regard her well—the austere face. Röntgen Photograph. Elisabeth Eybers. PeSA
Regard not then if wit be old or new. Pope. *Fr.* An Essay on Criticism. YAT
Regard, O reader, how it is with me. Look, in the Labyrinth of Memory. Delmore Schwartz. TrJP
Regard the capture here, O Janus-faced. Recitative. Hart Crane. FaBoMo
Regard the little needle. The Needle. Grace Cornell Tall. GoYe
Regarding (1) the U.S. and (2) New York. Franklin P. Adams. HBMV
Regeneration. Walter Savage Landor. ViBoPo, *abr.*
(Invocation, An: "We are what suns and winds and waters make us.") VA
Regeneration. Henry Vaughan. AnAnS-1; CABA; EP; ExPo; LoBV; MeLP; MeP; MePo; NoP; OBS; SCEP-1; SeEP
Regenesis. Ron Welburn. NBP
Regent-Bird and Girl. Clem Christesen. MoAuPo
Regent of song! who bringest to our shore. To Rosina Pico. William Wilberforce Lord. AA
Regent's Park. Rose Fyleman. SoPo
Regiment of Princes, The. Thomas Hoccleve. *See* De Regimine Principum.
Regina Angelorum. G. K. Chesterton. ISi
Regina Coeli. Coventry Patmore. ISi; JKCP; PoVP; VA
Regina Coeli. *Unknown, tr. fr. Latin.* ISi, *tr. by* Winfred Douglas; WHL
Regina Confessorum. *Unknown.* GoBC
Region of life and light! The Life of the Blessed. Luis de León, *tr. by* Bryant. AWP; SoP
Regions of soft clear air, of cold green leaves. Sonnet. Thomas Caulfield Irwin. IrPN
Regret [*or* Regrat]. William Drummond of Hawthornden. *See* In This World's Raging Sea.
Regret, A. Charles Harpur. BoAu
Regret. Richard Le Gallienne. VA
Regret. Mabel Murray. SoP
Regret Not Me. Thomas Hardy. GTBS-D; LO; MoVE; SeCeV
Regrets, *sels.* Joachim du Bellay, *tr. fr. French.*
Heureux qui, comme Ulysse, a fait un beau voyage, XXXI, *tr. by* G. K. Chesterton. AWP
(Happy Ulysses, The, *tr. by* G. K. Chesterton.) WoL
(Returning Home, *tr. by* William Stirling.) LiTW
(Translation from Du Bellay: "Happy, who like Ulysses or that lord," *tr. by* G. K. Chesterton.) InP

Regulation-skirted. Emergency. Isabel Fiske Conant. HBMV
Regulus, *sel.* John Crowne.
To Many Deaths Decreed. SeCL
Rehearsal, The, *sel.* George Villiers, Duke of Buckingham.
"I have made, too, one of the most delicate, dainty similes." Par
Reid at Fayal. John Williamson Palmer. PAH
Reid in the Loch Sayis, The. *Unknown. See* Reeds in the Loch Sayis, The.
Reign in my thoughts, fair hand, sweet eye, rare voice! To Delia, XXV. Samuel Daniel. ReIE
Reign of Chaos, The. Pope. *See* Conclusion: "In vain, in vain. . ."
Reign of Peace, The. Mary Starck. WBLP
Reign of Peace, The. Eliza Thornton. PEDC
Reign on, majestic Ville Marie! Montreal. William Douw Lighthall. VA
Reincarnation. Lloyd Frank Merrell. ChIP
Reincarnation. David Banks Sickels. AA
(It Cannot Be.) HBV
Reine d'Amour. Francis Turner Palgrave. GBV (1952 ed.)
Reinforcements. Thomas Toke Lynch. OBVV
Reivers they stole Fair Annie, The. Fair Annie. *Unknown.* CH; HBV; OBEV (1st ed.)
Rejected. Lord Alfred Bruce Douglas. PeVV
Rejected Member's Wife, The. Thomas Hardy. NoP
Rejected "National Hymns," The. "Orpheus C. Kerr."
By Dr. Ol-v-r W-nd-l H-lmes, III. BOHV; InMe
By H-y W. L-ngf-w, I. BOHV; InMe
By J-hn Gr-nl-f Wh-t-r, II. BOHV; InMe
By N. P. W-ll-is, VI. BOHV; InMe
By R-lph W-ldo Em-r-n, IV. BOHV; InMe
(Parodies.) ALV
By Th-m-s B-il-y Ald-ch, VII. BOHV; InMe
By W-ll-m C-ll-n B-y-nt, V. BOHV; InMe
Rejected Offer, The. Sir John Suckling. *See* Proffered Love Rejected.
Rejoice. Joaquin Miller. PAH
Rejoice,/ Ye woods and fountains. Epithalamium. *Unknown.* SeCL
Rejoice! Another revolutionist. The Imprisoned Revolutionist. Mihran Damadian. PoFr
Rejoice, Be Glad. Carlton Buck. SoP
Rejoice! He Liveth! Kathryn Blackburn Peck. BePJ
Rejoice in God. Christopher Smart. *Fr.* Jublilate Agno. AtBAP
("Rejoice in God, O ye tongues.") EiCP; EiPP
Rejoice in God, O ye. Psalm XXXIII. *Paraphrased by* Sir Philip Sidney. FCP
Rejoice in the Abyss. Stephen Spender. OnHM
Rejoice in the Lamb. Christopher Smart. *See* My Cat Jeoffry.
Rejoice, O Bridegroom! *Unknown, tr. fr. Hebrew by* Israel Abrahams. TrJP
Rejoice, O Youth, in the Lovely Hind. Moses ibn Ezra, *tr. fr. Hebrew by* Solomon Solis-Cohen. TrJP
Rejoice, rejoice, brave patriots, rejoice! Reparation or War. *Unknown.* PAH
Rejoice, rejoice, O soul, be glad. Rejoice, Be Glad. Carlton Buck. SoP
Rejoice, ye nations, vindicate the sway. British Commerce. John Dyer. *Fr.* The Fleece. OBEC
Rejoicing at the Arrival of Ch'en Hsiung. Po Chü-i, *tr. fr. Chinese by* Arthur Waley. AWP
Rejoicing in Hope. Augustus Montague Toplady. BePJ
Rejoicing in Hope. Charles Wesley. SoP
Rejoyce whyle in thy youth thou art. *Unknown.* SeCSL
Relapse, The. Thomas Stanley. AnAnS-2; OBEV; SeCL
Relapse, The. Henry Vaughan. AnAnS-1; MeP
Relating to Robinson. Weldon Kees. NaP; TwAmPo
Relating to the care of souls. Maximus to Gloucester, Letter 19. Charles Olson. NMP
Relation of the Late Royal Entertainment Given by the Lord Knowles, A, *sels.* Thomas Campion.
"Can you the author of our joy." SiCE
Night as Well as Brightest Day. TuPP
"Welcome to this flowery place." SiCE
Relations. Alessandro Tassoni, *tr. fr. Italian by* Lorna de' Lucchi. WoL
Relativity. Kathleen Millay. PoMa
Relativity. *Unknown. See* Limerick: "There was a young lady named Bright."
Relativity that cloaks the Word, The. Two Morsels of Profundity from the Minor Pre-Socratics. John Simon. SiTL
Relaxation. Dick Gallup. ANYP
Releas'd from the noise of the butcher and baker. Jinny the Just. Matthew Prior. CABL; CEP; OBEV (new ed.); PoEL-3
Release. D. H. Lawrence. CMoP
Release. Jean Grigsby Paxton. OQP
Release. Peter Schjeldahl. ANYP
Relent, my dear yet unkind Coelia. Coelia, XVII. William Percy. Sonn; TUPP
Relentless, black on white, the cable runs. T-Bar. P. K. Page. OBCV
Relentless press of little things. The Lien. Adelaide Love. MoSiPe
Reliance. Henry van Dyke. FaFP
Relic, The. John Donne. *See* Relique, The.
Relic, The. Robert Hillyer. GoYe; UnS
Relics. George Frederick Cameron. PeCV
Relics, The. Harry Mathews. ANYP
Relics of Saints. Cardinal Newman. JKCP
Relief of Lucknow, The. Robert Traill Spence Lowell. HBV; StPo
Relief on Easter Eve, The. Thomas Pestel. CBEP; OxBoCh; SeCL
Relieved, I let the book fall behind a stone. Depressed by a Book of Bad Poetry, I Walk toward an Unused Pasture and Invite the Insects to Join Me. James Wright. PIA
Relieving Guard. Bret Harte. RoGo
Religio Laici. John Dryden. AnAnS-2; CEP; EiPP; NoP; SeCV-2; SeEP
Sels.
"Dim, as the borrow'd beams of moon and stars." EiCL; OxBoCh; PeRV; ViBoPo, *br. sel.*
(Finite Reason.) LoBV
(Reason and Religion, *br. sel.*) FiP
(Reason and Revelation.) OBS, *longer sel.*; PoLi, *longer sel.*
Priestcraft and Private Judgement. OBS
Scriptures, The. OBS
"Thus man by his own strength." WGRP
Tradition. OBS; PoLi
Religio Medici, *sel.* Sir Thomas Browne.
Evening Hymn. MaRV; OxBoCh
(Colloquy with God, A.) OBS; SeCL
Religio Novissima. Aubrey Thomas De Vere. IrPN; NBM
Religion. Robert Browning. *Fr.* Mr. Sludge, "The Medium." MaRV; SoP
Religion. John Donne. *See* Satire III: "Kind pity chokes my spleen . . ."
Religion. Heine, *tr. fr. German by* Louis Untermeyer. LiTW
Religion. Henry Vaughan. AnAnS-1; MeP; OBS; OxBoCh
Religion. Jean Vauquelin de la Fresnaye, *tr. fr. French by* Wilfrid Thorley. CAW
Religion and Doctrine. John Hay. MaRV; StJW; WGRP
Religion Is a Fortune I Really Do Believe, *with music. Unknown.* BoAN-2
Religion is of faith indeed. Faith. Hugh O. Isbell. ChIP
Religion of Hudibras, The. Samuel Butler. *Fr.* Hudibras, I, i. BOHV; InMe
(For All Fanatics.) PoFr
("For his religion it was fit.") LoBV; ViBoPo
(Presbyterian, The.) FOL
(Sir Hudibras's Religion.) FaBoEn
Religion's all or nothing; it's no mere smile. Religion. Robert Browning. *Fr.* Mr. Sludge, "The Medium." MaRV; SoP
Religious faith is a most filling vapor. Innate Helium. Robert Frost. ImOP
Religious Isolation. Matthew Arnold. EPN; MBW-2
Religious Musings, *sels.* Samuel Taylor Coleridge.
Desultory Poem, A, Written on the Christmas Eve of 1794. EnRP
"There is one Mind, one omnipresent Mind." WGRP
"Toy-bewitched." WGRP
Religious Unity. Hartley Coleridge. MaRV
Religious Use of Taking Tobacco, A. *At. to* Robert Wisdome. ElL; HBV; OBS; SeEP
(Pipe and Can.) OBEV
Relique, The. John Donne. AnAnS-1; AnFE; AtBAP; MaMe; MBW-1; MeLP; MePo; OAEP; OBS; PoEL-2; ReIE; SCEP-1; SeCP; SeCV-1; SeEP; ViBoPo

Relique (continued)
(Relic, The.) CABA; CBEP; ElL; EnRePo; EP; ILP; LiTB; LiTG; LoBV; MaPo; MyFE; NoP; PoeP; ReEn; SeCeV; StP; TuPP; WHA
Reliques, *sel.* Edmund Blunden.
"And mathematics, fresh as May," 2 *ll.* ImOP
Reluctance. Robert Frost. AmPP; CMoP; ExPo; GTBS-D; MAP; MoAB; MoAmPo; OxBA; Po; PoFS
Reluctances. Harold Witt. NYTB
Reluctant Lady, The. *Unknown. See* Maiden's Denial, A.
Reluctantly I laid aside my smiles. The Journey. Mary Berri Hansbrough. AA
Relying on the disasters o' the war. March, 1941. Paul Goodman. LiTA
Remain, ah not in youth alone. Walter Savage Landor. *See* Appeal, The.
Remainder. Frederika Blankner. GoYe
Remains, The. Mark Strand. NYBP
Remarkable truly, is art! Limerick. Gelett Burgess. HBV
Rembrandt alone could paint this mammoth shed. The Roundhouse. William Rose Benét. PoMa
Remedy Worse than the Disease, The. Matthew Prior. ALV; BOHV; HBV; TrGrPo
(I Sent for Ratcliffe.) TOP
Remeidis of Luve. *Unknown.* OxBS
Remember. William Johnson Cory. OBVV; TOP
Remember. Georgia Douglas Johnson. PoNe
Remember [*parody on* Christina Rossetti]. "Judy." ALV
Remember. Christina Rossetti. AnEnPo; AnFE; AWP; BoLiVe; CH; EnLi-2; EnLoPo; FaBoEn; FaBV; GTBS; GTBS-D; GTSL; HBV; JAWP; MaRV; MCCG; MemP; NeHB; NoP; OAEP; OBEV; OBNC; OBVV; OQP; OuHeWo; PoLF; PoPo; PoRA; PoVP; TOP; TreFS; TrGrPo; VA; ViBoPo; ViPo; VP; WBP; WePo; WHA
(Remember Me.) MeWo
("Remember me when I am gone away.") EG
(Sonnet: "Remember me when I am gone away.") LoBV
"But if the darkness and corruption leave," *sel.* LO
Remember. *Unknown.* SoP
Remember Also Thy Creator. Ecclesiastes, Bible, *O.T. See* Remember Now Thy Creator.
Remember he was poor and country-bred. Abraham Lincoln. Mildred Plew Meigs. PAL; TiPo
Remember it, although you're far away. Remember. "Judy." ALV
Remember man that passeth by. An Epitaph and a Reply. *Unknown.* TreFS; TreFT
Remember May? Rhyme for Remembrance of May. Richard Burton. HBMV
Remember Me. Keith Douglas. NeBP; OnHM
(Simplify Me When I'm Dead.) NePoEA
Remember Me! Thomas Haweis. BePJ
Remember Me, Gulls! Joseph Auslander. YT
Remember Me. Christina Rossetti. *See* Remember.
Remember me when I am dead. Remember Me [*or* Simplify Me When I'm Dead]. Keith Douglas. NeBP; NePoEA; OnHM
Remember me when I am gone away. Remember [*or* Sonnet]. Christina Rossetti. AnEnPo; AnFE; AWP; BoLiVe; CH; EG; EnLi-2; EnLoPo; FaBoEn; FaBV; GTBS; GTBS-D; GTSL; HBV; JAWP; LoBV; MaRV; MCCG; MemP; MeWo; NeHB; NoP; OAEP; OBEV; OBNC; OBVV; OQP; OuHeWo; PoLF; PoPo; PoRA; PoVP; TOP; TreFS; TrGrPo; VA; ViBoPo; ViPo; VP; WBP; WePo; WHA
Remember, Mother, when I said right here. Look, the Soliders! Felix V. Ramos. PoFr
Remember Not. Helene Johnson. BANP; PoNe
Remember now, my Love, what piteous thing. A Carrion. Baudelaire. LiTW
Remember Now Thy Creator. Ecclesiastes, XII: 1-7, Bible, *O.T.* AWP; ChTr (1-8); EnLi-1 (1949 ed.) (1-8); JAWP; LiTW; MaRV; ShBV-1; TreF (1-14); WBP
(Remember Also Thy Creator.) ExPo
(Remember Then Thy Creator, 1-8.) TrJP
(Youth and Age.) OuHeWo (XI: 1-XII: 7); TrGrPo (XII: 1-8)
Remember or Forget. Hamilton Aïdé. HBV; VA
"Remember Pearse," he said; "If we/ Lose Irish we lose Ireland." The Orator. Roy McFadden. OnYI
Remember, Phyllis. Honeymoon. Samuel L. Albert. GoYe
Remember Richard, lately king of price. The Tudor Rose. Sebastian Brant, *tr. by* Alexander Barclay. *Fr.* The Ship of Fools. ACP
Remember September. May Justus. SiSoSe; YeAr
Remember that we are dust. It is said. Camel. W. S. Merwin. NePA
Remember the blackness of that flesh. Memento. Stephen Spender. AtBAP
Remember the covenant of our youth. A Dying Wife to Her Husband. Moses ibn Ezra. TrJP
Remember the Day of Judgment. *Unknown. See* Every Day Thou Might Lere.
Remember the day the sea turned red. Plankton. Ruth Miller. PeSA
Remember the Last Things. *Unknown.* MeEL
Remember the Promise, Dakotah. Robert V. Carr. PoOW
Remember the pure machine. Heart. MacKnight Black. AnAmPo
Remember the Source. Richard Eberhart. MoRP
Remember the spider. Tanist. James Stephens. NYTB; OnYI
Remember the sun in the autumn, its rays. Abraham Sutzkever. *Fr.* The Secret Town. TrJP
Remember Thee! Remember Thee! Byron. PoG; ViBoPo
Remember Then Thy Creator. Ecclesiastes, Bible, *O.T. See* Remember Now Thy Creator.
Remember three things come not back. Three Things Come Not Back. *Unknown.* MaRV; OQP
Remember, though the Telescope Extend. George Dillon. ImOP
Remember, though we cannot write it, the delicate dream. Rainy Summer. Ruth Pitter. MoVE; UnPo (3d ed.)
Remember Thy Covenant. Edith Lovejoy Pierce. MoRP
Remember us poor Mayers all! The Song of the Mayers. *Unknown.* CH
Remember what I promised you. Way Out in Idyho. *Unknown.* CoSo
Remember when you hear them beginning to say Freedom. Notes for My Son. Alex Comfort. *Fr.* The Song of Lazarus. LiTM (1970 ed.); MoBrPo (1950 ed.); NeBP; SeCePo
Remember Your Lovers. Sidney Keyes. WaP
Remember, youth will not last more. Advice to a Young Man (of Letters) Who Doesn't Know How to Take Care of Himself. Irwin Edman. InMe
Remembered Grace. Coventry Patmore. The Unknown Eros, I, xxiii. OxBoCh
Remembering. "Michael Lewis," *after the Chinese. Fr.* Cherry Blossoms. UnTE
Remembering Althea. William Stafford. NYBP
Remembering Calvary. Ethel Fanning Young. OQP
Remembering Day. Mary Wright Saunders. DD; HH; OTPC (1946 ed.); PEDC; YeAr
Remembering Golden Bells. Po Chü-i, *tr. fr. Chinese by* Arthur Waley. AtBAP; AWP; JAWP; WBP
Remembering his taste for blood. Of Baiting the Lion. Sir Owen Seaman. BOHV; NA
Remembering Lincoln. Frank Mundorf. GoYe
Remembering Nat Turner. Sterling A. Brown. PoNe
Remembering now, my love, what piteous thing. A Carrion. Baudelaire. AWP
Remembering one day when your wide eyes. Repeated in Thin Gold. Marya Zaturenska. NYTB
Remembering Snow. R. N. Currey. PeSA
Remembering That Island. Thomas McGrath. NePoEA; PPON
Remembering the past/ And gloating at it now. What the Bones Know. Carolyn Kizer. NePoAm-2
Remembering the Strait of Belle Isle or. Large Bad Picture. Elizabeth Bishop. MiAP; NYBP
Remembering the swan upon her nest. The Swan's Nest. Pamela Griffin. BoPe
Remembering the 'Thirties. Donald Davie. NePoEA; PP
Remembering the Winter. Rowena Bennett. SiSoSe
Remembering what passed. Old Scent of the Plum Tree. Fujiwara Ietaka. AWP
Remembrance. John Henry Boner. AA
Remembrance. Emily Brontë. BoPe; BWP; CH; EnLi-2; EnLit; EnLoPo; FaBoEn; FaFP; ForPo; GTBS-D; GTBS-W; GTSL; HBV; LiTB; LiTG; LiTL; LO; MasP; OAEP; OBEV (1st ed.); OBNC; OxBI; PoEL-5; PoIE; PoVP; TreFT; TrGrPo
(R. Alcona to J. Brenzaida, *complete vers.*) PeER
Remembrance. Margaret E. Bruner. PoToHe

Remembrance. John Bunker. JKCP (1955 ed.)
Remembrance, *sel.* John Clare.
Enclosure. NBM
Remembrance. Leslie Savage Clark. ChIP
Remembrance, A. Willis Gaylord Clark. AA
Remembrance. Walter de la Mare. CMoP
Remembrance. Ibnu'l-Farid, *tr. fr. Arabic by* R. A. Nicholson. LiTW
Remembrance. Aline Kilmer. CAW
Remembrance. George Parsons Lathrop. AA
Remembrance. Rainer Maria Rilke, *tr. fr. German by* Paul Engle. ReMP
Remembrance. Shakespeare. *See* Sonnets, XXX.
Remembrance. Antoni Slonimski, *tr. fr. Polish by* Frances Notley. TrJP
Remembrance. Grace V. Watkins. SoP
Remembrance. Sir Thomas Wyatt. *See* Lover Showeth How He Is Forsaken of Such as He Sometime Enjoyed.
Remembrance of Collins. Wordsworth. PeER
Remembrance of Some English Poets, A. Richard Barnfield. ReIE; SiCE; TuPP
Remembrance of that most heroic spirit. To the Right Honorable and Most Virtuous Lady, The Countess of Pembroke. Spenser. Sonn
Remembrance of Things Past. Shakespeare. *See* Sonnets, XXX.
Remembrancer of joys long passed away. To a Golden Heart, Worn round His Neck. Goethe. AWP; JAWP; LiTW; WBP
Remembrances. John Clare. CBEP; NCEP; PeER
Rememorised, Maurice Devane. Austin Clarke. *Fr.* Mnemosyne Lay in Dust. OPoP
Remind you, that there was darkness in my heart. Canticle of Darkness. Wilfred Watson. ACV; MoCV
Reminder, The. Léonie Adams. MoVE
Reminder. John Galsworthy. OQP
Reminder, The. Thomas Hardy. CMoP
Reminder. *Unknown.* STF
Reminiscence. Thomas Bailey Aldrich. AA; AnAmPo
Reminiscence, *sel.* Padraic Colum.
"I saw the wind to-day!" GoJo; LOW
(Wind, The.) PDV; RoGo; SUS
Reminiscence. Wallace Irwin. FiBHP
Reminiscence of 1820, A, *sel.* H. H. Dugmore.
"And this is now their home." ACV
Reminiscences of a Dancing Man. Thomas Hardy. MoVE
Reminiscences of a Day, *sel.* John Francis O'Donnell.
"O dim delicious heaven of dreams." IrPN
Reminiscences of a Landlord. Elizabeth J. Coatsworth. *See* After Christmas a Landlord Remembers.
Rémon, *with music.* *Unknown,* *tr. fr. French.* TrAS
Remonstrance. Sidney Lanier. AmePo
Remonstrance. Philodemos the Epicurean, *tr. fr. Greek by* Dudley Fitts. LiTW
Remonstrance to the King. William Dunbar. OxBS
R-e-m-o-r-s-e. George Ade. ALV; FiBHP; TreFT
Remorse. John Betjeman. MoBrPo (1962 ed.)
Remorse. Byron. *Fr.* On This Day I Complete My Thirty-sixth Year. MaRV
Remorse, (Osorio), *sel.* Samuel Taylor Coleridge.
Dungeon, The, *fr.* V, i. MCCG
Invocation, An. OAEP
(Hear, Sweet Spirit.) ViBoPo
(Song: "Hear, sweet spirit.") MCCG
(Song from "Osorio.") TOP
(Voice Sings, A.) CAW; CH
Remorse. Sydney Dayre. DD
Remorse. Pierre Louys, *tr. fr. French by* Horace M. Brown. *Fr.* The Songs of Bilitis. UnTE
Remorse. Shakespeare. *Fr.* Macbeth, V, iii. MaRV
("Canst thou not minister to a mind diseased?") TRV
(Mind Diseased, A, *longer sel.*) TreFT
Remorse. Shelley. *See* Stanzas—April, 1814.
Remorse. Tennyson. *Fr.* Idylls of the King: Guinevere. MaRV
Remorse after Death. Baudelaire, *tr. fr. French by* Arthur Symons. OnPM
Remorse for Time, The. Howard Nemerov. Sonn
Remorse is memory awake. Emily Dickinson. NoP
Remorsefully,/ Upon my bed. Forgiveness. Lois Duffield. SoP
Remote and ineffectual Don. Lines to a Don. Hilaire Belloc. MoBrPo; OtMeF
Remote Bermudas, The. Shakespeare. *See* Ariel's Song: "Come unto these yellow sands."
Remote from citys liv'd a swain. The Shepherd and the Philosopher. John Gay. *Fr.* Fables. CEP; EiCL
Remote from smoky cities, aged and grey. Sonnet. Thomas Caulfield Irwin. IrPN
Remote in the dream perspective of the street. Effect of Military Music on a Welfare-Worker. Laurence Whistler. MuSP
Remote, unfriended, melancholy, slow. The Traveller. Goldsmith. CEP; EiPP EnPE; OAEP; ViBoPo
Remove away that black'ning church. An Ancient Proverb. Blake. ERoP-1
"Remove this thorn, dear Lord," in vain I cried. God's Will. Oswald J. Smith. SoP
Renaissance. Robert Avrett. GoYe
Renascence. Muredach J. Dooher. OnYI
Renascence. Edna St. Vincent Millay. AmPP; FaFP; HBV; MAP; MoAB; MoAmPo; NeMA; NePA; OHFP; PFY; TIHL; TwAmPo, *sl. abr.*
Sels.
"All I could see from where I stood." PDV
"World stands out on either side, The." MaRV
Rencontre. Jessie Fauset. CDC
Rend America asunder. The Ship Canal from the Atlantic to the Pacific. Francis Lieber. PAH
Render unto Caesar. Rolfe Humphries. CrMA
Rendezvous, The. Jack Anderson. ThO
Rendezvous, The. Catullus, *tr. fr. Latin by* George Lamb. OnPM
Rendezvous. Mary Scott Fitzgerald. PoToHe (new ed.)
Rendezvous. Robert Hillyer. MoLP
Rendezvous. Antonia Pozzi, *tr. fr. Italian by* Glauco Cambon. OnPM
Rendezvous, The. Alan Seeger. *See* I Have a Rendezous with Death.
Rendezvous, The. Bernard Spencer. GTBS-P
Rendezvous with America, *sel.* Melvin Tolson.
"New Negro strides upon the continent, The." WOW
Rendezvous with God, *sel.* Mehdi Ali Seljouk.
"There was one in the myriad throngs." BoPe
Renegado, The, *sel.* Philip Massinger.
"Yet there's one scruple with which I am much," *fr.* V, i. ACP (1952 ed.)
Renewal. Gladys Cromwell. AnAmPo; NP
Renewal. "Michael Field." OBVV
Renewal, A. James Merrill. PoPl
Renounce those threads of twisted gold that close. To a Beautiful but Heartless Coquette. Francisco de Terrazas. LiTW
Renouncement. Alice Meynell. AnFE; BoLP; BoPe; CAW; EnLit; GTSL; HBV; LiTL; LO; MeWo; MoBrPo; OBEV; OBMV; OBNC; OBVV; PoVP; Sonn; TOP; TreFT; VA; ViBoPo
Renouncing of Hardly Escaped Love, A. Sir Thomas Wyatt. ReIE
("Farewell the reign of cruelty.") SiPS
Renouncing of Love, A. Sir Thomas Wyatt. BEL; EnLi-1 (1949 ed.); EnLit; FaBoEn; LiTL; OAEP; ReIE; Sonn; StP; TOP; TuPP
("Farewell, love, and all thy laws for ever.") EnPo; FCP; LiTB; ReEn; SiCE; SiPS; YAT
(Lover Renounceth Love, The.) TrGrPo
Renowned Generations, The. W. B. Yeats. OxBoLi
Renownèd Spenser [*or* Spencer], lie a thought more nigh. Elegy on Shakespeare [*or* on Mr. Wm. Shakespeare]. William Basse. CBEP; CLwM; EIL; OBS; SeEP; ViBoPo
Rented Garden, The. Bink Noll. ToPo
Renunciants. Edward Dowden. OBVV; VA
Renunciation. Wathen Mark Wilks Call. OBVV; WGRP
Renunciation, A. Thomas Campion. *See* Thou Art Not Fair.
Renunciation. Emily Dickinson. *See* There came a day at summer's full.
Renunciation. Henry King. OBEV
Renunciation. Richard Chenevix Trench. SoP
Renunciation, A. Edward de Vere, Earl of Oxford. *See* If Women Could Be Fair.
Reparation. Helen Hoyt. HBMV
Reparation or War. *Unknown.* PAH
Repartee. *Unknown.* *See* Epigram: "Loud brayed an Ass."

Repartee (continued)
Repast. Gertrude Tiemer-Wille. GoYe
Repeat That, Repeat. Gerard Manley Hopkins. *See* Cuckoo, The.
Repeated in Thin Gold. Marya Zaturenska. NYTB
Repeated Journey, The. Thomas McGrath. NePoEA
Repeated Pilgrimage. John Gilland Brunini. GoBC
Repent, O ye, predestinate to woe! The Conscience-Keeper. William Young. *Fr.* Wishmakers' Town. AA
Repentance. George Chapman. *Fr.* Hero and Leander, Third Sestiad. OBSC
Repentance. Thomas Curtis Clark. ChIP
Repentance. George Herbert. MaMe; OAEP
Repetitions. Carl Sandburg. HBMV; NP
Repetitions of a Young Captain. Wallace Stevens. WaP
Repetitive Heart, The, *sels.* Delmore Schwartz.
All Clowns Are Masked, III. LiTA; OxBA; ViBoPo
All of Us Always Turning Away for Solace, I. OxBA
"Calmly we walk through this April's day," IV. MoVE
(For Rhoda.) MoAB; MoAmPo; OxBA
(Time Is the Fire.) LiTA; LiTM
Dog Named Ego [the Snowflakes as Kisses], A, X. AmP; LiTA; LiTM; MiAP
Heavy Bear Who Goes with Me, The, IX. AmLP; AnAmPo; CBV; CrMA; FiMAP; LiTA; LiTG; LiTM; MiAP; MoPo; MoVE; NePA; PIA; ReMP; TrJP; TwCP; UnPo (3d ed.)
Will You Perhaps, II. FiMAP
("Mentrechè il Vento, Come Fa, Si Tace.") AnFE; CoAnAm; TwAmPo
Repine not, Gray, that our weak dazzled eyes. To Mr. Gray. David Garrick. OBEC
Reply. Janet Norris Bangs. OQP
Reply, A. Cecil Browne. SiTL
Reply. Hartley Coleridge. OBRV
Reply. Sidney Godolphin. OBS
Reply, The. John Norris. PeRV
Reply, A. Pope, *See* Epigram: "Sir, I admit your general rule." *also at. to* Matthew Prior.
Reply. Sir Walter Ralegh. *See* Nymph's Reply to the Shepherd, The.
Reply, The. Theodore Roethke. NoP; NYBP
Reply. Sir Ronald Ross. *See* Lines Written after the Discovery by the Author of the Germ of Yellow Fever.
Reply from the Akond of Swat, A. Ethel Talbot Scheffauer. FiBHP
Reply, in the Same Measure and Number of Lines, A [Horace, 2d Ode, 3d Book]. Walter Titley. EiCL
Reply of Socrates, The. Edith M. Thomas. WGRP
Reply to a Lady Editor. Theodore Roethke. TDP
Reply to an Imitation of the Second Ode in the Third Book of Horace, A. Richard Bentley. *See* Verses: "Who strives to mount Parnassus hill."
Reply to "In Flanders Fields." John Mitchell. BLPA; PAL
Reply to Lines by Thomas Moore, A, *sel.* Walter Savage Landor.
"Will you come to the bower I have shaded for you?" ChTr
Reply to Mr. Wordsworth, *sel.* Archibald MacLeish.
"Space-time, our scientists tell us, is impervious." ImOP
Reply to Nancy Hanks, A. Julius Silberger. TiPo
Reply to the Provinces. Galway Kinnell. NYBP
Re-plyed, extorted, oft transposed, and fleeting. Sea Voyage. William Empson. CMoP
Report, A. Ruth Fainlight. HYE
Report. Robert Finch. TwCaPo
Report. Archibald Fleming MacLiesh. *Fr.* The Jungle. NAMP
Report, The. Jon Swan. NYBP
Report Back. John Cotton. HYE
Report from California. Lois Moyles. NYBP
Report from the Carolinas, *sel.* Helen Bevington.
"It's a debatable land. The winds are variable." AmFN
Report of an Adjudged Case; Not to Be Found in Any of the Books. William Cowper. *See* Nose and the Eyes, The.
Report of the Meeting. Weldon Kees. TwAmPo
Report on Experience. Edmund Blunden. CBEP; FaBoEn; FaBoTw; GTBS-P; LO; MoPW; OBMV; POTE
Report on the Planet, Earth. James Oppenheim. PoMa
Report Song, A. Nicholas Breton. OBSC; SeCePo
(Country Song.) TrGrPo
Report to the Blue Guard. Robert Hershon. ThO
Reporters, The. Newman Levy. InMe
Reports Come In, The. J. D. Reed. NYBP
Repose. Adelaide Anne Procter. *See* Shadows of the Evening Hours, The.
Repose of Rivers. Hart Crane. AP; AWP; CMoP; CoBMV; ExPo; ForPo; FosPo; InPo; LiTM (rev. ed.); MoAB; MoAmPo (1950 ed.); NP; OxBA; PIA; PoIE; SeCeV; TDP
Representing nothing on God's earth now. Lines on the Back of a Confederate Note. Samuel Alroy Jonas. BLPA; PaA
Repression. Timothy Corsellis. WaP
Repression of War Experience. Siegfried Sassoon. BrPo; MMA
Reprieve. Barbara Villy Cormack. CaP
Reprisal[l], The. George Herbert. AnAnS-1; EP; MaMe; MeP; SCEP-1
(Second Thanksgiving, The.) OAEP
Reproach. Firdausi, *tr. fr. Persian by* E. G. Browne. LiTW
Reproach. Robert Graves. GTSL
Reproach to Dead Poets. Archibald MacLeish. CMoP
Reproach to Julia. Robert Graves. ELU
Reproach to Morvyth, A. Dafydd ab Gwilym, *tr. fr. Welsh by* H. Idris Bell. LiTW
Reproaches, The. *Unknown.* WHL
Reproof, A. Proverbs, VI: 6-11, Bible, *O.T.* TrGrPo
(Go to the Ant [Thou Sluggard].) FaPON (6-8); LiTW; TreFT; TrJP
(Sluggard, The—a Sonnet, *Moulton, Modern Reader's Bible.*) MaRV
Reproof. *Unknown.* STF
Reptilian green the wrinkled throat. Sir Gawaine and the Green Knight. Yvor Winters. AnFE; CoAnAm; MoVE; PoIE; PoRA (rev. ed.); QFR; TwAmPo
Republic, The. Longfellow. *See* Ship of State, The.
Republic, forever, the land of the free. Hymn of the Soviet Union. Sergei Mikhalkov *and* El-Registan. PoFr
Republic of the West. On a Rhine Steamer. James Kenneth Stephen. England and America, I. InMe; NBM
Republic of the World. Victor Hugo. *See* Universal Republic, The.
Republic to Republic. Witter Bynner. PAH
Republican Genius of Europe, The. Philip Freneau. AmPP (3d ed.)
Repulse, The. Thomas Stanley. AnAnS-2; LO; MeLP; MePo; OBS
Request, The. Abraham Cowley. AnAnS-2
Request. Barbara Marshall. TNV
Request for a Song. Julian Tuwim, *tr. fr. Polish by* Jack Lindsay. LiTW
Request for Requiems. Langston Hughes. ShM
Request Number. G. N. Sprod. FiBHP
Requests. Digby Mackworth Dolben. *See* I Asked for Peace.
Requiem. Carl Bode. ToPo
Requiem. Thomas Curtis Clark. PEDC
Requiem. Nathalia Crane. *Fr.* The Death of Poetry. MoAmPo (1942 ed.)
Requiem. Robert Davenport. *Fr.* King John and Matilda. SeCL
("Matilda, now go take thy bed.") TuPP
Requiem. Kenneth Fearing. CMoP
Requiem. Joseph Lee. DD; OHIP
Requiem. George Lunt. AA; PaA
Requiem. John Frederick Matheus. CDC
Requiem. Theodore Maynard. GoBC
Requiem, A. Herman Melville. *See* Requiem for Soldiers Lost in Ocean Transports, A.
Requiem. Ogden Nash. SiTL
Requiem. Conal O'Riordan. HBV
Requiem. Sir Joseph Noel Paton. VA
Requiem. Kathleen Raine. NeBP
Requiem. Christina Rossetti. *See* Song: "When I am dead, my dearest."
Requiem. William Stafford. NaP
Requiem. Robert Louis Stevenson. AnFE; ATP; BBV; BrPo; DD; EPN; FaBV; FaPL; GoTP; GoTS; GTSL; HBV; HBVY; ILP; InP; LiTG; MaRV; MCCG; MoBrPo; MPB; NeHB; NeMa; OBEV; OBNC; OBVV; OQP; OtMeF; OTPC; PCD; PoFS; PoIE; PoLF; PoPl; PoRA; PoSa; PoVP; ShBV-2; TIHL; TOP; TreF; TrGrPo; TSW; VA; ViBoPo; WaKn; WGRP; WHA; YAT; YT
Requiem, A. James Thomson. EnLit; HBV
Requiem. William Thomas Walsh. JKCP (1955 ed.)
Requiem. Hamilton Warren. GoYe
Requiem, *sels.* Humbert Wolfe.

"Feathers in a fan, The." POTE
Man. MoBrPo
Saint, The ("Do you remember, Joan"). CAW
Requiem for a Dead Warrior. Edgar McInnis. PEDC
Requiem for a Modern Croesus. Lew Sarett. MaRV
Requiem for a Young Soldier. Florence Earle Coates. OHIP
Requiem for an Abstract Artist. Jascha Kessler. AmPC
Requiem for "Bird" Parker. Gregory Corso. PoNe (1970 ed.)
Requiem for Soldiers Lost in Ocean Transports, A. Herman Melville. PoEL-5
(Requiem, A.) GTBS-D
Requiescat. Matthew Arnold. AWP; BEL; BoLiVe; BoPe; DD; ELP; EnLi-2; EnLit; EPN; FiP; GTBS; GTBS-D; GTBS-W; GTSL; HBV; ILP; InP; InPo; InvP; JAWP; LiTB; LiTG; LiTL; MaVP; MBW-2; NoP; OAEP; OBEV; OBVV; OHIP; OuHeWo; PG; PoFS; PoRA; PoSa; PoVP; TOP; TreFS; TrGrPo; ViBoPo; ViPo; ViPP; VP; WBP; WHA
Requiescat. Katherine Anne Porter. HBMV
Requiescat. Frederick George Scott. DD; OHIP
Requiescat. Rosamund Marriott Watson. HBV
Requiescat. Oscar Wilde. BrPo; EnLit; GTSL; HBV; InvP; MoBrPo; NeMA; OBNC; OBVV; OnYI; OxBI; PeVV; PoVP; TreF; TrGrPo; ViPP; WePo; WHA
Required Course. Frances Stoakley Lankford. GoYe
Required of You This Night. Peter Redgrove. NMP
Requirements: "Not for me a giantess." Nicarchus, *tr. fr. Greek by* Wallace Rice. ErPo
Requirements: "Not too chary, not too fast." Rufinus, *tr. fr. Greek by* Wallace Rice. ErPo
Requirements: "Not too lean, and not too fat." Rufinus, *tr. fr. Greek by* Wallace Rice. ErPo
Requirements: "Not too old, and not too young." Honestus, *tr. fr. Greek by* Wallace Rice. ErPo
Requirements: "Not too pallid, as if bleacht." Xenos Palaestes, *tr. fr. Greek by* Wallace Rice. ErPo
Requital. Adelaide Anne Procter. VA
Re-run. Winfield Townley Scott. FiMAP
Res Publica. J. A. R. McKellar. MoAuPo
Rescue. Olive Tilford Dargan. GoYe
Rescue, The. John Logan. CMoP; NYBP
Rescue. Dabney Stuart. NYBP
Rescue. James Tate. YAP
Rescuing gate is wide, The. Like a Mourningless Child. Kenneth Patchen. MoAmPo
Resembles life what once was deem'd of light. What Is Life? Samuel Taylor Coleridge. ERoP-1; FiP
Resentments Composed because of the Clamor of Town Topers Outside My Apartment. Sarah Kemble Knight. SCAP
Reservation. David McCord. WhC
Reserve. Richard Aldington. BrPo
Reserve. Lizette Woodworth Reese. AA
Reserve. Mary Ashley Townsend. AA
Reserved. Walter de la Mare. GTBS-P
Residence at Cambridge. Wordsworth. The Prelude, III. MBW-2
Residence in France. Wordsworth. *See* Prelude, The.
Residence in France (Continued). Wordsworth. *See* French Revolution, The.
Residence in London. Wordsworth. *See* Prelude, The.
Resident of Spider Hill, A. Spidersilk. John Nixon, Jr. NYTB
Resident Worm, The. James Hayford. NePoAm-2
Resignation. Matthew Arnold. MaVP; OAEP; PoVP; ViPP; VP
Resignation. Mother Francis d'Assisi. WHL
Resignation. Walter Savage Landor. *See* Why, Why Repine.
Resignation. Longfellow. CoBA; HBV; MaRV, *shorter vers.*
"There is no Death. What seems so is transition." SoP; TRV
Resignation. Seumas MacManus. JKCP
Resignation. Santob de Carrion, *tr. fr. Spanish by* George Ticknor. TrJP
Resignation. William L. Stidger. ChIP
Resignation. *Unknown.* OBSC
Resignation. Sir Thomas Wyatt. *See* In Faith Methinks It Is No Right.
Resist me/ Make me strong. Saga of Resistance. Sun-Ra. BF
Resisted by the tangle. Walking in Bush. Basil Dowling. AnNZ
Resolute Cat, The. Nancy Byrd Turner. RIS
Resolute Courtier, The. Thomas Shipman. ErPo; LO; SeCL
Resolution. Ted Berrigan. ANYP
Resolution. Carlton Buck. SoP
Resolution. W. S. Merwin. NYBP
Resolution, The. Vassar Miller. CoPo
Resolution. Henry More. OxBoCh
Resolution. Charles L. O'Donnell. GoBC; TrPWD
Resolution. "Wiolar." InMe
Resolution and Independence. Wordsworth. BEL; CABA; CBEP; ChER; DiPo; EnL; EnLi-2; EnLit; EnRP; EPN; ERoP-1; LiTB; MasP; MBW-2; MERP; OAEP; OBNC; OBRV; PAn; PeER; PIA; PoE; PoEL-4; ShBV-4
Sels.
"I thought of Chatterton, the marvellous boy." ML
"Now, whether it were by peculiar grace." Par
"There was a roaring in the wind all night," *first* 2 *sts.* BoNaP; FlW
(There Was a Roaring in the Wind All Night.) TreFT
Resolution in Four Sonnets, of a Poetical Question Put to Me by a Friend, Concerning Four Rural Sisters. Charles Cotton. CLwM; PeRV; PoEL-3; Sonn
Sels.
Alice. TrGrPo; UnTE
("Alice is tall and upright as a pine.") EG
(Two Rural Sisters.) EnLoPo
Margaret. TrGrPo; UnTE
("Margaret of humbler stature by the head.") EG
(Two Rural Sisters.) EnLoPo
Resolution of Dependence. George Barker. FaBoTw; LiTB; LiTM (rev. ed.)
Resolution; the Song of Hylobaris Concerning Divine Providence. Henry More. OxBoCh
Resolutions?—New and Old. Harvey E. Rolfe. STF
Resolve, The. Alexander Brome. CavP; LiTL; LO; OBEV; SeCL
("Tell me not of a face that's fair.") EG
Resolve, The. Mary, Lady Chudleigh. OBEC
Resolve. Charlotte Perkins Stetson Gilman. OQP; PoToHe; WGRP
Resolve, The. Denise Levertov. WIRo
Resolve. Vassar Miller. TPM
Resolve, The. Henry Vaughan. AnAnS-1; MeP; NCEP
Resolve me, Chloe, what is this. On Beauty; A Riddle. Matthew Prior. CEP
Resolve me, dearest, why two hearts in one. To His Mistresse on Her Scorne. Thomas Beedome. CavP
Resolved. Ottis Shirk. STF
Resolved in time, the sun's attractive force. Eadem Mutato Resurgo. Selden Rodman. OnHM
Resolved to dust, entombed here lieth Love. My Love Is Past [*or* Here Lieth Love *or* Love's Grave]. Thomas Watson. *Fr.* Hecatompathia. ElL; OBSC; TuPP
Resolved to Love, *sel.* Abraham Cowley.
"If Learned in other things you be." LO
Resolved to love, unworthy to obtain. Henry Constable. *Fr.* Diana. Sonn
Resolving Doubts. William Dickey. ErPo
Resonant Silence, A. David Llorens. TNV
Resound my voice, ye woods that hear me plain. Sir Thomas Wyatt. FCP; SiPS
Respect all surfaces. The skater is. In Defense of Superficiality. Elder Olson. NYBP
Respect for the Dead. Laura Riding. LiTA
Respect My Faith. Thomas Campion. TuPP
Respectabilities. Jon Silkin. NePoEA-2
Respectability. Robert Browning. EnLoPo; EPN; MBW-2; PoVP; VA; ViBoPo; ViPP
Respectable Burgher, The. Thomas Hardy. CMoP; ViPo (1962 ed.)
Respectable People. Austin Clarke. NMP
Respice Finem. Thomas Proctor. OBSC; ReIE; SiCE; TuPP
Respice Finem. Francis Quarles. *See* Epigram: Respice Finem.
Respite, The. Maria Gowen Brooks. *Fr.* Zophiel; or, The Bride of Seven. AA
Resplendent precinct of the skies. The Valley of the Heavens. Luis de León. CAW
Resplendent studs of heaven's frame. *Unknown.* SCAP
Respondez! Walt Whitman. AmePo; PoEL-5; WOW, *abr.*
Response. Bob Kaufman. BOLo; Kal

Response to Rimbaud's Later Manner. T. Sturge Moore. OBMV; SyP
Responsibilities. J. C. Hall. HaMV
Responsibilities, *sel.* W. B. Yeats.
"Pardon, old fathers, if you still remain," Prologue. PoEL-5
(Pardon, Old Fathers.) OAEP (2d ed.)
Responsibility. *Unknown.* PV
Responsible sound of the lawnmower, The. Elegy. William Stafford. OPoP
Responsive Reading. Pearl Cleage. WSL
Ressaif My Saul. R. Crombie Saunders. OxBS
Rest. "Æ." POTE
Rest. Annie Clarke. SoP
Rest. Goethe. *See* True Rest.
Rest. Mary Woolsey Howland. *See* In the Hospital.
Rest. George Macdonald. SoP
Rest. Cardinal Newman. OBRV; OBVV
(Refrigerium.) OBNC
Rest, The. Ezra Pound. AmP; AmPP (5th ed.); MAP; MoAB; MoAmPo; OxBA; PP; WOW
Rest. Christina Rossetti. EnLi-2; EPN; GTBS; HBV; OBEV; OBNC; OBVV; TOP; TrGrPo; VP
Rest. *At. to* Bayard Taylor. *See* Not So in Haste, My Heart.
Rest ("Are you very weary?"). *Unknown.* PoToHe
Rest. Margaret L. Woods. VA
Rest and Silence. Georg Trakl, *tr. fr. German by* Werner Heider. LiTW
(Peace and Silence. *tr. by* Glauco Cambon.) OnPM
Rest and Work. Anna Temple Whitney. *See* Kneeling Camel, The.
Rest from Loving and Be Living. C. Day Lewis. CoBMV; MoBrPo; OBMV; POTE; ReMP
Rest, Heart of the Tired World. Kenneth Patchen. ToPo
Rest here, at last. At Last. Philip Bourke Marston. VA
Rest Hour. George Johnston. WHW
Rest in Peace. Wilfred J. Funk. PoLF
Rest Is Not Here. Lady Nairne. HBV
Rest is not quitting. True Rest [*or* Rest]. Goethe. MaRV; OQP; SoP; TreFT; TRV; WBLP
Rest, little Guest. After Annunciation. Anna Wickham. MoBrPo
Rest O Sun I Cannot. Joseph Tusiani. GoYe
Rest of the Weary. *Unknown.* BePJ
Rest on Him. Frances Ridley Havergal. FaChP
(Unfailing One, The.) BLRP
Rest on, O heroes! in your silent slumber! Our Dead Heroes. Rose Terry Cooke. HH
Rest quietly—the world moves toward its end. Two Cats on the Hearth. Bernice Kenyon. CIV
Rest Remaineth. Robert Browning. *Fr.* Christmas-Eve and Easter-Day. OQP; PoRL
Rest! This little fountain runs. For a Fountain [*or* Inscription for a Fountain]. "Barry Cornwall." OBEV (new ed.); OBRV; OBVV
Rest Where You Are. *Unknown, at. to* Charles Poole Cleaves. OQP; SoP, *longer vers.*
Rest ye in peace, ye Flanders dead. America's Answer. R. W. Lillard. BLPA; HH; PAL; PEDC
Restatement of Romance. Wallace Stevens. LiTL; MoLP
Restful place, reviver [*or* renewer] of my smart, The. The Lover to His Bed, with Describing of His Unquiet State. Sir Thomas Wyatt. FCP; ReIE; SiPS; TuPP
Resting. A. B. Simpson. SoP
Resting Figure. Denise Levertov. TDP; ToPo
Restles streame thy self persuinge. *Unknown.* SeCSL
Restless and clamoured by unsparing birds. Christmas Dawn. Fleur Adcock. ACV
Restless as a Wolf. Moishe-Leib Halpern, *tr. fr. Yiddish by* Jacob Sloan. TrJP
Restless Heart, The. Earl of Surrey. SiPS
("Fancy, which that I have served long, The.") FCP
Restless Heart, The. *Unknown, tr. fr. Marathi.* WGRP
Restless sea is calling, and I would be away, The. Voices. James S. Hearst. MoSiPe
Restless State of a Lover, The. Earl of Surrey. GoTL
("Sun hath twice brought forth the tender green, The.") SiPS
Restless, to-night, and ill at ease. In the Dark. Frances Louisa Bushnell. AA
Restoration. Woodridge Spears. GoYe
Restrain your child; you'll soon beleive. The Old Hen and the Cock. John Gay. *Fr.* Fables. EiCP
Restrained/ with branch and young shoot undisclosed. Poplar. Gottfried Benn. PoPl
Restrained Passion. Lady Mary Wortley Montagu. MeWo
Restricted. Eve Merriam. TrJP
Restricted. Miriam Waddington. CaP
Rests Charidas beneath this tomb? Sinister Dialogue. Callimachus. OnPM
Résumé. Dorothy Parker. ALV; PoPl; PoPo; ShM; TrJP; WhC
(Some Beautiful Letters: Résumé.) InMe
Resurgam. W. Nelson Bitton. BLRP
Resurgam. Struthers Burt. HBMV
Resurgam. Emily Dickinson. *See* At last to be identified.
Resurgam. Theodosia Garrison. MaRV
Resurgam. John Richard Moreland. ChIP
Resurgam. Marjorie Pickthall. OBCV
Resurgam ("'I shall arise.' For centuries"). *Unknown.* WGRP
Resurgat. A. S. Cripps. BoSA
Resurge San Francisco. Joaquin Miller. PAH
Resurgence. John L. Bonn. JKCP (1955 ed.)
Resurgence. Laura Bell Everett. PGD
Resurgence. Jalal ed-Din Rumi, *tr. fr. Persian by* E. G. Browne. LiTW
Resurgence. Robert Louis Stevenson. MaRV
(Though He That Ever Kind and True.) BBV
(Verses Written in 1872.) BLPA; NeHB
Resurgent. Richard Linn Edsall. JKCP (1955 ed.)
Resurrection, The. Jonathan Henderson Brooks. AmNP; CDC; PoNe
Resurrection, The. John Gilland Brunini. MaRV
Resurrection. George Crabbe. OxBoCh
Resurrection. John Donne. AnAnS-1; MaMe; MeP; OBS; Sonn; StJW
Resurrection. William Henry Fanning. NYTB
Resurrection. Kenneth Fearing. CMoP
Resurrection. Henry W. Frost. SoP
Resurrection. Paula Giddings. WSL
Resurrection. George Herbert. *See* Peace.
Resurrection. Laurence Housman. *Fr.* Rue, III. MaRV
Resurrection, The. St. John of Damascus. *See* Day of Resurrection, The.
Resurrection. Harry Kemp. HBV
Resurrection. Sidney Lanier. PoEL-5
Resurrection. D. H. Lawrence. NP
Resurrection. Lloyd Frank Merrell. ChIP
Resurrection. Angela Morgan. OQP
Resurrection. Ida Norton Munson. ChIP
Resurrection. Robert Pack. NePoEA-2
Resurrection. Lady Margaret Sackville. HBMV
Resurrection. Agnes W. Storer. ChIP; OQP
Resurrection. Esther H. Turner. SoP
Resurrection. *Unknown.* ChIP; MaRV
Resurrection, The. Nathaniel Wanley. LoBV
Resurrection, The, *sel.* W. B. Yeats.
Two Songs from a Play. CABA; CMoP; ExPo; FosPo; ILP; LiTB; MBW-2; MoPo; NoP; PAn; PoDB; PoFS; PoIE; SeCeV; UnPo
"I saw a staring virgin stand," I. CoBMV
(Song from a Play.) FaBoTw
Resurrection—an Easter Sequence, *sel.* W. R. Rodgers.
"It was a deliberate moment, and O." ACV
Resurrection and Ascension. Earl D. Todd. ChIP
Resurrection and Immortality. Henry Vaughan. AnAnS-1; MeP
Resurrection and the Life, The. Robert Norwood. MaRV
Resurrection Hymn. Michael Weiss. BePJ
Resurrection Imperfect. John Donne. MaMe
Resurrection of Arp. A. J. M. Smith. MoCV
Resurrection Possible and Probable, The. Robert Herrick. ILP; PAn
Resurrection Song. Thomas Lovell Beddoes. ELU; ERoP-2; NBM; PoE
Resurrexit. Henry Longan Stuart. CAW
Retaliation. Margaret E. Bruner. PoToHe
Retaliation. Goldsmith. CEP; EiPP; LaA; OAEP; OxBoLi; TOP, *abr.*
Sels.
David Garrick ("Here lies David Garrick"). CBEP; OBEC; SeCeV

Edmund Burke ("Here lies our good Edmund"). InvP; OBEC; SeCeV
Sir Joshua Reynolds ("Here Reynolds is laid"). OBEC; SeCePo
Reticulations creep upon the slack stream's face. On Sturminster Foot-Bridge. Thomas Hardy. OAEP
Retinue. Paul Verlaine, *tr. fr. French by* C. F. McIntyre. ErPo
Retired Cat, The. William Cowper. BOHV; CIV; OTPC (1923 ed.), *sl. abr.*
Retired Colonel, The. Ted Hughes. CBV; NePoEA-2; PoIE (1970 ed.)
Retired Pork-Butcher and the Spook, The. G. E. Farrow. BOHV
Retired thoughts enjoy their own delights. Look Home. Robert Southwell. TuPP
Retirement, *sel.* James Beattie.
Solitude, *abr.* OBEC
Retirement, The. Charles Cotton. CEP; HBV; OBS
(To Mr. Izaak Walton, *abr.*) BoPe; ViBoPo
Retirement, *sels.* William Cowper.
Absence of Occupation. OBEC
"I praise the Frenchman, his remark was shrewd," *br. sel.* BLPA; NeHB
Statesman in Retirement. OBEC
Retirement ("Far from the world, O Lord, I flee"). William Cowper. SoP
Retirement, The. Thomas Flatman. PeRV
Retirement, The. John Norris. CavP; OBS
Retirement. Richard Chenevix Trench. EPN; OBVV
(Sonnet: "Wretched thing it were, to have our heart, A.") OQP
Retirement ("In youth I served my time"). *Unknown, tr. fr. Irish by* Frank O'Connor. ErPo; KiLC
Retirement, The ("'Tis weak and worldly to conclude"). *Unknown.* OBEC
Retirement, an Ode, *sel.* Thomas Warton, the Elder.
"Joy, rose-lipped dryad, loves to dwell." ViBoPo
Retort. Paul Laurence Dunbar. AA
Retort, The. George Pope Morris. BOHV; HBV
Retort Discourteous, The. Stephen Vincent Benét. HBMV
Retort on the Foregoing. John Scott of Amwell. *See* Drum, The.
Retort to the Anti-Abstractionists. Elizabeth Jennings. BoPe
Retracing Paul Blackburn's Transit, *sel.* Margaret Randall.
"He says we are beggars." WOW
Retractions, *sels.* James Branch Cabell. HBMV
"Although as yet my cure be incomplete," I.
"And therefore praise I even the most high," *closing st.*
"Cry Kismet! and take heart. Eros is gone," XII.
"I am contented by remembrances," II.
"It is in many ways made plain to us," V.
"Nightly I mark and praise, or great or small," XV.
"So, let us laugh—lest vain rememberings," XIV.
"With Love I garnered mirth and dreams, and shame," VI.
"You ask a sonnet? Well, it is your right," *introd. st.*
Retreat. J. K. Clark. NYTB
Retreat, The. Charles Cotton. CBEP; SeCL
Retreat, The. Henry King. AnAnS-2
Retreat, The. Sir Herbert Read. BrPo
Retreat[e], The. Henry Vaughan. AnAnS-1; AtBAP; ATP; AWP; BEL; BoC; BoLiVe; BWP; CABA; CAW; CBEP; CenL; CoBE; EnL; EnLi-1; EnLit; ExPo; FaBoEn; GTBS; GTBS-D; GTBS-P; GTBS-W; GTSE; GTSL; HBV; InPo; InvP; JAWP; LiTB; LiTG; LoBV; MaPo; MeLP; MeP; MePo; NoP; OAEP; OBEV; OBS; PAn; PoAn; PoEL-2; PoFS; PoIE; PoRA; ReEn; SCEP-1; SeCePo; SeCeV; SeCL; SeCP; SeCV-1; SeEP; StP; TOP; TreFT; TrGrPo; UnPo (1st ed.); ViBoPo; WBP; WHA
("Happy those early days when I.") EG; LO, 6 *ll.*
Retreat from Heaven, The. J. A. R. McKellar. MoAuPo
Retreat from Paradise, The. Milton. *Fr.* Paradise Lost, XII. PoEL-3
("He ended; and thus Adam last replied.") CoBE; MyFE
Retreate, The. Henry Vaughan. *See* Retreat, The.
Retribution. Friedrich von Logau, *tr. fr. German by* Longfellow. MaRV; PoToHe; TreF
Retrievers run through the meadow. Exercise in a Meadow. Jean Elliot. GoYe
"Retro Me, Sathana." Dante Gabriel Rossetti. The House of Life, XC. MaVP; NoP; PoVP; ViPo
Retrospect. Rupert Brooke. NP
Retrospect. Pearl Cleage. WSL
Retrospect. Roy Davis. WhC
Retrospect. "An Pilibin." OnYI
Retrospect. Agnes Mary Frances Robinson. OBVV
Retrospect. Chidiock Tichborne. *See* Elegy: "My prime of youth is but a frost of cares."
Retrospect—Love of Nature Leading to Love of Man. Wordsworth. *Fr.* The Prelude, VIII. MBW-2
Retrospection. Hubert Church. AnNZ
Retrospection. Sir Arthur Quiller-Couch. CenHV
Return, The. Conrad Aiken. NePA
Return, The. John Peale Bishop. LiTA; LiTM; MoPo; MoVE; OxBA; TwAmPo; UnPo (3d ed.); WaP
Return, The. Arna Bontemps. CDC; PoNe
Return. Sterling A. Brown. BALP; CDC
Return, The. John Burroughs. MaRV
Return. H. D. Carberry. PoNe
Return. C. P. Cavafy, *tr. fr. Modern Greek by* John Mavrogordato. ErPo
Return, The. Eleanor Rogers Cox. PAH
Return, The. Emily Dickinson. *See* Though I get home how late, how late!
Return! Sydney Dobell. LO; OBEV (1st ed.); OBVV
Return, The. Jessie Fauset. CDC
Return, The. Annie Fields. AA
Return, The. Lloyd Frankenberg. NYTB
Return. Mary S. Hawling. PoMa
Return. Robinson Jeffers. GoYe
Return, The. Kipling. MoBrPo; NeMA
England, *br. sel.* OtMeF
Return, The. George MacBeth. NYBP; OPoP
Return, The. Pittendrigh Macgillivray. GoTS; OxBS
Return. Sister Mary Madeleva. JKCP (1955 ed.)
Return, The. Edna St. Vincent Millay. GTBS-W; InP; LiTA; MAP; MoAB; MoAmPo; MoPo; OxBA; PoPl
Return. Vassar Miller. ToPo
Return, The ("The doors flapped open in Ulysses' house"). Edwin Muir. CMoP; MoPW
Return, The ("The veteran Greeks came home"). Edwin Muir. CMoP; MemP
Return. Adèle Naudé. ACV
Return, The. Martha Ostenso. CaP
Return, The. Ezra Pound. AmPP (5th ed.); AnEnPo; AP; APA; CMoP; CoAnAm; CoBMV; FaBoEn; MAP; MoAB; MoAmPo; MoPo; NAMP; NePA; NP; OxBA; PoAn; TwAmPo; ViBoPo
Return. Earl of Rochester. *See* Song, A: "Absent from thee, I languish still."
Return, The. Muriel Rukeyser. FiMAP
Return, The. Jon Silkin. NePoEA-2
Return, The. L. A. G. Strong. HaMV
Return, The. Swinburne. *See* Sea, The.
Return, The. Arthur Symons. Amor Triumphans, V. BrPo; HBMV
Return, The. Thomas Traherne. SCEP-1
Return, The. Tu Fu, *tr. fr. Chinese by* Robert Payne. LiTW
Return. *Unknown, tr. fr. Chinese by* Arthur Waley. LiTW
Return, The, *sels.* Margaret L. Woods.
Facing the Gulf. HBMV
"Father of Life, with songs of wonder." TrPWD
Return and go again and yet return! Repeated Pilgrimage. John Gilland Brunini. GoBC
Return, Content! for fondly I pursued. The River Duddon, XXVI. Wordsworth. EnLi-2
Return, dear Lord, to those who look. Jesus, Return. Henry van Dyke. SoP; TRV
Return from Egypt, The. Pope Leo XIII, *tr. fr. Latin by* H. T. Henry. CAW
Return from the Freudian Islands, The. A. D. Hope. MoAuPo
Return, Oh Shulamite, Return Return. Edward Taylor. *See* Preparatory Meditations: "My deare deare Lord, I know not. . ."
Return of a Reaper. Alan Creighton. CaP
Return of Autumn. "Pablo Neruda," *tr. fr. Spanish by* Lloyd Mallan. LiTW
Return of Belisarius, The; Mud Flat, 1860. Bret Harte. IHA
Return of Eve, The. G. K. Chesterton. ISi; PoLi
Return of Morgan and Fingal, The. E. A. Robinson. TOP

Return of Napoleon from St. Helena, The. Lydia Huntley Sigourney. AA
Return of Philista, The. Dick Gallup. ANYP
Return of the Fairy, The. Humbert Wolfe. PoMS
Return of the Native, The. Harley Matthews. PoAu-2
Return of the Prodigal. A. E. Johnson. JKCP (1955 ed.)
Return of Ulysses, The. Homer, *tr. fr. Greek by* Bryant. *Fr.* The Odyssey, XXI. BBV (1923 ed.)
Return often and take me. Return. C. P. Cavafy. ErPo
Return, return! all night my lamp is burning. Return! Sydney Dobell. LO; OBEV (1st ed.); OBVV
Return, Return, O Shulammite. The Song of Solomon, VII: 1-10, Bible, *O.T.* TrJP
Return, sad sister, Faith. Amen. A. C. Benson. OBVV
Return to Lane's Island. William H. Matchett. PoPl
Return to Life. Abbie Huston Evans. NePoAm
Return to My Native Land, *sel.* Aimé Césaire, *tr. fr. French by* Emile Snyders.
"I shall not regard my swelled head as a sign of real glory." TTY
Return to New York. John Hall Wheelock. HT
Return to Ritual. Mark Van Doren. MoVE
Return to Sirmio. Catullus. *See* Home to Sermio.
Return to Spring. Florence Ripley Mastin. GoYe
Return to the most human, nothing less. Santos: New Mexico. May Sarton. EaLo
Return to Work, The. William Carlos Williams. NYBP
Return'd from the opera, as lately I sat. A Bon Mot. *Unknown.* ErPo
Returne The, Hairt. Alexander Scott. OxBS
Returned, a wraith from her defrauded tomb. Transformation Scene. Constance Carrier. GoYe
Returned from Mehiko he'll grab. A Hex on the Mexican X. David McCord. FiBHP
Returned Soldier. E. G. Moll. MoAuPo
Returned to Frisco, 1946. W. D. Snodgrass. AP
Returned to Say. William Stafford. NaP
Returned Volunteer to His Rifle, The. Herman Melville. ThLM
Returned Warrior ("O saepe mecum"). Horace, *tr. fr. Latin by* John Wight. Odes, II, 7. LiTW
("Pompeius, best of all my comrades, you and I.") WaaP
Returning. Ruth Guthrie Harding. HBV
Returning/ to all the unsaid. The Charge. Denise Levertov. NePoEA-2
Returning after dark, I thought. Traditional Red. Robert Huff. NePoEA-2
Returning each morning from a timeless world. Autumn 1940. W. H. Auden. LiTA
Returning from Harvest. Vernon Watkins. NYBP; StP
Returning from its daily quest, my Spirit. To Dante. Guido Cavalcanti. AWP; JAWP; WBP
Returning from the movies we find. Building a House. Dick Gallup. ANYP
Returning Home. Joachim du Bellay. *See* Heureux qui, comme Ulysse, a fait un beau voyage.
Returning, I find her just the same. Passing Visit to Helen. D. H. Lawrence. CMoP
Returning Spring. Joseph von Eichendorff, *tr. fr. German by* George N. Shuster. CAW
Returning to the Fields. Tao Yuan-ming, *tr. fr. Chinese by* Arthur Waley. LiTW; PoFr
(Once More Fields and Gardens, *tr. by* Florence Ayscough *and* Amy Lowell.) AWP
Returning to the room. Margaret Atwood. *Fr.* The Circle Game. MoCV
Returning, We Hear the Larks. Isaac Rosenberg. BrPo; FaBoMo; MMA; WaaP
Retyred thoughts enjoy their owne delights. Looke Home. Robert Southwell. AnAnS-1; MeP
Reuben. Phoebe Cary. BOHV
Reuben Bright. E. A. Robinson. AmP; AnNE; MAP; MaPo; MoAB; MoAmPo; NePA; NoP; PAn; PoPo; Sonn; StP; TrGrPo
Reuben James. James Jeffrey Roche. PAH
Reuben Ranzo. *Unknown.* AmSS, *with music*; ShS, 2 *vers., with music*; SoAmSa, *with music*
(Poor Reuben Ranzo, *diff. vers.*) IHA
Reunion. Paul Dehn. PV
Reunion. John Gould Fletcher. MoLP
Reunion. W. S. Merwin. AmPC
Reunion, A. James Schuyler. ANYP
Reunited. Sir Gilbert Parker. *Fr.* A Lover's Diary. OBVV; OQP
(Envoy: "When you and I have played the little hour.") VA
Rev Owl. A. M. Klein. TrJP
Reveal Thy Presence now, O Lord. A Prayer for the Presence of Christ [*or* A Grace]. Thomas Tiplady. ChIP; MaRV; SoP; TrPWD; TRV
Revealed. Harry Lyman Koopman. AA
Revealer, The. E. A. Robinson. DD
Revealment. John Richard Moreland. ChIP
Reveillé. Audrey Alexandra Brown. CaP
Reveille, The. Bret Harte. GN; HBV; MC; OHIP; OtMeF; OTPC (1946 ed.); PaA; PAH; PAL; PoRL
Reveille. A. E. Housman. A Shropshire Lad, IV. BEL; CLwM; CMoP; CoBE; EnLi-2; EnLit; EPN; FaFP; GTBS-W; LiTB; LiTM (rev. ed.); MasP; MoAB; MoBrPo; NeMa; NoP; OAEP; OuHeWo; PG; PoLF; PoMa; PoPo; PoVP; TDP; TreF; ViPo
Reveille. Hughes Mearns. *Fr.* Later Antigonishes. InMe; SiTL
Reveille. Michael O'Connor. AA; HBV
Reveille. Lola Ridge. AnAmPo; HBMV; PoFr
Reveille. Louis Untermeyer. HBV; PaA
Revel, The. Bartholomew Dowling. BLPA; HBV; OnYI; VA
(Our Last Toast.) YaD
(Revelry for the Dying.) AnIV
(Stand to Your Glasses.) TreF
Revel, A. Donagh MacDonagh. NeIP
Revel pauses and the room is still, The. Pannyra of the Golden Heel. Albert Samain. AWP
Revelation, *sels.* Bible, *N.T.*
"And there appeared a great wonder in heaven," XII: 1-17. CAW
(Woman Clothed with the Sun, A. Apocalypse, XII: 1, 2, 5, 10, *Douay vers.*) ISi
Last Judgment, The, XX: 11-XXI: 7. TreF
New Jerusalem, The, XXI, *abr.* TrGrPo
There Shall Be No Night, XXII: 1-5. TrGrPo
Revelation. Verne Bright. BLRP; OQP; WBLP
Revelation. Alice Brown. *Fr.* The Road to Castaly. WGRP
Revelation. Warren F. Cook. BLRP
Revelation, The. Stanley Crouch. WSL
Revelation. Blanche Taylor Dickinson. CDC
Revelation. Robert Frost. InPo; PoDB
Revelation. Sir Edmund Gosse. OBEV; OBVV
Revelation. Nancy Keesing. PoAu-2
Revelation, The. Leslie Clare Manchester. OQP
Revelation. Edwin Markham. MaRV; OQP; WGRP
Revelation. John Masefield. *See* If I Could Come Again to That Dear Place.
Revelation. David Meltzer. NeAP
Revelation, The. Coventry Patmore. The Angel in the House, I, viii, 2. EnLoPo; GTBS-P; NBM; OBNC; PoG
("Idle poet, here and there, An.") EG; ViBoPo
"Love wakes men, once a life-time each," *sel.* LO
Revelation. John Jerome Rooney. JKCP
Revelation. William Soutar. HaMV
Revelation. Robert Penn Warren. AnFE; CoAnAm; FiMAP; LiTA; MoPo; NePA; TwAmPo
Revelation, The. William Carlos Williams. MoLP
Revelations. Sterling A. Brown. Kal
Revelry for the Dying. Bartholomew Dowling. *See* Revel, The.
Revenants. Joseph Auslander. NP
Revenge ("Audivere, Lyce") Horace, *tr. fr. Latin by* Louis Untermeyer. Odes, IV, 13. AWP; WoL
Revenge. Lord Nugent. PV
Revenge, The. Pierre de Ronsard, *tr. fr. French by* Thomas Stanley. AWP
Revenge, The [a Ballad of the Fleet]. Tennyson. BBV; BEL; BeLS; DTo; EnLi-2; EnLit; EPN; FaBoCh; FOL; HBV; HoPM; MaC; MCCG; OAEP; OnMSP; OTPC; PCD; PoRA; PoVP; ShBV-1; TOP; UnPo (1st ed.); ViPo
Revenge of Hamish, The. Sidney Lanier. AnEnPo; AP; CoBA; HoPM; PoEL-5; TOP
Revenge of Rain-in-the-Face, The. Longfellow. BBV; PaA; PAH
Revenge of the Hunted. R. A. D. Ford. MoCV

Revenge to Come. Propertius, *tr. fr. Latin by* Kirby Flower Smith. Elegies, III, 25. AWP; JAWP; LiTW; WBP
Revenger's Tragedy, The, *sels.* Cyril Tourneur.
"And now methinks I could e'en chide myself," *fr.* III, iv. ViBoPo
"Madame, his grace will not be absent long," III, iv. AtBAP; PoEL-2
"My study's ornament, thou shell of death," *fr.* I, i. ViBoPo
"O hour of incest!" *fr.* I, iii. AtBAP
"Ravish me in thine answere; art thou rare," *fr.* II, ii. AtBAP
Revered, beloved—O you that hold. To the Queen. Tennyson. MaVP
Rev. Chickenwing/ in his/ pulpit. Illusions. Kirk Hall. BF
Rev. Gabe Tucker's Remarks. *Unknown.* BOHV
Reverend Henry Ward Beecher, The. Limerick [*or* An Eggstravagance]. *At. to* Oliver Wendell Holmes. CenHV; ChTr; HBVY; PCD
Rev. Malcolm Lassiter. Free Wine on Communion Day. Linwood D. Smith. TNV
Reverend Mr. Higginson, The. Edward Johnson. SCAP
Rev. Nicholas Noyes to the Rev. Cotton Mather, The. Nicholas Noyes. SCAP
Reverie. Don Marquis. PoLF
Reverie, The. Egan O'Rahilly, *tr. fr. Modern Irish by* Frank O'Connor. AnIL
(Reverie at Dawn.) KiLC
Reverie of Poor Susan, The. Wordsworth. CBEP; CH; EnRP; ERoP-1; GTBS; GTBS-D; GTBS-P; GTBS-W; GTSE; GTSL; HBV; MBW-2; MCCG; MERP; OTPC (1923 ed.); OxBoLi; ShBV-1; WiR
Reverse the flight of Lucifer. The Task. Ruth Pitter. MoBrPo; TrGrPo (1942 ed.)
Reverses. Cardinal Newman. VA
Reversible Metaphor, The. "Troubadour." InMe
Reversion. Barry O. Higgs. PeSA
Reversions. Alfred Dorn. FiSC
Revery of a Business Man. Horace. *See* Country Life.
Review, The. Thomas Traherne. *See* Childhood.
Review from Staten Island. G. C. Oden. Kal; NNP
Review of a Cook Book. Louise Dyer Harris. WhC
Reviewing me without undue elation. A Choice of Weapons. Stanley Kunitz. LiTM (1970 ed.)
Revival, The. Henry Vaughan. BoLiVe; MaPo; MemP; OBS; OxBoCh; PoEL-2; PrWP; SeCL; SeEP; SoP; TrGrPo
(Unfold! Unfold!) ELP
Revival Hymn. Joel Chandler Harris. *Fr.* Uncle Remus, His Songs and His Sayings. HBV; MCCG
Revivalist in Boston, A. Adrienne Cecile Rich. EaLo
Revocation, A. Sir Thomas Wyatt. *See* Farewell: "What should I say."
Revolt of Islam, The, *sels.* Shelley.
"And they, and all, in one loud symphony," *fr.* V. PoFr
"Can man be free if woman be a slave?" *fr.* II. PoFr
Child of Twelve, A, *fr.* II. GN
Ever as We Sailed, *fr.* XII. SeCePo
"I could not choose but gaze; a fascination," *fr.* I. ChER
"Islands and the mountains in the day, The," *fr.* III. ChER
Laon and Cythna, *sels. fr.* I, III, VIII, *and* XII. MyFE
"Lifting the thunder of their acclamation," *fr.* V. ChER
To Mary; Dedication. EnRP; EPN
"Tyrants of the Golden City tremble, The," *fr.* IV. PoFr
Revolution. "Basil Dahl," *tr. fr. Yiddish by* Joseph Leftwich. PoFr
Revolution. Emily Dickinson. *See* Revolution is the pod.
Revolution. Lesbia Harford. PoAu-1
Revolution. A. E. Housman. BrPo; ImOP; NoP; VP
Revolution, The. Filip Stepanovich Shkulev, *tr. fr. Russian by* George Z. Patrick. PoFr
Revolution!! Richard W. Thomas. BF
Revolution is the pod. Emily Dickinson. AP; CoBA; MWA-2
Revolution Man Black. Linda Goss. WSL
Revolutionary, The. Vernon Watkins. NYTB
Revolutions. Matthew Arnold. EPN; PoVP
Revolutions. Shakespeare. *See* Sonnets, LX.
Revolutions. Sir Henry Taylor. *Fr.* Philip Van Artevelde. PoFr; VA
Revolving Door, The. Newman Levy. ShM
Revolving doors compete with sales-day traffic. Shoplifter. Solomon Edwards. NNP
Reward, The. Grace G. Bostwick. MaRV
Reward. Bert Leston Taylor. RIS
Reward Doth Not Always Answer Desert. Thomas Howell. SiCE
Reward of Innocent Love, The. William Habington. *See* To Castara: The Reward of Innocent Love.
Reward of Service. *St.* 1, *Unknown, at. to* Elizabeth Barrett Browning; *st.* 2, Elizabeth Barrett Browning, *fr.* A Drama of Exile. BLPA; FaBoBe; NeHB
(Sweetest Lives, The.) MaRV; TRV
Reward of Virtue. Arthur Guiterman. InMe
Rex Mundi. Davie Gascoyne. ChMP
Reynard the Fox, *sels.* John Masefield.
"Cobbler bent at his wooden foot, The," *fr.* II. ViBoPo
Countrymen, The ("Ock Gurney and old Pete were there"), *fr.* I.
Fox Awakes, The, *fr.* II. MoVE
"Fox knew well, that before they tore him, The," *fr.* II. OtMeF
"From the Gallows Hill to the Tineton Copse," *fr.* II. NAMP
"On old Cold Crendon's windy tops," *fr.* II. OA
"Past the gibbet-stock all stuck with nails," *fr.* II. ViBoPo
"They were a lovely pack for looks," *fr.* I. OtMeF
"Tom Dansey was a famous whip," *fr.* I. OtMeF
Reynard the Fox. *Unknown.* OnYI
Rhaicos was born amid the hills wherefrom. The Hamadryad. Walter Savage Landor. *Fr.* The Hellenics. EnRP; EPN; TOP; VA
Rhapsody. William Stanley Braithwaite. AmNP; BALP; BANP
(I Am Glad Daylong.) GoSl
Rhapsody, A ("Now, I confess, I am in love"). *Unknown.* SeCL
Rhapsody, A. Henry Vaughan. ReEn
Rhapsody of the Deaf Man. Tristan Corbière, *tr. fr. French by* Walter McElroy. LiTW; OnHM
Rhapsody on a Windy Night. T. S. Eliot. ACV; AmP; CMoP; ExPo; InPo; MAP; MoAmPo (1942 ed.)
Rhapsody to Milton. Sneyd Davies. WaPE
Rhetoric of a Journey. Roy Fuller. ToPo
Rheumatic old man in White Plains, A. Limerick. *Unknown.* LiBL
Rhine was red with human blood, The. Blake. *Fr.* Jerusalem. ViBoPo
Rhinoceros, The ("Rhinoceros, your hide looks all undone"). Hilaire Belloc. ChTr; FaPON; RIS
Rhinoceros, The ("The rhino is a homely beast"). Ogden Nash. CenHV; FiBHP; GoTP; MoAmPo; NeMA; RePo
Rhinocerostrich, The. Kenyon Cox. *Fr.* Mixed Beasts. RIS
Rhodanthe. Agathias Scholasticus, *tr. fr. Greek by* Andrew Lang. AWP
Rhode Island. T. Clarke Brown. PoRL
Rhododaphne, *sels.* Thomas Love Peacock. OBRV
Bacchus.
Larissa.
Rhodora, The [On Being Asked, Whence Is the Flower]. Emerson. AA; AmePo; AmLP; AmPo; AmPP; AnAmPo; AnEnPo; AnFE; AnNE; AP; APA; AWP; BoLiVe; BoNaP; CoAnAm; CoBA; DD; FaBV; FaFP; GN; GoTP; GTSE; HBV; HBVY; ILP; InPo; JAWP; LiTA; LiTG; MAmP; MCCG; MPB; MWA-1; NeHB; NoP; OHFP; OTPC; OxBA; PoIE; SeCeV; TOP; TreFS; TrGrPo; TRV; WBP; WHA; YT
Rhoecus. James Russell Lowell. MCCG
"Hear now this fairy legend," *sel.* AA
Rhotus on Arcadia. John Chalkhill. *Fr.* Thealma and Clearchus. OBS
Rhyme, The. Robert Creeley. AmPC
Rhyme about an Electrical Advertising Sign, A. Vachel Lindsay. InP
Rhyme-beginning Fragment, A. *Unknown.* AnIL
Rhyme for a Phonetician. Frances Cornford. YT
Rhyme for Musicians, A. E. Lemke. BOHV
Rhyme for Remembrance of May. Richard Burton. HBMV
Rhyme for Washing Hands, A. *Unknown.* BoTP
Rhyme from Grandma Goose. Annemarie Ewing. NePoAm
Rhyme o' The Raggedy Man's 'at's best, The. The Lugubrious Whing-Whang. James Whitcomb Riley. BOHV; NA
Rhyme of Joyous Garde, The, *sel.* Adam Lindsay Gordon.
"We were glad together in gladsome meads." PoAu-1
Rhyme of Life, A. Charles Warren Stoddard. HBV; MaRV
Rhyme of One, A. Frederick Locker-Lampson. HBV
Rhyme of Rain. John Holmes. OCS; WaKn

Rhyme of the Ancient Mariner, The. Samuel Taylor Coleridge. *See* Rime of the Ancient Mariner, The.
Rhyme of the Chivalrous Shark, The. Wallace Irwin. ShM
Rhyme of the Dream-Maker Man, A. William Allen White. PoLF
Rhyme of the Duchess May, The, *sel.* Elizabeth Barrett Browning.
Round Our Restlessness, *last st.* MaRV
Rhyme of the Kipperling, The. Sir Owen Seaman. CenHV
Rhyme of the poet, The. Merlin, II. Emerson. PoEL-4
Rhyme of the Rail[s]. John Godfrey Saxe. BOHV; InMe; MoShBr; PoLF
Rhyme of the Rain Machine, The. F. W. Clarke. BoNaP
Rhyme of the Three Captains, The. Kipling. BeLS
Rhyme Sheet of Other Lands, A. Hugh Chesterman. BoTP
Rhyme [*or* Rime] the rack of finest wits. A Fit of Rime Against Rime [*or* Rime against Rime]. Ben Jonson. AnAnS-2; InvP; NoP; PAn; PoEL-2; PoFS; PP; SCEP-2; SeCP; SeCV-1; TuPP
Rhymed Dance Calls. *Unknown.* CoSo
Rhymes. Y. Y. Segal, *tr. fr. Yiddish by* Miriam Waddington. WHW
Rhymes about a Little Woman. William Canton. PPL
Rhymes about the Weather. *Unknown. See* Weather Signs.
Rhymes and Rhythms, *sels.* W. E. Henley.
Epilogue: "These to you now, O, more than ever now." ViBoPo
"Trees and the menace of night," XXI. Po
Rhymes for a Modern Nursery, *sels.* Paul Dehn.
"Hey diddle diddle." FiBHP
"In a cavern, in a canyon." FiBHP; PV; ShM
"Jack and Jill went up the hill." FiBHP
"Little Miss Muffet." FiBHP; ShM
"Two blind mice." FiBHP
Rhymes of a Rolling Stone, *sel.* Robert W. Service.
"Thank God! there is always a Land of Beyond." TRV
Rhymes to Remember. *Unknown.* StaSt
Rhymester, A. Samuel Taylor Coleridge. BOHV; PV
Rhyming Riddle. *Unknown.* TreFT
Rhyming Riddles, *sels.* Mary Austin.
"First I am frosted." TiPo
"I come more softly than a bird." BoNaP; SoPo; TiPo
"I have no wings, but yet I fly." SoPo; TiPo
"I never speak a word." TiPo
Rhythm, The. Robert Creeley. CoPo; FRC; LiTM (1970 ed.); TPM
Rhythm. Emerson. OQP; TOP
Rhythm ("Rhythm in the pulse of Time"). Jean Percival Waddell. CaP
Rhythm and blues. The Blues Today. Mae Jackson. BOLo
Rhythm of His Life, The. Mary Hallet. ChIP
Ribald and unbuttoned air, A. Back Lane. R. D. Murphy. PoAu-2
Ribbon Two Yards Wide, A. Alfred Kreymborg. HBMV
Ribs and Terrors, The. Herman Melville. *See* Father Mapple's Hymn.
Rice Fields. Basho, *tr. fr. Japanese by* H. G. Henderson. OnPM
Rice Pudding. A. A. Milne. BBGG
Rice Seller, The. *Unknown, tr. fr. Chinese by* Isaac Taylor Headland. PCH
Rich. Aileen Fisher. GaP; MPB
Rich and Poor; or, Saint and Sinner. Thomas Love Peacock. SiTL
Rich and strange thy history. Dust. Sister Mary Angelita. JKCP (1926 ed.)
Rich arrived in pairs, The. The Garden Party. Hilaire Belloc. DTC; MoVE
Rich damask roses in fair cheeks do bide. Robert Tofte. *Fr.* Laura. EIL
Rich Days. W. H. Davies. BoNaP; BoTP
Rich Earth, The. Psalms, CIV: 16-24, Bible, *O.T.* GoTP
Rich folks 'cided to take a trip, De. De Titanic. *Unknown.* AS
Rich fools there be, whose base and filthy heart. Astrophel and Stella, XXIV. Sir Philip Sidney. FCP; MaPo (1969 ed.); OAEP; ReEn; ReIE; SiCE; SiPS; TuPP
Rich in her weeping country's spoils, Versailles. The Charms of Nature. Joseph Warton. *Fr.* The Enthusiast; or, The Lover of Nature. OBEC
Rich in the waning light she sat. Waiting. John Freeman. CH
Rich Interior Life, The. Richard Eberhart. MoRP
Rich king of a rainy country, The. The King in May. Michael Dennis Browne. NYBP
Rich labor is the struggle to be wise. The Discipline of Wisdom. George Meredith. EPN
Rich Lady from Dublin, The, *with music. Unknown.* BFSS
Rich Lazarus! richer in those gems, thy teares. Upon Lazarus His Teares. Richard Crashaw. MaMe; SeCV-1
Rich Man, The. Franklin P. Adams. FiBHP; InMe; MAP; MoAmPo (1942 ed.); PoMa
Rich Man and the Kingdom of Heaven, The. St. Matthew, XIX: 13-30, Bible, *N.T.* TreF
Rich man bought a swan and goose, A. The Swan and the Goose. Aesop. AWP; FaPON; JAWP; LiTW; UnS; WBP
Rich man has his motorcar, The. The Rich Man. Franklin P. Adams. FiBHP; InMe; MAP; MoAmPo (1942 ed.); PoMa
Rich man lay on his velvet couch, The. Mag's Song. *Unknown.* AS
Rich man, poor man, beggar-man, thief. Oberammergau. Leonora Speyer. AnAmPo; HBMV
Rich man's son inherits lands, The. The Heritage. James Russell Lowell. HBV; HBVY; OTPC
Rich men, trust not in wealth. Thomas Nashe. AnFE; EG
Rich Mine of Knowledge. George Chapman. SeCePo
Rich Old Lady, The, *with music. Unknown.* OuSiCo
Rich Statue, double-faced. To the New Yeere. Michael Drayton. AtBAP; PoEL-2
Rich the peace of the elements tonight on the Land-of-Joy. The Path of the Old Spells. Donald Sinclair. GoTS
Rich, voluptuous languor of dim pain, A. Vanitas Vanitatum. Israel Zangwill. TrJP
Rich Young Man, The. Laura Simmons. ChIP
Rich Young Ruler, The. *Unknown.* SoP
Richard and Robin were two pretty men. *See* Robin and Richard were two pretty men.
Richard Cory. E. A. Robinson. AmePo; AmP; AmPP; AnNE; CaFP; CBV; CMoP; CoBA; DiPo; DTC; ExPo; FaFP; ForPo; GTBS-W; ILP; LiTA; LiTG; LiTM; LoGBV; MAP; MasP; MoAB; MoAmPo; MoVE; NeMA; NePA; NP; OnPP; OxBA; PAn; PFY; PoLF; PoMa; PoPo; PoRA; StPo; TDP; TOP; TreF; TrGrPo
Richard Crashaw's Answer; for Hope. Richard Crashaw. *See* For Hope.
Richard Dick upon a stick. *Unknown.* OxNR
Richard Forest's Midsummer Night, *sel.* James Thomson.
Midsummer Courtship. OBVV
Richard has been sent to bed. Dirge for a Bad Boy. E. V. Rieu. BBGG
Richard Has Something to Say. Rose Fyleman. GaP
Richard Roe and John Doe ("Richard Roe wished himself Solomon"). Robert Graves. CMoP
Richard II. Shakespeare. *See* King Richard II.
Richard II as Captive. Samuel Daniel. *Fr.* The Civil Wars. SiCE
Richard II Banishes Bolingbroke. Shakespeare. King Richard II, *fr.* I, iii. PoFS
Richard II's Dejection. Shakespeare. *See* Death of Kings, The.
Richard Somers. Barrett Eastman. AA
Richard, thah thou be ever trichard. Against the Barons' Enemies. *Unknown.* MeEL
Richard the Second. Shakespeare. *See* King Richard II.
Richard the Third. Shakespeare. *See* King Richard III.
Richard Tolman's Universe. Leonard Bacon. ImOP
Riche Croesus, whylom king of Lyde, The. Croesus. Chaucer. *Fr.* The Canterbury Tales: The Monk's Tale. MyFE
Richelieu; or, The Conspiracy, *sel.* Sir Edward Bulwer-Lytton.
Cardinal's Soliloquy, The, *fr.* III, i. VA
Richer. Aileen Fisher. BiCB
Riches. Blake. BoLiVe; PoG; StaSt; TrGrPo
Riches. Robert Loveman. OQP
Riches. *Unknown, tr. fr. Greek by* William Cowper. AWP
Riches and honours Buckley layes aside. Onely the Reverend Grave and Godly Mr. Buckly Remaines. Edward Johnson. SCAP
Riches I hold in light esteem. The Old Stoic. Emily Brontë. CBV; EnLi-2; EnLit; FaPL; OAEP; OBEV (new ed.); OBNC; OBVV; OxBI; PoFr; PoLF; PoPl; PoPo; PoVP; TreFT; TrGrPo; VA; ViBoPo; YT
Riches of a nation are her dead, The. To Those Who Reproved

the Author for Too Sanguine Patriotism. George Woodberry. AmePo
Richest Woman, The. Elizabeth Madox Roberts. GaP
Richie Story. *Unknown.* BaBo; ESPB (A *and* B *vers.*)
Richly scattered temple ruins. Mysterious Landscape. Hans Carossa. LiTW
Rick of Green Wood, The. Edward Dorn. NeAP
Rid of the world's injustice, and his pain. The Grave of Keats. Oscar Wilde. PoVP
Riddle: "As I went over London Bridge." *Unknown.* ChTr
Riddle: "As I went over Tipple Tyne." *Unknown.* ChTr
Riddle: "At the end of my yard there is a vat." *Unknown.* ChTr
Riddle, A: Book, A. Hannah More. *See* Book, A.
Riddle: Book-Moth. *Unknown, tr. fr. Anglo-Saxon by* Richard L. Hoffman. YAT
Riddle, A: "Clothes make no sound when I tread ground." *Unknown, tr. fr. Anglo-Saxon.* ChTr
Riddle, The: "Down in a garden sits my dearest Love." *Unknown. See* Down in a Garden.
Riddle: "First it was a pretty flower, dressed in pink and white." Christina Rossetti. SoPo
Riddle, A: "Four stiff-standers." *Unknown.* ChTr; OxNR
Riddle: Gnats. *Unknown, tr. fr. Anglo-Saxon by* Richard L. Hoffman. YAT
Riddle, The: "He told himself and he told his wife." Ralph Hodgson. PoPl; WhC
Riddle: "Here is a riddle most abstruse." *Unknown.* SiTL
Riddle: "Highty, tighty, paradighty, clothed in green." *Unknown.* ChTr; OxNR
Riddle: "Hill full, a hole full, A." Mother Goose. SoPo
Riddle #14: Horn, A. *Unknown, tr. fr. Anglo-Saxon by* Burton Raffel. DiPo
Riddle, A: "I am just two and two, I am warm, I am cold." William Cowper. HBV
Riddle: "I am within as white as snow." *Unknown.* ChTr
Riddle: "I'm a strange creature, for I satisfy women." *Unknown, tr. fr. Anglo-Saxon by* Kevin Crossley-Holland. PV
Riddle: "I washed my face in water." *Unknown.* ChTr
Riddle: "In Mornigan's park there is a deer." *Unknown.* ChTr
Riddle: "It is in the rock, but not in the stone." *Unknown.* ChTr
Riddle: "Land was white, The." *Unknown.* ChTr; OxNR
Riddle, A: Letter "H," The. Catherine Fanshawe. *See* Riddle, A: "'Twas whispered in heaven . . ."
Riddle: "Long white barn, A." *Unknown.* ChTr
Riddle #29: Moon and the Sun, The. *Unknown, tr. fr. Anglo-Saxon by* Burton Raffel. CaFP; GoJo
Riddle, The: "No more, no more." Alexander Brome. OBS
Riddle: "Old Mother Twitchet had but one eye." Mother Goose. SoPo
Riddle: "On yonder hill there is a red deer." *Unknown.* ChTr
Riddle: "Shoemaker makes shoes without leather, A." *Unknown.* SoPo
Riddle, A: "'Twas whispered in heaven [*or* in heaven pronounced], 'twas muttered in hell." Catherine Maria Fanshawe. ChTr; OTPC
(Enigma.) LiTG; SiTL
(Enigma on the Letter H.) BOHV; GoTP
(Letter for You, A.) RIS
(Riddle, A: Letter "H," The.) GN
Riddle, The: "Underneath the leaves of life." W. H. Auden. EnLi-2 (1949 ed.)
Riddle: "Upon a bed of humble clay." Thomas Parnell. WaPE
Riddle, A: "We are little airy creatures." Swift. GN; OTPC
(A E I O U.) BoTP
(Five, The.) RIS
(Riddle, A; the Vowels.) OnYI
Riddle: "Wee man o' leather." *Unknown.* ChTr
Riddle: What Am I? Dorothy Aldis. *See* What Am I?
Riddle, The: "What it is, the literal size." Robert Creeley. OPoP
Riddle, The: "Where's an old woman to go when the years." "H. E. H." PoToHe
Riddle: "White bird featherless." *Unknown.* ChTr
(Riddle of Snow and Sun.) CBEP; NCEP
(Snow.) RIS
("White bird featherless.") OxNR
Riddle: "White bird floats down through the air, A." *Unknown.* ChTr
Riddle, A: "Yon laddie wi' the gowdan pow." William Soutar. OxBS
Riddle: "You are a riddle I would not unravel." Josephine Miles. FiMAP
Riddle, a riddle, as I suppose, A. Mother Goose. OxNR; TiPo
Riddle cum diddle cum dido [*or* doodle]. Kindness to Animals. Laura E. Richards. SoPo; TiPo
Riddle-me riddle-me riddle-me-ree. Mother Goose. BoChLi; OTPC (1946 ed.); OxNR; PPL
Riddle me, riddle me, what is that. *Unknown.* OTPC (1946 ed.)
Riddle of Snow and Sun. *Unknown. See* Riddle: "White bird featherless."
Riddle of the World. Pope. *See* Know Then Thyself.
Riddle of the World, The. Whittier. SoP; TRV
Riddle, A; the Vowels. Swift. *See* Riddle, A: "We are little airy creatures."
Riddles. Patrick F. Kirby. GoBC
Riddles. Sister Mary Madeleva. JKCP (1955 ed.)
Riddles Wisely Expounded. *Unknown.* NoP
Riddles, *sels. Unknown, formerly at. to* Cynewulf, *tr. fr. Anglo-Saxon.*
Anchor: "Oft I must strive with wind and wave," *tr. by* Charles W. Kennedy. AnOE
Bible, A: "A stern destroyer struck out my life," *tr. by* Stith Thompson. EnLi-1; OuHeWo
Bookworm, A: "A moth ate a word. To me that seemed," *tr. by* Stith Thompson. EnLi-1
(Book-Moth: "A moth ate a word. To me it seemed," *tr. by* Charles W. Kennedy.) AnOE
(Book-Worm, The: "A moth ate a word. Methought it.") CoBE
("Moth ate words, A. To me that seemed," *tr. by* Harold S. Stine.) EnLit
Cuckoo: "In former days my father and mother," *tr. by* Charles W. Kennedy. AnOE
Fish in River: "My house is not quiet, I am not loud," *tr. by* Charles W. Kennedy. AnOE
Honey-Mead: "I am valued by men, fetched from afar," *tr. by* Charles W. Kennedy. AnOE
Horn, A: "I was once an armed warrior," *tr. by* Stith Thompson. OuHeWo
(Horn: "Time was when I was weapon and warrior," *tr. by* Charles W. Kennedy.) AnOE
Plow: "My beak is bent downward, I burrow below," *tr. by* Charles W. Kennedy. AnOE
Riddle: "I am of value to men, variously am found," *tr. by* Harold S. Stine. EnLit
Riddle: "One of my foes deprived me of life," *tr. by* Harold S. Stine. EnLit
Shield: "A lonely wanderer, wounded with iron," *tr. by* Charles W. Kennedy. AnOE
Storm, A: "At times I am fast confined by my Master," *tr. by* Stith Thompson. EnLi-1; OuHeWo
Storm, A: "At times I travel in tracks undreamed of," *tr. by* Stith Thompson. OuHeWo
Storm, A: "What man is so clever, so crafty of mind," *tr. by* Stith Thompson. OuHeWo
Storm Riddles: "What man is so wise as to explain," *tr. by* William H. Matchett. FosPo
Swan, A: "My robe is noiseless when I roam the earth," *tr. by* Stith Thompson. OuHeWo
(Swan, The: "Silent my robe, when I rest on earth.") CoBE
(Swan, The: "Voiceless my robe when I dwell on the earth," *tr. by* F. B. Snyder.) BEL
(Wild Swan: "My attire is noiseless when I tread the earth," *tr. by* Charles W. Kennedy.) AnOE
Wind: "At times I resort, beyond man's discerning," *tr. by* Charles W. Kennedy. AnOE
Riddles (*18th century*). *Unknown.* CoBE
"Close in a cage a bird I'll keep."
"I saw five birds all in a cage."
"Once hairy scenter did transgress."
"Promotion lately was bestow'd."
"Take of letters the first."
"Vase which holds all fat'ning liquor, The."
"Wide mouth, no ears nor eyes, A."
Riddles Wisely Expounded. *Unknown.* BaBo (A, B, *and* C *vers.*); BEL; ESPB (3 *vers.*); HBV; ViBoFo (A *and* B *vers.*)

Riddles (continued)
(Jennifer Gentle and Rosemary.) OxBoLi
("There was a knicht riding frae the east.") CH
Riddling Knight, The. *Unknown.* AtBAP; FaBoCh; LoGBV; OBB; PoEL-1
Ride a cock-horse to Banbury Cross, To see a fine lady upon a white horse. Mother Goose. BoChLi; BoTP; ExPo; FaBoBe; FaFP; HBV; HBVY; OTPC; OxBoLi; OxNR; PCH; PPL; RIS; SAS; SiTL; SoPo; StVeCh; TiPo
Ride a cock-horse to Banbury Cross,/ To buy little Johnny a galloping horse. *Unknown.* OxNR
Ride a cock-horse to Banbury Cross/ To see what baby. *Unknown.* SAS
Ride a cock-horse to Banbury Cross,/ To see what Tommy can buy. *Unknown.* OxNR
Ride away, ride away,/ Johnny shall ride. Mother Goose. OxNR; TiPo
Ride away, ride away, baby shall ride. *Unknown.* SAS
Ride-by-Nights, The. Walter de la Mare. FaPON; SiSoSe; TiPo
Ride in a Blue Chevy from Alum Cave Trail to Newfound Gap, A. Jonathan Williams. NYTB
Ride of Colin Graves, The. John Boyle O'Reilly. PAH
Ride of Tench Tilghman, The. Clinton Scollard. MC
Ride On in Majesty. Henry Hart Milman. *See* For Palm Sunday.
Ride On, Moses, *with music.* *Unknown.* BoAN-1
Ride on! ride on in majesty! For Palm Sunday [*or* Ride On in Majesty]. Henry Hart Milman. OQP; VA
Ride, ride to Boston. *Unknown.* SAS
Ride round the Parapet, The. Friedrich Rüchert, *tr. fr. German by* James Clarence Mangan. AWP; JAWP; WBP
Ride to Cherokee, The. Amelia Walstien Carpenter. AA
Ride to Jerusalem, The. Norman Nicholson. StJW
Ride to the Lady, The. Helen Gray Cone. AA
Rider, The. William Burford. NYTB
Rider, The. Leah Bodine Drake. NePoAm-2
Rider, The. Horse & Rider. Wey Robinson. SD; WhC
Rider at the Gate, The. John Masefield. BrPo; ShBV-2
Rider Victory, The. Edwin Muir. CMoP; GTBS-W; LiTM; WaP
Riderless Horse, The. Harold Trowbridge Pulsifer. MaRV
Riders, The. Ann Stanford. TPM
Riders Held Back, The. Louis Simpson. PIA
Riders of the Stars. Henry Herbert Knibbs. SCC
Rides. Gene Derwood. LiTM; NePA
Ridge, The, 1919. W. W. Gibson. POTE
Ridiculous Excess. Shakespeare. *See* To Gild Refinèd Gold.
Ridiculous Optimist, The. Samuel Ellsworth Kiser. SoP; STF
Ridin'. Badger Clark. IHA
Ridin' up the Rocky from Town. *Unknown.* SCC
Riding. Harry Amoss. CaP
Riding across John Lee's Finger. Stanley Crouch. WSL
Riding against the east. To Beachey, 1912. Carl Sandburg. TiPo
Riding at dawn, riding alone. Gillespie. Sir Henry Newbolt. PeVV; ShBV-1
Riding at Daybreak. Sun Yün Fêng, *tr. fr. Chinese by* Henry H. Hart. FIW
Riding Down. Nora Perry. AA; HBV
Riding Down from Bangor. Louis Shreve Osborne. BLPA
Riding in a Motor Boat. Dorothy W. Baruch. FaPON; MPB
Riding in an Airplane. Dorothy W. Baruch. FaPON
Riding of the Kings, The. Eleanor Farjeon. ChBR; YeAr
Riding Stone. Isidor Schneider. PG
Riding Song. *Unknown.* SCC
Riding the "A." May Swenson. CAD
Riding the black express from heaven to hell. Lucifer in the Train. Adrienne Cecile Rich. EaLo; NePoEA-2; TwAmPo
Riding through Jerusalem. Marion Susan Campbell. ChIP
Riding through Ruwu swamp, about sunrise. Bête Humaine. Francis Brett Young. CH; HBMV
Riding Together. William Morris. ViPo; ViPP; WaKn
Riding with Kilpatrick. Clinton Scollard. PAH
Rienzi, *sel.* Mary Russell Mitford.
Rienzi to the Romans, *fr.* II, ii. PoFr; TreFS
"Rifleman, shoot me a fancy shot." Civil War. Charles Dawson Shanly. HBV; PAH
Rifleman's Song at Bennington, The. *Unknown.* PAH
Rift, The. Ruth Margaret Gibbs. SoP
Rig-Veda, The. *Unknown.* *See* Vedic Hymns.
Rigadoon, rigadoon, now let him fly. *Unknown.* OxNR
Rigger, The. Washington Jay McCormick. WhC
Righ Shemus he has gone to France. The Irish Rapparees. Sir Charles Gavan Duffy. AnIV; PoFr; VA
Right above the Wrong, The, 1857. William Cox Bennett. PoFr
Right Apprehension. Thomas Traherne. PoEL-2
Right as a rose that breaks out of its folds. The Proffered Rose. Wenceslas, King of Bohemia. LiTW
Right [*or* Ryght] as the stern of day begouth to shine [*or* schine *or* schyne]. The Golden [*or* Goldyn] Targe [*or* The Poet's Dream]. William Dunbar. OxBS; PoEL-1; SiCE
Right down the shocked street with a siren-blast. A Fire-Truck. Richard Wilbur. TPM
"Right fresshe flowr, whos I ben have and shal." The Sorrow of Troilus. Chaucer. *Fr.* Troilus Criseyde. PoEL-1
Right in the middle of the storm it was. The Storm. Elizabeth Jennings. NePoEA-2
Right Is Right. Frederick William Faber. SoP; TRV; WBLP
Right Kind of People, The. Edwin Markham. BLPA; PoPo; PoToHe; StaSt
Right many times with hand assured. Guillaume de Lorris. *Fr.* The Romance of the Rose. EnLi-1
Right merry lass, thy overweening joy. To Lilly. Hartley Coleridge. Sonn
Right mighty prince and redoubted sovereign. Here Beginneth the Pastime of Pleasure. Stephen Hawes. *Fr.* The Pastime of Pleasure. SiCE
Right Must Win. Frederick William Faber. JKCP; MaRV; VA
Right Now. William Stafford. NaP
Right of Asylum, The. Stephen Phillips. PoFr
Right of Way, The. William Carlos Williams. MoVE
Right-of-Way, A: 1865. William Plomer. DTC
Right On: White America. Sonia Sanchez. BOLo; WSL
Right on our flank the crimson sun went down. The Loss of the *Birkenhead.* Sir Francis Hastings Doyle. HBV
Right rigorous, and so forth! The Petition of Tom Dermody to the Three Fates in Council Sitting. Thomas Dermody. AnIV
Right Royal. John Masefield. OtMeF
Right Time, The. *Unknown, tr. fr. German by* Louis Untermeyer. UnTE
Right true it is, and said full yore ago. Sir Thomas Wyatt. FCP
Right under their noses, the green. The Dusk of Horses. James Dickey. AP; LiTM (1970 ed.); NYBP; ToPo
Right up into Bossy's eyes. Bossy and the Daisy. Maragret Deland. PPL
Right upward on the road of fame. Emerson. *Fr.* The Poet. PP
Right Use of Prayer, The. Aubrey De Vere (1788-1846). OBVV; OQP; WGRP
Right Way to Fish, The. *Unknown.* WhC
Righteous Anger. James Stephens. *See* Glass of Beer, A.
Righteous or not, here comes an angry man. A View of the Burning. James Merrill. NePoEA-2
Rights of Women, The. William Cowper. CBEP
Rigid Body Sings, *parody.* James Clerk Maxwell. BOHV; Par
(In Memory of Edward Wilson.) WhC
Rigmarole. William Carlos Williams. AnAmPo
Rigor Viris. Margaret Avison. CaP
Rigorists. Marianne Moore. PoIE
Rigs o' Barley, The. Burns. LiTB; LoBV; UnTE; ViBoPo
(Corn Rigs Are Bonny [*or* Bonnie].) CBEP; ErPo; OxBS
(Song: "It was upon a Lammas night.") EiCL
Rikki-tikki-tavy. Food for Thought. Michael Lewis. RIS
Rilke. Phyllis Webb. PeCV (1967 ed.)
Rilloby-Rill. Sir Henry Newbolt. HBVY
Rillons, Rillettes. Richard Wilbur. NYBP
Rimas, *sels.* Gustavo Adolfo Bécquer, *tr. fr. Spanish.*
"I am a passion; I am a flame," XI, *tr. by* Muna Lee. (Song.) OnPM
"I am ardorous, I am dark," *tr. by* Thomas Walsh. CAW
"Invisible atoms of the air, The," X, *tr. by* Harold Morland. (Three Rimas, 1.) LiTW
"Quivering, unseen atoms of air, The," X. *tr. by* Alice Jane McVan.
(Love Passing By.) OnPM
"Sighs are air, and are lost in air," XXXVIII, *tr. by* Harold Morland.
(Three Rimas, 2.) LiTW

"Tear was in here eye, A," *tr. by* Harold Morland. (Three Rimas, 3.) LiTW
"They closed her eyes," LXXIII, *tr. by* John Masefield. AWP; JAWP; WBP
Rimbaud. W. H. Auden. SyP
Rimbaud and Verlaine, Precious Pair of Poets. Conrad Aiken. Preludes for Memnon, LVI. LiTA; LiTM (rev. ed.); MoPo; NAMP; NePA; TwAmPo
(Prelude: "Rimbaud and Verlaine, precious pair of poets.") FaBoMo; NAMP; TwCP
Rimbaud in Africa. Edgell Rickword. ChMP
Rime nor mars nor makes, The. His Defense against the Idle Critic. Michael Drayton. ReIE
Rime of the Ancient Mariner, The. Samuel Taylor Coleridge. AnFE; AtBAP; ATP; BEL; BeLS; BoLiVe; CABA; CABL; CaFP; CBEP; CH; ChER; CoBE; DiPo; EnL; EnLi-2; EnLit; EnRP; EPN; ERoP-1; ExPo; FaBoBe; FaBoCh; FaBV; FaFP; FaPL; FiP; FosPo; GBV (1922 ed.); HBV; HoPM; ILP; LiTB; LiTG; LoGBV; MaPo; MasP; MBW-2; MCCG; MERP; MyFE, *much abr.*; NoP; OAEP; OBEV; OBNC; OBRV; OnSP; OtMeF, *abr.*; OTPC; OuHeWo; PAn; PeER; Po; PoAn; PoE; PoEL-4; PoFS; PoSa; PTK; RoGo; SeCeV; ShBV-2; StP; TOP; TreF; TrGrPo; UnPo (1st ed.); VaPo; ViBoPo; WePo; WHA; YAT;
Sels.
"Beyond the shadow of the ship," *fr.* IV. BoC
"Fair breeze blew, the white foam flew, The," *fr.* II. PoG
"For when it dawn'd—they dropp'd their arms," *fr.* V. UnS
"He prayeth best, who loveth best," *fr.* VII. FaPON; GoTP, 1 *st.*; LO, 1 *st.*; MaRV, 4 *sts.*; PCH, 1 *st.*; StVeCh, 1 *st.*; TRV, 1 *st.*; YT
(He Prayeth Well, 6 *ll.*) BoTP; SoP; ThGo
"Moving Moon went up the sky, The," *fr.* IV. LO
Rime of the Duchess May. Elizabeth Barrett Browning. *See* Rhyme of the Duchess May, The.
Rime of the Rood, A. Charles L. O'Donnell. GoBC
Rime the rack of finest wits. *See* Rhyme, the rack of finest wits.
Rin and rout, rin and rout. The Deevil's Waltz. Sidney Goodsir Smith. FaBoTw
Rinaldo. Henry Peterson. AA
Ring, The. Harry Mathews. ANYP
Ring-a-Ring. Kate Greenaway. FaPON; MoShBr; MPB
("Ring-a-ring of little boys.") TiPo (1952 ed.)
Ring-a-Ring o' Fairies. Madeleine Nightingale. GaP; GFA
Ring-a-ring o' roses. Plague Charm. *Unknown.* FOL; OxNR
Ring-a-ring of little boys. Ring-a-Ring. Kate Greenaway. FaPON; MoShBr; MPB; TiPo (1952 ed.)
Ring and rim, The/ Of tidal sleep. Sleep. A. S. J. Tessimond. POTE
Ring and the Book, The, *sels.* Robert Browning.
Giuseppe Caponsacchi, VI. PoVP; VP
"I have done with being judged," *fr.* VI. OAEP
"I never realized God's birth before," 3 *ll.* ChIP
"No one ever plucked," 4 *ll.* ChIP
"O lyric Love, half angel and half bird," *fr.* I. EPN; FiP; OAEP
(Dedication: "O lyric Love," *longer sel.*) CoBE
(Lyric Love.) OBVV; TOP
(Ring and the Book, The.) PoVP
Our Known Unknown, *br. sel. fr.* X. OQP
Pompilia, VII. MaVP; MBW-2; OAEP; PoVP; ViPo; ViPP
Pope, The, X. MBW-2; ViPo; ViPP
Old Pope is Comforted by the Thought of the Young Pompilia, The, *fr.* X. BoC
"Quis pro Domino," *fr.* X. OAEP
"There's a blessing on the hearth," *fr.* VIII. PoToHe
"You never know what life means till you die," *fr.* XI. OAEP
Ring-around-a-Rosy. Mother Goose. SoPo; TiPo
Ring around the World. Annette Wynne. GaP; StVeCh (1955 ed.); TiPo
Ring, bells, from every lofty height! Ring, Joyful Bells! Violet Fuller. PEDC
Ring Forth, Fair Nymphs, Your Joyful Songs for Gladness. Gaspar Gil Polo, *tr. fr. Spanish by* Bartholomew Young. *Fr.* Diana Enamorada. HW
Ring, Joyful Bells! Violet Fuller. PEDC
Ring out, O bells! ring silver-sweet o'er hill and moor fell. On the Threshold [*or* The New Year]. Augustus Henry Baldwin. DD; HH; PEDC
Ring out the joy bells! Once again. The Nation's Birthday. Mary E. Vandyne. DD; HH
Ring out to the stars the glad chorus! Our Nation Forever. Wallace Bruce. OHIP; PEDC
Ring Out the Old, Ring in the New. *See* In Memoriam A. H. H.: "Ring out, wild bells. . ."
Ring Out, Wild Bells. Tennyson. *Fr.* In Memoriam A. H. H., CV-CVI. WiR
Ring out, wild bells, to the wild sky. In Memoriam A. H. H., CVI. Tennyson. BEL; BoLiVe; CoBE; DD; DiPo; EnL; EnLi-2; EnLit; EPN; FaFP; FaPL; FaPON; FiP; GTBS; GTBS-W; GTSL; HBV; HH; InP; LiTB; LiTG; MaPo; MaRV; MCCG; MemP; MPB; NeHB; OAEP; OQP; OTPC; PEDC; PG (1945 ed.); PGD; PoE; PoIE; PoRL; SeCeV; ShBV-2; SoP; TiPo (1959 ed.); TOP; TreF; TrGrPo; TRV; UnPo; ViPo; VP; WBLP; YAT
Ring Out Your Bells. Sir Philip Sidney. CABA; EIL; EnRePo; NoP; PoFS; SiPS; TuPP; ViBoPo
(Astrophel's Love Is Dead.) ReIE
(Litany, A: "Ring out your bells.") CenL; FosPo; OBSC; PoIE; UnPo
(Love Is Dead.) BEL; EnLi-1
("Ring out your bells, let mourning shows be spread.") FCP; ReEn; SiCE
Ring out your name! O cherished land. National Anthem (Finland). Johan Ludvig Runeberg. PoFr
Ring round her! children of her glorious skies. The Foe at the Gates. John Dickson Bruns. PAH
Ring, sing! ring, sing! Pleasant Sabbath bells! The Green Gnome. Robert Buchanan. StPo
Ring slender bells an elfin tune. Harebells in June. Annette Wynne. SUS
Ring, so worn as you behold, The. A Marriage Ring [*or* His Wife's Wedding Ring *or* His Mother's Wedding Ring]. George Crabbe. CBEP; EnLoPo; LO; OBEV; OBNC; OBRV
Ring the bell! Baby at Play. *Unknown.* HBV; HBVY; OxNR; PPL
Ring the bells, nor ring them slowly. Cedar Mountain. Annie Fields. MC; PAH
Ring the bells, ring! *Unknown.* OxNR
Ring-ting! I wish I were a primrose. Wishing. William Allingham. BoChLi (1939 ed.); BoTP; DD; FaPON; GFA; HBV; HBVY; MPB; OHIP; OTPC; PCH; PRWS; TVC
Ringely, Ringely. Eliza Lee Follen. BiCB; SAS
Ringing the Bells. Anne Sexton. NMP
Ringleted Youth of My Love. *Unknown, tr. fr. Modern Irish by* Douglas Hyde. AnIL; AnIV; OnYI; OxBI
Rings. William Barnes. NBM
Rings in a Roundness. Carleton Drewry. NYTB
Rings of stars in sky turns. The Dancing Ploughmen. M. K. Joseph. ACV
Rings of the sun rise, The. Epithalamium. Anne Cluysenaar. HW
Ringsend. Oliver St. John Gogarty. AnIL; LiTM; OBMV
Rink. Dick Lourie. ThO
Rintrah roars and shakes his fires in the burden'd [*or* burdened] air. The Marriage of Heaven and Hell. Blake. CEP; EiCL; EiPP; EnRP; ERoP-1; FosPo; LoBV
Rio Bravo—a Mexican Lament. José de Saltillo, *tr. fr. Spanish by* Charles Fenno Hoffman. PAH
Rio Grande, The. Sacheverell Sitwell. SeCePo
Rio Grande ("Heave away, Rio!"), *with music. Unknown.* ShS
Rio Grande, The ("Oh, Johnny came over"), *with music. Unknown.* ABF
Rio Grande ("Oh, say, were you ever in Rio Grande?"), *with music. Unknown.* SoAmSa; TrAS
("Oh say, were you ever in Rio Grande.") LO
Rioupéroux. James Elroy Flecker. OBEV (new ed.); OBVV
Riot. Gwendolyn Brooks. BP
Riot! screamed the studs. A Black Cop's Communion. Arnold Kemp. WSL
Rip. James Wright. NaP
Ripe and Bearded Barley, The. *Unknown.* BoNaP; ChTr
Ripe apple, the banana and the pear. Rainer Maria Rilke. Sonnets to Orpheus, Pt. I, XIII. OnPM
Ripe apples were caught like red fish in the nets. The Great Scarf of Birds. John Updike. NYBP
Ripe cherries and ripe maidens. Cherries. Zalman Schneour. TrJP

Ripe Fruit, The. *Unknown, tr. fr. Breton by* Louis Untermeyer. UnTE
Ripe Grain. Dora Read Goodale. HBV
Ripe, the plums fall from the bough. Anxiety of a Young Lady to Get Married. *Unknown.* OuHeWo
Ripeness is all; her in her cooling planet. To an Old Lady. William Empson. AtBAP; CoBMV; FaBoTw; GTBS-P; MoAB; MoPW; NoP; SeCeV (1967 ed.); ToPo
Ripping Trip, A. *Unknown.* CoSo; SGR, *with music.*
Ripple of dust panicked across, A. Ghosts. Ethna MacCarthy. NeIP
Rippling in the ocean of that darkening room. Woman at the Piano. Marya Zaturenska. MoAmPo
Riprap. Gary Snyder. NeAP
Riquet of the Tuft, *sels.* Stopford Brooke. VA
Prince Riquet's Song.
Queen's Song.
Rise, A. Ernest McGaffey. AA
Rise! Francis Albert Rollo Russell. SoP
(Laborare Est Orare.) MaRV
Rise and Fall of Creede, The. Cy Warman. PoOW
Rise and Fall of Valentines. Fairfax Downey. InMe
Rose and hold up the curved glass. Pour Us Wine. Ibn Kolthúm. *Fr.* The Mu'allaqát. AWP
Rise and Shine. Richmond Lattimore. NYBP
Rise at 7:15. Good Morning Love! Paul Blackburn. NMP
Rise, brothers, rise; the wakening [*or* waking] skies pray to the morning light. The Coromandel Fishers. Sarojini Naidu. BBV; EtS; MCCG; RePo
Rise, Crowned with Light. Pope. *Fr.* Messiah. GoBC; WGRP
(Hymn: "Rise, crowned with light, imperial Salem, rise!") NeHB
Rise from the waves, my rivering one. Four Poems for April, II. Louis Adeane. NeBP
Rise, Glorious Conqueror! Rise. Matthew Bridges. BePJ
Rise, Happy Morn. Tennyson. *See* In Memoriam A. H. H.: "Time draws near the birth of Christ, The."
Rise, happy youth, this bright machine survey. John Gay. *Fr.* The Fan. ViBoPo
Rise heart; thy Lord is risen. Sing his praise. Easter. George Herbert. AnAnS-1; MaMe; MeP; SCEP-1; SeCV-1; SeEP
Rise, Heir[e] of fresh eternity. Easter Day. Richard Crashaw. MaMe; PoLi
Rise, Lady Mistress, Rise! Nathaniel Field. *Fr.* Amends for Ladies. ElL; TuPP
(Matin Song.) HBV
(Song: "Rise Lady Mistresse, rise.") OBS
Rise Love and with my heart's. Venus on a Sea Horse. Maurice Carpenter. FaBoTw
Rise, Magyar; 'tis the country's call! National Song. Alexander Petofi. PoFr
Rise Me Up from Down Below, *with music. Unknown.* ShS
Rise, Mourner, Rise, *with music. Unknown.* BoAn-2
Rise, My Soul. Robert Seagrave. SoP
Rise, my soul, thy God directs thee. Egypt Left Behind. John Nelson Darby. SoP
Rose, O earth from out thy slumber. Prayer for Rain. *Unknown. Fr.* Kalevala. WGRP
Rise, O My Soul! *Unknown, sometimes at. to* Sir Walter Ralegh. OxBoCh
(To Jesus.) MaRV
Rise Oedipeus, and if thou canst unfould. The Poem. Thomas Morton. SCAP
Rise of Man, The. John White Chadwick. AA
Rise of Shivaji, The. Zulfikar Ghose. MoBS
Rise Oot Your Bed. John Barr of Craigielee. AnNZ
Rise, rise princely shepherd & bee arbiter. *Unknown.* SeCSL
Rise, royall Sion! rise and sing. Lauda Sion Salvatorem. Richard Crashaw. MaMe
"Rise," said the Master, "come unto the feast." The Bride [*or* The Master's Call]. Henry Alford. OBEV (1st ed.); SoP
Rise! Sleep no more! 'Tis a noble morn! The Hunter's Song. "Barry Cornwall." BBV (1923 ed.); GN; OTPC; VA
Rise then, immortall maid! Religion rise! On a Treatise of Charity. Richard Crashaw. MaMe
Rise, thou best and brightest morning! New Year's Day. Richard Crashaw. MaMe; SeEP
Rise thou first and fairest morning. An Himne for the Circumcision Day of Our Lord. Richard Crashaw. MaMe
Rise up, my song! stretch forth thy wings and fly. A Greeting. Philip Bourke Marston. VA
Rise Up, O Men of God! William Pierson Merrill. MaRV
(Festal Song.) SoP; WGRP
Rise up, rise up,/ And, as the trumpet blowing. The Trumpet. Edward Thomas. HBMV; MMA; MoBrPo; OHIP; POTE; SiSw; TSW
Rise up, rise up, Jack Spratt. And you, his wife. Sonnet XIII. Winfield Townley Scott. ErPo
"Rise up, rise up, my seven brave sons." Earl Brand (A *vers.*). *Unknown.* ViBoFo
"Rise up, rise up, now, Lord Douglas," she says. The Douglas Tragedy [*or* Earl Brand]. *Unknown.* BoLiVe; ESPB (B *vers.*); HBV; MaC; MeWo; NoP; OBB; OnSP; OxBB; PAn; PoPo; TrGrPo
"Rise up, rise up, ye seven sleepers." The Seven Sleepers. *Unknown.* BFSS
Rise Up Shepherd an' Foller. *Unknown.* BoAN-2, *with music;* ChrBoLe
Rise up! the flute sounds in the distance. Ariosto. *Fr.* Song for the Third Marriage of Lucrezia Borgia. HW
Rise up, thou monstrous anthill on the plain. Residence in London. Wordsworth. *Fr.* The Prelude, VII. MBW-2
"Rise up, you seven bretherens." Earl Brand (B *vers.*). *Unknown.* BaBo
Rise with the Lamb of Innocence. *Unknown.* MeEL
Rise you up, my dearest dear. Shoot the Buffalo. *Unknown.* TrAS
Risen above the uncertain. To Her. Robert Mezey. NaP
Risen Lord, The. H. J. McKinnell. SoP
Risen with Healing in His Wings. St. John of Damascus, *tr. fr. Greek.* BePJ
Risest thou thus, dim dawn, again,/And howlest, issuing out of night. In Memoriam A. H. H., LXXII. Tennyson. EPN; GTBS-D; OBNC; PoEL-5; ViPo; VP
Risest thou thus, dim dawn, again,/ So loud with voices of the birds. In Memoriam A. H. H., XCIX. Tennyson. EnLi-2; EPN; OAEP; ViPo; VP
Rising, The. Thomas Buchanan Read. *Fr.* The Wagoner of the Alleghanies. PAH; TreFS
Rising, The. Julia Vinograd. YAP
Rising in the North, The. *Unknown.* ACP (1952 ed.); BaBo; ESPB
Rising moon has hid the stars, The. Endymion. Longfellow. AA; HBV
Rising of the Moon, The, A.D. 1798. John Keegan Casey. AnIV; IrPN; OnYI
Rising of the Session, The. Robert Fergusson. OxBS
Rising Sun, The. Lawrence Durrell. *Fr.* Eight Aspects of Melissa. NeBP
Rising Sun Blues, The, *with music. Unknown.* OuSiCo
Rising sun complies with our weak sight, The. To the King, upon His Majesty's Happy Return. Edmund Waller. SCEP-2
Rising Village, The, *sels.* Oliver Goldsmith, the Younger.
"How sweet it is, at first approach of morn." OBCV
"Not fifty summers yet have passed thy clime." OBCV
"What noble courage must their hearts have fired." FOL; OBCV; PeCV
"While now the Rising Village claims a name." CaP
Rising without names today. The Survivor. Stephen Berg. *Fr.* Entering the Body. NaP
Risks of the Game, The. Adam Lindsay Gordon. *Fr.* Ye Wearie Wayfarer, Fytte II. OtMeF
Rispetti: On the Death of a Child. Paul Heyse, *tr. fr. German by* E. H. Mueller. PoPl
Rispetto: "What good is there, ah me, what good is Love?" Agnes Mary Frances Robinson. Tuscan Cypress, II, XII, *and* XV. HBMV
Risposta. *Unknown.* HBV
Risselty Rosselty. *Unknown.* DiPo
Risus Dei. Thomas Edward Brown. PoVP
Rite and Fore-Time. David Jones. *Fr.* The Anathemata. AtBAP
Rite at a Brother's Grave. Catullus, *tr. fr. Latin by* George Lamb. OnPM
Rite of Spring. Leo Kennedy. CaP
Rites for a Demagogue. Anthony Thwaite. NePoEA-2
Ritratto. Ezra Pound. PP
Ritual. Gustav Davidson. NYTB
Ritual Not Religion. *Unknown.* WGRP
Ritual of Departure. Thomas Kinsella. OPoP
Ritual of the Grape. Omar Khayyám. *See* Omar and Death.

Ritual to Read to Each Other, A. William Stafford. NePA
Ritualists, The. William Carlos Williams. NYBP
Rival, The. Sir George Etherege. *See* Rivals.
Rival, The. Sylvia Plath. NoP
Rival, The. Sylvia Townsend Warner. BoLiVe (1939 ed.); MoAB; MoBrPo
Rival Curates, The. W. S. Gilbert. CenHV
Rival Friends, The, *sels.* Peter Hausted.
Have Pity, Grief. EG; SeCL
("Have pity, grief, I cannot pay.") TuPP
(Song, The: "Have pity (Grief) I can not pay.") SeEP
"Have you a desire to see." TuPP
Of His Mistress. EG; SeCL
Rival Sisters, The, *sel.* Robert Gould.
Song: "Fair, and soft, and gay, and young," *fr.* III. CEP; SeCL
(Fair, and Soft, and Gay, and Young.) UnTE
Rivals, The, *sel.* Sir William Davenant.
Song: "My lodging it is on the cold ground." PeRV; SeCL
Rivals, The. Paul Laurence Dunbar. IHA
Rivals, The. James Stephens. BiS; BoTP; FaPON; GTBS-D; InvP; MoVE; OBEV (new ed.); OBMV; OTPC (1946 ed.); PoPl; PoRh; SP; UTS
Rivals. *At. to* Sir George Etherege *and to* William Walsh. HBV; OBEV
(Rival, The.) CavP
(Song: "Of all the torments, all the cares.") LiTL; OBEC; ViBoPo
Rivals, The. Robert Whitaker. OQP
River, The. Matthew Arnold. CBEP; VP
River, The. Hart Crane. *Fr.* The Bridge: Powhatan's Daughter. AmP; AmPP; AnFE; AP; CMoP; CoAnAm; CoBA; CoBMV; LiTA; MoAB; MoAmPo; NAMP; OxBA; TwAmPo; ViBoPo (1958 ed.)
Sels.
"Down, down—born Pioneers in time's despite." TrGrPo
"You will not hear it as the sea." ViBoPo
River, The. Donald Davie. NYTB
River, The. Emerson. MAmP
River, The. Mary Sinton Leitch. HBMV
River, The, *sels.* Pare Lorentz.
"Black spruce and Norway pine." AmFN; NAMP
"Down the Yellowstone, the Milk, the White and Cheyenne." AmFN
River, The. Patrick MacDonogh. NeIP
River, The. Roy Macnab. PeSA
River, The. Dabney Stuart. NYBP
River Afram. Andrew Amankwa Opoku. PBA
River boat had loitered down its way, The. Gamesters All. DuBose Heyward. HBMV; InP
River Boats, The. Daniel Whitehead Hicky. AmFN
River Bridge, The. James S. Tippett. GFA
River brought down, The. How We Heard the Name. Alan Dugan. CaFP; CoAP; NMP
River Cherwell, The. William Lisle Bowles. Sonn
River Duddon, The, *sels.* Wordsworth.
After-Thought, XXXIV. EnL; EnRP; EPN; FaBoEn; MBW-2; OBNC; PeER; SeCePo
(After-Thought to "The River Duddon.") OAEP; OBRV
("I thought of thee, my partner and my guide.") EnLi-2
(Valedictory Sonnet to the River Duddon.) OBEV
"'Change me, some God, into that breathing rose!" VII. Sonn
"How shall I paint thee?—Be this naked stone," III. Wordsworth. MERP
"Not hurled precipitous from steep to steep," XXXII. Sonn
"Old inventive poets, had they seen, The," XX. EnLi-2
"Return, Content! for fondly I pursued," XXVI. EnLi-2
"Sole listner, Duddon! to the breeze that played," V. EnLi-2
"Take, cradled nursling of the mountain, take," IV. MERP
River Fight, The. Henry Howard Brownell. PaA; PAH; PAP
"Would you hear of the river-fight,"*sel.* AA; EtS
River-Fog. Kiyowara Fukayabu, *tr. fr. Japanese by* Arthur Waley. *Fr.* Shui Shu. by Arthur Waley. FaPON
("Because river-fog.") AWP; JAWP; LiTW; WBP
River Glideth in a Secret Tongue, The. Anthony Ostroff. NePoAm-2
River God, The. John Fletcher. *Fr.* The Faithful Shepherdess, III, i. BoC; TrGrPo, *sl. shorter*
(River God to Amoret, The.) CLwM
River God, The. Sacheverell Sitwell. MoBrPo
River God, The. Stevie Smith. FaBoTw
River god cries far, The. Tao. Alfred Goldsworthy Bailey. CaP
River God to Amoret, The. John Fletcher. *See* River God, The.
River-God's Song, The. John Fletcher. *Fr.* The Faithful Shepherdess, III, i. FaPON; MoShBr; PCH
("Do not fear to put thy feet.") CBEP; TuPP
(Song: "Do not fear to put thy feet.") EIL; OBS; ThWaDe
River God's Song. Anne Ridler. NYBP
River has not any care, The. Francis Thompson. *Fr.* Contemplation. FaBoEn
River, I am passing. River Afram. Andrew Amankwa Opoku. PBA
River in the Meadows, The. Léonie Adams. AnAmPo; MAP; MoAB; MoAmPo; NP
River Is a Piece of Sky, The. John Ciardi. PDV; PoPl; SoPo
River Lea, The, with music. Sam Peck. SoAmSa
River Map, The, and We're Done. Charles Olson. CoPo
River-Mates. Padraic Colum. AnIV; AWP; JAWP; WBP
(Otters.) OA
River meads of vanished Clonard hold, The. Clonard. Thomas S. Jones, Jr. HBMV
River Merchant's Wife, The; a Letter. Li Po, *tr. fr. Chinese by* Ezra Pound. AmP; AmPP; AnAmPo; AWP; BoLP; CABA; CoAnAm; DTC; InPo; LiTA; LiTL; LiTW; MoAB; MoAmPo (1950 ed.); MoPo; NAMP; NoP; NP; OBMV; OxBA; PG (1945 ed.); PIA; PoIE; PoSa; TwAmPo; TwCP; VaPo; WBP
River Moons. Carl Sandburg. FIW
River Night. Frances Frost. OCS
River of Grace, A. Molly Anderson Haley. ChIP
River of Heaven, The. *Unknown, tr. fr. Japanese by* Lafcadio Hearn. *Fr.* Manyo Shu. AWP; LiTW
River of Life, The. Thomas Campbell. FaFP; GTBS; GTBS-D; GTBS-P; GTBS-W; GTSE; GTSL; HBV; LiTB; LiTG
(Thought Suggested by the New Year, A.) OBNC
River of Life. Elayne Tedder. SoP
River of Stars, The. Alfred Noyes. OnMSP
River Roses. D. H. Lawrence. BrPo; CMoP; SiSw; ViBoPo
River Skater. Winifred Welles. SD
River Song. Elizabeth Brewster. CaP
River Song. Weldon Kees. TwAmPo
River that must turn full after I stop dying. All. Louis Zukofsky. CoPo
River, that rollest by the ancient walls. Stanzas to the Po. Byron. ERoP-2
River this November afternoon, The. The Double Vision. C. Day Lewis. AtBAP
River used to store up in its mouth, The. The River. Roy Macnab. PeSA
River Walk, The. Padraic Fallon. OxBI
River widens to a pathless sea, The. On a Ferry Boat. Richard Burton. AA
Riverdale Lion. John Robert Colombo. PeCV (1967 ed.)
Riverman, The. Elizabeth Bishop. NYBP
Rivers. Thomas Storer. EIL; FaBoCh
Rivers and Mountains. John Ashbery. ANYP; CoAP; FRC
Rivers Arise; a Fragment. Milton. ChTr
Rivers of the West. "Sunset Joe." PoOW
Rivers Remember, The. Nancy Byrd Turner. AmFN
Rivers rush into the sea, The. The Song of the Bird. Longfellow. BoTP
Rivers that flowed divided each from each. Chinese Poems: Arthur Waley. "C. A. Fair." PeSA
Rivers Till and Tweed, The. *Unknown.* *See* Two Rivers.
"Rivers Unknown to Song." Alice Meynell. HBMV; NP
Riverton. Edmund Wilson. AnFE; CoAnAm
Rivery field spread out below, A. W. B. Yeats. *Fr.* Let All Things Pass Away. ChTr
Riveter, The. Margaret E. Sangster. PEDC
Rivets. N. S. Olds. EtS
Rivulet, The. Lucy Larcom. PRWS
Rivulet-loving wanderer Abraham, The. Abraham. Edwin Muir. MoRP
Rivulet with rush of sound, The. Midwinter Thaw. Lenore Pratt. CaP
Rizpah. Tennyson. BEL; CABL; EnLi-2; EPN; PAn; PeVV; PoEL-5; PoVP; TOP; VA
Road, The. Conrad Aiken. AP; MAP; MoAmPo
Road, The. Patrick R. Chalmers. HBV
Road, The. John Gould Fletcher. HBMV; TSW

Road, The. Helene Johnson. AmNP; BANP; CDC; GoSl; PoNe
Road, The. Herbert Morris. NePoAm-2
Road, The. Edwin Muir. CMoP; FaBoEn; FaBoMo; FaFP; LiTB; LiTG; LiTM; ViBoPo (1958 ed.)
Road, The. Nikolay Platonovich Ogarev, *tr. fr. Russian by* P. E. Matheson. AWP
Road, The. Hyam Plutzik. FiMAP
Road, The. Siegfried Sassoon. MCCG
Road, The. Zalman Schneour, *tr. fr. Yiddish by* Joseph Leftwich. TrJP
Road, The. James Stephens. HBMV
Road and the End, The. Carl Sandburg. NP
Road at My Door, The. W. B. Yeats. Meditations in Time of Civil War, V. CABL; LiTB; PIA
Road at the top of the rise, The. The Middleness of the Road. Robert Frost. CrMA; LiTA
Road Back, The. Anne Sexton. NYBP
Road can't be as sad as a shoe is sad, A. Shoe. John Perreault. YAP
Road climbs from the valley past the public, The. A Visit to Brontëland. James Kirkup. POTi
Road deepening in the north, A. The Stone Harp. John Haines. ThO
Road Fellows. Barbara Young. BrR
Road from Election to Christmas, The. Oscar Williams. NAMP
Road-Hymn for the Start. William Vaughn Moody. MAP; MoAmPo (1942 ed.)
Road in the Weald, A. Richard Church. HaMV
Road is burnt to dust, like more dust meadow rue, The. Harvest Dust. Winifred Welles. MAP
Road is left that once was trod, The. The Old Road. Jones Very. AA
Road is thronged with women, The: soldiers pass. The Road. Siegfried Sassoon. MCCG
Road is wide and the stars are out and the breath of the night is sweet, The. Roofs. Joyce Kilmer. PoLF
Road like brown ribbon, A. September. Edwina Fallis. SUS; TiPo; YeAr
Road Makers. V. H. Friedlaender. MaRV
Road might lead to anywhere, A. Roads. Rachel Field. BrR; FaPON; PDV; SoPo; StVeCh; TiPo; WaKn
Road Not Taken, The. Robert Frost. AmPP; AnFE; AnNE; AP; APA; ChTr; CMoP; CoAnAm; CoBA; CoBMV; DiPo; EvOK; FaBoCh; FaFP; GTBS-D; GTBS-W; ILP; InP; LiTA; LiTG; LiTM; LoGBV; MAP; MAPA; MaPo (1969 ed.); MoAB; MoAmPo; NePA; OxBA; PAn; PG; PoE; PoLF; PoPl; PoPo; ReMP; SeCeV; TIHL; TreFT; TwAmPo; TwCP
Road of Ireland, A. Charles L. O'Donnell. HBMV
Road of Life, The. William Morris. *Fr.* The Earthly Paradise. OBNC
Road of Remembrance, The. Lizette Woodworth Reese. HBV
Road Song. Margaret E. Sangster. PoMa
Road Song. Louis Untermeyer. StaSt
Road Song of the Bandar Log, The. Kipling. *Fr.* The Jungle Book. BoPe; OAEP (2d ed.)
Road to Anywhere, The. Bert Leston Taylor. HBMV; MPB; TSW
Road to Babylon, The. Margaret Adelaide Wilson. HBMV
Road to Bethlehem, The. Watson Kirkconnell. MaRV
Road to Bologna, The. Roy Macnab. PeSA
Road to Castaly, The, *sel.* Alice Brown.
Revelation. WGRP
Road to China, The. Olive Beaupré Miller. MPB
Road to Cook's Peak, The. *Unknown.* CoSo
Road to Dieppe, The. John Huston Finley. MCCG
Road to Emmaus, The. Ida Norton Munson. ChIP
Road to France, The. Daniel Henderson. HBV; MC; PaA; PAH
Road to Granada, The. Arthur Ketchum. HT
Road to Nijmegen, The. Earle Birney. OBCV
Road to Raffydiddle, The. Mildred Plew Meigs. GoBP; TiPo (1952 ed.)
"Road to Ruin, The." *Unknown.* SCC
Road to the Bow, The. James David Corrothers. BANP
Road to the Pool, The. Grace Hazard Conkling. HBMV
Road to Town, The. H. M. Sarson. BoTP
Road to Vagabondia, The. Dana Burnet. OTD; PoLF
Road to Wisdom, The. Piet Hein. TIHL
Road was dreary and rough and long. The Emmaus Road. Avis B. Christiansen. SoP
Road was lit with moon and star, The. Emily Dickinson. MWA-2
Road winds up the hill to meet the height, The. Faith. Emma Carleton. MaRV
Roads. Ruth Dallas. AnNZ
Roads. Rachel Field. BrR; FaPON; PDV; SoPo; StVeCh; TiPo; WaKn
Road's End, The. Theodosia Garrison. HBMV
Roads Go Ever On and On. J. R. R. Tolkien. FaPON
(Roads Go Ever Ever On.) TiPo (1959 ed.)
Roads lead southward, blue, The. To Argos. Lawrence Durrell. MoPo
Roadside Fire, The. Robert Louis Stevenson. *See* Romance.
Roadside Flowers. Bliss Carman. HBMV
Roadside forests here and there were touched with tawny gold, The. Mistress Hale of Beverly. Lucy Larcom. PAH
Roadside inn this summer Saturday, A. Sonnet. Thomas Caulfield Irwin. IrPN
Roadside near Moscow. R. A. D. Ford. PeCV; TwCaPo
Roadside nut-tree planted, here I stand, A. The Mournful Nut-Tree. Antipater. OnPM
Roadside: Spleen. Arthur Freeman. NYTB
Roadside thistle, eager, The. Matsuo Basho, *tr. fr. Japanese by* Curtis Hidden Page. AWP; LiTW
Roadway has a flinten face, The. The Old Inn-Sign. Wilfrid Thorley. BrR
Roadways. John Masefield. BEL; BoTP; GTSL; HT; MCCG; PoPo; RePo
Roamer, The, *sel.* George Edward Woodberry.
"Love is the bread that feeds the multitudes." MaRV
Roaming the lonely garden, he and I. From a Chinese Vase. Winifred Welles. MAP
Roan Stallion. Robinson Jeffers. AmPP (4th ed.); BeLS; NAMP
Roar and gurgle of the ocean cave, The. Stradivarius to an Unfinished Violin (1710). Eugene Lee-Hamilton. Sonn
Roar drowns the reproach, facing him. Edwin Denby. ANYP
Roar of Niagara dies away, The. H. W. L. John Nichol. VA
Roar of the world is in my ears, The. Thanksgiving. Joyce Kilmer. MaRV
Roarers in a Ring. Ted Hughes. NePoEA-2; POTi
Roaring alongside he takes for granted, The. Sandpiper. Elizabeth Bishop. NYBP
Roaring, clanking. Broadway: Twilight. Tom Prideaux. OCS
Roaring company that festive night, A. The Dark and the Fair. Stanley Kunitz. PoCh
Roaring Days, The. Henry Lawson. BoAV; NeLNL
Roaring Lad and the Ranting Lass, The; or A Merry Couple Madly Met. *Unknown.* CoMu
Roaring Mad Tom. *Unknown.* *See* Tom o' Bedlam's Song.
Roaring of the wheels has filled my ears, The. A Cry from the Ghetto. Morris Rosenfeld. TrJP
Roast Beef of Old England, The. Henry Fielding. *Fr.* Don Quixote in England, I. CEP; OBEC
Roast Swan Song. *Unknown, tr. fr. Latin by* George F. Whicher. FlW; LiTW
Rob Roy. Eleanor *and* Herbert Farjeon. OnPP
Rob Roy, *sel.* Sir Walter Scott.
"Farewell to the land where the clouds love to rest," *fr. ch.* 36. NBM
Rob Roy. *Unknown.* BaBo; ESPB (A *and* B *vers.*)
Rob Roy Macgregor. Rob Roy. Eleanor *and* Herbert Farjeon. OnPP
Robben Island. Robert Dederick. PeSA
Robber, The. Ivy O. Eastwick. SiSoSe
Robber, The. W. J. Turner. MoBrPo
Robber Bridegroom, The. Allen Tate. TwAmPo
Robber Kitten, The. *At. to* George M. Baker. CIV; FTB
Robe of Grass, The. John Le Gay Brereton. BoAu
Robene and Makyne. Robert Henryson. GoTS
(Robin and Makin.) OAEP; PoEL-1
(Robin and Makyne.) OBEV
Robert Barnes, fellow fine. Mother Goose. OxNR; RIS
Robert Bruce to His Men at Bannockburn. Burns. *See* Scots Wha Hae.
Robert Bruce's Address to His Army, before the Battle of Bannockburn. Burns. *See* Scots Wha Hae.

Robert Burns. William Alexander. HBV
Robert E. Lee. Stephen Vincent Benét. *Fr.* John Brown's Body. AmFN
Robert E. Lee. Julia Ward Howe. DD; MC; PAH; PoRL
Robert Frost. Louis Untermeyer. BOHV
Robert Gould Shaw. Paul Laurence Dunbar. Kal
Robert Gould Shaw. William Vaughn Moody. *Fr.* An Ode in Time of Hesitation. AA
Robert Louis Stevenson. Lizette Woodworth Reese. HBV
Robert of Lincoln. Bryant. AmePo; AnNE; BoChLi; DD; FaBoBe; FaPON; GFA; HBV; HBVY; HH; MPB; OTPC (1946 ed.); PCH; PRWS; PTK; WBLP, *abr.*
Robert of Sicily, brother of Pope Urbane. King Robert of Italy. Longfellow. *Fr.* Tales of a Wayside Inn. AnNE; BeLS; MWA-1; OHIP; OnSP; PCD; YT
Robert Rowley rolled a round roll 'round. Mother Goose. OxNR; StVeCh
Robert, Second Duke of Normandy, *sel.* Thomas Lodge.
  Pluck the Fruit and Taste the Pleasure. ElL
  (Carpe Diem.) OBSC
  (Song: "Pluck the fruit and taste the pleasure.") CLwM; EnRePo
Robert the Bruce. Edwin Muir. OxBS
Robert Whitmore. Frank Marshall Davis. Kal; PoNe
Robes loosely flowing, and aspect as free. Seeing Her Dancing. Sir Robert Heath. OBS; SeEP
Robin, The. Laurence Alma-Tadema. BoTP; GFA; OTPC (1946 ed.)
Robin, The. O. M. Bent. BoTP
Robin, The. George Daniel. OBS; UnPo (1st ed.)
Robin, A. Walter de la Mare. BiS; ChTr; CMoP
Robin, The. Emily Dickinson. *See* Robin is the one, The.
Robin. Anne Blackwell Payne. GFA
Robin, The. *Unknown.* PoPo
Robin, The. Jones Very. AnNE; Sonn
Robin-a-bobbin. *Unknown.* OxNR
Robin Adair. Lady Caroline Keppel. FaBoBe; HBV
Robin and a robin's son, A. *Unknown.* OxNR
Robin and Gandelyn. *Unknown.* *See* Robyn and Gandeleyn.
Robin and Makin [*or* Makyne]. Robert Henryson. *See* Robene and Makyne.
Robin and Man. Ralph Gordon. NYTB
Robin and Richard [*or* Richard and Robin] were two pretty [*or* little] men. Mother Goose. BoTP; OTPC (1946 ed.); OxBoLi; OxNR; RIS; SAS
Robin and the Cows, The. William Dean Howells. GoTP
Robin and the red-breast, The. A Rule for Birds' Nesters. *Unknown.* DD; HBV; HBVY; OTPC; OxNR
Robin and the Wren, The. Popular Rhymes. Blake. ThGo
Robin and the wren, The. Four Birds. *Unknown.* ChTr
Robin and the wren, The. Greed. *Unknown.* OxNR
Robin, biped, beaked, worm-prober, The. Robin and Man. Ralph Gordon. NYTB
Robin chants when the thrush is done, The. To-Morrow. Florence Earle Coates. AA
Robin dwelt in greenë wood. The Death of Robin Hood. *Unknown.* EnSB
Robin Friend has gone to bed. Bed-Time. Laurence Alma-Tadema. BoTP
Robin Goodfellow ("From Oberon, in fairyland"). *Unknown.* FaBoCh; ViBoPo
  (Mad-Merry Pranks of Robin Good-Fellow, The.) CBEP; SeCL, *abr.*; SeEP
Robin Goodfellow, His Mad Prankes and Merry Jestes, *sels.* *Unknown.*
  And Can the Physician Make Sick Men Well, *fr.* Pt. II. AtBAP
  (Lily, Germander, and Sops-in-Wine.) AnFE
  (Song: "And can the physician make sick men well?") ElL; LoBV; ThWaDe
  Robin Good-Fellow's Song: "Round about, little ones," *fr.* Pt. II. ElL
Robin has flown away up in a tree, A. A May Basket. Lilian Bayne West. GFA
Robin he's gane to the wast. The Wife Wrapt in Wether's Skin (B *vers.*). *Unknown.* ESPB
Robin Hood. Keats. AWP; BEL; EnLi-2; EnLit; EnRP; EPN; InPo; OTPC (1946 ed.); PCD; PoeP
Robin Hood. Rachel MacAndrew. BoTP
Robin Hood, *wr. title.* John O'Keeffe. *See* Merry Sherwood.
Robin Hood. Patience Adrian Ross. PCH
Robin Hood/ Has gone to the wood. *Unknown.* OxNR
Robin Hood and Allen [*or* Allan *or* Alan *or* Allin] -a-Dale. *Unknown.* BaBo; BoChLi; BuBa; EnLit; ESPB; FaBoBe; GoTP; HBV; LoEn; MCCG; MoShBr; OBB; OnSP; StVeCh (1940 ed.)
Robin Hood and Guy of Gisborne. *Unknown.* ATP (1935 ed.); BaBo; BEL; BuBa; CoBE; ESPB; OAEP; OBB, *sl. diff., abr.*; TOP
Robin Hood and Little John. *Unknown.* BaBo (A *and* B *vers.*); OTPC (1946 ed.); StaSt; StVeCh; ViBoFo
Robin Hood and Maid Marian. *Unknown.* BaBo; ESPB
Robin Hood and Queen Katherine. *Unknown.* BaBo; ESPB (A *and* B *vers.*)
Robin Hood and the Beggar, I ("Come light and listen, you gentlemen all"). *Unknown.* BaBo; ESPB
Robin Hood and the Beggar, II ("Lyth and listen, gentlemen"). *Unknown.* BaBo; ESPB
Robin Hood and the Bishop of Hereford. *Unknown.* BaBo; BuBa; ESPB; OBB
  (Robin Hood and the Bishop, *sl. diff.*) BaBo; ESPB
Robin Hood and the Butcher. *Unknown.* BuBa; ESPB (A *and* B *vers.*); OBB; RG
Robin Hood and the Curtal Friar. *Unknown.* BaBo; BuBa; ESPB (A *and* B *vers.*); OBB
Robin Hood and the Golden Arrow. *Unknown.* ESPB
Robin Hood and the Monk. *Unknown.* BaBo; ESPB; MeEV, *tr. fr. Middle English*; OBB; ViBoFo
  (Robyn Hode and the Munke.) OxBB
  Sel.
  "In somer, when the shawes be sheyne," *first* 5 *sts.* ViBoPo
  (In Summer.) CH
  (In the Fair Forest, *first* 2 *sts., mod.*) BoTP
  (May in the Green-Wood.) OBEV
  (Morning of May, A, *mod.*) PoLi
Robin Hood and the Pedlars. *Unknown.* ESPB
Robin Hood and the Potter. *Unknown.* BaBo; ESPB
Robin Hood and the Prince of Aragon. *Unknown.* ESPB
Robin Hood and the Ranger. *Unknown.* ESPB; StVeCh
Robin Hood and the Scotchman (A *and* B *vers.*) *Unknown.* ESPB
Robin Hood and the Shepherd. *Unknown.* ESPB
Robin Hood and the Tanner. *Unknown.* BaBo; ESPB; MaC
Robin Hood and the Three Squires. *Unknown.* *See* Robin Hood and the Widow's Three Sons.
Robin Hood and the Tinker. *Unknown.* BaBo; ESPB
Robin Hood and the Two Priests. *Unknown.* *See* Robin Hood's Golden Prize.
Robin Hood and the Valiant Knight. *Unknown.* ESPB
Robin Hood and the Widow's Three Sons. *Unknown.* BuBa; OBB; OnMSP
  (How Robin Hood Rescued the Widow's Sons.) StPo
  (Robin Hood and the Three Squires.) EnSB
  (Robin Hood and the Widow's Sons.) GoTP
  (Robin Hood Rescuing the Widow's Three Sons.) EnLi-1; TiPo (1952 ed.)
  (Robin Hood Rescuing Three Squires.) ESPB (A *and* B *vers.*); ViBoFo
Robin Hood hee was and a tall young man. Robin Hood's Progress to Nottingham. *Unknown.* BaBo; ESPB
Robin Hood Newly Revived. *Unknown.* BaBo; ESPB
Robin Hood Rescuing Three Squires [*or* the Widow's Three Sons]. *Unknown.* *See* Robin Hood and the Widow's Three Sons.
Robin Hood Rescuing Will Stutly. *Unknown.* BaBo; ESPB
Robin Hood, Robin Hood,/ In the mickle wood! Mother Goose. BoTP; OTPC; OxNR
"Robin Hood, Robin Hood,"/Said Little John. Mother Goose. PCH
Robin Hood's Birth, Breeding, Valor, and Marriage. *Unknown.* ESPB
Robin Hood's Chase. *Unknown.* BaBo; ESPB
Robin Hood's Death, *diff. vers.* *Unknown.* BaBo; ESPB; TrGrPo; ViBoFo
  (Death of Robin Hood, The.) BuBa; EnSB; FlW; OBB; OnSP
  Sel.
  Death of Robin Hood: "I never hurt maid," *last* 3 *sts.* ViBoPo
Robin Hood's Delight. *Unknown.* ESPB
Robin Hood's End. *Unknown.* A Gest of Robyn Hode, Fytte VIII. GoTL
Robin Hood's Funeral. Anthony Munday *and* Henry Chettle. *See* Dirge for Robin Hood.
Robin Hood's Golden Prize. *Unknown.* BaBo; ESPB; OBB

Robin (continued)
(Robin Hood and the Two Priests.) BuBa
Robin Hood's Progress to Nottingham. *Unknown.* BaBo; ESPB
Robin is a Gabriel, The. Emily Dickinson. MWA-2
Robin is a lovely lad. The Dance. *Unknown, at. to* Thomas Campion. ElL; FaBoCh; LiTL; LoBV; LoGBV
Robin is the one, The. Emily Dickinson. BiS; FaBV; HBVY
Robin Knows Great A. *Unknown. See* Come Hither, Little Puppy-Dog.
Robin laughed in the orange tree, The. Tampa Robins. Sidney Lanier. PoRL
Robin of the Red Breast, The. *Unknown.* PoMS
Robin on my lawn, The. February. Francis Brett Young. HBMV; HBVY
Robin Redbreast. William Allingham. BiS; BoChLi; DD; FaBoBe; HBV; HBVY; MoShBr; MPB; OTPC; PEDC; PRWS; TVC; WePo
(Child's Song, A.) UTS
Robin Redbreast, A, *much abr.* Blake. *Fr.* Auguries of Innocence. SiSoSe; UTS
(Many Birds.) ThGo
("Robin redbreast in a cage, A.") OxBoLi, *sl. abr.*; TreFT, *much abr.*
(Things to Remember, *br. sel.*) RIS
(Three Things to Remember, *br. sel.*) FaPON; MoShBr; OTD; OTPC (1946 ed.); PCD
Robin Redbreast. George Washington Doane. AA; DD; HBV; HBVY
Robin Redbreast. John Banister Tabb. StJW
Robin Red Breast. Lula Lowe Weeden. CDC
Robin redbreast in a cage, A. A Robin Redbreast [*or* Three Things to Remember]. Blake. *Fr.* Auguries of Innocence. FaPON; MoShBr; OTD; OTPC (1946 ed.); OxBoLi; PCD; RIS; SiSoSe; ThGo; TreFT; UTS
Robin Redbreasts, The. Ann Hawkshaw. OTPC (1923 ed.); SAS
(I'll Try.) PPL
Robin rents a tree-top house. Honest Mr. Robin. Eleanor Hammond. GFA
Robin sang sweetly/ In the Autumn days. *Unknown.* BoTP
Robin [*or* Robene] sat on gude green hill. Robene [*or* Robin] and Makyne [*or* Makin]. Robert Henryson. GoTS; OAEP; OBEV; PoEL-1
Robin, sing to the rainbow! Sing-Time. Rose Waldo. GFA
Robin sings in the elm, The. The Robin and the Cows. William Dean Howells. GoTP
Robin sings of willow-buds, The. Bird Song. Laura E. Richards. HBV
Robin skimmed into the room, A. The Bird in the Room. Rudolph Chambers Lehmann. HBMV; HBVY
Robin the Bobbin. *Unknown.* OxNR
Robin to His Mate, The. Ann A. G. Carter. OTPC (1923 ed.); PPL; SAS
Robinets and Jenny Wrens. *Unknown.* OxNR
Robin's Come. William W. Caldwell. DD, *abr.*; HBVY
Robin's Cross. George Darley. OnYI
Robin's Egg, The. Annie Charlotte Dalton. CaP
Robin's Epitaph, A. Samuel Rogers. *See* Epitaph on a Robin Redbreast, An.
Robins in the treetop. Marjorie's Almanac. Thomas Bailey Aldrich. FaPON; GFA; MPB; PRWS
Robins sang in England. Robin's Song. Rodney Bennett. BoTP
Robin's Secret. Katharine Lee Bates. AA
Robin's Song. Rodney Bennett. BoTP
Robin's Song, The. *Unknown, at. to* C. Lovat Fraser. BoTP; MoShBr
Robin's Song. E. L. M. King. TiPo
Robins wait for early worms; bees will find their clover. Birds and Bees. *Unknown.* UnTE
Robinson. Weldon Kees. NaP; NYBP; TwAmPo
Robinson at cards at the Algonquin; a thin. Aspects of Robinson. Weldon Kees. CoAP; NaP; NYBP; TwAmPo
Robinson at Home. Weldon Kees. CoAP; NYBP; TwAmPo
Robinson Crusoe. Charles Edward Carryl. *See* Robinson Crusoe's Story.
Robinson Crusoe Returns to Amsterdam. Francis Jammes, *tr. fr. French by* Jethro Bithell. *Fr.* Amsterdam. FaPON
Robinson Crusoe's Story. Charles Edward Carryl. *Fr.* Davy and the Goblin, *ch.* 11. BeLS; BoChLi; BOHV; FiBHP; InMe; MCCG; OnPP; OTPC (1946 ed.); PCD; PoRA; PoRh; TSW
(Robinson Crusoe.) AA; HBV; HBVY; LHV; MPB; TreFT
Robyn and Gandeleyn. *Unknown.* BaBo; ESPB; OBB; OxBB
(Robin and Gandelyn.) EnSB
Robyn Hode and the Munke. *Unknown. See* Robin Hood and the Monk.
Roc, The. Richard Eberhart. CMoP
Rochester to the Post Boy. *At. to* the Earl of Rochester. PeRV
Rock, The, *sels.* T. S. Eliot.
"And now you live dispersed on ribbon roads." TiPo
Eagle Soars in the Summit of Heaven, The, *fr.* Chorus I. NAMP; OBMV; OnHM
(Knowledge without Wisdom.) MaRV
"Endless cycle of idea and action." TRV
"I have known two worlds." OxBoCh
"If humility and purity be not in the heart." TiPo
"In the beginning God created the world," *fr.* Chorus VII. OxBoCh
"In the land of lobelias and tennis flannels." SoP
"It is hard for those who have never known persecution," *fr.* Chorus VI. LiTM
(Why Should Men Love the Church?) MoRP
"Men have left God not for other gods, they say." SoP; TRV
Men Who Turn from God, *fr.* Chorus III. MaRV
"O Light Invisible, We praise Thee!" *fr.* Chorus X. MoRP; OxBoCh; TrPWD
"Son of Man, behold with thine eyes and hear with thine ears." PoDB
There Shall Always Be the Church. MaRV; TRV
When the Church Is No Longer Regarded, *fr.* Chorus VII. MaRV
"Where My Word is unspoken." TRV
"Word of the Lord came unto me, saying, The," *fr.* Chorus III. LiTB; TRV
"World turns and the world changes, The." TiPo
"You have seen the house built, you have seen it adorned, *fr.* Chorus X. PoDB
Rock, *sel.* Kathleen Raine.
"There is stone in me that knows stone." ImOP
Rock, The. Wallace Stevens. AP
Rock, The. *Unknown, tr. fr. Welsh.* ChTr
Rock, a leaf, mud, even the grass, A. The Concealment: Ishi, the Last Wild Indian. William Stafford. NaP
Rock and Hawk. Robinson Jeffers. MoVE; OxBA
Rock away, passenger, in the Third Class. *Unknown.* CenHV
Rock, Ball, Fiddle. *Unknown.* CBEP; CH; OxBoLi
("He that lies at the stock.") OxNR; SiTL
Rock, Be My Dream. MacKnight Black. NP
Rock Carving. Douglas Stewart. NeLNL; SeCePo
Rock Crumbles, The. Else Lasker-Schüler, *tr. fr. German by* Ralph Manheim. TrJP
Rock foundation of the fort was dread, The. Blockhouse. Olga Kirsch. PeSA
Rock-like mud unfroze a little and rills, The. The Manor Farm. Edward Thomas. ExPo; HaMV; NP; SeCeV
Rock-like the souls of men. Men Fade like Rocks. W. J. Turner. OBMV; POTE
Rock-lily's Pale Spray, The. Roland Robinson. BoAV
(Rock-Lily.) PoAu-2
Rock Me to Sleep. Elizabeth Akers Allen. AA; AmePo; BLPA; DD, *abr.*; FaBoBe; FaFP; NeHB; TreF; WBLP
(Rock Me to Sleep, Mother.) PaPo
Rock of Ages. Augustus Montague Toplady. BLRP; CBEP; FaFP; HBV; MaRV; NeHB; OTPC; OxBoCh; SoP; TOP; TreF; WGRP
(Prayer, Living and Dying, A.) CEP; EiCL; OBEC
Rock of Ages, let our song. Hanukkah Hymn. *Unknown.* TreFT
Rock of Cashel, The. Sir Aubrey De Vere. IrPN; NBM
Rock of My Salvation. Mordecai ben Isaac, *tr. fr. Hebrew by* Solomon Solis-Cohen. TrJP
Rock of Rubies, The. Robert Herrick. InMe
(Julia.) OTPC (1923 ed.)
(Rubies and Pearls.) HBV
Rock Painting. Jack Cope. PeSA
Rock Paintings, Drakensberg. Alan Ross. POTi
Rock Pool, The. Philip Hobsbaum. NYTB
Rock-a-by baby up in a tree. The Tree Buds. Kate L. Brown. TVC

Rock-a-by, hush-a-by, little papoose. Indian Lullaby. Charles A. Myall. MPB
Rock-a-by Lady, The. Eugene Field. BoChLi; BoTP; HBVY; MPB; PCH; PTK; RIS; TiPo
Rockaby, Lullaby. Josiah Gilbert Holland. *See* Lullaby: "Rock-aby, lullaby, bees in the clover."
Rock-a-bye, baby, on the tree top! *See* Hush-a-bye, baby, on the tree top.
Rock-a-bye [*or* Hush-a-bye], baby, thy cradle is green. Mother Goose. BoTP; FaFP; HBVY; OTPC; OxNR; PCH; PPL; RIS; SAS
Rock-a-bye Song, A. Helen Wing. GFA
Rocked in the Cradle of the Deep. Emma Hart Willard. AA; FaBoBe; FaFP; HBV; SoP; TreF; WBLP; WGRP
(Cradle of the Deep, The.) MaRV
Rockefeller Center. Charles Norman. CBV
Rocket Show. James K. Baxter. AnNZ
Rockets bubble upward and explode, The. Fourteen July 1956. Laurence D. Lerner. BoSA; PeSA
Rockferns. Norman Nicholson. MoBrPo (1950 ed.); NeMA
Rocking. *Unknown, tr. fr. Czech carol.* ChrBoLe
Rocking Chair, The. A. M. Klein. CaP; PeCV
Rocks flow and the mountain shapes flow, The. The Songs of the Birds. Edward Carpenter. WGRP
Rocks in de Mountens. *Unknown.* *See* My Old Hammah.
Rocks out in this bay, The. Rocks Partly Held in Mist. Arthur Gregor. NYTB
Rocky Acres. Robert Graves. LiTB; UnPo (3d ed.)
Rocky Mountain Sheep, The. Mary Austin. MPB
Rocky nook with [*or* and] hilltops three, The. Boston. Emerson. MC; PAP
Rococo. John Payne. OBVV
Rococo. Swinburne. HBV; ViBoPo
Roc's Brood. Samuel M. Bradley. FiSC
Rod, The. Robert Herrick. LiTB
Rod of Jesse, The. Isaiah XI:1-10, Bible, *O.T.* AWP; OuHeWo, XI: 1-9, LIII: 10-12
(And There Shall Come Forth, XI: 1-9.) TrJP
Rod Slemmon's Dream. William Hathaway. QAH
Rodeo Days. S. Omar Barker. PoOW
Roderick Dhu. Sir Walter Scott. *Fr.* The Lady of the Lake, V. OBRV
Rodney's Glory. Owen Roe O'Sullivan. OnYI
Rodney's Ride. Elbridge Streeter Brooks. MC; OTPC; PAH
Roe (and my joy to name) th'art now to go. To William Roe. Ben Johnson. BWP; OBS
Roethke. Howard Healy. NYTB
Rogation Days. Kenneth Rexroth. NaP
Roger and Dolly. Henry Carey. CoMu
("Young Roger came tapping at Dolly's window," *st.* 1, *sl. diff.*) OxNR
Roger Francis. Wilfrid Thorley. BrR
Roger Williams. Hezekiah Butterworth. PAH
Rogue Pearunners. R. G. Everson. PeCV (1967 ed.)
Roisin Dubh. Aubrey Thomas De Vere. AnIV
Roisin Dubh. *Unknown.* *See* Dark Rosaleen.
Rokeby, *sels.* Sir Walter Scott.
Allen-a-Dale, *fr.* III. EnRP; OTPC (1946 ed.); TOP
Brignal[l] Banks, *fr.* III. BEL; EnRP; EPN; OBEV; TOP
(Edmund's Song.) EnLi-2
(Outlaw, The.) GTBS; GTBS-D; GTBS-P; GTBS-W; GTSE; GTSL; OtMeF
(Song: "O Brignall banks are wild and fair.") HBV; OAEP; OBRV
Hunting Tribes of Air and Earth, The, *fr.* III. OA
Man the Enemy of Man, *fr.* III. WBLP
Song: "Weary lot is thine, fair maid, A," *fr.* III. OBNC; OBRV; ViBoPo
(Rover, The.) GTBS-P; GTSE; GTSL
(Rover's Adieu, The.) HBV; OBEV
(Rover's Farewell, The.) PoE
(Weary Lot Is Thine, A.) CH; EG
Roll a Rock Down. Henry Herbert Knibbs. AnAmPo; PFY
Roll-Call. Nathaniel Graham Shepherd. AA; BBV (1923 ed.); DD; HBV; OHIP; PaA
Roll de Ol' Chariot Along, *with music.* *Unknown.* BoAN-1
Roll forth, my song, like the rushing river. The Nameless One. James Clarence Mangan. ACP; EnRP; EPN; GoBC; GTBS; GTSE; HBV; IrPN; NBM; OBEV; OnYI; OxBI
Roll, Johnny Booger, *with music.* *Unknown.* BFSS
Roll, Jordan, Roll. *Unknown.* AA; BoAN-1; *with music*
Roll, *Julia,* Roll, *with music.* *Unknown.* ShS
(Row, Bullies, Row, *diff. vers., with music.*) SoAmSa
Roll of a chariot, The. *Unknown.* *Fr.* The Combat of Ferdiad and Cuchulain. OnYI
Roll on, and with thy rolling crust. One in the Infinite. George Francis Savage-Armstrong. VA
Roll on, roll on, you restless waves. The Waves on the Sea-Shore. Ann Hawkshaw. OTPC (1923 ed.)
Roll on, sad world! not Mercury or Mars. Elegy in Six Sonnets. Frederick Goddard Tuckerman. *Fr.* Sonnets. AnNE; AP; QFR; TreFS
Roll on, thou ball, roll on! To the Terrestrial Globe. W. S. Gilbert. BOHV; HBV; LiTG; OTD; PoPl; SiTL; TrGrPo; WhC
Roll on, thou deep and dark blue ocean—roll! The Ocean [*or* Address to the Ocean.] Byron. *Fr.* Childe Harold's Pilgrimage, IV. AtBAP; BoLiVe; EtS; FaPON; GN; OTD; PTK; TreFS; TrGrPo; UnPo (1st ed.); WBLP; WGRP
Roll on, ye stars! exult in youthful prime. Immortal Nature. Erasmus Darwin. *Fr.* The Botanic Garden: The Economy of Vegetation. OBEC
Roll Out, O Song. Frank Sewall. AA
Roll out ye drums, peal organs' loudest thunder. Elegy on Albert Edward the Peacemaker. *Unknown.* CoMu
"Roll out!" yell cookee. The Lumberyak. William F. Kirk. IHA
Roll the Chariot. *Unknown.* *See* We'll Roll the Golden Chariot Along.
Roll the Cotton Down, *with music.* *Unknown.* ShS, 3 *vers.*; SoAmSa
Rolled Over on Europe. Stephen Spender. CMoP
Rolled umbrella on my wrist, The. Waterloo Bridge. Christopher Middleton. *Fr.* Herman Moon's Hourbook. NePoEA-2
Roller, perched upon the wire, The. Driving Cattle to Casas Buenas. Roy Campbell. PeSA
Roller Skates. John Farrar. FaPON; GFA
Rollicking Bill the Sailor. *Unknown.* AmSS
Rollicking Mastodon, The. Arthur Macy. BOHV; NA
Rollicking Robin is here again. Sir Robin. Lucy Larcom. BoChLi; MPB; OTPC (1946 ed.); TiPo (1952 ed.)
Rolling clouds of greasy smoke. The Forest Fire. Arthur W. Monroe. PoOW
Rolling Down to Old Maui. *Unknown.* SoAmSa
Rolling Down to Rio. Kipling. HT
Rolling English Road, The. G. K. Chesterton. EvOK; FaBoCh; HBMV; LoGBV; OBEV (new ed.); OBMV; OtMeF; SeCeV; ShBV-2
(Before the Roman Came to Rye.) GTBS
Rolling Home, *with music.* *Unknown.* AmSS; ShS, 2 *vers.*
Rolling John, *sel.* A. J. Wood.
"Rolling John and night together." PoAu-2
Rolling King, *with music.* *Unknown.* SoAmSa
(South Australia, *with music.*) ShS
Rolling the Lawn. William Empson. MoBrPo (1962 ed.)
Rolling wave is on thy shore, Jerseyland, The. Ode to New Jersey. Elias F. Carr. PoRL
Roly! poly! pudding and pie! The Tale of a Tart. Frederic E. Weatherly. SUS
Rom. Cap. 8. Ver. 19. Henry Vaughan. AnAnS-1; MeP; SCEP-1; SeEP
(And Do They So?) ReEn
("And do they so? have they a sense?") MeLP; OBS
Roma. Rutilius, *tr. fr. Latin by* Ezra Pound. CTC
Roma Aeterna. Adelaide Crapsey. QFR
Roma Mater Sempaeterna. Shaemas O'Sheel. JKCP
Roman and Jew upon one level lie. In Galilee. Mary Frances Butts. AA
Roman had an, A/ artist, a freedman. The Jerboa. Marianne Moore. AtBAP; CMoP; MoPo
Roman host descended from the height, A. Mater Amabilis. Aubrey Thomas De Vere. ISi
Roman Legions, The. John Mitford. VA
Roman Lullaby. *Unknown, ad. by* Louis Untermeyer. RIS
Roman Mirror, A. Sir Rennell Rodd. OBVV; VA
Roman Officer Writes Home, A. C. M. Doughty. *Fr.* The Dawn in Britain. FaBoTw
Roman Road, The. Thomas Hardy. AWP; BrPo; GoJo; InPo; MoBrPo; PoeP
Roman Soldier on the Wall, A. W. H. Auden. *See* Over the Heather.

Roman soldiers come ridin' at full speed. The Man of Calvary. "Sin Killer" Griffin. OuSiCo
Roman Stage, The. Lionel Johnson. BrPo
Roman Virgil [*or* Vergil], thou that singest Ilion's lofty temples robed in fire. To Virgil [*or* Vergil]. Tennyson. ChTr; EPN; GTBS-P; InP; InPo; MBW-2; NoP; PoEL-5; PoFS; PoVP; StP; ViPo; ViPP; WHA
Roman Wall, The. Patric Dickinson. POTi
Roman Wall Blues. W. H. Auden. *See* Over the Heather.
Roman Women, *sel.* Thomas Edward Brown.
"O Englishwoman on the Pincian." OBNC
Romance. W. E. Henley. In Hospital, XXI. EnLit; MC; PAH
Romance. Mildred Howells. AA
Romance. Andrew Lang. HBV; PCD; PTK; VA
Romance. Poe. AmePo; AmPP; AnAmPo; AnFE; AP; APA; AtBAP; ATP; BoLiVe; CBEP; CoAnAm; FaBoEn; ILP; MWA-1; NePA; OxBA; PeER; PoE
Romance. "Gabriel Setoun." BoTP; OTPC; PRWS
Romance. Robert Louis Stevenson. GoTS; GTSL; HBV; LiTL; MeWo; MoBrPo; NeMA; OBEV; OBVV; OtMeF; PoFS; PoRA; PoSC; RG; TrGrPo
(Fine Song For Singing, The.) MemP
(I Will Make You Brooches.) PoE; PoVP
("I will make you brooches and toys for your delight.") BoLP; BrPo
(My Valentine, *st.* 1.) FaPON; MPB; PoRL; SiSoSe
(Roadside Fire, The.) GTSE
(Song of a Traveller, The.) BoTP
Romance. Walter James Turner. BiCB; CH; CLwM; GoJo; HBMV; HBVY; HT; ILP; LiTM; MemP, *abr.*; MoBrPo; OBMV; PoMS; PoRA; POTE; PTK; ShBV-1; ThWaDe; TrGrPo; WePo; WHA
Romance beside his unstrung lute. Realism. Thomas Bailey Aldrich. AnNE
Romance VIII. St. John of the Cross, *tr. fr. Spanish by* E. Allison Peers. ISi
Romance of a Christmas Card, The. Kate Douglas Wiggin. MaRV
(Christmas Eve.) OQP; TRV
Romance of the Carpet, The. Robert J. Burdette. BOHV
Romance of the Range. Robert V. Carr. PoOW
Romance of the Swan's Nest, The. Elizabeth Barrett Browning. GN; OTPC, *abr.*
Romance, who loves to nod and sing. Romance. Poe. AmePo; AmPP; AnAmPo; AnFE; AP; APA; AtBAP; ATP; BoLiVe; CBEP; CoAnAm; FaBoEn; ILP; MWA-1; NePa; OxBA; PeER; PoE
Romancer, far more coy than that coy sex! Hawthorne. Amos Bronson Alcott. AA
Romans, *sels.* Bible, *N.T.*
Duties of Man, The, XII: 3-21. TreF
To Him Be Glory, XII: 33-36. TRV
"Who shall separate us from the love of Christ?" VIII: 35-39. BoC
Romans Angry about the Inner World. Robert Bly. CBV; OPoP; PoIE (1970 ed.)
Romans, countrymen, and lovers! Brutus Explains Why He Murdered Caesar. Shakespeare. *Fr.* Julius Caesar, III, ii. TreFT
Romans first with Julius Caesar came, The. The English Race. Defoe. *Fr.* The True-Born Englishman, I. FOL; OBEC
Romans, rheumatic, gouty, came. La Condition Botanique. Anthony Hecht. NePoEA
Romantic, The. Louise Bogan. NP
Romantic Episode. Vincent Starrett. FiSC
Romantic subject of the Great White Queen. The Explorer. William Plomer. BoSA
Romantic to Burlesque. Byron. *See* Author's Purpose, The.
Romany Girl, The. Emerson. CoBA
Romany Gold. Amelia Josephine Burr. HBMV
Romanze, or the Music Students. Frank O'Hara. FRC
Romanzo to Sylvia. George Darley. *See* Song: "I've taught thee love's sweet lesson o'er."
Romaunt of Humpty Dumpty, The. Henry S. Leigh. BOHV
Romaunt of the Rose, The. Guillaume de Lorris *and* Jean de Meun. *See* Romance of the Rose, The .
Rome. Byron. *Fr.* Childe Harold's Pilgrimage, IV. BEL; MaPo; ShBV-3
("Oh Rome! my country! City of the soul!") InP
(Rome and Freedom.) EPN
Rome. Joachim du Bellay, *tr. fr. French by* Ezra Pound. Ruins of Rome, I. AWP; JAWP; WBP; LiTW, *tr. by* Spenser
("Thou stranger, which for Rome in Rome here seekest," *tr. by* Spenser.) OnPM
Rome. Thomas Hardy. CLwM; EnLi-2; MoAB; Sonn
Rome. Marcelino Menéndez y Pelayo, *tr. fr. Spanish by* Roderick Gill. CAW
Rome. Milton. *Fr.* Paradise Regained, IV. OBS
Rome and Freedom. Byron. *See* Rome.
Rome did its worst; thorns platted for his brow. Praetorium Scene; Good Friday. Elinor Lennen. PGD
Rome disappoints me still; but I shrink and adapt myself to it. Rome. Arthur Hugh Clough. *Fr.* Amours de Voyage, I. EPN
Rome had her Roscius and her theater. In Ed. Allen. John Weever. ReIE
Rome Is Fallen, I Hear. Arthur Hugh Clough. Amours de Voyage, Canto V, vi. BEL
Rome never looks where she treads. A Pict Song. Kipling. FOL
Rome Remember. Sidney Keyes. MoAB
Rome still holds her rod of power. Nazareth. Thomas Curtis Clark. ChIP
Romeo and Juliet. H. Phelps Putnam. ErPo
Romeo and Juliet, *parody.* Fred Newton Scott. InMe
Romeo and Juliet, *sels.* Shakespeare.
Come, Gentle Night, *fr.* III, ii. HW
Come Night, Come Romeo, *fr.* III, ii. BoLP; LiTL
("Come, night;—come, Romeo,—come, thou day in night.") MemP
Everlasting Rest, *fr.* V, iii. WHA
(Romeo's Last Words.) FiP
("How oft when men are at the point of death.") AtBAP; MemP
(Thus with a Kiss I Die.) TrGrPo
(Here Lies Juliet.) FaFP; TreFS
(With a Kiss I Die.) LiTL
Friar Laurence's Cell, *fr.* II, vi. GoBC
"He jests at scars that never felt a wound," *fr.* II, ii. BoC; LiTB; LiTG; LiTL; MasP
(Balcony Scene, The.) TreF
(Living Juliet, The.) TrGrPo
"If I profane with my unworthiest hand," *fr.* II, v. Sonn
Juliet's Yearning, *fr.* III, ii. TreFS
Music's Silver Sound, *fr.* IV, v. GN; HH
"O Romeo, Romeo, wherefore art thou Romeo!", *fr.* II, ii. WHA
"O, then, I see Queen Mab hath been with you," *fr.* I, iv. FIW
(Mercutio Describes Queen Mab.) TrGrPo
(Mercutio's Queen Mab Speech.) LiTB; TreF
(Queen Mab.) BoC; FaPON; FiP; GoTP; MPB; OTPC, *abr.*; PoFS
(Queene Mab.) BoW
(Shakespeare Gallery, A: Queen Mab.) MaC
Romeo and Juliet in the Orchard, *fr.* III, v. TreFT
"Soft, what light through yonder window breaks," *fr.* II, ii.
(Shakespeare Gallery, A: Juliet.) MaC
Rome's guns are spiked; and they'll stay so. Of Rome. Herman Melville. *Fr.* Clarel. OxBA
Romira, stay. The Call. John Hall. FaBoEn; LO; MeLP; MePo; OBS; SeCL; ViBoPo
Romish Lady, The, *with music.* *Unknown.* BFSS; OuSiCo
Romney, The. Harriet Monroe. HBMV
Romney and Aurora. Elizabeth Barrett Browning. *Fr.* Aurora Leigh, IX. VA
Romulus and Remus. Kipling. FOL
Ronald Wyn. Robert Bagg. TwAmPo
Rondeau: "Do you recall what I recall?" Louis Untermeyer. MeWo
Rondeau: "Help me to seek, for I lost it there." Sir Thomas Wyatt. *See* Help Me to Seek.
Rondeau: "Homage to change that scatters the poppy seed." Ronald Bottrall. MoVE
Rondeau: "Jenny kissed me when we met." Leigh Hunt. *See* Jenny Kissed Me.
Rondeau: "Lord, I'm done for: now Margot." William Jay Smith, *after* Vincent Voiture. FiBHP
Rondeau: "Thou fool! if madness be so rife." Charles Cotton. SeCL
Rondeau: "What no, perdie [*or* perdy]! ye may be sure!" Sir Thomas Wyatt. FCP; LoBV; MeEL; OBSC

Rondeau: "Year his winter cloak lets fall, The." Charles d'Orléans, *See* Spring.
Rondeau, The: "You bid me try, Blue-Eyes, to write." Austin Dobson, *after* Vincent Voiture. BOHV; HBV
(You Bid Me Try.) PoVP
Rondeau for You. Mário de Andrade, *tr. fr. Portuguese by* John Nist. TTY
Rondeau Humbly Inscribed to the Right Hon. William Eden, Minister Plenipotentiary of Commercial Affairs at the Court of Versailles. *At. to* George Ellis. OBEC
Rondeau in Wartime. James Bertram. AnNZ
Rondeau of Remorse, A. Burges Johnson. HBMV
Rondeau Redoublé. John Payne. HBV
Rondeau to Ethel, A. Austin Dobson. VA
Rondel: "Behold the works of William Morris." *Unknown.* Par
Rondel: Beside the Idle Summer Sea. W. E. Henley. OBNC
Rondel: "Good-by, the tears are in my eyes." Villon, *tr. fr. French by* Andrew Lang. AWP; JAWP; WBP
Rondel: "Kissing her hair, I sat against her feet." Swinburne. FaBoBe; HBV; Po; PoVP; ViBoPo; ViPP
Rondel: "Strengthen, my Love, this castle of my heart." Charles d'Orléans, *tr. fr. French by* Andrew Lang. AWP
Rondel: "These many years since we began to be." Swinburne. HBV
Rondel: To His Mistress, to Succor His Heart. Jean Froissart, *tr. fr. French by* Longfellow. AWP
Rondel for Middle Age. Louise Townsend Nicholl. NePoAm
Rondel for September. Karle Wilson Baker. HBMV
Rondel of Love [*or* Luve], A. Alexander Scott. OBEV; OxBS
Rondel of Merciless Beauty. Chaucer. *See* Merciles Beaute.
Rondel; the Wanderer. Austin Dobson. *See* Wanderer, The.
Rondelay: "Chloe found Amyntas lying." Dryden. CavP; DiPo; MaPo; PAn; PeRV; SeCL; ViBoPo
(Kiss Me, Dear.) UnTE
(Roundelay.) ALV; SeEP
Rondelay, A: "Man Is For Woman Made." Peter Anthony Motteux. *See* Man Is For Woman Made.
Rondo: "Did I love thee? I only did desire." George Moore. UnTE
Ronsard. Miriam Allen deFord. HBMV
Ronsard to His Mistress. Thackeray. HBV
Röntgen Photograph. Elisabeth Eybers, *tr. fr. Afrikaans by* Jack Cope, Uys Krige, *and* Ruth Miller. PeSA
Roo. Mary Oliver. NYTB
Rood is my name. Once long ago I bore. Brussels Cross Inscription. *Unknown.* InP
Roof, The. Gelett Burgess. *See* Lazy Roof, The.
Roof Garden. James Schuyler. ANYP
Roof is high and arched and blue, The. The Green Inn. Theodosia Garrison. HBMV
Roof it has a lazy time, The. The Lazy Roof [*or* Roof]. Gelett Burgess. BOHV; NA; RIS; TreFT
Roof of midnight, hushed and high, The. Nocturnal. Os Marron. NeBP
Roof-Tops. Charles Hanson Towne. *See* City Roofs.
Roofs. Joyce Kilmer. PoLF
Roofs are shining from the rain, The. April. Sara Teasdale. FaPON; GFA; OTPC (1946 ed.); PCH; PDV; PoSC; SoPo; StVeCh; TiPo; TSW; YeAr
Roofwalker, The. Adrienne Rich. CoAP
Rookery, The. Charles Tennyson Turner. VA
Rookhope Ryde. *Unknown.* ESPB
Rookie's Lament, A, *with music. Unknown.* ABF
Rooks. Charles Hamilton Sorley. HBMV; MoBrPo
Rooks are alive, The. What the Weather Does. Hamish Hendry. BoTP
Room, The. Conrad Aiken. AP; LiTG; LiTM (rev. ed.); MAP; MAPA; MoAmPo; NePA; PoDB
Room, The. C. Day Lewis. PoCh
Room. Robert Finch. MoCV
Room, The. Elizabeth Jennings. NePoEA-2
Room. Shirley Kaufman. QAH
Room, The. W. S. Merwin. FRC; NaP
Room, The. Vladimir Nabokov. NYBP
Room, The. Francis Webb. *Fr.* Leichhardt in Theatre. PoAu-2
Room a dying poet took, The. The Room. Vladimir Nabokov. NYBP
Room above the Square, The. Stephen Spender. ChMP; CMoP
Room after room. Love in a Life. Robert Browning. CBEP; EPN; HBV; InvP; LiTL; MaVP; OAEP; OBNC; OBVV; PoVP; TOP
Room after room, table after table. Public Library. Candace T. Stevenson. GoYe
Room and the Windows, The. Feng Chih, *tr. fr. Chinese by* Chu K'an. LiTW
Room dark and tight, The. Vestiges. Denis Devlin. OnHM
Room for a Jovial Tinker; Old Brass to Mend. *Unknown.* CoMu; OxBB
(Jovial Tinker, The.) UnTE
Room for a soldier! lay him in the clover. Dirge: For One Who Fell in Battle. Thomas William Parsons. AA; GN; HBV; PaA; PAH
Room for all else but love. Nor House nor Heart. Elinor Lennen. PGD
Room for Him! Room! Mary A. Lathbury. *See* Song of Hope.
Room for Jesus. Barbara H. Staples. STF
"Room for the leper! Room!" and as he came. The Leper. Nathaniel Parker Willis. StJW; WGRP
Room full of bones, A. The Parking Lot World of Sergeant Pepper. Charles Johnson. WSL
Room I Once Knew, A. Henry Birnbaum. GoYe
Room in Darkness. Mary Elizabeth Counselman. FiSC
Room in the Villa, A. William Jay Smith. NYBP
Room is full of gold, The. Jason. Anthony Hecht. CoPo
Room looks strange when moonlight falls, The. Summer Moonlight. Patience Strong. RePo
Room of peering shadows holds her fast, The. Sonnet of Departure. J. R. Hervey. AnNZ
Room of quiet, a temple of peace, A. Is This Your Church? *Unknown.* SoP
Room on a Garden, A. Wallace Stevens. NoP
Room, room for a blade of the town. The Bully [*or* Song]. *At. to* the Earl of Rochester *and to* Thomas D'Urfey. CBEP; InvP; SeCePo; SeCL
Room! room! [*or* Roome, roome,] make room for the bouncing belly. Hymn to Comus [*or* Hymn to the Belly]. Ben Jonson. *Fr.* Pleasure Reconciled to Virtue. AnAnS-2; ElL; OAEP; SeCePo; SeEP; SiTL
Room! room to turn round in, to breathe and be free. Kit Carson's Ride. Joaquin Miller. AmPP (3d ed.); TreFS
Room was a, The/ red, glow. We Dance Like Ella Riffs. Carolyn M. Rodgers. TNV
Room was low and small and kind, The. Bible Stories. Lizette Woodworth Reese. BrR; MoSiPe; MPB; StJW; TSW
Room was suddenly rich and the great bay-window was, The. Snow. Louis MacNeice. ExPo; GTBS-W; LiTM; ReMP; VaPo
Roome make roome you that are fled. *Unknown.* SeCSL
Roome, roome, make roome for the bouncing bellie. *See* Room! room!. . .
Rooming-House Melancholy. Eric Kästner, *tr. fr. German by* Howard Hugo. LiTW
Room's Width, The. Elizabeth Stuart Phelps Ward. AA
Roosevelt. Samuel Valentine Cole. PEDC
Roosevelt. Robert H. Davis. HH; PEDC
Roosevelt. Peter Fandel. PEDC
Roosevelt. T. E. Thomas. PEDC
Roosevelt and the *Antinoe,* The, *sel.* E. J. Pratt.
Burial at Sea. CaP
Roosevelt—Pilot and Prophet! Charles Hanson Towne. *See* Pilot and Prophet!
Roosevelt's in the White House, doing his best. The White House Blues. *Unknown.* OuSiCo
Rooster, The. Gil Orlovitz. ToPo
Rooster her sign. At the Sign of the Cock. Sir Owen Seaman. BOHV
Roosters. Elizabeth Bishop. AmLP; CrMA; FiMAP; LiTM; NePA; OnHM
Root, The. Francis Maguire. JKCP (1926 ed.)
Root Cellar. Theodore Roethke. AmPP (5th ed.); BoNaP; CBV; FiMAP; NoP; PoeP
Root Hog or Die, *parody.* Floyd B. Small. PoOW
Rooting in packing case of/ dirty straw. Digdog. Ruth Pitter. AnFE
Roots. Louis Ginsberg. TrJP

Roots. Harold Telemaque. PoNe
Roots and Leaves Themselves Alone. Walt Whitman. NePA
Roots, go deep: wrap your coils; fasten your knots. Wild Horses. Carl Sandburg. RePo
Roots Go Down. Lloyd Frankenberg. AnEnPo
Rope, The. Tania van Zyl. PeSA
Rope for Harry Fat, A. James K. Baxter. MoBS
Ropero, El ("Ropero, so sad and so forlorn"). Antonio de Montoro, *tr. fr. Spanish.* TrJP
Ropewalk, The. Longfellow. AP; MAmP
Ropin' of yearlin's and tyin' 'em down. Rodeo Days. S. Omar Barker. PoOW
Rory of the Hill. Charles Joseph Kickham. OnYI
Rory O'More; or, Good Omens. Samuel Lover. BOHV; HBV; VA
Rosa, *with music. Unknown, tr. fr. Dutch.* TrAS
Rosa Mystica. Gerard Manley Hopkins. ACP; GoBC
Rosa Mystica. Denis A. McCarthy. JKCP
Rosa Mystica. *Unknown.* CAW; GoBC; ISi; PoLi
("There is no rose of such vertu.") EG
(Two Carols to Our Lady, 2.) ACP
Rosa Nascosa. Maurice Hewlett. OBVV
Rosa Rosarum. Agnes Mary Frances Robinson. HBMV; VA
Rosabelle. Sir Walter Scott. *Fr.* The Lay of The Last Minstrel, VI. BeLS; GTBS; GTBS-D; GTBS-P; GTBS-W; GTSE; GTSL; HBV; OTPC (1923 ed.)
(Harold's Song.) EnLi-2; EnRP
Rosader's Sonnet ("In sorrow's cell"). Thomas Lodge. *Fr.* Rosalynde; or, Euphues' Golden Legacy. RelE
Rosader's Sonnet ("Turn I my looks"). Thomas Lodge. *Fr.* Rosalynde; or, Euphues' Golden Legacy. OBSC
(Rosader's Second Sonetto.) TuPP
("Turn I my looks unto the skies.") SiCE
Rosalie. Washington Allston. AA
Rosalind. Hubert Church. BoAu
Rosalind. Thomas Lodge. *See* Rosalynde: Rosaline.
Rosalind has come to town! Rosalind. Hubert Church. BoAu
Rosalind, in a negligee. Early Unfinished Sketch. Austin Clarke. ErPo
Rosalind; or, Euphues' Golden Legacy. Thomas Lodge. *See* Rosalynde; or, Euphues' Golden Legacy.
Rosalind's Scroll. Elizabeth Barrett Browning. *Fr.* The Poet's Vow. HBV; OBEV (1st ed.)
Rosalynde; or, Euphues' Golden Legacy, *sels.* Thomas Lodge.
Blith and Bonny Country Lass, A. ALV
(Coridon's Song.) UnTE
(Corydon's Song.) RelE
Contents of the Scedule Which Sir John of Bordeaux Gave to His Sons, The. RelE; SiCE
Fancy, A. EIL; LoBV; OBSC
("First shall the heavens want starry light.") SiCE
(Lover's Protestation, A.) GoBC
(Love's Protestation.) ACP
"Phoebe sat./ Sweet she sat." SiCE
(Montanus' Sonnet.) AtBAP; PoEL-2; TuPP
Rosader's Sonnet ("In sorrow's cell"). RelE
Rosader's Sonnet ("Turn I my looks"). OBSC
(Rosader's Second Sonetto.) TuPP
("Turn I my looks unto the skies.") SiCE
Rosalind's [*or* Rosalindes] Madrigal[l]. ALV; BEL; CoBE; EIL; EnLit; EnRePo; FaBoEn; GoBC; HBV; InvP; LoBV; NoP; OBEV; OBSC; PoIE; SeCePo; SiCE; TOP; TuPP; UnTE; ViBoPo
(Love in My Bosom like a Bee.) EG; LiTG; LiTL
(Rosalynde's [*or* Rosalynd's] Madrigal[l].) AtBAP; GTSL; PoEL-2; RelE; TrGrPo
Rosaline. GoBC; GTBS-P; GTSE; GTSL; LiTB; LiTG; LO; OBEV; UnTE
(Rosalind.) EIL; PoIE
(Rosalind's Description.) OBSC
(Rosalynde.) GTBS; GTBS-D; GTBS-W; TrGrPo
Sonetto: "Of all chaste birds the phoenix doth excel." RelE; SiCE
(Of Rosalind.) GoBC
(Of Rosalynd.) PoLi
Rosamond, *sel.* Swinburne.
Rosamond at Woodstock. VA
Rosamond's Appeal. Samuel Daniel. *Fr.* The Complaint of Rosamond. OBSC
Rosarie, The. Robert Herrick. InMe
Rosario d'Arabeschi; Poems and Rose Portraits, *sels.* Sacheverell Sitwell.
Belle Isis; Ballad of a Rose, I. POTE (1959 ed.)
O Rose with Two Hearts, II. POTE (1959 ed.)
Rosary, The, *abr.* Sister Maura. ISi
Rosary, The. Robert Cameron Rogers. AA; FaBoBe; HBV; TreF; WBLP
Rosary of My Tears, The. Abram J. Ryan. HBV
Rosciad, The, *sel.* Charles Churchill.
Critical Fribble, A. OBEC
(Criticaster, A.) FaBoEn
Rose, The. "Angelus Silesius," *tr. fr. German by* Thomas Walsh. CAW
Rose, A. Arlo Bates. HBV
Rose, The. William Browne. CH; HBV; OBEV; OTPC (1923 ed.)
("Rose, as fair as ever saw the north, A.") ViBoPo
(Vision, A.) SeCL; SeEP
Rose, The. Robert Creeley. AP; ToPo
Rose, A. Sir Richard Fanshawe, *after* Luis de Gongora. *Fr.* Il Pastor Fido (*after* Guarini). CavP; HBV; OBEV; OBS; PoEL-2; SeCePo; SeCL; SeEP
(Rose of Life, The.) AWP
Rose, The. Goethe, *tr. fr. German by* Andrew Lang. AWP; JAWP; WBP
Rose, The. William Hammond. OBS
Rose, The. George Herbert. AtBAP; LiTB; MaMe; PoEL-2; PoIE
Rose, The. Thomas Howell. EIL; OBSC; PrWP; RelE; TuPP
Rose, The. Thomas Lodge. *Fr.* The Life and Death of William Longbeard. OBSC
(Fancy, A.) EIL
Rose, The. Richard Lovelace. EG; HBV; SeCL; ViBoPo
(Ode: Rose, The.) SCEP-2
(To Lucasta: The Rose.) AnAnS-2; SeCV-1
Rose, The. Theodore Roethke. NaP; NYBP
Rose, The. Pierre de Ronsard, *tr. fr. French by* Andrew Lang. AWP; JAWP; WBP
Rose, The. G. A. Studdert-Kennedy. MaRV
Rose. Swinburne. YT
Rose. Lewis Thompson. AtBAP
Rose, The. Humbert Wolfe. MoBrPo; NP
Rose aloft in sunny air, The. Rose and Root. John James Piatt. AA
Rose and amber was the sunset on the river. The Syrian Lover in Exile Remembers Thee, Light of My Land. Ajan Syrian. LiTL; NP
Rose and God, The. Charles Wharton Stork. HBMV
Rose and Root. John James Piatt. AA
Rose and the Gardener, The. Austin Dobson. *See* Fancy from Fontenelle, A.
Rose and the Gauntlet, The. "Christopher North." BeLS
Rose and the lily, the moon and the dove, The. Rose, die Lilie, die Taube, die Sonne, Die. Heine. AWP; JAWP; WBP
Rose and the Thorn, The. Paul Hamilton Hayne. AA
(Rose and Thorn, The.) FaBoBe; HBV
Rose and the Wind, The. Philip Bourke Marston. OBVV; VA
Rose, as fair as ever saw the north, A. The Rose [*or* A Vision]. William Browne. *Fr.* Visions, V. CenL; CH; HBV; OBEV; OTPC (1923 ed.); SeCL; SeEP; ViBoPo
Rose Aylmer. Walter Savage Landor. AnFE; AWP; BEL; BoLiVe; CABA; CBEP; CH; ELP; EnLi-2; EnRP; EPN; ExPo; FaBoEn; FaFP; FaPL; FosPo; GTBS; GTBS-D; GTBS-W; GTSL; HBV; HoPM; ILP; InP; InPo; JAWP; LiTB; LiTG; LiTL; LO; LoBV; NoP; OAEP; OBEV; OBNC; OBRV; OBVV; OTPC (1923 ed.); PoAn; PoE; PoEL-4; RoGo; SeCeV; TOP; TreFS; TrGrPo; UnPo; VA; WBP; WHA; WoL
(Ah! what avails the sceptred race.) EG; EnLoPo; ViBoPo
Rose Aylmer's Hair, Given by Her Sister. Walter Savage Landor. VA
Rose-Bud. *See* Rosebud.
Rose-Bush. *See* Rosebush.
Rose, but one, none other rose had I, A. A Worm within the Rose. Tennyson. *Fr.* Idylls of the King: Pelleas and Ettarre. PAn; PoEL-5
Rose-cheeked [*or* cheek'd *or* cheekt] Laura [Come]. Thomas Campion. AtBAP; CaFP; EnL; EnLoPo; EnRePo; ExPo;

FosPo; InPo; InvP; LoBV; NoP; OAEP; PoE; PoEL-2; PoIE; ReEn; SeCeV; SiCE; SiSw; TrGrPo; TuPP; ViBoPo
(Laura.) AnFE; BoPe; EIL; GTSE; OBEV; OBSC; SeCePo; UnS
Rose, die Lilie, die Taube, die Sonne, Die. Heine, *tr. fr. German by* Richard Garnett. AWP; JAWP; WBP
Rose do you know. Joseph Cardarelli. *Fr.* The Marlborough Poems. QAH
Rose Family, The. Robert Frost. BoLP
Rose for a young head, A. The Watcher. James Stephens. HBV; MoBrPo; OBEV (new ed.); OBVV; PoDB
Rose, harsh rose. Sea Rose. Hilda Doolittle ("H. D."). FaBoMo
Rose in the breast. On Waking. Alida Carey Gulick. GoYe
Rose in the garden slipped her bud, The. A Fancy from Fontenelle [*or* The Rose and the Gardener]. Austin Dobson. HBV; MPB; OBVV
"Rose is a mystery, The"—where is it found? Rosa Mystica. Gerard Manley Hopkins. ACP; GoBC
Rose is a rose, The. The Rose Family. Robert Frost. BoLP
Rose Is a Royal Lady, The. Charles G. Blanden. HBMV
Rose is fairest when 'tis budding new, The. Sir Walter Scott. *Fr.* The Lady of the Lake. ViBoPo
Rose is made of little frills, The. Somebody's Garden. Margaret Steele Anderson. DD
Rose Is Not the Rose, The. Hafiz, *tr. fr. Persian by* Richard Le Gallienne. *Fr.* Odes. LiTW
("Rose is not the rose, unless thou see, The.") AWP
Rose is red, The. *See* Roses are red.
Rose is red, the grass is green, The. *Unknown.* OxNR
Rose is red, the rose is white, The. *Unknown.* OxNR
Rose is red, the violet blue, The/ The gillyflower sweet, and so are you. Easter Gloves. *Unknown.* PCH; SiTL
Rose is red, the violet's blue, The/ The honey's sweet, and so are you. *Unknown.* OxNR
Rose is weeping for her love, The. Helen's Song. Philip James Bailey. *Fr.* Festus. VA
"Rose, it is a royal flower, The." The Peace of the Roses. Thomas Philipps. ACP
Rose kissed me to-day. A Kiss. Austin Dobson. *Fr.* Rose-Leaves. ALV; CenHV; EnLit; HBV; InP; MoBrPo (1942 ed.); PoVP
Rose Leaf, The. Flora L. Osgood. SoP
Rose-Leaves. Austin Dobson. CenHV; PoVP
Greek Gift, A. MoBrPo (1942 ed.)
Kiss, A. ALV; EnLit; HBV; InP; MoBrPo (1942 ed.)
"Urceus Exit." ATP (1935 ed.); BoPe; GTSL; HBV; PTK; TOP
(I Intended an Ode.) OBEV
Rose Looks Fair, The. Shakespeare. *See* Sonnets, LIV.
Rose of Eden, The. Susan K. Phillips. BeLS
Rose of England, The. *Unknown.* ESPB
Rose of Flame, The. "Fiona Macleod." PoVP
Rose of Life, The. Sir Richard Fanshawe. *See* Rose, A.
Rose of May, The. Mary Howitt. HBV
Rose of Peace, The. W. B. Yeats. OBVV; PoDB
Rose of Stars, The. George Edward Woodberry. Wild Eden, IX. AA; HBV
Rose of that Garland! fairest and sweetest. To the Most Beautiful Lady, the Lady Bridget Manners. Barnabe Barnes. EnLoPo
Rose of the World, The. John Masefield. PoRA
Rose of the World, The. Coventry Patmore. The Angel in the House, I, iv, 1. HBV
Rose of the World, The. W. B. Yeats. BoLiVe; BrPo; CMoP; EnLi-2 (1949 ed.); EnLit; FaBoEn; HBV; MoAB; MoBrPo; OBVV; PoAn; PoeP; PoVP; VA; ViPo (1962 ed.)
Rose of the World, she came to my bed. The Dark Man. Nora Hopper. HBV
Rose of Tralee, The. William Pembroke Mulchinock, *also at. to* C. Mordaunt Spencer. OnYI; TreFT
Rose-petals fall without a touch. Reflections on the River. Andrew Young. ACV
Rose Pogonias. Robert Frost. MAmP
Rose-red, russet-brown. A Letter to Elsa. Grace Hazard Conkling. HBMV; HBVY
Rose, round whose bed. Rose. Swinburne. YT
Rose Song, The. Gil Vicente, *tr. fr. Spanish by* John Bowring. OnPM
Rose Still Grows beyond the Wall. A. L. Frink. BLPA
Rose that here our mortal eyes behold, The. The Rose. "Angelus Silesius." CAW
Rose that leans its chin, The. Sleep. J. P. McAuley. NeLNL
Rose the Red and White Lilly. *Unknown.* ESPB; OBB, *abr., sl. diff.*; OxBB
Rose Thou Gav'st, The. Charles Swain. VA
Rose to the Living, A. Nixon Waterman. HBV; MaRV; PoToHe
Rose to the roseburst break of day. The Cliff Rose. Ernest Fewster. CaP
Rose Tree, The. W. B. Yeats. CMoP; DiPo; ELP; GTBS-D; OBMV; PoFr
Rose was sick, and smiling died, The. The Funeral[l] Rites of the Rose. Robert Herrick. AnAnS-2; CABA; OBEV; PoSa
Rose, when I remember you. To Rose. Sara Teasdale. BiCB; HBV
Rose when shaken fragrance shed around, The. Inscription on an Ancient Bell. *Unknown.* ISi
Rose Will Fade, A. Dora Sigerson Shorter. HBV
Roseberry to his lady says. Suppertime. Burns. UnTE
Rose-Bud, The. William Broome. CEP; LoBV; OBEC; OBEV, *abr.*
Rose-Bud, A, [by my Early Walk]. Burns. OTPC
Within the Bush, *sel.* BiS
Rosebud that grew by the settle, The. The Gossips. Nathalia Crane. MAP
Rosebush and the Trinity, The. Alfred Barrett. GoBC
Rose-Marie of the Angels. Adelaide Crapsey. HBV
Rosemary and Thyme. *Unknown.* *See* Elfin Knight, The
Rosemary Spray, The. Luis de Góngora, *tr. fr. Spanish by* Edward Churton. AWP; LiTW
Roses. Thomas Campion. *Fr.* Lord Hay's Mask. OBSC
Roses. "George Eliot." BoTP
Roses. J. Corson Miller. CAW
Roses. Pierre de Ronsard, *tr. fr. French by* Andrew Lang. AWP; JAWP; WBP; LiTW, *tr. by* Vernon Watkins
Roses. Thomas Stanley, *after the Greek of* Anacreon AWP
Roses and butterflies snared on a fan. A Painted Fan. Louise Chandler Moulton. AA
Roses and gold. Places. Carl Sandburg. NP
Roses and pinks will be strewn where you go. Song. Sir William Davenant. *Fr.* The Unfortunate Lovers. ViBoPo
Roses and Rain. Archibald T. Strong. BoAu
Roses Are Beauty. John Masefield. *Fr.* Sonnets ("Long, long ago"). TOP
("Roses are beauty, but I never see.") EnLi-2 (1949 ed.); HBV
Roses are red [*or* The rose is red]. Mother Goose. OxNR; RIS; StVeCh
Roses are red,/ Violets are blue,/ What you need. *Unknown.* SiTL
Roses at first were white. How Roses Came Red. Robert Herrick. BEL; CavP; EnL; PoeP
Rose's crimson stain, A. Roses of Memory. A. C. Gordon. AA
Rose's Cup, The. Frank Dempster Sherman. AA
Roses have been his bed so long that he. Jeremiah. Witter Bynner. CrMA
Roses in breathing forth their scent. Celia Singing. Thomas Stanley. AnAnS-2
Roses in December. G. A. Studdert-Kennedy. BLPA
Roses in my garden, The. Ballad. Maurice Baring. HBV
Roses (Love's delight) let's join. Roses. Thomas Stanley. AWP
Roses of Memory. A. C. Gordon. AA
Roses of Sa'adi, The. Marceline Desbordes-Valmore, *tr. fr. French by* Barbara Howes. LiTW
Roses of Thy Cheeks, The. Rafi of Merv, *tr. fr. Persian by* R. A. Nicholson. LiTW
Roses of yesteryear, The. At Twilight. Peyton Van Rensselaer. AA
Roses on the Breakfast Table. D. H. Lawrence. BrPo
Roses Only. Marianne Moore. AnFE; CoAnAm; LiTM
Roses Red. Arno Holz, *tr. fr. German by* Jethro Bithell. AWP
Roses Red. *Unknown.* PCD; PCH
Roses red and jonquils gold. One, Two, Buckle My Shoe. Ogden Nash. BiCB
Roses red upon my neighbor's vine, The. My Neighbor's Roses.

Roses (continued)
Abraham L. Gruber. BLPA; NeHB; OQP; PoToHe
Rose's red, vi'let's blue. Roses Red. *Unknown.* PCD; PCH
Roses red wind themselves. Roses Red. Arno Holz. AWP
Roses, rose-red and white, and green. Alleluya. Rubén Darío. TTY
Rose's Scent, The. *Unknown. See* All Night by the Rose.
Roses' Song. Philip Bourke Marston. *Fr.* Garden Fairies. VA
Roses sweeter than red dates and grapes. The Beautiful Boy. *Unknown. Fr.* The Thousand and One Nights. LiTW
Roses, their sharp spines being gone. Bridal Song. Fletcher *and* Shakespeare. *Fr.* The Two Noble Kinsmen. CBEP; EG; ElL; HW; MyFE; NoP; OBEV; OBSC; SiCE; ViBoPo
Rosewood Vision. James Brodey. ANYP
Rosie, *with music. Unknown.* ABF
Rosie-fingerd morne, no sooner shone, The. The Sacrifice. Homer. *Fr.* The Odyssey, III. OBS
Rosie Nell, *with music. Unknown.* AS
Rosies. Agnes I. Hanrahan. HBV
Roslin and Hawthornden. Henry van Dyke. AA
Rostov. G. S. Fraser. LiTM (rev. ed.); WaP
Rosy Apple, Lemon or Pear. *Unknown.* CH; HH
(Wedding, A.) PCH
Rosy Bosom'd Hours, The. Coventry Patmore. EnLoPo
Rosy cloud of the dawn I see, A. Almond Blossoms. Charles Dalmon. *Fr.* Three Pictures. TSW
Rosy clouds float overhead, The. The Sandman. "Margaret Vandegrift." HBV; HBVY; PRWS; TVC
Rosy Days Are Numbered, The. Moses ibn Ezra, *tr. fr. Hebrew by* Solomon Solis-Cohen. *Fr.* Wine-Songs. TrJP
Rosy egret, sunset, The. The Old Bayou. Madison Cawein. PFY
Rosy mouth and rosy toe, The. A Bunch of Roses. John Banister Tabb. HBVY; PRWS; SP
Rosy Musk-Mallow, The. Alice E. Gillington. VA
Rosy plum-tree, think of me. A Little Girl's Song. Hilda Conkling. NP
Rosy shield upon its back, A. The Dead Crab. Andrew Young. FaBoTw; LoBV; OA
Rotation. Julian Bond. NNP
Rotten Lake Elegy. Muriel Rukeyser. MoPo; NePA
Rotten Row. Frederick Locker-Lampson. ALV
Rou-cou spoke the dove. Song of Fixed Accord. Wallace Stevens. NePoAm; OA
Rouge Bouquet. Joyce Kilmer. DD; HBV; MC; PaA; PAH; PFY; PoPl; TIHL; TreFS
Rough green wealth of wheaten fields that sway, The. Sonnet. Thomas Caulfield Irwin. IrPN
Rough pasture where the blackberries grow! A Pasture. Frederic Lawrence Knowles. AA
Rough, shaggy furze. Our Dog. Janet Vaughn. PCD
Rough wind, that moanest loud. A Dirge. Shelley. BEL; BoLiVe; CABA; ChTr; DiPo; EnLi-2; EnLit; EnRP; EPN; GTSL; MCCG; OAEP; PoFS; PoRA; TOP; TrGrPo; WHA; WiR
Rough Winds Do Shake. Louis Simpson. ErPo
Roughchin, the Pirate. Arthur Boswell. EtS
Roughly, so to say, you know. John William Mackail. *Fr.* The Masque of Balliol. CenHV
Round, A: "Hey nonny no!" *Unknown. See* Hey Nonny No!
Round, A: "Now that the spring hath filled our veins." William Browne. ViBoPo
Round: "'Wondrous life!' cried Marvell at Appleton House." Weldon Kees. CoAP; NaP
Round: "Worlds, you must tell me." Louis Untermeyer. WhC
Round, The. Philip Booth. BoNaP
Round, a round, a round, boys, a round, A. Richard Brome. *Fr.* A Jovial Crew; or, The Merry Beggars. TuPP
Round about in a fair ring-a. *Unknown, at. to* John Lyly *and to* Thomas Ravenscroft. *Fr.* The Mayde's Metamorphosis. BoTP
Round about, little ones, quick, quick and nimble. Robin Good-Fellow's Song. *Unknown.* ElL
Round about Me. Sappho, *tr. fr. Greek by* William Ellery Leonard. AWP; JAWP; WBP
Round about, round about. The Elves' Dance [*or* Fairy Dances]. *Unknown, at. to* John Lyly *and to* Thomas Ravenscroft. *Fr.* The Mayde's Metamorphosis. CH; ElL; FaPON; HH; MPB; PoRh
Round about, round about, catch a wee mouse. *Unknown.* OxNR
Round about, round about, here sits the hare. *Unknown.* OxNR
Round about, round about, maggotty pie. *Unknown.* OxNR
Round about the cauldron go. Witches' Charm [*or* Brew]. Shakespeare. *Fr.* Macbeth, IV, i. SiTL; TreFT
Round about the rosebush. *Unknown.* OxNR
Round about there/ Sat a little hare. *Unknown.* OxNR
Round among the quiet graves. Love's Resurrection Day. Louise Chandler Moulton. AA; HBV
Round and around on the glockenspiel. The Birthday-Cake Glockenspiel. Elizabeth Henley. BiCB
Round and Round. Dorothy Brown Thompson. BiCB; ChBR
Round and round our lavatory. The Thinker. Anthony Delius. PeSA
Round and round the garden. *Unknown.* OxNR
Round and round the rugged rock. *Unknown.* OxNR
Round as a biscuit. *Unknown.* RIS
Round Barrow, The. Andrew Young. SeCePo
Round, calm faces rosy with the cold, The. Japanese Children. James Kirkup. FIW
"Round Cape Horn." *Unknown.* EtS
Round Dance, & Canticle. Robert Kelly. CoPo
Round de meadows am a-ringing. Massa's in de Cold [Cold] Ground. Stephen Collins Foster. AA; IHA; TreF
Round her red garland and her golden hair. Of His Last Sight of Fiammetta [*or* Fiammetta]. Boccaccio. *Fr.* Sonnets. AWP; GoBC; JAWP; OnPM; WBP
Round-hoof'd, short-jointed, fetlocks shag and long. A Horse. Shakespeare. *Fr.* Venus and Adonis. ExPo
Round moon hangs above the rim, The. Moment Musicale. Bliss Carman. HBMV
Round moon hangs like a yellow lantern in the trees, The. The Ancient Thought. Watson Kerr. SoP; TRV; WGRP
'Round my Indiana homestead wave the cornfields. On the Banks of the Wabash, Far Away. Paul Dresser. PoRL; TreFT
Round Number, A. Keith Douglas. NeBP
Round Our Restlessness. Elizabeth Barrett Browning. *Fr.* Rhyme of the Duchess May. MaRV; TRV
Round Quebec's embattled walls. Montgomery at Quebec. Clinton Scollard. PAH
Round Robin. Bhartrihari, *tr. fr. Sanskrit by* Paul Elmer More. LiTW
Round Table, The. Layamon, *tr. fr. Middle English. Fr.* The Brut. EnLi-1, *pr. tr. by* Stith Thompson; MeEV
Round Table, The. Robert Mannyng. ACP
Round the Bay of Mexico, *with music. Unknown.* OuSiCo
Round the cape of a sudden came the sea. Parting at Morning. Robert Browning. AWP; BEL; CBEP; CBV; DiPo; EnL; EnLi-2; EnLit; EPN; FaBoEn; FaBV; FiP; GBV (1952 ed.); GTSL; HBV; JAWP; MaVP; MBW-2; MCCG; MemP; OAEP; OBEV; OBNC; OBVV; PAn; PCD; PoAn; PoVP; ShBV-3; TOP; TreFT; UnPo (3d ed.); VA; ViPo; ViPP; WBP; WiR
Round the Corner, *with music. Unknown.* SoAmSa
Round the island of Zipangu. The Mimshi Maiden. Hugh McCrae. MoAuPo; NeLNL
Round the wide earth, from the red field your valour has won. The Conquerors. Paul Laurence Dunbar. AmePo
Round the Year. Coventry Patmore. *See* Year, The.
Roundabout Turn, A. Robert E. Charles. MoShBr
Rounded Up in Glory, *with music. Unknown.* CoSo
Rounded world is fair to see, The. Nature. Emerson. ILP; MWA-1
Roundel: "My ghostly fadir, Y me confesse." Charles duc d'Orleans. *See* My Ghostly Father.
Roundel, A: "Now welcom somer, with thy sonne softe." Chaucer. *Fr.* The Parlement of Foules. ATP; CTC
(Foules Rondel, *orig., with mod. vers.* [The Birds' Rondel] *by* Louis Untermeyer.) TrGrPo
(Now Welcome Somer.) SeCePo
(Now Welcome Summer.) CBEP; PoLi
(Qui Bien Aime a Tard Oublie.) EnLoPo
(Welcome, Summer.) MeEL
Roundel, The: "Roundel is wrought as a ring or a starbright sphere, A." Swinburne. ATP (1935 ed.); EPN; PoIE; PoVP; TOP; VA
Roundel: "Your eyen two will slay me suddenly." Chaucer. *See* Merciles Beaute.

Roundel in the Rain. *Unknown.* FiBHP
Roundel of Farewell. Villon, *tr. fr. French by* John Payne. MeWo
Roundel of Passion-Tide. *Unknown.* CAW
Roundel of Rest, A. Arthur Symons. HBV
Roundelay: "Chloe found Amyntas lying." Dryden. *See* Rondelay: "Chloe found. . ."
Roundelay, A: "It fell upon a holy eve." *See* Perigot's and Cuddy's Roundelay.
Roundelay: "O Sorrow,/ Why dost borrow." *See* Song of the Indian Maid.
Roundelay, A: "Tell me, thou skilful shepherd's swain." Michael Drayton. *See* Sylvia.
Roundhouse, The. William Rose Benét. PoMa
Roundhouse in Cheyenne is filled every night, The. The Dreary Black Hills. *Unknown.* AS; CoSo
Rounding the Cape. Roy Campbell. BoSA; PeSA
Rounding the Horn. John Masefield. *Fr.* Dauber, VI. EtS; MoAB; MoBrPo; NeMA; WHA
(Dauber Rounds Cape Horn, The.) BBV
Round-up, The. Sarah Elizabeth Howard. PoOW
Roundup Cook, The. Robert V. Carr. PoOW
Rouse, Britons! at length. A New Ballad. *Unknown.* PAH
Rouse every generous, thoughtful mind. The Blasted Herb. Meshech Weare. PAH
Rousecastle. David Wright. MoBS
Rousing Canoe Song, The. Hermia Harris Fraser, *ad. fr. Haida Indian Song.* CaP; WHW
Rousing to rein his pad's head back. Song. Geoffrey Taylor. NeIP; OxBI
Rousseau. Schiller, *tr. fr. German by* Sir Edward Bulwer-Lytton. PoFr
Rousseau—Voltaire—our Gibbon—and De Staël. Sonnet to Lake Leman. Byron. Sonn
Roustabout Holler, *with music.* *Unknown.* OuSiCo
Rout of San Romano, The. Jon Manchip White. NePoEA
Route. Joseph Ceravolo. ANYP
Route March. Charles Hamilton Sorley. *See* All the Hills and Vales Along.
Route of evanescence, A. Emily Dickinson. AmePo; AmLP; AmP; AmPP; AP; CaFP; CoBA; DiPo; ForPo; GoTP; MaPo (1969 ed.); MWA-2; NeMA; NoP; PoE; PoEL-5
Routine, The. Paul Blackburn. ELU
Routine trickery of the examination, The. Examiner. F. R. Scott. PPON; TwCaPo
Rover, The, *sel.* Aphra Behn.
When Damon First Began to Love, *fr.* Pt. I, Act II, sc. i. UnTE
Rover, The. Sir Walter Scott. *See* Weary Lot Is Thine, A.
Rover killed the goat. Brave Rover. Max Beerbohm. OA
Rovers, The, *sel.* George Canning, George Ellis, *and* John Hookham Frere.
Song: "Whene'er with haggard eyes I view," *fr.* I. ALV; OBEC
(Song by Rogero.) EiCL
(Song by Rogero the Captive.) CEP; TOP
(Song of One Eleven Years in Prison.) BOHV; FiBHP
Rover's Adieu, The. Sir Walter Scott. *See* Weary Lot Is Thine, A.
Rover's Apology, The. W. S. Gilbert. *Fr.* Trial by Jury. ALV
Rover's Farewell, The. Sir Walter Scott. *See* Weary Lot Is Thine, A.
Roving Alley-Cat, A. Mary Cockburn Bomke. CIV
Roving breezes come and go, The. On Kiley's Run. Andrew Barton Paterson. BoAu
Roving Gambler, The. *Unknown.* ABF; AS; TrAS, *with music*
(Gamboling Man, The, *diff. vers.* AS
(Yonder Comes My Pretty Little Girl, *diff. vers.*) AS
Roving God, whose playfellows. To Dionysus. Anacreon. LiTW
Roving Worker, The. *Unknown,* *tr. fr. Modern Irish by* George Sigerson. OnYI
Row after row with strict impunity. Ode to the Confederate Dead. Allen Tate. AnFE; AP; ATP (1953 ed.); CABA; CoAnAm; FaBoMo; InPo; LiTA; LiTM; MAP; MoAB; MoAmPo; MoPo; MoVE; NoP; NP; OxBA; PIA; PoIE; ReMP; SeCeV; TwAmPo; UnPo; ViBoPo (1958 ed.)
Row, Bullies, Row. *Unknown.* *See* Roll, *Julia,* Roll.
Row-diddy, dow de, my little sis. Grampy Sings a Song. Holman F. Day. BOHV
Row Gently Here. Thomas Moore. HBV
"Row me o'er the strait, Douglas Gordon." Douglas Gordon. Frederic Edward Weatherly. VA
Row of Stalls, A, *sel.* Raymond Knister.
Nell. OBCV
Row of Thick Pillars, A. Stephen Crane. AmePo
Row, row, Manoli. Swing Song. *Unknown.* PCH
Row, row, row your boat. *Unknown.* SD
Row us out from Desenzano, to your Sirmione row! "Frater Ave atque Vale." Tennyson. ChTr; GTBS-P; MaPo (1969 ed.); MBW-2; NoP; PoVP; ViPo
Rowan County Crew, The, *with music.* *Unknown.* OuSiCo
Rowan routs the green eastern hills, The. In Autumn. Gene Derwood. NYTB
Rowan Tree, The. Lady Nairne. HBV
Rowdy, The, *with music.* John A. Stone. SGR
Rowers, The. Laura Benét. FiSC; GoYe
Rowers now are rowing. Song of the Three Angels. Gil Vicente. *Fr.* The Auto of the Bark of Purgatory. CAW
Rowing, I reach'd a rock — the sea was low. Gerard Manley Hopkins. *Fr.* A Vision of the Mermaids. ChTr
Rowland's Rhyme. Michael Drayton. *Fr.* The Shepherd's Garland, Eclogue II. OBSC
Rowley Powley. *Unknown.* OTPC
Rows of cells are unroofed, The. The Old Prison. Judith Wright. NeLNL; PoAu-2
Roxbury Garden, A, *abr.* Amy Lowell. LaNeLa
Roxie, Roxie, if you were mine. O Lawd, I Went up on the Mountain. *Unknown.* OuSiCo
Roy Bean. *Unknown, at. to* Charles J. Finger. ABF; BeLS; CoSo, *with music*
Roy Kloof. Sydney Clouts. BoSA
Roy Kloof Went Riding. Sydney Clouts. BoSA
Royal Adventurer, The. Philip Freneau. PAH
Royal and saintly Cashel! I would gaze. The Rock of Cashel. Sir Aubrey De Vere. IrPN; NBM
Royal banners forward go, The. Vexilla Regis [*or* Hymn to the Holy Cross]. Venantius Fortunatus. CAW; LiTW; WHL
Royal Charlie's now awa. Will He No Come Back Again? *Unknown.* MemP; OBEC; OBEV
Royal Crown, The, *abr.* Solomon ibn Gabirol, *tr. fr. Hebrew by* Israel Zangwill. AWP
My God, *sel., tr. by* Alice Lucas. TrJP
Royal feast was done; the King, The. The Fool's Prayer. Edward Rowland Sill. AA; AmePo; AnNE; BeLS; FaBoBe; HBV; LHV; MAP; MaRV; MoAmPo (1942 ed.); NeHB; OHFP; OnMSP; OTD; PFY; PG; PoLF; TIHL; TreF; WBLP; WGRP
Royal Fisherman, The. *Unknown.* ChTr
Royal Guest, A. *Unknown.* *See* Yet If His Majesty, Our Sovereign Lord.
Royal Love Scene, The, Ernest Dowson, *ad. fr.* Voltaire. UnTE
Royal Military Canal, The. Patric Dickinson. POTi
Royal Mummy to Bohemia, The. Charles Warren Stoddard. AA
Royal Palace of the Highest Heaven, The. *At. to* Alexander Montgomerie. GoTS
Royal Palm. Hart Crane. AP; CMoP; MAP; MoAB; MoAmPo; NoP; PoIE; TDP; TrGrPo
Royal Pickle, A. Carlton Talbott. ALV
Royal Presents. Nathaniel Wanley. MaRV; OxBoCh
(Royall Presents.) OBS
"Instead of incense (Blessed Lord) if wee," *sel.* TrPWD
Royal Slave, The, *sel.* William Cartwright.
Drinking Song. SeCL
Royal Tour, The. "Peter Pindar." OxBoLi
Royal Way of the Holy Cross, The. Thomas á Kempis, *tr. fr. Latin.* BoC
Royalist, The. Alexander Brome. CavP
Royall Presents. Nathaniel Wanley. *See* Royal Presents.
Roye Robert the Bruss the rayke he avowit, The. Sir Richard Holland. *Fr.* The Buke of the Howlat. OxBS
R-P-O-P-H-E-S-S-A-G-R. E. E. Cummings. AmPP (5th ed.); PoAn
Rub-a-dub-dub, /Three men in a tub. Mother Goose. HBV; HBVY; OTPC; OxNR; RIS
Rub and scrape of a city's feet, The. The Pavement Artist. James Kirkup. HaMV
Rubáiyát of Omar Khayyám of Naishápúr. Omar Khayyám, *tr. fr. Persian by* Edward Fitzgerald. AtBAP, *abr.*; AWP; BEL; EnL, *abr.*; EnLi-2; EPN; FaBoBe; FaFP; FaPL, *much abr.*; GTBS; GTSL, *abr*; HBV; ILP, *abr.*; JAWP, *abr.*; LiTB; LiTG; LoBV, *abr.*; MasP; NeHB, *abr.*; NoP; OtMeF; OuHeWo;

Rubáiyát (continued)
PeVV, *abr.*; PoEL-5; PoIE, *abr.*; PoVP; ShBV-4, *abr.*; TOP; TrGrPo; UnPo (1st ed.), *much abr.*; VA, *abr.*; ViBoPo; ViPo; ViPP; WBP, *abr.*; WHA, *abr.*; WoL, *abr.*
Sels.
"Ah Love! could you and I with Him conspire." PoPl
(Wish, A.) OnPM
"Ah, with the grape my fading life provide." GTBS-P; GTBS-W; OBEV; OBVV
(Omar and Death, *abr.*) GTSE
(Ritual of the Grape.) OnPM
"And those who husbanded the golden grain." PoFr
"Awake! for Morning in the bowl of Night." GTBS-D; MemP; OxBI; PoFS
Ball, The. OnPM
"Book of verses underneath the bough, A." AnFE; DiPo; EG; FosPo; GTBS-W; HoPM; LiTL; OBEV; OBVV; OQP; SeCeV; SiTL; YT
(Heart's Desire.) MeWo
(Paradise.) OnPM
(Quatrains.) SeCePo
Careless Delight. OnPM
"Come, fill the cup, and in the fire of spring." FaBV; InP; TreF; WGRP
(Bird of Time, The.) OnPM
(Fifteen Rubaiyat.) LiTW
"Dreaming when dawn's left hand was in the sky." PoSa
Equity with God. OnPM
("O Thou, who man of baser earth didst make.") EaLo; SeCeV
Fatalism. MaRV
"For in and out, above, about, below." TRV
"I sometimes think that never blows so red." EG; InP; LO
(So Red the Rose.) OnPM
Iram Indeed Is Gone. OnPM
Long While, The. OnPM
Master-Knot, The. OnPM
Minister of Wine, The. OnPM
"Moment's halt, A—a momentary taste." PoFr
"Moving finger writes, The." EG; GTBS-W
(Moving Finger, The.) OnPM
New Year, The. OnPM
Predestination. OnPM
Prefer the Cash. OnPM
("Some for the glories of this world; and some.") PoPl
Sleep Unbroken. OnPM
Soul Is All, The. OnPM
(Heaven and Hell.) MaRV
There Is No Sin. OnPM
("Think, in this batter'd Caravanserai.") ChTr; OBVV
This Life Flies. OnPM
"Awake! For the Sun, who scattered into flight." OBNC; SeCeV
(Wake!) FaPON
Waste Not Your Hour. OnPM
"Why, all the saints and sages who discuss'd." TRV
Worldly Hope, The. MaRV
(Like Snow.) OnPM
Worldly Wisdom. MaRV
(Great Argument.) OnPM
("Myself when young did eagerly frequent.") EaLo; EG; WGRP
"Yet Ah, that Spring should vanish with the Rose." SeCeV
Rubaiyat, The. Edwin Meade Robinson. Limericised Classics, III. HBMV
Rubber Boots. Rowena Bastin Bennett. GFA
Rubens, de Vos, Memling—room after room. Antwerp: Musée Des Beaux-Arts. Alan Ross. NYBP
Rubicon, The. William Winter. HBV
Rubies and Pearls. Robert Herrick. *See* Rock of Rubies, The.
Rubinstein Staccato Etude, The. R. Nathaniel Dett. BANP
Rubric. Josephine Preston Peabody. AA
Ruby wine is drunk by knaves. Heroism. Emerson. AtBAP; ViBoPo
Ruddigore, *sels.* W. S. Gilbert.
Darned Mounseer, The. TSW
Mad Margaret's Song. RIS
Sir Roderic's Song ("When the night wind howls in the chimney cowls"). GBV (1952 ed.); PoMS; ShM; WhC
Ruddy drop of manly blood, A. Friendship. Emerson. AmPP (3d ed.)
Ruddy poppies bend and bow, The. To Diane. Helen Hay Whitney. AA; HBV
Ruddy sunset lies, The. In November. Duncan Campbell Scott. VA
Rude architect, rich instinct's natural taste. The Mole. John Clare. SeCeV
Rude rebuffs of bay-besieging winds, The. Patrick Moloney. Sonnets—Ad Innuptam, II. BoAu
Rudel to the Lady of Tripoli. Robert Browning. LoBV; OtMeF; PoVP
Rudely blows the winter blast. Flora's Flower. *Unknown.* UnTE
Rudely forced to drink tea, Massachusetts, in anger. Epigram. *Unknown.* PAH
Rudely thou wrongest my dear heart's desire. Sonnet. Spenser. Amoretti, V. EIL; ReIE; SiCE; Sonn
Rudeness. Elizabeth Turner. OTPC (1923 ed.)
Ruder Italy laid bare, The. Captain Cook. Alfred Somett. *Fr.* Ranolf and Amohia. FOL
Rudolph Is Tired of the City. Gwendolyn Brooks. PDV; RePo; TiPo (1959 ed.)
Rue, *sel.* Laurence Housman.
Resurrection, *fr.* III. MaRV
Rue Bonaparte. Joseph Warren Beach. NP
Rue on me, Lord, for Thy goodness and grace. Psalm LI. *Paraphrased by* Sir Thomas Wyatt. FCP
Rue St. Honore. Peter Williamson. NYTB
Rueful Lamentation on the Death of Queen Elizabeth, A. Sir Thomas More. LiTB; LiTG; OBSC
Rufflecumtuffle. Annette Bishop. FTB
Rufty and Tufty. Isabell Hempseed. BoTP
Rufus, I trusted you. How vain that trust. Two Poems against His Rival, 2. Catullus. LiTW
Rufus is wondrous rich, but what of that? Henry Parrot. SiCE
Rufus Prays. L. A. G. Strong. MoBrPo
Rufus the courtier, at the theater. In Rufum. Sir John Davies. ReIE
Rufus's Mare, *with music.* George Calhoun. ShS
Rug, The. Michael McClure. NeAP
Rugby Chapel [November, 1857]. Matthew Arnold. ATP (1935 ed.); BEL; CBEP; EnL; EnLi-2; EnLit; EPN; GTBS; MaVP; MBW; OxBoCh; PoE; PoEL-5; PoVP; TOP; ViPo; ViPP; VP; WGRP
Sels.
Contagion of Courage. MaRV
"What is the course of the life." MaRV
Rugby League Game. James Kirkup. POTi
Rugged forehead that with grave foresight, The. Love. Spenser. *Fr.* The Faerie Queene, IV. OBSC
Rugged Pyrrhus, he whose sable arm, The. Shakespeare. *Fr.* Hamlet, II, ii Par
Ruin, The. Richard Hughes. OBMV; POTE
Ruin, The. Charles Tomlinson. NePoEA-2
Ruin, The. *Unknown, tr. fr. Anglo-Saxon.* AnOE, *tr. by* Charles W. Kennedy; EnLit, *tr. by* Harold S. Stine; YAT, *tr. by* Richard L. Hoffman
Ruin and death held sway. In Apia Bay. Sir Charles G. D. Roberts. PAH
Ruin of Bobtail Bend, The. James Barton Adams. PoOW
"Ruin seize thee, ruthless King." The Bard. Thomas Gray. BEL; CEP; EiCP; EiPP; EnL; EnLi-2; EnPE; EnRP; GTBS; GTBS-D; GTBS-P; GTBS-W; GTSE; GTSL; OAEP; OBEC; PAn; Po; PoFr; ShBV-4; StP; TOP
Ruined and ill—a man of two score. Remembering Golden Bells. Po Chü-i. AtBAP; AWP; JAWP; WBP
Ruined Cabin, The. Alfred Castner King. PoOW
Ruined Chapel, The. William Allingham. IrPN
Ruined Chapel, The. Andrew Young. POTE
Ruined City, The. Pao Chao, *tr. fr. Chinese by* Jerome Ch'en *and* Michael Bullock. FIW
Ruined Cottage, The. Wordsworth. *See* Margaret; or, The Ruined Cottage.
Ruined Farm, The. William Plomer. BoSA
Ruined House, A. Richard Aldington. BrPo
Ruined Maid, The. Thomas Hardy. BrPo; CABA; CMoP; ErPo; FiBHP; LiTB; MaPo; NoP; PeVV; PoeP; PoG; SeCeV; SiTL; ViPo (1962 ed.)
Ruins at Sunset. William Allingham. IrPN
Ruins for These Times. Theodore Weiss. OPoP

Ruins of a Great House. Derek Walcott. ToPo; TwCP
Ruins of Rome. Joachim du Bellay, *tr. fr. French by* Spenser. OnPM
"All that which Egypt whilom did devise," VIII.
"Such as the Berecynthian Goddess bright," III.
"Thou stranger, which for Rome in Rome here seekest," I. (Rome, *tr. by* Ezra Pound.) AWP; JAWP; WBP; LiTW, *tr. by* Spenser
"Thou that at Rome astonished dost behold," VII.
"When that brave honor of the Latin name," V.
"Who list the Roman greatness forth to figure," VI.
"Who lists to see whatever nature, art," II.
"Ye sacred ruins and ye tragic sights," IV.
Ruins of Rome, The. *sel.* John Dyer.
"Fall'n, fall'n, a silent heap." OBEC
Ruins of the City of Hay. Randolph Stow. PoAu-2
Ruins under the Stars. Galway Kinnell. NaP
"Sometimes I see them," *sel.* WIRo
Rule, A. John Wesley. *See* John Wesley's Rule.
Rule a Wife and Have a Wife, *sel.* John Fletcher.
"I cast my cloud off, and appear myself." MyFE
Rule, Britiannia! James Thomson. *Fr.* Alfred, a Masque, II, v (*by* Thomson *and* David Mallet). BEL; CEP; EiCP; EiPP; EnLi-2 (1949 ed.); EnLit; GTBS; GTBS-D; GTBS-P; GTBS-W; GTSE; GTSL; HBV; NoP; OAEP; OBEC; PoFr; TreF: WBLP; YAT
Rule for Birds' Nesters, A. *Unknown.* DD; HBV; HBVY; OTPC
("Robin and the redbreast, The.") OxNR
Rule of Fair Play. Solon, *tr. fr. Greek by* Henry Nelson Coleridge. PoFr
Rule of Money, The. *Unknown.* PoFr
Rule On. Phyllis C. Michael. SoP
Rule to Play, A. Sir John Harington. SiCE
Ruler of the Queen's Navee, The. W. S. Gilbert. *See* When I Was a Lad.
Ruler of warriors then called the wisest, The. Cynewulf. *Fr.* Elene. YAT
Rulers. Fenton Johnson. PoNe
(Rulers; Philadelphia.) AmFN; GoSl
Rulers. *Unknown, tr. fr. Spanish by* Havelock Ellis. OnPM
Rules and Lessons. Henry Vaughan. AnAnS-1; MeP
Sels.
Early Rising and Prayer. SoP
O Do Not Go. MemP; SoP
"Observe God in His works: here fountains flow." TRV
Rules and Regulations. "Lewis Carroll." PeVV
"A short direction," *sel.* OTD
Rules for Daily Life. *Unknown.* SoP; STF
Rules for the Road. Edwin Markham. OQP; OTPC (1946 ed.); PoRL; RePo; RIS; StaSt; TreFT
Rules of Behavior. *Unknown. See* Hearts, like Doors.
Rules of the Road. *Unknown. See* Sailor's Grace, The.
Ruling Passion, The. Pope. *Fr.* Moral Essays, Epistle I. BOHV, *br. sel.*
("Search then the ruling passion: there, alone.") ViBoPo
Rum Tum Tugger, The. T. S. Eliot. EvOK; FaBV; FaPON; PDV; TiPo
Rumba. José Zacarías Tallet, *tr. fr. Spanish by* Sangodare Akanji. TTY
Rumba of the Three Lost Souls. Charles Madge. NeBP
Rumble of distant thunder, The. The Christ. Edgar William Whan. ChIP
Rumble of guns, A—not earthly ones. Electric Storm. Michael C. Martin. WaP
Rumble on, machines of the gold mines. On the Gold Mines. B. W. Vilakazi. PeSA; TTY
Rumble, rumble, rumble, goes the gloomy "L." Roller Skates. John Farrar. FaPON; GFA
Rumbling and rattly good green Bus. Good Green Bus. Rachel Field. BrR
Rumbling under blackened girders, Midland, bound for Cricklewood. Parliament Hill Fields. John Betjeman. FaBoTw; HaMV
Rumination. Richard Eberhart. CBV; FiMAP; LiTA; LiTM (rev. ed.)
Rummle an' dunt o' watter. Sumburgh Heid. George Bruce. OxBS
Rumor came to Frei Egidio, The. Egidio of Coimbra (A. D. 1597). Thomas Walsh. JKCP
Rumor Letalis. *At. to* Peter Abelard, *tr. fr. Latin by* Kenneth Rexroth. LiTW
Rumoresque Senum Severiorum. Marcus Argentarius, *tr. fr. Greek by* Dudley Fitts. ErPo; LiTW
Rumors. Reginald Arkell. TreFT
(When the War Will End.) InMe
Rumpled sheet, a/ of brown paper. The Term. William Carlos Williams. InvP; LiTA; OCS; PoPo; RePo; ThWaDe
Rumpty-iddity, row, row, row. *Unknown.* OxNR
Run along, Bobby. Ego Sum. Gelett Burgess. InMe
Run Along, You Little Dogies. *Unknown. See* Whoopee, Ti Yi Yo.
"Run faster, love," you say and I. Of Love and Time. John Henderson. BoAV
Run from Manassas Junction, The. *Unknown.* PAH
Run, Kitty, Run! Jimmy Garthwaite. BBGG
Run, little rivulet, run! The Rivulet. Lucy Larcom. PRWS
Run, Mary, Run, *with music. Unknown.* BoAN-2
Run, Nigger, Run, *with music. Unknown.* ABF
Run on, run on, in a way causing shaking motion on the sidewalk. Autolycus' Song (in Basic English). Richard L. Greene. WhC
Run, run, run with the rising moon! Lynn Strongin. *Fr.* Paschal Poem. ThO
Run, shepherds, run where Bethlehem blest appears. The Angels. William Drummond of Hawthornden. GN; HBV; OBS; OxBoCh
Run with the Bullgine, *with music. Unknown.* SoAmSa
Runagate Runagate. Robert E. Hayden. BALP; BP; IDB; PoNe, *diff vers.*; PoNe (1970 ed.)
Runaway. Rhoda Coghill. NeIP; OxBI
Runaway, The. Robert Frost. AnNE; AWP; BBV (1951 ed.); BoChLi; CH; FaBoCh; FaPON; GoJo; GoTP; GTBS-D; HaMV; InPo; JAWP; LoGBV; MAP; MCCG; MoAB; MoAmPo; MPB; NeMA; PDV; PoRL; RePo; ShBV-3; StVeCh; TiPo; TSW; TwCP; WBP
Runaway, The. Daniel Whitehead Hicky. BrR
Runaway. Kim Kurt. NePoAm-2
Runaway, *sels.* James Whaler.
Boy in a Pond. OA
Pond, The. MAP; MoAmPo (1942 ed.)
Runaway Boy, The. James Whitcomb Riley. MPB
Runaway Brook. Eliza Lee Follen. GFA
Runaway Slave, The. Walt Whitman. *Fr.* Song of Myself, X. PoNe
("Runaway slave came to my house and stopt outside.") PoFr
Runaway Slave at Pilgrim's Point, The. Elizabeth Barrett Browning. PoNe
Runaway slave came to my house and stopt outside, The. The Runaway Slave. Walt Whitman. *Fr.* Song of Myself, X. PoFr; PoNe
Runaways, The. Mark Van Doren. PoRA
Rune for C., A. Barbara Howes. NYBP
Rune for the Disenchanted. William Wantling. WOW
Rune of Hospitality, The. *Unknown, tr. fr. Irish by* Thomas Walsh. CAW; WHL
Rune of Praise, A. *Unknown, tr. fr. Irish.* WHL
Rune of Riches, A. Florence Converse. BoTP; SUS
Runes. Emmett Jarrett. ThO
Runes. Howard Nemerov. PoCh; ToPo
Runes for an Old Believer. Rolfe Humphries. NYBP
Runes on Weland's Sword, The. Kipling. AtBaP; PoEL-5
Runic Ode, A. Thomas Warton, the Elder. CEP
Runilda's Chant. George Darley. *See* O'er the Wild Gannet's Bath.
Runnable Stag, A. John Davidson. AnFE; BrPo; EvOK; GoTS; GTSL; HBV; LiTG; OA; OBEV (new ed.); OBVV; OnSP; PoVP; SD; ShBV-2; WiR
Runner. W. H. Auden. SD
Runner, The. Alexandra Grilikhes. SD
Runner, The. Walt Whitman. PCH; SD; TSW
Runner in the Skies, The. James Oppenheim. AnEnPo; MAP; MoAmPo (1942 ed.); NP; PFY; TrJP
Runner with the Lots, The. Léonie Adams. MoPo; NePA
Running. Richard Wilbur. CoAP
Running along a bank, a parapet. The Path. Edward Thomas. BrPo; MoVE
Running the Batteries. Herman Melville. PaA; PAH; ThLM
Running the Blockade. Nora Perry. PAH

Running to Paradise. W. B. Yeats. BoLiVe; LOW; OxBoLi
Running Vines [in a Field]. H. L. Davis. AnAmPo; NP
Runs all day and never walks. Mother Goose. TiPo
Runs falls rises stumbles on from darkness into darkness. Runagate Runagate. Robert E. Hayden. BALP; BP; IDB; PoNe (1970 ed.)
Runs the wind along the waste. Were-Wolf. Julian Hawthorne. AA
Rupert Brooke ("Your face was lifted to the golden sky"). W. W. Gibson. HBMV
Rural Bliss. Anthony C. Deane. InMe
Rural Dance about the Maypole, The. *Unknown.* OxBoLi; SeCL
(May-Pole Dance.) WePo
Rural Dumpheap. Melville Cane. AmFN
Rural Legend. Mary Elizabeth Osborn. NePoAm
Rural Mail, The. John Glassco. MoCV
Rural Poesy. Sir Philip Sidney. *Fr.* Arcadia. EIL
(O Words Which Fall like Summer Dew on Me.) MaPo
Rural Raptures. *Unknown.* BOHV
Rural Sports, *sel.* John Gay.
Fly-fishing. SD
Rural Walk, The. William Cowper. *Fr.* The Task, I. TOP
("For I have lov'd the rural walk through lanes.") EnRP
Rus in Urbe. Clement Scott. HBV; VA
Rush City—the Hole. Eugene Redmond. TNV
Rush of the *Oregon*, The. Arthur Guiterman. PAH
Rushes in a Watery Place. Christina Rossetti. ChTr; PDV
Rushing along on a narrow reach. The Main-Sheet Song. Thomas Fleming Day. EtS
Rushing Panic in San Francisco. *Unknown.* SGR
Rushing thence, in one diffusive band. The Sheep Shearing. James Thomson. *Fr.* The Seasons: Summer. CoBE
Russet leaves of the sycamore, The. The Last Days. George Sterling. AnAmPo; HBMV; NP
Russia. Aleksandr Blok, *tr. fr. Russian by* Babette Deutsch *and* Avrahm Yarmolinsky. AWP; JAWP; WBP; WoL
Russia. Nathan Haskell Dole. AA
Russia. Elliott Napier. BoAu
Russia and America circle each other. A Woman Unconscious. Ted Hughes. StP
Russian and Turk. Robert J. Burdette. *See* "Soldier, Rest!"
Russian Cathedral. Claude McKay. CDC; PoNe
(St. Isaac's Church, Petrograd.) AmNP; Kal
Russian Cradle Song, A. David Nomberg, *tr. fr. Yiddish by* Alter Brody. TrJP
Russian Fantasy, A. Nathan Haskell Dole. AA
Russian New Year. Bill Berkson. ANYP
Russian sailed over the blue Black Sea, A. "Soldier, Rest!" Robert J. Burdette. BOHV
Russian Spring Song with Minaiev, A. Thomas Walsh. GoBC
Rust. Mary Caroline Davies. HBMV
Rust is ripeness, rust. Season. Wole Soyinka. FIW
Rustic at the Play, The. George Santayana. HBV; MAP; MoAmPo; OBVV
Rustic Childhood. William Barnes. OBNC
Rustic Song, A. Anthony C. Deane. FiBHP; InMe
Rustle of each falling leaf, The. Love. Samuele Romanelli. TrJP
Rustler, The. *Unknown.* CoSo
Rustling leaves of the willow-tree. Alone in April. James Branch Cabell. HBMV
Rustling of leaves under the feet in woods, The. Pleasant Sounds. John Clare. BoPe; CBEP
Rustling of the silk is discontinued, The. Liu Ch'e. Ezra Pound. AP
Rustling palms bend readily, The. Song in Exile. Alice Duer Miller. TIHL
Ruth. Bible, *O.T.* WoL, (I: 1-IV: 17)
(Story of Ruth, The.) EnLi-1 (I: 1-IV: 13); OuHeWo (I: 1-IV: 10)
Sels.
Intreat Me Not to Leave Thee, I: 16-17. InP; TreF
(Address of Ruth to Naomi.) GBV (1952 ed.)
("And Ruth said, Intreat me not to leave thee.") LO; PoPl
(Entreat Me Not to Leave Thee.) TRV
(Ruth to Naomi.) MaRV; TrGrPo
Naomi and Ruth, I: 8-17. TrJP
Ruth. Thomas Hood. EnLoPo; EnRP; EPN; ERoP-2; GN; GTBS-W; HBV; InP; LiTG; LiTL; LoBV; OBEV; OBNC; OBRV; OnPP; OTPC; TOP; TreFS; VA
Ruth. Wordsworth. ChER; EnRP; ERoP-1; GTBS; GTBS-D; GTBS-P; GTBS-W; GTSE; GTSL; MERP; PoEL-4
"And many an endless, endless lake," *br. sel.* MyFE
Ruth and Johnnie. *Unknown.* ShM
Ruth Goes By. Edna Tucker Muth. PEDC
Ruth had been moved out of her job in an/ Hawaiian school. Honolulu and Back. John Logan. AmPC
Ruth; or, The Influences of Nature. Wordsworth. *See* Ruth.
Ruth to Naomi. Ruth, Bible, *O.T.* *See* Intreat Me Not to Leave Thee.
Rutherford McDowell. Edgar Lee Masters. *Fr.* Spoon River Anthology. LiTA; NP; OxBA; TOP
Ruthless Moon, The. Byron Herbert Reece. NYTB
Ruthless unrest has urged slow feet. Rescue. Olive Tilford Dargan. GoYe
Ruthlessly 'twixt palm and thumb. For a Girl in Love. Florence Hynes Willette. GoBC
Rutt, to the suburb beauties full well known. On Rutt the Judge. Charles Cotton. PeRV
Rutterkin. W. Cornish. PoMS
Ruyter the while, that had our ocean curb'd. The Dutch in the Medway [or Thames]. Andrew Marvell. *Fr.* Last Instructions to a Painter. OBS; PeRV
Rwose in the Dark, The. William Barnes. AtBAP; CBEP
Rye Bread. William Stanley Braithwaite. CDC
Rye Whisky [*or* Whiskey]. *Unknown.* ABF, *with music*; CoSo (A *and* B *vers.*), *with music*; OxBoLi; SiTL; TrAS, *with music* (Way Up on Clinch Mountain, A *and* B *vers., with music.*) AS
Ryght as the stern of day begouth to schyne. *See* Right as the stern of day. . .

S

S, C, M. Ted Wilson. BF
SOS. Kenneth Fearing. AmP
S.P.C.A. Sermon. Stuart Hemsley. FiBHP
S.S. *Lusitania.* Matthew Arnold. CBEP
"S.S.R., Lost at Sea."—The *Times.* Ralph Gustafson. OBCV; PeCV
S. T. Coleridge Dismisses a Caller from Porlock. Gerard Previn Meyer. GoYe
Saadabad. James Elroy Flecker. SeCePo
Saadi. Emerson. AmP; OxBA
Saagin. Sidney Goodsir Smith. AtBAP
Sabbat, The. Lin Carter. FiSC
Sabbath, The, *sel.* James Grahame.
Sunday Morning. OBRV
Sabbath-Day Chace. Philip Freneau. WoL
Sabbath day has reached its close, The. Sunday Evening. Charlotte Elliott. SoP
Sabbath day was ending in a village by the sea, The. The Last Hymn. "Marianne Farningham." BLPA
Sabbath, My Love. Judah Halevi, *tr. fr. Hebrew by* Solomon Solis-Cohen. TrJP
Sabbath of Rest, A. Isaac Luria, *tr. fr. Hebrew by* Nina Davis Salaman. TrJP
Sabbath Reflection. Denis Wrafter. NeIP
Sabbath Sonnet. Felicia Dorothea Hemans. Sonn
Sabidi, I love thee not, nor why I wot. Translat. ex Martial. Martial, *tr. by* John Weever. TuPP
Sabina has a thousand charms. A Love-Song. *Unknown.* SeCL; SeEP
Sabine Farmer's Serenade, The. Francis Sylvester Mahony. BOHV; HBV
Sable garb of darkness clothes the land, The. Night on the Prairie. Rufus B. Sage. PoOW
Sable is my throat. Negro Spiritual. Perient Trott. PoNe
Sabrina ("There is a gentle nymph"). Milton. *Fr.* Comus. OBS ("There is a gentle nymph not far from hence.") MyFE; SeEP
Sabrina Fair. Milton. *Fr.* Comus. AtBAP; ATP (1935 ed.); CBEP; EG; ELP; FaBoCh; InPo; LoGBV; OBEV; PoEL-3; SeCL; TOP; ViBoPo
(Sabrina.) CH; UnPo (1st ed.)
(Song: "Sabrina fair.") LoBV; SeCeV
Sa-Cá-Ga-We-A. Edna Dean Proctor. PAH

Sacco Writes to His Son. Alun Lewis. DTC
Sachem voices cloven out of the hills, The. Miramichi Lightning. Alfred Goldsworthy Bailey. OBCV; TwCaPo
Sack of Baltimore, The. Thomas Osborne Davis. IrPN; VA
Sack of Deerfield, The. Thomas Dunn English. PAH
Sack of Old Panama, The, *abr.* Dana Burnet. PFY
Sack of straw suspended from a tree, A. The Barrack Yard. Nettie Palmer. NeLNL
Sacrament, The. John Donne. *See* This Is My Body.
Sacrament, The. Charles L. Ford. OQP
Sacrament. Una W. Harsen. ChIP
Sacrament of Sleep, The. John Oxenham. PoLF
Sacrament of the Altar, The. *Unknown.* MeEL
Sacrament of Work, The. John Oxenham. MaRV
(Gratitude for Work.) PGD
Sacramental Meditations. Edward Taylor. *See* Preparatory Meditations.
Sacramento. Jesse Hutchinson. *See* Ho! for California.
Sacramento Gals, *with music.* John A. Stone. SGR
Sacraments of Nature, The. Aubrey Thomas De Vere. ACP; CAW
Sacramentum Supremum. Sir Henry Newbolt. GTSL
Sacred ape, now, children, see, The. The Ape. Roland Young. PoPl; WhC
Sacred armies and the godly Knight, The. Tasso. *Fr.* Jerusalem Delivered, I. CAW
Sacred Book, The. Thomas Kelly. SoP
Sacred Book, The. *At. to* Zoroaster. *See* Zoroaster Devoutly Questions Ormazd.
Sacred day is this, A. Lincoln's Birthday. John Kendrick Bangs. DD; HH; PGD
Sacred Elegy V: "These errors loved no less than the saint loves arrows." George Barker. *See* Elegy: Separation of Man from God.
Sacred Emily, *sel.* Gertrude Stein.
"Noisy pearls noisy pearl coat." AtBAP
Sacred Flora crowne this feild. *Unknown.* SeCSL
Sacred Formula to Attract Affection. *Unknown, tr. fr. Cherokee by* James Mooney. LiTA
Sacred Formula to Destroy Life. *Unknown, tr. fr. Cherokee by* James Mooney. LiTA
Sacred Grove, A. Edward Cracroft Lefroy. *Fr.* Echoes from Theocritus. AWP
Sacred Heart, The. Adelaide Anne Procter. JKCP
Sacred Hearth, The. David Gascoyne. FaBoTw
Sacred keep of Ilion is rent, The. Homeric Unity. Andrew Lang. HBV
Sacred lake of Fundisi is an eye of moonstone, The. Fundisi. Ruth Miller. BoSA
Sacred lowe of weel-placed love, The. Burns. *Fr.* Epistle to Davie. PoG
Sacred muse that first made love divine, The. Gulling Sonnets, VI. Sir John Davies. Sonn; TuPP
Sacred Night. Michelangelo, *tr. fr. Italian by* John Addington Symonds. OnPM
Sacred Order, The. May Sarton. ImOP
Sacred Page, The. John Bowring. SoP
Sacred Poetry. "Christopher North." WBLP
Sacred Seasons, The, *sels.* Carl Bode. ToPo
Eastertide.
Feast of Saint Andrew the Apostle.
Sacred Trinity, The. *Unknown.* *See* Rann of the Three.
Sacrifice, The. Gerald William Barrax. Kal
Sacrifice. Emerson. *Fr.* Quatrains. HBV; HBVY; MaRV; TRV
(Faith.) OtMcF
(Quatrain: "Though love repine.") OQP
Sacrifice. Henry W. Frost. SoP
Sacrifice, The. George Herbert. AtBAP; MaMe; PoEL-2; ReEn; SCEP-1
Sacrifice, The. Homer, *tr. fr. Greek by* George Chapman. *Fr.* The Odyssey, III. OBS
Sacrifice, The. Norman Jordan. BF
Sacrifice. George Macdonald. FaChP
Sacrifice. Frederick Manning. NP
Sacrifice of a Rainbow Trout. Joseph Langland. TPM
Sacrifice of a Red Squirrel. Joseph Langland. NYBP
Sacrifice of Er-Heb, The. Kipling. PeVV
Sacrifice of Youth. Simonides, *tr. fr. Greek by* Robert Guthrie MacGregor. OnPM
Sacrifice to Apollo, The. Michael Drayton. OBS; SeEP
Sacrilege, The. Thomas Hardy. DTo
Sad, all alone, not long I musing sat. Licia, I. Giles Fletcher. ReIE; SiCE; Sonn; TuPP
Sad and dismal is the tale/ I now relate to you. Invasion Song. *Unknown.* PoOW
Sad and dismal is the tale I will relate to you. The *Persia*'s Crew. *Unknown.* SoAmSa
Sad and solemn night, The. Hymn to the North Star. Bryant. OTPC
Sad bells sound, The. Strangers. Walter de la Mare. POTE
Sad Day, The. Thomas Flatman. OBEV
(Death.) SeCL
(Song: "Oh the sad day.") PeRV
Sad eyes, that were patient and tender. The Eyes of Lincoln. Walt Mason. OQP
Sad Goat, The. *Unknown.* WaKn
Sad Green. Sylvia Townsend Warner. MoBrPo
Sad Hesper o'er the buried sun. In Memoriam A. H. H., CXXI. Tennyson. EPN; OAEP; ViPo; VP
Sad is my lot; among the shining spheres. Earth. William Caldwell Roscoe. VA
Sad Is Our Youth. Aubrey Thomas De Vere. *See* Human Life.
Sad is the fate of those. The Worst. *Unknown.* OnPM
Sad, lost in thought, and mute I go. Medieval Norman Songs, IX. *Unknown, tr. by* John Addington Symonds. AWP; JAWP; WBP
Sad Love and Sad Song. Homei Iwano, *tr. fr. Japanese by* Yone Noguchi. LiTW
Sad Lover, The. George Crabbe. *See* Dejected Lover, The.
Sad Memories. Charles Stuart Calverley. CIV
Cat, The, *sel.* ChTr
Sad Mother, The. Katharine Tynan. VA
Sad nymph, Gaho, followed to the shadie woods, The. *Unknown.* SeCSL
Sad One, The, *sel.* Sir John Suckling.
Song to a Lute, A. ReEn; SCEP-2; TrGrPo
Sad painter of the green midnight, A. The New Dummy. Geoffrey Grigson. LiTM (rev. ed.)
Sad, sad—lean with long illness. Illness. Po Chü-i. MoPW
Sad, Sad Story, A. *Unknown, at. to* John Gay. *See* Three Children.
Sad seamstress, The. House Guest. Elizabeth Bishop. NYBP
Sad searching eyes with benediction in their gaze. Galilean. Margielea Stonestreet. ChIP
Sad September Sentiments. Edwin Meade Robinson. YT
Sad Shepherd, The, *sels.* Ben Jonson.
Here She Was Wont to Go. CLwM; ILP; TuPP
(Aeglamour's Lament.) CH
Karolin's Song. AtBAP; LiTL; LoBV; PoEL-2; PoIE
(Love and Death.) CBEP; SeCL
(Song: "Though I am young and cannot tell.") EnRePo; SeCP
(Though I Am Young and Cannot Tell.) ELP; ILP; NoP; OAEP; TuPP
Mother Maudlin the Witch. ChTr
"Spring, A, now she is dead! of what? of thorns." GoBC
Sad Shepherd, The. W. B. Yeats. PP
Sad soft scars, childbitten, The. A Thanks That Flesh Is Sad. John Ciardi. ToPo
Sad Song, The. Beaumont *and* Fletcher. *See* Away, Delights!
Sad Song, A. Philip Massinger. *See* Song: "Why art thou slow, thou rest of trouble, Death."
Sad Song about Greenwich Village, A. Frances Park. OCS
Sad Story. Clarence Day. InMe
Sad Story of a Little Boy That Cried, The. *Unknown.* BBGG
Sad Strains of a Gay Waltz. Wallace Stevens. OxBA
Sad Tale of Mr. Mears, The. *Unknown.* HBV; PTK; StPo; TreFS; YaD
Sad Thyrsis weeps till his blue eyes are dim. Thyrsis. Edward Cracroft Lefroy. *Fr.* Echoes from Theocritus. AWP
Sad to fare from the hills of Fál. A Farewell to Fál. Gerald Nugent. OnYI
"Sad Years, The." Eva Gore-Booth. HBMV
Sadako, you have gone. A Hiroshima Lullaby. Joseph Langland. PPON
Sadder. *Unknown, tr. fr. Spanish by* Havelock Ellis. OnPM
Saddest fish that swims the briny ocean, The. The Catfish. Oliver Herford. BOHV
Saddest noise, the sweetest noise, The. Emily Dickinson. MWA-2
Saddest place that e'er I saw, The. Screaming Tarn. Robert Bridges. ExPo

Saddest Words, The. Whittier. *Fr.* Maud Muller. NePA; SiTL
Saddle! saddle! saddle! After the Comanches. *Unknown.* PAH
Saddled and briddled. Bonnie James Campbell (B *vers.*). *Unknown.* ESPB
Sadie. *Unknown. See* Frankie and Johnny.
Sadie's Playhouse. Margaret Danner. Kal
Sadly as some old mediaeval knight. My Books. Longfellow. AA
Sadly I walk't within the field. The Olive Branch. Robert Herrick. OnPM
Sadly talks the blackbird here. The Deserted Home [*or* The Ruined Nest]. *Unknown.* OnYI; OxBI
Sadly the dead leaves rustle in the whistling wind. The Church of a Dream. Lionel Johnson. OBMV; PoVP
Sadly through the factory doors. The Little Children. Irwin Granich. MaRV
Sadness. F. S. Flint. MoBrPo (1942 ed.)
Sadness. Barbara Guest. AmPC
Sadness, Glass, Theory. Roy Fuller. WaP
Sae rantingly, sae wantonly. M'Pherson's Farewell. Burns. MCCG
Safari. Worth Long. WOW
Safari to Bwagamoyo. Bwagamoyo. Lebert Bethune. BF
Safari West. John A. Williams. NBP
Safe despair it is that raves. Emily Dickinson. AP
"Safe for Democracy." L. A. G. Strong. HBMV
Safe home, safe home in port. The Finished Course. St. Joseph of the Studium. WGRP
Safe in his fortress. The Tortoise. Herbert Asquith. RIS
Safe in His Keeping. Edgar Cooper Mason. BLRP
Safe in their alabaster chambers. Emily Dickinson. AmPP (5th ed.); AnFE; AP; APA; CaFP; CBEP; CoAnAm; EG; MAmP, 2 *vers.*; MAPA; MasP; MoPo; MWA-2, *vers.*; NoP, 2 *vers.*; OxBA; TwAmPo
Safe sleeping on its mother's breast. The Baby. Ann Taylor. DD; OHIP
Safe stronghold our God is still, A. Luther's Hymn. Martin Luther, *tr. by* Thomas Carlyle. SoP
Safe upon the solid rock the ugly houses stand. Second Fig. Edna St. Vincent Millay. AmP
Safe where I cannot die yet. Is It Well with the Child? Christina Rossetti. OBEV (1st ed.)
Safely Home. *Unknown.* STF
Safety. Rupert Brooke. 1914, II. BrPo; EnLoPo; PoFr (1914.) HBV; NP
Sag' mir wer einst die Uhren erfund. Heine, *tr. fr. German by* Richard Garnett. AWP; JAWP; WBP
(Who Was It, Tell Me.) TrJP
Sag', wo ist dein schönes Liebchen. Heine, *tr. fr. German by* James Thomson. AWP; OuHeWo
(Ashes, *tr. by* Asa Hughes.) LiTW
(Love Dead, *tr. by* James Thomson.) OnPM
Saga of King Olaf, The, *sels.* Longfellow. *Fr.* Tales of a Wayside Inn: The Musician's Tale.
Sels.
Building of the *Long Serpent,* xiii. EtS
Challenge of Thor, The, i. AmPP (4th ed.)
Einar Tamberskelver, xx. AmPP (4th ed.); YT
King Olaf's Death-Drink, xxi. AmPP (4th ed.)
King Olaf's Return, ii. AmPP (4th ed.)
King Olaf's War-Horns, xix. AmPP (4th ed.); PFY
Saga of Leif the Lucky, *sel.* Hervey Allen.
"Leif was a man's name." EtS
Saga of Resistance. Sun-Ra. BF
Sagacity. William Rose Benét. MAP; MoAmPo; NeMA
Sagamore. Corinne Roosevelt Robinson. HBMV; PoRL
"Sage and rabbi, stoop to help us from the ban of our sorrow." Rabbi Loew. Rainer Maria Rilke. TwGP
Sage Counsel. Sir Arthur Quiller-Couch. HBV; HBVY; LBN; NA
("Lion is a beast to fight, The.") CenHV
Sage lectured brilliantly, The. The Black Riders, LVIII. Stephen Crane. AnAmPo; YaD
Sage once to a maiden sung, A. The Green Leaves All Turn Yellow. James Kenney. IrPN
Sages, The. Adam Mickiewicz, *tr. fr. Polish by* Dorothy Todd *and* George R. Noyes. CAW
Sagesse, *sels.* Paul Verlaine, *tr. fr. French.*
Chevalier Malheur, Le, *tr. by* John Gray. SyP
"Fairer is the sea," *tr. by* Arthur Symons.
(From "Sagesse.") AWP; JAWP; WBP
God Has Spoken, *tr. by* John Gray. SyP
(My God Has Spoken.) CAW
"Sky is up above the roof, The," *tr. by* Ernest Dowson. AWP; JAWP; SyP; WBP
(Sagesse.) EnLi-2
"Slumber dark and deep," *tr. by* Arthur Symons.
(From "Sagesse.") AWP; JAWP; WBP
Sagittarius or the Archer. Joseph Gordon Macleod. NP
Said ("Agatha Christie to"). George Starbuck. PV
Said ("J. Alfred Prufrock to"). George Starbuck. PV
Said ("President Johnson to"). George Starbuck. PV
Said a bad little youngster named Beauchamp. Limerick. *At. to* Carolyn Wells. TSW
Said a frog on a log. *Unknown.* BoTP
Said a girl from beyond Pompton Lakes. Limerick. Morris Bishop. LiBL
Said a great Congregational preacher. Limerick. *At. to* Oliver Wendell Holmes. GoTP; LiBL; SiTL; WhC
Said a precious little laddie. Too Little Children. *Unknown.* SoP
Said a pumpkin to me. A Pumpkin Speaks. Amanda Barris. PCH
Said a Snake to a Frog with a wrinkled skin. Hospitality. John Banister Tabb. PPL
Said Abner, "At last thou art come! Ere I tell, ere thou speak." Saul. Robert Browning. BEL; EnLi-2; EPN; FOL; GBV (1922 ed.); MaRV; MaVP; MBW-2; OAEP; OxBoCh; PoVP; TOP; ViPo; WHA
Said an ancient hermit, bending. The Olive Tree. Sabine Baring-Gould. GN; OTPC (1946 ed.); SoP
Said Aristotle unto Plato. Owen Wister. PoPl; WhC
Said Burgoyne to his men, as they passed in review. The Progress of Sir Jack Brag. *Unknown.* PAH
Said Christ our Lord, "I will go and see." A Parable. James Russell Lowell. ChIP; MaRV
Said Day to Night. Day and Night. Lady Anne Lindsay. ThGo
Said Death to Passion. Emily Dickinson. MoVE
Said Descartes, "I extol." Theological. Clifton Fadiman. FiBHP; PV
Said Fading-leaf to Fallen-leaf. Fading-Leaf and Fallen-Leaf. Richard Garnett. OBVV; TOP
Said Folly to Wisdom. On the Road. Tudor Jenks. NA
Said God, "You sisters, ere ye go." Hope and Despair. Lascelles Abercrombie. HBV; OBMV
Said Hanrahan. P. J. Hartigan. PoAu-1
Said he: "I can no longer sanction." Wisdom of the Abbot Macarius I. John Beecher. WOW
Said I to Lord & Taylor. A Father Does His Best. E. B. White. ALV; WhC
Said I to Myself, Said I. W. S. Gilbert. *Fr.* Iolanthe. PoVP
Said Jeremy Jonathan Joseph Jones. The Rhyme of the Rain Machine. F. W. Clarke. BoNaP
Said Judge Jessop, "The hyssop." Hyssop. Walter de la Mare. BoC
Said lady once to lover. The Three Bushes. W. B. Yeats. DTC; LiTG; LiTL
Said Life to Death: "Methinks, if I were you." Recrimination. Ella Wheeler Wilcox. AA
Said Lizzie the big blonde barmaid, "There." In the Township. Denis Glover. AnNZ
Said Mr. Smith, "I really cannot." Bones. Walter de la Mare. FiBHP; ShM
Said my landlord, white-headed Gil Gomez. Battle of the King's Mill. Thomas Dunn English. MC; PAH
Said Nero to one of his train. Limerick. *Unknown.* LiBL
Said Old Gentleman Gay, "On a Thanksgiving Day." A Good Thanksgiving. "Marian Douglas" PoLF; SoP; TRV; TVC
Said old Peeping Tom of Fort Lee. Limerick. Morris Bishop. LiBL; WhC
Said Opie Read. Julian Street *and* James Montgomery Flagg. BOHV; HBV
(To Be Continued.) FiBHP; InMe; PV
Said Orville Wright to Wilbur Wright. Wilbur Wright and Orville Wright. Rosemary *and* Stephen Vincent Benét. PoMa
Said Peter the Great to a Great Dane. Peterhof. Edmund Wilson. GoJo
Said, Pull her up a bit will you, Mac, I want to unload there.

Reason. Josephine Miles. FiMAP; PoCh
Said Robin to his pretty mate. The Robin to His Mate. Ann A. G. Carter. OTPC (1923 ed.); PPL; SAS
Said Simple Sam: "Does Christmas come." Simple Sam. Leroy F. Jackson. ChBR; GaP; PoSC
Said Sir Christopher Wren. *Unknown.* RIS
Said the Archangels, moving in their glory. Voice. Harriet Prescott Spofford. AA
Said the bird in search of a cage. A Bird in Search of a Cage. Robert Pack. NePoEA
Said the birds of America. The Birds of America. James Broughton. AmFN
Said the Captain: "There was wire." Our Modest Doughboys. Charlton Andrews. PAH
Said the child to the youthful year. The Child and the Year. Celia Thaxter. DD; HH
Said the corn to the lilies. The Corn and the Lilies. Emily A. Braddock. SoP
Said the Duck to the Kangaroo. The Duck and the Kangaroo. Edward Lear. BoChLi; GFA; OTPC (1946 ed.); PoRh; TiPo (1952 ed.)
Said the expert: "All right, let's call it a day." Rhapsody of the Deaf Man. Tristan Corbière. LiTW; OnHM
Said the first little chicken. The Five Little Chickens [*or* Chickens *or* Wishes]. *Unknown.* BoTP; FaPON; GFA; GoTP; MoShBr; OTPC (1946 ed.); PDV; SAS; UTS
Said the grave Dean of Westminster. A Refusal. Thomas Hardy. LiTB
Said the Innkeeper. Myles Connolly. SoP; TRV
Said the landlord to his lady. Bow Lamkin. *Unknown.* BFSS
Said the Lion to the Lioness—"When you are amber dust." Heart and Mind. Edith Sitwell. AtBAP; ChMP; FaBoTw; GTBS-D; MoPo; OAEP (2d ed.) Po; TwCP
Said the Lord God, "Build a house." The Kingdom of Heaven. G. K. Chesterton. OQP
Said the lord to his lady as he went away from home. False Linfinn. *Unknown.* BaBo
Said the monkey to the donkey. *Unknown.* FaFP; SiTL
Said the old deaf gardener. Lupin. Humbert Wolfe. ThGo
Said the Old Young Man to the Young Old Man. A Catch for Singing. W. W. Gibson. AnFE
Said the Poet to the Analyst. Anne Sexton. TwAmPo
Said the Raggedy Man on a hot afternoon. The Man in the Moon. James Whitcomb Riley. BOHV; HBV; HBVY; InMe; NA; OTPC; YT
Said the Reverend Jabez McCotton. Limerick. James Montgomery Flagg. LiBL
Said the Robin to the Sparrow. Overheard in an Orchard [*or* Feathered Faith]. Elizabeth Cheney. BLRP; FaChP; MaRV; SoP; STF; TRV
Said the Rose. George H. Miles. BLPA
Said the shark to the flying fish over the phone. The Flattered Flying Fish. E. V. Rieu. PDV; ShM
Said the sparrow to the robin. *See* Said the Robin to the Sparrow.
Said the Sword to the Axe, 'twixt the whacks and the hacks. Ned Braddock. John Williamson Palmer. MC; PAH
Said the Table to the Chair. The Table and the Chair. Edward Lear. BoChLi; GoTP; HBVY; MPB; OTPC (1946 ed.); PCH; PPL; SAS; SoPo; StVeCh; TreFT
Said the tooler to the driller, "Will you dance me a jig?" Turkey in the Straw (C *vers.*). *Unknown.* AS
Said the victory of Samothrace. Overheard in the Louvre. X. J. Kennedy. ELU
Said the Watcher by the Way. The Town down the River. E. A. Robinson. CoBA
Said the Whisky Flask. *Unknown.* STF
Said the Wind to the Moon, "I will blow you out." The Wind and the Moon. George Macdonald. GoJo; GoTP; HBV; HBVY; MoShBr; OnMSP; OTPC; StVeCh (1940 ed.); SUS; TreFS; TVC
Said this little fairy. The Five Little Fairies. Maud Burnham. HBVY; OTPC (1946 ed.); PCH; PPL
Saies, "Come here, cuzen Gawaine so gay." King Arthur and King Cornwall. *Unknown.* ESPB; OBB
Sail, A. Mikhail Yurevich Lermontov, *tr. fr. Russian by* Babette Deutsch. LiTW; OnPM; PoPl; WoL
—— *Tr. by* Max Eastman. AWP; JAWP; WBP
"Sail A! a sail! Oh, whence awa." Heart's Content. *Unknown.* HBV; OTPC (1923 ed.); PoLF
Sail-bellyer, exciter of boys, come bang. Autumnal Equinox on Mediterranean Beach. Robert Penn Warren. VaPo
Sail forth—steer for the deep waters only. Walt Whitman. *Fr.* Passage to India. TRV
Saîl of Claustra, Aelis, Azalais. The Alchemist. Ezra Pound. CMoP; LiTA; NePA; TwAmPo
Sail On! Joaquin Miller. *See* Columbus.
Sail On, O Ship of State! Longfellow. *See* Ship of State, The.
Sail on, sail on, fair cousin Cloud. The Cloud. Sidney Lanier. AmePo
Sail on, sail on, O Ship of State! The Ship of State [*or* Sail On, O Ship of State]. Longfellow. *Fr.* The Building of the Ship. HBVY; OHIP; OQP; PAP; PoFr; TreF
Sail Peacefully Home. Simeon Frug, *tr. fr. Yiddish.* TrJP
Sailboat, Your Secret. Robert Francis. SD
Sailing. Sidney Lanier. *See* Barnacles.
Sailing. Godfrey Marks. TreFS
Sailing after Lunch. Wallace Stevens. MoPo
Sailing at Dawn. Sir Henry Newbolt. EtS
Sailing beyond Seas. Jean Ingelow. VA
Sailing Homeward. Chan Fang-sheng, *tr. fr. Chinese by* Arthur Waley. AWP; FaBoCh; JAWP; LoGBV; WBP
Sailing of the Fleet, The. *Unknown.* PAH
Sailing of the *Sword*, The. William Morris. CoBE; ILP; OAEP; OBVV; PoVP
Sailing pine, The; the cedar, proud and tall. Kinds of Trees to Plant. Spenser. *Fr.* The Faerie Queene, I, i. OHIP
Sailing, Sailing. Gray Burr. CoPo; NYBP
Sailing ships with joy at length do touch the long-desired port, The. Wanting His Desire, He Complaineth. Richard Edwards. ReIE
Sailing to an Island. Richard Murphy. NMP
Sailing to Byzantium. W. B. Yeats. AnFE; AnIL; AtBAP; ATP (1953 ed.); BoPe; BWP; CABA; CaFP; CBEP; CBV; CMoP; CoBMV; DiPo; EnL; EnLi-2 (1949 ed.); EnLit; ExPo; FaBoEn; FaFP; ForPo; FosPo; GTBS-P; GTBS-W; HoPM; ILP; InPo; InvP; LiTB; LiTG; LiTM; MaPo; MasP; MBW-2; MoAB; MoBrPo; MoPo; MoPW; MoRP; MoVE; NAMP; NoP; OAEP (2d ed.); OBMV; OxBI; PAn; PIA; PoAn; PoDB; PoeP; PoFS; PoIE; PoPo; PoRA (rev. ed.); PoTE; PoVP; PP; ReMP; SeCePo; SeCeV; ShBV-4; StP; TreFT; UnPo (3d ed.); ViBoPo
Sailing upon the River. George Crabbe. *Fr.* The Borough. OBNC
Sailor, The. William Allingham. HBV; VA
Sailor. Eleanor Farjeon. BrR; PoRh
Sailor. Langston Hughes. GoSl
Sailor, The. Goodridge MacDonald. CaP
Sailor. P. K. Page. ACV
Sailor, The. Sylvia Townsend Warner. OBMV
Sailor and Inland Flower. Hamish Maclaren. EtS
Sailor and the Shark, The. Paul Fort, *tr. fr. French by* Frederick York Powell. OBMV
Sailor Ben had just been wed, The. Ballad of the Sailor Ben. Jack Mitchell. PCD
Sailor Boy, The. *Unknown.* BaBo; ShS, *with music*
Sailor boy who leant over the side, The. The Mermaid. Allen Upward. *Fr.* Scented Leaves from a Chinese Jar. NP
Sailor Girl, The. Alfred Perceval Graves. RIS
Sailor in his sailboat, homeward bound, The. Vacationer. Walker Gibson. SD
Sailor Man. H. Sewall Bailey. EtS
Sailor to His Parrot, The. W. H. Davies. EtS; ViBoPo
Sailor, What of the Isles? Edith Sitwell. ChMP
"Sailorman, I'll give to you." The Silver Penny. Walter de la Mare. CMoP; ExPo; OBMV
Sailors. Louis Simpson. NYBP
Sailors. *Unknown.* *See* Wrap Me Up in My Tarpaulin Jacket.
Sailors. *Unknown,* *tr. fr. Spanish by* Havelock Ellis. OnPM (Folk Songs, 2.) LiTW
(Spanish Folk Song.) AWP
Sailors, The. Karel van de Woestijne, *tr. fr. Dutch by* Adriaan J. Barnouw. OnPM
Sailor's Apology for Bow-Legs, A. Thomas Hood. EtS
Sailor's Carol. Charles Causley. AtBAP
Sailors come/ To the drum. Hornpipe. Edith Sitwell. *Fr.* Façade. GTBS-P; MoVE; SeCePo
Sailors' "Come-All-Ye". *Unknown.* SoAmSa
Sailor's Consolation, The. William Pitt, *wr. at. to* Charles Dibdin. BBV; BeLS; EtS; HBV; LBN; MemP, *abr.*; OTPC

Sailor's (continued)
(1946 ed.); StVeCh (1955 ed.); TreFS
Sailors for My Money. Martin Parker. SeCL; TuPP
(Saylors for My Money.) CoMu
Sailor's Grace, The. *Unknown.* ShS
(Blow the Man Down, *vers.* V.) ShS
(Rules of the Road.) SoAmSa
Sailor's Grave. Eliza Cook. BLPA
Sailor's Grave, The, *with music. Unknown, diff. vers. of song by* Eliza Cook. ShS; SoAmSa
Sailor's Harbor. Henry Reed. MoAB; MoBrPo (1962 ed.)
Sailor's Mother, The, *sel.* Wordsworth.
"And thus continuing, she said." Par
Sailors on Leave. Owen Dodson. AmNP
Sailor's Prayer, A. George Hornell Morris. TrPWD
Sailor's Return, The. *Unknown.* OxBoLi
("As I walked out one night.") LO
Sailor's Return, The, ("Madame, I come straight from sea battles"), *with music. Unknown, tr. fr. French by* Janet E. Tobitt. SaSa
Sailors' Song. Thomas Lovell Beddoes. *See* To Sea, to Sea!
Sailor's Song, A. Hazel Harper Harris. EtS
Sailor's Sweetheart, The. Duncan Campbell Scott. PeCV
Sailors there are of gentlest breed. Commemorative of a Naval Victory. Herman Melville. AP
Sailor's Way, The. *Unknown.* ShS
Sailors' Weather Proverbs. *Unknown.* PCH
Sailor's Wife, A. Clara Bernhardt. CaP
Sailor's Wife, The. William Julius Mickle, *also at. to* Jean Adam. BeLS; GTBS; GTBS-D; GTBS-P; GTBS-W; GTSL; HBV
("And are ye sure the news is true?") LO
(Mariner's Wife, The.) ViBoPo
(There's Nae Luck about the House.) GN; GTSE; OBEC
Sailor's Woman. Annette Patton Cornell. GoYe
Sailor's Yarn, A. James Jeffrey Roche. BOHV; NA
Sails. George Sterling. EtS
Sainclaire's Defeat. *Unknown.* PAH
Saint. Robert Graves. CMoP
Saint. Stéphane Mallarmé, *tr. fr. French by* Roger Fry. SyP
Saint. Kersti Merilaas, *tr. fr. Estonian by* W. K. Matthews. LiTW
Saint, The, *sel.* Humbert Wolfe. *Fr.* Requiem.
"Do you remember, Joan." CAW
St. Agnes' Eve. Tennyson. CoBE; EnL; EnLit; GoBC; GTBS-W; GTSL; HBV; ILP; LiTB; LiTG; MaVP; OAEP; OBEV; OBVV; OTPC; OxBoCh; PoVP; StJW; ViPo
(St. Agnes.) CAW
St. Agnes' Eve—ah, bitter chill it was! The Eve of St. Agnes. Keats. AtBAP; ATP; BEL; BeLS; BoLiVe; CABA; CABL; CaFP; ChER; CoBE; DiPo; DTo; EnL; EnLi-2; EnLit; EnRP; EPN; ERoP-2; ExPo; FiP; FosPo; GoTL; HoPM; ILP; LiTL; MBW-2; MERP; MyFE; NoP; OAEP; OBNC; OBRV; OnSP; PAn; PoAn; PoE; PoEL-4; PoIE; PoLF; SeCeV; ShBV-4; StP; TOP; TreF; TrGrPo; UnPo (1st ed.); WHA
St. Alphonsus Rodriguez. Gerard Manley Hopkins. *See* In Honor of St. Alphonsus Rodriguez.
St. Andrews by the Northern Sea. Almae Matres. Andrew Lang. OBVV; TOP
St. Andrew's Voyage to Mermedonia. *Unknown, tr. fr. Anglo-Saxon by* Charles W. Kennedy. *Fr.* Andreas. AnOE
Saint Anthony at church. St. Anthony's Sermon to the Fishes. "Abraham á Sancta-Clara." BOHV
Saint Anthony's Shirt, *sel.* C. Day Lewis.
"Saints and heroes, you dare say." BoPe
St. Anthony's Township. Gilbert Sheldon. CH
Saint Antony. R. S. Thomas. ToPo
Saint Apollinare in Classe. R. N. D. Wilson. CAW; CLwM
St. Augustine, Bishop of Hippo. Gerard Moultrie. SoP
Saint Augustine! well hast thou said. The Ladder of Saint Augustine. Longfellow. SoP
Saint Bernard's Prayer to Our Lady. Dante, *tr. fr. Italian by* Louis How. *Fr.* Divina Commedia: Paradiso, XXXIII. ISi
("Thou Virgin Mother, daughter of thy Son," *tr. by* Longfellow.) CAW
(Vision of the Divine Mystery, *longer sel., tr. by* Laurence Binyon.) LiTW
Saint Bernard's Verses. *At. to* St. Bernard of Clairvaux, *tr. fr. Latin by* Thomas Tusser. SiCE
Saint Brandan. Matthew Arnold. PoVP
Saint Brendan's Prophecy. *Unknown, tr. fr. Late Middle Irish by* Thomas Crofton Croker. OnYI
Saint Bridget was/ A problem child. The Giveaway. Phyllis McGinley. PoRA
St. Bridget's Lullaby. Dorothy Una Ratcliffe. CAW
Saint Brigid. Denis A. McCarthy. JKCP
St. Catherine, St. Catherine. The Milton Abbas Rhyme. *Unknown.* SiTL
Saint Cecilia. John Heath-Stubbs. MuSP
St. Cecilia's Day Epigram, A. Peter Porter. ELU
St. Colman came from Lindisfarne. Graves at Inishbofin. Richard Murphy. NYTB
St. Columcille the Scribe. *At. to* St. Columcille, *tr. fr. Middle Irish by* Kuno Meyer. AnIL
(Columcille the Scribe.) OnYI
St. Columcille's Island Hermitage. *Unknown, tr. fr. Middle Irish by* Kenneth Jackson. AnIL
St. Cuthbert Intervenes. "Thomas Ingoldsby." *Fr.* The Lay of St. Cuthbert. NBM
St. Dexter's Fire. Dave Etter. ThO
St. Dunstan, as the story goes. *Unknown.* OxNR
St. Enda. Laurence Lerner. PeSA
Saint Erkenwald. *Unknown, tr. fr. Middle English.* MeEV
Saint Francis. John Peale Bishop. EaLo
St. Francis. Vachel Lindsay. OQP
(Franciscan Aspiration.) CAW
Saint Francis. Roger Pfingston. NYTB
Saint Francis and Saint Benedight. A House Blessing. William Cartwright. ChTr; EaLo
Saint Francis and the Birds. Seamus Heaney. FlW
Saint Francis and the Birds. Roy McFadden. OxBI
St. Francis and the Cloud. Marie de L. Welch. MoRP
Saint Francis Borgia; or, A Refutation for Heredity. Phyllis McGinley. NePoAm-2
St. Francis, Buddha, Tolstoi, and Saint John. Above the Battle's Front. Vachel Lindsay. StJW
Saint Francis came to preach. With smiles he met. Sermon without Words. Elizabeth Patton Moss. MaRV
St. Francis Einstein of the Daffodils. William Carlos Williams. AtBAP; MoPo
Saint Francis? No indeed, although at that. Old Man in the Park. Mary Elizabeth Osborn. NePoAm-2
Saint Francis of Assisi. "Joan Ramsay." MaRV
St. Francis of the mountain cave and wattle hut. A Little Litany to St. Francis. Philip Murray. NePoAm
St. Francis' Prayer. St. Francis of Assisi. *See* Lord, Make Me an Instrument of Your Peace.
Saint Francis' Sermon to the Birds, *abr.* Longfellow. OTPC
Saint George and the Dragon ("Saint George he slew the dragon"). Alfred Noyes. RePo
St. George he was for England. The Englishman. G. K. Chesterton. WhC
Saint George of England. Cicely Fox Smith. BBV
St. George's Day—Ypres 1915. Sir Henry Newbolt. GTSL
Saint Germain-en-Laye. Ernest Dowson. SyP
St. Gervais. Michael Roberts. FaBoCh; LoGBV
St. Govan. A. G. Prys-Jones. ACV
St. Gregory's Day. *Unknown, tr. fr. Czech.* PCH
St. Helena Lullaby, A. Kipling. AtBAP; FaBoCh; FOL; MoVE; OAEP (2d ed.); OBMV; OtMeF; PoEL-5; POTE; ShBV-2; ViPP
Saint Hugh. Thomas Dekker. *See* Cold's the Wind.
Saint I heard of saw the world, A. The Plastic Glass. Josephine Miles. FiMAP
St. Isaac's Church, Petrograd. Claude McKay. *See* Russian Cathedral.
St. James, hover near him. In Extremis. Angelico Chavez. JKCP (1955 ed.)
St. James's Street. Frederick Locker-Lampson. HBV
Saint Jeanne. Theodosia Garrison. PEDC
(Sainte Jeanne.) HH
Saint Jerome and his lion. Leonardo Da Vinci's. Marianne Moore. NYBP
St. John, *sels.* Bible, *N.T.*
Be of Good Cheer; I Have Overcome the World, XVI. TreFS (19-33); WoL (1-33)
Children of the Light, XII: 23-36. WoL
Good Shepherd, The, X. TreFS (7-18); WoL (1-30)

Gospel According to Saint John, The ("For God so loved the world"), III: 16-17. LO
Gospel According to Saint John, The ("On the first day of the week cometh Mary Magdalene"), XX: 1-17. LO
Greater Love Hath No Man, XV: 13-16. TreFT
I Am the Bread of Life, VI: 35-40. TreFS
"In the beginning was the Word, and the Word was with God, and the Word was God," I. BoC (1-5); TreF (1-17)
(Word, The, I: 1-5.) MaRV; TrGrPo
Inscription on the Cross, XIX: 19-22. TreFT
Jesus and the Woman at the Well, IV: 5-26. TreFT
Jesus Answers the Pharisees, VIII: 12-32. TreFS
Last Supper, The, XIII: 1-XVI: 16. OuHeWo
Light of the World, The, XII: 44-50. WoL
Love One Another, XIII: 33-35. TreFT
My Peace I Give unto You, XIV: 1-31. WoL
(Peace of Christ, The, XIV: 1-27.) TreFS
"Then said Jesus to those Jews which believed on him," VIII; 31-36. PoFr
True Vine, The, XV: 1-27. WoL
Woman Taken in Adultery, The, VIII: 2-11. TreFT
Saint John, The. George Frederick Clarke. CaP
Saint John. Elizabeth J. Coatsworth. MoRP
St. John. Whittier. PAH
Saint John Baptist. William Drummond of Hawthornden. *See* For The Baptist.
St. John Baptist. Arthur O'Shaughnessy. HBV
Saint John Damascene. The Rosebush and the Trinity. Alfred Barrett. GoBC
St. John's, Cambridge. Longfellow. OBEV
St. Joseph, when the day was done. To St. Joseph. Charles L. O'Donnell. JKCP
Saint Judas. James Wright. CBV; NMP
St. Kevin. Samuel Lover. OnYI
St. Kilda. William Collins. *Fr.* Ode on the Popular Superstitions of the Highlands. FaBoEn
St. Kilda. Barrie Reid. BoAV
St. Lawrence and the Saguenay, The, *sels.* Charles Sangster.
"On, through the lovely Archipelago." PeCV
Thousand Islands, The. OBCV
Saint Leger. Clinton Scollard. PAH
St. Louis Blues. W. C. Handy. NAMP
St. Luke, *sels.* Bible, *N.T.*
Adoration of the Shepherds, The. ChrBoLe (II: 1-16)
(Angels of Bethlehem, The, II; 8-16.) BoC
(Christmas Eve, II: 8-14.) BiCB; ChBR; GaP; PCH; SiSoSe
(Christmas Story, The, II: 8-14.) MaRV
(First Christmas, The.) OTPC (1946 ed.) (II: 8-16); PoRL (II: 8-16); SoPo (II: 8-16); TreFS (II: 1-19)
(Tidings of Great Joy, II: 8-14.) FaPON
"And he said, A certain man had two sons," XV: 11-24. BoC
"And one of the malefactors which were hanged railed on him," XXIII: 39-43. BoC
"And when he was twelve years old, they went up after the custom of the feast," II: 42-52. BoC
Benedictus, I: 68-79. MaRV
Child of Nazareth, The, II: 40-52. ChrBoLe
Death of Jesus, The, XXIII: 1-46. TreF
(Gospel According to Saint Luke, The: "And there followed him a great company," XXIII: 27-44.) LO
Effective Prayer, XI: 9-13. TreFT
Good Samaritan, The, X: 25-37. TreF
Good Tidings, IV: 18-19. MaRV
Gospel According to Saint Luke, The ("One of the Pharisees desired [Jesus] that he would eat with him"), VII: 36-50. LO
Jesus' Parable of the Sower, VIII: 5-15. TreFT
Lost Sheep, The, XV: 4-7. TreF
Magnificat, The, I: 46-55. ISi (*Douay vers.*); MaRV; WGRP; WHL
(Hymn of the Blessed Virgin.) CAW
Mary and Elizabeth, I: 39-45, *Douay vers.* ISi
Mary and Gabriel, I: 26-38, *Douay vers.* ISi
Mary and Simeon, II: 34-35, *Douay vers.* ISi
Nunc Dimittis, II: 29-32. WGRP; WHL
On Taking up One's Cross, IX: 23-26. TreFT
On the Road to Emmaus, XXIV: 13-36. TreFS
Pharisee and the Publican, The, XVIII: 9-14. TreFT
Poems by the Roadside ("Fear not, little flock"), XII: 32-37. CAW
Prelude of the New Testament ("Hail Mary full of grace!"), I: 28, 38, 42, II: 10-11, 14, *Douay vers.* CAW
Prodigal Son, The, XV: 11-32. TreF
(Gospel According to Saint Luke, The: "And Jesus said. . .") LO
To His Disciples, XII: 24-25, 27-28. CAW
Widow's Mite, The, XXI: 1-4. TreFT
St. Luke the Painter. Dante Gabriel Rossetti. The House of Life, LXXIV. GoBC; MaVP; PoVP; ViPo
St. Magnus control thee, that martyr of treason. Claud Halcro's Invocation. Sir Walter Scott. *Fr.* The Pirate, *ch.* 23. NBM
St. Malachy. Thomas Merton. CoPo
St. Margaret's bells. London Voluntaries. W. E. Henley. Po; PoVP
St. Mark, *sels.* Bible, *N.T.*
Jesus and the Children, X: 13-16. TreFT
Jesus Eats with Sinners, II: 15-17. TreFT
St. Mark. Christopher Smart. *Fr.* Hymns and Spiritual Songs. EiCP
St. Martin and the Beggar. Thom Gunn. MoBS; ShBV-3
Saint Mary Magdalene. Richard Crashaw. *See* Weeper, The.
St. Matthew, *sels.* Bible, *N.T.*
"Ask, and it shall be given you; seek, and ye shall find," VII: 7-8. BoC
Come Unto Me, XI: 28-30. MaRV
(My Yoke Is Easy.) TreFS
Easter Morning, XXVIII: 1-10. TreF
Great Commandment, The, XXII: 34-40. TreFT
("Then one of them, which was a lawyer.") PoFr
Parable of the Talents, The, XXV: 14-30. EnLi-1
Poems by the Roadside, V: 14-16-XVI: 17-19. CAW
Rich Man and the Kingdom of Heaven, The, XIX: 13-30. TreF
Sermon on the Mount, The, V: 1-VII:29. GoTP (V: 3-10); OuHeWo; TreF; WoL
"And seeing the multitudes, he went up into a mountain." PoPl (V: 1-10); RelE (V: 1-48)
Beatitudes, The, V:3-12. MaRV; TrGrPo (V: 3-10)
(Blessed Are the Poor in Spirit.) ExPo
God Provides, VI: 26-34, *abr.* BLRP
Lord's Prayer, The, VI: 9-13. EaLo; MaRV; PoLF; TrGrPo; TRV
(Poem of the Our Father, The.) CAW
Treasures [in Heaven], VI: 19-21. GoTP; TrGrPo
Things That Are Caesar's, The, XXII: 15-22. TreF
Visit of the Wise Men, The, II: 1-12. ChrBoLe
When the Son of Man Shall Come in His Glory, XXV: 31-46. TreF
Wise and Foolish Virgins, The, XXV: 1-13. TreF
St. Matthias. Christopher Smart. *Fr.* Hymns and Spiritual Songs. EiCP
Saint Michael of the Flaming Sword. Ballade of the Harrowing of Hell. D. B. Wyndham Lewis. CoBE; JKCP (1955 ed.)
St. Michael the Weigher. James Russell Lowell. AnFE; AnNE; APA; CAW; CoAnAm
St. Michael's Mount. John Davidson. HBV
Saint Nicholas. Marianne Moore. NYBP; PoAn
Saint of the Uplands, The. W. S. Merwin. NoP
Saint on the pillar stands, The. Stylite. Louis MacNeice. MoPo
Saint Patrick. Henry Bennett. *See* St. Patrick Was a Gentleman.
St. Patrick, *sel.* Phyllis Garlick.
"Christ with me, Christ before me, Christ behind me." TRV
Saint Patrick. Edwin Markham. HH
St. Patrick of Ireland, My Dear! William Maginn. BOHV; InMe
Saint Patrick, slave to Milcho of the herds. The Proclamation. Whittier. PAH; ThLM
St. Patrick Was a Gentleman. Henry Bennett. DD, *abr.*; PoRL, *abr.*; SiSoSe, *abr.*
(Saint Patrick.) HBV
St. Patrick's Breastplate. *At. to* St. Patrick. *See* Deer's Cry, The.
St. Patrick's Day. Eleanor Hammond. GFA
Saint Patrick's day in 'sixty-five. Bound Down to Newfoundland. *Unknown.* ShS
St. Patrick's Day is with us. I'll Wear a Shamrock. Mary Carolyn Davies. BrR; SiSoSe; TiPo (1952 ed.); YeAr
St. Patrick's Day it is—it is. Dawn Song—St. Patrick's Day. Violet Alleyn Storey. YeAr
St. Patrick's dean, your country's pride. To Dr. Swift on His

St (continued)
Birthday. Esther Johnson ("Stella"). EnLoPo
St. Patrick's Hymn before Tara[h]. James Clarence Mangan, *after the Irish.* EnRP; GoBC
St. Patrick's Treasure. Patrick J. Carroll. JKCP
Saint Paul, *abr.* F. W. H. Myers. PGD
Sels.
Alpha and Omega. OQP
"Christ, I am Christ's and let the name suffice you." ChIP; TRV
(Christ, all-sufficient.) MaRV
Experience ("Oh could I tell ye surely would believe it!") MaRV
(St. Paul Speaks.) BoC
"Hark what a sound, and too divine for hearing." FaChP
Knowledge. OQP
("Whoso has felt the Spirit of the Highest.") FaChP; TRV
"Lo, as some bard on isles of the Aegean." VA
(Inner Light, The.) MaRV
"Lo! as some venturer, from his stars receiving." ChIP
(Advent.) MaRV
Not in Solitude. OQP
Saints, The ("So tho' our Daystar from our sight be taken"). BoC
"Whoso has felt the Spirit of the Highest." FaChP; TRV
St. Paul on Charity. First Corinthians, Bible, *N.T.* *See* Charity.
St. Paul's Church, Her Bill for the Parliament, *sel.* Henry Farley.
To See a Quaint Outlandish Fowl. ViBoPo
(Bounty of Our Age, The.) FaBoCh; SeCePo; SeCL
Saint Peray. Thomas William Parsons. HBV
St. Peter. Eileen Duggan. WHL
St. Peter at the Gate. Joseph Bert Smiley. BLPA
Saint Peter Relates an Incident of the Resurrection Day. James Weldon Johnson. Kal
Saint Peter sat by the celestial gate. The Vision of Judgment. Byron. EnRP; ERoP-2; MasP; MBW-2; MERP; OxBoLi; PIA; StP; TOP
St. Peter stood guard at the golden gate. St. Peter at the Gate. Joseph Bert Smiley. BLPA
Saint Peter's Complaint, *sel.* Robert Southwell.
Stanzas from Saint Peter's Complaint ("Weep balm and myrrh"). ACP; CAW
St. Peter's Shadow. Richard Crashaw. *See* Sicke Implore St. Peter's Shadow, The.
St. Philip and St. James, *sel.* Christopher Smart.
Spring. OBEC
("Now the winds are all composure.") LoBV
St. Philip in Himself. Cardinal Newman. GoBC
Saint R. L. S. Sarah Norcliffe Cleghorn. HBMV
Saint, Revolutionist. Delmore Schwartz. FiMAP
St. Saviour's, Aberdeen Park, Highbury, London, N. John Betjeman. MoVE
St. Simon and St. Jude's Day. Cecil Frances Alexander. IrPN
St. Stephen and [King] Herod. *Unknown.* BaBo, *Middle English vers.*; BoLiVe, *Middle English vers.*; ESPB, *Middle English vers.*; MeEV *mod. vers.*; NoP, *mod. vers.*; OBB, *mod. vers.*; OxBoCh, *Middle English vers.*; OxBoLi, *Middle English vers.*; TrGrPo, *mod. vers.*
(Carol for St. Stephen's Day, A, *Middle English vers.*) CH
(Saint Stephen Was a Clerk, *mod. vers.*) StJW
(Seynt Stevyn and Herowdes, *Middle English vers.*) OxBB
("Seynt Stevene was a clerk in Kyng Herowdes halle," *Middle English vers.*) EnPo
Saint Stephen in San Francisco. Melvin Walker La Follette. CoPo
St. Stephen's cloistered hall was proud. Columbus. Lydia Huntley Sigourney. AA; DD; HBV; HH; MC; OTPC; PAH
St. Stephen's Day. John Keble. CoBE
St. Stephen's Word. Rayner Heppenstall. ChMP
St. Swithin. Daniel Henderson. HBMV; ShM
St. Swithin's Day. *Unknown.* OTPC (1946 ed.)
("St. Swithin's Day, if thou do rain.") GoTP; RIS
(Signs and Charms.) StaSt
Saint Teresa's Book-Mark. Saint Teresa of Avila. *See* Lines Written in Her Breviary. *tr. by* Longfellow.
Saint Thomas Aquinas. Thomas S. Jones, Jr. CAW
St. Thomas Aquinas. J. Corson Miller. JKCP (1955 ed.)
St. Thomas the Apostle. John Keble. SoP
St. Thomas's Day is past and gone. *Unknown.* OxNR
St. Uncumber and St. Trunnion. The Palmer. John Heywood. *Fr.* The Four P's. ACP; CAW
St. Ursanne. Michael Roberts. LiTM
St. Valentine. Marianne Moore. NYBP
St. Valentine, though wide your fame. To St. Valentine. Jennie Betts Hartswick. DD
St. Valentine's Day. Wilfrid Scawen Blunt. The Love Sonnets of Proteus, LV. EnLoPo; NBM; OBEV (1st ed.); OBVV; ViBoPo
Saint Valentine's Day. Coventry Patmore. *Fr.* The Unknown Eros, XLIII. FaBoEn; GoBC; OBNC; PoLi
Saint Valentine's Day. Shakespeare. *See* Tomorrow Is Saint Valentine's Day.
St. Valentine's Way. Eleanor Farjeon. MemP
Saint Wears a Halo, The. "Peter." BoTP
Sainte Anne de Beaupre. Richard Eberhart. NePoAm
Sainte Jeanne. Theodosia Garrison. *See* Saint Jeanne.
Sainte Margérie. *Unknown.* BOHV
Sainte Mary Magdalene. Richard Crashaw. *See* Weeper, The.
Sainte Marye Virgine. A Cry to Mary. St. Godric. MeEL
Saints, The. Robert Creeley. NMP
Saints. George Garrett. EaLo
Saints, The (St. Paul). F. W. H. Myers. *Fr.* Saint Paul. BoC
Saints and heroes, you dare say. C. Day Lewis. *Fr.* Saint Anthony's Shirt. BoPe
Saint's Delight, The, *with music.* *Unknown.* TrAS
Saints have adored the lofty soul of you. Two Sonnets, 1. Charles Hamilton Sorley. HBMV; MMA; MoBrPo; NemA; TrGrPo (1942 ed.)
Saints, I give myself up to thee. Chorus. Jack Kerouac. *Fr.* Mexico City Blues. NeAP
Saints in Glory, The. Dante, *tr. fr. Italian by* Henry F. Cary. *Fr.* Divina Commedia: Paradiso, XXXI. WGRP
Saint's Parade. Robert Layzer. NePoEA
Saint's Tragedy, The, *sels.* Charles Kingsley.
Crusader Chorus, *abr.* FOL; VA
Song: "Oh! that we two were Maying." HBV; VA
Song: "When I was a greenhorn and young." NBM
(When I Was a Greenhorn and Young.) PoVP
Saints who love the Crucified, The. A Proud Song. Marguerite Wilkinson. HBMV
Saith man to man, We've heard and known. No Master. William Morris. PoFr; PoVP
Saki, for God's love, come and fill my glass. Odes. Hafiz. AWP
Sakunami. James Kirkup. POTi
Salaam Alaikum. *Unknown.* PoLF
Salad. Mortimer Collins. ALV; BOHV; Par
Salad, A. Sydney Smith. BOHV; HBV
Salad—after Tennyson. Mortimer Collins. CenHV
Salad of greens! Salad of greens! The Universal Favorite. Carolyn Wells. InMe
Salámán and Absál, *sel.* Jami, *tr. fr. Persian by* Edward Fitzgerald.
Bewildered Arab, The. WoL
Salamander. Muriel Rukeyser. WIRo
Salamis. Aeschylus, *tr. fr. Greek by* G. M. Cookson. *Fr.* Persians. WaaP
(Battle of Salamis, The, *tr. by* Gilbert Murray.) PoFr
Salamis. Lawrence Durrell. NYBP
Salangadou, *with music.* *Unknown,* *tr. fr. French.* ABF; TrAS
Salaziennes, Les, *sel.* Auguste Lacaussade, *tr. fr. French.*
"My lips from this day forgot how to smile." TTY
Salcombe Seaman's Flaunt to the Proud Pirate, The. *Unknown.* ChTr
(Pirate of High Barbary, The.) EtS
Sale. Josephine Miles. FiMAP
Sale began—young girls were there, The. The Slave Auction. Frances Ellen Watkins Harper. Kal; PoNe; TTY
Sale of Saint Thomas, The, *sel.* Lascelles Abercrombie.
Tormented by the World. POTE
Sale of the Pet Lamb, The. Mary Howitt. CH
Salem. Robert Lowell. AnNE; CABA; NePoEA; PoPo; Sonn; ToPo
Salem. Edmund Clarence Stedman. AA; PAH
Salem Witch, A. Ednah Proctor Clarke. PAH
Salems of Oppression. Joseph Joel Keith. FiSC
Salesman, The. Robert Mezey. NePoEA
Salesman Is an It That Stinks Excuse, A. E. E. Cummings. AmP; OxBA

Salley Gardens, The. W. B. Yeats. *See* Down by the Salley Gardens.
Sallie Jewel. Stanley Crouch. WSL
Sallow dawn is in the sky, A. Lola Ridge. *Fr.* The Ghetto. MAP; MoAmPo (1942 ed.)
Sallow waiter brings me six huge oysters, A. Storm on Fifth Avenue. Siegfried Sassoon. ILP; MoVE
Sallows like heads in Polynesia. Into the Salient. Edmund Blunden. ViBoPo
Sally and Manda. Alice B. Campbell. PoMa
Sally Birkett's Ale. *Unknown.* ChTr
Sally Brown, *with music. Unknown.* AmSS; ShS, 2 *vers.*; SoAmSa
Sally Centipede. Helen Cowles LeCron. GFA
Sally from Coventry, The. George Walter Thornbury. HBV
Sally Go Round the Sunshine, *with music. Unknown.* OuSiCo ("Sally go round the sun," *sl. diff.*) OxNR
Sally, having swallowed cheese. Cruel Clever Cat. Geoffrey Taylor. ChTr; LiTM; SiTL
Sally in Our Alley. Henry Carey. AWP; BOHV; CBEP; CoMu; EiCL; FaBoBe; FaFP; FaPL; GTBS; GTBS-D; GTBS-P; GTBS-W; GTSE; GTSL; HBV; InMe; JAWP; LiTG; LiTL; MemP; NeHB; OBEV; PG (1945 ed.); PTK; RIS; SiTL; TOP; TreF; ViBoPo; WBP
(Ballad of Sally in Our Alley, The.) CEP; EiPP; OBEC; PoE
("Of all the girls that are so smart.") LO; PoSC; TiPo (1952 ed.)
Sally is gone that was so kindly. Ha'nacker Mill. Hilaire Belloc. HBMV; MoBrPo
Sally Monroe, *with music. Unknown.* ShS
Sally, Sally Waters. *Unknown.* OxNR
Sally Salter, she was a young teacher who taught. The Lovers [*or* Love's Moods and Tenses]. Phoebe Cary. BOHV; HBV
Sally Simpkin's Lament. Thomas Hood. BOHV; EnRP; ShM
Sally Sweetbread. Henry Carey. CoMu
Salmon Drowns Eagle. Malcolm Lowry. MoCV; OBCV; TwCaPo
Salmon-fishing. Robinson Jeffers. AnEnPo; SD
Salonikan Grave. Kipling. *Fr.* Epitaphs of the War, 1914-18. OAEP (2d ed.)
Saloon is gone up the creek, The. Hemmed-in Males. William Carlos Williams. *Fr.* A Folded Skyscraper. AnAmPo; MoVE; PoRA (rev. ed.); PoSa
Saloon is sometimes called a Bar, The. The Bar. *Unknown.* PoToHe (new ed.)
Salopia Inhospitalis. Douglas Brooke Wheelton Sladen. VA
Salt. Robert Francis. NYTB
Salt. Monk Gibbon. OxBI
Salt and Pepper Dance. Jimmy Garthwaite. GFA
Salt creek mouths unflushed by the sea. The South Coast. Brother Antoninus. NeAP
Salt Flats, The. Sir Charles G. D. Roberts. CaP
Salt for white. Salt. Robert Francis. NYTB
Salt Garden, The. Howard Nemerov. FiMAP; NePoEA
Salt Lake City. Hayden Carruth. AmFN
Salt Marsh, The. James Dickey. FRC
Salt of the Earth, The. Swinburne. PoVP
Salt sea, sweet sea. Bring Back. Anne Ridler. ACV
Salt wave sings, The. Fingernail Sunrise. Vernon Watkins. NYBP
Salts were formed by acids combined with bases. Scientia Vincit Omnia? Merrill Moore. AnAmPo
Saltus goes booted to the dancing school. Videantur Quae Non Sunt. Henry Parrot. SiCE
Salty Dogs. *Unknown.* CoSo
Salut au Monde, *sel.* Walt Whitman.
"My spirit has pass'd in compassion and determination around the whole earth." AtBAP
Salutamus. Sterling A. Brown. CDC
Salutation. "Æ." OnYI
Salutation. T. S. Eliot. *See* Lady, Three White Leopards.
Salutation. Zerea Jacob. *See* Hymn to Mary.
Salutation. Ezra Pound. LoGBV; MoAB; MoAmPo (1950 ed.); MoPW; OxBA
Salutation, The. Thomas Traherne. AnAnS-1; AtBAP; InvP; MeP; OBS; PeRV; PoIE; SCEP-1; SeCL; SeCP; SeCV-2; SeEP
Sels.
"From dust I rise." FaBoEn
"These little limbs." OxBoCh
Salutation of the Blessed Virgin, The. John Byrom. ISi
Salutation of [*or* to] the Dawn, The. *Unknown, at. to* Kalidasa, *ad. fr. Sanskrit.* MaRV; PoLF; PoToHe (new ed.); TIHL; TreFT (Look to This Day.) OQP
Salutation the Second. Ezra Pound. OxBA
Salutation to Jesus Christ. John Calvin. MaRV; SoP; WGRP (I Greet Thee, *shorter and diff. vers.*) SoP
Salutations: To Mary, Virgin. *Unknown, tr. fr. Latin by* Raymond F. Roseliep. ISi
Salute. Archibald MacLeish. CMoP
Salute. Oliver Pitcher. Kal
Salute. James Schuyler. ANYP; NeAP
Salute the last and everlasting day. Ascention [*or* Ascension]. John Donne. AnAnS-1; MaMe; MeP; OBS; Sonn
Salute to Greece. "Clemence Dane." PoFr
Salute to the Modern Language Association, A, Convening in the Hotel Pennsylvania, December 28th-30th. Morris Bishop. WhC
Salute to Trees, A. Henry van Dyke. StVeCh
Salvation comes by Christ alone. An Evening Thought. Jupiter Hammon. PoNe
Salvation of Texas Peters, The. J. W. Foley. ShM
Salvation Prospect. LeRoy Smith, Jr. NePoAm
Salvation to all that will is nigh. Annunciation. John Donne. AnAnS-1; ISi; MaMe; MeP; OBS; Sonn
Salve! Thomas Edward Brown. HBV; OBEV; OBVV; TOP
Salve Regina ("Mary, we hail thee"). *At. to* Hermanus Contractus, *tr. fr. Latin by* Winfred Douglas. ISi
Salve Regina ("Hail, holy Queen"). *Unknown.* WHL
Salve, Virgo Florens. *Unknown.* WHL
Salvos for Randolph Bourne. Horace Gregory. CMoP; NAMP
Sam. Arthur St. John Adcock. WhC
Sam. Walter de la Mare. FaBV; MoAB; MoBrPo; NeMA; OnMSP; PoMS; PoPo; TiPo; WePo
Sam Bass. *Unknown.* ABF, *with music*; AS; BeLS; BFSS, *with music*; CoSo, *with music*; ViBoFo
Sam Brown was a fellow from way down East. In the Catacombs. Harlan Hoge Ballard. BOHV; YaD
Sam had spirits naught could check. Impetuous Samuel. Harry Graham. NA
Sam Hall, *with music. Unknown.* ABF; CoSo; ViBoFo (Samuel Hall, *sl. diff. vers.*) ChTr
Sam, Sam, the butcher man. *Unknown.* FaFP; SiTL
Samadhi. Conrad Aiken. MAPA
Samarian Nights. Yaakov Fichman, *tr. fr. Hebrew by* Dov Vardi. LiTW
Samaritan Woman. Mother Francis d'Assisi. JKCP (1955 ed.)
Sambo's Right to be Kilt. Charles Graham Halpine. AA
Same, The ("Milton! thou shouldst be living at this hour"). Wordsworth. *See* London, 1802.
Same Forever, The. Horatius Bonar. BePJ
Same great angel who had once, The. On the Death of Mary. Rainer Maria Rilke. ISi
Same in Blues. Langston Hughes. NoP
Same leaves over and over again, The. In Hardwood Groves. Robert Frost. AmLP; MWA-2
Same old charitable lie, The. The Lie of the Land. Margaret Fishback. SiTL
Same old fable, The. On Being Told That One's Ideas Are Victorian. Sara Henderson Hay. InMe
Same Old Jazz, The. Philip Whalen. NeAP
Same Old Law, The. Walt Whitman. *Fr.* Song of Myself. OA
Same Old Story, The. James J. Montague. HBMV
Same Old Story. Harry B. Smith. BOHV
Same Train, *with music. Unknown.* BoAN-2
Sam'el Down vrom Lon'on. William Barnes. PeVV
Samela. Robert Greene. *See* Doron's Description of Samela.
Samis Idyll. Dachine Rainer. NePoAm
Samisen. James Kirkup. NYTB
Samor, *sel.* Henry Hart Milman.
Beacons, The. OBRV
Sampan. *Unknown, tr. fr. Chinese.* WePo
Sampler, The. Rachel Field. BiCB
Sampler, The. Nancy Byrd Turner. BiCB
Sampling the books the moderns bring. Deep Stuff. Keith Preston. WhC
Samson. Frederick George Scott. VA
Samson, *with music. Unknown.* OuSiCo
Samson Agonistes. Milton. EnLi-1; ILP; MBW-1; PoEL-3
Sels.

Samson (continued)
"All is best, though we oft doubt." BoC; MyFE; OBEV; OBS; SeCePo; SeCeV
(Epilogue.) FaBoEn
(Final Chorus.) ExPo
(Last Chorus.) ShBV-4
Blindness of Samson, The. LiTB; UnPo
"I, dark in light, exposed," 5 *ll.* TrGrPo
"But who is this, what thing on sea or land?"
(Delilah.) SeCePo
"Come, come, no time for lamentation now." FiP
(Death of Samson.) ChTr
"It is not vertue, wisdom, valour, wit."
(Woman.) OBS
"Little onward lend thy guiding hand, A." AtBAP; ViBoPo
"Many are the sayings of the wise." SeCeV
(Ways of God to Men, The.) OBS
"O dearly-bought revenge, yet glorious!"
(Heroic Vengeance.) OBS
"Oh, how comely it is and how reviving." OBEV; SeCeV
(Deliverer, The.) OBS
"O wherefore was my birth from heaven foretold." AnFE
(O Dark, Dark, Dark, *abr.*) WHA
"Why was my breeding order'd and prescrib'd," 12 *ll.* PoFr
"Occasions drew me early to this city." FlW; FOL
Samson Fallen. OBS
("Can this be he," *shorter sel.*) InP
Samson Hath Quit Himself. LoBV
"This only hope relieves me, that the strife." TRV
Transcendence of God, The. OBS
Samson to His Delilah. Richard Crashaw. TrGrPo
(Sampson to His Dalilah.) MaMe
Samuel. Alan Paton. BoSA
Samuel, Book I. Bible, *O.T.* *See* First Samuel.
Samuel, Book II. Bible, *O.T.* *See* Second Samuel.
Samuel Hall. *Unknown.* *See* Sam Hall.
Samuel Hoar. Franklin Benjamin Sanborn. AA
Samuel Pepys. Allan M. Laing. FiBHP
Samuel, Samuel Palmer. In a Shoreham Garden. Laurence Lerner. NePoEA-2
Samuel Sewall. Anthony Hecht. LiTM (1970 ed.); NePoEA; PoPl; PoRA (rev. ed.); TwCP
Samuel Taylor Coleridge. Dante Gabriel Rossetti. Five English Poets, 3. PoVP
San Francisco. John Vance Cheney. PAH
San Francisco. Joaquin Miller. PAH
San Francisco. Walter Adolphe Roberts. PoNe
San Francisco/ gentle in storms of fiery fogbank shower. Rosewood Vision. James Brodey. ANYP
San Francisco Company, The. O! California. Isaac W. Baker. SGR
San Francisco Company, of which I've often told, The. Arrival of the San Francisco. Isaac W. Baker. SGR
San Gloria. "Tom Redcam." PoNe
San Juan Capistrano. Alice Cecilia Cooper. GoBC
San Lorenzo Giustiniani's Mother. Alice Meynell. HBV
San Marco Museum, Florence. Sister Maris Stella. GoBC
San Martino del Carso. Giuseppe Ungaretti, *tr. fr. Italian by* Glauco Cambon. OnPM
San Miguel de la Tumba. Gonzalo de Berceo, *tr. fr. Spanish by* Longfellow. *Fr.* The Miracles of Our Lady. CAW
San Sabas. Luis Palés Matos, *tr. fr. Spanish by* Muna Lee. CAW
San Terenzo. Andrew Lang. VA
Sanary. Katherine Mansfield. AnNZ
Sancho. William Edwin Collin. CaP
Sancta Maria Dolorum or The Mother of Sorrows. Richard Crashaw. MaMe
Sancta Silvarum. Lionel Johnson. BrPo
Sancte Confessor. Rhabanus Maurus, *tr. fr. Latin by* Alan G. McDougall. CAW
Sanctity. Patrick Kavanagh. ELU; FaBoTw
Sanctuary. J. B. Boothroyd. FiBHP
Sanctuary. Bruce Boyd. NeAP
Sanctuary. Louise Imogen Guiney. AA
Sanctuary, The. Howard Nemerov. NePoEA
Sanctuary. Clinton Scollard. MaRV; OQP
Sanctuary. *Unknown.* SoP
Sanctuary. Mildred Wojtalewicz. WHL
Sanctuary. Elinor Wylie. MAP; MoAB; MoAmPo; PoMa
Sanctum, The. T. A. Daly. TrPWD
Sanctus. David Gascoyne. *Fr.* Miserere. NeBP
Sand below the border-mountain lies like snow, The. On Hearing a Flute at Night from the Wall of Shou-hsiang. Li Yi. UnS
Sand-between-the-Toes. A. A. Milne. TiPo (1959 ed.)
Sand Castles. W. Graham Robertson. MPB
Sand Cooking. *Unknown.* PCH
Sand Dunes. Robert Frost. MAP; MoAB; MoAmPo
Sand Dunes and Sea. John Richard Moreland. HBMV
Sand Paintings. Alice Corbin. AnAmPo; NP
Sand, sand; hills of sand. The [Hidden] Mermaids. Walter de la Mare. BrPo; OTPC
Sandal and garment of yellow and lotus garlands upon his body of blue. Jayadeva. *Fr.* Gita Govinda. ErPo
Sandalwood Song. Sacheverell Sitwell. MuSP
Sandalled with morning and with evening star. To Pain. George Sterling. JKCP (1926 ed.)
Sandalphon. Longfellow. AmPP (3d ed.); AnNE
Sandgate Girl's Lamentation, The. *Unknown.* CoMu; ELP
Sandhill Crane, The. Mary Austin. TiPo
Sandhill People. Carl Sandburg. CMoP
Sandman, The ("I have a pair of boots so rare"). *Unknown, tr. fr. German by* Louis Untermeyer. RIS
Sandman, The. "Margaret Vandegrift." HBV; HBVY; PRWS; TVC
Sandpiper. Elizabeth Bishop. NYBP
Sandpiper, The. Witter Bynner. HBMV
Sandpiper, The. Celia Thaxter. AA; BBV (1923 ed.); BoChLi; DD; FaBoBe; FaPON; GN; HBV; HBVY; MPB; PTK; UTS; WBLP
Sandpipers. Helen Merrill Egerton. CaP
Sandpipers. Carl Sandburg. BiS
Sandra and that boy that's going to get her in trouble. Cora Punctuated with Strawberries. George Starbuck. NMP
Sands Are Alive with Sunshine, The. W. E. Henley. PoVP
Sands of [*or* o'] Dee, The. Charles Kingsley. *Fr.* Alton Locke. BBV (1923 ed.); BeLS; BoChLi; CH; FaPON; GBV (1952 ed.); GN; GTBS; GTBS-D; GTSE; GTSL; HBV; MCCG; MPB; NeHB; OBEV (1st ed.); OnSP; OTPC; PoMS; PoVP; PTK; RG; ShBV-2; TreF; TSW; VA; WBLP
Sands of Time, The. Robert E. Howard. FiSC
Sandstone. Anne Marriott. CaP
Sandwich Man, The. Louis Johnson. AnNZ
Sandwich Man, The. Ron Padgett. ANYP
Sandy—A Small Dog. Alan Anderson. PCD
Sandy cat by the Farmer's chair, The. Summer Evening. Walter de la Mare. MoAB; MoBrPo; MoShBr; NeMA; TiPo (1959 ed.); TSW
Sandy Dan he had red hair. The Erie Canal. *Unknown.* ABF
Sandy he belongs to the mill. *Unknown.* OxNR
Sandy Hook. George Houghton. AA
Sandy Kildandy. *Unknown.* OxNR
Sandy Lan', *with music.* *Unknown.* ABF
Sandy Star and Willie Gee (*Complete,* I-V). William Stanley Braithwaite. BANP
Sandy Star, *sel.,* V. HBMV
Sang: "My Peggy is a young thing". Allan Ramsay. *See* My Peggy.
Sang: Recoll o Skaith. Sidney Goodsir Smith. NeBP
Sang: "There's a reid lowe in yer cheek." Robert MacLellan. OxBS
Sang old Tom the lunatic. Tom the Lunatic. W. B. Yeats. OnYI
Sang Solomon to Sheba. Solomon to Sheba. W. B. Yeats. CMoP; ELP; GTBS-D
Sang the sunrise on an amber morn. An April Adoration. Sir Charles G. D. Roberts. HBV
Sangar. John Reed. NP
Sank through easeful. The Diver. Robert Hayden. AmPP (5th ed.); Kal
Sanna. Alan Paton. BoSA
Sans Equity and sans Poise. Confucius, *tr. fr. Chinese by* Ezra Pound. *Fr.* Yung Wind. CTC
Sans Souci. Lisel Mueller. NePoAm-2
Sant 'Angelo d'Ischia. Edwin Denby. ANYP
Santa Anna [*or* Ana] came storming, as a storm might come. The Defense [*or* Defence] of the Alamo. Joaquin Miller. BeLS; DD; FaBoBe; HBV; MC; OnMSP; PaA; PAH
Santa Anna; or, The Plains of Mexico, *with music.* *Unknown.* AmSS
(Santy Anna, *with music.*) ShS, 2 *vers.*; SoAmSa

(Santy Anna, *longer vers., with music.*) OuSiCo
Santa Barbara. Francis Fisher Browne. AA
Santa Barbara Beach. Ridgely Torrence. HBMV
Santa Claus ("He comes in the night!"). *Unknown.* BoTP; ChBR; HBVY; HH; PEDC; PRWS; TVC
Santa Claus (Little fairy snowflakes"). *Unknown.* OTPC (1946 ed.); SoPo
Santa Claus ("Old Santa Claus puts on his cap"). *Unknown.* GFA
Santa Claus and the Mouse. Emilie Poulsson. ChBR; GFA; UTS
Santa Claus comes when you're good. Belsnickel. Arthur Guiterman. BBGG
Santa Claus, I hang for you. A Real Santa Claus. Frank Dempster Sherman. ChBR; GaP
Santa Fe Trail, The. Effortlessly Democratic Santa Fe Trail. Martha Baird. PoPl
Santa Fé Trail. Barbara Guest. NeAP
Santa Fé Trail, The, *with music. Unknown.* CoSo
Santa-Fé Trail, The (A Humoresque). Vachel Lindsay. CoBA
"I am a tramp by the long trail's border," *sel.* LaNeLa
Santa Filomena. Longfellow. PEDC; PoRL
Santa Maria del Fiore. George Herbert Clarke. CaP
Santa Maria, well thou tremblest down the wave. The Triumph. Sidney Lanier. *Fr.* The Psalm of the West. PAH
Santa Teresa's Book-Mark. St. Teresa of Avila. *See* Lines Written in Her Breviary.
Santiago. Thomas A. Janvier. MC; PAH
Santorin. James Elroy Flecker. CLwM; FaBoTw; GoJo; OBMV
Santos: New Mexico. May Sarton. EaLo
Santy Anna [*or* Anno]. *Unknown. See* Santa Anna.
Sanyassi, The. Philip Gilbert Hamerton. VA
Saon of Acanthus. Callimachus, *tr. fr. Greek by* John Addington Symonds. AWP; TRV
Sap, The. Henry Vaughan. AnAnS-1; MeP
Sap Bucket Song. Louis Stoddard. NYTB
Sap dripped from a broken twig. Youth of the Mountain. Walter Hard. AnNE
Sap was liquid light from spout to pail, The. Dusk in the Sugar Woods. Charles Malam. NYTB
Saphire (Metamorpho's Chick). Joe Rosenblatt. MoCV
Sapho and Phao, *sels.* John Lyly.
Sapho's Song: "O cruel Love!" OBSC
Song in Making of the Arrows, The. LoBV; OBSC; TuPP
(Vulcan's Song.) ElL
Sapientia Lunae. Ernest Dowson. EnLi-2; HBV
Sapling. Yvette Johnson. TNV
Sapphic Dream, A. George Moore. SyP
Sapphic Stanzas. Aleksandr Radischev, *tr. fr. Russian by* V. de S. Pinto. LiTW
Sapphics. George Canning *and* John Hookham Frere. *See* Friend of Humanity and the Knife-Grinder, The.
Sapphics. Sir Philip Sidney. *Fr.* Arcadia. SiPS
Sapphics. Swinburne. AnEnPo; Po; PoEL-5; PoVP; TOP; ViPo
Sapphics upon the Passion of Christ. *Unknown.* ReIE
Sapphire, nor diamond, nor emerald. No Jewel so Worthy. Jacopo da Lentino. OnPM
Sappho, *sel.* Bliss Carman.
"When in the spring the swallows all return," XCIII. PeCV
Sappho. Catullus, *tr. fr. Latin by* William Ellery Leonard. AWP; JAWP; WBP
Sappho. Jack Cope. PeSA
Sappho. Swinburne. *Fr.* On the Cliffs. VA
Sappho and Phao. John Lyly. *See* Sapho and Phao.
Sappho, Be Comforted. William Carlos Williams. NePoAm-2
Sappho Rehung ("Sappho saw three stars"). LeRoy Smith, Jr. NePoAm
Sappho's Tomb. Arthur Stringer. CaP
Sarah. "Robin Hyde." AnNZ
Sarah Byng. Hilaire Belloc. CenHV; GoJo
Sarah Cynthia Sylvia Stout. Shelley Silverstein. BBGG
Sarah kissed me when we met. Osculation. Henry Sydnor Harrison. InMe
Sarah Lorton. Mary Finnin. BoAV
Sarah Threeneedles. Katharine Lee Bates. HBMV
Sarajevo. Lawrence Durrell. GTBS-P
Saratoga Ending. Weldon Kees. NaP
Saratoga Song. *Unknown.* PAH
Sarcophagi. Bernard Spencer. FaBoMo
Sarcophagus Cover. Ruth Feldman. NYTB
Sardanapulus. Earl of Surrey. EP; FOL; SiPS
("Assyrians' king in peace, with foul desire, Th'.") EnPo; FCP
(Portrait of Henry VIII, The.) ACP (1952 ed.)
Sardinian Lullaby. *Unknown.* RIS
(Sleep, Baby Boy.) FaPON
Sargent's Portrait of Edwin Booth at "The Players." Thomas Bailey Aldrich. AA
Sargon is dust, Semiramis a clod! The Dust Dethroned. George Sterling. *Fr.* Three Sonnets on Oblivion. HBV
Saris go by me from the embassies, The. The Woman at the Washington Zoo. Randall Jarrell. AP; CoAP; LiTM (1970 ed.); NMP; TwCP; UnPo (3d ed.)
Sarmed, whom they intoxicated from the cup of love. Quatrain. Sarmèd the Yahud. TrJP
Sarpedon to Glaukos. Homer, *tr. fr. Greek by* Richmond Lattimore. *Fr.* The Iliad, XII. WaaP
("Nor had great Hector and his friends the rampire overrun," *tr. by* George Chapman.) AtBAP
(Sarpedon's Speech, *tr. by* George Chapman.) OBS
Sarolla's women in their picture hats. Lawrence Ferlinghetti. Pictures of the Gone World, Sec. 8. NeAP
Sarrazine's Song to Her Dead Lover. Marie de France. *See* Song from "Chartivel."
Sarsfield went out the Dutch to rout. A Ballad of Sarsfield. Aubrey Thomas De Vere. GoBC; HBV
Sartorial Solecism. R. E. C. Stringer. FiBHP
Sarum Primer, *sel. Unknown.*
God Be in My Head. BoC; EaLo; MaRV; OxBoCh; PoLi; TRV
(God with Us.) TreFT
(Hymnus.) ChTr
(Knight's Prayer, The.) BoTP
(Mihi Adhaerere Deo Bonum Est.) PG (1955 ed.)
Sarvant, Marster! Yes, sah, dat's me. Uncle Gabe's White Folks. Thomas Nelson Page. AA
Sary "Fixes Up" Things. Albert Bigelow Paine. BOHV
Sassafras. Samuel Minturn Peck. AA
Sassafras Memories. Edward S. Spriggs. BF
Sassafras Tea. Mary Effie Lee Newsome. CDC; GoSl
Sat est Scripsisse. Austin Dobson. BoPe
Sat on a telephone pole talking to his girl. Lineman Calling. Josephine Miles. FiMAP
Sat Will & Kate. Those Troublesome Disguises. Jonathan Williams. NeAP
Satan. Michael Madhusudan Dutt. ACV
Satan. Milton. *Fr.* Paradise Lost, I. SeCePo, *Bk.* I, *ll.* 283-313, *Bk.* II, *ll.* 1010-1055; TreFT, *ll.* 36-75; TrGrPo, *ll.* 36-75, 221-237, 522-543
Satan and His Host. Milton. *Fr.* Paradise Lost, I. OBS
Satan and Pilate's Wife. *Unknown.* ACP (1952 ed.)
Satan and the Fallen Angels. Milton. *Fr.* Paradise Lost, I. LiTB; OBS
(Satan.) SeCePo
(Superior Fiend, The.) MaPo
Satan Beholds Eve. Milton. *Fr.* Paradise Lost, IX. PoFS
Satan Defiant. Milton. *Fr.* Paradise Lost, I. WHA
(Fallen Angels, The.) FaBoEn
(". . .Him the Almighty Power/ Hurl'd headlong flaming.") AnFE; MyFE
Satan Discovers Eden. Milton. *Fr.* Paradise Lost, IV. ExPo
Satan from hence now on the lower stair. The Panorama. Milton. *Fr.* Paradise Lost, III. WHA
Satan in Eden "was constrain'd." Error Pursued. Helen Pinkerton. QFR
Satan Is on Your Tongue. George Barker. MoAB; MoBrPo (1950 ed.)
Satan Journeys to the Garden of Eden. Milton. *Fr.* Paradise Lost, IV. ChTr
Satan Looks upon Adam and Eve in Paradise. Milton. *Fr.* Paradise Lost, IV. TreFS
Satan on War. Milton. *Fr.* Paradise Lost, II. MaRV
Satan Ponders His Fallen State. Milton. *See* Fall of the Angels, The.
Satan Views the World. Milton. *Fr.* Paradise Lost, II. WHA
Satan's a Liar [*or* Liah]. *Unknown.* AS, *with music*; IHA
Satan's Adjuration. Milton. *Fr.* Paradise Lost, I. FaBoEn
Satan's Guile. Milton. *Fr.* Paradise Regained, I. LiTB; OBS

Satan's (continued)
Satan's Metamorphosis. Milton. *Fr.* Paradise Lost, X. StP
Satan's Pride. Milton. *Fr.* Paradise Lost, IV. MaRV
Satan's Soliloquy. Milton. *Fr.* Paradise Lost, IV. LiTB; OBS
Satan's Speech. Milton. *Fr.* Paradise Lost, I. DiPo
Sathan, no woman, yet a wandering spirit. Caelica, XXI. Fulke Greville. NCEP
Sather Gate Illumination. Allen Ginsberg. NeAP
Satia Te Sanguine. Swinburne. PeVV
Satin Mice Creaking Last Summer's Grass, The. Robert P. Tristram Coffin. OA
Satin Shoes, The. Thomas Hardy. CoBMV
Satira Prima. Everard Guilpin. *Fr.* Skialetheia. ReIE
Satire, *sel.* John Marston. *Fr.* Certaine Satyres, V.
"Ambitious gorgons, wide-mouthed Lamians." ViBoPo
Satire [*or* Satyr] A, *sel.* John Oldham.
Dissuasive against Poetry, A. PeRV
("But, grant thy poetry should find success.") ViBoPo
Satire VI: "Another scorns the homespun thread of rhymes." Joseph Hall. *Fr.* Virgidemiarum. SiCE; TuPP
Satire: "Ask you what provocation I have had?" Pope. *Fr.* Epilogue to the Satires, Dialogue II. OBEC
(In Defence of Satire.) CoBE
Satire: "Away, thou fondling motley humorist." John Donne. Satires, I. OAEP
Satire VIII: "Curio, ay me! Thy mistress' monkey's dead!" John Marston. *Fr.* The Scourge of Villainy. ReEn; ReIE
Satire I: Garnet's Ghost Addressing to the Jesuits. John Oldham. *Fr.* Satires upon the Jesuits. SeEP
Satire: "Gentle squire would gladly entertain, A." Joseph Hall. *Fr.* Virgidemiarum. ReIE; TuPP
("Gentle squire would gladly entertain, A.") SiCE; ViBoPo
Satire: "Great is the folly of a feeble brain." Joseph Hall. *See* Love-sicke Poet, The.
Satire: "Great Osmond knows not how he shall be known." Joseph Hall. *Fr.* Virgidemiarum. ReIE
Satire X: Humors, *sel.* John Marston. *Fr.* The Scourge of Villainy.
"Sleep, grim reproof, my jocund muse doth sing." SICE, *longer sel.*; TuPP
Satire II: "I cannot hold, I cannot, I, indure." John Marston. *Fr.* The Scourge of Villainy. ReIE
Satire: "I wot not how the world's degenerate." Joseph Hall. *Fr.* Virgidemiarum. ReIE
Satire III: "Kind pity [*or* Kinde pitty] chokes my spleen; brave scorn forbids." John Donne. *Fr.* Satires. AnAnS-1; CABL; MaMe; MaPo; MBW-1; MeLP; MeP; OBS; PoEL-2; ReIE; SCEP-1; SeEP; TuPP
(Religion.) ReEn
(Satire III: Religion.) CABA; FosPo; NoP
(Satyre: Of Religion.) MePo
(Satyre III: On Religion.) SeCP
(Satyre III: "Kinde pitty chokes my spleene; brave scorn forbids.") SeCV-1
(Truth.) SeCePo
Satire: Maimed Debauchee, The. Earl of Rochester. *See* Maimed Debauchee, The.
Satire VII: "'Man, a man, a kingdom for a man, A!'" John Marston. *Fr.* The Scourge of Villainy. ReIE
Satire: "Mine own John Poynz." Sir Thomas Wyatt. *See* Of the Courtier's Life.
Satire I: "My verse is satire; Dorset, lend your ear." Edward Young. *Fr.* Love or Fame, the Universal Passion. EiCL
Satire I: "Nor lady's wanton love, nor wand'ring knight." Joseph Hall. *Fr.* Virgidemiarum. TuPP
("Nor ladies' wanton love, nor wandering knight.") SiCE
Satire: "Satire, my friend ('twixt me and you). Alexander Geddes. ACP
Satire: "Sir though (I thank God for it) I do hate." John Donne. Satires, II. PoFS; ViBoPo
Satire 3: To Sir Francis Brian. Sir Thomas Wyatt. *See* To Sir Frances Brian.
Satire IV: "Vice, from privation of that sacred grace." John Marston. *Fr.* The Scourge of Villainy. ReIE
Satire II: "Yes; thank my stars! as early as I knew." Pope. *Fr.* The Satires of Dr. John Donne, Versified. PoFS
Satire IV: "Well I may now receive, and die. My sin." John Donne. *Fr.* Satires. MBW-1; SeEP
Satire against Mankind, A. Earl of Rochester. CABL; EiPP; FosPo; LiTB, *abr.*; MasP; NoP; PIA; SiTL
(Satyr against Mankind, A.) CEP; EiCL; FaBoEn, *shorter sel.*; LiTB, *abr.*; OBS, *abr.*; PeRV *shorter sel.*; PoEL-3; SeCV-2
Wretched Man. SeCePo
Satire, be kind and draw a silent veil. Daniel Defoe. *Fr.* The True-Born Englishman, I. TOP
Satire, my friend ('twixt me and you). Satire. Alexander Geddes. ACP
Satire of Circumstance, A ("I stood at the back of the shop. ."). Thomas Hardy. *Fr.* Satires of Circumstance. NeMA
Satire of the Three Estates, The, *sel.* Sir David Lindsay.
"Have I nocht made ane honest shift." GoTS
Satire on London, A. Earl of Surrey. SiPS
(London, Hast Thou Accusèd Me.) FCP; OAEP; ReEn; TuPP
Satire on Paying Calls. Ch'eng Hsiao, *tr. fr. Chinese by* Arthur Waley. WoL
Satire on Riches. Pope. *See* Timon's Villa.
Satire on the People of Kildare, A. *Unknown, at. to* Friar Michael of Kildare, *mod. vers. by* St. John Seymour. OnYI
Satire Septimus Contra Sollistam. William Rankins. NCEP
Satire should be like the porcupine, The. Joseph Hall. *Fr.* Virgidemiarum. ReEn
Satires, *sels.* John Donne.
"Away thou fondling motley humorist," I. MaMe; OAEP
"Kind pity [*or* kinde pitty] chokes my spleen; brave scorn forbids," III. AnAnS-1; CABL; MaMe; MaPo MBW-1; MeLP; MeP; OBS; PoEL-2; ReIE; SCEP-1; SeEP; TuPP
(Religion.) ReEn
(Satire III: Religion.) CABA; FosPo; NoP
(Satyre: Of Religion.) MePo
(Satyre III: "King pitty chokes my spleene; brave scorn forbids.") SeCV-1
(Satyre III: On Religion.) SeCP
(Truth.) SeCePo
"Sir: though (I thank God for it) I do hate," II. MaMe; PoFS; ViBoPo
"Thou shalt not laugh in this leafe, Muse, nor they," V. MaMe
Upon Mr. Thomas Coryats Crudities. MaMe
"Well; I may now receive, and die; my sinne," IV. MaMe; MBW-1; SeEP
Satires, *sels.* Horace, *tr. fr.* Latin.
Bore, The, I.9. ATP, *tr. by* John Conington; EnLi-1, *tr. by* Sir Theodore Martin; OuHeWo, *tr. by* Sir Theodore Martin
Town and Country Mouse, The, II. 6. *sl. abr. tr. by* Francis Howes. WoL
Satires, The, *sels.* Juvenal, *tr. fr. Latin.*
Against Women, Satire VI, *abr., tr. by* Dryden. LiTW; UnTE, *abr.*
Celestial Wisdom, X, *tr. by* Samuel Johnson. AWP; JAWP; WBP
"Grieved though I am to see the man depart," III, *tr. by* William Gifford. EnLi-1
"Hear what Claudius suffered: When his wife knew he was asleep," *fr.* VI, *tr. by* Hubert Creekmore. ErPo
"In Saturn's reign, at Nature's early birth," *fr.* VI, *tr. by* Dryden. MBW-1
Tenth Satire of Juvenal, The, *tr. by* Dryden. WoL
Vices of Women, The, *fr.* VI, *tr. by* Dryden. PeRV
"We are led on," *fr.* X, *tr. by* L. R. Lind. PoPl
Satires, *sel.* Persius, *tr. fr. Latin. by* Dryden.
Prologue to the First Satire. AWP
Satires, *sels.* Sir Thomas Wyatt.
"My mother's maids, when they did sew and spin," II. SiPS
(Of the Mean and Sure Estate.) BEL; OA; ReIE; SiCE; TuPP
(To John Poynz.) FCP
"Mine [*or* Myne] own John Poins [*or* Poynz]," I. NoP; PoEL-1; ReEn; SiPS
(Epistle to John Poins: of the Courtier's Life.) FosPo
(Of the Courtier's Life.) CoBE; GoTL; OBSC; ReIE; SiCE; TuPP
(To John Poynz.) FCP
"Spending hand, A," III.
To Sir Francis Bryan, III. FCP; SiPS
Satires of Circumstance, I-XV. Thomas Hardy. BrPo
Sels.
At Tea, I. PoVP; VaPo
At the Altar-Rail, IX. MoAB; MoBrPo; PoVP

At the Draper's, XII. EnLi-2 (1949 ed.); MoAB; MoBrPo; NeMA; PoeP; VaPo
By Her Aunt's Grave, III. MoAB; MoBrPo; PoPo; PoVP; VaPo
In Church, II. DiPo; DTC; FosPo; MoAB; MoBrPo; PoDB; VaPo; VP
In the Restaurant, XI. MoAB; MoBrPo
In the Study, VIII. PoPo
Satires of Dr. John Donne, Versified, The, *sel.* Pope.
Satire II: "Yes; thank my stars! as early as I knew." PoFS
Satires [*or* Satyrs] upon the Jesuits, *sels.* John Oldham.
Garnet's Ghost Addressing to the Jesuits, I. SeEP
Loyola's Instructions to His Followers, III. PeRV
Prologue: "For who can longer hold?" CEP; SeCV-2
"When shaven crown, and hallow'd girdle's power," III. SeCV-2
"When the first traitor Cain," *fr.* II. PeRV
Satirical Elegy on the Death of a Late Famous General, A, 1722. Swift. CABA; CBV; EiCL; FosPo; HoPM; PAn; PoEL-3
(Satyrical Elegy on the Death of a Late Famous General, A, 1722.) ExPo; FOL; SeCeV; StP
Satirical Poems on Daimyos. Issa, *tr. fr. Japanese by* Max Bickerton. PoFr
Satirist, The. Harry Lyman Koopman. AA
Satisfaction. Avis B. Christiansen. SoP
Satisfied. Samuel Valentine Cole. BLRP
Satisfied. Edgar Cooper Mason. BLRP
Satisfied Tiger, The. Cosmo Monkhouse. *See* Limerick: "There was a young lady of Niger."
Satisfying Portion, The. *Unknown.* BLRP
Saturated meadow, A. Rose Pogonias. Robert Frost. MAmP
Saturday afternoon and sun—sifting. Beauty Then Is Being. James W. Thompson. WSL
Saturday. Dove calls to running wave. Beach Queen. David Campbell. BoAV
Saturday in the County Seat. Elijah L. Jacobs. AmFN
Saturday Market, *sel.* Charlotte Mew.
"In Saturday Market, there's eggs a-plenty." FaPON; HBMV
Saturday Morning. Richard Howard. ErPo
Saturday Night. Gail Dusenbery. ThO
Saturday Night. Langston Hughes. MAP; MoAmPo
Saturday Night. James Oppenheim. HBV; TSW
Saturday Night. *Unknown.* SAS
Saturday night she comes in her little boat. Music on the Water. George Johnston. MoCV
Saturday; or, The Flights. John Gay. *Fr.* The Shepherd's Week. EiCP; EiPP
Saturday Review, The. William Cole. PV
Saturday Shopping. Katherine Edelman. SoPo
Saturday Sundae. Francis Reginald Scott. CaP
Saturday Towels. Lysbeth Boyd Borie. UTS
Saturday's Child. Countee Cullen. Kal; LiTM (1970 ed.); PoNe
Saturday's Party in Fairyland, The. Mary Carolyn Davies. TVC
Saturn. Keats. *Fr.* Hyperion; a Fragment, I. LoBV; OBNC; TrGrPo
(Saturn Fallen.) AnEnPo
Saturnian mother! why dost thou devour. Russia. Nathan Haskell Dole. AA
Saturninus. Katherine Eleanor Conway. AA; JKCP
Satyr, The, *sel.* Ben Jonson.
Queen Mab. HBV; OTPC (1923 ed.)
(Mab.) WiR
(Mab the Mistress-Fairy.) EIL
("This is Mab, the mistress fairy.") SiCE
Satyr, A. John Oldham. *See* Satire, A.
Satyr. *At. to* the Earl of Rochester *and at. to* Sir Charles Sedley. PeRV
Satyr, The. James Stephens. OnYI
(Crackling Twig, The.) ELU
Satyr III: "When shaven crown, and hallow'd girdle's power." John Oldham. *Fr.* Satyrs upon the Jesuits. SeCV-2
Satyr Address'd to a Friend, That Is About to Leave the University, and Come Abroad in the World, A, *sel.* John Oldham.
"If you for Orders." OBS
Wolf and the Dog, The. PeRV
Satyr against Mankind, A. Earl of Rochester. *See* Satire against Mankind, A.
Satyr against Vertue, A, *sel.* John Oldham.
"Vertue! thou solemn gravé Impertinence." PeRV
Satyr in Imitation of the Third of Juvenal, A, *sel.* John Oldham.
Streets of London, The. PeRV
Satyr in the Periwig, The. Edith Sitwell. *Fr.* Façade. AnEnPo
Satyr nature riots in my blood, The. Sonnet. George Henry Boker. *Fr.* Sonnets: a Sequence on Profane Love. AmePo
Satyr once did run away for dread, A. Sir Philip Sidney. FCP
Satyr Scarabombardon, The. The Satyr in the Periwig. Edith Sitwell. *Fr.* Façade. AnEnPo
Satyra Quinta. Everard Guilpin. *Fr.* Skialetheia. TuPP
("Let me alone, I prithee, in this cell.") SiCE
Satyre Entituled the Witch, A. *Unknown.* CoMu
Satyre III: "Kinde pitty chokes my spleene; brave scorn forbids." John Donne. *See* Satire III: "Kind pity chokes my spleen. . ."
Satyre: Of [*or* On] Religion. John Donne. *See* Satire III: "Kind pity chokes my spleen. . ."
Satyretericall Charracter of a Proud Upstart, A. John Saffin. SCAP
(March 4th Anno 1698/9; a Charracteristicall Satyre.) SCAP
Satyrical Elegy on the Death of a Late Famous General, A, 1722. Swift. *See* Satirical Elegy. . .
Satyrs and the Moon, The. Herbert S. Gorman. HBV; PFY; TSW
Satyr's Farewell, The. John Fletcher. *Fr.* The Faithful Shepherdess, V, v. OBS
(Satyr's Leave-taking, The.) LoBV (2d ed)
("Thou divinest, fairest, brightest.") LO
Satyr's mouth is stained red with wine, The. Nymphs and Satyrs. Gavin Ewart. PV
Satyr's Song ("See, the day begins to break"). John Fletcher. *Fr.* The Faithful Shepherdess, IV, iv. OBS
Satyrs upon the Jesuits. John Oldham. *See* Satires upon the Jesuits.
Saucer-valley open oven, A. Hiroshima. Murray Noss. PoPo
Saucy Sailor, The, *with music. Unknown.* SaSa
Sauerkraut Talk Shreds in His Ear. Colette Inez. QAH
Saul. Nathan Alterman, *tr. fr. Hebrew by* Dov Vardi. TrJP
Saul. Robert Browning. BEL; EnLi-2; EPN; FOL, much abr.; GBV (1922 ed.); MaRV; MaVP; MBW-2; OAEP; OxBoCh; PoVP; TOP; ViPo; WHA
Sels.
David's Song, *fr.* IX. BoLive; FaBV
(Joy of Living, The.) ShBV-2
(Oh, the Wild Joy of Living.) TreFT
(Saul: "Oh, our manhood's prime vigor!") OtMeF
(Youth.) BoTP
"He who did most, shall bear most; the strongest shall stand the most weak," *fr.* XVIII. TRV
"I believe it! 'Tis thou, God, that givest, 'tis I who receive," XVIII. ChIP; StJW
"I know not too well how I found my way home in the night," XIX. LoBV
"Saul. . .sat out my singing,—one arm round the tent prop to raise," *fr.* XV. BoC
"Then I tuned my harp, took off the lilies we twine round its chords," V. BBV (1951 ed.); FiP (V-IX)
"Yea, my King," XIII-XIX, *sl. abr.* WGRP
Saul, *sels.* Charles Heavysege.
David Exorcising Malzah, the Evil Spirit from the Lord. VA
Flight of Malzah, The. VA
Malzah and the Angel Zelehtha. VA
Malzah's Song. OBCV
"To hunt and to be hunted make existence." CaP
"What now? Thou look'st surprised." PeCV
Zaph Describes the Haunts of Malzah. OBCV
Saul. George Sterling. HBMV
"Saul Kane," she said, "when next you drink." Another Cross. John Masefield. *Fr.* The Everlasting Mercy. MaRV
Saul. . .sat out my singing,—one arm round the tent-prop to raise. Robert Browning. *Fr.* Saul. BoC
Sauntering hither on listless wings. To a Sea-Bird. Bret Harte. EtS

Sauntering the pavement or riding the country by-road. Faces. Walt Whitman. Po; PoEL-5
Savage, A. John Boyle O'Reilly. AA
Savage I was sitting in my house, late, lone. The Householder. Robert Browning. *Fr.* Fifine at the Fair. LO
Savage loves his native shore, The. The Irishman. James Orr. DD
Savage Portraits. Don Marquis. HBMV
Savage the Daylight and Annihilate Night. Clifford Dyment. POTi
Savages, The. Josephine Miles. FiMAP; LiTM (1970 ed.)
Savannah. Alethea S. Burroughs. PAH
Save Me. Henry W. Frost. SoP
Save me, Lord, for why Thou art. Psalm XVI. *Paraphrased by* Sir Philip Sidney. FCP
Save me, O God, Thou God of my redemption. Save Me. Henry W. Frost. SoP
Save the Tiger! A. P. Herbert. OnSP
Saved, But—. *Unknown.* SoP; STF
Saved By Grace. Fanny J. Crosby. FaChP
Saving God, The. Fulke Greville. *See* Caelica: "Down in the depth of mine iniquity."
Saviour. *Unknown.* SoP
Saviour, The. Samuel Wesley. BePJ
Saviour, blessed Saviour. Jesus Christ the Lord. Godfrey Thring. SoP
Saviour, bowed beneath His cross, climbed up the dreary hill, The. Why the Robin's Breast Was Red. James Ryder Randall. AA; CAW; JKCP
Saviour, Breathe an Evening Blessing. James Edmeston. MaRV
(Evening Blessing, An.) BePJ
Saviour came, The. With trembling lips. The Second Coming. Norman Gale. HBV; MaRV
Saviour Can Solve Every Problem, The. Oswald J. Smith. BePJ; SoP
Saviour Comes, The. Philip Doddridge. *See* Prince of Peace, The.
Savior! I've no one else to tell. Emily Dickinson. AmePo; CoBA; MaRV; TrPWD
Saviour! like a shepherd lead us. The Good Shepherd. Dorothy Ann Thrupp. SoP
Saviour looked on Peter, The. Ay, no word. The Look [*or* "The Lord Turned, and Looked upon Peter"]. Elizabeth Barrett Browning. ChIP; MaRV; SoP; TRV
Saviour must have been, The. Emily Dickinson. MWA-2
Saviour of mankind, Man! Emmanuel! Lines Written at the Temple of the Holy Sepulchre. George Sandys. BePJ
Saviour of them that trust in thee. A Hymn for Family Worship. Henry Alford. SoP
Saviour Teach Me [Day by Day]. Jane Eliza Leeson. MaRV; SoP
Saviour, the world's and mine. Draw Me, Saviour, after Thee. Charles Wesley. BePJ
Saviour, Thou art always near me. Saviour. *Unknown.* SoP
Saviour! Thy dying love. Something for Jesus. S. D. Phelps. BLRP
Savior, While My Heart Is Tender. John Burton, Jr. SoP
Saviour, Who Died for Me. Mary J. Mason. BePJ
Saviour, Whose Love Is like the Sun. Howard Chandler Robbins. TrPWD
Saviors, The. *Unknown, tr. fr. Greek by* Lord Neaves. OnPM
Savonarola. E. C. Bentley. OxBoLi
Saw God Dead but Laughing. José Garcia Villa. AnFE; CoAnAm; TwAmPo
Saw-Mill, The. James Clarence Mangan. PeER
Saw Ye Bonny Lesley? Burns. *See* Bonnie Lesley.
Saw Ye Never in the Meadows, *abr.* Cecil Frances Alexander. OTPC (1923 ed.)
Saw You My True Love John? *with music.* *Unknown.* BFSS
Saw you never in the twilight. The Adoration of the Wise Men. Cecil Frances Alexander. HBVY; PRWS
Sawney Was Tall. Thomas D'Urfey. *Fr.* The Virtuous Wife. OAEP
Saws Were Shrieking, The. W. W. E. Ross. CaP; PeCV
Saxon Grit. Robert Collyer. HBV; OTPC (1923 ed.)
Saxon Song, A. V. Sackville-West. MoBrPo (1942 ed.)
Saxons of Flint, The. Lewys Glyn Clothi, *tr. fr. Welsh by* Mrs. M. C. Llewelyn. PrWP
Say, are you she that came to me last. The Second Vision. Tadhg Dall O'Huiginn. AnIL
"Say, bold but blessed thief." The Thief. *Unknown.* LO; OBS; OxBoCh; SeCL
Say, bud, ya got a cigarette? Refugee. Naomi Long Witherspoon. PoNe
Say, but did you love so long? An Answer. Sir Tobie Matthew. SeCL; SeCV-1
Say, crimson rose and dainty daffodil. A Nosegay [*or* The Garden's Queen]. John Reynolds. OBEV; SeCL
Say, darkeys [*or* darkies] hab you seen de massa. Year of Jubilo [*or* Jubliee]. Henry Clay Work. PAH; TrAS
Say day lay day may fay come some bum'll. Bludoo Baby, Want Money, and Alligator Got It to Give. LeRoi Jones. BF
Say, did his sisters wonder what could Joseph see. Regina Coeli. Coventry Patmore. ISi; JKCP; PoVP; VA
Say, earth, why hast thou got thee new attire. Easter Morn. Giles Fletcher, the Younger. *Fr.* Christ's Victory and Triumph. EIL
Say, fair maids maying. Of Life. Andrew Lang. VA
Say, fellers, that ornery thief must be nigh us. Denver Jim. Sherman D. Richardson. SCC
Say good-by er howdy-do. Good-by er Howdy-do. James Whitcomb Riley. CTC
Say Good-Bye to Big Daddy. Randall Jarrell. PoNe (1970 ed.)
Say goodnight to him and shut the door. Exquisite Lady. Mary Elizabeth Osborn. NePoAm-2
Say, guiltless pair. The Winged Worshippers. Charles Sprague. AA; HBV
Say he was sad, for there was none to love him. Epitaph. Robert Nathan. NoLP
Say—if men ask for him—he has gone home. Lincoln. Wendell Phillips Stafford. HH
Say, in a hut of mean estate. The Soul of Man. Dora Reed Goodale. AA
Say in what land, or where. Ballad for the Dead Ladies. Robert Lowell. TDP
Say, is it day, is it dusk in thy bower. The Song of the Bower. Dante Gabriel Rossetti. HBV; PoVP
Say it and cry aloud. I Am a Negro. Muhammad Al-Fituri. TTY
Say It Now. *Unknown.* BLPA; WBLP
(If You Have a Friend.) FaFP
(Seeds of Kindness.) PoToHe
Say it is life that matters. Say the bone. Address to the Doomed, I. George Dillon. NP
Say it were true that thou outliv'st us all. To My Tortoise Ananke. Eugene Lee-Hamilton. OBVV
Say, lad, have you things to do? A. E. Housman. A Shropshire Lad, XXIV. NeMa; PoVP
Say, Lovely Dream. Edmund Waller. OAEP
(Song: "Say, lovely dream! where couldst thou find.") CavP
Say, lovely nymph, where dost thou dwell? To the Echo; in a Clear Night upon Astrop Walks. Countess of Winchilsea. EiPP
Say, lovely Tory, why the jest. To Miss Eleanor Ambrose on the Occasion of Her Wearing an Orange Lily at a Ball in Dublin Castle on July the 12th. Earl of Chesterfield. EnLoPo
Say Me, Wiit in the Brom. *Unknown.* OAEP
Say, Moll, now don't you 'llow to quit. Cowboy's Valentine. Charles Fletcher Lummis. SCC
Say, Muse, who first, who last, on foot or steed. On the Road to Anster Fair. William Tennant. *Fr.* Anster Fair. OBRV
Say my love is easy had. Fighting Words. Dorothy Parker. InMe; NAMP
Say Nay. Sir Thomas Wyatt. *See* Earnest Suit to His Unkind Mistress Not to Forsake Him, An.
Say Not. Arthur Hugh Clough. *See* Say Not, the Struggle Nought Availeth.
Say not, "It matters not to me." Where Is Thy Brother? *Unknown.* MaRV
Say not, my soul, "From whence?" Comfort. J. J. Lynch. SoP
Say not of Beauty she is good. Beauty. Elinor Wylie. NP; OxBA
Say Not of Me That Weakly I Declined. Robert Louis Stevenson. OBNC; PeVV
Say Not that Beauty. Robin Flower. HBMV; HBVY

Say not that death is king, that night is lord. Easter. Thomas Curtis Clark. OQP
Say Not That the Past Is Dead. W. E. H. Lecky. EPN
(Unconscious Cerebration.) InP
Say Not the Struggle [Nought Availeth]. Arthur Hugh Clough. AnFE; ATP; AWP; BEL; CABA; CBEP; CBV; EaLo; EnLi-2; EnLit; EPN; FaBoEn; FaFP; FaPL; GTBS; GTBS-D; GTBS-P; GTBS-W; GTSL; HBV; HBVY; ILP; JAWP; LiTB; LiTG; LoBV; MaRV; OAEP; OBEV; OBNC; OBVV; OtMeF; PCD; PoFr; PoIE; PoVP; PTK; ShBV-3; StaSt; TOP; TreF; TrGrPo; TRV; ViBoPo; ViPo; ViPP; WaaP; WBP; WGRP
(Keeping On.) MoShBr
(Look!) SoP
(Say Not.) FaBV
Say not you love a roasted fowl. Loving and Liking. Dorothy Wordsworth. OTPC (1923 ed.)
"Say, O Fool, hast thou riches?" The Lover and the Belovèd. Ramon Lull. CAW
Say of them/ They knew no Spanish. To the Veterans of the Abraham Lincoln Brigade. Genevieve Taggard. PoFr
Say over again, and yet once over again. Sonnets from the Portuguese, XXI. Elizabeth Barrett Browning. HBV; ViPo
Say, pard, have you sighted a schooner. The Santa Fe Trail. *Unknown.* CoSo
Say puritan ist come to passe. *Unknown.* SeCSL
Say sheaphards boy who makes thee greeve soe sore. *Unknown.* SeCSL
Say-so is in a woe of shuddered leaves. Irritable Song. Russell Atkins. AmNP
Say something about still life. Body English. Ron Padgett. YAP
Say, sweet, my grief and I, we may not brook. Je ne veux de personne auprès de ma tristesse. Henri de Régnier. AWP; JAWP; WBP
Say (sweetest) whether thou didst use me well. To Cynthia on Her Being an Incendiary. Sir Francis Kynaston. NCEP
Say That He Loved Old Ships. Daniel Whitehead Hicky. EtS; PoMa
Say That I Should Say [I Love Ye]. Nicholas Breton. ElL; OBSC; PoIE; ReEn; TuPP
Say that she was young, awkward and bold. Small Elegy. Morris Weisenthal. NYTB
Say that the men of the old black tower. The Black Tower. W. B. Yeats. CMoP; NoP
Say that thou didst forsake me for some fault. Sonnets, LXXXIX. Shakespeare. CLwM; OAEP; SiCE
Say, the man's not a man. Perseverance. *Unknown.* SoP
Say there! P'r'aps. "Jim." Bret Harte. AA; BOHV; MAP; MoAmPo (1942 ed.); NeMA; WhC
Say this city has ten million souls. Refugee Blues [*or* Song]. W. H. Auden. InPo; LiTA; LiTM; NYBP; WePo
Say This of Horses. Minnie Hite Moody. PoLF
Say this when you return. The Wrong Road. Richard Church. POTE
Say well and do well. *Unknown.* OxNR
Say, what blinds us, that we claim the glory. Self-Deception. Matthew Arnold. MaVP; MBW-2; PoVP
Say! what is life? 'Tis to be born. The Story of Life. John Godfrey Saxe. PoToHe (new ed.)
Say, what is love? To live in vain. What is Love? John Clare. NCEP
Say, what is the spell, when her fledgings are cheeping. A Song of Love. "Lewis Carroll." GN
Say what you like. Nature's Friend. W. H. Davies. PoRL; RG; TSW
Say What You Will. Edna St. Vincent Millay. BoLiVe
(Sonnet: "Say what you will.") HBMV
Say what you will in two. Air: Sentir avec ardeur. Marie-Françoise-Catherine de Beauveau, Marquise de Boufflers. CTC
"Say, where did you get that spear there?" I asked of the hunter old. Smoke of the Camp Fire. Brian Brooke. BoSA
"Say, where have you been, Frank—say, where have you been?" The Old Man in the Moon. *Unknown.* PCH
"Say, where is the maiden sweet." Sag', wo ist dein schönes Liebchen [*or* Love Dead]. Heine, *tr. by* James Thomson. AWP; OnPM; OuHeWo
Say, where is your Love so lovely. Ashes. Heine, *tr. by* Asa Hughes. LiTW
Say, wilt thou go with me, sweet maid. An Invitation [*or* Invite] to Eternity. John Clare. NBM; NCEP; PoEL-4
Say, wilt thou more of scenes so sordid know. A Slum Dwelling. George Crabbe. *Fr.* The Borough. OBNC
Say, would'st thou be. The Last Hour. Henry Augustus Rawes. CAW
Say, wouldst thou guard thy son. Of Caution. Francesco da Barberino. AWP; JAWP; OnPM; WBP
Say, "You are lovely!" Second Night, or What You Will. Rolfe Humphries. MoLP
Say you, brother! Colonized Mind. Barbara Marshall. TNV
Say you, my life, that we shall ever love? Lesbia's Vow. Catullus. OnPM
Say you were the kid who could not sleep. The Actor. Thomas Snapp. NYBP
Saye, must wee part. *Unknown.* SeCSL
Sayes "Christ thee save, good Child of Ell!" Earl Brand (F *vers.*) *Unknown.* ESPB
Saying a Prayer. Rowena Bennett. MPB (1956 ed.)
Saying Not Meaning. William Basil Wake. BOHV
Saying "There is no hope," he stepped. A Generous Creed. Elizabeth Stuart Phelps Ward. WGRP
Saylors for My Money. Martin Parker. *See* Sailors for My Money.
Says Death: "I take your son." Inalienable, The. Rabindranath Tagore. MemP
Says Hyam to Moses. A Practical Answer. Shirley Brooks. SiTL
Says I to Myself. Edward Lear. FiBHP; WhC
Says my uncle, I pray you discover. Molly Mog; *or* The Fair Maid of the Inn. John Gay. CEP; CoMu
Says Phoebe Snow. The D.L. and W's Phoebe Snow. *Unknown.* TreF
Says Stonewall Jackson to "Little Phil": "Phil, have you heard the news?" Joined the Blues. John Jerome Rooney. AA
Says the master to me, is it true? I am told. My Master and I. *Unknown.* CoMu
Says the old man to the oak-tree. The Oak Tree. *Unknown.* CBEP
Says Tweed to Till. Two Rivers [*or* Tweed and Till]. *Unknown.* BoNaP; BuBa; CBEP; ChTr; OBEV; PV; ShBV-1; WhC
Scabby walls of tenements, The. John Henry in Harlem. M. B. Toleson. GoSl
Scala Coeli. Kathleen Raine. NYBP
Scale in May, A. W. S. Merwin. FRC
Scale of Things, The. Patric Dickinson. POTi
Scales, The. William Empson. CMoP; LiTM (rev. ed.)
Scales of Love, The. Hartman von Aue, *tr. fr. German by* Jethro Bithell. LiTW
Scales of the Eyes, The. Howard Nemerov. CMoP; NMP
Scaling small rocks, exhaling smog. Central Park. Robert Lowell. LiTM (1970 ed.)
Scampering over saucers. Yosa Buson, *tr. fr. Japanese by* Geoffrey Bownas *and* Anthony Thwaite. FIW
Scan with calm bloodshot eyes the world around us. The Spectacle. Walter de la Mare. BoPe
Scandal among the Flowers, A. Charles S. Taylor. BLPA
Scandalous Tale of Percival and Genevieve, The. Newman Levy. WhC
Scanderbeg. Longfellow. *Fr.* Tales of a Wayside Inn: The Spanish Jew's Second Tale, Pt. III. PFY
'Scaped. Stephen Crane. The Black Riders, LXV. AA
Scapegoats. Eleanor D. Breed. MaRV; PGD
Scar. Coleman Barks. *Fr.* Body Poems. QAH
Scar not earth's breast that I may have. The Last Camp-Fire. Sharlot Mabridth Hall. HBV
Scarabs for the Living. R. P. Blackmur. AnFE; CoAnAm; TwAmPo
Sels.
In the Wind's Eye, II. CrMA
On Common Ground, III. CrMA
Too Much for One: Not Enough to Go Around, I. CrMA
Scaramouche waves a threatening hand. Fantoche [*or* Puppets]. Paul Verlaine. AWP; OBMV; SyP
Scarborough Fair. *Unknown.* OxBoLi
("Where are you going? To Scarborough Fair.") LO
Scarce do I pass a day, but that I hear. Meditation 8. Philip Pain. QFR
Scarce lay the blossoms of her golden hair. Mary on Her Way to the Temple. Ruth Schaumann. ISi

Scarce sixteen years old was bold Robin Hood. Robin Hood and Little John (B *vers.*). *Unknown.* BaBo
Scarcely a street, too few houses. The Village. R. S. Thomas. HaMV
Scarcely Spring. Louis Untermeyer. GoTP; MAP; MoAmPo (1942 ed.)
Scarcity. Lizette Woodworth Reese. NP
Scarecrow, The. Walter de la Mare. MoBrPo; ShBV-1
Scarecrow, The. H. L. Doak. OnYI
Scarecrow, The. Michael Franklin. BoTP; SUS
Scarecrow, The. Andrew Young. FaBoTw
Scarf, The. Ivy O. Eastwick. BoTP
Scaring Crows. *Unknown.* BoTP
("O all you little blackey tops.") OxNR
Scarlet poppy smouldering in the fields, The. Narcissus. John Press. UnTE
Scarlet Tanager, The. Joel Benton. AA; AmLP
Scarlet Tanager, The. Mary Augusta Mason. AA
Scarlet Thread, The. Daniel Henderson. HBMV
Scarlet tide of summer's life, The. To an Autumn Leaf. Albert Mathews. AA
Scarlet Woman, The. Fenton Johnson. BANP; PoNe
Scarlet Woman, The. "Hugh MacDiarmid." ACV
Scarred. Bob Jones, Jr. SoP; STF
Scarred Girl, The. James Dickey. ToPo
Scars Remaining, The. Samuel Taylor Coleridge. *See* Broken Friendship.
Scatheless. Marguerite Wilkinson. HBMV
Scatter grey ash to the darkness, break. Shining Dark. Michael Roberts. FaBoMo
Scatter Seeds of Kindness. May Riley Smith. BLPA; WBLP
Scattered Moluccas. Mauberley, IV. Ezra Pound. *Fr.* Hugh Selwyn Mauberley. NoP
Scattering Flowers. St. Thérèse of Lisieux. WHL
Scel lem duib, *Tr. fr. Irish by* Brian O'Nolan. OxBI
Scenario. D. S. Savage. NeBP
Scene à Faire. Morton Dauwen Zabel. NP
Scène à Faire. John Gill. ThO
Scene, The: a public square in Ruritania. The Belle of the Balkans. Newman Levy. ALV; FiBHP
Scene around me disappears, The. A Visit to Bethlehem in Spirit. James Montgomery. SoP
Scene from a Play, Acted at Oxford, Called "Matriculation." Thomas Moore. NBM
Scene in a Garden. Robert Browning. *Fr.* Paracelsus, I. PCH
Scene in a Madhouse. Aubrey Thomas De Vere. OnYI
Scene in Paradise, A. Milton. *Fr.* Paradise Lost, IV. GN
Scene is different, and the place, The; the air. Arthur Hugh Clough. *Fr.* Dipsychus. PeVV
Scene of a Summer Morning. Irving Feldman. NYBP
Scene Pope John Wouldn't Let Fellini Film, The. Dan Georgakas. ThO
Scene-Shifter Death. Mary Devenport O'Neill. NeIP
Scene with Figure. Babette Deutsch. TrJP
Scenes, *sel.* Gertrude Stein.
"Pale rose is a smell that has no fountain, A." AtBAP
Scènes de la Vie de Bohème, sel. Arthur Symons.
Episode of a Night of May, I. BrPo; PeVV
Scenes from the Life of the Peppertrees. Denise Levertov. LiTM (1970 ed.); NeAP
Scenes of Childhood. James Merrill. CoAP
Scenic. John Updike. CAD
Scent, A, of beeswax, dust; the empty rooms. Meeting Myself. Edward Lucie-Smith. NePoEA-2
Scent of esparto grass—and again I recall, A. By the Weir. W. W. Gibson. MoVE; POTE
Scent of jasmines in the sultry air, The. Tropic Storm. Walter Adolphe Roberts. *Fr.* Boyhood Etchings. PoNe
Scent of guava-blossoms and the smell, A. At Set of Sun. Mary Ashley Townsend. AA
Scent of hyacinths, like a pale mist, lies between me and my book, The. Vernal Equinox. Amy Lowell. MAPA
Scent of ripeness from over a wall, A. Unharvested. Robert Frost. BoNaP
Scent of rotted apples, The. Late October. Sara King Carleton. GoYe
Scented, cool, and marble dark. Lemons. Ted Walker. NYBP
Scented Herbage of My Breast. Walt Whitman. AP; MAmP; MWA-1
Scented Leaves from a Chinese Jar. Allen Upward. NP
Schelynlaw Tower is fair on the brae. The Laird of Schelynlaw. John Veitch. VA
Scheme of Redemption, The. Milton. *Fr.* Paradise Lost, III. StJW
Schenectady, Schenectady. A Trip on the Erie. *Unknown.* ABF
Scherzando. W. E. Henley. London Voluntaries, III. BrPo
Schipman was ther, wonyng fer by weste, A. The Shipman. Chaucer. *Fr.* The Canterbury Tales: Prologue. EtS
Schir, though your grace has put great order. Ane Supplication in Contemptioun of Syde Taillis. Sir David Lindsay. GoTS
Schir William Wallace. Henry the Minstrel. *See* Wallace, The.
Schir, ye have mony servitouris. Remonstrance to the King. William Dunbar. OxBS
Schism, A/ Nurtured by foppery and barbarism. Keats. *Fr.* Sleep and Poetry. InP
Schlof, Bobbeli, *with music.* *Unknown,* *tr. fr. German.* TrAS
Schmaltztenor. M. W. Branch. FiBHP
Scholar, The. Robert Southey. *See* My Days among the Dead Are Past.
Scholar and His Dog, A. John Marston. BoPe
Scholar and the Cat, The. *Unknown.* *See* Monk and His Pet Cat, The.
Scholar Complains, The. *Unknown.* MeEL
Scholar-Gipsy, The. Matthew Arnold. AnFE; BEL; BWP; CABA; ChTr; EnL; EnLi-2; EnLit; EPN; FaBoEn; FiP; GoTL; GTBS; HBV; ILP; LoBV; MaPo; MasP; MaVP; MBW-2; NoP; OAEP; OBEV; OBNC; OBVV; Po; PoAn; PoE; PoEL-5; PoFS; PoVP; SeCeV; ShBV-4; TOP; UnPo (1st ed.); ViBoPo; ViPo; ViPP; VP
"And near me on the grass lies Glanvil's book," *sel.* ACV
Scholar in the Narrow Street, The. Tso Ssu, *tr. fr. Chinese by* Arthur Waley. AWP; JAWP; WBP
Scholar newly entered marriage life, A. Samuel Rowlands. TuPP
Scholars. *Unknown,* *tr. fr. Irish by* Frank O'Connor. KiLC
Scholars, The. W. B. Yeats. CaFP; CMoP; ML; NoP; TDP
Scholar's Life, The. Samuel Johnson. *Fr.* The Vanity of Human Wishes. FaBoEn; OBEC; SeCePo
Scholfield Huxley. Edgar Lee Masters. *Fr.* Spoon River Anthology. LiTA; MoPo; TrPWD
Schöne Rothraut. John Arthur Goodchild. VA
School. James Kenneth Stephen. BOHV
School after Christmas. Wymond Garthwaite. ChBR
School and Schoolfellows. Winthrop Mackworth Praed. OBRV
Schoolfellows, *sel.* NBM
School Begins. Nell Goodale Price. BrR
School-Bell. Eleanor Farjeon. BrR; FaPON; SiSoSe
School Boy. *See* Schoolboy.
School Days. Maltbie D. Babcock. MaRV
School Days. Will D. Cobb. TreFT
School Days in New Amsterdam. Arthur Guiterman. FaPON
School for Scandal, The, *sel.* Sheridan.
Let the Toast Pass, *fr.* III, iii. HBV; OnYI; OxBI
(Famous Toast, A.) TreF
(Here's to the Maiden.) ALV; ELP; LiTL; SiTL
(Song: "Here's to the maiden [*or* maid] of bashful fifteen.") CEP; NeHB; OBEC; OxBoLi; PoRA; ViBoPo
School Girl, The. William Henry Venable. AA
School Is Out. Frances Frost. RePo; SiSoSe
School is over. Kate Greenaway. TiPo
School is over. It is too hot. The Lonely Street. William Carlos Williams. TDP; TwCP
School of Desire, The. May Swenson. TwAmPo
School of Sorrow, The. Harold Hamilton. BLRP
School was out. The boys were quelling Mars. A Time of Light, a Time of Shadow. Samuel Yellen. NePoAm-2
Schoolboy [*or* School Boy], The. Blake. *Fr.* Songs of Experience. BoNaP; CBEP; CH; FaBoCh; FIW; GTBS-D; PeER
Schoolboy [*or* School Boy] Reads His Iliad, The. David Morton. MCCG; PoMa; PTK
Schoolboys in Winter. John Clare. CBEP; InvP; NBM; PoEL-4
Schoolfellows. Winthrop Mackworth Praed. *Fr.* School and Schoolfellows. NBM

Schoolgirl on Speech-Day in the Open Air. Iain Crichton Smith. NePoEA-2
Schoolgirls Hastening. John Shaw Neilson. BoAV
Schoolmaster, The. Goldsmith. *See* Village Schoolmaster, The.
Schoolmaster, The. Whittier. *Fr.* Snow-bound. GoTP
Schoolmaster. Yevgeny Yevtushenko, *tr. fr. Russian by* Robin Milner-Gulland *and* Peter Levi. FIW
Schoolmaster Abroad with His Son, The. Charles Stuart Calverley. BOHV
"Oh, what harper could worthily harp it," *sel.* MemP
Schoolmaster's Guests, The. Will M. Carleton. IHA
Schoolmistress, The. William Shenstone. CEP; EiPP; EnPE; GoTL; LaA
Schoolroom on a Wet Afternoon. Vernon Scannell. HaMV
Schoolroom: 158. James E. Warren, Jr. GoYe
Schools. George Crabbe. The Borough, Letter XXIV. CTC
School's Out. W. H. Davies. BoC; OBMV; POTE
School-Time. Wordsworth. The Prelude, II. BEL; ERoP-1; MBW-2
Schooner *Blizzard,* The, *with music.* Henry Burke. ShS
Schooner *Kandahar,* The, *with music. At. to* Sepley Collin. ShS
Schott and Willing did engage. The Duel. *Unknown.* ShM
Schubert's Ninth Symphony. Margaret Stanley-Wrench. MuSP
Science. Robinson Jeffers. AmPP; CoBA; OxBA
Science. Pope. *See* Epitaph Intended for Sir Isaac Newton.
Science drove his plow. Pasts. Alfred Kreymborg. NP
Science Fiction. Kingsley Amis. NePoEA-2
Science for the Young. Wallace Irwin. BBGG
"Arthur with a lighted taper," *sel.* ShM
Science in God. Robert Herrick. ImOP
Science is what the world is, earth and water. The Laboratory Midnight. Reuel Denney. ImOP; NePA
Science long watched the realms of space. A World Beyond. Nathaniel Ingersoll Bowditch. AA
Science of the Night, The. Stanley Kunitz. MoAmPo (1962 ed.); TDP; TwCP; UnTE
Science—so the savants say, A. Emily Dickinson. ImOP
Science, that simple saint, cannot be bothered. Dr. Sigmund Freud Discovers the Sea Shell. Archibald MacLeish. PPON
Science! thou fair effusive ray. Hymn to Science. Mark Akenside. CEP; PoEL-3
Science! true daughter of Old Time thou art! Sonnet to Science [*or* To Science]. Poe. Al Aaraaf: Prologue. AmePo; AmP; AmPP; AnAmPo; AnFE; AP; APA; CBEP; CBV; CoAnAm; CoBA; ILP; MAmP; MWA-1; NePA; NoP; OxBA; PPON; Sonn
Scientia Vincit Omnia? Merrill Moore. AnAmPo
Scientific Proof. J. W. Foley. BOHV
Scientific proof of how I know. Discovery. Carlton Buck. SoP
Scientist living at Staines, A. Genius. R. J. P. Hewison. FaFP; SiTL
Scientists have not made known. Those Who Soar. Margaret Lathrop Law. PoMa
Scientists removed their coats and hats, The. Report of the Meeting. Weldon Kees. TwAmPo
Scillaes [*or* Scilla's *or* Scylla's] Metamorphosis, *sels.* Thomas Lodge.
Earth, Late Choked with Showers, The. EIL; PoSa; SiCE; ViBoPo
(Sonnet: "Earth, late choked with showers, The.") TuPP
Melancholy. OBSC
Most Pithy and Pleasant History of Glaucus and Scylla, The. ReIE
Scintilla. William Stanley Braithwaite. AmNP; BANP; CDC
Scintillate, scintillate, globule orific. The Little Star. *Unknown.* BOHV; InMe
Scion of a noble stock! The Young American. Alexander H. Everett. PaPo
Scissor-Man. George MacBeth. OPoP
Scissor-Man, The. Madeleine Nightingale. BoTP; GaP; MPB; TiPo
Scissors and string, scissors and string. *Unknown.* OxNR
Scissors-Grinder, The. Vachel Lindsay. *Fr.* Poems about the Moon. MAPA; TwAmPo
Scissors Grinder, The. Raymond Roseliep. FiSC
Scobble for whoredome whips his wife; and cryes. Upon Scobble, Epigram. Robert Herrick. AnAnS-2
Scoffers, The. Blake. *See* Mock On, Mock On, Voltaire, Rousseau.
Scolding Wives Vindication, The; or, An Answer to the Cuckold's Complaint. *Unknown.* CoMu
Scoops in the sea rock full of natural water. Bathtubs. Richmond Lattimore. NYBP
Score of years had come and gone, A. John Underhill. Whittier. PAH
Scorn me as reason, who am always there. To a Friend. Charles Gullans. NePoEA
Scorn Not the Least. Robert Southwell. SiCE
(Where Wards Are Weak.) NCEP
Scorn Not the Sonnet. Wordsworth. ATP; BoLiVe; CLwM; DiPo; EnL; EnLit; EnRP; EPN; HBV; InP; MBW-2; NoP; OAEP; OBRV; PP; Sonn; TOP
(Sonnet, The: "Scorn not the Sonnet; critic, you have frowned.") OBEV; TrGrPo
"Scorn not the sonnet," though its strength be sapped. On a Magazine Sonnet. Russell Hilliard Loines. AA; BOHV; InP; SiTL
Scorna Boy [*or* Scorney Bwee], the Barretts' bailiff, lewd and lame. The Welshmen of Tirawley. Sir Samuel Ferguson. OBVV; OnYI; PoVP
Scorne then their censure, who gave out thy wit. Jasper Mayne. *Fr.* To the Memory of Ben Johnson. OBS
Scorned. Alexander Smith. OBVV
Scorner, The. Tchicaya U'Tamsi, *tr. fr. French by* Gerald Moore *and* Ulli Beier. TTY
Scorney Bwee, the Barretts' bailiff, lewd and lame. *See* Scorna Boy, the Barretts' bailiff. . .
Scorpion, The. William Plomer. AtBAP; BoSA; OBMV; POTE
Scot in the Desert. Laurie Lee. POTi; ToPo
Scot to Jeanne d'Arc, A. Andrew Lang. VA
Scotch Air. Thomas Moore. *See* Oft in the Stilly Night.
"Scotch over ice?" the Wolf said to the Tiger. Wolf and Tiger Dining, A. B. Joseph Joel Keith. FiSC
Scotch Rhapsody. Edith Sitwell. TwCP
Scotch Song. Thomas D'Urfey *Fr.* The Campaigners; or, The Pleasant Adventures at Brussels, III, i. CEP
Scotch Te Deum. William Kethe. *See* Hundredth Psalm, The.
Scotland. Alexander Gray. GoTS; OxBS
Scotland. William Soutar. OxBS
Scotland 1941. Edwin Muir. OxBS
Scotland, when it is given to me. With a Lifting of the Head. Hugh "MacDiarmid." MoBrPo
Scotland Yet. Henry Scott Riddell. HBV
Scotland Yet. *Unknown, at. to* John Galt. *Br. sel. fr.* The Canadian Boat Song. OtMeF
Scotland's Tribute to Wallace. James MacFarlan. PoFr
Scotland's Winter. Edwin Muir. OxBS
Scot's Farewell to His Golf Ball, A. James J. Montague. LHV; PoMa
Scots Wha Hae [wi' Wallace Bled]. Burns. ATP; BEL; CABA; CEP; CoBE; EiPP; EnLi-2; EnPE; EnRP; FOL; OAEP; OBEC; OuHeWo; OxBS; SeCeV; TOP; TrGrPo; WHA
(Bannockburn.) BBV (1923 ed.); GN; PoPo; RG; TreF; WBLP
(Before Bannockburn.) FaBoCh LoGBV
(Bruce to His Army.) OTPC
(Bruce to His Men at Bannockburn.) EnLit; HBV
(Bruce's Address to His Army at Bannockburn.) InP; YAT
(Bruce's March to Bannockburn.) BoLiVe; TrGrPo
(Robert Bruce to His Men at Bannockburn.) PTK
(Robert Bruce's Address to his Army before the Battle of Bannockburn.) PoFr
Scott and the Veteran. Bayard Taylor. PaA; PAP
Scott, your last fragments I arrange tonight. On Editing Scott Fitzgerald's Papers. Edmund Wilson. CrMA; NYBP
Scottish Hinds too poor to house, The. A Receipt to Restore Stella's Youth. Swift. Po
Scottish Merchant's Daughter, The, *with music. Unknown.* BFSS
Scourge, The. Stanley Kunitz. CrMA
Scourge of life, and death's extreme disgrace, The. Sir Philip Sidney. FCP
Scourge of Villainy [*or* Villanie *or* Villany], The, *sels.* John Marston.
Proemium in Librum Primum. ReIE
Satire VIII: "Curio, aye me! thy mistress' monkey's dead." ReEn; ReIE
Satire X: Humors. TuPP

Scourge (continued)
("Sleep grim Reproof; my jocund Muse doth sing," *longer sel.*) SiCE
Satire II: "I cannot hold, I cannot, I, indure." RelE
Satire VII: "Man, a man, a kingdom for a man, A!" RelE
Satire IV: "Vice, from privation of that sacred grace." RelE
To Detraction [I Present My Poesie]. LoBV; OBSC; RelE; SiCE; TuPP
To Everlasting Oblivion. CBEP; LoBV (1949 ed.); OBSC; RelE; SiCE; TuPP
Scow on Cowden Shore, The, 3 *vers., with music.* Larry Gorman. ShS
Scrape no more your harmless chins. Advice to the Old Beaux. Sir Charles Sedley. CEP; PeRV; SeCV-2
Scraping sound, A: The grasshopper. The Grasshopper's Song. H. N. Bialik. FaPON; YeAr
Scrapper, you don't refuse. Gull. Dabney Stuart. NYTB
Scratch, The. James Dickey. AP
Scratch a Jew and you'll find a Wailing Wall. The Wall. Eve Merriam. TrJP
Scream, The. Robert Lowell. TDP
Scream of teeth is contortion tied, The. Eskimoes Again. Dick Gallup. ANYP
Scream, the echo of a scream, A. The Scream. Robert Lowell. TDP
Screaming Tarn. Robert Bridges. ExPo
Screams/ screams. Interlude. Welton Smith. BF
Screams round the arch-druid's brow the sea-mew—white. Trepidation of the Druids. Wordsworth. *Fr.* Ecclesiastical Sonnets. Sonn
Screech Owl, The. *Unknown.* GFA
Screech-owl sings, The; death follows at her cries. Demophilus. Henry Wellesley. ALV
Screw-Guns. Kipling. ViBoPo
Screw Spring. William M. Hoffman. ThO
Scribe, The. Walter de la Mare. AnFE; AtBAP; CMoP; FaBoCh; LoGBV; MoRP; OBMV; TrPWD
Scribe, The. F. R. Higgins. JKCP (1926 ed.)
Scribe, The. *Unknown, tr. fr. Old Irish.* AnIL, *tr. by* Kuno Meyer; OnYI, *tr. by* Whitley Stokes *and* John Strachan, *arr. by* Kathleen Hoagland
Scribe's Prayer, The. Arthur Guiterman. TrPWD
Scribe's Prayer, The. Robert Service. TrPWD
Scrip Ant. Clark Coolidge. YAP
Script of trees before the hill, A. Winter Spring. Richard Wilbur. FiMAP
Scriptures, The. Dryden. *Fr.* Religio Laici. OBS
Scroll-Section. Robert Finch. PeCV
Scrub Oak. E. Merrill Root. MAP
Scrubber. W. E. Henley. *Fr.* In Hospital. PoVP
Scrutiny [*or* Scrutinie], The. Richard Lovelace. AnAnS-2; CavP; EG; EnLit; EnLoPo; EP; LO; MeLP; MePo; OBS; SCEP-2; SeCP; SeEP; TrGrPo
(Song: Scrutiny, The.) ReEn
(Song: "Why should you swear I am forsworn.") BOHV; InMe
(That Fond Impossibility.) McWo
(Why Should You Swear?) ELP
Sculptor, The. *Unknown. See* Piece of Clay, A.
Sculptor first in breath and blood, A. With Metaphor. Sarah Wingate Taylor. GoYe
Sculptor of the Soul. Toyohiko Kagawa. MaRV
Sculptor, wouldst thou glad my soul. Odes of Anacreon [*or* Design for a Bowl]. *Tr. by* Thomas Moore. OuHeWo; UnTE
Sculptors, The. Alfred Purdy. PeCV (1967 ed.)
Sculptors of Life. George Washington Doane. *See* Life Sculpture.
Sculpture. *Unknown. See* Piece of Clay, A.
Sculptured Worship. William Stanley Braithwaite. Sandy Star and Willie Gee, I. BANP
"Scum o' the Earth." Robert Haven Schauffler. HBV; PaA; PoFr; TIHL
Scunner. "Hugh MacDiarmid." FaBoTw
Scurrilous Scribe, The. Philip Freneau. AA
Scurvy-grass creeps down the strand, The. January. Daniel James O'Sullivan. NeIP
Scuttle, scuttle, little roach. Nursery Rhymes for the Tender-hearted, I. Christopher Morley. FaFP; HBMV; SiTL; YaD
Scylla and Charybdis. Homer, *tr. fr. Greek by* George Chapman. *Fr.* The Odyssey, XII. OBS
Scylla Toothless. *Unknown.* SiTL
Scylla's Lament. Thomas Hood. *Fr.* Hero and Leander. EnRP
Scylla's Metamorphosis. Thomas Lodge. *See* Scillaes Metamorphosis.
Scyros. Karl Shapiro. HoPM; ILP; LiTA; LiTM; MoVE; NePA; SeCeV; WaP
Scythe, The. Stanley Snaith. POTE
Scythe of Dreams, The. Joseph Payne Brennan. FiSC
Scythe Song. Andrew Lang. GN; HBV; PCD; PoVP; VA
Scythians, The. Aleksandr Blok, *tr. fr. Russian by* Babette Deutsch *and* Avrahm Yarmolinsky. AWP; WaaP
Sea, The. E. M. Adams. BoTP
Sea, The. Byron. *See* Ocean, The.
Sea, The. "Barry Cornwall." GN; HBV; HBVY; OTPC; TreFS; VA
Sea, The. Hart Crane. *See* Voyages, I.
Sea, The. Lloyd Frankenberg. AnFE; CoAnAm
Sea. Don Gordon. EtS
Sea, The. Herman Gorter, *tr. fr. Dutch by* A. J. Barnouw. LiTW
Sea, The. D. H. Lawrence. BoNaP; NAMP; POTE
Sea. Bernadette Mayer. ANYP
Sea, The. Richard Henry Stoddard. AA; HBV
Sea, The. Swinburne. *Fr.* The Triumph of Time. BoLiVe; TrGrPo; TSW
(Return, The.) EtS
(Stanzas: "I will go back to the great sweet mother.") HBV
(Triumph of Time.) GTSL; OAEP
Sea, The ("Behold the wonders of the mighty deep"). *Unknown.* NA
Sea, The ("Look, wild and wide"). *Unknown, tr. fr. Irish by* Frank O'Connor. KiLC
Sea, The. Francis Webb. PoAu-2
Sea and Land Victories. *Unknown.* PAH
Sea and Shore. Harry Lyman Koopman. AA
Sea and strand, and a lordlier land than sea-tides rolling. England; an Ode. Swinburne. ViPo
Sea and the Eagle, The. Sydney Clouts. BoSA; PeSA
Sea and the Hills, The. Kipling. FaBV; OtMeF
Sea and the Mirror, The, *sels.* W. H. Auden.
Alonso to Ferdinand. MoPo
Miranda's Song. FaBoMo
Preface. LiTA; SeCeV
Song of the Master and Boatswain. DTC
("At Dirty Dick's and Sloppy Joe's.") FaBoTw
Sea and the Skylark, The. Gerard Manley Hopkins. LiTB; NoP; OBMV; PoeP; PoVP
Sea and the Tiger, The. Laurence Collinson. PoAu-2
Sea at evening moves across the sand, The. Soldiers Bathing. F. T. Prince. ChMP; GTBS-P; LiTB; LiTM; MoBrPo (1962 ed.); MoVE; PeSA; WaP
Sea awoke at midnight from its sleep, The. The Sound of the Sea. Longfellow. AnFE; AP; APA; CoAnAm; EtS; Po; PoPo; TreFT
Sea Ballad. Sydney Dobell. *Fr.* Balder. VA
Sea Battle, The. Dryden. *Fr.* Annus Mirabilis. FiP
Sea Bird, The. Keith Douglas. ChMP
Sea Bird to the Wave, The. Padraic Colum. EtS; RePo; SUS
Sea-Birds. Elizabeth Akers Allen. AA; FaBoBe; HBV
Sea Birds, The. Van K. Brock. NYBP
Sea-Birds. Fray Angelico Chavez. ISi
Sea-Birds. James Thomson. EtS
Sea-birds are asleep. Sea Slumber-Song. Roden Noel. VA
Sea bluely gleaming. Dalmatian Nocturne. Aleksa Santic. LiTW
Sea Born. Harold Vinal. HBMV
Sea-born queen, who deigns to smile, The. On the Ladies' Head-Dresses. James Greenwood. WaPE
Sea-bound landsman looking back to shore, The. John Brown. Harry Lyman Koopman. AA
Sea Breeze. Stéphane Mallarmé. *See* Sea-Wind.
Sea Burial. Robina Monkman. EtS
Sea Burial from the Cruiser "Reve." Richard Eberhart. NYBP
Sea Call. Margaret Widdemer. TSW
Sea Calm. Langston Hughes. LOW
Sea-Captain, The. Gerald Gould. EtS
Sea Captain, The ("It was of a sea captain that followed the sea"). *Unknown.* ViBoFo

Sea-Captain, The ("There was a sea captain lately come to shore"). *Unknown.* BaBo
Sea Cathedral, The. E. J. Pratt. CaP
Sea-Change. John Masefield. AtBAP; FaBoTw; OBMV
Sea-Change. Genevieve Taggard. EtS; NP
Sea-Change, A: For Harold. Joseph Langland. LiTM (1970 ed.)
Sea-Chantey, A, *sel.* Derek Walcott.
"In the middle of the harbour." TTY
Sea Child, A. Bliss Carman. HBV; VA
Sea-Child, The. Eliza Cook. VA
Sea-Chronicles. Rex Ingamells. BoAV
Sea-coast of Bohemia, The. Perdita. James Hebblethwaite. BoAu
Sea contains a destiny, The. The Sea and the Eagle. Sydney Clouts. BoSA; PeSA
Sea cries with its meaningless voice, The. Pibroch. Ted Hughes. NePoEA-2; PoCh; PoDB
Sea Danceth, The. Sir John Davies. *See* Dancing Sea, The.
Sea Dawn. Francis Hackett. AnIV
Sea-Deeps, The. Thomas Miller. EtS
Sea Dialogue, A. Oliver Wendell Holmes. EtS
Sea Dike, The. M. Vasalis, *tr. fr. Dutch by* A. J. Barnouw. LiTW
Sea Dirge. Archias of Byzantium, *tr. fr. Greek by* Andrew Lang. AWP
Sea Dirge, A. "Lewis Carroll." CenHV; StaSt
Sea Dirge. Tom Scott. ACV
Sea Dirge, A. Shakespeare. *See* Ariel's Song: "Full fathom five thy father lies."
Sea drained off, my poverty's uncovered, The. All Gone. C. Day Lewis. FaBoMo
Sea Dreams, *sel.* Tennyson.
What Does Little Birdie Say? GFA; HBV; HBVY; HH; MPB; OTPC
(Cradle Song: "What does little birdie say.") BoTP; PPL; TVC
(Little Birdie.) SAS
Sea Eats the Land at Home, The. Kofi Awoonor. CAD
Sea Eclogue: "Otys, begin." William Diaper. Nereides; or, Sea-Eclogues, X. LoBV
Sea-Elephant, The. William Carlos Williams. LiTA; PoeP
Sea Fairies. Eileen Mathias. BoTP
Sea-Fairies, The. Tennyson. ViPP
Sea Fever. John Masefield. BEL; BoChLi; BoLiVe; CMoP; EnLi-2 (1949 ed.); EnLit; EtS; FaBoBe; FaBV; FaPON; GBV; GTBS; GTSL; HBV; HBVY; MCCG; MoAB; MoBrPo; MPB; NeHB; NeMA; OBVV; OHFP; OTD; OtMeF; OTPC (1946 ed.); PCD; PDV; PoLF; PoMa; PoPl; PoPo; RePo; RG; ShBV-1; SP; StVeCh; TIHL; TiPo; TOP; TreF; TrGrPo; WHA; YAT; YT
Sea Fog, The. Josephine Jacobsen. NYBP
Sea Fowler, The. Mary Howitt. VA
Sea Gipsy, The. Richard Hovey. *See* Sea Gypsy, The.
Sea gives her shells to the shingle, The. Dedication to Poems and Ballads. Swinburne. PoVP; ViPo
Sea go dark, go dark with wind. Wild Iron. Allen Curnow. AnNZ
Sea-Goddess, The. Margaret Cavendish, Duchess of Newcastle. *Fr.* The Convent of Pleasure. SeCL
(My Cabinets Are Oyster Shells.) ELP
(Song by Lady Happy, as a Sea-Goddess.) SiSw
Sea Gods. Hilda Doolittle ("H. D."). AtBAP; LiTA
Sea-God's Address to Bran, The. *Unknown, tr. fr. Middle Irish by* Kuno Meyer. OnYI
(Sea-God's Song to Bran, The, *tr. by* Howard Mumford Jones.) LiTW
Sea-Grief. Dowell O'Reilly. BoAu; PoAu-1
Sea guards warily its treasures, The. The Heart. Jacob Steinberg. TrJP
Sea-Gull, The. Mary Howitt. BoTP
Sea Gull, The. Leroy F. Jackson. GFA; UTS
Sea-Gull, The. Ogden Nash. FaFP; LiTM; NePA; PoPo; SiTL
Sea gull curves his wings, The. Elizabeth J. Coatsworth. TiPo
Seagull flying from the sea. A Feather for My Cap. Ivy O. Eastwick. BoTP
Sea gull poises, The. Things Not Seen. Mark Turbyfill. NP
Seagull, spreadeagled, splayed on the wind, The. Memorial (For Two Young Seamen Lost Overboard in a Storm in Mid-Pacific, January, 1940). George Barker. LiTG; LiTM; MasP; ReMP; WaP
Sea-Gulls. Norah M. Holland. MCCG
Seagulls. Patricia Hubbell. PDV
Seagulls, The. Sir John Morris-Jones, *tr. fr. Welsh by* Gwyn Williams. PrWP
Sea Gulls. E. J. Pratt. EtS; TwCaPo
Seagulls. John Updike. StP
Seagull's narrow sails of feather lift, The. Winged Mariner. Grace Clementine Howes. EtS
Seagulls on the Serpentine. Alfred Noyes. EtS
Sea-gulls whiten and dip, The. In the Bay. Arthur Symons. Amoris Exsul, III. OBNC; PoVP
Sea Gypsy, The. Richard Hovey. AmePo; BBV; FaPON; GBV; GoTP; HBVY; OQP; PDV; RePo; StaSt; TreFS; TSW; YT
(Sea Gipsy, The.) EtS; HBV; MCCG; TIHL
Sea has a laugh, The. The Frowning Cliff. Herbert Asquith. BrR
Sea has it this way, The: if you see. Cormorants. John Blight. FIW
Sea Hath Its Pearls, The. Heine, *tr. fr. German by* Longfellow. AWP; JAWP; OnPM; OuHeWo; WBP
Sea Hath Many Thousand Sands, The. *Unknown.* ElL; LiTB; OBSC; TuPP; ViBoPo
(Advice to a Lover.) GTSL; HBV
Sea hath tempered, The; the mighty sun. The Fountain. Mu'tamid, King of Seville. AWP; JAWP; WBP
Sea-Hawk. Richard Eberhart. NoP; WIRo
Sea here used to look, The. At Darien Bridge. James Dickey. NoP
Sea Holly. Conrad Aiken. AP; LiTM; MAPA; NePA
Sea House, The. William Goodreau. NYTB
Sea Hunger. John Hanlon Mitchell. EtS
Sea, The—in Calm. "Barry Cornwall." EtS
Sea Irony. John Langdon Heaton. AA
Sea is a circuit of holes, The. The Coral Reef. Laurence Lieberman. CoAP
Sea is a lonely thing, The. In Exile. Blanche Edith Baughan. ACV; AnNZ
Sea is an acre of dull glass, the land is a table, The. Lusty Juventus. Charles Madge. FaBoMo
Sea is awake, and the sound of the song of the joy of her waking is rolled, The. In the Water. Swinburne. *Fr.* A Midsummer Holiday. PoVP
Sea is calm tonight, The. Dover Beach. Matthew Arnold. AnEnPo; ATP; AWP; BEL; BoLiVe; BoLP; BoPe; BWP; CABA; CaFP; CBEP; CBV; CoBE; DiPo; DTC; EaLo; EnL; EnLi-2; EnLit; EPN; EtS; ExPo; FaBoBe; FaBoEn; FaBV; FaFP; FaPL; FiP; FlW; ForPo; FosPo; GBV; GTBS-D; GTBS-P; GTBS-W; GTSL; HBV; HoPM; ILP; InP; InPo; InvP; JAWP; LiTB; LiTG; LiTL; LoBV; MaPo; MaRV; MasP; MaVP; MBW-2; MCCG; MeWo; NeHB; NoP; OAEP; OBNC; OBVV; OTPC (1946 ed.); OuHeWo; PAn; PeVV; PG; PIA; Po; PoAn; PoE; PoEL-5; PoFS; PoIE; PoPl; PoPo; PoRA; PoSa; PoVP; PPON; PTK; SeCePo; SeCeV; StP; TDP; TIHL; TOP; TreFS; TrGrPo; TRV; UnPo; VA; VaPo; ViBoPo; ViPo; ViPP; WBP; WePo; WHA; YAT
Sea is flecked with bars of grey, The. Les Silhouettes. Oscar Wilde. *Fr.* Impressions. BrPo; Po; PoVP; SyP
Sea Is His, The. Edward Sandford Martin. EtS
Sea is never still, The. Young Sea. Carl Sandburg. RePo
Sea is strange, The. Waves. Mary Britton Miller. RePo
Sea is wild marble waiting a stonecutter's hand. Sea. Don Gordon. EtS
Sea Island Miscellany, *sels.* R. P. Blackmur.
Mirage, IX. GTBS-W; LiTM; MoVE
"One grey and foaming day," V. MoVE
"Where shall I go then," XIV. MoVE
Sea-King, The. L. Frank Tooker. EtS
Sea-kings' daughter from over the sea. A Welcome to Alexandra. Tennyson. PoVP
Sea laments, The. Echoes. Walter de la Mare. RePo
Sea-Lands, The. Orrick Johns. HBV
Sea Lavender. Louise Morey Bowman. CaP
Sea lies quieted beneath, The. At Dieppe: After Sunset. Arthur Symons. BrPo; SyP
Sea like a mirror. Wind Force. Bernadette Mayer. ANYP
Sea like a vast quicksilvered glass, The. Symphony in Gray Major. Rubén Darío. LiTW

Sea-Limits, The. Dante Gabriel Rossetti. AnEnPo; EPN; EtS; NBM; PoVP; TOP; VA
(Chime of the Sea, The.) BoC
Sea limps up here twice a day, The. Paphos. Lawrence Durrell. NYBP
Sea Longing. Harold Vinal. PoMa
Sea Love. Charlotte Mew. BoLP; ELU; MeWo; MoAB; MoBrPo; NeMA; TrGrPo; ViBoPo
Sea Lullaby. Elinor Wylie. BoNaP; NeMA
Sea Lyric. William Stanley Braithwaite. GoSl
Sea Lyric, A. William Hamilton Hayne. EtS
Sea-Maiden, The. J. W. De Forest. EtS
Sea-Maids' Music, The. Ernest Myers. VA
Sea-Marge. Alexander Smith. *Fr.* A Life-Drama. VA
(Autumn.) GTSE
Sea Mark. *See* Seamark.
Sea Memories. Longfellow. *Fr.* My Lost Youth. FaPON; MPB
Sea-Mew, The. Elizabeth Barrett Browning. HBV; OTPC
Sea Monsters. Spenser. *Fr.* The Faerie Queene, II, 12. ChTr; FaBoEn
("Waves come rolling, and the billowes rore, The.") AtBAP
Sea News. Eric Barker. NYTB
Sea-nurtured. Jean Ingelow. EtS
Sea-Nymph's Parting, The. Walter Savage Landor. *Fr.* Gebir. FaBoEn
Sea of Death, The. Thomas Hood. ERoP-2; FaBoEn; LiTB; LoBV; OBNC; PeER; PoEL-4
Sea of Death, The. *Unknown.* CH
Sea of Faith, The. Walt Whitman. *Fr.* Passage to India, XIII. OQP
Sea of Peace, The. Ruth McEnery Stuart. MaRV
Sea Pieces. Robert Fitzgerald. PoPl
Sea Princess, The. Katharine Pyle. PCH; SoPo; TVC
Sea—quick pugilist, The. Training. Demetrio Herrera S. TTY
Sea retains such images, The. Louis Dudek. *Fr.* Europe. OBCV; PeCV
Sea-Ritual, The. George Darley. *Fr.* Syren Songs. ERoP-2; OBNC; OBRV; OnYI; OxBI; SiSw; WiR
(Deadman's Dirge.) CH
Sea rocks have a green moss, The. Home Thoughts. Carl Sandburg. MoLP
Sea Rose. Hilda Doolittle ("H. D."). FaBoMo
Sea-Sand and Sorrow. Christina Rossetti. ChTr; OTD
Sea Sang sweetly to the shore, The. Hymn Written for the Two Hundredth Anniversary of the Old South Church, Beverly, Massachusetts. Lucy Larcom. OHIP
Sea Scape. *See* Seascape.
Sea School. Barbara Howes. NYBP
Sea Serpant, The. Wallace Irwin. FiBHP
Sea-Serpent, The. James Robinson Planché. NA
Sea Shell. Elizabeth Stanton Hardy. MaRV
Sea Shell. Amy Lowell. BoTP; BrR; FaPON; GFA; MPB; PCH; RePo; StVeCh; TSW
Sea Shell is a castle, A. Shell Castles. Rowena Bennett. GFA; UTS
Sea shell is a palace, A. Palace. Dorothy Vena Johnson. GoSl
Sea-Shell Murmurs. Eugene Lee-Hamilton. VA
Sea Shell, Sea Shell,/ Sing me a song, O please! Sea Shell. Amy Lowell. BoTP; BrR; FaPON; GFA; MPB; PCH; StVeCh; TSW
Sea Shells. Clinton Scollard. BrR
Sea Side. *See* Seaside.
Sea-Sleep. Thomas Lake Harris. AA
Sea Slumber-Song. Roden Noel. VA
Sea-smooth stones imprison a moon. Forgotten Objects on a Beach. Patricia Excell. BoAV
Sea Song. Thomas Lovell Beddoes. *See* To Sea, to Sea!
Sea Song, A. Allan Cunningham. *See* Wet Sheet and a Flowing Sea, A.
Seasong. Stefan George, *tr. fr. German by* Kenneth Gee. LiTW
Sea Song. Norah Holland. CaP
Sea-Song. Irene Rutherford McLeod. YT
Sea Song from the Shore, A. James Whitcomb Riley. BoTP; GaP; PRWS; TiPo; TVC
Sea Sonnet. Norma Lay. GoYe
Sea-Spell, A. Dante Gabriel Rossetti. SyP
Sea still plunges where as naked boys, The. The Grotto. Francis Scarfe. NeBP
Sea Story, A. Emily Henrietta Hickey. JKCP; VA
Sea sucks in the traveller, The. The Sea and the Tiger. Laurence Collinson. PoAu-2
Sea Surface Full of Clouds. Wallace Stevens. AmPP (5th ed.); AnAmPo; AnFE; AP; CMoP; CoAnAm; CoBA; CoBMV; MAP; MaPo (1969 ed.); MoAB; MoAmPo; TwAmPo
Sea tells something but it tells not all, The. Reserve. Mary Ashley Townsend. AA
Sea, the Sea, The. Rafael Alberti, *tr. fr. Spanish by* Eleanor L. Turnbull. OnPM
Sea Town. Frances Frost. EtS
Sea-Turtle and the Shark, The. Melvin B. Tolson. *Fr.* Harlem Gallery. BP
("Strange but true is the story.") Kal
Sea Urge. *Unknown.* PoMa
Sea Voyage. William Empson. CMoP
Sea-Voyage. John Hall Wheelock. EtS
Sea was born of the earth without sweet union of love, The. Maximus, from Dogtown, I. Charles Olson. CoPo
Sea was breaking at my feet, The. Faith. James Whitcomb Riley. SoP
Sea-Wash. Carl Sandburg. BrR
Sea-Watcher, The. Aubrey Thomas De Vere. IrPN
Sea waves are green and wet. Sand Dunes. Robert Frost. MAP; MoAB; MoAmPo
Sea-Way. Ellen Mackay Hutchinson Cortissoz. AA
Sea Weed. *See* Seaweed.
Sea-Wind. Stéphane Mallarmé, *tr. fr. French by* Arthur Symonds. AWP; JAWP; SyP; WBP
(Sea Breeze, *tr. by* Warren Carrier.) ReMP
(Sea Winds, *tr. by* Patricia Terry.) OnPM
Sea Wolf, The. Violet McDougal. FaPON;MPB
Sea Words. Mary Sinton Leitch. EtS
Sea would flow no longer, The. The Frozen Ocean. Viola Meynell. CH
Sea Wrack. "Moira O'Neill." OnYI
Seace o seace this hum of greiveing. *Unknown.* SeCSL
Seaconk or Rehoboths Fate. Benjamin Tompson. SCAP
Seaconk Plain Engagement. Benjamin Tompson. SCAP
Seafarer. Archibald MacLeish. NoP
Seafarer, The. Earl of Surrey. *See* Complaint of the Absence of Her Lover. . .
Seafarer, The ("May I for my own self song's truth reckon"). *Unknown, tr. fr. Anglo-Saxon by* Ezra Pound. AmP; AnAmPo; AnOE, Pt. I, *tr. by* Charles W. Kennedy; AP; CTC; EnL, Pt. I; EnLi-1 (1949 ed.), Pt. I, *tr. by* Stith Thompson; EtS, Pt. I, *tr. by* Charles W. Kennedy; ExPo; FaBoTw; LiTA; LiTW; OxBA; PoE; PoRA (rev. ed.), Pt. I, *tr. by* L. Iddings; SeCeV (1967 ed.); StP
Sels.
Afar on the Floodways, Pt. I, *mod. vers. by* Mother Margaret Williams. PoLi
Hour of Death, The, Pt. II, *abr., mod. vers. by* Mother Margaret Williams. PoLi
"I can tell a true story about myself," *fr.* Pt. I, *tr. by* Richard L. Hoffman. YAT
Seafarer, The ("Shall I thus ever long . . ."). *Unknown.* *See* Lady Prayeth the Return of Her Lover. . ., The.
Seafront. Laurie Lee. POTi
Seal, A. Oliver Herford. *Fr.* Child's Natural History. HBV HBVY
Seal. William Jay Smith. GoTP
Seal Lullaby. Kipling. *Fr.* The Jungle Book. FaPON; PRWS; TiPo (1959 ed.)
(Seal's Lullaby.) PoRA
Seal Rocks: San Francisco. Robert Conquest. PP
Seal thou the window! Yea, shut out the light. Cloistered. Alice Brown. AA; MaRV
Seal Up Her Eyes, O Sleep. William Cartwright. *Fr.* The Siege. EG; SeCL
Sealed Bags of Ducats. Martial, *tr. fr. Latin by* Paul Nixon. LiTW
Sealed in Vain. Shakespeare. *See* Take, O Take Those Lips Away.
Sealed inside the anemone. The Pulse. Denise Levertov. FRC
Sealed Orders. Richard Burton. HBV; OQP
Sealed with the seal of Life, thy soul and mine. The Inscription. Elsa Barker. *Fr.* The Spirit and the Bride. HBMV

Seals, The. Dorothy Aldis. *Fr.* At the Circus. TiPo (1952 ed.); UTS
Seals, The. L. A. G. Strong. LO; POTE
Seals all flap, The. The Seals. Dorothy Aldis. *Fr.* At the Circus. TiPo (1952 ed.); UTS
Seals and porpoises present. Off Spectacle Island. Richard Eberhart. ToPo
Seals at play off Western Isle, The. Seals, Terns, Time. Richard Eberhart. FiMAP; LiTM (1970 ed.); MoAB; MoAmPo (1962 ed.)
Seals in Penobscot Bay, The. Daniel Hoffman. TwCP
Seal's Lullaby. Kipling. *See* Seal Lullaby.
Seals of Love. Shakespeare. *See* Take, O Take Those Those Lips Away.
Seals, Terns, Time. Richard Eberhart. FiMAP; LiTM (1970 ed.); MoAB; MoAmPo (1962 ed.)
Seaman's Confession of Faith, A. Harry Kemp. TrPWD
Seaman's Happy Return, The. *Unknown.* ChTr
Sea-Man's Renown, The. John Playford. *See* Jovial Marriner, The.
Seaman's Tomb, A. Plato, *tr. fr. Greek by* Lord Neaves. OnPM
Seamark, A. Bliss Carman. PeCV
Sea Marke, The. John Smith. SCAP
Seamen shout once and together, The. A Leave-taking. Sir Frederick Napier Broome. AnNZ
Seamen Three. Thomas Love Peacock. *See* Three Men of Gotham.
Seamy Side of Motley, The. Sir Owen Seaman. InMe
Séance. William Abrahams. NYBP
Search. T. Moore Atkinson. ChIP
Search, The. Psalms, XLII *and* XLIII, Bible, *O.T.* *See* My Soul Thirsteth For God.
Search, The. Kwesi Brew. PBA
Search, The. Thomas Curtis Clark. MaRV; SoP; WGRP
Search, The. Ernest Crosby. AA; OQP
Search, The. Sara Henderson Hay. MaRV
Search, The. George Herbert. AnAnS-1; MaMe; MeP
Search, The. St. John of the Cross, *tr. fr. Spanish by* E. Allison Peers. BoC
Search, The. James Russell Lowell. MaRV; SoP; StJW; TRV
Search. Anne Marriott. MaRV; SoP; TRV
Search. Raymond Souster. ELU; OBCV
Search, The. Henry Vaughan. AnAnS-1; MeP; SCEP-1; SeCP
Search. Margaret Widdemer. TrPWD
Search after Happiness, The, *sel.* Hannah More.
  Solitude. WBLP
Search for God, The. Thomas Heywood. *Fr.* Hierarchie of the Blessed Angels, I. MaRV, *abr.*; OxBoCh, *abr.*
  ("I sought Thee round about, O Thou my God.") WGRP
Search for St. Truth, The. William Langland, *tr. fr. Middle English.* *Fr.* The Vision of Piers Plowman. MeEV
Search out in me all hidden sin. For Thee. *Unknown.* FaChP
Search then the ruling passion: there, alone. The Ruling Passion. Pope. *Fr.* Moral Essays. ViBoPo
Searcher of Hearts. George Pope Morris. SoP
Searcher of Hearts Is Thy Maker, The. Psalms, CXXXIX, 1-24, Bible, *O.T.* WGRP
  ("O Lord, thou hast searched me and known me.") BoC
Searchers of majesty shall all be slain by glory, The. Presumption. Eileen Duggan. CAW
Searching my heart for its true sorrow. Exiled. Edna St. Vincent Millay. EtS; HT; PoRA
Searching once I found a flower. Indian Pipe. Richard Eberhart. TDP
Searching the earth, with exile worn. I Said to the Leaf. Carleton Drewry. MoRP
Seas are quiet when the winds give o'er, The. Old Age [*or* Last Verses]. Edmund Waller. *Fr.* Of the Last Verses in the Book. BoC; MaRV; OBEV; OxBoCh; TreFT
Sea's Spell, The. Susan Marr Spalding. AA; EtS
Sea's Voice, The. William Prescott Foster. EtS
Seas were left behind, The. Taliessin's Return to Logres. Charles Williams. ACV
Seascape. W. H. Auden. GTBS-P
Seascape. Elizabeth Bishop. MoAB
Seascape. Langston Hughes. BrR
Seascape. Stephen Spender. AtBAP; ChMP; CoBMV; GTBS-D; NoP
Seascape shifts, The. Distinctions. Charles Tomlinson. CMoP
Sea Scape with Parable. Richard Eberhart. PoDB
Seashore [*or* Sea-Shore]. Emerson. AmPP (4th ed.); AnAmPo; EtS; LiTA; MAmP; OxBA
Sea Side. Robert Graves. MoPo
Seaside, The. Charles Tennyson Turner. Sonn
Seaside and the Fireside, The, *sel.* Longfellow.
  Dedication: "As one who, walking in the twilight gloom." MAmP
Seaside Golf. John Betjeman. PoPl; SD
Season. Wole Soyinka. FlW
Season into season, as the weathers go. The Wind Is Round. Howard Moss. WIRo
Season, The? Not yet Spring. The Place? Beside. Rabbit Cry. Edward Lucie-Smith. NePoEA-2
Season of love, The. Elegies, IV. Philippe Thoby-Marcelin. PoNe
Season of mists and mellow fruitfulness. To Autumn [*or* Ode to Autumn]. Keats. AnEnPo; AnFE; AtBAP; ATP; AWP; BEL; BoC; BoLiVe; BoNaP; BoPe; BoTP; BWP; CABA; CaFP; CBEP; CBV; CH; ChER; CoBE; DD; DiPo; EG; EnL; EnLi-2; EnLit; EnRP; EPN; ERoP-2; ExPo; FaBoEn; FaBV; FiP; ForPo; FosPo; GoTP; GTBS; GTBS-D; GTBS-P; GTBS-W; GTSE; GTSL; HBV; HBVY; ILP; InPo; InvP; JAWP; LiTB; LiTG; LoBV; MaPo; MBW-2; MCCG; MemP; MERP; MyFE; NoP; OAEP; OBEV; OBNC; OBRV; OuHeWo; PAn; PeER; PIA; Po; PoAn; PoE; PoEL-4; PoeP; PoFS; PoIE; PoLF; PoPo; PoSa; RoGo; SeCeV; ShBV-3; StP; TDP; TOP; TreFS; TrGrPo; UnPo; VaPo; ViBoPo; WBP; WePo; WHA
Season 'Tis, My Lovely Lambs, The. E. E. Cummings. UnPo (3d ed.)
Seasons. Hayden Carruth. NYTB
Seasons, The. John Vance Cheney. DD
Seasons, The. Rolfe Humphries. NYBP
Seasons, The, *sels.* Kalidasa, *tr. fr. Sanskrit by* Arthur W. Ryder.
  Autumn. AWP; JAWP; WBP
  Early Spring. AWP
  Rains, The. AWP
  Spring. AWP
  Summer. AWP
  Winter. AWP
Seasons, The. Lynette Roberts. MoPW
Seasons. Christina Rossetti. YeAr
Seasons. Spenser. *See* Mask of Mutability, The.
Seasons, The, *sels.* James Thomson.
  Autumn ("Crowned with the sickle"). CEP
    Autumn ("But see the fading many-coloured woods") EnRP; LoBV
    "Fled in the blasted verdure." OAEP
    Lavinia. OBEC
    Love of Nature. OBEC
    Moonlight in Autumn, *abr.* OBEC
  Hymn on the Seasons, A. EiCP; EnRP; OxBoCh; PoE
    (Hymn, A: "These, as they change, Almighty Father, these.") CEP; EiPP
  Spring. EiCP
    Birds in Spring. OBEC
    ("Blackbird whistles from the thorny brake, The.") PeER
    "Come, gentle Spring, ethereal mildness, come." PeER, 4 *ll.*
    Spring ("As rising from the vegetable world"). PoEL-3
    Spring ("At length the finished garden"). ViBoPo
    Spring Flowers. AtBAP; OBEC
    Woodland Choir, The. CoBE
  Summer. StP
    Happy Britannia. OBEC; SeCePo
    Sheep-washing, The. EnLi-2
    (Sheep Shearing, The.) CoBE
    Storm, The. LoBV
    Summer ("Still let me pierce into the midnight depth"). EnRP
    Summer Evening and Night. OBEC
    Summer Morning. OBEC
  Winter ("See, Winter comes, to rule the varied year"). BEL, *sl. abr.*; CABL; CEP; EiCL, 2 *versions*; EiPP; EnL, *shorter sel.*; EnLi-2, *shorter sel.*; EnLit, *shorter sel.*; OAEP, *abr.*; Po, *abr.*; YAT, *brief sel.*

Seasons (continued)
Approach of Winter. OBEC
"Clear frost succeeds, and thro' the blew serene." FaBoEn
"From all the livid east or piercing north." YAT
Frost at Night. OBEC
"Late, in the louring sky, red, fiery, streaks." FaBoEn
Lo! from the Livid East. AtBAP
("Lo! from the livid East, or piercing North.") FaBoEn; PeER, 26 *ll.*
Lost Shepherd, The. CoBE
"Now, solitary, and in pensive guise." FaBoEn
"See! Winter comes, to rule the varied year." PeER, 16 *ll.*
Storm, The. CoBE
Winter ("As thus the snows arise, and, foul and fierce"). SeCePo
Winter ("Now, when the cheerless empire of the sky"). OxBS
Winter ("The keener tempests come"). EnRP; NoP; ViBoPo
(Winter Storm, A.) TOP
Winter ("What art thou, frost? and whence are thy keen stores"). OxBS
Winter ("When from the pallid sky the sun descends"). OxBS
Winter Scene, A ("Through the hushed air"). OBEC
Winter Winds ("Nature, great parent"). UnPo (1st ed.)
Seasons Alter, The. Shakespeare. *Fr.* A Midsummer Night's Dream, II, i. BoW
Season's anguish, crashing whirlwind, ice, The. Winter Garden. David Gascoyne. ChMP; GTBS-D; GTBS-P
Seasons in North Cornwall, The. Charles Causley. ACV; POTi
Season's Lovers, The. Miriam Waddington. MoCV; OBCV; PeCV (1967 ed.)
Seasons of the Soul. Allen Tate. AP; CrMA; MoPo; NePA; OxBA
Autumn, II. MoVE
Seat for Three, A; Written on a Settle. Walter Crane. OBVV; VA
Seated in the cafeteria, you say. After the Concert. David Stapleton. MuSP
Seated once by a brook, watching a child. The Brook. Edward Thomas. MoVE; SeCeV
Seated One Day. Paul Jennings. MuSP
Seated one day at the organ / I jumped as if I'd been shot. The Lost Chord. D. B. Wyndham Lewis. MuSP; WhC
Seated one day at the organ / I was weary and ill at ease. A [*or* The] Lost Chord. Adelaide Anne Procter. CAW; FaFP; HBV; OTD; PaPo; SoP; TreF; WBLP; WGRP
Seated statue of himself he seems, A. Farm Boy after Summer. Robert Francis. PoIE; PoSa
Seated, the harpist waits. Marble Statuette Harpist. Sara Van Alstyne Allen. GoYe
Seattle weather: it has rained for weeks in this town. Homage to Arthur Waley. Weldon Kees. NaP
Seawall goes to show you can cut water, The. The Water Wants All Sea. Lloyd Frankenberg. NYTB
Seaward. Celia Thaxter. AA
Seaward. George Edward Woodberry. Wild Eden, XLI. AA
Seaward, at morn, my doves flew free. Three Doves. James Jeffrey Roche. JKCP
Seaward Bound. Alice Brown. TrPWD
Sea-Weed. D. H. Lawrence. BoNaP
Seaweed [*or* Sea Weed]. Longfellow. AmePo; AP; CoBA; HBV; MWA-1; OxBA; PCD
Equinox, The, *sel.* EtS
Sea-Weed, The. Elisabeth Cavazza Pullen. AA
Sea-weed sways and sways and swirls. Sea-Weed. D. H. Lawrence. BoNaP
Sebastian. Gene Baro. PoDB
Second after, A. The Settlers. Margaret Atwood. MoCV
2nd afternoon I come, The. A Poem for the Insane. John Wieners. NeAP
Second Air Force. Randall Jarrell. AP; CMoP; CoBMV; FiMAP; LiTM (1970 ed.); WaP
Second Angel, The. Philip Levine. NaP
Second Anniversary, The. John Donne. *See* Of the Progress of the Soul.
Second Asgard, The. Matthew Arnold. *Fr.* Balder Dead. FiP
Second Attempt, A. Thomas Hardy. MaPo (1969 ed.)
Second Benefit! Mary Ferguson. SoP
Second Best, The. Matthew Arnold. EPN
Second Best. Rupert Brooke. MoBrPo; OBVV
Second Birthday, A. Albert Kayper-Mensah. ACV
Second Blossoming. Ruth Lechlitner. NYTB
Second Brother, The, *sels.* Thomas Lovell Beddoes.
"I should not say." AtBAP
Song: "Strew not earth with empty stars." CBEP
Second Chap. of the Cant. from the 10. Verse to the 13. John Norris. *See* Canticle.
Second Coming, The. Dannie Abse. NMP
Second Coming, The. Stanton A. Coblentz. ChIP
Second Coming, The. Norman Gale. HBV; MaRV
Second Coming, The. W. B. Yeats. AtBAP; BWP; CABA; CBV; CMoP; CoBMV; DiPo; EaLo; EnL; ExPo; FaBoEn; FaBoMo; ForPo; GTBS-P; GTBS-W; HoPM; ILP; InPo; LiTB; LiTG; LiTM; LoBV; MaPo; MasP; MBW-2; MoAB; MoBrPo (1962 ed.); MoRP; MoVE; NoP; OAEP (2d ed.); OxBI; PAn; Po; PoAn; PoDB; PoE; PoeP; PoFS; PoIE; PoPo; ReMP; SeCePo; SeCeV; StP; TDP; UnPo (3d ed.); WaP
Second Corinthians, *sels.* Bible, *N.T.*
Glory of God Revealed in Jesus, The, IV: 6. MaRV
God Was in Christ, V: 18-21. TRV
Second Crucifixion. Victoria Beaudin Johnson. SoP
Second Crucifixion, The. Richard Le Gallienne. HBV; MaRV; OBEV (1st ed.); OBVV; WGRP
Second Cycle of Love Poems, *sels.* George Barker.
O Tender under Her Right Breast. MoAB; MoBrPo (1950 ed.); NeMA
(Love Poem: "O tender under her right breast.") NeBP
Verses for a First Birthday. MoAB; MoBrPo (1950 ed.)
Second Dance Poem. Gerald William Barrax. YAP
2nd Dance—Seeing Lines—6 February 1964. Jackson MacLow. CoPo
Second Dialogue between Crab and Gillian. Thomas Durfey. *Fr.* The Bath; or, The Western Lass. PeRV
Second Dirge. Thomas Lovell Beddoes. *See* Dirge: "We do lie beneath the grass."
Second Egloge Entituled Fortunatus, The. Mantuan, *tr. fr. Latin by* George Turberville. *Fr.* The Eglogs of the Poet B. Mantuan Carmelitan. ReIE
Second Epistle of the Essay on Man, The. Pope. GoTL
Second Epitaph, A. *Unknown.* MeEL
Second Fig. Edna St. Vincent Millay. AmP
Second Glance at a Jaguar. Ted Hughes. NYBP
Second Half. David McCord. SD
Second-hand sights, like crumpled. Newark, for Now (68). Carolyn M. Rodgers. WSL
Second Idyll, The. Theocritus. *See* Incantation, The.
Second Iron Age (1939-1945), The. Michael Harrington. CaP
Second Jungle Book, The, *sels.* Kipling.
Bagheera's Song. PoFr
Law of the Jungle, The. BoChLi; LiTB; OA; PoEL-5; PoVP; ShBV-1; VA
Song of the Little Hunter, The. ShBV-1
Second Life, The. Edwin Morgan. OxBS
Second Man, The. Julian Symons. WaP
Second Mask, Which Was of Beauty, The, *sel.* Ben Jonson.
Had Those That Dwell in Error Foul. TuPP
Second Mate, The. Fitz-James O'Brien. AA
Second Mile, The. Stephen Moore. SoP
Second News Item. *Unknown.* SiTL
Second Night, or What You Will. Rolfe Humphries. MoLP
Second Nimphall, The. Michael Drayton. *Fr.* The Muses' Elizium. AnAnS-2
"With full-leav'd lillies I will stick," *sel.* AtBAP
Second Nun's Tale, The, *sel.* Chaucer. *Fr.* The Canterbury Tales.
Invocatio ad Mariam, *mod. vers. by* Frank Ernest Hill, *fr. prologue.* ISi
("Thou maid and mother, daughter of thy Son," *mod. vers.*) GoBC
(Two Invocations of the Virgin, 1.) ACP
Second Ode in the Third Book of Horace, Imitated. Walter Titley. EiCL
Second Part of Absalom and Achitophel, The. Dryden. *See* Absalom and Achitophel, Pt. II.
Second Poem: "Morning again, nothing has to be done." Peter Orlovsky. NeAP

Second Quest, The. Joseph Rodman Drake. *Fr.* The Culprit Fay. AA
Second Rapture, The. Thomas Carew. UnTE
Second Review of the Grand Army, A. Bret Harte. HBV; MC; PAH
Second Samuel, *sels.* Bible, *O.T.*
David and Bathsheba, XI: 2-XII: 18. OuHeWo
David's Lament, I: 19-27. ChTr (17-27); TrGrPo; TrJP
("Beauty of Israel is slain upon thy high places, The," I: 19-26.) LO
(David's Lament for Saul and Jonathan.) AWP
(David's Lament over Saul and Jonathan.) ShBV-3
(How Are the Mighty Fallen.) LiTW; WaaP
"It came to pass after this, that Absalom the son of David had a fair sister," XIII: 1-19. LO
Leader, The, XXIII: 3-4. PCD; PCH
Second Seeing. Louis Golding. WGRP
Second Settler's Story, The. Will Carleton. IHA
Second Shepherds' Play, The. *Unknown.* EnLit, *mod Eng.*; MeEV, *mod. Eng.*; PoEL-1
Haylle, Comly and Clene, *sel.* OBEV (new ed.); OxBoLi
(Hayll, Comly and Clene.) AtBAP; BoW
(Shepherds at Bethlehem, The.) ChTr
Second Sight. W. S. Merwin. StP
Second Sight. H. S. Neill. FiSC
Second Sonnet on "Tetrachordon." Milton. *See* On the Detraction Which Followed. . . ("I did but prompt the age").
Second Stanza for Dr. Johnson, A. Donald Hall. FiBHP; ShM
Second Thanksgiving, The. George Herbert. *See* Reprisal, The.
Second Timothy, *sel.* Bible, *N.T.*
"For God hath not given us the spirit of fear," I: 7. TiPo (1952 ed.)
Second Vision, The. Robert Herrick. UnTE
(Vision, The.) CBEP
Second Vision, The. Tadhg Dall O'Huiginn, *tr. fr. Late Middle Irish by* the Earl of Longford. AnIL
Second Volume, The. Robert Mowry Bell. AA
Second Walk in the Garden, The. John Gould Fletcher. MAPA
Second Wisdom. Henry Morton Robinson. GoYe
Second Woman's Lament. Brenda Chamberlain. NeIP
(Fisherman Husband.) PrWP
Second Year in a Seminary. Peter Levi. MemP
Secrecy. Samuel Daniel. *See* Eyes, Hide My Love.
Secrecy [*or* Secresie] Protested. Thomas Carew. *See* Fear Not, Dear Love.
Secret, The. "Æ." MoBrPo
(Unity.) MoRP; PoVP
Secret. Gwendolyn B. Bennett. CDC
Secret, The. José Joaquin Casas, *tr. fr. Spanish by* Thomas Walsh. CAW
Secret, The. Marchette Chute. GoBP
Secret, The. Ralph Spaulding Cushman. FaChP; MaRV; SoP; STF; TRV
(His Presence Came like Sunrise.) BLRP
Secret, The ("A fuzzy fellow without feet"). Emily Dickinson. *See* Fuzzy fellow without feet, A.
Secret, The ("I have not told my garden yet"). Emily Dickinson. *See* I have not told my garden yet.
Secret, A ("A secret told"). Emily Dickinson. *See* Secret told, A.
Secret, The ("Some things that fly there be"). Emily Dickinson. *See* Some things that fly there be.
Secret. Esther Hull Doolittle. YeAr
Secret, The. Elizabeth Fleming. BoTP
Secret. Catherine Haydon Jacobs. GoYe
Secret, The. Denise Levertov. NaP
Secret, The. Cosmo Monkhouse. VA
Secret, The. John Richard Moreland. OQP
Secret, The. Arthur Wallace Peach. HBMV
Secret, The. Joan Suisted. SoP
Secret, The ("Hark, Celia, hark!"). *Unknown.* SeCL
Secret, A ("If I had wit for to indite"). *Unknown.* OBSC
Secret, The ("We have a secret"). *Unknown.* BoChLi; MPB (1956 ed.); OTPC (1946 ed.); SoPo; StVeCh (1940 ed.); TiPo; UTS
Secret, The. Mary Morison Webster. PeSA
Secret, The. George Edward Woodberry. Wild Eden, VI. AA; HBV
Secret Cavern, The. Margaret Widdemer. FaPON; MPB; RePo
Secret Combination, The. Ellis Parker Butler. BoHV
Secret Garden, The. Thomas Kinsella. TwCP
Secret Garden, The. Robert Nichols. WGRP
Secret Heart, The. Robert P. Tristram Coffin. OTD; PoRL; PoSC
Secret in bed the lustful with soft cries. Sonnet against the Too-facile Mystic. Elizabeth B. Harrod. NePoEA
Secret Joy, The. Mary Webb. BoTP
Secret Land, The. Robert Graves. BoC
Secret Laughter. Christopher Morley. FaBV; TreFS
Secret Love, The. "Æ." HBV
Secret Love. John Clare. CBEP; CLwM; ERoP-2; FaBV; FaPL; LiTL; NBM; PoEL-4; TrGrPo
(I Hid My Love.) AtBAP; NCEP; OBNC; PeER
(I Hid My Love When Young.) WePo
"And even silence found a tongue," *br. sel.* LO
Secret Love; or, The Maiden Queen, *sels.* Dryden.
"I feed a flame within, which so torments me." InPo; LO; MaPo; SeCL
(Hidden Flame, The.) OBEV
(I Feed a Flame Within.) PoIE; QFR
(Song.) AWP; JAWP; LiTL; MBW-1; WBP
Prologue: "He who writ this, not without pains and thought." MBW-1; SeCV-2; SeEP
(First Prologue.) PeRV
Secret Love or Two I Must Confess, A. Thomas Campion. ErPo
Secret Muse, The. Roy Campbell. BoC; PeSA
Secret of a Happy Day, The. Frances Ridley Havergal. SoP
Secret of Song. Christine White. STF
Secret of the Cross, The. M. J. Clarkson. BePJ
Secret of the Deeps, The. Sidney Royse Lysaght. EtS
Secret of the King possesses me, The. As One Finding Peace. Sister Mary Madeleva. JKCP
Secret of the Machines, The. Kipling. PoMa; StVeCh
Secret of the Nightingale, The. Roden Noel. VA
Secret of the Sea, The. Longfellow. AnNE; EtS; GoTP; RIS
(Galley of Count Arnaldos, The.) OBEV (new ed.); OBVV
Secret of these hills was stone, The. The Pylons. Stephen Spender. AWP; CMoP; EnLi-2 (1949 ed.); EnLit
Secret Parting. Dante Gabriel Rossetti. The House of Life, XLV. MaVP; PoVP; ViPo; VP
Secret People, The. G. K. Chesterton. OtMeF; PoFr
Secret Place, The. Henry Francis Lyte. VA
Secret Place, The. Adelaide A. Pollard. FaChP; SoP; STF
Secret Place of Prayer, The. Georgia B. Adams. STF
Secret Places. Irene Thompson. BoTP
Secret Prayer. Fanny J. Crosby. SoP
Secret Prayer. John Cross Belle. STF
Secret Sits, The. Robert Frost. LOW; SoPo
Secret Song, The. Margaret Wise Brown. PDV
Secret Thoughts. Christopher Morley. *Fr.* Translations from the Chinese. EvOK
Secret told, A. Emily Dickinson. CoBA
Secret Town, The, *sel.* Abraham Sutzkever, *tr. fr. Yiddish by* Jacob Sonntag.
"Remember the sun in the autumn, its rays." TrJP
Secret was the garden. The Mistress of Vision. Francis Thompson. BrPo; CH; OBVV
Secret Weapon. Ammonides, *tr. fr. Greek by* Dudley Fitts. LiTW
Secret Wood, The. Andrew Young. POTE
Secretary. Ted Hughes. ErPo; ToPo
Secretary, The. Matthew Prior. BWP; CEP; PoE; PoFS
(Written at The Hague, in the Year 1696.) EiCL
Secrets. Elsie Melchert Fowler. BiCB; ChBR
Secrets. Luisa Hewitt. PCH
Secrets of Angling, The, *sel.* John Dennys.
"Let me live harmlessly, and near the brink," 4 *sts.* MyFE
(Angler's Song, The, 6 *sts.*) EIL
Secrets of Cisterns, The. Stanley McNail. FiSC
Secrets of Life, The. N. P. Nielson. FaChP
Secrets of Our Garden, The. Rupert Sargent Holland. OTPC
Section and brick and grass. The Houses, VI. "Robin Hyde." AnNZ
Section men a-workin' there all side by side. Mike. *Unknown.* ABF
Secular Elegies. George Barker. ToPo

Secular (continued)
"O Golden Fleece she is where she lies tonight," V. ErPo; LiTM; MoAB; MoBrPo; NeBP
(Love Poem.) LiTL
Secular Litany. M. K. Joseph. AnNZ
Secular Masque, The. Dryden. DiPo; EiCL; ExPo; MaPo; MBW-1; PoEL-3; SeCeV; SeCV-2; SeEP
Sels.
All, All of a Piece Throughout. CBEP; ChTr; ELP; ELU; GTBS-W
(Chorus.) ViBoPo
(Chorus from "The Secular Masque.") OnPM
Diana's Hunting-Song. SeCePo; SeCL
(Songs from "The Secular Masque": Diana.) InPo
Song of Momus to Mars, The. CBEP
(Songs from "The Secular Masque": Momus.) InPo
Security. Denis Glover. AnNZ
Security. Michael Hamburger. NMP; OPoP; PoCh
Security. Charles L. O'Donnell. TrPWD
Security. Lina Sandell. SoP; STF
Security. Margaret E. Sangster. BLRP
Security. Robert Tucker. PPON
Sed Non Satiata. Baudelaire, *tr. fr. French by* Arthur Symons. OnPM
Seder-Night. Israel Zangwill. TrJP
Sedge Warblers. Edward Thomas. LO
"And sedge-warblers, clinging so light," *sel.* BiS
Sedges, The. "Seumas O'Sullivan." AnIV
Sediment. David Ignatow. NYBP
Seduced Girl. Hedylos, *tr. fr. Greek by* Louis Untermeyer. ErPo
(To Venus.) UnTE
("With wine and words of love and fervent vow.") MeWo
Seduction of Engadu. *Unknown, tr. fr. Babylonian tablets by* William Ellery Leonard. *Fr.* Gilgamesh. ErPo
See/ Me. A Pair of Wings. Stephen Hawes. MeEL
See a pin and pick it up. Old Superstitions [*or* Some Proverbs in Verse]. *Unknown.* FaBoBe; GoTP; HBV; HBVY; RIS; TreF
See, above this mortal cloudland. Gwel uwchlaw cymylau amser. Islwyn. PrWP
See, all the silver roads wind in, lead in. The Sufficient Place. Edwin Muir. BoPe
See an old unhappy bull. The Bull. Ralph Hodgson. AnFE; BrPo; EnLi-2 (1949 ed.); EnLit; LiTG; LiTM (rev. ed.); MoAB; MoBrPo; MoVE; OA; OBMV; ShBV-2; TOP; YT
See, as the Carver Carves a Rose. Conrad Aiken. Priapus and the Pool, XVI [XIX]. PFY
(Carver, The.) HBMV
("See, as the carver carves a rose.") AnAmPo
See, as the prettiest graves will do in time. Fame. Robert Browning. *Fr.* Earth's Immortalities. PoVP; PP
See, chil-dren, the fur-bear-ing seal. A Seal. Oliver Herford. *Fr.* Child's Natural History. HBV; HBVY
See, Chloris, how the clouds. To Chloris. William Drummond. CLwM
See, cold island, we stand. Clare Coast. Emily Lawless. OxBI
"See, Corydon, see, here's the stall." Corydon and Tityrus. *Unknown.* CAW
See! down the red road by the brown tree. The End of Exploring. David Campbell. SeCePo
See, Fairest! virgins gather dew. To Eliza, upon May Day Morning, 1649. Robert Baron. SeCL
See, far above the starry height. The Eagle Swift. Adam of St. Victor. BePJ
See! from the brake the whirring pheasant springs. The Pheasant. Pope. *Fr.* Windsor Forest. FaBoEn; FlW; GoTP; PoEL-3
See, from this counterfeit of him. On a Bust of Dante. Thomas William Parsons. AA; AnAmPo; HBV
See, gallants, see this gallery of delights. Anthony Munday unto All Young Gentlemen in Commendation of this Gallery and Workmen Thereof. Anthony Munday. ReIE
See God in Everything. A. E. Finn. SoP
See her caught in the throb of a drum. Agbor Dancer. John Pepper Clark. PBA
See here an easie feast that knowes no wound. On the Miracle of Multiplyed Loaves. Richard Crashaw. MaMe
See! Here, My Heart. *Unknown. See* O! Mankind.
See, here's the grand approach. On Blenheim [*or* Verses on Blenheim]. Swift. *after the Latin of* Martial. AWP; OnPM
"See here's the workbox, little wife." The Workbox. Thomas Hardy. PoeP
See him, the gentle Bible beast. The Toy Horse. Edwin Muir. FaBoMo
See how dark the night settles on my face. Nocturne. Naomi Long Madgett. BALP
See how Flora smiles to see. On Clarastella Walking in Her Garden. Robert Heath. CavP; OBS; SeCL
See how from far upon the eastern road. The Magi. Milton. *Fr.* On the Morning of Christ's Nativity. ChTr
See how he dives. Seal. William Jay Smith. GoTP
See how it flashes. In a Wine Cellar. Victor J. Daley. PoAu-1
See how it is teed up on the nest, enabling. A Flamingo's Egg. Terence Heywood. BoSA
See, how like twilight slumber falls. Song. Charles Cotton. OBS; SeCL
See how the arched earth does here. Upon the Hill and Grove at Bill-borrow. Andrew Marvell. MaMe
See how the dying west puts forth her song. Nocturne. Richard Church. ChMP
See how the flowers, as at parade. A Garden. Andrew Marvell. *Fr.* Upon Appleton House. CEP HBV; OBEV; TrGrPo
See how the orient dew. On a Drop of Dew [*or* A Drop of Dew]. Andrew Marvell. AnAnS-1; BWP; EnLi-1; FosPo; GoBC; GTBS-W; ILP; LiTB; LiTG; MaMe; MaPo (1969 ed.); MeLP; MeP; MePo; OBS; OuHeWo; OxBoCh; PoAn; PoFS; ReEn; SCEP-2; SeCP; SeCV-1; SeEP; UnPo (1st ed.); WoL
See how the sky. The Moon. Louise Ayres Garnett. SiSoSe
See how the sun has somewhat not of light. El Greco. E. L. Mayo. HoPM; MiAP
See how the Yellow River's waters move from heaven. Bringing in the Wine. Li Po. OuHeWo
See how this trim girl. Artemis. Peter Davison. ErPo
See how this violet which before. On a Violet in Her Breast. Thomas Stanley. OBS
See! Hymen comes; how his torch blazes. Song. Sir Charles Sedley. PeRV
See! I give myself to you, Beloved! A Gift. Amy Lowell. NP
See, I have bent thee by thy saffron hair. The Sunflower. Peter Quennell. AtBAP; POTE
See, I have set before thee this day life and good, and death and evil. Choose Life. Deuteronomy, Bible, *O.T.* TreFT
See, in the circle how we stand. In a Convex Mirror. Rosemary Dobson. MoAuPo
See, in the garden there, it hops and lurches about. On a Child with a Wooden Leg. Bertram Warr. OBCV
See in the Midst of Fair Leaves. Marianne Moore. MoAB
See, Lord,/ my coat hangs in tatters. The Prayer of the Old Horse. Carmen Bernos de Gasztold. PDV
See me with all the terrors on my roads. The Face. Edwin Muir. ChMP; FaBoMo; GTBS-P
See, Mignonne, hath not the rose. The Rose. Pierre de Ronsard. AWP; JAWP; WBP
See, my belovèd, how the sun. Nightfall. Kalidasa. LiTW
See my lov'd [*or* loved] Britons, see your Shakespeare rise. Prologue. Dryden. *Fr.* Troilus and Cressida. CEP; MBW-1; SeCV-2
See my mast, a pen! The Voyage. Vachel Lindsay. MAP
See my pretty little nest. Oriole. Marion Mitchell Walker. GFA
See now, dead friend. Duty to Death, LD. Dick Roberts. WaP
See, O see!/ How every tree. Song. George Digby, Earl of Bristol. *Fr.* Elvira. SeCL
See on Newmarket's turf, my lord. At Newmarket. Samuel Bishop. PV
See on what mighty draughts of life. O Spring, Come Prettily In. Adolf Strodtmann. CAW
See, one physician, like a sculler, plies. Two Heads Are Better than One. Joseph Jekyll. WhC
See represented here, in light and shade. The Salutation of the Blessed Virgin. John Byrom. ISi
See saw. *See also* Seesaw.
See-saw, down in my lap. *Unknown.* OxNR
See saw, Margery Daw. Mother Goose. BoChLi; OTPC; OxNR; RIS

See-saw, Margery Daw,/ The old hen flew over the malt house. *Unknown.* OxNR
See-saw, Margery Daw,/ Sold her bed and lay upon straw. *Unknown.* OxNR
See-saw, sacradown. Mother Goose. OTPC; OxNR; PCH; PPL
See, see, mine own sweet jewel. Canzonet. *Unknown.* EG; EIL; LO
See! see! she comes; with graceful ease she treads. On Her Entering Her Room. Richardson Pack. WaPE
See, see, she wakes! Sabina wakes! Song. Congreve. HBV
See! see the bright light shines. *Unknown.* SeCSL
See, see, what shall I see? *Unknown.* OxNR
See, see where royal Snowdon rears. Liberty. John Ceiriog Hughes. PoFr
See, Sir, here's the grand approach. On Blenheim House. Abel Evans. CBEP OBEC
See Sir, how as the suns hot masculine flame. To E. of D. with Six Holy Sonnets. John Donne. MaMe
See! some strange comfort every state attend. Life's Poor Play. Pope. *Fr.* An Essay on Man. OBEC; SeCePo; YAT
See, stretching yonder o'er that low divide. The Old Mackenzie Trail. John A. Lomax. SCC
See that building, which, when my mistress living. A Well-wishing to a Place of Pleasure. *Unknown.* SeCL
See That One? Robert Bagg. ErPo
See that satan pollarding a tree. Progression. Francis Scarfe. NeBP
See the bunnies sitting there. Timid Bunnies. Jeannie Kirby. BoTP
See the chariot at hand here of Love. The Triumph of Charis [*or* Her Triumph]. Ben Jonson. *Fr.* A Celebration of Charis. AnAnS-2; AnFE; AtBAP; BEL; CABA; CaFP; CBEP; CTC; EIL; ELP; ExPo; FaBoEn; GoBC; HBV; InPo; InvP; LiTB; LiTL; LoBV; MaPo; NoP; OAEP; OBEV; PAn; Po; PoEL-2; SeCeV; SeCP; SeCV-1; SeEP; SiCE; TOP; TuPP; ViBoPo; WHA
See the Crocus' Golden Cup. Joseph Mary Plunkett. OnYI
See the day begins to break. Satyr's Song. John Fletcher. *Fr.* The Faithful Shepherdess, IV, iv. OBS
See the dazzled stripling stand. Goliath and David. Louis Untermeyer. TrJP
See the far hills white with snow. Winter. Jean Jaszi. SoPo
See the fur coats go by! Poems. Hilda Conkling. ExPo; NP
See the happy moron. The Moron. *Unknown.* CenHV; MemP; TreFT; YaD
See the kitten on the wall. The Kitten at Play. Wordsworth. *Fr.* The Kitten and Falling Leaves. BoTP; FaPON; GoTP; MPB (1956 ed.); OTPC; PRWS; PTK
See the land, her Easter keeping. Easter Week. Charles Kingsley. DD; OHIP
See the little maunderer. A Love for Patsy. John Thompson, Jr. GTBS-W; LiTA; LiTL; LiTM; NePA; WaP
See the lovely morning rise. An Hymn to the Morning. Mary Leapor. WaPE
See the madly blowing dust. A Colorado Sand Storm. Eugene Field. PoOW
See! The Mother Corn comes hither, making all hearts glad! An Indian Hymn of Thanks to Mother Corn. *Unknown.* PCH
See, the pretty planet! Blowing Bubbles [*or* The Bubble]. William Allingham. GN; OnYI
See the pretty snowflakes. Falling Snow. *Unknown.* BoChLi; GFA; SoPo; TiPo (1952 ed.)
See the rivers flowing downward to the sea. Giving. Adelaide Anne Procter. SoP
See, the ruthless victor comes. Song for Peace. W. R. Rodgers. NeBP
See, the see, the Bishop's see, The. The Bishop's See. *Unknown.* CoMu
See the Smoking Bowl before Us. Burns. *Fr.* The Jolly Beggars. ALV, *abr.*; ATP (1935 ed.); GoTS
(Jolly Mortals, Fill Your Glasses.) EnLi-2 (1949 ed.)
See, the spring herself discloses. Spring. Thomas Stanley. AWP; JAWP; SeCL; WBP
See the star-breasted villain. Village-Born Beauty. *Unknown.* PaPo
See the stars, love. In a Boat. D. H. Lawrence. BoLP
See the white stillness of the unicorn. Sonnet. Roy Daniells. PeCV
See the yellow catkins cover. A Spring Song. Mary Howitt. BoTP
See them joined by strings to history. P. K. Page. MoCV
See there! God's signpost, standing at the ways. The Cross at the Crossways. John Oxenham. MaRV
See! There he stands; not brave, but with an air. Brothers. James Weldon Johnson. BANP
See, they are clearing the sawdust course. A Circus Garland. Rachel Field. SoPo; StVeCh
See, they return; ah, see the tentative. The Return. Ezra Pound. AmPP (5th ed.); AnEnPo; AP; CMoP; CoAnAm; CoBMV; FaBoEn; MoAB; MoAmPo; MoPo; NePA; OxBA; PoAn; TwAmPo; ViBoPo
See this house, how dark it is. The Empty House. Walter de la Mare. BrPo
"See this my garden." The Philosopher's Garden. John Oxenham. PoMa
See thou character. Give thy thoughts no tongue. Polonius' Advice to Laertes. Shakespeare. *Fr.* Hamlet, I, iii. BBV
See, though the oil be low, more purely still and higher. Terence MacSwiney [*or* A Prisoner]. "Æ." AnIL; AnIV; PoFr
See twilight standing on the brink. At the Edge of the Day. Clarence Urmy. HBMV
See What a Lovely Shell. Tennyson. *See* Shell, The.
See what a mass of gems the city wears. Impression de Nuit; London. Lord Alfred Douglas. OBEV (new ed.); OBVV; PoVP
See, when a fireship in mid ocean blazes. Surrender to Christ. Frederic William Henry Myers. OxBoCh
See where black water. Strip Mining Pit. Dan Gillespie. QAH
See where Calisto wheels about. Serenade, to Two Ladies. Thomas Porter. *Fr.* The Villain. SeCL
See where Capella with her golden kids. Edna St. Vincent Millay. Epitaph for the Race of Man, VI. CMoP; MAP; MoAB; MoAmPo
See where enamoured Thyrsis lies. The Amorist. Nahum Tate. SeCL
See Where My Love a-Maying Goes. *Unknown.* EIL
See where she sits upon the grassy green [*or* grassie greene]. A Ditty. Spenser. *Fr.* The Shepheardes Calender: April. FaBoCh; OBEV; ViBoPo
See where she stands! a mortal shape indued. Shelley. *Fr.* Epipsychidion. MBW-2
See, whilst thou weep'st, fair Cloe, see. To Cloe Weeping. Matthew Prior. CEP; EiCP; EiPP
See, Will, 'Ere's a Go. *Unknown.* ChTr
("Civile, si ergo," *sl. diff.*) WhC
See, Winter comes, to rule the varied year. Winter [*or* The Storm]. James Thomson. *Fr.* The Seasons. BEL; CABL; CEP; CoBE; EiCL; EiPP; EnL; EnLi-2; EnLit; OAEP; OBEC; PeER; Po; YAT
See! with what constant motion. Gratiana Dancing [*or* Dauncing] and Singing. Richard Lovelace. AnAnS-2; CavP; CLwM; LiTL; LoBV; MeLP; MePo; OAEP; OBS; ReEn; SCEP-2; SeCL; SeCV-1; SeEP
See with what simplicity. The Picture of Little T. C. in a Prospect of Flowers. Andrew Marvell. AnAnS-1; BWP; CBEP; ExPo; GTSL; HBV; LiTB; MaMe; MeLP; MemP; MeP; MePo; NoP; OBEV; OBS; PoE; SCEP-2; SeCeV; SeCP; SeCV-1
See yon blithe child that dances in our sight. The Child. Sara Coleridge. OBEV (1st ed.)
See yonder goes old Mendax, telling lies. Mendax. Gotthold Ephraim Lessing. BOHV; PV
See yonder hallow'd fane! the pious work. Church and Churchyard at Night. Robert Blair. *Fr.* The Grave. OBEC; ViBoPo
See yonder leafless trees against the sky. Transition. Emerson. MWA-1
See yonder melancholy gentleman. Meditations of a Gull. Sir John Davies. SiCE
See, yonder, the belfry tower. At Midnight. Frank Dempster Sherman. AA; MAP
See yonder, where a gem of night. Es fallt ein Stern herunter. Heine. AWP; JAWP
See you him yonder who sits o'er the stage. Of Cornelius.

See (continued)
Everard Guilpin. *Fr.* Skialetheia. SiCE; TuPP
See you the ferny ride that steals. Puck's Song. Kipling. *Fr.* Puck of Pook's Hill. FaBoCh; FaBV; LoGBV
Seed. H. C. Bosman. BoSA; PeSA
Seed-Eaters, The. Robert Francis. NePoAm-2
Seed Growing Secretly, The. Henry Vaughan. AnAnS-1; MeP; OxBoCh; SCEP-1; SeCV-1
Seed is dug under, A. Shekhinah. Karl Wolfskehl. TrJP
Seed Leaves. Richard Wilbur. BoNaP
Seed, Lord, falls on stony ground, The. Process. Charles L. O'Donnell. TrPWD
Seed of my day begins, The. Personal Jihad. Gaston Neal. BF
Seed Shop, The. Muriel Stuart. BoNaP; GoTP; GoTS; MemP; NP; POTE
Seed Time. *See* Seedtime.
Seeds. Walter de la Mare. RePo; StVeCh; TiPo (1959 ed.)
Seeds. John Oxenham. WGRP
Seeds. Thurmond Snyder. NNP
Seeds. Muriel Stuart. BoC
Seeds. Augusta Webster. OBVV
('Tween Earth and Sky.) VA
Seeds clutched in my hand. Hunting. "Yehoash." TrJP
Seeds I sowed, The. Seeds. Walter de la Mare. RePo; StVeCh; TiPo (1959 ed.)
Seeds in a dry pod, tick, tick, tick. Petit the Poet. Edgar Lee Masters. *Fr.* Spoon River Anthology. AnFE; APA; CMoP; CoAnAm; ILP; InPo; LaNeLa; LoGBV; MAP; MoAmPo; MoVE; NeMA; OxBA; PoSa; PPON
Seeds of Kindness. *Unknown. See* Say It Now.
Seeds of Love, The. *Unknown, at. to* Mrs. Fleetwood Habergham. CBEP; FaBoCh; LoGBV; OxBoLi, *sl. diff.*; WiR
(I Sowed the Seeds of Love.) ELP
Seeds of perversion, The. Scène à Faire. John Gill. ThO
Seeds with wings, between earth and sky. Seeds [*or* 'Tween Earth and Sky]. Augusta Webster. OBVV; VA
Seedsmen of Old Saturn's Land. Herman Melville. *Fr.* Clarel. AmPP (3d ed.)
Seed-Time. George Meredith. VP
Seed Time Hymn. John Keble. VA
Seedy Henry rose up shy in de world. The Dream Songs, LXXVII. John Berryman. NaP; TwCP
Seein' Things. Eugene Field. BoChLi; HBV; HBVY; MAP; MoAmPo (1942 ed.); MPB; NeMA; OTPC; PoMa; RIS; TreF
Seeing. John Lyle Donaghy. NeIP
Seeing/ the sky/ come down. Sunny Day. Alex Raybin. ThO
Seeing a Lady. John Tatham. *Fr.* Ostella. SeCL
("Oh, she is fair: fair as the eastern morn.") LO
Seeing at last how each thing here beneath. No Question. George Dillon. AmLP
Seeing Eye-Dog, A. Saundra Sharp. WSL
Seeing Her Dancing. Sir Robert Heath. OBS; SeEP
Seeing how the world suffered and bled. Angela Morgan. *Fr.* The Humanitarian. OQP
Seeing in illustrated magazines. Olduvai. Leroy Smith, Jr. NYTB
Seeing is believing. On Sir Henry Ferrett, M.P. J. B. Morton. PV
Seeing the Elephant, *with music.* David G. Robinson. SGR
Seeing the Frog. May Swenson. OPoP
Seeing the great moon rising. Moonrise. Abbie Huston Evans. NP
"Seeing the plum tree I thought of the Western Island." Ballad of the Western Island in the North Country. *Unknown.* SiSw
Seeing the size, the domed. Cat in the Long Grass. Alan Dixon. FIW
Seeing those mountains, distant and obscure. Mellin de Saint-Gelais. *See* Sonnet of the Mountain, The.
Seeing thou art fair, I bar not thy false playing. Advice to a Fair Wanton. Ovid. *Fr.* Amores. UnTE
Seeing you smile, the furies fail to stay angry. You. *Unknown.* MeWo
Seek a convenient time to take heed to thyself. Of Love of Silence and of Solitude. Thomas à Kempis. *Fr.* Imitation of Christ. TreF
Seek a Haven ("O navis referent"). Horace, *tr. fr. Latin by* Charles Stuart Calverley. Odes, I, 14. OnPM
Seek Flowers of Heaven. Robert Southwell. ReIE
Seek not afar for beauty. Lo! it glows. Earth's Common Things. Minot J. Savage. MaRV; OQP
Seek not for me within a tomb. L'Envoi. John G. Neihardt. *See also* Oh, seek me not within a tomb. MaRV.
Seek not, for thou shalt not find it, what my end, what thine shall be. To Leuconöe [*or* Mistrust To-Morrow]. Horace, *tr. by* Charles Stuart Calverley. Odes, I, ii. LoBV; OnPM
Seek not, Leuconöe, to know how long you're going to live yet. To Leuconöe. Horace, *tr. by* Eugene Field. AA; ALV
Seek not the tree of silkiest bark. Song. Aubrey Thomas De Vere. JKCP; OBVV; PoVP; VA
Seek not to know Love's full extent. The Ghost. W. H. Davies. BrPo
Seek not to know (the ghost replied with tears). Marcellus. Vergil, *tr. by* Dryden. *Fr.* The Aeneid, VI. OBS
Seek otherwhere for happiness? Answer. Harriet Hoock. WHL
Seek out reality, leave things that seem. W. B. Yeats. *Fr.* Vacillation. MBW-2
Seek the Lord. Thomas Campion. OxBoCh
Seek true religion. Oh, where? Mirreus. Truth. John Donne. *Fr.* Satires, III. SeCePo
Seek up and down, both fair and brown. Kate o' Belashanny. William Allingham. IrPN
Seek ye the Lord while he may be found. For Ye Shall Go out with Joy. Isaiah, Bible, *O.T.* TreFT
Seeke not to know my love, for shee. Song: To One That Desired to Know My Mistris. Thomas Carew. AnAnS-2; SeCP
Seeker, The. Lascelles Abercrombie. *Fr.* The Fool's Adventure. WGRP
Seeker after God, The. Harry Kemp. OQP
Seeker in the Marshes, The. Daniel Lewis Dawson. AA
Seeker in the Night, A. Florence Earle Coates. TrPWD
Seekers, The. Lucia Trevitt Auryansen. OQP
Seekers, The. John Masefield. BoPe; HBV; MaRV; OQP; WGRP
Seekers, The. Charles Hamilton Sorley. WGRP
Seekers, The. Victor Starbuck. MaRV; WGRP
Seeking. Mary Carolyn Davies. OQP
(Feet.) WGRP
Seeking and Finding God. John C. Earle. MaRV
Seeking God. Edward Dowden. MaRV; WGRP
Seeking Narcissus in my weariness. The Divine Narcissus. Sister Juana Inéz de la Cruz. CAW
Seeking the topic like a much needed bottle. O Please Read Backwards. Tyner White. YAP
Seele im Raum. Randall Jarrell. CoBMV; FiMAP
Seeming as though. Late Show. Issa. RePo
Seemingly as other men, yet always. Momist. Amy Groesbeck. GoYe
Seemingly lovely mourning dove is but a churl, The. Mourning Dove. Clinch Calkins. MeWo
Seemingly more/ Whistle than boy. Whistling Boy. John Robert Quinn. BiCB
Seems lak [*or* like] to me de stars don't shine so bright. Sence You Went Away. James Weldon Johnson. BALP; BANP; PoNe
Seems like We Must Be Somewhere Else. Denise Levertov. NePoEA-2
Seems not our breathing light? Renunciants. Edward Dowden. OBVV; VA
Seen from the Train. C. Day Lewis. BoC
Seen from these cliffs the sea circles slowly. Zennor. Anne Ridler. MoVE
Seen in a Glass. Kathleen Raine. ChMP
Seen my lady home las' night. A Negro Love Song. Paul Laurence Dunbar. BANP; PoNe
Seen on the sea, no sign; no sign, no sign. The Dead Wingman. Randall Jarrell. MiAP
Seen you down at chu'ch las' night. Discovered. Paul Laurence Dunbar. MAP; MoAmPo (1942 ed.)
Seene? and yet hated thee? they did not see. But Now They Have Seen, and Hated. Richard Crashaw. MaMe
Seer, The. Lewis Turco. FiSC
Seers have no monopoly. Communal. Mary Fullerton. PoAu-1
Sees not my love how time resumes. To a Lady in a Garden. Edmund Waller. NCEP
Seesaw. *See also* See saw.
Seesaw. Gerardo Diego, *tr. fr. Spanish by* Eleanor L. Turnbull. LiTW

Seesaw, The. Oscar Williams. LiTA; LiTG
See-Saw, Margery Daw. Mother Goose. SoPo
See'st Not My Love. William Bosworth. *Fr.* The Chaste and Lost Lovers. SeCL
Seest thou how gayly my young master goes. Joseph Hall. *Fr.* Virgidemiarum. SiCE
Seest thou, my friend, with envious eye. Martial Rage. Horace. OnPM
See'st thou not in clearest dayes. Philarete Praises Poetry. George Wither. *Fr.* The Shepherd's Hunting. OBS
Seest thou not nann to day my pretty nanny. *Unknown.* SeCSL
"See'st thou o'er my shoulders falling." Love Song. Judah Halevi. TrJP
Seest thou those dyamonds which she weares. *Unknown.* SeCSL
Seest thou yon woodland child. Gardening. John Keble. OTPC (1923 ed.)
Segovia and Madrid. Rose Terry Cooke. AA
Seguidilla. José de Valdivielso, *tr. fr. Spanish by* Thomas Walsh. CAW
Sehnsucht. Arthur Hugh Clough. EPN
Sehnsucht. Anna Wickham. MoBrPo
Sehnsucht; or, What You Will. "Corinna." FiBHP; InMe
Seicheprey. *Unknown.* PAH
Seil o' yer face! the send has come. The Fleggit Bride. "Hugh MacDiarmid." OxBS
Seismograph. A. M. Sullivan. JKCP (1955 ed.)
Seize, O seize the sounding lyre. The Hero of Bridgewater. Charles L. S. Jones. PAH
Seldom "can't." Christina Rossetti. *Fr.* Sing-Song. SAS
(Good Advice.) PPL
(Rules of Behavior.) HBV; HBVY
"Seldom we find," says Solomon Don Dunce. An Enigma. Poe. Sonn
Select Passages from a Coming Poet. "F. Anstey." BOHV
Selector's Wife, The. Mary Fullerton. MoAuPo
Selestial apoley which didest inspire. Odd to a Krokis. *Unknown.* NA
Self, The. *Unknown, tr. fr. Sanskrit by* Joseph Nadin Rawson. *Fr.* The Upanishads. OnPM
Self-Analysis. Anna Wickham. MoBrPo; TrGrPo (1942 ed.)
Self and the Weather, The. Reed Whittemore. NMP
Self[e] Banished, The. Edmund Waller. CavP; FaBoEn; MePo; OBS; SeEP
Self-composed Epitaph on a Doctor by the Name of I. Letsome. John Coakley Lettsom. *See* On Dr. Isaac Letsome.
Self-Condemnation. George Herbert. MaMe
Self-Control. Polly Chase Boyden. GoBP
Self-Criticism in February. Robinson Jeffers. AmPP
Self-Deception. Matthew Arnold. MaVP; MBW-2; PoVP
Self-Defense. Santob de Carrion, *tr. fr. Spanish by* George Ticknor. TrJP
Self-Dependence. Matthew Arnold. BBV; BEL; EnLi-2; EnLit; EPN; HBV; MaVP; MBW-2; MCCG; OAEP; OQP; Po; PoIE; PoVP; TreFS; ViPP; WGRP
Self-Discipline. "Æ." MoBrPo; VA
Self-Examination. *Unknown.* SoP
Self-exiled, The. Walter C. Smith. VA
Self, I want you now to be. The Thing Is Violent. Gwendolyn MacEwen. MoCV; PeCV (1967 ed.)
Self-Knowledge. Samuel Taylor Coleridge. ERoP-1; SeCePo
Self-Love. Shams Tabrez, *tr. fr. Persian by* Puran Singh. OnPM
Self-Love (which never rightly understood). Tyrannic Love: Prologue. Dryden. OAEP; ViBoPo
Self-made hero, marked by virtue man, The. Conversation in Clichés. James Edward Tobin. JKCP (1955 ed.)
Self-Mastery. Bayard Taylor. MaRV
Self-pleasing souls that play with beauty's bait. Robert Southwell. LO
Self-Portrait. William Cowper. *See* Stricken Deer, The.
Self Portrait. Edward Lear. *See* How Pleasant to Know Mr. Lear.
Self-Portrait. Moses Mendelssohn, *tr. fr. German.* TrJP
Self-Portrait. Robert Pack. CoPo
Self Portrait. Robert Louis Stevenson. CBV
Self-Portrait, as a Bear. Donald Hall. TPM
Self-Portrait, from Another Direction. Philip Whalen. FRC
Self-Portrait of the Laureate of Nonsense. Edward Lear. *See* How Pleasant to Know Mr. Lear.
Self-praise is a wonderful thing! The Unawkward Singers. David Ferry. NePoAm-2
Self-Reliance. Emily Dickinson. *See* We never know how high we are.
Self-reverence, self-knowledge, self-control. The Way to Power. Tennyson. *Fr.* Oenone. MaRV; OQP
Self-Righteousness. John Byrom. MaRV
Self-Sacrifice. Harry Graham. Some Ruthless Rhymes, IV. BBGG
Self-Slaved, The. Patrick Kavanagh. MoBrPo (1962 ed.)
Self Unsatisfied Runs Everywhere, The. Delmore Schwartz. FiMAP
Self-unseeing, The. Thomas Hardy. FaBoEn; GTBS-D; MoBrPo; MoPW; NoP; OBNC; PoeP; ViPP; VP
Selfe Accuser, A. John Donne. MaMe
Selfe Banished, The. Edmund Waller. *See* Self Banished, The.
Selfe Love. John Donne. MaMe
Selfe-pitties teares, wherein my hope lyes drown'd. Caelica, VIII. Fulke Greville. AtBAP
Selfishness. Margaret E. Bruner. MaRV;PoToHe
Selfsame Song, The. Thomas Hardy. CMoP; TOP
Selfsame song, The? I'm far south from the dale. For Keats and the Florentine Night. Gerta Kennedy. NYTB
Selfsame toothless voice for death or bridal, The. Bell Speech. Richard Wilbur. AP; CABA; MoAB; MoAmPo (1962 ed.); MoVE
Selindra, *sel.* Sir William Killigrew.
Beauty Paramount. SeCL
"Sell all thou hast and give it to the poor." A Certain Rich Man. Theodore Maynard. OQP
Selves of myself, these waning days. Out of November; Speaking for One. David McCord. MAP
Semblables, The. William Carlos Williams. AP
Semen. Coleman Barks. PV
Semi-private. Mabel MacDonald Carver. FiSC
Semi-Revolution, A. Robert Frost. LiTM; SiTL
Seminary. Constance Carrier. NePoAm
Semmes in the Garden ("Semmes waited under the still trees."). George Marion O'Donnell. NYBP
Sempronius,/ Sends greeting, warden of this Roman shore. A Roman Officer Writes Home. C. M. Doughty. *Fr.* The Dawn in Britain. FaBoTw
Sempronius, why, why wilt thou urge the fate. Addison. *Fr.* Cato, III, v. PoFr
Sen throw virtue increases dignitie. Good Counsel. James I, King of Scotland. ACP
Sence You Went Away. James Weldon Johnson. BALP; BANP; PoNe
Senchi Ferry; Gold Coast. Laurence D. Lerner. BoSA
Send Antipatra naked to meet the Parthian cavalry. Secret Weapon. Ammonides. LiTW
Send Back My Heart. Sir John Suckling. *See* I Prithee Send Me Back My Heart.
Send but a song oversea for us. To Walt Whitman in America. Swinburne. BEL; EnLi-2; EnLit; EPN; InP; PoVP; ViPo; ViPP
Send down thy truth, O God! For the Gifts of the Spirit. Edward Rowland Sill. TrPWD
Send Forth, O God, Thy Light and Truth. John Quincy Adams. MaRV; SoP
Send Forth the High Falcon. Léonie Adams. InPo; NP
Send Her a Valentine. Edgar A. Guest. ATP (1935 ed.)
Send Her On Along. *Unknown.* IHA
Send home my long-strayed [*or* stray'd] eyes to me. The Message. John Donne. ATP (1935 ed.); ElL; EnLit; GTBS-W; HBV; LiTG; MaMe; MBW-1; MeLP; OBS; PoeP; SCEP-1; TuPP; ViBoPo; WHA; YAT
Send Me. Christina Rossetti. FaChP; MaRV; SoP; TRV
Send Me. *Unknown.* MaRV
Send me no flowers, for they will die before they leave America. Junglegrave. S. E. Anderson. WSL
Send me O' Allah as a. An Angels Prayer. Lefty Sims. BF
Send me some token, that my hope may live. Sonnet: The Token. John Donne. MaMe
Send-off, The. Wilfred Owen. BrPo; LiTB; MoAB; MoBrPo (1950 ed.); MoVE
Send soldiers again to kill you, Garcia. Lines to Garcia Lorca. LeRoi Jones. NNP
Sending of the Magi, The. Bliss Carman. ChrBoLe
Senec. Traged. ex Thyeste Chor. 2. Seneca, *See* Chorus: "Climb

Senec (continued)
at Court for me that will." *tr. by* Andrew Marvell.
Seneca. Thomas Merton. CoPo
Seneca Lake. James Gates Percival. *See* To Seneca Lake.
Senex. John Betjeman. CBV; DTC
Senex to Matt. Prior. James Kenneth Stephen. *Fr.* Two Epigrams. BOHV; CenHV; FiBHP; WhC
Senlin, a Biography, *sels.* Conrad Aiken.
Evening Song of Senlin II, ix. HBMV
("It is evening, Senlin says, and in the evening.") LOW
Morning Song of Senlin, II, ii. AmP; CMoP; HBMV; InP; LiTA; LiTM; MAP; MoAB; MoAmPo; NeMA; NP; OxBA; PoMa; ReMP; TrGrPo; WoL
Sennacherib. Byron. *See* Destruction of Sennacherib, The.
Señora, it is true the Greeks are dead. Invocation to the Social Muse. Archibald MacLeish. LiTM; NAMP
Sensation. Arthur Rimbaud, *tr. fr. French by* Jethro Bithell. AWP; JAWP; WBP
—— *Tr. by* John Gray. SyP
—— *Tr. by* T. Sturge Moore. SyP
Sense and Spirit. George Meredith. EPN; PoVP; WGRP
Sense of an earnest will, A. Small Things. Richard Monckton Milnes. NeHB
Sense of Comedy, The: I. Jay Wright. ThO
Sense of danger must not disappear, The. Leap Before You Look. W. H. Auden. TPM
Sense of Death, The. Helen Hoyt. HBMV
(Since I Have Felt the Sense of Death.) LiTM (1946 ed.); NP
Sense of disguise is a, The. Follow That Stagecoach. Diane Wakoski. YAP
Sense of Humor, A. Vachel Lindsay. *Fr.* Poems about the Moon. MAPA; TwAmPo
Sense of Responsibility, The. Harry Mathews. ANYP
Sense of Smell, The. Louis MacNeice. NYBP
Sense of the Sleight-of-Hand Man, The. Wallace Stevens. AP; BWP; CABA; CoBMV; LiTM (rev. ed.); MoAB; MoAmPo (1950 ed.); MoPo; TwCP
Sense of the world is short, The. Eros. Emerson. AnNe; FaBoBe; HBV
Sense with keenest edge unused. Pater Filio. Robert Bridges. CMoP; OBEV; OBVV; PoVP; ViBoPo
Senseless school, where we must give, A. A Young Man's Epigram on Existence. Thomas Hardy. BrPo
Senses Festival, The. John Cleveland. *See* To the State of Love; or, The Senses Festival.
Senses loving Earth, or well or ill, The. Sense and Spirit. George Meredith. EPN; PoVP; WGRP
Sensible Is the Label. Eldon Grier. MoCV
Sensible Miner, The, *with music.* John A. Stone. SGR
Sensitive Plant, The. Shelley. EnRP; ERoP-2; GoTL
(Garden, A, *abr.*) OTPC
"In this life/ of error, ignorance, and strife," *fr.* Conclusion. LO
Sensitive Sydney. Wallace Irwin. FiBHP
Sensitiveness. Cardinal Newman. PoVP
(Yielded.) SoP
"Sensual will have its moment, The? The brain." Elder Tree. Conrad Aiken. AP
Sensualists, The. Theodore Roethke. ErPo; NePoAm-2; PoeP
(Sensualist, The.) UnTE
Sensuality. Coventry Patmore. *Fr.* The Angel in the House, I, xi, 2. OBVV
Sensuality. Kenneth Slessor. NeLNL
Sent Ahead. John Hay. NePoAm
Sent as a present from Annam. The Red Cockatoo. Po Chü-i. ChTr; LiTW; MoPW; OA; OuHeWo
Sent from Egypt with a Fair Robe of Tissue to a Sicilian Vinedresser. T. Sturge Moore. OBEV (new ed.); OBVV
Sent with a Rose to a Young Lady. Margaret Deland. AA
Sentence. Witter Bynner. HBV
Sentence undulates, The. The End of the Parade. William Carlos Williams. NYBP
Sentencing goes blithely on its way, The. In a Poem. Robert Frost. PoeP; PP
Sententious Man, The. Theodore Roethke. NoP
Sentimental Bloke, The, *sel.* C. J. Dennis.
Play, The. PoAu-1
Sentimental Colloquy. Paul Verlaine. *See* Colloque sentimental.
Sentimental Conversation. Paul Verlaine. *See* Colloque sentimental.
Sentimental Journey. "Elspeth." WhC
Sentimental Lines to a Young Man Who Favors Pink Wallpaper, While I Personally Lean to the Blue. Margaret Fishback. FiBHP
Sentimental Monologue. John Hall Wheelock. NYTB
Sentimentalist sends his mauve balloon, The. The Celebration in the Plaza. Adrienne Cecile Rich. NePoEA; TwAmPo
Sentinel, The. *Unknown.* BLRP; MaRV; OQP
Sentinel angel, A, sitting high in glory. A Woman's Love. John Hay. HBV
Sentinel Songs. Abram J. Ryan. DD, *abr.*; HBV
Sentry, The. Alun Lewis. DTC
Sentry, The. Wilfred Owen. AnEnPo; MMA
Separate Parties. Dabney Stuart. NYBP
Separate Peace. Harrison S. Morris. MC
Separate place between the thought and felt, A. The Corridor. Thom Gunn. NePoEA; ToPo
Separately I still recall. Portrait. Adèle Naudé. PeSA
Separation. Matthew Arnold. HBV; VP
Separation. Martha Dickinson Bianchi. AA
Separation. Alice Learned Bunner. Vingtaine, I. AA
Separation, A. William Johnson Cory. OBNC
Separation. Empress Kogyoku, *tr. fr. Japanese by* Ishii *and* Obata. OnPM
Separation. Walter Savage Landor. OBEV (1st ed.); TOP
Separation. W. S. Merwin. AmPC
Separation. D. S. Savage. NeBP
Separation, A. Stephen Spender. MoLP
Separation. John L. Sweeney. TwAmPo
Separation Deed, A. Sir Lewis Morris. OBVV
Sephestia's Song to Her Child [*or* Childe]. Robert Greene. *Fr.* Menaphon. AtBAP; CoBE; ELP; EnLi-1 (1949 ed.); EnLit; EnRePo; GTSL; LoBV; PoEL-2; PoIE; ReEn; ReIE; SiCE; TrGrPo; TuPP
(Sephestia's Lullaby.) HBV; OBEV
(Sephestia's Song.) OBSC
(Weep Not My Wanton.) CBEP; ElL; SeCePo; ViBoPo
Sept ans sur mer, *with music.* *Unknown.* OuSiCo
Septem contra Thebas. Aeschylus. *See* Seven against Thebes.
September. George Arnold. DD; HBV
September. Gabriele D'Annunzio, *tr. fr. Italian by* Glauco Cambon. OnPM
September. Edwina Fallis. SUS; TiPo; YeAr
September. Folgore da San Geminiano, *tr. fr. Italian by* Dante Gabriel Rossetti. *Fr.* Sonnets of the Months. AWP; SD
September. S. Frances Harrison. VA
September. Mary Howitt. BoTP; OTPC (1923 ed.)
September. Ted Hughes. SiSw
September. Helen Hunt Jackson. BoChLi; FaPON; GoJo; GoTP; MPB; OTD; PEDC; OTPC (1946 ed.); PoLF; PoRL; PRWS; TiPo (1959 ed.)
(September Days Are Here.) YeAr
September. Archibald Lampman. PeCV
September. Robert Lowell, *ad. fr. the Russian of* Boris Pasternak. NaP
September. Dorothy Frances McCrae. BoAu
September. Katharine Pyle. PCH
September. Edward Bliss Reed. DD; HBMV; HBVY; MPB
(September Is Here.) YeAr
September. Thomas Tusser. ReIE
September Afternoon. Margaret Haley Carpenter. GoYe
September Days Are Here. Helen Hunt Jackson. *See* September.
September, 1802; Near Dover. Wordsworth. *See* Near Dover, September, 1802.
September Evening, 1938. William Plomer. SeCePo
September evenings such as these. Watching the Moon. David McCord. RePo; YeAr
September 1, 1939. W. H. Auden. CMoP; CoBMV; ExPo; ForPo; InPo; LiTA; LiTM; MaPo; MasP; MoAB; MoBrPo (1950 ed.); MoVE; NePA; OAEP (2d ed.); OxBA; PIA; PoFS; ReMP; SeCeV; WaP
(1st September 1939.) FaBoEn
September Gale, The. Oliver Wendell Holmes.
"It chanced to be our washing day," *sel.* FiBHP
September in Australia. Henry C. Kendall. BoAu; OBVV; PoAu-1; VA
September in the Park. W. D. Snodgrass. ToPo
September Is Here. Edward Bliss Reed. *See* September.
September! Let us go, it's time to wander. September. Gabriele D'Annunzio. OnPM

Sept. 1957. Edward Marshall. CoPo
September 1, 1965. Paris Leary. CoPo
September, 1913. W. B. Yeats. BrPo; CMoP; CoBMV; GTBS-P; MoPW; PoIE; PoRA
September six o'clock. Sea Pieces. Robert Fitzgerald. PoPl
September sky expands, The. Death of a Hornet. D. G. Jones. PeCV
September Sun: 1947. David Gascoyne. AtBAP; FaBoMo; POTE (1959 ed.)
September twenty-second, Sir: today. After the Surprising Conversions. Robert Lowell. AmPP (5th ed.); AP; CABA; CoBMV; FiMAP; NePoEA; NoP; PIA; PoAn; PoeP; SeCeV
September was when it began. The Coming of the Plague. Weldon Kees. NaP
Sepulcher, The. Annie Johnson Flint. STF
Sepulcher in the Garden, The. John Finley. ChIP
Sepulchral Imprecation. Crinagoras, *tr. fr. Greek by* Dudley Fitts. LiTW
Sepulchre. George Herbert. AnAnS-1; MaMe; MeP; SCEP-1
Sequaire. Godeschalk, *tr. fr. Latin by* Ezra Pound. CTC
Sequel, The. Theodore Roethke. NYBP
Sequel, The. Delmore Schwartz. LiTM (1970 ed.)
Sequel to Finality. Patrick F. Kirby. GoBC; MaRV
Sequelula to "The Dynasts," A. Max Beerbohm. Par
Sequence. Edgar Daniel Kramer. BLRP
Sequence of Sonnets on the Death of Robert Browning, A, *sel.* Swinburne.
(On the Death of Robert Browning.) EnLit; EPN; PoVP
Sequence, with Strophes in Paraphrase Thereof, A. Francis Burke. CAW
Seraglio of the Sultan Bee! A Hollyhock. Frank Dempster Sherman. AA
Seraph and the Snob, The. May Kendall. CenHV
Seraph of Heaven. Shelley. *Fr.* Epipsychidion. ISi
Seraphion. James K. Baxter. AnNZ
Seraphs' Song, The. Matthew Bridges. SoP
Serenade, A: "Ah! County Guy, the hour is nigh." Sir Walter Scott. *See* County Guy.
Serenade: "Ah, sweet, thou little knowest how." Thomas Hood. HBV
Serenade: "Awake thee, my Lady-love." George Darley. *See* Morning-Song.
Serenade: "Blue waves are sleeping, The." Jeremiah Joseph Callanan. IrPN, *abr.*; OnYI
Serenade: "By day my timid passions stand." Richard Middleton. HBV
Serenade: "Come now, let us wake them; time." *Unknown, tr. fr. German by* Jethro Bithell. AWP; JAWP; WBP
Serenade: "Come on, don't be afraid you'll spoil me." Emanuel Carnevali. AnAmPo
Serenade: "Hide, happy damask, from the stars." Henry Timrod. HBV
Serenade: "High in the dark the moon rides white." Paul Fearon. CIV
Serenade: "I'm a gay tra, la, la." Bret Harte. LBN
(Swiss Air.) NA
Serenade, A: "Look out upon the stars, my love." Edward Coote Pinkney. AA; AmLP; AnFE; APA; CoAnAm; HBV
Serenade: "O beautiful Amaryllis." Theocritus. *See* Rustic Serenade.
Serenade: "Softly, O midnight hours!" Aubrey Thomas De Vere. HBV; OBEV
(Song: "Softly. . .") IrPN
Serenade: "Sometimes you seem a star." John Bunker. JKCP (1955 ed.)
Serenade: "Stars of the summer night!" Longfellow. *Fr.* The Spanish Student, I, iii. AA; AmPP (3d ed.); FaBoBe; HBV; LoBV; NeHB; OnPM; OuHeWo; PFY; PTK; ViBoPo
(Stars of the Summer Night.) MemP
Serenade, The: "This age-old church." Sister Mary Madeleva. Christmas in Provence, I. WHL
Serenade: "Western wind is blowing fair, The." Oscar Wilde. HBV
Serenade: "When maidens are young, and in their spring." Aphra Behn. *Fr.* The Emperor of the Moon. SeCL
Serenade: "While my lady sleepeth." John Gibson Lockhart. OBRV
Serenade of a Loyal Martyr. George Darley. *See* Song: "Sweet in her green dell. . ."
Serenade, to Two Ladies. Thomas Porter. *Fr.* The Villain. SeCL
Serenader. George Dillon. NP
Serendipity of Love, A. Richard Aldridge. NePoAm-2
Serene, cool and composed, and easygoing. "One in a Thousand of Years of the Nights." Delmore Schwartz. FiMAP
Serene, I fold my hands and wait. Waiting. John Burroughs. AA; AmePo; AnAmPo; AnFE; APA; BLPA; CoAnAm; DD; FaBoBe; FaPL; HBV; MaRV; NeHB; OHFP; OQP; PTK; TreF; TRV; WGRP
Serene Immediate Silliest and Whose. E. E. Cummings. MoVE
Serene, not as a prize for conflict won. On a Portrait of Mme. Rimsky-Korsakov. Kingsley Amis. MuSP; NePoEA-2
Serene the silver fishes glide. At the Aquarium. Max Eastman. AnAmPo; FaPON; HBMV; OTPC (1946 ed.); PoMa; PoPo; StaSt; WGRP
Serene, vast head, with silver cloud of hair. A Tribute of Grasses. Hamlin Garland. AnAmPo
Serenity of Faith, The. Psalms, XXVII, Bible, *O.T.* *See* My Light and My Salvation.
Serf, The. Roy Campbell. BoSA; CBV; GTBS-P; LiTB; LiTM; MoBrPo; NAMP; OBMV; ReMP; TrGrPo (1942 ed.)
Serf's Secret, The. William Vaughn Moody. HBV
Sergeant Champe. *Unknown.* PAH
Sergeant, He Is the Worst of All, The, *with music.* *Unknown.* AS
Sergeant-Major Money. Robert Graves. MMA
Sgt. stands so fluently in leather, The. On a Photo of Sgt. Ciardi a Year Later. John Ciardi. MiAP
Sergeant, the sergeant he is the worst of all, The. The Sergeant, He Is the Worst of All. *Unknown.* AS
Sergeant's Prayer, A. Hugh R. Brodie. *See* Airman's Prayer, An.
Sergey Yesenin Speaking Isadora Duncan. William Knott. YAP
Series 5.8, A. John Wieners. CoPo
Serio-Comic Elegy, A. Richard Whately. ShM
Serious and a Curious Night-Meditation, A. Thomas Traherne. SeCP
Serious Danger, A. R. A. Davenport. PV
Serious Omission. John Farrar. RIS; UTS
Serious over my cereals I broke one breakfast my fast. Breakfast with Gerard Manley Hopkins. Anthony Brode. FiBHP; Par
Serious Poem, A. Ernest Walsh. ErPo
Serious Question, A. Carolyn Wells. CIV
Sermon. Emanuel Carnevali. NP
Sermon, The. Richard Hughes. BoC; OBMV
Sermon. Bernadette Mayer. ANYP
Sermon, A. Lady Margaret Sackville. HBMV
Sermon educates, The. Sermon. Bernadette Mayer. ANYP
Sermon in a Churchyard. Macaulay. OBRV
Sermon in a Stocking. Ellen A. Jewett. BLPA
Sermon in the Hospital, The, *sel.* Harriet Eleanor Hamilton King.
"But yet one thought has often stayed by me." BoC
Sermon on the Mount, The. St. Matthew, V:1-VII:29, Bible, N.T. OuHeWo; TreF; WoL
Sels.
"And seeing the multitudes, he went up into a mountain," V: 1-48. RelE
Beatitudes, The, V: 3-10. TrGrPo
Blessed Are the Poor in Spirit, V. ExPo (3-12); GoTP (3-10)
Lord's Prayer, The, VI: 9-13. TrGrPo
Treasures, VI: 19-21. TrGrPo
Sermon on the Warpland, The. Gwendolyn Brooks. LiTM (1970 ed.)
Sermon to the Birds. St. Francis of Assisi, *tr. fr. Italian by* Thomas W. Arnold. TreF
Sermon to the Rebels at Blackheath. John Ball. PoFr
Sermon without Words. Elizabeth Patton Moss. MaRV
Sermonette. Ishmael Reed. WOW
Sermons We See. Edgar A. Guest. MaRV
(How Do You Live?) STF
(Living Sermon, The.) SoP
Serpent is shut out from paradise, The. Stanzas to Edward Williams [*or* To Edward Williams]. Shelley. OBNC; PeER
Serpent of God, The. Cerise Farallon. UnTE
Serpent Waits, The. Joseph Payne Brennan. FiSC

Serpent with a voyce, so slie and fine, The. Samuel Gorton. SCAP
Serpents exploded, open balconies. Morvin. John Fuller. NePoEA-2
Serpent's Nature, The. *Unknown, tr. fr. Middle English. Fr.* The Bestiary. MeEV
Serried hosts stood man to man, The. The Oranges. Abu Dharr. TTY
Servant, A. Kipling. *Fr.* Epitaphs of the War. PoVP
Servant. R. S. Thomas. POTi
Servant Girl and Grocer's Boy. Joyce Kilmer. LHV; YaD
Servant of Christ, stand fast amid the scorn. The Servant's Path. *Unknown.* SoP
Servant of God, well done! Well Done. James Montgomery. MaRV
Servant of the eternal Must. Pagan Epitaph. Richard Middleton. OBVV; TOP
Servant of the Nymphs, who loves the showers, The. The Bronze Frog. *Unknown.* OnPM
Servant to Servants, A. Robert Frost. BWP; CMoP
Servants, The. Richard Wightman. WGRP
Servants of the Great Adventure. Percy Dearmer. MaRV
Servant's Path, The. *Unknown.* SoP
Servants then (commanded) soone obaid, The. Nausicaa. Homer, *tr. by* George Chapman. *Fr.* The Odyssey, VI. OBS
Serve in Thy Post. Arthur Hugh Clough. *Fr.* Last Words; Napoleon and Wellington. PGD
Service. Sybil Leonard Armes. FaChP
Service. Robert Browning. *See* All Service Ranks the Same with God.
Service. Washington Gladden. *See* O Master, Let Me Walk with Thee.
Service. Hermann Hagedorn. OQP
Service, The. Burges Johnson. HBMV; StaSt
Service. Georgia Douglas Johnson. CDC
Service. Ellen H. Underwood. *See* I Shall Not Pass Again This Way.
Service. *Unknown.* SoP
Service Flag, The. William Herschell. PEDC
Service is joy, to see or swing. Tennis. Margaret Avison. PeCV
Service Is No Heritage. *Unknown.* CBEP
"Service Man, The." Kipling. Par
Service of All the Dead. D. H. Lawrence. NP
Service of the Lutherans, The. Feodor Tyutchev, *tr. fr. Russian by* Babette Deutsch. OnPM
Service, or Latin *sorbus,* European. The Life of Service. Donald Davie. NYBP
Service Supreme. *Unknown.* *See* Little Fellow Follows Me, A.
Serving Girl, The. Gladys May Casely Hayford (Aquah Laluah). CDC; GoSl; PoNe
Serving Men's Song, A. John Lyly. *Fr.* Alexander and Campaspe, I, iii. *Also in* A Mad World, My Masters (*by* Thomas Middleton). ALV; OBSC
(O for a Bowl of Fat Canary.) NoP; OnPM; ViBoPo
Sesostris. Lloyd Mifflin. AA; HBV
Session[s] of the Poets, A ("A session was held the other day."). Sir John Suckling. AnAnS-2; NCEP; SCEP-2; SeCV-1
Session with Uncle Sidney, A, *sel.* James Whitcomb Riley. It. PDV
Sessions of Sweet Silent Thought. Shakespeare. *See* Sonnets, XXX.
Sestina. James K. Baxter. Cressida, XV. AnNZ
Sestina. Richard Eberhart. FiMAP; TDP
Sestina. Sir Edmund Gosse. InP
Sestina. Donald Hall. NePoEA
Sestina. Donald Justice. *See* Dream Sestina, A.
Sestina. Sir Philip Sidney. *See* Double Sestine.
Sestina; Altaforte. Ezra Pound. AmP; CaFP; CMoP; CoBMV; FaBoTw; LiTA; LiTG; LiTM (1946 ed.); MoAB; MoAmPo (1950 ed.); PoIE; StP
Sestina for Cynthia, A. David Lougée. NePA
Sestina for Khasan Israelov. John Wain. *Fr.* Wildtrack. ToPo
Sestina in a Cantina. Malcolm Lowry. MoCV; TDP
Sestina; of the Lady Pietra degli Scrovigni. Dante, *tr. fr. Italian by* Dante Gabriel Rossetti. AWP; JAWP; SiSw; WBP
Sestina of the Tramp-Royal. Kipling. BrPo; LiTB; MoBrPo; OtMeF; PoVP; SiTL
Sestina on Her Portrait. Howard Nemerov. WaP
"Set back your watches—this is Mountain Time." Continental Crossing. Dorothy Brown Thompson. AmFN
Set Down, Servant, *with music.* *Unknown.* ABF
Set every stitch of canvas to woo the fresh'ning wind. The Slave Chase. *Unknown.* CoMu
Set forty thousand on a row. Constant Affection. *Unknown.* SeCL
"Set he that hat on his head?" Cardinal Fisher. John Heywood. ACP
Set high your head above the nameless flood. To a Survivor of the Flood. John Gould Fletcher. AnAmPo
Set in this stormy northern sea. Ave Imperatrix! Oscar Wilde. HBV; PeVV; VA
Set Love in order, thou that lovest me. Cantica: Our Lord Christ [*or* Of Order In Our Lord Christ]. *At. to* St. Francis of Assisi *and to* Jacopone da Todi. AWP; CAW; GoBC; JAWP; OnPM; WBP
Set Me as a Seal. Song of Solomon, Bible, *O.T.* *See* Love.
Set Me Where Phoebus' Heat. Petrarch, *tr. fr. Italian.* Sonnets to Laura: To Laura in Life, CXIII. TuPP
(Last Trial, The.) OBSC
Set Me Whereas the Sun Doth Parch the Green. Petrarch, *tr. by* the Earl of Surrey. *See* Vow to Love Faithfully.
Set not your heart to woo that basilisk. To a Lad Who Would Wed Himself with Music. Edward Doro. TwAmPo
Set of phrases learned [*or* learnt] by rote, A. The Furniture of a Woman's Mind. Swift. BWP; CaFP; CEP; PoIE
Set over against lust. The City. Emmett Jarrett. *Fr.* Design for the City of Man. ThO
Set silver cone to tulip flame! Inscription for a Mirror in a Deserted Dwelling. William Rose Benét. MAP; MoAmPo
Set where the upper streams of Simois flow. Palladium. Matthew Arnold. EPN; FaBoEn; GTBS-P; MaVP; NoP; OAEP; OBNC; PoVP; ViPP; VP
Set your face to the sea, fond lover. Refuge. William Winter. HBV
Seth Compton. Edgar Lee Masters. *Fr.* Spoon River Anthology. LiTA; NP
Sett to the sun, a diall that doth passe. *Unknown.* SeCSL
Settin' on de Fence. *Unknown.* WBLP
Settin' [*or* Sittin'] round the stove, last night. A Liz-Town Humorist. James Whitcomb Riley. AmePo; IHA
Setting a trotline after sundown. In the Deep Channel. William Stafford. NaP
Setting my bulbs a-row. Planting Bulbs. Katharine Tynan. JKCP
Setting Out. Jack Marshall. YAP
Setting Sun, The. George Moses Horton. BALP
Setting sun leaves the poet to the dreary night, The. Early Summer Night. Wen Yi-tuo. LiTW
Setting the Table. Dorothy Aldis. FaPON; MPB; TiPo
Settled Men, The. George M. Brady. NeIP
Settler, The. Roy Macnab. BoSA
Settler, The. Alfred Billings Street. AA; FaBoBe; MC; PAH
Settler in the olden times went forth, A. Charles Harpur. *Fr.* The Creek of the Four Graves. PoAu-1
Settlers, The. Margaret Atwood. MoCV
Settlers, The. Laurence Housman. HBV; OBVV
Settler's Lament, The. *Unknown.* PoAu-1
Settling Some Old Football Scores. Morris Bishop. SD
Seumas Beg. James Stephens. EvOK; FaPON; GaP; RoGo; TSW
Seurat. James Schevill. FiMAP
Seurat looked well to see these people. La Grande Jatte; Sunday Afternoon. Thomas Cole. NePoAm
Seven against Thebes, The, *sel.* Aeschylus, *tr. fr. Greek by* A. E. Housman.
Lament for the Two Brothers Slain by Each Other's Hand. AWP; JAWP; WBP
Seven Ages of Elf-Hood, The. Rachel Field. BiCB
Seven Ages of Man, The. Shakespeare. *See* All the World's a Stage.
Seven are the lights that wander in the skies. Licia, XXV. Giles Fletcher. ReEn; ReIE; SiCE; TuPP
Seven around the moon go up. The Pinwheel's Song. John Ciardi. PDV
Seven cities warred for Homer, being dead. On Homer's Birthplace. Thomas Heywood. ML

Seven Cuban/ army officers. Pornographic Poem. John Giorno. ANYP
Seven daughters had Lord Archibald. The Seven Sisters; or, The Solitude of Binnorie. Wordsworth. OTPC
Seven days he travelled. The Crowning of Dreaming John. John Drinkwater. HBMV
Seven Days of the Sun, The, *sels.* W. J. Turner.
"I had watched the ascension and decline of the moon." OBMV
"Spirits walking everywhere." BoPe
Seven Deadly Sins, The. Stephen Hawes. *Fr.* The Pastime of Pleasure. PoEL-1
Seven dog-days we let pass. Queens. J. M. Synge. ChTr; MoBrPo; OBMV; OnYI; PeVV
Seven Evils. Proverbs, VI:16-19, Bible, *O.T.* TrGrPo
(Sower of Discord, A, *Moulton, Modern Reader's Bible.*) MaRV
Seven Fiddlers, The. Sebastian Evans. OnMSP; PoMS; RIS
Seven Grecian cities vied for Homer dead. The Poet in Life and Death. *Unknown.* OnPM
Seven hundred and a half of years. The Old Woman Remembers. Lady Gregory. OnYI
Seven invasions, seven dynasties. Morocco. R. N. Currey. BoSA
Seven lang years I hae served the king. The Whummil Bore. *Unknown.* CH; ESPB
Seven Little Pigs. *Unknown.* BoTP
Seven Long Years in State Prison, *with music.* *Unknown.* AS
Seven lovely poplars. Poplars. Helen Leuty. BoTP
Seven Metal Mountains, The. Book of Enoch, LII: 6-9, Bible, Pseudepigrapha. TrJP
Seven notes of grief. Motif for Mary's Dolors. Sister Mary Madeleva. ISi
Seven of the Clock. Roy Macnab. PeSA
Seven Penitential Psalms, *sel.* Petrarch, *tr. fr. Italian by* George Chapman.
To Young Imaginaries in Knowledge. ReEn
Seven Pictures from China, *sels.* James Kirkup.
Autumn Grove after Rain, by Wen Tien. POTi
Landscape, by Ch'êng Sui. BoPe; POTi
Seven Sad Sonnets. Mary Aldis. HBMV
Seven Sisters, The; or, The Solitude of Binnorie. Wordsworth. OTPC
Seven Sleepers, The. Sir Herbert Read. FaBoMo; SeCePo
Seven Sleepers, The, *with music.* *Unknown.* *See* Douglas Tragedy, The.
Seven Sonnets, *sel.* Arthur Hugh Clough.
"But whether in the uncoloured light of truth," IV. ViPP
Seven South African Poems. David Wright. BoSA
Sels
"Each time I return to Johannesburg it is summer." ACV
"My countryman, the poet, wears a Stetson." PeSA
"My grandfather was an elegant gentleman." PeSA
Seven Spiritual Ages of Mrs. Marmaduke Moore, The. Ogden Nash. MoAmPo (1950 ed.)
Seven Stanzas at Easter. John Updike. EaLo
Seven stars in the still water. The Dole of the King's Daughter. *Unknown.* AWP
Seven sweet singing birds up in a tree. The Dream of a Girl [*or* Little Girl] Who Lived at Seven Oaks. William Brighty Rands. GaP; OTPC; PPL; RIS
Seven Themes from the Zoo, No.2 John Bennett. NYTB
Seven Times Five. Jean Ingelow. *Fr.* Songs of Seven. GBV (1922 ed.); HBV
Seven Times Four. Jean Ingelow. *Fr.* Songs of Seven. GBV (1922 ed.); HBV
(Heigh Ho!) BoTP
(Maternity.) OHIP
Seven times hath Janus ta'en new year by hand. A Sonnet upon the Author's First Seven Years' Service. Thomas Tusser. EIL; SiCE; TuPP
Seven Times One. Jean Ingelow. *Fr.* Songs of Seven. BiCB; BLPA; FaPON; GBV (1922 ed.); GoTP; HBV; MPB; OBNC; OTPC; PCH; PRWS; TreF; TVC
(Birthday Morning.) ThGo
Seven Times One Are Seven. Robert Hillyer. BiCB
Seven Times Seven. Jean Ingelow. *Fr.* Songs of Seven. GBV (1922 ed.); HBV
(Longing for Home.) WGRP
Seven times seven/ the beads I toll. To the Queen of Dolors. Sister Mary Maura. ISi
Seven Times Six. Jean Ingelow. *Fr.* Songs of Seven. GBV (1922 ed.); HBV
Seven times the centuple wheels of life have whirled. The Blessing of St. Francis. Sister Maura. CaP
Seven Times the Moon Came. Jessie B. Rittenhouse. HBMV
Seven Times Three. Jean Ingelow. *Fr.* Songs of Seven. GBV (1922 ed.); HBV; PoLF
Seven Times Two. Jean Ingelow. *Fr.* Songs of Seven. GBV (1922 ed.); GN; HBV; OTPC (1923 ed.)
Seven Today. Ivy O. Eastwick. BiCB
Seven Virgins, The. *Unknown.* CH, *sl. abr.*; ChTr; OBB; OBEV; OxBoCh
Seven we were, and two are gone. Two Long Vacations: Grasmere. Arthur Gray Butler. OBVV
Seven Wealthy Towns. *Unknown.* PP
(Cure for Poetry.) SiTL
Seven weeks of sea, and twice seven days of storm. Gibraltar. Wilfrid Scawen Blunt. ACP; GTSL; HBV; OBEV; OBVV; OTPC (1923 ed.); VA
Seven Whistlers, The. Alice E. Gillington. VA
Seven white peacocks against the castle wall, The. What the Orderly Dog Saw. Ford Madox Ford. CTC
Seven white roses on one tree. Seven Years Old. Swinburne. HBV
Seven Wise Men. Alfred Noyes. *Fr.* Tales of the Mermaid Tavern. InP
Seven Wonders of England, The. Sir Philip Sidney. FCP
Seven Wonders of the Ancient World, The. *Unknown.* TreFT
Seven-year-old Poet. Arthur Rimbaud, *tr. fr. French by* Norman Cameron. OnHM
Seven Years. Marquess of Crewe. OBVV
Seven Years at Sea. *Unknown.* *See* Sept ans sur mer.
Seven Years Old. Swinburne. HBV
Seven years ye shall be a stone. The Maid and the Palmer. *Unknown.* ACP; ESPB; OBS
Seventeen rosebuds in a ring. Lucy's Birthday. Thackeray. OTPC (1923 ed.)
1777, *sels.* Amy Lowell.
City of Falling Leaves, The, II. MAPA; SUS; TiPo; TwAmPo
Trumpet-Vine Arbour, The, I. MAPA; NP
Seventeen years ago, the sun so glaring. Cypress. John Peter. BoSA
Seventeen years ago you said. A Quoi Bon Dire. Charlotte Mew. HBMV
Seventh Day. Kathleen Raine. ChMP
Seventh Hell, The. Jerome Rothenberg. CoPo; NMP
Seventh Nimphall, The. Michael Drayton. *Fr.* The Muses Elizium. AnAnS-2
Seventh Property [*or* Properte], The. Sir Thomas More. *Fr.* The Twelve Properties or Conditions of a Lover. CoBE; EnRePo
Seventh Station. Paul Claudel, *tr. fr. French by* Henry M. Robinson. CAW
Seventy-five feet hoed rows equals. The Market, 2. Gary Snyder. *Fr.* Mts. & Rivers. NaP
Seventy-four and Twenty. Thomas Hardy. WhC
Seventy-six. Bryant. DD; HBV; MC; PAH
Several Questions Answered. Blake. PeER
Question Answer'd, The, *sel.* EiCL; ELU; ERoP; ErPo; ViBoPo
Several Voices Out of a Cloud. Louise Bogan. ExPo; MoVE
Severed Selves. Dante Gabriel Rossetti. The House of Life, XL. MaVP; PoVP; ViPo; VP
Severely now will we dance. Apollo Alone Approves. Mark Turbyfill. NP
Severn, The. Michael Drayton. *Fr.* The Baron's War, I. ChTr
Severus is extreme in eloquence. Samuel Rowlands. TuPP
Seville. L. D'O. Walters. HBMV
Sevin Seages, The, *sel.* John Rolland.
"In haist ga hy thee to sum hoill." OxBS
Sev'n skunks lumbering in a row. Black and White Shuffle. Harry Elmore Hurd. WhC
Sewanee Hills of dear delight. The Hills of Sewanee. George Marion McClellan. BANP
Sewing. William H. Hayne. *See* Pine Needles.
Sex is a spiritual sojourn. Love Song. Lynn Strongin. ThO
Sexes waking, now separate and sore, The. The Martyrs. Jay Macpherson. MoCV

Sexsmith the Dentist. Edgar Lee Masters. *Fr.* Spoon River Anthology. NePA
Sext. W. H. Auden. *Fr.* Horae Canonicae. PoDB
Sextains, *sels.* William Baylebridge. BoAV
Master-Foe, The.
Troubled Unquickening, The.
Sextant, The. A. M. Sullivan. GoBC
Sextant of the meetinouse, which sweeps, The. A Appeal for Are to the Sextant of the Old Brick Meetinouse. Arabella M. Willson. BOHV
Sextus the Usurer. Martial, *tr. fr. Latin by* Kirby Flower Smith. AWP
Seynt Stevyn [*or* Stevene] and Herowdes. *Unknown. See* Saint Stephen and Herod.
Sez Alderman Grady. Officer Brady. Robert W. Chambers. BOHV; InMe
Sez Corporal Madden to Private McFadden. The Recruit. Robert W. Chambers. AA; BOHV; HBV; PFY
"Sh." James S. Tippett. SUS; TiPo
Shabby fellow chanced one day to meet, A. An Actor. "Peter Pindar." BOHV
Shabby Old Dad. Anne Campbell. PoToHe (new ed.)
Shack, The. Nellie Burget Miller. PoOW
Shack Bully Holler, *with music. Unknown.* ABF
Shadbush. Christina Rainsford. GoYe
Shade. Theodosia Garrison. MaRV; OHIP
Shade. T. Harrison. SoP
Shade of His hand shall cover us, The. His Hand Shall Cover Us. Isaac ben Samuel of Dampière. TrJP
Shade once swept about your boughs, The. The Fallen Tree. Andrew Young. BoNaP
Shade, the light, the figures, the horizon as, The. October, 1942. Roy Fuller. WaP
Shaded lamp and a waving blind, A. An August Midnight. Thomas Hardy. BrPo; PoMa
Shaded Pool, The. Norman Gale. HBV; OBVV
Shades are half-drawn on classroom and hall, The. Discourse on the Real. Samuel Yellen. NePoAm
Shades of Callimachus, Coan ghosts of Philetas. Ezra Pound. *Fr.* Homage to Sextus Propertius. CMoP; MoAB; MoVE; OxBA; PP
Shades of eve had crossed the glen, The. The Pretty Girl of Loch Dan. Sir Samuel Ferguson. HBV
Shades of Night, The. A. E. Housman. ChTr; FiBHP
Shades of night were falling fast, The. Excelsior. Longfellow. AmePo; FaPON; HBV; HBVY; NeHB; OnMSP; OTPC; PaPo; PoFS; TreF; WBLP
Shadow. Guillaume Apollinaire, *tr. fr. French by* Jessie Degen *and* Richard Eberhart. WaaP
Shadow. Richard Bruce. CDC
Shadow. Mary Elizabeth Coleridge. PoVP
Shadow, The. Walter de la Mare. BoChLi (1950 ed.); CMoP
Shadow. Anthony Delius. PeSA
Shadow, The. Gail Dusenbery. ThO
Shadow, The. Ben Jonson. *See* Song: That Women Are but Men's Shadows.
Shadow. Ann Mars. GoYe
Shadow, The. Richard Henry Stoddard. AA
Shadow, The. Arthur Symons. OBVV
Shadow, A. *Unknown. See* I Heard a Noise.
Shadow, The. William Carlos Williams. NP
Shadow and Shade. Allen Tate. InPo; LiTA; TwAmPo; ViBoPo
Shadow and the Light, The, *sel.* Whittier.
"All souls that struggle and aspire." TrPWD
Shadow Boat, A. Arlo Bates. HBV
Shadow Child, The. Harriet Monroe. HBV
Shadow Dance. Ivy O. Eastwick. SoPo; TiPo
Shadow Dance, The. Louise Chandler Moulton. AA; HBV
Shadow-Evidence. Mary Mapes Dodge. AA
Shadow falls, the path I cannot trace, The. Satisfied. Samuel Valentine Cole. BLRP
Shadow gates are swinging, The. The Gates of the Year. John Mervin Hull. STF
Shadow House of Lugh, The. "Ethna Carbery." AnIV
Shadow, index of the sun. By Day and by Night. W. S. Merwin. AmPC
Shadow is floating through the moonlight, A. The Bird of Night. Randall Jarrell. BiS
Shadow, killer of doves. Shadow. Anthony Delius. PeSA
Shadow like a liquid lies. August Night. May Swenson. MoLP
Shadow-Love. Heine, *tr. fr. German by* Emma Lazarus. *Fr.* Songs to Seraphine. TrJP
Shadow of Cain, The. Edith Sitwell. CoBMV
Shadow of Darkness. Gladys May Casely Hayford (Aquah Laluah). PBA
Shadow of her profile lay stringent, The. Woman, Gallup, N.M. Karen Swenson. NYBP
Shadow of His Wings, The. Gerhardt Tersteegen, *tr. fr. German.* SoP
Shadow of Night, The. George Chapman. NCEP
Sels.
Hymnus in Noctem. PoEL-2; ReIE, *abr.*
"All you possessed with indepressed spirit." TuPP
"Great goddesse to whose throne in Cynthian fires." AtBAP
Night ("Kneel then with me"). OBSC
Shadow of Night, The. Coventry Patmore. CH
Shadow of the dwarf magnolia, The. The Magnolia's Shadow. Robert Lowell, *ad. fr. Italian of* Eugenio Montale. NaP
Shadow of the girl with the white, The. A Girl Skipping Rope in Flushing. Stephen Stepanchev. NYTB
Shadow of the little fishing launch, The. The Parrot Fish. James Merrill. NYTB
Shadow of the Night, A. Thomas Bailey Aldrich. AA
Shadow of the Rock, The. Frederick W. Faber. GoBC
Shadow on the Loom, The. Nellie Burget Miller. OQP
Shadow on the Stone, The. Thomas Hardy. QFR
Shadow People, The. Francis Ledwidge. GaP; MCCG; MPB; PCH; SP; TSW
Shadow Remains, The. Lynette Roberts. NeBP
Shadow River. Pauline Johnson. CaP
Shadow Rose, The. Robert Cameron Rogers. AA
Shadow streamed into the wall, The. Shadow and Shade. Allen Tate. InPo; LiTA; TwAmPo; ViBoPo
Shadow to Shadow. Hervey Allen. HBMV
Shadowed. Burnham Eaton. FiSC
Shadowed in midnight green. The Pond. James Whaler. *Fr.* Runaway. MAP; MoAmPo (1942 ed.)
Shadowgraphs, The. Richmond Lattimore. NYBP
Shadows. Paul Claudel, *tr. fr. French by* Joseph T. Shipley. CAW
Shadows. Samuel Daniel. *See* Are They Shadows?
Shadows, The. Mary Lundie Duncan. OTPC (1923 ed.)
Shadows. Sebastian Evans. PrWP
Shadows, The. Robert Finch. TwCaPo
Shadows. Henry W. Frost. SoP
Shadows. D. H. Lawrence. OAEP (2d ed.)
Shadows, The. George Macdonald. TRV
Shadows. Richard Monckton Milnes. HBV; OBEV (1st ed.)
Shadows. Arthur J. Peel. MoSiPe
Shadows, The. Frank Dempster Sherman. AA
Shadows. "Yehoash," *tr. fr. Yiddish by* Elias Lieberman. TrJP
Shadows are descending, The. Outgoing Sabbath. *Unknown.* TrJP
Shadows are long on Soldiers Field. Second Half. David McCord. SD
Shadows blown from trees, The. Vain Advice at the Year's End. James Wright. NYBP
Shadows do every where for substance passe. The Church-Windows. *Unknown. Fr.* A Poem, in Defence of the Decent Ornaments of Christ-Church, Oxon. . . OBS
Shadows gather round me, while you are in the sun, The. Next of Kin. Christina Rossetti. HBV
Shadows grazing eastwards melt. Last Meeting. Gwen Harwood. PoAu-2
Shadows in the Water. Thomas Traherne. AtBAP; EnLi-1; LiTB; MePo; NoP; OBS; PoEL-2; SCEP-1; SeCL; SeCP; UnPo (1st ed.)
Shadows lay along Broadway, The. Unseen Spirits [*or* Two Women]. Nathaniel Parker Willis. AA; AmePo; AnAmPo; BeLS; HBV; OBVV
Shadows of Chrysanthemums. E. J. Scovell. MoVE
Shadows of clouds. Clouds across the Canyon. John Gould Fletcher. *Fr.* The Grand Canyon of the Colorado. HT
Shadows of His Lady. Jacques Tahureau, *tr. fr. French by* Andrew Lang. AWP
Shadows of night were a-comin' down swift, The. Higher. *Unknown.* FiBHP
Shadows of Sails. John Anderson. EtS

Shadows of the Evening Hours, The. Adelaide Anne Procter. MaRV; TreFS
(Repose.) SoP
Shadows of the ships, The. Sketch. Carl Sandburg. AP; HBMV; NP
Shadows there are, mixed in the other shadows. The Shadows. Robert Finch. TwCaPo
Shadows To-Day. Christina Rossetti. OxBoCh
Shadows Worship, The. *Unknown, tr. fr. Arabic by* Sir Edwin Arnold. OnPM
Shadowy Horses, The. W. B. Yeats. *See* Michael Robartes Bids His Beloved Be at Peace.
Shadowy Swallows. Gustavo Adolfo Bécquer, *tr. fr. Spanish by* L. R. Lind. LiTW
Shadrach, Meshach, Abednego. Warm Babies. Keith Preston. FiBHP; HBMV; WhC
Shadwell. Dryden. *Fr.* MacFlecknoe. AnFE
("All human things are subject to decay.") CoBE; TrGrPo; ViBoPo
(Poet Shadwell, The.) FiP
(Primacy of Dullness, The.) OBS
Shadwell Stair. Wilfred Owen. FaBoTw
Shady friend for torrid days, A. Emily Dickinson. NePA
Shady Old Camp, The, *with music.* John A. Stone. SGR
Shady, Shady. Tao Yuan-ming, *tr. fr. Chinese by* Arthur Waley. AWP; JAWP; WBP; WoL
Shady Woods. E. M. Adams. BoTP
Shaemus. Conrad Aiken. OxBA
Shaftesbury. Dryden. *See* Achitophel.
Shag Rookery. William Hart-Smith. AnNZ
Shaggy, and lean, and shrewd, with pointed ears. The Woodman's Dog. William Cowper. *Fr.* The Task. BoTP; ELU; OTPC (1946 ed.); PCD; PCH
Shaggy camels kneel upon the sand, The. Caravans. Emily Patterson. ChIP
Shags or, they say, occasional a white. Incident at Matauri. Kendrick Smithyman. AnNZ
Shaka, King of the Zulus. *Unknown, tr. fr. Hlubi by* A. C. Jordan. PBA; TTY
Shake back your hair, O red-headed girl. Red-Headed Restaurant Cashier. Carl Sandburg. CMoP
Shake Hands. A. E. Housman. WePo
Shake, Mulleary, and Go-ethe. H. C. Bunner. ALV; AnAmPo; BOHV; FiBHP; InMe
Shake off thy sloth, my drowsy soul, awake. Thomas Traherne. *Fr.* On Christmas Day. OxBoCh
Shake Off Your Heavy Trance. Francis Beaumont. *Fr.* Masque of the Inner Temple and Gray's Inne. CBEP; ELU; OBS; OnPM; ViBoPo
(Fit Only for Apollo.) ChTr
(Song for a Dance.) ElL; FaBoCh; LoGBV
(Songs from a Masque.) TrGrPo
(Superlative Dance and Song.) UnS
(Three Songs, I.) GoBC
Shakespeare. Matthew Arnold. AnFE; ATP; BEL; BoLiVe; BoPe; CABA; CaFP; CBEP; CLwM; CoBE; EnLi-2; EnLit; EPN; FiP; GTBS; GTSE; GTSL; HBV; InP; InvP; MaVP; MBW-2; NoP; OAEP; OBEV; OBVV; OnPP; OTPC (1923 ed.); OuHeWo; PoIE; PoPo; PoRL; PoVP; Sonn; TOP; TrGrPo; ViBoPo; ViPo; ViPP; VP; WHA
Shakespeare. Henry Ames Blood. AA
Shakespeare. Emerson. AnNE
Shakespeare. Thomas Hood. *Fr.* The Plea of the Midsummer Fairies. OBRV
Shakespeare. Agnes Lee. NP
Shakespeare. Longfellow. AWP; InPo; MAmP; MWA-1; TOP
Shakespeare. John Sterling. VA
Shakespeare. Sir William Watson. HBV
Shakespeare; an Epistle to Mr. Garrick. Robert Lloyd. EiCL
Critics Rules, The, *sel.* OBEC
Shakespeare and Milton. Walter Savage Landor. VA
Shakespeare and Milton—what third blazoned name. Tennyson. Thomas Bailey Aldrich. AA
Shakespeare, at length thy pious fellows give. To the Memory of the Deceased Author Master W. Shakespeare. Leonard Digges. CLwM
Shakespeare Dead. Hugh Holland. ACP (1952 ed.)
(Sonnet to Shakespeare.) PrWP
(Upon the Lines and Life of the Famous Scenic Poet, Master William Shakespeare.) CLwM
Shakespeare is dust, and will not come. To and Fro about the City. John Drinkwater. MaRV; StJW
Shakespeare Might Have Boiled Othello. Edwin Meade Robinson. Limericised Classics, II. HBMV
Shakespeare Milton Keats are dead. Song of Allegiance. R. A. K. Mason. AnNZ
Shakespeare, Possibly, in California. Reed Whittemore. MoVE
Shakespeare, that nimble Mercury thy brain. To Master W. Shakespeare. Thomas Freeman. SiCE
Shakespeare: The Fairies' Advocate. Thomas Hood. *Fr.* The Plea of the Midsummer Fairies. OBNC
Shakespeare, thy legacy of peerless song. At Stratford-on-Avon. Mackenzie Bell. VA
Shakespeare, whose heartfelt scenes shall ever give. To Shakespeare. Thomas Edwards. Sonn
Shakespearean Bear, The. Arthur Guiterman. BOHV; CenHV; EvOK
Shakespearean fish swam the sea, far away from land. Three Movements. W. B. Yeats. CMoP; ELU
Shakespeare's Mourners. John Banister Tabb. AmP
Shako, The. Robert Lowell, *after the German of* Rainer Marie Rilke. OnHM; Sonn
Shall a Frown or Angry Eye. *Unknown.* ElL; EnRePo
Shall clammy clay shroud such a gallant gloze. A Mirror of Mortality. Thomas Proctor. ReIE
Shall dumpish melancholy spoil my joys. On Christmas-Day. Thomas Traherne. OBS; PoEL-2
Shall Earth No More Inspire Thee? Emily Brontë. ELP; GTBS-D
(Lines: "Shall earth no more inspire thee.") LoBV
Shall He come—and find me watching? Watching. *Unknown.* SoP
Shall hearts that beat no base retreat. The Enthusiast. Herman Melville. MAmP
Shall I be fearful thus to speak my mind. Irene Rutherfod McLeod. *Fr.* Sonnets. HBMV
Shall I Be Silent? George Herbert. *Fr.* Christmas. SoP; TRV
"Shall I be your first love, lady, shall I be your first?" Love-in-Idleness. Thomas Lovell Beddoes. LiTL; PeER; ViBoPo
Shall I begin by saying. Lafayette to Washington. Maxwell Anderson. *Fr.* Valley Forge. PAL
Shall I begin with Ah, or Oh? An Ode: Secundum Artem. William Cowper. FosPo; PP
Shall I call it fortune or my froward folly. How Jacke Cade Traiterously Rebelling agaynst His Kyng, Was for His Treasons and Cruell Doinges Wurthely Punyshed. *At. to* William Baldwin. *Fr.* A Mirror for Magistrates. SiCE
Shall I come, if I swim? wide are the waves, you see. Thomas Campion. EnLoPo
Shall I Come, Sweet Love, to Thee. Thomas Campion. EG; ElL; EnRePo; FaBoEn; LoBV; OAEP; OBSC; OxBoLi; PIA; PoEL-2; ViBoPo
Shall I compare thee to a summers day? Sonnets, XVIII. Shakespeare. AnFE; AtBAP; ATP; AWP; BEL; BoLiVe; BWP; CBEP; CBV; CoBE; CTC; DiPo; EG; ElL; EnL; EnLi-1; EnLit; EnLoPo; ExPo; FaBoBe; FaBoEn; FaBV; FaFP; FiP; GTBS; GTBS-D; GTBS-P; GTBS-W; GTSE; GTSL; HBV; ILP; InP; InvP; LiTB; LiTG; LiTL; LoBV; MaPo; MasP; MCCG; MeWo; NeHB; NoP; OAEP; OBEV; OBSC; OuHeWo; PAn; PoAn; PoE; PoEL-2; PoeP; PoFS; PoIE; PoLF; PoMa; PoPL; PoPo; PoRA; PoSa; PTK; ReEn; ReIE; SeCePo; SeCeV; ShBV-4; SiCE; Sonn; StP; TDP; TOP; TreFT; TrGrPo; ViBoPo; WePo; WHA; YAT
Shall I Complain? Louise Chandler Moulton. PoToHe
Shall I despaire of my resolv'd intent. *Unknown.* SeCSL
Shall I dip, Shall I dip it, Dolores? The Poets at a House-Party. Carolyn Wells. PA
Shall I Do This? Purohit. OBMV
Shall I get drunk or cut myself a piece of cake. Cairo Jag. Keith Douglas. NePoEA
Shall I Go Bound and You Go Free? Padraic Colum. AnFE; PoFr
Shall I, I wonder, ever find. Peace. Irwin Edman. TrJP
Shall I kill myself? Remorse. Tennyson. *Fr.* Idylls of the King: Guinevere. MaRV
Shall I let myself be caught. Pygmalion. Hilda Doolittle ("H. D."). AnAmPo

Shall I (like a hermit) dwell. His Further Resolution. *Unknown.* HBV
Shall I Look. *Unknown.* EnRePo
Shall I look on when states step on the stage. How Thomas Wolsey Did Arise unto Great Authority and Government. . . Thomas Churchyard. *Fr.* A Mirror for Magistrates. SiCE
Shall I look to ease my grief? What Remains but Only Dying? *Unknown.* ElL
Shall I Love Again. William Browne. ViBoPo
Shall I love God for causing me to be? The Proof. Richard Wilbur. EaLo
Shall I love him. A Young Girl's Song. Paul Heyse. PoPl
Shall I, mine affections slack. Answer to Master Wither's Song, "Shall I, Wasting in Despair?" Ben Jonson. BOHV; InMe
Shall I no way win you to grant my desire? Being Importunate, at the Length He Obtaineth. Richard Edwards. TuPP
Shall I Pray On? Edith L. Mapes. SoP
Shall I Repine. Swift. *See* Power of Time, The.
Shall I say that I love you. Of Disdainful Daphne. M. H. Nowell. ElL
Shall I say that what heaven gave. Sentence. Witter Bynner. HBV
Shall I sonnet-sing to you about myself? House. Robert Browning. CLwM; DiPo; MBW-2; OAEP; PoVP; PP; ViPo
Shall I spend the days of my youth in pride. God's Call. *Unknown.* STF
Shall I still miche in silence and give aim. Satira Prima. Everard Guilpin. *Fr.* Skialetheia. ReIE
Shall I stray/ In the middle air. John Fletcher. *Fr.* The Faithful Shepherdess, V, v. ViBoPo
Shall I strew on thee rose or rue or laurel. Ave atque Vale. Swinburne. EnLi-2; MaVP; OAEP; OBEV; OBNC; PoVP; StP; SyP; ViBoPo; ViPP; VP
Shall I stroke your thighs. "I Would Not Change for Thine." William Carlos Williams. PoeP
Shall I take thee, the Poet said. Emily Dickinson. DiPo; MWA-2
Shall I tell you what I saw? Wonder. Dawn Finlay. SoP
Shall I tell you who will come. Words from an Old Spanish Carol [*or* On Christmas Morn]. *Unknown, tr. by* Ruth Sawyer. BrR; ChBR; ChrBoLe; FaPON; PDV
Shall I Tell You Whom I Love? William Browne. *Fr.* Britannia's Pastorals, II, Song 2. ElL; SeEP
(Song: "Shall I tell you whom I love?") HBV
Shall I then weep or shall I sing. *Unknown.* SeCSL
Shall I thus ever long, and be no whit the near? The Lady Prayeth the Return of Her Lover Abiding on the Seas [*or* The Seafarer *or* To Her Sea-faring Lover]. *Unknown.* ElL; OBEV; OBSC
Shall I, Wasting in Despair. George Wither. *Fr.* Fair Virtue, the Mistress of Philarete, *and also* Fidelia. ALV; AnFE; BEL; BoLP; EG; ElL; EnLi-1; LiTB; LiTG; OBS; OuHeWo; PoIE; ReEn; WHA
(Author's Resolution in a Sonnet, The.) CLwM; NoP; ViBoPo
(Lover's Resolution, The.) AWP; EnLit; HBV; InMe; JAWP; LiTL; OBEV; PG; TOP; TreFS; WBP; YAT
(Manly Heart, The.) FaBV; GTBS; GTBS-D; GTBS-P; GTBS-W; GTSE; GTSL; MCCG
(Sonnet: "Shall I, wasting in despair.") SeCV-1; SeEP
(What Care I.) MeWo; TrGrPo
Shall I write pretty poetry. The Egoist. Anna Wickham. FaBoTw
Shall mine eyes behold thy glory, oh, my country? After Death [*or* Post Mortem]. Fanny Parnell. AnIV; OBVV; OnYI; OxBI; PoFr; VA
Shall not a man sing as the night comes on? Song on Reaching Seventy. John Hall Wheelock. TwAmPo
Shall one be sorrowful because of love. De Amore. Ernest Dowson. OBNC
Shall reason rule where reason hath no right? To His Love That Sent Him a Ring. George Turberville. EnPo; EnRePo; TuPP
Shall She Never Out of My Mind. *Unknown.* ReIE
Shall Simon Suckegg, simple Simkins' son. Henry Parrot. SiCE
Shall summer wood where we have laughed our fill. Apocalypse. Theodore Maynard. JKCP
Shall the great soul of Newton quit this earth. A Poem Sacred to the Memory of Sir Isaac Newton. James Thomson. CEP; EiPP
Shall the mole, in his dark underground, call the beasts from the day-glare to flee? Spiritual Vision. Solomon Solis-Cohen. MaRV
Shall these early fragrant hours. Henry Vaughan. LO
Shall they bury me in the deep. My Grave. Thomas Osborne Davis. ACV; OnYI
Shall this double anniversary, today, tonight. November 7th. "Pablo Neruda." PoFr
Shall we die, both thou and I. One and His Mistress a-Dying. *Unknown.* LO; SeCL
Shall We Forget. William Mitchell. BePJ
Shall we forget, when Nations meet. Forget-Me-Not Day. Nan Terrell Reed. HH
Shall we go dance the hay, the hay? Country Song [*or* A Report Song]. Nicholas Breton. OBSC; SeCePo; TrGrPo
Shall we go on with it? Driving ever seaward? Voyage of Discovery: 1935. Richmond Lattimore. TwAmPo
Shall we make love. A Bright Night. *Unknown. Fr.* Manyo Shu. AWP; LiTW; WoL
Shall we meet no more, my love, at the binding of the sheaves. Adonais. Will Wallace Harney. AA; HBV
Shall we not open the human heart. Give Way! Charlotte Perkins Gilman. WGRP
Shall we not weary in the windless days. Hereafter. Rosamund Marriott Watson. VA
Shall we say heaven is not heaven. One Kind of Humility. Jean Starr Untermeyer. MAP; MoAmPo (1942 ed.)
Shall we win at love or shall we lose. Hotel Transylvanie. Frank O'Hara. NeAP
Shall you complain who feed the world? To Labor. Charlotte Perkins Stetson Gilman. PoLF
Shallo Brown, *with music. Unknown.* ShS; SoAmSa
Shallow dark but mocks the eyes. Night's Ancient Cloud. Thomas Keohler. AnIV
Shallows of the Ford, The. Henry Herbert Knibbs. SCC
Shalom Aleichem. *Unknown, tr. fr. Hebrew.* TrJP
Shaman Songs, *sels.* Gene Fowler. ThO
"Rains are warm, The," 10.
"We have made hawks," 12.
"Word, The/ is in the hand," 2.
Shamash of the glade, The. The Venerable Bee. A. M. Klein. TrJP
Shambles come ready-made these years/ are found. On Common Ground. R. P. Blackmur. Scarabs for the Living, III. CrMA
Shame. Coventry Patmore. *Fr.* The Angel in the House. I, xi, 2. OBVV
Shame. Arthur Rimbaud, *tr. fr. French by* Louise Varèse. SyP
Shame checks our first attempts, but then 'tis proved. Sins Loathed, and Yet Loved. Robert Herrick. LiTB
Shame He suffered left its brand, The. Scarred. Bob Jones, Jr. SoP; STF
Shame Hitherto. Al Mutanabbi, *tr. fr. Arabic by* R. A. Nicholson. LiTW
Shame of thy mother soyle! ill-nurtur'd tree! Out of Horace. Richard Crashaw. MaMe
Shame on you! Indictment. Dorothy C. Parrish. TNV
Shame to my thoughts, how they stray from me! On the Flightiness of Thought. *Unknown.* OnYI
Shame upon you, Robin. Milkmaid's Song [*or* The Song of the Milkmaid]. Tennyson. *Fr.* Queen Mary. EPN; HBV
Shameful Death. William Morris. ChTr; GoTP; GSP; GTBS; GTBS-P; HBV; MaC; OAEP; OBVV; PAn; PeVV; PoVP; ShBV-2; SiSw; VA; ViPo; ViPP
Shameful Impotence. Ovid, *tr. fr. Latin by* Christopher Marlowe. *Fr.* Amores. ErPo
(Impotent Lover, The.) UnTE
Shamrock, The. Andrew Cherry. *See* Green Little Shamrock of Ireland, The.
Shamrock, The. Maurice Francis Egan. AA; DD; HBV
Shamrock, The. *Unknown.* HH
Shan Van Vocht, The. *Unknown.* AnIL; AnIV, 2 *sts.*; OnYI; OxBoLi, *diff. vers.*; PoFr
Shanadore, I love your daughter. Shenandoah. *Unknown.* ShS
Shancoduff. Patrick Kavanagh. OxBI
Shandon Bells, The. Francis Sylvester Mahony. *See* Bells of Shandon, The.

Shane O'Neill. Seumas MacManus. OnYI
Shaneen and Maurya Prendergast. Patch-Shaneen. J. M. Synge. LoBV
Shango ("Shango is an animal like the gorilla"). *Unknown, tr. fr. Yoruba by* Ulli Beier. PBA; TTY, *st.* 1
Shango ("Shango is the death who kills money with a big stick"). *Unknown, tr. fr. Yoruba by* Gbadamosi *and* Ulli Beier. TTY
Shankill. Eileen Shanahan. NeIP
Shannon and the *Chesapeake*, The. Thomas Tracy Bouvé. MC; PAH
Shannon and the *Chesapeake*, The. *Unknown.* AmSS (*Chesapeake* and *Shannon*.) PAH
Shanty-Boy and the Farmer's Son, The, *with music. Unknown.* ABF; IHA
Shantyboys' Song, The. Kenneth Zwicker. ShS
Shantyman's Life, The, *with music. Unknown.* AS; ShS, 2 *vers.*; TrAS, *diff. vers.*
Shao and the South, *sels.* Confucius, *tr. fr. Chinese by* Ezra Pound. CTC
"'Chkk! chkk!' hopper-grass."
"Three stars, five stars rise over the hill."
Shapcot! to thee the Fairy State. Oberon's Feast. Robert Herrick. BoLiVe; OAEP; OTPC (1923 ed.); PoeP; SeCV-1; TrGrPo
Shape alone let others prize, The. Song. Mark Akenside. HBV
Shape-Changer. Ella Young. BoChLi (1950 ed.)
Shape God Wears, The. Sara Henderson Hay. GoTP
Shape, like folded light, embodied air, A. Aishah Schechinah. Robert Stephen Hawker. ACP (1926 ed.); GoBC; ISi; OBNC; OxBoCh
Shape of a Bird, The. Laurence Whistler. MoVE
Shape of Autumn, The. Virginia Russ. GoYe
Shape of Fear, The. Sydney King Russell. FiSC
Shape of the Fire, The. Theodore Roethke. AmP; LiTA; MiAP; MoAB
Shape of the Heart, The. Louise Townsend Nicholl. ImOP
Shaped and vacated. The Event. T. Sturge Moore. OBMV
Shaped long and arrowy. Express Trains. MacKnight Black. PoMa
Shapes. Mark Turbyfill. NP
Shapes and Signs. James Clarence Mangan. ACV; OnYI
Shapes of Death [Haunt Life]. Stephen Spender. MoPW; OBMV
Shapes that frowned before the eyes, The. The Eclipse of Faith. Theodore Dwight Woolsey. AA
Shaping of a Disciple, The. Dale Martin Stone. SoP (God Knows What He's About.) STF
Shards. Aline Kilmer. PFY
Sharing Eve's Apple. Keats. ChER; ErPo
Sharing His Cross. Gracia L. Fero. BePJ
Shark, The. E. J. Pratt. WHW
Sharks, The. Denise Levertov. NeAP
Shark's Fin. Eithne Wilkins. NeBP
Shark's Parlor, The. James Dickey. NYBP
Sharks tooth is perfect for biting, The. Canticle. Michael McClure. NeAP
Sharp is the night, but stars with frost alive. Winter Heavens. George Meredith. BoLiVe; CABA; Po
Sharp smoke drifts, A. Landscape with Figures. Theodore Enslin. CoPo
Sharp triangles of red rubber and white. Consuelo at the Country Club. Selden Rodman. NAMP
Sharpeville Inquiry. Anne Welsh. PeSA
Shattered, O Lord, is each enclosing wall. Heart's Poverty. Gloria T. Stein. JKCP (1955 ed.)
Shattered water made a misty din, The. Once by the Pacific. Robert Frost. AmLP; AmPP; AnFE; BWP; CBV; CMoP; CoAnAm; CoBMV; GTBS-W; HT; ILP; InPo; LiTA; LiTM; MAP; MaPo (1969 ed.); MoAB; MoAmPo; NePA; NP; PoAn; PoDB; PoFS; PoPo; Sonn
Shawls, The. Monk Gibbon. NeIP; OxBI
She. Edward Field. FRC
She. Theodore Roethke. BoLP; ErPo
She. Richard Wilbur. AmPP (5th ed.); CoPo; ToPo
She/ wore/ her flossiest smile. Movie Queen. James P. Vaughn. NNP
She always leaned to watch for us. The Watcher [*or* Mother]. Margaret Widdemer. DD; HBMV; MaRV; OHIP; OQP; SoP; STF; TSW
"She always seems so tied," is what friends say. Just to Be Needed. Mary Eversley. PoToHe
She and He. Sir Edwin Arnold. *See* He and She.
She, as a veil down to the slender waist. Milton. *Fr.* Paradise Lost, IV. ErPo
She Asks for New Earth. Katharine Tynan. BoPe; HBMV
She bade me follow to her garden, where. Snap-Dragon. D. H. Lawrence. ErPo
She bade us listen to the singing lark. On a Lady Singing. Isaac Rosenberg. FaBoTw
She beat the happy pavement. Gratiana Dancing and Singing. Richard Lovelace. CBEP; OAEP; OBS
She Being Brand. E. E. Cummings. ErPo; OxBA; UnTE
She Began to Wash His Feet with Teares. Richard Crashaw. MaMe
She Bewitched Me. Thomas Burbidge. EnLoPo
She bites into the red skin. My Love Eats an Apple. Ralph Gustafson. MoCV
She brings Him, smiling, in her arms to me. Stella Matutina. Lillian Doherty. WHL
She brought a drinking-cup to him. Two. Hugo von Hofmannsthal. TrJP
She brought her gift of worship to adorn. Fragrance. Ruth Gibbs Zwall. SoP
She by the river sate, and sitting there. Upon Julia Weeping. Robert Herrick. ExPo
She called from her cell. Madness. Harry Lee. MaRV
She Called Him Mr. *Unknown. See* Limerick: "She frowned and called him Mr."
She came. Dirge. Alfred Kreymborg. NP
She came across the seas steerage class. My Grandmother's Funeral. Jascha Kessler. AmPC
She came among the gathering crowd. Common Sense. James Thomas Fields. AA
She came and stood in the Old South Church. In the "Old South." Whittier. AA
She Came and Went. James Russell Lowell. AA; CoBA; FaPL; HBV; ViBoPo
She came and went as comes and goes. Under the Red Cross. Chauncey Hickox. AA
She came bringing unlikely bloom. The Studio. Anthony Kerrigan. NYTB
She came in from the snowing air. Ice. Stephen Spender. AtBAP; FaBoMo; GTBS-P; SeCePo
She came on Earth soon after the creation. The Fairy Mamounè. John Moultrie. OBRV
She Came Out of the Frost. Aleksandr Blok, *tr. fr. Russian by* Babette Deutsch. PoPl
She came to him in dreams—her ears. The Tame Hare. Norman Nicholson. FaBoMo
She came to me in hidden guise. Mater Incognita. Sister Mary Benvenuta. ISi
She came to us recommended. For Louise, Age 17. Irving Layton. PeCV
She can be as wise as we. Marian. George Meredith. HBV
She cannot tell my name. Prayer. Edward Bliss Reed. HBMV
She carried me under her heart. My Mother. *Unknown.* SoP
She casts a spell, oh, casts a spell! My Love, Oh, She Is My Love. *Tr. by* Douglas Hyde. AnIV
She caught a butterfly. Patroness. Gerald William Barrax. Kal
She chops the meat with a golden knife. The Richest Woman. Elizabeth Madox Roberts. GaP
She comes, and straight therewith her shining orbs do move. Astrophel and Stella, LXXVI. Sir Philip Sidney. CABA; FCP; ReIE; SiPS
She Comes as Comes the Summer Night. Frank S. Williamson. BoAu
She comes like the hush and beauty of the night. Poetry. Edwin Markham. AA
She comes, majestic with her swelling sails. Homeward Bound. Robert Southey. EtS
She comes not: in the summer night. O Ubi? Nusquam. R. W. Dixon. LO
She Comes Not When Noon Is on the Roses. Herbert Trench. HBMV; OBEV (new ed.); OBVV
She comes. She's here. Dryden. *Fr.* All for Love, III. MyFE
She comes! the spirit of the dance! A Dancing Girl. Frances Sargent Osgood. AA

She could die laughing. Minnie and Mrs. Hoyne. Kenneth Fearing. AnEnPo; PoRA
She Crosses Her Knees. *Unknown.* SiTL
She crouched outside my door at break of dawn. Cruelty. Margaret E. Bruner. CIV
She danced, near nude, to tom-tom beat. Zalka Peetruza. Ray Garfield Dandridge. BANP
She dances, and I seem to be. Perdita. Florence Earle Coates. AA
She dared not wait my coming, and shall look. Canute the Great. "Michael Field." VA
She dealt her pretty words like blades. Emily Dickinson. NoP
She-Devil. Douglas Goldring. HBMV
She Died in Beauty. Charles Doyne Sillery. HBV
She died in the upstairs bedroom. Death in Leamington. John Betjeman. ACV; NoP; PoPl
She died—this was the way she died. Emily Dickinson. AA
She died when earth was fair beyond all price. On the Death of a Favorite Cat. *Unknown.* CIV
She dismisses me in late sunbeams. Dismissal. Peter Redgrove. NMP; OPoP
She does not know. No Images. Waring Cuney. AmNP; BANP; CDC; GoSl; PoNe; TTY
She dreamed death came to her one day in May. Prophecy. Walter Shedlofsky. FiSC
She dreams of Love upon the temple stair. A Sleeping Priestess of Aphrodite. Robert Cameron Rogers. AA
She drew back; he was calm. The Subverted Flower. Robert Frost. CMoP; MWA-2; OxBA
She dwells, pale midnight sun, beyond the river. Une Idole du Nord. Francis Stuart. NeIP
She Dwelt among the Untrodden Ways. Wordsworth. ATP; AWP; BEL; BoLiVe; CABA; CBEP; CoBE; DiPo; EG; ELP; EnL; EnLit; EnLoPo; EnRP; EPN; ERoP-1; GTSL; HBVY; ILP; InP; InPo; JAWP; LiTB; LiTG; LiTL; MaPo; MBW-2; MCCG; MERP; NoP; OAEP; OBNC; OBRV; OTPC; OuHeWo; PAn; PG; PoAn; PoE; PoeP; PoFS; PoIE; ShBV-4; TOP; ViBoPo; WBP; WHA
(Lost Love, The.) GTBS; GTBS-D; GTBS-P; GTBS-W; GTSE; PoPo
(Lucy.) AnFE; BLPA; EnLi-2; FaBoEn; FaBV; FiP; HBV; LoBV; MaC; NeHB; OBEV; TreF; TrGrPo
Violet, The, *sel.* PCH
She entered, and passionately, the eyes half closed. Desire. Pierre Louys. *Fr.* The Songs of Bilitis. UnTE
She even thinks that up in heaven [*or* She thinks that even. . .]. For a Lady I Know. Countee Cullen. Four Epitaphs, 4. AmNP; CDC; GoSL; IDB; Kal; MAP; MaRV; MoAmPo; PoNe; ShM; TRV
She fears him, and will always ask. Eros Turannos. E. A. Robinson. AmLP; AnAmPo; AnFE; AnNE; AP; APA; BWP; CMoP; CoAnAm; CoBA; CoBMV; CrMA; ForPo; ILP; LiTA; LiTM (rev. ed.); MAmP; MAP; MAPA; MaPo (1969 ed.); MoAB; MoAmPo; MoPo; MoVE; NePA; NoP; NP; OXBA; PIA; PoE; PoFS; PoIE; QFR; TDP; TwAmPo
She fell asleep on Christmas Eve. My Sister's Sleep. Dante Gabriel Rossetti. EnL; EPN; ExPo; LoBV; MaVP; MyFE; OAEP; PoVP; SeCeV; ViPo; ViPP
She fell away in her first ages spring. Spenser. *Fr.* Daphnaida. OBEV
She felt, I think, but as a wild-flower can. An Irish Wild-Flower. Sarah Morgan Bryan Piatt. AA
She fled in anguish; he pursued desire. First Love. Charles Gullans. NePoEA
She flourished in the 'Twenties, "hectic" days of Peace. Mews Flat Mona. William Plomer. FaBoTw
She flung the parlour window wide. Quite by Chance. Frederick Langbridge. BOHV
She frowned and called him Mr. Limerick [*or* She Called Him Mr.]. *Unknown.* FaPON; GoTP
She gamboll'd on the greens. Olivia. Tennyson. *Fr.* The Talking Oak. GN
She gave her life to love. She never knew. The Old Maid. George Barlow. VA
She gave him milk and incidental comfort. The Concert: Oratorio for a Season of Wrath. John L'Heureux. YAP
She gave me all that woman can. Monna Lisa. James Russell Lowell. AmLP
She-Goat and Glow-Worm. Christian Morgenstern, *tr. fr. German by* Christopher Middleton. OA
She goes but softly, but she goeth sure. Upon the Snail. Bunyan. BoPe; ChTr
She goes by many names; Diana of the sacred wood. The Goddess. Kathleen Raine. FaBoTw
She got her way by shedding tears. Child Wife. Joseph Joel Keith. FiSC
She grew up in bedeviled southern wilderness. The Ballad of Sue Ellen Westerfield. Robert Hayden. AmPP (5th ed.); Kal
She had a beautiful, bitter face. Devil Doll. Lisa Grenelle. FiSC
She had a cock hight Chaunteclere. The Poor Widow's Cock. Chaucer. *Fr.* The Canterbury Tales: The Nun's Priest's Tale. MyFE
She had a name among the children. A Cat. Edward Thomas. BrPo
She had cornflowers in her ear. Gipsy Jane. William Brighty Rands. BoTP; FaPON; SoPo; TiPo
She had green eyes, that excellent seer. Bast. William Rose Benét. HBMV
She had no business doin' it, but she come out o' the East. The Peeler's Lament. *Unknown.* CoSo
She had no saying dark enough. The Oft-repeated Dream. Robert Frost. *Fr.* The Hill Wife. NP; PG (1945 ed.)
She had not held her secret long enough. The Visitation. Elizabeth Jennings. MoBS
She had thought the studio would keep itself. Living in Sin. Adrienne Cecile Rich. NePoEA; NYBP
She has a beauty of her own. An Australian Girl. Ethel Castilla. VA
She has a bright and clever mind. A Disagreeable Feature. Edwin Meade Robinson. HBMV
She has a primrose at her breast. A Primrose Dame. Gleeson White. HBV; VA
"She has beauty, but [still] you must keep your heart cool." Dear Fanny. Thomas Moore. HBV; InMe
She has calld to her bower-maidens. Young Hunting (G *vers.*). *Unknown.* ESPB
She has dancing eyes and ruby lips. My Mistress's Boots. Frederick Locker-Lampson. BOHV; HBV; TOP
She has dusted the ornaments, rubbed down the chairs. Humbert Wolfe. *Fr.* The Uncelestial City. BoC
She has finished and sealed the letter. Parting, without a Sequel. John Crowe Ransom. DTC; LiTL; MAP; MoAB; MoAmPo; MoVE; NP; OxBA
She has gone out, she is far from me, but I see her. Absence. Pierre Louys. *Fr.* The Songs of Bilitis. UnTE
She has gone—she has left us in passion and pride. Brother Jonathan's Lament for Sister Caroline. Oliver Wendell Holmes. CoBA; HBV; PaA; PAH; ThLM
"She has gone to be with the angels." The Vision of the Snow. Margaret Junkin Preston. AA
She has gone to the bottom! the wrath of the tide. The *Alabama.* Maurice Bell. PAH
She has laughed as softly as if she sighed. A Woman's Shortcomings. Elizabeth Barrett Browning. BLPA HBV; NeHB
She has left me, my pretty. Song. Sylvia Townsend Warner. MoAB; MoBrPo
She has no need to fear the fall. Portrait. Louise Bogan. HBMV
She has not found herself a hard pillow. To Clarissa Scott Delany. Angelina W. Grimké. AmNP
She has not grown uncivil. Her Race. W. B. Yeats. Upon a Dying Lady, V. LiTB
She has opened an immense hole in the soft ground. The Goddess. Théodore de Banville. OnPM
She has put on a silver gown and gone. Mad Maid's Whim. Randolph Stow. ACV
She has returned from Paris, I am told. Fable of a Forgotten Woman. Louis Johnson. AnNZ
She has that quality of innocence. Virgin Country. Roy McFadden. NeIP
She has the strange sweet grace of violets. Elizabeth. George Brandon Saul. HBMV
She has tightened her cinch by another inch. Over the Hills with Nancy. Gelett Burgess. WhC
She hath the apple in her hand for thee. Venus. Dante Gabriel Rossetti. MaVP
She heard the children playing in the sun. Pain. Harriet Monroe. NP

She heard with patience all unto the end. Prince Arthur. Spenser. *Fr.* The Faerie Queene, I. OBSC
She Hears the Storm. Thomas Hardy. ATP; NP; PoeP; TOP
She hears, upon that water without sound. Sunday Morning, II [VIII]. Wallace Stevens. AnFE; AnNE; APA; CoAnAm; MAP; MAPA; MoAmPo
She hid herself in the soirée kettle. A Ballade of the Nurserie. John Twig. NA
She hung the cage at the window. Caprice. William Dean Howells. ALV
She hurries. Catherine Takes a Stroll. John Cournos. CLwM
She I love (alas in vain!). Walter Savage Landor. GTSE
She I love leaves me and I leave my friends. False Bay. F. T. Prince. BoSA
She, in dowdy dress and dumpy. Still Life: Lady with Birds. Quandra Prettyman. CAD
She in whose lipservice. The Goddess. Denise Levertov. AP; LiTM (1970 ed.); NeAP; PoCh
She is a nun, withdrawing behind her veil. The Desert. Charles E. S. Wood. *Fr.* The Poet in the Desert. AnAmPo; MAP
She is a person here in her own right. Memling's Virgin with Apple. Adèle Naudé. BoSA
She is a reed,/ straight and simple. The Reed. Caryll Houselander. ISi
She is a rich and rare land. My Land [*or* This Native Land]. Thomas Osborne Davis. BoTP; DD; HBV; MPB (1956 ed.); OTPC; PAL
She is a winsome wee thing. My Wife's a Winsome Wee Thing. Burns. HBV; LiTL
She is all so slight. After Two Years. Richard Aldington. GTSL; HBV; MoBrPo; PG; PoPl; WHA
She is as in a field a silken tent. The Silken Tent. Robert Frost. AmPP (5th ed.); BWP; CABA; CBV; ExPo; InPo; MaPo (1969 ed.); MeWo; MoPo; MWA-2; NePA; OnP; PoDB; PoIE; Sonn; TwCP
She is bravest and best of a cursed race. Chipeta. Eugene Field. PoOW
She is committed to the earth and the earth. Canaan. Muriel Spark. NYBP
She is dead; and all which die. The Dissolution. John Donne. ILP
She is dead, nor did she ever live! On a Dead Lady. Alfred de Musset. EnLi-2 (1949 ed.)
"She is dead!" they said to him; "come away." He and She [*or* She and He]. Sir Edwin Arnold. BLPA; HBV
She is devout and plump, but not happy. A Baroque Gravure. Thomas Merton. CoPo
She Is Far from the Land. Thomas Hood. DTC; WiR
She Is Far from the Land. Thomas Moore. AnIL; EnRP; FaPL; HBV; OBNC
She is foremost of those that I would hear praised. Her Praise. W. B. Yeats. Po
She is free of the trap and the paddle. The Half-Breed Girl. Duncan Campbell Scott. CaP
She is gentle [*or* gentil] and also wise. That Ever I Saw. *Unknown.* CBEP; EG; LO; TrGrPo
She is gone, she is lost, she is found, she is ever fair. My Woe Must Ever Last. Sir Walter Ralegh. EIL
She is like a cricket. For a Happy Girl. Philip Dow. QAH
She is like pearls, of course, and rubies, and other. Valentine. Hollis Summers. GoYe
She is more sparkling beautiful. A Bridal Song. Hugh McCrae. BoAu
She Is More to Be Pitied than Censured. William B. Gray. BeLS; BLPA; TreF
She Is My Dear. *Unknown, tr. fr. Irish by* Frank O'Connor. KiLC
She Is No Liar. Robert Graves. MemP
She Is Not Fair [to Outward View]. Hartley Coleridge. *See* Song: "She is not fair to outward view."
She is not mistress here, the arrows shake themselves. Lady with Arrows. Margaret Marks. MAP
She is not of the fireside. Revolution. Lesbia Harford. PoAu-1
She is not old, she is not young. The Woman with the Serpent's Tongue. Sir William Watson. HBV
She is not yet; but he whose ear. Dominion of Australia, The (a Forecast, 1877). Brunton Stephens. BoAu; PoAu-1; VA
She is now water and air. Sea Burial from the Cruiser "Reve." Richard Eberhart. NYBP
She is older than the rocks among which she sits. Mona Lisa. Walter Pater. OBMV
She Is Overheard Singing. Edna St. Vincent Millay. InMe
She is playing like a child. The End of Day. W. B. Yeats. Upon a Dying Lady, IV. LiTB
She is risen from the dead! America Resurgent. Wendell Phillips Stafford. MC
She is so proper and so pure. My Sweet Sweeting. *Unknown.* CH
She is so young, and never never before. Sonnet. Edward Davison. ErPo
She is so young, becoming a stranger. Waking. Jon Anderson. NYTB
She is so young, dear Lord, so very young. Prayer for a Bride's House. Christie Lund. SoP
She is standing at the gate. Mid-Forest Fear. Roderic Quinn. BoAu
She is still, she is cold. Shelley. *Fr.* Ginevra. ChER
She is submarine, she is an octopus, she is/ A biological process. Ezra Pound. *Fr.* Canto XXIX. MoPo
She is the clernesse and the verray light. Chaucer. *Fr.* The Legend of Good Women. LO
She is the fairies' midwife, and she comes. Queen Mab [*or* Mercutio Describes Queen Mab]. Shakespeare. *Fr.* Romeo and Juliet, 1, iv. GoTP; MaC; PoFS; TrGrPo
She is the Rose, the glorie of the day. Lament for Daphnaida. Spenser. FiP
She is too cruell, alas too cruell. *Unknown.* SeCSL
She is touching the cycle—her tender tread. Tennessee. Virginia Fraser Boyle. PAH
She is tougher than me, harder. For My Mother. Iain Crichton Smith. OxBS
She is up in the dark and out in the cowyard. The Milker. Eileen Duggan. CoBE
She Is Wise, Our Ancient Mother. Karle Wilson Baker. OQP
She is young. Have I the right. The Dance. R. S. Thomas. BoPe
She issues radiant from her dressing-room. Modern Love, VII. George Meredith. ViPo; VP
She keeps her clavichord. The Clavichord. May Sarton. UnS
She keeps her nook, sitting with folded hands. The Old Woman. John Bunker. CAW
She kept her secret well, oh, yes. My Angeline. Harry B. Smith. *Fr.* The Wizard of the Nile. BOHV; InMe
She kissed me on the forehead. Windle-Straws. Edward Dowden. HBV
She kneeled before me begging. Confession. Donald Jeffrey Hayes. CDC
She kneeled before the dead lamb weeping. Synekdechestai. C. M. Schmid. GoYe
She knelt upon her brother's grave. Dora. Thomas Edward Brown. OBEV (1st ed.); PoVP
She knew it not:—most perfect pain. The Mirror. Dante Gabriel Rossetti. SyP
She knew that she was growing blind. Blind Louise. George Washington Dewey. AA
She knows a cheap release. The Movies. Florence Kiper Frank. NP
She Lay All Naked [in Her Bed]. *Unknown.* ErPo; UnTE
She lay, and serving-men her lithe arms took. Abishag. Rainer Maria Rilke. AWP
She lay as if at play. Emily Dickinson. LiTA
She lay there in the stone folds of his life. Private Worship. Mark Van Doren. LiTL; MoVE
She leads me on through storm and calm. My Guide. George Francis Savage-Armstrong. VA
She leaned [*or* lean'd] her back unto [*or* upon] a thorn. The Cruel Mother. *Unknown.* ESPB (C *vers.*); NoP; OBB; ViBoFo
She leaned her cheek upon her hand. The Ballad of Oriskany. Obadiah Cyrus Auringer. AA
She leaves the puddle where she drinks. A Cow at Sullington. Charles Dalmon. TSW
She left me at the silent time. Lines Written in the Bay of Lerici. Shelley. ERoP-2
She let her golden ball fall down the well. The Frog and the Golden Ball. Robert Graves. NoP

She lies congealed in carven stone. The Medici Tombs. W. W. E. Ross. NYTB
She lies far inland, and no stick nor stone of her. Inland City. John Crowe Ransom. CMoP
She lies in her little bed. Little Spring. *Unknown.* GFA
She lies in silence. She Walks. Joseph Joel Keith. ISi
She lies on her left side her flank golden. Landscape as a Nude. Archibald MacLeish. Frescoes for Mr. Rockefeller's City, I. AmPP (4th ed.); CMoP; UnPo
She lies there, her full firm teats not denied. Force. "Nikolai Maksimovich Minski." LiTW
She lies upon the cold stone of her cell. The Nun. Arthur Symons. BrPo
She like the Moon Arises. James McAuley. MoAuPo
She, like the morning, is still fresh and fair. Her Praises. Anthony Scoloker. ElL
She limps with halting painful pace. Portrait of an Old Woman. Arthur Davison Ficke. MAP; NP
She listen'd like a cushat dove. Christina Rossetti. EG
She listen'd to the music of the spheres. *Λειριόεσσα Κάλυξ* (Leirioessa Kalyx). Maurice Baring. OBVV
She lived beside the Anner. The Irish Peasant Girl. Charles Joseph Kickham. AnIV; JKCP (1926 ed.)
She lived in storm and strife. That the Night Come. W. B. Yeats. CoBMV; MemP; NP; PoEL-5; PoeP
She lived, we knew not how. They Called Her Sunshine. Mary Gilmore. NeLNL
She lived where the mountains go down to the sea. Golden Rowan. Bliss Carman. VA
She lives a prisoner within. The Shut-in. Nellie De Hearn. PoToHe (new ed.)
She lives in a garret. A Sad Song About Greenwich Village. Frances Park. OCS
She lives in light, not shadow. Of One Who Neither Sees nor Hears. Richard Watson Gilder. AA
She lives in the porter's room; the plush is nicotined. Bitter Sanctuary. Harold Monro. FaBoMo; LiTB; OBMV
She Lives with the Furies of Hope and Despair. Delmore Schwartz. FiMAP
She looked on me with sadder eyes than Death. Never Again. Hugh McCrae. BoAu
She looked over his shoulder. The Shield of Achilles. W. H. Auden. GTBS-P; NePA; NoP; OAEP (2d ed.); PAn; PoDB; SeCeV (1967 ed.)
She looked over the hills for many a day. The Golden Ball. *Unknown.* BaBo
She looked to east, she looked to west. Mater Dei. Katharine Tynan. ISi
She looks out in the blue morning. The Window. Conrad Aiken. CMoP
She Loved Her Husband Dearly, *with music.* *Unknown, at. to* John Sinclaire *and* J. Simmonds. BFSS
She loved the Autumn, I the Spring. Spirit of Sadness. Richard Le Gallienne. HBV
She loves him; for her infinite soul is Love. True Woman, 2. Dante Gabriel Rossetti. The House of Life, LVII. EPN; MaVP; PoVP; ViPo; VP
She loves me! From her own bliss-breathing lips. Sonnet. Charles Harpur. BoAu
She made a little shadow-hidden grave. The Dead Faith. Fanny Heaslip Lea. HBV; WGRP
She made her appearance at noon. The Corn Dance. Fanny Howe. QAH
She Made Home Happy. Henry Coyle. DD
She makes thee seek, yet fear to find. Love's Servile Lot. Robert Southwell. ACP
She met a lion face to face. A Cautionary Tale. Anne Wilkinson. OBCV; PeCV (1967 ed.)
She met me, Stranger, upon life's rough way. True Love. Shelley. *Fr.* Epipsychidion. LoBV
She might have borne them had they come. Breaking Point. Sylvia Auxier. GoYe
She might have chosen cities, but the man. Droving Man. Thea Astley. PoAu-2
She might have known it in the earlier spring. Feminine. H. C. Bunner. AA
She might have stolen from his arms. Solitary Confinement. X. J. Kennedy. NePoEA-2
She mixes blue and mauve and green. The Patchwork Quilt. Elizabeth Fleming. BoTP
She Moved through the Fair. Padraic Colum. GTBS-D; InvP
She moved through the garden in glory because. Marigold. Richard Garnett. CIV
She moves across the unlit hall to greet me. Old Woman in a Cage. Christopher Hampton. NYTB
She moves in tumult; round her lies. The Teresian Contemplative. Robert Hugh Benson. ACP; CAW; JKCP
She must go back, she said. The Housewife. W. W. Gibson. *Fr.* The Battle. NP
She naked lies asleep beside the wine. From Titian's "Bacchanal" in the Prado at Madrid. T. Sturge Moore. QFR
She never climbed a mountain. Farm Wife. John Hanlon Mitchell. CaP
She never could sleep in the earth, in the cold dark grave. Fire Burial. Edgar McInnis. CaP
She never met a fairy. Mrs. C. (Or Any Other Too Practical Person). Rowena Bennett. GaP
She never puts her toys away. Patty-Poem. Nick Kenny. PoToHe
She Never Told Her Love. Shakespeare. *Fr.* Twelfth Night, II, iv. MemP; MeWo
(Love Concealed.) TreFS
(Patience on a Monument.) TrGrPo
She never was quite one of us. Sleep-Walking Child. Elisabeth Eybers. PeSA
She of the Garden. Emile Verhaeren, *tr. fr. French by* Alma Strettell. CAW
She of the Impudent Face. Proverbs, VII: 6-27, Bible, *O.T.* TrJP
She of whose soul, if we may say 'twas gold. John Donne. *Fr.* Of the Progress of the Soul. TuPP
She only knew the birth and death. At Dawn. Arthur Symons. OBNC
She oped the portal of the palace. In the Sultan's Garden. Clinton Scollard. InP
She paced the silent hall. Sleep. Robert Eyres Landor. *Fr.* The Impious Feast, VII. OBRV
She packs the flower beds with leaves. For Fran. Philip Levine. PoCh
She painfully holds back a fart. A Sweet Thing/ Last Thoughts. Lanon A. Fenner, Jr. WSL
She passed away, like morning dew. Early Death. Hartley Coleridge. HBV; MaRV; OBEV; TreFS
She passes in her beauty bright. The Secret. Cosmo Monkhouse. VA
She Plans Her Funeral. Louise Morey Bowman. CaP
She play'd me false, but that's not why. Our Photographs. Frederick Locker-Lampson. ALV
She played upon her music-box a fancy air by chance. Her Polka Dots. Peter Newell. NA
She plays her harp by hidden rills. The Muses of Australia. Victor Daley. BoAu
She prepares to walk. Taking Steps at Thirteen Months. Heather Ross Miller. NYTB
She Promised She'd Meet Me, *with music.* *Unknown.* AS
She put him on a snow-white shroud. The Little Shroud. Letitia E. Landon. PaPo
She rises clear to memory's eye. Red Jack. Mary Durack. PoAu-1
She rises from coiled song of shells. Genealogy of a Mermaid. Morris Weisenthal. NYTB
She rose amid the Nations, tall and fair. Australia. John Laurence Rentoul. PoFr
She rose among us where we lay. The Vampire. Conrad Aiken. HBMV
She rose from her untroubled sleep. Chamber Scene. Nathaniel Parker Willis. HBV
She rose to his requirement, dropped. Emily Dickinson. CABA; FaBoEn; NoP
She roves through shadowy solitudes. Tacita. James Benjamin Kenyon. AA
She runs away and gathers up her gown. The Giddy Maid. John Clare. Sonn
She Said . . . Jonathan Henderson Brooks. PoNe
She Said. Walter de la Mare. ELP
She said, "I was not born to mope at home in loneliness." The Ride round the Parapet. Friedrich Rückert AWP; JAWP; WBP
She said my father had whiskers and looked like god. Our Father. Ray Mathew. FlW
She said, "Not only music; brave men marching." She Said. . . Jonathan Henderson Brooks. PoNe

She said, "Now give me flesh to eat. Cherry. Gene Baro. ErPo
She Said the Same to Me, *with music. Unknown.* AS
She said: The world is empty that we loved. Eternal. Agnes Foley Macdonald. CaP
She said: then, raging to Sir Plume repairs. Pope. *Fr.* The Rape of the Lock. MyFE
She said, "They gave me of their best." After Aughrim. Emily Lawless. OBEV (new ed.); OxBI
She said to me, He lay there sleeping. The Watchers. Muriel Rukeyser. NMP
She sang beyond the genius of the sea. The Idea of Order at Key West. Wallace Stevens. AmLP; AmP; AmPP; AP; BWP; CMoP; CoBMV; ForPo; ILP; MAP; MaPo (1969 ed.); MoAB; MoAmPo; MoPo; NoP; OXBA; PIA; Po; PoIE; PP; SeCeV (1967 ed.)
She sang her little bedtime air. Evening Prayer. Hermann Hagedorn. GoBC
She sang of lovers met to play. A Casual Song. Roden Noel. HBV
She sat and sewed that hath done me the wrong. Of His Love That Pricked Her Finger with a Needle. Sir Thomas Wyatt. FCP; ReIE
She sat and wept beside His feet; the weight. "Multum Dilexit." Hartley Coleridge. EnRP; HBV; VA
She sat beside the mountain springs. The Forsaken. Hamilton Aïdé. VA
She sat down below a thorn. The Cruel Mother [*or* Fine Flowers in the Valley]. *Unknown.* BaBo (A *vers.*); CBEP; ESPB (B *vers.*); FosPo; OxBB
She sat on a shelf. Motherhood. May Swenson. CoAP
She sate upon her Dobie. The Cummerbund. Edward Lear. CenHV
She Saw Me in Church. *Unknown.* MeEL
She saw the bayonets flashing in the sun. Memorial Day. Richard Watson Gilder. OHIP
She says, "But in contentment I still feel." Sunday Morning, IV [V]. Wallace Stevens. AnFE; AnNE; APA; CoAnAm; MAP; MAPA; MoAmPo
She says: "I am content when wakened birds." Sunday Morning, III [IV]. Wallace Stevens. AnFE; AnNE; APA; CoAnAm; MAP; MAPA; MoAmPo
She Scorns Her Husband the Caliph. Lady Maisun, *tr. fr. Arabic by* R. A. Nicholson. LiTW
She seemed an angel to our infant eyes! A Mother's Picture. Edmund Clarence Stedman. OHIP
She seemed so bored. The Great Offence. Abu Nuwas. LiTW
She seems to come by wing. 2nd Dance—Seeing Lines—6 February 1964. Jackson MacLow. CoPo
She Sees Another Door Opening. Firman Houghton. Par
She sees her image in the glass. The Shadow Dance. Louise Chandler Moulton. AA; HBV
She served love well. Elegy, Montreal Morgue. Goodridge MacDonald. CaP
She Sews Fine Linen. Julia Johnson Davis. HBMV
She sharpened her knife both sharp and keen. Young Hunting. *Unknown.* OxBoLi
She, she is dead; she's dead: when thou knowst this. John Donne. *Fr.* An Anatomy of the World. MyFE
She Should Have Died Hereafter. Shakespeare. *See* Tomorrow and Tomorrow and Tomorrow.
"She should have had. . .," I said, and there I stopped. After Speaking of One Dead a Long Time. Padraic Colum. GoYe
She should have had the state. Requiescat. Katherine Anne Porter. HBMV
She should never have looked at me. Cristina. Robert Browning. EPN; MaVP; MBW-2; OAEP; PoVP; ViPo
She shuts her eyes and keeps them shut. Whenever We Happen to Kiss. Heine. MeWo
She sights a bird, she chuckles. Emily Dickinson. MWA-2; OA
She sings her wild dirges, and smiles 'mid the strain. Scene in a Madhouse. Aubrey Thomas De Vere. OnYI
She sits a queen whom none shall dare despoil. Australia, 1894. William Gay. BoAu
She sits on the recreation ground. Reading a Letter. D. H. Lawrence. NoP
She sits beneath the elder-tree. The Death Child. "Fiona Macleod." VA
She sits in Sarras, delicate and strange. Our Lady with Two Angels. Wilfred Rowland Childe. ISi
She sits upon the tumulus [*or* on tumulus Savoor] and stares. Flax. Ivan Bunin. AWP; JAWP; WBP
She sits with/ tears on. Young Woman at a Window. William Carlos Williams. OCS
She sits with a son on her nursery knee. Mother. Keith Sinclair. AnNZ
She sits within a subway car. Girl in the Subway. Sydney King Russell. StaSt
She sits within the white oak hall. Helen. Edward A. U. Valentine. AA
She sitteth still who used to dance. Today for Me. Christina Rossetti. PoVP
She sleeps: peace crown thine eyes, sweet dreams in deep. Sickness, Not Sleep. *Unknown.* LO; SeCL
She smil'd, and more of pleasure than disdain. The Sea-Nymph's Parting. Walter Savage Landor. *Fr.* Gebir. FaBoEn
She smiled behind a lawny cloud. Fancy Dress. Dorothea MacKellar. PoAu-1
She Smiled like a Holiday. *Unknown.* OxBoLi
She smiles and smiles, and will not sigh. Urania. Matthew Arnold. HBV
She softly droops her maiden eyes. A Russian Spring Song with Minaiev. Thomas Walsh. GoBC
She sought him east, she sought him west. Rare Willy Drowned in Yarrow (B *vers.*). *Unknown.* ESPB
She sought the Studios, beckoning to her side. Heiress and Architect. Thomas Hardy. PoVP; ViPo (1962 ed.)
She speaks always in her own voice. The Portrait. Robert Graves. CABA; CMoP
She spent her time recalling. Play-acting. Frances Barber. GoYe
She spoke to me gently with words of sweet meaning. Song. Patrick MacDonogh. NeIP
She stands full-throated and with careless pose. The Onondaga Madonna. Duncan Campbell Scott. PeCV
She stands in the dead center like a star. The Mother. S. S. Gardons. NePoEA-2
She stands, within the shadow, at the foot. Mater Dolorosa. John Fitzpatrick. JKCP
She stares from out the wagon as/ It trails the dimming road. The Woman in the Wagon. Clyde Robertson. PoOW
She stay'd not for her robes, but straight arose. Christopher Marlowe. *Fr.* Hero and Leander. UnTE
She stole his eyes because they shone. Kleptomaniac. Leonora Speyer. AnAmPo; HBMV
She stood alone amidst the April fields. The Spring Is Late. Louise Chandler Moulton. HBV
She stood at the bar of justice. "Guilty or Not Guilty?" *Unknown.* BeLS; BLPA
She stood beneath the mistletoe. Under the Mistletoe. George Francis Shults. BOHV
She stood breast high amid the corn. Ruth. Thomas Hood. EnLoPo; EnRP; EPN; ERoP-2; GN; GTBS-W; HBV; InP; LiTG; LiTL; LoBV; OBEV; OBNC; OBRV; OnPP; OTPC; TOP; TreFS; VA
She stood hanging wash before sun. Ghetto Lovesong—Migration. Carole Gregory. NBP
She Stoops to Conquer, *sel.* Goldsmith.
Song: "Let schoolmasters puzzle their brain[s]," *fr.* I, ii. OAEP; ViBoPo
("Let schoolmasters puzzle their brain.") EnLi-1 (1949 ed.)
(Three Jolly Pigeons, The.) PoRA
(Three Pigeons, The.) ELP
She suns on grass, my dark, my gifted mistress. Nude. Harold Witt. ErPo
She sweeps with many-coloured brooms. Evening. Emily Dickinson. BoTP
She Swims Back in the Crowning Hour. Bilhana, *formerly at. to* Chauras, *tr. fr. Sanskrit by* E. Powys Mathers. *Fr.* Black Marigolds. OnPM
She swings the lantern. Night around her. The Lantern. Richard Church. MoBrPo (1942 ed.)
She Tasted Death. John Giorno. ANYP
She tells her child to have no fear. A Christian Mother. Phyllis E. Parlett. SoP
She Tells Her Love [While Half Asleep]. Robert Graves. FaBoTw; WePo
She tells us an interminable story, from television. The Somerset Dam for Supper. John Holmes. NYBP

She that but little patience knew. On a Political Prisoner. W. B. Yeats. BWP; NoP; OBMV; PoE
She That Denies Me [I Would Have]. Thomas Heywood. *Fr.* The Rape of Lucrece. ErPo; UnTE
("She that denies me, I would have.") LO
(Valerius on Women.) HBV
She that has that is clad in cómplete steel. Milton. *Fr.* Comus; a Masque. InP
She that I pursue, still flies me. Les Amours. Charles Cotton. HBV
She That Is Memory's Daughter. Vernon Watkins. NYBP
She That with Love Is Not Possessed. Elkanah Settle. *Fr.* Cambyses. SeCL
She—the woman whom I loved. The Avenger. James Wright. TwAmPo
She, then, like snow in a dark night. Like Snow. Robert Graves. AtBAP
She thinks that even up in heaven. *See* She even thinks that up in heaven.
She, to Him. Thomas Hardy. BEL; OBEV (new ed.); OBVV; TOP
She told the story, and the whole world wept. Harriet Beecher Stowe. Paul Laurence Dunbar. AA; AmePo; DD; Kal
She, too, the voyaging in doors and Keys. This Alice. Herbert Morris. PoRA
She took the bone from her arm. The Empress. Diane Wakoski. CoPo
She took the dappled partridge flecked with blood. Sonnet. Tennyson. CABA
She touches me. Her fingers nibble gently. In Love. David Wevill. MoCV
She tripped and fell against a star. Innocence. Anne Spencer. CDC
She turn'd the fair page with her fairer hand. Home, in War-Time. Sydney Dobell. VA
She turned in the high pew, until her sight. A Church Romance. Thomas Hardy. FaBoTw
She Turns the Dolls' Faces to the Wall. W. B. Yeats. Upon a Dying Lady, III. LiTB
She turns the pillow, smoothes the rumpled bed. Rites for a Demagogue. Anthony Thwaite. NePoEA-2
She undressed slowly. Whore. Gene Fowler. ThO
She wadna bake, she wadna brew. The Wife Wrapt in Wether's Skin. *Unknown.* BaBo (A *vers.*); ESPB
She Waited. Tania van Zyl. PeSA
She waits in a white dress. The Rendezvous. Jack Anderson. ThO
She walked along the crowded street. Revelation. Blanche Taylor Dickinson. CDC
She walked among the lilies. Mary. Margaret E. Sangster. DD
She Walked Unaware. Patrick MacDonogh. BoLP; ErPo; FaBoTw; NeIP; OnYI; OxBI
She Walks. Joseph Joel Keith. ISi
She Walks in Beauty. Byron. AnFE; AtBAP; ATP; AWP; BEL; BLPA; BoLiVe; BWP; CABA; CBEP; CBV; ChER; CoBe; EG; ELP; EnL; EnLi-2; EnLit; EnRP; EPN; ExPo; FaBoBe; FaBoEn; FaFP; FiP; GBV (1952 ed.); GTSE; GTSL; HBV; HBVY; HoPM; ILP; InP; InPo; JAWP; LiTB; LiTG; LiTL; LO; LoBV; MaPo; MBW-2; MCCG; MERP; MeWo; NeHB; NoP; OAEP; OBEV; OBNC; OBRV; OnPP; OTPC; OuHeWo; PG; PoEL-4; PoFS; PoIE; PoPo; PTK; RePo; RoGo; SeCeV; ShBV-4; TreF; TrGrPo; UnPo (1st ed.); VaPo; WePo; WoL
("She walks in beauty, like the night.") GTBS-D; GTBS-P; GTBS-W; StP
She walks in beauty like a lake. The Bed, Robert Creeley. StP
She walks—the lady of my delight. The Shepherdess. Alice Meynell. ACP; AWP; DD; EnLit; GBV; GoBC; GTSE; HBV; HBVY; JAWP; JKCP; MoBrPo; OBVV; OnPP; PoVP; TreFS; TSW; WBP
She walks with stately grace. Lyric of Doubt. Donald Wandrei. FiSC
"She Wandered after Strange Gods." Laura Benét. HBMV
She wanders in the April woods. Agatha. Alfred Austin. HBV; VA
She wanders up and down the main. Derelict. Elisabeth Cavazza Pullen. AA
She Warns Him. Frances Cornford. Two Poems, I. EnLoPo
She Was a Beauty. H. C. Bunner. AA; HBV
She was a city of patience; of proud name. Ypres. Laurence Binyon. MMA
She was a gordian shape of dazzling hue. Keats. *Fr.* Lamia. FIW
She was a high-class bitch and a dandy. Epitaph. Theodore Spencer. LiTA
She was a little girl who smelled/ of nice cologne. Two Weeks. Nicolás Guillén. PoNe
She Was a Phantom of Delight. Wordsworth. AnFE; ATP (1935 ed.); BEL; CBEP; EnLi-2; EnLit; EnRP; EPN; ERoP-1; FaBoBe; FaBV; FaFP; FaPL; GTBS; GTBS-D; GTBS-P; GTBS-W; GTSE; GTSL; ILP; LiTB; LiTL; LoBV; MBV-2; MCCG; MERP; NeHB; NoP; OAEP; OBRV; OHFP; OnPP; OTPC; OuHeWo; PoEL-4; PoPl; StP; TOP; TrGrPo; ViBoPo
(Perfect Woman.) HBV; OBEV; TreF
She Was a Pretty Little Girl. Ramón Pérez de Ayala, *tr. fr. Spanish by* Alida Malkus. FaPON
She was a quiet little body. Silence. Winifred Welles. HBMV
She was a stately lady. Changeling. Barbara Young. MoSiPe
She was a sweet country lassie. Blackpool Breezes. *Unknown.* CoMu
She was a Texas maiden, she came of low degree. The Transformation of a Texas Girl. James Barton Adams. SCC
She Was a Treasure. William Canton. TVC
She was a Virgin of austere regard. Christ's Victory in Heaven. Giles Fletcher. *Fr.* Christ's Victory and Triumph. ViBoPo
She was a woman peerless in her station. On Mistress Nicely, a Pattern for Housekeepers. Thomas Hood. OBRV
She Was All That You Loved. Halldór Laxness, *tr. fr. Icelandic by* Magnús A. Árnason. LiTW; PoPl
She was as lovely as a flower. Dream Tryst. Richard Le Gallienne. HBMV
She was beautiful that evening and so gay. An Escape. Abu Nuwas. ErPo
She was built for the hard voyage. Tanker. Christopher Middleton. NMP
She was careerish in a gentle way. Domestic: Climax. Merrill Moore. ErPo
She Was Carrying the Lamp. Rafael Méndez Dorich, *tr. fr. Spanish by* Donald Devenish Walsh. OnPM
She was generous, helpful, went out of her way. Epitaph on a Career Woman. William Cole. PV
She was never a dog that had much sense. Of an Ancient Spaniel in Her Fifteenth Year. Christopher Morley. WaKn
She was not as pretty as women I know. My Kate. Elizabeth Barrett Browning. OBVV; OHFP; WBLP
She was only a woman, famished for loving. A Tragedy. Théophile Marzials. HBV
She Was Poor but She Was Honest. *Unknown.* *See* Poor but Honest.
She was really neat, man. Jazzy Vanity. Richard W. Thomas. BF
She was seated of her goodness on my knee. The Snake. Hilary Corke. PV
She was sitting on the rough embankment. The Companion. Yevgeny Yevtushenko. FIW
She was skilled in music and the dance. Alas! Poor Queen. Marion Angus. ACV; GoTS; OxBS; SiSw
She was so aesthetic and culchud. The Cultured Girl Again. Ben King. FiBHP
She was so little—little in her grave. The Mother Who Died Too. Edith M. Thomas. AA
She was the daughter of Glubstein the Glover. Villanelle of a Villaness. Edwin Meade Robinson. HBMV
She Was the Girl within the Picture Frame. Delmore Schwartz. FiMAP
She was the human chalice. Venite Adoremus. Margery Cannon. GoBC
She was urgent to speak of the moon: she offered delight. An Old Woman Speaks of the Moon. Ruth Pitter. BoC
She was wearing the coral taffeta trousers. Full Moon. V. Sackville-West. MoBrPo (1942 ed.); MoShBr
She Was Young and Blithe and Fair. Harold Monro. HBV
She wears, my beloved, a rose upon her head. Requiem.

John Frederick Matheus. CDC
She Weeps over Rahoon. James Joyce. NP; ViBoPo
She welcomes him with pretty impatience. The Visit. Ogden Nash. FiBHP
She went about accustomed tasks. Loss. Julia Johnson Davis. HBMV
She went along the road. Hagar. Francis Lauderdale Adams. OxBS
She went round and asked subscriptions. A Cosmopolitan Woman. Sam Walter Foss. BOHV
She went to buy a brand new hat. Red. Countee Cullen. GoSl
She Went to Stay. Robert Creeley. ToPo
She went up the mountain to pluck wild herbs. Old and New. *Unknown, tr. by* Arthur Waley. AWP; LiTW
She Wept, She Railed. Stanley Kunitz. ErPo
She, who could neither rest nor sleep. Alas! Sadi. *Fr.* The Gulistan. AWP; WoL
She who hath felt a real pain. John Gay. EnLoPo
She, who so long has lain. New Love, New Life. Amy Levy. OBVV
She who to Heaven more Heaven doth annex. On a Virtuous Young Gentlewoman That Died Suddenly. William Cartwright. OBEV
She who was easy for any chance lover. Effie. Sterling A. Brown. BANP
She who with innocent and tender hands. The Monstrous Marriage. William Carlos Williams. MoPo
She whom I love will sit apart. Song. Gerald Gould. MoBrPo (1942 ed.)
She whose matchless beauty staineth. *Unknown.* OBSC
She, wild with wantonness, to her two suitors. The Wanton's Death. Norman Cameron. FaBoTw
She will not hunt again. The Old Falcon. Eleanor Baldwin. NYTB
She with his sight made breathless haste to meet him. Homer, *tr. by* George Chapman. *Fr.* The Iliad, VI. ViBoPo
She with Young Limbs. Bilhana, *formerly at. to* Chauras, *tr. fr. Sanskrit by* E. Powys Mathers. *Fr.* Black Marigolds. OnPM
She woke at length, but not as sleepers wake. The Death of Haidée. Byron. *Fr.* Don Juan, IV. FiP
She Wolf, The. Muriel Spark. NYBP
She wore a new "terra-cotta" dress. A Thunderstorm in Town. Thomas Hardy. EnLoPo
She Wore a Wreath of Roses. Thomas Haynes Bayly. BeLS; VA
She Would. Dixie Willson. GFA
She Would if She Could, *sel.* Sir George Etherege.
To Little or No Purpose I Spent Many Days. SeCL; SeEP; UnTE
She yields: my Lady in her noblest mood. Modern Love, XXXIX. George Meredith. ViPo; VP
Sheaf, The. Andrew Young. ChTr
Sheaf-Tosser. Eric Rolls. PoAu-2
Sheafe of snakes used heretofore to be, A. To Mr. George Herbert. John Donne. MaMe
Shearer's Song, The. *Unknown.* PoAu-1
Shearer's Wife, The. Louis Esson. BoAu; PoAu-1
Shearing. David McKee Wright. AnNZ
Shearing Grass. Peter Redgrove. NePoEA-2
Shears and paper. The Kite. Fang Che Chai. OnPM
Sheath and Knife. *Unknown.* CH; ESPB (A *and* E *vers.*); ViBoFo
("One king's daughter said to anither.") LO
Sheaves, The. E. A. Robinson. AP; AWP; CMoP; CoBMV; DiPo; FaBV; ForPo; InPo; JAWP; MAmP; MAP; MaPo; MoAB; MoAmPo; NePA; OxBA; PoSa; PTK; ReMP; TOP; WBP; WHA; YT
Sheba, now let down your hair. The Puppet Dreams. Conrad Aiken. *Fr.* Punch, the Immortal Liar. MAP; MoAmPo
Shed, The. Charles L. O'Donnell. ISi
Shed in blue-grey weatherboard with a high, A. Hillside. Alexander Craig. PoAu-2
Shed no tear! oh shed no tear! Fairy Song [*or* Faery Song]. Keats. CH; FaPON; HBV; OTPC
Shed not a tear upon this burial place. Epitaph for Elizabeth Ranquet. Corneille. CAW
Shed Not Too Many Tears. *Unknown.* MaRV
Shee brought her to her joyous paradize. The Garden of Adonis. Spenser. *Fr.* The Faerie Queene, III. PoEL-1
Shee is dead; and all which die. The Dissolution. John Donne. MaMe; OAEP; SeCV-1
Shee with whom troopes of Bustuary slaves. A Satyre Entituled the Witch. *Unknown.* CoMu
Sheep. W. H. Davies. LiTM; MoBrPo; OA; PrWP; StPo
Sheep. Samuel Hoffenstein. AnAmPo; TrJP
Sheep, The. "Seumas O'Sullivan." OxBI
Sheep, The. Hal Porter. NeLNL; PoAu-2
Sheep, The. Ann Taylor. BoChLi; BoTP; MPB; OTPC; UTS
(Boy and the Sheep, The.) PRWS
Sheep!/ Unhappy connotation. Bleat of Protest. Mildred Weston. FiBHP
Sheep and Lambs. Katharine Tynan. AnIV; BoPe; BoTP; HBV; JKCP; OBEV; OBVV; OnYI; OTPC (1946 ed.); OxBI; PoRL *abr.;* PRWS; StJW; VA; WHL
Sheep are coming home in Greece, The. The Homecoming of the Sheep. Francis Ledwidge. EnLit; HBMV; YT
Sheep are yarded, an' I sit, The. The Old Black Billy an' Me. Louis Esson. BoAu; NeLNL
Sheep Beezness, The. S. Omar Barker. IHA
Sheep-boy whistled loud, and lo, The. Elegiac Verses. Wordsworth. PoeP
Sheep get up and make their many tracks, The. Sheep in Winter. John Clare. FlW
Sheep Herd. *See* Sheepherd.
Sheep in Fog. Sylvia Plath. NaP
Sheep in Winter. John Clare. FlW
Sheep is blind; The, a passing Owl. The Blind Sheep. Randall Jarrell. NYBP
Sheep move on the grass. The Kill. Donald Hall. WIRo
Sheep Shearing, The. James Thomson. *See* Sheep-washing, The.
Sheep shit and fever gold. Sierra Kid. Philip Levine. AmPC
Sheep-washing, The. James Thomson. *Fr.* The Seasons: Summer. EnLi-2
(Sheep Shearing, The.) CoBE
Sheepbells. Edmund Blunden. BrPo
Sheepfol', De ("Po' lil' brack sheep"). *At. to* Paul Laurence Dunbar, *also to* Sarah Pratt McLean Greene. MaRV
(Little Black Sheep, The.) WBLP
Sheepfol', De ("De Massa . . ."). Sarah Pratt McLean Greene. AA; HBV
(Massa ob de Sheepfol, De.) OQP
Sheepheards Daffadill, The. Michael Drayton. *See* Gorbo and Batte.
Sheep Herd, The. Sister Mariella. ChrBoLe; WHL
Sheep-Herder, The. Badger Clark. IHA; SCC
Sheepherder, The. Lew Sarett. AmFN; FaPON; GaP
Sheep Herders. Maurice Lesemann. NP
Sheepstor. L. A. G. Strong. HBMV
Sheer Joy. Ralph Spaulding Cushman. SoP; TRV
Sheer over to the other side,—for see. The Idiot. Hart Crane. CBV; PoFS
Sheer stillness of the water, that resembles, The. Liadov: "The Enchanted Lake." James Kirkup. MuSP
Sheer whistles, noon's rejoinder to the wheel's spin. Whistles and Wheels. Alfred G. Bailey. PeCV
Sheet Lightning. Edmund Blunden. HaMV
Sheet of water which reflects the house, The. Ornamental Water. Louise Townsend Nicholl. NePoAm
Sheets of night mist travel a long valley, The. Mist Forms. Carl Sandburg. CMoP
Sheets were frozen hard, and they cut the naked hand, The. Christmas at Sea. Robert Louis Stevenson. BBV (1951 ed.); BrPo; CH; EtS; FaBoBe; FaBV; HBV; MCCG; OBVV; OTPC (1946 ed.); PeVV; PoVP; ShBV-2; StaSt; StPo; YAT
Sheffield Apprentice, The, *with music. Unknown.* BFSS
Shekel in the Fish's Mouth, The. Francis Quarles. StJW
Shekhinah. Karl Wolfskehl, *tr. fr. German by* Carol North Valhope *and* Ernst Morwitz. TrJP
Sheldonian Soliloquy. Siegfried Sassoon. UnS
Shell, The. James Stephens. BoNaP; BoTP; CH; CMoP; FlW; MoAB; MoBrPo; MoShBr; MoVE; NeMA; POTE; YT
Shell, The. Tennyson. *Fr.* Maud, Pt. II, ii. BoTP; GN; VA
(See What a Lovely Shell.) GoJo
("See what a lovely shell.") BoNaP; PoEL-5
She'll Be Comin' round the Mountain (A *and* B *vers.*), *with music. Unknown.* AS
Shell Castles. Rowena Bennett. GFA; UTS
She'll come at dusky first of day. August. Francis Ledwidge. OxBI; SiSw

She'll Do It. Burns. *See* Muirland Meg.
Shell Secrets. *Unknown.* BoTP
Shellbrook. William Barnes. OBNC
Shelley. Robert Browning. *Fr.* Pauline. OBRV
Shelley. Alexander Hay Japp. VA
Shelley, madman, made his rhymes. Wiser than the Children of Light. Monk Gibbon. NeIP
"Shelley? Oh yes, I saw him often then." The General Public. Stephen Vincent Benét. ML
Shelley! whose song so sweet was sweetest here. To Shelley. Walter Savage Landor. ViBoPo
Shelley's *Arethusa* Set to New Measures. Robert Duncan. OPoP
Shelley's Centenary. Sir William Watson. PoVP
Shelley's loves/ on fancies ripened. For a Little Lady. Fred Saidy. InMe
Shelley's Skylark. Thomas Hardy. CoBMV; FaBV; PoVP; ViPo (1962 ed.); VP
Shellfish and octopus, and all the insane. Crab. John Blight. BoAV
Shellpicker, The. Ronald Perry. NePoEA-2
Shells. T. Sturge Moore. SeCePo
Shells. Kathleen Raine. ImOP
Shells. Wordsworth. *Fr.* The Excursion, IV. BoPe
("Curious child, who dwelt upon a tract, A.") WGRP
(Faith.) MaRV
("I have seen/ a curious child, who. . .") OBRV; TreFT
Shells in Rock. Elizabeth Madox Roberts. AnAmPo
Shell's Song, The. Keats. EtS
Shelly. James McIntyre. FiBHP
Shelter. Charles Stuart Calverley. PCD
Shelter. Gene Derwood. NePA
Sheltered beneath white hawthorn boughs. Anonymous Alba. *Unknown.* OuHeWo
Sheltered Garden. Hilda Doolittle ("H. D.") PG
Sheltering from the rain. *Unknown.* *tr. fr. Japanese by* Geoffrey Bowna *and* Anthony Thwaite. FIW
Shema Yisrael. *Unknown.* TrJP
Shemuel. Edward Ernest Bowen. HBV
Shenandoah. Carl Sandburg. PaA
Shenandoah, *sel.* Delmore Schwartz.
Let Us Consider Where the Great Men Are. MoAB; MoAmPo
Shenandoah, The ("It's of a famous American ship"). *Unknown.* SoAmSa
Shenandoah ("Oh, Shenandoah, I love your daughter [*or* long to hear you]"), *with music.* *Unknown.* ABF, diff. vers.; AmFN; AmSS; ShS; SoAmSa; TrAS; TreFT
(Wide Mizzoura, The, *with music.*) AS
(Wild Miz-zou-rye, The, *longer vers., with music.*) ABF
Shepard upon a hill he sat, The. *Unknown.* *See* Can I Not Sing.
Shepeheards [*or* Shepheardes] boye, A (no better doe him call). January [Eclogue]. Spenser. *Fr.* The Shepheardes Calender. FiP; PIA; ReIE
Shepheard and the Milkmaid, The. *Unknown.* *See* Shepherd and the Milkmaid, The.
Shepheardes boy, A (no better doe him call). *See* Shepeheards boye, A (no better doe him call).
Shepheardes [*or* Shepheards *or* Shepherd's] Calendar, The, *sels.* Spenser.
April [*or* Aprill]. EnLi-1; PoEL-1; ReEn; ReIE; SiCE
Ditty, A: "See where she sits upon the grassy green," 6 *sts.* FaBoCh; OBEV
("See where she sits upon the grassy green," 2 *sts.*) ViBoPo
Elisa. OBSC
("Ye dayntye nymphs, that in this blessed brooke.") AtBAP
August. OAEP; ReEn
Perigot's and Cuddy's Roundelay. EP
(It Fell upon a Holy Eve.) PoE
(Perigot and Willye.) LoBV
(Roundelay, A: "It fell upon a holy eve.") EIL
February.
Oak and the Brere, The. OBSC
January Eclogue. FiP
(January.) ReIE
(Januarye.) PIA
July. ReIE
June. EnLit
March Eclogue. FosPo
(March.) PIA
November. MaPo; PoEL-1
Dido My Dear, Alas, Is Dead. ChTr
"Up then Melpomene thou mournefulst muse of nyne." AtBAP
October. EnPo; ReEn; ReIE; SiCE
(Contempt of Poetry, The.) OBSC
(October Eclogue.) PP
"But, ah! Maecenas is yclad in clay," *br. sel.* MyFE
To His Book[e], *dedicatory sonnet.* CLwM; ReIE; SiCE
Shepheards, The. Henry Vaughan. AnAnS-1; MeP
(Shepherds, The.) FosPo
Shepheards boy (best knowen by that name), The. Spenser. *Fr.* Colin Clout's Come Home Again. CABL; ReIE
Shepheard's Hunting, The. George Wither. *See* Shepherd's Hunting, The.
Shepheards Sirena, The. Michael Drayton. *See* Shepherd's Sirena.
Shepheards, that wont, on pipes of oaten reed. Astrophel. Spenser. StP
Shepherd, The. Blake. *Fr.* Songs of Innocence. BoTP; CBEP; EiPP; EnRP; ExPo; GaP; GoTP; HBV; LoBV; OBEC; OTPC; PoRh; ThWaDe; TiPo (1959 ed.); TOP; TVC
Shepherd. Edmund Blunden. HBMV
Shepherd, The. Mary Gilmore. ACV; PoAu-1
Shepherd, The. *Unknown.* UnTE
Shepherd, The. Wordsworth. *See* Prelude, The.
Shepherd and Nymph. Walter Savage Landor. *See* Tamar and the Nymph.
Shepherd and Shepherdess. Nicholas Breton. *See* Merry Country Lad, The.
Shepherd and Shepherdess. Thomas Hennell. FaBoTw
Shepherd and the Hawk, The. William Hart-Smith. AnNZ
Shepherd and the King, The. Eleanor Farjeon. TiPo (1952 ed.)
Shepherd [*or* Shepheard] and the Milkmaid, The. *Unknown.* CoMu; UnTE
Shepherd and the Nymph, The. Walter Savage Landor. *See* Tamar and the Nymph.
Shepherd and the Philosopher, The. John Gay. *Fr.* Fables. CEP; EiCL
Shepherd Boy, The. Heine, *tr. fr. German.* BoTP
Shepherd Boy, The. Edward Joseph O'Brien. HBMV
Shepherd boy a kingdom rules, The. The Shepherd Boy. Heine. BoTP
Shepherd-Boy and the Wolf, The. Aesop, *rhymed tr. fr. Greek by* William Ellery Leonard. AWP; JAWP; MPB; WBP
Shepherd-boy his grief is brooding o'er, A. Stanzas Concerning Christ and the Soul. St. John of the Cross. BoC
Shepherd boy lies on the hill, The. Noontide. John Keble. OTPC (1923 ed.)
Shepherd Boy Sings [in the Valley of Humiliation], The. Bunyan. *See* Shepherd Boy's Song, The.
Shepherd-boy, that hastens now and then, The. John Clare. *Fr.* The Shepherd's Calendar. GTBS-D
Shepherd Boys, The. Nicolas Saboly, *tr. fr. Provençal.* OHIP
Shepherd Boy's Song, The. Bunyan. *Fr.* The Pilgrim's Progress. BoTP; MaRV; OTPC (1923 ed.); PCH, *st.* 1; SoP; ThGo TRV
(Enough.) BLRP
(He That Is Down.) CBEP
("He that is down, needs fear no fall.") SeEP
(Shepherd Boy Sings [in the Valley of Humiliation], The.) EaLo; EG; GBV; GN; GoTP; HBV; HBVY; OBEV; OQP; OTD; WGRP
(Shepherd's Boy's Song, The.) PeRV
(Shepherd's Song, The.) BoC; OxBoCh
(Song of Low Degree, A.) STF
(Song of the Shepherd in the Valley of Humiliation, The.) CavP; OBS
Shepherd Dog of the Pyrenees, The. Ellen Murray. PoRL
Shepherd: Echo, I ween, will in the wood reply. *See* Echo, I ween. . .
Shepherd Folk Go to Bethlehem, The. Nicolas Saboly, *tr. fr. Provençal by* Ann Macdonnell. CAW
Shepherd in Winter, The. Sir Walter Scott. *Fr.* Marmion, *introd. to* IV. OTPC (1923 ed.)
Shepherd Kept Sheep on a Hill So High, A. Thomas D'Urfey. CoMu; ErPo
Shepherd Left Behind, The. Mildred Plew Meigs. ChBR

Shepherd Maiden, A. Edward Cracroft Lefroy. *Fr.* Echoes from Theocritus. VA
Shepherd of Eager [*or* Tender] Youth. Clement of Alexandria, *tr. fr. Greek by* Henry M. Dexter. MaRV, 3 *sts.*
(Earliest Christian Hymn, The) BePJ
(Youth of Jesus, The) SoP
Shepherd of King Admetus, The. James Russell Lowell. HBVY; TOP
Shepherd of Meriador, The. Wilfred Rowland Childe. HBMV
Shepherd of souls, Thy sheep behold! Three Hymns, 2. Charles Wesley. WaPE
Shepherd of tender youth. The Youth of Jesus [*or* The Earliest Christian Hymn]. Clement of Alexandria. BePJ; SoP
Shepherd on the fell, The. On Dow Crag. Patric Dickinson. POTi
Shepherd sat 'neath a tree one day, A. The Shepherd. *Unknown.* UnTE
Shepherd saw thou not my fair lovely Philis. *Unknown.* SeCSL
Shepherd set him under a thorn, A. The Merry Bagpipes. *Unknown.* CoMu
Shepherd, Shepherd, Hark. St. Theresa of Avila, *tr. fr. Spanish by* Arthur Symons. AWP;CAW;LiTW
Shepherd Song. Sir Philip Sidney. *Fr.* Arcadia. SiPS
Shepherd Speaks, The. John Erskine. ChIP; MaRV; OQP
Shepherd! that [*or* who] with thine amorous, sylvan song. The Good Shepherd. Lope de Vega, *tr. by* Longfellow. BePJ; CAW
Shepherd to His Love, The. Christopher Marlowe. *See* Passionate Shepherd to His Love, The.
Shepherd, to yon tall poplars tune your flute. Song of Poplars. Aldous Huxley. MoBrPo (1942 ed.)
Shepherd upon a [*or* the] Hill, The. *Unknown.* *See* Can I Not Sing.
Shepherd, what's love, I pray thee tell? The Shepherd's Description of Love. *At. to* Sir Walter Ralegh. ViBoPo
Shepherd, who can pass such wrong. The Nymph Selvagia [*or* Song]. Jorge de Montemayor, *tr. by* Bartholomew Young. *Fr.* Diana. EIL; SiCE; TuPP
Shepherd Who Stayed, The. Theodosia Garrison. ChrBoLe; OHIP
Shepherd! who with thine amorous, sylvan song. *See* Shepherd! that with. . .
Shepherd, wilt thou take counsel of the bird. Philomel to Corydon. William Young. AA
Shepherd, wouldst thou here obtain. Inscription: On the Back of a Gothic Seat. William Shenstone. EiPP
Shepherdes Calender, The. Spenser. *See* Shepheardes Calender, The.
Shepherdess. Norman Cameron. Three Love Poems, III. FaBoTw; GTBS-P; OxBS
Shepherdess, The. Alice Meynell. ACP; AWP; DD; EnLit; GBV; GoBC; GTSE; HBV; HBVY; JAWP; JKCP; MoBrPo; OBVV; OnPP; PoVP; TreFS; TSW; WBP
(Lady of the Lambs, The.) GTSL; OBEV
Shepherdess' Valentine, *sel.* Francis Andrewes.
I Bear, in Sign of Love. BiS
Shepherds, The. Samuel Taylor Coleridge. *See* Christmas Carol, A: "Shepherds went their hasty way, The."
Shepherds, The. Sophie Jewett. ChBoLe
Shepherds, The. Laura Spencer Portor. PEDC
Shepherds, The. Beren Van Slyke. GoYe
Shepherds, The. Henry Vaughan. *See* Shepheards, The.
Shepherds all, and maidens fair. Evening Song [*or* Folding the Flocks]. John Fletcher. *Fr.* The Faithful Shepherdess, II, i. CH; EIL; GN; OBS; OTPC (1923 ed.)
Shepherds almost wonder where they dwell, The. November. John Clare. GoTP; PoG
Shepherds and stars are quiet with the hills. V. Sackville-West. *Fr.* The Land. ShBV-4
Shepherds and the nymphs were seen, The. Cadenus and Vanessa. Swift. EiCL
Shepherd's Anthem, The. Michael Drayton. ReIE
Shepherd's boy, A (he seeks no better name). Summer. Pope. *Fr.* Pastorals. CEP; EiPP
Shepherd's Boy's Song, The. Bunyan. *See* Shepherd Boy's Song.
Shepherds buried the sun in a naked forest. Rest and Silence. Georg Trakl, *tr. by* Werner Heider. LiTW
Shepherds buried the sun in the bare wood. Peace and Silence. Georg Trakl, *tr. by* Glauco Cambon. OnPM
Shepherd's Calendar, The, *sel.* John Clare.
February. OBNC
(February: a Thaw.) NCEP
"Milkmaid singing, The." OBRV
Hedgehog, The, *fr.* February. OA; SeCeV
"Loud is the summer's busy song," *fr.* July. GoTP; OBRV
"Shepherd-boy, that hastens now and then, The," *fr.* March. GTBS-D
Shepherd's Calendar, The. Spenser. *See* Shepheardes Calender, The.
Shepherd's Coat, A. Lilian Bowes-Lyon. ChMP; GTBS-D
Shepherd's Complaint, A. Richard Barnfield. *See* Unknown Shepherd's Complaint, The.
Shepherd's Complaint, The, *sel.* John Dickenson.
Tityrus to His Fair Phyllis. EIL
Shepherd's Daffodil, The. Michael Drayton. *See* Gorbo and Batte.
Shepherd's daughter watching sheep, A. The Knight and Shepherd's Daughter (B *vers.*) *Unknown.* BaBo
Shepherd's Description of Love, The. *At. to* Sir Walter Ralegh. ViBoPo
Shepherd's Despair, The. Thomas Dermody. OnYI
Shepherd's Dirge, The. George Peele. *See* Dirge: "Welladay, welladay, poor Colin."
Shepherd's Dochter, The. *Unknown.* OxBB
Shepherd's Dog and the Wolf, The. John Gay. *Fr.* Fables. OA
Shepherd's Dream, A. Nicholas Breton. ReIE
Shepherd's Garland, The, *sels.* Michael Drayton.
Batte's Song: "Love is the heaven's fair [*or* fayre] aspect," *fr.* Eclogue VII (1593 ed.) LO
Batte's Song: "What is love but the desire," *fr.* Eclogue VII (1606 ed.). LoBV
Cassamen and Dowsabell, *fr.* Eclogue VIII (1593 ed.). OBSC
(Ballad of Dowsabell, The.) LoBV
(Dowsabel.) UnTE
(Eighth Eclogue, The.) ReEn; TuPP
Eclogue IX: "Late 'twas in June" (1606 ed.). OBSC
Gorbo and Batte, *fr.* Eclogue IX (1606 ed.). LoBV
("Gorbo, as thou cam'st [*or* camest] this way.") ViBoPo
(Ninth Eclogue, The.) OAEP; TuPP
(Shepherd's Daffodil, The.) EIL
Ninth Eglog, The: "What time the weatherbeaten flocks" (1593 ed.). ReIE
Rowland's Rhyme, *fr.* Eclogue II (1606 ed.). OBSC
Song to Beta: "O thou fair silver Thames," *fr.* Eclogue III (1593 ed.). OBSC
("Stay, Thames, to heare my song," *fr.* Eclogue III, 1606 ed.) PoEL-2
Sylvia *fr.* Eclogue IX (1606 ed.). LoBV (1949 ed.)
(Roundelay, A: "Tell me, thou skilful shepherd's swain.") EIL
Shepherd's Gift, A. Anyte. *See* By the Fountain.
Shepherd's Gratitude, The. Vergil, *tr. fr. Latin.* Eclogues, I. AWP, *tr. by* Charles Stuart Calverley
Shepherds Had an Angel, The. Christina Rossetti. MaRV; OHIP
(Christmas Carol, A: "Shepherds had an angel, The.") BoChLi
Shepherd's Holiday, The, *sel.* Joseph Rutter.
Hymen. SeCL
Shepherd's Holiday. Elinor Wylie. CrMA; HBMV
Shepherd's Home, The. William Shenstone. *See* Hope.
Shepherd's Hunting, The, *sels.* George Wither.
Fourth Eglogue, The, *abr.* SeCV-1
Philarete Praises Poetry, *fr.* Eclogue IV. OBS
Shepherd's Hut, The. Andrew Young. DTC; ThWaDe
Shepherd's Hymn, The. Richard Crashaw. *See* Hymn Sung as by the Shepherds, A.
Shepherds Hymn Their Saviour. Richard Crashaw. *See* Hymn Sung as by the Shepherds, A.
Shepherds, I have lost my love. The Banks of Banna. George Ogle. IrPN
Shepherds, I sing you, this winter's night. For the Nativity. John Heath-Stubbs. BoPe
Shepherds in Judea, The. Mary Austin. ChrBoLe; DD
Shepherd's Lament, The. Goethe, *tr. fr. German by* Bayard Taylor. AWP; JAWP; WBP
Shepherd's Madrigal, The. Geraldine Farrar. StJW

Shepherd's Ode, The. Robert Greene. *Fr.* Tullie's Love. OBSC
Shepherds on the lawn, The. Milton. *Fr.* On the Morning of Christ's Nativity. BoC
Shepherd's Pipe, The, *sel.* William Browne.
Dawn of Day, *fr.* Eclogue III. EIL
Shepherd's Plea, The. Christopher Marlowe. *See* Passionate Shepherd to His Love, The.
Shepherd's Praise of Diana, The. Sir Walter Ralegh. *See* Praised Be Diana's Fair and Harmless Light.
Shepherd's Psalm, The. Psalms, XXIII, Bible, *O.T.* *See* Lord Is My Shepherd, The.
Shepherds sing, The; and shall I silent be? Shall I Be Silent? George Herbert. *Fr.* Christmas. SoP; TRV
Shepherd's [*or* Shepheards] Sirena, The, *sel.* Michael Drayton.
Sirena ("Near to the silver Trent"). CBEP; OBEV, *abr.*; SeCL
(Jovial Shepheard's Song, The.) PoEL-2
("Near to the silver Trent.") SeEP; TuPP
(Song to Sirena.) AtBAP
Shepherd's Song, The. Bunyan. *See* Shepherd Boy's Song, The.
Shepherd's Song. Norah M. Holland. ChrBoLe
Shepherd's Song. Tennyson. *See* Come Down, O Maid.
Shepherd's Song of Venus and Adonis, The. Henry Constable. TuPP
Shepherd's Star, The. Juan Ramón Jiménez, *tr. fr. Spanish by* Anna Pursche. LiTW
Shepherd's star with trembling glint, The. En Bateau. Paul Verlaine. AWP
Shepherd's Tale, The. James Kirkup. POTi
Shepherd's Tale, A. Sir Philip Sidney. *Fr.* Arcadia. SiPS
Shepherds that on this mountain ridge abide. Cleitagoras. Leonidas of Tarentum. AWP
Shepherds there were who in the fields by night. Peace on Earth. Helen Wieand Cole. ChIP; OQP
Shepherd's Week, The. John Gay. EiCL
Sels.
Ditty, The. LoBV
Friday; or, The Dirge. BWP; CEP; EiCP; EiPP
Blouzelinda's Funeral. OBEC
Saturday; or, The Flights. EiCP; EiPP
Thursday; or, The Spell. CEP; EiPP; PoEL-3
Wednesday; or, The Dumps. EiCP; FosPo, *abr.*
Shepherds went their hasty way, The. A Christmas Carol [*or* The Shepherds]. Samuel Taylor Coleridge. ISi; OxBoCh; SoP; StJW
Shepherd's Wife's Song, The. Robert Greene. *Fr.* Greene's Mourning Garment. EIL; EnLit; HBV; LoBV; OBSC; PG; PTK; ReEn; SiCE; TOP; TuPP; ViBoPo
("Ah what is love? It is a pretty thing.") EG
Shepherd's Wooing Dulcina, The. *At. to* Sir Walter Ralegh. *See* Dulcina.
Sheppard in faith tell me. *Unknown.* SeCSL
Sheridan at Cedar Creek. Herman Melville. BBV (1923 ed.); LiTA; PAH
Sheridan's Ride. Thomas Buchanan Read. BBV; BeLS; CoBA; DD; FaBoBe; FaBV; FaFP; GN; HBV; HBVY; MC; OHFP; OHIP; OnSP; OTPC; PaA; PAH; PAP; TreF; WBLP; YaD
Sheriff, The. William Morris. *Fr.* A Dream of John Ball. PoVP
Sheriff followed hard and fast, a muy hombre he. Dodge City, the End of the Trail. *Unknown.* CoSo
Sheriff is made a mighty lord, The. The Sheriff. William Morris. *Fr.* A Dream of John Ball. PoVP
Sherman. Richard Watson Gilder. AA
Sherman Cyclone, The, *with music.* *Unknown.* BFSS
(Brown-eyed Lee.) CoSo
Sherman's in Savannah. Oliver Wendell Holmes. MC; PAH
Sherman's March to the Sea. Samuel H. M. Byers. DD; PAH; PAP
(Song of Sherman's March to the Sea.) HBV; MC; OTPC
Sherpa gasped out as they mounted the slope, The. Poem, neither Hilláryous Norgay. Gardner E. Lewis. FiBHP
Sherwood. Alfred Noyes. *See* Song of Sherwood, A.
She's a saucy fast packet and a packet of fame. The *Dreadnought, vers.* II. *Unknown.* ShS
She's All My Fancy Painted Him. "Lewis Carroll." ALV; CenHV; LiTL; NA; StaSt
She's bin out here a-teachin' fer this winter now a-past. Romance of the Range. Robert V. Carr. PoOW
She's bitter to her country: hear me, Paris. Helen of Troy. Shakespeare. *Fr.* Troilus and Cressida, IV, i. TreFT
She's But a Lassie Yet. James Hogg. *See* My Love She's But a Lassie Yet.
She's funny, she's funny. Un-Birthday Cake. Aileen Fisher. BiCB
She's Hoy'd Me Out o' Lauderdale. *Unknown.* CoMu
She's just a little kiddie. He Takes My Hand. Louis Paul Lehman, Jr. SoP
She's learned to hold her gladness lightly. A Lesson in Detachment. Vassar Miller. NePoEA-2
She's loveliest of the festal throng. The Rose and the Thorn. Paul Hamilton Hayne. AA; FaBoBe
She's Pretty to Walk With. Sir John Suckling. *Fr.* The Discontented Colonel. ALV; SeCL
She's somewhere in the sunlight strong. Richard Le Gallienne. HBV; OBEV; OBVV
She's tall and gaunt, and in her hard, sad face. Scrubber. W. E. Henley. *Fr.* In Hospital. PoVP
She's up there—Old Glory—where lightnings are sped. The Old Flag Forever [*or* Our Flag Forever]. Frank L. Stanton. DD; HH; PGD
Sheskinbeg. Elizabeth Shane. HBMV
Shew me thy feet; shew me thy legs, thy thighes. To Dianeme. Robert Herrick. AnAnS-2
Shh! The Professor Is Sleeping. John Morris. CABA
Shi King [*or* Book of Odes *or* Book of Songs], *sels.* *Unknown, tr. fr. Chinese.*
Companion of Her Lord till Death, *tr. by* Arthur Waley. HW
Elms of the Eastern Gate, *tr. by* Arthur Waley. LiTW
Fallen Leaves, *tr. by* Arthur Waley. LiTW
Farming, *tr. by* Arthur Waley. LiTW
Fast Bundled Is the Firewood, *tr. by* Arthur Waley. HW
Girl in the Carriage, The, *tr. by* Arthur Waley. LiTW
Glimpse of a Plain Cap, The, *tr. by* Arthur Waley. LiTW
How Goes the Night, *tr. by* Helen Waddell. AWP; JAWP; WBP
I Wait My Lord, *tr. by* Helen Waddell. AWP; JAWP; WBP
If Along the Highroad, *tr. by* Arthur Waley. LiTW
In Our Lane, *tr. by* Arthur Waley. LiTW
In the Wicker Fish-Trap, *tr. by* Arthur Waley. HW
Maytime, *tr. by* L. Cranmer-Byng. AWP
Morning Glory, The, *tr. by* Helen Waddell. AWP; JAWP; WBP
Of Silk Is Her Fishing-Line, *tr. by* Arthur Waley. HW
Pear-Tree, The, *tr. by* Allen Upward. AWP; JAWP; WBP
Soldier Thought Dead Returns Home, The, *tr. by* Arthur Waley. LiTW
Sun in the East, *tr. by* Arthur Waley. LiTW
"There grows an elm tree," *tr. by* Arthur Waley.
(Book of Odes.) MoBrPo (1942 ed.)
Thick Grows the Tarragon, *tr. by* Arthur Waley. HW
To the Lady of Ch'i, *tr. by* Arthur Waley. HW
Under the Pondweed, *tr. by* Helen Waddell. AWP
Wedding Song, *tr. by* Arthur Waley. LiTW
Wife, The, *tr. by* Henry H. Hart. OnPM; WoL
Wind and Rain, *tr. by* Arthur Waley. HW
Woman, *tr. by* H. A. Giles. AWP; LiTW
You Will Die, *tr. by* H. A. Giles. AWP; JAWP; WBP
Shield. *Unknown,* *tr. fr. Anglo-Saxon by* Charles W. Kennedy. *Fr.* Riddles. AnOE
Shield from every dart, The. What Christ Is to Us. *Unknown.* BLRP; SoP
Shield of Achilles, The. W. H. Auden. GTBS-P; NePA; NoP; OAEP (2d ed.); PAn; PoDB; SeCeV (1967 ed.)
Shield of Heracles, The, *sel.* Hesiod, *tr. fr. Greek by* Arthur S. Way.
"These were men that in harness of battle fought." PoFr
Shifting his position to relieve a cramped limb. Christ. Theodore Holmes. CoPo
Shiftless and shy, gentle and kind and frail. An Epitaph. J. C. Squire. HBMV
Shifty limpet on his rocky shore, The. Every Earthly Creature. John Malcolm Brinnin. LiTA
Shillin' a Day. Kipling. OAEP (2d ed.); ViBoPo
Shilling life will give you all the facts, A. Who's Who. W. H. Auden. CABA; CoBMV; MoAB; MoBrPo (1950 ed.); MoPW; NeMA; PoPo; ReMP; Sonn
Shiloh; a Requiem. Herman Melville. AmFN; AP; CBEP; HT; LiTA; MAmP; MWA-1; NCEP; NoP; OxBA; PaA; PAL; PoFS; PoPo; StP; TDP; ViBoPo; WiR
"Shimmer of Evil, The." Theodore Roethke. NePoAm-2

Shine and shock, A. Sight. Anne Welsh. BoSA
Shine forth into the night, O Flame. Give Our Conscience Light. Aline Badger Carter. ChIP; TrPWD
Shine in, O sun, on this dull place! For Martha's Kitchen. Fay Inchfawn. OQP
Shine Just Where You Are. *Unknown.* STF
Shine On, *with music.* Luke Schoolcraft. TrAS
Shine on me, oh, you gold, gold sun. Vacation Song. Edna St. Vincent Millay. YeAr
Shine on Me, Secret Splendor. Edwin Markham. TrPWD
Shine Out, Fair Sun [with All Your Heat]. *Unknown, at. to* George Chapman. *Fr.* The Masque of the Twelve Months. ChTr; ELP; FIW
(Song: "Shine out, fair Sun, with all your heat.") EIL
Shine, Perishing Republic. Robinson Jeffers. AmLP; AmP; AmPP; AnAmPo; CBV; CMoP; InP; LiTA; LiTM; MAP; MoAB; MoAmPo; MoVE; NAMP; NePA; NoP; NP; OTD; OxBA; PoIE; UnPo (3d ed.); ViBoPo
"And Boys, be in nothing so moderate as in love of man." *sel.* TRV
Shine, Republic. Robinson Jeffers. AmFN; MoRP
Shingle, sand, sea, shells, the tracks. For Sheila. Margaret Allonby. BoSA
Shining black in the shining light. To a Black Greyhound. Julian Grenfell. OtMeF
Shining daggers of the harbor lights, The. Evening on the Harbor. Virginia Lyne Tunstall. HBMV
Shining Dark. Michael Roberts. FaBoMo
Shining Eye of Horus cometh, The. He Kindleth a Fire. *Unknown. Fr.* Book of the Dead. AWP
Shining Hope, A. Julia H. Thayer. OQP
Shining Lord He is my light, The. Psalm XXVII. *Paraphrased by* Sir Philip Sidney. FCP
Shining neutral summer has no voice, The. In Memory of Ernst Toller. W. H. Auden. AtBAP; NYBP
Shining Night, A; or Dick Daring, the Poacher. *Unknown.* CoMu
Shining Spaces of the South, The. Joseph Campbell. JKCP
Shining Things. Elizabeth Gould. BoTP
Shining waters rise and swell, The. The Drowning of Conaing. *Unknown.* AnIL
Shiny. James Reeves. RePo
Shiny Little House, The. Nancy M. Hayes. BoTP; SUS
Shiny record albums scattered over. As You Leave Me. Etheridge Knight. BP
Ship, The. Louise A. Doran. EtS
Ship, The. J. F. Hendry. NeBP
Ship, The. Charles Mackay. BLPA
Ship, The. Lloyd Mifflin. AA
Ship, The. J. C. Squire. CH
Ship, The. *Unknown.* PoLF
Ship, an Isle, a Sickle Moon, A. James Elroy Flecker. BrPo; SyP
Ship and Her Makers, The. John Masefield. CoBE
Ship and the Sea, The. B. E. Baughan. AnNZ
Ship a-Raging, The, *with music. Unknown.* BFSS
Ship Bottom. Richmond Lattimore. NePoAm-2
Ship-broken Men Whom Stormy Seas Sore Toss. William Fowler. GoTS
Ship Builders, The. Whittier. AnNE; EtS
Ship-building Emperors Commanded. Peter Levi. NePoEA-2
Ship Burning and a Comet All in One Day, A. Richard Eberhart. NYBP; ToPo
Ship Canal from the Atlantic to the Pacific, The. Francis Lieber. PAH
Ship Comes In, A. Oliver Jenkins. EtS; PCH
Ship for Singapore, A. Daniel Whitehead Hicky. MoSiPe
Ship from Thames. Rex Ingamells. MoAuPo; PoAu-2
Ship I have got [*or* have] in the North Country, A. The *Golden Vanity. Unknown.* FaBoCh; OBB; ShBV-1
Ship in the Midst of the Sea, The. Christopher Wordsworth. BePJ
Ship is floating in the harbour now, A. Shelley. *Fr.* Epipsychidion. OBRV
Ship is sailing for Singapore, A. A Ship for Singapore. Daniel Whitehead Hicky. MoSiPe
Ship, leaving or arriving, of my lover. After a Passage in Baudelaire. Robert Duncan. OPoP
Ship near Shoals. Anna Wickham. HBMV
Ship o' Bed, The. Robert P. Tristram Coffin. TSW
Ship of Death, The. D. H. Lawrence. CMoP; DTC; FaBoTw; GTBS-P; LiTB; LoBV; MasP; MoAB; MoBrPo (1962 ed.); NoP; OAEP (2d ed.); ViBoPo
"I sing of autumn and the falling fruit," *sel.* NAMP
Ship of Fools, The, *sels.* Sebastian Brant, *tr. fr. German by* Alexander Barclay.
Ballade to Our Lady. ISi
Geographers. ACP
Preachment for Preachers. ACP; CAW
Star of the Sea. ACP; CAW
Tudor Rose, The. ACP
Ship of my body has danced in the dance of the storm, The. The Voyage. Karl Shapiro. MoLP
Ship of Rio, The. Walter de la Mare. CenHV; EtS; PDV; TiPo; UTS
Ship of State, The ("O navis, referent"). Horace, *tr. fr. Latin by* William Ewart Gladstone. Odes, I, 14. AWP; JAWP; WBP; OuHeWo, *tr. by* Sir Stephen E. De Vere.
Ship of State, The. Longfellow. *Fr.* The Building of the Ship. FaBoBe; HBVY; MaRV; NeHB; OHIP; OQP; PAL; PAP
(O Ship of State.) FaFP
(Republic, The.) AA; DD; HH; MC; PAH; WGRP
(Sail On, O Ship of State!) FaPON; PoFr; TreF
("Thou, too, sail on, O Ship of State!") PaA; PGD; YaD
Ship of State, beware! The Ship of State. Horace, *tr. by* Sir Stephen E. De Vere. OuHeWo
Ship *Rambolee,* The, *with music. Unknown.* ShS
Ship Rock. Jones Very. PoIE
Ship Sails Up to Bideford, A. Herbert Asquith. BoTP; BrR
Ship set forth on a tranquil sea, A. Sovereignty. Henry W. Frost. SoP
Ship That Never Returned, The, *with music. Unknown, diff. vers. of song by* Henry Clay Work. AS
Ship That Never Returned, The. Henry Clay Work. BLPA
Ship That Sails, The. *Unknown.* PoToHe (new ed.)
Ship to the roadstead rolled. O Navis. Austin Dobson. VA
Ship was built in Glasgow, and oh, she looked a daisy, A. In Prize. Cicely Fox Smith. WhC
"Ship was cheered, the harbour cleared, The." Samuel Taylor Coleridge. *Fr.* The Rime of the Ancient Mariner. MyFE
Ship with shields before the sun, The [*or* A]. Near Avalon. William Morris. CBEP; PoVP
Shiperd-boy, what is yer trade? The Beggar-Laddie. *Unknown.* ESPB
Shipman, The. Chaucer. *Fr.* The Canterbury Tales: Prologue. ACP, *mod.*; EtS
Shipmates, if you'll listen to me. Can't They Dance the Polka! *Unknown.* ShS
Shipmen, The. William Hunnis. *See* No Pains Comparable to His Attempt.
Shipment to Maidenek. Ephim G. Fogel. TrJP
Ships, The. John Joy Bell. BoTP
Ships. John Masefield. NP
Ships, The. Theodore Maynard. EtS
Ships. Nancy Byrd Turner. SoPo; SUS
Ships are fitted, and the convoy sails, The. Convoy. William Jay Smith. WaP
Ships are lying in the bay, The. The Wanderer. Zoë Akins. HBMV; NP
Ships at Sea. Robert Barry Coffin. EtS
Ship's Bell. Glenn Ward Dresbach. BoC
Ship's Cook, a Captive Sings, The. Hugo von Hofmannsthal, *tr. fr. German by* Charles Wharton Stork. TrJP
Ships glide in at the harbor's mouth, The. Our Father's World. Margaret E. Sangster. MaRV
Ships in Harbour. David Morton. EtS
Ships of Arcady, The. Francis Ledwidge. EtS
Ships of Saint John, The. Bliss Carman. EtS
Ships of Yule, The. Bliss Carman. BiCB; CaP; HBVY; RePo; WHW
Ships That Pass in the Night. Paul Laurence Dunbar. BANP; CDC
Ships That Pass in the Night. Longfellow. *Fr.* Tales of a Wayside Inn: The Theologian's Tale. EtS; PoToHe (new ed.); PTK
(Ocean of Life, The.) TreFT
Ships with Your Silver Nets. Wade Oliver. EtS
Shipwreck, The. Byron. *Fr.* Don Juan, II. MCCG, *much abr.*; OBRV; WHA
Shipwreck, The, *sels.* William Falconer.
All Hands Unmoor! *fr.* I. EtS

Shipwreck (continued)
"But now Athenian Mountains they descry," *fr.* III. GoTL
"In vain the cords and axes were prepared," *fr.* III. OBEC
Shortening Sail, *fr.* II. EtS
Shipwreck, The. E. Harriet Palmer. BOHV; NA
Shipwrecked Heart. *Unknown, tr. fr. Greek by* Lord Neaves. OnPM
Shipwrecked I, a farmer he. Farmer and Sailor. Plato. LiTW
Shirley Temple Surrounded by Lions. Kenward Elmslie. ANYP
Shiv and the Grasshopper ("Shiv, who poured the harvest and made the winds to blow"). Kipling. BoPe
Shiva. Robinson Jeffers. NYTB; SiSw; Sonn
Shiver, The. Thomas Hardy. InPo
Sho-sho-ne Sa-ca-ga-we-a — captive and wife was she. Sa-Ca-Ga-We-A. Edna Dean Proctor. PAH
Shoal of idlers, A, from a merchant craft. Pelters of Pyramids. Richard Henry Horne. VA
Shock, The. Larry Eigner. CoPo
Shock-headed Peter! There he stands. Slovenly Peter. Heinrich Hoffmann. BBGG
Shocking Rape and Murder of Two Lovers. *Unknown.* CoMu
Shock's fate I mourn; poor Shock is now no more. An Elegy on a Lap Dog. John Gay. DiPo; HBV; PoE
Shoe. John Perreault. YAP
Shoe a little horse. *Unknown.* OxNR
Shoe Factory, The. Ruth Harwood. HBMV
Shoe the colt, shoe the colt. Mother Goose. OxNR; RIS
Shoe the [old] horse, and shoe the mare. *Unknown.* PPL; SAS
Shoe the steed with silver. Sheridan at Cedar Creek. Herman Melville. BBV (1923 ed.); LiTA; PAH
Shoemaker, The ("As I was a-walking the other day"). *Unknown.* FaPON; GFA; SoPo
Shoemaker, The ("I am a shoemaker by my trade"), *with music. Unknown.* TrAS
Shoemaker makes shoes without leather, A. Riddle. *Unknown.* OxNR; SoPo
Shoemakers, The. Whittier. AmPP (4th ed.); AnNE; CoBA
Shoemaker's Booth, The. Robert Hershon. ThO
Shoemaker's Holiday, The, *sels.* Thomas Dekker.
"Cold's the wind, and wet's the rain," *fr.* V, iv. ReEn; TuPP
(Cold's the Wind.) ViBoPo
(Drinking Song.) TrGrPo
(Hey Derry Derry.) SeCePo
(Saint Hugh.) OBSC
(Troll the Bowl!) ElL
Oh, the Month of May! *fr.* III, v. ElL; ViBoPo
(May.) OBSC
(Maytime.) TrGrPo
Shoes. Tom Robinson. SoPo; TiPo
Shoes. Louis Untermeyer. StaSt
Shoes have tongues. Ilo Orleans. RIS
Shoes, secret face of my inner life. My Shoes. Charles Simic. CoAP
Sholom Aleichem. Elias Lieberman. TrJP
Shoo, Shoo, Shoo-Lye, *with music. Unknown.* ABF
Shoogy-Shoo, The. Winthrop Packard. HBV
Shoon-a-shoon/ I sing no psalm/ Little Man. The Virgin's Slumber Song. Francis Carlin. ISi; YeAr
Shoot down the "rebels"—men who dare. Rebels. Ernest Crosby. MC; PAH
Shoot, false Love, I care not. Song. *Unknown.* OBSC
Shoot the Buffalo, *with music. Unknown.* ABF; TrAS, *incl.* Hunt the Buffalo
Shoot your dice and have your fun, sugar babe. Sugar Babe. *Unknown.* ABF
Shooter's Hill, *sel.* Robert Bloomfield.
"Health! I seek thee;—dost thou love." OBNC
Shooting, The. Robert Pack. CoPo
Shooting of Dan McGrew, The. Robert W. Service. BeLS; FaBoBe; FaFP; MaC; NeHB; PoLF; PoRA; TreF; WHW
Shooting of His Dear. *Unknown. See* Molly Bawn.
Shooting of John Dillinger outside the Biograph Theater, July 22, 1934, The. David Wagoner. CoAP
Shooting of the Cup, The. John G. Neihardt. *Fr.* The Song of Three Friends. PoOW
Shooting of Werfel, The. Vernon Watkins. WaP
Shooting Song, A. William Brighty Rands. OTPC (1923 ed.)
Shooting Stars. Grace Noll Crowell. BoChLi
Shooting the Sun. Amy Lowell. MoAmPo (1950 ed.)
Shop. Robert Browning. PoVP; ViPo
Shop, The. W. W. Gibson. BEL
Shop and Freedom. *Unknown.* PAH
Shop of Dreams. Mary Jane Carr. BrR
Shop Windows. Rose Fyleman. SoPo; TiPo; UTS
Shopgirls leave their work, The. Charles Reznikoff. OCS
Shoplifter. Solomon Edwards. NNP
Shopman, The. Eleanor Farjeon. HBVY; PCH
Shopping cart clatters out of the Safeway, The. The Dazzling Day. Lewis MacAdams. ANYP
Shopping Day. Orrick Johns. InMe
Shopping for Meat in Winter. Oscar Williams. GTBS-W; LiTA; LiTM; NePA
Shops. John Farrar. PCH
Shops. Winifred M. Letts. MoSiPe
Shops take down their awnings. An Almanac. James Schuyler. ANYP
Shore. Mary Britton Miller. SUS; TiPo (1952 ed.)
Shore Birds. Vi Gale. GoYe
Shore is always a shelf, The. Conjured. John Gill. ThO
Shore-lark soars to his topmost flight, The. Ecstasy. Duncan Campbell Scott. CaP
Shore Roads of April. Bill Adams. EtS
Shore Scene. John Logan. NMP
Shore Tullye. Robert Rendall. OxBS
Shoreham: Twilight Time. Samuel Palmer. ERoP-2; NBM
Shores of my native land. Farewell. Isaac Toussaint-L'Ouverture. PoNe; TTY
Shores of the Styx are lone forevermore, The. Idle Charon. Eugene Lee-Hamilton. OBVV
Short and sweet, and we've come to the end of it. Da Capo. H. C. Bunner. HBV
Short direction, A. Rules and Regulations. "Lewis Carroll" OTD; PeVV
Short Hymne to Venus, A. Robert Herrick. CavP
Short Is My Rest. *Unknown.* EnRePo
Short Lay of Sigurd, The. *Unknown, tr. fr. Icelandic by* William Morris *and* Eiríkur Magnússon. *Fr.* The Elder Edda. EnLi-1
(Lay Called the Short Lay of Sigurd, The.) OuHeWo
(Lay of Sigurd, The.) AWP
Short Measures. Ben Jonson. *See* It Is Not Growing like a Tree.
Short Poem for Frustrated Poets, A. Johnie Scott. WSL
Short Prayer to Mary, A. *Unknown.* MeEL
Short seemed the space 'twixt sunset and the night. Nineveh. Robert Eyres Landor. *Fr.* The Impious Feast, V. OBRV
Short Sermon. *Unknown, ad. fr. German by* Louis Untermeyer. *Fr.* Proverbs. RIS; TiPo
Short Short Story. Josephine Jacobsen. NePoAm-2
Short Song of Congratulation, A. Samuel Johnson. CABA; EiCL; EiCP; ELP; InvP; LoBV; MBW-1; OBEC; PoEL-3; StP
(Long-Expected One-and-twenty.) CLwM
(One-and-twenty.) OBEV
(To a Young Heir.) UnPo (3d ed.)
"Wealth, my lad, was made to wander," *sel.* OtMeF
(On the Coming of Age of a Rich Extravagant Young Man.) ViBoPo
Short Visit, A. *Unknown.* SeCL
Shorten Sail. George Bubb Dodington. *See* Ode: "Love thy country. . ."
Shortenin' Bread, *with music. Unknown.* ABF
Shortening Sail. William Falconer. *Fr.* The Shipwreck, II. EtS
Shortest Poem in the World, The. Eli Siegel. SiTL
Shorthand. Julia Vinograd. YAP
Shorty George, *with music. Unknown.* ABF
Shot at Random, A. D. B. Wyndham Lewis. FaFP; FiBHP; SiTL
Shot, A: from crag to crag. Hunting Season. W. H. Auden. CBV
Shot gold, maroon and violet, dazzling silver, emerald, fawn. A Prairie Sunset. Walt Whitman. CoBA
Shot My Pistol in de Heart of Town, *with music. Unknown.* ABF
Shot? so quick, so clean an ending? A. E. Housman. A Shropshire Lad, XLIV. PoVP
Shot Who? Jim Lane! Merrill Moore. MAP; MoAmPo
Should a monkey wear a crown. Swift. *Fr.* To a Lady Who Desired I Would Write Some Verses in the Heroic Style. PoFr

Should a plan we suggest, just that minute. Limerick. "R. K. B." LiBL
Should all the world so wide to atoms fall. Our Insufficiency to Praise God Suitably for His Mercy. Edward Taylor. *Fr.* God's Determinations. LiTA
Should any ask me on His form to dwell. He Hath No Parallel. Sadi. *Fr.* The Gulistan. AWP; LiTW
Should auld acquaintance be forgot. Auld Lang Syne. Burns. AWP; BEL; CEP; CoBE; EiCP; EiPP; EnLi-2; EnLit; EnPE; EnRP; FaFP; GoTS; GTBS-W; HBV; InP; InPo; JAWP; LiTB; LiTG; LiTL; MCCG; NeHB; OAEP; OBEC; OBEV; OuHeWo; OxBS; PAn; PoE; PoLF; PTK; SiTL; TOP; TreF; WBP; YAT
Should chance strike out of me some human heat. Gentleman of Fifty Soliloquizes. Don Marquis. HBMV
Should D——s print, how once you robb'd your brother. Epigram. Pope. CEP
Should he upon an evening ramble fare. Keats. *Fr.* Epistle to George Keats. ChER
Should I Be a Rabbi? Hayyim Nahman Bialik, *tr. fr. Hebrew by* Grace Goldin. TrJP
Should I get married? Should I be good? Marriage. Gregory Corso. CABA; CoAP; LiTM (1970 ed.); NeAP; PIA
Should I long that dark were fair? The Dark. "George Eliot." *Fr.* The Spanish Gypsy. VA
Should I not be ashamed. The Ending. Paul Engle. NYBP
Should I sing a requiem, as the trap closes? Perhaps. Bob Kaufman. Kal
Should I sigh out my dayes in griefe. Song. Matthew Stevenson. CavP
Should I thee ranke with Radamanthus fell. A Satyretericall Charracter of a Proud Upstart [*or* March 4th Anno 1698/9; a Charracteristicall Satyre]. John Saffin. SCAP, 2 *versions*
Should I tread with ease the path He trod with sorrow? Sharing His Cross. Gracia L. Fero. BePJ
Should I with silver tooles delve through the hill. Meditation LVI. Edward Taylor. *Fr.* Preparatory Meditations, Second Series. MAmP; OxBA; SCAP
Should Lanterns Shine. Dylan Thomas. FaBoMo; GTBS-W
Should man oppose a rash rigidity. Meditation on a March Wind. Sister Mary Gilbert. JKCP (1955 ed.)
Should no man write, say you, but such as do excel? That No Man Should Write but Such as Do Excel. George Turberville. EnRePo
Should not the glowing lilies of the field. In His Steps. Katharine Lee Bates. PGD
Should old acquaintance be forgot. Auld Lang Syne. Burns. *See* Should auld acquaintance . . .
Should old acquaintance be forgot. Old-long-syne. *Unknown.* OBS
Should the building totter, run for an archway! The Fallen Tower of Siloam. Robert Graves. WaP
Should the cold Muscovit, whose furre and stove. To the Right Honourable the Countesse of C. William Habington. AnAnS-2; SeCP
Should the shade of Plato. On Installing an American Kitchen in Lower Austria. W. H. Auden. NYBP
Should the wide world roll away. The Black Riders, X. Stephen Crane. AmPP (5th ed.); AP
Should Thy Love Die. George Meredith. ELP; GTBS-D
Should we our sorrows in this method range. An Elegy upon My Best Friend. Henry King. AnAnS-2
Should you ask me, whence these stories? The Song of Hiawatha: Introduction. Longfellow. AnNE; PG (1945 ed.)
Should You Go First. A. K. Rowswell. PoLF; PoToHe (new ed.)
Should you meet a little saint. Identity. Sister Mary Helen. GoBC
Should you, my lord, while you pursue my song. Phillis Wheatley. *Fr.* To the Right Honorable William, Earl of Dartmouth. Kal; TTY
Should you, of mirth and hope bereft. Song. Alfred de Musset. OnPM
Should you revisit us. New Approach Needed. Kingsley Amis. PPON
Shoulder, The ("The shoulder of a man is shaped like a baby pig"). Edwin Denby. ANYP
Shoulder up your gun and call your dog. Ground Hog. *Unknown.* TrAS
Shouldering shapes of the skies of Broceliande. Taliessin's Song of the Unicorn. Charles Williams. FaBoTw
Shouldn't I ask. Oscar. Bill Berkson. ANYP
Shout, A!/ A trumpet note! The Morning Cometh! Anne Catherine White. SoP
Shout All over God's Heaven. *Unknown.* IHA
Shout for the mighty men. Leonidas. George Croly. HBV
Shout from a clump of bathing boys. Bridge. S. Foster Damon. AnAmPo
Shouts shrink to a tense, The. This Baptism with Fire. A. X. Nicholas. WSL
Shovel-gnats gnaw at the open wound, The. On the Edge of the Copper Pit. Pauline Henson. GoYe
Shovellin' Iron Ore, *with music.* *Unknown.* AS
Show, The. Emily Dickinson. *See* The show is not the show.
Show, The. Wilfred Owen. LiTB; LiTG; LiTM (rev. ed.); MoAB; MoBrPo (1950 ed.); NAMP; WaaP; WaP
Show is not the show, The. Emily Dickinson. AmePo; AmPP (5th ed.); CBV; CoBA; DiPo; MemP
Show me again the time. Lines to a Movement in Mozart's E-flat Symphony. Thomas Hardy. BoLP; ELP
Show me, dear [*or* deare] Christ, thy spouse so bright and clear. Holy Sonnets, XVIII. John Donne. AnAnS-1; ExPo; ILP; MaMe; MasP; MBW-1; MeLP; MeP; NoP; OAEP; OBS; SCEP-1; SeEP; Sonn; TuPP
Show me himselfe, himselfe (bright Sir) O show. Come See the Place Where the Lord Lay. Richard Crashaw. MaMe
Show Me Lord Show Me. Yusef Iman. BF
Show Me More Love. *Unknown.* OxBoCh
Show me the face, cold mirror, that the world. Her Decision. James K. Baxter. Cressida, XI. AnNZ
Show Me Thy Feet. Robert Herrick. UnTE
Show Me Thyself. Margaret E. Sangster. TrPWD
"Show me your cloister," asks the Lady Poverty of the friars. Cloister. Charles L. O'Donnell. CAW
"Show me your God!" the doubter cries. Blind. John Kendrick Bangs. MaRV; OQP; PoToHe; SoP
Show-window manikins. Three Links of Light Armour. Richard Armour. SiTL
Shower, A. Izembo, *arr. by* Olive Beaupré Miller. SUS; TiPo
Shower, The. Henry Vaughan. AtBAP; BoNaP; ChTr; FlW; LiTB; MemP; OBS; ViBoPo
(Showre, The.) AnAnS-1; MeP; MePo; SeCP
Shower, a sprinkle, A. Summer Rain. Eve Merriam. PDV
Shower and Sunshine. Maud Morin. BoTP
Shower came. A Shower. Izembo. SUS; TiPo
Shower hath past, ere it hath well begun, The. After the Shower. Archibald Lampman. CaP
Shower in spring, A. Chums. Buson. GaP
Shower of green gems on my apple tree, A. May Garden. John Drinkwater. HBMV
Shower, Shower! Rain, Rain! *Unknown.* OnPM
Showers fall as softly, The. High and Low. Dora Read Goodale. PRWS
Showing How the Cavern Followed the Hut's Advice. John Hookham Frere. OTPC (1923 ed.)
Showing Off. *Unknown, tr. fr. Irish by* Frank O'Connor. KiLC
Showman comes with his box of dolls, The. The Puppet Play. Padraic Colum. RoGo
Showre, The. Henry Vaughan. *See* Shower, The.
Shredded sunset, The. Night Interpreted. Everett Hoagland. NBP
Shrew, The. Ogden Nash. CenHV
Shrill the fife, kettle the drum. Baldy Bane. W. S. Graham. NePoEA
Shrilling locust slowly sheathes, The. The Beetle. James Whitcomb Riley. FaPON; PCD
Shrimp, The. Moses Browne. WaPE
Shrimping boats are late today, The. Nocturne: Georgia Coast. Daniel Whitehead Hicky. AmFN
Shrine, The. Digby Mackworth Dolben. DD; GoBC; HBV
Shrine, The. Hilda Doolittle ("H. D.") AnAmPo; MAPA; NP
Shrine in Nazareth. Sister Mary St. Virginia. ISi
Shrine to What Should Be. Mari Evans. NNP
Shropshire Lad, A. John Betjeman. MoBS; ShBV-4
Shropshire Lad, A. A. E. Housman. *Poems indexed separately by titles and first lines.*
Shropshire Lad, A. *Unknown.* ChTr
Shroud, The. Edna St. Vincent Millay. NP

Shrouded Stranger, The. Allen Ginsberg. NeAP
Shrouding of the Duchess of Malfi, The. John Webster. *See* Hark, Now Everything Is Still.
Shrouds and Away. Alfred G. Bailey. PeCV
Shrubbery, The. William Cowper. BWP; CBEP; CEP; EiPP; FaBoEn; GTSL; NCEP; OBEC; PoIE; StP
Sh-ta-ra-dah-dey, *with music.* *Unknown.* AS
Shu is away in the hunting-fields. In Our Lane. *Unknown.* *Fr.* Shi King. LiTW
Shub-Ad. Robert H. Barlow. FiSC
Shudder, The. Donald Hall. NYBP
Shuffle-Shoon and Amber-Locks. Eugene Field. PTK
Shuffling along in her broken shoes from the slums. Douglas Stewart. *Fr.* Lady Feeding the Cats. FIW
Shui Shu, *sels.* *Tr. fr. Japanese by* Arthur Waley.
"Because river-fog." Kiyowara Fukuyabu. AWP; JAWP; LiTW; WBP
(River-Fog.) FaPON
"Deer which lives, The." Onakatomi Yoshinobu. AWP
("Deer on pine mountain, The," *tr. by* Kenneth Rexroth.) LiTW
"If it were not for the voice." Nakatsukasa. AWP
"Time I went to see my Sister, The." Tsurayuki. AWP
"When halting in front of it." Hitomaro. AWP; JAWP; WBP
"Winter has at last come." Minamoto no Shigeyuki. AWP
Shule, Agrah! "Fiona Macleod." OBVV
(Shule, Shule, Shule, Agrah!) PoVP
Shu-lin was a parrot who sat on the shoulder. Deprecating Parrots. Beulah May. EtS
Shun delays, they breed remorse. Loss in Delay. Robert Southwell. OBSC; SiCE
Shun Passion. Emerson. AmPP (3d ed.)
Shunting. Basil Dowling. AnNZ
Shut Door, The. *Unknown.* SoP
Shut fast again in beauty's sheath. Monochrome. Louise Imogen Guiney. AnAmPo
Shut-in, The. Nellie De Hearn. PoToHe (new ed.)
Shut In ("Shut in; a prisoner"). Henry W. Frost. SoP
Shut In ("Shut in? Ah, yes, that's so"). *Unknown.* SoP
Shut in from all the world without. Firelight. Whittier. *Fr.* Snow-bound. AA; LaNeLa
Shut In with God. *Unknown.* FaChP
Shut not so soon; the dull-eyed [*or* dull-ey'd] night. To Daisies, Not to Shut So Soon. Robert Herrick. AtBAP; BoLiVe; CH; EG; ELP; HBV; OBEV; OBS; SeCV-1; SeEP; TrGrPo
Shut Not Your Doors. Walt Whitman. ML; OxBA
Shut Out. Christina Rossetti. NoP
Shut Out That Moon. Thomas Hardy. BrPo; CMoP; MoVE; ViBoPo
Shut, shut the door, good John! Epistle to Dr. Arbuthnot [*or* An Epistle from Mr. Pope, to Dr. Arbuthnot]. Pope. BEL; CABA; CABL; CEP; CoBE; EiCL; EiPP; EnLi-1; EnLit; FosPo; HoPM; LoBV; MBW-1; NoP; OAEP; OxBoLi; PAn; PoE; PoEL-3; PoIE; TOP; WHA; WoL
Shut the Seven Seas against Us. George Barker. *Fr.* Third Cycle of Love Poems. MoAB; MoBrPo (1950 ed.); NeMA
Shut Up, I Said. Peggy Bennett. ELU
Shutter of time darkening ceaselessly, The. August. Louis MacNeice. CMoP; FaBoEn; LiTM
Shutters unhinge the bat, and brazen sun. Praise to Light. Thomas Cole. NePoAm-2
Shuttles of His purpose move, The. His Purposes. *Unknown.* FaChP
Shuttles of trains going north, going south, drawing threads of blue. Morning Sun. Louis MacNeice. MoAB; MoBrPo; NeMA; TwCP
Shy and timid, Gloom to me. The Outcast. James Stephens. MoBrPo
Shy as the April weather. Armor the Bud. Frances Frieseke. JKCP (1955 ed.)
Shy Geordie. Helen B. Cruickshank. ACV; GoTS; OxBS
Shy in their herding dwell the fallow deer. Deer. John Drinkwater. CH
Shy one, I said, you can take me away in a breath. I Spoke to the Violet. John Shaw Neilson. BoAV
Shy one, shy one. To an Isle in the Water. W. B. Yeats. AWP; JAWP; ThGo; WBP
Shylock's Defense. Shakespeare. *Fr.* The Merchant of Venice, III, i. TreFS
Shyly the silver-hatted mushrooms make. May. John Shaw Neilson. NeLNL; PoAu-1
Si Hubbard. *Unknown.* AS, *with music*; IHA
Si Jeunesse Savait! Edmund Clarence Stedman. AA
Si, senor, is halligators here, your guidebook say it. Sinalóa. Earle Birney. MoCV
Si talked with Dauber, standing by the side. John Masefield. *Fr.* Dauber. InP
Siamese twins: one, maddened by. Twins. Robert Graves. PV
Siasconset Song. Philip Booth. CaFP; NePoAm; StP
Siberia. James Clarence Mangan. FOL; IrPN; NBM; PeER; RoGo
Sibrandus Schafnaburgensis. Robert Browning. Garden Fancies, II. CTC; EnLi-2 (1949 ed.)
Sibyl, The. Thomas Gordon Hake. VA
Sibyl, The. Joan LaBombard. GoYe
Sibyl. John Payne. VA
Sibylla's Dirge. Thomas Lovell Beddoes. *See* Dirge: "We do lie beneath the grass."
Sibylline Prophecy, The. Vergil, *tr. fr. Latin by* Roderick Gill. *Fr.* Eclogues, IV. CAW; ISi, *tr. wr. at. to* Thomas Walsh
Sic a Wife as Willie Had. Burns. GoTS
Sic Ars Diluditur Arte. Henry Parrot. SiCE
Sic et Non. Sir Herbert Read. FaBoTw
Sic Itur. Arthur Hugh Clough. NCEP
Sic Transit. Thomas Campion. *See* Come, Cheerful Day!
Sic Transit. Joseph Mary Plunkett. ACP
Sic Transit. *Unknown.* *See* Proper Sonnet, A, How Time Consumeth . . .
Sic Transit Gloria Mundi. James Wreford Watson. CaP
Sic Vita. William Stanley Braithwaite. BANP; OQP
Sic Vita. Henry King. AnAnS-2; DiPo; ELP; HBV (8th ed.); MePo; OBS; PoFS; SeCP; UnPo (1st ed.); YAT
(Even Such Is Man.) BEL
(Like to the Falling of a Star.) EG; GTBS-W; LiTG, PoPo; SeCePo
(Of Human Life.) TrGrPo
(On the Life of Man.) GoBC; HBV (6th ed.); TOP; WHA
Sic Vita. Henry David Thoreau. *See* I Am a Parcel of Vain Strivings Tied.
Siccine separat amara mors? Knowledge after Death. Henry Charles Beeching. OBVV; VA
Sicelides, *sel.* Phineas Fletcher.
Woman's Inconstancy, *fr.* II, ii. EIL
Sicilian Cyclamens. D. H. Lawrence. ChMP; MoVE
Sicilian Muse, begin a loftier strain! The Messiah. Vergil, *tr. by* Dryden. Eclogues, IV. AWP; JAWP; OuHeWo; WBP
Sicilian Night, A. Edward Cracroft Lefroy. Echoes from Theocritus, IV. VA
Siciliana; the Landings at Gela. G. Stanley Koehler. NePoAm-2
Sicilian's Tale, The. Longfellow. *See* Monk of Casal-Maggiore, The.
Sicily and Naples, *sel.* Samuel Harding.
Of Death. CBEP; SeCL
Sick. Haldor Lillenas. SoP
Sick and used Cambridge in the sucking sound. The Morning Light for One with Too Much Luck. Delmore Schwartz. FiMAP
Sick Boy. Anne Ridler. NYTB
Sick Child, A. Randall Jarrell. InvP; TDP
Sick Child, The. Robert Louis Stevenson CH; PoSC
Sick, Cornificius, is thy friend. The Complaint. Catullus. OnPM
Sick King in Bokhara, The. Matthew Arnold. PoVP
Sick Leave. Siegfried Sassoon. NP
Sick Lion and the Fox, The. La Fontaine, *tr. fr. French by* Elizur Wright. OnPM
Sick Love. Robert Graves. CMoP; GTBS-P; PoTE
(O Love in Me.) FaBoMo
Sick Man and the Angel, The. John Gay. *Fr.* Fables. CEP
Sick man, though, had wit who thought you up, The. For Two Girls Setting Out in Life. Peter Viereck. MiAP
Sick Nought, The. Randall Jarrell. OxBA
Sick of pale European beauties spoiled. Black Marble. Arthur O'Shaughnessy. SyP
Sick of the day's heat, of noise. The Underground Gardens. Robert Mezey. NaP

Sick of the piercing company of women. A Country Walk. Thomas Kinsella. NMP; OPoP
Sick of thy Northern glooms, come, shepherd, seek. Philip Freneau. *Fr.* The Beauties of Santa Cruz. CoBA
Sick Room. Francis D. Clare. JKCP (1955 ed.)
Sick Rose, The. Blake. *Fr.* Songs of Experience. AtBAP; AWP; BEL; BoLiVe; BoW; BWP; CABA; CaFP; CBEP; CBV; ChER; ChTr; DiPo; EiCL; EiPP; EnL; EnLoPo; ERoP-1; ExPo; FaBoEn; ForPo; FosPo; GTBS-D; ILP; InPo; JAWP; LoBV; MaPo; NoP; OAEP; OBNC; OnPM; PeER; PIA; PoAn; PoEL-4; PoeP; PoFS; PoG; PoIE; PoSa; SeCeV; ShBV-4; StP; TOP; TrGrPo; ViBoPo; WBP
(“O Rose, thou art sick.”) EG; ELP
Sick Stockrider, The. Adam Lindsay Gordon. ACV; BoAu; FOL; OBVV; PoAu-1; VA
“I've had my share of pastime,” *sel.* OtMeF
Sick with the pangs that prompt the lover's moan. Thomas Russell. Sonn
Sicke Implore St. Peter's Shadow, The. Richard Crashaw. MaMe; SCEP-1
(St. Peter's Shadow.) ACP
Sickened with slaughter and weary of war. A New Year's Message. Martha Snell Nicholson. SoP
Sickle Pears. Owen Dodson. AmNP
Sickles sound. Harvest Song. Ludwig Hölty. AWP; JAWP; WBP; WoL
Sickness, The. Frederick Seidel. CoPo
Sickness, intending my love to betray. Sir John Davies. *Fr.* Sonnets to Philomel. SiPS
Sickness, Not Sleep. *Unknown.* SeCL
(“She sleeps: peace crown thine eyes, sweet dreams in deep.”) LO
Sickness of Adam, The. Karl Shapiro. *Fr.* Adam and Eve. AP; CoBMV; MoAB
Sickness of desire, that in dark days, The. Melancholia. Robert Bridges. CMoP
Sickness of Friends, The. Henri Coulette. NYBP
Sickness, 'tis true. Samuel Taylor Coleridge. *Fr.* A Tombless Epitaph. OBRV
Side by side in the crowded streets. The Cantelope. Bayard Taylor. BOHV
Side by side, their faces blurred. An Arundel Tomb. Philip Larkin. NePoEA-2
Side by side through the streets at midnight. April Midnight. Arthur Symons. SyP
Sidewalk cracks, gumspots, the water, the bits of refuse, The. The Silence at Night, Edwin Denby. ANYP
Sidewalk Orgy. Richard O'Connell. PV
Sidewalks of New York, The. James W. Blake. BLPA; FaBoBe; TreFS; YaD
Siding Near Chillicothe, A. Richmond Lattimore. AmFN
Sidney, according to report, was kindly hearted. Various Ends. Ruthven Todd. NeBP; SeCePo
Sidney Godolphin. Clinton Scollard. AA
Sidney Greenstreet Blues, The. Richard Brautigan. FRC
Sidrophel, the Rosicrucian Conjurer. Samuel Butler. *Fr.* Hudibras. OxBoLi
Siege, The, *sel.* William Cartwright.
Seal Up Her Eyes, O Sleep. SeCL
Siege, The. Sir John Suckling. *See* 'Tis Now, Since I Sat Down Before.
Siege of Belgrade, The. *Unknown, at. to* Alaric Alexander Watts. BLPA; BOHV; HBV; PTK; TreF
(Alliteration; or, The Siege of Belgrade.) ChTr
(Austrian Army, An.) FiBHP; PoPo; SiTL
Siege of Chapultepec, The. William Haines Lytle. MC; PAH
Siege of Corinth, The. Byron. GoTL
Siege of Ismail, The. Byron. *Fr.* Don Juan, VII *and* VIII. WoL
Siege of Plattsburg, *with music. Unknown.* ABF
Siege of Rhodes, The, *sel.* Sir William Davenant.
Jealousy. BoLP
(“This cursed jealousy, what is't?”) LO
Siege of Silence, A. Brother Antoninus. ToPo
Siege of Valencia, The, *sel.* Felicia Dorothea Hemans.
Dirge: “Calm on the bosom of thy God.” HBV, *longer sel.*; OBEV
(Death-Hymn, A.) OBRV
Siegfried. Randall Jarrell. MiAP; ReMP
Siena. Swinburne. ViPo
Laud of Saint Catherine, The, *sel.* CAW
“Siena Mi Fé; Disfecemi Maremma.” Ezra Pound. *Fr.* Hugh Selwyn Mauberley. CMoP; MoAmPo (1962 ed.)
Sierra Kid. Philip Levine. AmPC
Sierran Vigil. Ewart Milne. NeIP
Siesta. Samuel Hazo. NYTB
Siesta, The (“Airs! that wander and murmur round”). *Unknown, tr. fr. Spanish by* Bryant. AWP; JAWP; WBP
Siesta in Andalusia! Villafranca de Córdoba. Pedro Garfias. PoFr
Sieve, The. Sadi, *tr. fr. Persian by* Edward B. Eastwick. LiTW
Sifting. Victor E. Beck. GoYe
Sifting of Peter, The. Longfellow. SoP
Sigh. Stéphane Mallarmé, *tr. fr. French by* Arthur Symons. AWP; JAWP; SyP; WBP
—— *Tr. by* Alan Conder. OnPM
Sigh, A. Harriet Prescott Spofford. AA; HBV
Sigh, The. Nathaniel Wanley. OBS; OxBoCh
Sigh, A. Countess of Winchilsea. CEP
Sigh heart, and break not; rest, lark, and wake not. Nuptial Song. Lord De Tabley. GTBS-P; OBVV; PeVV
Sigh his name into the night. Love's Secret Name. John Arthur Blaikie. VA
Sigh no more, ladies, sigh no more. Shakespeare. AnFE; *Fr.* Much Ado About Nothing, II, iii. AWP; BoLP; CBEP; CTC; DiPo; EG; EIL; ELP; EnLi-1 (1949 ed.); EnLit; ExPo; HBV; InMe; InPo; JAWP; LiTB; LiTG; LiTL; MCCG; MeWo; OAEP; PAn; PoEL-2; SeCeV; SiCE; SiTL; TOP; TreFS; TrGrPo; ViBoPo; WBP
(Balthasar's Song.) ALV; BoLiVe; OBSC
(Song: “Sigh no more, ladies, sigh no more.”) FiP
Sigh Not for Love. Helen Hay Whitney. AA
Sigh of Silence, The. Keats. *See* I Stood Tiptoe.
Sigh That Heaves the Grasses, The. A. E. Housman. MoVE
Sigh, wind in the pine. Lament. Douglas Stewart. MoAuPo
Sighing, and sadly sitting by my love. Richard Barnfield. *Fr.* Cynthia. Sonn
Sighing Time, The. Edmund Blunden. BrPo
Sighs. *Unknown.* SeCL
(“All night I muse, all day I cry.”) LO
Sighs and Grones. George Herbert. AtBAP; MaMe; PoEL-2
Sighs are air, and are lost in air. Three Rimas, 2. Gustavo Adolfo Bécquer, *tr. by* Harold Morland. *Fr.* Rimas. LiTW
Sighs are my food, my drink are my tears. Wyatt Being in Prison, to Bryan. Sir Thomas Wyatt. FCP; SiCE; SiPS; TuPP
Sight, A. Robert Creeley. NaP
Sight. Sir John Davies. LoBV (2d ed.)
Sight. W. W. Gibson. MoBrPo; NeMA; PoMa
Sight. Cora Ball Moton. GoSl
Sight. Ida Norton Munson. ChIP
Sight. Anne Welsh. BoSA
Sight and Insight. Eleanor Slater. TrPWD
Sight in Camp [in the Daybreak Gray and Dim], A. Walt Whitman. AA; AmPP (4th ed.); AP; ExPo; GTBS-W; ILP; LO; OxBA; PoEL-5; PoPo; PoSa; TDP; TRV
Sight Unseen. Kingsley Amis. ErPo; NePoEA-2
Sighted Sub. *Unknown.* WhC
Sightings I. Jerome Rothenberg. CoPo
Sightless, I breathe and touch; this night of pines. The Cicadas. Aldous Huxley. POTE
Sightseers in a Courtyard. Nicolás Guillén, *tr. fr. Spanish by* Langston Hughes. PoNe; TTY
Sigismonda and Guiscardo, *sel.* Dryden.
Ave atque Vale. OBS
Sign, The. Bhartrihari, *tr. fr. Sanskrit by* Paul Elmer More. LiTW
Sign, The. Frederic Manning. NP
Sign of Spring, A. Eben Eugene Rexford. PCH
(Bluebird, The.) PEDC
Sign of the Cross, The. Cardinal Newman. GoBC; JKCP; PoVP; VA
Sign of the Love Divine. The Red Cross. Henry van Dyke. PEDC
Sign-Post. *See* Signpost.
Signal, The. Eugenio Florit, *tr. fr. Spanish by* H. R. Hays. OnPM
Signal Fire, The. Aeschylus, *tr. fr. Greek by* Dallam Simpson. *Fr.* Agamemnon. CTC
Signal Fires. Edward Everett Hale. From Potomac to Merrimac, II. PAH

Signals spelled summer but for me it was spring, The. Evergreen. Ewart Milne. OxBI
Signature. Dorothy Livesay. OBCV
Signature for Tempo. Archibald MacLeish. MoVE
Signature of All Things, The, *sel.* Kenneth Rexroth.
"When I dragged the rotten log." BoNaP
Signature of Pain, The. Alan Porter. POTE
Signatures. Candace Thurber Stevenson. AmFN
Significance of John Brown, The. Stephen Vincent Benét. *Fr.* John Brown's Body. PaA
Signpost. Robinson Jeffers. GoYe; PoPo; ViBoPo
Sign-Post, The. Edward Thomas. PoIE; ViBoPo
Signs. Beatrice M. Murphy. GoSl
Signs. William Soutar. ACV
Signs and Charms. *Unknown.* StaSt
Signs and Seasons. *Unknown.* RIS
Signs Everywhere of Birds Nesting, While. William Carlos Williams. *Fr.* Paterson. MoVE
Signs of Christmas. Edwin Lees. OHIP
Signs of Love. Petrarch. *See* If Amorous Faith.
Signs of Rain. Edward Jenner. BLPA; BoNaP; OTPC; PRWS; RIS, *abr.*
Signs of Rain. Alex Rogers, *after* Edward Jenner. StaSt
Signs of Winter. John Clare. BoNaP; ERoP-2; PoE; PoSC; WaKn; WiR
Signum Cui Contradicetur. Sister Mary Angelita. GoBC; JKCP (1926 ed.)
Sigurd of yore. The Short Lay of Sigurd [*or* The Lay of Sigurd]. *Unknown, tr. by* William Morris *and* Eiríkur Magnusson. *Fr.* The Elder Edda. AWP; EnLi-1; OuHeWo
Sigurd Rideth to the Glittering Heath. William Morris. *Fr.* The Story of Sigurd the Volsung, II. PoEL-5
Sigurd the Volsung. William Morris. *See* Story of Sigurd the Volsung, The.
Sigurd's Ride. William Morris. *See* Story of Sigurd the Volsung, The.
Silence. Mavis Clare Barnett. OQP
Silence. Robert Bly. NaP
Silence, The. John Gould Fletcher. Down the Mississippi, VII. HT; LiTA; NP
Silence. Samuel Miller Hageman. TRV
Silence. Thomas Hood. CBEP; CH; CoBE; EnLi-2 (1949 ed.); EnRP; ERoP-2; FaBoEn; GTSL; ILP; OBEV; OBRV; PeER; PoEL-4; ShBV-4; Sonn; TDP; ViBoPo
(Sonnet: Silence.) OBNC
Silence, The. Archibald MacLeish. HBMV
Silence. Edgar Lee Masters. LaNeLa; MAP; MoAmPo; NP; PoMa; PoToHe (new ed.)
Silence. Marianne Moore. CMoP; FaBoEn; FaBoMo; FIW; LiTA; PG (1955 ed.); PoIE; PoPo; PoSa; ViBoPo
Silence. T. Sturge Moore. QFR; SyP
Silence. James Herbert Morse. AA
Silence. John Lancaster Spalding. AA
Silence. Charles Hanson Towne. MaRV; OQP; TRV; WGRP
Silence. W. J. Turner. MoBrPo
Silence. Winifred Welles. HBMV
Silence. John Hall Wheelock. LiTM
Silence. Anna Wickham. BoLP; NP
Silence. William Carlos Williams. BiS
Silence/ we are given. The Eye. Sophia Castro-Leon. QAH
Silence. A while ago. A Sea Story. Emily H. Hickey. JKCP; VA
Silence all flesh, your selves prepare. A Judicious Observation of That Dreadful Comet. Ichabod Wiswall. SCAP
Silence—and a muted bell rings. Consecration. Patrick F. Kirby. GoBC
Silence and solitude may hint. An Uninscribed Monument on One of the Battlefields of the Wilderness. Herman Melville. AA; AmLP
Silence and Speech. Richard Garnett. *See* Epigram: "I hardly ever ope my lips."
Silence, and Stealth of Day[e]s! Henry Vaughan. SCEP-1; SeCV-1; WHA
("Silence, and stealth of dayes! 'tis now.") AnAnS-1; MeP; MePo; SeEP
(Since Thou Art Gone.) SeCL
Silence at Night, The. Edwin Denby. ANYP
Silence augmenteth grief, writing increaseth rage. Epitaph on [the Right Honorable] Sir Philip Sidney [*or* Another of the Same *or* Elegy on the Death of Sidney]. *At. to* Fulke Greville *and to* Sir Edward Dyer. AnFE; EnRePo; FCP; LiTG; LoBV; OBSC; ReIE; SiCE; TuPP
Silence before/ Sound. Zacchaeus in the Leaves. Vernon Watkins. FaBoTw
Silence here bears gunfire in its breath. Cozzo Grillo. H. B. Mallalieu. WaP
Silence holds for it, taut and true, The. Click o' the Latch. Nancy Byrd Turner. HBMV
Silence (in truth) would speak my sorrow best. Tears at the Grave of Sir Albertus Morton. Sir Henry Wotton. AnAnS-2; SeCP
Silence instead of thy sweet song, my bird. Lament of a Mocking-Bird. Frances Anne Kemble. AA; HBV
Silence Invoked. Richard Flecknoe. *See* Invocation of Silence.
Silence is strange when the voices eddy and fade, The. Wills Dies in Solitude. Colin Thiele. *Fr.* Burke and Wills. NeLNL
Silence My Heart. Avis B. Christiansen. SoP
Silence of God, The. Sir Osbert Sitwell. WaKn
Silence of our watching waiting springs, A. A View. Beverly Quint. NYBP
Silence slipping around like death, A. A Winter Twilight. Angelina W. Grimké. CDC; PoNe
Silence Spoke with Your Voice. Ryah Tumarkin Goodman. GoYe
Silence still and no sun burns above, The. Alone. Hubert Witheford. AnNZ
Silence. The man defined. The Hand at Callow Hill Farm. Charles Tomlinson. NePoEA-2
Silence was envious of the only voice. Robert Underwood Johnson. *Fr.* The Voice of Webster. AA
Silence, with its ragged edge of lost communication, The. Barbed Wire. Eithne Wilkins. NeBP
Silenced Singer, The. William James Linton. VA
Silences. Arthur O'Shaughnessy. OBNC; VA
Silences. E. J. Pratt. OBCV; PoCh
Silent. Iwan Goll, *tr. fr. French by* Claire Goll. OnPM
Silent, The. Jones Very. AmePo
Silent,/ Above the chaste bushes. Ulysses S. Grant. Paul Southworth Bliss. StaSt
Silent amidst unbroken silence deep. India. Florence Earle Coates. AA
Silent, and in face/ Confounded, long they sat, as stricken mute. Milton. *Fr.* Paradise Lost, IX. EnL
Silent are the singers in the purple halls of Emain. Death of Cuchulain. Eleanor Rogers Cox. JKCP
Silent are the woods, and the dim green boughs are. On Eastnor Knoll. John Masefield. CH; FIW; MCCG; ShBV-3
Silent at Joseph's side he stood. The Carpenter. Phyllis Hartnoll. ChIP
Silent bivouac of the dead, we say, A. Decorating the Soldiers' Graves. Minot J. Savage. OHIP
Silent, But. Tsuboi Shigeji, *tr. fr. Japanese by* Geoffrey Bownas *and* Anthony Thwaite. FIW
Silent Christmas stars shine cool and clear, The. Stars of Cheer. Caroline D. Swan. JKCP
Silent fell the rain. Fallen Rain. Richard Watson Dixon. NBM
Silent Generation, The. Louis Simpson. NePoAm-2; ThLM
Silent Hour. Rainer Maria Rilke, *tr. fr. German by* Jessie Lemont. AWP; OnPM; WoL
Silent I gaze at the cataract. By the Waterfall. Friedrich Adler. TrJP
Silent in America. Philip Levine. NaP
"I tell time," *sel.* TDP
Silent is Orpheus now, and silent now. Elegy VIII. William Bell. FaBoTw
Silent is the dark. Hope's Song. Francis Carlin. HBMV
Silent Is the House. Emily Brontë. *See* Visionary, The.
Silent Love. John Clare. EnRP
Silent Love. *Unknown, tr. fr. German by* Longfellow. LiTW
Silent Lover, The. Sir Walter Ralegh. EIL; LiTB; OBEV, *abr.*; PG, *abr.*; ViBoPo
(Merit of True Passion, The.) LiTB
(Sir Walter Raleigh to the Queen.) OAEP
(To His Mistress.) SiPS
(To Queen Elizabeth.) FCP; TuPP
(To the Queen.) CBEP; OBSC
Wrong Not, Sweet Empress of My Heart, *sel.* HBV, *abr.*; OBS, *sl. diff., at. to* Sir Robert Ayton

Silent moment comes at last, The. Scène à Faire. Morton Dauwen Zabel. NP
Silent my robe, when I rest on earth. The Swan. *Unknown. tr. fr. Anglo-Saxon. Fr.* Riddles. CoBE
Silent Night [Holy Night]. Joseph Mohr, *tr. fr. German.* ChrBoLe; FaFP; FaPL; MaRV; PTK; TreF; YaCaBo, *with music*
(Stille Nacht, *tr. by* Thomas Walsh.) CAW
Silent Noon. Dante Gabriel Rossetti. The House of Life, XIX. BEL; BoLiVe; ELP; EnLi-2; EnLit; EPN; GTBS-D; HBV; ILP; LiTL; LO; MaVP; MeWo; NoP; OAEP; OBNC; PAn; PoEL-5; PoVP; Sonn; TrGrPo; ViPo; ViPP; VP; WHA; YAT
Silent nymph, with curious eye! Grongar Hill. John Dyer. CEP; ChTr; EiCL; EiPP; EnRP; GoTL; LoBV; OBEC; PoE; PoEL-3; TOP
Silent, O Moyle, be the roar of thy water. The Song of Fionnuala. Thomas Moore. AnIL; OnYI
Silent One, The. Ivor Gurney. MMA
Silent Places, The. Harold M. Hildreth. OQP
Silent Pool, The. Harold Monro. BrPo
Silent Ranges, The. Stephen Moylan Bird. HBMV
Silent room, the heavy creeping shade, The. Fabien dei Franchi. Oscar Wilde. BrPo
Silent, Silent, Night. Blake. CBEP
Silent Slain, The. Archibald MacLeish. *See* Too-late Born, The.
Silent Snake, The. *Unknown.* BoTP; FaPON; TiPo (1959 ed.)
Silent Stars, The. Eric H. Daniell. MaRV
Silent Stars Go By, The. Harriet Hartridge Tompkins. MaRV
Silent Sufferer. John Gilland Brunini. JKCP (1926 ed.)
Silent tepees stand like shocked corn, The. Always the Melting Moon Comes. Margot Osborn. CaP
Silent Testimony. Catherine Parmenter. PGD
Silent Tower of Bottreau[x], The. Robert Stephen Hawker. GoBC; OBRV; VA
Silent Town, The. Richard Dehmel, *tr. fr. German by* Jethro Bithell. AWP; JAWP; WBP
"Silent upon a peak in Darien." Darien. Sir Edwin Arnold. MC; PAH
Silent Voices, The. Tennyson. MaRV; OQP; VA
Silent, with her eyes. Blind Girl. W. S. Merwin. NePoEA-2
Silent Woman, The. Ben Jonson. *See* Epicoene; or, The Silent Woman.
Silentium. Feodor Tyutchev, *tr. fr. Russian by* Babette Deutsch. LiTW; OnPM; PoPl; WoL
Silentium Altum. Blanche Mary Kelly. CAW
Silently I footed by an uphill road. The Last Signal. Thomas Hardy. ML
Silently my wife walks on the still wet furze. Berry Picking. Irving Layton. MoCV
Silently, slowly falls the snow from an ashen sky. Snowfall. Giosuè Carducci. AWP; JAWP; WBP
Silenus in Proteus. Thomas Lovell Beddoes. EnRP
Silet. Ezra Pound. MAP; MoAB; MoAmPo; Sonn
Silhouette. Violet Alleyn Storey. CIV
Silhouette in Sepia. Robert V. Carr. PoOW
Silhouette on the face of the moon. Shadow. Richard Bruce. CDC
Silk,/ Satin. *Unknown.* OxNR
Silk I have for you, Madonna—you shook your small dear head. Needs. Elizabeth Rendall. HBMV
Silk Merchant's Daughter, The, *with music. Unknown.* BFSS; ShS, 2 *vers.*
Silken-sheathed Angelica, The. Daily Paradox. Sara Henderson Hay. InMe
Silken Tent, The. Robert Frost. AmPP (5th ed.); BWP; CABA; CBV; ExPo; InPo; MaPo (1969 ed.); MeWo; MoPo; MWA-2; NePA; PoDB; PoIE; Sonn; TwCP
Silkie o' Sule Skerrie, The. *Unknown. See* Great Silkie of Sule Skerry, The.
Silkweed. Philip Henry Savage. AA
Silkworm, The. Marco Girolamo Vida, *tr. fr. Latin by* Francis Sylvester Mahony. *Fr.* De Bombycibus. CAW
Silkworms. Mary Elliott. OTPC (1923 ed.)
Silkworms, The. Douglas Stewart. FlW; PoAu-2
Siller Croun, The. Susanna Blamire. HBV
Silly Boy, there is no cause. Song. Thomas Pestel. ElL
Silly boy, 'tis full moon yet, thy night as day shines clearly. First Love. Thomas Campion. LO; OxBoLi; SiCE
Silly country maiden went, A. Leda in Stratford, Ont. Anne Wilkinson. MoCV
Silly Fool, The. W. H. Auden. OBMV
Silly girl! Yet morning lies. To a Pretty Girl. Israel Zangwill. TrJP
Silly heart forbeare. *Unknown.* SeCSL
Silly man that in the thickett lay, The. Spenser. *Fr.* The Faerie Queene, III. MBW-1
Silly Old Man, The. *Unknown.* CoMu
Silly shepherd lately sate, A. A Shepherd's Dream. Nicholas Breton. ReIE
Silly swain whose love breeds discontent, The. Tityrus to His Fair Phyllis. John Dickenson. *Fr.* The Shepherd's Complaint. ElL
Silly Sweetheart. *Unknown.* CH
Silly Willy. "R. L. B." ShM
Silly young cricket, accustomed to sing, A. The Ant and the Cricket. *Unknown.* GoTP; HBV; HBVY; OTPC (1923 ed.); PRWS
Silly Young Fellow Named Hyde, A. *Unknown.* ShM
(Limerick.) LiBL; WhC
Silus hath sold his crimson satin suite. Henry Parrot. SiCE
Silver. Walter de la Mare. AnEnPo; BoChLi; BoNaP; BoTP; BrR; CMoP; FaPON; GFA; GoTP; GTSL; MoAB; MoBrPo; NeMA; PCD; PoMa; PoMS; PoPl; PoRA (rev. ed.); ShBV-1; SiSoSe; StVeCh; SUS; TiPo; TreF; WaKn
Silver Age, The. Thom Gunn. ToPo
Silver Age, The, *sel.* Thomas Heywood.
Song: "With fair Ceres, Queen of grain." CLwM
(Praise of Ceres.) ElL
Silver bark of beech, and sallow. Counting-out Rhyme. Edna St. Vincent Millay. GoJo; MoShBr
Silver Bells. Hamish Hendry. BoTP
Silver birch is a dainty lady, The. Child's Song in Spring [*or* Bird's Song in Spring]. Edith Nesbit. BoTP; DD; HBV; HH; OHIP; OTPC; PRWS
Silver birch-tree like a sacred maid, A. Recollection. Amelia Walstien Carpenter. AA
Silver Bird of Herndyke Mill, The. Edmund Blunden. GoTL (1949 ed.)
Silver Bowl, The, *sel.* Joseph Ezobi, *tr. fr. Hebrew by* D. I. Friedmann.
Barren Soul, A. TrJP
Silver carolling of Matins woke, The. On the Annunciation of Fra Angelico. Manuel Machado. CAW
Silver Dagger, The. *Unknown.* BaBo
Silver dust. Pear Tree. Hilda Doolittle ("H. D."). AP; CMoP; HBMV; MAP; MoAmPo; NeMA; UnPo
Silver Herring Throbbed Thick in My Seine, The. Kenneth Leslie. ErPo; OBCV
(Sonnet.) PeCV; TwCaPo
Silver House, The. John Lea. BoTP
Silver Jack. *Unknown.* CoSo
Silver key of the fountain of tears. A Fragment: To Music [*or* Music]. Shelley. BoLiVe; TrGrPo
Silver Lamps. W. C. Dix. BePJ
Silver Lantern, A, Karle Wilson Baker. HBMV
Silver Leaf, The. John Hay. NePoAm
Silver Moon, The. Sappho, *tr. fr. Greek by* John Addington Symonds. EnLi-1
Silver moon's enamored beam, The. Kate of Aberdeen. John Cunningham. HBV
Silver Penny, The. Walter de la Mare. CMoP; ExPo; OBMV
Silver Question, The. Oliver Herford. NA
Silver rain, the shining sun, The. The Harvest. Alice Corbin. BoTP
Silver Road, The. Hamish Hendry. BoTP
Silver-scaled dragon with jaws flaming red, A. The Toaster. William Jay Smith. SoPo
Silver Sheep. Anne Blackwell Payne. GFA; SiSoSe; UTS
Silver Ships. Mildred Plew Meigs. FaPON; TiPo
Silver sky is faintly etched, A. Skiing Song [*or* January]. "Michael Lewis." GoTP; OTD
Silver Stag, The. Kathleen Raine. FaBoMo
Silver Sty, The. *Unknown. See* Lady Who Loved a Swine, The.
Silver Swan, The. *Unknown.* CBV; ChTr; DiPo; ElL; ELP; EnRePo; EP; ExPo; FaBoCh; LoGBV; NoP; OAEP; TuPP
(Silver Swan [*or* Swanne], Who Living Had No Note, The.) AtBAP; PoEL-2; ReEn; SiCE; SiSw
Silver Tassie, The. Burns. *See* My Bonnie Mary.

Silver that shies off the silver-leaf maple, The. The Silver Leaf. John Hay. NePoAm
Silver Treads among the Gold. Eben E. Rexford. FaFP; TreF
Silver-vested monkey trips, A. Cortège. Paul Verlaine. AWP; OnPM; WoL
Silver Wedding. Ralph Hodgson. HBMV; TrGrPo
Silvery dewdrops that in autumn light, The. Jewels. Asayasu. OnPM
Silvery the olives on Ravello's steeps. Above Salerno. Ada Foster Murray. HBV
Silvia. Sir George Etherege. CavP; SeCL
Silvia. Shakespeare. *See* Who Is Sylvia?
Silvia, let us from the crowd retire. To Silvia. Countess of Winchilsea. *Fr.* The Cautious Lovers. HBV
Silvy. *Unknown. See* On a Time the Amorous Silvy.
Sim Ines. Jane Stubbs. FiBHP
Simaetha. Hilda Doolittle ("H. D."). MAPA
Simchas Torah. Morris Rosenfeld, *tr. fr. Yiddish.* TRJP
Simeon's Light Remembered. John W. Simons. JKCP (1955 ed.)
Simhat Torah. Judah Leib Gordon, *tr. fr. Hebrew by* Alice Lucas *and* Helena Frank. TRJP
Similar Cases. Charlotte Perkins Stetson Gilman. BBV; HBV; PoLF
Simile. Sir Samuel Ferguson. *Fr.* Congal. IrPN
Simile, A. Matthew Prior. BOHV; CEP; CoBE; EiPP; FaBoEn
Simile for Her Smile, A. Richard Wilbur. CBV; FiMAP; HoPM; MiAP; MoLP
Similes. Edward Moxon. OBRV
Similes. *Unknown.* BOHV; HBVY
(Comparisons.) GoTP
Similes for Two Political Characters of 1819. Shelley. CBEP; PeER
Similia Similibus. John Hunt Morgan. ShM
Similitude, A. Charles Harpur. BoAu
(Love Sonnets, VIII.) PoAu-1
Simmer's a Pleasant Time. Burns. PoEL-4
Simon and Judas. Kenneth W. Porter. ChIP; OQP
Simon and Susan. *Unknown.* OxBoLi
"Simon Bar-Jona, lovest thou Me?" Upon This Rock. James L. Duff. JKCP
Simon, called Peter, and Andrew his brother. Fishers. Edwin Meade Robinson. LHV
Simon Danz. Longfellow. *See* Dutch Picture, A.
Simon Lee. Wordsworth. BEL; EnRP; EPN; GTBS; GTSE; GTSL; MERP
(Simon Lee the Old Huntsman.) GTBS-D; GTBS-P; GTBS-W
Simon Legree—a Negro Sermon. Vachel Lindsay. The Booker Washington Trilogy, I. CoBA; HBMV; InMe; LiTA; LoGBV; MoVE; NAMP; NePA; PFY; ShBV-2
(Negro Sermon, A: Simon Legree.) AnAmPo; ATP (1935 ed.); MAP; MoAmPo; PFY
Simon my son, son of my Nuptiall knott. A Lamentation on My Dear Son Simon. John Saffin. SCAP
Simon of Cyrene. Georgia Harkness. ChIP
Simon the Cyrenean. Lucy Lyttelton. HBV
Simon the Cyrenian Speaks. Glen Baker. ChIP
Simon the Cyrenian Speaks. Countee Cullen. AmNP; BBV (1951 ed.); MAP; MaRV; MoAmPo; NeMA; OQP; PoNe; StJW; TTY
Simple and fresh and fair from winter's close emerging. The First Dandelion. Walt Whitman. NePA; TSW
Simple Autumnal. Louise Bogan. MAP; MoAB; MoAmPo; QFR; Sonn
Simple bee that do's no harme, The. *Unknown.* SeCSL
Simple child, A/ That lightly draws its breath. We Are Seven. Wordsworth. BLPA; EnLi-2; EnRP; EPN; FaPL; GN; HBV; MBW-2; MERP; NeHB; OnPP; PoE; TreF; WBLP
Simple Duty, A. Poe. PoRL
Simple Faith. William Cowper. *Fr.* Truth. OBEC
Simple Field That I Shall Buy, The. Mildred I. McNeal Sweeney. PFY
Simple-hearted Child was He, A. The Little Child. Albert Bigelow Paine. AA; ChIP; MaRV
Simple her way of smiling was and coy. Ten of Chaucer's People: A Polite Nun. Chaucer. *Fr.* The Canterbury Tales. PoSa
Simple light from all contagion free, A. An Infant's Eye. Thomas Traherne. CoBE; SCEP-1
Simple Maid, A. Lord De Tabley. VA
Simple Nature. George John Romanes. HBV
Simple nosegay, A! was that much to ask? The Troll's Nosegay. Robert Graves. PoCh; Sonn
Simple Ploughboy, The. *Unknown.* FaBoCh; LoGBV; OBB
Simple ring with a single stone, A. A Pearl, a Girl. Robert Browning. CBEP; PoVP
Simple Sam. Leroy F. Jackson. ChBR; GaP; PoSC
Simple Simon. Harriet S. Morgridge. *Fr.* Mother Goose Sonnets. AA
Simple Simon met a pieman. Mother Goose. BoChLi; BoTP; FaBoBe; GaP; GoTP; HBV; HBVY; OTPC; OxNR; PoPl; PPL; RIS; SiTL; SoPo; StVeCh
Simple Things. Paul Jean Toulet, *tr. fr. French by* Joseph T. Shipley. CAW
Simple Verses, *sels.* José Martí, *tr. fr. Spanish by* Seymour Resnick. TTY
"I am a sincere man."
"I grow a white rose."
Simple weight attached, A. Stanky. Bill Berkson. ANYP
Simpler Thing, a Chair, A. Robert Mezey. NePoEA
Simples. James Joyce. HBMV; NP; PoPl
Simplex Munditiis. Ben Jonson, *tr. fr. the Latin of* Jean Bonnefons. *Fr.* Epicoene; or, The Silent Woman, I, i. AWP; CoBE; EnLi-1; EnLit; GoBC; HBV; HoPM; InPo; JAWP; OBEV; TDP; TOP; WBP
(Clerimont's Song.) BoLiVe; LoBV; PoIE; SeCP; SeCV-1; SiCE; TrGrPo; VaPo
(Song: "Still to be neat, still to be dressed [*or* drest].") AnAnS-2; AnEnPo; CBV; EnRePo; LiTL; NeHB; OBS; SCEP-2; ViBoPo; YAT
(Still to be Neat [Still to Be Dressed].) ALV; CABA; CBEP; EIL; EnL; GTBS-W; MaPo; NoP; OAEP; OuHeWo; PAn; PoE; PoFS; PoSa; SeCePo; StP; TreFT; TuPP; WHA
("Still to be neat, still to be dressed [*or* drest].") EG; ILP; LO; ReEn
(Such Sweet Neglect.) MeWo
Simplicity. Emily Dickinson. *See* How happy is the little stone.
Simplicity's Song. Robert Wilson. *Fr.* Three Ladies of London. CTC; OBSC
Simplification, A. Richard Wilbur. CMoP
Simplify Me When I'm Dead. Keith Douglas. *See* Remember Me.
Simplon Pass, The. Wordsworth. *Fr.* The Prelude, VI. InPo; PoeP; PoFS; SyP
(Alpine Descent: "Downwards we hurried.") WHA
("Brook and road, The.") OBRV
(Down the Simplon Pass: "Downwards we hurried.") EPN
("Melancholy slackening that ensued, The.") PoEL-4
Simply being drunk makes it. Drunk; on Crutches. Raymond Souster. PeCV
Simply by sailing in a new direction. Landfall in Unknown Seas. Allen Curnow. AnNZ
Simply one warm night, among much warmth and many nights: Arab Music. D. J. Enright. MuSP
Simply she stands on the cathedral's. Eve. Rainer Maria Rilke. MoRP
Simpson's Rest. George S. Simpson. PoOW
Simson settled in the timber when his arm was strong and true. Peter Simson's Farm. Edward Dyson. BoAu
Simulacra. Ezra Pound. NoP
Simultaneously. David Ignatow. TPM; TwCP
Simultaneously, as soundlessly. Prime. W. H. Auden. *Fr.* Horae Canonicae. CMoP; MaPo (1969 ed.); PoDB
Simultaneously, five thousand miles apart. Simultaneously. David Ignatow. TPM; TwCP
Sin. George Herbert. ViBoPo
Sin!/ O only fatal woe. Thomas Traherne. *Fr.* The Third Century. AnAnS-1; MeP
Sin, The; a Definition. Francis Maguire. JKCP (1955 ed.)
Sin and Its Cure. *Unknown.* STF
Sin, Despair, and Lucifer. Phineas Fletcher. *Fr.* The Locusts, or Apollyonists. OBS
Sin I fro Love escaped am so fat. Escape. Chaucer. *Fr.* Merciles Beaute. OBEV (1st ed.)
Sin of Omission, The. Margaret E. Sangster. BLPA; HBV; MaRV; PoToHe; SoP; TreFS; TRV
Sin of self-love [*or* Sinne of selfe-love] possesseth all mine eye [*or* al mine eie]. Sonnets, LXII. Shakespeare. EnRePo; EP; PoEL-2

Sin-satiate, and haggard with despair. Tannhäuser. William Morton Payne. AA
Sin that I have a nounparall maistress. A Mistress without Compare. Charles d'Orleans (?). MeEL
Sin! wilt thou vanquish me! The Recovery. Thomas Traherne. *Fr.* The Third Century. AnAnS-1; MeP
Sinalóa. Earle Birney. MoCV
Since/ Malcolm died. Aardvark. Julia Fields. BOLo
Since after all we were born to marry strangers. To Marry Strangers. Winfield Townley Scott. FiMAP
Since all my life out of my death derives. Ballata: Of Love's Power. Guido Cavalcanti. LiTW
Since all our keys are lost or broken. An Art of Poetry. James McAuley. ACV
Since all that beat about in Nature's range. Constancy to an Ideal Object. Samuel Taylor Coleridge. ERoP-1
Since all that I can ever do for thee. The Last Wish. "Owen Meredith." OBEV (1st ed.); OBVV
Since as in night's deck-watch ye show. Herman Melville. *Fr.* John Marr. ViBoPo
Since beauty is honored all over the empire. The Beautiful Hsi-shih. Wang Wei. OuHeWo
Since Bonny-boots Was Dead. *Unknown.* NCEP; OxBoLi; PoEL-2
(Madrigal: "Since Bonny boots was dead, that so divinely.") SiTL
Since brass[e], nor stone, nor earth, nor boundless[e] sea. Sonnets, LXV. Shakespeare. AtBAP; AWP; BEL; BoLiVe; BWP; CABA; CLwM; DiPo; EnLi-1 (1949 ed.); EnRePo; FaFP; FiP; GTBS; GTBS-D; GTBS-P; GTBS-W; GTSE; GTSL; JAWP; LiTB; LiTL; MaPo; MasP; MCCG; MemP; NoP; OuHeWo; PoeP; PoFS; PoIE; PoRA; SeCeV; SiCE; Sonn; TOP; UnPo (1st ed.); WBP
Since bundling very much abounds. A New Bundling Song. *Unknown.* ErPo
Since Celia's my foe. Celia. Thomas Duffett. SeCL
Since Christ embrac'd the Crosse it selfe, dare I. The Crosse. John Donne. MaMe
Since Christmas. Frederick R. McCreary. MAP
Since Christmas they have lived with us. Balloons. Sylvia Plath. TPM
Since clarity suggests simplicity. The Counterpart. Elizabeth Jennings. LiTM (1970 ed.)
Since Cleopatra Died. Thomas Wentworth Higginson. AA
Since counterfeit plots have affected this age. A Ballad upon the Popish Plot. John Gadbury. CoMu
Since earth has put you away, O sons of Barmak. Abu Nowas for the Barmacides. *Unknown.* *Fr.* The Thousand and One Nights. AWP
Since every quill is silent to relate. A Monumental Memorial of Marine Mercy. Richard Steere. SCAP
Since fate commands me hence, and I. The Farewell. Thomas Stanley. CavP
Since Feeling Is First. E. E. Cummings. MoAB; MoAmPo; NoP
Since First I Saw Your Face. *Unknown.* CBEP; ELP; LiTB; OBEV
("Since first I saw your face I resolved to honour and renown ye.") EG; LO; OBSC
Since first the stone was rolled away. This Easter Day. Martha Snell Nicholson. BePJ
Since for kissing thee, Minguillo, my mother scolds me all the day. Minguillo's Kiss. *Unknown, tr. fr. Spanish.* BOHV
Since fortune's wrath envieth the wealth. Earl of Surrey. FCP; SiPS
Since fret and care are everywhere. Capsule Conclusions. *Unknown.* MeWo
Since God Is There. Mme Guyon, *tr. fr. French by* William Cowper. MaRV
Since God's eye is on the sparrow. God's Eye Is on the Sparrow. Bertha Meyer. STF
Since gratious Lord if thou withhold thy hand. *Unknown.* SeCSL
Since he weighs nothing. Postscript. W. H. Auden. FIW
Since he will call some night to sup. Most Honored Guest. Walter Shea. ChIP
Since his death, nothing removes my fear. The Weasel. Robert Pack. CoPo
Since honour from the honourer proceeds. Of Books. John Florio. EIL
Since hopeless of thy love I go. Hopeless Love. *Unknown.* IrPN
Since I am coming [*or* comming] to that holy room. Hymn [*or* Hymne] to God My God, in My Sicknesse. John Donne. AnAnS-1; AtBAP; BoC; BWP; CABA; ChTr; DiPo; DTC; EnL; EnRePo; EP; FaBoEn; GoBC; LoBV; MaMe; MaPo; MasP; MBW-1; MeLP; MeP; MePo; NoP; OAEP; OBS; OxBoCh; PoEL-2; PoIE; ReEn; SCEP-1; SeCL; SeCP; SeCV-1; SeEP; TDP; TrPWD; TuPP; UnS
Since I am convinced. Saigyo Hoshi, *tr. fr. Japanese by* Arthur Waley. AWP; LiTW
Since I am free,/ Offending no just law, let no law make. George Chapman. *Fr.* Bussy d'Ambois, II, i. MyFE
Since I believe in God the Father Almighty. Johannes Milton, Senex. Robert Bridges. CMoP; LiTB; NAMP; PoEL-5; PoPl
Since I did leave the presence of my love. Amoretti, LXXXVI. Spenser. EG; ReEn
Since I do trust Jehova still. Psalm XI. *Paraphrased by* Sir Philip Sidney. FCP
Since I emerged that day from the labyrinth. The Labyrinth. Edwin Muir. CMoP; MoBrPo (1962 ed.); PoIE
Since I have been so quickly done for. On an Infant Eight Months Old. *Unknown.* SiTL; WhC
Since I Have Felt the Sense of Death. Helen Hoyt. *See* Sense of Death, The.
Since I have lacked the comfort of that light. Amoretti, LXXXVIII. Spenser. EnRePo
Since I have learned Love's shining alphabet. Ignorance. John Masefield. BEL
Since I have seen a bird one day. The Truth. W. H. Davies. FaBoTw
Since I have set my lips to your full cup, my sweet. More Strong than Time. Victor Hugo. AWP; JAWP; WBP
Since I heard/ Faintly the voice. Mitsune. *Fr.* Kokin Shu. AWP
Since I in storms us'd most to be. The Wreath. Henry Vaughan. SCEP-1
Since I keep only what I give away. Sonnet. George Hetherington. NeIP
Since I lost you, my darling, the sky has come near. Call into Death. D. H. Lawrence. BoPe
Since I must love your north. To My Mountain. Kathleen Raine. OxBS; PoPl
Since I no longer speak I. Silent in America. Philip Levine. NaP
Since I noo mwore do zee your feace. The Wife a-Lost. William Barnes. ELP; EnLoPo; GTBS; GTBS-D; OBEV; OBVV
Since I Saw My Love. Anna Wickham. *See* Song: "I was so chill, and overworn, and sad."
Since I was a child. Rebel. Irene Rutherford McLeod. HBMV
Since I was in Syracuse is a month ago. Quarries in Syracuse. Louis Golding. TrJP
Since I was ten I have not been unkind. The Final Word. Dom Moraes. BoPe; MemP; NePoEA-2
Since in a land not barren still. Love and Discipline. Henry Vaughan. TrPWD
Since Jesus freely did appear. Wedding. *Unknown.* SoP
Since Jesus is my friend. My Friend. Paul Gerhardt. SoP
Since Just Disdain. *Unknown.* EnRePo
(Being Scorned, and Disdained, He Inveighs against His Lady.) SiCE
Since last September I've been trying to describe. Edward Lear in February. Christopher Middleton. TwCP
Since, Lord, to thee/ A narrow way and little gate. Holy [*or* H.] Baptism[e]. George Herbert. HBV; PoEL-2; MaMe; SCEP-1; SeCV-1
Since love is such that, as ye wot. Sir Thomas Wyatt. FCP; SiPS
Since love will needs that I shall love. Sir Thomas Wyatt. FCP; SiPS
Since lovers' joys then leave so sick a taste. Henry King. *Fr.* Paradox: That Fruition Destroys Love. ErPo; LO
Since man has been articulate. Every Thing. Harold Munro. AnEnPo; MoBrPo; NeMA
Since men grow diffident at last. Youth Sings a Song of Rosebuds. Countee Cullen. BANP; NoP; PoLF; PoNe
Since more than half my hopes came true. Contented at Forty. Sarah N. Cleghorn. HBMV
Since musick so delights the sense. Musick Commended, and

Since (continued)
Scraping Ridiculed, etc. Thomas D'Urfey. MuSP
Since My Birth. Iwan Goll, *tr. fr. French by* Claire Goll. OnPM
Since my life's been spent. Côte d'Azur. Katherine Hoskins. NYBP
Since Nature's works be good, and death doth serve. Why Fear to Die? Sir Philip Sidney. *Fr.* Arcadia. SiPS
Since neither Bach nor Paganini speak. Morning Concert—Nantucket. Isabel Harriss Barr. JKCP (1955ed.)
Since nothing so much is. Old Song. Louis Dudek. ACV
Since nought avails, let me arise and leave. Love's Last Resource. Sadi. *Fr.* The Gulistan. AWP; LiTW
Since now, at last, we understand. Finis? Michael Lewis. MeWo
Since now my Silvia is as kind as fair. The Happy Night. John Sheffield, Duke of Buckingham and Normanby. UnTE
Since ocean rolled and ocean winds were strong. Sonnets on the Sea's Voice. George Sterling. EtS
Since o'er thy footstool here below. Heaven's Magnificence. William Augustus Muhlenberg. AA
Since one anthologist put in his book. Anthologistics. Arthur Guiterman. InMe; WhC
Since our hair was plaited and we became man and wife. Su Wu, *tr. fr. Chinese by* Arthur Waley. LO
Since Pa put in the radio we have a lot of fun. The Radio. Edgar A. Guest. PEDC
Since perfect happiness, by princes sought. George Chapman. *Fr.* Epistle Dedicatory to Chapman's Translation of the Iliad. CLwM; ReEn; ReIE
Since recombination's not. Central Park: It's About This Eden Thing. John Morgan. YAP
Since reverend doctors now declare. The Respectable Burgher. Thomas Hardy. CMoP; ViPo (1962 ed.)
Since Robin Hood. *Unknown.* NCEP
Since, Senora, you torment me. The Challenge. *Unknown.* UnTE
Since She Is Gone. William Browne. *See* Memory ("So shuts the marigold. . .").
Since she must go, and I must mourn, come night. His Parting From Her. John Donne. Elegies, XII. MaMe; OBS
Since she whom I lov'd [*or* loved] hath payd [*or* paid] her last debt. Holy Sonnets, XVII. John Donne. AnAnS-1; MaMe; MaPo (1969 ed.); MasP; MeP; MePo; OAEP; SCEP-1; SeEP; Sonn
Since shunning pain, I ease can never find. Sir Philip Sidney. FCP
Since, Sir, you have made it your study to vex. The Lady's Receipt for a Beau's Dress. *Unknown.* CoMu
Since So Mine Eyes. Sir Philip Sidney. *Fr.* Arcadia. SiPS
Since so ye please to hear me plain. Sir Thomas Wyatt. FCP; SiPS
Since succour to the feeblest of the wise. Remembered Grace. Coventry Patmore. OxBoCh
Since that this thing we call the world. An Epicurean Ode. John Hall. EG; MeLP; MePo; SeEP; SiSw
Since the Conquest none of us. The Conquest. Oliver St. John Gogarty. OBMV
Since the wise men have not spoken, I speak that am only a fool. The Fool. Padraic Pearse. OnYI
Since there are saints in the islands still. To Ultima Thule. George Dangerfield. CAW
Since There Is No Escape. Sara Teasdale. AnAmPo
Since there's no help, come let us kiss and part. Idea, LXI [*or* The Parting *or* Sonnet *or* Love's Farewell]. Michael Drayton. AnEnPo; AtBAP; ATP; AWP; BEL; BoLP; BWP; CABA; CaFP; CBEP; CBV; DiPo; EG; EIL; EnL; EnLi-1; EnLit; EnLoPo; EnRePo; ExPo; FaBoEn; FaPL; ForPo; FosPo; GTBS; GTBS-D; GTBS-P; GTBS-W; GTSE; GTSL; HBV; HoPM; ILP; InP; JAWP; LiTB; LiTG; LiTL; LO; LoBV; MemP; MeWo; NoP; OAEP; OBEV; OBSC; OtMeF; OuHeWo; PoAn; PoE; PoEL-2; PoIE; PoSa; ReEn; ReIE; SeCePo; SeCeV; ShBV-4; SiCE; Sonn; StP; TOP; TreFS; TrGrPo; TuPP; ViBoPo; WBP; WePo; WHA
Since this ingenious earth began. In Praise of Diversity. Phyllis McGinley. SiTL
Since Those We Love and Those We Hate. W. E. Henley. OBMV
Since Thou Art Gone. Henry Vaughan. *See* Silence, and Stealth of Days!
Since thou art gone, my friend, I seek in vain for peace. On Parting with Moses ibn Ezra. Judah Halevi. TrJP
Since thou desirest, I will then unveil. The Demon Speaks. Calderón de la Barca. *Fr.* El Mágico prodigioso. CAW
Since Thou Hast Given Me This Good Hope, O God. Robert Louis Stevenson. TrPWD
Since thou hast view'd some Gorgon, and art grown. The Double Rock [*or* Sonnet: The Double Rock]. Henry King. AnAnS-2; AtBAP; BoW; CLwM; SeCP
Since thou wilt goe fond hart and I, must lye. *Unknown.* SeCSL
Since thou wou'dst needs, bewitcht with some ill charms. To One Married to an Old Man. Edmund Waller. SeCP
Since thou'rt condemn'd to wed a thing. A Wife. Alexander Brome. PeRV
Since through vertue encreaseth dignity. Good Counsel. James I, King of Scotland. ACP
Since 'tis resolvd that I must dy. *Unknown.* SeCSL
Since to be loved endures. Robert Bridges. GTSL
Since tonight the wind is high. The Viking Terror. *Unknown.* KiLC
Since we agreed to let the road between us. No Road. Philip Larkin. MoBrPo (1962 ed.); OPoP
Since we are born in blood to be convinced. La Ci Darem la Mano. John Frederick Nims. MiAP
Since We Are Property. Lilith Lorraine. FiSC
Since we had changed. Message. Allen Ginsberg. NeAP
Since We Parted. "Owen Meredith." HBV
Since who'd begin must make an end. "I Die Daily." Phil. J. Fisher. MaRV
Since without Thee we do no good. Hymn. Elizabeth Barrett Browning. TrPWD
Since ye delight to know. Sir Thomas Wyatt. FCP; SiPS
Since you all will have singing, and won't be said nay. The King's Own Regulars. *Unknown.* PAH
Since you have come thus far. Chorus. C. Day Lewis. *Fr.* Noah and the Waters. OAEP (2d ed.)
Since you have turned unkind. To a Lady Friend. W. H. Davies. MoBrPo
Since you lie buried in the hill. To Senna Hoy. Else Lasker-Schüler. OnPM
Since you must go, and I must bid farewell. An Elegy. Ben Jonson. EnRePo; LoBV
Since you remember Nimmo, and arrive. Nimmo. E. A. Robinson. HBMV
Since You Will Needs. Sir Thomas Wyatt. ReIE; TuPP ("Since you will needs [*or* Sins you will nedes] that I shall sing.") SiCE; SiPS
Since you desire of me to know. The Reply. John Norris. PeRV
Since you must go and I must bid farewell. An Elegy. Ben Jonson. CLwM
Since you will needs that I shall sing. Sir Thomas Wyatt. FCP
Since Youth Is All for Gladness. Glenn Ward Dresbach. HBMV
Since youth is wise, and cannot comprehend. Inscription for Arthur Rackham's Rip Van Winkle. James Elroy Flecker. BrPo
Sincere Flattery of R. B. James Kenneth Stephen. *See* Imitation of Robert Browning.
Sincere Flattery of W. W. (Americanus). James Kenneth Stephen. HBV; InMe; Par
(Of W. W.—Americanus.) FiBHP; WhC
Sincere Man, The. Alfred Grant Walton. PoToHe (new ed.)
Sincere Praise. Isaac Watts. CEP
"Almighty Maker God!" *sel.* TrPWD
Sincerest Critic of my Prose, or Rhyme. Letter to Viscount Cobham. Congreve. LoBV
Sindbad, *with music.* *Unknown.* SoAmSa
Sinfonia Domestica. Jean Starr Untermeyer. HBMV; MAP; MoAmPo; NP
Sinfonia Eroica. Alice Archer James. AA
Sinful father, The/ Seem'd not to strike. Shakespeare. *Fr.* Pericles, I, ii. PoFr
Sing! *Unknown.* SoP
Sing a little as the feet unwearied. Voyageur. R. E. Rashley. CaP
Sing a song of cobbler! Jeremy Hobbler. *Unknown.* BoTP
Sing a song of hollow logs. Song of Summer Days. J. W. Foley. BoTP
Sing a Song of Joy, *sel.* Thomas Campion.
"Sing a song of joy!" UnS

Sing a Song of Juniper. Robert Francis. LOW
Sing a song of laughter. The Giraffe and the Woman. Laura E. Richards. PDV
Sing a song of mincemeat. Mincemeat. Elizabeth Gould. BoTP
Sing a song of monkeys. The Monkeys. Edith Osborne Thompson. TiPo; UTS
Sing a Song of Moonlight. Ivy O. Eastwick. SiSoSe
Sing a song of picnics. Picnic Day. Rachel Field. SiSoSe; SoPo; TiPo
Sing a song of pop corn. A Pop Corn Song. Nancy Byrd Turner. FaPON; GFA; MPB
Sing a song of rockets. Fourth of July Song. Lois Lenski. SiSoSe
Sing a song of scissor-men. The Scissor-Man. Madeleine Nightingale. BoTP; GaP; MPB; TiPo
Sing a Song of Seasons! Robert Louis Stevenson. OTPC (1946 ed.)
Sing a song of sixpence. Mother Goose. BoChLi; FaBoBe; FTB; HBV; HBVY; LiTG; OTPC; OxBoLi; OxNR; PCH; PoPl; PPL; RIS; SAS; SiTL; SoPo; StVeCh; TiPo
Sing a Song of Sixpence, *parody.* Frank Sidgwick. WhC
Sing a song of Spring-time. The Song of the Seasons. Cosmo Monkhouse. DD; HBV
Sing a Song of Sunshine. Ivy O. Eastwick. SiSoSe
Sing a Song of the Cities. Morris Bishop. CAD; WhC
Sing a song of washing-up. The Washing-up Song. Elizabeth Gould. BoTP
Sing a song of whisky. A Whisky Song. *Unknown.* STF
Sing a song of winter. A Sledding Song. Norman C. Schlichter. FaPON
Sing Again. Marie van Vorst. AA
Sing again the song you sung. Egyptian Serenade. George William Curtis. HBV
Sing all the earth, ye hills break forth with singing! Rejoice! He Liveth! Kathryn Blackburn Peck. BePJ
Sing All Ye Joyful. J. R. R. Tolkien. PoRh
Sing aloud, harmonious spheares. William Strode. SeCSL
Sing aloud, his praise rehearse. The Philosopher's Devotion. Henry More. SeCL
Sing and heave, and heave and sing. The Banks of the Sacramento. *Unknown.* AmSS
Sing, Ballad-singer, raise a hearty tune. The Ballad Singer. Thomas Hardy. At Casterbridge Fair, I. BEL; EnLi-2 (1949 ed.); EnLit; LO; MeWo; NoP; PoVP
Sing bird, on green Missouri's plain. The Death of Lyon. Henry Peterson. PAH
Sing, Brothers, Sing! W. R. Rodgers. MoAB; MoBrPo (1950 ed.)
Sing care away with sport and play. A Song to the Tune of Heart's Ease. *Unknown. Fr.* Misogonus. ReEn; TuPP
Sing, children, sing! A Song of Easter. Celia Thaxter. HH
Sing clear, O! throstle. To a Thrush. T. A. Daly. CAW; JKCP
Sing Cuccu. *Unknown. See* Sumer Is Icumen In.
Sing for the Garish Eye. W. S. Gilbert. BOHV; NA
Sing forth a hymn sublime and solemn, grateful to glorious Varuna, imperial ruler. Hymn to Varuna, God of Fire and Light. *Unknown. Fr.* The Rigveda. LiTW
Sing, Goddess, of Achilles, Peleus' Son. The Quarrel. Homer, *tr. by* Sir William Marris. *Fr.* The Iliad, I. WoL
Sing Heigh-ho! Charles Kingsley. ALV; HBV
(There Sits a Bird.) GBV (1952 ed.)
Sing hey, and sing ho, and sing down-a-down-derry. The Ballad of the Merry Ferry. Emma Rounds. MPB; RIS
Sing hey diddle diddle, the cat and the fiddle. *See* Hey, diddle, diddle. . .
Sing hey! for bold George Washington. George Washington. Rosemary Benét *and* Stephen Vincent Benét. FaPON; MaC
Sing hey! Sing hey!/ For Christmas Day. Christmas Greeting [*or* An Old Christmas Greeting]. *Unknown.* BrR; ChBR; FaPON; MPB; SiSoSe; TiPo
Sing His Praises. John Fletcher. *See* Hymn to Pan.
Sing ho! for a brave and a gallant ship. Ten Thousand Miles Away. *Unknown.* SoAmSa
Sing; how 'a would sing! Julie-Jane. Thomas Hardy. MoVE
Sing how the uncreated Light. Carmen Genesis. Francis Thompson. CoBE; PoLi
Sing I for a brave and gallant barque, and a stiff and a rattling breeze. Ten Thousand Miles Away. *Unknown.* AS
Sing, I pray, a little song. Golden-tressed Adelaide. "Barry Cornwall." VA
Sing in my love's ear tonight. The Guitar. Gail Dusenbery. ThO
Sing in the Silent Sky. Christina Rossetti. *Fr.* A Summer Wish. BiS
Sing Ivy. *Unknown. See* Mad Farmer's Song.
Sing jigmijole, the pudding bowl. *Unknown.* OxNR
Sing Little Bird. Maria Hastings. SoPo
Sing low, my heart, lest we be overheard. The Heart Has Its Reasons. *Unknown.* GoBC
Sing Lullaby, as Women Do. George Gascoigne. *See* Lullaby of a Lover, The.
Sing, magnarello, merrily. The Leaf-Picking. Frédéric Mistral. AWP; JAWP; WBP
Sing Me a Song. Christina Rossetti. *Fr.* Sing-Song. BoChLi
Sing Me a Song. Robert Louis Stevenson. InP; MemP; PoVP
(Lad That Is Gone, A.) HBV
(Over the Sea to Skye.) EtS; ShBV-1
("Sing me a song of a lad that is gone.") BrPo
Sing me a sweet, low song of night. A Song. Hildegarde Hawthorne. AA; FaBoBe; HBV
Sing me at morn but only with your laugh. Song of Songs. Wilfred Owen. NAMP
Sing me no song! Give me one silent hour! The Musician to His Love. Percy French. MuSP
Sing me the men ere this. He Would Have His Lady Sing [*or* Heaven]. Digby Mackworth Dolben. BoC; CAW; GoBC
Sing, my tongue, the Saviour's glory. Hymn [*or* Pange Lingua Gloriosa]. St. Thomas Aquinas. CAW; WGRP; WHL
Sing, nigger in the distance, coming up the hill. Night Song. Wallace Gould. AnAmPo
Sing, O goddess, the wrath, the ontamable dander of Keitt. The Fight over the Body of Keitt. *Unknown.* PAH
Sing of the brave and the miracles they wrought. Song of the Brave. Laurence Altgood. PAL
Sing On, Blithe Bird! William Motherwell. DD; GN; HBV; HBVY; OTPC (1923 ed.)
Sing out, my soul, thy songs of joy. Songs of Joy. W. H. Davies. MoBrPo; OBVV; YT
Sing out pent Soules, sing cheerefully! The Vintage to the Dungeon. Richard Lovelace. SCEP-2; SeCV-1
Sing Sally O! *with music. Unknown.* SoAmSa
Sing, Sing for Christmas. J. H. Egar. OHIP
Sing sing Syren though thy notes bring death. *Unknown.* SeCSL
Sing, sing! what shall I sing? Mother Goose. OTPC; OxNR
Sing, sing, what shall we sing? A Musical Evening. Joseph G. Francis. CIV
Sing-Song. *See* Singsong.
Sing, soul of mine, this day of days. Easter. *Unknown.* OQP
"Sing sweet, my bird; oh! sing, I pray." Lucy's Canary. Adelaide O'Keefe. OTPC (1923 ed.)
Sing the old song, amid the sounds dispersing. Song. Aubrey Thomas De Vere. HBV
Sing the song of wave-worn Coogee, Coogee in the distance white. Coogee. Henry Clarence Kendall. VA
Sing Thou, My Soul. Theodosia Garrison. CAW
Sing-Time. Rose Waldo. GFA
Sing to Apollo, god of day. Song to Apollo. John Lyly. *Fr.* Midas. AtBAP; OBSC
Sing to Ashtaroth and Bel. To Ashtaroth and Bel. Saul Tchernichowsky. TrJP
Sing to God, my spirit, sing. He Shall Bear the Glory. William Blane. SoP
Sing to the Lord of Harvest. John Samuel Bewley Monsell. SoP
Sing unto Jehovah [*or* the Lord]. Psalms, XCVIII, Bible, *O.T.* *See* Floods Clap Their Hands, The.
Sing unto the Lord with Thanksgiving. Psalm CXL VII, Bible, *O.T.* OHIP; PoRL; SoPo
Sing we all merrily. A Catch by the Hearth [*or* Christmas Hearth Rhyme]. *Unknown.* ChBR; OHIP; PCH
Sing We and Chant It. *Unknown.* EnRePo; EP
("Sing we and chant it.") OBSC
(To Live in Pleasure.) TrGrPo
Sing we for love and idleness. An Immorality. Ezra Pound. CMoP; ForPo; GoJo; HBV; LiTL; LiTM; MAP; MoAB; MoAmPo; NeMA; NePA; PoPl; PoSa; SiTL

Sing we the two lieutenants, Parer and M'Intosh. Flight [to Australia.] C. Day Lewis. CMoP; MoVE; ShBV-3
Sing We Yule. *Unknown.* MeEL
Sing while you may, O bird upon the tree! Dark Wings. James Stephens. NP
"Sing while you work" and be full of cheer. To a Young Woman on the *World* Staff. Franklin P. Adams. ALV
Sing, Woods and Rivers All. Claudian, *tr. fr. Latin by* Maurice Platnauer *and* Virginia Tufte. *Fr.* Fescennine Verses in Honor of the Marriage of the Emperor Honorius. HW
Sing, ye ripening fields of wheat. Song of the Golden Sea. Jean Blewett. PTK
Singee a songee sick a pence. Nursery Song in Pidgin English. *Unknown.* BOHV; WhC
Singer, The. James Danner. BF
Singer, The. Edward Dowden. IrPN
Singer, The. Edmund Clarence Stedman. PRWS
Singer, The. Anna Wickham. HBMV; MoBrPo; NeMA; NP; TSW
Singer, The. Keith Wilson. ThO
Singer Asleep, A. Thomas Hardy. OAEP; POTE
Singer in the Prison, The. Walt Whitman. BeLS
Singer of One Song, The. Henry Augustin Beers. AA
Singer within the little streets. Song. Monk Gibbon. NeIP
Singers, The. George Bruce. OxBS
Singers, The. Longfellow. SoP
Singers are gone from the cornmarket-place, The. After the Fair. Thomas Hardy. At Casterbridge Fair, VII. BEL; CMoP; EnLi-2 (1949 ed.); EnLit; PoVP
Singers have hushed their notes of clear song, The. The Harper of Chao. Po Chü-i. MoPW; UnS
Singers in a Cloud, The. Ridgely Torrence. AnAmPo; HBMV; UnS
Singers in the Snow, The. *Unknown.* OHIP
Singers of serenades, The. Mandoline. Paul Verlaine. AWP; JAWP; OBMV; WBP
Singer's Prelude, The. William Morris. *See* Apology, An: "Of Heaven or Hell. . ."
Singers, sing! The hoary world. The Servants. Richard Wightman. WGRP
Singin' wid a Sword in Ma Han', *with music.* *Unknown.* BoAN-1
Singing. Dorothy Aldis. GFA
Singing. Robert Louis Stevenson. GaP; GFA; PCH; SUS; ThGo
Singing Bush, The. William Soutar. ACV
Singing Cat, The. Stevie Smith. BoC
Singing Children: Luca Della Robbia (T. H.). C. Day Lewis. MuSP
Singing Fairy, The. Rose Fyleman. BoChLi
Singing Girl, The. Joyce Kilmer. JKCP
Singing Huntsman, The. Witter Bynner. MAP; MoAmPo (1942 ed.)
Singing in the Dark. Irma Wassall. PoNe
Singing is sweet; but be sure of this. Art, III. James Thomson. EnLi-2
Singing Leaves, The. James Russell Lowell. GN; LoEn; MPB; OnSP; OTPC; StVeCh
Singing Lesson, The. Jean Ingelow. DD; HBV; OTPC (1946 ed.)
Singing Lesson, A. Swinburne. HBV; MuSP
Singing Maid, The. *Unknown.* *See* Now Springs the Spray.
Singing Man, The. Josephine Preston Peabody. HBV; PoFr, *abr.*
Singing my days. Passage to India. Walt Whitman. AmePo; AmPP (4th ed.); CoBA; DiPo; MWA-1; Po; PoEL-5
Singing My Doubts Away. *Unknown.* BePJ
Singing of your words is to be heard on a bended knee, The. Your Mouth. Jenab Shehabuddin. LiTW
Singing Saviors, The. Clement Wood. MaRV; OQP
Singing Stars. Katharine Tynan. VA
Singing the Reapers Homeward Come. *Unknown.* OHIP; PoRL
Singing through the forests. Rhyme of the Rail[s]. John G. Saxe. BOHV; InMe; MoShBr; PoLF
Singing-Time. Rose Fyleman. SiSoSe; TiPo
Singing Water. Rudolph Chambers Lehmann. MBMV
Singing-Woman from the Wood's Edge, The. Edna St. Vincent Millay. HBMV
Single Candle as the Presence of God, A. Gregory Orr. QAH
Single cause why you invite, The. Dinner with Ligurinus. Martial. OnPM
Single clenched fist lifted and ready, The. Choose. Carl Sandburg. NP
Single flow'r he sent me, since we met, A. One Perfect Rose. Dorothy Parker. ALV; FiBHP
Single Girl, The. *Unknown.* *See* When I Was Single.
Single-handed, and surrounded by Lecompton's black brigade. Lecompton's Black Brigade. Charles Graham Halpine. PAH
Single man stands like a bird-watcher, A. The Mouth of the Hudson. Robert Lowell. AmFN; CAD; CoPo; FRC; NaP; OCS; TDP; TPM
Single sleeper lying here, The. Epitaph for the Poet. George Barker. PoIE
Single Sonnet. Louise Bogan. AnEnPo; Sonn
Single step, that freed me from the skirts, A. Sky after Storm. Wordsworth. *Fr.* The Excursion. BoLiVe
Single Stitch, A. "Susan Coolidge." SoP
Single touch of a gentle hand, A. Transformed. Henry W. Frost. SoP
Single tree there was, A. Wordsworth. *Fr.* The Prelude, VI. OBRV
Single Woman, The. Frances Cornford. ELU
Sing Song. Robert Creeley. NMP
Sing-Song; a Nursery Rime Book. Christina Rossetti.
Sels.
"All the bells were ringing." TiPo
(Broken Doll, The.) MPB
"And timid, funny, brisk little bunny." TiPo
Baby, Sleep. OTPC (1946 ed.)
Boats Sail on the Rivers. BoChLi; BoTP; BrR; CoBE; OTPC (1946 ed.); PCH; PoVP; RIS; StVeCh; TiPo; TSW
(Rainbow, The.) GFA
Break and Milk [for Breakfast]. CBEP; SAS
(Winter.) PCH
Brownie, Brownie, Let Down Your Milk. RIS
"But give me holly, bold and jolly." BrR; ChBR; TiPo
Caterpillar, The. BoChLi (1950 ed.); BoTP; FaPON; GFA; GoTP; GoJo; MPB; OTPC (1946 ed.); RIS; SoPo; StVeCh
(Brown and Furry.) SUS; UTS
City Mouse and the Garden Mouse, The. BoChLi; BoTP; FaBoBe; FaPON; GoTP; HBV; HBVY; MPB; OTPC; PPL; StVeCh; UTS
(City Mouse and the Country Mouse, The.) PCH
("City mouse lives in a house, The.") SUS; TiPo
Daisies. RIS
"Days are clear, The." RIS; TiPo
(Stay, June, Stay!) YeAn
"Eight o'clock/ The postman's knock." RIS; SAS; TiPo
(Postman, The.) GaP; GFA; PCH
"Emerald is as green as grass, An." TiPo
(Precious Stones.) GoTP
Ferry Me across the Water. ChTr; GaP; GoJo; PDV; PoRh; SUS
(Boatman, The.) PCH
(Ferryman, The.) BoTP; SoPo
"Fly away, fly away over the sea." CoBE; PoVP; SUS
(Swallow, The.) GoTP; OTPC (1946 ed.); StVeCh
Frisky Lamb, A. BoTP
Growing in the Vale. BrR; GFA; RIS; TiPo
(Sweet Daffadowndilly.) BoChLi
Horses of the Sea, The. FaPON; GFA; GoJo; PCD; PoRh; SUS; UTS
House of Cards, The. OTD; PCH; PoPl
Hurt No Living Thing. FaPON; PCH; PDV; PoRL; RIS; SiSoSe; SoPo; ThGo
If a Pig Wore a Wig. BoChLi
If I Were a Queen. CoBE; GaP; PoVP; SiSoSe
"If stars dropped out of heaven." RIS
Is The Moon Tired? BoTP; StVeCh
"Kookoorookoo! Kookoorookoo." RIS
Lesson, A. RIS
"Lily has a smooth stalk, The." OuHeWo
Love Me—I Love You. BoTP
(Mother's Song, A.) OTPC (1946 ed.)
Lullaby: "Lullaby, oh lullaby." BoChLi; OTPC (1946 ed.); RIS
Minnie and Mattie. BoTP; GaP; GoJo; InvP; SUS; TiPo
(Minnie, Mattie and May.) TSW
Mix a Pancake. GFA; OTPC (1946 ed.); PoRh; SoPo; SUS; TiPo (1952 ed.)
(Pancake, The.) BoTP; HBVY; PCH

Months, The ("January cold"). FaPON; RIS
"Mother shake the cherry-tree." PoVP; TiPo
(Let's Be Merry.) FaPON
Motherless Soft Lambkin, A. RIS
Neighboring. GaP; PCH
Oh, Fair to See. DD; FaPON; MPB; OHIP; OTPC (1946 ed.); TiPo; YeAr
O Lady Moon. PRWS
(Lady Moon.) PCH
O Sailor, Come Ashore. BoTP; BrR; GaP
(Coral.) GFA
O Wind, Where Have You Been? BoTP
"O wind, why do you never rest." TiPo
On the Grassy Banks. UTS
(Lambs at Play.) BoTP
(Woolly Lambkins.) StVeCh
Phases of the Moon, The. MemP
Pin Has a Head, A. RIS
(Paradoxes.) OTPC (1946 ed.)
Pocket Handkerchief to Hem, A. RIS; SAS
(Stitching.) OTPC (1946 ed.); PPL
"Pussy has a whiskered face." TiPo
(Four Pets.) PPL
Rainbow, The. SoPo
"Seldom 'can't.' " SAS
(Good Advice.) PPL
(Rules of Behavior.) HBV; HBVY
Sing Me a Song. BoChLi
Skylark and Nightingale. RIS
(Heaven Is Heaven.) YeAr
Stars, The. OTPC (1946 ed.)
"There is but one May in the year." TiPo
(May-Time.) BoTP
"There is one that has a hèad without an eye." OTPC (1946 ed.); PPL
There's Snow on the Fields. BoTP
Three Plum Buns. BoTP
(Snack, A.) PCH
"Twist me a crown of wind-flowers." VA
Watching Angels. PPL
What Does the Bee Do? BoTP; RIS; SUS; TiPo
What Is Pink? GoJo; SUS; TiPo
(Color.) SoPo
When the Cows Come Home. OTPC (1946 ed); UTS
(Do You Know?) StVeCh
(Milking Time.) GFA; MPB; PRWS
Who Has Seen the Wind? BoTP; BrR; CoBE; FaPON; GoJo; HBV; HBVY; MPB; OTD; OTPC; OuHeWo; PCH; PDV; PoPl; PoRh; PoVP; PPL; StVeCh; SUS; TiPo; TreFT; TSW
(Wind, The.) BoChLi; FaBoBe; GFA; MaRV; NeHB; RIS
"Wind has such a rainy sound, The." BrR; PoVP; TiPo
(Sound of the Wind, The.) BoTP
"Wrens and robins in the hedge." GFA; SUS; TiPo
Sing-Song of Old Man Kangaroo, The. Kipling. FaPON; TiPo (1952 ed.)
Sing-Song Rhyme ("One! two! three!/ Outside the school"). *Unknown.* BoTP; SiSoSe
Singular Sangfroid of Baby Bunting, The. Guy Wetmore Carryl. NA
Sinister Dialogue. Callimachus, *tr. fr. Greek by* Robert Guthrie MacGregor. OnPM
Sinister presence changed life in a twelvemonth, A. Mountain Convent. Laura Benét. GoYe
Sink the world! Can that dismay us? A Pair. Karl Gjellerup. OnPM; PoPl
Sinking of the Mendi, The. S. E. K. Mqhayi, *tr. fr. Xhosa by* C. M. Mcanyangwa *and* Jack Cope. PeSA
Sinking of the *Merrmac[k].* Lucy Larcom. MC; PAH
Sinks the sun and fades the light. Am I Nearer Heaven Tonight? Henry Dobbs Holt. SoP
Sinks the sun below the desert. Cleopatra Dying. Thomas Stephens Collier. BLPA; FaBoBe; NeHB; OTD; TreFT
Sinless Child, The, *sel.* Elizabeth Oakes Smith
"Her ways were gentle." AA
Sinne ("Lord, with what care hast thou begirt us round"). George Herbert. MaMe; SCEP-1
Sinne ("O that I could a sinne once see!"). George Herbert. MaMe
Sinne of selfe-love possesseth al mine eie. *See* Sin of self-love possesseth all mine eye.
Sinner, The. Margaret E. Bruner. PoToHe
Sinner, The. George Herbert. MaMe; SCEP-1; Sonn
Sinner. Norman Jordan. BF
Sinner, Please Don't Let Dis Harves' Pass, *with music.* *Unknown.* BoAN-2
Sinner-Saint, The. Wilfrid Scawen Blunt. ACP; CAW
Sinners. D. H. Lawrence. CBV; ViBoPo
Sinner's Lament, A. Lord Herbert of Cherbury. SeCP
Sinner's Rue. A. E. Housman. PeVV
Sinners, turn; why will he die? Why Will Ye Die? Charles Wesley. SoP
Sinnes Heavie Loade. Robert Southwell. AnAnS-1; MeP
Sinnes Round. George Herbert. *See* Sins' Round.
Sins Loathed, and Yet Loved. Robert Herrick. LiTB
Sins of Youth, The. Thomas, Lord Vaux. ACP (1952 ed.)
Sins' [*or* Sinnes] Round. George Herbert. ExPo; LoBV; MaMe; ReEn
Sinuous among the reeds. Water Snake. Ethel Jacobson. NYTB
Sion. George Herbert. AnAnS-1; MaMe; MeP
Sion lies [*or* Syon lyes] waste, and thy Jerusalem. Fulke Greville. Caelica, CIX [CX]. EnRePo; NoP; OxBoCh; PoEL-1; QFR; ReIE; SiCE; TuPP
Sion the son of Evan sang. Microcosmos, XLVI. Nigel Heseltine. NeBP
Sion, thy bridal-bower prepare. The Purification. St. Cosmas. *Fr.* Menaion. ISi
Sioux, The. Eugene Field. FiBHP; GoJo
Sioux Indians, *with music.* *Unknown.* BFSS; CoSo
Sipping judiciously, he saw come near. Narcissus in a Cocktail Glass. Frances Minturn Howard. GoYe
Sir,/ Our times are much degenerate from those. To His Noble Friend, Mr. Richard Lovelace, upon His Poems. Andrew Marvell. PP
Sir, after you have wip'd the eyes. A Consolatory Poem Dedicated unto Mr. Cotton Mather. Nicholas Noyes. SCAP
Sir Aldingar. *Unknown.* BaBo (A *vers.*); ESPB (A, B, *and* C *vers.*); OBB; OxBB
(Ravngard and Memering, B *vers.*) BaBo
Sir Andrew Bart[t]on. *Unknown.* BaBo; EnSB; ESPB; OBB; OxBB; ViBoFo
Sir Andrew Barton said, I'm hurt. Determination. *Unknown.* TreFT
Sir Andrew Bartton. *Unknown.* *See* Sir Andrew Barton.
Sir Antony Love; or, The Rambling Lady, *sel.* Thomas Southerne.
Song: "Pursuing beauty, men descry." PeRV; SeCL
(Song in the Second Act, A.) SeEP
Sir, as your mandate did request. The Inventory. Burns. CABL
Sir Bailey Barre. W. S. Gilbert. *Fr.* Utopia, Limited. PCD
Sir Beelzebub. Edith Sitwell. *Fr.* Façade. CoBMV; HoPM; MoAB; MoBrPo
(When Sir Beelzebub.) FaBoMo
Sir, can you tell where my young master lives. Henry Parrot. SiCE
Sir Cawline. *Unknown.* ESPB; OBB
Sir Christopher Wren. E. C. Bentley. *Fr.* Clerihews. BOHV; CenHV; FiBHP; InMe; LiTG; MoShBr; PV; ShBV-3; SiTL; WhC
(Important People, 8.) StaSt
Sir Cock, to you the first place I award. Fortitude. Reinmar von Zweter. LiTW
Sir Colin. *Unknown.* OxBB
Sir Drake, whom well the world's end knew. Epigram: On Sir Francis Drake [*or* Sir Francis Drake]. Unknown. CBEP; OBS
Sir Eglamore. *Unknown.* OnSP
Sir Eglamour, *parody.* Samuel Rowlands. *Fr.* The Melancholy Knight. EIL; FaBoCh; InvP; LoGBV; WaKn
Sir Egrabell had sonnes three. Sir Lionel. *Unknown.* BaBo (A *vers.*); ESPB
Sir Eustace Grey. George Crabbe. MyFE
Sels.
"Peace, peace, my friend; these subjects fly." PoEL-4
"Then those ill-favour'd Ones, whom none." ELP
Sir Fopling Flutter. Dryden. DiPo
Sir Francis Drake, *sels.* Charles Fitzgeffrey.
Bee, The ("Look how the industrious bee"). EIL
Sir Francis, Sir Francis, Sir Francis is come. Upon Sir Francis Drake's Return from His Voyage about the World, and the

Sir (continued)
Queen's Meeting Him. *Unknown.* CoMu; EIL; FaBoCh; FOL
Sir Galahad. Tennyson. BEL; EPN; GTBS; HBV; LiTG; OBVV; OnPP; OTPC; PoVP; VA; ViPo; ViPP
Pure Heart, The ("My good blade carves the casques of men") *br. sel.* MaRV; TreF
Sir Gawain and the Green Knight. *Unknown, tr. fr. Middle English.* BEL *tr. by* Jessie L. Weston; EnL,*tr. by* George B. Pace; EnLi-1,*tr. by* Theodore Howard Banks; EnLit. *tr. by* Jessie L. Weston, MeEV *tr. by* Theodore Howard Banks; OuHeWo *tr. by* Theodore Howard Banks
Sels.
"Now will I tell you no more of their serving," *tr. by* Richard L. Hoffman. YAT
Passage of a Year, The, *fr.* II. PoEL-1
Temptation of Sir Gawain, The. ACP
Sir Gawain Encounters Sir Priamus. *Unknown.* *Fr.* Morte Arthure. PoEL-1
Sir Gawaine and the Green Knight. Yvor Winters. AnFE; CoAnAm; MoVE; PoIE; PoRA (rev. ed.); QFR; TwAmPo
Sir Geoffrey Chaucer. Robert Greene. *See* Description of Sir Geoffrey Chaucer, The.
Sir George Prevost, with all his host. The Battle of Plattsburg. *Unknown.* PAH
Sir Giles's War-Song. William Morris. PoVP; ViPo
Sir Guy the Crusader. W. S. Gilbert. BOHV
Sir Halewyn. Alexander Gray. OxBB
Sir Helmer Blaa and His Bride's Brothers. *Unknown.* BaBo
Sir Henry Clinton's Invitation to the Refugees. Philip Freneau. PAH
Sir Hudibras. Samuel Butler. *Fr.* Hudibras. UnPo (1st ed.)
Sir Hudibras his passing worth. Samuel Butler. *Fr.* Hudibras, Pt. I. FosPo
Sir Hudibras's Religion. Samuel Butler. *See* Religion of Hudibras, The.
Sir Hugh; or, The Jew's Daughter. *Unknown.* BaBo (A, B, *and* D *vers.*); BFSS, *with music*; CH; ESPB (A, B, C, *and* N *vers.*); ViBoFo (A, B, *and* C *vers.*)
(Hugh of Lincoln.) ACP; EnSB; OBB; OxBB
(Jewish Lady, The.) BaBo (C *vers.*)
Sir Humphrey Gilbert. Longfellow. EtS; HBV; HBVY; MC; OnSP; OTPC; PAH; TOP
Sir Humphry Davy. E. C. Bentley. *Fr.* Clerihews. CenHV; ImOP; ShBV-3
Sir, I Admit Your General Rule. Pope. *See* Epigram: "Sir, I admit your general rule."
Sir, I commend to you the spirit. José Garcia Villa. *Fr.* Divine Poems. MoRP
Sir, I pray you, be you not master god? John Heywood. *Fr.* The Play of the Weather. CoBE
Sir; I read of late. Four Questions Addressed to His Excellency the Prime Minister. James P. Vaughn. AmNP
Sir, I shall tell you news, except you know it. Of Don Pedro and His Poetry. Sir John Harington. SiCE
Sir J.S. Sir John Suckling. *See* Constant Lover, The ("Out upon it").
Sir James the Rose. *Unknown.* ESPB
Sir John addressed the Snake-god in his temple. Robert Graves. *Fr.* Grotesques. DTC
Sir John Barleycorn. *Unknown.* CBEP
Sir John Butler. *Unknown.* ESPB
Sir John Franklin; On the Cenotaph in Westminster Abbey. Tennyson. InP
Sir John Graeme and Barbara Allen. *Unknown.* *See* Barbara Allen.
Sir John Wingefield. John Donne. MaMe
Sir Joseph's Song. W. S. Gilbert. *See* When I Was a Lad.
Sir Joshua praises Michael Angelo. Blake. EiCL
Sir Joshua Reynolds. Blake. ELU; FiBHP; LiTG; OxBoLi (Epigram.) SiTL
Sir Joshua Reynolds. Goldsmith. *Fr.* Retaliation. OBEC; SeCePo
Sir Lancelot beside the mere. Lancelot and Guinevere. Gerald Gould. HBV
Sir Lark and King Sun. George Macdonald. *Fr.* Adela Cathcart, *ch.* 16. HBV; HBVY; OTPC
Sir Launcelot and Queen Guinevere. Tennyson. ACV; VA
Sir Launfal. Thomas Chester, *tr. fr. Middle English by* Jessie L. Weston. ATP
Sir Launfal, *sel.* John Moultrie.
"But here at starting." OBRV
Sir Launfal and the Leper. James Russell Lowell. *Fr.* The Vision of Sir Launfal, I. GN; OTPC
Sir Lionel. *Unknown.* BaBo (A *vers.*); ESPB (A, B, *and* C *vers.*)
(Old Bangham, *with music.*) OuSiCo
(Old Bangum.) BaBo (B *vers.*); BFSS, *with music*
Sir Magnus and the Elf-Maid. *Unknown.* BaBo
Sir Marmaduke. George Colman. GoTP
Sir Marmaduke's Musings. Theodore Tilton. AA
Sir Martyn. William Julius Mickle. *See* Concubine, The.
Sir, more then kisses, letters mingle soules. To Sir Henry Wotton. John Donne. MaMe; ReEn
Sir Moses, Sir Aaron, Sir Jamramajee. A New Order of Chivalry. Thomas Love Peacock. CenHV
Sir Nameless, once of Athelhall, declared. The Children and Sir Nameless. Thomas Hardy. NoP
Sir Nicketty Nox. Hugh Chesterman. BoTP
Sir, No Man's Enemy [Forgiving All]. W. H. Auden. BWP; FaBoMo; NAMP
(Petition.) CMoP; CoBMV; GTBS-W; LiTB; LiTM; MoPo; OAEP (2d ed.); PoDB; PoIE; ReMP; Sonn
Sir Ogey and Lady Elsey. *Unknown.* *See* Sweet William's Ghost.
Sir Olaf. Johann Gottfried von Herder, *tr. fr. German by* Elizabeth Craigmyle. AWP; JAWP; PoMS; WBP
Sir Oluf he rideth over the plain. The Elected Knight. *Unknown.* AWP; JAWP; WBP
Sir, or madam, choose you whether. Upon an Hermaphrodite. John Cleveland. AnAnS-2
Sir Orfeo. *Unknown, ad. fr. Middle English by* Edward Eyre Hunt. MeEV
"His harp, whereon was al his gle," *orig. vers.* AtBAP
Sir Patrick Spens [*or* Spence]. *Unknown.* AnFE; AtBAP; ATP; AWP; BaBo (A, B, *and* C *vers.*); BBV (1923 ed.); BEL; BoChLi; BoLiVe; BuBa; CABA; CABL; CaFP; CBEP; CBV; CH; CoBE; DiPo; ELP; EnL; EnLi-1; EnLit; EnRP; EnSB; ESPB, (A, B, *and* G *vers.*); ExPo; FaBoCh; FIW; ForPo; FosPo; GN; GoJo; GoTS; HBV; HoPM; ILP; InP; InPo; InvP; JAWP; LiTB; LoBV; LoGBV; MCCG; NoP; OAEP; OBB; OBEV; OnSP; OtMeF; OTPC (1946 ed.); OuHeWo; OxBB; OxBS; PAn; PIA; PoAn; PoEL-1; PoIE; PoMa; PoPo; PoRA; PoSA; RG; SeCeV; ShBV-1; StP; TiPo (1952 ed.); TOP; TreF; TrGrPo; UnPo; ViBoFo, (A *vers.*, with music; B *vers.*); ViBoPo; WBP; WHA; YAT
(Ballad of Sir Patrick Spens, The.) EtS; RoGo
Sir Peter's Leman. *Unknown.* *See* Lord Thomas and Fair Annet.
Sir Philip Sidney. Eleanor *and* Herbert Farjeon. OnPP
Sir Richard's Song. Kipling. OtMeF
Sir Robert Bolton had three sons. Sir Lionel (C *vers.*). *Unknown.* ESPB
Sir Robin. Lucy Larcom. BoChLi; MPB; OTPC (1946 ed.); TiPo (1952 ed.)
Sir Roderic's Song. W. S. Gilbert. *Fr.* Ruddigore. GBV (1952 ed.); PoMS; ShM; WhC
Sir, say no more. Dramatic Fragment. Trumbull Stickney. CBEP; ELU; OxBA
Sir Sidrophel, the Conjuror. Samuel Butler. *See* Portrait of Sidrophel.
Sir, since the last Elizabethan died. A Letter to a Live Poet. Rupert Brooke. BrPo
Sir T. J.'s Speech to His Wife and Children. *Unknown.* CoMu
Sir, the night is darker now. A Nightly Deed. Charles Madge. NeBP
Sir Thomas, stark green until he crept acurl. A Contempt for Dylan Thomas. Wilfred Watson. PeCV
Sir Thomas was a merry man, he laughed deep in his throat. A Ballad of St. Thomas. Charles A. Brady. JKCP (1955 ed.)
Sir Thopas. Chaucer. *Fr.* The Canterbury Tales. BEL; Par
Sir: though (I thank God for it) I do hate. Satires II. John Donne. MaMe; PoFS; ViBoPo
Sir Tristram was a Bear, in listed field. Tristram and Isolt. Don Marquis. HBMV
Sir Tristrem, *sel.* *At. to* Thomas of Erceldoune.
Tristrem and the Hunters. OxBS
Sir Turlough; or, The Churchyard Bride. William Carleton. IrPN

Sir Walter, oh, oh, my own Sir Walter. Lady Ralegh's Lament. Robert Lowell. NoP
Sir Walter Ralegh the Night before His Death. Sir Walter Ralegh. *See* Conclusion, The.
Sir Walter Ralegh to His Son. Sir Walter Ralegh. *See* Wood, the Weed, the Wag, The.
Sir Walter Raleigh. E. C. Bentley. *Fr.* Clerihews. CenHV
Sir Walter Raleigh. William Carlos Williams. *Fr.* In the American Grain. OnHM
Sir Walter Raleigh has built a ship. The Sweet Trinity; or, The Golden Vanity (A *vers.*). *Unknown.* BaBo
Sir Walter Raleigh Sailing in the Low-lands. *Unknown. See* Golden Vanity, The.
Sir Walter Raleigh to a Caged Linnet. Eugene Lee Hamilton. VA
Sir Walter Raleigh to His Son. Sir Walter Ralegh. *See* Wood, the Weed, the Wag, The.
Sir Walter Raleigh to the Queen. Sir Walter Ralegh. *See* Silent Lover, The.
Sir Walter Raleigh's Verses, Found in His Bible in the Gatehouse at Westminster. Sir Walter Ralegh. *See* Conclusion, The.
Sir Walter Rauleigh His Lamentation. *Unknown.* CoMu
Sir Walter Scott's Tribute. Sir Walter Scott. *See* Book of Books, The.
Sir, welcome. Shakespeare. *Fr.* The Winter's Tale, IV, iii. AtBAP
Sir. whatsoever you are pleas'd to do. Dedications [*of* Orchestra]. II; To the Prince. Sir John Davies. SiPS
Sir! when I flew to seize the bird. Beau's Reply. William Cowper. EiCL;FaBoCh;OA;OTPC(1923 ed.);PRWS
Sir, when you say. 15th Raga: For Bela Lugosi. David Melter. NeAP
Sir, while at the helm of state you ride. A Letter to Sir Robert Walpole. Henry Fielding. CEP
Sir William of Deloraine at the Wizard's Tomb. Sir Walter Scott. *See* Melrose Abbey.
Sir Wind, why blow so rough? The Squirrel and the Wind. *Unknown.* PCH
Sir, you should [shall, *wr.*] notice me: I am the Man. Epitaph. Lascelles Abercrombie. MoBrPo; POTE; ViBoPo
Sire. W. S. Merwin. CoAP; NaP
Sire of the rising day. An Ode. Lord De Tabley. OBVV; PoVP
Siren Chorus. George Darley. *See* Mermaidens' Vesper-Hymn.
Siren cries that ran like mad and naked screaming women, The. Eine Kleine Nachtmusik. Robert E. Hayden. PoNE
Siren sang, and Europe turned away, A. To the Western World. Louis Simpson. CoAP; LiTM (1970 ed.); NePoAm-2; NePoEA-2; PoPl
Siren Song. William Browne. *See* Siren's Song, The.
Sirena. Michael Drayton. *Fr.* The Shepherd's Sirena. CBEP; OBEV, *abr.*; SeCL
(Jovial Shepheard's Song, The.) PoEL-2
("Near to the silver Trent.") SeEP; TuPP
(Song to Sirena.) AtBAP
Sirens, The, *sels.* Laurence Binyon. GoTL (1949 ed.)
"Mystery of Dawn, ere yet the glory streams."
"World-besieging storm, from horizon heaped and menacing."
Sirens, The. Donald Finkel. NePoEA
Sirens, The. John Manifold. LiTB; LiTM; MoBrPo (1962 ed.); Sonn; VaPo; WaP
Sirens, Scylla and Charybdis, The. Homer, *tr. fr. Greek by* Pope. *Fr.* The Odyssey, XII. LiTW
Sirens' Song, The. William Browne. *Fr.* The Inner Temple Masque. EtS; OBEV
(Siren Song.) EG
(Song of the Sirens.) ElL
(Song of the Syrens.) ChTr; OBS, *sl. abr.*
("Steer hither, steer your wingèd pines.") ViBoPo
Sirmio. Catullus, *tr. fr. Latin by* Charles Stuart Calverley. AWP; JAWP; WBP
Sirocco at Deyá. Robert Graves. MoVE
Sirs—though we fail you—let us live. To Men. Anna Wickham. MoBrPo
Sirs, when you are in your last extremity. Gone Away Blues. Thomas McGrath. WOW
Sirventes: "I have made a sirventes against the city of Toulouse." Paul Blackburn. NeAP
Sis Joe, *with music. Unknown.* OuSiCo
Sisiphus is he, whom noise and strife, The. The Fear of Death. Lucretius, *tr. by* Dryden. *Fr.* De Rerum Natura. LoBV
Sissinghurst. V. Sackville-West. POTE
Sister. Whittier. *Fr.* Snow-bound; a Winter Idyl. AA
Sister and mother and diviner love. To the One of Fictive Music. Wallace Stevens. AnAmPo; AnFE; AP; APA; CoAnAm; CoBMV; MAP; MoAB; MoAmPo; MoVE; TwAmPo
Sister Anne, Sister Anne. Perspectives Are Precipices. John Peale Bishop. LiTA; LiTM; MoVE; NePA
Sister Anne, Sister Anne. The Ballad of Sister Anne. Sir Osbert Sitwell. AtBAP
Sister, Awake! *Unknown.* CH; DD; ElL; HBV; OBEV; PoSC; RG
(Madrigal: "Sister, awake, close not your eyes.") BoTP
Sister, come to the chestnut toll. The Last Night. Alfred Austin. PeVV
Sister false is, A. Masque. Jewel C. Latimore. WSL
Sister Helen. Dante Gabriel Rossetti. BEL; BeLS; EnL; EnLi-2; EnLit; EPN; MaVP; OAEP; PoE; PoVP; ShBV-2; TOP; ViPo; ViPP
Sister Lou. Sterling A. Brown. AmNP; GoSl; PoNe
Sister Mary of the Love of God. Rosa Mulholland. VA
Sister Nell. *Unknown.* BBGG; FaPON
Sister Simplicitie. Fragment of a Sleep-Song. Sydney Dobell. VA
"Sister, sister, go to bed!" Brother and Sister. "Lewis Carroll." BBGG; ChTr; ShM
Sister Songs, *sels.* Francis Thompson.
"But lo! at length the day." OBMV
We Poets Speak. FaBV
Sister Speaks of Rapping, A. Shirley Staples. WSL
Sister, the bride-bed waits: sister for thee. Epithalamium. Arthur Symons. FaBoTw
Sister to sister said. The Avenging Daughters. *Unknown.* LiTW
Sistern and Brethren, *with music. Unknown.* TrAS
Sisters, The. Roy Campbell. ChMP; ErPo; FaBoTw; MoVE; OBMV
Sisters. Eleanor Farjeon. FaPON
Sisters. "Robin Hyde." AnNZ
Sisters, The. Amy Lowell. AnNE; MAP; MoAmPo
Sisters. Dorothy Roberts. CaP
Sisters, The, *sel.* Swinburne.
Lyric, A. HBV
Sisters, The. John Banister Tabb. AA; MaRV
Sisters, The ("We were two daughters of one race"). Tennyson. InvP
Sisters, The. Whittier. AWP; InPo
Sisters, it will be necessary. Mother Superior. George MacBeth. HYE; NMP
Sisters Kastemaloff, The. Carlton Talbott. ALV
Sisyphus. Josephine Miles. NYBP
Sit Down, Sad Soul. "Barry Cornwall." CAW; TreFT; VA
Sit further, and make room for thine own fame. To His Worthy Friend Doctor Witty upon His Translation of the Popular Errors. Andrew Marvell. MaMe; PP
Sit on the bed. I'm blind, and three parts shell. A Terre. Wilfred Owen. LiTM (rev. ed.); MMA; WaP
Sit quiet in my lap while solemnly. Evensong. Carleton Drewry. GoYe
Sit tight, little hills, little valleys. Dame Liberty Reports from Travel. Dorothy Cowles Pinkney. GoYe
Sit under a pine on Christmas Eve. Ballad of the Unmiraculous Miracle. Vassar Miller. ToPo
Sitalkas. Hilda Doolittle ("H. D."). ViBoPo
Sitar Player, The. Julian Cooper. MuSP
Sith earth is stage whereon we play our parts. Man's Life Likened to a Stage Play. Thomas Howell. SiCE
Sith fortune favors not and all things backward go. A Refusal. Barnabe Googe. EnRePo; NoP
Sith, in dark, speech, Carvilios hymn unfolds. Druids' Hymn to the Sun. C. M. Doughty. *Fr.* The Dawn in Britain. FaBoTw
Sith my desire is prest to please. Reward Doth Not Always Answer Desert. Thomas Howell. SiCE
Sith my life from life is parted. Marie Magdalens Complaint at Christs Death. Robert Southwell. AnAnS-1; MeP; MePo

Sith (continued)
Sith sickles and the shearing scythe. Hawking for the Partridge. Thomas Ravenscroft. NCEP; OxBoLi
Sith that you both are like in life. To a Married Couple That Could Not Agree. Martial, *tr. by* Timothe Kendall. TuPP
Sit-in, The. Darwin T. Turner. BALP
Sits by a fireplace, the seducer talks. Sonnet. Leonard Wolf. ErPo
Sitteth alle stille and herkneth to me! The Song of Lewes [*or* the Barons' Enemies]. *Unknown.* MeEL; OxBoLi
Sittin' around the stove last night. A Liz-Town Humorist. James Whitcomb Riley. IHA
Sittin' on the Porch. Edgar A. Guest. TreFS
Sitting, The. C. Day Lewis. FaBoMo
Sitting Alone. Robert Herrick. *See* Vision, The.
Sitting at evening in the warm grass. For My Wife. Julian Symons. NeBP; WaP
Sitting at her [*or* a] window in her cloak and hat. Mother Tabbyskins [*or* Old Mother Tabbyskins]. *Unknown, at. to* Elizabeth Anna Hart. CenHV; CIV; FTB
Sitting by a river [*or* river's] side. Philomela's Ode [That She Sung] in Her Arbor. Robert Greene. *Fr.* Philomela, the Lady Fitzwater's Nightingale. LO; NoP; OBSC; ReIE; SiCE; TuPP
Sitting down near him in the shade. The Smoker. Robert Huff. NePoEA-2
Sitting, He travels afar. Tranquility. *Unknown. Fr.* The Upanishads. OnPM
Sitting Here. Elizabeth J. Coatsworth. *See* It's Pleasant to Think.
Sitting in his rocker waiting for your tea. The View at Gunderson's. Joseph Warren Beach. NP
Sitting in our garden you cannot escape symbols. *See* Sitting in this garden. . .
Sitting in the disorder of my silence. Fulfillment. Vassar Miller. NePoEA-2
Sitting in this [*or* our] garden you cannot escape symbols. Of the Unscathing Fire [*or* The Phoenix Answered]. Anne Ridler. ChMP; LiTL; MoLP; POTE
Sitting on the flower-bed beneath the hollyhocks. The Fairy Tailor. Rose Fyleman. PoRh; TVC
Sitting Pretty. Margaret Fishback. PoLF
Sittinge downe to her repast. *Unknown.* SeCSL
Situation, The. Sydney Clouts. BoSA
Situation is blue and white, The. The Crucifixion of Noel. Marsden Hartley. AnAmPo
Situation Normal. Hank Chernick. WhC
Six!/ Such different minds and faces! Mistresses. *Unknown.* KiLC
Six and Thirty. D. E. Stevenson. BiCB
Six Badgers, The. Robert Graves. GoJo
Six Bards, The, *sel.* James Macpherson.
"Night is dull and dark." PeER
Six Birthday Candles Shining. Mary Jane Carr. BiCB
Six Carpenters' Case, The. Sir Frederick Pollock. VA
Six decent lines can make a man immortal. Six Lines Unheard. Diana der Hovanessian. NYTB
Six Epigrams, *sel.* Gerard Manley Hopkins.
"No, they are come; their horn is lifted up." SeCePo
Six feet beneath. Jerry Jones. *Unknown.* ShM
Six Feet of Earth. *Unknown.* BLPA
Six-foot nest of the sea-hawk, The. Sea-Hawk. Richard Eberhart. NoP; WIRo
Six in June. Mary Carolyn Davies. BiCB
Six Jolly Wee Miners. *Unknown.* CoMu
Six Lines Unheard. Diana der Hovanessian. NYTB
Six [*or* Some *or* Ten] little mice sat down [*or* in a barn] to spin. Mother Goose. BoTP; HBV; OTPC; OxNR; PPL; RIS; SAS
Six men drove up to his house at midnight. Arturo Giovannitti. *Fr.* When the Cock Crows. WOW
Six month child, The. Slippery. Carl Sandburg. BiCB; FaPON; TiPo
Six o'Clock. Owen Dodson. PoNe
Six o'Clock. Trumbull Stickney. NCEP; OxBA
Six of Cups. Diane Wakoski. CoPo
Six Poets in Search of a Lawyer. Donald Hall. NYBP; SiTL
Six-Quart Basket, The. Raymond Souster. MoCV; PeCV (1967 ed.)
Six Questions. *Unknown.* *See* Captain Wedderburn's Courtship.
Six Religious Lyrics, *sel.* Karl Shapiro.
"I sing the simplest flower," I. CMoP
Six Rubaiyat. Abu Said ibn Abi-l-Khair, *tr. fr. Persian by* E. G. Browne. LiTW
Six seven, 6, 7. Alice 1963. G. Bishop-Dubjinsky. ThO
Six Silver Handles. Sydney King Russell. FiSC
Six street-ends come together here. Blue Island Intersection. Carl Sandburg. MAP; MoAmPo
Six Sunday. Hart Leroi Bibbs. NBP
Six thousand years in these dull regions pass'd. Discovery. Philip Freneau. WoL
Six times faster than the fool can weep. The Peasant. Leonard Wolf. NYBP
Six to Six. *Unknown, tr. fr. Xhosa by* A. C. Jordan. PBA
Six Variations. Denise Levertov. AmPP (5th ed.); CoPo
Six Weeks Old. Christopher Morley. BiCB
Six Winters. Ruthven Todd. NeBP
Six-Year-Old Marjory Fleming Pens a Poem. Marjory Fleming. *See* Melancholy Lay, A.
Six Young Men. Ted Hughes. POTi
"Sixpence a week," says the girl to her lover. By Her Aunt's Grave. Thomas Hardy. *Fr.* Satires of Circumstance. MoAB; MoBrPo; PoPo; PoVP; VaPo
Sixt Nimphall, The. Michael Drayton. *See* Fine Day, A.
Sixteen Dead Men. Dora Sigerson Shorter. ACP; OnYI
Sixteen Dead Men. W. B. Yeats. PIA
1643 "Veritas" 1878. Oliver Wendell Holmes. *Fr.* Two Sonnets: Harvard. AP
Sixteen years ago I built this house. A World within a War. Sir Herbert Read. MoPo
Sixth Book of the Aeneis, The, *sel.* Vergil, *tr. fr. Latin by* Dryden. *Fr.* The Aeneid.
Destiny of Rome, The. PeRV
("Let others better mold the running mass.") SeCV-2
Sixth-Month Song in the Foothills. Gary Snyder. FRC; WIRo
Sixth Nymphal, The. Michael Drayton. *See* Fine Day, A.
Sixth Pastoral, The ("How still the sea!"). Ambrose Philips. *Fr.* Pastorals. CEP
(Pastoral Landscape, *abr.*) OBEC
Sixth was August, being rich arrayed, The. August. Spenser. *Fr.* The Faerie Queene, VII, 7. GN
Sixty-eighth Birthday. James Russell Lowell. PoEL-5; StP
Sixty seconds make a minute. *Unknown.* RIS
Siyalila, siyalila, inkomo yetu ifile! Lament for a Dead Cow. F. C. Slater. BoSA; TDP
Size, The. George Herbert. MaMe
Size balls are saddens Lamarck, The. Edwin Denby. ANYP
Size of a cavern for men to crouch in, The. Dawn Hippo. Sydney Clouts. PeSA
Skaian Gate, The, *sel.* Geoffrey Scott.
"Hector, the captain bronzed." OBMV
Skater of Ghost Lake, The. William Rose Benét. PoPo
Skaters, The. John Gould Fletcher. MAP; MoAmPo; NeMA; PFY; PoMa; SD
Skaters, The. John Williams. NePoAm-2; SD
Skaters upon thin ice. Black Water and Bright Air. Constance Carrier. SD
Skater's Valentine, A. Arthur Guiterman. SiSoSe
Skater's Waltz, A. Gray Burr. CoPo
Skating. Herbert Asquith. BoChLi; BrR; FaPON; SoPo; StVeCh; SUS; TiPo
Skating. Kipling. SD
Skating. Wordsworth. *See* On the Frozen Lake.
Skating Song. Christopher Morley. PCH
'Skeeters am a-hummin' on de honeysuckle vine. Kentucky Babe. Richard Henry Buck. AA; HBV
Skeleton, The. G. K. Chesterton. FaBoTw
Skeleton at the Feast, The. James Jeffrey Roche. AA
Skeleton in Armor, The. Longfellow. AA; AmePo; AmPP; AnNE; AP; AWP; BeLS; CoBA; FaBoBe; GBV (1922 ed.); GoTP; HBV; HBVY; LoEn; MaC; MCCG; MWA-1; OnSP; PAH; PoPo; RG; TOP; TreF
Skeleton in the Cupboard, The. Frederick Locker-Lampson. HBV; VA
Skeleton of the Future, The. "Hugh MacDiarmid." GoTS; MoBrPo; OBMV; ShBV-4
Skeleton of the moa on iron crutches, The. Attitudes for a New Zealand Poet, III. Allen Curnow. AnNZ
Skeleton Once in Khartoum, A. *Unknown.* ShM
Skelton Laureate, upon a Dead Man's Head. John Skelton. *See* Upon a Dead Man's Head.
Skeltoniad, A. Michael Drayton. PoEL-2; PP

Skeptic, The. Robert Service. PV
Skeptic, The. Loring Williams. FiSC
Skerryvore ("For love of lovely words"). Robert Louis Stevenson. ILP
Skerryvore: The Parallel ("Here all is sunny"). Robert Louis Stevenson. ILP
Sketch. Burns. EiCL
Sketch, A. Byron. ERoP-2; OBRV
(Sketch from Private Life, A.) OBNC
Sketch. "Seumas O'Sullivan." AnIV
Sketch, A. Christina Rossetti. GTBS-P
Sketch. Carl Sandburg. AP; HBMV; NP
Sketch, A. Wordsworth. *See* Old Man, An.
Sketch from Private Life, A. Byron. *See* Sketch, A.
Sketch from the Life, A. Arthur Guiterman. BOHV
Sketch of His Own Character. Thomas Gray. BEL; CEP; EiCP; EnLit; TOP
Sketch of Lord Byron's Life, *sel.* Julia A. Moore.
"Lord Byron' was an Englishman." FiBHP
Sketches of Harlem. David Henderson. Kal; NNP; PoNe (1970 ed.)
Skew-Ball Black, The. *Unknown.* CoSo
Ski Train. Patrick Anderson. TwCaPo
Skialetheia, *sels.* Everard Guilpin.
"As in the greatest of societies." SiCE
(Proemium I.) ReIE
De Ignoto. ReIE
"Fie on these Lydian tunes which blunt our sprights." SiCE
"Let me alone, I prithee, in this cell." SiCE
(Satyra Quinta.) TuPP
Of Cornelius. SiCE; TuPP
Of Pansa. ReIE
Of Titus. ReIE; SiCE; TuPP
Of Zeno. SiCE
Satira Prima: "Shall I still miche in silence and give aim." ReIE
To Clodius. ReIE
To Deloney. ReIE
To Licus. SiCE
To the Reader. ReIE; SiCE
Skier. Robert Francis. SD
Skiers, The. Anthony Frisch. TwCaPo
Skies are brass and the plains are bare, The. Song of the Darling River. Henry Lawson. ACV
Skies are low, the winds are slow, The. Under the Blue. Francis Fisher Browne. AA
Skies cant keep their secret, The! Emily Dickinson. DiPo
Skies contain still groves of silver clouds, The. Spring 1943. Roy Fuller. LiTB; LiTM; WaP
Skies gan scowl, o'ercast with misty clouds, The. Gascoigne's De Profundis. George Gascoigne. TuPP
Skies have sunk, and hid the upper snow, The. Ite Domum Saturae, Venit Hesperus [*or* Les Vaches]. Arhur Hugh Clough. BEL; EnLit; OAEP; PoVP; VA
Skies is different than they was, The. A Spring Lay. Oliver Opdyke. InMe
Skies they were ashen and sober, The. Ulalume. Poe. AA; AmePo; AmP; AmPP; AnAmPo; AnEnPo; AnFE; AP; APA; ATP; AWP; CoAnAm; CoBA; DiPo; JAWP; LiTA; LiTG; LO; MAmP; MWA-1; NePA; OuHeWo; OxBA; PoFS; PoIE; PoPo; TDP; TOP; TreF; UnPo; ViBoPo; WBP; WHA
Skies they were ashen and sober, The, *parody.* The Willows. Bret Harte. BOHV; InMe
Skies to the West are stained with madder. Gloaming. Robert Adger Bowen. HBV
Skiing Song. "Michael Lewis." OTD
(January.) GoTP
Skilful Listener, The. John Vance Cheney. AA
Skill'd to deceive our ears and eyes. The County Member. Winthrop Mackworth Praed. *Fr.* The County Ball. OBNC
Skimbleshanks; the Railway Cat. T. S. Eliot. FaBoCh; LoGBV
Skimmers. Ted Walker. NYBP
Skimming lightly, wheeling still. Shiloh, a Requiem. Herman Melville. AmFN; AP; CBEP; HT; LiTA; MAmP; MWA-1; NCEP; NoP; OxBA; PaA; PAL; PoFS; PoPo; StP; TDP; ViBoPo; WiR
Skin creamy as the furled magnolia bud. The Dancer. Ednah Proctor Clarke. AA
Skin-flakes, repetitions, erosions. Ezra Pound. *Fr.* Canto XV. MoPo
Skin more pure than Ida's snow. My Mistress. Richard Brathwaite. *Fr.* The English Gentlewoman. SeCL
Skin transparent as water. Bearings. Jack Marshall. YAP
Skindivers, The. George Starbuck. NYBP; TDP
Skin Diving in the Virgins. John Malcolm Brinnin. NYBP
Skinful of bowls, he bowls them. Second Glance at a Jaguar. Ted Hughes. NYBP
Skinny Mrs. Snipkin. Mrs. Snipkin and Mrs. Wobblechin. Laura E. Richards. PoRh; SoPo; StVeCh (1955 ed.); TiPo
Skinny Poem. Lou Lipsitz. YAP
Skip-Scoop-Anellie. Tom Prideaux. FiBHP
Skip to My Lou, *with music. Unknown.* ABF; TrAS
Skipper-Hermit, The. Hiram Rich. EtS
Skipper Ireson's Ride. Whittier. AmePo; AmP; AmPP; AnNE; AP; BeLS; BOHV; CoBA; GBV; HBV; InMe; InP; OnSP; OTPC; OxBA; PAH; PFY; PoLF; PoPo; StPo; StVeCh (1940 ed.); ThLM, *sl. abr.*; TreFS; YaD; YT
Skippery Boo, The. Earl L. Newton. GoTP
Skippets, the Bad One. Christine E. Bradley. BoTP
Skipping Along Alone. Winifred Welles. SoPo; TiPo
Skipping Ropes. Dorothy Aldis. StVeCh
Skirting the river road, (my forenoon walk, my rest). The Dalliance of the Eagles. Walt Whitman. AA; AmPP (5th ed.); BWP; CABA; FaBoEn; MWA-1; NoP; TDP
Skottles out of Berwik and of Aberdene. A Song of Laurence Minot. Laurence Minot. BEL
Skreak and skritter of evening gone, The. Autumn Refrain. Wallace Stevens. LiTA; Sonn; TDP
Skull. Coleman Barks. *Fr.* Body Poems. QAH
Skull, The. Mary E. Fullerton. BoAu
Skull of Haydn returned to his bones, The. The Turtle. James Schevill. FiMAP
Skunk, The. Dorothy Baruch. SoPo
Skunk, The. Robert P. Tristram Coffin. FaPON; TiPo
Skunk, The. Alfred Noyes. RePo
Skunk cabbage, bloodroot. The Round. Philip Booth. BoNaP
Skunk Hour. Robert Lowell. AmPP (5th ed.); AP; CMoP; CoAP; FRC; MaPo (1969 ed.) MoAmPo (1962 ed.); NMP; PoAn; PoeP; PoIE; TDP
Sky, The. Elizabeth Madox Roberts. GFA; MAP; MoAmPo
Sky, The. Richard Henry Stoddard. AA
Sky, The. *Unknown, tr. fr. Ewe by* Ulli Beier. TTY
Sky, The/ is that beautiful old parchment. Old Manuscript. Alfred Kreymborg. MAP; NeMA; NP
Sky above London, The. London Night. Kathleen Raine. NeBP
Sky above us here is open again, The. Traveling Storm. Mark Van Doren. MoSiPe
Sky after Storm. Wordsworth. *Fr.* The Excursion, II. BoLiVe
Sky at night is like a big city, The. The Sky. *Unknown.* TTY
Sky, be blue, and more than blue. Denouement. Kenneth Fearing. OnHM
Sky came tripping, The. Ilo Orleans. RIS
Sky can still remember, The. His Birth. Phillips Brooks. SoP
Sky can't get in, The. Room. Shirley Kaufman. QAH
Sky Full of Dead. Robert Mezey. TDP
Sky grew darker with each minute, The. Before the Storm. Richard Dehmel. AWP; JAWP; WBP
Sky hangs heavy tonight, The. Negro Woman. Lewis Alexander. CDC
Sky in its lucent splendor lifted. A Tropical Morning at Sea. Edward Rowland Sill. EtS
Sky is a blue, coiled serpent, The. Francis Carey Slater. *Fr.* Drought. ACV
Sky is a drinking-cup, The. The Sky. Richard Henry Stoddard. AA
Sky is changed, The!—and such a change! Oh night. Sky, Mountains, River! Byron. *Fr.* Childe Harold's Pilgrimage, III. WHA
Sky is cold as pearl, The. Ancient. "Æ." SeCePo
Sky is cut into sections and put on a frame, The. Poem. Tony Towle. ANYP
Sky is dark, and the hills are white, The. Norse Lullaby. Eugene Field. BoTP; MPB; SUS
Sky is dotted like th' unleavened bread, The. Haggadah. A. M. Klein. TrJP
Sky is full of clouds to-day, The. Clouds. Frank Dempster Sherman. PRWS
Sky is glad that stars above, The. A Morisco [*or* Song].

Sky (continued)
Jasper Fisher. *Fr.* Fuimus Troes. SeCL; SeEP; TuPP
Sky is gray with rain that will not fall, The. At the Zoo. Israel Zangwill. TrJP
Sky is heavy, it is raining stars, The. The Cannibal Hymn. *Unknown.* TTY
Sky is hid in a snowy shroud, The. The Snowstorm. Frederick George Scott. PeCV
Sky is his ceiling, grass is his bed. Speaking of Cowboy's Home. *Unknown.* CoSo
Sky is just the top of day, The. The Top of Day. Anne Blackwell Payne. GFA
Sky is laced with fitful red, The. Impression: Le Rèveillon. Oscar Wilde. PoVP
Sky is low, the clouds are mean, The. Emily Dickinson. AA; AmPo; AmPP; BoNaP; CBEP; CoBA; DiPo; ELU; FaBoEn; FaBV; MAP; MoAmPo; MoPW; NeMA; OnPM; OxBA; PoEL-5
Sky is overcast, The. A Night-Piece. Wordsworth. EnRP
Sky is perfectly clear, The. Maximian Elegy V. Kenneth Rexroth. CrMA
Sky is ruddy in the East, The. The Ship-Builders. Whittier. AnNE; EtS
Sky is such [a] softness, is such dark. No Moon, No Star. Babette Deutsch. NYBP; WIRo
Sky Is Up above the Roof, The. Paul Verlaine, *tr. fr. French by* Ernest Dowson. *Fr.* Sagesse. AWP; FaPON; JAWP; SyP; WBP
(Sagesse.) EnLi-2
Sky, lazily disdaining to pursue, The. Georgia Dusk. Jean Toomer. AmNP; AnAmPo; BP; CDC; Kal; MAP; PoNe
Sky-like limpid eyes, The. Brennbaum. Ezra Pound. Hugh Selwyn Mauberley, VIII. AmPP (5th ed.); CABA; MoAmPo (1962 ed.)
Sky looks half-erased, The. Winter Twilight. Jack Anderson. ThO
Sky-making. Mortimer Collins. BOHV
Sky, Mountains, River ("The sky is changed"). Byron. *Fr.* Childe Harold's Prilgrimage, III. WHA
Sky of deepening bronze, A. Moon Rider. William Rose Benét. YT
Sky of Late Summer, A, *sel.* Henry Rago.
"Fountains of fire, The." NMP
Sky Pair, A. Robert Frost. MAP; MoAB; MoAmPo
Sky Pictures. Mary Effie Lee Newsome. CDC; GoSl
Sky sags low with convoluted cloud, The. Rain. W. E. Henley. SyP
Sky seemed so small that winter day, The. Two Illustrations That the World Is What You Make of It. Wallace Stevens. NePoAm
Sky so bright. A Song in Praise of the Lord of Heaven and Earth. *Unknown.* GBV
Sky so pale, and the trees, such frail things, The. A la Promenade. Paul Verlaine. AWP
Sky that has never known sun, moon, or stars, A. Rear Porches of an Apartment Building. Maxwell Bodenheim. AnAmPo; NP
Sky unfolding its blankets to free, The. Morning Workout. Babette Deutsch. NePoAm-2; SD
Sky was battened down, The. On Galveston Beach. Barbara Howes. MoAmPo (1962 ed.)
Sky was blue, so blue, that day, The. For the Candle Light. Angelina W. Grimké. CDC; PoNe
Sky was cold December blue, The. Steelhead. Robinson Jeffers. WoL
Sky was like a waterdrop, The. Remembrance. Walter de la Mare. CMoP
Sky was on the hill, The. When You Reach the Hilltop the Sky Is on Top of You. Etta Blum. GoYe
Sky was violet hued, The. The Shepherd's Star. Juan Ramón Jiménez. LiTW
Sky where the white clouds stand in prayer. Easter. Mary Carolyn Davies. OHIP
Sky-wide an Estuary. C. Day Lewis. POTE
Sky widens to Cornwall, The. A sense of sea. In Memoriam: A.C., R.J.O., K.S. John Betjeman. NYBP
Sky with clouds was overcast, The. Washing Day. *Unknown.* CoMu
Sky Writer. *See* Skywriter.
Skylark, The. Richard Watson Dixon. *Fr.* Mano; a Poetical History. VA
Skylark, The. James Hogg. ATP; DD; GN; HBV; HBVY; OTPC; PTK
Skylark, The. Christina Rossetti. *See* Green Cornfield, A.
Skylark, The. Frederick Tennyson. GN, *abr.*; HBV
Skylark and Nightingale. Christina Rossetti. *Fr.* Sing-Song. RIS
(Heaven Is Heaven.) YeAr
Skylarks are far behind that sang over the down, The. Good-Night. Edward Thomas. NoP
Skylark's Nest, The. R. H. Long. BoAu; PoAu-1
Skylark's nest among the grass, The. Birds' Nests. *Unknown.* BoTP; MPB
Sky Lark's Song, The. John Bennett. *Fr.* Master Sky-Lark. AA
Skyline of New York does not excite me, The. Review from Staten Island. G. C. Oden. Kal; NNP
Sky's a faded blue and taut-stretched flag, The. Jardin du Palais Royal. David Gascoyne. MoPo
Sky's lip and the sea's lip shut in peace, The. Lines on the Sea. Dilys Bennett Laing. NYBP
Sky's unresting cloudland, that with varying play, The. Robert Bridges. *Fr.* The Testament of Beauty. MoVE
Skyscraper. Carl Sandburg. PoMa; PoPl
Skyscraper. Byron Vazakas. OnHM
Skyscraper Is a City's House. Clara Lambert. MPB
Skyscrapers. Rachel Field. FaPON; GFA; StVeCh
Sky-Writer. Vincent Starrett. PoPo
Skywriting. Mary Maxtone. BrR
Slabs of the Sunburnt West, *sel.* Carl Sandburg.
Finale. NeMA
"Slack your rope, hangs-a-man [*or* hangsaman]." The Maid Freed from the Gallows [*or* Hangsaman]. *Unknown.* AS; ExPo; TOP; TrAS
Slacker Apologizes, The. Peter Viereck. MiAP
Slain enemy resembled, The. The Story of White Man Leading Viet Cong Patrol. Eric Torgersen. QAH
Slain eye has not died, The. Cries Out of Blindness. Tristan Corbière. LiTW
Slainthe! Patrick MacGill. AnIV
(Dedication: "I speak with a proud tongue.") OnYI
Slanderer, A. *Unknown, tr. fr. Greek by* Lord Neaves. OnPM
Slant of Sun [on Dull Brown Walls], A. Stephen Crane. *Fr.* War is Kind, XIV. AmePo; AmP; AmPP; VaPo
'Hymn: "Slant of sun on dull brown walls, A.") LiTM (1970 ed.); MAP; MoAmPo
Slant-windowed belt-footed enormously long-boomed, A. Bucyrus. John Holmes. CrMA; NePoAm
Slanting the ragged peaks of the mind, Eagles. Calling Eagles. Leo Kennedy. TwCaPo
Slapandergosheka. *Unknown.* *See* Snapoo.
Slaughter-House, The. Alfred Hayes. LiTA; LiTM
Slaughter of Grendel by Beowulf, The. *Unknown, tr. fr. Anglo-Saxon by* Charles W. Kennedy. *Fr.* Beowulf. LiTW
Slaughter of the Innocents by Order of King Herod, The. Caelius Sedulius, *tr. fr. Latin by* George Sigerson. *Fr.* Carmen Paschale. OnYI
Slaughter of the Laird of Mellerstain, The. *Unknown.* ESPB
Slav Ho! *with music.* *Unknown.* SoAmSa
Slave, The. Richard Henry Horne. VA
Slave. Langston Hughes. LiTM (1970 ed.)
Slave, The. James Oppenheim. MAP; MaRV; MoAmPo (1942 ed.); NP; PFY; PoFr; PoMa; TrJP
Slave, The. Jones Very. AP
Slave and the Iron Lace, The. Margaret Danner. AmNP
Slave Auction, The. Frances E. W. Harper. Kal; PoNe; TTY
Slave Chase, The. *Unknown.* CoMu
Slave in the Dismal Swamp, The. Longfellow. MWA-1
Slave Quarter. Carl Carmer. MoSiPe
Slave Quarters. James Dickey. NYBP
Slave Story. Hodding Carter. PoNe (1970 ed.)
Slaver, The. Stephen Vincent Benét. *Fr.* John Brown's Body. AmPP
Slavery. William Cowper. *Fr.* The Task. CoBE
("Oh for a lodge in some vast wilderness.") EnRP; OAEP
Slaves. James Russell Lowell. *Fr.* Stanzas on Freedom. NeHB; OQP; PCD; SoP; TRV; WBLP
(Commitment.) TreFT
(On Freedom.) PAL
(Stanza on Freedom, A.) AA; WaKn

Slaves Cannot Breathe in England. William Cowper. *Fr.* The Task. OBEC
Slave's Dream, The. Longfellow. AnNE; CoBA; GTBS; MemP; OBVV; PoNe; TSW; WePo
Slaves of Thy Shining Eyes. Hafiz, *tr. fr. Persian by* Gertrude L. Bell. LiTW
Slaves to London. Peter Anthony Motteux. *Fr.* Love's a Jest. OAEP
(London.) SeCL
(Song, A: "Slaves to London, I'll deceive you.") SeEP
Slaves to the World. *Unknown.* CBEP
Slav'ry Chain, *with music. Unknown.* TrAS
Slay fowl and beast; pluck clean the vine. Cavalier. Richard Bruce. CDC
Slayer of the winter, art thou here again? March. William Morris. *Fr.* The Earthly Paradise. HBV; OtMeF
Slayer standeth where his stroke is sure, The. Ajax, Before His Suicide. Sophocles. *Fr.* Ajax. LiTW
Slaying of multitudes should be mourned with sorrow, The. *Unknown. Fr.* Tao Teh King. TRV
Sledburn Fair. *Unknown.* CH
Sledding Song, A. Norman C. Schlichter. FaPON
Sleek and lax as a slug in the grass. The Sun-Bather. Kim Kurt. NePoAm-2
Sleep. Thomas Bailey Aldrich. AA
Sleep ("Come, Sleep, and with thy sweet deceiving"). Beaumont *and* Fletcher. *See* Come, Sleep.
Sleep. Alice Brown. AA
Sleep, The. Elizabeth Barrett Browning. HBV; MaRV; SoP; TRV; VA; WGRP
Sleep. Ella Conrad Cowherd. SoP
Sleep, *sel.* Abraham Cowley.
"Sleep is a god too proud to wait in palaces.' ChTr
Sleep. Emily Dickinson. *See* Sleep is supposed to be.
Sleep, A. Larry Eigner. CoPo
Sleep. Bartholomew Griffin. Fidessa, More Chaste than Kind, XV. OBSC
("Care-charmer sleep, sweet east in restless misery.") ReEn; ReIE; SiCE; Sonn; TuPP
Sleep. William Knott. YAP
Sleep. Robert Eyres Landor. *Fr.* The Impious Feast, VII. OBRV
Sleep. J. P. McAuley. NeLNL
Sleep. "Fiona Macleod." GBV; TSW
Sleep. Ada Louise Martin. HBV
Sleep. Charles Péguy, *tr. fr. French by* Julian Green. TIHL
Sleep. Thomas Sackville. *Fr.* The Induction to "The Mirror for Magistrates." WHA
Sleep ("Methought I heard a voice"). Shakespeare. *Fr.* Macbeth, II, ii. TreFS
(Conscience.) MaRV
(Macbeth Does Murder Sleep.) FiP
("Methought I heard a voice cry, 'Sleep no more!' ") MemP
(Murderers, The.) WHA
("That which hath made them drunk hath made me bold.") AtBAP; MyFE
Sleep ("Come, sleep! O Sleep") Sir Philip Sidney. *See* Astrophel and Stella, XXXIX.
Sleep ("Lock up, fair lids"). Sir Philip Sidney. *Fr.* Arcadia. OBSC; SiPS
("Lock up, fair lids, the treasure of my heart.") SiCE
(Sonnet: "Lock up, fair lids.") EG; EIL
Sleep. Charles Simic. CoAP
Sleep. Kenneth Slessor. BoAV; MoAuPo
Sleep. Publius Papinius Statius, *tr. fr. Latin by* W. H. Fyfe. AWP
Sleep. A. S. J. Tessimond. POTE
Sleep. Lewis Frank Tooker. AA
Sleep. Théophile de Viau, *tr. fr. French by* Sir Edmund Gosse. AWP
Sleep a little, a little little. The Sleep Song of Diarmaid and Grainne [*or* The Sleep Song of Grainne over Dermuid]. *Unknown.* AnIV; OnYI
Sleep after Toil. Spenser. *Fr.* The Faerie Queene, I, 9. ChTr
("He there does now enjoy eternal rest.") MyFE
Sleep: and between the Closed Eyelids of Sleep. Conrad Aiken. Preludes for Memnon, III. LiTA; LiTG; PoDB; TwAmPo
"Sleep and His Brother Death." William Hamilton Hayne. AA
Sleep; and my song shall build about your bed. Slumber Song. Siegfried Sassoon. MCCG
Sleep and Poetry. Keats. ATP, *abr.*; EnRP; ERoP-2; MERP; PP
Sels.
"Could all this be forgotten? Yes, a schism." ChER
"Is there so small a range." BEL
"Schism, A/ Nurtured by foppery and barbarism." InP
"Stop and consider! life is but a day." OBRV; SeCePo; TreFT
"What is more gentle than a wind in summer?" AtBAP; ATP
Sleep, Angry Beauty. Thomas Campion. EIL; EnRePo; ErPo; GTSE; HBV; NCEP; TrGrPo
("Sleep, angry beauty, sleep, and fear not me.") EG; GTSL; LO
Sleep at Sea. Christina Rossetti. NBM; PoEL-5
Sleep, Baby Boy. *Unknown. See* Sardinian Lullaby.
Sleep, Baby Jesukin. Mary Sings. Norah M. Holland. ChrBoLe
Sleep baby mine, desire, nurse beauty singeth. Sir Philip Sidney. FCP
Sleep, Baby, Sleep ("Sleep, baby, sleep!/ Thy father watches [*or* father's watching] the sheep"), 2 *sts. Unknown, tr. fr. German at. to* Elizabeth Prentiss. BoChLi; FaPON; GFA; MPB; OTPC; PPL; SAS
(Cradle Song, A.) BoTP, 5 *sts.*; PCH, 3 *sts.*
Sleep, Baby, Sleep. George Wither. HBV; OTPC (1923 ed.)
Sleep, baby, sleep./ Thy father guards the sheep. Holy Lullaby. *Unknown.* GoTP
Sleep, baby, sleep!/ Your father herds his sheep. Nurse's Song. *Unknown.* ThWaDe
Sleep, baby, sleep,/ Thy father herds the sheep. Old German Lullabies, 1. *Unknown, ad. by* Louis Untermeyer. RIS
Sleep, baby, sleep! The Mother sings. A Christmas Lullaby. John Addington Symonds. PRWS
Sleep, baby, sleep! what ails my dear. Sleep, Baby, Sleep. George Wither. HBV; OTPC (1923 ed.)
Sleep Brings No Joy. Emily Brontë. ViBoPo
Sleep brought me vision of my lady dead. John Peale Bishop. Sonn
Sleep, calm winter sleep, the rides are woollen. Calm Winter Sleep. Hilary Corke. NYBP
Sleep, child, lie quiet, let be. A Lullaby. James Agee. OnHM
Sleep, comrades, sleep and rest. Decoration Day. Longfellow. DD; HH; MC; MPB; OTD; PoSC
Sleep enfold thee,/ Jesukin. Cradle Song. James L. Duff. ISi
Sleep evades me, there's no light. Verses Written during a Sleepless Night. Pushkin. PoPl
Sleep falls, with limpid drops of rain. Bells in the Rain. Elinor Wylie. YT
Sleep, gray brother of death. On Waking. Joseph Campbell. AnIV; NP
Sleep, grim Reproof, my jocond muse doth sing. Satire X: Humors. John Marston. *Fr.* The Scourge of Villainy. SiCE; TuPP
Sleep, Holy Babe. Edward Caswall. BePJ
Sleep Impression. Carl Sandburg. RePo
Sleep in your silent glory. The Cliff Dwelling. Arthur W. Monroe. PoOW
Sleep is a god too proud to wait in palaces. Abraham Cowley. *Fr.* Sleep. ChTr
Sleep Is a Reconciling. *Unknown. See* Weep You No More, Sad Fountains.
Sleep Is a Suspension. Carl Sandburg. *Fr.* The People, Yes. NAMP
Sleep is death's image,—poets tell us so. Absence. James Russell Lowell. CBV
Sleep is great. To be. Stationery Motion. Tom Clark. YAP
Sleep is supposed to be. Emily Dickinson. OnPM
Sleep, kinsman thou to death and trance. In Memoriam A. H. H., LXXI. Tennyson. ViPo; VP
Sleep late with your dream. For My Brother. Owen Dodson. Poems for My Brother Kenneth, VII. BALP; IDB; PoNe
Sleep, little baby, sleep and rest. Lullaby. Elinor Chipp. HBMV
Sleep, little Baby, sleep; the holy angels love thee. Holy Innocents. Christina Rossetti. HBV; HBVY
Sleep, little brother, you must not awaken. The Little Sister Left in Charge. Cecil Frances Alexander. OTPC (1923 ed.)
Sleep, little one, sleep. Schlof, Bobbeli. *Unknown.* TrAS
Sleep, little one, sleep for me. Response. Bob Kaufman. BOLo; Kal
Sleep, little pigeon, and fold your wings. Little Blue Pigeon. Eugene Field. GBV (1922 ed.)

Sleep, love, sleep! Watching. "Fanny Forester." AA
Sleep, love, sleep. Lullaby. Quandra Prettyman. BOLo
Sleep, Madame, Sleep. Annemarie Ewing. NePoAm
Sleep, Mr. Speaker; it's surely fair. Stanzas on Seeing the Speaker Asleep in His Chair. Winthrop Mackworth Praed. EnRP; NBM
Sleep, mouseling, sleep. Lullaby. Elizabeth J. Coatsworth. SiSoSe
Sleep, my babe, lie still and slumber. All through the Night [*or* Welsh Lullaby]. *Unknown.* FaPON; GoTP
Sleep, my baby, while I sing. Bed-Time Song. Emilie Poulsson. HBV; HBVY
Sleep, My Child. Sholom Aleichem, *tr. fr. Yiddish by* Alter Brody. TrJP
Sleep, my child; because of you. Night. "Gabriela Mistral." LiTW
Sleep, my child, my joy, my treasure. Sleep, My Child. Sholom Aleichem. TrJP
Sleep, my child, my little daughter. Cradle Song. *Unknown.* TrJP
Sleep, my darling, sleep. Cradle Song. Louis MacNeice. OxBI; PoPl
Sleep, my little baby, sleep. Lullaby. Samuel Hoffenstein. TrJP
Sleep, my love, and peace attend thee. All through the Night. Harold Boulton. TreFS
Sleep, my own darling. Home and Mother. Mary Mapes Dodge. BOHV
Sleep, My Treasure. Edith Nesbit. PRWS
Sleep Not, Dream Not, *sel.* Emily Brontë. LoBV, 2 *sts.*
Sleep, Now that the charge is won. Taps. Lizette Woodworth Reese. DD; HH; OHIP
Sleep, O sleep. Song. John Gay. Polly, Air XXIII. EG; FaBoEn; ViBoPo
Sleep of Spring, The. John Clare. ERoP-2
Sleep of the Brave, The. William Collins. *See* How Sleep the Brave.
Sleep of the Just. *Unknown, tr. fr. Greek by* Lord Neaves. OnPM
Sleep on, and dream of Heaven awhile. The Sleeping Beauty. Samuel Rogers. GTBS; GTBS-D; GTBS-P; GTBS-W; GTSE; GTSL; HBV
Sleep on, beloved, sleep, and take thy rest. The Christian's "Good-Night." Sarah Doudney. BLPA
Sleep on, brave heart; thy broken sword beside thee! Requiem for a Dead Warrior. Edgar McInnis. PEDC
Sleep on, dear, now. The Dead Child. Ernest Dowson. BrPo
Sleep on, I lie at heaven's high oriels. Nirvana. John Hall Wheelock. HBMV; MAP; MoAmPo; NP; TSW
Sleep on my Love, in thy cold bed. Henry King. *Fr.* The Exequy. CH; PoFS; TrGrPo
Sleep, our lord, and for thy peace. Night Song for a Child! Charles Williams. OBEV (new ed.)
Sleep serene, avoid the backward. Louis MacNeice. *Fr.* Autumn Journal. CMoP
Sleep, Silence' Child. William Drummond of Hawthornden. *See* Sonnet: "Sleep, Silence' Child."
Sleep, Sleep, Beauty Bright. Blake. *See* Cradle Song, A: "Sleep! sleep! beauty bright."
Sleep, Sleep, come to me, Sleep. A Charm to Call Sleep. Henry Johnston. PRWS
Sleep, sleep, lovely white soul. Lullaby. Walter de la Mare. GBV
Sleep, sleep mine Holy One! The Virgin Mary to the Child Jesus. Elizabeth Barrett Browning. ISi
Sleep, Sleep, My Soul. *Unknown.* SeCL
Sleep, sleep, my treasure. Sleep, My Treasure. Edith Nesbit. PRWS
Sleep sleep old Sun, thou canst not have repast. Resurrection [Imperfect]. John Donne. MaMe; StJW
Sleep, sleep, sleep, in thy folded waves, O Sea! Sea-Sleep. Thomas Lake Harris. AA
Sleep, sleep softe, you colde clay cindars that late clad. *Unknown.* SeCSL
Sleep, sleep, sweetly sleep. Lady Day in Harvest. Sheila Kaye-Smith. ISi
Sleep softly. . .eagle forgotten. . .under the stone. The Eagle That Is Forgotten. Vachel Lindsay. AmP; AnFE; APA; ATP; AWP; CMoP; CoAnAm; HBV; InP; JAWP; LiTA; MAP; MoAB; MoAmPo; MoRP; NeMA; NePA; NP; OTD; OxBA; PFY; Po; PoFr; TOP; TwAmPo; ViBoPo (1958 ed.); WBP; WHA; WOW
Sleep Song of Diarmaid and Grainne, The. *Unknown, tr. fr. Late Middle Irish by* Eoin MacNeill. OnYI
(Sleep-Song of Grainne over Dermuid, The, *tr. by* Eleanor Hull.) AnIV
Sleep sound, O soldier, through the night. Pillow Cases. Richard Armour. WhC
Sleep stands off to watch me brood the curse. "All My Pretty Ones? Did You Say All?" Bink Noll. ToPo
Sleep Sweet. Ellen M. Huntington Gates. BLPA; BLRP; FaBoBe; MaRV; NeHB
Sleep sweetly in your humble graves. Ode [*or* At Magnolia Cemetery]. Henry Timrod. AA; AmePo; AmP; AmPP; AnAmPo; AP; DD; HBV; MAmP; MC; OxBA; PaA; PAL; StP; TreFT
Sleep That like the Couchèd Dove. Gerald Griffin. *See* Nocturne: "Sleep that like the couched dove."
Sleep the Mother. Florence Kiper. NP
Sleep, this is the time for sleep. Old German Lullabies, 2. *Unknown, ad. by* Louis Untermeyer. RIS
Sleep, Thou little Child of Mary. The Song of a Shepherd-Boy at Bethlehem. Josephine Preston Peabody. ChrBoLe; OHIP; StJW
Sleep Unbroken. Omar Khayyám, *tr. fr. Persian by* Edward Fitzgerald. *Fr.* The Rubáiyát. OnPM
Sleep upon the World. Alcman. *See* Fragment: "Mountain summits sleep, The."
Sleep walks over the hill. Lady Sleep. Rowena Bastin Bennett. GaP
Sleep, wayward thoughts, and rest you with my love. So Sleeps My Love. *Unknown.* EG; EnRePo; ReEn; TrGrPo
Sleep Will Come Singly. W. H. Oliver. AnNZ
Sleepe, close not up mine eyes, and if thou doe. *Unknown.* SeCSL
Sleepe in your lidds thou loved shades. *Unknown.* SeCSL
Sleepe O sleepe thou sacred dust. *Unknown.* SeCSL
Sleepe, sleepe faire virgin, sleepe in peace. *Unknown.* SeCSL
Sleeper, The. Sydney Clouts. BoSA; PeSA
Sleeper, The. Walter de la Mare. MoAB; MoBrPo; SeCeV; YT
Sleeper, The. "Isobel Hume." HBMV
Sleeper, The. Poe AA; AmePo; AmPo; AmPP; AnFE; AP; APA; CBEP; CoAnAm; CoBA; InP; LiTA; MWA-1; NePA; OBVV; OxBA; PoEL-4; PoFS; TDP; TrGrPo; UnPo (1st ed.)
Sleeper, The. Clinton Scollard. HBV
Sleeper, The. *Unknown, tr. fr. Arabic by* E. Powys Mathers. *Fr.* The Thousand and One Nights. AWP; LiTW
Sleeper from the Amazon, A. *Unknown. See* Limerick: "Sleeper from the Amazon, A."
Sleeper Hood-winked, The. John Skelton. *See* Lullay, Lullay.
Sleeper of the Valley, The. Arthur Rimbaud, *tr. fr. French by* Ludwig Lewisohn. AWP; JAWP; WBP
(Sleeper in the Valley, The, *tr. by* Selden Rodman.) WaaP
Sleeper, the palm-trees drink the breathless noon. The Sleeper. *Unknown. Fr.* The Thousand and One Nights. AWP; LiTW
Sleepers, The. W. H. Davies. AnFE; WoL
Sleepers, The. F. W. Harvey. MMA
Sleepers, The. Louis Untermeyer. MoLP
Sleepers, The. Walt Whitman. AmP; AmPP (5th ed.); MAmP; MWA-1
Indian Woman, The, *sel.* PCD; PCH
Sleepers are mangled by the scythe of dreams. The Scythe of Dreams. Joseph Payne Brennan. FiSC
Sleepers, Wake, *with music.* Philip Nicolai, *tr. by* Catherine Winkworth. YaCaBo
Sleepest or wakest thou, jolly shepherd? The Jolly Shepherd. Shakespeare. *Fr.* King Lear, III, vi. PCH
Sleepin' at the Foot of the Bed. Luther Patrick. BLPA
Sleeping at Last. Christina Rossetti. PoVP; TrGrPo; VP
Sleeping-Bag, The. Herbert George Ponting. CenHV
Sleeping Beauty. William Drummond of Hawthornden. LiTL
Sleeping Beauty, The. Robert Layzer. NePoEA
Sleeping Beauty, The. Samuel Rogers. GTBS; GTBS-D; GTBS-P; GTBS-W; GTSE; GTSL; HBV
Sleeping Beauty, The, *sels.* Edith Sitwell.
"Fairies all received an invitation, The." FIW
"When we come to that dark house." MoVE; OBMV

Sleeping Beauty, The; Variation of the Prince. Randall Jarrell. FiMAP
Sleeping butterfly, A. The Butterfly. Kikaku. SoPo
Sleeping Child, A. Arthur Hugh Clough. PRWS
Sleeping Fury, The. Louise Bogan. LiTM
Sleeping Giant, The. Donald Hall. CaFP; NePoEA; NYBP; TwCP
Sleeping, he is not blind. The Blind Man's Morning. Viola Meynell. MemP; MoBrPo (1942 ed.)
Sleeping Heroes. Edward Shanks. OBMV
Sleeping House, The. Tennyson. *Fr.* Maud. FaBoEn; OBNC
Sleeping in a cabin is as jolly as can be. The Boat. Rose Fyleman. BrR
Sleeping in fever, I am unfit. For God While Sleeping. Anne Sexton. CABA; NePoEA-2; PoDB
Sleeping on Her Couch. Richard Leigh. FaBoEn; MePo (Thus Lovely Sleep.) ELP
Sleeping on Horseback. Po Chü-i, *tr. fr. Chinese by* Arthur Waley. LiTW
Sleeping on the Ceiling. Elizabeth Bishop. MiAP
"Sleeping or waking, thou sweet face." Popular Songs of Tuscany. *Unknown.* AWP; JAWP; WBP
Sleeping Priestess of Aphrodite, A. Robert Cameron Rogers. AA
Sleeping Saint, The. Melvin Walker La Follette. CoPo
Sleeping They Bear Me. Alfred Mombert, *tr. fr. German by* Jethro Bithell. AWP; JAWP; WBP
Sleeping Together. Katherine Mansfield. *Fr.* Two Nocturnes. HBMV
Sleeping Village. Harold Vinal. FiSC
Sleeping, waking. Issa, *tr. fr. Japanese by* Lewis Mackenzie. FIW
Sleeping with One Eye Open. Mark Strand. NYBP
Sleeping with Women. Kenneth Koch. ANYP
Sleeping woman dreams she wakes, A. Nightmare. Isabella Gardner. CoAP
Sleeping Youth, A. Keats. *Fr.* Endymion, II. SeCePo
Sleepless Dreams. Dante Gabriel Rossetti. The House of Life, XXXIX. MaVP; OAEP; PoVP; ViPo; VP
Sleepless hours who watch me as I lie, The. Hymn of [*or* to] Apollo. Shelley. EnL; EnLit; EnRP; ERoP-2; HBV; MBW-2; OAEP; OBRV
Sleepless in the dark I lie. Verses Written during a Sleepless Night. Pushkin. OnPM
Sleepless Night, A. Egan O'Rahilly, *tr. fr. Modern Irish by* Frank O'Connor. AnIL; KiLC
Sleepmonger,/ deathmonger. The Addict. Anne Sexton. TPM
Sleeps tranquilly the lake—a slender throat. Bohernabreena. Leslie Daiken. OnYI
Sleepwalker, The. Nelly Sachs, *tr. fr. German by* Michael Hamburger. NYBP
Sleep-Walking Child. Elisabeth Eybers, *tr. fr. Afrikaans by* Jack Cope, Uys Krige, *and* Adèle Naudé. PeSA
Sleepy Harry. Ann *or* Jane Taylor. SAS
Sleepy Harry. *Unknown.* OTPC (1923 ed.)
Sleepy Hollow. William Ellery Channing. SoP
Sleepy Maple Trees, The. Eleanor Hammond. GFA
Sleepy Song. Thomas Bailey Aldrich. GoTP
Sleepy Song, The. Josephine Dodge Daskam Bacon. OTPC (1946 ed.); PCH; PPL; StVeCh; SUS; UTS
Sleepy Song, A. Charles Buxton Going. SP
Sleepy Tulips, The. Marion Mitchell Walker. GFA
Sleepy vines on the chalk-white houses. Sancho. William Edwin Collin. CaP
Sleepyhead. Walter de la Mare. TiPo
Sleepyland. Laura E. Richards. SAS
Sleepytown Express, The. James J. Montague. HBMV
Sleet Storm. James S. Tippett. BrR; SiSoSe
Sleet Storm on the Merritt Parkway. Robert Bly. CBV
Sleigh Bells at Night. Elizabeth J. Coatsworth. SiSoSe
Sleighride. Patrick Anderson. CaP; OBCV
Sleigh-Ride. A. Laura E. Richards. GFA
Sleighing Song. John Shaw. AA
Slender beech and the sapling oak, The. Beech and Oak. Thomas Love Peacock. CBEP
Slender goblet wreathed in flame, A. Tulip. William Jay Smith. RePo
Slender I saw her stand, stooped a little, her arms akimbo. The White Sand. Edmund Wilson. NePoAm
Slender one, white one. Alcibiades to a Jealous Girl. Arthur Davison Ficke. HBMV
Slender young blackbird built in a thorn-tree, A. The Blackbird. Dinah Maria Mulock Craik. BoTP; GoTP
Slender's Ghost. William Shenstone. *See* O Sweet Anne Page.
Slepynge Long in Greet Quiete Is Eek a Greet Norice to Leccherie. John Hollander. AmPC; ErPo
Sliced with shade and scarred with snow. Inverberg. J. F. Hendry. NeBP
Slide at the Empire Mine, The. Harriet L. Wason. PoOW
Slide, Kelly, Slide. J. W. Kelly. FaFP; TreFS
Sliding. Marchette Chute. TiPo (1959 ed.)
Sliding. Myra Cohn. SiSoSe
Sliding down the banisters. On the Banisters. Margaret E. Gibbs. BoTP
Slieve Gua. *Unknown, tr. fr. Old Irish.* ChTr
Slievenamon. *Unknown, tr. fr. Irish by* Frank O'Connor. KiLC
Slight, The. Thomas Flatman. LO; PeRV; SeCL
Slight as thou art, thou art enough to hide. To a Daisy. Alice Meynell. JKCP; MoBrPo; Sonn; WGRP
Slight-boned animal, young, A. Small Colored Boy in the Subway. Babette Deutsch. PoNe (1970 ed.)
Slight stirring darkness, A. Upon Which to Rejoice. "Luke." QAH
Slim Cunning Hands. Walter de la Mare. ELU; SeCePo
Slim dragonfly. Arthur Mitchell. Marianne Moore. PoNe (1970 ed.)
Slim feet than lilies tenderer. Sainte Margérie. *Unknown.* BOHV
Slim Greer. Sterling Brown. BALP; BANP
Slimy obscene creatures, insane. The Nigga Section. Welton Smith. BF
Sling, The. Roy Campbell. BoSA
Slings. Rubén Darío, *ad. fr. Spanish by* William Rose Benét. PoFr
Slinky and black. Our Cat. Janet Vaughn. PCD
Slip of loveliness, slim, seemly. In Praise of a Girl. Huw Morus. PrWP
Slip off the husk of gravity to lie. The New Icarus. Vassar Miller. ToPo
Slip-Shoe Lovey. Edgar Lee Masters. NP
Slippery. Carl Sandburg. BiCB; FaPON; TiPo
Slipping in blood, by his own hand, through pride. To an Artist, to Take Heart. Louise Bogan. NYBP
Sliprails and the Spur, The. Henry Lawson. BoAu; PoAu-1
Slog brute streets [*or* the squares] with rebel tramping! Our March. Vladimir Mayakovsky. AWP; PoFr
Sloth, The. Theodore Roethke. FiBHP; NePA; NePoAm; PoPo; SiTL; WaKn
Slough. John Betjeman. MoBrPo (1962 ed.)
Slough of Despond, The. Robert Lowell. SyP
Slovenly Peter. Heinrich Hoffmann, *tr. fr. German.* BBGG
Slow are the years of light. Lachrymae. David Gascoyne. *Fr.* Miserere. AtBAP; BoW; NeBP; POTE
Slow bells at dawn. Bells. Duncan Campbell Scott. CaP
Slow bleak awakening from the morning dream. Living. Harold Monro. FaBoMo; LiTB; LiTM; SeCePo
Slow breaks the hushed June dawn. The Voices. *Unknown.* MCCG; PoMa
Slow burn, A. Pit Viper. George Starbuck. NYBP; TDP
Slow Death. Hazel Hall. MAP; MoAmPo (1942 ed.)
Slow dripping of a fountain, The. Impression of a Fountain. Hakushu Kitahara. LiTW
Slow freight wriggles along the rail, The. The Freight Train. Rowena Bastin Bennett. PDV; RePo
Slow, groping giant, whose unsteady limbs. Doubt. Robert Cameron Rogers. AA
Slow heave of the sleeping sea, The. A Dead Calm and Mist. "Fiona Macleod." SyP
Slow-hooved across the carrion sea. Bombay Arrival. Laurie Lee. POTi; ToPo
Slow, horses, slow. Night of Spring. Thomas Westwood. BoTP; CBEP; OBVV; TOP
Slow Me Down. *Unknown.* STF
Slow Me Down, Lord! Orin L. Crane. TreFT
Slow Me Down, Lord. *Unknown.* SoP
Slow Movement. Louis MacNeice. FaBoMo
Slow Movement. William Carlos Williams. NP

Slow moves the acid breath of noon. Field of Autumn. Laurie Lee. LiTM (1970 ed.); POTi; ToPo
Slow Pacific Swell, The. Yvor Winters. CBV; ForPo; QFR
Slow Race, The. Andrew Young. MemP
Slow Rhythm. Ethel Livingston. ThO
Slow sail'd the weary mariners and saw. The Sea-Fairies. Tennyson. ViPP
Slow sift the sands of Time; the yellowed leaves. The Sands of Time. Robert E. Howard. FiSC
Slow sinks, more lovely ere his race be run. Summer [*or* Sunset over the Aegean]. Byron. *Fr.* The Corsair, III OBNC; OBRV
Slow, Slow, Fresh Fount. Ben Jonson. *Fr.* Cynthia's Revels, I, ii. ChTr; EIL; ELP; EnLi-1 (1949 ed.); MaPo (1969 ed.); NoP; SeCeV; TuPP; UnPo; WHA
(Echo's Lament of Narcissus.) AnEnPo
(Echo's [*or* Eccho's] Song.) BoLiVe; LoBV; PoIE; SeCV-1; TrGrPo
("Slow, slow, fresh fount; keep time with my salt tears.") CH; EG; ExPo; ILP; OAEP; OBS; ReEn; SiCE
(Song: "Slow, slow, fresh fount, keep[e] time with my salt tear [e]s.) AnAnS-2; AtBAP; CBV; EnRePo; EP; FaBoEn; PoEL-2; SeCP; ViBoPo
(Song of Echo.) GoBC
Slow Spring. Katharine Tynan. BoTP; MemP
Slow spring between two wheat-fields, A. The Old Are Sleepy. H. L. Davis. NP
Slow Summer Twilight. John Hall Wheelock. LiTM (1970 ed.)
Slow the Kansas sun was setting o'er the wheat fields far away. Towser Shall Be Tied Tonight. *Unknown.* BLPA
Slow the moon rises, wraith of a moon long drowned. Fog-Horn. George Herbert Clarke. CaP
Slow to resolve, but in performance quick. King James II. Dryden. *Fr.* The Hind and the Panther, III. ACP
Slow turns the water by the green marshes. Virginiana. Mary Johnston. HBMV
Slowly a floor rises, almost becomes a wall. A Hurricane at Sea. May Swenson. WIRo
Slowly a hundred miles through the powerful rain. You Drive in a Circle. Ted Hughes. NYBP
Slowly by God's hand unfurled. Evening Hymn [*or* The Light of Stars]. William Henry Furness. AA; FaBoBe; HBV; TrPWD
Slowly comes a hungry people, as a lion creeping nigher. Tennyson. *Fr.* Locksley Hall. PoFr
Slowly England's sun was setting o'er the hilltops far away. Curfew Must Not Ring Tonight. Rose Hartwick Thorpe. BeLS; BLPA; FaBoBe; FaPON; GSP; HBV; NeHB; PaPo; WBLP
Slowly flutters the snow from ash-coloured heavens in silence. Snowfall. Giousè Carducci, *tr. by* G. A. Greene. PoPl
Slowly forth from the village church. Little Christel. William Brighty Rands. PRWS
Slowly he rode home at the end of day. The Captain. Jon Manchip White. NePoEA
Slowly I mount the stairs to have/ my picture taken. The Progress of Photography. Byron Vazakas. MoPo
Slowly I smoke and hug my knee. Ballade by the Fire. E. A. Robinson. InP
Slowly, my lords, go slowly. The Case of Thomas More. Sister Mary St. Virginia. GoBC
Slowly Nan the widow goes. Planter's Charm. Fay M. Yauger. InP
Slowly, O so slowly, longing rose up. Christ Walking on the Water. W. R. Rodgers. AnIL; MoAB; OxBI
Slowly, silently, now the moon. Silver. Walter de la Mare. AnEnPo; BoChLi; BoNaP; BoTP; BrR; CMoP; FaPON; GFA; GoTP; GTSL; MoAB; MoBrPo; NeMA; PCD; PoMa; PoMS; PoPl; PoRA (rev. ed.); ShBV-1; SiSoSe; StVeCh; SUS; TiPo; TreF; WaKn
Slowly, Slowly. Ovid, *tr. fr. Latin by* Kirby Flower Smith. Elegies, I, 14. WoL
(Lente, Lente.) AWP; LiTW
Slowly, slowly, swinging low. Swinging. Irene Thompson. BoTP
Slowly the Bible of the race is writ. The Bible of the Race. James Russell Lowell. OQP
Slowly the black earth gains upon the yellow. Odes, IV. George Santayana. AmePo; AnFE; APA; CoAnAm; TwAmPo
Slowly the daylight left our listening faces. Early Chronology. Siegfried Sassoon. FaBoTw
Slowly the flakes come down through the ash-gray skies and the shouting. First Snowfall. Giosuè Carducci. LiTW
Slowly the great head turned. Elephant. N. H. Brettell. BoSA
Slowly the mist o'er the meadow was creeping. Lexington. Oliver Wendell Holmes. DD; MC; PAH
Slowly the moon is rising out of the ruddy haze. Aware. D. H. Lawrence. BoNaP; MoBrPo
Slowly the night blooms, unfurling. Flowers of Darkness. Frank Marshall Davis. AmNP; IDB; PoNe
Slowly the poison the whole blood stream fills. Missing Dates. William Empson. CBV; ChMP; CMoP; CoBMV; FaBoEn; FaBoMo; ForPo; LiTB; LiTM; MoAB; MoBrPo (1962 ed.); MoPo; PoIE; ViBoPo (1958 ed.)
Slowly the roses bleed into the water. The Vase. Terence Tiller. ChMP
Slowly the sun descends at fall of night. Twilight. Joaquín A. Pagaza. CAW
Slowly the thing comes. Panic. Archibald MacLeish. MAP; MoAmPo
Slowly the women file to where he stands. Faith Healing. Philip Larkin. PoeP
Slowly the world contracts about my ears. The Flagpole Sitter. Donald Finkel. CoAP
Slowly they pass. The Sheep. "Seumas O'Sullivan." OxBI
Slowly through the tomb-still streets I go. The Lover's Farewell. James Clarence Mangan. IrPN
Slowly thy flowing tide. The Ebb Tide. Robert Southey. OBNC
Slowly ticks the big clock. The Big Clock. *Unknown.* SoPo; TiPo
Slowly we learn; the oft repeated line. On National Vanity. J. E. Clare McFarlane. PoNe
Slowly, without force, the rain drops into the city. The Bombardment. Amy Lowell. YT
Slug in Woods. Earle Birney. CaP; OBCV; PeCV; TDP
Sluggard, The. A. E. Coppard. MoBrPo (1942 ed.)
Sluggard, The. W. H. Davies. OBMV
Sluggard, The. Lucilius, *tr. fr. Greek by* Humbert Wolfe. SD
Sluggard, The. Isaac Watts. CEP; CH; EiCL; HBV; HBVY; MoShBr; OBEC; OnPP; OTD; OTPC; OxBoLi; PaPo; Par; PoEL-3; ThGo; TreFS
Sluggard, The—a Sonnet. Proverbs, Bible, *O.T.* *See* Reproof, A.
Sluggish morn[e] as yet undrest [*or* undressed], The. Upon Phyllis [*or* Phillis] Walking in a Morning before Sun-rising. John Cleveland. AnAnS-2; EG; LiTL; MeLP
Sluggish smoke curls up from some deep dell, The. Smoke in Winter. Henry David Thoreau. AnNE; BWP; MAmP
Sluice gates of sleep are open wide, The. Viaticum. Ethna MacCarthy. NeIP
Slum Dwelling, A. George Crabbe. *Fr.* The Borough. OBNC
Slumber dark and deep. Paul Verlaine. *Fr.* Sagesse. AWP; JAWP; WBP
Slumber Did My Spirit Seal, A. Wordsworth. AnEnPo; AWP; BEL; BoLiVe; BWP; CABA; CaFP; CBEP; CBV; DiPo; EG; ELP; EnL; EnLit; EnLoPo; EnRP; EPN; ERoP-1; ExPo; FaBoCh; FaBoEn; FlW; ForPo; FosPo; GTBS; GTBS-D; GTBS-P; GTBS-W; GTSE; GTSL; ILP; InPo; InvP; JAWP; LiTB; LiTG; LoGBV; MaPo; MBW-2; MERP; NoP; OAEP; OBRV; OnPM; OuHeWo; PAn; Po; PoAn; PoE; PoEL-4; PoeP; PoFS; PoIE; PoRA; SeCeV; ShBV-4; TOP; TreFS; TrGrPo; UnPo (3d ed.); ViBoPo; WBP; WePo
(Lines.) LoBV
(Lucy.) AnFE; EnLi-2; FiP; HBV; LiTL; OBEV; OBNC
Slumber in Spring. Elizabeth Gould. BoTP
Slumber, Jesu, lightly [*or* o'er Thy] dreaming. Lullaby [*or* Latin Lullaby]. *Unknown.* CAW; ISi
Slumber, my darling, no danger is near. The Mother to Her Infant. Thomas Miller. OTPC (1923 ed.)
Slumber, Small One. Though She Slumbers. Joseph Joel Keith. ISi
Slumber Song: "Drowsily come the sheep." Louis V. Ledoux. FaPON; HBMV; MPB; UTS
Slumber Song: "Sleep; and my song shall build about your bed." Siegfried Sassoon. MCCG

Slumber-Song of the Blessed Mother. *Unknown, tr. fr. Tuscan folk song by* Grace Warrack. ChrBoLe
Slumnight. Colette Inez. QAH
Slung between the homely poplars at the end. Ursa Major. James Kirkup. ImOP
Slurred and drawled and crooning sounds, The. A Toast. Louis MacNeice. CMoP; GTBS-D
Slushy snow splashes and sploshes, The. Mary Ann Hoberman. TiPo (1959 ed.)
Sly Beelzebub took all occasions. Job. Samuel Taylor Coleridge. BOHV
Sly merchants plotted newer, greater gains. Renaissance. Robert Avrett. GoYe
Smack in School, The. William P. Palmer. BOHV; HBV
Small, The. Theodore Roethke. NoP
Small activity of mice, The. Mad Boy's Song. Leo Kennedy. TwCaPo
Small and Early. Tudor Jenks. AA; PCD
Small and emptied woman you lie here a thousand years dead. In the Museum. Isabella Gardner. ELU; NYBP
Small April sobbed. April Fool. Eleanor Hammond. GFA; SoPo
Small as a breath, so drawn together. Winter Aconites. Robert Gittings. MemP
Small baker carried bread, The. Rue St. Honore. Peter Williamson. NYTB
Small bird hops about in branches, A. November Light, Short Days Dark Fiery Sunsets. William Knott. YAP
Small Birds. Peter Quennell. BiS; MoVE
Small birds swirl around, The. The Small. Theodore Roethke. NoP
Small birds who sweep into a tree. Small Birds. Peter Quennell. BiS
Small Boy, Dreaming, A. Albert Herzing. NYBP
Small boy drove the shaggy ass, The. Turf Carrier on Aranmore. John Hewitt. PoRA (rev. ed.)
Small boy has thrown a stone at a statue, A. The Statue. Robert Finch. OBCV; PeCV
Small Boy's Loquitur, The. *Unknown.* CH
Small, busy flames play through the fresh laid coals. To My Brothers. Keats. EnLi-2; Sonn
Small Celandine, The. Wordsworth. *See* Lesson, A.
Small City on a Rock, A. Phocylides, *tr. fr. Greek by* C. M. Bowra. WoL
Small Cleodemus. Antistius, *tr. fr. Greek by* Robert Guthrie MacGregor. OnPM
Small Colored Boy in the Subway. Babette Deutsch. PoNe (1970 ed.)
Small Comment. Sonia Sanchez. NBP
Small Dragon, A. Brian Patten. HYE
Small Elegy. Morris Weisenthal. NYTB
Small Fountains. Lascelles Abercrombie. *Fr.* Emblems of Love: Epilogue. CH
Small Game. Philip Levine. AmPC
Small gnats that fly. Song: One Hard Look. Robert Graves. MoAB; MoBrPo
Small Hours, The. Mary Ursula Bethell. OnPM
Small house with a pointed roof, A. Epiphany. Eileen Shanahan. NeIP
Small householder now comes out warily, The. Spring Voices. Louis MacNeice. Sonn; WePo
Small is Eumenes' Cleodemus, yet. Small Cleodemus. Antistius. OnPM
Small lights pirouette. Peterhead in May. Burns Singer. OxBS
Small Man Orders His Wedding, The. C. S. Lewis. HW
Small moon. Prayer to the Young Moon. *Unknown.* PeSA
Small offender, small innocent child. To a Small Boy Who Died at Diepkloof Reformatory. Alan Paton. BoSA
Small on the skylit plain. Birds in the Flax. Stanley Snaith. HaMV
Small Perfect Manhattan. Peter Viereck. MiAP
Small Quiet Song. Robert Paul Smith. CAD
Small Rain. Alice Lawry Gould. MoSiPe
Small red-painted helicopter, A. Precision. Peter Collenette. FIW
Small room with one table and one chair, A. Poet in Winter. Edward Lucie-Smith. TwCP
Small Sad Song. Alastair Reid. NYBP
Small service is true service while it lasts. To a Child [*or* In a Child's Album]. Wordsworth. GN; HBV; HBVY; MemP; OBNC; OBRV; PCH
Small shining drop, no lady's ring. For a Dewdrop. Eleanor Farjeon. HBVY; YT
Small Silver-coloured Bookworm, The. Thomas Parnell. OnYI
Small skill is gained by those who cling to ease. *Unknown.* GoTP
Small Soldiers with Drum in Large Landscape. Robert Penn Warren. Mexico Is a Foreign Country, IV. FiMAP
Small Song. Frances Frost. RePo
Small Song. Daniel Whitehead Hicky. MaRV
Small Talk. Don Marquis. *Fr.* Archy Does His Part. StPo
Small Things. Richard Monckton Milnes. NeHB
Small Thought Speaks for the Flesh, A. Carleton Drewry. MoRP
Small town bears the mark of Cain, A. Estevan, Saskatchewan. E. W. Mandel. PeCV
Small traveler from an unseen shore. To a New-born Child. Cosmo Monkhouse. HBV
Small type of great ones, that do hum. A Fly Caught in a Cobweb. Richard Lovelace. SCEP-2; SeCP
Small wasp lies in state, The. Dead Wasp. Kenneth Slade Alling. NePoAm
Small wind whispers through the leafless hedge, The. Winter. John Clare. ATP
Small Woman on Swallow Street. W. S. Merwin. CoAP
Smallest Angel, The. Elsie Binns. ChBR
Smart Yankee packet lay out in the bay, A. A Long Time Ago (B *vers.*). *Unknown.* SoAmSa
Smashed, and brought up against. After an Accident. Donald Davie. OPoP
Smatterers. Samuel Butler. BOHV
Smear of blue peat smoke, The. The Shepherd's Hut. Andrew Young. DTC
Smell. William Carlos Williams. MoAB; MoAmPo
Smell of arnica is strong, The. When Father Played Baseball. Edgar A. Guest. PEDC
Smell of cigar smoke, Sunday, after dinner. Cigar Smoke, Sunday, after Dinner. Louise Townsend Nicholl. NePoAm
Smell of death was in the air, The. Farewell. John Press. PoRA
Smell of the heat is boxwood, The. To Daphne and Virginia. William Carlos Williams. CrMA
Smell of woodyards in the rain is strong, The. Woodyards in the Rain. Anne Marriott. CaP; TwCaPo
Smell on the Landing, The. Peter Porter. NMP
Smell the rug. Smell the wire that holds the chair together. On Blindness. Joseph Cardarelli. QAH
Smelling or feeling of the several holes. Dishonor. Edwin Denby. ErPo
Smelling the End of Green July. "Peter Yates." ChMP
Smells. Christopher Morley. PoMa; ShBV-1; YT
Smells. Kathryn Worth. BrR; RePo
Smells are surer than sounds or sights. Lichtenberg. Kipling. EnLit
Smells—how many. The Sense of Smell. Louis MacNeice. NYBP
Smells (Junior). Christopher Morley. BoChLi; GFA; MPB; TiPo
Smile, The. Blake. OBRV
Smile, The. Anthony Euwer. *See* Limerick: "No matter how grouchy you're feeling."
Smile, The. Robert Frost. *Fr.* The Hill Wife. NP
Smile, A ("Let others cheer"). *Unknown.* BLPA; WBLP
Smile ("Like a bread"). *Unknown.* BLPA; WBLP
Smile, A ("Smile costs nothing but gives much, A"). *Unknown.* PoToHe; SoP
Smile ("Thing that goes the farthest, The"). Wilbur D. Nesbit. *See* Let Us Smile.
Smile and Never Heed Me. Charles Swain. HBV
Smile, and the world smiles with you. Hustle and Grin. *Unknown.* WBLP
Smile at us, pay us, pass us; but do not quite forget. The Secret People. G. K. Chesterton. OtMeF; PoFr
Smile costs nothing but gives much, A. A Smile. *Unknown.* PoToHe; SoP
Smile is quite a funny thing. Growing Smiles. *Unknown.* PoLF
Smile, Massachusetts, Smile. A Song. *Unknown.* PAH

Smile not, nor think the legend vain. Contentment. Sadi. LiTW
Smile of one face is like a fierce mermaid, The. Soldiers. Maxwell Bodenheim. MAPA
Smile of the Goat, The. Oliver Herford. FiBHP
Smile of the Walrus, The. Oliver Herford. FiBHP
(Two Smiles.) PV
Smile then, children, hand in hand. Epithalamion. James Elroy Flecker. BrPo
Smiles. Peter Schjeldahl. ANYP
Smiles of the Bathers, The. Weldon Kees. NaP
Smiling. Dixie Willson. GFA
Smiling Demon of Notre Dame, A. Sophie Jewett. AA
Smiling girls, rosy boys. Mother Goose. GaP; OxNR
Smiling Morn, the breathing Spring, The. The Birks of Endermay. David Mallet. OBEC
Smiling morne had newly wak't the day, The. The Beginning of Heliodorus. Richard Crashaw. MaMe
Smiling Mouth, The. Charles d'Orléans. NoP
Smiling Phyllis has an air. Phyllis. *Unknown.* SeCL
Smith, The. Juana de Ibarbourou, *tr. fr. Spanish by* Beatrice Gilman Proske. OnPM
Smith/ a refugee from the Black Country. One Race, One Flag. A. R. D. Fairburn. AnNZ
Smith at the organ is like an anvil being. The Sound of Afroamerican History Chapt II. S. E. Anderson. BF
Smith makes me, A. The Runes on Weland's Sword. Kipling. AtBAP; PoEL-5
Smith of Maudlin. Walter Thornbury. PeVV
Smithfield Market Fire, The. Fred Dallas. WePo
Smiths of the heavens are mending the weather, The. Thunderstorm. Arthur Guiterman. PoMa
Smith's Song. George Sigerson, *ad. fr. the Irish.* OnYI
Smoke. Henry David Thoreau. *Fr.* Walden, *ch.* 13. AA; AmePo; AmLP; AmPP; AnAmPo; AnFE; AnNE; APA; AWP; CBV; CoAnAm; CoBA; InPo; JAWP; MWA-1; NoP; OxBA; TOP; VaPo; WBP
(Light-winged Smoke.) ViBoPo
(Light-winged Smoke, Icarian Bird.) AP; OnPM
Smoke. Charles Wright. NYBP
Smoke and Steel, *sel.* Carl Sandburg.
"Smoke of the fields in spring is one." MAP; MoAmPo; NeMA; PoMa
Smoke Animals. Rowena Bennett. PDV; RePo
Smoke-blackened Smiths. *Unknown. See* Blacksmiths, The.
Smoke-blue Plains, The. Badger Clark. YaD
Smoke color. August. Brother Antoninus. ToPo
Smoke-eyed lover, mouth. Home-Made Peach Ice Cream. Sandford Lyne. QAH
Smoke from the train-gulf hid by hoardings blunders upward. Birmingham. Louis MacNeice. CMoP; ILP; MoAB; MoBrPo
Smoke in Winter. Henry David Thoreau. AnNE; BWP
Smoke of the Camp Fire. Brian Brooke. BoSA
Smoke of the fields in spring is one. Carl Sandburg. *Fr.* Smoke and Steel. MAP; MoAmPo; NeMA; PoMa
Smoke Rose Gold. Carl Sandburg. NeMA; YT
Smoke Stack. A. M. Sullivan. WaKn
Smoker, The. Robert Huff. NePoEA-2
Smokin' my pipe on the mountings. Screw-Guns. Kipling. ViBoPo
Smoking Flax. Mary Josephine Benson. CaP
Smoky blue of evening wreathes from fields, The. Living. D. S. Savage. NeBP
Smoky sighes, the bitter teares, The. The Lover Accusing Hys Love for Her Unfaithfulnesse. *Unknown.* EnPo
Smoky Smirr o' Rain, The. George Campbell Hay. ACV
Smoky sunset, A. I dab my eyes. Required of You This Night. Peter Redgrove. NMP
Smooth between Sea and Land. A. E. Housman. MaPo; MoPo; NoP
Smooth Divine, The. Timothy Dwight. *Fr.* The Triumph of Infidelity. AA; AnAmPo; PPON; WGRP
(Minister, New Style, A.) AmPP
Smooth hill is bare, and the cannons are planted, The. At Fredericksburg. John Boyle O'Reilly. MC; PAH
Smooth was the water, calm the air. Song. Sir Charles Sedley. CBV; CEP; PeRV; SeCV-2
Smooth-worn coin and threadbare classic phrase, The. Andromeda. Thomas Bailey Aldrich. AA; AmePo
Smoothing a cypress beam. The Builder. Willard Wattles. AnAmPo; HBMV; OQP
Smoothly riding. The Carpenter's Plane. Vasily Kazin. OnPM
Smothered streams of love, which flow, The. The Atlantides. Henry David Thoreau. BWP; ViBoPo
Smothering dark engulfs relentlessly, The. A Child's Winter Evening. Gwen John. CH
Smudged eyeballs. Breakfast in a Bowling Alley in Utica, New York. Adrienne Rich. CoPo
Smuggler, The. *Unknown.* WhC
Smuggler's Song, A. Kipling. *Fr.* Puck of Pook's Hill. ShBV-1
Snack, A. Christina Rossetti. *See* Three Plum Buns.
Snagtooth Sal. Lowell O. Reese. ABF, *with music;* SCC, *abr.*
Snail, The ("The frugal snail with forecast of repose"). Vincent Bourne, *See* Housekeeper, The. *tr. fr. Latin by* Charles Lamb.
Snail, The ("To grass, or leaf, or fruit, or wall"). Vincent Bourne, *tr. fr. Latin by* William Cowper. BoTP; EiCL; GFA; GoTP; HBV; HBVY; OTPC (1923 ed.); PoRh; WaKn
Snail, The. Grace Hazard Conkling. SUS; UTS
Snail. John Drinkwater. GoJo; SoPo
Snail. Elisabeth Eybers, *tr. fr. Afrikaans by* Elisabeth Eybers. PeSA
Snail. Langston Hughes. FaPON; GoSl; TiPo
Snail. David McCord. RePo
Snail. C. Lindsay McCoy. GFA
Snail, The. James Reeves. RePo
Snail, The ("Little snail"). *Unknown, tr. fr. Chinese by* Isaac Taylor Headland. PCH
Snail, The ("The snail he lives in his hard round house"). *Unknown.* OTPC (1946 ed.); PPL
Snail is very odd and slow, The. The Snail. Grace Hazard Conkling. SUS; UTS
Snail pushes through a green, The. Considering the Snail. Thom Gunn. FIW; LiTM (1970 ed.); NePoEA-2; TDP; TwCP; WIRo
Snail, The, says, "Alas!" The Poor Snail. J. M. Westrup. BoTP
Snail, snail, put out your horns. *Unknown.* OxNR
Snail upon the wall. Snail. John Drinkwater. GoJo; SoPo
Snail who had a way, it seems, A. The Snail's Dream. Oliver Herford. PCH; UTS
Snail's a lucky fellow, he can go, The. The Lucky Snail. Winifred Welles. StVeCh (1940 ed.)
Snail's Dream, The. Oliver Herford. PCH; UTS
Snake, The. Roy Campbell. AtBAP
Snake, The. Hilary Corke. PV
Snake, A [*or* The]. Emily Dickinson. *See* Narrow fellow in the grass, A, *and* Sweet is the swamp. . .
Snake, The. Kyoshi, *tr. fr. Japanese by* Harold G. Henderson. RePo
Snake. D. H. Lawrence. AtBAP; BBV (1951 ed.); BrPo; CBV; CMoP; CoBMV; DiPo; FaBoMo; GoTL (1949 ed.); HoPM; LiTB; LiTM; LoBV; MoAB; MoPo; MoPW; MoVE; NoP; OAEP (2d ed.); PIA; PoRA (rev. ed.); PoSa; ReMP; SeCeV; ShBV-3; StP; VaPo
Snake, The. Kenneth Mackenzie. BoAV
Snake, The. Thomas Moore. HBV
Snake. Theodore Roethke. NYBP; OA; PoeP; PoPl; TDP
Snake, The. Robert Penn Warren. CBV
Snake and the Mouse, The. Bhartrihari, *tr. fr. Sanskrit by* Paul Elmer More. OnPM
Snake came to my water-trough, A. Snake. D. H. Lawrence. AtBAP; BBV (1951 ed.); BrPo; CBV; CMoP; CoBMV; DiPo; FaBoMo; GoTL (1949 ed.); HoPM; LiTB; LiTM; LoBV; MoAB; MoPo; MoPW; MoVE; NoP; OAEP (2d ed.); PIA; PoRA (rev. ed.); PoSa; ReMP; SeCeV; ShBV-3; StP; VaPo
Snake Charmer, The. Muriel Earley Sheppard. IHA
Snake emptied itself into the grass, A. Monsoon. David Wevill. NYBP
Snake Eyes. LeRoi Jones. Kal
Snake fled, The. Takahama Kyoshi, *tr. fr. Japanese by* Geoffrey Bownas and Anthony Thwaite. FIW
Snake Story. Henry Johnstone. PPL
Snake, A! Though it passes. The Snake. Takahama Kyoshi, *tr. fr. Japanese by* Harold G. Henderson. RePo
Snake Trying, The. W. W. E. Ross. MoCV; OBCV
Snakecharmer. Sylvia Plath. NepoEA-2; PP
Snakes and Snails. Grace Taber Hallock. RePo

Snakes, Mongooses, Snake-Charmers and the Like. Marianne Moore. CMoP; ExPo
Snakeskin and Stone. Keith Douglas. NePoEA
Snap back the canopy. Parachute Descent. David Bourne. WaP
Snap-Dragon. D. H. Lawrence. ErPo
Snapdragon. Cardinal Newman. GoBC
Snap-Dragon will never snap, A. A Lucky Thing. Dorothy Aldis. RePo
Snap Judgement on the Llama, A. Peggy Bennett. ELU
Snapoo (Slapandergosheka: "Oh, a little Dutch soldier from over the Rhine") (*orig. vers. of* Mademoiselle from Armentières). *Unknown.* SoAmSa
Snapshot. John Fuller. NePoEA-2
Snapshot: Ambassadress. George Garrett. NePoAm-2
Snapshot for Miss Bricka Who Lost in the Semi-final Round of the Pennsylvania Lawn Tennis Tournament at Haverford, July, 1960, A. Robert Wallace. SD
Snapshot of a Pedant. George Garrett. NePoAm-2
Snapshot: Politician. George Garrett. NePoAm-2
Snare, The. Edward Davison. PG (1955 ed.); ViBoPo (1941 ed.)
Snare, The. Patrick MacDonogh. NeIP
Snare, The. James Stephens. BoTP; CH; CMoP; HBMV; MoSiPe; OxBI; PDV; PoRL; ShBV-1; TiPo; UTS; YT
Snare me the soul of a dragon-fly. Miyoko San. Mary McNeil Fenollosa. AA
Snare of sleep held fast his struggling will, The. Epitaph on a Sentry. L. A. G. Strong. NeMA
Snares, The. Nahab Koutchak, *tr. fr. Armenian by* Thomas Walsh. CAW
Snark, The. "Lewis Carroll." *See* How to Recognize a Snark.
Snarlers, The. Arthur Guiterman. PaA
Snarleyyow; or, The Dog Fiend, *sel.* Frederick Marryat.
Captain Stood on the Carronade, The. BBV (1923 ed.); EtS; HBV; OTPC; RePo
(Old Navy, The.) PaPo
Snatch the departing mood. To a Town Poet. Lizette Woodworth Reese. AA
Snayl, The. Richard Lovelace. AtBAP; PoEL-3; SCEP-2
Sneel, Snaul. *Unknown.* OTPC
Sneeze on a Monday, you sneeze for danger. *See* If you sneeze on Monday. . .
Sneezing. Marie Louise Allen. SoPo
Sneezing. Leigh Hunt. HBV
Sniff. Frances Frost. BrR; SiSoSe; TiPo (1959 ed.)
Sniffle, The. Ogden Nash. RePo; WePo
Snips and Snails. Susan Axelrod. QAH
Snore in the foam: the night is vast and blind. Tristan da Cunha. Roy Campbell. MoBrPo; MoVE; OnHM; PeSA; RoGo
Snore on in your front-row chair! Let not my voice. To an Old Lady Asleep at a Poetry Reading. James Kirkup. BoPe; POTi
Snoring. Aileen Fisher. SoPo
Snorting his pleasure in the dying sun. Landscape, Deer Season. Barbara Howes. GoJo
Snow. Elizabeth Akers Allen. HBV
Snow. Dorothy Aldis. TiPo
(On a Snowy Day.) PDV
Snow. Ecclesiasticus, Bible, Apocrypha. BoC
Snow. Margaret Avison. PeCV
Snow, The. Joseph Beaumont. StJW
Snow. Madison Cawein. MAP; PFY
Snow. Elizabeth J. Coatsworth. SiSoSe
Snow. Adelaide Crapsey. QFR
Snow, The. Robert Creeley. AP
Snow, The. Emily Dickinson. *See* It sifts from leaden sieves.
Snow, The. Clifford Dyment. MoVE; POTE
Snow, The. F. Ann Elliott. BoTP
Snow, The. W. W. Gibson. BEL
Snow, The. Donald Hall. NePoEA-2; NMP; OPoP
Snow. John Kelleher. ELU
Snow, The. Sidney Keyes. NeBP
Snow, The. Vista. Alfred Kreymborg. BoLP
Snow. Archibald Lampman. PeCV
Snow. Longfellow. *See* Snow-Flakes.
Snow. Louis MacNeice. ExPo; GTBS-W; LiTM; ReMP; VaPo
Snow, The. Nellie Burget Miller. GFA
Snow. Munetake, *tr. fr. Japanese by* Asataro Miyamori. OnPM
Snow. W. R. Rodgers. LiTG; LiTM (rev. ed.)
Snow. Ruth Stone. NYBP
Snow. Jane Taylor. OTPC (1923 ed.); PCH; PPL
Snow. Edward Thomas. FaBoTw; MoVE
Snow. *Unknown.* *See* Riddle: "White bird featherless."
Snow. David Wevill. MoCV
Snow, The. Whittier. *See* Winter Day.
Snow. Alice Wilkins. GFA; TiPo
Snow/ is an anthology. Snow Anthology. Arthur S. Bourinot. GoYe; TwCaPo
Snow Advent. Joseph Auslander. MoSiPe
Snow, The, Ah, yes; ah, yes, indeed. Vista. Alfred Kreymborg. MAPA
Snow and stars, the same as ever. Age. William Winter. HBV
Snow Anthology. Arthur S. Bourinot. GoYe; TwCaPo
Snow Ball, The. Petronius Arbiter. *tr. fr. Latin by* Soame Jenyns. LiTW
Snow-Ball, The. Thomas Stanley. CavP
Snow-beaten, winter-bound, all that I see. First Words before Spring. Louis Untermeyer. MAP
Snow breaks the hushed June dawn. The Voices. *Unknown.* MCCG
Snow by Morning. May Swenson. NYBP
Snow came down last night like moths, The. First Snow in Alsace. Richard Wilbur. AP; NoP
Snow came down like stars tonight, The. Fall of Stars. George Dillon. NP
Snow can come as quietly, A. Snow. Elizabeth J. Coatsworth. SiSoSe
Snow cannot melt too soon for the birds left behind, The. Rag Doll and Summer Birds. Owen Dodson. PoNe
Snow-Dance for the Dead. Lola Ridge. AnAmPo
Snow Country. Dave Etter. AmFN
Snow Curlew, The. Vernon Watkins. NYBP
Snow dissolv'd, no more is seen, The. Horace. Odes IV, 7. CLwM; EiCL
Snow-dust driven over the snow. Winter Noon. Sara Teasdale. RePo; YeAr
Snow falling and night falling fast, oh, fast. Desert Places. Robert Frost. AmPP (4th ed.); AnFE; AP; AtBAP; CABA; CBV; CMoP; CoAnAm; CoBMV; DiPo; ForPo; MAP; MaPo (1969 ed.); MoAB; MoAmPo; MoVE; MWA-2; OxBA; PAn; PoAn; PoIE; PoPo; ReMP; TwAmPo; UnPo
Snow falls/ flake on flake. Winter in the Wood. Ivy O. Eastwick. YeAr
Snow falls deep; the forest lies alone, The. Gipsies [*or* Gypsies *or* The Gipsy Camp]. John Clare. CBEP; CH; ChTr; NBM; NoP; PoEL-4; ShBV-2
Snow falls on the cars in Doctors' Row and hoods the headlights. Doctors' Row. Conrad Aiken. AP; PoPl
Snow fell as for Wenceslas. Roarers in a Ring. Ted Hughes. NePoEA-2; POTi
Snow fell slowly over the long sweep, The. Landscape. Alfred W. Purdy. CaP
Snow fell softly all the night, The. Snow. Alice Wilkins. GFA; TiPo
Snow Fell with a Will. Richard Gillman. NePoAm-2
Snow Globe, The. Howard Nemerov. FiMAP
Snow-Gum, The. Douglas Stewart. PoAu-2
Snow had begun in the gloaming, The. The First Snow-Fall. James Russell Lowell. AA; AnNE; BLPA; FaBoBe; FaPON; GFA; HBV; MCCG; NeHB; OTD; PCD; PoSC; TreF; WBLP
Snow had buried Stuyvesant, The. Inauguration Day: January 1953. Robert Lowell. PoeP; ToPo
Snow had fallen many nights and days, The. The End of the World. Gordon Bottomley. BrPo; CH; MoBrPo; MoVE
Snow Harvest. Andrew Young. BoNaP
Snow has come back to make of weeds. Annunciation. D. G. Jones. PeCV (1967 ed.)
Snow has covered the next line of tracks. Looking at New-Fallen Snow from a Train. Robert Bly. FRC; NaP
Snow has fallen all night. The Snow Curlew. Vernon Watkins. NYBP
Snow has fallen lightly on the earth, The. Prose Poem: Sadness of the Husbandman. Judith Gautier. OnPM
Snow has left [*or* is gone from] the cottage top [*or* tops], The. February. John Clare. *Fr.* The Shepherd's Calendar. NCEP; OBNC
Snow-hills all about. Ice-Skaters. Elder Olson. SD

Snow in April. Leonora Speyer. PG (1955 ed.)
Snow in August, and people. When Beulah Did the Hula in Missoula. William Hathaway. QAH
Snow, in bitter cold, The.. The Snow. F. Ann Elliott. BoTP
Snow in Europe. David Gascoyne. MoPW
Snow in October. Alice Dunbar Nelson. CDC
Snow in Spring. Ivy O. Eastwick. PDV
Snow in the Caucasus. Yetza Gillespie. NYTB
Snow in the Suburbs. Thomas Hardy. BoNaP; CMoP; GoJo; MoAB; MoBrPo; OBMV; PoVP; ShBV-3; ThWaDe; ViPP; VP; WePo
Snow in Town. Rickman Mark. BoTP; TVC
Snow is a strange white word. On Receiving News of the War. Isaac Rosenberg. MMA; MoBrPo
Snow, The, is for sale. No takers. Winter Indian. James Welch. YAP
Snow is gone from cottage tops, The. *See* Snow has left the cottage top, The.
Snow is in the oak. The Snow. Donald Hall. NePoEA-2; NMP; OPoP
Snow is lying very deep, The. Convention. Agnes Lee. HBMV; PoMa
Snow is out of fashion. Snow in the City. Rachel Field. TiPo
Snow, The, is soft, and how it squashes! Thaw. Eunice Tietjens. BrR
Snow is white, the wind is cold, The. Night. Mary Frances Butts. OTPC (1946 ed.); PRWS
Snow Lay on the Ground, The, *with music*. *Unknown*. YaCaBo
Snow-Leopard, The. Randall Jarrell. LiTM (1970 ed.); MoPo; TwCP
Snow, less intransigeant than their marble, The. At the Grave of Henry James. W. H. Auden. LiTA; MoPo
Snow lies crisp beneath the stars, The. Christmas Pastoral. Robert Hillyer. MaRV
Snow lies deep, The: nor sun nor melting shower. Winter at Tomi. Ovid. AWP; JAWP; WBP
Snow Lies Light, The, *sel*. W. W. Christman.
"Snow lies light upon the pine, The." BiS
Snow Lies Sprinkled on the Beach, The. Robert Bridges. PoVP
Snow Line. John Berryman. The Dream Songs, XXVIII. NaP
Snow makes whiteness where it falls. First Snow. Marie Louise Allen. SoPo; TiPo
Snow Man. *See* Snowman.
Snow-masked and bell-bewitched the village. Christmas on Three Continents. John Peter. BoSA
Snow may come as quietly, A. January. Elizabeth J. Coatsworth. BoChLi (1950 ed.); PoSC
Snow Meditation. Francis Beauchesne Thornton. JKCP (1955 ed.)
Snow melting! Kato Gyodai, *tr. fr. Japanese by* Geoffrey Bownas *and* Anthony Thwaite. FIW
Snow on ground and. January. James Applewhite. YAP
Snow on the East Wind. Lord Dunsany. MoBrPo (1942 ed.)
Snow Queen comes on dazzling feet, The. The North Wind. Dorothy Gradon. BoTP
Snow-Shower, The. Bryant. AnNE; HBV
Snow, snow faster. *Unknown*. OxNR
Snow Storm. *See* Snowstorm.
Snow Story. L. A. MacKay. TwCaPo
Snow thaws, The. Issa, *tr. fr. Japanese by* Lewis Mackenzie. FIW
Snow toward Evening. Melville Cane. MAP; MoAmPo; PDV; SUS; TiPo
Snow upon my lifeless mountains, The. The Day of Love. Shelley. *Fr.* Prometheus Unbound. EPN
Snow was falling soft and slow, The. Winter Night. Boris Pasternak. PoPl
Snow whispers about me, The. Chinoiseries: Falling Snow. Amy Lowell. AnAmPo; NP
Snow wind-whipt to ice. Winter. Richard Hughes. OBMV; ThWaDe
Snow-Bird, The. Hezekiah Butterworth. PCH; PRWS
Snow-Bird, The. Frank Dempster Sherman. SiSoSe; SoPo; TiPo; UTS
Snow-Bird's Song, The. Francis C. Woodworth. PPL; SAS
Snow-bound; a Winter Idyl. Whittier. AmePo; AmPP; AnNE; AP; CoBA; GN, *sels.*; MAmP; MCCG, *abr.*; OxBA; TOP; WiR
Sels.
"Alas for him who never sees." InP
"And yet, dear heart! remembering thee." MaRV
"As night drew on, and, from the crest." YT
(Winter Night, The.) PTK; TrGrPo
Life and Love. BLRP
Mother. AA; OHIP; PFY
Prophetess ("Another guest that winter night"). AA
Schoolmaster, The ("Brisk wielder of the birch and rule"). GoTP
"Shut in from all the world without." LaNeLa
(Firelight.) AA
Sister ("As one who held herself apart"). AA
"Sun that brief December day, The." AtBAP
(Lines.) BBV (1951 ed.)
(Snow, The.) StVeCh
(Storm, The.) FaBV
(Winter Day.) TrGrPo
Uncle, The ("Our uncle, innocent of books"). GoTP
"Unwarmed by any sunset light." BBV (1923 ed.); GBV
(World Transformed, The.) AA
Yet Love Will Dream. MaRV
Snow-bound in woodland, a mournful word. Postponement. Thomas Hardy. PoVP; ViPo (1962 ed.)
Snow-bound mountains, snow-bound valleys. Carol of the Russian Children. *Unknown*. OHIP
Snowball. *See* Snow Ball.
Snowdrop. Anna Bunston de Bary. BoTP; HBMV; MaRV
Snowdrop, A, *abr.* Harriet Prescott Spofford. GN
Snowdrop. William Wetmore Story. HBV
Snowdrop. Tennyson. OTPC (1946 ed.); PCH; PoRL
Snow-drop of dogs, with ear of brownest dye. Sonnet: To Tartar, a Terrier Beauty. Thomas Lovell Beddoes. OBNC
Snowdrops. Laurence Alma-Tadema. BoTP; PRWS
Snowdrops. W. Graham Robertson. OTPC; PPL
Snowdrops. Mary Vivian. BoTP
Snowfall: Four Variations. George Amabile. NYBP
Snowfall. Giosuè Carducci, *tr. fr. Italian by* Romilda Rendel. AWP; JAWP; WBP; PoPl, *tr. by* G. A. Greene.
(First Snowfall, *tr. by* Asa Hughes.) LiTW
Snowfall, The. Donald Justice. NePoEA-2
Snow Fall, The. Archibald MacLeish. LOW; PoPl
Snowfall. "I. V. S. W." InMe
Snowfall in the Afternoon. Robert Bly. NMP
Snowfall on Plum Trees After They Had Bloomed, A. Charles Dalmon. *Fr.* Three Pictures. TSW
Snowflake, The. Mary Mapes Dodge. *See* Snowflakes ("Whenever a snowflake").
Snowflake on Asphodel. Conrad Aiken. CMoP
Snow-flake Song. Hilda Conkling. NP
Snowflake Which Is Now and Hence Forever, The. Archibald MacLeish. NoP
Snowflakes. Ruth M. Arthur. BoTP
Snowflakes. Alice Behrend. GoYe
Snowflakes. Marchette Chute. PDV
Snowflakes ("Little white feathers"). Mary Mapes Dodge. MPB
Snowflakes ("Whenever a snowflake"). Mary Mapes Dodge. HBVY; OTPC (1946 ed.); PRWS
(Snowflake, The.) AA
(Winter, *st.* 1.) GFA
Snow-Flakes. Longfellow. AmLP; AnNE; AP; BBV (1951 ed.); ChTr; MAmP; NoP; PCH, *st.* 1; PoEL-5; WiR
(Snow, *st.* 1.) BoTP
Snow-flakes come in fleets. Snow-flake Song. Hilda Conkling. NP
Snowing of the Pines, The. Thomas Wentworth Higginson. AA; GN
Snowman, The. E. M. Adams. BoTP
Snow Man, The. Wallace Stevens. AnEnPo; AP; BWP; CoBMV; CrMA; ForPo; GoJo; NoP; NP; Po; PoFS; PoIE; QFR; ReMP; TDP
Snowman. *Unknown*. GFA
Snowman's Resolution, The. Aileen Fisher. SoPo
Snow's a snuggly blanket, The. The Snow. Nellie Burget Miller. GFA
Snows are fled away, leaves on the shaws, The. Diffugere Nives. Horace, *tr. by* A. E. Housman. Odes, IV, 7. MaPo (1969 ed.); NoP
Snows cloaked/ Mountain cliffs. Lament. Gudmundur Gudmundsson. LiTW

Snows have fled, the hail, the lashing rain, The. Diffugere Nives, 1917. Maurice Baring. HBMV; POTE
Snows have joined the little streams and slid into the sea, The. One Morning When the Rain-Birds Call. Lloyd Roberts. CaP
Snows of Yester-Year, The. Villon. *See* Ballad of Dead Ladies, The.
Snowshoeing Song. Arthur Weir. VA
Snowstorm. John Clare. BoNaP; WiR
"What a night! The wind howls, hisses, and but stops," *sel.* FIW
Snowstorm, The. Pearl Riggs Crouch. PoOW
Snow-Storm, The. Emerson. AA; AmePo; AmP; AmPP; AnNE; AP; BoLiVe; BoNaP; CoBA; DiPo; FaBoBe; GN; GTBS-D; GTBS-W; InP; LaNeLa; LiTA; LiTG; MAmP; MWA-1; NePA; NoP; OHFP; OTPC; OuHeWo; OxBA; PG (1945 ed.); PoE; PoEL-4; PoFS; PoLF; PoPo; PTK; StP; TDP; TreFT; TrGrPo; VaPo; WiR; YT
"Announced by all the trumpets of the sky," *sel.* PCH; TiPo
Snow Storm. Sister Mary Madeleva. GoBC
Snowstorm, The. Frederick George Scott. PeCV
Snow Storm. Tu Fu, *tr. fr. Chinese by* Kenneth Rexroth. NaP
Snow Storm, The. Ethelwyn Wetherald. VA
Snowstorm in the Midwest. James Wright. FRC
Snowy Day in School, A. D. H. Lawrence. FIW
Snowy, flowy, blowy. The Twelve Months. "Gregory Gander." TreFT
Snowy path for squirrel and fox, A. The Brook in February. Sir Charles G. D. Roberts. BoNaP; OBCV; WHW
Snowy-smooth beneath the pen. White Paper. Sydney Jephcott. BoAu
Snub nose, the guts of twenty mules are in your cylinders and transmission. New Farm Tractor. Carl Sandburg. FaPON
Snuff-Boxes, The. *Unknown.* StPo
Snug in My Easy Chair. W. W. Gibson. EPN
(Proem: "Snug in my easy chair.") HBMV
Snugly upon the equal heights. The Old Feminist. Phyllis McGinley. ThLM
So? James P. Vaughn. AmNP
So/ Went this little pig from the mainland to the market. Mother Goose Up-to-Date. Louis Untermeyer. MoAmPo
So Abram rose, and clave the wood, and went. The Parable of the Old Men and the Young. Wilfred Owen. BoPe; FIW; MemP
So active they seem passive, little sheep. Grace. Richard Wilbur. LiTA
So all day long I followed through the fields. Gentian. Elizabeth Green Crane. AA
So all day long the noise of battle roll'd. Morte d'Arthur. Tennyson. AnEnPo; ATP; BBV; BEL; BoLiVe; DTo; EnL; EnLi-2; FaBoBe; FiP; HBV; ILP; MBW-2; NoP; OAEP; OnSP; PoAn; PoE; PoEL-5; PoVP; SeCeV; ShBV-3; TOP; UnPo (1st ed.); ViPo; ViPP; VP; WHA
So all men come at last to their Explorers' Tree. Burke and Wills. Ken Barratt. BoAV; PoAu-2
So am I as the rich, whose blessed key. Sonnets, LII. Shakespeare. OBSC
So-and-So Reclining on Her Couch. Wallace Stevens. AmPP (5th ed.); LiTM; PoeP; SiTL
So, April, here thou art again. Lady April. Richard Le Gallienne. YeAr
So are you to my thoughts as food to life. Sonnets, LXXV. Shakespeare. PoEL-2
So as I was saying to you. Talk. John Perreault. ANYP
So as they traveild, lo they gan espy. The Cave of Despair. Spenser. *Fr.* The Faerie Queene, I, 9. LoBV; MBW-1
So as they travellèd, the drouping night. Spenser. *Fr.* The Faerie Queene, IV, 5. MBW-1
So, back again? To a Dog. Josephine Preston Peabody. BLPA; WGRP
So bandit-eyed, so undovelike a bird. Blue Jay. Robert Francis. ELU
So Be My Passing. W. E. Henley. *See* Margaritae Sorori.
So Beautiful You Are, Indeed. Irene Rutherford McLeod. HBMV
So blest are they who round a family board. The Family. Donna R. Lydston. PoToHe (new ed.)
So brief a time I have them, Lord. Prayer at a Nursery Window. Frances Stoakley Lankford. FaChP
So brilliant a moonshine. Harvest Moon. Ryota. RePo
So by your edict Christ once more lies slain. Word to a Dictator. Adelaide Love. MaRV
So careful is Isa, and anxious to last. On a Valetudinarian. Ibn al-Rumi. LiTW
"So careful of the type?" but no. In Memoriam A. H. H., LVI. Tennyson. AnFE; CoBE; DiPo; EnL; EPN; FosPo; HBV; InP; LoBV; MaPo; OAEP; OBEV (1st ed.); OBNC; OuHeWo; SeCeV; TOP; ViPo; VP
So Castlereagh has cut his throat! The worst. Epigrams on Castlereagh, I. Byron. ExPo
So clear a season, and so snatch'd from storms. On the Fair Weather just at the Coronation. Katherine Philips. PeRV
So cold the first Thanksgiving came. The First Thanksgiving. Nancy Byrd Turner. YeAr
So Cruel Prison. Earl of Surrey. *See* Prisoned in Windsor, He Recounteth His Pleasure There Passed.
So Deep Is Death. Frank Kendon. MoBrPo (1942 ed.)
So delicate, so airy,/ The almond on the tree. Pink Almond. Katharine Tynan. BoTP
So detached and cool she is. The Mask. Clarissa Scott Delany. CDC; PoNe
So did the world from the first hour decay. John Donne. *Fr.* An Anatomy of the World. TuPP
So does the sun withdraw his beames. On His Mistress Going from Home. *Unknown.* OBS
So down the silver streams of Eridan. Giles Fletcher. *Fr.* Christ's Victory and Triumph: Christ's Triumph over Death. LoBV
So dream thy sails, O phantom bark. The Phantom Bark. Hart Crane. CMoP
So earnest with thy God, can no new care. Of His Majesties Receiving the News of the Duke of Buckingham's Death. Edmund Waller. SeCV-1
So endlessly the gray-lipped sea. The Dead Aviator. Francis Hackett. JKCP (1926 ed.)
So fair, so dear, so warm upon my bosom. The Firstborn. John Arthur Goodchild. HBV
So Fair, So Fresh. Charles d'Orléans. NoP
So Fair, So Sweet, Withal So Sensitive. Wordsworth. EnRP; NoP
So faire a church as this, had Venus none. Love at First Sight. Christopher Marlowe. *Fr.* Hero and Leander, First Sestiad. FaBoEn
So faith is strong. The Tide of Faith. "George Eliot." *Fr.* A Minor Prophet. MaRV; OQP; TRV; WGRP
So fallen! so lost! the light withdrawn. Ichabod. Whittier. AA; AmePo; AmP; AmPP; AnAmPo; AnFE; AnNE; AP; APA; CBEP; CoAnAm; CoBA; DD; HBV; LiTA; OxBA; PAH; PG; Po; PoEL-4; PoIE (1970 ed.); TOP
So far as I can see. Meditations of a Tortoise Dozing under a Rosetree near a Beehive at Noon While a Dog Scampers About and a Cuckoo Calls from a Distant Wood. E. V. Rieu. FiBHP
So far as our story approaches the end. A Light Woman. Robert Browning. CLwM; HBV; PoVP
So Far, So Near. Christopher Pearse Cranch. MaRV; TrPWD
So fare ye well, my darlin', so fare ye well, my dear. Fare Ye Well, My Darlin'. *Unknown.* OuSiCo
"So Farewell." Wang Wei, *tr. fr. Chinese by* W. J. B. Fletcher. OnPM
So Fast Entangled. *Unknown.* MeWo; TrGrPo
(Her Hair.) LiTL
("Her hair the net of golden wire.") EG
So feeble is the thread that doth the burden stay. In Spain. Petrarch, *tr. by* Sir Thomas Wyatt. FCP
So fell our statesman-for he stood sublime. Everett. Thomas William Parsons. DD
"So fleet the works of men, back to the earth again." The Curtain (Old Tabor Grand Opera House). Jean Milne Gower. PoOW
So flies love's meteor to her shroud of winds. The Dead Words. Vernon Watkins. LiTM (rev. ed.)
So Fly by Night. Charles Osborne. BoAV
So, forth issew'd [*or* issued] the Seasons of the year. The Mask of Mutability [*or* Seasons]. Spenser. *Fr.* The Faerie Queene, VII, 7. GN; OBSC
So frail our life, perchance to-morrow's sun. An Elegy. Tsurayuki. OnPM
So, Freedom, thy great quarrel may we serve. Our Cause. William James Linton. VA

So, friend, your shop was all your house! Shop. Robert Browning. PoVP; ViPo
So frisky and fit. Simchas Torah. Morris Rosenfeld. TrJP
So from the ground we felt that virtue branch. The Transfiguration. Edwin Muir. BoPe; FaBoMo; MasP; OxBS
So from the years the gifts were showered. W. H. Auden. *Fr.* In Time of War. CMoP
So gay on your lovely head. Relaxation. Dick Gallup. ANYP
So gentle Ellen now no more. Samuel Taylor Coleridge. *Fr.* The Three Graves. ChER
So glad I done done. I Done Done What Ya' Tol' Me to Do. *Unknown.* BoAN-1
So good-luck came, and on my roofe did light. The Coming [*or* Comming] of Good Luck. Robert Herrick. AtBAP; CBEP; ELU
So goodbye, Mrs. Brown. On Leaving Mrs. Brown's Lodgings. Sir Walter Scott. NBM
So Handy, *with music. Unknown.* ShS; SoAmSa
So happy the song he sings. Bluebird. Hilda Conkling. GFA
So happy were Columbia's eight. A Crew Poem. Edward Augustus Blount, Jr. AA
So hath he fallen, the Endymion of the air. Chavez. Mildred I. McNeal Sweeney. HBV
So have I seen a little silly fly. A Quarrel with Fortune. Benjamin Colman. SCAP
So have I seen a silver swan. A Song. *At. to* John Webster. CBEP; LO; SeCL
So having said, a while he stood, expecting. Satan's Metamorphosis. Milton. *Fr.* Paradise Lost, X. StP
So having said, Aglaura him bespake. Colin Clout at Court. Spenser. *Fr.* Colin Clout's Come Home. OBSC
So he died for his faith. That is fine. How Did He Live [*or* Life and Death]. Ernest H. Crosby. MaRV; OQP
So he droned on, of parish work and claims. City Priest. Anne Higginson Spicer. OQP
So He has cut his throat at last! He? Who? Epigrams on Castlereagh, II. Byron. ExPo
So he said then: I will make the poem. The Maker. R. S. Thomas. ELU
So he sat down and slowly, slowly. Foreclosure. Mark Van Doren. CrMA
So he sits down. His host will play for him. Concert Scene. John Logan. NePoEA-2
So he won't talk to me when we meet? Confucius. *Fr.* Songs of Cheng. CTC
So heavy and so fraught with pain. The Cross. Shirley Dillon Waite. ChIP; OQP
So Hector spake; the Trojans roar'd applause. Night Encampment outside Troy. Homer. *Fr.* The Iliad. RoGo
So here hath been dawning. To-Day. Thomas Carlyle. HBV; HBVY; MaRV; NeHB; OQP; OTD; OTPC (1946 ed.); WGRP
So here I sit behind my nasty desk. Any Man to His Secretary. Hilary Corke. ErPo
So here is my desert and here am I. In Paris. Thomas MacDonagh. OnYI
So here, twisted in steel, and spoiled with red. Trapped Dingo. Judith Wright. NeLNL
So here we are in April, in showy, blowy April. April. Ted Robinson. GoTP
So, here we meet—after long seeking. Linota Rufescens. Lyle Donaghy. OnYI
So he's got there at last, been received as a partner. Security. Michael Hamburger. NMP; OPoP; PoCh
So his bold tube, Man, to the sun apply'd. To the King. Andrew Marvell. MaMe
So huge a burden to support. Ill Luck. Baudelaire. PoPl
So I am your "darling girl"! Remonstrance. Philodemos the Epicurean. LiTW
So I arm thee for the final night. The Page of Lancelot. May Kendall. VA
So I came down the steps to Lenin. Dorothy Wellesley. *Fr.* Lenin. OBMV
So I go on, not knowing. Faith and Sight. Mary Gardiner Brainard. *Fr.* Not Knowing. FaChP; MaRV
So I have known this life. Lollingdon Downs. John Masefield. LiTB
So, I have seen a man killed! Arthur Hugh Clough. Amours de Voyage, II. PeVV
So I live in my nook, turning my face from the world. The Poet in His Poverty. Nizami. LiTW
So I may gain thy death, my life I'll give. Qui Perdiderit Animam Suam. Richard Crashaw. ACP
So I possess a perfect thing. A Bed of Campanula. "John Crichton." CaP
So, I shall see her in three days. In Three Days. Robert Browning. EPN; PoVP
So I Stay Near the Door; an Apologia for My Life. Samuel M. Shoemaker. SoP
So I, who love, with all this outward. The Meaning. Ralph Gustafson. OBCV
So I would hear out those lungs. Buckdancer's Choice. James Dickey. NoP; NYBP; PoAn; PoNe (1970 ed.)
So in a one man Europe I sit here. George Barker. NeBP
So, in the Evening, to the Simple Cloister. Conrad Aiken. *See* Cloister.
So in the empty sky the stars appear. John Masefield. BoPe
So in the sinful streets, abstracted and alone. Easter Day, II. Arthur Hugh Clough. EPN; OAEP; PoVP; ViPP
So innocent, so quiet—yet. The Pond. W. H. Davies. ChMP
So is it not with me as with that Muse. Sonnets, XXI. Shakespeare. InvP; OBSC; ReEn; SiCE
So is the child slow stooping beside him. The Gardeners. David Ignatow. NYTB
So It Begins. James Agee. Sonnets, I. ATP (1953 ed.)
("So it begins. Adam is in his earth.") MAP; MoAmPo
So it happened, exactly as I tell you. Being. Jacob Glatstein. *Fr.* The Bratzlav Rabbi to His Scribe. LiTW
So it is, my dear. Even So. Dante Gabriel Rossetti. OBNC
So it is, they say, that the men in the bay. Merrimac Side, and Agiochook. Edward Everett Hale. From Potomac to Merrimac, III. PAH
So it was true. Elastic air could fill. Ash. George MacBeth. NMP
So it was when Jesus came in his gentleness. Jesus. Robert Bridges. *Fr.* The Testament of Beauty. MaRV
So large a morning, so itself, to lean. Song. W. H. Auden. NePoAm-2
So Late into the Night. Byron. *See* So We'll Go No More a-Roving.
So late one eve as they sat courting. The Bramble Briar. *Unknown.* BFSS
So Late Removed from Him She Swore. Walter Savage Landor. OBRV
So late, so late, so haunting. On the Threshold. Karl Kraus. TrJP
So lately one evening as I rambled. Dixie's Green Shore. *Unknown.* BFSS
So leave her and cast care from thy heart. His Camel. Alqamah. *Fr.* The Mufaddiliyat. AWP; JAWP; WBP
So Let Me Hence. W. E. Henley. EnLit
So let our lips and lives express. Prove the Doctrine. *Unknown.* SoP
So let the month end: the new fiscal year. William Harmon. *Fr.* Treasury Holiday. QAH
So, let us laugh—lest vain rememberings. Retractions, XIV. James Branch Cabell. HBMV
So light no one noticed. The Song. Edward Dorn. CoPo
So like a god I sit here. The Sitting. C. Day Lewis. FaBoMo
So like a queen she moves/ among the rabble. Our Lady on Calvary. Sister Michael Marie. ISi
So Little and So Much. John Oxenham. BLRP
So little time, time's guest. In the Year's Morning. David Ross. PG (1955 ed.)
So Live. Bryant. *Fr.* Thanatopsis. PoToHe
(Be Ye Also Ready.) MaRV
("So live, that when thy summons comes.") DD; OQP; OTD; SoP; TRV
So lively, so gay, my dear mother, I'm grown. Taste and Spirit. Christopher Anstey. *Fr.* The New Bath Guide. CEP; EiCL
So Long! Walt Whitman. AmP; MWA-1
So long,/ So far away. Afro-American Fragment. Langston Hughes. NoP; PoNe
So Long Ago. Morris Rosenfeld, *tr. fr. Yiddish by* Elbert Aidline. TrJP
So Long As There Are Homes. Grace Noll Crowell. MaRV
So long as Time & Space are the stars. Michael Silverton. PV
So long as you live and move. Teach Us to Mark This, God. Franz Werfel. TrJP

So Long Folks, Off to the War. Anthony Ostroff. NePoAm-2; PoPl
So long he rode he drew anigh. The King's Visit. William Morris. *Fr.* The Earthly Paradise. VA
So long I sat and conned. The Elm Beetle. Andrew Young. LoBV
So long you wandered on the dusky plain. To His Friend in Elysium. Joachim du Bellay. AWP; JAWP; WBP
So Look the Mornings. Robert Herrick. ELP
So looks Anthea, when in bed she lyes. To Anthea Lying in Bed. Robert Herrick. SeCP
So loud the deer cries, calling to his mate. Deer and Echo. Otomo Yakamochi. OnPM
So Love, emergent out of chaos, brought. Love. Ben Jonson. UnTE
So Love is dead that has been quick so long! Hic Jacet. Louise Chandler Moulton. AA; AnAmPo; AnFE; APA; CoAnAm
So lucky I was in being born. Yankee Cradle. Robert P. Tristram Coffin. EvOK
So make your impassive passage to the act. Poem in Time of War. William Abrahams. WaP
So, Man? Gene Derwood. NePA
So Man, grown vigorous now. Prelude to Space. C. S. Lewis. HW
So Many! Frank L. Stanton. MaRV
So many cares to vex the day. Summer Magic. Leslie Pinckney Hill. BANP
So many evenings, on the red-tiled terrace. Lost Garden. "Katherine Hale." CaP
So many folk are happy folk. A Song of Happiness. Muna Lee. NP
So many girls vague in the yielding orchard. The Greenhouse. James Merrill. TwAmPo
So many hearts are like old battlefields. The Path. Sybil Leonard Armes. FaChP
So many little flowers. Cycle. Langston Hughes. FaPON; GoSl
So Many Monkeys. Marion Edey. SoPo; TiPo
So many moral matters, and so little used. John Skelton. *Fr.* Speak, Parrot. CoBE; ViBoPo
So Many stars in the infinite space. So Many! Frank L. Stanton. MaRV
So many thousands for a house. On a Certain Lord Giving Some Thousand Pounds for a House. David Garrick. PV
"So many unlived lives," she said; and idle. An Idyl in Idleness. Robert Pack. NePoEA
So many worlds, so much to do. In Memoriam A. H. H., LXXIII. Tennyson. EPN; HBV; ViPo; VP
So may the auspicious Queen of Love. To the Ship in Which Virgil Sailed to Athens. Horace. Odes, I, 3. AWP
So men, who once have cast the truth away. Leaving Me, and Then Loving Many. Abraham Cowley. AnAnS-2
So merrily singeth the nightingale! John Skelton. *Fr.* Magnificence. PoFr
So Might is Right, you say; I fight in vain. "Might Is Right." Israel Zangwill. TrJP
So Might It Be. John Galsworthy. PoLF
So Miss Myrtle is going to marry? The Charming Woman. Helen Selina Sheridan. ALV; OBRV
So, Mistress Anne, faire neighbor myne. *See* Soe, Mistress Anne. . .
So moping flat and low our valleys lie. Winter in the Fens. John Clare. BoNaP; FlW
So much depends. The Red Wheelbarrow [*or* Spring and All]. William Carlos Williams. AmLP; CMoP; EvOK; FlW; ForPo; FosPo; HoPM; LiTA; LiTM (1970 ed.); MoAB; MoAmPo; NoP; PoAn; PoeP; ThWaDe; UnPo (3d ed.); VaPo
So much have I forgotten in ten years. Flame-Heart. Claude McKay. AmNP; BALP; BANP; CDC; NoP; PoNe
So much that I would give you hovers out. For a Birthday. Elaine V. Emans. BiCB
So much to tell you. 2 Variations: All About Love. Philip Whalen. NeAP
So music flowed for them, and left. A Closing Music. Laurence Whistler. MusP
So music was "left out" of your make-up. To a Mute Musician. E. Margaret Clarkson. SoP
So must he be, who in the crowded street. "Is Thy Servant a Dog?" John Banister Tabb. JKCP
So near to death yourself. For a Very Old Man on the Death of His Wife. Jane Cooper. NePoEA-2
So Nigh Is Grandeur. Emerson. *See* Duty.
So nigh is grandeur to man. ——Cook. YaD
So nigh is grandeur to our dust. Duty [*or* Heroism]. Emerson. *Fr.* Voluntaries, III. FaFP; GN; HBV; OQP; TreF; TRV; YaD
So Not Seeing I Sung. Arthur Hugh Clough. *Fr.* Amours de Voyage. OBNC
("Tibur is beautiful, too, and the orchard slopes, and the Anio.") GTBS-P
So, now I have confessed [*or* confest] that he is thine. Sonnets, CXXXIV. Shakespeare. CBEP; InvP
So, Now Is Come Our Joyful'st Feast. *See* Christmas Carol, A: "So, now is come our joyfullest feast."
So now my summer task is ended, Mary. To Mary. Shelley. *Fr.* The Revolt of Islam. EnRP; EPN
So now the very bones of you are gone. Doricha. E. A. Robinson. AWP; JAWP; WBP
So now, this poet, who forsakes the stage. Prologue to "Love Triumphant." Dryden. OxBoLi; SiTL
So oft as I her beauty do behold. Amoretti, LV. Spenser. BoLiVe; HBV; PoIE; SiCE; Sonn; TrGrPo
So oft as I with state of present time. Prologue. Spenser. *Fr.* The Faerie Queene, V. PoFS
So oft our hearts, belovèd lute. Dream and the Song. James David Corrothers. BANP
So often we praise our mothers here and merit all their ways. Dear Old Dad. Eva Gilbert Shaver. STF
So on he fares, and to the border comes. Satan Discovers Eden. Milton. *Fr.* Paradise Lost, IV. ExPo
So, on the bloody sand, Sohrab lay dead. Matthew Arnold. *Fr.* Sohrab and Rustum. GTBS-P; PeVV
So once again the trouble's o'er. The Matron-Cat's Song. Ruth Pitter. MemP
So Paradise was brightened, so 'twas blest. To Philomela. Benjamin Colman. SCAP
So pass my Days. But when Nocturnal Shades. The Thirsty Poet. John Philips. *Fr.* The Splendid Shilling. OBEC
So passed the morning away. The Church Scene. Longfellow. *Fr.* Evangeline. TreF
So passed they naked on, nor shunned the sight. Adam and Eve [or Hail, Wedded Love]. Milton. *Fr.* Paradise Lost, IV, HW; SeCePo
So passeth, in the passing of a day. The Song. Spenser. *Fr.* The Faerie Queene, II, 12. MyFE
So, passing through the rustic gate. The Burnt Bridge. Louis MacNeice SiSw
So Pleasant It Is to Have Money. Arthur Hugh Clough. *Fr.* Dipsychus. SeCePo
So poor old Prunes has cashed in.—Too bad. Me and Prunes. Rupe Sherwood. PoOW
So prayis me as ye think caus quhy. Remeidis of Luve. *Unknown.* OxBS
So questioning, I was bold to dare. The Shape God Wears. Sara Henderson Hay. GoTP
So Quick, So Hot [So Mad Is Thy Fond Sute]. Thomas Campion. NCEP; PoEL-2
So quickly to have lost the summertime. Mint by Night. Alfred Barrett. JKCP (1955 ed.)
So Quietly. Leslie Pinckney Hill. BANP; IDB
So Ranolf felt when over wood and wild. Alfred Domett. *Fr.* Ranolf and Amohia. AnNZ
So rare, so mere. Presence of Snow. Melville Cane. GoYe
So Red the Rose. Omar Khayyám, *tr. fr. Persian by* Edward Fitzgerald. *Fr.* The Rubáiyát. OnPM
("I sometimes think that never blows so red.") EG; InP; LO
So rest, forever rest, O princely pair! The Tomb. Matthew Arnold. *Fr.* The Church of Brou. PoVP
So restless Cromwell could not cease. Andrew Marvell. *Fr.* A Horatian Ode upon Cromwell. ViBoPo
So Runs Our Song. Mary Eva Kitchel. ChIP; PGD
So sang he: and as meeting rose and rose. Willowwood, 4. Dante Gabriel Rossetti. The House of Life, LII. MaVP; OAEP; PoVP; ViPo; VP
So sang I in the springtime of my years. Morton Luce. Thysia, XXXVI. HBV
So sang the hierarchies: meanwhile the Son. The First Day of Creation. Milton. *Fr.* Paradise Lost, VII. OxBoCh
So sat the Muses on the banks of Thames. Caelia, IV. William Browne. Sonn

So Satan spake, and him Beelzebub. The Council of Satan. Milton. *Fr.* Paradise Lost, I. PoEL-3
"So say the foolish! Say the foolish so, Love?" Poetics. Robert Browning. PoVP
So Separate and Strange. Felix Stefanile. FiSC
So shall I live, supposing thou art true. Sonnets, XCIII. Shakespeare. InvP; MasP
So shall it ever be. As Thy Days. Grant Colfax Tullar. BLRP
So shalt thou come to a court as clear as the sun. The Palace of Truth. *At. to* William Langland. *Fr.* The Vision of Piers Plowman. ACP
So she became a bird and bird-like danced. Procne. Peter Quennell. ChMP; FaBoMo; GTBS-W; LiTB; LiTM; MoBrPo
So she was gently glad to see him laid. Keats. *Fr.* Endymion. BoPe
So she went into the garden. The Great Panjandrum [Himself]. Samuel Foote. FaBoCh; LoGBV; MoShBr; Par; PoLF; RIS; WhC
So shoots a star as doth my mistress glide. Sonnet. John Davies of Hereford. ElL; Sonn
So short the road from Bethlehem. "The Way." Leslie Savage Clark. PGD
So Shuts the Marigold Her Leaves ("Marina's gone. . ."). William Browne. *See* Memory ("Marina's gone. . .").
So shuts the marigold her leaves. Memory [*or* Since She Is Gone]. William Browne. *Fr.* Britannia's Pastorals. EG; LiTL; OBEV; ViBoPo
So Shy Shy Shy (and with a). E. E. Cummings. TPM
So, sick at heart, we watched the piccanins. Outside Kimberley. N. H. Brettell. BoSA
So sleep undoes itself and I arrive. For My Twenty-fifth Birthday in Nineteen Forty-one. John Ciardi. WaP
So Sleeps My Love. *Unknown.* TrGrPo
("Sleep, wayward thoughts, and rest you with my love.") EG; ReEn
So Slow to Die. George Edward Woodberry. Wild Eden, XXXVIII. AA
So slowly you walk, and so quickly you eat. To a Slow Walker and Quick Eater. Gotthold Ephraim Lessing. BOHV
So smell those odours that do rise. To the Most Fair and Lovely Mistress, Anne Soame, Now Lady Abdie. Robert Herrick. AtBAP; ViBoPo
So smile the heavens upon this holy act. Friar Laurence's Cell. Shakespeare. Romeo and Juliet, II, vi. GoBC
So smooth and clear the Fountain was. To a Lady Sitting before Her Glass. Elijah Fenton. OBEC
So smooth, so sweet, so silvery [*or* silv'ry] is thy voice. Upon Julia's Voice. Robert Herrick. AtBAP; BoW; CABA; CBV; ExPo; MyFE; PoeP; SeCePo; SeCL; SeCP
So, So. William Clerke. ELP
(Song: "So so,/ Lo, lilies fade before the roses fade.") SeCL
So, so, break[e] off this last lamenting kiss[e]. The Expiration. John Donne. AtBAP; ATP; CBEP; EG; ElL; MaMe; MBW-1; MeLP; MePo; SCEP-1; SeCP
So, so; I feel the signal. Malzah and the Angel Zalehtha. Charles Heavysege. *Fr.* Saul. VA
So soberly and softly. Nature No Self-Acting Instrument. Elizabeth Rundle Charles. SoP
So soft and gentle falls the rain. Rain in the Spring. "Gabriel Setoun." PPL
So soft in the hemlock wood. Pastoral. Robert Hillyer. MAP; MoAmPo
So soft streams meet, so springs with gladder smiles. The Welcome to Sack. Robert Herrick. AnAnS-2; SCEP-2; SeCP; SeCV-1
So soon as day, forth dawn from the East. Artegall and Radigund. Spenser. *Fr.* The Faerie Queene, V, 5 OBSC
So soon my body will have gone. Immortal. Sara Teasdale. WGRP
So spake our Mother Eve, and Adam heard. The Banishment. Milton. *Fr.* Paradise Lost, XII. OBS
So spake the archangel Michael; then paused. Milton. *Fr.* Paradise Lost, XII. EnL; MBW-1
So spake the Enemy of mankind, enclosed. Eve's Temptation and Fall. Milton. *Fr.* Paradise Lost, IX. DiPo
So still. The Stillness. Basho. RePo
So still the night swinging. Mariners' Carol. W. S. Merwin. EaLo; PoDB
So Still the World. Gerald Bullett. *Fr.* Winter Solstice. POTE
So stood [of old] the holy Christ. The Healer. Whittier. MaRV; PGD; SoP
So straight, so slender, and so tall. The Heaven's Mould. William Cavendish, Duke of Newcastle. LO; SeCL
So summer comes in the end to these few stains. The Beginning. Wallace Stevens. TPM
So Sweet a Kiss. Shakespeare. *Fr.* Love's Labour's Lost, IV, iii. ElL; InvP
So Sweet Is She. Ben Jonson. *See* Have You Seen a Bright Lily Grow.
So sweet is thy discourse to me. Thomas Campion. SiCE
So Sweet Love Seemed [That April Morn]. Robert Bridges. EG; EnLit; EPN; FaBV; GTSL; HBV; LiTL; PoVP; VA
So sweet, so sweet the roses in their blowing. In June. Nora Perry. YeAR
So sweet the plum trees smell! Plum Trees [*or* Plum Blossoms]. Ranko. FaPON; MPB; SoPo; SUS
So swete a kis yistrene fra thee I reft. To His Maistres. Alexander Montgomerie. OxBS
So swift to bloom, so soon to pass, Love's flower! Ulysses Returns, II. Roselle Mercier Montgomery. HBMV
So take a happy view. A Happy View. C. Day Lewis. CMoP
So talked the spirted sly snake; and Eve. Milton. *Fr.* Paradise Lost, IX. EnL
So tall she is, and slender, and so fair. The Poet Describes His Love. Robert Nathan. HBMV
So tame, so languid looks this drowsing sea. Calm. Stanton A. Coblentz. EtS
So That Even a Lover. Louis Zukofsky. CoPo
So that soldierly legend is still on its journey. Kearney at Seven Pines. Edmund Clarence Stedman. AA; DD; HBV; HBVY; MC; OTPC (1923 ed.); PaA; PAH; PAP
So that the vines burst from my fingers. Canto XVII. Ezra Pound. ExPo; LoBV; NAMP; OBMV; Po; ReMP
So That Women Will Talk to Trees. William Hunt. YAP
So that's Cleopathera's Needle, bedad. Reflections on Cleopathera's Needle. Cormac O'Leary. BOHV
So That's Who I Remind Me Of. Ogden Nash. PoLF
So that's your diary—that's your private mind. On Reading the War Diary of a Defunct Ambassador. Siegfried Sassoon. CMoP
So, the All-great were the All-loving too. The All-loving. Robert Browning. *Fr.* An Epistle Containing the Strange Medical Experience of Karshish, the Arab Physician. ChIP; MaRV; OQP; TRV
So the church Christ was hit and buried. Le Christianisme. Wilfred Owen. BrPo
So the committee met again, and again. The Committee. C. Day Lewis. CMoP
So the distances are Galatea. The Distances. Charles Olson. NeAP
So the eyes accost and sunder. Emily Dickinson. CoBA
"So the foemen have fired the gate, men of mine." The Knight's Leap. Charles Kingsley. PCD; StPo
So the last day's come at last, the close of my fifteen year. The Old Place (New Zealand). Blanche Edith Baughan. AnNZ; BoAu
So the long absent winter sun. A Short Visit. *Unknown.* SeCL
So the man spread his blanket on the field. A Tall Man Executes a Jig. Irving Layton. MoCV; PoCh
So, the powder's low, and the larder's clean. The Last Cup of Canary. Helen Gray Cone. AA; PFY
So the red Indian, by Ontario's side. Lords of the Wilderness. John Leyden. OBRV
So the silver-feathered swan. Song to a Viol. Jasper Fisher. *Fr.* Fuimus Troes. LO; SeCL; SeEP; TuPP
So the soldier replied to the poet. The Volunteer's Reply to the Poet. Roy Campbell. *Fr.* Talking Bronco. ViBoPo (1958 ed.)
So the wind blew all that night. A Bucket of Bees. David McCord. MAP; MoAmPo (1942 ed.)
So, the year's done with! Love. Robert Browning. *Fr.* Earth's Immortalities. EnLoPo; PoVP
So then, at last, let me awake this sleep. Purpose. Langdon Elwyn Mitchell. *Fr.* To a Writer of the Day. AA
So Then, I Feel Not Deeply! Walter Savage Landor. EnRP; EPN
So, then, we were no new device at all. America. Donald C. Babcock. NePoAm

"So then you won't fight?" Dooley Is a Traitor. James Michie. NePoEA-2
So there stood Matthew Arnold and this girl. The Dover Bitch. Anthony Hecht. CBV; NePoEA-2; PP
"So there we were stuck." The Life of. . . Theodore Weiss. NYBP
So, there, when sunset made the downs look new. Charles Hamilton Sorley. *Fr.* Marlborough. WGRP
So there you lie. In a Museum. Anne Elizabeth Wilson. CIV
So these two faced each other there. A Portrait in the Guards. Laurence Whistler. GTBS-P
So. They and I are back from the outside. Requiem. Carl Bode. ToPo
So they begin. With two years gone. Poem. Boris Pasternak. TrJP
So they came riding. The Warrior Bards. Henry Treece. ML
So they carried the dead man out of the fighting. Patroclus' Body Saved. Homer. *Fr.* The Iliad. XVII. WaaP
So they in Heav'n their Odes and Vigils tun'd. The Messiah. Milton. *Fr.* Paradise Regained, I. OBS
"So they went deeper into the forest," said Jacob Grimm. Deeper into the Forest. Roy Daniells. TwCaPo
So they were married, and lived/ Happily for ever? Marriage of Two. C. Day Lewis. ChMP
So they *will* have it! Sumter. Henry Howard Brownell. MC; PaA; PAH
So they would go a long while in the solid dark. David Jones. In Parenthesis, III. FlW
So This Is Autumn. W. W. Watt. OTD; PoPl
So this is life, the ranger said. Optimism. Blanaid Salkeld. NeIP
So this is life, this world with all its pleasures. By Life, or by Death. Will H. Houghton. SoP
So This Is Middle Age! Francis Whiting Hatch. WhC
So this is the red? Tanka, V. Lewis Alexander. CDC
So tho' our Daystar from our sight be taken. The Saints (St. Paul). F. W. H. Myers. *Fr.* Saint Paul. BoC
So thou art come again, old black-winged Night. To Night. Thomas Lovell Beddoes. LoBV; Sonn
So thou hast left us and our meadows. Ascension Day. Sheila Kaye-Smith. CAW
So through the darkness and the cold we flew. Skating. Wordsworth. *Fr.* The Prelude, I. CH; SD
So through the sun-laced woods they went. The Sphere of Glass. John Lehmann. ChMP
So thy rare virtues fixed in mine eyes. In Caium. Thomas Bastard. SiCE
So Tir'd Are All My Thoughts. Thomas Campion. LoBV
So to Fatness Come. Stevie Smith. PoG
So to his perch appropriate with owls. Alexander Pope at Stanton Harcourt. Sidney Keyes. *Fr.* Sour Land. FaBoTw
So to Sion's hill there come up together. The Human Race Comes to Be Judged. Cynewulf. *Fr.* Christ. PoLi
So to the sea we came; the sea, that is. Her Heards Be Thousand Fishes. Spenser. *Fr.* Colin Clout's Come Home Again. ChTr
So Unwarely Was Never No Man Caught. Sir Thomas Wyatt. FCP; NoP; SiPS
So up and up they journeyed, and ever as they went. Sigurd's Ride. William Morris. *Fr.* The Story of Sigurd the Volsung. NBM
So very like a painter drew. The Painter Who Pleased Nobody and Everybody. John Gay. CEP
So Wags the World. Ellen Mackay Hutchinson Cortissoz. AA
So was He framed; and such his course of life. Margaret; or, The Ruined Cottage. Wordsworth. *Fr.* The Excursion. EnRP
So was it even then. So soundlessly. A Trysting. Richard Dehmel. AWP
So wayward is the wind tonight. Wind in the Dusk [*or* The Wind]. Harold Monro. NeMA; OBVV
So we ride, and ride through milked heaven. Rides. Gene Derwood. LiTM; NePA
So we set signs over the world to say. Bell Buoy. W. S. Merwin. OPoP
So we some antique hero's strength. On the Head of a Stag. Edmund Waller. Po
So we who've supped the self-same cup. After the Quarrel. Paul Laurence Dunbar. CDC
So We'll Go No More a-Roving. Byron. AnFE; AtBAP; AWP; BEL; BoW; BWP; CaFP; CBV; EG; ELP; EnL; EnLi-2; EnRP; EPN; ERoP-2; ExPo; FaBoEn; FaFP; FaPL; FiP; HoPM; ILP; InPo; JAWP; LiTB; LO; LoBV; MaPo; MBW-2; MERP; MyFE; NoP; OAEP; OBRV; OxBS; PAn; PeER; PG (1955 ed.); Po; PoEL-4; PoIE; PoRA; PoSa; SeCeV; ShBV-3; TOP; TreFS; ViBoPo; WBP; WHA; YAT
(So Late into the Night.) WiR
(Song.) BoLP; EnLoPo
(We'll Go No More a-Roving.) ATP; CBEP; CH; DiPo; FaBV; HBV; MemP; MeWo; OBEV; OnPM; OtMeF; PoFS; PoG; PoLF; TrGrPo
So Well I Love Thee. Michael Drayton. EnRePo; FaPL
(Looking-Glass, The.) CLwM
So well that I can live without. Emily Dickinson. CoBA
So what do you do? What. How the Friends Met. James Tate. PIA
So what said the others and the sun went down. Mrs. Alfred Uruguay. Wallace Stevens. AP; MoPo; NePA; TwCP
So when the old delight is born anew. Immortality. Frederic William Henry Myers. VA
So when the Queen of Love rose from the seas. To a Very Young Gentleman at a Dancing-School. Elizabeth Rowe. SeCL; SeEP
So when the shadows laid asleep. The Kingfisher. Andrew Marvell. *Fr.* Upon Appleton House. AtBAP; FaBoEn
So where have you been, my good old man? Where Have You Been, My Good Old Man? *Unknown.* OuSiCo
So White, So Soft, So Sweet. Ben Jonson. *See* Have You Seen a Bright Lily Grow.
So wild yet candle-calm. The Grave's Cherub. Sydney Clouts. PeSA
So, with the wan waste grasses on my spear. G. K. Chesterton. *Fr.* The Wild Knight. MaRV
So, without overt breach, we fall apart. Estrangement. Sir William Watson. MoBrPo (1942 ed.)
So work the honey-bees. The Commonwealth of the Bees. Shakespeare. *Fr.* King Henry V, I, ii. GN
So ye're runnin' fer Congress, mister? le' me tell ye 'bout my son. Whisperin' Bill. Irving Bacheller. PoLF
So you are gone, and are proved bad change, as we had always known. Address Not Known. John Heath-Stubbs. ChMP
So you are gone, dear Chalse! Chalse a Killey. Thomas Edward Brown. PoVP
So you are married, girl. It makes me sad. Epithalamium. Roy McFadden. NeIP
So you beg for a story, my darling, my brown-eyed Leopold. How He Saved St. Michael's. Mary A. P. Stansbury. BLPA
So you came/ with a hyacinth, a poem and a thousand kisses. Meeting. Sam Harrison. NeIP
So you go back—because they bid you come. Sonnets of a Portrait Painter, XXXVI. Arthur Davison Ficke. AnAmPo
So you think it is all a matter of love? Venus' Speech. Louis MacNeice. CMoP
So Young ane King. Sir David Lindsay. SeCePo
So you're back from your travels, old fellow. The Return of Belisarius; Mud Flat, 1860. Bret Harte. IHA
So, you're stretched on the planks, you schemer. The Nails. Charles Wharton Stork. StJW
So, you've come to the tropics, heard all you had to do. Down and Out. Clarence Leonard Hay. BeLS; BLPA
So zestfully canst thou sing? The Blinded Bird. Thomas Hardy. AnFE; CMoP; EaLo; LiTM (rev. ed.); PAn; VP
Soak your lungs with wine, for now. Two Drinking Songs. Alcaeus. LiTW
Soap is green. Ilo Orleans. RIS
Soap, the Oppressor. Burges Johnson. PoLF
Soapship went a-rocking, A. The Voyage of Jimmy Poo. James A. Emanuel. AmNP; NNP; NYTB
Soar up, my soul, unto thy rest. Seek Flowers of Heaven. Robert Southwell. ReIE
Soaring hawk from fist that flies, The. The Lover Compareth Himself to the Painful Falconer. *Unknown.* EnPo
Sob, Heavy World. W. H. Auden. DTC
Sob of fall, and song of forest, come you here on haunting quest. The Trail to Lillooet. E. Pauline Johnson. CaP
Sober and gray the afternoon. Afternoon in the Tropics. Rubén Darío. LiTW
Social Future, The. John Kells Ingram. OnYI
Social Note. Dorothy Parker. BOHV
(Some Beautiful Letters: Social Note.) InMe

Society. George Meredith. EPN
Society in my head, The. The Sense of Responsibility. Harry Mathews. ANYP
Society upon the Stanislaus [*or* Stanislow], The. Bret Harte. AA; BeLS; BOHV; GSP; HBV; InMe; MaC; SiTL
Sockeye Salmon. Ronald Hambleton. CaP; OBCV; PeCV
Socrates' Ghost Must Haunt Me Now. Delmore Schwartz. AnFE; CoAnAm; LiTM; TwAmPo
Socrates Prays a Day and a Night. George O'Neil. AnAmPo
Socrates Snooks. Fitz Hugh Ludlow. BLPA
Socratic. Hilda Doolittle ("H. D."). AnEnPo; HoPM
Sod-Breaker, The. Arthur Stringer. CaP
Soda clock flange flume slim. Blue Kinds. Clark Coolidge. YAP
Sodden bumping of caisson wheels, The. Red Atlantis. John Haines. ThO
Sodenly Afraide. *Unknown.* *See* Suddenly Afraid.
Sodom. Chaim Grade, *tr. fr. Yiddish by* Joseph Leftwich. TrJP
Sodom. Herman Melville. *Fr.* Clarel. AmPP (5th ed.)
Sodoma's Christ Scourged. George Edward Woodberry. StJW
Soe I may gaine thy death, my life I'le give. Whosoever Shall Loose His Life. Richard Crashaw. MaMe
Soe, Mistress Anne, faire neighbour myne. Salem. Edmund Clarence Stedman. AA; PAH
Soe Phebus rose as if hee had last night. *Unknown.* SeCSL
Soe Well I Love Thee. Michael Drayton. AtBAP
(Last Verses.) FaBoEn
Soeur Marie Emilie. Caryll Houselander. BoC
Sofa, The. William Cowper. The Task, I. EiCP; NoP, *first* 209 *ll.*
Soffermati sull' arida sponda, *sel.* Alessandro Manzoni, *tr. fr. Italian by* Lorna de' Lucchi.
"With humble and discouraged mien." PoFr
Soft and pale is the moony beam. Joseph Rodman Drake. *Fr.* The Culprit Fay. PFY
Soft and pure fell the snow. Infant Spring. Fredegond Shove. HBMV
Soft answer turneth away wrath, A. The Lips of the Wise [*or* A Merry Heart]. Proverbs, Bible, *O.T.* StVeCh; TiPo (1952 ed.); TrGrPo
Soft Answers. Robert Bagg. UnTE
Soft as the bed in the earth. The Shadow. William Carlos Williams. NP
Soft as the voice, as the voice of a/ Zephyr. Hope. *Unknown.* MaRV
Soft as the wind your hair. Love Song. Joseph Gordon Macleod. NeBP; OnHM
Soft calls/ Hello, yes it is. The Claes Oldenburg Story. Lewis Mac Adams. YAP
Soft child of love, thou balmy bliss. To a Kiss. "Peter Pindar." HBV
Soft crying of the dawn while cockatoos. 'Morning, Morning. Ray Mathew. PoAu-2
Soft Day, A. Winifred M. Letts. AnIV; OnYI
Soft deceit & idleness. Blake. EiCL
Soft fall the February snows, and soft. Bereavement of the Fields. Wilfred Campbell. CaP
Soft falls the night. Evening Song. Edith King. BoTP
Soft floods of moonlight. Dominion. Martha Snell Nicholson. FaChP
Soft from the linden's bough. A Legend of the Dove. George Sterling. NP
Soft, gray buds on the willow. The Turn of the Road. Alice Rollit Coe. HBV
Soft gray hands of sleep, The. Forgotten Dreams. Edward Silvera. PoNe
Soft hangs the opiate in the brain. An Opium Fantasy. Maria White Lowell. AnFE; APA; CoAnAm
Soft is the collied night, and cool. Summer Song II. George Barker. ToPo
Soft Job. William C. Summers. STF
Soft Letter. Peter Schjeldahl. YAP
Soft light from a stable door, The. Never Night Again. Lilian Cox. ChIP; MaRV
Soft lights, the companionship, the beers, The. The Pick-up. J. V. Cunningham. UnTE
Soft little hands that stray and clutch. Little Hands. Laurence Binyon. HBV; MaRV
Soft, lovely, rose-like lips, conjoined with mine. Barnabe Barnes. *Fr.* Parthenophil and Parthenophe. EnLoPo
Soft malice of the silence. Per Amica Silentia Lunae. Ronald de Carvalho. LiTW
Soft-Man 1. Ed Sanders. ANYP
Soft-Man 3. Ed Sanders. ANYP
Soft Musick. Robert Herrick. SeEP
Soft new grass is creeping o'er the graves, The. By the Potomac. Thomas Bailey Aldrich. PAH; Sonn
Soft on the sunset sky. Ashes of Roses. Elaine Goodale Eastman. AA; HBV
Soft Rain. Sophia Castro-Leon. QAH
Soft-sandalled twilight, handmaid of the night. Winter Twilight. George Tracy Elliot. AA
"Soft Sell." Lorna Beers. FiSC
Soft sleep, profoundly pleasing power. Ode to Sleep. Tobias George Smollett. WaPE
Soft Snow. Blake. AtBAP; BoW; CBV; ERoP-1
Soft! what light through yonder window breaks? A Shakespeare Gallery: Juliet. Shakespeare. *Fr.* Romeo and Juliet, II, ii. MaC
Soft, where the shadow glides. Autumnal. James Wright. TPM
Soft Wood. Robert Lowell. LiTM (1970 ed.); NoP
Soft you; a word or two before you go. Death of Othello [*or* Othello's Farewell]. Shakespeare. *Fr.* Othello, V, ii. FiP; TreFS
Soft-throated South, breathing of summer's ease. South-Wind. George Parsons Lathrop. AA
Softë season, that bud and bloom forth brings, The. Spring. Earl of Surrey. CBEP
Softening of her face which comes, The. At Only That Moment. Alan Ross. ErPo
Softer than silence, stiller than still air. The Snowing of the Pines. Thomas Wentworth Higginson. AA; GN
Softest whisperings of the scented South, The. An Old Battle-Field. Frank L. Stanton. OQP
Softly along the road at evening. Nod. Walter de la Mare. AtBAP; BoLiVe; BoTP; EnLit; GoTP; HBMV; MoAB; MoBrPo; ThWaDe; TSW
Softly and gently, dearly-ransom'd soul. Angel. Cardinal Newman. *Fr.* The Dream of Gerontius. OxBoCh
Softly and humbly to the Gulf of Arabs. Beach Burial. Kenneth Slessor. BoAV; MoAuPo; PoAu-2
Softly at dawn a whisper stole. Spring Song. William Griffith. MPB
Softly blow lightly. Nocturne. Donald Jeffrey Hayes. CDC
Softly, drowsily. Walter de la Mare. *Fr.* A Child's Day. SoPo; StVeCh; SUS; TiPo (1952 ed.)
Softly I closed the book as in a dream. The Book. Winfred Ernest Garrison. OQP; TRV
Softly, in the dusk, a woman is singing to me. Piano. D. H. Lawrence. BWP; CBEP; CBV; CMoP; GTBS-P; InvP; LiTB; MoAB; MoBrPo; MuSP; NeMA; NoP; OAEP (2d ed.); PoE; PoIE; UnPo (3d ed.); VaPo
Softly, let the measure break. Harp Music. Rolfe Humphries. UnS
Softly now the burn is rushing. Lullaby. Seumas MacManus. AnIV; BOL
Softly Now the Light of Day. George Washington Doane. TreFS
(Evening.) AA; HBV; SoP
(Evening Contemplation.) BLPA; FaBoBe; NeHB
Softly, O midnight hours! Serenade [*or* Song]. Aubrey Thomas De Vere. IrPN; HBV; OBEV
Softly rustled the oaks, whispered low in my ear. The Graveyard. Hayyim Nahman Bialik. TrJP
Softly! She is lying. Dirge. Charles Gamage Eastman. AA
Softly sighs the April air. Bel m'es quan lo vens m'alena. Arnaut Daniel. AWP; JAWP; LiTW; WBP
Softly sinking through the snow. Roses' Song. Philip Bourke Marston. *Fr.* Garden Fairies. VA
Softly, softly, through the darkness. Christmas Night. B. E. Milner. BoTP
Softly the car goes with the music in it. Mollesse. Josephine Jacobsen. NePoAm-2
Softly the day dies out behind the pines. Evening Landscape. Pol de Mont. LiTW
Softly the dews upon my forehead light. Stars as Spray. *Unknown.* OnPM
Softly the waters ripple. Ares. Albert Ehrenstein. TrJP

Softly through the Mellow Starlight. *Unknown.* OHIP; PoRL
Softly Woo Away Her Breath. "Barry Cornwall." HBV
Soggarth Aroon. John Banim. GoBC; VA
Sohrab and Rustum. Matthew Arnold. BEL; CABL; DTo; EPN; MaVP; PoVP; ShBV-2, *abr.*; TOP; ViPo; ViPP; VP
Sels.
Combat, The. VA
Oxus ("But the majestic river floated on"). VA
"So, on the bloody sand, Sohrab lay dead." GTBS-P; PeVV
Sohrab's Death. WHA
(Death of Sohrab, The, *shorter sel.*) FiP
"Then, at the point of death, Sohrab replied." MBW-2
Soil is quick with dust of men, The. What Far Kingdom. Arthur S. Bourinot. CaP
Soil now gets a rumpling soft and damp, The. The Strong Are Saying Nothing. Robert Frost. CMoP; NoP; PoDB; PoE
Soil of man's escape, The. Suburbia. Maurice Martinez. PoNe (1970 ed.)
Soil ysowpit into water wak, The. Winter. Gawin Douglas. *Fr.* Prologues to the Aeneid. SeCePo
Soiled city oblongs stand sprawling, The. City Number. Carl Sandburg. OCS
Soiree. Ezra Pound. DTC
Sois sage, o ma douleur. Baudelaire, *tr. fr. French by* Lord Alfred Douglas. AWP; JAWP; WBP
Sojourn in the Whale. Marianne Moore. PoIE
Sojourners, The. Emmett Jarrett. *Fr.* Design for the City of Man. ThO
Sojourning alone in Paris. Straining. Kathleen Spivack. YAP
Sol, Bronze Age come first Sol. The Windows of Waltham. John Wieners. CoPo
Solace. Clarissa Scott Delany. AmNP; CDC; PoNe
Solace in Age. Sir Richard Maitland. OxBS
Solace to my Thoughts. *Unknown.* MuSP
Solar Creation. Charles Madge. FaBoMo; OBMV
Solar Myth. Genevieve Taggard. MAP; MoAmPo
Solar Road, The. Francis Carlin. JKCP
Soldier, The, *sels.* Conrad Aiken.
I. The Wars. WaaP
II. The Unknown Soldier. WaaP; WaP
Soldier, The. Rupert Brooke. AnFE; BBV; BEL; BoLiVe; BrPo; CBV; EnLit; EPN; ExPo; FaBoEn; FaBV; FaFP; FaPL; GTBS; GTBS-W; GTSL; InP; LiTB; LiTM; MaC; MaRV; MCCG; MoBrPo; MoVE; NeHB; NeMA; OBEV (new ed.); OTPC (1946 ed.); PoLF; PoMa; PoPl; PoPo; PoRA; POTE; ShBV-3; Sonn; TOP; TreF; TrGrPo; ViBoPo; WaP; WHA; YT
(1914.) HBV; NP
(Soldier, The, 1914-1918.) BoC
Soldier, A. Robert Frost. CBV; ILP; MoPo; NePA; PoPo; SeCeV; ThLM; WaaP; WaP
Soldier, The. Gerard Manley Hopkins. WaaP
Soldier, The. Uys Krige, *tr. fr. Afrikaans by* Uys Krige. PeSA
Soldier, A. Sir John Suckling. SeCV-1
Soldier, A ("In obedience to the imperial command"). *Unknown, tr. fr. Japanese by* Ishii *and* Obata. OnPM
Soldier and a Sailor, A. Congreve. *Fr.* Love for Love. CoMu
(Buxom Joan.) BOHV; InMe
(Song: "Soldier and a sailor, A.") OAEP
Soldier and a Scholar, A, *sel.* Swift.
"Thus spoke to my Lady the Knight full of care." OBEC
Soldier and singer of Erin. In Memoriam; Francis Ledwidge. Norreys Jephson O'Conor. HBMV
Soldier and statesman, rarest unison. Washington [*or* Ours, and All Men's]. James Russell Lowell. *Fr.* Under the Old Elm. DD; GN; HH; MC; OHIP; OQP; OTPC; PAL; PEDC; PGD; RePo
Soldier and the Sailor, The, *with music.* *Unknown.* ShS
Soldier-Boy, The. William Maginn. *See* I Give My Soldier Boy a Blade.
Soldier Boy, The. Johan Ludvig Runeberg, *tr. fr. Swedish by* Charles W. Stork. WoL
Soldier brave, sailor true. *Unknown.* OxNR
Soldier-Dead. Gilbert Emery. PEDC
Soldier from Missouri, A, *with music.* *Unknown.* BFSS
Soldier from the Wars Returning. A. E. Housman. LiTB; OBMV
Soldier, A: His Prayer. Gerald Kersh. TreFS
(Soldier, The, 1939-1945.) BoC
Soldier I watch so proudly pass. In a London Terminus. John Lehmann. AtBAP
Soldier loves his rifle, The. Foxtrot from a Play. W. H. Auden. LiTM
Soldier, The, 1939-1945. Gerald Kersh. *See* Soldier, A: His Prayer.
Soldier of the Cromwell stamp, A. Heredity. Thomas Bailey Aldrich. AA; AnAmPo; MAP; PFY
Soldier of the cross, arise! Onward. Jared Bell Waterbury. SoP
Soldier of the Legion lay dying in Algiers, A. Bingen on the Rhine. Caroline Norton. BeLS; BLPA; HBV; NeHB; TreF; WBLP
Soldier of the Russians, A. A New Version. William James Lampton. BOHV
Soldier of the Silences, The. William Herschell. PEDC
"Soldier of the Union mustered out, A." A Nameless Grave. Longfellow. PoIE (1970 ed.)
Soldier of Weight, A. John Kendall. WhC
Soldier Overseas. Leonard Mann. BoAu
Soldier passed me in the freshly-fallen snow, A. To a Conscript of 1940. Sir Herbert Read. ChMP; ExPo; LiTB; LiTM; WaP
Soldier Poet, A. Rossiter Johnson. AA
"Soldier, Rest!" Robert J. Burdette. BOHV
(Russian and Turk.) NA
Soldier, Rest! [Thy Warfare O'er]. Sir Walter Scott. *Fr.* The Lady of the Lake, I. ATP (1935 ed.); AWP; BEL; CoBE; DD; EnLi-2; EnLit; EPN; GN; HBV; HBVY; HH; JAWP; MoShBr; OTPC (1946 ed.); PoRA; TOP; TreFS; TrGrPo; WaKn; WBP
(Song: "Soldier rest! thy warfare o'er.") OAEP; OBNC; OBRV
Soldier rode from east to west, The. The Soldier's Farewell. *Unknown.* BFSS
Soldier-Statesman Returns, The. Tu Fu, *tr. fr. Chinese by* Arthur Christy. OnPM
Soldier (T. P.). Randall Jarrell. WaP
Soldier, There Is a War [between the Mind]. Wallace Stevens. *Fr.* Notes toward a Supreme Fiction. LiTM (rev. ed.); NePA
Soldier Thought Dead Returns Home, The. *Unknown, tr. fr. Chinese by* Arthur Waley. *Fr.* Shi King. LiTW
Soldier to His Wife, A. Liu Chi, *tr. fr. Chinese by* Henry H. Hart. OnPM
Soldier; Twentieth Century. Isaac Rosenberg. ChMP; MMA
Soldier Walks under the Trees of the University, The. Randall Jarrell. OxBA; PoPl; WaP
Soldier, What Did You See? Don Blanding. BBV (1951 ed.); MaRV
Soldier, Won't You Marry Me? *Unknown.* OxBoLi
Soldiers. Maxwell Bodenheim. MAPA
Soldiers, The. Giuseppe Ungaretti, *tr. fr. Italian by* Glauco Cambon. OnPM
Soldiers are citizens of death's grey land. Dreamers. Siegfried Sassoon. BrPo; CMoP; HBMV; MCCG; MoBrPo; NeMA; Sonn
Soldiers are weapons of evil. Weapons of Evil. *Tr. by* Lin Yutang. *Fr.* Tao Teh King. MaRV
Soldiers, as we come to lay. More than Flowers We Have Brought. Nancy Byrd Turner. SiSoSe
Soldiers Bathing. F. T. Prince. ChMP; GTBS-P; LiTB; LiTM; MoBrPo (1962 ed.); MoVE; PeSA; WaP
Soldier's Death, A. Cyril Tourneur. *Fr.* The Atheist's Tragedy. SeCePo
Soldier's Death, The. Countess of Winchilsea. MemP; OtMeF
(Trail All Your Pikes [Dispirit Every Drum].) ExPo; StP
Soldier's Dirge. A. Elizabeth Harman. DD; HH
Soldier's Dove. James Forsyth. WaP
Soldier's Dream, The. Thomas Campbell. BeLS; EnRP; FaPL; GTBS; GTBS-D; GTBS-P; GTBS-W; GTSE; GTSL; HBV; MCCG; RoGo; TreFS
Soldier's Farewell, The. *with music.* *Unknown.* BFSS
Soldier's Farewell to Manchester. The. *Unknown.* CoMu
Soldiers fight by land and air. Ilo Orleans. RIS
Soldier's Friend, The. George Canning *and* John Hookham Frere. OBEC; Par
Soldiers fuzz the city in khaki confusion. Habana. Julian Bond. NNP
Soldier's Grave, A. John Albee. AA

Soldier's Grave. The. Henry D. Muir. OHIP
Soldiers have to fight and swear. Unequal Distribution. Samuel Hoffenstein. TrJP
Soldiers of Christ, arise. The Whole Armor. Charles Wesley. SoP
Soldiers of the Cross, Arise. William Walsham How. SoP
Soldier's Prayer, A. Robert Freeman. *See* Prayer: "White Captain of my soul, lead on."
Soldier's Song. David Campbell. BoAV; NeLNL
Soldier's Song. Goethe, *tr. fr. German by* Bayard Taylor. *Fr.* Faust. AWP
Soldier's Song. Tobias Hume. WiR
Soldier's Song, The. Peadar Kearney. OnYI
Soldier's Song. Sir Walter Scott. *Fr.* The Lady of the Lake, VI. NBM; ViBoPo
Soldier's Song, The ("I sing the praise of honored wars"). *Unknown.* ReEn; TuPP
Soldiers suddenly struck by love, The. In Postures That Call. Oscar Williams. WaP
Soldier's Wife, The. George Canning *and* John Hookham Frere. Par
Soldier's Wife, A. Li Po, *tr. fr. Chinese by* Henry H. Hart. OnPM
Soldier's Wife, The. Robert Southey. OBEC
Soldier's Wife to Her Husband. Liu Chi, *tr. fr. Chinese by* Henry H. Hart. OnPM
Soldier's Wound, The. Wallace Stevens. *See* How Red the Rose That Is the Soldier's Wound.
Sole listener, Duddon! to the breeze that played. The River Duddon, V. Wordsworth. EnLi-2
Sole Lord of Lords and very King of Kings. Sesostris. Lloyd Mifflin. AA; HBV
Sole positive of night! Ne Plus Ultra. Samuel Taylor Coleridge. ERoP-1
Sole thing I hate is Hate, The. Love and Hate. Longfellow. *Fr.* Christus; a Mystery. MaRV
Sole true something—This! In Limbo's den, The. Limbo. Samuel Taylor Coleridge. ERoP-1
Solemn and lovely visions and holy dreams. But My Neighbor Is My Treasure. Ruth Pitter. BoPe
Solemn and slow they move. The Sod-Breaker. Arthur Stringer. CaP
Solemn Conceit, A. Nicholas Breton. SiCE
Solemn he paced upon that schooner's deck. The Captain. John G. C. Brainard. EtS
Solemn Hour. Rainer Maria Rilke, *tr. fr. German by* C. F. MacIntyre. PoPl; TrJP
Solemn Meditation, A. Ruth Pitter. OxBoCh
Solemn Noon of Night, The. Thomas Warton, the Younger. *Fr.* The Pleasures of Melancholy. OBEC; SeCePo
Solemn Rondeau. Charles Dent Bell. OBVV
Solemn, solemn the coachman gets ready to go. To His Wife. Ch'in Chia. LiTW
Solemn thing—it was—I said, A. Emily Dickinson. AmePo
Solemn thing within the soul, A. Emily Dickinson. MWA-2
Solemn whip-poor-will, The. The Queens. Robert Fitzgerald. NYBP
Solemnly, mournfully,/ Dealing its dole. Curfew. Longfellow. AA; MCCG; OxBA; PCD; TDP
Soles Occidere et Redire Possunt, *sel.* Aldous Huxley.
"'Misery,' " he said, 'to have no chin,' " VIII. ViBoPo (1941 ed.)
Solid citizens, The. Undertow. Langston Hughes. LiTM (1970 ed.)
Solid ocean and the liquid land, The. The Planet. Carl Bode. ToPo
Soliloquy. Frederick E. Laight. *See* Drought.
Soliloquy. Francis Ledwidge. EnLit
Soliloquy. Dorothy C. Parrish. TNV
Soliloquy by the Shore. Martin Scholten. GoYe
Soliloquy from "Hamlet." Shakespeare. *See* To Be or Not to Be.
Soliloquy in an Air-Raid. Roy Fuller. LiTM
Soliloquy of a Tortoise on Revisting the Lettuce Beds after an Interval of One Hour While Supposed to Be Sleeping in a Clump of Blue Hollyhocks. E. V. Rieu. FiBHP
Soliloquy of a Water-Wagtail. James Montgomery. OTPC (1923 ed.)
Soliloquy of Lincoln before Manassas. Stephen Vincent Benét. *Fr.* John Brown's Body. PaA
Soliloquy of the Returned Gold Adventurer. *Unknown.* PoOW
Soliloquy of the Spanish Cloister. Robert Browning. ATP; BEL; BoLiVe; CABA; CaFP; CBV; DiPo; DTo; EnL; EnLi-2; EnLit; EPN; ExPo; ForPo; ILP; LiTB; MaVP; MBW-2; NoP; OAEP; OtMeF; PAn; PeVV; PIA; PoAn; PoE; PoIE; PoVP; SeCeV; ShBV-4; TDP; TOP; TrGrPo; UnPo (1st ed.); ViPo; ViPP; VP
Soliloquy on Death. F. K. Fiawoo. PBA
Soliloquy on Sleep. Shakespeare. *See* Cares of Majesty, The.
Soliloquy I. Richard Aldington. BrPo
Soliloquy to Absent Friends. D. G. Jones. MoCV
Soliloquy to Imogen, *sels.* Christopher Hassall. LO
"I heard a voice say 'Look into your heart.' "
"We danced/ Shyly, not speaking, more as partial friends."
Soliloquy II. Richard Aldington. BrPo; MMA
Solipsism. George Santayana. AnFE; APA; CoAnAm
Solitaire. Amy Lowell. LaNeLa; MAP; MAPA; MoAmPo; NeMA; NP
Solitariness. Sir Philip Sidney. *See* O Sweet Woods.
Solitary, The. Jason Miller. ThO
Solitary, The. Nietzsche, *tr. fr. German by* Ludwig Lewisohn. AWP
Solitary, The. Rainer Maria Rilke, *tr. fr. German by* C. F. MacIntyre. TrJP
Solitary, The. Sara Teasdale. MAP; MoAmPo; NeMA; WHA
Solitary, The. Wordsworth. *Fr.* The Excursion, II. EnRP
Solitary bird of night, The. Ode to Wisdom. Elizabeth Carter. OBEC
Solitary Confinement. X. J. Kennedy. NePoEA-2
Solitary egret, The. Early Morning. Philip Dow. QAH
Solitary-hearted, The. Hartley Coleridge. HBV; OBEV; OnPP (1st ed.)
Solitary Life, A. William Drummond of Hawthornden. *See* Thrice Happy He.
Solitary Lyre, The. George Darley. GTBS-W; LiTB; LiTG; OBEV (new ed.)
(Enchanted Lyre, The.) OBNC
(Lyre, The, 1.) OBVV
(Wherefore, Unlaurelled Boy.) ERoP-2; OBRV; PeER
Solitary Pine. Prince Ichihara, *tr. fr. Japanese by* Ishii *and* Obata. OnPM
Solitary Place, The. Carlton Buck. SoP
Solitary prospector, A. Sunstrike. Douglas Livingstone. PeSA
Solitary Reaper, The. Wordsworth. AnEnPo; AnFE; AtBAP; ATP; AWP; BEL; BoLiVe; BoPe; BWP; CABA; CaFP; CBEP; CBV; CH; ChER; CoBE; DiPo; EnL; EnLi-2; EnLit; EnRP; EPN; ERoP-1; ExPo; FaBoCh; FaBoEn; FiP; ForPo; GBV; GN; HBV; HoPM; ILP; InP; InPo; JAWP; LiTB; LiTG; LiTL; LoBV; MaPo; MBW-2; MCCG; MERP; NoP; OAEP; OBEV; OBNC; OBRV; OnPP; OTPC; OuHeWo; PAn; PCD; PoAn; PoE; PoEL-4; PoeP; PoFS; PoIE; PoRA; PoSa; PTK; RG; RoGo; SeCeV; ShBV-3; StP; TDP; ThWaDe; TOP; TreF; TrGrPo; UnPo; UnS; WBP; WHA; YAT
("Behold her, single in the field.") EG
(Reaper, The.) GTBS; GTBS-D; GTBS-P; GTBS-W; GTSE; GTSL
Solitary Shepherd's Song, The. Thomas Lodge. *See* Sonnet: "O shady vales. . ."
Solitary wayfarer! Hoopoe. George Darley. *Fr.* Nepenthe. OBNC; OBRV
Solitary Woodsman, The. Sir Charles G. D. Roberts. CaP; OBCV
Solitude. James Beattie. *Fr.* Retirement. OBEC
Solitude. John Clare. EnRP
Solitude. Walter de la Mare. CMoP; FaBoEn
Solitude. Babette Deutsch. HBMV
Solitude, *sel.* James Grainger. CEP; OBEC, *abr.*
Ode to Solitude ("O solitude, romantic maid"). ViBoPo
Solitude. Keats. EnRP
(O Solitude! If I Must with Thee Dwell.) MERP
Solitude. Archibald Lampman. BoNaP; CBEP; ExPo; OBCV; PeCV
Solitude, A. Denise Levertov. NePoEA-2
Solitude. Mary Mollineux. CavP
Solitude. Harold Monro. MoBrPo; StaSt; TrGrPo; TSW
Solitude. Hannah More. *Fr.* Search after Happiness. WBLP
Solitude. Cardinal Newman. SoP

Solitude. Frederick Peterson. AA
Solitude. Pope. *See* Ode on Solitude.
Solitude. Rainer Maria Rilke. *tr. fr. German.* OnPM, *tr. by* Jessie Lemont;TrJP, *tr. by* C. F. MacIntyre.
Solitude. Philip Henry Savage. AA
Solitude. Edward Rowland Sill. AnNE
Solitude. Thomas Traherne. OBS; SeEP
"I do believ," *sel.* FaBoEn
Solitude. Ella Wheeler Wilcox. AmePo; FaFP; HBV; OHFP; PaPo; PoLF; YaD
(Way of the World, The.) TreF; WBLP
Solitude and the Lily. Richard Henry Horne. OBVV; VA
Solitude is like rain. Solitude. Rainer Maria Rilke. TrJP
Solitude of Alexander Selkirk, The. William Cowper. *See* Verses Supposed to Be Written by Alexander Selkirk. . .
Solitude that unmakes me one of men. Compensation. Robinson Jeffers. MAP; MoAB; MoAmPo; NeMA
Solitudes. John Hall Wheelock. MoLP
Solo for Bent Spoon. Donald Finkel. NePoEA-2
Solo for Ear-Trumpet. Edith Sitwell. MoAB; MoBrPo; NeMA
Solomon. Hermann Hagedorn. GoBC
Solomon. Heine, *tr. fr. German by* Emma Lazarus. TrJP
Solomon. Matthew Prior. *See* Solomon on the Vanity of the World.
Solomon, *sels.* *Unknown.* WGRP
Inspiration, VI.
To Truth, XXXVIII.
Solomon and the Bees. John Godfrey Saxe. GN; GoTP; OTPC
Solomon, Clown, put by your crown. Conrad Aiken. *Fr.* Punch; the Immortal Liar. NP
Solomon Grundy/ Born on a Monday. Mother Goose. BiCB; HBV; HBVY; OTPC; OxBoLi; OxNR; PPL; RIS; SiTL; TreFT
Solomon Judges between Two Women Disputing over a Child. First Kings, III: 16-27, Bible, *O.T.* TreFT
Solomon on the Vanity of the World, *sels.* Matthew Prior.
Love and Reason, *fr.* Bk. II. OBEC
"Pass we the ills, which each man feels or dreads," *fr.* Bk. III. PoEL-3
(Power.) LoBV
"Ye sons of men, with just regard attend." EiCP
Solomon Pease. *Unknown.* WhC
Solomon to Sheba. W. B. Yeats. CMoP; ELP; GTBS-D
Solomon, where is thy throne? It is gone in the wind. Gone in the Wind. James Clarence Mangan. ACP; CAW; CBEP; GoBC; IrPN; MaRV; OBVV; OnYI; OxBI; PoLi; SeCePo
Solon's Song. Thomas D'Urfey. *See* Hunting Song.
Solsequium, The. Alexander Montgomerie. GoTS; OxBS
Solstice. Charles Weekes. OnYI
Solstices. Richard Church. POTE
Solstitium Saeculare. Robert Fitzgerald. MoVE
Solutions. Edmund Blunden. FaBoTw
Solvitur Acris Hiems. Francis Sylvester Mahony. IrPN
Solway Sands. Elizabeth Craigmyle. VA
Solyman and Almena, *sel.* John Langhorne.
Farewell Hymn to the Valley of Irwan, A. CEP
Som tyme this world was so stedfast and stable. *See* Sometime this world. . .
Sombre and rich, the skies. By the Statue of King Charles at Charing Cross. Lionel Johnson. BoC; BrPo; CoBE; HBV; JKCP; MoBrPo; NBM; OBEV (new ed.); OBMV; OBNC; OBVV; PeVV; PIA; PoEL-5; PoVP; RoGo; ShBV-4; ViPP
Sombre the night is. Returning, We Hear the Larks. Isaac Rosenberg. BrPo; FaBoMo; MMA; WaaP
Some act of Love's bound to rehearse. Why I Write Not of Love. Ben Jonson. EnLit; FosPo; OAEP; TuPP
Some ages hence, for it must not decay. Under a Lady's Picture. Edmund Waller. EnLoPo
Some are sick for spring and warm winds blowing. The Hound. Babette Deutsch. HBMV
Some are stout. Professors. Harold A. Larrabee. InMe
Some are teethed on a silver spoon. Saturday's Child. Countee Cullen. Kal; LiTM (1970 ed.); PoNe
Some are too difficult to win. Dinah. A. R. Ammons. PV
Some are too much at home in the role of wanderer. Poem. Denise Levertov. NeBP
Some asked [*or* ask'd] me where the rubies grew? The Rock of Rubies [*or* Rubies and Pearls *or* Julia]. Robert Herrick. HBV; InMe; OTPC (1923 ed.)
Some Beautiful Letters. Dorothy Parker. InMe
Comment. ALV
News Item. TreF; YaD
Observation. FiBHP
Résumé. ALV; WhC
Social Note. BoHV
Some Bird. *Unknown.* STF
Some blaze the precious beauties of their loves. John Davies of Hereford. Sonn
Some Blesseds. John Oxenham. WGRP
Some blind themselves, 'cause possibly they may. Reason, the Use of It in Divine Matters. Abraham Cowley. AnAnS-2
Some bloodied sea-bird's hovering decay. The Lie. Howard Moss. AtBAP; LiTM (1970 ed.); MoAB; NePoAm
Some Bombs, *sel.* Ron Padgett.
"Pied quarts of Chevrolets trim blent Sir her eyes on, The." ANYP
Some *bon vivant* of the heart might have come for her. "There'll Be Others but Non So for Me." Delmore Schwartz. FiMAP
Some books are lies frae end to end. Death and Doctor Hornbook. Robert Burns. OxBS
Some Brave, awake in you to-night. Fancy Dress. Siegfried Sassoon. BrPo
Some Brothers Cry. Alan Weeks. WSL
Some, by their monarch's fatal mercy grown. Lord Shaftesbury. Dryden. *Fr.* Absalom and Achitophel, Pt. I. LoBV
Some candle clear burns somewhere I come by. The Candle Indoors. Gerard Manley Hopkins. BWP; DiPo; FaBoMo; FlW; GTBS-W; LiTB; LiTM; OxBoCh; PoEL-5; ReMP; ViPP
Some children like gay weather. A Preference. John Farrar. GFA
Some children live in palaces. Other Children. Helen Wing. GFA; OTPC (1946 ed.)
Some clerks aver that as the tree doth fall. The Utmost. "Owen Meredith." VA
Some Contemplations of the Poor, and Desolate State of the Church at Deerfield. John Williams. SCAP
Some Cook! John Ciardi. PDV
Some cry up Haydn, some Mozart. Free Thoughts on Several Eminent Composers. Charles Lamb. MuSP; OBRV; OxBoLi
Some Day. *See* Someday.
Some days are fairy days. The minute that you wake. Sometimes. Rose Fyleman. SiSoSe
Some days I go with Daddy for a walk. Six and Thirty. D. E. Stevenson. BiCB
Some days my thoughts are just like cocoons. Days. Karle Wilson Baker. GFA; OQP; RePo; SP; TiPo
Some days, you say, are good days. Warp and Woof. Harry Halbisch. BLRP
Some die too late and some too soon. The Lost Occasion. Whittier. CoBA
Some doleful thing there is at hand. Egloga Quinta. Barnabe Googe. ReIE
Some dreams we have are nothing else but dreams. The Haunted House. Thomas Hood. AnEnPo
Some eat the countries; these are kings. *Unknown.* *Fr.* The Panchatantra. LiTW
Some Europeans. *Unknown.* SiTL
Some evening, when the forest is a mist. Song to Say a Farewell. Howard McKinley Corning. NP
Some evening when you are sitting alone. The White Dress. Humbert Wolfe. NP
Some Faith at Any Cost. Harriet Du Autermont. MaRV
Some Feathers. Dick Gallup. ANYP
Some fell away to westward with the wind. Caesar's Lost Transport Ships. Robert Frost. AmePo
Some Few, Some Very Few. "Luke." QAH
Some few yards from the hut the standing beeches. Poem in the Matukituki Valley. James K. Baxter. AnNZ
Some find love late, some find him soon. When Will Love Come? Pakenham Beatty. HBV
Some Fishy Nonsense. Laura E. Richards. SoPo; TiPo
Some Flowers o' the Spring. Shakespeare. *Fr.* The Winter's Tale, IV, iii. ChTr
Some folk like the chaffinch. The Robin. O. M. Bent. BoTP
Some folks are drunk, yet do not know it. An English Ballad, on the Taking of Namur by the King of Great Britain,

Some (continued)
1695. Matthew Prior. PoEL-3
Some folks as can afford. Under a Wiltshire Apple Tree. Anna Bunston de Bary. CH
Some Folks I Know. Samuel Hoffenstein. ALV
Some folks in looks take so much pride. *Unknown.* PoToHe (new ed.)
Some folks say dat de worry blues ain' bad. Dink's Blues. *Unknown.* ABF
Some fools keep ringing the dumb waiter bell. Chant Royal of the Dejected Dipsomaniac. Don Marquis. HBMV
Some for everyone. Snow by Morning. May Swenson. NYBP
Some for the glories of this world; and some. Prefer the Cash. Omar Khayyám, *tr. by* Edward Fitzgerald. *Fr.* The Rubáiyát. OnPM; PoPl
Some Foreign Letters. Anne Martin. MoAmPo (1962 ed.); PoCh; ToPo
Some fowls there be that have so perfect sight. How the Lover Perisheth in His Delight, As the Fly in the Fire. Sir Thomas Wyatt. FCP; Sonn
Some Friends. John Gill. ThO
Some from their income tithe the gross. Unpayable Debt. Barbara Drake Johnston. SoP
Some Future Day When What Is Now Is Not. Arthur Hugh Clough. Songs in Absence, VI. EPN
Some gain a universal fame. A Ballade of Lawn Tennis. Franklin P. Adams. SD
Some Geese. Oliver Herford. *See* Geese.
Some glory in their birth, some in their skill. Sonnets, XCI. Shakespeare. CBEP
Some gypsies are like her. The Ballad of Adam's First. Leland Davis. HBMV
Some had in courts been great, and thrown from thence. The Earl of Shaftesbury. Dryden. *Fr.* Absalom and Achitophel. FaBoEn StVeCh
Some hae meat and [*or* that] canna eat. A Child's Grace. Burns. BrR; FaBoCh; FaPON; LoGBV; MoShBr; MPB; PCH; PRWS; StVeCh
Some Hallucinations. "Lewis Carroll." *See* Gardener's Song, The.
Some hang above the tombs. On Such a Day. Mary Elizabeth Coleridge. GTBS-D; LO; MoVE
Some hearts go hungering thro' the world. Hungering Hearts. *Unknown.* PoToHe
Some hot, some cold. Thomas Campion. LO
Some in my speedy pace I must outrun. Dryden. *Fr.* Absalom and Achitophel, Pt. II. PIA
Some in the town go betimes to the Downs. The Hunt. *Unknown.* CoMu
Some innocent girlish kisses by a charm. Wild Rose. William Allingham. GN; OTPC
Some keep the Sabbath [*or* Sunday] going to church. Emily Dickinson. AmePo; CoBA; DiPo; MoAB; MoAmPo (1950 ed.); WGRP
Some Ladies. Frederick Locker-Lampson. BOHV; InP
Some ladies love the jewels in Love's zone. Love's Lovers. Dante Gabriel Rossetti. The House of Life, VIII. MaVP; PoVP; ViPo; VP
Some ladies now make pretty songs. Some Ladies. Frederick Locker-Lampson. BOHV; InP
Some lasses are nice and strange. The Innocent Country-Maid's Delight; or, A Description of the Lives of the Lasses of London. *Unknown.* CoMu
Some Late Lark Singing. W. E. Henley. *See* Margaritae Sorori.
Some laws there are too sacred for the hand. Liberty of the Press. Sir Aubrey De Vere. PoFr;
Some leaders lead too far ahead. Leaders. *Unknown.* WBLP
Some like drink. Not I. Robert Louis Stevenson. NA; WePo
"Some likes picturs o' women," said Bill, "an' some likes 'orses best." Pictures. Cicely Fox Smith. EtS
Some Lines in Three Parts. Peter Viereck. MiAP; MoAmPo (1950 ed.)
I. "One tawny paw is all it takes to squash."
II. "But 'I' being less than soul."
III. "What hubbub rocks the nest?"
Some lit theirs at both end. Despair. W. S. Merwin. AmPC
Some Litanies. Michael Benedikt. CoAP; TwCP; YAP
Some little boys get shushed all day. Mokie's Madrigal. Ronald McCuaig. NeLNL
Some Little Bug. Roy Atwell. BOHV; PoLF
"In these days of indigestion," *sel.* ShM
Some little mice sat in a barn to spin. *See* Six little mice. . .
Some look at nature for the surface: eye. Nature Lover. John Frederick Nims. CBV
Some love Marce and some love Venus. *Unknown.* SeCSL
Some lovers speak, when they their muses entertain. Astrophel and Stella, VI. Sir Philip Sidney. FCP; PIA; ReEn; ReIE; SiPS; Sonn; TuPP
Some lucky day each November great waves awake and are drawn. November Surf. Robinson Jeffers. CrMA; MoPo; NoP; OxBA
Some man unworthy to be possessor. Confined Love. John Donne. AnEnPo; MaMe; TuPP
Some may wish for city streets, jewels or silken gown. Wishes. A. C. Child. PoToHe
Some men are born, while others seem to grow. Great Oak. Bennet Chapple. HH
Some men break your heart in two. Experience. Dorothy Parker. BoLP; InMe; PoPl; WhC
Some men deem. Ideals. Robert Greene. PoToHe (new ed.)
Some men for sudden joy do weep. *Unknown.* SiCE
Some men live for warlike deeds. John James Audubon. Stephen Vincent Benét. ThLM
Some men marriage do commend. De Se. John Weever. TuPP
Some men there be which like my method well. Idea, XLII. Michael Drayton. SiCE; TuPP
Some Minutes in the Morning. *Unknown.* SoP
Some misbelieving and profane in love. To Miracle. Michael Drayton. Idea, XXXV. SiCE; TuPP
Some modest windfalls from the tree. Vacation Trip. Donald C. Babcock. NePoAm
Some morning I shall rise from sleep. The Last Voyage. Katharine Tynan. HBMV
Some Murmur When Their Sky Is Clear. Richard Chenevix Trench. HBVY; SoP
Some must delve when the dawn is nigh. The King of Dreams. Clinton Scollard. HBV
Some names there are of telling sound. The *Cumberland.* Herman Melville. PAH
Some Negatives: X. at the Chateau. James Merrill. NePoEA-2
Some night I think if you should walk with me. The Lover Praises His Lady's Bright Beauty. Shaemas O'Sheel. BoLP
Some night, John Carter, you will dream of hands. No Envy, John Carter. Merrill Moore. NeMA
Some of our dead are famous, but they would not care. W. H. Auden. *Fr.* Commentary. MoPo
Some of the hurts you have cured. *See* Some of your hurts you have cured.
Some of the roofs are plum-color. Not Three—but One. Esther Lillian Duff. HBMV
Some of their chiefs were princes of the land. Zimri. Dryden. *Fr.* Absalom and Achitophel, Pt. I. AnFE; AWP; InPo; JAWP; WBP
Some of Wordsworth. Walter Savage Landor. ChTr
Some of your [*or* the] hurts you have cured. Borrowing [*or* Needless Worry]. Emerson. *Fr.* Anxiety. MaRV; TreFT; WhC
Some officers take them away: good guard. Lear and Cordelia. Shakespeare. *Fr.* King Lear, V, iii. FiP
Some one. *See* Someone.
Some opulent force of genius, soul, and race. Abraham Lincoln. Joel Benton. DD
Some painters paint the sapphire sea. The Clean Platter. Ogden Nash. BOHV
Some passionate hour before my own deep stripe. To an Enemy. E. J. Pratt. MaRV
Some People. Rachel Field. FaPON; PDV
Some people hang portraits up. A Likeness. Robert Browning. CTC; PoVP
Some people, now like mountains, where the shafts. Horizontal World. Thomas Saunders. CaP
Some people say the world's all a stage. The Gate at the End of Things. *Unknown.* BLPA
Some people shave before bathing. And Three Hundred and Sixty-six in Leap Year. Ogden Nash. NePA

Some people think I think I'm good. Oh, if They Only Knew! Edith L. Mapes. BLRP; WBLP
Some people understand all about machinery. Up from the Wheelbarrow. Ogden Nash. FaBoBe
Some poets sing of sweethearts dead. Ballade of Forgotten Loves. Arthur Grissom. BOHV
Some praise the looks, and others praise the locks. Phyllis, XX. Thomas Lodge. Sonn
Some primal termite knocked on wood. The Termite. Ogden Nash. CenHV; PoPl; PoPo; ShM; WhC
Some prisoned moon in steep cloud-fastnesses. The Soul's Sphere. Dante Gabriel Rossetti. The House of Life, LXII. MaVP; PoVP; ViPo
Some Questions to Be Asked of a Rajah, Perhaps by the Associated Press. Preston Newman. FiBHP
Some rainbow shreds of hope and joy. Patchwork. Clinton Scollard. OQP
Some reckon their age by years. The Rosary of My Tears. Abram J. Ryan. HBV
Some Refrains at the Charles River. Peter Viereck. PoCh
Some say, compar'd to Bononcini. Epigram on [*or* on the Feuds between] Handel and Bononcini. Byrom. CBEP; CEP; MuSP; OBEC; UnS
Some say, good Will (which I in sport do sing). To Our English Terence, Mr. Will: Shakespeare. John Davies of Hereford. SiCE
Some say he's from Georgia. John Henry. *Unknown.* GoSl
Some say kissin's ae [*or* that kissing's a] sin. Kissin' [*or* Kissing's No Sin]. *Unknown.* BoLP; FiBHP; HBV; LiTG; LiTL; MeWo; SiTL; TreF; UnTE
Some say Love. Menaphon's Song. Robert Greene. *Fr.* Menaphon. LoBV; OBSC; ReIE
Some say my satires over-loosely flow. Joseph Hall. *Fr.* Virgidemiarum. SiCE
Some say no evil thing that walks by night. Milton. *Fr.* Comus. LO
Some say that ever 'gainst that season comes. The Gracious Time [*or* Christmas]. Shakespeare. *Fr.* Hamlet, I, i. ChIP; ChrBoLe; ChTr; GN; MaRV; TiPo (1952 ed.)
Some say that kissing's a sin. *See* Some say kissin's ae sin.
Some say the dead are lonely where they lie. Sonnets to My Mother. Arthur S. Bourinot. CaP
Some say the deil's deid. *Unknown.* FaBoCh; LoGBV
Some say the Phoenix dwells in Aethiopia. The Phoenix. Siegfried Sassoon. ChTr
Some say the sun is a golden earring. Natalia M. Belting. PDV
Some say the world will end by fire. Frostbite. Conrad Aiken. PoPo; SiTL
Some say the world will end in fire. Fire and Ice. Robert Frost. AmPP; AnFE; AnNE; APA; CABA; CaFP; CBV; CMoP; CoAnAm; CoBMV; DiPo; FaFP; GTBS-W; HBMV; ILP; LiTA; LiTM; MAP; MaPo (1969 ed.); MoAB; MoAmPo; MoVE; NePA; OnPM; OxBA; PoDB; PoeP; PoPl; PoPo; SiTL; TDP; TreFS; TrGrPo; TwAmPo; ViBoPo (1958 ed.); WePo; WHA; WoL
Some say we're bound for Liverpool. Heave Away. *Unknown.* SoAmSa
Some say, when nights are dry and clear. The Fatal Vision. Shelley. *Fr.* The Two Spirits. LO
Some say you dye your hair. But I deny it. To Chloe. *Unknown.* UnTE
Some seek a heaven for rest. Heaven. Edwin Hatch. MaRV
Some seek for ecstasies of joy. The One Thing Needful. Max Isaac Reich. BLRP
Some sit and stare. The Common Grave. James Dickey. CoAP
Some space beyond the garden close. The Hollyhocks. Craven Langstroth Betts. AA
Some speakis of lords, some speakis of lairds. *See* Sum speiks of lords, sum speiks of lairds.
Some Stories of the Beauty Wapiti. Ebbe Borregaard. NeAP
Some take to liquor, some turn to prayer. A La Carte. Kenneth Fearing. CMoP
Some talk of Alexander, and some of Hercules. The British Grenadiers. *Unknown.* CBEP; EiCL; HBV; OBEC; OxBoLi
Some tell us 'tis a burnin' shame. Sambo's Right to be Kilt. Charles Graham Halpine. AA
Some ten or twelve old friends of yours and mine. A Gentleman of Fifty Soliloquizes. Don Marquis. HBMV
Some ten or twenty times a day. Ballade of a Friar. Clement Marot. HBV
Some that have deeper digged [*or* digg'd] love's mine [*or* myne] than I. Love's Alchemy [*or* Alchymie]. John Donne. AnAnS-1; CABA; LiTL; MaMe; MePo; NoP; OAEP; ReEn; SCEP-1; SeCP; TuPP; ViBoPo
Some That Report. Thomas Watson. *Fr.* Hecatompathia; or, Passionate Century of Love. TuPP
Some, the great Adepts, found it. The Adepts. Lawrence Durrell. *Fr.* Eight Aspects of Melissa. ErPo; NeBP
Some there are as fair to see to. Her Commendation [*or* Madrigal]. Francis Davison. ElL; OBSC; TuPP
Some there are who are present at such occasions. On the Suicide of a Friend. Reed Whittemore. NMP
Some there be that sow the seed and reap the golden grain. The Mother. Sarah Louise Arnold. PEDC
Some they will talk of bold Robin Hood. Robin Hood and the Bishop of Hereford. *Unknown.* BaBo; ESPB; OBB
Some things a man must surely know. Recipe for Living. Alfred Grant Walton. PoToHe (new ed.)
Some things a man should tell his wife. *Unknown.* *Fr.* The Panchatantra. LiTW
Some things are hard to understand. God Is. Phyllis C. Michael. SoP
Some things are very dear to me. Sonnets, II. Gwendolyn B. Bennett. AmNP; BANP; CDC; PoNe
Some things go to sleep in such a funny way. How They Sleep. *Unknown.* PPL
Some things persist by suffering change, others. Homage to the Philosopher. Babette Deutsch. ImOP; TrJP
Some Things That Easter Brings. Elsie Parrish. PCH; SoPo
Some things that fly there be. Emily Dickinson. AmP; AmPP (4th ed.); MaPo; NoP; OnPM; OxBA
Some Things You Cannot Will to Men. Walter E. Isenhour. STF
Some think the world is made for fun and frolic. Funiculi, Funicula. Luigi Denza. TreFT
Some time. *See also* Sometime.
Some time ago from Rome, in smart array. The Cudgelled but Contented Cuckold. La Fontaine. UnTE
Some time ago — two weeks or more. The Cowboy at Church. *Unknown.* CoSo
Some Time at Eve. Elizabeth Clark Hardy. HBV; PoLF (When I Sail Away.) MaRV
Some time now past in the autumnal tide. Contemplations. Anne Bradstreet. AmPP; AnFE; AnNE; AP; APA; CoAnAm; MAmP; Po; PoEL-3; SCAP
Some time some ordinary day will come. The Day Before. *Unknown.* SoP
Some time there ben a lyttel boy. The Lyttel Boy. Eugene Field. AA
Some Tips on Watching Birds. Deatt Hudson. NYBP
Some to conceit alone their taste confine. Pope. *Fr.* An Essay on Criticism. YAT
Some, too fragile for winter winds. Emily Dickinson. MWA-2
Some twenty cats repose. A Philosophical Poem on Cats. Fillmore Hyde. CIV
Some vast amount of years ago. Gemini and Virgo. Charles Stuart Calverley. WhC
Some Verses to Snaix. *Unknown.* NA
Some Verses upon the Burning of Our House, July 10th, 1666. Anne Bradstreet. *See* Upon the Burning. . .
Some vex their souls with jealous pain. On One Who Died Discovering Her Kindness. John Sheffield, Duke of Buckingham and Normanby. LO; OBEV
Some want a vault, some want a grave. Madrigal Macabre. Samuel Hoffenstein. ShM
Some water—about a half a cup. Mud Cakes. Mildred D. Shacklett. GFA
Some we see nor more, tenements of wonder. Emily Dickinson. MoVE
Some weep because they part. The Difference. Thomas Bailey Aldrich. TOP
Some were unlucky. Blown a mile to Shoreward. Moonlight Night on the Port. Sidney Keyes. DTC
Some who are uncertain compel me. At This Moment of Time. Delmore Schwartz. TwAmPo
Some Who Do Not Go to Church. *Unknown.* WBLP
Some will talk of bold Robin Hood. *See* Some they will talk of bold Robin Hood.

Some wit of old—such wits of old there were. Paper. Benjamin Franklin. LHV
Some winter night, shut snugly in. Ronsard to His Mistress. Thackeray. HBV
Some women herd such little things. Women. Lizette Woodworth Reese. MAP; MoAmPo; NP
Some words are tall white candles to honor Mary's name. Ad Mariam. Sister M. Edwardine. WHL
Some would know. His Answer to a Question. Robert Herrick. ReEn
Some wretched creature, savior take. Emily Dickinson. MoVE
Some write for pleasure. *Unknown.* SiTL
Some years ago, ere time and taste. The Vicar. Winthrop Mackworth Praed. *Fr.* Every-Day Characters. EnRP; InMe; NBM; OBEV (new ed.); OBNC; OBRV; OBVV; PoEL-4; VA
Some years ago you heard me sing. Sarah Byng [Who Could Not Read and Was Tossed into a Thorny Hedge by a Bull]. Hilaire Belloc. CenHV; GoJo
Some years of late, in eighty-eight. The Defeat of the Armada [*or* The Spanish Armado]. *Unknown, at. to* William Warner. CoBE; FaBoCh; LiTG; LoGBV
Some young and saucy dandelions. The Dandelions. *Unknown.* BoTP
Somebody ("Och hon for somebody!"). *Unknown.* OxBS
Somebody ("Somebody did a golden deed"). *Unknown.* FaFP
Somebody ("Somebody's tall and handsome"), *with music.* *Unknown.* AS
Somebody,/ Cut his hair. Young Poet. Myron O'Higgins. PoNe
Somebody called Walt Whitman. Witter Bynner. *Fr.* The New World. InP
Somebody did a golden deed. Somebody. *Unknown.* FaFP
Somebody has got to tell me something real. Runaway. Rhoda Coghill. NeIP
Somebody Knew Lincoln Somebody Xerxes. E. E. Cummings. NoP
Somebody knocked. Who's There? Frances Frost. RePo
Somebody left a mirror. Twenty Foolish Fairies. Nancy Byrd Turner. SUS
Somebody Prayed. *Unknown.* STF
Somebody said that it couldn't be done. It Couldn't Be Done. Edgar A. Guest. BLPA; FaBoBe; FaFP; NeHB; OTD; PTK; SoP; STF; TreFS; WBLP; YaD
Somebody stole my myths. Song to the Tune of "Somebody Stole My Gal." X. J. Kennedy. CoPo
Somebody up in the rocky pasture. The Ant Village. Marion Edey. FaPON; TiPo
Somebody's Birthday. Abbie Farwell Brown. BiCB
Somebody's Boy. Katharine Lee Bates. PEDC
Somebody's Child. Louise Chandler Moulton. HBV
Somebody's Darling. Marie La Coste [*or* La Conte]. BLPA; DD; HBV; TreF; WBLP
Somebody's Garden. Margaret Steele Anderson. DD
Somebody's knockin' at th' door. The Collier's Wife. D. H. Lawrence. HaMV
Somebody's Knockin' at Yo' Do', *with music.* *Unknown.* BoAN-1
Somebody's Mother. Mary Dow Brine. BeLS; BLPA; FaFP; OTPC (1946 ed.); TreF; WBLP
Somebody's tall and handsome. Somebody. *Unknown.* AS
Some Day. Medora Addison. HBMV
Someday/ Jane shall/ Have. Skipping Ropes. Dorothy Aldis. StVeCh
Some day, all unawares, alone in the deep forest. My Death. Carl Zuckmayer. TrJP
Someday I'd like to climb the Puig. Balearic Idyll. Frederick Packard. FiBHP
Someday I'm going to have a store. General Store. Rachel Field. BoChLi; GaP; MPB (1956 ed.); SoPo; StVeCh (1955 ed.); SUS
Some day my spirit will grow up tall and wise. My Spirit Will Grow Up. Ruth Evelyn Henderson. OQP
Some Day of Days. Nora Perry. HBV
Some day our town will grow old. The Springfield of the Far Future. Vachel Lindsay. MoRP
Some day perhaps I too may speak your name. Some Day. Medora Addison. HBMV
Someday somebody will say that. Turko-Persian Bazaar-Boutique. Eugene Lesser. FRC
Some Day, Some Day (Alguna Vez). Cristóbal de Castillejo, *tr. fr. Spanish by* Longfellow. AWP; JAWP; ViBoPo; WBP
Some day, some day of days, threading the street. Some Day of Days. Nora Perry. HBV
Some day, some happy day. The Reign of Peace. Mary Starck. WBLP
Some day the silver cord will break. Saved by Grace. Fanny J. Crosby. FaChP
Some day there would be an escape, she knew. Escape. Daniel Whitehead Hicky. JKCP (1955 ed.)
Some day, when trees have shed their leaves. After the Winter. Claude McKay. BANP; GoSl; IDB; PoNe
Somehow, but God knows how, we'll meet again. Somehow, Somewhere, Sometime. Winifred M. Letts. HBMV
Somehow come to the calm of this present, a Sunday in summer. To Lighten My House. Alastair Reid. NePoEA
Somehow, not only for Christmas. The Joy of Giving. Whittier. ChBR; OTD
Somehow, Somewhere, Sometime. Winifred M. Letts. HBMV
Somehow You Know When It Arrives. Ethel Livingston. ThO
Someone. John Ciardi. BiCB
Someone [*or* Some One]. Walter de la Mare. BoChLi; BoTP; FaPON; GaP; MoBrPo; MoShBr; MPB; PDV; SoPo; SP; StVeCh; SUS; TiPo
Someone approaches to say his life is ruined. The Dream. David Ignatow. CoAP
Someone came knocking. Someone [*or* Some One]. Walter de la Mare. BoChLi; BoTP; FaPON; GaP; MoBrPo; MoShBr; MPB; PDV; SoPo; SP; StVeCh; SUS; TiPo
Some one complained to the Master. The Estuary. Allen Upward. *Fr.* Scented Leaves from a Chinese Jar. NP
Someone Could Certainly Be Found. Anne Hébert, *tr. fr. French by* F. R. Scott. CaP
Someone had been walking in and out. The Origin of Baseball. Kenneth Patchen. Po
Someone has got to tell me something real. Runaway. Rhoda Coghill. OxBI
Someone has idly set a record turning. In a Liberal Arts Building. Ruth Stone. TwAmPo
Someone has left a stack. The Stack. Stanley Snaith. ChMP
Someone has lived here where twin chimneys. The Grapevine. Zoe Kincaid Brockman. GoYe
Someone has opened and undone. Beyond the Tapestries. Norma Farber. GoYe
Someone has shut the shining eyes, straightened and folded. Beside the Bed. Charlotte Mew. AnEnPo; MoAB; MoBrPo; NeMA; NP; TrGrPo
Someone I Lost. Jon Silkin. OPoP
Some one is always sitting there. The Little Green Orchard. Walter de la Mare. EvOK; TiPo (1952 ed.)
Someone Is Harshly Coughing as Before. Delmore Schwartz. WOW
Someone is knocking at the door. The Rice Seller. *Unknown, tr. by* Isaac Taylor Headland. PCH
Someone is walking through the snow. Hearing Steps. Charles Simic. YAP
Someone painted pictures on my. Jack Frost. Helen Bayley Davis. GFA; SoPo
Some one started the whole day wrong—was it you? Was It You? Stewart I. Long. WBLP
Some one within my hearing said tonight. Sonnet. George Henry Boker. *Fr.* Sonnets: a Sequence on Profane Love. AmePo
Someone's Bible. E. C. Kurtz. SoP
Somersault. Dorothy Aldis. SoPo
Somerset Dam for Supper, The. John Holmes. NYBP
Something. Robert Creeley. NaP
Something befell. At the Bottom of the Well. Louis Untermeyer. GoJo; MAP
Something Beyond. Mary Clemmer. OQP
Something calls and whispers, along the city street. Song. Georgiana Goddard King. *Fr.* The Way of Perfect Love. HBV
Something Childish, but Very Natural. Samuel Taylor Coleridge. *See* If I Had but Two Little Wings.
Something Else. Michael Brownstein. ANYP
Something far off buried deep and free. The Flash. James Dickey. FRC
Something for Jesus. S. D. Phelps. BLRP
Something forgotten for twenty years: though my fathers. A Map

of the Western Part of the County of Essex in England. Denise Levertov. CoAP; ToPo
Something goes wrong with my synthetic brain. The Case for the Miners. Siegfried Sassoon. PoFr
Something hangs in back of me. The Wings. Denise Levertov. FRC
Something happened the other day, that never happened before. Shovellin' Iron Ore. *Unknown.* AS
Something has ceased to come along with me. Death of a Son. Jon Silkin. GTBS-P; NePoEA; POTE (1959 ed.); TwCP
Something has spoken to me in the night. Thomas Wolfe. *Fr.* You Can't Go Home Again. TRV
Something I saw or thought I saw. On the Heart's Beginning to Cloud the Mind. Robert Frost. CMoP
Something in Common. Richard Church. MoRP
Something in the climate of a hammer. Because Going Nowhere Takes a Long Time. Kenneth Patchen. NaP
Something inspires the only cow of late. The Cow in Apple Time. Robert Frost. CABA; MAP; MoAB; MoAmPo; OA; PoeP; PoLF
Something Is Bound to Happen. W. H. Auden. *See* Doom Is Dark.
Something is dead. Prologue to "Rhymes and Rhythms." W. E. Henley. PoVP
Something is happening—that he seems to sense. The Summer Cat. Ella Augusta Fanning. CIV
Something lives in this house. Tenant. Frances Angevine Gray. FiSC
Something more than the lilt of the strain. Poetry. Lucius Harwood Foote. AA
Something of glass about her, of dead water. Circe. Louis MacNeice. LO; OBMV
Something of how the homing bee at dusk. Southern Gothic. Donald Justice. TwAmPo
Something one day occurr'd about a bill. George Crabbe. *Fr.* Tales of the Hall. Par
Something slithers on the beach. The Monster. Dorothy Quick. FiSC
Something, so great a sweetness, came. Poem. Jean Garrigue. NYTB
Something so noble in that lifted brow. Clio. Ernest Rhys. POTE
Something Starting Over. Thomas Hornsby Ferril. AnAmPo
Something startles me where I thought I was safest. This Compost. Walt Whitman. AWP; CABA; LiTA; MAmP; MoAmPo (1950 ed.); MWA-1
Something tapped at my window pane. April. Theodosia Garrison. DD; HBMV; MPB
Something there is that doesn't love a wall. Mending Wall. Robert Frost. AmFN; AmP; AmPP; AnNE; AP; CaFP; CMoP; CoBA; CoBMV; DiPo; ExPo; FaBV; FaFP; GTBS-W; HBV; ILP; InP; InPo; LaNeLa; LiTA; LiTM; MAP; MaRV; MCCG; MoAB; MoAmPo; MoPW; MoVE; NeMA; NePA; NoP; NP; OHFP; OtMeF; OxBA; PAn; PFY; PoAn; PoE; PoeP; PoMa; PoPo; PoSa; PTK; RePo; SeCeV; TDP; TOP; ViBoPo; WHA
Something to Be Thankful For. Clara J. Denton. HH
Something to do with territory makes them sing. Birds All Singing. Norman MacCaig. ChMP
Something to Eat. Tom Veitch. ANYP
Something to live for came to the place. Only. Harriet Prescott. HBV
Something Told the Wild Geese. Rachel Field. BrR; PDV; PoSC; SiSoSe; SoPo; StVeCh (1955 ed.); TiPo; WaKn; YeAr
Something Very Elegant. Aileen Fisher. BiCB
Something wakes and stirs within me. On Hearing Jazz. Alice Phelps-Rider. PoMa
Something You Can Do. *Unknown.* STF
Sometime. *See also* Some Time.
Sometime. May Riley Smith. BLPA; HBV; MaRV; SoP
Sometime [*or* Some time] at eve when the tide is low. Some Time at Eve [*or* When I Sail Away]. Elizabeth Clark Hardy. HBV; MaRV
Sometime, I feel, I'll hear. Duke of Parma's Ear. Eli Siegel. ELU
Sometime I sigh, sometime I sing. Sir Thomas Wyatt. FCP; SiPS
Sometime It May Be. Arthur Willis Colton. HBV
(To Faustine.) AA
Sometime it may be pleasing to remember. Olim Meminisse Juvabit. Aline Kilmer. JKCP
Sometime, it may be, you and I. Sometime It May Be [*or* To Faustine]. Arthur Willis Colton. AA; HBV
Sometime Lively Gerald. Richard Stanyhurst. NCEP
Sometime, should I no longer flee forever. To His Dead Brother. Ugo Foscolo. OnPM
Sometime, Somewhere. Ophelia Guyon Browning. BLRP; STF
(Pray without Ceasing.) BLPA; NeHB
Sometime [*or* Somtyme *or* Sometimes] this [*or* the] world was so steadfast [*or* stedfast] and stable. Chaucer. Lack of Steadfastness [*or* Lak of Stedfastnesse]. AWP; CBEP; ILP; NoP; PoLi
Sometime, We'll Understand. *At. to* Maxwell N. Cornelius *and to* James McGranahan. BLRP; SoP; WBLP
Sometime, when all life's lessons have been learned. Sometime. May Riley Smith. BLPA; HBV; MaRV; SoP
Sometimes. Annie Johnson Flint. STF
Sometimes. Rose Fyleman. SiSoSe
Sometimes. Thomas S. Jones, Jr. HBV; InP; MaRV; OQP; PoMa; TreFT; TRV
Sometimes/ I help my dad. Automobile Mechanics. Dorothy Baruch. FaPON; SoPo; TiPo
Sometimes,/ I wish I knew the magic word. A Sometimes Wish. Mildred D. Shacklett. GFA
Sometimes a crumb falls. Luck. Langston Hughes. MoLP
Sometimes a lantern moves along the night. The Lantern out of Doors. Gerard Manley Hopkins. CMoP; LiTB; OxBoCh
Sometimes a light surprises. Joy and Peace in Believing [*or* In Him Confiding]. William Cowper. MaRV; SoP; TRV
Sometimes a Little House Will Please. Elizabeth J. Coatsworth. BrR
Sometimes a right white mountain. Sky Pictures. Newsome. CDC; GoSl
Sometimes, apart in sleep, by chance. The Trance. Stephen Spender. ChMP; CoBMV
Sometimes, as if forewarned, before we die. Views of Boston Common and Nearby. R. P. Blackmur. MoVE
Sometimes at evening travellers have heard. Delusions IV. Charles Madge. FaBoMo
Sometimes at night when human-kind. Sorrow Turned into Joy. John Alexander Bouquet. MaRV
Sometimes at night the heart stumbles and stops. Caesura. Kenneth Mackenzie. BoAV
Sometimes deeply immured in white-washed tower. The Tingling Back. Karl Shapiro. FiMAP
Sometimes Even My Knees Smile. Diane Wakoski. YAP
Sometimes, exhausted. The Cure for Exhaustion. Piet Hein. TIHL
Sometimes, for sport, the men of the crew. The Albatross. Baudelaire. ReMP
Sometimes God seems so far away. The Fault Is Mine. Edith M. Lee. SoP
Sometimes God, who knoweth best. God Knoweth Best. Emily Donaghy. SoP
Sometimes goldfinches one by one will drop. Goldfinches. Keats. GN
Sometimes he roars among the leafy trees. The Wind. W. H. Davies. SeCePo
Sometimes he was cool like an eternal. Lester Young. Ted Joans. AmNP
Sometimes I am a tapster new. The Jolly Trades-Men. *Unknown.* CoMu
Sometimes I envy others, fear them. The Cure. William Carlos Williams. ML
Sometimes I fain would find in thee some fault. The Lamp's Shrine. Dante Gabriel Rossetti. The House of Life, XXXV. MaVP; PoVP; ViPo; VP
Sometimes I Feel like a Motherless Child. *Unknown.* BoAN-2, *with music*
Sometimes I Feel Like an Eagle in de Air. *Unknown.* NAMP
Sometimes I feel like I will never stop. To Satch [*or* American Gothic]. Samuel Allen. AmNP; IDB; Kal; PoNe (1970 ed.); SD; TTY
Sometimes I have supposed seals. Soft Wood. Robert Lowell. LiTM (1970 ed.); NoP
Sometimes I have to cross the road. Bobby Blue. John Drinkwater. FaPON; GaP; SoPo
Sometimes, I know not why, nor how, nor whence. Inspirations. William James Dawson. MaRV; WGRP

Sometimes I know the way. Absence. Charlotte Mew. ChMP; MoAB; MoBrPo
Sometimes I like to go. Memorandum. Rudy Bee Graham. PoNe (1970 ed.)
Sometimes I pause and sadly think. It Might Have Been Worse. G. J. Russell. PoToHe (new ed.)
Sometimes I see, against a storm-whipped sky. In the Storm. Stanton A. Coblentz. ChIP
Sometimes I see them. Galway Kinnell. *Fr.* Ruins under the Stars. WIRo
Sometimes I seem to see gliding the green. Nilotic Elegy. G. S. Fraser. WaP
Sometimes I think God grew tired of making. The Soul of a Mother. Margaret Sangster. PEDC
Sometimes I think it's here too. East End. Bill Berkson. YAP
Sometimes I think my woman, she too sweet to die. Cornfield Holler. *Unknown.* ABF
Sometimes I think the hills. The Hills. Rachel Field. GFA; RePo
Sometimes, I think, the things we see. Phoebe Cary. *Fr.* Dreams and Realities. MaRV
Sometimes I walk in the shadow. Walking with God. *Unknown.* BLRP
Sometimes I wish that I his pillow were. Sonnet. Richard Barnfield. ReIE
Sometimes I wish that I might do. Patience. G. A. Studdert-Kennedy. OQP; TrPWD
Sometimes, I wonder if my life. Her Mother. Worral G. Sonastine. SoP
Sometimes I write with the stub of a pencil. The Poet Confides. Herbert T. J. Coleman. CaP
Sometimes, in a woman's brow. In a Woman's Face. Richard Church. LO
Sometimes in bonnet that she. Heart-summoned. Jesse Stuart. FiSC; GoYe
Sometimes, in morning sunlights by the river. Resurrection. Sidney Lanier. PoEL-5
Sometimes in summer months, the matrix [*or* gestate] earth. Summer Idyll. George Barker. FaBoMo; MoPo
Sometimes in the hills. Burma Hills. Bernard Gutteridge. WaP
Sometimes in the summer. Sprinkling. Dorothy Mason Pierce. SUS; TiPo
Sometimes it is like a beast. A Trucker. Thom Gunn. TPM
Sometimes it seems as though some puppet player. The Puppet Player. Angelina Weld Grimké. CDC
Sometimes I've seen. A Little Bird's Song. Margaret Rose. BoTP
Sometimes Life Is Not a Literary Experience. Eugene Lesser. FRC
Sometimes my brother lets me look. Neighbors. Helen Wing. GFA
Sometimes, old pal, in the morning. Is It Really Worth the While? *Unknown.* BLPA
Sometimes on My Way back down to the Block. Victor Hernandez Cruz. BOLo
Sometimes, riding in a car, in Wisconsin. Three Kinds of Pleasures. Robert Bly. FRC
Sometimes she is a child within mine arms. Heart's Haven. Dante Gabriel Rossetti. The House of Life, XXII. EPN; MaVP; OAEP; PoVP; Sonn; ViPo; VP
Sometimes that promised glory haunts my sleep. Two Married, II. Helen Frazee-Bower. HBMV
Sometimes the girl on boyhood's silver screen. She Was the Girl within the Picture Frame. Delmore Schwartz. FiMAP
Sometimes the light falls here too as at Florence. The Old Age of Michelangelo. F. Templeton Prince. PeSA
Sometimes the lions' mouths are shut. Sometimes. Annie Johnson Flint. STF
Sometimes the Man of Nazareth. When Spring Came to Nazareth. Mary Sinton Leitch. ChIP
Sometimes the pencil, in cool airy halls. James Thomson. *Fr.* The Castle of Indolence. PoEL-3
Sometimes the road was a twisted riddle. The Road's End. Theodosia Garrison. HBMV
Sometimes this world was so steadfast and stable. *See* Sometimes this world. . .
Sometimes thou seem'st not as thyself alone. Heart's Compass. Dante Gabriel Rossetti. The House of Life, XXVII. EPN; MaVP; Po; PoVP; ViPo; VP
Sometimes, tired, I imagine your death. To L. B. S. Winfield Townley Scott. FiMAP
Sometimes, to entertain themselves, the men of the crew. The Albatross. Baudelaire. WoL
Sometimes up out of this land. Bi-focal. William Stafford. NoP
Sometimes waking, sometimes sleeping. Nestus Gurley. Randall Jarrell. NoP; TwCP
Sometimes we feel uncertain. In Hours of Discouragement God Is Our Encouragement. Helen Rice Steiner. FaChP
Sometimes we find we have nothing to give. Black Judgement. Nikki Giovanni. TNV
Sometimes we go our carefree. Rebirth. Margaret E. Bruner. PoToHe
Sometimes we peep beneath the blinds. The Tide. Marjorie Wilson. OTPC (1946 ed.); PCH
Sometimes we're bound to New York town and others we're bound to France. Heave Away, *vers.* II. *Unknown.* ShS
Sometimes when all the world seems gray and dun. While Loveliness Goes By. Anna Hempstead Branch. MAP; MoAmPo (1942 ed.)
Sometimes when alone. The Outcast. "Æ." LO; OxBI; POTE
Sometimes when fragrant summer dusk comes in with scent of rose and musk. Night for Adventures. Victor Starbuck. HBV
Sometimes when I/ am walking the street. New York in the Spring. David Budbill. CAD
Sometimes when I am at tea with you. Things. Aline Kilmer. MCCG
Sometimes when I am very sick. His Promises. Martha Snell Nicholson. BePJ
Sometimes when I feel hurried or dismayed. For One Who Is Serene. Margaret E. Bruner. PoToHe (new ed.)
Sometimes when I lie all alone. A Child-Thought. Wilfrid Thorley. PCH
Sometimes When I Sit Musing All Alone. Agnes Mary Frances Robinson. WHA
Sometimes when I think of things. Evidence. Arthur Kober. InMe
Sometimes when I wake up I lie. Roughchin, the Pirate. Arthur Boswell. EtS
Sometimes when it is bedtime. The Critic. John Farrar. GaP; SoPo
Sometimes, when Nature falls asleep. Night Mists. William Hamilton Hayne. AA
Sometimes when on night-herd I'm ridin', and the stars are a-gleam in the sky. The Range Rider's Soliloquy. Earl Alonzo Brininstool. PoOW
Sometimes when the day is ended. The City Beautiful. *Unknown.* SoP
Sometimes, when the grind of the city beats on my heart. Memories. Charles Hanson. OQP
Sometimes, when winding slow by brook and bower. Frederick Goddard Tuckerman. *Fr.* Sonnets. AnNE; MAmP; PoIE
Sometimes when you are gone. Suite from Catullus. Vincent McHugh. ErPo
Sometimes when you watch the fire. Long Distance. William Stafford. ELU
Sometimes wind and sometimes rain. Children's Song. Ford Madox Ford. HBV
Sometimes Wish, A. Mildred D. Shacklett. GFA
Sometimes with One I Love. Walt Whitman. CBEP; CBV
Sometimes, with Secure Delight. Milton. *Fr.* L'Allegro. MPB
Sometimes you hear, fifth-hand. Poetry of Departures. Philip Larkin. CMoP; NePoEA; NMP; PoeP; ToPo; TwCP
Sometimes you seem a star. Serenade. John Bunker. JKCP (1955 ed.)
Sometimes your voices call me back. Alleyway. Salvatore Quasimodo. FIW
Somewhat apart from the village, and nearer the Basin of Minas. Evangeline in Acadie. Longfellow. *Fr.* Evangeline. AA
Somewhat back from the village street. The Old Clock on the Stairs. Longfellow. CoBA; HBV; OTPC; WBLP
Somewhere. Sir Edwin Arnold. *See* Destiny.
Somewhere. J. C. Cochrane. OQP
Somewhere. Walter de la Mare. BrR; FaPON

Somewhere a hungry muzzle rooted. Design for Mediaeval Tapestry. A. M. Klein. CaP
Somewhere afield here something lies. Shelley's Skylark. Thomas Hardy. CoBMV; FaBV; PoVP; ViPo (1962 ed.); VP
Somewhere around Christmas. John Smith. FlW
Somewhere beneath the sun. Amaturus. William Johnson Cory. GTBS; HBV
Somewhere between Crewkerne. Seen from the Train. C. Day Lewis. BoC
Somewhere—but where I cannot guess. Arthur Hugh Clough. *Fr.* Songs in Absence. EPN
Somewhere he failed me, somewhere he slipt away. The Lost Shipmate. Theodore Goodridge Roberts. CaP
"Somewhere," he mused, "its dear enchantments wait." The Land of Heart's Desire. Emily Huntington Miller. HBV
Somewhere I Chanced to Read. Gustav Davidson. HBMV
Somewhere I Have Never Travelled [Gladly Beyond]. E. E. Cummings. AmPP; AnNE; AP; AtBAP; BoLiVe (1939 ed.); BoLP; CoBMV; FaBoEn; GTBS-W; LiTA; LiTL; LiTM; MeWo; MoAB; MoAmPo; MoPo; NoP; TrGrPo; TwAmPo; TwCP
Somewhere I read a strange old rusty tale. Sangar. John Reed. NP
Somewhere I read, in an old book whose name. With the Tide. Edith Wharton. PEDC
Somewhere in California. Hiroshima Crewman. Dan Georgakas. ThO
Somewhere in Chelsea, early summer. Relating to Robinson. Weldon Kees. NaP; TwAmPo
Somewhere—in desolate wind-swept space. Identity. Thomas Bailey Aldrich. AA; AnNE; MAP; PFY
Somewhere-in-Europe-Wocky. F. G. Hartswick. BOHV
"Somewhere in France," upon a brown hillside. The First Three. Clinton Scollard. MC; PAH
Somewhere in India, upon a time. An Oriental Apologue. James Russell Lowell. PoEL-5
Somewhere in Tuscany. David Holbrook. NYTB
Somewhere inside of me. Altar Smoke. Rosalie Grayer. GoTP
Somewhere Is Such a Kingdom. John Crowe Ransom. CMoP; LiTA
Somewhere it is always light. The Sun. Thomas Miller. OTPC (1923 ed.)
Somewhere Jack-in-the-Pulpit stands. Where the Wood-Thrush Calls. Jessie Wallace Hughan. TSW
Somewhere lost in the haze. Lord Dunsany. Songs from an Evil Wood, II. MoBrPo (1942 ed.)
Somewhere near the end of a snowshoe trail. A Baby Ten Months Old Looks at the Public Domain. William Stafford. NYBP
Somewhere on these bare rocks in some bare hall. For a College Yearbook. J. V. Cunningham. CBV
Somewhere or Other. Christina Rossetti. ViPo
Somewhere, out on the blue seas sailing. When My Ship Comes In. Robert Jones Burdette. FaFP
Somewhere she waits to make you win, your soul in her firm, white hands. The Woman Who Understands. Everard Jack Appleton. PoLF
Somewhere, somewhen I've seen. The Parrots. W. W. Gibson. CH; RoGo
Somewhere the Equation Breaks Down. Daniel Berrigan. NYBP
Somewhere the sun is shining. Beautiful Isle of Somewhere. Jessie B. Pounds. TreFT
Somewhere the world has a place for you. Take Your Place. *Unknown.* STF
Somewhere there lies the dust. Somewhere. J. C. Cochrane. OQP
Somewhere there waiteth in this world of ours. Destiny [*or* Somewhere]. Sir Edwin Arnold. MaRV; PoLF; PoToHe (new ed.)
Somewhere upon a battlefield. In Memory of Two Sons. Russell Stellwagon. STF
Somewhile before the dawn I rose, and stept. A Memory. Rupert Brooke. BrPo
Somnambulistic Ballad. Federico García Lorca, *tr. fr. Spanish by* Roy Campbell *and* Mary Campbell. LiTW; OnHM
(Somnambulant Ballad, *tr. by* Warren Carrier.) ReMP
Somnolent through landscapes and by trees. The Permanent Tourists. P. K. Page. LiTM (1970 ed.)
Somnus. Sir John Denham. *Fr.* The Sophy. SeCL
Somtyme [*or* Somtime] this [*or* the] world was so stedfast and stable. *See* Sometime this world . . .
Son, The. George Herbert. EP; Sonn
(Sonne, The.) MaMe; SeCP
Son, A. Kipling. *Fr.* Epitaphs of the War. ChMP; PoVP
Son. Josephine Miles. FiMAP
Son, The. Edwin Muir. PoDB
Son, The. Ridgely Torrence. HBMV; InP; InvP; MAP; MoAmPo (1942 ed.); NP; PFY; WaKn
"Son,"/ My father used to say. Out in the Woods with Father. David McCord. ThGo
Son, a son, a son, A! I wanted a son of yours. Poem of the Son. "Gabriela Mistral." PoPl
Son am I of the rolling plain, A. The Departure of Martín Fierro. José Hernández. PoFr
Son and Father. C. Day Lewis. EaLo
Son and Surf. Julia Hurd Strong. GoYe
Son Cotton! these light idle brooks. Izaac Walton, Cotton, and William Oldways. Walter Savage Landor. NBM; PoEL-4
Son David. *Unknown.* OxBB; OxBS
Son-Dayes. Henry Vaughan. AtBAP; SeCP
(Sun-Days.) MemP
"Son, fit grooves and join them well." The Carpenter's Son. Kathryn Blackburn Peck. BePJ
Son in December, A. Frank Kendon. POTE
Son just born, A. Mary Britton Miller. TiPo (1959 ed.)
Son. my son! Lament of a Man for His Son. *Tr. fr. Paiute Indian* AWP;JAWP;WBP;WOW
Son of a Gambolier, The. *with music. Unknown.* AS
Son of a Gun. *Unknown.* CoSo
Son of a mystic race, he came. Heinrich Heine. Ludwig Lewisohn. TrJP
Son of a whore, God dam you: Can you tell. Rochester to the Post Boy. *At. to* the Earl of Rochester. PeRV
Son of Erebus and Night. William Browne. *Fr.* The Inner Temple Masque. ViBoPo
Son of God, The. Charles L. O'Donnell. JKCP
"Son of God am I, The," he humbly said. Good Friday. Alice B. Jurica. ChIP
Son of God goes forth for Peace, The. A Hymn of Peace. Ernest Bourner Allen. MaRV
Son of God Goes Forth to War, The. Reginald Heber. HBV; MaRV; OTPC; TreFS
(Who Follows in His Train?) SoP; WGRP
Son of Man. Leslie Savage Clark. ChIP
Son of Man, The. Dorothy J. Langford. BePJ
Son of Man, behold with thine eyes, and hear with thine ears. Chorus. T. S. Eliot. *Fr.* The Rock. PoDB
Son of the King of Moy, The. *Unknown, tr. fr. Old Irish by* Myles Dillon. AnIL
Son of the lightning and the light that glows. For the Feast of Giordano Bruno. Swinburne. PoFr; ViPo
Son of the Mountain. Eifion Wyn, *tr. fr. Welsh by* Gwyn Williams. PrWP
Son of the ocean isle! England's Dead. Felicia Dorothea Hemans. HBV
Son of the old moon-mountains African. To the Nile. Keats. HBV
Son of the righteous one, he who thunders on the ground. Praises of the King Tshaka. *Unknown.* PeSA
Son of the Sea, A. Bliss Carman. EtS
Son of the thundercloud. Song of the Thunder. *Unknown.* PeSA
"Son," said my mother. The Ballad of the Harp-Weaver. Edna St. Vincent Millay. MaC; StPo; YT
Sonata. Hal Summers. MuSP
Sonata by Scarlatti, A. John Heath-Stubbs. MuSP
Sonatina. Rubén Daró, *tr. fr. Spanish by* G. W. Umphrey *and* Laura Forsberg. WoL
Sonet. *See also* Sonnet.
Sonet: "Fra bank to bank [*or* banc to banc], fra wood to wood [*or* wod to wod] I rin." Mark Alexander Boyd. *See* Sonnet: "Fra bank to bank. . ."
Sonet, A: "Her face, her tongue, her wit." *At. to* Sir Walter Ralegh. *See* Her Face, Hen Tongue, Her Wit.
Sonet, A: "His golden lockes, Time hath to silver turn'd." George Peele. *See* His Golden Locks. . .
Sonet to Sleepe. William Drummond. *See* Sonnet: "Sleep, Silence child, sweet father of soft rest."

Sonet to the Tune of A Hone a Hone, A. Nicholas Breton. SiCE
Sonet Written in Prayse of the Browne Beautie, A. George Gascoigne. EnPo
Sonetto: "Of all chaste birds the phoenix doth excel." Thomas Lodge. *See* Of Rosalind.
Sonetto XXXV: To Guido Orlando. Guido Cavalcanti, *tr. fr. Italian by* Ezra Pound. CTC
Sonetto VII: "Who is she that comes, makyng turn every man's eye." Guido Cavalcanti, *tr. fr. Italian by* Ezra Pound. (Chi è questa.) ReMP
Song: "A ho! A ho!/ Love's horn doth blow. Thomas Lovell Beddoes. *Fr.* The Bride's Tragedy. BiS; ChER
(Love Goes a-Hawking.) VA
Song, A: "Absent from thee I languish still." Earl of Rochester. CavP; ELP; EnLoPo; FaBoEn; LoBV; MePo; OBS; PeRV; PoFS; SeCePo; SeCV-2; SeEP; ViBoPo
(Absent from Thee.) SeCL
("Absent from thee, I languish still!") LO
(Return.) OBEV
Song: "Across the Sea." William Allingham. IrPN
(Song: "I walk'd in the lonesome evening.") EnLoPo
Song: "Adieu, farewell, earth's bliss." Thomas Nashe. *See* Adieu, Farewell, Earth's Bliss!
Song: "After the pangs of a desperate lover." Dryden. *See* After the Pangs of a Desperate Lover.
Song: "Again rejoicing Nature sees." Burns. BoNaP; HBV
(Composed in Spring.) CBEP
Song: "Ah Cloris! that I now could sit." Sir Charles Sedley. *See* Child and Maiden.
Song: "Ah! County Guy, the hour is nigh." Sir Walter Scott. *See* County Guy.
Song: "Ah, fading joy! how quickly art thou past!" Dryden. *See* Ah, Fading Joy.
Song: "Ah, how sweet it is to love." Dryden. *See* Ah, How Sweet It Is to Love.
Song: "Ah stay! ah turn! ah whither would you fly." Congreve. *Fr.* The Fair Penitent (*by* Nicholas Rowe). AtBAP; LoBV; OBEC
Song: "Ah, vale of woe, of gloom and darkness moulded." Rachel Morpurgo, *tr. fr. Hebrew by* Nina Davis Salaman. TrJP
Song: "All in green went my love riding." E. E. Cummings. *See* All in Green. . .
Song: "All my love for my sweet." John Hall Wheelock. NP
Song: "All service ranks the same with God." Robert Browning. *See* All Service Ranks the Same with God.
Song: "All the flowers of the spring." John Webster. *See* All the Flowers of the Spring.
Song: "Always before your voice my soul." E. E. Cummings. *See* Always before Your Voice.
Song: "And can the physician make sick men well?" *Unknown.* *See* And Can the Physician Make Sick Men Well.
Song: "And did those feet in ancient time." Blake. *See* And Did Those Feet in Ancient Time.
Song: "April, April,/ Laugh thy girlish laughter." Sir William Watson. DD; HBV; HBVY; MoBrPo (1942 ed.); OBVV; PoRL; PoSC; TreF; TrGrPo; TSW; YT
(April.) BoTP; FaBV; GoTP
(Song to April.) GN
Song: "Are they shadowes that we see?" Samuel Daniel. *See* Are They Shadows?
Song, A: "As Chloris [*or* Cloris] full of harmless thoughts." Earl of Rochester. ErPo; UnTE
Song: As I Walked Out One Evening. W. H. Auden. *See* As I Walked Out One Evening.
Song: "As the holly groweth green." Henry VIII, King of England. *See* Green Groweth the Holly.
Song, A: "Ask me no more where Jove bestows." Thomas Carew. *See* Ask Me No More Where Jove Bestows.
Song: "At setting day and rising morn." Allan Ramsay. HBV
Song: "Awake thee, my Bessy, the morning is fair." Jeremiah Joseph Callanan. IrPN; OnYI
Song: "Balkis was in her marble town." Lascelles Abercrombie. *See* Balkis.
Song: "Beautiful Mistress, A. Thomas Carew. *See* Beautifull Mistress, A.
Song: "Beauty clear and fair." John Fletcher. *See* Beauty Clear and Fair.
Song: "Beauty no more the subject be." Thomas Nabbes. *Fr.* Hannibal and Scipio. SeCL; TuPP
Song: "Because he was gone, without a goodbye." Lysander Kemp. NYTB
Song: "Because the rose must fade." Richard Watson Gilder. HBV
Song: "Bee to the heather, The." Sir Henry Taylor. OBVV
Song: "Before the barn-door crowing." John Gay. *See* Before the Barn-Door Crowing.
Song: "Before we shall again behold." Sir William Davenant. MeLP; SeEP
(Endimion Porter and Olivia.) MePo
(Song; Endymion Porter and Olivia.) OBS
Song: "Bells of Sunday rang us down, The." John Ciardi. WaP
Song: "Belovèd, it is morn!" Emily Henrietta Hickey. *See* Belovèd, It Is Morn.
Song: "Bird in my bower, A." Francis Howard Williams. AA
Song: "Blow, blow, thou winter wind." Shakespeare. *See* Blow, Blow, Thou Winter Wind.
Song: "Blow there, sweet Zephyrus!" *Unknown.* SeCL
Song: "Blushing rose and purple flower, The." Philip Massinger. *Fr.* The Picture, III, v. LiTL; ViBoPo
(Song of Pleasure, A.) SeCL; UnTE
Song, A: "Boast no more fond love, thy power." Thomas D'Urfey. CavP
Song: "Boat is chafing at our long delay, The." John Davidson. OBEV; OBVV
Song: "Bone-aged is my white horse." Brenda Chamberlain. NeIP
(Song—Talysarn.) NeBP
Song: "Bring from the craggy haunts of birch and pine." John Todhunter. OBVV; PoVP
(O Mighty, Melancholy Wind.) OnYI
Song: Bunthorne. W. S. Gilbert. *See* Bunthorne's Song.
Song: "Call for the robin redbreast and the wren." John Webster. *See* Call for the Robin Redbreast.
Song: "Calm was the even, and cleer was the sky." Dryden. *See* Calm Was the Even, and Clear Was the Sky.
Song: "Can life be a blessing." Dryden. *See* Can Life Be a Blessing.
Song: "Can love be controll'd by advice?" John Gay. *Fr.* The Beggar's Opera, I, viii. LoBV
Song: "Care charming Sleep, thou easer of all woes." John Fletcher. *See* Care-charming Sleep.
Song: Catch a Falling Star. John Donne. *See* Song: Go and Catch a Falling Star.
Song: Celia Singing. Thomas Carew. *See* Celia Singing ("You that think Love can convey").
Song, A: "Celia, that I once was blest." Dryden. *Fr.* Amphitrion. CavP
Song, A: "Celimena, of my heart." Dryden. *Fr.* An Evening's Love. CavP; PeRV
(Damon and Celimena.) InvP; SeCL
Song: "Celinda, by what potent art." Thomas Stanley. CavP
Song: "Chloris! farewell. I now must go." Edmund Waller. CavP; CEP; SCEP-2
(Chloris Farewell.) OBS
Song, A: "Chloris, when I to thee present." *Unknown.* OBS
("Cloris when I to thee present.") SeCSL
Song: "Christ keep the Hollow Land." William Morris. *Fr.* The Hollow Land. NBM; PoEL-5; ThWaDe
(Hollow Land, The.) AtBAP; ChTr
Song: "Circle and wheel of. Who cares what I'll." Robert Kelly. YAP
Song: "Cloris, it is not thy disdaine." Sidney Godolphin. MeLP
("Cloris, it is not thy disdaine.") EG
(To Chloris.) SeCL
(To the Tune of, In Fayth I Cannot Keepe My Fathers Sheepe.) OBS
Song: "Closes and courts and lanes." John Davidson. BrPo; HBV; PoVP
Song: Colonel. W. S. Gilbert. *Fr.* Patience. PoVP
Song: "Come away, come away death." Shakespeare. *See* Come Away, Come Away, Death.
Song: "Come, Celia, let's agree at last." John Sheffield. HBV
Song, A: "Come, cheer up, my lads, like a true British band." *Unknown.* PAH
Song: "Come down, O maid, from yonder mountain height." Tennyson. *See* Come down, O Maid.

Song: "Come into the garden, Maud." Tennyson. *See* Come into the Garden, Maud.
Song: "Come, rest in this bosom, my own stricken deer." Thomas Moore. *See* Come, Rest in This Bosom.
Song: "Cupid and my Campaspe played." John Lyly. *See* Apelles' Song.
Song: "Daughter of Egypt, veil thine eyes!" Bayard Taylor. AA
Song: "Day is come, I see it rise, The." Dryden. *Fr.* Amboyna. HW
Song: "Day will rise and the sun from eastward." George Campbell Hay. OxBS
Song: "Deftly, admiral, cast your fly." W. H. Auden. GTBS-P
Song: "Delicious beauty, that doth lie." *At. to* John Marston. *See* Delicious Beauty.
Song: Dissembler, The. Matthew Prior. *See* Ode, An: "Merchant, to secure his treasure, The."
Song: "Do I venture away too far." Keith Douglas. NePoEA
Song: "Do not fear to put thy feet." John Fletcher. *See* River God's Song, The.
Song: "Don't Tell Me What You Dreamt Last Night." Franklin P Adams. FiBHP
Song: "Dorinda's sparkling wit, and eyes." Charles Sackville. CavP; CEP; OBS; SeCV-2; SeEP
(Dorinda.) CEP; OBEV (new ed.); SeCePo; SeCL
Song: "Down lay in a nook my lady's brach." Sir Henry Taylor. *Fr.* Philip van Artevelde. VA
Song: "Down the dimpled green-sward dancing." George Darley. OnYI
Song: "Draw near, and see." *Unknown.* SeCL
Song: "Dressed up in my melancholy." M. Carl Holman. AmNP; Kal; PoNe
Song: "Drink about till the day find us." Earl of Rochester. PeRV
Song: "Drink to me only with thine eyes." Ben Jonson. *See* To Celia ("Drink to me only. . .").
Song: "Drink today, and drown all sorrow." John Fletcher, *See* Drink To-Day. *and others.*
Song, The: "Drinke and be merry, merry, merry boyes." *See* Songe, The: "Drink and be merry. . ."
Song: "D'ye ken John Peel with his coat so gay?" John Woodcock Graves. *See* John Peel.
Song: "Earl March looked on his dying child." Thomas Campbell. *See* Maid of Neidpath, The.
Song: "Echo, tell me, while I wander." Addison. BOHV
Song: Endimion Porter and Olivia. Sir William Davenant. *See* Song: "Before we shall again behold."
Song: Eternity of Love Protested. Thomas Carew. *See* Eternity of Love Protested.
Song: "Faiery beame upon you, The." Ben Jonson. *See* Gipsy Song.
Song: "Fain would I change that note." *Unknown. See* Fain Would I Change That Note.
Song: "Fair, and soft, and gay, and young." Robert Gould. *Fr.* The Rival Sisters. CEP; SeCL
("Fair and Soft, and Gay, and Young.") UnTE
Song: "Fair Iris I love, and hourly I die." Dryden. *Fr.* Amphitryon, IV, i. AWP; JAWP; LiTL; WBP; WoL
(Fair Iris I Love.) InPo; OnPM
(False and Fickle.) MeWo
(Hourly I Die.) UnTE
(Mercury's Song to Phaedra.) CEP; MBW-1; PoEL-3; SeCV-2
Song: "Fair is the night, and fair the day." William Morris. *Fr.* The Earthly Paradise. HBV
Song: "Fair, sweet and young, receive a prize." Dryden. LiTL; OBS; SeEP
(Fair, Sweet, and Young.) SeCL
Song: "Fair Sylvia, cease to blame my youth." Francis Atterbury. WaPE
Song: "Fairy band are we, A." Alfred Noyes. GBV (1922 ed.)
Song: "Fall, leaves, fall; die, flowers, away." Emily Brontë. *See* Fall, Leaves, Fall.
Song: "False though she be to me and love." Congreve. *See* False Though She Be.
Song, A: "Fame let thy trumpet sound." Joel Barlow. AmPP (5th ed.)
Song: "Farewell, adieu, that courtly [*or* court-like] life!" John Pickering. *See* Haltersick's Song.
Song: "Farewell, ungrateful traitor!" Dryden. *See* Farewell, Ungrateful Traitor.
Song: "Fear no more the heat o' the sun." Shakespeare. *See* Fear No More the Heat o' the Sun.
Song: "Fearless follow, thou sad soul." *Unknown.* SeCL
Song: "Feathers of the willow, The." Richard Watson Dixon. BoNaP; CBEP; CH; FaBoCh; GTBS-D; GTBS-P; LoBV; LoGBV; OBNC; OBVV; ThWaDe; YeAr
(Feathers of the Willow, The.) ShBV-4
(November.) GTSL
(Willow.) OBEV (new ed.)
Song: "Few more windy days, A." Helen Dudley. NP
Song: Fie My Fum. Allen Ginsberg. ErPo
Song: "Find me a lonely cave." *Unknown.* SeCL
Song: "Fine young folly, though you were." William Habington. *See* Fine Young Folly.
Song: "First month[s] of his absence, The." Alun Lewis. ChMP; DTC; LiTM; WaaP
Song: Fish in the Unruffled Lakes. W. H. Auden. *See* Fish in the Unruffled Lakes.
Song: "Flame at the core of the world." Arthur Upson. HBV
Song: "Floods come o'er the meadow leas, The." John Clare. PeER
Song: "Flowers that in thy garden rise, The." Sir Henry Newbolt. FaBoTw
Song: "Fly, fly, you happy shepherds, fly." Sir John Vanbrugh. *See* Philira.
Song: "Fly hence, shadows, that do keep." John Ford. *See* Fly Hence Shadows.
Song: "Fond affection, hence, and leave me!" *At. to* Robert Parry. *Fr.* The Mirror of Knighthood. EIL
Song: "Fond men! whose wretched care the life soon ending." Phineas Fletcher. *Fr.* Brittain's Ida. EIL
Song: "Fool, take up thy shaft again." Thomas Stanley. EnLoPo
Song: "Fooles, they are the onely nation." Ben Jonson. *See* Nano's Song.
Song: "For a shape, and a bloom, and an air, and a mien." Edward Moore. WaPE
Song: "For her gait, if she be walking." William Browne. *See* Complete Lover, The.
Song: "For me the jasmine buds unfold." Florence Earle Coates. HBV; PoMa
(World Is Mine, The.) AA
Song, A: "For Mercy, Courage, Kindness, Mirth." Laurence Binyon. BoTP; HBMV; MoBrPo
Song: "For the tender beech and the sapling oak." Thomas Love Peacock. *Fr.* Maid Marian. OHIP; PRWS
(For the Slender Beech and the Sapling Oak.) EnRP
(Greenwood Tree, The.) GTSE
(Oak and the Beech, The.) OTPC
Song: "Forgive, fair creature, form'd to please." *Unknown.* EiCL
Song: "Fortunate are the feet of the swallow." Walter James Turner. LO
Song: "Four arms, two necks, one wreathing." *Unknown.* EIL
Song: "Fresh from the dewy hill, the merry year." Blake. CoBE; EiPP; EnLit; EnRP
Song: "Friend and lover mine." Dinis, King of Portugal, *tr. fr. Portuguese by* Aubrey F. G. Bell. CAW
Song: "Fringéd vallance of your eyes advance, The." Thomas Shadwell. *Fr.* Timon of Athens. ViBoPo
(Good-Morrow, A.) SeCL
Song: "From White's and Will's." Ambrose Philips. CEP
Song: "Full fathom [*or* fadom] five thy father lies." Shakespeare. *See* Ariel's Song: "Full fathom five. . ."
Song, A: "Gay Florimel, of generous birth." *Unknown.* WaPE
Song: "Give her but a least excuse to love me." Robert Browning. *Fr.* Pippa Passes, sc., ii. EPN; GTBS; GTSL; ViBoPo
Song, A: "Give me leave to rail at you." Earl of Rochester. EG
Song: "Give me more love or more disdain." Thomas Carew. *See* Mediocrity in Love Rejected.
Song: "Glories of our blood and state, The." James Shirley. *See* Glories of Our Blood and State.
Song: "Glories, pleasures, pomps, delights, and ease." John Ford. *See* Glories, Pleasures.
Song: "Go and Catch a Falling Star." John Donne. ATP; AWP; BOHV; BoLiVe; CABA; CaFP; CBEP; CBV; CLwM; DiPo; EIL; ELP; EnL; EnLi-1; EnRePo; FaFP; FosPo; HBV; ILP; InMe; InPo; JAWP; LoBV; MaPo; MBW-1; NoP; OAEP;

Song (continued)
OBEV; OuHeWo; PAn; PG (1945 ed.); PoIE; PoSa; PPON; ReEn; ReIE; SeCeV; SeEP; SiTL; StP; TDP; TOP; TrGrPo; TuPP; ViBoPo; WBP; WHA
(Go and Catch a Falling Star.) BEL; EG; EnLit; FaBV; GTBS-W; LiTB; LiTG; LiTL; PoAn; PoeP; PoRA
(Goe, and Catche a Falling Starre.) AtBAP; TreFT
(Song: Catch a Falling Star.) MeWo
(Song: "Goe, and catche a falling starre.") AnAnS-1; AnFE; HoPM; MaMe; MeLP; MePo; PoEL-2; PoPl; SCEP-1; SeCP; SeCV-1; YAT
Song: "Go, lovely rose!" Edmund Waller. *See* Go, Lovely Rose.
Song: "Go not, happy day." Tennyson. *See* Go Not, Happy Day.
Song, A: "Go tell Amynta gentle swain." Dryden. *Fr.* Sylvoe. CavP
Song: "Go with your tauntings, go." John Clare. OBRV
Song: "Goe, and catche a falling starre." John Donne. *See* Song: "Go and catch a falling star."
Song: "Going down the old way." Margaret Widdemer. HBMV
Song: "Gold wings across the sea!" William Morris. *See* Gold Wings across the Sea.
Song: "Good morrow, 'tis Saint Valentine's day." Shakespeare. *See* Tomorrow Is Saint Valentine's Day.
Song: Grace and beauty has the maid. Gil Vicente, *tr. fr. Spanish by* Alice Jane McVan. LiTW
Song: "Great is the rose." Nathalia Crane. *Fr.* Tadmor. MAP; MoAmPo (1942 ed.)
Song: Green Grow the Rashes. Burns. *See* Green Grow the Rashes.
Song: "Gross sun squats above, The." Dom Moraes. NePoEA-2
Song: "Had I a heart for falsehood framed." Sheridan. *Fr.* The Duenna, I, v. CEP; HBV; OBEV
Song: "Hang sorrow, cast away care." *Unknown.* OBS
Song: "Hark, hark, the lark at heaven's gate sings." Shakespeare. *See* Hark! Hark! the Lark.
Song, A: "Hark! 'tis Freedom that calls, come, patriots, awake!" *Unknown.* PAH
Song: "Has summer come without the rose?" Arthur O'Shaughnessy. HBV
(Has Summer Come without the Rose?) VA
Song, A: "Hast thou seen the down in the air." Sir John Suckling. *See* Song to a Lute, A.
Song, The: "Have pity (Grief) I can not pay." Peter Hausted. *See* Have Pity, Grief.
Song: "He came unlook'd for, undersir'd." Sara Coleridge. *See* He Came Unlook'd For.
Song: "He found me sitting among flowers." Aubrey Thomas De Vere. IrPN
Song: "He or she that hopes to gain." *Unknown.* SeCL
Song: "He that will court a wench that is coy." *Unknown.* ErPo
Song: "Heap cassia, sandal-buds and stripes." Robert Browning. *See* Heap Cassia, Sandal-Buds and Stripes.
Song: "Hear, sweet spirit." Samuel Taylor Coleridge. *See* Invocation, An: "Hear, sweet spirit."
Song: "Heare ye Ladies that despise." John Fletcher. *See* Hear, Ye Ladies.
Song: "Hears not my Phyllis how the birds." Sir Charles Sedley. *See* Hears Not My Phyllis.
Song: "Heavy hours are almost past, The." George Lyttelton. WaPE
Song: "Hence, all you vain delights." John Fletcher *and (at.)* Thomas Middleton. *See* Melancholy.
Song: "Here's to the maiden of bashful fifteen." Sheridan. *See* Let the Toast Pass.
Song: "Heron is harsh with despair." Brenda Chamberlain. NeBP; NeIP
Song: "Hither haste, and gently strew." Thomas Lovell Beddoes. EG
Song: "Home they brought her warrior dead." Tennyson. *See* Home They Brought Her Warrior Dead.
Song: Hopeless Comfort, The. Robert Gould. CEP
Song: "Hound was cuffed, The." Sidney Lanier. *See* Hound, The.
Song: "How blest are lovers in disguise!" George Farquhar. *Fr.* Love and a Bottle. SeCL
Song: "How blest he appears." Thomas Otway. *Fr.* Friendship in Fashion. SeCL
Song: "How can that tree but withered be." *Unknown.* ElL
Song: "How delicious is the winning." Thomas Campbell. *See* Freedom and Love.
Song: "How do I love you?" Irene Rutherford McLeod. HBV
Song: "How happy the lover." Dryden. *See* How Happy the Lover.
Song: "How happy were my days." Isaac Bickerstaffe. *Fr.* Love in a Village. BEC
Song: "How many times do I love thee, dear?" Thomas Lovell Beddoes. *Fr.* Torrismond. AnFE; ERoP-2; LiTB; LiTG; LiTL; NBM; OBEV (1st ed.); OBRV; PCD; PoEL-4; TrGrPo; VA; ViBoPo
(How Many Times?) MeWo; TSW
(How Many Times Do I Love Thee, Dear?) EnRP; GTBS-D; NeHB
Song: "How pleasant it is that always." Florence Smith. BLPA
Song: "How should I your true love know." Shakespeare. *See* How Should I Your True Love Know.
Song: "How sweet I roamed [*or* roam'd] from field to field." Blake. AtBAP; BoLiVe; CABA; CH; ChER; ChTr; EiCL; EiPP; EnL; EnLi-2; EnLoPo; EnRP; ERoP-1; FaBoEn; GTBS-D; LiTB; LiTG; LiTL; MeWo; NoP; OAEP; OBEC; OBNC; PIA; PoE; PoEL-4; SeCeV; TrGrPo; ViBoPo; WHA
(How Sweet I Roamed.) CBEP; FosPo; OTPC (1923 ed.); TreFT
(How Sweet I Roam'd from Field to Field.) EG; GTBS-W; MaPo; SeCePo
Song: "I am a passion; I am a flame." Gustavo Adolfo Bécquer, *tr. fr. Spanish by* Muna Lee. Rimas, XI. OnPM
Song: "I came to the door of the House of Love." Alfred Noyes. HBV
Song: "I cannot change as others do." Earl of Rochester. *See* Constancy.
Song: "I can't be talkin' of love, dear." Esther Mathews. FaFP; LiTL; LiTM; NePA; SiTL
Song: "I come from haunts of coot and hern." Tennyson. *See* Brook, The; an Idyl.
Song: "I could make you songs." Dorothy Dow. HBMV
Song: "I dream'd that I woke from a dream." George Macdonald. VA
Song: "I feed a flame within, which so torments me." Dryden. *Fr.* Secret Love; or, The Maiden Queen. AWP; JAWP; LiTL; LO; MBW-1; WBP
(Hidden Flame, The.) OBEV
(I Feed a Flame Within [Which So Torments Me].) InPo; MaPo; PoIE; QFR; SeCL
Song: "I had a dove and the sweet dove died." Keats. *See* I Had a Dove.
Song: "I have halted my horse by the trees of the doves." "St.-J. Perse", *tr. fr. French by* T. S. Eliot. *Fr.* Anabasis. LiTW
Song: "I have twelve oxen that be fair and brown." *Unknown.* *See* I Have Twelve Oxen.
Song: "I kept neat my virginity." Glyn Jones. NeBP
Song: "I know that any weed can tell." Louis Ginsberg. TrJP
Song: "I love the jocund dance." Blake. EiPP
("I love the jocund dance.") EG
Song: "I made another garden, yea." Arthur O'Shaughnessy. HBV; OBEV; OBVV; PoVP
(New Love and the Old, The.) GTSL; MoBrPo (1942 ed.)
Song: "I make my shroud but no one knows." Adelaide Crapsey. AmLP; AnAmPo; HBV; MAP; MoAmPo (1942 ed.); NP; TOP
Song, The: "I met a ragged man." Theodore Roethke. AP; CrMA; FiMAP
Song: "I once had a sweet little doll, dears." Charles Kingsley. *See* Lost Doll, The.
Song: "I pass all my hours in a shady old grove." *At. to* Charles II, King of England. SeCL
Song: "I prithee [*or* prethee] let my heart alone." Thomas Stanley. AnAnS-2; ViBoPo
Song: "I prithee send me back my heart." Sir John Suckling. *See* I Prithee Send Me Back My Heart.
Song: "I prithee spare me, gentle boy." Sir John Suckling. BWP
Song: I Promised Sylvia. Earl of Rochester. CavP
(Song: "I promised Sylvia to be true.") SeCePo
Song: "I saw a staring virgin stand." W. B. Yeats. *Fr.* The Resurrection. MBW-2
Song: "I saw the day's white rapture." Charles Hanson Towne. HBV
Song: "I sowed my wild oats." Dom Moraes. BoPe

Song, A: I Thought No More Was Needed. W. B. Yeats. AtBAP
Song: "I try to knead and spin, but my life is low the while." Louise Imogen Guiney. *See* In Leinster.
Song: "I walk'd in the lonesome evening." William Allingham. *See* Song: "Across the Sea."
Song: "I was so shill and overworn, and sad." Anna Wickham. MoBrPo; NeMA
(Since I Saw My Love.) MeWo
Song: "I went to her who loveth me no more." Arthur O'Shaughnessy. OBNC
(Enchainment.) HBV
Song, A: "I will not tell her that she's fair." Matthew Coppinger. CavP
Song: "I who love you bring." Theodore Spencer. AnFE; CoAnAm; TwAmPo
Song: "If a daughter you have, she's the plague of your life." Sheridan. *Fr.* The Duenna, I, iii. CEP; NeHB
Song: "If any wench Venus's girdle wear." John Gay. *Fr.* The Beggar's Opera, I, i. PoEL-3
Song: "If everywhere in the street." Denis Glover. Songs, II. AnNZ
Song, A: "If for a woman I would die." Countess of Winchilsea. ViBoPo
Song: "If I freely may discover." Ben Jonson. *See* If I Freely May Discover.
Song: "If I only had loved your flesh." V. Sackville-West. HBMV
Song: "If love were but a little thing." Florence Earle Coates. HBMV
Song: "If once I could gather in song." W. W. Gibson. OBVV; TOP
Song: "If she be not as kind as fair." Sir George Etherege. *See* If She Be Not as Kind as Fair.
Song: "If the scorn of your bright eyne." Shakespeare. *Fr.* As You Like It, IV, iii. CTC
Song: "If thou art sleeping, maiden." Gil Vicente, *tr. fr. Spanish by* Longfellow. AWP; JAWP; LiTW; WBP
Song: "If to be absent were to be." Richard Lovelace. *See* To Lucasta, [on] Going beyond the Seas.
Song, A: "If wine and music have the power." Matthew Prior. ATP (1935 ed.); CEP; LoBV
Song: "If you love God, take your mirror between your hands and look." Mahmud Djellaladin Pasha, *tr. fr. Turkish by* E. Powys Mathers. ErPo; LiTW
Song: "I'll tell her the next time, said I." George Granville. *See* I'll Tell Her.
Song: "In crystal towers and turrets richly set." Geffrey Whitney. *See* Content.
Song, A: "In her fair cheeks two pits do lie." Thomas Carew. UnTE
Song: "In his last bin Sir Peter Lies." Thomas Love Peacock. *Fr.* Headlong Hall. OBRV; ViBoPo
(In His Last Binn Sir Peter Lies.) EnRP
Song: "In pity for man's darkening thought." W. B. Yeats. *Fr.* The Resurrection. MBW-2
Song: "In summer when the rose-bushes." Edith Sitwell. NP
Song, A: "In the air there are no coral-/ Reefs." Duncan Campbell Scott. PeCV
Song, A: In the Name of a Lover, to His Mistress; Who Said, She Hated Him for His Grey Hairs, Which He Had at Thirty. William Wycherley. *See* To His Mistress, Who Said She Hated Him for His Grey Hairs.
Song: "In thy white bosom Love is laid." John Arthur Blaikie. VA
Song, A: "In vain you tell your parting lover." Matthew Prior. HBV
Song: "Indeed, my Caelia, 'tis in vain. Sir John Henry Moore. LO; OBEC
Song: Inviting the Influence of a Young Lady upon the Opening Year. Hilaire Belloc. *See* Song: "You wear the morning like your dress."
Song: "Is it dirty/ does it look dirty." Frank O'Hara. CAD
Song: "It autumne was, and on our hemispheare." William Drummond of Hawthornden. OBS
Song: "It is all one in Venus' wanton school." John Lyly. SeCePo
Song, A: "It is not beauty I demand." George Darley. *See* Loveliness of Love, The.
Song: "It is the miller's daughter." Tennyson. *See* Miller's Daughter, The.
Song: "It was a friar of orders free." Thomas Love Peacock. *Fr.* Maid Marian. ViBoPo
Song: "It was a lover and his lass." Shakespeare. *See* It Was a Lover and His Lass.
Song: "It was upon a Lammas night." Burns. *See* Rigs o' Barley, The.
Song: "I've taught thee love's sweet lesson o'er." George Darley. *Fr.* Sylvia, or, The May Queen. OBRV
(Romanzo to Sylvia.) VA
Song: "Johnnie Crack and Flossie Snail." Dylan Thomas. *See* Johnnie Crack and Flossie Snail.
Song: "Join once again, my Celia." Charles Cotton. ViBoPo
Song: "Keep the dream alive and growing always." Edwin Rolfe. TrJP
Song: "Kind lovers, love on." John Crowne. *Fr.* Calisto. ALV; SeCL
(Kind Lovers, Love On.) InvP
Song: "Kiss me, sweet; the wary lover." Ben Jonson. *See* To Celia ("Kiss me, sweet. . .").
Song: "Know, Celadon, in vain you use." "Ephelia." CavP
Song: "Ladies, though to your conquering eyes." Sir George Etherege. *Fr.* The Comical Revenge, V, iii. HBV; LO; OBEV (1st ed.); OBS
Song: "Lady, you are with beauties so enriched." Francis Davison. ElL
Song: "Lake and a fairy boat, A." Thomas Hood. HBV; OTPC (1946 ed.); PCH
(Lake and a Fairy Boat, A.) MPB (1956 ed.)
Song: Landskip, The. William Shenstone. CEP; OBEC
(Landscape, The.) SeCePo
(Landskip, The.) CBEP
Song: "Lark now leaves his wat'ry nest, The." Sir William Davenant. *See* Lark Now Leaves. . ., The.
Song: "Lay your sleeping head, my love." W. H. Auden. *See* Lay Your Sleeping Head.
Song: "Lean out of the window." James Joyce. *See* Goldenhair.
Song: "Let it be forgotten, as a flower is forgotten." Sara Teasdale. *See* Let It Be Forgotten.
Song: "Let my voice ring out and over the earth." James Thomson. *Fr.* Sunday up the River, XVII. HBV; MaRV; OBVV; TreFT
Song, A: "Let not the sluggish sleep." *Unknown.* *See* Let Not the Sluggish Sleep.
Song: "Let schoolmasters puzzle their brains." Goldsmith. *Fr.* She Stoops to Conquer, I, ii. OAEP; ViBoPo
("Let schoolmasters puzzle their brain.") EnLi-1 (1949 ed.)
(There Jolly Pigeons, The.) PoRA
(Three Pigeons, The.) ELP
Song: "Let the bells ring, and let the boys sing." John Fletcher. *Fr.* The Spanish Curate, III, ii. OBS; TuPP
Song: "Let's sing a song together once." Louis Simpson. NePoAm
Song: "Life, in one semester." Charles G. Blanden. OQP
Song: "Life with her weary eyes." Mary Zaturenska. NMP
Song: "Life with its weariness." E. Margaret Clarkson. SoP
Song: Lift Boy. Robert Graves. DTC
Song: "Light of spring, The." Alice Duer Miller. AA
Song: "Like violets pale i' the spring o' the year." James Thomson. Sunday up the River, IX. OBVV
Song: "Linnet in the rocky dells, The." Emily Brontë. EnLit; HBV; OAEP; OBNC; PoVP; VA
(Linnet in the Rocky Dells, The.) OTPC
(My Lady's Grave.) OBEV (1st ed.); OBVV; TOP
Song: "Little Black Rose shall be red at last, The!" Aubrey Thomas De Vere. *See* Little Black Rose, The.
Song: "Lo! here we come a-reaping." George Peele. *Fr.* The Old Wives' Tale. OBSC
Song: "Long betwixt love and fear Phillis tormented." Dryden. *See* Long betwixt Love and Fear.
Song: "Lord, when the sense of thy sweet grace." Richard Crashaw. CBV; MaMe; PoE; SeCeV; TrPWD; ViBoPo
(Divine Love.) MaRV
(Song of Divine Love, A.) GoBC
Song: "Lost is my quiet for ever." *Unknown.* SeCL
Song: "Love a thousand sweets distilling." James Shirley. *See* Love, a Thousand Sweets Distilling.
Song: "Love a woman! y'are an ass." Earl of Rochester. PeRV
(Love a Woman.) CavP

Song: "Love and harmony combine." Blake. EnRP; LiTL
Song: Love Arm'd [*or* Armed]. Aphra Behn. *See* Song: "Love in fantastic triumph sate."
Song: "Love, by that loosened hair." Bliss Carman. HBV; VA
Song: "Love for such a cherry lip." Thomas Middleton. *Fr.* Blurt, Master Constable. EG; ElL; ViBoPo
(Lips and Eyes.) HBV
Song: "Love in fantastic [*or* fantastique] triumph sate [*or* satt]." Aphra Behn. *Fr.* Abdelazer. AtBAP; HBV; OBEV; TrGrPo; ViBoPo
(Love Armed.) SeCL
(Love in Fantastic Triumph [Sate].) CBEP; OAEP; OnPM
(Song: Love Arm'd.) CavP; OBS
Song: "Love in her eyes sits playing." John Gay. *See* Love in Her Eyes Sits Playing.
Song: "Love in my heart: oh, heart of me, heart of me." "Fiona Macleod." AA
Song: "Love is a sickness full of woes." Samuel Daniel. *See* Love Is A Sickness.
Song: "Love is cruel, Love is sweet." Thomas MacDonagh. ACP
Song: Love Is like a Lamb. Thomas Middleton. *Fr.* Blurt, Master Constable. AtBAP
("Love is like a lamb, and love is like a lion.") BoLP
Song: "Love laid his sleepless head." Swinburne. BoLiVe; MeWo; TrGrPo
Song: Love Lives beyond the Tomb. John Clare. NoP; OBVV; TOP
(Love.) ChTr
("Love lives beyond.") GTBS-D
(Love Lives beyond the Tomb.) FaBoEn; OBNC
Song: "Love, love me only." Robert Crawford. BoAu
Song: "Love, love today, my dear." Charlotte Mew. MoBrPo
Song: "Love me because I am lost." Louise Bogan. NP; PG (1955 ed.)
Song: "Love still has something of the sea." Sir Charles Sedley. CavP; CEP; FaBoEn; HBV; OBS; PeRV; SeCV-2; SeEP; ViBoPo
(Love Still Has Something of the Sea.) EtS; LoBV; SeCL
Song: "Love that is hoarded, moulds at last." Louis Ginsberg, *wr. at. to* Harold C. Sandall. MaRV; PoToHe (new ed.)
Song: "Love, that looks still on your eyes." William Browne. EG
Song, A: "Love, thou art best of human joys." Countess of Winchilsea. *See* On Love.
Song: "Love took my life and thrill'd it." Lewis Morris. OBVV; VA
(Surface and the Depths, The.) HBV
Song: "Love was true to me." John Boyle O'Reilly. ACP
Song: "Lovely hill-torrents are." W. J. Turner. GoJo; MoBrPo
Song: "Lovely kind and kindly loving." Nicholas Breton. *See* Odd Conceit, An.
Song; "Love's but the frailty of the mind." Congreve. *See* Love's but the Frailty of the Mind.
Song: "Love's on the highroad." Dana Burnet. HBV; PoMa
Song: "Low whispers the wind from Malaya." Jayadeva, *tr. fr. Sanskrit by* Sir Edwin Arnold. *Fr.* The Gita Govinda. LiTW
Song: "Maidens came, The." *Unknown. See* Maidens Came, The.
Song: "Man's a poor deluded bubble." Robert Dodsley. CEP
Song: Mary Morison. Burns. *See* Mary Morison.
Song: "Mary, the mother, sits on the hill." Langdon Elwyn Mitchell. *See* Carol: "Mary, the mother. . ."
Song: "Me Cupid made a happy slave." Sir Richard Steele. OBEC
Song: "Memory, hither come." Blake. EG; EiPP; EnLit; PoEL-4
Song: "Men of thought! be up and stirring." Charles Mackay. PoFr
Song: "Merchant, to secure his treasure, The." Matthew Prior. *See* Ode, An: "Merchant to secure his treasure, The."
Song: "Methinks the poor town has been troubled too long." Charles Sackville. CavP; CEP; PeRV; SECV-2
(Bonny Black Bess.) SeCL
Song: "Mighty thoughts of an old world, The." Thomas Lovell Beddoes. *See* Mighty Thoughts of An Old World, The.
Song: "Moth's kiss, first! The." Robert Browning. *See* Moth's Kiss, First, The.
Song: Murdring Beautie. Thomas Carew. AnAnS-2; SeCP
Song: "My dark-headed Käthchen, my spit-kitten darling." John Manifold. BoLP; DTC
Song: "My days have been so wondrous free." Thomas Parnell. *See* My Days Have Been So Wondrous Free.
Song: "My dear mistress has a heart." Earl of Rochester. HBV; LiTL; LoBV; PeRV; SeCV-2
(My Dear Mistress.) SeCL
Song: "My dreams were doleful and drear." Thomas Caulfield Irwin. IrPN
Song: "My Fair, no beauty of thine will last." Alice Meynell. VA
Song: "My limbs I will fling." William Strode. *Fr.* The Floating Island. SeCL
Song: "My lodging it is on the cold ground." Sir William Davenant. *Fr.* The Rivals. PeRV; SeCL
Song: "My love bound me with a kiss." *At. to* Thomas Campion. *See* Kisses.
Song: "My love is the flaming sword." James Thomson. Sunday up the River, XVI. OBVV
Song: "My luve is like a red, red rose." Burns. *See* Red, Red, Rose, A.
Song: My Nanie, O. Burns. *See* My Nanie, O.
Song: "My silks and fine array." Blake. BEL; CEP; CoBE; EG; EiCL; EiPP; EnLi-2; EnLit; EnRP; ERoP-1; FaBoEn; GTBS-D; HBV; LoBV; OAEP; OBEC; OBEV (1st ed.); OBNC; PAn; PoE; PoPo; TOP; TrGrPo
(My Silks and Fine Array.) BoLiVe; CBEP; ChTr; CLwM; ELP
Song: "My spirit like a shepherd boy." V. Sackville-West. HBMV
Song: "My true love hath my heart, and I have his." Sir Philip Sidney. *See* My True Love Hath My Heart.
Song: "Naomi looks for her child." William Knott. YAP
Song: "Nay but you, who do not love her." Robert Browning. AnFE; BoLiVe; BoLP; EPN; GTBS-W; HBV; LiTL; MaPo; OBEV (1st ed.); PoVP; TrGrPo; ViBoPo
Song: "Neath blue-bell or streamer." Poe. *Fr.* Al Aaraaf. AnFE; APA; CoAnAm; OxBA
('Neath Blue-Bell or Streamer.) AmPP
(Song from "Al Araaf.") NePA
Song: "Neither sighs, nor tears, nor mourning." *Unknown.* SeCL
Song: "Never seek to tell thy love." Blake. *See* Love's Secret.
Song, A: "Night her blackest sables wore, The." Thomas D'Urfey. CavP
Song: "Night is an ancient sorceress, The." Simeon S. Frug, *tr. fr. Yiddish by* Isaac Goldberg. LiTW
Song: "Night is darkening round me, The." Emily Brontë. *See* Night Is Darkening round Me, The.
Song: "No, no, fair heretic[k], it needs must be." Sir John Suckling. *Fr.* Aglaura, IV, i. AnAnS-2; AtBAP; CABA; LiTL; LoBV; OBS; PoIE; ReEn; SeEP
(No, No, Fair Heretic.) CBEP
Song: "No, no, no, no, I cannot hate my foe." Sir Philip Sidney. SiPS
("No, no, no, no, I cannot hate my foe.") FCP
Song: "No, no, no, no, resistance is but vain." Anthony Henly. SeCL
Song: "No, no, poor suff'ring heart no change endeavour." Dryden. *See* No, No, Poor Suffering Heart.
Song: "No, no, the falling blossom is no sign." George Meredith. EnLit
Song: Noble Name of Spark, The. *At. to* the Earl of Rochester *and to* Thomas D'Urfey. *See* Bully, The.
Song: "Noe more unto my thoughts appeare." Sidney Godolphin. MeLP; MePo
(Quatrains.) OBS
Song: "Not, Celia, that I juster am." Sir Charles Sedley. *See* To Celia.
Song: "Not from the whole wide world I chose thee." Richard Watson Gilder. The New Day, Pt. IV, Song IV. AA
Song, A: "Not he, that knows how to acquire." Thomas May. *See* Not He That Knows.
Song: "Nothing I have is worth a tear." E. N. da Costa Andrade. POTE
Song: "Now are the Tritons heard, to Loving-land to call." Michael Drayton. *Fr.* Polyolbion. AtBAP

Song: "Now do the birds in their warbling words." Patrick Hannay. SeCL
Song: "Now I see thy looks were feigned." Thomas Lodge. *See* Ode, An: "Now I find thy looks were feigned."
Song: "Now is the month of maying." *Unknown.* EG; OBSC
Song: "Now let us honor with violin and flute." May Sarton. MoRP
Song: "Now, now the fight's done, and the great god of war." Nathaniel Lee. *Fr.* Theodosius; or, The Force of Love. PeRV
Song: "Now sleeps the crimson petal." Tennyson. *See* Now sleeps the Crimson Petal.
Song: "Now that Fate is dead and gone." Edith Sitwell. MoAB; MoBrPo (1950 ed.); NeMA
Song: "Now the lusty spring is seen." John Fletcher. *See* Love's Emblems.
Song: "Nymphs and shepherds, dance no more." Milton. *Fr.* Arcades. AtBAP; FiP; SeCL; ViBoPo
Song: "O bird, thou dartest to the sun." Maria White Lowell. AA
Song: "O Brignall banks are wild and fair." Sir Walter Scott. *See* Brignall Banks.
Song: "O come soft rest of cares! come, Night!" George Chapman. *See* Bridal Song ("O come. . .").
Song, A: "Oh do[e] not wanton with those eyes." Ben Jonson. AnAnS-2; HBV; NoP; OBS; ReEn; SCEP-2; SeCP
Song: "O fair! O sweet! when I do look on thee." Sir Philip Sidney. SiPS
(O Faire! O Sweete!) AtBAP
("O fair, O sweet, when I do look on thee.") FCP
Song: "O fair[e] sweet face, O eyes celestial[l] bright." John Fletcher. *Fr.* Women Pleas'd. OBS; PoEL-2
Song: "O fly not, Pleasure, pleasant-hearted Pleasure." Wilfrid Scawen Blunt. *Fr.* The Love Lyrics of Proteus: A Rhapsody. JKCP; OBEV (1st ed.); OBVV; ViBoPo
Song: "O harmless feast." Barten Holyday. *Fr.* Technogamia. ElL
Song: "Oh, how hard it is to find." Thomas Campbell. CLwM
Song: "O, inexpressible as sweet." George E. Woodberry. *See* O, Inexpressible as Sweet.
Song: "O, it was out by Donnycarney." James Joyce. Chamber Music, XXXI. MoBrPo; OBVV
Song: "O lady, leave thy silken thread." Thomas Hood. HoPM
Song: "O lady, when the tipped cup of the moon blessed you." Ted Hughes. BoPe; POTi
Song: "O let the solid ground." Tennyson. Maud, I, xi. HBV
(I Shall Have Had My Day.) MeWo
Song: "O, like a queen's her happy tread." Sir William Watson. HBV
Song: "O Love, how strangely sweet." John Marston. *See* O Love, How Strangely Sweet.
Song: "Oh Love! that stronger art than wine." *At. to* Aphra Behn, *also to*—— Ousley. *Fr.* The Lucky Chance (*by* Alphra Behn). LO
(Of Love.) SeCL
Song: "'Oh! Love,' they said, 'is King of Kings.'" Rupert Brooke. HBV; TSW
Song: "O lovely April, rich and bright." Gustave Kahn, *tr. fr. French by* Ludwig Lewisohn. TrJP
Song: "O lovers, this song I give to you." A. R. D. Fairburn. *Fr.* To Daphnis and Chloe in the Park. AnNZ
Song: "O memory, thou fond deceiver." Goldsmith. *See* Memory.
Song: "O mistress mine, where are you roaming?" Shakespeare. *See* O Mistress Mine, Where Are You Roaming?
Song: "O Nancy, wilt thou go with me?" Thomas Percy. *See* O Nancy, Wilt Thou Go with Me?
Song: "Oh, no more, no more, too late." John Ford. *Fr.* The Broken Heart, IV, iii. LO; LoBV; OBS; PoEL-2; SeCePo; SeEP; ViBoPo
(Now Love Dies.) SeCL
(Oh No More, No More, Too Late.) AtBAP; ELP; TuPP
Song: "O ruddier than the cherry." John Gay. *See* O Ruddier than the Cherry.
Song: "Oh roses for the flush of youth." Christina Rossetti. GTBS; GTBS-P; LoBV; ViBoPo; ViPo; VP
(Oh Roses for the Flush of Youth.) ELP
Song: "Oh! say not woman's love [*or* heart] is bought." Isaac Pocock, *wr. at. to* Thomas Love Peacock. *Fr.* The Heir of Vironi. HBV
Song: "O sing unto my roundelay." Thomas Chatterton. *See* Minstrel's Song.
Song: "O Sorrow,/ Why dost borrow." Keats. *See* Song of the Indian Maid.
Song: "O spirit of the Summertime!". William Allingham. IrPN
Song: "O, strew the way with rosy flowers." James Clarence Mangan. IrPN
Song; "O Swallow, Swallow, flying, flying South." Tennyson. *See* O Swallow, Swallow...
Song: "O sweet delight, O more than human bliss." Thomas Campion. *See* O Sweet Delight.
Song: "O, that joy so soon should waste." Ben Jonson. *Fr.* Cynthia's Revels, IV, iii. LiTL; ViBoPo
(Kiss, The.) HBV; UnTE
(Oh, That Joy So Soon Should Waste.) TuPP
Song: "Oh! that we two were Maying." Charles Kingsley. *Fr.* The Saint's Tragedy. HBV; VA
Song: "Oh, the fickle state of lovers!" Francis Quarles. SeCL
Song: "Oh the sad day." Thomas Flatman. *See* Sad Day, The.
Song: "O thou that sleep'st like pig in straw." Sir William Davenant. *Fr.* News from Plymouth. EG; SeCL; SeEP
(O Thou That Sleep'st like Pig in Straw.) CBEP; InvP
Song: "'O where are you going?' said reader to rider." W. H. Auden. *See* O Where Are You Going?
Song: "Oh, why did e'er my thoughts aspire." Charles Sackville. SeCL
Song: "O'er desert plains, and rushy meers." William Shenstone. FaBoEn
Song: "O'er [*or* O're] the smooth enamel[l]ed green." Milton. *Fr.* Arcades. BoLiVe; LoBV; OBEV; SeCL; ThWaDe; TrGrPo; ViBoPo
(O'er [*or* O're] the Smooth Enamelled Green.) AtBAP; InPo
Song: "Of all the torments, all the cares." *At. to* Sir George Etherege. *See* Rivals.
Song: "Of thee (kind boy) I ask no red and white." Sir John Suckling. *See* Sonnet: "Of thee (kind boy). . ."
Song: " Often I have heard it said." Walter Savage Landor. *See* Her Lips.
Song: "Old Adam, the carrion crow." Thomas Lovell Beddoes. *Fr.* Death's Jest Book, V, iv. ChER; ERoP-2; LiTB; OBRV; PoEL-4; TOP
(Carrion Crow, The.) TrGrPo; WiR
(Old Adam, the Carrion Crow.) EnRP; PoMS
(Song That Wolfram Heard in Hell, The.) PeER
(Wolfram's Song.) CBEP; GTBS-D; OBEV; OBVV; SiTL
Song: "Old England is eaten by knaves." Alexander McLachlan. *Fr.* The Emigrant. OBCV
Song: "Old Farmer Oats and his son Ned." John Jay Chapman. PoEL-5
Song: "Old friends/ when I was young." Louis Zukofsky. NYTB
Song: On Captain Barney's Victory over the Ship *General Monk.* Philip Freneau. PAH
Song: On May Morning. Milton. *See* Song on May Morning.
Song: "Once my heart was a summer rose." Edith Sitwell. ChMP; GTBS-D
Song: "One day the god of fond desire." James Thomson. EnLoPo
Song: "One gloomy eve I roam'd about." John Clare. EG
Song: One Hard Look. Robert Graves. MoBrPo
Song: "Only a little while since first we met." Brian Hooker. HBMV
Song: "Only tell her that I love." Lord Cutts. HBV; OBEV (1st ed.)
(Only Tell Her That I Love.) SeCL
Song: "Or love me less [*or* mee lesse], or love me more." Sidney Godolphin. CavP; MePo; OBS; SeCL; SeEP
Song: "O're the smooth enamel'd green." Milton. *See* Song: "O'er the smooth enameled green."
Song: "Orpheus with his lute made trees." *At. to* John Fletcher, *also to* Shakespeare. *See* Orpheus with His Lute.
Song: "Out upon it, I have loved." Sir John Suckling. *See* Constant Lover, The.
Song: "Over hill, over dale." Shakespeare. *See* Over Hill, over Dale.
Song: "Over the sea our galleys went." Robert Browning. *Fr.* Paracelsus, Pt. IV. OBRV; VA
(Over the Sea Our Galleys Went.) PoVP
(Wanderers, The.) OBEV; OBVV

Song: Owl, The. Tennyson. *See* Owl, The.
Song: "Pardon, goddess of the night." Shakespeare. *Fr.* Much Ado about Nothing, V, iii. CTC
("Pardon, goddess of the night.") OBSC; SiCE; ViBoPo
Song: "Peace, wayward barne! O cease thy moan!" Richard Brome. *Fr.* The Northern Lass. SeCL
Song: "Peasant sun went crushing grapes, The." Laurence Dakin. *Fr.* Tancred, I, i. CaP
Song: Perswasions to Enjoy. Thomas Carew. *See* Persuasions to Joy.
Song: "Phillis, be gentler I advise [*or* advice]." Earl of Rochester. CavP; EiCL; PeRV
Song: "Phillis, for shame let us improve." Charles Sackville. *See* Song: "Phyllis, for shame. . ."
Song: "Phillis is my only joy." Sir Charles Sedley. *See* Song: "Phyllis is my only joy."
Song: "Phillis, let's shun the common fate." Sir Charles Sedley. PeRV; SeCV-2
("Phillis, let's shun the common fate.") LO
Song: "Phillis, men say that all my vows." Sir Charles Sedley. PeRV
Song: "Phoebus, arise." William Drummond of Hawthornden. *See* Phoebus, Arise!
Song: "Phyllis [*or* Phillis], for shame, let us improve." Charles Sackville. CEP; SeCV-2
(Advice, The.) SeCL
(Phillis for Shame Let Us Improve.) CavP; OBS
Song: "Phyllis [*or* Phillis] is my only joy." Sir Charles Sedley. ATP; CavP; CEP; CLwM; EnLoPo; InMe; OBS; SeCV-2; SeEP
(Phyllis.) SeCL
(Phyllis Is My Only Joy.) EG
(To Phillis.) BoLP
Song: "Pious Selinda goes to prayers." Congreve. *See* Pious Selinda.
Song: "Place in thy memory, dearest, A." Gerald Griffin. *See* Place in Thy Memory, A.
Song: "Pleasures of love, and the joys of good wine, The." Sir George Etherege. *Fr.* The Man of Mode, IV, i. CEP
Song: "Pluck the fruit and taste the pleasure." Thomas Lodge. *See* Pluck the Fruit and Taste. . .
Song: "Poppies paramour the girls." Haniel Long. HBMV
Song, A: "Pouring music, soft and strong, The." Frederic William Henry Myers. VA
Song: "Pride and ambition, and peevishness too." *Unknown.* SeCL
Song: "Primrose in the green forest, The." Thomas Deloney. *Fr.* The Gentle Craft. TiPo (1959 ed.); ViBoPo
Song: "Pursuing beauty, men descry." Thomas Southerne. *Fr.* Sir Antony Love; or, The Rambling Lady. PeRV; SeCL
(Song in the Second Act, A.) SeEP
Song: "Quoth tongue of neither maid nor wife." Sir Henry Taylor. *See* Elena's Song.
Song: "Rarely, rarely, comest thou." Shelley. EnRP; EPN; ERoP-2; HBV; OAEP; OBNC; OBRV; TrGrPo
(Invocation: "Rarely, rarely, comest thou.") GTBS; GTBS-D; GTBS-P; GTBS-W; GTSE
(Rarely, Rarely Comest Thou.) CBEP; CH
(Spirit of Delight.) BoLiVe
"I love snow and all the forms," 3 *ll.* TiPo (1959 ed.)
Song: "Rise Lady Mistresse, rise." Nathaniel Field. *See* Rise, Lady Mistress, Rise!
Song: "Roses and pinks will be strewn where you go." Sir William Davenant. *Fr.* The Unfortunate Lovers. ViBoPo
Song: "Rousing to rein his pad's head back." Geoffrey Taylor. NeIP; OxBI
Song: "Sabrina fair." Milton. *See* Sabrina Fair.
Song: "Say, lovely dream! where couldst thou find." Edmund Waller. *See* Say, Lovely Dream.
Song: "Say this city has ten million souls." W. H. Auden. *See* Refugee Blues.
Song: "See! Hymen comes; how his torch blazes." Sir Charles Sedley. PeRV
Song: Scrutiny, The. Richard Lovelace. *See* Scrutiny, The.
Song: "See, how like twilight slumber falls." Charles Cotton. SeCL
(Song; Set by Mr. Coleman.) OBS
Song: "See, O see!/ How every tree." George Digby, Earl of Bristol. *Fr.* Elvira. SeCL
Song: "See, see, she wakes! Sabina wakes." Congreve. HBV
Song: "Seek not the tree of silkiest bark." Aubrey Thomas De Vere. JKCP; OBVV; PoVP; VA
Song: "Shall I tell you whom I love?" William Browne. *See* Shall I Tell You Whom I Love?
Song: "Shape alone let others prize, The." Mark Akenside. HBV
Song: "She has left me, my pretty." Sylvia Townsend Warner. MoAB; MoBrPo
Song: "She is not fair to outward view." Hartley Coleridge. BBV (1951 ed.); EG; EnRP; GTSE; GTSL; HBV; MCCG; OBEV; OBRV; OBVV; TreFS; VA; ViBoPo
(She Is Not Fair.) FaBV
(She Is Not Fair to Outward View.) GTBS; GTBS-D; GTBS-P; GTBS-W; LiTL; TOP
Song: "She spoke to me gently with words of sweet meaning." Patrick MacDonogh. NeIP
Song: "She whom I love will sit apart." Gerald Gould. MoBrPo (1942 ed.)
Song: "Shepherd, who can pass such wrong." Jorge de Montemayor. *See* Nymph Selvagia, The, Her Song.
Song: "She's somewhere in the sunlight strong." Richard Le Gallienne. HBV; OBEV; OBVV
Song: "Shine out, fair Sun, with all your heat." *Unknown.* *See* Shine Out, Fair Sun. . .
Song: "Shoot, false Love, I care not." *Unknown.* OBSC
Song: "Should I sigh out my dayes in griefe." Matthew Stevenson. CavP
Song: "Should you, of mirth and hope bereft." Alfred de Musset, *tr. fr. French by* Alan Conder. OnPM
Song: "Sigh no more, ladies, sigh no more." Shakespeare. *See* Sigh No More.
Song: "Silly boy, there is no cause." Thomas Pestel. ElL
Song: "Sing his praises that doth keep." John Fletcher. *See* Hymn to Pan.
Song, A: "Sing me a sweet, low song of night." Hildegarde Hawthorne. AA; FaBoBe; HBV
Song: "Sing the old song, amid the sounds dispersing." Aubrey Thomas De Vere. HBV
Song: "Sing we and chant it." *Unknown.* *See* To Live in Pleasure.
Song: "Singer within the little streets." Monk Gibbon. NeIP
Song, A: "Slaves to London, I'll deceive you." Peter Motteux. *See* Slaves to London.
Song: "Sleep, O sleep." John Gay. Polly, Air XXIII. FaBoEn
("Sleep, O sleep.") EG; ViBoPo
Song: "Slow, slow, fresh fount, keep time with my salt tears." Ben Jonson. *See* Slow, Slow, Fresh Fount.
Song, A: "Smile, Massachusetts, smile." *Unknown.* PAH
Song: "Smooth was the water, calm the air." Sir Charles Sedley. CBV; CEP; PeRV; SeCV-2
Song: "So have I seen a silver swan." *At to* John Webster. CBEP; SeCL
Song: "So large a morning, so itself, to lean." W. H. Auden. NePoAm-2
Song, The: "So light no one noticed." Edward Dorn. CoPo
Song, The: "So passeth, in the passing of a day." Spenser. *Fr.* The Faerie Queene, II, 12. MyFE
Song: "So, so,/ Lo, lilies fade, before the roses show." William Clerke. *See* So, So.
Song: "So, we'll go no more a-roving." Byron. *See* So We'll Go No More a-Roving.
Song: "Softly, O midnight hours!" Aubrey Thomas De Vere. *See* Serenade: "Softly, O midnight hours."
Song: "Soldier and a sailor, A." Congreve. *See* Soldier and a Sailor, A.
Song: "Soldier, rest! thy warfare o'er." Sir Walter Scott. *See* Soldier, Rest!
Song: "Something calls and whispers, along the city street." Georgiana Goddard King. *Fr.* The Way of Perfect Love. HBV
Song: "Song is so old." Hermann Hagedorn. HBV
Song, The: "Song lay silent in my pen, A. John Erskine. AA
Song, A: "Song of grass, A,/ A song of earth." "Yehoash," *tr. fr. Yiddish by* Isidore Goldstick. TrJP
Song: Souldier Going to the Field The. Sir William Davenant. *See* Souldier Going to the Field, The.
Song: "Soules joy, now I am gone." *Unknown, at. to* The Earl of Pembroke. AnAnS-1; MeP; OBS
Song: "Spirit haunts the year's last hours, A." Tennyson. AtBAP; GTBS-P; GTSL; ILP; NoP; OAEP; OBNC; PeER; PoEL-5; PoVP; TOP; ViPP
(Spirit Haunts the Years Last Hours, A.) InvP

Song: "Spirit! that dwellest where." Poe. *Fr.* Al Aaraaf. CoBA
Song: "Splendour falls on castle walls, The." Tennyson. *See* Bugle Song.
Song: "Spouse I do hate, A." William Wycherley. *See* Spouse I Do Hate.
Song: Spring and Winter. Shakespeare. *See* When Daisies Pied and Violets Blue.
Song: "Spring lights her candles everywhere." Fredegond Shove. HBMV
Song: "Spring, the sweete spring, is the year's pleasant king." Thomas Nashe. *See* Spring, the Sweet Spring.
Song: "Star that bids the shepherd fold, The." Milton. *See* Star That Bids the Shepherd Fold, The.
Song: "Stay Phoebus, stay." Edmund Waller. AnAnS-2; ILP; SCEP-2; SeCP
Song: "Stay, stay at home, my heart, and rest." Longfellow. *See* Home Song.
Song, A: "Steal from the meadows, rob the tall green hills." Lord Alfred Douglas. JKCP (1926 ed.); PoVP
Song: "Still to be neat, still to be dressed." Ben Jonson. *See* Simplex Munditiis.
Song: "Stop all the clocks." W. H. Auden. *See* Stop All the Clocks.
Song: "Stranger, you who hide my love." Stephen Spender. FaBoTw
Song: "Streams that wind among the hills, The." George Darley. *Fr.* Sylvia; or, The May Queen. NBM
Song: "Strew not earth with empty stars." Thomas Lovell Beddoes. *Fr.* The Second Brother. CBEP; ViBoPo
Song: "Sun is mine, The." Robert Hogg. WHW
Song: "Sunny shaft did I behold, A." Samuel Taylor Coleridge. *See* Glycine's Song.
Song: "Sweet and low, sweet and low." Tennyson. *See* Sweet and Low.
Song: "Sweet are the charms of her I love." Barton Booth. OBEC
Song: "Sweet are the thoughts that savor of content." Robert Greene. *See* Sweet Are the Thoughts. . .
Song: "Sweet beast, I have gone prowling." W. D. Snodgrass. MoAmPo (1962 ed.); NYBP
Song: "Sweet Cupid, ripen her desire." *Unknown.* LoBV; OBSC; ViBoPo
Song: "Sweet Echo, sweetest nymph, that liv'st unseen." Milton. *See* Sweet Echo.
Song: "Sweet in her green dell the flower of beauty slumbers." George Darley. GTBS-D; LO; OBEV; OBVV
(Flower of Beauty.) HBV; VA
(Serenade of a Loyal Martyr.) OBNC; OBRV; OnYI
Song: "Sweet, yet cruel unkind is she." *Unknown.* SeCL
Song: "Sweetest love, I do not go[e]." John Donne. AnAnS-1; ATP; AWP; BoLiVe; CBEP; EG; EIL; ELP; EnL; EnLit; EnRePo; FaBoEn; InvP; LiTL; MaMe MaPo; MBW-1; MeLP; MePo; NoP; OAEP; OBS; PAn; PoE; PoEL-2; ReEn; ReIE; SCEP-1; SeCP; SeCV-1; SeEP; TOP; ViBoPo
(Sweetest Love [I Do Not Go].) BEL; EnLi-1; FaPL; MeWo; PoeP; PTK; TreFT; TrGrPo
"O how feeble is man's power," *br. sel.* LO
Song: "Sylvia the fair, in the bloom of fifteen." Dryden. ErPo; LiTG; LiTL; ViBoPo
(Sylvia the Fair.) CBEP; SiTL; UnTE
Song: "Take it love!" Richard Le Gallienne. HBV
Song: "Take, O take those lips away." Shakespeare. *See* Take, O Take Those Lips Away.
Song: "Tears, idle tears." Tennyson. *See* Tears, Idle Tears.
Song: "Tell me no more I am deceived." Congreve. ALV
(Better Bargain, The.) UnTE
Song: "Tell me no more I am deceived." Sir George Etherege. CavP
Song: "Tell me not I my time misspend." *At. to* Sir John Eaton *and to* Phillip King. SeCL
Song: "Tell me where is fancy bred." Shakespeare. *See* Tell Me Where Is Fancy Bred.
Song, The: "That day, in the slipping of torsos and straining flanks." Lola Ridge. NP
Song: That Women Are but Men's Shadows [*or* Shaddowes]. Ben Jonson. EnLit; FaBoEn; HBV; LiTL; NoP; OBS; PoIE; ReIE; SCEP-2; SeCP
(Follow a Shadow.) ALV
(Shadow, The.) OBEV
(That Women Are but Men's Shadows [*or* Shaddowes].) AtBAP; CBEP; EIL; ViBoPo
(Women Men's Shadows.) WBLP
Song: "There is many a love in the land, my love." Joaquin Miller. HBV
Song: "There is no joy in water apart from the sun." R. N. Currey. BoSA; MemP; PeSA
Song: "There is no land like England." Tennyson. *Fr.* The Foresters, II, i. VA
Song: "There stands a lonely pine-tree." Heine, *tr. fr. German by* Emma Lazarus. TrJP
Song: "There was a jolly miller once." Isaac Bickerstaffe. *See* There Was a Jolly Miller.
Song: "There was a Knight of Bethlehem." Henry Neville Maugham. *See* Knight of Bethlehem, A.
Song: "There's one great bunch of stars in heaven." Théophile Marzials. OBVV
Song: "These songs will not stand." Denis Glover. Songs, I. AnNZ
Song: "Think of dress in ev'ry light." John Gay. *See* Think of Dress in Every Light.
Song: "This is the song of those who live alone." William Justema. NYBP
Song: "This peach is pink with such a pink." Norman Gale. HBV; VA
Song: This Tress. Robert Browning. MeWo
Song, A: "Thou art the soul of a summer's day." Paul Laurence Dunbar. AmNP
Song: "Though I am young and cannot tell." Ben Jonson. *See* Though I Am Young.
Song: "Though regions farr devided." Aurelian Townshend. *See* Though Regions Far Divided.
Song: "Though richer swains thy love pursue." Joanna Baillie. *Fr.* The Country Inn. OBRV
Song: "Three little maidens they have slain." Maurice Maeterlinck, *tr. fr. French by* Jethro Bithell. AWP; JAWP; WBP
Song: "Three Moorish girls I loved." *Unknown, tr. fr. Spanish by* Jean Willard Burnham. LiTW
Song: "Three score and ten by common calculation." James Robinson Planché. BOHV
Song: "Thus the Mayne glideth." Robert Browning. *See* Thus the Mayne Glideth.
Song: "Thus when the swallow, seeking prey." John Gay. *Fr.* The Beggar's Opera, II, ii. PoEL-3
Song: "Thy face I have seen as one seeth." Sophie Jewett. AA
Song: "Thy fingers make early flowers of all things." E. E. Cummings. MAP; MoAmPo
Song: "Thy voice is heard thro rolling drums." Tennyson. *See* Thy Voice is Heard. . .
Song: "Thrysis, when we parted, swore." Thomas Gray. OAEP
Song: "'Tis said that absence conquers love!" Frederick William Thomas. AA; HBV
Song: "'Tis sweet to hear the merry lark." Hartley Coleridge. *See* Lark and the Nightingale, The.
Song: To a Lady with Many Names. John Wickham. JKCP (1955 ed.)
Song: "To all you ladies now at land." Charles Sackville. BEL; CavP; HBV; SeCV-2; TOP
(Song: Written at Sea, in the First Dutch War, 1665, the Night before an Engagement.) CEP; EnLoPo; LiTG; OBEV; OBS
(Song Written at Sea.) CoMu; EnLi-1 (1949 ed.); SiTL
(Written at Sea, in the First Dutch War.) SeCL; SeEP
Song: To Althea, from Prison. Richard Lovelace. *See* To Althea from Prison.
Song: To Celia ("Come, my Celia, let us prove"). Ben Jonson. *See* Come, My Celia, Let Us Prove.
Song: To Celia ("Drink to me only with thine eyes"). Ben Jonson. *See* To Celia ("Drink to Me. . .").
Song: To Celia ("Kiss me, sweet; the wary lover"). Ben Jonson. *See* To Celia ("Kiss me, sweet. . .").
Song: To Comus. Ben Jonson. *See* Hymn to Comus.
Song: To Cynthia. Ben Jonson. *See* Hymn to Diana.
Song: "To fix her—'twere a task as vain." Tobias George Smollett. WaPE
Song: "To friend and to foe." *Unknown.* *See* To Friend and Foe.
Song: To Her Againe, She Burning in a Feaver. Thomas Carew. AnAnS-2; SeCP
Song: To Lucasta, Going beyond the Seas. Richard Lovelace. *See* To Lucasta, Going beyond the Seas.

Song: To Lucasta, Going to the Warres. Richard Lovelace. *See* To Lucasta, Going to the Wars.
Song: To My Inconstant Mistress. Thomas Carew. *See* To My Inconstant Mistress.
Song: To My Mistris, I Burning in Love. Thomas Carew. AnAnS-2; SCEP-2; SeCP
Song: To Myra. George Granville. *See* Happiest Mortals Once Were We, The.
Song: To One That Desired to Know My Mistris. Thomas Carew. AnAnS-2; SeCP
Song: To Psyche. William Morris. *Fr.* The Earthly Paradise. VA
Song: To the Masquers Representing Stars. Thomas Campion. *Fr.* The Lords' Mask. LoBV
(Stars Dance, The.) OBSC
Song: "To the ocean now I fly." Milton. *See* To the Ocean Now I Fly.
Song: "Tomorrow is [*or* Good morrow, 'tis] Saint Valentine's day." Shakespeare. *See* Tommorrow Is Saint Valentine's Day.
Song: "Too late, alas! I must confess." Earl of Rochester. HBV
Song: "Trip it gipsies, trip it fine." Thomas Middleton *and* William Rowley. *See* Trip It Gipsies.
Song: "Trust the form of airy things." Henry Harington. *See* Trust the Form of Airy Things.
Song, A: "Turn on and sing my happy song." Michael McClure. FRC
Song: "Turn, turn thy beauteous face away. Beaumont *and* Fletcher. *See* Turn, Turn Thy Beauteous Face Away.
Song: "'Twas a dispute 'twixt heav'n and earth." Earl of Rochester. PeRV
Song: "Under a southern wind." Theodore Roethke. CrMA
Song: "Under the bronze leaves a colt was foaled." "St.-J. Perse," *tr. fr. French by* T. S. Eliot. *Fr.* Anabasis. AtBAP; LiTW; PoPl
Song: "Under the greenwood tree." Shakespeare. *See* Under the Greenwood Tree.
Song: "Under the winter, dear." Eugene Lee-Hamilton. OBVV
Song: "Urnes and odours bring away!" Fletcher *and* Shakespeare. *See* Funeral Song.
Song: "Victor was a little baby." W. H. Auden. AnFE
Song: "Victorious men of earth, no more." James Shirley. *See* Victorious Men of Earth.
Song: "Violet in her lovely hair, A." Charles Swain. HBV
Song: "Virtue's branches wither, virtue pines." Thomas Dekker. *See* Priest's Song, A.
Song: "Wait but a little while." Norman Gale. HBV; VA
Song: "Wake all the dead! What hoa! What hoa!" Sir William Davenant. *See* Wake All the Dead. . .
Song: "Wake not, but hear me, love!" Lew Wallace. *Fr.* Ben-Hur. AA
Song: "Warm are the still and lucky miles." W. H. Auden. FaBoMo; GTBS-D; POTE
Song: "Was it a form, a gait, a grace." Henry Reynolds. LO; SeCL
(Was It a Form?) TuPP
("Was it a forme, a gate, a grace.") SeCSL
Song: "We break the glass, whose sacred wine." Edward Coote Pinkney. AmLP; HBV
Song: "We came to Tamichi in 1880." Scott Judy *and* "Doc" Hammond. PoOW
Song: "We have bathed, where none have seen us." Thomas Lovell Beddoes. *See* Bridal Song to Amala.
Song: "We only ask for sunshine." Helen Hay Whitney. HBV
Song: "We sail towards evening's lonely star." Celia Thaxter. AA
Song: "We, who are men, how shall we know?" R. S. Thomas. ToPo
Song: "Weary lot is thine, fair maid, A." Sir Walter Scott. *See* Weary Lot Is Thine, A.
Song: "Weep, weep, ye woodmen, wail." Anthony Munday *and* Henry Chettle. *See* Dirge for Robin Hood.
Song: "Were I laid on Greenland's coast." John Gay. *Fr.* The Beggar's Opera, I, i. CEP; OBEC; OxBoLi; PoEL-3; SeCeV
(Macheath and Polly.) LoBV
(Over the Hills and Far Away.) ATP (1935 ed.); EnLi-1 (1949 ed.)
(Were I Laid on Greenland's Coast.) AtBAP; CBEP; EnLoPo; NoP
Song: "Westron wynde when wyll thou blow." *Unknown.* *See* Western Wind, When Wilt Thou Blow?
Song: "What a dainty life the milkmaid leads!" Thomas Nabbes. *Fr.* Tottenham Court. EG; SeCL
Song: "What have the years left us?" Charles G. Blanden. OQP
Song: "What is there hid in the heart of a rose." Alfred Noyes. CH
Song: "What shall he have that kill'd the deer?" Shakespeare. *See* What Shall He Have That Killed the Deer?
Song: "What trees were in Gethsemane." Charles G. Blanden. ChIP; OQP
Song: "Whaur yon broken brig hings owre." William Soutar. GoTS; OxBS
Song: "When all the world is young, lad." Charles Kingsley. *See* Young and Old.
Song: "When as the rye [*or* rie] reach to the chin." George Peele. *See* Whenas the Rye Reach to the Chin.
Song: "When Britain really ruled the waves." W. S. Gilbert. *See* House of Peers, The.
Song: "When daffodils begin to peer." Shakespeare. *See* When Daffodils Begin to Peer.
Song: "When daisies pied and violets blue." Shakespeare. *See* When Daisies Pied and Violets Blue.
Song: "When, dearest, I but think of thee." *At. to* Sir John Suckling *and to* Owen Felltham. *See* When, Dearest, I but Think of Thee.
Song: "When Delia on the plain appears." George Lyttelton. CEP; OBEC
(Tell Me, My Heart, if This Be Love.) HBV; OBEV (1st ed.)
(When Delia on the Plain Appears.) CBEP
Song: "When I am dead, my dearest." Christina Rossetti. ATP; AWP; CBEP; CH; EnLi-2; FaFP; ForPo; FosPo; GTBS; GTSL; HBV; JAWP; LiTG; LiTL; MemP; MeWo; NoP; OAEP; OBEV; OBVV; OuHeWo; PCD; PoE; PoFS; PoLF; PoRA; PoVP; TIHL; TOP; TreFS; ViBoPo; ViPo; VP; WBP; WHA
(Requiem.) OtMeF
(When I Am Dead [My Dearest].) BoLiVe; BoLP; ELP; FaPL; GTBS-D; GTBS-W; LiTB; MCCG; NeHB; PG (1955 ed.); PoSa; TrGrPo; WePo
Song: "When I behold my mistress' face." *Unknown.* SeCL
Song: "When I lie burning in thine eye." Thomas Stanley. CavP; ViBoPo
Song: "When I was a greenhorn and young." Charles Kingsley. *Fr.* The Saint's Tragedy. NBM
(When I Was a Greenhorn and Young.) PoVP
Song: "When I was young, I said to Sorrow." Aubrey Thomas De Vere. GTBS-D
(Sorrow.) WiR
Song, The: "When I would sing of crooked streams and fields." Jones Very. MAmP
Song: "When icicles hang by the wall." Shakespeare. *See* When Icicles Hang by the Wall.
Song: "When love at first did move." Ben Jonson. *Fr.* The Masque of Beauty. GoBC
Song: "When love on time and measure makes his ground." *At. to* John Lilliat. EIL; LO
(False Love.) OBSC
Song: "When lovely woman stoops to folly." Goldsmith. *Fr.* The Vicar of Wakefield, *ch.* 24. AWP; BEL; CBV; CEP; EiPP; GTBS; GTSE; GTSL; ILP; JAWP; LiTL; OBEC; PoFS; PoPl; SeCePo; TOP; TrGrPo; VaPo; ViBoPo; WBP
(Stanzas on Woman.) ELP; EnLit; ExPo; OnYI; OxBI
(When Lovely Woman [Stoops to Folly].) CBEP; EnLi-1; GTBS-D; GTBS-P; GTBS-W; HBV; InP; NoP; PoIE; SeCeV; StP; TreF
(Woman.) LiTB; LiTG; OBEV
Song: "When that I was and a little tiny boy." Shakespeare. *See* When That I Was and a Little Tiny Boy.
Song: "When the echo of the last footstep dies." E. W. Mandel. MoCV; OBCV
Song: "When the rose came I loved the rose." Arthur O'Shaughnessy. PoVP
Song: "When thy beauty appears." Thomas Parnell. EiCL; EiPP; LO; OBEC; OBEV; UnTE
(When Thy Beauty Appears.) CBEP
Song: "When Time, who steals our years away." Thomas Moore. TreFS
Song: "When working blackguards come to blows." Ebenezer Elliott. NBM

Song: "Whenas the rye reach to the chin." George Peele. *See* Whenas the Rye Reach to the Chin.
Song: "Whene'er with haggard eyes I view." George Canning, George Ellis, *and* John Hookham Frere. *Fr.* the Rovers, I. ALV; OBEC
(Song by Rogero.) EiCL
(Song by Rogero the Captive.) CEP; TOP
(Song of One Eleven Years in Prison.) BOHV; FiBHP
Song: "Where did you come from, baby dear?" George Macdonald. *See* Baby, The.
Song: "Where is the nymph, whose azure eye." Thomas Moore. EnLoPo
Song: "Where shall Celia fly for shelter." Christopher Smart. EnLoPo
Song: "Where shall the lover rest." Sir Walter Scott. *See* Where Shall the Lover Rest.
Song: "Where the bee sucks, there suck I." Shakespeare. *See* Ariel's Song: "Where the bee sucks."
Song: "Wherever I am, and whatever I doe." Dryden. *See* Wherever I Am, and Whatever I Do.
Song, A: "While in the bower, with beauty blessed." Joseph Warton. WaPE
Song: "While Morpheus thus doth gently lay." Henry Killigrew. CH
Song: "While on those lovely looks I gaze." Earl of Rochester. *See* While on Those Lovely Looks I Gaze.
Song, A: "Whil'st Alexis lay prest." Dryden. *See* Whilst Alexis Lay Prest.
Song: "Who calls me bold because I won my love." Cosmo Monkhouse. VA
Song: "Who can say." Tennyson. FaBoCh; LoGBV
Song: "Who has robbed the ocean cave [*or* wave]." John Shaw. AA; AmLP; HBV
Song: "Who hath his fancy pleasèd." Sir Philip Sidney. *See* Who Hath His Fancy Pleasèd.
Song: "Who is it that, this dark night." Sir Philip Sidney. *See* Astrophel and Stella: Eleventh Song.
Song: "Who is lord of lordly fate." Charles Heavysege. *Fr.* Count Filippo. PeCV
Song: "Who is Silvia? what is she". Shakespeare. *See* Who Is Silvia?
Song: "Who tames the lion now?" Thomas Lovell Beddoes. PoE; ViBoPo
Song: "Why art thou slow, thou rest of trouble, Death." Philip Massinger. *Fr.* The Emperor of the East, V, iii. ViBoPo
(Death Invoked.) ACP (1952 ed.)
(Sad Song, A.) OBS; SeCL
("Why art thou slow, thou rest of trouble, Death.") SeEP; TuPP
Song: "Why canst thou not, as others do." *Unknown.* *See* Why Canst Thou Not.
Song: "Why do the bells of [*or* do bells for] Christmas ring?" Eugene Field. *See* Christmas Song.
Song: "Why do the houses stand." George Macdonald. OBVV
Song: "Why fadest thou in death." Richard Watson Dixon. ChTr
Song: "Why, lovely charmer, tell me why." Sir Richard Steele. *Fr.* The Tender Husband. LiTL; ViBoPo
(Why, Lovely Charmer.) HBV
Song: "Why should a foolish marriage vow." Dryden. *See* Why Should a Foolish Marriage Vow.
Song: "Why should you swear I am forsworn." Richard Lovelace. *See* Scrutiny, The.
Song: "Why should your face so please me." Edwin Muir. BoPe
Song: "Why so pale and wan, fond lover?" Sir John Suckling. *See* Why So Pale and Wan?
Song: "Widow bird sate mourning for her love, A." Shelley. *See* Widow Bird, A.
Song: "Wind blows out of the gates of the day, The." W. B. Yeats. *See* Fairy Song.
Song: Wit and Beauty. Robert Gould. CavP
Song: "With fair Ceres, Queen of grain." Thomas Heywood. *Fr.* The Silver Age. CLwM
(Praise of Ceres.) ElL
Song, A: "With love among the haycocks." Ralph Hodgson. GoJo
Song: "With whomsoever I share the spring." Jan Burroway. NePoAm-2
Song: "Woman's face is full of wiles, A." Humphrey Gifford. *Fr.* A Delectable Dream. ElL; SiCE; TuPP
Song: "World is full of loss, The; bring, wind, my love." Muriel Rukeyser. MiAP
Song, A: "World is young today, The." Digby Mackworth Dolben. LoBV; OBNC
Song: "Would you know what's soft? I dare." Thomas Carew. BEL; EG; EnLi-1; TOP
Song: Written at Sea, in the First Dutch War. Charles Sackville. *See* Song: "To all you ladies now at land."
Song: "Ye happy swains, whose hearts are free." Sir George Etherege. HBV; LiTL; ViBoPo
Song: "Year's at the spring, The." Robert Browning. *See* Year's at the Spring, The.
Song, A: "Years have flown since I knew thee first." Richard Watson Gilder. The New Day, Pt. IV, Song VII. AA
Song: "You are as gold." Hilda Doolittle ("H. D."). AnFE; APA; CoAnAm; CoBA; LiTA; LiTM; MAP; MAPA; MoAmPo; TwAmPo
Song, A: "You charm'd me not with that fair face." Dryden. *Fr.* An Evening's Love, II, i. CavP; CEP; SeCV-2
(You Charm'd Me Not.) ATP (1935 ed.); DiPo; EiCL
Song: "You spotted snakes with double tongue." Shakespeare. *See* You Spotted Snakes.
Song: "You virgins that did late despair." James Shirley. *See* Piping Peace.
Song: "You wear the morning like your dress." Hilaire Belloc. OBEV (new ed.)
(Song: Inviting the Influence of a Young Lady upon the Opening Year.) OBVV
Song: "You wrong me, Strephon, when you say." "Ephelia." CavP; LiTL
Song: "You'll love me yet! and I can tarry." Robert Browning. *See* You'll Love Me Yet.
Song: "Young Philander woo'd me long." *Unknown.* ErPo
Song: Your hay it is mow'd and your corn is reap'd. Dryden. *Fr.* King Arthur, V, i. CEP; SeCV-2
Song: "Your heart is a music-box, dearest!" Frances Sargent Osgood. AA
Song: "Youth's the season made for joys." John Gay. *Fr.* The Beggar's Opera, II, i. CEP; OBEC
Song; a Morisko. Jasper Fisher. *See* Morisco, A.
Song, a poem of itself—the word itself a dirge, A. Yonnondio. Walt Whitman. MCCG
Song about Charleston, A. *Unknown.* PAH
Song about Great Men, A. Michael Hamburger. NePoEA
Song about Major Eatherly, A. John Wain. CABL; ToPo
Song about Myself, A. Keats. BoTP, *sts.* 1-2; CoBE; DiPo, *st.* 4; InvP; PoEL-4; PoeP; PP
(Naughty Boy, The, st. 4) GaP; OTPC (1946 ed.); RIS
(There Was a Naughty Boy.) FaBoCh, *sts.* 1 *and* 4; LiTB, *st.* 4; LiTG, *st.* 4; LoGBV, *sts.* 1 *and* 4; ML, *st.* 2; MoShBr, *st.* 4; SiTL, *sts.* 1 *and* 4; YAT
Song about Singing, A. Anne Reeve Aldrich. AA
Song about Whiskers. P. G. Wodehouse. FiBHP
Song above Death. James Edward Tobin. JKCP (1955 ed.)
Song against Children. Aline Kilmer. SP; TSW
Song against Grocers, The. G. K. Chesterton. CenHV
Song against Servants. Gertrude Jane Codd. JKCP (1926 ed.)
Song against Songs, The. G. K. Chesterton. ALV
Song against Women. Willard Huntington Wright. HBV
Song A-la-Mode. Sir Charles Sedley. PeRV
Song and Science. Milicent Washburn Shinn. AA
Song and Wine. Bacchylides, *tr. fr. Greek by* C. M. Bowra. LiTW
Song as Yet Unsung, A. "Yehoash," *tr. fr. Yiddish by* Isidore Goldstick. TrJP
Song at Amala's Wedding. Thomas Lovell Beddoes. *See* Bridal Song to Amala.
Song at Easter, A. Charles Hanson Towne. BLRP; ChIP; MaRV
Song at Morning, A. Edith Sitwell. CMoP
Song at Night. Norman Nicholson. FaBoTw
Song at Santa Cruz. Francis Brett Young. HBMV
Song at Summer's End. A. R. D. Fairburn. AnNZ
Song at the Feast of Brougham Castle. Wordsworth. EnRP
Song at the Moated Grange, A. Shakespeare. *See* Take, O Take Those Lips Away.
Song at the Ruin'd Inn. Tennyson. *Fr.* The Vision of Sin. PoEL-5
Song at the Well, The. George Peele. *Fr.* The Old Wives' Tale. AtBAP; ExPo; SeCeV

Song (continued)
(Celanta at the Well of Life.) LoBV; ThWaDe
(Fair Maiden.) PoEL-2
(Gently Dip.) ELP
(Voice from the Well [of Life Speaks to the Maiden], The.) CBEP; ChTr; FaBoEn
(Voice Speaks from the Well, A.) FaBoCh; LoGBV; OBSC; OxBoLi; SiTL
Song Be Delicate. John Shaw Neilson. BoAV; PoAu-1
Song before Action, *sel.* Kipling.
O Mary Pierced with Sorrow. ISi
Song before Grief, A. Rose Hawthorne Lathrop. AA; CAW; JKCP
Song before Night. Richard Dehmel, *tr. fr. German by* Babette Deutsch *and* Avrahm Yarmolinsky. OnPM
Song between the Queen's Majesty and England, A. William Birche. TuPP
(Songe betwene the Quenes Majestie and Englande, A.) CoMu
Song between two silences Life sings, A. The Silence. Archibald MacLeish. HBMV
Song-Bird. Brian Vrepont. NeLNL
Song-birds, The? are they flown away? Flight. Madison Cawein. AA
Song-Books. *See* Songbooks.
Song by Apelles. John Lyly. *See* Apelles' Song.
Song by Fairies. John Lyly. *Fr.* Endymion. OAEP; ReEn; TuPP
(Fairy Song, A.) OBSC
Song by Isbrand. Thomas Lovell Beddoes. *See* Isbrand's Song.
Song by Lady Happy, as a Sea-Goddess. Margaret Cavendish, Duchess of Newcastle. *See* Sea-Goddess, The.
Song by Mr. Cypress. Thomas Love Peacock. *See* There Is a Fever of the Spirit.
Song by Rogero [the Captive]. George Canning, George Ellis *and* John Hookham Frere. *See* Song: "Whene'er with haggard eyes I view."
Song by the Deaths. Thomas Lovell Beddoes. PeER
Song by Two Voices. Thomas Lovell Beddoes. PeER
Song for a Ball-Game. Wilfrid Thorley. BoTP
Song for a Blue Roadster. Rachel Field. FaPON; TiPo (1950 ed.)
Song for a Camper. John Farrar. YeAr
Song for a Child. Helen B. Davis. SoPo
Song for a Dance. Francis Beaumont. *See* Shake Off Your Heavy Trance.
Song for a Dark Girl. Langston Hughes. AmPP (5th ed.); CDC; IDB; PoNe
Song for a Departure. Elizabeth Jennings. NMP
Song for a Girl. Dryden. ELP; ErPo
(Sung by a Young Girl.) UnTE
Song for a Hot Day. Elizabeth J. Coatsworth. StVeCh (1955 ed.)
Song for a Jewess. Iwan Goll, *tr. fr. French by* Joseph T. Shipley. TrJP
Song for a Listener, *sel.* Leonard Feeney.
Because of Her Who Flowered So Fair. ISi
Song for a Little Cuckoo Clock. Elizabeth J. Coatsworth. SiSoSe
Song for a Little House. Christopher Morley. BoTP; FaPON; MPB; OTD; StVeCh; TreF; TSW
Song for a Lyre. Louise Bogan. LiTA
Song for a Man in Doubt. Kathleen Fraser. YAP
Song for a Marriage. Vassar Miller. HW; ToPo
Song for a Proud Relation. Patrick MacDonogh. OnYI
Song for a Slight Voice. Louise Bogan. AmLP; NP
Song for a Suicide. Langston Hughes. PoNe (1970 ed.)
Song for All Seas, All Ships. Walt Whitman. CH; FaBoBe; HBV; HBVY; MCCG; MoRP; NePA
Song for an Allegorical Play. John Ciardi. PoCh
Song for Apollo. Matthew Arnold. *See* Callicles' Song.
Song for Beauty, A. P. Lal. ACV
Song for December Thirty-first. Frances Frost. YeAr
Song for Decoration Day. Helen C. Bacon. HH
Song for Fine Weather. *Tr. fr. Haida Indian by* Conatance Lindsay Skinner. AWP; JAWP; WBP
Song for Flag Day, A. Lydia Avery Coonley Ward. *See* Flag Song.
Song for Government. Raymond Holden. PoFr
Song for Heroes, A. Edwin Markham. PEDC
Song for Ishtar. Denise Levertov. NaP; PoIE (1970 ed.)
Song for Lexington, A. Robert Kelley Weeks. AA
Song for Lovers. T. I. Moore. MoAuPo
Song for Love's Coming of Age. J. Corson Miller. JKCP (1955 ed.)
Song for Mariana. Shakespeare. *See* Take, O Take Those Lips Away.
Song for May Day, A. Frederick Herbert Adler. DD
Song for Memorial Day. Clinton Scollard. OHIP
Song for Midsummer Night. Elizabeth J. Coatsworth. YeAr
Song for Mother's Day. T. S. Matthews. ELU
Song for Music. G. S. Fraser. ChMP
Song for Music. Sir Edmund Gosse. VA
Song for Music, A. *Unknown.* *See* Weep You No More, Sad Fountains.
Song for My Lady. A. Godwhen. OxBoLi
("Now wolde I faine sum merthes make.") CH, *abr.*; EG, *abr.*; LO
(Song in His Lady's Absence, A.) MeEL
Song for My Mother, A: Her Hands. Anna Hempstead Branch. *See* Her Hands.
Song for My Mother, A: Her Stories. Anna Hempstead Branch. *Fr.* Songs for My Mother. OHIP
Song for My Mother, A: Her Words. Anna Hempstead Branch. *Fr.* Songs for My Mother. BoChLi; OHIP; SiSoSe; TiPo (1959 ed.); YeAr
(Her Words.) FaPON
(Songs for My Mother: Her Words.) HH; OnPP; YT
Song for Naomi. Irving Layton. WHW
Song for New Year's Eve, A. Bryant. DD; MPB; PoRL
Song for Old Apis, A. James Schevill. FiMAP
Song for Our Flag, A. Margaret E. Sangster. FaFP
Song for Peace. W. R. Rodgers. NeBP
Song for St. Cecilia's Day. W. H. Auden. FaBoTw
(Anthem for St. Cecilia's Day.) TwCP
Song for St. Cecilia's Day, A, 1687. Dryden. AtBAP; ATP; AWP; BEL; BoLiVe; BWP; CABA; CBEP; CBV; CEP; DiPo; EiCL; EiPP; EnL; EnLi-1 (1949 ed.); EnLit; ExPo; FaBoEn; FosPo; GoBC; GTBS; GTBS-D; GTBS-P; GTBS-W; GTSE; GTSL; HBV; ILP; InPo; JAWP; LiTB; LiTG; MaPo; MasP; MBW-1; MuSP; OAEP; OBEV; PAn; Po; PoEL-3; PoIE; PoLi, *much abr.*; SeCV-2; SeEP; TOP; TreFT; TrGrPo; UnS, *abr.*; WBP
Instruments, The, *sel.* PoPo
(Fife and Drum, 8 *ll.*) GN
Song for Simeon, A. T. S. Eliot. BoLiVe; CoBE; EaLo; LiTB; MAP; MaRV; MoAmPo (1942 ed.); OxBoCh; POTE
Song for Souls under Fire, A. Mark Turbyfill. NP
Song for the Asking, A. Francis Orrery Ticknor. AA
Song for the beautiful trees, A. Forest Song. William Henry Venable. PEDC
Song for the Clatter-Bones. F. R. Higgins. LiTB; LiTM; OBMV; OnYI; OxBI; SiTL
Song for the Dead, III. *Unknown,* *tr. by* Frances S. Herskovits. TTY
Song for the Divine Bride and Mother. Lope de Vega, *tr. fr. Spanish by* Virginia Tufte. HW
Song for the Flag, A. Denis A. McCarthy. PEDC
Song for the Greenwood Fawn. I. L. Salomon. GoYe
Song for the Heroes. Alex Comfort. MoBrPo (1950 ed.); NeBP
Song for the heroes who saw the sign, A. A Song for Heroes. Edwin Markham. PEDC
Song for "The Jacquerie" ("The hound was cuffed"). Sidney Lanier. *See* Hound, The.
Song for the Last Act. Louise Bogan. AmLP; NePoAm; NYBP
Song for the Least of All Saints, A. Christina Rossetti. BePJ
Song for the Luddites. Byron. PoFr
Song for the New Year. W. H. Auden. EnLi-2 (1949 ed.)
Song for the Old, A. The New Year. George Cooper. DD; PEDC
Song for the Passing of a Beautiful Woman. *Unknown,* *tr. fr. Paiute Indian by* Mary Austin. LiTA
Song for the Pike's Peaker. *Unknown.* PoOW
Song for the Seasons, A. "Barry Cornwall." HBV
Song for the Sick Emperor. John Fletcher. *See* Care-charming Sleep.
Song for the Spanish Anarchists, A. Sir Herbert Read. ChMP
Song for the Spinning Wheel. Wordsworth. OBRV
Song for the Squeeze-Box. Theodore Roethke. NePoAm
Song for the States, A. Walt Whitman. PoRL

Song for the Sun That Disappeared behind the Rainclouds. *Unknown, tr. fr. Hottentot by* Ulli Beier. TTY
Song for the Third Marriage of Lucrezia Borgia, *sel.* Ariosto, *tr. fr. Latin by* Birgitta Wohl *and* Virginia Tufte.
"Rise up! the flute sound in the distance." HW
Song for the unsung heroes who rose in the country's need, A. The Unsung Heroes. Paul Laurence Dunbar. PoFr
Song for the Virgin Mother, A. Lope de Vega, *tr. fr. Spanish by* Ezra Pound. LiTW
Song for the Wandering Jew. Wordsworth. ERoP-1
Song for These Days. Patrick F. Kirby. GoBC
Song for Thrift Week. Mildred Weston. WhC
Song for Tomorrow. Lucia Trent. PGD
Song for Two Voices, A. *Unknown. See* What Can We Poor Females Do.
Song for Unbound Hair. Genevieve Taggard. PG; PoRA
Song for War. W. R. Rodgers. NeBP
Song for Youth. Dana Burnet. MPB
Song for Zarathustra. Lawrence Durrell. ToPo
Song from a Booke of Ayres, A. Thomas Campion. *See* Follow Thy Fair Sun, Unhappy Shadow.
Song from a Country Fair. Léonie Adams. GoJo
Song from a Drama. Edmund Clarence Stedman. AA
Song from a Play. W. B. Yeats. *See* Two Songs from a Play.
Song from a Two-Desk Office. Byron Buck. NYBP
Song from "Aella." Thomas Chatterton. *See* Minstrel's Song.
Song from "Al Aaraaf." Poe. *See* Song: "Neath blue-bell or streamer."
Song from "April." Irene Rutherford McLeod. SUS
Song from "Chartivel." Marie de France, *tr. fr. French by* Arthur O'Shaughnessy. *Fr.* Chartivel. AWP; JAWP; LiTW; WBP
("Hath any loved you well, down there.") EnLoPo; PoVP
(Sarrazine's Song [to Her Dead Lover].) HBV
Song from Cyprus, A. Hilda Doolittle ("H. D."). *See* Songs from Cyprus.
Song from Fragment of an Eccentric Drama. Henry Kirke White. OBRV
Song from "Maud" ("Come into the garden, Maud"). Tennyson. *See* Come into the Garden, Maud.
Song from "Maud" ("Go not, happy day"). Tennyson. Maud, Pt. I, xvii. ATP
Song from "Ogier the Dane." William Morris. *Fr.* The Earthly Paradise. OAEP; PoVP
(Antiphony.) VA
("In the white-flowered hawthorn brake.") EG; ViBoPo
Song from Old Spain, A. Alice Corbin. NP
Song from "Osorio." Samuel Taylor Coleridge. *See* Invocation, An: "Hear, sweet, spirit."
Song from "Pippa Passes." Robert Browning. *See* Year's at the Spring, The.
Song from Shakespeare's "Cymbeline," A ("To fair Fidele's grassy tomb"). William Collins. BEL; CEP; EiCL; EiCP; EiPP; EnRP; ForPo; OAEP; TOP
(Dirge in "Cymbeline.") ATP; ELP; EnLi-2 (1949 ed.); HBV; OBEC; PoFS; SeCePo; ViBoPo
(Fidele.) CLwM; OBEV
Song from "Sylvan," A. *Unknown. See* Out in the Fields with God.
Song from the End of the Earth. William Hunt. YAP
Song from the Gulf. Rolfe Humphries. MoLP
Song from "The Hill of Venus." William Morris. *Fr.* The Earthly Paradise. PoVP
Song from the Italian, A. Dryden. *Fr.* Limberham; or, The Kind Keeper, III, i. CEP; SeCV-2
Song from "The Only Jealousy of Emer." W. B. Yeats. *Fr.* The Only Jealousy of Emer. MoAB
Song from the Ship. Thomas Lovell Beddoes. *See* To Sea, to Sea!
Song I sing of my sea-adventure, A. The Seafarer. *Unknown.* AnOE; EtS
Song I sing of sorrow unceasing, A. The Wife's Lament. *Unknown.* AnOE; LiTW
Song in a Siege. Robert Heath. CavP; OBS
Song in a suffocating night, A. The Toad. Tristan Corbière [*wr.* Jules Laforgue], *tr. by* Patricia Terry. OnPM
Song in a windless night, A. The Toad. Tristan Corbière, *tr. by* Vernon Watkins. SyP
Song in a Winter Night. Bink Noll. ToPo
Song in Camp, The. Bayard Taylor. *See* Song of the Camp, The.
Song in Exile. Alice Duer Miller. TIHL
Song in His Lady's Absence, A. A. Godwhen. *See* Song for My Lady.
Song in Humility, A. Carleton Drewry. MoRP
Song in Imitation of the Elizabethans. Sir William Watson. VA
Song in Leinster. Louise Imogen Guiney. *See* In Leinster.
Song in Making of the Arrows, A. John Lyly. *Fr.* Sapho and Phao. LoBV; OBSC; TuPP
(Vulcan's Song.) ElL
Song in March. William Gilmore Simms. AA; DD; HBV
Song In Plague-Time. Thomas Nashe. *See* Adieu, Farewell, Earth's Bliss.
Song, in Praise of a Beggers Life, A. "A. W." *See* In Praise of a Beggar's Life.
Song in Praise of Old English Roast Beef, A. Richard Leveridge. OBEC
Song in Praise of Paella. C. W. V. Wordsworth. FiBHP
Song in Praise of the Lord of Heaven and Earth, A. *Unknown.* GBV
Song in Spite of Myself. Countee Cullen. BALP
Song in Spring. Louis Ginsberg. YeAr
Song in the Dell, The. Charles Edward Carryl. AA
Song in the Front Yard, A. Gwendolyn Brooks. IDB
Song in the Second Act, A. Thomas Southerne. *See* Song: "Pursuing beauty, men descry."
Song in the Songless. George Meredith. ACV; GTSL; OTPC; PCD; PoVP
Song in the Valley of Humiliation. Bunyan. *See* Shepherd Boy's Song, The.
Song in the valley of Nemea, A. Nemea. Lawrence Durrell. ChMP; FaBoTw; GTBS-P
Song in the Wood. John Fletcher. *Fr.* The Little French Lawyer. ElL; ThWaDe
Song in Time of Order, A. Swinburne. PoVP
Song is a violence. Spindle. A. R. Ammons. NYTB
Song is but a little thing, A. The Poet and His Song. Paul Laurence Dunbar. PoRL
Song is gone, The; the dance. Bora Ring. Judith Wright. NeLNL
Song is not singing. Kissing the Dancer. Robert Sward. CoPo
Song is such a curious thing, A. Written in a Song Book. Lizette Woodworth Reese. NP
Song lay silent in my pen, A. The Song. John Erskine. AA
Song Made by F.B.P., A. *Unknown. See* New Jerusalem, The.
Song-Maker, The. Kingsley Fairbridge. ACV; BoSA
Song-Maker, The. Anna Wickham. MoBrPo
Song Making. Sara Teasdale. WGRP
Song My Paddle Sings, The. E. Pauline Johnson. CaP; FaPON; HBV; OTPC; PoRL; PTK; VA
Song of a boat, A. Songs of Seven: Seven Times Seven [*or* Longing for Home]. Jean Ingelow. GBV (1922 ed.); HBV; WGRP
Song of a Common Lover. Flavien Renaivo. *tr. fr. French by* Alan Ryder. TTY
Song of a Factory Girl. Marya Zaturenska. HBMV; NP
Song of a Fool. W. B. Yeats. *See* Two Songs of a Fool.
Song of a Happy Rising, The. John Thewlis. ACP
Song of a Heathen, The. Richard Watson Gilder. AA; BePJ; ChIP; MaRV; OQP; StJW; TRV; WGRP
Song of a Jewish Boy. "M. J.," *tr. fr. Polish by* A. Glanz-Leyeless. TrJP
Song of a Man Who Has Come Through. D. H. Lawrence. BoPe; ChMP; CMoP; CoBMV; FaBoMo; GTBS-P; LiTM; MoPo; PoIE; SeCeV; ViBoPo
Song of a Second April. Edna St. Vincent Millay. CMoP; OxBA
Song of a Shepherd-Boy at Bethlehem, The. Josephine Preston Peabody. ChrBoLe; OHIP; StJW
Song of a Thousand Years. Don Marquis. WePo
Song of a Train. John Davidson. BrPo
Song of a Traveller, The. Robert Louis Stevenson. *See* Romance.
Song of a Young Lady to Her Ancient Lover, A. Earl of Rochester. CavP; CBV; EP; ErPo; MePo; PeRV
Song of Accius and Silena. John Lyly. *See* O Cupid! Monarch over Kings.
Song of Aerial Spirits. Sir Robert Howard *and* John Dryden. *See* Poor Mortals.
Song of Albert Graeme. Sir Walter Scott. *See* It Was an English Ladye Bright.

Song of Ale, A. *At. to* William Stevenson. *See* Back and Side Go Bare, Go Bare.
Song of Allegiance. R. A. K. Mason. AnNZ
Song of Always, A. Efraim Rosenzweig. TiPo (1952 ed.)
Song of American Freedom, A. John Dickinson. *See* Liberty Song, The.
Song of an Australian. Flexmore Hudson. BoAu
Song of Angiola in Heaven, A. Austin Dobson. HBV
Song of Apelles. John Lyly. *See* Apelles' Song.
Song of Arno, A. Grace Ellery Channing. AA
Song of Autumn, A. Joseph Ceravolo. ANYP
Song of Autumn, A. Adam Lindsay Gordon. BoAu
Song of Autumn, A. Sir Rennell Rodd. HBV
Song of Autumn. Paul Verlaine. *See* Chansons d'Automne.
Song of Basket-weaving. Constance Lindsay Skinner. AnAmPo
Song of Battle. Bertrand de Born. *See* Well Pleaseth Me the Sweet Time of Easter.
Song of Braddock's Men, The. *Unknown.* MC; PAH
Song of Bread and Honey, A. Richard Le Gallienne. PCH
Song of Breath, A. Stephen Vincent Benét. *See* Song of the Breath, The.
Song of Breath. Peire Vidal, *tr. fr. French by* Ezra Pound. AWP; JAWP; WBP
Song of Callicles, The ("Far, far from here"). Matthew Arnold. *See* Cadmus and Harmonia.
Song of Callicles, The ("Through the black, rushing smoke-bursts"). Matthew Arnold. *Fr.* Empedocles on Etna, II GTBS; OBEV; OBVV; ShBV-3
(Apollo.) ViPo
(Callicles' Song.) ChTr; LoBV
(Song for Apollo.) FiP
(Song of the Muses, The.) WiR
("Through the black, rushing smoke-bursts.") PoVP
Song of canaries, The. The Canary. Ogden Nash. FiBHP
Song of Carroll's Sword, The. *At. to* Dallan MacMore, *tr. fr. Middle Irish by* Kuno Meyer. OnYI
(Carroll's Sword, *tr. by* Frank O'Connor.) KiLC
Song of Casyor Brioschi, The. Thomas Hanna. QAH
Song of Chess, The. *At. to* Abraham ibn Ezra, *tr. fr. Hebrew by* Nina Davis Salaman. TrJP
Song of Christian Workingmen. Thomas Curtis Clark. OQP
Song of Clover, A. Helen Hunt Jackson. GN; OTPC
Song of Colours, A. Theodore Maynard. JKCP
Song of Coridon and Melampus. George Peele. *Fr.* The Hunting of Cupid. OBSC
(Coridon and Melampus' Song.) TuPP
Song of Cradle-making. Constance Lindsay Skinner. CaP
Song of Crede, The. *Unknown, tr. fr. Middle Irish by* Howard Mumford Jones. LiTW
(Song of Crede, Daughter of Gooary, The, *tr. by* Kuno Meyer.) OnYI
Song of Dagger-Dancing, A, *sel.* Tu Fu, *tr. fr. Chinese by* Witter Bynner.
"There lived years ago the beautiful Kung-sun." UnS
Song of Dalliance, A. William Cartwright. ALV; ErPo
Song of Daphne to the Lute, A. John Lyly. *See* Daphne.
Song of Dark Waters, The. Roy Helton. IHA
Song of David, The. Christopher Smart. *See* Catholic Amen, The.
Song of Deborah [and Barak], The. Judges, V: 2-31, Bible, *O.T.* AWP; LiTW
(Then Sang Deborah and Barak, 1-31.) TrJP
Song of Denmark, *sel.* Soeren Haller, *tr. fr. Danish by* Joy Davidman.
"This is the ironhard winter foretold." PoFr
Song of Derivations, A. Alice Meynell. MaRV; PoVP; WGRP
(Modern Poet, The.) VA
Song of Desire, A. Frederic Lawrence Knowles. HBV
Song of Diana's Nymphs, A. John Lyly. *See* Cupid's Indictment.
Song of Diego Valdez, The. Kipling. OtMeF
Song of Diligence, A. Helen Frazee-Bower HBMV
Song of Divine Love, A. Richard Crashaw. *See* Song, A: "Lord, when the sense of Thy sweet grace."
Song of Doubt, A. Josiah Gilbert Holland. WGRP
Song of Dust, A. Lord De Tabley. EnLoPo
Song of Early Autumn, A. Richard Watson Gilder. DD; HBV
Song of Easter. Celia Thaxter. HH
Song of Echo. Ben Jonson. *See* Slow, Slow, Fresh Fount.
Song of Egla. Maria Gowen Brocks. AA; AnAmPo
Song of Emptiness to Fill up the Empty Pages Following, A. Michael Wigglesworth. *See* Vanity of Vanities.
Song of Enchantment, A. Walter de la Mare. GTSL; PG (1955 ed.)
Song of Enion. Blake. *Fr.* Vala; or, The Four Zoas. ERoP-1
(Price of Experience, The.) EnRP
Song of Enitharmon. Blake. *Fr.* Vala; or, The Four Zoas. ERoP-1
Song of Eros. George Edward Woodberry. *Fr.* Agathon. AA; HBV
Song of Exile, A. Psalms, CXXXVII, Bible, *O.T.* TrGrPo
(Psalm CXXXVII.) AWP; ExPo; JAWP; LiTW; OnPM; StaSt (1-6, *ad.*)
Song of Exile, *sel.* Antônio Gonçalves Dias, *tr. fr. Portuguese by* Frances Ellen Buckland.
"There are palm trees in my homeland." TTY
Song of Fairies Robbing an Orchard. Thomas Randolph. *See* Fairies' Song.
Song of Fairly Utter Despair. Samuel Hoffenstein. CIV
Song of Faith. William Croswell. SoP
Song of Faith, A. Josiah Gilbert Holland. *Fr.* Bitter-sweet. WGRP
Song of Faith Forsworn, A. Lord De Tabley. PeVV; VA
Song of Farewell, A. Dora Greenwell. VA
Song of Fate. Friedrich Hölderlin, *tr. fr. German by* Emery Neff. WoL
Song of Finis, The. Walter de la Mare. MoBrPo
Song of Finn, The. *Unknown. See* In Praise of May.
Song of Fionnuala, The. Thomas Moore. OnYI
Song of Fire, The. Rolland Snellings. BF
Song of Fixed Accord. Wallace Stevens. NePoAm; OA
Song of Fleet Street, A. Alice Werner. HBV
Song of Flight, A. Christina Rossetti. CAW
Song of Four Priests Who Suffered Death at Lancaster, A. *Unknown.* ACP
Song of Freedom, A. Alice Milligan. AnIV; OnYI; PoFr
Song of Glenann, A. "Moira O'Neill." HBV
Song of grass, A,/ A song of earth. A Song. "Yehoash." TrJP
Song of Greatness, A. *Tr. fr. Chippewa Indian by* Mary Austin. AmFN; BiCB; BoChLi; FaPON; RePo; TiPo
Song of Grief. Liu Hsi-Chun, *tr. fr. Chinese by* David Rafael Wang. HW
Song of Gwythno. Thomas Love Peacock. *Fr.* The Misfortunes of Elphin. OBRV
Song of Handicrafts, A. Annie Matheson. OBVV
Song of Hannah, The. First Samuel, Bible, *O.T. See* Hannah's Song of Thanksgiving.
Song of Hannibal; Rome. Marcus B. Christian. GoSl
Song of Happiness, A. Muna Lee. NP
Song of Happiness, A. Ernest Rhys. NP
Song of Hate. Jacob ben David Frances, *tr. fr. Hebrew by* A. B. Rhine. TrJP
Song of Hiawatha, The, *sels.* Longfellow.
As Brothers Live Together, *fr.* I. TreFT
"As the bow unto the cord is," *fr.* X. TRV
Death of Minnehaha, The, *fr.* XX. AA
Firefly Song, *fr.* III. PCD
Four Winds, The, II. AnNE
Ghosts, The, XIX. LoBV
Hiawatha and Mudjekeewis, IV. AnNE
Hiawatha's Brothers, *fr.* III. BoTP; PCH, *br. sel.*
(Hiawatha's Chickens, *br. sel.*) PCH
Hiawatha's Childhood, III. AnNE; BoChLi, *sel.*; BoTP, *sel.*; FaBV; FaPON, *sel.*; GFA, *sel.*; MPB, *sel.*; OHFP, *sel.*; PoRh, *sel.*; RePo; RIS, *abr.*; ShBV-1, *sel.*; StVeCh, *sel.*; TiPo, *sel.*; TreF, *sel.*; WBLP, *sel.*
Hiawatha's Fishing, *fr.* VIII. PoG
Hiawatha's Sailing, VII. BBV; PCH, *sel.*
(Hiawatha's Canoe.) OHIP, *sel.*; StVeCh, *abr.*
Hiawatha's Wooing, X. BeLS; TreFS
Hunting of Pau-Puk-Keewis, The, XVII. CoBA
Introduction. AnNE; PG (1945 ed.)
Lullaby of Nokomis, *abr., fr.* III. PCH
Pau-Puk-Keewis, XVI. CoBA
Peace-Pipe, The, I. AnNE
Song of Honour [*or* Honor], The. Ralph Hodgson. AtBAP; CAW, *abr.*; GTSL; MCCG; MoBrPo; OtMeF; TSW
Sels.
"I climbed a hill as light fell short." MemP, *abr.*
"I heard the hymn of being sound." LO
Song of Hope. Thomas Hardy. VP

Song of Hope. Mary A. Lathbury. BLPA; MaRV; SoP
(Room for Him! Room!) ChIP
Song of Igor's Campaign, The. *sel.* *Unknown.* *tr. fr. Russian by* Vladimir Nabokov.
Igor's Escape. FOL
Song of Impossibilities, A. Winthrop Mackworth Praed. BOHV; InMe; NA
Song of Industrial America. Sherwood Anderson. NP
Song of Iowa, The. S. H. M. Byers. PoRL
Song of Ithamore, The. Christopher Marlowe. *Fr.* The Jew of Malta, IV. WHA
Song of January. Gerta Kennedy. PoPl
Song of Jehane du Castel Beau, The. William Morris. *See* Gold Wings across the Sea.
Song of Jonah in the Whale's Belly, The. Michael Drayton. *Fr.* The Harmony of the Church. ReIE
Song of Labor, The. Ninette M. Lowater. PEDC
Song of Laughter, A. Theodore Maynard. JKCP
Song of Laurence Minot. Laurence Minot. BEL
Song of Lewes, The. *Unknown.* OxBoLi
(Against the Barons' Enemies.) MeEL
Song of Liberty, A. Blake. EiPP; EnLi-2; EnRP
Song of Liberty, *sel.* Louise Ayres Garnett.
"Lead on, lead on, America." PGD
Song of Life, A. Lizette Woodworth Reese. *See* Little Song of Life, A.
Song of Life, A. Franz Werfel, *tr. fr. German by* Edith Abercrombie Snow. TrJP
Song of Living, A. Amelia Josephine Burr. HBV
Song of Lo-fu, The. *Unknown, tr. fr. Chinese.* AWP, *tr. by* Arthur Waley
Song of Loneliness. Judah Halevi, ' *tr. fr. Hebrew by* Nina Davis Salaman. TrJP
Song of Louisiana. Vashti R. Stopher. PoRL
Song of Love, A. "Lewis Carroll." GN
Song of Love, The. Rainer Maria Rilke, *tr. fr. German by* Ludwig Lewisohn. AWP
Song of Love for Jesus, A. Richard Rolle. MeEL
Song of Low Degree, A. Bunyan. *See* Shepherd Boy's Song, The.
Song of Maelduin. Thomas William Rolleston. HBMV
Song of Marion's Men. Bryant. AmePo; AnNE; CoBA; DD; HBV; HBVY; MC; PAH; PAP; ThLM; TreF
Song of Mary the Mother of Christ, The. *At. to* Henry Walpole. ISi
Song of May Morning. Milton. *See* Song on May Morning.
Song of Mehitabel, The. Don Marquis. *Fr.* Archy and Mehitabel. FiBHP; TreFS
Song of Milkanwatha, The, *parody, sel.* George A. Strong.
Modern Hiawatha, The. BBV (1951 ed.); BOHV; FaFP; FaPON; FiBHP; HBV; InMe; LiTG; MoShBr; NA; Par; SiTL; TreFS; WhC; YaD
(Hiawatha's Mittens.) ShBV-1
Song of Mr. Toad, The. Kenneth Grahame. *See* World Has Held Great Heroes, The.
Song of Momus to Mars, The. Dryden. *See* Secular Masque, The
Song of Moses, The. Exodus, Bible, *O.T.* *See* Triumphal Chant.
Song of My Heart, A. Robert Bridges. ACV
Song Of Myself. Walt Whitman. AmP; AmPP; AnFE; AP; APA; ATP (1935 ed.), *much abr.*; BoLiVe, *much abr.*; CoAnAm; CoBA, *abr.*; LiTA; MAmP; MAP, *abr.*; MoAmPo, *abr.*; MWA-1; NeMA, *abr.*; OxBA; PoIE, *much abr.*; TrGrPo, *abr.*; ViBoPo, *much abr.*
(Walt Whitman, *much abr.*) WHA
Sels.
"All truths wait in all things," *fr.* XXX-XXXI. PFY
"Alone far in the wilds and mountains I hunt," X. SeCeV
Animals, *fr.* XXXII. FaFP; GTBS-W; LiTG; MCCG; NePA; PoPl; PPON; SiTL
(Beasts, The.) CBEP; HBV; OBVV
("I think I could turn and live with animals.") AnEnPo; BoC; LoBV (1949 ed.); PDV; PG (1955 ed.); PoG; PoMa; TrGrPo; WGRP
Battle of the *Bonhomme Richard* and the *Serapis*, XXXV-XXXVI. UnPo (3d ed.)
(John Paul Jones, *fr.* XXXV.) PAL
(Old-Time Sea-Fight, An, XXXV.) MaC; OnMSP
("Would you hear of an old-time sea-fight?") CoBA; SeCeV; TrGrPo
Dazzling and Tremendous How Quick the Sun-Rise Would Kill Me, *fr.* XXV. AtBAP
Drayman, The, *fr.* XIII. PoNe
Encountering God, XLVIII. TreFT
"Gigantic beauty of a stallion, fresh and responsive to my caresses," *fr.* XXXII. PDV
Grass, The, VI. GTBS-W; LiTG; NePA
("Child said, *What is the Grass?*, A.") AtBAP; BoLiVe; InP; MaPo; PG (1955 ed.); TrGrPo
(From "Walt Whitman.") PFY
(Leaves of Grass, *fr.* VI *and* XX.) AA
(Lines from "Song of Myself.") BBV (1951 ed.)
(What is the Grass?) PCD, *abr.*; PCH; TSW, *sel.*
I Am He That Walks with the Tender and Growing Night, *fr.* XXI. AtBAP; ChTr; ExPo; MCCG; TSW
"I am the poet of the body," XXI. CoBA; SeCeV; TrGrPo
"I am the teacher of athletes," XLVII. CoBA
"I celebrate myself, and sing myself," I. PoFS (I-XLVIII, *much abr.*); PP
(I Celebrate Myself.) NePA
(Myself.) AA; FaBoBe
I Dote upon Myself, *fr.* XXIV. AnEnPo
"I have said that the soul is not more than the body," XLVIII. CoBA; TrGrPo
(Hub for the Universe, A.) FaFP
(I Hear and Behold God in Every Object.) MoRP
"I hear and behold God in every object," *fr.* XLVIII. WGRP
I Know I Am Deathless, *fr.* XX. MaRV
"I open my scuttle at night and see the far-sprinkled systems," *fr.* XLV. PFY
I Tramp a Perpetual Journey, *fr.* XLVI. OQP
"I understand the large hearts of heroes," *fr.* XXXIII. PoFr
(Heroes, *fr.* XXXIII *and* XXXV.) AA
Infinity ("My feet strike an apex"), *fr.* XLIV-XLV. AA
"It is time to explain myself—let us stand up," XLIV. DiPo: MaRV, *abr.*
"Little one sleeps in its cradle, The," VIII. MaPo
Miracles, *fr.* XXXI. MaRV
("I believe a leaf of grass is no less than the journey-work of the stars.") PDV; PG (1955 ed.); SeCeV; TiPo; TRV
(Leaf of Grass, A.) OQP
(Leaves of Grass.) YT
My Barbaric Yawp, LII. NePA
("Spotted hawk swoops by and accuses me, The.") CoBA; PP; TrGrPo
"Now I will do nothing but listen," XXVI. HoPM; MaPo
Press Close Bare-Bosom'd Night, *fr.* XXI. MeWo
"Pure contralto sings in the organ loft, The", XV. MaPo
Runaway Slave, The, *fr.* X. PoNe
("Runaway slave came to my house, The.") PoFr
Same Old Law, The, *fr.* XIV. OA
Twenty-eight Young Men Bathe by the Shore, XI. ExPo; MaPo
"Walt Whitman, a kosmos, of Manhattan the son," XXIV. PoFr, 11 *ll.*
With Music Strong I Come, *fr.* XVIII-XIX. AtBAP
Wounded Person, The, *fr.* XXXIII. PoNe
Song of Mystic Unity, The. Jami, *tr. fr. Persian by* R. A. Nicholson. LiTW
Song of Nature. Emerson. AnNE; HBV
Song of Nidderdale, The. Dorothy Una Ratcliffe. HBMV
Song of Nu-Numma-Kwiten, The. *Unknown, tr. fr. Bushman.* PeSA
Song of Nuns, A. James Shirley. *See* O Fly My Soul.
Song of Oenone and Paris. George Peele. *See* Fair and Fair.
Song of One Eleven Years in Prison. George Canning, George Ellis, *and* John Hookham Frere. *See* Song: "Whene'er with haggard eyes I view."
Song of O'Ruark, Prince of Breffni, The. Thomas Moore. OnYI
Song of Panama, A. Damon Runyon. PAH; ThLM
Song of Parting, A. Compton Mackenzie. HBV; OBVV
Song of Perfect Propriety. Dorothy Parker. InMe
Song of Phillida and Coridon. Nicholas Breton. TuPP
Song of Pleasure, A. Philip Massinger. *See* Song: "Blushing rose and purple flower, The."
Song of Poplars. Aldous Huxley. MoBrPo (1942 ed.)
Song of Power, A. Berton Braley. PoMa
Song of Praise, A. Psalms, VIII, Bible, *O.T.* *See* What Is Man?
Song of Praise, A. Psalms, CXLVIII, Bible, *O.T.* TrGrPo

Song (continued)
(Praise Ye the Lord.) TrJP
Song of Praise, A. Countee Cullen. NP
Song of Praise to Mary. "Angelus Silesius," *tr. fr. German by* Mary E. Mannix. CAW
Song of Quetzalcoatl, *sels.* *Unknown*, *tr. fr. Aztec by* John Hubert Cornyn. LiTW
Hymn to the Wind God.
White Kite, The.
Song of Quoodle, The. G. K. Chesterton. GoJo; SiTL; WePo
Song of Renunciation, A. Sir Owen Seaman. CenHV
Song of Resignation. Yehuda Amichai, *tr. fr. Hebrew by* Assia Gutmann. NYBP
Song of Riches, A. Katharine Lee Bates. AA
Song of Right and Wrong, The. G. K. Chesterton. *See* Feast on Wine or Fast on Water.
Song of Robin Goodfellow, A. Shakespeare. *See* Now the Hungry Lion Roars.
Song of Roland, The, *sels.* *Unknown*, *tr. fr. Old French*.
Last Battle, The, *tr. by* C.K. Scott Moncrieff. LiTW
Ready They Make Hauberks Sarrazinese, *tr. by* C. K. Scott Moncrieff. WaaP
"When Roland saw that life had fled," *tr. by* John O'Hagan. EnLi-1; OuHeWo
Song of Sack, A. *Unknown*. OBS
Song of Safety, A. Psalms, CXXI, Bible, *O.T.* *See* I Will Lift Up Mine Eyes unto the Hills.
Song of Satisfaction on Completing an Overhauling of Fishing Tackle, A. Leslie P. Thompson. WhC
Song of Saul before His Last Battle. Byron. Po
Song of Self-Pity, A. Geoffrey Vivien. TwCaPo
Song of Shadows, The. Walter de la Mare. BoLiVe; CMoP; CoBE; MoBrPo; ShBV-3; TrGrPo
Song of Sherman's Army, The. Charles Graham Halpine. MC; PAH; PAP
Song of Sherman's March to the Sea. Samuel H. M. Byers. *See* Sherman's March to the Sea.
Song of Sherwood, A. Alfred Noyes. BBV; FaPON; HBV; HBVY; MCCG; MPB; OTPC (1946 ed.); PCD; RG; SP; TiPo (1959 ed.)
(Sherwood.) BoTP; MoBrPo; ShBV-1
Song of Sighing, A. James Thomson. EnLit
Song of Slaves in the Desert. Whittier. AmPP; AnAmPo; OBVV; OxBA
(Song of the Slaves in the Desert.) PFY
Song of Solomon, The. Bible, *O.T.*
(Song of Songs, The.) AWP; TrGrPo; UnTE
Sels.
"Awake! Oh, north wind," IV: 16. FaPON; SUS
Behold, Thou Art Fair, IV. MeWo (1-16); TrJP (1-7)
(Song of Songs, 1-16.) WoL
"For, lo, the winter is past," II: 11-12. PDV; SUS; TiPo
(For, Lo, the Winter Is Past, 10-13.) TreF
(Hark! My Beloved! 8-13.) TrJP
(Lo, the Winter Is Past.) FaPON (11-12); ShBV-3 (11-13)
(Spring, 11-12.) PCD; PCH
(Time of the Singing of Birds, The, 11-12) ThGo
(Winter is Past, The, II: 11-12.) SoPo; YeAR
"I adjure you, O daughters of Jerusalem," V: 8-16 (*King James Version, Revised*). LiTW
I Am My Beloved's, VII: 11-14. TrJP
"I am the flower of the field," II: 1,2,14, *Douay vers.*
(Canticle of Canticles.) ISi
I Am the Rose of Sharon, II. ChTr
(Song of Songs.) GBV, *abr.*; PG
I Sleep, but My Heart Waketh, V: 2-VI: 3. TrJP
"My beloved spake, and said unto me," II: 10-III: 4. LO
On My Bed I Sought Him, III: 1-5. TrJP
Return, Return, O Shulammite, VII:1-10. TrJP
"Set me as a seal upon thine heart," VIII: 6-7. LiTW (*King James Version, Revised*)
(As a Seal upon Thy Heart.) TrJP
(Love.) MaRV
"Song of songs, which is Solomon's, The." I-IV. HW
"Thou art beautiful, O my love," VI:3,8,9, *Douay vers.*
(Canticle of Canticles.) ISi
"Voice of my beloved, The," II:8-14. EnLi-1; LiTW (*King James Version, Revised*); PoPL (8-13)
(Love Lyrics.) OuHeWo
Song of Solomon, A. Josephine Preston Peabody. NP
Song of Songs, The. Bible, *O.T.* *See* Song of Solomon, The.
Song of Songs, The. Heine, *tr. fr. German by* Louis Untermeyer. UnTE
Song of Songs. Wilfred Owen. NAMP
Song of songs, which is Solomon's, The. The Song of Solomon, Bible, *O.T.* HW
Song of Sorrow, A. Charles Battell Loomis. BOHV
Song of Spring. Keats. *Fr.* At Teignmouth. BoTP
Song of Springbok Does. *Unknown*, *tr. fr. Bushman by* W. H. I. Bleek. PeSA
Song of Street Labor, A. Caroline A. Lord. DD
Song of Summer. Paul Laurence Dunbar. MCCG; OTPC (1946 ed.); TSW
Song of Summer Days. J. W. Foley. BoTP
Song of sunshine through the rain, A. Calvary and Easter [*or* Easter Song]. "Susan Coolidge." BLRP; OQP; PGD; SoP; TRV; WBLP
Song of Supplication, A. Psalms, CXXX, Bible, *O.T.* *See* De Profundis.
Song of Switzerland. Stoddard King. WhC
Song of Texas. William Henry Cuyler Hosmer. PAH
Song of Thanatos, The. Thomas Lovell Beddoes. *See* Mighty Thoughts of an Old World, The.
Song of Thanks, A. Edward Smyth Jones. BANP
Song of Thanksgiving. John Richard Moreland. PGD
Song of the All-Wool Shirt. Eugene Field. StPo
Song of the Ancient People, The, *sel.* Edna Dean Proctor.
"We are the Ancient People." AA
Song of the Angels. Nahum Tate. *See* While Shepherds Watched Their Flocks by Night.
Song of the Answerer, *sel.* Walt Whitman.
"Indications and tally of time, The." PP
Song of the Argonauts. William Morris. *See* O Bitter Sea.
Song of the Argonauts, *with music.* Sam C. Upham. SGR
Song of the Arrow, The. Isabella Valancy Crawford. *Fr.* Gisli, the Chieftain. OBCV; PeCV (1967 ed.)
Song of the Artesian Water. A. B. Paterson. ACV
Song of the Ascension. William Drummond of Hawthornden. *See* Hymn of the Ascension, An.
Song of the Ballet. J. B. Morton. FiBHP
Song of the Banishment of the Two Dukes, A. Thomas Deloney. SiCE
Song of the Banjo, The. Kipling. FaBoCh; OtMeF; PoVP
Song of the Basket Maker. Thomas Dekker. *Fr.* The Patient Grissill, I, i. PTK
Song of the Bath, The. Margaret Gibbs. BoTP
Song of the Beasts, The. Anthony Hecht. CBV
Song of the Bees. Hannah Flagg Gould. OTPC
Song of the Beggars. Richard Brome. *Fr.* A Jovial Crew, I, i. SeCL
Song of the Bird, The. Wilhelm Müller, *tr. fr. German by* Longfellow. BoTP
Song of the Borderguard, The. Robert Duncan. NeAP
Song of the Bow, The. Sir Arthur Conan Doyle. *Fr.* The White Company. HBV; MCCG
Song of the Bower, The. Dante Gabriel Rossetti. HBV; PoVP
Song of the Brave. Laurence Altgood. PAL
Song of the Breath, The. Stephen Vincent Benét. *Fr.* John Brown's Body. AmP
(Song of Breath, A.) MoVE
Song of the Broad-Axe. Walt Whitman. WoL
Broad-Axe, The, *fr.* I. MAP; MoAmPo
Song of the Brook. Tennyson. *See* Brook, The; an Idyl.
Song of the Builders. Jessie Wilmore Murton. AmFN
Song of the Bush Shrike. *Unknown*, *tr. fr. Zulu*. PeSA
Song of the Camels. Elizabeth J. Coatsworth. FaPON; RIS
(Twelfth Night.) ChBR
Song of the Camp, The. Bayard Taylor. AA; BeLS; GN; HBV; HBVY; OTPC; WBLP
(Song in Camp, The.) BBV (1923 ed.)
Song of the Captured Woman. James Devaney. PoAu-1
Song of the Cattle Trail. John Milton Hagen. *See* Cowboy and His Love, The.
Song of the Chattahoochee. Sidney Lanier. AA; AmePo; AmFN; AmP; AmPP; AnAmPo; AnEnPo; AP; BBV (1923 ed.); BoNaP; CoBA; DiPo; FaBoBe; FaBV; HBV; InP; LaNeLa; LiTA; MAP; MCCG; MoAmPo (1942 ed.); NePA; OHFP; OTPC (1946 ed.); PCD; RG; TreF; YaD; YT
Song of the Chickadee. *Unknown*. OTPC (1946 ed.); PCH

Song of the Christmas Trees. Blanche Elizabeth Wade. OHIP
Song of the Clouds. Aristophanes, *tr. fr. Greek. Fr.* The Clouds. AWP, *tr. by* Oscar Wilde
(Chorus of the Clouds, *tr. by* T. F. Higham.) LiTW
Song of the Colorado, The. Sharlot Mabridth Hall. HBV
Song of the Cornpopper, The. Laura E. Richards. BoChLi
Song of the Corsairs. Byron. *Fr.* The Corsair, I. EtS
Song of the Creatures, The. St. Francis of Assisi. *See* Canticle of the Sun.
Song of the Crusaders. *Unknown. See* Fairest Lord Jesus.
Song of the Cyclops, The. Thomas Dekker. ShBV-1
("Brave iron! brave hammer! from your sound.") TuPP
Song of the Darling River. Henry Lawson. ACV
Song of the Dawn, *sel.* John Ruskin.
"Awake! awake! the stars are pale, the east is russet gray." HBV; PoFr
Song of the Demented Priest, The. John Berryman. MoPo
Song of the Derelict, The. John McCrae. EtS
Song of the Dew. *Unknown, tr. fr. Hebrew by* Solomon Solis-Cohen. TrJP
Song of the Dial, The. Peter Airey. OQP
Song of the Drift Weed. Jessie Mackay. BoAu
Song of the Dying Gunner A.A.1. Charles Causley. POTi
Song of the Elfin Miller. Allan Cunningham. OTPC (1946 ed.)
Song of the Elfin Steersman. George Hill. AA
Song of the Emigrants in Bermuda. Andrew Marvell. *See* Bermudas.
Song of the Engine, The. H. Worsley-Benison. BoTP
Song of the Exposition, *sel.* Walt Whitman.
Muse in the New World, The, II, III, *abr.* MAP; MoAmPo
("Come, Muse, migrate from Greece and Ionia.") PP
Song of the Fairies. Shakespeare. *See* You Spotted Snakes.
Song of the Fairies. *Unknown, tr. fr. Middle Irish by* A. H. Leahy. OnYI
Song of the Fairy ("Over hill, over dale"). Shakespeare. *See* Over Hill, over Dale.
Song of the fields and a song of the woods, A. Lord De Tabley. *Fr.* A Song of the Rolling Wind. GTBS-D
Song of the Fire. Edward Fitzgerald. OTPC (1923 ed.)
Song of the Fishes, *with music. Unknown.* AmSS
Song of the Flags, The. S. Weir Mitchell. PAH
Song of the Flea. Judah Al-Harizi, *tr. fr. Hebrew.* TrJP
Song of the Foot-Track. Elsie Cole. BoAu
Song of the Forest Ranger, The. Herbert Bashford. HBV; OHIP
Song of the Forest Trees. *Unknown, tr. fr. Middle Irish by* Standish Hayes O'Grady. OnYI
Song of the Four Seasons, A. Austin Dobson. BoC; HBV
Song of the Four Winds, The. Thomas Love Peacock. *Fr.* The Misfortunes of Elphin. ERoP-1; OBRV; WiR
Song of the Full Catch. Constance Lindsay Skinner. *Fr.* Songs of the Coast Dwellers. CaP
Song of the Galley, The. *Unknown, tr. fr. Spanish by* John Gibson Lockhart. AWP; PoFr
Song of the Galley-Slaves. Kipling. *Fr.* Many Inventions. ChTr; GTBS-P; PoEL-5; PoFr
Song of the General Strike. Mario Bravo, *tr. fr. Spanish by* Alice Stone Blackwell. PoFr
Song of the Ghost, The. Alfred Perceval Graves. AnIV
Song of the Golden Sea. Jean Blewett. PTK
Song of the Good Samaritan, The. Vernon Watkins. LiTM (rev. ed.)
Song of the Grass, The. Sarah Roberts Boyle. *See* Voice of the Grass, The.
Song of the Graves, The. *Unknown, tr. fr. Welsh by* Ernest Rhys. OBMV
Song of the Gulf Stream. Francis Alan Ford. EtS
Song of the Happy Shepherd, The. W. B. Yeats. PoFS; ViPo (1962 ed.)
Song of the Harlot. Isaiah, XXIII: 16, Bible, *O.T.* TrJP
Song of the Harper. *Unknown, tr. fr. Egyptian by* T. Eric Peet. LiTW
Song of the Harvest. Henry Stevenson Washburn. OHIP
Song of the Hatteras Whale, A. *Unknown.* EtS
Song of the Heads, The. *Unknown, tr. fr. Irish by* Frank O'Connor. KiLC
Song of the Hesitations. Paul Blackburn. NMP
Song of the Highest Tower. Arthur Rimbaud, *tr. fr. French by* Edgell Rickword. AWP; JAWP; WBP
Song of the Hill. Edith Lodge. GoYe
Song of the Horse. *Tr. fr. Navajo Indian by* Natalie Curtis. AWP; JAWP; WBP
Song of the Hunt, The. John Bennett. *Fr.* Master Sky-Lark. AA
Song of the Indian Maid. Keats. *Fr.* Endymion. OAEP; OBEV
(O Sorrow! *abr.*) CH
(Roundelay: "O Sorrow.") ATP (1935 ed.)
(Song: "O Sorrow," *shorter sel.*) LoBV
Song of the Jellicles, The. T. S. Eliot. FaBoCh; LoGBV
Song of the King's Minstrel, The. Richard Middleton. HBV
Song of the Kings of Gold. Ebenezer Jones. VA
Song of the Leadville Mine Boss. Don Cameron. PoOW
Song of the Lilies, The. Lucy Wheelock. OHIP
Song of the Little Hunter, The. Kipling. *Fr.* The Second Jungle Book. ShBV-1
Song of the Little Villages. James B. Dollard. CAW; JKCP
Song of the Lotos-Eaters. Tennyson. *See* Choric Song.
Song of the Love of Jesus, A. Richard Rolle of Hampole. PoEL-1
Song of the Lower Classes, The. Ernest Charles Jones. CoMu; OBVV
Song of the Lute in the Praise of God and Dispraise of Idolatry, A. John Hall. ReIE
Song of the Mad Prince, The. Walter de la Mare. AtBAP; FaBoCh; GoJo; LoGBV; MoVE; OAEP (2d ed.); ShBV-4
Song of the Mariner's Needle. C. R. Clarke. EtS
Song of the Master and Boatswain. W. H. Auden. *Fr.* The Sea and the Mirror. DTC
Song of the Mayers: "Remember us poor Mayers all." *Unknown.* CH
Song of the Mermaids. George Darley. *See* Mermaidens' Vesper-Hymn.
Song of the Micmac, The. Joseph Howe. CaP
Song of the Midnight Rain. John Gould Fletcher. MoLP
Song of the Milkmaid. Tennyson. *See* Milkmaid's Song.
Song of the Mischievous Dog, The. Dylan Thomas. FaFP; SiTL
Song of the Moderns. John Gould Fletcher. AWP; InPo
Song of the Moon, A. Claude McKay. PoNe
(Moon Song.) TSW
Song of the Mound. Wincenty Pol, *tr. fr. Polish by* Paul Soboleski. PoFr
Song of the Movie Mexican, A. Edwin Meade Robinson. LHV
Song of the Muses, The. Matthew Arnold. WiR
Song of the Musicians. Shakespeare. *Fr.* Cymbeline. *See* Hark! Hark! the Lark.
Song of the Musicians. Shakespeare. *Fr.* Two Gentlemen of Verona. *See* Who Is Silvia.
Song of the Mystic. Abram J. Ryan. *See* Valley of Silence, The.
Song of the Narcissus, The. *Unknown, tr. fr. Arabic by* E. Powys Mathers. *Fr.* The Thousand and One Nights. AWP
Song of the Navajo. Albert Pike. PoOW
Song of the Negro Boatman. Whittier. *Fr.* At Port Royal. GN
Song of the New World. Angela Morgan. HBMV; HBVY; OQP
Song of the Nibelungs, The. *sel. Unknown, pr. tr. fr. Middle High German by* Margaret Armour.
Fall of Siegfried, The, *abr.* WoL
Song of the Night at Daybreak. Alice Meynell. CH; PoVP; VA
Song of the Nudge. Marge Piercy. ThO
Song of the Old Days, A. Patrick MacGill. MaRV
Song of the Old Love. Jean Ingelow. *Fr.* Supper at the Mill. HBV
Song of the Old Man in Chains. Anatoli Vasilyevich Lunacharsky, *tr. fr. Russian by* L. A. Magnus *and* K. Walter. *Fr.* Faust and the City. PoFr
Song of the Old Mother, The. W. B. Yeats. AnIV; BEL; GTSL; LOW; MCCG; MoBrPo; NeMA; PoPo; VA
Song of the Open Road. Ogden Nash. LiTM; NAMP; PoPo; SiTL; TreFS; WhC
Song of the Open Road, A. *Unknown, tr. fr. Latin by* John Addington Symonds. AWP; JAWP; WBP; WHA
Song of the Open Road. Walt Whitman. FaFP; MAP, *abr.*; MoAmPo, *abr.*; NePA; PoMa; ViBoPo, *abr.*; WHA, *sl. abr.*
(Open Road, The, *much abr.*) StaSt
Sels.
"Afoot and light-hearted I take to the open road." AtBAP; HBVY; NeMA; OQP; TiPo; TreFT

Song (continued)
(Open Road, The.) GTSE
Be Not Afraid. MaRV
"Listen! I will be honest with you." PoFr
Song of the Outlaws. Joanna Baillie. *See* Outlaw's Song, The.
Song of the Palm. Tracy Robinson. AA
Song of the Parrot. Elizabeth J. Coatsworth. StVeCh
Song of the Passion, A. Richard Rolle of Hampole. OxBoCh
(My Trewest Tresowre.) AtBAP
Song of the Pen, The. Judah Al-Harizi, *tr. fr. Hebrew by* Joseph Chotzner. TrJP
Song of the Pilgrims, The, *sel.* Rupert Brooke.
"O Thou/ God of all desirous roaming." TrPWD
Song of the Pilgrims. Thomas Cogswell Upham. MC; PAH
Song of the Plow, The, *sels.* Maurice Hewlett.
"He loathed his bond, but could not stir," *fr.* V. PoFr
Hodge in the Strife, *fr.* VIII. PoFr
London, *abr., fr.* V. PoFr
Man on the Hill, The. POTE
1914 Autumn and Winter, *fr.* Envoy. PoFr
Old Thought, An, *abr., fr.* Envoy. PoFr
Poll Tax (1378), *fr.* V. PoFr
Song of the Poor Man. *Unknown, tr. by* Anselm Hollo. TTY
Song of the Pop-Bottlers. Morris Bishop. FaPON; FiBHP
Song of the Queen Bee. E. B. White. NYBP
Song of the Rain. Hugh McCrae. BoAV; MoAuPo; PoAu-1
Song of the Rain Chant. *Tr. fr. Navajo Indian by* Natalie Curtis. AWP; JAWP; WBP
Song of the Redwood-Tree. Walt Whitman. AmPP (5th ed.)
"Flashing and golden pageant of California, The," *sel.* HT
Song of the Reim-Kennar, The. Sir Walter Scott. *Fr.* The Pirate. OAEP; OBNC
(Song of the Tempest, The.) PeER
Song of the Riders. Stephen Vincent Benét. *Fr.* John Brown's Body. MAP; MoAmPo
Song of the River Thames, A. Dryden. *Fr.* Albion & Albanius. FaBoEn
Song of the Road, A. Fred G. Bowles. MaRV; OQP
Song of the Road, A. Robert Louis Stevenson. BrPo; OTPC (1946 ed.); PoVP; YT
Song of the Robin, The. Beatrice Bergquist. SUS
Song of the Rolling Wind, A, *sel.* Lord De Tabley.
"Song of the fields and a song of the woods, A." GTBS-D
Song of the saw, The. Busy Carpenters. James S. Tippett. SoPo; StVeCh
Song of the Screw. *Unknown.* NA
Song of the Sea. Richard E. Burton. EtS
Song of the Sea. *Unknown, at. to* Rumann MacColmain, *tr. fr. Middle Irish.* OnYI, *tr. by* Kuno Meyer.
Song of the sea-adventurers, that never were known to fame, The. The Pageant of Seamen. May Byron. HBV
Song of the sea was an ancient song, The. Song of the Sea. Richard E. Burton. EtS
Song of the Seasons. Blanche De Good Lofton. YeAr
Song of the Seasons, A. Cosmo Monkhouse. DD; HBV
Song of the Seaweed, *sel.* Eliza Cook.
"Many a lip is gaping for drink." FiBHP
Song of the Settlers. Jessamyn West. FaPON
Song of the Shepherd in the Valley of Humiliation, The. Bunyan. *See* Shepherd Boy's Song, The.
Song of the Shirt, The. Thomas Hood. BEL; CABL; CoBE; EnLi-2; EnLit; EnRP; EPN; FaPL; FOL; HBV; MaC; MCCG; OBVV; OHFP; OTD; OTPC (1946 ed.); PaPo; PCD; PoFr; PoPo; PPON,*abr.*; StaSt; TreF; VA; WBLP
Sels.
Sweated Labor. MaRV
"With fingers weary and worn." YAT
Song of the Siberian Exiles, The, *abr.* Nikolai Alekseyevich Nekrasov, *tr. fr. Russian by* Martha Dickinson Bianchi. PoFr
Song of the Silent Land. Johann Gaudenz von Salis-Seewis, *tr. fr. German by* Longfellow. AWP; HBV; JAWP; OQP; WBP
Song of the Sirens. William Browne. *See* Sirens' Song, The.
Song of the Ski, The. Wilson MacDonald. CaP
Song of the Slaves in the Desert. Whittier. *See* Song of Slaves in the Desert.
Song of the Sleepy Bridegroom. Theocritus, *tr. fr. Greek by* Dryden. *Fr.* Idylls, XVIII. HW
Song of the Snowflakes. Annette Wynne. GFA
Song of the Sojourner. Paul Gerhardt, *tr. fr. German by* Jane Borthwick. SoP
Song of the Soldier. Charles G. Halpine. PAP
Song of the Son. Jean Toomer. AmNP; BP; CDC; Kal; MAP; PoNe
Song of the Sons of Esau, The. Bertha Runkle. AA
Song of the sorrow of Melisande is a weary song and a dreary song, The. The Song against Songs. G. K. Chesterton. ALV
Song of the Spanish Main, The. John Bennett. HBV
Song of the Spirits, The. Joseph Sheridan Le Fanu. *Fr.* The Legend of the Glaive. OnYI
Song of the Springtide. *Unknown.* BOHV
Song of the Squatter. Robert Lowe. *See* Songs of the Squatters.
Song of the Standard, The. Swinburne. PoVP
Song of the Storm-Finch, The. Maxim Gorki, *tr. fr. Russian by* Alice Stone Blackwell. PoFr
Song of the Strange Ascetic, The. G. K. Chesterton. HBMV
Song of the Stygian Naiades. Thomas Lovell Beddoes. EnRP; ERoP-2; PeER
Song of the Syrens. William Browne. *See* Sirens' Song, The.
Song of the Tempest. Sir Walter Scott. *See* Song of the Reim-Kennar.
Song of the Three Angels. Gil Vicente, *tr. fr. Spanish by* Aubrey F. G. Bell. *Fr.* The Auto of the Bark of Purgatory. CAW
Song of the Three Minstrels. Thomas Chatterton. *Fr.* Aella. TrGrPo
("Budding floweret blushes at the light, The.") ViBoPo
(Mynstrelles Songe.) EnRP
Song of the Thrush, The. T. A. Daly. MAP; NeMA
Song of the Thunder. *Unknown, tr. fr. Hottentot.* PeSA
Song of the Toad, The. John Burroughs. FaPON
Song of the Tortured Girl, The. John Berryman. CoAP
Song of the Train. David McCord. FaPON; SoPo
Song of the Trees. Mary Colborne-Veel. BoAu
Song of the Truck. Doris Frankel. AmFN
Song of the Turnkey, The. Harry Bache Smith. AA
Song of the Turtle and Flamingo. James Thomas Fields. *See* Turtle and Flamingo, The.
Song of the Two Brothers. Shakespeare. *See* Fear No More the Heat o' the Sun.
Song of the Two Pages. Shakespeare. *See* It Was a Lover and His Lass.
Song of the Ungirt Runners, The. Charles Hamilton Sorley. EnLit; HBMV; MoBrPo; NeMA; OBEV (new ed.); ShBV-2; TreFT; TrGrPo (1942 ed.); TSW
Song of the Universal, *sels.* Walt Whitman.
"All, all for immortality," *fr.* IV. MaRV
"And thou, America," *fr.* IV. PGD
Song of the Unloved. *Unknown, tr. fr. Sotho by* Jack Cope *and* Dan Kunene. PeSA
Song of the Unsuccessful, The. Richard Burton. OQP; WGRP
Song of the Valkyries, The. *Unknown, tr. fr. Norse by* Lee M. Hollander. LiTW; WaaP
Song of the Virgin Mother, A. Lope de Vega, *tr. fr. Spanish by* Ezra Pound. AWP; JAWP; WBP
Song of the Vivandiere. Heine, *tr. fr. German by* Louis Untermeyer. UnTE
Song of the Wage-Slave, The. Ernest Charles Jones. PoFr
Song of the Wave, The. George Cabot Lodge. AA; AmePo; EtS
Song of the Well. Numbers, XXI: 17-18, Bible, *O.T.* TrJP
Song of the Western Men, The. Robert Stephen Hawker. CBEP; EnRP; FOL; GoBC; HBV; OBNC; OBRV; OBVV; PaPo; PoFr; RoGo; VA
(And Shall Trelawn[e]y Die?) EvOK; GTBS; GTSL; OtMeF; ShBV-1
(Trelawny.) ACP (1926 ed.)
Song of the White Lady of Avenel. Sir Walter Scott. *Fr.* The Monastery, *ch.* 5. NBM
Song of the Wild Storm-Waves, The. Percy F. Sinnett. VA
Song of the Wind and the Rain. Solomon ibn Gabirol, *tr. fr. Hebrew by* Solomon Solis-Cohen. TrJP
Song of the Wise Men. Edith Lovejoy Pierce. PGD
Song of the Withy Greatcoat. Norma Farber. NYTB
Song of the Woman-Drawer, The. Mary Gilmore. PoAu-1
Song of the Wood, The. Frederic Edward Weatherly. OTPC (1946 ed.)
Song of the Wulfshaw Larches. Ernest Rhys. VA

Song of the Young Girls. *Unknown, tr. fr. Sanskrit by* Puran Singh. OnPM
Song of the Zambra Dance. Dryden. *Fr.* The Conquest of Granada, Pt. I. AtBAP; OAEP; PoEL-3
(Beneath a Myrtle Shade.) UnTE
(Zambra Dance, The.) CEP; ErPo; MBW-1; SeCV-2
Song of the Zincali. "George Eliot." *Fr.* The Spanish Gypsy. VA
Song of Three Friends, The, *sel.* John G. Neihardt.
Shooting of the Cup, The. PoOW
Song of Three Smiles. W. S. Merwin. CoAP
Song of Thyrsis. Philip Freneau. *Fr.* Female Frailty. AA; AnFE; APA; CoAnAm; HBV; LiTA; OnPM; ViBoPo
Song of Tom. Kirk Hall. BF
Song of Troilus. Chaucer, *after* Petrarch. *Fr.* Troilus and Criseyde. AWP
(Canticus Troili.) AtBAP
("If no love is, O God, what fele I so?") LO
(Troilus Soliloquizes.) EG
Song of Trust, A. Psalms, CXXI, Bible, *O.T. See* I Will Lift Up Mine Eyes unto the Hills.
Song of Twilight, A. *Unknown.* HBV
Song of Two Angels, A. Laura E. Richards. AA
Song of Two Wanderers, A. Marguerite Wilkinson. HBMV
Song of Venus. Dryden. *Fr.* King Arthur, V, i. LoBV; OxBoLi; PoEL-3; SeCeV
(Fairest Isle.) CBEP
Song of Waking, A. Katharine Lee Bates. DD; OHIP
Song of Wandering Ængus, The. W. B. Yeats. BoLiVe; BoLP; BrPo; CH; CLwM; CMoP; DiPo; EnLi-2 (1949 ed.); EnLit; FaBoCh; GoJo; GoTP; InP; LoGBV; LOW; MaPo; MemP; MoAB; MoBrPo; OnSP; PG; PoEL-5; PoeP; PoMS; PoRA; PoSa; RG; SiSw; SP; TDP; ThWaDe; TiPo; ViPo (1962 ed.); WaKn; YAT
Song of Welcome. Hermia Harris Fraser, *ad. fr. Haida Indian song.* CaP
Song of Whip-plaiting. Constance Lindsay Skinner. *Fr.* Songs of the Coast Dwellers. NP
Song of White and Red, A. Sister Mary Benvenuta. JKCP (1926 ed.)
Song of White Snow, A. Ts'en Ts'an, *tr. fr. Chinese by* Witter Bynner. LiTW
Song of Winter, A. Emily Davis Pfeiffer. ACV; PrWP; VA
Song of Winter, A. *Unknown, tr. fr. Middle Irish by* Kuno Meyer. AnIL; CH; OnYI
Song of Work, A. Mary Blake. HH
Song-Offering, A. Rabindranath Tagore, *tr. fr. Bengali by* Rabindranath Tagore. LiTW
Song on a May Morning. Milton. *See* Song on May Morning.
Song on a Young Lady Who Sung Finely. Earl of Roscommon. CavP
Song on King William, A. *Unknown. See* As I Walked by Myself.
Song on May Morning. Milton. BoLiVe; CH; DD; GN HBV; HBVY; NoP; OTPC; TrGrPo
(May Morning.) OTD; YeAr
(On a May Morning.) ExPo
(On May Morning.) RG
(Song of May Morning.) PoPl
(Song: On May Morning.) BoNaP
(Song on a May Morning.) PoRL
Song on Reaching Seventy. John Hall Wheelock. TwAmPo
Song, on Reading that the Cyclotron Has Produced Cosmic Rays, *sel.* Samuel Hoffenstein.
"Be gay, be merry, and don't be wary of milking the modest minute." ShM
Song (on Seeing Dead Bodies Floating off the Cape). Alun Lewis. *See* Song: "First month of his absence, The."
Song on the Water. Thomas Lovell Beddoes. EG; FaBoCh; LoGBV; PoE
Song on the Way The. *Unknown.* BrR MPB
Song, Set by H. Purcell, and Sung by Mrs. Hodgson, A. Thomas Southerne. *See* Though You Make No Return.
Song Set by John Farmer. *Unknown.* CTC
("Take time while time doth last.") OBSC; SiCE
Song; Set by Mr. Coleman. Charles Cotton. *See* Song: "See, how like twilight slumber falls."
Song; Set by Mr. John Eccles. Congreve. *See* Nymph and a Swain, A.
Song Set by Nicholas Yonge. *Unknown. See* Brown Is My Love.
Song soars from a sordid city street, A. A Street Melody. Belle Copper. GoBC
Song Sparrow, The. Henry van Dyke. MPB
Song-Talysarn. Brenda Chamberlain. *See* Song: "Bone-aged is my white horse."
Song that I'm going to sing, The. The Crafty Farmer. *Unknown.* BaBo; ESPB; TiPo (1952 ed.)
Song That Wolfram Heard in Hell, The. Thomas Lovell Beddoes. *See* Song: "Old Adam, the carrion crow."
Song the Body Dreamed in the Spirit's Mad Behest, The. Brother Antoninus. ErPo
Song the Eighth: "That Jenny's my friend." Edward Moore. CEP
Song the Grass Sings, A. Charles G. Blanden. HBV
Song the Ninth: "You tell me I'm handsome." Edward Moore. CEP
Song the Oriole Sings, The. William Dean Howells. AmePo; HBV
Song—the Owl. Tennyson. *See* Owl, The.
Song-Throe, The. Dante Gabriel Rossetti. The House of Life, LXI. MaVP; PoVP; ViPo
Song, 'tis my will that thou do seek out Love. Dante, *Fr.* La Vita Nuova. AWP
Song to a Fair, Young Lady, Going Out of [the] Town in the Spring. Dryden. BWP; CABA; HBV; LiTL; MaPo; MBW-1; OBEV; OBS; PoIE; SeEP
(To a Fair Young Lady Going Out of [the] Town in the Spring.) SeCL
Song to a Lute, A. Sir John Suckling. *Fr.* The Sad One. ReEn; SCEP-2; TrGrPo
(Song, A: "Hast thou seen the down in the air?") AnAnS-2; EnLoPo; SeEP
Song to a Minuet. Dryden. *See* How Happy the Lover.
Song to a Negro Wash-woman. Langston Hughes. GoSl
Song to a Tree. Edwin Markham. FaPON; MPB
Song to a Viol. Jasper Fisher. *Fr.* Fuimus Troes. LO; SeCL
("So the silver-feathered swan.") SeEP; TuPP
Song to Amoret, A. Henry Vaughan. HBV; LiTL; ViBoPo
Song to Apollo. John Lyly. *Fr.* Midas. AtBAP; OBSC
Song to Bacchus. John Fletcher. *See* God Lyaeus.
Song to Be Sung by the Father of Infant Female Children. Ogden Nash. MoAmPo
Song to Beta ("O thou fair silver Thames"). Michael Drayton. *Fr.* The Shepherd's Garland, Eclogue III (1593 ed.). OBSC
(Third Eclogue, The: "Stay, Thames to heare my song" [1606 ed.].) AtBAP; PoEL-2
Song to Celia ("Come, my Celia, let us prove"). Ben Jonson. *See* Come, My Celia, Let Us Prove.
Song to Celia ("Drink to me only with thine eyes"). Ben Jonson. *See* To Celia ("Drink to me . . .").
Song to Celia. Sir Charles Sedley. *See* To Celia.
Song to Cloris, A. Earl of Rochester. ErPo
Song to David, A. Christopher Smart. AtBAP; CEP; ChTr; EiCL; EiCP; EiPP; EnPE; GoTL; LaA; LoBV, *abr.*; MasP; OBEC; PeER; PoEL-3; TrGrPo, *abr.*; WoL, *abr.*
Sels.
Beauteous, Yea Beauteous More than These. EaLo
"For adoration, David's psalms," 23 *sts.* AnFE
"For adoration seasons change."
(Adoration, 12 *sts.*) FaBoEn
Glorious the Sun in Mid Career, *last* 3 *sts.* FaBoCh; LiTG; LoGBV
"He sang of God — the mighty source." GBV, 3 *sts.*; GTSL, 3 *sts.*; LiTG, 3 *sts.*; TRV
(Catholic Amen, The, 15 *sts.*) GoBC
(Song of David, The, 3 *sts.*) GTBS-W
"O David, highest in the list," 38 *sts.* OxBoCh
"O servant of God's holiest charge," 45 *sts.* ViBoPo
"O thou, that sit'st upon a throne." UnS, 2 *sts.*
"Strong is the horse upon his speed." MyFE, 3 *sts.*
(Man of Prayer, The, 3 *sts.*) BBV (1951 ed.); LiTB; LiTG
(Strength, 3 *sts.*) OtMeF
"Sublime—invention ever young," 18 *sts.* HBV; OBEV
"Sweet is the dew that falls betimes." Po, 15 *sts.*
"Tell them, I am, Jehovah said," 14 *sts.*) wGRP
Song to Death. Juan Escrivá. *See* Welcome Death.
Song to Five Toes. *Unknown.* OTPC (1946 ed.); PCH
Song to His Cynthia. Fulke Greville. *See* Of His Cynthia.

Song to His Purse for the King, A. Chaucer. *See* Compleint of Chaucer to His Empty Purse, The.
Song to Imogen. Shakespeare. *See* Hark! Hark! the Lark.
Song to Imogen (in Basic English). Richard L. Greene. WhC
Song to John, Christ's Friend, A. *Unknown.* MeEL
Song to Mary, A. William of Shoreham(?). MeEL
Song to Mithras, A. Kipling. FOL
Song to My Love. Laurence McKinney. InMe
Song to Night. Elizabeth J. Coatsworth. WaKn
Song to One, A. T. A. Daly. YT
Song to Our Lady. *Unknown.* *See* Hymn to the Virgin, A.
Song to Say a Farewell. Howard McKinley Corning. NP
Song to Silvia. Shakespeare. *See* Who Is Silvia?
Song to Sirena. Michael Drayton. *See* Sirena.
Song to Sleep. John Fletcher. *See* Care-charming Sleep.
Song to the Evening Star ("Gem of the crimson-colour'd even"). Thomas Campbell. *See* To the Evening Star.
Song to the Evening Star ("Star that bringest . . ."). Thomas Campbell. GTBS; GTSE; GTSL; HBV
(To the Evening Star.) GTBS-D; GTBS-P; GTBS-W; TRV
"Song, to the Gods, Is Sweetest Sacrifice." Annie Fields. AA
Song to the Lute in Music, A. Richard Edwards. MuSP
Song to the Men of England. Shelley. AnFE; EnL; EnLi-2 (1949 ed.); EnRP; ExPo; FiP; ILP; PAn; PeER; PoFr; PoPo; SeCeV; TrGrPo; ViBoPo; WoL
Song to the Mountains. *Tr. fr. Pawnee Indian by* Alice C. Fletcher. AWP; JAWP; WBP
Song to the oak, the brave old oak, A. The Brave Old Oak. Henry Fothergill Chorley. FaBoBe; HBV
Song to the Soviet Union. Manuel Crespo, *tr. fr. Spanish by* Muna Lee. PoFr
Song to the Tune of Heart's Ease, A. *Unknown.* *Fr.* Misogonus. TuPP
("Sing care away with sport and play.") ReEn
Song to the Tune of "Somebody Stole My Gal." X. J. Kennedy. CoPo
Song to the Virgin, A. *Unknown.* *See* Hymn to the Virgin, A.
Song to the Virgin Mary. Pero López de Ayala, *tr. fr. Spanish by* Thomas Walsh. CAW
Song to the Wind, A. Taliesin, *tr. fr. Welsh by* A. P. Graves. FaBoCh
Song Tournement: New Style. Louis Untermeyer. CrMA
Song under Shadow. William Rose Benét. MoRP
Song unto Liberty's brave buccaneer, A. Paul Jones. *Unknown.* PAH
Song, A? What goes to make a poet's song? Plea. Eileen Duggan. JKCP (1955 ed.)
Song, A! What songs have died. A Song for the Asking. Francis Orrery Ticknor. AA
Song with a Discord, A. Arthur Colton. AA
Song with Words. James Agee. MAP; MoAmPo
Song without a Sound. Sir Edwin Arnold. *Fr.* With Sa'di in the Garden. VA
Song, Written at Sea, in the First Dutch War. Charles Sackville. *See* Song: "To all you ladies now at land."
Song you sang you will not sing again, The. Local Places. Howard Moss. NePoEA-2
Song, Youth, and Sorrow. William Cranston Lawton. AA
Songbooks of the War. Siegfried Sassoon. InP
Songe, The: "Drinke and be merry, merry, merry boyes." Thomas Morton. *Fr.* New English Canaan. AmPP; SCAP
Songe betwene the Quenes Majestie and Englande, A. William Birche. *See* Song between the Queen's Majesty and England, A.
Songe of Seyncte Warburghe. Thomas Chatterton. PeER
Songs, The ("Continuous, a medley of old pop numbers"). Martin Bell. MuSP
Songs ("I would make songs for you"). Babette Deutsch. HBMV
Songs. Denis Glover. AnNZ
"These songs will not stand," I.
"If everywhere in the street," II.
Songs ("How are songs begot and bred?"). Richard Henry Stoddard. AA
Songs: Spring and Winter. Shakespeare. *See* When Daisies Pied *and* When Icicles Hang by the Wall.
Songs above the Dust. Grantland Rice. PaA
Songs and Lyrics. Sir Thomas Wyatt. *Poems indexed separately by titles and first lines.*
Song's Apostasy. Sir William Watson. EPN
Songs Ascending. Witter Bynner. *Fr.* To Celia. HBV; NP
Songs at Amala's Wedding. Thomas Lovell Beddoes. *See* Bridal Sang to Amala.
Songs' End. John Payne. VA
Song's Eternity. John Clare. CBEP; FaBoCh; LoGBV; NCEP; PG; WaKn
Songs for a Colored Singer. Elizabeth Bishop. MiAP; PoNe
Songs for a Three-String Guitar. Léopold Sédar-Senghor, *tr. fr. French by* Miriam Koshland. PBA
Songs for Fragoletta. Richard Le Gallienne. HBV
Songs for My Mother, *sels.* Anna Hempstead Branch.
Her Hands. MPB
(My Mother's Hands.) DD
(Song for My Mother, A: Her Hands.) OHIP; RG
(Songs for My Mother: Her Hands.) HH; OnPP; PoRL; YT
Her Words. FaPON
(Song for My Mother, A: Her Words.) BoChLi; OHIP; SiSoSe; TiPo (1959 ed.); YeAr
(Songs for My Mother: Her Words.) HH; OnPP; YT
Song for My Mother, A: Her Stories. OHIP
Songs from a Masque. Francis Beaumont. *See* Masque of the Inner Temple and Gray's Inne, The.
Songs from an Evil Wood. Lord Dunsany. MoBrPo (1942 ed.)
Songs from Cyprus, *sels.* Hilda Doolittle ("H. D.").
"Gather for festival." MAP; MoAmPo
"Where is the nightingale." MAP; MoAmPo
(Song from Cyprus, A.) NeMA
Songs from "The Princess." Tennyson. *See* Princess, The.
Songs from "The Secular Masque." Dryden. *See* Secular Masque, The.
Songs I Sing, The. Charles G. Blanden. HBV
Songs in Absence, *sels.* Arthur Hugh Clough.
O Ship, Ship, Ship, XIV. PoVP
Some Future Day When what Is Now Is Not, VI. EPN
Where Lies the Land [to Which the Ship Would Go], VII. AWP; BEL; BoTP; ChTr; EtS; FaBoBe; FaBoCh; GN; HBV; ILP; JAWP; LoGBV; MCCG; OBVV; OTPC (1946 ed.); PoIE; TOP; TreFT; VA; ViPo; ViPP; WBP; WGRP
(Songs in Absence.) OQP
("Where lies the land to which the ship would go?") EPN; GTBS; GTBS-D; GTSL
Ye Flags of Piccadilly, II. PoVP
Songs in the Night. J. Lyall. SoP
Songs light as these may sound, though deep and strong. Dedication to Christina G. Rossetti. Swinburne. StP
Songs of adolescence, The. Lyric. John Thompson. BoAu
Songs of an Empty House, *sel.* Marguerite Wilkinson.
End, The. HBMV
Songs of Autolycus. Shakespeare. *See* Jog On, Jog On *and* Lawn as White as Driven Snow *and* When Daffodils Begin to Peer *and* Will You Buy Any Tape.
Songs of Bilitis, The, *sels.* Pierre Louys, *tr. fr. French by* Horace M. Brown. UnTE
Absence.
Bilitis.
Desire.
Despairing Embrace, The.
Endearments.
Kiss, The.
Little House, The.
Remorse.
Songs of Ch'en, *sels.* Confucius, *tr. fr. Chinese by* Ezra Pound. CTC
Aliter.
"Marsh bank, lotus rank."
Songs of Cheng, *sels.* Confucius, *tr. fr. Chinese by* Ezra Pound. CTC
"Be kind, good sir, and I'll lift my sark."
"Hep-Cat Chung, 'ware my town."
"In chariot like an hibiscus flower at his side."
"So he won't talk to me when we meet?"
Songs of Conn the Fool, The, *sel.* Fannie Stearns Davis.
Moon Folly. RG; SP
Songs of Education, *sel.* G. K. Chesterton.
Geography. HBMV
Songs of Experience, *sels.* Blake.
Ah! Sun-Flower. AtBAP; AWP; CABA; CBEP; CBV; DiPo; EiCL; EiPP; ELP; ELU; EnLi-2; EnLit; EnRP; ERoP-1; ExPo; ForPo; GTBS-D; GTBS-W; InPo; JAWP; MaPo; NoP; OAEP;

OBEC; OBNC; OuHeWo; PAn; PoE; PoEL-4; SeCeV; ShBV-4; TOP; UnPo; ViBoPo; WBP
(Ah! Sunflower, Weary of Time.) EG
(Sunflower, The.) BEL; BoLiVe; ChTr; PoFS; TrGrPo
Angel, The. CH; EiPP; EnRP
Chimney Sweeper, The ("A little black thing among the snow"). AtBAP; BoW; BWP; CABA; EiCL; EiPP; EnL; EnLi-2 (1949 ed.); EnLit; EnPE; ERoP-1; ForPo; PAn; PoeP; PoIE; TDP; YAT
Clod and the Pebble, The. AWP; BEL; BoLiVe; CABA; CBEP; EiPP; EnL; EnLi-2; EnLit; EnLoPo; EnRP; FaBoEn; FaBV; ForPo; JAWP; LoBV; MaPo (1969 ed.); OAEP; OBEC; OBNC; OnPM; OtMeF; PeER; PoAn; PoeP; TOP; TrGrPo; ViBoPo; WBP
("Love seeketh not itself to please.") LO
Divine Image, A ("Cruelty has a human heart"). NoP; PoeP
Earth's Answer. CBEP; EiPP; EnPE; EnRP; ERoP-1
Fly, The. BoLiVe; CBEP; DiPo; EiPP; EnL; GoTP; MaPo; OTPC (1923 ed.); PoSa; TrGrPo; YAT
Garden of Love, The. AWP; CABA; CBEP; DiPo; EiCL; EnLi-2 (1949 ed.); EnLoPo; EnRP; ERoP-1; ExPo; FaBV; FosPo; InPo; JAWP; LiTB; LiTG; LiTL; LO; LoBV; MeWo; NoP; OAEP; PoE; PoFS; PoIE; SeCeV; StP; TOP; VaPo; ViBoPo; WBP
Holy Thursday ("Is this a holy thing to see"). CEP; CoBE; EiPP; EnL; EnLi-2 (1949 ed.); EnPE; EnRP; ERoP-1; ILP; NoP; OAEP; PeER; PoE; PoeP; PoIE; StP
Human Abstract, The. DiPo; EiPP; EnRP; ERoP-1; MaPo; PoEL-4 PTK
Infant Sorrow. BoLiVe; BWP; CBEP; DiPo; EiCL; EiPP; EnL; FaBoEn; MaPo (1969 ed.); OBNC; PeER; PoEL-4; PoeP; PoFS
Introduction: "Hear the voice of the bard!" BWP; EiPP; EnPE; EnRP; ERoP-1; LoBV; OAEP; PeER; PoEL-4; PoeP
(Bard, The.) TRV; WGRP
(Hear the Voice of the Bard.) CBEP; ELP; GTBS-D; OBEC; OBEV
(Introduction to "Songs of Experience.") ExPo
Little Boy Lost, A ("Nought loves another as itself"). CBEP; CEP; EnLi-2; EnLit; EnRP; OAEP; PeER; PoIE; ViBoPo
Little Girl Found, The. CBEP; DiPo
Little Girl Lost, The. DiPo; ERoP-1
London. AtBAP; AWP; BWP; CABA; CaFP; CBEP; CBV; CEP; ChER; DiPo; EiCL; EiPP; EnL; EnLi-2 (1949 ed.); EnPE; EnRP; ERoP-1; ExPo; FaBoEn; ForPo; ILP; InPo; LiTB; MaPo; NoP; OBNC; OnPM; PAn; PeER; PIA; PoAn; PoE; PoEL-4; PoeP; PoFS; PoIE; PoSa; PPON; SeCePo; SeCeV; StP; TDP; UnPo; ViBoPo; WoL
("I wander thro' each chartered street.") LO
("I wander thro' each dirty street," *sel., sl. diff.*) ChTr
My Pretty Rose Tree. PoeP
Nurse's Song ("When the voices of children are heard on the green/ And whisperings"). CEP; EiPP; EnLi-2 (1949 ed.); EnRP; PoFS; TOP
Poison Tree, A. AnFE; AWP; BoLiVe; BWP; CABA; CaFP; CBEP; CBV; DiPo; EiCL; EnL; EnLi-2; EnLit; EnRP; ERoP-1; FaFP; HoPM; InPo; JAWP; LiTB; LiTG; MaPo; NoP; OAEP; OtMeF; PoAn; PoEL-4; PoeP; PoFS; PoMS; SiSw; TOP; TreFS; TrGrPo; VaPo; WBP
("I was angry with my friend.") EG; GTBS-W
Schoolboy, The. BoNaP; CBEP; CH; FaBoCh; FIW; GTBS-D; PeER
Sick Rose, The. AtBAP; AWP; BEL; BoLiVe; BoW; BWP; CABA; CaFP; CBEP; CBV; CheR; ChTr; DiPo; EiCL; EiPP; EnL; EnLoPo; ERoP-1; ExPo; FaBoEn; ForPo; FosPo; GTBS-D; ILP; InPo; JAWP; LoBV; MaPo; NoP; OAEP; OBNC; OnPM; PeER; PIA; PoAn; PoEL-4; PoeP; PoFS; PoG; PoIE; PoSa; SeCeV; ShBV-4; StP; TOP; TrGrPo; ViBoPo; WBP
(O Rose, Thou Art Sick!) EG; ELP
Tiger, The. ATP; AWP; BBV; BEL; BoC; BoLiVe; BWP; CBEP; ChTr; EiPP; EnL; EnLi-2; EnLit; EnPE; FaBoBe; FaFP; FaPON; ForPo; GN; GoTP; GTBS-W; HBV; JAWP; LiTB; LiTG; MaPo; MaRV; MCCG; MPB; MyFE; NeHB; OA; OAEP; OBEC; OBEV; OnPM; OtMeF; OTPC; OuHeWo; PAn; PG; Po; PoAn; PoFS; PoLF; PoPl; PoPo; PoRA; PoSa; PTK RG; RoGo; ShBV-2; StaSt; StP; TIHL; TOP; TreF; TRV; VaPo; ViBoPo; WBP; WGRP; WHA; WoL
(Tyger, The.) AnFE; AtBAP; BoTP; CABA; CaFP; CBV; CEP; CH; DiPo; EaLo; EiCL; EnRP; ERoP-1; ExPo; FaBoCh; FaBoEn; FaBV; FosPo; GTBS-D; HoPM; ILP; InPo; LoBV; LoGBV; MasP; MemP; NoP; OBNC; PeER; PIA; PoE; PoEL-4; PoeP; PoIE; SeCePo; SeCeV; TrGrPo; WaKn; YAT
("Tyger, Tyger, burning bright.") EG
To Tirzah. EiPP; EnRP; ERoP-1; LO; OxBoCh
Songs of Guthrum and Alfred, The. G. K. Chesterton. *Fr.* The Ballad of the White Horse. HBV
Songs of Innocence, *sels.* Blake.
Blossom, The. CBEP; EiCL; FosPo; GoJo; OTPC (1923 ed.); ThWaDe
Chimney Sweeper, The ("When my mother died I was very young"). AtBAP; BoW; BWP; CaFP; CBEP; CEP CH; DiPo; EiCL; EiPP; EnPE; EnRP; ERoP-1; FosPo; ILP; PAn; PoeP; PoIE
Cradle Song, A: "Sweet dreams, form a shade." AnFE; BEL; CBEP; EiPP; EnLi-2; EnLit; EnRP OAEP; RIS; ViBoPo
(Sweet Dreams Form a Shade.) OTPC
Divine Image, The ("To mercy, pity, peace, and love"). BoPe; BoTP; CBEP; CEP; EiPP; EnL; EnLit; EnPE; EnRP; ERoP-1; FaBoEn; LiTG; MaPo; MaRV; MemP; NoP; OAEP; OBEC; OBNC; OnPM; OxBoCh; PoEL-4; PoeP; PoIE; SoP; TRV; ViBoPo; WGRP
("To Mercy Pity Peace and Love.") LO
Dream, A. CBEP; CH; EnRP; MPB; OA; PoRh; TVC
Echoing [*or* Ecchoing] Green, The. BoTP; BWP; CaFP; CBEP; CBV; CEP; CH; DiPo; EiPP; ERoP-1; GBV (1952 ed.); OBEC; OTPC; PAn; PCH; PeER; PoeP; PoRh; PoSC; WiR
Holy Thursday ("'Twas on a Holy Thursday"). AnFE; BoC; CBEP; CEP; CH; CoBE; DiPo; EiCL; EiPP; EnL; EnPE; EnRP; ERoP-1; HBV; MemP; NoP; OAEP; OBEC; OTPC; PeER; PoE; PoeP; PoFS; PoIE; StP; YAT
Infant Joy. BiCB; CBEP; EiPP; EnLi-2; EnLit; FaPON; GoJo; GoTP; GTSL; HBV; HBVY; LoBV; MaPo (1969 ed.); MemP; NeHB; OTPC; PoeP; PoLF; PRWS; SiSoSe; ThWaDe; TiPo; ViBoPo
Lamb, The. AnFE; BEL; BoChLi; BoLiVe; BoTP; BWP; CABA; CaFP; CAW; CBEP; CBV; CEP; CH; CoBE; DiPo; EaLo; EiCL; EiPP; EnL; EnLi-2; EnLit; EnPE; EnRP; ERoP-1; ExPo; FaBoBe; FaBoCh; FaPON; ForPo; GoJo; GoTP; HBV; ILP; LiTB; LiTG; LoBV; LoGBV; MaPo; MaRV; MemP; MPB; NeHB; NoP; OAEP; OBEC; OTPC; OuHeWo; OxBoCh; PAn; PG (1945 ed.); PIA; PoAn; PoeP; PoFS; PoIE; PoPl; PoPo; PoRh; PRWS; RIS; SeCeV; SoP; StaSt; StVeCh; SUS; TIHL; TOP; TreF; TrGrPo; TRV; TVC; UTS; WaKn; WGRP; WHA; YAT
Laughing Song. BoTP; BrR; CBEP; DiPo; EiPP; EnLi-2; EnRP; GoJo; GoTP; OTPC; PCH; PoRh; PoSC; SoPo; SUS; TiPo; ThWaDe; WaKn
(When the Green Woods Laugh.) CH
Little Black Boy, The. AnFE; AtBAP; AWP; BEL; BoC; CABA; CaFP; CBEP; CBV; CEP; CH; DiPo; EiPP; EnL; EnLi-2; EnLit; EnPE; EnRP; ERoP-1; ForPo; HBV; ILP; InPo; LoGBV; MyFE; NoP; OAEP; OBEC; OBEV; OBNC; OxBoCh; PAn; PoEL-4; PoeP; PoFr; PoIE; PoNe; SeCeV; TDP; TOP; TreFS; TrGrPo
Little Boy Found, The. CBEP; EnRP; TiPo (1952 ed.)
Little Boy Lost ("Father! father! Where are you going?"). CBEP; EnRP; TiPo (1952 ed.)
Night. AnFE; AtBAP; BoNaP; BoTP; CBEP; CEP; CH; CoBE; EnRP; FaBoBe; FaPON; GoTP; GTBS-D; HBV; HBVY; MaPo; MyFE; OBEC; OBEV; OTPC (1923 ed.); OxBoCh; PoE; PoLF; RIS; SAS; ShBV-3; StaSt, *abr.*; TreFT; WiR
(Guardian Angels of the Creatures.) BoC
Nurse's Song ("When the voices of children are heard on the green/ And laughing"). AWP; BoChLi; CBEP; CEP; CH; EiCL; EiPP; EnRP; FaBoBe; GaP; GoTP; HBV; HBVY; InPo; MPB; OBEC; OnPM; OTPC (1923 ed.); RG; ThWaDe; TiPo; WoL
On Another's Sorrow. AWP; CBEP; CEP; EiCL; EnRP; FaBV; LiTG; MaRV; OTPC (1923 ed.); PeER; PoEL-4; SoP; ViBoPo
Piping down the Valleys Wild. CBEP; FaBoCh; FaBV; GBV; InvP; LoGBV; OBEC; PAn; PoRh; PRWS; TreFS; UnS
(Happy Songs.) GoTP; RIS
(Introduction: "Piping down the valleys wild.") AnFE; BEL; BWP; CEP; DiPo; EiCL; EiPP; EnLit; EnPE; EnRP; ERoP-1; FosPo; GoJo; ILP; OAEP; OBNC; PeER; PoAn; PoE; PoEL-4; PoeP; PoIE; SeCeV; ThWaDe; TrGrPo; YAT
(Introduction to "Songs of Innocence.") CoBE; EnLi-2; ExPo; FaBoBe; NeHB; OuHeWo; PG (1945 ed.); Po; TiPo; ViBoPo; WHA
(Piper, The.) AWP; BoChLi; BoTP; GaP; InPo; JAWP; MPB; OTPC; PDV; RoGo; TOP; WBP
(Reeds of Innocence.) GTBS-W; HBV; HBVY; LiTB; LiTG; OBEV
(Songs of Innocence: Introduction.) EiPP; LoBV
"Piper, sit thee down and write," *last 2 sts.* YT

Songs (continued)
Shepherd, The. BoTP; CBEP; EiPP; EnRP; ExPo; GaP; GoTP; HBV; LoBV; OBEC; OTPC; PoRh ThWaDe; TiPo (1959 ed.); TOP; TVC
(Innocence.) BoPe
Spring. BoChLi; BoTP; FaBoCh; FaPON; GoTP; LoGBV; MoShBr; OTPC; PoPl; RIS; SUS; TiPo (1952 ed.); YeAr
Songs of Jesus. Louis F. Benson. MaRV
Songs of Joy. W. H. Davies MoBrPo; OBVV; YT
Songs of Kabir. Kabir, *tr. fr. Hindi by* Rabindranath Tagore.
"How could the love between Thee and me sever?"
(Two Songs, 2.) LiTW
"Moon shines in my body, but my blind eyes cannot see it, The." WGRP
(Two Songs, 1.) LiTW
"Tell me, O Swan, your ancient tale." WGRP
Songs of Labor: Dedication. Whittier. *See* Dedication: "I would the gift I offer here."
Songs of Maximus, The. Charles Olson. NeAP
Songs of Selma, The. James MacPherson.
Alpin. CEP
Argument. CEP
Colma. CEP
(From "Songs of Selma," *abr.*) BEL
Ryno. CEP
Songs of Seven. Jean Ingelow. GBV (1922 ed.); HBV
Seven Times Five. GBV (1922 ed.); HBV
Seven Times Four. GBV (1922 ed.); HBV
(Heigh Ho!) BoTP
(Maternity.) OHIP
Seven Times One. BiCB; BLPA; FaPON; GBV (1922 ed.); GoTP HBV; MPB; OBNC; OTPC; PCH; PRWS; TreF; TVC
(Birthday Morning.) ThGo
Seven Times Seven. GBV (1922 ed.); HBV
(Longing for Home.) WGRP
Seven Times Six. GBV (1922 ed.); HBV
Seven Times Three. GBV (1922 ed.); HBV
(Seven Times Three—Love.) PoLF
Seven Times Two. GBV (1922 ed.); GN; HBV; OTPC (1923 ed.)
Songs of shepherds and rustical roundelays. The Hunting of the Gods. Walter Wasse. OxBoLi; SeCL
Songs of T'ang, *sel.* Confucius, *tr. fr. Chinese by* Ezra Pound.
Alba. CTC
Songs of the Birds, The. Edward Carpenter. WGRP
Songs of the Blue-Light Dakini. Lenore Kandel. FRC
Songs of the Coast Dwellers, *sels.* Constance Lindsay Skinner.
Chief's Prayer after the Salmon Catch, The. NP
Song of the Full Catch. CaP
Song of Whip-plaiting. NP
Songs of the Greenwood. Shakespeare. *See* Blow, Blow, Thou Winter Wind *and* Under the Greenwood Tree.
Songs of the Night Watches, *sel.* Jean Ingelow.
Apprenticed. LiTL; OBVV
Songs of the People, *sels.* Hayyim Nahman Bialik, *tr. fr. Hebrew by* Maurice Samuel.
"On a hill there blooms a palm," 2. AWP; JAWP; WBP
"Two steps from my garden rail," 1. AWP; JAWP; WBP
Songs of the Plains, I-IV. Glenn Ward Dresbach. NP
Songs of the Sea-Children, *sels.* Bliss Carman. OBCV
"I see the golden hunter go," LIV.
"What is it to remember?" LXVI.
Songs of the Slave, *sel.* Svatopluk Cech, *tr. fr. Czech by* Otto Koutouc.
"Here and there, Freedom is an empty name." PoFr
Songs of the Squatters. Robert Lowe. PoAu-1
(Song of the Squatter.) VA
Songs of the Three Minstrels. Thomas Chatterton. *Fr.* Aella. PeER
Songs, so old and bitter, The. The Coffin. Heine. AWP; JAWP; WBP
Songs to a Woman. Maxwell Bodenheim. NP
Songs to Seraphine, *sel.* Heine, *tr. fr. German by* Emma Lazarus. TrJP
Shadow-Love.
Waves Gleam in the Sunshine, The.
Songs We Need, The. Bernard Freeman Trotter. MaRV
"Songs without Words." Robert J. Burdette. BOHV
Song's Worth, A. Susan Marr Spalding. AA
Songstress, in all times ended and begun. To Christina Rossetti. Sir William Watson. InP
Sonic Boom. John Updike. TPM
"Sonja Henie," the young girl. Preface. Theodore Weiss. NMP
Sonne, The. George Herbert. *See* Son, The.
Sonnet, The ("A sonnet is a moment's monument"). Dante Gabriel Rossetti. The House of Life, *introd.* BEL; CoBE; EnL; EnLi-2; EnLit; EPN; GTBS-W; HBV; ILP; InP; MaVP; NoP; OAEP; PoVP; Sonn; StP; TOP; ViBoPo; ViPo; ViPP; VP; YAT
(Introductory.) VA
(Sonnet Is a Moment's Monument, A.) PP
Sonnet: "Academy of the future is opening its doors, The." Ted Berrigan. FRC
Sonnet: "Accuse me not, beseech thee, that I wear." Elizabeth Barrett Browning. Sonnets from the Portuguese, XV. PoVP
Sonnet: "Across the shaken bastions of the year." Arthur Davison Ficke. Sonnets of a Portrait Painter, XLVII. AnAmPo
Sonnet: Addressed by a Father Mourning His Recently Deceased Married Daughter to the Father Whose Daughter Had Entered a Convent. Jacopo Vittorelli. *See* On a Nun.
Sonnet: Addressed to Haydon. Keats. *See* Addressed to Haydon.
Sonnet: "After dark vapours have oppress'd our plains." Keats. *See* After Dark Vapours.
Sonnet: "After long storms and tempests' sad assay." Spenser. *See* Amoretti, LXIII.
Sonnet: "Against my love shall be as I am now." Shakespeare. Sonnets, LXIII. OBSC; ReEn; SiCE
Sonnet: "Against that time, if ever that time come." Shakespeare. *See* Sonnets, XLIX.
Sonnet: Age. Richard Garnett. *See* Age.
Sonnet: "Ah, could I grow in some remote degree." George Henry Boker. *Fr.* Sonnets; a Sequence on Profane Love. AmePo
Sonnet: "Ah, sweet Content, where is thy mild abode?" Barnabe Barnes. Parthenophil and Parthenophe, LXVI. EIL; ReEn; TuPP
(Content.) OBSC
Sonnet: "Ah, we are neither heaven nor earth, but men." John Masefield. *Fr.* Sonnets ("Long long ago"). EPN
Sonnet: "Ah wherefore with infection should he live." Shakespeare. Sonnets, LXVII. SiCE
Sonnet: "Alack! what poverty my Muse brings forth." Shakespeare. *See* Sonnets, CIII.
Sonnet: "Alas, 'tis true I have gone here and there." Shakespeare. *See* Sonnets, CX.
Sonnet: "Alexis, here she stayed; among these pines." William Drummond of Hawthornden. EIL; OBS
(Alexis, Here She Stay'd.) HBV
(Spring Bereaved.) LO; OBEV
Sonnet: "All beautiful things bring sadness, nor alone." Richard Chenevix Trench. VA
Sonnet: " All men,—the preacher saith,—whate'er or whence." Frederick Goddard Tuckerman. PoIE
Sonnet: "All other joys of life he strove to warm." George Meredith. Modern Love, IV. GTBS-D; OAEP; VA; ViPo
Sonnet: "Along the garden terrace." George Meredith. Modern Love, XXXVII. ViPo
Sonnet: "Altarwise by owl-light in the halfway-house." Dylan Thomas. *See* Altarwise by Owl-Light.
Sonnet: "Am I failing? For no longer can I cast." George Meredith. Modern Love, XXIX. ViPo
Sonnet: "And change with hurried hand has swept these scenes." Frederick Goddard Tuckerman. NoP; QFR
Sonnet: "And faces, forms and phantoms, numbered not." Frederick Goddard Tuckerman. QFR
Sonnet: "And from the windy West came two-gunned Gabriel." Dylan Thomas. Altarwise by Owl-Light, V. CoBMV; LiTM; MasP
Sonnet: "And I have seen again the marvellous child." Paul Verlaine, *tr. fr. French by* Vernon Watkins. LiTW
Sonnet: "And me my winter's task is drawing over." Frederick Goddard Tuckerman. QFR
Sonnet: "And now there is nothing left to celebrate." George Barker. LiTM (1970 ed.)

Sonnet: "And she, her beauty never made her cold." Frederick Goddard Tuckerman. AmePo
Sonnet: "And so the day drops by; the horizon draws." Frederick Goddard Tuckerman. AmePo; AnNE; PoIE
Sonnet: "And then I sat me down, and gave the rein." Gustav Rosenhane. *tr. fr. Swedish by* Sir Edmund Gosse. *Fr.* Sonnets. AWP; JAWP; WBP
Sonnet: "And what were roses." E. E. Cummings. NP
Sonnet: "And wilt thou have me fashion into speech." Elizabeth Barrett Browning. Sonnets from the Portuguese, XIII. PoVP
Sonnet: "And yet, because thou overcomest so." Elizabeth Barrett Browning. Sonnets from the Portuguese, XVI. OAEP; PoVP; ViPo
Sonnet: "And yet I cannot reprehend the flight." Samuel Daniel. *See* To Delia: "And yet I cannot . . ."
Sonnet: "And you as well must die, beloved dust." Edna St. Vincent Millay. Unnamed Sonnets, VIII. NP; MasP
Sonnet: Anniversary, February 23, 1795. William Mason. OBEC
Sonnet: "Apples ripen under yellowing leaves, The." Thomas Caulfield Irwin. IrPN
Sonnet: Army Surgeon, The. Sydney Thompson Dobell. NCEP
Sonnet: "As an unperfect actor on the stage." Shakespeare. *See* Sonnets, XXIII.
Sonnet: "As due by many titles I resigne." John Donne. Holy Sonnets, II. AnAnS-1; MaMe; MasP; MeP; MePo; OBS; PIA; SCEP-1; SeEP; Sonn
Sonnet: "As Eponina brought, to move the king." Frederick Goddard Tuckerman. AmePo
Sonnet: "As fast as thou shalt wane, so fast thou grow'st." Shakespeare. *See* Sonnets, IX.
Sonnet: "As in a duskie and tempestuous night." William Drummond of Hawthornden. *See* As in a Dusky and Tempestuous Night.
Sonnet: "As in the midst of battle there is room." George Santayana. Sonnets, XXV. AnFE; APA; AWP; CoAnAm; JAWP; LiTM; MAP; MoAmPo; WBP
Sonnet: "As one who walks and weeps by alien brine." Frederick Goddard Tuckerman. AmePo
Sonnet: "As when the scepter dangles from the hand." George Santayana. Sonnets, XLII. ATP
Sonnet: "Ashamed at times that I am silent." Petrarch. *See* Praises of Laura Transcend His Poetic Power, The.
Sonnet: At Dover Cliffs, July 20, 1787. William Lisle Bowles. *See* Dover Cliffs.
Sonnet: At Ostend, July 22, 1787. William Lisle Bowles. OBEC
(At Ostend.) ERoP-1
(Bells of Ostend, The.) EnRP
(Bells, Ostend, The.) Sonn
Sonnet: "At the round earths imagin'd [*or* imagined] corners, blow." John Donne. AnAnS-1; AnEnPo; AtBAP; ATP (1953 ed.); BWP; CABA; CBEP; CBV; CoBE; DiPo; EaLo; EnRePo; EP; ExPo; FaBoEn; FlW; ForPo; FosPo; ILP; InPo; LiTB; LiTG; LoBV; MaMe; MaPo; MasP; MBW-1; MeLP; MeP; MePo; MyFE; NoP; OAEP; OBS; OxBoCh; PAn; PIA; Po; PoAn; PoEL-2; PoFS; PoIE; QFR; ReEn; SCEP-1; SeCeV; SeCP; SeCV-1; SeEP; ShBV-4; Sonn; StP; TDP; TreFT; TuPP; VaPo; ViBoPo YAT
(Blow Your Trumpets, Angels.) ChTr
Sonnet: Avenge O Lord Thy Slaughter'd Saints. Milton. *See* On the Late Massacre in Piedmont.
Sonnet: "Awakened, I behold through dewy leaves." Thomas Caulfield Irwin. IrPN
Sonnet: "Away with these self-loving lads." Fulke Greville. *See* Of His Cynthia.
Sonnet: "Azured vault, the crystal circles bright, The." James I, King of England. *See* Heaven and Earth.
Sonnet: "Batter my heart, three person'd God; for, you." John Donne. Holy Sonnets, XIV. AnAnS-1; AnEnPo; AnFE; BoLiVe; BWP; EnL; ExPo; ForPo; FosPo; GoBC; GTBS-W; LiTB; LiTG; MaMe; MaPo; MaRV; MasP; MBW-1; MeLP; MeP; OAEP; OBS; OxBoCh; PAn; PIA; PoAn; PoEL-2; PoFS; SCEP-1; SeCeV; SeCV-1; SeEP; Sonn; TrGrPo; TrPWD; TuPP
Sonnet: "Be secret, heart, and if your dreams have come." Anna Virginia Mitchell. OQP
Sonnet: "Beatrice is gone up into high Heaven." Dante, *tr. fr. Italian by* Dante Gabriel Rossetti. *Fr.* La Vita Nuova. GoBC
Sonnet: "Beauty, sweet love, is like the morning dew." Samuel Daniel. To Delia, XLII [XLVII]. ElL; FaBoEn; HBV; OBSC; TuPP; ViBoPo
(Beauty, Sweet Love.) EnRePo
(Beauty, Time, and Love, 5.) OBEV
Sonnet: "Because I breathe not love to every one." Sir Philip Sidney. *See* Astrophel and Stella, LIV.
Sonnet: "Because mine eyes can never have their fill." Dante. *See* Ballata: He Will Gaze upon Beatrice.
Sonnet: "Because my faltering feet may fail to dare." Hilaire Belloc. *See* Because My Faltering Feet.
Sonnet: "Because my grief seems quiet and apart." Robert Nathan. *See* Because My Grief Seems Quiet and Apart.
Sonnet: "Because thou hast the power and own'st the grace." Elizabeth Barrett Browning. Sonnets from the Portuguese, XXXIX. PoVP; VA
Sonnet: "Beckie, my luve!—What is't, ye twa-faced tod?" George Campbell Hay. OxBS
Sonnet: "Beehould a cluster to itt selfe a vine." William Alabaster. AnAnS-1; MeP
Sonnet: "Being myeself [*or* my selfe] captyved here in care." Spenser. *See* Amoretti, LXXIII.
Sonnet: "Being your slave, what should I do but tend." Shakespeare. *See* Sonnets, LVII.
Sonnet: "Belovèd, my Belovèd, when I think." Elizabeth Barrett Browning. *See* Sonnets from the Portuguese; "Belovèd, my Belovèd..."
Sonnet: "Belovèd, thou hast brought me many flowers." Elizabeth Barrett Browning. Sonnets from the Portuguese, XLIV. OAEP; PoVP; ViPo
Sonnet: "Beshrew that heart that makes my heart to groan." Shakespeare. Sonnets, CXXXIII. CBEP; InvP; ReIE
Sonnet: "Between my love and me there runs a thread." Irene Rutherford McLeod. *Fr.* Sonnets. HBMV
Sonnet: "Beyond the sphere which spreads to widest space." Dante, *tr. fr. Italian by* Dante Gabriel Rossetti. *Fr. La* Vita Nuova. AWP; JAWP; OuHeWo; WBP
(Beyond the Sphere.) OnPM
Sonnet: "Bird that discoursest from yon poplar bough." James Clarence Mangan. IrPN
Sonnet: "Black pitchy night, companion of my woe." Michael Drayton. Idea's Mirrour, LXX [XLV]. LoBV; OBSC; ReIE; SiCE; TuPP
Sonnet: "Blast of wind, A, a momentary breath." Barnabe Barnes. *Fr.* A Divine Century of Spiritual Sonnets. SiCE; TuPP
Sonnet: "Bow down, my song, before her presence high." Morton Luce. *Fr.* Thysia. HBV
Sonnet: "Breeze is sharp, the sky is hard and blue, The." Frederick Goddard Tuckerman. AP
Sonnet: "Bright star of beauty, on whose eyelids sit." Michael Drayton. Idea, IV. HBV; SiCE
Sonnet: "Bright star, would I were steadfast as thou art." Keats. *See* Bright Star, Would I Were. . .
Sonnet: "But be contented when that fell arrest." Shakespeare. Sonnets, LXXIV. CBEP; OBSC; Sonn
Sonnet: "But love whilst that thou may'st [*or* maist] be loved again." Samuel Daniel. *Fr.* To Delia, XXXVII. AtBAP; ElL; OBSC; SiCE; TuPP
Sonnet: "But now my muse, toil'd with continual care." Richard Barnfield. ReIE
Sonnet: "But only three in all God's universe." Elizabeth Barrett Browning. Sonnets from the Portuguese, II. PoVP
Sonnet: "But unto him came swift calamity." Frederick Goddard Tuckerman. AP
Sonnet: "But where began the change; and what's my crime?" George Meredith. Modern Love, X. NBM
Sonnet: "But wherefore do not you a mightier way." Shakespeare. Sonnets, XVI. FaBoEn
Sonnet: "But whether in the uncoloured light of truth." Arthur Hugh Clough. Seven Sonnets, IV. ViPP
Sonnet: "By this he knew she wept with waking eyes." George Meredith. Modern Love, I. AnEnPo; BEL; EnLi-2; EnLit; EnLoPo; HBV; HoPM; NBM; OAEP; Po; PoEL-5; PoVP; ViPo; ViPP
Sonnet: "By this low fire I often sit to woo." Frederick Goddard Tuckerman. AP; Sonn
Sonnet: "Caelica, I overnight was finely used." Fulke Greville. *See* Caelica: "Caelica, I overnight. . ."

Sonnet: "Can it be right to give what I can give?" Elizabeth Barrett Browning. Sonnets from the Portuguese, IX. HBV; PoVP; VA
Sonnet: "Captain or Colonel, or Knight in Arms." Milton. *See* When the Assault Was Intended to the City.
Sonnet: "Care-charmer Sleep, son of the sable Night." Samuel Daniel. *See* Care-Charmer Sleep.
Sonnet: "Cartoons of slashes on the tide-traced crater." Dylan Thomas. Altarwise by Owl-Light, VI. CoBMV; LiTM; MasP
Sonnet VI: "Chasten your fears, I have not been destroyed." Mark Van Doren. MoLP
Sonnet: "Cherish you then the hope I shall forget." Edna St. Vincent Millay. NP
Sonnet: "Chloris, whilst thou and I were free." Charles Cotton. PeRV; ViBoPo
Sonnet: "Cleare moving cristall, pure as the sunne beames." Earl of Stirling. Aurora, XXV. OxBS
Sonnet, A: "Cold are the crabs that crawl on yonder hills." Edward Lear. *See* Cold Are the Crabs.
Sonnet: "Come back to me, who wait and watch for you." Christina Rossetti. Monna Innominata, I. ViPo
Sonnet: "Come, sleep, O sleep, the certain knot of peace." Sir Philip Sidney. *See* Astrophel and Stella, XXXIX.
Sonnet: "Comes the New Year; wailing the north winds blow." Morton Luce. Thysia, XVI. HBV
Sonnet: "Comming to kisse her lyps (such grace I found)." Spenser. *See* Amoretti, LXIV.
Sonnet: Common Grave, The. Sydney Thompson Dobell. NCEP
Sonnet: "Companions were we in the grove and glen!" Frederick Goddard Tuckerman. AP
Sonnet: Composed after a Journey across the Hamilton Hills, Yorkshire. Wordsworth. ChER
Sonnet: Composed While the Author Was Engaged in Writing a Tract Occasioned by the Convention of Cintra. Wordsworth. ChER
Sonnet: Corpse, The. George Moore. SyP
Sonnet: "Could then the babes from yon unshelter'd cot." Thomas Russell. OBEC
Sonnet: "Cupid laid by his brand and fell asleep." Shakespeare. *See* Sonnets, CLIII.
Sonnet: "Cupid, thou naughty boy, when thou wert loathed." Fulke Greville. *See* Caelica: "Cupid, thou naughty boy . . ."
Sonnet: "Cynthia, because your horns look divers ways." Fulke Greville. Caelica, LV. SiCE
Sonnet: "Cyriack, this three years' day." Milton. *See* To Cyriack Skinner ("Cyriack, this three years' day").
Sonnet: "Cyriack, whose grandsire on the royal bench." Milton. *See* To Cyriak Skinner ("Cyriak, whose grandsire . . .").
Sonnet: "Daughter of her whose face, and lofty name." Sir William Watson. Sonnets to Miranda, I. HBV
Sonnet: "Daughter to that good Earl, once President." Milton. *See* To the Lady Margaret Ley.
Sonnet: "Dead men of 'ninety-two, also of 'ninety-three." Arthur Rimbaud, *tr. fr. French by* Norman Cameron. WaaP
Sonnet, A: "Dear, if you love me, hold me most your friend." Alice Duer Miller. AA
Sonnet: "Dear Marge, hello. It is 5:15 a.m." Ted Berrigan. FRC
Sonnet: "Dear quirister, who from those shadows sends." William Drummond of Hawthornden. ViBoPo
(To the Nightingale.) HBV; LO
Sonnet: "Dear to my soul! then leave me not forsaken!" Henry Constable. *Fr.* Diana. EIL; OBSC; ReEn; ReIE; SiCE; Sonn; TuPP
Sonnet: "Dear [*or* Deare], why should you command me to my rest." Michael Drayton. *See* Idea: "Dear, why should you . . ."
Sonnet: Death. William Walsh. *See* Sonnet on Death.
Sonnet: "Death, be not proud, though some have called thee." John Donne. *See* Death, Be Not Proud.
Sonnet: "Death is all metaphors, shape in one history." Dylan Thomas. Altarwise by Owl-Light, II. CMoP; CoBMV; LiTM; MasP; MoAB; MoBrPo (1950 ed.); Sonn
Sonnet: Death Is Not without but within Him. Cino da Pistoia, *tr. fr. Italian by* Dante Gabriel Rossetti. AWP
Sonnet: Death Warnings. Francisco de Quevedo y Villegas, *tr. fr. Spanish by* John Masefield. AWP; JAWP; WBP; WoL
(Death Warnings, *tr. by* Thomas Walsh.) CAW
Sonnet I: Dedication of These Rimes to His First Love. Francis Davison. ReIE
Sonnet: "Deep in a vale where rocks on every side." Gustav Rosenhane, *tr. fr. Swedish by* Sir Edmund Gosse. *Fr.* Sonnets. AWP; JAWP; WBP
Sonnet: "Devouring Time, blunt thou the lion's paws." Shakespeare. *See* Sonnets, XIX.
Sonnet: "Did not the heavenly rhetoric of thine eye." Shakespeare. *See* Did Not the Heavenly Rhetoric . . .
Sonnet: "Distraction is the panacea, Sir!" George Meredith. Modern Love, XXVII. ViPo
Sonnet: "Divers doth use (as I have heard and know)." Sir Thomas Wyatt. *See* Divers Doth Use. . .
Sonnet: "Do'st see how unregarded now?" Sir John Suckling. AnAnS-2; ELP; SCEP-2
Sonnet: Double Rock, The. Henry King. *See* Double Rock, The
Sonnet: "Down [*or* Downe] in the depth of mine iniquity." Fulke Greville. *See* Caelica: "Down in the depth. . ."
Sonnet: "Drawn with th' attractive virtue of her eyes." Samuel Daniel. To Delia, XLVIII. ReIE
Sonnet VII: "Dull day darkens to its close, The. The sheen." "Fiona Macleod." SyP
Sonnet: "Each man me telleth I change most my devise." Sir Thomas Wyatt. SiPS
Sonnet: "Each tree stands alone in stillness." Ted Berrigan. FRC
Sonnet: "Earth, late choked [*or* chok'd] with showers, The." Thomas Lodge. *See* Earth, Late Choked with Showers, The.
Sonnet: "Earth with thunder torn, with fire blasted, The." Fulke Greville. Caelica, LXXXVII. SiCE; Sonn; TuPP
Sonnet: England in 1819. Shelley. *See* England in 1819.
Sonnet: "England! the time is come." Wordsworth. *See* England! The Time Is Come.
Sonnet: "Envious wits, what hath been mine offence." Sir Philip Sidney. *See* Astrophel and Stella, CIV.
Sonnet: "Eternal [*or* Eternall] Truth, almighty, infinite." Fulke Greville. Caelica, XCVII [XCVIII]. OBS; OxBoCh; SiCE
Sonnet: "Euclid alone has looked on beauty bare." Edna St. Vincent Millay. *See* Euclid ,Alone Has Looked on Beauty Bare.
Sonnet: "Even as a lover, dreaming, unaware." Frederick Goddard Tuckerman. AP
Sonnet: "Even as love grows more, I write the less." Robert Hillyer. Sonnets, XVI. HBMV
Sonnet: "Evening, as slow thy placid shades descend." William Lisle Bowles. CEP
Sonnet: "Evil spirit, your beauty haunts me still, An." Michael Drayton. Idea, XX. CoBE; EIL; LoBV; OAEP; OBSC; SiCE; TuPP
Sonnet: "Expense of spirit in a waste of shame, The." Shakespeare. *See* Sonnets, CXXIX.
Sonnet: "Face of all the world is changed, I think, The." Elizabeth Barrett Browning. *See* Sonnets from the Portuguese: "Face of all the world . . ."
Sonnet: "Fair and lovely maid, look from the shore." Samuel Daniel. To Delia, XLII. ReIE
Sonnet: "Fair is my Love, and cruel as she's fair." Samuel Daniel. *See* To Delia: "Fair is my Love. . ."
Sonnet: "Fair is my love, for April in her face." Robert Greene. *See* Fair Is My Love, for April in Her Face.
Sonnet: "Fair [*or* Faire] is my Love that feeds among the lilies." Bartholomew Griffin. Fidessa, More Chaste than Kind, XXXVII. EG; EIL; ErPo; LO; SiCE; Sonn; TuPP; ViBoPo
(Fair [*or* Faire] Is My Love.) CBEP; PoEL-2
(My Love.) TrGrPo
Sonnet: "Fair is my love, when her fair golden hairs [*or* heares]." Spenser. *See* Amoretti, LXXXI.
Sonnet: "Fair star of evening, splendor of the west." Wordsworth. *See* Composed by the Sea-Side, near Calais, August, 1802.
Sonnet: "Farewell, Love, and all thy laws forever." Sir Thomas Wyatt. *See* Renouncing of Love, A.
Sonnet: "Farewell, sweet boy; complain not of my truth." Fulke Greville. *See* Caelica: "Farewell, sweet boy. . ."
Sonnet: "Farewell, thou art too dear for my possessing." Shakespeare. *See* Sonnets, LXXXVII.
Sonnet: "Father in heaven! after the days misspent." Petrarch,

tr. fr. Italian by Lady Dacre. Sonnets to Laura: To Laura in Life. CAW
Sonnet: "Father, part of his double interest." John Donne. Holy Sonnets, XVI. AnAnS-1; MaMe; MasP; MeP; OBS; SCEP-1; Sonn
Sonnet: "Fie, foolish earth, think you the heaven wants glory." Fulke Greville. *See* Love's Glory.
Sonnet: "First there was the lamb on knocking knees." Dylan Thomas. Altarwise by Owl-Light, III. CMoP; CoBMV; LiTM; MasP
Sonnet: "First time he kissed me, he but only kissed." Elizabeth Barrett Browning. *See* Sonnets from the Portuguese: "First time he kissed . . ."
Sonnet: "First time that the sun rose on thine oath, The." Elizabeth Barrett Browning. *See* Sonnets from the Portuguese: "First time that the sun . . ."
Sonnet: "Flesh, I have knocked at many a dusty door." John Masefield. *Fr.* Sonnets ("Long long ago"). GTSL; LiTM; MoBrPo; SeCePo
Sonnet; "Flower of the dust am I: for dust will flower." Clement Wood. Eagle Sonnets, VII. HBMV
Sonnet: "For Nature daily through her grand design." Frederick Goddard Tuckerman. AP; MAmP
Sonnet: "For shame! deny that thou bear'st love to any." Shakespeare. Sonnets, X. MasP
Sonnet: "For this true nobleness I seek in vain." James Russell Lowell. CoBA
Sonnet: "Forward violet thus did I chide, The." Shakespeare. *See* Sonnets, XCIX.
Sonnet: "Fountain of sorrow, inn of cursed ire." Petrarch, *tr. fr. Italian by* Joseph Auslander. Sonnets to Laura: To Laura in Life, CVII. PoFr
Sonnet [*or* Sonet]: "Fra bank to bank [*or* banc to banc], fra wood to wood [*or* wod to wod], I rin." Mark Alexander Boyd. AnFE; LO; LoBV (2d ed.); NCEP; OBEV; OxBS; PIA; SeCeV; Sonn
(Cupid and Venus.) GoTS
Sonnet: French and Spanish Guerrillas, The. Wordsworth. *See* French and the Spanish Guerrillas, The.
Sonnet: "Fresh spring, the herald of love's mighty king." Spenser. *See* Amoretti, LXX.
Sonnet: "From fairest creatures we desire increase." Shakespeare. *See* Sonnets, I.
Sonnet: "From the oracular archives and the parchment." Dylan Thomas. Altarwise by Owl-Light, IX. CMoP; CoBMV; LiTM; MasP; Sonn
Sonnet: "From you have I been absent in the spring." Shakespeare. *See* Sonnets, XCVIII.
Sonnet: "Full faith I have she holds that rarest gift." George Meredith. Modern Love, XXXII. ViPo
Sonnet: "Full many a glorious morning have I seen." Shakespeare. *See* Sonnets, XXXIII.
Sonnet: "Gertrude and Gulielma, sister-twins." Frederick Goddard Tuckerman. AP; MAmP; QFR
Sonnet: "Give me the darkest corner of a cloud." R. W. Dixon. LO
Sonnet: "Give to imagination some pure light." George Meredith. Modern Love, XXXVIII. ViPo
Sonnet: "Go from me. Yet I feel that I shall stand." Elizabeth Barrett Browning. *See* Sonnets from the Portuguese: "Go from me . . ."
Sonnet: "Go you, O winds that blow from north to south." Alexander Craig. *See* To Pandora.
Sonnet: "Golden spring redeems the withered year, The." Robert Hillyer. Sonnets, II. HBMV
Sonnet: "Haile gracefull morning of eternall daye." William Alabaster. AnAnS-1; MeP
Sonnet: "Happy ye leaves when as those lilly hands." Spenser. *See* Amoretti, I.
Sonnet: "Have patience; it is fit that in this wise." George Santayana. Sonnets, IX. WGRP
Sonnet: "Having this day my horse, my hand, my lance." Sir Philip Sidney. *See* Astrophel and Stella, XLI.
Sonnet: He Argues His Case with Death. Cecco Angiolieri da Siena, *tr. fr. Italian by* Dante Gabriel Rossetti. AWP
Sonnet I: "He came in silvern armor, trimmed with black." Gwendolyn B. Bennett. AmNP; CDC; PoNe
Sonnet: He Compares All Things with His Lady. Guido Cavalcanti, *tr. fr. Italian by* Dante Gabriel Rossetti. AWP
Sonnet: He Craves Interpreting of a Dream of His. Dante da Maiano, *tr. fr. Italian by* Dante Gabriel Rossetti. AWP; LiTW
Sonnet I: He Demands Pardon for Looking, Loving, and Writing. Walter Davison. ReIE
Sonnet: "He felt the wild beast in him between whiles." George Meredith. Modern Love, IX. ViPo
Sonnet: "He found her by the ocean's moaning verge." George Meredith. Modern Love, XLIX. BEL; EnLi-2; HBV; OAEP; PoE; ViPo
Sonnet: He Is Out of Heart with His Time. Guerzo di Montecanti, *tr. fr. Italian by* Dante Gabriel Rossetti. AWP
Sonnet: He Is Past All Help. Cecco Angiolieri da Siena. *See* Past Help.
Sonnet: He Jests Concerning His Poverty. Bartolomeo di Sant' Angelo, *tr. fr. Italian by* Dante Gabriel Rossetti. AWP
Sonnet: He Rails against Dante. Cecco Angiolieri da Siena, *tr. fr. Italian by* Dante Gabriel Rossetti. AWP; JAWP; WBP
Sonnet: He Speaks of a Third Love. Guido Cavalcanti, *tr. fr. Italian by* Dante Gabriel Rossetti. AWP
Sonnet: He Will Not Be Too Deeply in Love. Cecco Angiolieri da Siena, *tr. fr. Italian by* Dante Gabriel Rossetti. AWP
(Not Too Deeply in Love.) OnPM
Sonnet: He Will Praise His Lady. Guido Guinicelli, *tr. fr. Italian by* Dante Gabriel Rossetti. AWP
(Praise.) OnPM
Sonnet: Head Next to Mine. Carl Bode. ToPo
Sonnet: "Hear, O Self-Giver, infinite as good." Morton Luce. Thysia, XXXVII. HBV
Sonnet: "Here in the self is all that man can know." John Masefield. *Fr.* Sonnets ("Long long ago"). AWP; BoPe; JAWP; WBP
Sonnet: "Here Jack and Tom are paired with Moll and Meg." George Meredith. Modern Love, XVIII. NBM
Sonnet: "Here lies, and none to mourn him but the sea." Edna St. Vincent Millay. *See* Epitaph for the Race of Man.
Sonnet: "Highway, since you my chief Parnassus be." Sir Philip Sidney. *See* Astrophel and Stella, LXXXIV.
Sonnet: "Him not the golden fang of furious heaven." Edna St. Vincent Millay. AtBAP
Sonnet, A: "His golden locks time hath to silver turn'd." George Peele. *See* His Golden Locks. . .
Sonnet: "His heart was in his garden; but his brain." Frederick Goddard Tuckerman. AP
Sonnet: "Holy, holy, holy Lord unnamed." William Alabaster. MeP
Sonnet: "How all men wrongly death to dignify." A. J. M. Smith. *See* Wisdom of Old Jelly Roll, The.
Sonnet: "How can I then return in happy plight." Shakespeare. Sonnets, XXVIII. OBSC
Sonnet: "How can my Muse want subject to invent." Shakespeare. Sonnets, XXXVIII. EnLit; ReEn; Sonn
Sonnet: "How do I love thee? Let me count the ways." Elizabeth Barrett Browning. *See* Sonnets from the Portuguese: "How do I love thee . . ."
Sonnet: "How heavy do I journey on the way." Shakespeare. Sonnets, L. ReEn; ReIE; SiCE
Sonnet: "How like a winter hath my absence been." Shakespeare. *See* Sonnets, XCVII.
Sonnet: "How many paltry, foolish, painted things." Michael Drayton. *See* Idea: "How many paltry, foolish, painted things."
Sonnet: "How most unworthy, echoing in mine ears." Frederick Goddard Tuckerman. AP
Sonnet: "How oft in schoolboy-days, from the school's sway." Frederick Goddard Tuckerman. MAmP; Sonn
Sonnet: "How oft, when thou, my music, music play'st." Shakespeare. *See* Sonnets, CXXVIII.
Sonnet: "How shall I tell the measure of my love?" Morton Luce. Thysia, XLV. HBV
Sonnet: "How soon hath Time, the subtle thief of youth." Milton. *See* On His Having Arrived at the Age of Twenty-three.
Sonnet: "How sweet and lovely dost thou make the shame. Shakespeare. *See* Sonnets, XCV.
Sonnet: "How sweet only to delight in lambs." Rex Warner. LO
Sonnet: "How that vast heaven intitled First is rolled." William Drummond of Hawthornden. ElL
Sonnet: "I abide and abide and better abide." Sir Thomas Wyatt. EnLoPo; FCP; SiPS

Sonnet: "I am a little world made cunningly." John Donne. Holy Sonnets, V. AnAnS-1; EnL; MaMe; MaPo (1969 ed.); MasP; MeP; MyFE; OBS; OxBoCh; PIA; ReEn; SCEP-1; SeEP; Sonn
Sonnet: "I am a tongue for beauty. Not a day." Clement Wood. Eagle Sonnets, XIX. HBMV
Sonnet: "I am ashamed through this thick husk of clay." George Henry Boker. *Fr.* Sonnets; a Sequence on Profane Love. AmePo
Sonnet: "I, being born a woman and distressed." Edna St. Vincent Millay. *See* I, Being Born a Woman.
Sonnet: "I cannot tell what charms my lady finds." George Henry Boker. *Fr.* Sonnets; a Sequence on Profane Love. AmePo
Sonnet: "I cast these lyric offerings at your feet." Sir William Watson. Sonnets to Miranda, V. HBV
Sonnet: "I could not sleep for thinking of the sky." John Masefield. *See* I Could Not Sleep for Thinking of the Sky.
Sonnet: "I dare but sing of you in such a strain." Sir William Watson. Sonnets to Miranda, III. HBV
Sonnet: "I did but prompt the age to quit their clogs." Milton. *See* On the Detraction Which Followed Upon My Writing Certain Treatises ("I did but prompt the age").
Sonnet: "I envy not Endymion now no more." Earl of Stirling. Aurora, XXIX. ElL; Sonn
Sonnet: "I fear to me such fortune be assign'd." William Drummond of Hawthornden. NCEP
Sonnet: "I find no peace, and all my war is done." Petrarch, *See* Description of the Contrarious Passions in a Lover. *tr. by* Sir Thomas Wyatt.
Sonnet: "I grant thou wert not married to my Muse." Shakespeare. Sonnets, LXXXII. CBEP
Sonnet: "I had no thought of violets of late." Alice Dunbar Nelson. BANP; CDC; PoNe
Sonnet: "I have been sure of three things all my life." Clement Wood. Eagle Sonnets, III. HBMV
Sonnet: "I have not spent the April of my time." Bartholomew Griffin. *Fr.* Fidessa, More Chaste than Kind, XXXV. ElL; ReEn; SiCE; TuPP
(Youth.) OBSC
Sonnet: "I have seen beauty where light stabs the hills." Arthur Davison Ficke. Sonnets of a Portrait Painter, XVI. AnAmPo
Sonnet: "I hereby swear that to uphold your house." Elinor Wylie. *See* I Hereby Swear . . .
Sonnet: "I hope, I fear, resolved, and yet I doubt." Earl of Stirling. Aurora, LXVIII. Sonn
Sonnet: "I know I am but summer to your heart." Edna St. Vincent Millay. *See* I Know I Am But Summer to Your Heart.
Sonnet: "I know that every note and chord of woe." George Henry Boker. *Fr.* Sonnets; a Sequence on Profane Love. AmePo
Sonnet: "I lift my heavy heart up solemnly." Elizabeth Barrett Browning. *See* Sonnets from the Portuguese: "I lift my heavy heart . . ."
Sonnet: "I lived with visions for my company." Elizabeth Barrett Browning. *See* Sonnets from the Portuguese: "I lived with visions . . ."
Sonnet: "I might—unhappy word!—oh me, I might." Sir Philip Sidney. *See* Astrophel and Stella, XXXIII.
Sonnet: "I move amid your throng, I watch you hold." Sir William Watson. Sonnets to Miranda, VI. HBV
Sonnet: "I must not grieve my Love, whose eyes would read." Samuel Daniel. To Delia, XLVIII. ElL; HBV
(Beauty, Time and Love, VI.) OBEV
Sonnet: "I never drank of Aganippe well." Sir Philip Sidney. *See* Astrophel and Stella, LXXIV.
Sonnet: "I never gave a lock of hair away." Elizabeth Barrett Browning. *See* Sonnets from the Portuguese: "I never gave . . ."
Sonnet: "I never see the red rose crown the year." John Masefield. *See* I Never See the Red Rose.
Sonnet: "I never swung a staff and deep, oh deep." Roy Daniells. PeCV
Sonnet: "I once may see when years shall wreck my wrong." Samuel Daniel. To Delia, XXXIV. ReIE
Sonnet: "I said I splendidly loved you; it's not true." Rupert Brooke. CBEP
Sonnet: "I saw the figure of a lovely maid." Wordsworth. *See* I Saw the Figure of a Lovely Maid.
Sonnet: "I saw the object of my pining thought." Thomas Watson. *Fr.* The Tears of Fancy. ElL; Sonn; TuPP
Sonnet: "I stood beside a pool, from whence ascended." Richard Chenevix Trench. IrPN
Sonnet: "I strive to live my life in whitest truth." George Henry Boker. *Fr.* Sonnets; a Sequence on Profane Love. AmePo
Sonnet: "I thank all who have loved me in their hearts." Elizabeth Barrett Browning. Sonnets from the Portuguese, XLI. CoBE; PoVP; VA; ViPo
Sonnet: "I thought once how Theocritus had sung." Elizabeth Barrett Browning. *See* Sonnets from the Portuguese: "I thought once . . ."
Sonnet: "I wake and feel the fell of dark, not day." Gerard Manley Hopkins. *See* I Wake and Feel the Fell of Dark.
Sonnet: "I walk of grey noons by the old canal." Thomas Caulfield Irwin. IrPN
Sonnet XIV: "I was confused; I cannot promise more." Mark Van Doren. MoLP
Sonnet: "I watch beside you in your silent room." Morton Luce. Thysia, VII. HBV
Sonnet: "I watched the sea for hours blind with sun." Winfield Townley Scott. MiAP
Sonnet: "I will fling wide the windows of my soul." Robert Hillyer. Sonnets, XII. HBMV
Sonnet: "I, with whose colors Myra dressed her head." Fulke Greville. *See* Caelicia: "I, with . . ."
Sonnet: "I would not have this perfect love of ours." James Russell Lowell. CoBA
Sonnet: "Idly she yawned, and threw her heavy hair." George Moore. ErPo
Sonnet: "If ever Sorrow spoke from soul that loves." Henry Constable. *Fr.* Diana. ElL; SiCE
Sonnet: "If faithfull soules be alike glorifi'd." John Donne. Holy Sonnets, VIII. AnAnS-1; MaMe; MasP; MeP; OBS; SCEP-1; SeEP; Sonn
Sonnet: "If I could get within this changing I." John Masefield. *Fr.* Sonnets ("Long, long ago"). WGRP
Sonnet: "If I had never known your face at all." Sir William Watson. Sonnets to Miranda, VIII. FaBoBe; HBV
Sonnet: "If I leave all for thee, wilt thou exchange." Elizabeth Barrett Browning. *See* Sonnets from the Portuguese: "If I leave all . . ."
Sonnet: "If I might choose where my tired limbs shall lie." John Anster. *See* If I Might Choose.
Sonnet: "If it must be; if it must be, O God!" David Gray. *Fr.* In the Shadows. OxBS
Sonnet: "If life on earth be less than is a day." Joachim du Bellay. *See* Sonnet to Heavenly Beauty, A.
Sonnet: "If, of a wretched state and all forlorn." Leonard Digges. LO; SeCL; SeEP
Sonnet: "If of our life the span be not a day." Joachim du Bellay. *See* Sonnet to Heavenly Beauty, A.
Sonnet: "If poisonous minerals, and if that tree." John Donne. *See* If Poisonous Minerals . . .
Sonnet: "If she should give me all I ask of her." George Henry Boker. *Fr.* Sonnets; a Sequence on Profane Love. AmePo
Sonnet: "If the dull substance of my flesh were thought." Shakespeare. *See* Sonnets, XLIV.
Sonnet: "If there be nothing new, but that which is." Shakespeare. Sonnets, LIX. FaBoEn; ReEn
Sonnet: "If thou art sinful, there are thousands then." George Henry Boker. *Fr.* Sonnets; a Sequence on Profane Love. AmePo
Sonnet: "If thou must love me, let it be for nought." Elizabeth Barrett Browning. *See* Sonnets from the Portuguese: "If thou must love me . . ."
Sonnet: "If thou survive my well-contented day." Shakespeare. *See* Sonnets, XXXII.
Sonnet: "If thy soul check thee that I come so near." Shakespeare. *See* Sonnets, CXXXVI.
Sonnet: "If you had lived in that more stately time." Sir William Watson. Sonnets to Miranda, II. HBV
Sonnet: "Ile give thee leave my love, in beauties field." Earl of Stirling. Aurora, XXVI. OxBS
Sonnet: In Absence from Becchina. Cecco Angiolieri de Siena, *tr. fr. Italian by* Dante Gabriel Rossetti. AWP; JAWP; WBP
Sonnet: "In faith, I do [*or* doe] not love thee with mine eyes." Shakespeare. Sonnets, CXLI. CBEP; MaPo; PoEL-2; TrGrPo

Sonnet: "In heaven there is a star I call my own." Irene Rutherford McLeod. *Fr.* Sonnets. HBMV
Sonnet: "In highest way of heaven the sun did ride." Sir Philip Sidney. *See* Astrophel and Stella, XXII.
Sonnet: "In Joe Brainard's collage its white arrow." Ted Berrigan. FRC
Sonnet: "In loving thee thou know'st I am forsworn." Shakespeare. Sonnets, CLII. ReIE; Sonn
Sonnet: "In minds pure glasse when I my selfe behold." William Drummond of Hawthornden. OBS
Sonnet: "In night, when colors all to black are cast." Fulke Greville. *See* Caelica: "In night, when colors. . ."
Sonnet: "In the old age black was not counted fair." Shakespeare. Sonnets, CXXVII. CBEP; ReIE; Sonn
Sonnet: "In truth, O Love, with what a boyish kind." Sir Philip Sidney. *See* Astrophel and Stella, XI.
Sonnet: "In vain to me the smiling mornings shine." Thomas Gray. *See* Sonnet on the Death of Mr. Richard West.
Sonnet: "Indeed this very love which is my boast." Elizabeth Barrett Browning. Sonnets from the Portuguese, XII. HBV; PoVP
Sonnet: "Innumerable Beauties, thou white haire." Lord Herbert of Cherbury. BoW; PoEL-2
(Innumerable Beauties.) AtBAP
Sonnet: "Into the closed air of the slow." Ted Berrigan. FRC
Sonnet: "Into the golden vessel of great song." Edna St. Vincent Millay. *Fr.* Unnamed Sonnets. NP
Sonnet: "Into the wood at close of rainy day." Thomas Caulfield Irwin. IrPN
Sonnet: "Into these loves, who but for passion looks." Michael Drayton. Idea, *introd. sonnet.* BEL; HBV; ViBoPo
Sonnet XI: "Is God invisible? This very room." Adele Greeff. GoYe
Sonnet: "Is it for fear to wet a widow's eye?" Shakespeare. Sonnets, IX. MasP; Sonn
Sonnet: "Is it indeed so? If I lay here dead." Elizabeth Barrett Browning. Sonnets from the Portuguese, XXIII. PoVP; VA
Sonnet: "Is it thy will thy image should keep open." Shakespeare. Sonnets, LXI. LO; PoEL-2
Sonnet: "Is there a great green commonwealth of Thought." John Masefield. *Fr.* Sonnets ("Long, long ago"). ILP; LiTM; MoBrPo
Sonnet: "Isle of trees full foliaged in a meadow, An." Thomas Caulfield Irwin. IrPN
Sonnet: "It is a beauteous evening, calm and free." Wordsworth. *See* It Is a Beauteous Evening . . .
Sonnet: "It is as true as strange, else trial feigns." John Davies of Hereford. EIL
Sonnet: "It is most true that eyes are formed to serve." Sir Philip Sidney. *See* Astrophel and Stella, V.
Sonnet: "It is not death." Thomas Hood. *See* Death.
Sonnet: "It is not to be thought of that the flood." Wordsworth. *See* It Is Not to Be Thought Of.
Sonnet: "It is the season of the sweet wild rose." George Meredith. Modern Love, XLV. NBM
Sonnet: "It shall be said I died for Coelia!" William Percy. Coelia, XIX. EIL; ReEn; ReIE
Sonnet: "It was the time, when rest, soft sliding downe." Joachim du Bellay, *tr. fr. French by* Spenser. *Fr.* Visions. AWP; OnPM
("It was the time, when rest, soft sliding down.") Sonn
Sonnet: "Italia, O Italia, upon whom." Vincenzo da Filicaja. *See* Italy.
Sonnet: "Jesu thie love within mee is soe maine." William Alabaster. MeP
("Jesu, thie love within mee is soe maine.") AnAnS-1
Sonnet: "Joy of my life! full oft for loving you." Spenser. *See* Amoretti, LXXXII.
Sonnet: "Keen, fitful gusts are whisp'ring here and there." Keats. *See* Keen, Fitful Gusts Are Whisp'ring Here and There.
Sonnet: "Lacking my love, I go from place to place." Spenser. *See* Amoretti, LXXVIII.
Sonnet: "Lady, if grace to me so long be lent." Petrarch. *See* He Hopes That Time Will Render Her More Merciful.
Sonnet: Lady Laments, A. *Unknown, tr. fr. Italian by* Dante Gabriel Rossetti. AWP
Sonnet: "Lame, impotent conclusion to youth's dreams." Wilfrid Scawen Blunt. The Love Sonnets of Proteus, LII. ViBoPo
Sonnet: "Languid, and sad, and slow, from day to day." William Lisle Bowles. CEP
Sonnet: "Last All Saints' holy-day, even now gone by." Dante. *See* Sonnet: Of Beatrice de Portinari on All Saints' Day.
Sonnet: "Last night I dreamed we parted once again." Frederick Goddard Tuckerman. MAmP
Sonnet: "Last night I kissed you with a brutal might." Arthur Davison Ficke. Sonnets of a Portrait Painter, XXXVII. AnAmPo
Sonnet: "Late tired with woe, even ready for to pine." Sir Philip Sidney. Astrophel and Stella, LXII. EnLit; HBV; ReEn; SiPS
Sonnet: "Lawrence, of virtuous father virtuous son." Milton. *See* To Mr. Lawrence.
Sonnet: "Leave me, all sweet refrains my lip hath made." Luis de Camoes, *tr. fr. Portuguese by* Richard Garnett. AWP; CAW; JAWP; WBP
Sonnet: "Leave me, O Love, which reachest but to dust." Sir Philip Sidney. *See* Leave Me, O Love.
Sonnet: Leaves. William Barnes. *See* Leaves.
Sonnet: "Let all men see the ruins of the shrine." Robert Hillyer. Sonnets, XIV. HBMV
Sonnet: "Let dainty wits cry on the sisters nine." Sir Philip Sidney. *See* Astrophel and Stella, III.
Sonnet: "Let me confess that we two must be twain." Shakespeare. Sonnets, XXXVI. CBEP; OAEP
Sonnet: "Let me not to the marriage of true minds." Shakespeare. *See* Sonnets, CXVI.
Sonnet: "Let others of the world's decaying tell." Earl of Stirling. Aurora, XCVIII. EIL; Sonn
Sonnet: "Let others sing of knights and paladins." Samuel Daniel. *See* To Delia: "Let others sing . . ."
Sonnet: "Let the world's sharpness, like a clasping knife." Elizabeth Barrett Browning. Sonnets from the Portuguese, XXIV. PoVP
Sonnet: "Let the tale's sailor from a Christian voyage." Dylan Thomas. Altarwise by Owl-Light, X. CMoP; CoBMV; LiTM; MaSP
Sonnet: "Let those who are in favor with their stars." Shakespeare. *See* Sonnets, XXV.
Sonnet: "Let us leave talking of angelic hosts." Elinor Wylie. *Fr.* One Person. OxBA
Sonnet: "Lift not the painted veil." Shelley. EnRP; FaBoEn; OBNC; SyP
(Lift Not the Painted Veil.) EPN
("Lift not the painted veil which those who live.") Sonn
Sonnet: "Like as a huntsman after weary chase." Spenser. *See* Amoretti, LXVII.
Sonnet: "Like as the waves make toward the pebbled shore." Shakespeare. *See* Sonnets, LX.
Sonnet: "Like as, to make our appetites more keen." Shakespeare. Sonnets, CXVIII. CBEP; UnPo
Sonnet: "Like Memnon's rock, touched [*or* touch'd] with the rising sun." Giles Fletcher. Licia, XLVII. EIL; ReEn; ReIE; SiCE; TuPP
Sonnet: "Like some lone miser, dear, behold me stand." Morton Luce. Thysia, XXIII. HBV
Sonnet: "Like to an hermit poor, in place obscure." *At. to* Sir Walter Ralegh. *See* Like to a Hermit.
Sonnet: "Little Love-god lying once asleep, The." Shakespeare. Sonnets, CLIV. ReIE; Sonn
Sonnet: "Lo, as a careful housewife runs to catch." Shakespeare. Sonnets, CXLIII. CBEP; OAEP; ReEn
Sonnet: "Lo, in the orient when the gracious light." Shakespeare. Sonnets, VII. ReIE; SiCE
Sonnet: "Lock up, fair lids, the treasure of my heart." Sir Philip Sidney. *See* Sleep.
Sonnet: London 1802. Wordsworth. *See* London, 1802.
Sonnet: "Long time a child, and still a child, when years." Hartley Coleridge. *See* Long Time a Child.
Sonnet: "Look, Delia, how we esteem the half-blown rose." Samuel Daniel. *Fr.* To Delia. EIL; EnLit; HBV; SiCE; TuPP; WHA
Sonnet: "Look how the flower which lingeringly doth fade." William Drummond of Hawthornden. *See* No Trust in Time.
Sonnet: "Look in thy glass, and tell the face thou viewest." Shakespeare. Sonnets, III. BWP; EG; GTBS-W; LiTB; OBSC; SiCE
Sonnet: "Looking into the windows that doom has broken." George Woodcock. NeBP
Sonnet: "Lord of my love, to whom in vassalage." Shakes-

Sonnet (continued)
peare. Sonnets, XXVI. PoFS; ReEn
Sonnet: "Lord, what a change within us one short hour." Richard Chenevix Trench. *See* Prayer: "Lord, what a change . . ."
Sonnet: "Love born in Greece, of late fled from his native place." Sir Philip Sidney. Astrophel and Stella, VIII. Sonn
Sonnet: "Love, by sure proof I may call thee unkind." Sir Philip Sidney. Astrophel and Stella, LXV. Sonn
Sonnet: "Love guards the roses of thy lips." Thomas Lodge. *See* Love Guards the Roses . . .
Sonnet: "Love, how ignobly hast thou met thy doom!" Wilfrid Scawen Blunt. The Love Sonnets of Proteus, XIV. ViBoPo
Sonnet: "Love is not all: it is not meat nor drink." Edna St. Vincent Millay. AmLP; BoLP; CMoP; MasP; MoLP; OxBA; Sonn
Sonnet: "Love is too young to know what conscience is." Shakespeare. Sonnets, CLI. CBEP; PoEL-2; ReEn
Sonnet: "Love still a boy, and oft a wanton is." Sir Philip Sidney. *See* Astrophel and Stella, LXXIII.
Sonnet: "Loving in truth, and fain in verse my love to show." Sir Philip Sidney. *See* Astrophel and Stella, I.
Sonnet: "Lyke as a huntsman after weary chace." Spenser. *See* Amoretti, LXVII.
Sonnet: "Lyke as a ship, that through the ocean wyde." Spenser. *See* Amoretti, XXXIV.
Sonnet: Mackado, Fustian and Motley. John Taylor. *Fr.* Odcomb's Complaint. CBEP
Sonnet: "Man, dreame no more of curious mysteries." Fulke Greville. Caelica, LXXXVIII. MePo; OBS
Sonnet: "Mark when she smiles with amiable cheer." Spenser. *See* Amoretti, XL.
Sonnet: "Mark where the pressing wind shoots javelin-like." George Meredith. Modern Love, XLIII. NBM
Sonnet: "Master and the slave go hand in hand, The." E. A. Robinson. PP
Sonnet: "Matthew, whose skilful hand and well-worn spade." Thomas Edwards. EiCL
Sonnet: "Men call you fair, and you do credit it." Spenser. *See* Amoretti, LXXIX.
Sonnet XCIV: "Men, that delight to multiply desire." Fulke Greville. Caelica, XCIV [XCV]. OBS; SiCE
Sonnet: "Merry cuckoo, messenger of spring, The." Spenser. *See* Amoretti, XIX.
Sonnet: "Methought I saw my late espousèd saint." Milton. *See* On His Deceased Wife.
Sonnet: "Milton, thou shouldst be living at this hour." Wordsworth. *See* London, 1802.
Sonnet: "Mine eyes beheld the blessed pity spring." Dante. *See* Mine Eyes Beheld the Blessed Pity.
Sonnet: "More my own poor wishes would commend me, The." Petrarch, *tr. fr. Italian by* Joseph Auslander. Sonnets to Laura: To Laura in Life, CVIII. PoFr
Sonnet: "Morning comes, The; not slow, with reddening gold." Frederick Goddard Tuckerman. AmePo; AP
Sonnet: "Most glorious Lord of life [*or* lyfe]! that on this day." Spenser. *See* Amoretti, LXVIII.
Sonnet: Most Men Know Love. Henry Timrod. *See* Quatorzain.
Sonnet: "Muses that sing love's sensual empery." George Chapman. A Coronet for His Mistress Philosophy, I. CoBE; EIL; LoBV; PoE; TuPP
(Love and Philosophy.) OBSC; SeCePo
Sonnet: "Music to hear, why hear'st thou music sadly?" Shakespeare. *See* Sonnets, VIII.
Sonnet: "My Anna! though thine earthly steps are done." Frederick Goddard Tuckerman. AP
Sonnet: "My Anna! When for her my head was bowed." Frederick Goddard Tuckerman. AP
Sonnet: "My darling, now the slumber of the night." George Henry Boker. *Fr.* Sonnets; a Sequence on Profane Love. AmePo
Sonnet: "My duchess was the werst she laffed she bitte." Ernest Walsh. ErPo
Sonnet: "My future will not copy fair my past." Elizabeth Barrett Browning. Sonnets from the Portuguese, XLII. PoVP
Sonnet: "My glass shall not persuade me I am old." Shakespeare. Sonnets, XXII. EG; OBSC; Sonn
Sonnet: "My God, where is that ancient heat towards thee." George Herbert. *See* To His Mother.
Sonnet: "My heart the anvil where my thoughts do beat." Michael Drayton. Idea, XL. HBV
Sonnet: "My honoured lord, forgive the unruly tongue." Elinor Wylie. *Fr.* One Person. NP
Sonnet: "My lady looks so gentle and so pure." Dante, *tr. fr. Italian by* Dante Gabriel Rossetti. *Fr.* La Vita Nuova. AWP; JAWP; WBP
Sonnet: "My lady's presence makes the roses red." Henry Constable. *Fr.* Diana. CoBE; EIL; HBV; OBSC; ReIE; SiCE
Sonnet: "My lady's senses are so pure and fine." George Henry Boker. *Fr.* Sonnets; a Sequence on Profane Love. AmePo
Sonnet: "My letters all dead paper, mute and white!" Elizabeth Barrett Browning. *See* Sonnets from the Portuguese: "My letters. . ."
Sonnet: "My Love, I cannot thy rare beauties place." William Smith. *See* My Love, I Cannot. . .
Sonnet: "My love is as a fever, longing still." Shakespeare. *See* Sonnets, CXLVII.
Sonnet: "My love is like to ice, and I to fire." Spenser. *See* Amoretti, XXX.
Sonnet: "My love is strengthen'd, though more weak in seeming." Shakespeare. *See* Sonnets, CII.
Sonnet: "My love took scorn my service to retain." Sir Thomas Wyatt. SiPS
Sonnet: "My lute, be as thou wast when thou didst grow." William Drummond of Hawthornden. EG; EIL; LoBV; OBS; ViBoPo
("My lute, be as thou wast when thou didst grow.") Sonn
(To His Lute.) GTBS; GTBS-D; GTBS-P; GTBS-W; GTSE; GTSL; UnS
Sonnet: "My mistress' eyes are nothing like the sun." Shakespeare. *See* Sonnets, CXXX.
Sonnet: "My mouth doth water, and my breast doth swell." Sir Philip Sidney. Astrophel and Stella, XXXVII. Sonn
Sonnet XXXIII: "My only need—you ask me, and I tell you." Mark Van Doren. MoLP
Sonnet: "My own Belovèd, who hast lifted me." Elizabeth Barrett Browning. Sonnets from the Portuguese, XXVII. PoVP
Sonnet: "My Phyllis [*or* Phillis] hath the morning sun." Thomas Lodge. *See* To Phyllis, the Fair Shepherdess.
Sonnet: "My poet, thou canst touch on all the notes." Elizabeth Barrett Browning. *See* Sonnets from the Portuguese: "My poet. . ."
Sonnet: "My simple heart, bred in provincial tenderness." G. S. Fraser. NeBP
Sonnet: "My soul surcharged with grief now loud complains." Rachel Morpurgo, *tr. fr. Hebrew by* Nina Davis Salaman. TrJP
Sonnet: "My soule a world is by contraccion." William Alabaster. MeP
("My soule a world is by contraccion"). AnAnS-1
Sonnet: "My spotless love hovers, with purest wings." Samuel Daniel. *See* To Delia: "My spotless love. . ."
Sonnet: "My tameless will doth recklessly pursue." Petrarch. *See* Of His Foolish Passion for Laura.
Sonnet: "My tongue-tied Muse in manners holds her still." Shakespeare. Sonnets, LXXXV. Sonn
Sonnet: "My true love hath my heart, and I have his." Sir Philip Sidney. *See* My True Love Hath My Heart.
Sonnet: Netley Abbey. William Lisle Bowles. CEP
Sonnet: "Night, the starlesse night of passion, The." William Alabaster. MeP
("Night, the starless night of passion, The.") AnAnS; Sonn
Sonnet: "No longer mourn for me when I am dead." Shakespeare. *See* Sonnets, LXXI.
Sonnet: "No more be grieved at that which thou hast done." Shakespeare. *See* Sonnets, XXXV.
Sonnet: "No more, my dear, no more these counsels try." Sir Philip Sidney. *See* Astrophel and Stella, LXIV.
Sonnet: "No, Time, thou shalt not boast that I do change." Shakespeare. *See* Sonnets, CXXIII.
Sonnet: "No worst, there is none. Pitched past pitch of grief." Gerard Manley Hopkins. *See* No Worst, There Is None.
Sonnet: "Nor idle all, though naught he sees in thine." Frederick Goddard Tuckerman. MAmP
Sonnet: "Nor looks that backward life so bare to me." Frederick Goddard Tuckerman. PoIE

Sonnet: "Nor mine own fears, nor the prophetic soul." Shakespeare. *See* Sonnets, CVII.
Sonnet: "Not at first sight, nor yet with a dribbed shot." Sir Philip Sidney. *See* Astrophel and Stella, II.
Sonnet: "Not from the stars do I my judgment pluck." Shakespeare. Sonnets, XIV. SiCE; Sonn
Sonnet: "Not, I'll not, carrion comfort, Despair, not feast on thee." Gerard Manley Hopkins. *See* Carrion Comfort.
Sonnet: "Not marble, nor the gilded monuments." Shakespeare. *See* Sonnets, LV.
Sonnet: "Not mine own fears, nor the prophetic soul." Shakespeare. *See* Sonnets, CVII.
Sonnet: "Not proud of station, nor in worldly pelf." Frederick Goddard Tuckerman. AmePo
Sonnet: "Not the round natural world, not the deep mind." Frederick Goddard Tuckerman. AmePo; NoP
Sonnet: "Not with libations but with shouts and laughter." Edna St. Vincent Millay. HBMV; NP
(Not with Libations.) WHA
Sonnet: "Not with vain tears, when we're beyond the sun." Rupert Brooke. BrPo
Sonnet: "Not wrongly moved by this dismaying scene." William Empson. ToPo; WaP
(Not Wrongly Moved.) LiTM (rev ed.)
Sonnet: November. Hartley Coleridge. *See* November.
Sonnet VI: "Now from the world the light of God is gone." Robert Nathan. *See* Now from the World the Light of God Is Gone.
Sonnet: "Now I have found thee, I will ever more." William Alabaster. *See* Upon the Crucifix.
Sonnet: "Now keep that long revolver at your side." George Hetherington. NeIP
Sonnet: "Now stamp the Lord's Prayer on a grain of rice." Dylan Thomas. Altarwise by Owl-Light, VII. CoBMV; GTBS-W; LiTM; MasP; Sonn
Sonnet: "Now stands our love on that still verge of day." James Agee. Sonnets, XX. MoAmPo
Sonnet: "Now that the midd day heate doth scorch my shame." William Alabaster. MeP
("Now that the midd day heate doth scorch my shame.") AnAnS-1
Sonnet: "Now they are gone with all their songs and sins." John Masefield. *Fr.* Sonnets ("Like bones the ruins of the cities stand"). InP
Sonnet: "Now, winter's dolorous days are o'er, and through." Thomas Caulfield Irwin. IrPN
Sonnet: "Nuns fret not at their convent's narrow room." Wordsworth. *See* Nuns Fret Not. . .
Sonnet: "O bitter moon, O cold and bitter moon." Clement Wood. Eagle Sonnets, IX. HBMV
Sonnet: "O call not me to justify the wrong." Shakespeare. Sonnets, CXXXIX. ReIE
Sonnet: "Oh! Death will find me, long before I tire." Rupert Brooke. MoBrPo; NeMA
(Oh! Death Will Find Me.) HBV; PoRA
("Oh! Death will find me, long before I tire.") Sonn
Sonnet: "O eyes, which do the spheres of beauty move." Sir Philip Sidney. Astrophel and Stella, XLII. Sonn
Sonnet: "O false and treacherous Probability." Fulke Greville. Caelica, CIII [CIV]. OBS; OxBoCh
Sonnet: "Oh for a poet—for a beacon bright." E. A. Robinson. *See* Oh for a Poet—for a Beacon Bright.
Sonnet: "O for my sake do you with Fortune chide." Shakespeare. *See* Sonnets, CXI.
Sonnet: "Oh, for some honest lover's ghost." Sir John Suckling. *See* Doubt of Martyrdom, A.
Sonnet: "Oh for the face and footstep!—Woods and shores!" Frederick Goddard Tuckerman. AP
Sonnet: "O Friend! I know not which way I must look." Wordsworth. *See* Written in London, September, 1802.
Sonnet: "O had she not been fair and thus unkind." Samuel Daniel. To Delia, VII. ReIE
Sonnet: "O happy Thames that didst my Stella bear!" Sir Philip Sidney. *See* Astrophel and Stella, CIII.
Sonnet: "O hard endeavor, to blend in with these." Frederick Goddard Tuckerman. QFR
Sonnet: "O how I faint when I of you do write." Shakespeare. Sonnets, LXXX. ReEn; SiCE
Sonnet: O! how much more doth beauty beauteous seem." Shakespeare. *See* Sonnets, LIV.
Sonnet: "Oh, if thou knew'st how thou thyself dost harm." Earl of Stirling. *See* To Aurora.
Sonnet: "O kiss which dost those ruddy gems impart." Sir Philip Sidney. Astrophel and Stella, LXXXI. Sonn
Sonnet: "Oh! leave the Past to bury its own dead." Wilfrid Scawen Blunt. The Love Sonnets of Proteus, LXII. ViBoPo
Sonnet: "O little self, within whose smallness lies." John Masefield. *Fr.* Sonnets ("Long long ago"). HBV; POTE; SoP; WGRP
Sonnet: "O me, what eyes hath Love put in my head." Shakespeare. *See* Sonnets, CXLVII.
Sonnet: "O might those sighs and tears return again." John Donne. Holy Sonnets, III. AnAnS-1; AnEnPo; MaMe; MasP; MeP; OBS; SCEP-1; SeEP; Sonn
Sonnet: "Oh, my beloved, have you thought of this." Edna St. Vincent Millay. Unnamed Sonnets, X. HBMV
Sonnet: "Oh my black soul! now thou art summoned." John Donne. Holy Sonnets, IV. AnAnS-1; MaMe; MasP; MeP; MePo; MyFE; OBS; SCEP-1; Sonn
Sonnet: "O! never say that I was false of heart." Shakespeare. *See* Sonnets, CIX.
Sonnet: "O Nightingale, that on yon bloomy spray." Milton. *See* To the Nightingale.
Sonnet: "O patience, that dost wait eternally!" Pedro Malon de Chaide, *tr. fr. Spanish by* E. Allison Peers. CAW
Sonnet: "O shady vales, O fair enriched meads." Thomas Lodge. *Fr.* A Margarite of America. ElL; OBSC
(Solitary Shepherd's Song, The.) ReIE
Sonnet: "Oh! sigh no more, no longer paint the air." George Henry Boker. Sonnets, LXXIX. AmLP
Sonnet: "Oh spring, that hides the wrinkled earth in green." George Henry Boker. Sonnets, CXV. AmLP
Sonnet: "O starry temple of unvalted space." William Alabaster. *See* O Starry Temple of Unvalted Space.
Sonnet: "O sweete, and bitter monuments of paine." William Alabaster. *See* Upon the Ensignes of Christes Crucifyinge.
Sonnet: "O tears, no tears, but rain from beauty's skies." Sir Philip Sidney. *See* Astrophel and Stella, C.
Sonnet: "O that you were yourself! but, love, you are." Shakespeare. Sonnets, XIII. OAEP; SiCE
Sonnet: "Oh, think not I am faithful to a vow!" Edna St. Vincent Millay. *See* Oh, Think Not I Am Faithful to a Vow.
Sonnet: "O thou, my lovely boy, who in thy power." Shakespeare. *See* Sonnets, CXXVI.
Sonnet: "O Thou to whom the musical white springs." E. E. Cummings. *See* O Thou to Whom the Musical White Springs.
Sonnet: "O Time! who know'st a lenient hand to lay." William Lisle Bowles. *See* Time and Grief.
Sonnet: "Oh, to vex me, contraries [*or* contraryes] meet in one." John Donne. Holy Sonnets, XIX. AnAnS-1; EP; MaMe; MasP; MBW-1; MeP; NoP; PoEL-2; SCEP-1; Sonn
(Devout-Fits.) SeCePo
(Inconstancy.) MaRV
Sonnet: "O truant Muse, what shall be thy amends." Shakespeare. Sonnets, CI. Sonn
Sonnet: O World. George Santayana. *See* O World.
Sonnet: Of All He Would Do. Cecco Angiolieri da Siena, *tr. fr. Italian by* Dante Gabriel Rossetti. AWP; JAWP; WBP
(Of All He Would Do.) OnPM
Sonnet: Of an Ill-favored Lady. Guido Cavalcanti, *tr. fr. Italian by* Dante Gabriel Rossetti. AWP; JAWP; WBP
Sonnet: Of Beatrice de Portinari on All Saints' Day. Dante, *tr. fr. Italian by* Dante Gabriel Rossetti. AWP; JAWP; WBP
(Sonnet: "Last All Saints' holy-day, even now gone by.") GoBC
(To Beatrice on All Saints' Day.) OnPM
Sonnet: Of Beauty and Duty. Dante, *tr. fr. Italian by* Dante Gabriel Rossetti. AWP; JAWP; WBP
Sonnet: Of Becchina in a Rage. Cecco Angiolieri da Siena, *tr. fr. Italian by* Dante Gabriel Rossetti. AWP; JAWP; WBP
Sonnet: Of Becchina, the Shoemaker's Daughter. Cecco Angiolieri da Siena, *tr. fr. Italian by* Dante Gabriel Rossetti. AWP
Sonnet: Of His Lady in Heaven. Jacopo da Lentino, *tr. fr. Italian by* Dante Gabriel Rossetti. AWP; JAWP; WBP
Sonnet: Of His Lady's Face. Jacopo da Lentino. *See* Of His Lady's Face.

Sonnet: Of His Lady's Weeping. Walter Davison. ReIE
Sonnet: Of His Pain from a New Love. Guido Cavalcanti, *tr. fr. Italian by* Dante Gabriel Rossetti. AWP
Sonnet: Of Love, in Honor of His Mistress Becchina. Cecco Angiolieri da Siena, *tr. fr. Italian by* Dante Gabriel Rossetti. AWP
(In Honor of His Mistress.) OnPM
Sonnet: Of Love in Men and Devils. Cecco Angiolieri da Siena, *tr. fr. Italian by* Dante Gabriel Rossetti. AWP
(Love in Men and Devils.) OnPM
Sonnet: Of Moderation and Tolerance. Guido Guinicelli, *tr. fr. Italian by* Dante Gabriel Rossetti. AWP; JAWP; WBP
Sonnet: Of the Eyes of a Certain Mandetta. Guido Cavalcanti, tr. fr. Italian by Dante Gabriel Rossetti. AWP
Sonnet: Of the Grave of Selvaggia. Cino da Pistoia, *tr. fr. Italian by* Dante Gabriel Rossetti. AWP; JAWP; WBP
(At the Grave of Selvaggia.) OnPM
Sonnet: Of the Making of Master Messerin. Rustico di Filippo, *tr. fr. Italian by* Dante Gabriel Rossetti. AWP; JAWP; LiTW; WBP
(Making of Master Messerin, The.) OnPM
Sonnet: Of the 20th June 1291. Cecco Angiolieri da Siena, *tr. fr. Italian by* Dante Gabriel Rossetti. AWP
Sonnet: "Of thee (kind boy) I ask no red and white." Sir John Suckling. AnAnS-2; LO; MeLP; MePo; OBS; OxBoLi; ReEn; SCEP-2; SeCP; SeCV-1; SeEP
(Of Thee, Kind Boy.) SeCL
(Song.) LoBV
(To Cupid.) CBEP
Sonnet: "Of this fair volume which we World do name." William Drummond of Hawthornden. *See* Book of the World, The.
Sonnet: Of Virtue. Folgore da San Geminiano, *tr. fr. Italian by* Dante Gabriel Rossetti. AWP; JAWP; WBP
Sonnet: Of Why He Is Unhanged. Cecco Angiolieri da Siena, *tr. fr. Italian by* Dante Gabriel Rossetti. AWP
Sonnet: Of Why He Would Be a Scullion. Cecco Angiolieri da Siena, *tr. fr. Italian by* Dante Gabriel Rossetti. AWP
Sonnet: Oft o'er My Brain. Samuel Taylor Coleridge. ChER
(Composed on a Journey Homeward.) Sonn
Sonnet: "Oft when my spirit doth spread her bolder wings." Spenser. *See* Amoretti, LXXII.
Sonnet: On a Distant View of England. William Lisle Bowles. CEP
Sonnet: On a Picture of Leander. Keats. *See* On a Picture of Leander.
Sonnet: On First Looking into Chapman's Homer. Keats. *See* On First Looking into Chapman's Homer.
Sonnet: On His Being Arrived at the Age of Twenty-three. Milton. On His Having Arrived at the Age of Twenty-three.
Sonnet: On King Arthur's Round Table at Winchester. Thomas Warton, the Younger. Sonnets, VIII. EiPP
(On King Arthur's Round Table, at Winchester.) Sonn
Sonnet: On the Death of Richard West. Thomas Gray. *See* Sonnet on the Death of Richard West.
Sonnet: On the Detection of a False Friend. Guido Cavalcanti, *tr. fr. Italian by* Dante Gabriel Rossetti. AWP
Sonnet: On the Late Massacre in Piedmont. Milton. *See* On the Late Massacre in Piedmont.
Sonnet: On the 9th of June 1290. Dante, *tr. fr. Italian by* Dante Gabriel Rossetti. AWP
Sonnet XIV: On the Religious Memorie of Mrs. Catherine Thomason My Christian Friend Deceased Dec. 16, 1646. Milton. *See* On the Religious Memory of Mrs. Catherine Thomason.
Sonnet: "One day I wrote her name upon the strand." Spenser. *See* Amoretti, LXXV.
Sonnet: "One still dark night, I sat alone and wrote." Frederick Goddard Tuckerman. AmePo; AP
Sonnet: "Open wound which has been healed anew," An. Richard Chenevix Trench. TrPWD
Sonnet: "Or I shall live your epitaph to make." Shakespeare. Sonnets, LXXXI. OAEP; OBSC
Sonnet: "Orgasm completely, The." Tom Clark. ANYP; CoAP; YAP
Sonnet: "Our doom is in our being." James Agee. Sonnets, II. MAP; MoAmPo
Sonnet: "Out of the dusk into whose gloom you went." Arthur Davison Ficke. Sonnets of a Portrait Painter, L. AnAmPo
Sonnet: "Over the waters but a single bough." Robert Hillyer. Sonnets, XXIII. HBMV
Sonnet: Ozymandias. Shelley. *See* Ozymandias.
Sonnet: "Passing glance, a lightning long the skies, A." William Drummond of Hawthornden. ViBoPo
Sonnet: "Patience, hard thing! the hard thing but to pray." Gerard Manley Hopkins. FaBoEn; OBNC
(Patience.) BoC
(Patience, Hard Thing!) CoBMV; ViPo (1962 ed.)
("Patience, hard thing! the hard thing but to pray.") Sonn; VP
Sonnet: "Penelope, for her Ulysses' sake." Spenser. *See* Amoretti, XXIII.
Sonnet: "Perhaps a dream; yet surely truth has beamed." Frederick Goddard Tuckerman. AP; MAmP
Sonnet: "Phoebe runs in from the warm rain." Lewis Mac Adams. YAP
Sonnet: Pity Me Not. Edna St. Vincent Millay. *See* Pity Me Not.
Sonnet: "Point where beauty and intelligence meet, The." Gavin Ewart. WaP
Sonnet: "Ponder thy cares, and sum them all in one." Sir David Murray. *Fr.* Caelia. EIL
Sonnet: "Poor soul, the center of my sinful earth." Shakespeare. *See* Sonnets, CXLVI.
Sonnet: "Quickly and pleasantly the seasons blow." Robert Hillyer. Sonnets, I. HBMV
Sonnet: "Rainbow o'er the sea of afternoon, The." Thomas Caulfield Irwin. IrPN
Sonnet: Rapture Concerning His Lady, A. Guido Cavalcanti, *tr. fr. Italian by* Dante Gabriel Rossetti. AWP
Sonnet: "Regions of soft clear air, of cold green leaves." Thomas Caulfield Irwin. IrPN
Sonnet: "Reign in my thoughts, fair hand, sweet eye, rare voice!" Samuel Daniel. To Delia, XXV. ReIE
Sonnet: "Remember me when I am gone away." Christina Rossetti. *See* Remember.
Sonnet: "Remote from smoky cities, aged and grey." Thomas Caulfield Irwin. IrPN
Sonnet XIII: "Rise up, rise up, Jack Spratt. And you, his wife." Winfield Townley Scott. ErPo
Sonnet: "Roadside inn this summer Saturday, A." Thomas Caulfield Irwin. IrPN
Sonnet: "Roll on, sad world! Not Mercury or Mars." Frederick Goddard Tuckerman. AnNE; AP; QFR; TreFS
Sonnet: "Rough green wealth of wheaten fields that sway, The." Thomas Caulfield Irwin. IrPN
Sonnet: "Rudely thou wrongest my dear heart's desire." Spenser. Amoretti, V. EIL; ReIE; SiCE; Sonn
Sonnet: "Saints have adored the lofty soul of you." Charles Hamilton Sorley. Two Sonnets, I. HBMV; MoBrPo; NeMA; TrGrPo
Sonnet: "Satyr nature riots in my blood, The." George Henry Boker. *Fr.* Sonnets; a Sequence on Profane Love. AmePo
Sonnet: "Say over again, and yet once over again." Elizabeth Barrett Browning. Sonnets from the Portuguese, XXI. HBV; PoVP; ViPo
Sonnet: "Say that thou didst forsake me for some fault." Shakespeare. *See* Sonnets, LXXXIX.
Sonnet: "Say what you will, and scratch my heart to find." Edna St. Vincent Millay. *See* Say What You Will.
Sonnet, The: "Scorn not the Sonnet." Wordsworth. *See* Scorn Not the Sonnet.
Sonnet: "See the white stillness of the unicorn." Roy Daniells. PeCV
Sonnet: September, 1815. Wordsworth. ChER
Sonnet: September, 1802. Wordsworth. *See* Near Dover, September, 1802.
Sonnet: September 1, 1802. Wordsworth. ChER
Sonnet: "Set me whereas the sun doth parch the green." Petrarch. *See* Vow to Love Faithfully, Howsoever He Be Rewarded, A.
Sonnet: "Shall I be fearful thus to speak my mind." Irene Rutherford McLeod. *Fr.* Sonnets. HBMV
Sonnet: "Shall I compare thee to a summer's day?" Shakespeare. *See* Sonnets, XVIII.
Sonnet: "Shall I, wasting in despair." George Wither. *See* Shall I, Wasting in Despair.
Sonnet: "She is so young, and never never before." Edward Davison. ErPo
Sonnet: "She loves me! From her own bliss-breathing lips." Charles Harpur. BoAu

Sonnet: "She took the dappled partridge flecked with blood." Tennyson. CABA
Sonnet: "Show me deare Christ, thy spouse, so bright and clear." John Donne. Holy Sonnets, XVIII. AnAnS-1; ExPo; ILP; MaMe; MasP; MBW-1; MeLP; MeP; NoP; OAEP; OBS; SCEP-1; SeEP; Sonn; TuPP
Sonnet: Silence. Thomas Hood. *See* Silence.
Sonnet: Silence. Poe. AP; MAmP; MWA-1
Sonnet: "Silver herring throbbed thick in my seine, The." Kenneth Leslie. *See* "Silver Herring Throbbed . . ."
Sonnet: "Sin of self-love [*or* Sinne of selfe-love] possesseth all mine eye [*or* al mine eie]." Shakespeare. Sonnets, LXII. EnRePo; EP; PoEL-2
Sonnet: "Since brass, nor stone, nor earth, nor boundless sea." Shakespeare. *See* Sonnets, LXV.
Sonnet: "Since I keep only what I give away." George Hetherington. NeIP
Sonnet: "Since she whom I lov'd [*or* loved] hath payd [*or* paid] her last debt." John Donne. Holy Sonnets, XVII. AnAnS-1; MaMe; MaPo (1969 ed.); MasP; MeP; MePo; OAEP; SCEP-1; SeEP; Sonn
Sonnet: "Since there's no help, come let us kiss and part." Michael Drayton. *See* Idea: "Since there's no help . . ."
Sonnet: "Sinne of selfe-love possesseth al mine eie." Shakespeare. *See* Sonnet: "Sin of self-love possesseth all mine eye."
Sonnet: "Sion lies [*or* Syon lyes] waste, and thy Jerusalem." Fulke Greville. Caelica, CIX [CX]. OxBoCh; PoEL-1; ReIE; SiCE; TuPP
Sonnet: "Sits by a fireplace, the seducer talks." Leonard Wolf. ErPo
Sonnet: "Sleep, Silence' child, sweet father of soft rest." William Drummond of Hawthornden. EIL; OBS
(Sleep, Silence' Child.) HBV
(Sleep, silence' child, sweet father of soft rest.) Sonn
(Sonet to Sleep.) OxBS
Sonnet: "So am I as the rich, whose blessed key." Shakespeare. Sonnets, LII. OBSC
Sonnet: "So are you to my thoughts as food to life." Shakespeare. Sonnets, LXXV. PoEL-2
Sonnet: "So is it not with me as with that Muse." Shakespeare. Sonnets, XXI. InvP; OBSC; ReEn; SiCE
Sonnet: "So it begins. Adam is in his earth." James Agee. Sonnets, I. ATP (1953 ed.); MAP; MoAmPo
Sonnet: "So, now I have confest that he is thine." Shakespeare. Sonnets, CXXXIV. CBEP; InvP
Sonnet: "So oft as I her beauty do behold." Spenser. *See* Amoretti, LV.
Sonnet: "So sang I in the springtime of my years." Morton Luce. Thysia, XXXVI. HBV
Sonnet: "So shall I live, supposing thou art true." Shakespeare. Sonnets, XCIII. InvP; MasP
Sonnet: "So shoots a star as doth my mistress glide." John Davies of Hereford. EIL
("So shoots a star as doth my mistress glide.") Sonn
Sonnet: "So you go back—because they bid you come." Arthur Davison Ficke. Sonnets of a Portrait Painter, XXXVI. AnAmPo
Sonnet: "Sole listener, Duddon! to the breeze that played." Wordsworth. The River Duddon, V. EnLi-2
Sonnet: "Some glory in their birth, some in their skill." Shakespeare. Sonnets, XCI. CBEP
Sonnet: "Some lovers speak, when their muses entertain. Sir Philip Sidney. *See* Astrophel and Stella, VI.
Sonnet: "Some one within my hearing said tonight." George Henry Boker. *Fr.* Sonnets; a Sequence on Profane Love. AmePo
Sonnet II: "Some things are very dear to me." Gwendolyn B. Bennett. AmNP; BANP; CDC; PoNe
Sonnet: "Sometimes I wish that I his pillow were." Richard Barnfield. ReIE
Sonnet: "Sometimes, when winding slow by brook and bower." Frederick Goddard Tuckerman. AnNE; MAmP; PoIE
Sonnet, The: "Sonnet is a fruit which long hath slept, The." John Addington Symonds. HBV; VA
Sonnet, The: "Sonnet is a moment's monument, A." Dante Gabriel Rossetti. *See* Sonnet, The ("A sonnet is a moment's monument").
Sonnet: "Soul's Rialto hath its merchandise, The." Elizabeth Barrett Browning. Sonnets from the Portuguese, XIX. PoVP
Sonnet: "Spit in my face you Jewes, and pierce my side." John Donne. Holy Sonnets, XI. AnAnS-1; MaMe; MasP; MeP; OBS; OxBoCh; SCEP-1; SeEP; Sonn
Sonnet: "Star of my mishap impos'd this paining, The." Samuel Daniel. To Delia, XXXI. OBSC; ReIE
Sonnet: "Stella! since thou so right a Princess art." Sir Philip Sidney. *See* Astrophel and Stella, CVII.
Sonnet: "Stella, think not that I by verse seek fame." Sir Philip Sidney. *See* Astrophel and Stella, XC.
Sonnet: "Still craves the spirit: never Nature solves." Frederick Goddard Tuckerman. MAmP
Sonnet: "Still pressing through these weeping solitudes." Frederick Goddard Tuckerman. AmePo; AP
Sonnet: "Stoics think, The (and they come near the truth)." Richard Barnfield. ReIE
Sonnet: "Such, such is Death: no triumph: no defeat." Charles Hamilton Sorley. Two Sonnets, II. HBMV; MoBrPo; NeMA; TrGrPo
Sonnet: "Sunne begins uppon my heart to shine, The." William Alabaster. MeP
Sonnet: Suppos'd to Be Written at Lemnos. Thomas Russell. CEP; OBEC
(Philoctetes.) LoBV
Sonnet: "Sure Lord, there is enough in thee to dry." George Herbert. AnAnS-1; MaMe; MeP
Sonnet: "Surprised by joy — impatient as the wind." Wordsworth. *See* Surprised by Joy — Impatient as the Wind.
Sonnet: "Sweet is the rose, but grows upon a brere." Spenser. *See* Amoretti, XXVI.
Sonnet: "Sweet love, renew thy force; be it not said." Shakespeare. *See* Sonnets, LVI.
Sonnet: "Sweet poets of the gentle antique line." John Hamilton Reynolds. OBRV
Sonnet: "Sweet semi-circled Cynthia played at maw." John Taylor. *Fr.* Odcomb's Complaint. EIL
Sonnet: "Sweet Spring, thou turn'st with all thy goodly train." William Drummond of Hawthornden. EIL; FaBoEn
(Spring Bereaved, 2.) OBEV
("Sweet Spring, thou turn'st with all thy goodly train.") Sonn
Sonnet: "Sweet, when I think how summer's smallest bird." Irene Rutherford McLeod. *Fr.* Sonnets. HBMV
Sonnet: "Take all my loves, my love, yea, take them all." Shakespeare. Sonnets, XL. CBEP; InvP; OBSC
Sonnet, A: "Take all of me—I am thine own, heart, soul." Amélie Rives. AA
Sonnet: "Tall stately plants with spikes and forks of gold." Frederick Goddard Tuckerman. AnNE
Sonnet: "Tell me no more how fair she is." Henry King. *See* Tell Me No More.
Sonnet: "That boy, the farmer said, with hazel wand." Frederick Goddard Tuckerman. MAmP
Sonnet: "That learned Grecian (who did so excel)." William Drummond of Hawthornden. OBS; SeEP
Sonnet: "That thou hast her, it is not all my grief." Shakespeare. Sonnets, XLII. CBEP; InvP
Sonnet: "That time of year thou mayst in me behold." Shakespeare. *See* Sonnets, LXXIII.
Sonnet: "That you were once unkind befriends me now." Shakespeare. Sonnets, CXX. InvP
Sonnet: "Then hate me when thou wilt; if ever, now." Shakespeare. *See* Sonnets, XC.
Sonnet: "Then judge me as thou wilt I cannot flee." Robert Hillyer. Sonnets, III. HBMV
Sonnet: "Then let not winter's ragged hand deface." Shakespeare. Sonnets, VI. MasP; SiCE; Sonn
Sonnet: "Then whilst that Latmos did contain her bliss." Earl of Stirling. Aurora, XXVIII. ViBoPo
Sonnet: "There are strange shadows fostered of the moon." Arthur Davison Ficke. MAP
Sonnet: "There have been many cats I loved and lost." Margaret E. Bruner. CIV
Sonnet: There Is a Bondage Worse. Wordsworth. ChER
Sonnet: "There was an Indian, who had known no change." J. C. Squire. *See* There Was an Indian.
Sonnet: "They say that shadows [*or* shadowes] of deceasèd ghosts." Joshua Sylvester. EIL; OBS; SeEP
("They say that shadows of deceasèd ghosts.") Sonn
Sonnet: "They that have power to hurt and will do none." Shakespeare. *See* Sonnets, XCIV.
Sonnet: "Thine eyes I love, and they, as pitying me." Shakespeare. Sonnets, CXXXII. OAEP; OBSC; SiCE

Sonnet, A: "Think, when a starry night of bitter frost." Conrad Aiken. AnEnPo
Sonnet: "This fellow calls me sordid, that one poor." George Henry Boker. *Fr.* Sonnets; a Sequence on Profane Love. AmePo
Sonnet: "This infant world has taken long to make." George Macdonald. *See* This Infant World.
Sonnet: "This is my play's [*or* playes] last scene, here heavens appoint." John Donne. Holy Sonnets, VI. AnAnS-1; AnEnPo; LoBV; MaMe; MasP; MeLP; MeP; MePo; MyFE; OAEP; OBS; OxBoCh; PoFS; SCEP-1; SeCP; SeEP; Sonn; TuPP
Sonnet: "This is the garden: colours come and go." E. E. Cummings. *See* This Is the Garden.
Sonnet: "This is the golden book of spirit and sense." Swinburne. SyP
Sonnet XV: "This is the way we say it in our time." Winfield Townley Scott. ErPo
Sonnet: "This virgin, beautiful and lively day." Stéphane Mallarmé, *tr. fr. French by* Roger Fry. PoPl
Sonnet: "This was the crucifixion on the mountain." Dylan Thomas. Altarwise by Owl-Light, VIII. CMoP; CoBMV; LiTM; MasP
Sonnet, A: "Those eyes that hold the hand of every heart." Nicholas Breton. ReIE
Sonnet: "Those former loves wherein our lives have run." James Agee. Sonnets, XIX. MAP; MoAmPo
Sonnet: "Those hours that with gentle work did frame." Shakespeare. Sonnets, V. ReEn; SiCE
Sonnet: "Those lines that I before have writ do lie." Shakespeare. Sonnets, CXV SiCE
Sonnet: "Those lips that Love's own hand did make." Shakespeare. Sonnets. CXLV. Sonn
Sonnet: "Those parts of thee that the world's eye doth view." Shakespeare. Sonnets, LXIX. CBEP
Sonnet: "Those pretty wrongs that liberty commits." Shakespeare. Sonnets, XLI. CBEP;InvP;PoeP;ReEn
Sonnet: "Thou art indeed just, Lord." Gerard Manley Hopkins. *See* Thou Art Indeed Just, Lord.
Sonnet: "Thou blind man's mark, thou fool's self-chosen snare." Sir Philip Sidney. *See* Thou Blind Man's Mark.
Sonnet: "Thou comest! all is said without a word." Elizabeth Barrett Browning. Sonnets from the Portuguese, XXXI. PoVP
Sonnet: "Thou fair-haired angel of the evening." Blake. *See* To the Evening Star.
Sonnet: "Thou hast made me, and shall thy work decay?" John Donne. Holy Sonnets, I. AnAnS-1; AnEnPo; BWP; EG; EnRePo; EP; FaBoEn; MaMe; MaPo; MasP; MBW-1; MeLP; MeP; NoP; OAEP; OBS; OxBoCh; PAn; Po; PoEL-2; PoFS; SCEP-1; SeCP; SeEP; Sonn
Sonnet: "Thou hast thy calling to some palace floor." Elizabeth Barrett Browning. Sonnets from the Portuguese, IV. EnLi-2; PoVP; VA
Sonnet: "Though dusty wits dare scorn astrology." Sir Philip Sidney. *See* Astrophel and Stella, XXVI. Sonn
Sonnet: "Thought of a Briton on the Subjugation of Switzerland. Wordsworth. *See* Thought of a Briton on the Subjugation of Switzerland.
Sonnet: "Three seasons only in his calendar." George Henry Boker. Sonnets, CXCIV. AmLP
Sonnet: "Three sortes of teares doe from myne eies distraine." William Alabaster. MeP
("Three sortes of teares doe from myne eies distraine.") AnAnS-1
Sonnet: "Thus can my love excuse the slow offense." Shakespeare. Sonnets, LI. PoFS
Sonnet: "Thus ends my love, but this doth grieve me most." Lord Herbert of Cherbury. LiTL; ViBoPo
(Loves End.) AnAnS-2; SeCP
Sonnet: "Thus in her absence is my fancy cool." George Henry Boker. *Fr.* Sonnets; a Sequence on Profane Love. AmePo
Sonnet: "Thus is his cheek the map of days outworn." Shakespeare. Sonnets, LXVIII. OBSC; PoeP; ReIE; UnPo (1st ed.)
Sonnet: "Thus piteously love closed what he begat." George Meredith. Modern Love, L. NBM
Sonnet: "Thy baby, too, the child that was to be." Frederick Goddard Tuckerman. AP
Sonnet: "Thy bosom is endearèd with all hearts." Shakespeare. Sonnets, XXXI. OBEV; OBSC
(Sonnet: "Thy bosome is indeared with all hearts.") PoEL-2
Sonnet: "Thy glass will show thee how thy beauties wear." Shakespeare. Sonnets, LXXVII. EnRePo; QFR
Sonnet: "Time and the mortal will stand never fast." Luís de Camoes, *tr. fr. Portuguese by* Richard Garnett. AWP
Sonnet: "Tired with all these, for restful death I cry." Shakespeare. *See* Sonnets, LXVI.
Sonnet: "'Tis better to be vile than vile esteemed." Shakespeare. *See* Sonnets, CXXI.
Sonnet: To ——. Wordsworth. ChER
Sonnet: To a Friend. Hartley Coleridge. *See* To a Friend.
Sonnet: To a Friend Who Does Not Pity His Love. Guido Cavalcanti, *tr. fr. Italian by* Dante Gabriel Rossetti. AWP
Sonnet: To Brunetto Latini. Dante, *tr. fr. Italian by* Dante Gabriel Rossetti. AWP
Sonnet: To Certain Ladies. Dante, *tr. fr. Italian by* Dante Gabriel Rossetti. AWP
Sonnet: To Dante Alighieri (He Commends the Work of Dante's Life). Giovanni Quirino, *tr. fr. Italian by* Dante Gabriel Rossetti. AWP
(To Dante Alighieri.) OnPM
Sonnet: To Dante Alighieri (He Conceives of Some Compensation in Death). Cino da Pistola, *tr. fr. Italian by* Dante Gabriel Rossetti. AWP
Sonnet: To Dante Alighieri (He Interprets Dante Alighieri's Dream). Dante da Maiano, *tr. fr. Italian by* Dante Gabriel Rossetti. AWP
Sonnet: To Dante Alighieri (He Interprets Dante's Dream). Guido Cavalcanti, *tr. fr. Italian by* Dante Gabriel Rossetti. AWP
Sonnet: To Dante Alighieri (He Interprets Dante's Dream). Cino da Pistoia, *tr. fr. Italian by* Dante Gabriel Rossetti. AWP
Sonnet: To Dante Alighieri (He Mistrusts the Love of Lapo Gianni). Guido Cavalcanti, *tr. fr. Italian by* Dante Gabriel Rossetti. AWP
Sonnet: To Dante Alighieri (He Reports the Successful Issue of Lapo Gianni's Love). Guido Cavalcanti, *tr. fr. Italian by* Dante Gabriel Rossetti. AWP
Sonnet: To Dante Alighieri (He Writes to Dante, Defying Him). Cecco Angiolieri da Siena, *tr. fr. Italian by* Dante Gabriel Rossetti. AWP
Sonnet: To Dante Alighieri (On the Last Sonnet of the "Vita Nuova"). Cecco Angiolieri da Siena, *tr. fr. Italian by* Dante Gabriel Rossetti. AWP
Sonnet: To Guido Cavalcanti. Dante, *tr. fr. Italian by* Shelley. AWP; JAWP; WBP
Sonnet: To His Lady Joan, of Florence. Guido Cavalcanti, *tr. fr. Italian by* Dante Gabriel Rossetti. AWP; JAWP; WBP
Sonnet: To Homer. Keats. *See* To Homer.
Sonnet: To Love, in Great Bitterness. Cino da Pistoia, *tr. fr. Italian by* Dante Gabriel Rossetti. AWP
(In Great Bitterness.) OnPM
Sonnet: "To me, fair friend, you never can be old." Shakespeare. *See* Sonnets, CIV.
Sonnet: To Mr. H. Lawes, on His Aires. Milton. *See* To Mr. H. Lawes on His Airs.
Sonnet: "To nothing fitter can I thee compare." Michael Drayton. Idea, X. BEL; EIL; HBV; OBSC; SiCE; TrGrPo; TuPP; ViBoPo
Sonnet: "To one who has been long in city pent." Keats. *See* To One Who Has Been Long in City Pent.
Sonnet: To Oxford. Thomas Russell. ATP; CEP; OBEC
(To Oxford.) Sonn
Sonnet: "To rail or jest, ye know I use it not." Sir Thomas Wyatt. FCP; SiPS
Sonnet: To Science. Poe. *See* Sonnet to Science.
Sonnet: To Sleep. Keats. *See* To Sleep.
Sonnet: To Tartar, a Terrier Beauty. Thomas Lovell Beddoes. OBNC
Sonnet: To the Critic. *See* Idea: "Methinks I see . . ."
Sonnet: To the Lady Beaumont. Wordsworth. ChER
Sonnet: To the Lady Pietra degli Scrovigni. Dante, *tr. fr. Italian by* Dante Gabriel Rossetti. AWP
Sonnet: To the River Lodon [*or* Loddon]. Thomas Warton, the Younger. Sonnets, IX. CEP; OBEC; ViBoPo
(To the River Lodon.) CoBE; Sonn

Sonnet: To the River Otter. Samuel Taylor Coleridge. ChER; ERoP-1
(To the River Otter.) Sonn
Sonnet: "Tonight I walked with the grim Florentine." George Henry Boker. Sonnets, LXVI. AmLP
Sonnet: To the Same Ladies. Dante, *tr. fr. Italian by* Dante Gabriel Rossetti. AWP
Sonnet: "To travel like a bird, lightly to view." C. Day Lewis. *Fr.* O Dreams O Destinations. ChMP; GTBS-P; Sonn
Sonnet: To Valclusa. Thomas Russell. CEP; OBEC
Sonnet: Token, The. John Donne. MaMe
Sonnet: Trance of Love, A. Cino da Pistoia, *tr. fr. Italian by* Dante Gabriel Rossetti. AWP
Sonnet: True Ambition. Benjamin Stillingfleet. OBEC
Sonnet: "Twin songs there are, of joyance, or of pain." Morton Luce. Thysia, II. HBV
Sonnet: "Two loves I have of comfort and despair." Shakespeare. *See* Sonnets, CXLIV.
Sonnet, A: "Two voices are there: one is of the deep." James Kenneth Stephen. FiBHP; Par; VA; WhC
(Sonnet on Wordsworth, A.) CenHV; ML
(Two Voices Are There.) EnLi-2 (1949 ed.)
(Wordsworth.) HBV
Sonnet: "Tyr'd with all these for restfull death I cry." Shakespeare. *See* Sonnets, LXVI.
Sonnet: "Under a throne I saw a virgin sit." Fulke Greville. Caelica, LXXXI [LXXXII]. ReIE; SiCE; TuPP
Sonnet: "Under the bark remembers now my heart." Roy Daniells. PeCV
Sonnet: "Under the mountain, as when first I knew." Frederick Goddard Tuckerman. AmePo; AP; MAmP; NoP; QFR
Sonnet: "Understanding of a medical man, The." Rex Warner. ChMP
Sonnet: "Unlike are we, unlike, O princely Heart." Elizabeth Barrett Browning. *See* Sonnets from the Portuguese: "Unlike are we . . ."
Sonnet: "Unto the boundless ocean of thy beauty." Samuel Daniel. To Delia, I. LiTL; LoBV; OAEP; OBSC; ReIE; SiCE
Sonnet: "Upon an upland orchard's sunny side." Thomas Caulfield Irwin. IrPN
Sonnet III: Upon His Absence from Her. Francis Davison. ReIE
Sonnet: "Upon our fullness shines the dawning day." Francis Lyman Windolph. MaRV
Sonnet: "Upper chamber in a darkened house, A." Frederick Goddard Tuckerman. AmePo; AnNE; MAmP; NoP
Sonnet XII: "Virgins terrify too many men." Winfield Townley Scott. ErPo
Sonnet: "Warm rain whispers, but the earth knows best, A." Kenneth Leslie. By Stubborn Stars, II. PeCV; TwCaPo
Sonnet: "Was it the proud full sail of his great verse." Shakespeare. *See* Sonnets, LXXXVI.
Sonnet: "Way feare with thy projectes, noe false fyre, A." William Alabaster. MeP
Sonnet: "We are the singing shadows beauty casts." Clement Wood. Eagle Sonnets, XX. HBMV
Sonnet: "We will not whisper, we have found the place." Hilaire Belloc. Sonnets, XIX. MoBrPo
Sonnet: "Weary with toil, I haste me to my bed." Shakespeare. *See* Sonnets, XXVII.
Sonnet: "Weary yeare his race now having run, The." Spenser. Amoretti, LXII. OBSC; ReIE; SiCE
Sonnet: "Were I as base as is the lowly plain." *At. to* Joshua Sylvester. *See* Were I as Base . . .
Sonnet: "What are we first? First, animals; and next." George Meredith. Modern Love, XXX. NBM
Sonnet: "What can I give thee back." Elizabeth Barrett Browning. *See* Sonnets from the Portuguese; "What can I give thee back . . ."
Sonnet: "What doth it serve to see sun's burning face." William Drummond of Hawthornden. ElL; Sonn
Sonnet: "What if this present were the world's last night?" John Donne. Holy Sonnets, XIII. AnAnS-1; ExPo; GTBS-W; LiTB; MaMe; MaPo (1969 ed.); MasP; MBW-2; MeLP; MeP; OAEP; OBS; SCEP-1; SeCeV; SeEP; Sonn; TuPP
Sonnet, The: "What is a sonnet? 'Tis the pearly shell." Richard Watson Gilder. AA; HBV
Sonnet: "What is the metre of the dictionary?" Dylan Thomas. Altarwise by Owl-Light, IV. CMoP; CoBMV; LiTM; MasP
Sonnet: "What is your substance, whereof are you made." Shakespeare. *See* Sonnets, LIII.
Sonnet: "What lips my lips have kissed, and where, and why." Edna St. Vincent Millay. *See* What Lips My Lips Have Kissed.
Sonnet: "What meaneth this, that Christ an hymne did singe." William Alabaster. MeP
Sonnet: "What potions have I drunk of Siren tears." Shakespeare. Sonnets, CXIX. CBEP; ReIE; WHA
Sonnet: "When as mans life, the light of human lust." Fulke Greville. *See* Sonnet: "Whenas man's life . . ."
Sonnet: "When down the windy vistas of the years." Clement Wood. Eagle Sonnets, XI. HBMV
Sonnet: "When far spent night persuades each mortal eye." Sir Philip Sidney. *See* Astrophel and Stella, XCIX. Sonn
Sonnet: "When forty winters shall besiege thy brow." Shakespeare. *See* Sonnets, II.
Sonnet: "When, from the tower whence I derive love's heaven." *Unknown. Fr.* Zepheria. ElL
Sonnet: "When I consider everything that grows." Shakespeare. *See* Sonnets, XV.
Sonnet: "When I consider how my light is spent." Milton. *See* On His Blindness.
Sonnet: "When I do count the clock that tells the time." Shakespeare. *See* Sonnets, XII.
Sonnet: "When I entreat, either thou wilt not hear." Henry King. AnAnS-2
Sonnet: "When I had turned Catullus into rhyme." Thomas Caulfield Irwin. IrPN
Sonnet: "When I have fears that I may cease to be." Keats. *See* When I Have Fears.
Sonnet: "When I have seen by time's fell hand defaced." Shakespeare. *See* Sonnets, LXIV.
Sonnet: "When I look back upon my early days." George Henry Boker. *Fr.* Sonnets; a Sequence on Profane Love. AmePo
Sonnet: "When I perceive the sable of your hair." Elinor Wylie. *Fr.* One Person. NP
Sonnet: "When I was marked for suffering, Love forswore." Cervantes. *tr. fr. Spanish by* Sir Edmund Gosse. AWP; PoFr
Sonnet: "When, in disgrace with fortune and men's eyes." Shakespeare. *See* Sonnets, XXIX.
Sonnet: "When in the chronicle of wasted time." Shakespeare. *See* Sonnets, CVI.
Sonnet: "When men shall find thy flower, thy glory, pass." Samuel Daniel. *See* To Delia: "When men shall find . . ."
Sonnet: "When most I wink, then do mine eyes best see." Shakespeare. Sonnets, XLIII. CBEP
Sonnet: "When my love swears that she is made of truth." Shakespeare. *See* Sonnets, CXXXVIII.
Sonnet: "When nature made her chief work, Stella's eyes." Sir Philip Sidney. *See* Astrophel and Stella, VII. Sonn
Sonnet: "When our two souls stand up erect and strong." Elizabeth Barrett Browning. *See* Sonnets from the Portuguese: "When our two souls . . ."
Sonnet: "When Phoebe form'd a wanton smile." William Collins. EnLoPo
Sonnet: "When sane men gather in to talk of love." Irene Rutherford McLeod. *Fr.* Sonnets. HBMV
Sonnet: "When sorrow (using mine own fire's might)." Sir Philip Sidney. *See* Astrophel and Stella, CVIII.
Sonnet: "When thou hast taken thy last applause." E. E. Cummings. NP
Sonnet: "When thou shalt be dispos'd to set me light." Shakespeare. Sonnets, LXXXVIII. CLwM
Sonnet: "When to his class the surgeon's skilful blade." George Henry Boker. *Fr.* Sonnets; a Sequence on Profane Love. AmePo
Sonnet: "When to the sessions of sweet silent thought." Shakespeare. *See* Sonnets, XXX.
Sonnet: "When we are old and these rejoicing veins." Edna St. Vincent Millay. ErPo
Sonnet: "When we met first and loved, I did not build." Elizabeth Barrett Browning. Sonnets from the Portuguese, XXXVI. PoVP
Sonnet: "When winter snows upon thy sable hairs [*or* golden hears]." Samuel Daniel. To Delia, XXXVIII [XXXIX]. OBSC; ReIE; TuPP

Sonnet: "When without tears I looke on Christ, I see." William Alabaster. MeP
Sonnet: "Whenas [*or* When as] man's life, the light of human lust." Fulke Greville. Caelica, LXXXVII [LXXXVIII]. EP; GTBS-W; LiTB; MePo; OxBoCh; PoIE ("When as mans life, the light of human lust.") OBS; PoEL-1
Sonnet: "Where are we to go when this is done?" Alfred A. Duckett. AmNP; PoNe
Sonnet: "Where art thou, Muse, that thou forget'st so long." Shakespeare. Sonnets, C. OBSC
Sonnet: Where Lies the Land. Wordsworth. *See* Where Lies the Land to Which Yon Ship Must Go?
Sonnet: "Whether the Turkish new moon minded be." Sir Philip Sidney. *See* Astrophel and Stella, XXX.
Sonnet: "Whilst I alone did call upon thy aid." Shakespeare. Sonnets, LXXIX. Sonn
Sonnet: "White as this paper was my lady's mind." George Henry Boker. *Fr.* Sonnets; a Sequence on Profane Love. AmePo
Sonnet: "Who will believe my verse in time to come." Shakespeare. *See* Sonnets, XVII.
Sonnet: "Whoever hath her wish thou hast thy Will." Shakespeare. Sonnets, CXXXV. PAn; ReEn
Sonnet: "Whoso list to hunt, I know where is an hind." Sir Thomas Wyatt. *See* Hind, The.
Sonnet: "Why are wee by all creatures waited on?" John Donne. Holy Sonnets, XII. AnAnS-1; CABA; MaMe; MaPo; MasP; MeP; OBS; PoEL-2; SCEP-1; Sonn; TuPP
Sonnet: "Why didst thou promise such a beauteous day." Shakespeare. Sonnets, XXXIV. CBEP; OBSC; PoE
Sonnet: "Why is my verse so barren of new pride." Shakespeare. *See* Sonnets, LXXVI.
Sonnet: "Why practise, love, this small economy?" Wilfrid Scawen Blunt. The Love Sonnets of Proteus, LVIII. ViBoPo
Sonnet: "Why should I hate you, love, or why despise." Wilfrid Scawen Blunt. The Love Sonnets of Proteus, XXVIII. ViBoPo
Sonnet: Wild Duck's Nest, The. Wordsworth. ChER
Sonnet: "Wilt thou love God, as he thee! then digest." John Donne. Holy Sonnets, XV. AnAnS-1; MaMe; MasP; MeP; OBS; SCEP-1; Sonn
Sonnet: "Wind has blown the rain away and blown, A." E. E. Cummings. AmPP; AnNE; MAP; MoAB; MoAmPo
Sonnet: Window, The. Carl Bode. ToPo
Sonnet: "Winter deepening, the hay all in, The." Richard Wilbur. PoPl; TDP
Sonnet: "With how sad steps, O Moon, thou climb'st the skies." Sir Philip Sidney. *See* Astrophel and Stella, XXXI.
Sonnet: "With sighs my bosom always laboureth." Dante, *tr. fr. Italian by* Dante Gabriel Rossetti. *Fr.* La Vita Nuova. GoBC, *sl. abr.*
Sonnet: "With what sharp checks I in myself am shent." Sir Philip Sidney. *See* Astrophel and Stella, XVIII.
Sonnet: "Within her hair Venus and Cupid sport them." "E. C." Emaricdulfe, VI. ElL
Sonnet: "Witless gallant, a young wench that wooed, A." Michael Drayton. Idea, XXI. SiCE; TuPP
Sonnet: "Woman's face, with Nature's own hand painted, A." Shakespeare. Sonnets, XX. CBEP; ErPo; InvP; MasP; ReEn
Sonnet: "Wonderfully out of the beautiful form." Dante, *tr. fr. Italian by* Dante Gabriel Rossetti. *Fr.* La Vita Nuova. GoBC
Sonnet, A: "World is too much with us, The; late and soon." Wordsworth. *See* World Is Too Much with Us, The.
Sonnet: "World, that all contains, is ever moving, The." Fulke Greville. *See* Change.
Sonnet: "World's bright comforter, whose beamsome light, The." Barnabe Barnes. *See* World's Bright Comforter, The.
Sonnet: "Wretched thing it were, to have our heart, A." Richard Chenevix Trench. *See* Retirement.
Sonnet: Written after Seeing Wilton-House. Thomas Warton, the Younger. Sonnets, V. OBEC
Sonnet: Written at Stonehenge. Thomas Warton, the Younger. Sonnets, IV. CEP; EiPP (Written at Stonehenge.) Sonn
Sonnet: Written at the End of "The Floure and the Lefe." Keats. EnRP
Sonnet: Written in a Blank Leaf on Dugdale's "Monasticon." Thomas Warton, the Younger. Sonnets, III. EiPP; OBEC; SeCePo (Written in a Blank Leaf of Dugdale's "Monasticon.") Sonn
Sonnet: Written in January, 1818. Keats. *See* When I Have Fears.
Sonnet: Written in London, September 1802. Wordsworth. *See* Written in London, September 1802.
Sonnet: Written on the Day That Mr. Leigh Hunt Left Prison. Keats. ChER (Written on the Day That Mr. Leigh Hunt Left Prison.) MERP; PoFr; Sonn
Sonnet: "Ye tradeful merchants that, with weary toil." Spenser. *See* Amoretti, XV.
Sonnet: "Ye two fair trees that I so long have known." Thomas Caulfield Irwin. IrPN
Sonnet: "Yea, Love is strong as life; he casts out fear." Lady Blanche Elizabeth Lindsay. VA
Sonnet: "Yet even mid merry boyhood's tricks and scapes." Frederick Goddard Tuckerman. MAmP
Sonnet: "Yet love, mere love, is beautiful indeed." Elizabeth Barrett Browning. *See* Sonnets from the Portugese: "Yet Love, Mere Love . . ."
Sonnet: "Yet vain, perhaps, the fruits our care applaud." Frederick Goddard Tuckerman. AnNE
Sonnet: "Yet wear we on; the deep light disallowed." Frederick Goddard Tuckerman. AmePo
Sonnet: "You ask my love. What shall my love then be?" Wilfrid Scawen Blunt. The Love Sonnets of Proteus, XXII. ViBoPo
Sonnet: "You little stars that live in skies." Fulke Greville. *See* You Little Stars That Live in Skies.
Sonnet: "You say my love no marvel is to you." George Henry Boker. Sonnets, CLIII. AmLP
Sonnet: "You that do search for every purling spring." Sir Philip Sidney. *See* Astrophel and Stella, XV.
Sonnet: "You that in love find luck and abundaunce." Sir Thomas Wyatt. SiPS (May Time.) OBSC (You That in Love Find Luck [and Abundance].) CBEP; MaPo ("You that in love finde luck[e] and abundance [*or* habundance].") EnPo; FCP
Sonnet: "You waken slowly. In your dream you're straying." William Bell. NePoEA
Sonnet: "You were born; must die." Stephen Spender. EnLit; MoAB; MoBrPo (1950 ed.)
Sonnet: "You whispered, 'still the stars shine cold above me.'" William Bell. FaBoTw
Sonnet: "Your words, my friend (right healthful caustics), blame." Sir Philip Sidney. *See* Astrophel and Stella, XXI.
Sonnet: "You're [*or* You] not alone when you are still alone." Michael Drayton. *See* Idea: "You're not alone . . ."
Sonnet Addressed to Haydon. Keats. *See* Addressed to Haydon ("Great Spirits now on earth . . .")
Sonnet against the Too-facile Mystic. Elizabeth B. Harrod. NePoEA
Sonnet and Limerick. Morris Bishop. FiBHP
Sonnet at Christmas. Allen Tate. *See* Sonnets at Christmas.
Sonnet at Easter. Howard Nemerov. FiMAP
Sonnet Entitled How to Run the World. E. E. Cummings. NePA
Sonnet for a Picture. Swinburne. *Fr.* The Heptalogia. OAEP; VP
Sonnet for Christmas. Vincent G. Burns. MaRV
Sonnet for Dick Gallup, A. Ted Berrigan. ANYP
Sonnet for My Son. Melanie Gordon Barber. GoYe
Sonnet for the Broken Windows. Anne Waldman. YAP
Sonnet for the Madonna of the Cherries. A. P. Wavell. OtMeF
Sonnet Found in a Deserted Madhouse. *Unknown.* BOHV; InvP; NA; SiTL
Sonnet from "Idea." Michael Drayton. *See* Idea: "Since there's no help . . ."
Sonnet from " One Person." Elinor Wylie. *See* I Hereby Swear That to Uphold Your House.
Sonnet in a Garden. Josephine Preston Peabody. AA
Sonnet in a Pass of Bavaria. Richard Chenevix Trench. OBRV
Sonnet in Autumn. Donald Petersen. NePoEA-2
Sonnet in Dialogue, A. Austin Dobson. YT

Sonnet is a fruit which long hath slept, The. The Sonnet. John Addington Symonds. HBV; VA
Sonnet Is a Moment's Monument, A. Dante Gabriel Rossetti. *See* Sonnet, The ("A sonnet is a moment's monument").
Sonnet, July 18th, 1787. William Lisle Bowles. *See* Time and Grief.
Sonnet Made on Isabella Markham, A. John Harington. ElL; OBSC; TuPP
Sonnet of Black Beauty. Lord Herbert of Cherbury. AnAnS-2; AtBAP; BoW; EP; MePo; SeCL; SeEP
Sonnet of Brotherhood. R. A. K. Mason. AnNZ
Sonnet of Departure. J. R. Hervey. AnNZ
Sonnet of Fishes. George Barker. FaBoMo; FlW; Sonn
Sonnet of the Moon, A. Charles Best. CH; HBV; TuPP
(Looke How the Pale Queene.) EtS
(Moon, The.) OBSC
(Of The Moon.) ElL
Sonnet of the Mountain, The. Mellin de Saint-Gelais, *tr. fr. French by* Austin Dobson. AWP
("Seeing those mountains, distant and obscure," *tr. by* Alan Conder.) LO
Sonnet on a Family Picture. Thomas Edwards. CEP; EiCL; OBEC
Sonnet on a Monkey, A. Marjory Fleming. FaFP; FiBHP; LiTG; SiTL
(Sonnet to a Monkey, A.) ALV; MemP
(To a Monkey.) GoTP
Sonnet on a Picture of Leander. Keats. *See* On a Picture of Leander.
Sonnet on a Somewhat Inferior Radio Outfit. Cary Ross. AnAmPo
Sonnet on Chillon. Byron. *Fr.* The Prisoner of Chillon. AnEnPo; ATP; BEL; BoLiVe; CABL; EnLi-2; EnLit; EnRP; EPN; ExPo; FiP; ILP; InP; LiTB; LoBV; MBW-2; MERP; OAEP; OBRV; PoFr; PoFS; SeCeV; Sonn; TOP; TreFS; TrGrPo; YAT
("Eternal Spirit of the Chainless Mind!") PoPl
(Freedom's Hero.) MaRV
(On the Castle of Chillon.) GTBS; GTBS-D; GTBS-P; GTBS-W; GTSE; GTSL
(Prisoner of Chillon, The, *introd. sonnet.*) MCCG
Sonnet on Death. William Walsh. ViBoPo
(Death.) CBEP
(Death; a Sonnet.) SeCL
(Sonnet: Death.) SeEP
Sonnet on Hearing the *Dies Irae* Sung in the Sistine Chapel. Oscar Wilde. TrPWD
Sonnet on His Blindness. Milton. *See* On His Blindness.
Sonnet on His Deceased Wife. Milton. *See* On His Deceased Wife.
Sonnet on Holy Week. Oscar Wilde. JKCP (1926 ed.)
Sonnet on Life. Sir Brooke Boothby. ViBoPo
Sonnet on Sir William Alexander's Harsh Verses, A. James I, King of England. Sonn
Sonnet on Stewed Prunes. William F. Kirk. WhC
Sonnet on the Death of His Wife. John Masefield. BoPe
Sonnet on the Death of Robert Riddell of Glenriddell. Burns. Sonn
Sonnet on the Sea. Keats. *See* On the Sea.
Sonnet on the Sonnet. Lord Alfred Douglas. MoBrPo (1942 ed.)
Sonnet on the Sonnet. Keats. *See* On the Sonnet.
Sonnet on Turning a Radio Dial. Anderson M. Scruggs. PoMa
Sonnet on Wordsworth, A. James Kenneth Stephen. *See* Sonnet: "Two voices are there . . ."
Sonnet or Dittie: "Mars in a fury gainst love's brightest queen." Robert Greene. *See* Mars and Venus.
Sonnet Sequence. Darwin T. Turner. BALP
Sonnet Series of French Canada, A, *sels.* Frank Oliver Call. CaP
Blue Homespun.
Old Habitant, An.
Sonnet—Silence. Poe. *See* Sonnet: Silence.
Sonnet Suppos'd to be Written at Lemnos. Thomas Russell. FaBoEn
Sonnet to ——. John Hamilton Reynolds. OBRV
Sonnet to a Cat. Heine, *tr. fr. German.* CIV
Sonnet to a Clam. John Godfrey Saxe. AnNE; BOHV
Sonnet to a Friend Who Asked How I Felt When the Nurse First Presented My Infant to Me. Samuel Taylor Coleridge. EnRP
Sonnet to a Monkey. Marjorie Fleming. *See* Sonnet on a Monkey, A.
Sonnet to a Negro in Harlem. Helene Johnson. AmNP; BANP; CDC
Sonnet to a Young Lady Who Sent Me a Laurel Crown. Keats. EnRP
Sonnet to Byron. Shelley. *See* To Byron.
Sonnet to Chatterton. Keats. ERoP-2
Sonnet to Edgar Allan Poe ("On our lone pathway"). Sarah Helen Whitman. *Fr.* Sonnets from the Series Relating to Edgar Allan Poe. AnAmPo
(Sonnets.) AA
Sonnet to Gath. Edna St. Vincent Millay. CMoP; CoBA; MAP; MoAB; MoAmPo
Sonnet to Hampstead. Leigh Hunt. Sonn
Sonnet to Heavenly Beauty, A. Joachim du Bellay, *tr. fr. French by* Andrew Lang. Olive, CXIII. AWP; CTC; JAWP; WBP
(Sonnet: "If life on earth be less than is a day," *tr. by* Armel O'Conner.) CAW
(Sonnet: "If of our life the span be not a day," *tr. by* Eleanor L. Turnbull.) WoL
Sonnet to Lake Leman. Byron. Sonn
Sonnet to Liberty. Oscar Wilde. PoFr
Sonnet to Mrs. Reynolds' Cat. Keats. *See* To a Cat.
Sonnet to Mrs. Unwin. William Cowper. *See* To Mary Unwin.
Sonnet to My Mother. George Barker. FaFP; GTBS-W; LiTB; LiTM; MemP; MoAB; PG (1955 ed.); SeCePo; VaPo; ViBoPo (1958 ed.); WaP
(To My Mother.) BoC; DTC; FaBoMo; FlW; GTBS-D; MoPW; Sonn; TwCP
Sonnet to My Mother, A. Heine. *See* To My Mother.
Sonnet to Robert Graham, Esq. Burns. Sonn
Sonnet to Science. Poe. Al Aaraaf: Prologue. AmePo; AmP; AmPP; AnAmPo; AnFE; AP; APA; CBV; CoAnAm; CoBA; ILP; MAmP; MWA-1; NePA; NoP; OxBA; PPON
(To Science.) CBEP; Sonn
Sonnet to Shakespeare. Hugh Holland. *See* Shakespeare Dead.
Sonnet to Sleep. Keats. *See* To Sleep.
Sonnet to the Moon. Yvor Winters. TwAmPo
Sonnet, to the Noble Lady, the Lady Mary Worth, A. Ben Jonson. AnAnS-2
Sonnet to the Prince Regent. Byron. MBW-2
Sonnet to the Sea Serpent. John G. C. Brainard. EtS
Sonnet to the Virgin. Wordsworth. *See* Virgin, The.
Sonnet to Vauxhall. Thomas Hood. PoEL-4
Sonnet to William Wilberforce, Esq. William Cowper. CEP; ILP; OAEP; PoIE (1970 ed.)
(To William Wilberforce.) CoBE; Sonn
Sonnet—To Zante. Poe. MAmP
Sonnet upon a Stolen Kiss. George Wither. *See* Stolen Kiss, A.
Sonnet upon Sonnets, A. Burns. Sonn
Sonnet upon the Author's First Seven Years' Service, A. Thomas Tusser. SiCE; TuPP
(Upon the Author's First Seven Years' Service.) ElL
Sonnet upon the Pitiful Burning of the Globe Playhouse in London, A. *Unknown.* TuPP
Sonnet with her Mona Lisa smile, The. Sonnet and Limerick. Morris Bishop. FiBHP
Sonnet Written at the Close of Spring. Charlotte Smith. OBEC
(Elegiac Sonnet.) FaBoEn
Sonnet Written in Disgust of Vulgar Superstition. Keats. ERoP-2
Sonneteering Made Easy. S. B. Botsford. NYBP
Sonnets, *sels.* James Agee. MAP; MoAmPo
"Now stands our love on that still verge of day," XX.
"Our doom is in our being," II.
"So it begins," I.
"Those former loves wherein our lives have run," XIX.
Sonnets, *sels.* Hilaire Belloc.
"Almighty God, whose justice like a sun," XXI. TrPWD
"Because my faltering feet may fail to dare," XVII. OxBoCh; POTE
(Her Faith.) GoBC
"We will not whisper, we have found the place," XIX. MoBrPo
Sonnets, *sels.* Gwendolyn B. Bennett.

Sonnets (continued)
"He came in silvern armour," I. CDC; PoNe
"Some things are very dear to me," II. BANP; CDC; PoNe
Sonnets, *sels.* Boccaccio, *tr. fr. Italian by* Dante Gabriel Rossetti.
Inscription for a Portrait of Dante. AWP; JAWP; WBP
(Inscription for Portrait of Dante.) OnPM
(Tribute to Dante, A.) GoBC
Of Fiammetta Singing. AWP
(Fiammetta.) GoBC
Of His Last Sight of Fiammetta. AWP; JAWP; OnPM; WBP
(Fiammetta.) GoBC
Of Three Girls and [of] Their Talk. AWP; JAWP; OnPM; WBP
To Dante in Paradise, after Fiammetta's Death. AWP
(Fiammetta.) GoBC
To One Who Had Censured His Public Exposition of Dante. AWP
(Tribute to Dante, A.) GoBC
Sonnets, *sels.* George Henry Boker. AmLP
"Oh! sigh no more, no longer paint the air," LXXIX.
"Oh spring, that hides the wrinkled earth in green," CXV.
"Three seasons only in his calendar," CXCIV.
"Tonight I walked with the grim Florentine," LXVI.
"You say my love no marvel is to you," CLIII.
Sonnets. Samuel Daniel. *See* To Delia.
Sonnets. Michael Drayton. *See* Idea *and* Idea's Mirrour.
Sonnets, *sels.* Robert Hillyer. HBMV
"Even as love grows more, I write the less," XVI.
"Golden spring redeems the withered year, The," II.
"I will fling wide the windows of my soul," XII.
"Let all men see the ruins of the shrine," XIV.
"Long after both of us are scattered dust," XXXIV.
"Over the waters but a single bough," XXIII.
"Quickly and pleasantly the seasons blow," I.
"Then judge me as thou wilt, I cannot flee," III.
Sonnets (I-XIV). Thomas Caulfield Irwin. IrPN
Sonnets, *sels.* Muna Lee.
"Along my ways of life you never came," XII. HBMV; NP
"I have a thousand pictures of the sea," IV. HBMV
"I make no question of your right to go," III. HBMV
"It were easiest to say: the moon and lake." NP
"It will be easy to love you when I am dead," XI. HBMV
"Life of itself will be cruel and hard enough," V. HBMV
"What other form were worthy of your praise," Foreward. HBMV
Sonnets, *sels.* Irene Rutherford McLeod. HBMV
"Between my love and me there runs a thread."
"In heaven there is a star I call my own."
"Shall I be fearful thus to speak my mind."
"Sweet, when I think how summer's smallest bird."
"When sane men gather in to talk of love."
Sonnets ("Like bones the ruins of the cities stand"), *sel.* John Masefield.
"Now they are gone with all their songs and sins," II. InP
Sonnets ("Long long ago"), *sels.* John Masefield.
"Ah we are neither heaven nor earth, but men." EPN
"Flesh, I have knocked at many a dusty door." GTSL; LiTM; MoBrPo; SeCePo
"Here in the self is all that man can know." AWP; BoPe; JAWP; WBP
"How many ways, how many times." WGRP
(How Many Ways.) LiTB
"I never see the red rose crown the year." CMoP; EnLi-2 (1949 ed.); GoYe; InP
"If I could come again to that dear place." HBV
"If I could get within this changing I." WGRP
"Is there a great green commonwealth of Thought." ILP; LiTM; MoBrPo
"It may be so with us that in the dark." ATP; TOP
"Let that which is to come be as it may." HBV
"Long long ago, when all the glittering earth." HBV
"Men are made human by the mighty fall." EPN
"O little self, within whose smallness lies." HBV; POTE; SoP; WGRP
"Roses are beauty, but I never see." HBV
(Roses Are Beauty.) TOP
"There is no God, as I was taught in youth." HBV; WGRP
(There Is No God, As I Was Taught.) CMoP
What Am I, Life? ImOP; NP
Sonnets. Gustav Rosenhane, *tr. fr. Swedish by* Sir Edmund Gosse. AWP; JAWP; WBP
"And then I sat me down and gave the rein," II.
"Deep in a vale where rocks on every side," I.
Sonnets, *sels.* George Santayana.
"After gray vigils, sunshine in the heart," XLIX. MAP; MoAmPo; WHA
"As in the midst of battle there is room," XXV. AnFE; APA; AWP; CoAnAm; JAWP; LiTM; MAP; MoAmPo; NePA; WBP
"As when the sceptre dangles from the hand," XLII. ATP
"Deem not, because you see me in the press," XI. TrGrPo
(Deem Not.) AnEnPo
"Have patience; it is fit that in this wise," IX. WGRP
"I sought on earth a garden of delight," I. AnEnPo
(Sorrow.) WGRP
"I would I might forget that I am I," IV. AWP; JAWP; TOP; WBP
"O world, thou choosest not the better part," III. ATP; InP; MAP; MoAmPo; TreFS
(Faith.) OQP; WGRP
(O World.) HBMV; MaRV; TrGrPo
"We needs must be divided in the tomb," XXXV. ViBoPo
What Riches Have You? HBV; TrGrPo
Sonnets, *sels.* Shakespeare.
I. "From fairest creatures we desire increase." AtBAP; CTC; EG; FaBoEn; LiTB; LiTL; MasP; OAEP; OBSC; SiCE; TrGrPo
II. "When forty winters shall besiege thy brow." EG; LiTB; OBSC; ReEn; ReIE; SiCE; Sonn
III. "Look in thy glass and tell the face thou viewest." BWP; CABA; EG; EnRePo; GTBS-W; LiTB; MasP; OBSC; SiCE
V. "Those hours that with gentle work did frame." ReEn; SiCE
VI. "Then let not winter's ragged hand deface." MasP; SiCE; Sonn
VII. "Lo, in the orient when the gracious light." ReIE; SiCE
VIII. "Music to hear, why hear'st thou music sadly?" MuSP; PoEL-2; ViBoPo
IX. "Is it for fear to wet a widow's eye?" MasP; Sonn
X. "For shame! deny that thou bear'st love to any." MasP
XI. "As fast as thou shalt wane, so fast thou grow'st." Sonn
XII. "When I do count the clock that tells the time." AWP; BEL; CBEP; DiPo; EG; ElL; EnLi-1; EnRePo; EP; FaFP; InPo; JAWP; MasP; NoP; OBSC; OuHeWo; Po; PoeP; ReEn; ReIE; Sonn; SiCE; TOP; ViBoPo; WBP
XIII. "O! that you were yourself; but, love, you are." OAEP; SiCE
XIV. "Not from the stars do I my judgment pluck." MasP; SiCE; Sonn
XV. "When I consider every thing that grows." AWP; BEL; BWP; CoBE; DiPo; EnLi-1; MasP; OAEP; OBSC; OuHeWo; PoFS; ReEn; ReIE; SiCE; Sonn; TrGrPo
XVI. "But wherefore do not you a mightier waie." FaBoEn
XVII. "Who will believe my verse in time to come." DiPo; EnLi-1; OBSC; SiCE; Sonn
XVIII. "Shall I compare thee to a summer's day?" AnFE; AtBAP; ATP; AWP; BEL; BoLiVe; BWP; CBEP; CBV; CoBE; CTC; DiPo; EG; ElL; EnL; EnLi-1; EnLit; EnLoPo; ExPo; FaBoBe; FaBoEn; FaBV; FaFP; FiP; HBV; ILP; InP; InvP; LiTB; LiTG; LiTL; LoBV; MaPo; MasP; MCCG; MeWo; NeHB; NoP; OAEP; OBEV; OBSC; OuHeWo; PAn; PoAn; PoE; PoEL-2; PoeP; PoFS; PoIE; PoLF; PoPl; PoPo; PoRA; PoSa; PTK; ReEn; ReIE; SeCePo; SeCeV; ShBV-4; SiCE; Sonn; StP; TDP; TOP; TreFT; TrGrPo; ViBoPo; WHA; YAT
(To His Love.) GTBS; GTBS-D; GTBS-P; GTBS-W; GTSE; GTSL; PoMa; WePo
XIX. "Devouring Time, blunt thou the lion's paw." AtBAP; AWP; BWP; CBEP; ChTr; DiPo; EG; EP; GTBS-W; InPo; OBSC; PoEL-2; ReIE; SiCE; Sonn; TrGrPo; WHA
(Devouring Time.) MeWo
XX. "Woman's face, with Nature's own hand painted, A." CBEP; ErPo; InvP; MasP; ReEn
XXI. "So is it not with me as with that Muse." InvP; OBSC; ReEn; SiCE
XXII. "My glass shall not persuade me I am old." EG; OBSC; Sonn
XXIII. "As an unperfect actor on the stage." BEL; EnL; HBV; InvP; OAEP; ReEn; SiCE; Sonn
XXV. "Let those who are in favour with their stars." CBEP; EnL; EnLi-1; OBSC; ReIE; SiCE; Sonn; WoL
XXVI. "Lord of my love, to whom in vassalage." PoFS; ReEn

XXVII. "Weary with toil, I haste me to my bed." DiPo; OBSC; PoFS; ReEn; SiCE
XXVIII. "How can I then return in happy plight." OBSC
XXIX. "When, in disgrace with fortune and men's eyes." AnFE; AtBAP; ATP; AWP; BEL; BoLiVe; BoLP; BWP; CBEP; CBV; CoBE; CTC; DiPo; ElL; EnL; EnLi-1; EnLit; ExPo; FaBoEn; FaBV; HBV; ILP; InP; InPo; InvP; JAWP; LiTB; LiTG; LiTL; LoBV; MaPo; MasP; MemP; NoP; OAEP; OBEV; OBSC; OuHeWo; PAn; PG; Po; PoAn; PoE; PoEL-2; PoFS; PoIE; PoPl; PoPo; PoRA; PoSa; ReEn; ReIE; SeCeV; SiCE; Sonn; TIHL; TOP; TreF; TrGrPo; TRV; ViBoPo; WBP; WHA
(Consolation, A.) GTBS; GTBS-D; GTBS-P; GTBS-W; GTSE; GTSL; PoMa
(For Thy Sweet Love.) MaRV
(Fortune and Men's Eyes.) MeWo
XXX. "When to the sessions of sweet silent thought." AnFE; ATP; BEL; CABA; CaFP; CBEP; CBV; CoBE; CTC; DiPo; EG; ElL; EnL; EnLi-1; EnLit; EnRePo; EP; ExPo; FaBoEn; FaBV; GTBS-W; HBV; ILP; InPo; JAWP; LiTB; LiTG; LoBV; MaPo; MasP; MemP; NeHB; NoP; OAEP; OBEV; OBSC; OuHeWo; PAn; PIA; PoE; PoEL-2; PoFS; PoIE; PoLF; PoPo; PoRA; PTK; ReEn; ReIE; SeCeV; ShBV-4; SiCE; Sonn; TDP; TOP; TreFS; TrGrPo; ViBoPo; WBP; WHA; WoL
(Memory.) GTSL
(Remembrance.) FaFP; GTBS; GTBS-D; GTBS-P; GTSE; TRV
(Sessions of Sweet Silent Thought.) BoLiVe
XXXI. "Thy bosom is endeared with all hearts." OBEV; OBSC; PoEL-2
XXXII. "If thou survive my well-contented day." CBEP; BEL; BoLiVe; ElL; EnL; EnLit; HBV; LiTL; ML; OBSC; PP; SiCE; TOP
(Post Mortem.) GTBS; GTBS-D; GTBS-P; GTBS-W; GTSE; GTSL
XXXIII. "Full many a glorious morning have I seen." ATP; AWP; BEL; BoLiVe; BWP; CBEP; CoBE; EG; ElL; EnL; EnLi-1; FaBoEn; FaFP; HBV; ILP; InPo; JAWP; LiTB; LiTG; LoBV; NoP; OAEP; OBSC; OtMeF; OuHeWo; PoRA; ReEn; ReIE; SeCePo; SeCeV; SiCE; Sonn; TOP; TreFS; TrGrPo; UnPo (1st ed.); ViBoPo; WBP
XXXIV. "Why didst thou promise such a beauteous day." CBEP; OBSC; PoE
XXXV. "No more be grieved at that which thou hast done." CABA; CBEP; NoP; UnPo
XXXVI. "Let me confess that we two must be twain." CBEP; OAEP
XXXVIII. "How can my Muse want subject to invent." EnLit; ReEn; Sonn
XL. "Take all my loves, my love, yea, take them all." CBEP; InvP; OBSC
XLI. "Those pretty wrongs that liberty commits." CBEP; InvP; PoeP; ReEn
XLII. "That thou hast her, it is not all my grief." CBEP; InvP
XLIII. "When most I wink, then do mine eyes best see." CBEP
XLIV. "If the dull substance of my flesh were thought." CBEP; PoeP; Sonn
XLIX. "Against that time, if ever that time come." BWP; Sonn
L. "How heavy do I journey on the way." ReEn; ReIE; SiCE
LI. "Thus can my love excuse the slow offense." PoFS
LII. "So am I as the rich, whose blessed key." OBSC
LIII. "What is your substance, whereof are you made." AtBAP; BWP; CTC; ElL; EnRePo; FaFP; GTBS-W; LiTB; LiTG; LiTL; MasP; OAEP; OBEV; OBSC; ViBoPo
LIV. "O, how much more doth beauty beauteous seem." AWP; ElL; EnLi-1 (1949 ed.); JAWP; OBEV; OBSC; PoeP; ReEn; ReIE; SiCE; TOP; ViBoPo; WBP
(Rose Looks Fair, The.) LiTG
LV. "Not marble, nor the gilded monuments." AnEnPo; AnFE; ATP; AWP; BEL; BWP; CABA; CBEP; CoBE; CTC; DiPo; EG; EnL; EnLi-1; EnLit; EnRePo; EP; ExPo; FaBoEn; FaFP; ForPo; GTBS-W; ILP; InPo; JAWP; LiTB; LiTG; LiTL; LoBV; MaPo (1969 ed.); MasP; NoP; OAEP; OBSC; OuHeWo; PAn; PoE; PoEL-2; PoeP; PoPo; PoRA; PoSa; PP; ReEn; ReIE; SeCeV; SiCE; Sonn; TDP; TOP; TrGrPo; VaPo; ViBoPo; WBP
(After Horace.) CLwM
LVI. "Sweet love, renew thy force; be it not said." CBEP; LO; PoLF; UnPo (1st ed.)
LVII. "Being your slave, what should I do but tend." BoLP; CLwM; EG; LiTL; OBEV; PoEL-2; ViBoPo; WoL
(Absence.) GTBS; GTBS-D; GTBS-P; GTBS-W; GTSE; GTSL
LIX. "If there be nothing new, but that which is." FaBoEn; ReEn
LX. "Like as the waves make towards the pebbled shore." AnFE; ATP; BEL; BoLiVe; BWP; CBEP; ChTr; CoBE; ElL; EnL; EnLi-1; EnLit; EnRePo; ExPo; FaBoEn; FaFP; HBV; LiTB; LiTL; LoBV; OBSC; Po; PoRA; ReEn; ReIE; SeCeV; ShBV-4; SiCE; Sonn; UnPo; ViBoPo
(Revolutions.) GTBS; GTBS-D; GTBS-P; GTBS-W; GTSE; GTSL
LXI. "Is it thy will thy image should keep open." LO; PoEL-2
LXII. "Sin of self-love [*or* Sinne of selfe-love] possesseth all mine eye [*or* al mine eie]." EnRePo; EP; PoEL-2
LXIII. "Against my love shall be, as I am now." OBSC; ReEn; SiCE
LXIV. "When I have seen by Time's fell hand defaced." AWP; BEL; BWP; CABA; CLwM; ElL; EnL; EnLi-1 (1949 ed.); EnLit; EnLoPo; EnRePo; EP; FaFP; ILP; InP; InPo; JAWP; LiTB; LiTL; LO; MCCG; NoP; OBSC; OuHeWo; PoAn; PoeP; PoFS; PoIE; PoPo; PoRA; ReEn; ReIE; SeCeV; SiCE; Sonn; TOP; ViBoPo; WBP
(Time and Love, 1.) GTBS; GTBS-D; GTBS-P; GTBS-W; GTSE; GTSL
LXV. "Since brass, nor stone, nor earth, nor boundless sea." AtBAP; AWP; BEL; BoLiVe; BWP; CABA; CLwM; DiPo; EnLi-1 (1949 ed.); EnRePo; FaFP; FiP; JAWP; LiTB; LiTL; MaPo; MasP; MCCG; MemP; NoP; OuHeWo; PoeP; PoFS; PoIE; PoRA; SeCeV; SiCE; Sonn; TOP; UnPo (1st ed.); WBP
(Time and Love, 2.) GTBS; GTBS-D; GTBS-P; GTBS-W; GTSE; GTSL
LXVI. "Tired with all these, for restful death I cry." AnFE; AWP; BEL; BoLiVe; CBEP; CLwM; CTC; EnL; EnLi-1; ExPo; FaFP; InPo; JAWP; LiTB; LiTG; MemP; MyFE; OBSC; PAn; PoIE; ReEn; SeCeV; SiCE; Sonn; TOP; TrGrPo; ViBoPo; WBP; WHA
("Tyr'd with all these for restfull death I cry.") PoEL-2
(World's Way, The.) GTBS; GTBS-D; GTBS-P; GTBS-W; GTSE; GTSL
LXVII. "Ah, wherefore with infection should he live." SiCE
LXVIII. "Thus is his cheek the map of days outworn." OBSC; PoeP; ReIE; UnPo (1st ed.)
LXIX. "Those parts of thee that the world's eye doth view." CBEP
LXXI. "No longer mourn for me when I am dead." AWP; BEL;BoLiVe;CBEP;CoBE;ElL;EnL;EnLi-1;EnLit;EnRePo; EP; HBV; ILP; InPo; JAWP; LiTB; LO; NoP; OAEP; OBSC; OuHeWo; PIA; PoE; PoIE; PoRA; PTK; ReEn; ReIE; SeCeV; SiCE; Sonn; TOP; TreFT; TrGrPo; ViBoPo; WBP; WHA
(Triumph of Death, The.) GTBS; GTBS-D; GTBS-P; GTBS-W; GTSE; GTSL
LXXII. "O! lest the world should task you to recite."
"O, lest your true love may seem false in this," *sel.* LO
LXXIII. "That time of year thou may'st in me behold." AnFE; ATP (1935 ed.); AWP; BEL; BoLiVe; BWP; CABA; CaFP; CBEP; CBV; ChTr; CLwM; CoBE; CTC; DiPo; EG; ElL; EnL; EnLi-1; EnLit; EnLoPo; EnRePo; EP; ExPo; FaBoEn; FaBV; FiP; ForPo; FosPo; GTBS; GTBS-D; GTBS-P; GTBS-W; GTSE; GTSL; HBV; HoPM; ILP; InPo; InvP; JAWP; LiTB; LoBV; MaPo; MasP; NoP; OAEP; OBEV; OBSC; OHFP (1958 ed.); OuHeWo; PAn; PG (1955 ed.); PoAn; PoE; PoeP; PoEL-2; PoFS; PoIE; PoMa; PoPo; PoRA; PoSa; QFR; ReEn; ReIE; SeCeV; SiCE; Sonn; StP; TrGrPo; VaPo; ViBoPo; WBP
(Where Late the Sweet Birds Sang.) LiTG
LXXIV. "But be contented: when that fell arrest." CBEP; OBSC; PoeP; Sonn
LXXV. "So are you to my thoughts as food to life." PoEL-2
LXXVI. "Why is my verse so barren of new pride." CLwM; EnLi-1 (1949 ed.); InvP; PP; ReEn; ReIE; SiCE
LXXVII. "Thy glass will show thee how thy beauties wear." EnRePo; QFR
LXXIX. "Whilst I alone did call upon thy aid." Sonn
LXXX. "Oh how I faint when I of you do write." ReEn; SiCE
LXXXI. "Or I shall live your epitaph to make." OAEP; OBSC
LXXXII. "I grant thou wert not married to my Muse." CBEP

Sonnets (continued)
LXXXV. "My tongue-tied Muse in manners holds her still." Sonn
LXXXVI. "Was it the proud full sail of his great verse." CBEP; InvP; ML; OAEP; ReEn; ReIE; SiCE; Sonn
LXXXVII. "Farewell! thou art too dear for my possessing." AnFE; BoLiVe; BWP; CLwM; CoBE; EIL; GTBS; GTBS-D; GTBS-P; GTBS-W; GTSE; GTSL; InvP; LiTB; LiTG; MasP; MeWo; OAEP; OBEV; OBSC; PG (1955 ed.); PoAn; PoEL-2; PoeP; PoFS; QFR; ReIE; SiCE; Sonn; StP; TOP; TrGrPo; ViBoPo
LXXXIX. "Say that thou didst forsake me for some fault." CLwM; OAEP; SiCE
XC. "Then hate me when thou wilt; if ever, now." ATP; AWP; CLwM; EIL; JAWP; LO; MaPo; OBEV; OBSC; PG; PoEL-2; ReIE; TOP; WBP; WHA; WoL
XCI. "Some glory in their birth, some in their skill." CBEP
XCIII. "So shall I live, supposing thou art true." InvP; MasP
XCIV. "They that have power to hurt and will do none." AnFE; BoLiVe; BWP; CABA; CBEP; EIL; ExPo; FaBoEn; FosPo; LiTB; LiTG; MaPo; MasP; MemP; NoP; OBEV; PG (1955 ed.); PoEL-2; PoeP; PoG; PoIE; PoSa; ReEn; Sonn; TrGrPo; ViBoPo
(Life without Passion, The.) GTBS; GTBS-D; GTBS-P; GTBS-W; GTSE; GTSL
XCV. "How sweet and lovely dost thou make the shame." CBEP; EP; MasP; PoeP; ReEn; TrGrPo
XCVII. "How like a winter hath my absence been." ATP; AWP; BEL; CABA; CBEP; CLwM; DiPo; EIL; EnLi-1; EnLoPo; EnRePo; FaBoEn; GTBS; GTBS-D; GTBS-P; GTBS-W; GTSE; GTSL; JAWP; LiTG; MeWo; NoP; OBEV; OBSC; PAn; PoeP; PoFS; PoRA; ReIE; Sonn; TOP; TrGrPo; VaPo; WBP
XCVIII. "From you I have been absent in the spring." AWP; BEL; BoC; BWP; ChTr; DiPo; EG; EIL; EnLi-1; InPo; JAWP; LiTB; LiTG; NoP; OBEV; OBSC; PoAn; ReEn; ReIE; SiCE; TOP; ViBoPo; WBP
XCIX. "Forward violet thus did I chide, The." EG; EnLi-1; OAEP; OBSC
C. "Where art thou, Muse, that thou forget'st so long." OBSC
CI. "O truant Muse, what shall be thy amends." Sonn
CII. "My love is strengthen'd, though more weak in seeming." AWP; CLwM; EIL; LiTG; LiTL; OAEP; OBEV; OBSC; SiCE; TOP; ViBoPo
CIII. "Alack! what poverty my Muse brings forth." CLwM
CIV. "To me fair friend, you never can be old." BEL; BWP; EG; EIL; EnLi-1 (1949 ed.); EnLit; EnRePo; FaBoEn; GTBS; GTBS-D; GTBS-P; GTBS-W; GTSE; GTSL; HBV; InP; MaPo (1969 ed.); OAEP; OBEV; OBSC; PoIE; ReEn; ReIE; SiCE; TOP; ViBoPo
(You Never Can Be Old.) LiTL
CVI. "When in the chronicle of wasted time." AnFE; AWP; BEL; BoLiVe; CBEP; CBV; CLwM; CoBE; CTC; DiPo; EG; EIL; EnL; EnLi-1; EnLit; EnLoPo; EnRePo; ExPo; FaBoCh; FaBoEn; FaBV; FiP; HBV; InPo; JAWP; LiTB; LiTG; LiTL; LoBV; LoGBV; MaPo; MasP; MCCG; NoP; OAEP; OBEV; OBSC; OuHeWo; PAn; PIA; Po; PoE; PoeP; PoFS; PoIE; PoPo; PoRA; ReEn; ReIE; SeCeV; ShBV-3; SiCE; Sonn; StP; TOP; TreFT; TrGrPo; ViBoPo; WBP; WHA
(Her Beauty.) GTSL
(To His Love.) GTBS; GTBS-D; GTBS-P; GTBS-W; GTSE
CVII. "Not mine own fears, nor the prophetic soul." AWP; CABA; CBEP; CTC; DiPo; EG; EnLi-1; FiP; InPo; JAWP; LiTB; LoBV; MaPo; MasP; NoP; OAEP; OBSC; OuHeWo; PoFr; PoIE; ReEn; ReIE; SeCeV; SiCE; TOP; WBP
(I'll Live in This Poor Rime.) LiTG
CIX. "O! never say that I was false of heart." BEL; CLwM; EIL; HBV; LiTG; LiTL; LO; OBEV; OBSC; SiCE; WoL
(Unchangeable, The.) GTBS; GTBS-D; GTBS-P; GTBS-W; GTSE; GTSL
CX. "Alas, 'tis true I have gone here and there." CBEP; EnLi-1 (1949 ed.); EP; MaPo; OAEP; OBSC; PoE; ReEn; ReIE; SiCE; ViBoPo
CXI. "O, for my sake do you with fortune chide." SiCE; TOP
CXV. "Those lines that I before have writ do lie." SiCE
CXVI. "Let me not to the marriage of true minds." AnFE; ATP; AWP; BEL; BoC; BoPe; CABA; CaFP; CBEP; CBV; CLwM; CoBE; DiPo; EG; EIL; EnL; EnLi-1; EnLit; EnLoPo; EnRePo; EP; ExPo; FaBoEn; FaBV; FaFP; FosPo; HBV; ILP; InPo; InvP; JAWP; LiTB; LiTG; LO; LoBV; MaPo; MasP; MCCG; NoP; OAEP; OBEV; OBSC; OnP; OuHeWo; PAn; PG; PIA; Po; PoE; PoEL-2; PoeP; PoIE; PoPl; PoPo; PoRA; PoSa; ReEn; ReIE; SeCePo; SeCeV; ShBV-4; SiCE; Sonn; TOP; TrGrPo; TRV; UnPo; ViBoPo; WBP; WePo; WHA
(Love's Not Time's Fool.) LiTL; TreF
(Marriage of True Minds, The.) AnEnPo; BoLiVe; MeWo
(True Love.) BBV; GBV; GoBC; GTBS; GTBS-D; GTBS-P; GTBS-W; GTSE; GTSL; MaRV
CXVIII. "Like as, to make our appetites more keen." CABA; CBEP; UnPo (1st ed.)
CXIX. "What potions have I drunk of Siren tears." CBEP; ReIE; WHA
CXX. "That you were once unkind befriends me now." InvP
CXXI. "'Tis better to be vile than vile esteemed." BWP; CBEP; InvP; MaPo; PAn; PoEL-2; Sonn
CXXIII. "No, Time, thou shalt not boast that I do change." BoLiVe; OAEP; OBSC; SiCE; Sonn; TrGrPo
CXXVI. "O thou, my lovely boy, who in thy power." MyFE; ReIE; Sonn
CXXVII. "In the old age black was not counted fair." CBEP; DiPo; ReIE; Sonn
CXXVIII. "How oft, when thou, my music, music play'st." EIL; EnLit; EnLi-1 (1949 ed.); ILP; MemP; ReEn; ReIE
CXXIX. "Expense [*or* Expence] of spirit in a waste of shame, The." AWP; BWP; CABA; CaFP; CBEP; CBV; CoBE; DiPo; EnL; EnRePo; EP; ErPo; ExPo; FaBoEn; ForPo; FosPo; GTBS-W; InPo; JAWP; LiTB; LiTG; LiTL; LO; LoBV; MaPo; MasP; NoP; OBEV; OBSC; OtMeF; PAn; PoAn; PoE; PoEL-2; PoeP; PoFS; PoIE; QFR; ReEn; ReIE; SeCePo; SeCeV; ShBV-4; Sonn; StP; TOP; TrGrPo; UnPo (3d ed.); VaPo; ViBoPo; WBP
(Lust.) AnEnPo
CXXX. "My mistress' eyes are nothing like the sun." ATP; AWP; BEL; BoLP; CABA; CaFP; CBEP; CBV; CoBE; DiPo; EnL; EnLi-1 (1949 ed.); EnLit; ExPo; HBV; HoPM; ILP; InvP; JAWP; LiTB; LiTL; MaPo (1969 ed.); NoP; OtMeF; PAn; PIA; PoAn; PoE; PoeP; PoIE; PP; ReEn; ReIE; SeCeV; SiCE; Sonn; StP; TOP; WBP
CXXXII. "Thine eyes I love, and they, as pitying me." OAEP; OBSC; SiCE
CXXXIII. "Beshrew that heart that makes my heart to groan." CBEP; InvP; ReIE
CXXXIV. "So, now I have confessed that he is thine." CBEP; InvP
CXXXV. "Whoever hath her wish thou hast thy Will." PAn; ReEn
CXXXVI. "If thy soul check thee that I come so near." MaPo (1969 ed.)
CXXXVIII. "When my love swears that she is made of truth." AWP; CABA; InPo; JAWP; MeWo; NoP; OAEP; PoEL-2; PoeP; ReEn; TrGrPo; ViBoPo; WBP
(When My Love Swears.) MeWo
CXXXIX. "O, call not me to justify the wrong." ReIE
CXLI. "In faith, I do not love thee with mine eyes." CBEP; MaPo; PoEL-2; TrGrPo
CXLIII. "Lo, as a careful housewife runs to catch." CBEP; OAEP; ReEn
CXLIV. "Two loves I have of comfort and despair." CABA; CBEP; InvP; LoBV; OAEP; PoEL-2; ReEn; ReIE; Sonn
CXLV. "Those lips that Love's own hand did make." Sonn
CXLVI. "Poor soul, the centre [*or* center] of my sinful earth." AtBAP; ATP; AWP; BEL; BoLiVe; BWP; CABA; CaFP; CAW; CBEP; CBV; CoBE; DiPo; EaLo; EIL; EnL; EnLi-1; EnRePo; ExPo; FaBoEn; ForPo; HBV; InPo; JAWP; LiTB; LiTG; LO; MaPo; MasP; MemP; MyFE; NoP; OBEV; OBSC; OxBoCh; PAn; PIA; PoAn; PoEL-2; PoeP; PoIE; ReEn; ReIE; SeCeV; SiCE; Sonn; StP; TOP; TrGrPo; UnPo (1st ed.); ViBoPo; WBP; WHA
(Death of Death, The.) TreFS
(Outer and the Inner Man, The.) MaRV
(Soul and Body.) GoBC; GTBS; GTBS-D; GTBS-P; GTBS-W; GTSE; GTSL
CXLVII. "My love is as a fever, longing still." CBEP; DiPo; HoPM; LO; NoP; PoEL-2; ReEn; ReIE
CXLVIII. "O me! what eyes hath Love put in my head."
(Blind Love.) GTBS; GTBS-D; GTBS-P; GTBS-W; GTSE; GTSL
CLI. "Love is too young to know what conscience is." CBEP; PoEL-2; ReEn
CLII. "In loving thee thou know'st I am forsworn." ReIE; Sonn
CLIII. "Cupid laid by his brand and fell asleep." Sonn

CLIV. "Little Love-god, lying once asleep, The." ReIE; Sonn
Sonnets. Spenser. *See* Amoretti.
Sonnets. Dylan Thomas. *See* Altarwise by Owl-Light.
Sonnets, *sels.* Frederick Goddard Tuckerman.
"All men,—the preacher saith,—whate'er or whence," I, xvii. PoIE
"And change with hurried hand has swept these scenes," II, xviii. NoP; QFR
"And faces, forms and phantoms, numbered not," II, xix. QFR
"And me my winter's task is drawing over," V, xiv. QFR
"And she, her beauty never made her cold," I, xv. AmePo
"And so the day drops by; the horizon draws," I, v. AmePo; AnNE; PoIE
"As Eponina brought, to move the king," II, xxxvii. AmePo
"As one who walks and weeps by alien brine," I, xiii. AmePo
"Breeze is sharp, the sky is hard and blue, The," II, xiv. AP
"But unto him came swift calamity," II, ix. AP
"By this low fire I often sit to woo," I, xxv. AP; Sonn
"Companions were we in the grove and glen!" II, viii. AP
"Even as a lover, dreaming, unaware," II, xiii. AP
"For Nature daily through her grand design," I, xxvi. AP; MAmP
"Gertrude and Gulielma, sister-twins," II, xv. AP; MAmP; QFR
"His heart was in his garden; but his brain," II, vii. AP
"How most unworthy, echoing in mine ears," II, xii. AP
"How oft in schoolboy-days, from the school's sway," II, xxix. MAmP; Sonn
"Last night I dreamed we parted once again," II, xxi. MAmP
"Morning comes, The; not slow, with reddening gold," I, xxii. AmePo; AP
"My Anna! though thine earthly steps are done," II, xxxiv. AP
"My Anna! When for her my head was bowed," II, xxxi. AP
"Nor idle all, though naught he sees in thine," II, ii. MAmP
"Nor looks that backward life so bare to me," I, iv. PoIE
"Not proud of station, nor in worldly pelf," I, xiv. AmePo
"Not the round natural world, not the deep mind," I, xxviii. AmePo; NoP
"Oh for the face and footstep!—Woods and shores!" II, xxxii. AP
"O hard endeavor, to blend in with these," II, xx. QFR
"One still dark night, I sat alone and wrote," II, xxxiii. AmePo; AP
"Perhaps a dream; yet surely truth has beamed," I, xxiv. AP; MAmP
"Roll on, sad world! Not Mercury or Mars," II, xvii. AnNE; AP; QFR; TreFS
"Sometimes, when winding slow by brook and bower," I, i. AnNE; MAmP; PoIE
"Still craves the spirit: never Nature solves," I, xx. MAmP NoP
"Still pressing through these weeping solitudes," II, xi. AmePo; AP
"Tall stately plants with spikes and forks of gold," I, xii. AnNE
"That boy, the farmer said, with hazel wand," II, i. MAmP
"Thy baby, too, the child that was to be," II, x. AP
"Under the mountain, as when first I knew," II, xvi. AmePo; AP; MAmP; NoP; QFR
"Upper chamber in a darkened house, An," I, x. AmePo; AnNE; MAmP; NoP
"Yet even mid merry boyhood's tricks and scapes," II, xxx. MAmP
"Yet vain, perhaps, the fruits our care applaud," I, xix. AnNE
"Yet wear we on; the deep light disallowed," I, ix. AmePo
Sonnets, *sels.* Thomas Warton, the Younger.
Sonnet: On King Arthur's Round Table at Winchester, VIII. EiPP
(On King Arthur's Round Table.) Sonn
Sonnet: To the River Lodon [*or* Loddon], IX. CEP; OBEC; ViBoPo
(To the River Lodon.) CoBE; Sonn
Sonnet: Written after Seeing Wilton-House, V. OBEC
Sonnet: Written at Stonehenge, IV. CEP; EiPP
(Written at Stonehenge.) Sonn
Sonnet: Written in a Blank Leaf of Dugdale's "Monasticon," III. EiPP; OBEC; SeCePo
(Written in a Blank Leaf of Dugdale's "Monasticon.") Sonn
To Mr. Gray, VI. Sonn
Written at Winslade, in Hampshire, I. Sonn
Sonnets; a Sequence on Profane Love, *sels.* George Henry Boker. AmePo
"Ah! could I grow in some remote degree."
"I am ashamed through this thick husk of clay."
"I cannot tell what charms my lady finds."
"I know that every note and chord of woe."
"I strive to live my life in whitest truth."
"If she should give me all I ask of her."
"If thou art sinful, there are thousands then."
"My darling, now the slumber of the night."
"My lady's senses are so pure and fine."
"Satyr nature riots in my blood, The."
"Some one within my hearing said tonight."
"This fellow calls me sordid, that one poor."
"Thus in her absence is my fancy cool."
"When I look back upon my early days."
"When to his class the surgeon's skilful blade."
"White as this paper was my lady's mind."
Sonnets—Actualities, *sels.* E. E. Cummings.
"I like my body when it is with your." ErPo; LiTG; Sonn; UnTE
"Notice the convulsed orange inch of moon." AnAmPo
Sonnets—Ad Innuptam (I-VII). Patrick Moloney. BoAu
Sonnets after the Italian. Richard Watson Gilder. HBV
"I know not if I love her overmuch."
"I like her gentle hand that sometimes strays."
Sonnets are full of love, and this my tome. To My First Love, My Mother. Christina Rossetti. OHIP
Sonnets at Christmas (I-II). Allen Tate. AmP; AP; GTBS-W; LiTA; LiTM; NePA; OxBA; ReMP; Sonn
"Ah, Christ I love you rings to the wild sky," I. PoDB; PoNe (1970 ed.)
Sonnets Attempted in the Manner of Contemporary Writers. Samuel Taylor Coleridge. Sonn
House That Jack Built, The, *sel.* BOHV
(On a Ruined House in a Romantic Country.) Par
Sonnets for a Dying Man, *sels.* Burns Singer. NePoEA-2
"Christ comes to mind and comes across the mind," XXXIX.
"I promise you by the harsh funeral," XLVIII.
"Old man dozed, The. The hospital quietened," XV.
"Those flaming Christians with their hygienic rose," XXXIII.
"To see the petrel cropping in the farmyard," XXX.
Sonnets from a Sequence, *sels.* Shirley Barker. AnAmPo
"Thin rain seeps along the apple boughs, A," XXI.
"Down the black highway where no whisper stirs," XXIV.
Sonnets from Greece, *sels.* Trumbull Stickney.
Mt. Lykaion. AmLP; AnAmPo; AnFE; APA; CoAnAm; MoVE; NePA; OxBA; Sonn; TrGrPo
(Alone on Lykaion.) MAP; MoAmPo (1942 ed.)
Near Helikon. AnFE; CoAnAm; LiTA; TwAmPo
Sonnets from "One Person." Elinor Wylie. *See* One Person.
Sonnets from the Portuguese (*Complete,* I-XLIV). Elizabeth Barrett Browning. PoVP
Sels.
"And yet, because thou overcomest so," XVI. OAEP; PoVP; ViPo
"Because thou hast the power and own'st the grace," XXXIX. PoVP; VA
"Belovèd, my Belovèd, when I think," XX. CoBE; MaRV; OAEP; PoVP; Sonn; TOP; VA; ViPo
"Beloved, thou hast brought me many flowers," XLIV. ILP; OAEP; OBNC; PoVP; ViPo
"Can it be right to give what I can give?" IX. CTC; PoVP; Sonn; VA
"Face of all the world is changed, I think, The," VII. ATP; BEL; CoBE; CTC; EnLi-2; EnLit; EPN; HBV; OAEP; OuHeWo; PoVP; TOP; ViPo
"First time he kissed me, he but only kissed," XXXVIII. BLPA; CTC; FaBoBe; HBV; NeHB; PoPl; PoVP; VA; ViBoPo; ViPo
"First time that the sun rose on thine oath, The," XXXII. PoVP; ViBoPo; ViPo
"Go from me. Yet I feel that I shall stand," VI. DiPo; EPN; GBV; GTSL; HBV; MemP; OBEV; OBVV; PG (1955 ed.); PoVP; SoP; TreFS; TrGrPo; VA; ViBoPo; ViPo
(Nevermore Alone.) MaRV
"How do I love thee? let me count the ways," XLIII. AnFE;

Sonnets (continued)
ATP; BBV (1951 ed.); BEL; BoLP; CoBE; CTC; EnLi-2; EnLit; EPN; FaBoBe; FaBV; FaFP; FaPL; GTBS; GTBS-W; GTSL; HBV; HoPM; ILP; InP; LiTB; LiTG; LiTL; LO; MaRV; MeWo; OAEP; OQP; OTD; OuHeWo; PG; Po; PoFS; PoLF; PoMa; PoPl; PoPo; PoRA; PoRL; PoToHe (new ed.); PoVP; PTK; ShBV-4; Sonn; SoP; TIHL; TreF; TrGrPo; TRV; UnPo; Va; ViBoPo; ViPo; WHA; YAT; YT
(Wife to a Husband, A.) BoC
"I lift my heavy heart up solemnly," V. PoVP; TOP; VA; ViPo
"I lived with visions for my company," XXVI. BEL; CoBE; EnLi-2; EnLit; OAEP; PoVP; TOP; VA; ViPo
"I never gave a lock of hair away," XVIII. HBV; PoVP; VA
"I thank all who have loved me in their hearts," XLI. CoBE; PoVP; VA; ViPo
"I think of thee!—my thoughts to twine and bud," XXIX. EPN; PoVP
"I thought once how Theocritus had sung," I. AnFE; BEL; CoBE; EnLi-2; EnLit; EPN; GTBS; GTBS-D; GTSL; HBV; OAEP; OBEV; OBNC; OuHeWo; PoE; PoVP; TOP; TreFT; ViBoPo; ViPo
"If I leave all for thee, wilt thou exchange," XXXV. BEL; EnLi-2; EnLit; PoVP; Sonn; TOP; VA; ViBoPo; ViPo
"If thou must love me, let it be for naught," XIV. AnFE; ATP (1935 ed.); BEL; BoLP; CoBE; CTC; EnLi-2; EnLit; EPN; FaFP; GTBS; GTBS-W; GTSE; GTSL; HBV; LiTG; LiTL; MaRV; MemP; MeWo; OBEV; OBNC; OBVV; PG; PoPo; PoVP; Sonn; TOP; TreFS; TrGrPo; ViBoPo; ViPo; WHA; YAT
(For Love's Sake Only.) PoToHe (new ed.)
"Indeed this very love which is my boast," XII. HBV; PoVP
"Is it indeed so? If I lay here dead," XXIII. PoVP; VA
"My letters! all dead paper, mute and white!" XXVIII. CoBE; EnLi-2; EnLit; HBV; PoVP; ViBoPo; ViPo
"My poet, thou canst touch on all the notes," XVII. HBV; PoVP; WHA
"Say over again, and yet once over again," XXI. HBV; PoVP; ViPo
"Thou hast thy calling to some palace floor," IV. EnLi-2; PoVP; Sonn; VA
"Unlike are we, unlike, O princely Heart," III. AnFE; EnLi-2; GTSL; HBV; OAEP; OBEV; OBVV; PoVP; TrGrPo; ViPo
"What can I give thee back, O liberal," VIII. GTBS; GTSL; HBV; OBVV; PoVP; ViPo
"When our two souls stand up erect and strong," XXII. AnFE; BEL; EnLi-2; EnLit; EPN; GTSE; GTSL; HBV; LiTL; MeWo; OAEP; OBEV; PoVP; TreFT; TrGrPo; ViBoPo; ViPo; WHA
"Yet, love, mere love, is beautiful indeed," X. CTC; GTBS; HBV; PoVP
Sonnets from the Series Relating to Edgar Allan Poe, *sels.* Sarah Helen Whitman.
"If thy sad heart, pining for human love," VI. AA
"Oft since thine earthly eyes have closed on mine," III. AA
"On our earthly pathway bloomed no hope," V. AA
(Sonnet to Edgar Allan Poe.) AnAmPo
"When first I looked into thy glorious eyes," II. AA
(To Edgar Allan Poe.) DD
Sonnets in Quaker Language. Hildegarde Flanner. NP
Sonnets of a Portrait Painter, *sels.* Arthur Davison Ficke.
"Across the shaken bastions of the year," XLVII. AnAmPo
April Moment. HBMV
Her Pedigree, IX. HBMV
I Am in Love with High Far-seeing Places, XIII. NP; OQP
(View from Heights.) HBMV
"I have seen beauty where light stabs the hills," XVI. AnAmPo
"Last night I kissed you with a brutal might," XXXVII. AnAmPo
"Out of the dusk into whose gloom you went," L. AnAmPo
"So you go back—because they bid you come," XXXVI. AnAmPo
Sonnet: "There are strange shadows fostered of the moon," XLV. MAP
Spring Landscape, XII. HBMV
Summons, XIV. HBMV
Troubadours, X. HBMV
Sonnets of Christian Passions; or, Sundry Christian Passions, *sels.* Henry Lok.
"It is not, Lord, the sound of many words." SiCE; Sonn; TuPP
"Words may well want, both ink and paper fail." ReEn; SiCE; Sonn; TuPP
Sonnets of the Empire, *sels.* Archibald T. Strong.
Australia, 1905. BoAu
Australia, 1914. BoAu
Australia to England. BoAu; PoFr
Dawn at Liverpool. BoAu
Gloriana's England. BoAu
Hawke. BoAu
Nelson. BoAu
Oxford. BoAu
Sonnets of the Months; or, Of the Months. Folgore da San Gemignano, *tr. fr. Italian by* Dante Gabriel Rossetti. AWP
Sels.
August. CTC
September. SD
Sonnets on English Dramatic Poets (1590-1650), *sels.* Swinburne.
Beaumont and Fletcher, IV. PoVP
Ben Jonson, III. BEL; PoVP; Sonn
Christopher Marlowe, I. BEL; PoVP; Sonn; TOP; TrGrPo
James Shirley, XIV. Sonn
John Marston, XII. Sonn
John Webster, VII. InvP; Sonn
Many, The, XIX. PoVP
William Shakespeare. PoVP; TrGrPo
Sonnets on the Divina Commedia. Longfellow. *See* Divina Commedia.
Sonnets on the Sea's Voice. George Sterling. EtS
Sonnets on the Seasons, *sel.* Hartley Coleridge.
November, XII. LoBV; OBRV; PeER; PoRL
Sonnets pour Hélène, *sels.* Pierre de Ronsard, *tr. fr. French by* Humbert Wolfe.
"Hate me, or love, my Helen, as you list."
(Four Sonnets to Helen, 2.) LiTW
"In these long winter nights when moon doth steer."
(Four Sonnets to Helen, 3.) LiTW
Of His Lady's Old Age, *tr. by* Andrew Lang. AWP; CTC; JAWP; WBP
(To Helen.) OuHeWo
"Tossed by the seas of love how have I striven."
(Four sonnets to Helen, 1.) LiTW
"When you are old, at evening candle-lit."
(Four Sonnets to Helen, 4.) LiTW
"When you are very old, at evening," *tr. by* Andrew Lang. AWP; CTC; JAWP; OuHeWo; WBP
Sonnets—Realities, *sels.* E. E. Cummings.
"Cambridge ladies who live in furnished souls, The." AmPP (5th ed.); AnAmPo; CBEP; CoBA; MoPW; MoVE; NoP; OxBA; PoSa; PPON; Sonn; ViBoPo (1958 ed.)
"My girl's tall with hard long eyes." UnTE
Sonnets Relating to Edgar Allan Poe. Sarah Helen Whitman. *See* Sonnets from the Series Relating to Edgar Allan Poe.
Sonnets to Aurelia, *sels.* Robert Nichols. OBMV
"But piteous things we are—when I am gone," III.
"Come, let us sigh a requiem over love, IV.
"Though to your life apparent stain attach," II.
"When the proud World does most my world despise," I.
Sonnets to Delia. Samuel Daniel. *See* To Delia.
Sonnets to "Idea." Michael Drayton. *See* Idea.
Sonnets to Laura, *sels.* Petrarch, *tr. fr. Italian.*
To Laura in Death.
"First day she passed up and down through the Heavens, The," LXXV, *pr. tr. by* J. M. Synge.
(Laura Waits for Him in Heaven.) OBMV
"In the years of her age the most beautiful," X, *pr. tr. by* J. M. Synge.
(He Wishes H Might Die and Follow Laura.) OBMV
"My flowery and green age was passing away, XLVII, *pr. tr. by* J. M. Synge.
(He Understands the Great Cruelty of Death.) OBMV
"Now of my life each gay and greener year," XLVII, *tr. by* Thomas LeMesurier.
(Jealous Enemy, The.) LiTW
"Sorrow and love did thrust me in the way," LXXIV, *tr. by* Agnes Tobin.
(Flying Lesson, The.) CAW
"That nightingale, whose strain so sweetly flows," XLIII, *tr. by* Thomas LeMesurier.
(Nightingale, The.) LiTW; PoPl
"What a grudge I am bearing the earth," XXXII, *pr. tr. by* J. M. Synge.
(Translation from Petrarch, A.) MoBrPo; NeMA

"When my heart was the amorous worms' meat," XXXVI, *tr. by* Anna Maria Armi.
(Amorous Worms' Meat, The.) LiTW
To Laura in Life.
"Ashamed at times that I am silent," XVIII, *tr. by* Robert Guthrie MacGregor.
(Praises of Laura Transcend His Poetic Power, The.) EnLi-1; OuHeWo
"Father in heaven! after the days misspent," XLVIII, *tr. by* Barbarina Lady Dacre.
(Sonnet.) CAW
"Fountain of sorrow, inn of cursèd ire," CVII, *tr. by* Joseph Auslander.
(Sonnet.) PoFr
"I find no peace, and all my war is done," CIV, *tr by* Sir Thomas Wyatt. FCP; ReEn
(Contrarious Passions in a Lover, The.) LiTL
(Description of the Contrarious Passions [in a Lover].) EnLi-1 (1949 ed.); OAEP; PoFS; ReIE; Sonn; TrGrPo; TuPP
(I Find No Peace.) DiPo; LiTB; PoAn; PoIE
(Love's Inconsistency.) AWP; JAWP; OuHeWo; WBP
(Sonnet: "I find no peace. . .") SiPS
"If amorous faith, a heart of guileless ways," CLXXXVIII, *tr. by* C. B. Cayley.
(If Amorous Faith.) OnPM
("If amour's faith, an heart unfeigned," *tr. by* Sir Thomas Wyatt.) FCP
(Signs of Love.) AWP; JAWP; WBP
"If it be destined that my life, from thine," XI, *tr. by* Edward Fitzgerald. AWP; JAWP; OnPM; WBP
"Lady, if grace to me so long be lent," XI, *tr. by* Robert Guthrie MacGregor.
(He Hopes That Time Will Render Her More Merciful.) EnLi-1; OuHeWo
"Long love that in my thought doth harbor, The," CIX, *tr. by* Sir Thomas Wyatt. CABA; FCP; NoP; PIA; ReEn; SiCE
(Long Love, The.) CBV; ILP
(Lover for Shamefastness Hideth His Desire Within His Faithful Heart, The.) CoBE; ReIE; Sonn; STP; TuPP
"Love that liveth and reigneth in my thought," CIX, *tr. by* the Earl of Surrey. PIA; ReEN; SiPS; StP
(Complaint of a Lover Rebuked.) AWP; BEL; CABA; CoBE; EnLi-1 (1949 ed.); EnLit; LiTW; OAEP; OnPM; ReIE; SiCE; Sonn; TrGrPo; TuPP
(Love That Doth Reign.) CBV; FCP; ILP; NoP
"More my own poor wishes would commend me, The," CVIII, *tr. by* Joseph Auslander.
(Sonnet.) PoFr
"My galley charged with forgetfulness," CLVI, *tr. by* Sir Thomas Wyatt. BWP; CABA; CBEP; DiPo; EnL; EnPo; FCP; ILP; LiTB; MaPo; NoP; PAn; PoAn; ReEn; SiCE; SiPS
(Galley, The.) OBSC
(Lover Compareth His State to a Ship [in Perilous Storm Tossed on the Sea], The.) BEL; CoBE; ElL; EnLi-1; EnLit; PoE; PoEL-1; PoFS; ReIE; Sonn; StP; TuPP
(Lover like to a Ship Tossed on the Sea.) EtS
"My tameless will doth recklessly pursue," VI, *tr. by* Susan Wollaston.
(Of His Foolish Passion for Laura.) EnLi-1; OuHeWo
"Set me where phoebus's heat the flowers slayeth," CXIII, *tr. unknown.* TuPP
(Last Trial, The.) OBSC
"Set me whereas the sun doth parch the green," CXIII, *tr. by* the Earl of Surrey. CBEP; EnPo; FCP; ForPo; ILP; OnPM; ReEn; SiPS
(Love's Fidelity.) AWP; JAWP; WBP
(To His Lady.) OBSC
(Vow to Love Faithfully, Howsoever He Be Rewarded, A.) ElL; EnLi-1 (1949 ed.); EnLit; PoFS; SiCE; Sonn; TrGrPo; TuPP; ViBoPo
"Thou green and blooming, cool and shaded hill," CCV, *tr. by* C. B. Cayley.
(Heart on the Hill, The.) AWP
"Vengeaunce must fall on thee, thou filthie whore," CVII, *tr. by* Sir Thomas Wyatt.
(Against the Court of Rome.) LiTW
Songs.
Canzone: "Clear, fresh, sweet waters." To Laura in Life, Canzone XIV, *tr. by* William D. Foulke. LiTW
"Fair Virgin,/ Vestured with the sun!" To Laura in Death, Canzone VIII, *tr. by* Helen Lee Peabody.
(Ode to the Virgin.) ISi
(To the Virgin Mary, *abr., tr. by* Robert Guthrie MacGregor.) CAW
Visions, The. To Laura In Death, Canzone III, *tr. by* Spenser. AWP; EnLi-1; JAWP, *abr.*; WBP, *abr.*
I Saw a Phoenix in the Wood Alone, *sel.* ChTr
Sonnets to Miranda, *sels.* Sir William Watson.
"Daughter of her whose face, and lofty name," I. HBV
"I cast these lyric offerings at your feet," V. HBV
"I dare but sing of you in such a strain," III. HBV
"I move amid your throng, I watch you hold," VI. HBV
"If I had never known your face at all," VIII. FaBoBe; HBV
"If you had lived in that more stately time," II HBV
Sonnets to My Mother. Arthur S. Bourinot. CaP
Sonnets to Orpheus, *sels.* Rainer Maria Rilke, *tr. fr. German.*
"All we have achieved, the machine threatens to rule,' Pt. II, X, *tr. by* Jessie Lemont. OnPM
"All we have gained the machine threatens," Pt. II, X, *tr. by* M. D. Herter Norton. PoFr
"Almost a girl it was and issued forth," Pt. I, II, *tr. by* M. D. Herter Norton.
(Four Sonnets to Orpheus.) LiTW
"Almost a girl it was, then, issuing," Pt. I, II, *tr. by* W. D. Snodgrass. ReMP
"Dancer: O you translation," Pt. II, XVIII, *tr. by* Jessie Lemont. OnPM
"Hark, already you can hear the working song," Pt. II, XXV, *tr. by* Jessie Lemont. OnPM
"Mirrors; never yet has anyone described," Pt. II, III, *tr. by* M. D. Herter Norton.
(Four Sonnets to Orpheus.) LiTW
"Oh, come and go, you almost child, entrancing," Pt. II, XXVIII, *tr. by* J. B. Leishman. UnS
"O fountain-mouth, O giving, O mouth that speaks," Pt. II, XX, *tr. by* M. D. Herter Norton.
(Four Sonnets ot Orpheus.) LiTW
"O this is the beast that does not have being!" Pt. II, IV, *tr. by* W. D. Snodgrass. ReMP
"Only one who has lifted the lyre," Pt. I, IX, *tr. by* M. D. Herter Norton.
(Four Sonnets to Orpheus.) LiTW
Poet, The, Pt. I, III, *tr. by* Selden Rodman. OnHM
"Ripe apple, the banana and the pear," Pt. I, XIII, *tr. by* Jessie Lemont. OnPM
"Though the world is changing fast," Pt. I, XIX, *tr. by* Jessie Lemont. OnPM
"Tree ascending there, A, O pure transcension!" Pt. I, I, *tr. by* J. B. Leishman. UnS
"Tree rose up, A. O clear transcendency!" Pt. I, I, *tr. by* W. D. Snodgrass. ReMP
Sonnets to Philomel, *sels.* Sir John Davies. SiPS
"If you would know the love which I you bear."
"Oft did I hear our eyes the passage were."
"Once did my Philomel reflect on me."
"Sickness, intending my love to betray."
Sonnets to the Fairest Coelia. William Percy. *See* Coelia.
Sonnets — Unrealities, *sel.* E. E. Cummings.
It May Not Always Be So; and I Say. AnAmPo; FaBV; MoLP
Sonnet's Voice, The. Theodore Watts-Dunton. EtS; HBV; InP; TOP; VA
Sonnets Written in the Fall of 1914. George Edward Woodberry. HBV; MC; PAH
Sonnets Written in the Orillia Woods, *sel.* Charles Sangster.
"Blest Spirit of Calm that dwellest in these woods!" PeCV
Sonora Filibusters, The, *with music.* John A. Stone. SGR
Sons. Jack Cope. PeSA
Sons of Belial. Lola Ridge. PFY
Sons of Failure. Edith Lovejoy Pierce. MaRV
Sons of Indolence. James Thomson. *Fr.* The Castle of Indolence, I. OBEC
Sons of Martha, The. Kipling. EPN; HBV; WGRP
Sons of New England, in the fray. Treason's Last Device. Edmund Clarence Stedman. PAH
Sons of Our Sons, The. Ilya Ehrenburg, *tr. fr. Russian by* Babette Deutsch. TrJP
Sons of Patrick, The. James B. Dollard. JKCP
Sons of Promise. Thomas Curtis Clark. PoToHe

Sons of the Empire, bond and free. The Hands-across-the-Sea Poem. J. C. Squire. HBMV
Sons of the Greeks, arise! Greek War Song. *Unknown, tr. fr. Greek by* Byron. FOL; PoFr
Sons of the King[s]. Joan Agnew. BiCB; BoTP
Sons of the prophet are brave men [*or* valiant] and bold, The. Abdul A-Bul-Bul A-Mir [*or* Ivan Skavinsky Skavar *or* Ye Ballade of Ivan Petrofsky Skevar]. *Unknown.* ABF; AS; BLPA; GSP; StPo; TreF
Sons of the youth and the truth of a nation. The Name of Washington. George Parsons Lathrop. DD; HH
Sons of valor, taste the glories. Off from Boston. *Unknown.* MC; PAH
"Sooeep!" Walter de la Mare. BoTP
Soomtyme liv'lye Girald in grave now liv'les is harbourd. Sometime Lively Gerald. Richard Stanyhurst. NCEP
Soon as the azure-colored gates of th' east. Diella, II. Richard Lynche. Sonn; TuPP
Soon as the day begins to waste. The Constant Swain and Virtuous Maid. *Unknown.* HBV
Soon as the sound had ceased whose thunder filled. Shelley. *Fr.* Prometheus Unbound, III, iv. ChER
Soon at Last My Sighs and Moans. Louis Ginsberg. TrJP
Soon may a noble offspring. Wishes for a Bridal Couple and Their Unborn Child. Statius. *Fr.* Epithalamium for Stella and Violentilla. HW
Soon One Mornin' Death Come Creepin', *with music.* *Unknown.* OuSiCo
Soon one mornin', was mistin' rain. The Wreck on the Somerset Road. *Unknown.* OuSiCo
Soon shall thy arm, Unconquered Steam! afar. Steam Power. Erasmus Darwin. *Fr.* The Botanic Garden: The Economy of Vegetation. OBEC
"Soon—soon—soon" the prophet stars foretell. Strong Arms. Frances O'Connell Corridan. JKCP (1926 ed.)
Soon the night in mantle dark. The Ploughboy. John Clare. PoEL-4
Soon the wind will be gentle. A Hermit Advises a Monk When Things Are Bleak Indeed. William Hathaway. QAH
Soon Thou Wilt Come. J. W. H. Nichols. FaChP
Soon we heard a challenge—trumpet. The Battle of Killiekrankie. W. E. Aytoun. FOL
Soon with the Lilac Fades Another Spring. Patrick MacDonogh. OxBI
Soote [*or* Sweet] season, that bud and bloom forth brings, The. Description of Spring, Wherein Each Thing Renews Save Only the Lover [*or* Summer Comes]. Earl of Surrey. AnEnPo; AtBAP; AWP; BEL; CoBE; EG; EIL; EnLi-1; EnLit; EnRePo; FCP; FIW; ILP; JAWP; LiTB; LoBV; NoP; OA; OAEP; OBEV; OBSC; OnPM; OuHeWo; PoE; ReEn; ReIE; SeCePo; SeCeV; SiCE; SiPS; Sonn; STP; TOP; TuPP; WBP; YAT
Soothd by the murmurs of a plaintive streame. A Wild Romantic Dell. William Julius Mickle. *Fr.* The Concubine. OBEC
Sooth-Sayer, The. Sadi, *tr. fr. Persian by* Sir Edwin Arnold. *Fr.* The Gulistan. AWP
Sop, The. *Unknown.* StJW
Sophia, her age between. Wisdom of the Gazelle. George P. Solomos. GoYe
Sophia Nichols. Robin Blaser. CoPo
Sophisticate. Barbara Young. BiCB; SiSoSe
Sophisticated, worldly-wise. I Found God. Mary Afton Thacker. MaRV; SoP; TRV
Sophy, The, *sel.* Sir John Denham.
Somnus. SeCL
Sopolis. Callimachus, *tr. fr. Greek by* William M. Hardinge. AWP
Sops of Light. Fredegond Shove. ChMP
Sorcerer, The, *sel.* W. S. Gilbert.
My Name Is John Wellington Wells. PoMS
Sorcerer, The. A. J. M. Smith. PeCV (1967 ed.)
Sorceress. Gertrude Claytor. FiSC
Sorceress, The. Vachel Lindsay. PDV
Sorceress, The. Eugene Marais, *tr. fr. Afrikaans by* Jack Cope *and* Uys Krige. PeSA
Sordello, *sels.* Robert Browning. MyFE
And What Sordello Would See There.
At Ecelin.
How a Poet's Soul Comes into Play.
Sordello's Birth-Place.
Vault inside the Castle at Goito, A.
Sorrie, I am, my God, sorrie I am. *See* Sorry I am, my God. . .
Sorrow. Samuel Daniel. *See* Had Sorrow Ever Fitter Place.
Sorrow ("Count each affliction, whether light or grave"). Aubrey Thomas De Vere. BLPA;EPN;GoBC;HBV;JKCP;MaRV; NeHB; OBEV (1st ed.); OQP; VA; WGRP
Sorrow ("When I was young, I said to Sorrow"). Aubrey Thomas De Vere. *See* Song: "When I was young I said to Sorrow."
Sorrow. Emily Dickinson. *See* They say that 'Time assuages.'
Sorrow. Helen Parry Eden. JKCP
Sorrow. Reginald C. Eva. OQP
Sorrow. Goethe, *tr. fr. German by* Gretchen Warren. MaRV
(Who Never Ate with Tears His Bread, *tr. by* Farnsworth Wright.) WGRP
Sorrow. D. H. Lawrence. CMoP; GTBS-P; OBMV
Sorrow. Marie Tello Phillips. GoYe
Sorrow. George Santayana. *See* I Sought on Earth.
Sorrow. Katrina Trask. AA
Sorrow ("I will not gather the vervain sweet"). *Unknown, tr. fr. Spanish by* Sir John Bowring. OnPM
Sorrow ("Whither shall I, the fair maiden, flee from sorrow?"). *Unknown, tr. fr. Russian by* W. R. S. Ralston. AWP
Sorrow and love did thrust me in the way. The Flying Lesson. Petrarch. Sonnets to Laura: To Laura in Death, LXXIV. CAW
Sorrow can wait. Folded Power. Gladys Cromwell. HBMV; NP
Sorrow has a harp of seven strings. The Harp of Sorrow. Ethel Clifford. HBV; WGRP
Sorrow heaped on sorrow, ruin on disaster. On My Sorrowful Life. Moses ibn Ezra. TrJP
Sorrow in my own yard. *See* Sorrow is my own yard.
Sorrow, in vain why dost thou seek to tempt. To Sorrow. *Unknown.* SeCL
Sorrow is [*or* in] my own yard. The Widow's Lament in Springtime. William Carlos Williams. AP; CMoP; CoBMV; ForPo; LiTM (1970 ed.); MoLP; NP; PIA; PoIE
Sorrow is over the fields. The Land War. "Seumas O'Sullivan." OxBI
Sorrow Is the Only Faithful One. William Stanley Braithwaite. BALP
Sorrow Is the Only Faithful One. Owen Dodson. AmNP; IDB
Sorrow lay upon my breast more heavily than winter clay. Desolation Is a Delicate Thing. Elinor Wylie. MAP; MoAmPo
Sorrow, lie still and wear. Dirge. Thomas Lovell Beddoes. ERoP-2
Sorrow, my friend. A Song before Grief. Rose Hawthorne Lathrop. AA; CAW; JKCP
Sorrow of Kodio, The. *Unknown, tr. fr. Baule by* Miriam Koshland. PBA
Sorrow of Love, The. W. B. Yeats. MoAB; MoBrPo; PeVV; PoEL-5; PoeP; ViPo (1962 ed.)
Sorrow of Mydath. John Masefield. MoBrPo
Sorrow of Troilus, The. Chaucer. *Fr.* Troilus and Criseyde, V. PoEL-1
Sorrow of Unicume, The. Sir Herbert Read. BrPo; ChMP
Sorrow on the acres. Winter Field. A. E. Coppard. BiS; MoBrPo (1942 ed.)
"Sorrow seldom killeth any." Francis Davison. EG
Sorrow shared divides the trouble, A. Rhymes to Remember. *Unknown.* StaSt
Sorrow Shatters My Heart. Moses ibn Ezra, *tr. fr. Hebrew by* Solomon Solis-Cohen. LiTW
Sorrow Turned into Joy. John Alexander Bouquet. MaRV
Sorrow, who to this house scarce knew the way. Elegy [*or* Elegie] on the L. C. John Donne. ATP (1953 ed.); MaMe
Sorrowful Verses Made on the Death of Our Most Sovereign Lady Queen Elizabeth My Gracious Mistress. Thomas Churchyard. ReIE
Sorrows Humanize Our Race. Jean Ingelow. MaRV; WGRP
Sorrow's Ladder. Gertrude Callaghan. CAW
Sorrows of my heart enlarged are, The. Some Contemplations of the Poor, and Desolate State of the Church at Deerfield. John Williams. SCAP
Sorrows of Werther, The. Thackeray. ALV; BLPA; BOHV; CenHV; EnLi-2; FiBHP; HBV; InMe; InP; LiTL; NA; NBM;

NeHB; OnSP; PoVP; ShM; SiTL; TOP; TreF; VA; WePo
Sorry [*or* Sorrie] I am, my God, sorry I am. Sins' [*or* Sinnes] Round. George Herbert. ExPo; LoBV; MaMe; ReEn
Sorry world is sighing now, The. Fin de Siècle. Newton Mackintosh. NA
Sort of a Song, A. William Carlos Williams. CBV; HoPM; NoP; PoIE; PP; SeCeV
Sort of girl I like to see, The. The Olympic Girl. John Betjeman. SD
Sorting out letters and piles of my old. Mementos, I. W. D. Snodgrass. MeWo; MoAmPo (1962 ed.); NePoEA-2; PoIE (1970 ed.)
Sory beuerech it is and sore it is abouth, A. Christ's Prayer in Gethsemane. *Unknown.* SeCePo
Sospetto d'Herode, sels. Richard Crashaw, *after the Italian of* Giambattista Marini.
"Casting the times with their strong signs." MaMe; SCEP-1
"Mongst all the palaces in Hells command." SeCV-1
Sospiri di Roma, *sels.* "Fiona Macleod."
Red Poppies. VA
Susurro. VA
White Peacock, The. PoVP; VA
Sotus hates wise men, for himself is none. Impar Impares Odit. Henry Parrot. SiCE; TuPP
Sou'-sou'east of the Woods of Penn. The Blue Hen's Chickens. Arthur Guiterman. PaA
Sought by the World. *Unknown.* TuPP
(Love's Ending.) OBSC
Soul, The. George Barlow. OBVV
Soul. Austin Black. NBP
Soul, The. Madison Cawein. AA
Soul, The. Hartley Coleridge. Sonn
Soul, The. Abraham Cowley. AnAnS-2
Soul. D. L. Graham. Kal
Soul, A. Randall Jarrell. CMoP
Soul, A. Christina Rossetti. EPN
Soul. Barbara Simmons. BF
Soul, The. *Unknown.* STF
Soul, A. Bertha Prince Vander Ark. SoP
Soul, A! a soul! a soul-cake! The Souling Song. *Unknown.* SiSw
Soul Alone, The. Emily Dickinson. *See* Departed to the judgment.
Soul alone, like a neglected harp, The. Harriet Beecher Stowe. *Fr.* Abide in Me. ChIP
Soul and Body. Shakespeare. *See* Sonnets, CXLVI.
Soul and Body. Samuel Waddington. OBVV; VA
Soul and Body of John Brown, The. Muriel Rukeyser. MoAmPo
Soul and Country. James Clarence Mangan. VA
Soul and Sense. Hannah Parker Kimball. AA
Soul and the Body, The. John Davies. *Fr.* Nosce Teipsum. CTC; OBSC
(In What Manner the Soul[e] Is United to the Body.) LiTB; PoEL-2
Soul, art thou sad again. Triumphalis. Bliss Carman. HBMV; PG
Soul as full of Worth, A, as void of Pride. To James Craggs, Esq., Secretary of State. Pope. CEP
Soul, be your own. The Outcast. John Davidson. MoBrPo (1942 ed.)
Soul before God, The. Cardinal Newman. *Fr.* The Dream of Gerontius. OxBoCh
Soul, do you hear the trumpets down in the valley. Reveillé. Audrey Alexandra Brown. CaP
Soul dust with particles of. Music of the Other World. Ted Wilson. BF
Soul Eternal, The. Sir John Bowring. MaRV
Soul-feeding Hyacinths. Corinne Farley. ChIP
Soul Growth. Annerika Fries. OQP
Soul has bandaged moments, The. Emily Dickinson. MAmP
Soul, he said, is composed, The. Anecdote of Men by the Thousand. Wallace Stevens. Po
Soul has many motions, body one, The. The Motion. Theodore Roethke. SeCeV (1967 ed.)
Soul, heart, and body, we thus singly name. Love's Trinity. Alfred Austin. OBVV
Soul in the Body, The. Edith M. Thomas. AA
Soul Is All, The. Omar Khayyám, *tr. fr. Persian by* Edward Fitzgerald. *Fr.* The Rubáiyát. OnPM
(Heaven and Hell.) MaRV
Soul Is Form. Spenser. *See* Beauty.
Soul Lifted. Albert Durrant Watson. CaP
Soul-Light. Dante Gabriel Rossetti. The House of Life, XXVIII. CoBE; MaVP; PoVP; ViPo; VP
Soul lonely comes and goes; for each our theme. Lachesis. Kathleen Raine. NYBP
Soul Longs to Return Whence It Came, The. Richard Eberhart. AmP; CBV; CMoP; ExPo; LiTM; ToPo
Soul must have, for its great need, The. Neoplatonic Soliloquy. Donald C. Babcock. NePoAm
Soul of a Child, The. Unknown. SoP
Soul of a Mother, The. Margaret E. Sangster. PEDC
Soul of a tree ungrown, new life out of God's life proceeding. Yosemite. Milicent Washburn Shinn. *Fr.* The Washington Sequoia. AA
Soul of Christ, be my sanctification. Anima Christi. St Ignatius Loyola. WHL
Soul of Dante, The. Michelangelo, *tr. fr. Italian by* John Addington Symonds. GoBC
(On Dante Alighieri.) OnPM
Soul of Jesus Is Restless, The. Cyprus R. Mitchell. ChIP; OQP
Soul of Karnaghan Buidhe, The. James B. Dollard. JKCP
Soul of Lincoln, The. Chauncey R. Piety. PGD
Soul of Man, The. Dora Reed Goodale. AA
Soul of man is larger than the sky, The. To Shakespeare. Hartley Coleridge. VA
Soul of mine, pretty one, flitting one. Emperor Hadrian's Dying Address to His Soul. Emperor Hadrian. TreFT
Soul of my soul! it cannot be. The Sympathy. Owen Feltham. LO; SeCL
Soul of the deceased, although it live, The. Euripides. *Fr.* Helen. MaRV
Soul of the muses! and supreme in verse! Rhapsody to Milton. Sneyd Davies. WaPE
Soul of the World, The. Ernest Crosby. AA
Soul of Time, The. Trumbull Stickney. LiTA; NePA
Soul Remembers, The. Richard Burdick Eldridge. GoYe
Soul selects her own society, The. Emily Dickinson. AmePo; AmP; AmPP; AnFE; AnNE; AP; APA; AWP; CABA; CaFP; CBV; CMoP; CoAnAm; CoBA; DiPo; GTBS-W; InPo; JAWP; MAmP; MAP; MaPo; MeWo; MoAB; MoAmPo; MWA-2; NePA; NoP; OnPM; OxBA; PoEL-5; PoeP; PoIE; TreFT; TrGrPo; UnPo; WBP; WHA
Soul shall burn her fetters, The. The Soul. George Barlow. OBVV
Soul-Sickness. Jones Very. AP
Soul-Smiles. S. E. Anderson. BF
Soul Speaks, The. Edward H. Pfeiffer. HBMV
Soul Stithy, The. James Chapman Woods. VA
Soul to the Body, The. *Unknown.* PoLi
Soul unto itself, The. Emily Dickinson. MWA-2
Soul unto Soul Glooms Darkling. Charles Leonard Moore. AA
Soul, Wherefore Fret Thee? "Stuart Sterne." AA
Soul Wherein God Dwells, The. "Angelus Silesius," *tr. fr. German.* CAW; SoP
Soul Winner's Prayer, The. Eugene M. Harrison. STF
Souldier Going to the Field, The. Sir William Davenant. MePo
(Song: Souldier Going to the Field, The.) CavP
Souldiers Farewel to His Love, The. *Unknown.* CoMu
Soules Ignorance in This Life and Knowledge in the Next, The. John Donne. *Fr.* Of the Progresse of the Soule. OBS
Soules joy, now I am gone. Song. *Unknown, at. to* the Earl of Pembroke. AnAnS-1; MeP; OBS
Soulless, colorless strain, thy words are the words of wisdom. The Didactic Poem. Richard Garnett. VA
Souling Song, The. *Unknown.* SiSw
Souls. Fannie Stearns Davis. HBMV; SP
Souls. Paul Wertheimer, *tr. fr. German by* Jethro Bithell. TrJP
Soul's Adventure. Stanley J. Kunitz. NP
Soul's Beauty. Dante Gabriel Rossetti. The House of Life, LXXVII. CoBE; EnLit; MaVP; OAEP; OBEV (new ed.); OBVV; PAn; PoVP; ViPo; ViPP
Soul's Bitter Cry, The. *Unknown.* WGRP
Soul's Dark Cottage, The. Edmund Waller. *Fr.* Of the Last Verses in the Book. ChTr
Soul's Defiance, The. Lavinia Stoddard. AA
Soul's Desire, The. *Tr. fr. Irish by* Eleanor Hull. OxBI
Soul's Errand, The. Sir Walter Ralegh. *See* Lie, The.
Soul's Garment, The. Margaret Cavendish, Duchess of Newcastle. OxBoCh; SeCePo; SeCL

Souls Groan to Christ for Succour, The. Edward Taylor. *Fr.* God's Determinations. MAmP; PoEL-3
Soul's Harmony, The, *sels.* Nicholas Breton. SiCE
"What is the gold of all this world but dross."
"Worldly prince doth in his scepter hold, The."
Souls in the east, awake. An Easter Reveille. John R. Slater. MaRV
Soul's joy, bend not those morning stars from me. Astrophel and Stella, XLVIII. Sir Philip Sidney. FCP; MaPo; NoP; SiPS
Souls joy, when thou art gone. A Parodie. George Herbert. AnAnS-1; MaMe; MeP; OBS; SCEP-1
Soul's Kiss. Samuel Greenberg. LiTA
Souls Lake. Robert Fitzgerald. MoPo; TwCP
Soul's Liberty. Anna Wickham. MoBrPo
Souls of Black and White, The. Gladys May Casely Hayford (Aquah Laluah). PoNe
Souls of men! why will ye scatter. God Our Father. Frederick W. Faber. WGRP
Souls of Poets dead and gone. Lines on the Mermaid Tavern [*or* The Mermaid Tavern]. Keats. ATP; AWP; BEL; CoBE; DiPo; EnLi-2; EnLit; EnRP; EPN; FaBoBe; GTBS; GTBS-D; GTBS-P; GTBS-W; GTSE; GTSL; HBV; ILP; InMe; InPo; InvP; LoBV; MERP; ML; OAEP; OBRV; OTPC (1923 ed.); PoeP; PoFS; PoRA; PP; SeCeV; TOP; TreFS; ViBoPo
Souls of the righteous are in the hand of God, and there shall no torment touch them, The. The Wisdom of Solomon, Bible, Apocrypha. BoC
Souls of the Slain, The. Thomas Hardy. CMoP; LiTB; PoEL-5; PoVP; ViPo (1962 ed.)
Souls of the patriot dead. The Kidnapping of Sims. John Pierpont. PAH
Soul's Prayer, The. Sarojini Nidu. MaRV
Soul's Response, The. Annie Clarke. SoP
Soul's Soliloquy, A. Wenonah Stevens Abbott. BLPA; NeHB
Soul's Sphere, The. Dante Gabriel Rossetti. The House of Life, LXII. MaVP; PoVP; ViPo
Soul's superior instants, The. Emily Dickinson. MWA-2
Soul's Tendency towards Its True Centre, The. John Byrom. CEP
Sound, A, a sigh; a whip of rushing air. As It Began to Dawn. George Edward Hoffman. ChIP
Sound and Sense ("True ease in writing. . ."). Pope. *Fr.* An Essay on Criticism, Pt. II. UnPo, 14 *ll.*
(Craft of Verse, The, 12 *ll.*) BoLiVe
("True ease in writing comes from art, not chance.") ExPo, 12 *ll.*; TrGrPo, 22 *ll.*
Sound as if from bells of silver, A. The Pageant. Whittier. AmLP
Sound came booming through the air, A. The Philosopher and Her Father. Shirley Brooks. CenHV
Sound Country Lass, The. *Unknown.* CoMu; ErPo
Sound from Leopardi. Bill Berkson. ANYP
Sound in Cambridge, Mass., A. Ruth Whitman. NYTB
Sound me brass trumpets of the sun! Song for Love's Coming of Age. J. Corson Miller. JKCP (1955 ed.)
Sound must seem an echo to the sense, The. Pope. *Fr.* An Essay on Criticism. PoPo
Sound-Noise. Memory as Memorial in the Last. Edward Marshall. CoPo
Sound of Afroamerican History Chapt I, The. S. E. Anderson. BF
Sound of Afroamerican History Chapt II, The. S. E. Anderson. BF
Sound of Breaking. Conrad Aiken. AnAmPo; AWP; InPo; MAPA; PoDB
Sound of her silk skirt has stopped, The. Li Fu-jen. Wu Ti. AtBAP; BoW; LO
Sound of many waters, A!—now I know. Sonnet in a Pass of Bavaria. Richard Chenevix Trench. OBRV
Sound of Morning in New Mexico, The. Reeve Spencer Kelley. AmFN
Sound of Night, The. Maxine W. Kumin. BoNaP
Sound of the closing outside door was all, The. The Valley's Singing Day. Robert Frost. UnS
Sound of the Horn, The. Alfred de Vigny, *tr. fr. French by* Wilfrid Thorley. AWP; JAWP; WBP
Sound of the Sea, The. Longfellow. AnFE; AP; APA; CoAnAm; EtS; Po; PoPo; TreFT
Sound of the Sea, The. John Hall Wheelock. EtS
Sound of the Trees [*or* of Trees], The. Robert Frost. AnFE; APA; AtBAP; CoAnAm; MAPA; MWA-2; OxBA; PG; TwAmPo
Sound of the Wind, The. Christina Rossetti. *See* Wind Has Such a Rainy Sound, The.
Sound of Thy Sweet Name, The. Francis Davison. TuPP
(Madrigal: "Sound of thy sweet name, my dearest treasure, The.") EIL
Sound of Trees. Robert Frost. *See* Sound of the Trees.
Sound out, proud trumpets. Sir Osbert Sitwell. *Fr.* England Reclaimed. ViBoPo
Sound smashes through the dark. It is a wall. Joseph Schull. *Fr.* I, Jones, Soldier. TwCaPo
Sound, sound forever, clarions of thought! The Trumpets of the Mind. Victor Hugo. WoL
Sound, Sound the Clarion. Thomas Osbert Mordaunt, *formerly at. to* Sir Walter Scott. *Fr.* Old Mortality (*by* Scott), *ch.* 34. AnFE; OQP; TOP
(Answer.) OBEV (1st ed.)
(Call, The.) GTBS-W; MemP; OBEV (new ed.)
(Clarion.) BEL; EnLit
(One Crowded Hour.) MaRV; TrGrPo
("Sound, sound the clarion, fill the fife!") InP; OAEP
(Sound the Clarion.) TreFS
Sound the deep waters. Sleep at Sea. Christina Rossetti. NBM; PoEL-5
Sound the flute! Spring. Blake. *Fr.* Songs of Innocence. BoChLi; BoTP; FaBoCh; FaPON; GoTP; LoGBV; MoShBr; OTPC; PoPl; RIS; SUS; TiPo (1952 ed.); YeAr
Sound the Loud Timbrel. Thomas Moore. GoBC; MaRV
(Miriam's Song.) SoP
Sound which silence makes all you could hear. Cousin Emily and the Night Visitor. Kendrick Smithyman. ACV
Soundest of all literary legal tenders. Old Bill's Memory Book. William Rose Benét. InMe
Sounding, The. Conrad Aiken. CrMA
Sounding. Doris Ferne. CaP
Sounding battles leave him nodding still, The. The School-Boy Reads His Iliad. David Morton. MCCG; PoMa; PTK
Sounding brass and tinkling cymbal. Music. G. K. Chesterson. JKCP (1955 ed.)
Sounding cataract, The. Wordsworth. *Fr.* Lines Composed a Few Miles above Tintern Abbey. BoPe; FaBoEn; WGRP
Sounding Fog, The. Susan Nichols Pulsifer. PDV
Sounding Portage, The. Annie Charlotte Dalton. CaP
Soundings. Kathleen Fraser. YAP
Soundless the moth-flit, crisp the death-watch tick. Maerchen. Walter de la Mare. CoBMV
Sounds. Mary Austin. NP
Sounds are heard too high for ears. Watching Television. Robert Bly. CoAP; FRC; TPM
Sounds in the Morning, The. Eleanor Farjeon. BoChLi; SUS
Sounds of Dawn, The. Efraín Huerta, *tr. fr. Spanish by* Dudley Fitts. LiTW
Soup. Carl Sandburg. RePo
Soupy, soupy, soupy, without a single bean. Words for Army Bugle Calls: Mess Call. *Unknown.* TreF
Sour fiend, go home and tell the Pit. Ghoul Care. Ralph Hodgson. AnEnPo; MoBrPo
Sour Land, *sel.* Sidney Keyes.
Alexander Pope at Stanton Harcourt. FaBoTw
Source, The. Phyllis Harris. ThO
Source immaterial of material naught. The Rejected "National Hymns," IV. "Orpheus C. Kerr." ALV; BOHV; InMe
Source of News. *Unknown.* TreF
Sourdough mountain called a fire in. Burning, XVII. Gary Snyder. *Fr.* Myths & Texts. NaP
Sourdough Mountain Lookout. Philip Whalen. NeAP
Sourwood Mountain (*diff. versions*). *Unknown.* ABF, *with music;* AS, *with music;* IHA; TrAS, *with music*
(I Got a Gal at the Head of the Holler, *with music.*) AS
Sousa. Edward Dorn. CoPo
South, The. Wang Chien, *tr. fr. Chinese by* Arthur Waley. AWP
South African Broadsheets, *sel.* David Wright.
"Under the African lintel, Table Mountain." PeSA
South and west winds joined, and, as they blew, The. John Donne. *Fr.* The Storm. EtS
South atlantic clouds rode low, The. Safari West. John A. Williams. NBP
South Australia. *Unknown.* *See* Rolling King.
South Carolina, The. *Unknown.* PAH

South Carolina to the States of the North. Paul Hamilton Hayne. PAH
South Coast, The. Brother Antoninus. NeAP
South Coast Idyll, A. Rosamund Marriott Watson. OBVV
South Country, The. Hilaire Belloc. ACP (1952 ed.); GoBC; HBV; HT; JKCP; MoBrPo; OBVV; POTE; ShBV-3
South Cumberland, 16th May 1943 ("The sun has set"). Norman Nicholson. POTi
South Cumberland, 10th May 1943 ("The fat flakes fall"). Norman Nicholson. POTi
South End. Conrad Aiken. CMoP; MoVE; OxBA
South-Folk in Cold Country. Ezra Pound. CrMA
South, in the town, the sun had spread. The Brothers. John Holloway. NMP
South is green with coming spring, The. The Trial. Muriel Rukeyser. NAMP; PoNe
South of Guardafui with a dark tide flowing. The Dhows. Francis Brett Young. EtS
South of My Days. Judith Wright. NeLNL; PoAu-2
South of success and east of gloss and glass are. The Wall. Gwendolyn Brooks. BP; PoNe (1970 ed.)
South of the bridge on Seventeenth. Fifteen. William Stafford. CAD
South of the fabled pillars of Hercules. Volubilis, North Africa. R. N. Currey. PeSA
South of the Line, inland from far Durban. A Christmas Ghost-Story. Thomas Hardy. EnLi-2
South of the Thames by Chelsea Reach. Power Station. T. W. Ramsey. HaMV
South Sea Bubble, The. Countess of Winchilsea. CBEP
South Street. Francis E. Falkenbury. EtS; PFY
South Street. Edward S. Silvera. CDC
South Wind, The. Robert Bridges. OBNC
South Wind. George Parsons Lathrop. AA
South Wind. Siegfried Sassoon. BoTP
South Wind. Tu Fu, *tr. fr. Chinese by* Kenneth Rexroth. FlW
South-wind brings, The,/ Life, sunshine. Threnody. Emerson. AA; AmePo; AnNE; AP; MAmP; MWA-1; StP; TOP
South wind brings wet weather, The. Weather Wisdom [*or* Country Proverbs *or* Winds and Weathers]. *Unknown.* HBV; HBVY; RIS; StaSt; TreF
South Wind laid his moccasins aside, The. Isabella Valancy Crawford. *Fr.* Malcolm's Katie. OBCV
South wind rose at dusk of the winter day, The. The South Wind. Robert Bridges. OBNC
South-wind strengthens to a gale, The. Low Barometer. Robert Bridges. CMoP; CoBMV; ForPo; LiTB; LoBV (2d ed.); PoIE; QFR; UnPo (3d ed.)
South wind's molded by a spine of hill, The. Another Kind of Burning. Ruth Fox. NYBP
Southbound on the Freeway. May Swenson. AmFN; NYBP
Southdown Summer. "Sagittarius." HT
Southeast, and storm, and every weathervane. Hatteras Calling. Conrad Aiken. BoNaP
Southerly. E. J. Brady. NeLNL
Southerly Wind, *with music. Unknown.* ShS
Southern Cross. Hart Crane. *Fr.* The Bridge: Three Songs. LiTA
Southern Cross, The. Robert Stephen Hawker. *See* Mystic Magi, The.
Southern Cross. Herman Melville. AnFE; CoAnAm; LiTA
Southern Girl, A. Samuel Minturn Peck. AA
Southern Gothic. Donald Justice. TwAmPo
Southern Mansion. Arna Bontemps. AmFN; AmNP; BALP; BANP; IDB; Kal; LiTM (1970 ed.); PoNe; TTY
Southern Road. Sterling A. Brown. BALP; BANP
Southern Road, The. Dudley Randall. NNP
Southern Ships and Settlers. Stephen Vincent Benét. AmFN
Southern Snow-Bird, The. William Hamilton Hayne. AA
Southern Summer. Francis Stuart. NeIP
Southerner, The. Karl Shapiro. FiMAP; NYBP; PoNe
Southey and Wordsworth. Byron. *See* Dedication: "Bob Southey! You're a poet—Poet laureate."
Southrons, hear your country call you! Dixie. Albert Pike. AA; HBV; MC; PaA; PAH
Southward and eastward had our seamen steered. The Dutch Seamen and New Holland. William Pember Reeves. AnNZ
Southward Sidonian Hanno. Hervey Allen. EtS
Southward through Eden went a river large. Milton. *Fr.* Paradise Lost, IV. ViBoPo
Southward with fleet of ice. Sir Humphrey Gilbert. Longfellow. EtS; HBV; HBVY; MC; OnSP; OTPC; PAH; TOP
Southwest wind blows in from the sea unceasing, The. Return to Life. Abbie Huston Evans. NePoAm
South-west wind is blowing, The. Autumn Morning. Adeline White. BoTP
Southwestern Night. Angelico Chavez. JKCP (1955 ed.)
South-westward, where th' autumnal sun went down. Ruins at Sunset. William Allingham. IrPN
Soutine the Sour. A Story of Soutine. James Schevill. PoCh
Souvenir, The. Robert Creeley. FRC
Souvenir. Alfred de Musset, *tr. fr. French by* George Santayana. AWP; WoL
Souvenir. E. A. Robinson. InP
Souvenirs. Margaret E. Bruner. CIV
Souvenirs. Dudley Randall. Kal
Sovereign [*or* Soverayne] beauty which I do[o] admire [*or* admyre], The. Amoretti, III. Spenser. ATP; HBV; OAEP; PAn; PoEL-1; SiCE
Sovereign Emblem, The. James Russell Lowell. *Fr.* The Cathedral. MaRV
("Whatsoe'er/ The form of building or the creed professed.") ChIP
Sovereign Poet, The. Sir William Watson. PoVP; WGRP
Sovereigns, The. Lloyd Mifflin. AA; AnAmPo; HBV
(Sovereign Poets.) WGRP
Sovereignty. Leslie Savage Clark. ChIP
Sovereignty. Henry W. Frost. SoP
Soviet Union, immense resplendence of blood. Song to the Soviet Union. Manuel Crespo. PoFr
Sow came in with the saddle, The. *Unknown.* OxNR
Sow love, and taste its fruitage pure. Harvest. Horatius Bonar. FaChP
Sow ye by all waters. Fear Not. J. Bullock. STF
Sower, The. Laurence Binyon. MMA
Sower, The. R. Olivares Figueroa, *tr. fr. Spanish by* Dudley Fitts. FaPON; OnPM
Sower, The. Sir Charles G. D. Roberts. CaP; OBCV
Sower of Discord, A. Proverbs, Bible, *O.T.* *See* Seven Evils.
Sower trudged and swung, leaning, The. Dust. Stanley Snaith. POTE
Sower went out to sow his seed. Jesus' Parable of the Sower. St. Luke, Bible, *N.T.* TreFT
Sower's Song, The. Thomas Carlyle. OBVV; VA
Sowing. Edward Thomas. HBMV; NP; POTE
Sowing and Reaping. Adoniram Judson. *See* In Spite of Sorrow.
Sowing Seed. Laurence Binyon. POTE
Sowing Seeds. Ursula Cornwall. BoTP
Space. William Hart-Smith. *Fr.* Christopher Columbus. MoAuPo; PoAu-2
(Columbus Goes West.) BoAV; NeLNL
Space. Inez Hogan. RePo
Space and Dread and the Dark. W. E. Henley. PoVP; WHA
Space, and the twelve clean winds of heaven. The Most-sacred Mountain. Eunice Tietjens. HBMV; HT; MoRP
Space and Time! now I see it is true, what I guess'd at. Song of Myself, XXXIII. Walt Whitman. CoBA
Space beats the ruddy freedom of their limbs, The. Daughters of War. Isaac Rosenberg. BrPo
Space in the Air, A. Jon Silkin. NePoEA; TrJP
Space-time, our scientists tell us, is impervious. Archibald MacLeish. *Fr.* Reply to Mr. Wordsworth. ImOP
Space Travel. Jane W. Krows. SoPo
'Spacially Jim. Bessie Morgan. BOHV; HBV
Spacious Firmament on High, The. Joseph Addison. EaLo; ELP; FaBoBe; GN; HBV; HBVY; MCCG; OTPC; Po; PoEL-3; ShBV-2
(Heavens, The.) SoP
(Hymn: "Spacious firmament on high, The.") AWP; CBV; JAWP; LiTG; OBEV; TOP; WBP
(Hymn to the Creation.) DD; OHIP
(Ode: "Spacious firmament on high, The.") BWP; BLPA; CoBE; CEP; EiCL; MaRV; NeHB; NoP; OBEC; OxBoCh; PoIE; VaPo
(Psalm XIX.) WGRP
(Spacious Firmament, The. GTBS-W; TreFT
Spacious hive well stocked with bees, A. The Grumbling Hive;

Spacious (continued)
or, Knaves Turned Honest. Bernard Mandeville. *Fr.* The Fable of the Bees. CEP; EiCL; EiPP
Spade, A! a rake! a hoe! The Lay of the Laborer. Thomas Hood. DD; HH; VA
Spades take up leaves. Gathering Leaves. Robert Frost. LOW; RePo
Spading earth. Animal Kingdom. Sydney Clouts. PeSA
Spaewife, The. Robert Louis Stevenson. BrPo; OxBS; PoVP; VA
Spain. W. H. Auden. *See* Spain, 1937.
Spain drew us proudly from the womb of night. Full Cycle. John White Chadwick. PAH
Spain, 1809. F. L. Lucas. HaMV
Spain 1937. W. H. Auden. CABL; EnLit; LiTB
(Spain.) LiTG; WAP
Spain. The wild dust, the whipped corn. Teresa of Avila. Elizabeth Jennings. NePoEA-2
Spain's Last Armada. Wallace Rice. PAH
Spake full well in language quaint and olden. Flowers. Longfellow. DD; HBV
Spake the Lord Christ—"I will arise." An Easter Hymn. Richard Le Gallienne. OHIP
Span of Life, The. Robert Frost. DiPo; FlW; HoPM; LiTM; SiTL
(Old Dog, The.) RIS
Spangled Pandemonium, The. Palmer Brown. TiPo (1959 ed.)
Spaniel, Beau, that fares like you, A. On a Spaniel, Called Beau, Killing a Young Bird. William Cowper. EiCL; FaBoCh; OA; PRWS
Spaniel's Sermon. Colin Ellis. PV
(Bishop Spaniel's Sermons.) MemP
Spanish Alleluja. James J. Galvin. JKCP (1955 ed.)
Spanish Armado, The. *Unknown, at. to* William Warner. *See* Defeat of the Armada, The.
Spanish Bawd, The. James Mabbe, *after the Spanish of* Fernando de Rojas. *See* Celestina.
Spanish Blue. Herbert Morris. NYBP
Spanish Curate, The, *sels.* John Fletcher.
Dearest, Do Not You Delay Me, *at. to* Fletcher, *fr.* II, iv. SeCL; ViBoPo
Song: "Let the bells ring, and let the boys sing," *fr.* III, ii. OBS
("Let the bells ring, and let the boys sing.") TuPP
Spanish Folk Songs. *Unknown, tr. fr. Spanish by* Havelock Ellis.
"Let the rich man fill his belly." AWP; JAWP; WBP
"My father was a sailor." AWP
(Folk Songs, 2.) LiTW
(Sailors.) OnPM
Spanish Friar, The, *sel.* Dryden.
Farewell, Ungrateful Traitor, *fr.* V, i. CBEP; ELP; InPo; LiTB; LiTG; PAn; SeCL; ViBoPo
("Farwell ungratfull traytor.") EnLoPo
(Love's Despair.) ACP
(Song: "Farewell ungrateful[l] traitor.") CavP; EiPP; FaBoEn; FiP; MBW-1; OBS; PeRV; SeCV-2; SeEP
Spanish Gipsy, The, *sel.* Thomas Middleton *and* William Rowley.
Trip It, Gipsies [Trip It Fine], *fr.* III, i. OAEP; SeCL
(Song: "Trip it gipsies, trip it fine.") OBS
Spanish Gypsy, The, *sels.* "George Eliot."
Dark, The. VA
I Am Lonely. GN; HBV
Spring Song. PRWS
Song of the Zincali. VA
Spanish is the lovin' tongue. Border Affair. Badger Clark. SCC
Spanish Johnny. Willa Cather. ABF, *with music;* FaPON; HBMV; MPB; NP; OTD; PFY; RePo; WaKn
Spanish Ladies. *Unknown.* AmSS, *with music;* FaBoCh; LoGBV
Spanish Lady's Love, The. *Unknown.* OBB
Spanish Lions, The. Phyllis McGinley. NYBP
Spanish Lullaby. *Unknown, ad. by* Louis Untermeyer. RIS
Spanish Man, The. F. R. Higgins. JKCP (1926 ed.)
Spanish Needle, The. Claude McKay. GoSl
Spanish sculptor named Cherino, A. Who Has Seen the Wind? Bob Kaufman. Kal
Spanish Song. Charles Divine. HBMV
Spanish Student, The, *sel.* Longfellow.
Serenade: "Stars of the summer night," *fr.* I, iii. AA; AmPP (3d ed.); FaBoBe; HBV; LoBV; NeHB; OnPM; OuHeWo; PFY; PTK; ViBoPo
(Stars of the Summer Night.) MemP
Spanish War, The. "Hugh MacDiarmid." NMP
Spanish Waters. John Masefield. BeLS; FaBoBe; FaPON; MCCG; OnMSP; PCD; PoMa; PTK; ShBV-3; WaKn
Spanking is something that must go. Character Building. Edward Anthony. GoTP
Spare!/ There is one, yes I have one. The Golden Echo. Gerard Manley Hopkins. *Fr.* The Leaden Echo and the Golden Echo. LiTM; LoBV; MoAB; MoBrPo; OBMV; ViPo
Spare all who yield; alas, that we must pierce. The Death of Hampden. Pakenham Beatty. VA
Spare, Gen'rous Victor, spare the Slave. To a Lady; She Refusing to Continue a Dispute with Me, and Leaving Me in the Argument. Matthew Prior. CEP; EiCL; EiPP; LiTL; SeCL; WHA
Spare my sweetheart, boar, whether in grass-sweet meadow. Sulpicia's Rival. Tibullus. LiTW
Spare us this silence after the guns. Map Reference T994724. John Pudney. WaP
Sparhawk proud did hold in wicked jail, A. A Sparrow-Hawk. *Unknown.* CH
Spark, The. Joseph Plunkett. AnIV; AWP; JAWP; WBP
Spark of Laurel. Stanley Kunitz. ML
Sparkle up, little tired flower. Tired. Hilda Conkling. NP
Sparkles from the Wheel. Walt Whitman. AP; DiPo; FaBoEn; MWA-1
Sparkling and Bright. Charles Fenno Hoffman. AA; HBV; LHV
Sparkling Bowl, The. John Pierpont. AnAmPo
Sparkling sunset, oranged to gold, A. First Frost. Edwin Curran. HBMV; TSW
Sparrow, The. Psalms, LXXXIV: 3, Bible, *O.T., and* St. Matthew, X: 29, Bible, *N.T.* FaPON
Sparrow dips in his wheel-rut bath, The. The Five Students. Thomas Hardy. CMoP; ExPo; GTBS-P; PoEL-5
Sparrow has gone home into the tree, The. 1914. Frank Wilmot. BoAu; MoAuPo
Sparrow hath found an house, The. The Sparrow. Psalm LXXXIV, Bible, *O.T.* FaPON
Sparrow-Hawk, A. *Unknown.* CH
Sparrow Hills. Robert Lowell, *ad. fr. the Russian of* Boris Pasternak. NaP
Sparrow in the cherry-tree. The Child and the Sparrow. Thomas Westwood. BiS
Sparrow told it to the robin, The. Early News. Anna Maria Pratt. AA
Sparrows among Dry Leaves. William Carlos Williams. NYBP
Sparrows at the Airport, The. Anthony Ostroff. NePoAm-2
Sparrow's Dirge, The ("Pla ce bo"). John Skelton. *Fr.* Phyllyp Sparowe. OBSC
("Pla ce bo/ Who is there, who?") AtBAP; CoBE, *abr.*; EnLo; OxBoLi, *abr.*; PoEL-1; ReEn; ReIE; TuPP
Sparrow's Dirge, The ("When I remember again"). John Skelton. *Fr.* Phyllyp Sparowe. FaBoCh; LoGBV
("When I remember again".) SeCePo
Sparrow's Feather, A. George Barker. NYBP
Sparrows in gossip outside the bedroom eaves. Come Not Near. Mary Elizabeth Osborn. NePoAm-2
Sparrow's Nest, The. Wordsworth. EnRP
Sparrows quarreled outside our window. Waking an Angel. Philip Levine. NaP
Sparrow's Skull, The. Ruth Pitter. EaLo
Sparrow's Song, The. *Unknown.* STF
Sparrows through the winters flying. Flight of the Sparrows. Marya Zaturenska. TPM
Sparse mists of moonlight hurt our eyes. Festubert: The Old German Line. Edmund Blunden. MMA
Sparta. Terpander, *tr. fr. Greek by* C. M. Bowra. WoL
Spate in Winter Midnight. Norman MacCaig. BoC; GTBS-P
Spatial depths of being survive. The Lost Dancer. Jean Toomer. BALP
Spattering of the rain upon pale terraces, The. Irradiations, I. John Gould Fletcher. AnFE; APA; CoAnAm; MAPA; TwAmPo
Spawn of fantasies. Love Songs. Mina Loy. AnAmPo
Speak! Wordsworth. *See* Why Art Thou Silent?
Speak and tell us, our Ximena, looking northward far away. The

Angels of Buena Vista. Whittier. BeLS; PAH
Speak, gentle heart, where is thy dwelling place? Thomas Watson. LO
Speak Gently. David Bates. PaPo; Par; PoToHe, *wr. at. to* G. W. Langford
Speak gently, Spring, and make no sudden sound. Four Little Foxes. Lew Sarett. FaPON; GoTP; NP; OTD; PCD; PDV; PoMa; PoSC; PTK; RePo; WaKn; YeAr
Speak gently to the herring and kindly to the calf. Kindness to Animals. Joseph Ashby-Sterry. BOHV; InMe; NA
Speak, gracious Lord, oh speak; Thy servant hears. A Paraphrase on Thomas à Kempis. Pope. GoBC; OBEC; TrPWD
Speak, History! Who are life's victors? William Wetmore Story. *Fr.* Io Victis. ChIP
Speak holy words—too many blasphemies. To Pulpit and Tribune. Amos N. Wilder. MaRV
Speak low to me, my Saviour, low and sweet. Comfort. Elizabeth Barrett Browning. HBV; SoP; TRV
Speak No Evil. *Unknown.* GoTP
Speak no more of life. The Dying Enthusiast. James Clarence Mangan. IrPN
Speak not ill of womankind. Against Blame of Women. Gerald, Earl of Desmond. AnIL
"Speak not of niceness when there's chance of wreck." Sir Walter Scott. *Fr.* Peveril of the Peak. NBM
Speak not too much lest speech make thee speechless. Of the Senses. John Heywood. ReIE
Speak not—whisper not. The Sunken Garden. Walter de la Mare. HBMV
"Speak, O man, less recent! Fragmentary fossil!" To the Pliocene Skull. Bret Harte. BOHV
Speak of the birds, he lifts a listening finger. The Blind Man. Andrew Young. BiS
Speak Out. Maltbie D. Babcock. SoP
Speak Out for Jesus. *Unknown.* STF
Speak [*or* Speke], Parrot, *sels.* John Skelton.
"My name is Parrot, a byrd of paradyse." OxBoLi
(Parrot, The.) ACP
(Parrot's Soliloquy.) PoEL-1
"So many moral matters, and so little used." CoBE; ViBoPo
Speak, quiet lips, and utter forth my fate. An English Girl. F. Wyville Home. VA
Speak Roughly to Your Little Boy. "Lewis Carroll." *Fr.* Alice's Adventures in Wonderland. FaBoCh; LoGBV; Par
(Dutchess' Lullaby, The.) BBGG
Speak, Satire; for ther's none can tell like thee. The Introduction. Daniel Defoe. *Fr.* The True-born Englishman. BEL
"Speak! speak! thou fearful guest." The Skeleton in Armor. Longfellow. AA; AmePo; AmPP; AnNE; AP; AWP; BeLS; CoBA; FaBoBe; GBV (1922 ed.); GoTP; HBV; HBVY; LoEn; MaC; MCCG; MWA-1; OnSP; PAH; PoPo; RG; TOP; TreF
Speak the speech, I pray you, as I pronounced it to you. Hamlet's Instruction to the Players. Shakespeare. *Fr.* Hamlet, III, ii. TreFS
Speak the Truth to the People. Mari Evans. WSL
Speak the Word. Charles Wesley. BePJ
Speak them slowly, space them so. For a Wordfarer. Rolfe Humphries. ML
Speak This Kindly to Her. Robert Bagg. NePoAm-2
Speak Thou and Speed. Sir Thomas Wyatt. EnRePo; FCP
(That Speaking or Proffering Brings Alway Speeding.) TuPP
Speak Thou for me, against wrong-speaking foes. Psalm XXXV. Sir Philip Sidney. EP; FCP
Speak to her heart! Ars Amoris. J. V. Cunningham. QFR
Speak to me. Take my hand. What are you now? Effort at Speech between Two People. Muriel Rukeyser. MoAB; MoAmPo; TrGrPo (rev. ed.); TrJP; TwCP; WOW
Speak to the Sun. Dedie Huffman Wilson. GoYe
Speak to us, Music, for the discord jars. A Cry to Music. John Masefield. MuSP
Speak to us only with the killer's tongue. Sursum Corda. Conrad Aiken. ReMP
Speak to us who/ are also split. Tiresias. George Garrett. NePoAm-2
Speak when you're spoken to,/ Come for one call. *Unknown.* OxNR
Speak when you're spoken to,/ Do as you're bid. *Unknown.* CenHV
Speak with contempt of none, from slave to king. Speak No Evil. *Unknown.* GoTP
Speak with the Sun. David Campbell. ACV; NeLNL; SeCePo
Speake, speake, at last replye. *Unknown.* SeCSL
Speake you that heare, now Cloris sings. *Unknown.* SeCSL
Speakers, Columbus Circle. Raymond Souster. CaP
Speakin' in general, I'ave tried 'em all. Sestina of the Tramp-Royal. Kipling. BlPo;LiTB;MoBrPo;OtMeF;PoVP;SiTL
Speaking of Cowboy's Home. *Unknown.* CoSo
Speaking of Joe, I should have said. Fred. David McCord. TiPo (1959 ed.)
Speaking of Poetry. John Peale Bishop. LiTA; LiTM (rev. ed.); OxBA; PP; TwAmPo
Speaking of wine. The Grapes of Wrath. Christopher Morley. WhC
Speaking: The Hero. Felix Pollak. WOW
Spear-points of young men blossom there. Sparta. Terpander. WoL
Speargrass crackles under the billy and overhead is the winter sun, The. While the Billy Boils. David McKee Wright. AnNZ
Spearmen heard the bugle sound, The. Beth Gêlert. William Robert Spencer. BeLS; BLPA; GoTP; GSP; OnSP; TreFS
Special Delivery. Elizabeth Winton. PCH
Special Section for the Niggas on the Lower Eastside or: Invert the Divisor and Multiply. Welton Smith. BF
Special Starlight. Carl Sandburg. MoRP
Special tenderness and love, A. For the Blind. Martha Snell Nicholson. SoP
Specialist. Theodore Roethke. PV
Speck that would have been beneath my sight, A. A Considerable Speck. Robert Frost. AmP; AmPP; MoAB; MoAmPo; WhC
Speck went blowing up against the sky, A. A Visit from Abroad. James Stephens. LOW; PoMS
Speckeldy hen, speckeldy hen. *Unknown, tr. fr. the German.*
Speckled bird sings in the tree, The. The Nightingale. Katharine Tynan. BoTP
Speckled cat and a tame hare, A. Responsibilities. J. C. Hall. HaMV
Speckled cat and a tame hare, A. Two Songs of a Fool. W. B. Yeats. CMoP; OA; PoDB; PoG
Speckled sky is dim with snow, The. Midwinter. John Townsend Trowbridge. AA; AnAmPo; AnFE; APA; CoAnAm; GN; HBV; OTPC
Speckled with glints of star and moonshine. Mr. Walter de la Mare Makes the Little Ones Dizzy. Samuel Hoffenstein. Par; SiTL
Spectacle, The. Walter de la Mare. BoPe
Spectator ab Extra. Arthur Hugh Clough. GTB-P; OxBoLi; PeVV; SiTL
Sels.
"As I sat at the cafe I said to myself," *also in* Dipsychus. ALV; ELP; FiBHP; LiTG; NBM; WePo
"I cannot but ask, in the park and the streets." NBM
Specter, The. Ernst Hardt, *tr. fr. German by* Jethro Bithell. AWP
Spectra, *sel.* Witter Bynner.
"If I were only dafter," *st.* 1 *fr.* Opus 6. LiTM
Spectre, The. Walter de la Mare. WhC
Spectre. Sydney King Russell. FiSC
Spectre is haunting Europe, with no name, A. Manifesto. Paris Leary. CoPo
Spectre Is on the Move, The. G. Allana. ACV
Spectre Ship, The. Thomas Stephens Collier. EtS
Spectrum. William Dickey. ELU
Spectrum, The. Cosmo Monkhouse. VA
Specula. Thomas Edward Brown. OQP
Speculative. Robert Browning. EPN; PoVP
Speculative Evening. Marguerite Young. LiTA
Speech after long silence; it is right. After Long Silence. W. B. Yeats. BWP; CBV; CMoP; DiPo; ELU; EnLoPo; GTBS-W; HoPM; LiTL; LiTM; MBW-2; OBMV; PoAn; PoeP; PoPl; POTE; UnPo
Speech, both pithy and concise, A. "Exactly So." Lady T. Hastings. BOHV
Speech by Romelio. John Webster. *See* All the Flowers of the Spring.
Speech for the Repeal of the McCarran Act. Richard Wilbur. CMoP; NePoAm
Speech of Abbot Stephen. Petar Petrovic Njegos, *tr. fr. Serbian*

Speech (continued)
by James William Wiles. *Fr.* The Mountain Wreath. PoFr
Speech of Night, The. Michelangelo, *tr. fr. Italian by* John Addington Symonds. OnPM
Speech of the Dead, The. Anne Ridler. ChMP
Speech of the Salish Chief. Earle Birney. *Fr.* Damnation of Vancouver. OBCV
"Speech, or dark cities screaming." Johnie Scott. *Fr.* The American Dream. NBP
Speech to a Crowd. Archibald MacLeish. MoAB; MoAmPo; NePA
Speech to the Court. Walter Lowenfels. PPON
Speech to Those Who Say Comrade. Archibald MacLeish. AmPP; OxBA
Speechless Sorrow sat with me. The Guest. Harriet McEwen Kimball. AA
Speechless tree and animal and bird. A Lesson from Van Gogh. Howard Moss. MoAB
Speed. W. H. Davies. MoRP
Speed, bonny boat, like a bird on the wing. Flora MacDonald and the King. *Unknown.* BFSS
Speed on, speed on, good Master! The Walker of the Snow. Charles Dawson Shanly. OnYI; PTK; VA
Speed Track, The. "Peter." BoTP
Speke, Parrot. John Skelton. *See* Speak, Parrot.
Spell, The. Medora Addison. HBMV
Spell, A. Dryden. *See* Incantation to Oedipus.
Spell, The. John Gay. DD
Spell, The. Henry Martyn Hoyt. HBMV
Spell, A. George Peele. *Fr.* The Old Wives' Tale. ChTr
Spell before Winter, A. Howard Nemerov. LiTM (1970 ed.); ToPo; WIRo
Spell Eva back and Ave shall you find. The Virgins [*or* Lady's] Salutation. Robert Southwell. ISi; MeP
Spell is past, the dream is o'er, The. We Never Speak as We Pass By. *Unknown.* TreFS
Spell of Creation. Kathleen Raine. FaBoCh; LoGBV; OxBS; PoIE; WaKn
Spell of France, The. Edmund Blunden. POTE
Spell of Invisibility, A. *At. to* Christopher Marlowe. ChTr
Spell of Sleep. Kathleen Raine. HaMV
Spell of the Yukon, The. Robert W. Service. BLPA; FaBoBe; FaFP; NeHB; OTD; PoPl; TreF
Spelling Bee at Angels, The. Bret Harte. StPo
Spelling with love the Word among the flowers. Holy Thursday. Leonard McCarthy. JKCP (1955 ed.)
Spells. James Reeves. PoMS
Spels, *sels.* Robert Kelly. *Fr.* Thor's Thrush. YAP
"And all these years I have hidden it," IV.
"Mood passes/ spring comes," VI.
"Now the meadow drinks," V.
"Sun spell/ rooves spread," VII.
Spelt from Sibyl's Leaves. Gerard Manley Hopkins. BrPo; CMoP; CoBMV; FaBoMo; LiTM; MaPo; MoPo; PoAn; PoDB; ViPo (1962 ed.); ViPP; VP
Spend and God will send, but wot ye what follow. John Davies of Hereford. SiCE
Spending hand that alway poureth out, A. To Sir Francis Brian [*or* Bryan]. Sir Thomas Wyatt. *Fr.* Satires, III. EnPo; EnRePo; FCP; SiPS
Spendthrift. I. A. Richards. PoPl
Spenser! a jealous honorer of thine. To Spenser. Keats. CoBE; MaPo (1969 ed.); MBW-2
Spenserian Stanzas on Charles Armitage Brown. Keats. InMe
(Portrait, A.) BOHV
Spenser's Ireland. Marianne Moore. GTBS-W; LiTA; LiTG; LiTM (rev. ed.); MasP; NePA; OxBA
Spent purpose of a perfectly marvellous, The. In Favor of One's Time. Frank O'Hara. NeAP
Spent Wave. John Hall Wheelock. LiTM (1946 ed.)
Sphere of Glass, The. John Lehmann. ChMP
Sphere, which is as many thousand spheres, A. Shelley. *Fr.* Prometheus Unbound. ImOP
Sphinx, The. Henry Howard Brownell. AA
Sphinx, The. Emerson. AmePo; AmPP (3d ed.); AP; DiPo; MAmP; MWA-1; OxBA
Sphinx, The. Agnes Repplier. *See* Le Repos en Egypte.
Sphinx, The. James Thomson. The City of Dreadful Night, XX. EPN
("I sat me weary on a pillar's base.") NBM; OAEP
Sphinx, The. Oscar Wilde. PoVP; ViPP
"How subtle-secret is your smile," *sel.* MoBrPo; UnTE
Sphinx is drowsy, The. The Sphinx. Emerson. AmePo; AmPP (3d ed.); AP; DiPo; MAmP; MWA-1; OxBA
Sphinx Speaks, The. Francis Saltus. AA; HT
Sphinx with lion's feet, The. The Phoenix. Theodore Spencer. CrMA
Spicewood. Lizette Woodworth Reese. MAP; MoAmPo; NeMA
Spider, The. Robert P. Tristram Coffin. ImOP; OTPC (1946 ed.)
Spider. Padraic Colum. RoGo
Spider, The. Richard Eberhart. ToPo
Spider, The. A. P. Herbert. RIS
Spider, The. Mary Jones. WaPE
Spider. Richmond Lattimore. PP
Spider, The. David McCord. MAP
Spider, The. Walt Whitman. *See* Noiseless, Patient Spider, A.
Spider and His Wife, The. Jane Taylor. OTPC (1923 ed.)
Spider and the Fly, The, *abr.* John Heywood. ReIE
Spider and the Fly, The. Mary Howitt. BeLS; FaFP; FaPON; GFA; HBV; HBVY; OHFP; OnSP; OTPC; Par; RIS; TreFS; TVC; WBLP
Spider as an artist, The. Emily Dickinson. NoP
Spider Danced a Cosy Jig, A. Irving Layton. WHW
Spider expects the cold of winter, The. The Spider. Richard Eberhart. ToPo
Spider, from his flaming sleep. Little City. Robert Horan. CrMA; LiTM (rev. ed.); NePA
Spider glints, The. The Assassin. Donald Hall. TPM
Spider in the bath, A. The image noted. The Image. Roy Fuller. ChMP; GTBS-P; ToPo
Spider Silverlegs. Carolyn Sherwin Bailey. PCH
Spider, Sir Spider. Spider. Padraic Colum. RoGo
Spider! Spider! The Spider's Web. Charlotte Druitt Cole. GFA
Spider weaves his silver wire, The. Of a Spider. Wilfrid Thorley. BrR; FaPON; PDV
Spider Web, The. Mattie Lee Hausgen. GFA
Spider Webs. James S. Tippett. UTS
Spider works across the wall, The. The Huntress. George Johnston. WHW
Spiders. David Wevill. MoCV
Spiders are spinning their webs. Mid-August. Louise Driscoll. YeAr
Spider's Nest, The. George MacBeth. NMP
Spider's Web, The. Charlotte Druitt Cole. GFA
Spidersilk. John Nixon, Jr. NYTB
Spiel of the Three Mountebanks. John Crowe Ransom. MAP; MoAB; MoAmPo
Spies, you are lights in state, but of base stuff. On Spies. Ben Jonson. NoP
Spiked sun. The Hudson's. Early December in Croton-on-Hudson. Louise Glück. YAP
Spikenard. Laurence Housman. TrPWD
Spikes of new smell driven up nostrils. Burning, XIII. Gary Snyder. *Fr.* Myths & Texts. NaP
Spilled into the cup. Bubbling Wine. Abu Zakariya. TTY
Spin, a hardy spin, and here's the globe, A. A Small Boy, Dreaming. Albert Herzing. NYBP
Spin cheerfully. Leave the Thread with God. *Unknown.* BLRP
Spin, Dame, spin. *Unknown.* OxNR
Spin, daughter Mary, spin. The Making of Viola. Francis Thompson. PoVP
"Spin, oh my darling daughter, I'll give you a hat." Spinning Song. *Unknown.* UnTE
Spindle. A. R. Ammons. NYTB
Spindle-wood, spindle-wood, will you lend me, pray. Alms in Autumn. Rose Fyleman. PCH
Spindrift. Galway Kinnell. NaP; NYBP
Spined and gullet shaped. Free me. Oh Bright Oh Black Singbeast Lovebeast Catkin Sleek. Michael McClure. CoPo
Spinet, The. Andrew Lang. MuSP
Spinner, The. "Madeline Bridges." AA
Spinner, The. Charles L. O'Donnell. GoBC; ISi
Spinners at Willowsleigh. Marya Zaturenska. HBMV
Spinning Song. *Unknown, tr. fr. German by* Louis Untermeyer. UnTE
Spinning. Helen Hunt Jackson. HBV; OQP

Spinning Heart, The. John Berryman. LiTM (1946 ed.)
Spinning in April. Josephine Preston Peabody. HBV
Spinning Song, A. John Francis O'Donnell. IrPN
Spinning Song. Edith Sitwell. MoAB; MoBrPo
Spinning Top, The. Sister Mary Angelita. WHL
Spinning Top. Frank Dempster Sherman. GFA
Spinning Wheel, The. A. M. Klein. CaP
Spinning-Wheel, The. John Francis Waller. AnIV; ChTr; StPo
(Spinning-Wheel Song, A.) BoLP; VA
Spinning Woman, The. Leonidas of Tarentum, *tr. fr. Greek by* Andrew Lang. AWP; JAWP; WBP
Spinozaism, A. John Swanwick Drennan. IrPN
Spinster Song. Virginia Lyne Tunstall. HBMV
Spinsterish/ silver/ Before the shuttered window. Men Walked To and Fro. Blanaid Salkeld. NeIP
Spiral, The. John Holmes. MiAP
Spiral Landscape. Michael Brownstein. ANYP
Spiralwise it spins. Time. Ralph Hodgson. BrPo; GTBS-P
Spires of Oxford, The. Winifred M. Letts. BEL; EnLit; FaFP; HBV; InP; MaRV; MCCG; NeHB; OHFP; OnYI; PoLF; PoMa; PoRA; TIHL; TOP; TreF; WGRP
Spirit, The. Harold Lenoir Davis. NP
Spirit, The. Lon Woodrum. SoP
Spirit and nature beat in one breast-bone. The Sententious Man. Theodore Roethke. NoP
Spirit and the Bride, The, *sels.* Elsa Barker. HBMV
Caresses.
Confession.
Consummation.
Fulfilment.
Inscription, The: "Sealed with the seal of Life, thy soul and mine."
Love's Immortality.
Spirit breathes upon the Word, The. The Light and Glory of the World [*or* The Spirit's Light]. William Cowper. BLRP; SoP; TRV
Spirit came in childhood, The. The Four Calls. Lydia Hadley. SoP; STF
Spirit from Perfecter Ages, A. Arthur Hugh Clough. *Fr.* Amours de Voyage, II. OBNC
("Is it illusion? or does there a spirit from perfecter ages.") EPN
Spirit from Whom Our Lives Proceed. Howard Chandler Robbins. TrPWD
Spirit haunts the year's last hours, A. Song. Tennyson. AtBAP; GTBS-P; GTSL; ILP; InvP; NoP; OAEP; OBNC; PeER; PoEL-5; PoVP; TOP; ViPP
Spirit in me/ why are you so sad? Sadness. F. S. Flint. MoBrPo (1942 ed.)
Spirit, in Our Hearts, The. H. U. Onderdonk. BePJ
Spirit is caged, they said, its prison flesh. The Master-Welder. Sarah Wingate Taylor. JKCP (1955 ed.)
Spirit-Land, The. Jones Very. AmLP; AnAmPo
Spirit moves, The. A Light Breather. Theodore Roethke. NoP
Spirit of Britannia, The. Ode to the Germans. Thomas Campbell. PoFr
Spirit of Christ my sanctification. Prayer. *Unknown.* CAW
Spirit of Delight. Shelley. *See* Song: "Rarely, rarely comest thou."
Spirit of Earth, with still, restoring hands, The. The Last Furrow. Edwin Markham. AA
Spirit of "fire and dew." To O. S. C. Annie Eliot Trumbull. AA
Spirit of Freedom, The, *abr.* *Unknown.* PoFr
Spirit of Freedom, Thou Dost Love the Sea. Henry Nehemiah Dodge. EtS
Spirit of God, Descend Upon My Heart. George Croly. MaRV
(Prayer in the Spirit, 4 *sts.*) SoP
Spirit of man shall triumph and reign o'er all the earth, The. A Psalm of Confidence. Horace Westwood, *at. also to* Stanton Coit. MaRV
Spirit of Night, The. Thomas Rogers. EIL
Spirit of Plato. *Unknown,* *tr. fr. Greek by* Shelley. AWP; JAWP; WBP
(Epigram: "Eagle! why soarest thou above that tomb?") EnLi-1
(Plato's Tomb.) FaBoCh; LoGBV
Spirit of Poetry, The. Longfellow. CoBA; PP
Spirit of Sadness. Richard Le Gallienne. HBV
Spirit of self-sacrifice, The. Christ's Giving. Anna E. Hamilton. ChIP; OQP
Spirit of Shakespeare, The. George Meredith. EPN; PoVP; VA; ViPo
Spirit of song, whose shining wings have borne. Song and Science. Milicent Washburn Shinn. AA
Spirit of Spring, thy coverlet of snow. The Waking of Spring. Olive Custance. VA
Spirit of the Birch, The. Arthur Ketchum. MPB; OHIP; SP
Spirit of the *Bluenose,* The. Claire Harris MacIntosh. CaP
Spirit of the Fall, The. Danske Dandridge. AA
Spirit of the Lord is upon me, The. Good Tidings. St. Luke, Bible, *N.T.* MaRV
Spirit of the *Maine,* The. Tudor Jenks. AA; MC; PAH
Spirit of the Time-to-be, The. Resurgence. Laura Bell Everett. PGD
Spirit of the Wheat, The. Edward A. U. Valentine. AA
Spirit of Twilight, through your folded wings. Twilight. Olive Custance. CAW; HBV; JKCP; VA
Spirit of Victory, The. William H. Hudnut, Sr. SoP
Spirit of Wine, The. W. E. Henley. Echoes, XLI. HBV
Spirit of wordless love! that in the lone. Love. James Clarence Mangan. IrPN
Spirit seems to pass, A. Lausanne. Thomas Hardy. FaBoTw; ViPo
Spirit, Silken Thread. Margot Ruddock. OBMV
Spirit speeding down on All Soul's Eve, A. The One Forgotten. Dora Sigerson Shorter. PoRL
Spirit that breathest through my lattice, thou. The Evening Wind. Bryant. AA; AnNE; AP; CoBA; LaNeLa; MCCG
Spirit! that dwellest where. Song. Poe. *Fr.* Al Aaraaf. CoBA
Spirit that moves the sap in spring. A Prelude. Maurice Thomson. AmePo; HBV
Spirit who sweepest the wild Harp of Time. Ode to the Departing Year. Samuel Taylor Coleridge. EnRP; MERP
Spiritism. Robert Hillyer. WHL
Spirits. Robert Bridges. *See* Angel Spirits of Sleep.
Spirits and illusions have died. Life from the Lifeless. Robinson Jeffers. CMoP
Spirits and Men, *sel.* Ebenezer Elliott.
"I sing of men and angels." OBRV
Spirits, Dancing. Arthur Gregor. NYBP
Spirit's Epochs, The. Coventry Patmore. The Angel in the House, I, viii, 3. GoBC
("Not in the crises of events.") EG
Spirits Everywhere. Ludwig Uhland, *tr. fr. German by* James Clarence Mangan. AWP
Spirit's Grace, The. Janie Screven Heyward. HBMV
Spirit's House. Sara Teasdale. Interlude: Songs Out of Sorrow, I. OQP
Spirit's Light, The. William Cowper. *See* Light and Glory of the World, The.
Spirits of patriots, hail in heaven again. The Flag. George Henry Boker. HH
Spirits of the Dead. Poe. MAmP
Spirits of the dead are with us still, The. The Unseen World. Craven Langstroth Betts. OQP
Spirits of well-shot woodcock, partridge, snipe. "New King Arrives in His Capital by Air . . ."—Daily Newspaper. John Betjeman. OxBoLi; WhC
Spirit's Song. Louise Bogan. NYBP
Spirit's Song, The. Arthur Hugh Clough. *See* "There Is No God," the Wicked Saith.
Spirits walking everywhere. W. J. Turner. *Fr.* The Seven Days of the Sun. BoPe
Spiritual Conflict. Henry W. Frost. SoP
Spiritual Gifts. First Corinthians, XII: 1-XIII: 13, Bible, *N.T.* WoL
Spiritual Isolation. Isaac Rosenberg. TrJP
Spiritual Love. William Caldwell Roscoe. OBVV
Spiritual Passion. George Barlow. OBVV
Spiritual, the carnal, are one, The. Dorothy Wellesley. *Fr.* Matrix. OBMV
Spiritual Vision. Solomon Solis-Cohen. MaRV
Spirituality. Samuel Greenberg. LiTA
Spirk Troll-Derisive. James Whitcomb Riley. BOHV; LBN; NA
Spit-Bug, The. William H. Matchett. WaKn

Spit in my face you [*or* yee] Jew[e]s, and pierce my side. Holy Sonnets, XI. John Donne. AnAnS-1; MaMe; MasP; MeP; OBS; OxBoCh; SCEP-1; SeEP; Sonn
Spite hath no power to make me sad. Sir Thomas Wyatt. FCP; SiPS
Spite o' the tempests a-blowin'. "Tollable Well!" Frank L. Stanton. FaFP
Spite of Thy Godhead, Powerful Love. Anne Wharton. CavP
Spiteful snow spit through the bitter day, A. Labor and Capital. William Dean Howells. AmePo
Spitz, dear Spitz, for a moment come here. Pug-Dog and Spitz. F. Hey. SAS
Splashing along the boggy woods all day. Together. Siegfried Sassoon. BrPo
Spleen ("Old Pluvius, month of rains, in peevish mood"). Baudelaire, *tr. fr. French by* Kenneth O. Hanson. PIA
Spleen ("When the dull dire sky weighs a heavy cover"). Baudelaire, *tr. fr. French by* Arthur Symons. SyP
Spleen. Ernest Dowson. BrPo; CBEP; MoBrPo; NCEP; SyP
Spleen, The. Matthew Green. EiPP
Sels.
"And may my humble dwelling stand." LoBV
"But now more serious let me grow." PoEL-3
Cure for the Spleen, A. OBEC
On Even Keel, with Gentle Gale. OBEC
"This motley piece," *abr.* CEP
Spleen. Paul Verlaine, *tr. fr. French by* Ernest Dowson. AWP; EnLi-2; JAWP; OnPM; SyP; WBP
Spleen LXXV: "January, angry at the whole damned town." Baudelaire, *tr. fr. French by* Warren Carrier. ReMP
Splendid and Terrible [Your Love]. "Seumas O'Sullivan." HBMV; NP
Splendid arc of fishnet cast wide upon the sea, The. Feast of Saint Andrew the Apostle. Carl Bode. ToPo
Splendid burns the huge house with bronze. An Armoury. Alcaeus. WaaP
Splendid Fellow, A. H. C. Dodge. BOHV
Splendid Flower, The. Etta May Van Tassel. JKCP (1955 ed.)
Splendid Isolation. Katharine Lee Bates. LHV
Splendid Lover, The. John Richard Moreland. ChIP; PGD
Splendid Shilling, The. John Philips. BOHV; CEP; EiCL; EiPP; Par
Thirsty Poet, The, *sel.* OBEC
Splendid Spur, The. Sir Arthur Quiller-Couch. HBV; HBVY; VA
Splendid Village, The, *sels.* Ebenezer Elliott. NBM
Bailiff, The.
Steward, The.
Splendidis Longum Valedico Nugis. Sir Philip Sidney. *See* Leave Me, O Love . . .
Splendor [*or* Splendour] Falls [on Castle Walls], The. Tennyson. *See* Bugle Song.
The Splendor of the kindling day, The. Fluttered Wings. Christina C. Rossetti. VA
Splendor of Thine Eyes, The. Moses ibn Ezra, *tr. fr. Hebrew by* Solomon Solis-Cohen. TrJP
Splendor-throned Queen, immortal Aphrodite. Ode to Aphrodite. Sappho. EnLi-1; OuHeWo
Splendour of my Spring I destroy here, The. Abishag. Jacob Fichman. TrJP
Splendour recurrent. Fraternitas. Confucius. *Fr.* Deer Sing. CTC
Splendours of this passing world, The. "Peace Is the Tranquillity of Order." Robert Wilberforce. GoBC; JKCP (1955 ed.)
Splib Odyssey, A. Quincy Troupe. WSL
Spliced between Milan and Carthage this strip of days. Moment in Ostia. Sister Mary Thérèse. JKCP (1955 ed.)
Splinter. Carl Sandburg. FaPON; RePo; SUS; TiPo; UTS
Splinter, The. James Kenneth Stephen. CenHV
Splinter, flicked, A. New Moon in January. Ted Hughes. ToPo
Split Standard. Hart Leroi Bibbs. BF
Split the lark—and you'll find the music. Emily Dickinson. AP; MWA-2
Spoils. Robert Graves. MoLP; Sonn
(Spoils of Love, The.) NYBP
Spoils of War, The. Vernon Watkins. WaP
Spoke my heart in the dearth of the night. John Francis O'Donnell. *Fr.* Ossian. IrPN
Spoken at a Castle Gate. Donald Davidson. MAP; MoAmPo (1942 ed.)
Spoken by the God Pan. *Unknown, tr. fr. Greek by* Lord Neaves. OnPM
Spoken Extempore. Earl of Rochester. SeCePo
Spoken through Glass. Eithne Wilkins. NeBP
"Spoken Word, The." Christopher Morley. PoFr
Spontaneous Me. Walt Whitman. MWA-1; OxBA
Spontaneous Us! Presto Furioso. Sir Owen Seaman. BOHV
Spooks. Nathalia Crane. ShM; StaSt
Spool of Thread, A. Sophie E. Eastman. PAH
Spoon River Anthology, *sels.* Edgar Lee Masters.
Aaron Hatfield. LiTA; NP
Anne [*or* Ann] Rutledge. AmFN; AmLP; AmP; CMoP; FaFP; ILP; InPo; LiPo; LiTA; LiTM (rev. ed.); MAP; MoAmPo; MoVE; NeHB; NeMA; NePA; NP; OHFP; OxBA; PaA; PG (1945 ed.); PoPl; PoSa; PoSC; PTK; ThLM; TrGrPo
Archibald Higbie. InP; NP
Arlo Will. LiTA; NP
Bert Kessler. AnFE; APA; CoAnAm
"Butch" Weldy. NePa; PoPo
Carl Hamblin. AmP; CMoP; ILP; LiTA; LiTM (rev. ed.)
Cassius Hueffer. OxBA
Daisy Fraser. CMoP; MoVE; NP
Davis Matlock. LiTA; LiTM (rev. ed.)
Doc Hill. NP
Editor Whedon. CMoP; CrMA; NP; OxBA
Edmund Pollard. AnFE; APA; CoAnAm; ErPo
Elliott Hawkins. OxBA
Elsa Wertman. OxBA
English Thornton. OxBA
Father Malloy. NP; OxBA; PoPo
Fiddler Jones. AmP; CMoP; LiTA; LoGBV; NP; OxBA; TDP; TrGrPo; UnS
George Gray. TOP
Hamilton Greene. OxBA
Hannah Armstrong. LiPo
Hare Drummer. TOP
Harry Wilmans. PPON; WOW
Henry C. Calhoun. AmP; LiTA; LiTM (rev. ed.); NP
Herman Altman. OxBA
Hill, The. AmLP; AmP; CMoP; ExPo; LiTA; LiTM; NePA; NP; OxBA; ReMP; SeCeV; ViBoPo
J. Milton Miles. CrMA
Jacob Godbey. LiTA
James Garber. ILP
John Hancock Otis. PoFr; TOP
John Horace Burleson. CrMA
John Wasson. LaNeLa
Jonathan Houghton. OxBA; TDP
Julia Miller. MoVE
Knowlt Hoheimer. OxBA
Lucinda Matlock. CMoP; FaBV; ILP; InP; LaNeLa; LiTA; LiTL; LiTM; MAP; MCCG; MoAmPo; MoVE; NeMA; NP; OnPP; OxBA; PoPo; ReMP
Mrs. Williams. NAMP
Mollie [*or* Ollie] McGee. NP
Percy Bysshe Shelley. ML
Perry Zoll. CrMA; NP
Petit, the Poet. AnFE; APA; CMoP; CoAnAm; ILP; InPo; LaNeLa; LoGBV; MAP; MoAmPo; MoVE; NeMA; OxBA; PoSa
Rutherford McDowell. LiTA; NP; OxBA; TOP
Scholfield Huxley. LiTA; MoPo; TrPWD
Seth Compton. LiTA; NP
Sexsmith the Dentist. NePA
Thomas Rhodes. NP
Thomas Trevelyan. AnFE; APA; CoAnAm; MoPo
Village Atheist, The. AmP; EaLo; LiTA; MaRV; PoPo
Webster Ford. NP
William H. Herndon. LiPo; NP; TOP
William Jones. ImOP
Spoon River Anthology. Edwin Meade Robinson. Limericised Classics, V. HBMV
Sport, an adventitious sprout, A. Perspective. Margaret Avison. OBCV; PeCV
Sport for Gods. Jewell Bothwell Tull. CIV
Sport is absurd, and sad. Rugby League Game. James Kirkup. POTi
Sportif. David McCord. NYBP
(Ascot Waistcoat.) FiBHP

Sporting Beasley. Sterling A. Brown. Kal
Sporting Cowboy, The, *with music.* *Unknown.* OuSiCo
Sporting through the forest wide. Little Children. Mary Howitt. PRWS
Sportive Love-god in this worldly sea, The. The Angler. Bhartrihari. LiTW
Sports and gallantries, the stage, the arts, the antics of dancers. Boats in a Fog. Robinson Jeffers. AmPP; NoP; OxBA
Sportsman's Prayer, A. *Unknown.* MaRV
Sportsmanship. Thackeray. OTD
Sportsmen in Paradise. T. P. Cameron Wilson. PoMa
Sporus. Pope. *Fr.* Epistle to Dr. Arbuthnot. AWP; ChTr; JAWP; MaPo; WBP
(Characters from the Satires: Sporus.) InPo
("Let Sporus tremble—What? that thing of silk.") ViBoPo
Spotless Maid, The. Vincent McNabb. ISi
Spotted cow that's light and freckled. The Woman of Lyn y Fan's Call to Her Cattle. *Unknown.* PrWP
Spotted hawk swoops by and accuses me, The. My Barbaric Yawp. Walt Whitman. *Fr.* Song of Myself. CoBA; NePA; PP; TrGrPo
Spouse. Witter Bynner. AnFE; CoAnAm
Spouse I Do Hate. William Wycherley. *Fr.* Love in a Wood. OAEP
(Song: "Spouse I do hate, A.") PeRV
Spouse of Christ, The. D. A. Casey. JKCP
Spouse! Sister! Angel! Pilot of the Fate. Shelley. *Fr.* Epipsychidion. ChER
Spouse to the Beloved, The. William Baldwin. *See* Christ, My Beloved.
Sprawed on the bags and crates [*or* crates and sacks] in the rear of the trunk. El Aghir [*or* Green, Green Is El Aghir]. Norman Cameron. FaBoTw; MoBS
Spray. D. H. Lawrence. BoNaP
Spray of Honeysuckle, A. Mary Emily Bradley. AA
Spray of song that springs in April, light of love that laughs through May. Swinburne. EPN
Spraying the Potatoes. Patrick Kavanagh. OxBI
Spread beneath me it lies—lean upland. Flying above California. Tom Gunn. ToPo
Spread the board with linen snow. Invitation to the Dance. Sidonius Apollinarius. AWP
Spread the Word. Hugh Stowell. SoP
Spread thy close curtain, love-performing night. Juliet's Yearning. Shakespeare. *Fr.* Romeo and Juliet, III, ii. TreFS
Spread We Our Nets. Bilhana, *formerly at. to* Chauras, *tr. fr. Sanskrit* by E. Powys Mathers. Fr. Black Marigolds. OnPM
Spreeng ees com', Da; but oh, da joy. Da Leetla Boy. T. A. Daly. HBV; YT
'Spress. Jimmy Garthwaite. GFA
Sprig Fever. Margaret Fishback. BOHV
Sprig of Lime, The. Robert Nicholas. GTBS-S; POTE
Sprightly the cockcrowing. A Little Song in Assisi. George Barker. ToPo
Sprin' Fevah. Ray Garfield Dandridge. BANP
Spring. William Allingham. IrPN
Spring, The. William Barnes. BoNaP; HBV
Spring. Harry Behn. TiPo
Spring. Song of Solomon, Bible, *O.T.* *See* For, Lo, the Winter Is Past.
Spring. Blake. *Fr.* Songs of Innocence. BoChLi; BoTP; FaBoCh; FaPON; GoTP; LoGBV; MoShBr; OTPC; PoPl; RIS; SUS; TiPo (1952 ed.); YeAr
Spring. Anne Bradstreet. *Fr.* The Four Seasons of the Year. AnNE
Spring, The. Thomas Carew. *See* Now That the Winter's Gone.
Spring. John Alden Carpenter. RIS
Spring. Catullus, *tr. fr. Latin by* L. R. Lind. PoPl
Spring, The. Chang Chung-sur, *tr. fr. Chinese by* W. J. B. Fletcher. OnPM
Spring. Marchette Chute. TiPo (1959 ed.)
Spring. William Cornish. *See* Pleasure It Is.
Spring, The. Abraham Cowley. *Fr.* The Mistress. BWP; CLwM; LO; MeLP; OBS; ReEn; SeEP
(Love's Absence in the Spring.) LiTL
Spring. E. E. Cummings. *See* Spring Is like a Perhaps Hand.
Spring. Aubrey Thomas De Vere. *Fr.* The Year of Sorrow: Ireland—1849. IrPN; OBNC
Spring. John Gould Fletcher. PFY
Spring, The. Rose Fyleman. BrR; FaPON
Spring. Caroline Giltinan. HBMV
Spring. Giovanni Battista Guarini, *tr. fr. Italian by* Leigh Hunt. AWP; JAWP; OnPM; WBP
Spring. Gerard Manley Hopkins. ACV; BoLiVe; BoNaP; BrPo; CaFP; DiPo; FaBoEn; FaBV; ForPo; ILP; InvP; JKCP; LiTM; MaPo; MoAB; MoBrPo; MoVE; OAEP (2d ed.); OBMV; OBNC; OnHM; OxBoCh; PoDB; PoLi; SoP; StP; ViPP; VP
("Nothing is so beautiful as spring.") EG; LO
Spring, *sels.* Richard Hovey.
"I said in my heart, 'I am sick of four walls and a ceiling'." BBV (1951 ed.); PoMa; RePo
Stein Song, A. AmePo; HBV; MAP; MoAmPo (1942 ed.); NeMA; PFY
("Give a rouse, then, in the Maytime.") AnAmPo
Spring. Thomas Caulfield Irwin. IrPN
Spring. Orrick Johns. InMe
Spring. Kalidasa, *tr. fr. Sanskrit by* Arthur W. Ryder. *Fr.* The Seasons. AWP
Spring. Karla Kuskin. PDV
Spring. Philip Larkin. ACV; MoBrPo (1962 ed.)
Spring. Robert Loveman. AA
Spring ("I, country-born an' bred, know where to find"). James Russell Lowell. *Fr.* The Biglow Papers, 2nd Series, No. VI: Sunthin' in the Pastoral Line. FaBV
Spring ("O little city-gals, don't never go it"). James Russell Lowell. *Fr.* The Biglow Papers, 2nd Series, No. VI: Sunthin' in the Pastoral Line. MCCG
Spring, The. John Lyly. *See* Trico's Song.
Spring. Hugh McCrae. ACV
Spring. Anne Elizabeth Maddock. OQP
Spring. Vladimir Mayakovsky, *tr. fr. Russian by* Babette Deutsch. CAD
Spring ("Now Winter's winds are banished from the sky"). Meleager, *tr. fr. Greek by* William M. Hardinge. AWP; JAWP; WBP
Spring. W. S. Merwin. NaP
Spring. Charlotte Mew. *See* In the Fields.
Spring. Edna St. Vincent Millay. MAP; MoAB; MoAmPo; NePA; NP
Spring, *sel.* William Miller.
"Spring comes linking and jinking through the woods, The." PoSC
Spring. Thomas Nashe. *See* Spring, the Sweet Spring.
Spring, The. John Francis O'Donnell. IrPN
Spring ("The year has changed his mantle cold"). Charles d'Orleans, *tr. fr. French by* Andrew Lang. AWP; CTC; WBP
(Rondeau: "Year his winter cloak lets fall, The." *tr. by* J. G. Legge.) LiTW
(Spring: "Time hath laid his mantle by, The." *tr. unknown.*) DD
Spring ("How many buds"). Boris Pasterak, *tr. fr. Russian by* Babette Deutsch. LiTW
Spring, The. Ezra Pound. Po
Spring. W. R. Rodgers. AnIL; OnYI
Spring. Isaac Rosenberg. TrJP
Spring. Christina Rossetti. OBNC
Spring. Shakespeare. *See* When Daisies Pied and Violets Blue.
Spring. Edith Sitwell. OAEP (2d ed.)
Spring. Christopher Smart. *Fr.* St. Philip and St. James. OBEC
("Now the winds are all composure.") LoBV
Spring. Robert Southey. Sonn
Spring. Andre Spire, *tr. fr. French by* Jethro Bithell. AWP; BoLP
Spring. Thomas Stanley, *after the Greek of* Anacreon. AWP; JAWP; SeCL; WBP
Spring. Earl of Surrey. *See* Description of Spring.
Spring ("Dip down upon the northern shore"). Tennyson. *See* In Memoriam A. H. H.: "Dip down upon. . ."
Spring ("Now fades the last long streak of snow"). Tennyson. *See* In Memoriam A. H. H.: "Now Fades. . ."
Spring. Celia Thaxter. BoChLi; DD; HH; OTPC (1946 ed.); PRWS
Spring. James Thomson. *Fr.* The Seasons. EiCP
Sels.
"As rising from the vegetable world." PoEL-3
"At length the finished garden to the view." ViBoPo
Birds in Spring. OBEC

Spring (continued)
("Blackbird whistles from the thorny brake, The.") PeER, 10 *ll.*
"Come gentle Spring, ethereal mildness, come." PeER, 4 *ll.*
Spring Flowers. AtBAP; OBEC
Woodland Choir, The. CoBE
Spring. Henry Timrod. AP; HBV
Spring ("Lenten ys come with love to toune"). *Unknown. See* Lenten Is Come.
Spring ("When from her winter-prison"). *Unknown, tr. fr. Japanese.* SUS
Spring. Paul Verlaine, *tr. fr. French by* Roland Gant *and* Claude Apcher. ErPo
Spring. Oscar Williams. LiTA
Spring: "Now I know why I dream." Allen Van Newkirk. YAP
Spring: "Orpheus was a sadist." Allen Van Newkirk. YAP
Spring: "There are nothing but pipes and dripping faucets here." Allen Van Newkirk. YAP
Spring Afternoon. John Morgan. YAP
Spring Air. Gene Derwood. FaFP; GTBS-W; LiTL
Spring all the Graces of the age. Chorus. Ben Jonson. *Fr.* Neptune's Triumph. OBS; SeCL
Spring and all ("By the road to the contagious hospital"). William Carlos Williams. AP; CABA; CMoP; CoBMV; ExPo; ForPo; LiTM (1970 ed.); MoVE; OxBA; PoeP; PoIE; PoSA; QFR
(Contagious Hospital, The.) VaPo
(Poem: "By the road to the contagious hospital.") MAP; MoAB; MoAmPo; NeMa; UnPo (3d ed.)
Spring and All ("So much depends"). William Carlos Williams. *See* Red Wheelbarrow, The.
Spring and Autumn. William James Linton. VA
Spring and Death. Gerard Manley Hopkins. BrPo; FosPo; NoP; SyP
Spring and Fall. Gerard Manley Hopkins. AnFE; BrPo; BWP; CaFP; CBV; ChTr; CMoP; DiPo; ELP; EnL; ExPo; FosPo; GoJo; GTBS-P; GTBS-W; ILP; LiTB; LiTM; MaPo (1969 ed.); MoAB; MoPo; MoVE; NoP; OAEP; PAn; PeVV; PIA; PoAn; PoE; PoEL-5; PoeP; PoFS; PoIE; PoPl; PoRA; PoSa; PPON; ReMP; SeCeV; SoP; TDP; ThWaDe; ViPo (1962 ed.); ViPP
Spring and Summer. "A." PRWS
Spring and Summer. Tennyson. *Fr.* Vastness. OQP
Spring! and the buds against the sky. Spring. Caroline Giltinan. HBMV
Spring and the Fall, The. Edna St. Vincent Millay. BoLP
Spring and Winter ("When daisies pied. . ."). Shakespeare. *See* When Daisies Pied and Violets Blue.
Spring and Winter ("When icicles hang. . ."). Shakespeare. *See* When Icicles Hang by the Wall.
Spring Arithmetic. *Unknown.* FiBHP
Spring at her height on a morn at prime. Ballade of Youth and Age. W. E. Henley. PoVP
Spring Beauties, The. Helen Gray Cone. AA
Spring, beautiful spring! Spring Song. *Unknown, tr. fr. Russian.* PCH
Spring Bereaved ("Alexis, here she stayed"). William Drummond of Hawthornden. *See* Sonnet: "Alexis, here she stayed. . ."
Spring Bereaved ("Sweet Spring, thou turn'st with all thy goodly train"). William Drummond of Hawthornden. *See* Sonnet: "Sweet Spring, thou turn'st. . ."
Spring Bereaved ("That zephyr every year"). William Drummond of Hawthornden. OBEV
Spring blew trumpets of color, The. Blind. Harry Kemp. HBMV; PFY; PoMa
Spring Breeze. Buson, *tr. fr. Japanese by* Harold G. Henderson. RePo
Spring Burning. Patrick Roland. PeSA
Spring bursts to-day. An Easter Carol. Christina Rossetti. DD; HH; MaRV; MPB; OHIP; PoRL
Spring came earlier on, The. A Song for Lexington. Robert Kelley Weeks. AA
Spring came round, and still he was not dead, The. The Neurotic. C. Day Lewis. ACV
Spring came with tiny lances thrusting. Blossom Time. Wilbur Larremore. AA
Spring Cellar. Gladys McKee. GoYe
Spring comes early to the gardens. Green Jade Plum Trees in Spring. Ou Yang Hsiu. NaP
Spring comes hither. Spring Song. "George Eliot." *Fr.* The Spanish Gypsy. OTPC (1946 ed.); PRWS
Spring comes hurrying. Hello! Louise Ayres Garnett. SiSoSe
Spring comes laughing down the valley. New Life. Amelia Josephine Burr. HBV
Spring comes linking and jinking through the woods, The. William Miller. *Fr.* Spring. PoSC
Spring Comes to Murray Hill. Ogden Nash. FiBHP
Spring Comes to Our Garden. Sister Mary Immaculata. JKCP (1955 ed.)
Spring comes with silent rush of leaf. Resurrection. Laurence Housman. *Fr.* Rue. MaRV
Spring Cricket. Frances Rodman. FaPON; SiSoSe
Spring Days. Basho, *tr. fr. Japanese by* H. G. Henderson. OnPM
Spring Doggerel. Rhoda Coghill. NeIP
Spring Ecstasy. Lizette Woodworth Reese. MAP; MoAmPo
Spring Equinox, The. Anne Ridler. NeBP
Spring, etc. Reed Whittemore. WaKn
Spring Families. Frances Frost. RePo
Spring Fever. Alice Hansche Mortenson. SoP
Spring Flowers. James Thomson. *Fr.* The Seasons: Spring. AtBAP; OBEC
Spring Flowers from Ireland. Denis Florence MacCarthy. ACP; GoBC
Spring for All Seasons. James Welch. YAP
Spring, for Julian, was amber in the hand. In the Henry James Country. William Abrahams. WaP
Spring for Travelers. *Unknown, tr. fr. Greek by* Lord Neaves. OnPM
Spring-germs, spring-germs. Tyranny. Sidney Lanier. MAmP
Spring Goeth All the White. Robert Bridges. BoNaP; BoTP; ChTr; HBMV
Spring Grass. Carl Sandburg. FaPON
Spring Has Come ("Hark! the tiny cowslip bell"). *Unknown.* BoTP
Spring Has Come [To Town with Love]. *Unknown. See* Lenten Is Come.
Spring has come and the snow has gone. Captive. Peretz Hirshbein. TrJP
Spring has darkened with activity, The. Time and the Garden. Yvor Winters. MoAmPo (1962 ed.); QFR
Spring has returned again this year. Spring Fever. Alice Hansche Mortenson. SoP
Spring Holidays. Catullus, *tr. fr. Latin by* George Lamb. OnPM
Spring in England. Charles Buxton Going. HBMV
Spring in Hiding. Frances Frost. YeAr
Spring in his death abounds among the lily islands. Elegy on My Father. Allen Curnow. AnNZ
Spring in My Hut. Sodo, *tr. fr. Japanese by* H. G. Henderson. OnPM; RePo
Spring in New Hampshire. Claude McKay. BANP; GoSl; Kal; PoNe
Spring in New Zealand. Hubert Church. BoAu
Spring in the Jungle. Eugene Redmond. TNV
Spring in the Students' Quarter. Henry Murger, *tr. fr. French by* Andrew Lang. AWP
Spring in War Time. Sara Teasdale. OHIP
Spring Is a Looping-free Time. Martin Robbins. SD
Spring is a requiem rehearsed. Spring Song. LeRoy Smith, Jr. NePoAm
Spring Is at Work with Beginnings of Things. Greta Leora Rose. CaP
Spring is come to town with love. Spring Song. *Unknown.* EnLi-1
Spring Is Coming. Mary Howitt. PEDC, *abr.*
(Voice of Spring, The, *st.* 2.) OTPC (1923 ed.); PRWS
Spring is coming by a many signs, The. Young Lambs. John Clare. EG; GoTP; TrGrPo
Spring is coming, spring is coming. May Song [*or* Oxfordshire Children's May Song]. *Unknown.* BoTP; HH; OTPC
Spring is growing up. Spring and Summer. A. PRWS
Spring Is Hard on Us. *Unknown.* ErPo; PV
Spring is in her eyes. A Little Girl. Charles Angoff. GoYe
Spring Is in the Making. Nona Keen Duffy. YeAr
Spring Is Late, The. Louise Chandler Moulton. HBV
Spring Is Like a Perhaps Hand. E. E. Cummings. AmPP (5th ed.); FIW; GTBS-W; NePA; NoP
(Spring.) AnEnPo

Spring is not so beautiful there, The. Water-Front Streets. Langston Hughes. OCS
Spring is showery, flowery, bowery. Mother Goose. SoPo; TiPo
Spring is the morning of the year. The Golden Rod. Frank Dempster Sherman. BoChLi; FaPON
Spring it is cheery. Ballad. Thomas Hood. VA
Spring Journey, A. Alice Freeman Palmer. HBV
Spring Landscape. Arthur Davison Ficke. Sonnets of a Portrait Painter, XII. HBMV
Spring Landscape. Melvin Walker La Follette. NePoEA-2
Spring Lay, A. Oliver Opdyke. InMe
Spring lights her candles everywhere. Song. Fredegond Shove. HBMV
Spring Lilt, A. *Unknown.* HBV; MPB; OTPC
"June! June! June!" *sel.* PCH
Spring made little promise. Portrait of an Indian. R. E. Rashley. CaP
Spring Malediction, *sel.* John Gill.
"Oh gentlemen gentlemen don't worry." WOW
Spring Market. Louise Driscoll. HBMV; HBVY
Spring Morning. Frances Cornford. BoTP
Spring Morning! Galante Garden, I. Juan Ramón Jiménez. PoPl
Spring Morning. D. H. Lawrence. BoLP; BrPo; CMoP; MoAB; MoBrPo
Spring Morning—Sante Fé. Lynn Riggs. HT
Spring Mountain Climb. Richard Eberhart. GoYe
Spring, my dear, The. Out of Tune. W. E. Henley. MoBrPo
Spring Night. Richard Aldridge. NePoAm
Spring Night, A. Robert Beloof. PoPo
Spring Night. Sidney Keyes. POTE
Spring Night. "Rana Mukerji." UnTE
Spring Night. Sara Teasdale. BoLP; FaBoBe; HBMV; LiTA; LiTL; LiTM (1946 ed.); MAP; MoAmPo; NeMA; PG (1945 ed.)
Spring night, the owls crying. Spring Night. Sidney Keyes. POTE
Spring 1940. W. H. Auden. OAEP (2d ed.)
Spring MCMXL. David Gascoyne. MoVE
Spring 1943. Roy Fuller. LiTB; LiTM; WaP
Spring 1942. Roy Fuller. LiTM; NeBP; WaaP
Spring Nocturne. Abraham Liessin, *tr. fr. Yiddish.* TrJP
Spring, A, now she is dead! of what? of thorns. Ben Jonson. *Fr.* The Sad Shepherd. GoBC
Spring Oak. Galway Kinnell. BoNaP; ELU; NePoAm
Spring of God, The. William Alexander Percy. *Fr.* In April Once. OQP
Spring of Joy. Vera E. Guerard. TNV
Spring of Joy Is Dry, The. *Unknown.* ElL; EnRePo
Spring of the Year, The. Allan Cunningham. HBV; OBEV (1st ed.)
(Gone Were But the Winter Cold.) CH
Spring of Work Storm. Joseph Ceravolo. ANYP
Spring Offensive. Wilfred Owen. BrPo; GTBS-P; LiTB; MoVE
Spring Offensive, 1941. Maurice Biggs. PoAu-2
Spring Omnipotent Goddess. E. E. Cummings. OxBA
Spring on the Ochils. J. Logie Robertson. OBVV
Spring once said to the nightingale. The Birds' Ball. William Bardeen. BLPA
Spring Passion. Joel Elias Spingarn. HBV
Spring Pastoral. Elinor Wylie. AnEnPo
Spring Poem. Julian Symons. NeBP
Spring Poem. Colleen Thibaudeau. TwCaPo
Spring Pools. Robert Frost. AmPP (5th ed.); BWP; DiPo; MoAB; NoP; OxBA; PIA
Spring Prayer. *Unknown, See* We Thank Thee.
Spring Questions. Clara Doty Bates. PPL
Spring Quiet. Christina Rossetti. BiS; BoNaP; BoTP; CH; GTBS-P; LoBV; PoEL-5; ThGo; ThWaDe
("Gone were but the winter.") EG
Spring Rain. Harry Behn. TiPo
Spring Rain. Marchette Chute. TiPo
Spring Rain. William Hawkins. MoCV
Spring rain:/ Everything just grows. Kaga no Chiyo, *tr. fr. Japanese by* R. H. Blyth. FlW
Spring rain! And as yet. Taniguchi Buson, *tr. fr. Japanese by* Harold G. Henderson. LiTW
Spring rain is soft rain, The. Rainy Day Song. Violet Alleyn Storey. YeAr
Spring Returns, The. Charles Leonard Moore. HBV
Spring returns, and blended meet. Spring Holidays. Catullus. OnPM
Spring returns, The. What matters then that war. The Spring Returns. Charles Leonard Moore. HBV
Spring rides down, The; from Judith and the Larb. A Missouri Traveller Writes Home, 1830. Robert Bly. NePoEA
Spring Ring-Jingle. Michael Lewis. RIS
Spring Sailing. Leonidas of Tarentum, *tr. fr. Greek by* Robert Guthrie MacGregor. OnPM
Spring, St. Stephen's Green. Leslie Daiken. OnYI
Spring Scene. Taniguchi Buson, *tr. fr. Japanese by* Harold G. Henderson. PoPl
Spring Scene at River Town. *Unknown, tr. fr. Korean by* Grace W. Mitchell. OnPM
Spring Serpent, A. Ivor Winters. CBV; ExPo
Spring shakes the windows; doors whang to. A Spring Wind. Bernard Spencer. GTBS-P
Spring shall rouse my buried Lord, The. Easter Poem. Kathleen Raine. LiTB
Spring Signs. Rachel Field. InMe
Spring Snow and Tui. Mary Ursula Bethell. AnNZ
Spring Song. Robert Browning. *See* Year's at the Spring, The.
Spring Song. Bliss Carman. HBV; VA; YT
Make Me Over, Mother April, *sel.* HBVY
Spring Song. Hilda Conkling. GBV (1922 ed.); HH; MPB; PoSC; TSW
Spring Song. Aubrey Thomas De Vere. IrPN
Spring Song. "George Eliot." *Fr.* The Spanish Gypsy. OTPC (1946 ed.); PRWS
Spring Song. Donald Finkel. NYBP
Spring Song. William Griffith. MPB
Spring Song. Rayner Heppenstall. NeBP
Spring Song. Hermann Hesse, *tr. fr. German by* Ludwig Lewisohn. AWP; JAWP; WBP
Spring Song, A. Mary Howitt. BoTP
Spring Song. Rod McKuen. CAD
Spring Song. Nahum, *tr. fr. Hebrew by* Emma Lazarus. TrJP
Spring Song. Katharine O'Brien. GoYe
Spring Song. Helen Steiner Rice. FaChP
Spring Song. George Brandon Saul. GoYe
Spring Song ("When daisies pied . . ."). Shakespeare. *See* When Daisies Pied and Violets Blue.
Spring Song. LeRoy Smith, Jr. NePoAm
Spring Song. Theodore Spencer. AnFE; CoAnAm; TwAmPo
Spring Song. Swinburne. PCD
Spring Song ("Lenten is come with love to towne"). *Unknown. See* Lenten Is Come.
Spring Song, A ("Old Mother Earth woke up from her sleep"). *Unknown.* PoLF
Spring Song ("Spring, beautiful spring!"). *Unknown, tr. fr. Russian.* PCH
Spring Song ("Spring is come to town with love"), *mod. vers. of* Lenten Is Come. *Unknown.* EnLi-1
Spring Song ("Storks fly over the fields"). *Unknown, tr. fr. Czech.* PCH
Spring Song in the City. Robert Buchanan. HBV; OTPC (1923 ed.); VA
Spring Song of a Super-Blake. Louis Untermeyer. HBMV
Spring Song of Aspens. Lilian White Spencer. PoOW
Spring Song of the Birds. James I, King of Scotland. *Fr.* The Kingis Quair. OBEV
("Worshipe, ye that lovers been, this May.") TrGrPo
Spring, Spring. Pussy-Willows. Aileen Fisher. RePo
Spring still makes spring in the mind. We Are Never Old. Emerson. *Fr.* The World-Soul. OQP; PoRL
Spring Stops Me Suddenly. Valentin Iremonger. OnYI
Spring, summer, autumn, winter. The Builders. Ebenezer Elliott. VA
Spring: The Lover and the Birds. William Allingham. *See* Lover and Birds, The.
Spring, the Sweet Spring. Thomas Nashe. *Fr.* Summer's Last Will and Testament. CH; EnLi-1 (1949 ed.); FlW; GTBS; GTSE; GTSL; HBV; LiTB; NoP; OBEV; PoRA; TOP; ViBoPo
(Birds in Spring.) PRWS
(Song: "Spring, the sweete spring, is the yeres pleasant King.") YAT
(Spring.) AtBAP; BoNaP; CBEP; ElL; GTBS-D; GTBS-P; GTBS-W; LiTG; MCCG; MemP; OTPC; PCH; PoIE; RG; RIS; ShBV-2; TrGrPo; WiR

Spring (continued)
("Spring, the sweet spring, is the year's pleasant king.") EG; MyFE; ReEn; SiCE; TuPP
Spring, the Travelling Man. Winifred M. Letts. BoTP
Spring Thunder. Mark Van Doren. WIRo
Spring to Winter. George Crabbe. *Fr.* The Ancient Mansion. ChTr
Spring too, very soon! Harbingers. Basho. PoPl; RePo
Spring Trip of the Schooner *Ambition,* The, *with music.* *Unknown.* ShS
Spring under a Thorn, The. *Unknown.* MeEL
(At a Spring-Well.) NoP
Spring Up, O Well! *Unknown.* SoP
Spring up, O well—sing ye into it. Song of the Well. Numbers, Bible, *O.T.* TrJP
Spring Voices. Louis MacNeice. Sonn; WePo
Spring Voices. Jesse Stuart. FiSC
Spring Walk, The. Thomas Miller. OTPC (1923 ed.)
Spring Was Late That Year, The. V. Sackville West. *Fr.* The Land. AtBAP
Spring which has its appeal in ghosts. The Seasons. Lynette Roberts. MoPW
Spring Will Come, The. H. D. Lowry. BoNaP
Spring will come again, dear friends, The. A Song of Farewell. Dora Greenwell. VA
Spring Wind, A. Bernard Spencer. GTBS-P
Spring Wind. Nancy Byrd Turner. SiSoSe
Spring Wish. John Farrar. GFA
Spring, with that nameless pathos in the air. Spring. Henry Timrod. AP; HBV
Spring with the lark, most comely bride, and meet. A Nuptial Verse to Mistress Elizabeth Lee Now Lady Tracy. Robert Herrick. HW
Spring Work at the Farm. Thirza Wakley. BoTP
Spring Workman. Alan Creighton. CaP; TwCaPo
Springboard, The. Louis MacNeice. ChMP
Springbok. *Unknown, tr. fr. Hottentot.* PeSA
Springbok doe mothers sang, The. Song of the Springbok Does. *Unknown.* PeSA
Springfield Calibre Fifty, The. Joseph Mills Hanson. PoOw
Springfield Mountain (*diff. versions*). *Unknown.* BaBo; Po; TrAS, *with music*; ViBoFo (A, B, *and* C *vers.*; D *vers., with music*)
(In Springfield Mountain.) IHA
Springfield of the Far Future, The. Vachel Lindsay. MoRP
Springful of larks in a rolling, A. October. Dylan Thomas. *Fr.* Poem in October. YeAr
Spring's Arrival. *Unknown.* FaPON
Spring's Delights. Joseph Ashby-Sterry. CenHV
Spring's Glory, The, *sel.* Thomas Nabbes.
On a Mistress of Whose Affections He Was Doubtful. SeCL
Spring's Immortality. Mackenzie Bell. VA
Spring's on the Curb. Hildegarde Flanner. AnAmPo
Spring's Welcome. John Lyly. *See* Trico's Song.
Spring-Tide. *Unknown.* *See* Lenten Is Come.
Springtide of spirits, at the Altar rail. Nam Semen Est Verbum Dei. Louise Imogen Guiney. CAW
Springtime. Alfred Kreymborg. MAPA
Springtime, The. Denise Levertov. CoAP
Springtime in Cookham Dean. Cecil Roberts. HBMV
Springtime in Donegal. Mabel Rose Stevenson. StVeCh
Springtime is a green time. Four Seasons. Rowena Bennett. SiSoSe; TiPo (1959 ed.)
Springy motion in her gait, A. Charles Lamb. *Fr.* Hester. LO
Sprinkling. Dorothy Mason Pierce. SUS; TiPo
Sprinters, The. Lee Murchison. SD
Spritely Dead, The. Oscar Williams. *Fr.* Variations on a Theme. LiTA; NePA; Sonn
Sprouting flowers and leaves and the May time, The. Fealty. Wolfram von Eschenbach. LiTW
Sprouts the Bitter Grain. Phyllis Webb. PeCV
Spruce Macaronis, and pretty to see. The Maryland Battalion. John Williamson Palmer. AA; HBV; MC; PaA; PAH
Sprung from a race that had long till'd the soil. The Adventures of Simon Swaugum, a Village Merchant. Philip Freneau. PoEL-4
Spur, The. W. B. Yeats. ELU
Spur is red upon the briar, The. An Outdoor Litany. Louise Imogen Guiney. TrPWD
Spurn the temerity. Emily Dickinson. MWA-2
Spurning the Earth. Giordano Bruno. *See* Philosophic Flight, The.
Sputter, city! Bead with fire. To Chicago at Night. Mildred Plew Meigs. HBMV
Spyglass. Horace Gregory. TPM
Squalid village set in wintry mud, A. Born without a Chance. Edmund Vance Cooke. BLPA
Squall. Stanley Moss. CoAP
Squanderings. Witter Bynner. MoLP
Square-Cap. John Cleveland. AnAnS-2
Square in Savannah. Jason Miller. ThO
Square sheets—they saw the marble into. Island Quarry. Hart Crane. CrMA
Square, squat room, A. Waiting. W. E. Henley. In Hospital, II. NBM; PoVP
Square-stanced hind-legs; body rectangular. Mantis. Terence Heywood. BoSA
Square-Toed Princes. Robert P. Tristram Coffin. AmFN
Square, with gravel paths and shabby lawns, The. Charleville. Arthur Rimbaud. SyP
Squares and Angles. Alfonsina Storni, *tr. fr. Spanish by* Seymour Resnick. OCS
Squaring the Circle. Louis O. Coxe. NYBP
Squat in swamp shadows. Burning. Gary Snyder. Myths & Texts, III. NeAP
Squats on a Toad-Stool under a Tree. Thomas Lovell Beddoes. *See* Isbrand's Song.
Squatter's Children. Elizabeth Bishop. NePoAm-2
Squeak the fife, and beat the drum. Independence Day. Royall Tyler. HS, *abr.*; PAH
Squeak's heard in the orchestra, A. Quatrain. George T. Lanigan. WhC
Squeal. Louis Simpson. FiBHP; Par
Squeal of car wheels braking, The. The Accident. Raymond Richard Patterson. CAD
Squealing under city stone. Rapid Transit. James Agee. AnAmPo; MoAmPo; NAMP
Squealshrilling mosquitoes, fraternity lost to shame. Against Mosquitoes. Meleager. LiTW
Squire, A. Chaucer, *mod. by* Louis Untermeyer. *Fr.* The Canterbury Tales: Prologue. GoTP; WePo, *mod. by* Nevill Coghill
Squire Adams had two wives, they say. Ballade of My Lady's Beauty. Joyce Kilmer. HBV
Squire and Milkmaid; or, Blackberry Fold. *Unknown.* CoMu; OxBB
Squire her hent in arms two, The. Medieval Mirth. *Unknown.* *Fr.* The Squire of Low Degree. ACP
Squire Meldrum at Carrickfergus. Sir David Lindsay. *Fr.* The Historie of Squyer William Meldrum. OxBS
Squire of Alsatia, The, *sels.* Thomas Shadwell.
Expostulation, The. OAEP
Victory in Hungary, The. SeCL
Squire of Low Degree, The, *sel.* *Unknown.*
Medieval Mirth. ACP
Squirrel, The. Bernard Barton. OTPC (1923 ed.)
Squirrel, The. William Cowper. GoTP
Squirrel. Frances Frost. BoChLi
Squirrel, The. Mary Howitt. BoTP
Squirrel, The. Ogden Nash. CenHV
Squirrel. James S. Tippett. RePo
Squirrel, The ("Whisky Frisky"). *Unknown.* BoChLi; FaPON; PDV; RIS; SoPo; StVeCh; SUS; TiPo; UTS
(Whisky Frisky.) GFA; OTPC (1946 ed.)
Squirrel, The ("The winds they did blow"). *Unknown.* BoTP; OxNR
Squirrel and the Wind, The. *Unknown.* PCH
Squirrel, dear Squirrel, up there on the tree. The Boy and the Squirrel. F. Hey. SAS
Squirrel, flippant, pert, and full of play, The. The Squirrel. William Cowper. GoTP
Squirrel in the Rain. Frances Frost. RePo
Squirrel is happy, the squirrel is gay, The. The Squirrel. Bernard Barton. OTPC (1923 ed.)
Squirrel is the curliest thing, The. The Curliest Thing. *Unknown.* BoTP
Squirrel to some is a squirrel, A. The Squirrel. Ogden Nash. CenHV
Squirrels' Christmas, The. Winifred Howard. ChBR
Stab, The. Will Wallace Harney. AA

Stabat Mater. Jozef Wittlin, *tr. fr. Polish by* Joy Davidman. PoFr
Stabat Mater Dolorosa [*or* Stabat Mater],*sels.* *At. to* Jacopone da Todi. *tr. fr. Latin.*
"At the cross her station keeping." *Tr. by* Richard Mant *and* Edward Caswall. TreFS; WGRP; WHL
"By the cross of expiation/ The Mother stood, and kept her station." *Tr. by* Aubrey Thomas De Vere. ISi
"Near the cross her vigil keeping." *Comp. by* Louis F. Benson. MaRV
"Stood the afflicted mother weeping." *Tr. by* Abraham Coles. HBV
"Stood the Mother in her anguish." *Tr. by* Thomas Walsh. CAW
Stabat Mater Speciosa. *At. to* Jacopone da Todi, *tr. fr. Latin by* Thomas Walsh. CAW
Stable-lamp is lighted, A. A Christmas Hymn. Richard Wilbur. CoPo; MoRP
Stable-Talk. Raymond Knister. CaP
Staccato! Staccato! The Rubinstein Staccato Etude. R. Nathaniel Dett. BANP
Stack, The. Stanley Snaith. ChMP
"Stack Arms!" Joseph Blynth Alston. PAH
Stacked houses on either side, The. The Languages We Are. F. J. Bryant. NBP
Staff and Scrip, The. Dante Gabriel Rossetti. OAEP; PoVP
Staff-Nurse: New Style. W. E. Henley. In Hospital, X. NBM; PoVP
Staff-Nurse: Old Style. W. E. Henley. In Hospital, VIII. InP; PoVP
Staff of Aesculapius, The. Marianne Moore. ImOP
Staff Officer, The. Shakespeare. *See* My Liege, I Did Deny No Prisoners.
Staff slips from the hand, The. Outward. Louis Simpson. NYBP
Staffa. Keats. SiSw
Stag does not lay his side to sleep. Grania. *Unknown.* KiLC
Stag of the Ogura Mountain, The. Cry of the Stag. Emperor Jomei. OnPM
Stage Directions. William Rose Benét. ShBV-2
Stage Driver's Story, The. *Unknown.* IHA
Stage is about to be swept of corpses, The. Horatian Epode to the Duchess of Malfi. Allen Tate. FaBoMo
Stage is lighted, the first act half over, The. Third Row, Centre. William Rose Benét. WhC
Stage Love. Swinburne. NoP; PoEL-5; ViPP
Stages. Roy Macnab. ACV
Stages on a Journey Westward. James Wright. AmPC; NaP
Staggering down the road at midnite. The Encounter. Paul Blackburn. NeAP
Stagnant tower foretold the doom, The. The Kind Look. Willard Maas. LiTM (1946 ed.)
Stagolee. *Unknown.* ABF (2 *vers.*), *with music*; BaBo (A *and* B *vers.*); OxBoLi; TTY; ViBoFo (A *and* B *vers.*)
Stainless Fair Appearance, The. Bilhana, *formerly at. to* Chauras, *tr. fr. Sanskrit by* E. Powys Mathers. *Fr.* Black Marigolds. OnPM
Stainless soldier on the walls. Emerson. *Fr.* Voluntaries. WGRP
Stair, The ("The stair is curved, the railing high"). Gertrude Clayton. FiSC
Stains. Theodosia Garrison. HBV; MaRV; WGRP
Stair-carpet is Turkey red, The. On the Staircase. Eleanor Farjeon. SiSoSe
Stairs. Oliver Herford. FiBHP; InMe; RePo; WhC
Stairway is not, The. The Jacob's Ladder. Denise Levertov. AmPP (5th ed.); CaFP; CoPo; ToPo
Stairway to the Stars, The. William Ludlum. SoP
Stalky Jack. William Brighty Rands. BoTP; RIS
Stalled on the sidelines we must hope and wait. We Who Build Visions. Stanton A. Coblentz. PGD
Stallions I must have, The, good wife! the red one and the brown. At Welbedacht. A. M. Buckton. BoSA
Stalwart soldier comes, the spring, A. The Seasons: Spring. Kalidasa. AWP
Stamp Battalion. E. V Lucas. StVeCh (1955 ed.)
Stampede, The. Earl Alonzo Brininstool. PoOW
Stampede, The. Wallace D. Coburn. PoOW
Stampede, The. *Unknown.* CoSo
Stampede of machine and the avarice of man. Swan Song. Som Parkash Ranchan. ACV
Stamp's a tiny, flimsy thing, A. Stamp Battalion. E. V. Lucas. StVeCh (1955 ed.)
Stan' Still Jordan, *with music.* *Unknown.* BoAN-1
Stance. Theodore Enslin. CoPo
"Stand aside." Sun and Cloud. Melville Cane. PoPl
Stand at my window. Apology for Youth. Sister Mary Madeleva. PoPl
Stand By. *Unknown.* STF
Stand by the Flag. John Nichols Wilder. GN, *abr.*; HH; PGD, *abr.*
"Stand by the flag," 2 *sts.* PEDC
Stand close around, ye Stygian set. Dirce. Walter Savage Landor. *Fr.* Pericles and Aspasia. AnFE;AWP;BoLiVe;CBEP;CBV;ChTr;CTC;EG;EnRP;ExPo;f-aBoEnGTBS-D;InPo;JAWP;LiTB;LoBV;MemP;NoP;OAEP;-OBEV;OBNC;OBRV;PoEL-4;PoRA;SeCeV;StP;TOP;TreFT;-TrGrPo;VA;ViBoPo;WBP;HA;WhC
Stand Fast. O My Heart. *Unknown* *tr. fr. Egyptian by* Alan H. Gardiner. LiTW
Stand Forth! Angela Morgan. MaRV
Stand forth, Seithenyn: winds are hight. Song of Gwyntho. Thomas Love Peacock. *Fr.* The Misfortunes of Elphin. OBRV
Stand here by my side and turn, I pray. The Snow-Shower. Bryant. AnNE; HBV
Stand Not Uttering Sedately. Victor Plarr. *See* Epitaphium Citharistriae.
Stand off, and let me take the air. A Fair Nymph Scorning a Black Boy Courting Her. John Cleveland. AnAnS-2
Stand on the highest pavement of the stair. La Figlia Che Piange. T. S. Eliot. APA; BoLiVe; BWP; CLwM; CoAnAm; FaBoTw; LiTA; MAP; MaPo (1969 ed.); MWA-2; MoAmPo (1942 ed.); NP; PG (1945 ed.); PoIE; POTE; ReMP; ViBoPo
Stand, Stately Tavie. *Unknown.* ErPo; PV
(Stand statly Tavie out of the codpis rise.) SeCSL
Stand still, and I will read to thee. A Lecture upon the Shadow. John Donne. AnAnS-1; AnEnPo; AtBAP; AWP; CABA; CaFP; DiPo; EnRePo; InPo; MaMe; OBS; PAn; Po; PoeP; ReEn; SCEP-1; SeCP; SeEP; TuPP
"Stand still in bright array ye saints, here stand." War in Heaven. Milton. *Fr.* Paradise Lost. DiPo
"Stand still," my soul, for so thy Lord commands. Be Still. *Unknown.* SoP
Stand still, true poet that you are! Popularity. Robert Browning. PoVP; PP
Stand still you floods doe not deface. On Sight of a Gentlewomans Face in the Water. Thomas Carew. SeCV-1
Stand straight:/ Step firmly, throw your weight. Rules for the Road. Edwin Markham. OQP; OTPC (1946 ed.); PoRL; RePo; RIS; StaSt; TreFT
Stand! the ground's your own, my braves! Warren's Address to the American Soldiers [*or* at Bunker Hill]. John Pierpont. AA; AmePo; AnNE; DD; FaBoBe; GN; HBV; HBVY; MC; PaA; PAH; PAL; PAP; PEDC; PoFr; PTK; TreF; WBLP
Stand there hours, Casyor Brioschi. The Song of Casyor Brioschi. Thomas Hanna. QAH
Stand-to; Good Friday Morning. Siegfried Sassoon. FaBoTw
Stand to Your Glasses. Bartholomew Dowling. *See* Revel, The.
"Stand to your guns, men!" Morris cried. On Board the *Cumberland.* George Henry Boker. PAH
Stand Up for Jesus. George Duffield, Jr. TreFS
Stand, Whoso List. Seneca. *See* Stond Who So List Upon the Slipper Toppe.
Stand ye calm and resolute. Shelley. *Fr.* The Masque of Anarchy. LoBV
Standard Forgings Plant. William Stephens. NAMP
Standardization. A. D. Hope. BoAV
Standards. Nathalia Crane. *See* Colors, The.
Standin' on the Walls of Zion, *with music.* *Unknown.* AS
Standing aloof in giant ignorance. To Homer [*or* Sonnet: To Homer]. Keats. BWP; CABA; CBEP; ChER; MBW-2; NCEP; NoP; OBRV; Sonn
Standing at my writing desk. Difficult Times. Bertolt Brecht. ELU
Standing at the Foot of the Steps at Night. Yüan Mei, *tr. fr. Chinese by* David Mackay. FIW
Standing at the portal. At the Portal. Frances Ridley Havergal. BLRP

Standing between the sun and moon preserves. Einstein. Archibald MacLeish. AnFE; APA; CMoP; CoAnAm; MoPo; TwAmPo
Standing in silence. Blow Fish. A. Kirby Congdon. NYTB
Standing on Earth. Milton. *Fr.* Paradise Lost, VII. ChTr
Standing on 127th the. Langston. Mari Evans. BOLo
Standing on the mountaintop. Lost Silvertip. J. D. Reed. NYBP
Standing on the Streetcorner. Edwin Denby. ANYP
Standing on Tiptoe. George Frederick Cameron. CaP; OBCV; PeCV (1967 ed.); VA
Standing on top of the hay. The Farm. Donald Hall. LiTM (1970 ed.)
Standing there. Just Sixteen. Hsü Chien. OnPM
Standing upon the margent of the Main. The Tempest. Charles Cotton. PeRV; SeCePo
Standing with folded wings of mystery. The New Year. Lillian Gilchrist Gard. OQP
Stands a lady/ on a mountain. David Jones. *Fr.* The Anathemata. PrWP
Stanky. Bill Berkson. ANYP
Stanley Meets Mutesa. James D. Rubadiri. PBA
Stans Puer and Mensam. Sir Walter Raleigh. WhC
Stanza: "Often rebuked, yet always back returning." *At. to* Emily Brontë. *See* Stanzas: "Often rebuked. . ."
Stanza: "When a man hath no freedom to fight for at home." Byron. *See* When a Man Hath No Freedom.
Stanza from an Early Poem. Christopher Pearse Cranch. *See* Gnosis.
Stanza on Freedom, A. James Russell Lowell. *See* Stanzas on Freedom.
Stanzas: "Away! the moor is dark beneath the moon." Shelley. *See* Stanzas—April, 1814.
Stanzas: "Black absence hides upon the past." John Clare. EnLoPo
Stanzas: "Could love for ever." Byron. HBV; NoP; ViBoPo, *abr.*
Stanzas: "Dead leaves strew the forest walk, The." John G. C. Brainard. AnAmPo
Stanzas: "Farewell, Life! my senses swim." Thomas Hood. *See* Farewell, Life!
Stanzas: "How beautiful this hill of fun swells on!" John Clare. *Fr.* Child Harold. OBNC
Stanzas: "I will go back to the great sweet mother." Swinburne. *See* Sea, The.
Stanzas: "If, Marchioness, you can descry." Corneille, *tr. fr. French by* Henry Carrington. LiTW
Stanzas: "I'll not weep that thou art going to leave me." Emily Brontë. LoBV
Stanzas: "In a drear-nighted December." Keats. ChER; HBV; OBEV; OBNC; OBRV
(December.) GN; OTPC
(Happy Insensibility.) GTBS; GTBS-D; GTBS-P; GTBS-W; GTSE; GTSL
(In a Drear-nighted December.) CBEP; CH; EG; ELP; EnRP; EPN; ERoP-2; PoE; TOP
Stanzas: "In youth have I known one with whom the Earth." Poe. MAmP
Stanzas: "Mighty thought of an old world, The." Thomas Lovell Beddoes. *See* Mighty Thoughts of an Old World, The.
Stanzas: "My life is like the summer rose." Richard Henry Wilde. *See* My Life Is like the Summer Rose.
Stanzas: "Nature doth have her dawn each day." Henry David Thoreau. AmLP
Stanzas: "No tongue can tell, no pen describe." Philip Freneau. CoBA
Stanzas: "Often rebuked, yet always back returning." *At. to* Emily Brontë. BoPe; ChER; FaBoEn; HBV; LiTB; LoBV; OAEP; OBNC; OBVV; VA
(Often Rebuked Yet Always Back Returning.) EnLit; PoIE; PoVP
(Stanza: "Often rebuked. . .") OBEV (new ed.)
Stanzas: "When a man hath no freedom to fight for at home." Byron. *See* When a Man Hath No Freedom.
Stanzas: "Where forlorn sunsets flare and fade." W. E. Henley. *See* Over the Hills and Far Away.
Stanzas: "With tears thy grief thou dost bemoan." Solomon ibn Gabirol, *tr. fr. Hebrew by* Emma Lazarus. TrJP
Stanzas—April, 1814. Shelley. ChER; EnRP; FiP; MBW-2; MyFE; OAEP; OBNC
(Remorse.) OBEV
(Stanzas: "Away! the moor is dark beneath the moon." ERoP-2; LoBV
Stanzas Cancelled from the Elegy. Thomas Gray. ViBoPo
Stanzas Concerning Christ and the Soul. St. John of the Cross, *tr. fr. Spanish by* E. Allison Peers. BoC
Stanzas concerning Love. Stefan George, *tr. fr. German by* Ludwig Lewisohn. AWP; JAWP; WBP
Stanzas for Lent. James Howell. PrWP
Stanzas for Music ("I speak not, I trace not"). Byron. MERP
(I Speak Not, I Trace Not, I Breathe Not Thy Name.) FaPL
Stanzas for Music ("There be none of beauty's daughters"). Byron. BEL; ChER; DTC; EnL; EnLi-2 (1949 ed.); EnLit; EnRP; EPN; FiP; ForPo; HBV; ILP; MBW-2; MCCG; NeHB; NoP; OAEP; OBRV; OuHeWo; PoE; PoFS; PoRA; TOP; TrGrPo
(For Music.) CBEP; OBEV (1st ed.)
(There Be None of Beauty's Daughters.) ELP; GTBS; GTBS-D; GTBS-P; GTBS-W; GTSE; GTSL; LiTB; LoBV; LiTG; LiTL
Stanzas for Music ("There's not a joy"). Byron. BEL; CoBE; EnLi-2; EnLit; EnRP; EPN; HBV; MaPo; OAEP; OuHeWo; PoFS; TOP
(There's Not a Joy the World Can Give.) FosPo
(Youth and Age.) GTBS; GTBS-D; GTBS-P; GTBS-W; GTSE; GTSL
Stanzas for Music ("They say that hope is happiness"). Byron. ForPo
Stanzas for My Daughter. Horace Gregory. *See* Poems for My Daughter.
Stanzas for the Harp. *Unknown, tr. fr. Welsh by* Gwyn Williams. PrWP
Stanzas from "Elegy for Edward Thomas." Charles Dalmon. POTE
Stanzas from "Milton." Blake. *See* And Did Those Feet in Ancient Time.
Stanzas from "Saint Peter's Complaint." Robert Southwell. *Fr.* Saint Peter's Complaint. ACP; CAW
Stanzas from the Grande Chartreuse. Matthew Arnold. BWP; CoBE; EPN; MaVP; MBW-2; OAEP; PoEL-5; PoVP; ViPo; ViPP; VP
"For rigorous teachers seized my youth," *sel.* ViBoPo
Stanzas from "The Ivory Gate." Thomas Lovell Beddoes. *See* Mighty Thoughts of an Old World, The.
Stanzas in Memory of the Author of "Obermann." Matthew Arnold. EPN; MaVP; PoVP; ViPo; ViPP
Stanzas Occasioned by the Ruins of a Country Inn, Unroofed and Blown Down in a Storm. Philip Freneau. OxBA
(On the Ruins of a Country Inn.) AA
Stanzas on a Visit to Longleat House in Wiltshire, October 1953. George Barker. ToPo
Stanzas on Freedom. James Russell Lowell. CoBA; GN, 2 *sts.*; MaRV, *abr.*; MC; OHIP; PGD, *abr.*; PoFr; PoNe
Slaves, *last st.* NeHB; OQP; PCD; SoP; TRV; WBLP
(Commitment.) TreFT
(On Freedom.) PAL
(Stanza on Freedom, A.) AA; WaKn
Stanzas on Mutability. Hugo von Hofmannsthal, *tr. fr. German by* Jethro Bithell. AWP; TrJP
Stanzas on Seeing the Speaker Asleep in His Chair. Winthrop Mackworth Praed. EnRP
(Stanzas to the Speaker Asleep.) NBM
Stanzas on Woman. Goldsmith. *See* Song: "When lovely woman stoops to folly."
Stanzas to——("Well, some may hate"). Emily Brontë. LoBV
Stanzas to Augusta ("Though the day of my destiny's over"). Byron. EnRP; ERoP-2
Stanzas to Edward Williams. Shelley. OBNC
(To Edward Williams.) PeER
Stanzas to Mr. Bentley. Thomas Gray. EiPP; NoP
Stanzas to Pale Ale. *Unknown.* BOHV
Stanzas to the Memory of Thomas Hood. Bartholomew Simmons. VA
Stanzas to the Po. Byron. ERoP-2
Stanzas to the Speaker Asleep. Winthrop Mackworth Praed. *See* Stanzas on seeing the speaker asleep in his chair.
Stanzas Written in Dejection, near Naples. Shelley. BEL; BWP; CABA; CBEP; ChER; CoBE; EnL; EnLi-2; EnLit; EnRP; EPN; ERoP-2; FaBV; FiP; GTBS; GTBS-D; GTBS-P; GTBS-W; GTSE; GTSL; MCCG; MERP; NoP; OAEP; OBRV; PeER; PoRA; ViBoPo; WHA

Stanzas Written in My Pocket Copy of Thomson's "Castle of Indolence." Wordsworth. EnRP
Stanzas Written on Battersea Bridge during a Southwesterly Gale. Hilaire Belloc. GoBC
Stanzas Written on the Road between Florence and Pisa. Byron. EnLi-2 (1949 ed.); EnRP; HBV; MCCG; MERP; OBRV; PoFS; YAT
(All for Love.) GTBS; GTBS-D; GTBS-P; GTBS-W; GTSE; GTSL; LiTL; PoPo; TreFT
(O Talk Not to Me.) InP
Star, The. Grace Hazard Conkling. HBMV
Star. Gene Derwood. NePA; TwAmPo
Star, The. Bertha Palmer Lane. ChrBoLe
Star, A. George MacBeth. NYBP
Star, The. Ida Norton Munson. ChIP
Star. Plato. *See* Morning and Evening Star.
Star, The. Beatrice Redpath. CaP
Star, The. William Soutar. NeBP
Star, The. Jane Taylor. *See* Twinkle, Twinkle, Little Star.
Star, The ("This other night so cold"). *Unknown.* ChrBoLe
Star, The. Willoughby Weaving. HBMV; HBVY
Star,/ If you are. A Christmas Tree. William Burford. NePA
Star, A—a star in the west! Hymn of the New World. Percy MacKaye. PEDC; PoRL
Star and Face. *Unknown, tr. fr. Spanish by* Havelock Ellis. OnPM
Star, bright morning star, the shining sun, A. Meditation CXIV [*or* The Bright and Morning Star]. Edward Taylor. *Fr.* Preparatory Meditations, Second Series. MAmP; MWA-1
Star bright, starlight. *See* Star light, star bright.
Star, The; Dedicated to Theodore Roosevelt, Following His Death, January 6, 1919. Marion Couthouy Smith. DD; PAH
Star Drill. T. Inglis Moore. PoAu-2
Star-dust and vaporous light. Noel. Richard Watson Gilder. AA
Star-Fear. Leonora Speyer. AnEnPo
Star-filled seas are smooth tonight, The. The Isle of Portland. A. E. Housman. A Shropshire Lad, LIX. MoBrPo; PoVP
Star from out the heavens, A. Star and Face. *Unknown.* OnPM
Star-gaze Poem. Sandford Lyne. QAH
Star-gazing, O my Star; would I could be. My Star. Plato, *tr. by* Alexander Lothian. EnLi-1; OuHeWo
Star in the Hills, The ("A star hit in the hills behind our house"). William Stafford. PoAn
Star in the West, The. Eliza Cook. PEDC
Star, A, is gone! a star is gone! The Fallen Star. George Darley. AnFE; ERoP-2; HBV; OBEV
Star Light. *See also* Starlight.
Star light, star bright [*or* Star bright, starlight). Star Wish [*or* Signs and Charms]. *Unknown.* HBVY; OxNR; PCH; RIS; SiTL; SoPo; StaSt; StVeCh (1955 ed.); TiPo
Star looked down on Bethlehem, A. Holier Night. Leslie Savage Clark. ChIP
Star looks down at me, A. Waiting Both. Thomas Hardy. MoAB; MoBrPo; NeMA; OxBoLi; PoeP; PoPo; WaKn; WHA
Star Morals. Nietzsche, *tr. fr. German by* Ludwig Lewisohn. AWP
Star must cease to burn with its own light, The. Et Mori Lucrum. John Lancaster Spalding. *Fr.* God and the Soul. AA
Star of Bethlehem. Florence Van Cleve. OQP
Star of Bethelhem, The; a Nativity Play for Children. Alice Corbin Henderson. ChrBoLe
Star of Calvary, The. Nathaniel Hawthorne. AA
Star of Columbia, *with music.* Timothy Dwight. *See* Columbia.
Star of Descending night! fair is thy light in the west! The Songs of Selma. James MacPherson. CEP
Star of Eternal Possibles and Joy. "Peter Yates." ChMP
Star of Ethiopia. Lucian B. Watkins. BANP
Star of My Heart. Vachel Lindsay. OQP
Star of my mishap imposed [*or* impos'd] this pain [*or* paining], The. To Delia, XXXI. Samuel Daniel. OBSC;ReIE
Star of ocean fairest. Ave Maris Stella. *Unknown.* ISi
Star of Sangamon, The. Lyman Whitney Allen. PGD
Star of the East. Eugene Field. HH; OQP; PGD; PoRL
Star of the Evening. James M. Sayles. Par
Star of the Morning. D. V. Johnstone. BePJ
Star of the Nativity. Boris Pasternak, *tr. fr. Russian by* Eugene M. Kayden. PoPl
(Christmas Star, *tr. by* Lydia Pasternak.) FIW
Star of the North! though night winds drift. The Fugitive Slave's Apostrophe to the North Star. John Pierpont. AA
Star of the Sea. Sebastian Brant, *tr. fr. German by* Alexander Barclay. *Fr.* The Ship of Fools. ACP; CAW
Star of the Sea. Richard Webb Sullivan. ISi
Star of the Sea, to whom, age after age. To Ask Our Lady's Patronage for a Book on Columbus. Thomas D'Arcy McGee. JKCP
Star proves never traitor and a weed, A. Thrift. Lizette Woodworth Reese. NP
Star-Pudding. Robert P. Tristram Coffin. PoPo
Star Sirius, The. George Meredith. VP
Star Sirius and the Pole Star dwell afar. Christina Rossetti. *Fr.* Later Life. VA
Star Song. Robert Underwood Johnson. HBV
Carol to the King. Robert Herrick. OxBoCh
(Star Song, The, *abr.*) GN
Star Song of the Bushman Women. *Unknown, tr. fr. Bushman by* W. H. I. Bleek. PeSA
Star-spangled Banner, The. Francis Scott Key. AA; BBV; BLPA; DD; FaBoBe; FaFP; FaPL; FaPON; HBV; HBVY; HH; InP; MaRV; MC; NeHB; NePA; OTD; OTPC; PaA; PAH; PAL; PAP; PEDC; PoFr; PoRL; PTK; ThLM; TreF; WBLP; YaD
(Defence of Fort M'Henry.) AmePo
Star-spangled Ode. Phyllis McGinley. ThLM
Star-Splitter, The. Robert Frost. ImOP
Star, star, shining bright. Star. Gene Derwood. NePA; TwAmPo
"Star stood over where the young child was, The." A Christmas Prayer. Molly Anderson Haley. PGD
Star-Talk. Robert Graves. BoNaP; GoJo; HBMV; MoBrPo; RG
Star That Bids the Shepherd Fold, The. Milton. *Fr.* Comus. EG; FaBoCh; LoGBV; OBEV, *abr.*; TOP; ViBoPo; WHA
(Comus' Invocation to His Revelers.) BoLiVe; TrGrPo
(Invocation of Comus, The.) OBS
(Mask, A.) FiP
(Song: "Star that bids the shepherd fold, The.") SeCeV
Star that bringest home the bee. Song to the Evening Star [*or* To the Evening Star]. Thomas Campbell. GTBS; GTBS-D; GTBS-P; GTBS-W; GTSE; GTSL; HBV; TRV
Star that guided the wise men, The. The Eternal Light. William C. Fisher. SoP
Star that shone on Bethlehem, shine on London City. A Christmas Carol. Gilbert Thomas. MoRP
Star that watched above your sleep has just put out his light, The. The Child's Star. John Banister Tabb. PPL
Star There Fell, A. Zalman Schneour, *tr. fr. Hebrew by* Harry H. Fein. TrJP
Star Thought. Frances Shaw. NP
Star-throned, incorruptible Aphrodite. Ode to Aphrodite. Sappho. AWP
Star Watcher, The. Peter Davison. TwCP
Star Wish. *Unknown.* HBVY; PCH
(Signs and Charms.) StaSt
("Star-light, star-bright.") OxNR; RIS; SiTL; TiPo
Stare at the monster: remark. Famous Poet. Ted Hughes. LiTM (1970 ed.)
Stare at the stars, the stars say. Ego. Norman MacCaig. GTBS-P
Stared Story, A. William Stafford. TPM
Stare's Nest by My Window, The. W. B. Yeats. Meditations in Time of Civil War, VI. CABL; GTBS-P; LiTB; PIA
Starfish, The. Robert P. Tristram Coffin. ImOP
Starfish. Winfred Welles. FaPON; SiSoSe
Stark by the Eastern gate. Two Men in Armour. John Heath-Stubbs. NeBP
Stark day corrodes the silver of the dream. Naomi Long Madgett. *Fr.* Trinity: a Dream Sequence. Kal
Stark in the pasture of the skull-shaped hill. Pieta. David Gascoyne. *Fr.* Miserere. NeBP; POTE
Starless and chill is the night. A Night by the Sea. Heine, *tr. by* Howard Mumford Jones. *Fr.* The North Sea. AWP
Starless and cold is the night. Night on the Shore. Heine, *tr. by* Emma Lazarus. *Fr.* The North Sea. LiTW
Starlight. John White Chadwick. AA

Starlight. Harold Lewis Cook. NP
Starlight. William Meredith. NePoEA
Starlight like Intuition Pierced the Twelve. Delmore Schwartz. AmP; LiTM (1946 ed.); MiAP; MoRP; NMP; TwAmPo
(Starlight's Intuitions Pierced the Twelve, The.) MoPo; NePA; PoCh
(Starlight's Intuitions Pierced the Twelve.) PoDB
Starlight Night, The. Gerard Manley Hopkins. ACP; BrPo; BWP; CAW; DiPo; GoBC; GTBS; GTBS-P; GTBS-W; JKCP; LiTM; MoAB; MoBrPo; MoPW; MoVE; OBVV; OxBoCh; PoVP; SeCePo; ShBV-4; Sonn; ThWaDe; ViBoPo; ViPo (1962 ed.); VP; WoL
(Starlit Night, The.) BoC
Starlight through the curve of space. Starlight. Harold Lewis Cook. NP
Starlighter, The. Arthur Guiterman. GaP; MoSiPe; SiSoSe
Starlight's Intuitions Pierced the Twelve, The. Delmore Schwartz. *See* Starlight like Intuition Pierced the Twelve.
Starling, The ("The Starling is my darling, although"). John Heath-Stubbs. FIW
Starling Lake, The. "Seumas O'Sullivan." AnIV; AWP; JAWP; WBP
(My Sorrow.) HBV; NP
Starlings. Ted Olson. PV
Starling's Spring Rondel, A. James Cousins. HBV; HBVY
Starlit Night, The. Gerard Manley Hopkins. *See* Starlight Night, The.
Starre, The. George Herbert. AnAnS-1; AtBAP; MaMe; MeP
Starre, The. Henry Vaughan. AnAnS-1; MeP; MePo
Starred Mother, The. Robert Whitaker. PGD
Starry Host, The. John Lancaster Spalding. *Fr.* God and the Soul. AA; HBV
Starry hosts whose far-flung cohorts gleam, The. Human Greatness. Edwin Barclay. PBA
Starry Night. Hermann Hagedorn. MaRV
Starry Night, The. Anne Sexton. NMP; OPoP; ToPo
Starry Night, The. George Starbuck. NYBP
Starry Sky. *Unknown, tr. fr. Old Irish by* Seán O'Faoláin. AnIL
Stars. Rhoda W. Bacmeister. BrR
Stars. George Mackay Brown. OxBS
Stars, The. "Barry Cornwall." OTPC
Stars, The. Mary Carolyn Davies. DD; HH
Stars, The. Mary Mapes Dodge. AA
Stars. Florence S. Edsall. MoSiPe
Stars. Robert Frost. MAmP
Stars, The. Dafydd ap Gwilym. BoPe
Stars. Carolyn Hancock. RIS
Stars. Martha Hird. SoP
Stars. Langston Hughes. OCS
Stars. Dowell O'Reilly. BoAu
Stars, The. Christina Rossetti. *Fr.* Sing-Song. OTPC (1946 ed.)
Stars. Kenneth Slessor. BoAV
Stars, The, *sel.* Christopher Smart.
"Stars of the superior class," *sel.* ChTr
Stars. Sara Teasdale. BoChLi; FaPON; HBMV; MoRP; NP; PoPo; SP; TiPo; YT
Stars ("A little boy"). *Unknown.* GFA
Stars ("I'm glad the stars"). *Unknown.* GFA
Stars, The. Andrew Young. MemP
Stars and atoms have no size. Measurement. A. M. Sullivan. RePo; WaKn
Stars and Silence. *Unknown, tr. fr. Spanish by* Havelock Ellis. OnPM
Stars and Stripes, The. James T. Fields. HH
Stars are dimly seen among the shadows of the bay, The. Barcarolle. Arthur O'Shaughnessy. NBM
Stars are everywhere to-night, The. Daisies. Andrew Young. GoJo
Stars are forth, the moon above the tops, The. The Coliseum. Byron. *Fr.* Manfred, III, iv. MCCG
Stars Are Glittering in the Frosty Sky, The. Charles Heavysege. *See* Winter Galaxy, The.
Stars are gone out spark by spark, The. At Cockcrow. Lizette Woodworth Reese. TrPWD
Stars are hidden, The. A Group of Verse. Charles Reznikoff. NP
Stars are lighted candles, The. The Stars. Mary Carolyn Davies. DD; HH
Stars Are Lit, The. Hayyim Nahman Bialik, *tr. fr. Hebrew by* Florence L. Friedman. TrJP
Stars are of mighty use: the night. God's Saints. Henry Vaughan. SoP
Stars are only a backdrop for, The. Notes on a Life to Be Lived. Robert Penn Warren. NYBP
Stars are pale, The. The Break of Day. Shaw Neilson. BoAu; BoAV; PoAu-1
Stars Are True, The. *Unknown.* MaRV
Stars Are with the Voyager, The. Thomas Hood. EnRP
Stars as Spray. *Unknown, tr. fr. Japanese by* Basil Hall Chamberlain. OnPM
Stars at Night, The. Jane Taylor. *See* Twinkle, Twinkle, Little Star.
Stars began to peep, The. The Little Ghost. Katharine Tynan. HBV
Stars Begin to Fall. *Unknown.* AA
Stars burnt out in the pale blue air, The. Shelley. *Fr.* The Boat on the Serchio. MyFE
Stars by night are the candles which light up my soul, The. My Life. Henrietta C. Parks. TNV
Stars catch my eyes, The. A Thought for My Love. Bruce Williamson. NeIP
Stars Dance, The. Thomas Campion. *See* Song: To the Masquers Representing Stars.
Stars Fade. Peretz Hirshbein, *tr. fr. Yiddish by* Joseph Leftwich. TrJP
Stars Go By, The. Lilian Bowes-Lyon. ChMP
Stars Go over the Lonely Ocean, The. Robinson Jeffers. GTBS-W; LiTA; LiTM (rev. ed.); NePA; WaP
Stars had the look of dogs to him sometimes. The Star Watcher. Peter Davison. TwCP
Stars Have Not Dealt Me, The. A. E. Housman. EnLi-2 (1949 ed.); ELU; OxBoLi; PoPo; SeCeV
("Stars have not dealt me the worst they could do, The.") GTBS-P
Stars have their glory and, or near or far. The Sun Men Call It. John Hall Wheelock. NePoAm-2
Stars have ways I do not know. I Look into the Stars. Jane Draper. HBMV
Stars, I Have Seen Them Fall. A. E. Housman. More Poems, VII. ChTr; EnLi-2 (1949 ed.); MaPo; NoP; VP
Stars know a secret, The. Force. Edward Rowland Sill. AA
Stars lie broken on a lake. Reflections. Edna Becker. SoP; TRV
Stars Look at Love, The. Heine. *See* When Young Hearts Break.
Stars must make an awful noise, The. One Blackbird. Harold Monro. *Fr.* Strange Meetings. RIS; StaSt
Stars never had any mystery for me, The. Sailor and Inland Flower. Hamish Maclaren. EtS
Stars of Cheer. Caroline D. Swan. JKCP
Stars of Night contain the glittering Day, The. The Dying Words of Stonewall Jackson. Sidney Lanier. PAH
Stars of the early dawning, set in a field of blue. Ode to the Flag. Charles C. Crellin. PEDC
Stars of the morn, The/ On our banner borne. The Flag of the *Constellation.* Thomas Buchanan Read. EtS; PaA
Stars of the Summer Night. Longfellow. *See* Serenade: "Stars of the summer night."
Stars of the superior class. The Stars. Christopher Smart. ChTr
Stars over snow. Night [*or* It Is Not Far]. Sara Teasdale. BrR; FaPON; MoSiPe; SoPo; StVeCh; SUS; TiPo
Stars rushed forth to-night, The. The Stars. Andrew Young. MemP
Stars Sang in God's Garden, The. Joseph Mary Plunkett. JKCP
Stars shine over the mountains, the stars shine over the sea, The. When the Stars Are Gone. Robert Louis Stevenson. SoP
Stars, Songs, Faces. Carl Sandburg. FIW; OTD
Stars Stand Up in the Air, The. *Tr. fr. Irish by* Thomas MacDonagh. AnIV
Stars that open and shut, The. Nonentity. D. H. Lawrence. BoPe

Stars that swing from twilight to far dawn, The. Sanctuary. Mildred Wojtalewicz. WHL
Stars trembling o'er us and sunset before us. In Our Boat. Dinah Maria Mulock Craik. HBV
Stars wheel in purple, yours is not so rare. Let Zeus Record. Hilda Doolittle ("H. D."). MAP; MoAmPo
Stars wheel past the windows, The. For the New Year. Norman Nicholson. NeBP; POTi
Stars with their laughter are shaken, The. A Song of Laughter. Theodore Maynard. JKCP
Starscape, A. John Bellenden. ACP
Starshine on the Arch is silver white, The. Villanelle of Washington Square. Walter Adolphe Roberts. PoNe
Start, The. *Unknown.* SD
Start, A. Transfigured Swan. Louis Untermeyer. MAP
Start not—nor deem my spirit fled. Lines Inscribed upon a Cup Formed from a Skull. Byron. PeER
Start Where You Stand. Berton Braley. PoToHe
Starting from Paumanok. Walt Whitman. AtBAP; PIA
Sels.
Necessity of Religion, The. MaRV
"Starting from fish-shape Paumanok." ViBoPo
Startled/ By a single scream. Saigyo Hoshi, *tr. fr. Japanese by* Arthur Waley. AWP
Startled stag, the blue-grey night, A. The Dark Stag. Isabella Valancy Crawford. PeCV (1967 ed.)
Startling all spirits, dreams, and secrets. To Our Catchment Board. Edmund Blunden. MoPW
Starvation Peak Evening. David O'Neil. AnAmPo
Starved lost frozen. La Belle Saison. Jacques Prévert. CAD
Starved, scarred, lenten, amidst ash of air. The Sugaring. A. M. Klein. OBCV
Starving, savage, I aspire. The Tiger of Desire. Tom Maclnnes. OBCV
Starving to Death on a Government Claim. *Unknown. See* Lane County Bachelor, The.
Stasis in darkness. Ariel. Sylvia Plath. NMP; OPoP
State, The. Randall Jarrell. LiTM (1970 ed.); MiAP
State of Arkansas, The, *with music. Unknown.* BFSS; CoSo; TrAS, *abr.*
(Arkansaw Traveler, The, *diff vers.) ViBoFo*
State of Maine Song. Roger Vinton Snow. PoRL
State of the Nation (1680). The. *Unknown.* PeRV
State Street is lonely today. Aunt Jane Allen. Fenton Johnson. GoSl; IDB; PoNe
State the alternative preferred. F. H. Townsend. PV
State We Honor, The. Fanny J. Crosby. PoRL
State with the prettiest name, The. Florida. Elizabeth Bishop. AmP; TwCP
Stately homes of England, The. The Homes of England. Felicia Dorothea Hemans. PaPo; WhC
Stately Homes of England, The, *parody.* E. V. Knox. WhC
Stately, kindly, lordly friend. To a Cat. Swinburne. CIV
Stately Lady, The. Flora Sandstrom. BoTP
Stately rainbow came and stood, A. The Rainbow. Coventry Patmore. *Fr.* The Angel in the House. GTBS-P
Stately Southerner, The. *Unknown. See* Yankee Man-of-War, The.
Stately the feast, and high the cheer. The Grave of King Arthur. Thomas Warton, the Younger. CEP; EnRP; GoTL
Stately Verse. *Unknown.* FaPON; TiPo (1959 ed.)
Statement. John Unterecker. ThO
States when they black out and lie there rolling, The. Falling. James Dickey. NYBP
Statesman in Retirement. William Cowper. *Fr.* Retirement. OBEC
Statesman's Holiday, The. W. B. Yeats. AtBAP; CMoP
Static. Rolfe Humphries. UnS
Static. Gertrude Van Winkle. GFA
Station, The. Mary Catherine Parsons. PCH
Stationary Journey, The. Edwin Muir. POTE
Stationed Scout, The. Lyman H. Sproull. PoOW
Stationery Motion. Tom Clark. YAP
Stationmaster's Lament, The. Jerome Rothenberg. CoPo
Stations of the Cross, The. Padraic Colum. GoBC
Stations of the Cross, The, *sels.* William A. Donaghy.
Fourth Station. ISi
He Falls. JKCP (1955 ed.)
He Is Buried. JKCP (1955 ed.)
Thirteenth Station. ISi
Statistician, The. Charles Wharton Stork. PoMa
Statistics. Stephen Spender. MoBrPo
Statuary Christ bleeds sweating grief, A. Book Buying in the Tenderloire. Robert Hass. YAP
Statue, The. Hilaire Belloc. ACP (1952 ed.); MoVE
Statue, The. John Berryman. LiTM (1946 ed.)
Statue, The. Robert Finch. OBCV; PeCV
Statue, The. John Fuller. NePoEA-2
Statue and Birds. Louise Bogan. MAP; MoAB; MoAmPo
Statue and the Bust, The. Robert Browning. BEL; EnLi-2 (1939 ed.); EPN; OAEP; PoVP; TOP; ViPP; VP
Statue and the Perturbed Burghers, The. Denis Devlin. OnYI
Statue at Charing Cross, The. Andrew Marvell. MaMe
Statue, The—Buonarroti said—doth wait. Epigram. Sir William Watson. MoBrPo (1942 ed.)
Statue in a Blizzard. Ruth Douglas Keener. NYTB
Statue in a Garden, A. Agnes Lee. HBMV; NP
Statue in Stocks-Market, The. Andrew Marvell. MaMe
Statue of a Libertine, The. Ron Padgett. YAP
Statue of Liberty, The. Sheila Jane Crooke. YaD
Statue of Liberty, The. Thomas Hardy. EPN; LiTB
Statue of Lorenzo de' Medici, The. J. E. Nesmith. AA
Statue of Shadow, The. John Peale Bishop. LiTA
Statue, The, stood/ Of Newton. Newton. Wordsworth. *Fr.* The Prelude, III. ImOP
Statue, tolerant through years of weather, The. The Statue. John Berryman. LiTM (1946 ed.)
Statues, The. Laurence Binyon. OBEV (new ed.); OBVV
Statues. Kathleen Raine. NYBP
Statues. Richard Wilbur. TPM
Statues, The. W. B. Yeats. AnIL
Statuette; Late Minoan. C. Day Lewis. EnLit; OxBI
Status Quo. Binga Dismond. PoNe
Status Symbol. Mari Evans. IDB
Statute. Josephine Miles. FiMAP
Stavin' Chain, *with music. Unknown.* OuSiCo
Stay as the tree—go as the wind. Motto for a Tree-planting. Richard Watson Gilder. PoRL
Stay beautiful. For Poets. Al Young. WSL
Stay, Christmas! Ivy O. Eastwick. SiSoSe
Stay, Fortunatus, once more hear me speak. Thomas Dekker. *Fr.* Old Fortunatus. ViBoPo
Stay, June, Stay! Christina Rossetti. *Fr.* Sing-Song. YeAr ("Days are clear, The.") RIS; TiPo
"Stay, lady, stay, for mercy's sake." The Orphan Boy's Tale. Amelia Opie. PaPo
Stay Little Always. Jessie Corrigan Pegis. JKCP (1955 ed.)
Stay near me—do not take thy flight! To a Butterfly. Wordsworth. EnRP
Stay near me. Speak my name. Oh, do not wander. Midcentury Love Letter. Phyllis McGinley. MoLP; ViBoPo (1958 ed.)
Stay now with me, and list to my sighs. Dante. *Fr.* La Vita Nuova. AWP
Stay, Nymph. *Unknown.* EnRePo
Stay, O Stay. A. E. Coppard. MoBrPo (1942 ed.)
Stay O stay why dost thou fly me. *Unknown.* SeCSL
Stay, oh, stay, ye wingëd hours! At the Florists' Feast in Norwich. Matthew Stevenson. SeCL
Stay, O sweet, and do not rise! Break of day [*or* Daybreak]. John Donne. EG; ElL; MeWo; OBEV; TOP; TrGrPo
Stay Phoebus, stay. Song. Edmund Waller. AnAnS-2; ILP; SCEP-2; SeCP
Stay, ship from Thames, with fettered sails. Ship from Thames. Rex Ingamells. MoAuPo; PoAu-2
Stay, speedy Time, behold, before thou pass. To Time. Michael Drayton. Idea, XVII. EnRePo; OBSC; SiCE
Stay, Spring. Andrew Young. FaBoTw
Stay, Stay, Old Time. *Unknown.* SeCL
Stay, stay, sweet Time! Behold, or ere thou pass. Michael Drayton. Idea's Mirrour, VII. ReIE
Stay, stay, thou lovely, fearful snake. An American Love Ode. Thomas Warton, the Elder. CEP
Stay, stay, ye greedy merchants, stay. Chloris a Constant Comfort. Henry Hughes. SeCL
Stay, Thames, to heare my song, thou great and famous flood. Michael Drayton. *fr.* The Third Eclogue. AtBAP; PoEL-2
Stay thy Soft Murmuring. Erasmus Darwin. *Fr.* The Botanic Gardens. OA
Stay, Time. James Wreford Watson. CaP

Stay we here/ With the wild hawks? Robert Browning. *Fr.* Pauline. MyFE
Stay weary traveler, stay! The Fountain at the Tomb. Nicias. AWP; JAWP; WBP
Stay with me, God. The night is dark. A Soldier—His Prayer [*or* The Soldier, 1939-1945]. Gerald Kersh. BoC; TreFS
Stay yet, my friends, a moment stay. A Song for New Year's Eve. Bryant. DD; MPB; PoRL
Staye, staye Aeneas, for thyne owne sake staye. *Unknown.* SeCSL
Stayed where he was. The Boar. Robert Kelly. CoPo
Staying Alive. David Wagoner. BoNaP; CoAP; NYBP
Staying in bed and being sick. Being Sick. Jimmy Garthwaite. BrR
Steadfast. Arthur Hugh Clough. *See* "With Whom Is No Variableness, neither Shadow of Turning."
Steadfast Cross! *Unknown.* *See* Holy Cross.
Steadfast Mind, The. Thomas Carew. *See* Disdain Returned.
Steadfastness. Sir Thomas Wyatt. *See* Forget Not Yet.
Steady heart, which in its steadiness, The. Angina Pectoris. W. R. Moses. LiTA
Steal Away to Jesus, *Unknown.* BoAN-1, *with music* (Steal Away.) TrGrPo
Steal from the meadows, rob the tall green hills. A Song. Lord Alfred Douglas. JKCP (1926 ed.); PoVP
Stealing. James Russell Lowell. MaRV; TreF (International Copyright.) AA; PV
Stealing Trout. Ted Hughes. NYBP
Stealthy the silent hours advance, and still. On a Sundial. Hilaire Belloc. MoVE
Steam Navigation Thieves, The, *with music.* John A. Stone. SGR
Steam Power. Erasmus Darwin. *Fr.* The Botanic Garden: The Economy of Vegetation, I. OBEC
Steam Shovel. Charles Malam. PoMa; PoPo
Steam Shovel, The. Eunice Tietjens. NP
Steamshovel, seen from afar, The. James Brodey. *Fr.* Identikit. ANYP
Steam Threshing-Machine, The. Charles Tennyson Turner. OBNC; PoVP
Steamboat is a slow poke, The. Boats. Rowena Bennett. GFA; SoPo; TiPo
Steamboat's coming 'round the bend. *Unknown.* LaNeLa
Steamer left the black and oozy wharves, The. Alexander Smith. *Fr.* A Boy's Poem. PeVV
Steamfitter had no notion of buying an opal, The. Opal. Josephine Miles. FiMAP
Steamshovel. *See* Steam shovel.
Steddefast Crosse, inmong alle other. A Hymn to the Cross. *Unknown.* MeEL
Steed, a steed of matchless speed, A. The Cavalier's Song. William Motherwell. GN; HBV; OTPC
Steed bit his master, The. On a Clergyman's Horse Biting Him. *Unknown.* GoTP; LiTG; OxBoLi; SiTL; TreFT; WhC
Steeds. Paul Hiebert. WHW
Steel. Henri DeWitt Saylor. PoMa
Steel fibrous slant & ribboned glint, The. The Turncoat. LeRoi Jones. NeAP; NoP
Steel Glass, The, *sels.* George Gascoigne.
"Behold him, priests, and though he stink of sweat." ReEn
"But that my lord may plainly understand." ReEn
"For whiles I mark this weak and wretched world." ReIE; SiCE; TuPP
Steel Laying Holler, *with music.* *Unknown.* ABF
Steel Mills after Midnight. Louise Crenshaw Ray. JKCP (1955 ed.)
Steel the Flint abused, The. The Flint and the Steel. Tomás de Iriarte. BoChLi
Steelhead. Robinson Jeffers. WoL
Steep, Stone Steps. Norman Cameron. MoPW
Steeped in ecstasies of perfume. Spring Nocturne. Abraham Liessin. TrJP
Steepies for the bairnie. Supper. William Soutar. OxBS
Steeple-Jack, The. Marianne Moore. *Fr.* Part of a Novel, Part of a Poem, Part of a Play. AmLP; AmPP; AP; CMoP; CoBMV; CrMA; ExPo; FaBoMo; ILP; MoPo; NoP; OnPM; OxBA; TwAmPo
Steer, Bold Mariner, On! Schiller, *tr. fr. German.* MC
Steer hither, steer, your wingèd pines. The Siren's Song [*or* Song of the Sirens]. William Browne. *Fr.* The Inner Temple Masque. ChTr; EG; ElL; EtS; OBEV; OBS; ViBoPo
Stein Family, The. *Unknown.* BOHV
Stein Song, A. Richard Hovey. *Fr.* Spring. AmePo; HBV; MAP; MoAmPo (1942 ed.); NeMA; PFY ("Give a rouse, then, in the Maytime.") AnAmPo
Stella. Charles Henry Crandall. AA
Stella Flammarum. Wilfred Campbell. WoL
Stella is sick, and in that sick-bed lies. Astrophel and Stella, CI. Sir Philip Sidney. FCP; SiPS
Stella Maris, *sels.* John Addington Symonds.
"Give me thyself! It were as well to cry." PoVP (Thyself.) VA
"How often have I now outwatched the night." PoVP
"Venice, thou Siren of sea-cities, wrought." PoVP; VA
Stella Matutina. Lillian Doherty. WHL
Stella oft sees the very face of woe. Astrophel and Stella, XLV. Sir Philip Sidney. FCP; PoE; ReEn; SiCE; SiPS; TuPP
Stella, since thou so right a princess [*or* princesse] art. Astrophel and Stella, CVII. Sir Philip Sidney. FCP; HBV; MaPo; NoP; ReEn; SiPS
Stella Sleeping. Sir Philip Sidney. Astrophel and Stella: Second Song. SiPS
Stella, the fullness of my thoughts of thee. Astrophel and Stella, L. Sir Philip Sidney. FCP; ReEn; SiPS
Stella, the only planet of my light. Astrophel and Stella, LXVIII. Sir Philip Sidney. FCP; OBSC; ReEn; SiPS
Stella, think not that I by verse seek fame. Astrophel and Stella, XC. Sir Philip Sidney. EnLit; FCP; OBSC; ReEn; SiCE; SiPS; TuPP
Stella this day is thirty four. Stella's Birthday, Written in the Year 1718. Swift. BWP; CEP; EiPP; EnLoPo
Stella, whence doth these new assaults arise. Astrophel and Stella, XXXVI. Sir Philip Sidney. FCP; SiPS
Stella, while now by Honour's cruel might. Astrophel and Stella, XCI. Sir Philip Sidney. FCP; SiPS
Stella's Birthday ("As, when a beauteous nymph decays"). Swift. PP
Stella's Birthday; March 13, 1726/7 ("This day whate'er the fates decree"). Swift. BWP; CEP; EiCL; EiPP; LoBV; NoP; OBEC; PoEL-3
Stella's Birthday, 1720 ("All travellers at first incline"). Swift. ILP; OxBI; PoEL-3
Stella's Birthday, Written in the Year 1718 ("Stella this day is thirty-four"). Swift. BWP; CEP; EiPP; EnLoPo
Stenographers, The. P. K. Page. CaP; LiTM (1970 ed.); OBCV; PeCV; TwCaPo
Step. Jason Miller. ThO
Step/ and pattern becomes. To Dance in a Loving ring. Sister Mary Norbert Körte. ThO
Step Away from Them, A. Frank O'Hara. ANYP
Step by Step. Barbara C. Ryberg. STF
Step into my room tonight. People Trying to Love. Stephen Berg. NaP
Step lightly on this narrow spot! Emily Dickinson. NePA
Step Mother, The. Helen Adam. FiSC
Step-stream pavement bears. Victoria Dancing. Anne Welsh. BoSA
Step to silence taken, The. Wild Philomela. William Rose Benét. NP
Step to the garden from the cool-roomed house. Weekend Stroll. Frances Cornford. BoNaP
Stephen is just five years old. Blanket Street. Inez Hogan. BiCB
Stephano's Song. Shakespeare. *See* Master, the Swabber, The.
Stepney Green. John Singer. WaP
Stepping Ashore. Robert E. Selle. SoP
Stepping Stones, The. Conrad Aiken. CrMA
Stepping Westward. Wordsworth. BEL; CH; EnLi-2; EnRP; ERoP-1; ExPo; HBV; MaPo (1969 ed.); MERP; OBRV; PoEL-4; SeCeV; ShBV-4
Steps. Bernadette Mayer. ANYP
Steps. Frank O'Hara. ANYP; FRC
Steps, The. Paul Valéry, *tr. fr. French by* Donald Petersen. ReMP
Steps from the Stream, *sels.* James Applewhite.
Church and Clouds. YAP
Lawn and Light. YAP

Steps, shops noses, ears, eyes steps. Steps. Bernadette Mayer. ANYP
Sterile these stones. The Corner Stone. Walter de la Mare. BrPo
Sterkfontein. Ruth Miller. PeSA
Stern be the pilot in the dreadful hour. To Abraham Lincoln [*or* Sonnet in 1862]. John James Piatt. AA
Stern Daughter of the Voice of God! Ode to Duty. Wordsworth. AWP; BEL; EnLit; EnRP; EPN; ERoP-1; GTBS; GTBS-D; GTBS-P; GTBS-W; GTSE; GTSL; HBV; HBVY; InPo; JAWP; MaRV; MBW-2; MERP; NoP; OBEV; OBRV; PoFS; TOP; TreFS; TRV; WBP; WGRP
Stern destroyer struck out my life, A. A Bible. *Unknown. Fr.* Riddles. EnLi-1; OuHeWo
Stern Duty said, "Go walk a mile." The Second Mile. Stephen Moore. SoP
Stern eagle of the far north-west. The Song of the Reim-Kennar. Sir Walter Scott. *Fr.* The Pirate. OAEP; OBNC; PeER
Stern lover in your helm of steel. The Only Pretty Ringtime. A. V. Bowen. POTE
Stern Parent, The. Harry Graham. Some Ruthless Rhymes, I. BBGG; CenHV; ChTr; TreFT
Stethoscope tells what everyone fears, The. Academic. Theodore Roethke. CrMA; ELU; MiAP; PoeP; StP
Stevedore. Leslie M. Collins. AmNP
Stevedores, The. John Gould Fletcher. Down the Mississippi, V. HT; LiTA; NP
Stevenson's Birthday. Katherine Miller. AA
Steward, The. Ebenezer Elliott. *Fr.* The Splendid Village. NBM
Steward of God. Martha Snell Nicholson. FaChP
Stewball *with music. Unknown.* ABF
Stick, The. May O'Rourke. HBMV
Stick to It. Edgar A. Guest. FaFP
Stick your patent name on a signboard. The River. Hart Crane. *Fr.* The Bridge: Powhatan's Daughter. AmP; AmPP; AnFE; AP; CMoP; CoAnAm; CoBA; CoBMV; LiTA; MoAB; MoAmPo; NAMP; OxBA; TwAmPo; ViBoPo (1958 ed.)
Stiff are the warrior's muscles. Lines Written after a Battle. *Unknown.* BOHV; InMe
Stiff spokes of this wheel, The. July in Washington. Robert Lowell. NaP; TDP
Stiff wind off the chanel, A. Wet Thursday. Weldon Kees. NaP; NYBP
Stigmata. *At. to* Edwin McNeill Poteat. *See* He Cannot Heal.
Stigmata. Charles Warren Stoddard. JKCP; TrPWD
Stiles. John Pudney. NYBP
Still a bare, silent, solitary glen. Thalaba and the Banquet. Robert Southey. *Fr.* Thalaba the Destroyer. SeCePo
"Still alive—" the message ran. The Emergency Maker. David Wagoner. NePoEA-2
Still am I haunting. Come Down. George Macdonald. TrPWD
Still Amathea thou art fayre. *Unknown.* SeCSL
Still and All. Burns Singer. NePoEA-2; OxBS
Still and blanched and cold and lone. The Mountains. Walter de la Mare. BrPo
Still and calm. The Blue Ridge. Harriet Monroe. HBMV
Still and dark along the sea. Twilight on Sumter. Richard Henry Stoddard. PAH; PAP
Still are the meadowlands, and still. In September. Francis Ledwidge. POTE
Still as/ On windless nights. Moon Shadows. Adelaide Crapsey. AnAmPo; NeMA
Still as I move thou movest. Her Shadow. Elisabeth Cavazza Pullen. AA
Still as of Old. Hester H. Cholmondeley. *See* Betrayal.
Still as the holy of holies breathes the vast. Dawn. "Æ." BEL
Still Barred Thy Doors. Aru Dutt. ACV
Still blooming on, when Summer flowers all fade. Autumn Flowers. Jones Very. MAmP
Still blue stones. Park Pigeons. Melville Cane. CAD
Still by meadow and stream. The Whisperer. Arthur Bullen. HBMV (2d ed.)
Still, Citizen Sparrow. Richard Wilbur. AmPP (5th ed.); AP; CMoP; ILP; LiTM (1970 ed.); MiAP; MoAB; MoPo; NePA; NoP; ReMP; ToPo
Still craves the spirit: never Nature solves. Frederick Goddard Tuckerman. *Fr.* Sonnets. MAmP
Still Day, A. Joseph Cherwinski. RePo
Still do the stars impart their light. Falsehood. William Cartwright. OBEV
Still drifting together. The Unpossessed. Adèle Naudé. PeSA
Still dripping, I grabbed it. The Bestfriend. Dick Lourie. *Fr.* Calls on the Dream Telephone. ThO
Still Falls the Rain. Edith Sitwell. ChMP; CoBMV; DTC; FaBoEn; FaBoMo; LiTM; MoAB; MoBrPo (1950 ed.); MoPo; MoRP; POTE; SeCePo; TrGrPo; TwCP; WaaP
Still farther would I fly, my child. An Aboriginal Mother's Lament. Charles Harpur. ACV; VA
Still for the world he lives, and lives in bliss. Written on the Anniversary of Our Father's Death. Hartley Coleridge. Sonn
Still glides the stream, slow drops the boat. The River. Matthew Arnold. CBEP; VP
Still glowing from the red-lipped kiss of noon. Twilight. Virginia McCormick. HBMV
Still-Heart. Frank Pearce Sturm. OBMV
Still heavy with may, and the sky ready to fall. Before Invasion, 1940. John Betjeman. MoVE
Still herald of the morn, whose ray. The Morning Star. John Hall. SeCL
Still I am patient, tho' you're merciless. The Patriarchal Home. Charles Jeremiah Wells. *Fr.* Joseph and His Brethren. VA
Still I complain; I am complaining still. Meditation Forty [*or* He is the Propitiation for Our Sin]. Edward Taylor. *Fr.* Preparatory Meditations, First Series. AP; MAmP; MeP; MWA-1; OxBA; PoEL-3
Still in an amorphous world she moves. The Idiot. Adèle Naudé. PeSA
Still in her native glory, unsubdued. Babylon. Robert Eyres Landor. *Fr.* The Impious Feast. OBRV
Still, in some hidden towns of our Dispersion. The Talmud Student. Hayyim Nahman Bialik. TrJP
Still is the toiling hand of Care. The Peopled Air. Thomas Gray. *Fr.* Ode on the Spring. OA
Still, it is dear defiance now to carry. Love Note II [*or* Flags]. Gwendolyn Brooks. AmNP; PoNe
Still let me pierce into the midnight depth. Summer. James Thomson. *Fr.* The Seasons. EnRP
"Still let my tyrants know, I am not doom'd to wear." Emily Brontë. *Fr.* The Prisoner. ChER; EG; MemP; OBEV; OBNC; OBVV
Still let us go the way of beauty. A Prayer for the Old Courage. Charles Hanson Towne. TrPWD
Still-Life. Elizabeth Daryush. QFR
Still-Life. Ted Hughes. NYBP
Still-Life. Ronald Perry. NePoEA-2
Still Life. Kathleen Raine. NeBP
Still Life. Reed Whittemore. CoAP
Still Life: Lady with Birds. Quandra Prettyman. CAD
Still like his Master, known by breaking bread. Epitaph on a Worthy Clergyman. Benjamin Franklin. TRV
Still more, still more: I feel the demon move. David Exorcising Malzah, the Evil from the Lord. Charles Heavysege. *Fr.* Saul. VA
Still must I hear?—shall hoarse Fitzgerald bawl. Byron. *Fr.* English Bards and Scotch Reviewers. AtBAP
Still, no one had paid much tribute to the man. Cocteau's *Opium*: 1. Donald Finkel. CoPo
Still, O Lord, for Thee I Tarry. Charles Wesley. OxBoCh
Still of Andromache the wail we hear. Life through Verse. Alpheus of Mitylene. OnPM
Still on my cheeks I feel their fondling breath. Stanzas on Mutability. Hugo von Hofmannsthal. AWP; TrJP
Still on the tower stood the vane. The Letters. Tennyson. HBV
Still onward winds the dreary way. In Memoriam A. H. H., XXVI. Tennyson. EnLi-2; EPN; ViPo; VP
Still Poem 9. Philip Lamantia. NeAP
Still poised, as if in prayer. My House. Robert Pack. PoDB
Still Pond, No More Moving. Howard Moss. NYBP
Still Pool, The. Kathleen Raine. MoAB
Still pressing through these weeping solitudes. Frederick Goddard Tuckerman. *Fr.* Sonnets. AmePo; AP
Still round thy towers descend the fertile rain! Cordova. Ibn Zaydun. AWP; LiTW
Still shall the tyrant scourge of Gaul. Ode to the Inhabitants of Pennsylvania. *Unknown.* PAH

Still sits the school-house by the road. In School-Days. Whittier. AA; AnNE; BLPA; CoBA; FaBoBe; FaPON; MPB (1956 ed.); NeHB; OTPC (1946 ed.); PCD; PoPl; PTK; StVeCh (1940 ed.); TreF
Still sleeps the unknown soldier. Memorial. Mae Winkler Goodman. PGD
Still Small Voice, The. A. M. Klein. OBCV; PeCV
Still Small Voice, The. Alexander Smart. PRWS
Still small voice spake unto me, A. The Two Voices. Tennyson. MasP; PoVP
Still south I went and west and south again. Prelude. J. M. Synge. AWP; BoNaP; ChTr; HBMV; JAWP; MoBrPo; NeMA; OBMV; PoFr; TSW; WBP
Still, still my eye will gaze long fixed on thee. The Columbine. Jones Very. AP
Still, Still with Thee. Harriet Beecher Stowe. BLRP; MaRV
(Still with Thee.) SoP
(When I Awake I Am Still with Thee.) OQP; TrPWD
Still tell me no, my God, and tell me no. Though He Slay Me. Vassar Miller. NePoEA-2
Still the Cross. E. Merrill Root. MaRV; StJW
Still the faint harps & silver voices calm the weary couch. Night. Blake. *Fr.* The Four Zoas. BoW
Still the ghost of Joseph Alston. Theodosia Burr. Myra Burnham Terrell. GoYe
Still the heat of mid-July. July 14, at Night. Feodor Invanovich Tyutchev. OnPM
Still the mighty mountains stand. Epilogue to Alun Mabon. John Ceiriog Hughes. PrWP
Still the Mind Smiles. Robinson Jeffers. CMoP
Still the same function, still the same habit come. Preludes to Definition, III. Conrad Aiken. TwAmPo
Still the Wonder Grew. Goldsmith. *Br. sel. fr.* The Deserted Village. TreF
Still the wood I knocked on. An Afterword to My Father. Marvin Bell. YAP
Still the world is wondrous large, seven seas from marge to marge. The Wide, Wide World. Kipling. OtMeF
Still thirteen years: 'tis autumn now. Palinode. James Russell Lowell. AA
Still Thou Art Question. *Unknown.* ChIP; PGD; StJW
Still Though the One I Sing. Walt Whitman. AA
Still Thy Sorrow, Magdalena! *Tr. by* E. A. Washburn. BePJ
Still to Be Neat, Still to Be Dressed [*or* Drest]. Ben Jonson. *See* Simplex Munditiis.
Still Voice of Harlem, The. Conrad Kent Rivers. IDB; Kal; NNP
Still Undaunted. George B. Ryan. CIV
Still was the night, serene and bright. The Day of Doom. Michael Wigglesworth. SCAP
Still we who follow Christ in deed. Eucharist. E. Merrill Root. ChIP; OQP
Still Will I Trust. Albert Simpson Reitz. SoP
Still wilt thou sigh, and still in vain. The Expostulation. Thomas Shadwell. *Fr.* The Squire of Alsatia. OAEP
Still with Thee. Harriet Beecher Stowe. *See* Still, Still with Thee.
Stillborn Love. Dante Gabriel Rossetti. The House of Life, LV. EnLi-2; EPN; MaVP; PoVP; ViPo; VP
Stillborn Silence, thou that art. Invocation of Silence [*or* Silence Invoked]. Richard Flecknoe. GoBC; SeCL
Stille Nacht. Joseph Mohr. *See* Silent Night.
Stillness, The. Basho, *tr. fr. Japanese by* Harold G. Henderson. RePo
Stillness. James Elroy Flecker. BrPo; CH; GoJo; GTBS-D; MoBrPo; SyP
Stillness and splendour of the night. Canticle. James McAuley. PoAu-2
Stillness midst the ever-changing. God's Eternal Now. Gerhard Tersteegan. FaChP
Stillness of the Poem, The. Ron Loewinsohn. NeAP
Stimulus of Friendship, The. *Unknown.* OQP
Sting of Death, The. Frederick George Scott. OBCV; PeCV
Stinger and Gonoph and Peterman. Another Villon-ous Variation. Don Marquis. HBMV
Stinginess, Sin, Stupidity, shall determine. To the Reader. Baudelaire. SyP
Stinging/ gold swarms. Sunset [*or* Impression]. E. E. Cummings. MAP; MoAB; MoAmPo; PIA
Stinging Nettle, The. A. E. Housman. POTE
(With Seed the Sowers Scatter.) EnLi-2 (1949 ed.)
Stings. Sylvia Plath. NaP
Stir Me. *Unknown.* STF
(Stir Into Flame.) SoP
Stir Us, Oh, Stir Us, Lord, 1st *st., sl. diff.* FaChP
Stir not the sand too much, for there lies Stuyvesant. Epitaph for Peter Stuyvesant. Henricus Selyns. SCAP
Stir not, whisper not. The River. Patrick MacDonogh. NeIP
Stir—shake off sleep. Love Lyric. Max Michelson. NP
Stir the pot and mix the brew. Devil's Cauldron. Monk Gibbon. HaMV
Stir the Wallaby Stew. *Unknown.* FOL
Stir Us, Oh, Stir Us, Lord. *Unknown.* *See* Stir Me.
Stirring porch pots up with greenfingered witchcraft. Aspects of Spring in Greater Boston. George Starbuck. NYBP
Stirring suddenly from long hibernation. Mid-Winter Waking. Robert Graves. BoPe; MoAB
Stirrup Cup, The. Douglas Ainslie. GoTS
Stirrup-Cup, The. John Hay. AA; HBV
Stirrup Cup, The. Aline Kilmer. CAW
Stirrup-Cup, The. Sidney Lanier. AA; AmePo; AmP; AmPP (5th ed.); CoBA; OQP; PFY; TOP
Stirrup Cup, The. William Alexander Percy. WHA
Stitches over and over. Lesbia Sewing. Harold Vinal. HBMV
Stitching. Christina Rossetti. *See* Pocket Handkerchief to Hem, A.
Stock-Taking. Joan Suisted. SoP
Stock whom Cromwell planted here, The. Lines Written in a Country Parson's Orchard. Leslie Daiken. OnYI
Stockdove, The. Ruth Pitter. HaMV; SeCePo
Stockdoves, The. Andrew Young. POTE
Stocking Fairy. Winifred Welles. BoChLi; FaPON; SoPo; TiPo
Stocking Song on Christmas Eve. Mary Mapes Dodge. ChBR; OHIP
Stockings are a trouble; so many times my toes. Troubles. Dorothy Aldis. StVeCh
Stockman, The. David Campbell. MoAuPo
Stocky woman at the door, The. The Last Day and the First. Theodore Weiss. TwCP
Stoic. Lawrence Durrell. NYBP
Stoic, The; for Laura von Courten. Edgar Bowers. CoAP; NePoEA; QFR
Stoics think, The (and they come near the truth). Sonnet. Richard Barnfield. ReIE
Stolen Boat, The. Wordsworth. *See* Prelude, The: "One summer evening. . ."
Stolen Child, The. W. B. Yeats. BEL; CMoP; EnLi-2 (1949 ed.); MPB; OnYI; OxBI; PoMS; POTE; PoVP; ViPo (1962 ed.)
Stolen Fifer, The. Padraic Fiacc. NeIP
Stolen Kiss, A. George Wither. *Fr.* Fair Virtue, the Mistress of Philarete. HBV; LiTL; SeCL
(Kiss, The.) UnTE
(Sonnet upon a Stolen Kiss, A.) PoIE (1970 ed.)
(Theft, The.) MeWo
Stolen Pleasure. William Drummond of Hawthornden. EnLoPo
Stol'n to this paradise, and so entranced. Keats. *Fr.* The Eve of St. Agnes. LO
Stomach. Coleman Barks. *Fr.* Body Poems. QAH
"Stond well, moder, under Rode." The Mother and Her Son on the Cross. *Unknown.* MeEL
Stood Who So List upon the Slipper Toppe. Seneca, *tr. fr. Latin by* Sir Thomas Wyatt. *Fr.* Thyestes. EnPo; PoEL-1
(Of the Mean and Sure Estate.) SiCE
(Stand Whoso List.) NoP
("Stand whoso list upon the slipper top.") FCP; SiPS
Stone, The. Paul Blackburn. NYBP
Stone, The. Emily Dickinson. *See* How happy is the little stone.
Stone, A. Richard Eberhart. NePoAm-2
Stone, The. W. W. Gibson. GSP; MoBrPo; NeMA; PoPo
Stone, The. Walter H. Kerr. FiSC
Stone, The. Kenneth W. Porter. ChIP
Stone. Charles Simic. YAP
Stone, The. Thomas Vaughan. OBS; PrWP
Stone, The/ would like to be. Evolution. May Swenson. TrGrPo (rev. ed.)
Stone, a Leaf, a Door, A. Thomas Wolfe. PoPl
Stone-Age Sea, The. Helen Hoyt. NP
Stone and the Shell, The. Wordsworth. *Fr.* The Prelude, V. ERoP-1

Stone Angel. Anne Ridler. EaLo
Stone, bronze, stone, steel, stone, oakleaves, horses' heels. Triumphal March. T. S. Eliot. *Fr.* Coriolan. BWP; MBW-2; ShBV-4; WaaP
Stone cries from the wall, The. Epitaph. *Unknown.* TrJP
Stone Crop, The. Robert P. Tristram Coffin. PaA
Stone Fleet, The. Herman Melville. EtS
Stone-flake and salmon. Burning, XV. Gary Snyder. *Fr.* Myths & Texts. NaP
Stone found me in bright sunlight, The. The Stone. Paul Blackburn. NYBP
Stone Frog, The. Glenn Pritchard. NYTB
Stone from the Gods. Irma Wassall. GoYe
Stone goes straight, The. Washington Monument by Night. Carl Sandburg. CMoP; FaPON; OHIP; PoSC
Stone-gray roses by the desert's rim, The. The Princess. W. J. Turner. HBMV
Stone Harp, The. John Haines. ThO
Stone Horse Shoals. Malcolm Cowley. NYBP; TwAmPo
Stone jug and a pewter mug, A. The Kavanagh. Richard Hovey. HBV
Stone lips to the unspoken cave. Orpheus. W. D. Snodgrass. CABA; ToPo
Stone the size of man was my stone, A. A Stone. Richard Eberhart. NePoAm-2
Stone Too Can Pray. Conrad Aiken. EaLo; MoRP
Stone Trees. John Freeman. BoNaP
Stone Venus, fixed and still. The Venus of Bolsover Castle. Sacheverell Sitwell. HBMV
Stone Walls. Julie Mathilde Lippmann. AA
Stone Walls. Richard Lovelace. *Fr.* To Althea from Prison. WePo
("Stone walls do not a prison make.") MaRV; OQP
Stone-cutters fighting time with marble, you foredefeated. To the Stone-Cutters. Robinson Jeffers. AmP; AmPP; ILP; InP; MAP; MoAB; MoAmPo; MoVE; NeMA; NoP; OxBA; PoCh; PoPl; PoRA (rev. ed.); PP; TrGrPo; VaPo
Stoned dogs crawl back through the blood, The. The Contours of Fixation. Weldon Kees. NaP
Stonefish and Starfish. John Blight. BoAV; NeLNL
Stones. William Jeffrey. OxBS
Stones and Blossoms. *Unknown, tr. fr. Spanish by* Havelock Ellis. OnPM
Stones in Jordan's stream, The. Stones. William Jeffrey. OxBS
Stones only, the *disjecta membra* of this Great House. Ruins of a Great House. Derek Walcott. ToPo; TwCP
Stones towards the earth descend. The Soul's Tendency towards Its True Centre. John Byrom. CEP
Stonewall Jackson. Stephen Vincent Benét. OTD
Stonewall Jackson. Henry Lynden Flash. AA; DD; PAH
Stonewall Jackson. Herman Melville. AmePo
Stonewall Jackson's Way. John Williamson Palmer. AA; DD; HBV; MC; OTPC (1946 ed.); PaA; PAH
Stoney Ridge Dance Hall. Alden Nowlan. MoCV
Stony Limits. "Hugh MacDiarmid." CABL
Stony Town. John Shaw Neilson. BoAV; NeLNL
Stood, at the closed door, and remembered. Preludes for Memnon, LII. Conrad Aiken. LiTM
Stood straight/ holding the choker high. Logging, III. Gary Snyder. *Fr.* Myths & Texts. NaP; NMP
Stood the afflicted mother weeping. Stabat Mater Dolorosa. *At. to* Jacopone da Todi, *tr. by* Abraham Coles. HBV
Stood the lovely Mother smiling. Stabat Mater Speciosa. *At. to* Jacopone da Todi, *tr. by* Thomas Walsh. CAW
Stood the Mother in her anguish. Stabat Mater Dolorosa. *At. to* Jacopone da Todi, *tr. by* Thomas Walsh. CAW
Stood the tall Archangel weighing. St. Michael the Weigher. James Russell Lowell. AnFE; AnNE; APA; CAW; CoAnAm
Stool Ball. *Unknown.* CH
Stop. Richard Wilbur. WIRo
Stop a Minute! *Unknown.* STF
Stop All the Clocks. W. H. Auden. MeWo; NeMA; WePo
(Song: "Stop all the clocks.") MoBrPo (1950 ed.)
Stop and consider! life is but a day. Keats. *Fr.* Sleep and Poetry. OBRV; SeCePo; TreFT
Stop, Christian passer-by!—Stop, child of God. Epitaph [on Himself]. Samuel Taylor Coleridge. CH; EnRP; EPN; ERoP-1; FiP; MaRV; NoP; OAEP; OBRV; OxBoCh; PeER
"Stop, Cuckoo," said the Bee. The Bee and the Cuckoo. Tomás de Iriarte. BoChLi

Stop, feathered bullies! To Sparrows Fighting. W. H. Davies. BiS
Stop!—for thy tread is on an empire's dust! Byron. *Fr.* Childe Harold's Pilgrimage, III. ILP
Stop—Go. Dorothy W. Baruch. FaPON; SUS; TiPo
Stop, let me have the truth of that! Dis Aliter Visum; or, Le Byron de Nos Jours. Robert Browning. ViPP
Stop look &/ listen Venezia. Memorabilia. E. E. Cummings. OnHM
Stop look listen. Crossing. Philip Booth. AmFN
Stop, mortal! Here thy brother lies. A Poet's Epitaph. Ebenezer Elliott. VA
Stop!—not to me, at this bitter departing. Separation. Matthew Arnold. HBV; VP
Stop on the Appian Way. On the Campagna. Elizabeth Stoddard. AA
Stop playing, poet! May a brother speak? Transcendentalism; a Poem in Twelve Books. Robert Browning. DiPo; PoVP; PP
Stop, Science—Stop! A. P. Herbert. FiBHP
Stop still on the stair. Sops of Light. Fredegond Shove. ChMP
"Stop, stop!" The Maid Freed from the Gallows (B *vers.*). *Unknown.* ViBoFo
Stop, stop and listen for the bough top. The Blackbird of Derrycairn. Austin Clarke. NeIP
"Stop, stop, pretty water!" Runaway Brook. Eliza Lee Follen. GFA
Stopped. Allen Polite. NNP
Stopping at an otel with an Ibernian. Dropping your Aitches. Joseph Warren Beach. NYBP
Stopping by Woods on a Snowy Evening. Robert Frost. AmLP; AmP; AmPP; AnFE; AnNE; AP; APA; BoLiVe; BoNaP; CABA; CaFP; CBV; CMoP; CoAnAm; CoBA; CoBMV; DiPo; ExPo; FaBoCh; FaBV; FaFP; FaPON; FlW; ForPo; GBV (1952 ed.); GoJo; GTBS-W; HBMV; HoPM; ILP; InP; InPo; LiTA; LiTG; LiTM; LoGBV; MAP; MaPo; MasP; MoAB; MoAmPo; MoShBr; MoVE; MWA-2; NeMA; NePA; NoP; NP; OTPC (1946 ed.); OxBA; PAn; PCD; PDV; PG (1955 ed.); PoAn; PoE; PoeP; PoFS; PoPo; PoRA; PoSa; PoSC; PTK; ReMP; RePo; ShBV-1; SiSoSe; StaSt; StVeCh; SUS; TDP; ThWaDe; TiPo; TreFS; TSW; TwAmPo; TwCP; UnPo (3d ed.); UTS; ViBoPo (1958 ed.); WaKh; WHA
"Woods are lovely, dark and deep, The, *sel.*" TRV
Stopwatch and an Ordnance Map, A. Stephen Spender. MoBS
Store cattle from Nelanjie! The mob goes feeding past. From the Gulf. Will H. Ogilvie. BoAu; PoAu-1
Store we like best is Emma's store, The. Emma's Store. Dorothy Aldis. OCS
Store-House, A. Louis Dudek. CaP
Stories of Snow. Patricia K. Page. OBCV
Stork in Jerez. Laurie Lee. BoPe; POTi
Stork questioned the swan whose moving song, The. Aria Senza da Capo. Robert Finch. MoCV
Storks fly over the fields. Spring Song. *Unknown.* PCH
Storm, The. Alcaeus. *tr. fr. Greek by* John Herman Merivale. AWP; JAWP; OnPM; WBP
Storm, The. Chora, *tr. fr. Japanese by* Harold G. Henderson. RePo
Storm, The. "Robin Christopher." RIS
Storm, The. Robert David Cohen. NYBP
Storm, The. Emily Dickinson. See There came a wind like a bugle.
Storm, The. John Donne. CABL; ReIE; SeEP
(Storme, The.) MaMe
"South and west winds joined, and, as they blew, The, *sel.*" EtS
Storm. Hilda Doolittle ("H. D."). TiPo; TSW
Storm, The. Heine, *tr. fr. German by* Louis Untermeyer. AWP; JAWP; WBP
Storm, The. George Herbert. AnAnS-1; MaMe; MeP
Storm, The. Imr el Kais, *tr. fr. Arabic by* Sir Charles Lyall. LiTW
Storm, The, *sel.* Islwyn, *tr. fr. Welsh by* Gwyn Williams. "For everything is sacred, poetry." PrWP
Storm, The. Elizabeth Jennings. NePoEA-2
Storm, The, *sel.* Egan O'Rahilly, *tr. fr. Modern Irish by* P. S. Dinneen *and* T. O'Donoghue.
"Pitiful the playing of the flood with dire destruction!" OnYI
Storm, The. Coventry Patmore. EnLoPo

Storm. Ruth Pitter. BoPe
Storm, The. Edward Shanks. BoNaP
Storm, The ("Behold, slow-settling . . ."). James Thomson. *Fr.* The Seasons: Summer. LoBV
Storm, The ("See, winter comes . . ."). James Thomson. *Fr.* The Seasons: Winter. CoBE
Storm, The. Richard Untermeyer *and* Louis Untermeyer. RIS
Storm, A. *Unknown.* *See* Storm Riddles.
Storm, The. Henry Vaughan. AnAnS-1; CBEP; MeP
Storm, The. Robert Wallace. NYBP
Storm, The. Whittier. *Fr.* Snow-bound. FaBV
Storm. Judith Wright. PoAu-2
Storm at Nightfall, The. Morton Dauwen Zabel. NP
Storm at Sea. Sir William Davenant. *See* Winter Storms, The.
Storm at Sea, A. *Unknown, tr. fr. Middle Irish by* Robin Flower. AnIL; KiLC, *tr. by* Frank O'Connor
Storm-beaten old watch-tower, A. Symbols. W. B. Yeats. OBMV
Storm broke, and it rained, The. Frogs. Louis Simpson. TDP
Storm came home too blind to stand, The. One A.M. X. J. Kennedy. ELU; NYTB
Storm came up so very quick, The. Spring Rain. Marchette Chute. TiPo
Storm-Child, The. May Byron. HBV
Storm Cone, The. Kipling. ChMP; POTE; PoVP
Storm cries every night, The. Spring Song. Hermann Hesse. AWP; JAWP; WBP
Storm-dances of gulls, the barking game of seals, The. Divinely Superfluous Beauty. Robinson Jeffers. LiTL; MAP; MoAmPo; MoLP; PoPl
Storm Fear. Robert Frost. CMoP; HBV; NP; OxBA; ViBoPo
Storm from the East, A. Reed Whittemore. NYBP; PoPl
Storm had strong intention in its flow, The. Cleavage. Louise Townsend Nicholl. NePoAm
Storm in Childhood, A. T. H. Jones. FIW
Storm in the Distance, A. Paul Hamilton Hayne. AA
Storm Is Over, The. Robert Bridges. LiTB; LiTM (rev. ed.); MoPo; OBMV
("Storm is over, the land hushes to rest, The.") BrPo; GTBS-P
Storm is riding on the tide, A. The Tragedienne. Zoë Akins. NP
Storm not, brave friend, that thou hast never yet. To Scilla. Sir Charles Sedley. PeRV; PV
Storm of Love, A. Hilary Corke. NYBP
Storm on Fifth Avenue. Siegfried Sassoon. ILP; MoVE
Storm over Rockefeller Center. Raymond Holden. AnAmPo
Storm Riddles. *Unknown, tr. fr. Anglo-Saxon by* William H. Matchett. *Fr.* Riddles. FosPo
(Storm, A, I, II, *and* III, *tr. by* Stith Thompson.) OuHeWo
Storm, A, *sel.* EnLi-1
Storm Snapped Its Fingers, The. Elizabeth J. Coatsworth. BrR
Storm Song. Bayard Taylor. BBV (1923 ed.); EtS; HBV; OTD
Storm-sudden summer filled the dongas with thunder. Estrangement. John Peter. BoSA
Storm Thrush, The. Mrs. C. L. de Cheney. SoP
Storm tossed and driv'n. Derelict, The. SoP
Storm upon the mountain. The Lost Lamb. Thomas Westwood. OTPC (1923 ed.); PCH
Storm-wind blows, A. The Storm. Chora. RePo
Storm Windows. Howard Nemerov. PoIE
Stormalong, *with music.* *Unknown.* AmSS; ShS; SoAmSa
Stormcock in Elder. Ruth Pitter. BoC
Storme, The. John Donne. *See* Storm, The.
Storming of Stony Point, The. Arthur Guiterman. MC; PAH
Storms are past, the [*or* these] clouds are overblown, The. Bonum Est Mihi Quod Humiliasti Me. Earl of Surrey. FCP;SiPS
Storms come and sorrows come. Security. Margaret E. Sangster. BLRP
Storms once hurled my howls about. The Lighthouse Keeper's Offspring. James Broughton. CrMA
Stormy Day. W. R. Rodgers. LiTB
Stormy March is come at last, The. March. Bryant. DD;GN;OTPC
Stormy Night. Barbara Drake Johnston. SoP
Stormy Night. W. R. Rodgers. OxBI
Storny Nights. Robert Louis Stevenson. BrPo
Stormy Petrel, The. "Barry Cornwall." EtS;HBV;OTPC;VA
Stormy Sea. Janet Vaughn. PCD
Stormy sea. A! Waves dashing high! He Shall Speak Peace unto the Nations. Lila V. Walters. BePJ;FaChP;WBLP
Stormy the night and the waves roll high. Asleep in the Deep. Arthur J. Lamb. TreFT
Story, A. Margaret Avison. MoCV
Story Dorothy Parker. InMe;MaC
Story, a story to you I will tell, A. The Cunning Cobbler Done Over. *Unknown* CoMu
Story about Chicken Soup, A. Louis Simpson. NMP
Story, as now we see, was over-written, The. Thermopylae. Michael Twaites. PoAu-2
Story for a Child, A. Bayard Taylor. HBV; HBVY; OTPC (1923 ed.); PCD
(Night with a Wolf, A.) GN; GoTP; TVC
Story from Russian Author. Peter Redgrove. NePoEA-2
Story from the Bushmen, A. Joseph Ceravolo. ANYP
Story I Have to Tell, The. Richard Murphy. *Fr.* The Battle of Aughrim. OPoP
Story in the Snow, A. Pearl Riggs Crouch. MPB; SoPo; TiPo
Story of a fisher lad, The. An Incident of French History. James I. Whitman. PCD
Story of a Stowaway, The. Clement Scott. PaPo
Story of Augustus Who Would Not Have Any Soup, The. Heinrich Hoffmann, *tr. fr. German at. to* J. R. Planché. BBGG; GoJo; HBV; HBVY; MoShBr; OTPC; ShM; TiPo
Story of Baby's Blanket, The. Emilie Poulsson. PPL
Story of Baby's Pillow, The. Emilie Poulsson. PPL
Story of Cruel Psamtek. *Unknown.* NA
Story of Flying Robert, The. Heinrich Hoffmann, *tr. fr. German at. to* J. R. Planché. RIS
Story of Frederick Gowler, The. The King of Canoodle-Dum. W. S. Gilbert. CenHV
Story of Johnny Head-in-Air, The. Heinrich Hoffmann, *tr. fr. German at. to* J. R. Planché. BBGG; TiPo
Story of Life, The. John Godfrey Saxe. PoToHe (new ed.)
Story of Little Suck-a-Thumb, The. Heinrich Hoffmann, *tr. fr. German at. to* J. R. Planché. EvOK; HBV; HBVY
Story of Macha, The. *Unknown, tr. fr. Middle Irish by* Sir Samuel Ferguson. *Fr.* Dinnshenchas. OnYI
Story of Phoebus and Daphne Applied, The. Edmund Waller. InvP; OBS; SeEP
Story of Ponce de Leon, A. The Fountain of Youth. Hezekiah Butterworth. PAH
Story of Prince Agib, The. W. S. Gilbert. BOHV; InMe; LBN; NA
Story of Pyramid Thothmes, The. *Unknown.* NA
Story of Rimini, The, *sels.* Leigh Hunt.
Places of Nestling Green. OBRV
("Noble range it was, of many a rood, A.") EnRP
"Ready she sat with one hand to turn o'er." EvOK
Story of Ruth, The. Bible, *O.T.* *See* Ruth.
Story of Samuel Jackson, The. Charles Godfrey Leland. StPo
Story of Sigurd the Volsung, The, *sels.* William Morris.
Brooding of Sigurd, The. SeCePo
Gunnar in the Pit of Adders, *fr.* IV. PoVP; ViPo
Of the Passing Away of Brynhild, *fr.* III. PoVP; VA
Sigurd Rideth to the Glittering Heath, *fr.* II. PoEL-5
Sigurd's ride, *fr.* II. NBM
Story of Soutine, A. James Schevill. PoCh
Story of Svetaketu, The. *Unknown, tr. fr. Sanskrit by* F. Max Müller. *Fr.* The Upanishads. WoL
Story of the Alchemist, The. Eugene Williams. PCD
Story of the Ashes and the Flame, The. E. A. Robinson. MaPo (1969 ed.)
Story of the Baby Squirrel, The. Dorothy Aldis. TiPo
Story of the Corn. K. Fisher. BoTP
Story of the Flowery Kingdom. James Branch Cabell. HBMV; OnMSP; PCD
Story of the Little Rid Hin, The. F. W. Sweetser. SAS
Story of the Shepherd, The. *Unknown, tr. fr. Spanish.* OHIP
Story of the Wild Huntsman, The. Heinrich Hoffmann, *tr. fr. German at. to* J. R. Planché. NA
Story of Two Gentlemen and the Gardener, The. Christopher Logue. CABL
Story of Ug, The. Edwin Meade Robinson. HBMV; LHV; YaD
Story of Uriah, The. Kipling. BrPo; PeVV

Story of Vinland, The. Sidney Lanier. *Fr.* Psalm of the West. PAH; ThLM
Story of White Man Leading Viet Cong Patrol, The. Eric Torgersen. QAH
Storys to rede ar delitabill. John Barbour. *Fr.* The Bruce. OxBS
Story-Teller, The. Mark Van Doren. LOW
Stoush o' Day, The. C. J. Dennis. NeLNL
Stout. Rue Carpenter. RIS
Stout Affirmation. Kenneth Burke. TwAmPo
Stove Pipe Hole, De. William Henry Drummond. IHA
Stowaway. Bill Adams. EtS
Stowed away in a Montreal lumber room. O God! O Montreal! [*or* A Psalm of Montreal]. Samuel Butler. CBEP; DTC; NBM; OxBoLi
Stradivarius, *sel.* "George Eliot."
  Working with God. MaRV; TRV
Stradivarius to an Unfinished Violin (1710). Eugene Lee-Hamilton. Sonn
Stragglers. Pietro Aretino, *tr. fr. Italian by* Samuel Putnam. ErPo
Straight and swift the swallows fly. Rococo. John Payne. OBVV
Straight from a mighty bow this truth is driven. The Arrow. Clarence Urmy. HBMV
Straight from the feast, Akhti, you went to Hell. Epitaph for a Tyrannous Governor Who Choked on Wine. Adib-i Sabir. LiTW
Straight-jacketing sprang to every lock. Austin Clarke. *Fr.* Mnemosyne Lay in Dust. OPoP
Straight Road, The. Ellen Hooper. HBV
Straight strength pitched into the surliness of the ditch. To a Discarded Steel Rail. Maxwell Bodenheim. NP; PFY
Straight, the swift, the debonair, The. Magnets. Countee Cullen. BALP
Straight to his heart the bullet crushed. Apocalypse. Richard Realf. PaA; PAP
Straight to Syr Martins hall the Hunters bend. Sunset. William Julius Mickle. *Fr.* The Concubine. OBEC
Straightly sliced half-moon. Summer Night. Jason Miller. ThO
Strain, strain thine eyes, this parting is for aye! Lohengrin. William Morton Payne. AA
Straining. Kathleen Spivack. YAP
Strains of Sight. Robert Duncan. NMP; OPoP
Strains upraise of joy and praise, The. Cantemus Cuncti Melodum. Notker Balbulus. CAW
Straiten'd am I, O Lord, upon a pillar. Liberty. Leopold Staff. PoFr
Strampin' the bent, like the Angel o' Daith. Molecatcher. Albert D. Mackie. GoTS
Strand, The. Louis MacNeice. AnIV
Strand-Thistle. Gustav Falke, *tr. fr. German by* Jetro Bithell. AWP
Strange. Stanley Burnshaw. TrJP
Strange. Kirby Doyle. NeAP
Strange/ that we wake. For Poki. A. X. Nicholas. WSL
Strange, All-absorbing Love. Digby Mackworth Dolben. GoBC; TrPWD
Strange and unnatural! lets stay and see. Destinie. Abraham Cowley. MeLP
Strange are the feelings arising within me. The Love of Hell. Abraham Burstein. TrJP
Strange—as I sat brooding here. Lucy. Walter de la Mare. CMoP
Strange as it seems, the smallest mammal. The Shrew. Odgen Nash. CenHV
Strange atoms we unto ourselves. Lovelight. Georgia Douglas Johnson. AmNP
Strange beauty, eight-limbed and eight-handed. Octopus. Arthur Clement Hilton. CenHV; Par
Strange bed, whose recurrent dream we are, The. Hotel de l'Univers et Portugal. James Merrill. MoAB; NePoAm; NePoEA-2
Strange bird,/ His song remains secret. Youth. James Wright. NaP
Strange, bright dancers, The. Poppies. P. A. Ropes. BoTP
Strange, but he cheats his master. Man of the World. Michael Hamburger. NePoEA-2
Strange but true is the story. The Sea-Turtle and the Shark. Melvin B. Tolson. *Fr.* Harlem Gallery. BP; Kal
Strange Companion, The. Harold Monro. NP
Strange Description of a Rare Garden-Plot, A. Nicholas Breton. ReIE
Strange, fantastic claims abound. Christ Alone. Shel Helsley. STF
Strange Fits of Passion Have I Known. Wordsworth. CBEP; CoBE; EG; EnL; EnLit; EnRP; EPN; ERoP-1; ILP; LiTB; LiTG; LiTL; MBW-2; MERP; OAEP; OBRV; PAn; PIA; Po; PoE; PoeP; PoFS; ViBoPo
  (Lucy.) EnLi-2; FiP; HBV; LO; OBEV; OBNC; TrGrPo
Strange foreboding is o'er me, A. The Lorelei. Heine. PoMS
Strange Fortunes of Two Excellent Princes, The, *sel.* Nicholas Breton.
  His Wisdom. ALV; OBSC
  (I Would Thou Wert Not Fair [*or* I Were Wise].) EIL; InvP
Strange friend, past, present and to be. Tennyson. *Fr.* In Memoriam A. H. H., CXXIX. LO
Strange Fruit. Randolph Stow. PoAu-2
Strange Funeral in Braddock, A. Michael Gold. WOW
Strange gift indeed! a thorn to prick. Thorns. J. Danson Smith. SoP
Strange grows the river on the sunless evenings! Vesperal. Ernest Dowson. OBMV
Strange Guest. Gertrude Jane Codd. JKCP (1955 ed.)
Strange, how the moon will come. Moon Magic. Leigh Hanes. StaSt
Strange, how this smooth and supple joint can be. Hands. Louis Untermeyer. AnAmPo; MoLP
Strange how you go along all day. Strange. Kirby Doyle. NeAP
Strange Interlude, A. Margaret Fishback. BOHV
Strange, Is It Not. Edward D. Kennedy. HBMV
Strange is it not if scholars yell. Scholars. *Unknown.* KiLC
Strange, is it not, that youth will always sing. Strange, Is It Not. Edward D. Kennedy. HBMV
Strange is my story, passing prodigy. The Mock Caliph. *Unknown.* EnLi-1
Strange is this thing! My horse I cannot make. Robert Tofte. *Fr.* Laura. ReIE; Sonn; TuPP
Strange justice walks abroad tonight. Woodrow Wilson. Donald Gillies. DD
Strange land holds thy bones, A. Lost at Sea. Simonides. WoL
Strange Lands. Laurence Alma-Tadema. DD; HBVY; OTPC; PRWS
Strange Legacies. Sterling A. Brown. Kal; TTY
Strange lesson taught by war. Lessons. Helen Weber. PGD
Strange little tune, so thin and rare. To a Scarlatti Passepied. Robert Hillyer. HBMV
Strange Love. Moses ibn Ezra, *tr. fr. Hebrew by* Solomon Solis-Cohen. TrJP
Strange Man, The. *Unknown.* FaPON; MPB; OTPC (1946 ed.); StVeCh (1940 ed.)
Strange Meeting. Wilfred Owen. AnFE; AtBAP; BoPe; BrPo; ChMP; CMoP; CoBE; CoBMV; DTC; EnLi-2 (1949 ed.); ExPo; FaBoEn; FaBoMo; FaPL; GTBS-P; GTBS-W; ILP; LiTB; LiTM; LoBV; MMA; MoAB; MoBrPo; MoPo; MoVE; NAMP; NP; OAEP (2d ed.); PoE; PoIE; POTE; SeCeV; ShBV-4; TreFT; TrGrPo; Waap; WaP
Strange Meetings, *sels.* Harold Monro.
  Flower Is Looking, A. MoBrPo
  If Suddenly a Clod of Earth. MoBrPo
  One Blackbird. RIS; StaSt
Strange Music, The. G. K. Chesterton. OtMeF
Strange news! a cittie full? will none give way. Upon Christ His Birth. Sir John Suckling. NCEP
Strange now to think of you, gone without corsets & eyes. Kaddish. Allen Ginsberg. AmPC; NeAP; OPoP
Strange Pangs of a Poor Passionate Lover, The. *Unknown.* TuPP
Strange Passion of a Lover, A. George Gascoigne. EnLit; EnRePo; EP; ReIE; SiCE; TuPP
  ("Amid my bale I bathe in bliss.") ReEn
Strange pie that is almost a passion. A Melton Mowbray Pork Pie. Richard Le Gallienne. BOHV; Par
Strange power, I know not what thou art. To Memory. Mary Elizabeth Coleridge. CBEP
Strange rumours gripped Olympus. Apollo's hand. Home Thoughts. Guy Butler. BoSA

Strange spirit with inky hair. The Lion. W. J. Turner. MoBrPo; TrGrPo (1942 ed.)
Strange, strange thing it is to know, A. The Sampler. Rachel Field. BiCB
Strange Talk. L. E. Yates. BoTP
Strange Teeth, The. Nancy Birckhead. RIS
Strange that I did not know him then. An Old Story. E. A. Robinson. AnNE; HBMV; MAP; MaRV; MoAmPo; NeMA; TreFS
Strange, that in this nigger place. Esthete in Harlem. Langston Hughes. BANP
Strange that such horror and such grace. To a Fair Lady Playing with a Snake. Edmund Waller. HoPM; NCEP; PoEL-3; SCEP-2
Strange that the spring has come. Only a Flower. Toyohiko Kagawa. MaRV
Strange that you let me come so near. The Rat. Andrew Young. WePo
Strange the world about me lies. World-Strangeness. Sir William Watson. MoBrPo (1942 ed.); PoVP
Strange to be torn away from your embrace. Strange. Stanley Burnshaw. TrJP
Strange Tree. Elizabeth Madox Roberts. BoChLi; BoNaP; FaPON; MPB; NP; SP
Strange violin! Dost thou follow me? The Neighbor. Rainer Maria Rilke. OnPM
Strange Visitor, The. *Unknown.* ChTr; FaBoCh
Strange walkers! See their processional. The Mushroom Gatherers. Donald Davie. NePoEA-2
Strange wanderer out of the deeps. Stella Flammarum. Wilfred Campbell. WoL
Strange wares are handled on the wharves of sleep. The Wharf of Dreams. Edwin Markham. HBV
Strange was the wooing! Lullaby of the Catfish and the Crab. William Rose Benét. WhC
Strange Western town at the round edge of night. Western Town. Karl Shapiro. NYBP
Strange Wild Song, A. "Lewis Carroll." *See* Gardener's Song, The.
Strangely/ my mother's sad eyes. X-Ray. David Ray. NePoEA-2
Strangely assorted, the shape of song and the bloody man. The Military Harpist. Ruth Pitter. FaBoTw; MoVE; MuSP
Strangeness of Heart. Siegfried Sassoon. MoRP; TrJP
Stranger, The. Brother Antoninus. CBV; ToPo
Stranger, The. John Clare. OxBoCh
Stranger, The. Walter de la Mare. BrPo; MoVE; OAEP (2d ed.)
Stranger, The. Helen Frazee-Bower. SoP
Stranger, The. Jean Garrigue. LiTA; LiTM; TwCP
Stranger, The. Daniel Henderson. HBMV
Stranger. Thomas Merton. EaLo
Stranger, The. John Richard Moreland. ChIP; OQP
Stranger, The. Adrienne Rich. CoPo
Stranger. Elizabeth Madox Roberts. MAP; MoAmPo
Stranger, The. Richard Sullivan. JKCP (1955 ed.)
Stranger and countryman to me. Greet All Equally. Macedonius. OnPM
Stranger and His Friend, The. James Montgomery. SoP
Stranger, approach this spot with gravity. Epitaph on a Dentist [*or* A Dentist *or* On a Dentist]. *Unknown.* GoTP; LiTG; OxBoLi; TreFS; TreFT; WhC
Stranger at the Peace Table. Esther Baldwin York. MaRV
Stranger! awhile upon this mossy bank. Inscription for a Tablet on the Banks of a Stream. Robert Southey. OBEC
Stranger Bride. Jocelyn Macy Sloan. FiSC
Stranger Call This Not. *Unknown.* ShM
Stranger came one night to Yussouf's tent, A. Yussouf. James Russell Lowell. BBV (1951 ed.); BeLS; BLPA; BoTP; FaBoBe; MPB; NeHB; OTPC (1946 ed.)
Stranger came to Bethlehem, A. Helen Frazee-Bower. SoP
Stranger came to the door at eve, A. Love and a Question. Robert Frost. MoBS
Stranger here, as all my fathers were, A. A Motect. *Unknown.* SeEP
Stranger, I threaded sunken-hearted, A. The Woman I Met. Thomas Hardy. AtBAP
Stranger, if thou hast learned a truth which needs. Inscription for the Entrance to a Wood. Bryant. AmLP; AmP; AmPP; AnNE; AP; CoBA; ILP; MAmP; MCCG; MWA-1; OxBA
Stranger in his own element. Penguin on the Beach. Ruth Miller. PeSA
Stranger in my gates, The—lo! that am I. Omnia Exeunt in Mysterium. George Sterling. AnAmPo; NP; WGRP
Stranger in Scythopolis, A. Katharine Lee Bates. StJW
Stranger it was never meant for, A. Mine. Frank Polite. NYBP
Stranger, may I button-hole you. Something in Common. Richard Church. MoRP
Stranger pass by and waste no time. Suffolk Epitaph. *Unknown.* MemP; SiTL
Stranger, tell the Spartans we lie here. Variations on Simonides. Gladys Ely. NYTB
Stranger, the bark you see before you says. The Yacht. Catullus. AWP; JAWP; WBP
Stranger, the world expected You for long days. Messias. Thomas Merton. JKCP (1955 ed.)
Stranger to Europe. Guy Butler. ACV; BoSA
Stranger walls, that shell no violent prescence. F. D. Sinclair. Zimbabwe. PeSA
Stranger, where thy feet now rest. The Grove of Colonus. Sophocles. *Fr.* Oedipus at Colonus. WoL
Stranger! whoe'er thou art, whose restless mind. Verses Copied from the Window of an Obscure Lodging-House. *Unknown.* LiTL; ViBoPo
Stranger, Why Do You Wonder So? K. B. Jones-Quartey. PBA
Stranger, you freeze to this: there ain't no kinder gin-palace. Home, Sweet Home, with Variations, II. H. C. Bunner. CenHV
Stranger, you who hide my love. Song. Stephen Spender. FaBoTw
Strangers, The. Audrey Alexandra Brown. WHW
Strangers. Walter de la Mare. POTE
Strangers. R. S. Thomas. NMP
Strangers. Mark Turbyfill. NP
Strangers, The. Jones Very. CBEP; OxBA
Strangers Are We All upon the Earth. Franz Werfel, *tr. fr. German by* Edith Abercrombie Snow. TrJP
Strangers ask. The Tower. Philip Booth. NePoEA-2
Stranger's Gift, The. Jones Very. AmePo
Stranger's Grave, The. Emily Lawless. OnYI
Stranger's Song, The. Thomas Hardy. BrPo
Strangers! your eyes are on that valley fixed. The Field of the Grounded Arms. Fitz-Greene Halleck. PoEL-4
Strangest of adventures, The. Lord Arnaldos. James Elroy Flecker. StPo
Strangled Prayer, The. Vernon Watkins. PoIE (1970 ed.)
Strappado for the Devil, A, *sels.* Richard Brathwaite.
Of Maids' Inconstancy. EIL
To the Precision. SiCE
Strapped at the center of the blazing wheel. A Pilot from the Carrier. Randall Jarrell. MoPo; TPM
Strapping young stockman lay dying, A. The Dying Stockman. *Unknown.* PoAu-1; ViBoFo
Stratagem. Allen Curnow. AnNZ
Strategies. Welton Smith. NBP
Stratton Water. Dante Gabriel Rossetti. OxBB
Stravinsky. Julian Cooper. MuSP
Straw, The. Robert Graves. MoVE
Strawberries in Mexico. Ron Padgett. ANYP
Strawberries in November. John Shaw Neilson. PoAu-1
Strawberries Mit Cream. Rochelle Owens. CoPo
Strawberries that in gardens grow. Wild Strawberries. Robert Graves. FaBoCh; LoGBV
Strawberry Blond. Bill Berkson. ANYP
Strawberry Jam. May Justus. FaPON
Strawberry Plant, The. Ruth Pitter. POTE
Strawberry Roan, The, *with music.* *Unknown.* ABF
Strawberry shortcake, blueberry pie. *Unknown.* LoGBV
Strawberry Shrub, The. Edna St. Vincent Millay. CMoP
Straws. Elizabeth Coatsworth. AmFN
Straws like tame lightnings lie about the grass. Summer Farm. Norman MacCaig. ACV
Stray deer, A/ pursued by four Newark policemen. John Giorno. *Fr.* The American Book of the Dead. ANYP
Stray Dog. Charlotte Mish. PoLF
Stray Dog by the Summerhouse, The. Donald Justice. CBV
Stray Dog, near Ecully, Valley of the Rhône. Margaret Avison. OBCV

Stray Memories of Natal and Zululand, *sels.* Charles Barter. BoSA
Changes.
Dingaan and Retief.
Strayed Reveller, The. Matthew Arnold. LoBV; MBW-2; MyFE, *abr.*; ViPo; ViPP; VP
Sels.
Strayed Reveller to Ulysses, The. OBEV (new ed.)
"These things, Ulysses." PoG
Straying Sheep, The. *Unknown, tr. by* Eleanor Hull. JKCP (1962 ed.)
Straying Student, The. Austin Clarke. AnIL; MoAB; NeIP; OxBI
Streaks of green and yellow iridescence. An Aquarium. Amy Lowell. PFY
Stream, The. William Cowper. *See* To a Young Lady.
Stream, The. Lula Lowe Weeden. CDC
Stream/ piles out of the pile, The. The Crossing. Paul Blackburn. NYBP
Stream and Sun at Glendalough. W. B. Yeats. MaPo; MoPW
Stream descends on Meru mountain, A. Robert Southey. *Fr.* The Curse of Kehama. OBRV
Stream flowing steadily over a stone does not wet its core, A. An Elder's Reproof to His Wife. 'Abdillaahi Muuse. TTY
Stream is frozen hard, The. Going by. Antenora. "Hugh MacDiarmid." SeCePo
Stream of Faith, The. William Channing Gannett. OQP; WGRP
Stream of Life, The. Bryant. AnNE
Stream of tender gladness, A. Shadow River. E. Pauline Johnson. CaP
Stream swirls, The. The wind moans in. Jade Flower Palace. Tu Fu. NaP
Stream was smooth as glass, we said, The. The Ballad of the Boat. Richard Garnett. HBV; VA
Streamlined Stream-Knowledge. Arthur W. Bell. WhC
Streams. Clinton Scollard. PoMA
Streams fall down and through the darkness bear, The. Spate in Winter Midnight. Norman MacCaig. BoC; GTBS-P
Streams of Lovely Nancy, The. *Unknown.* LO; OxBoLi
Stream's Song, The. Lascelles Abercrombie. OBMV; POTE
Streams that wind among the hills, The. Song. George Darley. *Fr.* Sylvia; or, The May Queen. NBM
Streams would wander, bridges stay. The Bridge. Willibald Köhler. CAW
Street, The. Gene Baro. NYBP
Street. Alan Brown. TwCaPo
Street, The. James Russell Lowell. OQP; Sonn
Street, The. Octavio Paz, *tr. fr. Spanish by* Muriel Rukeyser. OCS
Street Beggar. Anderson M. Scruggs. PoMa
Street climbs upward steeply, The. The Street. Gene Baro. NYBP
Street Corner College. Kenneth Patchen. MoAmPo
Street Fight. Harold Monro. FaBoTw
Street in April, A. Louis Dudek. OBCV
Street in our town, A. The Watchmaker's Shop. *Unknown.* BoTP
Street is quiet, The. Where the Blue Horses. Raymond Souster. PeCV (1967 ed.)
Street Lamps. D. H. Lawrence. BoPe
Street Lanterns. Mary Elizabeth Coleridge. BoTP; PoRA (rev. ed.)
Street light, The. Late Corner. Langston Hughes. Kal; NePoAm-2
Street Melody, A. Belle Cooper. GoBC
Street Musician. *Unknown.* TSW
Street of Doctors, The. Thomas Walsh. PoMa
Street of Named Houses, The. Robert David Cohen. NYBP
Street Performers, 1851. Terence Tiller. GTBS-P
Street Scene. W. E. Henley. BoTP
Street Scene. Robert Mezey. LiTM (1970 ed.); ToPo
Street Scene, A. Lizette Woodworth Reese. PCH; TSW
Street Scene—1946. Kenneth Porter. PoNe
Street Song. Edith Sitwell. CMoP; CoBMV; MoPo; MoVE; OnHM; POTE
Street Sounds to the Soldiers' Tread, The. A. E. Housman. A Shropshire Lad, XXII. PoVP
Street, the store, the station especially the bar, The. The Pioneers; or, Twenty Years After. William Plomer. BoSA
Street there is in Paris famous, A. The Ballad of Bouillabaisse. Thackeray. ALV; BOHV; HBV; InMe; OBEV (new ed.); OBVV; PoVP; VA; ViBoPo
Street-Walker in March. Samuel L. Albert. NePoAm-2
Street Window. Carl Sandburg. OCS
Streetcleaner's Lament, The. Patricia Hubbell. OCS
Streets. Douglas Goldring. HBMV
Streets of Baltimore. *Unknown.* BLPA
Streets of Laredo, The. Louis MacNeice. ChTr; MoBS
Streets of Laredo, The. *Unknown. See* Cowboy's Lament, The.
Streets of London, The. John Oldham. *Fr.* A Satyr in Imitation of the Third of Juvenal. PeRV
Streets of San Miguel, The. Keith Wilson. ThO
Streets of the roaring town. On a Soldier Fallen in the Philippines. William Vaughn Moody. AmPP (3d ed.); AP; HBV; MAP; MC; MoAmPo (1942 ed.); PaA; PAH; ThLM
Streets that slept all afternoon in sun, The. Camptown. John Ciardi. ThLM; WaP
Strength. Jessie Wilmore Murton. ChIP; MaRV; OQP
Strength. Christopher Smart. *See* Strong Is the Horse upon His Speed.
Strength and dignity [*or* honour] are her clothing. The Mother of the House. Proverbs, Bible, *O.T.* GoTP; OQP; PGD; PoSC
Strength—Human. Tennyson. *Fr.* Ode on the Death of the Duke of Wellington. SoP
Strength in Weakness. Richard Burton. MaRV
Strength leaves the hand I lay on this beech bole. The Beech. Andrew Young. BoNaP
Strength, Love, Light. Robert II, King of France. WGRP
Strength of Fate, The. Euripides, *tr. fr. Greek by* A. E. Housman. *Fr.* Alcestis. AWP; JAWP; WBP
Strength of Willows, The. Alex Raybin. ThO
Strength to War. Stephen Stepanchev. WaP
Strengthen, my Love, this castle of my heart. Rondel to His Mistress. Charles d'Orléans. AWP
Strengthened to live, strengthened to die. In Distrust of Merits. Marianne Moore. AmPP; AP; CoBMV; EaLo; LiTA; LiTM; MoAB; MoAmPo (1950 ed.); NePA; OxBA; PoAn; PoRL; SeCeV; TreFT; TrGrPo (rev. ed.); UnPo (3d ed.); ViBoPo (1958 ed.); WaaP; WaP
Strephon. John Smith. SeCL; UnTE
Strephon kissed me in the spring. The Look. Sara Teasdale. ALV; BoLP; HBV; LiTL; LiTM; WePo
Strephon the brisk and gay. Strephon. John Smith. SeCL; UnTE
Stretch'd and still lies the midnight. Song of Myself, XXXVI. Walt Whitman. CoBA
Stretched in the shadow of the broad beech. The Shepherd's Gratitude. Vergil. Eclogues, I. AWP
Stretched out full length, his eighty years too ripe. The Old Peasant in the Billiard Saloon. Huw Menai. ACV
Stretchin' Out. Mari Evans. *See* Vive Noir!
Strew lightly o'er the soldier's grave. The Soldier's Grave. Henry D. Muir. OHIP
Strew me with blossoms when I die. Popular Songs of Tuscany. *Unknown.* AWP; JAWP; WBP
Strew not earth with empty stars. Song. Thomas Lovell Beddoes. *Fr.* The Second Brother. CBEP; ViBoPo
Strew on her roses, roses. Requiescat. Matthew Arnold. AWP; BEL; BoLiVe; BoPe; DD; ELP; EnLi-2; EnLit; EPN; FiP; GTBS; GTBS-D; GTBS-W; GTSL; HBV; ILP; InP; InPo; InvP; JAWP; LiTB; LiTG; LiTL; MaVP; MBW-2; NoP; OAEP; OBEV; OBVV; OHIP; OuHeWo; PG; PoFS; PoRA; PoSa; PoVP; TOP; TreFS; TrGrPo; ViBoPo; ViPo; ViPP; VP; WBP; WHA
Strew the fair garlands where slumber the dead. Memorial Day. Samuel F. Smith. *Fr.* Our Honored Heroes. OQP
Stricken Colts, The. Louise D. Peck. NYTB
Stricken Deer, The. William Cowper. *Fr.* The Task, III. FiP; LoBV
("I was a stricken deer.") EnRP; MaRV; OAEP; OxBoCh; PeER
(In His Mental Illness, William Cowper Finds He Is Not Alone.) BoC
(Self-Portrait.) CoBE
Stricken Deer, The. Thomas Moore. *See* Come, Rest in This Bosom.
Stricken South to the North, The. Paul Hamilton Hayne. PAH

Stricken (continued)
Stricken to earth, the sword snapped in his hand. I Am the Last [*or* One Love]. Edward Shillito. MaRV; OQP
Strict hairshirt of circumstance wears the flesh. The Veterans. Donagh MacDonagh. JKCP (1955 ed.); OnYI
Strictly Germ-proof. Arthur Guiterman. BLPA; BOHV; HBV; TreF; TrJP; YaD
Strife is grown between Virtue and Love, A. Astrophel and Stella, LII. Sir Philip Sidney. FCP; ReEn; SiPS
Strife Is O'er, The. *Unknown, tr. fr. Latin by* Francis Pott. OQP
(Victory.) MaRV
Strike among the Poets, A. *Unknown.* BOHV; FiBHP; PP; SiTL
Strike, churl; hurl, cheerless wind, then; heltering hail. Fragment. Gerard Manley Hopkins. NAMP
Strike down into my breast, O sun, and cleanse my soul. Hymn to the Sun. William Alexander Percy. TrPWD
Strike home, strong-hearted man! Down to the root. To Ronge. Whittier. AnEnPo
Strike It Up, Tabor. *Unknown.* NCEP
Strike the Blow. "F. McK." PAH
Strike the concertina's melancholy string! The Story of Prince Agib. W. S. Gilbert. BOHV; InMe; LBN; NA
"Strike the sails!" King Olaf said. King Olaf's War-Horns. Longfellow. *Fr.* Tales of a Wayside Inn, Pt. I. AmPP (4th ed.); PFY
Strike up, you lusty gallants, with musick and sound of drum. Captain Ward and the *Rainbow.* *Unknown.* BaBo; EsPB
Striking. Charles Stuart Calverley. CenHV
Striking a Lead, *with music.* John A. Stone. SGR
Striking like lightning to the quick of the real world. Duns Scotus. Thomas Merton. CoPo
String Quartet. Babette Deutsch. UnS
String Stars of Pearls. J. U. Nicholson. HBMV
Strings' Excitement, The. W. H. Auden. MoAB; MoBrPo
(Family Ghosts.) ReMP
Strings in the Earth and Air. James Joyce. Chamber Music, I. CLwM; FIW; HBMV; HW; LOW; MoBrPo; OnYI; ReMP
Strings of camels come in single file, The. He Cometh Late. *Unknown.* OQP
Strip Mining Pit. Dan Gillespie. QAH
Strip of Blue, A. Lucy Larcom. AA; HBV; MaRV, *abr.*; OQP; OTPC; WGRP
Striped blouse in a clearing by Bazille, A. Ceremony. Richard Wilbur. CoAP; FiMAP; MiAP; Po; PP; ReMP
Stripped almond of the plane is gone, The. Between Two Worlds. Rosemary Thomas. NYBP
Stripping an almond tree in flower. Little Joke. Elinor Wylie. LHV
Strive No More. Thomas Lodge. CoBE; TuPP
Strive Not, Vain Lover, to Be Fine. Richard Lovelace. OAEP
Striving is past. Ah, I must sink and drown. Fidessa, More Chaste than Kind, XXIV. Bartholomew Griffin. ReIE
Striving to sing glad songs, I but attain. Two Sonnets, II. James Thomson. PoVP
Stroke of One. Jorge Carrera Andrade, *tr. fr. Spanish by* Muna Lee. OnPM
Strokes of mania on this vanilla, The. Comanche. Tom Clark. ANYP
Strolling fox, famished and underfed, A. The Greedy Fox and the Elusive Grapes. Aesop. MaC
Strolling on the green grass. *Unknown.* RIS
Strolling one afternoon along a street. Monody on the Demolition of Devonshire House. Siegfried Sassoon. FaBoTw
Strong, The. John Vance Cheney. AA
Strong, The. John Curtis Underwood. MaRV
Strong and slippery, built for the midnight grass-party confronted by four cats. Peter. Marianne Moore. AnAmPo; CMoP; NoP; OxBA
Strong Are Saying Nothing, The. Robert Frost. CMoP; NoP; PoDB; PoE
Strong Arms. Frances O'Connell Corridan. JKCP (1926 ed.)
Strong as Death. H. C. Bunner. HBV
Strong, but with gentleness. Variations on a Medieval Theme. Geoffrey Dutton. PoAu-2
Strong City, The. Alfred Noyes. *Fr.* The Last Voyage. GoBC
Strong extreme speed, that the brain hurries with. Boulogne to Amiens and Paris. Dante Gabriel Rossetti. *Fr.* A Trip to Paris and Belgium. PeVV
Strong God which made the topmost stars. The Prophet Lost in the Hills at Evening. Hilaire Belloc. JKCP; OxBoCh
Strong Hand, A. Aaron Hill. HBV
Strong Heroic Line, The. Oliver Wendell Holmes. AA
Strong imagination from my youth has been combined, A. The Caulker. M. A. Lewis. StPo
Strong in a dream of perfect bloom. To the Brave Soul. Wilbur Underwood. WGRP
Strong in thy steadfast purpose, be. Purpose. John James Piatt. AA
Strong Is the Horse upon His Speed. Christopher Smart. *Fr.* A Song to David. MyFE
(Man of Prayer, The.) BBV (1951 ed.); GTBS-W; LiTB; LiTG
(Strength.) OtMeF
Strong Love. A. E. Housman. OtMeF
Strong man awhile in his kingdom is lord, The. The Eternal. Esaias Tegnér. LiTW
Strong Men. Sterling Brown. BANP; PPON; TTY; WOW
Strong men keep coming on, The. Upstream. Carl Sandburg. HBMV; MAP; MoAB; MoAmPo; MoRP; NeMA; PoFr
Strong Men, Riding Horses. Gwendolyn Brooks. Kal
Strong rods for scepters to bear sway. On the Decease of the Religious and Honourable Jno Haynes Esqr. John James. SCAP
Strong shock, A. Wordsworth. *Fr.* The Prelude, XI. MaPo (1969 ed.)
Strong-shouldered mole. A Dead Mole. Andrew Young. GTBS-P
Strong sob of the chafing stream, The. Orara. Henry C. Kendall. BoAu; PoAu-1
Strong Son of God, immortal Love. In Memoriam A. H. H., Proem. Tennyson. BBV; BEL; BoLiVe; ChIP; CoBE; EaLo; EnL; EnLit; EPN; FaPL; GTBS-W; HBV; ILP; LiTB; MaRV; MaVP; MBW-2; NeHB; OAEP; OQP; OuHeWo; OxBoCh; PAn; PoFS; PoIE; PoVP; SeCeV; SoP; StJW; TOP; TreF; TrGrPo; TrPWD; TRV; UnPo (1st ed.); ViPo; ViPP; VP; WGRP; WHA
Strong, still light upon the verge of Being. To the Angel. Rainer Maria Rilke. LiTW
Strong sun across the sod can make. Song for the Passing of a Beautiful Woman. *Unknown.* LiTA
Strong Swimmer, The. William Rose Benét. PoNe
Strong Wind, A. Austin Clarke. BoNaP
Strong wind is gathering the storm-clouds together, The. The Song of the Storm-Finch. Maxim Gorki. PoFr
Stronger Faith, A. Tennyson. *Fr.* In Memoriam A. H. H., XCVI. MaRV
("Perplext in faith, but pure in deeds.") TRV
Strongest, The. "Yehoash," *tr. fr. Yiddish by* Marie Syrkin. TrJP
Strongest and the noblest argument, The. Dedication II. Sir John Davies. *Fr.* Nosce Teipsum. SiPS
Strophes: "There is one who takes all men within his hand." Rainer Maria Rilke, *tr. fr. German by* Jessie Lemont. OnPM
Struck into a mountain one black cross. Saint. Kersti Merilaas. LiTW
Struck was I, nor yet by lightning. Emily Dickinson. AnNE
Struck with huge love, of what to be possest. A Prefatory Poem on. . .*Magnalia Christi Americana.* Nicholas Noyes. SCAP
Structural Iron Workers. MacKnight Black. NP
Structure of Rime XXIII. Robert Duncan. FRC
Struggle. Sidney Lanier. CBEP; LiTA; OxBA
Struggle, The. Sully-Prudhomme, *tr. fr. French by* Arthur O'Shaughnessy. AWP; PoPl
Struggle is over, the boys are defeated, The. Bold Robert Emmet. Tom Maguire. OnYI
Struggle is strong and splendid, The. Sounding. Doris Ferne. CaP
Struggling Fancies. Bhartrihari, *tr. fr. Sanskrit by* Arthur W. Ryder. OnPM
Strumbo, Dorothy, Trumpart, Cobbling Shoes. *At. to* George Peele. *See* Cobblers' Song, The.
Strut and wiggle. To Midnight Nan at LeRoy's. Langston Hughes. AnAmPo
Strutting cock, with swelling chest. The Cock [*or* For a Cock.] Eleanor Farjeon. PoRh; RIS
Stubborn Fool, The. Bhartrihari, *tr. fr. Sanskrit by* Arthur W. Ryder. OnPM
Stud Groom. John Glassco. OBCV

Student, The. Marianne Moore. TwCP
Student, The. *Unknown, tr. fr. Early Modern Irish by* Frank O'Connor. AnIL; KiLC; OBMV
Student, at his book so placed, A. Of a New-Married Student. *Unknown.* CBV; SiCE; TuPP
Student came from Oxford town also, A. Seven Pilgrims. Chaucer. *Fr.* The Canterbury Tales. TrGrPo
Students. Florence Wilkinson Evans. HBV
Students, *much abr.* Haniel Long. AnAmPo
Student's Kiss, A. *Unknown, tr. fr. Spanish by* Havelock Ellis. OnPM
Student's life is pleasant, The. The Student. *Unknown.* AnIL; KiLC; OBMV
Students, like students, form and fly. "When the Students Resisted, a Minor Clash Ensued." David Knight. MoCV
Students of Justice, The. W. S. Merwin. NaP
Studies at Delhi, *sels.* Sir Alfred Comyn Lyall.
Badminton. OBVV; PeVV
Hindu Ascetic, The. OBVV
Studio, The. Anthony Kerrigan. NYTB
Studios Photographic, The, *sel.* Paul Shivell.
In God's Eternal Studios. HBV
Study in a Late Subway. Muriel Rukeyser. OnHM
Study in a Minor Key, *sel.* Philip Hobsbaum.
Chopin in London. MuSP
Study in Aesthetics, The. Ezra Pound. CMoP; NoP; NP
Study it carefully. The Bible. *Unknown.* SoP
Study No. X. Pierre Coupey. PeCV (1967 ed.)
Study of an Elevation, in Indian Ink. Kipling. BOHV; InMe
Study of Images, I. Wallace Stevens. ReMP
Study of Two Pears. Wallace Stevens. AmPP (4th ed.); AP; MaPo (1969 ed.); OxBA; PoeP; TDP
Study this violent and trembling woman. How Music's Made. Dilys Laing. ELU
Stuff of Dreams, The. Shakespeare. *See* Our Revels Now Are Ended.
Stuff of the moon. Nocturne in a Deserted Brickyard. Carl Sandburg. AnPP; CoBA; MAP; MoAmPo; NP
Stuffed Owl, The. Wordsworth. Par
Stumbling/ in our own curriculum. Bound Together. Ruth Lisa Schechter. WOW
Stumbling over fallen logs. Lost in a Blizzard. Arthur W. Monroe. PoOW
Stun. James Schuyler. ANYP
Stung. *Unknown, tr. fr. Greek by* Thomas Stanley. OuHeWo
Stung by the tail of a scorpion. Jet Plane. A. M. Sullivan. JKCP (1955 ed.)
Stunned in the stone light, laid among the lilies. Ophelia. Vernon Watkins. MoVE
Stuntman. Lionel Kearns. MoCV
Stupendious love! All saints astonishment! Edward Taylor. *Fr.* Preparatory Meditations, First Series. OxBA
Stupid Kite, The. Allen Upward. *Fr.* Scented Leaves from a Chinese Jar. NP
Stupid men, forever prone. Redondillas. Sister Juana Ines de la Cruz. CAW
Stupid Old Body, The. Edward Carpenter. WGRP
Stupidity Street. Ralph Hodgson. AtBAP; BrPo; CH; EnLit; HBV; LiTM (rev. ed.); LOW; MoAB; MoBrPo; NeMA; NP; PDV; PoFr; SiSoSe; SP; TOP; TreFS; UTS
Sturdiest of forest trees, The. The Holly. Walter de la Mare. CMoP
Sturdy rock, for all his strength, The. Man's Flitting Life Finds Surest Stay, Where Sacred Virtue Beareth Sway. John Thorn. SiCE
Stutterer. Alan Dugan. NYBP
"Styles that at present are regnant, The." Limerick. *Unknown.* LiBL
Stylite. Louis MacNeice. MoPo
Styro. Clark Coolidge. ANYP; YAP
Styx River Anthology. Carolyn Wells. BOHV
Suave body of the Queen, she gave me you. Body of the Queen. Donald Evans. AnAmPo
Suave Mari Magno. Lucretius, *tr. fr. Latin by* W. H. Mallock. *Fr.* De Rerum Natura. AWP
Sub-average *Time* Reader, The. Ernest Wittenberg. FiBHP
Sub Pondere Crescit. James Russell Lowell. MaRV
Sub Specie Aeternitatis. Robert Hayden. AmPP (5th ed.)
Sub Terra. William Carlos Williams. NP
Subalterns, The. Thomas Hardy. CMoP; MaPo; MoAB; MoBrPo; TDP
Subaltern's Love-Song, A. John Betjeman. EvOK; MeWo; ShBV-4; TwCP
Subject chosen for tonight's discussion, The. An Evening of Russian Poetry. Vladimir Nabokov. NYBP
Subject for Prophecy. Gemma D'Auria. JKCP (1955 ed.)
Subject of Heroic Song, The. Milton. *Fr.* Paradise Lost, IX. OBS
("No more of talk where God or Angel guest.") SeEP
Subject of the Bishop's Miracle, The. John Philip. BoAV
Subject to All Pain. *Unknown.* MeEL
Subject today, my friends, is stinted praise, The. "The Art of Our Necessities Is Strange." Forrest Izard. WhC
Subject was put to bed at midnight, The. Operative No. 174 Resigns. Kenneth Fearing. NYBP
Subject, with Apologies. Phillip Hey. YAP
Subjectivity at Sestos. P. M. Hubbard. NYBP
Subjects' Joy, The. *Unknown. See* England's Triumph.
Sublimation. Alex Comfort. ErPo; UnTE
Sublime—invention ever young. Christopher Smart. *Fr.* A Song to David. HBV; OBEV
Sublimer strains, O rustic Muse, prepare. Saturday; or, The Flights. John Gay. *Fr.* The Shepherd's Week. EiCP; EiPP
Sublimity! Sublimity! I lay thee down. Wilfred Campbell. *Fr.* Lines on a Re-reading of Parts of the Old Testament. InP
Submarine Bed, The. John Peale Bishop. LiTA
Submarine Mountains. Cale Young Rice. EtS
Submarine Voyage, The, *sel.* Thomas Heyrick.
"There lies a broken anker, on whose trust." PeRV
Submerged, silent, rooted in water. Foetus. Phyllis Haring. PeSA
Submerged Village, The. James Kirkup. POTi
Submergence. Hazel Hall. NP
Submission. George Herbert. MaMe
Submission. *Unknown, tr. fr. Siamese by* E. Powys Mathers. ErPo
Submission. Jessie E. Williams. OQP
Submission and Rest. Anna Temple Whitney. *See* Kneeling Camel, The.
Submission in Affliction. *Unknown.* STF
Submite submitted to her heavenly king. *Unknown.* WhC
Submitting to a sentry's fate. Common Dawn. Guy Butler. PeSA
Subsiding from those heavenly wings the air. Hymn for the Feast of the Annunciation. Aubrey Thomas De Vere. ISi
Substance and Shadow. Cardinal Newman. GoBC
Substitution. Elizabeth Barrett Browning. MaRV; WGRP
Substitution. Anne Spencer. CDC
Subterranean City, A. Thomas Lovell Beddoes. HoPM; StP
(Lines: "I followed once a fleet and mighty serpent.") NBM
Subtle almost beyond thought are these dim colours. Dun-Colour. Ruth Pitter. MoVE; PoRA (rev. ed.)
Subtle chain of countless rings, A. Emerson. *Fr.* Nature (essay). AmePo; AmLP; AmPP; AWP; ILP; InPo
Subtle tracery of the leafless bough, The. Ad Matrem in Coelis. Linda Lyon Van Voorhis. GoBC
Suburb. Harold Monro. HBV
Suburb Hilltop. Richard Moore. NYBP
Suburban Homecoming. John Ciardi. ToPo
Suburban Lullaby. J. S. Manifold. BoAV
Suburban Wife's Song. Robert Hutchinson. NYBP
Suburbia. Maurice Martinez. PoNe (1970 ed.)
Suburbs, The. Enid Derham. BoAu
Suburbs Is a Fine Place, The. *Unknown.* CoMu
Suburbs on a Hazy Day. D. H. Lawrence. OBMV
Subversive. William Rose Benét. MoRP
Subverted Flower, The. Robert Frost. CMoP; MWA-2; OxBA
Subway, The. Conrad Kent Rivers. Kal
Subway, The. Allen Tate. AP; TDP
Subway Builders. Lawrence Lee. PoMa
Subway Rush Hour. Langston Hughes. OCS
Success ("It's doing your job. . ."). Berton Braley. WBLP
(That's Success!) PoToHe
Success. C. C. Cameron. PoToHe (new ed.)
Success. Barbara E. Cornet. SoP
Success. Emily Dickinson. *See* Success is counted sweetest.
Success. William Empson. ToPo
Success. Edgar A. Guest. TreF

Success ("Before God's footstool to confess"). *Unknown.* PoToHe
(Judgment.) TreFT
Success ("Success is speaking words of praise"). *Unknown.* FaFP; PoToHe (new ed.)
Success. Wang Chi, *tr. fr. Chinese by* Henry H. Hart. WoL
Success is counted sweetest. Emily Dickinson. AmePo; AmP; AmPP (4th ed.); AP; AWP; CABA; CBEP; CBV; CMoP; CoBA; DiPo; GoJo; GTBS-W; InPo; JAWP; LiTA; LiTM; MAmP; MCCG; MoAB; MoAmPo (1950 ed.); MWA-2; NeMA; OxBA; PG; PoeP; PoIE; PoPo; PoRA; StP; TreFT; WaaP; WBP
Success is speaking words of praise. Success. *Unknown.* FaFP; PoToHe (new ed.)
Success of the Gospel. Samuel F. Smith. *See* Morning Light Is Breaking, The.
Succession, The. Frances Laughton Mace. AA
Succession, The. Edwin Muir. PoDB
Succession of the Four Sweet Months, The. Robert Herrick. OTPC (1946 ed.); PCH; YeAr
(Four Sweet Months, The.) BoTP; WiR
(July; the Succession of the Four Sweet Months.) FaPON
Succumbing. Paul Eaton Reeve. ErPo
Such a Blustery Day! Elizabeth Gould. BoTP
Such a fine pullet ought to go. A Blue Ribbon at Amesbury. Robert Frost. NePA
"Such a little king's eye," said my mother. Roy Kloof. Sydney Clouts. BoSA
Such a morning it is when love. Day of These Days. Laurie Lee. AtBAP; BoNaP; FaBoMo; MoVE
Such a Parcel of Rogues in a Nation. Robert Burns. OxBS
Such a Pleasant Familee. Wallace Irwin. ShM
Such a Starved Bank of Moss. Robert Browning. The Two Poets of Croisic: Prologue. EPN
(Apparitions.) TSW
Such a time of it they had. Stanley Meets Mutesa. James D. Rubadiri. PBA
Such a wide, still landscape, all cold and white! A Greenland Winter. Lucy Diamond. BoTP
Such age how beautiful! O lady bright. To——, in Her Seventieth Year. Wordsworth. BWP
Such are the stillness and peace that prevail through the Sultan's dominions. A Triplet on the Reign of the Great Sultan. James Clarence Mangan. IrPN
Such as it is. Such as two men. The Clothing's New Emperor. Donald Finkel. NePoEA
Such as, retired from sight of men, like thee. To St. Mary Magdalen. Henry Constable. CoBE; Sonn; TuPP
Such as the Berecynthian Goddess bright. Ruins of Rome, III. Joachim du Bellay. OnPM
Such beautiful, beautiful hands. Beautiful Hands [*or* My Mother's Hands]. *Unknown, at. to* Ellen M. H. Gates. TreF; TreFS
Such darkness as when Jesus died! San Francisco. Joaquin Miller. PAH
Such dubious nomenclatures crowding in. Basic Communication. Thomas Hornsby Ferril. NePoAm-2
Such fame as I have drops from me in a flash. The Perturbations of Uranus. Roy Fuller. ErPo
Such folly of margins that may retaliate. Gil Orlovitz. *Fr.* Art of the Sonnet. ToPo
Such hap as I am happed in. Sir Thomas Wyatt. FCP; SiPS
Such happiness—and all amongst the dead. Elegy in a Museum. Pamela Griffin. BoPe
Such hints as untaught Nature yields! Nature, the Artist. Frederic Lawrence Knowles. AA
Such Is Holland! Petrus Augustus de Genestet, *tr. fr. Dutch by* Adriaan J. Barnouw. FIW
Such Is Love. Rodrigo Cota de Maguaque, *tr. fr. Spanish by* Thomas Walsh. OnPM
Such is the course that nature's kind hath wrought. Sir Thomas Wyatt. FCP
Such Is the Death the Soldier Dies. Robert Burns Wilson. AA; HBV
Such is the mode of these censorious days. On Mr. Hobbs, and His Writings. John Sheffield, Duke of Buckingham and Normanby. PoEL-3
Such is the mystery of man's freedom, says God. Charles Péguy. *Fr.* Freedom. PoFr
Such Is the Sickness of Many a Good Thing. Robert Lowell. NoP
Such Is the Way of the World. "St.- J. Perse," *tr. fr. French by* T. S. Eliot. Anabasis, Pt. IV. AtBAP
(Thus Was the City Founded.) OnHM
Such light is in sea-caves. Musica No. 3. Richard Duerden. NeAP
Such little, puny things are words in rhyme. Quickening. Christopher Morley. HBMV
Such love is like a smoky fire. George Chapman. LO
Such lovers as shall haunt this grove. *Unknown.* SeCSL
Such majestic rhythms, such tiny disturbances. A Grain of Rice. F. R. Scott. PeCV
Such marvellous ways to kill a man! The Bofors A. A. Gun. Gavin Ewart. WaP
Such moving sounds from such a careless touch. Of My Lady Isabella Playing on the Lute. Edmund Waller. MePo; SeCP
Such natural depths of love our Oxford knows. Martyr's Memorial. Louise Imogen Guiney. AA
Such old, illustrious tidings you proclaim. To a Young Priest. Anne Blackwell Payne. MaRV
Such perfect bliss, fair Cloris, we. To a Lady in a Letter. Earl of Rochester. PeRV; SeEP
Such pictures of the heavens were never seen. The Invisible. Richard Watson Gilder. WGRP
Such special sweetness was about. That Day You Came. Lizette Woodworth Reese. HBV
Such splendid icecaps and hard rills, such weights. Piano Practice. Howard Moss. NYBP
"Such Stuff as Dreams." Franklin P. Adams. FiBHP
"Such Stuff as Dreams Are Made Of." Thomas Wentworth Higginson. AA
Such Stuff as Dreams Are Made On. Shakespeare. *See* Our Revels Now Are Ended.
Such subtle filigranity and nobless of construccion. Wellcome, to the Caves of Arta! Robert Graves. NYBP
Such, such is death: no triumph: no defeat. Two Sonnets [on Death], II. Charles Hamilton Sorley. HBMV; MMA; MoBrPo; NeMA; TrGrPo (1942 ed.)
Such Sweet Neglect. Ben Jonson. *See* Simplex Munditiis.
Such times as windy moods do Stir. The Spirit of the Wheat. Edward A. U. Valentine. AA
Such trivial things. Trivia. Beatrice M. Murphy. TNV
Such vain thought as wonted to mislead me. Sir Thomas Wyatt. FCP
Such was he, our Martyr-Chief. Abraham Lincoln [*or* Our Martyr-Chief *or* Lincoln]. James Russell Lowell. *Fr.* Ode Recited at the Harvard Commemoration, July 21, 1865. AnNE; InP; OHIP; PAP; PEDC
Such was old Chaucer. Such the placid mien. For a Statue of Chaucer at Woodstock. Mark Akenside. SeCePo
Such was the boy—but for the growing youth. Communion. Wordsworth. *Fr.* The Excursion, I. MaRV; OBRV
Such wayward ways hath love that most part in discord. Earl of Surrey. FCP; SiPS
Such were the notes, thy once-lov'd poet sung. Epistle to Robert Earl of Oxford. Pope. EiCL
Such were those epigrams of elder times. Henry Parrot. SiCE
Such Wisdom. *Unknown.* GFA
"Suck, baby, suck, mother's love grows by giving." The Gypsy's Malison. Charles Lamb. Sonn
Suck Creek, Lover's Leap. Ear Lobe. Coleman Barks. *Fr.* Body Poems. QAH
Suck the bare sob out of the heart. Microcosmos, X. Nigel Heseltine. NeBP
Sucking Cider through a Straw, *with music.* *Unknown.* AS
Sudbury Fight, The. Wallace Rice. PAH
Sudden amid the slush and rain. In the City. Israel Zangwill. WGRP
Sudden autumn winds, like hounds, The. Mary Gilmore. *Fr.* The Disinherited. PoAu-1
Sudden, before my inward, open vision. Compassion for the Lost. *Unknown.* SoP
Sudden blow, A: the great wings beating still. Leda and the Swan. W. B. Yeats. AnIL; AtBAP; BWP; CABA; CaFP; CBV; CMoP; CoBMV; DiPo; EnL; EnLi-2 (1949 ed.); ErPo; ExPo; FaBoEn; FosPo; GTBS-P; ILP; InPo; LiTM; MaPo; MBW-2; MoAB; MoBrPo; MoVE; NoP; OAEP (2d ed.); PAn; PIA; PoAn; PoE; PoeP; PoFS; PoIE; SeCeV; Sonn; StP; TDP; TrGrPo; VaPo

Sudden Frost. David Wagoner. PoPl
Sudden Light. Dante Gabriel Rossetti. CBEP; ELP; FaBoEn; GTBS-D; InP; LO; LoBV; MeWo; NBM; NoP; OAEP, *sl. diff.*; OBNC; Po; PoLF; PoVP; TrGrPo; VA
(Song IV: Sudden Light.) CTC
Sudden night is here at once, The. Poppies. Charles Weekes. OnYI
Sudden refreshment came upon the school. Physical Geography. Louise Townsend Nicholl. ImOP
Sudden Shower. John Clare. CBEP; OBRV; PoSC
Sudden Shower, A. James Whitcomb Riley. PRWS
Sudden Spring. Margaret Coulby. TwCaPo
Sudden storms that heave me to and fro. Introduction to Psalm LXXIII. Earl of Surrey. FCP; PoLi
Sudden sun, and the white spring rain, The. Picnic. Ray Mathew. BoAV
Sudden swallows swiftly skimming. Susan Simpson. *Unknown.* BOHV
Sudden the desert changes. Bridge-Guard in the Karroo. Kipling. BoSA
Sudden thrust of speech is no mean test, The. The Fire i' the Flint. Lucy Catlin Robinson. AA
Sudden wakin', a sudden weepin', A. Man's Days. Eden Phillpotts. HBV; OBEV (new ed.); OBVV
Sudden waking when a saffron glare, A. A Transvaal Morning. William Plomer. BoSA
Suddenly. Leonora Speyer. PG (1945 ed.)
Suddenly/ out of the faint gray smother. White Fox. Elizabeth Alsop Shepard. GoYe
Suddenly./ Suddenly and certainly, as I watched elsewhere, locked. The First Morning of the Second World. Delmore Schwartz. FiMAP
Suddenly Afraid. *Unknown.* CBEP; NCEP
(Sodenly Afraide.) EnLit
Suddenly, after the quarrel, while we waited. The Quarrel. Conrad Aiken. LiTL; MAP; MoAB; MoAmPo; MoLP; PoPl
Suddenly all the fountains in the park. The Fountains. W. R. Rodgers. MoVE
Suddenly as I came. Ducks. Roy Daniells. TwCaPo
Suddenly flickered a flame. Suddenly. Leonora Speyer. PG (1945 ed.)
Suddenly from a wayside station. In the Train. Clifford Bax. InP
Suddenly, from the rocky spring. Sacrifice of a Rainbow Trout. Joseph Langland. TPM
Suddenly he awoke and was running—raw. Bayonet Charge. Ted Hughes. POTi
Suddenly I remember the holes. The Holes. Stephen Berg. NaP; NYBP
Suddenly I saw the cold and rook-delighting Heaven. The Cold Heaven. W. B. Yeats. AWP; CTC; GTBS-P; InPo; JAWP; MoVE; NAMP; NP; OAEP (2d ed.); WBP
Suddenly I was in the act of soaping my head. Spiral Landscape. Michael Brownstein. ANYP
Suddenly in the midnight on mortal men. The Last Judgment. Cynewulf. *Fr.* Christ. AnOE
Suddenly into my dream why should they come. Lament for the Great Yachts. Patric Dickinson. HaMV; PoTi
Suddenly light shone out from the dark window. Snow Story. L. A. MacKay. TwCaPo
Suddenly night crushed out the day and hurled. The Unreturning. Wilfred Owen. MoBrPo
Suddenly night flung wide the sapphire gate. Charles Erskine Scott Wood. *Fr.* The Poet in the Desert. PoFr
Suddenly, out of dark and leafy ways. Tenants. W. W. Gibson. HBV; NP
Suddenly, out of my darkness, shines Thy beauty, O Brother. A Psalm to the Son. Marguerite Wilkinson. TrPWD
"Suddenly she slapped me, hard across the face." In Memoriam II: Elizabeth in Italy. Richard Weber. ErPo
Suddenly, stroke of vertigo, a lightning-flash where, cast. Lightning of the Abyss. Jules Laforgue. SyP
Suddenly the sky turned gray. Snow toward Evening. Melville Cane. MAP; MoAmPo; PDV; SUS; TiPo
Suddenly they came flying, like a long scarf of smoke. The Thing. Theodore Roethke. TDP
Suddenly to become John Benbow, walking down William Street. Metempsychosis. Kenneth Slessor. ViBoPo (1958 ed.)
Suddenly with intense. The Runner. Alexandra Grilikhes. SD
Sudds launders bands in pisse; and starches them. Upon Sudds a Laundresse. Robert Herrick. AnAnS-2
Suffenus, whom so well you know. To Varus. Catullus. AWP
Suffer, Poor Negro. David Diop, *tr. fr. French by* Langston Hughes. PBA
Sufferance of her race is shown, The. "Formerly a Slave." Herman Melville. PoNe
Suffering. Albert Ehrenstein, *tr. fr. German by* Babette Deutsch. TrJP
Suffering. Jane W. Lauber. SoP
Suffering God, The. Raymond Kresensky. ChIP
Suffering God, The. G. A. Studdert-Kennedy. MaRV
Sels.
Christian Soldier, The. MaRV, 3 *sts.*; TRV, 2 *sts.*
Peace and Joy. MaRV; OQP
Suffering has settled like a sly disguise. A Korean Woman Seated by a Wall. William Meredith. NePoEA
Suffering in sorrow in hope to attain. Sir Thomas Wyatt. FCP
Sufferings of the Poor, The. William Langland, *mod. by* Henry W. Wells. *Fr.* The Vision of Piers Plowman. PoLi
("Needy are our neighbors, The," *mod. by* Henry W. Wells.) PoFr
(Poor, The, *shorter sel., Middle English vers.*) PoEL-1
Sufficed not, madam, that you did tear. Sir Thomas Wyatt. FCP; SiPS
Sufficeth it to you, my joys interred. Sir Walter Ralegh. The Ocean [*or* The Ocean's Love] to Cynthia, XI. FCP; NCEP; OBSC; ReIE; SiPS
Sufficiency. Avis B. Christiansen. SoP
Sufficiency. Gleeson White. VA
Sufficient Place, The. Edwin Muir. BoPe
Suffolk Epitaph. *Unknown.* MemP; SiTL
Suffolk Miracle, The. *Unknown.* BaBo (A *and* B *vers.*); ESPB; OBB
Sugar Babe, *with music. Unknown.* ABF
Sugar-Plum Tree, The. Eugene Field. FaFP; HBV; HBVY; MPB; OTPC (1946 ed.); PCH; SoPo; TreF
Sugar Weather. Peter McArthur. CaP
Sugaring, The. A. M. Klein. OBCV
Suggested Device of a New Western State. John James Piatt. AnAmPo
(Farther.) AA; AmePo
Suggestions by Steam. Thomas Hood. NBM
Suibne Geilt. *Unknown. See* Sweeney the Mad.
Suicidal Cat, The. *Unknown.* CIV
Suicide. Louis MacNeice. DTC
Suicide in Trenches. Siegfried Sassoon. BrPo; MMA
Suicide of the night—ah, flotsam. Strange Fruit. Randolph Stow. PoAu-2
Suicide off Egg Rock. Sylvia Plath. NMP
Suicide Rates, The, *sel.* Lewis Warsh.
"Like small foreign villages whose gates have been." YAP
Suicide's Grave, The. W. S. Gilbert. *Fr.* The Mikado. ALV; LiTG; LiTL; TreF; WhC
(Ko-Ko's Song.) FaFP
(Ko-Ko's Winning Song.) LiTB
(Tit-Willow.) SiTL
(Willow, Titwillow.) PoVP
Suicide's Note. Langston Hughes. CDC
Suilven. Andrew Young. OxBS
Suilven and the Eagle, *sel.* Gordon Bottomley.
Eagle Song. MoBrPo
Suire, The. Thomas Caulfield Irwin. IrPN
Suit of Nettles, A, *sels.* James Reaney.
Branwell's Sestina. MoCV
Drunken Preacher's Sermon, The. PeCV (1967 ed.)
January. OBCV; PIA
November. OBCV; PIA
Suit of sheep's clothing, A. Policy. Carolyn Wells. WhC
Suite from Catullus. Vincent McHugh. ErPo
Suits hang half a year in. Tyburn and Westminster. John Heywood. ACP
Sukey, you shall be my wife. *Unknown.* OxNR
Sulk when you're spoken to. *Unknown.* CenHV
Sullen and dark [*or* dull], in the September day. The Last Reservation. Walter Learned. AA; PaA; PAH
Sulky witch and a surly cat, A. Hallowe'en Indignation Meeting. Margaret Fishback. PoSC
Sullen carre why dost thou keepe. *Unknown.* SeCSL

Sullen clouds are gathering fast over the black fringe. The Rainy Day. Rabindranath Tagore. FlW
Sullen Moods. Robert Graves. StP
Sullen skies today. Joy and Sorrow. Aubrey Thomas De Vere. OQP
Sullen, the stream gives no clear image back. Henley on Taieri. Charles Brasch. AnNZ
Sulpicia's Rival. Tibullus, *tr. fr. Latin by* Hubert Creekmore. LiTW
Sultan's Harem, The ("The Sultan got sore on his harem") *Unknown.* TreFT
Sultry air, the smoke of shavings. A Night in a Village. Ivan Savvich Nikitin. AWP; JAWP; WBP
Sultry and brazen was the August day. Saint R. L. S. Sarah N. Cleghorn. HBMV
Sultry, summer evening, the children playing jacks, A. Death of a Cat. James Schevill. NMP; OPoP
Sultry Sunday, noon. Tropic Siesta. Luis Carlos López. WoL
Sum, Es, Est ("Sum—I am a gentleman"). *Unknown.* ChTr
Sum of All Known Reverence, The. Walt Whitman. MoRP
Sum of him is not here, The. Book Review. David Ross. PG (1945 ed.)
Sum of Kisses, A. Juan Meléndez Valdés, *tr. fr. Spanish by* Thomas Walsh. OnPM
Sum of Life, The. Ben King. *See* Pessimist, The.
Sum of Things, The. Arthur W. Jose. BoAu
Sum of Wisdom, The. Milton. *Fr.* Paradise Lost, XII. MaPo
Sum [*or* Some] speiks of Lords, sum speiks of Lairds. Johnie Armstrang. *Unknown.* ESPB (C vers.); OBB; OxBB; ViBoFo (B *vers.*)
Sumach and Birds. Carl Sandburg. YT
Sumburgh Heid. George Bruce. OxBS
Sumer Is Icumen In. *Unknown.* AWP; BEL; CBEP; ILP; InPo; InvP; JAWP; MeEL; PIA; PoAn; PoIE; SeCePo; SeCeV; SiTL; TOP; TreFT; WBP; YAT
(Cuckoo.) ShBV-1
(Cuckoo [*or* Cuccu] Song.) ChTr; EnL; EnLi-1; EnLit; FlW; LiTG; NoP; OBEV; TrGrPo
(Sing Cuccu.) ViBoPo
(Summer Has Come.) PoLi
(Summer Is a-Coming In, *st.* 1.) PCH
(Summer Is Y-Comen In.) MemP
Summa contra Gentiles. Paris Leary. CoPo
Summa is i-cumen in. Baccalaureate, *parody.* David McCord. WhC
Summah night and sighn' breeze. Lover's Lane. Paul Laurence Dunbar. BANP
Summary. Sonia Sanchez. BF
Summary of the Distance between the Bomber and the Objective. Walter Benton. WaP
Summer. Johannes Carl Andersen. BoAu
Summer. Byron. *Fr.* The Corsair, III. OBRV
(Sunset over the Aegean.) OBNC
Summer. John Clare. BoNaP; CBEP
Summer. John Davidson. BoNaP
Summer. Edwin Denby. ANYP
Summer. Kalidasa. *Fr.* The Seasons. AWP
Summer. P. K. Page. PeCV
Summer. Pope. *Fr.* Pastorals. CEP
(Summer; the Second Pastoral, or Alexis.) EiPP
Summer. Christina Rossetti. CBEP; BoNaP; ELP; NBM
(Summer Days.) MCCG; OTPC; PRWS
Summer. Spenser. *Fr.* The Faerie Queene, VII, 7. GN
Summer, *sels.* James Thomson. *Fr.* The Seasons. StP
Happy Britannia. OBEC
Sheep-washing, The. EnLi-2
(Sheep Shearing, The.) CoBE
"Still let me pierce into the midnight depth." EnRP
Storm, The. LoBV
Summer Evening and Night. OBEC
Summer Morning. OBEC
Summer ("The cock's on the housetop.) *Unknown.* *See* Busy Day, A.
Summer ("Summer is icumen in"). *Unknown.* *See* Summer Is Icumen In.
Summer,/ the plain's vehement season. Cicada. Libero de Libero. LiTW
Summer Acres. Anne Wilkinson. CaP
Summer Afternoon. Basil Dowling. AnNZ
Summer Afternoon. Elizabeth B. Harrod. NePoEA
Summer Afternoon. Raymond Souster. BoNaP; NYTB
Summer again. Margaret Atwood. *Fr.* The Circle Game. MoCV
Summer and autumn had been so wet, The. God's Judgement on a Wicked Bishop [*or* Bishop Hatto]. Robert Southey. ChTr; EnRP; HBV; HBVY; OBRV; OnMSP; OTPC (1923 ed.); PaPo; StPo
Summer and spring the lovely rose. Not Quite Fair. H. S. Leigh. InMe
Summer and Winter. G. S. Fraser. FaBoMo
Summer and Winter. Shelley. BoNaP; UnPo (3d ed.)
Summer as it passes owes to night, The. Incense. Louise Townsend Nicholl. NePoAm-2
Summer, autumn, winter, spring. The Changing Year. Lloyd Roberts. DD
Summer Beach. Frances Cornford. ChMP
Summer Breeze. *Unknown.* BoTP
(Breeze, The.) PCH
Summer Cat, The. Ella Augusta Fanning. CIV
Summer cloud in summer blue, The. Cloud and Flame. John Berryman. AP
Summer Comes. Edith Agnew. SiSoSe
Summer comes. Magalu. Helene Johnson. CDC; PoNe
Summer Comes. Earl of Surrey. *See* Description of Spring.
Summer Commentary, A. Yvor Winters. LiTM; QFR; UnPo (3d ed.)
Summer Concert. Reed Whittemore. AmFN
Summer Dawn. William Morris. AtBAP; CBEP; FaBoEn; GTBS; GTBS-D; GTSL; LoBV; OBEV; OBNC; OBVV; ViBoPo; ViPo
Summer Day, A. Henry Charles Beeching. VA
Summer Day, A. Florence Harrison. BoTP
Summer Day. Alexander Hume. LoBV; OBEV (1st ed.), *much abr.*
(Of the Day Estivall.) OxBS
Summer's Day, A, *br. sel.* CH
Summer Day, A. Li Po, *tr. fr. Chinese by* Shigeyoshi Obata. OnPM
Summer Day in Old Sicily, A. Edward Cracroft Lefroy. *Fr.* Echoes from Theocritus. OBVV
Summer day is closed, The—the sun is set. An Evening Revery. Bryant. AA
Summer Days. Wathen Marks Wilks Call. VA
Summer Days. Roy Daniells. CaP
Summer Days, *sel.* Thomas Moult.
Prelude to Cricket. POTE
("Before we came the moon-soaked dews were here.") MemP
Summer Days. Christina Rossetti. *See* Summer.
Summer Days Are Come Again. Samuel Longfellow. SoP; TRV
Summer days moved with the pace of a caged lion, The. July in the Jardin des Plantes. Claire McAllister. NePA
Summer Deaths, The, *sel.* Jon Anderson.
"Christ, I was twelve," III. YAP
Summer dieth: o'er his bier. A Dirge for Summer. Sebastian Evans. VA
Summer ends now; now, barbarous in beauty, the stooks arise. Hurrahing in Harvest. Gerard Manley Hopkins. BoC; BoNaP; BrPo; CBEP; ChTr; CMoP; FlW; InvP; LO; MoAB; MoBrPo; MoPo; MoVE; PoeP; PoIE; PoVP; ViPo (1962 ed.); VP
Summer Evening. John Clare. BoTP
Let Ye Then My Birds Alone, *sel.* BiS
Summer Evening. Charles Cotton. *See* Evening Quatrains.
Summer Evening. Walter de la Mare. MoAB; MoBrPo; MoShBr; NeMA; TiPo (1959 ed.); TSW
Summer Evening. Sara Henderson Hay. PoMa
Summer Evening, A. Archibald Lampman. PeCV
Summer Evening and Night. James Thomson. *Fr.* The Seasons: Summer. OBEC
Summer Fable, from Montaigne, A. Helen Bevington. NYTB
Summer Farm. Norman MacCaig. ACV
Summer flows in golden waves, The. Invasion Weather. Douglas Newton. NeBP
Summer Gone, A. Howard Moss. NePoEA
Summer gone. A Frost Fancy. Richard Le Gallienne. OTPC (1946 ed.)
Summer grasses grow, The. The Afterglow. Basho, *tr. by* Harold Gould Henderson. WoL

Summer harvest day begun, The. July. *At. to* Whittier. YeAr
Summer Has Come ("Summer has come"). *Unknown, tr. fr. Middle Irish by* Kuno Meyer. LiTW; OnYI
Summer Has Come ("Summer is i-cumen in"). *Unknown. See* Sumer Is Icumen In.
Summer has doft his latest green. Winter. W. D. Landor. BoTP
Summer has two beginnings. Emily Dickinson. InPo; MaPo (1969 ed.); StP
Summer Holiday. Robinson Jeffers. CrMA; MAP; MoAmPo; MoVE; OxBA
Summer Holidays. W. R. Rodgers. LiTB
Summer Idyll. George Barker. FaBoMo; MoPo
Summer Images. John Clare. OBNC
Sels.
"Green lane now I traverse, where it goes, The." OBRV
"I love at early morn, from new-mown swath." CBEP; ChTr; EG
Summer Interlude. Lionel Stevenson. CaP
Summer Invocation. William Cox Bennett. *See* Invocation to Rain in Summer.
Summer is/ coming. The Cure All. Don L. Lee. CAD
Summer Is a-Coming In. *Unknown. See* Sumer Is Icumen In.
Summer is all a green air. Summer Music. May Sarton. NePoAm
Summer Is Come. Earl of Surrey. *See* Description of Spring.
Summer is come. The beetle's wings. Plenitude. A. M. Sullivan. JKCP (1926 ed.)
Summer Is Coming, The. Bryan Guinness. OxBI
"Summer is coming, summer is coming." The Throstle. Tennyson. BoChLi; BoNaP; DD; EPN; FaPON; HBV; HBVY; MCCG; OTPC; PoPo; PoRL; PoSC; PoVP; ShBV-1; WaKn
Summer Is Ended, The. Christina Rossetti. HBV
Summer is fading. Afternoons. Philip Larkin. TDP
Summer is fading; the broad leaves that grew. Farewell to Summer. George Arnold. AA; DD
Summer is full of things that are good. Belonging to Summer. Mildred Shacklett. GFA
Summer Is Gone. *Unknown, tr. fr. Old Irish by* Seán O'-Faoláin. AnIL; PoPl
—— *Tr. by* Kuno Meyer. FaBoCh; LoGBV; OnYI
Summer Is Icumen In. *Unknown. See* Sumer Is Icumen In.
Summer Is Nigh. *Unknown.* BoTP
Summer is over, The. October. Rose Fyleman. RePo; SiSoSe; TiPo (1959 ed.)
Summer is over, the old cow said. Moo! Robert Hillyer. WhC
Summer is sadness and its vivid light. Old Montague. M. K. Joseph. *Fr.* The Lovers and the City. AnNZ
Summer Is Y-Comem In. *Unknown. See* Sumer Is Icumen In.
Summer Landscape, The; or, The Dragon's Teeth. Rolfe Humphries. NYBP
Summer Lightning. Horatio Colony. TwAmPo
Summer Lightning. T. Sturge Moore. BrPo; SyP
Summer, like a dread disease. Thredbo River. Sydney Jephcott. PoAu-1
Summer lilies, sweet and rare. Sacrifice. Henry W. Frost. SoP
Summer Longings. Denis Florence MacCarthy. HBV
Summer Lullaby, A. Eudora S. Bumstead. BoTP
Summer Magic. Leslie Pinckney Hill. BANP
Summer Malison, The. Gerard Manley Hopkins. CMoP; PoEL-5
Summer Matures. Helene Johnson. CDC; PoNe
Summer Moods. John Clare. OTD
Summer Moonlight. Patience Strong. RePo
Summer Morning. John Clare. CBEP; PoSC
Summer Morning, A. Rachel Field. BoChLi; PDV; SoPo; StVeCh (1955 ed.); SUS; TiPo
Summer Morning. Jean Ingelow. ThGo
Summer Morning. Charles Simic. YAP
Summer Morning. James Thomson. *Fr.* The Seasons: Summer. OBEC
Summer Music. May Sarton. NePoAm
Summer near the River. Carolyn Kizer. CoAP
Summer Night, A. Matthew Arnold. CBEP; EnLi-2; EPN; ExPo; GTBS; GTSE; GTSL; MBW-2; MCCG; NoP; OAEP; PoVP; SeCePo; SeCeV; ViPo; ViPP; VP
Summer Night. Victor Contoski. ThO
Summer Night. Jason Miller. ThO
Summer Night. Ranko, *tr. fr. Japanese by* Harold G. Henderson. RePo
Summer Night, A. Elizabeth Stoddard. AA
Summer Night. Tennyson. *See* Now Sleeps the Crimson Petal.
Summer Noon at Sea, A. Epes Sargent. EtS
Summer Noon, 1941. Yvor Winters. CrMA
Summer of 'sixty-three, sir, and Conrad was gone away. Kentucky Belle. Constance Fenimore Woolson. BeLS; BLPA; FaBoBe; GoTP; MaC; PAH; StPo
Summer on the Great American Desert. Rufus B. Sage. PoOW
Summer Palace burnt, the Winter Palace, wherever it was, The. 10:X:5, 45 Years Since the Fall of the Ch'ing Dynasty. Philip Whalen. FRC; NeAP
Summer Pool, The. Robert Buchanan. VA
Summer Rain. Elizabeth J. Coatsworth. *See* What Could Be Lovelier than to Hear.
Summer Rain. Laurie Lee. MoVE
Summer Rain. Eve Merriam. PDV
Summer Rain. Sir Herbert Read. LiTM; POTE
Summer Rain, The. Henry David Thoreau. AmP; AnNE (My Books I'd Fain Cast Off, I Cannot Read.) AP
Summer Resort. P. K. Page. CaP
Summer Sabbath. Jessie E. Sampter. TrJP
Summer Sanctuary, A. John Hall Ingham. AA
Summer season at Tyne Dock, The. Tyne Dock. Francis Scarfe. NeBP
Summer set lip to earth's bosom bare. The Poppy. Francis Thompson. MoBrPo; OBEV (1st ed.); PoVP
Summer Shower. Emily Dickinson. *See* Drop fell on the apple tree, A.
Summer Shower. Selma Robinson. MoSiPe
Summer Shower, A ("'Hurry!' said the leaves"). *Unknown.* BoTP
Summer sits wilting like a lilac woman. The Garden. Marvin Solomon. NePoAm
Summer Sky. Ruth McKee Gordon. TiPo (1959 ed.)
Summer so histrionic, marvelous dirty days. Ted Berrigan. ANYP
Summer Song I ("I looked into my heart to write"). George Barker. ChMP; FaBoTw; GTBS-D; ToPo
Summer Song II ("Soft is the collied night, and cool"). George Barker. ToPo
Summer Song. Edith Nesbit. PoSC
Summer Song, A. George Peele. *See* Whenas the Rye Reach to the Chin.
Summer Song. W. W. Watt. FiBHP
Summer Song. William Carlos Williams. WIRo
Summer Stars. Carl Sandburg. LOW; RePo; YeAr
Summer still plays across the street. Dying: An Introduction. L. E. Sissman. NYBP
Summer Storm, A. Lord Alfred Douglas. JKCP (1926 ed.)
Summer Storm. Lionel Johnson. BrPo
Summer Storm. Louis Simpson. CBV; ErPo
Summer Storm. Louis Untermeyer. UnTE
Summer Storm, A. Charles Whitehead. OBRV
Summer Storm (circa 1916) and God's Grace. Robert Penn Warren. CBV; PoDB
Summer Sun. Robert Louis Stevenson. MoBrPo
Summer sun is falling soft on Carbery's hundred isles, The. The Sack of Baltimore. Thomas Osborne Davis. IrPN; VA
Summer sun is sinking low, The. Sunset. Longfellow. BoTP
Summer Sunday morning, A. A Battle Ballad. Francis Orrery Ticknor. PAH
Summer Sunshine. Mary A. Lathbury. YeAr
Summer that I was ten, The. The Centaur. May Swenson. NePoAm-2; TwAmPo; TwCP
Summer; the Second Pastoral, or Alexis. Pope. *See* Summer.
Summer, this is our flesh. Seasons of the Soul. Allen Tate. AP; CrMA; MoPo; NePA; OxBA
Summer Time on Bredon. A. E. Housman. *See* Bredon Hill.
Summer Twilight, A. Charles Tennyson Turner. OBRV; PeER
Summer Vacation. Wordsworth. *See* Prelude, The.
Summer vapours, soft and white. A May Sunday. Thomas Caulfield Irwin. IrPN
Summer Walk, A. Elizabeth Winton. PCH

Summer was another country, where the birds. Holiday. Adrienne Cecile Rich. MoLP
Summer was dead and autumn was expiring. Shelley. *Fr.* The Zucca. ERoP-2
Summer Wind. Bryant. AA; AP; PoEL-4
Summer Winds. George Darley. VA
Summer Wish. Louise Bogan. AnFE; CoAnAm; TwAmPo
Summer Wish. John Farrar. GFA
Summer Wish, A. Christina Rossetti. OBNC
Sing in the Silent Sky, *sel.* BiS
Summer Wooing, A. Louise Chandler Moulton. HBV
Summerhouse. Melvin Walker La Follette. NePoEA
Summers and summers have come, and gone with the flight of the swallow. Tantramar Revisited. Sir Charles G. D. Roberts. CaP; OBCV
Summer's Day, A. Alexander Hume. *See* Summer Day.
Summer's Early End at Hudson Bay. Hayden Carruth. NYBP
Summer's End. Ethel Kirk Grayson. TwCaPo
Summer's Farewell. Thomas Nashe. *Fr.* Summer's Last Will and Testament. PoEL-2
Summer's gone brown, and, with it. Me to You. Alastair Reid. NYBP
Summer's Last Will and Testament, *sels.* Thomas Nashe.
Adieu, Farewell, Earth's Bliss [*or* Blisse]! AtBAP; CaFP; CBV; CH; ElL; ELP; InvP; LoBV; OAEP; PoE; PoG, 3 *sts.*; PoIE; PoSa; QFR; SiCE; TuPP; ViBoPo
(Death's Summons.) HBV; SoP
(Dust Hath Closed Helen's Eye.) SeCePo
(In Plague Time.) FaBoCh; LoGBV; OBSC
(In Time of Pestilence 1593.) CBEP; DTC; HoPM; LiTG; MemP; OBEV; OtMeF; PoFS; TrGrPo
(In Time of Plague.) EnRePo; EP
(Litany in Plague Time, A.) FosPo
(Litany in Time of Plague, A.) BEL; BWP; CABA; EnLi-1 (1949 ed.); ForPo; NoP; PoRA; ReEn
(Lord, Have Mercy on Us.) ChTr
(Song: "Adieu, farewell earth's blisse.") DiPo; FaBoEn; MyFE; PoEL-2; StP
(Song in Plague-Time.) FOL
A-Maying, a-Playing. ElL
(Clownish Song, A.) OBSC
Autumn. ElL; EnRePo; LoBV; OBSC; QFR; TrGrPo; TuPP
"Beauty is But a Flower." LO
Fair Summer Droops. ElL; LoBV; TuPP
(Waning Summer.) OBSC
Harvest. OBSC
Spring, the Sweet Spring. CH; EnLi-1 (1949 ed.); FIW; GTBS; GTSE; GTSL; HBV; LiTB; NoP; OBEV; PoRA; TOP; ViBoPo
(Birds in Spring.) PRWS
(Song: "Spring, the sweete spring, is the yeres pleasant King.") YAT
(Spring.) AtBAP; BoNaP; CBEP; ElL; GTBS-D; GTBS-P; GTBS-W; LiTG; MCCG; MemP; OBSC; OTPC; PCH; PoIE; PCH; RG; RIS; ShBV-2; TrGrPo; WiR
("Spring, the sweet spring, is the year's pleasant king.") EG; MyFE; ReEn; SiCE; TuPP
Summer's Farewell. PoEL-2
Summer's pleasures they are gone like to visions every one. Remembrances. John Clare. CBEP; NCEP; PeER
Summer's residue, The. Lines with a Gift of Herbs. Janet Lewis. QFR
Summer's Revel, The. Pierre de Ronsard. Odes, II, 18. WoL
Summers Sun, The. Dennis Schmitz. YAP
"Summertime and the Living." Robert Hayden. Kal; PoIE (1970 ed.); TwCP
Summery Windermere, sweet lake! From Four Lakes' Days. Richard Eberhart. MiAP
Summing-Up, The. Stanley Kunitz. ELU; PoPl
Summit, The. Kathleen Raine. *Fr.* Beinn Naomh, IV. OxBS
Summit gained, behold the proud alcove, The. Landscape. William Cowper. *Fr.* The Task. CoBE
Summit Redwood, The. Robinson Jeffers. AmPP (3d ed.)
Summit Temple, The. Li Po, *tr. fr. Chinese by* Shigeyoshi Obata. OnPM
Summits and vales, slim cypresses and pines. Santa Maria del Fiore. George Herbert Clarke. CaP
Summon the Workers. Clara Lambert. MPB
Summoned by Bells, *sel.* John Betjeman.
"Deal out again the dog-eared poetry books." ML
Summoned by love and heat and God knows what. News from the Court. David Wagoner. NePoAm-2; NePoEA-2
Summoning sun, the sun that looks on London, The. The Hours of the Planets. Charles Madge. FaBoMo
Summons. Arthur Davison Ficke. Sonnets of a Portrait Painter, XIV HBMV
Summons, The. James Laughlin. ExPo; LiTA
Summons, The. Elizabeth Roberts MacDonald. CaP
Summons, The. Milton. *Fr.* Paradise Lost, I. WHA
Summons, The. W. W. E. Ross. CaP
Summons to Execution. John Webster. *See* Hark, Now Everything Is Still.
Summons to Love. William Drummond of Hawthornden. *See* Phoebus, Arise!
Summons was urgent; and forth I went, The. Her Death and After. Thomas Hardy. PoVP
Summum Bonum. Abu-l-Ala al-Maarri, *tr. fr. Arabic by* R. A. Nicholson. LiTW
Summum Bonum. Robert Browning. BoLP; CBV; ELU; EnLi-2 (1949 ed.); EPN; GTSL; HBV; LiTL; NeHB; OHFP; PG (1955 ed.); PoVP; TIHL; YAT
Sumter. Henry Howard Brownell. MC; PaA; PAH
Sumter. Edmund Clarence Stedman. MC; PAH
Sumter—a Ballad of 1861. *Unknown.* PAH
Sumter's Band. James Wright Simmons. PAH
Sun, The. John Davis. NA
Sun. James Dickey. TPM
Sun, The. Emily Dickinson. *See* I'll tell you how the sun rose.
Sun, The. John Drinkwater. FaPON; SoPo; TiPo
Sun. Langston Hughes. *Fr.* A House in Taos. CDC
Sun, The. Thomas Miller. OTPC (1923 ed.)
Sun! Marianne Moore. NP
Sun. Henry Rowe. OBEV
Sun, The. Anne Sexton. NYBP
Sun, The. Francis Thompson. *Fr.* Ode to the Setting Sun. MoAB; MoBrPo
Sun, The. W. J. Turner. MoBrPo
Sun about to set. Face in the Rock Wall. Robert Kelly. YAP
Sun and Cloud. Melville Cane. PoPl
Sun and Moon. Charlotte Druitt Cole. BoTP
Sun and moon must make their haste, The. Emily Dickinson. MWA-2
Sun and moon, that ceaselessly obey, The. Immortal Israel. Judah Halevi. TrJP
Sun and Rain. Christina Rossetti. PPL
Sun and Rain and Dew from Heaven. Adam Lindsay Gordon. *Fr.* Ye Wearie Wayfarer. PoLF
Sun and rain at work together. Orange Tree by Day. Sacheverell Sitwell. *Fr.* The Red-gold Rain. AtBAP; MoBrPo
Sun and skies and clouds of June. October's Bright Blue Weather. Helen Hunt Jackson. BBV; BLPA; DD; GN; HBVY
Sun and the Rain, The. Lizette Woodworth Reese. *See* Little Song of Life, A.
Sun and Wind. Eleanor Farjeon. OTPC (1946 ed.)
Sun and Wind, The. Owen Felltham. CavP
Sun and wind and beat of sea. Adventure. Adelaide Crapsey. NP
Sun appeared so smug and bright, The. The Silver Question. Oliver Herford. NA
Sun arises from its ocean bed. Man's Life. Henry W. Frost. SoP
Sun, as hot as he was bright, The. In Search of the Picturesque. William Combe. *Fr.* Dr. Syntax in Search of the Picturesque. OBRV
Sun at noon to higher air, The. March. A. E. Housman. A Shropshire Lad, X. FaBoCh; LoGBV; PoVP
Sun, autumnly thin and timid. Whispered to the Afternoon. Georg Trakl. OnPM
Sun-Bather, The. Kim Kurt. NePoAm-2
Sunbather, The. Vernon Watkins. MoPo; MoVE
Sun became a small round moon, The. Climbing in Glencoe. Andrew Young. SD
Sun blazed while the thunder yet, The. The Mill Pond. Edward Thomas. POTE
Sun blazing slowly in its last hour, The. An Evening. Robert Mezey. NaP
Sun-bleached skeleton, A. The Dead Branch. Douglas Gibson. NYTB
Sun bombed the happy fields, The. Airborn. Louis Grudin. PG (1955 ed.)

Sun breaks over the eucalyptus. Marin-An. Gary Snyder. FRC
Sun burns bright in the azure sky, The. Shadows. Henry W. Frost. SoP
Sun burns on its sultry wick, The. Elegy Written on a Front-porch. Karl Shapiro. MoPo
Sun Came Out in April, The. C. Day Lewis. MoBS
Sun comes up and the sun goes down, The. The Fallow Field. Julia C. R. Dorr. AA
Sun departing, kissed the summer sky, The. A Sunset. Robert Loveman. AA
Sun descending in the west, The. Night. Blake. *Fr.* Songs of Innocence. AnFE; AtBAP; BoC; BoNaP; BoTP; CBEP; CEP; CH; CoBE; EnRP; FaBoBe; FaPON; GoTP; GTBS-D; HBV; HBVY; MaPo; MyFE; OBEC; OBEV; OTPC (1923 ed.); OxBoCh; PoE; PoLF; RIS; SAS; ShBV-3; StaSt; TreFT; WiR
Sun does [*or* doth] arise, The. The Echoing [*or* Ecchoing] Green. Blake. *Fr.* Songs of Innocence. BoTP; BWP; CaFP; CBEP; CBV; CEP; CH; DiPo; EiPP; ERoP-1; GBV (1952 ed.); OBEC; OTPC; PAn; PCH; PeER; PoeP; PoRh; PoSC; WiR
Sun drew off at last his piercing fires, The. Witchcraft; New Style. Lascelles Abercrombie. MoBrPo
Sun drops luridly into the west, The. Augusta Webster. *Fr.* Circe. PeVV
Sun Drops Red, The. Nellie Burget Miller. PoOW
Sun five times the earth had compassed, The. The Cape of Tempests. Luís de Camoes. *Fr.* The Lusiads. LiTW
Sun from the east tips the mountains with gold. A Hunting Song. Paul Whitehead. *Fr.* Apollo and Daphne. EiCL; OBEC; OxBoLi
Sun gas coughed, A. A million miles of flame. In the Year of Many Conversions and the Private Soul. John Ciardi. MiAP
Sun gathers, The. Morning, in the Pastures Near Suisun. Philip Dow. QAH
Sun God, The. Aubrey Thomas De Vere. ACP; OBVV; PoVP; Sonn
Sun god came upon her in a day, The. Daphne. David Galler. NYTB
Sun, God's eye, The. The Nature of Love. James Kirkup. EaLo
Sun goes down, The. Midsummer Night. Elizabeth Gould. BoTP
Sun goes down and over all, The. Low Tide on Grand-Pré. Bliss Carman. CaP; OBCV; PeCV
Sun goes down, and with him takes, The. The Romany Girl. Emerson. CoBA
Sun goes lime in a throng of oak. First Reader. Paris Leary. CoPo
Sun Gonna Shine in My Door Some Day, *with music.* *Unknown.* OuSiCo
Sun had clos'd the winter-day, The. The Vision. Robert Burns. OxBS
Sun had gone down o'er the hills in the west, The. Amanda. *Unknown.* BFSS
Sun had left the western road, The. The Spider. Mary Jones. WaPE
Sun had set behind yon hill, The. To Be a Farmer's Boy. *Unknown.* BFSS
Sun had set, The; the leaves with dew. Keenan's Charge. George Parsons Lathrop. AA; BBV (1923 ed.); HBV; MC; PAH; PAP; PFY
Sun had sunk beneath the west, The. The Ocean-Fight. *Unknown.* PAH
Sun had shrunk to a dime, The. Cold August. Jim Harrison. NYTB
Sun has come, I know, The. The Sun. W. J. Turner. MoBrPo
Sun has gane down o'er the lofty Benlomond, The. Jessie, the Flower o' Dunblane [*or* The Flower o' Dumblane]. Robert Tannahill. HBV
Sun has gone from the shining skies, The. A Summer Lullaby. Eudora S. Bumstead. BoTP
Sun has kissed the violet sea, The. Betrayal. Sidney Lanier. *Fr.* The Jacquerie. AA
Sun Has Long Been Set, The. Wordsworth. PoG; YeAr
Night in June, A, *sel.* BoTP
Sun has risen on the eastern brim of the world, The. The Song of Lo-fu. *Unknown.* AWP
Sun Has Set, The. Emily Brontë. ViBoPo
Sun has set, The. South Cumberland, 16th May 1943. Norman Nicholson. POTi
Sun has set, The; the curtain stirs. The Onset. Patric Dickinson. POTi
Sun has set, the stars are still, The. The Fair-haired Girl. *Unknown.* OnYI
Sun has sucked and beat the encircling hills. In Hospital: Poona (II). Alun Lewis. DTC
Sun has sunk within the west, The. Good-Night. Henry W. Frost. SoP
Sun has turned the dusky hill, The. The Voice. Richard Mansfield. POTE
Sun hath twice brought forth his [*or* the] tender green, The. The Restless State of a Lover. Earl of Surrey. FCP; GoTL; SiPS
Sun, his journey ending in the west, The. Henry Constable. *Fr.* Diana. OBSC
Sun in the East. *Unknown, tr. fr. Chinese by* Arthur Waley. *Fr.* Shi King. LiTW
Sun in the heavens, The. The Young Reaper. Aleksey Koltsov. WoL
Sun, in wanton pride, The. In the Barn. Josephine Pinckney. NP
Sun is a glorious thing, The. Common Things. Ann Hawkshaw. OTPC (1923 ed.)
Sun is a huntress young, The. An Indian Summer Day on the Prairie. Vachel Lindsay. SoPo; StVeCh; WaKn; YT
Sun is always in the sky, The. Breakfast Time. James Stephens. SUS
Sun is blue and scarlet on my page, The. Falling Asleep over the Aeneid. Robert Lowell. AP; CoBMV; CrMA; FiMAP; MoAmPo (1962 ed.); OxBA; ToPo; TwAmPo
Sun is careering in glory and might, The. Joy of Life. Mary Russell Mitford. OTPC
Sun is clear of bird and cloud, The. Alulvan. Walter de la Mare. GBV (1952 ed.); MoVE
Sun is down, and time gone by, The. Good-Night. Joanna Baillie. OTPC (1923 ed.)
Sun Is First to Rise, The. Elizabeth J. Coatsworth. StVeCh (1955 ed.)
Sun is gone: those glorious chariot-wheels, The. Evening. Edward Rowland Sill. AnAmPo
Sun is hidden from our sight, The. The Little Boy's Good-Night. Eliza Lee Follen. OTPC (1923 ed.)
Sun is high, The. Young Saxons shouldering oars. North Shore. Peter Davison. CoPo
Sun is in the sky, mother, the flowers are springing fair, The. The Biter Bit. William E. Aytoun. BOHV; InMe
Sun is lord and god, sublime, serene, The. The Lake of Gaube. Swinburne. PAn; PoVP
Sun is low, to say the least, The. The Sunset [*or* Nonsense Rhymes]. Gelett Burgess. HBVY; TSW
Sun is mine, The. Song. Robert Hogg. WHW
Sun is nigh the verge, The. Soon we must part. A Walk. Hedwig Lachmann. TrJP
Sun, The, is not a-bed, when I. The Sun's Travels. Robert Louis Stevenson. FaPON; GFA; MPB; StVeCh (1940 ed.)
Sun is not in love with us, The. Isles of Greece, The. Demetrios Capetanakis. GTBS-P
Sun is set, The; the swallows are asleep. Evening; Ponte al Mare, Pisa. Shelley. CBEP; SyP
Sun is sinking over hill and sea, The. At Night. George Edward Montgomery. AA
Sun is warm, the sky is clear, The. Stanzas Written in Dejection, Near Naples. Shelley. BEL; BWP; CABA; CBEP; ChER; CoBE; EnL; EnLi-2; EnLit; EnRP; EPN; ERoP-2; FaBV; FiP; GTBS; GTBS-D; GTBS-P; GTBS-W; GTSE; GTSL; MCCG; MERP; NoP; OAEP; OBRV; PoRA; ViBoPo; WHA
Sun Is warm to-day, The. Roma Aeterna. Adelaide Crapsey. QFR
Sun itself was cheering, so they said, The. Independence. Roy McFadden. OxBI
Sun lay warm on tawny fields, The. Remembrance. Leslie Savage Clark. ChIP
Sun lies light on a jade-green hill, The. Spring. Anne Elizabeth Maddock. OQP
Sun like a stone, The. The Gardeners. Asa Benveniste. HYE
Sun looked from his everlasting skies, The. My Old Counselor. Gertrude Hall. AA
Sun makes music as of old, The. Prologue in Heaven. Goethe. *Fr.* Faust. AWP; JAWP; WBP

Sun may set and rise, The. Lines from Catullus. Sir Walter Ralegh. EnRePo; FCP; SiPS
Sun Men Call It, The. John Hall Wheelock. NePoAm-2
Sun, Moon and Stars. Ecclesiasticus, Bible, Apocrypha. BoC
Sun, moon and stars. *Unknown.* ThGo
Sun, Moon and Thunder. *Unknown. tr. fr. Russian by* W. R. S. Ralston. OnPM
Sun of Ivera, The. *See* Sun on Ivera, The.
Sun of life has crossed the line, The. Equinoctial. Adeline D. H. Whitney. HBV
Sun of my soul, Thou Saviour dear. Evening Hymn. John Keble. BePJ; MaRV; SoP
Sun of the Center. Robert Kelly. CoPo
Sun of the moral world; effulgent source. To Freedom. Joel Barlow. AnAmPo; AnNE; PAL; PoFr
Sun of the Sleepless! Byron. AtBAP
Sun of the stately day. The National Ode. Bayard Taylor. PAH
Sun, of whose terrain we creatures are, The. Solar Creation. Charles Madge. FaBoMo; OBMV
Sun on [*or* upon *or* of] Ivera, The/ No longer shines brightly. The Lament for [*or* of *or* Dirge of] O'Sullivan Bear[e]. *Tr. by* Jeremiah Joseph Callanan. AnIV; IrPN; NBM
Sun on the tree-tops no longer is seen, The. Queen Sabbath. Hayyim Nahman Bialik. TrJP
Sun Orchids. Douglas Stewart. NeLNL
Sun over all and air over all and clover. Merrill's Brook. Winfield Townley Scott. FiMAP
Sun rises, The/ The Goldenrod blooms. In Fields of Summer. Galway Kinnell. BoNaP; WIRo
Sun Rises Bright in France, The. Allan Cunningham. HBV; OBEV (1st ed.); OBRV
Sun rises in south east corner of things, The. A Ballad of the Mulberry Road. Ezra Pound. LOW
Sun [*or* Sunne] Rising, The. John Donne. AnAnS-1; AnFE; AtBAP; BoLiVe; BWP; CABA; CBEP; CBV; DiPo; EnRePo; EP; ExPo; GTSE; ILP; InvP; LiTB; LiTG; LiTL; LoBV; MaMe; MaPo (1969 ed.); MBW-1; MeLP; MePo; MeWo; NoP; OAEP; PoAn; PoE; PoEL-2; PoeP; PoFr; PoFS; PoIE; ReEn; ReIE; SCEP-1; SeCePo; SeCeV; SeCP; SeCV-1; SeEP; TrGrPo; TuPP; UnTE; VaPo
("Busie old foole, unruly sun.") EG
Sun, The, rushed up the sky; the taxi flew. Parting as Descent. John Berryman. LiTA; MoAmPo (1950 ed.)
Sun saw on that widening shore, The. Sainte Anne de Beaupre. Richard Eberhart. NePoAm
Sun set, and up rose the yellow moon, The. 'Tis Sweet to Hear. Byron. *Fr.* Don Juan, I. MCCG
Sun set, but set not his hope, The. Character. Emerson. AnFE; AnNE; CoAnAm; LiTA
Sun sets in the cold without friends, The. Dusk in Winter. W. S. Merwin. NaP
Sun shines, The. Tommies in the Train. D. H. Lawrence. MMA
Sun shines bright in the [*or in our or* on my] old Kentucky home, The. My Old Kentucky Home [Good-Night]. Stephen Collins Foster. AA; AnAmPo; AnFE; APA; CoAnAm; FaBoBe; FaBV; FaFP; FaPL; HBV; OTPC; PoLF; PoRL; StaSt; TrAS; TreF; TrGrPo
Sun shines bright on Arlington, the drowsy sheep creep by, The. Arlington. David McKee Wright. AnNZ
Sun shines high on yonder hill, The. The False Lover [Won Back]. *Unknown.* ESPB; OxBB
Sun shines on the chamber wall, The. The Death of Marlborough. George Walter Thornbury. VA
Sun shines, The. The coltsfoot flowers. Tommies In the Train. D. H. Lawrence. NP
Sun shines warm on seven old soldiers, The. The Oldest Soldier. Robert Graves. DTC
Sun shone in my hut, The. He Who Has Lost All. David Diop. TTY
Sun strikes gold the dirty street, The. Brest Left Behind. John Farrar. PAH
Sun-Shower, The. George Amabile. YAP
Sun sinks down, the tremulous daylight dies, The. Plainte Eternelle. Lord Alfred Douglas. PoVP
Sun sinks softly to his Ev'ning Post, The. The Rejected "National Hymns," V. "Orpheus C. Kerr." BOHV; InMe
Sun sought thy dim bed and brought forth light, The. Africa. Claude McKay. BALP
Sun spell/ rooves spread. Spel VII. Robert Kelly. *Fr.* Thor's Thrush. YAP
Sun streaked the coffee urn. The Deaths at Paragon, Indiana. John Woods. CoPo
Sun strikes those windows blind. The Library. Mary Mills. NePoAm
Sun strikes through the windows, up the floor, The. Sursum Corda. Elizabeth Barrett Browning. *Fr.* Casa Guidi Windows. VA
Sun, stun me, sustain me. On Looking into Henry Moore. Dorothy Livesay. OBCV
Sun that brief December day, The. Snow-bound; a Winter Idyl. Whittier. AmePo; AmPP; AnNE; AP; AtBAP; BBV; CoBA; FaBV; GN; MAmP; MCCG; OxBA; StVeCh; TOP; TrGrPo; WiR
Sun that shines all day so bright, The. Night. *Unknown.* BoTP
Sun, the moon, the stars, the seas, the hills and the plains, The. The Higher Pantheism. Tennyson. BEL; BoPe; EnLi-2; MaRV; MaVP; PoVP; TRV; ViPo; ViPP; VP; WGRP
Sun, the Rose, the Lily, the Dove, The. Love's Résumé. Heine. TrJP
Sun This March, The. Wallace Stevens. BWP
Sun-treader—life and light be thine for ever. Shelley. Robert Browning. *Fr.* Pauline. OBRV
Sun-up in March. Abbie Huston Evans. NePoAm
Sun upon Ivera, The. *See* Sun on Ivera, The.
Sun upon the lake is low, The. Datur Hora Quieti. Sir Walter Scott. *Fr.* The Doom of Devorgoil, I. GTBS; GTBS-D; GTBS-P; GTBS-W; GTSE; GTSL
Sun upon the Weirdlaw Hill, The. The Dreary Change. Sir Walter Scott. EPN; ERoP-1; OBNC; PeER
Sun Used to Shine, The. Edward Thomas. FaBoTw; ML
Sun was black with judgment, and the moon, The. Femina contra Mundum. G. K. Chesterton. MoRP
Sun was bright when we went in, The. At the Theater. Rachel Field. FaPON
Sun was down, and twilight grey, The. In the Room. James Thomson. OBVV; PeVV
Sun was gold over the water and the voices golden, The. The Flower. John Holmes. LiTL
Sun was in the summer grass, The. The Stockman. David Campbell. MoAuPo
Sun was now withdrawn, The. Damon and Cupid. John Gay. EnLoPo; SeCeV
Sun was setting, and its golden glow, The. The Throne of the King. Francis Clement Kelley. JKCP
Sun was setting, and vespers done, The. Thursday. Frederick E. Weatherly. BOHV
Sun was shining on the sea, The. The Walrus and the Carpenter. "Lewis Carroll." *Fr.* Through the Looking-Glass. BeLS; BoChLi; BOHV; FaBoBe; FaBV; FaFP; FaPON; FiBHP; GN; GSP; HBV; HBVY; InMe; LBN; LiTB; LiTG; MaC; MCCG; NA; NeHB; OnSP; OTPC; PoRA; PoRh; PoVP; SAS; ShBV-1; SoPo; StVeCh; TreF; TVC; YT
Sun was sinking in the west, The. The Dying Ranger [*or* Soldier]. *Unknown.* BFSS; CoSo; ShS
Sun Was Slumbering in the West, The. Thomas Hood. FiBHP
Sun was strong enough today, The. A Courtyard Thaw. Richard Wilbur. FosPo
Sun was warm but the wind was chill, The. Early April. Robert Frost. YeAr
Sun was witness when his eyes appeared, The. Glitter of Pebbles. Dom Moraes. ACV
Sun, when it shines on traffic, has a look. Noon on Alameda Street. Hildegarde Flanner. LiTM
Sun, which doth the greatest comfort bring, The. Master [*or* Mr.] Francis Beaumont's Letter to Ben Jonson [*or* A Letter to Ben Jonson]. Francis Beaumont. BEL; LoBV; OBS; SeCP; SeEP; ViBoPo
Sun-Witch to the Sun, The. George Howe. NYBP
Sun, with his great eye, The. Daisy's Song. Keats. BoNaP; OTPC; PRWS
Sun woke me this morning loud, The. A True Account of Talking to the Sun at Fire Island. Frank O'Hara. ANYP
Sun, yon glorious orb of day, The. The Sun. John Davis. NA
Sunbather. *See* Sun Bather.
Sunbeam, The ("I dined with a friend"). *Unknown.* NA
Sun-beams in the east are spread, The. Epithalamion Made at

Lincolnes [*or* Lincoln's] Inn[e]. John Donne. HW; MaMe; OBS; PAn; SeCP
Sunbeams streamed without, The. In the Morgue. Israel Zangwill. TrJP
Sunbows, The. Swinburne. EPN
Sunday. Elizabeth J. Coatsworth. AmFN; OCS; WaKn
Sunday, A. Walter de la Mare. NYTB; POTE
Sunday. James Edmeston. SoP
Sunday. George Herbert. MaMe; OBS; SCEP-1; SeCV-1; SeEP
Sunday Afternoon. Philip Levine. NaP
Sunday afternoon. Veracruz. Robert Hayden. AmNP
Sunday Afternoon in Italy. D. H. Lawrence. BrPo
Sunday Afternoon Service in St. Enodoc Church, Cornwall. John Betjeman. MoVE
Sunday Again. David Hilton. QAH
Sunday and sunlight ashen on the Square. The Self Unsatisfied Runs Everywhere. Delmore Schwartz. FiMAP
Sunday at Hampstead, *sel.* James Thomson.
"As we rush, as we rush in the train," X. GTBS; GTBS-W; LiTG; PoVP; ViBoPo
(In the Train.) BoTP; OBEV; PCD
Sunday at the End of Summer. Howard Nemerov. BoNaP
Sunday Bells. William Allingham. IrPn
Sunday Edition. Joseph Joel Keith. FiSC
Sunday Evening. Charlotte Elliott. SoP
Sunday Evening. Barbara Guest. NeAP
Sunday Evening in the Common. John Hall Wheelock. CLwM; HBV; MAP; MoAmPo; NP; PFY
Sunday evening. The thick-lipped men binoculared. Merthymawr. George Woodcock. NeBP
Sunday Evenings. John Hollander. NYBP
Sunday gardening, hoeing, trying to think of nothing but. For the Death of Anton Webern Particularly. Nathaniel Tarn. MuSP
Sun-Day Hymn, A. Oliver Wendell Holmes. *Fr.* The Professor at the Breakfast Table, *ch.* 12. AmePo; AnNE; InP; MaRV; SoP; TrPWD; TRV; WGRP
Sunday in Old England. *Kearsarge.* S. Weir Mitchell. PAH
Sunday in the Country. May Swenson. NePoAm-2
Sunday in the Park. William Carlos Williams. *Fr.* Paterson. CrMA
Sunday is the dullest day, treating. Sweeney in Articulo. "Myra Buttle." Par
Sunday, July 14th; a Fine Day at the Baths. Julian Symons. WaP
Sunday Morning. James Grahame. *Fr.* The Sabbath. OBRV
Sunday Morning. Louis MacNeice. CoBMV; FaBoMo; LiTB; MoAB; MoBrPo; MoVE; NeMA; PoE; Sonn
Sunday Morning. Isidor Schneider. AnAmPo
Sunday Morning (Complete, I-VIII). Wallace Stevens. AmLP; AmP; AmPP (4th ed.); AP; BWP; CABA; CABL; CaFP; CBV; CMoP; CoBA; CoBMV; CrMA; FaBoEn; ForPo; FosPo; InPo; LiTA; LiTG; LiTM; MaPo (1969 ed.); MasP; MoAB; MoVE; NePA; NoP; OxBA; PAn; PoAn; PoDB; PoeP; PoIE; QFR; ReMP; SeCeV; StP; TDP; TwAmPo
Sels.
"Complacencies of the peignoir, and late," I. AnFE; AnNE; APA; CoAnAm; MAP; MAPA; MoAmPo
"She hears, upon that water without sound," VIII. AnFE; AnNE; APA; CoAnAm; MAP; MAPA; MoAmPo
"She says, 'But in contentment I still feel,'" V. AnFE; AnNE; APA; CoAnAm; MAP; MAPA; MoAmPo
"She says: 'I am content when wakened birds,'" IV. AnFE; AnNE; APA; CoAnAm; MAP; MAPA; MoAmPo
"Supple and turbulent, a ring of men," VII. AnFE; AnNE; APA; CoAnAm; GTBS-W; MAP; MAPA; MoAmPo
Sunday Morning. L. A. G. Strong. WhC
Sunday Morning Apples. Hart Crane. NAMP
Sunday morning just at nine. Down Went McGinty. Joseph Flynn. TreF; YaD
Sunday Morning, King's Cambridge. John Betjeman. BoC; EaLo; POTi
Sunday: New Guinea. Karl Shapiro. AmFN; PoPl
Sunday night and the park policemen. The Picnic Boat. Carl Sandburg. WoL
Sunday Night Walk. Raymond Souster. CaP
Sunday on Hampstead Health. George Woodcock. NeBP
Sunday: Outskirts of Knoxville, Tennessee. James Agee. ErPo
Sunday School Teacher Speaks, A. *Unknown.* STF
Sunday shuts down on a twentieth-century evening. Boy with His Hair Cut Short. Muriel Rukeyser. ExPo; FiMAP; LiTM (1970 ed.); MoAB; NAMP; PoPl; RoGo; TwAmPo; TwCP
Sunday the sea made morning worship, sang. Half-Tide Ledge. R. P. Blackmur. AnFE; CoAnAm; TwAmPo
Sunday, the shout of hosannas. His Last Week. Elinor Lennen. PGD
Sunday up the River, *sels.* James Thomson.
"Church bells are ringing, The," IV. OAEP
"Give a man a horse he can ride," XV. EnLi-2; GTSL; PoVP
(Gifts.) BBV; HBV; OBEV; OBVV; TOP; TreF
"I looked out into the morning," I. OAEP; PoVP; ViBoPo
"Let my voice ring out and over the earth," XVII. PoVP
(Song.) HBV; MaRV; OBVV; TreFT
"Like violets pale i' the spring o' the year," IX.
(Song.) OBVV
"My love is the flaming sword," XVI.
(Song.) OBVV
"My Love o'er the water bends dreaming," XII. OBEV (1st ed.)
(Reflection.) EnLit
"'Oh, what are you waiting for here, young man?'" II. PoVP
(Bridge, The.) OBVV; TOP
"Were I a real poet, I would sing," X. OAEP
"Wine of Love is music, The," XVIII. PoVP; ViBoPo
(Vine, The.) HBV; OBEV; OBVV
Sun-Days. Henry Vaughan. *See* Son-Dayes.
Sundays too my father got up early. Those Winter Sundays. Robert Hayden. BP; IDB
Sunder me from my bones, O sword of God. The Sword of Surprise. G. K. Chesterton. MoBrPo; MoRP
Sundered. Israel Zangwill. TrJP
Sundered from this beauty is its fond lover. Elegy in the Orongorongo Valley. Hubert Witheford. AnNZ
Sundew, The. Swinburne. ELP; NoP; OBNC; PeVV; WePo
Sundial, The. Jane Cooper. AmPC
Sun-Dial, The. Thomas Love Peacock. *Fr.* Melincourt. OBNC
Sundown. Léonie Adams. AmLP; MAP; MoAB; MoAmPo; TrGrPo; TwAmPo
Sundown. Bert Leston Taylor. OQP
Sundowner, The. John Shaw Neilson. PoAu-1
Sundry Christian Passions. Henry Lok. *See* Sonnets of Christian Passions.
Sunflower, The. Blake. *See* Ah! Sunflower.
Sunflower. André Breton, *tr. fr. French by* Edouard Roditi. LiTW
Sunflower, The. Eugenio Montale, *tr. fr. Italian by* Glauco Cambon. OnPM
Sunflower, The. Peter Quennell. AtBAP; POTE
Sunflower. John Updike. BoNaP
Sunflower ain't de daisy, De. Doan't You Be What You Ain't. Edwin Milton Royle. BLPA
Sunflower, of flowers. Sunflower. John Updike. BoNaP
Sunflower Sutra. Allen Ginsberg. AmPP (5th ed); CoAP; NeAP
Sunflower to the Sun, The. Mary Elizabeth Hewitt Stebbins. AA
Sunflowers. Clinton Scollard. HBMV; MPB
Sunflowers, The. Douglas Stewart. BoAV
Sung by a Young Girl. Dryden. *See* Song for a Girl.
Sung by the nightingale to birth. Pomegranates. Roy Campbell. AtBAP
Sung on a By-Way. "Æ." TOP
Sung on a Sunny Morning. Jean Starr Untermeyer. TrPWD
Sunglasses. Tom Clark. ANYP
Sunk earlier in the silence of grey cashmere. Slepynge Long in Greet Quiete Is Eek a Greet Norice to Leccherie. John Hollander. AmPC; ErPo
Sunk Lyonesse. Walter de la Mare. CoBMV; FaBoCh; LiTM (1970 ed.)
Sunken Evening [in Trafalgar Square]. Laurie Lee. LiTM (1970 ed.); NYBP; POTi; ToPo
Sunken Garden, The. Walter de la Mare. HBMV
Sunken Gold. Eugene Lee-Hamilton. EtS; NCEP; VA
Sunlicht still on me, you row'd in clood, The. At My Father's Grave. "Hugh MacDiarmid." ELU; GTBS-P; PoIE
Sunlight and summer wind are never sure. The Attic. Charles Bruce. CaP *Fr.* The Flowing Summer.
Sunlight doesn't go on making. The Wall. Alan Brownjohn. NYTB

Sunlight drawing from shadow, up and down the street. Passages. Larry Eigner. NeAP
Sunlight falls happily upon this sea. Tranquil Sea. Claire Aven Thomson. EtS
Sunlight from the sky's own heart. A Song of Handicraft. Annie Matheson. OBVV
Sunlight laughs along the serried stone, The. Dawn at Liverpool. Archibald T. Strong. *Fr.* Sonnets of the Empire. BoAu
Sunlight lies along my table. The Weather of Six Mornings. Jane Cooper. NYBP
Sunlight, moonlight. Dream-Song. Walter de la Mare. RePo
Sunlight on the Garden, The. Louis MacNeice. CMoP; CoBMV; GTBS-P; LiTB; MemP; MoPo; NoP; OAEP (2d ed.); OxBI; PoIE; TwCP; VaPo
Sun-light recedes on the mountains, in long gold shafts. Interlude. Maxwell Bodenheim. MAPA
Sunlight speaks, and its voice is a bird, The. The Humming Bird. Harry Hibbard Kemp. FaPON; HBMV; MPB
Sunlight the tall women may never have seen. Children, the Sandbar, That Summer. Muriel Rukeyser. FiMAP
Sunlit Vale, The. Edmund Blunden. CBEP; ChMP; GTBS-D; MoVE
Sunly the day streams. Evening. Robert Wallace. PoPo
Sunne begins uppon my heart to shine, The. William Alabaster. AnAnS-1; MeP
Sunne Rising, The. John Donne. *See* Sun Rising, The.
Sunning. James S. Tippett. SiSoSe; SUS; TiPo
Sunny Day. Alex Raybin. ThO
Sunny hair and eyes of wonder. A Little Person. Brian Hooker. HBMV
Sunny Prestatyn. Philip Larkin. PoeP
Sunny rounds of earth contain, The. Proletaria. Bernard O'-Dowd. BoAu
Sunny shaft did I behold, A. Glycine's Song. Samuel Taylor Coleridge. *Fr.* Zapolya. BoTP; CEP; LO; OBEV; OTPC (1946 ed.); PoPl; PoSC; PTK
Sunrise. Rowena Bennett. TiPo (1959 ed.)
Sunrise. Robert Browning. *Fr.* Pippa Passes. OQP
("Day!/ Faster and more fast.") GTSL; PoVP; ViPP
Sunrise. Sidney Lanier. Hymns of the Marshes, I. AA; AmePo; PoEL-5
"Tide's at full, The: the marsh with flooded streams," *sel.* FaBoEn
Sunrise. Lizette Woodworth Reese. TWS
Sunrise. Margaret E. Sangster. SoP; TRV
Sunrise!! Rolland Snellings. BF
Sunrise. Charles Erskine Scott Wood. *Fr.* The Poet in the Desert, III. GoTP; MAP; PFY
Sunrise and Sunset. Emily Dickinson. *See* I'll tell you how the sun rose.
Sunrise at Sea. Edwin Atherstone. EtS
Sunrise at Sea. Epes Sargent. EtS
Sunrise at Sea. Swinburne. *Fr.* Tristram of Lyonesse: The Sailing of the Swallow. EtS
Sunrise in the Hills of Satsuma. Mary McNeil Fenollosa. AA
Sunrise of the Poor, The. Robert Burns Wilson. AA
Sunrise on Mansfield Mountain. Alice Brown. HBV
Sunrise on Rydal Water. John Drinkwater. GBV; HBV; LiTM; NP
Sunrise on the Sea. Shakespeare. *Fr.* A Midsummer Night's Dream, III, ii. ChTr
Sunrise on the Sunset. Wally Ford. WSL
Sunrise tints the dew, The. Crocuses. Josa. MPB; TiPo
Sunrise Trumpets. Joseph Auslander. AnAmPo; TrJP
Sunrise wakes the lark to sing, The. Bird Raptures. Christina Rossetti. ViPo
Sun's a bright-haired shepherd boy, The. Silver Sheep. Anne Blackwell Payne. GFA; SiSoSe
Suns and Clouds. Shakespeare. *See* Sonnets, XXXIII.
Sun's Darling, The, *sels.* Thomas Dekker *and* John Ford.
"Cast away care, he that loves sorrow." ReEn; TuPP
Haymakers, Rakers, *fr.* III, i. ELP; ViBoPo
Live with Me Still. SeCL
Sun's Golden Bowl, The. Mimnermus, *tr. fr. Greek by* Kirby Flower Smith. LiTW
Sun's gone dim, The. Two-Volume Novel. Dorothy Parker. InMe
Suns in a skein, the uncut stones of night. Roy Fuller. Mythological Sonnets, VIII. GTBS-P
Sun's low light splinters in a plastic gleam, The. On a Scooter. D. A. Greig. PeSA
Sun's noon throne is hid in hazy cloud, The. "A View of the Present State of Ireland." Edmund Blunden. BrPo
Sun's over the Foreyard, The. Christopher Morley. EtS
Sun's Perpendicular Rays, The. W. L. Mansel. ChTr
Suns, planets, stars, in glorious array. Victor J. Daley. *Fr.* Night. PoAu-1
Sun's Shame, The. Dante Gabriel Rossetti. The House of Life, XCII-XCIII. MaVP; PoVP; ViPo
Sun's snow, conversing, lowly slides from limbs. To a Young Lady Swinging Upside Down on a Birch Limb over a Winter-swollen Creek. James H. Koch. GoYe
Sun's Travels, The. Robert Louis Stevenson. FaPON; GFA; MPB; StVeCh (1940 ed.)
Sunset. Laurence Alma-Tadema. *See* Blessing for the Blessed, A.
Sunset. Herbert Bashford. AA
Sunset. Arthur Bayldon. PoAu-1
Sunset. Hayyim Nahman Bialik, *tr. fr. Hebrew by* Helena Frank. TrJP
Sunset, The. Gelett Burgess. HBVY
(Nonsense Rhymes.) TSW
Sunset. Amy Carmichael. FaChP
Sunset, A. Samuel Taylor Coleridge. BWP; ERoP-1
Sunset. E. E. Cummings. MAP; MoAmPo
(Impression.) MoAB; PIA
Sunset, A. Victor Hugo, *tr. fr. French by* Francis Thompson. AWP; JAWP; WBP
Sunset, A. Aldous Huxley. MoBrPo (1942 ed.)
Sunset. Longfellow. BoTP
Sunset, A. Robert Loveman. AA
Sunset. William Julius Mickle. *Fr.* The Concubine. OBEC
Sunset. Edwin Muir. BoPe
Sunset and evening star. Crossing the Bar. Tennyson. BEL; BLRP; BoLiVe; CABA; CBV; DD; DiPo; EnL; EnLi-2; EnLit; EPN; ETS; FaBoEn; FaBV; FaFP; FaPL; FiP; GTBS-W; GTSL; HBV; HBVY; ILP; InP; LiTB; LiTG; MaRV; MaVP; MBW-2; MCCG; NeHB; NoP; OAEP; OBEV (new ed.); OBNC; OBVV; OHFP; OQP; OTD; OTPC (1946 ed.); OuHeWo; PG (1945 ed.); PoAn; PoE; PoLF; PoPo; PoRA; PoVP; ShBV-3; SoP; STJW; TIHL; TOP; TreF; TrGrPo; TRV; TSW; UnPo (1st ed.); VA; ViBoPo; ViPo; ViPP; VP; WBLP; WGRP; WHA; YAT; YT
Sunset and silence! A man: around him earth savage, earth broken. The Plougher [*or* Plower]. Padraic Colum. AnFE; GoBC; GTSL; HBMV; MoBrPo; NeMA; OHIP; OnYI
Sunset and Sunrise. Emily Dickinson. *See* I'll tell you how the sun rose.
Sunset; and the mountain tops are afire. Mountain Evenings. Jamie Sexton Holme. PoOW
Sunset at Les Eboulements, A. Archibald Lampman. OBCV
Sunset City, The. Henry Sylvester Cornwell. HBV
Sunset Garden, The. Marion St. John Webb. TVC
Sunset—God's face from which grief radiates. Sodom. Chaim Grade. TrJP
Sunset Horn. Myron O'Higgins. AmNP; PoNe
Sunset in the Lake Country. Wordsworth. *Fr.* An Evening Walk. EPN
Sunset in the rosy west, The. A Little Song. Duncan Campbell Scott. VA
Sunset is always disturbing. Afterglow. Jorge Luis Borges. NYBP
Sunset is golden on the steep. The Flock at Evening. Odell Shepard. HBMV
Sunset on Calvary. *Unknown. See* Now Goeth Sun under Wood.
Sunset on the Cunimbla Valley, Blue Mountains. Douglas Brooke Wheelton Sladen. VA
Sunset on the Spire. Elinor Wylie. CoBA
Sunset over the Aegean. Byron. *See* Summer.
Sunset; St. Louis. Sara Teasdale. HT; PoMa
Sunset was a crown of spiked flame, The. Montezuma. Witter Bynner. *Fr.* Chapala Poems. NP
Sunset, when the eyes suddenly closed. Death of an Elephant. Bertram J. Warr. TwCaPo
Sunset Wings. Dante Gabriel Rossetti. HBV
Sunsets. Florence Boyce Davis. OQP
Sunsets. Carl Sandburg. MAP; MoAmPo
Sunset's kiss, with lingering desire, The. The Wind in the Elms. J. Corson Miller. HBMV

Sunset's mounded cloud, A. An Evening. William Allingham. EnLoPo; IrPN
Sunshine. *Unknown.* FaChP
Sunshine after a Shower. Thomas Warton, the Younger. *Fr.* On the Approach of Summer. OTPC
Sunshine after rain, The. Spring of Joy. Vera E. Guerard. TNV
Sunshine and Music. Ripley Dunlap Saunders. PoToHe (new ed.)
Sunshine, and the grace of falling rain, The. Mozart. Maurice Baring. MuSP
Sunshine, come softly here. Prayer for a Play House. Elinor Lennen. TrPWD
Sunshine let it be or frost. After St. Augustine. Mary Elizabeth Coleridge. MaRV; SoP; TrPWD; TRV
Sunshine melts away in twilight golden-red, The. Angelus. "Yehoash." LiTW
Sunshine of the Gods, The, *sel.* Bayard Taylor.
"Ah, moment not to be purchased." AA
Sunshine of Thine Eyes, The. George Parsons Lathrop. AA
Sunshine set to music! The First Song-Sparrow. *Unknown.* PCH
Sunshine to the flower may give, The. Despise Not Thou the Chastening of the Almighty. Bernard Barton. SoP
Sunshiny shower, A. Weather Signs [*or* Signs and Charms *or* Rhymes about the Weather]. *Unknown.* FaBoBe; GoTP; HBV; HBVY; OTPC; OxNR; PCH; PPL; RIS; StaSt; TreF
Sunstrike. Douglas Livingstone. PeSA
Sunstruck spray sifts back breakwater waves, A. The Pavilion on the Pier. Byron Vazakas. NePA
Sunthin' in the Pastoral Line. James Russell Lowell. The Biglow Papers, 2d Series, No. VI. AmPP (3d ed.); AP; CoBA; MWA-1; PFY, *abr.*
Sels.
Spring ("I, country-born an' bred, know where to find"). FaBV
Spring ("O little city-gals, don't never go it"). MCCG
Super-cool. But He Was Cool. Don L. Lee. BP
Super Flumina Babylonis. Swinburne. AnFE; MaVP; OBVV; PoEL-5; PoFr, *abr.*; PoVP; ViPo
Unto Each [Man] His Handiwork, *sel.* OQP, 2 *sts.* ("Whoso Loseth His Life," 4 *sts.*) MaRV
Super-Lark, The. R. H. Long. BoAu
Superb and sole, upon a plumèd spray. The Mocking Bird. Sidney Lanier. AA; AmPP (3d ed.)
Superb creator,/ All being that wrought. Hymn to Satan. Giosuè Carducci. PoFr
Superballs. Tom Clark. ANYP
Superbus sold a gallant manor place. In Superbum. Thomas Freeman. SiCE
Supercilious nabob of the East, A. A Modest Wit. Selleck Osborne. BLPA; BOHN; HBV
Superfluous Bite. Heine. *See* Mir träumte wieder der alte Traum.
Superfluous Saddle, The. La Fontaine. UnTE
Superintindint wuz Flannigan. Finnigin to Flannigan. Strickland Gillilan. BOHV; FaBoBe; HBV; StPo; TreF; YaD
Superior Fiend, The. Milton. *See* Satan and the Fallen Angels.
Superior Nonsense Verses. *Unknown.* NA
Superiorities. Richard Wilbur. CBV
Superlative Dance and Song. Francis Beaumont. *See* Shake Off Your Heavy Trance.
Superliminare. George Herbert. AnAnS-1; MaMe; MeP; SeCP
Superman, The. Albert Bigelow Paine. MaRV
Supermarket in California, A. Allen Ginsberg. AmPP (5th ed.); CBV; CoAP; LiTM (1970 ed.); NaP; NeAP; PIA; TwCP
Supernal Dialogue. Harriet Monroe. NP
Superscription, A. Dante Gabriel Rossetti. The House of Life, XCVII. BEL; CBEP; EnL; EnLi-2; EnLit; FaBoEn; GTBS-P; HBV; LO; MaVP; NoP; OBNC; PG (1955 ed.); PoEL-5; PoVP; SeCePo; TOP; VA; ViPo; ViPP; WHA; YAT
Superseded, The. Thomas Hardy. TOP
Supersensual. Evelyn Underhill. WGRP
Superstition. John Norris. PeRV
Superstitious Ghost, The. Arthur Guiterman. ShM
Supine the wanderer lay. The Ruined Cottage. Wordsworth. *Fr.* The Excursion. MBW-2
Supper. Walter de la Mare. NYBP
Supper. William Soutar. OxBS
Supper after the Last, The. Galway Kinnell. PoCh; TwAmPo
Supper at the Mill, *sel.* Jean Ingelow.
Song of the Old Love. HBV
Supper Club meets in the evening, The. The Furniture Man. Dick Gallup. ANYP
Supper is o'er, the hearth is swept, The. Sermon in a Stocking. Ellen A. Jewett. BLPA
Supper with Lindsay. Theodore Roethke. ML
Supper time. Burns. UnTE
Supplanting, The. Wendell Berry. NYTB
Supple and turbulent, a ring of men. Sunday Morning, V [VII]. Wallace Stevens. AnFE; AnNE; APA; CoAnAm; GTBS-W; MAP; MAPA; MoAmPo
Supplement, A. Benjamin Tompson. SCAP
Supplement of an Imperfect Copy of Verses of Mr. Wil. Shakespeare, A. Sir John Suckling. SeEP
Suppliant. Florence Earle Coates. TrPWD
Suppliant, The. Georgia Douglas Johnson. BALP; CDC; PoNe
Suppliant. Alan Sullivan. CaP
Suppliants, *sel.* Euripides, *tr. fr. Greek by* Arthur S. Way.
"Eloquent herald this, a speech-crammed babbler, An." PoFr
Supplication, A. Nicholas Breton. *See* Coridon's Supplication to Phillis.
Supplication. Joseph Seamon Cotter, Jr. BANP; CDC; PoNe
Supplication, A. Abraham Cowley. *Fr.* Davideis. III. GTBS; GTBS-D; GTBS-P; GTBS-W; GTSE; GTSL; SCEP-2; SeCL
Supplication. Josephine Johnson. TrPWD
Supplication. Edgar Lee Masters. TrPWD
"Dost Thou not see about our feet," *sel.* MaRV
Supplication. Edith Lovejoy Pierce. TrPWD
Supplication. Louis Untermeyer. HBMV
Supplication, A. Sir Thomas Wyatt. *See* Forget Not Yet.
Supplication of the Black Aberdeen. Kipling. BLPA
Supplices. Euripides. *See* Suppliants.
Suppose. Anne Reeve Aldrich. HBV
Suppose. Phoebe Cary. BLPA
Suppose. Walter de la Mare. TSW
Suppose. Epes Sargent, *sometimes at. to* Fanny Crosby. *See* Deeds of Kindness.
Suppose . . . and suppose that a wild little horse of magic. Suppose. Walter de la Mare. TSW
Suppose he had been tabled at thy teats. Blessed Be the Paps Which Thou Hast Sucked [*or* Luke 11]. Richard Crashaw. CABA; MaMe
Suppose in Perfect Reason. Howard Griffin. CrMA
Suppose it, for the last time, in that moment. The Coming of the White Man. Patrick Anderson. *Fr.* Poem on Canada. MoCV
Suppose it is nothing but the hive. Davis Matlock. Edgar Lee Masters. *Fr.* Spoon River Anthology. LiTA; LiTM (rev. ed.)
Suppose, my little lady. Suppose. Phoebe Cary. BLPA
Suppose it's true. Where's It's At: A Melody for Breath. Lenore Kandel. FRC
Suppose that Christ Had Not Been Born. Martha Snell Nicholson. BePJ
Suppose that what's now sky and wind for you. The Prisoner. R. M. Rilke. BoPe
Suppose the little cowslip. Deeds of Kindness [*or* Suppose]. Epes Sargent, *sometimes at. to* Fanny Crosby. HBV; HBVY; OTPC; PPL; TVC
Suppose there's a cranky woman inside me who. Edwin Denby. ANYP
Suppose you screeve? or go cheep-jack? Villon's Straight Tip to All Cross Coves. W. E. Henley, *after* Villon. AWP; BOHV; CenHV; HBV; InMe; InvP; NA; SeCePo
Supposed Confessions of a Second-rate Sensitive Mind. Tennyson. ViPP
Supposed of Phamphylax the Antiochene. A Death in the Desert. Robert Browning. GoTL; OxBoCh; PoVP; StJW
Supposed to be Written at Lemnos. Thomas Russell. *See* Sonnet: Suppos'd to Be Written at Lemnos.
Supposition at 2 A.M. Phillip Hey. YAP
Supreme Sacrifice, The. John Stanhope Arkwright. WGRP
Supreme Surrender. Dante Gabriel Rossetti. the House of Life, VII. MaVP; PoVP; ViPo; VP
Supreme, the Best Being of all, the Source of Light, The. Divine Songs to Ahura Mazda. Zoroaster. LiTW
Surabaja [*or* Surabaya]. Bill Berkson. ANYP; YAP

Sure. Ted Robinson. MaRV
Sure and erect, the master's quiet touch. The Dead Player. Robert Burns Wilson. AA
Sure, deck your lower limbs in pants. What's the Use. Ogden Nash. PoPl
Sure, I am a wild young Irish boy and from Dubalin town I came. I Am a Wild Young Irish Boy. *Unknown.* ShS
Sure, it takes a lot of courage. Trust. Betsey Kline. SoP
Sure, it was so. Man in those early days. Corruption. Henry Vaughan. AnAnS-1; CAW; FaBoEn; MeP; OBS; OxBoCh; SCEP-1; SeCP; SeCV-1
Sure Lord, there is enough in thee to dry. Sonnet. George Herbert. AnAnS-1; MaMe; MeP
Sure maybe ye've heard the storm-thrush. Birds. "Moira O'-Neill." HBV
Sure my sparrows are my own. Let Ye Then My Birds Alone. John Clare. *Fr.* Summer Evening. BiS
Sure Promise, A. Herbert G. Tovey. SoP
Sure Sign, A. Nancy Byrd Turner. PCH; SoPo; TiPo
Sure Signs. Thad Stem, Jr. PoNC
Sure, such a day as this was never seen! The Tragedy of Tragedies. Henry Fielding. EiCL
Sure there are poets which did never dream. Cooper's Hill. Sir John Denham. AnAnS-2; CEP; EiCL; SeCP; SeCV-1; SeEP
Sure, There's a Tie of Bodies! Henry Vaughan. NCEP
Sure, this world is full of trouble. "Ain't It Fine Today!" [*or* It's Fine Today]. Douglas Malloch. BLPA; SoP; WBLP
Sure thou didst flourish once! and many springs. The Timber. Henry Vaughan. EP; NoP; OBEV; SCEP-1; SeCP; SeCV-1
Sure Trust, A. *Unknown.* SoP
Sure 'twas by Providence design'd. On a Beautiful Youth Struck Blind with Lightning. Goldsmith. OAEP
"Sure we can," said the man. Heartbeat of Democracy. Virginia Brasier. StVeCh (1955 ed.)
Surely among a rich man's flowering lawns. Ancestral Houses. W. B. Yeats. Meditations in Time of Civil War, I. CABL; ChMP; LiTB; MoVE; PIA
Surely I dreamt to-day, or did I see. Keats. *Fr.* Ode to Psyche. LO
Surely I think the wild beasts fear your white bones. Epitaph of a Thessalian Hound. Simonides. LiTW
Surely it is not you! Sit, nevertheless. Conversation Galante. Humbert Wolfe. HBMV; MAP
Surely My Soul. Jacob Cohen, *tr. fr. Hebrew by* I. M. Lask. TrJP
Surely that is not a man. Acrobat. Rachel Field. *Fr.* A Circus Garland. SoPo; StVeCh
Surely that moan is not the thing. Fog-Horn. W. S. Merwin. NMP
Surely the finger of God that governs the stars. Yeats' Tower. Vernon Watkins. NeBP
Surely the saints you loved visibly came. Joyce Kilmer. Amelia Josephine Burr. DD; HBMV
Surely the toothpaste magnate who controls. The Broadcast. John W. Simons. JKCP (1955 ed.)
Surely there is a vein for the silver. The Price of Wisdom. Job, Bible, *O.T.* TrGrPo
Surely you would not ask me to have known. Question to Life. Patrick Kavanagh. MoBrPo (1962 ed.)
Surety. Lizette Woodworth Reese. MAP; MoAmPo
Surface and the Depths, The. Lewis Morris. *See* Song: "Love took my life and thrill'd it."
Surface Fishing. W. R. Moses. NYTB
Surfers at Santa Cruz. Paul Goodman. CBV
Surge mea sponsa, swete in sight. Veni, Coronaberis. *Unknown.* AtBAP; BoW
Surgeon, The. W. J. Funk. PoMa
Surgeon's Hands, The. Ida Norton Munson. OQP
Surgeons must be very careful. Emily Dickinson. CBEP; DiPo; ImOP
Surging sea of human life forever onward rolls, The. A Hundred Years from Now. Mary A. Ford. BLPA
Surnames. James Smith. BOHV
Surprise, The. William Barnes. PoVP
Surprise. Harry Behn. BiCB; TiPo (1959 ed.)
Surprise, The. *Unknown, tr. fr. Greek by* Louis Untermeyer. UnTE
Surprise, A. Elizabeth Winton. PCH
Surprise at Ticonderoga, The. Mary A. P. Stansbury. MC; PAH
Surprised by Evening. Robert Bly. NaP
Surprised by Joy [Impatient as the Wind]. Wordsworth. BWP; CBEP; EnRP; EPN; ERoP-1; ExPo; HBV; LiTB; LO; MaPo (1969 ed.); NoP; OBRV; PeER; PIA; PoeP; SeCeV; Sonn
(Desideria.) GTBS; GTBS-D; GTBS-P; GTBS-W; GTSE; GTSL; OBEV
(Sonnet: Surprised by Joy.) ChER; ViBoPo
(To Catherine Wordsworth 1808-1812.) FaBoEn; OBNC
Surprised by Me. Walter Darring. NYBP
Surprises. Jean Conder Soule. BiCB
Surprises. *Unknown.* STF
Surprises are round. Surprises. Jean Conder Soule. BiCB
Surrender. Amelia Josephine Burr. HBV
Surrender. Henry W. Frost. SoP
Surrender. Angelina W. Grimké. CDC
Surrender. Ruth Guthrie Harding. HBMV
Surrender, The. Henry King. AnAnS-2; LO; MePo; TrGrPo
Surrender. "S. M. M." JKCP
Surrender. Anna L. Waring. SoP
Surrender at Appomatox, The. Herman Melville. MC; PAH
Surrender of Cornwallis, The. *Unknown.* PAH
Surrender of New Orleans, The. Marion Manville. PAH
Surrender of Spain, The. John Hay. AA
Surrender to Christ. Frederic William Henry Myers. OxBoCh
Surrounded by beakers, by strange coils. The Naked World. Sully-Prudhomme. ImOP
Surrounded by unnumbered foes. His Banner over Me. Gerald Massey. HBV; VA; WGRP
Surrounding woods are burning with subdued fire, The. Treason. Lora Dunetz. NePoAm
Sursum. Guillermo Valencia, *tr. fr. Spanish by* Thomas Walsh. CAW
Sursum Corda. Conrad Aiken. ReMP
Sursum Corda. Elizabeth Barrett Browning. *Fr.* Casa Guidi Windows. VA
Sursum Corda. Annie Lake Townsend. OQP
Survey, my fair! that lucid stream. Ode to a Young Lady, Somewhat too Sollicitous about Her Manner of Expression. William Shenstone. CEP
Survey of Literature. John Crowe Ransom. FaBoCh; LiTA; LoGBV; SiTL; TwCP
Survey our progress from our birth. John Webster. LO
Surveyor. Guy Butler. PeSA
Surview. Thomas Hardy. ChMP
(Surview; Cogitavi Vias Meas.) LO
Survival, The. Edmund Blunden. OBEV (new ed.); OBMV
Survival. Florence Earle Coates. AA
Survival. Margaret Moore Meuttman. MaRV
Survival of the Fittest, The. Sarah N. Cleghorn. HBMV
Survival of the Fittest Groceries. William Knott. YAP
Survivor, The. Stephen Berg. *Fr.* Entering the Body. NaP
Survivor, The. Robert Graves. CMoP; MoVE
Survivor, The. Frederic L. Knowles. OQP
Survivor sole, and hardly such, of all. Yardley-Oak. William Cowper. LaA; NCEP; PeER
Survivors, The. S. S. Gardons. AmPC
Survivors, The. Daryl Hine. TwCP
Survivors, The. Adrienne Cecile Rich. NYBP
Survivors. Alan Ross. POTi
"Susaddah!" exclaimed Ibsen. Clerihews. E. C. Bentley. PV
Susan. Frederick Locker-Lampson. BOHV
Susan. *Unknown.* NA
Susan; a Poem of Degrees, *sel.* Arthur Joseph Munby. Sweet Nature's Voice. VA
Susan Blue. Kate Greenaway. MPB; OTPC (1946 ed.) ("Oh, Susan Blue.") TiPo
Susan poisoned her grandmother's tea. Susan. *Unknown.* NA
Susan Simpson. *Unknown.* BOHV
Susan to Diana. Frances Cornford. MoVE
Susan Van Dusan. *Unknown.* ABF
Susanna and the Elders. Adelaide Crapsey. AnAmPo; MAP; MoAmPo (1942 ed.); NP
Susanna Fair, Sometime of Love Requested. *Unknown.* ReIE
Susannah and the Elders ("Susannah the fair with her Beauties all bare"). *Unknown.* ALV; ErPo
Susceptible Chancellor, The. W. S. Gilbert. *Fr.* Iolanthe. ALV; PoVP

Susiana, *with music.* *Unknown.* ShS
Susie's galoshes. Galoshes. Rhoda W. Bacmeister. BrR; SoPo; TiPo
Suspecting hollow trees, the barn to be. Play-wright. John Woods. CoPo
Suspended in a moving night. Corner Seat. Louis MacNeice. MoVE
Suspended Moment. Mariana B. Davenport. GoYe
Suspense. Emily Dickinson. *See* Elysium is as far as to.
Suspense. William J. Grace. JKCP (1955 ed.)
Suspense. D. H. Lawrence. MoBrPo
Suspense. Adrien Stoutenburg. WIRo
Suspicious Sweetheart. Heine, *ad. fr. German by* Louis Untermeyer. MeWo
Suspiria. Longfellow. ViBoPo
Suspiria. *Unknown.* OBEV (new ed.)
Suspition upon His Over-much Familiarity with a Gentlewoman, The. Robert Herrick. CavP
Sussex. Kipling. HT; ViPP
Sussex Legend, A. Charles Dalmon. BoTP
Sustaining Power, The. Anna-Modine Moran. SoP
Sustainment. *Unknown.* SoP
Susurro. "Fiona Macleod." *Fr.* Sospiri di Roma. VA
Susy Miller. Elizabeth Prentiss. SAS
Suum Cuique Pulchrum. Henry Parrot. TuPP
Svetasvatara Upanishad. *Unknown.* *See* Upanishads, The.
Swaggering Damsel, The, *sel.* Robert Chamberlain.
"Farewell this company." TuPP
Swallow, The. Thomas Aird. VA
Swallow, The. Abraham Cowley. BEL; CoBE; OBEV; SeCL; TOP
Swallow, A. Euenus, *tr. fr. Greek by* William Cowper. WoL
Swallow, The. Carmen Bernos de Gasztold, *tr. fr. French by* Rumer Godden. BiS
Swallow, The. Christina Rossetti. *Fr.* Sing-Song. GoTP; OTPC (1946 ed.); StVeCh
("Fly away, fly away over the sea.") CoBE; PoVP; SUS
Swallow, The. Thomas Stanley, *after the Greek of* Anacreon. AWP
Swallow, bonny birdie, comes sharp twittering o'er the sea, The. The Swallow. Thomas Aird. VA
Swallow, The, comes! She comes, she brings. Folk Song. *Unknown,* *tr. fr. Greek.* PCH
Swallow flew like lightning over the green, The. Solutions. Edmund Blunden. FaBoTw
Swallow Flight. Sara Teasdale. NP
Swallow has come again, The. The Children's Song [*or* Greek Children's Song]. *Unknown.* FaPON; OTPC (1946 ed.)
Swallow has set her six young on the rail, The. In the Doorway. Robert Browning. *Fr.* James Lee's Wife. NCEP
Swallow is a mason, The. Bird Trades. *Unknown.* DD; HH
Swallow is flying over, The. Tears in Spring. William Ellery Channing. AA
Swallow Leaves Her Nest, The. Thomas Lovell Beddoes. *See* Dirge: "Swallow leaves her nest, The."
Swallow, my sister, O sister swallow. Itylus. Swinburne. ChTr; EnLi-2; GTBS; GTSL; HBV; NoP; OBEV (1st ed.); PoVP; StP; ViPo; ViPP; VP; WHA
Swallow-shell that eases birth, The. Hunting, IV. Gary Snyder. *Fr.* Myths & Texts. NaP
Swallow skims low over the field, A. Barn Swallow. Charles G. Bell. NYTB
Swallow Song. Marjorie Pickthall. CaP
Swallow Tails. Tom Robinson. FaPON
Swallowed thud of cattle shouldering through, The. Enigma. Joseph Auslander. NP
Swallowing snow. Near Mons. Neil Myers. NYTB
Swallows, The. Sir Edwin Arnold. DD; PoRL
Swallows, The. Patric Dickinson. ChMP
Swallows. Afanasi Afanasievich Fet, *tr. fr. Russian by* Babette Deutsch. OnPM
Swallows, The. Agathias Scholasticus, *tr. fr. Greek by* Dudley Fitts. LiTW
Swallows, The/ returned at dawn today. John Giorno. *Fr.* The American Book of the Dead. ANYP
Swallows, The; an Elegy. Richard Jago. CEP
Swallow's Flight, The. Louis Levy, *tr. fr. Danish by* Martin S. Allwood *and* Sanford Kaufman. TrJP
Swallows in their torpid state, The. To the Rev. Mr. Newton. William Cowper. LoBV
Swallow's Nest, The. Sir Edwin Arnold. OTPC (1946 ed.); PRWS
Swallows Over the Camp. Uys Krige, *tr. fr. Afrikaans by* Uys Krige *and* Jack Cope. PeSA
Swamp Fox, The. William Gilmore Simms. AA; AmePo; BeLS; DD; FaBoBe; MC; PaA; PAH
Swampstrife and spatterdock. The Marsh. W. D. Snodgrass. BoNaP; NePoEA; OTD; ToPo; WIRo
Swan, The. Baudelaire, *Tr. fr. French by* F. P. Sturm. SyP
Swan, The. John Gould Fletcher. OTPC (1946 ed.)
Swan, The. F. S. Flint. NP
Swan, The. Edmund Gosse. SyP
Swan. D. H. Lawrence. CMoP
Swan. Edward Lowbury. GTBS-P
Swan, The. Jay Macpherson. PeCV
Swan, The. Stéphane Mallarmé, *tr. fr. French by* T. Sturge Moore. SyP
Swan, The. W. R. Rodgers. NeBP; NMP
Swan, The. Stephen Spender. UnS
Swan, The. *Unknown.* ChTr; FaPON
("Swan swam over the sea.") BoChLi; OxNR
Swan, The. *Unknown,* *tr. fr. Anglo-Saxon.* *Fr.* Riddles. BEL, *tr. by* F. B. Snyder; CoBE; OuHeWo, *tr. by* Stith Thompson
Swan and the Cook, The. La Fontaine, *tr. fr. French.* BoChLi
Swan and the Goose, The. Aesop, *rhymed tr. fr. Greek by* William Ellery Leonard. AWP; FaPON; JAWP; LiTW; UnS; WBP
Swan Bathing, The. Ruth Pitter. MoBrPo
Swan Boat, A. Robert Palfrey Utter. PCH
Swan Curse. A. W. Sullivan. NYTB
Swan existing, The. Voyage à l'Infini. Walter Conrad Arensberg. AnAmPo
Swan has a neck that is curly and long, The. Necks. Rowena Bennett. RePo
Swan Song. Samuel Taylor Coleridge. *See* On a Bad Singer.
Swan Song. Som Parkash Ranchan. ACV
Swan Song. Swinburne. *Fr.* The Garden of Proserpine. OtMeF
Swan Song of Parson Avery, The. Whittier. AA; AmePo
Swansong on the Moorlands. Steingrímur Thorsteinsson, *tr. fr. Icelandic by* Jakobina Johnson. LiTW
Swan swam over the sea. The Swan. *Unknown.* BoChLi; ChTr; FaPON; OxNR
Swan switches its tail and plugs, The. And Other Poems. R. S. Morgan. FIW
Swan, the Pike, and the Crab, The. Ivan Andreyevich Krylov, *tr. fr. Russian by* I. Henry Harrison. BoChLi
Swan, The—Vain Pleasures. George Moses Horton. BALP
Swanee River. Stephen Collins Foster. *See* Old Folks at Home.
Swans. Lawrence Durrell. FaBoMo; MoBrPo (1962 ed.); SeCePo
Swans, The. Clifford Dyment. MoVE; POTi
Swans, The. Catulle Mendès, *tr. fr. French by* Stuart Merrill. OnPM
Swans, The. Edith Sitwell. ACV; CMoP; FaBoMo; GTBS-D; MoVE
Swans, The. Randall Swingler. POTE
Swans. Wordsworth. *Fr.* An Evening Walk. OBEC
Swans, The. Andrew Young. MoBrPo (1942 ed.); POTE; WePo
Swans at Night, *sel.* Mary Gilmore.
"Within the night, above the dark." MoAuPo; PoAu-1
Swan's Feet, The. E. J. Scovell. FaBoMo
Swan's Nest, The. Pamela Griffin. BoPe
Swans of Vadstena, The. Ralph Gustafson. MoCV
Swans of Worcester with their lifted wings, The. Depression. "Michael Field." SyP
Swans rise up with their wings in day, The. The Boy and the Geese. Padraic Fiacc. NeIP
Swans Sing. Samuel Taylor Coleridge. *See* On a Bad Singer.
Swan's Singing, The. *Unknown,* *tr. fr. Spanish by* Havelock Ellis. OnPM
"Swans, whose pens as white as ivory, The." Robert Greene. *Fr.* A Madrigal. ViBoPo
Swansea Town, *with music.* *Unknown.* ShS
Swansong. *See* Swan Song.
Swapping Song, The. *Unknown.* RIS
("My father he died, but I can't tell you how.") OxNR

Swapping yarns, two Mountain Men. Mountain Liars. Ann Woodbury Hafen. PoOW
Swarm of bees in May, A. Weather Signs [*or* Proverbs *or* Rhymes about Months and Days]. *Unknown.* FaBoBe; HBV; OTPC; OxNR; PPL; RIS; SiTL; StaSt
Swarms of minnows show their little heads. Minnows. Keats. *Fr.* I Stood Tiptoe upon a Little Hill. FaPON; GN; GoTP; RIS
Swart[e], sweaty [*or* smeked] smith[e]s [*or* Black-smocked Smiths], smutched [*or* smattered] with smoke. The Blacksmiths [*or* Smoke-blackened Smiths]. *Unknown.* CABA; EnL; MeEL; WiR
Swarthy bee is a buccaneer, The. A More Ancient Mariner. Bliss Carman. VA
Swashbuckler's Song, The. James Stuart Montgomery. HBMV
Swathe Uncut, The. John Hewitt. NeIP
Swear by what the sages spoke. Under Ben Bulben. W. B. Yeats. AnIV; CMoP; CoBMV; LiTM (rev. ed.); LoBV; NoP; OxBI
Swear, "Rather death than tyrants in the land." Manuel José Quintana. *Fr.* Ode to Spain—after the Revolution of March. PoFr
Swearing. Henry Fitzsimon. ACP (1952 ed.)
Sweated Labor. Thomas Hood. *Fr.* The Song of the Shirt. MaRV
Swedes. Edward Thomas. BrPo; MoVE
Swedish Angel. Winfield Townley Scott. LiTM
Swedish Folk Song: "Three ships I saw come sailing." *Unknown, tr. fr. Swedish by* Florence Christine Svenson. PCH
Swedish National Hymn. Karl Vilhelm August Strandberg, *tr. fr. Swedish by* Charles W. Stork. PoFr
Sweeney among the Nightingales. T. S. Eliot. AmPP (5th ed.); AnEnPo; AnFE; AP; APA; BoLiVe; BWP; CABA; CaFP; ChMP; CMoP; CoAnAm; CoBMV; DiPo; EnL; EnLit; FaBoMo; ILP; InPo; InvP; LiTA; LiTM; MAP; MAPA; MaPo; MBW-2; MoAmPo (1942 ed.); MoVE; NePA; NoP; NP; OAEP (2d ed.); OBMV; OxBA; PoAn; ReMP; SeCeV; TwAmPo
Sweeney in Articulo. "Myra Buttle." Par
Sweeney the Mad. *Unknown, tr. fr. Old Irish by* J. G. O'-Keeffe.
(Mad Sweeney.) AnIL
"He came to me in his swift course," *sel.* OnYI
Sweeney to Mrs. Porter in the Spring. L. E. Sissman. NYBP
Sweep the house clean. Love Song. William Carlos Williams. MoAB; MoAmPo (1950 ed.)
Sweep thy faint strings, Musician. The Song of Shadows. Walter de la Mare. BoLiVe; CMoP; CoBE; MoBrPo; ShBV-3; TrGrPo
Sweeper, The. Agnes Lee. HBMV; NP; QFR
Sweeper of the Floor, The. George Macdonald. MaRV
Sweeping the Skies. Elizabeth Anna Hart. CenHV
Sweet. *Unknown, tr. fr. Spanish by* Havelock Ellis. OnPM
Sweet, a delicate white mouse, A. The Waltzer in the House. Stanley Kunitz. ErPo; NYBP
Sweet Adeline. Richard H. Gerard. TreFT
Sweet Adon. Robert Greene. *See* Infida's Song.
Sweet after showers, ambrosial air. In Memoriam A. H. H., LXXXVI. Tennyson. BEL; EPN; OAEP; TOP; ViPo; VP
Sweet Afton. Burns. *See* Flow Gently, Sweet Afton.
Sweet Alice S. Morris, I am pleased, of course. Reply to a Lady Editor. Theodore Roethke. TDP
Sweet and Bitter. Bhartrihari, *tr. fr. Sanskrit by* Arthur W. Ryder. OnPM
Sweet and goodly fellowship. There's No Lust like to Poetry. *Unknown.* AWP
Sweet and Low [Sweet and Low]. Tennyson. *Fr.* The Princess, Pt. II. BEL; BoChLi; BoTP; CoBE; EnLi-2; EnLit; EPN; EtS; FaBoBe; FaPON; GFA; GoTP; ILP; InP; MBW-2; MCCG; MPB; NeHB; OTPC; PG (1945 ed.); PoE; PoPl; PoVP; PRWS; ShBV-1; StVeCh; TreF; TrGrPo; TSW; VA; ViPP
(Lullaby.) GBV (1922 ed.); HBV; HBVY; PoRh; PoLF; TVC
(Lyrics from "The Princess.") OuHeWo
(Song: "Sweet and low, sweet and low.") ThWaDe; YAT
(Songs From "The Princess".) ViPo
Sweet and Sour. Spenser. *See* Amoretti, XXVI.
Sweet-and-Twenty. Shakespeare. *See* O Mistress Mine.
Sweet and Various the Woodlark. Lawrence Ferlinghetti. NoP
Sweet Apple. James Stephens. CMoP
Sweet are the charms of her I love. Song. Barton Booth. OBEC
Sweet are the moonbeams, sweet the grass-grown wood. Sweet and Bitter. Bhartrihari. OnPM
Sweet are the rosy memories of the lips. "Owen Meredith." *Fr.* A Night in Italy. OBEV (1st ed.)
Sweet Are the Thoughts That Savor of Content. Robert Greene. *Fr.* Farewell to Folly. BEL; CoBE; EG; PoToHe; ReIE; SiCE; TuPP
(Content.) EnLit; OnPM; WoL
(Maesia's Song.) CTC; HBV; OBSC; ReEn
(Mind Content, A.) EIL; ViBoPo
(Poor Estate, The.) TrGrPo
(Song: "Sweet are the thoughts that savor of content.") EnLi-1; OuHeWo; PoEL-2
Sweet are the thoughts where hope persuadeth hap. Sir Walter Ralegh. FCP
Sweet Are the Uses of Adversity. Shakespeare. *See* Uses of Adversity, The.
Sweet are the ways of death to weary feet. Chorus. Lord de Tabley. *Fr.* Medea. NBM; OBEV (new ed.); OBVV
Sweet are the whispers of yon pine that makes. The Death of Daphnis. Theocritus. Idylls, I. AWP; JAWP; WBP
Sweet as violets to a weary heart. The Pleiades. Elizabeth J. Coatsworth. ImOP
Sweet, at this morn I chanced. Buen Matina. Sir John Salusbury. EIL
Sweet Auburn! loveliest village of the plain. The Deserted Village. Goldsmith. BEL; BeLS; CEP; CoBE; EiCL; EiPP; EnL; EnLi-1; EnLit; EnPE; EnRP; FaFP; FOL; GoTL; HBV; ILP; LaA; LiTB; LoBV; MasP; MCCG; NoP; OAEP; OBEC; OnYI; OTPC; OuHeWo; OxBI; Po; PoE; PoEL-3; SeCePo; TOP; TreFS; TrGrPo; ViBoPo
Sweet Auburn! parent of the blissful hour. Blest Retirement. Goldsmith. *Fr.* The Deserted Village. OBEC
Sweet babe! a golden cradle holds thee. The Fairy Nurse. Edward Walsh. OnYI
Sweet baby, sleep; what ails my dear? A Rocking Hymn [*or* A Lullaby]. George Wither. *Fr.* Hallelujah. OxBoCh [*wr. at. to* William Austin]; SeCV-1
Sweet, Be No Longer Sad. Charles Webbe. SeCL
Sweet, be not proud of those two eyes. To Dianeme. Robert Herrick. CBEP; EG; FaBoEn; GTBS; GTBS-D; GTBS-P; GTBS-W; GTSE; GTSL; HBV; LiTL; LoBV; OBEV; OBS; OnPM; PoeP; PoPo; SCEP-2; SeCV-1; SeEP; TOP; TrGrPo; ViBoPo; WoL
Sweet beast, I have gone prowling. Song. W. D. Snodgrass. MoAmPo (1962 ed.); NYBP
Sweet bell of Stratford, tolling slow. The Passing Bell at Stratford. William Winter. AA
Sweet Benjamin, since thou art young. John Hoskins to His Little Child Benjamin, from the Tower. John Hoskins. TuPP
Sweet Betsy from Pike, *with music. Unknown.* ABF; AmPP (4th ed.); AS; BFSS; CoSo; TrAS; TreFT; ViBoFo
(Betsy from Pike.) BaBo
(Sweet Betsey from Pike.) OxBoLi
(Sweet Betsey from Pike, *sl. diff. vers., with music, by* John A. Stone.) SGR
Sweet bird that shunn'st the noise of folly. Milton. *Fr.* Il Penseroso. CH
Sweet birds! that sit and sing amid the shady valleys. A Pastoral [*or* Phyllis]. Nicholas Breton. EG; EIL; OBSC; ReIE; SiCE; TrGrPo
Sweet blackbird is silenced with chaffinch and thrush. Winter. Christina Rossetti. BoTP
Sweet-breathed and young. A Woman's Execution. Edward King. AA
Sweet brother, if I do not sleep. For My Brother. Thomas Merton. InPo; TreFS
"Sweet boy," she says, "this night I'll waste in sorrow." Shakespeare. *Fr.* Venus and Adonis. ErPo
Sweet cake tongue, The. Song for a Man in Doubt. Kathleen Fraser. YAP
Sweet, can I sing you the song of your kisses? Your Kisses. Arthur Symons. MeWo
Sweet Chance, that led my steps abroad. A Great Time. W. H. Davies. AnFE; ExPo; LiTB; MemP; MoBrPo; MoVE; POTE; WePo; WHA; YT

Sweet chestnuts brown, like soling leather, turn. The Winter's Come. John Clare. ERoP-2
Sweet child of April, I have found thy place. The Pyxidanthera. Augusta Cooper Bristol. AA
Sweet clavichord. Sacheverell Sitwell. MuSP
Sweet Clover. Wallace Rice. HBV
Sweet Content. Thomas Dekker. *See* Happy Heart, The.
Sweet Cupid, Ripen Her Desire. *Unknown.* EnRePo; EP; LoBV; OBSC; ViBoPo
Sweet cyder is a great thing. Great Things. Thomas Hardy. GTBS-P; GTSL; MoVE; TreFT
Sweet Cynthia, take the book away. To Cynthia, Not to Let Him Read the Ladies' Magazines. P. M. Hubbard. FiBHP
Sweet Daffadowndilly. Christina Rossetti. *See* Growing in the Vale.
Sweet day of Christ, earth's perfect peace. The Lord's Day. Henry W. Frost. SoP
Sweet day, so cool, so calm, so bright. Virtue [*or* Vertue]. George Herbert. AnAnS-1; AtBAP; ATP; AWP; BEL; BoLiVe; BWP; CABA; CaFP; CBEP; CBV; CH; CoBE; EG; ELP; EnLi-1; EnLit; EP; ExPo; FaBoEn; ForPo; FosPo; HBV; InPo; InvP; JAWP; LoBV; MaMe; MaPo (1969 ed.); MeLP; MeP; MePo; NoP; OBEV; OBS; OnPM; PAn; PG (1955 ed.); PIA; Po; PoAn; PoE; PoFS; PoIE; PoRA; PoSa; SCEP-1; SeCeV; SeCL; SeCP; SeCV-1; SeEP; ShBV-4; TOP; TreFT; TrGrPo; UnPo (1st ed.); ViBoPo; WBP; WGRP; WHA
Sweet death com vissit my sicke hart. *Unknown.* SeCSL
Sweet dimness of her loosened hair's downfall. Love-Sweetness. Dante Gabriel Rossetti. The House of Life, XXI. BEL; EnLit; EPN; MaVP; OAEP; PoVP; TOP; ViPo; VP
Sweet disorder in the dress, A. Delight in Disorder. Robert Herrick. AnAnS-2; AnFE; AWP; CABA; CavP; CBEP; CBV; EG; EP; ErPo; FaBV; GTBS-P; ILP; InPo; JAWP; MemP; MeWo; NoP; PAn; PIA; PoAn; PoeP; PoIE; PoSa; PP; SCEP-2; SeCP; ShBV-4; StP; TDP; TOP; VaPo; WBP
Sweet, doe not frowne on me though I must goe. *Unknown.* SeCSL
Sweet Dreams Form a Shade. Blake. *See* Cradle Song: "Sweet dreams form a shade."
Sweet Echo [Sweetest Nymph, That Liv'st Unseen]. Milton. *Fr.* Comus. AtBAP; ELP; ExPo; SeCL
(Echo.) CBEP; OBEV; OBS
(Lady's Song.) BoLiVe; TrGrPo
(Song: "Sweet Echo, sweetest Nymph, that liv'st unseen.") LoBV
(Songs from Comus.) SeCeV
("Sweet Echo, sweetest nymph, that liv'st unseen.") EG; TOP; ViBoPo
Sweet Eden was the arbor of delight. In Gethsemane. Giles Fletcher. MaRV; StJW
Sweet Emma Moreland of yonder town. Edward Gray. Tennyson. OBVV
Sweet England, call for grace! The Four Wonders. *Unknown.* TuPP
Sweet, exclude me not, nor be divided. Bar Not the Door. Thomas Campion. UnTE
Sweet eyes by sorrow still unwet. Wonderland. Harry Thurston Peck. AA
Sweet father I have shrunk a bit. Father Father Son and Son. Jon Swan. NYBP
Sweet fellow, whom I sware such sure, affected love. The Preamble to Nicholas Breton His Garden-Plot. Nicholas Breton. ReIE
Sweet flower, that art so fair and gay. Medieval Norman Songs, XI. *Unknown, tr. fr. French by* John Addington Symonds. AWP
Sweet for a little even to fear, and sweet. Erotion. Swinburne. PoEL-5
Sweet friend, when you and I are gone. Patience with the Living. Margaret Elizabeth Sangster. PoToHe
Sweet Genevieve. George Cooper. TreFS
Sweet gentle angel, not that I aspire. To Miss M——Written by Moonlight. Sir Samuel Edgerton Brydges. Sonn
Sweet girl graduate, lean as a fawn, A. Nancy Hanks, Mother of Abraham Lincoln. Vachel Lindsay. ATP (1935 ed.); CMoP; LiPo; MAP; ThLM
Sweet glove, the witness of my secret bliss. Sir Philip Sidney. *Fr.* Arcadia. FCP
Sweet hand! the sweet yet cruel bow thou art. Love's Francis-can. Henry Constable. ACP; GoBC
Sweet, harmless [*or* harmles] live[r]s! (on whose holy leisure). The Shepheards. Henry Vaughan. AnAnS-1; FosPo; MeP
Sweet Harmony. Shakespeare. *See* How Sweet the Moonlight Sleeps upon This Bank.
Sweet harmony of life, just musick flows. John Banks. *Fr.* The Innocent Usurper. PeRV
Sweet have I known the blossoms of the morning. Because of You. Sophia Almon Hensley. HBV
Sweet Highland Girl, a very shower. To a Highland Girl [*or* To the Highland Girl of Inversneyde]. Wordsworth. CABL; EnRP; EPN; GTBS; GTBS-D; GTBS-P; GTBS-W; GTSE; GTSL; LoBV; TreFT, *abr.*
Sweet Hour of Prayer. William W. Walford. BLRP; TreFT; WBLP
Sweet I am not come too soone. *Unknown.* SeCSL
Sweet if thou wilt be. Come Turn to Mee, Thou Pretty Little One. *Unknown.* CoMu
Sweet in goodly fellowship. There's No Lust Like to Poetry. *Unknown.* AWP
Sweet in goodly fellowship. Wine and Love and Lyre. *Unknown.* UnTE
Sweet in her green dell [*or* cell] the Flower of Beauty slumbers. Song [*or* Flower of Beauty]. George Darley. GTBS-D; HBV; LO; OBEV; OBNC; OBRV; OBVV; OnYI; VA
Sweet in your antique body, not yet young. To a Child. Wilfred Owen. Sonn
Sweet infancy:/ O heavenly fire! The Rapture. Thomas Traherne. NoP; OBS; SCEP-1
Sweet Innisfallen. Thomas Moore. HBV; OBNC
Sweet Is Childhood. Jean Ingelow. TreFS
Sweet is my sleep, but more to be mere stone. The Speech of Night. Michelangelo. OnPM
Sweet is the dew that falls betimes. Christopher Smart. *Fr.* A Song to David. Po
Sweet is the music of yon whispering pine. The Song of the Death of Daphnis. Theocritus. EnLi-1
Sweet is the rose, but grows upon a brere [*or* brier]. Amoretti, XXVI. Spenser. EIL; HBV; EP; ILP; ReEn
Sweet is the solemn voice that calls. Delight in God's House. Henry Francis Lyte. SoP
Sweet is the swamp with its secrets. Emily Dickinson. MAPA; TwAmPo
Sweet is the time for joyous folk. Hora Christi. Alice Brown. HBV; MaRV; TrPWD; WGRP
Sweet is the voice that calls. September. George Arnold. DD; HBV
Sweet is true love tho' given in vain, in vain. Elaine's Song [*or* Song of Love and Death]. Tennyson. *Fr.* Idylls of the King: Lancelot and Elaine. FaBoEn; OBNC
Sweet it is to see the sun. Every Day Thanksgiving Day. Harriet Prescott Spofford. DD; OHIP; PEDC
Sweet Jesus. Friar Michael of Kildare, *mod. vers. by* Russell K. Alspach. OnYI
Sweet Jesus with Thy Mother mild. England's Prayer. William Blundell of Crosby. GoBC
Sweet kiss, thy sweets I fain would sweetly indite. Astrophel and Stella, LXXIX. Sir Philip Sidney. FCP; ReEn; SiPS
Sweet Kitty Wells. *Unknown. See* Kitty Wells.
Sweet lady & sole mistres of my love. *Unknown.* SeCSL
Sweet Land. Francis Maguire. JKCP (1955 ed.)
"Sweet land"/ at last! St. Francis Einstein of the Daffodils. William Carlos Williams. AtBAP; MoPo
Sweet land of song, thy harp doth hang. The War Ship of Peace. Samuel Lover. PAH
Sweet, Let Me Go! *Unknown.* EIL; InvP; LO; MeWo; OnPM; PV; TrGrPo; UnTE; ViBoPo
Sweet, let us love enjoy. Love Play. William Cavendish, Duke of Newcastle. ErPo
Sweet lips, there are songs about kisses now. Counting. Carl Sandburg. MoLP
Sweet little bell. The Bell of the Hermitage. *Unknown.* AnIL; CAW; OnYI
Sweet little bird in russet coat. The Autumn Robin. John Clare. BoTP
Sweet little maid with winsome eyes. The Other One. Harry Thurston Peck. AA
Sweet Love,—but oh! most dread Desire of Love. Love's Fatal-

Sweet (continued)
ity. Dante Gabriel Rossetti. The House of Life, LIV. MaVP; PoVP; ViPo; VP
Sweet love has twined his fingers in my hair. Love's Prisoner. Mariana Griswold Van Rensselaer. HBV
Sweet Love, If Thou Wilt Gain a Monarch's Glory. *Unknown.* EG
(Picture, A.) GTSL
Sweet Love, mine only treasure. Where His Lady Keeps His Heart. "A. W." CTC
Sweet love, renew thy force; be it not said. Sonnets, LVI. Shakespeare. CBEP; LO; PoLF; UnPo (1st ed.)
Sweet Lullaby, A. Nicholas Breton. EIL; GTSL; OBSC; SiCE; TOP; TuPP; ViBoPo
(Come, Little Babe.) PoIE
(Cradle Song, A: "Come little babe, come silly soul.") HBV; OBEV
Sweet Lydia take this maske, and shroud. A Maske for Lydia. Thomas Randolph. AnAnS-2
Sweet maid, if thou wouldst charm my sight. A Persian Song [of Hafiz]. Hafiz. AWP; OBEC; OuHeWo; PrWP
Sweet maiden of Passamaquoddy. Lines to Miss Florence Huntington [*or* The Maiden of Passamaquoddy]. *Unknown, at. to* James De Mille. BOHV; NA; WhC; WHW
Sweet Marie. Cy Warman. TreFS
Sweet Mary primping for the prom. What Makes Life Interesting. Marion Montgomery. NYTB
Sweet Mary was a servant girl. Young Edwin in the Lowlands Low (B *vers.*). *Unknown.* BaBo
Sweet mouth, that send'st a musky-rosed breath. Joshua Sylvester. EnLoPo
Sweet Muse. Isaac Watts. OxBoCh
(Meditation in a Grove.) CEP
Sweet music, sweeter far. A Carol. Edmund Bolton. OxBoCh
Sweet my musings used to be. Mot eran dous miei cossir. Arnaut Daniel. AWP
Sweet names, the rosary of my evening prayer. Love's Rosary. George Edward Woodberry. AA
Sweet Nature's Voice. Arthur Joseph Munby. *Fr.* Susan; a Poem of Degrees. VA
Sweet Nea!—for your lovely sake. Because. Edward Fitzgerald. HBV
Sweet "No, no," A—with a sweet smile beneath. Yes and No [*or* A Love Lesson]. Clément Marot. AWP; JAWP; OnPM; WBP
Sweet nymphs, if, as ye stray. Love Vagabonding [*or* Madrigal: Love Vagabonding]. William Drummond of Hawthornden. EG; LoBV
Sweet o' the Year, The. George Meredith. BoNaP
Sweet Old Chapters. *Unknown.* SoP
Sweet orange grove, the fairest of the isle. The Beauties of Santa Cruz. Philip Freneau.
Sweet Pastoral, A. Nicholas Breton. LO; SiCE
(To His Muse.) OBSC
Sweet peace, where dost thou dwell? I humbly crave. Peace [*or* Resurrection]. George Herbert. AnAnS-1; AWP; BoPe; ChTr; ELP; ExPo; InPo; JAWP; MaMe; MeP; OxBoCh; ReEn; SCEP-1; SeCeV; SeEP; WBP
Sweet Peas. Keats. *Fr.* I stood Tiptoe Upon a Little Hill. GN; MPB (1956 ed.); PCH
Sweet peas and roses, strawberries on the vine. Way Over in the Blooming Garden. *Unknown.* ABF
Sweet Peril. George Macdonald. BLPA; FaBoBe; NeHB; TreFS
Sweet Phillis [*or* Phyllis], if a silly swain. Coridon's Supplication to Phillis [*or* A Supplication]. Nicholas Breton. OBSC; SiCE
Sweet Pity, Wake. *Unknown.* EIL
Sweet poets of the gentle antique line. Sonnet. John Hamilton Reynolds. OBRV
Sweet pretty fledglings, perched on the rail arow. Flycatchers. Robert Bridges. MoVE; POTE
Sweet procession, rose-blue. Seems like We Must Be Somewhere Else. Denise Levertov. NePoEA-2
Sweet reader, whom I've never seen. Apostrophic Notes from the New-World Physics. E. B. White. ImOP
Sweet Red Rose, The. Mary Mapes Dodge. BiCB
Sweet Riley. *Unknown. See* Willy Reilly.
Sweet Risen Christ! They shall not gag our song. Spanish Alleluja. James J. Galvin. JKCP (1955 ed.)
Sweet Robin, I have heard them say. Robin Redbreast. George Washington Doane. AA; DD; HBV; HBVY
Sweet Robinette. *Unknown.* CoMu
Sweet Rose, Fair Flower. *At. to* Shakespeare. The Passionate Pilgrim, X. EIL
Sweet rose [*or* Sweit roiss] of virtue [*or* vertew] and of gentleness [*or* gentilnes]. To a Lady. William Dunbar. CLwM; EG; GoBC; MeEL; OAEP; OBEV; OxBS
Sweet, sacred hill! on whose fair brow. Mount of Olives. Henry Vaughan. Po
Sweet—safe—houses. Emily Dickinson. MWA-2
Sweet Saint, thou better canst declare to me. To Saint Mary Magdalen. Henry Constable. ACP
Sweet saint! whose rising dawned upon the sight. Ariana. Franklin Benjamin Sanborn. AA
Sweet season, that bud and bloom forth brings, The. *See* Soote season, that bud. . .
Sweet secrecy, what tongue can tell thy worth? Idea's Mirrour, XLVI. Michael Drayton. SiCE; ViBoPo
Sweet semi-circled Cynthia played at maw. Sonnet: Mackado, Fustian and Motley. John Taylor. *Fr.* Odcomb's Complaint. CBEP; EIL
Sweet September. George Arnold. GN
Sweet serene skye-like flower. To Lucasta, the Rose [*or* The Rose, *or* Ode: The Rose]. Richard Lovelace. AnAnS-2; EG; HBV; SCEP-2; SeCL; SeCV-1; ViBoPo
Sweet she was, as kind a love. She Smiled like a Holiday. *Unknown.* OxBoLi
Sweet Silence after Bells. Christopher Brennan. BoAV
Sweet Simplicity. Timothy Dwight. *Fr.* Greenfield Hill. AmPP
Sweet singer of the Spring, when the new world. On a Thrush Singing in Autumn. Sir Lewis Morris. OBVV; VA
Sweet sixteen is shy and cold. Growing Old. Walter Learned. HBV
Sweet sleep a spider of dreams. "Everywhere I Wander." Philip Whalen. FRC
Sweet! sleep, lie still, my dear! A Cavalier's Lullaby for His Mistress. Thomas Jordan. *Fr.* An Alarm in 1645. SeCL
Sweet smiling village, loveliest of the lawn. Goldsmith. *Fr.* The Deserted Village. AnFE; PoFr; PPON
Sweet Soldier of the Silences! The Soldier of the Silences. William Herschell. PEDC
Sweet Solitude, thou placid queen. Solitude. Hannah More. *Fr.* The Search after Happiness. WBLP
Sweet soul, do with me as thou wilt. In Memoriam A. H. H., LXV. Tennyson. EPN; ViPo; VP
Sweet sounds, oh, beautiful music, do not cease! On Hearing a Symphony of Beethoven. Edna St. Vincent Millay. GTBS-W; InP; LiTA; LiTM; MAP; MasP; MoAB; MoAmPo; NeMA; NePA; NP; TrGrPo; TwAmPo; UnS
Sweet Spirit! Sister of that orphan one. Epipsychidion. Shelley. EnRP; EPN; ERoP-2
Sweet spring, like man in his minority. Spring. Anne Bradstreet. *Fr.* The Four Seasons of the Year. AnNE
Sweet Spring, thou turn'st with all thy goodly train. Sonnet [*or* Spring Bereaved, 2]. William Drummond of Hawthornden. EIL; FaBoEn; OBEV; Sonn
Sweet Stay-at-Home. W. H. Davies. *Fr.* Foliage. AtBAP; CH; GTBS; HBMV; POTE
Sweet stream-fed glen, why say "farewell" to thee. Farewell to the Glen. Dante Gabriel Rossetti. The House of Life, LXXXIV. MaVP; PoVP; ViPo
Sweet stream, that dost with equal pace. On His Mistress Drowned. Thomas Sprat. ATP; EnLoPo; SeCL
Sweet stream that winds through [*or* thro'] yonder glade. To a Young Lady [*or* The Stream]. William Cowper. EiPP; EnRP; GTBS; GTBS-D; GTBS-P; GTBS-W; GTSE; GTSL; HBV; LiTL; LO
Sweet Suffolk Owl. *Unknown.* CBEP; CH; ChTr; EIL; EnRePo; HBV
Sweet summer breeze. Kiss Me Again. Henry Blossom. TreFT
Sweet Sunday Bells! your measured sound. Sunday Bells. William Allingham. IrPN
Sweet Surprises. S. Doudney. BoTP
Sweet Swan of Avon! what a sight it were. Ben Jonson. *Fr.* To the Memory of My Beloved; the Author Mr. William Shakespeare. ChTr
Sweet sweet Robinette all the shepherds do declare. Sweet Robinette. *Unknown.* CoMu

Sweet, sweet, sweet is the wind's song. Harvest. Ellen Mackay Hutchinson Cortissoz. AA; HBV
Sweet-swelling lip, well mayst thou swell in pride. Astrophel and Stella, LXXX. Sir Philip Sidney. FCP; SiPS
Sweet Teviot, fare thee well! Less gentle themes. The Emigrants: Introductory Stanzas. Thomas Pringle. BoSA
Sweet Teviot! on thy silver tide. A Father's Notes of Woe. Sir Walter Scott. *Fr.* The Lay of the Last Minstrel. OBNC; OBRV
Sweet Thing, *with music.* *Unknown.* OuSiCo
(Crawdad Song, The, *diff. vers.*) OuSiCo
Sweet Thing, A/ Last Thoughts. Lanon A. Fenner, Jr. WSL
"Sweet, thou art pale." The Three Enemies. Christina Rossetti. CoBE; PoVP; ViPo
Sweet thought—sweet model—that gloweth for all. The Opponent Charm Sustained. Samuel Greenberg. MoPo
Sweet timber land. Homing. Arna Bontemps. CDC
Sweet to the morning traveller. The Traveller's Return. Robert Southey. BoTP; OTPC
Sweet Tooth, The. Katharine Pyle. BBGG
Sweet twining hedgeflowers wind-stirred in no wise. The Lovers' Walk. Dante Gabriel Rossetti. The House of Life, XII. MaVP; OAEP; PoVP; TOP; ViPo; VP
Sweet Unsure. Sir Walter Ralegh. SiPS
Sweet upland, to whose walks, with fond repair. To Hampstead. Leigh Hunt. EnRP
Sweet upland! where, like hermit old. In Mortem Venerabilis Andreae Prout Carmen. Francis Sylvester Mahoney. IrPN; NBM
Sweet, use your time, abuse your time. Kingston Church. Thomas D'Urfey. SeCL
Sweet Violets, Love's Paradise. *Unknown.* ElL
(Violets and Roses.) OBSC
Sweet wantton wagg whose chaire of state. *Unknown.* SeCSL
Sweet warrior when shall I have peace with you? Amoretti, LVII. Spenser. StP
Sweet Was the Song. Walter Savage Landor. ViBoPo
Sweet Was the Song. *Unknown.* PoSC
Sweet was the sound when oft at evening's close. Goldsmith. *Fr.* The Deserted Village. FaBoEn; ShBV-2
Sweet were the dayes, when thou didst lodge with Lot. Decay. George Herbert. AnAnS-1; MaMe; MeP; SeCP; SeCV-1
Sweet were the joys that both might like and last. Sweet Unsure. Sir Walter Ralegh. SiPS
Sweet were the sauce would please each kind of taste. In Commendation of The [*or* George Gascoigne's] Steel Glass. Sir Walter Ralegh. FCP; SiPS
Sweet Western Wind, whose luck it is. To the Western Wind. Robert Herrick. HBV; OBEV; SeCV-1; SeEP
Sweet, when I think how summer's smallest bird. Irene Rutherford McLeod. *Fr.* Sonnets. HBMV
Sweet Wild April. William Force Stead. HBV; HBVY
Sweet William ("It was in the merry, merry month of May.") *Unknown.* *See* Douglas Tragedy, The.
Sweet William ("Sweet William he rose on last May morning.") *Unknown.* *See* Fair Margaret and Sweet William.
Sweet William ("Sweet William on a fine summer day"). *Unknown.* *See* Lady Isabel and the Elf Knight.
Sweet William and Lady Marget. *Unknown.* *See* Fair Margaret and Sweet William.
Sweet William and May Margaret. *Unknown.* *See* Sweet William's Ghost.
Sweet William arose [*or* rose] one morning bright [*or* merry May morning]. Fair Margaret and Sweet William. *Unknown.* BFSS
Sweet William he married a wife. The Wife Wrapped in Wether's Skin. *Unknown.* ESPB (F *vers.*); ViBoFo (B *vers.*)
Sweet William would a-wooing ride. Fair Margaret and Sweet William. *Unknown.* BaBo (A *vers.*); OBB; ViBoFo
Sweet William's Farewell to Black-eyed Susan. John Gay. *See* Black-eyed Susan.
Sweet William's Ghost. *Unknown.* BaBo (A *vers.*); BuBa; ESPB (A, B, F, *and* G *vers.*); InPo; ViBoFo (A *and* B *vers.*)
(Sir Ogey and Lady Elsey, B *vers.*) BaBo
(Sweet William and May Margaret.) CH; HBV, *abr.*
Sweet William's gone over seas. Lord William; or, Lord Lundy. *Unknown.* BaBo; ESPB
Sweet Willie. *Unknown.* *See* Willie's Lady.
Sweet Willie was a widow's son. Willie and Lady Maisry [*or* Margerie]. *Unknown.* ESPB; OxBB
Sweet Willy's ta'en him o'er the faem. Willy's [*or* Willie's] Lady. *Unknown.* BaBo; ESPB; OBB; OxBB; ViBoFo
Sweet, wooded way in life, forgetful Sleep! To Sleep. Maybury Fleming. AA
Sweet World, if you will hear me now. Envoy. Sarah Morgan Bryan Piatt. AA
Sweet Yak, I do adore you for your hair. The Yak. Nathalia Crane. StaSt
Sweet, yet cruel unkind is she. Song. *Unknown.* SeCL
Sweeter Far than the Harp, More Gold than Gold. "Michael Field." OBMV; PEVV
Sweeter Saint I Serve, A. Sir Philip Sidney. *Fr.* Arcadia. SiPS
Sweeter than honey and the honeycomb. The Shed. Charles L. O'Donnell. ISi
Sweeter than sour apples flesh to boys. Ted Berrigan. ANYP
Sweeter than water or cream or ice. The Watch on the Rhine. Gertrude Stein. *Fr.* Accents in Alsace. AtBAP
Sweetes' Li'l' Feller. Frank L. Stanton. FaFP; TreFS
Sweetest Bud of Beauty! may. To a Very Young Lady. Sir George Etherege. CEP; SeCL; ViBoPo
Sweetest Cloris lend a kisse. *Unknown.* SeCSL
Sweetest Home, The. *Unknown.* STF
Sweetest! if thy fairy hand. To a Little Girl Gathering Flowers. Mary Tighe. OTPC (1923 ed.)
Sweetest Jesus, gracious, free. Sweet Jesus. Friar Michael of Kildare. OnYI
Sweetest Lives, The ("The sweetest lives are those to duty wed"). *At. to* Elizabeth Barrett Browning. *See* Reward of Service.
Sweetest Love, I Do Not Go. John Donne. *See* Song: "Sweetest love, I do not go."
Sweetest Melancholy. John Fletcher. *See* Melancholy.
Sweetest melody, The. Two Songs, 1. Abraham Reisen. LiTW
Sweetest Name, The. *At. to* St. Bernard of Clairvaux. *See* Jesus, The Very Thought of Thee.
Sweetest of all childlike dreams. The Vanishers. Whittier. AA; SoP
Sweetest of sweets, I thank you: when displeasure. Church-Musick. George Herbert. AnAnS-1; EP; MaMe; MeP; MuSP; SCEP-1; SeCV-1; UnS
Sweetest Place, The. Mary Frances Butts. PPL
Sweetest Saviour, if my soul. Dialogue. George Herbert. MaMe; MePo; OBEV; OBS; SeCV-1
Sweetest Story Ever Told, The. R. M. Stults. TreFS
Sweetest sweets that time hath rifled. Song in Imitation of the Elizabethans. Sir William Watson. VA
Sweetest Thing, The. *Unknown,* *tr. fr. Susu by* Ulli Beier. TTY
Sweetgrass Range. Edwin Ford Piper. MAP; PFY
Sweetheart Gate, Th'. Edwin Waugh. VA
Sweetheart in the Army, A (A *and* B *vers.*). *Unknown.* BaBo
(Pretty Fair Maid, A, *with music.*) AS
Sweethearts. Mary Gilmore. BoAu
Sweetly-favored face, The. Canzonetta: Of His Lady in Absence. Giacomino Pugliese. AWP
Sweetly (my dearest) I left thee asleep. John Saffin. SCAP
Sweetly Sleep. *At. to* Eliza Lee Follen, *also to* Jane Taylor. *See* Lullaby: "Sleep, my baby, sleep my boy."
Sweetmeat, The. Sir Edward Sherburne. SeCL
Sweetness of Nature, The. *Unknown,* *tr. fr. Irish by* Frank O'Connor. KiLC
Sweetness of poverty like this, The. Aspiration. Mário de Andrade. TTY
Sweetness of Spring memories bring. When it's Iris Time in Tennessee. Willa Mae Waid. PoRL
Sweets That Die. Langdon Elwyn Mitchell. AA
Sweit roiss of vertew and of gentilnes. *See* Sweet rose of virtue. . .
Swell Me a Bowl. Ben Jonson. *Fr.* The Poetaster. TuPP
Swell People. Carl Sandburg. LOW
Swell's Soliloquy. *Unknown.* FiBHP
Swept by the hot wind, stark, untrackable. Mohammed and Seid. Harrison Smith Morris. AA
Swept clean of leaves, with stripped boughs, the garden. Sestina. James K. Baxter. Cressida, XV. AnNZ
"Swerve to the left, son Roger," he said. The Judgment of God. William Morris. OBVV; PeVV; ViPP

Swerving east, from rich industrial shadows. Here. Philip Larkin. OPoP
Swet Jesus/ Is cum to us. Welcome! Our Messiah. *Unknown.* MeEL
Swete Ihesu King of Blisse. *Unknown.* OxBoCh
Swetnam, the Woman-Hater, *sel.* *Unknown.*
Ding Dong. EIL
Swift, *sel.* Thomas Caulfield Irwin.
"Two women loved him, shapes of Heaven." IrPN
Swift across the palace floor. Little Guinever. Annie Fields. AA
Swift as a spirit hastening to his task. The Triumph of Life. Shelley. ChER; ERoP-2; MasP; PoEL-4
Swift as an arrow in the wind he goes. Polo Player. Daniel Whitehead Hicky. MoSiPe
Swift boomerang, come get! December 18th. Anne Sexton. MeWo
Swift Bullets, The. Carolyn Wells. ShM
Swift had pains in his head. January 1940. Roy Fuller. HoPM; LiTM; OnHM; PP; SeCePo; WaP
Swift had sailed into his rest. Swift's Epitaph. W. B. Yeats. CMoP; NAMP
Swift in his step and careless of his speech. Native Son. Gertrude Callaghan. JKCP (1955 ed.)
Swift is't in pace, light poiz'd, to look in clear. Description of a New England Spring. John Josselyn. SCAP
Swift kindnesses are best: a long delay. Be Kind Promptly. *Unknown.* OnPM
Swift o'er the sunny grass. Shadow Evidence. Mary Mapes Dodge. AA
Swift red flesh, a winter king, The. The Dance. Hart Crane. *Fr.* The Bridge: Powhatan's Daughter. AnAmPo; AnFE; CoAnAm; LiTA; LiTM; MoAB; MoAmPo; OxBA; SeCeV; TwAmPo
Swift swallows sailing from the Spanish main. Homing Swallows. Claude McKay. TSW
Swift Things Are Beautiful. Elizabeth J. Coatsworth. StVeCh; TiPo (1952 ed.)
Swift through some trap mine eyes have never found. The Harlequin of Dreams. Sidney Lanier. AA; AP
Swift through the eyes unto the heart within. Carnal and Spiritual Love. Michelangelo. OnPM
Swift through the yielding air I glide. The Lark. *Unknown.* OBS; SeCL
Swift to the western bounds of this wide land. On the Completion of the Pacific Telegraph. Jones Very. AP
Swift was sweet on Stella. Us Poets. Franklin P. Adams. PoPl; WhC
Swiftly Relight the Flame. Hilda Doolittle ("H. D."). *Fr.* A Tribute to the Angels. FaBoTw
Swiftly the dews of the gloaming are falling. The Bugles of Dreamland. "Fiona Macleod." OTPC (1946 ed.)
Swiftly the world retreats. Departure. L. A. G. Strong. HaMV
Swiftly turn the murmuring wheel! Song for the Spinning Wheel. Wordsworth. OBRV
Swiftly walk o'er [*or* over] the western wave. To Night [*or* To the Night *or* Night]. Shelley. AnFE; AtBAP; ATP; AWP; BEL; BoC; BoLiVe; CBEP; CH; ChER; CoBE; EG; EnL; EnLi-2; EnLit; EnRP; EPN; ERoP-2; ExPo; GTBS; GTBS-D; GTBS-P; GTBS-W; GTSE; GTSL; HBV; HBVY; ILP; InP; InPo; JAWP; LoBV; MaPo; MCCG; MemP; MyFE; NoP; OAEP; OBNC; OBRV; PCD; PoE; PoFS; PoIE; PoLF; PoRA; SeCeV; ShBV-4; TOP; TreFS; TrGrPo; UnPo (1st ed.); ViBoPo; WBP; WHA; WiR
Swift's Epitaph. W. B. Yeats. CMoP; NAMP
Swim off the Rocks, A. Howard Moss. TDP
Swim with the stream! Sleep as you swim! Dance Band. A. S. J. Tessimond. MuSP
Swimmer. Robert Francis. CrMA; NePoAm
Swimmer, The. Irving Layton. PeCV
Swimmer, The. Roden Noel. OBVV
Swimmer, The. John Crowe Ransom. PFY; SD
Swimmer of Nemi, The. "Fiona Macleod." SyP
Swimmers, The. Allen Tate. AP; MoAmPo (1962 ed.); MoVE
Swimmers. Louis Untermeyer. PFY
Sels.
"O the swift plunge unto the cool, green dark." TSW
"Then, the quick plunge into the cool, green dark." SD
Swimming. Byron. *Fr.* The Two Foscari. GN
Swimming. Clinton Scollard. FaPON; GFA; MPB; UTS
Swimming. Swinburne. *Fr.* Tristram of Lyonesse. GN
Swimming by Night. James Merrill. NYBP
Swimming Lady, The; or, A Wanton Discovery. *Unknown.* ErPo; UnTE
Swineherd, let us make for the moorland. The Wry Rowan. *Unknown.* OnYI
Swing, The. Mary I. Osborn. BoTP
Swing, The. Robert Louis Stevenson. BoChLi; FaBoBe; FaFP; GFA; GoBP; GoJo; NeHB; OTPC; PCH; PDV; SoPo; StVeCh; SUS; TiPo; TreF
Swing back the gate till it stumbles over the furrows. Chance Met. Rosemary Dobson. NeLNL
Swing dat hammer—hunh—. Southern Road. Sterling Brown. BALP; BANP
Swing high, Iscariot. The Sacrifice. Gerald William Barrax. Kal
Swing Low, Sweet Chariot ("Oh, de good ole chariot swing so low"). *Unknown.* AA
Swing Low, Sweet Chariot ("I looked over Jordan, and what did I see"). *Unknown.* ABF, *with music;* AmPP; AmFN; BoAN-1, *with music;* FaPON; GoSl; InP; LoGBV; MaRV
Swing on the Corner, *with music.* *Unknown.* TrAS
Swing on the cripple and hit the dying quail. An Astonished Listener Hears the Radio Announcer Bat Out the Long Balls of Verbs, Nouns and Adjectives. James Schevill. FiMAP
Swing out, oh bells. The Bells of Peace. Aileen Fisher. SiSoSe
Swing Ship, The. Mildred D. Shacklett. GFA
Swing Song, A. William Allingham. BrR; FaPON; MoShBr; MPB; OTPC (1946 ed.); PCD; PoRh; SUS
Swing Song. *Unknown,* *tr. fr. Turkish.* PCH
Swing! Swing! Swing! Skating Song. Christopher Morley. PCH
Swing thee low in thy cradle soft. Indian Cradle Song. *Unknown.* BoChLi
Swinging. Irene Thompson. BoTP
Swinging mill bell changed its rate, The. A Lone Striker. Robert Frost. NoP
Swinging Song, A. Mary Howitt. OTPC (1923 ed.)
Swinging Stair, The. Nathalia Crane. YT
Swinging toward the Light. Georgia Harkness. MaRV
Swiss Air. Bret Harte. *See* Serenade: "I'm a gay tra, la, la."
Swiss Peasant, The. Wordsworth. OBEC
(On the Swiss.) PoFr
Swiss they are a hardy race, The. Song of Switzerland. Stoddard King. WhC
Switch Blade, The; or, John's Other Wife. Jonathan Williams. NeAP
Switch Cut in April, A. Clifford Dyment. MoVE; POTi
Switzerland. Matthew Arnold. MaVP; OAEP; ViPP; VP
Sels.
Absence, VI. CBEP; MBW-2; PoVP
Farewell, A: "My horse's feet beside the lake," III. MBW-2
Isolation: To Marguerite, IV. MBW-2; PoVP; TreFT
(To Marguerite.) CBEP
Meeting, I. ELP; MBW-2
(Lake, The.) CBEP
To Marguerite—Continued, V. BWP; CABA; CaFP; CBV; ELP; EnL; EnLi-2; EPN; FaBoEn; FiP; GTBS-D; GTBS-P; HBV; ILP; MaPo; MBW-2; NoP; OBEV; OBNC; PAn; PoAn; PoEL-5; PoVP; SeCeV; TOP; VaPo; ViPo
(Isolation.) OBVV
Switzerland. James Sheridan Knowles. *Fr.* William Tell. PoFr
Swollen to bursting like a pod, her ripeness. Beets. Alden Nowlan. PeCV (1967 ed.)
Swoon of noon, a trance of tide, A. In a Bye-Canal. Herman Melville. MAmP; PoFS
Sword, The. Abu Bakr, *tr. fr. Arabic by* A. J. Arberry. TTY
Sword, a sword, and a sword, A. Which Sword? Jason Noble Pierce. PGD
Sword and the Sickle, The. Blake. *Fr.* Gnomic Verses. BoLiVe; ChTr; TrGrPo
("The sword sung on the barren heath.") ERoP-1
Sword fell down, The: I heard a knell. The Leader. Hilaire Belloc. ACP (1952 ed.)
Sword in a Cloud of Light, A. Kenneth Rexroth. NMP
Sword in length a reaping-hook amain. King Harald's Trance. George Meredith. PeVV

Sword of Bunker Hill, The. William Ross Wallace. PEDC
Sword of Robert Lee, The. Abram Joseph Ryan. JKCP; PaA; PoRL
Sword of silver cuts the fields asunder, A. Vigil of the Immaculate Conception. Maurice Francis Egan. CAW; JKCP
Sword of Surprise, The. G. K. Chesterton. MoBrPo; MoRP
Sword of Tethra, The. William Larminie. *Fr.* Moytura. OnYI
Sword sang [*or* sung] on the barren heath, The. The Sword and the Sickle. Blake. *Fr.* Gnomic Verses. BoLiVe; ChTr; ERoP-1; TrGrPo
Sword was sheathed, The: in April's sun. The Vow of Washington. Whittier. DD; MC; PAH
Swords crossed, but not in strife! The Crossed Swords. Nathaniel Langdon Frothingham. AA
Swordy Well. John Clare. WHA
Sybilla's Dirge. Thomas Lovell Beddoes. *See* Sibylla's Dirge.
Sycophantic Fox and the Gullible Raven. Guy Wetmore Carryl. AA; AnAmPo; BLPA; CenHV; FaFP; FiBHP; HBV; InMe; LHV; MAP; MoAmPo (1942 ed.); ShBV-3; TreFT
Syghes ar my foode, drynke are my teares. Sir Thomas Wyatt. *See* Sighs are my food. . .
Sylla declares the world shall know. A Serious Danger. R. A. Davenport. PV
Syllables of grief are small, The. Text for Today. Phyllis McGinley. WhC
Sylly boy wert thou but wise. *Unknown.* SeCSL
Sylvan meant savage in those primal woods. Woods. W. H. Auden. NePA; NePoAm
Sylvan Muses, can ye sing. Aglaia. Nicholas Breton. *Fr.* The Passionate Shepherd. OBSC
Sylvan Ode. José Santos Chocano, *tr. fr. Spanish by* John Pierrepont Rice. WoL
Sylvan Revel, A. Edward Cracroft Lefroy. Echoes from Theocritus, XXV. AWP; JAWP; WBP
Sylvester Vermicelli was a conscientious clerk. Ballad of the Faithful Clerk. Albert Stillman. InMe
Sylvia. Michael Drayton. *Fr.* The Shepherd's Garland, Eclogue IX. LoBV (1949 ed.)
(Roundelay, A: "Tell me, thou skilful shepherd's swain.") EIL
Sylvia. Robert Lowell, *ad. fr. the Italian of* Giacomo Leopardi. NaP
Sylvia and the Bee. Mary Leapor. WaPE
Sylvia, do you remember the minutes. Sylvia. Robert Lowell, *ad. fr. Italian of* Giacomo Leopardi. NaP
"Sylvia, hush!" I said, "come here." Dove's Nest. Joseph Russell Taylor. HBV
Sylvia; or, The May Queen, *sels.* George Darley.
Chorus of Spirits, I. OnYI; VA
Dirge: "Wail! wail ye o'er the dead!" OBRV
Morning-Song, II. VA
(Serenade.) HBV
Nephon's Song, III. VA
(Elfin Pedlar, The.) BoTP
Song: "I've taught thee Love's sweet lesson o'er." OBRV
(Romanzo to Sylvia, IV.) VA
Song: "The streams that wind among the hills." NBM
Sylvia the fair, in the bloom of fifteen. Song. Dryden. CBEP; ErPo; LiTG; LiTL; SiTL; UnTE; ViBoPo
Sylvie and Bruno, *sels.* "Lewis Carroll."
Gardener's Song, The. EvOK; HBV; OTPC
(He Thought He Saw.) GBV (1952 ed.); HBVY
(He Thought He Saw a Banker's Clerk.) LBN; NA
("He thought he saw an Elephant.") EnLi-2; MemP
(Mad Gardener's Song, The.) FiBHP; NBM; PoRh; SiTL; TreFS; WiR
(Some Hallucinations.) BOHV
(Strange Wild Song, A.) StVeCh
Melancholy Pig, The. FaPON; OTPC (1946 ed.); PPL
Sylvie and Bruno Concluded, *sels.* "Lewis Carroll."
King-Fisher Song, The. RIS
Little Birds. WhC
Little Birds Are Playing, *shorter sel.* OxBoLi
Pig-Tale, A. OA; WiR
Sylvoe, *sel.* Dryden.
Song, A: "Go tell Amynta gentle swain." CavP
Sym of Lyntoun, be the ramis horn. King Berdok. *Unknown.* OxBS
Symbol, The. James Hebblethwaite. BoAu
Symbol. David Morton. HBMV; MaRV; OQP; StJW
Symbol from the first, of mastery, A. The Staff of Aesculapius. Marianne Moore. ImOP
Symbol inside this poem is my father's feet, The. The Pawnbroker. Maxine Kumin. TDP
Symbol of Hope. Carl S. Weist. *See* Cross on a Hill, A.
Symbol of star or lily of the snows. The Cloud of Carmel. Jessica Powers. ISi
Symbolism. Karen Swenson. NYTB
Symbolisms, *sel.* Richard Realf.
Word, The. AA; AmLP; TRV; WGRP
(O Earth!) AnEnPo
(World, The.) MaRV
Symbols. John Richard Moreland. ChIP; PGD
Symbols. Vance Thompson. AA
Symbols. W. B. Yeats. OBMV
Symbols of gross experience!—our grief. C. Day Lewis. *Fr.* Oh Dreams, Oh Destinations. Sonn
Symmetries and Asymmetries, *sel.* W. H. Auden.
"Deep in earth's opaque mirror." FIW
"Leaning out over," 3 *ll.* FIW
Sympathizers, The. Josephine Miles. CrMA; FiMAP
Sympathy. Emily Brontë. OAEP
Sympathy. Elizabeth Barrett Browning. *Fr.* A Reed. SoP
Sympathy. Paul Laurence Dunbar. AmNP; CDC; IDB; PoNe
Sympathy, The. Owen Felltham. LO; SeCL
Sympathy. Althea Gyles. HBV
Sympathy. Anna E. Hamilton. OQP
Sympathy. Reginald Heber. BeLS; BOHV
Sympathy. Henry David Thoreau. *See* Lately, Alas, I Knew a Gentle Boy.
Sympathy, The. *Unknown.* SeCL
Sympathy, a Welcome, A. John Berryman. NYBP
Symphony. Christopher Hassall. MuSP
Symphony. Frank Horne. AmNP
Symphony, The. Sidney Lanier. AmPP; AP; ATP (1935 ed.); CoBA; LiTA
Sels.
"For the outside leagues of liberty." PoFr
"I speak for each no-tonguéd tree." ViBoPo
"O Trade! O Trade! would thou wert dead!" PoPo
Symphony, The. Charlotte Grant MacIntyre. FaChP
Symphony, The. Herman W. Stillman. PEDC
Symphony; First Movement. John Hall Wheelock. UnS
Symphony in Blue. Raymond F. Roseliep. ISi
Symphony in Gray Major. Rubén Darío, *tr. fr. Spanish by* Alice Jane McVan. LiTW
Symphony in Yellow. Oscar Wilde. MoBrPo; OTPC (1946 ed.); PCH; SyP
Symphony of the Soul. Carlton Buck. SoP
Symphony Orchestra. James Kirkup. MuSP
Synce my joyes thoroughe Phillis frownes. *Unknown.* SeCSL
Synchronized. Larry Rubin. FiSC
Synekdechestai. C. M. Schmid. GoYe
Synge's Grave. Winifred M. Letts. AnIV
Synnöve's Song. Björnstjerne Björnson, *tr. fr. Norwegian by* Charles Wharton Stork. LiTW; PoPl
Synods are whelps of th' Inquisition. Presbyterian Church Government. Samuel Butler. *Fr.* Hudibras, I, 3. OBS
Synonym for God, A. John Fandel. JKCP (1955 ed.)
Syon lyes waste, and thy Jerusalem. *See* Sion lies waste. . .
Syracusan Women, The. Theocritus, *tr. fr. Greek by* J. M. Chapman. Idylls, XV. WoL
Syracuse. Elizabeth Coatsworth. HT
Syren Songs, *sels.* George Darley.
Mermaiden's Vesper Hymn, The, VI. LoBV; OBNC; OBRV; PeER; PoEL-4
(Chorus of Sirens.) NBM
(Siren Chorus: "Troop home to silent grots and caves.") OxBI; ViBoPo
(Song of the Mermaids.) ChTr
Sea-Ritual, The, V. ERoP-2; OBNC; OBRV; OnYI; OxBI; SiSW; WiR
(Deadman's Dirge.) CH
Syrian Evening, A. Thomas Moore. *Fr.* Lalla Rookh. PeER
Syrian Lover in Exile Remembers Thee, Light of My Land, The. Ajan Syrian. LiTL; NP
Syrian's Tale, The. Leslie Savage Clark. ChIP
Syrinx. John Lyly. *See* Pan's Song.
Syro-Phoenician Woman, The. *Unknown.* StJW

System. Robert Louis Stevenson. PoVP; RIS
Systole and Diastole. Conrad Aiken. CrMA
Systolic city noise denies the thrush. Rural Legend. Mary Elizabeth Osborn. NePoAm

T

T. A. H. Ambrose Bierce. AA; AnAmPo; YaD
T-Bar. P. K. Page. OBCV
T is for turkey so crispy and brown. The Feast Day. Amy McDonall. PCH
T. S. Eliot. Thomas Whitbread. NYTB
T.V.A., The, *with music.* *Unknown.* TrAS
T. V. gunning down. Slumnight. Colette Inez. QAH
Tabernacle Thought, A. Israel Zangwill. TrJP
Tabernacles. Gerrit Lansing. CoPo
Tabitha Soliloquizes. Minnie Leona Upton. CIV
Table and the Chair, The. Edward Lear. BoChLi; GoTP; HBVY; MPB; OTPC (1946 ed.); PCH; PPL; SAS; SoPo; StVeCh; TreFT
Table-Birds. Kenneth Mackenzie. PoAu-2
Table D'Hote. Richard Curry Esler. NYTB
Table for One. John Holmes. WhC
Table Manners. Gelett Burgess. BBGG
Table Manners for the Hostess. Jean de Meun, *tr. fr. French by* Bernard D. N. Grebanier. *Fr.* The Romance of the Rose, *ch.* 73. EnLi-1
Table Richly Spread, A. Milton. *Fr.* Paradise Regained, II. FaBoCh; LoGBV
Table Talk, *sels.* William Cowper.
Fragment. WGRP
"Freedom has a thousand charms to show." PoFr
"I know the mind that feels indeed the fire." PP
Table Talk. Donald Mattam. FiBHP
Table Talk. Wallace Stevens. NoP
Tableau. Countee Cullen. AmFN; BANP; Kal
Tableau at Twilight. Ogden Nash. FiBHP
Table's long and gleaming, The. The Board Meets. John Gloag. FiBHP
Tables Turned, The. Wordsworth. BEL; CBEP; DiPo; EnL; EnLi-2; EnLit; EnRP; EPN; ERoP-1; HBV; MBW-2; MERP; OAEP; OBRV
(Up! Up! My Friend, and Quit Your Books.) PoMa
Let Nature Be Your Teacher, *sel.* MaRV
Taboo to Boot. Ogden Nash. FiBHP
Taborer beat/ Your little drum. Jig for Sackbuts. D. B. Wyndham Lewis. ErPo
Tacita. James Benjamin Kenyon. AA
Tacking Ship off Shore. Walter Mitchell. AA; EtS; FaBoBe; GN; HBV; PFY
Tact. Harry Graham. ALV
Tact. Paul Pascal. PV
Tactic. Margaret Marks. MAP
Taddeo Gaddi built me. I am old. The Old Bridge at Florence. Longfellow. HT
Tadmor, *sel.* Nathalia Crane.
Song: "Great is the rose." MAP; MoAmPo (1942 ed.)
Tadoussac. Charles Bancroft. BLPA
Tadpole, The. Elizabeth Gould. BoTP
Tae be wan o them kings. Stars. George Mackay Brown. OxBS
Tae titly. *Unknown.* OxNR
Taedium Vitae. Oscar Wilde. SyP
Taffy, the topaz-colored cat. In Honor [*or* Honour] of Taffy Topaz. Christopher Morley. CIV; PoMa; TiPo
Taffy was a Welshman, Taffy was a thief. Mother Goose. BBGG; OTPC; OxNR; RIS; SiTL
Taffy was born. *Unknown.* OxNR
Tagus, Farewell. Sir Thomas Wyatt. *See* Of His Return from Spain.
Tahiti, Tahiti. Vor a Gauguin Picture zu Singen. Kurt M. Stein. FiBHP
Tail behind, a trunk in front, A. The Elephant, or the Force of Habit. A. E. Housman. FaBV; PoPo; PV; WhC
Tail for the Horse, A. *Unknown.* SiTL
Tail toddle, tail toddle. Tommie Makes My Tail Toddle. Burns. ErPo
Taill of the Foxe, That Begylit the Wolf, in the Schadow of the Mone. Robert Henryson. OxBS
Tailor, The. "S. Ansky," *tr. fr. Yiddish by* Joseph Leftwich. TrJP
Tailor, The. Thomas Lovell Beddoes. *See* Oviparous Tailor, The.
Tailor, The. Joseph Leftwich. TrJP
Tailor, A, a man of an upright dealing. Of a Precise Tailor. Sir John Harington. BOHV
Tailor of Bicester, The. *Unknown.* OxNR
Tailor That Came from Mayo, The. Denis A. McCarthy. OnYI
Tails. Rowena Bennett. RePo
Tailspinning from the shelves of sky. Jubilo. Allen Tate. WaP
Tak tyme in tym, or tym will not be tane. A Description of Tyme. Alexander Montgomerie. OxBS
Tak' Your Auld Cloak about Ye. *Unknown.* *See* Old Cloak, The.
Take a blessing from my heart to the land of my birth. The Fair Hills of Eirè, O! Donogh Mac-Con-Mara (Macnamara), *tr. by* James Clarence Mangan. IrPN; OBVV
Take a common little bronco. The Cowboy up to Date. Charles S. Thomas, Jr. CoSo
Take a dainty paradox. Finale. A. P. Herbert. *Fr.* Perseverance; or, Half a Coronet. InMe
Take a father's admonition, from a heart disturbed. A Father's Testament. Judah ibn Tibbon. TrJP
Take a harp. Song of the Harlot. Isaiah, Bible, *O.T.* TrJP
Take a Man. Carlton Buck. SoP
Take a robin's leg. Homoeopathic Soup. *Unknown.* BOHV
Take a walk in my head. Gerald Butler. *Fr.* This Side of Orion. QAH
Take all my loves, my love, yea, take them all. Sonnets, XL. Shakespeare. CBEP; InvP; OBSC
Take all of me—I am thine own heart, soul. A Sonnet. Amélie Rives. AA
Take Any Bird. Chaucer. *Fr.* The Canterbury Tales: The Manciple's Tale. OA
Take as a gift. Giving and Taking. James Kirkup. EaLo
Take as gold this old tradition. Schöne Rothraut. John Arthur Goodchild. VA
Take Away. Margot Ruddock. OBMV
Take away your soft hair and your softer lips. Supplication. Louis Untermeyer. HBMV
Take back into thy bosom earth. Stanzas to the Memory of Thomas Hood. Bartholomew Simmons. VA
Take Back the Heart. Charlotte Alington Barnard. TreFT
Take Back the Virgin Page. Thomas Moore. HBV; OBNC
Take Back Your Gold. Louis W. Pritzkow. TreF
Take back your suit. A Song of Faith Forsworn. Lord De Tabley. PeVV; VA
Take Care. Rose Waldo. GFA
Take care, O wisp of a moon. To the Afternoon Moon, at Sea. Cale Young Rice. EtS
Take, cradled nursling of the mountain, take. The River Duddon, IV. Wordsworth. MERP
Take Frankincense, O God. Charles Fitzgeffrey. *Fr.* Holy Transportations. ChTr
Take from the earth its tragic hunger, Lord. Prayer. Hazel J. Fowler. TrPWD
Take from your head the garland too, Menechtenus. After the Festival. Stefan George. LiTW
Take hand and part with laughter. Rococo. Swinburne. HBV; ViBoPo
Take Heart. Edna Dean Proctor. HBV
Take heed betime lest ye be spied. Sir Thomas Wyatt. FCP; SiPS
Take heed, my love. H. G. Andrews. LO
Take Heed of Gazing Overmuch. Thomas Richardson. *Fr.* A Proper New Song Made by a Student in Cambridge. ElL
Take heed of loving me[e]. The Prohibition. John Donne. EG; ElL; MaMe; MBW-1; MeLP; OBS; SCEP-1; TuPP
Take heed of this small child of earth. The Poor Children [*or* The Children of the Poor]. Victor Hugo. AWP; JAWP; LiTW; WBP
Take Him. Horatius Bonar. FaChP
Take him, earth, for cherishing. The Burial of the Dead. Prudentius. LiTW
Take him up tendahly. Parody on Thomas Hood's "The Bridge of Sighs." *Unknown.* FiBHP
Take Home This Heart. John Holmes. LiTL

Take home Thy prodigal child, O Lord of Hosts! Birthday Sonnet. Elinor Wylie. BoLiVe; MAP; MoAB; MoAmPo; OnPM
Take in good part these trifling toys. To the Reader [*or* Quip to the Reader]. Timothe Kendall, *after* Martial. OnPM; TuPP
Take It from Me. Kenneth O. Hanson. CoAP
Take it from me kiddo. Poem, or Beauty Hurts Mr. Vinal. E. E. Cummings. AmP; MoAB; MoAmPo; MoVE; OxBA; PoIE
Take it, love. Song. Richard Le Gallienne. HBV
Take it, my dear. Keep it beneath your pillow. Gift of a Mirror to a Lady. David Wagoner. NePoAm-2
Take me aboard your barque, where the valuable water. Fauré. Charles Causley. MuSP
Take me as I drive alone. White Blossoms. Robert Mezey. NaP
Take me away, and in the lowest deep. The Dream of Gerontius: The Soul before God. Cardinal Newman. OxBoCh
Take me back to old Montana. *Unknown.* CoSo
Take me down from this cross, for now my body is broken. Golgotha. John Hall Wheelock. MoRP
Take Me in Your Arms, Miss Moneypenny-Wilson. Patrick Barrington. WhC
Take Me, Mother Earth. Anna Jameson. VA
Take me upon thy breast. O Sleep. Grace Fallow Norton. HBV
Take My Hand, O Blessed Master. Connie Calenberg. BePJ
Take My Heart. St. Augustine, *tr. fr. Latin.* TRV
Take My Heart. Lon Woodrum. SoP
Take My Life. Frances Ridley Havergal. FaChP; MaRV
(Take My Life and Let It Be.) BLRP; TreFT
Take my right hand. Evangelist. Dave Etter. ThO
Take My Wings and Dance with Me. Aristophanes, *tr. fr. Greek by* Ann Stanford. *Fr.* The Birds. HW
Take Nothing for Granite. Nate Salsbury. InMe
Take Notice. Ralph Robin. NYTB
Take, O Take Those Lips Away. Shakespeare. *Fr.* Measure for Measure, IV, i; *also given, with add. st., in* The Bloody Brother (*by* John Fletcher, *and others*), V, ii. AnFE; AtBAP, 2 *sts.*; BEL; CBEP; DiPo; ElL; ELP; EnLi-1; EnLit; EnLoPo, 2 *sts.*; EnRePo; ExPo; FaBV; HBV, 2 *sts.*; ILP; InPo; LiTB; LiTG; LiTL; LO; NoP; OAEP; OBEV; OnPM; OuHeWo; PoeP; PoIE; SeCeV; SiCE; TOP; TuPP, 2 *sts.*; ViBoPo; WHA
(Boy's Song to Mariana.) BoLiVe
(Frustra.) GTSL
(Love Forsworn.) MCCG
(Love Song.) FaBoEn, 2 *sts.*
(Madrigal.) GTBS; GTBS-D; GTBS-P; GTBS-W; GTSE
(Sealed in Vain.) WoL
(Seals of Love.) MeWo; TrGrPo
(Song: "Take, O take those lips away.") FiP; ForPo; MemP; PoEL-2, 2 *sts.*
(Song at the Moated Grange, A.) OBSC
(Song for Mariana.) EG
(Songs from the Plays.) AWP; JAWP; WBP
(Three Songs, 2.) UnPo (1st ed.)
Take of English earth as much. A Charm. Kipling. OtMeF
Take of letters the first. *Unknown.* *Fr.* Riddles. CoBE
Take of me what is not my own. Envoi. Kathleen Raine. NeBP
Take off your hat. Pass Office Song. *Unknown.* PBA; TTY
Take old Amyntor to thy heart, dear soil. The Good Farmer. *Unknown.* OnPM
Take one bowl, one valley. Florence; Design for a City. Elizabeth Jennings. HaMV
Take I, 4: II: 58. Philip Whalen. NeAP
Take One Home for the Kiddies. Philip Larkin. ELU
Take out of time that moment when you stood. The Sundial. Jane Cooper. AmPC
Take Physic, Pomp. Shakespeare. *Fr.* King Lear, III, iv. TrGrPo
(Discovery of Pity.) UnPo (1st ed.)
Take pity, signors, ye who pass me by. For a Blind Beggar's Sign. Clemente Biondi. CAW
Take stock, citizen bacillus. Citizen Bacillus. John Brunner. HYE
Take strands of speech, faded and broken. Maker of Songs. Hazel Hall. HBMV
Take the back off the watch. Time Piece. William Cole. ELU
Take the cloak from his face, and at first. After [*or* The Avenger Speaks]. Robert Browning. BoLiVe; EG; TrGrPo
Take the cloak of all my love. Song for a Jewess. Iwan Goll. TrJP
Take the Crust. Sadi, *tr. fr. Persian by* L. Cranmer-Byng. *Fr.* The Gulistan. AWP
Take the Glass Away. *Unknown.* SiTL
Take the good and cast the evil. Crusaders' Song. *Unknown.* CAW
Take the Supreme Climb! *Unknown.* SoP
Take the World as It Is. Charles Swain. VA
"Take the world as it is!—with its smiles and its sorrow," *sel.* PoToHe (new ed.)
Take them, O Death! and bear away. Suspiria. Longfellow. ViBoPo
Take then the music; plunge in the thickest of it. Samadhi. Conrad Aiken. MAPA
Take, then, your paltry Christ. To the Christians. Francis Lauderdale Adams. OxBS; WGRP
Take these flowers which, purple waving. To a Lady with Flowers from the Roman Wall. Sir Walter Scott. OAEP
Take these stripes from, stripes from around my shoulder, huh! Lord It's All, Almost Done. *Unknown.* OuSiCo
Take these, times tardy truants, sent by me. Upon Two Greene Apricockes Sent to Cowley by Sir Crashaw. Richard Crashaw. MaMe
Take these who will as may be. Permit Me Voyage. James Agee. MAP; MoAmPo
Take This Hammer, *with music.* *Unknown.* OuSiCo
Take this kiss upon the [*or* thy] brow! A Dream within a Dream. Poe. AmP; AmPP; AnFE; AP; APA; BoLiVe; CBEP; CoAnAm; CoBA; LO; MAmP; MeWo; OxBA; SyP; TDP; TrGrPo
Take Thou My Hand. Phyllis C. Michael. SoP
Take Thou, O Lord. Oswald J. Smith. SoP
Take Thou the burden, Lord. The Burden. Toyohiko Kagawa. MaRV
Take Thy Bliss, O Man. Blake. *Fr.* Visions of the Daughters of Albion. EnRP
Take Thy Old Cloak about Thee. *Unknown.* *See* Old Cloak, The.
Take time, my dear, e're time takes wing. Fading Beauty. *Unknown.* PeRV; SeCL; SeEP
Take Time to Be Holy. W. D. Longstaff. BLRP
Take Time to Live. Thomas Curtis Clark. PoToHe
Take Time to Talk with God. Helen Frazee-Bower. STF
Take time to work. Old English Prayer. *Unknown.* TreFT
Take time while time doth last. Song Set by John Farmer. *Unknown.* CTC; OBSC; SiCE
Take Tools Our Strength. Gerald L. Simmons, Jr. NBP
Take up the oxen, boys, and harness up the mules. The Gold Seeker's Song. *Unknown.* PoOW
Take up the White Man's burden. The White Man's Burden. Kipling. EnLi-2 (1949 ed.); InP; PoVP; StP
Take Up Thy Cross. Francis Turner Palgrave. MaRV
Take us on the quest of beauty. The Prayer of the Quest. Eleanor B. Stock. MaRV
Take us size for size and he. A Fledgling Robin. Leonard Feeney. JKCP (1926 ed.)
Take weapon away, of what force is a man? The Preface to the Book of Housewifery. Thomas Tusser. SiCE
Take what God gives, O heart of mine. Your House of Happiness. Thomas Campion. MaRV
Take wings of fancy, and ascend. In Memoriam A. H. H., LXXVI. Tennyson. EPN; ViPo; VP
Take yesterday's worries and sort them all out. Worries. *Unknown.* PoToHe (new ed.)
Take Yo' Time, Miss Lucy. *Unknown.* GoSl
Take you my brushes, child of light, and lay. Spring Landscape. Arthur Davison Ficke. *Fr.* Sonnets of a Portrait Painter, XII. HBMV
Take your bucket, and take your spade. The Sea. E. M. Adams. BoTP
Take Your Gun. Jacob Bronowski. POTE
Take your meals, my little man. The Little Gentleman. *Unknown.* *Fr.* Little Derwent's Breakfast. HBV; HBVY
Take Your Place. *Unknown.* STF
Take your pleasure, dance and play. Invitation to Youth. *Unknown.* OnPM; UnTE

Taking a charity. Confession in Holy Week. Christopher Morley. HBMV
Taking a Walk with You. Kenneth Koch. AmPC; ANYP
Taking Down the Tree. Aileen Fisher. RePo
Taking Leave of a Friend. Li Po, *tr. fr. Chinese by* Ezra Pound. CoAnAm; PoFS; TwAmPo
Taking Long Views. May Kendall. CenHV
Taking my walk the other day. Commination. Walter Savage Landor. ALV
Taking of the Name. *Unknown, tr. fr. Omaha Indian.* PCH
Taking Off. Mary McB. Green. SoPo; TiPo
Taking pity on this scrag-end of the city. One Kingfisher and One Yellow Rose. Eileen Brennan. BiS; NeIP
Taking Steps at Thirteen Months. Heather Ross Miller. NYTB
Taking the air rifle from my son's hand. Cain. Irving Layton. MoCV; PeCV (1967 ed.)
Taking the Hands. Robert Bly. PoIE (1970 ed.)
Taking Turns. Emilie Blackmore Stapp. GFA
Taking us by and large, we're a queer lot. The Sisters. Amy Lowell. AnNE; MAP; MoAmPo
Taking your life as one long Eucharist. Imitation of Christ. Wilma C. Ludlow. ChIP
Takings. Tom Hood. BOHV
(What He Took.) CoMu
Talbragar. Henry Lawson. PoAu-1
Tale, A. Edward Thomas. ChTr
Tale for Husbands, A. Sir Philip Sidney. *Fr.* Arcadia. SiPS
Tale from the Garden, A. Margaret Wynne Jones. GFA
Tale half told and hardly understood, A. Exodus for Oregon. Joaquin Miller. AmPP (3d ed.); FaPL
Tale is every time the same, The. Fable. Maurice James Craig. NeIP
Tale of a Citizen and His Wife, A. John Donne. Elegies, XIV. MaMe
Tale of Calidore, The. Spenser. The Faerie Queene, VI, 9. StP
Tale of a Dog and a Bee, The. *Unknown.* BoTP
Tale of a Little Pig. *Unknown.* ABF
Tale of a Tart, The. Frederic E. Weatherly. SUS
Tale of Custard the Dragon, The. Ogden Nash. FaPON; GoTP; PoPl; PoRA; ShBV-1; TiPo (1959 ed.)
(Tale of the Custard Dragon, The.) WePo
Tale of Hugelin, Count of Pisa, The. Chaucer. *Fr.* The Canterbury Tales: The Monk's Tale. MyFE
Tale of Jorkyns and Gertie, The; or, Vice Rewarded. R. P. Lister. NYBP
Tale of Margaret, The. Wordsworth. *See* Margaret; or, The Ruined Cottage.
Tale of One Hill. Franklin D. Elmer, Jr. ChIP
Tale of Sigemund, The. *Unknown, tr. fr. Anglo-Saxon by* Charles W. Kennedy. *Fr.* Beowulf. AnOE
Tale of the Custard Dragon, The. Ogden Nash. *See* Tale of Custard the Dragon, The.
Tale of the Dixie-Belle, The. Frank Chase. InMe
Tale of the little Cossack, The. The Little Cossack. Laura E. Richards. PoRh
Tale of the Skunk and Poor Jez, The. John Becker. RePo
Tale of the times of old, A!/ Why, thou wanderer unseen! James Macpherson. *Fr.* Cath-Loda. BEL
Tale of the times of old, A! The deeds of days of other years! Carthon, a Poem. James Macpherson. EiPP; EnRP
Tale the Hermit Told, The. Alastair Reid. NePoEA-2
Tale Told by a Head, A. Lois Moyles. NYBP
Tale was this, The. The Wind in the Pines. Henry Taylor. *Fr.* Edwin the Fair. VA
Talented Man, The. Winthrop Mackworth Praed. ALV; CoBE; EnRP; FiBHP; HBV
"Talents Differ." Laura E. Richards. TiPo
Tales, *sel.* Alden Van Buskirk.
"Not after but within this poem I stalk my lovers." YAP
Tales and talismans I have chronicled. The Task. Robert Bhain Campbell. MoPo
Tales from a Family Album. Donald Justice. NePoEA-2; TwAmPo
Tales of a Wayside Inn, *sels.* Longfellow.
Azrael (The Spanish Jew's Tale), *fr.* Pt. III. AnAmPo; MWA-1
Birds of Killingworth, The (The Poet's Tale), *fr.* Pt. I. OnMSP; OxBA
"Do you ne'er think what wondrous beings these," 2 *sts.* WBLP
Charlemagne (The Poet's Tale), *fr.* Pt. III. AnAmPo; FaFP; MWA-1
Emma and Eginhard (The Student's Tale), *fr.* Pt. III. AmPP (5th ed.); MWA-1
King Robert of Sicily (The Sicilian's Tale), *fr.* Pt. I. AnNE; BeLS; MWA-1; OHIP; OnSP; PCD; YT
Legend of Rabbi Ben Levi, The (The Spanish Jew's Tale), *fr.* Pt. I. AnNE; GBV (1952 ed.)
Monk of Casal-Maggiore, The (The Sicilian's Tale), *fr.* Pt. III. AmPP (4th ed.); OxBA
(Sicilian's Tale, The.) AP
Paul Revere's Ride (The Landlord's Tale), *fr.* Pt. I. AmePo; AmPP (4th ed.); AnNE; BBV; BeLS; BLPA; CaFP; CoBA; DD; FaBoBe; FaBV; FaFP; FaPON; GoTP; HBV; HBVY; LoGBV; MC; NeHB; OHFP; OnSP; OTD; PaA; PAH; PAL; PAP; PEDC; PoFr; PoRL; PTK; RePo; RIS; StPo; StVeCh; ThLM; TiPo (1952 ed.); TreF; TrGrPo; WBLP; YaD
(Midnight Ride of Paul Revere.) PaPo
Saga of King Olaf (The Musician's Tale), *fr.* Pt. I.
(Building of the *Long Serpent,* xiii.) EtS
(Challenge of Thor, The.) AmPP (4th ed.)
("Dawn is not distant, The," *fr.* xxii.) TRV
(Einar Tamberskelvar, xx.) AmPP (4th ed.); YT
(King Olaf's Death-Drink, xxi.) AmPP (4th ed.)
(King Olaf's Return, ii.) AmPP (4th ed.)
(King Olaf's War-Horns, xix.) AmPP (4th ed.); PFY
Scanderbeg (The Spanish Jew's Second Tale), *fr.* Pt. III. PFY
Ships That Pass in the Night (The Theologian's Tale, iv), 4 *ll. fr.* Pt. III. EtS; PoToHe (new ed.) PTK
(Ocean of Life, The.) TreFT
Wayside Inn, The. Prelude to Pt. I. CoBA
Tales of the Hall, *sels.* George Crabbe.
Dejected Lover, The, *fr.* XIII. FaBoEn
(Sad Lover, The.) OBNC
"George loved the cause of freedom, but reproved," *fr.* I. PoFr
"Something one day occurr'd about a bill," *fr.* VII. Par
Tales of the Mermaid Tavern, *sel.* Alfred Noyes.
Seven Wise Men. InP
Tales the Barbers Tell, The. Morris Bishop. ALV
Taliesin, *sel.* Richard Hovey.
"Here falls no light." AA
Taliesin and Melanghel. Thomas Love Peacock. PeER
Taliessin's Return to Logres. Charles Williams. ACV
Taliessin's Song of the Unicorn. Charles Williams. FaBoTw
Talisman, A. Marianne Moore. AnFE; APA; CoAnAm; GoJo; MAP; MoAB; MoAmPo; NP; ViBoPo
Talisman, The, *sel.* Sir Walter Scott.
"You talk of gayety and innocence," *fr. ch.* 13. NBM
Talk. John Perreault. ANYP
Talk. Philip A. Stalker. FiBHP
Talk about de lates', de lates' of this song. The Ballet of the Boll Weevil (B *vers.*). *Unknown.* ViBoFo
Talk Faith. Ella Wheeler Wilcox. OQP
Talk Happiness. Ella Wheeler Wilcox. PoToHe
(Optimism.) BLPA; FaBoBe; SoP
Talk not of justice and her scales of woe. The Cross. Eva Gore-Booth. ChIP; MaRV
Talk not of strength, till your heart has known. Ella Wheeler Wilcox. PoToHe
Talk not of wasted affection! affection never was wasted. Longfellow. *Fr.* Evangeline. PoToHe (new ed.)
Talk not to me of all the frowns of fate. Woman's Jealousy. Baltasar del Alcázar. OnPM
Talk of Chocolate! Bacchus on Beverages. Francesco Redi. *Fr.* Bacchus in Tuscany. LiTW
Talk of energy. Mayan sub-flower. Dangers of the Journey to the Happy Land. Joseph Ceravolo. ANYP
"Talk of pluck!" pursued the sailor. Romance. W. E. Henley. In Hospital, XXI. EnLit; MC; PAH
Talk of the Greeks at Thermopylae! A Ballad of Redhead's Day. Richard Butler Glaenzer. MC; PAH
Talk of the Town, The. Ed Fisher. FiBHP
Talk to Me Tenderly. Vivian Yeiser Laramore. HBMV
Talk with prudence to a beggar. Emily Dickinson. MWA-2
Talk with strangers and fence. Drink Wine in the Corner Store. Clive Matson. ThO
Talk with Us, Lord. Charles Wesley. SoP
Talker, The. Benjamin Appel. TrJP

Talking Bronco, *sel.* Roy Campbell.
Volunteer's Reply to the Poet, The. ViBoPo (1958 ed.)
Talking Drums, The. Kojo Gyinaye Kyei. PBA
Talking in Their Sleep. Edith M. Thomas. BoNaP; DD; OHIP; PEDC; PTK
Talking Oak, The, *sel.* Tennyson.
Olivia. GN
Talking oak, The/ To the ancients spoke. Be Different [*or* Deferent] to Trees. Mary Carolyn Davies. DD; FaPON; HBMV; MPB; OHIP
Talking of sects till [*or* quite] late one eve. No Sect [*or* Sects] in Heaven. Elizabeth H. Jocelyn Cleaveland. BLPA; TreFS
Talking to her, he knew it was the end. Hector. Valentin Iremonger. NeIP; OxBI
Talking to Myself, *sel.* Vincent McHugh.
"I am very fond of the little ribs of women." ErPo
Talking with Soldiers. W. J. Turner. ChMP; FaBoTw; GTBS-D; MoBrPo
Tall/ Poetic/ Loud. Washiri (Poet). Kattie M. Cumbo. BOLo
Tall Ambrosia. Henry David Thoreau. PoEL-4
Tall and clothed in samite. A White Iris. Pauline B. Barrington. PoLF
Tall and thin. The Thin Man, a Sculpture. George Murray. NYTB
Tall Atlas, Jupiter, Hercules, Thor. Deities and Beasts. John Updike. ELU
Tall Axe-Man, The. Robert P. Tristram Coffin. PoFr
Tall Braunighrindas left her bed. A Legend of Camelot. George du Maurier. CenHV
Tall camels of the spirit, The. A World without Objects Is a Sensible Emptiness. Richard Wilbur. FiMAP; LiTM (1970 ed.); MoAmPo (1962 ed.); Po
Tall City. Susan Nichols Pulsifer. OCS
Tall clock is striking twelve, The. A Roxbury Garden. Amy Lowell. LaNeLa
Tall, cool and gentle, you are here. The Guest. Harold Monro. BoPe; NeMA
Tall dancer dances, The. The Dancer. Joseph Campbell. OBMV; OxBI; POTE
Tall ears. What Is It? Marie Louise Allen. TiPo
Tall elm, The. The Connecticut Elm. Emma Swan. PoPl
Tall Girl, The. John Crowe Ransom. Sonn; TDP
Tall Jane is dark who was burnished bright. For Jane Kane, Whom We Knew in Our Young Marriages. Bink Noll. ToPo
Tall, majestic monarch of the wood, The. The Mountain to the Pine. Clarence Hawkes. AA
Tall Man Executes a Jig, A. Irving Layton. MoCV; PoCh
Tall Men, The *sel.* Donald Davidson.
Fire on Belmont Street, *Epilogue.* MAP; MoAmPo (1942 ed.)
Tall Nettles. Edward Thomas. BoTP; BrPo; CBEP; ChTr; ELU; FaBoTw; HBMV; MoAB; MoBrPo; NeMA; POTE
Tall Oaks from Little Acorns Grow. David Everett. FaFP; OTD; TreF
(Boy Reciter, The.) BLPA
(Lines Spoken by a Boy of Seven Years.) AmePo
Tall palm tree sixty feet high, The. Prayer to the God Thot. *Unknown.* TTY
Tall people, short people. People. Lois Lenski. FaPON; OCS; SoPo
Tall pines wave, and the winds loudly roar, The. My Log Cabin Home. John A. Stone. SGR
Tall ships were wrecked here, and exotic cargoes. The Beachcomber. W. H. Oliver. AnNZ
Tall, somber [*or* sombre], grim, against the morning sky. Aspects of the Pines. Paul Hamilton Hayne. AA; AmPP (3d ed.); AnAmPo; HBV
Tall Stately Plants with Spikes and Forks of Gold. Frederick Goddard Tuckerman. *Fr.* Sonnets. AnNE
Tall Tale, A; or, A Moral Song. Phyllis Webb. OBCV
Tall Tale God. Mark Van Doren. CrMA
Tall Toms, The. Edwin Honig. NePA
Tall-topped acacia, you, full of branches. Elephant. *Unknown.* PeSA
Tall Trees. Edgar Daniel Kramer. PEDC
Tall Trees. Eileen Mathias. BoTP
Tall unpopular men. Dedication. Oliver St. John Gogarty. OBMV
Tall, with tow-hair, the texture of hide. Aubade: Dick, the Donkey-Boy. Sir Osbert Sitwell. HaMV
Tallahassee, *sel.* Andrew Merkel.
"Ann stood and watched the combers race to shore." CaP
Taller Today, We Remember. W. H. Auden. FaBoMo
(As Well as Can Be Expected.) CMoP
Talmud, The, *sels.* *Tr. fr. Hebrew.* TrJP
God to Man.
Good Man, The.
Why?
Talmud, The. Simeon Frug, *tr. fr. Yiddish by* Alice Stone Blackwell. TrJP
Talmud Student, The. Hayyim Nahman Bialik, *tr. fr. Hebrew by* Helena Frank. TrJP
Tam Glen. Burns. ALV; AWP; BEL; CEP; EnLi-2; InPo; JAWP; OAEP; OBEC; OxBS; TOP; WBP
Tam i' the Kirk. Violet Jacob. GoTS; HBMV; POTE
Tam Lin. *Unknown.* BaBo; CABL; ESPB; OBB, *longer vers.*; OBEV (new ed.), *longer vers.*; OxBB; OxBS; ViBoFo
(Tamlane.) BuBa
Tam o' Shanter. Burns. BEL; BeLS; BOHV; BoLiVe, *sl. abr.*; CABL; CEP; EiCL; EiPP; EnL; EnLi-2; EnLit; EnRP; GoTL; GoTS; HBV; NoP; OAEP; OBEC; OnSP; OuHeWo; OxBS; PeER; PoE; SeCePo; ShBV-3; TOP; TrGrPo, *sl. abr.*; UnPo (1st ed.), *sl. abr.*; ViBoPo; WHA
Tam o' the linn cam up the gait. *Unknown.* FaBoCh
Tam Samson's Elegy. Burns. PoEL-4
Tamar, *sel.* Robinson Jeffers.
"They two had unbridled the horses." AnAmPo
Tamar and the Nymph. Walter Savage Landor. *Fr.* Gebir. VA
(Shepherd and the Nymph, The.) OBNC; PeER
(Tamar's Wrestling.) EnRP
Tamazunchali. Witter Bynner. NYTB
Tamburlaine the Great, *sels.* Christopher Marlowe.
"Ah faire Zenocrate, divine Zenocrate," *fr.* Pt. I, Act V, sc. ii. AtBAP; PoEL-2; ViBoPo
"And ride in triumph through Persepolis!" *fr.* Pt. I, Act II, sc. v. FOL; MyFE; TrGrPo; WHA
(Persepolis.) CLwM
"Black[e] is the beauty of the brightest day," *fr.* Pt. II, Act II, sc. iv. AtBAP; BoW; ViBoPo
(Divine Zenocrate.) WHA
(To Entertain Divine Zenocrate.) ChTr
"Disdains Zenocrate to live with me," *fr.* Pt. I, Act. I, sc. ii. ViBoPo
(Tamburlaine to Zenocrate, *shorter sel.*) WHA
Emperor of the Threefold World, *fr.* Pt. II, Act IV, sc. iii. TrGrPo
(Bloody Conquests of Mighty Tamburlaine, The.) ChTr
("Forward, then, ye jades," *longer sel.*) ViBoPo
Fair Is Too Foul an Epithet, *fr.* Pt. I, Act V, sc. ii. LiTB
"Nature that framed us of four elements," *fr.* Pt. I, Act II, sc. vii. MyFE; PoEL-2; TrGrPo
(Perfect Bliss and Sole Felicity.) SeCePo
Now Clear the Triple Region of the Air, *fr.* Pt. I, Act IV, sc. ii. TrGrPo
Tamburlaine's Love. ShBV-4
"Thirst of reign and sweetness of a crown, The," *fr.* Pt. I, Act II, sc. vii. ViBoPo
"Those walléd garrisons will I subdue," *fr.* Pt. I, Act III, sc. iii. ViBoPo
"Virgins, in vain you labour to prevent," *fr.* Pt. I, Act V, sc. i. MyFE
"What is beauty, saith my sufferings, then?" *fr.* Pt. I, Act V, sc. ii. MyFE
(Beauty.) TrGrPo
(If All the Pens That Ever Poets Held.) ChTr
Tame Cat. Ezra Pound. ELU
Tame Hare, The. Norman Nicholson. FaBoMo
Tame Stag, The. John Gay. *Fr.* Fables. CBEP; EiCP
Tamed by Miltown, we lie on Mother's bed. Man and Wife. Robert Lowell. AmPP (5th ed.); MaPo (1969 ed.); OPoP
Tameless in his stately pride, along the lake of islands. The Loon. Alfred Billings Street. AA
Tamely, fraile body, 'abstaine to day: to day. The Annuntiation and Passion. John Donne. MaMe
Tamer and Hawk. Thom Gunn. NePoEA
Tamerlane. Victor J. Daley. PoAu-1
Tamerlane. Poe. AmP; AP; MAmP
"I have no words—alas!—to tell," *sel.* LO
Taming of the Shrew, The, *sels.* Shakespeare.

Taming (continued)
Petruchio Is Undaunted by Katharina, *fr.* I, ii. TreFT
"Why, then thou canst not break her to the lute?" *fr.* II, i. UnS
Tamlane. *Unknown. See* Tam Lin.
Tammuz. Rayner Heppenstall. WaP
Tampa Robins. Sidney Lanier. PoRL
Tampico. Grace Hazard Conkling. HBMV
"Tan Ta Ra, Cries Mars . . ." David Wagoner. NePoAm-2
Tan Ta Ra Ran Tan Tant: Cries Mars on Bloody Rapier. *Unknown.* NCEP
Tanagra! think not I forget. Corinna [from Athens] to Tanagra. Walter Savage Landor. *Fr.* Pericles and Aspasia. OBEV (new ed.); OBNC; OBRV; OBVV; TOP; ViBoPo
Tancred, *sels.* Laurence Dakin. CaP
"All night I raced the moon," *fr.* II, i.
"How gently sings my soul and whets its wings," *fr.* III, i.
Song: "Peasant sun went crushing grapes, The," *fr.* I, i.
Tandaradei ("Under der Linden"). Walther von der Vogelweide, *tr. fr. German by* Ford Madox Ford. AWP; LiTW
(Under the Lime Tree.) ErPo, *tr. by* Thomas Lovell Beddoes; UnTE, *tr. by* Gillian Barker *and* Kenneth Gee
(Under the Lindens.) CTC
Tang! tang! went the gong's wild roar. Night Quarters. Henry Howard Brownell. GN
Tangere. Theodore Enslin. CoPo
Tangle of iron rods and spluttered beams, A. Les Halles d'Ypres. Edmund Blunden. MMA
Tangled I Was in Love's Snare. Sir Thomas Wyatt. *See* Lover Rejoiceth, The.
Tangled in nets. Fishers. Albert Reginald Gold. ChIP; OQP
Tangled in sea weed minutes. The Baroness and the Black Musician. Larry Neal. BF
Tangled Was I in Love's Snare. Sir Thomas Wyatt. *See* Lover Rejoiceth, The.
Tanglewood. Francis Sweeney. JKCP (1955 ed.)
Tangmalangaloo. P. J. Hartigan. PoAu-1
Tanist. James Stephens. NYTB; OnYI
Tank, The. Roland Robinson. PoAu-2
Tank Town. John Atherton. NYBP
Tanka (I-VIII). Lewis Alexander. CDC
Tanka: "Blossoms of the plum." *Unknown, tr. fr. Japanese by* Eunice Tietjens. InP
Tanka: Cry of the Crane, The. Tsurayuki, *tr. fr. Japanese by* Arthur Waley. InP
Tanka: "In the evening/ Quiet of the country town." Noin Hoshi, *tr. fr. Japanese by* Nobuyuki Yuasa. Po
Tanka: "Men of valor, The." Akahito, *tr. fr. Japanese by* Arthur Waley. *Fr.* Manyo Shu. InP
("Men of valór, The.") AWP
Tanka: Reflection, A. Saigyo Hoshi, *tr. fr. Japanese by* Arthur Waley. InP
("Those ships which left.") AWP; LiTW
Tanker. Christopher Middleton. NMP
Tanned blonde, The. The Once-over. Paul Blackburn. ErPo; NeAP
Tannhäuser, *sel.* Heine, *tr. fr. German by* Emma Lazarus.
Best Religion, The. TrJP
Tannhäuser. William Morton Payne. AA
Tansy for August. Theodore Enslin. CoPo
Tant' Amare. *Unknown, tr. fr. Spanish by* Paul Blackburn. ErPo
Tantalus. Paulus Silentiarius, *tr. fr. Greek by* Dudley Fitts. LiTW
(Tantalos.) ErPo
Tantalus; Texas. *Unknown, at. to* Joaquin Miller. HBV
(Llano Estacado, The.) CoSo
Tantanoola Tiger, The. Max Harris. MoBS; PoAu-2
Tantivee [*or* Tantivy], tivee, tivee, tivee, high and low. Hunting Song [*or* Solon's Song *or* Brother Solon's Hunting Song]. Thomas D'Urfey. *Fr.* The Marriage-Hater Match'd. CavP; CEP; SeCL; SeEP
Tantramar Revisited. Sir Charles G. D. Roberts. CaP; OBCV
Tantum Ergo Sacramentum. *Unknown, tr. fr. Latin.* WHL
Tao. Alfred Goldsworthy Bailey. CaP
Tao Teh King. *sels. Unknown. tr. to* Lao-tzu, *tr. fr. Chinese.*
Endless Self. *tr. by* Witter Bynner. OnPM
Gentle Touch, A, *tr. by* Witter Bynner. OnPM
He Walks at Peace. TRV
He Who Feels Punctured, *tr. by* Witter Bynner. OnPM
"How can a man's life keep its course," *tr. by* Witter Bynner. WaKn
In a Land, *tr. by* Witter Bynner. OnPM
Knowledge Studies Others, *tr. by* Witter Bynner. OnPM
Lesson of Water, *tr. by* Witter Bynner. OnPM
Life, *tr. by* Witter Bynner. OnPM
"Slaying of multitudes should be mourned with sorrow, The." TRV
Those Who Know Do Not Tell, *tr. by* Witter Bynner. OnPM
To Be, *tr. by* Witter Bynner. OnPM
True Freedom, *tr. by* Witter Bynner. OnPM
Weapons of Evil, *tr. by* Lin Yutang. MaRV
Taoist Monk, The. Tu Hsün Hao, *tr. fr. Chinese by* Henry H. Hart. OnPM
Tape collage sound bursts. The Scene Pope John Wouldn't Let Fellini Film. Dan Georgakas. ThO
Tape for the Turn of the Year, *sel.* A. R. Ammons.
"Two jays in the sumac." FRC
Taped to the wall of my cell are 47 pictures: 47 black. The Idea of Ancestry. Etheridge Knight. BALP
Tapering stars glint cool. Challengers. Alfred Dorn. GoYe
Tapers. Frances Angevine Gray. FiSC
Tapers in the great God's hall, The. By Night. Philip Jerome Cleveland. MaRV; TRV
Tapestry, The. Stefan George, *tr. fr. German by* Carol North Valhope *and* Ernst Morwitz. LiTW
Tapestry for Bayeux, A. George Starbuck. TDP
Tapestry Trees. William Morris. BoNaP; FaPON; MPB; OHIP
Tapestry Weavers, The. Anson G. Chester. BLPA; BLRP; WBLP
Taps. Lizette Woodworth Reese. DD; HH; OHIP
Tapster, fille another ale! Drinking Song. *Unknown.* EnLit
Tar for All Weathers, The. Charles Dibdin. OTPC (1923 ed.)
Tara. *Unknown, tr. fr. Middle Irish by* Edward Gwynn. *Fr.* Dinnshenchas. OnYI
Tara Is Grass. *Unknown, tr. fr. Modern Irish by* Padraic Pearse. AnIL; AnIV
Tarantella. Hilaire Belloc. CH; FaBoCh; GoBC; HT; LoGBV; MoBrPo; MoShBr; MoSiPe; NeMA; OBMV; OtMeF; ShBV-2; WePo
Tarantula, The. Reed Whittemore. CoAP
Tarantula or the Dance of Death. Anthony Hecht. CoAP
Tarantula rattling at the lily's foot, The. O Carib Isle! Hart Crane. AP; MoPo; NePA; OnHM
Tardiness. Gelett Burgess. BBGG
Tardy George. *Unknown.* GA, *abr.*; PAH
Tardy Spring. George Meredith. OBEV (1st ed.)
Target of the hunting shepherd boys. Zebra Stallion. *Unknown.* PeSA
Target Practice. Donald Finkel. NePoEA-2
Tarpauling Jacket. *Unknown.* DTC; OxBoLi; PeVV
Tarras Moon. James K. Baxter. AnNZ
Tarry a moment, happy feet. The Statues. Laurence Binyon. OBEV (new ed.); OBVV
Tarry Buccaneer, The. John Masefield. MCCG
Tarry sweete love. *Unknown.* SeCSL
Tarry with me, O my Saviour! The Final Struggle. Caroline Sprague Smith. SoP
"Tarry Ye." *Unknown.* STF
Tartars led in chains. The Prisoner. Po Chü-i. PoFr
Tartary. Walter de la Mare. GaP; GoTP; HBMV; PoRh; SP
(Lord of Tartary.) ShBV-1
Tarye [*or* Tary] no lenger [*or* longer]; toward thyn herytage [*or* heritage]. Vox Ultima Crucis. John Lydgate. OBEV; OxBoCh; StJW
Task, The. Robert Bhain Campbell. MoPo
Task, The, *sels.* William Cowper.
City and Country Life, *fr.* I. CoBE
Discipline in Education, *fr.* II. CoBE
England, *fr.* II. FiP, *shorter sel.*; OBEC; TOP
(Love of England.) LoBV
"For I have lov'd the rural walk through lanes," *fr.* I. EnRP
(Rural Walk, The.) TOP
Garden, The, III. CEP; EiCL; EiPP; EnPE
God Made the Country, *fr.* I. FiP; PoEL-3
("God made the country, and man made the town.") AnFE; EnRP
(Town and Country.) FaBoEn

"I say the pulpit (in the sober use)," *fr.* II. TRV
"I was a stricken deer, that left the herd," *fr.* III. EnRP; MaRV; OAEP; OxBoCh; PeER
(In His Mental Illness, William Cowper Finds He Is Not Alone.) BoC
(Self-Portrait.) CoBE
(Stricken Deer, The.) FiP; LoBV, *longer sel.*
Landscape, *fr.* I. CoBE
Nature and God, *fr.* I. CoBE
"Night was winter in his roughest mood, The," *fr.* VI. EnRP
(Winter Scene.) OBEC
"Oh for a lodge in some vast wilderness," *fr.* II. EnRP; OAEP, *longer sel.*
(Slavery.) CoBE
Of Preachers, *fr.* II. SoP
Poetic Pains, *fr.* II. FiP
(Poetry; Satire and Pulpit.) CoBE
("There is a pleasure in poetic pains.") PP
Postman, The, *fr.* IV. CoBE
(Post-Boy, The.) FiP
Preachers; the True vs. the Insincere, *fr.* II. MaRV
Slaves Cannot Breathe in England, 7 *ll. fr.* II. OBEC
Sofa, The, I. CEP; EiCP; NoP, *shorter sel.*; OAEP, *abr.*
Time-Piece, The, II. BEL
True Preacher, The, *fr.* II. MaRV
"Who loves a garden, loves a greenhouse too," *fr.* III. BoPe
"Whose freedom is by suff'rance, and at will," *fr.* V. EnRP; PoFr
Winter, *fr.* IV. OBEC
("Oh Winter, ruler of th' inverted year," *longer sel.*)
Winter Evening ("Come, Evening"), *fr.* IV. CoBE
(Evening.) OBEC
Winter Evening, The ("Hark! 'tis the twanging horn"), IV. EiPP; EnLi-2; EnLit; OAEP; SeCePo, *sel.*9; TOP, *sel.*
Winter Morning Walk, The, V. EiCP; PoEL-3
Wisdom ("Knowledge and wisdom, far from being one"), *fr.* VI. MaRV
Woodman's Dog, The, *fr.* V. BoTP; ELU; OTPC (1946 ed.); PCD; PCH
"Would I describe a preacher, such as Paul," *fr.* II. TRV
Task, The. Ruth Pitter. MoBrPo; TrGrPo (1942 ed.)
Task That Is Given to You, The. Edwin Markham. WBLP
Tasker Norcross. E. A. Robinson. CMoP
Taste and Spirit. Christopher Anstey. The New Bath Guide, X. CEP; EiCL
Taste of Prayer, The. Ralph W. Seager. TrPWD
Taste of Space, The. A. J. M. Smith. PV
Tasting the Earth. James Oppenheim. MAP; MoAmPo (1942 ed.); PFY
Tattered outlaw of the earth, The. The Donkey. G. K. Chesterton. HBVY; TOP; WGRP
Tattering of rain and then the reign, A. Darkling Summer, Ominous Dusk, Rumerous Rain. Delmore Schwartz. WIRo
Tattoo. Wallace Stevens. AnFE; APA; CoAnAm; LiTA; NP
Tattooed. William Plomer. ChMP
Tattooed Man, The. Harry B. Smith. *Fr.* The Idol's Eye. InMe
Taught by no priest, but by our beating hearts. Faith to Each Other. *Unknown.* OQP
Taught early that his mother's skin was the sign of error. Mr. Z. M. Carl Holman. Kal
Taught from your artfull straines my faire. *Unknown.* SeCSL
Taught Me Purple. Evelyn Tooley Hunt. OCS
Tavern. Edna St. Vincent Millay. GaP; OTPC (1946 ed.)
Tawny are the leaves turned, but they still hold. Antique Harvesters. John Crowe Ransom. AnFE; AP; APA; CoAnAm; CoBMV; CrMA; FaBoEn; InPo; MAP; MoAB; MoAmPo; NoP; OxBA; WoL
Tawny gleam in the sunlight, A. The First Robin. Lilian Leveridge. CaP
Tawny in a pasture by the true sea. The Forgotten Rock. Richard Eberhart. NePA
Tawny iris, The—oh! the slim-necked swan. Flowers. Stéphane Mallarmé. SyP
Tax-Gatherer, The. John Banister Tabb. GN; UTS
Tax not the royal saint with vain expense. Inside of [*or* Within] King's College Chapel, Cambridge. Wordsworth. *Fr.* Ecclesiastical Sonnets. EnLi-2; EnRP; EPN; GoBC; GTBS; GTBS-D; GTBS-P; GTBS-W; GTSE; GTSL; MaRV; MBW-2; OAEP; OBNC; OBRV; OxBoCh; PeER
Taxes. Don L. Lee. BOLo
Taxes. Tu Hsün Hao, *tr. fr. Chinese by* Henry H. Hart. OnPM
Taxi, The. Amy Lowell. MAP; MoAmPo
Taxicabs scuttle by on the wet streets. Whaddaya Do for Action in This Place? George Starbuck. NePoEA-2
Taxis. Rachel Field. FaPON; GFA; MPB; PoRh; SoPo; StVeCh (1940 ed.); TiPo
Tay Bridge Disaster, The. William McGonagall. EvOK
Te Deum. Charles Reznikoff. TrJP
Te Deum Laudamus. *Unknown, tr. fr. Latin.* MaRV; WGRP; WHL, *sl. diff. tr.*
(Te Deum, The, *tr. by* Dryden.) AWP; JAWP; OuHeWo; WBP
Te Deum of the Commonplace, A. John Oxenham. *See* Little Te Deum of the Commonplace, A.
"Te Judice." Frederick George Scott. PeCV
Te Martyrum Candidatus. Lionel Johnson. ACP; BoC; CAW; HBV; JKCP; OBMV; OxBoCh; PoLi
Te-whit! te-whit [*or* To-whit! to-whit]! te-whee!/ Will you listen to me? Who Stole the Bird's Nest? Lydia Maria Child. OTPC; PRWS; SAS
Tea. Jacqueline Embry. HBMV; YaD
Tea at the Palaz of Hoon. Wallace Stevens. CBEP; FaBoMo; NP
Tea Flowers. Rito, *tr. fr. Japanese by* William N. Porter. MPB
Tea garden shows you how, A. Bridge. A. R. Ammons. CoAP
Tea in a Space-Ship. James Kirkup. POTi
Tea-Party, A [*or* The]. Kate Greenaway. MPB; OTPC; PPL
("In the pleasant green garden.") TiPo (1952 ed.)
Tea party at Le Cannet, The. Bonnard: A Novel. Richard Howard. CoAP; NYBP
Tea-rose tea gown, etc., The. Ezra Pound. *Fr.* Hugh Selwyn Mauberley. CMoP; FaBoMo; ILP; LiTG; MoAmPo (1962 ed.); MoVE; NePA; OxBA; SeCeV; UnPo (3d ed.)
Tea Shop, The. Ezra Pound. WePo
Tea-Tree and the Lyrebird, The. Roland Robinson. NeLNL
Teach Me. Freda Hanbury Allen. SoP
Teach me, Father, how to go. A Prayer. Edwin Markham. BoTP; DD; HBMV; HBVY; MaRV; OTPC (1946 ed.); PGD; PoRL; RG; SoP; StVeCh; TrPWD; TRV; TSW; WGRP
Teach me, life. Only the Heart. Marjorie Freeman Campbell. CaP
Teach me, my God and King. The Elixir. George Herbert. AnAnS-1; BoLiVe; BoTP; FaBoCh; GN; LoGBV; MaMe; MaRV; MeP; NoP; OHIP; PCH; SeCV-1; SoP; ThGo; TrGrPo; WGRP
Teach Me, O Lord. Grand Duke Constantine of Russia. SoP
Teach me some prayer. For Instruction. Vassar Miller. ToPo
Teach me the ritual that runs beyond. Worship. Robert Whitaker. TrPWD
Teach me the secret of thy loveliness. To a Wind Flower. Madison Cawein. AA; HBV
Teach Me to Live. *Unknown.* SoP
(Harder Task, The.) BLRP; MaRV
Teach me to love—for what is wealth or fame? My Prayer. Flora Emily Smith. SoP
Teach me to love? Go teach thy self more wit. The Prophet. Abraham Cowley. TrGrPo
Teach not thy parent's mother to extract. *Unknown.* WhC
Teach the child to pray to the blue waves. The Child's Prayer. Robert de Montesquiou-Fezensac. CAW
Teach us, good Lord, to serve Thee as Thou deservest. Teach Us to Serve Thee, Lord. St. Ignatius Loyola. SoP; TRV
Teach Us to Die. Arthur Penrhyn Stanley. VA
Teach Us to Mark This, God. Franz Werfel, *tr. fr. German by* Jacob Sloan. TrJP
Teach Us to Serve Thee, Lord. St. Ignatius Loyola, *tr. fr. Latin.* SoP; TRV
Teacher, The. Leslie Pinckney Hill. BANP; FaChP; MaRV; PoNe; SoP; TrPWD
Teacher, The. Hildegarde Hoyt Swift. ChIP; MaRV; OQP
Teacher, The. Annette Wynne. GaP
Teacher, The. Virginia Brady Young. GoYe
Teacher Sees a Boy, The. Margaret Morningstar. STF
Teacher should impart what's true, A. Flower for a Professor's Garden of Verses. Irwin Edman. InMe

Teachers, The. C. V. Pilcher. OQP
Teacher's Dream, The. William Henry Venable. BeLS
Teacher's Prayer, A. Frances Ridley Havergal. *See* Lord, Speak to Me That I May Speak.
Teacher's Prayer, The. "Gabriela Mistral," *tr. fr. Spanish by* James H. McLean. MaRV
Teacher's Prayer, The. Nancy Byrd Turner. SoP
Teaching, I Am Taught. Hazel M. Lindsey. SoP
Teaching of Mohammed, The. Mohammed, *tr. fr. Arabic by* J. M. Rodwell. *Fr.* The Koran. WoL
Teak Forest, The, *sel.* "Laurence Hope."
For This Is Wisdom. PoLF; TreFT
(Wisdom?) OtMeF
Teams, The. Henry Lawson. BoAu; NeLNL; PoAu-1
Teamster's Farewell, A. Carl Sandburg. CoBA
Teamster's Song, *with music.* *Unknown.* TrAS
Teapot Dragon, The. Rupert Sargent Holland. OTPC; UTS
Teapots and Quails. Edward Lear. GoJo
Tear, The. Byron. Par
(Hours of Idleness.) EvOK
Tear [*or* Teare], The. Richard Crashaw. EnLi-1; GTBS-W; LiTB; MaMe; MasP; OAEP; SeCP; UnPo
Tear. Arthur Rimbaud, *tr. fr. French by* James McMichael. PIA
Tear bedews my Delia's eye, A. The Kid. William Shenstone. OTPC (1923 ed.)
Tear down the Ivory Tower! Bring Torches. A. M. Stephen. CaP
Tear Down the Walls. Edgar Cooper Mason. OQP
Tear out my tongue: I shall still have hands. The Forest. Paul Zech. OnPM
Tear was in her eye, A. Three Rimas, 3. Gustavo Adolfo Bécquer. *Fr.* Rimas. LiTW
Teare, The. Richard Crashaw. *See* Tear, The.
Teares doe not spare. *Unknown.* SeCSL
Tearin' Out-a Wilderness, *with music.* *Unknown.* ABF
Tears. Elizabeth Barrett Browning. OQP; SoP
Tears. George Rostrevor Hamilton. POTE
Tears. Khansa, *tr. fr. Arabic by* R. A. Nicholson. AWP; JAWP; WBP
Tears. Lizette Woodworth Reese. AA; HBV; HBVY; InP; MAP; MaRV; MCCG; MoAmPo; NeMA; OQP; PFY; TreFS; WGRP; WHA
Tears. Edith Sitwell. CMoP; MoPo
Tears. Edward Thomas. CBEP; GTBS-P; LiTB; MoPW; PoE
Tears. Feodor Ivanovich Tyutchev, *tr. fr. Russian by* Babette Deutsch. OnPM
Tears ("Ashamed of tears?"). *Unknown.* SoP
Tears ("Weep you no more. . ."). *Unknown.* *See* Weep You No More, Sad Fountains.
Tears. Walt Whitman. AnAmPo; NePA
Tears against the Moon. Thomas Walsh. CAW
Tears and a Dream. Marsha Ann Jackson. TNV
Tears and Rain. Paul Verlaine. *See* Il pleut doucement sur la ville.
Tears and Song. *Unknown, tr. fr. Spanish by* Havelock Ellis. OnPM
Tears at the Grave of Sir Albertus Morton. Sir Henry Wotton. AnAnS-2; SeCP
Tears cannot wash the horror from our faces. J.F.K. D. L. O'Neill. OTD
Tears, ere thy death, for many a one I shed. Tears. Khansa. AWP; JAWP; WBP
Tears Fall within Mine Heart. Paul Verlaine. *See* Il pleut doucement sur la ville.
Tears, Flow No More. Lord Herbert of Cherbury. AnAnS-2; AtBAP; CBEP; ElL; OBS; SeCP
Tears for my lady dead. Heliodore Dead. Meleager. VA
Tears for Sale. Leonora Speyer. HBMV
Tears, human tears, that pour forth beyond telling. Tears. Feodor Ivanovich Tyutchev. OnPM
Tears, Idle Tears [I Know Not What They Mean]. Tennyson. *Fr.* The Princess, Pt. IV. AnFE; AtBAP; BEL; BoLiVe; BWP; CABA; CaFP; CBV; DiPo; EG; ELP; EnL; EnLi-2; EnLit; EPN; FaFP; FiP; ForPo; FosPo; GTBS; GTBS-P; GTBS-W; GTSL; HBV; InvP; LiTB; LiTG; MaPo; MasP; MBW-2; MCCG; NeHB; NoP; OBNC; OBVV; PG (1945 ed.); PoAn; PoE; PoEL-5; PoFS; PoIE; PoPo; PoSa; PoVP; ShBV-4; StP; TreF; TrGrPo; UnPo; VA; ViBoPo; ViPP; WePo; WHA
(Lyrics from "The Princess.") OuHeWo
(Song: "Tears, idle tears, I know not what they mean".) FaBoEn; PoPl; TOP
(Songs from "The Princess.") AWP; InPo; JAWP; OAEP; SeCeV; ViPo; WBP
Tears in my heart that weeps. Paul Verlaine. *See* Il pleut doucement sur la ville.
Tears in Spring. William Ellery Channing. AA
Tears in the eyes of the surgeon. To My Friends. Peter De Vries. FiBHP
Tears, long-stayed, that well. Rain at Night. Helen Walker Homan. JKCP (1955 ed.)
Tears of a Muse in America, The. F. T. Prince. FaBoMo
Tears of Amynta, The, for the Death of Damon. Dryden. MaPo
Tears of Fancy, The, *sels.* Thomas Watson.
"Each tree did boast the wished springtime's pride." Sonn; TuPP
"Go idle lines unpolished rude and base." Sonn
"I saw the object of my pining thought." Sonn; TuPP
(Sonnet.) ElL
"In clouds she shines, and so obscurely shineth." Sonn; TuPP
Tears of Peace, The. George Chapman. *See* Euthymiae Raptus; or, The Teares of Peace.
Tears of Scotland, The. Tobias Smollett. CEP; OBEC
Tears of the Poplars, The. Edith M. Thomas. AA; AnAmPo
Tears of the widower, when he sees. In Memoriam A. H. H., XIII. Tennyson. EnLi-2; EPN; ViPo; VP
Tears of the World. Mu'tamid, King of Seville, *tr. fr. Arabic by* Dulcie L. Smith. AWP
Tears on my pillow—who has wept. Tears against the Moon. Thomas Walsh. CAW
Tears on the Death of Meliades, *sel.* William Drummond of Hawthornden.
Lament: "Chaste maids which haunt fair Aganippe's well." LoBV
Tears pouring from the [*or* this] face of stone. The Vase of Tears. Stephen Spender. AtBAP; LO; POTE
Tears! tears! tears! Tears. Walt Whitman. AnAmPo; NePA
Tears that never quite touch earth. White Violets. Benjamin R. C. Low. HBMV
Tears that weep for shattered Sunday schools. The Song of Fire. Rolland Snellings. BF
Tears through the earth I send you, Heliodora. To Heliodora, Dead. Meleager, *tr. fr. Greek by* L. R. Lind. LiTW
Tears will betray all pride, but when ye mourn him. Parnell [*or* Parnell's Memory]. Thomas Kettle. ACP; AnIV; JKCP (1926 ed.)
Teased and titillated by the need. Beyond Biology. Robert Francis. NePoAm
Teasing Lovers, The. Horace. *See* Reconciliation, The.
Technique. Burnham Eaton. GoYe
Technique. Langdon Elwyn Mitchell. *Fr.* To a Writer of the Day. AA
Technique of Laughter, The. Jascha Kessler. AmPC
Technique of Love, The. Jascha Kessler. AmPC
Technique of Power, The. Jascha Kessler. AmPC
Technogamia, *sels.* Barten Holyday.
Song: "O harmless feast." ElL
"Tobacco's a musician." TuPP
Technologies. George Starbuck. NYBP
Tecumseh, *sels.* Charles Mair.
Buffalo Herds, *fr.* IV, vi. VA
"Tell me more of those unrivaled wastes." CaP
"He comes! Yohewah! the Great Spirit, comes," *fr.* V, ii. PeCV
Iena's Song, *fr.* II, iv. VA
Lefroy in the Forest, *abr.* VA
"Once we were strong," *fr.* II, iv. PeCV
"There was a time on this fair continent," *fr.* I, ii. OBCV
"We left/ The silent forest," *fr* IV, vi. OBCV
Tecumseh and the Eagles. Bliss Carman. PoFr
Teddy unt Me unt Gott. *Unknown.* BLPA
Teddy's Wonderings. John Kendrick Bangs. BiCB
Tee Roo, *with music.* *Unknown.* *See* Farmer's Curst Wife, The.
Teeming the host, the ash-tree budding. Tercets. Llywarch Hen. LiTW
Teemothy Hatch. Wilson MacDonald. WhC
Teeney and Weeney together are going. Green Grass and White Milk. Winifred Welles. TiPo

Teeny Cow, The. *Unknown.* *See* Father Grumble.
Teeters on the top of the stairs. The Aquarium Dream. Florence Trefethen. NYTB
Teeth on the saw. Piney Woods. Malcolm Cowley. NYBP
Teeth you see up here, The. Oisin. *Unknown.* KiLC
Teignmouth. Keats. PeER
Telegram. William Wise. TiPo (1959 ed.)
Telegram One. Adrian Mitchell. PV
Telegraph, The. Annette Wynne. GFA
Telephone, The. Hilaire Belloc. MoVE
Telephone, The. Edward Field. CAD
Telephone, The. Robert Frost. AnFE; APA; CLwM; CoAnAm; HBV
Telephone Conversation. Wole Soyinka. FIW; TTY
Telephone line goes cold, A. The Farm on the Great Plains. William Stafford. PIA; PoCh
Telephone Pole, The. Karel van den Oever, *tr. fr. Dutch by* Adriaan J. Barnouw. OnPM
Telephone Poles. John Updike. FIW
Telephone poles, The. Crossing Kansas by Train. Donald Justice. NYBP
Telescope, The. J. C. Hall. HaMV
Television-Movie. Kirby Congdon. WOW
Tell all my mourners. Wake. Langston Hughes. ShM
Tell all the truth but tell it slant. Emily Dickinson. AmPP (5th ed.); AP; DiPo; LiTA; LiTM; MAmP; MaPo; MWA-2; NePA; NoP; PAn; PoeP; PoPo
Tell All the World. Harry Kemp. HBMV
Tell Forth His Fame. *Unknown.* BePJ
Tell Freedom, *sel.* Peter Abrahams.
Me, Colored. PBA
Tell her I love/ she will remember me. Poems [*or* Stanzas] for My Daughter. Horace Gregory. MAP; MoAmPo; MoVE
Tell Her So. *Unknown.* PoToHe (new ed.)
Tell him it's all [*or* the tale is] a lie. A Learned Mistress. *Unknown.* KiLC; OBMV
Tell Him, O Night. *Unknown, tr. fr. Arabic by* E. Powys Mathers. *Fr.* The Thousand and One Nights. AWP; LiTW
Tell Him So. James Arthur Edgerton. MaRV
Tell Him So. *Unknown.* BLPA; WBLP
Tell him the tale is a lie! *See* Tell him it's all a lie.
Tell hir he that sent hir this. *Unknown.* SeCSL
Tell it to the forest fire, tell it to the moon. The Dream Songs, XLIV. John Berryman. NaP
Tell Jesus. *Unknown.* BePJ; STF
Tell Me. Edith M. Thomas. *Fr.* The Inverted Torch. AA
Tell me a story, Father, please do. Request Number. G. N. Sprod. FiBHP
Tell Me a Word. D. H. Lawrence. SiTL
Tell me, abandon'd miscreant, prithee tell. Upon the Author of a Play Call'd Sodom. John Oldham. PeRV
Tell me about soul. Soul. Barbara Simmons. BF
Tell me about that harvest field. Real Property. Harold Monro. BoNaP; BoPe
Tell me about the good things. How Long Has Trane Been Gone? Jayne Cortez. WSL
Tell Me about the Master! *Unknown.* SoP
Tell me Beatrice. The Van Gogh Influence. Shel Silverstein. ELU
"Tell me, Belinda, prithee do." Celia and Belinda. Colley Cibber. *Fr.* Woman's Wit. SeCL
Tell me bright boy, tell me my golden lad. On the Prodigall. Richard Crashaw. MaMe
Tell me, dear, in terms laconic. The Conservative Shepherd to His Love. Jack D'Arcy. InMe
Tell Me, Dearest, What Is Love? 3 *sts.* Beaumont *and* Fletcher. *Fr.* The Captain, II, ii. ElL; SeEP; ViBoPo
(What Is Love?) HBV
Tell me, Dorinda, why so gay. On the Countess of Dorchester. Charles Sackville. CavP
Tell me, Echo fair! Lover and Echo. Carrol O'Daly. OnYI
Tell me, Fancy, sweetest child. Fancy's Home. W. H. Davies. AtBAP
"Tell me, good dog, whose tomb you guard so well." The Tomb of Diogenes. *Unknown.* AWP; JAWP; OnPM; WBP
Tell me, good Hobbinoll, what garres thee greete? April[l]. Spenser. *Fr.* The Shepheardes Calender. EnLi-1; PoEL-1; ReEn; ReIE; SiCE
Tell me, hair of her head, where I should lie. The Hair's Breadth. Nicholas Moore. NeBP
Tell me is there anything lovelier. Greenness. Angelina Weld Grimké. CDC
Tell me, is there sovereign cure. Edith M. Thomas. *Fr.* The Inverted Torch. AA
Tell Me, Lydia ("Cum tu, Lydia"). Horace, *tr. fr. Latin by* William Boscawen. Odes, I, 13. OnPM
Tell me more of those unrivalled wastes. Charles Mair. *Fr.* Tecumseh, IV, vi. CaP
Tell Me, Mother. Sybil Leonard Armes. FaChP
Tell Me, My Heart, if This Be Love. George Lyttelton. *See* Song: "When Delia on the plain appears."
Tell me (my love) since Hymen ty'de. An Hymeneall Dialogue. Thomas Carew. AnAnS-2; SeCP
Tell me, my patient friends — awaiters of messages. Speech to a Crowd. Archibald MacLeish. MoAB; MoAmPo; NePA
Tell Me No More. William Drummond of Hawthornden. TrGrPo
Tell Me No More. Henry King. SeCL
(Sonnet: "Tell me no more how fair she is.") AnAnS-2; CavP; EnLoPo; MeLP; MePo; OBS; SeCP; SeEP; ViBoPo
("Tell me no more how fair she is.") EG
(That Distant Bliss.) TrGrPo
Tell me no more I am deceived. Song [*or* The Better Bargain]. Congreve. ALV; UnTE
Tell me no more I am deceived. Song. Sir George Etherege. CavP
Tell me no more of gives of brasse. *Unknown.* SeCSL
Tell me no more of minds embracing minds. No Platonic [*or* Platonique] Love. William Cartwright. CABA; ErPo; FosPo; ILP; InvP; LiTB; PoEL-2; SiTL
Tell me no secret, friend. The Burden. Francesca Yetunde Pereira. PBA
Tell me noe more tis love. *Unknown.* SeCSL
Tell Me Not Here [It Needs Not Saying]. A. E. Housman. CBEP; ChMP; CoBMV; ELP; FaBoEn; GTBS-D; GTBS-P; LiTM; MaPo; MoPo; MoPW; MoVE; OBNC
Tell me not I my time misspend. Song. *At. to* Sir John Eaton *and to* Phillip King. SeCL
Tell me not in joyous numbers. Stephen Crane. MWA-2
Tell me not, in mournful numbers. A Psalm of Life. Longfellow. AA; AmePo; AnNE; CoBA; FaBoBe; DiPo; FaPL; HBV; HBVY; MaRV; NeHB; OHFP; OTD; PaPo; PoLF; PoPl; SoP; TreF; UnPo; WBLP; YaD
Tell me not, O Soul that slumbers, *parody.* A Psalm of Life. Andrew Lang. CenHV
Tell me not of a face that's fair. The Resolve. Alexander Brome. CavP; EG; LiTL; LO; OBEV; SeCL
Tell me not of joy: there's none. The Dead Sparrow [*or* Lesbia on Her Sparrow]. William Cartwright. CavP; CH; LO
Tell Me Not of Morrows, Sweet. Augusta Davies Webster. VA
Tell me not sweet I am unkind[e]. To Lucasta, [on] Going to the Wars [*or* Warres]. Richard Lovelace. ALV; AnAnS-2; AnFE; AtBAP; AWP; BBV (1923 ed.); BEL; CABA; CavP; CBEP; CBV; CLwM; CoBE; ELP; EnL; EnLi-1; EnLit; EnLoPo; EP; ExPo; FaBoEn; FaBV; FaFP; FaPL; GTBS; GTBS-D; GTBS-P; GTBS-W; GTSE; GTSL; HBV; HoPM; InPo; JAWP; LiTB; LiTG; LiTL; LoBV; MCCG; MeLP; MePo; MeWo; NeHB; NoP; OAEP; OBEV; OBS; OuHeWo; PG (1945 ed.); Po; PoAn; PoEL-3; PoIE; PoPl; PoRA; ReEn; SCEP-2; SeCePo; SeCeV; SeCL; SeCP; SeCV-1; SeEP; ShBV-3; TOP; TreF; TrGrPo; UnPo (1st ed.); ViBo
Tell me not what too well I know. On Catullus. Walter Savage Landor. OBEV; TOP; ViBoPo
Tell Me Now. Wang Chi, *tr. fr. Chinese by* Arthur Waley. FaBoCh; LoGBV
(What Should a Man Want?) OuHeWo
Tell me now in what hidden way is. The Ballad of Dead Ladies [*or* The Snows of Yester-Year]. Villon, *tr. by* Dante Gabriel Rossetti. ALV; ATP (1935 ed.); AWP; BEL; CTC; EnLi-2; ExPo; FaFP; GoBC; HBV; InP; JAWP; LO; OuHeWo; PoFS; PoRA; PoVP; TOP; VA; ViBoPo; ViPP; WBP; WiR
"Tell me now, what should a man want." Tell Me Now [*or* What Should a Man Want?]. Wang Chi. FaBoCh; LoGBV; OuHeWo
Tell Me, O Love. William Hammond. CBEP
(Cruel Mistress, The.) SeCL
Tell me, Oh Muse (for thou, or none canst tell). The Power of Numbers. Abraham Cowley. *Fr.* Davideis. OBS
Tell me, O Octopus, I begs. The Octopus. Ogden Nash. NePA; SoPo; TiPo; WePo

Tell me, O Swan, your ancient tale. Songs of Kabir. Kabir. WGRP
Tell me, O tell, what kind of thing is wit. Ode: Of Wit [*or* Of Wit]. Abraham Cowley. AnAnS-2; CEP; MeLP; MePo; OAEP; OBS; ReEn; SCEP-2; SeCP; SeCV-1; SeEP
Tell me of love, sweet Love, who is thy sire? Fidessa, More Chaste than Kind, XLIII. Bartholomew Griffin. TuPP
Tell me of progress if you will. Mountain Air. John Galsworthy. OQP
Tell me of that Treasure State. Montana. Charles C. Cohan. PoRL
Tell me once, dear, how it does prove. To the Unconstant Cynthia. Sir Robert Howard. CavP
Tell me one thing; why do you follow Jesus? Conversion. Andrew Young. *Fr.* Nicodemus. MaRV
Tell me Perigot, what shalbe the game. August. Spenser. *Fr.* The Shepheardes Calender. OAEP; ReEn
Tell me, Praise, and tell me, Love. Praise and Love. William Brighty Rands. OBVV
Tell me, Pyrrha, what fine youth. Another to the Same. Horace. Odes, I, 5. WiR
Tell me, sage Will, thou that the town around. A Dialogue between Fleet Shepard and Will the Coffee Man. *Unknown.* PeRV
Tell me, shepherd, tell me, pray. Country Gods. Cometas. FaBoCh; LoGBV
Tell me, some pitying angel, quickly say. The Blessed Virgin's Expostulation. Nahum Tate. ISi
Tell Me Some Way. Lizette Woodworth Reese. PG
"Tell me, tell me." The Galliass. Walter de la Mare. FaBoTw
Tell Me, Tell Me. Marianne Moore. LiTM (1970 ed.); NYBP
Tell me, tell me everything. Curiosity. Harry Behn. SoPo
Tell me, tell me, gentle Robin. Cat and the Bird, The. George Canning. BiS; ChTr
Tell Me, Tell Me, Smiling Child. Emily Brontë. OAEP
(Tell Me, Tell Me.) LoBV (1949 ed.); ViBoPo
Tell me that the snow is red. Belief. Ruth Fitch Bartlett. InMe
Tell me the auld, auld story. The Parrot Cry. "Hugh MacDiarmid." OxBS
Tell Me the Stories of Jesus. William Henry Parker. MaRV
Tell me the tales that to me were so dear. Long, Long Ago. Thomas Haynes Bayly. TreF
Tell me, Thou common Father,—tell me why. Not of This World. Bartolomé Leonardo de Argensola. OnPM
Tell me, thou skilful shepherd's swain. Sylvia [*or* A Roundelay]. Michael Drayton. *Fr.* The Shepherd's Garland, Eclogue IX. EIL; LoBV (1949 ed.)
Tell me, thou soul of her I love. Ode. James Thomson. OBEC
Tell me, thou Star whose wings of light. The World's Wanders. Shelley. BEL; EnLit; EPN; ViBoPo
Tell me today, when all my tides are gone. Sea Sonnet. Norma Lay. GoYe
Tell me, was Venus more beautiful. Venus Transiens. Amy Lowell. NP
Tell me, what is a poet's thought? A Poet's Thought. "Barry Cornwall." VA
Tell me what is that Lucifer thy Lord. Christopher Marlowe. *Fr.* Doctor Faustus. YAT
Tell me what is that only thing. Women's Longing. John Fletcher. *Fr.* Women Pleased. HBV
Tell me what is this innumerable throng. A Christmas Hymn. Richard Watson Gilder. MaRV; StJW
Tell me what sail the seas. Under the Stars. Wallace Rice. AA; OHIP
Tell me what shapes your mind. The light grows less. Autumnal. Louis O. Coxe. TwAmPo
"Tell me what you're doing over here, John Gorham." John Gorham. E. A. Robinson. MAP; MAPA; MoAB; MoAmPo; NP
Tell me, where doth whiteness grow. Whiteness, or Chastity. Joseph Beaumont. LiTL; LoBV
Tell Me Where Is Fancy Bred. Shakespeare. *Fr.* The Merchant of Venice, III, ii. AnFE; AtBAP; BEL; CH; DiPo; EG; EIL; ELP; EnLi-1; EnLit; EnRePo; FaPON; ILP; InPo; LiTB; LiTG; LO; NoP; OAEP; SeCeV; SiCE; TOP; ViBoPo; WHA
(Casket Song, A.) OBSC
(Fancy.) TreFS; TrGrPo
(Love.) OBEV
(Madrigal: "Tell me where is fancy bred.") GTBS; GTBS-D; GTBS-P; GTBS-W; GTSE
(Song, A: "Tell me, where is fancy [*or* fancie] bred.") BoLiVe; CTC; MemP; PoEL-2; YAT
(Where Is Fancy Bred?) WePo
(Young Love.) GTSL
Tell me where thy lovely love is. Heine. *Fr.* Die Heimkehr. AWP
Tell me whither, maiden June. The Reaper. John Banister Tabb. ACP
Tell me, why Heav'n at first did suffer sin? Sir William Davenant. *Fr.* The Philosopher's Disquisition Directed to the Dying Christian. PeRV
Tell me, wide wandering soul, in all thy quest. But Once. Theodore Winthrop. AA
Tell Me, Wight in the Broom. *Unknown, tr. fr. Middle English by* Mabel Van Duzee. MeEV
Tell Me, Ye Wingèd Winds. Charles Mackay. VA
Tell me you/ That sing in the black-thorn. You That Sing in the Blackthorn. Alfred Noyes. *Fr.* The Last Voyage. GoBC
Tell me, you anti-saintes, why glasse. Upon Faireford Windowes. Richard Corbett. AnAnS-2
Tell Me, You Wandering Spirits [of the Air]. *Unknown.* OBS; SeCL; SeEP
"Tell me your name," I challenged Christ. The Bargain. Anna Bunston de Bary. MaRV
Tell me your secrets, pretty shell. Shell Secrets. *Unknown.* BoTP
Tell mee shepherd dost thou love? *Unknown.* SeCSL
Tell my priests, when I am gone. *Unknown.* WhC
Tell, O Tell. Thomas Campion. *See* When Thou Must Home.
Tell old Bill, when [*or* before] he leaves home dis mornin'. Dis Mornin', Dis Evenin', So Soon [*or* Old Bill]. *Unknown.* ABF; AS
Tell Our Daughters. Besmilr Brigham. ThO
Tell, tell our fortune, Mirabel. Fortune for Mirabel. Horace Gregory. TwAmPo
Tell the story to your sons. The Fight of the *Armstrong* Privateer. James Jeffrey Roche. PAH
Tell them, I am, Jehovah said. Christopher Smart. *Fr.* A Song to David. WGRP
Tell them in Lakedaimon, passer-by. At Thermopylae. Simonides. ChTr; OnPM; WaaP; WoL
Tell them, O Sky-born, when I die. Farewell. Harry Kemp. HBMV
Tell them to go away. Insomnia. Ethna MacCarthy. NeIP
Tell them, when you are home again. Love's Caution. W. H. Davies. ChMP
Tell this to ladies: how a hero man. Man without Sense of Direction. John Crowe Ransom. LiTM (rev. ed.); NoP; OxBA
Tell thou the world, when my bones lie whitening. The Nameless One. James Clarence Mangan. ACP; EPN; GTBS; GTSE; HBV; OBEV
Tell us, tell us, holy shepherds. Flowers for the Altar. Digby Mackworth Dolben. GoBC
Tell us that love/ returns. Horace Gregory. *Fr.* Chorus for Survival, I. CMoP
Tell us, thou clear and heavenly tongue. The Star Song; a Carol to the King. Robert Herrick. GN; OxBoCh
"Tell Ye the Faint of Heart." Francis J. Rock. JKCP (1955 ed.)
Tell you I chyll. John Skelton. *Fr.* The Tunning [*or* Tunnynge] of Elinour Rumming [*or* Elynour Rummynge]. EnPo; PoFS; ReIE; SiTL; StP; TrGrPo
Tell you what I like the best. Knee-Deep in June. James Whitcomb Riley. AmePo; OHFP
Tell youth to play with wine and love and never bear away the scars! Compensation. Ridgely Torrence. *Fr.* The House of a Hundred Lights. AA
Tell-a me who dat had a rod? Mone, Member, Mone. *Unknown.* ABF
Telling the Bees. Andrew Lang, *after the Greek.* VA
Telling the Bees. Lizette Woodworth Reese. AA
Telling the Bees. Whittier. AmePo; AmPP (3d ed.); AnNE; AP; AWP; CoBA; GBV (1952 ed.); HBV; InP; InPo; LaNeLa; PFY; PoIE; TOP
Tellus. William Reed Huntington. AA
Temagami. Archibald Lampman. OBCV
Temair noblest of hills. Tara. *Unknown.* *Fr.* Dinnshenchas. OnYI
Temeraire, The. Herman Melville. WaaP
Temper, The ("How should I praise thee, Lord!"). George

Herbert. AnAnS-1; AtBAP; FosPo; MaMe; MeP; MePo; NoP; OBS; OxBoCh; PoEL-2; PoFS; SCEP-1; SeCL; WHA
Temper, The ("It cannot be. Where is that mightie joy"). George Herbert. MaMe; SCEP-1
Temper. *Unknown.* PoToHe (new ed.); SoP
Temper, blood and speech divide. Tears. George Rostrevor Hamilton. POTE
Temper in October. V. L. Edminson. BoPe
Temper my spirit, O Lord. The Passionate Sword. Jean Starr Untermeyer. HBMV; MaRV; TrJP; TrPWD
Temperament. Martial, *tr. fr. Latin by* Addison. AWP; ELU; JAWP; WBP
(In All the Humors.) OnPM
(To a Capricious Friend.) BOHV
Temperaments, The. Ezra Pound. ErPo
Temperance ("Wine taken with excess"). *Unknown.* ACP; CAW
Temperance and Virginity. Milton. *Fr.* Comus. OBS
Temperance, exercise, and air. To His Son. John Dyer. PrWP
Temperance Note; and Weather Prophecy. James Agee. *Fr.* Two Songs on the Economy of Abundance. MAP; MoAmPo
Temperance, or the Cheap Physitian. Richard Crashaw. MaMe; SeCV-1
(In Praise of Lessius His Rule of Health. MaMe
Temperate Drinking. Anacreon, *tr. fr. Greek by* Thomas Moore. OnPM
Temperature. Gerard Malanga. NYBP
Tempest, The. Charles Cotton. PeRV; SeCePo
Tempest, A. Emily Dickinson. *See* Awful tempest mashed the air, An.
Tempest, The. James Thomas Fields. *See* Ballad of the Tempest.
Tempest, The. Mabuchi, *tr. fr. Japanese by* Asataro Miyamori. OnPM
Tempest, The, *sels.* Shakespeare.
Ariel's Song: "Come unto these yellow sands," *fr.* I, ii. CTC; EG; FaBoCh; GN; GoJo; LoBV; LoGBV; MCCG; MPB (1956 ed.); PCH; PTK; ThWaDe
("Come unto these yellow sands.") AnFE; AtBAP; BEL; BoTP; CBEP; CH; EIL; InPo; MaPo (1969 ed.); NoP; OBSC; OTPC (1923 ed.); PoEL-2; PoIE; SiCE; TOP; ViBoPo
(Fairy Land.) OBEV
(Fairy Life, The, 2.) GTSL
(Fairy Songs.) HBV
(Remote Bermudas, The.) CLwM
Ariel's Song: "Full fathom five thy father lies," *fr.* I, ii. BoLiVe; EG; FaBoEn; FlW; GN; LoBV; PTK; SeCePo; TreFT
(Ariel's Dirge.) EvOK; GoJo; ThWaDe
(Fairy Land.) OBEV
("Full fathom five thy father lies.") AnFE; AtBAP; ATP; BEL; CABA; CaFP; CBEP; ChTr; DiPo; EIL; ELP; EnLi-1; ExPo; FaBoCh; GTSL; HoPM; ILP; InPo; LiTB; LiTG; LoGBV; MaPo; NoP; OAEP; OBSC; OTPC; OuHeWo; PAn; PIA; PoEL-2; PoeP; PoIE; PoRA; SeCeV; ShBV-1; SiCE; TOP; ViBoPo; WHA
(Sea Dirge, A.) AnEnPo; EtS; GTBS; GTBS-D; GTBS-P; GTBS-W; GTSE; HBV; MCCG; TrGrPo
Song: "Full Fathom Five Thy Father Lies." CBV; ForPo; FosPo; NeHB; YAT
(Songs from the Plays.) AWP; JAWP; WBP
Ariel's Song: "Where the bee sucks," *fr.* V, i. AnEnPo; EG; GN; MCCG; PCD; PDV; PTK
(Fairy Land.) OBEV
(Fairy Life, The, 1.) GTSL
(Fairy Songs.) HBV; HBVY; RIS
(Fairy's Life, A.) PCH; PoPl
Song: "Where the bee sucks, there suck I." YAT
(Songs from the Plays.) AWP; JAWP; WBP
("Where the bee sucks, there suck I.") AnFE; BEL; BoTP; CABA; CBEP; CH; CTC; DiPo; EIL; EnLi-1; EnLit; EnRePo; FaBV; ILP; InPo; MaPo (1969 ed.); MPB; NoP; OBSC; OTPC; PoRh; SeCeV; SiCE; ThWaDe; TiPo; TOP; TreFT; UTS; ViBoPo; WHA
"Be not afeard; the isle is full of noises," *fr.* III, ii. AtBAP; FlW; UnS
(Caliban.) FiP
(To Dream Again.) TrGrPo
Brave New World, *fr.* V, i. TrGrPo
"Ceres, most bounteous lady, thy rich leas," *fr.* IV, i. AtBAP
Epilogue: "Now my charms are all o'erthrown," *fr.* V, i. CTC
"Had I plantation of this isle, my lord," *fr.* II, i. PoFr
Honour, Riches, Marriage Blessing, *fr.* IV, i. HW
Magic, *after* Ovid, *fr.* V, i. AWP; JAWP; WBP
No More Dams I'll Make, *fr.* II, ii. ViBoPo
"Now I want/ Spirits to enforce, art to enchant," *fr.* Epilogue. MyFE
Our Revels Now Are Ended, *fr.* IV, i. DiPo; GTBS-W; LiTB; LiTG; MaRV; PG; ShBV-3; WHA
("Cloud-capp'd towers, the gorgeous palaces, The.") PoPl
(Clouds.) BoC
(Our Little Life.) OQP
(Prospero.) FiP
(Prospero Ends the Revels.) TreF
(Stuff of Dreams, The.) FaBV
(Such Stuff as Dreams Are Made On.) TrGrPo
Stephano's Song, *fr.* II, ii. WhC
("Master, the swabber, the boatswain, and I, The.") InPo; ViBoPo
(None of Us Cared for Kate.) OnPM
"Where should this music be? I' the air, or the earth?" *fr.* I, ii. UnS
You Nymphs, Call'd Naiads, *fr.* IV, i. ViBoPo
Tempest, The. William Jay Smith. MoAmPo (1962 ed.)
Tempest, The. Henry Vaughan. AnAnS-1; MeP
Tempest, The. Marya Zaturenska. MoAmPo; TrGrPo (1942 ed.)
Tempest cracked on the theatre, A. Repetitons of a Young Captain. Wallace Stevens. WaP
Tempest on the great seaborders! A Storm at Sea. *Unknown.* AnIL
Tempest on the plain of Lir. Storm at Sea. *Unknown.* KiLC
Tempest without: within the mellow glow. Hands. W. W. Gibson. PoMa
Temple. John Donne. AnAnS-1; MaMe; MeP; OBS; Sonn
(Jesus in the Temple.) StJW
Temple, The. Clifford Dyment. ChMP
Temple, The. Josephine W. Johnson. MoRP
Temple, The. Po Chü-i, *tr. fr. Chinese by* Arthur Waley. OBMV
Temple, The. Tennyson. OQP
Temple, The. Tu Fu, *tr. fr. Chinese by* Chi Hwang Chu *and* Edna Worthley Underwood. OnPM
Temple Bar. Rose Fyleman. UTS
Temple by the Sea, The. Geoffrey Dutton. ACV
Temple Fever: Sounion. Joanne de Longchamps. NYTB
Temple Garlands. Agnes Mary Frances Robinson. HBV
Temple is clean, The. A Song of Always. Efraim Rosenzweig. TiPo (1952 ed.)
Temple of Fame, The, *sel.* Pope.
Honest Fame. OBEC
Temple of Infamy, The, *sel.* Charles Harpur.
"But hark! What hubbub now is this that comes." PoAu-1
Temple of the Trees, The. J. D. C. Pellow. PGD
Temple of Venus, The. Spenser. *Fr.* The Faerie Queene, IV, 10. WHA
Temple Offering. Leslie Savage Clark. ChIP
Temple That Charged Admission, The. Issa, *tr. fr. Japanese by* Max Bickerton. PoFr
Temple to Friendship, A. Thomas Moore. BeLS; HBV; NeHB
Templeogue. Blanaid Salkeld. NeIP
Temples, yes, there are temples, dung-coloured. Agrigento. Alan Ross. POTi
Tempora Acta. "Owen Meredith." *Fr.* Babylonia. OBVV; VA
Tempt Me No More. C. Day Lewis. *Fr.* The Magnetic Mountain, XXIV. AnFE; MoAB; MoBrPo; OAEP (2d ed.); OBMV; PoDB; PoPl; PoFr; POTE
("Tempt me no more: for I.") EnLit; NAMP
Temptation. William Cowper. EiCP
Temptation. Winfred Ernest Garrison. ChIP
Temptation. Robert Herrick. LiTB
Temptation. *Unknown.* ELU
Temptation and Fall of Man, The. *Unknown, tr. fr. Anglo-Saxon by* Charles W. Kennedy. *Fr.* Genesis. AnOE
Temptation of Saint Anthony, The. Arthur Symons. BrPo
Temptation of Sir Gawain, The. *Unknown.* *Fr.* Sir Gawain and the Green Knight. ACP
Temptation, temptation, temptation. Temptation. *Unknown.* ELU
Tempted. Katharine Lee Bates. ChIP; StJW

Tempted. Edward Rowland Sill. AA
Tempus Edax Rerum. Henry Parrot. SiCE
Ten Brothers. *Unknown, ad. fr. Yiddish by* Louis Untermeyer. MaC; RePo
Ten Commandments, The. Exodus, Bible, *O.T.* OHFP (XX: 2-26); TreF (XX: 1-17); WBLP (XX: 2-26)
Ten Commandments, Seven Deadly Sins, and Five Wits. *Unknown.* ChTr
Ten cuckolds slain without confession. Ballad of Don Juan Tenorio and the Statue of the Comendadar. Roy Campbell. PeSA
Ten Days Leave. W. D. Snodgrass. MoAmPo (1962 ed.); UnPo (3d ed.)
Ten Definitions of Poetry. Carl Sandburg. MAP; MoAmPo
Ten Lepers, The. Katharine Tynan. MaRV; StJW
Ten leprous men, condemned to die. The Cry of Faith. M. Allen Gibson. SoP
Ten little children/ Dancing on the shore. Dancing on the Shore. M. M. Hutchinson. BoTP
Ten Little Christmas Trees. Rodney Bennett. BoTP
Ten Little Dicky-Birds. A. W. I. Baldwin. BoTP
Ten Little Indian Boys. M. M. Hutchinson. BoTP; SoPo
Ten Little Injuns. *Unknown.* OTPC (1946 ed.); RIS
Ten little mice sat down to spin. *See* Six little mice. . .
Ten Little nigger boys went out to dine. *Unknown.* OxNR
"Ten little toes, ten little toes." The Ideal Age for a Man. Monica Shannon. BiCB
Ten met the Master in a field. The Living Tithe. Mabel Munns Charles. ChIP
Ten miles of flat land along the sea. Sandpipers. Carl Sandburg. BiS
Ten O'Clock. Patricia Hubbell. OCS
Ten of Chaucer's People. Chaucer. *See* Canterbury Tales, The: Prologue.
Ten of the night is Talavera tolling. The Field of Talavera. Thomas Hardy. *Fr.* The Dynasts. CMoP
Ten pound hammer kill John Henry. John Henry (F *vers.*). *Unknown.* ViBoFo
Ten snowy white pigeons are standing in line. The Pigeons. Maud Burnham. PCH
Ten South Sea Island boys. Fun with Fishing. Eunice Tietjens. FaPON; GaP
Ten Thousand Cattle (A *vers.*), *with music. Unknown.* CoSo
Ten thousand flakes about my window blow. Fame. Walter Savage Landor. PV
Ten thousand Fords are idle here in search. Concord. Robert Lowell. MaPo (1969 ed.); TDP
Ten Thousand God-damn Cattle (B *vers. of* Ten Thousand Cattle), *with music. Unknown.* CoSo
Ten Thousand Miles Away, *with music. Unknown.* AS; SoAmSa
Ten Thousand Miles Away from Home, *with music. Unknown.* AS
Ten thousand tomes with pendant discs of jade. In an Old Library. Yuan Mei. LiTW
10:X:5, 45 Years Since the Fall of the Ch'ing Dynasty. Philip Whalen. FRC
Ten Years After, *sel.* Lucia Trent *and* Ralph Cheyney.
Toward a True Peace. PGD
Ten years!—and to my waking eye. The Terrace at Berne. Matthew Arnold. Switzerland, VII. OAEP; ViPP; VP
Ten years being enough of copra, he souvenired a/ whalestooth. Trader's Return. Sylvia Lawson. PoAu-2
Ten Years Old. Louis Untermeyer. TSW
Ten years together without yet a cloud. Firelight. E. A. Robinson. CMoP; InP; NP
Tenacious foliage; burgundy. Nothing Lovely as a Tree. Frederick J. Bryant, Jr. BF
Tenancy, The. Mary Gilmore. BoAV; PoAu-1
Tenant. Frances Angevine Gray. FiSC
Tenant, The. Frederic Lawrence Knowles. SoP
(My Faith.) OQP
Tenants. W. W. Gibson. HBV; NP
Tend me my birds, and bring again. A Prayer. Norman Gale. TrPWD
Tended by Faustina. Faustina, or Rock Roses. Elizabeth Bishop. NMP
Tendency, The. Heine, *tr. fr. German by* Louis Untermeyer. PoFr
Tender Babes. Thomas Hood. *Fr.* The Plea of the Midsummer Fairies. OBRV
Tender bud within herself [*or* itselfe] doth close, The. On a Rosebud Sent to Her Lover. *Unknown.* AtBAP; LO; SeCL
Tender-handed stroke a nettle. A Strong Hand. Aaron Hill. HBV
Tender he was, perplexed and jealous; yet. The White Bird. "Anna Akhmatova." LiTW
Tender Husband, The, *sel.* Sir Richard Steele.
Song: "Why, lovely charmer, tell me why." LiTL; ViBoPo
(Why, Lovely Charmer.) HBV
Tender is the night and clear, and without wind. The Evening of the Feast-Day. Giacomo Leopardi. LiTW
Tender, Slow. *Unknown, tr. fr. Greek by* Wallace Rice. ErPo
Tender softness! infant mild! A Mother's Soliloquy. Hetty Wright. WaPE
Tender, the young auburn woman. Spring. Paul Verlaine. ErPo
Tenderfoot, The. D. J. O'Malley. *See* Horse Wrangler, The.
Tenderheartedness. Harry Graham. Some Ruthless Rhymes, II. ALV; CenHV; FaFP; NA; SiTL; TreFT; WePo; WhC
(Billy.) LiTM; MaC
Tenderly as a/ barber. For the Barbers. Joel Oppenheimer. CoPo
Tenderly as a bee that sips. Escalade. Arthur Symons. UnTE
Tenderly, day that I have loved, I close your eyes. Day That I Have Loved. Rupert Brooke. BEL; GTSL; PoLF
Tenderness of dignity of souls, The. Crass Times Redeemed by Dignity of Souls, II. Peter Viereck. HoPM
Tenderness so hard to swallow, The. View from a Window. Eldon Grier. PeCV (1967 ed.)
Tenebrae. Austin Clarke. AnIL; NeIP
Tenebrae. David Gascoyne. *Fr.* Miserere. NeBP
Tenebris. Angelina W. Grimké. CDC; PoNe
Tenebris Interlucentem. James Elroy Flecker. CBEP; MoBrPo
Tenement Room; Chicago. Frank Marshall Davis. GoSl
Teneriffe, *sel.* Frederic William Henry Myers.
"Atlantid islands, phantom-fair." OBVV
Tennessee. Virginia Frazer Boyle. PAH
Tennessee. Francis Brooks. *Fr.* Intaglios. AA
Tennis. Margaret Avison. PeCV
Tennis Court Oath, The. John Ashbery. FRC
Tennis in San Juan. Reuel Denney. SD
Tennyson. Thomas Bailey Aldrich. AA
Tennyson. Alan Ansen. CoAP
Tennyson. Florence Earle Coates. AA
Tennyson. Thomas Henry Huxley. HBV; VA
Tennyson. Henry van Dyke. AA; InP
Tenour which my life, holds, The. Wordsworth. *Fr.* The Excursion, III. OBRV
Tense and whittled thundershaft he pulls, A. Herakles Archer. Morton Dauwen Zabel. NP
Tense with infallibility. The Opposition. Samuel Hazo. NYTB
Tensed/beneath a shaft. Discobolus. David A. Locher. NYTB
Tension in the tendons of her wing, The. Soldier's Dove. James Forsyth. WaP
Tent-lights glimmer on the land, The. At Port Royal. Whittier. PAH; PAP
Tent with rustling breezes cool, A. She Scorns Her Husband the Caliph. Lady Maisun. LiTW
Tentative Description of a Dinner to Promote the Impeachment of President Eisenhower. Lawrence Ferlinghetti. CoPo
10th Dance—Coming On as a Horn—20 February 1964. Jackson MacLow. CoPo
Tenth Elegy: Elegy in Joy. Muriel Rukeyser. MiAP
Tenth Muse. Robert Lowell. MaPo (1969 ed.); PoeP
Tenth Nimphall, The. Michael Drayton. *Fr.* The Muses Elizium. AnAnS-2
Tenth Properte, The. Sir Thomas More. *Fr.* The Twelve Properties or Condicions of a Lover. CoBE
Tenth Reunion. Edward Steese. GoYe
Tenth Satire of Juvenal, The, *abr.* Juvenal, *tr. fr. Latin by* Dryden. WoL
Tenting on the Old Camp Ground. Walter Kittredge. TreFS
(Tenting To-Night, *with music.*) TrAS
(We're Tenting To-Night.) PaA; PAL
Tenure of Kings and Magistrates, The, *sel.* Milton.

"There can be slain/ No sacrifice," 3 *ll.*, *tr. fr. the Latin of* Seneca. PoFr
Tercets. Llywarch Hen, *tr. fr. Welsh by* Owen Masters. LiTW
Terence, if I could return. To Myself, after Forty Years. T. H. White. NYBP
Terence McDiddler. *Unknown.* OxNR
Terence MacSwiney. "Æ." AnIV; PoFr
(Prisoner, A.) AnIL
Terence, This Is Stupid Stuff. A. E. Housman. A Shropshire Lad, LXII. CABA; CaFP; CMoP; CoBMV; EnL; EnLit; LiTB; LiTM (rev. ed.); ILP; MaPo; MasP; NAMP; NoP; OAEP; PoAn; PoVP; PP; SeCeV; ViPo; VP; WHA; YAT
(Epilogue: "Terence, this is stupid stuff.") MoAB; MoBrPo; OuHeWo; ReMP; TrGrPo
Power of Malt, The, *sel.* HBV
Terenure. Blanaid Salkeld. NeIP
Teresa of Avila. Elizabeth Jennings. NePoEA-2
Teresa was God's familiar. She often spoke. Conversation in Avila. Phyllis McGinley. EaLo; PoPo
Teresian Contemplative, The. Robert Hugh Benson. ACP; CAW; JKCP
Teresina's Face. Margaret Widdemer. HBMV; NP
Terly Terlow. *Unknown.* AtBAP; CBEP
Term, The. William Carlos Williams. InvP; LiTA; OCS; PoPo; RePo; ThWaDe
Term of Death, The. Sarah Morgan Bryan Piatt. AA
Terminal. Karl Shapiro. AmLP
Terminal Days at Beverly Farms. Robert Lowell. FRC
Terminal Theater. Robert Sward. CoPo
Terminus. Emerson. AA; AmePo; AmPo; AmPP; AnNE; AP; AWP; CoBA; HBV; InPo; MWA-1; NoP; OuHeWo; OxBA; PoEL-4; PoIE (1970 ed.); PoLF
Termite, The. Ogden Nash. CenHV; PoPl; PoPo; ShM; WhC
Termites. Charles G. Bell. NePoAm-2
Termites, The. Robert Hillyer. OA
Ternarie [*or* Ternary] of Littles, upon a Pipkin of Jellie [*or* Jelly] Sent to a Lady, A. Robert Herrick. ALV; BOHV; FaBoCh; GoJo; HBV; HBVY; LoGBV; MaPo; MyFE, 2 *sts.*; OTPC (1923 ed.); PG (1955 ed.); PoEL-3; PoRA; WhC
(Littles, *sl. abr.*) BoTP
Ternissa! You Are Fled! Walter Savage Landor. *Fr.* The Hellenics. ExPo; GTSE; LoBV; OBNC; PoEL-4; SeCeV
(On Ternissa's Death.) ELP
(Ternissa.) FaBoEn
Terra Australis. Douglas Stewart. BoAV; MoAuPo
Terrace, The. Richard Wilbur. MiAP
Terrace at Berne, The. Matthew Arnold. Switzerland, VII. OAEP; ViPP; VP
Terrace in the Snow, The. Su Túng-po, *tr. fr. Chinese by* Kenneth Rexroth. NaP
Terraces rise and fall, The. Going to Sleep in the Country. Howard Moss. PoCh; StP
Terrapin War. *Unknown.* PAH
Terrible. Lawrence Ferlinghetti. CBV
Terrible/ is the soft sound of a hardboiled egg. Late Rising. Jacques Prévert. CAD; OnHM
Terrible and splendid trust, A. Ways of War. Lionel Johnson. AnIV
Terrible Beauty. Kingsley Amis. ErPo; NePoEA-2; PV
Terrible Dead, The. Mary Carolyn Davies. HBMV
Terrible Door, The. Harold Monro. EnLoPo; FaBoTw
Terrible Infant, A. Frederick Locker-Lampson. ALV; BoHV; FiBHP; HBV; InMe; TreFS; WhC
Terrible Meek, The, *sel.* Charles Rann Kennedy.
"Already our kingdoms are beginning to totter." ChIP
Terrible People, The. Ogden Nash. NePA; SiTL
Terrible Robber Men, The. Padraic Colum. HBMV LOW; RG
Terrible Sonnets, The. Gerard Manley Hopkins. *See* Carrion Comfort; I Wake and Feel the Fell of Dark; *and* No Worst, There Is None.
Terrible Sons, The. Eleazar ben Kalir, *tr. fr. Hebrew by* Israel Zangwill. TrJP
Terrible Thought, A. Eliezer Steinberg, *tr. fr. Yiddish by* Joseph Leftwich. TrJP
Terrible wrath I say, The. Achilles and the King. John Logan. AmPC
Terrifying are the attent sleek thrushes on the lawn. Thrushes. Ted Hughes. GoYe; NePoEA-2; PoIE; POTi
Terrifying Tell-Tale, The. Antipater, *tr. fr. Greek by* Lord Neaves. OnPM
Terror. Thomas O'Brien. NeIP
Terror. Robert Penn Warren. MoPo; NePA; WaP
Terror. "Yehoash," *tr. fr. Yiddish by* Isidore Goldstick. TrJP
Terror Conduction. Philip Lamantia. NeAP
Terror does not belong to open day. Counterpoint. Owen Dodson. PoNe
Terror in Beauty. M. Eugenie Perry. TwCaPo
Terror of Death, The. Keats. *See* When I Have Fears That I May Cease To Be.
Tess's Lament. Thomas Hardy. FaBoTw
Test, The. Emerson. AA; PP
Test, The. Walter Savage Landor. *Fr.* Ianthe. HBV; VA
(Epigram: "I held her hand, the pledge of bliss.") ALV
Test. Helen Pursell Roads. OQP
Test, The. John Banister Tabb. AnAmPo
Test of Manhood, The. *sel.* George Meredith.
"In fellowship religion has its founts." WGRP
Test of Men, The. Ecclesiasticus, XXVI: 5-8, Bible, Apocrypha. TrJP
Testament. John Holmes. MoRP
Testament. Langston Hughes. NePoAm-2
Testament. Sister M. Thérèse. MoRP
Testament, A. *Unknown.* OBSC
Testament of Beauty, The, *sels.* Robert Bridges.
"But love's true passion is of immortal happiness," *fr.* III. LO
Friendship, *fr.* IV. MaRV
"How was November's melancholy endear'd to me," *fr.* III. MoVE
"In higher natures, poetic or mystical," *fr.* III. LO
Introduction: "'Twas late in my long journey, when I had clomb to where," *fr.* I. MoVE
Jesus, *fr.* I. MaRV
"Our happiest earthly comradeships hold a foretaste," *fr.* IV. MaRV
"Sky's unresting cloudland, that with varying play, The," *fr.* I. MoVE
"'Twas at thatt hour of beauty when the setting sun," *fr.* IV. MoVE; OxBoCh
Testament of Cathaeir Mor, The. *Unknown, tr. fr. Middle Irish by* James Clarence Mangan. *Fr.* Book of Rights. OnYI
Testament of Cresseid, The. Robert Henryson. CABL; GoTS; MeEV, *sl. abr., tr. fr. Middle English by* Marshall W. Stearns; OxBS
Sels.
Assembly of the Gods, The. PoEL-1
Cresseid's Complaint against Fortune. MeEL
Cressida's Leprosy. SeCePo
Testament of John Davidson, The, *sel.* John Davidson.
Last Journey, The. GoTS
Testament of Mr. Andro Kennedy, The. William Dunbar. OxBS
Testified that Miss McNair. For Denise McNair. Colette Inez. QAH
Testimony. Mark Bullock. SoP
Testimony. Beverly Connelly. FiSC
Testimony. Eva Moad Turner. OQP
Testimony to an Inquisitor. William Stafford. NePoAm-2
Testing, The. Edwin Markham. MaRV; OQP
(Man-Test.) MoRP
Testing, Testing. Dan Dillon. PV
Tetélestai. Conrad Aiken. CMoP; LiTA; LiTM (rev. ed.); MAP; MAPA; MoAB; MoAmPo; PoDB
Tethys' Festival, *sel.* Samuel Daniel.
Are They Shadow[e]s [That We See]? AtBAP; ATP; EIL; ExPo; InvP; LoBV; NoP; PoIE; SeCeV; TuPP
("Are they shadows that we see?") CH; SiCE
(Eidola.) LO
(Shadows.) OBSC
(Song: "Are they shadowes that we see?") PoEL-2
Teufelsdröckh Minor. Morton Dauwen Zabel. NP
Teuton sang the "Wacht am Rhein," The. "Il Est Cocu—le Chef de Gare!" H. S. Mackintosh. WhC
Tewkesbury Road. John Masefield. BoTP; EPN; GBV; MCCG; StaSt; TreFT; TSW
Texas. James Daugherty. TiPo (1959 ed.)
Texas. Amy Lowell. AmFN; InP; PoMa
Texas. Whittier. PAH
Texas Cowboy, The ("Oh, I am a Texas cowboy"), *with music.* *Unknown.* CoSo

Texas Cowboy and the Mexican Greaser, The. *Unknown.* SCC
Texas cowboy [lay down] on a barroom floor, A. The Hell-bound Train. *Unknown.* BeLS; BLPA; CoSo
Texas Cowboys, The ("It's of those Texas cowboys. . ."). *Unknown.* *See* Lone Buffalo Hunter, The.
Texas has nothing so abundant. The All Girls Drill Team. Marvin Bell. TDP
Texas, Our Texas. Gladys Yoakum Wright. PoRL
Texas Rangers, The, *with music.* *Unknown.* BFSS; CoSo, *with music;* OuSiCo, *with music*
Texas Song, The: "I'm going to leave old Texas now." *Unknown.* CoSo
Texas Trains and Trails. Mary Austin. SoPo; TiPo
Texas Types—"The Bad Man." William Lawrence Chittenden. PoOW
Texian Boys. *Unknown.* *See* Kansas Boys.
Text, The. Gary Snyder. *Fr.* Myths & Texts: Burning. NaP
Text for Today. Phyllis McGinley. WhC
Thaba Bosio. S. D. R. Sutu, *tr. fr. Sotho by* Dan Kunene *and* Jack Cope. PeSA
Thaddeus Stevens. Phoebe Cary. PAH
Thaddeus Stevens was a burning scandal. Old Thad Stevens. Kenneth Porter. NePoAm-2
Thai passit in thare pilgramage. *Unknown.* *Fr.* Golagros and Gawane. OxBS
Thair Is Nocht ane Winche. *Unknown.* OxBS
Thais. Newman Levy. BOHV; FiBHP; InMe
Thaisa's Dirge ("Thaisa fair, under the cold sea lying"). Herman Charles Merivale. VA
Thalaba the Destroyer, *sels.* Robert Southey.
  Night [in the Desert], *fr.* I. GN; OTPC
  Thalaba and the Banquet, *fr.* VI. SeCePo
  Thalaba and the Magic Thread, *fr.* VIII. SeCePo
Thalamos. Peter Kane Dufault. ErPo
Thalassius. Swinburne. PoVP
Thalatta. Willis Boyd Allen. EtS
Thalatta! Thalatta! Joseph Brownlee Brown. AA; HBV
Thalia. Thomas Bailey Aldrich. AA; HBV; InMe; LHV
Thames, The. Sir John Denham. *Fr.* Cooper's Hill. FaBoEn
Thames, The. M. M. Hutchinson. BoTP
Thames Doth the Medway Wed. Spenser. *Fr.* The Faerie Queene, IV. HW
Thames from Cooper's Hill, The. Sir John Denham. *Fr.* Cooper's Hill. OBS; SeCePo
  ("My eye descending from the hill, surveys.") ReEn; ViBoPo
Thames nocturne of blue and gold, The. Impression du Matin. Oscar Wilde. BrPo; CABA; CBV; MoBrPo; PoVP; SyP
Thames, the most lov'd of all the Ocean's sons. The Thames. Sir John Denham. *Fr.* Cooper's Hill. FaBoEn
Thames will take us to London town, The. The Thames. M. M. Hutchinson. BoTP
Thammuz. William Vaughn Moody. AP
Than forth I went into a meadow green. Stephen Hawes. *Fr.* The Pastime of Pleasure. ReIE
Than Perseverance, in all goodly haste. Of the Great Marriage between Grand Amour and La Belle Pucelle. Stephen Hawes. *Fr.* The Pastime of Pleasure. ReIE
Than this great universe no less. Rowland's Rhyme. Michael Drayton. *Fr.* The Shepherd's Garland, Eclogue II. OBSC
Thanatopsis. Bryant. AA; AmePo; AmLP; AmP; AmPP; AnAmPo; AnFE; AnNE; AP; APA; AWP; BoLiVe; BoNaP; CoAnAm; CoBA; DiPo; FaBoBe; FaFP; FaPL; GTBS-W; HBV; HBVY; LaNeLa; LiTA; LiTG; MAmP; MCCG; MWA-1; NeHB; NePA; OBEV (new ed.); OBRV; OBVV; OHFP; OTPC (1946 ed.); OxBA; PFY; PG (1945 ed.); PoFS; TIHL; TreF; TrGrPo; UnPo (1st ed.); ViBoPo; WBLP; WGRP; WHA
  Sels.
  "Earth that nourished thee." YT
  "So live that when thy summons comes to join." DD; OQP; OTD; SoP; TRV
    (Be Ye Also Ready.) MaRV
    (So Live.) PoToHe
  "Yet not to thine eternal resting-place." PTK
Thank God. Joseph Rolnik, *tr. fr. Yiddish by* Joseph Leftwich. TrJP
Thank God! *Unknown.* MaRV; OQP; PoToHe
Thank God, a man can grow! Per Aspera. Florence Earle Coates. FaChP; HBMV
Thank God, bless God, all ye who suffer not. Tears. Elizabeth Barrett Browning. OQP; SoP
Thank God for dirty dishes. Thanks. *Unknown.* SoP
Thank God for Fools! *Unknown.* OQP; PoToHe (1941 ed.)
Thank God for Life. *Unknown.* PGD
Thank God for Life!/ E'en though it bring much bitterness and strife. Thank God. *Unknown.* MaRV; OQP; PoToHe
Thank God for life!/ There! A meadowlark sings! The Things of the Spirit. Douglas Malloch. MaRV
Thank God for life; life is not sweet always. Thank God for Life. *Unknown.* PGD
Thank God for life, with all its endless store. Thomas Durley Landels. *Fr.* At Eighty-three. MaRV
Thank God for sleep! The Sacrament of Sleep. John Oxenham. PoLF
Thank God for sleep in the long quiet night. Morning Thanksgiving. John Drinkwater. BoTP
Thank God! for that lovely spirit. Wondrous Motherhood. *Unknown.* PGD
Thank God for the Country. Mrs. Major Arnold. WBLP
Thank God my brain is not inclined to cut. The Menagerie. William Vaughn Moody. AmPP (3d ed.); AP; PFY; TOP; YaD
Thank God our liberating lance. The Road to France. Daniel Henderson. HBV; MC; PaA; PAH
Thank God that God shall judge my soul; not man! The Eternal Justice. Anne Reeves Aldrich. AA
Thank God! there is always a Land of Beyond. Robert W. Service. *Fr.* Rhymes of a Rolling Stone. TRV
Thank God we do not live by bread alone. Twice Fed. A. A. Bassett. HBV
Thank God who seasons thus the year. The Fall of the Leaf. Henry David Thoreau. AmP; AP
Thank Goodness, the moving is over. "When the World Was in Building. . ." Ford Madox Ford. CTC
Thank Heaven! the crisis. For Annie. Poe. AmP; AmPP; AnFE; AP; APA; CoAnAm; HBV; LiTA; LO; MWA-1; NePA; OBEV; OBVV; OxBA; TreFS
Thank him who isled us here, and roughly set. Tennyson. *Fr.* Ode on the Death of the Duke of Wellington. PoFr
Thank Thee. Thomas Wentworth Higginson. *See* Things I Miss, The.
Thank Thee, Lord. Georgia B. Adams. SoP; STF
Thank Thee, O Giver of life, O God! Thanksgiving. Angela Morgan. TrPWD; TRV
Thank-You, A. William Canton. ThGo
Thank You. Kenneth Koch. NeAP
Thank You for Friends, A. Rodney Bennett. BoTP
Thank you for the world so sweet. E. Rutter Leatham. ThGo
Thank you for your letter. Ilford Rose Book. James Schuyler. ANYP
Thank You, God. Nina Stiles. PoToHe (new ed.)
Thank You, Pretty Cow. Ann *or* Jane Taylor. *See* Cow, The.
Thank you very much indeed. Thanks. Norman Gale. GoTP; OQP; OTPC (1946 ed.); YT
"Thank you, whatever comes." And then she turned. Erat Hora. Ezra Pound. CBV
Thankful Acknowledgment of God's Providence, A. John Cotton. SCAP
Thankful Country Lass, The; or, The Jolly Batchelor Kindly Entertained. *Unknown.* CoMu
Thankful Heart. F. W. Davis. STF
Thankful Heart, A. Robert Herrick. *See* Thanksgiving to God for His House, A.
Thankful Hearts. Helena Isabella Tupper. *See* Give Thanks.
Thankfulness. Albert Leonard Murray. SoP
Thankfulness. Adelaide Anne Procter. MaRV; SoP; TrPWD
Thanks. Norman Gale. GoTP; OQP; OTPC (1946 ed.); YT
Thanks. *Unknown.* SoP
Thanks and a Plea to Mary. *Unknown.* MeEL
Thanks Be to God. Janie Alford. MaRV; PGD; PoToHe
Thanks be to God for the light and the darkness. The Irish Te Deum. *Unknown.* WHL
Thanks, fair Urania; to your scorn. The Indifference. Sir Charles Sedley. BWP; CEP; SeCV-2
Thanks for Everything. Helen Isabella Tupper. *See* Give Thanks.

Thanks for Laughter. *Unknown.* OQP
Thanks from Earth to Heaven. John Hall Wheelock. HBMV
"Holy Poet, I have heard," *sel.* TrPWD
Thanks, Gentle Moon, for Thy Obscured Light. *Unknown.* NCEP
Thanks, I will. Phono, at the Boar's Head. Henri Coulette. *Fr.* The War of the Secret Agents. NePoEA-2
Thanks in Old Age. Walt Whitman. MCCG
Thanks Just the Same. *Unknown.* PoLF
Thanks, my Lord, for your venison, for finer or fatter. The Haunch of Venison. Goldsmith. CEP
Thanks: not for thoughts that give the mind more mirth. To Thomas Hardy. Laurence Housman. MaRV
Thanks, thanks! With the Muse is always love and light. Philip James Bailey. *Fr* Festus. VA
Thanks That Flesh Is Sad, A. John Ciardi. ToPo
Thanks to God. J. A. Hultman. STF
Thanks to much industry and pains. Shakespeare; an Epistle to Mr. Garrick. Robert Lloyd. EiCL
Thanks to Saint Matthew, who had been. Comrade Jesus. Sarah N. Cleghorn. AnAmPo; HBMV; MaRV; NAMP; OQP; PoFr; StJW; WGRP
Thanks to Spring. Mary Anderson. BoTP
Thanks to the morning light. The World-Soul. Emerson. AmePo; MWA-1
Thanksgiving. David Abenatar Melo, *tr. fr. Spanish by* Henry Hart Milman. TrJP
Thanksgiving, A. John Kendrick Bangs. MaRV
Thanksgiving. Amelia E. Barr. PEDC
Thanksgiving. Susie M. Best. TrPWD
Thanksgiving. Psalms, XCV: 1-7, C: 1-5, CXXXVI: 1-9, 26, Bible, *O.T.* BoChLi (1950 ed.)
Thanksgiving. Psalms, C, Bible, *O.T.* StVeCh
(Be Thankful unto Him.) FaPON
(Psalm of Praise.) SiSoSe; SUS
(Psalm C.) MPB; OHIP; OnPM; PG (1955 ed.); TiPo (1952 ed.); UnS
Thanksgiving. Alice Williams Brotherton. PGD
Thanksgiving. Florence Earle Coates. PEDC; TrPWD
Thanksgiving. Louise Driscoll. YeAr
Thanksgiving. Emerson. PCH
Thanksgiving, A. Annie Johnson Flint. SoP
Thanksgiving, The. George Herbert. AnAnS-1; MaMe; MeP; SCEP-1
Thanksgiving. Robert Herrick. LiTB
Thanksgiving. William Dean Howells. *See* Undiscovered Country, The.
Thanksgiving. Arthur Ketchum. STF
Thanksgiving. Joyce Kilmer. MaRV
Thanksgiving. Grenville Kleiser. SoP
Thanksgiving, A. Lucy Larcom. OHIP
"For the rosebud's break of beauty," *sel.* TrPWD
Thanksgiving. Angela Morgan. TrPWD; TRV
Thanksgiving. Margarete Münsterberg. GFA
Thanksgiving, A. Cardinal Newman. TrPWD
Thanksgiving. Robert Nichols. MMA
Thanksgiving. Gene H. Osborne. PGD
Thanksgiving. John Oxenham. BLRP; OQP; WBLP
Thanksgiving ("For all true words that have been spoken"). Margaret E. Sangster. SoP; TRV
Thanksgiving ("For the days when nothing happens"). Margaret E. Sangster. BLRP
Thanksgiving ("I think God loves simplicity"). Margaret E. Sangster. PEDC
Thanksgiving. Odell Shepard. PEDC
Thanksgiving. A. B. Simpson. STF
Thanksgiving, A. Jane Taylor. ThGo
Thanksgiving. Charles Hanson Towne. PoMa
Thanksgiving ("I thank Thee, dear Lord, for my eyes"). *Unknown.* SoP
Thanksgiving ("O precious Father, as we bow"). *Unknown.* SoP
Thanksgiving. *Unknown, at. to* Emerson. *See* We Thank Thee.
Thanksgiving, A. Carolyn Wells. PEDC
Thanksgiving. Amos Niven Wilder. MaRV
Thanksgiving. "Yehoash," *tr. fr. Yiddish by* Isidore Goldstick. TrJP
Thanksgiving and Praise. Neva Brien. SoP
Thanksgiving Day. John Kendrick Bangs. TrPWD
Thanksgiving Day. Robert Bridges. MaRV; OHIP
Thanksgiving Day. Lydia Maria Child. DD; FaPON; GFA; GoTP; HH; MPB; OHIP; OTD; OTPC; PCH, *sl. abr.*; PEDC; PRWS; PTK; SAS; SiSoSe; StVeCh; TreFS
Thanksgiving Day. James J. Montague. HH; PEDC
Thanksgiving Day. Annette Wynne. OHIP
Thanksgiving Day I like to see. Thanksgiving Magic. Rowena Bennett. BrR; SiSoSe; TiPo
Thanksgiving Day will soon be here. Turkey Time. *Unknown.* PCH
Thanksgiving Fable, A. Oliver Herford. HH; PRWS; UTS
Thanksgiving for a former, doth invite. Thanksgiving. Robert Herrick. LiTB
Thanksgiving for a Habitat. W. H. Auden. NYBP
Thanksgiving for America, The. Hezekiah Butterworth. PAH
Thanksgiving for National Peace. Anne Steele. SoP
Thanksgiving for Thanksgiving. Amos R. Wells. PEDC
Thanksgiving for the Body. Thomas Traherne. ImOP
Thanksgiving for the Earth. Elizabeth Goudge. YeAr
Thanksgiving for the ranks of corn. Thanksgiving Song. Clinton Scollard. PEDC
Thanksgiving Hymn ("The Lord above, in tender love"). *Unknown.* PAH
Thanksgiving in Boston Harbor, The. Hezekiah Butterworth. AA; DD, *abr.*; MC; OHIP; PAH
Thanksgiving Magic. Rowena Bennett. BrR; SiSoSe; TiPo
Thanksgiving Night. Wilbur D. Nesbit. DD; HH; PEDC
Thanksgiving, 1963. Molly Kazan. TreFT
Thanksgiving Psalm, A. *Unknown.* SoP
Thanksgiving Rosary, A. Edwin Markham. PEDC
Thanksgiving Song. Clinton Scollard. PEDC
Thanksgiving stirs her ruddy fire. Two Festivals. Lucy Larcom. DD
Thanksgiving Time. *Unknown.* OTPC (1946 ed.); PCH; SoPo
Thanksgiving to God, for His House, A. Robert Herrick. AnAnS-2; BEL; BoC; ChTr; EnLi-1; EnLit; FaBoBe; HBV; InPo; MaRV, *much abr.*; NeHB; NoP; OBS; OHIP; OTPC; PGD, *much abr.*; Po; PoE; PoRA; ReEn; SCEP-2; SeCeV; SeCP; SeCV-1; SeEP; SoP; TiPo (1952 ed.); TOP; TreFT; TrPWD; UnPo (1st ed.); ViBoPo; WGRP; WoL
(Thankful Heart, A, *much abr.*) OQP; PoToHe
Thanksgiving to the gods! The Seeker in the Marshes. Daniel Lewis Dawson. AA
Thanksgiving Wishes. Arthur Guiterman. PoSC
Thanksgiving for the Beauty of His Providence. Thomas Traherne. FaBoCh; LoGBV
Thanksliving. Chauncey R. Piety. OQP PGD
Thar she goes a-lopin', stranger. Our Little Cowgirl. *Unknown.* SCC
Thar was an ol' man who lived in de West. De Ol' Man. Alonzo W. Combs. IHA
Thar's lots o' music in 'em—the hymns o' long ago. The Old Hymns. Frank L. Stanton. BLRP
Thar's More in the Man than Thar Is in the Land. Sidney Lanier. AmePo; AP; CoBA
Thar's the bread, thar's the meat. Cowboy Grace. *Unknown.* CoSo
Tha'rt welcome, little bonny brid. Welcome, Bonny Brid! Samuel Laycock. VA
Thass a funny title, Mr. Bones. April Fool's Day, or, St. Mary of Egypt. John Berryman. The Dream Songs, XLVII. NaP
That after horror that was Us. Emily Dickinson. MoPo
That aged woman with the bass voice. The Great-Grandmother. Robert Graves. DTC; MoPW
That all should change to ghost and glance and gleam. The Transmutation. Edwin Muir. FaBoEn
That All Things Are as They Are Used. George Turberville. EnRePo
That all things should be mine. Amendment. Thomas Traherne. SCEP-1; SeCV-2
That amazing holiday. The Unscarred Fighter Remembers France. Kenneth Slade Alling. HBMV
That American Poet's future. The Line of an American Poet. Reed Whittemore. MoVE; PPON
That angel whose charge was Eiré sang thus. The Three Woes. Aubrey Thomas De Vere. AnIV
That any thing should be. Axle Song. Mark Van Doren. MoPo
That autumn when the partridges called in the stubble. Microcosmos, XLI. Nigel Heseltine. NeBP

That balmy eve, within a trellised bower. The Marriage of Pocahontas. Mrs. M. M. Webster. MC; PAH
That Beauty I Ador'd Before. Aphra Behn. UnTE
That best portion of a good man's life. Wordsworth. *Fr.* Lines Composed a Few Miles above Tintern Abbey. PoToHe
That blessed sunlight, that once showed to me. Sonnet on the Death of His Wife. John Masefield. BoPe
That boat has killed three people. Unlucky Boat. George Mackay Brown. NePoEA-2
That boy, the farmer said, with hazel wand. Frederick Goddard Tuckerman. *Fr.* Sonnets. MAmP
That Bright Chimeric Beast. Countee Cullen. AmNP; PoNe
That bull-necked blotch-faced farmer from Drumlore. Ghosts' Stories. Alastair Reid. NePoEA-2
That by which we have lost and still shall lose. Lost and Found. Edwin Muir. PoDB
That Cat. Ben King. FiBHP
That celestial power, to whom the care. Spenser. *Fr.* The Faerie Queene, II. MyFE
That childish thoughts such joys inspire. The Approach. Thomas Traherne. *Fr.* The Third Century. AnAnS-1; MeP; OxBoCh
That civilisation may not sink. Long-Legged Fly. W. B. Yeats. CaFP; CMoP; FaBoEn; FaBoTw; ForPo; LiTM; NoP; PoE; PoeP; PoIE
That Corner. Blanaid Salkeld. OnYI; OxBI
That corner of earth. Aware Aware. Tram Combs. TwCP
That "Craning of the Neck." Isabella Gardner. NePA
That crazed girl improvising her music. A Crazed Girl. W. B. Yeats. Sonn
That dark brown rabbit, lightness in his ears. John Berryman. *Fr.* The Dream Songs. TwCP
That Dark Other Mountain. Robert Francis. SD
That Day. Mark Van Doren. WaP
That day everything went wrong. Poetry Defined. John Holmes. PP
That day I oft remember, when from sleep. Eve's Speech to Adam. Milton. *Fr.* Paradise Lost, IV. DiPo
That day, in the slipping of torsos and straining flanks. The Song. Lola Ridge. NP
That day of wrath, that dreadful day/ Shall the whole world in ashes lay. Dies Irae. Thomas of Celano, *tr. by* Wentworth Dillon. WGRP
That day of wrath, that dreadful day/ When heaven and earth. Dies Irae. Thomas of Celano, *par. by* Sir Walter Scott. *Fr.* The Lay of the Last Minstrel, VI. GoBC; MaRV
That day of wrath, that dreadful day,/ When heaven and earth. Dies Irae. Thomas of Celano, *tr. by* Father Wingfield *and* Father Alward. WHL
That day the doves with burnished breasts. Told in the Market-Place. Edwina Stanton Babcock. StJW
That day the eggshell of appearance split. Transfigured Bird. James Merrill. MoAB
That day the sunlight lay on the farms. On Heaven. Ford Madox Ford. CTC
That Day You Came. Lizette Woodworth Reese. HBV
That Death Is Not So Much to Be Feared as Daily Diseases Are. George Turberville. ReIE
That Delightful Time. Mark Akenside. *Fr.* The Pleasures of Imagination. SeCePo
"That Did in Luve So Lively Write." Georgine M. Adams. InMe
That Distant Bliss. Henry King. *See* Tell Me No More.
That dog with daisies for eyes. The Dog of Art. Denise Levertov. FRC
That dolphin-torn, that gong-tormented face. The Death of Yeats. George Barker. LiTB
That dusky child upon your knee. Guardianship. Georgia Douglas Johnson. GoSl
That Each Thing Is Hurt of Itself. *Unknown.* EIL
That each, who seems a separate whole. In Memoriam A. H. H., XLVII. Tennyson. EnLi-2; EPN; ViPo; VP
That England lost, that learning lov'd, that every mouth commended. An Epitaph upon the Death of Sir Philip Sidney, Knight, Lord-Governor of Vlissing. Richard Barnfield. ReIE
That epigram that last you did rehearse. To Sextus, an Ill Reader. Sir John Harington. TuPP
That Eureka of Archimedes out of his bath. Voluptuaries and Others. Margaret Avison. MoCV
That evening all in fond discourse was spent. The Dejected Lover [*or* The Sad Lover]. George Crabbe. *Fr.* Tales of the Hall. FaBoEn; OBNC
That evening the stranger was carried to the chamber of death. On the Way. Georg Trakl. LiTW
That evening, when the fire was lit. The Dream. Helen Spalding. ChMP
That Ever I Saw. *Unknown.* CBEP; TrGrPo
("She is gentil and al so wise.") EG
("She is gentle and also wise.") LO
That face which no man ever saw. Sargent's Portrait of Edwin Booth at "The Players." Thomas Bailey Aldrich. AA
That Familiar Stranger. Felix Stefanile. FiSC
That Far Lone Mountain. Sister Mary Stephanie. JKCP (1955 ed.)
That far-off day the leaves in flight. The Wind and the Rain. Robert Frost. MWA-2
That fearful day, that day of speechless dread. The Canon for Apocreos. St. Theodore of Studium. CAW
That firewood pale with salt and burning green. Gigha. W. S. Graham. FaBoMo; NeBP
That first Christmas night of all. First Christmas Night of All. Nancy Byrd Turner. BiCB; PEDC
That flame is borne of earthly fire. *Unknown.* SeCSL
That Fond Impossibility. Richard Lovelace. *See* Scrutiny, The.
That for seven lusters I did never come. To the Reverend Shade of His Religious Father. Robert Herrick. AnAnS-2; OBS; SeCV-1; SeEP
That force is lost. Snake Eyes. LeRoi Jones. Kal
That, Fragoletta, is the rain. Songs for Fragoletta, III. Richard Le Gallienne. HBV
That Freedom and the Law are identical. In the Place of a Passage 22. Robert Duncan. FRC
That Garden of sedate Philosophy. The Garden of Epicurus. George Meredith. ATP (1953 ed.); EPN
That Gentle Man from Boston Town. Joaquin Miller. BOHV
That girl from the sun is bathing in the creek. The Dosser in Springtime. Douglas Stewart. ErPo; TDP
That girl who always wore the Harris tweeds. The English Rider. "Robin Hyde." AnNZ
That God doth live, enthroned in heaven above. My Creed. Henry W. Frost. SoP
That God, which ever lives and loves. The Truths That Never Can Be Proved. Tennyson. *Fr.* In Memoriam A. H. H., Epilogue. MaRV
That grave small face, but twelve hours here. The Chart. Walter de la Mare. CoBMV
That great tree covered with snow. Cardinal. Jim Harrison. WIRo
That gusty spring, each afternoon. Love's Calendar. William Bell Scott. HBV
That Harp You Play so Well. Marianne Moore. HBMV; MAP; MoAB; MoAmPo
(Harp You Play So Well, The.) NP
That haughty tyranny of thine. Love Song. Luis de León. TrJP
That He Findeth [*or* Finds] Others as Fair, but Not So Faithful as His Friend. George Turberville. EIL; SiCE; TuPP
That he to his unmeasur'd mightie acts. Praise of Homer. George Chapman. OBS
That He Who lay on Mary's knee. Rabboni! Master! Mother Loyola. WHL
That he would never have any rest this side of his death. Hagiograph. Rayner Heppenstall. NeBP
That Heart My Heart. *Unknown.* NoP
That heavens are void, and that no gods there are. Against an Atheist. Sir John Harington. SiCE
That her serene influence should spread. Two Loves. Richard Eberhart. CMoP; FiMAP
That Hill. Blanche Taylor Dickinson. CDC
That Hollow space, where now in living rowes. Fairies. Thomas Tickell. *Fr.* Kensington Garden. OBEC
That holy night when stars shone bright. A Child Is Born. *Unknown.* STF
That Holy Thing. George Macdonald. *Fr.* Paul Faber, Surgeon, *ch.* 49. ChIP; FaChP; HBV; MaRV; OBEV; OBVV; OQP; StJW; TRV; TrPWD; WGRP
That horse whose rider fears to jump will fall. Masters. Kingsley Amis. NePoEA; PoPl
That house, a stone's throw from the shell-strewn shore. Boat-Haven, Co. Mayo. Geoffrey Taylor. NeIP

That houses forme within was rude and strong. The House of Richesse. Spenser. *Fr.* The Faerie Queene, II. CH
"That humble, simple duty of the day." Serve in Thy Post. Arthur Hugh Clough. *Fr.* Last Words: Napoleon and Wellington. PGD
That I did always love. Emily Dickinson. FaPL
That I have felt the rushing wind of Thee. The Poet's Prayer. Stephen Phillips. WGRP
That I may know, yet more and more. Heart Wish. Henry W. Frost. SoP
That I may not in blindness grope. A Little Prayer. Samuel Ellsworth Kiser. MaRV
"That I might have unto my paramour." Christopher Marlowe. *Fr.* Dr. Faustus. FaPL
That I might make your cabinet my tombe. Epitaph on Himselfe. John Donne. MaMe
That I should have a joyous life. A Gift of God. *Unknown.* STF
That I so slenderly set forth my mind. William Drummond of Hawthornden. Sonn
That I went to warm my self in Lady Betty's chamber, because I was cold. To Their Excellencies the Lords Justices of Ireland, the Humble Petition of Frances Harris [*or* Mrs. Frances Harris's Petition]. Swift. BWP; CEP; ILP; Par; PoEL-3
That in Jesus' heart should be. In the Heart of Jesus. Murdoch O'Daly. CAW
That innocence is not a shield. The Wolf and the Lamb. La Fontaine. OuHeWo
That insect, without antennae, over its. The Crane. Charles Tomlinson. MoBrPo (1962 ed.)
That Is All I Heard. "Yehoash," *tr. fr. Yiddish by* Isidore Goldstick. TrJP
That Is Even So! *with music.* John A. Stone. SGR
"That is important. I do not watch the birds." He Said the Facts. Merrill Moore. CrMA
That is no country for old men. Sailing to Byzantium. W. B. Yeats. AnFE; AnIL; AtBAP; ATP (1953 ed.); BoPe; BWP; CABA; CaFP; CBEP; CBV; CMoP; CoBMV; DiPo; EnL; EnLi-2 (1949 ed.); EnLit; ExPo; FaBoEn; FaFP; ForPo; FosPo; GTBS-P; GTBS-W; HoPM; ILP; InPo; InvP; LiTB; LiTG; LiTM; MaPo; MasP; MBW-2; MoAB; MoBrPo; MoPo; MoPW; MoRP; MoVE; NAMP; NoP; OAEP (2d ed.); OBMV; OxBI; PAn; PIA; PoAn; PoDB; PoeP; PoFS; PoIE; PoPo; PoRA (rev. ed.); POTE; PoVP; PP; ReMP; SeCePo; SeCeV; ShBV-4; StP; TreFT; UnPo (3d ed.); ViBoPo
That is rain on dry ground. We heard it. Rain. Christopher Fry. *Fr.* The Boy with a Cart. BoC
That Is Tad. Sister Mary Norbert Körte. ThO
That is what they say, who were broken off from love. Children's Elegy. Muriel Rukeyser. *Fr.* Eighth Elegy. FiMAP
That it will never come again. Emily Dickinson. MWA-2
That Jenny's my friend, my delight, and my pride. Song the Eighth. Edward Moore. CEP
"That just reminds me of a yarn," he said. The Jester in the Trench. Leon Gellert. PoAu-1
That knot in the wood if wood. The Man with the Hollow Breast. Tania van Zyl. PeSA
That lady of all gentle memories. Dante. *Fr.* La Vita Nuova. AWP
That lamp thou fill'st in Eros' name to-night. Hero's Lamp. Dante Gabriel Rossetti. The House of Life, LXXXVIII. MaVP; PoVP; ViPo
That Learned Graecian (who did so excel). Sonnet. William Drummond of Hawthornden. OBS; SeEP
That (like the man sd) Booth. Charles Olson. *Fr.* Anecdotes of the Late War. LiPo
That little grey-haired lady. The Little Old Lady. Rodney Bennett. BoTP
That Love—whose power and sovranty we own. The Creation of My Lady. Francesco Redi. AWP
That lovely spot which thou dost see. Upon a Mole in Celias Bosome. Thomas Carew. AnAnS-2
That lover of a night. Crazy Jane on God. W. B. Yeats. AtBAP; CMoP; MoAB; PoDB
That man/ there. The Poet's Guilt. Arthur Pfister. WSL
That man,/ this man, never. Night Song for Two Mystics. Paul Blackburn. NeAP
That man is great, and he alone. True Greatness. "Owen Meredith." MaRV
That man must lead a happy life. Panegyric on the Ladies. *Unknown.* BOHV
That man or woman which will look. To the Reader. *Unknown.* SeCL
That man's a fool who tries by art and skill. Woman's Will. *Unknown.* HBV
That matter of the murder is hushed up. The Cenci. Shelley. EnRP
That Men Should Fear. Shakespeare. *See* Cowards ("Cowards die many times before their deaths").
That missel-thrush. The Missel Thrush. Andrew Young. BiS
That moment all the world respired. First Communion. José Asunción Silva. CAW
That morn which saw me made a bride. Upon a Maid That Died the Day She Was Married. Meleager. AWP
That morning, after the storm. After the Storm. Elizabeth Bartlett. GoYe
That my old bitter heart was pierced in this black doom. A Grey Eye Weeping. Egan O'Rahilly. AnIL; KiLC; OBMV; OxBI
That Nantucket Limerick, and What Followed. *Unknown.* TreF
Sels.
Limerick: "But he [*or* He *or* Pa] followed the pair to Pawtucket." HBV (8th ed.); LiBL; LiTG
Limerick: "Then the pair followed Pa to Manhasset." LiBL
Limerick: "There was [*or* once was] an old man of [*or* a man from] Nantucket." HBV (8th ed.); LiBL; LiTG
That Nature Is a Heraclitean Fire and of the Comfort of the Resurrection. Gerard Manley Hopkins. AtBAP; BrPo; CABA; CoBMV; DiPo; FaBoMo; GTBS-P; LiTB; MaPo; MoAB; MoPo; MoVE; NoP; OAEP (2d ed.); PAn; PoEL-5; ViPo (1962 ed.); ViPP
Of a Death in Winter, *sel.* BoW
That neither fame nor love might wanting be. To Sir Henry Cary. Ben Jonson. NoP
That night I think that no one slept. The Last Fight. Lewis Frank Tooker. AA; FaBoBe
That night, letting lie the copper kettle, she was saying. The Invasion of Greece. Jeremy Ingalls. PoFr
That night my angel stooped and strained. My Angel. Jonathan Henderson Brooks. PoNe
That night, when I woke suddenly, was sweet. Conversation with Rain. Louise D. Gunn. GoYe
That Night When Joy Began. W. H. Auden. CBV
That night, when through the mooring-chains. The Ballad of Fisher's Boardinghouse. Kipling. PoRA
That night will long delight us, Nealca. Three Lyrics. Petronius Arbiter, *tr. fr. Latin by* Kenneth Rexroth. LiTW
That night your great guns, unawares. Channel Firing. Thomas Hardy. BrPo; CABA; CBV; CMoP; CoBMV; EnL; ExPo; ForPo; ILP; LiTB; MaPo; MoPo; NoP; OAEP (2d ed.); PAn; PoAn; PoEL-5; PoeP; PoFS; PoIE; PoRA; PPON; SeCeV; StP; TDP; UnPo; ViPP; VP; WaaP
That nightingale, whose strain so sweetly flows. The Nightingale. Petrarch, *tr. by* Thomas LeMesurier. Sonnets to Laura: To Laura in Death, XLIII. LiTW; PoPl
That No Man Should Write but Such as Do Excel. George Turberville. EnRePo
That noise that Time makes in passing by. The Noise That Time Makes. Merrill Moore. TrGrPo (rev. ed.)
That None Beguiled Be. Sir John Suckling. PoEL-3; SeCL
That nose is out of drawing. With a gasp. Sonnet for a Picture. Swinburne. *Fr.* The Heptalogia. OAEP; VP
That Nova was a moderate star like our good sun. Robinson Jeffers. CMoP
That Odd Little Sparrow. *Unknown.* SoP
That odyssey? We three left Amherst late. To My Fellow-Mariners, March' 53. Thomas Whitbread. NYBP
That old man at the farm near Norman's Lane. The Farm near Norman's Lane. Mary Finnin. PoAu-2
That old monk confined in his cell. Monasteries. Charles David Webb. NePoAm-2
That Old Time Religion. Marvin E. Jackmon. BF
That on her lap she casts her humble eye. On the Blessed Virgin's Bashfulness. Richard Crashaw. EnLi-1; ILP; ISi; MaMe; OAEP
That once the gentle mind of my dead wife. William Ellery Leonard. *Fr.* Two Lives, Pt. III. AnAmPo

That once this life was really mine. A Song of Life. Franz Werfel. TrJP

That One Face. Robert Browning. *Fr.* Dramatis Personae: Epilogue. ChIP; MaRV

That overnight a rose could come. Overnight, a Rose. Caroline Giltinan. HBMV; SoP

That Path. *Unknown, tr. fr. Japanese by* Ishii *and* Obata. OnPM

That poets are far rarer births than kings. To Elizabeth, Countess of Rutland. Ben Jonson. NoP

That Pretty Little Gal. *Unknown* ABF

That Providence which had so long the care. A Poem upon the Death of O. C. Andrew Marvell. MaMe

That prudent Prince who ends Shakespearian plays. Elizabethan Tragedy; a Footnote. Howard Moss. NePoEA

That Radio Religion. William Ludlum. WBLP

"That rake up near the rafters, why leave it there so long?" Rory of the Hill. Charles Joseph Kickham. OnYI

That Rama whom the Indian sung. Of Rama. Herman Melville. AnFE; CoAnAm; LiTA

That Reminds Me. Ogden Nash. FiBHP; MeWo

That same first fiddler who leads the orchestra tonight. At Madame Tussaud's in Victorian Years. Thomas Hardy. MuSP

That scything wind has cut the rich corn down. John Knox. Iain Crichton Smith. OxBS

That sea was greater than we knew. The Voyage. Edwin Muir. GTBS-W; LiTM (rev. ed.)

That season when the leaf deserts the bole. October 1. Karl Shapiro. FiMAP; MoAB; MoAmPo (1950 ed.)

That seat of science, Athens. Free America. *At.* to Joseph Warren. PAP; PoFr

That second time they hunted me. The Italian in England. Robert Browning. MaVP; OAEP; PoVP; ViPo

That selfsame tongue which first did thee entreat. The Constancy of a Lover. George Gascoigne. EnRePo; QFR

That she hath gone to Heaven suddenly. Dante. *Fr.* La Vita Nuova, III. CTC

That son of Cain, let him have no more power. A Wish. Vidal de Nicolas. BoC

That son of Italy who tried to blow. Austerity of Poetry [*or* Jacopone da Todi]. Matthew Arnold. BEL; CAW; CLwM; EnLi-2; EPN; GoBC; OAEP; OBVV; PoFS; PoVP; TOP; VP

That sovereign thought obscured? That vision clear. On a Great Man Whose Mind Is Clouding. Edmund Clarence Stedman. AA

That Speaking or Proffering Brings Alway Speeding. Sir Thomas Wyatt. *See* Speak Thou and Speed.

That spot of blood on the drawing room wall. The Conversation in the Drawing Room. Weldon Kees. TwAmPo

That spring in Palestine when airs went forth. The Annunciation. Margaret D. Conway. JKCP (1955 ed.)

That spring night I spent. Lady Suo, *tr. fr. Japanese by* Kenneth Rexroth. LiTW

That story which the bold Sir Bedivere. The Passing of Arthur. Tennyson. *Fr.* Idylls of the King. CoBE; EPN; OBNC

That Strain Again. Ronald Hambleton. CaP

That strange companion came on shuffling feet. The Strange Companion. Harold Monro. NP

That stream ran through the sunny grass so clear. The Ancestors. Judith Wright. BoAV

That such have died enables us. Emily Dickinson. AA; AmPP

That Summer. Henry Treece. NYBP

That summer we saw the Blue Horse. The Blue Horse. Melvin Walker La Follette. NePoEA

That Summer's Shore. John Ciardi. ErPo

That Sunday morning, at half past ten. The Ballad of Longwood Glen. Vladimir Nabokov. NYBP

That Sunday, on my oath, the rain was a heavy overcoat. Mary Hynes. Padraic Fallon, *after* Anthony Raftery. AnIV; OxBI

That Texan Cattle Man. Joaquin Miller. BOHV

That! That! There I was told. The Bible. Thomas Traherne. LoBV (1949 ed.)

That the dread happenings of myths reveal. *Fr.* Mythological Sonnets. Roy Fuller. Sonn

That the glass would melt in heat. The Glass of Water. Wallace Stevens. AP AtBAP; CABA; CoBMV; MoAB; MoAmPo (1950 ed.); MoPo; OxBA

That the green angel of nature. The Leader. Thomas Hanna. QAH

That the high sheen of death could blot. Midsummer. James Scully. NYBP; TwCP

That the mere glimpse of a plain cap. The Glimpse of a Plain Cap. *Unknown. Fr.* Shi King. LiTW

That the Night Come. W. B. Yeats. CoBMV; MemP; NP; PoEL-5; PoeP

That the Soul Is Immortal, and Cannot Die. Sir John Davies. *Fr.* Nosce Teipsum. TuPP

That thee is sent, receyve in buxumnesse. Chaucer. *Fr.* The Canterbury Tales: The Clerk's Tale PoG

That There Are Powers above Us I Admit. Arthur Hugh Clough. ViPP

That there is falsehood in his looks. The Parson's Looks. Burns. OxBoLi

That there should be a barren garden. A House in Taos: Sun. Langston Hughes. CDC

"That They All May Be One." Roden Noel. VA

That Things Are No Worse, Sire. Helen Hunt Jackson. OHIP

That thou hast her, it is not all my grief. Sonnets, XLII. Shakespeare. CBEP; InvP

That thou so often held Him to thine arms. Mother Most Powerful. Giovanni Dominici. CAW

That Time and Absence Proves Rather Helps than Hurts to Loves. John Hoskins. *See* Absence.

That time of revolution being come. Reflections in Bed. Julian Symons. LiTM; WaP

That time of year thou may'st in me behold. Sonnets, LXXIII [*or* A Twilight of Love]. Shakespeare. AnFE; ATP (1935 ed.); AWP; BEL; BoLiVe; BWP; CABA; CaFP; CBEP; CBV; ChTr; CLwM; CoBE; CTC; DiPo; EG; EiL; EnL; EnLi-1; EnLit; EnLoPo; EnRePo; EP; ExPo; FaBoEn; FaBV; FiP; ForPo; FosPo; GTBS; GTBS-D; GTBS-P; GTBS-W; GTSE; GTSL; HBV; HoPM; ILP; InPo; InvP; JAWP; LiTB; LiTG; LoBV; MaPo; MasP; NoP; OAEP; OBEV; OBSC; OHFP (1958 ed.); OuHeWo; PAn; PG (1955 ed.); PoAn; PoE; PoEL-2; PoeP; PoFS; PoIE; PoMa; PoPo; PoRA; PoSa; QFR; ReEn; RelE; SeCeV; SiCE; Sonn; StP; TOP; TrGrPo; VaPo; ViBoPo; WBP

That time that mirth did steer my ship. Sir Thomas Wyatt. FCP; SiPS

That time we went to Suffolk Downs to see. The Beautiful Horses. Donald Hall. NePoAm-2

That time when Bob got throwed. When Bob Got Throwed. *Unknown.* SCC

That 'tis well to be off with the old love. Dictum Sapienti. Charles Henry Webb. ALV

That twilight, dearest, as I spoke with thee. In the Face of Grief. Sister Juana Inéz de la Cruz. CAW

That unripe side of earth, that heavy clime. To the Countesse of Huntington. John Donne. MaMe

That vengeance [*or* vengeaunce] I ask and cry. Cursing of the Cat [*or* O Cat of Carlish Kind]. John Skelton. *Fr.* Phyllyp Sparowe. ChTr; OA; SiCE

That very time I saw, but thou couldst not. Love-in-Idleness. Shakespeare. *Fr.* A Midsummer Night's Dream, II, i. MemP; TrGrPo

That very time I saw (but thou couldst not). Reuben. Phoebe Cary. BOHV

That voice, that presence, or that face. To His Mistress. T. Beaumont. SeCL

That war should bankrupts make of merchants is no wonder. Upon the Bankruptcy of a Physician. Henricus Selyns. SCAP

That was a brave old epoch. The Battle of La Prairie. William Douw Lighthall. MC; PAH; VA

That was a shocking day. Beasts. Paul Engle. PoCh; ReMP

That Was All! *Unknown.* SoP

That was her beginning, an apparition. First Love. Laurie Lee. ChMP; ToPo

That Was My Woe. Robert Fairfax. TuPP

That was once her casement. In the Mind's Eye. Thomas Hardy. SiSw

That was the chirp of Ariel. Wind on the Lyre. George Meredith. CaFP; EG; NBM

That was the day they killed the Son of God. The Killing. Edwin Muir. ACV; BoPe; ChMP; MoRP; PoPl

That was the night, Love, Bird came back and blew. Ballade of the Session after Camarillo. David Galler. NMP

"That was the thrush's last good-night," I thought. The Singer. Edward Dowden. IrPN
That was the top of the walk, when he said. The Gypsy. Ezra Pound. ThWaDe
That was the year. A Poem to Delight My Friends Who Laugh at Science-Fiction. Edwin Rolfe. NePA; NePoAm; PPON; ThLM
That Way. Anne Welsh. PeSA
That way look, my infant, lo! The Kitten and Falling Leaves. Wordsworth. CIV; HBVY
That we are mortals and on earth must dwell. A Garden Prayer. Thomas Walsh. OQP
That we may never lack two Sundays in a week. Secular Litany. M. K. Joseph. AnNZ
That week the fall was opulent. Vendanges. 1956. Daniel G. Hoffman. PoCh
That which hath made them drunk, hath made me bold. The Murder. Shakespeare. *Fr.* Macbeth, II, ii. AtBAP; MyFE; WHA
"That Which Hath Wings Shall Tell." Linda Lyon Van Voorhis. GoBC
That which her slender waste confined. On a Girdle. Edmund Waller. ALV; AnAnS-2; AWP; BEL; CABA; CavP; CEP; EG; EnLi-1; EnLit; GTBS; GTBS-D; GTBS-P; GTBS-W; GTSE; GTSL; HBV; InMe; InPo; JAWP; LiTB; LiTG; LiTL; LoBV; MeWo; NoP; OAEP; OBEV; OBS; PG (1945 ed.); PoAn; PoFS; PoIE; PoRA; SCEP-2; SeCePo; SeCL; SeCV-1; SeEP; StP; TOP; TreFS; TrGrPo; UnTE; ViBoPo; WBP; WHA
"That which I have myself seen and the fighting." Bernál Díaz's Preface to His Book. Archibald MacLeish. *Fr.* Conquistador. AmPP (3d ed.)
That which is, being the only answer. Question and Answer. Kathleen Raine. MoBrPo (1962 ed.)
That which is marred at birth time shall not mend. Gertrude's Prayer. Kipling. FaBoEn
That Which Made Us. Tennyson. *Fr.* Locksley Hall Sixty Years After. OQP
That which my fault has made me, O paint not. A Poet to a Painter. Aubrey Thomas De Vere. Sonn
That which shall last for aye can have no birth. Or Ever the Earth Was. Charles Leonard Moore. AA
That which the long scythe whispered to the grass. Ruth Gilbert. *Fr.* And There Shall Be No More Death. AnNZ
That which we dare invoke to bless. In Memoriam A. H. H., CXXIV. Tennyson. EnL; EPN; FosPo; GTSL; MaRV; OAEP; ViPo; VP; WGRP
That Whitsun, I was late getting away. The Whitsun Weddings. Philip Larkin. NePoEA-2; PoeP; TDP
That Wind. Emily Brontë. CH
That winter love spoke and we raised no objection. Jig. C. Day Lewis. OxBI; WePo
That with this bright believing band. The Impercipient. Thomas Hardy. MaPo; MaRV; OAEP; TrGrPo; ViBoPo; ViPo; WGRP
That wolf, shivering by the palisade. Colonial Set. Alfred Goldsworthy Bailey. OBCV
That Women Are but Men's Shadows. Ben Jonson. *See* Song: That Women Are but Men's Shadows.
That wooded face of cliffs and shadows. Remembering Lincoln. Frank Mundorf. GoYe
That year no wondering shepherds came. Christmas, the Year One, A.D. Sara Henderson Hay. PoRA
That year they fought in the snow. Rostov. G. S. Fraser. LiTM (rev. ed.); WaP
That year? Yes, doubtless I remember still. The World Well Lost. Edmund Clarence Stedman. AA; OBRV
That you like me not. Referring to Flowers. *Unknown.* *Fr.* Manyo Shu. OnPM
That you, struck down by fortune's angry hand. Letter to Manlius Torquatus. Catullus. LiTW
That you were once unkind befriends me now. Sonnets, CXX. Shakespeare. InvP
That zephyr every year. Spring Bereaved. William Drummond of Hawthornden. OBEV
Thatcher of Thatchwood went to Thatchet a-thatching, A. *Unknown.* OxNR
"That's a detestable thing you did!" A Deep Discussion. Richard Moore. HoPM
That's a pint of red daisies. Liquid'll. Alfred Starr Hamilton. QAH
That's All. *Unknown.* SoP
That's Ethan Allen on the monument. Green Mountain Boy. Florida Watts Smyth. GoYe
That's Faith. S. N. Leitner. STF
That's his saddle across the tie-beam, an' them's his spurs up there. My Mate Bill. G. H. Gibson. PoAu-1
That's Jesus! Grace B. Renfrow. BePJ
That's July. Mary F. Butts. YeAr
That's June. Mary F. Butts. YeAr
That's my last Duchess painted on the wall. My Last Duchess. Robert Browning. ATP; AWP; BEL; BeLS; BoLiVe; CABA; CaFP; CBEP; CBV; CoBE; DiPo; EnL; EnLi-2; EnLit; EPN; ExPo; FaBoEn; FaFP; FiP; ForPo; FosPo; GTBS-P; HBV; HoPM; ILP; InP; InPo; JAWP; LiTB; MasP; MaVP; MBW-2; MCCG; NoP; OAEP; OBNC; OnPP; OtMeF; OuHeWo; PAn; PeVV; PIA; PoAn; PoE; PoEL-5; PoIE; PoLF; PoPo; PoSa; PoVP; SeCeV; ShBV-4; StP; TOP; TreFS; TrGrPo; UnPo (1st ed.); VA; VaPo; ViPo; ViPP; VP; WBP; WHA; YAT
That's not a broom you're using, soldier. The Bayonet. Shawn O'Leary. MoAuPo
That's slowish work, Bob. What'st a-been about? The Best Man in the Vield. William Barnes. PeVV
That's Success! Berton Braley. *See* Success.
That's the cuckoo, you say. I cannot hear it. The Cuckoo. Edward Thomas. BrPo
That's the queer life, said the chair. Chair, Dog, and Clock. Hilary Corke. NYBP
That's the Way to Talk It. Mart Taylor. SGR
That's what misery is. Poetry Is a Destructive Force. Wallace Stevens. OxBA
T'have written then, when you writ, seem'd to mee. To the Countesse of Bedford. John Donne. MaMe
Thaw. Walker Gibson. ELU; NePoAm
Thaw, The. Jack Matthews. WIRo
Thaw. Edward Thomas. BiS; ELU; FaBoTw; FIW; GTBS-P; HaMV; MoAB; MoBrPo; NeMA
Thaw. Eunice Tietjens. BrR
Thaw. Jean Starr Untermeyer. AtBAP
Thaw in the City. Lou Lipsitz. YAP
Thay walkit furth so derk oneith they wist. The Entrance to Hell. Vergil, *tr. by* Gawin Douglas. *Fr.* The Aeneid, VI. GoTS
The/ Voice of Jesus I. Poem Beginning "The". Louis Zukofsky. CoPo
"The: the"/ matter-of-factness, plural. James Brodey. *Fr.* Identikit. ANYP
Thealma and Clearchus, *sel.* John Chalkhill. Rhotus on Arcadia. OBS
Theater is still, and Duse speaks, The. Eleonora Duse as Magda. Laurence Binyon. SyP
Theatre, The. Horace Smith *and* James Smith. Par
"John Richard William Alexander Dwyer." OBRV
Thebes of the Seven Gates. Sophocles, *tr. fr. Greek by* Dudley Fitts *and* Robert Fitzgerald. *Fr.* Antigone. WaaP
Thee finds me in the garden, Hannah—come in! The Quaker Widow. Bayard Taylor. AA
Thee for my recitative. To a Locomotive in Winter. Walt Whitman. AmLP; AmPP; AP; DiPo; FaBV; ILP; InP; MCCG; MoAmPo (1950 ed.); NoP; PoE; PoEL-5; PoFS; StP
Thee, God, O thee, we sing, we celebrate. Psalm LXXV. Countess of Pembroke. EP
Thee, holiest minister of Heaven—thee, envoy, usherer, guide at last of all. Peaceful Death. Walt Whitman. OQP
Thee I Adore. Baudelaire, *tr. fr. French by* Arthur Symons. OnPM
"Thee, Mary, with this ring I wed." To His Wife on the Fourteenth [*or* Sixteenth] Anniversary of Her Wedding-Day [*or* To Mary]. Samuel Bishop. HBV; LO; ViBoPo
Thee, May and Mother, I entreat. Author's Entreaty for His Lay. Eysteinn Asgrímsson. *Fr.* Lilya. ISi
Thee, O Mary, will I praise. Song of Praise to Mary. "Angelus Silesius." CAW
Thee sets a bell to swinging in my soul. Sonnets in Quaker Language. Hildegarde Flanner. NP
Thee, Sovereign God, our grateful accents praise. Te Deum. *Unknown, tr. by* Dryden. AWP; JAWP; OuHeWo; WBP
Thee, Thee, Only Thee. Thomas Moore. OBNC
Thee too, modest tressèd maid. Moon. Henry Rowe. OBEV

Thee too the years shall cover. Anactoria. Swinburne. ViBoPo
Thee will I love, O Lord, with all my heart's delight. Psalm XVIII. *Paraphrased by* Sir Philip Sidney. FCP
Theft, The. George Wither. *See* Stolen Kiss, A.
Thefts of the Morning. Edith M. Thomas. AA
Their Banishment. Milton. *Fr.* Paradise Lost, XII. SeCePo
Their belongings were buried side by side. The Drawer. George MacBeth. NePoEA-2
Their brown, harmless flack. The Sparrows at the Airport. Anthony Ostroff. NePoAm-2
Their cheeks are blotched for shame, their running verse. The Bards [*or* Lust in Song]. Robert Graves. DTC; FaBoMo; GTBS-W; LiTM (rev. ed.); OxBI; SeCePo. *See also* Bards falter in shame, their running verse, The.
Their Conscience as Their King. Tennyson. *Fr.* Idylls of the King: Guinevere. MaRV
Their country's need is more to them than personal demands. The Medical Corps. Beatrice Barry. PEDC
Their dufflebags sprawl like a murder. Words without Music. Irving Layton. CaP
Their eyelids are drooping, no tears lie beneath. Weavers. Heine. TrJP
Their eyes had known the quiet color blue. Prisoner of War. Gertrude May Lutz. GoYe
Their faces, safe as an interior. The Middle-aged. Adrienne Rich. NePoEA-2
Their feet on London, their heads in the gray clouds. Whitmonday. Louis MacNeice. NYBP
Their hearts are filled with Pity's mead. A Gaelic Christmas. Liam P. Clancy. ISi
Their heels slapped their bumping mules. Merchants from Cathay. William Rose Benét. HBMV; MAP; MoAmPo; NeMA
Their height in heaven comforts not. Emily Dickinson. NePA
Their horses are black, the shoes of their horses are black. Ballad of the Spanish Civil Guard. Federico García Lorca. LiTW
Their house faces east, is protected by trees. A Storm from the East. Reed Whittemore. NYBP; PoPl
Their Last Will and Testament. Louis MacNeice. NAMP
Their learned kings bent down to chat with frogs. Nursery Rhyme. W. H. Auden. SiSw
Their little room grew light with cries. Proper Clay. Mark Van Doren. PoRA; TrGrPo
Their Lonely Betters. W. H. Auden. GoJo; LOW
Their memories behind them. Salvation Prospect. LeRoy Smith, Jr. NePoAm
Their mockery brought him double force. Blind Samson. William Plomer. PeSA
Their mouths have drunken the eternal wine. The Night of Gods. George Sterling. MAP; MoAmPo (1942 ed.); PFY; WHA
Their noonday never knows. Fame. John Banister Tabb. AA; AmLP
Their Party, Our House. Jon Swan. NYBP
Their poet, a sad trimmer, but no less. The Isles of Greece, Ways of Poets. Byron. *Fr.* Don Juan, III. EPN
Their prayers still swarm on me like lost bees. The Saint of the Uplands. W. S. Merwin. NoP
Their quick feet pattered on the grass. Night Dancers. Thomas Kennedy. MoSiPe
Their sense is with their senses all mixed in. Modern Love, XLVIII. George Meredith. EnLi-2; ViPo; VP
Their shoulders you shook. The Preacher. Al-Mahdi, *tr. fr. Arabic by* A. J. Arberry. TTY
Their spare, fanatic sentry comes. Ants and Others. Adrien Stoutenburg. NYBP
Their Thanksgiving Day. Louise Driscoll. PCH
Their time past, pulled down. Burning the Christmas Greens. William Carlos Williams. AP; CABL; CoBMV; LiTM (1970 ed.); MoPo; NePA; TwAmPo
Their verdure dare not show. Valediction. Louis MacNeice. AnIL; MoVE
Their Victory Won. Florence Earle Coates. PEDC
Their voices heard, I stumble suddenly. One More New Botched Beginning. Stephen Spender. NYBP
Their war-boots said big shots to the plank floor. Behold, One of Several Little Christs. Kenneth Patchen. NaP
Their Wedded Love. Milton. *See* Wedded Love.
Theirs is a white a green life, a smooth. Red Cross Nurses. Gervase Stewart. WaP
Theirs is the courage of flesh and bone. Of Things Not Seen. Leslie Savage Clark. ChIP
Theirs is the house whose windows—every pane. On the Asylum Road. Charlotte Mew. MoBrPo (1950 ed.)
Thekla's Song. Schiller, *tr. fr. German by* Samuel Taylor Coleridge. *Fr.* The Piccolomini. AWP; JAWP; WBP
Thel's Motto. Blake. *Fr.* The Book of Thel. ChTr; DiPo ("Does the eagle know what is in the pit?") LO
Them ez wants, must choose. A Baker's Duzzen uv Wize Sawz. Edward Rowland Sill. FaBoBe; FaFP; HBV; HBVY; InMe; SiTL; TreFS
Theme. Carl Spitteler, *tr. fr. German by* Margarete Münsterberg. PoPl
Theme. James Stephens. ACV; POTE
Theme and Variation. Peter De Vries. NYBP
Theme Brown Girl. Elton Hill. NBP
Theme for English B. Langston Hughes. BALP
Theme in Yellow. Carl Sandburg. MPB; RePo; StVeCh (1955 ed.); TiPo; YeAr
Theme of morning was the sound of rain, The. Rain. Sam Harrison. NeIP
Theme Song for a Songwriters' Union. Al Graham. WhC
Theme tune occurs again, The. Das Liebesleben. Thom Gunn. ErPo
Theme with Variations, *sel.* James Stephens.
"No pride hath he who sings of escape from love." POTE
Themes. Denis Glover. AnNZ
Themes of love and death I have rehearsed, The. Judges, Judges. Gene Baro. NePoEA-2
Then. Dorothy Aldis. BiCB
Then. Rose Terry Cooke. HBV
Then. Walter de la Mare. GaP; TVC
Then. Edwin Muir. CMoP
Then a partridge-shaped cloud over dust storm. Ezra Pound. *Fr.* Canto CXIII. NYBP
Then a ploughman said, speak to us of work. On Work. Kahlil Gibran. *Fr.* The Prophet. PoToHe (new ed.)
Then a thousand men thronged together. The Search for St. Truth. William Langland. *Fr.* The Vision of Piers Plowman. MeEV
Then Ag'in. Sam Walter Foss. BOHV; HBV
Then all the minutes of my life to come. Thomas Lovell Beddoes. *Fr.* Death's Jest Book, II. LO
Then and Now. A. E. Housman. *See* Oh, When I Was in Love with You.
Then and Now. Charles Frederick Johnson. AA
Then and Now. Sir Rennell Rodd. VA
Then and Now. George Sterling. PoMa
Then are the trackless copses alive with the trilling of birds. Vergil. *Fr.* The Georgics, II. FlW
Then as Now. Walter de la Mare. WaKn
Then As to Feasting. Oliver Wendell Holmes. WhC
Then, at the point of death, Sohrab replied. Matthew Arnold. *Fr.* Sohrab and Rustum. MBW-2
Then bold Robin Hood to the north he would go. Robin Hood and the Scotchman. *Unknown.* ESPB
Then came fair May, the fairest maid on the ground. May. Spenser. *Fr.* The Faerie Queene, VII. GN; PoRL
Then Came I to the Shoreless Shore of Silence. Conrad Aiken. Preludes for Memnon, XXXIII. LiTA; NePA; OxBA; TwAmPo
Then came old January, wrapped well. Old January. Spenser. *Fr.* The Faerie Queene, VII, 7. YeAr
Then came the Autumn all in yellow clad. Autumn. Spenser. *Fr.* The Faerie Queene, VII, 7. GN
Then came the cry of "Call all hands on deck!" Rounding the Horn [*or* Dauber Rounds Cape Horn]. John Masefield. *Fr.* Dauber. BBV; EtS; MoAB; MoBrPo; NeMA; WHA
Then came there two women, that were harlots. Solomon Judges between Two Women Disputing over a Child. First Kings, Bible, *O.T.* TreFT
Then comes the Winter, like a hale old man. Winter. James Hurnard. PoSC
Then cometh he to a city of Samaria. Jesus and the Woman at the Well. St. John, Bible, *N.T.* TreFT
Then Constantine, mindful of the Holy Cross. Helena Embarks for Palestine. Cynewulf. *Fr.* Elene. AnOE
Then, couched at night in hunter's wattled shieling. Thomas Pringle. *Fr.* The Desolate Valley. BoSA

Then, day by day, her broidered gown. The Earth in Spring. Judah Halevi. TrJP
Then did Siddartha raise his eyes, and see. The End Which Comes. Sir Edwin Arnold. *Fr.* The Light of Asia. LoBV
Then die! Outside the prison gawk. For St. Bartholomew's Eve. Malcolm Cowley. NAMP
Then first I observe from the French-man Des Cartes. A Character of the Dutch. *At. to* Henry Nevile Payne. *Fr.* A Description of Holland by Mr. Nevell. PeRV
Then fled, O brethren, the wicked juba. The Ballad of Nat Turner. Robert E. Hayden. BALP
Then forth issewed (great goddesse) great Dame Nature. Dame Nature. Spenser. *Fr.* The Faerie Queene, VII, 7. PoEL-1
Then from a Ruin. Ferid ed-Din Attar, *tr. fr. Persian by* Edward Fitzgerald. BiS
Then from the moor, under misty hills. Beowulf's Fight with Grendel. *Unknown. Fr.* Beowulf. YAT
Then from the seas [*or* sea] the dawning 'gan arise. Dido's Hunting [*or* The Fourth Book of Virgil]. Vergil, *tr. by* the Earl of Surrey. *Fr.* The Aeneid, IV. OBSC; ReEn
Then, from the skeletons of trams. Kenneth Slessor. *Fr.* Last Trams. MoAuPo
Then from their poverty they rose. The Ordinary Women. Wallace Stevens. OxBA
Then gently scan your brother man. Burns. *Fr.* Address to the Unco Guid, or the Rigidly Righteous. MaRV
Then Glutton got ready to go to confession. Glutton and Bat the Brewer. William Langland. *Fr.* The Vision of Piers Plowman, Passus V. CoBE
Then God Bends Low. Dorothy Conant Stroud. SoP
Then had passed by, in the course of years. Cynewulf. *Fr.* Elene. YAT
Then haste ye, Prescott and Revere! The Battle of Lexington. Sidney Lanier. *Fr.* The Psalm of the West. PAP
Then hate me when thou wilt; if ever, now. Sonnets, XC. Shakespeare. ATP; AWP; CLwM; EIL; JAWP; LO; MaPo; OBEV; OBSC; PG; PoEL-2; ReIE; TOP; WBP; WHA; WoL
Then have mercy upon me. Mercury. Josephine Miles. FiMAP
Then he lived among wild lands. Stages. Roy Macnab. ACV
Then he made of the stars, in my mind. Baiamai's Never-failing Stream. William Hart-Smith. BoAV
Then He summoned an archangel. Romance VIII. St. John of the Cross. ISi
Then he who had formerly worked many crimes. The Defeat of Grendel. *Unknown. Fr.* Beowulf. YAT
Then heavenly branches did I see arise. The Visions of Petrarch. *Tr. by* Spenser. EnLi-1
Then here's an end of me: fare-well day-light. John Webster. *Fr.* The White Devil. AtBAP
Then hey for a song of Sussex. Southdown Summer. "Sagittarius." HT
Then Hrothgar's minstrel rehearsed the lay. The Lay of Finn. *Unknown. Fr.* Beowulf. AnOE
Then Hurrah for Home! *with music.* John A. Stone. SGR
Then hush! oh, hush! for the Father knows what thou knowest not. Hush! Frances Ridley Havergal. SoP
Then I cried out upon him: Cease. Christina Rossetti. *Fr.* Despised and Rejected. PeVV
Then I Saw What the Calling Was. Muriel Rukeyser. FiMAP
Then I turned my harp—took off the lilies we twine round its chords. Robert Browning. *Fr.* Saul. BBV (1951 ed.); FiP
Then I was crazy. The Monument to Resignation. Jon Anderson. YAP
Then I was sealed, and like the wintering tree. Alas, Kind Element. Léonie Adams. MoVE
Then I'll Believe. B. W. Vilakazi, *tr. fr. Zulu by* Jack Cope. PeSA
Then I'll say this—life is so still. Endymion. Humbert Wolfe. NP
Then, indeed, did I yearn to die. The Parting. Sappho. LiTW
Then is there mirth in heaven. High Wedlock Then Be Honoured. Shakespeare. *Fr.* As You Like It, V, iv. HW
Then it came to pass that a pestilence fell on the city. The Finding of Gabriel. Longfellow. *Fr.* Evangeline, II. AA
Then it was dusk in Illinois, the small boy. First Song. Galway Kinnell. GoJo; LiTM (1970 ed.); NePoAm; TPM; TwCP
Then it was hound. Its force compelled the jaw. Famine. Georg Heym. LiTW
Then it was ordered that hands should make ready. The Feasting and Giving of Treasure in the Hall. *Unknown. Fr.* Beowulf. YAT
Then it's a hooraw, and a hooraw. Standin' on the Walls of Zion. *Unknown.* AS
Then Job answered and said. Not Flesh of Brass. Job, Bible, *O.T.* TrJP
Then Job arose, and rent his mantle. The Lord Gave. Job, Bible, *O.T.* TreF
Then judge me as thou wilt, I cannot flee. Sonnets, III. Robert Hillyer. HBMV
Then, lady, at last thou art sick of my sighing. A West-Country Lover. Alice Brown. HBV
Then Laugh. Bertha Adams Backus. BLPA; NeHB; PoToHe (new ed.); TreFT; WBLP; YaD
Then Lelex rose, an old experienced man. Baucis and Philemon. Ovid. *Fr.* Metamorphoses. AWP; JAWP; MBW-1; WBP
Then let not winter's ragged hand deface. Sonnets, VI. Shakespeare. MasP; SiCE; Sonn
Then let the chill sirocco blow. The Winter Glass. Charles Cotton. HBV
Then lift up the head with a song! Praise. *Unknown.* PCH
Then, like a miracle, the violets came out. Bay Violets. Sister Maris Stella. GoBC
Then like the ship at rest in the bay. Love Poem. George Barker. First Cycle of Love Poems, IV. FaBoMo; MoPo
Then listen, as I listened unto you. Thomas Lovell Beddoes. *Fr.* Death's Jest Book, III. PoFr
Then Lose in Time Thy Maidenhead. *Unknown.* ErPo
Then Mahoney, standing in the surf. Mahoney. Seán Jennett. NeIP
Then Mercury 'gan bend him to obey. Vergil, *tr. by* the Earl of Surrey. *Fr.* The Aeneid, IV. ViBoPo
Then muster thy folk, play the captain thyself. July. Thomas Tusser. ReIE
Then next a merry woodsman, clad in green. The Green Dryad's Plea. Thomas Hood. *Fr.* The Plea of the Midsummer Fairies. OBNC
Then night throbs on; O, let me pray, dear Lord! Motherhood. Josephine Dodge Daskam Bacon. HBV
Then once more men's ears were full of "Yankee Doodle." Harry Brown. *Fr.* The Poem of Bunker Hill. PoFr
Then one of them, which was a lawyer. St. Matthew, Bible, *N.T.* PoFr
Then our music is in prime. A Good Eating Song. William Cartwright. *Fr.* The Ordinary. SeCL
Then out spake brave Horatius. Horatius at the Bridge. Macaulay. *Fr.* Lays of Ancient Rome. PoFr
Then out-streamed a Light. Death of Saint Guthlac. Cynewulf. *Fr.* Guthlac. ACP
Then piped a tiny voice hard by. Chickadee. Emerson. *Fr.* The Titmouse. PCH
Then roll the swag and blanket up. The Golden Gullies of the Palmer. *Unknown.* PoAu-1
Then rose the King and moved his host by night. Tennyson. *Fr.* Idylls of the King: The Passing of Arthur. PeVV
Then round the Bay of Mexico. Round the Bay of Mexico. *Unknown.* OuSiCo
Then said Almitra, speak to us of love. Of Love. Kahlil Gibran. *Fr.* The Prophet. PoLF
Then said Jesus to those Jews which believed on him. St. John, Bible, *N.T.* PoFr
Then said Jesus unto them again, Verily, verily, I say unto you, I am the door of the sheep. The Good Shepherd. St. John, Bible, *N.T.* TreFS
Then said the Cid, who in good hour had girded on the steel. Pawning the Coffers of Sand. *Unknown. Fr.* The Cid. LiTW
Then saith another, "We are kindly things." Tender Babes. Thomas Hood. *Fr.* The Plea of the Midsummer Fairies. OBRV
Then saith the timid Fay—"Oh, mighty Time!" The Fairy's Reply to Saturn. Thomas Hood. *Fr.* The Plea of the Midsummer Fairies. OBNC
Then Sang Deborah and Barak. Judges, Bible, *O.T.* *See* Song of Deborah, The.
Then Sang Moses. Exodus, Bible, *O.T.* *See* Triumphal Chant.

Then Saturn thus:—"Sweet is the merry lark." The Melodies of Time. Thomas Hood. *Fr.* The Plea of the Midsummer Fairies. OBNC
Then saw I, with gray eyes fulfilled of rest. In Hades. Anna Callender Brackett. AA
Then saw they how there hove a dusky barge. Tennyson. *Fr.* Idylls of the King: The Passing of Arthur. VA
Then settle, frost! Otomo Oemaru, *tr. fr. Japanese by* Geoffrey Bownas *and* Anthony Thwaite. FIW
Then shall the kingdom of heaven be likened unto ten virgins. The Wise and Foolish Virgins. St. Matthew, Bible, *N.T.* TreF
Then Shall We See. Charles Leonard Moore. AA
Then she came to the pillar of the bed. The Tyrant's Death. Judith, Bible, Apocrypha. PoFr
Then since from God those lesser lives began. From God to God. Vergil. MaRV
Then sing, ye birds, sing, sing a joyous song! The Gladness of the May. Wordsworth. YeAr
"Then sleep, Thou little Child." Thus sweet and high. Choir-Boys on Christmas Eve. Louise Townsend Nicholl. TSW
Then spake Jesus unto them, saying, I am the light of the world. Jesus Answers the Pharisees. St. John, Bible, *N.T.* TreFS
Then spoke the Lord. Cædmon (?). *Fr.* Genesis. YAT
Then step by step walks Autumn. Autumn's Processional. Dinah Maria Mulock Craik. GN
Then strip, lads, and to it, though sharp be the weather. Football Song. Sir Walter Scott. SD
Then that dread angel near the awful throne. Fiat Lux. Lloyd Mifflin. AA; AnAmPo; PFY
Then the air was perfect. And his descent. The Parachutist. Jon Anderson. NYBP
Then the Ermine. Marianne Moore. NePoAm
Then the glorious King, Constantine. Cynewulf. *Fr.* Elene. YAT
Then the golden hour. Length of Moon. Arna Bontemps. CDC; LiTM (1970 ed.); PoNe
Then the little Hiawatha. Hiawatha's Brothers [*or* Hiawatha's Chickens]. Longfellow. *Fr.* The Song of Hiawatha, III. BoTP; PCH
Then the Lord Answered. Job, XXXVIII, Bible, *O.T.* *See* Voice Out of the Whirlwind.
Then the Lord God spoke and said unto Noah. Noah's Flood. *Unknown.* *Fr.* Genesis. AnOE
Then the Master/ With a gesture. Longfellow. *Fr.* The Building of the Ship. OHFP
Then the pair followed Pa to Manhasset. Limerick. *Unknown.* *Fr.* That Nantucket Limerick. LiBL; TreF
Then, the quick plunge into the cool, green dark. Louis Untermeyer. *Fr.* Swimmers. SD
Then the son of Weohstan, stalwart in war. The Funeral Pyre. *Unknown.* *Fr.* Beowulf. AnOE
Then the wisest, before the assembly. Cynewulf. *Fr.* Elene. YAT
Then there came at that time a valiant man riding. Arthur's Dream. Layamon. *Fr.* The Brut. MeEV
Then there is this civilizing love of death, by which. Ignorance of Death. William Empson. CMoP; CoBMV; LiTM (rev. ed.); ReMP; ToPo
Then there shall be signs in heaven. The Fifteen Days of Judgement. Sebastian Evans. NBM
Then there were the grapes turned purple in the sun. Grapes. Sister Maris Stella. GoBC
Then they saw/ Forth and forward faring. The Approach [*or* Coming] of Pharaoh. Cædmon (?). *Fr.* Genesis. ACP; CAW; WaaP
Then those ill-favour'd ones, whom none. George Crabbe. *Fr.* Sir Eustace Grey. ELP
Then thus we have beheld. Chorus. Samuel Daniel. *Fr.* Cleopatra. OBSC
Then to Emmaus with him I, too, walked. Contemporary. Sara Bard Field. ChIP
Then to the bar all they drew near. The Infants' Petition. Michael Wigglesworth. *Fr.* The Day of Doom. AnNE
Then to the bees one said. The Bees. Monk Gibbon. OnYI
Then touch then park; the leaves are stained to lure you. Counter-Serenade; She Invokes the Autumn Instant. Peter Viereck. CrMA
Then Twist the Neck of This Delusive Swan. Enrique Gonzaález Martínez, *Tr. fr. Spanish by* John Peale Bishop. LiTW
Then up aloft this yard must go. A Long Time Ago, *vers.* VI. *Unknown.* ShS
Then was earth made anew where'er He went. The Law of Love. John Oxenham. OQP
Then was Gunnar silent a little. Gunnar in the Pit of Adders. William Morris. *Fr.* The Story of Sigurd the Volsung. PoVP; ViPo
Then was not non-existent nor existent. The Creation Hymn. *Unknown.* *Fr.* The Rig-Veda. OuHeWo
Then watching the unposed beggars pose. Et Quid Amabo Nisi Quod Aenigma Est. Stephen Sandy. NYBP
Then wear the gold hat, if that will move her. Epitaph from "The Great Gatsby." F. Scott Fitzgerald. ELU
Then we'll sing of Lydia Pinkham. Lydia Pinkham. *Unknown.* AS
Then went the Pharisees, and took counsel. The Things That Are Caesar's. St. Matthew, Bible, *N.T.* TreF
Then were brought near with trembling fear, a number numberless. The Heathen and the Infants. Michael Wigglesworth. *Fr.* The Day of Doom. AmPP (3d ed.)
Then were brought nigh a company. Men of Good Works. Michael Wigglesworth. *Fr.* The Day of Doom. AmPP
Then were there brought unto him little children. The Rich Man and the Kingdom of Heaven. St. Matthew, Bible, *N.T.* TreF
Then what does it avail me, that you once. What Does It Avail Me? Louise Labé. LiTW
Then what is the answer?—Not to be deluded by dreams. The Answer. Robinson Jeffers. CMoP; GoYe; MoRP
Then, when an hour was twenty hours, he lay. Lost Days. Stephen Spender. NYTB
Then, When I Am Thy Captive, Talk of Chains. Milton. *Fr.* Paradise Lost, IV. WHA
Then When the Ample Season. Richard Wilbur. MiAP
Then, when the child was gone. The Empty House. Stephen Spender. NYBP; WePo
Then whilst that Latmos did contain her bliss. Sonnet. Earl of Stirling. Aurora, XXVIII. ViBoPo
Then You'll Remember Me. Alfred Bunn. *See* When Other Lips and Other Hearts.
Then you'll see our oars with feathered spray. In Measure Time We'll Row. *Unknown.* ShS
Thence onward by the well-known road. Changes. Charles Barter. *Fr.* Stray Memories of Natal and Zululand. BoSA
Thence passing forth, they shortly do arrive. The Bower of Bliss. Spenser. *Fr.* The Faerie Queene, II. ATP; FiP
Thenot Protests. "C. N. S." InMe
Theobalds' Roads. Charles Williams. LO
Theocritus. Annie Fields. AA
Theocritus. Sir Edmund Gosse. VA
Theocritus. Charles Hartley Langhorne. VA
Theocritus. Oscar Wilde. HBV; OxBI; ShBV-4; StP
Theocritus! Theocritus! ah, thou hadst pleasant dreams. Theocritus. Charles Hartley Langhorne. VA
Theodor Herzl. Israel Zangwill. TrJP
Theodore and Honoria. Dryden, *paraphrased fr. the Italian of* Boccaccio. SeEP
Theodore Roosevelt. William W. Peavyhouse. HH
Theodosia Burr. Myra Burnham Terrell. GoYe
Theodosia Burr; the Wrecker's Story. John Williamson Palmer. PAH
Theodosius; or, The Force of Love, *sel.* Nathaniel Lee.
Song: "Now, now the fight's done, and the great god of war." PeRV
Theologians. Walter de la Mare. EaLo
Theological. Clifton Fadiman. FiBHP; PV
Theology. Paul Laurence Dunbar. AmePo; TRV
Theology. Joyce Kilmer. TSW
Theology. William Langland, *mod. by* Henry W. Wells. *Fr.* The Vision of Piers Plowman. PoLi
(Grace for Theology.) GoBC
Theology of Bongwi, the Baboon, The. Roy Campbell. PeSA
Theology of Jonathan Edwards, The. Phyllis McGinley. MoAmPo (1962 ed.)
Theophany. Evelyn Underhill. MaRV; WGRP
Theophila; or, Love's Sacrifice, *sels.* Edward Benlowes.
Evening Prayer. FaBoEn
Life and Death. FaBoEn
To His Muse. SeCL

Theophilus Thistledown, the successful thistle sifter. *Unknown.* OxNR
Theoretikos. Oscar Wilde. BrPo
Theory. Dorothy Parker. BOHV
Theory of Poetry. Archibald MacLeish. AP
Ther is at the west syde of Ytaille. Chaucer. *Fr.* The Canterbury Tales: The Clerk's Tale. MBW-1
Ther was a lady fair an rear. The Kitchie-Boy. *Unknown.* ESPB
Ther was also a Nonne, a Prioresse. *See* There also was a nun, a Prioress.
Ther was in Asie [or Asye], in a greet citee. The Prioress's Tale. Chaucer. *Fr.* The Canterbury Tales. BEL; LoBV; MBW-1; OAEP. *See also* There was in Asia. . .
There. Robert Mezey. NaP
There actually stood the fabled riders. Roy Fuller. *Fr.* Mythological Sonnets. Sonn
There ain' no liars there in my Father's house. In My Father's House. *Unknown.* AS
There ain' no mo' cane on de Brazis. Ain' No Mo' Cane on de Brazis. *Unknown.* ABF
There aince was a very pawky duke. The Pawky Duke. David Rorie. GoTS
There all the golden codgers lay. News for the Delphic Oracle. W. B. Yeats. CMoP; CoBMV; LiTB; LiTM; MoPo; OAEP (2d ed.)
There also was a nun [*or* Ther was also a Nonne], a Prioress. A Prioress [*or* The Portrait of the Prioresse]. Chaucer. *Fr.* The Canterbury Tales: Prologue. MaC; MaPo (1969 ed.); TrGrPo
There always is a noise when it is dark! In the Night. James Stephens. OBMV
There Always Will Be God. A. L. Murray. SoP
There—and Back. Rodney Bennett. BoTP
There are/ No clocks on the wall. End. Langston Hughes. CBV
There are a few things I shall not forget. 1917-1919. Henry Martin Hoyt. HBMV
There are a number of us creep. Horace Paraphrased. Isaac Watts. LoBV; UnPo (3d ed.)
There are abandoned corners of our exile. The Mathmid. Hayyim Nahman Bialik. AWP; PoFr
There are all kinds of men. A Thank You for Friends. Rodney Bennett. BoTP
There Are Big Waves. Eleanor Farjeon. BoTP
There are blind eyes. A Prayer in Time of Blindness. Clement Wood. TrPWD
There are brightest apples on those trees. The Fertile Muck. Irving Layton. OBCV; PeCV (1967 ed.)
There are certain things—as, a spider, a ghost. A Sea Dirge. "Lewis Carroll." CenHV; StaSt
There Are Children in the Dusk. Bertram Warr. PeCV
There are dealers in pictures named Agnew. Tom Agnew, Bill Agnew. Dante Gabriel Rossetti. ChTr
There are eight people in this room. Song of the Nudge. Marge Piercy. ThO
There are fairies at the bottom of our garden! The Fairies. Rose Fyleman. FaPON; HBMV; HBVY; MPB; OTPC (1946 ed.); SoPo; StVeCh; TSW; TVC
There are figures like the dark figures. Microcosmos, XXXII. Nigel Heseltine. NeBP
There Are Four Doors Which Open on the Skies. Robert Nathan. MaRV
There are four men mowing down by the Isar. A Youth Mowing. D. H. Lawrence. MoAB; MoBrPo; TrGrPo
There are four vibrators, the world's exactest clocks. Four Quartz Crystal Clocks. Marianne Moore. AmPP (5th ed.); ImOP; TwCP
There Are Gains for All Our Losses. Richard Henry Stoddard. *See* Flight of Youth, The.
"There are gains for all our losses." An Old Song Reversed. Richard Henry Stoddard. AA
There are glories up in Heaven. The House of Many Mansions. Oswald J. Smith. SoP
There are harps that complain to the presence of night. Music of the Night. John Neal. AA; AmePo
There are hearts that are crushed by the cares of the road. Sing! *Unknown.* SoP
There are hermit souls that live withdrawn. The House by the Side of the Road. Sam Walter Foss. AmePo; BLPA; FaBoBe; FaFP; HBV; HBVY; MaRV; NeHB; OHFP; OQP; OTD; SoP; TIHL; TreF; TRV; WBLP; WGRP
There are human beings who seem to regard the place as craftily. Dock Rats. Marianne Moore. AnAmPo
There are (I scarce can think it, but am told). The First Satire of the Second Book of Horace. Pope. EiCL; MBW-1
There are in our existence spots of time. Imagination and Taste, How Impaired and Restored. Wordsworth. *Fr.* The Prelude, XII *and* XIII. FosPo; LO; MBW-2; PoEL-4
There are in Paradise. The Shepherd Who Stayed. Theodosia Garrison. ChrBoLe; OHIP
There are jasmine-petaled hands that droop. Hands. Margaret Lathrop Law. PoMa
There are lions and roaring tigers, and enormous camels and things. At the Zoo. A. A. Milne. FaPON; TiPo (1959 ed.)
There are little eyes upon you, and they're watching night and day. To Any Daddy. *Unknown.* SoP; STF
There are lonely cemeteries. Death Alone. "Pablo Neruda." OnHM
There are lonely hearts to cherish. While the Days Are Going By. George Cooper. BLRP; STF; WBLP
There are lots of queer things that discoverers do. Christopher Columbus. Rosemary Benét *and* Stephen Vincent Benét. PoRh; RePo
There are loved ones who are missing. The Blessings That Remain. Annie Johnson Flint. BLRP
There are loyal hearts, there are spirits brave. Life's Mirror [*or* Give]. "Madeline Bridges." BLPA; FaBoBe; FaChP; MaRV; NeHB; PoToHe; TreF; WBLP
There are many dead in the brutish desert. First Elegy [for the Dead in Cyrenaica]. Hamish Henderson. ChMP; OxBS
There are many desert places. Missions. *Unknown.* STF
There are many flags in many lands. Our Flag. Mary H. Howliston. GFA
There are many like him there—unsymbolled heap. A Grave in Ukraine. Saul Tchernichowsky. TrJP
There are many monsters that a glassen surface. The Octopus. James Merrill. CoAP; TwAmPo
There are many more Good Fridays. Unkept Good Fridays. Thomas Hardy. MoRP
There are many ways to die. History among the Rocks. Robert Penn Warren. Kentucky Mountain Farm, III. MAP; MoVE
There are many who go to the Vineyard. The Vineyard. *Unknown.* STF
There are many who say that a dog has his day. The Song of the Mischievous Dog. Dylan Thomas. FaFP; SiTL
There are men in the village of Erith. The Village of Erith [*or* Erith]. *Unknown.* CBEP; ChTr
There are men making death together in the wood. The Delta. Michael Dennis Browne. NYBP
There are moments a man turns from us. Drowning with Others. James Dickey. CoPo
There are monsters who are very good. Monsters. Quillevic. OnPM
There are moons like continents. Moons. John Haines. ThO
There are more problems to a woodchuck. On Looking into Robert Frost in Kanji. William Meredith. ML
There are mushrooms in the paddock. The Wagon in the Barn. John Drinkwater. MoSiPe
There are no bells in all the world. Sleigh Bells at Night. Elizabeth J. Coatsworth. SiSoSe
There are no fairy-folk in our Southwest. Western Magic. Mary Austin. AmFN
There are no frontiers in the air. "Nation Shall Speak Peace. . ." William Soutar. POTE
There Are No Gods. Euripides, *tr. fr. Greek by* John Addington Symonds. *Fr.* Bellerophon. EaLo
There are no hills for climbing. Lucifer at Leisure. Sister Mary Maura. JKCP (1955 ed.)
There are no hollows any more. Ironic: LL.D. William Stanley Braithwaite. BANP
There are no instructions here for that dazzling man. Old Iron. Douglas Stewart. BoAV
There are no red leaves in yellow Oxford. Views of the Oxford Colleges. Paris Leary. CoPo
There are no rocks. Geography: A Song. Howard Moss. CAD; PV
There are no stars to-night. My Grandmother's Love Let-

There (continued)
ters. Hart Crane. CMoP; FaBoBe; MoAB; PG (1945 ed.)
There are no stars which fell on Alabama. Elements of Grammar. Calvin C. Hernton. NBP
There are no trenches dug in the park, not yet. Nightmare at Noon. Stephen Vincent Benét. OxBA
There are no upper hands in love. After You, Madam. Alex Comfort. ErPo; UnTE
There Are No Wolves in England Now. Rose Fyleman. HBMV; UTS
There are nothing but pipes and dripping faucets here. Spring. Allen Van Newkirk. YAP
There are one or two things I should just like to hint. To His Countrymen. James Russell Lowell. *Fr.* A Fable for Critics. AA
There are only two things now. New Year's Eve. D. H. Lawrence. ErPo
There are open fields. The Summers Sun. Dennis Schmitz. YAP
There are palm trees in my homeland. Antônio Gonçalves Dias. *Fr.* Song of Exile. TTY
There are people go to Carmel. At Carmel. Mary Austin. AmFN
"There are people so dumb," my father said. Plain Talk. William Jay Smith. FiBHP; MoAmPo (1962 ed.)
There Are Places. Myra Von Riedemann. OBCV
There are portraits and still-lifes. Paring the Apple. Charles Tomlinson. CMoP; NePoEA-2; NMP; PoIE
There are pumpkins in the field. Fall Days. Marion Conger. SiSoSe
There are questions that must be asked. Incidents in Playfair House. Nicholas Moore. ErPo; NeBP
There are rivers. Wilderness Rivers. Elizabeth J. Coatsworth. AmFN
There Are Roughly Zones. Robert Frost. CMoP
There Are Seeds to Sow. Bernette Golden. TNV
There are seven hills. The Windy Bishop. Wilfred Watson. OBCV
There are seven men in Moy Castle. Moy Castle. *Unknown.* GoTP; OnSP
"There are sixteen lang miles, I'm sure." The Bent Sae Brown. *Unknown.* ESPB
There are so many things I have forgot. The Word. Edward Thomas. NP
There are so many things to do to-day. Every Day. Mary I. Osborn. BoTP
There Are So Many Ways of Going Places. Leslie Thompson. FaPON; SoPo
There are solemn figures walking up the Tocaïma roadway. The Feast of Padre Chala. Thomas Walsh. CAW
There are some birds in these valleys. The Decoys. W. H Auden. CMoP; SyP
There are some critics say our verse is bad. Your Teeth Are Ivory Towers. William Empson. ToPo
There are some days the happy ocean lies. Seascape. Stephen Spender. AtBAP; ChMP; CoBMV; GTBS-D; NoP
There are some heights in Wessex, shaped as if by a kindly hand. Wessex Heights. Thomas Hardy. CMoP; FaBoEn; OBNC; PoEL-5; UnPo
There are some qualities—some incorporate things. Sonnet: Silence. Poe. AP; MAmP; MWA-1
There are some quiet crossings in his city. Water Color. Stephen Mooney. NYBP
There are some quiet ways. The Wayside. James Herbert Morse. AA
There are some very ghastly faces. Conspiracy in Iowa. William Hathaway. QAH
There are some who believe the Bible. It Means Just What It Says [*or* Believe the Bible]. A. B. Simpson. SoP; STF
There are strange shadows fostered of the moon. November Dusk. Arthur Davison Ficke. Sonnets of a Portrait Painter, XLV. MAP
There are strange things done in the midnight sun. The Cremation of Sam McGee. Robert W. Service. FaFP; GSP; MaC; PoLF; ShM; StPo; TreF; TwCaPo; YT
There are strange ways of serving God. Service. Hermann Hagedorn. OQP
There are sunsets who whisper a good-by. Sunsets. Carl Sandburg. MAP; MoAmPo
There Are Sweet Flowers. Walter Savage Landor. EnRP
There are the fair-limbed nymphs o' the woods. Leigh Hunt. *Fr.* The Nymphs. OBNC; OBRV
There are things/ Feet know. Feet. Dorothy Aldis. BoChLi; SUS
There are things/ Hands do. Hands. Dorothy Aldis. SUS
There are things you almost see. Almost. Rachel Field. SUS
There are thirteen months in all the year. *See* There are twelve months. . .
There are those to whom place is unimportant. The Rose. Theodore Roethke. NaP; NYBP; PoIE (1970 ed.)
There are three central figures preoccupied by toplighting. Composition for a Nativity. John Ciardi. MiAP
There are three green eggs in a small brown pocket. At Little Virgil's Window. Edwin Markham. TRV
There are three lessons I would write. Three Words of Strength [*or* Three Lessons]. Schiller. MaRV; OQP
There are three things which are too wonderful for me. Too Wonderful. Proverbs, Bible, *O.T.* TrJP
There are three valleys where the warm sun lingers. The Long Harbour. Mary Ursula Bethell. ACV; AnNZ
There are three ways in which men take. The Music Grinders. Oliver Wendell Holmes. WhC
There are times when I wish I could poet a poem. Dry Wishing Well. Wally Ford. WSL
There are, to whom too poignant I appear. The Bold Satirist. Horace. WoL
There are too many heart-shaped words for one. Too Much for One; Not Enough to Go Around. R. P. Blackmur. Scarabs for the Living, I. CrMA
There are too many of you. Presidential Address to a Party of Exiles Leaving for the Moon. Howard Nemerov. ML
There are too many poems with the word. Testament. John Holmes. MoRP
There are tracks which belong to wheels. In the Lupanar at Pompeii. James Dickey. ToPo
There are trails that a lad may follow. Silver Ships. Mildred Plew Meigs. FaPON; TiPo
There are truths you Americans need to be told. James Russell Lowell. *Fr.* A Fable for Critics. AmePo
There are twelve [*or* thirteen] months in all the year. Robin Hood and [*or* Rescuing] the Widow's Three Sons [*or* the Three Squires]. *Unknown.* BuBa; EnLi-1; EnSB; ESPB (B *vers.*); GoTP; OBB; OnMSP; StPo; TiPo (1952 ed.); ViBoFo
There are twelve months throughout the year. September. Mary Howitt. BoTP; OTPC (1923 ed.)
There are twenty dead who're sleeping near the slopes of Bud Dajo. The Fight at Dajo. Alfred E. Wood. PAH
There are two births; the one when light. William Cartwright. *Fr.* To Chloe, Who Wished Herself Young Enough for Me. GTBS-W; LO; OBEV; PoToHe (new ed.)
There are two different kinds, I believe, of human attraction. Arthur Hugh Clough. *Fr.* Amours de Voyage. GTBS-P
There are two kinds of people on earth today. Lifting and Leaning [*or* Leaners or Lifters *or* Two Kinds of People]. Ella Wheeler Wilcox. BLPA; MaRV; PoToHe; SoP; WBLP
There are two sights that make my heart feel gay. Good Morning, America. Harry Kemp. PEDC
There are two ways now. Progress. Edith Agnew. AmFN
There are two women; one I love, and one. Twins. "Owen Meredith." ErPo
There are veils that lift, there are bars that fall. Song of Maelduin. Thomas William Rolleston. HBMV
There are veins in the hills where jewels hide. The Best Treasure. John J. Moment. MaRV; TRV
There are white moon daisies in the mist of the meadow. Summer Song. Edith Nesbit. PoSC
There Are Who Say. Walter Savage Landor. EPN
There are willow pussies. Pussy Willows. *Unknown.* GFA
There are wolves in the next room waiting. The Wolves. Allen Tate. LiTA; LiTG; LiTM; OxBA
There are words like Freedom. Refugee in America. Langston Hughes. AmFN; WaKn
There are words that slip out of you. Jonathan Cott. YAP
There are words that wait. Words to Sleep Upon. Leonora Speyer. NP
There are wrongs done in the fair face of heaven. The Deeds That Might Have Been. Wilfrid Scawen Blunt. *Fr.* In Vinculis. TrGrPo
There are youngsters now. Furniture. Phyllis Harris. NYBP; TPM

There, as she sewed, came floating through her head. Past. Winifred Howells. AA
There at the top of the world. Harlem in January. Julia Fields. CAD
There Atin fownd Cymochles sojourning. Spenser. *Fr.* The Faerie Queene, II. MBW-1
There be four things which are little upon the earth. Four Things. Proverbs, Bible, *O.T.* FaPON; GoTP; PoG
There be many kinds of parting-yes, I know. Separation. Martha Dickinson Bianchi. AA
There Be None of Beauty's Daughters. Byron. *See* Stanzas for Music.
There be six things which the Lord hateth. A Sower of Discord. Proverbs, Bible, *O.T.* (*Moulton, Modern Reader's Bible*). MaRV
There be the greyhounds! lo'k! an' there's the heäre. The Heäre. William Barnes. VA
There be three things seeking my death. Prayer for the Speedy End of Three Great Misfortunes. *Tr. by* Frank O'Conner. DTC; OBMV
There be two men of all mankind. Two Men. E. A. Robinson. BOHV; GoTP; LaNeLa; WhC
There beams no light from thy hall to-night. The Dark Palace. Alice Milligan. AnIV
There Blooms No Bud in May. Walter de la Mare. MoAB; MoBrPo; NeMA
There breaks upon my sight. Frank Wilmot. *Fr.* The Gully. BoAV; NeLNL
There breathes a sense of Spring in the boon air. Accidian. Henry Charles Beeching. OBVV
There by the window in the old house. William H. Herndon. Edgar Lee Masters. *Fr.* Spoon River Anthology. LiPo; NP; TOP
There calleth me ever a marvelous horn. Home-Sickness. Justinus Kerner. AWP; JAWP; WBP
There cam' seven Egyptians on a day. The Gypsy Countess. *Unknown.* OBB
There came a bird out o' a bush. Lady Isabel and the Elf-Knight (B *vers.*). *Unknown.* ESPB
There came a day at summer's full. Emily Dickinson. AmePo; AP; FaPL; MAmP; MoAmPo (1950 ed.); MWA-2
There came a ghost to Margaret's [*or* Margret's] door. Sweet William's Ghost [*or* Sweet William and May Margaret]. *Unknown.* BaBo; BuBa; CH; ESPB; HBV; InPo; ViBoFo (A *vers.*)
There came a knight from out the west. Clootie. *Unknown.* BuBa
There came a knocking at the front door. A Person from Porlock. R. S. Thomas. BoC
There came a little light-foot breeze a-dancing down the bay. The Isle of Apple-Trees. Fritz S. Burnell. BoAu
There came a satyr creeping through the wood. The Satyr [*or* The Crackling Twig]. James Stephens. ELU; OnYI
There came a seaman up from the sea. The Drowned Seaman. Maude Goldring. HBMV
There came a soul to the gate of Heaven. The Self-exiled. Walter C. Smith. VA
There came a wind like a bugle. Emily Dickinson. AmPP (4th ed.); AtBAP; CMoP; FaBoEn; ILP; LoBV; MAPA; MoAB; NePA; NoP; OxBA; PoE; PoIE; TSW; TwAmPo
There came a youth upon the earth. The Shepherd of King Admetus. James Russell Lowell. HBVY; TOP
There Came an Ancient Huron. *Unknown.* IHA
There came an ancient man and slow. The Call to a Scot. Ruth Guthrie Harding. HBV
There came an image in Life's retinue. Death-in-Love. Dante Gabriel Rossetti. The House of Life, XLVIII. MaVP; PoVP; SyP; ViPo; VP
There came by the post. Special Delivery. Elizabeth Winton. PCH
There came, for lack of sleep. New York in August. Donald Davie. NMP
There came from an alley and into the street. God's Instrument. Sir William Herschel. OTD
There came three men from out the West. Sir John Barleycorn. *Unknown.* CBEP
There came tidings to Arthur the king. The Battle of Bath. Layamon. *Fr.* The Brut. MeEV
There came to port last Sunday night. The New Arrival. George Washington Cable. AA; HBV
There came to the beach a poor Exile of Erin. Exile of Erin. Thomas Campbell. HBV
There Came You Wishing Me. José Garcia Villa. TwAmPo
There can be slain/ No sacrifice. Milton, *tr. fr. the Latin of* Seneca. *Fr.* The Tenure of Kings and Magistrates. PoFr
There chanced to be a pedlar bold. The Bold Pedlar and Robin Hood. *Unknown.* BaBo; ESPB
There comes a moment late in Summer. Prognostic. Samuel Yellen. NePoAm
There comes a moment when to believe is not enough. Action. James Oppenheim. TrJP
There comes a night when the once full-orbed moon. *Unknown.* LO
There comes a wail of anguish. A Cry for Light. *Unknown.* BLRP
There comes an end to summer. To His Mistress. Ernest Dowson. BoLP
There comes Emerson first, whose rich words, every one. Emerson. James Russell Lowell. *Fr.* A Fable for Critics. AmPP (4th ed.); AnNE; AP; CoBA; MWA-1; OuHeWo; OxBA; PP
There comes Poe, with his raven, like Barnaby Rudge. Poe and Longfellow. James Russell Lowell. *Fr.* A Fable for Critics. AmePo; AmPP (5th ed.); AnNE; AP; CoBA; MWA-1; OxBA
There died a myriad. Ezra Pound. *Fr.* Hugh Selwyn Mauberley. CBV; CMoP; FaBoMo; ILP; LiTG; MoAmPo (1962 ed.); MoVE; NePA; NP; OxBA; PoIE; SeCeV; UnPo (3d ed.); WaaP
There dwelt a fair maid in the West. James Harris. *Unknown.* BaBo (A *vers.*); ESPB
There dwelt a man in faire Westmerland [*or* fair Westmoreland]. Johnie Armstrong. *Unknown.* BaBo; BoLiVe; EnLi-1 (1949 ed.); ESPB; HoPM; NoP; PoPo; TOP; TrGrPo; UnPo; VaPo; ViBoFo (A *vers.*)
There dwelt a miller hale and bold. The Miller of the Dee. Charles Mackay. HBV; OTPC
There dwelt the man, the flower of human kind. Mount Vernon, the Home of Washington. William Day. DD; OHIP; PoRL
There Falls with Every Wedding Chime. Walter Savage Landor. VA
(Last Fruit off an Old Tree, The.) SeCePo
There fared a mother driven forth. The House of Christmas. G. K. Chesterton. GoBC; HBV; HBVY; MaRV; MoBrPo; MoRP; TSW
There fell red rain of spears athwart the sky. Last Judgment. John Gould Fletcher. AWP
There flames the first gay daffodil. Daffodils. Ruth Guthrie Harding. HBMV
There flourished once a potentate. The King of Yvetot. Pierre Jean de Béranger. AWP; JAWP; WBP; WoL
There, from its entrance, lost in matted vines. The Covered Bridge. Madison Cawein. YT
There go the grownups. A Lazy Thought. Eve Merriam. OCS
There, go to sleep, Dolly, in own mother's lap. The Little Girl to Her Dolly. Ann Taylor. SAS
There goes the clock; there goes the sun. Epitaph for John and Richard. Karl Shapiro. TwAmPo
There goes the dog of the mind. Soliloquy by the Shore. Martin Scholten. GoYe
There goes the grandson, run off to the beach! The Grandson. James Scully. NYBP
There goes the Wapiti. The Wapiti. Ogden Nash. MoShBr
There grew a goodly tree him faire beside. Balme. Spenser. *Fr.* The Faerie Queene, I, 11. CH
There grew a lowly flower by Eden-gate. Eden-Gate. Sydney Dobell. OBVV
There grew an aged tree on the green. The Oak and the Brere. Spenser. *Fr.* The Shepheardes Calender: February. OBSC
There grows an elm-tree on the hill. *Unknown, tr. by* Arthur Waley. *Fr.* The Book of Odes. MoBrPo (1942 ed.)
There had been years of passion—scorching, cold. "And There Was a Great Calm." Thomas Hardy. ChTr; CMoP; LiTM; MoRP; TDP
There hangs the long bow, the strong bow, once was bent. The Death of Robin Hood. William Rose Benét. OTPC (1946 ed.)
There hangs this bellied pear, let no rake doubt. The Pear. Ruth Stone. TwAmPo
There hartes ware so roted in the popes lawes. Fragment of an

There (continued)
Anti-Papist Ballad. *Unknown.* CoMu
There has a question been of late. Up-Tails All. *Unknown.* UnTE
There has been a light snow. In a Train. Robert Bly. NaP
There has something gone wrong. Keep a Stiff Upper Lip. Phoebe Cary. FaFP
There hath come an host to see Thee. Lullaby to Bethlehem. Henry Howarth Bashford. HBV; HBVY
There haunts in Time's bare house an active ghost. Polonius. Walter de la Mare. AtBAP
There have been many cats I loved and lost. Sonnet. Margaret E. Bruner. CIV
There have been poets that in verse display. To Wordsworth. Hartley Coleridge. Sonn
There have been three storms in my heart. Summerhouse. Melvin Walker La Follette. NePoEA
There have been times when I have looked at life. Vision. Elizabeth N. Hauer. PoToHe
There have been times when I well might have passed. In Tenebris, III. Thomas Hardy. ViPo
There have been times when on a city street. On City Streets. Margaret E. Bruner. PoToHe
There he goes, tacking against the fields. The Labourer. R. S. Thomas. BoPe; POTi
"There he is, woman!" The Seduction of Engadu. *Unknown. Fr.* Gilgamesh. ErPo
There he lies—the saviour, the lord of the earth. The Iron Messiah. Vladimir Timofeevich Kirillov. PoFr
There he moved, cropping the grass at the purple canyon's lip. The Horse Thief. William Rose Benét. BBV (1951 ed.); HBMV; MAP; MoAmPo; OnMSP; TSW
There he stands, see? Two Jazz Poems. Carl Wendell Hines, Jr. AmNP
There He Was. Alan Dugan. CBV
There headlong into the calm black night. Orestes Pursued. Charles David Webb. NePoAm-2
There in a bare place, in among the rocks. The Little Lough. John Hewitt. NeIP
There in his room, whene'er the moon looks in. Ode for a Master Mariner Ashore. Louise Imogen Guiney. AA; GoBC; JKCP
There in the bracken was the ominous spoor mark. The Tantanoola Tiger. Max Harris. MoBS; PoAu-2
There in the dusty alcove of the room. The Waiting Harp. Gustavo Adolfo Bécquer. CAW
There, in the earliest and chary spring, the dogwood flowers. Sunday: Outskirts of Knoxville, Tennessee. James Agee. ErPo
There in the fane a beauteous creature stands. Woman. Kalidasa. HBV
There, in the night, where none can spy. Robert Louis Stevenson. *Fr.* The Land of Story-Books. YT
There is/ One great society alone on earth. The Noble. Wordsworth. *Fr.* The Prelude, IX. ChTr
There Is a Beauty. Archibald Lampman. *Fr.* The Largest Life. MaRV
There is a bird bath on our grass. The Bird Bath. Florence Hoatson. BoTP
There is a bird I know so well. The Song Sparrow. Henry van Dyke. MPB
There is a bird in the poplars. Metric Figure. William Carlos Williams. MAP; MoAB; MoAmPo; NeMA; NP
There is a bird that comes and sings. The Song the Oriole Sings. William Dean Howells. AmePo; HBV
There is a bird, who by his coat. The Jackdaw. Vincent Bourne. HBV; HBVY; OTPC (1923 ed.)
There is a blessed home. Heaven. Sir Henry Williams Baker. SoP
There is a blue star, Janet. Baby Toes. Carl Sandburg. FaPON; LaNeLa; SUS; TSW
There is a bondage worse, far worse, to bear. Sonnet: There Is a Bondage Worse. Wordsworth. ChER
There is a book, who runs may read. Who Runs May Read. John Keble. *Fr.* The Christian Year. FaChP; SoP; VA
There is a bridge, whereof the span. The Unseen Bridge. Gilbert Thomas. FaChP; HBMV; MaRV; SoP
There is a brook I must hear. Morning. Hilda Conkling. NP
There is a budding morrow in midnight. "Found." Dante Gabriel Rossetti. PoVP
There is a change—and I am poor. A Complaint. Wordsworth. ATP; CBEP; OBRV; PoEL-4
There Is a Charming Land. Adam Oehlenschläger, *tr. fr. Danish by* Robert Hillyer. AWP; FaPON
There Is a City. *At. to* "The Jewish Sibyl," *tr. fr. Greek by* Bohn. *Fr.* The Fourth Book of Sibylline Oracles. TrJP
There is a city, builded by no hand. Paradisi Gloria. Thomas William Parsons. AA; OQP
There is a city, Chaldean Ur. There Is a City. *At. to* "The Jewish Sibyl." *Fr.* The Fourth Book of Sibylline Oracles. TrJP
There is a city where God's happy children. The Life to Come. Edward Shillito. OQP
There is a close companionship of pain. Sons of Failure. Edith Lovejoy Pierce. MaRV
There is a clouded city, gone to rest. The Aztec City. Eugene Fitch Ware. AA; HBV; HT; PTK
There is a coarseness. Jungle Taste. Edward S. Silvera. CDC
There is a cool river. Detroit. Donald Hall. AmFN
There is a country full of wine. Two Voices. Alice Corbin. HBMV; NP
There is a creator named God. Limerick. James McNeill Whistler. BOHV; LiBL
There is a dale in Ida, lovelier. *See* There lies a vale in Ida, lovelier.
There is a day that comes in spring. Apple Blossoms. Ralph Bergengren. GFA
There is a delight in singing tho' none hear. To Robert Browning. Walter Savage Landor. ILP
There is a desert island of the heart. "What Five Books Would You Pick to Be Marooned with on a Desert Island?" Paris Leary. CoPo
There is a destiny that makes us brothers. A Creed. Edwin Markham. BLPA; FaBoBe; FaFP; MaRV; NeHB; PoPl; TreFS
There is a dish to hold the sea. Imagination. John Davidson. *Fr.* New Year's Eve. MoBrPo
There is a far country where there is a hall for dreams. The Far Country. Robert Greacen. NeIP
"There is a fashion in this land." The Knight's Ghost. *Unknown.* ESPB
There is a feast in your father's house. Leesome Brand. *Unknown.* ESPB (B *vers.*); OBB
There Is a Fever of the Spirit. Thomas Love Peacock. *Fr.* Nightmare Abbey, *ch.* 11. EPN; GTSE
(Mr. Cypress's Song.) LO
(Song by Mr. Cypress.) ERoP-1; OBNC; OBRV; Par
There is a fine stuffed chavender. A False Gallop of Analogies. Warham St. Leger. CenHV; FiBHP; WhC
There is a fish, that quivers in the pool. In the Beck. Kathleen Raine. CMoP
There is a flash packet, flash packet [*or* 'n' a packet] of fame. The *Dreadnought. Unknown.* ShS (*vers.* I); SoAmSa
There Is a Floure Sprung of a Tree. *Unknown.* AtBAP
There is a flower, a little flower. The Daisy [*or* A Field Flower]. James Montgomery. BoTP; HBV; OTPC (1923 ed.)
There is a flower I wish to wear. Hearts-Ease. Walter Savage Landor. EnRP; VA
There is a flower that bees prefer. Emily Dickinson. MoAmPo (1950 ed.)
There is a flower, the lesser celandine. A Lesson [*or* The Small Celandine]. Wordsworth. BWP; ERoP-1; GTBS; GTBS-D; GTBS-P; GTBS-W; GTSE; GTSL; HBV; OBRV; PeER
There is a flower within my heart. Daisy Bell. Harry Dacre. TreF
There is a fountain filled with blood. Praise for the Fountain Opened [*or* The Fountain Opened]. William Cowper. CEP; EiPP; SoP
There is a fountain in a wood. The Puppet Dreams. Conrad Aiken. *Fr.* Punch; the Immortal Liar. MAP; NeMA
There is a fountain in the forest called. The Fountain of the Fairies. Robert Southey. OTPC
There is a friendship that exists between. A Dog's Vigil. Margaret E. Bruner. PoToHe
There is a funny little man. Mr. Nobody. *Unknown.* HBVY; OTPC
There is a garden enclosed. Wild Eden, III. George Edward Woodberry. HBV
There Is a Garden in Her Face. Thomas Campion. AtBAP; CABA; CBV; DiPo; EG; ElL; ELP; EnL; EnRePo; FaBoEn;

ForPo; GoJo; ILP; InPo; NoP; OAEP; OBSC; PAn; PoAn; PoEL-2; PoFS; PTK; ReEn; SiCE; SiTL; StP; ThWaDe; TrGrPo; TuPP; ViBoPo; WHA
(Cherry-ripe.) BEL; CBEP; CH; CoBE; EnLi-1; EnLit; ExPo; GTBS; GTBS-D; GTBS-P; GTBS-W; GTSE; GTSL; HBV; LiTB; LiTG; LiTL; MemP; OBEV; PG (1955 ed.); PoIE; SeCeV; TreFT
There is a garden where lilies. Eutopia. Francis Turner Palgrave. OBVV; TOP
There is a garden, which I think He loves. The Garden. Digby Mackworth Dolben. GoBC
There is a general idiom to all rime. Karl Shapiro. *Fr.* Essay on Rime. PP
There is a gentle nymph not far from hence. Sabrina. Milton. *Fr.* Comus. MyFE; OBS; SeEP
There is a great amount of poetry in unconscious/ fastidiousness. Critics and Connoisseurs. Marianne Moore. AmPP (5th ed.); AnAmPo; AnEnPo; CMoP; NePA; OxBA; PIA
There Is a Green Hill Far Away. Cecil Frances Alexander. BLRP; HBV; MaRV; VA; WGRP
There is a green light which pets feel. The Animals. Lewis MacAdams. ANYP; YAP
There is a harp set above us. Harp in the Rigging. Hamish Maclaren. EtS
There is a hawk that is picking the birds out of our sky. Shiva. Robinson Jeffers. NYTB; SiSw; Sonn
There is a heaven, for ever, day by day. Theology. Paul Laurence Dunbar. AmePo; TRV
There is a heigh-ho in these glowing coals. Heigh-ho on a Winter Afternoon. Donald Davie. NePoEA-2
There is a hill and on that hill is a stone. The Heart of the World. Nahman of Bratzlav. TrJP
There Is a Hill Beside the Silver Thames. Robert Bridges. BrPo; OAEP; PoVP
There is a hill in England. Three Hills. Everard Owen. StJW
There is a hole. A Bar at Night. Sakutaro Hagiwara. LiTW
There is a honey none shall taste. The Bees of Christ. Clifford J. Laube. JKCP (1955 ed.)
There is a hornet in the room. Buried at Springs. James Schuyler. ANYP; CoAP
There is a house in New Orleans, they call the Rising Sun. The Rising Sun Blues. *Unknown.* OuSiCo
There is a hunger in my heart tonight. Music. Charles Phillips. CAW; JKCP
There is a hush that comes on Christmas Eve. Christmas Eve Meditation. Margaret E. Bruner. MaRV
There is a hush this golden afternoon. Classroom in October. Elias Lieberman. GoYe
There is a jewel which no Indian mines. Risposta. *Unknown.* HBV
There is a joy I have not known, a splendor. After Reading Saint Teresa, Luis de Leon and Ramon Lull. Muna Lee. CAW
There is a joyful night in which we lose. When the Dumb Speak. Robert Bly. FRC
There is a knack in doing many a thing. The Pilgrims and the Peas. "Peter Pindar." BOHV
There Is a Lady [Sweet and Kind]. *Unknown.* BoLP; CBEP; CH, *abr.*; EG, *abr.*; EIL; ELP; EP; FaFP; GoBC; GTBS-W; LiTB; LiTL; MemP; MeWo; NeHB; NoP; OAEP; OBEV, *abr.*; OBS; SiTL; TreFS; TrGrPo
(Passing By.) OTPC (1946 ed.); ShBV-4
There Is a Lady Conquering with Glances. Walther von der Vogelweide, *tr. fr. German by* Jethro Bithell. AWP; OnPM; WoL
There Is a Land. James Montgomery. PAL; PEDC; PGD
There is a land of Dream. Dream Fantasy. "Fiona Macleod." WGRP
There is a land, of every land the pride. There Is a Land. James Montgomery. PAL; PEDC; PGD
There is a land of pure delight. Heaven [*or* A Prospect of Heaven]. Isaac Watts. EiCL; EiPP; ELP; NoP; OBEC; SoP; WGRP
There is a language in a naval log. E. J. Pratt. *Fr.* Behind the Log. MoCV
There is a life deep hid in God. Peace. Henry W. Frost. SoP
There is a little church in France to-day. Saint [*or* Sainte] Jeanne. Theodosia Garrison. HH; PEDC
There is a little garden path. A Garden Path. May Justus. PCH
There is a little gentleman. The Bee. *Unknown.* PCH
There is a little man. The Merry Man of Paris. Stella Mead. SUS
There Is a Little Unpretending Rill. Wordsworth. EPN
There is a lobster in the ocean. Pretty Beads. Dick Gallup. ANYP
There is a locust. Dislike of a Governor. Issa. PoFr
There Is a Loneliness. Margaret E. Bruner. PoToHe
There is a lonely mountain-top. Jephthah's Daughter. "Yehoash." TrJP
There is a lonely stream in a lone dim land. The Washer of the Ford. "Fiona Macleod." PoVP
There is a loud noise of Death. To Dear Daniel. Samuel Greenberg. LiTA; MoPo
There Is a Love. Philip Jerome Cleveland. TRV
There is a loved one, far away. My Mother. J. F. Cuthriell. SoP
There is a magic melting pot. The Melting Pot. Dudley Randall. BALP
There Is a Man on the Cross. Elizabeth Cheney. ChIP; MaRV; OQP; PGD; SoP; TRV
There is a manner of growing old. On Growing Old. Srinavas Rayaprol. ACV
There is a melody for which I would surrender. Fantasy. Gerard de Nerval. SiSw
There is a memory stays upon old ships. Old Ships. David Morton. BBV; EtS; StVeCh; TSW
There is a mighty, magic tree. The Tree of Life. Thomas Lovell Beddoes. ERoP-2
There is a mirror in my room. My Mirror. Aline Kilmer. AnAmPo; NP
There is a moment country children know. Village before Sunset. Frances Cornford. BoNaP; LoGBV
There is a moment in midsummer when the earth. Midsummer Pause. Fred Lape. PoSC
There is a morn by men unseen. Emily Dickinson. MWA-2; OxBA
There is a mountain and a wood between us. Separation. Walter Savage Landor. OBEV (1st ed.); TOP
There is a mountain everyone must climb. The Mountain. Robert Finch. CaP
There Is a Mystery in Human Hearts. *Unknown.* PoToHe
There is a mystery too deep for words. Silence. John Hall Wheelock. LiTM
There Is a Mystic Borderland. Helen Field Fischer. *See* Mystic Borderland.
There Is a Mystic Splendor. Raymond Barrow. PoNe
There is a myth, a tale men tell. The Pearl. Hans Christian Andersen. LiTW
There is a name, a wondrous name. The Name. Henry W. Frost. SoP
There is a name all names above. The Name of Jesus. Annie Johnson Flint. BePJ
There Is a Name I Love to Hear. Frederick Whitfield. BePJ; SoP
There is a niche provided. For Every Man. Max I. Reich. STF
There is a niland on a river lying. Collusion between a Alegaiter and a Water-Snaik. J. W. Morris. NA
There Is a Nook Among the Alders. Robert Frost. AmePo
There is a painted bus. The Bus. "Peter." BoTP
There is a panther caged within my breast. The Black Panther. John Hall Wheelock. HBMV; LiTG; LiTM; PFY; TPM
There is a path which no fowl knoweth. Not Weighing. . .But Pardoning. Amy Carmichael. FaChP
There is a peace which cometh after sorrow. Peace [after Sorrow]. Jessie Rose Gates. MaRV; SoP
There is a people mighty in its youth. Tribute to America. Shelley. PaA; PAL
There is a pity in forgotten things. The Triumph of Forgotten Things. Edith M. Thomas. HBV
There Is a Place. Alma Hoellein. STF
There is a place of safe retreat. The Everlasting Arms. William M. Scholfield. SoP
There is a place that some men know. The Cross. Allen Tate. AP; AWP; MAP; MoAmPo; MoVE; OxBA; PoDB
There is a place where love begins and a place where love

There (continued)
ends. Explanations of Love. Carl Sandburg. LiTL; MoLP
There is a place where thou canst touch the eyes. The Secret Place. Adelaide A. Pollard. FaChP; SoP; STF
There is a place where, wisdom won, right recorded. Elegy for Our Dead. Edwin Rolfe. WaP
There is a plan far greater than the plan you know. There Is No Death. *Unknown.* BLPA; NeHB; SoP
There is a pleasure in poetic pains. Poetic Pains [*or* Poetry; Satire and Pulpit]. William Cowper. *Fr.* The Task. CoBE; FiP; PP
There is a pleasure in the pathless woods. The Ocean [*or* The Sea]. Byron. *Fr.* Childe Harold's Pilgrimage, IV. BEL; ChTr; EPN; FaBoBe; FaBV; FiP; HBV; InP; LiTB; LiTG; MaPo; MaRV; MCCG; OBRV; OHFP; PoIE; ShBV-3; TreF; ViBoPo; WHA
There is a poem I have read, and which is quoted far. If We Could Only Be! Lee Shippey. PEDC
There is a poem on the way. Invocation. Kathleen Raine. CMoP
There Is a Pool on Garda. Clinton Scollard. HBV
There is a poverty that trees may show. City Trees. Anderson M. Scruggs. PoMa
There is a pretty piece of work. The Naughty Lord & the Gay Young Lady. *Unknown.* CoMu
There is a private tension that endears. The Crack. Michael Goldman. NYBP
There is a quality of pain. A Quality of Pain. Barbara D. Holender. NYTB
There is a quest that calls me. The Mystic. Cale Young Rice. MaRV; WGRP
There is a quiet kingdom's strand. The Quiet Kingdom. Carl Busse. AWP; JAWP; WBP
There is a quiet spirit in these woods. The Spirit of Poetry. Longfellow. CoBA; PP
There is a race from eld descent. Hey Nonny No. Marguerite Merington. AA
There is a reaper whose name is Death. The Reaper and the Flowers. Longfellow. AnNE; HBV
There is a rest that deeper grows. Rest. George Macdonald. SoP
There is a river clear and fair. Fragment in Imitation of Wordsworth [*or* An Imitation of Wordsworth]. Catherine Fanshawe. ALV; BOHV; HBV; NA; Par
There is a road that turning always. The Road. Edwin Muir. CMoP; FaBoEn; FaBoMo; FaFP; LiTB; LiTG; LiTM; ViBoPo (1958 ed.)
There is a rumour hereabout of summer. The Overgrown Back Yard. John Holmes. CrMA; NePoAm
There is a sad carnival up the valley. Are They Dancing. Edward Dorn. NeAP
There is a safe and secret place. The Secret Place. Henry Francis Lyte. VA
There is a secret laughter. Secret Laughter. Christopher Morley. FaBV; TreFS
There is a secret that the sober mood. Unison. John Hall Wheelock. MoRP
There is a sentinel before the gate. The City Church. "E. H. K." WGRP
There is a serpent in perfection tarnished. True Vine. Elinor Wylie. AnFE; APA; CoAnAm; LiTA
There is a shame of nobleness. Emily Dickinson. NePA
There is a sheeling hidden in the wood. The Lay of Prince Marvan. *Tr. by* Eleanor Hull. AnIV
There is a ship we understand. An Invitation to Lubberland. *Unknown.* CoBE
There is a shrine whose golden gate. The Shrine. Digby Mackworth Dolben. DD; GoBC; HBV
There is a sighing in the wood. The Silent. Jones Very. AmePo
There is a silence. Christmas. Catherine Parmenter. DD
There is a silence I carry about with me always. The Silence. John Gould Fletcher. Down the Mississippi, VII. HT; LiTA; NP
There is a silence where hath been no sound. Silence [*or* Sonnet: Silence]. Thomas Hood. CBEP; CH; CoBE; EnLi-2 (1949 ed.); EnRP; ERoP-2; FaBoEn; GTSL; ILP; OBEV; OBNC; OBRV; PeER; PoEL-4; ShBV-4; Sonn; TDP; ViBoPo
There is a singer everyone has heard. The Oven Bird. Robert Frost. AmPP (4th ed.); AP; AWP; BWP; CoBMV; CrMA; ForPo; FosPo; InPo; JAWP; MAPA; MaPo; NoP; OxBA; Po; Sonn; TwAmPo; UnS; VaPo
There is a singing in the summer air. The Summer Pool. Robert Buchanan. VA
There is a small store-house of knowledge in which I sit sometimes on hard wooden cases. A Store-House. Louis Dudek. CaP
There is a smile of love. The Smile. Blake. OBRV
There is a solitude in seeing you. Lightning. Witter Bynner. MoLP
There is a solitude of space. Emily Dickinson. AP; MWA-2
There is a sorcerer in Lachine. The Sorcerer. A. J. M. Smith. PeCV (1967 ed.)
There is a soul above the soul of each. Humanity. Richard Watson Dixon. EPN; OBVV; OQP; VA
There is a Soul Gethsemane. Easter Sacraments. Henry Park Schauffler. OQP
There is a sound I would not hear. Fear. Langdon Elwyn Mitchell. AA
There is a sound of going. Sounds. Mary Austin. NP
There is a sound that's dear to me. The Lay of the Levite. William E. Aytoun. HBV
There Is a Spell, for Instance. Hilda Doolittle ("H. D."). MoPo
There is a spray the bird clung to. Misconceptions. Robert Browning. EPN; GTBS; OBEV; OBVV; TOP; VA
There is a stane in yon water. Burd Isabel and Earl Patrick. *Unknown.* BaBo; ESPB
There is a star that runs very fast. Moon Song. Hilda Conkling. SP; TiPo
There Is a Stillness. *Unknown.* SoP
There is a stranger in the council hall. Stranger at the Peace Table. Esther Baldwin York. MaRV
There is a stream, I name not its name, lest inquisitive tourist. The Bathers. Arthur Hugh Clough. *Fr.* The Bothie of Tober-na-Vuolich. BoNaP; VA
There is a stream that flowed before the first beginning. Kathleen Raine. *Fr.* Water. ImOP
There is a strength in knowing that it can be borne. Emily Dickinson. MaPo
There is a stubblefield, where a black rain falls. De Profundis. Georg Trakl. OnPM
There is a supreme God in the ethnological section. Homage to the British Museum. William Empson. CMoP; FaBoMo; LiTM (rev. ed.); MoAB; MoBrPo (1962 ed.); NoP
There is a tale, beloved of old Japan. The Chrysanthemum Legend. Arthur Davison Ficke. PoMa
There Is a Tavern in the Town. *Unknown.* FaFP; TreF; YaD
There is a temple in my heart. Temple Garlands. Agnes Mary Frances Robinson. HBV
There is a thing that much is us'd. *Unknown.* SeCSL
There is a thing which in the light. A Candle. Sir John Suckling. ErPo
"There is a Thorn—it looks so old." The Thorn. Wordsworth. EnRP
There Is a Tide. Shakespeare. *Fr.* Julius Caesar, IV, iii. MaRV; PoPl
(Time to Strike, The.) TreFS
("There is a tide in the affairs of men.") TRV
There Is a Time. Frederic J. Osborn. MemP
There is a time to mount; to humble thee. On the Fitness of Seasons. Enzo, King of Sardinia. OnPM
There is a time, we know not when. The Hidden Line [*or* The Doomed Man]. Joseph Addison Alexander. BLPA; MaRV; NeHB; SoP; TRV
There is a time wherein eternity. The Last Communion. Leo Ward. CAW; GoBC
There is a Top Secret room in the White House. A Gothic Tale. William Witherup. QAH
There is a treasure. God's Treasure. "A. M. N." SoP; STF
There is a tree, by day. Tenebris. Angelina W. Grimké. CDC; PoNe
There is a tree native in Turkestan. Note on Local Flora. William Empson. AtBAP; FaBoMo; MoVE; ToPo
There is a tree of praise and dower. The Year. *Unknown.* OTPC (1946 ed.)
There is a truck that rumbles by. The Grumbling Truck. Rowena Bennett. MPB (1956 ed.)
There is a wall of which the stones. The Rebel. Hilaire Belloc. CoBE; PoFr

There is a walled garden where the flowers never pale or turn dark. Paradise. E. N. Sargent. NYBP
"There is a way I cannot take." The Cup. Martha Snell Nicholson. SoP
There Is a Way of Life. Merrill Moore. OnPM
There is a way of seeing that is not seeing. Trompe l'Oeil. Daryl Hine. MoCV
There is a way, that sages tell. The Advantage of the Outside. Richard Eberhart. NePA
There is a way which man hath trod. Gethsemane. Charles Russell Wakeley. OQP
There is a well, a willow-shaded spot. The Cherwell Water Lily [*or* Waterlily]. Frederick W. Faber. CAW; GoBC
There is a white mare that my love keeps. The Postures of Love, II. Alex Comfort. ErPo; FaBoMo; NeBP
There is a wild boar in these woods. Old Bangum. *Unknown.* BaBo
There is a wild flower growing. Jean. Paul Potts. NeBP
There is a willow grows aslant a brook. Ophelia's Death. Shakespeare. *Fr.* Hamlet, V, i. ChTr
There is a wind where the rose was. Autumn [*or* The Lost Playmate]. Walter de la Mare. GTBS-D; OTPC (1923 ed.); POTE
There is a wolf in me. . .fangs pointed for tearing gashes. Wilderness. Carl Sandburg. AnAmPo; AP
There is a woman like a seed. Another Generation. J. C. Squire. HBMV
There is a wonderful family called Stein. Limerick. *Unknown. See also* Wonderful family is Stein, A. BOHV.
There is a world deep in the seas of night. Dark Yuggoth. Lin Carter. FiSC
There is a world of wonder in this rose. The Rose. G. A. Studdert-Kennedy. MaRV
There is a worm in the world, well man knoweth him. The Serpent's Nature. *Unknown. Fr.* The Bestiary. MeEV
There is a yew-tree, pride of Lorton Vale. Yew-Trees. Wordsworth. BEL; CABA; EnLi-2; EnRP; ERoP-1; UnPo (3d ed.)
There is a young artist called [*or* named] Whistler. Limerick. Dante Gabriel Rossetti. BOHV; LiBL
There is a young lady whose nose/ Continually prospers and grows. Limerick. Edward Lear. *See also* There was a young lady whose nose/ Was so long . . . OTPC (1946 ed.).
There is always a first flinging. Variations on a Theme. Anne Wilkinson. MoCV
There Is Always a Place for You. Anne Campbell. PoToHe
There is always the sound of falling water here. Night Piece. Robert Hillyer. MAP; MoAmPo
There is an air for which I would disown. An Old Tune. Gérard de Nerval, *tr. by* Andrew Lang. AWP; HBV; JAWP; WBP
There is an air for which I'd gladly give. Fantasy. Gérard de Nerval, *tr. by* Anthony Bower. LiTW
There is an altar and a throne. The Choice. Avis B. Christiansen. SoP
There is an ape in Paris. The Ape. La Fontaine. OnPM
There is an architecture grander far. The Builders. Henry van Dyke. OQP
There is an end of joy and sorrow. Ilicet. Swinburne. MaVP; PoVP
There is an evening coming in. Going. Philip Larkin. CMoP; ToPo
There is an exquisite torture in living with dull people. Always Battling. Thomas O'Brien. NeIP
There is an eye that never sleeps. God the Omniscient. *At. to* James Cowden Wallace, *also to* John Aikman Wallace. BLRP SoP; STF; WGRP
There is an hour of calm relief. Secret Prayer. Fanny J. Crosby. SoP
There is an hour of peaceful rest. The Hour of Peaceful Rest. William Bingham Tappan. AA; HBV
There is an inevitability. Fable. Norman Harris. NYBP
There is an island in a far-off sea. Where the Single Men Go in Summer. Nina Bourne. FiBHP
There is an isle beyond our ken. The Isle of Lost Dreams. "Fiona Macleod." VA
There is an ode in every swaying tree. Reflection. Kurt M. Stein. InMe
There is an old and very cruel god. Vicarious Atonement. Richard Aldington. WGRP
There is an Old City. Karl Bulcke, *tr. fr. German by* Ludwig Lewisohn. AWP; JAWP; WBP
There is an old Cook in N. Y. *Unknown.* SiTL
There is an old he-wolf named Gambart. Limerick. Dante Gabriel Rossetti. CenHV
There is an old woman/ Who lives in the town. The Old Woman Who Lives in the Town. Pringle Barret. PCH
There is an old woman/ Who ought to die. The Old Woman. Marjorie Allen Seiffert. AnAmPo; NP
There is an Order by a northern sea. Religio Novissima. Aubrey Thomas De Vere. IrPN; NBM
There is at least one thing I would less rather have in the neighborhood than a gangster. What's the Matter, Have't You Got Any Sense of Humor? Ogden Nash. SiTL
There is beauty in the bellow of the blast. Ko-Ko's Song. W. S. Gilbert. *Fr.* The Mikado. PCD
There is beauty in the forest. When the Heart Is Full of Love. *Unknown.* MaRV
There is, besides the warmth, in this new love. Scarabs for the Living, V. R. P. Blackmur. TwAmPo
There is blood on thy desolate shore. Apostrophe to the Island of Cuba. James Gates Percival. PAH
There is bound to be a certain amount of. Trouble. Don Marquis. *Fr.* Archy and Mehitabel. TreFT
There is bright light. Its Name Is Known. Daniel Lawrence Kelleher. NeIP
There is Bryant, as quiet, as cool, and as dignified. Bryant. James Russell Lowell. *Fr.* A Fable for Critics. AmePo; AnNE; AP; CoBA; MWA-1
There is but one great sorrow. The Shadow. Richard Henry Stoddard. AA
There is but one May in the year. May-Time. Christina Rossetti. *Fr.* Sing-Song. BoTP; TiPo
There is comfort in old houses. Old Houses. Homer D'Lettuso. PoToHe (new ed.)
There is dark. Trying to Sleep. Ralph Pomeroy. ELU
There is death enough in Europe without these. Dead Ponies. Brenda Chamberlain. NeBP
There is delight in singing, tho' none hear. To Robert Browning. Walter Savage Landor. BEL; EnLi-2; EnRP; EPN; GTBS; GTSL; InP; MCCG; MyFE; NoP; OAEP; PoRL; ViBoPo
There is fear in. Eskimo Song. *Unknown.* PeCV
There is fire in the lower hold, there's fire down below. Fire Down Below. *Unknown.* SoAmSa
There is great mystery, Simone. Hair. Remy de Gourmont. AWP; ErPo
There Is Hallelujah Hannah. A. E. Housman. WhC
There is hardly a mouthful of air. Nelson Street. "Seumas O'-Sullivan." OxBI
There is Hawthorne, with genius so shrinking and rare. Hawthorne. James Russell Lowell. *Fr.* A Fable for Critics. AmPP (4th ed.); AnNE; AP; CoBA; MWA-1; OxBA
There is health in thy gray wing. To a Marsh Hawk in Spring. Henry David Thoreau. PoEL-4
There is heard a hymn when the panes are dim. The Feast of the Snow. G. K. Chesterton. HBV
There is here an ancient anchorite. San Sabas. Luis Palés Matos. CAW
There is immortal living now and here. Immortal Living. Harold T. Pulsifer. MaRV
There is in all the sons of men. God's Altar. Emerson. MaRV
There is in stillness oft a magic power. Solitude. Cardinal Newman. SoP
There is in this world something. The Sweetest Thing. *Unknown.* TTY
There is joy in. Eskimo Chant. *Unknown.* WHW
There is lightning on the edge of the water. Poem. Lewis Mac Adams. YAP
There is Lowell, who's striving Parnassus to climb. Lowell [*or* On Himself]. James Russell Lowell. *Fr.* A Fable for Critics. AA; AmePo; AmPP (4th ed.); AP; CoBA; OxBA
There is majesty in rose. Tuesday 7:00 P.M. John Wieners. FRC
There is many a love in the land, my love. Song. Joaquin Miller. HBV
There is many a slipton. Lady Tree. WhC
There is many a wild Canadian boy who leaves his happy home. Harry Dunne, *vers.* II. *Unknown.* ShS
There is midsummer. Midsummer. Stephen Spender. AtBAP
There is much to be said. Mac Diarmod's Daughter. Francis Carlin. HBMV
There is much to be said for the portrait painted in winter. Portrait in Winter. Katherine Garrison Chapin. GoYe

There is music in me, the music of a peasant people. The Banjo Player. Fenton Johnson. AnAmPo; BANP; GoSl; Kal; PoNe
There is naught for thee by thy haste to gain. The Created. Jones Very. AmP; QFR
There is Never a Day So Dreary. *Unknown, at. to* Lilla M. Alexander. BLRP
(Consolation.) STF
There is never an open door to the wild beasts' home. The Uninvited. William D. Mundell. NYBP
There is never any trusting. Foam. *Unknown.* OnPM
There is no balm on earth. Invocation. Gilbert Thomas. TrPWD
There is no beauty. The World I See. Mari Evans. Kal
There is no bountie to be shew'd to such. Ben Jonson. *Fr.* The Poetaster. PoEL-2
There is no chance, no destiny, no fate. Will. Ella Wheeler Wilcox. BLPA; NeHB; PoToHe
There is no chapel on the day. Capital Punishment. Oscar Wilde. *Fr.* The Ballad of Reading Gaol. OxBl; WePo
There is no cock crowing in our bedroom. No Cock Crows at Morning. Horace Gregory. CMoP
There Is No Country. Juljan Tuwim, *tr. fr. Polish by* Watson Kirkconnell. TrJP
There is no dearer lover of lost hours. Idleness. Silas Weir Mitchell. AA
There Is No Death. John Luckey McCreery. BLPA; FaBoBe; HBV; NeHB; TreF; WBLP
"There is no death! The stars go down," *sel.* MaRV
There Is No Death. *Unknown.* BLPA; NeHB; SoP
('Tis Immortality.) SoP
There is no death, O child divine. The Great Victory. R. V. Gilbert. BLRP
There is no death! The stars go down. There Is No Death. John Luckey McCreery. BLPA; FaBoBe; HBV; MaRV; NeHB; TreF; WBLP
There is no death! What seems so is transition. Longfellow. *Fr.* Resignation. MaRV; SoP; TRV
There Is No Dream. Margaret E. Sangster. PEDC
There is no end to the/ Deception of quiet things. The Chinese Banyan. William Meredith. NePoEA
There is no escape by the river. At the End of the Day. Richard Hovey. HBVY; StaSt; YT
There is no fire of the crackling boughs. Glenaradale. Walter Chalmers Smith. OBEV (new ed.); OBVV; PeVV
There is no fitter end than this. In Memoriam, S.C.W., V.C. Charles Sorley. MMA
There is no flock, however watched and tended. Resignation. Longfellow. CoBA; HBV
There is no frigate like a book. Emily Dickinson. ATP; BBV (1951 ed.); CoBA; FaPON; GoJo; HH; InP; MAP; MoAmPo; MPB; NeMA; PoLF; PoMa; PoPl; SiSoSe; TreFS; TrGrPo; YeAr
There Is No God. Arthur Hugh Clough. *See* "There Is No God," the Wicked Saith.
There Is No God, As I Was Taught. John Masefield. *Fr.* Sonnets ("Long long ago"). CMoP
("There is no God, as I was taught in youth.") HBV; WGRP
"There is no God," the foolish saith. Convinced by Sorrow. Elizabeth Barrett Browning. *Fr.* The Cry of the Human. BLRP; MaRV; OQP; PoVP; WBLP
"There Is No God," the Wicked Saith. Arthur Hugh Clough. *Fr.* Dipsychus, Pt. I, sc. V. EPN; NBM; PoVP; TreFS; ViPP
(Spirit's Song, The.) LoBV
(There Is No God.) FaPL
There is no great and no small. The Informing Spirit [*or* No Great, No Small]. Emerson. *Fr.* History. AmLP; AWP; BBV (1951 ed.); InPo; MaRV; WGRP
There is no happy [*or* happier] life. Love's Matrimony [*or* Love's Vision]. Duke of Newcastle. BoPe; LO; MeWo; SeCePo; SeCL
There is no Job but cries to God and hopes. A Copy of Verses. John Wilson. SCAP
There is no joy in water apart from the sun. Song. R. N. Currey. BoSA; MemP; PeSA
There is no land like England. Song. Tennyson. *Fr.* The Foresters. VA
There is no land upon the earth. You Who Don't Believe It. John A.Stone. SGR
There is no last step. Step. Jason Miller. ThO
There is no laughter in the natural world. Laughter and Death. Wilfrid Scawen Blunt. The Love Sonnets of Proteus, XCI. MoBrPo (1942 ed.); PoMa; Sonn; VA
There is no light in any path of Heaven. The Dark Road. Ethel Clifford. HBV
There is no love like the love of Jesus. The Heart of God. W. E. Littlewood. BePJ
There is no lover he[e] or she[e]. A Paradox. Aurelian Townshend. AnAnS-2; EP; SeCP
There is no memorial site. For Brother Malcolm. Edward S. Spriggs. CAD
There is no music now in all Arkansas. Variations for Two Pianos. Donald Justice. NYBP; TDP
There is no music that man has heard. A Sea Lyric. William Hamilton Hayne. EtS
There is no mystery. Black Woman. R. Ernest Holmes. WSL
There is no name in all our country's story. Abraham Lincoln. Robert Whitaker. HH
There is no name so sweet on earth. The Blessed Name. George W. Bethune. BLRP
There Is No Nearer Nearness. Cha Liang-cheng, *tr. fr. Chinese by* Cha Liang-cheng. LiTW
There is no need to flirt with him today. A Seeing Eye-Dog. Saundra Sharp. WSL
There is no need to run outside. To Be. *Unknown, at. to* Lao-tzu. *Fr.* Tao Teh King. OnPM
There is no one among men that has not a special failing. Madly Singing in the Mountains. Po Chü-i. CBEP; MoPW; OuHeWo
There Is No Opera like "Lohengrin." John Wheelwright. NYBP; OnHM; WhC
There is no page or servant, most or least. The Seventh Property. Sir Thomas More. *Fr.* The Twelve Properties or Conditions of a Lover. CoBE; EnRePo
There is no path in this desert waste. My Guide. Robert Jones Burdette. MaRV
There is no peace with you. Enigma. Jessie Redmond Fauset. PoNe
"There is no permanence," you sagely said. Two Sonnets for a Lost Love, I. Samuel A. De Witt. GoYe
There is no person lonelier. Visit the Sick. James J. Metcalfe. PoToHe (new ed.)
"There is no place to turn," she said. The Sensualists. Theodore Roethke. ErPo; NePoAm-2; PoeP; UnTE
There is no poetry when you live there. The Flowering Past. Malcolm Lowry. NYTB
There is no point in work. The World of Work, as a Poet Would Like It to Be. D. H. Lawrence. BoC; OBMV; ShBV-3
There is no polemic between East and West. Eurasian Girl. Anthony Kerrigan. NYTB
There is no power to change. Permanence. Francis Meynell. HBMV; MoBrPo (1942 ed.)
There is no quenching of the other thirst. Hagar. Elisabeth Eybers. PeSA
There is no Rachel any more. One Shall Be Taken and the Other Left. Aline Kilmer. NP
There Is No Reason Why Not to Look at Death. Robert Sward. CoPo
There is no rest for the mind. Interior; the Suburbs. Horace Gregory. AnAmPo; NP
There is no rest in falling, even so. Snow Meditation. Francis Beauchesne Thornton. JKCP (1955 ed.)
There is no rhyme that is half so sweet. Proem. Madison Cawein. AA; BoNaP
There is no roof in all the world. Waiting for the Morning. *Unknown.* STF
There is no rose of such virtue. Rosa Mystica [*or* Two Carols to Our Lady]. *Unknown.* ACP; CAW; EG; GoBC; ISi; PoLi
There is no sense in asking those who fought. Anabasis. Eithne Wilkins. NeBP
There is no siding for the brain. Listening to a Broadcast. John Manifold. WaP
There is no silence upon the earth or under the earth like the silence under the sea. Silences. E. J. Pratt. OBCV; PoCh
There Is No Sin. Omar Khayyám, *tr. fr. Persian by* Edward Fitzgerald. *Fr.* The Rubáiyát. OnPM
There is no sinning against God, what does God care about sin! God and the Holy Ghost. D. H. Lawrence. MoRP

There is no small work unto God. Anna Hempstead Branch. *Fr.* The Monk in the Kitchen. MaRV
There is no soft beatitude in Death. Death Is but Death. Will Dyson. BoAV; MoAuPo
There is no sorrow. Away. Walter de la Mare. CMoP; NoP
There is no sorrow anywhere. Homeward Bound. L. Frank Tooker. EtS
There is no sound. Portent. Richard Church. MoBrPo (1942 ed.)
"There is no sun!" the blind man said. Unfaith. Ted Robinson. MaRV
There is no sweeter sight, I swear; in Heaven. The Crimson Cherry Tree. Henry Treece. LiTM (1946 ed.); WaP
There is no thing in all the world but love. The Camel Rider. *Unknown.* AWP; FaBoTw
There Is No Trumpet like the Tomb. Emily Dickinson. *See* Immortality she gave, The.
There Is No Unbelief. Elizabeth York Case. HBV; NeHB; OQP; TreFS; WBLP; WGRP
(Faith, *wr. at. to* Edward Bulwer-Lytton.) TRV
(Unbelief.) MaRV
There is no vacant chair. The loving meet. Afterward. Elizabeth Stuart Phelps Ward. HBV
There is no way in this starless night. Christ. Robert Jones Burdette. *Fr.* My Guide. BePJ
There is no whispering of any friend. No Friend like Music. Daniel Whitehead Hicky. PoToHe
There is no word of thanks to hear. Pioneers. Arthur W. Jose. BoAu
There is no wrath in the stars. Songs from an Evil Wood, I. Lord Dunsany. MoBrPo (1942 ed.)
There Is None like Her. Tennyson. *Fr.* Maud FaBoEn; OBNC
There Is None, O None but You. Thomas Campion, *wr. at. to* Robert Devereux, Earl of Essex. AtBAP; ElL; HBV; OBSC
There is not a grand inspiring thought. Mother. Emily Taylor. PGD
There is not half so warm a fire. Against Fulfillment of Desire. *Unknown.* TrGrPo
There is not in the wide world a valley so sweet. The Meeting of the Waters. Thomas Moore. AnIL; NBM; OxBoLi; PoEL-4
"There is not much that I can do." At the Railway Station, Upway. Thomas Hardy. FlW
There is nothing as sweet as independence. Independence. Adebayo Faleti. PBA
There Is Nothing False in Thee. Kenneth Patchen. PoPl
There is nothing more perky. The Turkey. Ogden Nash. RePo
There is nothing moving there, in that desert of silence. Conrad Aiken. *Fr.* Priapus and the Pool, IX. CMoP
There is nothing new to be written of tears and man's shuddering breath. On a Fly-Leaf of Schopenhauer's "Immortality." Ruth Guthrie Harding. MaRV
There is nothing on the. The Pilgrimage. Ed Sanders. ANYP
There is nothing the Blood cannot cover. Nothing the Blood Cannot Cover. F. E. Robinson. SoP
There is nought for thee by thy haste to gain. The Created. Jones Very. MAmP; PoIE
There is one/ race of men. Nemean Ode, VI. Pindar. *Fr.* Odes. LiTW
There Is One Creed, and Only One. E. A. Robinson. MaRV
There is one form of life to which I unconditionally surrender. Oh, Please Don't Get Up! Ogden Nash. NePA; SiTL
There is one Mind, one omnipresent Mind. Samuel Taylor Coleridge. *Fr.* Religious Musings. WGRP
There is one sin: to call a green leaf grey. Ecclesiastes. G. K. Chesterton. MoBrPo
There is one story and one story only. To Juan at the Winter Solstice. Robert Graves. CMoP; CoBMV; FaBoMo; ILP; LiTB; LiTM (rev. ed.); MoBrPo (1962 ed.); MoPo; OnHM; PIA; PoIE; PoSa; SeCeV; TwCP; UnPo (3d ed.)
There is one that has a head without an eye. Christina Rossetti. *Fr.* Sing-Song. OTPC (1946 ed.); PPL
There is one who takes all men within his hand. Strophes. Rainer Maria Rilke. OnPM
There is only one love. Sappho, Be Comforted. William Carlos Williams. NePoAm-2
There Is Pleasure in the Pathless Woods. Byron. *See* Ocean, The.
There is Power in a Union. *Unknown, at. to* Joe Hill. ThLM
There Is Shrill Music in High Winds at Night. Jesse Stuart. Man with a Bull-Tongue Plow. PoMa
There is silence that saith, "Ah me!" Golden Silences. Christina Rossetti. NBM
There is so much good in the worst of us. Charity [*or* Good and Bad]. *Unknown, at. to* Edward Wallis Hoch. BLPA; NeHB; TreFS
There is so much loveliness gone out of the world. The Triumph of Doubt. John Peale Bishop. EaLo
There is so much of loneliness. *Unknown.* PoToHe
There is some that like the city. Ridin'. Badger Clark. IHA
There is some will talk of lords and knights. Robin Hood's Delight. *Unknown.* ESPB
There is something/ In me so cruel, so. The New Sheriff. LeRoi Jones. NoP
There is something about a Martini. A Drink with Something in It. Ogden Nash. PoPl
There is something in the autumn that is native to my blood. A Vagabond Song. Bliss Carman. FaPON; GBV; GN; GoTP; HBV; HBVY; MAP; MCCG; MoAmPo (1942 ed.); MPB; NeMA; OTPC (1946 ed.); PoMa; PoSC; RePo; StaSt; StVeCh (1940 ed.); YT
There is something in the word home. Home. *Unknown.* HBV
There is somewhere a secret garden, which none hath seen. The Secret Garden. Robert Nichols. WGRP
There is sorrow enough in the natural way. The Power of the Dog. Kipling. BLPA
There is stone in me that knows stone. Kathleen Raine. *Fr.* Rock. ImOP
There Is Strength in the Soil. Arthur Stringer. OHIP
There Is Sweet Music Here. Tennyson. *See* Choric Song: "There is sweet music here that softer falls."
There is that whispering gallery where. Letter to a Young Poet. George Barker. ChMP
There is the caw of a crow. Jonathan Houghton. Edgar Lee Masters. *Fr.* Spoon River Anthology. OxBA; TDP
There is the loneliness of peopled places. Solitude. Babette Deutsch. HBMV
There is the quaintest little girl. A Little Girl in Bloom. Anne Blackwell Payne. GFA
There is the sign of/ the flower. The Rhyme. Robert Creeley. AmPC
There is the star bloom of the moss. Forest. Jean Garrigue. LiTM
There is this cave. The Jewel. James Wright. CoAP; FRC
There is this distance between me and what I see. Still Poem 9. Philip Lamantia. NeAP
There is this infinite energy, the power of God forever working. Look, How Beautiful. Robinson Jeffers. MoRP
There is unknown dust that is near us. Surprised by Evening. Robert Bly. NaP
There is waiting a work where only his hands can avail. The Day and the Work. Edwin Markham. OQP; PEDC
There is Whittier, whose swelling and vehement heart. Whittier. James Russell Lowell. *Fr.* A Fable for Critics. AmePo; AmPP (4th ed.); AnNE; AP; CoBA; OxBA
There is wind where the rose was. The Lost Playmate. Walter de la Mare. OTPC (1923 ed.)
There is wisdom in the Bible. The Bible. Dorothy Conant Stroud. STF
There Is Yet Time. Arvel Steece. PGD
There isn't a prettier sight, I think. Bare-Back Rider. Dorothy Aldis. *Fr.* At the Circus. UTS
There Isn't Time. Eleanor Farjeon. BoTP; FaPON; RePo
There it is, a block of leaping marble. Cousin Florence. Richard Eberhart. ToPo
There it lies. The Foundered Tram. Harold Monro. BrPo
There it was I saw what I shall never forget. The Fawn. Edna St. Vincent Millay. LaNeLa
There it was, word for word. The Poem That Took the Place of a Mountain. Wallace Stevens. ML
There leeft a may, an a weel-far'd may. Katharine Jaffray (C *vers.*). *Unknown.* ESPB
There leeved a wee man at the fit o' yon hill. Get Up and Bar the Door (B *vers.*). *Unknown.* ESPB
There Let Thy Bleeding Branch Atone. Emily Brontë. SeCePo
There lies a broken anker, on whose trust. Thomas Heyrick.

There (continued)
Fr. The Submarine Voyage. PeRV
There lies a city inaccessible. The Unknown City. Sir Charles G. D. Roberts. CaP
There lies a cold corpse upon the sands. Death Song. Robert Stephen Hawker. OBNC; OBRV; OBVV
There lies a little city in the hills. Home. Edward Rowland Sill. AnNE; HBV
There lies a little city leagues away. The Deserted City. Sir Charles G. D. Roberts. VA
There lies a lone isle in the tropic seas. Easter Island. Frederick George Scott. OBCV
There lies a somnolent lake. In the Past. Trumbull Stickney. MAP; MoAmPo (1942 ed.); OxBA
There lies a vale [*or* There is a dale] in Ida, lovelier. Oenone. Tennyson. BEL; EnLi-2; EnLit; EPN; MaVP; MBW-2; OAEP; OBRV; PoVP; ViBoPo; ViPo; ViPP; VP
There lies afar behind a western hill. The Town without a Market. James Elroy Flecker. MoBrPo
There lies no magic in this bit of bread. Sacrament. Una W. Harsen. ChIP
There lies the port; the vessel puffs her sail. Tennyson. *Fr.* Ulysses. EtS; MaRV; OQP; OTPC
There! little girl, don't cry! A Life-Lesson. James Whitcomb Riley. AA; HBV; PoLF; TreFS
There liv'd a lady in Lauderdale. She's Hoy'd Me Out o' Lauderdale. *Unknown.* CoMu
There livd a laird down into Fife. The Wife Wrapt in Wether's Skin (D *vers.*). *Unknown.* ESPB
There livd a lass in yonder dale. *See* There lived a lass . . .
There livd a lord on yon sea-side. Fair Annie (B *vers.*). *Unknown.* ESPB
There liv'd a man in yonder glen. Johnie Blunt. *Unknown.* OxBB
There liv'd of late in Luteners Lane. A Westminster Wedding; or, Like unto Like, Quoth the Devil to the Collier. *Unknown.* CoMu
There lived a carl in Kellyburnbraes. Kellyburnbraes. *Unknown.* OxBB
There Lived a King. W. S. Gilbert. *Fr.* The Gondoliers. FiBHP; StPo; WhC
(King Goodheart.) ALV; InMe
There lived a king into the east. King Orpheo. *Unknown.* BuBa
There Lived a Lady in Milan. William Rose Benét. HBMV; OnPP
There lived [*or* livd] a lass in yonder dale. Katharine Jaffray. *Unknown.* BaBo; ESPB; InP; ViBoFo (A *vers.*)
There Lived a Man. Thomas Curtis Clark. ChIP
There lived a man at the foot of a hill. Get Up and Bar the Door. *Unknown.* EnSB
There lived a sage in days of yore. A Tragic Story. Adelbert von Chamisso, *tr. by* Thackeray. BoChLi (1950 ed.); BOHV; BoTP; FaPON; GaP; GoTP; HBV; HBVY; MoShBr; MPB; OnMSP; OTPC; RePo; RIS; StVeCh (1940 ed.)
There lived a singer in France of old. A Farewell. Swinburne. *Fr.* The Triumph of Time. GTSL
There lived a wife at Usher's Well. The Wife of Usher's Well. *Unknown.* AnFE; AtBAP; AWP; BaBo (A *vers.*); BEL; BoLiVe; BuBa; CBEP; CH; ChTr; DiPo; EnL; EnLi-1; EnRP; EnSB; ESPB; ExPo; GoTS; HBV; ILP; InP; InPo; JAWP; LiTB; LoBV; NoP; OAEP; OBB; OBEV; OnMSP; OuHeWo; OxBB; OxBS; PIA; PoAn; PoEL-1; PoIE; SeCeV; ShBV-2; StP; TiPo (1952 ed.); TOP; TreF; TrGrPo; UnPo; ViBoFo (A *vers.*); WBP
There lived a young squire in ten months a year. The Jolly Farmer. *Unknown.* BFSS
There lived a youth, and a well-beloved youth. The Bailiff's Daughter of Islington. *Unknown.* BFSS
There lived an honest man and true. The Cruel Sister. *Unknown.* BaBo
There lived an old lord by the Northern Sea. The Two Sisters. *Unknown.* PoMa
There lived an old man in the Kingdom of Tess. The New Vestments. Edward Lear. BOHV; OnPP
There lived in a laburnum tree. The Yellow Fairy. Charlotte Druitt Cole. BoTP
There lived once Svetaketu Aruneya, the grandson of Aruna. The Story of Svetaketu. *Unknown.* *Fr.* The Upanishads. WoL
There lived years ago the beautiful Kung-sun. Tu Fu. *Fr.* A Song of Dagger-Dancing. UnS
There lives a cat across the way. A Parlor Cat. Louella C. Poole. CIV
There lives a lassie i' the braes. Lizzy Liberty. John Skinner. PoFr
There lives a maid down under yon brae. Katherine Jaffray. *Unknown.* OxBB
There lives a man in Rynie's land. Lang Johnny More. *Unknown.* ESPB
There lives a pig in Georgia's far land. Pipes in the Sty. John Kendall. WhC
There lives beside me here an unknown woman. The Ascension and the Assumption. Ramón López Velarde. HW
There may be agony in furnished rooms. The Room. Francis Webb. *Fr.* Leichhardt in Theatre. PoAu-2
There mounts in squalls a sort of rusty mire. The Exile's Return. Robert Lowell. AmPP (5th ed.); AP; MiAP; NePA; OxBA
There mournful cypress grew in greatest store. The Garden of Proserpina. Spenser. *Fr.* The Faerie Queene, II, 7. ChTr
There Must Be a Lone Ranger!!! Leroi Jones. WOW
There must be fairy miners. Buttercups. Wilfrid Thorley. DD; FaPON; GaP; HBV; HBVY; OBVV
There must be magic. Otherwise. Aileen Fisher. SoPo; SUS
There must be many Theobalds' Roads in the universe. Theobalds' Roads. Charles Williams. LO
There Must Be Silence. Anne Tansey. JKCP (1955 ed.)
There, my blessing with thee [*or* you]! Polonius' Advice to Laertes [*or* To Thine Own Self Be True]. Shakespeare. *Fr.* Hamlet, I, iii. FaFP; LiTB; LiTG; MaRV; OHFP; OQP; OTD; PoPl
There, my lad, lie the Articles. Scene from a Play, Acted at Oxford, Called "Matriculation." Thomas Moore. NBM
There never breathed a man, who, when his life. Gabriello Chiabrera. Epitaphs, IV. AWP; JAWP; WBP
There never shall be the strange beauties of Vignettes. The Ideal. Baudelaire. SyP
There never were such radiant noons. Then and Now. Sir Rennell Rodd. VA
There never yet was honest man. Loving and Beloved. Sir John Suckling. FaBoEn; OBS; SeEP
There never yet was woman made. Sir John Suckling. AnAnS-2
There no more partying, no more pain. With Him. Christina Rossetti. FaChP
There, on the darkened deathbed, dies the brain. The End. John Masefield. CMoP; LiTB
"There, on the left!" said the colonel. Marthy Virginia's Hand. George Parsons Lathrop. MC; PAH
There on the top of the down. June Bracken and Heather. Tennyson. EnLoPo; PoVP
There once did live in days of old. Florent and the Loathly Hag. John Gower. *Fr.* Confessio Amantis. MeEV
There once the walls. A Tale. Edward Thomas. ChTr
There once was a bonnie Scotch laddie. Limerick. *Unknown.* LiBL; WhC
There once was a boring young Rev. *Unknown.* SiTL
There once was a boy of Bagdad. Limerick [*or* New Limericks]. *Unknown.* RIS; StaSt
There once was a cobbler. The Kind Mousie. Natalie Joan. BoTP
There Once was a Cow with a Double Udder. The Cow. Theodore Roethke. FiBHP
There once was a Dormouse who lived in a bed. The Dormouse and the Doctor. A. A. Milne. WhC
There once was a frog. A Legend of Lake Okeefinokee [*or* A Legend of Okeefinokee]. Laura E. Richards. BoChLi; PoRh; RIS; StPo
There once was a girl of New York. Limerick. Cosmo Monkhouse. LiBL; NA
There once was a girl of Pitlochry. Limerick. *Unknown.* CenHV
There once was a guy named Othello. Shakespeare Might Have Boiled Othello. Edwin Meade Robinson. *Fr.* Limericised Classics. HBMV
There once was a happy hyena. The Happy Hyena. Carolyn Wells. PCH
There once was a maid with such graces. *Unknown.* SiTL
There once was a man from Nantucket. *See* There was an old man of Nantucket.
There once was a man, named Power. Clock Time by the Geyser. John White. ShM

There once was a man of Bengal. Limerick. *Unknown.* CenHV
There once was a man of Calcutta. Limerick. *Unknown.* LiBL; WhC
There once was a man [*or* There was a young man] who said: "Damn!" Limerick. Maurice Evan Hare. CenHV; LiBL; OxBoLi
There once was a man [*or* There was a young man] who said, "God." Limerick [*or* Rhyme]. Ronald Arbuthnott Knox. LiBL; OxBoLi
There once was a man who said, "How." Limerick. *Unknown.* LiBL; NA
There once was a monarch, a pompous old Persian. The King and the Clown. *Unknown.* MaC
There once was a noble ranger. Mustang Gray. *Unknown.* ABF; BFSS; CoSo
There once was a painter named Scott. Limerick. Dante Gabriel Rossetti. CenHV
There once was a peach on a tree. The Peach. Abbie Farwell Brown. GFA
There once was a person of Benin. Limerick. Cosmo Monkhouse. LiBL; NA
There once was a popular crooner. Limerick. M. B. Thornton. LiBL
There Once Was a Puffin. Florence Page Jaques. SoPo; TiPo
There once was a sculptor called [*or* named] Phidias. Limerick. Oliver Herford. BOHV; LiBL
There once was a Shah had a second son. Noureddin, the Son of the Shah. Clinton Scollard. BOHV
There once was a Warden of Wadham. The Folkways of Sodom. "E. W." SiTL
There once was a Willow, and he was very old. The Willow-Man. Juliana Horatia Ewing. TVC
There once was a witch of Willowby Wood. The Witch of Willowby Wood. Rowena Bennett. PoMS; RePo
There once was a woman named Jacqueline Gray. Jacqueline Gray. Kenneth Pitchford. *Fr.* Good for Nothing Man. CoPo
There once was a wood, and a very thick wood. The First Tooth. William Brighty Rands. HBV; HBVY
There Once Was a Young Man Named Hall. *Unknown.* ShM
There once was an arch armadillo. The Arch Armadillo. Carolyn Wells. PCH
There once was an Ichthyosaurus. The Ichthyosaurus. *Unknown.* OTPC (1946 ed.)
There once was an old man of Lyme. *Unknown, at. to* Edward Lear, *also to* Cosmo Monkhouse. *See also* There was an old party of Lyme. NA.
There once were some learned M.D.'s. Limerick. Oliver Herford. BOHV; LiBL
There once were some people called Sioux. The American Indian [*or* The Indian]. *Unknown.* FiBHP; LiTG; SiTL
There once were two cats of Kilkenny. *See* There wanst was two cats of Kilkenny.
There our murdered brother lies. The Wake of William Orr. William Drennan. OnYI; OxBI
There out of hell the Old One bellows. Lamentations of the Fallen Angels. Cædmon (?). *Fr.* Christ and Satan. AnOE
There overtook me and drew me in. The Gum-Gatherer. Robert Frost. MWA-2
There pass the careless people. A. E. Housman. A Shropshire Lad, XIV. PoVP; ViPo
There passed the low door of the Nazareth home. The Open Door. Ida Norton Munson. ChIP
There, pay it, James! 'tis cheaply earned. Vers de Société. H. D. Traill. Par
There piped a piper in the wood. The Magic Piper. E. L. Marsh. BoTP; SiSoSe
There rolls the deep where grew the tree. In Memoriam A. H. H., CXXIII. Tennyson. CoBE; EPN; GTSL; MaPo; OAEP; OuHeWo; SeCePo; SeCeV; TOP; ViPo; VP
There runs a rhythm thro' the woods and seas. The Woodland Singer. John Jerome Rooney. MaRV
"There!" Said a Stripling Pointing with Meet Pride. Wordsworth. BEL; EPN
There sat a happy fisherman. The Reed. Mikhail Yurevich Lermontov. AWP; JAWP; WBP
There sat an old man on a rock. Too Late. Fitz Hugh Ludlow. BOHV; PoLF
There sat down, once, a thing on Henry's heart. The Dream Songs, XXIX. John Berryman. NMP; OPoP
There sat two glasses, filled to the brim. The Two Glasses. Ella Wheeler Wilcox. BLPA
There sat upon the linden tree. The Linden Tree. Dietmar von Aist. PoPl
There Shall Always Be the Church. T. S. Eliot. *Fr.* The Rock. MaRV; TRV
There shall be beds full of light odours blent. The Lovers' Death. Baudelaire. SyP
"There Shall Be More Joy." Ford Madox Ford. MoBrPo (1942 ed.)
There Shall Be No Night. Revelation, XXII: 1-5, Bible, *N.T.* TrGrPo
There Shall Be Wars. Anna Williams. SoP
There shall come from out this noise of strife and groaning. Sir Lewis Morris. *Fr.* Brotherhood. PGD
There She Blows! *Unknown.* EtS; SoAmSa, *with music*
There she sits in her Island-home. England. Gerald Massey. HBV
There should be no despair for you. Sympathy. Emily Brontë. OAEP
There should be two words, dearest, one made up. Alone. Carolyn Wells. PoToHe
There Sits a Bird. Charles Kingsley. *See* Sing Heigh-ho!
There sits a piper on the hill. The Piper on the Hill. Dora Sigerson Shorter. HBV; HBVY; OnYI; OTPC (1923 ed.)
There Sleeps in the Churchyard. Peter Hopegood. MoAuPo
There smiled the smooth Divine, unused to wound. The Smooth Divine [*or* A Minister, New Style]. Timothy Dwight. *Fr.* The Triumph of Infidelity. AA; AmPP (3d ed.); AnAmPo; PPON; WGRP
There souls of men are bought and sold. London. Blake. *Fr.* The Human Image. ChTr
There, spring lambs jam the sheepfold. In air. Water Color of Grantchester Meadows. Sylvia Plath. NYBP
There stands a lady on a mountain. Kiss in the Ring. *Unknown.* OxBoLi
There stands a lonely pine-tree. Song. Heine. TrJP
There stood an unsold captive in the mart. Parrhasius. Nathaniel Parker Willis. AA
There sunk the greatest, nor the worst of men. Napolean. Byron. *Fr.* Childe Harold's Pilgrimage. OBRV
There the black river, boundary to hell. The Southern Road. Dudley Randall. NNP
There the moon leans out and blesses. In a September Night. F. Wyville Home. VA
There the voluptuous nightingales. Shelley. *Fr.* Prometheus Unbound, II, ii. ViBoPo
There the wrinkled, old Nokomis. Hiawatha's Childhood. Longfellow. *Fr.* The Song of Hiawatha. RIS
There, there is no mountain within miles. Nebraska. Jon Swan. PoPo; WIRo
There they all were. Learning Family. Dell Washington. WSL
There they are./ Thirty at the corner. The Blackstone Rangers. Gwendolyn Brooks. BALP; CAD
There they are, my fifty men and women. One Word More. Robert Browning. FiP; HBV; OtMeF; PoEL-5; PoVP; VA; ViBoPo; ViPP
There they are now. Three Sentences for a Dead Swan. James Wright. NaP
There they dismounting, drew their weapons bold. Britomart in the House of Busirane. Spenser. *Fr.* The Faerie Queene, III. FiP; MBW-1
There they stand, on their ends, the fifty faggots. Fifty Faggots. Edward Thomas. BrPo; MoAB; MoBrPo
There 'tis the Shepherd's task the winter long. The Shepherd. Wordsworth. *Fr.* The Prelude, VIII. OBNC
There used to be a time when, like Kate now in the lane. Dead Metaphors. David Holbrook. NYTB
There used to be gods in everything, and now they're gone. The Companions. Howard Nemerov. NYBP
There Uther the king took Ygerne for queen. The Birth of Arthur. Layamon. *Fr.* The Brut. MeEV
There walked on Plover's shady banks. Driving Saw Logs on the Plover. *Unknown.* AS; IHA
There wanst was [*or* once were] two cats of [*or* at] Kilkenny. The Kilkenny Cats [*or* Limerick]. *Unknown.* BOHV; CenHV; CIV; FaFP; LiTG; ShM; TreF
There wanted yet the Master work, the end. The Creation of

There (continued)
Man. Milton. *Fr.* Paradise Lost. PeRV
There was a battle in her face. The Battle. W. H. Davies. BrPo
There was a battle in the north. Geordie. *Unknown.* BaBo (A *vers.*); ESPB; OxBB
There was a Being whom my spirit oft. Shelley. *Fr.* Epipsychidion. EnLi-2
There was a big bear. Honey Bear. Elizabeth Lang. BoTP
There was a bird. Tom's Sleeping Song. Mark Van Doren. *Fr.* Jonathan Gentry. LOW
There was a bonny blade. The Dumb Wife Cured. *Unknown.* MaC
There Was a Boy. Wordsworth. *Fr.* The Prelude, V. BoLiVe; BWP; ChER; FaBoCh; FaBoEn; LoGBV; MaPo; MCCG; MyFE; OBNC; OBRV; PoEL-4; PoeP
(Boy of Winander, The.) ERoP-1
(Echoes.) BoPe
(Winander Lake.) FiP
There was a Boy bedded in bracken. Carol. John Short. DTC; FaBoCh; FaBoTw; LoGBV
There was a boy just one year old. Someone. John Ciardi. BiCB
There was a boy of other days. Lincoln. Nancy Byrd Turner. FaPON; MPB; TiPo
There was a boy whose name was Jim. Jim Who Ran Away from His Nurse, and Was Eaten by a Lion. Hilaire Belloc. BBGG; CenHV; ChTr; EvOK; HBMV; MaC; OnSP; ShBV-2; ShM; TSW
There was a boy whose name was Phinn. A Fishing Song. William Brighty Rands. CenHV
There was a brave girl of Connecticut. Benjamin. Ogden Nash. NePA; SiTL
There was a bride; she lived abroad. The Three Little Babes. *Unknown.* BFSS
There was a bride (the Gospel goes). Nuptial. Mary Fabyan Windeatt. JKCP (1955 ed.)
There was a bright and happy tree. The Happy Tree. Gerald Gould. MoBrPo (1942 ed.); WGRP
There Was a Brisk Girle. *Unknown.* CoMu
(The Brisk Girl, *shorter vers.*) UnTE
There was a butcher cut his thumb. *Unknown.* PPL
There was a Cameronian cat. The Cameronian Cat. *Unknown.* BOHV; CIV
There was a captain-general who ruled in Vera Cruz. El Capitan-General. Charles Godfrey Leland. AA; HBV; YaD
There was a chalice in the ancient East. Two Chalices. Edwin McNeill Poteat. ChIP
There Was a Chandler. *Unknown.* OTPC (1923 ed.)
There was a chap—I forget his name. The Gemlike Flame. R. P. Lister. FiBHP
There was a child, as I have been told. The Comical Girl. M. Pelham. BOHV
There Was a Child Went Forth. Walt Whitman. AmePo; AmPP; AWP; BiCB; CoBA; GoTP; InPo; LaNeLa; MAmP; MWA-1; OnPP; OQP; OxBA; Po; StP; WoL
There was a Christmas Brownie. Christmas Brownie. Rowena Bennett. ChBR
There was a company of young folk living. The Pardoner's Tale. Chaucer. *Fr.* The Canterbury Tales. EnL
There was a crooked man, and he went [*or* walked] a crooked mile. Mother Goose. BoChLi; BoTP; CBEP; FaBoBe; FaFP; HBV; HBVY; OTPC; OxBoLi; OxNR; PPL; RIS; SiTL; SoPo; StVeCh
There was a cruel naughty [*or* darkey] boy. The Cruel Naughty [*or* Naughty Darkey] Boy. *Unknown.* BBGG; BOHV
There was a dark and awful wood. Wood. Thomas Hornsby Ferril. PoRA
There Was a Darkness in this Man. John Gould Fletcher. *Fr.* Lincoln. PAL
("There was a darkness in this man; an immense and hollow darkness.") PoFr
There was a dear lady of Eden. Limerick. *Unknown.* LiBL; NA
There was a devil and his name was I. Malzah's Song. Charles Heavysege. *Fr.* Saul. OBCV
There was a dreamer once, whose spirit trod. The Seeker after God. Harry Kemp. OQP
There was a duke's daughter lived in York. The Cruel Mother (P *vers.*). *Unknown.* ESPB
There was a fair lady far crossed in love. The Fair Maid by the Seashore. *Unknown.* BaBo
There was a fair maid from Decatur. Limerick. *Unknown.* LiBL
There was a fair maiden who dwelt on the plains. The Fair Lady of the Plains. *Unknown.* BFSS
There was a fairy once. The Singing Fairy. Rose Fyleman. BoChLi
There was a faith-healer of Deal. Limerick [*or* Mind and Matter *or* Faith-Healer]. *Unknown.* CenHV; FaFP; GoTP; LiBL; LiTM; SiTL; WhC
There was a farmer had two sons. Bohunkus. *Unknown.* YaD
There was a fat canon of Durham. Limerick. *Unknown.* WhC
There was a fat man of Bombay. Limerick. *Unknown.* BoChLi; RIS
There Was a Frog. *Unknown.* NA
("There was a froge swum in the lake.") SeCSL
There Was a Frog Lived in a Well. *Unknown.* OTPC (1923 ed.)
There was a frog[e] swum in the lake. *Unknown.* There Was a Frog. NA; SeCSL
There was a funny little man. Fussy. Laura E. Richards. MPB
There was a gallant ship, and a gallant ship was she. The Golden Vanity [*or* The Sweet Trinity]. *Unknown.* AtBAP; CH; ESPB (B *vers.*); OnSP; ViBoFo
There Was a Garden. Marie Barton. OQP
There was a gather'd stillness in the room. My Mother. William Bell Scott. VA
There was a gay damsel of Lynn. Limerick. *Unknown.* LiBL; NA
There was a gay maiden lived down by the mill. The Ferry. George Henry Boker AA
There was a gentle hostler. Gates and Doors. Joyce Kilmer. ChrBoLe; GBV (1952 ed.); HBV; HBVY
There was a giant by the Orchard Wall. In the Orchard. James Stephens. LOW; RoGo
There was a giant in times of old. The Dorchester Giant. Oliver Wendell Holmes. FaPON; MPB; OnMSP
There was a gifted Mexican who came up here to paint. Sad Story. Clarence Day. InMe
There Was a Girl I Used to Go With. Stephen Vincent Benét. *Fr.* John Brown's Body. LOW
There was a girl in our town. Riddles. *Unknown.* HBV; HBVY; OTPC (1946 ed.); OxNR; PPL; RIS
There was a girl with us in our carriage. The Girl in the Carriage. *Unknown.* *Fr.* Shi King. LiTW
There was a glorious time. He Fears His Good Fortune. Thomas Hardy. VP
There was a good Canon of Durham. Limerick. William Ralph Inge. CenHV
There was a gray rat looked at me. Rat Riddles. Carl Sandburg. OCS
There was a great commotion. The Lollypops. Cordia Thomas. SoPo
There was a green branch hung with many a bell. The Dedication to a Book of Stories Selected from the Irish Novelists. W. B. Yeats. NAMP
There Was a Guinea-Pig. *Unknown.* OTPC (1946 ed.)
(Guinea-Pig, The.) GoTP; NA
("There was a little guinea-pig.") OxNR
There was a Hag who kept two chambermaids. The Hag and the Slavies. La Fontaine. AWP
There was a hardness of stone. The Harsh Country. Theodore Roethke. TDP
There was a Jewish bandit who lived in a wood. Bandit. A. M. Klein. WHW
There was a jolly beggar, and a begging he was born [*or* bound]. The Jolly Beggar. *At. to* James V, King of Scotland. CoMu; OxBB
There was a jolly blade that married a country maid. Dumb, Dumb, Dumb. *Unknown.* OnYI
There was a jolly harper-man. The Lochmaben Harper. *Unknown.* BaBo
There Was a Jolly Miller. Isaac Bickerstaffe. *Fr.* Love in a Village, I. GoTP; HBV; OnPP; OTPC (1946 ed.), *st.* 1; ViBoPo, *st.* 1
(Jolly Miller, The.) RIS, *st.* 1
(Song: "There was a jolly miller once," *st.* 1.) OBEC; OnYI
("There was a jolly miller once," *st.* 1.) OxNR

There was a jolly student with a medical degree. Similia Similibus. John Hunt Morgan. ShM
There was a jovial beggar. The Jovial Beggar. *Unknown.* BoTP
There was a jury sat at Perth. The Earl of Errol. *Unknown.* ESPB
There was a kind curate of Kew. Limerick. *Unknown.* CenHV
There Was a King. *Unknown.* OxBoLi
There was a king, and a very great king. Lady Diamond. *Unknown.* BaBo; ESPB
There was a king, and he had three daughters. *Unknown.* OxNR
There was a king in Brentford, of whom no legends tell. The King of Brentford. Thackeray, *after* Béranger. HBV; OtMeF
There was a king met a king. *Unknown.* OxNR
There was a king of the north countree. The Twa Sisters (C *vers.*). *Unknown.* ViBoFo
There was a king of Yvetot. The King of Yvetot. Thackeray, *after* Béranger. OnPP; RIS
There was a knicht riding frae the east. Riddles Wisely Expounded [*or* Jennifer Gentle and Rosemary *or* The Riddling Knight]. *Unknown.* AtBAP; BEL; CH; ESPB (C *vers.*); HBV; NoP; OxBoLi; ViBoFo (A *vers.*)
There Was a Knight. *Unknown. See* Baffled Knight, The.
There was a Knight, a most distinguished man. Ten of Chaucer's People: A Perfect Knight. Chaucer. *Fr.* The Canterbury Tales. PoSa
There was a knight, an he had a daughter. Erlinton (B *vers*). *Unknown.* ESPB
There was a knight and a lady bride. A Knight and a Lady Bride. *Unknown.* BFSS
There was a knight and a lady bright. The Broomfield Hill. *Unknown.* BaBo; ESPB; OBB; OxBB; ViBoFo
There Was a Knight and He Was Young. *Unknown. See* Baffled Knight, The.
There was a knight, in a summer's night. The Bonny Birdy. *Unknown.* ESPB
There was a Knight of Bethlehem. A Knight of Bethlehem [*or* Song]. Henry Neville Maugham. *Fr.* The Husband of Poverty. BoTP; ChIP; MaRV; OQP
There was a lad was born in Kyle. Rantin, Rovin Robin. Robert Burns. OxBS
There Was a Lady ("There was a lady all skin and bone"). *Unknown.* CBV
There was a lady fair and gay. The Wife of Usher's Well. *Unknown.* ESPB (D *vers.*); ViBoFo (C *vers.*)
There was a lady fine and gay. Willie o Winsbury (D *vers.*). *Unknown.* ESPB
There was a lady in this land. The Tinker. *Unknown.* CoMu
There was a lady liv'd at Leith. The Irishman and the Lady. William Maginn. BOHV; HBV; VA
There was a lady lived in a hall. Two Red Roses across the Moon. William Morris. CBEP; EnLit; PoIE; PoRA; PoVP
There was a lady lived in York. The Cruel Mother (C *vers.*). *Unknown.* BaBo
There Was a Lady Loved a Swine. *Unknown. See* Lady Who Loved a Swine, The.
There was a lady of Erskine. *Unknown.* SiTL
There was a lady of the North Country. Riddles Wisely Expounded. *Unknown.* BaBo (B *vers.*); ESPB
There was a lame soldier in time of the war. The Lame Soldier. *Unknown.* OuSiCo
There was a land where lived no violets. The Violets. Stephen Crane. War Is Kind, XXIII. AA; AnAmPo; AP
There was a lass and a bonnie lass. The Nut-gathering Lass. Burns. UnTE
There was a lass of Islington. The Lass of Islington [*or* The Fair Lass of Islington]. *Unknown.* CoMu; OxBB
There was a lily and rose sea-maiden. The Sea-Maiden. J. W. De Forest. EtS
There was a little Baby once. A Child's Christmas Carol. Christine Chaundler. BoTP
There was a little boy. Sir Hugh; or, The Jew's Daughter (D *vers.*). *Unknown.* BaBo
There was a little boy and a little girl. Mother Goose. OTPC (1923 ed.); OxNR; RIS. *See also* Little boy and a little girl, A.
There was a little boy, and he had a little dog. Tumbling Doggie. *Unknown.* SAS
There was a little boy, and he had a piece of bread. Walter and His Dog. Eliza Lee Follen. SAS
There was a little boy went into a barn. *Unknown.* OxNR
There was a little dog, and he had a little tail. *Unknown.* BoTP
There was a little, Elvish man. The Man Who Hid His Own Front Door. Elizabeth MacKinstry. FaPON; GaP; TiPo
There was a little family. The Little Family. *Unknown.* BaBo; BFSS
There Was a Little Girl. *St.* 1, Mother Goose; *sts.* 2 *and* 3, *unknown, at. to* Longfellow. BoChLi; BOHV; BLPA, *st.* 1; EvOK; FaFP; HBV; HBVY; LBN; LiTG, *st.* 1; NA; NeHB, *st.* 1; OnPP; OTPC; RIS, *st.* 1; SAS, *st.* 1; TreF; YaD, *st.* 1
(Jemima, *diff. vers.*) BBGG; FaBoCh; GoTP; LoGBV
("There was a little girl, and she had a little curl.") OxNR
There was a little goblin. Agnes Grozier Herbertson. GFA
There was a little guinea-pig. There Was a Guinea-Pig [*or* The Guinea Pig]. *Unknown.* GoTP; NA; OTPC (1946 ed.); OxNR
There was a little hobby-horse. A Little Hobby-Horse. Eliza Grove. OTPC
There was a little lawny islet. The Isle. Shelley. SyP
There was a little maid, and she was afraid. *Unknown.* OxNR; SiTL
There was a little maiden. The Singing Girl. Joyce Kilmer. JKCP
There was a little man and he had a little can. No More Booze [*or* Fireman Save My Child]. *Unknown.* AS; TrAS; TreF
There was a little man, and he had a little gun. Mother Goose. FaFP; HBV; HBVY; OTPC; OxNR; PPL
There was a little man and he had a little wife. The Crabfish. *Unknown.* SaSa
There was a little man, and he woo'd a little maid. Mother Goose. OTPC (1923 ed.); OxNR; SiTL
There Was a Little Nobby Colt. *Unknown.* OTPC (1923 ed.); PPL
There was a little old woman, as I've heard tell. The Old Woman Who Went to Market. *Unknown.* BFSS
There was a little old woman, in London she did dwell. She Loved Her Husband Dearly. *Unknown.* BFSS
There was a little one-eyed gunner. *Unknown.* OxNR
There was a little postage stamp. The Postage Stamp Lesson. *Unknown.* STF
There Was a Little Rabbit Sprig. *Unknown.* BoTP; OTPC (1923 ed.)
(True Story, A.) RIS
There was a little serpent and he wouldn't go to school. Snake Story. Henry Johnstone. PPL
There Was a Little Ship, *with music. Unknown.* BFSS
There was a little turtle. The Little Turtle. Vachel Lindsay. BoChLi; FaPON; GFA; GoJo; PCH; PDV; SoPo; SP; StVeCh; SUS; TiPo; UTS
There was a little woman, as I've heard tell. *See* There was an old woman, so I've heard tell.
There was a locked door. Don Marquis. *Fr.* I Have Looked Inward. PFY
There was a long, old road anear the town. The Ghost's Promenade. Thomas Caulfield Irwin. IrPN
There was a lovely lady Gnu. The Gnu Wooing. Burges Johnson. HBVY
There was a mad lad had an acre of ground. Mirth. *Unknown.* SeCL
There Was a Maid. *Unknown. See* Maid of Kent, A.
There was a maid, and a well-favoured maid. Katherine Johnstone. *Unknown.* BuBa
There was a maid of Edinburgh. Kath'rine Jaffrey. *Unknown.* BFSS
There was a maid, richly arrayd. Blancheflour and Jellyflorice. *Unknown.* ESPB
There Was a Man. Thomas Curtis Clark. ChIP
There Was a Man. Stephen Crane. *See* There Was a Man with a Tongue of Wood.
There Was a Man. *Unknown.* Po
("There was a man of double deed.") OxNR
There was a man,/ And his name was Dob. *Unknown.* OxNR
There was a man/ Named Iky Small. The Sad Goat. *Unknown.* WaKn
There was a man/ Whose name was Peter. The Tragedy of Pete.

There (continued)
Joseph Seamon Cotter, Sr. CDC; PoNe
There was a man and he had nought. *Unknown.* OxNR
There Was a Man and He Went Mad. *Unknown.* OTPC (1923 ed.)
("There was a man, he went mad.") OxNR; SiTL
"There was a man in Arkansaw." A Great Fight. Robert Henry Newell. BOHV
There was a man in Denver. The Man Who Thought He Was a Horse. Thomas Hornsby Ferril. NePoAm-2
There Was a Man in Our Toone. *Unknown.* OTPC (1923 ed.)
There was a man in [*or* of] our town [*or* of Newington],/ And he was wondrous wise. Mother Goose. FaFP; HBV; HBVY; OTPC; PPL; RIS; SAS; StVeCh (1940 ed.); YT
There was a man in our town whose Christian name was Jim. It Happens, Often. Edwin Meade Robinson. HBMV
There was a man in Westmoreland. Johnny Armstrong. *Unknown.* MaC; StaSt
There was a man lived in the moon. Aiken Drum. *Unknown.* FaBoCh; LoGBV; OxNR
There was a man lived in the west. Dandoo. *Unknown.* TrAS
There was a man lived under the hill. The Devil and the Farmer's Wife. *Unknown.* TrAS
There was a man named Ferguson. The Suicidal Cat. *Unknown.* CIV
There was a man, now please to note. The Goat and the Three Red Shirts [*or* The Goat]. *Unknown.* GSP; PoLF
There was a man of double deed. There Was a Man. *Unknown.* OxNR; Po
There was a man of Newington. *See* There was a man in our town.
There was a man of our town. *See* There was a man in our town.
There was a man of Thessaly. The [*or* A] Man of Thessaly. *Unknown.* CBEP; LiTG; OxNR; SiTL
There was a man—or was he but a man? There Was a Man. Thomas Curtis Clark. ChIP
There was a man rode through our town. *Unknown.* OxNR
There was a man was half a clown. Auvergnat. Hilaire Belloc. MemP
There was a man who had a clock. The Sad Tale of Mr. Mears. *Unknown.* HBV; PTK; StPo; TreFS; YaD
There was a man who had no eyes. *Unknown.* OxNR
There was a man who [*or* and he] lived in England. The Turkish Lady. *Unknown.* BaBo; MaC
There was a man who married a maid. She laughed as he led her home. I Love My Love. Helen Adam. NeAP
There was a man who saw God face to face. To Love, at Last the Victory. David Starr Jordan. OQP
There was a man who watched the river flow. The Cranes of Ibycus. Emma Lazarus. AA; PFY
There was a man whom Sorrow named his friend. The Sad Shepherd. W. B. Yeats. PP
There Was a Man with a Tongue of Wood. Stephen Crane. War Is Kind, XVI. LiTA; NePA
(There Was a Man.) MoAmPo (1950 ed.)
There was a man within our tenement. The Spritely Dead. Oscar Williams. *Fr.* Variations on a Theme. LiTA; NePA; Sonn
There was a mayde cam [*or* maid came] out of Kent. The Maid of Kent. *Unknown.* ElL; LO; OxBoLi
There was a Monk, a leader of the fashions. Ten of Chaucer's People: A Sporting Monk. Chaucer. *Fr.* The Canterbury Tales. PoSa
There Was a Monkey. *Unknown.* NA; OTPC (1923 ed.)
("There was a monkey climbed a tree.") OxNR
There was a most odious yak. The Yak. Theodore Roethke. TDP
There was a music throbbed athwart the street. Hubert Church. *Fr.* A Fugue. AnNZ
There was a naked greatness in those times. The Festival. Robert Eyres Landor. *Fr.* The Impious Feast. OBRV
There Was a Naughty Boy. Keats. *See* Song about Myself, A.
There was a negro preacher, I have heard. The Learned Negro. *Unknown.* BOHV
There was a noble ranger. Mustang Gray. *Unknown.* ABF
There was a perfect tree. 229. José Garcia Villa. PoPl
There was a Pig that sat alone. The Melancholy Pig [*or* The Pig-Tale]. "Lewis Carroll." *Fr.* Sylvie and Bruno. FaPON; OA; OTPC (1946 ed.); PPL; WiR
There was a piper had [*or* he had] a cow. Mother Goose. OTPC (1946 ed.); OxNR; RIS
There was a pond on which we learned to skate. A Skater's Waltz. Gray Burr. CoPo
There was a poor chap called Rossetti. Limerick. Dante Gabriel Rossetti. CenHV
There was a Presbyterian cat. The Auld Seceder Cat. *Unknown.* FaBoCh; LoGBV; SiTL
There was a pretty dandelion. Dandelion. *Unknown.* GFA
There was a pretty young lady, so handsome, brave, and bold. Pretty Mary. *Unknown.* BFSS
There was a priest in the land; Layamon was he called. The Prolog. Layamon. *Fr.* The Brut. MeEV
There was a princess of Bengal. Limerick. Walter Parke. NA
There was a prudent grave physician. The Doctor and His Patients. Sir Charles Sedley. PeRV
There was a pussy in the stable. In the Stable. Elizabeth Goudge. ChBR
There was a queen that fell in love with a jolly sailor bold. The Sailor and the Shark. Paul Fort. OBMV
There was a queer fellow named Woodin. Limerick. "Cuthbert Bede." CenHV
There was a ragman and a madman. The Ragman. *Unknown.* FTB
There was a rat, for want of stairs. *Unknown.* OxNR; SiTL
There was a rich Dutchman. Villkins and His Dinah (B *vers.*). *Unknown.* BaBo
There was a rich lady, from Dublin she came. The Rich Lady from Dublin. *Unknown.* BFSS
There was a rich lady, from England she came. The Brown Girl (B *vers.*). *Unknown.* BaBo
There was a rich lord, and he lived in Forfar. Bonnie Annie. *Unknown.* ESPB; OBB
There was a rich old farmer [*or* rancher]. The Rambling Cowboy. *Unknown.* BFSS; CoSo
There was a rift tonight. The Rift. Ruth Margaret Gibbs. SoP
There was a road ran past our house. The Unexplorer. Edna St. Vincent Millay. LOW; MoShBr; RePo; SUS
There Was a Roaring in the Wind All Night. Wordsworth. *See* Resolution and Independence.
There was a Romish lady, brought up in poverty [*or* popery]. The Romish Lady. *Unknown.* BFSS; OuSiCo
There was a rose-tree grew so high. White Roses. Cora Randall Fabbri. AA
There was a round pond, and a pretty pond too. The Pond. Jane Taylor. OTPC (1923 ed.)
There was a rover from a western shore. Mother England. Edith M. Thomas. AA; HBV
There was a Russian came over the sea. Russian and Turk. Robert J. Burdette. NA
There was a score of likely girls. Cerelle. Margaret Bell Houston. PoMa
There was a sea captain lately come to shore. The Sea-Captain. *Unknown.* BaBo
There was a shepherd's daughter/ Came tripping on the way. The Knight and Shepherd's Daughter (A *vers.*). *Unknown.* ESPB
There was a shepherd's dochter/ Kept sheep upon yon hill. The Knight and Shepherd's Daughter. *Unknown.* BaBo (A *vers.*); ESPB (B *vers.*); OxBB; ViBoFo
There was a shepherd's son. Blow the Winds, I-ho! *Unknown.* OxBoLi
There was a ship, and a ship of fame. William Glen [*or* Captain Glen]. *Unknown.* BaBo
There was a ship called *The Golden Vanitie.* The Golden Vanitie. *Unknown.* EnSB
There was a ship came [*or* sailed] from the north country [*or* countree]. The Golden Vanity. *Unknown.* CBEP; WiR
There was a ship of Rio. The Ship of Rio. Walter de la Mare. CenHV; EtS; PDV; TiPo; UTS
There was a silk merchant. Jackaro. *Unknown.* IHA
There was a Slug who ate and ate. A Tale from the Garden. Margaret Wynne Jones. GFA
There was a small boy [*or* young man] of [*or* from *or* in] Quebec. Limerick. Kipling. HBV; HBVY; LiBL; NA
There was a snake that dwelt in Skye. The Fastidious Serpent. Henry Johnstone. BOHV; HBV; HBVY; OTPC (1946 ed.); PPL
There was a sound of hunting in the mountains. Incident on

a Front Not Far from Castel di Sangro. Harry Brown. NYBP
There was a sound of revelry by night. Waterloo [*or* The Eve of Waterloo]. Byron. *Fr.* Childe Harold's Pilgrimage. AnFE; BBV; BeLS; FaBoBe; FaBoCh; FaBoEn; FaBV; FaFP; FiP; FOL; GN; HBV; MCCG; OBNC; OBRV; OnSP; OtMeF; OTPC; PoG; PTK; ShBV-3; TreF; TrGrPo; ViBoPo; WaaP; WBLP; WHA
There was a squire lived in this town. The Suffolk Miracle (B *vers.*). *Unknown.* BaBo
There was a strange and unknown race. The New World. Paul Engle. AmFN
There was a strife 'twixt man and maid. Kipling. PV
There was a student out of Oxford town. The Clerk of Oxenford. Chaucer. *Fr.* The Canterbury Tales: Prologue. OnPP
There was a stunted handpost just on the crest. Near Lanivet, 1872. Thomas Hardy. AWP; CMoP; LoBV
There was a thick-headed marine. *Unknown.* GoTP
There was a thing a full month old. *Unknown.* OxNR
There Was a Time. Edward Thomas. MMA
There was a time before our time. Clipper Ships and Captains. Rosemary Benét *and* Stephen Vincent Benét. RePo; StVeCh (1955 ed.)
There was a time in former years. She Hears the Storm. Thomas Hardy. ATP; NP; PoeP; TOP
There was a time, O Lesbia, when you said Catullus. Transformation. Catullus. LiTW
There was a time on this fair continent. Charles Mair. *Fr.* Tecumseh. OBCV
There was a time, so ancient records tell. Revolutions. Sir Henry Taylor. *Fr.* Philip Van Artevelde. PoFr; VA
There was a time when Death and I. Beyond Recall. Mary E. Bradley. AA
There was a time when I was very small. Childhood. Jens Baggesen. AWP; JAWP; WBP
There was a time when I would magnify. Elegy for an Unknown Soldier. James K. Baxter. AnNZ
There was a time when meadow, grove, and stream. Ode: Intimations of Immortality from Recollections of Early Childhood. Wordsworth. AnFE; AtBAP; ATP; AWP; BEL; BoC; BoLiVe; CABA; CaFP; ChER; CoBE; DiPo; EnL; EnLi-2; EnLit; EnRP; EPN; ERoP-1; ExPo; FaFP; FiP; ForPo; FosPo; GTBS; GTBS-D; GTBS-P; GTBS-W; GTSE; GTSL; HBV; ILP; InP; InPo; InvP; JAWP; LiTB; LiTG; LoBV; MaPo; MaRV; MasP; MBW-2; MCCG; MERP; NoP; OAEP; OBEV; OBNC; OBRV; OHFP; OQP; OuHeWo; PAn; PeER; PIA; Po; PoAn; PoEL-4; PoeP; PoFS; PoIE; SeCeV; ShBV-4; StP; TOP; TreF; TrGrPo; VaPo; ViBoPo; WBP; WHA; WoL
There was a time when men for love did marry. Nuptiae post Nummos. Henry Parrot. SiCE; TuPP
There was a time when Mother Nature made. First Miracle. Genevieve Taggard. HBMV
There was a time when this poor frame was whole. There Was a Time. Edward Thomas. MMA
There was a tinker liv'd of late. The Jovial Tinker; or, The Willing Couple. *Unknown.* CoMu
There was a trampling of horses from Calvary. It Is Finished. John Hall Wheelock. MoRP
There was a tree stood in the ground. The Green Grass Growing All Around. *Unknown.* HBVY; MoShBr; MPB
There was a trim maiden named Wood. Limerick. William A. Lockwood. LiBL
There was a troop of merry gentlemen. The Broom of Cowdenknows (A *vers.*). *Unknown.* ESPB
There was a tumult in the city. *See* There was tumult in the city.
There was a wealthy merchant. Lily Munro [*or* Jackie Frazier]. *Unknown.* BFSS; OuSiCo
There was a weasel lived in the sun. The Gallows. Edward Thomas. GTBS-D; HaMV; LiTB; MoAB; MoBrPo; PoE; UnPo (3d ed.)
There Was a Wee Bit Mousikie. *Unknown.* MoShBr (Cheetie-Poussie-Cattie, O.) FaBoCh
There was a wee bit wifie. *Unknown.* OxNR
There was a wee cooper who lived in Fife. The Wife Wrapt [*or* Wrapped] In Wether's Skin. *Unknown.* BaBo (B *vers.*); ViBoFo (A *vers.*)
There was a whispering in my hearth. Miners. Wilfred Owen. BrPo; GTBS-D; MoAB; MoBrPo; NoP
There was a widow-woman lived in far Scotland. The Wife of Usher's Well. *Unknown.* ESPB (C *vers.*); ViBoFo (B *vers.*)
There was a Wife from Bath, a well-appearing. The Wife of Bath and the Parson [*or* Seven Pilgrims]. Chaucer. *Fr.* The Canterbury Tales: Prologue. TrGrPo
There was a wild colonial boy, Jack Dollin was his name. The Wild Colonial Boy. *Unknown.* OuSiCo
There was a wild Montana boy, Jack Nolan was his name. The Wild Montana Boy. *Unknown.* CoSo
There was a winter. Alba after Six Years. Christopher Middleton. NePoEA-2
There was a woman lived in Ardell. The Wife of Usher's Well (B *vers.*) *Unknown.* BaBo
There Was a Wyly Ladde. *Unknown.* ErPo
There was a yellow pumpkin. Coach. Eleanor Farjeon. PoRh
There was a young bard of Japan. Limerick. *Unknown.* CenHV
There was a young belle of Old Natchez. Requiem [*or* Limerick]. Ogden Nash. LiBL; SiTL
There was a young chap not so nice. *Unknown.* SiTL
There was a young critic of King's. Limerick. Arthur Clement Hilton. CenHV
There was a young curate of Hants. Limerick. E. V. Knox. CenHV
There was a young curate of Salisbury. Limerick. *Unknown, at. to* George Libaire. LiBL
There was a young farmer of Leeds. Limerick [*or* New Limericks]. *Unknown.* RIS; StaSt
There was a young fellow called Green. Limerick. *Unknown.* CenHV
There was a young fellow from Fife. Limerick. T. R. Ybarra. LiBL
There was a young fellow named Clyde. Limerick. *Unknown.* BOHV
There was a young fellow named Dice. Limerick. *Unknown.* LiBL
There was a young fellow named Hall. Limerick [*or* A Happy Time]. *Unknown.* LiTG; LiTM; SiTL; WhC
There was a young fellow named Hatch. Limerick. *Unknown.* LiBL
There was a young fellow named Sydney. Limerick [*or* A Young Fellow Named Sydney]. Don Marquis. LiBL; SiTL
There was a young fellow [*or* person] named Tate [*or* Tait]. *At. to* Carolyn Wells. GoTP; HBV; HBVY; LiBL; TSW; WhC
There was a young fellow of Ceuta. Limerick. *Unknown.* CenHV
There was a young fellow of Lyme. *See* There was an old party of Lyme.
There was a young fellow of Perth. Limerick [*or* New Limericks]. *Unknown.* RIS; StaSt; WhC
There was a young genius of Queens'. Limerick. Arthur Clement Hilton. CenHV
There was a young girl of Asturias. Limerick. *Unknown.* BBGG; GoTP
There was a young girl of Lahore. Limerick. Cosmo Monkhouse. HBV
There was a young girl of Majorca. Limerick. Edward Lear. LiBL
There was a young gourmand of John's. Limerick. Arthur Clement Hilton. CenHV
There was a young king who was sad. Our Story. Thomas MacDonagh. MemP
There was a young lady at Bingham. Limerick. *Unknown.* LiBL
There was a young lady called Starky. *See* There was a young woman called Starkie.
There was a young lady from Joppa. Limerick. *Unknown.* BOHV; LiBL
There was a young lady from Woosester. *See* There was a young lady of Woosester.
There was a young lady in white. Limerick. Edward Lear. NBM
There was a young lady [*or* woman] named [*or* called] Bright. Limerick [*or* Relativity]. *Unknown, at. to* Arthur Buller. CenHV; FaFP; FaPON; ImOP; LiBL; LiTM; OxBoLi; SiTL; WhC
There was a young lady named Rood. *Unknown.* SiTL
There was a young lady of Bute. Limerick [*or* Nonsense Verses]. Edward Lear. OTPC (1946 ed.); StVeCh

There was a young lady of Byde. Limerick. *Unknown.* LiBL
There was a young lady of Corsica. Limerick. Edward Lear. CenHV; ChTr
There was a young lady of Ealing. Limerick. *Unknown.* CenHV
There was a young lady of Firle. Limerick. Edward Lear. RePo
There was a young lady of Flint. Limerick. *Unknown.* CenHV
There was a young lady of Hull. Limerick. Edward Lear. MoShBr
There was a young lady of Kent. Limerick. *Unknown.* CenHV; LiBL; SiTL
There was a young lady of Limerick. Limerick. Andrew Lang. CenHV
There was a young lady of Lynn,/ Who was deep in original sin. Limerick. *Unknown.* BOHV; LiBL
There was a young lady of Lynn/ Who was so exceedingly thin. Limerick [*or* The Young Lady of Lynn]. *Unknown.* CenHV; ChTr; InP; OnPP
There was a young lady of Milton. Limerick. *Unknown.* NA
There Was a Young Lady of Niger. *Unknown, at. to* Cosmo Monkhouse. *See* Limerick: "There was a young lady of Niger."
There was a young lady of Norway. Limerick [*or* A Young Lady of Norway]. Edward Lear. FaPON; OTPC (1946 ed.); StVeCh; TiPo; TSW
There was a young lady of Oakham. Limerick. *Unknown.* BBGG; BOHV
There was a young lady of Portugal. Limerick. Edward Lear. LiTG; OxBoLi
There was a young lady of Rheims. Moonshine. Walter de la Mare. FiBHP
There was a young lady of Riga. Limerick. *Unknown.* CenHV
There was a young lady of Russia. Limerick. Edward Lear. MoShBr
There Was a Young Lady of Ryde. *Unknown. See* Limerick: "There was a young lady of Ryde/ Who ate a green apple and died."
There was a young lady of Ryde/ Whose shoe-strings were seldom untied. Limerick. Edward Lear. OxBoLi; WhC
There was a young lady of Spain. Limerick [*or* A Young Lady of Spain]. *Unknown.* LiTG; LiTM (rev. ed.)
There was a young lady of station. Limerick. "Lewis Carroll." BOHV; CenHV; GoTP
There was a Young Lady of Sweden. Edward Lear. PeVV
There was a young lady of Truro. Limerick. *Unknown.* BOHV
There was a young lady of Twickenham. Limerick. Oliver Herford. BOHV; LiBL; WhC
There was a young lady of Venice. Limerick. *Unknown.* BOHV; LiBL
There was a young lady of Wales. Limerick. *Unknown.* NA
There was a young lady of Wantage. Real Estate. *Unknown.* SiTL
There was a young lady of Wilts. Limerick. *Unknown.* HBV
There was a young lady of [*or* from] Woosester. *Unknown.* GoTP; LiBL; WhC
There was a young lady whose bonnet. Limerick. Edward Lear. GFA; PCH; StVeCh
There was a young lady whose chin. Limerick. Edward Lear. BoChLi; RePo; RIS; SoPo; StaSt; TiPo
There was a young lady whose eyes. Limerick. Edward Lear. GoJo; RIS; StaSt; TSW
There was a young lady whose nose/ Was so long . . . Limerick. Edward Lear. BoChLi; FaPON; RePo; SAS. *See also* There is a young lady whose nose/ Continually prospers . . .
There was a young maid from Madras. *Unknown.* SiTL
There was a young maid of Manila. Limerick. *Unknown.* OnPP
There was a young maid who said, "Why." Limerick [*or* New Limericks]. *Unknown.* LiBL; NA; RIS; StaSt
There was a young maiden, a Sioux. Limerick. *Unknown.* LiBL
There was a young man. Victory. Mary Britton Miller. RePo
There was a young man at St. Kitts. *See* There was a young man of St. Kitts.
There was a young man down in Ga. Limerick. *Unknown.* OnPP
There was a young man from Chapultepec. A Dublin Limerick. Ray Bradbury. SiTL
There was a young man from Cornell. Limerick. *Unknown.* BOHV
There was a young man from Japan. Limerick. *Unknown.* LiBL; LiTM; SiTL
There was a young man from Port Jervis. At the Tennis Clinic. I. L. Martin. SD
There was a young man from Quebec. *See* There was a small boy of Quebec.
There was a young man from the city. Limerick. *Unknown.* TreFT
There Was a Young Man from Trinity. *Unknown.* ImOP
There was a young man named Achilles. How Homer Should Have Written the Iliad. Edwin Meade Robinson. HBMV
There was a young man named Willie the Weeper. Willie the Weeper. *Unknown.* ABF; BLPA
There was a young man of Bengal. Limerick. *Unknown.* GoTP; OxBoLi
There was a young man of Cohoes. Limerick. Robert J. Burdette. BOHV; NA
There was a young man of Devizes. Limerick. *Unknown, at. to* Archibald Marshall. CenHV; WhC
There was a young man of Fort Blain[e]y. Limerick. *Unknown.* BOHV; LiBL
There was a young man of Hong Kong. Limerick. *Unknown.* LiBL
There was a young man of Laconia. Limerick. *Unknown.* BOHV
There was a young man of Madrid. Limerick. *Unknown.* LiBL; WhC
There was a young man of Montrose. Limerick [*or* It Pays]. Arnold Bennett. CenHV; FaFP; LiTM; OxBoLi; SiTL
There was a young man of Ostend. Limerick. *Unknown.* BOHV; LiBL
There was a young [*or* an old] man of St. Bees. Limerick [*or* Old Man of St. Bees]. W. S. Gilbert. BOHV; InvP; LBN; LiBL; LiTG; SiTL
There was a young man of [*or* at] St. Kitts. Limerick. *Unknown.* BOHV; LiBL; NA
There was a young man of Sid. Sussex. Limerick. Arthur C. Hilton. WhC
There was a young man of the Cape. *See* There was an old man of the Cape.
There was a young man of the Clyde. Just for the Ride. *Unknown.* FaFP; SiTL
There was a young man so benighted. Limerick. *Unknown.* HBV; OnPP; PTK
There was a young man who said, "Damn!" *See* There once was a man who said: "Damn!"
There was a young man who said, "God." *See* There once was a man who said, "God."
There was a young who said, "Run." Limerick. *Unknown.* LiBL
There was a young man who was bitten. Limerick. *Unknown, at. to* Walter Parke. LiBL; NA
There was a young monk of Siberia. Limerick. *Unknown.* TreFT
There was a young person named Tate. *See* There was a young fellow named Tate.
There was a young person of Crete. Limerick. Edward Lear. OTPC (1946 ed.)
There was a young person of Smyrna. Limerick. Edward Lear. NBM; OxBoLi
There was a young poet of Thusis. Limerick. *Unknown.* OxBoLi
There was a young poet of Trinity. Limerick. *Unknown.* HBMV
There was a young woman, and what do you think? A Lost Illusion. George Du Maurier. CenHV
There was a young woman [*or* lady] called Starkie [*or* Starky]. Mendelian Theory [*or* Limerick]. *Unknown.* CenHV; LiTM; SiTL
There was a young woman named Bright. *See* There was a young lady named Bright.
There was a youth, and a well-belovèd [*or* well belovd] youth.

The Bailiff's Daughter of Islington. *Unknown.* BaBo (A *vers.*); ESPB; GN; GoTP; HBV; LoEn; NoP; OAEP; OBB; OnSP; OTPC; OxBB; OxBoLi; PoPo; RePo; SaSa; ViBoFo
There was airy music and sport at the fair. The Fair at Windgap. Austin Clarke. OnYI; SeCePo
There was also a Nun, a Prioress. *See* There also was a nun, a Prioress.
There was an ancient carver that carved of a saint. The Figure-Head. Crosbie Garstin. EtS; StPo
There was an ancient craftsman once, who made. The Leaf-Makers. Harold Stewart. PoAu-2
There was an ancient Grecian boy. A Tiger's Tale. John Bennett. TiPo (1959 ed.)
There was an Archbishop named Tait. Archbishop Tait. *Unknown.* ChTr
There was an Archdeacon who said. Limerick. *Unknown.* OxBoLi
There was an Auchtergaven mouse. A Whigmaleerie. William Soutar. OxBS
There was an auld birkie ca'ed Milton. Limerick. Andrew Lang. CenHV
There was an ease of mind that was like being alone in a boat at sea. Prologues to What Is Possible. Wallace Stevens. NePoAm
There Was an Indian. J. C. Squire. AmFN; InP; ShBV-2
(Discovery, The.) PoMa; PoSC; WaKn
(Sonnet: "There was an Indian, who had known no change.") CH; FaPON
There was an island in the sea. Atlantis. Conrad Aiken. Priapus and the Pool, XV. CMoP; SiSw
There was an old crow. *Unknown.* OxNR; SiTL
There was an old farmer in Sussex did dwell. The Farmer's Curst Wife. *Unknown.* BaBo (A *vers.*); ESPB; ViBoFo
There was an old fellow of Lynn. Limerick. *Unknown.* LiBL
There was an old Fellow of Trinity,/ A doctor well versed in Divinity. Limerick. *Unknown.* CenHV; LiBL
There was an old fellow of Trinity/ Who solved the square root of Infinity. Limerick. *Unknown.* LiBL; WhC
There was [*or* There was once] an old Fox. The Owl and the Fox [*or* The Tragic Tale of Hooty the Owl]. *Unknown.* BLPA; FTB
There was an old lady. Godmother. Phyllis B. Morden. BrR; MoSiPe; SoPo
There Was an Old Lady Named Crockett. William Jay Smith. ShM
There was an old lady of Chertsey. Limerick. Edward Lear. RePo
There was an old lady of Wales. Limerick. *Unknown.* RIS
There was an old lady who lived in Dundee. A Long Time Ago, *vers.* V. *Unknown.* ShS
There was an old lady who said. Limerick [*or* New Limericks]. *Unknown.* RIS; StaSt
There was an old lady whose folly. Limerick. Edward Lear. RIS; StaSt
There was an old looney of Rhyme. An Old Looney of Rhyme. *Unknown.* SiTL
There was an old-man and a jolly old-man. The Old Man and Young Wife. *Unknown.* CoMu
There Was an Old Man and He Had a Calf. *Unknown.* OTPC
("There was an old man.") OxNR; PPL; RIS; SiTL
There was an old man and he lived in a wood. *See* There was an old man lived out in the wood.
There was an old man from Antigua. *Unknown.* SiTL
There was an old man from [*or* of] Peru/ Who dreamt he was eating his shoe. Limerick [*or* An Old Man from Peru]. *Unknown.* CenHV; FaFP; LiTG; LiTM (rev. ed.); PDV; SiTL
There was an old man from the Rhine. *See* There was an old man of the Rhine.
There was an old man in a barge. Limerick [*or* Nonsense Pictures in Rhyme]. Edward Lear. MPB; PoVP
There was an old man in a boat. Limerick [*or* Nonsense Verses *or* The Floating Old Man]. Edward Lear. BoChLi (1950 ed.); HBV; OTPC; StVeCh; WiR
There was an old man in a pew. Limerick. Edward Lear. MoShBr
There was an old man in a pie. Limerick. *Unknown.* BOHV
There Was an Old Man in a Tree. Edward Lear. *See* Limerick: "There was an old man in a tree."
There was an old man in a trunk. Limerick. Ogden Nash. CenHV
There was an old man in a velvet coat. *Unknown.* OxNR
There was an old man in the North Countrie. The Twa Sisters (D *vers.*) *Unknown.* ViBoFo
There was an old man lived out in the wood [*or* and he lived in a wood]. Green Broom [*or* Broom, Green Broom]. *Unknown.* ALV; CH; LiTB; LiTG; LoEn; OnSP; OxBoLi; PoRA (rev. ed.); SiTL; StPo
There was an old man lived under the hill. Father Grumble. *Unknown.* ViBoFo
There was an old man named Michael Finnegan. *Unknown.* GoTP; TiPo
There was an old man of Bengal. Limerick. "F. Anstey." CenHV
There was an old man of Berlin. Limerick. Edward Lear. PoVP
There was an old man of Blackheath. Limerick. *Unknown.* CenHV; PDV
There was an old man of Boulogne. Limerick [*or* An Old Man of Boulogne]. *Unknown.* CenHV; LiTM; OxBoLi; SiTL
There was an old man of Calcutta. Arthur. Ogden Nash. FiBHP
There was an old man of Cape Horn. Limerick. Edward Lear. TSW
There was an old man of Corfu. Limerick. Edward Lear. RePo
There was an old man of Dumbree. Edward Lear. GoTP; NBM
There was an old man of Hawaii. *Unknown.* SiTL
There was an old man of Hong Kong. Limerick. Edward Lear. NBM; RePo
There was an old man of Ibreem. Limerick. Edward Lear. RePo
There was an old man of Kamschatka. Limerick. Edward Lear. NA
There was an old man of Khartoum. Limerick. *Unknown.* LiBL; OxBoLi
There was an old man of Leghorn. Limerick. Edward Lear. NA
There was an old man of Melrose. Limerick. Edward Lear. LBN
There was an old man of [*or* once was a man from] Nantucket. Limerick. *Unknown, at. to* Dayton Voorhees. *Fr.* That Nantucket Limerick. HBV (8th ed.); LiBL; LiTG; TreF
There was an old man of Peru/ Who dreamt he was eating his shoe. *See* There was an old man from Peru. . .
There was an old man of St. Bees. *See* There was a young man of St. Bees.
There was an old man of Tarentum. Limerick. *Unknown.* HBV; LiBL; WhC
There was an old [*or* a young] man of the Cape. Limerick. *At. to* Robert Louis Stevenson. BOHV; LiBL
There was an old man of the coast. Limerick. Edward Lear. CenHV; LiBL; MoShBr; PoVP; RIS; StaSt
There was an old man of the Dargle. Edward Lear. ChTr
There was an old man of the Dee. Limerick. Edward Lear. RePo
There was an old man of The Hague. Limerick. Edward Lear. EvOK
There was an old man of the Isles. Limerick. Edward Lear. OTPC (1946 ed.); StVeCh
There was an old man of [*or* from] the Rhine. Limerick. *Unknown.* BOHV; GoTP
There was an old man of the West. Limerick. Edward Lear. RIS; StaSt
There was an old man of Thermopylae. Limerick. Edward Lear. CenHV; EvOK; LBN; LiBL; NA; NBM
There was an old man of Tobago. Limerick. *Unknown.* BoHV; LiBL; RIS
There was an old man of Vesuvius. Limerick. Edward Lear. LiBL
There was an old man of Whitehaven. Limerick. Edward Lear. NBM
There was an old man on the Border. Limerick. Edward Lear. CenHV; PoVP
There Was an Old Man, on Whose Nose. Edward Lear. *See* Limerick: "There was an old man on whose nose."
There was an old man who lived in a wood. The Old Man Who Lived in a Wood. *Unknown.* MoShBr; MPB; StVeCh
There was an old man who lived in Middle Row. *Unknown.* OxNR

There was an old man who lived in the West. The Wife Wrapt in Wether's Skin (C *vers.*). *Unknown.* BaBo
There was an old man who lived on a common. The Wonderful Old Man. *Unknown.* NA
There was an old man who owned a small farm. The Farmer's Curst Wife (B *vers.*). *Unknown.* BaBo
There was an old man who said, "Do." Limerick [*or* New Limericks]. *Unknown.* FaPON; ImOP; LiBL; NA; RIS; StaSt
There was an old man who said. "Gee!" Limerick. *Unknown.* BOHV
There was an old man who said, "How." Limerick [*or* Nonsense Verses]. Edward Lear. BoChLi; EvOK; GFA; SAS; StVeCh; TSW
There was an old man who said: "Hush!" Limerick [*or* Nonsense Verses]. Edward Lear. GoJo; GoTP; HBV; LiTG; NA; NBM; OTPC; OxBoLi; StVeCh
There was an old man who said, "Well!" Limerick. Edward Lear. OTPC (1946 ed.); RIS; StaSt
There was an old man who supposed. Limerick. Edward Lear. LBN; LiBL; NA; RIS; StaSt; WhC
There was an old man who was very well known. The Miller That Made His Will. *Unknown.* BFSS
There was an old man, who when little. Limerick. Edward Lear. GoTP; RePo
There was an old man with a beard,/ Who said, "It is just as I feared!" Limerick [*or* Old Man with a Beard]. Edward Lear. BoChLi; ChTr; FaPON; HBV; LBN; LiBL; NA; OTPC; PDV; PoVP; RePo; SoPo; StVeCh; TiPo; TSW
There was an old man with a beard,/ Who sat on a horse when he reared. Limerick. Edward Lear. LiBL
There was an old man with a gong. Limerick. Edward Lear. GoJo
There was an old man with a poker. Limerick [*or* Nonsense Verses]. Edward Lear. HBV; OTPC
There was an old miser named Clarence. Fragonard. Ogden Nash. RePo
There was an old monk of great renown. The Monk of Great Renown. *Unknown.* CoMu
There was an old monk of Siberia. Limerick. *Unknown.* LiBL
There Was an Old Owl. *Unknown.* GFA
("There was an old owl [who] lived in an oak.") CenHV; GoTP
There was an old party called Pennycomequick. Mr. Pennycomequick. P. M. Stone. BoTP
There was an old party [*or* old person *or* a young fellow] of Lyme. Limerick. *Unknown.* CenHV; LiBL; LiTG; OxBoLi; SiTL. *See also* There once was an old man of Lyme.
There was an old person of Anerly. Limerick. Edward Lear. LiBL
There Was an Old Person of Bradley. Edward Lear. UnS
There was an old person of Bromley. Limerick. Edward Lear. NBM
There was an old person of Burton. Limerick. Edward Lear. RIS; StaSt
There was an old person of Dean. Limerick. Edward Lear. BoChLi; MoShBr; PCH
There was an old person of Diss. Limerick. Edward Lear. GoJo
There was an old person of Dover. The Eel. Walter de la Mare. ShM
There was an old person of Gretna. Limerick. Edward Lear. ChTr
There was an old person of Hurst. Limerick. Edward Lear. RePo
There was an old person of Ickley. Limerick. Edward Lear. EvOK
There was an old person of Leeds. Limerick. *Unknown.* WhC
There was an old person of Lyme. *See* There was an old party of Lyme.
There was an old person of Minety. Limerick. Edward Lear. RePo
There was an old person of Shoreham. Limerick. Edward Lear. NBM
There was an old person of Skye. Edward Lear. ChTr
There was an old person of Sparta. Limerick. Edward Lear. BoChLi (1939 ed.)
There was an old person of Stroud. Limerick. Edward Lear. RePo
There was an old person of Tring/ Who, when somebody asked her to sing. Limerick. *Unknown.* LiBL; WhC
There was an old person of Ware. Limerick [*or* The Moppsikon Floppsikon Bear]. Edward Lear. BoChLi; CenHV; GoTP; LiBL; NA; PCH; PoPl; RePo; SAS
There was an old person of Wick. Limerick. Edward Lear. NA
There was an old person of Woking. Limerick. Edward Lear. NA
There was an old person whose habits. Limericks. Edward Lear. BoChLi (1950 ed.); FaPON; LBN
There was an old skinflint of Hitching. Buttons. Walter de la Mare. DTC
There Was an Old Soldier, *with music.* *Unknown.* AS; TrAS, *with* Old Zip Coon
There was an old soldier of Bister. Limerick. *Unknown.* BOHV
There was an old stump of an old tree standing. The New View. John Holmes. MiAP
There was an old stupid who wrote. Limerick. Walter Parke. LiBL; NA
There was an old tailor of Bicester. Limerick. *Unknown.* CenHV
There was an old wife and she lived all alone. The Old Wife and the Ghost. James Reeves. PDV; PoMS; ShM
There Was an Old Woman. *Unknown.* BFSS
There was an old woman/ Lived down in a dell. Was She a Witch? Laura E. Richards. PDV; SoPo
There was an old woman/ Lived under a hill. Mother Goose. HBV; HBVY; OTPC; RIS; SAS; StVeCh
There was an old woman/ Lived up on a hill. Mother Goose. RIS
There was an old woman,/ And nothing she had. *Unknown.* OxNR
There was an old woman/ Sold puddings and pies. *Unknown.* OxNR
There was an old woman/ Who lived in Dundee. *Unknown.* OxNR
There was an old woman/ Went blackberry picking. Berries. Walter de la Mare. AtBAP; BoChLi; MoBrPo; OnSP; RG; StaSt; TiPo
There was an old woman/ Went out one morning. Fairies. Louis Untermeyer. StaSt
There was an old woman all skin and bone. Old Woman All Skin and Bone. *Unknown.* TrAS
There was an old woman and she had a little pig. Tale of a Little Pig. *Unknown.* ABF
There was an old woman and she lived in a shoe. The Old Woman Who Lived in a Shoe. *Unknown.* LiTG; OxBoLi. *For* Mother Goose *vers., see* There was an old woman who lived in a shoe.
There was an old woman, and what do you think. Mother Goose. FaBoCh; HBV; LoGBV; OTPC; OxNR
There was an old woman, as I've heard tell. *See* There was an old woman, so I've heard tell.
There was an old woman called Nothing-at-all. Mother Goose. OxNR; RIS
There was an old woman had three cows. *Unknown.* OxNR
There was an old woman, her name was Peg. *Unknown.* OxNR
There was an old woman in Ireland, in Ireland she did dwell. The Wife of Kelso. *Unknown.* ShS
There was an old woman in Surrey. Mother Goose. BoChLi
There was an old woman lived down in a dell. Was She a Witch? Laura E. Richards. MPB
There was an old woman lived on the sea shore. The Twa Sisters (B *vers.*) [*or* The Two Sisters]. *Unknown.* BaBo; BFSS
There was an old woman lived under a hill/ And if she's not gone. Mother Goose. HBV; HBVY; OTPC; OxNR; RIS; SAS; StVeCh (1940 ed.)
There was an old woman lived under a hill/ She put a mouse in a bag. Mother Goose. OxNR
There was an old woman of Leeds. Limerick. *Unknown.* RIS
There was an old woman sat spinning. *Unknown.* GoTP; OxNR
There was an old [*or* a little] woman, so [*or* as] I've heard tell. Mother Goose. BoChLi; GoTP; InvP; MoShBr; OnMSP; OTPC; OxNR; PoSC; RIS; SAS; SiTL; StPo; TiPo
There was an old woman tossed [*or* went] up in a basket. Mother Goose. BoChLi; EvOK; OTPC; OxNR; PCH; PDV; PPL; RIS; SAS; SiTL; SoPo; StVeCh
There was an old woman who bought a pig, uh-uh-huh! The

Old Woman Who Bought a Pig. *Unknown.* BFSS
There was an old woman who lived all alone. There Was an Old Woman. *Unknown.* BFSS
There was an old woman who lived in a shoe. Mother Goose. BoChLi; FaBoBe; FaFP; HBV; HBVY; OTPC; OxNR; PPL; RIS; SAS; SiTL; StVeCh; TiPo. *See also* There was an old woman and she lived in a shoe.
There was an ould man down by Killyburn brae. Killyburn Brae. *Unknown.* OnYI
There was an owl lived in an oak. *Unknown.* GFA; OxNR; RIS
There was an ox, there was a flea. Partners. Jaime Castiello. WaKn
There was another, too. Graph. William Carlos Williams. CBV
There was, before me. The Black Riders, XXI. Stephen Crane. AP
There was blood on the saddle. Trail End. *Unknown, at. to* Everett Chatham. CoSo
There Was Crimson Clash of War. Stephen Crane. The Black Riders, XIV. AP; NoP
There was Dai Puw. He was no good. On the Farm. R. S. Thomas. POTi
There was feasting in the hall. King Edwin's Feast. John White Chadwick. OTPC (1923 ed.)
There was fire & the people were yelling. running crazy. Urban Dream. Victor Hernandez Cruz. NBP
There was Hep and Texas an' Bronco Jack. Campfire and Bunkhouse. *Unknown.* CoSo
There was in Arll a little cove. The Piper of Arll. Duncan Campbell Scott. PeCV
There was in Asia, in a city great [*or* great city]. The Prioress's Tale (*mod. vers.*). Chaucer. *Fr.* The Canterbury Tales. ACP; ISi. *See also* Ther was in Asie...
There was in him a vital scorn of all. Byron. *Fr.* Lara. OBRV
There was king's daughter lived in the north. The Cruel Mother (B *vers.*). *Unknown.* BaBo
There was lifted up one voice of woe. A Lamentation for the Death of Sir Maurice Fitzgerald, Knight of Kerry. Pierce Ferriter. IrPN
There was monie a braw noble. Glenlogie. *Unknown.* GN
There was movement at the station, for the word had passed around. The Man from Snowy River. A. B. Paterson. NeLNL; PoAu-1; WePo
There was music in the air. Music in the Air. Ronald McCuaig. ErPo
There was never a leaf on bush or tree. A Winter Morning [*or* January]. James Russell Lowell. *Fr.* The Vision of Sir Launfal. GN; PoRL
There was never a sound beside the wood but one. Mowing. Robert Frost. AmPP; AnFE; AnNE; APA; BWP; CMoP; CoAnAm; DiPo; ExPo; HBMV; HoPM; LiTA; MAmP; NeMA; NP; OxBA; ShBV-3; TwAmPo; UnPo (3d ed.); YT
There Was Never Nothing More Me Pained. Sir Thomas Wyatt. CBEP; FCP; SiPS
There was no ceremony. Lion. Mary Fullerton. PoAu-1
There was no glory on the hills that day. Good Friday. Martha Provine Leach Turner. MaRV; OQP
There was no hunted one. The Baying Hounds. Mary Gilmore. BoAV; PoAu-1
There was no lady more refined. Mrs. Brown and the Famous Author. Stoddard King. ATP
There was no land, they used to tell. At the Grave of a Land-Shark. Ernest G. Moll. WhC
There was no leaf upon its wood. The Singing Bush. William Soutar. ACV
There was no one like 'im, 'Orse or Foot. "Follow Me 'Ome." Kipling. OAEP (2d ed.)
There Was No Place Found. Mary Elizabeth Coleridge. OxBoCh
There was no reason to go back now. Ember Grease. Dick Gallup. ANYP
There was no repose. Hero Song. Robert Duncan. CrMA
There was no road at all to that high place. The Grove. Edwin Muir. LiTM (rev. ed.); MoPo
There Was No Room on the Cross. *Unknown.* GoBC
There was no song nor shout of joy. The Ship. J. C. Squire. CH
There was no trace of Heaven. Bivouac. Alun Lewis. ChMP
There was no union in the land. Gettysburg. James Jeffrey Roche. MC; PaA; PAH
There was no west, there was no east. The Demon of the Gibbet. Fitz-James O'Brien. PoMS
There was (not certain[e] when) a certain[e] preacher. Of a Certain[e] Man. Sir John Harington. BOHV; SiCE
There was once a boat on a billow. Longing for Home. Jean Ingelow. *Fr.* Songs of Seven. WGRP
There was once a Filipino hombre. A Filipino Hombre. *Unknown.* AS
There was once a heron in a certain place on the edge of a pond. The Heron That Liked Crab-Meat. *Unknown.* *Fr.* The Panchatantra. OuHeWo
There was once a little animal. Similar Cases. Charlotte Perkins Stetson Gilman. BBV; HBV; PoLF
There was once a little man, and his rod and line he took. The Usual Way. Frederic E. Weatherly. BOHV
There was once a maiden of Siam. Limerick. *Unknown.* TreFT
There was once a man who smiled. The Ridiculous Optimist. Samuel Ellsworth Kiser. SoP; STF
There was once a pirate, greedy and bold. A Message of Peace. John Boyle O'Relly. OnYI
There was once a young lady of Ryde. See Limerick: "There was a young lady of Ryde/ Who ate a green apple and died."
There was once an old fox. *See* There was an old fox.
There was once an old sailor my grandfather knew. The Old Sailor. A. A. Milne. CenHV
There was once two Irish labouring men; to England they came over. How Paddy Stole the Rope. *Unknown.* BLPA
There was once upon a time a man who lost the/ Dictionary. Doctor Bill Williams. Ernest Walsh. InvP
There was once't upon a time. The Story of the Little Rid Hin. F. W. Sweetser. SAS
There Was One I Met upon the Road. Stephen Crane. EaLo
There was one in the myriad throngs. Mehdi Ali Seljouk. *Fr.* Rendezvous with God. BoPe
There was one little Jim. Dirty Jim. Jane Taylor. HBV; HBVY
There was rain without, and lightning stalked into the room. Song of the Midnight Rain. John Gould Fletcher. MoLP
There was revel of heroes and high carouse. The Slaughter of Grendel by Beowulf. *Unknown.* *Fr.* Beowulf. LiTW
There was silence in heaven, as if for half an hour. Mary's Assumption. Alfred J. Barrett. ISi
There was some jolly drivers on the Denver City Line. Root Hog or Die. Floyd B. Small. PoOW
There was such speed in her little body. Bells for John Whiteside's Daughter. John Crowe Ransom. AmLP; AmP; AmPP; AnFE; AP; CaFP; CBV; CMoP; CoAnAm; CoBMV; CrMA; DTC; FosPo; GTBS-D; ILP; InP; InPo; LiTA; LiTM (rev. ed.); MAP; MoAB; MoAmPo; MoVE; NePA; NoP; NP; OxBA; PIA; PoAn; PoIE; PoPo; PPON; ReMP; StP; TDP; TreFT; TwAmPo; UnPo (3d ed.); VaPo
There was that fall the fall of desire. Two. Winfield Townley Scott. NYBP
There was the butcher's hand. Force of Illusions. Wallace Stevens. NYTB
There was the sonne of Ampycus of great forecasting wit. Meleager. Ovid. *Fr.* Metamorphoses. CTC
There was the star of course. Christmas Comes. Earle Birney. ACV
There was the world that Jackson always found. Obituary. Louis Untermeyer. MAP
There was this empty bird cage in the garden. A Sparrow's Feather. George Barker. NYBP
There was this road. The Legs. Robert Graves. FaBoMo; HaMV; LiTB; LiTM; PoSa
There was three crows sat on a tree. Blow the Man Down, *vers.* IV. *Unknown.* ShS
There was [*or* were] three Kings into the east. John Barleycorn. Burns. BOHV; EiCL; FaBoCh; HBV; LoGBV; SeCeV; ShBV-1
There was three ladies play'd at the ba'. *See* There were three ladies play'd at the ba'.
There was three travelers, travelers three. The Three Travelers. *Unknown.* UnTE
There was, 'tis said, and I believe, a time. Burials. George Crabbe. *Fr.* The Parish Register: Burials. EiCL; EiPP
There was too much swamp, too much blue in the sky. Nature

There (continued)
Poem. Ruth Herschberger. OnHM
There was tumult [*or* a tumult] in the city. Independence Bell [*or* Liberty and Independence]. *Unknown.* BLPA; DD; FaBoBe; MC; PAL; PEDC; TreFS
There was twa sisters in a bowr. *See* There were twa sisters. . .
There was two little boys going to the school. The Twa Brothers (B *vers.*). *Unknown.* ESPB; ViBoFo
There was two lofty ships, from old England they set sail. High Barbaree. *Unknown.* SoAmSa
There went out in the dawning light. A Pastoral [*or* Pastoral Dialogue]. *Unknown.* AWP; OnPM; UnTE
There went three children down to the shore. The Black Pebble. James Reeves. PDV
There were bees about. From the start I thought. Shore Scene. John Logan. NMP
There were estrangements on the road of love. The Altar. Jean Starr Untermeyer. HBMV
There were footsteps on the stairway, uncertain. Night-Piece. John Hall Wheelock. CBV
There were four [red] apples on the bough. August. Swinburne. AtBAP; WiR
There were four dogs one summer day. Four Dogs. *Unknown.* SoP
There were four of us about that bed. Shameful Death. William Morris. ChTr; GoTP; GSP; GTBS; GTBS-P; HBV; MaC; OAEP; OBVV; PAn; PeVV; PoVP; ShBV-2; SiSw; VA; ViPo; ViPP
There were four red apples on the bough. *See* There were four apples. . .
There were hours when life was bitter. Now and Then. Margaret E. Sangster. TRV
There were ladies, they lived in a bower. Mary Hamilton. *Unknown.* CBEP; ESPB
There Were Many Who Went. Stephen Crane. OTD
There were more dirty. Route. Joseph Ceravolo. AnYP
There Were Ninety and Nine. Elizabeth Cecilia Clephane. WGRP
(Lost Sheep, The.) HBV; OTPC; VA
(Ninety and Nine, The.) FaChP; TreF, 4 *sts.*
There were no footprints left upon the waters. Dies Irae. James L. Duff. ChIP; JKCP; MaRV
There were no men and women then at all. Then. Edwin Muir. CMoP
There were none of my blood in this battle. Wildwest. Archibald MacLeish. Frescoes for Mr. Rockefeller's City, II. ReMP; UnPo
There were once two cats of Kilkenny. The Cats of Kilkenny. *Unknown.* GoTP
There were only two or three of us. At Prayer Meeting. Margaret E. Sangster. SoP
There were saddened hearts in Mudville for a week or even more. Casey's Revenge. James Wilson. BLPA; OnMSP; TreFS
There were sights to be seen at the flaming end of summer. End of Summer. Jean Starr Untermeyer. YT
There were some kings, in number three. Jumbo Jee. Laura E. Richards. GaP; SUS
There were sparkles on the window-pane, and sparkles in the sky. The Waits. Madeline Nightingale. SUS
There were strange riders once, came gusting down. Earth-Visitors. Kenneth Slessor. BoAV
There were the roses, in the rain. The Act. William Carlos Williams. CBV; ELU
There were three brothers in merry Scotland. Henry Martyn. *Unknown.* ViBoFo
There were three brothers in old Scotland. Andrew Bardeen. *Unknown.* BFSS
There were three cherry trees once. The Three Cherry Trees. Walter de la Mare. CMoP; GBV; SiSw
There were three cooks of Colebrook. *Unknown.* OxNR
There were three crows sat on a tree. The Three Ravens (The Twa Corbies) (C *vers.*). *Unknown.* BaBo; ViBoFo
There were three gipsies [*or* gypsies] a-come to my door. The Wraggle Taggle Gipsies [*or* The Raggle, Taggle Gypsies] *Unknown.* BoTP; CH; EvOK; FaPON; MPB; OnSP; OTPC (1946 ed.); PCD; StVeCh; ThWaDe; TiPo (1952 ed.); WiR
There were three hills that stood alone. The Three Hills. J. C. Squire. HBMV; InP
There were three in the meadow by the brook. The Code. Robert Frost. MaC; NP; YT
There were three jolly hunters, a-hunting all alone. Three Jovial Huntsmen; or, The Owl and the Jay Bush. *Unknown.* BFSS
There were three jovial Welshmen [*or* huntsmen]. The Three Jovial Welshmen [*or* The Three Jovial Huntsmen]. *Unknown.* BoChLi; BOHV; GaP; HBVY; MoShBr; NA; OnMSP; OTPC; OxBoLi; OxNR; SiTL; StVeCh
There were three kings cam frae the East. The Kings from the East. Heine, *tr. into Scottish* by Alexander Gray. ACV; GoTS
There were three kings into the East. *See* There was three kings. . .
There were three ladies [*or* laides] lived in a bower. Babylon; or, The Bonnie Banks o' Fordie. *Unknown.* BaBo (A *vers.*); EnLi-1; ESPB; OBB; OxBB; SeCePo; TOP
There were [*or* was] three ladies playd [*or* play'd] at the ba. The Cruel Brother. *Unknown.* BaBo (A *vers.*); EnLit; ESPB; LoEn; OBB; OxBB; ViBoFo; YAT
There were three lights that night. God with Us. Nancy Byrd Turner. ChIP; OQP
There were three little birds in a wood. *Unknown.* GoTP
There were three maidens who loved a king. Three Loves. Lucy H. Hooper. BeLS
There were three maids lived in a barn. Babylon; or, The Bonnie Banks o Fordie (B *vers.*). *Unknown.* BaBo
There were three ravens sat on a tree. The Three Ravens. *Unknown.* AtBAP; BaBo (A *vers.*); BEL; CABA; CaFP; CBV; ChTr; ESPB; ExPo; HBV; NoP; OAEP; OBB; OBEV; OxBB; OuHeWo; PAn; PoAn; PoEL-1; PoG; PoPo; SeCeV; TrGrPo; UnPo; ViBoFo (A *vers.*); ViBoPo
There were three sailors of Bristol city. Little Billee [*or* The Three Sailors]. Thackeray. BOHV; CenHV; EtS; FaBoCh; GaP; HBV; HBVY; LBN; LoGBV; MPB; NA; OnSP; OTPC; OxBB; PoVP; ShM; TreFS; TSW
There were three sisters fair and bright. The Riddling Knight. *Unknown.* FaBoCh; LoGBV; OBB; PoEL-1
There were three sisters in a hall. *Unknown.* OxNR
There were three sisters lived in a bower. The Bonnie Banks of Fordie. *Unknown.* BuBa
There were three young maids of Lee. A Bird in the Hand. Frederic E. Weatherly. BOHV; VA
There were three young women of Birmingham. Limerick. *Unknown.* HBV
There were twa brethren in the north. The Twa Brothers. *Unknown.* ATP; BaBo (A *vers.*); CH; ESPB; OBB; OxBB; ViBoFo (A *vers.*)
There were twa knights in fair Scotland. The Twa Knights. *Unknown.* ESPB
There were [*or* was] twa [*or* two] sisters in [*or* sat in] a bour [*or* bower *or* bowr]. The Twa [*or* Two] Sisters [*or* Binnorie *or* The Cruel Sister]. *Unknown.* AnFE; BaBo; BEL; BoLiVe; BuBa; CBEP; CH; CoBE; EnLit; EnSB; ESPB (B *vers.*); GBV (1952 ed.); HBV; NoP; OBB; OBEV; OnSP; OuHeWo; OxBB; OxBS; ShBV-1; StaSt; TOP; TrGrPo; ViBoFo (B *vers.*); WHA
There were two birds sat on a stone. Mother Goose. OxNR; PPL
There were two birds today. The Two Freedoms. Jon Silkin. PoDB
There were two blackbirds sitting on a hill. Mother Goose. HBV; HBVY; OTPC
There were two little girls, neither handsome nor plain. Jane and Eliza. Ann Taylor. HBV; HBVY; OnPP
There were two little skeezucks who lived in the isle. The Two Little Skeezucks. Eugene Field. MPB
There were two lofty ships from old England came. The High Barbaree [*or* High Barbary]. *Unknown.* AmSS; BaBo; OuSiCo; ViBoFo
There were two men of holy will. The Marvellous Bear Shepherd. *Unknown.* FlW
There were two of us left in the berry patch. Robert Frost Relates "The Death of the Tired Man." Louis Untermeyer. BOHV
There were two sisters sat in a bower. *See* There were twa sisters . . .
There were two sisters, they went playing. The Twa Sisters. *Unknown.* ESPB; ViBoFo (A *vers.*)
There were two wrens upon a tree. *Unknown.* OxNR
There were years vague of measure. Her Apotheosis. Thomas Hardy. ViPP
There when the water was not potable. Chloride of Lime and

Charcoal. Louis Zukofsky. CoPo
There where he sits, in the cold, in the gloom. The Hidden Weaver. Odell Shepard. WGRP
There where the course is. At Galway Races. W. B. Yeats. SD
There where the hackles of the Rocky Mountains. Observe the Whole of It. Thomas Wolfe. TreFT
There where the rusty iron lies. Rooks. Charles Hamilton Sorley. HBMV; MoBrPo
There where the sottish ignoraunt adore. Satire Septimus Contra Sollistam. William Rankins. NCEP
There, where the sun shines first. The Azalea. Coventry Patmore. ELP; GoBC; PoVP
There will always be monkeys and peacocks. Swell People. Carl Sandburg. LOW
There will be a rusty gun on the wall, sweetheart. A. E. F. Carl Sandburg. CMoP; CoBA; HBMV; MAP; MoAB; MoAmPo; WaaP
There will be butterflies. Butterflies. Haniel Long. HBMV
There will be news tomorrow. Tomorrow's News. "George Klingle." OQP
There will be no holyman crying out this year. Jitterbugging in the Streets. Calvin C. Hernton. BF; WOW
There Will Be No Peace. W. H. Auden. NePoAm-2
There will be no simple. The Window. Robert Creeley. OPoP
There Will Be Peace. Margaret Miller Pettengill. PGD
There will be rose and rhododendron. Elegy before Death. Edna St. Vincent Millay. AnFE; APA; CMoP; CoAnAm; GTBS-W; LiTA; LiTM
There will be the cough before the silence, then. Dictum: For a Masque of Deluge. W. S. Merwin. AP
There will be those to-day who weep their own. Woodrow Wilson. S. Omar Barker. DD
There will come a day. The Punching Clock. Milos Macourek. LiTW
There Will Come Soft Rains. Sara Teasdale. LiTA; NP
There, wrapped in his own roars, the lone airman. The Raider. W. R. Rodgers. AnIL; MoBrPo (1950 ed.)
There you are once more near me. Shadow. Guillaume Apollinaire. WaaP
There you sit. Shelley Silverstein. PoSC
There'd Be an Orchestra. F. Scott Fitzgerald. *Fr.* Thousand-and-First Ship. ELU; GoJo
Therefore all seasons shall be sweet to thee. All Seasons Shall Be Sweet. Samuel Taylor Coleridge. *Fr.* Frost at Midnight. BoTP
Therefore doth heaven divide. Commonwealth of the Bees. Shakespeare. King Henry V, *fr.* I, ii. GN
Therefore I cannot think thee wholly gone. James Russell Lowell. *Fr.* Elegy on the Death of Dr. Channing. MaRV
Therefore I Must Tell the Truth. Torlino, *tr. fr. Navajo Indian by* Washington Matthews. ExPo
"Therefore Is the Name of It Called Babel." Sir Osbert Sitwell. MMA
Therefore Philippi saw once more the Roman battalions. We Have Paid Enough Long Since in Our Own Blood. Vergil. *Fr.* Georgics. WaaP
Therefore the Lord Himself/ shall give you a sign. Isaias, Bible, *O.T.* (*Douay vers.*). ISi
Therefore thus saith the Lord; Ye have not hearkened unto me. Jeremiah, Bible, *O.T.* PoFr
Therefore, to be possess'd with double pomp. Ridiculous Excess. Shakespeare. *Fr.* King John, IV, ii. TreFT
Therefore to whom turn I but to thee, the ineffable Name? Robert Browning. *Fr.* Abt Vogler. MaRV
Therefore We Preserve Life. Shen Ch'an. *tr. fr. Chinese by* William C. White. TrJP
Therefore, We Thank Thee, God. Reuben Grossman, *tr. fr. Hebrew by* L. V. Snowman. TrJP
Therefore, when restless rage of wind and wave. Marcus Tullius Cicero's Death. Nicholas Grimald. ReIE
Therefore, when thou wouldst pray, or dost thine alms. The Right Use of Prayer. Sir Aubrey De Vere. OBVV; OQP; WGRP
"There'll Be Others but Non So for Me." Delmore Schwartz. FiMAP
There'll Never Be Peace. Burns. CBEP
There's a barrel-organ caroling across a golden street. The Barrel-Organ. Alfred Noyes. EnLit; FaBV; HBV; MCCG; MoBrPo; NeMA; PoRA; TreF
There's bear in yon hill, and he is a brave fellow. The Bear in the Hill. *Unknown.* ABF
There's a beautiful island away in the West. The Land of the Evening Mirage. *Unknown.* WGRP
There's a beautiful legend, that's never been told. The Three Children. Charles W. H. Bancroft. SoP
There's a big fat turkey. *Unknown.* GFA
There's a bit of sky across the street. My "Patch of Blue." Mary Newland Carson. BLPA; NeHB
There's a black fog hiding London. Promise. Florence Lacey. BoTP
There's a blessing on the hearth. Robert Browning. *Br. sel. fr.* The Ring and the Book, VIII. PoToHe
There's a book. Seven Today. Ivy O. Eastwick. BiCB
There's a Bower of Bean-Vines. Phoebe Cary. BOHV
There's a bower of roses by Bendemeer's stream. By Bendemeer's Stream [*or* Bendemeer]. Thomas Moore. *Fr.* Lalla Rookh. OBRV; OTPC (1946 ed.); RG
There's a brand new wind a-blowin' down that Lincoln road. A New Wind a-Blowin'. Langston Hughes. TrAS
There's a breathless hush in the Close to-night. Vitaï Lampada. Sir Henry Newbolt. BBV; BLPA; MaRV; NeHB; OQP; PaPo; PTK; TreF; YT
There's a brief spring in all of us and when it finishes. To S.T.C. on His 179th Birthday, October 12th, 1951. Maurice Carpenter. FaBoTw
There's a brook on the side of Greylock that used to be full of trout. Dave Lilly. Joyce Kilmer. JKCP (1926 ed.)
There's a Catholic church on the corner. Young Buck's Sunday Blues. Kenneth Pitchford. *Fr.* Good for Nothing Man. CoPo
There's a certain slant of light. Emily Dickinson. AmePo; AmP; AmPP; AnFE; AP; APA; AtBAP; ATP (1953 ed.); CABA; CBEP; CMoP; CoAnAm; DiPo; ExPo; ForPo; FosPo; GTBS-W; ILP; LiTA; LiTG; LiTM (rev. ed.); LoGBV; MAmP; MAP; MasP; MoAB; MoAmPo; MoPo; MWA-2; NePA; NoP; OnPM; OxBA; PAn; PIA; PoEL-5; PoeP; PoFS; PoSa; QFR; ReMP; TreFT
There's a certain young lady. A Certain Young Lady. Washington Irving. FaBoBe; HBV; OnPP
There's a chirrupy cricket as guest in my room. The Chirrupy Cricket. Martha Banning Thomas. GFA; PCH
There's a church in the valley by the wildwood. Little Brown Church in the Vale. William S. Pitts. TreFT
There's a circus in the sky. Winter Circus. Aileen Fisher. YeAr
There's a city that lies in the Kingdom of Clouds. The Sunset City. Henry Sylvester Cornwell. HBV
There's a colleen fair as May. Pearl of the White Breast. *Unknown, tr. by* George Petrie. AnIV; OnYI
There's a combative artist named Whistler. Limerick. Dante Gabriel Rossetti. CenHV
There's a comforting thought at the close of the day. Touching Shoulders. *Unknown.* BLPA; MaRV
There's a Convent garden across the way. From My Window. Mother M. Columba. WHL
There's a crack in the city—down that sharp street. Brogan's Lane. Louis Esson. BoAu
There's a crackle of brown on the leaf's crisp edge. Romany Gold. Amelia Josephine Burr. HBMV
There's a craze among us mortals that is cruel hard to name. The Other Fellow's Job. Strickland W. Gillilan. WBLP
There's a dandy little fellow. Dandelion. Nellie M. Garabrant. GFA
There's a dear little plant that grows in our isle. The Green Little Shamrock of Ireland [*or* The Shamrock]. Andrew Cherry. DD; HBV; HH; MPB; PoRL
There's a death-dealing custom/ Abroad in the land. Drilling Missed Holes. Don Cameron. PoOW
There's a door at the end of our garden. The Door at the End of Our Garden. Frederic E. Weatherly. OTPC (1946 ed.)
There's a dragon on our teapot. The Teapot Dragon. Rupert Sargent Holland. OTPC; UTS
There's a faerie at the bottom of my garden. My Garden. Janice Appleby Succorsa. HoPM
There's a family nobody likes to meet. The Grumble Family. *Unknown.* WBLP
There's a Fire in the Forest. W. W. E. Ross. WHW
There's a flash packet, a flash packet of fame. The Dreadnought. *Unknown.* AmSS
There's a flower in the garden. *Unknown.* OTPC (1946 ed.)

There's a Friend for Little Children. Albert Midlane. OTPC (1923 ed.)
There's a game much in fashion—I think it's called Euchre. The Game of Life. John Godfrey Saxe. BLPA; NeHB
There's a gathering in the village, that has never been outdone. The Country Doctor. Will M. Carleton. BLPA
There's a girl in these parts. No Names. *Unknown.* KiLC
There's a girl out in Ann Arbor, Mich. *Unknown.* GoTP
There's a glade in Aghadoe, Aghadoe, Aghadoe. Aghadoe. John Todhunter. AnIL; AnIV; BoLP; OBEV (1st ed.); OBVV; OxBI; PoVP
There's a good time coming, boys. The Good Time Coming. Charles Mackay. PaPo
There's a grass-grown road from the valley. Threnody. Ruth Guthrie Harding. HBV
There's a graveyard near the White House. The Unknown Soldier. Billy Rose. BLPA; PAL
There's a green hollow where a river sings. The Sleeper of the Valley. Arthur Rimbaud. AWP; JAWP; WBP
There's a grim one-horse hearse in a jolly round trot. The Pauper's Drive. Thomas Noel. PaPo
There's a hard wind yet and a sad road. The Walking Woman. Sidney Keyes. *Fr.* Against a Second Coming. AtBAP; POTE
There's a heap o' love in the human heart. The Human Heart. Frank Carleton Nelson. PoToHe (new ed.)
There's a hill above the harbor. In the Cove. Mary Fanny Youngs. HH
There's a hill somewhere, and a tree and birds. Town Child. Barbara Young. PoMa
There's a hole in the fence. Dorothy Dickinson. GFA
There's a humming in the sky. Aeroplane. Mary McBride Green. SoPo; TiPo
There's a joy without canker or cark. Ballade of Blue China [*or* Of Blue China]. Andrew Lang. PoVP; TSW; VA
There's a land bears a well-known name. The Englishman. Eliza Cook. PaPo
There's a land that is fairer than day. In the Sweet By and By. S. F. Bennett. TreFT
There's a lemondrop monkey that whistles and sings. The Land Where the Taffy Birds Grow. Margaret McBride Hoss. GFA
There's a Light upon the Mountains. Henry Burton. TRV (Light upon the Mountains, A.) MaRV; SoP
There's a little black train a-comin'. The Little Black Train. *Unknown.* OuSiCo
There's a little grey friar in yonder green bush. The Grey Linnet. James McCarroll. CaP
There's a little secret. Keep Sweet. A. B. Simpson. SoP; STF
There's a lone [*or* low] green valley by [*or* on] the old Kentucky shore. Darling Nelly Gray. B. R. Hanby. TrAS; TreFS
There's a lonely stretch of hillocks. Anzac Cove. Leon Gellert. PoAu-1
There's a lot of music in 'em—the hymns of long ago. The Old Hymns. Frank L. Stanton. BLRP
There's a low green valley on the old Kentucky shore. *See* There's a lone green valley by the old Kentucky shore.
There's a man goin' roun' takin' names. Man Goin' Round. *Unknown.* ABF; AS
There's a mellower light just over the hill. Morning Song. Karle Wilson Baker. HBMV; PCD
There's a merry brown thrush sitting up in the tree. The Brown Thrush. Lucy Larcom. BoChLi; BoTP; DD; FaPON; HBV; HBVY; MPB; OTPC; PEDC; PPL; RIS; TVC; UTS
There's a message, sweet and tender. Christmas Still Lives. William Hawkes. BePJ
There's a Nation. Alfred Kreymborg. PG (1945 ed.)
There's a never dying chorus. Toil. *Unknown.* PEDC
There's a nice green little gully on the Numerella shore. The Numerella Shore. "Cockatoo Jack." PoAu-1
There's a noise of coming, going. Ballade of Spring. W. E. Henley. TSW
There's a Notable Clan Yclept Stein. *Unknown.* SiTL
There's a one-eyed yellow idol to the north of Khatmundu. The Green Eye of the Yellow God. J. Milton Hayes. BLPA; PaPo
There's a package. The Package. Aileen Fisher. SoPo
There's a palace in Florence, the world knows well. The Statue and the Bust. Robert Browning. BEL; EnLi-2 (1939 ed.); EPN; OAEP; PoVP; TOP; ViPP; VP
There's a part of the sun in the apple. Out of the Vast [*or* Each a Part of All]. Augustus Wright Bamberger. MaRV; OQP; WBLP
There's a patch of old snow in a corner. A Patch of Old Snow. Robert Frost. CMoP; OCS; PoFS
There's a path that leads to Nowhere. The Path that Leads to Nowhere. Corinne Roosevelt Robinson. BLPA; HBMV; NeHB
There's a pathos in the solemn desolation. The Ruined Cabin. Alfred Castner King. PoOW
There's a piping wind from a sunrise shore. Off to the Fishing Ground. L. M. Montgomery. CaP
There's a place called Far-away Meadow. The Last Mowing. Robert Frost. InP
There's a place the man always say. Where? Kenneth Patchen. LiTM (1970 ed.); ToPo
There's a plump little chap in a speckled coat. Bob White. George Cooper. DD; GoTP; HBVY; MPB; OTPC (1946 ed.); StVeCh (1940 ed.)
There's a Portuguese person named Howell. Limerick. Dante Gabriel Rossetti. CenHV
There's a pretty fuss and bother both in country and in town. A New Song on the Birth of the Prince of Wales. *Unknown.* CoMu
There's a puckle lairds in the auld house. The Auld House. William Soutar. OxBS
There's a quaint little place they call Lullaby Town. Lullaby Town. John Irving Diller. BLPA; NeHB
There's a race of men that don't fit in. The Men That Don't Fit In. Robert W. Service. BLPA
There's a ragged old man in the garden to-day. Mr. Scarecrow. Sheila Braine. BoTP
There's a red light on the track for Bolsum Brown. Bolsum Brown. *Unknown.* AS
There's a Regret. W. E. Henley. AnEnPo
There's a regret that from my bosom aye. A Regret. Charles Harpur. BoAu
There's a reid lowe in yer cheek. Sang. Robert MacLellan. OxBS
There's a road to heaven, a road to hell. My Road. Oliver Opdyke. HBV
There's a rosie-show in Derry. Rosies. Agnes I. Hanrahan. HBV
There's a schooner out from Kingsport. Arnold, Master of the *Scud.* Bliss Carman. EtS
There's a silver house in the lovely sky. The Silver House. John Lea. BoTP
There's a Song in the Air! Josiah Gilbert Holland. *See* Christmas Carol, A.
There's a stairway leading upward. The Stairway to the Stars. William Ludlum. SoP
There's a star in the west, that shall never go down. The Star in the West. Eliza Cook. PEDC
There's a stir among the trees. The Christmas Trees. Mary Frances Butts. OHIP; PRWS
There's a streak across the sky line. The Unfurling of the Flag. Clara Endicott Sears. PEDC
There's a sweet little bird in a far-off isle. The Storm Thrush. Mrs. C. L. de Cheney. SoP
There's a sweet old story translated for men. The Gospel According to You. *Unknown.* BLRP; SoP
There's a sweetness in surrender. The Blessings of Surrender. Mary J. Helphingtine. STF
There's a tender hand that guides me. Guidance. Avis B. Christiansen. SoP
There's a trade you all know well. The Overlander. *Unknown.* PoAu-1
There's a Three-penny Lunch on Dover Street. Eat and Walk. James Norman Hall. BLPA
There's a thrush that sings in a shadowy wood. City Bird. Theda Kenyon. PoMa
There's a time each year that we always hold dear. In the Good Old Summer Time. Ren Shields. TreF
There's a town called Don't-You-Worry. The Town of Don't-You-Worry. I. J. Bartlett. BLPA; WBLP
There's a tramping of hoofs in the busy street. The Troop of the Guard. Hermann Hagedorn. HBV; OHIP
There's a tree out in our garden which is very nice to climb. The Tree in the Garden. Christine Chaundler. BoTP
There's a tree that is growing alone on the hill. The All Alone

Tree. F. O'Neil Gallagher. PCH
There's a vaporish maiden in Harrison. Limerick. Morris Bishop. LiBL; WhC
There's a voice on the wind of the world. The Prophecy. Lon Woodrum. MaRV
There's a whisper down the field where the year has shot her yield. The Long Trail [*or* L'Envoi]. Kipling. FaBV; HBV; OBEV; OBVV; OtMeF; PoVP; ViBoPo
There's a whisper down the line at 11:39. Skimbleshanks; the Railway Cat. T. S. Eliot. FaBoCh; LoGBV
There's a whisper of life in the grey dead trees. The White Canoe. Alan Sullivan. CaP
There's a Wideness in God's Mercy. Frederick William Faber. *Fr.* God Our Father. ThGo, *abr.*; TRV; WBLP, *abr.*
(All-embracing, The.) BLRP; TRV, *sl. diff.*
(God's Mercy.) MaRV
(Heart of the Eternal, The.) OQP
(Hymn.) NBM
There's a woman like a dew-drop, she's so purer than the purest. Earl Mertoun's Song. Robert Browning. *Fr.* A Blot in the Scutcheon. HBV; OBEV; PTK; UnTE
There's a wonderful family, called Stein. The Stein Family. *Unknown.* BOHV
There's a wonderful weaver. The Wonderful Weaver. George Cooper. BoChLi; OTPC (1946 ed.); StVeCh (1940 ed.)
There's a wondrous peace lies on this earth. Christmas. Elizabeth Stanton Rice. StJW
There's a yellow rose of Texas. *Unknown.* TreFT
There's About Two Million Fellows. Albert Jay Cook. PaA
There's all of pleasure and all of peace. A Friend or Two. Wilbur D. Nesbit. PoLF
There's an end to the duel long fought in the Dark. The End of the Duel. Rachel Annand Taylor. CAW
There's an [*or* the] Irishman, Arthur O'Shaughnessy. Limerick [*or* On the Poet O'Shaughnessy]. Dante Gabriel Rossetti. CenHV; ChTr
There's an Italy of Titian-colours here. Black and White Spring. Christopher Hampton. NYTB
There's an odd fellow (I'll not tell his name). De Ignoto. Everard Guilpin. *Fr.* Skialetheia. ReIE
There's Asia on the avenue. Manhattan. Morris Abel Beer. AmFN
There's beauty in the deep. The Deep. John Gardiner Calkins Brainard. AA; EtS
There's been a death in the opposite house. Emily Dickinson. BoLiVe; NCEP
"There's been an accident," they said. Mr. Jones [*or* Common Sense]. Harry Graham. Some Ruthless Rhymes, VIII. CenHV; FaFP; FiBHP; LiTG; MaC; OtMeF; SiTL
There's black grief on the plains, and a mist on the hills. Roisin Dubh. *Unknown.* OnYI
There's blood between us, love, my love. The Convent Threshold. Christina Rossetti. MasP; PoEL-5; PoVP
There's but one stirrer-up of the crafts, Diophantus. Idylls, XXI. Theocritus. FosPo
There's comfort in a horse's lean brown thighs. The Thoroughbred. Helen Magaret. StaSt
There's folks that like the good dry land, an' folks that like the sea. When the Drive Goes Down. Douglas Malloch. AmFN; StVeCh
There's ghosts on the road here. Wilderness Road. Martha Keller. FiSC
There's good cooks and there's bad ones. The Roundup Cook. Robert V. Carr. PoOW
There's Gowd in the Breast. James Hogg. HBV
There's half a god in many a man. Inspiration. Mary Fullerton. PoAu-1
There's hardly a wheel rut left to show. The Old Coach Road. Rachel Field. GFA
There's heaven above, and night by night. Johannes Agricola in Meditation. Robert Browning. MaVP; OBVV; PoVP; ViPo; ViPP
There's Holmes, who is matchless among you for wit. James Russell Lowell. *Fr.* A Fable for Critics. AmePo; AnNE; CoBA
"There's just one Book!" cried the dying sage. Just One Book. *Unknown.* BLRP
There's light in the west, o'er the rims of the walnut. By the Turnstile. John Francis O'Donnell. IrPN; NBM
There's little in taking or giving. Coda. Dorothy Parker. BOHV; InMe; TreFS
There's little joy in life for me. On the Death of Anne Brontë. Charlotte Brontë. ViBoPo
There's little wildness in my city head. The Wind Blows. Donagh MacDonagh. NeIP
There's lots o' friendly fellers in this here fine ole town. Friendly People. John G. Herndon. MPB
There's lots of things I'd like to be. The Hurdy Gurdy Man. Elizabeth Fleming. BoTP
There's Lowell, who's striving Parnassus to climb. On Himself. James Russell Lowell. *Fr.* A Fable for Critics. AA
There's Many a Man Killed on the Railroad, *with music.* *Unknown.* AS
There's many a strong farmer. The Happy Townland. W. B. Yeats. ThWaDe
There's many a young Canadian boy leaves home and friends so dear. Harry Dunne, *vers.* I. *Unknown.* ShS
There's moaning somewhere in the dark. Voice in Darkness. Richard Dehmel. AWP; JAWP; WBP
There's Money in Mother and Father. Morris Bishop. FiBHP
There's mony a man loves land and life. The Tyneside Widow. Swinburne. PoVP
There's More. *Unknown.* FaChP
There's much afoot in heaven and earth this year. The Rainy Summer. Alice Meynell. GoJo; MemP; MoVE; SiSw
There's music in a hammer. *Unknown.* SiTL
There's music in the air. Music in the Air. Fanny Crosby. OTD
There's nae lark loves the lift, my dear. A Lyric. Swinburne. HBV
There's Nae Luck about the House. William Julius Mickle, *also at. to* Jean Adam. *See* Sailor's Wife, The.
There's nae mair lands to tyne, my dear. A Jacobite's Farewell. Swinburne. PoVP; TOP
There's Nae Place like Otago Yet. John Barr of Craigielee. AnNZ
There's naught but care on ev'ry han'. Green Grow the Rashes. Burns. HBV. *See also* Green Grow the Rashes.
"There's no a bird in a' this foreste." Johnie Cock (K *vers.*). *Unknown.* ESPB
There's no arrangement. It is a thicket in little. Bunch of Wild Flowers. Luke Zilles. RePo
There's no defeat in life. *Unknown.* PoToHe (new ed.)
There's no dew left on the daisies and clover. Seven Times One [*or* Birthday Morning]. Jean Ingelow. *Fr.* Songs of Seven. BiCB; BLPA; FaPON; GBV (1922 ed.); GoTP; HBV; MPB; OBNC; OTPC; PCH; PRWS; ThGo; TreF; TVC
There's No Lust like to Poetry. *Unknown, tr. fr. Latin by* John Addington Symonds. AWP
There's no respect for youth or age. California Stage Company. John A. Stone. CoSo; SGR
"There's no sense of going further-it's the edge of cultivation." The Explorer. Kipling. WHA
There's no smoke in the chimney. The Deserted House. Mary Elizabeth Coleridge. BoTP; CH; MoVE; PCD; PoG; ThWaDe
There's no time left to write poems. To American Poets. William Knott. YAP
There's no way out. In the Suburbs. Louis Simpson. ELU; PoIE (1970 ed.)
There's not a breath the dewy leaves to stir. Moonlight in Italy. Elizabeth Clementine Kinney. AA
There's not a craving in the mind. He Satisfies. Frederick William Faber. BePJ
There's not a joy the world can give like that it takes away. Stanzas for Music [*or* Youth and Age]. Byron. BEL; CoBE; EnLi-2; EnLit; EnRP; EPN; FosPo; GTBS; GTBS-D; GTBS-P; GTBS-W; GTSE; GTSL; HBV; MaPo; OAEP; OuHeWo; PoFS; TOP
There's not a nook within this solemn Pass. The Trosachs. Wordsworth. EnLi-2; EPN; GTSL; HBV; MBW-2; OBEV; OBRV; SeCePo
There's not a pair of legs so thin, there's not a head so thick. The Job That's Crying to Be Done. Kipling. TRV
There's not a person in the street. Empty Houses. Mary Colborne-Veel. BoAu
There's not a spider in the sky. A Love-Song by a Lunatic. *Unknown.* NA

There's not a tear that brims thine eye unshed. Faithless. Louis Lavater. PoAu-1
There's not on earth a thing more vile and base. A Prayer for Faith. Michelangelo. OnPM
There's not the smallest orb which thou behold'st. Shakespeare. *Fr.* The Merchant of Venice, V, i. LO
There's nothing grieves me but that age should haste. Idea, VIII. Michael Drayton. ReEn; ReIE; SiCE
There's Nothing like the Rose. Christina Rossetti. PRWS
There's Nothing like the Sun. Edward Thomas. FaBV; NP; YT
There's nothing very beautiful and nothing very gay. Little Things. Orrick Johns. AnAmPo; MAP; NP; PG (1945 ed.); PoToHe (new ed.)
There's nought but care on ev'ry han'. Green Grow the Rashes, O! Burns. EiCL; SiTL. *See also* Green Grow the Rashes.
There's one great bunch of stars in heaven. Song. Théophile Marzials. OBVV
There's one joins sweetly in the quavering hymn. Sunday Morning. L. A. G. Strong. WhC
There's one that I have loved so much. I Give Thanks. Grace Fallow Norton. NP
There's pain in parting, and a kind of hell. Robert Herrick. *Fr.* To His Dying Brother. LO
There's panic in Paris. Bicycalamity. Edmund W. Peters. SD
There's part of the sun in an apple. Out of the Vast [*or* Each a Part of All]. Augustus Wright Bamberger. OQP; TRV; WBLP
There's recompense to balm your spirit's ire. Da Silva Gives the Cue. Walter Hart Blumenthal. TrJP
There's room for most things: Tropic seas. A Sermon. Lady Margaret Sackville. HBMV
There's room on the bus. Jittery Jim. William Jay Smith. BBGG
There's scarce a point whereon mankind agree. On the Phrase "To Kill Time." Voltaire. ALV; MemP; PV
There's snakes on the mountain. Wanderin'. *Unknown.* AS
There's snow in every street. Winter. J. M. Synge. OBMV
There's Snow on the Fields. Christina Rossetti. *Fr.* Sing-Song. BoTP
There's soap-suds on the waves. Morning at the Beach. John Farrar. RIS
There's some is born with their legs straight by natur. A Sailor's Apology for Bow-Legs. Thomas Hood. EtS
"There's someone at the door," said gold candlestick. Green Candles. Humbert Wolfe. HBMV; MoBrPo; NeMA; PoMS
There's Somethin'. Adam Small, *tr. fr. Afrikaans.* PeSA
There's something about the going down of the sun. Any Sunset. Louis Untermeyer. GoTP
There's something in a flying horse. The Crescent Boat [*or* Among the Stars]. Wordsworth. *Fr.* Peter Bell. GoTP; ThWaDe
There's something in a noble boy. The Torn Hat. Nathaniel Parker Willis. AA
There's something in a noble tree. The Trees. Samuel Valentine Cole. OHIP
There's something in a stupid ass. Epilogue. Byron. Par
There's something in the air. The Coming of [the] Spring. Nora Perry. DD; HBVY; HH; PRWS; SoPo; YeAr
There's somewhat on my breast, father. The Confession. "Thomas Ingoldsby." BOHV; FiBHP
There's such a tiny little mouse. The Mouse. Thirza Wakley. BoTP
There's ten of ye now, and twenty long years in between. Johneen. Patrick J. Carroll. WHL
There's that old hag [*or* thik wold hag] Moll Brown, look, see, just past! A Witch [*or* A Country Witch]. William Barnes. GoTP; PoMS
There's the field. I can see it. The Word. Neil Weiss. NYBP
There's the gals at the bar, there's the beer. The Homeward Bound. Bill Adams. EtS
There's the Irishman Arthur O'Shaughnessy. *See* There's an Irishman, Arthur O'Shaughnessy.
There's the old, the waves that harvested. The Fisherman. Leonidas of Tarentum. AWP
There's thik wold hag, Moll Brown, look zee, jus' past! *See* There's that old hag Moll Brown, look, see, Just past!
There's time for the mending and making. No Time for My Lord? Beth Coombe Harris. SoP
There's trampling of hoofs in the busy street. A Troop of the Guard. Hermann Hagedorn. HBV; OHIP
There's Wisdom in Women. Rupert Brooke. BoLP; HBV
Theresienstadt Poems, *sel.* Robert Mezey.
"In your watercolor, Nely Silvínová." NaP
Therewith she left the cave, and with her went. Thetis and Achilles. Homer. *Fr.* The Iliad, XVIII. LiTW
Therewith when he was ware, and gan behold. Chaucer. *Fr.* Troilus and Criseyde. LO
Therfore to thee and thine auspitious ray. The Close. Richard Crashaw. MaMe
Thermopylae. Robert Hillyer. AnAmPo
(Thermopylae and Golgotha.) MaRV
Thermopylae ("Go tell the Spartans, thou that passest by"). Simonides, *tr. fr. Greek by* William Lisle Bowles. AWP; JAWP; WBP
(At Thermopylae, *tr. unknown.*) OnPM; WaaP; WoL
(Inscription to Spartans Dead at Thermopylae, *tr. by* William Lisle Bowles.) TreF
(On the Army of Spartans, Who Died at Thermopylae, *tr. unknown.*) ChTr
Thermopylae ("Of those at famed Thermopylae who lie"). Simonides. *See* Thermopylae Ode, The.
Thermopylae. Michael Thwaites. PoAu-2
Thermopylae and Golgotha. Robert Hillyer. *See* Thermopylae.
Thermopylae Ode, The. Simonides, *tr. fr. Greek by* Richmond Lattimore. WaaP
(On Those Who Fell at Thermopylae, *tr. by* Robert Bland.) PoFr
(Thermopylae, *tr. by* Lord Neaves.) OnPM
Thesaurus Nightmare, A. J. Willard Ridings. WhC
These. William Carlos Williams. AP; CoBMV; MoAB; MoAmPo; NoP; OxBA; PIA
These acres, always again lost. Lost Acres. Robert Graves. FaBoMo; LiTG; MoPW
These acres breathe my family. Summer Acres. Anne Wilkinson. CaP
These alternate nights and days, these seasons. Prologue. Archibald MacLeish. MAP; MoAmPo
These Apple Trees. Valentin Iremonger. NeIP
These are an airport's bones: the pairs of lovers. "Boarding of Pan American Flight 207 Will Be Delayed Ten Minutes." Barbara L. Greenberg. QAH
These are arrows that murder sleep. The Song of Crede, Daughter of Gooary. *Unknown.* LiTW; OnYI
These are my legs. I don't have to tell them, legs. Walter Jenks' Bath. William Meredith. CBV
These are my murmur-laden shells that keep. On Some Shells Found Inland. Trumbull Stickney. AnFE; APA; CoAnAm; LiTA; LiTG; NCEP; NePA; Sonn; TwAmPo
These Are My People. Lucia Trent. PGD
These are my scales to weigh reality. Reality. Martha Dickinson Bianchi. AA
These are my tears that now you see. M. Kirwan. LO
These are my thoughts on realizing. Anniversary. John Wain. NePoEA-2; ToPo
These Are Not Lost. *At. to* Richard Metcalf. PoToHe
These are not words set down for the rejected. A Communication to Nancy Cunard. Kay Boyle. PoNe
These are our brave, these with their hands in on the work. Citation for Horace Gregory. Muriel Rukeyser. NAMP
These are stale tidings I foreknew. Prometheus in the Earthquake. Aeschylus. *Fr.* Prometheus Bound. LiTW
These are stirring times for the editors of newspapers. Powers and Times Are Not Gods. W. H. Auden. *Fr.* For the Time Being. MoRP
These are the best of him. On a Flyleaf of Burns's Songs. Frederick Lawrence Knowles. HBV; PoMa
These Are the Chosen People. Robert Nathan. TrJP
These are the days of falling leaves. Autumn Song. Elizabeth-Ellen Long. SiSoSe
These are the days of our youth, our days of glory and honor. The Days of Our Youth. *Unknown.* AWP; JAWP; WBP
These are the days when birds come back. Emily Dickinson. AmePo; AnNE; AP; BoLiVe (1945 ed.); CaFP; CoBA; ForPo; GoTP; HBV; MAmP; MAP; MoAmPo; NeMA; PoIE; TDP
These are the desolate, dark weeks. These. William Carlos Williams. AP; CoBMV; MoAB; MoAmPo; OxBA
These are the eggs that were put in a nest. The Story of Baby's Pillow. Emilie Poulsson. PPL
These are the fellows who smell of salt to the prairie. Words Are

Never Enough. Charles Bruce. CaP; OBCV
These are the fields of light, and laughing air. The Pea-Fields. Sir Charles G. D. Roberts. OBCV; PeCV
These are the first shapes: stonefish and starfish. Stonefish and Starfish. John Blight. BoAV; NeLNL
"These are the floating berries of the night." Stars. Kenneth Slessor. BoAV
These are the flowers for a mad bride. Indian Pipes. Winifred Welles. AnAmPo
These are the gardens of the desert, these. The Prairies. Bryant. AmePo; AmP; AmPP (3d ed.); AnAmPo; AP; CoBA; InP; MAmP; OxBA; Po; PoE; PoEL-4
These are the generations of the heavens and of the earth. The Garden of Eden. Genesis, Bible, *O.T.* EnLi-1; OuHeWo
These are the ghosts of the unwilling dead. Ghosts, Fire, Water. James Kirkup. BoPe; POTi
These Are the Gifts I Ask. Henry van Dyke. *Fr.* God of the Open Air. FaBoBe; NeHB; OQP; TreFT
These are the green paths trodden by patience. The Rural Mail. John Glassco. MoCV
These are the heroes, for their country's weal. Epitaph on Those Who Fell at the Battle of Chaeronea. Demosthenes. PoFr
These are the letters which Endymion wrote. On the Sale by Auction of Keats' Love Letters. Oscar Wilde. AnEnPo
These are the live! Kenneth Fearing. NAMP
These are the saddest of possible words. Baseball's Sad Lexicon. Franklin P. Adams. FaFP; InMe; SD; TreFS
These are the signs in which my days endure. Museum Piece. Lawrence P. Spingarn. GoYe
These are the sins for which they cast out angels. Annotation for an Epitaph. Adrienne Rich. TwAmPo
These Are the Subtle Rhythms. Glenway Wescott. NP
These are the things I prize. The Things I Prize. Henry van Dyke. TreFT
These are the things men seek at dusk. Dusk. Helen Welshimer. PoToHe
These are the things our Christmas Day should leave. Sonnet for Christmas. Vincent G. Burns. MaRV
These are the things that make me laugh. Villanelle of Things Amusing. Gelett Burgess. BOHV
These are the things which once possessed. True Happiness. Morris Talpalar. PoToHe (new ed.)
These are the trees for hill folk—men that toil. Pines. Anderson M. Scruggs. PoMa
These are the Victoria Falls, whose noisy gushing. The Victoria Falls. William Plomer. BoSA
These are the wells of incredible wonder. Honey for the Heart. Louis J. Sanker. JKCP (1955 ed.)
These are the women whom no man has loved. The Unloved. Arthur Symons. PoVP
These are the words. Stone from the Gods. Irma Wassall. GoYe
These Are the Young. Vachel Lindsay. ATP (1935 ed.)
These are thy glorious works, Parent of good. Adam's Morning Hymn [*or* Morning Hymn of Adam and Eve]. Milton. *Fr.* Paradise Lost, V. MaRV; OxBoCh; TrPWD; WGRP
These, as they change, Almighty Father, these. A Hymn on the Seasons [*or* A Hymn]. James Thomson. *Fr.* The Seasons. CEP; EiCP; EiPP; EnRP; OxBoCh; PoE
These barrows of the century-darkened dead. Prehistoric Burials. Siegfried Sassoon. MoBrPo
These be/ Three silent things. Triad. Adelaide Crapsey. InP; MAP; MCCG; MoAmPo (1942 ed.); NeMA; NP; PFY; PoPl
These be two men of all mankind. Two Men. E. A. Robinson. BOHV
These Beasts and the Benin Bronze. Margaret Danner. Kal
These being the haunts of those. The Death of Friends. Adele Levi. GoYe
These buildings are too close to me. Rudolph Is Tired of the City. Gwendolyn Brooks. PDV; RePo; TiPo (1959 ed.)
These bunched soldiers, just now shooting the emperor. Manet: The Execution of Emperor Maximilian. W. D. Snodgrass. AmPC
These burning fits but meteors be. A Fever. John Donne. MyFE
These butterflies, in twos and threes. Flying Blossoms. W. H. Davies. BrPo
These by the streams of famed Eurymedon. On Those Who Fell. Simonides, the younger. OnPM
These caverns yield. The Bats. Robert Hillyer. GoYe
These children of the sun which summer brings. Wild Bees. John Clare. BoPe
These Children of the Wind. Carl Sandburg. *Fr.* The People, Yes. BiS
(Children of the Wind.) StVeCh; WePo
These children playing at statues fill. Statues. Richard Wilbur. TPM
These Children Singing in Stone a. E. E. Cummings. NoP
These chill pillars of fluted stone. Winter Homily on the Calton Hill. Douglas Young. OxBS
These clouds are soft fat horses. Clouds. James Reaney. WHW
These days are misty, insulated, mute. Louis MacNeice. *Fr.* Autumn Journal. CMoP
These days, continually fuddled with drink. On Going to a Tavern. Wang Chi. OnPM
These days of disinheritance, we feast. Cuisine Bourgeoise. Wallace Stevens. LiTA
These discords and these warring tongues are gales. A Solemn Meditation. Ruth Pitter. OxBoCh
These dreams abound. Prelude for Spring. Dorothy Livesay. PeCV
These dreary hours of hopeless gloom. The Face. Ebenezer Jones. VA
These droll slices of spring like a novel similar. The Busted Lute: a Baedeker. Raymond Dipalma *and* Stephen Shrader. QAH
These errors loved no less than the saint loves arrows. Elegy V: Separation of Man from God [*or* Sacred Elegy V]. George Barker. FaBoTw; GTBS-W; LiTB; MoPo
These evenings since the Child was born. Since Christmas. Frederick R. McCreary. MAP
These eyes, dear [*or* deare] Lord, once brandons of desire. For the Magdalene. William Drummond of Hawthornden. AtBAP; LoBV; PoEL-2
These Faithful Verses. Richard Elwes. MemP
These fallen boughs now never more will weave. The Fallen Tree. Patrick Maybin. NeIP
These fell miasmic rings of mist. Prejudice. Georgia Douglas Johnson. AmNP
These fishes take their own trip, scrape. Average. P. K. Page. TwCaPo
These flowers in their symmetry. Flower Arrangement. Samuel Yellen. NYTB
"These foreigners with strange and avid faces." Immigrants. Nancy Byrd Turner. AmFN
These fought in any case. Ezra Pound. *Fr.* Hugh Selwyn Mauberley. CMoP; FaBoMo; LiTG; MoAmPo (1962 ed.); MoVE; NePA; NP; OxBA; PoIE; PoSA; SeCeV; ThLM; UnPo (3d ed.); WaaP
These going home at dusk. French Peasants. Monk Gibbon. HaMV; NeIP; OxBI; POTE
These golden heads, these common suns. Dandelions. Howard Nemerov. NePA; TwAmPo
"These Gothic windows, how they wear me out." The Young Glass-Stainer. Thomas Hardy. CTC
These grand and fatal movements toward death. Rearmament. Robinson Jeffers. OxBA
These grasses, ancient enemies. Poem. Keith Douglas. NeBP
These green painted park benches are. In a Season of Unemployment. Margaret Avison. MoCV
These had been together from the first. Leolin and Edith. Tennyson. *Fr.* Aylmer's Field. GN
These hands are shaped like God's, and so. Warning. Sara Henderson Hay. MaRV
These hands shall beate upon my pensive brest. *Unknown.* SeCSL
These have forsaken other lives and ways. The Monks at Ards. Patrick Maybin. NeIP
These have no Christ to spit and stoop. Black Magdalens. Countee Cullen. BANP
These hearts were woven of human joys and cares. The Dead. Rupert Brooke. 1914, IV. AnFE; ATP; BrPo; CH; EnLit; GTBS-W; GTSL; HBV; LiTB; LiTG; MCCG; MMA; NP; OtMeF; PoRL; POTE; SeCeV; ShBV-4; Sonn; TOP; YT
These hemp-clothes which you take. Who Will Mend Them? *Unknown.* OnPM
These houres, and that which hover's o'er my end. The Recommendation. Richard Crashaw. MaMe; PoLi

These hours of spring are jolly. The Lover and the Nightingale. *Unknown.* UnTE
These I assume were words so deeply meant. The Ingenuities of Debt. Robert Frost. MWA-2
These I have loved. Rupert Brooke. *Fr.* The Great Lover. NAMP; ShBV-2; WePo
These I have loved with passion, loved them long. Quiet Things. Grace Noll Crowell. PoLF
These I have seen with my eyes. The Banished. Arturo Serrano Plaja. PoFr
These Images Remain. May Sarton. MoLP
These, in the day when heaven was falling. Epitaph on an Army of Mercenaries. A. E. Housman. BrPo; CBV; CMoP; CoBMV; ForPo; GTBS; MMA; MoAB; MoVE; OBEV (new ed.); OtMeF; PoAn; PoFS; PoIE; POTE; StP; UnPo; ViBoPo; WaaP
These jewel-coloured walls, gemmed Salomé. "L'Apparition" of Gustave Moreau. Gordon Bottomley. BrPo
These Lacustrine Cities. John Ashbery. ANYP
These lands are clothed in burning weather. The Arid Lands. Herbert Bashford. AA
These larger-than-life comic characters. Homage to Our Leaders. Julian Symons. NeBP
These leaves, so deeply and so lately green. Color. Melville Cane. RePo
These lines are a discipline he would avoid. Notes on a Child's Coloring Book. Robert Patrick Dana. PoPl
These lions, each by a daisy queen. Dandelions. Sacheverell Sitwell. RIS
These little firs today are things. A Young Firwood. Dante Gabriel Rossetti. GN; PoRL
These little limbs [*or* limmes]. The Salutation. Thomas Traherne. AnAnS-1; AtBAP; InvP; MeP; OBS; OxBoCh; PeRV; PoIE; SCEP-1; SeCL; SeCP; SeCV-2; SeEP
These little songs. Day and Night Songs. William Allingham. VA
These locks on doors have brought me happiness. Locks. Kenneth Koch. CoAP
These London wenches are so stout. The Sound Country Lass. *Unknown.* CoMu; ErPo
These lovely groves of fountain-trees that shake. Golden Bough. Elinor Wylie. MAP; MoAmPo
These magnificent senses. A Hymn of Touch. Gordon Bottomley. BrPo
These many years since we began to be. Rondel. Swinburne. HBV
These market-dames, mid-aged, with lips thin-drawn. Former Beauties. Thomas Hardy. *Fr.* At Casterbridge Fair, II. BEL; EnLi-2 (1949 ed.); EnLit; FaBoEn; OBMV; OBNC; PoVP
These Men. Leon Gellert. BoAV; MoAuPo; PoAu-1
These morning airs. Spring Breeze. Buson. RePo
These mountains forget rough color. Running. Montana, Nothing like Boston. James Welch. YAP
These mountains of up-pointed spears. Rock Paintings, Drakensberg. Alan Ross. POTi
These native angles of decay. Deserted Buildings under Shefford Mountain. John Glassco. OBCV
These never knew or had a hint. Bones of a French Lady in a Museum. Richard Gillman. NePoAm
These new night. Ivory Masks in Orbit. K. William Kgositsile. BF
These nights we fear the aspects of the moon. Full Moon; New Guinea. Karl Shapiro. MiAP; PoPo
These nuts, that I keep in the back of the nest. My Treasures. Robert Louis Stevenson. SAS
These nymphs I would perpetuate. The Afternoon of a Faun. Stéphane Mallarmé. ReMP; SyP
These panting damsels, dancing for their lives. The Mother's Choice. *Unknown.* OxBoLi
These pearls of thought in Persian gulfs were bred. In a Copy of Omar Khayyam. James Russell Lowell. AA
These People. Howard McKinley Corning. AnAmPo
These people have not heard your name. In a Cathedral City. Thomas Hardy. EnLoPo
These pines, these fall oaks, these rocks. After Drinking All Night with a Friend, We Go Out in a Boat at Dawn to See Who Can Write the Best Poem. Robert Bly. NaP
These places abound in the old. Limerick. George Libaire. LiBL
These plaintive verse, the posts of my desire. To Delia, IV. Samuel Daniel. OBSC; ReEn; SiCE
These Poems. Doug Palmer. ThO
These Poems I Have So Loved. Leonora Speyer. PG (1955 ed.)
These pools that, though in forests, still reflect. Spring Pools. Robert Frost. AmPP (5th ed.); BWP; DiPo; MoAB; NoP; OxBA; PIA
These pretty little birds, see how. Human [*or* Humaine] Cares. Nathaniel Wanley. OBS; SeCL
These rioters, of whom I make my rime. Chaucer. *Fr.* The Canterbury Tales: The Pardoner's Tale. WHA
These royal kings that rear up to the sky. Thomas Sackville in Commendation of the Work to the Reader. Thomas Sackville. ReIE
These set a crown of glory on their land. On the Lacedaemonian Dead at Plataea. Simonides. WaaP
These seven houses have learned to face one another. On a Painting by Patient B [of the Independence State Hospital for the Insane]. Donald Justice. CoAP; NePoEA-2
These six things doth the Lord Hate. Seven Evils. Proverbs, Bible, *O.T.* TrGrPo
These songs will not stand. Songs, I. Denis Glover. AnNZ
These Stoic Romans had a flair for dying. In the Annals of Tacitus. Philip Murray. NePoAm
These Stones. Menander, *tr. fr. Greek by* E. F. Watling. LiTW
These suggestions by Asians are not taken seriously. Asian Peace Offers Rejected without Publication. Robert Bly. NaP
These summer birds did with thy master stay. To His Maid Prew. Robert Herrick. OBS
These Sunday mornings Londoners delight. In Regent's Park. Anne Ridler. POTE
These sweeter far than lilies are. Thanksgivings for the Beauty of His Providence. Thomas Traherne. FaBoCh; LoGBV
These tenants sleeping under ground. Brief Biography. Marguerite George. FiSC
These the assizes: here the charge, denial. Epigraph from *The Judge Is Fury.* J. V. Cunningham. QFR
These things have I spoken unto you. Be of Good Cheer. St. John, Bible, *N.T.* WoL
These Things I Do Remember. Solomon Ephraim ben Aaron of Lenczicz, *tr. fr. Hebrew by* Nina Davis Salaman. TrJP
These things I wish you for our friendship's sake. Wishes for William. Winifred M. Letts. OnYI
These Things Shall Be. John Addington Symonds. *See* Loftier Race, A.
These things, Ulysses. Matthew Arnold. *Fr.* The Strayed Reveller. PoG
These thoughts of mine. Thoughts. Duncan Campbell Scott. PeCV
These three robust black-sheeted sybils. Roadside: Spleen. Arthur Freeman. NYTB
These Times. Gertrude Ryder Bennett. MaRV; OQP
These to His Memory—since he held them dear. Dedication. Tennyson. *Fr.* Idylls of the King. CABA; PoVP; ViPP
These to their country brought an endless name. Not to Die. Simonides. OnPM
These to you now, O, more than ever now. Epilogue to Rhymes and Rhythms. W. E. Henley. ViBoPo
These Trees Stand. W. D. Snodgrass. ToPo
These trees that fling their leafy boughs aloft. London Trees. Beryl Netherclift. BoTP
These trucks and coaches, only yesterday. Shunting. Basil Dowling. AnNZ
These truly are the Brave. The Negro Soldiers. Roscoe Conkling Jamison. BANP
These umbered cliffs and gnarls of masonry. Rome. Thomas Hardy. Sonn
These urns beside the river are not full. To the Roman Bridge on Michigan Avenue. Reuel Denney. TDP
These walls will not forget, through later days. In a Girls' School. David Morton. PoRL
These were men that in harness of battle fought. Hesiod. *Fr.* The Shield of Heracles. PoFr
These were my end: a fierce down-squall from the east. Epitaph of a Sailor. Leonidas of Tarentum. LiTW
These were our fields. Dust Bowl. Robert A. Davis. GoSl; IDB
These were the distant fruits of a garden childhood. Fruit. Ruth Miller. BoSA

These were the ones who thanked their God. Psalm XII. A. M. Klein. *Fr.* The Psalter of Avram Haktani. PeCV
These were the seas that you knew, and these were the ways that you followed. To Columbus. John Gould Fletcher. AnAmPo
These Women All. ——Heath. TuPP
(Women.) CTC; OBSC
These wonderful things. A Last World. John Ashbery. ANYP
These Words I Write on Crinkled Tin. Lynette Roberts. ChMP
These words spake Don Henriquez. The Last Words of Don Henriquez. Zalman Schneour. TrJP
These words the poet heard in Paradise. President Garfield. Longfellow. PAH
Theseus and Ariadne. Lloyd Mifflin. AA
Thesis and Antithesis. Arthur Hugh Clough. ViPP
Thesis, Antithesis, and Nostalgia. Alan Dugan. CAD
Thesmophoriazusae, The, *sel.* Aristophanes, *tr. fr. Greek by* Benjamin Bickley Rogers.
Women Speak out in Defense of Themselves, The. TreFT
(Chorus of Women, *tr. by* W. I. Collins.) BOHV
Thespians at Thermopylae, The. Norman Cameron. ChMP; GTBS-P
Thetis and Achilles. Homer, *tr. fr. Greek by* Sir William Marris. *Fr.* The Iliad, XVIII. LiTW
Thevet waited in his workshop. Noël de Thevet. *Unknown.* ChrBoLe
"They." Siegfried Sassoon. CMoP; HBMV; MaRV
They/ were/ our leaders. Ode to the Idiots. Arthur Pfister. WSL
They Accuse Me. Byron. SiTL
They, after the slow building of the house. Asmodai. Geoffrey Hill. NePoEA
They All Belong to Me. Eliza Cook. PGD
They All Love Jack, *with music. Unknown.* ShS
They all see the same movies. Powwow. W. D. Snodgrass. NYBP
They All Want to Play Hamlet. Carl Sandburg. PFY
They all were looking for a king. That Holy Thing. George Macdonald. *Fr.* Paul Faber, Surgeon. ChIP; FaChP; HBV; MaRV; OBEV; OBVV; OQP; StJW; TrPWD; TRV; WGRP
They Also. Basho, *tr. fr. Japanese by* H. G. Henderson. OnPM
(Beauty.) SoP
They Also Stand. . . Merrill Moore. CrMA
They Answer Back; to His Ever-worshipped Will from W. H. "Francis." FiBHP
(To His Ever-worshipped Will from W. H.) ErPo
They are able, with science, to measure. C Stands for Civilization. Kenneth Fearing. TrJP
They are all dying. Death as History. Jay Wright. ThO
They Are All Gone. Henry Vaughan. *See* They Are All Gone into the World of Light.
They are all gone away. The House on the Hill. E. A. Robinson. AA; AnNE; CoBA; GoJo; FaPON; HBMV; InP; LaNeLa; MAP; MPB; OTD; PCD; PG; PIA; PoSa; PTK; TDP; TreFT; TrGrPo; TSW; WHA; YT
They Are All Gone into the World of Light. Henry Vaughan. AnAnS-1; BoC; ChTr, *abr.*; CoBE; EG; EP; GTBS-W; LiTB; LiTG; MaPo; MeP; MePo; NoP; OAEP; OBS; OxBoCh; PAn; PoE; PoEL-2; PoIE; ReEn; SCEP-1; SeCePo; SeCL; SeCP; SeCV-1; SeEP; StP; ViBoPo; WHA
(Ascension-Hymn.) MeLP; PrWP; SeCeV
(Beyond the Veil.) FaPL
(Departed Friends.) ATP (1935 ed.); AWP; EnLi-1 (1949 ed.); InPo; MaRV; TreFS
(Friends Departed.) FaBoEn; HBV; OBEV
(Friends in Paradise, *abr.*) GTSL
(World of Light, The.) CBEP; CH; OHIP; SoP; WGRP
They are all riders: Spring on a two-year-old. The Seasons. Rolfe Humphries. NYBP
They are asleep: the utmost crests and the cracks in the mountains. Asleep. Alcman. LiTW
They are at rest. Rest [*or* Refrigerium]. Cardinal Newman. OBNC; OBRV; OBVV
They are at rest, the heroes brave. Apotheosis. Joseph Bajza. PoFr
They are at their places, straining. The Boat Race. Vergil. *Fr.* The Aeneid. SD
They are bearing him home through the old Virginia valley. Passing of the Unknown Soldier. Vilda Sauvage Owens. DD; MC
They are bringing him down. Casualty. Robert Nichols. MMA
They are by nature lonely things. Ideal Angels. John R. Colombo. MoCV
They Are Closing In. Ethel Livingston. ThO
They are crying salt tears. Repetitions. Carl Sandburg. HBMV; NP
They are curious things that hide in the woods. Forest Shapes. Donald Wandrei. FiSC
They are cutting down the great plane trees at the end of the gardens. The Trees Are Down. Charlotte Mew. BoNaP; MoAB; MoBrPo
They are dying! they are dying! where the golden corn is growing. Ireland. Denis Florence MacCarthy. PoFr
They are gathered, astounded and disturbed. The Last Supper. Rainer Maria Rilke. MoRP
They are gathering round. A Concert Party. Siegfried Sassoon. EnLit; MMA; MuSP
They are given to. Knee Lunes. Robert Kelly. CoPo
They are gone who were the sum of summer. For a Parting. Keith Sinclair. AnNZ
They are heard as a choir of seven. The Pleiades. Mary Barnard. NYBP
They are immortal, voyagers like these. Flight. Harold Vinal. FaPON; MPB; WaKn
They are inspecting hearts again. A Glimpse of the Body Shop. Stephen Berg. NaP
They are lang deid, folk that I used to ken. Elegy. Robert Garioch. OxBS
They are left alone in the dear old home. They Two. Mrs. Frank A. Breck. WBLP
They are like tightrope walkers, unable to fall. The People at the Party. Lisel Mueller. NePoAm-2
They are living the poems we write. Hymn to Labor. Angela Morgan. MaRV
They are moving inwards, the circle is closing. Man Meeting Himself. Howard Sergeant. *Fr.* The Leaves of Europe. ToPo
They are murdering all the young men. Kenneth Rexroth. *Fr.* Thou Shalt Not Kill. WOW
They are my laddie's hounds. My Laddie's Hounds. Marguerite Elizabeth Easter. AA
They are not all sweet nightingales. Not All Sweet Nightingales. Luis de Góngora, *tr. by* Sir John Bowring. CAW
They are not born secret, moon-eyed and still. Cats. Edith Richmond Blanchard. CIV
They are not dead, the soldiers fallen here. On a World War Battlefield. Thomas Curtis Clark. PGD
They are not dead, those loved ones who have passed. Waiting Yonder. "H. A. C." SoP
They are not given much to laughter. Hill People. Harriet Gray Blackwell. AmFN
They are not gone who pass. They Softly Walk. Hugh Robert Orr. MaRV; OQP
They are not here. And we, we are the Others. The Absent. Edwin Muir. MoRP
They are not long, the weeping and the laughter. Vitae Summa Brevis Spem Nos Vetat Incohare Longam [*or* Envoy]. Ernest Dowson. AWP; BrPo; CBV; ChTr; EnLit; HBV; InPo; JAWP; LoBV; MoBrPo; NeMA; NoP; OBEV (new ed.); OQP; PeVV; PoRA; PoSa; PoVP; StP; TOP; TreFT; TrGrPo; ViBoPo; ViPP; WBP; WGRP; WHA
They are not those who used to feed us. The Puzzled Game-Birds. Thomas Hardy. ViPo (1962 ed.); VP
They are ordinary men like you and me. The Reporters. Newman Levy. InMe
They Are Ours. A. B. Magil. PoNe
They are rattling breakfast plates in basement kitchens. Morning at the Window. T. S. Eliot. AmPP; AnEnPo; AWP; CABA; CAD; CoBA; InPo; JAWP; MAP; MoAmPo (1942 ed.); NeMA; NePA; OnPM; WBP; WePo
They are rhymes rudely strung with intent less. A Dedication. Adam Lindsay Gordon. BoAu; PoAu-1
They are slaves who fear to speak. Slaves [*or* Commitment *or* On Freedom]. James Russell Lowell. *Fr.* Stanzas on Freedom. AA; NeHB; OQP; PAL; PCD; SoP; TreFT; TRV; WaKn; WBLP
They are such dear familiar feet that go. Be Patient. "George Klingle." PoToHe

They are the angels of that watery world. Goldfish. Harold Monro. BrPo
They are the foes of silence and of time. Sonnet on Turning a Radio Dial. Anderson M. Scruggs. PoMa
They are the proudest who have met defeat. The Proud. Frances M. Frost. OQP
They are unholy who are born. Wild Plum. Orrick Johns. HBMV; MAP; NP; PG (1945 ed.)
They are walking. Postcard: Two Figures from an Oriental Print. Ethel Livingston. ThO
They are working, beneath the sun. A Song of Street Labor. Caroline A. Lord. DD
They argued on till dead of night. Theologians. Walter de la Mare. EaLo
They ask me where I've been. Back. W. W. Gibson. GTSL; MaRV; TreFT
They bade me cast the thing away. Doubt. Helen Hunt Jackson. WGRP
They bade me to my spinning. The Warrior Maid. Anna Hempstead Branch. HBV; LoEn
They bear him through the channels of the crowd. Anno Santo. Stephen Spender. FaBoMo
They bear no laurels on their sunless brows. Failures. Arthur W. Upson. HBV; OQP; PoToHe (1941 ed.); WGRP
They beat the tom-tom, they plucked the guitar. Fandango. "Stanley Vestal." IHA
They beat their drums with a loud noise. The Soldier Thought Dead Returns Home. *Unknown. Fr.* Shi King. LiTW
They bid us live each day afresh. On Looking Backward. Ernestine Mercer. MaRV
They bled a bullock, and stripped the hide. Res Publica. J. A. R. McKellar. MoAuPo
They borrowed a bed to lay His head. The Cross Was His Own [*or* "Borrowed"]. *Unknown.* BePJ; BLPA; BLRP; MaRV
They bowed to him: "O man of God, we'll crown thy head." The Prophet. "Yehoash." TrJP
They bring me gifts, they honour me. If They Honoured Me, Giving Me Their Gifts. "Michael Field." OBMV
They bring with them their burden. Some Friends. John Gill. ThO
They brought me ambrotypes. Rutherford McDowell. Edgar Lee Masters. *Fr.* Spoon River Anthology. LiTA; NP; OxBA; TOP
They brought thy body back to me quite dead. Luca Signorelli to His Son. Eugene Lee-Hamilton. PeVV
They call her fair. I do not know. Love's Blindness. William James Linton. VA
They call him Bill, the hired man. William Brown of Oregon. Joaquin Miller. BOHV
They call it regional, this relevance. Lake Chelan. William Stafford. NaP
They call me and I go. Complaint. William Carlos Williams. QFR
They call me cruel. Do I know if mouse or songbird feels? The Cat. Charles Stuart Calverley. *Fr.* Sad Memories. ChTr
They call me Hanging Johnny. Hanging Johnny. *Unknown.* AmSS
They call streets "boulevards" and build them huge. Big Crash Out West. Peter Viereck. PoPl
They call thee rich; I deem thee poor. Treasure. Lucilius. AWP; LiTW
They call them pussy willows. The Willow Cats. Margaret Widdemer. BrR; OTPC (1946 ed.); RIS
They call us aliens, we are told. On Behalf of Some Irishmen Not Followers of Tradition. "Æ." AnIL; PoFr
They called her "Angel," sardonic. "Angel." Robin Skelton. NMP
They Called Her Sunshine. Mary Gilmore. NeLNL
They called him King; and I would have no King. Judas. Gamaliel Bradford. OQP
"They called it Annandale—and I was there." How Annandale Went Out. E. A. Robinson. AmP; AP; CBV; CoBMV; HBMV; ILP; MAP; MoAB; MoAmPo
They called me to the window, for. Emily Dickinson. MoVE
They called my love a poor blind maid. On a Blind Girl. Baha Ad-din Zuhayr. AWP
They came for Him with sword and stave. He Was Alone. Lois Duffield. SoP
They came from only God knows where. Three Tarry Men. Edmund Leamy. PoMa
They came from Persia to the Sacred Way. Peacocks. Walter Adolphe Roberts. PoNe
They came on to fish-hook Gettysburg in this way, after this fashion. The Battle of Gettysburg. Stephen Vincent Benét. *Fr.* John Brown's Body. BeLS
They came out of the sun undetected. The Raid. William Everson. OnHM
They Came This Evening. Léon Damas, *tr. fr. French by* Seth L. Wolitz. TTY
They came to catch the stars. At the Ebony Circle. Helen G. Quigless. TNV
They Came to the Wedding. Babette Deutsch. NePoAm
They cannot shell His temple. There Always Will Be God. A. L. Murray. SoP
They cannot wholly pass away. The Departed. John Banister Tabb. AA
"They carry on/ though sorrows completely." Floodtide. Askia Muhammad Touré. PoNe (1970 ed.)
They carry their lean bread. In Brittany. Nancy Willard. ThO
They caught the jetting sperm in a set of ice-cold. My Species. D. M. Black. HYE
They chained her fair young body to the cold and cruel stone. Andromeda. James Jeffrey Roche. AA; HBV; JKCP
They chose me from my brothers: "That's the." What Am I? [*or* Riddle]. Dorothy Aldis. OTPC (1946 ed.); RIS; SoPo; StVeCh (1955 ed.)
They claim no guard of heraldry. Aristocrats of Labor. W. Stewart. *Fr.* The True Aristocrat. OQP; PGD
They clear away the grass, the trees. Farming. *Unknown. Fr.* Shi King. LiTW
They Closed Her Eyes. Gustavo Adolfo Bécquer, *tr. fr. Spanish by* John Masefield. Rimas, LXXIII. AWP; JAWP; WBP
They come/ each one. Circus Maximus. George Bowering. PeCV (1967 ed.)
They come again, those monsters of the sea. Icebergs. William Prescott Foster. EtS
They come, beset by riddling hail. Albuera. Thomas Hardy. *Fr.* The Dynasts. WaaP
They come close together, vines. Who Walks There? Kenneth Patchen. WIRo
They come from beds of lichen green. The Assembling of the Fays. Joseph Rodman Drake. *Fr.* The Culprit Fay. GN
They come in ones and twos and threes. The Carol Singers. Eleanor Farjeon. MemP
They come into. Feeding the Lions. Norman Jordan. BOLo; NBP
They come!—they come!—the heroes come. Evacuation of New York by the British. *Unknown.* PAH
They come to me and talk about God's will. Soliloquy of Lincoln before Manassas. Stephen Vincent Benét. *Fr.* John Brown's Body. PaA
They come with, ah, fell footfall. Fêtes, Fates. John Malcolm Brinnin. LiTA
They commune at 7:30 where I walked my arid hands. Two Poems on the Emotions. David Shapiro. ANYP
They could not shut you out of heaven. To——. Katharine Duncan Morse. HBMV
They cowered inert before the study fire. Certain American Poets. Odell Shepard. InP
They Crucified My Lord. *Unknown.* STF
They crucified my Lord. Crucifixion. *Unknown.* BoAN-1; TrGrPo
They crushed the thorns into His brow. Second Crucifixion. Victoria Beaudin Johnson. SoP
They cut down the old pine tree in Tunisia. Guitar Lament for a Mountain Boy. Carl De Suze. CaFP
"They cut it in squares." Socratic. Hilda Doolittle ("H. D."). AnEnPo; HoPM
They danced by the roadside on Saturday night. The Dance by the Roadside. Gustaf Fröding. WoL
They deployed military troops. White Weekend. Quincy Troupe. NBP
They did not crucify the Lord. Golgotha. Katherine Greenleaf Pedley. ChIP
They did not know that the moon had shone. Moon-Madness. Victor Starbuck. HBMV
They did not know this face. Job. Elizabeth Sewell. EaLo
They do but grope in learning's pedant round. Substance and

Shadow. Cardinal Newman. GoBC
They do me wrong who say I come no more. Opportunity. Walter Malone. BLPA; FaBoBe; HBV; MaRV; NeHB; OQP; WBLP; YaD
They do neither plight nor wed. The City of the Dead. Richard Burton. HBV
They do not care, the dying, whether it be dawn or dusk or daylight full and clear. Illi Morituri. Mary Morison Webster. PeSA
They do not count the mountains that they climb. These People. Howard McKinley Corning. AnAmPo
They do not live in the world. The Animals. Edwin Muir. CMoP; MoBrPo (1962 ed.); MoPW; PoDB
They do not speak but into their empty mood. Two Old Men Look at the Sea. J. R. Hervey. AnNZ
They do you wrong who paint you, wondrous Man. To the Master Poet. Thomas Curtis Clark. ChIP
They dogged him all one afternoon. On the Way to the Mission. Duncan Campbell Scott. CaP
They don't like strangers. Stoney Ridge Dance Hall. Alden Nowlan. MoCV
They dragged you from homeland. Strong Men. Sterling A. Brown. BANP; PPON; TTY; WOW
They dream of hoop-snakes in the darkened house. Children at Night. Samuel French Morse. NYTB
They Dream Only of America. John Ashbery. FRC
They dressed us up in black. The Funeral. Walter de la Mare. CMoP; MoVE
They drift away. Ah, God! they drift for ever. Drifting Away. Charles Kingsley. OxBoCh
They drop with periodic regularity. The Preacher Sought to Find Out Acceptable Words. Richard Eberhart. WaP
They dropped like flakes, they dropped like stars. Emily Dickinson. AA; OHIP
They drove the hammered nails into His hands. Sequel to Finality. Patrick F. Kirby. GoBC; MaRV
"They dug ten streets from that there hole," he said. Millom Old Quarry. Norman Nicholson. ChMP; HaMV
They eat beans mostly, this old yellow pair. The Bean Eaters. Gwendolyn Brooks. Kal; NoP; TTY
They enter the bare wood, drawn. The Novices. Denise Levertov. NaP
They err who count it glorious to subdue. Milton. *Fr.* Paradise Regained, III. PoFr
They err who say this long-withdrawing line. Paul Veronese: Three Sonnets, III. Sir Samuel Ferguson. IrPN
They find the way who linger where. The Way. Sidney Henry Morse. HBV
They fished and they fished. The Fish with the Deep Sea Smile. Margaret Wise Brown. PDV
They Flee from Me. Sir Thomas Wyatt. *See* Lover, The, Showeth How He Is Forsaken. . .
They fling their flags upon the morn. Spain's Last Armada. Wallace Rice. PAH
They flutter out of white, and run. Bathers. Terence Tiller. ChMP; FaBoMo; NeBP
They fought last year by the upper Valley of Son-Kan. The Long War. Li Po. WaaP
They fought like demons of the night. Cats. John Banister Tabb. CIV
They fought south of the Castle. Fighting South of the Castle. *Unknown.* AWP; JAWP; WaaP; WBP
They fought south of the ramparts. Fighting South of the Ramparts. *Unknown.* FIW; LiTW
They found a taxi. He took her home. The Moral Taxi Ride. Erich Kästner. ErPo
They found him deep within an ancient cave. The Prehistoric Huntsman. Donald Wandrei. FiSC
They Found Him Sitting in a Chair. Horace Gregory. MoAmPo
They found it in her hollow marble bed. A Roman Mirror. Sir Rennell Rodd. OBVV; VA
They founded in the turbulent stream their bridge. The Bridge. Albert Verwey. LiTW
They gathered around and told him not to do it. Noah. Roy Daniells. PeCV (1967 ed.); WHW
They gave him his orders at Monroe, Virginia. The Wreck of the Old 97. *Unknown.* ViBoFo
They gave his flesh the sting of knout. The Greater Guilt. John Richard Moreland. ChIP
They gave me advice and counsel in store. Heinrich Heine, *tr. fr. German.* OTD
They get drunk, these Great Sled-Makers. The Great Sled-Makers. Kenneth Patchen. ToPo
They glare—those stony eyes! The Sphinx. Henry Howard Brownell. AA
They glide upon their endless way. The Stars. "Barry Cornwall." OTPC
They go along the graveled walks. Seminary. Constance Carrier. NePoAm
"They got pictures of V stamped on letter stamps." Conversation on V. Owen Dodson. Kal
They Got You Last Night. Aaron Kurtz. *Fr.* Behold the Sea. PPON
They grew and charcoal bundle shakes itself. Brothers. Solomon Edwards. NNP
They grew in beauty, side by side. The Graves of a Household. Felicia Dorothea Hemans. HBV; WBLP
They guided birds and came to hear their story. Of History More Like Myth. Jean Garrigue. NYBP
They had a Cook with them who stood alone. Ten of Chaucer's People: A Tasty Cook. Chaucer. *Fr.* The Canterbury Tales. PoSa
They had a picnic in the woods. The Picnic. Elizabeth Madox Roberts. RIS
They had a pocketful of stories that they told. A High Place. Eithne Wilkins. NeBP
They had a tale on which to gloat. No Miracle. Daniel Corkery. AnIV
They had brought in such sheafs of hair. The Last Bowstrings. Edward Lucas White. AA
They had known it all before, routine. New Wine, Old Bottles. Colin Newbury. AnNZ
They hadn't noticed her coming, too busy with loud. An Aftermath. Thomas Blackburn. NMP
They hail you as their morning star. Men. Dorothy Parker. BoLP
They hailed him King as he passed by. He — They — We. John Oxenham. ChIP
They hailed him, trembling, to the Judgment Seat. Judgment. Kenneth W. Porter. ChIP
They hanged the King of Ai at eventide. The King of Ai. Hyam Plutzik. LiTM (1970 ed.)
They hasten, still they hasten. The Were-Wolves. Wilfred Campbell. VA
They Have Been with Jesus. *Unknown.* SoP
They have been with us a long time. Telephone Poles. John Updike. FIW
They have burned to Thee many tapers in many temples. Psalm. Jessie E. Sampter. OQP
They have carried the mahogany chair. Mourning Picture. Adrienne Rich. CoAP
They have chiseled on my stone the words. Cassius Hueffer. Edgar Lee Masters. *Fr.* Spoon River Anthology. OxBA
They have come by carloads. Surfers at Santa Cruz. Paul Goodman. CBV
They have connived at those jewelled fascinations. Auspice of Jewels. Laura Riding. FaBoMo; LiTA
They have dreamed as young men dream. Old Black Men. Georgia Douglas Johnson. CDC; PoNe
They have dressed me up in a soldier's dress. The Jewish Conscript. Florence Kiper Frank. OQP
They have gone over, the god, the friend, the lover. The Purification. Richard Church. MoBrPo (1942 ed.); POTE
They have hanged Roger Casement to the tolling of a bell. On the Death of Roger Casement. Padraic Colum. PoFr
They have laid the penthouse scenes away. Elegy in a Theatrical Warehouse. Kenneth Fearing. NYBP
They have [*or* They've] left Thee naked, Lord; O that they had! Upon the Body of Our Blessed Lord, Naked and Bloody [*or* On Our Crucified Lord Naked, and Bloody]. Richard Crashaw. ACP; CABA; EnLi-1; EP; ILP; InvP; MaMe; OAEP; OBS; Po; SeCP; SeCV-1; VaPo
They have made for Leonora this low dwelling in the ground. Leonora. E. A. Robinson. MaPo; NePA
They have met at last—as storm clouds. Manassas. Catherine Anne Warfield. MC; PAH
They have no pact to sign—our peaceful dead. The Pact. Alfred Noyes. MaRV
They have no song, the sedges dry. Song in the Songless. George Meredith. ACV; GTSL; OTPC (1946 ed.); PCD; PoVP

They have not fought in vain, our dead. Carry On! Thomas Curtis Clark. OQP
They have not gone from us. O no! they are. Our Dead. Robert Nichols. WGRP
They have pictured Peace at the wheel and loom. Peace Must Come as a Troubadour. Marie Drennan. OQP
They have said evil of my dear. Medieval Norman Songs, XIV. *Unknown, tr. by* John Addington Symonds. AWP; JAWP; WBP
They have said, "too risky." To Words. Ralph Pomeroy. CoPo
They have slain you, Sean MacDermott. Lament for Sean MacDermott. "Seumas O'Sullivan." AnIV
They Have Taken It from Me. Timothy Corsellis. WaP
They have taken the gable from the roof of clay. Swedes. Edward Thomas. BrPo; MoVE
They have taken the maps and spread them out. Still Pond, No More Moving. Howard Moss. NYBP
They have taken the tomb of our Comrade Christ. Crusaders. Elizabeth Waddell. ChIP; OQP
They have triumphed who have died. The Victors. Charles Hanson Towne. OQP
They have vanished, the immortal horses of Achilles. The Deathless Ones. Eleanor Glenn Wallis. NePoAm
They Have Yarns. Carl Sandburg. *Fr.* The People, Yes, Sec. 45. AmFN; LiTA; MoAmPo; RePo
(American Yarns.) StVeCh (1955 ed.)
(Yarns.) GoTP
(Yarns of the People.) NeMA
They haven't got no noses. The Song of Quoodle. G. K. Chesterton. GoJo; SiTL; WePo
They head the list. Horses. Richard Armour. PoPl; WhC
They held her south to Magellan's mouth. The Rush of the *Oregon.* Arthur Guiterman. PAH
They helped every one his neighbour; and everyone said to his brother. Comfort When Work Seems Difficult. Isaiah, Bible, *O.T.* BoC
They hold their hands over their mouths. The Poets Agree to Be Quiet by the Swamp. David Wagoner. CoAP
They howled 'til Pilate. Crucifixion. Waring Cuney. BANP; GoSl
They huddle in groups on shingle, aiming. Winter Boats at Brighton. Alan Ross. POTi
They hunt chameleon worlds with cameras. Adina. Harold Telemaque. PoNe; TTY
They hunt, the velvet tigers in the jungle. India. W. J. Turner. MoBrPo; PDV
They journeyed. Ode. Ibn al-Arabi. AWP; LiTW
They kill me for the death within them. Mihailovich. Roy McFadden. NeIP
They knew they were fighting our war. As the months grew to years. Pershing at the Tomb of Lafayette. Amelia Josephine Burr. PAH
They Know. Ryah Tumarkin Goodman. FiSC
They know the lion's power. Killed in Action. Terence Tiller. NeBP
They know the time to go! Time to Go. "Susan Coolidge." GN; OTPC (1946 ed.)
They landed and could. The English in Virginia (April, 1607). Charles Reznikoff. SiSw
They lean over the path. Orchids. Theodore Roethke. NMP; OPoP
They lean upon their windows. It is late. Ladies by Their Windows. Donald Justice. TwAmPo
They leave their love-lorn haunts. Wedded. Isaac Rosenberg. FaBoEn; LO
They leave us nothing. Gray Matter. Ford Madox Ford. MoBrPo (1942 ed.)
They left behind the insistent strain. Retrospect. Roy Davis. WhC
They left him hanging for the deed. Once the Wind. Mark Van Doren. TwAmPo
They left the fury of the fight. Sportsmen in Paradise. T. P. Cameron Wilson. PoMa
They left the vine-wreathed cottage and the mansion on the hill. The Women of the West. G. Essex Evans. PoAu-1
They left their Babylon bare. The Destruction of Jerusalem by the Babylonian Hordes. Isaac Rosenberg. SiSw
They lie in the Sunday street. The Dead. C. Day Lewis. TwCP
They lie on beaches and are proud to tan. Summer Resort. P. K. Page. CaP
They lie who say that love must be. No Sufferer for Her Love. *Unknown.* AnIL
"They lied, those lying traitors all." Medieval Norman Songs, XV. *Unknown, tr. fr. French by* John Addington Symonds. AWP
They lined the long perches like a living color spectrum. The Finches. Philip Murray. NePoAm
They list for me the things I can not know. Knowledge. Thomas Curtis Clark. OQP
They Live. Randall Swingler. WaP
They live in their country. Restricted. Miriam Waddington. CaP
They live 'neath the curtain. Puk-Wudjies. Patrick R. Chalmers. BoTP; DD; HBVY
They lived alone. The Romney. Harriet Monroe. HBMV
They lived in elaborate systems. Legends. Eric Torgersen. QAH
They look so solemn and fine. Who are they? The Unknown Soldier. Arthur B. Rhinow. OQP
They look up with their pale and sunken faces. Elizabeth Barrett Browning. *Fr.* The Cry of the Children. NBM
They look'd on each other and spake not; but Gunnar gat him gone. Of the Passing Away of Brynhild. William Morris. *Fr.* The Story of Sigurd the Volsung. VA
They looked up to the sky, whose floating glow. The Lovers. Byron. LiTL
They made a feast in the banquet hall. The Prodigal. Sara Henderson Hay. StaSt
They made a myth of you, professor. Mr. Attila. Carl Sandburg. ImOP; TPM
"They made her a grave, too cold and damp." The Lake of the Dismal Swamp. Thomas Moore. BLPA
They made the chamber sweet with flowers and leaves. A Pause [*or* A Meeting]. Christina Rossetti. GTBS-D; HBV
They made them idols in the elder days. Idols. Richard Burton. TrPWD
They made them ready and we saw them go. The Travellers. Mark A. De Wolfe Howe. AA
They Make a Lovely Pretense. Philip Legler. NYTB
They make it only more immortal still. The Cathedral of Rheims. Edmond Rostand. CAW
They marched,/ That sun-gold summer day. Via Dolorosa. Phoebe Smith. PGD
They may get better. A Lynching for Skip James. Rudy Bee Graham. BF
They May Rail at This Life. Thomas Moore. NBM; PoEL-4
They may talk of love in a cottage. Love in a Cottage. Nathaniel Parker Willis. HBV; LHV
They meet but with unwholesome springs. Against Them Who Lay Unchastity to the Sex of Women. William Habington. *Fr.* Castara, II. AnAnS-2; CLwM; MePo; OBS; SeCP; SeEP
They meet over water. 3rd Dance—Making a Structure with a Roof or under a Roof—6-7 February 1964. Jackson MacLow. CoPo
They met inside the gateway that gives the view. Wind and Mist. Edward Thomas. BrPo
They met me in the day of successe. Shakespeare. *Fr.* Macbeth, I, v. AtBAP
They might not need me; but they might. Emily Dickinson. PoToHe (new ed.); TRV
They mock'd the Sovereign of Ghaznin: one saith. Mahmoud and Ayaz; a Paraphrase of Sa'di. Sir Edwin Arnold. *Fr.* With Sa'di in the Garden. VA
They more than we are what we are. Statues. Kathleen Raine. NYBP
They mouth love's language. A Memory of the Players in a Mirror at Midnight. James Joyce. InvP; ViBoPo
They move on tracks of never-ending light. The Master Singers. Rhys Carpenter. WGRP
They must to keep their certainty accuse. The Leaders of the Crowd. W. B. Yeats. EnLit; MoAB; MoBrPo; PoAn; PoPo
They nailed my Saviour to the cross. They Crucified My Lord. *Unknown.* STF
They named it Aultgraat—Ugly Burn. The Black Rock of Kiltearn. Andrew Young. FaBoTw
They named your name and suddenly. Again for You. Sister Mary Catherine. JKCP (1955 ed.)

They nearly strike me dumb. My Mistress's Boots. Frederick Locker-Lampson. BOHV; HBV; InP; TOP
They never credit us. The Critics. Lawrence Durrell. ToPo
They never fail who die/ In a great cause. Triumph of the Defeated. Byron. MaRV
They Never Quite Leave Us. Margaret Elizabeth Sangster. WBLP
They never seem to be far away. Within the Veil. Margaret Elizabeth Sangster. BLRP
They never sought; nay, they but woke and came. The Shepherds. Laura Spencer Portor. PEDC
They nod at me and I at stems. Open. Larry Eigner. NeAP
They noticed that virginity was needed. The Presumptuous. W. H. Auden. CMoP
They of the Mean Estate Are Happiest. *Unknown.* SiCE
They offered barter—love. Transaction on the Roman Exchange. Henrietta A. Burke. JKCP (1955 ed.)
They often haunt me, these substantial ghosts. The Hymn Tunes. Edward Lucie-Smith. MuSP
They only seem to forget. Old Women Remember. Rosalie Boyle. NYTB
They paper the walls of their world. The Recluses. Stuart Z. Perkoff. NeAP
They Part. Dorothy Parker. ALV
They pass me by like shadows, crowds on crowds. The Street. James Russell Lowell. OQP; Sonn
They pass so close, the people on the street. Footsteps. Hazel Hall. HBMV
They pass through the great iron gates. The Legion of Iron. Lola Ridge. NAMP
They pass too fast. Ships, and there's time for sighing. Earth Has Shrunk in the Wash. William Empson. CMoP
They pass upon their old, tremulous feet. The Old Women. Arthur Symons. PoVP
They pity me. Lonely. André Spire. AWP; JAWP; TrJP; WBP
They planned for Christ a cruel death. Revealment. John Richard Moreland. ChIP
They played him home to the House of Stones. The Burial of Sir John McKenzie. Jessie Mackay. AnNZ
They played till the dusk of summer in the wood. Coogan's Wood. Francis Stuart. NeIP
They pluck their palm branches and hail him as King. Palm Sunday and Monday. Edwin McNeill Poteat. ChIP; MaRV
They pointed me out on the highway, and they said. The Traveller. John Berryman. CBV
They pushed him straight against the wall. At Sunrise. Rosa Zagnoni Marinoni. PoToHe
They put their finger on their lip. Eros. Emerson. HBV
They put up big wooden gods. Manufactured Gods. Carl Sandburg. WGRP
They put us far apart. Emily Dickinson. AP
They questioned my theology. Orthodox. Mark Guy Pearse. MaRV
They ran through the streets of the seaport town. Greyport [*or* Grayport] Legend. Bret Harte. EtS; GN
They reached the Maryland bridge of Harper's Ferry. John Brown. Stephen Vincent Benét. *Fr.* John Brown's Body. WoL
They rear'd their lodges in the wilderness. The First Fathers. Robert Stephen Hawker. OBVV
They require of us a song. In Search of a God. Charles Thomas. WSL
They rise like sudden fiery flowers. Fireworks. James Reeves. PoSC
They rise to mastery of wind and snow. Pioneers. Hamlin Garland. AA
They roamed between/ Delicious dells. Prose and Poesy; a Rural Misadventure. Thomas R. Ybarra. WhC
They rode along the road till they come to two stacks of oats. A Man and a Maid. *Unknown.* BFSS
They rode from the camp at morn. Sidney Godolphin. Clinton Scollard. AA
They rose in Freedom's rare sunrise. The Men of "Forty-eight." Gerald Massey. PoFr
They rode north. Black Thinks of His Brothers. Stanley Crouch. BF
They rose to where their sovran eagle sails. Montenegro. Tennyson. PoVP
They rose up in a twinkling cloud. The Stockdoves. Andrew Young. POTE
They roused him with muffins—they roused him with ice. The Baker's Tale. "Lewis Carroll." *Fr.* The Hunting of the Snark. BoChLi; PoVP
They said, It will be like snow falling. The Snow. Sidney Keyes. NeBP
They said, It will be like snow falling. Variations on a Theme by Sidney Keyes. Eithne Wilkins. NeBP
They said: "Now here is gold." Pioneers. Frederick William Ophel. BoAu
They said, "The Master is coming." Unawares. Emma A. Lent. PoLF; SoP
They said this mystery shall never cease. Blake. TrGrPo
They said to him, "It is a very good thing." Homage. Kenneth Fearing. CMoP
They said "Wait." Well, I waited. Alabama Centennial. Naomi Long Madgett. BALP
They sailed away in a gallant bark. Dublin Bay. *Unknown.* BFSS
They sat in a tavern in wicked Port Royal. Dana Burnet. *Fr.* The Sack of Old Panama. PFY
They sat. They stood about. Of Commerce and Society. Geoffrey Hill. NePoEA-2
They Saw and Believed. Esther Lloyd Hagg. ChIP
They saw the sun looke pale, and cast through aire. Presage of Storme. George Chapman. *Fr.* Eugenia. FaBoEn
They Say. Ella Wheeler Wilcox. WBLP
They say a snake the other day. On Jean Fréron. Voltaire. OnPM
They say a tropic river threads the seas. The Gulf Stream. Henry Bellamann. EtS
They say a wife and husband, bit by bit. A Bridge Instead of a Wall. *Unknown.* PoToHe (new ed.)
They Say, and I Am Glad They Say. Hilaire Belloc. ALV
They say: he lives with colours. Sons. Jack Cope. PeSA
They say He was a serious child. The Gentlest Lady. Dorothy Parker. ISi
They say I do not love thee. The American Flag. Charles Constantine Pise. CAW
They say in Harlan County. Which Side Are You On? Mrs. Sam. Reece. WOW
They say La Jac Brite Pink Skin Bleach avails not. Government Injunction [Restraining Harlem Cosmetic Co.]. Josephine Miles. FiMAP; PoNe
They Say My Verse Is Sad. A. E. Housman. EnLit; WePo (Dedication.) EnLi-2 (1949 ed.)
("They say my verse is sad: no wonder.") VP
They say old man your horse will die. The Dead Horse. *Unknown.* AmSS; AS
They Say on Leaving Eden. Mark Dunster. NYTB
They say that, afar in the land of the west. The Green Isle of Lovers. Robert Charles Sands. AA
They say that dead men tell no tales! Dead Men Tell No Tales. Haniel Long. HBMV; MCCG; NP
They say that God lives very high! A Child's Thought of God. Elizabeth Barrett Browning. FaPON; MPB; OTPC; PCH; PRWS; SoP; TRV
They say that hope is happiness. Stanzas for Music. Byron. ForPo
They say that I am growing old. Not Growing Old. *Unknown.* SoP
They say that I was in my youth. Limerick. *Unknown.* CenHV
They Say That in the Unchanging Place. Hilaire Belloc. *Fr.* Dedicatory Ode. PoLF
They say that man is mighty. What Rules the World. William Ross Wallace. DD; OHIP; OTPC (1946 ed.); PoRL
They say that old age. Unbeliever. Dorothy Dow. HBMV
They say, that Pity in Love's service dwells. Modern Love, XLIV. George Meredith. VA; ViPo; VP
They say that shadows of deceasèd ghosts. Sonnet. Joshua Sylvester. ElL; OBS; SeEP; Sonn
They say that the year is old and gray. New Year Song. Emily Huntington Miller. DD; PoRL
They say that thou wert lovely on thy bier. Death's Alchemy. William Sidney Walker. VA
They say that "Time assuages." Emily Dickinson. AmePo; WGRP
They Say That Time Is Swift. "Angelus Silesius," *tr. fr. German by* Paul Carus. OnPM

They say that when a murder victim dies. Crime Story. Charles Higham. NYTB
They say that when they burned young Shelley's corpse. The Fishes and the Poet's Hands. Frank Yerby. AmNP; PoNe (1970 ed.)
They say the experimental. Nothing. Burns Singer. OxBS
They say the Lion and the Lizard keep. Sleep Unbroken. Omar Khayyám, *tr. by* Edward Fitzgerald. *Fr.* The Rubáiyát. OnPM
They say the men are. The Men Are Coming Back! Barry Cole. HYE
They say the most of mothers. My Mother. *Unknown.* STF
They say the phoenix is dying, some say dead. News of the Phoenix. A. J. M. Smith. ELU; MoCV; PeCV (1967 ed.)
They say the sea is cold, but the sea contains. Whales Weep Not! D. H. Lawrence. CMoP; PoIE
They say the Spanish ships are out. The Dragon of the Seas. Thomas Nelson Page. PAH
They say the war is over. But water still. Redeployment. Howard Nemerov. LiTM (1970 ed.); NePA; ThLM; TrJP
They say the world is round, and yet. Life's Scars. Ella Wheeler Wilcox. BLPA
They say there is/ A still pool. Whirlpool. *Unknown.* LiTW; WoL
They say there is a sweeter air. A Carriage from Sweden. Marianne Moore. LiTA; LiTM (rev. ed.); MoAB; NePA; TwCP
They say there is no hope. Sea Gods. Hilda Doolittle ("H. D."). AtBAP; LiTA
They say there's a high windless world and strange. Mutability. Rupert Brooke. BrPo
They say this is His mother. Fourth Station. Ruth Schaumann. ISi
They say Thou art a Myth. Per Contra. Mahlon Leonard Fisher. ChIP; MaRV
They say your lady friends have no long life. Epigram. Martial, *tr. by* J. A. Pott *and* F. A. Wright. ALV
They say you're in love with that keck-eyed lad. Braggart! Denis Wrafter. OnYI
They scoured the hill with steel and living brooms. Mine No. 6. Malcolm Cowley. *Fr.* Blue Juniata. InP; MAP; MoAmPo (1942 ed.)
They See Dark Skies. Roy Fuller. NYTB
They see Gods wonders that are call'd. Roger Williams. SCAP
They seemed, to those who saw them meet. Shadows. Richard Monckton Milnes. HBV; OBEV (1st ed.)
They sell good beer at Haslemere. West Sussex Drinking Song. Hilaire Belloc. MoBrPo
They sent him back to her. The letter came. Not to Keep. Robert Frost. AmPP; AnAmPo; CMoP; OxBA
They sent me to bed, dear, so dreadfully early. Cuddle Down, Dolly. Kate Douglas Wiggin. PPL
They served tea in the sandpile. The Party. Reed Whittemore. CAD; CoAP
They set the fish upon the table. Pesci Misti. L. Aaronson. FaBoTw
They set the slave free, striking off his chains. The Slave. James Oppenheim. MAP; MaRV; MoAmPo (1942 ed.); NP; PoFr; PoMa; TrJP
They shall come in the black weathers. The Waiting Watchers. Henry Treece. NeBP
"They shall not die in vain," we said. Dedication. Ralph Gustafson. CaP; TwCaPo
They shall not return to us, the resolute, the young. Mesopotamia. Kipling. MMA
They shall sink under water. The Cities. "Æ." OBMV
They shot young Windebank just here. Young Windebank. Margaret L. Woods. HBV; HBVY; VA
They shouldn't call me "little boy" anymore. When a Fellow's Four. Mary Jane Carr. BiCB
They shut me up in prose. Emily Dickinson. MAmP
They shut the road through the woods. The Way through the Woods. Kipling. CH; FaBoCh; FaPON; GTBS-D; LoGBV; MCCG; MoVE; OBEV (new ed.); OBNC; OBVV; Po; PoSa; POTE; SeCeV; ShBV-2; StP; TDP; ThWaDe; WePo
They sin who tell us Love can die. Love Indestructible. Robert Southey. *Fr.* The Curse of Kehama. OBNC; OBRV
They Sing. Theodore Roethke. NYBP
They sing their dearest songs. During Wind and Rain. Thomas Hardy. CBV; CMoP; ELP; ExPo; ForPo; GTBS-P; PeVV; PIA; PoIE; PoSa; QFR; SeCeV; ViPP
They Sing, They Sing. Theodore Roethke. *Fr.* The Dying Man. PoDB
They sit and smoke on the esplanade. At a Watering-Place. Thomas Hardy. CMoP
They sit at home and they dream and dally. The Adventurers. May Byron. HBV
They sit at the green baize table. Congress, 1878. Victor Alexis de la Montagne. WoL
They sit in the roots. The Lost Tribe. Robert Finch. CaP
They sleep beneath no immemorial yews. We Shall Remember Them. James Terry White. PEDC
They sleep, eyeing the mountain peaks and clefts. After Alcman. Dick Gallup. ANYP
They slept on the field which their valor had won. Beyond the Potomac. Paul Hamilton Hayne. PAH
They slew a god in a valley. Gluskap's Hound. T. G. Roberts. WHW
They sneaked into the limbo of time. Ancestral Faces. Kwesi Brew. PBA
They Softly Walk. Hugh Robert Orr. MaRV; OQP
They sold me candles by the pound. Candlemas. Hugh Francis Blunt. JKCP (1955 ed.)
They spat in his face and hewed him a cross. Men Follow Simon. Raymond Kresensky. ChIP; OQP
They Speak o' Wiles. William Thom. HBV
They speak of time, as if the hour were split. Madaket Beach. Isabel Harriss Barr. GoYe
They splayed him scientifically on the rock. Prometheus, with Wings. Michael Ondaatje. PeCV (1967 ed.)
They spoke of Progress spiring round. A Ballade of an Anti-Puritan. G. K. Chesterton. BOHV
They spoke of the horse alive. The Horse. Philip Levine. CoAP
They stand like penitential Augustines. Gothic Landscape. Irving Layton. TrJP
They step through the moonlight. In the Moonlight. Kenneth Patchen. ToPo
They stood above the world. Yes. Richard Doddridge Blackmore. HBV
They stood on the bridge at midnight. How Often. Ben King. BOHV; HBV
They strolled down the lane together. A Farmer's Boy. *Unknown.* MemP
They sung how God spoke out the worlds vast ball. The Creation. Abraham Cowley. *Fr.* Davideis. OBS
They take no shame for dark defeat. The Fortitude of the North. Herman Melville. AmePo
They take their stand, each rising. The Boxing Match. Vergil. *Fr.* The Aeneid. SD
They talk about you as if you were alive. To a War Poet, on Teaching Him in a New Country. D. J. Enright. ML
They talk as slow as legends grow. Emily Dickinson. MWA-2
They talk of short-lived pleasure—be it so. Mutation. Bryant. AmPP (3d ed.)
They talked of their concerts, and singers, and scores. The Fancy Concert. Leigh Hunt. MuSP
They teeter with an inane care among the skewbald stones. The Sheep. Hal Porter. NeLNL; PoAu-2
They tell me (but I really can't). My Aunt's Spectre. Mortimer Collins. BOHV
They tell me I am beautiful: they praise my silken hair. Sad Memories. Charles Stuart Calverley. CIV
They tell me, Liberty! that, in thy name. Liberty for All. William Lloyd Garrison. AA; AmePo
They tell me she is beautiful, my City. Dusk. DuBose Heyward. HBMV; HT
They tell me that euphoria is the feeling of feeling wonderful. No Doctors Today, Thank You. Ogden Nash. ShBV-4
They tell me that I must not love. Love Unsought. Emma Catherine Embury. AA
They tell me 'tis decided; you depart. Byron. *Fr.* Don Juan, I. ViBoPo
They tell themselves so many little lies, my beloved. Song of Industrial America. Sherwood Anderson. NP
They tell us of an Indian tree. To My Mother. Thomas Moore. OHIP; PEDC; PoRL
They tell you Lincoln was ungainly, plain? His Face. Florence Earle Coates. OHIP
They tell you that Death's at the turn of the road. The Unillu-

mined Verge. Robert Bridges. AA
They tell you the poet is useless and empty the sound of his lyre. The Poet. Bernard O'Dowd. BoAu
They That Go Down to the Sea in Ships. Psalms, CVII, Bible, *O.T.* BBV (1951 ed.) (23-31); ChTr (23-31); EtS (23-30); FaPON (23-24); GaP (23-24); WaKn (23-30)
(Ocean, The, 23-32, *Moulton, Modern Readers Bible.*) WGRP
They that have power to hurt, and will do none. Sonnets, XCIV. Shakespeare. AnFE; BoLiVe; BWP; CABA; CBEP; ElL; ExPo; FaBoEn; FosPo; GTBS; GTBS-D; GTBS-P; GTBS-W; GTSE; GTSL; LiTB; LiTG; MaPo; MasP; MemP; NoP; OBEV; PG (1955 ed.); PoEL-2; PoeP; PoG; PoIE; PoSa; ReEn; Sonn; TrGrPo; ViBoPo
They, that in course of heavenly spheres are skilled. Amoretti, LX. Spenser. Sonn
They that never had the use. An Apologie [*or* Apology] for Having Loved Before. Edmund Waller. MePo; OAEP
They That Wait upon the Lord. Isaiah, XL: 28-31, Bible, *O.T.* TRV
("Hast thou not known? hast thou not heard, that the everlasting God," XL: 28-31; XLIX: 13-16.) BoC
(Power from God.) TreFT
They that wash on Monday. Mother Goose. FaBoBe; HBV; HBVY; OTPC (1946 ed.); PPL; TreF
They thought to kill old Socrates: instead. Bringers of the Hemlock. Stanton A. Coblentz. ChIP
They threw a stone, you threw a stone. After the Martyrdom. Scharmel Iris. ChIP; MaRV
They throw in Drummer Hodge, to rest. Drummer Hodge. Thomas Hardy. AWP; BrPo; CoBMV; EnL; GTBS-P; ILP; InPo; JAWP; MaPo (1969 ed.); NoP; PoE; PoeP; POTE; PoVP; SeCeV; ViPo; VP; WBP
They tied my mother's legs when I was born. Years Later. Laurence Lerner. PeSA
They tinkle laughter at the solemn hills. Spring Song of Aspens. Lilian White Spencer. PoOW
They Toil Not neither Do They Spin. Christina Rossetti. *See* Prayer, A: "Clother of the lily. . ."
They told her she had hair the colour. Daphne. Hildegarde Flanner. HBMV
They told him gently he was made. Man's Place in Nature. *Unknown.* BOHV
They told me first she was a tree. Girl. Dom Moraes. NePoEA-2
They told me, Heraclitus, they told me you were dead. Heraclitus. William Johnson Cory, *after* Callimachus. AWP; CBEP; ELU; EnLi-1; GTBS; GTBS-D; GTSE; GTSL; HBV; JAWP; ML; OBEV; OBNC; OBVV; OuHeWo; PCD; PoRA; SeCePo; ShBV-4; TOP; TreF; VA; ViBoPo; WBP; WePo; WoL
They told me I was heir: I turned in haste. My Legacy. Helen Hunt Jackson. HBV
They told me in their shadowy phrase. To Alfred Tennyson. Robert Stephen Hawker. VA
They told me that Life could be just what I made it. Life. Nan Terrell Reed. BLPA
They told me when I came. The Shoe Factory. Ruth Harwood. HBMV
They told me you had been to her. Evidence Read at the Trial of the Knave of Hearts. "Lewis Carroll." *Fr.* Alice's Adventures in Wonderland. FaFP; GTBS-P; LiTG; NBM; OxBoLi; SiTL
They told us that the King was coming up to see the base. The Inspection. Frederick B. Watt. CaP
They took him out to die. "And When He Had Scourged Jesus, He Delivered Him to Be Crucified." W. H. Rodgers. WePo
They took him to a mountain top to see. Temptation. Winfred Ernest Garrison. ChIP
They took John Henry to the steep hillside. If I Die a Railroad Man. *Unknown.* AS
They took me from the white sun and they. "A Little Boy Lost." Jerome Rothenberg. CoPo
They tore down the toll-gate. The Toll-Gate Man. Wilson MacDonald. CaP
They tore me down and flushed. Body Job. John Stevens Wade. ThO
They travelled like a blue pencil against the stars. In Praise of Antonioni. Stephen Holden. NYBP
They tried to evolve a sphere. Succumbing. Paul Eaton Reeve. ErPo
They trod the streets and squares where now I tread. London Poets. Amy Levy. OBVV
They Two. Mrs. Frank A. Breck. WBLP
They two had unbridled the horses. Robinson Jeffers. *Fr.* Tamar. AnAmPo
They visit me and I attempt to keep. The Visitors. Elizabeth Jennings. BoPe
They wait all day unseen by us, unfelt. The Stars. Mary Mapes Dodge. AA
They walk against a hueless sky. Farm Couple, after Norman Rockwell. Barry Spacks. NYTB
They walk dangerously. The Home. Susan Axelrod. QAH
They walk with surer step the paths of men. Motherhood. Karl M. Chworowsky. PGD
They walked along together side by side. My Boy and His Saviour. William C. Fisher. SoP
They walked by the frolicking sea. Amber. Holger Drachmann. LiTW
They walked in the green wood, wild snows, soft, unchilling. The Flowering Forest. Edith Sitwell. SiSw
They warned Our Lady for the Child. Our Lord and Our Lady. Hilaire Belloc. GoBC; HBMV; ISi; JKCP; WHL
They was a lawyer from Fredericton came. Perigoo's Horse. *At. to* George Calhoun *and to* John Calhoun. ShS
They was twenty men on the Cabbage Rose. The Fate of the Cabbage Rose. Wallace Irwin. FiBHP
They Watched Him There. Shirley Elizabeth Reitz. SoP
They wear air. Naked in Borneo. May Swenson. NYBP
They wear their evening light as women wear. Fields at Evening. David Morton. AnAmPo; HBMV
They Went Forth to Battle, but They Always Fell. Shaemas O'Sheel. AnAmPo; AnFE; APA; CoAnAm; HBV; JKCP; LiTM (1946 ed.); MaRV; OQP; WaaP; WGRP
They went off on the buckboard in the rain. Ranchers. Maurice Lesemann. NP
They went to sea in a Sieve, they did. The Jumblies. Edward Lear. BOHV; ChTr; EnLi-2 (1949 ed.); EvOK; FaBoBe; FaFP; GFA; GoJo; HBV; HBVY; LBN; LiTB; NA; OnMSP; OtMeF; OTPC; OxBoLi; PeVV; PoE; PoRA; PoVP; RIS; SAS; SeCeV; SiTL; SoPo; TiPo; VA; WiR
They went with axe and rifle, when the trail was still to blaze. Western Wagons. Stephen Vincent Benét. WaKn
They went with songs to the battle. Laurence Binyon. *Fr.* For the Fallen. ViBoPo
They were a lovely pack for looks. John Masefield. *Fr.* Reynard the Fox. OtMeF
They Were All like Geniuses. Horace Gregory. The Passion of M'Phail, IV. NYBP
("Lunchroom bus boy who looked like Orson Welles, The.") TwAmPo
They were approaching the region where reigns perpetual summer. Longfellow. *Fr.* Evangeline. FaBoEn
They were at play, she and her cat. Femme et chatte [*or* Woman and Cat]. Paul Verlaine. AWP; JAWP; OnPM; WBP; WoL
They were hopeful of a curtain raiser. Because in This Sorrowing Statue of Flesh. Kenneth Patchen. NaP
They were islanders, our fathers were. Knowledge. Frederick George Scott. VA
They were met in the Last Inn's tap-room, where the road strikes hands with the sea. Wayfarers. Dana Burnet. EtS
They Were Only Playing Leapfrog. *Unknown.* SiTL
They were the people, those who. The Broken String. *Unknown.* PeSA
They Were Welcome to Their Belief. Robert Frost. AtBAP
They wheeled me up the snow-cleared gardenway. Elfin Skates. Eugene Lee-Hamilton. OBVV
They which read Horace, Virgil, and the rest. Thomas Bastard. SiCE
They whispered when she passed—gave knowing looks. The Sinner. Margaret E. Bruner. PoToHe
They whisted all, with fixèd face attent. Certain Books of Virgil's Aeneis. Vergil, *tr. by* the Earl of Surrey. *Fr.* The Aeneid, II. EnLi-1; FCP; LiTB; SiCE; SiPS; TuPP
They who create rob death of half its stings. The Sovereigns [*or* Sovereign Poets]. Lloyd Mifflin. AA; AnAmPo; HBV; WGRP
They, who have best succeeded on the stage. Epilogue. Dryden. *Fr.* The Conquest of Granada, Pt. II. CEP; EiCL; EiPP; FiP; MBW-1; SeCV-2; SeEP
They who once probed and doubted now believe. Beyond Elec-

They (continued)
trons. Adelaide P. Love. OQP
They Who Possess the Sea. Marguerite Janvrin Adams. EtS
They Who Tread the Path of Labor. Henry van Dyke. SoP; TRV
They Who Wait. Charles Buxton Going. HBMV
They whose life is given utterly over to valor. Epitaph: Inscription from Anticyra. *Unknown.* WaaP
They will be telling you soon who you are. Arsenic. Howard Moss. CoAP; NYBP
They will come no more. I Vecchi. Ezra Pound. PoIE
They Will Look for a Few Words. Nancy Byrd Turner. AmFN
They will never die on that battlefield. Uccello. Gregory Corso. NeAP
They will take us from the moorings, they will tow us down the Bay. Homeward Bound. D. H. Rogers. AnNZ; BoAu; EtS
They wind a thousand soldiers round the king. A Ribbon Two Yards Wide. Alfred Kreymborg. HBMV
They wondered why the fruit had been forbidden. W. H. Auden. *Fr.* In Time of War. CMoP; Sonn
They wore it walking Sunday, three small men. Spanish Blue. Herbert Morris. NYBP
They would have fought again/ Had not the Major stepped between the men. The Shooting of the Cup. John G. Neihardt. *Fr.* The Song of Three Friends. PoOW
They wove for me a little cloak. Codes. Lois Seyster Montross. HBMV
They wrought a pillar from the rock of sacred stone. The High Place at Marib. Grant Code. FiSC
They'd make you believe that your problem is one of sex. The New Being. Kenneth Patchen. ToPo
They'll come again to the apple tree. The Building of the Nest. Margaret Elizabeth Sangster. DD; HBV; HBVY
They'll never fish again in quiet inland lakes. Pearl Harbor. John C. Frolicher. OTD
They'll None of 'em Be Missed. W. S. Gilbert. *See* Ko-Ko's Song ("As some day it may happen").
They'll soon be flying to Mars, I hear. Progress. Samuel Hoffenstein. ThLM
They'll Tell You about Me. Ian Mudie. PoAu-2
They'll walk no longer to Mass on Sunday. The Shawls. Monk Gibbon. NeIP; OxBI
They're altogether otherworldly now. Grandparents. Robert Lowell. LiTM (1970 ed.); ToPo
They're always abusing the women. Chorus of Women. Aristophanes. *Fr.* Thesmophoriazusae. BOHV
They're big. Grownups. William Wise. TiPo (1959 ed.)
They're building a skyscraper. Building a Skyscraper. James S. Tippett. MPB
They're changing guard at Buckingham Palace. Buckingham Palace. A. A. Milne. PDV
They're hiding by the pebbles. Sea Fairies. Eileen Mathias. BoTP
They're holding a revival at New Hope Meeting house. The Mourner's Bench. Edgar Lee Masters. CMoP
They're nice—one would never dream of going over. A Healthy Spot. W. H. Auden. EnLit
They're out of the dark's ragbag, these two. Blue Moles. Sylvia Plath. NePoEA-2; PoAn
They're Shifting Father's Grave. *Unknown.* CoMu
They're taking down a tree at the front door. Learning by Doing. Howard Nemerov. TwCP
They're taking me to the gallows, mother—they mean to hang me high. Death-Doomed. Will Carleton. PaPo
They're tunin' up the orchestray down at old Bill Haller's. Bill Haller's Dance. Robert V. Carr. PoOW
They've builded wooden timber tracks. Progress. Frank Wilmot. BoAu
They've Crucified Our Lord. Alice Mortenson. BePJ
They've got a brand-new organ, Sue. The New Church Organ. Will M. Carleton. BOHV; PoLF
They've got some pretty horses up in the long dark mountains. Now I Went Down to the Ringside and Little Henry Armstrong was There. Kenneth Patchen. ToPo
They've left Thee naked, Lord; O that they had. *See* They have left thee naked, Lord; O that they had!
They've marched them out of old Yorktown, the vanquished redcoat host. The Ride of Tench Tilghman. Clinton Scollard. MC
They've paid the last respects in sad tobacco. Padraic O'Conaire —Gaelic Storyteller. F. R. Higgins. OBMV; OnYI; OxBI
They've putten her into prison strang. Sir Aldingar (C *vers.*). *Unknown.* ESPB
They've taken the cosy bed away. Kit's Cradle. Juliana Horatia Ewing. CIV; SAS
They've turned at last! Good-by, King George. Haarlem Heights. Arthur Guiterman. PAH
Thick and stormy was the night. My Delight. Gamaliel Bradford. HBMV
Thick Grows the Tarragon. *Unknown, tr. fr. Chinese by* Arthur Waley. *Fr.* The Book of Songs. HW
Thick in its glass. Poor Henry. Walter de la Mare. HBMV
Thick lids of Night closed upon me, The. The Souls of the Slain. Thomas Hardy. CMoP; LiTB; PoEL-5; PoVP; ViPo (1962 ed.)
Thick rise the spear-shafts o'er the land. The Burghers' Battle. William Morris. PoVP; VA
Thick trees swallow a mountain trail. The Temple. Tu Fu. OnPM
Thick wool is muslin to-night and the wire. A Cold Night. Bernard Spencer. WaP
Thickness of paint or flesh cannot deface. Sestina on Her Portrait. Howard Nemerov. WaP
Thief, The. Abraham Cowley. *Fr.* The Mistress. BEL; EnLi-1; EnLit; OAEP; SeCL; WHA
Thief. Robert Graves. POTE
Thief, The. Stanley Kunitz. MoAmPo (1962 ed.)
Thief, The. Irene F. Pawsey. BoTP
Thief ("A maiden caught stealing a dahlia"). *Unknown.* BBGG
Thief, The ("Say, bold but blessed thief"). *Unknown.* LO; OBS; OxBoCh; SeCL
Thief, The, in me is running a/ round in circles. Zapata & the Landlord. Alfred B. Spellman. NNP
Thief on the Cross, The. Harriet Monroe. OQP
Thiepval Wood. Edmund Blunden. AnFE; MMA
Thieves. Perseus Adams. ACV
Thieves, The. Robert Graves. CBV; CMoP; GTBS-P; GTBS-W; LiTM (rev. ed.); OxBI
Thieves and the Ass, The. La Fontaine, *tr. fr. French by* Elizur Wright. OnPM
Thieves of Love, The. R. A. D. Ford. PeCV (1967 ed.)
Thieving locksmith died of late, A. On a Thieving Locksmith. *Unknown.* GoTP
Thin air I breathe and birds use for flying. Air. Edwin Denby. ANYP; CrMA
Thin are the night-skirts left behind. Insomnia. Dante Gabriel Rossetti. PoVP
Thin birches stood on Stockholm's nesses. Visual Memory. Harry Martinson. LiTW
Thin, erect and silent. Alone. Elsie Laurence. CaP
Thin Facade for Edith Sitwell, A. John Malcolm Brinnin. FiBHP; NYBP
Thin Fox/ sidled by with his stingy shadow, A. Dead Center. Ruth Whitman. NYBP
Thin gray shadow on the edge of thought, A. Apparitions. Alice Corbin. NP
Thin ice/ Free advice. David McCord. TiPo (1959 ed.)
Thin-legged, thin-chested, slight unspeakably. Apparition. W. E. Henley. *Fr.* In Hospital. BEL; EnLi-2 (1949 ed.); PoVP; TrGrPo
Thin Man, a Sculpture, The. George Murray. NYTB
Thin Potomac scarcely moves, The. The Potomac. Karl Shapiro. AP; CoBMV; ToPo
Thin rain seeps along the apple boughs, A. Sonnets from a Sequence, XXI. Shirley Barker. AnAmPo
Thin rank at regular intervals lines, A. The Proud Trees. Walter H. Kerr. NePoAm-2
Thin steel in paired lines, forever mated, cuts. North Philadelphia, Trenton, and New York. Richmond Lattimore. NYBP
Thin under the arc lights. Tennis in San Juan. Reuel Denney. SD
Thin wind seemed uneasy, The. The Gallows Tree. F. R. Higgins. OnYI
Thin wool coat was the jew of him, A. The Victim. Barbara L. Greenberg. QAH
Thine arms, O Mother, be outspread. Inscription on a Shrine near Ischl. Elizabeth, Empress of Austria-Hungary. CAW
Thine be those motions strong and sanative. To Coleridge in

Sicily. Wordsworth. *Fr.* The Prelude, XI. OBNC
Thine elder that I am, thou must not cling. Sweeter Far Than the Harp, More Gold Than Gold. "Michael Field." OBMV; PeVV
Thine emulous, fond flowers are dead too. Robert Frost. AmePo
Thine eyes, dear one, dot dot, are like, dash, what? Lovelilts. Marion Hill. BOHV
Thine eyes I love, and they, as pitying me. Sonnets, CXXXII. Shakespeare. OAEP; OBSC; SiCE
Thine eyes shall see the light of distant skies. To Cole, the Painter, Departing for Europe. Bryant. AmePo; AmPP (4th ed.); AP; MAmP; MWA-1
Thine is the mystic melody. Coleridge. George Sidney Hellman. AA
Thine old world eyes—each one a violet. On a Miniature. Henry Augustin Beers. AA
Thine was the corn and the wine. The Bells of San Gabriel. Charles Warren Stoddard. CAW; JKCP
Thing, The. Theodore Roethke. TDP
Thing could barely stand, The. Yet taken. The Bull Calf. Irving Layton. OBCV; PeCV
"Thing is but a statue after all, The!" W. S. Gilbert. *Fr.* Pygmalion and Galatea. VA
Thing Is Violent, The. Gwendolyn MacEwen. MoCV; PeCV (1967 ed.)
Thing itself was rough and crudely done, The. The Knight in the Wood. Lord De Tabley. NCEP; PeVV
Thing Made Real, The. Ron Loewinsohn. NeAP
Thing of Beauty, A [Is a Joy Forever]. Keats. *Fr.* Endymion, I. ATP; BBV (1951 ed.), *br. sel.*; BEL; BoC; BoLiVe; CoBE; CTC; EnLi-2; EnLit; EnRP; FaBV; FaFP; FiP; ILP; LiTB; LiTG; MaRV; MBW-2; MCCG; MERP; NeHB, 6 *ll.*; OAEP; OBNC; OBRV; OTPC; OuHeWo; PG; PoeP; PoPl; PTK; SoP; StVeCh, 5 *ll.*; TOP; TreF; TrGrPo; TRV; ViBoPo; YAT
Thing one learns too much, The. Learning. Mary Fullerton. NeLNL
Thing Remembered, A. *Unknown. tr. fr. Arabic by* E. Powys Mathers. ErPo
Thing that goes the farthest towards making life worth while, The. Let Us Smile [*or* Smile]. Wilbur D. Nesbit. SoP; WBLP
Thing that numbs the heart is this, The. Firm Belief. *Unknown.* PoToHe (new ed.)
Thing that's rich in tears is sweet, A. Born of Tears. W. H. Davies. GTBS-D
Thing We Long For, The. James Russell Lowell. *Fr.* Longing. OQP
Thing which fades, A. Ono no Komachi. *Fr.* Kokin Shu. AWP; JAWP
Thing You Leave Undone, The. *At. to* Adelaide Procter. FaChP
Things. Dorothy Dow. HBMV
Things. Aline Kilmer. MCCG
Things. William Jay Smith. TiPo (1959 ed.)
Things being what they are do not imply necessity. Theodore Enslin. Forms, LXXVII. CoPo
Things come out. City Summer. Lou Lipsitz. YAP
Things concentrate at the edges; the pond-surface. Marginalia. Richard Wilbur. CMoP; NMP
Things Dead. Marcel Schwob, *tr. fr. French by* William Brown Meloney. TrJP
Things did not vibrate so when I was young. Lines Written in a Moment of Vibrant Ill-Health. Morris Bishop. WhC
Things I Like. Marjorie H. Greenfield. BoTP
Things I Miss, The. Thomas Wentworth Higginson. TrPWD (Thank Thee.) SoP
Things I Prize, The. Henry van Dyke. TreFT
Things I Used to Do, *with music. Unknown.* AS
Things Kept. William Dickey. NYBP
Things Lovelier. Humbert Wolfe. MoBrPo; TrJP
Things native sweetly grew. Thomas Traherne. *Fr.* Christendom. FaBoEn
Things never changed since the Time of the Gods. Four Folk-Songs in Hokku Form, 1. *Unknown.* LiTW
Things Not Seen. Mark Turbyfill. NP
Things of every day are all so sweet, The Life's Common Things. Alice E. Allen. WBLP
Things of the Spirit, The. Douglas Malloch. MaRV
Things of worth we pay for not at all, The. Worthwhile Things Are Free. Charles E. Glazer. SoP
Things That Are Caesar's, The. St. Matthew, XXII: 15-22, Bible, *N.T.* TreF
Things that are lovely. Things. Dorothy Dow. HBMV
"Things That Are More Excellent, The." Sir William Watson. OHFP
Things that can bless a life, and please. Contentment. Martial. CavP
Things That Cause a Quiet Life, The. Martial. *See* Means to Attain Happy Life, The.
Things That Count. *Unknown.* SoP
Things That Endure, The, *sel.* Florence Wilkinson Evans. "What wish you, immortality?" OQP
Things That Endure. Ted Olson. WBLP
Things that make a life to please, The. The Means to Attain Happy Life. Martial. WoL
Things that make a virgin please, The. The Virgin. Katherine Philips. LO
Things that make the happier life, are these, The. Epigram. Martial. EP
Things That Never Die. Charles Dickens. MaRV; SoP
Things to Do around a Lookout. Gary Snyder. NaP
Things to Do around Kyoto. Gary Snyder. NaP
Things to Learn About. John Becker. RePo
Things to Remember. Blake. *See* Robin Redbreast, A.
Things We Can't Afford. *Unknown.* SoP
Things We Dreamt We Died For. Marvin Bell. CoAP; YAP
Things you heard that blessed be. Grenstone River. Witter Bynner. PFY
Things You Left Behind. Gregory Orr. QAH
Thingumbob, The. *Unknown.* BOHV
Think. Charles Weekes. AnIV; OnYI
Think before You Act. Mary Elliott. HBVY
Think from how many trees. The Compost Heap. Vernon Watkins. NYBP
Think, in this batter'd Caravanserai. Omar Khayyám, *tr. by* Edward Fitzgerald. *Fr.* The Rubáiyát. ChTr; OBVV
Think it not idolatry. In Gusts of Music. Sister Davida. JKCP (1955 ed.)
Think It Not Strange. Amy Carmichael. MaRV
Think It Over. *Unknown.* SoP; STF
Think, Man of Flesh, and be not proud. Speed. W. H. Davies. MoRP
Think me not unkind and rude. The Apology. Emerson. AmePo; AmPP (3d ed.); AP; CLwM; CoBA; PG (1945 ed.)
Think naught a trifle. *Unknown.* PoToHe (new ed.)
Think no evil, have no fear. Phyllis. *Unknown.* UnTE
Think No More Lad [Laugh, Be Jolly]. A. E. Housman. A Shropshire Lad, XLIX. CABA; CMoP; InP; InPo; PoPo; PoVP (Laugh, Be Jolly.) WePo
Think not, because I wonder where you fled. Another Dark Lady. E. A. Robinson. CLwM
Think not I may not know thee kneeling there. Dusk. Archibald MacLeish. HBMV
Think not, my dearest, though I love to speak. Gothic. Louis Untermeyer. AnAmPo
Think not, my Phoebe [*or* Phebe], 'cause a cloud. To His Mistress [*or* Mistris] Confined. James Shirley. LO; OBS; SeCL
Think not, O man that dwells therein. Upon the New-built House at Appleton. Thomas, Lord Fairfax. SeCL
Think not on me, as countless men have thought. Christ Speaks. Wade Oliver. MaRV
Think not that I for pride and stubbornness. Prometheus the Teacher of Men. Aeschylus. *Fr.* Prometheus Bound. LiTW
Think not that incense-smoke has had its day. Incense. Vachel Lindsay. MoRP
Think of—/ Stepping on shore, and finding it Heaven! Heaven. *Unknown.* PoLF
Think of all the games you play. Trees Used in Games and Sports. Mary Isabel Curtis. GFA
Think of all the people. The World's So Big. Aileen Fisher. SoPo
Think of Dress in Every Light. John Gay. *Fr.* Achilles. InvP (Song.) OBEC
Think of each house you stay in as a tent. Campers. Robert Finch. TwCaPo
Think of Eight Numbers. Shelley Silverstein. BBGG
Think of me as your friend. The Heart's Anchor. William Winter. PoToHe
Think of only now, and how this pencil. The Promontory Moment. May Swenson. NYBP

Think of the jungle. What to Think Of. Mark Strand. YAP
Think of the storm roaming the sky uneasily. Little Exercise [at 4 A.M.]. Elizabeth Bishop. CBV; CoAP; CrMA; MoAB; MoAmPo (1950 ed.); NYBP; UnPo (3d ed.)
Think of the things that make you happy. Thinking Happiness. Robert E. Farley. PoToHe
Think on St. Francis' feathered friends, dear heart. "That Which Hath Wings Shall Tell." Linda Lyon Van Voorhis. GoBC
Think on These Things. Philippians, IV: 8, Bible, *N.T.* TreFT
("Whatsoever things are true.") TiPo (1952 ed.)
Think that this world against the wind of time. Signature for Tempo. Archibald MacLeish. MoVE
Think, the ragged turf-boy urges. Think. Charles Weekes. AnIV; OnYI
Think [*or* Thinke] then, my soul, that death is but a groom. John Donne. *Fr.* Of the Progresse of the Soule; the Second Anniversary. OBS; OxBoCh
Think thou and act; tomorrow thou shalt die. The Choice, 3. Dante Gabriel Rossetti. The House of Life, LXXIII. ATP; BEL; EnL; EnLi-2; GTBS-P; HBV; MaVP; MyFE; OBEV (new ed.); OBVV; OHIP; PoVP; TOP; ViBoPo; ViPo; WHA
Think upon death, 'tis good to think of death. Hartley Coleridge. Sonn
Think what you like, but. You and It. Mark Strand. NYBP
Think, when a starry night of bitter frost. A Sonnet. Conrad Aiken. AnEnPo
Think ye the joys that fill our early day. Life. George Crabbe. OBEC
Think you I am not fiend and savage too? To the White Fiends. Claude McKay. BANP
Think you 'mid all this mighty sum. Communion with Nature. Wordsworth. *Fr.* Expostulation and Reply. MaRV
Think you the dead are lonely in that place? The Dead. David Morton. PAH
Think you to escape. Immunity. Thomas à Kempis. *Fr.* Imitation of Christ. ChIP; OQP
Thinke not cause men flatt'ring say. To A.L.: Perswasions to Love. Thomas Carew. AnAnS-2; SeCP
Thinke then, my soule, that death is but a groome. *See* Think then, my soul, that death is but a groom.
Thinker, The. Berton Braley. BLPA; NeHB; OQP; PEDC; PoMa; StVeCh (1940 ed.); WBLP
Thinker, The. Anthony Delius. PeSA
Thinker, The. William Carlos Williams. MoLP
Thinkers and airmen—all such. To Poets and Airmen. Stephen Spender. WaP
Thinking. Walter D. Wintle. WBLP
(Man Who Thinks He Can.) PoLF
Thinking about the Unthinkable. Barbara Gibson. WOW
Thinking Happiness. Robert E. Farley. PoToHe
Thinking of a Master. Richard Church. HaMV
Thinking of Hölderlin. Christopher Middleton. NePoEA-2
Thinking of My Brothers. Tu Fu, *tr. fr. Chinese by* W. J. B. Fletcher. OnPM
Thinking of Our Visits. Craig Sterry. QAH
Thinking of words that would save him, slanting. Finding Them Lost. Howard Moss. CoAP; NYBP
Thinking of you, and all that was, and all. Monna Innominata, IX. Christina Rossetti. ViPo; VP
Thinking of you, I think of the *coureurs de bois.* Coureurs de Bois. Douglas Le Pan. CaP; MoCV
Thinking on thee, thy beauties then. Sir John Suckling. LO
Thinking tomorrow remains, thou heart's frail flower-of-cherry. Four Folk-Songs in Hokku Form, 2. *Unknown.* LiTW
Think'st Thou, Kate? Unknown. TuPP
Think'st thou that this love can stand. Ametas and Thestylis Making Hay-Ropes. Andrew Marvell. ALV; CavP; InvP; MaMe; SeCL; SeCP
Think'st Thou to Seduce Me Then. Thomas Campion. EIL; NoP
Thir Lenterne Dayis Ar Luvely Lang. *At. to* William Stewart. OxBS
Third and Fourth. Keidrych Rhys. NeBP
Third Avenue in Sunlight. Anthony Hecht. CoAP; NePoEA-2
Third Century, The, *sels.* Thomas Traherne.
"Life of Sabbaths here beneath, A!" MeP
On News. MeP
Recovery, The. AnAnS-1; MeP
"Sin!/ O only fatal Woe." AnAnS-1; MeP
"That childish thoughts such joys inspire." AnAnS-1; MeP
(Approach, The.) OxBoCh
Third Continent, The. Mary Erulkar. ACV
Third Cycle of Love Poems, *sels.* George Barker.
Shut the Seven Seas against Us. MoAB; MoBrPo (1950 ed.); NeMA
"This is that month, Elizabeth." NeBP
3rd Dance—Making a Structure with a Roof or under a Roof—6-7 February 1964. Jackson MacLow. CoPo
Third Day, The. Edith Lovejoy Pierce. MoRP
Third Dimension, The. Denise Levertov. NeAP
Third Duino Elegy, The. Rainer Maria Rilke, *tr. fr. German by* Stephen Spender and J. B. Leishman. LiTW
Third Eclogue, The, Michael Drayton. *See* Song to Beta.
Third Enemy Speaks. C. Day Lewis. *Fr.* The Magnetic Mountain. EaLo
Third Eye, The. Jay Macpherson. MoCV
Third Generation, The. Denise Levertov. CBV
Third-grade angels, two by two, The. Christmas Pageant. Margaret Fishback. PoSC
Third hour's deafen'd with the cry, The. Richard Crashaw. *Fr.* The Office of the Holy Cross. PoG
Third in our Borough's list appears the sign. The Caroline. George Crabbe. *Fr.* The Borough. SeCePo
Third Limick. Ogden Nash. NePA
Third Madrigal. Gene Derwood. NePA
Third night after wedding, The. The Newlyweds' Cuisine. Wang Chien. HW
Third of February, The, 1852. Tennyson. PoFr
Third Proposition, The. "Madeline Bridges." BOHV
Third Row, Centre. William Rose Benét. WhC
Third Sunday after Easter, The, and the first dominical day of the white month of Mary. Ave Maria. Henriette Charasson. CAW; ISi
Third Wonder, The. Edwin Markham. MAP
(Breathless Awe.) MaRV
Thirsis a youth of the inspired train. *See* Thyrsis, a youth . . .
Thirst. Emily Dickinson. *See* We thirst at first—'tis nature's act.
Thirst of reign and sweetness of a crown, The. Christopher Marlowe. *Fr.* Tamburlaine the Great. ViBoPo
Thirst Song. Denise Levertov. FRC
Thirsty earth soaks up the rain, The. Drinking [*or* Anacreontic on Drinking]. Abraham Crowley. ALV; CEP; EG; EnLi-1 (1949 ed.); HBV; LoBV; MePo; NoP; OBEV; OtMeF; PG; PoFS; ReEn; SCEP-2; SeCePo; SeCV-1; SeEP; ShBV-4; TDP; TrGrPo; WhC; WiR
Thirsty Flowers. Arthur A. Knipe. GFA
Thirsty Poet, The. John Philips. *Fr.* The Splendid Shilling. OBEC
Thirteen o'Clock. Kenneth Fearing. ExPo
Thirteen Sisters, The. Stephen Vincent Benét. *Fr.* John Brown's Body, I. TreF
Thirteen Ways of Looking at a Blackbird. Wallace Stevens. AP; CABA; CMoP; CoBMV; DiPo; LiTM; MAPA; MaPo (1969 ed.); PoeP; PoFS; PoSa; TDP; TwAmPo
Thirteen's no age at all. Thirteen is nothing. Portrait of a Girl with Comic Book. Phyllis McGinley. CrMA
13th Dance—Matching Parcels—21 February 1964. Jackson MacLow. CoPo
Thirteenth one returns, The. . .Yet she's the first. Artemis. Gérard de Nerval, *tr. by* Hubert Creekmore. LiTW
Thirteenth Song, The, *abr.* Michael Drayton. *Fr.* Polyolbion. ReEn
Sels.
Forest of Arden ("My native country then, which so brave spirits hast bred"). SeEP
"Forest so much fallen from what she was before, The." SeCePo
"Of all the beasts." OBS
"Upon the midlands now th' industrious muse doth fall." ReIE; TuPP
"When Phoebus lifts his head." OBS
Thirteenth Station. William A. Donaghy. *Fr.* The Stations of the Cross. ISi
Thirty Bob a Week. John Davidson. CABL; FaBoTw; FaFP; LiTB; LiTG; LiTM (rev ed.); NBM; OBNC; OxBS; PoFr, *abr.*; PoVP; TIHL

"I step into my heart and there I meet," *sel.* ELU
Thirty days hath September. Mother Goose. FaBoBe; GoTP; HBV; HBVY; OTPC (1946 ed.); OxNR; PCH; PPL; RIS; SiTL; SoPo; StVeCh; TreFT
.38, The. Ted Joans. NNP
Thirty elongated seconds. For Dinah, the Adeneys' Cat. Anne Wilkinson. PeCV
Thirty-first of May. Frederick Tennyson. VA
Thirty Pieces of Silver. William Blane. SoP
Thirty Pieces of Silver for Jesus. Helene Mullins. StJW
37th Dance—Banding—22 March 1964. Jackson MacLow. CoPo
33. Adrienne Rich. CoPo
Thirty-three Ring Circus, The. John Logan. FRC
Thirty today, I saw. A Birthday Candle. Donald Justice. NYBP
Thirty-two years since, up against the sun. Zermatt: To the Matterhorn. Thomas Hardy. OBNC
Thirty [*or* Twenty] white horses upon a red hill. Mother Goose. HBV; HBVY; OTPC; OxNR; PPL; RIS; SiTL; SoPo; StVeCh; TiPo
Thirty years after. A Second Attempt. Thomas Hardy. MaPo (1969 ed.)
Thirty years ago lying awake. Cornet Solo. C. Day Lewis. MuSP
This/ ocean tougher than anything. At the Edge. Sister Mary Norbert Körte. ThO
This:/ That is my straight-flying fury. Witch Hazel. Theodore Enslin. CoPo
This a tale that the coachman told. The Coachman's Yarn. E. J. Brady. PoAu-1
This Above All. Shakespeare. *See* Polonius' Advice to Laertes.
This above All Is Precious and Remarkable. John Wain. LiTM (1970 ed.); ToPo
This Advent moon shines cold and clear. Advent. Christina Rossetti. PoVP
This ae nighte, this ae nighte. A Lyke-Wake Dirge [*or* Cleveland Lyke-Wake Dirge *or* Final Dirge]. *Unknown.* ACP; AnFE; AtBAP; BuBa; CBEP; CH; ChTr; EaLo; EnSB; EvOk; FaBoCh; FIW; GoBC; HBV; HoPM; LoBV; NoP; OBB; OBEV; OtMeF; OxBoCh; PoEL-1; PoLi; SeCeV; ShBV-2
This afternoon. The Giving-In. Jon Anderson. YAP
This afternoon I swam with a school of fish. Sea School. Barbara Howes. NYBP
This afternoon I take the path alone. In Loco. Peter Jackson. BoSA
This afternoon in loud Jerusalem. Fourth Station. William A. Donaghy. *Fr.* The Stations of the Cross. ISi
This age it is the same with less remembered. The Rape of Europa. R. P. Blackmur. CrMA
This age-old church, dream-stricken yesterday. The Serenade. Sister Mary Madeleva. Christmas in Provence, I. WHL
This Age, This Faust. George Reavey. SiTL
This ain't Torquemada. Dialect Quatrain. Marcus B. Christian. AmNP
This Air That Blows In from the Sea. Elizabeth J. Coatsworth. BrR
This Alice. Herbert Morris. PoRA
This almost bare tree is racing. November Through a Giant Copper Beech. Edwin Honig. NYBP
This also said Phocylides. A Small City on a Rock. Phocylides. WoL
This alum crystal. Alum. Richard Burns. NYTB
This Amber Sunstream. Mark Van Doren. GoYe; LiTA; LiTM (1946 ed.); MoPo; MoVE; TrGrPo (1942 ed.)
This America is an ancient land. Edgar Lee Masters. *Fr.* The New World. AmFN
This ancient hag. Mexican Market Woman. Langston Hughes. GaP; TiPo (1952 ed.)
This ancient silver bowl of mine, it tells of good old times. On Lending a Punch-Bowl. Oliver Wendell Holmes. AA; CAP; CoBA
This and More. Glenn Siebert. HW
This and That. Florence Boyce Davis. FaPON; GaP; TiPo (1952 ed.)
This animal, this sleek and beautiful ox ambling along the pleasant road. The Ox. Mary Morison Webster. PeSA
This Arrow. Dorothy Livesay. PeCV
This autumn day the new cross is set up. The Church. Edwin Muir. MoRP
This autumn, just before Thanksgiving hurries. Armistice. Margaret E. Sangster. PEDC
This autumn rainfall. November Rain. Maud E. Uschold. YeAr
This Bantu on a bicycle racing the sunset. Bantu on a Bicycle. Alan Ross. POTi
This Baptism with Fire. A. X. Nicholas. WSL
This baseness follows your profession. John Day. *Fr.* The Parliament of Bees. ViBoPo
This Be Our Revenge. Saul Tchernichowsky, *tr. fr. Hebrew by* Shalom Spiegel. TrJP
This bears the seal of immortality. The Living Book. Charlotte Fiske Bates. AA
This beauty made me dream there was a time. Sedge Warblers. Edward Thomas. LO
This bird is the keel-billed toucan. Limerick. Howard Ketcham. LiBL
This birthday man. It's Somebody's Birthday. Leslie Norris. NYTB
This black life. Spring Rain. William Hawkins. MoCV
This Blatant Beast was finally overcome. Saint. Robert Graves. CMoP
This Blessed Christ of Calvary. *Unknown.* STF
This Blessed Plot . . . This England. Shakespeare. *See* This England ("This royal throne").
This Blonde Girl. Kendrick Smithyman. AnNZ
This blue half circle of sea. Mersa. Keith Douglas. FaBoMo
This blue-washed, old, thatched summerhouse. The Old Summerhouse. Walter de la Mare. CMoP; GTBS-P; MoPo
This body is my house, it is not I. The Tenant [*or* My Faith]. Frederic Lawrence Knowles. OQP; SoP
This body of my mother, pierced by me. Epithalamium. Leo Kennedy. OBCV
This book is all that's left me now. My Mother's Bible. George Pope Morris. AA; BLRP; PaPo; SoP; WBLP
This book may seem, as it sorteth in suit. An Epigram on This Book of Epigrams. John Heywood. ReIE
This bookplate, that thou here seest put. Book & Bookplate. John Masefield. WhC
This Bread I Break [Was Once the Oat]. Dylan Thomas. FaBoTw; PAn; PoAn; PoIE
This brief common youth I was once in dread for it. Youth. Blanaid Salkeld. OxBI
This bronze doth keep the very form and mold. On the Life-Mask of Abraham Lincoln. Richard Watson Gilder. AA; HBV; PoRL
This busy, vast, inquiring soul. Insatiableness [*or* The Enquiring Soul]. Thomas Traherne. MaRV; VaPo
This California is a humbug state. California Humbugs. Mart Taylor. SGR
This careful head, with divers thoughts distressed. Parthenophil and Parthenophe, XCIX. Barnabe Barnes. TuPP
This case befell at four of the clock. The Six Carpenters' Case. Sir Frederick Pollock. VA
This celestial seascape, with white herons got up as angels. Seascape. Elizabeth Bishop. MoAB
This chair I trusted, lass, and I looted the leaves. Aristotle to Phyllis. John Hollander. PoCh
This Chauntecleer stood hye up-on his toos. Chaucer. *Fr.* The Canterbury Tales: The Nun's Priest's Tale. FiP
This cheerful picture shows the fate. The Jungle Pest. Roland Young. BOHV
This Child. Norman Rosten. TrJP
This child that God has given you. A Sunday School Teacher Speaks. *Unknown.* STF
This, chil-dren, is the famed Mon-goos. The Mongoos. Oliver Herford. *Fr.* Child's Natural History. AA; AmePo; HBV
This city and this country has brought forth many mayors. Good English Hospitality [*or* The Mayors]. Blake. *Fr.* An Island in the Moon. CH; CoMu
This city is the child of France and Spain. Vieux Carré. Walter Adolphe Roberts. PoNe
This claw remains alive. Painting of a Lobster by Picasso. Hy Sobiloff. NePA; TwAmPo
This clearing day. Blue on White. Elizabeth J. Coatsworth. RePo

This cluck of water in the tangles. The Voices of Nature. Thomas Edward Brown. PoVP
This Compost. Walt Whitman. AWP; CABA; LiTA; MAmP; MoAmPo (1950 ed.); MWA-1
This conduit stream that's tangled here and there. Zillebeke Brook. Edmund Blunden. MMA
This consciousness that is aware. Emily Dickinson. AP; MWA-2
This cool night is strange. Nocturne. Gwendolyn Bennett. BANP
This Corruptible. Elinor Wylie. AnFE; CoAnAm; MAP; MoAB; MoAmPo; MoRP
This could I paint my inward sight. Lines for a Drawing of Our Lady of the Night. Francis Thompson. ISi
This country might have. Right On: White America. Sonia Sanchez. BOLo; WSL
This country was not strange to me. Mirage at Mickleham. Francis Meynell. MemP
This Cross-Tree Here. Robert Herrick. BEL
This cruising caballero of the deep. Flying Fish. J. Corson Miller. EtS
This cursèd jealousy, what is't? Jealousy. Sir William Davenant. *Fr.* The Siege of Rhodes. BoLP; LO
This curve I'm plotting? The Parabola. H. Reynolds Goodwin. PoMa
This damsel was brought up to read and to write. The Female Warrior. *Unknown.* ShS
This darksome burn, horseback brown. Inversnaid. Gerard Manley Hopkins. ACP; BrPo; CABA; CMoP; FaBoMo; GTBS-P; GTBS-W; LiTB; LiTG; LiTM (rev. ed.); LoBV; MoAB; MoBrPo; PeVV; PIA; PoIE; PoRA; PoVP; ShBV-3; TDP; UnPo (3d ed.)
This dawn when the mountain-cherry lifts. Easter in the Woods. Frances Frost. BrR; SiSoSe
This Day. William Dean Howells. OTD
This day a year ago, to me. February Birthday. Nancy Byrd Turner. BiCB
This day day dawes. The Lily-white Rose. *Unknown.* MeEL
This day, I think, will be a common day. Help Me Today. Elsie Robinson. PoToHe
This day is for Israel light and rejoicing. A Sabbath of Rest. Isaac Luria. TrJP
This Day Is Thine. Verna Whinery. BLRP
This day might be. This Day. William Dean Howells. OTD
This day must Tita married be. Prothalamion. Michael Drayton. *Fr.* The Muses Elizium. HW
This day, O Father, give us daily bread. Francis Jammes. *Fr.* Géorgiques Chrétiennes. CAW
This day our Savior Christ was born. *Unknown.* SeCSL
This day relenting God. Lines Written after the Discovery by the Author of the Germ of Yellow Fever [*or* Reply]. Sir Ronald Ross. ImOP; InP; MaRV
This Day That's Mine. Theresa Gamble Head. SoP
This day upon the bitter tree. Good Friday. A. J. M. Smith. CaP; MaRV; StJW
This day, whate'er the fates decree. Stella's Birthday; March 13, 1726/7. Swift. BWP; CEP; EiCL; EiPP; LoBV; NoP; OBEC; PoEL-3
This day winding down now. Prologue. Dylan Thomas. GTBS-W
This daylit doll, this dim divinity. Neo-classical Poem. William Jay Smith. WaP
This death-mask is my portrait by my son. For a Child's Drawing. Anton Vogt. AnNZ
This deep of night, with nature's law complying. Hazard. Nils Petersen. LiTW
This delightful young man. Heine. *Fr.* Die Heimkehr. AWP
This Dim and Ptolemaic Man. John Peale Bishop. CrMA; ImOP; LiTA; LiTM (rev. ed.); NePA
This dirty little heart. Emily Dickinson. PoEL-5
This Discord in the Pact of Things. Boethius, *tr. fr. Latin by* Helen Waddell. LiTW
This Do in Remembrance of Me, *sel.* Horatius Bonar.
"Here, O my Lord, I see Thee face to face." TrPWD
This Do in Remembrance of Me. James Montgomery. *See* According To Thy Gracious Word.
"This Do in Remembrance of Me." *Unknown.* STF
This drop of ink chance leaves upon my pen. A Drop of Ink. Joseph Ernest Whitney. AA
This Dust Was Once the Man. Walt Whitman. *Fr.* Memories of President Lincoln. CBV; LiPo; PoRL
(Epitaph for Lincoln.) WoL
This dust was Timas; and they say. The Dust of Timas. E. A. Robinson, *after* Sappho. AWP; JAWP; WBP
This earth is not the steadfast place. William Vaughn Moody. *Fr.* Gloucester Moors. PoFr; WGRP
This earth Pythonax and his brother hides. On Two Brothers. Simonides. AWP
This Easter, Arthur Winslow, less than dead. Death from Cancer. Robert Lowell. In Memory of Arthur Winslow, I. AP; FiMAP; MiAP; PoSa; TDP; TwCP
This Easter Day. Martha Snell Nicholson. BePJ
This endless gray-roofed city, and each heart. London Despair. Frances Cornford. OBMV
This Endris Night. *Unknown.* NoP
This England ("This England never did"). Shakespeare. *Fr.* King John, V., vii. BoTP
(England, 2.) OTPC
This England ("This royal throne of kings"). Shakespeare. *Fr.* King Richard II, II, i. HT; PTK; TreF; TrGrPo
(England.) OTPC
(John of Gaunt's Dying Speech, *longer sel.*) FiP
(This Blessed Plot. . .This England.) FaBV
("This royal throne of kings, this scept'red isle.") ShBV-2; YAT
This evening, motherly summer moves in the pond. Mayday on Holderness. Ted Hughes. ToPo
This evening, our father. Prayer. *Unknown.* OuSiCo
This existence has, without the azure sphere, no reality. Quatrain. Sarmèd the Yahud. TrJP
This fable is a very short one. Showing How the Cavern Followed the Hut's Advice. John Hookham Frere. OTPC (1923 ed.)
This face you got. Phizzog. Carl Sandburg. RePo; TiPo (1952 ed.)
This fairest lady, who, as well I wot. Sonnet: Death Is Not without but within Him. Cino da Pistoia. AWP
This fairest one of all the stars, whose flame. Ballata: One Speaks of the Beginnings of His Love. *Unknown.* AWP
This fat woman in canvas knickers. Tourist Time. F. R. Scott. PoPl; WhC
This feast-day of the sun, his altar there. The Hill Summit. Dante Gabriel Rossetti. The House of Life, LXX. MaVP; MoAmPo; NoP; PoVP; ViPo
This Feast of the Law. *Unknown, tr. fr. Hebrew by* Israel Zangwill. TrJP
This feather-soft creature. A Goldfinch. Walter de la Mare. BiS
This Fevers Me. Richard Eberhart. FiMAP; MoRP
This field-grass brushed our legs. In the Field. Richard Wilbur. NYBP
This figure, that thou here seest put. On the Portrait of Shakespeare Prefixed to the First Folio Edition, 1623 [*or* To the Reader]. Ben Jonson. EnRePo; HBV; OTPC (1923 ed.)
This first year/ Of the atom. There Is Yet Time. Arvel Steece. PGD
This flesh is but the symbol and the shrine. Hail Man! Angela Morgan. WGRP
This flying angel's torrent cry. Eastern Tempest. Edmund Blunden. MoBrPo
This, for my soul's peace, have I heard from thee. The Transfiguration. *Unknown. Fr.* Bhagavad-Gita. OuHeWo
This fossil in my hand. Geologic. Patric Dickinson. POTi
This fountain sheds her flowery spray. The Fountain. A. J. M. Smith. CaP
This fourteen six and fiftieth year. The Lesser Testament. Villon. WoL
This Fresshe Flour. Chaucer. *Fr.* The Legend of Good Women. SeCePo
This from that soul incorrupt whom Athens had doomed to the death. The Reply of Socrates. Edith M. Thomas. WGRP
This fugue must be hummed, found. Dumb Dick. Leslie A. Fiedler. ErPo
This fullness that is emptiness. Definition. May Sarton. MoLP
This gapes for marriage, yet his fickle head. John Hall. *Fr.* On an Hour-Glass. LO
This garden does not take my eyes. The Garden. James Shirley. CavP; OBS
This garden too pleasant. Concert. Helen Quigless. NBP
This gentle and half melancholy breeze. An Autumn Breeze. William Hamilton Hayne. AA

This gentleman the charming duck. A Trueblue Gentleman. Kenneth Patchen. OA
This girl gave her heart to me. Conrad Aiken. *Fr.* Improvisations: Light and Snow. BoLP
This gives support to insects. 12th Dance—Getting Leather by Language—21 February 1964. Jackson MacLow. CoPo
This glorious title hath in it exprest. George Wither. *Fr.* The Protector. PoFr
This golden cockerel summer sun ruffles his feathers into sleep. Cockerel Sun. Rosemary Dobson. MoAuPo
This golden head has wit in it. Modern Love, XXXI. George Meredith. ViPo; VP
This grave-yard with its umbrella pines. The Island Cemetery. W. H. Auden. NePoAm-2
This great purple butterfly. Another Song of a Fool. W. B. Yeats. OA
This green wall to which I turn for sleep. Green Wall My Grave. Martin Seymour-Smith. MoPW
This grove is too secret: one thinks of murder. The Grove beyond the Barley. Alden Nowlan. MoCV
This handsome pair. Sarcophagus Cover. Ruth Feldman. NYTB
This Happy Day. Harry Behn. TiPo
This Heart That Flutters near My Heart. James Joyce. Chamber Music, XXIII. AnIV
This heaven is too clear and bright. Macrocosm. Philip Child. CaP
This helmet, I suppose. Arac's Song. W. S. Gilbert. *Fr.* Princess Ida. FiBHP; WhC
This Here Is Hell. Samuel M. Bradley. FiSC
This Heritage to the Race of Kings. Joseph Mary Plunkett. AnIV; PoFr
(Our Heritage.) OnYI
This high-caught hooded Reason broods upon my wrist. The Falcon and the Dove. Sir Herbert Read. BrPo; FaBoMo; POTE
This high-way beheld at break of day. March of the Three Kings. *Unknown.* OHIP
This Hill. Otomo Yakamochi, *tr. fr. Japanese by* Ishii *and* Obata. OnPM
This hill indents my soul. Champ de Manoeuvres. Sir Herbert Read. BrPo
This hinder year [*or* yeir] I heard [*or* hard] be tauld [*or* tald]. The Bludy Serk. Robert Henryson. OBEV (1st ed.); OxBoCh
This Holy Night. Eleanor Farjeon. ChBR
This Holy Night. Gertrude Hanson. ChIP
This holy season fit to fast and pray. Amoretti, XXII. Spenser. ReEn; SiCE
This honorable body is hard to be beat. California Legislature. John A. Stone. SGR
This hound has had his day, and is content. Old Dog. Leonard Twynham. StaSt
This Hour. Oliver La Grone. NNP; PoNe (1970 ed.)
This hour was set the time for heaven's descent. Twilit Revelation. Léonie Adams. MAP; MoAB; MoAmPo
This Houre Her Vigill. Valentin Iremonger. *See* Recollection in Autumn.
This house has been far out at sea all night. Wind. Ted Hughes. FIW
This house I know—though never seen before. House of Yesterday. Walter Shedlofsky. FiSC
This house is built within a sheltering. Back Road Farm. Charles Bruce. CaP
This house is haunted, this house is haunted. Calliope. *Unknown.* AS
This house of flesh was never loved of me! Protest in Passing. Leonora Speyer. HBMV
This house that has been our home has been condemned. Packing a Photograph from Firenze. William H. Matchett. NePoEA
This House Where Once a Lawyer Dwelt. William Erskine. HBV; TreF; WhC
This huge and purged trust I have. My Love behind Walls. Heather Spears. OBCV
This humanist whom no beliefs constrained. J. V. Cunningham. ELU
This hungry flesh and bone. The Son. Edwin Muir. PoDB
This I admit, Death is terrible to me. Pure Death. Robert Graves. AWP; InPo
This I ask Thee—tell it to me truly, Lord! Zoroaster Devoutly Questions Ormazd [*or* The Sacred Book]. *At. to* Zoroaster, *tr. by* A. V. Williams Jackson. *Fr.* Gathas. AWP; WGRP
This I beheld, or dreamed it in a dream. Opportunity [*or* The Broken Sword]. Edward Rowland Sill. AnNE; BBV; BLPA; GN; GoTP; HBV; HBVY; MAP; MaRV; MCCG; MoAmPo (1942 ed.); NeHB; NeMA; OHFP; PCD; PoMa; PoToHe; StP; TreFS; TSW; WGRP; YaD
This I Can Do. H. T. Lefevre. STF
This I got on the day that Goring. The Three Scars. George Walter Thornbury. VA
This I have read in some old book and wise. To Elizabeth. Mary Dixon Thayer. JKCP (1955 ed.)
This I Know. E. Margaret Clarkson. SoP
(Best for Me, The.) STF
This I Know. Eliza M. Hickok. SoP
(Prayer: "I know not by what methods rare.") BLRP; STF
This I Know. Grace V. Watkins. SoP
This I trow be truth—who can teach thee better. William Langland. *Fr.* The Vision of Piers Plowman. EG
This I would like to be—braver and bolder. Lord, Make a Regular Man Out of Me. Edgar A. Guest. BLPA; NeHB
This idol with black eyes and yellow hair. Childhood, I. Arthur Rimbaud. *Fr.* Illuminations. SyP
This Infant World. George Macdonald. *Fr.* A Memorial of Africa. EPN
(Sonnet: "This infant world has taken long to make.") OBVV
(World and Soul.) VA
This is a blossom of the brain. Emily Dickinson. MWA-2; PoeP
This is a breath of summer wind. On Reading a Poet's First Book. H. C. Bunner. AA
This is a cat that sleeps at night. Cat. Sinclair Lewis. GoTP
This is a civilization at war, and. The Shadow. Gail Dusenbery. ThO
This is a colder winter than last year. Ugga Byan. *Fr.* Her Absent Lord. LiTW
This is a country where there are no mountains. Morning on the St. John's. Jane Cooper. NYBP
This is a difficult land. Here things miscarry. The Difficult Land. Edwin Muir. BoPe
This is a fair in Magh Eala of the king. The Headless Phantoms. *Unknown.* AnIL
This is a fearful thing to bear. Horror. Peter Baum. AWP
This is a good dream, even if the falling is. In a Rented Room. Denis Johnson. QAH
This is a night to be out. Street-Walker in March. Samuel L. Albert. NePoAm-2
This is a piece too fair. What Is the World [*or* Design]. Dryden. *Fr.* To My Honor'd Friend Sir Robert Howard. MaRV; TRV
This is a poem about Iowa. Subject, with Apologies. Phillip Hey. YAP
This is a pool which bears deep looking into. A Pool. Thomas Whitbread. NYBP
This is a rocksaw seacoast. Memento. Winfield Townley Scott. FiMAP
This is a rune I ravelled in the still. The Cow. Bernard O'Dowd. BoAu; PoAu-1
This is a salt steep-cobbled town. Sea Town. Frances Frost. EtS
This Is a Sin-tryin' World, *with music. Unknown.* TrAS
This is a song. The Gift. Keith Wilson. ThO
This is a song to celebrate banks. Bankers Are Just like Anybody Else, except Richer. Ogden Nash. ATP (1953 ed.); LiTA
This is a spray the bird clung to. Misconceptions. Robert Browning. AtBAP; CBEP; EnLi-2 (1949 ed.); EPN; GTBS; OBEV; OBVV; PoVP; TOP; VA
This is a spyglass: it. Spyglass. Horace Gregory. TPM
This is a still life. Entrance to a Mirror. Jon Anderson. YAP
This is a strange twilit country, but full of peace. A Dream. Ruth Pitter. BoPe
This is a tale for a night of snow. The Fair Young Wife. Helen Adam. FiSC
This is a tale that true gold from dross tells. Aldhelm. Edgar Lee Masters. CMoP
This is a tale to tell your sons. Wayne at Stony Point. Clinton Scollard. MC; PAH
This is a theme for muted coronets. The Plot against Proteus. A. J. M. Smith. OBCV; PeCV

This is a wild land, country of my choice. Rocky Acres. Robert Graves. LiTB; UnPo (3d ed.)
"This is a wonderful error we live in." Rockefeller Center. Charles Norman. CBV
This is a world of picket fences, knowing. American Nights. Richmond Lattimore. TPM
This is a wrong that needs not my bespeaking. New Testament, Revised Edition. Sister Mary Catherine. ISi
This is about the size of it, Dad. The Beat. James R. Lucas. WSL
This is about the stillness in moving things. Runes. Howard Nemerov. PoCh; ToPo
This Is after All Vacation. Louis Zukofsky. CoPo
This is all we ever say. Christopher Morley. WhC
This Is America. Thomas Curtis Clark. PGD
This Is America. Katharine Janeway Conger. PaA
This is an ancient pattern on these hills. American Vineyard. Mildred Cousens. GoYe
This is an evening for a hallowed landfall. Pattern of Saint Brendan. Francis MacManus. AnIV; OxBI
This is an old and very cruel god. Vicarious Atonement. Richard Aldington. MoBrPo; WGRP
This is Anacreon's tomb: the Teian swan. Man at Peace. Antipater of Sidon. OnPM
This is Charles Ives. Muriel Rukeyser. *Fr.* Ives. UnS
This is enchanted country, lies under a spell. Bonac. John Hall Wheelock. HT; MoVE
This Is England. Laurence Binyon. BoTP
This is Flag Day. Hang Out the Flags. James S. Tippett. SiSoSe
This Is for Freedom, My Son. Charles Stewart. TNV
This is for poets. . .Reasoner and empiric. God Said: Let There Be Sky. James J. Donohue. JKCP (1955 ed.)
This is God's hive; the bees. Saint Apollinare in Classe. R. N. D. Wilson. CAW; CLwM
This is God's house—the blue sky is the ceiling. In the Woods. Frederick George Scott. ACV; CaP
This Is Halloween. Dorothy Brown Thompson. BrR; TiPo; YeAr
This is he, who, felled by foes. Worship. Emerson. MWA-1
This is her picture as she was. The Portrait. Dante Gabriel Rossetti. GTSE; MaVP; OAEP; PoVP; VA; ViPo; VP
This is her picture—Dolladine. Dolladine. William Brighty Rands. PRWS
This is high saintliness, I know. Earth-canonized. Henry Morton Robinson. CAW
This is how snowflakes play about. A Finger Play for a Snowy Day. *Unknown.* BoTP
This is how the flowers grow. How the Flowers Grow. "Gabriel Setoun." MPB; SoPo
This Is Indeed the Blessed Mary's Land. Longfellow. *Fr.* The Golden Legend. ISi
This is Independence Day. Stephen Vincent Benét. *Fr.* Listen to the People: Independence Day, 1941. PoSC
This is just the weather, a wet May and blowing. A Memory. Katharine Tynan. OxBI
This Is Just to Say. William Carlos Williams. AmP; FlW; ForPo; GoJo; HoPM; PIA; PoIE
This is like the nave of an unfinished cathedral. Broadway's Canyon. John Gould Fletcher. InP
This is Mab, the mistress-fairy. Queen Mab [*or* Mab the Mistress-Fairy]. Ben Jonson. *Fr.* The Satyr. EIL; HBV; OTPC (1923 ed.); SiCE; WiR
This is Mister Beers. Mister Beers. Hugh Lofting. FaPON; GaP; RePo
This is Morgan's country: now steady, Bill. Morgan's Country. Francis Webb. BoAV
This Is My Beloved, *sels.* Walter Benton. UnTE
"I saw autumn today . . . incipiently, on the sunset."
"It was like something done in fever, when nothing fits."
"White full moon like a great beautiful whore, The."
This Is My Body. John Donne. ChIP; OQP
(Sacrament, The.) TRV
"This is my body, which is given for you." The Sacrament. Charles L. Ford. OQP
This Is My Country. Robert P. Tristram Coffin. HT
This is my country's flag. My Country's Flag. Juniata Stafford. HH
This is my creed: To do some good. My Creed. Samuel Ellsworth Kiser. PoToHe
This is my curse on thee. God send thou love. A Curse. Rabi'a, Daughter of Ka'b. LiTW
This is my curse, Pompous, I pray. Epigram. J. V. Cunningham. PV
This Is My Father's World. Maltbie D. Babcock. MaRV; SoP; TRV
(My Father's World.) BLRP
This Is My Hour. Zoë Akins. HBV
This is my hour between the flight and the flight. Remember Me, Gulls! Joseph Auslander. YT
This is my letter to the World. Emily Dickinson. AmPP (4th ed.); AnNE; AP; DiPo; MWA-2; OxBA; TreFT
(Letter to the World.) OnPM
This Is My Love for You. Grace Fallow Norton. HBV
This is my play's [*or* playes] last scene, here heavens appoint. Holy Sonnets, VI. John Donne. AnAnS-1; AnEnPo; LoBV; MaMe; MasP; MeLP; MeP; MePo; MyFE; OAEP; OBS; OxBoCh; PoFS; SCEP-1; SeCP; SeEP; Sonn; TuPP
This is my prayer to Thee, my Lord. Prayer for Strength [*or* For Strength]. Rabindranath Tagore. Gitanjali, XXXVI. MaRV; MoRP
This Is My Rock. David McCord. FaPON; PDV; SiSoSe; SoPo; StVeCh; TiPo (1959ed.)
This is my secret, this is the chord most perfectly strung. The Beaches, V. "Robin Hyde." AnNZ
This Is My Song. Norma Davis. NeLNL
This is my world! within these narrow walls. My Study. Paul Hamilton Hayne. AmPP (3d ed.)
This is my wrong to you, O man that I love. A Woman's Song. Muna Lee. NP
This is Nevada, near the end of one. You Are on U.S. 40 Headed West. Vera White. AmFN
This is no book. To a Poet. Sister Mary Angelita. GoBC
This is no dreamworld, no nightmare country. Letter from the South. Robert E. Hayden. PoNe
This is no fallow field through which we travel. Golden Wedding. William W. Pratt. MaRV
"This is no place for a tree," said the sour black soil. The Mountain Tree. Hugh Connell. NeIP
This is no place for lovers. Advice from a Nightwatchman. Ian Healy. Poems from the Coalfields, II. PoAu-2
This is no time for fear, for doubts of good. Challenge. Thomas Curtis Clark. MaRV; PGD
This is no wood for me to walk. Forest. Harriet Gray Blackwell. GoYe
This is not all I would have said. Arlington Cemetery Looking toward the Capitol. Winthrop Palmer. GoYe
This Is Not Death. Humbert Wolfe. MoBrPo
This is not hell. Loss. Richard Aldington. BrPo
This is not poetry, he said. Some Tips on Watching Birds. Deatt Hudson. NYBP
This is not sorrow, this is work: I build. The Tomb of Lieutenant John Learmonth, A.I.F. John Manifold. BoAV; LiTM; NeLNL; PoAu-2
This is not the classic torso. All the Farewells. Byron Vazakas. MoPo
This is not the man that women choose. Act of Love. Vernon Scannell. ErPo
This is not the wind in the weeping willow tree. Spring Voices. Jesse Stuart. FiSC
This is not you? These phrases are not you? Prelude VI. Conrad Aiken. *Fr.* Preludes for Memnon. MAP; MoAB; MoAmPo
This is of green—unclassic shade. The Final Green. Leah Bodine Drake. NePoAm
This is our love, these wheels and chains. The Night Loves Us. Louis Adeane. NeBP
This is our place of meeting; opposite. At the Saturday Club. Oliver Wendell Holmes. AmePo; AmPP (3d ed.); CoBA
This is Palm Sunday; mindful of the day. To a Young Girl Dying. Thomas William Parsons. AA
This Is Pioneer Weather. William Carlos Williams. NePoAm-2
This is Popilia's tomb: my husband's care. Sleep of the Just. *Unknown.* OnPM
This is Proteus, a god. He comes from the ocean. Proteus; or, The Shapes of Conscience. Rolfe Humphries. LiTM (1946 ed.)
This is Scotch William Wallace. It was he. William Wallace. Francis Lauderdale Adams. OxBS
This Is She. Arthur Guiterman. LHV
This is that [*or* the] blessed Mary, pre-elect. 'Mary's Girl-

hood. Dante Gabriel Rossetti. CAW; GBV; GoBC; ISi; MaVP; PoVP; VP; WGRP
This is that month, Elizabeth. George Barker. *Fr.* Third Cycle of Love Poems. NeBP
This is the anniversary of the day. Wedding Anniversary. Margaret E. Bruner. PoToHe
This is the arsenal. From floor to ceiling. The Arsenal at Springfield. Longfellow. AmPP; AnNE; AP; CoBA; DD; GTBS; HBV; MCCG; MWA-1; WaaP
This is the best world that we live in. The World [*or* The Best and the Worst]. *Unknown.* ALV; TreFT
This is the birthday of our land. Prayer on Fourth of July. Nancy Byrd Turner. OTD; YeAr
This is the black sea-brute bulling through wave-wrack. Leviathan. W. S. Merwin. NePoEA
This is the blessed Mary, pre-elect. *See* This is that blessed Mary, pre-elect.
This is the breed that followed the tails. Nantucket Whalers. Daniel Henderson. EtS
This is the bricklayer; hear the thud. Sanctuary. Elinor Wylie. MAP; MoAB; MoAmPo; PoMa
This is the case of a high-school land. Canada: Case History. Earle Birney. TwCaPo
This is the cave of which I spoke. The Caves. Michael Roberts. ChMP
This is the chapel: here, my son. Clifton Chapel. Sir Henry Newbolt. OBEV (new ed.); OBVV
This is the charge I keep as mine. My Charge. Leslie Pinckney Hill. MaRV
This is the children's playground, the home of the inner eye. The Children's Playground. Oscar Williams. SiTL
This Is the City. Yvette Johnson. TNV
This Is the City Children Made. Frank Ernest Hill. PoMa
This is the convent where they tend the sick. Sister Mary of the Love of God. Rosa Mulholland. VA
This is the country of the Norman tower. A Warning to Conquerors. Donagh MacDonagh. OxBI
This is the dance America wanted! the dance of death. The Lotus Eaters. Floyce Alexander. QAH
This is the Darkness that they told us of. In Tenebris. Sister Mary of the Visitation. JKCP (1955 ed.)
This is the day His hour of life draws near. Sonnets at Christmas, I. Allen Tate. AmP; AP; GTBS-W; LiTA; LiTM; NePA; OxBA; ReMP; Sonn
This is the day the circus comes. Parade. Rachel Field. *Fr.* A Circus Garland. SoPo; StVeCh; UTS
This is the day the Lord hath made. An Hosanna for the Lord's Day. Isaac Watts. SoP
This is the day the prophets have foretold. Without Regret. Lilith Lorraine. PGD
This is the day when all through the town. Sunday. Elizabeth J. Coatsworth. AmFN; OCS; WaKn
This is the day when the fairy kind. Friday. Sir Walter Scott. BoTP
This is the day, which down the void abysm. Demogorgon's Song [*or* The Final Victory]. Shelley. *Fr.* Prometheus Unbound, IV. EnLit; LoBV; MaPo (1969 ed.); OQP; PoIE; SeCeV; ShBV-3
This is the dead fiddle. Look where the wood. The Dead Fiddle. Humbert Wolfe. TrJP
This is the death by water. This is dying. Dead Marine. Louis O. Coxe. WaP
This is the debt I pay. The Debt. Paul Laurence Dunbar. AmNP; BANP; CDC; Kal; MaRV; NoP; TRV
This is the depth, the end of all despair. Street Beggar. Anderson M. Scruggs. PoMa
This is the dust of Timas, whom unwed/ Persephone locked. Timas. Sappho, *tr. by* John Addington Symonds. LiTW
This is the earth he walked on. Holy Land. Richard Watson Gilder. StJW
This is the end of him, here he lies. Epitaph. Amy Levy. TrJP
This is the end of the book. Written at the End of a Book. Langdon Elwyn Mitchell. AA
"This is the end": the anguished word. The End. Walter de la Mare. OAEP (2d ed.)
This is the feast time of the year. The Feast Time of the Year. Dora Read Goodale. OHIP; PEDC
This is the female form. Walt Whitman. *Fr.* I Sing the Body Electric. ErPo
This is the final man. The Final Man. Basil McFarlane. PoNe
This is the football hero's moment of fame. Settling Some Old Football Scores. Morris Bishop. SD
This is the forest primeval. The murmuring pines and the hemlocks. Evangeline. Longfellow. AmPP (3d ed.); AnNE; BeLS; CoBA; InP; MWA-1; OTD; PCD; TreF; WBLP
This is the forest primeval. To What Base Uses! *parody.* Bert Leston Taylor. WhC
This is the fruit of that forbidden tree. On the Photograph of a Lynching. Wendell Phillips Stafford. PoFr
This Is the Garden. E. E. Cummings. BoLiVe; MoAmPo (Sonnet: "This is the garden: colours come and go.") MoAB
This is the garden; its twenty paths. Geraldine's Garden. John Francis O'Donnell. IrPN
This is the gay cliff of the nineteenth century. Brooklyn Heights. John Wain. LiTM (1970 ed.); ToPo
This is the gladness of our Easter morning. The Day of Joy. Lucy Larcom. HH
This is the glamour of the world antique. Sibyl. John Payne. VA
This is the golden book of spirit and sense. Sonnet. Swinburne. SyP
This is the golden goddess; friend is she. Aphrodite Pandemos. *Unknown.* UnTE
This is the gospel of labour, ring it, ye bells of the kirk! Henry van Dyke. *Fr.* The Gospel of Labour. OQP; WBLP
This is the grave of Mike O'Day. Mike O'Day. *Unknown.* LiTG; LiTM (rev. ed.); SiTL; TreFT; WhC
This is the greatest proof of power. Who Can Forget? Leslie Savage Clark. ChIP
This is the hand. At Cambridge. Audrey McGaffin. NePoAm
This is the haunted wood, where no man goes. Warning. Sydney King Russell. FiSC
This Is the Hay That No Man Planted. Elizabeth J. Coatsworth. BrR
This is the height of our deserts. Deservings. *Unknown.* HBV
This is the hero; he is black or white. Fairy Tale. John Frederick Nims. MiAP
This is the hidden place that hiders know. Stephen Vincent Benét. *Fr.* John Brown's Body. ViBoPo
This is the horrible tale of Paul. The Revolving Door. Newman Levy. ShM
This is the hour of magic, when the Moon. The Hour of Magic. W. H. Davies. MoBrPo; NeMA
This is the hour that we must mourn. Tenebrae. Austin Clarke. AnIL; NeIP
This is the house. On one side there is darkness. Portrait of One Dead. Conrad Aiken. *Fr.* The House of Dust. HBMV; NP; WHA
This is the house of Bedlam. Visits to St. Elizabeths. Elizabeth Bishop. CoAP
This is the house that Jack built. Mother Goose. BoTP; FaBoBe; HBV; HBVY; OxNR; Po; RIS; SiTL; SoPo; StVeCh *See also* This is the knife with a handle of horn.
This is the house we used to know so well. I. M. H. Maurice Baring. ACP (1952 ed.)
This is the house where Jesse White. Lowery Cot. L. A. G. Strong. MoBrPo
This is the huge dream of us that we are Heroes. The Flowers of Politics, I. Michael McClure. NeAP
This is the ironhard winter foretold. Soeren Haller. *Fr.* Song of Denmark. PoFr
This is the journey of this night. Journey, IV. Erik Lindegren. LiTW
This Is the Key. *Unknown.* CH; FaBoCh; FaFP; GBV (1952 ed.); LoGBV; MoShBr; OTPC (1946 ed.); OxBoLi; SiTL; ThWaDe; TreFS
(Key of the Kingdom, The.) CBEP; OtMeF
("This is the key of the kingdom.") BoTP; OxNR; PPL
This is the key to the playhouse. The Playhouse Key. Rachel Field. BoTP; FaPON; MPB
This is the knife with a handle of horn. The House that Jack Built. *Unknown.* OxBoLi. *For* Mother Goose *vers., see* This is the house that Jack built.
This is the land our fathers came to find. New World. Brewster Ghiselin. MoVE
This—is the land—the sunset washes. Emily Dickinson. MWA-2
This is the land where hate should die. The Land Where Hate Should Die. Denis A. McCarthy. PGD

This Is the Last. Gilbert Waterhouse. PGD
This is the last hotel. Irish Hotel. David Wevill. NYBP
This is the last stroke my toungs clock must strike. Summer's Farewell. Thomas Nashe. *Fr.* Summer's Last Will and Testament. PoEL-2
This is the law of the Yukon, and ever she makes it plain. The Law of the Yukon. Robert W. Service. CaP; HBV; TreFS
This is the light of the mind, cold and planetary. The Moon and the Yew Tree. Sylvia Plath. CoAP; NaP; NYBP
This is the loggia Browning loved. Browning at Asolo. Robert Underwood Johnson. AA
This is the magic morning. Christmas Morning. Elsie Melchert Fowler. ChBR
This is *The Making of America in Five Panels.* Empire Builders. Archibald MacLeish. Frescoes for Mr. Rockefeller's City, V. AmP; NoP; OxBA; Po; UnPo
This Is the Making of Man. Priscilla Leonard. OQP
(Making of Man, The.) MaRV
This is the measured moment. More than the Moment. Sister Claude of Jesus. JKCP (1955 ed.)
This is the metre Columbian. The soft-flowing trochees and dactyls. The Metre Columbian. *Unknown.* Par
This is the mew of God set high. Hawkesyard. Sister Mary Benvenuta. JKCP (1926 ed.)
This is the midnight—let no star. The Storm Cone. Kipling. ChMP; POTE; PoVP
This is the month and this is the happy morn. On [*or*Ode on] the Morning of Christ's Nativity. Milton. AnFE; AtBAP; BEL; CEL; CoBE; ExPo; GBV; GoTL; GTBS; GTBS-D; GTBS-P; GTBS-W; GTSE; GTSL; HBV; LiTB; LiTG; MaRV; MasP; MBV-1; MeLP; MeP; NoP; OBS; OxBoCh; PAn; PoE; PoEL-3; PoFS;; SeCeV; SeEP; SoP; TOP; UnPo; WGRP
This is the month of the Thunder Moon. The Month of the Thunder Moon. Marion Doyle. YeAr
This is the month of weeds. Weed Month. V. Sackville-West. *Fr.* The Land. MoBrPo (1942 ed.)
This is the month when hills turn white. The Long Night Moon; December. Frances Frost. OTD; YeAr
This is the mouth-filling song of the race that was run by a Boomer. The Sing-Song of Old Man Kangaroo. Kipling. FaPON; TiPo (1952 ed.)
This is the moving nakedness that swirls once and is night. Corliss Engine-Wheel. MacKnight Black. AnAmPo
This is the naked unsurmountable truth. The True Lover. Abbie Huston Evans. NP
This is the need/ Of every seed. What Every Gardener Knows. *Ad. by* Louis Untermeyer. StaSt
This is the night. Harlem '67. Clarence Reed. BF
This is the night mail crossing the border. The Night Mail. W. H. Auden. ChTr; PoSa; ShBV-3; WePo
"This is the night," the dark-faced stranger leered. The Sabbat. Lin Carter. FiSC
This is the order of the music of the morning. The Santa-Fé Trail. Vachel Lindsay. CoBA
This is the pathway where she walked. Amy. James Matthew Legaré. AA
This is the pedigree of degradation. Charles Erskine Scott Wood. *Fr.* The Poet in the Desert. PoFr
This is the place. In a Meadow. John Swinnerton Phillimore. OBEV (new ed.)
This is the place, as wild as summer snow. The Track into the Swamp. Samuel French Morse. CrMA
This is the place. Even here the dauntless soul. William Blake. Dante Gabriel Rossetti. Five English Poets, 2. PoVP
This is the place I love. Here I belong. Mountain Creed. Medora Addison Nutter. GoYe
This Is the Place to Wait. Horace Gregory. The Passion of M'Phail, V. MoAmPo
("When you are caught breathless in an empty station.") CMoP
This is the place where André met that death. André. Charlotte Fiske Bates. MC; PAH
This is the place where far from the unholy populace. In a Meadow. J. S. Phillimore. OBVV
This is the pool that Plato visited. The Pool. E. L. Mayo. MiAP
This is the prettiest motion. To a Lady That Desired Me I Would Bear My Part with Her in a Song. Richard Lovelace. MuSP
This is the promise that hangs on the tree. Christmas 1945. Al Hine. ThLM
This is the realm no man dares. The World Looks On. Louis Newman. PoNe (1970 ed.)
This is the river that had to be damned. Pentagonia. G. E. Bates. NYBP
This is the road to somewhere. To Somewhere. Leonard E. Nathan. NYTB
This is the room to which she came that day. Her Pity. Philip Bourke Marston. VA
This is the safest prayer to pray. Thy Will Be Done. Annie Johnson Flint. STF
This is the season when I long for a pen as sadly eloquent as Verlaine's. Who Wants to Travel All Over Europe and See Nothing but a Lot of American Tourists? I Do. Ogden Nash. SiTL
This is the secret love. Joy. Sister Mary Irma. JKCP (1955 ed.)
This is the shack where the old man died. Post Mortem. Verna Loveday Harden. CaP
This Is the Shape of the Leaf. Conrad Aiken. Priapus and the Pool IV [V]. AnAmPo; AtBAP; HBMV; MAPA; NePA; OxBA; TrGrPo; WHA
(Portrait of a Girl.) GoJo; MAP; MoAB; MoAmPo; TSW
("This is the shape of the leaf, and this of the flower.") CMoP
This is the ship of pearl, which, poets feign. The Chambered Nautilus. Oliver Wendell Holmes. *Fr.* The Autocrat of the Breakfast-Table. AA; AmePo; AmLP; AmP; AmPP; AnAmPo; AnNE; AP; DD; DiPo; EtS; FaBoBe; FaFP; GN; GTBS; GTBS-W; HBV; HBVY; HoPM; IHA; LiTA; MaRV; MCCG; NeHB; NePA; NoP; OBVV; OHFP; OQP; OTPC; OuHeWo; PCD; PG (1955 ed.); PoEL-5; PoLF; PTK; TIHL; TreF; UnPo (1st ed.); WGRP; YT
This is the sin against the Holy Ghost. The Unpardonable Sin. Vachel Lindsay. CMoP; LiTM (rev. ed.); MaRV; NePA
This is the song I rested with. Mammy Hums. Carl Sandburg; PoNe
This is the song of Mehitabel. The Song of Mehitabel. Don Marquis. *Fr.* Archy and Mehitabel. FiBHP; TreFS
This is the song of the Empire Builder. The Empire Builder. John Jerome Rooney. JKCP
This is the song of the waters churning. A Song of Power. Berton Braley. PoMa
This is the song of the wave! The mighty one! The Song of the Wave. George Cabot Lodge. AA; AmePo; EtS
This is the song of the wind as it came. The Avenue of the Allies. Alfred Noyes. PoFr
This is the song of those who live alone. Song. William Justema. NYBP
This is the song that the truck drivers hear. Song of the Truck. Doris Frankel. AmFN
This is the sorrowful story. The Legends of Evil, I. Kipling. MemP; MoShBr
This is the Space Age. The Cosmic Age. Sun-Ra. BF
This is the stagnant hour. Drunken Lover. Owen Dodson. AmNP
This is the story of/ The brawny Brady riflemen. Brady's Bend. Martha Keller. StPo
This is the story of a coal miner's child. The Coal Miner's Child. *Unknown.* OuSiCo
This is the story the Coxswain told. The Coxswain's Line. H. E. Cressman. RePo
This is the sum of things. . .that we. The Sum of Things. Arthur W. Jose. BoAu
This is the surest death. Mortality. Naomi Long Madgett. NNP; PoNe (1970 ed.)
This is the tale from first to last. Simon the Cyrenian. Lucy Lyttelton. HBV
This is the tale that Cassidy told. The Mornin's Mornin'. Gerald Brennan. BLPA
This is the tale that was told to me. A Sailor's Yarn. James Jeffrey Roche. BOHV; NA
This is the terminal: the light. At the San Francisco Airport. Yvor Winters. ForPo; QFR
This is the time lean woods shall spend. Sundown. Léonie Adams. AmLP; MAP; MoAB; MoAmPo; TrGrPo; TwAmPo

This is the time of wonder, it is written. It Rolls On. Morris Bishop. ImOP
This is the time of year. The Armadillo—Brazil. Elizabeth Bishop. NYBP
This is the time, the appointed place. The Impetuous Lover. A. R. D. Fairburn. AnNZ
This is the time when bit by bit. Turn o' the Year. Katharine Tynan. HBV
This is the time when larks are singing loud. The End of April. Robert Fuller Murray. CenHV
This is the toll of the desert. The Toll of the Desert. Arthur W. Monroe. PoOW
This Is the Tragedy. Helen Frazee-Bower. MaRV
This is the twilight of the summer dead. George Moore. *Fr.* A Parisian Idyl. SyP
This is the Violin. Trumbull Stickney. NCEP
This is the voice of high midsummer's heat. The Mowing. Sir Charles G. D. Roberts. ExPo; OBCV
This is the way a tree: from the rain down. From the Rain Down. Rhina P. Espaillat. GoYe
This is the way it is. We see. Ingmar Bergman's Seventh Seal. Robert Duncan. NMP
This is the way the baby slept. The Way the Baby Slept. James Whitcomb Riley. AA
This is the way the ladies are. Cantata for Two Lovers. Helga Sandburg. UnTE
This is the way the ladies ride. Rhymes about a Little Woman. William Canton. PPL
This is the way the ladies ride,/ Nim, nim, nim, nim. *Unknown.* OxNR
This is the way the ladies ride: Tri-tre-tre-tree! Mother Goose. PPL; TiPo
This is the way we dress the doll. Dressing the Doll. William Brighty Rands. PRWS; VA
This is the way we make our hay. Haymaking. A. P. Graves. BoTP
This is the way we say it in our time. Sonnet XV. Winfield Townley Scott. ErPo
This is the way we wash our clothes. Wash-Day. Lilian McCrea. BoTP
This is the weather the cuckoo likes. Weathers. Thomas Hardy. ALV; AnEnPo; BoLiVe; BoTP; CH; EvOK; FaBoCh; FaBV; GTSL; LoGBV; MemP; MoAB; MoBrPo; OBMV; OtMeF; PoIE; POTE; ReMP; RePo; SeCePo; ShBV-1; WePo; YT
This is the week when Christmas comes. In the Week When Christmas Comes. Eleanor Farjeon. ChBR; PDV; SiSoSe; TiPo (1952 ed.)
This is the wild huntsman that shoots the hares. The Story of the Wild Huntsman. Heinrich Hoffmann. NA
This is the wisdom of the ape. The Theology of Bongwi, the Baboon. Roy Campbell. PeSA
This is the word whose breaking heart. Mathematics or the Gift of Tongues. Anna Hempstead Branch. ImOP
This is the Yak, so neg-li-gee. The Yak. Oliver Herford. *Fr.* Child's Natural History. HBV; HBVY
This is their image: the desert and the wild. Pyramis; or, The House of Ascent. A. D. Hope. PoAu-2
This is their moment, when the brimming skies. Evening in the Great Smokies. DuBose Heyward. HT
This is their third parting. Now she goes. The Adventurers. John Thompson. PoAu-2
This is thy hour, O Soul, thy free flight into the wordless. A Clear Midnight. Walt Whitman. NeMA
This Is Today. Phyllis C. Michael. SoP
This is true liberty, when free-born men. Milton, *tr. fr. the Greek of* Euripides. *Fr.* Areopagitica. PoFr
This is true love, by that true Cupid got. The Dance of Love. Sir John Davies. *Fr.* Orchestra. ElL; SeCePo
This Is War. Richard Le Gallienne. OQP (War.) MaRV
This is what it was like? God on a donkey. The Palms. David Knight. MoCV
This is what the fiddle said to the bow. The Fiddle and the Bow. Humbert Wolfe. BoPe
This Is What the Watchbird Sings, Who Perches in the Lovetree. Bruce Boyd. NeAP
This is what we really want. By Fiat of Adoration. Oscar Williams. GTBS-W; LiTL; LiTM; NePA
This is where the scarlet lords-and-ladies. Under the Cliff. Geoffrey Grigson. WaP
This is where the serpent lives, the bodiless. Wallace Stevens. *Fr.* The Auroras of Autumn. CMoP
This is Willy Walker, and that's Tam Sim. *Unknown.* OxNR
This is your home to which you are returning. Return. Sister Mary Madeleva. JKCP (1955 ed.)
This Is Your Hour. Herbert Kaufman. PoToHe
This is your loveliest moment; now the song. On Her Twenty-fifth Birthday. Louis Hasley. JKCP (1955 ed.)
This island is the world's end. The Island. Seán Jennett. JKCP (1955 ed.); NeIP; SeCePo
This Kansas boy who never knew the sea. Kansas Boy. Ruth Lechlitner. AmFN
This kind o' sogerin' aint a mite like our October trainin'. A Letter from Mr. Hosea Biglow to the Hon. J. T Buckingham. James Russell Lowell. *Fr.* The Biglow Papers. OxBA
This kiss upon your fan I press. Two Triolets: What He Said. Harrison Robertson. HBV
This labouring, vast, Tellurian galleon. To My Godchild. Francis Thompson. JKCP
This lady, curled like a shell. The Shellpicker. Ronald Perry. NePoEA-2
This Land. Ian Mudie. BoAu
This land grows the oldest living things. Karl Shapiro. *Fr.* California Winter. AmFN
This land whose streams seem as the lives of men. The Connecticut River. Reuel Denney. TwAmPo
This landscape demands: open vowels. Campi Flegrei. Barend Toerien. PeSA
This Landscape, These People. Zulfikar Ghose. ACV
This last October working to a day of sun. Voyage. John Lyle Donaghy. OxBI
This Last Pain. William Empson. ChMP; CMoP; CoBMV; FaBoMo; GTBS-P; LiTM; MoAB; MoBrPo; MoVE; SeCePo; SeCeV 1967 ed.); ToPo
This Latest Poet. *Unknown.* LiTM (rev. ed.); SiTL
This legend is told of me. Actaeon. Rayner Heppenstall. FaBoTw
This let who hate me know, and much admire. The Master-Foe. William Baylebridge. *Fr.* Sextains. BoAV
This Life [a Bubble]. William Drummond of Hawthornden. *See* Madrigal: "This life which seems so fair."
This Life a Dream and Shadow. Sir Thomas More. *Fr.* The Twelve Weapons of Spiritual Battle. EnRePo
This Life Flies. Omar Khayyám, *tr. fr. Persian by* Edward Fitzgerald. *Fr.* The Rubáiyát. OnPM
This Life Is All Chequer'd with Pleasures and Woes. Thomas Moore. ELP
This life is but a game of cards. Life's a Game. *Unknown.* BLPA
This life is full of numbness and of balk. Later Life, XXVI. Christina Rossetti. Sonn
This life is like a garden place. Friendships. Mary Edith Halladay. SoP
This life were brutish did we not sometimes. Life's Purpose. James Russell Lowell. *Fr.* The Cathedral. MaRV
This Life Which Seems So Fair. William Drummond of Hawthornden. *See* Madrigal: "This life, which seems so fair."
This life's a hollow bubble. Fin de Siècle. Edmund Vance Cooke. BLPA
This light is loss backward; delight by hurt and by bias gained. March Twilight. Louise Bogan. NePoAm-2
This Lime-Tree Bower My Prison. Samuel Taylor Coleridge. BWP; CBEP; EnRP; ERoP-1; LoBV; MBW-2; MERP; PeER; PoEL-4; PoIE; ShBV-4
This little book, my God and King. Dedication. Sir James Chamberlayne. CavP
This Little Bride & Groom Are. E. E. Cummings. AmPP (5th ed.); HW
This little bunny said, "Let's play." Finger Play. *Unknown.* BoTP
This little child, so white, so calm. Challenge. Kenton Foster Murray. HBV
This Little Earth. Leslie Savage Clark. ChIP
This little fellow, we call him a thumb. To Be Said to Baby's Fingers. *Unknown.* SAS
This little flag to us so dear. The Union Jack. Jeannie Kirby. BoTP
This little flickering planet. Housemates. Odell Shepard. MoRP
This little house is sugar. Winter Sweetness. Langston Hughes. GoSl

This little instrument of art. Upon a Needle. William Pattison. WaPE
This little pig had a rub-a-dub. *Unknown.* OxNR OxNR
This little pig went to market. Mother Goose. BoChLi; HBV; HBVY; OTPC; OxNR; PPL; RIS; SAS; SiTL; SoPo; StVeCh; TiPo
This little runt whom I outplay. Down the Field. Rolfe Humphries. AnAmPo
This little talent goes to market. Rhyme from Grandma Goose. Annemarie Ewing. NePoAm
This little vault, this narrow room. An Epitaph [*or* Epitaph on the Lady Villiers]. Thomas Carew. AnAnS-2; BEL; EnLi-1; LiTL; OBEV; SeCP; SeCV-1; SeEP; UnPo (1st ed.)
This Little Vigil. Charles G. Bell. MoLP; NePoAm
This Living Hand. Keats. *See* Lines Supposed to Have Been Addressed to Fanny Brawne.
This Loneliness for You Is like the Wound. Dunstan Thompson. WaaP; WaP
This lonely figure of not much fun. Absent-Minded Professor. Howard Nemerov. ELU
This lonely hill has always/ Been dear to me. The Infinite. Giacomo Leopardi, *tr. by* Kenneth Rexroth. LiTW
This lonely hill was always dear to me/ And this hedge too. The Infinite. Giacomo Leopardi, *tr. by* Glauco Cambon. OnPM
This lonely hill was always dear to me,/ And this hedgerow. L'Infinito (The Infinite). Giacomo Leopardi, *tr. by* John Heath-Stubbs. Po
This lonely traveller longs for grace. The Wanderer. *Unknown.* PoAn
This long and lonely month. The Lonely Month. Ruthven Todd. NeBP
This, Lord, was an anxious brother and. Funeral Oration for a Mouse. Alan Dugan. AP
This lovely flower fell to seed. For My Grandmother. Countee Cullen. Four Epitaphs, 1. AmNP; CDC; GoSl; MAP; MoAmPo
This Lunar Beauty. W. H. Auden. MoAB; MoBrPo; OBMV
This luxury they call the Flesh. Phineas Pratt. Gloria MacArthur. GoYe
This lyfe, I see, is but a cheyre feyre. A Cherry Fair. *Unknown.* ChTr
This Mad Carnival of Loving. Heine, *tr. fr. German by* Emma Lazarus. *Fr.* To Angélique. TrJP
This man escaped the dirty fates. Flyer's Fall. Wallace Stevens. MoAB
This man has written songs. Fellow-Passengers. Frank Wilmot. BoAu
This man is O so. Item. E. E. Cummings. MoAB; MoAmPo
This man likes to dive. Cold Logic. Barney Hutchinson. SD
This man on bended knee thanked God for much. Blessing. John Frederick Nims. CBV
This man sowed faith wherever he moved. The White-haired Man. May Sarton. MoRP
This man swaying dully before us. The Muck Farmer. R. S. Thomas. POTi
This man, this poet, said. Spark of Laurel. Stanley Kunitz. ML
This man was strong, and like a seacape parted. C. Day Lewis. Sonn
This man, who his own fatherland forgets. He Is My Countryman. Antoni Slonimski. TrJP
This man whose homely face you look upon. Abraham Lincoln [*or* Lincoln's Birthday]. Richard Henry Stoddard. DD; GN; HH; OHIP; OTPC (1946 ed.); PEDC; PGD; PoRL
This man's uncertain; he's afraid. Portrait of a Certain Gentleman. Sara Henderson Hay. NYTB
This mast, new-shaved, through whom I rive the ropes. Choosing a Mast. Roy Campbell. BoC; FaBoTw; GTBS-D; PeSA
This matter of baldness: we do it badly. Baldness and the Swan. Winfield Townley Scott. FiMAP
This Measure. Léonie Adams. MAP; MoAB; MoAmPo
This memory of my mother stays with me. Remembrance. Margaret E. Bruner. PoToHe
This merry pleasant springe. *Unknown.* SeCSL
This midnight breathing. A House Divided. Michael Ondaatje. MoCV
This might have been a place for sleep. Thistledown. Harold Monro. BrPo; GTBS-D
This mighty empire hath but feet of clay. Theoretikos. Oscar Wilde. BrPo
This mild September mist recalls the soul. The Origin of Centaurs. Anthony Hecht. NePoEA
This miracle in me I scan. William Baylebridge. *Fr.* Life's Testament. PoAu-1
This mist has followed on an all-day rain. Spring Night. Richard Aldridge. NePoAm
This Moment. Annie Johnson Flint. BLRP
This moment is precious. Urgency. Sarah E. Wright. PoNe (1970 ed.)
This Moment Yearning and Thoughtful. Walt Whitman. MCCG; OTPC (1946 ed.); PoMa; RePo
This month of May, one pleasant eventide. Medieval Norman Songs, VI. *Unknown, tr. by* John Addington Symonds. AWP
This Monument Will Outlast. Horace, *tr. fr. Latin by* Ezra Pound. CTC
This music which you made, Domenico. A Sonata by Scarlatti. John Heath-Stubbs. MuSP
This Native Land. Thomas Davis. *See* My Land.
This Needle. Kurahashibe Otome, *tr. fr. Japanese by* Ishii *and* Obata. OnPM
This never-ended searching for the eyes. Egg-and-Dart. Robert Finch. OBCV
This new Diana makes weak men her prey. Diana. Ernest Rhys. OBVV; VA
This night is pure and clear as thrice refinèd silver. Fountains. Sacheverell Sitwell. MoBrPo
This night of frosty wind and stars. The Wind of Time. Joseph Payne Brennan. FiSC
This night sees Eire desolate. The Flight of the Earls. *Unknown.* AnIL
This night there is a child born. Three Christmas Carols, 3. *Unknown.* ACP
This night while sleep begins with heavy wings. Astrophel and Stella, XXXVIII. Sir Philip Sidney. BWP; FCP; NoP; SiPS
This noiseless ball and top so round. Philocles. Leonidas of Tarentum. AWP
This nycht befoir the dawing cleir. Followis How Dumbar Wes Desyrd to Be Ane Freir. William Dunbar. OAEP
This, of all fates, would be the saddest end. Tragedy. "Æ." MoRP
This of that and the that of this, The. The Reckoning. Naomi Long Madgett. Kal
This old crabbed man, with his wrinkled, fusty clothes. Old Crabbed Men. James Reeves. ChMP; ErPo
This old hammer killed John Henry. John Henry (E *vers.*). *Unknown.* ViBoFo
This Old Man. *Unknown.* SoPo
This old tree in a/ blaze of Spring. Wild Willow. James Wreford Watson. TwCaPo
This on thy posy-ring I've writ. The Posy Ring. Clément Marot. AWP; JAWP; WBP
This one deceives her husband with her eyes. Hostia. Irving Layton. PV
This one fellow calls me sordid, that one poor. Sonnet. George Henry Boker. *Fr.* Sonnets: Sequence on Profane Love. AmePo
This One Heart-shaken. Sister Maris Stella. GoBC
This one request I make to him that sits the clouds above. Love and Debt Alike Troublesome. *At. to* Sir John Suckling. AnAnS-2; CavP
This one sits shivering in Fortune's smile. Pessimist and Optimist. Thomas Bailey Aldrich. AnNE; TOP
This one was put in a jacket. Counting the Mad. Donald Justice. NePoEA; PPON; UnPo (3d ed.; WOW
This One's on Me. Phyllis Gotlieb. MoCV
This onion-dome holds all intricacies. Greenwich Observatory. Sidney Keyes. MoAB; MoBrPo (1962 ed)
This Only Do I Know. *Unknown.* BePJ
This only grant me, that my means may lie. Of Myself [*or* A Wish]. Abraham Cowley. *Fr.* A Vote. OAEP; OBS; SeCL; SeEP; TreFT
This only hope relieves me, that the strife. Milton. *Fr.* Samson Agonistes. TRV
This Other Night. *Unknown.* ISi
This other night so cold. The Star. *Unknown.* ChrBoLe
This ought to be in Russian. Alcohol. Peter Schjeldahl. YAP
This, our first night apart. For Kathleen, Gone on a Brief

Journey. Jack Marshall. YAP
This Page My Pigeon. Earle Birney. PeCV
This painful love dissect to the last shred. The Lovers. Conrad Aiken. MeWo
This palace standeth in the air. The Palace of the Fairies. Michael Drayton. OTPC (1923 ed.)
This Pardoner had hair as yellow as wax. Ten of Chaucer's People: A Girlish Pardoner. Chaucer. *Fr.* The Canterbury Tales. PoSa
This passeth yeer by yeer, and day by day. The Knight's Tale. Chaucer. *Fr.* The Canterbury Tales. BEL; TOP
This pathway marked No Thoroughfare. Spiritism. Robert Hillyer. WHL
This Peace He Gives. Alice Hansche Mortenson. SoP
This peach is pink with such a pink. Song. Norman Gale. HBV; VA
This pennant new. Poems of My Lambretta. Paul Goodman. NMP; OPoP
This person in the gaudy clothes. Captain Kidd. Stephen Vincent Benét. ThLM
This picture placed these busts between. On Beau Nash's Picture, Which Once Stood between the Busts of Newton and Pope. Jane Brereton. InP
This pig got in the barn. *Unknown.* OxNR
This pinched face of the moon. September in the Park. W. D. Snodgrass. ToPo
This Pine-Tree. Elizabeth Morrow. PEDC
This Place in the Ways. Muriel Rukeyser. MiAP
This place is so much. Rain on South-East England. Donald Davie. NYTB
This Place Rumord to Have Been Sodom. Robert Duncan. NeAP
This pleasant tale is like a little copse. Sonnet: Written at the End of "The Floure and the Lefe." Keats. EnRP
This plot of ground. Dedication for a Plot of Ground. William Carlos Williams. PoeP
This plot, which failed for want of common sense. Dryden. *Fr.* Absalom and Achitophel, Pt. I. CoBE
This ploughman dead in battle slept out of doors. A Private. Edward Thomas. GTBS-P; MMA
This Poem for Black Women. Reginald Lockett. BF
This Poem Is for Bear. Gary Snyder. *Fr.* Myths & Texts: Hunting. NaP
This Poem Is for Birds. Gary Snyder. *Fr.* Myths & Texts: Hunting. NaP
This Poem Is for Deer. Gary Snyder. *Fr.* Myths & Texts: Hunting. NaP
This poem is for my wife. Poem in Prose. Archibald MacLeish. LiTL; MoLP; PoPl
This Poem Will Never Be Finished. Raymond Souster. CaP
This points through place. Canoe. Patrick Anderson. SD
This pool, the quiet sky. March Evening. L. A. G. Strong. MoBrPo
This porthole overlooks a sea. Bendix. John Updike. NYBP
This portrait painter boasted twenty sons. The Artist as Cuckold. *Unknown.* UnTE
This powder-box might seem to be. Her Powder Box. William F. Stead. NYTB
This Prayer I Make. Wordsworth. *Fr.* Lines Composed a Few Miles above Tintern Abbey. PoToHe
This prophecy came by mail. Requiem for "Bird" Parker. Gregory Corso. PoNe (1970 ed.)
This Quiet Dust. Emily Dickinson. *See* This quiet dust was gentlemen and ladies.
This Quiet Dust. John Hall Wheelock. AnEnPo; MAP; MoAmPo; WHA
This quiet dust was gentlemen and ladies. Emily Dickinson. AP; CMoP; EG; InP; MAP; MoAB; MoAmPo; NeMA; OxBA; TOP; ViBoPo
This rain like silver corn, this northern rain. Count Orlo in England. Jon Manchip White. NePoEA
This realm is sacred to the silent past. In a Garret. Elizabeth Akers Allen. AA
This red nun on my left hand leans away. Red Right Returning. Louis O. Coxe. MoVE; WaP
This red scabbard of rock. The Phoenix. W. H. Oliver. AnNZ
This region is as lavish of its flowers. Lefroy in the Forest. Charles Mair. *Fr.* Tecumseh. VA
This relative of mine. To My Grandmother. Frederic Locker-Lampson. ALV; HBV; InMe; OBVV; TOP; VA
This reverend shadow cast that setting sun. Upon Bishop Andrewes His Picture Before His Sermons. Richard Crashaw. MaMe; OBS
This rich marble doth inter [*or* enter]. An Epitaph on the Marchioness of Winchester. Milton. CavP OBS
This rite perform'd, all inly pleas'd and still. A Wondrous Show. James Thomson. *Fr.* The Castle of Indolence, I. OBEC
This road is like a tomb. On Passing Two Negroes on a Dark Country Road Somewhere in Georgia. Conrad Kent Rivers. IDB; NNP
This road isn't passable. Warning. Jesse Douglas. WhC
This room I know so well becomes. The Room. Elizabeth Jennings. NePoEA-2
This room is very old and very wise. Poem. Sam Harrison. NeIP
This rose-tree is not made to bear. Envy. Charles *and* Mary Lamb. OTPC (1923 ed.)
This Royal Throne of Kings. Shakespeare. *See* This England ("This royal throne of kings").
This rudely sculptured porter-pot. Undying Thirst. Antipater of Sidon. AWP; OuHeWo
This rusty mound of cans. Rural Dumpheap. Melville Cane. AmFN
This said; he (begging) gather'd clouds from land. Ulysses in the Waves. Homer, *tr. by* George Chapman. *Fr.* The Odyssey, V. OBS
This said: he high Olympus reacht, the king then left his coach. Priam and Achilles. Homer, *tr. by* George Chapman. *Fr.* The Iliad, XXIV. OBS
This said, he left her there, and forth did to his bellows go. Achilles' Shield. Homer, *tr. by* George Chapman. *Fr.* The Iliad, XVIII. ReEn; TuPP
This said, he turned about his steed. Sidrophel, the Rosicrucian Conjurer. Samuel Butler. *Fr.* Hudibras. OxBoLi
This said, he went to see. The Parting of Hector and Andromache. Homer, *tr. by* George Chapman. *Fr.* The Iliad, VI. SeEP
This said unanimous, and other rites. Wedded Love. Milton. *Fr.* Paradise Lost, IV. PoFS
This sailor knows of wondrous lands afar. The Child and the Mariner. W. H. Davies. CH
This saith my Cloris bright. Madrigal. *Unknown.* LO
This Satyr was not carved, but laid asleep. Peace to the Statue. *Unknown.* OnPM
This saying good-by on the edge of the dark. Good-bye and Keep Cold. Robert Frost. CMoP; GoTP
This Scenery. Leo Connellan. WOW
This scheme of worlds, which vast we call. Turris Eburnea. Aubrey Thomas de Vere. *Fr.* May Carols. PoVP
This scored tissue. Snips and Snails. Susan Axelrod. QAH
This shabby, pencil-annotated text. For My Shakespeare Class. Vonna Hicks Adrian. NYTB
This shade-bestowing pear-tree, thou. The Pear-Tree. *Unknown.* *Fr.* Shi King. AWP; JAWP; WBP
This shadow flesh of risen man. Night. Glyn Jones. NeBP
This shall be called the laying on of hands. A Necessary Miracle. Eda Lou Walton. NYBP
This Shall Be Sufficient. Kenneth Rexroth. CAD
This Sharpening Tension. Sister Mary St. Virginia. JKCP (1955 ed.)
This shell, this slender spiral in the hand. The Enduring Music. Harold Vinal. EtS
This short straight sword. Prelude. R. A. K. Mason. AnNZ
This side of madness, while the flames abate. Two Sonnets from a Sequence. Edgar Holt. BoAV
This Side of Orion, *sels.* Gerald Butler. QAH
"But usually, words fill our heads, which we bring."
"Morphine combined with scopolamine is called."
"Reason why all colors look deeper, The."
"'Take a walk in my head.'"
"Winter/ the cockroach."
This Side of the Truth. Dylan Thomas. GTBS-W
This silken wreath, which circles in mine arme. Upon a Ribband. Thomas Carew. AnAnS-2; SCEP-2
This sky is unmistakable. Not lurid, not low, not black. Haying before Storm. Muriel Rukeyser. WIRo
This Smoking World. Graham Lee Hemminger. InMe
This song is of no importance. Evensong. Conrad Aiken. HBMV; PG
This song of lament I sing for my sorrow. The Wife's Lament.

This (continued)
Unknown, tr. fr. Anglo-Saxon by John F. Adams. FosPo
This song of late autumn. Autumn. Itzig Manger. TrJP
This song of mine. Catawba Wine. Longfellow. LHV
This song of mine sets my soul free. Vusumzi's Song. L. T. Manyase. PeSA
This song of mine will wind its music around you, my child, like the fond arms of love. My Song. Rabindranath Tagore. OHIP
This speech all Trojans did applaud; who from their traces loos'd. The Trojans outside the Walls. Homer, *tr. by* George Chapman. *Fr.* The Iliad, VIII. OBS
This spot is the sweetest I've seen in my life. From a Churchyard in Wales. *Unknown.* FiBHP; ShM; WhC
This Spring of Love. Shakespeare. *Fr.* The Two Gentlemen of Verona, I, iii. ChTr
This starry world, and I in it. Death. James Oppenheim. WGRP
This statue of Liberty, busy man. The Statue of Liberty. Thomas Hardy. EPN; LiTB
This sticky trail. Snail. David McCord. RePo
This still roof where the doves walk slowly, waves. The Cemetery by the Sea. Paul Valéry. OnHM
This Stone. *Unknown, tr. fr. Greek by* Goldwin Smith. AWP
This story's strange, but altogether true. "R. B." SCAP
This sturdy squire, he had, as well. Samuel Butler. *Fr.* Hudibras, I. ViBoPo
This sudden cockerel who stood. Cock-Crow. R. N. Currey. PeSA
This Suite. David Mus. YAP
This summer is your perfect summer. Never will the skies. To a Child before Birth. Norman Nicholson. ChMP
This Summer's Love, *sel.* Mikhail Alekseyevich Kuzmin, *tr. fr. Russian by* Babette Deutsch.
"Night was done; we rose and after." OnPM
This sunlight shames November where he grieves. Autumn Idleness. Dante Gabriel Rossetti. The House of Life, LXIX. ILP; MaVP; PoVP; ViPo; ViPP
This sweet and merry month of May. *Unknown.* SiCE
This sweetness built our beauty. America Is Corn. Robert P. Tristram Coffin. WaKn
This sycamore, oft musical with bees. Inscription for a Fountain on a Heath. Samuel Taylor Coleridge. ERoP-1; MCCG; OAEP
This tempest sweeps the Atlantic! Night Storm. William Gilmore Simms. EtS
This that I give you now. Bread. Stanley Burnshaw. TrJP
This that is washed with weed and pebblestone. The Figurehead. Léonie Adams. NP
This the downgoing, this. Downgoing. Gustav Davidson. FiSC
This the house of Circe, queen of charms. Circe. Lord De Tabley. VA
This the last refuge I can give you. Love Beleaguered. Katherine Garrison Chapin. MoLP
This the law of all war through all ages. The Waste of War. William L. Stidger. PGD
This the road I tread today. The Death of Moses. *Unknown.* TrJP
This the true sign of ruin to a race. The Decay of a People. William Gilmore Simms. AA
This, then, is she. The Daguerreotype. William Vaughn Moody. AnAmPo
This thief the gallows mounting, there to die. Of Labienus. John Owen. *Fr.* Four Epigrams. PrWP
This thin elastic stick was plucked. A Switch Cut in April. Clifford Dyment. MoVE; POTi
This thing I pray, dearest Night, thou Mother of all the gods. A Lover's Curse. Meleager. LiTW
This thing you see, this brightly gay deceit. To Her Portrait. Sister Juana Inés de la Cruz. LiTW
This, this is he; softly a while. Samson Fallen. Milton. *Fr.* Samson Agonistes. OBS
This tiger is not Blake's tiger burning bright. The Wooden Tiger. Samuel Yellen. NePoAm
This tilted jar. Honey. Melville Cane. NYTB
This time/ in the darkness. Stuntman. Lionel Kearns. MoCV
This time, I mean it. A Little Tumescence. Jonathan Williams. ErPo; NeAP
This time of year a twelvemonth past. A. E. Housman. Shropshire Lad, XXV. PoVP
This time the snow came fiercely down. Of Snow. Norman Brick. WaP
This to the crown and blessing of my life. A Letter to Daphnis. Countess of Winchilsea. EnLoPo
This Tokyo. Gary Snyder. NeAP
This told, strange Teras touched her lute, and sung. The Wedding of Alcmane and Mya. George Chapman. *Fr.* Hero and Leander. OBSC
This tomb, by loving hands up-piled. At the Lincoln Tomb. John H. Bryant. PGD
This, too, be your glory great. Primroses. Alfred Austin. OBVV
This too is an experience of the soul. Isis Wanderer. Kathleen Raine. FaBoMo; OxBS
This, Too, Shall Pass Away. *Ad. fr. var. sources by* A. L. Alexander. PoToHe
This, Too, Shall [*or* Will] Pass Away. Lanta Wilson Smith. BLPA; NeHB; STF
This torch, still burning in my hand. Crinagoras. SD
This town has docks where channel boats come sidling. Arrivals, Departures. Philip Larkin. MoBrPo (1962 ed.)
This tragical tale, which, they say, is a true one. Pyramus and Thisbe. John Godfrey Saxe. HBV; OnMSP
This Train. *Unknown.* ABF, *with music*; OxBoLi; SiTL
This tranquil roof whereon the white dove looms. The Marine Cemetery. Paul Valéry, *tr. by* Sidney Alexander. ReMP
This tranquil roof, with walking pigeons, looms. The Cemetery by the Sea. Paul Valéry, *tr. by* Barbara Gibbs. LiTW; PIA
This tree, here fall'n, no common birth or death. On the Site of a Mulberry-Tree; Planted by Wm. Shakespeare; Felled by the Rev. F. Gastrell. Dante Gabriel Rossetti. CBEP; NCEP
This triolet. A Cubic Triolet. *Unknown.* PV
This troubled world is sighing now. *Unknown.* GoTP
This truth came borne with bier and pall. In Memoriam. A. H. H., LXXXV. Tennyson. EPN; ViPo; VP
This tuft that thrives on saline nothingness. The Air Plant. Hart Crane. MAP; MoAB; MoAmPo; NoP; PoIE
This twilight of two years, not past nor next. To the Countesse of Bedford on New-Yeares Day. John Donne. MaMe; OBS; SeEP
This ultimate austerity. Desert Claypan. Frederick T. Macartney. PoAu-1
This Unimportant Morning. Lawrence Durrell. NeBP
This urge, wrestle, resurrection of dry sticks. Cuttings, Later. Theodore Roethke. AP; PoIE
This valley wood is hedged. An English Wood. Robert Graves. BrPo; YT
This vast web, of Nature's weaving. The Cosmic Fabric. Yakov Polonsky. EaLo
This verse be thine, my friend, nor thou refuse. To Mr. Jervas, with Fresnoy's Art of Painting, Translated by Mr. Dryden. Pope. OBEC
This Very Hour. Lizette Woodworth Reese. AnAmPo; HBMV
This very remarkable man. On Monsieur Coué. Charles Inge. FaFP; SiTL
This vestige of woman's animalness is the open secret. Second Dance Poem. Gerald William Barrax. YAP
This vibrant, all-embracing, all-pervading. Psalm for Sonny Rollins. Walt Delegall. BF
This virgin, beautiful and lively day. Sonnet. Stéphane Mallarmé. PoPl
This wall-paper has lines that rise. Missing My Daughter. Stephen Spender. AtBAP; BoC; GTBS-P
This warning, Gallus, for thy love I send. Hylas. Propertius. *Fr.* Elegies. AWP
This was a love in which there was always. Brief Farewell. Anthony Delius. PeSA
This was a man of mighty mould. On a Bust of Lincoln. Clinton Scollard. PEDC
This was a mouse who played around. Tracks in the Snow. Marchette Chute. SiSoSe
This was a poet—it is that. Emily Dickinson. AmePo; AmPP (5th ed.); AP; MAmP; MaPo (1969 ed.); ML; MWA-2; PP
This was a thing the saints never knew. Park Avenue Cat. Frances Frost. CIV
This was Briseis' way: she was a bridge. The Postures of Love, IV. Alex Comfort. NeBP
This was decreed by superior powers. Tower of Ivory. Leonard Bacon. WhC
This was different. To a Suicide. Craig Sterry. QAH

This was her table, these her trim outspread. On the Toilet Table of Queen Marie-Antoinette. J. B. B. Nichols. MemP
"This was Mr. Bleaney's room. He stayed." Mr. Bleaney. Philip Larkin. NePoEA-2; PolE
This Was My Brother. Mona Gould. CaP
This was of old my wishes' utmost bound. The Town and the Country Mouse. Horace. *Fr.* Satires. WoL
This was our heritage. An Ode on the Despoilers of Learning in an American University (1947). Yvor Winters. ExPo; StP
This was our valley, yes. The Dam. Patric Dickinson. POTi
This was that mystery of clearest light. The Statue of Shadow. John Peale Bishop. LiTA
This was the color of coolness. Spring Cellar. Gladys McKee. GoYe
This was the crucifixion on the mountain. Altarwise by Owl-Light, VIII. Dylan Thomas. CMoP; CoBMV; LiTM; MaSP
This was the end and yet, another start. Merlin in the Cave; He Speculates without a Book. Thom Gunn. NePoEA
This was the fire that ran in the wake of the promise. In a Class of Moral Theology. Francis Sweeney. JKCP (1955 ed.)
This was the first world, where the wild dove cries. Creation. Louise Townsend Nicholl. GoYe
This was the hand that knew to swing. The Hand of Lincoln. Edmund Clarence Stedman. PGD
This was the hawk's way. This way the hawk. Hawk's Way. Ted Olson. HoPM
This was the man God gave us when the hour. George Washington. John Hall Ingham. AA; HH; OHIP; OTD; PAH; PAL
This was the noblest Roman of them all. Portrait of Brutus [*or* Brutus *or* The Noblest Roman]. Shakespeare. *Fr.* Julius Caesar, V, v. FaFP; GoTP; MaC; PTK; TreFS; TrGrPo
This was the song of the wakeupworld. The Wakeupworld. Countee Cullen. GoSl
This was the stroke that fired the stacks. Poll Tax (1378). Maurice Hewlett. *Fr.* The Song of the Plow. PoFr
This was the summer when the tired girls. Now Kindness. Peter Viereck. LiTA
This was the Temple of the Mysteries. Eleusis and Beethoven. John Press. MuSP
This was the woman; what now of the man? Modern Love, III. George Meredith. Sonn; ViPo; VP
This was the year of the blackbird. Annals. Maxine Cassin. TDP
This was your butterfly, you see. After Wings. Sarah M. B. Piatt. AA; HBV
This watchful nurse and bundled boy at play. A Matter of Life and Death. Richard Aldridge. NePoAm
This water, like a sky that no one uses. Waters. Kenneth Slessor. NeLNL
This wax-mannequin nude, the florist rose. The Florist Rose. Robert Graves. AtBAP; CBV
This Way Only. Lesbia Harford. PoAu-1
This Way Out. Margaret Fishback. ALV
This way, this way, come and hear. Song in the Wood. John Fletcher. *Fr.* The Little French Lawyer. ElL; ThWaDe
This weather's like my troubled mind and eyes. In Rainy-gloomy Weather. John Davies of Hereford. CBEP
This Were to Pray. Richard Chenevix Trench. MaRV
This while we are abroad. An Ode Written in the Peak[e]. Michael Drayton. OBS; ReIE
This White and Slender Body. Heine. *tr. fr. German by* Louis Untermeyer. UnTE
This whirlwind sounds a larger dissonance. Mid-Century. Mary Elizabeth Osborn. NePoAm
This wild night, gathering the washing as if it were flowers. From the Roof. Denise Levertov. NoP
"This will not do," he said. If It Offend Thee. Horace Gregory. NMP
This wind brings all dead things to life. A Windy Day. Andrew Young. GoTP; MoPW; ThWaDo
This winter air is keen and cold. Le Jardin des Tuileriers. Oscar Wilde. JKCP (1926 ed.)
This winter day, we build our fire. The Fire. William Burford. NePA
This winter eve how soft! how mild! Elegy. Richard Chenevix Trench. IrPN
This winter's morning, turning the other way. Turning. Robert Finch. MoCV; OBCV
This Winter's Weather It Waxeth Cold. *Unknown.* *see* Old Cloak, The.
This World. Abu-l-Ala al-Maarri, *tr. fr. Arabic by* R. A. Nicholson. LiTW
This World. Abbie Huston Evans. NePoAm
This World a Hunting Is. William Drummond of Hawthornden. CBEP; CBV
(World a Hunt, The.) OBS
(World a Hunting Is, The.) FaBoEn
This world and life are battered and shattered. Philosophy. Heine, *tr. by* James Thomson. OnPM
This world and this life are so scattered, they try me. Zu fragmentarisch ist Welt und Leben. Heine, *tr. by* Charles G. Leland. AWP; ELU
This World Is All a Fleeting Show. Thomas Moore. HBV
This world is not conclusion. Emily Dickinson. AmePo; EaLo; MaPo
This world is so full of a number of bugs. Happy Thought. Bert Leston Taylor. RIS
This world is unto God a work of art. Robert Bridges. *Fr.* The Growth of Love. PoVP
This world, O my friend, is like a carcase unsepulchred. This World. Abu-l-Ala al-Maarri. LiTW
This world of ours awakes the human will. Speech of Abbot Stephen. Petar Petrovic Njegos. *Fr.* The Mountain Wreath. PoFr
This world was not. The Golden Age. Ernest Francisco Fenollosa. AA
This world was once a fluid haze of light. Tennyson. *Fr.* The Princess. ImOP
This world we see, O Lord, is made so fair. Canto Espiritual. Juan Maragall. CAW
This worlde is ful of variaunce. Duplicity of Woman [*or* of Doubleness]. John Lydgate. EnPo; MeEL
This World's Joy. *Unknown.* *See* Wynter Wakeneth Al My Care.
This worthy limitour, this noble frere. Prologue. Chaucer. *Fr.* The Canterbury Tales: The Friar's Tale. EnLi-1 (1949 ed.)
This would be spring, if seasons could be found. Perhaps the Best Time. William Meredith. NePoEA
This wretched life, the trust and confidence. This Life a Dream and Shadow. Sir Thomas More. *Fr.* The Twelve Weapons of Spiritual Battle. EnRePo
This year,/ Next year. *Unknown.* OxNR
This Year, before It Ends. Eve Langley. BoAV
This year of fourteen fifty-six. The Little Testament. Villon. OuHeWo
This year (so I hear). A Year without Seasons. Mance Williams. NNP
This year, till late in April, the snow fell thick and light. The Nineteenth of April. Lucy Larcom. MC; PAH
This yellow velvet visitor. Caterpillar. R. E. Rashley. CaP
This Young Girl. C. Day Lewis. NYTB
This Yris, fro the high stage. The House of Sleep. John Gower. *Fr.* Confessio Amantis: Ceix and Alceone. AtBAP
Thisbe. Helen Gray Cone. AA
Thise olde gentil Britouns in hir dayes. The Franklin's Prologue and Tale. Chaucer. *Fr.* The Canterbury Tales. CABL; MBW-1; OAEP
Thise ryotoures three, of which I telle. Quest for Death. Chaucer. *Fr.* The Canterbury Tales: The Pardoner's Tale. MyFE
Thistle and darnel and dock grew there. Nicholas Nye. Walter de la Mare. BoChLi; BoTP; HBMV; OA
Thistle, Yarrow, Clover. Kenneth Porter. NePoAm
Thistle-Down. Clara Doty Bates. AA
Thistledown. Denis Glover. AnNZ
Thistledown. Harold Monro. BrPo; GTBS-D
Thistledown. Lizette Woodworth Reese. YeAr
Thistledown's flying, The. Autumn. John Clare. BoNaP; NBM; PoEL-4
Tho'. *See also* Though.
Tho' actors cannot much of learning boast. Prologue to the University of Oxford, 1676. Dryden. MBW-1
Tho' cruel fate should bid us part. My Jean! Burns. CBV
Tho' endowed with all the virtues of a Daniel. Tact. Harry Graham. ALV

Tho' grief and fondness in my breast rebel. London. Samuel Johnson. GoTL; PoEL-3
Tho' Grief had nipp'd her early bloom. The Maniac. Thomas Russell. OBEC
Tho' I am very old and wise. To Dick, on His Sixth Birthday. Sara Teasdale. TSW
Tho' I can not your cruelty constrain. Sir Thomas Wyatt. SiPS
Tho' I take the wings of the morning. Wings of the Morning. Mabel Curtis. SoP
Tho' if an eye that's downward cast. In Memoriam A. H. H., LXII. Tennyson. EPN; ViPo; VP
Tho' ill at ease, a stranger and alone. Thoughts on Pausing at a Cottage near the Paukataug River. Sarah Kemble Knight. SCAP
Tho' I'm no Catholic. The Catholic Bells. William Carlos Williams. CMoP; OxBA
Tho' my verse is exact. Hence These Rimes. Bert Leston Taylor. FiBHP
Tho' the road may be rough where He leads me. My Saviour's Face. *Unknown.* SoP
Tho' truths in manhood darkly join. In Memoriam A. H. H., XXXVI [*or* The Word *or* The Word Incarnate]. Tennyson. ChIP; EPN; GoBC; MaRV; ViPo; VP
Tho' world on world in myriad myriads roll. What Know We Greater than the Soul? Tennyson. *Fr.* Ode on the Death of the Duke of Wellington. MaRV
Tho' you make no return to my passion. *See* Though You Make No Return.
Tho' You May Boast You're Fairer. *Unknown.* OBS
Thocht, The. William Soutar. NeBP
Thocht raging stormes movis us to schaik. *See* Though raging stormes movis us to shake.
Thocht that this warld be verie strange. Solace in Age. Sir Richard Maitland. OxBS
Thomalin, why sytten we soe? March Eclogue. Spenser. *Fr.* The Shepheardes Calendar. FosPo; PIA
Thomas à Becket, *sel.* George Darley.
Queen Eleanor and Her Dwarf. PeER
Thomas A. Edison/ Never took medicine. Important people. Louis Untermeyer, *and others.* StaSt
Thomas à Kempis. Richard Rogers Bowker. AA
Thomas à Kempis. Lizette Woodworth Reese. AA
Thomas a Tattamus took two T's. Riddles. *Unknown.* HBV; HBVY; OTPC; RIS
Thomas at Chickamauga. Kate Brownlee Sherwood. PAH
Thomas Carlyle. *Unknown.* FiBHP
Thomas Chatterton. Dante Gabriel Rossetti. Five English Poets, 1. PoVP
Thomas Cromwell. *Unknown.* ESPB
Thomas Dudley, Ah! Old Must Dye. *Unknown.* SCAP
Thomas Gray in Patterdale. Norman Nicholson. ACV
Thomas Hardy in the stars. Winter's Dregs. George Bowering. PeCV (1967 ed.)
Thomas Hardy, Poet. Mark Van Doren. ML
Thomas Heywood. Swinburne. CLwM
Thomas Hood. E. A. Robinson. HBMV; ML
Thomas Hood. Sir William Watson. PoVP
Thomas in the Fields. Lois Moyles. NYBP
Thomas Jefferson. Stephen Vincent Benét. FaPON; NAMP; PoPl; RePo; TiPo
Thomas lay on the Huntlie bank. Thomas the Rimer [*or* Thomas Rymer]. *Unknown.* EnSB; ESPB
Thomas MacDonagh. Francis Ledwidge. OnYI; OxBI
(Lament for Thomas MacDonagh.) AnIV
Thomas More to Them That Seek Fortune. Sir Thomas More. EnRePo
Thomas o Yonderdale. *Unknown.* ESPB
Thomas of Erceldoune. *Unknown, tr. fr. Middle English.* MeEV
Thomas Rhodes. Edgar Lee Masters. *Fr.* Spoon River Anthology. NP
Thomas Rymer. *Unknown. See* Thomas the Rhymer.
Thomas Sackville in Commendation of the Work to the Reader. Thomas Sackville. ReIE
Thomas Shadwell the Poet. Dryden. *Br. sel. fr.* Absalom and Achitophel, Pt. II. ChTr
Thomas Stuart was a lord. Lord Thomas Stuart. *Unknown.* BaBo; ESPB
Thomas the Rhymer. *Unknown.* AnFE; BuBa; ELP; FaBoCh; GoTS; HBV; LiTB; LiTG; OBB; OBEV; OnMSP; OxBB; PoAn; SeCeV; ViBoPo
(Thomas Rymer.) ATP; BaBo (A *and* B *vers.*); BoChLi (1939 ed.); BoLiVe; CBEP; CH; CoBE; EnLi-1; ESPB (A *and* C *vers.*); FlW; InP; NoP; OAEP; ViBoFo
(Thomas Rymer and the Queen of Elfland.) ChTr
(Thomas the Rimer.) EnSB
(True Thomas.) GBV (1952 ed.); GoTP; MaC; OtMeF; OxBS; StPo; TrGrPo
"'Harp and carp, Thomas!' she said," *sel.* LO
Thomas, the vagrant piper's son. Mother Goose Up-to-Date. Louis Untermeyer. MoAmPo
Thomas Trevelyan. Edgar Lee Masters. *Fr.* Spoon River Anthology. AnFE; APA; CoAnAm; MoPo
Thomas was a little glutton. Little Thomas. F. Gwynne Evans. BBGG
Thomas Winterbottom Hance. W. S. Gilbert. InMe
Thompson Street. Samuel McCoy. HBMV
Thoralf and Synnöv. Hjalmar Hjorth Boyesen. AA
Thorberg Skafting, master-builder. The Building of the *Long Serpent.* Longfellow. *Fr.* Tales of a Wayside Inn. EtS
Thoreau. Amos Bronson Alcott. AA
Thoreau,/ grabbing on, hard. The Distances to the Friend. Jonathan Williams. NeAP
Thoreau, you've come into your own. To Henry David Thoreau. Irwin Edman. WhC
Thoreau's Flute. Louisa May Alcott. AA; DD; HBV
Thorgerda. John Payne. VA
Thorn, The. Wordsworth. EnRP
Sels.
"And they had fixed the wedding day." EvOK
"High on a mountain's highest ridge." Par
Thorn Leaves in March. W. S. Merwin. TwCP
Thorns. J. Danson Smith. SoP
Thorns Arm the Rose. Claudian, *tr. fr. Latin by* Maurice Platnauer *and* Virginia Tufte. HW
Thorns we see just up ahead, The. If You Believe. Phyllis C. Michael. SoP
Thoroughbred, The. Helene Magaret. StaSt
Thoroughgoing, The. Josephine Miles. FiMAP
Thorowe the halle the belle han sounde. The Accounte of W. Canynge's Feast. Thomas Chatterton. EnLi-2
Thor's Thrush, *sel.* Robert Kelly. YAP
Spels, IV—VII.
Those animals that follow us in dream. Lupus in Fabula [*or* Xochitepec]. Malcolm Lowry. MoCV; OBCV; PeCV; TDP
Those arts which common beauties move. To Corinna. John Oldmixon. SeCL
Those Beauteous Maids. Moses ibn Ezra, *tr. fr. Hebrew by* Solomon Solis-Cohen. TrJP
Those Being Eaten by America. Robert Bly. CoAP; FRC; NaP
Those charming eyes within whose starry sphere. On the Death of Catarina de Attayda. Luís de Camoes. AWP; JAWP; WBP
Those clarities detached us, gave us form. The Tourist and the Town. Adrienne Rich. NePoEA-2
Those Dancing Days Are Gone. W. B. Yeats. AtBAP
Those days we spent on Lebanon. On Lebanon. David Gray. AA
Those—dying then. Emily Dickinson. AmePo; CABA; NoP
Those earlier men that owned our earth. The After-Comers. Robert Traill Spence Lowell. AA
Those envied places which do know her well. Day of Love, A. Dante Gabriel Rossetti. The House of Life, XVI. MaVP; PoVP; ViPo; VP
Those evening clouds, that setting ray. On the Setting Sun. Sir Walter Scott. MaRV
Those eyes that hold the hand of every heart. A Sonnet. Nicholas Breton. ReIE
Those Eyes Which Set My Fancy on Afire. Philippe Desportes, *tr. fr. French.* ReIE; SiCE
(Conquest.) AWP
(His Lady's Might.) OBSC
Those famous men of old, the Ogres. Ogres and Pygmies. Robert Graves. CABA; CBV; CMoP; FaBoMo; LiTB; LiTM; SeCePo; SeCeV
"Those fantastic forms, fang-sharp." City Without Walls. W. H. Auden. NYBP
Those fireflies sparkling in the willows. The Code. Christopher Morley. LHV
Those flaming Christians with their hygienic rose. Burns Sing-

er. *Fr.* Sonnets for a Dying Man. NePoEA-2
Those former loves wherein our lives have run. Sonnets, XIX. James Agee. MAP; MoAmPo
Those Gambler's Blues. *Unknown.* *See* Gambler's Blues.
Those graves, with bending osier bound. A Night-Piece on Death. Thomas Parnell. SeCePo
Those great rough ranters, Branns. A Simplification. Richard Wilbur. CMoP
Those groans men use. The Mutes. Denise Levertov. NaP
Those hands, which you so clapped [*or* clapt], go now and wring. Shakespeare Dead [*or* Sonnet to Shakespeare]. Hugh Holland. ACP (1952 ed.); CLwM; PrWP
Those heav'nly rayes of thyne. *Unknown.* SeCSL
Those hewers of the clouds, the winds—that lair. The Winds. Madison Cawein. MAP
Those horns, the envy of the moon. Death of the Bull. Roy Campbell. FaBoTw
Those hours that with gentle work did frame. Sonnets, V. Shakespeare. ReEn; SiCE
Those houses haunt in which we leave. Ghosts. Elizabeth Jennings. MemP; NePoEA-2
Those Images. W. B. Yeats. CMoP; POTE; PP
Those in the vegetable rain retain. Stories of Snow. P. K. Page. OBCV
Those joys that us'd to flatter me. Corydon's Complaint. Samuel Pordage. CavP
Those lathered horses galloping past. The Horsemen. Gene Baro. NePoEA-2
Those lean and salty sires of ours. The Stone Crop. Robert P. Tristram Coffin. PaA
Those lines that I before have writ do lie. Sonnets, CXV. Shakespeare. SiCE
Those lips that Love's own hand did make. Sonnets, CXLV. Shakespeare. Sonn
Those long uneven lines. MCMXIV. Philip Larkin. PoeP
Those looks, whose beams be joy, whose motion is delight. Astrophel and Stella, LXXVII. Sir Philip Sidney. FCP; SiPS
Those lovers only hapye are. *Unknown.* SeCSL
Those lumbering horses in the steady plough. Horses. Edwin Muir. CMoP; FaBoCh; LoGBV; MoVE; SeCePo
Those make thunder though taking pigs somewhere. 13th Dance —Matching Parcels—21 February 1964. Jackson MacLow. CoPo
Those moon-gilded dancers. The Gay. "Æ." OBMV; POTE
Those nights we said "Goodbye! goodbye!" and then. Decent Burial. Lois Seyster Montross. HBMV
Those Not Elect. Léonie Adams. MoVE; PoDB
Those not live yet. Emily Dickinson. MAmP
Those occasions involving the veering of axles. Munich Elegy No. 1. George Barker. LiTG; LiTM; SeCePo; WaP
Those on the top say they know you, Earth—they are liars. The Miner. Maxwell Bodenheim. NP
Those parts of thee that the world's eye doth view. Sonnets, LXIX. Shakespeare. CBEP
Those pretty wrongs that liberty commits. Sonnets, XLI. Shakespeare. CBEP; InvP; PoeP; ReEn
Those ravens black that rested. Heavy-hearted. Judah Al-Harizi. TrJP
Those reckless hosts rush to the wells. Elegy. Baruch of Worms. TrJP
Those red men you offended were my brothers. In My First Hard Springtime. James Welch. YAP
Those rules of old discover'd, not devis'd. Pope. *Fr.* An Essay on Criticism. PoFS
Those saints, which God loves best. Temptation. Robert Herrick. LiTB
Those ships which left. Tanka: A Reflection [*or* Seven Poems, 5]. Saigyo Hoshi. AWP; InP; LiTW
Those souls that of His own good life partake. Eternal Life. Henry More. TRV
Those stopped by the barrage. Dirge for the Barrel-Organ of the New Barbarism. Louis Aragon. OnHM; WaaP
Those things which might be counted gain. God's Best. Avis B. Christiansen. SoP
Those trackless deeps, where many a weary sail. The Trackless Deeps. Shelley. *Fr.* The Daemon of the World. EtS
Those Troublesome Disguises. Jonathan Williams. NeAP
Those Two Boys. Franklin P. Adams. ALV; FiBHP; MAP; MoAmPo (1942 ed); TrJP
Those upon whom Almighty doth intend. The Frowardness of the Elect in the Work of Conversion. Edward Taylor. SCAP
Those Various Scalpels. Marianne Moore. LoBV
Those walléd garrisons will I subdue. Christopher Marlowe. *Fr.* Tamburlaine the Great, Pt. I. ViBoPo
Those we have loved the dearest. The Fallen. Duncan Campbell Scott. TrPWD
Those We Love the Best. Ella Wheeler Wilcox. PoToHe
Those we love truly never die. Forever. John Boyle O'Reilly. CAW; HBV; MaRV; OnYI; OQP; WGRP
Those were good times, in olden days. Written on a Fly-Leaf of Theocritus. Maurice Thompson. AA
Those were the conquered, still too proud to yield. The Battle-field. Lloyd Mifflin. PAH
Those which have travelled o'er the earth's round ball. John Heath. SiCE
Those who are not mine. The Feast. Nora B. Cunningham. OQP
Those who fling off, toss head. Meeting Together of Poles & Latitudes: In Prospect. Margaret Avison. OBCV; PeCV
Those who have chosen to pass the night. Violent Storm. Mark Strand. NYBP
Those who have descended to the nethermost deeps. Bathymeter. William Hart-Smith. BoAV
Those who have laid the harp aside. To Wordsworth. Walter Savage Landor. ERoP-1; PeER
Those who have visited the North Pole. The World's End. Michael Roberts. FaBoMo
Those Who Know Do Not Tell. *Unknown, at. to* Lao-tzu, *tr. fr. Chinese by* Witter Bynner. *Fr.* Tao Teh King. OnPM
Those who live in country places. Epiphany. Eileen Duggan. ISi
Those who lived here are gone. A Ruined House. Richard Aldington. BrPo
Those Who Lost Everything. David Diop, *tr. fr. French by* Langston Hughes. PBA
Those Who Love. Sara Teasdale. MoLP
Those who love cats which do not even purr. Cats. Francis Scarfe. NeBP
Those who love Thee may they find. A Prayer. George F. Chawner. BLRP
Those who said God is praised. For the New Railway Station in Rome. Richard Wilbur. NePoEA; PoDB
"Those who speak know nothing." Lao-tzu [*or* The Philosopher]. Po Chü-i, *tr. by* Arthur Waley. LiTW; OnPM; WhC; WoL
Those Who Soar. Margaret Lathrop Law. PoMa
Those who win are those who try. Ahead. *Unknown.* SoP
Those Winter Sundays. Robert Hayden. BP; IDB
Thothmes, who loved a pyramid. The Story of Pyramid Thothmes. *Unknown.* NA
Thou alive on earth, sweet boy. Three Epitaphs upon the Death of a Rare Child of Six Years Old, 3. Francis Davison. OBSC; ReIE
Thou Alone Art Good. Michelangelo, *tr. fr. Italian by* John Addington Symonds. OnPM
(Prayer for Purification, A.) AWP
Thou Alone Canst Save. Amelia Wakeford. BePJ
Thou ancient oak! whose myriad leaves are loud. Eliot's Oak. Longfellow. AmePo
Thou and I and he are not gods made men for a span. Swinburne. *Fr.* The Hymn of Man. WGRP
Thou are not, Penshurst, built to envious show. *See* Thou art not, Penshurst . . .
"Thou art a fool," said my head to my heart. Retort. Paul Lawrence Dunbar. AA
Thou art all fair, O Mary. A Prayer of Praise to Mary. *Unknown.* WHL
Thou art as a lone watcher on a rock. England. Richard Edwin Day. AA
Thou art beautiful, O my love. Canticle of Canticles (The Song of Solomon), Bible, *O.T. (Douay vers.).* ISi
Thou art come at length. Sitalkas. Hilda Doolittle ("H. D."). ViBoPo
Thou Art Coming! Frances Ridley Havergal. WGRP
Thou Art Coming to a King. John Newton. FaChP; SoP; TRV
Thou art God, and all things formed are Thy servants. The Royal Crown, VIII. Solomon ibn Gabirol. AWP
Thou art God's sky. Mary. Robert Farren. ISi

Thou art great, and compared with Thy greatness all greatness. The Royal Crown, V. Solomon ibn Gabirol. AWP
Thou art heav'n Olimpia. *Unknown.* SeCSL
Thou art in danger, Cincius, on my word. Epigram. Marcus Argentarius. ALV
Thou Art Indeed Just, Lord. Gerard Manley Hopkins. AWP; BrPo; BWP; CABA; CaFP; CBV; CMoP; CoBMV; EaLo; EnLit; GTBS-P; GTBS-W; ILP; InPo; LiTM; LoBV; MaPo (1969 ed.); MoAB; MoBrPo (1950 ed.); NeMA; NoP; OAEP (2d ed.); OxBoCh; PG (1945 ed.); PoeP; PoDB; TrPWD, 4 *ll*; UnPo (3d ed.); VaPo; ViPo (1962 ed.); ViPP; VP
(Justus Quidem Tu Es, Domine.) CAW
(Sonnet: "Thou art indeed just, Lord.") MoVE
Thou art King of Israel and of Davides kunne. A Palm-Sunday Hymn. William Herebert. MeEL
Thou art Light celestial, and the eyes of the pure shall. The Royal Crown, VII. Solomon ibn Gabirol. AWP
Thou art like to [*or* unto] a flower. The Translated Way. Franklin P. Adams. BOHV; FiBHP
Thou art lost to me forever!—I have lost thee, Isadore! The Widowed Heart. Albert Pike. AA
Thou art mine, thou hast given thy word. Song from a Drama. Edmund Clarence Stedman. AA
Thou art more than a clod. More Than. Fay Inchfawn. SoP
Thou art my God, sole object of my love. Prayer of St. Francis Xavier. Pope. TrPWD
Thou art my Hiding Place. My Hiding Place. Kathryn T. Bowsher. STF
Thou art my hiding place, O Lord! O Lord! My Hiding Place. Thomas Raffles. BePJ
Thou art my very own. The Unborn. Julia Neely Finch. AA
Thou Art My Victory. Avis B. Christiansen. SoP
Thou art not, and thou never canst be mine. To Imperia. Thomas Burbidge. VA
Thou art not dead, although the spoiler's hand. Africa. Lewis Alexander. CDC
Thou art not dead, my Prote! thou art flown. To Prote. Simmias. AWP
Thou Art Not Fair. Thomas Campion. AtBAP; EIL; EnRePo; InvP; NoP; ReIE; TuPP; ViBoPo
(Renunciation.) GTSL; OnPM
("Thou art not fair for all thy red and white.") EG; EnLoPo; OBSC; ReEn
Thou Art Not in a Place. "Angelus Silesius," *tr. fr. German by* Paul Carus. OnPM
Thou Art Not Lovelier Than Lilacs. Edna St. Vincent Millay. BoLiVe; CMoP
Thou art not, Penshurst, built to envious show. To Penhurst. Ben Jonson. AnAnS-2; AtBAP; BWP; CABA; CABL; LoBV; NoP; OBS; PoEL-2; PoFS; ReEn; ReIE; SCEP-2; SeCP; SeCV-1; SeEP; TuPP
Thou art not so black, as my heart. A Jeat Ring Sent. John Donne. MaMe; PoEL-2
Thou art, O God, the life and light. The Glory of God in Creation [*or* Thou Art, O God]. Thomas Moore. MaRV; OHIP; TrPWD
Thou Art of All Created Things. Pedro Calderón de la Barca, *tr. fr. Spanish.* WGRP
Thou art One, the first of every number and the foundation. The Royal Crown, II. Solomon ibn Gabirol. AWP
Thou art our Master! Thou of God the Son. The Master. S. D. Robbins. BePJ
Thou art repriv'd old yeare, thou shalt not die. Epithalamion: the Time of the Mariage. John Donne. MaMe
Thou art so fair, and yong withall. Youth and Beauty. Aurelian Townshend. AnAnS-2; EP; MePo; SeCP
Thou art the essence of all created things. Thou Art of All Created Things. Pedro Calderón de la Barca. WGRP
Thou art the flower of grief to me. The Woodruffe. Isa Craig Knox. VA
Thou art the joy of age. Light. George Macdonald. VA
Thou art the rock of empire, set mid-seas. At Gibraltar, II. George Edward Woodberry. AA; AnAmPo; GN
Thou art the sky and thou art the nest as well. Rabindranath Tagore. *Fr.* Gitanjali. BoPe; OBMV
Thou art the soul of a summer's day. A Song. Paul Laurence Dunbar. AmNP
Thou are the Star, blazing with beames bright. Star of the Sea. Sebastian Brant, *tr. by* Alexander Barclay. *Fr.* The Ship of Fools. ACP; CAW
Thou art the star for which all evening waits. Aldebaran at Dusk. George Sterling. PFY
Thou art the Way. "I Am the Way." Alice Meynell. ACP; CAW; GoBC; JKCP; MaRV; OBMV; OQP; PoVP; TRV
Thou art the Way! The Way, the Truth, and the Life. *Unknown.* BePJ
Thou art the Way, to Thee alone. Christ, the Way [*or* The Way, the Truth, the Life]. George Washington Doane. BePJ; MaRV
Thou art the wind and I the lyre. Wind and Lyre. Edwin Markham. SoP; TRV
"Thou art! Thou art!!" Lavater says. "Thou art!!" On Lavater's Song of a Christian to Christ. Johann Wolfgang von Goethe. ELU
Thou art to all lost love the best. To the Willow-Tree. Robert Herrick. HBV; OBEV
Thou art too hard for me in love. Love. George Herbert. MaMe
Thou art wise. And wisdom is the fount of life. The Royal Crown, IX. Solomon ibn Gabirol. AWP
"Thou Art Worthy." *Unknown.* SoP
Thou, att whose feete I waste mie soule in sighes. To Mie Tirante. George Darley. Sonn
Thou barren waste; unprofitable strand. Winter in Lower Canada. Standish O'Grady. *Fr.* The Emigrant. OBCV
Thou beauteous off-spring of a syre as fair. On a Sunbeam. Thomas Heyrick. MePo
Thou Beautiful Sabbath. *Unknown. tr. fr. Yiddish by* Isidore Myers. TrJP
"Thou beel amy, thou Pardoner," he sayde. Introduction. Chaucer. *Fr.* The Canterbury Tales: The Pardoner's Tale. FosPo
Thou bent and only motion of our lives. Lyttelton Harbour, XXXIII. D'Arcy Cresswell. AnNZ
Thou bidst me come away. To Death. Robert Herrick. CoBE; InPo
Thou Black, wherein all colours are composed. Another Sonnet to Black Itself. Lord Herbert of Cherbury. EP; SeEP
Thou bleedest, my poor Heart! and thy distress. On a Discovery Made Too Late. Samuel Taylor Coleridge. EnRP; Sonn
Thou Blind Man's Mark. Sir Philip Sidney. *Sometimes considered Sonnet CIX of* Astrophel and Stella; *also in* Certain Sonnets. BWP; CABA; EnRePo; ErPo; FCP; FosPo; NoP; PoSa; ReEn; ReIE; SiCE; Sonn; TuPP; VaPo; ViBoPo
(Desire.) LiTB; LiTG; MasP; SiPS; TrGrPo
Thou blossom bright with autumn dew. To the Fringed Gentian. Bryant. AA; AmePo; AmP; AmPP (3d ed.); AnAmPo; AnFE; AnNE; AP; APA; AWP; CoAnAm; CoBA; FaBoBe; GN; HBV; MPB; NeHB; NePA; NoP; OBRV; OTD; OTPC; PoLF; StP; TOP; TreFT; YT
Thou born to match the gale (thou art all wings). Walt Whitman. *Fr.* To the Man-of-War-Bird. InP
Thou, born to sip the lake or spring. On a Honey Bee [*or* To a Honey Bee *or* The Honey Bee]. Philip Freneau. AA; AmPP; AP; CoBA; TDP; YaD
Thou Bounteous Giver of the Light. St. Hilary of Arles, *tr. fr. Latin.* BePJ
Thou burden of all songs the earth hath sung. Autumn. Sir William Watson. OBVV
Thou call'st me effeminate, for I love women's joys. Manliness. John Donne. CLwM
Thou canst hold my nose to the grindstone. Of Holding of a Nose. John Heywood. ReIE
Thou canst not die whilst any zeal abound. To Delia, XL. Samuel Daniel. EnLi-1 (1949 ed.); OAEP; OBSC; Sonn; TuPP
Thou canst not prove that thou art body alone. Tennyson. *Fr.* The Ancient Sage. EPN
Thou canst not prove the Nameless, O my Son. Faith. Tennyson. *Fr.* The Ancient Sage. MaRV
Thou canst not wave thy staff in air. Rhythm. Emerson. OQP; TOP
Thou cheat'st us Ford, mak'st one seem two by Art. Upon Ford's Two Tragedies, "Love's Sacrifice" and "The Broken Heart." Richard Crashaw. MaMe; OBS
Thou Christ, my soul is hurt and bruised. The Doubter [*or* Christ

the Answer]. Richard Watson Gilder, *also at. to* George Macdonald. MaRV; TrPWD
Thou comest, Autumn, heralded by the rain. Autumn. Longfellow. OBVV
Thou comest by. 10th Dance—Coming On as a Horn—20 February 1964. Jackson MacLow. CoPo
Thou comest, much wept for; such a breeze. In Memoriam A. H. H., XVII. Tennyson. EnLi-2; EPN; OBEV (1st ed.); ViPo; VP
Thou comest to me, thou exultest, seeing my beauty. Hymn of Victory: Thutmose III. Amon-Re. WaaP
Thou cruel fair, I go. Virelay. Charles Cotton. LO; SeCL
Thou cursed cock, with thy perpetual noise. On a Cock at Rochester. Sir Charles Sedley. PeRV
Thou dancer of two thousand years. The Dancing Faun. Robert Cameron Rogers. AA
Thou dear and mystic semblance. Lines to the Blessed Sacrament. James Joseph Callanan. OnYI
Thou Dear Redeemer. John Cennick. SoP
Thou, Death, alone art kind, helpest men give. To Azrael. Baudelaire. SyP
Thou didst deign to pluck us. The Soul as a Plucked Flower. Bhai Vir Singh. OnPM
Thou Didst Delight My Eyes. Robert Bridges. ELP; GTBS-D; MoAB; MoBrPo; VA
Thou didst, O mighty God, exist. Three Hymns, 1. Elizabeth Rowe. WaPE
Thou Didst Say Me. Miriam Waddington. OBCV; PeCV (1967 ed.)
Thou didst teach the thronging people. Prayer for Purity. Jemima Luke. SoP
Thou divinest, fairest, brightest. The Satyr's Farewell [*or* The Satyr's Leave-taking]. John Fletcher. *Fr.* The Faithful Shepherdess, V, v. LO; LoBV (2d ed.); OBS
Thou Dome, where Edward first enroll'd. An Ode Inscribed to the Earl of Sunderland at Windsor. Thomas Tickell. OBEC
Thou dreamer with the million moods. A Song of Desire. Frederic Lawrence Knowles. HBV
Thou dreges of Lethey O thou dull. *Unknown.* SeCSL
Thou dusky spirit of the wood. The Crow. Henry David Thoreau. BiS
Thou Easer of All Woes. John Fletcher. *Fr.* The Tragedy of Valentinian, V, ii. TreFT
Thou enemy of love, how slow you creep. Dawn. *Unknown.* UnTE
Thou ever young! Persephone but gazes. To Demeter. Maybury Fleming. AA
Thou existest, but hearing of ear cannot reach Thee. The Royal Crown, III. Solomon ibn Gabirol. AWP
Thou fair-haired [*or* -hair'd] angel of the evening. To the Evening Star. Blake. BoNaP; CEP; CH; ChER; ChTr; CoBE; EiPP; EnLit; EnRP; ERoP-1; FaBV; GBV (1952 ed.); HW; LoBV; MCCG; NoP; OAEP; PoFS; PoLF; PoPo; SiSw; StaSt; TrGrPo; WiR
Thou fillest all of South America. To Bolívar. Rafael Pombo. PoFr
Thou Flower of Spring. John Clare. LO
Thou fool! if madness be so rife. Rondeau. Charles Cotton. SeCL
Thou fool profane, be silent! Epigram II. *Unknown. Fr.* Duel with Verses over a Great Man. TrJP
Thou foolish blossom, all untimely blown! To a Wild Rose Found in October. Ednah Proctor Clarke. AA
Thou for whose birth the whole creation yearned. The Rise of Man. John White Chadwick. AA
Thou foul-mouthed wretch! Why dost thou choose. The Sailor to His Parrot. W. H. Davies. EtS; ViBoPo
Thou from th' enthroned martyrs blood-stain'd line. Henry King. *Fr.* An Elegy upon the Most Incomparable King Charles the First. OBS
Thou gallant chief whose glorious name. Washington. Denis O'Crowley. OHIP; PoRL
Thou gavest me leave to kiss. *See* Thou gav'st me leave to kiss.
Thou gavest steel to us, Thou gavest brain. Frank Wilmot. *Fr.* To God, from the Warring Nations. BoAV
Thou gav'st me late to eat. The Sweetmeat. Sir Edward Sherburne. SeCL
Thou gav'st [*or* gavest] me leave to kiss. Chop-Cherry. Robert Herrick. ALV; CBEP; EnLoPo; MyFE; SeEP; UnTE
Thou gav'st us learning, lit with many an hour. Oxford. Archibald T. Strong. *Fr.* Sonnets of the Empire. BoAu
"Thou Ghost," I said, "and is thy name Today?" The Morrow's Message. Dante Gabriel Rossetti. The House of Life, XXXVIII. GTSE; MaVP; PoVP; ViPo; VP
Thou glorious mocker of the world! I hear. To the Mocking-Bird. Albert Pike. AA
Thou God of all, whose presence dwells. Hymn. John Haynes Holmes. TrPWD
Thou God of all, whose spirit moves. Hymn of At-One-Ment. John Haynes Holmes. MaRV
Thou God, whose high, eternal love. Wedding Prayer [*or* Wedding-Hymn]. Sidney Lanier. SoP; TrPWD
Thou goest more and more. Ode on Advancing Age. Richard Watson Dixon. NBM
Thou goest; to what distant place. Farewell. John Addington Symonds. HBV
Thou Great God. *Unknown, tr. fr. Xhosa by* A. C. Jordan. PBA
Thou great Supreme, whom angel choirs adore. Unseen. Fanny Crosby. TrPWD
Thou green and blooming, cool and shaded hill. The Heart on the Hill. Petrarch. Sonnets to Laura: To Laura in Life, CCV. AWP
Thou Guide to doubt, be silent evermore. Epigram I. *Unknown. Fr.* Duel with Verses over a Great Man. TrJP
Thou half-unfolded flower. The Blossom of the Soul. Robert Underwood Johnson. AA
Thou happiest thing alive. To the Boy. Elizabeth Clementine Kinney. AA
Thou, happy creature, art secure. On the Death of a Lady's Dog. Earl of Roscommon. CavP
Thou happy, happy elf! A Parental Ode to My Son, Aged Three Years and Five Months [*or* To My Son]. Thomas Hood. BOHV; FaPON; FiBHP; HBV; PoLF; PTK; RIS
Thou hast a lap full of seed. Blake. ERoP-1
Thou hast beauty bright and fair. Hermione. "Barry Cornwall." OBVV
Thou hast been very tender to the moon. Malvolio. Walter Savage Landor. Par
Thou has burst from thy prison. The Butterfly's First Flight. *Unknown.* OTPC
Thou hast clothed thy steepest hillsides/ With the fragrant fir and pine. To Pikes Peak. Elijah Clarence Hlls. PoOW
Thou hast come from the old city. The Old City. Ruth Manning-Sanders. CH
Thou hast conquered, O pale Galilean; the world has grown gray from thy breath. Swinburne. *Fr.* Hymn to Proserpine. WHA
Thou Hast Diamonds. Heine, *tr. fr. German by* Emma Lazarus. *Fr.* Homeward Bound. TrJP
Thou hast done evil. The Judgment. Dora Read Goodale. AA; AnAmPo
Thou hast fill'd me a golden cup. To Christina Rossetti. Dora Greenwell. VA
Thou hast [*or* that hast] given so much to me. A Heart to Praise Thee [*or* Our Prayer]. George Herbert. MaMe; MaRV; PGD; SoP; TRV
Thou hast lived in pain and woe. A Requiem. James Thomson. EnLit; HBV
Thou hast lost thy love, poor fool. A Simple Maid. Lord De Tabley. VA
Thou hast made me, and shall thy worke decay? Holy Sonnets, I. John Donne. AnAnS-1; AnEnPo; BWP; EnRePo; EP; FaBoEn; MaMe; MaPo; MasP; MBW-1; MeLP; MeP; NoP; OAEP; OBS; OxBoCh; PAn; Po; PoEL-2; PoFS; SCEP-1; SeCP; SeEP; Sonn
Thou has made me known to friends whom I knew not. When One Knows Thee. Rabindranath Tagore. Gitanjali, LXIII. NP; OQP
Thou Hast Made Us for Thyself. St. Augustine, *tr. fr. Latin.* TRV
Thou hast no faith of him that hath none. Sir Thomas Wyatt. FCP
Thou hast not drooped thy stately head. Savannah. Alethea S. Burroughs. PAH
Thou hast not that, my child, but thou hast Me. Content with Thee. Amy Carmichael. SoP
Thou hast not toiled, sweet Rose. To a Rose. John Banister Tabb. CAW

Thou hast on earth a Trinity. To the Christ. John Banister Tabb. ChIP; TrPWD
Thou Hast Put All Things under His Feet. Bryant. SoP
Thou hast stirred! Song of Cradle-making. Constance Lindsay Skinner. CaP
Thou hast the art on't Peter; and canst tell. On St. Peter Casting Away His Nets at Our Saviours Call. Richard Crashaw. MaMe
Thou hast thine eyrie in the lifted lands. Colorado. John D. Dillenback. PoOW
Thou hast thy calling to some palace floor. Sonnets from the Portuguese, IV. Elizabeth Barrett Browning. EnLi-2; VA
Thou hast thy ponds, that pay thee tribute fish. Ben Jonson. *Fr.* To Penshurst. FaBoEn
Thou Hast Wounded the Spirit That Loved Thee. Mrs. David Porter. BLPA
Thou hearest the nightingale begin the song of spring. Nightingale and Flowers [*or* Birdsong *or* The Choir of Day *or* Vision of the Lamentation of Beulah]. Blake. *Fr.* Milton, II. EnRP; ERoP-1; FaBoEn; LoBV; OBNC; OBRV; WiR
Thou hear'st me say that I do dote on thee. *Unknown. Fr.* Edward the Third. LO
Thou heavenly quivering beneath the deathlike above! To a Lark in War-Time. Franz Werfel. TrJP
Thou heaven-threat'ning rock, gentler then she! Echo to a Rock. Lord Herbert of Cherbury. AtBAP; PoEL-2
Thou, heedless Albion, what, alas, the while. England, Unprepared for War. Mark Akenside. *Fr.* An Ode to the Country Gentlemen of England. OBEC
Thou, Hesper, bringest homeward all. Evening. Sappho. WoL
Thou hidden love of God, whose height. Hymn. John Wesley. CEP; OBEC
Thou honeysuckle of the hawthorn hedge. *Unknown.* LO
Thou hope of all the lowly! Thy Kingdom Come. St. Bernard of Clairvaux. CAW; SoP
Thou huntress swifter than the Moon! thou terror. Shelley. *Fr.* Ode to Liberty. PoFr
Thou ill-form'd offspring of my feeble brain. The Author to [*or* and] Her Book. Anne Bradstreet. AmPP; AP; MAmP; NePA; OxBA; SCAP; StP
Thou in the fields walkst out thy supping howers. The Lier. John Donne. MaMe
Thou in this wide cold church art laid. On the Dead. Walter Savage Landor. NBM
Thou inmost, ultimate. To the Body. Alice Meynell. ACP; PeVV
"Thou jestedst when thou swor'st that thou betrothedst." Tudor Aspersions. R. A. Piddington. FiBHP
Thou Joy'st, Fond Boy. Thomas Campion. OAEP
Thou Knowest. Katharine Lee Bates. TrPWD
Thou Knowest, Lord! *Unknown.* MaRV
Thou knowest, love, I know that thou dost know. Love's Entreaty. Michelangelo. AWP
Thou knowest my years entire, my life. Walt Whitman. *Fr.* Prayer of Columbus. TrPWD
Thou knowest, Thou who art the soul of all. Thou Knowest. Katharine Lee Bates. TrPWD
Thou knowest what is best. Trust and Obedience. *Unknown.* BLRP
Thou laverock that springs frae the dews o' the lawn. My Nannie's Awa' [*or* My Nanie's Awa']. Burns. GN; HBV; OTPC (1923 ed.)
Thou layest thy hand on the fluttering heart. Thy Presence [*or* Be Quiet: Fear Not *or* Confidence]. Frances Ridley Havergal. FaChP; MaRV; OQP
Thou Life within My Life. Eliza Scudder. MaRV
Thou Light of Ages. Rolland W. Schloerb. ChIP; MaRV; TrPWD
Thou Light of Life. *At. to* St. Bernard of Clairvaux. *See* Jesus, Thou Joy of Loving Hearts.
Thou lily-leaf, thou roseal-bud. To Mary. Gottfried von Strassburg. ISi
Thou lingerest, Spring! still wintry is the scene. Spring. Robert Southey. Sonn
Thou Lingering Star. Burns. *See* To Mary in Heaven.
Thou little bird, thou dweller by the sea. The Little-Beach Bird. Richard Henry Dana. AA; AmLP; AnAmPo; AnFE; AnNE; APA; CoAnAm; HBV; OTPC (1923 ed.)
Thou livest, but not from any restricted season. The Royal Crown, IV. Solomon ibn Gabirol. AWP
Thou Livest, O Soul! Charles Leonard Moore. AA
Thou lookest up with meek, confiding eye. The Wind-Flower. Jones Very. AnNE
Thou Lord of Life and glorious King of Heaven. The Holy Viaticum Comes to Me. Giovanni Prati. CAW
Thou lovely and belovèd, thou my love. Mid-Rapture. Dante Gabriel Rossetti. The House of Life, XXVI. BEL; FaBoBe; HBV; MaVP; OAEP; PoE; PoVP; TOP; ViPo; VP
Thou lowly, meek and lovely flower. The Passion Flower. Charles G. Blanden. ChIP; OQP
Thou maid and mother, daughter of thy Son. The Canterbury Tales: Prologue to the Second Nun's Tale. Chaucer. GoBC
Thou man, first-comer, whose wide arms entreat. Veneration of Images. Alice Meynell. GTBS
Thou mastering me. The Wreck of the *Deutschland.* Gerard Manley Hopkins. AtBAP; BoC; BrPo; CABL; CMoP; CoBMV; DiPo; FaBoMo; LiTB; LiTM (rev. ed.); MasP; MoVE; OAEP (2d ed.); OBNC; OxBoCh; PAn; PoEL-5; PoVP; ReMP; SeCeV; ViPP; VP
Thou mayest retire, but think of me. To a Departing Favorite. George Moses Horton. BALP
Thou met'st, Euripides, a mournful fate! On Euripides. *Unknown.* OnPM
Thou mighty gulf, insatiate cormorant. To Everlasting Oblivion. John Marston. *Fr.* The Scourge of Villainy. CBEP; LoBV (1949 ed.); OBSC; ReIE; SiCE; TuPP
Thou mighty Mars, the god of soldiers brave. An Epitaph on Sir Philip Sidney. James I, King of England. Sonn
Thou monarch of eight parts of speech. To a Schoolmaster. Martial. OnPM
Thou Moon, that aidest us with thy magic might. A Charm. Dryden. ChTr
Thou more than most sweet glove. The Glove. Ben Jonson. *Fr.* Cynthia's Revels. ElL
Thou Mother with Thy Equal Brood. Walt Whitman. AmePo; CoBA
"Beautiful world of new, superber birth," *sel.* PoFr
Thou Must Be True. Horatius Bonar. *See* Be True.
Thou Needst Not. Walter Savage Landor. EPN
Thou need'st not flutter from thy half-built nest. The Robin. Jones Very. AnNE; Sonn
Thou ne're wilt [*or* wutt] riddle, neighbour John [*or* Jan]. A Devonshire Song. *Unknown, at. to* William Strode. OBS; PoEL-2
Thou noblest monument of Albion's isle! Sonnet: Written at Stonehenge. Thomas Warton, the Younger. Sonnets, IV. CEP; EiPP; Sonn
Thou of the hill Heliconian. Bridal Hymn. Catullus. WoL
Thou only bird that singest as thou flyest. The Skylark. Richard Watson Dixon. *Fr.* Mano; a Poetical History. VA
Thou pain, the only guest of loathed constraint. Sir Philip Sidney. FCP
Thou perceivest the flowers put forth their precious odors. The Wild Thyme. Blake. *Fr.* Milton, II. WiR
Thou priest that art behind the screen. Ipsissimus. Eugene Lee-Hamilton. PeVV
Thou, proud man, look upon yon starry vault. Man's Littleness in Presence of the Stars. Henry Kirke White. WBLP
Thou Remainest. Annie Johnson Flint. BLRP
Thou robb'st [*or* rob'st] my days of business [*or* bus'ness] and delights. The Thief. Abraham Cowley. *Fr.* The Mistress. BEL; EnLi-1; EnLit; OAEP; SeCL; WHA
Thou sai'st I swore I lov'd thee best. The Variety. John Dancer. CavP
Thou say'st, "Take up thy cross." Take Up Thy Cross. Francis Turner Palgrave. MaRV
Thou Seemest like a Flower. Heine. *See* Du bist wie eine Blume.
Thou seest me here at midnight, now all rest. John Donne. *Fr.* Obsequies to the Lord Harrington. MyFE
Thou seest me the meanest thing, and so I am indeed. The Worm. Blake. *Fr.* The Book of Thel. FlW
Thou seest the under side of every leaf. Omniscience. Blanche Mary Kelly. TrPWD
Thou seest this world is but a thoroughfare. Eternal Reward, Eternal Pain. Sir Thomas More. *Fr.* The Twelve Weapons of Spiritual Battle. CoBE; EnRePo
Thou sent to me [*or* mee] a heart was crowned [*or* crown'd]. Upon a Diamond Cut in Form of a Heart. . .Sent in a New Year's Gift. Sir Robert Ayton. ElL; OBS

Thou servant of the living God. Deliverance. "M. E. B." SoP
Thou shalt have no other gods before Me. The Ten Commandments. Exodus, Bible, *O.T.* OHFP; WBLP
Thou shalt have one God only. The Latest Decalogue. Arthur Hugh Clough. BEL; BOHV; CABA; CaFP; CBEP; CBV; ChTr; EnLi-2 (1949 ed.); EnLit; EPN; ExPo; FosPo; GTBS-P; HoPM; ILP; InMe; LiTG; LoBV NBM; OAEP; OBNC; OBVV; OtMeF; PoE; PoFS; PoIE; PoVP; SiTL; TOP; TreFT; TRV; VaPo; ViBoPo; ViPo; ViPP; WGRP
Thou Shalt Not Kill, *sel.* Kenneth Rexroth.
"They are murdering all the young men." WOW
Thou shalt not laugh in this leafe, Muse, nor they. John Donne. *Fr.* Satires. MaMe
"Thou Shalt Purge Me with Hyssop and I Shall Be Clean." Anna Bunston de Bary. MaRV
Thou Shalt See the Field-Mouse Peep. Keats. *Fr.* Fancy. OA
"Thou shalt seek the beach of sand." The Fay's Sentence. Joseph Rodman Drake. *Fr.* The Culprit Fay. GN
Thou shinest beautiful on the horizon of heaven. Hymn to the Sun. Ikhnaton (Amenhotep IV). LiTW
Thou should'st be living at this hour. Heathcote William Garrod. CenHV
"Thou Shouldst Be Living at This Hour!" Kenyon West. PGD
Thou shouldst have sung the swan song for the choir. James Russell Lowell. Oliver Wendell Holmes. DD
Thou, Sibyl rapt! whose sympathetic soul. Margaret Fuller. Amos Bronson Alcott. AA
Thou simple bird what mak'st thou here to play? Upon the Lark and the Fowler. Bunyan. CH
Thou Sleepest Fast. *Unknown.* ElL
Thou snowy farm with thy five tenements. Elinda's Glove [*or* The Glove]. Richard Lovelace. ALV; EG; OBS; SiSw
Thou, so far, we grope to grasp thee. So Far, So Near. Christopher Pearse Cranch. MaRV; TrPWD
Thou sorrow, venom elf[e]. Upon a Spider Catching a Fly. Edward Taylor. AmP; AmPP (4th ed.); AP; CBEP; GTBS-W; MAmP; NePA; NoP; OA; OxBA; PoEL-3; SCAP
Thou spark of life that wavest wings of gold. Ode to a Butterfly. Thomas Wentworth Higginson. AA; FaBoBe; HBV
Thou sparkling bowl! thou sparkling bowl! The Sparkling Bowl. John Pierpont. AnAmPo
Thou speaker of all wisdom in a word. A Prologue. Coventry Patmore. PoLi
Thou speakest always ill of me. To an Acquaintance. *Unknown.* FaFP; SiTL
Thou speak'st the word (thy word's a law). The Blind Cured by the Word of Our Saviour. Richard Crashaw. MaMe
Thou stately stream that with the swelling tide. The Lover to the Thames [of London to Favour His Lady Passing Thereon]. George Turberville. ChTr; ElL; OBSC; ReIE
Thou still unravish'd bride of quietness. Ode on a Grecian Urn. Keats. AnEnPo; AnFE; AtBAP; ATP; AWP; BEL; BoC; BoLiVe; BWP; CABA; CaFP; CBEP; CBV; ChER; CoBE; DiPo; EnL; EnLi-2; EnLit; EnRP; EPN; ERoP-2; ExPo; FaBoBe; FaBoEn; FaFP; FaPL; FiP; ForPo; FosPo; GTBS-W; GTSL; HBV; HBVY; HoPM; ILP; InP; InPo; JAWP; LiTB; LiTG; LoBV; MaPo; MasP; MBW-2; MCCG; MemP; MERP; NoP; OAEP; OBEV; OBNC; OBRV; OHFP; OuHeWo; PAn; PeER; PIA; Po; PoAn; PoE; PoEL-4; PoeP; PoFS; PoIE; PoMa; PoPo; PoSa; PTK; SeCeV; ShBV-4; StP; TOP; TreF; TrGrPo; UnPo; ViBoPo; WBP; WHA
Thou stranger, which for Rome in Rome here seekest. Ruins of Rome, I [*or* Rome]. Joachim du Bellay. LiTW; OnPM
Thou swearst thou'lt drink no more: kind heaven, send. To Julius [*or* Epigram *or* The Mistaken Resolve]. Martial. ALV; PeRV; PV
Thou sweet, beloved will of God. The Will of God. Gerhardt Tersteegen. SoP
Thou sweetly-smelling fresh red rose. Dialogue; Lover and Lady. Ciullo d'Alcamo. AWP
Thou talkest much, so soon to yield thy breath. Muse on Death. Palladas. OnPM
Thou that art by fates degree. New Canaans Genius; Epilogus. Thomas Morton. SCAP
Thou that art wise, let wisdom minister. Sonnet: He Craves Interpreting of a Dream of His. Dante de Malano. AWP; LiTW
Thou that at Rome astonished dost behold. Ruins of Rome, VII. Joachim du Bellay. OnPM
Thou that didst grant the wise King his request. The Sins of Youth. Thomas, Lord Vaux. ACP (1952 ed.)
Thou that didst leave the ninety and the nine. Missing. John Banister Tabb. TrPWD
Thou that didst mark from Heircte's spacious hill. Hamilcar Barca. Roger Casement. JKCP (1926 ed.)
Thou that dost save through pain. Thanksgiving. Florence Earle Coates. PEDC
Thou that from the heavens art. Wanderer's Night-Songs. Goethe, *tr. by* Longfellow. AWP; InP; JAWP; OnPM; WBP; WoL
Thou that hast a daughter. The Sailor. William Allingham. HBV; VA
Thou that hast given so much to me. *See* Thou hast given so much to me.
Thou that in prâyeres hes bene lent. Rise with the Lamb of Innocence. *Unknown.* MeEL
Thou that mak'st gain thy end, and wisely well. To My Bookseller. Ben Jonson. TuPP
Thou that once, on mother's knee. A Little Child's Hymn. Francis Turner Palgrave. VA
Thou that spendst thy time to knowe. *Unknown.* SeCSL
Thou, that wouldst find the habit of true passion. In Authorem. Ben Jonson. Sonn
Thou thy calling to some palace floor. Sonnets from the Portuguese, IV. Elizabeth Barrett Browning. Sonn
Thou Thyself. Christina Rossetti. *See* Prayer: "Lord, grant us eyes to see. . ."
Thou tiny solace of these prison days. Sir Walter Raleigh to a Caged Linnet. Eugene Lee-Hamilton. VA
Thou to wax fierce. The Zeal of Jehu. Cardinal Newman. OBRV
Thou, to whom my name bears witness. Be Not Silent. David ben Meshullam. TrJP
Thou, to whom the world unknown. Ode to Fear. William Collins. CEP; EiCL; EiCP; EiPP; EnPE; OAEP; Po; TrGrPo
Thou too hast traveled, little fluttering thing. To a Swallow Building under Our Eaves. Jane Welsh Carlyle. HBV; OBRV; OTPC (1923 ed.); VA
"Thou, too, my Lancelot," ask'd the King, "my friend." Lancelot and the Grail. Tennyson. *Fr.* Idylls of the King. GoBC
Thou, too, O bronze-eyed darling of the feast. In an Autumn Wood. William Alexander Percy. HBMV
Thou, Too, Sail On! Longfellow. *See* Ship of State, The.
Thou trim'st a prophets tombe, and dost bequeath. Yee Build the Sepulchres of the Prophets. Richard Crashaw. MaMe
Thou unrelenting Past The Past. Bryant. AA; TOP
Thou vague dumb crawler with the groping head. To My Tortoise Chronos. Eugene Lee-Hamilton. VA
"Thou Virgin Mother, daughter of thy Son." Dante. *Fr.* Divina Commedia: Paradiso. CAW
Thou visitest the earth, and waterest it. *Fr.* Psalm LXV, Bible, *O.T.* OHIP
Thou wast all that [*or* that all] to me, love. To One in Paradise. Poe. *Fr.* The Assignation. AA; AmLP; AmPP; AnFE; AP; APA; BoLiVe; CoAnAm; CoBA; GTBS-D; HBV; LiTA; LiTL; LO; MeWo; MWA-1; NePA; OBEV (new ed.); OBRV; OBVV; OxBA; PG; PoIE; PoLF; PoPo; TrGrPo; ViBoPo; WHA; YT
Thou wast not born for death, immortal bird! The Nightingale [*or* Magic Casements]. Keats. *Fr.* Ode to a Nightingale. DD; FaBV
Thou water turn'st to wine (faire friend of life). To Our Lord, upon the Water Made Wine. Richard Crashaw. MaMe; MePo; SCEP-1
Thou we adore, eternal name. Worthington. *Unknown.* AS
Thou wert fair, Lady Mary. Lady Mary. Henry Alford. VA
Thou wert out betimes, thou busy, busy bee! To a Bee. Robert Southey. OTPC
Thou wert the morning-star among the living. Morning and Evening Star [*or* Aster *or* Star *or* To Stella]. Plato, *tr. by* Shelley. AWP; EnLoPo; InPo; JAWP; LiTW; LO; MBW-2; OnPM; ViBoPo; WBP; WoL
Thou which art I, ('tis nothing to be soe). The Storm. John Donne. CABL; MaMe; ReIE; SeEP
Thou who art clothed in silk, who drawest on. Man Is a Weaver. Moses ibn Ezra. TrJP

Thou who art Lord of the wind and rain. A Hymn of Thanksgiving. Wilbur D. Nesbit. OHIP
Thou who condemnest Jewish hate. Self-Condemnation. George Herbert. MaMe
Thou, who didst lay all other bosoms bare. To Shakespeare. Richard Edwin Day. AA
Thou who didst multiply, by Galilee. Prayer. Frances Crosby Hamlet. ChIP
Thou, who didst stoop below. Looking unto Jesus. Sarah Elizabeth Miles. SoP
Thou, who dost dwell alone. Desire. Matthew Arnold. WGRP
Thou who dost dwell and linger here below. The Water-Course. George Herbert. MaMe
Thou, who dost feel life's vessel strand. Edmund Clarence Stedman. *Fr.* The Ordeal by Fire. WGRP
Thou, who dost flow and flourish here below. The Garland. Henry Vaughan. AnEnPo
Thou who hast fled from life's enchanted bowers. To a Clôistress. Juan dé Tassis. CAW
Thou who hast made this world so wondrous fair. At High Mass. Robert Hugh Benson. CAW
Thou who hast [*or* has] slept all night upon the storm. To the Man-of-War Bird. Walt Whitman. AA; AmP; AmPP (4th ed.); EtS; FaBoBe; HBV; NePA
Thou who loved Juvenal, and filed. Indignation. Victor Hugo. WoL
Thou who on Sin's wages starvest. Barnfloor and Winepress. Gerard Manley Hopkins. ACP; CAW
Thou who ordainest, for the land's salvation. God Save the Nation! Theodore Tilton. AA
Thou Who Taught the Thronging People. Henry S. Minde. TRV
Thou who, when fears attack. Ode to Tobacco. Charles Stuart Calverley. ALV; BOHV; FiBHP; HBV; InMe; TOP; WhC
Thou who wilt not love, doe this. Upon Some Women. Robert Herrick. AnAnS-2
Thou who wouldst see the lovely and the wild. Monument Mountain. Bryant. BeLS
Thou who wouldst wear the name. The Poet. Bryant. AA; AmPP (3d ed.); AP; CoBA; InP; MAmP; PP
Thou whom I lifted from her pallid lips. Crucifix. Alphonse de Lamartine. CAW
Thou whom of all the beings I have seen. To——. George Darley. Sonn
Thou, Whom rich and poor adore. An Offer. Arthur Guiterman. TrJP
Thou, whom the former precepts have. Superliminare. George Herbert. AnAnS-1; MaMe; MeP; SeCP
Thou whom these eyes saw never, say friends true. Epitaph. Robert Browning. VA
Thou whose birth on earth. Christmas Antiphon [*or* The Peace-Giver]. Swinburne. ChIP; MaRV; OTPC (1946 ed.); PGD; TrPWD; TRV
Thou whose chaste song simplicity inspires. To Mrs. Smith, Occasioned by the First of Her Sonnets. William Hayley. Sonn
Thou, whose diviner soule hath caus'd thee now. To Mr. Tilman After He Had Taken Orders. John Donne. MaMe
Thou—whose endearing hand once laid in sooth. Invocation. Edmund Clarence Stedman. AA
Thou whose prayer doth vice destroy. Lux Advenit Veneranda. Adam of St. Victor. CAW
Thou, whose sad heart, and weeping head lyes low. Easter-Day. Henry Vaughan. AnAnS-1; MeP
Thou, whose sweet youth and early hopes inhance. The Church-Porch. George Herbert. AnAnS-1; MaMe; MeP; SCEP-1; YAT
Thou whose thrilling hand in mine. George Darley. *Fr.* Nepenthe. OBRV
Thou, whose unmeasured temple stands. Dedication. Bryant. BLRP; MaRV; SoP; TrPWD; TRV
Thou wilt come with suddenness. Spring in New Zealand. Hubert Church. BoAu
"Thou wilt forget me." "Love has no such word." Spring and Autumn. William James Linton. VA
Thou wilt keep him in perfect peace. Perfect Peace. Isaiah, Bible, *O.T.* TRV
Thou wilt not cower in the dust. James Ryder Randall. *Fr.* Maryland, My Maryland. PoRL
Thou wilt not look on me? A Farewell. Alice Brown. HBV
Thou Wilt Revive Me. Psalms, CXXXVIII: 6-8, Bible, *O.T.* TreFT
Thou wilt to us Thy Name impart. Full Redemption. John Wesley. SoP
Thou winst thy wealth by war. To the Roving Pirate. George Turberville. EnRePo
Thou, with thy looks, on whom I look full oft. The Looks of a Lover Enamoured. George Gascoigne. EIL; SeCePo
Thou wommon boute fere. The Devout Man Prays to His Relations. William Herebert. MeEL
Thou wonder of the Atlantic shore. To Aaron Burr, under Trial for High Treason. Sarah Wentworth Morton. PAH
Thou wouldst be greate and to such height wouldst rise. Greatness. *Unknown.* OBS
Thou wouldst be loved?—then let thy heart. A Simple Duty. Poe. PoRL
Thou youngest virgin-daughter of the skies. To the Pious Memory of the Accomplisht Young Lady Mrs. Anne Killgrew [*or* Ode to the Pious Memory...]. Dryden. AtBAP; CEP; EiCL; EiPP; HBV; LoBV; MBW-1; OBEV; PeRV; PIA; PoEL-3; PoFS; SeCV-2; SeEP
Thou, Zion, old and suffering. David Levi. *Fr.* The Bible. TrJP
Though. *See also* Tho'.
Though All the Fates Should Prove Unkind. Henry David Thoreau. AP; MAmP
(Lines.) ILP
Though all we made depart. Who Dies If England Live? Kipling. PTK
Though Amaryllis Dance in Green. *Unknown.* EIL; OAEP; ReEn; SiCE
Though an ill mind appear in simulation. Ariosto. *Fr.* Orlando Furioso, IV. EnLi-1
Though art be on vacation. Leonard Feeney. WhC
Though aware of our rank and alert to obey orders. Which Side Am I Supposed to Be On? [*or* Ode: To My Pupils]. W. H. Auden. CoBMV; MoBrPo
Though beauty [*or* beautie] be the mark of praise. An Elegy [*or* Elegie]. Ben Jonson. BWP; EnRePo; NoP; OBEV; QFR; SCEP-2; SeCV-1
Though Bodies Are Apart. C. Day Lewis. POTE
Though brave your beauty be. The Lover Exhorteth His Lady to Take Time While Time Is. George Turbervile. EnRePo; ReIE
Though buds still speak in hints. Field-Glasses. Andrew Young. CBEP; ChMP
Though by thy bounteous favor I be in. The Examination of His Mistress' Perfections. Francis Beaumont. GoBC
Though Christ a thousand times. In Thine Own Heart. "Angelus Silesius." ChIP; MaRV; TRV
Though clasp'd and cradled in his nurse's arms. William Cowper. *Fr.* Hope. PoEL-3
Though clock,/ To tell how night draw[e]s hence, I've none. His Grange, or Private Wealth. Robert Herrick. AnAnS-2; EG; EnLit; GoJo; NoP; OAEP; OTPC (1923 ed.); SCEP-2; SeCV-1; SeEP; YAT
Though come down in the world to pulling a cart. Camel. Jon Stallworthy. NYTB
Though Cupit be a god. *Unknown.* SeCSL
Though decked the tray, two things afar and near. Fragment. Jami. *Fr.* Baharistan. CIV
Though doubters doubt and scoffers scoff. Christmas, 1898. Edward Sandford Martin. DD
Though dusty wits dare scorn astrology. Astrophel and Stella, XXVI. Sir Philip Sidney. FCP; ReEn; SiPS; Sonn
Though dusty wits of this ungrateful time. To Master Bastard, a Minister That Made a Pleasant Book of English Epigrams. Sir John Harington. SiCE
Though earth and man were gone. Emily Brontë. *Fr.* Last Lines. TRV
Though expedition bids, yet never stray. Of Narrow Streets. John Gay. *Fr.* Trivia; or, The Art of Walking the Streets of London. EnLi-1 (1949 ed.)
Though fast youth's glorious fable flies. Lone Founts. Herman Melville. AnFE; CoAnAm; LiTA; OnPM; ViBoPo
Though folks no more go Maying. The May Day Garland. Edmund Blunden. HBMV
Though frost, and snow, lockt from mine eyes. To Saxham. Thomas Carew. AnAnS-2; OBS

Though gifts like thine the fates gave not to me. To Hafiz. Thomas Bailey Aldrich. AA
Though God, as one that is an householder. Old and New Art, 3: The Husbandman. Dante Gabriel Rossetti. The House of Life, LXXVI. MaVP; PoVP; ViPo
Though grief and fondness in my breast rebel. London. Samuel Johnson. EiCP; EnPE
Though haunches of whales. Snowstorm in the Midwest. James Wright. FRC
Though he hung dumb upon her wall. And One Shall Live in Two. Jonathan Henderson Brooks. PoNe
Though he lift his voice in a great O. One Sort of Poet. A. J. M. Smith. NYTB
Though He Slay Me. Vassar Miller. NePoEA-2
Though He That Ever Kind and True. Robert Louis Stevenson. *See* Resurgence.
Though heart grows faint and spirits sink. The Word of God. Annie Johnson Flint. BLRP
Though Heaven be high, the gate is low. Humility. Thomas Washbourne. *Fr.* God's Two Dwellings. MaRV
Though her mother told her. Leda and the Swan. Oliver St. John Gogarty. AnIL; OnYI
Though here and there a man is left. Heroics. Elinor Wylie. CoBA
Though Here in Flesh I Be. Philip Howard, Earl of Arundel. CoBE
(Through Thy Cross and Passion.) PoLi
Though here on earth men differ, in the grave. Of Death. Samuel Sheppard. SeCL
Though I am Chateaulaire who sings. Chanson de Chateaulaire. Herbert S. Gorman. AnAmPo
Though I am humble, slight me not. The Moss Supplicateth for the Poet. Richard Henry Dana. AA
Though I am little as all little things. Not Overlooked. James Oppenheim. NP
Though I am native to this frozen zone. Reminiscence. Thomas Bailey Aldrich. AA; AnAmPo
Though I am to-day against the breast of battle. Knightsbridge of Libya. Sorley Maclean. NeBP
Though I Am Young [and Cannot Tell]. Ben Jonson. *Fr.* The Sad Shepherd, I, v. ELP; NoP; OAEP; TuPP
(Karolin's Song.) AtBAP; LiTL; LoBV; PoEL-2; PoIE
(Love and Death.) CBEP; SeCL
(Song: "Though I am young and cannot tell.") EnRePo; SeCP
("Though I am young and cannot tell.") ILP
Though I be dead, and buried, yet I have. To the Countesse of Bedford. John Donne. MaMe
Though I be foul, ugly, lean, and misshape. Death. Sir Thomas More. EnRePo
Though I be now a gray [*or* grey], gray friar. Friar's Hunting Song. Thomas Love Peacock. *Fr.* Maid Marian. GoTP; SD, 4 *ll.*
Though I be wooden Priapus (as thou see'st). Epigrams on Priapus. *Unknown.* ErPo
Though I cannot your cruelty constrain. Sir Thomas Wyatt. FCP
Though I get home how late, how late! Emily Dickinson. MoAmPo (1950 ed.); NeMA
Though I have an admiration for your charming resignation. Not Tonight, Josephine. Colin Curzon. ErPo
Though I have given. Lines Written in a Mausoleum. Lillian Grant. GoYe
Though I have not seen the milk snake. Five Serpents. Charles Burgess. NePoAm-2
Though I have twice been [*or* beene] at the doors [*or* doores] of death. To Sir William Alexander. William Drummond of Hawthornden. OBS; PoEL-2; SeEP
Though I march until I drop. Soldier's Song. David Campbell. BoAV; NeLNL
Though I met her in the summer. The Ballad of Cassandra Brown. Helen Gray Cone. BOHV; InMe
Though I must live here, and by force. To My Mistresse in Absence. Thomas Carew. AnAnS-2
Though I regarded not. Earl of Surrey. SiPS
Though I see the white azaleas on the shore. An Elegy. *Unknown.* *Fr.* Manyo Shu. OnPM
Though I should be maligned by those. Prayer for Strength. Margaret E. Bruner. MaRV; PoToHe
Though [*or* If I should] speak with the tongues of men and of angels. Charity [*or* The Gospel of Love *or* St. Paul on Charity *or* The Greatest of These]. First Corinthians, Bible, *N.T.* LO; OuHeWo; PG (1955 ed.); ShBV-4; StVeCh; TIHL; TreF; TrGrPo; TRV
Though I walk through the valley of the shadow of death. Psalm XXIII, Bible, *O.T.* BoC
Though I was born a Londoner. Oak and Olive. James Elroy Flecker. HBMV
Though I with strange desire. Kisses Desired. William Drummond of Hawthornden. EnLoPo
Though I would take comfort against sorrow. The Cry of the Daughter of My People. Jeremiah, Bible, *O.T.* TrJP
Though it be some divorce to thinke of you. Raysing of the Bridegroome. John Donne. MaMe
Though joy is better than sorrow, joy is not great. Joy. Robinson Jeffers. CMoP; NeMA; NP
Though leaves are many, the root is one. The Coming of Wisdom with Time. W. B. Yeats. DiPo
Though little be the god of love. Love's Victories. James Shirley. *Fr.* Cupid and Death. GoBC
Though loath to grieve. Ode Inscribed to W. H. Channing. Emerson. AmePo; AmP; AmPP; AnNE; AP; CoBA; ILP; MAmP; MWA-1; NoP; OxBA; PPON; TOP; WoL
"Though logic-choppers rule the town." Tom O'Roughley. W. B. Yeats. CMoP
Though, Lord, to Israel thy graces plenteous be. Psalm LXXIII. *Paraphrased by* the Earl of Surrey. FCP
Though love repine, and reason chafe. Sacrifice [*or* Faith *or* Quatrain]. Emerson. HBV; HBVY; MaRV; OQP; OtMeF; TRV
Though lovely are the tombs of the dead nymphs. Panope. Edith Sitwell. NP
Though many a year above his dust. His Living Monument. Minna Irving. PGD
Though many men had passed the ford, not one. Fight with a Water-Spirit. Norman Cameron. HaMV
Though men may build their bridges high and plant their piers below the sea. John Curtis Underwood. *Fr.* Central. PoMa
Though mild clear weather. There Will Be No Peace. W. H. Auden. NePoAm-2
Though Mine Eye Sleep Not. *Unknown, tr. fr. Hebrew by* Theodor H. Gaster. *Fr.* The Dead Sea Scrolls. TrJP
Though moonlight dapples. Traditional Tune. Robert D. Fitzgerald. BoAV
Though my bodye be restrained. *Unknown.* SeCSL
Though My Carriage. *Unknown.* TuPP
Though my interest in viands is easy to whet up. Tirade on Tea. Phyllis McGinley. InMe
Though my soul may set in darkness, it will rise in perfect light. Sarah Williams. *Fr.* The Old Astronomer. MaRV; TRV
Though naked trees seem dead to sight. Hopeless Desire Soon Withers and Dies. "A. W." ReIE
Though no kin to those fine glistening. Christening-Day Wishes for My God-Child, Grace Lane Berkley II. Robert P. Tristram Coffin. BiCB
Though not apparently, you choose it well. Poet with Sea Horse. Alastair Reid. ML
Though now 'tis neither May nor June. Two Dedicatory Poems [*or* Love's Nightingale]. Richard Crashaw. LoBV; MaMe
Though now you are bereft and ways seem black. For One Lately Bereft. Margaret E. Bruner. PoToHe
Though old the thought and oft exprest. For an Autograph. James Russell Lowell. InP
Though one with all that sense or soul can see. Transcendence. Richard Hovey. OQP; TRV; WGRP
Though others far exceed me. My Best. Annabelle Jones. SoP
Though others may her brow adore. Love's Insight. *Unknown.* GTSL
Though our great love a little wrong his fame. Charles Lamb. Pakenham Beatty. VA
Though pain and care are everywhere. Vita Brevis. *Unknown.* UnTE
Though prejudice perhaps my mind befogs. I Think I Know No Finer Things than Dogs. Hally Carrington Brent. BBV (1951 ed.); BLPA; NeHB
Though pride in damsels is a hateful vice. The Author to a Daughter of Nine Years Old. Sir John Harington, *after* Martial. SiCE
Though [*or* Thocht] raging stormes movis us to shake [*or*

Though (continued)
schaik]. The Reeds in the Loch Sayis. *Unknown.* GoTS; OxBS
Though Regions Far Divided. Aurelian Townsend. LoBV
(Constant Lover, The.) OxBoLi
(Song: "Though regions farr devided.") MePo
(Though Regions Farr Devided.) PoEL-2
Though richer swains thy love pursue. Song. Joanna Baillie. *Fr.* The Country Inn. OBRV
Though Rulers Fall. Christopher Caudwell. CBV
Though rulers spend a million men. Conquest. Leslie Savage Clark. ChIP
Though Shakespeare's Mermaid, ocean's mightiest daughter. On a Prohibitionist Poem. G. K. Chesterton. ViBoPo
Though She Slumbers. Joseph Joel Keith. ISi
Though short her strain nor sung with mighty boast. Erinna. Antipater of Sidon. AWP
Though Sin too oft, when smitten by Thy rod. Doubt and Prayer. Tennyson. EPN
Though singing but the shy and sweet. Content. Norman Gale. HBV; VA
Though sitting beside the brazier. Buried Fire. Emperor Meiji. OnPM
Though the bee. In Him. James Vila Blake. WGRP
Though the Clerk of the Weather insist. Pebbles. Herman Melville. AP; MAmP
Though the cover is worn. My Old Bible. *Unknown.* BLRP; SoP; STF
Though the crocuses poke up their heads in the usual places. Vernal Sentiment. Theodore Roethke. ELU; MiAP
Though the day be never so long. Evensong. George Tankervil. TRV
Though the day of my destiny's over. Stanzas to Augusta. Byron. EnRP; ERoP-2
Though the Earth Be Removed. Psalms, XLVI, Bible, *O.T.* *See* Our Refuge.
Though the evening comes with slow steps and has signalled for all songs to cease. The Bird. Rabindranath Tagore. *Fr.* The Gardener. LiTW; PoPl
Though the fairies meet by night. At Dawn. Rose Fyleman. BoChLi
Though the fig tree shall not ripen. Trust. Avis B. Christiansen. SoP
Though the great song return no more. The Nineteenth Century and After. W. B. Yeats. MBW-2
Though the great waters sleep. Emily Dickinson. EaLo; MWA-2
Though the hands be raised to kill. A War-Time Prayer. Anna Bunston de Bary. MaRV
Though the long seasons seem to separate. Harvest. Eva Gore-Booth. HBMV; OQP; WGRP
Though the Lord be high, yet hath he respect unto the lowly. Thou Wilt Revive Me. Psalms, Bible, *O.T.* TreFT
Though the midnight found us weary. Sunrise. Margaret E. Sangster. SoP; TRV
Though the mills of God grind slowly, yet they grind exceeding small. Retribution. Friedrich von Logau, *tr. by* Longfellow. MaRV; PoToHe; TreF
Though the muse be gone away. Persistency of Poetry. Matthew Arnold. MBW-2; PoVP
Though the pale white within your cheeks compos'd. The Green-Sickness Beauty. Lord Herbert of Cherbury. AnAnS-2
Though the rain may fall and the wind is blowing. Trust. *Unknown.* SoP
Though the rough, bitter-sweet haw of pioneering. American History. W. R. Moses. LiTA
Though the roving bee, as lightly. The Bridal Pair. William Young. *Fr.* Wishmakers' Town. AA
Though the stars riot and the heavens fall. Arise! Arise! Louis Untermeyer. StaSt
Though the times be dark and dreary. Bide a Wee! John Oxenham. TRV
Though the torrents from their fountains. Song for the Wandering Jew. Wordsworth. ERoP-1
Though the world has slipped and gone. Lullaby. Edith Sitwell. AtBAP; ChMP; CMoP; LiTM; POTE; WaP
Though the world is changing fast. Rainer Maria Rilke. *Fr.* Sonnets to Orpheus. OnPM
Though the world is torn with care. To a Woman. Denis Glover. AnNZ
Though there are wild dogs. Orpheus and Eurydice. Geoffrey Hill. NePoEA-2; PoIE
Though there was nothing final then. The Parting. Elizabeth Jennings. NePoEA-2
Though they have loved me as the gentle roebuck. Deirdre and the Poets. Ewart Milne. NeIP
Though this the port and I thy servant true. Sir Thomas Wyatt. FCP; SiPS
Though thou indeed hast quite forgotten ruth. Ballata: Of a Continual Death in Love. Guido Cavalcanti. AWP
Though thou, my ring, be small. To His Ring, Given to His Lady. George Turberville. EIL
Though three men dwell on Flannan Isle. Flannan Isle. W. W. Gibson. CH; GoTL (1949 ed.); MoVE; OBVV; PoRA; ShBV-2; StPo; TOP; WePo
Though thy constant love I share. To M. T. Bayard Taylor. AA
Though Time's black mountain overhangs. Night Song. A. R. D. Fairburn. AnNZ
Though tiny things, ants must see very well. Such Wisdom. *Unknown.* GFA
Though to talk too much of heaven. Japanese Fan. Margaret Veley. NBM
Though to the root you eat me, goat, I swear. The Vine to the Goat. Euenus. LiTW
Though to think. Love Song. Margot Ruddock. OBMV
Though to your life apparent stain attach. Sonnets to Aurelia, II. Robert Nichols. OBMV
Though troubles assail, and dangers affright. The Lord Will Provide. John Newton. SoP
Though tuneless, stringless, it lies there in dust. The Old Violin. Maurice Francis Egan. AA; JKCP
Though virtue be the same when low she stands. To the Lady Lucy, Countess of Bedford. Samuel Daniel. OBSC; ReIE; SiCE; TuPP
Though waves and billows o'er me pass. The Thread and the Cable. Annie Johnson Flint. FaChP
Though we boast of modern progress as aloft we proudly soar. A Paradox. *Unknown.* ShM
Though we love and suffer together. Meditation. Paul Géraldy, *tr. by* Joseph T. Shipley. ALV
Though we may waver, He remaineth steadfast. The Everlasting Love. Annie Johnson Flint. BLRP
Though when I cry. To Mistress Sarah Hickford. —— Chambers. SeCL
Though when I lov'd thee thou wert fair. A Deposition from Beauty [*or* When I Loved Thee]. Thomas Stanley. EG; HBV; LiTL
Though, when other maids stand by. Smile and Never Heed Me. Charles Swain. HBV
Though winter come with dripping skies. A Song with a Discord. Arthur Colton. AA
Though Winter's Barricade Delays. C. Day Lewis. *Fr.* The Magnetic Mountain. EnLit
Though with the North we sympathize. Shop and Freedom. *Unknown.* PAH
Though wolves against the silver moon do bark. To the Detracted. John Andrews. *Fr.* The Anatomy of Baseness. EIL; LO; SeEP
Though Ye Suppose. John Skelton. CBEP
Though ye were hard-hearted. To Mistress Gertrude Statham. John Skelton. *Fr.* The Garlande of Laurell. OAEP
Though You Are Young. Thomas Campion. EnRePo
("Though you are young, and I am old.") OBSC; SiCE
(Youth and Age.) CBEP
Though you be absent here, I needs must say. The Spring [*or* Love's Absence in the Spring]. Abraham Cowley. *Fr.* The Mistress. BWP; CLwM; LiTL; LO; MeLP; OBS; ReEn; SeEP
Though you be scholarly, beware. Bigot. Eleanor Slater. MaRV
Though you desire me I will still feign sleep. Reserve. Richard Aldington. BrPo
Though you determine not to love. *Unknown.* SeCSL
Though you Diana-like have liv'd still chaste. Lutea Allison. Sir John Suckling. ErPo
Though you regret it. Out of Your Hands. Theodore Weiss. CoPo
Though You Make No Return. Thomas Southerne. *Fr.* The Maid's Last Prayer. SeCL

(Song, A, Set by H. Purcell, and Sung by Mrs. Hodgson.) SeEP
Though you on seas in stormes have bin. *Unknown.* SeCSL
Though you serve richest wines. A Total Abstainer. Martial. LiTW
Though you should build a bark of dead men's bones. Cancelled First Stanza of the Ode on Melancholy. Keats. *Fr.* The Ode on Melancholy. ERoP-2; SyP
Though you should whisper. Dirge. Muna Lee. NP
Though your eyes with tears were blind. A Leader. "Æ." HBMV
Thought, A. W. H. Davies. GTSL; MoShBr; POTE
Thought. Emerson. AmePo; AmPP (3d ed.); CoBA
Thought, The. Lord Herbert of Cherbury. AnAnS-2; InvP; LoBV (2d ed.); SeCL; SeEP
Thought, A. Walter Savage Landor. VA
Thought, A. Mikhail Yurevich Lermontov, *tr. fr. Russian by* Max Eastman. AWP; WoL
Thought, A. Michael McClure. FRC
Thought, A. A. A. Milne. ThGo
Thought, The. William Brighty Rands. OBEV; OBVV
Thought, A. Margaret E. Sangster. SoP; TRV
Thought, A. James Kenneth Stephen. BOHV; FiBHP; VA
Thought, A. Robert Louis Stevenson. OTPC; PCH; PPL
Thought. Walt Whitman. MaRV
Thought, The. Humbert Wolfe. BoPe
Thought and the Poet. "Peter Yates." ChMP
Thought beneath so slight a film, The. Emily Dickinson. AmP; AmPP; OxBA
Thought does not crush to stone. The Adamant. Theodore Roethke. NYTB
Thought Eternal, The. Goethe, *tr. fr. German by* Ludwig Lewisohn. AWP; JAWP; WBP
Thought for a Lonely Death-Bed, A. Elizabeth Barrett Browning. MaRV
Thought for a New Year. Gail Brook Burket. PGD
Thought for a Sunshiny Morning. Dorothy Parker. PoMa
Thought for Easter. Mary E. McCullough. MaRV
Thought for My Love, A. Bruce Williamson. NeIP
Thought for the Winter Season. Mary Elizabeth Osborn. NePoAm
Thought-Fox, The. Ted Hughes. NePoEA-2; NYBP
Thought from Cardinal Newman, A. Matthew Russell. CAW; JKCP
Thought in Time, A. Robert Hillyer. NYBP
Thought in Two Moods, A. Thomas Hardy. EPN
Thought is deeper than all speech. Gnosis [*or* Thought *or* Stanza from an Early Poem]. Christopher Pearse Cranch. AmePo; AmLP; AnAmPo; HBV; ILP; PoIE; WGRP
Thought is false happiness: the idea. Crude Foyer. Wallace Stevens. LiTM (rev. ed.); NePA
Thought is with me sometimes, and I say, A. Wordsworth. *Fr.* The Prelude. PeER
Thought may, at times, be a very dangerous thing. A Tragedy of the Deep. Don Marquis. LHV
Thought of a Briton on the Subjugation of Switzerland. Wordsworth. BEL; BoLiVe; EnLi-2; EnRP; EPN; MBW-2; MERP; PoFr; SeCeV; TOP
(England and Switzerland, 1802.) GTBS; GTBS-D; GTBS-P; GTBS-W; GTSE; GTSL; MCCG
(On the Subjugation of Switzerland.) ShBV-3
(Sonnet: Thought of a Briton on the Subjugation of Switzerland.) ChER
(Thoughts of a Briton on the Subjugation of Switzerland.) EnL; OBRV
Thought of Death, A. Thomas Flatman. CEP; OBS
Thought of Marigolds, A. Janice Farrar. GoYe
Thought of the Nile, A. Leigh Hunt. *See* Nile, The.
Thought on a News Item. Lucia Trent. ChIP
Thought rattles along the empty railings. Respectable People. Austin Clarke. NMP
Thought Suggested by the New Year, A. Thomas Campbell. *See* River of Life, The.
Thought went up my mind today, A. Emily Dickinson. AmP; AmPP; AnFE; APA; CoAnAm; CoBA; DiPo
Thought, with good cause thou likest so well the night. Astrophel and Stella, XCVI. Sir Philip Sidney. FCP; ReEn; SiPS
Thoughtful little Willie Frazer. Science for the Young. Wallace Irwin. BBGG
Thoughtful nights, and restless waking. To Myra. George Granville. CEP
Thoughts. Roy Davis. WhC
Thoughts. Duncan Campbell Scott. PeCV
Thoughts are broken in my memory, The. Dante. *Fr.* La Vita Nuova. AWP; JAWP; WBP
Thoughts are strange that crowd into my brain, The. The Fall of Niagara. John G. C. Brainard. AmePo
Thoughts at the Museum. Eileen Brennan. OnYI
Thoughts by the Shore. George Crabbe. *Fr.* The Borough. PoG
Thoughts during an Air Raid. Stephen Spender. MoBrPo (1950 ed.); NeMA; ViBoPo
Thought's End. Léonie Adams. MAP; MoAB; MoAmPo
Thoughts for St. Stephen. Christopher Morley. ShM; WhC
Thoughts from Abroad. Patrick Maybin. NeIP
Thoughts in a Garden. Andrew Marvell. *See* Garden, The ("How vainly men themselves amaze").
Thoughts in a Summer Garden. Andrew Marvell. *See* Garden, The.
Thoughts in Separation. Alice Meynell. ACP; GoBC
Thoughts in the Gulf Stream. Christopher Morley. EtS
Thoughts like an empty cage. The Cage. Elizabeth Bartlett. NePoAm-2
Thoughts of a Briton on the Subjugation of Switzerland. Wordsworth. *See* Thought of a Briton on the Subjugation of Switzerland.
Thoughts of a Little Girl. María Enriqueta, *tr. fr. Spanish by* Emma Gutiérrez Suárez. FaPON
Thoughts of Death, The. Thomas à Kempis. *Fr.* Imitation of Christ. OuHeWo
Thoughts of Him. Georgia Adams. SoP
Thoughts of Loved Ones. Margaret Fishback. FiBHP
Thoughts of men appear, The. Consummation. Thomas Traherne. SCEP-1; SeCV-2
Thoughts of Thomas Hardy. Edmund Blunden. PoCh
Thoughts on Being Invited to Dinner. Christopher Morley. HBMV
Thoughts on Editors. Thomas Moore. WhC
Thoughts on One's Head. William Meredith. SiTL
Thoughts on Pausing at a Cottage near the Paukataug River. Sarah Kemble Knight. SCAP
Thoughts on Progress. David Daiches. SiTL
Thoughts on the Christian Doctrine of Eternal Hell. Stevie Smith. PPON
Thoughts on the Commandments. George Augustus Baker. AA; HBV
Thoughts on the Cosmos. Franklin P. Adams. HBMV
Thoughts on the Shape of the Human Body. Rupert Brooke. BrPo
Thoughts on the Sight of the Moon. Sarah Kemble Knight. SCAP
Thoughts That Move the Heart of Man, The. Ebenezer S. Oakley. TrPWD
Thoughts that rain their steady glow, The. Despondency. Matthew Arnold. PoVP
Thoughts Thought While Waiting for a Pronouncement from a Doctor, a Big Executive, the Department of Internal Revenue, or Any Other Momentous Pronouncer. Ogden Nash. SiTL
Thoughts upon a Walk with Natalie, My Niece, at Houghton Farm. Harold Trowbridge Pulsifer. HBMV
Thou'rt my sleeping. The Island Boatman's Love-Croon. Robert Farren. CoBE
Thou's welcome, wean! mishanter fa' me. The Poet's Welcome to His Love-begotten Daughter [*or* to His Illegitimate Child]. Burns. BoC; LiTB; OxBoLi; PoEL-4; SiTL; ViBoPo
Thousand-and-First Ship, *sel.* F. Scott Fitzgerald.
There'd Be an Orchestra. ELU; GoJo
Thousand and One Nights, The, *sels.* *Unknown,* *tr. fr. Arabic by* E. Powys Mathers.
Abu Nowas for the Barmacides. AWP
Beautiful Boy, The. LiTW
Birds. AWP; LiTW
Dates. AWP; FaPON; JAWP; LiTW; WBP
Death. AWP; JAWP; WBP
Drinking Song. LiTW
Haroun al-Rachid for Heart's-Life. AWP
Haroun's Favorite Song. AWP
Her Rival for Aziza. AWP
Inscription on a Chemise. ErPo
Inscriptions at the City of Brass. AWP; PG (1945 ed.); PoFr, 2 *sts.*; WaaP, 3 *sts.*
(Inscription at the City of Brass, 1 *st.*) LiTW

Thousand (continued)
Laments. AWP; JAWP; WBP
Love. AWP; LiTW
Mock Caliph, The. EnLi-1
Of Women. ErPo; PV
Pearls Seen through Amber. LiTW
Poems of the Arabic, *tr. by* Sir Richard Burton. ErPo
Power of Love, The. LiTW
Psalm of Battle. AWP; JAWP; WBP
Sleeper, The. AWP; LiTW
Song of the Narcissus, The. AWP
Tell Him, O Night. AWP; LiTW
To Lighten My Darkenss. AWP
Tumadir al-Khansa for Her Brother. AWP; JAWP; PG (1945 ed.); WBP
Wazir Dandan for Prince Sharkan, The. AWP; JAWP; WBP
Thousand and Second Night, The. James Merrill. NYBP
Thousand burdened burros filled, A. The Rise and Fall of Creede. Cy Warman. PoOW
Thousand guileless sheep have bled, A. Song from the Bride of Smithfield. Sylvia Townsend Warner. MoBPo
Thousand Hairy Savages, A. Spike Milligan. PV
Thousand Islands, The. Charles Sangster. *Fr.* The St. Lawrence and the Saguenay. OBCV
Thousand knights have rein'd their steeds, A. Calais Sands. Matthew Arnold. OAEP
Thousand lights their glory shed, A. The Return from Egypt. Pope Leo XIII. CAW
Thousand Martyrs I Have Made, A. Aphra Behn. *See* Libertine, The.
Thousand miles from land are we, A. The Stormy Petrel. "Barry Cornwall." EtS; HBV; OTPC; VA
Thousand Nights and One Night, The. *Unknown. See* Thousand and One Nights, The.
Thousand silent years ago, A. Praxiteles and Phryne. William Wetmore Story. AA; BeLS
Thousand sounds, and each a joyful sound, A. Omnipresence. Edward Everett Hale. SoP; TRV; WGRP
Thousand summers ere the time of Christ, A. The Ancient Sage. Tennyson. EPN; ViPP
Thousand Things, The. Christopher Middleton. NePoEA-2; OPoP
Thousand thoughts of tender vague regret, A. Autumn Moon. Chisato. OnPM
Thousand times you've seen that scene, A. Country Burying (1919). Robert Penn Warren. LiTM (1970 ed.)
Thousand years from this tonight, A. Survival. Margaret Moore Meuttman. MaRV
Thousand Years Have Come, A. Thomas T. Lynch. BLRP
(Jesus Christ the Lord.) SoP
Thousand years now had his breed, A. E. J. Pratt. *Fr.* The Cachalot. MoCV; OBCV
Thousand Years with Solitude, A. Charles Simic. YAP
Thousands/ of weird little figurines. Semen. Coleman Barks. PV
Thousandth Poem for Dylan Thomas, A. John Ciardi. ToPo
Thou'st Had Thy Day. Anacreon, *tr. fr. Greek by* Thomas Moore. OnPM
Thouzandz of thornz there be. The Bees' Song. Walter de la Mare. OTPC (1946 ed.); WhC; YT
Thow thou be kyng of tour and town. A Warning. *Unknown.* EnLit
Thracian Wonder, The, *sels. Unknown, at. to* John Webster *and* William Rowley.
Art Thou Gone in Haste? ElL; ELP; LO; OxBoLi; ThWaDe
("Art thou gon in haste Ile not forsake thee," *longer vers.*) SeCSL
(Chase, The.) CH
(Pursuit of Love.) ChTr
Love Is a Law. ElL
("Love is a law, a discord of such force.") TuPP
Thraldome, The. Abraham Cowley. *Fr.* The Mistress. SCEP-2; SeCV-1
Thrash away, you'll hey to rattle. A Letter from Mr. Ezekiel Biglow of Jaalam to the Hon. Joseph T. Buckingham. James Russell Lowell. *Fr.* The Biglow Papers, 1st Series, No. I. AmePo; AmPP; AnNE; CoBA; OxBA; PAH
Thrasymedes and Eunoe, *sel.* Walter Savage Landor. *Fr.* The Hellenics.
Overture. VA
Thre Prestis of Peblis, The, *sel. At. to* John Reid of Stobo.
"In Peblis town sum tyme, as I heard tell." OxBS
Thread and the Cable, The. Annie Johnson Flint. FaChP
Thread of Life, The, *sel.* Christina Rossetti.
Aloof, I. OBEV; OBVV; TrGrPo; YT
(Thread of Life, The.) FaBoEn; OBNC; VA
Thread the nerves through the right holes. Resurrection Song. Thomas Lovell Beddoes. ELU; ERoP-2; NBM; PoE
Threading the dance was one who trod. Legend of Ramapo Mountain. Jennie M. Palen. FiSC
Threads You Use, The. Alice Hansche Mortenson. SoP
Thredbo River. Sydney Jephcott. PoAu-1
Three. Roger Aplon. YAP
Three accomplishments well regarded in Ireland: a clever/ verse. *Tr. by* Thomas Kinsella. *Fr.* The Triads of Ireland. OxBI
Three Acres of Land. *Unknown. See* Mad Farmer's Song.
Three American Women and a German Bayonet. Winfield Townley Scott. FiMAP; NMP; OnHM
Three ancient men in Bethlehem's cave. The Mystic Magi [*or* The Southern Cross]. Robert Stephen Hawker. ChTr; OxBoCh
Three around the Old Gentleman. John Berryman. AP
Three Arrows, The. Edward Fitzgerald. OBVV
Three Awful Picnics. John L'Heureux. YAP
Three Bad Ones. *Unknown.* BBGG
Three Ballate. Angelo Poliziano, *tr. fr. Italian by* John Addington Symonds.
"He who knows not what thing is Paradise," II. AWP
(Ballata of Myrrha's Eyes.) LiTW
"I found myself one day all, all alone," I. AWP
"I went a roaming, maidens, one bright day," III. AWP
Three Barrows Down. Jocelyn Brooke. ChMP
Three Beggars, The. Walter de la Mare. RIS
Three Bells, The. Whittier. EtS
Three Best Things, The, Henry van Dyke.
Sels.
Life ("Let me but live my life from year to year"). MaRV; OQP; TRV
(Let Me But Live from Year to Year.) TreFT
Work. MaRV; OQP; OTD; PoMa; PoRL; SP; TIHL; YT
Three Black Crows, The. John Byrom. BOHV
Three Blessings. *Unknown.* ALV
Three Blessings. *Unknown, tr. fr. Gaelic by* Alexander Carmichael. BoPe
Three blind mice, see how they run! Mother Goose. OxNR; RIS; SiTL; StVeCh (1940 ed.)
Three blind mice, three blind mice/ Dame Julian, Dame Julian. *Unknown.* OBS
Three bold brothers of merrie Scotland. Henry Martyn (E *vers.*). *Unknown.* ESPB
Three brightest blessings of this thirsty race. Three Blessings. *Unknown.* ALV
Three brothers in old Scotland did dwell. Henry Martyn (A *vers.*). *Unknown.* ViBoFo
Three Brown Girls Singing. M. Carl Holman. Kal
Three Bushes, The. W. B. Yeats. DTC; LiTG; LiTL
Lady's Third Song, The, *sel.* FaBoTw
Three Butchers, The. *Unknown.* BFSS; PeVV, *diff. vers.*
Three Canterbury Pilgrims. Chaucer. *See* Canterbury Tales, The: Prologue.
Three Captains, The. *Unknown, tr. fr. French by* Andrew Lang. AWP
Three carrion crows in yonder tree. The Three Crows. *Unknown.* BFSS
Three Characteristic Epitaphs. *Unknown.* SoP
Three Cherry Trees, The. Walter de la Mare. CMoP; GBV; SiSw
Three Children, The. Charles W. H. Bancroft. SoP
Three Children. *Unknown, at. to* John Gay. BOHV; NA
(Sad, Sad Story, A.) RIS
("Three children sliding on the ice.") OxNR; PPL; StVeCh (1940 ed.)
Three children dancing around an orange tree. Coins and Coffins under My Bed. Diane Wakoski. CoPo
Three children dash in the dim dooryard. Tree Tag. Mary E. Caragher. GoYe
Three Children near Clonmel. Eileen Shanahan. OnYI; OxBI
Three children sliding on the ice. Three Children [*or* A Sad, Sad Story]. *Unknown, at. to* John Gay. BOHV; NA; OxNR; PPL; RIS; StVeCh (1940 ed.)

Three Christmas Carols, *Unknown.* ACP
"Babe is born all of a May, A," I.
"Man, be merry, I thee rede," II.
"This night there is a child born," III.
Three Cities. George Rostrevor Hamilton. POTE
Three City Cantos. Charles A. Wagner. GoYe
Three Colts Exercising in a Six-Acre. Joseph Campbell. OnYI
Three Companions, The. W. H. Auden. *See* O Where Are You Going?
Three Corners of Reality, The. Marvin Bell. YAP
Three Cottage Girls, The. Wordsworth. HBV
Three counties blacken and vanish. L'Aurore Grelottante. Peter Levi. NePoEA-2
Three crests against the saffron sky. Twilight on Tweed. Andrew Lang. OBVV; PoVP
Three crooked cripples went through Cripplegate. *Unknown.* OxNR
Three Crosses, The. Edmund Vance Cook. PEDC
Three Crosses. Helen Frazee-Bower. SoP
Three Crosses. Leila Avery Rotherburger. ChIP; MaRV; StJW
Three crosses rose on Calvary against the iron sky. The Thief on the Cross. Harriet Monroe. OQP
Three Crows, The. *Unknown.* *See* Twa Corbies, The.
Three Dangers. *Unknown,* *tr. fr. Spanish by* Havelock Ellis. OnPM
Three dark maids—I loved them when. Villancico. *Unknown.* AWP; JAWP; OnPM; WBP
Three Days. W. Boyd Carpenter. MaRV
Three days ago I found my love, and it's not so long. Je caresserai la belle par amitié. *Unknown.* OuSiCo
Three days from the Luapula still. The Explorer. Anthony Delius. BoSA
Three days I dreamed her. Proposal. Robert Sward. ELU
Three days, I ween, make up our life. Three Days. W. Boyd Carpenter. MaRV
Three days through sapphire seas we sailed. The Bay Fight. Henry Howard Brownell. PaA; PAH; PAP; PFY
Three Dead and the Three Living, The. George Barker. LiTB
Three Dogs. E. C. Brereton. BoTP
Three doors are in the temple. The Doors in the Temple. George Matheson. OQP
Three Doves. James Jeffrey Roche. JKCP
Three Dreams. James Michie. NePoEA-2
Three Elements. Stephen Vincent Benét. *Fr.* John Brown's Body. EaLo
Three Enemies, The. Christina Rossetti. CoBE; PoVP; ViPo
Three Epitaphs upon the Death of a Rare Child of Six Years Old. Francis Davison. OBSC; RelE
"Lovely boy, thou art not dead," II.
"Thou alive on earth, sweet boy," III.
"Wit's perfection, Beauty's wonder," I.
Three fellows were marching over the Rhine. The Hostess' Daughter. Ludwig Uhland. AWP; JAWP; WBP
Three Fields. Adolf Heyduk, *tr. fr. Czech by* Paul Selver. LiTW
Three fishermen/ fished in the old Round Pond. Fishes. Humbert Wolfe. RIS; StaSt
Three Fishers, The. Charles Kingsley. BBV; BeLS; EtS; HBV; MCCG; NeHB; OnMSP; OTPC (1923 ed.); PoLF; PoVP; ShBV-1; TreF; VA; WBLP
(Three Fishers Went Sailing.) OtMeF
Three folds in my garment, yet only one garment I bear. The Rann of the Three. *Unknown,* *tr. by* Thomas Walsh. CAW; WHL
Three folds of the cloth, yet one only napkin is there. The Sacred Trinity [*or* Four Prayers]. *Unknown,* *tr. by* Eleanor Hull. JKCP (1926 ed.); OnYI
Three for Robert Bly, *sel.* William Witherup.
"In Minnesota the barns are black." QAH
3 for 25. William Jay Smith. WaP
Three Foxes, The. A. A. Milne. GoJo; MoShBr; StVeCh (1955 ed.)
Three Fragments. William Allingham. IrPN
"And from a northern coast the Lovers watch'd," I.
"Black texture of the leafy trees," III.
"Night a spongy dimness fill'd with moonshine, The," II.
Three Fragments, William Collins. WaPE
Lament for Tintoretta, III.
Limitations of Human Art, II.
Luckless Collins, I.
Three Friends. *Unknown,* *tr. fr. Yoruba by* Ulli Beier. PBA
Three Friends of Mine. Longfellow. MAmP
Three gables; clustered chimney stacks; a wall. The Vacant Farmhouse. Walter de la Mare. HaMV
Three Gates. Beth Day, *after the Arabic.* BLPA; MaRV; NeHB; OQP; TreFS
(Three Gates of Gold.) PoToHe
Three ghosts on the lonesome road, The. Stains. Theodosia Garrison. HBV; MaRV; WGRP
Three Gifts. Edward Judson Hanna. ChIP; OQP
Three gipsies [*or* gypsies] stood at the Castle gate. The Wraggle Taggle Gipsies. *Unknown.* CBEP; LiTL; OtMeF; SaSa; ShBV-1
Three Graves, The, *sel.* Samuel Taylor Coleridge.
"So gentle Ellen now no more." ChER
Three Green Trees. Angela Morgan. HBMV
Three Green Windows. Anne Sexton. NYBP
Three grey geese in a green field grazing. *Unknown.* OxNR
Three gypsies stood at the Castle gate. *See* Three gipsies . . .
Three Haitian Creole Moods. Emile Roumer, *tr. fr. French by* Selden Rodman. OnHM
Three hand-spike raps on the forward hatch. Reefing Topsails. Walter Mitchell. EtS
Three Helpers in Battle. Mary Elizabeth Coleridge. EaLo
Three Hermits, The. W. B. Yeats. AtBAP; CMoP; FlW; PoDB; TDP
Three Hills. Everard Owen. StJW
Three Hills, The. J. C. Squire. HBMV; InP
Three horsemen galloped the dusty way. On the Road to Chorrera. Arlo Bates. AA
Three Hours. Vachel Lindsay. ATP
Three hours ago he blundered up the trench. A Working Party. Siegfried Sassoon. CMoP; MMA
305 Honda. Gene Fowler. ThO
306. E. E. Cummings. AnEnPo
Three Hundred Thousand More. James Sloan Gibbons. PaA; PAH; PoFr
Three hundred years the world has looked at it. Raphael's San Sisto Madonna. George Henry Miles. CAW
Three Huntsmen, The. *Unknown.* *See* Three Jovial Welshmen, The.
Three Hymns, Elizabeth Rowe. WaPE
On the Sacrament. II.
"Thou didst, O mighty God, exist." I.
"Ye pure inhabitants of light." III.
Three Hymns. Charles Wesley. WaPE
For One in Doubt, III.
Shepherd of Souls, Thy sheep behold! II.
"'Twas thus the subtle foe," I.
Three Jet Planes. May Swenson. PoPo
Three jolly farmers. Off the Ground. Walter de la Mare. RG; StaSt; StPo; YT
Three jolly gentlemen. The Huntsmen. Walter de la Mare. CenHV; HBMV; InP; SiSoSe; StVeCh; TiPo
Three Jolly Hunters, The. James Whitcomb Riley. WaKn
Three Jolly Huntsmen, The. *Unknown.* *See* Three Jovial Welshmen, The.
Three Jolly Pigeons, The. Goldsmith. *See* Song: "Let schoolmasters puzzle their brains."
Three Jovial Gentlemen. Daniel Hoffman. MoBS
Three Jovial Welshmen, The. *Unknown.* GaP; HBVY; SiTL
(Jovial Welshmen, The.) OTPC
("There were three jovial Welshmen.") BoChLi; OxNR; StVeCh
(Three Huntsmen, The.) OnMSP; OxBoLi
(Three Jolly Huntsmen.) GoTP
(Three Jovial Huntsmen, The.) BOHV, *abr.*; NA, *abr.*
(Three Jovial Huntsmen; or, The Owl and the Jay Bush, *with music.*) BFSS
(Three Welshmen, The.) MoShBr
Three Khalandeers, The. James Clarence Mangan. OBVV
Three Kinds of Pleasures. Robert Bly. FRC
Three Kings, The. Eugene Field. *See* Three Kings of Cologne, The.
Three Kings, The. Longfellow. ChrBoLe; GBV (1952 ed.); GN; GoTP; HBV; HBVY; OnMsP; PTK
(Three Kings Came Riding.) StVeCh
Three Kings. James P. Vaughn. NNP; PoNe (1970 ed.)
Three Kings, The. *Unknown.* OBB
Three Kings Came. Thomas W. Shapcott. PoAu-2
Three Kings Came Riding. Norah M. Holland. ChrBoLe

Three Kings came riding from far away. The Three Kings. Longfellow. ChrBoLe; GBV (1952 ed.); GN; GoTP; HBV; HBVY; OnMSP; PTK; StVeCh
Three Kings of Cologne, The. Eugene Field. StJW
(Three Kings, The.) GN
Three Kings of Orient. John Henry Hopkins, Jr. *See* We Three Kings of Orient Are.
Three Kings stepped out of my body. Poem for Epiphany. Norman Nicholson. PoPl; StJW
Three kings there were from Orient who came. Gifts. Helen Wieand Cole. ChIP; OQP
Three kings went down to the soul of the sea. Three Kings. James P. Vaughn. NNP; PoNe (1970 ed.)
Three Knights from Spain. *Unknown.* AtBAP; CH
("We are three brethren out of Spain.") OxNR; RIS, *much abr.*
Three Ladies, The. Robert Creeley. NeAP
Three Ladies of London, The, *sels.* Robert Wilson.
New Brooms. ElL
(Conscience's Song.) OBSC
Simplicity's Song. CTC; OBSC
Three ladies played at cup and ball. The Cruel Brother. *Unknown.* BaBo (B *vers.*)
Three Landscapes, *sel.* Jerome Rothenberg.
"Dark bull quartered in my eye, The." CoPo
Three Lessons. Schiller. *See* Three Words of Strength.
Three Links of Light Armour. Richard Armour. SiTL
Three Little Babes, The, *with music.* *Unknown.* BFSS
Three little chickens/ And one little worm. A Tug-of-War. M. M. Hutchinson. BoTP
Three little children sitting on the sand. All, All a-Lonely. *Unknown.* ChTr; ExPo; OxBoLi
Three little ghostesses. *Unknown.* OxNR
Three Little Girls. Richard Aldington. BrPo
Three Little Kittens, The ("Three little kittens, they lost their mittens"). *Unknown, at. to* Eliza Lee Follen *and to* Eliza Cook. BoTP; CIV; FaPON; GFA; OTPC (1946 ed.); OxNR; PCH; SAS; SoPo; StVeCh; TreFS; UTS
(Careless Kittens, The, *abr.*) RIS
("Three little kittens they lost their mittens.") PPL
Three little maidens they have slain. Song. Maurice Maeterlinck. AWP; JAWP; WBP
Three Little Maids from School. W. S. Gilbert. *Fr.* The Mikado. PoVP; TreFT
Three Little Men in a Boat. Rodney Bennett. BoTP
Three little mice sat down to spin. Pussy and the Mice. *Unknown.* MoShBr
Three little mice walked into town. Three Mice. Charlotte Druitt Cole. BoTP
Three Little Pigs, The. Sir Alfred Scott-Gatty. BoTP
Three Little Puffins. Eleanor Farjeon. TiPo (1959 ed.)
Three little words you often see. Grammar in a Nutshell [*or* Grammer in Rhyme *or* The Parts of Speech]. *Unknown.* HBV; HBVY; OTPC; TreFS
Three long nights, an' three long days. Walk, Mary, down de Lane. *Unknown.* BoAN-2
Three Love Poems. Norman Cameron.
From a Woman to a Greedy Lover, I. FaBoTw; GTBS-P
In the Queen's Room, II. FaBoTw; GTBS-P
Shepherdess, III. FaBoTw; GTBS-P; OxBS
Three Lovely Holes. Winifred Welles. StVeCh
Three lovely notes he whistled, too soft to be heard. The Unknown Bird. Edward Thomas. ACV; DTC; FaBoEn
Three Loves. Lucy Hamilton Hooper. BeLS
Three maidens in their chamber. Sir Ogey and Lady Elsey. *Unknown.* BaBo
Three Maids a-Milking Would Go. *Unknown.* CoMu
3 Meditations. Gene Fowler. ThO
Three Memorial Sonnets. George Barker. *See* Memorial (For Two Young Seamen. . .).
Three men came talking up the road. Nightpiece. John Manifold. LiTM; MoBrPo (1950 ed.); WaP
Three men coming down the winter hill, The. Winter Landscape. John Berryman. AP; LiTA; LiTG; LiTM (1970 ed.); MoAmPo (1950 ed.); PoPl; TwCP
Three men in a limousine travelling westward. The Three Dead and the Three Living. George Barker. LiTB
Three men lived yet when this dead man was young. After Looking into Carlyle's Reminiscences. Swinburne. ViPo
Three Men of Gotham. Thomas Love Peacock. *Fr.* Nightmare Abbey. FaBoCh; GTBS; GTBS-D; GTSL; LiTG; MyFE, *st.* 1; OBEV; SiTL; TOP
(Catch, A: "Seamen three! What men be ye?") ViBoPo
(Men of Gotham, The.) CH; OTPC (1946 ed.)
(Seamen Three.) OBRV; PeER; WiR
("Seamen three, what men be ye?") EG
(Wise Men of Gotham, The.) LoBV
Three men shared death upon a hill. Upon a Hill. Miriam LeFevre Crouse. ChIP
Three men were walking on a wall. Feeling, Faith and Fact. *Unknown.* SoP
Three Mice. Charlotte Druitt Cole. BoTP
Three miles extended around the fields of the homestead. Frithiof's Homestead. Esias Tegnér. *Fr.* Frithiof's Saga. AWP
Three miles from town to town over the snow. E. J. Pratt. *Fr.* Brebeuf and His Brethren. ACV
Three Mirrors, The. Edwin Muir. PoIE
Three Monkeys ("Three monkeys once dining in a cocoanut tree"). *Unknown.* STF
Three Moorish girls I loved. Song. *Unknown.* LiTW
Three Movements, The. Donald Hall. NePoEA-2
Three Movements. W. B. Yeats. CMoP; ELU
Three Movements and a Coda. LeRoi Jones. BF
Three Musicians, The. Aubrey Beardsley. ACP (1926 ed.); JKCP (1926 ed.); MuSP; PeVV
Three Nights Drunk (*diff. vers. of* Our Goodman), *with music.* *Unknown.* OuSiCo
3/19—"just a day's march." Conquistador. Georgia Lee McElhaney. CoPo
Three Nocturns. Sir Osbert Sitwell. POTE
"Milky clouds, dispersing, The." III.
"Owl, horned wizard of the night, An," II.
"Valleys that we knew in sunlit hours, The," I.
Three o'Clock in the Morning. R. S. Palfrey. DD; MPB
Three o'Clock—Morning. Ridgely Torrence. NP
Three of us afloat in the meadow by the swing. Pirate Story. Robert Louis Stevenson. BeLS; FaPON; GFA; GoTP; OTPC (1946 ed.); PoVP; TiPo; VA
Three Old Brothers. Frank O'Connor. OnYI
Three Old Cattlemen. Monica Shannon. GaP
Three old hermits took the air. The Three Hermits. W. B. Yeats. AtBAP; CMoP; FIW; PoDB; TDP
Three Organ Rituals for Erik Satie. Robert Kelly. YAP
Three ounces are necessary, first of Patience. Recipe for a Happy Life. Margaret of Navarre. PoMa
Three outas from the bleak Karoo. Christmas Carol. D. J. Opperman. PeSA
Three Paintings by Arthur Dove. Ronald Johnson. YAP
Three Part Invention. Paul Blackburn. CoPo
Three Persons. Louise Townsend Nicholl. CAW
Three Peters, The. Molly Michaels. RIS
Three Phases of Africa. Francis Ernest Kobina Parkes. PBA
Three Pictures. Charles Dalmon. TSW
Almond Blossoms.
Snowfall on Plum Trees after They Had Bloomed, A.
Wistaria Blossoms.
Three Pigeons, The. Goldsmith. *See* Song: "Let schoolmasters puzzle their brains."
Three pigeons down-swing. Possibilities. Peter Kane Dufault. NYBP
Three Pigs, *with music.* *Unknown.* ABF
Three Pipes, The. *Unknown, tr. fr. Russian by* W. R. S. Ralston. OnPM
Three Plum Buns. Christina Rossetti. *Fr.* Sing-Song. BoTP
(Snack, A.) PCH
Three Poems. Stephen Crane. AP
"Chant you loud of punishments," II.
"Man adrift on a slim spar, A," I.
"Naked woman and a dead dwarf, A," III.
Three Poems about Mark Twain, *sel.* Vachel Lindsay.
When the Mississippi Flowed in Indiana, II. CMoP
Three Poems of the Atomic Age, *sel.* Edith Sitwell.
Dirge for the New Sunrise. AtBAP; CMoP; MoAB; MoBrPo (1950 ed.); SeCePo
Three poets, in three different ages born. Lines Printed Under the Engraved Portrait of Milton [*or* Epigram on Milton]. Dryden. ACP; BEL; BoLiVe; CEP; EiPP; EnLi-1 (1939 ed.); EnLit; HBV; InP; MBW-1; SeCeV; SeCV-2; SeEP; TOP; TrGrPo; WHA; YAT
Three Poplars, The. Philip Francis Little. OxBI

Three Portraits of Prince Charles. Andrew Lang. PoVP; VA
Three Prayers, The. Annie Johnson Flint. SoP
Three Prison Portraits, *sel.* Miriam Waddington.
Drug Addict, The. ACV
Three Proverbs. James Clarence Mangan, *after the Ottoman (Turkish).* IrPN
"Hour of Good, a day of Ill, An," I.
"Nought, I hear thee say," III.
"Steed to the man who bestrides it newly, The," II.
Three Ravens, The ("As I was walking all alane"). *Unknown. See* Twa Corbies, The.
Three Ravens, The, ("There were three ravens sat on a tree"). *Unknown.* AtBAP; BEL; CABA; CaFP; CBV; ChTr; ESPB; HBV; NoP; OAEP; OBB; OBEV; OuHeWo; OxBB; PAn; PoAn; PoEL-1; PoG; PoPo; SeCeV; TrGrPo; UnPo; ViBoFo (A, B, *and* C *vers.*); ViBoPo
Three Rimas. Gustavo Adolfo Bécquer, *See* Rimas.
Three roads led out to Calvary. The Blessed Road. Charles Buxton Going. ChIP
Three roads were shadowy and the sky over. Vanessa Vanessa. Ewart Milne. NeIP
Three Roses, The. Walter Savage Landor. CLwM
Three Roundels of Love Unreturned. Chaucer. *See* Merciles Beaute.
Three Sailors, The. Thackeray. *See* Little Billee.
Three Scars, The. George Walter Thornbury. VA
Three score and ten by common calculation. Song. James Robinson Planché. BOHV
Three score and ten! The tumult of the world. Life's Evening. William Dudley Foulke. OQP; WGRP
Three Seamstresses, The. Isaac Leibush Peretz, *tr. fr. Yiddish by* Joseph Leftwich. TrJP
Three Seasons. Christina Rossetti. CBV; HBV
Three seasons only in his calendar. Sonnet. George Henry Boker. *Fr.* Sonnets. AmLP
Three Sections from "Anabasis." "St. J. Perse." *See* Anabasis.
Three Sentences for a Dead Swan. James Wright. NaP
Three Sermons to the Dead. Laura Riding.
Nor Is It Written, III. FaBoMo; LiTA
Not All Immaculate, II. LiTA
Way of the Air, The, I. LiTA
Three Shadows. Dante Gabriel Rossetti. HBV; PoVP; ViBoPo
Three ships I saw come sailing. Swedish Folk Song. *Unknown.* PCH
Three ships of war had Preble when he left the Naples shore. Reuben James. James Jeffrey Roche. PAH
Three Silences of Molinos, The. Longfellow. AmPP; AnFE; APA; CoAnAm; CoBA; Sonn
Three Singing Birds, The. James Reeves. PDV; PoMS
Three Sisters, The. Arthur Davison Ficke. HBV; MAP
Three slender things that best support the world. *Unknown. Fr.* The Triads of Ireland. OnYI
Three Songs. Hart Crane. *Fr.* The Bridge. LiTA
National Winter Garden, *sel.* OxBA
Three Songs, The. Bayard Taylor. StPo
Three Sonnets, *sels.* Hartley Coleridge.
"Hast thou not seen an aged rifted tower," I. EnRP
How Shall a Man Fore-Doomed, II. NCEP
Three Sonnets on Oblivion. George Sterling. HBV
Three Sorrowful Things. *Unknown, tr. fr. Middle English by* Mabel Van Duzee. MeEV
Three sortes of teares doe from myne eies distraine. Sonnet. William Alabaster. AnAnS-1; MeP
Three sorts of serpents do resemble thee. Idea, XXX. Michael Drayton. EnRePo
Three spirits came to me. April. Ezra Pound. CMoP
Three Spring Notations on Bipeds. Carl Sandburg. AWP; InPo; JAWP; WBP
Three Springs. Pushkin, *tr. fr. Russian by* Babette Deutsch. OnPM
Three Star Final. Conrad Aiken. OxBA
Three stars, five stars rise over the hill. Confucius. *Fr.* Shao and the South. CTC
Three Stars of Prophecy, The. David Gascoyne. POTE
Three Steps. Katharine Lee Bates. OQP
Three steps and I reach the door. Fate. Louis James Block. AA
Three steps there are our human life must climb. Three Steps. Katharine Lee Bates. OQP
Three strange men came to the inn. A Lady Comes to an Inn. Elizabeth J. Coatsworth. MAP; MoAmPo; NeMA; StPo
Three students/ sitting in the shade. Something Else. Michael Brownstein. ANYP
Three students once tarried over the Rhine. From the German of Uhland. *Tr. by* James Weldon Johnson. CDC
Three summers since I chose a maid. The Farmer's Bride. Charlotte Mew. ErPo; HBMV; MoAB; MoBrPo; NP; OnPP; PoRA; TrGrPo
Three Sweethearts. Heine, *tr. fr. German by* Louis Untermeyer. UnTE
Three Tarry Men. Edmund Leamy. PoMa
Three Taverns, The, *sel.* E. A. Robinson.
Out of Wisdom Has Come Love. MoRP
Three then came forward out of darkness, one. The Road. Conrad Aiken. AP; MAP; MoAmPo
Three Things. Joseph Auslander. HBMV; MPB; TrJP
Three Things. Gertrude B. Gunderson. OQP
Three Things ("I Know three things must always be"). *Unknown.* SoP
Three Things ("Three things there are that will never come back"). *Unknown, ad. fr. Persian by* Louis Untermeyer. GoTP
Three Things. W. B. Yeats. AtBAP; DTC; FaBoEn; OBMV
Three things are of the Evil One. Charm against Enemies. *Unknown.* JKCP (1926 ed.)
Three Things Come Not Back. *Unknown, tr. fr. Arabic.* MaRV; OQP
Three things filled this day for me. Three Things. Joseph Auslander. HBMV; MPB; TrJP
Three things I beg of Life to let me keep. Three Things. Gertrude B. Gunderson. OQP
Three Things Jeame Lacks. *Unknown.* MeEL
Three things must a man possess if his soul would live. The New Trinity. Edwin Markham. PGD
Three things seek my death. Inheritance. *Unknown.* KiLC
Three things the Master hath to do. Pray—Give—Go [*or* The Threefold Work]. Annie Johnson Flint. BLRP; SoP; STF
Three things there are more beautiful. The Beautiful. W. H. Davies. ELU; POTE
"Three things there are," said one. "And I, If I Be Lifted Up, Shall Draw All Men." E. P. Dickie. ChIP; MaRV
Three things there are that will never come back. Three Things. *Unknown.* GoTP
Three things there are, worth living for. The Swashbuckler's Song. James Stuart Montgomery. HBMV
Three Things There Be. Fulke Greville. Caelica, CV [CVI]. LiTG
("Three things there be in man's opinion dear.") LiTB; OBS; PoEL-1; SiCE
Three Things There Be That Prosper Up Apace. Sir Walter Ralegh. *See* Wood, the Weed, the Wag, The.
Three Things to Remember. Blake. *See* Robin Redbreast, A.
Three thousand for my brand new car. A Dollar I Gave. *Unknown.* STF
Three times a day my prayer is. *Unknown.* OBSC
Three times, all in the dead of night. Colin and Lucy [*or* Lucy and Colin]. Thomas Tickell. CEP; OBEC; OTPC (1923 ed)
Three times he crossed our way. Old Man Pondered. John Crowe Ransom. MAP; MoAmPo
Three times in Bethany, that hallowed spot. At His Feet. Lois R. Carpenter. BePJ
Three times round the cuckoo waltz. Cuckoo Waltz. *Unknown.* AS
Three times sitting down to bread. Daily Round. Lizette Woodworth Reese. *Fr.* After. ThGo
Three times we heard it calling with a low. The Ground-Swell. E. J. Pratt. CaP
Three Travelers, The. *Unknown.* UnTE
Three Trees. Charles H. Crandall. OHIP
Three Trees at Solstice. Mary Finnin. BoAV
Three Troopers, The. George Walter Thornbury. BeLS; HBV; VA
Three turkeys fair their last have breathed. A Melancholy Lay [*or* Six-Year-Old Marjory Fleming Pens a Poem]. Marjory Fleming. FaBoCh; FiBHP; LoGBV; SiTL; ThWaDe; TreFT
Three twangs of the horn, and they're all out of cover. The Glory of Motion. R. St. John Tyrwhitt. VA
3/26/66. James Schuyler. ANYP
Three Variations. Boris Pasternak, *tr. fr. Russian by* Babette Deutsch. TrJP

Three virgins at the break of day. The Golden Net. Blake. ERoP-1; SiSw
Three Warnings, The. Hester Thrale. BeLS; HBV
Three weeks gone and the combatants gone. Vergissmeinicht. Keith Douglas. ChMP; GTBS-P; NePoEA
Three Welshmen, The. *Unknown.* *See* Three Jovial Welshmen, The
Three White Birds of Angus. Eleanor Rogers Cox. HBMV
Three Winds, The. Laurie Lee. FaBoMo; POTi
Three Wise Couples, The. Mrs. E. T. Corbett. BLPA
Three Wise Kings. William E. Brooks. ChIP; PGD
Three Wise Men, The. John Finley. ChIP; OQP
Three wise men of Gotham. Mother Goose. BoChLi; FaBoBe; FaFP; HBV; HBVY; OTPC; OxNR; PPL; RIS; SiTL
Three Wise Monkeys, The. Florence Boyce Davis. WBLP
Three wise old couples were they, were they. The Three Wise Couples. Mrs. E. T. Corbett. BLPA
Three Wise Women, The. Mrs. E. T. Corbett. BLPA, *abr.*
Three with the Moon and His Shadow. Li Po, *tr. fr. Chinese by* Shigeyoshi Obata. WoL
Three without slumber ride from afar. Five Carols for Christmastide, III. Louise Imogen Guiney. ISi
Three Woes, The. Aubrey Thomas De Vere. AnIV
Three Women. Alan Dienstag. ErPo
Three women have slept with my books. Conon in Exile. Lawrence Durrell. ToPo
Three words fall sweetly on my soul. Mother, Home, Heaven. William Goldsmith Brown. DD; FaBoBe; HBV
Three Words of Strength. Schiller, *tr. fr. German.* OQP
(Three Lessons.) MaRV
Three workmen fashioning a cross. Cross Makers [*or* Free Enterprise]. Clyde McGee. ChIP; MaRV
Three Years She Grew [in Sun and Shower]. Wordsworth. AtBAP; AWP; BeL; CBEP; EnL; EnLit; EnRP; EPN; ERoP-1; FosPo; GBV (1922 ed.); HBVY; ILP; LoBV; MBW-2; MERP; NoP; OAEP; OBRV; OnPP; OuHeWo; PAn; PoE; PoEL-4; PoFS; PoIE; SeCeV; TOP; TreFS
(Education of Nature, The.) GTBS; GTBS-D; GTBS-P; GTBS-W; GTSE; GTSL
(Lucy.) EnLi-2; FiP; GN; HBV; LiTL; OBEV; OBNC; OTPC (1923 ed.); TrGrPo
Three young heifers were at Summer supper, The. The Gracious and the Gentle Thing. Robert P. Tristram Coffin. OA
Three Young Rats ("Three young rats with black felt hats"). *Unknown.* ChTr; InvP; LiTG; OxBoLi; OxNR; SiTL
Three youths went a-fishing. The Banished Duke of Grantham. *Unknown.* EnSB
Threefold the stride of Time, from first to last. Time. Schiller. OQP
Threefold Work, The. Annie Johnson Flint. *See* Pray—Give—Go.
Threes. Carl Sandburg. CMoP; OxBA; PoLF
Threescore and Ten. Richard Henry Stoddard. HBV
Threescore o' nobles rade to the king's ha! Glenlogie. *Unknown.* HBV
Threnody, A: Ahkoond of Swat, The. George Thomas Lanigan. *See* Threnody, A: "What, what, what."
Threnody: "Far away." Thomas Lovell Beddoes. StP
Threnody: "I have been a snob to-day." Alfred Kreymborg. MAPA
Threnody, A: In Memory of Albert Darasz, *sel.* William James Linton.
"O Blessed Dead! beyond all earthly pains." VA
Threnody: "In Plimmerton, in Plimmerton." Denis Glover. AnNZ
Threnody: "Let happy throats be mute." Donald Jeffrey Hayes. AmNP
Threnody: "Lilacs blossom just as sweet." Dorothy Parker. InMe
Threnody: "No sunny ray, no silver night." Thomas Lovell Beddoes. EnRP
Threnody: "Only quiet death." Waring Cuney. AmNP; BANP
Threnody: "Red leaves fall upon the lake, The." John Farrar. BoChLi; BrR; GFA; SUS
Threnody: "South-wind brings, The." Emerson. AA; AmePo; AnNE; AP; MAmP; MWA-1; StP; TOP
"Wilt thou not ope thy heart to know, *sel.*" MaRV
Threnody: "There's a grass-grown road from the valley." Ruth Guthrie Harding. HBV
Threnody: "Truth is a golden sunset far away." I. O. Scherzo. HoPM
Threnody, A: "What, what, what." George T. Lanigan. AA; CBEP; FiBHP; HBV; InMe; LHV; NA; PeCV; WHW
(Ahkoond of Swat, The.) BOHV; CaP; TreFS
(Threnody on the Ahkoond of Swat, A.) CenHV
Threnody for a Pet Cat. Mazie V. Caruthers. CIV
Threnody for a Poet. Bliss Carman. CaP
Threnody on the Ahkoond of Swat, A. George Thomas Lanigan. *See* Threnody: "What, what, what."
Threnos. J. R. Hervey. AnNZ
Threnos. Shelley. *See* Lament, A: "O world! O life! O time!"
Thresh seed and go fan, for the plow may not lie. September. Thomas Tusser. ReIE
Threshing Machine, The. Alice Meynell. SeCePo
Threshold. Edmund Blunden. HBMV
Threshold. Charles David Webb. NePoAm-2
Thrice, and above, blest (my soules halfe) art thou. A Country Life; to His Brother, M. Tho. Herrick. Robert Herrick. SeCP; SeCV-1
Thrice Armed. Shakespeare. King Henry VI, Pt. II, *fr.* III, ii. MaRV
Thrice at the huts of Fontenoy the English column failed. Fontenoy. Thomas Osborne Davis. HBV; OnYI
Thrice cruel fell my fate. In Rebellion. J. M. Synge. SyP
Thrice-cruel maid, may Heaven frown on thee. The Elusive Maid. Abraham ibn Chasdai. TrJP
Thrice hail, thou prince of jovial fellows. An Ode to Myself. Thomas Dermody. OnYI
Thrice happy day which sweetly dost combine. On the Coincidence of the Feasts of the Annunciation and the Resurrection in 1627. Sir John Beaumont. ACP (1926 ed.)
Thrice happy days! in rural business past. Blest Winter Nights. John Armstrong. *Fr.* The Art of Preserving Health, III. OBEC
Thrice Happy He. William Drummond of Hawthornden. BoNaP; HBV
(Solitary Life, A.) OBS
("Thrice happy he who by some shady grove.") Sonn
Thrice happy maid; supremely blest. The Wedding Night. Johannes Secundus. *Fr.* Epithalamium. UnTE
Thrice happy, who free from ambition and pride. The Fire Side; a Pastoral Soliloquy. Isaac Hawkins Browne. *Fr.* The Foundling Hospital for Wit, IV. OBEC
Thrice Holy. Reginald Heber. *See* Holy, Holy, Holy.
Thrice-holy thorns, encircling with thy fire. To the Most Holy Crown of Thorns. Sister Miriam Teresa. JKCP (1955 ed.)
Thrice the brinded cat hath mewed. The Witches' Song [*or* The Charm]. Shakespeare. *Fr.* Macbeth, IV, i. EIL; InvP; MyFE; PoMS
Thrice the crested cock has crowed. The Glory of Early Rising. Frank Sidgwick. WhC
Thrice Toss These Oaken Ashes [in the Air]. Thomas Campion. AnFE; AtBAP; EIL; EnLoPo; FaBoCh; LoBV; LoGBV; NoP; OBSC; PoRA; TuPP; ViBoPo
(Thrice Tosse These Oaken Ashes in the Ayre.) PoEL-2; SiSw
Thrice with her lips she touched my lips. Parting [*or* For Ever]. William Caldwell Roscoe. HBV; OBVV
Thrift. Lizette Woodworth Reese. NP
Thriftles thred which pampred beauty spinnes, The. A Sonet Written in Prayse of the Browne Beautie. George Gascoigne. EnPo
Thrifty Elephant, The. John Holmes. NYBP
Thrissil and the Rois, The, *sel.* William Dunbar.
"Quehn Merche wes with variand windis past." HW
Thro'. *Ee also* Through.
Thro' Grief and thro' Danger. Thomas Moore. *See* Irish Peasant to His Mistress, The.
Thro' the hushed air the whitening shower descends. A Winter Scene. James Thomson. *Fr.* The Seasons: Winter. OBEC
Thro' the night of doubt and sorrow. Pilgrim's Song. Bernhard S. Ingemann. WGRP
Thro' the night Thy angels kept. A Child's Prayer. William Canton. BoTP
Throat of thunder, a tameless heart, A. A Cyclone at Sea. William Hamilton Hayne. AA
Throat-to throat surgery. James Brodey. *Fr.* Vice, 1966. ANYP
Throats of the little trumpet-flowers are wide open, The. The

Trumpet-Vine Arbor. Amy Lowell. *Fr.* 1777. MAPA; NP
Throb, throb from the mixer. The Pigeon. Richard Church. WePo
Throb, throb, throb . . . the tall ship. Night Boat. Audrey Alexandra Brown. CaP
Throbs the Night with Mystic Silence. Hayyim Nahman Bialik, *tr. fr. Hebrew by* Bertha Beinkinstadt. TrJP
Thron'd in the sun's descending car. Benevolence. Mark Akenside. *Fr.* Against Suspicion. OBEC
Throne of the King, The. Francis Clement Kelley. JKCP
Throne of the Lily-King, The. Joseph Rodman Drake. *Fr.* The Culprit Fay. GN
Throned are the gods, and in. Chorus. Lord de Tabley. *Fr.* Philoctetes. NBM
Thronged boughs of the shadowy sycamore, The. The Day-Dream. Dante Gabriel Rossetti. SyP
Throstle, The. Tennyson. BoChLi; BoNaP; DD; EPN; FaPON; HBV; HBVY; MCCG; OTPC; PoPo; PoRL; PoSC; PoVP; ShBV-1; WaKn
Through. *See also* Thro'.
Through a dark drizzle of rain. The Mailman and Das Ewig Weibliche. James Schevill. FRC
Through a Fog of Stars. John Nixon, Jr. MaRV
Through a Glass Darkly. Arthur Hugh Clough. PoVP
(What We, When Face to Face We See.) ViPP
Through a green gorge the river like a fountain. The Sleeper in the Valley. Arthur Rimbaud. WaaP
Through a Porthole. Leon Gellert. BoAu
Through a Shop Window. Eleanor Farjeon. ChBR; GaP
Through a wild midnight all my mountainous past. The Monster. Henry Rago. SiTL
Through a window in the attic. Burglar Bill. "F. Anstey." CenHV; FiBHP
Through all the early morning hours. The Workers. Mary Blake Woodson. PEDC
Through All the Employments of Life. John Gay. *Fr.* The Beggar's Opera, I, i. CEP; StP
(Employments of Life, The.) PV
Through all the frozen winter. Smells. Kathryn Worth. BrR; RePo
Through all the long midsummer day. Midsummer. John Townsend Trowbridge. AA; DD; HBV; HBVY
Through all the pleasant meadow-side. The Hayloft. Robert Louis Stevenson. GFA; PCH; TSW
Through all the wind-blown aisles of May. A Benedictine Garden. Alice Brown. HBV
Through All the World, *with music.* *Unknown.* TrAS
Through all the years, dear, you would not reprove me. Aja's Lament over His Dead Wife. Kalidasa. LiTW
Through all this new-born day, O Lord. Hymn for the Day. "Gabriela Mistral." MaRV
Through Alpine meadows soft-suffused. Stanzas from the Grande Chartreuse. Matthew Arnold. BWP; CoBE; EPN; MaVP; MBW-2; OAEP; PoEL-5; PoVP; ViPo; ViPP; VP
Through an Embrace. Paul Eluard, *tr. fr. French by* Stephen Spender *and* Frances Cornford. LiTW
Through and through the inspired leaves. The Book-Worms. Burns. ChTr; ELU; FiBHP
Through Baltimore. Bayard Taylor. PAH
Through broken arches moonbeams softly shine. San Juan Capistrano. Alice Cecilia Cooper. GoBC
Through calm and storm the years have led. Centennial Hymn. Bryant. PAH
Through carnage, blood, and mire. The Army of the Red Cross. Katrina Trask. PEDC
Through Dangly Woods the aimless Doze. The Doze. James Reeves. GoTP
Through darkening pines the cavaliers marched on their sunset way. The Legend of Waukulla. Hezekiah Butterworth. PAH
Through Death to Love. Dante Gabriel Rossetti. The House of Life, XLI. MaVP; PoVP; SyP; ViPo; VP
Through drowsy stillness drifts a sound of mowing. Summer Afternoon. Basil Dowling. AnNZ
Through every minute of this day. A Prayer [*or* The Golden Cord *or* Be with Me, Lord!]. John Oxenham. BLRP; FaChP; SoP; TRV
Through every night we hate. Mothers, Daughters. Shirley Kaufman. QAH
Through every sort of trouble Joe. Contrary Joe. L. A. G. Strong. PoMa
Through ev'ry age eternal God. Highbridge. *Unknown.* AS
Through Fire in Mobile Bay. *Unknown, at. to* David Glascoe Farragut. PAH
Through grass, through amber'd cornfields, our slow stream. Meadowsweet. William Allingham. OBNC
Through great Earl Norman's acres wide. Earl Norman and John Truman. Charles Mackay. VA
Through [*or* Thro'] grief and through danger thy smile hath cheer'd my way. The Irish Peasant to His Mistress. Thomas Moore. ACP; AnIV; OBEV (1st ed.); PoFr
Through his iron glades. Winter the Huntsman. Sir Osbert Sitwell. AtBAP; BoW; POTE; ShBV-2; WePo
Through his million veins are poured. William Bull Wright. *Fr.* The Brook. AA
Through His Name. *Unknown.* SoP
Through intricate motions ran. Stream and Sun at Glendalough. W. B. Yeats. MaPo; MoPW
Through lane it lay—thro' bramble. Emily Dickinson. MWA-2; SiSw
Through laughing leaves the sunlight comes. In the Wood. Herbert Edwin Clarke. VA
Through life's dull road, so dim and dirty. On My Thirty-third Birthday. Byron. MBW-2; OBRV
Through love to light! O, wonderful the way. After-Song. Richard Watson Gilder. AA; TrPWD
Through meadow-ways as I did tread. A May Burden. Francis Thompson. HBV
Through miles of mist the lighthouse candle sweeps. Gentle Storm. Martha Banning Thomas. PoMa
Through my open window comes the sweet perfuming. Attainment. Algernon Tassin. AA
Through my small town I roamed, a taunting ghost. Rimbaud in Africa. Edgell Rickword. ChMP
Through naked sticks, his winter bones. Deliverance. Laurie Lee. BoPe
Through Nightmare. Robert Graves. BoPe; Po
Through Nurseryland. *Unknown.* BoTP
Through or over the deathless feud. Pacific Door. Earle Birney. PeCV; TwCaPo
Through rain falling on us no faster. Goodbye to Serpents. James Dickey. NYBP
Through reedy banks. The Nima. Jorge Isaacs. TrJP
Through sepia air the boarders come and go. Landlady. P. K. Page. CaP; TwCaPo
Through shattered galleries, 'mid roofless halls. Composed among the Ruins of a Castle in North Wales. Wordsworth. BWP
Through some strange sense of sight or touch. Death. Madison Cawein. AA
Through Sorrow to Service. *Unknown.* MaRV
Through storm and fire and gloom, I see it stand. The Celtic Cross. Thomas D'Arcy McGee. OnYI; VA
Through storm and wind. *Unknown.* OxNR
Through storms you reach them and from storms are free. The Enviable Isles. Herman Melville. AA; AmLP; AnAmPo; FaBoBe; MAmP
Through that pure virgin-shrine. The Night. Henry Vaughan. AnAnS-1; BWP; LiTB; MeLP; MeP; MePo; NoP; OBEV (new ed.); OBS; OxBoCh; PoEL-2; PoFS; ReEn; SCEP-1; SeCeV; SeCL; SeCV-1; SeEP; UnPo (1st ed.); VaPo
Through that window all else being extinct. The Room. Conrad Aiken. AP; LiTG; LiTM (rev. ed.); MAP; MAPA; MoAmPo; NePA; PoDB
Through the Ages. Margaret Hope. PGD
Through the ample open door of the peaceful country barn. A Farm Picture. Walt Whitman. OnPM; WoL
Through the Appalachian valleys, with his kit a buckskin bag. A Ballad of Johnny Appleseed. Helmer O. Oleson. SiSoSe; TiPo (1959 ed.)
Through the Barber Shop Window. Violet Anderson. CaP
Through the black, rushing smoke-bursts. Callicles' Song (*or* Apollo). Matthew Arnold. *Fr.* Empedocles on Etna, II. ChTr; FiP; GTBS; LoBV; OBEV; OBVV; PoVP; ShBV-3; ViPo; WiR
Through the Blowing Leaves. Glenn Ward Dresbach. BoC
Through the blue and frosty heavens. The Angel's Story. Adelaide Anne Procter. DD
Through the bound cable strands, the arching path. Atlantis.

Through (continued)
Hart Crane. *Fr.* The Bridge. AmLP; AnFE; AtBAP; CoAnAm; LiTA; LiTM; MoPo; NePA; TwAmPo
Through the clangor of the cannon. Defeat and Victory. Wallace Rice. MC; PAH
Through the dark aisles of the wood. Poem. Henry Treece. NeBP
Through the dark pine trunks. Images. Richard Aldington. NP; TOP
"Through the Dear Might of Him That Walked the Waves." John Heath-Stubbs. BoPe
Through the deep monastic halls. The Abbey. José M. Eguren. CAW
Through the deep woods, at peep of day. The Canadian Herd-Boy. Susanna Moodie. OBCV
Through the dim pageant of the years. Lincoln. Julia Ward Howe. PoRL
Through the dim window, I could see. In Passing. Roy Helton. HBMV
Through the eyes. Tanka. Lewis Alexander. CDC
Through the faintest filigree. The Ships of Arcady. Francis Ledwidge. EtS
Through the fierce fever I nursed him, and then he said. Little Wild Baby. "Margaret Vandegrift." AA HBV
Through the Forest Have I Gone. Shakespeare. *Fr.* A Midsummer Night's Dream, II, ii. CTC
Through the forest the boy wends all day long. The Boy and the Flute. Bjornstjerne Bjornson. AWP; JAWP; PoPl; WBP
Through the frosty air to the woods we go. Autumn Gloves. Mildred D. Shacklett. GFA
Through the gate. The Colt. Raymond Knister. TwCaPo
Through the grasses tall and slim. Snakes and Snails. Grace Taber Hallock. RePo
Through the great sinful streets of Naples as I passed. Easter Day. Arthur Hugh Clough. EPN; OAEP; PoVP; ViP; ViPP
Through the green boughs I hardly saw thy face. Saint Germain-en-Laye. Ernest Dowson. SyP
Through the green tassels of the weeper tree. Triumphal Ode MCMXXXIX. George Barker. LiTB; WaP
Through the haze of exhaustion. After the Japanese. Lynn Strongin. ThO
Through the hill by the Rite Nite Motel. A Water Glass of Whisky. X. J. Kennedy. CoPo
Through the House ("Through the house give glimmering light"). Shakespeare. *See* Oberon and Titania to the Fairy Train.
Through the house what busy joy. The First Tooth. Charles *and* Mary Lamb. OTPC (1923 ed.)
Through the long August day, mantled blue with a sky of Our Lady. Lady Day in Ireland. Patrick J. Carrol. JKCP
Through the long winter. And Fall Shall Sit in Judgment. Audre Lorde. NNP
Through the Looking-Glass. "Lewis Carroll."
Humpty Dumpty's Recitation, *fr. ch.* 6. BOHV; ChTr; FiBHP; GoTP; NBM; PeVV; SiTL
(Humpty Dumpty's Song.) GTBS-P; OnMSP; OxBoLi; SAS
"I'll tell thee everything I can," *fr. ch.* 8. Par
Jabberwocky, *fr. ch.* 1. ALV; BoChLi; CABA; CaFP; CBEP; CBV; DiPo; EnLi-2 (1949 ed.); FaBoBe; FaBV; FaFP; FaPON; FiBHP; GoJo; GoTP; HBV; HoPM; InP; LBN; LiTB; LiTG; NA; NAMP; NBM; OnSP; OTPC; PeVV; PIA; PoIE; PoPl; PoPo; PoRA; PoVP; RIS; SeCeV; ShBV-2; SiTL; TiPo; TreF; TrGrPo; VaPo; WhC
"To the Looking-Glass world it was Alice that said," *fr. ch.* 9. Par
Walrus and the Carpenter, The, *fr. ch.* 4. BeLS; BoChLi; BOHV; FaBoBe; FaBV; FaFP; FaPON; FiBHP; GN; GSP; HBV; HBVY; InMe; LBN; LiTB; LiTG; MaC; MCCG; NA; NeHB; OnSP; OTPC; PoRA; PoRh; PoVP; SAS; ShBV-1; SoPo; StVeCh; TreF; TVC; YT
"'Time has come, The,' the Walrus said," 1 *st.* TiPo
White Knight's Song, The, *fr. ch.* 8. EnLi-2; FaBoCh; GoTP; LoGBV
(Aged, Aged Man, The.) OnPP
(A-Sitting on a Gate.) PoE; PoRA (rev. ed.)
(I'll Tell Thee Everything I Can.) InvP
(Ways and Means.) BOHV; FiBHP; NA
(White Knight's Ballad, The.) PoRh
(White Knight's Tale, The.) RIS; ShBV-4
Through the Maze. *Unknown.* BLRP
Through the Metidja to Abd-el-Kadr. Robert Browning. PoVP
Through the night, through the night. The Sea. Richard Henry Stoddard. AA; HBV
Through the night thy Angels kept. A Thank-You. William Canton. ThGo
Through the Open Door. Patrick Kavanagh. AnIV
Through the open French window the warm sun. Still-Life. Elizabeth Daryush. QFR
Through the Parklands, through the Parklands. The Parklands. Stevie Smith. MoBS
Through the Porthole. Marjorie Wilson. BoTP
Through the pregnant universe rumbles life's terrific thunder. Exhortation; Summer, 1919. Claude McKay. CDC
Through the purple dusk on this pathless heath. The Heath. Thomas Boyd. OnYI
Through the revolving door. Alligator on the Escalator. Eve Merriam. OCS
Through the sea of money-changers he stormed. The Whip of Anger. Mary Ross. ChIP
Through the seedling grass. Red Poppies. "Fiona Macleod." *Fr.* Sospiri di Roma. VA
Through the shine, through the rain. Twilight Song. E. A. Robinson. HBV
Through the shrubs as I can crack[e]. Doron's Jig (*or* Jigge). Robert Greene. *Fr.* Menaphon. AtBAP; ElL; PoEL-2; TuPP
Through the silver mist. A Spring Lilt. *Unknown.* HBV; MPB; OTPC
Through the soft evening air enwinding all. Italian Music in Dakota. Walt Whitman. AmePo; AmP
Through the starred Judean night. Mary Tired. Marjorie Pickthall. ACV; PeCV (1967 ed.)
Through the still air of night. Night Coming Out of a Garden. Lord Alfred Douglas. MoBrPo (1942 ed.)
Through the straight pass of suffering. Emily Dickinson. MoRP
Through the street as I trot when the weather is hot. The Hottentot Tot [*or* Midsummer Fantasy]. Newman Levy. PoSC; RIS
Through the sunny garden. Chillingham. Mary Elizabeth Coleridge. BoTP
Through the thatched roof. Emperor Tenchi, *tr. fr. Japanese by* I. W. Furukami. LiTW
Through the thick morning steam they took shape. A Papuan Shepherd. Francis Webb. *Fr.* A Drum for Ben Boyd. PoAu-2
Through the trees, with the moon underfoot. The Owl King (*or* The Call). James Dickey. CoPo; NePoEA-2
Through the vague morning, the heart preoccupied. Bombers. C. Day Lewis. CMoP; MoAB
Through the Varied Patterned Lace. Margaret Danner. Kal
Through the Waters. Annie Johnson Flint. STF
Through the windmills. Fairy Wings. Winifred Howard. SUS
Through the Year. Julian S. Cutler. BLPA
Through the yesterday of ages. The Unchanging One. Frances Ridley Havergal. SoP
Through thee, Virginity, endure. Ad Castitatem. Francis Thompson. PoLi
Through these green Parthenons. In the Redwood Forest. Ralph Pomeroy. CoPo
Through These Pale Cold Days. Isaac Rosenberg. TrJP
Through thick Arcadian woods a hunter went. Atalanta's Race (*or* Atalanta's Victory). William Morris. BEL; DTo; VA; ViPo
Through this our city of delight. Chiffons. William Samuel Johnson. HBV
Through this toilsome world, alas! I Shall Not Pass This Way Again. *Unknown.* BLPA; NeHB; SoP; TreFS
Through throats where many rivers meet, the curlews cry. In the White Giant's Thigh. Dylan Thomas. AtBAP; LiTB; ReMP; ToPo
Through Thy Cross and Passion. Philip Howard. *See* Though Here in Flesh I Be.
Through torrid entrances, past icy poles. To Shakespeare. Hart Crane. Sonn
Through tranquil years they watched the changes. Clearing for the Plough. E. G. Moll. MoAuPo
Through Unknown Paths. Frederick L. Hosmer. TrPWD
Through verdant banks where Thames's branches glide. The Assault on the Fortress. Timothy Dwight. PAH

Through villages of yelping tykes. Dreaming Spires. Roy Campbell. BoSA
Through water, his own waterfall. Cold Fire. George Starbuck. NYBP
Through weary days and sleepless nights. One Gift I Ask. Virginia Bioren Harrison. HBV
Through what fierce incarnations, furled. The Beatific Vision. G. K. Chesterton. MoRP
Through what long heaviness, assayed in what strange fire. Carthusians. Ernest Dowson. JKCP; PoVP
Through what rock-strewn tunnels, O companions. The D Minor. E. L. Mayo. MiAP
Through winter streets to steer your course aright. Trivia; or, The Art of Walking the Streets of London (*or* Of the Implements for Walking the Streets, and Signs of the Weather). John Gay. CEP; EiCP
Through winter-time we call on spring. The Wheel. W. B. Yeats. GTBS-P; MoVE; PoPo
Through years our minds have wrestled and how vain! Disillusioned. Thomas Curtis Clark. ChIP
Through your eyes' round and perfect pupils. Narrative. Louis Dudek. CaP
Through your grey eyes evasive heaven. Four Poems for April, III. Louis Adeane. NeBP
Throughe a forest as I can ryde. Crow and Pie. *Unknown.* ESPB
Throughout a garden greene and gay. The Rose of England. *Unknown.* ESPB
Throughout His sojourn here below. I Had a Part. David F. Nygren. SoP
Throughout the day our sweet bells chime. Bluebells. P. A. Ropes. BoTP
Throughout the field I find no grain. Winter in Durnover Field. Thomas Hardy. MoBrPo
Throughout the soft and sunlit day. The Pines. Julie Mathilde Lippmann. AA
Throughout the World. Sir Thomas Wyatt. *See* Honesty.
Throw away Thy rod. Discipline. George Herbert. BoLiVe; CoBE; EG; ExPo; HBV; LiTB; LoBV; MaMe; MeLP; MemP; MePo; NoP; OBEV; OBS; OxBoCh; PAn; PG (1945 ed.); PoFS; PoLF; SeCePo; SeCeV; SeEP; TrGrPo; ViBoPo
Throw Him Down M'Closkey. John W. Kelly. TreF
Throw me, and yet I stand. The Celt Speaks. Arthur Stringer. PoFr
Throw Out the Lifeline. Edward Smith Ufford. TreF
Throw something to the gulls, any old scrap. Writing on the Wall. Padraic Fallon. NeIP
Throw your little dreams away. The Man of Science Speaks. Harriet Monroe. MaRV
Thrown. Ralph Hodgson. HBMV
Thrown backwards first, head over heels in the wind. To My Friend Whose Parachute Did Not Open. David Wagoner. TwAmPo
Thrush, The. Laura Benét HBMV
Thrush, The. Timothy Corsellis. LiTM; WaaP; WaP
Thrush, The. John Duffy. JKCP (1955 ed.)
Thrush before Dawn, A. Alice Meynell. HBMV; MoBrPo
Thrush for Hawk. John Fandel. NYTB
Thrush in February, The. George Meredith. OBNC
"Love born of knowledge, love that gains," *sel.* FaBoEn
Thrush is tapping a stone, A. Dawn. Gordon Bottomley. *Fr.* Night and Morning Songs. BiS; BoTP; MoBrPo; NP
Thrush, linnet, stare, and wren. In Glencullen. J. M. Synge. BiS; ELU; OBMV; OxBI; ThWaDe
Thrush Sings, A. W. E. Henley. YT
Thrush, the lark, and, chief, the nightingale, The. David ap Gwillam's Mass of the Birds. Padraic Colum. CAW
Thrushes. Ted Hughes. GoYe; NePoEA-2; PoIE; POTi
Thrushes. Humbert Wolfe. MoBrPo
Thrushes sing as the sun is going, The. Proud Songsters. Thomas Hardy. FlW; PoSa
Thrush's Nest, The. John Clare. BoTP; FlW; GoJo; GoTP; MemP; PoRL; PoSa; ThWaDe
Thrush's Song, The. *Unknown, tr. fr. Gaelic by* William Macgillivray. CH; GoTP
Thrust back by hands of air from the sanctuary door. Maria Aegyptiaca. John Heath-Stubbs. FaBoMo
Thrustararorum. Henry Nehemiah Dodge. EtS
Thrusting glance grows dim, The. Portrait of a Very Old Man. Sara E. Carsley. CaP
Thrusting of It, The. Burns. *See* Duncan Gray.
Thu sikest sore. Christ's Tear Breaks My Heart. *Unknown.* MeEL
Thule, the Period of Cosmography. *Unknown. See* Wonders.
Thumb bold. *Unknown.* OxNR
Thumb he. *Unknown.* OxNR
Thumbikin, Thumbikin, broke the barn. *Unknown.* OxNR
Thumbkin says, I'll dance. *Unknown.* OxNR
"Thumbs in the thumb-place." The Mitten Song. Marie Louise Allen. BrR; SoPo; SUS; TiPo
Thump—thud! Who is throwing. Nutting Time. Emilie Poulsson. BrR
Thumpin' sound o' hosses' hoffs, the clack o' runnin' cows, The. Hot Ir'n! S. Omar Barker. PoOW
Thumping old tunes give a voice to its whereabouts. Fairground. W. H. Auden. NYBP
Thunder. Walter de la Mare. BoNaP
Thunder,/ The gallop of innumerable Walkyrie. Barrage. Richard Aldington. BrPo
Thunder clouds are sweeping, shrouding. A Russian Cradle Song. David Nomberg. TrJP
Thunder of riotous hoofs over the quaking sod. The Maid. Theodore Goodridge Roberts. HBV; MoShBr
Thunder of the Rain God. A House in Taos: Rain. Langston Hughes. CDC
Thunder our thanks to her—guns, hearts, and lips. *Mayflower.* John Boyle O'Reilly. AA; PAH
Thunder over Earth. Horatio Colony. TwAmPo
Thunder Pools. Robert P. Tristram Coffin. LOW
Thunder Shower. Hilda Conkling. NP
Thunder-Shower, The. John Hall Wheelock. NP
Thunder, the flesh quails, and the soul bows down. John Webster. Swinburne. *Fr.* Sonnets on English Dramatic Poets. InvP; Sonn
Thunderdrums, *sel.* Lew Sarett.
Iron-Wind Dances, V. MAP
Thunderer, The. Phyllis McGinley. EaLo
Thundering, shimmering, silvery gray. Summer Shower. Selma Robinson. MoSiPe
Thundering sound, A/ He hears. All Hands Unmoor! William Falconer. *Fr.* The Shipwreck. EtS
Thunder-Storm, A. Emily Dickinson. *See* Wind began to rock the grass, The.
Thunderstorm. Arthur Guiterman. PoMa
Thunderstorm, A. Archibald Lampman. CaP
Thunderstorm in Town, A. Thomas Hardy. EnLoPo
Thunderstorms. W. H. Davies. HBV; POTE; TSW
Thursday. Edna St. Vincent Millay. InMe
Thursday. Frederic E. Weatherly. BOHV
Thursday; or, The Spell. John Gay. *Fr.* The Shepherd's Week. CEP; EiPP; PoEL-3
Thus all is here in motion, all is life. The Wool Trade. John Dyer. *Fr.* The Fleece, III. OBEC; SeCePo
Thus Bonny-Boots the Birthday Celebrated. *Unknown.* NCEP
Thus briefly sketch'd the sacred Rights of Man. To a Republican [*or* On Mr. Paine's "Rights of Man"]. Philip Freneau. AmPP (5th ed.); PoFr
Thus by himself compell'd to live each day. Peter Grimes. George Crabbe. *Fr.* The Borough. FaBoEn; OBNC; SeCePo
Thus, by the way, to human loves interring. George Chapman. *Fr.* Euthymiae Raptus; or, The Tears of Peace. LoBV
Thus can my love excuse the slow offence. Sonnets, LI. Shakespeare. PoFS
Thus chydand with her drery desteny. Cressida's Leprosy. Robert Henryson. *Fr.* The Testament of Cresseid. SeCePo
Thus com, lo! Engelond in-to Normandies hond. *At. to* Robert of Gloucester. *Fr.* Chronicle. YAT
Thus dark sett of my light, which like a ray. *Unknown.* SeCSL
Thus deaths hand clos'd his eyes. The Death of Hector. Homer, *tr. by* George Chapman. *Fr.* The Iliad, XXII. OBS
Thus did I think: I well will mark my way. Psalm XXXIX. *Paraphrased by* Sir Philip Sidney. FCP
Thus doth the Great Foresightless mechanize. The Overworld. Thomas Hardy. *Fr.* The Dynasts, Pt. III. WoL
Thus ends my love, but this doth grieve me most. Sonnet [*or* Loves End]. Lord Herbert of Cherbury. AnAnS-2; LiTL; SeCP; ViBoPo
Thus ere another noon they emerged from the shades. The

Thus (continued)
Lakes of the Atchafalaya. Longfellow. *Fr.* Evangeline. PoEL-5
Thus Etough looked; so grinned the brawling fiend. *See* Thus Tophet look'd . . .
Thus Eve to Adam. Milton. *Fr.* Paradise Lost, IV. FaBV
Thus far, O Friend! Have we though leaving much. School-Time. Wordsworth. The Prelude, II. BEL; ERoP-1; MBW-2
Thus far the Lord hath led us on—in darkness and in day. Light Shining Out of Darkness. Jane Borthwick. BLRP
Thus far the muse has traced in useful lays. Of Walking the Streets by Day. John Gay. *Fr.* Trivia; or, The Art of Walking the Streets of London, II. CEP; EiPP; EnLi-1 (1949 ed.)
Thus far, with rough and all-unable pen. Epilogue. Shakespeare. *Fr.* King Henry V. CTC
Thus Glory hath her being! thus she stands. Glory and Enduring Fame. William Gilmore Simms. Sonn
Thus grief still treads upon the heels of pleasure. William Congreve. *Fr.* The Old Bachelor, V, iii. TreF
Thus groan the old, till, by disease oppress'd. George Crabbe. *Fr.* The Village. PoFS
Thus have I back again[e] to thy bright name. An Apologie for the Precedent [*or* Fore-going]. Richard Crashaw. AnAnS-1; MaMe; MeP; SCEP-1
Thus have I waded through a worthless task. Epilogus. Henry Parrot. SiCE
Thus having past all perill, I was come. The Happy Isle. Spenser. *Fr.* The Faerie Queene, IV. OBSC
Thus having said, brave Hector went to see. The Last Parting of Hector and Andromache. Homer. *Fr.* The Iliad, VI. SeEP
Thus I/ Pass by. Upon His Departure. Robert Herrick. PCD; QFR
Thus I awaked and wrote what I had dreamed. The Vision of Jesus. William Langland. *Fr.* The Vision of Piers Plowman. ACP; CAW
Thus I come to you. Author Unknown. William Montgomerie. OxBS
Thus I sat one night by a blue-eyed girl. Categorical Courtship. *Unknown.* BOHV; CIV
Thus I woke, God wot, when I dwelt on Cornhill. Langland's Life. William Langland. *Fr.* The Vision of Piers Plowman. MeEV
Thus I would walk abroad when gentle night. Walking at Night. Henry Treece. WaP
Thus in her absence is my fancy cool. Sonnet. George Henry Boker. *Fr.* Sonnets; a Sequence on Profane Love. AmePo
Thus is his cheek the map of days outworn. Sonnets, LXVIII. Shakespeare. OBSC; PoeP; ReIE; UnPo (1st ed.)
Thus Kitty, beautiful and young. The Female Phaeton. Matthew Prior. HBV
Thus Lovely Sleep. Richard Leigh. *See* Sleeping on Her Couch.
Thus man by his own strength to Heaven would soar. Dryden. *Fr.* Religio Laici. WGRP
Thus much the fates have allotted me. Turning Aside from Battles. Sextus Propertius. WaaP
Thus, near the gates conferring as they drew. Ulysses and His Dog. Homer, *tr. by* Pope. *Fr.* The Odyssey, XVII. FiP; OBEC
Thus now, as on the face of one new-dead. Benediction. Frederick Ebright. NYTB
Thus pass the glories of the world. The Symbol. James Hebblethwaite. BoAu
Thus piteously Love closed what he begat. Modern Love, L. George Meredith. AnFE; BEL; CaFP; EnLi-2; EnLit; EnLoPo; FaBoEn; FaPL; GTBS-D; GTBS-P; GTSL; HBV; ILP; InPo; LoBV; NBM; OAEP; OBNC; PoAn; PoE; PoEL-5; PoIE; SeCePo; SeCeV; Sonn; TreFT; TrGrPo; UnPo (1st ed.); ViBoPo; ViPo; VP; WHA
Thus quoth Alfred: "If thou hast sorrow." Proverbs of King Alfred. *At. to* Alfred, King of England. WaKn
Thus reader, by our astrologick art. Almanac Verse. *Unknown.* SCAP
Thus re-inforc'd, against the adverse fleet. The Fourth Day's Battle. Dryden. *Fr.* Annus Mirabilis. OBS
Thus sadly I thought/ As that bird unsought. L'Envoy to W. L. H. Ainsworth, Esq. Francis S. Mahony. OnYI
Thus safely low, my friend, thou can'st not fall. To the Reverend Mr. Murdoch. James Thomson. OBEC
Thus said the Lord in the Vault above the Cherubim. The Last Chantey. Kipling. AnFE; BoLiVe; EPN; EtS; FaBoCh; GTBS; LoGBV; MoBrPo; OBVV; OtMeF; PoVP; VA
Thus sailing, sailing on forevermore. The Lake. Alphonse Marie Louis de Lamartine. WoL
Thus saith the great god Thoth. He Is Declared True of Word. *Unknown.* *Fr.* Book of the Dead. AWP; JAWP; WBP
Thus saith the Lord:/ I return unto Zion. I Return unto Zion. Zechariah, Bible, *O.T.* TrJP
Thus saith the Lord,/ The Redeemer of Israel. Proclamation. Isaiah, Bible, *O.T.* StaSt
Thus Sang Orpheus to His Strings. *Unknown.* *See* Thus Sung Orpheus to His Strings.
Thus sang she. The Wedding. *Unknown.* SAS
Thus saying, from her husbands hand her hand. The Fall. Milton. *Fr.* Paradise Lost, IX. PoEL-3
Thus says the prophet of the Turk. The Love of the World Reproved; or, Hypocrisy Detected. William Cowper. EiCL
Thus she sat weeping. The Animals Mourn with Eve. Christina Rossetti. *Fr.* Eve. OA
Thus should have been our travels. Over 2000 Illustrations and a Complete Concordance. Elizabeth Bishop. FiMAP; PoDB
Thus, some tall tree that long hath stood. On the Death of [Dr.] Benjamin Franklin. Philip Freneau. DD; PAH; ThLM
Thus spake the Lord. The Word of the Lord from Havana. Richard Hovey. HBV; PAH
Thus Speak the Slain. Carl Holliday. PGD
Thus Speaketh Christ Our Lord. *Unknown.* *tr. fr. German.* ChIP; PGD
Thus Spoke My Love. Pieter Corneliszoon Hooft, *tr. fr. Dutch by* A. J. Barnouw. LiTW
Thus spoke Priam's shining son with words supplicating. Achilles to Lycaon. Homer. *Fr.* The Iliad, XXI. LiTW; WaaP
Thus spoke the lady underneathe tree[s]. Colonel Fantock. Edith Sitwell. AnFE; MoAB; MoBrPo; MoVE; OBMV
Thus spoke to my Lady the Knight full of care. Swift. *Fr.* A Soldier and a Scholar. OBEC
Thus Sung [*or* Sang] Orpheus to His Strings. *Unknown.* NCEP; SeCSL
Thus systole addressed diastole. Systole and Diastole. Conrad Aiken. CrMA
Thus the heavens and the earth were finished. Genesis, Bible, *O.T.* LO
Thus the Mayne Glideth. Robert Browning. *Fr.* Paracelsus Pt. V. OBEV; PoVP
(Song: "Thus the Mayne glideth.") OBRV
Thus the poor bird, by some disast'rous fate. Time's Balm. Cuthbert Shaw. *Fr.* Monody to the Memory of a Young Lady. OBEC
Thus then, one beautiful day, in the sweet, cool air of October. Beauty at the Plough. Arthur Joseph Munby. *Fr.* Dorothy; a Country Story. VA
Thus therefore, he who feels the fiery dart. Concerning the Nature of Love. Lucretius. *Fr.* De Rerum Natura. PeRV; UnTE
Thus thou descend'st to our infirmitie. Her Apparrelling. John Donne. MaMe
Thus, thus begin the yearly rites. Pan's Anniversary. Ben Jonson. AnAnS-2; OBS; TuPP
Thus, thus I steer my bark, and sail. On Even Keel, with Gentle Gale. Matthew Green. *Fr.* The Spleen. OBEC
Thus Tophet [*or* Etough] look'd; so grinn'd the brawling fiend. Tophet; an Epigram. Thomas Gray. MyFE; NCEP
Thus, usually, when he was asked to sing. Byron. *Fr.* Don Juan, III. EnLi-2
Thus Was the City Founded. "St.-J. Perse." *See* Such Is the Way of the World.
Thus was this place/ A happy rural seat of various view. Eden. Milton. *Fr.* Paradise Lost, IV. ATP; DiPo; FaBoEn
Thus, when soft love subdues the heart. Goldsmith, *after the French of* Paul Scarron. LO
Thus when the silent grave becomes. Belinda's Recovery from Sickness. William Broome. OBEV (1st ed.)
Thus when the swallow, seeking prey. Song. John Gay. *Fr.* The Beggar's Opera. PoEL-3
Thus while he spoke, each eye grew big with tears. The Pyre of Patroclus. Homer, *tr. by* Pope. *Fr.* The Iliad, XXIII. OBEC
Thus while I ape the measure wild. To William Erskine,

Esq. Sir Walter Scott. *Fr.* Marmion, *Introd. to* III. OBRV
Thus will I have the woman of my dream. Dawn of Womanhood. Harold Monro. HBV
Thus wisely they taught the victorious King. Cynewulf. *Fr.* Elene. YAT
Thus with a Kiss I Die. Shakespeare. *Fr.* Romeo and Juliet, V, iii. TrGrPo
(Here Lies Juliet.) FaFP; TreFS
Thus with the year. Inner Light. Milton. *Fr.* Paradise Lost, III. MaRV
Thus would I have it. Exit. John Gould Fletcher. InP; PoPo
Thus writeth Meer Djafrit. To the Ingleezee Khafir, Calling Himself Djann Bool Djenkinzun. James Clarence Mangan. OnYI
Thy arms with bracelets I will deck. Homage. Gustave Kahn. TrJP
Thy azure robe I did behold. Julia's Petticoat [*or* Upon Julia's Petticoat]. Robert Herrick. AnAnS-2; PoeP; UnTE
Thy baby, too, the child that was to be. Frederick Goddard Tuckerman. *Fr.* Sonnets. AP
Thy beard and head are of a different dye. To a Rogue. Joseph Addison. PV
Thy Beauty Fades. Jones Very. AP
Thy beauty haunts me heart and soul. The Moon. W. H. Davies. BrPo; MoBrPo; MoVE; NeMA; POTE; StaSt
Thy beauty, O Israel, upon thy high places is slain! David's Lament. Second Samuel, Bible, *O.T.* TrJP
Thy Blessing, Lord, on All Vacation Days! Molly Anderson Haley. OQP
Thy blessing on the boys—for time has come. Prayer. Haim Guri. TrJP
Thy Blood was shed for me. In My Place. Esther Archibald. SoP; STF
Thy blue waves, Patapsco, flowed soft and serene. Fort McHenry. *Unknown.* MC; PAH
Thy books shou'd, like thy friends, not many be. Advice to a Young Friend on the Choice of His Library. William Wycherley. PeRV
Thy bosom is endearèd [*or* indeared] with all hearts. Sonnets, XXXI. Shakespeare. OBEV; OBSC; PoEL-2
Thy braes were bonny, Yarrow stream. The Braes of Yarrow. John Logan. GTBS; GTBS-D; GTBS-P; GTBS-W; GTSE; GTSL; HBV; OBEC
"Thy breath is far sweeter than honey." Far Sweeter than Honey. Abraham ibn Ezra. TrJP
Thy Brother. Theodore Chickering Williams. MaRV
Thy Brother's Blood. Jones Very. AP; MAmP; PoEL-4; QFR
Thy Conquering Name. Charles Wesley. BePJ
Thy converse drew us with delight. In Memoriam A. H. H., CX. Tennyson. EPN; ViPo; VP
Thy coral-colored lips how should I portray. *Unknown.* *Fr.* Zepheria. ReIE
Thy country, Wilberforce, with just disdain. Sonnet to [*or* To] William Wilberforce, Esq. William Cowper. CEP; CoBE; ILP; OAEP; PoIE (1970 ed.); Sonn
Thy cruise is over now. Mr. Merry's Lament for "Long Tom." John Gardiner Calkins Brainard. AA
Thy dawn, O Master of the world, thy dawn. James Elroy Flecker. *Fr.* Hassan, II, ii. OtMeF; WePo
Thy dawn, O Ra, opens the new horizon. Adoration of the Disk by King Akhnaten and Princess Nefer Neferiu Aten. *Unknown.* *Fr.* Book of the Dead. AWP; JAWP; WBP
Thy dawning is beautiful in the horizon of heaven. Hymn to the Sun. Ikhnaton (Amenhotep IV). WoL
Thy epigrams are of no bastard race. Ad Tho. Bastardum Epigrammatistam. John Heath. TuPP
Thy face I have seen as one seeth. Song. Sophie Jewett. AA
Thy Faithful Sons. Eleazar, *tr. fr. Hebrew.* TrJP
Thy fan is as a butterfly. The Fan. Serafín Alvarez Quintero *and* Joaquín Alvarez Quintero. OnPM
Thy father all from thee, by his last will. Disinherited. John Donne. MaMe
Thy filed words that from thy mouth did flow. Of Mistress D. S. Barnabe Googe. EnRePo
Thy flattering picture, Phryne, is like thee. Phryne. John Donne. MaMe; TuPP
Thy forests, Windsor! and thy green retreats. Windsor Forest. Pope. EiCL; FosPo; MBW-1
Thy friend, whom thy deserts to thee enchaine. To Mr. C.B. John Donne. AnAnS-1; MaMe
Thy friendship oft has made my heart to ache. To Hayley. Blake. TrGrPo
Thy Garden. Mu'tamid, King of Seville, *tr. fr. Arabic by* Dulcie L. Smith. AWP
Thy garden, orchard, fields. Francis Daniel Pastorius. SCAP
Thy gifts to us mortals fulfil all our needs. Rabindranath Tagore. Gitanjali, LXXV. InP
Thy gifts without Thy grace are lacking still. Grace for Grace. Mark Guy Pearse. OQP
Thy glass will show thee how thy beauties wear. Sonnets, LXXVII. Shakespeare. EnRePo; QFR
Thy Glorious Face Above. Charles Wesley. BePJ
Thy glory alone, O God, be the end of all that I say. Ad Majorem Dei Gloriam. Frederick George Scott. MaRV; VA
Thy Glory dawns, Jerusalem, awake, thy bells to ring! Palm Sunday. John J. Moment. MaRV
Thy God was making hast into thy roofe. I Am Not Worthy That Thou Should'st Come Under My Roofe. Richard Crashaw. MaMe
Thy grace, dear Lord's my golden wrack, I find. Meditation XXXII [*or* Whether Paul or Apollos, or Cephas]. Edward Taylor. *Fr.* Preparatory Meditations, First Series. EP; MAmP; MeP; MWA-1; NoP; SCAP
Thy greatest knew thee, Mother Earth. The Spirit of Shakespeare. George Meredith. EPN; PoVP; VA; ViPo
Thy hands are washt, but O the waters spilt. To Pontius Washing His Hands. Richard Crashaw. MaMe; SeEP
Thy Heart. *Unknown.* NA
Thy heart is like some icy lake. Thy Heart. *Unknown.* NA
Thy hue, dear pledge, is pure and bright. To a Lock of Hair. Sir Walter Scott. GTBS; GTBS-D; GTBS-P; GTBS-W; GTSE
Thy human[e] frame, my glorious Lord, I spy. Meditation Seven. Edward Taylor. *Fr.* Preparatory Meditations, First Series. LiTA; VaPo
Thy husband to a banquet goes with me. The Possessive Lover. Ovid. *Fr.* Amores. UnTE
Thy impious finger, would it, then, reborrow. Christ to Thomas. Richard Crashaw. StJW
Thy Joy in Sorrow. Chauncey Hare Townshend. VA
Thy Kingdom Come. St. Bernard of Clairvaux, *tr. fr. Latin by* Hamilton Montgomerie Macgill. CAW; SoP
Thy Kingdom Come! Thomas Curtis Clark. ChIP
Thy Kingdom Come. Frederick Lucian Hosmer. WGRP
Thy Kingdom Come. A. B. Simpson. BePJ
Thy Kingdom Come! Willard Wattles. OQP
"Thy Kingdom Come!" O Lord. Henry Warburton Hawkes. MaRV
Thy Kingdom Come, O Lord. Frederick Lucian Hosmer. MaRV; WGRP
(Prophecy Sublime, The.) TrPWD
Thy kingdom come — on bended knee. Thy Kingdom Come. Frederick Lucian Hosmer. WGRP
Thy Kingdom, Lord, We Long For. Vida D. Scudder. MaRV; WGRP
Thy kisses dost thou bid me count. To Lesbia. Catullus. UnTE
Thy knights, O Queen, ride forth by east and west. Regina Confessorum. *Unknown.* GoBC
Thy laugh's a song an oriole trilled. Kitty's Laugh. Arlo Bates. *Fr.* Conceits. AA
Thy leopard legs and python thighs. The Zoo of You. Arthur Freeman. ErPo
Thy life is someone's Bible, where. Someone's Bible. E. C. Kurtz. SoP
Thy little footsteps on the sands. To William Shelley. Shelley. ChER
Thy Look. Spencer. SoP
Thy Love Alone. Horatius Bonar. FaChP
Thy Mercies. Joseph Addison. *See* When All Thy Mercies.
Thy mercy, Lord, to us dispense. A Missionary Prayer. Martin Luther. SoP
Thy merits, Wolfe, transcend all human praise. The Death of Wolfe. *Unknown.* PAH
Thy Mother Was like a Vine. Ezekiel, XIX: 10-14, Bible, *O.T.* TrJP
Thy mouth, whereof the worm was amorous. Memorial. Clark Ashton Smith. FiSC
Thy Nail-pierced Hands. Kathryn Bowsher. STF

Thy name, O Washington renowned. Washington's Song. Edmond S. Meany. PoRL
Thy name of old was great. To My Totem. Henry Charles Beeching. VA
Thy Name We Bless and Magnify. John Power. BLRP
Thy need is great. For the Earth God. *Unknown.* EaLo
Thy Neighbor. *Unknown.* OQP; SoP
Thy nights moan into my days. Psalms of Love. Peter Baum. AWP
Thy one white leaf is open to the sky. To a Cherokee Rose. William Hamilton Hayne. AA
Thy Peace. Emily Huntington Miller. FaChP
Thy Peace, O God. *Unknown.* SoP
Thy praise, O Lord, will I proclaim. Palms and Myrtles. Eleazar ben Kalir. TrJP
Thy praise or dispraise is to me alike. To Fool or Knave. Ben Jonson. NoP
Thy Presence. Frances Ridley Havergal. MaRV
(Be Quiet; Fear Not.) OQP
(Confidence.) FaChP
Thy restless feet now cannot go. Christ Crucified. Richard Crashaw. GoBC; OBEV; PoRL
Thy Saints are comforted, I know. William Cowper. *Fr.* The Contrite Heart. MyFE
Thy Sea Is Great, Our Boats Are Small. Henry van Dyke. *See* Voyagers.
Thy Sea So Great. Winfred Ernest Garrison. MaRV; TrPWD
Thy shades, thy silence, now be mine. Solitude. James Beattie. *Fr.* Retirement. OBEC
Thy shadow, Earth, from Pole to Central Sea. At a Lunar Eclipse. Thomas Hardy. POTE; TOP
Thy sinnes and haires may no man equall call. A Licentious Person. John Donne. MaMe
Thy sorrow, and the sorrow of the sea. Ireland. Lionel Johnson. HBV
Thy soul is not enchanted by the moon. The Lilies of the Field. Compton Mackenzie. OBVV
Thy soul shall find itself alone. Spirits of the Dead. Poe. MAmP
Thy soul within such silent pomp did keep. A Quiet Soul. John Oldham. *Fr.* To the Memory of Mr. Charles Morwent. OBEV
Thy span of life was all too short. To a Withered Rose. John Kendrick Bangs. AA
Thy spear rent Christ, when dead for me He lay. To My Patrons. Lionel Johnson. JKCP
Thy spirit ere our fatal loss. In Memoriam A. H. H., XLI. Tennyson. EPN; ViPo; VP
Thy spirit, Independence, let me share! Independence [*or* Ode to Independence]. Tobias Smollett. OBEC; PoFr
Thy stricken daughter, now, O Lord, prepares. Hymn for the Eve of the New Year. Abraham Gerondi. TrJP
Thy summer voice, Musketaquit. Two Rivers. Emerson. AmePo; AmLP; AmPP; AnNE; AP; CoBA; MAmP; MWA-1; NoP; OxBA; TrGrPo
Thy Sun Posts Westward. William Drummond of Hawthornden. *See* No Trust in Time.
Thy sword within the scabbard keep. The Song of Momus to Mars [*or* Songs from "The Secular Masque": Momus]. Dryden. *Fr.* The Secular Masque. CBEP; InPo
Thy thoughts are here, my God. The Book of God. Horatius Bonar. SoP
Thy thoughts, dear Keats, are like fresh-gathered leaves. To Keats. John Hamilton Reynolds. Sonn
Thy throne is ringed by amorous cavaliers. Patrick Moloney. Sonnets — Ad Innuptam, III. BoAu
Thy trivial harp will never please. Merlin. Emerson. AA; AmePo; AmP; AmPP (4th ed.); AnNE; AP; BoLiVe; MAmP; OxBA
Thy various works, imperial queen, we see. On Imagination. Phillis Wheatley. AmPP (5th ed.); PoNe
Thy victory is in the heart. Victoria. Henry van Dyke. SoP; TRV
Thy Voice is Heard [thro' Rolling Drums]. Tennyson. *Fr.* The Princess: Interlude. OBVV; PoVP; TrGrPo
(Songs from "The Princess.") ViPo
Thy voice is hovering o'er my soul—it lingers. To Constantia Singing. Shelley. EnRP
Thy voice is on the rolling air. In Memoriam A. H. H. [*or* Truths That Never Can Be Proved] CXXX. Tennyson. DiPo; EnL; EnLi-2; EPN; FaPL; FosPo; HBV; MaPo; MaRV; OAEP; PoFS; TOP; TRV; UnPo; ViPo; VP
Thy vowes are heard, and thy Castara's fame. His Muse Speakes to Him. William Habington. AnAnS-2
Thy Way, Not Mine. Horatius Bonar. OxBoCh; SoP; TrPWD; TRV; VA
(God's Way.) FaChP; MaRV
Thy Will. Christina Rossetti. *Fr.* Christ Our All in All. SoP
Thy Will be Done! Charlotte Elliott. SoP
Thy Will Be Done. Annie Johnson Flint. STF
Thy Will Be Done. John Hay. *See* Not in Dumb Resignation.
Thy Will Be Done. Hugh Thomson Kerr. BLRP; MaRV
Thy Will Be Done. Albert Simpson Reitz. STF
Thy Will Be Done. Louise Peabody Sargent. OQP
Thy Will Be Done. G. A. Studdert-Kennedy. MaRV
Thy Will Be Done. *Unknown.* BePJ
Thy Will Be Done in Me. Fanny Crosby. MaRV
Thy Will be done. No greater words than these. Thy Will Be Done. G. A. Studdert-Kennedy. MaRV
"Thy will be done." Why always bow the head. Thy Will Be Done. Louise Peabody Sargent. OQP
Thy Will is best for me. God's Will Is Best. *Unknown.* BLRP
Thy will, O God, is best. Thy Will Be Done. Hugh Thomson Kerr. BLRP; MaRV
Thy wisdom and Thy might appear. The Burning Bush. Henry van Dyke. TRV
Thy Word. T. H. Gill. *See* Thy Word Is Like a Garden, Lord.
Thy Word. Isaac Watts. *See* Heavens Declare Thy Glory, Lord, The.
Thy Word Is Like a Garden, Lord. T. H. Gill. FaChP
(Thy Word.) SoP
Thy words are compounded of sweet-smelling myrrh. Words Wherein Stinging Bees Lurk. Judah Halevi. TrJP
Thyestes, *sels.* Seneca, *tr. fr. Latin.*
"Climb at court for me that will," *tr. by* Andrew Marvell. MaMe
(Chorus: "Climb at Court for me that will.") OnPM
(Quiet Life, The.) LiTW
(Senec. Traged. ex Thyeste Chor. 2.) SeCV-1
Stond Who So List upon the Slipper Toppe, *tr. by* Sir Thomas Wyatt. EnPo; PoEL-1
(Of the Mean and Sure Estate.) SiCE
(Stand Whoso List.) NoP
("Stand whoso list upon the slipper top.") FCP; SiPS
Thyrsis. Matthew Arnold. EnLi-2; EnLit; FiP; GTSL; ILP; MaVP; MBW-2; NoP; OAEP; OBEV (new ed.); OBNC; OBVV; PAn; PoAn; PoE; PoVP; StP; TOP; ViPo; ViPP; VP
Thyrsis. Edward Cracroft Lefroy. Echos from Theocritus, XXVI. AWP
Thyrsis [*or* Thirsis], a youth of the inspired train. The Story of Phoebus and Daphne Applied. Edmund Waller. InvP; OBS; SeEP
Thyrsis and Milla, arm in arm together. The Never-certain Male. *Unknown.* EG
Thyrsis' Praise of His Mistress. William Browne. ReIE
"Thyrsis, Sleep'st Thou?" *Unknown.* InvP; OBSC
Thyrsis, the musick of that murm'ring spring. Winter. Pope. *Fr.* Pastorals. EiCL
Thyrsis, when we parted, swore. Song. Thomas Gray. OAEP
Thys ender nyght [*or* endris nygth]. A Christmas Carol. *Unknown.* OAEP; TrGrPo
Thyself. John Addington Symonds. *Fr.* Stella Maris. VA
("Give me thyself! It were as well to cry.") PoVP
Thyself and thy belongings. Not Thine Own. Shakespeare. *Fr.* Measure for Measure, I, i. MaRV
Thyself from love Thy heart didst not defend. To Jesus. Jacopone da Todi. MaRV
Thysia, *sels.* Morton Luce. HBV
"Bow down, my song, before her presence high," III.
"Comes the New Year; wailing the north winds blow," XVI.
"Hear, O Self-Giver, infinite as good," XXXVII.
"How shall I tell the measure of my love?" XLV.
"I watch beside you in your silent room," VII.
"Like some lone miser, dear, behold me stand," XXIII.
"So sang I in the springtime of my years," XXXVI.
"Twin songs there are, of joyance, or of pain," II.
Tiara Tahiti. Rupert Brooke. BrPo; SeCeV
Tibetan Comforter, *sel.* Robert K. Ekvall.
Put Grief Away. MaRV
Tibur is beautiful, too, and the orchard slopes, and the Anio. So

Not Seeing I Sung. Arthur Hugh Clough. *Fr.* Amours de Voyage. GTBS-P; OBNC
Tic. Vito Hannibal Acconci. YAP
Tic-tic-tic!/ The sound of the sleet. Sleet Storm. James S. Tippett. BrR; SiSoSe
Tichborne's Elegy, Written [with His Own Hand] in the Tower before His Execution. Chidiock Tichborne. *See* Elegy: "My prime of youth is but a frost of cares."
"Tick can live, A." Mandylion. Phyllis Harris. ThO
"Tick-tock," said the nursery clock. Christmas Eve. Florence Hoatson. GFA
Tick, tock, tick, tock/ Merrily sings the clock. The Clock. *Unknown.* OTPC (1946 ed.); PCH
"Tick-Tock! Tick-Tock!"/ Sings the great time-clock. The Time-Clock. Charles Hanson Towne. HBMV
Ticket, The. John Ashbery. ANYP
Ticket Agent, The. Edmund Leamy. HBMV; PoMa; StVeCh
Ticking Clocks. Rachel Field. TiPo (1959 ed.)
Tickle Rhyme, The. Ian Serraillier. SoPo
Tickly, tickly, on your knee. *Unknown.* OxNR
Ticktacktoe. John Stevens Wade. ThO
Ticonderoga. V. B. Wilson. OTPC; PaA; PAL; PAP
Tiddle liddle lightum. *Unknown.* OxNR
Tide, The. Longfellow. *See* Tide Rises, the Tide Falls, The.
Tide, The. Marjorie Wilson. OTPC (1946 ed.); PCH
Tide be runnin' the great world over. Sea Love. Charlotte Mew. BoLP; ELU; MeWo; MoAB; MoBrPo; NeMA; TrGrPo; ViBoPo
Tide comes in, and out goes tide, The. In Robin Hood Cove. Marsden Hartley. AnFE; CoAnAm
Tide, high tide of golden air, A. Homage to the Weather. Michael Hamburger. NMP; OPoP
Tide in the river, The. Eleanor Farjeon. TiPo
Tide of Faith, The. "George Eliot." *Fr.* A Minor Prophet. MaRV; OQP; TRV; WGRP
Tide of Life, The, *sel.* Watson Kirkconnell.
"Ah, Flood of Life on which I am a wave." CaP
Tide Rises, the Tide Falls, The. Longfellow. AA; AmePo; AmLP; AmPP (4th ed.); AnNE; AP; CBEP; CBV; ChTr; FaFP; MAmP; MWA-1; NePA; NoP; OxBA; PG (1955 ed.); PoRA; TreFT
(Tide, The.) WiR
Tide River, The. Charles Kingsley. *Fr.* The Water Babies. BoNaP; HBV; PoVP; PTK
(Clear and Cool.) GN
Tide slips up the silver sand, The. Sea-Way. Ellen Mackay Hutchinson Cortissoz. AA
Tide Trapped. Floris Clark McLaren. TwCaPo
Tide Will Win, The. Priscilla Leonard. MaRV; TRV
Tides, The. Thomas Tapper. GFA
Tides. Josephine Williams. PCD
Tide's at full, The: the marsh with flooded streams. Sunrise. Sidney Lanier. *Fr.* Hymns of the Marshes. FaBoEn
Tides of Love, The. T. A. Daly. InMe; PoPl; WhC; YaD
Tides Run up the Wairau, The. Eileen Duggan. AnNZ
Tidewash. . .Memories. Lament of the Flutes. Christopher Okigbo. PBA
Tidings of Great Joy. St. Luke, Bible, *N.T.* *See* Adoration of the Shepherds, The.
Tidewater born he was, and ever. The Rivers Remember. Nancy Byrd Turner. AmFN
Tie a bandage over his eyes. A Rebel. John Gould Fletcher. MAP; MoAmPo
Tie-shuffling Chant, *with music.* *Unknown.* ABF
Tie-tamping Chant, *with music.* *Unknown.* ABF
Tie the moccasin, bind the pack. Young Washington. Arthur Guiterman. FaPON; MPB; OHIP; PoSC
Tie Your Tongue, Sir? Robert Paul Smith. CAD
Tien Shan snowed soon after the cold sea wind came, The. Following the Army to the North. Li I. OnPM
Ties. Raymond Souster. MoCV; OBCV
Tiffany, Tiffany. Captain Kelly Lets His Daughter Go to Be a Nun. Thomas Butler Feeney. PoPl
Tiger, The. Hilaire Belloc. MoBrPo
Tiger, The. Blake. *Fr.* Songs of Experience. ATP; AWP; BBV; BEL; BoC; BoLiVe; BWP; CBEP; ChTr; EiPP; EnL; EnLi-2; EnLit; EnPE; FaBoBe; FaFP; FaPON; ForPo; GN; GoTP; GTBS-W; HBV; JAWP; LiTB; LiTG; MaPo; MaRV; MCCG; MPB; MyFE; NeHB; OA; OAEP; OBEC; OBEV; OnPM; OtMeF; OTPC; OuHeWo; PAn; PG; Po; PoAn; PoFS; PoLF; PoPl; PoPo; PoRA; PoSa; PTK; RG; RoGo; ShBV-2; StaSt; StP; TIHL; TOP; TreF; TRV; VaPo; ViBoPo; WBP; WePo; WGRP; WHA; WoL
(Tyger, The.) AnFE; AtBAP; BoTP; CABA; CaFP; CBV; CEP; CH; DiPo; EaLo; EiCL; EnRP; ERoP-1; ExPo; FaBoCh; FaBoEn; FaBV; FosPo; GTBS-D; HoPM; ILP; InPo; LoBV; LoGBV; MasP; MemP; NoP; OBNC; PeER; PIA; PoE; PoEL-4; PoeP; PoIE; SeCePo; SeCeV; TrGrPo; WaKn; YAT
("Tyger, Tyger, burning bright.") EG
Tiger, The. Laura Riding. FaBoMo
Tiger-Cat Tim. Edith Newlin Chase. SoPo; TiPo
Tiger Christ unsheathed his sword. For the One Who Would Take Man's Life in His Hands. Delmore Schwartz. FiMAP; LiTA; LiTM; MiAP; MoAB; MoAmPo; MoVE; NePA; ThLM; WaP
Tiger in me I know late, not burning bright, The. The Tiger. Laura Riding. FaBoMo
Tiger in the tiger-pit, The. Lines for an Old Man. T. S. Eliot. FaBoTw; MoPW; MWA-2
Tiger-Lilies. Thomas Bailey Aldrich. GN; GoTP
Tiger Lily. David McCord. GoJo; PDV
Tiger of Desire, The. Tom MacInnes. OBCV
Tiger, on the other hand, is kittenish and mild, The. The Tiger. Hilaire Belloc. MoBrPo
Tiger stalking in the night, The. Edward Newman Horn. ELU
"Tiger, strolling at my side." Triumph of Sensibility. Sylvia Townsend Warner. MoAB; MoBrPo
Tiger! Tiger [*or* Tyger]! burning bright. The Tiger [*or* The Tyger]. Blake. Fr. Songs of Experience
AnFE; ATP; AtBAP; AWP; BBV; BEL; BoC; BoLiVe; BoTP; BWP; CABA; CaFP; CBEP; CBV; CEP; CH; Ch; ChTr; DiPo; EaLo; EG; EiCL; EiPP; EnL; EnLi-2; EnLit; EnPE; EnRP; ERoP-1; ExPo; FaBoBe; FaBoCh; FaBoEn; FaBV; FaFP; FaPON; ForPo; FosPo; GN; GoTP; GTBS-D; GTBS-W; HBV; HoPM; ILP; InPo; JAWP; LiTB; LiTG; LoBV; LoGBV; MaPo; MaRV; MasP; MCCG; MemP; MPB; MyFE; NeHB; NoP; OA; OAEP; YAT OBEV; OnPM; OtMeF; OTPC; OuHeWo; PAn; PeER; PG; PIA; Po; PoAn; PoE; PoEL-4; PoeP; PoFS; PoIE; PoLF; PoPl; PoPo; PoRA; PoSa; PTK; RG; RoGo; SeCePo; SeCeV; ShBV-1; StaSt; StP; TiHL; TOP; TreF; TrGrPo; TRV; VaPo; ViBoPo; WaKn; WBP; WePo; WGRP; WHA; WoL; YAT
Tiger, when a man goes by, The. The Dignity of Man—Lesson #1. Walter H. Kerr. NePoAm-2
Tiger's Tale, A. John Bennett. TiPo (1959 ed.)
Tiggady Rue. David McCord. RIS; TiPo (1959 ed.)
Tight-sphinctered and inhibited. Peace Delegate. Douglas Livingstone. PeSA
Tightly-folded bud. Born Yesterday. Philip Larkin. HaMV
Tigress, The. Ruth Pitter. FaBoTw; HaMV; NYTB
Till Christ. *Unknown.* *Fr.* The Gude and Godlie Ballatis. OxBS
Till dawn the wind drove round me. It is past. Dawn on the Night-Journey. Dante Gabriel Rossetti. NCEP
Till dawn the winds' insuperable throng. In Extremis. George Sterling. HBV
"Till death" is narrow loving. Emily Dickinson. CoBA
Till Eve was brought to Adam, he. Nearest the Dearest. Coventry Patmore. *Fr.* The Angel in the House. HBV
"Till He Come!" Bishop of Exeter. SoP
Till He Come. "L. R." SoP
"Till He come!" Oh, let the words. "Till He Come!" Bishop of Exeter. SoP
Till I have peace with thee, warr other men. Loves Warre. John Donne. Elegies, XX. MaMe
Till now the doubtful dusk reveal'd. Tennyson. *Fr.* In Memoriam A. H. H., XCV. GTBS-P
Till one dawn, above the green bloom of a gleaming lawn. The Death of Urgan. Swinburne. *Fr.* Tristram of Lyonesse. WHA
Till thinking had worn out my enterprise. Spring Mountain Climb. Richard Eberhart. GoYe
Till We Have Built Jerusalem. Blake. *See* And Did Those Feet in Ancient Time.
Tillaquils, The. Laura Riding. FaBoMo
Tillie. Walter de la Mare. PoMS; TiPo
Tilly. James Joyce. PoIE
Tim, an Irish Terrier. Winifred M. Letts. BoC

Tim and Tilly sauntered on. The Pussy-Cat Who Visited the Queen. Carolyn Wells. CIV
Tim Finnigan [*or* Finigan] lived in Walker Street. Finnegan's [*or* Finigan's] Wake. *Unknown.* BLPA; TrAS
Tim the Dragoon. Sir Arthur Quiller-Couch. WhC
Tim, the Fairy. Florence Randal Livesay. CaP
Tim Turpin. Thomas Hood. BOHV; WiR
Timareté, her wedding-day now near. A Girl's Treasures. *Unknown, tr. by* Lord Neaves. OnPM
Timas. Sappho, *tr. fr. Greek by* John Addington Symonds. LiTW
Timber, *with music. Unknown.* AS
Timber, The. Henry Vaughan. EP; NoP; SCEP-1; SeCP; SeCV-1
"Sure thou didst flourish once," *sel.* OBEV
Timber Line Trees. Jamie Sexton Holme. PoOW
Timbers heaving to heaven we sailed at seven. Crabbing. Norman Levine. CaP; OBCV
Time. Bhartrihari, *tr. fr. Sanskrit by* Paul Elmer More. AWP; JAWP; WBP
Time. Thomas Stephens Collier. AA
Time. Allen Curnow. AnNZ
Time. Giles Fletcher. *See* In Time the Strong and Stately Turrets Fall.
Time, The. G. S. Fraser. WaP
Time. Robert Graves. AtBAP; FaBoMo; LiTM (rev. ed.)
Time. George Herbert. EP; MaMe; SeCL
Time. Ralph Hodgson. BrPo; GTBS-P
Time. Jasper Mayne. *Fr.* The Amorous War. OBEV; SeCL
(First Song, Sung by Two Amazons, The.) SeEP
(Time Is a Feathered Thing.) CLwM
("Time is the feather'd thing.") EG
Time. Sir Thomas More. EnRePo
Time. Schiller, *tr. fr. German.* OQP
Time. Frederick George Scott. VA
Time. Shelley. BEL; EnLi-2; EPN; Par; PoIE (1970 ed.); PoLF; YAT
(Unfathomable Sea!) EtS
Time ("If I had time to find a place"). *Unknown.* SoP
Time ("Time is/ Too slow for those who wait"). *Unknown.* TreFT
Time. Thomas Watson. *Fr.* Hecatompathia. OBSC
("Time wasteth years, and months, and hours.") SiCE
Time. Marguerite Wilkinson. HBMV
Time and again, time and again I tie. The Edge. Louise Glük. YAP
Time and Death. William Henry Whitworth. VA
Time and Eternity. Bunyan. WiR
Time and Eternity. Fulke Greville. Caelica, LXXXIII. OBSC
Time and Eternity. Stephen Hawes. *Fr.* The Pastime of Pleasure. PoEL-1
Time and Grief. William Lisle Bowles. HBV; OBEV
(Influence of Time on Grief.) ATP; EnRP
("O Time! who know'st a lenient hand to lay.") LO
(Sonnet: "O Time!") CEP; OBEC
(Sonnet, July 18th, 1787.) FaBoEn
Time and Love. Shakespeare. *See* Sonnets, LXIV *and* LXV.
Time and the Garden. Yvor Winters. MoAmPo (1962 ed.); QFR
Time and the mortal will stand never fast. Sonnet. Luís de Camoes. AWP
Time and the World, whose magnitude and weight. Epitaph. Robert Southey. OBNC
Time as Variable. Lucian, *tr. fr. Greek by* Lord Neaves. OnPM
Time-Bomb. Earle Birney. TwCaPo
Time breaks our passion but the Virgin smiles. Our True Beginnings. Wrey Gardiner. NeBP
Time brings not death, it brings but changes. A Comrade Rides Ahead. Douglas Malloch. HBMV
Time can [*or* will] say nothing but I told you so. Villanelle [*or* If I Could Tell You]. W. H. Auden. LiTA; MoAB; MoBrPo; TDP
Time cannot age thy sinews, nor the gale. Albatross. Charles Warren Stoddard. AA; EtS
Time cannot break the bird's wing from the bird. To a Young Poet. Edna St. Vincent Millay. CrMA
Time-Clock, The. Charles Hanson Towne. HBMV
Time consumes each word. Feather. Francesco Bianco. CLwM
Time cost, time lost, time lusty I was. Englynion. *Unknown.* PrWP
Time, cruel Time, come and subdue that brow. To Delia, XXIII. Samuel Daniel. AtBAP; OBSC
Time demands a rolling eye, The. The Time. G. S. Fraser. WaP
Time Does Not Bring Relief. Edna St. Vincent Millay. FaBV
Time draws near the birth of Christ, The. In Memoriam A. H. H., XXVIII. Tennyson. BePJ; ChIP; EnLi-2; EnLit; EPN; MaRV; OAEP; OQP; PGD; TOP; ViPo; VP
Time draws near the birth of Christ, The. In Memoriam A. H. H., CIV. Tennyson. EnLi-2; EnLit; EPN; OAEP; PoE; ViPo; VP
Time drops in decay. The Moods. W. B. Yeats. CTC
Time Eating. Keith Douglas. FaBoMo; NeBP
Time ends when vision sees its lapse in liberty. Beata l'Alma. Sir Herbert Read. LiTG
Time erodes the hills? Tale of One Hill. Franklin D. Elmer, Jr. ChIP
Time flies. On an Old Sun Dial [*or* Love over All]. *Unknown.* OQP; TreFT
Time flies, hope flags, life plies a wearied wing. Monna Innominata, X. Christina Rossetti. ViPo; VP
Time flits away, time flits away, lady. Variation on Ronsard. T. Sturge Moore. OBMV
Time for Building, A. Myra Cohn Livingston. PDV
Time for Everything, A. Ecclesiastes, XII: 1-8, Bible, *O.T.* TrGrPo
Time for rain! for your long hot dry Autumn. The Englishman in Italy. Robert Browning. SeCePo
Time for toil is past, and night has come, The. Bringing Our Sheaves. Elizabeth Akers Allen. HBV
Time for Us to Leave Her. *Unknown. See* Leave Her Johnny.
Time Goes by Turns. Joel Chandler Harris. *Fr.* Uncle Remus, His Songs and His Sayings. IHA
Time goes, you say? Ah, no! The Paradox of Time. Austin Dobson. AWP; HBV; JAWP; PG (1945 ed.); WBP
Time had come to kill himself, he said, The. Epitaph on a Madman's Grave. Morris Gilbert. YaD
Time has a magic wand! On an Old Muff. Frederick Locker-Lampson. CenHV; VA
Time has been that these wild solitudes, The. A Winter Piece. Bryant. AmPP (4th ed.); AP; CoBA; OxBA
Time has come for a wench to wed, The. Ballad of the Double Bed. Eve Merriam. UnTE
Time Has Come, the Clock Says Time Has Come, The. Conrad Aiken. Preludes for Memnon, XXVIII. NePA; OxBA
"Time has come, The," the walrus said. "Lewis Carroll." *Fr.* The Walrus and the Carpenter. TiPo
Time has come to call a halt, The. Songs for a Colored Singer, II. Elizabeth Bishop. PoNe
Time has its ends and its beginnings. The Jungle. Louis Dudek. PeCV
Time has no flight—'tis we who speed along. Time. Thomas Stephen Collier. AA
Time has stored all, but keeps his chronicle. History. Laurence Binyon. POTE
Time hath laid his mantle by, The. Spring. Charles d'Orléans. DD
Time hath, my Lord, a wallet at his back. Ulysses Advises Achilles [Not to Let Slip Opportunity]. Shakespeare. *Fr.* Troilus and Cressida, III, iii. LiTB; LiTG
Time holds no purring hour-glass to your face. The Day. George M. Brady. NeIP
Time, I ever must complain. To Time. John Hagthorpe. SeCL
Time I went to see my sister, The. Tsurayuki. *Fr.* Shui Shu. AWP
Time in the Rock, *sels.* Conrad Aiken.
"And there I saw the seed upon the mountain," I.
(Preludes to Definition, I.) TwAmPo
"And you who love, you who attach yourselves." ViBoPo
"But no, the familiar symbol, as that the," XCII *and* XCIII. FaBoMo
"On that wild verge in the late night he stood," XXXIX.
(Preludes to Definition, II.) TwAmPo
"Or else, in an afternoon of minor reflection," XCIII. MoVE
Poem: "And this digester, this digester of food." VaPo
"Still the same function, still the same habit come," XLV.

(Preludes to Definition, III.) TwAmPo
"What without speech we knew and could not say," XLVI.
(Preludes to Definition, IV.) TwAmPo
Time in the Sun. Louise Townsend Nicholl. NePoAm-2
Time is, The. Anger. Robert Creeley. CoPo; NaP
Time is/ Too slow for those who wait. Time. *Unknown.* TreFT
Time is a [*or* the] feathered thing. Time [*or* The First Song, Sung by Two Amazons]. Jasper Mayne. *Fr.* The Amorous War. CLwM; EG; OBEV; SeCL; SeEP
Time is a fox on quick, velvet feet. Earthly Illusion. Louise Leighton. GoYe
Time is a heavy legend to be told. French Clock. Hortense Flexner. HBMV
Time is a thing. Epilogue. Stephen Spender. MoBrPo
Time is a treasure. New Time. *Unknown.* BLRP
Time is after dinner, The. The Boarder. Louis Simpson. PoPl
Time is come to speak, I think, The. Mrs. Golightly. Gertrude Hall. AA
Time is God's tenderness. Time. Marguerite Wilkinson. HBMV
Time is moving, people move up and down. The Parade. Ashton Greene. NePoAm
Time is never wasted, listening to the trees. The Trees. Lucy Larcom. OHIP
Time is no measure, there is only light. Villanelle of Light. A. M. Sullivan. JKCP (1955 ed.)
Time Is Not Mocked. Francis Meynell. MemP
Time is not remote, when I, The. Swift. *Fr.* Verses on the Death of Dr. Swift. OBEC; OxBoLi; SiTL; ViBoPo; WoL
Time is of the essence. This is a highly skilled. Polo Grounds. Rolfe Humphries. HoPM; SD
Time is our sculptor. He of earth and air. In Praise of Unfamous Men. Francis Meynell. MemP
Time is short, The. Linger Not! Horatius Bonar. SoP
Time is swiftly rolling on, The. Hicks's Farewell. *Unknown.* BFSS
Time is the feather'd thing. *See* Time is a feathered thing.
Time Is the Fire. Delmore Schwartz. The Repetitive Heart, IV. LiTA; LiTM
("Calmly we walk through this April's day.") MoVE
(For Rhoda.) MoAB; MoAmPo; OxBA
Time is the rest of all this earth. Time. Bhartrihari. AWP; JAWP; WBP
Time Is Today, The. John Farrar. GoYe
Time I've Lost in Wooing, The. Thomas Moore. ALV; BEL; BoLP; EnLi-2; EnLit; EnRP; EPN; HBV; HoPM; InP, *st.* 1; LiTL; MeWo; OAEP; OnYI; PG (1945 ed.); PoFS
Time Lags Abed. D'Arcy Cresswell. AnNZ
Time like an Ever-rolling Stream. P. G. Wodehouse. FiBHP
Time like the repetitions of a child's piano. The Reconciliation. Archibald MacLeish. MoAmPo
Time Long Past. Shelley. EPN; HBV
Time nor place did I want, what held me tongue-tied. Phaleuciaks I. *Unknown.* SiCE
Time of gifts has come again, The. The Pressed Gentian. Whittier. AnAmPo
Time of Light, a Time of Shadow, A. Samuel Yellen. NePoAm-2
"Time of Man, The." Phyllis Webb. MoCV
Time of Roses, The. Thomas Hood. MeWo; OBEV; OBVV; PG (1945 ed.)
(Ballad: "It was not in the winter.") TOP, *abr.*; VA
(It Was Not in the Winter.) ELP
(It Was the Time of Roses.) CH
Time of the Barmecides, The. James Clarence Mangan. EnRP
(Time of the Barmacides, The.) RoGo,*abr.*
Time of the Singing of Birds, The. The Song of Solomon, Bible, *O.T.* *See* For, Lo, the Winter Is Past.
Time Out. Frances Westgate Butterfield. GoYe
Time Out. Oliver Jenkins. GoYe
Time Out. John Montague. NYTB
Time out of mind I have stood. The Old Grey Wall. Bliss Carman. CaP
Time Passes. R. P. Lister. NYBP
Time Passing, Beloved ("Time passing, and the memories of love"). Donald Davie. NePoEA-2
Time Piece. *See* Timepiece.
Time Poem. Quentine Hill. NBP
Time present and time past. Burnt Norton. T. S. Eliot. *Fr.* Four Quartets. AnFE; AtBAP; CABL; CMoP; CoAnAm; LiTG; LiTM (rev. ed.); MoAB; MoAmPo (1950 ed.); MoPo; PAn; PoE; TwAmPo
Time, Real and Imaginary. Samuel Taylor Coleridge. EnRP; ERoP-1; MERP; OBEV; OBRV
Time Regained. Sir Herbert Read. FaBoMo
Time rolls his ceaseless course. The Gathering. Sir Walter Scott. *Fr.* The Lady of the Lake. OBNC; ViBoPo
Time runs wild on the hilltops. Wild Thyme. Eleanor Farjeon. SiSoSe
Time seems not now beneath his years to stoop. Dryden. *Fr.* To His Sacred Majesty, a Panegyrick on His Coronation, 1661. OBS
Time-Servers. Judah Halevi, *tr. fr. Hebrew by* Solomon Solis-Cohen. TrJP
Time shall come, when, free as seas or wind, The. Pope. *Fr.* Windsor Forest. PoFr
Time shall come when wrong shall end, The. Chartist Song. Thomas Cooper. VA
Time sitting on the throne of memory. October XXIX, 1795. William Stanley Braithwaite. CDC
Time smiling on this sundial of a world. Winter in Dunbarton. Robert Lowell. ToPo
Time so tranquil is and still, The. A Summer Day. Alexander Hume. OBEV
"Time stands still." The Unbeseechable. Frances Cornford. MoBrPo
Time stands still, with gazing on her face! *Unknown.* EnLoPo
Time taken by the forelock as he flies. Bluebell. Geoffrey Taylor. NeIP
Time takes the summer's loveliness. While Immortality Endures. Ernest Briggs. NeLNL
Time, that anticipates eternities. A Prayer to Time. Siegfried Sassoon. MemP
Time that bringes all things to light. Epitaph. Thomas Morton. SCAP
Time that brings children from the wizard den. Clock Symphony. John Frederick Nims. MiAP
Time that is moved by little fidget wheels. Five Bells. Kenneth Slessor. BoAV; MoAuPo; OnHM; PoAu-2; PoRA; SeCePo
Time, the Faithless. Valentine Iremonger. *See* Evening in Summer.
Time ticks away the centre of my pride. The Empty Glen. R. Crombie Saunders. OxBS
Time time said old King Tut. Don Marquis. FiBHP
Time to Be Wise. Walter Savage Landor. *See* Yes; I Write Verses.
Time to Choose a Lover. Horace. *See* To Chloe.
Time to Dance, A, *sels.* C. Day Lewis.
Flight, The. FaBoMo, *shorter sel.*; MoVE
(Flight to Australia.) CMoP; ShBV-3
"For those who had the power." FaBoMo; POTE
Time to Die. Ray Garfield Dandridge. BANP
Time to Get Up. Robert Louis Stevenson. *See* Time to Rise.
Time to Go. "Susan Coolidge." GN; OTPC (1946 ed.)
Time to Leave Her. *Unknown.* *See* Leave Her Johnny.
"Time to put off the world and go somewhere." Beggars to Beggar Cried. W. B. Yeats. CMoP
Time to Rise. Robert Louis Stevenson. BoChLi; InP; OTPC (1946 ed.); PCH; PoVP; RIS; SiSoSe; StVeCh; UTS
(Time to Get Up.) ThGo
Time to Strike, The. Shakespeare. *See* There Is A Tide.
Time to Talk, A. Robert Frost. CoBA; LaNeLa
Time to Trust, The. *Unknown.* BLRP
Time tryeth truth convicting all that strive. T. Street. SCAP
Time was, and that was termed the time of gold. The Olden Days. Joseph Hall. *Fr.* Virgidemiarum. OBSC; SiCE
Time was away and somewhere else. Meeting Point. Louis MacNeice. ChMP; MemP; POTE; WePo
Time was come when he must choose, The. 1914 Autumn and Winter. Maurice Hewlett. *Fr.* The Song of the Plow. PoFr
Time was he sang the British Brute. Ballade of Expansion. Hilda Johnson. PAH
Time was, I shrank from what was right. Sensitiveness [*or* Yielded]. Cardinal Newman. PoVP; SoP
Time was I was a plowman driving. Plowman. Sidney Keyes. MoAB; PoRA
Time was long and long ago, The. Ditty. Ted Robinson. MaRV

Time was, no archer with impunity. Archers of the King. Sister Mary Genoveva. GoBC
Time was upon. Upon Time. Robert Herrick. OBS
Time was when his half million drew. Bewick Finzer. E. A. Robinson. AnNE; AP; BoLiVe (1945 ed.); CMoP; CoBMV; ForPo; MAP; MoAB; MoAmPo; NeMA
Time was when I could weep; but now all care. Hartley Coleridge. Sonn
Time was when I was weapon and warrior. Horn. *Unknown. Fr.* Riddles. AnOE
Time was when ye were powerless. The Young Priest to His Hands. Edward F. Garesché. CAW
Time wasted and time spent. The Times. Charles Madge. OBMV
Time wasteth years, and months, and hours. Time. Thomas Watson. *Fr.* Hecatompathia. OBSC; SiCE
Time went away, and left him lingering. The Last Romantic. Alexander Laing. AnAmPo
Time When First, The. *Unknown.* TuPP
Time! Where Didst Thou Those Years Inter. William Habington. OxBoCh
(Recogitabo Tibi Omnes Annos Meos.) ACP (1926 ed.)
Time will assuage. To the Reader. J. V. Cunningham. QFR
Time will come when, looking in a glass, The. The Frailty of Beauty. "J. C." *Fr.* Alcilia. ElL
Time Will Not Grant. Sidney Keyes. SeCePo
Time Will Say Nothing but I Told You So. W. H. Auden. *See* Villanelle.
Time winnows beauty with a fiery wind. The Harvest of Time. Harold Trowbridge Pulsifer. HBMV
Time worketh; let me work too. Work. Horatius Bonar. SoP
Time-worn, the soldier lays aside the steel. Propertian. L. A. MacKay. *Fr.* Erotica Antiqua. PeCV
Time, wouldst thou hurt us? Never shall we grow old. The Double Fortress. Alfred Noyes. GoBC
Time, You Old Gipsy [*or* Gypsy] Man. Ralph Hodgson. BoLiVe; BoTP; BrPo; CH; EnLi-2 (1949 ed.); EnLit; FaPON; GaP; GBV (1952 ed.); HBV; HT; InP; LiTM (rev. ed.); MemP; MoAB; MoBrPo; MoShBr; NeMA; NP; OTD; PCD; PG; RG; ShBV-1; SiSoSe; StaSt; ThWaDe; TIHL; TOP; TreF; TrGrPo; ViBoPo; WaKn
Time you won your town the race, The. To an Athlete Dying Young. A. E. Housman. A Shropshire Lad, XIX. ATP; BEL; BoLiVe; BrPo; CABA; CAFP; CBV; CMoP; CoBE; EnL; EnLi-2; ExPo; GTBS-W; ILP; InP; LiTB; LiTG; LiTM (rev. ed.); MaC; MaPo; MasP; MoAB; MoBrPo; NBM; NeMA; NoP; OAEP (2d ed.); PAn; Po; PoEL-5; PoFS; PoIE; PoMa; PoPl; PoPo; PoRA; PoSa; PoVP; SD; SeCeV; TDP; TreF; TrGrPo; UnPo; VaPo; ViPo; VP; WHA; YAT
Time Zones for Forty-four. Donald A. Stauffer. WaP
Timely blossom, infant fair. To Miss Charlotte Pulteney, in Her Mother's Arms [*or* To Charlotte Pulteney]. Ambrose Philips. CEP; EiPP; ELP; FaBoEn; GTBS; GTBS-D; GTBS-P; GTBS-W; GTSE; GTSL; HBV; OBEC
Timely Warning, A. *Unknown.* PoMa
Time Piece. William Cole. ELU
Time-Piece, The. William Cowper. The Task, II. BEL
"Oh for a lodge in some vast wilderness, *sel.*" EnRP
Timepiece, A. James Merrill. NePoEA-2
Timers. Flora J. Arnstein. GoYe
Times, The. Charles Madge. OBMV
Times, The. Marcus Manilius, *tr. fr. Latin by* Thomas Creech. LiTW
Times, The. *Unknown.* PAH
Times's a circumference. The Soul of Time. Trumbull Stickney. LiTA; NePA
Times are nightfall, look, their light grows less, The. Gerard Manley Hopkins. BoPe
Time's Balm, *abr.* Cuthbert Shaw. *Fr.* Monody to the Memory of a Young Lady. OBEC
Time's Bright Sand. Robert Finch. CaP
Time's Changes. James Bramston. *Fr.* The Art of Politicks. OBEC
Times come round again, The. To a Military Rifle [1942]. Yvor Winters. MoAmPo (1962 ed.); WaP
"Time's Conscience!" cried the allerion. Forever Morning. Laura Riding. LiTA
Time's Flying. *Unknown. See* Lauriger Horatius.
Time's Fool. Ruth Pitter. ChMP; MoBrPo; PoRA
Times Gettin' Hard, Boys, *with music. Unknown.* AS
Times's Glory. Shakespeare. *Fr.* The Rape of Lucrece. ChTr
Times Go [*or* Goe] by Turns. Robert Southwell. ACP; CoBE; ElL; EP; GoBC; GTBS-W; HBV; LiTB; LiTG; OBEV (1st ed.); OBSC; OxBoCh; PG; PoEL-2; SiCE
(Tymes Goe by Turnes.) FaBoEn
Time's Hand Is Kind. Margaret E. Bruner. PoToHe
Times Have Altered, The. *Unknown.* CoMu
Times is mighty dull at Squawville, an' we've nothin' else to do. Patriotism at Squawville. *Unknown.* PAP
Time's Long Ago. Herman Melville. PoFS
Time's Mutability. Bertolt Brecht, *tr. fr. German by* Martin Esslin. ELU
Times o' Year. William Barnes. BoNaP
Time's Revenge. Walter Learned. HBV
Time's Revenges. Robert Browning. PoVP; VP
Time's sea hath been five years at its slow ebb. To ——. Keats. SyP
Times she'll sit quiet by the hearth. The Woodcutter's Wife. William Rose Benét. AnAmPo; AWP; InPo
Time's Song. Winthrop Mackworth Praed. EnRP; NBM
Times wherein old Pompion was a Saint, The. New-Englands Crisis. Benjamin Tompson. SCAP
Times without Number Have I Pray'd. Charles Wesley. MaRV; OxBoCh
Timid Ash Tree, The. Kathleen Millay. PEDC
Timid Bunnies. Jeannie Kirby. BoTP
Timid child with heart oppressed, A. Buffalo Creek. John Le Gay Brereton. BoAu; PoAu-1
Timid Gazelle, The. Kasmuneh, *tr. fr. Arabic.* TrJP
Timid Hortense. Peter Newell. NA
Timid little night moth, The. Moth Miller. Aileen Fisher. UTS
Timid Lover. Countee Cullen. BANP
Timidly/ Against a background of brick tenements. A City Park. Alter Brody. OCS
Timon of Archimedes. Charles Battell Loomis. NA
Timon of Athens, *sel.* Thomas Shadwell.
Good-Morrow, A. SeCL
Timon of Athens, *sels.* Shakespeare.
"Ah, when the means are gone that buy this praise," *fr.* II, ii. MyFE
"Here lies a wretched corse," *fr.* V, iv. MyFE
"How came the noble Timon to this change?" *fr.* IV, iii. MyFE
"If Alcibiades kill my countrymen," *fr.* V, i. MyFE
Timon's Epitaph. Callimachus, *tr. fr. Greek by* Shakespeare. AWP; JAWP; WBP
Timon's Villa. Pope. *Fr.* Moral Essays, Epistle IV. MaPo; OBEC
(At Timon's Villa.) ExPo
(Satire on Riches.) PoLi
Timor Mortis. *Unknown.* NoP
Timothy. Rose Fyleman. UTS
Timothy Boon. Ivy O. Eastwick. SoPo; TiPo
Timothy Tiggs and Tomothy Toggs. Some Fishy Nonsense. Laura E. Richards. SoPo; TiPo
Timothy Tim was a very small cat. Tiger-Cat Tim. Edith Newlin Chase. SoPo; TiPo
Timothy Titus took two ties. *Unknown.* OxNR
Timothy Winters. Charles Causley. BoC
Tin-bright and whistle-sharp the world occurs. The Body's Eye. Anne Welsh. BoSA
Tin-tinkle-tinkle-tinkle, went the bell. The Shop. W. W. Gibson. BEL
Tin-Whistle Player, The. Padraic Colum. UnS
Ting! ring! the sleigh bells jingle. A Sleigh-Ride. Laura E. Richards. GFA
Tinged with the blood of Aztec lands. El Vaquero. Lucius Harwood Foote. AA
Tingling Back, The. Karl Shapiro. FiMAP
Tingling, misty marvel, A. November Morning. Evaleen Stein. YeAr
Tink-a-tink, tink-a-tink. The Minaret Bells. Thackeray. RIS
Tinker, The. *Unknown.* CoMu
Tinker and the Monks, The. Nathaniel Whiting. *Fr.* Le Hore di Recreatione; or, The Pleasant Historie of Albiano and Bellama. SeCL
Tinker, Tailor. *Unknown.* OxNR
Tinkers, The. Joseph Campbell. OnYI
Tinker's Moon. Ewart Milne. OnYI

Tinkle, tinkle! The Waterfall. Frank Dempster Sherman. BoChLi; OTPC (1946 ed.); PRWS
"Tinkle, tinkle, tinkle": 'tis the muffin-man you see. The Muffin-Man's Bell. Ann Hawkshaw. BoTP; OTPC
Tint I cannot take is best, The. Emily Dickinson. CoBA; MAmP; MAP; MoAmPo
Tintadgel bells ring o'er the tide. The Silent Tower of Bottreau [*or* Bottreaux]. Robert Stephen Hawker. GoBC; OBRV; VA
Tintern Abbey. Wordsworth. *See* Lines Composed a Few Miles above Tintern Abbey.
Tiny bell the tree-toad has, A. The Tree-Toad. Orrick Johns. NP
Tiny Bird, The. *Unknown. tr. fr. Irish by* Robin Flower. BiS
Tiny fleece of my own flesh. Close to Me. "Gabriela Mistral." PoPl
Tiny fly fell down on my page, A. A Death to Us. Jon Silkin. NePoEA
Tiny moon as small and white as a single jasmine flower, A. A White Blossom. D. H. Lawrence. MoBrPo; NeMA
Tiny shoes so trim and neat. The Fairy Shoemaker. Phyllis Garlick. BoTP
Tiny slippers of gold and green. To a Pair of Egyptian Slippers. Sir Edwin Arnold. HBV; OBVV
Tiny spill of bird-things in a swirl, A. The Finches. Thomas W. Shapcott. PoAu-2
Tiny stone, a jasper, here displays, A. A Carved Stone. *Unknown.* OnPM
Tipperary. Mary Kelly. VA
Tipperary Recruiting Song. *Unknown.* OnYI
Tipperty-Toes, the smallest elf. Red in Autumn. Elizabeth Gould. BoTP
Tiptoe. Karla Kuskin. PDV
Tiptoe Night. John Drinkwater. GaP; SiSoSe
Tip-Toe Tale. Dixie Willson. GFA
Tiptoeing twilight. Twilight. Hazel Hall. AnAmPo; HBMV
Tir-Nan-Og. J. F. Hendry. NeBP
Tirade on Tea. Phyllis MacGinley. InMe
"Tiraha, Te Ra!" The Noosing of the Sun-God. Jessie Mackay. ACV
Tir'd Nature's sweet restorer, balmy sleep! *See* Tired Nature's sweet restorer. . .
Tir'd with all these, for restful death I cry. *See* Tired with all these. . .
"Tired." Helen Burnside. SoP
Tired. Hilda Conkling. NP
Tired. Fenton Johnson. BANP; IDB; Kal; PoLF; PoNe; TTY
Tired air groans as the heavies swing over, The. Thiepval Wood. Edmund Blunden. AnFE; MMA
Tired and thirsty, weary of the way. After the Hunt. Detlev von Liliencron. AWP
Tired and Unhappy, [You Think of Houses]. Delmore Schwartz. LiTM; MoAB; MoAmPo; NePA
Tired brain, there is a place of rest. Quiet. Ernest Radford. OBVV
Tired cars go grumbling by, The. When Dawn Comes to the City; New York. Claude McKay. GoSl; OCS
Tired Caterpillar, The. *Unknown.* UTS
Tired Man, The. Anna Wickham. HBMV; MeWo; NP; ViBoPo (1941 ed.)
Tired Mothers. May Riley Smith. HBV
Tired [*or* Tir'd] Nature's sweet restorer, balmy sleep! Night. Edward Young. *Fr.* Night Thoughts, I. CEP; EiPP; EnPE; EnRP; OBEC; SeCePo
"Tired!" Oh yes! so tired, dear. "Tired." Helen Burnside. SoP
Tired of being my dog, and with grave anger. A Dog Who Ate a Pond Lily. Winifred Welles. NP
Tired of Eating Kisses. Edward Vincent Swart. PeSA
Tired of play! Tired of play! On the Picture of a "Child Tired of Play." Nathaniel Parker Willis. HBV
Tired Petitioner, The, *sel.* George Wither.
"It may be 'tis observ'd, I want relations." SeCV-1
Tired. Sick and tired. Burn, Baby, Burn. Marvin E. Jackmon. BF
Tired swimmer in the waves of time, A. Sissinghurst. V. Sackville-West. POTE
Tired Tim. Walter de la Mare. ALV; BoTP; FaPON; GaP; MoShBr; MPB; OnPP; SoPo; TiPo; TSW
Tired vulture, A, nibbles at the bleak/ Flesh it thought ageless. Anatole France at Eighty. Gladys Oaks. AnAmPo
Tired [*or* Tir'd] with all these, for restful death I cry. Sonnets, LXVI. Shakespeare. AnFE; AWP; BEL; BoLiVe; CBEP; CLwM; CTC; EnL; EnLi-1; ExPo; FaFP; GTBS; GTBS-D; GTBS-P; GTBS-W; GTSE; GTSL; InPo; JAWP; LiTB; LiTG; MemP; MyFE; OBSC; PAn; PoIE; ReEn; SeCeV; SiCE; Sonn; TOP; TrGrPo; ViBoPo; WBP; WHA
Tired with dull grief, grown old before my day. 1916 Seen from 1921. Edmund Blunden. MMA
Tired with the noisome follies of the age. Earl of Rochester. *Fr.* Farewell to the Court. TrGrPo
Tired Woman, The. Anna Wickham. MeWo; MoBrPo
Tired Worker, The. Claude McKay. BANP
Tireless budding and flowering of women. Image in a Lilac Tree. Terence Tiller. NeBP
Tireless flight of a pursuing gull, The. A Christmas Dawn at Sea. Evan Morgan. EtS
Tiresias. George Garrett. NePoAm-2
Tiresias' Lament. Ellen de Young Kay. NePoEA
Tiring of rest, of plain and fruitless toil. The Dreamer. Dorothy Gould. PGD
'Tis a dull sight. Old Song [*or* The Meadows in Spring]. Edward Fitzgerald. GN; HBV; OBEV; OBVV
"'Tis a hundred years," said the bosun bold. The Whale. *Unknown.* EtS
'Tis a lesson you should heed. Try Again [*or* Try, Try, Again]. *Unknown, at. to* William Edward Hickson, *also to* T. H. Palmer. FaFP; FaPON; PTK; RePo; TreF; TVC
'Tis a Little Journey. *Unknown.* PoToHe
'Tis a little thing. A Friend. Sir Thomas Noon Talfourd. *Fr.* Ion. PoToHe
'Tis a long, long way to my waiting home. Home-Bound. Henry W. Frost. SoP
Tis a moon-tinted primsoes, with a well. Another (Fantastic Simile). Thomas Lovell Beddoes. Sonn
'Tis a new life;—thoughts move not as they did. The New Birth. Jones Very. AP; FaChP; MAmP
'Tis a region calm of sunny groves. *Unknown. Fr.* The Phoenix. LiTW
'Tis a sad land, that in one day. Death. Henry Vaughan. NCEP
'Tis a sad sight to see the year dying. Song of the Fire. Edward Fitzgerald. OTPC
'Tis a soft rogue, this Lycias. Lycias. Earl of Rochester. ErPo
'Tis a stern and startling thing to think. Her Death. Thomas Hood. *Fr.* Miss Kilmansegg and Her Precious Leg. VA
'Tis a substantial thing, and not a word. Fletcher *and* Massinger. *Fr.* The Double Marriage. PoFr
"'Tis a wonderful story," I hear you say. The Boy Columbus. *Unknown.* HH; PEDC
'Tis a world of silences. I gave a cry. Silences. Arthur O'Shaughnessy. OBNC; VA
'Tis advertised in Boston, New York and Buffalo. Blow, Ye Winds. *Unknown.* AmSS; IHA; SoAmSa
'Tis all a libel-Paxton (Sir) will say. One Thousand Seven Hundred and Thirty Eight, Dialogue II. Pope. CEP
'Tis all a myth that Autumn grieves. Autumn's Mirth. Samuel Minturn Peck. GN
'Tis all the way to Toe-town. Foot Soldiers. John Banister Tabb. HBV; HBVY; PPL
'Tis always love in Arles the old. In Provence. Jean Aicard. CAW
'Tis an honorable thought. Emily Dickinson. *See* It is an honourable thought.
'Tis an old maxim in the schools. Flattery. Swift. PV; TreFT
'Tis bad enough in man or woman. Epigram: On Inclosures. *Unknown.* OxBoLi
'Tis bedtime; say your hymn, and bid, "Good-night." Bedtime. Francis Robert St. Clair Erskine. HBV; HBVY; PRWS; VA
'Tis better to be vile than vile esteemed. Sonnets, CXXI. Shakespeare. BWP; CBEP; InvP; MaPo; PAn; PoEL-2; Sonn
'Tis Better to Have Loved and Lost. Tennyson. *See* In Memoriam A. H. H.: "I envy not in any moods."
Tis braul I cudgel, ranters, Quakers braul. Claudius Gilbert. John Wilson. SCAP
'Tis but a foil at best, and that's the most. Emblem. Francis Quarles. Emblems, II, 14. LoBV
'Tis but a frowne, I prithee let me dye. *Unknown.* SeCSL
'Tis But a Little Faded Flower. Ellen Clementine Howarth. AA; HBV
'Tis but a Wanton Trick. *Unknown. See* Wanton Trick, The.

'Tis (continued)
'Tis Christmas, and the North wind blows. A Christmas Letter from Australia. Douglas Brooke Wheelton Sladen. VA
'Tis Christmas night! The snow. The Light of Bethlehem. John Banister Tabb. CAW; ChIP; MaRV; PoRL
Tis Christmas now, 'tis Christmas now. *Unknown.* SeCSL
'Tis Christmas weather, and a country house. Modern Love, XXIII. George Meredith. ViPo; VP
"'Tis dead night round about: horror [*or* horrour] doth creepe. The Lampe. Henry Vaughan. AnAnS-1; MeP; QFR; SeCL
'Tis death! and peace, indeed, is here. Youth and Calm. Matthew Arnold. MBW-2; PoVP
'Tis done:—I tow'r to that degree. On Taking a Bachelor's Degree. Christopher Smart. VaPo
'Tis done, the edict past, by Heaven decreed. Ode to the Fourth of July. Daniel George. TrAS
'Tis "Done"—the wondrous throughfare. The Pacific Railway. C. R. Ballard. OTD; PAH
'Tis easy enough to be twenty-one. Responsibility. *Unknown.* PV
'Tis education forms the common mind. As the Twig Is Bent. Pope. *Fr.* Moral Essays. TreF
'Tis endless, Sir, to tell the many ways. John Oldham. *Fr.* A Letter from the Country to a Friend in Town. PeRV
'Tis Evanoe's. The House of Splendour. Ezra Pound. InPo
'Tis evening now! Abide with Us. Horatius Bonar. BePJ; VA
'Tis fatal to tyrannic power, when they. Defoe. *Fr.* The Kentish Petition, 1701. PoFr
'Tis fine to play. A Boy's Summer Song. Paul Laurence Dunbar. OTD; RePo; SiSoSe
'Tis fine to see the Old World, and travel up and down. America for Me. Henry van Dyke. BLPA; FaFP; HBVY; MC; MPB; OHFP; OTPC (1946 ed.); PaA; PAL; PCD; PTK; RePo; SP; TreFS; WBLP
'Tis Finished! Samuel Stennett. SoP
'Tis from high life high characters are drawn. The Gem and the Flower. Pope. *Fr.* Moral Essays, Epistle I. OBEC
'Tis God that girds our armor on. The American Soldier's Hymn. *Unknown.* PAH
'Tis gone, that bright and orbed blaze. John Keble. *Fr.* Evening. TrPWD
'Tis gone, the land of dreams! a grayer sky. Conclusion. Lord De Tabley. PoVP
'Tis hard, my friend, to write in such an age. To My Friend Mr. Motteux. Dryden. MBW-1
'Tis Hard to Find God. Robert Herrick. LiTB
'Tis hard to find in life. True Friendship. *Unknown.* *Fr.* Panchatantra. AWP; JAWP; LiTW; WBP
'Tis hard to say, if greater want of skill. An Essay on Criticism. Pope. ATP; BEL; CABA; CEP; CoBE; EiCL; EiPP; EnLi-1; EnLit; FaBoEn; FiP; MBW-1; OAEP; OuHeWo; PoEL-3; PP; TOP; WHA
'Tis held that sorrow makes us wise. In Memoriam A. H. H., CXIII. Tennyson. EPN; ViPo; VP
'Tis highly rational, we can't dispute. Epigram. Richard Garnett. HBV
'Tis human fortune's happiest height, to be. Epigram. Sir William Watson. TreFT
'Tis I Go Fiddling, Fiddling. Nora Hopper. *See* Fairy Fiddler, The.
'Tis Immortality. *Unknown.* *See* There Is No Death.
'Tis, in good truth, a most wonderful thing. Love. Sir William Davenant. *Fr.* The Unfortunate Lovers. SeCL
'Tis known, at least it should be, that throughout. Beppo. Byron. BEL; CABL; ERoP-2
'Tis Late and Cold. John Fletcher. *See* Dead Host's Welcome, The.
'Tis late at night, and in the realm of sleep. To-Morrow. Longfellow. SoP
'Tis late; the astronomer in his lonely height. The Appointment. Sully-Prudhomme. OxBI
'Tis Life Beyond. *Unknown.* MaRV
'Tis life in a half-breed shack. Life in a Half-Breed Shack. *Unknown.* CoSo
'Tis like stirring living embers when, at eighty, one remembers. Grandmother's Story of Bunker Hill Battle. Oliver Wendell Holmes. GoTP; PAH; PAP
'Tis little I can give you, yet I can give you these. Oblation. A. Newberry Choyce. HBMV
'Tis little I could care for pearls. Emily Dickinson. AmPP
'Tis long since, long since, since I heard. The Tin-Whistle Player. Padraic Colum. UnS
T'is madnesse to give physicke to the dead. Upon Castara's Absence. William Habington. *Fr.* Castara. AnAnS-2
'Tis March. Hope Nelson. GFA
'Tis Merry in Greenwood. Sir Walter Scott. *Fr.* Harold the Dauntless. FaPON; MPB; OHIP
'Tis Midnight. *Unknown.* BOHV; NA; RIS
'Tis Midnight; and on Olive's Brow. William Bingham Tappan. SoP
(Gethsemane.) STF
(Jesus Prays Alone.) BePJ
'Tis midnight, and the moonbeam sleeps. The Romaunt of Humpty Dumpty. Henry S. Leigh. BOHV
'Tis midnight, and the setting sun. 'Tis Midnight. *Unknown.* BOHV; NA; RIS
T'is midnight now—athwart the murky air. Epithalamium for Charlotte Corday and Francis Ravaillac. Shelley. HW
'Tis mirth that fills the veins with blood. Mirth [*or* Laugh and Sing]. Beaumont *and* Fletcher. *Fr.* The Knight of the Burning Pestle. EIL; SiCE; TrGrPo
'Tis more than Spaniel's place is worth. Spaniel's Sermon [*or* Bishop Spaniel's Sermons]. Colin Ellis. MemP; PV
'Tis morning; and the sun, with ruddy orb. The Winter Morning Walk. William Cowper. *Fr.* The Task, V. EiCP; PoEL-3
'Tis morning; well; I fain would yet sleep on. Abraham Cowley. *Fr.* Ode upon Liberty. PoFr
'Tis mute, the word they went to hear on high Dodona mountain. The Oracles. A. E. Housman. AnFE; NoP; PoFr; RoGo
'Tis my happiness below. William Cowper. SoP
'Tis mystic union, man and wife. For the Right Honorable Lucy, Countess of Huntingdon, 1649. Thomas Pestel. ReEn
'Tis nearing the noonday on Massabielle. The Canticle of Bernadette. *Unknown.* WHL
'Tis nigh two thousand years. Sir Lewis Morris. *Fr.* Christmas 1898. TrPWD
'Tis no wonder if my songs. Troubadour Song. Bernart of Ventadorn. EnLi-1
Tis noe shame to yeild. *Unknown.* SeCSL
'Tis noonday by the buttonwood, with slender-shadowed bud. The Minute-Men of North-Boro'. Wallace Rice. PAH
'Tis not a freedom that, where all command. Andrew Marvell. *Fr.* The First Anniversary of the Government under His Royal Highness the Lord Protector. PoFr
'Tis not a game that plays at mates and mating. The Flame. Ezra Pound. CoAnAm
'Tis not a pyramid of marble stone. On the Praise of Poetry. Abraham Cowley. CLwM
Tis not Boy the amorous looke. *Unknown.* SeCSL
'Tis not by brooding on delight. Marcus Curtius. Oliver St. John Gogarty. OBMV
'Tis not by guilt the onward sweep. Edward Rowland Sill. *Fr.* The Fool's Prayer. TrPWD
'Tis not enough for one that is a wife. Chorus. Lady Elizabeth Carew. *Fr.* Mariam. LiTL
'Tis not enough that Christ was born. Day Dawn of the Heart. Mary T. Lathrop. ChIP; PGD
'Tis not every [*or* ev'ry] day, that I. Not Every Day Fit for Verse. Robert Herrick. PoRA; SeEP
'Tis not for man to trifle! Life is brief. Life. Horatius Bonar. OQP
'Tis not for works which I have wro't. Accepted. *Unknown.* SoP
'Tis not great, what I solicit. Address to Plenty. John Clare. OBRV
'Tis not her birth, her friends, nor yet her treasure. Why I Love Her. Alexander Brome. HBV; LO
'Tis not how witty, nor how free. Upon Kind[e] and True Love. Aurelian Townsend. CavP; CBEP; EG; MeLP; MePo; OBS; SeCL
'Tis not in blood that Liberty inscribes her civil laws. True Freedom. Charles Mackay. PGD
'Tis not my lady's [*or* ladies] face that makes me love her. Love's without Reason. Alexander Brome. OBS; SeEP
'Tis not so much, these men more forms survey. Charles Lloyd. *Fr.* An Essay on the Genius of Pope. OBRV
'Tis not that both my eyes are black. The Penalties of Baldness. Sir Owen Seaman. FiBHP

'Tis not that dying hurts us so. Emily Dickinson. DiPo
'Tis not that I am weary grown. Upon [His] Leaving His Mistress. Earl of Rochester. EnLoPo; TrGrPo; UnTE; ViBoPo
'Tis not that I design to rob. An Epistle to Robert Lloyd, Esq. William Cowper. FiP
'Tis not the babbling of a busy world. Conscience. Charles Churchill. *Fr.* The Conference. OBEC
'Tis not the President alone. McKinley. *Unknown.* MC; PAH
'Tis not the stones that conquer now, nor the knotted flails. Seventh Station. Paul Claudel. CAW
Tis not the world not what can please. *Unknown.* SeCSL
Tis not thy well-mixd red & whyte. *Unknown.* SeCSL
'Tis not to be told/ What servile villainies men will do for gold. Ben Jonson. *Fr.* The Case Is Altered. LO
'Tis not too late to build our young land right. To Reformers in Despair. Vachel Lindsay. InP
'Tis not what I am fain to hide. My Secret. John Banister Tabb. WaKn
'Tis not your beauty can engage. To Flavia. Edmund Waller. HBV
'Tis now cleare day: I see a rose. The Search. Henry Vaughan. AnAnS-1; MeP; SCEP-1; SeCP
'Tis now since I began to die. To Mris. M[ary] A[wbrey] upon Absence. Katherine Phillips. PeRV
Tis Now Since I Sat[e] Down Before. Sir John Suckling. AnAnS-2; CavP; EnL; PoEL-3; SCEP-2; SeCV-1; SeEP
(Besieged Heart, The.) TrGrPo
(Siege, The). OxBoLi; ReEn; SeCP; ViBoPo
'Tis now the very witching time of night. The Witching Time of Night. Shakespeare. *Fr.* Hamlet, III, ii. TreFT
'Tis now we'd want to be wary, boys. Tipperary Recruiting Song. *Unknown.* OnYI
'Tis of a brisk young Farmer, in Derbyshire did dwel. The Frolicksome Farmer. *Unknown.* CoMu; UnTE
'Tis of a fearless Irishman. Brennan on the Moor. *Unknown.* BaBo
'Tis of a gallant Yankee ship that flew the stripes and stars. The Yankee Man-of-War. *Unknown.* AA; AmSS; EtS; FaBoBe; LaNeLa; PAH; PaPo
'Tis of a little drummer. The Little Drummer. Richard Henry Stoddard. AA; PAH
'Tis of a silk merchant in London I write. The Silk Merchant's Daughter, *vers.* II. *Unknown.* ShS
'Tis of a stately Southerner who flew the Stripes and Stars. The Stately Southerner. *Unknown.* ShS
'Tis of a wild Colonial boy, Jack Doolan was his name. The Wild Colonial Boy. *Unknown.* NeLNL; PoAu-1; ViBoFo
'Tis of Aucassin and Nicolete. Aucassin and Nicolete. *Unknown.* OuHeWo; WoL
'Tis of the Father Hilary. World's Worth. Dante Gabriel Rossetti. GoBC; PoVP
'Tis on Eilanowen. The Faery Reaper. Robert Buchanan. OBVV
'Tis only a half truth the poet has sung. Crowded Ways of Life. Walter J. Gresham. BLPA
'Tis only saints in youth. *Unknown.* *Fr.* The Panchatantra. LiTW
'Tis only with the Bible or with Walt Whitman's verse. To Roosevelt. Rubén Darío. WoL
'Tis pleasant on a fine spring morn. Merry Autumn Days. Charles Dickens. PCH
'Tis pleasant, stretched on grassy lawn. Thomas Caulfield Irwin. *Fr.* Elizabethan Days. IrPN
'Tis pleasing to be schooled in a strange tongue. Byron. *Fr.* Don Juan. ViBoPo
'Tis queer, it is, the ways o' men. The Ways o' Men. Angelina Weld Grimké. CDC
'Tis religion that can give. The Satisfying Portion. *Unknown.* BLRP
'Tis right for her to sleep between. In Memoriam. Richard Monckton Milnes. HBV
'Tis sad to see the sons of learning. He That Never Read a Line. *Unknown.* AnIL
'Tis said, as Cupid danced among. How Roses Came Red. Robert Herrick. ChTr
'Tis said that absence conquers love! Song. Frederick William Thomas. AA; HBV
'Tis Said, That Some Have Died for Love. Wordsworth. EnRP; LO; MERP
'Tis said that the gods on Olympus of old. The Mint Julep. Charles Fenno Hoffman. AA; AmePo
'Tis said the Gods lower down that chain above. George Alsop. SCAP
'Tis Sair to Dream. Robert Gilfillan. VA
'Tis so appalling-it exhilirates. Emily Dickinson. MWA-2
'Tis so old and ugly, and yet so convenient. On Gaulstown House. Swift. CBEP
'Tis solemn darkness; the sublime of shade. Night. Charles Heavysege. OBCV
'Tis something from that tangle to have won. Icarus. Harry Lyman Koopman. AA
'Tis Sorrow Builds the Shining Ladder Up. James Russell Lowell. *Fr.* On the Death of a Friend's Child. MaRV; WGRP
'Tis splendid to live so grandly. Washington's Birthday. Margaret E. Sangster. HH; PEDC
'Tis spring; come out to ramble. The Lent Lily. A. E. Housman. A Shropshire Lad, XXIX. MPB; OHIP; PoRL; PoSC; PoVP
'Tis spring, warm glows the south. Bird's Nests. John Clare. ERoP-2
'Tis strange how my head runs on! 'tis a puzzle to understand. The City Clerk. Thomas Ashe. OBVV
'Tis strange that absence often does. At the Garden Rail. A. M. Buckton. BoSA
'Tis strange, the miser should his cares employ. Of [*or* On] the Use of Riches [*or* To Richard Boyle, Earl of Burlington]. Pope. *Fr.* Moral Essays. BWP; CABL; EiCL; EiPP; MBW-1; PoEL-3
'Tis Strange to Me. Hartley Coleridge. NCEP
(From Country to Town.) CBEP; OBRV
'Tis sweet to trace the setting sun. The Setting Sun. George Moses Horton. BALP
'Tis sweet to view, from half-past five to six. The Theatre. James Smith. Par
'Tis Sunday at home. Vespers. Louis Mercier. CAW
'Tis Sweet [to Hear]. Byron. *Fr.* Don Juan, I. MaPo; MCCG
(First Love.) OBRV
(Pleasant Things, *shorter sel.*) OTPC (1923 ed.)
("Tis sweet to hear.") ViBoPo
'Tis sweet at dewy eve to rove. Rural Raptures. *Unknown.* BOHV
. . .'Tis sweet to hear,/ At midnight on the blue and moonlit deep. 'Tis Sweet [*or* First Love]. Byron. *Fr.* Don Juan, I. MaPo; MCCG; OBRV; OTPC (1923 ed.); ViBoPo
'Tis sweet to hear of heroes dead. The Great Adventure. Henry David Thoreau. HBV; OBVV
'Tis sweet to hear the merry lark. The Lark and the Nightingale [*or* Song]. Hartley Coleridge. HBV; OTPC (1923 ed.)
'Tis Sweet to Roam. *Unknown.* BOHV; NA
'Tis the Arabian bird alone. The Chaste Arabian Bird. Earl of Rochester. ErPo; SiTL
'Tis the blithest, bonniest weather for a bird to flirt a feather. Robin's Secret. Katharine Lee Bates. AA
'Tis the cause of my anguish and grief of heart. The Maiden's Complaint. Brian Merriman. *Fr.* The Midnight Court. LiTW
'Tis the hour of fairy ban and spell. Fairy Dawn. Joseph Rodman Drake. *Fr.* The Culprit Fay. GN
'Tis the hour when white-horsed Day. Morning. Charles Stuart Calverley. FiBHP; NBM
'Tis the human touch in this world that counts. The Human Touch. Spencer Michael Free. FaBoBe; MaRV; NeHB; PoToHe
'Tis the Last Rose of Summer. Thomas Moore. ATP; BEL; BLPA; BoNaP; ELP; EnLi-2 (1949 ed.); EnLit; HBV; NeHB; PG (1945 ed.); PoEL-4; PoPl; TreF; WBLP; WHA
(Last Rose of Summer, The.) FaBoBe; FaFP; OnYI; OxBoLi
'Tis the laughter of pines that swing and sway. The Phantom Light of the Baie des Chaleurs. Arthur Wentworth Hamilton Eaton. CaP; PoMS
'Tis the little kindly acts you do. Little Things. Maud Rose. SoP
'Tis the merry nightingale. The Nightingale. Samuel Taylor Coleridge. OBRV
'Tis the middle of night by the castle clock. Christabel. Samuel Taylor Coleridge. BEL; CH; CoBE; EnL; EnLi-2; EnLit; EnRP; EPN; ERoP-1; FiP; GoTL; MBW-2; MERP; OAEP; OBRV; SeCePo; ShBV-3; TOP; WHA

'Tis the rose of the desert. Written to a Young Lady. Jeremiah Joseph Callanan. IrPN
'Tis the voice of a sluggard . . . *See* 'Tis the voice of the sluggard . . .
'Tis the voice of the Lobster; I heard him declare. The Voice of the Lobster. "Lewis Carroll." *Fr.* Alice's Adventures in Wonderland. EvOK; Par; SAS; SiTL
'Tis the voice of the [*or* a] sluggard; I heard him complain. The Sluggard. Isaac Watts. CEP; CH; EiCL; HBV; HBVY; MoShBr; OBEC; OnPP; OTD; OTPC; OxBoLi; PaPo; Par; PoEL-3; ThGo; TreFS
'Tis the white anemone, fashioned so like the stars of the winter snow. "Owen Meredith." *Fr.* The White Anemone. GN; OTPC
'Tis the White Plum Tree. John Shaw Neilson. BoAV; PoAu-1
'Tis the year's [*or* yeares] midnight, and it is the day's [*or* dayes]. A Nocturnal[l] upon St. Lucy's [*or* S. Lucies] Day, Being the Shortest Day. John Donne. AnAnS-1; AtBAP; BoW; CBEP; EnLP; EnRePo; EP; FaBoEn; GTBS-W; LiTB; LiTG; MaMe; MaPo; MBW-1; MeLP; MeP; MePo; NoP; OBS; PIA; PoE; PoEL-2; ReIE; SCEP-1; SeCP; SeCV-1; SeEP; TuPP
'Tis these that free the small entangled fly. Shakespeare: The Fairies' Advocate. Thomas Hood. *Fr.* The Plea of the Midsummer Fairies. OBNC
'Tis they, of a veritie. Deid Folks' Ferry. Rosamund Marriott Watson. VA
'Tis Time, I Think, by Wenlock Town. A. E. Housman. *See* Wenlock.
'Tis time this heart should be unmoved. On This Day I Complete My Thirty-sixth Year. Byron. AnFE; BEL; CABA; CoBE; EnL; EnLi-2; EnLit; EnRP; EPN; ERoP-2; FiP; HBV; ILP; MaPo; MBW-2; MCCG; MERP; NoP; OAEP; OnPP; PAn; PeER; TreFT; ViBoPo; YAT
Tis to yourself I speak; you cannot know. Yourself. Jones Very. AA; AmLP; MAmP; NePA; OxBA; PoEL-4; Sonn
'Tis told by one whom stormy waters threw. Wordsworth. *Fr.* The Prelude, VI. ImOP
'Tis Too Late for a Coach. *Unknown.* SeCL
Tis true (deare Ben:) thy just chastizing hand. To Ben Jonson [*or* Johnson]. Thomas Carew. AnAnS-2; MePo; SCEP-2
'Tis true, fair Celia, that by thee I live. Against Platonick Love. *Unknown.* OBS
'Tis true. I am fettered. Chains. Patrick Carey. SeCL
'Tis true, I never was in love. A Mock Song. Alexander Brome. SeCL
'Tis true, I'm broke! Vowes, oathes, and all I had. An Elegie. Ben Jonson. AnAnS-2
'Tis true, no lover has that pow'r. The Art of Love. Samuel Butler. *Fr.* Hudibras. FaBoEn
'Tis true, one half of woman's life is hope. Her Horoscope. Mary Ashley Townsend. AA
Tis true that he is dead: but yet to chuse. An Elegy upon the Death of My Lord Francis Villiers. Andrew Marvell. MaMe
'Tis true the beauteous star. A Paradox. Richard Lovelace. Po
'Tis true, then why should I repine. In Sickness. Swift. CEP; OBEC
'Tis true, 'tis day; what though it be? Break [*or* Breake] of Day. John Donne. CABA; EG; EnRePo; ErPo; LiTB; LiTG; LiTL; MaMe; PoeP; TuPP
'Tis twelve o'clock! Within my prison dreary. New Year's Eve. F. A. Bartleson. PAP
'Tis Uha has hair looped and twisty like horns of the kine. Una Bhan. Robert Farren. JKCP (1955 ed.)
"'Tis very sad," the onion said. The Onion. C. C. Ward. PCH
'Tis weak and worldly to conclude. The Retirement. *Unknown.* OBEC
'Tis well; 'tis something; we may stand. In Memoriam A. H. H., XVIII. Tennyson. EnLi-2; EPN; ViPo; VP
'Tis well, 'tis well with them, say I. All-over Love. Abraham Cowley. *Fr.* The Mistress. LiTL; SeCL
'Tis well you think me truly one of those. To John Keats. Leigh Hunt. Sonn
'Tis what they say. The Red Man's Wife. *Unknown, tr. by* Douglas Hyde. OnYI; OxBI; SeCePo
'Tis where the road-side rivulet expands. Girls Going to the Fair. William Allingham. IrPN
'Tis wine that inspires. The Excellency of Wine. Roger Boyle Earl of Orrery. SeCL; SeEP
'Tis with our judgments as our watches. Pope. *Fr.* An Essay on Criticism. ViBoPo
'Tis years since last we met. Her Bright Smile. *Unknown.* SoAmSa
'Tis you that are the music, not your song. Listening. Amy Lowell. PoPo
Tisket, a Tasket, A. *Unknown. See* Itiskit, Itaskit.
Tit for Tat. Esther Antin. RIS
Tit for Tat. Walter de la Mare. UTS
Tit-tat-toe,/ My first go. A Baby Verse. *Unknown.* BoTP; OxNR
Tit-Willow. W. S. Gilbert. *See* Suicide's Grave, The.
Titan! to whose immortal eyes. Prometheus. Byron. EnRP; EPN; ERoP-2; VaPo
Titania. Thomas Hood. *Fr.* The Plea of the Midsummer Fairies. OBRV
Titania's Bower. Shakespeare. *See* Violet Bank, A.
Titanic, The, sels. E. J. Pratt.
  Iceberg, The. TwCaPo
  Isador and Ida Strauss. TwCaPo
  "Out on the water was the same display." PeCV
Titanic, The ("It was on one Monday morning"). *Unknown.* ViBoFo
Titanic, De ("De rich folks 'cided to take a trip"), *with music. Unknown.* AS
Titan's Lament. Alex Raybin. ThO
Tithonus. Tennyson. BWP; CABA; CABL; CBEP; CBV; DiPo; EnL; EPN; FaBoEn; ForPo; FosPo; GTBS-D; ILP; LiTB; LoBV; MaPo (1969 ed.); MBW-2; NoP; OAEP; OBNC; PAn; PoAn; PoE; PoEL-5; PoFS; PoVP; TOP; ViPo; ViPP; VP; WHA
Tithonus. D. M. Thomas. HYE
Title divine—is mine! Emily Dickinson. AmePo; AP; ViBoPo
Titles. Justin Richardson. ShBV-3
  (What'll Be the Title?) FiBHP
Titmouse. Walter de la Mare. BrPo
Titmouse, The. Emerson. PRWS
  Chickadee, *sel.* FaPON; GFA; OTPC (1946 ed.); PCH
Titty cum tawtay. *Unknown.* OxNR
Titus and Berenice. John Heath-Stubbs. GTBS-P
Titus oft vaunts his gentry everywhere. Of Titus. Everard Guilpin. *Fr.* Skialetheia. ReIE; SiCE; TuPP
Titus reads neither prose nor rhyme. The Writer. Hildebrand Jacob. SiTL
Titus, the brave and valorous young gallant. In Titum. Sir John Davies. ReIE; TuPP
Titwillow. W. S. Gilbert. *See* Suicide's Grave, The.
Tityrus to His Fair Phyllis. John Dickenson. *Fr.* The Shepherd's Complaint. EIL
To/ The territory of the non-memory. The Image Reach. Sun-Ra. BF
To ——: "All good things have not kept aloof." Tennyson. OBRV
To ——: "Asleep within the deadest hour of the night." Robert Nichols. HBMV
To ——: "Ay, thou art for the grave; thy glances shine." Bryant. Sonn
To ——: "Broken moon lay, The." Alexander Smith. VA
To ——: "Had I a man's fair form, then might my sighs." Keats. Sonn
To ——: "Half in the dim light from the hall." William Stanley Braithwaite. BALP
To ——: "I fear thy kisses, gentle maiden." Shelley. *See* I Fear Thy Kisses . . .
To ——? "I have baptized thee Withy, because of thy slender limbs." Richard Dehmel, *tr. fr. German by* Jethro Bithell. AWP
To ——, in Her Seventieth Year. Wordsworth. BWP
To ——: "Lady — the lyre thou bid'st me take." Jeremiah Joseph Callanan. IrPN
To ——, M.D. Leigh Hunt. Sonn
To ——: "Music, when soft voices die." Shelley. *See* Music, When Soft Voices Die.
To ——: "Not long ago, the writer of these lines." Poe. MWA-1
To ——: "Oh! there are spirits of the air." Shelley. *See* To Coleridge.
To ——: "One word is too often profaned." Shelley. *See* One Word Is Too Often Profaned.

To ——: "Take this kiss upon thy brow!" Poe. *See* Dream within a Dream.
To ——: "They could not shut you out of heaven." Katharine Duncan Morse. HBMV
To ——: "Thou whom of all the beings I have seen." George Darley. Sonn
To ——: "Time's sea hath been five years at its slow ebb." Keats. SyP
To ——: "We met but in one giddy dance." Winthrop Mackworth Praed. HBV
To ——: "When I loved you, I can't but allow." Thomas Moore. *See* When I Loved You.
To ——: "When passion's trance is overpast." Shelley. EnRP
To ——: With the Following Poem. Tennyson. *Introd. poem to* The Palace of Art. MBW-2; ViPo; ViPP; VP
To a Baffled Idealist. J. G. E. Hopkins. JKCP (1926 ed.); MaRV
To a Baked Fish. Carolyn Wells. FiBHP
To a Beautiful but Heartless Coquette. Francisco de Terrazas, *tr. fr. Spanish by* Peter H. Goldsmith. LiTW
To a Bee. Robert Southey. OTPC
To a Believer. Marjorie Pickthall. PeCV
To a Bird after a Storm. Henry Vaughan. *See* Bird, The.
To a Black Dog, Bereaved. Elizabeth J. Coatsworth. PCD
To a Black Greyhound. Julian Grenfell. OtMeF
To a Blockhead. Pope. BOHV
(Epigram: "You beat your pate, and fancy wit will come.") HBV; SiTL; TreFT
(You Beat Your Pate.) MemP
To a Blue Flower. John Shaw Neilson. BoAV; PoAu-1
To a Blue Hippopotamus. Ellen Kay. ForPo; NePoEA
To a Book. Elinor Wylie. LiTA
To a Boon Companion. Oliver St. John Gogarty. OBMV
(Boon Companion, The.) OtMeF
To a Boy. *Unknown, tr. fr. Irish by* Frank O'Connor. KiLC
To a Boy-Poet of the Decadence. Sir Owen Seaman. CenHV; FiBHP
To a Bride. Sappho, *tr. fr. Greek by* Walter Headlam. WoL
(Fragment of Sappho, *tr. by* Ambrose Philips.) OBEC
(Ode: "Peer of gods he seemeth to me, the blissful," *tr. by* John Addington Symonds.) LiTW
(Ode to Anactoria.) AWP, *tr. by* William Ellery Leonard
(Peer of the Gods, *tr. by* John Addington Symonds.) EnLi-1
To a Butterfly. Lady Flora Hastings. OTPC (1923 ed.)
To a Butterfly ("I've watched you"). Wordsworth. BWP; GoTP; HBV; OTPC; SeCeV
("I've watched you now a full half-hour.") EG
To a Butterfly ("Stay near me . . .") Wordsworth. EnRP
To a Candle. Walter de la Mare. ChMP; ELP; GTBS-D
To a Capricious Friend. Martial. *See* Temperament.
To a Captious Critic. Paul Laurence Dunbar. Kal
To a Carmelite Postulant. Michael Earls. CAW; JKCP
To a Cat. Samuel Hoffenstein. CIV
To a Cat. Keats. BoC; FaBoCh
(Sonnet to Mrs. Reynold's Cat.) CIV
(To Mrs. Reynold's Cat.) DiPo
To a Cat. Fanny Elizabeth Perkins. CIV
To a Cat. Swinburne. CIV
To a Cat Purring. Florence Small Edsall. CIV
To a Caty-did. Philip Freneau. AA; AmP; AmPP; CoBA; LHV
To a Certain Civilian. Walt Whitman. CoBA
To a Certain Lady, in Her Garden. Sterling A. Brown. CDC
To a Certain Woman. Albert Rice. CDC
To a Chameleon. Marianne Moore. GoYe; PoPl
To a Cherokee Rose. William Hamilton Hayne. AA
To a Child. S. S. Gardons. NePoEA-2
To a Child. Robert Herrick. *See* To His Saviour, a Child; a Present by a Child.
To a Child. Charles Kingsley. BoTP
To a Child, *sel.* Longfellow.
"By what astrology of fear or hope." FaBoEn
To a Child. David McCord. AnAmPo
To a Child. George Edgar Montgomery. AA
To a Child. Christopher Morley. BiCB; HBMV
To a Child. Norreys Jephson O'Conor. HBMV
To a Child. Wilfred Owen. Sonn
To a Child. John Sterling. VA
To a Child. Wordsworth. HBV; HBVY
(In a Child's Album.) GN; PCH
(Small Service.) MemP
(Written in the Album of a Child, *diff.*) OBNC; OBRV
To a Child. Judith Wright. BoAV
To a Child at the Piano. Alastair Reid. MuSP
To a Child before Birth. Norman Nicholson. ChMP
To a Child in Death. Charlotte Mew. MoAB; MoBrPo; POTE
To a Child of Fancy. Lewis Morris. HBV
To a Child of Noble Birth. Matthew Prior. *See* Letter to the Honourable Lady Miss Margaret Cavendish-Holles-Harley, A.
To a Child of Quality [of Five Years Old]. Matthew Prior. CBEP; CoBE; EiCL; EiCP; EiPP; ExPo; GN; GTBS-W; HBV; InP; LiTB; OBEC; OBEV; PoEL-3; SeCeV; VaPo
To a Child Who Inquires. Olga Petrova. BLPA
To a Child with Eyes. Mark Van Doren. LOW; PCH
To a Cloistress. Juan de Tassis, *tr. fr. Spanish by* Felicia Dorothea Hemans. CAW
To a Cloud. Manuel Altolaguirre, *tr. fr. Spanish by* Harold Morland. LiTW
To a Commencement of Scoundrels. Samuel Hazo. WOW
To a Common Prostitute. Walt Whitman. AnAmPo; MAP; MoAmPo; ViBoPo
To a Comrade in Arms. Alun Lewis. FaBoTw; MoBrPo (1962 ed.)
To a Conscript of 1940. Sir Herbert Read. ChMP; ExPo; LiTB; LiTM; WaP
To a Contemporary Bunkshooter. Carl Sandburg. CoBA; WGRP
To a Coquet Beauty. John Sheffield, Duke of Buckingham and Normanby. CEP
To a Cricket. William Cox Bennett. BoTP; GN; HBV; OTPC
To a Crow. Robert Burns Wilson. AA
To a Crucifix. Anna Wickham. MoBrPo
To A. D. W. E. Henley. Echoes, XVIII. AnFE; BEL; HoPM; OuHeWo; PoVP; TOP; ViBoPo
(Blackbird, The.) HBV; MoBrPo; NeMA; TrGrPo; TSW
(Nightingale, The.) MeWo
To a Cyclamen. Walter Savage Landor. VA
To a Daisy. John Hartley. VA
To a Daisy. Alice Meynell. JKCP; MoBrPo; Sonn; WGRP
To a Dark Girl. Gwendolyn B. Bennett. BANP; CDC
To a Dead Cricket. Mnasalcas, *ad. fr. Greek by* Louis Untermeyer. RIS
To a Dead Elephant. Douglas Livingstone. PeSA
To a Dead Journalist. William Carlos Williams. QFR
To a Dead Poet, His Book. Daniel Berrigan. ML
To a Deaf and Dumb Little Girl. Hartley Coleridge. PoEL-4
To a Dear Friend Lately Given Over to Covetousness. Thomas Lodge. *Fr.* A Fig for Momus. SiCE
To a Defeated Saviour. James Wright. NePoEA
To a Departing Favorite. George Moses Horton. BALP
To a Depraved Lying Woman. Sorley Maclean. NeBP
To a Desolate Friend. William James Dawson. VA
To a Discarded Steel Rail. Maxwell Bodenheim. NP; PFY
To a Distant Friend. Wordsworth. *See* Why Art Thou Silent!
To a Dog. Anna Hempstead Branch. MAP; MoAmPo (1942 ed.)
To a Dog. Josephine Preston Peabody. BLPA; WGRP
To a Dog Barking at Night. Francis Maguire. NYTB
To a Dog Injured in the Street. William Carlos Williams. LiTM (1970 ed.); MoAB; NePoAm; PP; SeCeV
To a Dog's Memory. Louise Imogen Guiney. AnAmPo
To A. E. Housman. Witter Bynner. NYTB
To a Fair Gentlewoman, False to Her Friend. George Turberville. TuPP
To a Fair Lady Playing with a Snake. Edmund Waller. HoPM; NCEP; SCEP-2
(Of a Fair Lady Playing with a Snake.) PoEL-3
To a Fair Young Lady, Going Out of [the] Town in the Spring. Dryden. *See* Song to a Fair Young Lady . . .
To a Faithless Lover. Robert Greacen. OnYI
To a Fat Lady Seen from the Train. Frances Cornford. BLPA; ELU; GoJo; LiTM; MoBrPo; NeMA; OBMV; OnPP; SiTL; WePo; YT
To a Field Mouse. Burns. *See* To a Mouse.
To a Fish. Leigh Hunt. *Fr.* The Fish, the Man, and the Spirit. BoC; FiBHP; OA
To a Flea in a Glass of Water. D. A. Greig. PeSA

To a Fly. William Oldys. *See* On a Fly Drinking Out of His Cup.
To a Fly. "Peter Pindar." BOHV
To a Foil'd European Revolutionaire, *sel.* Walt Whitman.
"Not songs of loyalty alone are these." PoFr
To a Friend. Matthew Arnold. EnLi-2; EPN; MBW-2; OAEP; PoVP; Sonn; ViPo; ViPP; VP
To a Friend. William Lisle Bowles. Sonn
To a Friend. Hartley Coleridge. CBEP; HBV; OBRV; PoLF
(Friendship.) NBM; OBEV
(Sonnet: To a Friend.) ERoP-2; OBNC
To a Friend. Grace Strickler Dawson. BLPA; NeHB
To a Friend. Charles Gullans. NePoEA
To a Friend. Amy Lowell. PoLF
To a Friend. Jean Valentine. TPM
To a Friend in Praise of Music and Poetry. Richard Barnfield. *See* To His Friend Master R. L.
To a Friend in the Country. Oliver St. John Gogarty. OnYI
To a Friend in the Wilderness, *sel.* A. R. D. Fairburn.
"Old friend, dear friend." AnNZ
To a Friend, Inviting Him to a Meeting Upon Promise. William Habington. AnAnS-2
To a Friend, on Her Examination for the Doctorate in English. J. V. Cunningham. EiCP; TwAmPo
To a Friend on His Marriage. F. T. Prince. LiTM
To a Friend on His Nuptials. Matthew Prior. HW
To a Friend Whose Work Has Come to Nothing. W. B. Yeats. AnFE; AWP; BoC; DiPo; ForPo; GTBS-W; InPo; JAWP; LiTG; LiTM (rev. ed.); MBW-2; MoAB; MoBrPo; NP; OBMV; WBP
To a Fugitive. James Wright. TPM
To a Gardener. Robert Louis Stevenson. AnEnPo
To a Gentleman in Love with a Negro Woman. Sneyd Davies. WaPE
To a Gentlewoman Objecting to Him His Gray Hairs. Robert Herrick.
(Age Not to Be Rejected, *sl. diff.*) OBS
To a Gipsy Child by the Sea-Shore. Matthew Arnold. PAn; ViPP
To a Giraffe. Marianne Moore. TDP
To a Girl. Horace, *tr. fr. Latin by* Milton. Odes, I, 5. WiR
To a Girl. Edmund Waller. *See* To a Very Young Lady.
To a Gnat. *Unknown. tr. fr. Greek by* Louis Untermeyer. UnTE
To a Golden-haired Girl in a Louisiana Town. Vachel Lindsay. MAP; MoAmPo; MoLP; NeMA
To a Golden Heart, Worn round [*or* around] His Neck. Goethe, *tr. fr. German by* Margaret Fuller Ossoli. AWP; JAWP; LiTW; WBP
To a good man of most dear memory. Wordsworth. *Fr.* Written after the Death of Charles Lamb. CoBE
To a Good Physician. William Wycherley. ACP
To a Goose. Robert Southey. Sonn
To a Greek Girl. Austin Dobson. HBV; VA
To a Greek Ship in the Port of Dublin. William Bedell Stanford. NeIP
To a Happy Warrior. Wilfrid Scawen Blunt. AnEnPo
To a Hedge-Sparrow. *Unknown.* OTPC (1923 ed.)
To a Highland Girl. Wordsworth. CABL; EnRP; EPN; LoBV; TreFT, *abr.*
(To the Highland Girl of Inversneyde.) GTBS; GTBS-D; GTBS-P; GTBS-W; GTSE; GTSL
To a Honey Bee. Philip Freneau. *See* On a Honey Bee.
To a History Professor. *Unknown, tr. fr. Greek by* Louis Untermeyer. UnTE
To a Human Skeleton. Richard Armour. WhC
To a Humble Bug. Linda Lyon Van Voorhis. GoYe
To a Humming Bird in a Garden. George Murray. VA
To a Hurt Child. Grace Denio Litchfield. AA
To a Jack Rabbit. S. Omar Barker. IHA
To a Japanese Girl Grieved over the War on China. Belle Chapman Morrill. MaRV
To a June Breeze. H. C. Bunner. AA
To a Junior Waiter. A. P. Herbert. FiBHP
To a king who had. King Rufus. Y. Y. Segal. WHW
To a Kiss. "Peter Pindar." HBV
To a Kitten. Martha Haskell Clark. CIV
To a Kitten. Rena M. Manning. CIV
To A. L.: Perswasions to Love. Thomas Carew. AnAnS-2; SeCP
To a Lad Who Would Wed Himself with Music. Edward Doro. TwAmPo
To a Lady. Franklin P. Adams. FiBHP
To a Lady. William Dunbar. CLwM; GoBC, *mod. vers. by* Belle Cooper; OBEV
(Sweet Rose of Virtue.) EG; MeEL
(To a Ladye.) OAEP; OxBS
To a Lady. Sir George Etherege. *See* To a Lady Asking Him How Long He Would Love Her.
To a Lady. John Gay. OBEC; OBEV (new ed.)
To a Lady. Thomas William Parsons. AA
To a Lady. John James Piatt. AA
To a Lady. Pope. *See* Of the Characters of Women.
To a Lady across the Way. E. B. White. InMe
To a Lady Asking [Him] How Long He Would Love Her. Sir George Etherege. CEP; HBV; LiTL; LO; LoBV; MeWo; OBEV; OBS, *diff. vers.*; SeCL; SeEP; ViBoPo
(Lines to a Lady, Who Asked of Him How Long He Would Love Her.) EG
(To a Lady.) OnPM
To a Lady Friend. W. H. Davies. MoBrPo
To a Lady Holding the Floor. Mildred Weston. FiBHP
To a Lady in a Garden. Edmund Waller. NCEP
To a Lady in a Letter. Earl of Rochester. PeRV; SeEP
To a Lady; of the Characters of Women. Pope. *See* Of the Characters of Women.
To a Lady on Her Marriage. William Bell. NePoEA
To a Lady on Her Passion for Old China. John Gay. EiPP; FaFP; LiTB; LoBV; PoE; SiTL
To a Lady Playing and Singing in the Morning. Thomas Hardy. TOP
To a Lady; She Refusing to Continue a Dispute with Me, and Leaving Me in the Argument. Matthew Prior. CEP; EiCL; EiPP; LiTL; SeCL; WHA
To a Lady Singing a Song of His Own Composing. Edmund Waller. ReEn; SeCL; SeEP
To a Lady Sitting before Her Glass. Elijah Fenton. OBEC
To a Lady That Desired I Would Love Her. Thomas Carew. AnAnS-2; BWP; CavP; EP; LiTL; LoBV; MeLP; MePo; OBS; SCEP-2; SeCL; SeCV-1; SeEP
To a Lady That Desired Me I Would Bear My Part with Her in a Song. Richard Lovelace. MuSP
To a Lady to Answer Directly with Yea or Nay. Sir Thomas Wyatt. CLwM; ElL; PoFS; ReIE; TuPP
(Madam, withouten Many Words.) CBEP; EnRePo; NoP
(Madame, withouten Many Words.) CABA; EP
("Madame, withouten many words.") EG; EnLoPo; FCP; LO; ReEn; SiPS
(To His Lady.) OBSC; SeCePo
To a Lady Troubled by Insomnia. Franklin P. Adams. InMe
To a Lady Who Desired I Would Write Verses in the Heroic Style, *sel.* Swift.
"Should a monkey wear a crown." PoFr
To a Lady Who Did Sing Excellently. Lord Herbert of Cherbury. AnAnS-2; OBS; SeCP
To a Lady Who Sent Me a Copy of Verses at My Going to Bed. Henry King. PP
To a Lady with a Guitar. Shelley. *See* With a Guitar, to Jane.
To a Lady with Flowers from the Roman Wall. Sir Walter Scott. OAEP
To a Ladye. William Dunbar. *See* To a Lady.
To a Lark in War-Time. Franz Werfel, *tr. fr. German by* Edith Abercrombie Snow. TrJP
To a Lily. James Matthew Legaré. AA; AnAmPo
To a Linnet in a Cage. Francis Ledwidge. OnYI; RoGo
To a Little Girl. Helen Parry Eden. HBV; OTPC (1923 ed.)
To a Little Girl. Gustav Kobbé. HBV
To a Little Girl Gathering Flowers. Mary Tighe. OTPC (1923 ed.)
To a Little Girl, One Year Old, in a Ruined Fortress. Robert Penn Warren. FiMAP
Colder Fire, *sel.* LiTM (1970 ed.)
("It rained toward day. The morning came sad and white.") MoVE
To a Little Sister, Aged Ten. Alison Elizabeth Cummings. BiCB
To a Living Author. *Unknown.* SiTL
To a Lock of Hair. Sir Walter Scott. GTBS; GTBS-D; GTBS-P; GTBS-W; GTSE
To a Locomotive in Winter. Walt Whitman. AmLP; AmPP;

AP; DiPo; FaBV; ILP; InP; MCCG; MoAmPo (1950 ed.); NoP; PoE; PoEL-5; PoFS; StP
To a lodge that stood. Wordsworth. *Fr.* The Prelude: Vaudracour and Julia. EvOK
To a Lofty Beauty, from Her Poor Kinsman. Hartley Coleridge. OBVV
To a Lost Sweetheart, *sels.* Don Marquis.
"I oft stand in the snow at dawn." FiBHP
"When Whistler's Mother's Picture's frame." FiBHP
To a Louse [On Seeing One on a Lady's Bonnet at Church]. Burns. BLPA; CEP; CoBE; EiCL; EnL; EnLit; EnRP; FaFP; ILP; InvP; LiTB; LiTG; OAEP; OxBS; PAn; Po; PoE; PoPo; SeCeV; SiTL; TreF; ViBoPo; WoL; YAT
As Others See Us, *sel.* MaRV
To a lovely mirtle bound. To My Mirtle. Blake. HW
To a Madonna. John Gray, *after* Baudelaire. SyP
To a Magnolia Flower in the Garden of the Armenian Convent at Venice. Silas Weir Mitchell. AA
To a Man in a Picture Window Watching Television. Mildred Weston. ELU
To a Man on His Horse. F. T. Prince. MoPW
To a Maple Seed. Lloyd Mifflin. AA
To a Married Couple That Could Not Agree. Martial, *tr. fr. Latin by* Timothe Kendall. TuPP
To a Marsh Hawk in Spring. Henry David Thoreau. PoEL-4
To a Mate. Roland Robinson. NeLNL
To a Mayflower. William E. Marshall. CaP
To a' men living be it kend. The Rising of the Session. Robert Fergusson. OxBS
To a Military Rifle. Yvor Winters. MoAmPo (1962 ed.); WaP
To a Mistress Dying. Sir William Davenant. BWP; GoBC; OBEV
(Lover and Philosopher.) ACP
(Philosopher and the Lover, The.) FaBoEn; LO; MePo
To a Mole. Louise Darcy. NYTB
To a Monkey. Marjory Fleming. *See* Sonnet on a Monkey, A.
To a Mosquito. Bryant. AnNE
To a Moth. Charles Edward Thomas. AA
To a Moth That Drinketh of the Ripe October. Emily Pfeiffer. VA
To a Mountain. Henry Clarence Kendall. NeLNL, *abr.*; VA
To a Mountain Daisy [On Turning One Down, with the Plow, in April, 1786]. Burns. AnEnPo; ATP; BEL; CEP; EiCL; EiPP; EnLi-2; EnLit; EnRP; GN, *abr.*; HBV; MPB; OAEP; OTPC (1923 ed.), *much abr.*; PoLF; UnPo (1st ed.); WBLP
(Daisy, The.) BoNaP
To a Mouse [on Turning Her Up in Her Nest with the Plough, November, 1785]. Burns. AnEnPo; AnFE; ATP; BBV (1923 ed.); BEL; BoLiVe; CBV; CEP; CoBE; DiPo; EiCL; EiCP; EiPP; EnL; EnLi-2; EnLit; EnRP; FaFP; FosPo; GoTS; GTBS; GTBS-D; GTBS-W; GTSL; HBV; HBVY; ILP; LiTG; LoBV; MCCG; MPB; NoP; OA; OAEP; OBEC; OTPC; OuHeWo; OxBS; PAn; PoAn; PoFS; PoIE; PoLF; PoMa; RG; SeCeV; ShBV-2; TIHL; TOP; TreFS; TrGrPo; WaKn; WHA
(To a Field Mouse.) CBEP; GTBS-P; GTSE
To a Musician. George Wither. *See* For a Musician.
To a Mute Musician. E. Margaret Clarkson. SoP
To a Negro Boy Graduating. Eugene T. Maleska. PoNe (1970 ed.)
To a New-born Baby Girl. Grace Hazard Conkling. HBV
To a New-born Child. Cosmo Monkhouse. HBV
To a New Daughter-in-Law. *Unknown.* PoToHe (new ed.)
To a New York Shop Girl Dressed for Sunday. Anna Hempstead Branch. HBV
To a Nightingale. William Drummond of Hawthornden. OBS
To a Nightingale. Keats. *See* Ode to a Nightingale.
To a Painted Lady. Alexander Brome. CavP
To a Pair of Egyptian Slippers. Sir Edwin Arnold. HBV; OBVV
To a Passer-by. Baudelaire, *tr. fr. French by* C. F. MacIntyre. SyP
To a Perjur'd Mistress. Sir Francis Fane. PeRV
To a Persistent Phantom. Frank Horne. AmNP; BANP; CDC
To a Pet Cobra. Roy Campbell. AtBAP
To a place of ruined stone we brought you, and sea-reaches. To a Little Girl, One Year Old, in a Ruined Fortress. Robert Penn Warren. FiMAP
To a Plagiarist. Moses ibn Ezra, *tr. fr. Hebrew by* Solomon Solis-Cohen. TrJP
To a Phoebe Bird. Witter Bynner. HBMV; YT
To a Photograph. John Banister Tabb. AmP
To a Photograph. Parker Tyler. NePA
To a Plain Sweetheart. T. A. Daly. JKCP
To a Poet. Walter Conrad Arensberg. AnAmPo
To a Poet. Sister Mary Angelita. GoBC
To a Poet. Carolyn Wells. PoMa
To a Poet a Thousand Years Hence. James Elroy Flecker. ChTr; HBV; InP; MemP; MoBrPo; MoPW; PoRA; ShBV-4; TrGrPo (1942 ed.)
To a Poet Breaking Silence. Francis Thompson. VA
To a Poet Who Has Had a Heart Attack. Richard Eberhart. ML
To a Poet Who Has Never Travelled. Charles Causley. POTE (1959 ed.)
To a Poet, Who Would Have Me Praise Certain Bad Poets, Imitators of His and Mine. W. B. Yeats. CTC; ML; PV
To a Poetic Lover. Martial, *tr. fr. Latin by* W. Hay. ALV
To a Polish Mother. Adam Mickiewicz, *tr. fr. Polish.* CAW, *tr. by* Jewell Parish *and* George R. Noyes; LiTW, *tr. by* Watson Kirkconnell
To a Poor Old Woman. William Carlos Williams. OnPM; TDP
To a Portrait. Arthur Symons. VA
To a Portrait of Whistler in the Brooklyn Art Museum. Eleanor Rogers Cox. HBMV
To a Post-Office Inkwell. Christopher Morley. InP; PoLF
To a Pretty Girl. Israel Zangwill. TrJP
To a Primrose. John Clare. FIW; GTSE; OTPC (1923 ed.)
To a Prince of the Church. Kenneth W. Porter. MaRV
To a Publisher. . .Cut-out. LeRoi Jones. NeAP
To a Recalcitrant Virgin. Asclepiades, *tr. fr. Greek by* L. R. Lind. LiTW
To a Recruiting Sergent. James Russell Lowell. *See* Letter from Mr. Ezekiel Biglow of Jaalam to the Hon. Joseph T. Buckingham, A.
To a Republican. Philip Freneau. AmPP (5th ed.)
(On Mr. Paine's "Rights of Man.") PoFr
To a Republican Friend, 1848. Matthew Arnold. EPN; MBW-2; PoFr; PoVP; Sonn; ViPP
To a Republican Friend, 1848, Continued. Matthew Arnold. EPN; MBW-2; Sonn; ViPP
(Continued.) PoVP
To a Revolutionist. Harold E. Fey. ChIP
To a River in the South. Sir Henry Newbolt. CH
To a Robin. T. A. Daly. JKCP
To a Rogue. Joseph Addison. PV
To a Roman. J. C. Squire. HBMV
To a Rose. Frank Dempster Sherman. AA
To a Rose. John Banister Tabb. CAW
To a Sacred Cow. *Unknown, tr. fr. Toda by* W. E. Mashiel. WGRP
To a Salesgirl, Weary of Artificial Holiday Trees. James Wright. NYBP
To a Saxon Poet. Jorge Luis Borges, *tr. fr. Spanish by* Norman Thomas di Giovanni. ML
To a Scarlatti Passepied. Robert Hillyer. HBMV
To a School-Girl. John Shaw Neilson. PoAu-1
To a Schoolmaster. Martial, *tr. fr. Latin by* John Hay. OnPM
To a Sea-Bird. Bret Harte. EtS
To a Seabird. Sir William Watson. VA
To a Sea Eagle. "Hugh MacDiarmid." MoBrPo
To a Sea-Gull. Arthur Symons. PoVP
To a Seamew. Swinburne. EtS
To a Severe Nun. Thomas Merton. CoPo
To a Shade. W. B. Yeats. AnIL; LiTB; PoE; PoEL-5
To a Single Shadow without Pity. Sam Cornish. NBP
To a Sinister Potato. Peter Viereck. OnHM
To a Skeleton. *Unknown.* BLPA
To a Skull, *sel.* Thomas Caulfield Irwin.
"Dumb are the heavens: sphere controlling sphere." IrPN
To a Skull. Joshua Henry Jones. BANP
To a Skylark. George Meredith. EnLit
To a Skylark. Shelley. AnFE; AtBAP; ATP; BEL; BoLiVe; CoBE; DD, *abr.*; DiPo; EnL; EnLi-2; EnLit; EnRP; EPN; ERoP-2; FaBoBe; FaBV; FaFP; FaPON, *abr.*; GBV; GN; GTBS; GTBS-D; GTBS-P; GTBS-W; GTSE; GTSL; HBV; HH; InP; InvP; LiTB; LiTG; LoBV; MBW-2; MCCG; MERP; MPB; MyFE; NoP; NP; OAEP; OBEV; OBNC; OBRV; OHFP; OTD; OTPC; OuHeWo; PoFS; PoIE; PoLF; PTK;

To (continued)
RoGo; ShBV-4; TOP; TreFS; TrGrPo; VaPo; WHA
Our Sweetest Songs ("We look before and after"), *sel.* MaRV
To a Skylark ("Etheral minstrel!"). Wordsworth. BEL; BoLiVe; EnLi-2; EnLit; EnRP; EPN; HBV; HBVY; MERP; OAEP; PoIE (1970 ed.); PTK; TrGrPo
(To the Skylark.) FaFP; GTBS; GTBS-D; GTBS-P; GTBS-W; GTSE; GTSL
To a Sky-Lark ("Up with me!"). Wordsworth. BEL; DD; HBV; MERP; TOP
To a Slow Walker and Quick Eater. Gotthold Ephraim Lessing. BOHV
To a Small Boy Standing on My Shoes While I Am Wearing Them. Ogden Nash. ALV; FiBHP
To a Small Boy Who Died at Diepkloof Reformatory. Alan Paton. BoSA
To a Snail. Marianne Moore. CMoP; FaBoMo; OnPM
To a Snowflake. Francis Thompson. BoLiVe; BoNaP; FaBV; GoTP; HBV; ImOP; InP; LoBV; MoAB; MoBrPo; NeMA; PoPl; SeCePo; ThWaDe; TrGrPo; TSW
To a Solitary Disciple. William Carlos Williams. PP
To a Songster. John Banister Tabb. InP
To a Spanish Poet. Stephen Spender. CMoP; OAEP (2d ed.)
To a Sparrow. Francis Ledwidge. HBMV; TSW
To a Sparrow. Sir Philip Sidney. Astrophel and Stella, LXXXIII. SiPS
("Good brother Philip, I have borne you long.") FCP
To a Squirrel at Kyle-na-no. W. B. Yeats. FaPON; PDV; ThWaDe
To a Steam Roller. Marianne Moore. CMoP; MAP; MoAB; MoAmPo; OxBA; PP
To a Suicide. Craig Sterry. QAH
To a Survivor of the Flood. John Gould Fletcher. AnAmPo
To a Swallow Building under Our Eaves. Jane Welsh Carlyle. HBV; OBRV; OTPC (1923 ed.); VA
To a "Tenting" Boy. Charles Tennyson Turner. OBNC
To a Thesaurus. Franklin P. Adams. BOHV; PoPl; SiTL; WhC
To a Thrush. T. A. Daly. CAW; JKCP
To a Town Poet. Lizette Woodworth Reese. AA
To a Traveler. Lionel Johnson. AnEnPo; MoBrPo; NBM
To a Traveler. Su T'ung-po, *tr. fr. Chinese by* Kenneth Rexroth. HoPM
To a Vagabond. Constance Davies Woodrow. CaP
To a Very Beautiful Lady. Ruthven Todd. NeBP
To a Very Wise Man. Siegfried Sassoon. BrPo
To a Very Young Gentleman. Christopher Morley. PoMa
To a Very Young Gentleman at a Dancing-School. Elizabeth Rowe. SeCL; SeEP
To a Very Young Lady. Sir George Etherege. CEP; SeCL; ViBoPo
To a Very Young Lady. Edmund Waller. AnAnS-2; LO; OBS; PoFS; SeCL; SeCP; TrGrPo; ViBoPo
(To a Girl.) WiR
(To My Young Lady, Lucy Sidney.) MePo; OAEP; SeEP
(To the Younger Lady Lucy Sydney.) CBEP
("Why came I so untimely forth.") EG
To a Virtuous Young Lady. Milton. *See* Lady That in the Prime.
To a Wanton. William Habington. AnAnS-2; SeCP
To a War Poet, on Teaching Him in a New Country. D. J. Enright. ML
To a Waterfowl. Bryant. AA; AmePo; AmLP; AmP; AmPP; AnAmPo; AnFE; AnNE; AP; APA; AWP; BoLiVe; CBEP; CH; CoAnAm; CoBA; DD; DiPo; ExPo; FaBoBe; FaBoEn; FaFP; FaPL; ForPo; GN; GTBS; GTBS-D; HBV; HBVY; HoPM; InP; LiTA; LiTG; MAmP; MaRV; MCCG; MWA-1; NeHB; NePA; NoP; OBRV; OHFP; OQP; OTPC; OxBA; PG (1945 ed.); Po; PoE; PoEL-4; PoLF; PoPo; PTK; SeCeV; SoP; TDP; TOP; TreF; TrGrPo; TRV; UnPo (1st ed.); WBLP; WGRP; YT
To a Weeping Willow. Louis Untermeyer. MeWo
To a Western Bard Still a Whoop and a Holler Away from English Poetry. William Meredith. PP
To a Wild Goose over Decoys. Lew Sarett. MAP; NP
To a Wild Rose Found in October. Ednah Proctor Clarke. AA
To a Wind Flower. Madison Cawein. AA; HBV
To a Withered Rose. John Kendrick Bangs. AA
To a Witty Man of Wealth and Quality; Who, after His Dismissal from Court, Said, He Might Justly Complain of It. William Wycherley. SeCV-2
To a Woman. Denis Glover. AnNZ
To a woman that I knew. Her Eyes. John Crowe Ransom. LiTM (rev. ed.); NePA; PoPl
To a Wood-Violet. John Banister Tabb. HBV
To a Wreath of Snow. Emily Brontë. PeER
To a Writer of the Day. Langdon Elwyn Mitchell. AA
To a Young Artist. Robinson Jeffers. CoBA
To a Young Ass. Samuel Taylor Coleridge. EnRP; MBW-2; OBEC
To a Young Beauty. W. B. Yeats. CMoP
To a Young Child. Eliza Scudder. AA
To a Young Friend, *br. sel.* Samuel Taylor Coleridge.
"And haply, bason'd in some unsunn'd cleft," 3 *ll.* ChER
To a Young Gentle-Woman, Councel Concerning Her Choice. Richard Crashaw. AtBAP; OBS
To a Young Girl Dying. Thomas William Parsons. AA
To a Young Girl Leaving the Hill Country. Arna Bontemps. CDC; Kal
To a Young Heir. Samuel Johnson. *See* Short Song of Congratulation, A.
To a Young Lady. William Cowper. GTBS; GTBS-D; GTBS-P; GTBS-W; GTSE; GTSL; HBV
(Addressed to a Young Lady.) EiPP; EnRP
(Stream, The.) LiTL; LO
To a Young Lady. Pope. *See* Epistle to Miss Blount.
To A Young Lady. Richard Savage. CBEP; OBEC
To a Young Lady. Wordsworth. EnRP
("Dear Child of Nature, let them rail!") EG
To a Young Lady on Her Leaving the Town after the Coronation. Pope. *See* Epistle to Miss Blount.
To a Young Lady Swinging Upside Down on a Birch Limb over a Winter-swollen Creek. James H. Koch. GoYe
To a Young Lady That Told Me My Fortune in the Cards. Thomas Catesby Paget. WaPE
To a Young Lady, Who Asked Me to Write Something Original for Her Album. Thomas Campbell. StP
To a Young Lady, with the Works of Voiture. Pope. *See* To Miss Blount with the Works of Voiture.
To a Young Leader of the First World War. Stefan George, *tr. fr. German by* E. B. Ashton. WaaP
To a Young Lover. Amur Mu'izzi, *tr. fr. Persian by* R. A. Nicholson. LiTW
To a Young Poet. Harry M. Meacham. GoYe
To a Young Poet. Edna St. Vincent Millay. CrMA
To a Young Poet Who Killed Himself. Joyce Kilmer. YT
To a Young Priest. Anne Blackwell Payne. MaRV
To a Young Woman on the *World* Staff. Franklin P. Adams. ALV
To a Young Wretch. Robert Frost. NeMA; PoDB
To Aaron Burr, under Trial for High Treason. Sarah Wentworth Morton. PAH
To Abraham Lincoln. John James Piatt. AA
To Adhiambo. Gabriel Okara. PBA
To Aenone. Robert Herrick. HBV
(To Oenone.) OBEV
To Age. Walter Savage Landor. BEL; EnRP; EPN; FaPL; HBV; OQP, *abr.*; TreFS; VA
To Ailsa Rock. Keats. EnRP; OBNC
To Alexander Neville. Barnabe Googe. EnRePo; NoP
To Alfred Tennyson. Robert Stephen Hawker. VA
To Alison Cunningham. Robert Louis Stevenson. PoVP
To All Angels and Saints. George Herbert. MaMe; SeCV-1
To All Hog-Raisers, My Ancestors. Charles Simic. YAP
To all Musicians. Richard Church. MuSP
To All Sisters. Sonia Sanchez. BF
To all the heart-wounds touched afresh this day. Memorial Day. Emerette H. Dunning. OQP
To all the humble beasts there be. Prayer for Gentleness to All Creatures. John Galsworthy. BoTP
To all the spirits of love that wander by. Supreme Surrender. Dante Gabriel Rossetti. The House of Life, VII. MaVP; PoVP; ViPo; VP
To all who hope for Freedom's gleam. Our Country. Anna Louise Strong. MaRV; OQP
To all you ladies now at Bath. Lady M. M——'s Farewel to Bath. Lady Mary Wortley Montagu. CEP; EiCL
To all you ladies now at land. Song [*or* Written at Sea, in the First Dutch War]. Charles Sackville. BEL; CavP; CEP; CoMu; EnLi-1 (1949 ed.); EnLoPo; HBV; LiTG; OBEV; OBS; SeCL; SeCV-2; SeEP; SiTL; TOP
To all young men that love to wooe. To Chuse a Friend, but Never

Marry. *At. to* the Earl of Rochester. CoMu
To Althea, from Prison. Richard Lovelace. AnAnS-2; AnEnPo; AnFE; ATP; AWP; BEL; BLPA; CABA; CavP; CBEP; CBV; CoBE; EnL; EnLi-1; EnLit; FaBoBe; FaBoEn; FaPL; GTBS; GTBS-D; GTBS-P; GTBS-W; GTSE; GTSL; HBV; ILP; InPo; JAWP; LiTB; LiTG; LiTL; LoBV; MCCG; MeLP; MemP; MePo; MeWo; NeHB; NoP; OAEP; OBEV; OBS; OuHeWo; PCD; PG (1945 ed.); PoAn; PoE; PoFS; PoIE; PoPo; PoRA; PoSa; SCEP-2; SeCeV; SeCL; SeCP; SeCV-1; SeEP; TOP; TreF; TrGrPo; ViBoPo; WBP; WHA; YAT
(Song.) ReEn
"Stone walls do not a prison make," 1 *st.* MaRV; OQP
(Stone Walls.) WePo
To Amanda Walking in the Garden. Nicholas Hookes. SeCL
To Amarantha, That She Would Dishevell Her Haire. Richard Lovelace. AnAnS-2; EP; HBV; HoPM; LO; MePo; MeWo; NoP; OBEV; PoFS; SCEP-2; SeCP; SeCV-1, *longer vers.*; TrGrPo
(To Amarantha.) LiTL; UnTE; ViBoPo
(To Amarantha, to Dishevel Her Hair.) EG
To Amasia, Tickling a Gentleman. John Hopkins. PeRV
To America. Alfred Austin. GN; HBV
(Britannia to Columbia.) PAH
To America. Richard Garnett. VA
To American Poets. William Knott. YAP
To Amine. James Clarence Mangan. OBEV (new ed.); OBVV
To Amoret [Gone from Him]. Henry Vaughan. CBEP; EnLoPo; MeLP; OBS; SeCP
To Amoret. Edmund Waller. SCEP-2; SeCV-1
To an Acquaintance. *Unknown.* FaFP; SiTL
To an Ambitious Friend ("Quid bellicosus"). Horace, *tr. fr. Latin by* Matthew Arnold. Odes, II, 11. AWP
To an American Poet Just Dead. Richard Wilbur. ML
To an Andalusian Fan. J. Rodríguez la Orden, *tr. fr. Spanish by* Thomas Walsh. OnPM
To an Anti-poetical Priest. Giolla Brighde MacNamee, *tr. fr. Middle Irish by* the Earl of Longford. AnIV
To an Artful Theatre Manager. Lorenzo da Ponte, *tr. fr. Italian by* John Mazzinghi. *Fr.* Il Capriccio Dramatico. TrJP
To an Artist, to Take Heart. Louise Bogan. NYBP
To an Athlete Dying Young. A. E. Housman. A Shropshire Lad, XIX. ATP; BEL; BoLiVe; BrPo; CABA; CaFP; CBV; CMoP; CoBE; EnL; EnLi-2; ExPo; GTBS-W; ILP; InP; LiTB; LiTG; LiTM (rev. ed.); MaC; MaPo; MasP; MoAB; MoBrPo; NBM; NeMA; NoP; OAEP (2d ed.); PAn; Po; PoEL-5; PoFS; PoIE; PoMa; PoPl; PoPo; PoRA; PoSa; PoVP; SD; SeCeV; TDP; TreF; TrGrPo; UnPo; VaPo; ViPo; VP; WHA; YAT
To an Author. Philip Freneau. AmPP; CoBA; MAmP; OxBA
To an Autumn Leaf. Albert Mathews. AA
To an Avenue Sport. Helen Johnson Collins. PoNe
To an Aviator. Daniel Whitehead Hicky. MoSiPe
To an Early Primrose. Henry Kirke White. HBV; OBNC; OBRV; OTPC (1923 ed.)
To an ebbing tide, all sail apeak. A Song of the Hatteras Whale. *Unknown.* EtS
To an Egyptian Boy. H. W. Berry. WhC
To an Enchantress. Alice Brown. CIV
To an Enemy. Maxwell Bodenheim. NP; TrJP
To an Enemy. E. J. Pratt. MaRV
To an English Setter. Thomas Walsh. PFY
To an Icicle. Blanche Taylor Dickinson. CDC
To an Imperilled Traveller. Nathan Haskell Dole. AA
To an Inconstant One. Sir Robert Ayton. *See* I Loved Thee Once.
To an Independent Preacher. Matthew Arnold. *See* In Harmony with Nature.
To an Indian Skull, *sel.* Alexander McLachlan.
"And art thou come to this at last." CaP
To an Insect. Oliver Wendell Holmes. HBV; HBVY; OTPC; StaSt; TreF
To an Irish Blackbird. James MacAlpine. HBMV; HBVY
To an Isle in the Water. W. B. Yeats. AWP; JAWP; ThGo; WBP
To an Oak Tree. Sir Walter Scott. *Fr.* Waverley. OBNC
To an Obscure Poet Who Lives on My Hearth. Charles Lotin Hildreth. AA
To an Old Danish Song-Book. Longfellow. OBVV
To an Old Fraud. Martial, *tr. fr. Latin by* L. R. Lind. LiTW
To an Old Gentlewoman. George Turberville. CBV; EnRePo
(To an Olde Gentlewoman, That Painted Hir Face.) EnPo
To an Old Lady. William Empson. AtBAP; CoBMV; FaBoTw; GTBS-P; MoAB; MoPW; NoP; SeCeV (1967 ed.); ToPo
To an Old Lady Asleep at a Poetry Reading. James Kirkup. BoPe; POTi
To an Old Lady Dead. Siegfried Sassoon. MemP
To an Old Philosopher in Rome. Wallace Stevens. AP
To an Old Tenor. Oliver St. John Gogarty. WhC
To an Old Tune. William Alexander Percy. HBMV
To an Old Venetian Wine-Glass. Lloyd Mifflin. AA
To an Olde Gentlewoman, That Painted Hir Face. George Turberville. *See* To an Old Gentlewoman Who Painted Her Face.
To an open house in the evening. Home at Last. G. K. Chesterton. *Fr.* The House of Christmas. BoPe; FaChP; OQP; TRV; WGRP
To an Oriole. Edgar Fawcett. HBV; OTPC
(Oriole.) GoTP
To an Unborn Pauper Child. Thomas Hardy. CoBMV; GTBS-P; LiTB; MaPo (1969 ed.); ReMP; ViBoPo
To an Ungentle Critic. Robert Graves. HBMV; InMe
To an Unknown Neighbor at the Circus. Rosemary Benét. InMe
To and Fro about the City. John Drinkwater. MaRV; StJW
To and fro from the city I go. A City Flower. Austin Dobson. BoPe
To and on Other Intellectual Poets on Reading That the U.S.A.F. Had Sent a Team of Scientists to Africa. Ramon Guthrie. NMP
To Andrew Lang. Robert Louis Stevenson. PoVP
To Angélique, *sel.* Heine, *tr. fr. German by* Emma Lazarus.
This Mad Carnival of Loving. TrJP
To Ann Scott-Moncrieff. Edwin Muir. *See* For Ann Scott-Moncrieff.
To Anne. Clément Marot, *tr. fr. French by* Louisa S. Costello. OnPM; WoL
To Anne. Sir William Stirling Maxwell. HBV
To Anthea ("Ah my Anthea! Must my heart still break?"). Robert Herrick. SCEP-2
(What Shame Forbids To Speak.) UnTE
To Anthea ("Bid me to live"). Robert Herrick. *See* To Anthea Who May Command Him Anything.
To Anthea ("If dear Anthea"). Robert Herrick. OBS; SeEP
To Anthea ("Now is the time"). Robert Herrick. OAEP; OBS; PoEL-3; SeEP
To Anthea Lying in Bed. Robert Herrick. SeCP
To Anthea, Who May Command Him Any Thing. Robert Herrick. AnAnS-2; BoC; BoLiVe; CavP; CBEP; CoBE; EnLit; GTBS-D; GTBS-P; GTBS-W; HBV; LoBV; MeWo; NeHB; PoeP; ReEn; SCEP-2; SeCL; SeCP; SeCV-1; SeEP; TOP; TrGrPo; ViBoPo
(To Anthea.) GTBS; GTSE; GTSL; OAEP; OBEV; OBS
To Anthea, Who May Command Him Anything (New Style). Alfred Cochrane. HBV
To Any Daddy. *Unknown.* SoP; STF
To Any Member of My Generation. George Barker. LiTM (rev. ed.); Sonn; ViBoPo (1958 ed.); WaP
To Aphrodite; with a Mirror. Aline Kilmer. HBMV
To Apollo Making Love. Bernard le Bovier de Fontenelle, *tr. by* Thomas Tickell. WaPE
To Arcady. Charles Buxton Going. HBV
To Archaeanassa, on whose furrow'd brow. On Archaeanassa. Plato. AWP
To Archbishop Stepinac. Sister Mary Eulalia. JKCP (1955 ed.)
To Archinus. Callimachus, *tr. fr. Greek by* F. A. Wright. AWP
To Argos. Lawrence Durrell. MoPo
To Ariake Kambara. Norman Rosten. NYBP
To Aristius Fuscus. Horace. *See* Integer Vitae.
To Arms. Park Benjamin. PAH
To arms, to arms! my jolly grenadiers! The Song of Braddock's Men. *Unknown.* MC; PAH
To Arolilia, *sel.* Herbert Trench.
"Ay, since beyond these walls no heavens there be." LO
To Ashtaroth and Bel. Saul Tchernichowsky, *tr. fr. Hebrew by* L. V. Snowman. TrJP
To Ask for All Thy Love. *Unknown.* EIL
To Ask Our Lady's Patronage for a Book on Columbus.

To (continued)
Thomas D'Arcy McGee. JKCP
To assassinate the Chase Manhattan Bank. The Plot to Assassinate the Chase Manhattan Bank. Carl Larsen. PPON
To Astraea. Sir John Davies. *Fr.* Hymns of Astraea. SiCE
To Atalanta. Dorothy Dow. HBMV
To Auden on His Fiftieth. Richard Eberhart. ML
To Augustus. Pope. *See* First Epistle of the Second Book of Horace, The.
To Aunt Rose. Allen Ginsberg. LiTM (1970 ed.); NoP
To Aurora. Earl of Stirling. Aurora, Sonnet XXXIII. FaFP; GTBS; GTBS-D; GTBS-P; GTBS-W; GTSE; GTSL
("Oh, if thou knew'st how thou thyself dost harm.") EIL; Sonn
To Autumn. Blake. BoNaP; CLwM; ERoP-1; WiR
To Autumn. Keats. AnEnPo; AnFE; AtBAP; ATP; AWP; BEL; BoC; BoNaP; BoPe; BoTP; BWP; CaFP; CBV; CH; ChER; CoBE; DD; DiPo; EnL; EnLi-2; EnRP; ERoP-2; EPN; FaBoEn; FiP; ForPo; FosPo; GoTP; HBV; HBVY; ILP; InPo; InvP; JAWP; LiTB; LiTG; MaPo; MBW-2; MERP; MyFE; NoP; OAEP; OBEV; OBNC; OBRV; OuHeWo; PAn; PeER; PIA; Po; PoAn; PoE; PoEL-4; PoeP; PoFS; PoIE; PoLF; PoPo; PoSa; RoGo; SeCeV; ShBV-3; StP; TDP; TOP; TreFS; UnPo; VaPo; ViBoPo; WBP; WHA
(Ode to Autumn.) BoLiVe; CABA; CBEP; EnLit; ExPo; FaBV; GTBS; GTBS-D; GTBS-P; GTBS-W; GTSE; GTSL; MemP; TrGrPo
("Season of mists and mellow fruitfulness.") EG
To Avisa. *At. to* Henry Willoby. *Fr.* Willobie His Avisa. EIL
To Baby. Kate Greenaway. MPB
To banish your shape from my mind. Exorcism. Oliver St. John Gogarty. AnIL
To Be. *Unknown, at. to* Lao-tzu, *tr. fr. Chinese by* Witter Bynner. *Fr.* Tao Teh King. OnPM
To be a birth there must be a begetting. Begetting. Dorothea Spears. PeSA
To Be a Farmer's Boy, *with music. Unknown.* BFSS
To be a giant and keep quiet about it. Trees. Howard Nemerov. BoNaP
To Be a Jew in the Twentieth Century. Muriel Rukeyser. *Fr.* Letter to the Front. TrJP
To be a Negro in a day like this. At the Closed Gate of Justice. James David Corrothers. BANP
To Be a Nurse. A. H. Lawrence. PoToHe (new ed.)
To be a poet and not know the trade. Sanctity. Patrick Kavanagh. ELU; FaBoTw
To be a poet is to be vanquished. Ars Poetica. Victor van Vriesland. TrJP
To be a sweetness more desired than Spring. True Woman, 1. Dante Gabriel Rossetti. The House of Life, LVI. EPN; MaVP; PoVP; ViPo; ViPP; VP
To Be a Woman. Jackie Earley. WSL
To be able to see every side of every question. Editor Whedon. Edgar Lee Masters. *Fr.* Spoon River Anthology. CMoP; CrMA; NP; OxBA
To be alive in such an age! To-Day [*or* In Such an Age]. Angela Morgan. BLPA; MaRV; OQP; TRV
To Be and Not to Be. *Unknown, tr. fr. Greek by* Robert Guthrie MacGregor. OnPM
To Be Answered in Our Next Issue. *Unknown.* WaKn
To Be Black Is to Suffer. Austin D. Washington. TNV
To Be Black, to Be Lost. Hannah Kahn. GoYe
To be born in the shadow of a mighty oak. Lu Yün's Lament. Herbert Read. ML
To Be Continued. Julian Street *and* James Montgomery Flagg. *See* Said Opie Read.
To Be Engraven on a Dial. Samuel Sewall. SCAP
To be forever young. Immortality. Frank Home. BANP
To-be-forgotten, The. Thomas Hardy. PoVP
To be Himself a star most bright. Childhood. John Erskine. MaRV
To be homeless is a pride. A Jealous Man. Robert Graves. CMoP
To Be Honest, to Be Kind. Robert Louis Stevenson. *Fr.* A Christmas Sermon. PoLF
To Be, or Not to Be. Shakespeare. *Fr.* Hamlet, III, i. AtBAP; DiPo; FaFP; FiP; GTBS-W; HoPM; LiTB; LiTG; MasP; MemP; OTD; PoPl; PoSa; TrGrPo; WHA; YAT
(Hamlet Contemplates Death.) MaRV
(Hamlet Contemplates Suicide.) TreF
(Hamlet's Soliloquy.) NeHB; PTK; WBLP
(Soliloquy from "Hamlet.") OHFP; OQP
To Be or Not to Be. Spenser. *See* Despair.
To Be or Not to Be. *Unknown.* BOHV; FaFP; LiTM; MoShBr; SiTL; WePo
(I Sometimes Think.) GoTP
To be redeemed the worlds Redeemer brought. The Presentation. Robert Southwell. MeP
To Be Said at the Seder. Karl Wolfskehl, *tr. fr. German by* Carol North Valhope *and* Ernst Morwitz. TrJP
To Be Said to Baby's Fingers ("Peedy, Peedy; Pally, Ludy"). *Unknown.* SAS
To Be Said to Baby's Fingers ("This little fellow, we call him a thumb"). *Unknown, tr. fr. German.* SAS
To Be Sung. Peter Viereck. FaBV
To Be Sung on the Water. Louise Bogan. MoVE
To be the father of the fatherless. Sonnet to the Prince Regent. Byron. MBW-2
To be unloved brings sweet relief. Lovers. Mary Fullerton. BoAV; PoAu-1
To Beachey, 1912. Carl Sandburg. TiPo
To bear, to nurse, to rear. Seven Times Six. Jean Ingelow. *Fr.* Songs of Seven. GBV (1922 ed.); HBV
To Beatrice on All Saints' Day. Dante. *See* Sonnet: Of Beatrice de Portinari on All Saints' Day.
To Beauty. Baudelaire, *tr. fr. French by* Frances Winwar. EnLi-2
To Becky in France. John Arey. LO
To Bed, to Bed. Beaumont *and* Fletcher. *Fr.* The Maid's Tragedy. UnTE
"To bed, to bed," says Sleepy-Head. *See* Come, let's to bed.
To Begin the Day. *Unknown. See* Moment in the Morning, A.
To begin with she wouldn't have fallen in. Our Silly Little Sister. Dorothy Aldis. EvOK; FaPON
To Ben Johnson. Thomas Carew. AnAnS-2; MePo; SCEP-2
To Benjamin West. Washington Allston. AnAmPo
To Bethlehem town in the long ago. Three Wise Kings. William E. Brooks. ChIP; PGD
To Bethlehem's silly shed, methinks I see. The Bee. Henry Hawkins. ACP
"To Bethlem did they go, the shepherds three." Masters, in This Hall. William Morris. ChTr
To Betsey-Jane, on Her Desiring to Go Incontinently to Heaven. Helen Parry Eden. HBMV
To Betty. "E. G. B." PCH
To Blossoms. Robert Herrick. BoNaP; BWP; EG; GTBS; GTBS-D; GTBS-P; GTBS-W; GTSE; GTSL; HBV; LoBV; OBEV; OBS; SCEP-2; SeCL; SeCP; SeCV-1; SeEP; UnPo (1st ed.)
To Bolívar. Rafael Pombo, *tr. fr. Spanish by* Alice Stone Blackwell. PoFr
To Borglum's Seated Statue of Abraham Lincoln. Charlotte B. Jordan. OHIP
To Boston. John Collins Bossidy. *See* Boston Toast, A.
To Bran around his coracle the billows crawl the crystal sea. The Sea-God's Song to Bran. *Unknown, tr. by* Howard Mumford Jones. LiTW
To Bran in his coracle it seems. The Sea-God's Address to Bran. *Unknown, tr. by* Kuno Meyer. OnYI
To Brander Matthews. Austin Dobson. *See* In Vain Today.
To brave and to know the unknown. The Unknown. John Davidson. MoBrPo
To break bolt and bar. Christmas Amnesty. Edith Lovejoy Pierce. PGD
To break the stillness of the hour. At Evening. Dora Wilcox. BoAu
To Bring the Dead to Life. Robert Graves. FaBoMo; MoBrPo (1962 ed.)
To Brooklyn Bridge. Hart Crane. *Fr.* The Bridge. AmPP; AP; CABA; CBV; CMoP; CoBMV; CrMA; DiPo; ExPo; FaBoEn; GTBS-W; HT; ILP; LiTA; LiTM; MoAB; MoAmPo (1950 ed.); MoPo; NePA; NoP; OxBA; PIA; PoDB; PoE; PoIE; PoPl; ReMP; SeCeV; TDP; ThLM
(Proem: To Brooklyn Bridge.) AmP
To build the trout a crystal stair. The Whole Duty of Berkshire Brooks. Hilda Conkling. HBMV; HBVY
To burn is surely bad, to be. House of Fire. Theodore Weiss. CoPo
To Butterfly. William Alexander Percy. HBMV
To buy, or not to buy; that is the question. Investor's Solilo-

quy. Kenneth Ward. FaFP; SiTL
To Byron. Keats. MBW-2
(Sonnet to Byron.) ERoP-2
To C., Crossing the Park. Pamela Millward. FRC
To C. L. M. John Masefield. POTE
To C. T. C. Joseph Bennett. LiTM (rev. ed.)
To Calista. Charles Cotton. LO
To Calliope. Robert Graves. CMoP; NYTB
To Carry the Child. Stevie Smith. NYBP
To Castara ("Doe not their prophane orgies heare"). William Habington. AnAnS-2
To Castara ("Give me a heart where no impure"). William Habington. AnAnS-2
To Castara, of True Delight. William Habington. AnAnS-2
To Castara: The Reward of Innocent Love. William Habington. *Fr.* Castara, II. ACP; CavP; LoBV
To Castara, upon an Embrace. William Habington. AnAnS-2
To Castara, upon Beautie. William Habington. *Fr.* Castara, II. AnAnS-2; CoBE; SeCP
To Castara, Ventring to Walke Too Farre in the Neighbouring Wood. William Habington. AnAnS-2
To catch some fragment from her hands. Beauty. Kenneth Slade Alling. HBMV
To catch the meaning out of the air. Hardening into Print. Richard Eberhart. NoP
To Catherine Wordsworth 1808-1812. Wordsworth. *See* Surprised by Joy.
To Cattraeth's vale in glittering row. Aneirin, *tr. fr. Welsh by* Thomas Gray. *Fr.* Gododdin. PrWP
To cause accord or to agree. Sir Thomas Wyatt. FCP; MaPo; PAn; SiPS
To Celebrate My Body. Diane Wakoski. YAP
To Celia, *sels.* Witter Bynner.
Consummation. NP
During a Chorals by César Granck. AmAmPo; HBMV; NP
Night. NP
Songs Ascending. HBV; NP
To Celia. Charles Cotton. HBV
(To Coelia.) OBEV
To Celia ("Come my Celia, let us prove"). Ben Jonson. *See* Come, My Celia, Let Us Prove.
To Celia ("Drinke to me, onely, with thine eyes"). Ben Jonson. AnAnS-2; ALV; AnFE; ATP; BoLiVe; CBEP; EnLi-1; EnLit; EnLoPo; FaBoBe; FaBoEn; FaBV; FaFP; GTBS; GTBS-D; GTBS-P; GTBS-W; GTSE; GTSL; HBV; LiTB; LiTG; MasP; MCCG; NeHB; OBEV; OBS; OTPC (1946 ed.); OuHeWo; PG; PoIE; PoLF; PoPo; PTK; ReEn; SeCeV; ShBV-3; SiTL; TIHL; TrGrPo; ViBoPo; WHA
(Drink to Me Only with Thine Eyes.) EG; LiTL; MeWo
(Song, 1 *st.*) FosPo
(Song to Celia.) AtBAP; AWP; BEL; CABA; CBV; CoBE; DiPo; ElL; ELP; EnL; EnRePo; ForPo; ILP; InP; InPo; JAWP; NoP; PAn; PoE; PoEL-2; PoFS; PoPl; PoSa; ReIE; SCEP-2; SeCP; SeCV-1; SeEP; TOP; TreF; TuPP; WBP; YAT
(To Celia: Song.) MaPo
To Celia ("Kiss me, sweet; the wary lover"). Ben Jonson. AWP; EnRePo; JAWP; LoBV; WBP
("Kiss me, sweet; the wary lover.") LO; UnTE
(Song: "Kiss me, sweet . . .") LiTL
(Song: to Celia.) ElL
(To the Same.) AnAnS-2; SCEP-2; SeCP; SeCV-1
To Celia ("I spend my sad life in sighs and in cries"). Daniel Kenrick. SeCL
To Celia. Sir Charles Sedley. AWP; HBV; JAWP; LiTL; OBEV; SeCL; TOP; WBP
(My Heart at Rest.) MeWo
("Not, Celia, that I juster am.) EnLi-1 (1949 ed.); GTBS-D; GTBS-P; GTBS-W; LO
(Song: "Not, Celia, that I juster am.") FaBoEn; GTBS; GTSE; GTSL; SeEP; ViBoPo
(Song to Celia, A.) CavP; OBS; SeCePo
To Celia ("When, Celia, I intend to flatter you"). *Unknown. See* When, Celia, I Intend.
To Celia Pleading Want of Merit. Thomas Stanley. *See* To One That Pleaded Her Own Want of Merit.
To Celia, upon Love's Ubiquity. Thomas Carew. AnAnS-2
To Celio. Sister Juana Inés de la Cruz, *tr. fr. Spanish by* Pauline Cook. LiTW
To Censorious Courtling. Ben Jonson. ReIE
To Charles Cowden Clarke. Keats. EnRP
To Charlotte Corday. Sir Osbert Sitwell. ChMP
To Charlotte Pulteney. Ambrose Philips. GTBS; GTBS-D; GTBS-P; GTBS-W; GTSE; GTSL; HBV
(To Miss Charlotte Pulteney in Her Mother's Arms.) CEP; EiPP; ELP; FaBoEn; OBEC
To Chaucer. Thomas Hoccleve. *Fr.* De Regimine Principum. ACP
To Cheng on His Deposal. Tu Fu, *tr. fr. Chinese by* Chi Hwang Chu *and* Edna Worthley Underwood. OnPM
To Cherry-Blossomes. Robert Herrick. SeCV-1
To Chicago at Night. Mildred Plew Meigs. HBMV
To Chile's coast we are bound away. Bangidero. *Unknown.* SoAmSa
To China. Leroy F. Jackson. StVeCh (1940 ed.)
To Chloe. William Cartwright. *See* To Chloe Who Wish'd Herself Young Enough for Me.
To Chloe. Thomas Cheek. SeCL
To Chloe. Earnest Albert Hooton. UnTE
To Chloe ("Vitas hinnuleo"). Horace, *tr. fr. Latin by* Austin Dobson. Odes, I, 23. AWP; JAWP; WBP; LiTW, *tr. by* Patrick Branwell Brontë; OuHeWo, *tr. by* Goldwin Smith
(Time to Choose a Lover, *tr. by* Patrick Branwell Brontë.) OnPM; UnTE
To Chloe. *Unknown, tr. fr. Greek by* Louis Untermeyer. UnTE
To Chloe Jealous [a Better Answer]. Matthew Prior. *See* Answer to Chloe Jealous.
To Chloë Who Wished Herself Young Enough for Me. William Cartwright. EP; LiTL, 4 *sts.*; MePo; OBS; SeCL; SeEP; ViBoPo
(To Chloe.) GTBS-W, 2 *sts.*; LiTB, 4 *sts.*; PoToHe (new ed.), 1 *st.*
(To Chloe Who for His Sake Wished Herself Younger.) HBV; LO, 2 *sts.*; OBEV, 2 *sts.*
To Chloris. John Cobbes. SeCL
To Chloris. Charles Cotton. CavP
To Chloris. William Drummond. CLwM
To Chloris. Sidney Godolphin. *See* Song: "Cloris, it is not thy disdaine."
To Chloris. Sir Charles Sedley. *See* Child and Maiden.
To Chloris. *At. to*—— Waldren. SeCL
To Christ. John Donne. *See* Hymn to God the Father, A.
To Christ Crucified. *Unknown, at. to* St. John of the Cross *and to* Miguel de Guevara, *tr. fr. Spanish by* Thomas Walsh. CAW; OnPM
To Christ Our Lord. Galway Kinnell. TwCP; WIRo
To Christ, the Lord, let every tongue. Majestic Sweetness. Samuel Stennett. SoP
To Christina Rossetti. Dora Greenwell. VA
To Christina Rossetti. Sir William Watson. InP
To Christopher North. Tennyson. EvOK; FiBHP
To Chuck—Concerning a Rendezvous in Siam. Jack Charles. WaKn
To church! I heard a sermon once in spring. God. Harold Monro. *Fr.* Dawn. WGRP
To Chuse a Friend, but Never Marry. *At. to* the Earl of Rochester. CoMu
To Clarastella on St. Valentines Day Morning. Robert Heath. OBS
To Clarinda. *Unknown.* SeCL
To Clarissa Scott Delany. Angelina W. Grimké. AmNP
To Claude McKay. Vivian L. Virtue. PoNe
To Claudia Homonoea. Elinor Wylie. TOP
To Clelia. Matthew Coppinger. CavP; SeCL
To climb a hill that hungers for the sky. Fulfillment. Helene Johnson. CDC; PoNe
To Clio. John Dyer. WaPE
To Clodius. Everard Guilpin. *Fr.* Skialetheia. ReIE
To Cloe. George Granville. PV
To Cloe. Thomas Moore, *after the Latin of* Martial. AWP; OuHeWo
To Cloe. John Oldmixon. PeRV
To Cloe Jealous [a Better Answer]. Matthew Prior. *See* Answer to Chloe Jealous.
To Cloe Weeping. Matthew Prior. CEP; EiCP; EiPP
To Cloris ("Cloris, I cannot say your eyes"). Sir Charles Sedley. CEP; PeRV
("Chloris, I cannot say your eyes.") LO
To Cloris ("Cloris, I justly am betray'd"). Sir Charles Sedley. PeRV

To clothe the fiery thought. Poet. Emerson. *Fr.* Quatrains. AnNE; OnPM; OxBA
To Coelia. Charles Cotton. *See* To Celia.
To Cole, the Painter, Departing for Europe. Bryant. AmePo; AmPP (4th ed.); AP; MAmP; MWA-1
To Coleridge. Shelley. CBEP
(To——"Oh! there are spirits of the air.") ERoP-2
To Coleridge in Sicily. Wordsworth. *Fr.* The Prelude, XI. OBNC
To Colin Clout. Anthony Munday. *See* Beauty Sat Bathing by a Spring.
To Columbus. Rubén Darío, *tr. fr. Spanish by* Lysander Kemp. TTY
To Columbus. John Gould Fletcher. AnAmPo
To come back from the sweet South, to the North. Italia, Io Ti Saluto! Christina Rossetti. LO; OBVV
To Come Out Singing. Jon Silkin. PoDB
To come to the river. The Resolve. Denise Levertov. WIRo
To communicate with Mars, converse with spirits. The Dry Salvages, V. T. S. Eliot. *Fr.* Four Quartets. AmPP; ATP (1953 ed.)
To conclude, I announce what comes after me. So Long! Walt Whitman. AmP; MWA-1
To Constantia, Singing. Shelley. EnRP
To Cordelia. Joseph Stansbury. CaP
To Corinna. John Oldmixon. SeCL
To Corinna's Chamber-maid. Ovid, *tr. fr.* Latin by Thomas Creed. *Fr.* Amores, I, 8. PeRV
To Cotton Mather once there came. Ben Franklin's Head (1728). M. A. De Wolfe Howe. WaKn
To couple is a custom. *Unknown.* EG
To: Coymistress/ From: Marvell. Telegram One. Adrian Mitchell. PV
To Crinog. *Unknown, tr. fr. Middle Irish by* Kuno Meyer. AnIL; OnYI
To Critics. Robert Herrick. PV
To Critics. Walter Learned. AA; AnAmPo; HBV
To Cupid. Francis Davison. OBSC; TuPP
("Love, if a god thou art.") EG
(Madrigal I: To Cupid.) SiCE
To Cupid. Michael Drayton. ElL
To Cupid. Sir John Suckling. *See* Sonnet: "Of thee (kind boy) I ask no red and white."
To Cynara. Ernest Dowson. *See* Non Sûm Qualis Eram Bonae sub Regno Cynarae.
To Cynthia. George Clifford. *See* My Thoughts are Winged With Hopes.
To Cynthia: a Song. Thomas D'Urfey. CavP
(Born with the Vices.) OBS
To Cynthia, Not to Let Him Read the Ladies' Magazines. P. M. Hubbard. FiBHP
To Cynthia, on Concealment of Her Beauty. Sir Francis Kynaston. CavP; HBV; LiTL; LO; MeLP; MePo; OBS; SeCL; SeEP; ViBoPo
("Do not conceal thy radiant eyes.") EG
To Cynthia on Her Being an Incendiary. Sir Francis Kynaston. NCEP
To Cynthia, on Her Changing. Sir Francis Kynaston. MePo; SeCL
("Dear Cynthia, though thou bear'st the name.") EG
To Cynthia, on Her Embraces. Sir Francis Kynaston. LO; NCEP
("If thou a reason dost desire to know.") EG
To Cynthia on His Love after Death. Sir Francis Kynaston. SeEP
To Cynthia Weeping and Not Speaking. Congreve. LiTL; LO
To Cypros she passed and entered the fragrant temple. Hymn to Aphrodite. *Unknown. Fr.* Homeric Hymns. LiTW
To Cyriack Skinner ("Cyriack, this three years' day"). Milton. AnEnPo; ATP (1935 ed.); BEL; EnLi-1; TOP; TrGrPo
(To Cyriack Skinner, upon His Blindness.) PoIE
(To Mr. Cyriack Skinner upon His Blindness.) BWP; DiPo; MBW-1; OBS; Sonn
To Cyriack Skinner ("Cyriack, whose grandsire, on the royal bench"). Milton. GTBS; GTBS-D; GTBS-P; GTBS-W; GTSE; GTSL; OBEV
(Sonnet: "Cyriack, whose grandsire on the royal bench.") LoBV; SeEP
(Sonnet XVIII.) OBS
To Daffodils. Austin Dobson. InP
To Daffodills [*or* Daffadills]. Robert Herrick. AnAnS-2; AnEnPo; AtBAP; AWP; BEL; BoLiVe; BoNaP; CBEP; CBV; CoBE; ELP; EnL; EnLi-1; EnLit; EvOK; ExPo; FaBoCh; FaBoEn; FosPo; GBV; GN; GoJo; GTBS; GTBS-D; GTBS-P; GTBS-W; GTSL; HBV; HBVY; InPo; JAWP; LiTB; LoBV; MaPo; NoP; OAEP; OBEV; OBS; OTPC; OuHeWo; PAn; PIA; PoE; PoEL-3; PoeP; PoFS; PoIE; PoPo; PoRA; QFR; ReEn; SCEP-2; SeCeV; SeCL; SeCP; SeCV-1; SeEP; ShBV-3; TOP; TrGrPo; ViBoPo; WBP; WePo; WHA
(Daffodils, The.) EP
("Fair daffodils, we weep to see.") EG
To Daisies. Francis Thompson. HBV
To Daisies, Not to Shut so Soon[e]. Robert Herrick. AtBAP; BoLiVe; CH; EG; ELP; HBV; OBEV; OBS; SeCV-1; SeEP; TrGrPo
To Dance in a Loving Ring. Sister Mary Norbert Körte. ThO
To D'Annunzio; Lines from the Sea. Robert Nichols. OBMV
To Dante. Vittorio Alfieri, *tr. fr. Italian by* Lorna de' Lucchi. AWP; JAWP; WBP
To Dante. Guido Cavalcanti, *tr. fr. Italian by* Shelley. AWP; JAWP; WBP
To Dante Alighieri. Giovanni Quirino. *See* Sonnet: To Dante Alighieri.
To Dante in Paradise, after Fiammetta's Death. Boccaccio, *tr. fr. Italian by* Dante Gabriel Rossetti. *Fr.* Sonnets. AWP
(Fiammetta.) GoBC
To Daphne. Sir Walter Besant. HBV; VA
To Daphne and Virginia. William Carlos Williams. CrMA
To Daphnis and Chloe in the Park, *sel.* A. R. D. Fairburn.
Song: "O lovers, this song I give to you." AnNZ
To Dean-bourn, a Rude River in Devon. Robert Herrick. *See* Dean-bourn, a Rude River. . .
To Dear Daniel. Samuel Greenberg. LiTA; MoPo
To Death. Caroline Anne Bowles. OBEV (1st ed.)
To Death. Oliver St. John Gogarty. MaRV; OBMV; OtMeF
To Death. Robert Herrick. CoBE; InPo
To Death. Padraic Pearse, *tr. fr. Modern Irish by* Thomas MacDonagh. AnIV
To Death. Countess of Winchilsea. HBV
To Death, Castara Being Sicke. William Habington. AnAnS-2
To Death of His Lady. Villon, *tr. fr. French by* Dante Gabriel Rossetti. AWP; OuHeWo
To Deck a Woman, *sel.* Ralph Hodgson.
And Every Sky Was Blue and Rain, II. LOW
To deities of gauds and gold. Ad Patriam [*or* Land of Our Fathers]. Clinton Scollard. MC; PaA; PAH; PEDC
To Delia, *sels.* Samuel Daniel.
"And yet I cannot reprehend the flight," XXX [XXXII]. HBV; OAEP
(Beauty, Time and Love, 3.) OBEV
"Beauty [*or* Beautie], sweet love, is like the morning dew," XLII *or* XLV [XLVII]. BWP; ElL; EnRePo; FaBoEn; HBV; OBSC; TuPP; ViBoPo
(Beauty, Time and Love, 5.) OBEV
"But love whilst that thou may'st be loved again," XXXVII. AtBAP; ElL; NoP; OBSC; SiCE; TuPP
"Care-charmer Sleep, son of the sable Night," XXXV *or* XLIV *or* XLV *or* XLIX *or*LII *or* LIV [LI]. AtBAP; ATP; CaFP; CBEP; CBV; CoBE; EG; EnLi-1; EnLit; EnRePo; FaBoEn; ForPo; GTBS; GTBS-D; GTBS-P; GTBS-W; GTSE; GTSL; HBV; LiTB; LiTG; LoBV; NoP; OAEP; PoIE; ReEn; ReIE; SiCE; Sonn; TOP; TreFS; TrGrPo; TuPP; VaPo; ViBoPo
(Sonnet.) ElL; PoEL-2
(Sonnets to Delia.) BEL; OBSC
"Drawn with th' attractive virtue of her eyes," XLVIII. ReIE
"Fair and lovely maid, look from the shore," XLII. ReIE
"Fair is my love, and cruel as she's fair," VI. ElL; EnRePo; GTBS-W; HBV; HoPM; LiTB; LiTG; LiTL; NoP; OAEP; OBSC; PoEL-2; ReEn; ReIE; SiCE; Sonn; TrGrPo; TuPP; ViBoPo
(Beauty, Time and Love, 1.) OBEV
"I must not grieve my Love, whose eyes would read," XLVI [XLVIII]. ElL; HBV
(Beauty, Time and Love, 6.) OBEV
"I once may see when years shall wreck my wrong," XXXIV. ReIE

(Beauty's Glass, *sl. diff., after the French of* Philippe Desportes.) OnPM
"If it so hap this offspring of my care," III. ReEn
"If this be love, to draw a weary breath," IX. OBSC; ReEn; SiCE; TrGrPo
"Let others sing of knights and paladins," XLVI *or* L *or* LIII *or* LV [LII]. BEL; CoBE; EIL; EnLi-1 (1949 ed.); FaBoEn; HBV; NoP; OAEP; OBSC; ReEn; ReIE; SiCE; Sonn; TuPP; ViBoPo
(Beauty, Time and Love, 7.) OBEV
"Like as the lute delights, or else dislikes," LIV. OAEP
"Lo, here the impost of a faith entire," LV [LVII]. Sonn; TuPP
"Look, Delia, how we esteem [*or* 'steem] the half-blown rose," XXXI *or* XXXIX [XXXVI]. AtBAP; EIL; EnLit; HBV; NoP; ReEn; SiCE; TuPP
(Sonnet: "Look, Delia.") WHA
"Most fair and lovely maid, look from the shore," XLI [XLIII]. Sonn; TuPP
"My cares draw on mine everlasting night," XXX (1592 ed.). AtBAP; OBSC; PoIE
"My spotless love hovers with purest [*or* white] wings," XII. HBV; OBSC; SiCE
(Beauty, Time and Love, 2.) OBEV
(Most Unloving One, The.) SeCePo
"None other fame mine unambitious muse," XLVIII [LV *or* LIII]. ReEn; SiCE; Sonn; TuPP
"O had she not been fair and thus unkind," VII. ReIE
"Read in my face a volume of despairs," XLIV. EnRePo
"Reign in my thoughts, fair hand, sweet eye, rare voice," XXV. ReIE
"Star of my mishap imposed this pain [*or* paining], The," XXXI. OBSC; ReIE
"These plaintive verse, the posts of my desire," IV. OBSC; ReEn; SiCE
"Thou canst not die whilst any zeal abound," XL [XXXVIII]. EnLi-1 (1949 ed.); OAEP; OBSC; Sonn; TuPP
"Time, cruel Time, come and subdue that brow, " XXIII. AtBAP; OBSC
To the Right Honorable, the Lady Mary, Countess of Pembroke. SiCE; TuPP
"Unto the boundless ocean of thy beauty," I. LiTL; LoBV; OAEP; OBSC; ReIE; SiCE
"When men shall find thy flow'r, thy glory pass," XXXVI [XXXVIII]. EG; EIL; HBV; LiTL; MeWo; NoP; OBSC; PoE; ReEn; SiCE; Sonn; TrGrPo; TuPP
(Beauty, Time and Love, 4.) LO; OBEV
"When winter snows upon thy sable hairs," XXXVII [XXXIX]. CTC; EnRePo; OBSC; ReIE; Sonn; TuPP
"Why should I sing in verse, why should I frame," XVII. Sonn; TuPP
To Delmore Schwartz. Robert Lowell. NMP; OPoP
To Deloney. Everard Guilpin. *Fr.* Skialetheia. ReIE
To Demeter. Maybury Fleming. AA
To Destiny. *Unknown, tr. fr. Dahomean song by* Frances Herskovits. EaLo
To Detraction [I Present My Poesie]. John Marston. *Fr.* The Scourge of Villainy. LoBV; OBSC; ReIE; SiCE; TuPP
To Diana. Ben Jonson. *See* Hymn to Diana.
To Diane. Helen Hay Whitney. AA; HBV
To Dianeme. Robert Herrick. AnAnS-2; CBEP; FaBoBe; FaBoEn; GTBS; GTBS-D; GTBS-P; GTBS-W; GTSE; GTSL; HBV; LiTL; LoBV; NeHB; OBEV; OBS; OnPM; PoeP; PoPo; SCEP-2; SeCV-1; SeEP; TOP; TrGrPo; ViBoPo; WoL
("Sweet, be not proud of those two eyes.") EG
To Dianeme, Again. Robert Herrick. LiTL
To Dick, on His Sixth Birthday. Sara Teasdale. BiCB; TSW
To Die. Paul Eluard, *tr. fr. French by* Glauco Cambon. OnPM
To die be given us, or attain! Resignation. Matthew Arnold. MaVP; OAEP; PoVP; ViPP; VP
To die with a forlorn hope, but soon to be raised. The Survivor. Robert Graves. CMoP; MoVE
To die—without the dying. Emily Dickinson. MWA-2
To Dionysus. Anacreon, *tr. fr. Greek by* T. F. Higham. LiTW
To dive for the nimbus on the sea-floor. Nimbus. Douglas Le Pan. MoCV; OBCV; PeCV
To Dives. Hilaire Belloc. CAW; HBMV
To do God's will from day to day. Abundant Life. Henry W. Frost. SoP
To Dr. Arbuthnot. Pope. *See* Epistle to Dr. Arbuthnot.
To Doctor Bale. Barnabe Googe. EnRePo; EP; ReIE; TuPP
To Dr. Delany, *sel* Swift.
"How oft am I for rhyme to seek?" PP
To Doctor Empirick [*or* Empiric]. Ben Jonson. BOHV; NoP; SeCP; TuPP
To Dr. Swift on His Birthday. Esther Johnson ("Stella"). EnLoPo
To Donnybrook steer, all you sons of Parnassus. The Humours of Donnybrook Fair. *Unknown.* OnYI
To draw no envy, Shakespeare, on thy name. To the Memory of My Beloved Master [*or* the Author, Mr.] William Shakespeare (and, What He Hath Left Us). Ben Jonson. AnAnS-2; BEL; BoLiVe; CABA; CLwM; CoBE; EnL; EnLi-1; EnLit; EnRePo; GoTL; HBV; ILP; LiTB; MaPo; MyFE; NoP; OAEP; OBS; PoEL-2; PoFS; PoIE; PP; ReEn; SCEP-2; SeCeV; SeCP; SeCV-1; SeEP; TOP; TreFS; TrGrPo; TuPP; ViBoPo; WHA
To Dream Again. Shakespeare. *See* Caliban.
To dream of rats in childhood. Who Is the Ratman? Stuart Peterfreund. QAH
To Dream of Thee. Keats. *Fr.* Lines to Fanny. MeWo
To dreamy languors and the violet mist. Dogwood Blossoms. George Marion McClellan. BANP
To drift with every passion till my soul. Hélas! Oscar Wilde. AnIV; BrPo; GTSL; MoBrPo; PoVP; Sonn; UnTE; ViPP
To drink a toast. The Man for Galway. Charles James Lever. OnYI
To drink in moderation, and to smoke. Party Knee. John Updike. FiBHP
To drive Paul out of any lumber camp. Paul's Wife. Robert Frost. AnAmPo; CABL
To drive the kine one summer's morn. The Cow-Chace. John André. PAH
To drum-beat and heart-beat. Nathan Hale. Francis Miles Finch. DD; MC; PAH; PAL; PAP; ThLM
To Duncan. Jessica Nelson North. NP
To Duty. Thomas Wentworth Higginson. AA; AnAmPo
To Dwell Together in Unity. Psalms, CXXXIII, Bible, *O.T.* TrJP
(Psalm CXXXIII.) AWP; JAWP; OnPM
To E. A. R. Lola Ridge. NP
To E. FitzGerald. Tennyson. PoEL-5
(To Edward Fitzgerald.) LoBV
To E. L., on His Travels in Greece. Tennyson. SeCePo
To E. M. O. Thomas Edward Brown. WhC
To E. of D. with Six Holy Sonnets. John Donne. MaMe
To E. T. Robert Frost. ML
To Each His Own. Margaret Root Garvin. HBV
To each his sufferings; all are men. Where Ignorance Is Bliss. Thomas Gray. *Fr.* On a Distant Prospect of Eton College. TreF
To each man is given a day and his work for the day. The Day and the Work. Edwin Markham. OQP; PEDC
To each one is given a marble to carve for the wall. The Task That Is Given to You. Edwin Markham. WBLP
To Earth, the Mother of All. *Unknown.* *See* Hymn to Earth the Mother of All.
To Earthward. Robert Frost. AnFE; AP; APA; BoLiVe; CABA; CoAnAm; CoBMV; GTBS-D; HBMV; InPo; LiTA; LO; MAP; MoAB; MoAmPo; MoPo; MoVE; MWA-2; NePA; NoP; OxBA; PIA; PoIE; ReMP; TwAmPo; WoL
To eastward ringing, to westward winging, o'er mapless miles of sea. When the Great Gray Ships Come In. Guy Wetmore Carryl. AA; EtS; FaBoBe; HBV; MC; PAH
To Edgar Allan Poe. Sarah Helen Whitman. *See* Sonnets from the Series Relating to Edgar Allan Poe.
To Edom. Heine, *tr. fr. German.* TrJP
To Edward Allen (Alleyne). Ben Jonson. OAEP; OBS; ReIE
To Edward Fitzgerald. Tennyson. *See* To E. FitzGerald.
To Edward Thomas. Alun Lewis. WaP
To Edward Williams. Shelley. *See* Stanzas to Edward Williams.
To Egypt. Gloria Davis. NBP
To Electra ("I dare not ask a kiss"). Robert Herrick. ALV; BEL; CavP; EnLit; HBV; HoPM; LoBV; OBEV; OBS; PG (1945 ed.); PoeP; SeCV-1; YAT
("I dare not ask a kiss.") EG
"No, no, the utmost share," *sel.* LO
To Electra ("More white than whitest lilies far"). Robert Herrick. ExPo

To Eliza, Duchess of Dorset. Joseph Bennett. LiTA; NePA
To Eliza, upon May Day Morning, 1649. Robert Baron. SeCL
To Elizabeth. Mary Dixon Thayer. JKCP (1955 ed.)
To Elizabeth, Countess of Rutland. Ben Jonson. NoP
To Elizabeth she came. The Visitation. Calvin Le Compte. ISi
To Ellen. Emerson. TOP
To Ellen at the South. Emerson. LaNeLa
Wind in the Grass, The, *st.* 1. BoTP
To Elsie. William Carlos Williams. *See* Pure Products of America, The.
To Emily Dickinson. Hart Crane. CMoP; ForPo; ML; Sonn
To Emily Dickinson. Yvor Winters. Sonn
To employ her. Europe. John Ashbery. CoPo
To End Her Fear. John Freeman. OBMV
To England. George Henry Boker. AA; AnAmPo; HBV; OTPC
To England. Byron. *Fr.* Childe Harold's Pilgrimage, IV. WHA
To England. Charles Leonard Moore. AA
To English Connoisseurs. Blake. OxBoLi
(Epigram: To English Connoisseurs.) SiTL
To Entertain Divine Zenocrate. Christopher Marlowe. *See* Divine Zenocrate.
To Envy. Sir John Davies. *Fr.* Hymns of Astraea. SiCE
To Eros. Anacreon, *tr. fr. Greek by* John Ounsted. LiTW
To Ethelinda. Christopher Smart. CLwM
To Eva. Emerson. GTBS
To Evening. William Collins. *See* Ode to Evening.
To Everlasting Oblivion. John Marston. *Fr.* The Scourge of Villainy. CBEP; LoBV (1949 ed.); OBSC; ReIE; SiCE; TuPP
To every class we have a school assign'd. Schools. George Crabbe. *Fr.* The Borough. CTC
"To every form of being is assigned." Discourse of the Wanderer, and an Evening Visit to the Lake. Wordsworth. *Fr.* The Excursion. EnRP
To Every Heart. Dante, *tr. fr. Italian by* Dante Gabriel Rossetti. La Vita Nuova, 1. AWP; OnPM
To every hearth a little fire. A Christmas Wish. Rose Fyleman. BoTP
To every man. The Treehouse. James A. Emanuel. AmNP; NNP
To every man there openeth. The Ways [*or* A High Way and a Low]. John Oxenham. HBMV; MaRV; OQP; PoLF; PoMa; TIHL; TRV
To every one on earth. The Burden. "Marianne Farningham." OQP
To everything there is a season. A Time for Everything. Ecclesiastes, Bible, *O.T.* PoPl; TrGrPo
To F. C. Mortimer Collins. HBV; TreFS
To F. C. in Memoriam Palestine. G. K. Chesterton. HBMV
To F. W. Edith Wyatt. NP
To failing strength a stick is given. The Stick. May O'Rourke. HBMV
To fair Fidele's grassy tomb. A Song from Shakespeare's "Cymbeline" [*or* Dirge in "Cymbeline" *or* Fidele]. William Collins. ATP; BEL; CEP; CLwM; EiCL; EiCP; EiPP; ELP; EnLi-2 (1949 ed.); EnRP; ForPo; HBV; OAEP; OBEC; OBEV; PoFS; SeCePo; TOP; ViBoPo
To fall in love, though classically human. Advice to Colonel Valentine. Robert Graves. NYBP
To Fancy. Keats. *See* Fancy.
To Fanny. Keats. CLwM; EnRP; ERoP-2; Sonn; TrGrPo; UnTE
(I Cry Your Mercy.) MeWo
To Fanny. Thomas Moore. HBV
To Father Gerard Manley Hopkins, S.J. George Barker. Sonn
To Faunus ("Faune, Nympharum"). Horace, *tr. fr. Latin by* Alfred Noyes. Odes, III, 18. LiTW
To Fausta. Matthew Arnold. PoVP
To Faustine. Arthur Colton. *See* Sometime It May Be.
To Favonius. Edmund Bolton. OBSC
To Fear. Clifford J. Laube. JKCP (1926 ed.)
To fear a violent good, abuseth goodness. George Chapman. *Fr.* The Conspiracy of Charles, Duke of Byron. MyFE
To February. Ethelwyn Wetherald. VA
To Felicity Who Calls Me Mary. Frances Chesterton. HBMV
To Fidentinus. Martial, *tr. fr. Latin by* Timothe Kendall. TuPP
To fight aloud is very brave. Emily Dickinson. AmePo; AmP; AmPP; AP; CoBA; DiPo; LiTA
To fill the gap, to bear the brunt. St. George's Day—Ypres, 1915. Sir Henry Newbolt. GTSL
To find out Tom of Bedlam ten thousand years I'll travel. Mad Maudlin to Find Out Tom of Bedlam. *Unknown.* SiTL
To find the western path. Morning. Blake. BoLiVe; EG; ERoP-1; FaBoCh; LoBV; LoGBV; OBRV; PeER
To Finde God. Robert Herrick. WGRP
To Fine Lady Would-Be. Ben Jonson. NoP
To fish for pearls in Lethe. The Great Magicians. C. Day Lewis. EaLo
To fix her— 'twere a task as vain. Song. Tobias George Smollett. WaPE
To Flavia. Edmund Waller. HBV
To Flaxman. Blake. OxBoLi
(Epigram: To Flaxman.) SiTL
To flee from memory. Emily Dickinson. Po
To fleece the Fleece from golden sheep. The Scales of the Eyes. Howard Nemerov. CMoP; NMP
To Fletcher Reviv'd. Richard Lovelace. OBS
To fling my arms wide. Dream Variation[s]. Langston Hughes. AmNP; BALP; CDC; IDB; OTD; PoNe; PoPl
To Flood Stage Again. James Wright. FRC
To Flossie. William Carlos Williams. NePoAm-2
To fly off, a ripe pear in a storm. Definition of the Soul. Boris Pasternak. TrJP
To Fool or Knave. Ben Jonson. NoP
To Ford Madox Ford in Heaven. William Carlos Williams. AmPP (5th ed.)
To Foreign Lands. Walt Whitman. AmPP (3d ed.)
To Forget Me. Theodore Weiss. CoAP
To form a just and finish'd piece. Directions for a Birth-Day Song. Swift. EiCL
To Fortune. Robert Herrick. SeCV-1
To Fortune. Sir Thomas More. ACP
To France. Ralph Chaplin. HBMV
To Francelia. Thomas Duffett. CavP
To Francis Beaumont. Ben Jonson. OAEP; OBS; SeEP; TuPP
To Francis Sauf Que. Ron Padgett. YAP
To Frankfort I on *Schobbas* came. The Best Religion. Heine. *Fr.* Tannhäuser. TrJP
To Franz Kafka. Edwin Muir. BoPe
To free me from domestic strife. On Susan Pattison. *Unknown.* CBEP
To Freedom. Joel Barlow. AnAmPo; PoFr
(Freedom.) AnNE; PAL
To Friend and Foe. *Unknown.* CoMu
(Song: "To friend and to foe.") PeRV
To further this, Achitophel unites. The Malcontents. Dryden. *Fr.* Absalom and Achitophel, Pt. I. OBS
To Fuscus Aristus. Horace, *tr. Latin by* Abraham Cowley. Epistles, I, 10. AWP; JAWP; WBP
To G. A. W. Keats. Sonn
To G. H. B. James Bayard Taylor. Sonn
To G. K. Chesterton. Joseph Mary Plunkett. OnYI
To Gabriel of the Annunciation. Peter Abelard, *tr. fr. Latin by* H. T. Henry. CAW
To gallop off to town post-haste. Friar Lubin. Clément Marot. AWP; WoL
To "Garryowen" upon an organ ground. In the Dials. W. E. Henley. BrPo
To gather flowers Sappha went. The Apron of Flowers. Robert Herrick. SeCV-1
To George Barker. Gene Derwood. NePA
To George Chapman. Thomas Freeman. SiCE
To Germany. Charles Hamilton Sorley. MoBrPo
To get home from some scene of gayety. Twelve P.M. William Dean Howells. AmePo
To get off the ground has always been difficult. Dialectics of Flight. John Hall Wheelock. NePoAm-2
To Gild Refinèd Gold. Shakespeare. *Fr.* King John, IV, ii. LiTB; LiTG
(Ridiculous Excess.) TreFT
To Giotto. Wesley Trimpi. NePoEA
To Giulia Grisi. Nathaniel Parker Willis. AA; AmLP
To give a little from a shining store. Giving. William F. Kirk. MaRV
To give—and forgive. Short Sermon. *Unknown. Fr.* Proverbs. RIS; TiPo
To Give My Love Good-Morrow. Thomas Heywood. *See* Pack, Clouds, Away.
To Give One's Life. Mary Carolyn Davies. PoToHe

To gladden one poor heart of man is more. Six Rubaiyat. Abu Said ibn Abi-l-Khair. LiTW
To Glorify My God. A. B. Simpson. SoP
To Glow-Worms. Andrew Marvell. *See* Mower to the Glow-worms, The.
To go, to leave the classics and the buildings. Poem. Gavin Ewart. NeBP
To go to Rome. The Pilgrim at Rome [*or* A Word of Warning]. *Unknown.* AnIL; KiLC
To God. Blake. CBV
To God ("Come to me God; but do not come"). Robert Herrick. AnAnS-2
To God ("Lord, I am like the mistletoe"). Robert Herrick. TrPWD; TRV; WGRP
(Holding to God.) BoPe
To God alone, the only donour. Francis Daniel Pastorius. SCAP
To God and Ireland True. Ellen O'Leary. VA
To God, from the Warring Nations. Frank Wilmot. BoAu
Sels.
"Thou gavest steel to us, Thou gavest brain," XV. BoAV
"We have been cruel in thought. Life's not so sweet," V. BoAV
"We pray for pity, Lord, not justice, we," II. BoAV; NeLNL
"We've smashed the tablets and the songs, forsworn," III. BoAV
To God, on His Sickness. Robert Herrick. OxBoCh
To God, the Architect. Harry Kemp. *See* God the Architect.
To God, the everlasting, who abides. An Invocation. John Addington Symonds. WGRP
To God the Father. Henry Constable. GoBC; PoLi
To God the Son. Henry Constable. OBSC
To God, Ye Choir Above. Philip Skelton. OxBoCh
To God's anointed and his chosen flock. "Christo et Ecclesiae" 1700. Oliver Wendell Holmes. *Fr.* Two Sonnets: Harvard. AP
To Gottfried Benn. Else Lasker-Schüler, *tr. fr. German by* Glauco Cambon. OnPM
To grasp it; say that you have seized that hour. César Franck. Joseph Auslander. HBMV
To grasp, to grasp the evening, the pear and the statue. Grasp. Jules Supervielle. OnPM
To grass, or leaf, or fruit, or wall. The Snail. Vincent Bourne, *tr. by* William Cowper. BoTP; EiCL; GFA; GoTP; HBV; HBVY; OTPC (1923 ed.) PoRh; WaKn
To Grow Older. "Jan Struther." LO
To grow unguided at a time when none. A Tough Generation. David Gascoyne. LiTM (1970 ed.)
To H. C. Wordsworth. ChER; EnRP; ERoP-1; MBW-2; OBRV; PoEL-4
(To Hartley Coleridge.) HBV
To Hafiz. Thomas Bailey Aldrich. AA
To Hampstead. Leigh Hunt. EnRP; OBRV
To Harold Jacoby. Irwin Edman. InMe
To Harriett. John Clare. AtBAP
To Hartley Coleridge. Wordsworth. *See* To H. C.
To Hasekawa. Walter Conrad Arensberg. HBV
To have a friend who follows all my thought. Friendship. Henry W. Frost. SoP
To have even a portion of you is the highest. The Idea of a University. David Shapiro. ANYP
To have known him, to have loved him. Monody. Herman Melville. AnFE; AP; CoAnAm; GTBS-W; LiTA; MAmP; MWA-1; NCEP; PoEL-5; PoIE
To have liv'd eminent in a degree. Upon the Death of My Ever Desired Friend Doctor Donne Dean of Pauls. Henry King. AnAnS-2; SeCP
To have stepped lightly among European marbles. Hark Back. Richard Eberhart. ToPo
To Haydon. Keats. *See* Addressed to Haydon.
To Hayley. Blake. TrGrPo
To hear an oriole sing. Emily Dickinson. AmePo; AmPP; AnFE; AP; CoAnAm; CoBA; MAmP; PoEL-5; UnS
To Hear Him Tell It. *Unknown.* SCC
To Heaven. Ben Jonson. AnAnS-2; BWP; EnRePo; EP; ExPo; ForPo; LiTB; LoBV; OBS; PIA; PoIE; QFR; ReIE; SCEP-2; SeCeV; SeCP; TrPWD; UnPo
(Good and Great God.) OxBoCh
To Helen ("Helen, thy beauty is to me"). Poe. AA; AmePo; AmP; AmPP; AnAmPo; AnFE; AP; APA; AtBAP; ATP; AWP; BoLiVe; BoLP; CABA; CaFP; CBEP; CBV; CH; ChTr; CLwM; CoAnAm; CoBA; DD; ExPo; FaBoBe; FaBoEn; FaBV; FaFP; FaPL; GTBS-D; GTBS-W; GTSE; HBV; HBVY; HoPM; ILP; InP; InPo; InvP; JAWP; LaNeLa; LiTA; LiTG; LiTL; LoBV; MAmP; MCCG; MemP; MeWo; MWA-1; NeHB; NePA; NoP; OBEV; OBRV; OtMeF; OTPC; OuHeWo; OxBA; PFY; Po; PoEL-4; PoFS; PoIE; PoLF; PoPo; PoRA; PTK; SeCeV; StP; TIHL; TOP; TreF; TrGrPo; TSW; UnPo (1st ed.); VaPo; ViBoPo; WBP; WHA; YT
("Helen, thy beauty is to me.") EG
To Helen. Winthrop Mackworth Praed. HBV; LoBV
To Helen. Pierre de Ronsard. *See* Of His Lady's Old Age.
To Helen. Delmore Schwartz. NYTB
To Helene. George Darley. OBEV (1st ed.)
To Heliodora. Meleager. *See* Heliodore.
To Heliodora; a Fretful Monody. Meleager, *tr. fr. Greek by* Dudley Fitts. LiTW
To Heilodora, Dead. Meleager, *tr. fr. Greek by* L. R. Lind. LiTW
To hell with holy relics. Ruins for These Times. Theodore Weiss. OPoP
To Hell with It. Frank O'Hara. NeAP
To Henry Constable and Henry Keir. Alexander Montgomerie. OxBS
To Henry David Thoreau. Irwin Edman. WhC
To Henry Reynolds, of Poets and Poesy, *sel.* Michael Drayton.
Christopher Marlowe. ChTr
To Henry Vaughan. A. J. M. Smith. OBCV
To Her. Robert Mezey. NaP
To Her Body, against Time. Robert Kelly. CoPo
To Her Eyes. Lord Herbert of Cherbury. OBS
To Her Hair. Lord Herbert of Cherbury. NoP; SeEP
To Her Husband, at the Wedding. Kaga no Chiyo, *tr. fr. Japanese by* Curtis Hidden Page. LiTW
To Her Portrait. Sister Juana Inés de la Cruz, *tr. fr. Spanish by* Pauline Cook. LiTW
To Her Sea-faring Lover. *Unknown.* *See* Lady Prayeth the Return of Her Lover . . ., The.
To Her—Unspoken. Amelia Josephine Burr. HBV
To her who first unmade a poet and gave. Offering. Thomas MacDonagh. ACV
To Hermes, this fair ball of pleasant sound. Boy's Playthings. Leonidas. OnPM
To Hero nightly, wet and rather cold. Subjectivity at Sestos. P. M. Hubbard. NYBP
To Hiero the Syracusan. Pindar, *tr. fr. Greek by* Abraham Moore. Olympian Ode I. EnLi-2; OuHeWo
(First Olympionique to Hiero of Syracuse, Victorious in the Horse-Race, The, *tr. by* Ambrose Philips.) ATP
To Him All Life Was Beauty. "A. L. C." ChIP
To Him Be Glory. Romans, XII: 33-36, Bible, *N.T.* TRV
To Him be praise who made. Deus Noster Ignis Consumens. Laurence Housman. HBMV
To him she hasted; in her face excuse. Milton. *Fr.* Paradise Lost, IX. EnL
To him that overcometh. Victory. Marguerite Wilkinson. ChIP
To him that smote Egypt in their firstborn. Psalm CXXXVI, Bible, *O.T.* PoFr
To Him That Was Crucified. Walt Whitman. AnEnPo; MaRV; MoRP; StJW
To him the moon was a silver dollar, spun. Requiem for a Modern Croesus. Lew Sarett. MaRV
To Him Who Ever Thought with Love of Me. Gerard Manley Hopkins. PoIE
(Christ Speaks.) BoC
To him who felt a human sea. Ballad of the Common Man. Alfred Kreymborg. PAL; PoFr
To him who in an hour must die. Two Poems to Miss Lucy Fortescue. George Lyttelton. WaPE
To him who in the love of Nature holds. Thanatopsis. Bryant. AA; AmePo; AmLP; AmP; AmPP; AnAmPo; AnFE; AnNE; AP; APA; AWP; BoLiVe; BoNaP; CoAnAm; CoBA; DiPo; FaBoBe; FaFP; FaPL; GTBS-W; HBV; HBVY; LaNeLa; LiTA; LiTG; MAmP; MCCG; MWA-1; NeHB; NePA; OBEV (new ed.); OBRV; OBVV; OHFP; OTPC (1946 ed.); OxBA; PFY; PG (1945 ed.); PoFS; TIHL; TreF; TrGrPo; UnPo (1st ed.); ViBoPo; WBLP; WGRP; WHA
To Him Who Is Feared. Eleazar ben Kalir, *tr. fr. Hebrew by* Lady Katie Magnus. TrJP
To Him Who Walks the Water. E. Merrill Root. ChIP

To Himself. Richard Aldridge. NePoAm
To Himself. Anacreon, *tr. fr. Greek by* John Ounsted. LiTW
To Himself. Catullus, *tr. fr. Latin by* William Ellery Leonard. AWP; LiTW
To Himself. Ben Jonson. *See* Ode to Himself, An ("Where do'st thou careless lie").
To Himselfe and the Harpe, *abr.* Michael Drayton. OBS
To His Book. Martial, *tr. fr. Latin by* Robert Herrick. AnAnS-2; AWP; LiTW
To His Book ("Go, little book: thyself present"). Spenser. The Shepheardes Calendar, *Dedicatory sonnet.* CLwM; RelE; SiCE
To His Book. William Walsh. CEP; CLwM
To His Booke. Martial. *See* To His Book.
To His Books. Henry Vaughan. EP; QFR
To His Book's End. Robert Herrick. EnLit
(End-Piece for His Book, An.) InP
("To his book's end this last line he'd have placed.") AnAnS-2; ReEn
To his castle Lord Fothergay bore his young bride. High-Life Low-Down. Justin Richardson. PV
To His Chi Mistress. George Starbuck. NYBP
To His Conscience. Robert Herrick. AnAnS-2; MaPo; OxBoCh; PoEL-3
To His Countrymen. James Russell Lowell. *Fr.* A Fable for Critics. AA
To His Cousin. Martial, *tr. fr. Latin.* PoFr
To his cousin the Bat. An Inconvenience. John Banister Tabb. UTS
To His Coy Love. Michael Drayton. ElL; ErPo; HBV; LiTL; LO; OBEV; OBS; RelE; SeEP; ViBoPo
(I Pray Thee Leave, Love Me No More.) ELP; InvP
To His Coy Mistress. Andrew Marvell. AnAnS-1; AnFE; AtBAP; ATP; AWP; BoLiVe; BWP; CABA; CaFP; CavP; CBEP; CBV; CEP; CLwM; CoBE; DiPo; ELP; EnL; EnLi-1 (1949 ed.); EnLit; EnLoPo; EP; ErPo; ExPo; FaBoEn; FaBV; FaFP; ForPo; FosPo; GTBS-W; HBV; HoPM; ILP; InPo; InvP; JAWP; LiTB; LiTG; LiTL; LO; LoBV; MaMe; MaPo; MasP; MeLP; MeP; MePo; MeWo; NeHB; NoP; OAEP; OBEV; OBS; OtMeF; PAn; PIA; PoAn; PoE; PoEL-2; PoFS; PoIE; PoLF; PoPl; PoRA; PoSa; ReEn; SCEP-2; SeCePo; SeCeV; SeCL; SeCP; SeCV-1; SeEP; ShBV-4; SiTL; StP; TDP; TreFT; TrGrP
("Had we but world enough.") EG
To His Cup Bearer. Catullus, *tr. fr. Latin by* George Lamb. OnPM
To His Cup-Bearer. Horace. *See* Persian Fopperies.
To His Darrest Freind. John Stewart of Baldynneis. OxBS
To His Dead Brother. Ugo Foscolo, *tr. fr. Italian by* Glauco Cambon. OnPM
To His Disciples. St. Luke, XII: 24-25, 27-28, Bible, *N.T.* CAW
To His Dying Brother, Master William Herrick. Robert Herrick. OAEP; SeCV-1
"There's pain in parting," 2 *ll.* LO
To His Ever-loving God. Robert Herrick. AnAnS-2; TrPWD
To His Ever-worshipped Will from W. H. "Francis." *See* They Answer Back; to His Ever-worshipped. . .
To His Excellency Joseph Dudley. John Saffin. SCAP
To His Familiar Friend. Nicholas Grimald, *after the Latin of* Marc-Antoine Muret. TuPP
To His Forsaken Mistress. *At. to* Sir Robert Ayton. ElL; ErPo; HBV; LO; OBEV; OBS; SeCePo
(Inconstancy Reproved.) LiTL
To His Friend. George Turberville. *See* To His Friend, Promising That Though Her Beauty Fade . . .
To His Friend ——. Henry Vaughan. PP
To His Friend Ben. Johnson, of His Horace Made English. Lord Herbert of Cherbury. AnAnS-2
To His Friend in Absence. Walafrid Strabo, *tr. fr. Latin by* Helen Waddell. LiTW
To His Friend in Elysium. Joachim du Bellay, *tr. fr. French by* Andrew Lang. AWP; JAWP; WBP
To His Friend J. H. Alexander Brome. CavP
To His Friend Master [*or* Maister] R. L., in Praise of Music and Poetry. Richard Barnfield. CLwM; ElL; ReEn; RelE; SiCE; Sonn; TuPP; UnS
(If Music and Sweet Poetry.) ViBoPo
(To a Friend in Praise of Music and Poetry.) MuSP
To His Friend, Promising That Though Her Beauty Fade, Yet His Love Shall Last. George Turberville. OBSC; SiCE; TuPP
(To His Friend.) CTC
To His Friend Riding to Londonward. George Turberville. RelE
To His Girl. Martial, *tr. fr. Latin by* Louis Untermeyer. UnTE
To His Godson Gerald C. A. Jackson. A. E. Housman. WhC
To His Good Friend, Sir Anthony Cooke. Sir John Davies. *Fr.* Gulling Sonnets. TuPP
To His Heart. Sir Thomas Wyatt. OBSC
("Ah my heart, ah, what aileth thee?") FCP; SiPS
To His Heart Bidding It Have No Fear. W. B. Yeats. BoPe
To His Honoured Kinsman, Sir William Soame. Robert Herrick. AtBAP; BoW
To His Inconstant Mistress. Thomas Carew. *See* To My Inconstant Mistress.
To His Lady. Sir John Davies. SiPS
To His Lady. Fulke Greville. *See* More than Most Fair.
To His Lady. Henry VIII, King of England. *See* Whereto Should I Express.
To His Lady. Petrarch. *See* Vow to Love Faithfully, Howsoever He Be Rewarded, A.
To His Lady. Sir Thomas Wyatt. *See* To a Lady to Answer Directly . . .
To His Lady, of Her Doubtful Answer. Thomas Howell. TuPP
To His Lady, Who Had Vowed Virginity. Walter Davison. OBSC
To His Late Majesty, Concerning the True Form of English Poetry. Sir John Beaumont. OBS, *abr.*; SeEP
"He makes sweet music who, in serious lines," *sel.* PP
To His Love. Ivor Gurney. MMA
To His Love. Shakespeare. *See* Sonnets, XVIII *and* CVI.
To His Love. *Unknown.* *See* Come Away, Come, Sweet Love.
To His Love That Sent Him a Ring. George Turberville. EnPo; EnRePo; TuPP
To His Love When He Had Obtained Her. Sir Walter Ralegh. FCP
To His Lovely Mistresses. Robert Herrick. CTC; OAEP; SeCP
To His Lute. William Drummond of Hawthornden. *See* Sonnet: "My lute, be as thou wast . . ."
To His Lute. Sir Thomas Wyatt. *See* Lover Complaineth the Unkindness of His Love, The.
To His Lyre. Franklin P. Adams. LHV
To His Maid Prew. Robert Herrick. OBS
To His Maistres. Alexander Montgomerie. OxBS
To His Mistress. Richard Barnfield. *Fr.* Cynthia. SiCE; TuPP
To His Mistress. Thomas Beaumont. SeCL
To His Mistress. *At. to* George Villiers, Duke of Buckingham. CavP; SeCL
To His Mistress. Samuel Butler. SeCL
To His Mistress. Henry Constable. *Fr.* Diana. TuPP
("Miracle of the world, I never will deny.") OBSC; ReEn
To His Mistress. Abraham Cowley. SeCL
("Tyrian dye why do you wear.") EG
To His Mistress. Ernest Dowson. BoLP
To His Mistress. Robert Herrick. ViBoPo
To His Mistress. Ovid, *tr. fr. Latin by* Dryden. ErPo
To His Mistress. Sir Walter Ralegh. *See* Silent Lover, The.
To His Mistress. Earl of Rochester. BoLP; LO; OBEV
My Light Thou Art, *sel.* MeWo; PG
(To His Mistress.) LiTL
To His Mistress Confined. James Shirley, *also at. to* Thomas Carew *and to* Samuel Pick. LO; SeCL
(To His Mistris Confined.) OBS
To His Mistress for Her True Picture. Lord Herbert of Cherbury. AnAnS-2; SeCP
To His Mistress Going to Bed. John Donne. *See* Going to Bed.
To His Mistress in Absence. Tasso, *tr. fr. Italian by* Thomas Stanley. AWP; JAWP; WBP
(Far from My Dearest Self.) OnPM
To His Mistress Objecting to Him neither Toying or Talking. Robert Herrick. *See* You Say I Love Not.
To His Mistress, Sending Her the Arcadia. Thomas Beaumont. SeCL
To His Mistress, the Queen of Bohemia. Sir Henry Wotton. *See* On His Mistress, the Queen of Bohemia.
To His Mistress, Who Said She Hated Him for His Grey Hairs. William Wycherley. SeCL

(Song, A: In the Name of a Lover, to His Mistress . . .) SeCV-2
To His Mistresse on Her Scorne. Thomas Beedome. CavP
To His Mistresses. Robert Herrick. ErPo; SCEP-2; SeCP; UnTE
To His Mistris Confined. James Shirley. *See* To His Mistress Confined.
To His Mother. Heine. *See* To My Mother.
To His Mother. George Herbert. PoFS; Sonn
("My God, where is that ancient heat towards thee.") SeEP
(Sonnet: "My God, where is that ancient heat towards thee.") AnAnS-1; MaMe; MeP
To "His" Mother. Minnie Price. SoP
To His Mother. John Banister Tabb. The Child, III. AA
To His Mother, C. L. M. John Masefield. *See* C. L. M.
To His Muse. Edward Benlowes. *Fr.* Theophila; or, Love's Sacrifice. SeCL
To His Muse. Nicholas Breton. *See* Sweet Pastoral, A.
To His Muse. Robert Herrick. OAEP
To His Noble Friend, Mr. Richard Lovelace, upon His Poems. Andrew Marvell. MaMe; PP
To His Pandora, from England. Alexander Craig. Sonn; TuPP
To His Pen. Sir Thomas Wyatt. *See* My Pen, Take Pain.
To His Posterity. Henry Parker, Baron Morley. TuPP
To His Reader. Samuel Daniel. OBSC
To His Retired Friend, *sel.* Henry Vaughan.
"Come! leave this sullen state, and let us wine." ViBoPo
To His Ring, Given to His Lady. George Turberville. ElL
To His Rival. Michael Drayton. ReEn
To His Sacred Majesty, a Panegyrick on His Coronation, 1661, *sel.* Dryden.
"Time seems not now beneath his years to stoop." OBS
To His Saviour, a Child; a Present by a Child. Robert Herrick. OTPC (1923 ed.); OxBoCh; PRWS; SeCP
(Child's Present to His Child-Saviour, A.) OHIP
(Go, Pretty Child.) BoTP
(To a Child.) EG
To His Servant. Horace. *See* Persian Fopperies.
To His Son. Richard Corbet. *See* To His Son, Vincent Corbet . . .
To His Son. John Dyer. PrWP
To His Son. Sir Walter Ralegh. *See* Wood, the Weed, the Wag, The.
To His Son, Vincent Corbet [on His Birth-Day, November 10, 1630, Being Then Three Years Old]. Richard Corbet. AnAnS-2; BoC; BWP; FaBoCh; LoGBV; OBS; SeCL; SeEP; TrGrPo
(To His Son.) CBEP
To His Soul. Emperor Hadrian, *tr. fr. Latin by* Matthew Prior. InP; SeCL; PoPl, *tr. by* Elinor Wylie.
(Adriani Morientis ad Animam Suam, *tr. by* Matthew Prior.) CEP
(Animula Blandula Vagula, *tr. by* Charles Glenn Wallis.) LiTW
(Emperor Hadrian's Dying Address to His Soul.) TreFT
(On the Soul, *tr. by* Byron.) WoL
To his sweet lute Apollo sung the motions of the spheres. Phoebus and Pan. Thomas Campion. MuSP
To His Tomb-Maker. Robert Herrick. SeCV-1
To His Tutor. John Hall. EG
To His Unconstant Friend. Henry King. AnAnS-2
To His Valentine. Michael Drayton. AtBAP; PoEL-2
To His Verse. Walter Savage Landor. OBVV
To His Very Friend, Master Richard Martin. Sir John Davies. Orchestra, Dedication I. SiPS
To His Watch. Gerard Manley Hopkins. MoAB; MoBrPo
To His Watch, When He Could Not Sleep. Lord Herbert of Cherbury. EP; MePo; PoEL-2
To His Wife. Decimus Magnus Ausonius. *tr. fr. Latin by* Terrot Reaveley Glover. AWP; JAWP; WBP
—— *Tr. by* Helen Waddell. LiTW
To His Wife. Ch'in Chia, *tr. fr. Chinese by* Arthur Waley. LiTW
To His Wife. Daniel Henry Deniehy. BoAV
To His Wife. John Skelton. CBEP
To His Wife, on the Fourteenth Anniversary of Her Wedding-Day, with a Ring. Samuel Bishop. LO; ViBoPo
(To Mary.) HBV
To His Worthy Friend Doctor Witty upon His Translation of the Popular Errors. Andrew Marvell. MaMe; PP
To His Young Mistress. Anacreon, *tr. fr. Greek by* Abraham Cowley. UnTE
To His Young Mistress. Pierre de Ronsard, *tr. fr. French by* Andrew Lang. *Fr.* Amours de Marie. AWP; OuHeWo
To Hold in a Poem. A. J. M. Smith. ACV
To Holy Jesus. Princess Philipa, *tr. fr. Portuguese by* Thomas Walsh. CAW
To Homer. John Malcolm Bulloch. ATP (1935 ed.)
To Homer. Keats. BWP; CABA; CBEP; MBW-2; NCEP; NoP; OBRV; Sonn
(Sonnet: To Homer.) ChER
To Honora Sneyd, April 1773. Anna Seward. Sonn
To Hope. Helen Maria Williams. *Fr.* Julia, a Novel. OBEC
To hope is good, but with such wild applause. Hope. Sir Richard Fanshawe. *Fr.* Il Pastor Fido. CBEP; OBS
To Houston at Gonzales town, ride, Ranger, for your life. The Men of the Alamo. James Jeffrey Roche. PAH; ThLM
To Hunt. Blake. OxBoLi
(Epigram: To Hunt.) SiTL
To hunt and to be hunted make existence. Charles Heavysege. *Fr.* Saul. CaP
To hurt the Negro and avoid the Jew. University. Karl Shapiro. AmPP (4th ed.); CoBA; LiTA; OxBA
To Ianthe. Byron. *Fr.* Childe Harold's Pilgrimage. FaBoEn; OBNC
To Ianthe ("Past ruined Ilion Helen lives"). Walter Savage Landor. *See* Past Ruined Ilion Helen Lives.
To Ianthe ("You smiled, you spoke, and I believed"). Walter Savage Landor. PV; VA
("You smiled, you spoke, and I believed.") OAEP
To Ianthe. Shelley. ATP
To Imagination. Emily Brontë. *See* Plead for Me.
To Imagination. Edith M. Thomas. AA
To Imperia. Thomas Burbidge. VA
To —— in Church. Alan Seeger. HBV
To Inez. Byron. *Fr.* Childe Harold's Pilgrimage, I. MBW-2
To infancy, O Lord, again I com. The Return. Thomas Traherne. SCEP-1
To intoxicate you with the wine of things. The Mangoes. Duraciné Vaval. PoNe
To Ireland in the Coming Times. W. B. Yeats. OxBI
(Apologia Addressed to Ireland in the Coming Days.) BrPo
To Iron-Founders and Others. Gordon Bottomley. GTSL; OBEV (new ed.); OBMV; OBVV
To Italy. Giovanni Guidiccioni, *tr. fr. Italian by* Longfellow. PoFr
To Italy. Giacomo Leopardi, *tr. fr. Italian by* Romilda Rendel. AWP; WoL
To J. M. George Meredith. EPN
To J. M. K. Tennyson. PoVP; ViPo
To J. S. Robert J. Misch. ALV
To J. S. Bach. Michael Thwaites. MoRP
To J. S. Collis. Ruth Pitter. OxBoCh
To James. Frank Horne. *Fr.* Letters Found near a Suicide. BANP; BiCB; GoSl; Kal
To James Craggs, Esq., Secretary of State. Pope. CEP
To James McNeill Whistler. W. E. Henley. PoVP; SyP
To James Smith. Burns. *See* Epistle to James Smith.
To James the VI, King of Scotland. Sir John Harington. SiCE
To James Whitcomb Riley. Kipling. YT
To Jane: The Invitation. Shelley. ERoP-2; HBV; MBW-2; OBRV; SeCeV
(Invitation, The.) GTBS; GTBS-D; GTBS-P; GTBS-W; GTSE; GTSL; OBEV; OTPC
(Invitation to Jane, The.) CH
(To Jane.) EPN
Sels.
Away, Away! GoTP
"Radiant Sister of the Day." ThWaDe
To Jane: The Keen Stars Were Twinkling. Shelley. EPN; NoP; ThWaDe
To Jane: The Recollection. Shelley. *See* Recollection, The.
To Janet. Ralph Pomeroy. NYBP
To Jann, in Her Absence. C. J. Driver. PeSA
To Jessie's Dancing Feet. William De Lancey Ellwanger. AA
To Jesus. Iacopone da Todi., *tr. fr. Italian.* MaRV
To Jesus. *Unknown.* *See* Rise, O My Soul!
To Jesus of Nazareth. Frederic Lawrence Knowles. TrPWD

To Jesus on His Birthday. Edna St. Vincent Millay. LiTG; MaRV; StJW; TrGrPo
To Jesus on the Cross. Juan Manuel Garciá Tejada. *tr. fr. Spanish by* Thomas Walsh. CAW
To John C. Frémont. Whittier. MC; PAH
To John Clare. John Clare. *See* Well, Honest John.
To John Donne ("Donne, the delight of Phoebus, and each Muse"). Ben Jonson. AnAnS-2; MaPo; OAEP; OBS; ReEn; SCEP-2; SeCV-1; SeEP; StP
To John Donne ("Who shall doubt, Donne, where I a poet be"). Ben Jonson. AnAnS-2; MaPo; NoP; ReIE; SeCP; SeCV-1; TuPP
To John Greenleaf Whittier. William Hayes Ward. AA
To John I owed great obligation. Epigram [*or* More than Quit *or* Quits]. Matthew Prior, *after* Martial. ALV; AWP; CEP; FaFP; LiTG; OnPM; SiTL
To John Keats. Leigh Hunt. Sonn
To John Keats, Poet. At Springtime. Countee Cullen. BANP; CDC
To John Lamb, Esq. of the South-Sea House. Charles Lamb. Sonn
To John Poynz ("Mine own John Poynz, since ye delight to know"). Sir Thomas Wyatt. *See* Of the Courtier's Life.
To John Poynz ("My mother's maids when they do sew and spin"). Sir Thomas Wyatt. *See* Of the Mean and Sure Estate.
To John Taylor. Burns. WhC
To join the ages they have gone. Seven Years. Marquess of Crewe. OBVV
To Joseph. Harriet Hoock. WHL
To Juan at the Winter Solstice. Robert Graves. CMoP; CoBMV; FaBoMo; ILP; LiTB; LiTM (rev. ed.); MoBrPo (1962 ed.); MoPo; OnHM; PIA; PoIE; PoSa; SeCeV; TwCP; UnPo (3d ed.)
To Judith Asleep. John Ciardi. LiTL; LiTM (1970 ed.); MiAP; MoLP; ToPo
To Julia in Shooting Togs. Sir Owen Seaman. BOHV
To Julian. Robert Gould. PeRV
To Julius. Martial, *tr. fr. Latin by* Sir Charles Sedley. PeRV
(Epigram: "Thou swearst thou'lt drink no more: kind heaven, send.") ALV
(Mistaken Resolve, The.) PV
To K. de M. W. E. Henley. PoVP
To K. H. Thomas Edward Brown. OBNC
To K. M. Walter de la Mare. *See* Horse in a Field.
Tò kanóv. Arthur Hugh Clough. PoVP; ViPo
(I Have Seen Higher, Holier Things than These.) OAEP
To Kate, Skating Better than Her Date. David Daiches. FiBHP; NYBP; SD
To K[atharine] de M[attos]. Robert Louis Stevenson. OBNC
To Keats. John Hamilton Reynolds. Sonn
To Keep a True Lent. Robert Herrick. AnAnS-2; BEL; EnLi-1; HBV; MaRV; SCEP-2; TOP; TRV
(True Lent, A.) DD; OHIP; PoRL
To keep my health! Resolve. Charlotte Perkins Gilman. OQP; PoToHe; WGRP
To keep through life the posture of the grave. To the Muse. Eugene Lee-Hamilton. Sonn
To kinder skies, where gentler manners reign. France. Goldsmith. *Fr.* The Traveller. OBEC
To King James. Ben Jonson. OAEP
To kiss a fan! Two Triolets: What She Thought. Harrison Robertson. HBV
To kiss my Celia's fairer breast. On Snow-Flakes Melting in [*or* on] His Lady's Breast. William Martin Johnson. AA; AmLP
"To Know All Is to Forgive All." Nixon Waterman. BLPA; NeHB; SoP; TreFT
(If I Knew You and You Knew Me.) PoToHe
(Understanding, *st.* 1.) MaRV
To know just how He suffered—would be dear. Emily Dickinson. DiPo; InvP
To know thy bent and then pursue. Ella Wheeler Wilcox. CenHV
To Kosciusko. Keats. MERP; PoFr
To L——. D'Arcy Cresswell. AnNZ
To L. B. C. L. M. Robert Bridges. *See* I Love All Beauteous Things.
To L. B. S. Winfield Townley Scott. FiMAP
To L. C. Lucy Hawkins. HBMV
To L. H. B. Katherine Mansfield. AnNZ; HBMV
To La Sanscoeur. William Caldwell Roscoe. VA
To Labor. Charlotte Perkins Gilman. PoLF
To Laddie. Anne Robinson. SUS
To Ladies' Eyes. Thomas Moore. OxBoLi; PoEL-4; SiTL
To Lady Anne Fitzpatrick, When about Five Years Old [with a Present of Shells]. Horace Walpole. CEP; OBEC
To Lady Jane Wharton, on Her Studying the Globe. Nicholas Rowe. LO
To Lake Aghmoogenegamook. The American Traveller. "Orpheus C. Kerr." BOHV; WhC
To Landrum Guy, Beginning to Write at Sixty. James Dickey. PP
To Larr. Robert Herrick. BoW; SeCV-1
To Laughter, to Leering. Richard Eberhart. ToPo
To Laura W——, Two Years Old. Nathaniel Parker Willis. HBV
To Laurels. Robert Herrick. ExPo; SeCV-1
To leave behind a picture, fine to see. To One Who after Death Would Leave His Lively Picture. Thomas Howell. TuPP
To leave the old with a burst of song. A Way to a Happy New Year. Robert Brewster Beattie. OQP
To Leigh Hunt, Esq. Keats. EnRP; Sonn
(Dedication: To Leigh Hunt.) OBNC; ViBoPo
To Lesbia ("My sweetest Lesbia.") Thomas Campion. *after* Catullus. *See* My Sweetest Lesbia.
To Lesbia ("I hate, and yet I love thee too"). Catullus. *See* Odi et Amo.
To Lesbia ("Let us, my Lesbia! live and love"). Catullus. *See* Love Is All.
To Lesbia ("Thy kisses dost thou bid me count"). Catullus, *tr. fr. Latin by* George Lamb. UnTE
To Lesbia. John Godfrey Saxe. HBV; UnTE
To Let. D. Newey-Johnson. BoTP
To Leuconöe ("Tu ne quaesieris"). Horace, *tr. fr. Latin.* Odes, I, 11. AA, *tr.* I *by* Roswell Martin Field, *tr.* II *by* Eugene Field; ALV, *tr. by* Eugene Field; LoBV, *tr. by* Charles Stuart Calverley
(Ad Leuconoen, *par. by* Franklin P. Adams.) AWP; JAWP; WBP
(Ask Not Ungainly, *tr. by* Ezra Pound.) CTC
(Mistrust To-Morrow, *tr. by* Charles Stuart Calverley.) OnPM
To Leven Water. Tobias George Smollett. OBEV
To Liane-Neila. Iwan Goll, *tr. fr. German by* Claire Goll. OnPM
To Liberality. *Unknown, tr. fr. Vedic by* Ralph T. H. Griffith. *Fr.* Vedic Hymns: Rig-Veda, Bk. X, Hymn 117. PoFr
To Liberty. Casimir Sarbiewski, *tr. fr. Polish by* Sir John Bowring. PoFr
To Li Chièn ("The province I govern is humble and remote"). Po Chü-i, *tr. fr. Chinese by* Arthur Waley. AWP
To Li Chien ("Wordly matters again draw my steps"). Po Chü-i, *tr. fr. Chinese by* Arthur Waley. LiTW
To Licinius ("Rectius vives"). Horace, *tr. fr. Latin by* William Cowper. Odes, II, 10. AWP; JAWP; WBP
(Golden Mean, The.) HBV
(To Licinius Murena.) EnLi-1; OuHeWo
(Translated out of Horace Which Begins Rectius Vives, *tr. by* Sir Philip Sidney.) FCP; ReIE
To Licus. Everard Guilpin. *Fr.* Skialetheia. SiCE
To Life. Thomas Hardy. TOP
To Life I Said Yes. Chaim Grade, *tr. fr. Yiddish by* Joseph Leftwich. TrJP
To Lighten My Darkness. *Unknown, tr. fr. Arabic by* E. Powys Mathers. *Fr.* The Thousand and One Nights. AWP
To Lighten My House. Alastair Reid. NePoEA
To Ligurinus. Horace, *par. fr. Latin by* Sir Edward Sherburne. Odes, IV, 10. CavP
To Lillian Russell. Bert Leston Taylor. WhC
To Lilly. Hartley Coleridge. Sonn
To Little or No Purpose [I Spent Many Days]. Sir George Etherege. *Fr.* She Would if She Could. SeCL; SeEP; UnTE
To Little Renée on First Seeing Her Lying in Her Cradle. William Aspenwall Bradley. HBV
To live a life, free from gout, pain, and phthisic. Athletic Employment. *Unknown.* SD
To live as gently as I can. My Creed. Edgar A. Guest. MaRV
To live illusionless, in the abandoned mineshaft. Double Monologue. Adrienne Rich. NePoEA-2; NoP

To live in hell, and heaven to behold. If This Be Love. Henry Constable. *Fr.* Diana. HBV; InvP; LiTL; OBSC; ReEn; ReIE; SiCE; Sonn; TuPP

To Live in Pleasure. *Unknown. See* Sing We and Chant It.

To live in Wales is to be conscious. Welsh Landscape. R. S. Thomas. POTi

To Live Merrily, and to Trust to Good Verses. Robert Herrick. AnAnS-2; AWP; BEL; InPo; InvP; LoBV; MaPo (1969 Head.); MyFE, *st.* 1; OBS; PP; ReEn; SCEP-2; SeCP; SeCV-1; SeEP

To live with saints in heaven. Living. *Unknown.* SoP

To live within a cave—it is most good. Salve! Thomas Edward Brown. HBV; OBEV; OBVV; TOP

To live without you, seems to me. Little Mother. "M. P. D." PEDC

To live's a gift, to dye's a debt what we. The Porch. Philip Pain. SCAP

To Lizard Head. Clifford J. Laube. CAW

To Lizbie Browne. Thomas Hardy. DTC; ELP; EnLit; LO

To locate a person hidden in this room. Identity. Hyam Plutzik. FiMAP

To London once my steps I bent. London Lickpenny. *Unknown.* GoTL; MeEV

To London the Train Gallops, Its Shrill Steel Hooves. Clifford Dyment. HaMV

To loosen with all ten fingers held wide and limber. Mossgathering. Theodore Roethke. CoBMV; FiMAP; ILP

To Lord Byron in the wilderness. The Ghost of Abel. Blake. ERoP-1

To Losers. George Dillon. NP

To Lou Gehrig. John Kieran. SD

To Love; a Sonnet. Philip Ayres. CEP

To love and to remember; that is good. Later Life, VII. Christina Rossetti. LO; Sonn

To Love, at Last, the Victory. David Starr Jordan. OQP

"To love is to give," said the crooked old man. Cupidon. William Jay Smith. NePoEA

To Love, my lord, I do knight's service owe. Gulling Sonnets, IX. Sir John Davies. Sonn

To love one woman, or to sit. Woman and Tree. Robert Graves. CBV; ErPo

To love our God with all our strength and will. The Whole Duty of Man. Henry Vaughan. OQP

To love some one more dearly every day. My Task. Maude Louise Ray. FaChP; MaRV

To love unloved it is a pain. To Luve Unluvit. Alexander Scott. LO

To love with no return. Sadder. *Unknown.* OnPM

To Lovers of Earth: Fair Warning. Countee Cullen. CDC

To Lucasta ("Ah Lucasta, why so bright!"). Richard Lovelace. AnAnS-2

To Lucasta ("I laugh and I sing but cannot tell"). Richard Lovelace. OBS

To Lucasta ("Tell me not, sweet, I am unkind"). Richard Lovelace. *See* To Lucasta, Going to the Wars.

To Lucasta, from Prison. Richard Lovelace. AnAnS-2; PoFr; SCEP-2

To Lucasta: Her Reserved Looks. Richard Lovelace. SeCV-1

To Lucasta, [on] Going beyond the Seas. Richard Lovelace. AnAnS-2; AtBAP; FaBoEn; GTBS-D; GTBS-P; GTBS-W; GTSE; GTSL; HBV; ILP; LiTB; LiTG; LiTL; LO; LoBV; MeLP; OAEP; OBEV; OBS; SCEP-2; SeCL; SeCP; SeCV-1; SeEP; TreFT; ViBoPo
("If to be absent were to be.") GTBS
(Song.) ReEn

To Lucasta, [on] Going to the Wars [*or* Warres]. Richard Lovelace. ALV; AnAnS-2; AtBAP; AWP; BBV (1923 ed.); BEL; CABA; CavP; CBEP; CBV; CLwM; CoBE; ELP; EnL; EnLi-1; EnLit; EnLoPo; EP; ExPo; FaBoEn; FaBV; FaFP; FaPL; GTBS; GTBS-D; GTBS-P; GTBS-W; GTSE; GTSL; HBV; HoPM; InPo; JAWP; LiTB; LiTG; LiTL; LoBV; MCCG; MeLP; MePo; MeWo; NeHB; NoP; OAEP; OBEV; OuHeWo; PG (1945 ed.); Po; PoAn; PoEL-3; PoIE; PoPl; PoRA; SCEP-2; SeCePo; SeCeV; SeCL; SeCP; SeCV-1; SeEP; ShBV-3; TOP; TreF; UnPo (1st ed.); ViBoPo; WBP; WHA; YAT
(Going to the Warres [*or* Wars].) AnFE; OBS
(Song: To Lucasta, Going to the Wars). ReEn

"To Lucasta, on Going to the Wars." Edwin Meade Robinson. Limericised Classics, IV. HBMV

To Lucasta: The Rose. Richard Lovelace. *See* Rose, The.

To Lucia Playing on Her Lute. Samuel Pordage. SeCL

To Lucius Sestius ("Solvitur acris hiems"). Horace, *tr. fr. Latin by* Sir Theodore Martin. Odes, I, 4. OuHeWo

To Lucy, Countess[e] of Bedford, with Mr. Donne's Satires [*or* Satyres]. Ben Jonson. AnAnS-2; OBS; ReIE; SCEP-2; SeCV-1; SeEP; TuPP

To Luve Unluvit. Alexander Scott. GoTS; OxBS
("To love unloved it is a pain.") LO

To "Lydia Languish." Austin Dobson. NBM; PoVP

To M. William Gay. BoAu

To M. E. W. G. K. Chesterton. HBV

To M. H. Wordsworth. EiCP

To M. T. Bayard Taylor. AA

To Mackinnon of Strath. Iain Lom, *tr. fr. Gaelic.* GoTS

To Madame A. P. Kern. Pushkin, *tr. fr. Russian by* V. de S. Pinto. LiTW

To Madame la Duchesse de Bauffremont. Louis Morpeau, *tr. fr. French by* Edna Worthley Underwood. PoNe

To Maecenas ("Tyrrhena regum progenies"). Horace, *paraphrased fr. Latin by* Dryden. Odes, III, 29. AWP; JAWP; PoFr, *sel.;* WBP
(Horat. Ode 29. Book 3.) CEP; SeCV-2
Sel.
Happy the Man, *br. sel.* MaRV
(Happiness, 4 *ll.*) TreF
("Happy the man, and happy he alone.") OTD; PeRV
(Twenty-ninth Ode of the Third Book of Horace, The.) MBW-1

To Maia. Keats. *See* Fragment of an Ode to Maia.

To Make a Bridge. Charles Madge. NeBP

To make a final conquest of all me. The Fair Singer. Andrew Marvell. CavP; CBEP; EG; EnLoPo; LiTL; LO; MaMe; MeLP; MemP; MePo; PoEL-2; PoIE (1970 ed.); ReEn; SeCL; UnPo (3d ed.)

To Make a Home. Lon Woodrum. SoP

To make a juju of my own. A Juju of My Own. Lebert Bethune. BF; PoNe (1970 ed.)

To make a lover known by plain anatomy. The Anatomy of a Lover. George Gascoigne. ReIE

To make a prairie it takes a clover and one bee. Emily Dickinson. AmePo; AmPP (4th ed.); AnNE; CoBA; DiPo; HBVY; MAmP; NoP; OxBA; Po; PoPl; WoL; YT

To make a resurrection there must be a death. Twin. Phyllis Haring. PeSA

To make a start. Preface. Wiliiam Carlos Williams. *Fr.* Paterson, I. AP; CMoP; CoBMV

To make an end of all this strife. Sir Thomas Wyatt. FCP

To make the best of Fate's inordinate demands. The Bowl of Goldfish: a Fable. James Kirkup. POTi

To make the doubt cleare, that no woman's true. The Expostulation. John Donne. Elegies, XV. MaMe

To Make the People Happy. Victor Hugo, *tr. fr. French.* PPON

To make this condiment, your poet begs. A Salad. Sydney Smith. BOHV; HBV

To make your candles last for aye. *Unknown.* OxNR

To man that was i'th ev'ninge mad. *Unknown.* SeCSL

To Man Who Goes Seeking Immortality. Adelaide Crapsey. QFR

To Manon, as to His Choice of Her. Wilfrid Scawen Blunt. The Love Sonnets of Proteus, VIII. HBV ViBoPo
(As to His Choice of Her.) Sonn; ViBoPo

To Manon, Comparing Her to a Falcon. Wilfrid Scawen Blunt. The Love Sonnets of Proteus, II. OBVV; VA
(Falcon, The.) ACP

To Manon on Her Lightheartedness. Wilfrid Scawen Blunt. The Love Sonnets of Proteus, XI. NBM; VA

To Manon, on His Fortune in Loving Her. Wilfrid Scawen Blunt. The Love Sonnets of Proteus, III. GTSL; OBEV (1st ed.)

To Many Deaths Decreed. John Crowne. *Fr.* Regulus. SeCL

To Mareta. Herschell Johnson. WSL

To Marguerite ("We were apart"). Matthew Arnold. *See* Isolation: To Marguerite.

To Marguerite ("Yes! in the sea of life enisled"). Matthew Arnold. Switzerland, V. BWP; ELP; EnL; EnLi-2; EPN; FaBoEn; FiP; GTBS-D; HBV; ILP; MaPo; NoP; OAEP; OBEV; OBNC; PAn; PoAn; PoEL-5; SeCeV; TOP; ViPo
(Isolation.) OBVV

To (continued)
(To Marguerite—Continued.) CABA; CaFP; CBV; GTBS-P; MBW-2; PoVP; VaPo; ViPP; VP
To Marie. John Bennett. BOHV; NA
To market, to market. Saturday Shopping. Katherine Edelman. SoPo
To market, to market, to buy a fat pig. Mother Goose. BoTP; FaBoBe; FaFP; HBV; HBVY; OTPC; OxNR; PCH; PPL; RIS; SoPo; StVeCh; TiPo
To market, to market, to buy a plum bun. Mother Goose. OxNR; SAS
To Marry Strangers. Winfield Townley Scott. FiMAP
To Mars. *Unknown, tr. fr. Latin by* George Chapman. *Fr.* Homeric Hymns. LoBV
To Mary. Samuel Bishop. *See* To His Wife, on the Fourteenth Anniversary of Her Wedding-Day . . .
To Mary ("I sleep with thee and wake with thee"). John Clare. EnLoPo
To Mary ("The twentieth year is well nigh past"). William Cowper. BEL; CBEP; EiCP; EiPP; EnLi-2 (1949 ed.); EnLoPo; EnRP; FiP; LO; OAEP; OBEC
(My Mary.) LiTL; OBEV; TreFS
(To Mary Unwin.) FaPL
(To the Same.) GTBS; GTBS-D; GTBS-P; GTBS-W; GTSE; GTSL
To Mary. Gottfried von Strassburg, *tr. fr. German by* E. M. Sweetman. ISi
To Mary ("So now my summer task is ended, Mary"). Shelley. The Revolt of Islam: Dedication. EnRP; EPN
To Mary. Charles Wolfe. GTSL; HBV; LO; OBEV; OBRV; ViBoPo
To Mary—A Dedication. Louis MacNeice. BoPe
To Mary at Christmas. John Gilland Brunini. ISi
To Mary; at the Thirteenth Station. Raymond F. Roseliep. ISi
To Mary in Heaven. Burns. ATP; BEL; CoBE; EnLit; HBV; OAEP; OuHeWo
(Thou Lingering Star.) EiPP; EnRP; OBEC
To Mary: It Is the Evening Hour. John Clare. *See* Mary.
To Mary Lady Wroth. Ben Jonson. OBS
To Mary Lamb. Walter Savage Landor. *See* To the Sister of Elia.
To Mary Magdalen. Bartolomé Leonardo de Argensola, *tr. fr. Spanish by* Bryant. CAW
To Mary, Mother of Christ. Una W. Harsen. ChIP
To Mary, of Sailing. Richard Snyder. NYTB
To Mary our Queen, that flower so sweet. The Marigold. William Forrest. ACP; CAW
To Mary Unwin ("Mary! I want a lyre with other strings"). William Cowper. CoBE; GTBS; GTBS-D; GTBS-P; GTBS-W; GTSE; GTSL; HBV; OBEV; TrGrPo
(Sonnet to Mrs. Unwin.) BEL; OAEP; OBEC
To Mary Unwin ("The twentieth year is well-nigh past"). William Cowper. *See* To Mary.
To Master Bastard, a Minister That Made a Pleasant Book of English Epigrams. Sir John Harington. SiCE
To Master Bastard, Taxing Him of Flattery. Sir John Harington. SiCE
To Master Denham, on His Prospective Poem. Robert Herrick. AnAnS-2
To Master Edward Cobham. Barnabe Googe. EnRePo
To Master Everard Digby. Thomas Lodge. ReIE
To Master Henrye Cobham, of the Most Blessed State of Lyfe. Barnabe Googe. EnPo; SiCE
To Master John Davies. Sir John Harington. SiCE
To Master Michael Drayton. Thomas Lodge. ReIE
To Master W. Shakespeare. Thomas Freeman. SiCE
To Maystres Isabell Pennell. John Skelton. *See* To Mistress Isabel Pennell.
To Me. William Barnes. NBM; PoEL-4
To me, fair friend, you never can be old. Sonnets, CIV. Shakespeare. BEL; BWP; EG; EIL; EnLi-1 (1949 ed.); EnLit; EnRePo; FaBoEn; GTBS; GTBS-D; GTBS-P; GTBS-W; GTSE; GTSL; HBV; InP; LiTL; MaPo (1969 ed.); OAEP; OBEV; OBSC; PoIE; ReEn; ReIE; SiCE; TOP; ViBoPo
To me, O Lord, be thou "The Way." The Christian Life. *Unknown.* SoP
To me, one silly task is like another. Cassandra. Louise Bogan. AnAmPo; MAP; MoAmPo; MoVE; NP
To me the earth once seemed to be. Then and Now. Charles Frederick Johnson. AA
To me way-ay-ay-yah!/ We'll pay Paddy Doyle for his Boots! Paddy Doyle. *Unknown.* SoAmSa
To me, whom in their lays the shepherds call. Inscription for a Grotto. Mark Akenside. BWP; CEP; OBEC; PoEL-3; SeCePo
To Meadows. Robert Herrick. AWP; BWP; CBEP; CH; EG; HBV; InPo; LoBV; OBEV; OTPC (1923 ed.); PoeP; QFR; SeCL; ViBoPo
(To Meddowes.) AtBAP; FaBoEn; OBS; PoEL-3; SeCP; SeCV-1
"Ye have been fresh and green," *sel.* MyFE
To Meath of the pastures. A Drover. Padraic Colum. AnIL; AnIV; AWP; HBV; HT; JAWP; MoBrPo; NP; OBMV; OxBI; ViBoPo; WBP
To Meddowes. Robert Herrick. *See* To Meadows.
To meditate upon the tiger, turn. Scarabs for the Living, II. R. P. Blackmur. CoAnAm; TwAmPo
"To meet and then to part," and that is all. The Close of Day. Wesley Curtwright. CDC
To Meet, or Otherwise. Thomas Hardy. OBNC
To meet the fountain of true life I run. Longing. Judah Halevi. TrJP
To Melité. Rufinus Domesticus, *tr. fr. Greek by* Dudley Fitts. LiTW
To Melody. George Leonard Allen. CDC
To Memory. Mary Elizabeth Coleridge. CBEP
To Men. Anna Wickham. MoBrPo
To Men Unborn. David Osborne Hamilton. HH; PEDC
To mend their every hurt, to heal all their ills. Mountain Medicine. Elizabeth-Ellen Long. AmFN
To Mercy, Pity, Peace, and Love. The Divine Image. Blake. *Fr.* Songs of Innocence. BoPe; BoTP; CBEP; CEP; EiPP; EnL; EnLit; EnPE; EnRP; ERoP-1; FaBoEn; LiTG; LO; MaPo; MaRV; MemP; NoP; OAEP; OBEC; OBNC; OnPM; OxBoCh; PoEL-4; PoeP; PoIE; SoP; TRV; ViBoPo; WGRP
To Midnight; an Epitaph. *Unknown.* CoSo
To Midnight Nan at LeRoy's. Langston Hughes. AnAmPo
To Mie Tirante. George Darley. Sonn
To Miguel de Cervantes Saavadra. Richard Kendall Munkittrick. AA
To Milton. Oscar Wilde. BrPo
To Milton ("Milton! thou should'st be living . . .") Wordsworth. *See* London, 1802.
To mine own self I am a wilderness. Stéphane Mallarmé. *Fr.* Hérodiade. SyP
To Minerva. Thomas Hood. BOHV; ChTr; FiBHP; HBV; InMe; OxBoLi; SiTL; ToP; WhC
(Fewer Books, More Salad.) OnPM
To Miracle. Michael Drayton. *See* Idea: "Some misbelieving and profane in love."
To Miss ——. Samuel Johnson. CABA
To Miss Arundell. Walter Savage Landor. OBVV
To Miss Blackett on Her First Ascent to the Summit of Helvellyn. Wordsworth. CLwM
To Miss Blount, with the Works of Voiture. Pope. PIA
(To a Young Lady, with the Works of Voiture.) EiCL
To Miss Charlotte Pulteney in Her Mother's Arms. Ambrose Philips. *See* To Charlotte Pulteney.
To Miss Eleanor Ambrose on the Occasion of Her Wearing an Orange Lily at a Ball in Dublin Castle on July the 12th. Earl of Chesterfield. EnLoPo
To Miss Ferrier. Burns. CBEP
To Miss Georgiana. Ambrose Philips. WaPE
To Miss M——, Written by Moonlight. Sir Samuel Egerton Brydges. Sonn
To Miss Margaret Pulteney. Ambrose Philips. CEP; EiCL
To Mr. Alexander Ross. James Beattie. OxBS
To Mr. B. B. John Donne. MaMe
To Mr. C. B. John Donne. AnAnS-1; MaMe
To Mr. Cyriack Skinner upon his Blindness. Milton. *See* To Cyriack Skinner ("Cyriack, this three years' day").
To Mr. E. G. John Donne. MaMe
To Mr. George Herbert. John Donne. MaMe
To Mr. Gray. David Garrick. OBEC
To Mr. Gray. Thomas Warton, the Younger. Sonnets, VI. Sonn
To Mr. H. Lawes on His Airs. Milton. AWP; InPo; JAWP; LoBV; NoP; WBP
(Sonnet XIII: To Mr. H. Lawes on His Aires.) OBS

(To My Friend, Mr. Henry Lawes [on His Airs].) MuSP; Sonn
To Mr. Henry Lawes [Who Had Then Newly Set a Song of Mine in the Year 1635]. Edmund Waller. AnAnS-2; CLwM; CTC; PP; SCEP-2; SeCP; SeCV-1
To M. Henry Lawes, the Excellent Composer, of His Lyrics. Robert Herrick. OAEP
To Mr. Hobbes [*or* Hobs]. Abraham Cowley. LoBV; ReEn; SCEP-2; SeCV-1
To Mr. I. L. ("Blest are your North parts"). John Donne. MaMe; SeCP
To Mr. I. L. ("Of that short roll of friends"). John Donne. MaMe
To Mr. Izaak Walton. Charles Cotton. *See* Retirement, The.
To Mr. Jervas, with Fresnoy's "Art of Painting," Translated by Mr. Dryden. Pope. OBEC
To Mr. John Davies. Sir John Harington. TuPP
To Mr. Lawrence. Milton. AWP; DiPo; GTBS; GTBS-D; GTBS-P; GTBS-W; GTSE; GTSL; InPo; JAWP; MyFE; OBEV; WBP
(Lawrence, of Virtuous Father.) NoP
(Lawrence, of Virtuous Father Virtuous Son.) CABA; MaPo; PoE
(Sonnet XVII: "Lawrence of vertuous father . . ."). MBW-1; OBS; SeEP
To Mr. Pope. Walter Harte. EiCL
To Mr. R. W. ("If, as mine is, thy life a slumber be"). John Donne. MaMe
To Mr. R. W. ("Kindly I envy thy songs perfection"). John Donne. AnAnS-1; MaMe
To Mr. R. W. ("Muse not that by thy mind"). John Donne. MaMe
To Mr. R. W. ("Zealously my Muse"). John Donne. MaMe
To Mr. Rowland Woodward ("Like one who'in her third widdowhood doth professe"). John Donne. AnAnS-1; MaMe; MeP; MePo
To Mr. S. B. John Donne. MaMe
To Mr. T. W. ("All haile sweet poet"). John Donne. MaMe
To Mr. T. W. ("At once, from hence . . ."). John Donne. MaMe; PP
To Mr. T. W. ("Hast thee harsh verse"). John Donne. MaMe
To Mr. T. W. ("Pregnant again with th'old twins"). John Donne. MaMe
To Mr. Tilman after He Had Taken Orders. John Donne. MaMe
To Mr. William Long, on his Recovery from a Dangerous Illness. William Hayley. Sonn
To Mrs. Ann Flaxman. Blake. OBRV
To Mistress Anne. John Skelton. EnRePo
To Mistress Anne Cecil, upon Making Her a New Year's Gift, January 1, 1567-8. William Cecil, Lord Burghey. ElL; OBSC; PrWP
To Mrs. Boteler. Mary Chandler. WaPE
To Mrs. Diana Cecyll. Lord Herbert of Cherbury. AnAnS-2
To Mistress Gertrude Statham. John Skelton. *Fr.* The Garlande of Laurell. OAEP
To Mistress [*or* Maystres] Isabel[l] Pennell. John Skelton. *Fr.* The Garlande of Laurell. AtBAP; CBEP; EnPo; FlW; LiTG; LiTL; LO; OAEP; OBEV (new ed.); OBSC; OxBoLi; PoEL-1; PoFS; PoIE; SeCeV; StP; TrGrPo; TuPP; YAT
("By Saint Mary, my lady.") EG
(In Praise of Isabel Pennell.) CH
To Mrs. L. H. Leigh Hunt. Sonn
To Mrs. Leigh upon Her Wedding-Day. George Canning. ALV
To Mrs. M. B. on Her Birthday [*or* Birth-Day]. Pope. CEP; EnLoPo; FaBoEn; OBEC
To Mrs. M. H. John Donne. MaMe
To Mistress Margaret Hussey. John Skelton. *Fr.* The Garlande of Laurell. ACP; AnFE; AtBAP; CBEP; DiPo; EnLoPo; GN; GoBC; GoJo; HBV; HoPM; InPo; LiTL; LoBV; NoP; OAEP; OBEV; OBSC; OTPC (1923 ed.); PG (1955 ed.); PoEL-1; PoIE; PoRA; PoSa; ReEn; SeCeV; SiCE; ThWaDe; TreFT; TrGrPo; TuPP; ViBoPo
(Merry Margaret.) GoTP; RIS
(Mistress Margaret Hussey.) FaBoCh; LoGBV
To Mistress Margaret Tilney. John Skelton. *Fr.* The Garlande of Laurell. MeEL
To Mistress Margery Wentworth. John Skelton. *Fr.* The Garlande of Laurell. BoPe; CBEP; EnLoPo; EnRePo; LoBV; OBEV; OBSC; TrGrPo; ViBoPo
("With margerain gentle.") EG
To Mris. M[ary] A[wbrey] upon Absence. Katherine Philips. PeRV
To Mrs. Reynolds's Cat. Keats. *See* To a Cat.
To Mistress Sarah Hickford. —— Chambers. SeCL
To Mrs. Smith, Occasioned by the First of Her Sonnets. William Hayley. Sonn
To Modigliani to Prove to Him That I Am a Poet. Max Jacob, *tr. fr. French by* Wallace Fowlie. TrJP
To Mollidusta. James Robinson Planché. NA
To Monsieur de la Mothe le Vayer. Molière, *tr. fr. French by* Austin Dobson. AWP; JAWP; WBP
To Morfydd. Lionel Johnson. AnIV; MoBrPo; OBMV; PIA; PoVP; ThWaDe; ViPP
To Morning. Blake. EnRP; ERoP-1
To mortal men Peace giveth these good things. Peace on Earth. Bacchylides. AWP; JAWP; WBP
To Mother. Thomas W. Fessenden. MaRV
(Mother.) SoP
To Mother Fairie. Alice Cary. OTPC (1946 ed.); PCH
To Mother—in Heaven. Bennett Weaver. OQP
To Mother Nature. Frederic Lawrence Knowles. HBV
To move the springs of nature as we please. To Mr. Pope. Walter Harte. EiCL
To murder one so young! Alfred Domett. *Fr.* A Christmas Hymn; New Style. VA
To Music. William Kean Seymour. HBMV
To Music. Shelley. *See* Fragment, A: To Music.
To Music Bent Is My Retired Mind. Thomas Campion. CoBE; EnRePo; OxBoCh; ReEn; SiCE; UnS
(To Music [*or* Musicke] Bent.) TrPWD; TuPP
To Music [*or* Musique], to Becalm[e] His Fever. Robert Herrick. ATP; EG; GoJo; HBV; MuSP; OBEV; OBS; QFR; ReEn; SeCL; SeCV-1
"Charm me asleep, and melt me so," *sel.* UnS
To Musick ("Begin to charme"). Robert Herrick. MuSP
To Musick ("Musick, thou Queen of Heaven, care-charming-spel"). Robert Herrick. UnS
To mute and material things. Nelson and Pitt [*or* Nelson, Pitt, Fox]. Sir Walter Scott. *Fr.* Marmion, *Introd. to* I. FOL; OBEV
To my,/ Aye. Paddy Doyle. *Unknown.* AmSS
To My Auld Dog Dash. John Barr of Craigielee. AnNZ
To My Blackthorn Stick. F. R. Higgins. POTE
To My Book[e]. Ben Jonson. AnAnS-2; EP; MaPo; OAEP; Po; ReIE; SCEP-2; SeCV-1; TuPP
To My Bookseller. Ben Jonson. TuPP
To My Brother. Louise Bogan. NYBP
To My Brother George. Keats. *See* Epistle to My Brother George.
To My Brothers. Norman Gale. VA
To My Brothers. Keats. EnLi-2; Sonn
To My Cat. Rosamund Marriott Watson. VA
To My Child Carlino. Walter Savage Landor. NoP; OBRV
To My Children. Marion Strobel. NP
To My Cosen Mrs. Ellinor Evins. George Alsop. SCAP
To My Country. "Rachel," *tr. fr. Hebrew by* Sholom J. Kahn. LiTW
To My Countrymen. Robert Underwood Johnson. OQP
To My Cousin (C. R.) Marrying My Lady (A.). Thomas Carew. AnAnS-2; SeCP
To My Daughter. Stephen Spender. BoC
To My Daughter Betty [The Gift of God]. Thomas Michael Kettle. CAW; HBMV; JKCP (1955 ed.); OnYI
To My Dead Friend Ben: Johnson. Henry King. AnAnS-2; SeCP
To My Dear and Loving Husband. Anne Bradstreet. AmP; AmPP; AP; CBEP; ForPo; HW; MAmP; NePA; OxBA; PoEL-3; PoLF; SCAP
To My Dear and Most Worthy Friend, Mr Isaac Walton. Charles Cotton. FaBoEn
To My Dear Friend Mr. Congreve [on His Comedy Call'd "The Double-Dealer"]. Dryden. CEP; EiCL; EiPP; FiP; MBW-1; OBS; PoE; PoEL-3; SeCV-2; SeEP
To My Distant Beloved. Alois Jeitteles, *tr. fr. German by* the Reverend Doctor Troutbeck. TrJP
To My Dog "Blanco." Josiah Gilbert Holland. PoLF
To My Empty Purse. Chaucer. *See* Compleint of Chaucer to His Empty Purse, The.

To My Excellent Lucasia, on Our Friendship. Katherine Phi-
lips. CavP; LO; MeLP; OBS; SeCL; SeEP
("I did not live until this time.") EG
To my fancy, idly roaming, comes a picture of the gloaming. The
Echo of a Song. James W. Foley. PEDC
To My Father. James K. Baxter. AnNZ
To My Father. W. S. Graham. FaBoTw
To My Father. Iris Tree. HBMV
To my father went and shyly asked consent. May I Woo the
Lassie? *Unknown.* SaSa
To My Fellow-Mariners, March '53. Thomas Whitbread.
NYBP
To My First Love, My Mother. Christina Rossetti. OHIP
To My Firstborn. Bernard Isaac Durward. JKCP (1926 ed.)
To My Friend. Anne Campbell. PoToHe
To My Friend. Martha Snell Nicholson. SoP
To My Friend. Wilfred Owen. NAMP
To My Friend, behind Walls. Carolyn Kizer. NePoAm-2
To My Friend Butts I Write. Blake. EnRP
To My Friend, Dr. Charleton. Dryden. *See* To My Honor'd
Friend, Dr. Charleton.
To My Friend G. N. from Wrest. Thomas Carew. AnAnS-2
To My Friend, Grown Famous. Eunice Tietjens. HBMV
To My Friend Mr. Henry Lawes [on His Airs]. Milton. *See* To
Mr. H. Lawes on His Airs.
To My Friend Mr. John Anderson. Charles Cotton. PeRV
To My Friend Mr. Motteux. Dryden. MBW-1
To My Friend Whose Parachute Did Not Open. David Wag-
oner. TwAmPo
To My Friends. Stephen Berg. NaP; NYBP
To My Friends. Peter De Vries. FiBHP
To My Friends. Peter Levi. NePoEA-2
To My Friends. Schiller, *tr. fr. German by* James Clarence
Mangan. AWP; LiTW
To My Generation. Benyamin Galai, *tr. fr. Hebrew by* Jacob
Sonntag. TrJP
To My God. George Macdonald. FaChP; TrPWD; TRV
To My Godchild—Francis M. W. M. Francis Thompson. JKCP
To My Grandmother. Frederick Locker-Lampson. ALV;
HBV; InMe; OBVV; TOP; VA
To My Hairdresser. Warham St. Leger. CenHV
To My Honor'd Friend, Dr. Charleton. Dryden. CEP; EiCL;
EiPP; EnL; MBW-1; SeEP
(To My Friend, Dr. Charleton, on His Learned and Useful
Works.) SeCV-2
To My Honoured Friend Mr. George Sandys. Henry King.
AnAnS-2
To My Honor'd Friend Sir Robert Howard, on His Excellent
Poems. Dryden. EiPP
What Is the World, 4 *ll.* TRV
(Design.) MaRV
To My Honored Kinsman, John Dryden [*or* Driden], of Chesterton
[in the County of Huntingdon, Esquire]. Dryden. MBW-1;
OBS, *abr.*; SeEP
To My Honoured Patron Humphery Davie. Benjamin Tomp-
son. SCAP
To My Inconstant Mistress [*or* Mistris]. Thomas Carew. EnLit;
EnLoPo; HBV; LO; LoBV; MeLP; MePo; OBS; SeCePo; SeCL;
SeCV-1; TrGrPo
(Song: To My Inconstant Mistris [*or* Mistress]. AnAnS-2;
BWP; CavP; SCEP-2; SeCP; SeEP
(To His Inconstant Mistress.) OBEV
("When thou, poor excommunicate.") EG
To My Lady. George Henry Boker. *Fr.* Sonnets. AA
To My Lady Mirriel Howard. John Skelton. *Fr.* The Garlande
of Laurell. LoBV
To My Little Son. Julia Johnson Davis. HBMV
To My Love. John Godfrey Saxe. HBV
To My Love. Sir John Suckling. *See* I Prithee Send Me
Back My Heart.
To My Lucasia, in Defence of Declared Friendship. Katherine
Philips. MeLP
To My Mere English Censurer. Ben Jonson. TuPP
To My Mirtle. Blake. HW
To My Mistress. Frederick Locker-Lampson. VA
To My Mistresse in Absence. Thomas Carew. AnAnS-2
To My Mistris Sitting by a Rivers Side. Thomas Carew.
AnAnS-2
To My Most Dearly-Loved [Friend] Henry Reynolds, Esquire, of
Poets and Poesie. Michael Drayton. AnAnS-2; OAEP;
OBS; ReEn; SeEP; TuPP

"For from my cradle you must know that I," *sel.* PP
To My Most Gracious Dread Sovereign. Sir John Davies.
See Dedication: "To that clear majesty which in the
north."
To My Mother. George Barker. *See* Sonnet to My Mother.
To My Mother. Edwin Brock. NMP
To My Mother. Louis Ginsberg. PoSC
To My Mother. Heine, *tr. fr. German by* Matilda Dick-
son. AWP; JAWP; WBP
(Sonnet to My Mother, A, *tr. by* Emma Lazarus.) TrJP
(To His Mother, *tr. by* Ralph Marcus.) OnPM
To My Mother. W. E. Henley. PoVP
To My Mother. Thomas Moore. OHIP; PEDC; PoRL
To My Mother. Poe. AnAmPo; AP; DD; LaNeLa; MAmP;
MaRV; MCCG; NePA; OxBA; PoPo
To My Mountain. Kathleen Raine. OxBS; PoPl
To My Mouse-colored Mare. Tristan Corbière, *tr. fr. French by*
C. F. MacIntyre. ErPo
To My Native Land. James Clarence Mangan. AnIL
"Awake! arise! shake off thy dreams!" *sel.* IrPN
To My New Mistress. Beverly Bowie. PoPl
To My Ninth Decade. Walter Savage Landor. BEL; EnRP
(On His Ninth Decade.) TrGrPo
To My Nose. Alfred A. Forrester. BLPA; BOHV
To My Old, and Most Worthy Friend, Mr. Izaak Walton.
Charles Cotton. SeEP
To My Patrons. Lionel Johnson. JKCP
To My People. Edwin Seaver. TrJP
To my quick ear the leaves conferred. Emily Dickinson. AnFE;
APA; CoAnAm; GTBS-D; MAPA; TwAmPo
To My Readers. Oliver Wendell Holmes. AmPP (3d ed.)
To My Retired Friend Wei. Tu Fu, *tr. fr. Chinese by* Witter
Bynner. LiTW
To My Reverend Dear Brother M. Samuel Stone. John Cot-
ton. SCAP
To My Setter, Scout. Frank H. Seldon. BLPA
To my short-sighted eyes. On My Short-Sightedness. Prem
Chaya. FIW
To My Sister. Wordsworth. EnRP; MBW-2; OBRV; PoE
Change in the Year, A, *sel.* BoTP
To My Son, *sel.* George Barker.
"My darkling child the stars have obeyed," I. TwCP
To My Son. Margaret Johnston Grafflin. *See* Like Mother, like
Son.
To My Son. Thomas Hood. *See* Parental Ode to My Son
[Aged Three Years and Five Months], A.
To My Son, *sel.* Helen Selina Sheridan.
Love Hath a Language. HBV
To My Son. *Unknown.* PoLF; PoMa
To My Son, Aged Three Years and Five Months. Thomas
Hood. *See* Parental Ode to My Son, [Aged Three Years and
Five Months], A.
To My Son Parker, Asleep in the Next Room. Bob Kauf-
man. Kal; TwCP
To My Soul. Phineas Fletcher. OxBoCh
(To My Soul in Its Blindness.) SeCL
To My Successor. George Herbert. MaMe, 2 *versions*
To My Tortoise Ἀνάγκη (Ananke). Eugene Lee-Hamilton.
OBVV
To My Tortoise Chronos. Eugene Lee-Hamilton. VA
To My Totem. Henry Charles Beeching. VA
To my true king I offered free from stain. A Jacobite's Epitaph
[*or* Epitaph on a Jacobite]. Macaulay. GTBS; InP;
NBM; OBNC; OBNV; VA; ViBoPo
To My Truly Valiant, Learned Friend, Who in His Book Resolv'd
the Art Gladiatory into the Mathematics. Richard Love-
lace. PoEL-3
To my twin who lives in a cruel country. The Dual Site.
Michael Hamburger. NePoEA-2
To My Unborn Son. Cyril Morton Horne. BLPA
To My Valentine. *Unknown.* PCH; SoPo
To my village fair no lass can compare. The Lovely Village Fair;
or, I Dont Mean to Tell You Her Name. *Unknown.* CoMu
To My Wife. Ausonius, *tr. fr. Latin by* Garrett Stewart.
HW
To My Wife. John Bayliss. POTE
To My Wife. William Rose Benét. PoMa
To My Wife. Peter Firth. BoPe
To My Wife. James Forsyth. WaP
To My Wife. Robert Louis Stevenson. *See* My Wife.
To My Worthy Friend Master Geo. [*or* George] Sands [On His

Translation of the Psalmes]. Thomas Carew. AnAnS-2; MePo; SCEP-2; SeCV-1; SeEP
(To My Worthy Friend Mr. George Sandys.) MeLP; OBS
To My Worthy Friend, Mr. James Bayley. Nicholas Noyes. SCAP
To My Young Lady, Lucy Sidney. Edmund Waller. *See* To a Very Young Lady.
To Myra. Fulke Greville. *See* I, with Whose Colors Myra Dressed Her Head.
To Myself, after Forty Years. T. H. White. NYBP
To Myself on the Occasion of My Twenty-first Century. John Brunner. HYE
To N. V. de G. S. Robert Louis Stevenson. BrPo; VA
To Naples. H. B. Mallalieu. WaP
To Naso. Catullus, *tr. fr. Latin by* Jack Lindsay. ErPo
To Natalie. Morrie Ryskind. HBMV
To Nature. Samuel Taylor Coleridge. BWP; ERoP-1; MaRV
To Nature. Mahlon Leonard Fisher. AnAmPo
To Nature. Friedrich Hölderlin, *tr. fr. German by* Frederick Prokosch. LiTW
To Nature Seekers. Robert W. Chambers. MoShBr
To Ned. Herman Melville. MWA-1; PoEL-5; ViBoPo
To New Haven. Frederick Scheetz Jones. *See* On the Democracy of Yale.
To New Haven and Boston. Walter Foster Angell. TreFS
To New Jerusalem. Dan Gillespie. QAH
To New York. Léopold Sédar-Senghor, *tr. fr. French by* Ulli Beier. PBA
To Night. Thomas Lovell Beddoes. LoBV; Sonn
To Night. Shelley. AnFE; AtBAP; ATP; AWP; BEL; BoLiVe; CBEP; ChER; CoBE; EnL; EnLi-2; EnLit; EnRP; EPN; ERoP-2; ExPo; GTSL; HBV; HBVY; ILP; InP; InPo; JAWP; LoBV; MaPo; MCCG; MemP; MyFE; OAEP; OBNC; OBRV; PCD; PoE; PoFS; PoIE; PoLF; PoRA; SeCeV; TOP; TreFS; TrGrPo; UnPo (1st ed.); ViBoPo; WBP; WHA; WiR
(Night.) BoC; OAEP
("Swiftly walk o'er the western wave.") EG
(To the Night.) CH; GTBS; GTBS-D; GTBS-P; GTBS-W; GTSE; ShBV-4
To Night. *Unknown.* *See* O Night, O Jealous Night.
To Night. Joseph Blanco White. CBEP; GoBC; GTBS-W; HBV; MaRV; OBEV (new ed.); OBRV; RoGo; Sonn; TreFS; ViBoPo; WGRP
(Mysterious Night.) AnFE
("Mysterious night, when our first parent knew.") EG
(Night.) AnIV; BoC; JKCP (1926 ed.)
(Night and Death.) EPN
"Hesperus with the Host of Heaven came," *sel.* MyFE
To Night, the Mother of Sleep and Death. John Addington Symonds. Sonn
To Nobodaddy. Blake. DiPo; ERoP-1
To nothing fitter can I thee compare. Idea, X. Michael Drayton. BEL; ElL; HBV; OBSC; SiCE; Sonn; TrGrPo; TuPP; ViBoPo
To Nowhere. David Ignatow. CAD
To Nysus. Sir Charles Sedley. PeRV
To O. E. A. Claude McKay. BANP; PoNe
To O. S. C. Annie Eliot Trumbull. AA
To O. W. Holmes. Paul Hamilton Hayne. DD
To Oenone. Robert Herrick. *See* To Aenone.
To Old Age. Walt Whitman. InP
To Old John Heywood the Epigrammatist, Wheresoever. John Davies of Hereford. SiCE
To Olive. Lord Alfred Douglas. OBEV (new ed.); OBVV
To Oliver Cromwell. Milton. *See* To the Lord General Cromwell.
To Olivia. Francis Thompson. MoBrPo
To One. Gustaf Munch-Petersen, *tr. fr. Danish by* Carl Nesjar *and* Martin S. Allwood. LiTW
To One Admiring Herself [*or* Her Selfe] in a Looking-Glass. Thomas Randolph. AnAnS-2; CLwM; LiTL; ViBoPo
To One alone my thoughts arise. Longfellow. *Fr.* Coplas de Manrique. ChIP
To One Being Old. Langdon Elwyn Mitchell. AA
To one fair lady out of court. The Challenge. Pope. PIA; PoEL-3
To one full sound and silently. The Man with Three Friends. Dora Greenwell. OBVV
To One in Bedlam. Ernest Dowson. ACP; BrPo; EnLi-2; MoBrPo; NeMa; OBMV; PoVP; Sonn; ViPP; WHA
To One in Paradise. Poe. AA; AmLP; AmPP; AnFE; AP; APA; BoLiVe; CoAnAm; CoBA; GTBS-D; HBV; LiTA; LiTL; LO; MeWo; MWA-1; NePA; OBEV; OBRV; OBVV; OxBA; PG; PoIE; PoLF; PoPo; TrGrPo; ViBoPo; WHA; YT
To one kneeling down no word came. In a Country Church. R. S. Thomas. ToPo
To One Long in City Pent. Keats. *See* To One Who Has Been Long in City Pent.
To One Married to an Old Man. Edmund Waller. SeCP
To One of Little Faith. Hildegarde Flanner. HBMV
To One Older. Marion M. Boyd. HBMV
To One on Her Waste of Time. Wilfrid Scawen Blunt. The Love Sonnets of Proteus, LVIII. ViBoPo
To One Persuading a Lady to Marriage. Katherine Philips. OBEV
(Answer to Another Persuading a Lady to Marriage, An.) CavP
To One Shortly to Die. Walt Whitman. CBEP
To One That Had Little Wit. George Turberville. EnRePo
To One That Pleaded Her Own Want of Merit. Thomas Stanley. OBS
(To Celia Pleading Want of Merit.) MeLP
To One Unknown. Helen Dudley. NP
To One Who after Death Would Leave His Lively Picture. Thomas Howell. TuPP
To One Who Denies the Possibility of a Permanent Peace. Lady Margaret Sackville. HBMV; MaRV
To One Who Died in Autumn. Virginia McCormick. HBMV
To One Who Had Censured His Public Exposition of Dante. Boccaccio, *tr. fr. Italian by* Dante Gabriel Rossetti. *Fr.* Sonnets. AWP
(Tribute to Dante, A.) GoBC
To One Who Has Been Long in City Pent. Keats. BEL; BoLiVe; CBEP; CoBE; EnLi-2; EnLit; EnRP; GTBS-W; GTSL; HBV; LiTB; LiTG; MBW-2; MCCG; MERP; PoFS; SeCeV; Sonn; TreFT; TrGrPo
(Nature's Enchantment.) BoPe
(Sonnet: "To one who has been long in city pent.") BLPA; FaBoBe; LoBV; NeHB
(To One Long in City Pent.) PAn
To One Who Worshipped Gods of Gold. John Richard Moreland. MaRV
To One Who Would Make a Confession. Wilfrid Scawen Blunt. The Love Sonnets of Proteus, LXII. HBV; ViBoPo
To onpreise women it were a shame. Women Are Worthy. *Unknown.* LO; MeEL
To others he was a presence—perhaps only. Matthew. Clive Sansom. HaMV
To Our Blessed Lady. Henry Constable. ACP; CAW; GoBC; ISi; OBSC
(To Our Lady.) CoBE
To Our Blessed Lord upon the Choice of His Sepulchre. Richard Crashaw. *See* Upon the Savior's Tomb.
To Our Catchment Board. Edmund Blunden. MoPW
To our country's soldiers. Tribute to Our Soldiers. Marion Kennedy. PEDC
To Our English Terence, Master William Shakespeare. John Davies of Hereford. SiCE
To Our First Born. Ebon. BP
To Our Friends. Lucian B. Watkins. BANP
To Our House-Dog Captain. Walter Savage Landor. NBM; PoEL-4
To Our Ladies of Death. James Thomson. GoTS
To Our Lady. Henry Constable. *See* To Our Blessed Lady.
To Our Lady. Robert Henryson. ACP; CAW
To Our Lady. Mary Dixon Thayer. TreFS
To Our Lady, the Ark of the Covenants. Raymond E. F. Larsson. ISi
To Our Lord. Francisco Galvam, *tr. fr. Portuguese by* Thomas Walsh. CAW
To Our Lord in the Sacrament. St. Anselm, *tr. fr. Latin by* Romano Rios. CAW
To Our Lord, upon the Water Made Wine. Richard Crashaw. MaMe; MePo; SCEP-1
To Our Saviour. Agostinho da Cruz, *tr. fr. Portuguese by* Thomas Walsh. CAW
To outer senses there is peace. La Fuite de la Lune. Oscar Wilde. *Fr.* Impressions. Po; PoVP; SyP

To own nothing, but to be. Words Spoken Alone. Dannie Abse. NYBP
To Oxford. Gerard Manley Hopkins. BrPo
To Oxford. Thomas Russell. *See* Sonnet: To Oxford.
To Pain. George Sterling. JKCP (1926 ed.)
To Paint a Water Lily. Ted Hughes. PP
To Paint the Portrait of a Bird. Jacques Prévert, *tr. fr. French by* Lawrence Ferlinghetti. FlW
To Pan. John Fletcher. *See* God of Sheep, The.
To Pandora. Alexander Craig. Sonn; TuPP
(Sonnet: "Go you, O winds that blow from north to south.") ElL
To Paris, to Paris, to Paris. The Hobby Horse. *Unknown.* PCH
To Pass the Place Where Pleasure Is. *Unknown.* CoMu
To Paths Unknown. Whittier. *See* At Last.
To Patricia on Her Christening Day. Edith Ballinger Price. BiCB
To Pensacola town we'll bid adieu. Homeward Bound. *Unknown.* AmSS
To Penshurst. Ben Jonson. AnAnS-2; AtBAP; AWP; BWP; CABA; CABL; LoBV; NoP; OBS; PoEL-2; PoFS; ReEn; ReIE; SCEP-2; SeCP; SeCV-1; SeEP; TuPP
"Thou hast thy ponds, that pay thee tribute fish," *sel.* FaBoEn
To people who allege that we. The Uses of Ocean. Sir Owen Seaman. ALV; FiBHP
To Percy Shelley. Leigh Hunt. Sonn
To Perilla. Robert Herrick. AnAnS-2; AtBAP; NoP; OBS; SCEP-2; SeCP; SeCV-1; SeEP; UnPo (1st ed.)
To Petronilla Who Has Put Up Her Hair. Henry Howarth Bashford. HBV
To Petronius Arbiter. Oliver St. John Gogarty. OBMV
To Phidyle ("Caelo supinas"). Horace, *tr. fr. Latin by* Austin Dobson. Odes, III, 23. AWP
To Philip Levine, on the Day of Atonement. Robert Mezey. AmPC
To Phillis. Robert Herrick. *See* To Phyllis, to Love and Live with Him.
To Phillis. Sir Charles Sedley. *See* Song: "Phyllis is my only joy."
To Phillis. Edmund Waller. *See* To Phyllis.
To Phillis, the Fair Shepherdess. Thomas Lodge. *See* To Phyllis, the Fair Shepherdess.
To Philomel. John Tatham. SeCL
To Philomela. Benjamin Colman. SCAP
To Phoebe. W. S. Gilbert. BOHV; InMe; InP
To Phoebus Seeing a Lady before Sunrise. Edmund Prestwich. SeCL
To Phyllis ("Est mihi"). Horace, *tr. fr. Latin by* Eugene Field. Odes, IV, 11. InMe
To Phyllis. Thomas Lodge. *See* Love Guards the Roses of Thy Lips.
To Phyllis. *Unknown.* SeCL
To Phyllis. Edmund Waller. CavP; NoP; SCEP-2; TrGrPo
(Plea for Promiscuity, A.) UnTE
(To Phillis.) AnAnS-2; CEP; OAEP; SeCP
(Why Should We Delay.) MeWo
To Phyllis, the Fair Shepherdess. Thomas Lodge. Phyllis, XV. ViBoPo
("My Phyllis [*or* Phillis] hath the morning sun.") SiCE; TuPP
(Phillis.) LoBV; OBEV, 12 *ll.* OBSC
(Phyllis.) ACP; ElL
To Phyllis [*or* Phillis], to Love and Live with Him. Robert Herrick. CavP; CLwM; LiTL; OAEP; PAn
(To Phillis.) AnEnPo
To Pi Ssu Yao. Tu Fu, *tr. fr. Chinese by* Kenneth Rexroth. ML
To Pikes Peak. Elijah Clarence Hills. PoOW
To pile like thunder to its close. Emily Dickinson. MAmP; MWA-2
To Ping-ku, Asleep. Lawrence Durrell. ChMP; NeBP
To Pius X at Easter. John Hazard Wildman. JKCP (1955 ed.)
To place the precisely slippered toes. Portraits. Robert Fitzgerald. OnHM
To plant a seed and see it grow. Lesson. Harry Behn. TiPo (1959 ed.)
To plant a tree! How small the twig. Arbor Day. Dorothy Brown Thompson. SiSoSe
To plant corn here was a futile whim. Playground of the Pixie. Grant Code. FiSC
To Plautia. Sir Aston Cokayne. CavP
To Plead My Faith. Earl of Essex. TuPP
To Pledge or Not to Pledge. *Unknown.* STF
To Poets. George Darley. Sonn
To Poets. Walter Savage Landor. ViBoPo
To Poets. Charles Hamilton Sorley. LO
To Poets All. Thomas Curtis Clark. MaRV
To Poets and Airmen. Stephen Spender. WaP
To Polla. John Owen, *tr. fr. Latin by* Thomas Harvey. *Fr.* Four Epigrams. PrWP
To Pontius Washing His Hands. Richard Crashaw. MaMe; SeEP
To Pontius Washing His Blood-Stained Hands. Richard Crashaw. MaMe
To popularize the mule, its neat exterior. The Labors of Hercules. Marianne Moore. AnAmPo; OxBA
To Posterity. Bertolt Brecht, *tr. fr. German by* H. R. Hays. OnHM
To Postumus ("Eheu, fugaces"). Horace, *tr. fr. Latin by* Sir Stephen Edward De Vere. Odes, II, 14. LiTW; OuHeWo
To Potapovitch. Hart Crane. UnS
To praise men as good, and to take them for such. Charity in Thought. Samuel Taylor Coleridge. WhC
To praise the blue whale's crystal jet. The Whale His Bulwark. Derek Walcott. TTY
To praise thy life or wail thy worthy death. An Epitaph upon the Right Honorable Sir Philip Sidney, Knight, Lord Governor of Flushing [*or* Epitaph on Sir Philip Sidney]. *At. to* Sir Walter Ralegh. FCP; ReIE; SiCE; SiPS; TuPP
To Primroses Filled [*or* Fill'd] with Morning-Dew. Robert Herrick. AnAnS-2; EG; HBV; OBS; PoPl; SCEP-2; SeCL; SeCV-1; SeEP; ViBoPo
To prink me up, and make me higher placed. Seven Sonnets in Sequence, IV. George Gascoigne. Sonn
To print, or not to print—that is the question. Hamlet's Soliloquy Imitated. Richard Jago. SiTL
To Promise Is One Thing, to Perform Is Another. La Fontaine. UnTE
To Prote. Simmias, *tr. fr. Greek by* John Addington Symonds. AWP
To Psyche. Keats. *See* Ode to Psyche.
To Puck. Beatrice Llewellyn Thomas. HBMV
To Pulpit and Tribune. Amos N. Wilder. MaRV
To purge what I am pleased to call my mind. Ataraxia. Bert Leston Taylor. HBMV; InMe
To Purity and Truth. *Unknown, tr. fr. Chinese by* William C. White. TrJP
To put new shingles on old roofs. A Little Brother of the Rich. Edward Sandford Martin. AA; HBV
To Pyrrha ("Quis multa tracilis"). Horace, *tr. fr. Latin by* Milton. Odes, I, 5. AWP; CLwM; EnLi-1, *tr. by* Goldwin Smith; JAWP; OuHeWo, *tr. by* Goldwin Smith; WBP
(Fifth Ode of Horace, *tr. by* Milton.) EnLoPo; MaPo (1969 ed.); PoEL-3
(For Whom, Pyrrha? *tr. by* Milton.) LiTW
(Horace to Pyrrha, *tr. by* Eugene Field.) LHV
To Queen Elizabeth. Sir John Davies. *See* Dedication: "To that clear majesty which in the north."
To Queen Elizabeth. Sir Walter Ralegh. *See* Silent Lover, The.
To Quintius. Catullus, *tr. fr. Latin by* George Lamb. OnPM
To Quintus Dellius ("Aequam memento"). Horace, *tr. fr. Latin by* John Herman Merivale. Odes, II, 3. OuHeWo
To R. B. Gerard Manley Hopkins. CBEP; CMoP; CoBMV; GTBS-P; InvP; ML; PoVP; ViPP
To R. H. S. James Bayard Taylor. Sonn
To R. Hudson. Alexander Montgomerie. OxBS
To R. K. James Kenneth Stephen. CenHV; EnLi-2 (1949 ed.); NBM; OtMeF; Par; WhC
(Lapsus Calami.) VA
(Millennium, The.) BOHV
To R. W. E. Ellen Hooper. AnAmPo
To rail or jest, ye know I use it not. Sonnet. Sir Thomas Wyatt. FCP; SiPS
To Rathlin's Isle I chanced to sail. The Enchanted Island. Luke Aylmer Conolly. OBRV
To reach it. Waterfall. Anne Welsh. PeSA

To read my book[e] the virgin shie [*or* shy]. To His Book[e]. Martial. AnAnS-2; AWP; LiTW
To Reformers in Despair. Vachel Lindsay. InP
To Remain. C. P. Cavafy, *tr. fr. Modern Greek by* John Mavrogordato. ErPo
To reply, in face of a bad season. The Ill Wind. Jay Macpherson. MoCV
To Retirement. Luís de Léon, *tr. fr. Spanish by* Thomas Walsh. TrJP
To Rich Givers. Walt Whitman. AnAmPo
To Richard Boyle, Earl of Burlington. Pope. *See* Of the Use of Riches
To Richard Wright. Conrad Kent Rivers. AmNP; IDB
To ride piggy-back. Slave. Langston Hughes. LiTM (1970 ed.)
To Rimbaud in Hell. Joseph Cardarelli. QAH
To rise up and get away from all this. Escape. Leonard Mann. NeLNL
To Robert Browning. Walter Savage Landor. BEL; EnLi-2 (1949 ed.); EnRP; EPN; GTBS; GTSL; ILP; InP; MCCG; NoP; OAEP; PoRL; ViBoPo
"There is delight in singing, though none hear," *sel.* MyFE
To Robert Earl of Oxford and Earl Mortimer. Pope. CEP; OBEC
To Robert Louis Stevenson. W. E. Henley. Echoes, XXIX. MoBrPo
To Robin Redbreast. Robert Herrick. OBS; SeEP; TrGrPo
To Ronge. Whittier. AnEnPo
To Roosevelt. Rubén Darío, *tr. fr. Spanish by* Elijah Clarence Hills. WoL
"United States are rich, they're powerful and great, The," *fr.* II. PoFr
To Rosamond [*or* Rosemounde]. Chaucer. CABA; CBEP; InP; NoP; PAn; PIA; PoLi
(Ballade to Rosamund.) MeEL
To Rose. Sara Teasdale. BiCB; HBV
To Rosemary. Stephen Vincent Benét. LaNeLa
To Rosemounde. Chaucer. *See* To Rosamond.
To Roses in the Bosome of Castara. William Habington. *Fr.* Castara, I. AnAnS-2; CavP; CLwM; EnLoPo; GoBC; HBV; LoBV; MeLP; OBEV; PoAn; SeCL; SeCP; SeEP; UnTE; ViBoPo
To Rosina Pico. William Wilberforce Lord. AA
To Ruin. Burns. CoBE
To Rupert Brooke. W. W. Gibson. *See* Going, The.
To Russia. Joaquin Miller. AA; AmePo; AnAmPo
To S. C. Robert Louis Stevenson. PeVV
To S. R. Crockett. Robert Louis Stevenson. FaBoEn; GTBS-D; LO; OBNC; ShBV-4
(Blows the Wind To-Day.) CH; GTSE; LoBV
(Whaups, The.) VA
To S.T.C. on His 179th Birthday, October 12th, 1951. Maurice Carpenter. FaBoTw
To Sabidius. Martial, *tr. fr. Latin by* Timothe Kendall. DiPo; TuPP
To Saint Catherine. Henry Constable. GoBC
To St. Joseph. Charles L. O'Donnell. JKCP
To Saint Margaret. Henry Constable. ACP; GoBC
To St. Mary Magdalen. Henry Constable. ACP; CoBE; LoBV (2d ed.); PoEL-2; Sonn; TuPP
To St. Mary Magdalen. Benjamin Dionysius Hill. AA
To St. Peter and St. Paul. Henry Constable. ReEn; Sonn; TuPP
To St. Valentine. Jennie Betts Hartswick. DD
To Sally. John Quincy Adams, *after the Latin of* Horace. AA; ALV; AWP; JAWP; LHV; WBP
To Samuel Daniel, Prince of English Poets. Francis Davison. ReIE
To San Francisco. S. J. Alexander. PAH
To Satch. Samuel Allen. AmNP; Kal; PoNe (1970 ed.); SD; TTY
(American Gothic.) IDB
To Saxham. Thomas Carew. AnAnS-2; OBS
To Science. Poe. *See* Sonnet to Science.
To Scilla. Sir Charles Sedley. PeRV; PV
To Scott. Winifred Letts. PoLF
To Sea, to Sea! Thomas Lovell Beddoes. *Fr.* Death's Jest Book, I, i. EtS; OTPC; PCD; VA
(Mariners' Song.) OBVV; YT
(Sailors' Song.) HBV
(Sea Song.) GoTP
(Song from the Ship.) GTBS-D; OBRV; PeER
(To Sea.) CH
To search our souls. Lent. Jane Mckay Lanning. MaRV; TRV
To See a Quaint Outlandish Fowl. Henry Farley. *Fr.* St Paul's Church, Her Bill for the Parliament. ViBoPo
(Bounty of Our Age, The.) FaBoCh; SeCePo; SeCL
To see a [*or* the] world in a grain of sand. Auguries of Innocence. Blake. AnFE; AtBAP; BEL; BoLiVe; CABA; CABL; CoBE; DiPo; EG; EiCL; EiPP; EnLi-2; EnLit; EnRP; ERoP-1; FaBoCh; FaBoEn; FaBV; FaFP; GoTP; GTBS-W; ILP; ImOP; InP; LiTB; LiTG; LO; LoBV; LoGBV; MaRV; MasP; NoP; OAEP; OBNC; OBRV; OnPM; OtMeF; PeER; Po; PoEL-4; PoFr; PoFS; RePo; SeCeV; TOP; TreFS; TrGrPo; TRV; ViBoPo; WGRP; WHA; WoL; YAT
To see both blended in one flood. Upon the Infant Martyrs. Richard Crashaw. MaMe; NoP
To See God's Bleedin' Lam', *with music. Unknown.* BoAN-2
To see the Lord the shepherds. We Would See Jesus. *Unknown.* STF
To see my coat hanging there limp as a scarecrow's. On the Couch. Oscar Williams. WaP
To see the Kaiser's epitaph. The Laughing Willow. Oliver Herford. BOHV; HBV
To see the moment hold a madrigal. Sonnet on the Sonnet. Lord Alfred Douglas. MoBrPo (1942 ed.)
To see the petrel cropping in the farmyard. Burns Singer. *Fr.* Sonnets for a Dying Man. NePoEA-2
To see the world in a grain of sand. *See* To see a world in a grain of sand.
To see them coming headstrong. In Love with the Bears. Greg Kuzma. NYBP
To see you every hour. A Divided Thought. *Unknown.* OnPM
To see you standing in the sagging bookstore door. The Visit of the Professor of Aesthetics. Margaret Danner. Far from Africa: Four Poems, 3. AmNP
To seek each where, where man doth live. Sir Thomas Wyatt. FCP; SiPS
To seeke new worlds, for golde, for prayse, for glory. Sir Walter Ralegh. *Fr.* The Last Booke of the Ocean to Scinthia. FaBoEn
To Seem the Stranger Lies My Lot. Gerard Manley Hopkins. BrPo; CoBMV; MaPo (1969 ed.); ViPP
To Seignora Cuzzoni. Ambrose Philips. *See* To Signora Cuzzoni.
To Seneca Lake. James Gates Percival. BoTP
(Seneca Lake.) AnNE
To Senna Hoy. Else Lasker-Schüler, *tr. fr. German by* Glauco Cambon. OnPM
To Sextus. Martial, *tr. fr. Latin by* J. A. Pott *and* F. A. Wright. ALV
To Sextus, an Ill Reader. Sir John Harington. TuPP
To Shades of Underground. Thomas Campion. *See* When Thou Must Home.
To shaggy Pan, and all the wood-nymphs. A Shepherd's Gift. Anyte, *tr. by* John William Burgon. AWP
To shaggy Pan, and to the Fold-nymphs fair. By the Fountain. Anyte, *tr. by* Lord Neaves. OnPM
To Shakespeare. Hartley Coleridge. VA
To Shakespeare. Hart Crane. Sonn
To Shakespeare. Richard Edwin Day. AA
To Shakespeare. Thomas Edwards. Sonn
To Shakespeare. Frances Anne Kemble. Sonn
To Sheila Playing Haydn. Sylvia Lynd. LO
To Shelley. Walter Savage Landor. ViBoPo
To Shelley. John Banister Tabb. AA
To shoot, to shoot, would be my delight. A Shooting Song. William Brighty Rands. OTPC (1923 ed.)
To show that Africa is more than breadth. The Giraffe. Marvin Solomon. NePoAm-2
To show their love, the neighbours far and near. Blouzelinda's Funeral. John Gay. *Fr.* The Shepherd's Week: Friday. OBEC
To shred them: a narrow labor, and simply toss. Destruction of Letters. Babette Deutsch. HoPM
To Signora Cuzzoni. Ambrose Philips. CEP; LoBV; OBEC
(To Seignora Cuzzoni.) EiCL
To Silence. Thomas Lovell Beddoes. Sonn
To Silence. T. Sturge Moore. BrPo
To Silvia. Shakespeare. *See* Who Is Silvia?
To Silvia ("You I love, by all that's true"). *Unknown.* SeCL

To (continued)
To Silvia. Countess of Winchilsea. *Fr.* The Cautious Lovers. HBV
To Simplicity. Samuel Taylor Coleridge. Sonn
To sin, unshamed, to lose, unthinking. Russia. Aleksandr Blok. AWP; JAWP; WBP; WoL
To sing of wars, of captains, and of kings. Prologue. Anne Bradstreet. AmPP (3d ed.); AP; OxBA; SCAP
To Sir Edward Herbert, at Julyers. John Donne. MaMe; SCEP-1; SeCV-1
To Sir Francis Brian [*or* Bryan]. Sir Thomas Wyatt. *Fr.* Satires, III. FCP; SiPS
(Satire 3: To Sir Francis Brian.) EnRePo
To Sir George Etheridge. William Wycherley. PeRV
To Sir Green-eyes Grimalkin de Tabby de Sly. The Dandy Cat. Laura E. Richards. CIV
To Sir H. W. at His Going Ambassador to Venice. John Donne. MaMe; MeLP; SeEP
To Sir Henrie Saville [upon His Translation of Tacitus]. Ben Jonson. OBS; SeCV-1
To Sir Henry Cary. Ben Jonson. NoP
To Sir Henry Goodyear. Ben Jonson. NoP
To Sir Henry Goodyere. John Donne. MaMe; SeEP
To Sir Henry Vane the Younger. Milton. OBS; Sonn
To Sir Henry Wotton ("Here's no more news than virtue"). John Donne. MaMe; Tupp
(Verse-Letter: To Sir Henry Wootton.) EP
To Sir Henry Wotton ("Sir, more than kisses, letters mingle souls"). John Donne. MaMe; ReEn
To Sir Philip Sidney's Soul. Henry Constable. *See* On the Death of Sir Philip Sidney.
To Sir Robert Wroth. Ben Jonson. SeCV-1
To Sir Thomas Egerton. Samuel Daniel. OBSC
To Sir Toby. Philip Freneau. AP; CoBA
To Sir William Alexander. William Drummond of Hawthornden. OBS; SeEP
(To Sir W. A.) PoEL-2
To Sir William Davenant upon His Two First Books of Gondibert. Abraham Cowley. AnAnS-2; CEP; SeCV-1
To Sit in Solemn Silence. W. S. Gilbert. *Fr.* The Mikado. FiBHP; SiTL; WhC
To Sleep. Giovanni della Casa, *tr. fr. Italian by* John Addington Symonds. AWP; JAWP; WBP
To Sleep. Maybury Fleming. AA
To Sleep. John Fletcher. *See* Care-Charming Sleep.
To Sleep. Robert Graves. MoVE
To Sleep. Keats. BoLiVe; BWP; ChTr; EnLi-2; EnRP; EPN; ERoP-2; GTBS-W; LoBV; MBW-2; OAEP; OBEV; OBRV; PAn; PIA; PoE; PoEL-4; PoeP; Sonn; TDP; WHA
(Sonnet to Sleep.) AtBAP; FlW; ViBoPo
(World of Sleep, The.) BoC
To Sleep. Jan Kochanowski, *tr. fr. Polish by* Watson Kirkconnell. LiTW
To Sleep. Walter Savage Landor. VA
To Sleep. Percy MacKaye. HBMV
To Sleep. Frances Sargent Osgood. AA
To Sleep. Sir Philip Sidney. *See* Astrophel and Stella, XXXIX.
To Sleep. Charlotte Smith. Sonn
To Sleep ("A flock of sheep that leisurely pass by"). Wordsworth. BoLiVe; EnRP; EPN; GBV; GTBS; GTBS-D; GTBS-P; GTBS-W; GTSE; GTSL; HBV; InPo; MBW-2; MyFE; OBRV; PoFS; ShBV-4; Sonn; TrGrPo; ViBoPo
To Sleep ("Fond words have oft been spoken to thee, Sleep"). Wordsworth. Sonn
To Sleep ("O gentle Sleep! do they belong to thee.") Wordsworth. Sonn
To sleep easy all night. *Unknown.* OxNR
To Sleep I give my powers away. In Memoriam A. H. H., IV. Tennyson. EnLi-2; EPN; MaPo; OAEP; ViPo; VP
To Sleep, to Sleep. Claire Goll, *tr. fr. French by* Claire Goll. OnPM
To smash the simple atom. Atomic Courtesy. Ethel Jacobson. FaFP; LiTM (rev. ed.); ShM; SiTL
To So-kin of Rakuyo, ancient friend, Chancellor of Gen. Exile's Letter. Li Po. CTC; FaBoMo; NP; OxBA; PoE; SeCeV
To Some Builders of Cities. Stanley Snaith. HaMV
To Some I Have Talked With by the Fire. W. B. Yeats. PoDB
To Some Reviewers Who Have Wilfully Abused Certain True Poets. Herbert Palmer. FaBoTw
To some the fat gods give money. Humoresque. Alice Corbin. NP
To some, the pattering raindrops on the roof. Reprieve. Barbara Villy Cormack. CaP
To Someone Who Insisted I Look Up Someone. X. J. Kennedy. PV
To Somewhere. Leonard E. Nathan. NYTB
To Sorrow. *Unknown.* SeCL
To Song. Thomas S. Jones, Jr. HBV
To soothe a mad king's fevered brain. A Ballade of Playing Cards. Gleeson White. VA
To soothe and mild your lowland airs. Margaret's Song. Lascelles Abercrombie. *Fr.* The New God; a Miracle. GTBS
To Sorrow, I bade good-morrow. Keats. *Fr.* Endymion. OBRV
To Spain—a Last Word. Edith M. Thomas. MC
To Sparrows Fighting. W. H. Davies. BiS
To speak of every day things with ease. The Shadow Remains. Lynette Roberts. NeBP
"To Speak of Woe That Is in Marriage." Robert Lowell. MaPo (1969 ed.)
To speed my brother. Journeying Alone. Princess Oku. OnPM
To spend the long warm days. Rest. Margaret L. Woods. VA
To Spend Uncounted Years of Pain. Arthur Hugh Clough. *See* "Perchè Pensa? Pensando S'Invecchia."
To Spenser. Keats. CoBE; MaPo (1969 ed.); MBW-2
To Spenser. John Hamilton Reynolds. Sonn
To Spring. Blake. ATP; BoC; BoNaP; BoTP; CBEP; CEP; EnRP; ERoP-1; HBV; OBEC; OBEV; PoEL-4; PoLF; UnPo; WiR
("O thou with dewy locks who lookest down.") EG
To Spring. Virginia Moore. AnEnPo
To Spring, *sel.* John Francis O'Donnell.
"From the grey wicket of the morn." IrPN
To Spring. William Stanley Roscoe. UnPo (1st ed.)
(To Spring; on the Banks of the Cam.) OBVV
To spring belongs the violet, and the blown. A Petition. Thomas Bailey Aldrich. AA
To Spring; on the Banks of the Cam. William Stanley Roscoe. *See* To Spring.
To stab my youth with desperate knives, to wear. Taedium Vitae. Oscar Wilde. SyP
To stand here in the wings of Europe. On a Return from Egypt. Keith Douglas. NeBP; NePoEA
To Stand Up Straight and Tread the Turning Mill. A. E. Housman. EnLi-2 (1949 ed.); EnLit
To stand within a gently gliding boat. The Haunts of the Halcyon. Charles Henry Luders. AA
To Start a Controversy. Peter Porter. HYE
To Stella. Hester Chapone. OBEC
To Stella. Plato. *See* Morning and Evening Star.
To Stella. Sir Philip Sidney. *See* Astrophel and Stella: First Song.
To Stella. Swift. EiCP
To Stella; March 13, MDCCXXIII-IV. Swift. Po
To Stephen Spender. Timothy Corsellis. WaP
To stone memorials of a bitter loss. November Eleventh. Katherine Burton. PoRL
To stones trust not your monument. To W. B. Yeats Who Says That His Castle of Ballylee Is His Monument. Oliver St. John Gogarty. AnIL
To streets (the people's region) early fame. Sir William Davenant. *Fr.* Gondibert, II, ii. SeEP
To Strike for Night. Lebert Bethune. NBP
To Summer. Blake. CEP; ERoP-1; WiR
To sup with thee thou didst me home invite. The Invitation. Robert Herrick. OAEP
To sweat a slave to a race of slaves. G. K. Chesterton. *Fr.* The Ballad of the White Horse. PoFr
To Sydney. Louise Mack. BoAu
To T. H. a Lady Resembling My Mistresse. Thomas Carew. AnAnS-2
To T. S. Eliot on His Sixtieth Birthday. W. H. Auden. ML
To take things as they be. A Philosopher. John Kendrick Bangs. HBV
To take thy calling thankfully. The Ladder to Thrift. Thomas Tusser. ReIE; SiCE

To talk with God. Wait On. Dnyanodaya. MaRV; STF
To Tan Ch'iu. Li Po, *tr. fr. Chinese by* Arthur Waley. AWP
To taste/ Wild wine of the mountain-spring. Five Prayers. Blanche Edith Baughan. BoAu
To tell strange feats of daemons, here I am. To the Much Honoured R. F. Esq. Richard Chamberlain. SCAP
To th' Minstrel Girl. T. A. Daly. BOHV
To Thaliarchus ("Vides ut alta"). Horace, *tr. fr. Latin by* Dryden. Odes, I, 9. AWP; JAWP; WBP
("Behold yon mountains hoary height.") CavP; MBW-1; PeRV
(Ode to Thaliarchus.) LiTW
To thank with a phrase. Old German Mottos [*or* Proverbs]. *Unknown.* RIS; StaSt
To that clear majesty which, in the north. Dedication I [*or* To Queen Elizabeth *or* To My Most Gracious Dread Sovereign]. Sir John Davies. *Fr.* Nosce Teipsum. OBSC; ReIE; SiCE; SiPS
To that gaunt House of Art which lacks for naught. Athanasia. Oscar Wilde. BrPo
To the Accuser Who Is the God of This World. Blake. The Gates of Paradise: Epilogue. NoP; PeER; TrGrPo; UnPo (1st ed.); ViBoPo
(Epilogue: "Truly, my Satan, thou art but a dunce.") CABA; EiCL; ERoP-1; FaBoEn; OBNC
To the Afternoon Moon, at Sea. Cale Young Rice. EtS
To the Ancestral North. James Kirkup. POTi
To the Angel. Rainer Maria Rilke, *tr. fr. German by* J. B. Leishman. LiTW
To the Anxious Mother. Valente Malangatana, *tr. fr. Portuguese by* Dorothy Guedes *and* Philippa Rumsey. PBA
To the Author. George Peele. *Fr.* Hecatompathia (*by* Thomas Watson). ReIE
To the Author of *Clarissa.* Thomas Edwards. Sonn
To the Author of Hesperides and Noble Numbers. Mark Van Doren. ML
To the Avon River above Stratford, Canada. James Reaney. MoCV
To the Balliol Men Still in Africa. Hilaire Belloc. JKCP
To the banks of the Moldau River. How They Made the Golem. John R. Colombo. MoCV
To the Bat. Edith King. BoTP
To the Bell-Ringer. Robert Farren. OnYI
To the Best and Most Accomplished Couple. Henry Vaughan. HW
To the Blacksmith with a Spade. *Unknown, tr. fr. Irish by* Frank O'Connor. KiLC
To the Blessed Sacrament. Henry Constable. ACP; CAW
To the Blessed Virgin Mary. Gerald Griffin. *See* Nightingale, The.
To the Blest Evanthe. John Fletcher. *Fr.* A Wife for a Month. SeCL; SeEP
To the Body. Alice Meynell. ACP; PeVV
To the Body. Coventry Patmore. The Unknown Eros, II, vii. GoBC; OxBoCh; PoEL-5; PoLi
To the Boy. Elizabeth Clementine Kinney. AA
To the brave all homage render. Ashby. John Reuben Thompson. AA
To the Brave Soul. Wilbur Underwood. WGRP
To the Bride. Sappho, *tr. fr. Greek by* Virginia Tufte. HW
To the Bridegroom. Judah Halevi, *tr. fr. Hebrew by* Ephraim Sando *and* William Cutter. HW
To the Bridegroom. Sappho, *tr. fr. Greek by* Virginia Tufte. HW
To the Cambro-Britons [*or* Britains] and Their Harp, His Ballad of Agincourt. Michael Drayton. *See* Agincourt.
To the Canary Bird. Jones Very. AP
To the Child Jesus. Henry van Dyke. TrPWD
Nativity, The, *sel.* MaRV
To the Choice Bridegroom. Judah Halevi, *tr. fr. Hebrew by* Ephraim Sando *and* William Cutter. HW
To the Christ. John Banister Tabb. ChIP; TrPWD
To the Christian Reader. Robert Southwell. SiCE
To the Christians. Francis Lauderdale Adams. OxBS; WGRP
To the Christians. Blake. *Fr.* Jerusalem, *prologue to ch.* 4. EnRP; WGRP
(Epigraph: "I give you the end of a golden string.") OBNC
(I Give You the End of a Golden String.) OBRV; ShBV-4
(I Will Give You.) OTPC (1946 ed.)
To the City in the Snow. Agnes O'Gara Ruggeri. MoSiPe
To the City of London. William Dunbar. *See* In Honour of the City of London.
To the cold peak without their careful women. The Climbers. Elizabeth Jennings. NePoEA
To the Contemporary Muse. Edgar Bowers. ELU
To the Countesse of Bedford ("Honour is so sublime perfection"). John Donne. MaMe; MeLP
(Verse Letter to the Countess of Bedford.) MBW-1
To the Countesse of Bedford ("Reason is our soul's left hand"). John Donne. ATP (1953 ed.); MaMe
To the Countesse of Bedford ("T'have written then, when you writ"). John Donne. MaMe
To the Countesse of Bedford ("Though I be dead"). John Donne. MaMe
To the Countesse of Bedford ("You have refin'd mee"). John Donne. MaMe
To the Countesse of Bedford on New-Yeares Day. John Donne. MaMe; OBS; SeEP
To the Countesse of Huntingdon ("Man to Gods image"). John Donne. MaMe
To the Countesse of Huntington ("That unripe side of earth"). John Donne. MaMe
To the Countesse of Salisbury. John Donne. MaMe
To the Countesse of Salisbury. Aurelian Townsend. AnAnS-2; MePo; OBS; SeCP
(Loves Victory.) MeLP
To the Cowpens riding proudly, boasting loudly, rebels scorning. The Battle of the Cowpens. Thomas Dunn English. PAH; PAP
To the Critic. Michael Drayton. *See* Idea: "Methinks I see. . ."
To the Crocus—with My Love. Marion Sturges-Jones. BOHV
To the Cuckoo. Michael Bruce, *revised by* John Logan. HBV; OBEV; ViBoPo
(Ode: To the Cuckoo.) DD; EiCL; OBEC; OTPC
To the Cuckoo. F. H. Townsend. ChTr
To the Cuckoo. Wordsworth. BEL; BoLiVe; BoTP; CBEP; CoBE; ELP; EnLit; EnRP; EPN; ERoP-1; FaFP; FiP; GoTP; GTBS; GTBS-D; GTBS-P; GTBS-W; GTSE; GTSL; LiTG; LoBV; MBW-2; MCCG; MERP; OuHeWo; PeER; PoeP; PoLF; PTK; ShBV-2; TOP; TreFT; TrGrPo
To the Daemon Sublimity. Clark Ashton Smith. FiSC
To the Daisy ("Bright flower! whose home is everywhere"). Wordsworth. CoBE; EnRP; EPN; MERP
To the Daisy ("In youth from rock to rock I went"). Wordsworth. EnRP; MERP
To the Daisy ("With little here to do or see"). Wordsworth. EPN; GTBS; GTBS-D; GTBS-P; GTBS-W; GTSE; GTSL; HBV; HBVY
(To the Same Flower.) EnRP
To the Dandelion. James Russell Lowell. AP; CoBA; DD, *abr.*; GN; HBV; HBVY
"Dear common flower, that grow's beside the way," *sel.* FaPON; YT
To the Dead. William Bell Scott. VA
To the Dead Cardinal of Westminster. Francis Thompson. PeVV; PoVP
To the Dead of '98. Lionel Johnson. HBV
To the Dead of the Revolution. Ernst Toller, *tr. fr. German by* R. Ellis Roberts. PoFr
To the Dear Child of the Muses and His Ever Kind Maecenas, Master Anthony Cooke, Esquire. Michael Drayton. *Fr.* Idea's Mirrour. ReIE; SiCE; TuPP
To the Defenders of New Orleans. Joseph Rodman Drake. DD; PAH
To the Detracted. John Andrews. *Fr.* The Anatomy of Baseness. EIL; LO; SeEP
To the dim light and the large circle of shade. Sestina, of the Lady Pietra degli Scrovigni. Dante. AWP; JAWP; WBP
To the Driving Cloud. Longfellow. ChTr; FaBoEn; MWA-1; Po; PoEL-5
To the Duke of Buckingham, a Man of a Great Mind, Reduc'd to a Little Fortune, *sel.* William Wycherley.
"He is not great who gives to others law." PeRV
To the Earl of Dorset. Ambrose Philips. LoBV
To the Earl of Warwick on the Death of Mr. Addison. Thomas Tickell. CEP; EiPP; HBV; OBEC
To the Echo; in a Clear Night upon Astrop Walks. Countess of Winchilsea. EiPP

To the edge of the wood I am drawn, I am drawn. Sidney Lanier. *Fr.* The Marshes of Glynn. BBV (1951 ed.)
To the Editor of Mr. Pope's Works. Thomas Edwards. Sonn
To the End. John E. Bode. BLRP
(O Jesus, I Have Promised.) SoP
To the English Martyrs. Francis Thompson. JKCP
To the Eternal Feminine. Tristan Corbière, *tr. fr. French by* C. F. MacIntyre. ErPo
To the Evening Star. Mark Akenside. *See* Ode to the Evening Star.
To the Evening Star. Blake. BoNaP; CEP; CH; ChER; ChTr; CoBE; EiPP; EnLit; EnRP; ERoP-1; FaBV; GBV (1952 ed.); HW; LoBV; MCCG; NoP; OAEP; PoFS; PoLF; SiSw; StaSt; TrGrPo; WiR
(Sonnet: "Thou fair-haired angel of the evening".) PoPo
To the Evening Star ("Gem of the crimson-colour'd even"). Thomas Campbell. GTBS; GTBS-D; GTBS-W; GTSE; GTSL
(Caroline, II: To the Evening Star.) OBNC
To the Evening Star ("Star that bringest home the bee"). Thomas Campbell. *See* Song to the Evening Star.
To the Evening Star: Central Minnesota. James Wright. NaP
To the Evening Wind. Bryant. *See* Evening Wind, The.
To the Excellent and Most Accomplish'd Lady, Lucy, Countess of Bedford. Michael Drayton. *Fr.* Mortimeriados. ReIE
To the Excellent Pattern of Beauty and Virtue, Lady Elizabeth, Countess of Ormond. James Shirley. GoBC
To the fair fields where loves eternal dwell. John Fletcher. *Fr.* The Mad Lover. MyFE
To the Fair Unknown. William Taylor. WaPE
To the fairest. Winchester. Lionel Johnson. OBVV
To the Faithful. Marcos Ana, *tr. fr. Spanish by* Chloe Vulliamy *and* Stephen Sedley. BoC
To the Father of the Bride. Tasso, *tr. fr. Italian by* David Rafael Wang. HW
To the Federal Convention. Thomas Dwight. PAH
To the field I carried my milking pail. I Want to Be Married and Cannot Tell How. *Unknown.* OnYI
To the figures bathing at the river. A Bodhisattva Undoes Hell. Jerome Rothenberg. CoPo
To the Five Members of the Honourable House of Commons. Sir John Denham. NCEP
To the Flag of Stars. Thomas Curtis Clark. PEDC
To the Forgotten Dead. Margaret L. Wood. VA
To the Fountain of Bandusia ("O fons Bandusiae"). Horace, *tr. fr. Latin by* Eugene Field. Odes, III, 13. AA; AWP; JAWP; WBP
(Bandusia, Stainless Mirror, *tr. by* Charles Stuart Calverley.) OnPM
(Fountain of Bandusia, The, *tr. by* Austin Dobson.) OuHeWo
(O Fons Bandusiae, *tr. by* Austin Dobson.) VA
To the Four Courts, Please. James Stephens. HBMV; MoAB; MoBrPo; NeMA
To the Fringed Gentian. Bryant. AA; AmePo; AmP; AmPP (3d ed.); AnAmPo; AnFE; AnNE; AP; APA; AWP; CoAnAm; CoBA; FaBoBe; GN; HBV; MPB; NeHB; NePA; NoP; OBRV; OTD; OTPC; PoLF; StP; TOP; TreFT; YT
To the Frivolous Muse. George Meason Whicher. InMe
To the galleys, thief, and sweat your soul out. Thief. Robert Graves. POTE
To the Garden God. Catullus, *tr. fr. Latin by* John Nott. OnPM
To the Garden the World. Walt Whitman. AP
To the Gentleman in Row D. Virginia Graham. MuSP
To the Ghost of a Kite. James Wright. NePoEA
To the Ghost of John Milton. Carl Sandburg. PP; ReMP
To the Ghost of Martial. Ben Jonson. OAEP
To the Girls of My Graduating Class. Irving Layton. ErPo
To the God of all [sure] mercies let my blessing rise to-day. Cassandra Southwick. Whittier. PAH; PoIE
To the God of Love. Edmund G. V. Knox. ALV; HBMV
To the Goddess of Liberty. George Sterling. PoFr
To the Gossamer-Light. Charles Tennyson Turner. VA
To the Grasshopper and the Cricket. Leigh Hunt. EnLi-2; EnRP; EPN; GBV (1922 ed.); GN; HBV; OBNC; OTPC (1946 ed.); PCD; Sonn
(On the Grasshopper and Cricket.) GoTP
To the Greatest City in the World. Rolfe Humphries. PoMa
To the green wood where I found my love. These Words I Write on Crinkled Tin. Lynette Roberts. ChMP
To the Guardian Angel. *Unknown.* WHL
To the Guelf Faction. Folgore da San Geminiano, *tr. fr. Italian by* Dante Gabriel Rossetti. FOL
To the Harbormaster. Frank O'Hara. ANYP; CBV; CoAP
To the Harpies. Arthur Davison Ficke. HBV
To the Hawks. Donald Justice. TDP
To the heavens above us. An Astrologer's Song. Kipling. MoBrPo; NeMA
To the Heirs of the Pilgrims. Benjamin Church. PoFr
To the Herald Honeysuckle. Emily Pfeiffer. VA
To the High-born Prince of Men, Henry. George Chapman. *Fr.* The Epistle Dedicatory to Chapman's Translation of the Iliad. ReIE
("Since perfect happiness, by princes sought.") ReEn
To the Highland Girl of Inversneyde. Wordsworth. *See* To a Highland Girl.
To the Holy Spirit. Yvor Winters. ForPo; MoAmPo (1962 ed.); MoVE; PoIE; QFR
To the Holy Trinitie. Ben Jonson. SCEP-2
To the Honorable Charles Montague, Esq. Matthew Prior. EiCP; PeRV
To the house on the grassy hill. The Presence. Denise Levertov. NaP; NePoEA-2
To the Immortal[l] Memory [*or* Memorie] and Friendship of That Noble Pair[e], Sir Lucius Cary and Sir Henry Morison. Ben Jonson. AnAnS-2; MaPo (1969 ed.); NoP; OBS; PoEL-2; PoFS; SCEP-2; SeCP; SeCV-1; SeEP; TuPP
(Pindaric Ode, A.) StP
Sels.
"He stood a soldier to the last right end." CoBE
It Is Not Growing like a Tree. BBV (1951 ed.); CABA; DiPo; EnLi-1 (1949 ed.); LiTB; LiTG; OQP
("It is not growing like a tree.") AnFE, 3 *sts.*; BEL; ChTr; CoBE; OBEV; OTD; PoIE; TOP; YAT
(Noble Nature, The.) GN; GoBC; GTBS; GTBS-D; GTBS-P; GTBS-W; GTSE; GTSL; HBV; HBVY; MaRV; MCCG; OTPC; PG; PoPo; TreFT
(Oak and Lily.) BoLiVe; TrGrPo
(Proportion.) FaBoEn
(Short Measures.) WePo
To the Immortal Memory of the Halibut on which I Dined This Day, Monday, April 26, 1784. William Cowper. SeCePo
To the Infant Martyrs ("Goe, smiling soules, your new built Cages break"). Richard Crashaw. MaMe; NoP; SCEP-1; SeCV-1
To the Ingleezee Khafir, Calling Himself Djann Bool Djenkinzun. James Clarence Mangan. OnYI
To the International Brigade. Rafael Alberti, *tr. fr. Spanish by* Katherine Garrison Chapin. PoFr
To the Ivy. John Clare. CBEP
To the Jews. Blake. *See* Fields from Islington to Marybone, The.
To the "JFK" Quintet. Al Fraser. BF
To the kind, the tall Carpenter. Carpenter. Isabel Fiske Conant. StJW
To the King. Andrew Marvell. MaMe
. . . to the King./ Thou art the Wall-stone the workers rejected. Advent Lyrics, I. *Unknown.* *Fr.* Christ 1. AnOE
To the King on His Navy. Edmund Waller. CEP; EiCL; NoP; SCEP-2
To the King, Upon His Comming with His Army into the West. Robert Herrick. AnAnS-2
To the King, upon His Majesty's Happy Return. Edmund Waller. SCEP-2
To the King, upon His Welcome to Hampton-Court. Robert Herrick. AnAnS-2
To the Ladies. Arnold Kenseth. PPON
To the Lady Bedford. John Donne. MaMe
To the Lady Lucy, Countess of Bedford. Samuel Daniel. OBSC; ReIE; SiCE; TuPP
To the Lady Magdalen Herbert. John Donne. MaMe
To the Lady Margaret, Countess of Cumberland. Samuel Daniel. LoBV; OBSC; ReIE; SiCE; TuPP
(High Mind, The.) AnEnPo
"Knowing the heart of man is set to be," *sel.* FaBoEn
To the Lady Margaret Ley. Milton. GTBS; GTBS-D; GTBS-P; GTBS-W; GTSE; GTSL; OBEV; Sonn
(Sonnet: "Daughter to that good Earl, once President.") OBS
To the Lady May. Aurelian Townsend. MePo; SeCL; SeEP
To the Lady Rogers, of Her Unprofitable Sparing. Sir John Harington. SiCE
To the Lady of Ch'i. *Unknown,* *tr. fr. Chinese by* Arthur

Waley. *Fr.* The Book of Songs. HW
To the Lady with a Book. *Unknown, tr. fr. Irish by* Frank O'Connor. KiLC
To the Ladybird. Caroline Anne Bowles. *See* Lady-Bird.
To the Laggards. Joseph Bovshover, *tr. fr. Yiddish by* Joseph Bovshover. TrJP
To the Lakes. Wilfred Campbell. VA
To the Lark. Sir John Davies. *Fr.* Hymns of Astraea. SiCE
To the last moment of his breath. Hope. Goldsmith. *Fr.* The Captivity. OBEC
To the Last Wedding Guest. Horace Gregory. NYBP
To the Laud and Praise of a Shock Bitch. Samuel Wesley. PeRV
To the Leanán Shee. Thomas Boyd. OnYI
To the Learned and Accomplish'd Gentleman Maister Nicholas Blackleech of Gray's Inn. Richard Barnfield. ReIE
To the Learned and Reverend Mr. Cotton Mather, on His Excellent Magnalia. Grindall Rawson. SCAP
To the Learned Critic. Ben Jonson. PP
To the Leaven'd Soil They Trod. Walt Whitman. AP
To the Liffey with the Swans. Oliver St. John Gogarty. AnIL; OxBI
To the Lighted Lady Window. Marguerite Wilkinson. CAW; ISi; WHL
To the Little House. Christopher Morley. HBMV
To the Living. Ernst Toller, *tr. fr. German by* R. Ellis Roberts. PoFr
To the Looking Glass world it was Alice that said. "Lewis Carroll." *Fr.* Though the Looking-Glass. Par
To the Lord Chancellor, *sel.* Shelley.
"Oh, let a father's curse be on thy soul." ViBoPo
To the Lord General Cromwell (May, 1652). Milton. AnEnPo; BEL; EnLit; MBW-1; NoP; OBS; OuHeWo; Sonn; TrGrPo; ViBoPo
(Cromwell, Our Chief of Men.) CABA; MaPo; PAn
(To Oliver Cromwell.) SeCeV
To the Lord General Fairfax. Milton. *See* Fairfax, Whose Name in Arms through Europe Rings.
To the Lord Love. "Michael Field." OBMV
To the Lords of Convention 'twas Claver'se who spoke. Bonny [*or* Bonnie] Dundee. Sir Walter Scott. *Fr.* The Doom of Devorgoil. BEL; EnRP; FaBoCh; HBV; LoGBV; OBRV; OTPC (1923 ed.); OxBoLi; OxBS; Par; SeCeV; TOP
To the lucky now who have lovers or friends. Alexandria. Lawrence Durrell. MoVE; ToPo
To the Maiden in the East. Henry David Thoreau. MWA-1; OxBA
To the Maids Not to Walk in the Wind. Oliver St. John Gogarty. AnIL; ErPo
To the Man after the Harrow. Patrick Kavanagh. GTBS-P
To the man-in-the-street, who, I'm sorry to say. Note on Intellectuals. W. H. Auden. FiBHP; PoPl; SiTL
To the Man-of-War-Bird. Walt Whitman. AA; AmP; AmPP (4th ed.); EtS; FaBoBe; HBV; NePA
"Thou born to match the gale (thou art all wings)," *sel.* InP
To the Mannequins. Howard Nemerov. CBV
To the Marchesana of Pescara. Michelangelo. *See* Love's Justification.
To the Master Poet. Thomas Curtis Clark. ChIP
To the me of my own making, seeing I am here. Sound from Leopardi. Bill Berkson. ANYP
To the Memory of a Lady, *abr.* George Lyttelton. OBEC
To the Memory of a Young Man. *Unknown.* WhC
To the Memory of Abraham Lincoln. Bryant. *See* Abraham Lincoln.
To the Memory of Ben Johnson, *sel.* Jasper Mayne.
"Scorne then their censure." OBS
To the Memory of John Burroughs. Catherine Parmenter. PEDC; PoRL
To the Memory of Master W. Shakespeare. I. M., *at. to* John Milton. CLwM
To the Memory of Mr. Charles Morwent, *sel.* John Oldham.
Quiet Soul, A. OBEV
To the Memory of Mr. Oldham. Dryden. ATP; AWP; BWP; CABA; CaFP; DiPo; EiCL; EiPP; ExPo; FaBoEn; FiP; ForPo; InPo; JAWP; LoBV; MBW-1; NoP; OBS; PAn; PeRV; PIA; PoEL-3; PoIE; PP; SeCeV; SeCV-2; SeEP; StP; UnPo (1st ed.); VaPo; ViBoPo; WBP
To the Memory of My Beloved Master William Shakespeare [and What He Hath Left Us]. Ben Jonson. BEL; BoLiVe; CABA; EnLi-1; GoTL; HBV; MyFE, *abr.*; PoFS; TOP; TreFS; TrGrPo; WHA
(To the Memory of My Beloved, the Author Mr. [*or* Master] William Shakespeare [and What He Hath Left Us].) AnAnS-2; CLwM; CoBE; EnL; EnLit; ILP; LiTB; NoP; OAEP; OBS; PoEL-2; PoIE; PP; ReEn; SCEP-2; SeCeV; SeCP; SeCV-1; SeEP; TuPP; ViBoPo
(To the Memory of My Beloved William Shakespeare and What He Hath Left Us.) EnRePo
(To the Memory of . . . William Shakespeare.) MaPo
Sels.
"I therefore will begin: soule of the age!" ML
"Sweet Swan of Avon! what a sight it were." ChTr
To the Memory of Sir Isaac Newton, *sel.* James Thomson.
"All-intellectual eye, our solar round." ImOP
To the Memory of the Brave Americans. Philip Freneau. AmP; AmPP; AP; CoBA; PaA; PAL; PoLF
(Eutaw Springs.) AA; BeLS; NeHB; PAH
(To the Memory of the Americans Who Fell at Eutaw.) PAP
To the Memory of the Deceased Author Master W. Shakespeare. Leonard Digges. CLwM
To the Memory of the Learned and Reverend, Mr. Jonathan Mitchell. Francis Drake. SCAP
To the Memory of Yale College. Phelps Putnam. AnAmPo
To the Men Who Lose. George L. Scarborough. BLPA
To the Merchantis of Edinburgh. William Dunbar. OxBS
To the Milkweed. Lloyd Mifflin. AA
To the Mocking-Bird. Albert Pike. AA
To the Mocking-Bird. Richard Henry Wilde. AA; AnAmPo
To the Modern Man. John Hall Wheelock. HBMV
To the Moon. George Darley. Sonn
To the Moon. Thomas Hardy. BoNaP; ChTr; CoBE
To the Moon. Pierre de Ronsard, *tr. fr. French by* Andrew Lang. *Fr.* Amours de Marie. AWP
To the Moon. Shelley. *See* Moon, The ("Art thou pale. . .").
To the Moon. Sir Philip Sidney. *See* Astrophel and Stella, XXXI.
To the Moon. Charlotte Smith. Sonn
To the Moon. Wordsworth. *See* "With How Sad Steps, O Moon, Thou Climb'st the Sky."
To the Moonflower. Craven Langstroth Betts. AA
To the Morning. Satisfaction for Sleepe. Richard Crashaw. MaMe
To the Most Beautiful Lady, the Lady Bridget Manners. Barnabe Barnes. EnLoPo
To the Most Excellent and Learned Shepherd, Colin Clout. William Smith. *Fr.* Chloris. Sonn; TuPP
("Colin, my dear and most entire beloved.") ReEn
To the Most Fair and Lovely Mistress [*or* Mistris], Anne Soame, Now Lady Abdie. Robert Herrick. AtBAP; ViBoPo
To the Most Holy Crown of Thorns. Sister Miriam Teresa. JKCP (1955 ed.)
To the Most Holy Mother of God. *Unknown, tr. fr. Greek by* Shane Leslie. ISi
To the Most Learned, Wise, and Arch-Antiquary, M. John Selden. Robert Herrick. SeCV-1
To the Mother of Christ, the Son of Man. Alice Meynell. ISi
To the Mothers. Ernst Toller, *tr. fr. German by* E. Ellis Roberts. TrJP
To the Mountains. Henry David Thoreau. PoEL-4
To the Much Honoured R. F. Esq. Richard Chamberlain. SCAP
To the much-tossed Ulysses, never done. Ulysses. Robert Graves. ChMP; CMoP; FaBoTw; OxBI
To the Muse. Eugene Lee-Hamilton. Sonn
To the Muse of the North. William Morris. PoVP
To the Muses. Blake. AnFE; BoLiVe; CBEP; CEP; ChER; ChTr; CoBE; EiCL; EiPP; EnLi-2; EnLit; EnRP; ERoP-1; GTBS-W; GTSL; HBV; LiTB; LiTG; LoBV; NoP; OAEP; OBEC; OBEV; OnPM; OuHeWo; PeER; PoFS; SeCeV; TrGrPo; ViBoPo; WHA
To the Mutable Fair. Edmund Waller. AnAnS-2; SeCP
To the Name above Every Name, the Name of Jesus, [a Hymn]. Richard Crashaw. MaMe; SCEP-1; SeCV-1
(On the Name of Jesus.) AnAnS-1; MeP
To the National Arts Council. Peter Schjeldahl. ANYP
To the Nautilus. Hartley Coleridge. VA
To the New Men. John Davidson. EPN; PoVP; TOP
To the New Owner. Lucile Hargrove Reynolds. PoToHe

To the new wick/ Of freedom's torch. My Thread. David Hofstein. TrJP
To the New Women. John Davidson. PoVP
To the New Yeere. Michael Drayton. AtBAP; PoEL-2
To the Night. Shelley. *See* To Night.
To the Nightingale. Philip Ayres. CEP
To the Nightingale. Richard Barnfield. *See* Nightingale, The.
To the Nightingale. William Cowper. PeER
To the Nightingale. Sir John Davies. *Fr.* Hymns of Astraea. OBSC; SiCE; TrGrPo
To the Nightingale ("Dear quirister, who from those shadows sends"). William Drummond of Hawthornden. *See* Sonnet: "Dear quirister. . ."
To the Nightingale. Milton. ATP (1953 ed.); DiPo; HBV; MyFE
(O Nightingale.) SeCePo
(O Nightingale That on Yon Bloomy Spray.) EG; Sonn
(Sonnet: "O Nightingale, that on yon bloomy spray.") OBS; SeCL; ViBoPo
To the Nightingale. Countess of Winchilsea. BWP; CEP; EiPP; PoIE
To the Nile. Keats. OBRV
To the Nile. Shelley. OBRV; Sonn
To the Noble Sir Francis Drake. Thomas Beedome. SeEP
(Epitaph on Drake.) MemP
To the Noble Woman of Llanarth Hall. Evan Thomas, *tr. fr. Welsh by* Anthony Conran. PV
To the Noblest and Best of Ladies [*or* Ladyes], the Countess[e] of Denbigh. Richard Crashaw. MaMe; MeLP; ReEn
(Against Irresolution, *diff. vers.*) MaMe; OxBoCh
(Letter to the Countess of Denbigh [against Irresolution and Delay in Matters of Religion], A.) MePo; SeCP
(Verse-Letter to the Countess of Denbigh, A.) EP
To the Oaks of Glencree. J. M. Synge. ELU; MoBrPo; OxBI
To the Ocean. Byron. *See* Ocean, The.
To the Ocean Now I Fly. Milton. *Fr.* Comus. AtBAP; OBEV; OBS; ViBoPo
(Farewell of the Attendant Spirit.) BoLiVe; TrGrPo
(Song: "To the ocean now I fly.") SeCeV
To the old, long life and treasure. Gipsy Song. Ben Jonson. *Fr.* The Gypsies Metamorphosed. SeCL
To the One I Love Most. *Unknown.* *See* Lines from Love Letters.
To the One of Fictive Music. Wallace Stevens. AnAmPo; AnFE; AP; APA; CoAnAm; CoBMV; MAP; MoAB; MoAmPo; MoVE; TwAmPo
To the Painter Preparing to Draw M. M. H. James Shirley. CavP
To the Parotid Gland. —— Schlesinger. WhC
To the Parted One. Goethe, *tr. fr. German by* Christopher Pearse Cranch. AWP; JAWP; WBP
To the Peoples of Earth. Sun-Ra. BF
To the Pious Memory of the Accomplished [*or* Accomplisht] Young Lady, Mrs. Anne Killigrew. Dryden. CEP; EiCL; EiPP; HBV; LoBV; MBW-1; PeRV; PIA; PoEL-3; PoFS; SeEP
(Ode to the Pious Memory of the Accomplished [*or* Accomplisht] Young Lady, Mrs. Anne Killigrew, Excellent in the Two Sister Arts of Poesy and Painting.) AtBAP; OBEV, *abr.*; SeCV-2
Poet's Resurrection, *sel.* WHA
To the Pliocene Skull. Bret Harte. BOHV
To the Poet T. J. Mathias. Walter Savage Landor. PV
To the Poets. Keats. *See* Ode: "Bards of Passion and of Mirth."
To the Poets of India. F. R. Scott. NYTB
To the Polyandrous Lydia. Franklin P. Adams, *after the Latin of Horace.* HBMV
To the Portrait of "A Gentleman." Oliver Wendell Holmes. BOHV; InMe
To the Portrait of an Unknown Man. Anderson M. Scruggs. NYTB
To the Potter's house I went down one day. The Potter's Hand. M. F. Clarkson. SoP
To the Powers of Desolation. Genevieve Taggard. WOW
To the Preacher, *sel.* Charlotte Perkins Gilman.
"Preach about the old sins, Preacher!" MaRV
To the Precision. Richard Brathwaite. *Fr.* A Strappado for the Devil. SiCE
To the Prince. Sir John Davies. Orchestra: Dedication II. SiPS
To the Princess Margaret Tudor. William Dunbar. SiSw
To the Queen. Blake. *See* Door of Death, The.
To the Queen. Lord Darnley. OxBS
To the Queen. Sir William Davenant. *See* To the Queen, Entertain'd at Night by the Countess of Anglesey.
To the Queen. Sir Walter Ralegh. *See* Silent Lover, The.
To the Queen ("O loyal to the royal in thy self"). Tennyson. *Fr.* Idylls of the King. PoVP
To the Queen ("Revered, beloved—O you that hold"). Tennyson. MaVP
To the Queen: an Apologie for the Length of the Following Panegyrick. Richard Crashaw. MaMe
To the Queen, Entertain'd at Night by the Countess of Anglesey. Sir William Davenant. FaBoEn; MeLP; MePo; OBS; SeCL
(To the Queen.) SeEP
To the Queen of Dolors. Sister Mary Maura. ISi
To the Queen: Upon the Duke of Yorke His Birth A Panegyricke. Richard Crashaw. MaMe
To the Queen's Majesty. Richard Crashaw. MaMe
To the quick brow Fame grudges her best wreath. The Guerdon. John James Piatt. AA
To the Rainbow. Thomas Campbell. HBV
To the Reader. Baudelaire, *tr. fr. French by* Arthur Symons. SyP
To the Reader. J. V. Cunningham. QFR
To the Reader. Samuel Daniel. PP; SiCE
To the Reader. Everard Guilpin. *Fr.* Skialetheia. ReIE; SiCE
To the Reader. Thomas Howell. SiCE
To the Reader. Ben Jonson. EnRePo; MaPo; NoP; OAEP; ReIE; SCEP-2; SeCV-1; TuPP
To the Reader. Timothe Kendall, *after the Latin of* Martial. TuPP
(Quip to the Reader.) OnPM
To the Reader. Denise Levertov. AmPP (5th ed.); CoPo
To the Reader. Urian Oakes. SCAP
To the Reader. *Unknown.* SeCL
To the Reader of These Sonnets. Michael Drayton. *See* Idea: "Into these loves. . ."
To the Redbreast. John Bampfylde. Sonn
To the Returning Brave. Robert Underwood Johnson. PAH
To the Rev. F. D. Maurice. Tennyson. GTBS-P
To the Rev. John M'Math. Burns. EiPP
To the Rev'd Mr. Jno. Sparhawk on the Birth of His Son. Samuel Sewall. SCAP
To the Reverend Mr. Murdoch. James Thomson. OBEC
To the Rev. Mr. Newton. William Cowper. LoBV
To the Reverend Shade of His Religious Father. Robert Herrick. AnAnS-2; OBS; SeCV-1; SeEP
To the Reverend W. L. Bowles. Samuel Taylor Coleridge. EnRP; Sonn
To the Right Honorable and Most Virtuous Lady, the Countess of Pembroke. Spenser. Sonn
To the Right Honourable Robert Walpole, Esq. Ambrose Philips. CEP
To the Right Honourable the Countesse of C. William Habington. AnAnS-2; SeCP
To the Right Honorable, the Lady Mary, Countess of Pembroke. Samuel Daniel. *Fr.* Delia. SiCE; TuPP
To the Right Honourable William, Earl of Dartmouth. Phillis Wheatley. AmPP (5th ed.); PoFr
"Should you, my lord, while you pursue my song," *sel.* Kal; TTY
To the Right Noble and Valorous Knight, Sir Walter Ralegh. Spenser. Sonn
To the Right Worshipful, My Singular Good Friend, M[aster] Gabriel Harvey, Doctor of the Laws. Spenser. ReIE
To the Right Worthy and Judicious Favorer of Virtue, Master [*or* Maister] Fulke Greville. Samuel Daniel. *Fr.* Musophilus. ReIE; SiCE
To the Right Worthy Knight Sir Fulke Greville. Samuel Daniel. EnRePo
To the River Anker. Michael Drayton. *See* Idea: "Our flood's queen, Thames. . ."
To the River Arun. Charlotte Smith. Sonn
To the River Duddon. Norman Nicholson. FaBoMo
To the River Itchin, near Winton. William Lisle Bowles. ERoP-1
To the River Lodon. Thomas Warton, the Younger. *See* Sonnet: To the River Lodon.

To the River Otter. Samuel Taylor Coleridge. *See* Sonnet: To the River Otter.
To the Roman Bridge on Michigan Avenue. Reuel Denney. TDP
To the Rose. Sir John Davies. *Fr.* Hymns of Astraea. OBSC; SiCE; TuPP
To the Rose. Robert Herrick. HBV; OBS; SeCP
To the Rose upon the Rood of Time. W. B. Yeats. OAEP (2d ed.); Po; ViPo (1962 ed.)
To the Rosella in the Poinsettia Tree. James Picot. BoAV
To the Roving Pirate. George Turberville. EnRePo
To the Royal Society. Abraham Cowley. AnAnS-2; CEP; SCEP-2
To the Ruins of Troy and Greece. George Chapman. ReIE
To the Rulers. John Frederick Nims. JKCP (1955 ed.)
To the Same. William Cowper. *See* To Mary.
To the Same. Ben Jonson. *See* To Celia ("Kiss me, sweet. . .").
To the Same Flower (Celandine). Wordsworth. EnRP
To the Same Flower (Daisy). Wordsworth. *See* To the Daisy ("With little here to do or see").
To the Same Party, Councel Concerning Her Choise. Richard Crashaw. MaMe
To the Same Purpos [He, Not Long Before]. Thomas Traherne. SCEP-1; SeCV-2
To the sea they came. Pure Products. Denise Levertov. NMP
To the sea-shell's spiral round. Appreciation. Thomas Bailey Aldrich. AA
To the Senses. Michael Drayton. *See* Idea: "When conquering love. . ."
To the Ship in Which Virgil Sailed to Athens ("Sic te diva potens Cypri"). Horace, *tr. fr. Latin by* Dryden. Odes, I, 3. AWP
To the Shore. May Swenson. NePoAm-2
To the Sister of Elia. Walter Savage Landor. HBV
(To Mary Lamb.) TOP
To the Sistine Madonna. Cornelia Otis Skinner. ISi
To the Sky-Council on Star, Riga, Milky Way. Report on the Planet, Earth. James Oppenheim. PoMa
To the Skylark. Wordsworth. *See* To a Skylark ("Ethereal minstrel!").
To the Small Celandine. Wordsworth. EPN; HBV; MERP; NoP; OBRV; OTPC
To the Snake. Denise Levertov. AmPP (5th ed.); LiTM (1970 ed.); NePoEA-2; PoIE; ToPo
To the Snipe. John Clare. NCEP; OBNC
To the Soul. Sir Frederick Napier Broome. ACV
To the Soul. John Collop. TrGrPo
To the sound of the strange hooves on the midnight cobbles. The Ostler. Hyam Plutzik. Horatio, II. FiMAP
To the Soure Reader. Robert Herrick. AnAnS-2; OAEP; SeCP
To the South. Brewster Ghiselin. LiTA; LiTM (rev. ed.); NePA
To the south-east—three thousand leagues. Civilization. Yüan Chieh. LiTW
To the Spanish Main we are bound away. Slav Ho! *Unknown.* SoAmSa
To the Spider. Thomas Russell. Sonn
To the Spirit Great and Good. Leigh Hunt. TrPWD
To the Spirit of Keats. James Russell Lowell. Sonn
To the Spirit of Poetry. Philip Bourke Marston. VA
To the Spring. Sir John Davies. *Fr.* Hymns of Astraea. EIL; SiCE; TuPP
To the Spring Sun. Freda Laughton. NeIP
To the State of Love; or, The Senses Festival. John Cleveland. MePo
(Senses Festival, The.) AnAnS-2
To the States. Walt Whitman. CTC
To the Stationer. Thomas Freeman. SiCE; TuPP
To the Stone-Cutters. Robinson Jeffers. AmP; AmPP; ILP; InP; MAP; MoAB; MoAmPo; MoVE; NeMA; NoP; OxBA; PoCh; PoPl; PoRA (rev. ed.); PP; TrGrPo; VaPo
To the Sun. Ingeborg Bachmann, *tr. fr. German by* Michael Hamburger. BoNaP
To the Sun. Roy Campbell. *Fr.* Mithraic Emblems. EaLo; FaBoTw
To the Sun. Guido Gezelle, *tr. fr. Flemish by* Jethro Bithell. LiTW
(To the Sun from a Flower.) FaPON
To the Sun. Pattericke Jenkyn. SeCL
To the sun. Last Song. James Guthrie. PDV; TiPo
To the (Supposed) Patron. Geoffrey Hill. NePoEA-2
To the Supreme Being. Michelangelo. *See* For Inspiration.
To the Terrestrial Globe. W. S. Gilbert. HBV; LiTG; OTD; PoPl; SiTL; TrGrPo; WhC
To the Thawing Wind. Robert Frost. LOW; OxBA; RIS
To the Thirty-ninth Congress. Whittier. PAH
To the Tomb. Raymond Kresensky. ChIP
To the Translation of Palingenius. Barnabe Googe. EnRePo
To the Translator of Lucan's Pharsalia (1614). Sir Walter Ralegh. SiPS
(To the Translator of Lucan.) FCP
To the Trinity. Richard Stanyhurst. *See* Prayer to the Trinity, A.
To the Tune of, In Fayth I Cannot Keepe My Fathers Sheepe. Sidney Godolphin. *See* Song: "Cloris, it is not thy disdaine."
To the Tune of the Coventry Carol. Stevie Smith. FaBoTw
To the Unconstant Cynthia. Sir Robert Howard. CavP; SeCL
To the Ungentilized Censurer. Henry Parrot. SiCE
To the United States of America. Robert Bridges. HBV; PaA; PAH; PoFr
To the University of Cambridge, in New-England. Phillis Wheatley. AmPP (5th ed.); BALP
To the University of Oxford, 1674. Dryden. *See* Epilogue Spoken at Oxford by Mrs. Marshall.
To the Unknown Eros. Coventry Patmore. The Unknown Eros, II, i. LO; OxBoCh; PoEL-5
To the Unknown God. *Unknown, tr. fr. Vedic by* Max Müller. The Rig-Veda, X, Hymn 121. OuHeWo
To the Unknown Light. Edward Shanks. TrPWD
To the Unknown Warrior. G. K. Chesterton. MMA
To the Veld. Arthur Shearly Cripps. ACV
To the Veterans of the Abraham Lincoln Brigade. Genevieve Taggard. PoFr
To the Victor. William Ellery Leonard. MAP; MoAmPo (1942 ed.); PoFr
To the Virgin. John Lydgate. ACP; CAW; GoBC; PoLi
To the Virgin. Rodríquez del Padrón, *tr. fr. Spanish by* Roderick Gill. OnPM
To the Virgin Mary, *abr.* Petrarch, *tr. fr. Italian by* Robert Guthrie MacGregor. Sonnets to Laura: To Laura in Death, Canzone VIII. CAW
(Ode to the Virgin, *tr. by* Helen Lee Peabody.) ISi
To the Virginian Voyage. Michael Drayton. AtBAP; CBEP; CoBE; EnRePo; HBV; MC, *sl. abr.*; NoP; OAEP; OBEV; OBS; PaA; PAH; PoEL-2; PoFr; ReEn; ReIE; SeCePo; SeEP; StP; ThLM; TuPP; ViBoPo, *sl. abr.*
(Ode to the Virginian Voyage.) EnLi-1 (1949 ed.)
(Virginian Voyage, The.) LoBV
To the Virgins, to Make Much of Time. Robert Herrick. ALV; AnAnS-2; AnFE; AWP; BEL; BLPA; BoLiVe; CABA; CavP; CBV; ChTr; DiPo; EG; ELP; EnL; EnLi-1; EnLit; EnLoPo; EP; ExPo; FaBoEn; FaBV; FaFP; ForPo; HBV; ILP; InMe; InP; InPo; JAWP; LiTB; LiTG; LiTL; LoBV; MaPo; MasP; MemP; NeHB; NoP; OAEP; OBEV; OBS; OuHeWo; PAn; PG; PoAn; PoE; PoEL-3; PoeP; PoFS; PoIE; PoPl; QFR; ReEn; SeCeV; SeCL; SeCP; SeCV-1; SeEP; ShBV-2; StP; TOP; TreFS; TrGrPo; ViBoPo; WBP; WHA; YAT
(Counsel to Girls.) GTBS; GTBS-D; GTBS-P; GTBS-W; GTSE; GTSL; PoMa; WePo
(Gather Ye Rosebuds [While Ye May].) AnEnPo; LoPo; MCCG; MeWo; PoPo; PoSa
(To the Virgins to Make Much of Their Time.) ErPo
To the wake of Tim O'Hara. The Wake of Tim O'Hara. Robert Buchanan. VA
To the wall of the old green garden. A Yellow Pansy. Helen Gray Cone. DD; GFA; HBMV
To the Virtuosos. William Shenstone. EiCL
To the Water Nymphs, Drinking at the Fountain. Robert Herrick. AnAnS-2; EG; PoFS; ViBoPo
To the Wayfarer. *Unknown.* SiSoSe
To the west of the towering mountain is a red cloud. The Soldier-Statesman Returns. Tu Fu. OnPM
To the Western Wind. Judah Halevi, *tr. fr. Hebrew by* Solomon Solis-Cohen. TrJP
To the Western Wind. Robert Herrick. HBV; OBEV; SeCV-1; SeEP
To the Western World. Louis Simpson. CoAP; LiTM (1970 ed.); NePoAm-2; NePoEA-2; PoPl
To the White Fiends. Claude McKay. BANP

To the White Man. Valerie Tarver. TNV
To the wild wild beat of a tom tom tom. Reversion. Barry O. Higgs. PeSA
To the Willow-Tree. Robert Herrick. HBV; OBEV
To the Wind at Morn. W. H. Davies. ELU
To the Winds. Philip Ayres. CEP
To the winds give our banner! St. John. Whittier. PAH
To the Winter Wind. John Gould Fletcher. TSW
To the Woman in Bond Street Station. Edward Weismiller. LiTA; NePA; WaP
To the World: A Farewell for a Gentlewoman, Virtuous and Noble. Ben Jonson. EnRePo; EP; QFR; SeCP
(Farewell to the World, A, *much abr.*.) OBEV (1st ed.)
To the World, the Perfection of Love. William Habington. AnAnS-2
To the Yew and Cypress to Grace His Funeral. Robert Herrick. QFR
To the Young Man Jesus. Annie Charlotte Dalton. CaP
To the Younger Lady Lucy Sydney. Edmund Waller. *See* To a Very Young Lady.
To the Younger Old-Americans, *sel.* Kenneth Porter.
Oration, An ("Too long we have cheated our bellies with crumbs of tradition"). PoFr
To Thee. *Unknown.* BePJ
"To thee, Constantine, the King of Angels." Cynewulf. *Fr.* Elene. YAT
To thee, fair freedom! I retire. Written at [*or* in] an Inn at Henley. William Shenstone. AWP; CEP; EiCL; EiPP; HBV; JAWP; LoBV; OBEC; OBEV (new ed.); OTPC (1923 ed.); PoE; TOP; ViBoPo; WBP
To thee I dedicate this green retreat. To the Garden God. Catullus. OnPM
To Thee, Lord, my cry I send. Psalm XXVIII. *Paraphrased by* Sir Philip Sidney. FCP
To Thee, O Lord most just. Psalm XXV. *Paraphrased by* Sir Philip Sidney. FCP
To thee my way in epigrams seems new. To My Mere English Censurer. Ben Jonson. TuPP
To thee now, Christes dere derling. A Song to John, Christ's Friend. *Unknown.* MeEL
To thee, O Father of the stately peaks. To a Mountain. Henry Kendall. NeLNL; VA
To thee that art the summer's nightingale. To the Right Noble and Valorous Knight, Sir Walter Ralegh. Spenser. Sonn
To thee these first fruits of my growing death. Our Lord in His Circumcision to His Father. Richard Crashaw. MaMe
To Their Excellencies the Lords Justices of Ireland, the Humble Petition of Frances Harris [Who Must Starve and Die a Maid if It Miscarries]. Swift. ILP; Par; PoEL-3
(Frances Harris's Petition.) NoP
(Humble Petition of Frances Harris, The.) BWP; CEP
(Mrs. Frances Harris's Petition.) CBEP; OxBI
To Theocritus, in Winter. Andrew Lang. *See* Ballade to Theocritus, in Winter.
To these I turn, in these I trust. The Kiss. Siegfried Sassoon. MMA; NP
To these, the gentle South, with kisses smooth and soft. Michael Drayton. *Fr.* Polyolbion. OBS
To these [*or* those] whom death again did wed. An Epitaph upon [*or* on] Husband and Wife [*or* a Young Married Couple] Who Died and Were Buried Together. Richard Crashaw. ELP; FaBoEn; ILP; LiTL; LO; MaMe; MaRV; OAEP; OBEV; OBS; SeCePo; SeCL; SeCP; SeEP; TreFS; TrGrPo; WHA
To Thine Own Self Be True. Shakespeare. *See* Polonius' Advice to Laertes.
To Think. Elizabeth J. Coatsworth. *See* Counters.
To think I once saw grocery shops. Counters [*or* To Think]. Elizabeth J. Coatsworth. GaP; MPB; PoRh; SoPo; SUS
To think of it! He knows me. And Yet. Arthur B. Rhinow. BLRP
To Think of Time. Walt Whitman. AnFE; APA; CoAnAm; LiTA; MAmP; MWA-1
"To think of time. . . to think through the retrospection," *sel.* AP
To think that Keats once held tnis volume dear. Association Copy. Paula Kurth. JKCP (1955 ed.)
To Think That Two and Two Are Four. A. E. Housman. ImOP
To think that where young Jesus lay. Thought on a News Item. Lucia Trent. ChIP
To think the face we love shall ever die. Etruscan Tombs. Agnes Mary Frances Robinson. PeVV; WHA
To think to know the country and not know. A Hillside Thaw. Robert Frost. CMoP; DiPo; ExPo; NP; StP; TSW
To this Khan, and from this Khan. The World; a Ghazel. James Clarence Mangan. OBVV
To This Lilac-Scented Room. Alice Hansche Mortenson. SoP
To this man, to his boned shoulders. The Sympathizers. Josephine Miles. CrMA; FiMAP
To this room—it was somewhere at the palace's. The Room. C. Day Lewis. PoCh
To this sad shrine, whoe'er thou art, draw near. On the Hon. Simon Harcourt. Pope. OnPM; WoL
To this the Panther, with a scornful[l] smile. Dryden. *Fr.* The Hind and the Panther. SeCV-2; SeEP
To this thin man in gray. Monotone. Alfred Kreymborg. WOW
To Thomas Hardy. Laurence Housman. MaRV
To Thomas Lord Chancellor. Ben Jonson. OBS
To Thomas Moore ("My boat is on the shore"). Byron. ATP; EnLi-2 (1949 ed.); EnLit; EnRP; InP; MCCG; ML; OAEP; TOP; TreFT
(Friendship.) OTPC (1946 ed.)
(My Boat Is on the Shore.) BEL; EPN
To those who died for her on land and sea. Prepared for a Soldiers' and Sailors' Monument in Boston. James Russell Lowell. InP; TOP
To those who have tried and seemingly have failed. Courage to Live. Grace Noll Crowell. PoToHe
To Those Who Reproved the Author for Too Sanguine Patriotism. George Woodberry. AmePo
To those whom death again did wed. *See* To these whom death again did wed.
To those whose bosomes harbours woes. *Unknown.* SeCSL
To Those Who've Failed. Walt Whitman. TOP
To throw away the key and walk away. Chorus [*or* The Walking Tour]. W. H. Auden. *Fr.* Paid on Both Sides. CMoP; MoBrPo
To Thy continual Presence, in me wrought. A Prayer. William Ellery Channing. TrPWD
To thy lover. Out of the Italian; a Song. Richard Crashaw. MaMe; SeCV-1
To Time. Michael Drayton. Idea, XVII. SiCE
("Stay, speedy Time, behold, before thou pass.") EnRePo; OBSC
To Time. John Hagthorpe. SeCL
To Time. "A. W." ElL; TuPP
To Time it never seems that he is brave. I Could Give All to Time. Robert Frost. MoRP
To Tirzah. Blake. *Fr.* Songs of Experience. EiPP; EnRP; ERoP-1; LO; OxBoCh
"To-to" pour down. Raindrops. *Unknown.* PCH
To Tomas [*or* Tomaus] Costello at the Wars. *At. to* Tomas O'Higgins, *tr. fr. Irish by* Frank O'Connor. AnIV; KiLC
To touch the cup with eager lips and taste, not drain it. Living. *Unknown.* BLPA; FaBoBe; NeHB; TreFS
To Toussaint L'Ouverture. Wordsworth. AnEnPo; BEL; EnL; EnLi-2; EnLit; EnRP; ERoP-1; ExPo; FOL; LoBV; MBW-2; OAEP; OBNC; OBRV; PAn; PeER; PoNe; PoRA; Sonn; TrGrPo; TRV
To toy with living. The Strength of Willows. Alex Raybin. ThO
To travel like a bird, lightly to view. Sonnet. C. Day Lewis. *Fr.* O Dreams O Destinations. ChMP; GTBS-P; Sonn
To tremble in prayer and trepidation. The Revelation. Stanley Crouch. WSL
To tremble, when I touch her hands. Divine Awe. George Edward Woodberry. Wild Eden, XVI. AA
To Truth. *Unknown.* *Fr.* Solomon. WGRP
To Turn Back. John Haines. BoNaP
To turn my volumes o'er nor find. How to Read Me. Walter Savage Landor. VA
To Two Bereaved. Thomas Ashe. OBEV (1st ed.)
To Ultima Thule. George Dangerfield. CAW
To Urania. Benjamin Colman. SCAP
To Urn, or not to Urn? that is the question. Cremation. William Sawyer. BOHV
To us, goddess, who are in barbary. Charles Madge. *Fr.* Poem by Stages. BoSA
To Vanity. Darwin T. Turner. PoNe (1970 ed.)

To Varus. Catullus, *tr. fr. Latin by* Walter Savage Landor. AWP
To Venus ("Intermissa, Venus"). Horace, *tr. fr. Latin by* Ben Jonson. Odes, IV, 1. AWP
To Venus. Hedylos. *See* Seduced Girl.
To Venus garlands—braids of clustering hair. A Happy Woman. Agathias. OnPM
To Vergil. Tennyson. *See* To Virgil.
To Vernon Lee. Amy Levy. VA
To Verse Let Kings Give Place. Ovid, *tr. fr. Latin by* Christopher Marlowe. Elegies, XV. ChTr
To Victor Hugo. Swinburne. OBVV
To view these walls each night I come alone. Complains, Being Hindered the Sight of His Nymph. Philip Ayres. SeCL
To Vineyarders in cold Korea. Pinkletinks. Grace Elisabeth Allen. GoYe
To Violets. Robert Herrick. EG; HBV; OBEV; OBS; PoeP; RG; SeCP; TrGrPo; ViBoPo
(Violets.) OTPC (1923 ed.)
"Welcome, Maids of Honour," *sel.* MyFE, 2 *sts.*
To Virgil. Tennyson. ChTr; EPN; GTBS-P; InP; MBW-2; NoP; PoEL-5; PoFS; PoVP; StP; ViPo; ViPP; WHA
(To Vergil.) AWP; InPo
To Virgins ("Hear ye virgins. . ."). Robert Herrick. UnTE; ViBoPo
To Vittoria Colonna. Michelangelo, *tr. fr. Italian by* Longfellow. AWP; JAWP; WBP
To W. A. W. E. Henley. Echoes, XXXVII. EnLi-2; OuHeWo; PoVP
(Echoes.) BLPA; TreF
("Or ever the knightly years were gone.") HBV
(When I Was a King in Babylon.) PaPo
To W. B. Yeats Who Says That His Castle of Ballylee Is His Monument. Oliver St. John Gogarty. AnIL
To W. H. Auden on His Fiftieth Birthday. Barbara Howes. ML
To W. M. Alice Meynell. *See* At Night.
To W. P., *sel.* George Santayana.
"With you a part of me," II. TrGrPo
"To wade the sea-mist, then to wade the sea." Stone Horse Shoals. Malcolm Cowley. NYBP; TwAmPo
To wake the soul by tender strokes of art. Prologue to Mr. Addison's Tragedy of Cato. Pope. CEP; EiCL
To Waken a Small Person. Donald Justice. NYBP
To Waken an Old Lady. William Carlos Williams. InPo; NoP; PoeP; PoIE; QFR
To Walk Abroad. Thomas Traherne. *See* Walking.
To walk in the muck of uncertainty. Uncertainty. Henrietta C. Parks. TNV
To Walk on Hills. Robert Graves. SD
To walk with God, O fellowship divine! Walking with God. "C. H. I." SoP
To Wallace Stevens. Daniel Berrigan. ML
To Walt Whitman. Tom MacInnes. CaP
To Walt Whitman in America. Swinburne. BEL; EnLi-2; EnLit; EPN; PoVP; ViPo; ViPP
"Send but a song oversea for us," *sel.* InP
To wear out heart, and nerves, and brain. Life Is Struggle. Arthur Hugh Clough. BEL; EnLi-2; PoVP
To wear the arctic fox. The Arctic Ox. Marianne Moore. NYBP
To weary hearts, to mourning homes. The Angel of Patience. Whittier. WGRP
To Weland came woes and wearisome trail. Deor's Lament. *Unknown.* EnLi-1; OuHeWo
To western woods, and lonely plains. On the Emigration to America and Peopling the Western Country. Philip Freneau. AmPP (3d ed.); PAH
To wet your eye withouten tear. Sir Thomas Wyatt. FCP; SiPS
To what a cumbersome unwieldiness. Love's Diet. John Donne. ILP; MaMe; OAEP; PoFS; SCEP-1
To What Base Uses! Bert Leston Taylor. WhC
To what dark purpose was the will employed. Sea-Voyage. John Hall Wheelock. EtS
To what intent or purpose was Man made. As concerning Man. Alexander Radcliffe. PeRV
To what new fates, my country, far. Unmanifest Destiny. Richard Hovey. AA; AmePo; AnAmPo; HBV; HBVY; MAP; MaRV; MoAmPo (1942 ed.); NeMA; PaA; PAL; PFY; PoFr; TRV; WGRP
To what purpose, April, do you return again? Spring. Edna St. Vincent Millay. MAP; MoAB; MoAmPo; NePA; NP
To What Serves Mortal Beauty? Gerard Manley Hopkins. PoeP
To what shall a woman liken her beloved. A Woman's Beloved. Marguerite Wilkinson. NP
To what shall I liken this life? A Boat Lost. *Unknown.* OnPM
To What Strangers, What Welcome, *sel.* J. V. Cunningham.
"You have here no otherness," 4. TDP
To while the long, long road away. The Shepherd Folk Go to Bethlehem. Nicolas Saboly. CAW
To-whit! to-whit! to-whee! *See* Te-whit! te-whit! te-whee!
To-Whit To-Who. Shakespeare. *See* When Icicles Hang by the Wall.
To Whittier. James Russell Lowell. CoBA
To Whom Else? Robert Graves. FaBoMo
To whom our Saviour calmly thus replied. True and False Glory. Milton. *Fr.* Paradise Regained. LiTB; OBS
To whom shall I this dancing poem send. Dedications [*or* Orchestra], I: To His Very Friend, Master Richard Martin. Sir John Davies. SiPS
To Whom Shall the World Hence forth Belong? John Oxenham. OQP; WBLP
To Whom Shall They Go? *Unknown.* STF
To whom should I speak today? A Dispute over Suicide. *Unknown.* TTY
To whom the wingèd Hierarch replied. Milton. *Fr.* Paradise Lost, V. MBW-1
To whom thus also th' angel last replied. Milton. *Fr.* Paradise Lost, XII. FiP
To whome shall I complaine, to men or gods. *Unknown.* SeCSL
To William Allen White. Edna Ferber. InMe
To William Blake. Olive Tilford Dargan. HBMV
To William Camden. Ben Jonson. AnAnS-2; AWP; InPo; OBS; PoFS; ReEn; ReIE; SCEP-2; SeCV-1; SeEP; TuPP
To William Carlos Williams. Galway Kinnell. NePoAm
To William Earle of Pembroke. Ben Jonson. SCEP-2; SeCP
To William Erskine, Esq. Sir Walter Scott. Marmion, *Introd. to* III. OBRV, *abr.*
To William Hayley, Esq. William Cowper. Sonn
To William Lloyd Garrison ("Champion of those"). Whittier. CoBA; PAH
To William Roe. Ben Jonson. BWP; OBS; SeCV-1
To William Sharp. Clinton Scollard. HBV
To William Shelley. Shelley. ChER
To William Simpson of Ochiltree. Burns. MCCG; OxBS
To William Stanley Braithwaite. Georgia Douglas Johnson. BALP
To William Wilberforce. William Cowper. *See* Sonnet to William Wilberforce, Esq.
To William Wordsworth. Samuel Taylor Coleridge. EnRP; ERoP-1; MBW-2; PeER
To Win the World. John Oxenham. MaRV
To Winter. Blake. AnEnPo; ERoP-1; WiR
To wish and want and not obtain. Sir Thomas Wyatt. FCP; SiPS
To Woman. Byron. HBV
"Woman! experience might have told me," *sel.*, 10 *ll.* ViBoPo
To wonder, Plato told, revealed the wise. The Astronomer. Kevin F. Doherty. JKCP (1955 ed.)
To Worcester Gardens next they strolled. Maggie's Visit to Oxford. "Lewis Carroll." CIV
To Words. Ralph Pomeroy. CoPo
To Wordsworth. John Clare. ERoP-2; Sonn
To Wordsworth. Hartley Coleridge. Sonn
To Wordsworth. Walter Savage Landor. ERoP-1; PeER
To Wordsworth. Shelley. EnRP; EPN; ERoP-2; FiP; MCCG; NoP; PoPo; PoRL; Sonn
To worship Him who is my Father-God. Prayer. Henry W. Frost. SoP
To write a verse or two is all the praise. Praise. George Herbert. MaMe
To write as your sweet mother does. Advice. Walter Savage Landor. HBV; VA
To write down all I contain at this moment. The Moment. Kathleen Raine. MoPW
To write of war and wot not what it is. The Fruits of War. George Gascoigne. ReIE
To yon fause stream that, by the sea. The Mermaid. *Unknown.* CH
To You ("Stranger, if you passing meet me"). Walt Whitman. MWA-1
To you, holding in spent hands all seasons' memories. To a Faith-

To (continued)
less Lover. Robert Greacen. OnYI
To you I hurrying come, O sacred arms. To Jesus on the Cross. Juan Manuel Tejada. CAW
To you I'll sing a good old song, made by a Quaker pate. Ye Ancient Yuba Miner, of the Days of '49. Sam C. Upham. SGR
To you, little girl-child, the fairies do give. To a Little Sister, Aged Ten. Alison Elizabeth Cummings. BiCB
To you, my lordis, that standis by. So Young ane King. Sir David Lindsay. SeCePo
To you, my purse [*or* purs], and to non [*or* no *or* noon] other wight. The Compleint [*or* Complaint] of Chaucer to his [Empty] Purse. Chaucer. BEL; BOHV; CABA; CLwM; CoBE; EnL; EnLi-1; EnLit; GoBC; MeEL; NoP; PAn; PoIE; SiTL; TrGrPo; ViBoPo; WHA; YAT
To you, that know the touch of true conceit. To the Learned and Accomplish'd Gentleman Maister Nicholas Blackleech of Gray's Inn. Richard Barnfield. ReIE
"To you the torch we fling." The Torch. Arthur B. Dale. OQP
To You! To You! Sir Philip Sidney. *See* Astrophel and Stella: First Song.
To you, troop [*or* who troop] so fleet. Hymn to the Winds. Joachim du Bellay. AWP; WoL
To You Who Wait. John Pudney. WaP
To you, whose temperate pulses flow. On the Fly-Leaf of Manon Lescaut. Walter Learned. AA
To Young Dreamers. Lucia Trent. OQP
To Young Imaginaries in Knowledge. Petrarch, *tr. fr. Italian by* George Chapman. *Fr.* Seven Penitential Psalms. ReEn
To Youth. Walter Savage Landor. BEL; EnRP; EPN; HBV; VA
To youths, who hurry thus away. On a Painted Woman. Shelley. SiTL
To Yvor Winters, 1955. Thom Gunn. GTBS-P
To zig-zag with the ant. Summer Afternoon. Raymond Souster. BoNaP; NYTB
To Zion. Judah Halevi, *tr. fr. Hebrew by* Maurice Samuel. AWP; JAWP; WBP
Toad, The. Tristan Corbiere, *tr. fr. French.* OnPM, *wr. at. to* Jules Laforgue, *tr. by* Patricia Terry; SyP, *tr. by* Vernon Watkins
Toad, The. Louis Kent. WaKn
Toad and the Frog, The. *Unknown.* RIS
("Croak! Said the Toad.) PCH
Toad beneath the harrow knows, The. Pagett, M.P. Kipling. BrPo
Toad Man, The. Howard McCord. YAP
Toad that lived on Albury Heath, A. A Roundabout Turn. Robert E. Charles. MoShBr
Toad the power mower caught, A. The Death of a Toad. Richard Wilbur. AmP; AP; CABA; CaFP; CMoP; ForPo; LiTM (1970 ed.); MiAP; MoVE; NMP; NoP; TwAmPo; VaPo
Toad the Tailor. N. E. Hussey. BoTP
Toads. Philip Larkin. CMoP; NePoEA; NMP; PoeP
Toads are tamping down cakes of moss. Firewood Hill. Dave Etter. ThO
Toads Revisited. Philip Larkin. PoeP
Toadstool comes up in a night, A. A Lesson. Christina Rossetti. RIS
Toadstool towers infest the shore, The. Windscale. Norman Nicholson. POTi
Toadstools. Elizabeth Fleming. BoTP
Toast, A. John Byrom. *See* Jacobite Toast.
Toast. Frank Horne. BANP; PoNe
Toast, A. Louis MacNeice. CMoP; GTBS-D
Toast, The. Charles Warren Stoddard. CAW
Toast ("Here's to those who love us"). *Unknown.* SiTL
Toast, A ("Here's to ye absent lords"). *Unknown.* ALV; WhC
Toast, A ("Here's to you and here's to me"). *Unknown.* PV
Toast ("Up to my lips and over my gums"). *Unknown.* CoSo
Toast to a Departing Duchess. Clément Marot, *tr. fr. French by* Cécile Schreiber *and* Virginia Tufte. HW
Toast to Omar Khayyám. Theodore Watts-Dunton. VA
Toast to our Native Land, A. Robert Bridges ("Droch"). MC; PAH; PAL
Toast to that lady over the fireplace, A. Drinking Song. Anthony Hecht. NMP
Toast to the Flag, A. John Daly. PAL; PoLF
Toaster, The. William Jay Smith. SoPo
Tobacco. Graham Lee Hamminger. PoLF; WhC
(This Smoking World.) InMe
Tobacco, Tobacco. *Unknown.* TuPP
("Tobacco, tobacco, sing sweetly for tobacco!") ReEn
Tobacconist of Eighth Street, The. Richard Eberhart. MiAP; ToPo
Tobacco's a musician. Barten Holyday. *Fr.* Technogamia; or, The Marriage of the Arts. TuPP
Tobit, *sel.* Bible, Apocrypha.
Blessed Is God, XIII, *tr. fr. Greek by* D. C. Simpson. TrJP
Toccata of Galuppi's, A. Robert Browning. AnFE; ATP (1935 ed.); CBEP; EnLi-2 (1949 ed.); GTBS-P; HBV; LiTB; LoBV; MaVP; MBW-2; NCEP; NoP; OAEP; OtMeF; PoAn; PoE; PoFS; PoVP; ViPo; ViPP; VP; WHA
Today. John Kendrick Bangs. PoToHe
Today. Mary Frances Butts. MaRV; SoP; TreFT; TRV
(Build a Fence of Trust.) OQP
Today. Thomas Carlyle. HBV; HBVY; MaRV; NeHB; OQP; OTD; OTPC (1946 ed.); WGRP
Today. Thomas Curtis Clark. ChIP
Today. Ozora Stearns Davis. OQP
Today. Ethel Romig Fuller. PoToHe (new ed.)
To-Day. Benjamin R. C. Low. HBV
Today. Clive Matson. ThO
To-Day. Angela Morgan. BLPA; MaRV; TRV
(In Such an Age.) OQP
Today. Gaston Neal. BF
To-Day. John Boyle O'Reilly. OnYI
To-Day. Sybil F. Partridge. *See* Just for Today.
To-Day. Sister Mary Philip. GoBC
Today. James Schuyler. ANYP
Today ("And if tomorrow shall be sad"). *Unknown.* OQP
To-Day. Lydia Avery Coonley Ward. HBV; MaRV
Today. Nixon Waterman. *See* What Have We Done Today?
Today,/ Hark! Heaven sings. On Christmas Day. Clement Paman. OBS; OxBoCh; SeCL
Today, a fellow in the mirror. "Today Well, Tomorrow Cold in the Mouth." John Gill. ThO
To-day a rude brief recitative. Song for All Seas, All Ships. Walt Whitman. CH; FaBoBe; HBV; HBVY; MCCG; MoRP; NePA
To-Day a Shepherd. St. Teresa of Avila, *tr. fr. Spanish by* Arthur Symons. AWP
To-day, all day, I rode upon the down. St. Valentine's Day. Wilfrid Scawen Blunt. *Fr.* The Love Sonnets of Proteus. EnLoPo; NBM; OBEV (1st ed.); OBVV; ViBoPo
To-Day and Thee. Walt Whitman. NePA
Today and Tomorrow. Horace, *See* Happy the Man. *par. by* Dryden.
Today and Tomorrow. Edward N. Pomeroy. MaRV; OQP
To-day as I went down the road. Turtle Town. Helen Wing. GFA
To-day as I went out to play. The Brown Frog. Mary K. Robinson. BoTP
To-day chance drove me to the wood. A Moment. Stopford Augustus Brooke. IrPN
Today, dear heart, but just today. Her Answer. John Bennett. AA; BLPA; NeHB
To-day Death seems to me an infant child. Newborn Death, 1. Dante Gabriel Rossetti. The House of Life, XCIX. MaVP; PoVP; ViPo
Today ees com' from Eetaly. Da Boy from Rome. T. A. Daly. FaPON; MPB
Today for Me. Christina Rossetti. PoVP
Today from the Aurora's bosom. The Nativity of Christ. Luis de Góngora. CAW
Today I am in the room watching the sun evaporate. News. Frank Lima. ANYP
Today I found lean winter's. The Coming. Anthony Delius. ACV; BoSA
Today I get this letter from you and the sun. You (III). Tom Clark. ANYP
Today I have a birthday. Birthday Candles. Louise Binder Scott *and* J. J. Thompson. BiCB
Today I have been happy. All the day. One Day. Rupert Brooke. MoLP
Today I have been thinking of very old men. Old Men. Nancy Keesing. BoAV
Today I have grown taller from walking with the trees. Good

Company. Karle Wilson Baker. FaPON; HBV; OQP; WGRP
Today I Have Touched the Earth. William Jay Smith. WaP
Today I met my woman in the subway. The Woman. Frank Lima. ANYP
To-day I saw a butterfly. Teresa Hooley. TiPo (1959 ed.)
Today I saw a group of children running. Green Branches. "Joan Ramsay." MaRV
Today I saw a picture of the cancer cells. The Cancer Cells. Richard Eberhart. HoPM; LiTM (1970 ed.); MiAP; ToPo
Today I saw a slender locust tree. Autumn Days. Margaret Knowled Speidel. SoP
Today I saw a thing of arresting poignant beauty. Snow in October. Alice Dunbar Nelson. CDC
Today I saw a woman wrapped in rags. At the Slackening of the Tide. James Wright. AmPC; CABA; UnPo (3d ed.)
To-Day I Saw Bright Ships. Eloise Robinson. HBMV
To-day, I saw the catkins blow. February. Dorothy Una Ratcliffe. BoTP
"To-day I saw the dragon-fly." The Dragon-Fly. Tennyson. *Fr.* The Two Voices. OA
To-day I saw the shop-girl go. To a New York Shop-Girl Dressed for Sunday. Anna Hempstead Branch. HBV
Today I sing a song to Atlantis in the glory of the sky. Ode to the Sky of the New Atlantis. Emilio Oribe. PoFr
Today I think. Digging. Edward Thomas. MoAB; MoBrPo
Today I think of a boy in the Transvaal. Remembering Snow. R. N. Curry. PeSA
Today I walk in and out of the doors of your death. On the Anniversary of the Death of Frank O'Hara. Sotère Torregian. YAP
Today, I will see some empty spaces. Today: the Idea Market. Michael Nicholas. NBP
Today in Bethlehem Hear I. St. John of Damascus, *tr. fr. Greek.* BePJ; MaRV
Today Is a Day of Great Joy. Victor Hernandez Cruz. TTY
Today is a holiday in the Western heart. Today Is Armistice, a Holiday. Delmore Schwartz. TrJP
Today is a thought, a fear is tomorrow. Dirge Written for a Drama. Thomas Lovell Beddoes. EnRP
Today Is Armistice, a Holiday. Delmore Schwartz. TrJP
Today is Candlemas, and by the light. Simeon's Light Remembered. John W. Simons. JKCP (1955 ed.)
"Today is hard. Tomorrow will/ Be harder still." The Kindly Screen. Belle Chapman Morrill. MaRV
Today Is Ours. Abraham Cowley. *See* Epicure, The ("Fill the bowl with rosy wine").
Today Is Sun. Arnold Adoff. CAD
Today, looking at the flowering peach. To My Father. James K. Baxter. AnNZ
To-day my heart is heavy. Cologne. John Bate. NeBP
To-day my thoughts/ Are swift and cool. To-Day. Sister Mary Philip. GoBC
Today, new-born from all my yesterdays. Today. Ozora Stearns Davis. OQP
Today, O Lord. Maltbie D. Babcock. *See* Not to Be Ministered To.
To day old Janus opens the new yeare. A New-Yeares-Gift Sung to King Charles, 1635. Ben Jonson. SeCP
Today, should you let fall a glass, it would. Tramontana at Lerici. Charles Tomlinson. GTBS-P
Today six slender fruit trees stand. Planting Trees. V. H. Friedlaender. BoNaP
Today, the first dead leaf in the hall. A Dead Leaf. Howard Moss. NYBP
Today: the Idea Market. Michael Nicholas. NBP
Today the journey is ended. A Soul's Soliloquy. Wenonah Stevens Abbott. BLPA; NeHB
Today the leaves cry, hanging on branches swept by wind. The Course of a Particular. Wallace Stevens. ForPo; PoIE; QFR
Today the peace of autumn pervades the world. Autumn. Rabindranath Tagore. BoPe; WGRP
To-day "the pines of Ramoth wood." John Greenleaf Whittier. John Cameron Grant. DD
Today the rain. Rain. Frank Marshall Davis. GoSl
Today the swards of heaven are merry. The First of April. Geoffrey Johnson. PoRL
Today the wind is from the south. I Make Fallout Too. Thomas Hanna. QAH
To-day the woods are trembling through and through. Corn. Sidney Lanier. AP; CoBA; LaNeLa; MAmP
Today the world is bound in blue. First Geography. Gladys McKee. JKCP (1955 ed.)
Today they brought me a message: Wordsworth was dead. Bells for William Wordsworth. Dom Moraes. BoPe; ML
To-day they laid him in the earth's cold colour. For Angus MacLeod. Iain Crichton Smith. OxBS
Today, this moment, here, you love me. In Defense of Marriage. John Gill. ThO
Today this town is dull, my world confin'd. The Wilderness. Gyula Juhasz. LiTW
Today unnumbered church bells ring. Easter. John Van Brakle. ChIP
Today upon a bus, I saw. Forgive Me When I Whine. *Unknown.* STF
Today we carted home the last brown sheaf. Load. John Hewitt. OnYI
To-day we have naming of parts. Naming of Parts. Henry Reed. *Fr.* Lessons of the War, I. CaFP; CBV; DTC; GoJo; HoPM; ILP; LiTB; LiTM (rev. ed.); MoAB; MoBrPo (1962 ed.); MoVE; NoP; PoPl; PoRA (rev. ed.); SeCePo; SeCeV (1967 ed.); ShBV-3; SiTL; StP; TrGrPo (rev. ed.); ViBoPo (1958 ed.); WaP; WePo
Today we think of that great man. For February Twelfth. Muriel M. Gessner. RePo; YeAr
"Today Well, Tomorrow Cold in the Mouth." John Gill. ThO
Today, what is there in the air. Carpe Diem. Théophile Marzials. BA
Today, whatever may annoy. Today. John Kendrick Bangs. PoToHe
Today when I heard. Retrospect. "An Pilibin." OnYI
Today, while thousands stared with captured eyes. Sky-Writer. Vincent Starret. PoPo
Today while walking in the wood. Where a Dogwood Stood. Earle J. Grant. SoP
To-day you shall have but little song from me. Irradiations, X [XXXII]. John Gould Fletcher. MAPA; TwAmPo
To-day's house makes to-morrow's road. The Survival. Edmund Blunden. OBEV (new ed.); OBMV
Todlen Butt, and Todlen Ben. *Unknown.* OBS
Todlin' Hame. *Unknown.* HBV
Toe Queen Poems, *sels.* Ed Sanders. ANYP
  "Dragged to her cell."
  "Good God / a 3 & 1/2 inch bony."
  "'I shall return!'"
Toe sticking out from under the hem, The. On a Fifteenth-Century Flemish Angel. David Ray. NePoEA-2
Toe Tipe. *Unknown.* OxNR
Toe, trip and go. *Unknown.* OxNR
Toe upon toe, a snowing flesh. Nude Descending a Staircase. X. J. Kennedy. CoAP; NePoEA-2; PIA
Together. Ludwig Lewisohn. HBMV; PoToHe; TrJP
Together. Siegfried Sassoon. BrPo
Together how many hours. Tant' Amare. *Unknown.* ErPo
Together in infinite shade. Too Much Coffee. E. A. Robinson. MAP; MoAmPo
Together, Lord. *Unknown.* SoP
Together we laughed and talked in the warm lit room. November. Laurence Binyon. SyP
Together, we looked down. Wedding Procession [from a Window]. James A. Emanuel. Kal; NNP
Together with my wife I passed. Passing the Cape. Otomo Tabito. OnPM
Toil. *Unknown.* PEDC
Toil and grow rich. The Witch. W. B. Yeats. ELU; FaBoTw
Toil Away. John Jay Chapman. HBMV
Toil is the Sun-God's portion, toil all the livelong day. The Sun's Golden Bowl. Mimnermus. LiTW
Toil of day is ebbing, The. Before Sleep. Prudentius. LiTW
Toil of the Trail, The. Hamlin Garland. HBV
Toil on, poor muser, to attain that goal. The Ideal. Francis Saltus Saltus. AA
Toiler, The, *sel.* Edwin Markham.
  "Behold, O world, the toiling man." PGD
Toiler, Canst Thou Dream? Lulu W. Mitchell. DD
Toilet, The. Pope. *Fr.* The Rape of the Lock. OBEC (Belinda's Morning.) ExPo
Toilette, The. Chu Ching-Yü, *tr. fr. Chinese by* David Rafael Wang. HW

Toilette, The; a Town Eclogue. John Gay. CEP
Toiling in Town now is "horrid." In Town. Austin Dobson. InP
Toiling of Felix, The, *sels.* Henry van Dyke.
Angler's Reveille, The. BBV (1923 ed.); GN; StVeCh
Envoy to "The Toiling of Felix." BLPA
"Never in a costly palace did I rest on golden bed." ChIP
Toils Are Pitched, The. Sir Walter Scott. *See* Hunter's Song.
Toils of the Road, The. *Unknown.* SoP
(End of the Way, The.) BLRP
Toil-worn I stood and said. Unique. Frances Bent Dillingham. SoP
Token. Peggy Bacon. PV
Token, The. F. T. Prince. FaBoTw
Tokens. William Barnes. NBM; PoEL-4
Tokens. John Richard Moreland. IHA
Tokens, The. Francis Thompson. *Fr.* Daisy. OtMeF
Told by Seafarers. Galway Kinnell. NePoAm-2
Told in the Market-Place. Edwina Stanton Babcock. StJW
Toledo ("Perched on its yellow peak"). Gómez Restrepo, *tr. fr. Spanish by* Thomas Walsh. CAW
Toledo ("No more the jousts"). José Zorrilla, *tr. fr. Spanish by* Thomas Walsh. CAW
Toledo, July 1936. Roy Campbell. FaBoTw; MoBrPo
Tolerance. Thomas Hardy. MoRP
Tolerance. Sir Lewis Morris. OBVV
Toll-a-Winker, *with music. Unknown.* OuSiCo
Toll for the brave! On the Loss [*or* The Loss] of the *Royal George.* William Cowper. AnFE; BEL; BWP; CBEP; EtS; FiP; GN; GTBS; GTBS-D; GTBS-P; GTBS-W; GTSE; GTSL; HBV; InPo; MyFE; OAEP; OBEC; RoGo; TrGrPo; WHA
Toll-Gate Man, The. Wilson MacDonald. CaP
Toll no bell for me, dear Father, dear Mother. The Changeling. Charlotte Mew. CH; MPB
Toll of the Desert, The. Arthur W. Monroe. PoOW
Toll! Roland, toll! The Great Bell Roland. Theodore Tilton. PAH
Toll the bell, fellow. The Red Cow Is Dead. E. B. White. NYBP
Toll the Bell for Damon. Maxwell Anderson. InMe
"Tollable Well!" Frank L. Stanton. FaFP
Tolling. Lucy Larcom. OHIP
Tolling Bells. Lady Kasa, *tr. fr. Japanese by* Ishii *and* Obata. OnPM
Tolstoy Seeks the Peasant Rhythm. James Schevill. FRC
Tom a Bedlam. *Unknown. See* Tom o' Bedlam's Song.
Tom-a-Bedlam's Poem. *Unknown. See* Tom o' Bedlam's Song.
Tom Agnew, Bill Agnew. Dante Gabriel Rossetti. ChTr
Tom Bolyn[n], *with music. Unknown.* OuSiCo; TrAS
Tom Bowling. Charles Dibdin. CBEP; EtS; HBV
(Poor Tom, or the Sailor's Epitaph.) OBEC; OxBoLi
(Tom Bowline, *with music.*) AmSS
Tom Brainless at College. John Trumbull. *Fr.* The Progress of Dulness. AmPP (3d ed.); ATP (1935 ed.)
(Tom Brainless as Student and Preacher.) AmPP (4th ed.)
Tom Brainless Seeks a Wife. John Trumbull. *Fr.* The Progress of Dulness. AmPP (3d ed.)
(Amorous Temper, An.) AmPP (4th ed.)
Tom Brown's two little Indian boys. *Unknown.* OxNR
Tom Child had often painted death. This Morning Tom Child, the Painter, Died. Samuel Sewall. SCAP
Tom Dansey was a famous whip. John Masefield. *Fr.* Reynard the Fox. OtMeF
Tom Dixon, *with music. Unknown.* ShS
Tom Dooley. *Unknown.* ViBoFo
Tom Ducket. Jean Jaszi. RePo
Tom Dunstan; or, The Politician. Robert Buchanan. HBV; PoFr, *abr.*
Tom Farley. Colin Thiele. PoAu-2
Tom Fool at Jamaica. Marianne Moore. AP; NYBP
Tom Gage's Proclamation. Thomas Flucker. PAH
Tom—garlanded with squat and surly steel. Tom's Garland. Gerard Manley Hopkins. BrPo; Sonn
Tom he was the [*or* a *or* Tom, Tom, the] piper's son. Over the Hills and Far Away [*or* Tom, the Piper's Son]. *Unknown.* GaP; OTPC; OxNR; PCH; PPL; RIS; TiPo (1952 ed.)
Tom Hight is my name, and old bachelor I am. Greer County [*or* Hurrah for Greer County]. *Unknown.* ABF; BFSS; CoSo
Tom, if they loved thee best who called thee Tom. Thomas Heywood. Swinburne. CLwM
Tom Joad, *with music.* Woody Guthrie. TrAS
Tom May's Death. Andrew Marvell. MaMe
Tom Moore has sung of '49. The Good Old Days of '50, '1, and '2. J. Riley Mains. SGR
Tom o' Bedlam's Song (*diff. versions*). *Unknown.* AnFE; AtBAP; CBEP; ChTr; EG; EvOK; FosPo; HoPM; InvP; LiTB; LiTG; MemP; OtMeF, *sl. abr.*; PoEL-2; PoFS; PoSa; PTK; SeCeV; ShBV-4; StP; TrGrPo; ViBoPo, *at. to* Giles Earle
(Loving Mad Tom.) EnSB
(Roaring Mad Tom.) WiR
(Tom a Bedlam.) SeEP
(Tom-a-Bedlam's Poem.) HBV
(Tom o' Bedlam.) BoW; CH, *much abr.*; FaBoCh; LoGBV; OxBoLi; PoRA (rev. ed.); SiTL; WaKn
"Moon's my constant mistress, The," *sel.*, 5 *ll.* LO
Tom of Bedlam ("From the top of high Caucasus"). *Unknown.* SiTL
Tom O'Roughley. W. B. Yeats. CMoP
"Tom Pearse, Tom Pearse, lend me your gray mare." Widdicombe [*or* Widdecombe] Fair. *Unknown.* BBV (1951 ed.); CH; MoShBr; OBB; OnSP; PoMS
Tom Potts. *Unknown.* ESPB
Tom Pringle. Louis Simpson. NePoAm-2
Tom sang for joy, and Ned sang for joy, and old Sam sang for joy. The Quartette. Walter de la Mare. BoC; CBEP; MuSP
Tom Tatter's Birthday Ode. Thomas Hood. LoBV
Tom the Lunatic. W. B. Yeats. OnYI
Tom, the Piper's Son. *Unknown. See* Over the Hills and Far Away.
Tom the Porter. John Byrom. CEP
Tom Thomson. Arthur S. Bourinot. CaP
Tom Thumbkin. *Unknown.* OxNR
Tom Thumb's Alphabet. *Unknown.* HBV; HBVY; OTPC; SiTL
("A was an archer, who shot at a frog.") OxNR
Tom tied a kettle to the tail of a cat. Three Bad Ones. *Unknown.* BBGG
Tom told his dog called Tim to beg. Tom's Little Dog. Walter de la Mare. TiPo
Tom-tom sun awakens day's jungle with heat beats, A. Midsummer Morn. Frank Marshall Davis. GoSl
Tom, Tom, the Piper's Son. John Crowe Ransom. ViBoPo
Tom, Tom, the piper's son/ Stole a pig and away he run. Mother Goose. BoChLi; OTPC; OxNR; RIS; SiTL
Tom, Tom, the piper's son,/ He learned to play when he was young. Over the Hills and Far Away. *Unknown. See* Tom he was the piper's son.
Tom Twist. William Allen Butler. OTPC (1946 ed.)
Tom Tyler and His Wife, *sel. Unknown.*
"Proverb reporteth, no man can deny, The." EIL; SiCE; TuPP
Tomah Stream, *with music.* Larry Gorman. ShS
Tomato Juice. A. P. Herbert. WhC
Tomb, The. Matthew Arnold. *Fr.* The Church of Brou. PoVP
Tomb. Besmilr Brigham. ThO
Tomb/ A hollow hateful word. Agamemnon's Tomb. Sacheverell Sitwell. LiTB; OBMV
Tomb at [*or* of] Akr Çaar, The. Ezra Pound. APA; CoAnAm; TwAmPo
Tomb of a shipwrecked mariner am I. Pass On. Theodorides. WoL
Tomb of Crethon, The. Leonidas of Tarentum, *tr. fr. Greek by* John Herman Merivale. AWP; JAWP; WBP
Tomb of Diogenes, The. *Unknown, tr. fr. Greek by* John Addington Symonds. AWP; JAWP; OnPM; WBP
Tomb of God before us, The. Crusader Chorus. Charles Kingsley. *Fr.* The Saint's Tragedy. FOL; VA
Tomb of Honey Snaps Its Marble Chains, The. Derek Stanford. NeBP
Tomb of Lieutenant John Learmonth, A.I.F., The. John S. Manifold. BoAV; LiTM; NeLNL; PoAu-2
Tomb of Michael Collins, The. Denis Devlin. OPoP; OxBI
Tomb of the Brave, The. Joseph Hutton. PAH
Tomb, thou shalt not hold Him longer. Easter Morning. Phillips Brooks. MaRV; SoP
Tombe, The. Thomas Stanley. OBS
Tombless Epitaph, A, *sel.* Samuel Taylor Coleridge.
"Sickness 'tis true." OBRV
Tomboy, The. William Burford. NePA

Tombs. Louise Webster. ChIP
Tombs in Westminster, The. *At. to* Francis Beaumont, *also to* William Basse. *See* On the Tombs in Westminster Abbey.
Tombstone Told When She Died, The. Dylan Thomas. FaBoTw
Tombstone with Cherubin. Horace Gregory. NAMP
Tomcat, The. Don Marquis. CIV; PoMa; PoRA
Tomlinson. Kipling. BeLS; OtMeF, *abr.*; PoVP
Tommie Makes My Tail Toddle. Burns. ErPo
Tommies in the Train. D. H. Lawrence. MMA; NP
Tommy. Kipling. BrPo; CABA; EnLi-2 (1949 ed.); EnLit; FaBV; MoBrPo; NeMA; NoP; PeVV; PoVP; TreFS; ViPP
Tommy for his evening game. *Unknown.* WhC
Tommy kept a chandler's shop. *Unknown.* OxNR
Tommy O'Linn was a Scotsman born. *Unknown.* OxNR
Tommy Tibule. *Unknown.* OxNR
Tommy Trot, a man of law. *Unknown.* OxNR
Tommy was a silly boy. Kate Greenaway. TiPo
"Tommy" you was when it began. "The Service Man." Kipling. Par
Tommy's Dead. Sydney Dobell. HBV; PeVV; VA
Tommy's Gone to Hilo, *with music.* *Unknown.* AmSS; ShS
(Tom's Gone to Hilo, *with music.*) SoAmSa
Tommy's tears and Mary's fears. Mother Goose. HBV; HBVY
To-Morrow. Florence Earle Coates. AA
To-Morrow. John Collins. GTBS; GTBS-D; GTBS-P; GTBS-W; GTSE; GTSL; HBV; TreFT
Tomorrow. Kenneth Fearing. CMoP
Tomorrow. Della Adams Leitner. STF
To-Morrow. Longfellow. SoP
Tomorrow. Lope de Vega, *tr. fr. Spanish by* Longfellow. AWP; CAW; SoP; TrPWD
To-Morrow. Martial. *See* Procrastination.
Tomorrow. John Masefield. MoBrPo; NeMA; OtMeF; POTE; StaSt; TrGrPo; YT
Tomorrow. Regino Pedroso, *tr. fr. Spanish by* Dudley Fitts. PoFr
Tomorrow. Shakespeare. *See* Tomorrow and Tomorrow and Tomorrow.
To-Morrow. Shelley. EPN
Tomorrow. *Unknown.* SoP
(Do It Now.) STF
Tomorrow,/ hurry, hurry, do! Hurry Tomorrow. Ivy O. Eastwick. BiCB
Tomorrow and Tomorrow. Sir William Davenant, *revision of* Shakespeare. UnPo
Tomorrow and Tomorrow and Tomorrow. Shakespeare. *Fr.* Macbeth, V, v. FaFP; LiTB; MasP; OQP; PG; PoPl; PTK; TrGrPo; TRV; WHA; YAT
(Empty Life, The.) MaRV
(Macbeth Learns of His Wife's Death.) TreF
(Out, Out, Brief Candle!) ChTr
(She Should Have Died Hereafter.) FiP; InP; MemP
(Tomorrow and Tomorrow.) DiPo; NeHB; UnPo
Tomorrow at dawn. A Soldier's Wife. Li Po. OnPM
"Tomorrow, friend, will be another day." Faith for Tomorrow. Thomas Curtis Clark. PoToHe
Tomorrow Is a Birthday. Gwendolen Haste. GoYe
Tomorrow Is [*or* Good Morrow, 'Tis] Saint Valentine's Day. Shakespeare. *Fr.* Hamlet, IV, v. EnLoPo; InPo; PV; ViBoPo
(Ophelia's Song.) UnTE
(Saint Valentine's Day.) LiTB; LiTG
(Song.) FaPON; HH; MPB; SiSoSe
Tomorrow is the Marriage Day. *Unknown.* NCEP
Tomorrow let loveless, let lover tomorrow make love. The Vigil of Venus (Pervigilium Veneris). *Unknown.* LiTW
To-Morrow Shall Be My Dancing Day. *Unknown.* PoEL-1
(My Dancing Day.) CBEP; OxBoLi
Tomorrow the Heroes. A. B. Spellman. BF
Tomorrow, tomorrow's the circus parade. The Circus Parade. Olive Beaupré Miller. GFA; SoPo
Tomorrow when I go to shop. Pretense. Helen Welshimer. PoMa
Tomorrow you are born again. December Twenty-fourth. Eleanor Slater. ChIP; MaRV; OQP
To-morrow you will live, you always cry. Procrastination [*or* To-Morrow]. Martial. AWP; JAWP; LiTW; OnPM; OuHeWo; WBP
Tomorrow's Men. Georgia Douglas Johnson. GoSl
Tomorrow's Way. *Unknown.* SoP
Tom's album was filled with the pictures of belles. The unattainable. Harry Romaine. BOHV
Tom's Angel. Walter de la Mare. BoC; POTE
Tom's Garland. Gerard Manley Hopkins. BrPo; Sonn
Tom's Gone to Hilo. *Unknown.* *See* Tommy's Gone to Hilo.
Tom's Little Dog. Walter de la Mare. TiPo
Tom's Sleeping Song. Mark Van Doren. *Fr.* Jonathan Gentry. LOW
Tom-tom, c'est moi. The blue guitar. Wallace Stevens. *Fr.* The Man with the Blue Guitar. CMoP
Tone Arm, *sel.* Ron Padgett.
"Clouds go rolling over, The." YAP
Tone de Bell Easy, *with music.* *Unknown.* ABF
Tone of my life takes, The. Today. Gaston Neal. BF
Tone of Voice, The. *Unknown.* PoToHe (new ed.)
Tone's Grave. Thomas Osborne Davis. OnYI
Tongue, The. *Unknown.* PoToHe (new ed.); WBLP
Tongue-doughty pedant; whose ambitious mind. Thomas Edwards. Sonn
Tongue of England, that which myriads, The. Shakespeare and Milton. Walter Savage Landor. VA
Tongue that mothered such a metaphor, The. Hogwash. Robert Francis. PoIE (1970 ed.)
Tongues. T. Sturge Moore. HBMV
Tongues of dying men, The. Dying Men. Shakespeare. King Richard II, *fr.* II, i. MaRV
Tongues there are that naught can say. Tongues. T. Sturge Moore. HBMV
Tonight. Franklin P. Adams. FiBHP
To-Night. Louise Chandler Moulton. AA
To Night. Shelley. NoP
Tonight. *Unknown.* *See* For All Who Need.
Tonight/ when the moon comes out. Proposition. Nicolás Guillén. FaPON; PoNe; TTY
Tonight a blackout. Christmas Eve under Hooker's Statue. Robert Lowell. AP; NePA; OxBA; PoDB; ThLM
Tonight and forever I shall be yours so says the oleo king. Some Stories of the Beauty Wapiti. Ebbe Borregaard. NeAP
To-night from deeps of loneliness I wake in wistful wonder. Bluebells. Lucia Clark Markham. HBMV
Tonight, grave sir, boeth my poor house and I. Inviting a Friend to Supper [*or* Epigram]. Ben Jonson, *after* Martial. AnAnS-2; AWP; BWP; EnRePo; EP; JAWP; LiTB; LoBV; MaPo; MyFE; NoP; OAEP; OBS; OxBoLi; Po; PoE; PoEL-2; ReEn; SCEP-2; SeCP; SeCV-1; SeEP; TuPP; WBP
To-night her lids shall lift again, slow, soft, with vague desire. Heart's Wild-Flower. William Vaughn Moody. TOP
Tonight I could die as easily as the grass. In the Soul Hour. Robert Mezey. NaP
To-night I do not come to conquer thee. Anguish. Stéphane Mallarmé. AWP; SyP
Tonight I sat on my back porch. Sometimes Life Is Not a Literary Experience. Eugene Lesser. FRC
To-night I saw three maidens on the beach. Ibant Obscurae. Thomas Edward Brown. OBNC
To-night I sing, though all mankind forbid it. Night Piece to Another Julia. Paul Fearon. CIV
To-night I stay at the Summit Temple. The Summit Temple. Li Po. OnPM
Tonight I walked with the grim Florentine. Sonnet. George Henry Boker. *Fr.* Sonnets. AmLP
Tonight in Chicago. *Unknown.* AmFN
To-night in million-voiced London I. The Telephone. Hilaire Belloc. MoVE
Tonight in our secret town. Right Now. William Stafford. NaP
Tonight is so coarse with chocolate. Ode. Louis MacNeice. CMoP
Tonight is the night. Hallowe'en. Harry Behn. FaPON; GBV (1952 ed.); OTD; PDV; PoSC; RePo; SiSoSe; StVeCh (1955 ed.); TiPo; YeAr
Tonight my children hunch. "It Out-Herods Herod, Pray You Avoid It." Anthony Hecht. CoAP
To-night retir'd the queen of heaven. Ode to the Evening Star [*or* The Nightingale *or* To the Evening Star]. Mark Akenside. CEP; HBV; OBEC; OBEV; PoEL-3
Tonight the Christmas landscape of the skull. Carol for His Darling on Christmas Day. Derek Stanford. NeBP
To-night, the gaudy auditorium. After the Show. Sam Harrison. NeIP

Tonight the hut grows menacing, the walls. This Is My Song. Norma Davis. NeLNL
Tonight the moon is high, to summon all. Elegy XII. William Bell. FaBoTw
Tonight the Pacifist Moon. Sidney Alexander. NYTB
Tonight the rain sheets down. After an hour. Cheshire Cat. Kenneth Allott. NeBP
Tonight the schools disperse. On the Breaking-up of a School. Tadhg O'g O'Huiginn. AnIL
To-night the stranger city and the old. The Cruel Solstice. Sidney Keyes. POTE
To-night the very horses springing by. Winter Evening. Archibald Lampman. OBCV; PeCV
Tonight the wind gnaws. Christmas Landscape. Laurie Lee. BoPe; FIW; POTi
Tonight the winds begin to rise. In Memoriam A. H. H., XV. Tennyson. AnFE; EnLi-2; EPN; FaBoEn; GTBS-D; GTBS-P; LiTB; OAEP; OBEV (1st ed.); OBNC; PoEL-5; PoFS; PoSa; ShBV-4; ViPo; VP
Tonight this city seated on a hill. Midnight Mass. Sister Mary Madeleva. Christmas in Provence, II. WHL
To-night this sunset spreads two golden wings. Sunset Wings. Dante Gabriel Rossetti. HBV
To-night ungathered let us leave. In Memoriam A. H. H., CV. Tennyson. EnLi-2; EPN; OAEP; ViPo; VP
To-night we strive to read, as we may best. Prologue. Longfellow. *Fr.* John Endicott. PAH
Tonight when the hoar frost falls on the wood. Christmas in the Woods. Frances Frost. ChBR; TiPo (1952 ed.)
To-night while I was pondering in my chair. A Midnight Interior. Siegfried Sassoon. MoRP
To-night's a moonlit cup. The Offensive. Keith Douglas. NeBP
Tonite, thriller was. Beware: Do Not Read This Poem. Ishmael Reed. NoP
Tonversation with Baby, A. Morris Bishop. FiBHP; WhC
Tony O! Colin Francis. CH; PV
Too Anxious for Rivers. Robert Frost. CBEP; MoPW
Too avid of earth's bliss, he was of those. Byron the Voluptuary. Sir William Watson. VA
Too beautiful this earth is! Weep I must. The Troubled Unquickening. William Baylebridge. *Fr.* Sextains. BoAV
Too Bright a Day. Norman MacCaig. GTBS-P
Too Busy. Avis B. Christiansen. SoP
Too Busy? Ralph S. Cushman. SoP
Too Busy. *At. to* Paul Laurence Dunbar. *See* Get Somebody Else.
Too Busy ("Too busy this morning"). *Unknown.* STF
Too Busy ("Too busy to read a chapter a day"). *Unknown.* STF
Too Candid by Half. John Godfrey Saxe. HBV
Too cold this night for Hugh Maguire. Hugh Maguire. Eochadh O'Hussey. AnIL; KiLC
Too dearly had I bought my green and youthful years. Earl of Surrey. FCP; SiPS
Too fair, I may not call thee mine. Parting. Gerald Massey. HBV
Too far afield thy search. Nay, turn. Nay, turn. To Man Who Goes Seeking Immortality. Adelaide Crapsey. QFR
Too far, too far, though hidden in thine arms. Pandora's Song. William Vaughan Moody. *Fr.* The Fire-Bringer. MOAP
Too green the springing April grass. Spring in New Hampshire. Claude McKay. BANP; GoSl; Kal; PoNe
Too happy had I been indeed, if Fate. The Parting. John Oldham. PeRV
Too honest for a gypsy, too lazy for a farmer. Shepherd's Holiday. Elinor Wylie. CrMA; HBMV
Too Late. Matthew Arnold. VP
Too Late. Robert Browning. PoVP
Too Late. Dinah Maria Mulock Craik. *See* Douglas, Douglas, Tender and True.
Too Late. Emily Dickinson. *See* Delayed till she had ceased to know.
Too Late. William James Linton. VA
Too Late? Longfellow. *See* It Is Too Late!
Too Late. Fitzhugh Ludlow. BOHV; PoLF
Too Late. Philip Bourke Marston. OBNC
Too Late. Nora Perry. PoToHe
Too Late. Tennyson. *Fr.* Idylls of the King: Guinevere. MaRV; OQP
Too Late. R. S. Thomas. NMP; POTi
Too Late, *with music. Unknown.* BoAN-2
Too late, alas! I must confess. Song. Earl of Rochester. HBV
Too-late Born, The. Archibald MacLeish. AmP; AnFE; APA; CoAnAm; GoJo; GTBS-W; LiTM; MAP; MoAB; MoAmPo; NAMP; OxBA; SeCeV; TwAmPo; WaP
(Silent Slain, The.) CABA; CMoP; CoBMV; ExPo; MoVE; NePA
Too Late for Love. Christina Rossetti. *See* Bride Song.
Too late, too late! I did not know my fairness. A Beauty's Soliloquy during Her Honeymoon. Thomas Hardy. PoVP
Too late, too late, sinnah. Too Late. *Unknown.* BoAN-2
Too late, when you show some. Warm Tea. Lewis MacAdams. ANYP
Too Literal Pupil, The. Martial, *tr. fr. Latin by* Louis Untermeyer. UnTE
Too Little Children. *Unknown.* SoP
Too long a sacrifice. W. B. Yeats. *Fr.* Easter, 1916. PoPo
Too long I followed have my fond desire. William Drummond of Hawthornden. Sonn
Too long outside your door I have shivered. The Terrible Door. Harold Monro. EnLoPo; FaBoTw
Too long we have cheated our bellies with crumbs of tradition. An Oration. Kenneth Porter. *Fr.* To the Younger Old-Americans. PoFr
Too many summers out of the way of a trowel. The Lawn Roller. Robert Layzer. NePoEA
Too Much. Edwin Muir. LiTB
Too Much Coffee. E. A. Robinson. MAP; MoAmPo
Too Much for One: Not Enough to Go Around. R. P. Blackmur. Scarabs for the Living, I. CrMA
Too much good luck no less than misery. Joy May Kill [*or* Fearful Joy]. Michelangelo. AWP; JAWP; OnPM; WBP
Too Much Sex. *Unknown.* MeEL
Too much thought. Proverbs: Day-Dreamer. *Unknown.* RIS; TiPo
Too Near the Waves. Poseidippus, *tr. fr. Greek.* OnPM
Too Old to Work. Joe Glazer. ThLM
Too poor for a bribe, and too proud to importune. Sketch of His Own Character. Thomas Gray. BEL; CEP; EiCP; EnLit; TOP
Too popular is tragic poesy. Joseph Hall. *Fr.* Virgidemiarum. ReEn; SiCE
Too powerful a drug is Hope. "Bottle Should Be Plainly Labeled Poison.'" Sara Henderson Hay. GoYe
Too solemn for day, too sweet for night. William Sidney Walker. OBEV
Too Soon the Lightest Feet. Amanda B. Hall. HBMV
Too soothe and mild your lowland airs. Margaret's Song. Lascelles Abercrombie. *Fr.* The New God; a Miracle. GTBS
Too swiftly my coracle flies on her way. On His Exile to Iona. St. Columcille. CAW; LiTW
Too tight, it is running over. Fence Wire. James Dickey. NYBP
Too warm, my friend, your anger waxes. The Peace. Henry Luttrell. *Fr.* Advice to Julia. OBRV
Too wearily had we and song. To a Poet Breaking Silence. Francis Thompson. VA
Too well, O Christ, we know Thee; on your eyes. He Is Not Risen. W. S. Handley Jones. MaRV
Too Wonderful. Proverbs, XXX: 18-19, Bible, *O.T.* TrJP
Too Young for Love. Horace, *tr. fr. Latin by* Louis Untermeyer. Odes, II, 5. UnTE
Took Bladyn then his crowth, anew, and toucht. Bladyn's Song of Cloten. Charles M. Doughty. *Fr.* The Dawn in Britain. PoEL-5
Tool of Fate, The. "Yehoash," *tr. fr. Yiddish by* Isidore Goldstick. TrJP
Tools with the comely names. A Saxon Song. V. Sackville-West. MBP; MoBrPo (1943 ed.)
Top Hand. *Unknown.* CoSo
Top Hat and Tales. Lorna Beers. FiSC
Top of a hill, The. How to Tell the Top of a Hill. John Ciardi. SoPo
Top of Day, The. Anne Blackwell Payne. GFA
Tophet; an Epigram. Thomas Gray. MyFE; NCEP
Topsy-turvy Land. Phyllis M. Stone. BoTP
Topsy-turvy Land. H. E. Wilkinson. BoTP; SoPo

Topsy-turvy World. William Brighty Rands. MPB; OTPC (1946 ed.); TSW; VA
Tor House. Robinson Jeffers. AnAmPo; LoBV
Tora's Song. Knut Hamsun, *tr. fr. Norwegian by* Charles Wharton Stork. PoPl
Torch, The. Arthur B. Dale. OQP
Torch, The. Theodosia Garrison. BLPA
Torchbearer. Humbert Wolfe. BoPe
Torch-Bearers, *sel.* Arlo Bates.
America. AA; PaA; PAL
("America, last hope of man and truth," 8 *ll.*) PGD
Torch Bearers, The. Alfred Noyes. *See* Last Voyage, The, *and* Watchers of the Sky.
Torch-Light in Autumn. John James Piatt. AA
Torch of Liberty, The. Thomas Moore. DD
Torches Have Gone Out, The. Putinas, *tr. fr. Lithuanian by* W. K. Matthews. LiTW
Tormented by the World. Lascelles Abercrombie. POTE
Tormented with incessant pains. To Stella; March 13, MDCCXXIII-IV. Swift. Po
Tormenting Virgin. *Unknown, tr. fr. Greek by* Louis Untermeyer. UnTE
Torn between hunger and maternal cares. A Mother with Young Kittens. Richard Hart. CIV
Torn book we burn, and the dead tree, The. The Broken One. John Holmes. MiAP
Torn Down from Glory Daily. Anne Sexton. WIRo
Torn from his country bed. The Settler. Roy Macnab. BoSA
Torn Hat, The. Nathaniel P. Willis. AA
Torn Nightgown, The. Joel Oppenheimer. CoPo
Torn upon Thy wheel. Out of the Depths. Frederic Lawrence Knowles. TrPWD
Tornado, The. Charles de Kay. EtS
Tornado. William Stafford. NaP; WIRo
Toro. W. S. Merwin. NePA
Toronto Crossing. Robert Finch. TwCaPo
Torrent, The. E. A. Robinson. MaPo; NePA
Torrismond, *sels.* Thomas Lovell Beddoes.
In a Garden by Moonlight. VA
Song: "How many times do I love thee, dear?" *fr.* sc. iii. AnFE; ERoP-2; LiTB; LiTG; LiTL; NBM; OBEV (1st ed.); OBRV; PCD; PoEL-4; TrGrPo; VA; ViBoPo
(How Many Times?) ELP; MeWo; TSW
(How Many Times Do I Love Thee, Dear?) EnRP; GTBS-D; NeHB
Tortoise, The. Herbert Asquith. RIS
Tortoise Family Connections. D. H. Lawrence. BrPo; ChMP; HaMV
Tortoise Gallantry. D. H. Lawrence. CMoP
Tortoise in Eternity, The. Elinor Wylie. FaPON; ImOP; OA
Tortoise Shell. D. H. Lawrence. BoPe; CMoP; ExPo
Tortoiseshell Cat, The. Patrick Reginald Chalmers. CenHV
Tortoise Shout. D. H. Lawrence. LiTM
Tortured body, lie at rest alone. Unknown Man in the Morgue. Merrill Moore. MAP; MoAmPo
Tossed by the seas of love how have I striven. Four Sonnets to Helen, 1. Pierre de Ronsard. *Fr.* Sonnets pour Hélène. LiTW
Tossed on a Sea of Trouble. Archilochus, *tr. fr. Greek by* William Hay. PoPl
Tossing his mane of snows in wildest eddies and tangles. In Earliest Spring. William Dean Howells. AA; FaBoBe; PFY
Total Abstainer, A. Martial, *tr. fr. Latin by* Paul Nixon. LiTW
Total Calm, The. Philip Booth. WIRo
Total Revolution, A. Oscar Williams. LiTM; SiTL
Totem. Jon Anderson. YAP
T'other day, as I was twining. Cupid Drowned. Leigh Hunt. HBV
Tottenham Court, *sel.* Thomas Nabbes.
Song: "What a dainty life the milkmaid leads!" EG; SeCL
Tottering brick volcanoes. Rush City—The Hole. Eugene Redmond. TNV
Tottingham Frolic. *Unknown.* UnTE
Totus Mundus in Maligno Positus. *Unknown.* SiCE; TuPP
Touch. Joseph Auslander. MAP; MoAmPo (1942 ed.)
Touch, The. James Graham, Marquess of Montrose. *See* My Dear and Only Love.
Touch but thy lire (my Harrie) and I heare. To Mr. Henry Lawes, the Excellent Composer, of His Lyrics. Robert Herrick. OAEP
Touch Divine, The. Jennie Wilson-Howell. SoP
Touch him ne'er so lightly, into song he broke. Epilogue. Robert Browning. *Fr.* Dramatic Idyls. MBW-2; PoVP
Touch It. Robert Mezey. NaP
Touch me, touch me. Grass Fingers. Angelina W. Grimké. CDC
Touch not that maid. Salopia Inhospitalis. Douglas B. W. Sladen. VA
Touch of cold in the autum night, A. Autumn. T. E. Hulme. CBV; FaBoMo; LoBV; LOW; MoBrPo (1942 ed.); SeCePo; ViBoPo
Touch of His Hand, The. Horatius Bonar. *See* Master's Touch, The.
Touch of Human Hands, The. Thomas Curtis Clark. OQP; PoToHe
Touch of the Master's Hand, The. Myra Brooks Welch. FaChP; PoToHe (new ed.); SoP; STF; TRV
Touch once more a sober measure. Lament For Capt. Paton. John Gibson Lockhart. OBRV
Touch our bodies, wind. A House in Taos: Wind. Langston Hughes. CDC
Touch us gently, Time! A Petition to Time. "Barry Cornwall." VA
Touché. Jessie Fauset. CDC
Touched with a certain silver light. In My Time. Edmund Blunden. MoPW
Touching me, you touch. The Wind. Charles Simic. YAP
Touching Shoulders. *Unknown.* BLPA; MaRV
Touchstone, The. Samuel Bishop. HBV; MeWo
(Epigram: "Fool and Knave with different views, A.") ALV
Touchstone, The, *sels.* Kalonymos ben Kalonymos, *tr. fr. Hebrew by* Joseph Chotzner. TrJP
Hypocrite, The.
Unfortunate Male, The.
Yoke, The.
Touchstone on a Bus, *sel.* Alfred Noyes.
New Duckling, The. BoTP; FaPON; MPB
Tough Cuss from Bitter Creek, A. James Barton Adams. PoOW
Tough Generation, A. David Gascoyne. LiTM (1970 ed.)
Tough hand closes gently on the load, The. Man Carrying Bale. Harold Monro. BrPo; MoBrPo
Toujours Amour. Edmund Clarence Stedman. HBV
Tour de Force. Peter Kane Dufault. ErPo
Tour in Rain. Raymond Roseliep. FiSC
Touring. David Morton. TrPWD
Touring the old miles again. Baldpate Pond. E. F. Weisslitz. NYBP
Tourist. Mark Van Doren. NePoAm-2
Tourist and the Town, The. Adrienne Rich. NePoEA-2
Tourist came in from Orbitville, A. Southbound on the Freeway. May Swenson. AmFN; NYBP
Tourist from Syracuse, The. Donald Justice. TwCP
Tourist, spare the avid glance. The Attic Landscape. Herman Melville. MWA-1
Tourist Time. F. R. Scott. PoPl; WhC
Tourists. Howard Moss. FiBHP; NYBP
Tourists in a Sacred Place. Sir Herbert Read. MoBrPo (1942 ed.)
Tourists in the courtyard. Sightseers in a Courtyard. Nicolás Guillén. PoNe
Tournament of Man, The. Ernest Crosby. PGD
Tournament of Tottenham, The. *Unknown.* OxBoLi
Toussaint L'Ouverture. E. A. Robinson. PoNe
Toussaint, the most unhappy man of men! To Toussaint L'Ouverture. Wordsworth. AnEnPo; BEL; EnL; EnLi-2; EnLit; EnLP; EnRP; ERoP-1; ExPo; FOL; LoBV; MBW-2; OAEP; OBNC; OBRV; PAn; PeER; PoNe; PoRA; Sonn; TrGrPo; TRV
"Towanda Winooski? Gowanda!" Sing a Song of the Cities. Morris Bishop. CAD; WhC
Toward a True Peace. Lucia Trent *and* Ralph Cheyney. *Fr.* Ten Years After. PGD
Toward Avernus. Harold Vinal. FiSC
Toward dawn I came awake hearing a crow. The Answer. John Hall Wheelock. WIRo
Toward evening/ When it stops snowing. A Thousand Years with Solitude. Charles Simic. YAP
Toward God in heaven spacious. The Child in Our Soul. Björnstjerne Björnson. WoL
Toward Harvest. Samuel French Morse. NYTB

Toward Jerusalem. Amy Carmichael. MaRV
Toward sun, the sun flared suddenly red. Summer Storm (circa 1916), and God's Grace. Robert Penn Warren. CBV; PoDB
Toward the sea turning my troubled eye. The Huge Leviathan. Spenser. *Fr.* Visions of the World's Vanity. ChTr
Towards a Walk in the Sun. K. William Kgositsile. BF
Towards nightfall when the wind. Winter Mask. Allen Tate. AmLP; NePA; OxBA
Toward the end he sailed into an extraordinary mildness. Herman Melville. W. H. Auden. GTBS-W; LiTA; LiTM (rev. ed.); NePA; OAEP (2d ed.); OxBA
Towards the Last Spike, *sels.* E. J. Pratt.
  Gathering, The. MoCV; OBCV
  Precambrian Shield, The. MoCV; OBCV
Towards the North Star. John Gould Fletcher. LaNeLa
Towards the Source, *sels.* Christopher Brennan. PoAu-1
  I Saw My Life as Whitest Flame.
  Let Us Go Down, the Long Dead Night Is Done.
Towards the South. Guillaume Apollinaire, *tr. fr. French by* Glauco Cambon. OnPM
Towart the evyn, amyd the symmyris heit. Vergil, *tr. by* Gawin Douglas. Aeneid: Prologue to Book XIII. OxBS
Tower, The. Philip Booth. NePoEA-2
Tower, The. Agnes Lee. NP
Tower, The. Mark Van Doren. MoPo
Tower, The. W. B. Yeats. CMoP; CoBMV; FaBoMo; HoPM; LiTB; LiTM (rev. ed.); MoPo; OAEP (2d ed.); SeCeV
  "It is time that I wrote my will," *sel.* MBW-2; MoVE
Tower high, The. Butterfly. Kwaso. OnPM
Tower is broken, the house, The. La Torre. Charles Olson. FRC
Tower of Genghis Khan, The. Hervey Allen. HT
Tower of Ivory. Leonard Bacon: WhC
Tower of Refuge is our God, A! Ein feste Burg ist unser Gott. Martin Luther, *tr. by* M. Woolsey Stryker. CTC
Tower of the Dream, The, *sel.* Charles Harpur.
  "Yes, wonderful are dreams: and I have known." PoAu-1
Towering it stood. Starvation Peak Evening. David O'Neil. AnAmPo
Towering o'er the Wrecks of Time. Sir John Bowring. *See* In the Cross of Christ I Glory.
Towers at Evening, The. Frank Wilmot. *Fr.* Melbourne and Memory. NeLNL
Towers of Song. Malcolm Cowley. NP
Towery city and branchy between towers. Duns Scotus's Oxford. Gerard Manley Hopkins. CoBE; GTBS-P; MaPo; NAMP; OBMV; PoE; PoEL-5; PoIE; VP
Town. Alfred Starr Hamilton. QAH
Town, The. David Rowbotham. PoAu-2
Town and Country. William Cowper. *See* God Made the Country.
Town and the Country Mouse, The, *sl. abr.* Horace, *tr. fr. Latin by* Francis Howes. Satires, II, 6. WoL
Town Betrayed, The. Edwin Muir. CMoP
Town Called Providence, Its Fate, The. Benjamin Tompson. SCAP
Town Child, The. Irene Thompson. BoTP
Town Child. Barbara Young. PoMa
Town Clerk's Views, The. John Betjeman. CMoP
Town Damascus and the lands about, The. Armida, the Sorceress. Tasso. *Fr.* Jerusalem Delivered. EnLi-1
Town does not exist, The. The Starry Night. Anne Sexton. NMP; OPoP; ToPo
Town down the River, The. E. A. Robinson. CoBA
Town Dump, The. Howard Nemerov. CMoP
Town froze, close as a fist, The. Operation. A. Alvarez. NMP
Town has opened to the sun, The. Bombardment. D. H. Lawrence. MMA
Town lies in the valley, A. The Silent Town. Richard Dehmel. AWP; JAWP; WBP
Town Maid. Clifford Bax. POTE
Town Meeting. John Hay. NePoAm
Town Meeting, The, *abr.* John Trumbull. *Fr.* M'Fingal, I *and* II. AnNE
Town of Don't-You-Worry, The. I. J. Bartlett. BLPA; WBLP, *st.* 1
Town of Hay, The. Sam Walter Foss. AA
Town of Nice, The. Herman C. Merivale. BOHV
Town of Nogood, The. William Edward Penney. BLPA
Town of Passage, The/ Is both large and spacious. The Attractions of a Fashionable Irish Watering-Place. Francis Sylvester Mahony. IrPN; NBM
Town of Passage, The. *Unknown.* OxBoLi
Town, our hero's scene of action, The. The Town Meeting. John Trumbull. *Fr.* M'Fingal. AnNE
Town Owl. Laurie Lee. POTi; ToPo
Town-Rakes, The. *At. to* P. A. Motteux. CoMu
Town, the churchyard, and the setting sun, The. On Visiting the Tomb of Burns. Keats. BWP
Town was full of bells, where I grew up, The. The Childhood Church. Pat Wilson. AnNZ
Town Window, A. John Drinkwater. BoTP; GTBS; NeMA
Town without a Market, The. James Elroy Flecker. MoBrPo
Towneley Plays. *Unknown. See* Second Shepherds' Play, The.
Townsman on his yielding bed, The. Note-Book of a European Tramp, XI. Michael Hamburger. NePoEA
Tow'rds the lofty walls of Balbi, lo! Durand of Blonden here hies. Durand of Blonden. Ludwig Uhland. AWP; JAWP; WBP
Towser Shall Be Tied Tonight. *Unknown.* BLPA
Toxicologist's report, The. My Brother's Death. Howard McCord. YAP
Toy Band, The. Sir Henry Newbolt. BoTP
Toy-bewitched. Samuel Taylor Coleridge. *Fr.* Religious Musings. WGRP
Toy Cross, The. Roden Noel. VA
Toy Horse, The. Edwin Muir. FaBoMo
Toy of the Titans! Tiny harp! again. Ebenezer Elliott. *Fr.* The Year of the Seeds. Sonn
Toys, The. Coventry Patmore. The Unknown Eros, I, x. ACP; AnFE; BeLS; BoC; CAW; CBEP; EnLit; EPN; FaFP; FaPL; GoBC; GTBS; GTBS-W; GTSL; HBV; JKCP; MaRV; MemP; OBEV; OBVV; PG; PoToHe (new ed.); PoVP; SoP; TIHL; TreFS; TrGrPo; TrPWD; TRV; VA; ViBoPo; YT
Toys, and treats, and pleasures pass. Love and the Child. William Brighty Rands. PRWS
Trace-horse, watch her move, The. Duchess. Lilian Bowes Lyon. HaMV; POTE
Tracer of wind's contour by line of flight. The Butterfly. Gray Burr. CoPo
Track into the Swamp, The. Samuel French Morse. CrMA
Trackless Deeps, The. Shelley. *Fr.* The Daemon of the World, Pt. II. EtS
Tracks. John Farrar. GFA
Tracks. Elaine Schwager. CAD
Tracks in the Snow. Marchette Chute. SiSoSe
Tracks in the Snow. Elizabeth J. Coatsworth. BoChLi (1950 ed.)
Tract. William Carlos Williams. AmP; AmPP; AP; CABL; CoBMV; ILP; LiTA; LiTM; MoAB; MoAmPo; NePA; PoeP; StP; TDP; TrGrPo; TwAmPo; TwCP; WoL
Tract for Autos, A. Arthur Guiterman. MPB; RePo
Traction: November 22, 1963. Howard Moss. AmFN
Tractor. William Hart-Smith. AnNZ
Tractor now is an essential, A. Horatian Variation. Leonard Bacon. NYBP
"Trade" Rat. Eleanor Glenn Wallis. NePoAm
Trade Winds. John Masefield. FaBoCh; OBMV; ShBV-4
Trader's Return. Sylvia Lawson. PoAu-2
Trades. Amy Lowell. OTPC (1946 ed.)
Tradesman, The. *Unknown.* PCH
Tradition. Dryden. *Fr.* Religio Laici. OBS; PoLi
Tradition of Conquest. Sara Morgan Bryan Piatt. AA
Traditional Red. Robert Huff. NePoEA-2
Traditional Tune. Robert D. Fitzgerald. BoAV
Traditions. Ramón Campoamor, *tr. fr. Spanish by* Thomas Walsh. OnPM
Trafalgar. Thomas Hardy. *See* Night of Trafalgar, The.
Trafalgar. Francis Turner Palgrave. BeLS; FaBoBe
Trafalgar Square. Rose Fyleman. UTS
Trafique is earth's great Atlas, that supports. George Alsop. SCAP
Tragedia de Heraclio Bernal, *with music. Unknown, tr. fr. Spanish.* ABF
Tragedie of Edward the Second, The. Christopher Marlowe. *See* Edward the Second.
Tragedie of Philotas, The, *sels.* Samuel Daniel.
  Chorus: "How dost thou wear and weary out thy days." OBSC
Tragedienne, The. Zoë Akins. NP

Tragedies that entertained the burghers of antiquity, The. The New Hellas. Irwin Edman. InMe
Tragedy. "Æ." MoBrPo; MoRP
Tragedy, The. Thomas Curtis Clark. ChIP
Tragedy, A. Théophile Marzials. HBV
Tragedy. Howard Moss. NePoEA
Tragedy, A. Edith Nesbit. HBV
Tragedy. Jill Spargur. BLPA
Tragedy. Mark Van Doren. NePoAm-2
Tragedy of Caesar and Pompey, The, *sel.* George Chapman.
"Poor slaves, how terrible this Death is to them!" ViBoPo
Tragedy of Charles, Duke of Byron, The, *sels.* George Chapman.
"And so, farewell for ever." MyFE
Tragedy of Cleopatra, The. Samuel Daniel. *See* Cleopatra.
Tragedy of Cleopatra, The, *sel.* Thomas May.
Not He That Knows. SeCL
("Not he that knows how to acquire.") TuPP
(Song, A: "Not he, that knows how to acquire.") SeEP
Tragedy of Dido, The, *sel.* Christopher Marlowe *and* Thomas Nashe.
I Have an Orchard. ChTr
Tragedy of King Lear, The. Shakespeare. *See* King Lear.
Tragedy of Orestes, The, *sel.* Thomas Goffe.
"Lullaby, lullaby baby." TuPP
Tragedy of Pete, The. Joseph Seamon Cotter, Sr. CDC; PoNe
Tragedy of Pompey the Great, The, *sels.* John Masefield.
Chief Centurions, The. POTE
("Man is a sacred city, built of marvellous earth.") WGRP
Tragedy of Rollo, Duke of Normandy, The. John Fletcher, *and others.* *See* Bloody Brother, The.
Tragedy of the Deep, A. Don Marquis. LHV
Tragedy of the Duchess of Malfy, The. John Webster. *See* Duchess of Malfi, The.
Tragedy of Tragedies, The. Henry Fielding. EiCL
Tragedy of Valentinian, The, *sels.* John Fletcher.
Care-charming Sleep, *fr.* V, ii. BEL; ELP; OnPM; TrGrPo; ViBoPo
("Care-charming sleep, thou easer of all woes.") AtBAP; OAEP; SeEP; TuPP
(Into Slumbers.) SeCePo
(Invocation to Sleep.) AnEnPo; WHA
(Song.) LoBV (2d ed.); PoEL-2
(Song for the Sick Emperor.) FaBoEn
(Song to Sleep.) OxBoLi
(To Sleep.) EnLi-1
God Lyaeus, *fr.* V, viii. OBEV
("God Lyaeus, ever young.") OnPM; TuPP; ViBoPo
(Song of Bacchus.) BEL; TOP
Hear, Ye Ladies [That Despise], *fr.* II, v. EIL; ELP; LiTG; OAEP; OBEV; PoEL-2; ViBoPo
(Mighty Love.) TrGrPo
(Power of Love, The.) HBV; UnTE
"Now the lusty spring is seen," *fr.* II, v. EG; ELP; ErPo; ViBoPo
(Love Song.) FaBoEn
(Love's Emblems.) EIL; HBV; OBEV; UnTE
(Song.) SeEP
Thou Easer of All Woes, *fr.* V, ii. TreFT
Tragic Guilt. Keidrych Rhys. WaP
Tragic Love. W. J. Turner. LO; OBMV
Tragic Mary Queen of Scots, The. "Michael Field." OBMV
("Ah me, if I grew sweet to man.") EnLoPo
Tragic Memory. *Unknown, tr. fr. Japanese by* Ishii *and* Obata. *Fr.* Manyo Shu. OnPM
Tragic, said I. Oh, tragicker, says she. Noël Tragique. Ramon Guthrie. ErPo
Tragic Story, A. Adelbert von Chamisso, *tr. fr. German by* Thackeray. BoChLi (1950 ed.); BOHV; BoTP; FaPON; GaP; GoTP; HBV; HBVY; MoShBr; MPB; OnMSP; OTPC; RePo; RIS; StVeCh (1940 ed.)
Tragic Tale of Hooty the Owl, The. *Unknown.* *See* Owl and the Fox, The.
Tragic Verses. *Unknown.* CoMu
Tragical History of Dr. Faustus, The. Christopher Marlowe. *See* Dr. Faustus.
Trail, The. Edward Weismiller. WaP
Trail All Your Pikes. Countess of Winchilsea. *See* Soldier's Death, The.
Trail Breakers. James Daugherty. AmFN; RePo
Trail End. *Unknown, at. to* Everett Chatham. CoSo
Trail of the Bird, The. William John Courthope. HBVY
Trail to Lillooet, The. Pauline Johnson. CaP
Trail to Mexico, The. *Unknown.* AS, *with music;* CoSo (A *and* B *vers., with music*); IHA
Trailer Park. Lewis MacAdams. ANYP
Trailing Arbutus, The. Whittier. AnAmPo; CoBA
Trails of Smoke. Rowena Bennett. MPB (1956 ed.)
Train, The. Mary Elizabeth Coleridge. BoTP
Train, The. Emily Dickinson. *See* I like to see it lap the miles.
Train, The. *Unknown, tr. by* D. F. van der Merwe. TTY
Train at night, A. Night Train. Adrien Stoutenburg. PDV
Train Butcher, The. Thomas Hornsby Ferril. GoYe
Train Dogs, The. E. Pauline Johnson. TwCaPo; WHW
Train has stopped for no apparent reason, The. En Route. Duncan Campbell Scott. OBCV
Train in the Night, The. Elizabeth Riddell. NeLNL
Train is a dragon that roars through the dark, A. A Modern Dragon. Rowena Bastin Bennett. GFA; PDV; PFY; SoPo; TiPo; UTS
Train-Mates. Witter Bynner. MAP; MoAmPo (1942 ed.); PFY
Train pulled out of Palestine, eighteen coaches long. Dirty Mistreatin' Women. *Unknown.* ABF
Train Ride. John Wheelwright. AnFE; CoAnAm; MoPo; TwAmPo
Train Runs Late to Harlem, The. Conrad Kent Rivers. IDB
Train takes me away from the northern valleys. Rhetoric of a Journey. Roy Fuller. ToPo
Train, The! The twelve o'clock for paradise. Week-End, I. Harold Monro. MemP; MoBrPo (1950 ed.); YT
Train through the night of the town, The. City Nights: In the Train. Arthur Symons. SyP
Train Tune. Louise Bogan. NePoAm
Train-whistles have a lonesome sound. Who-o-o-o-o! Harry Silleck Grannatt. StaSt
Train Will Fight to the Pass, The. Ruth Pitter. HaMV
Train Window. Robert Finch. OBCV; PeCV
Training. Demetrio Herrera S., *tr. fr. Spanish by* Dudley Fitts. TTY
Training-ship *Eurydice,* The. The Last of the *Eurydice.* Sir Joseph Noel Paton. VA
Trains, The. "Seumas O'Sullivan." BoTP
Trains. Hope Shepherd. BoTP
Trains. James S. Tippett. FaPON; GFA; OTPC (1946 ed.); SoPo; SUS; TiPo
Trains are for going. Things. William Jay Smith. TiPo (1959 ed.)
Trains are not coming as often now, The. Tracks. Elaine Schwager. CAD
Trains at Night. Frances Frost. TiPo
Trains of thought, The. La Bête Humaine. James Kirkup. NeBP
Trains that scream past every day, The. Traveler. Frances Frost. BoChLi
Trainwrecked Soldiers. John Frederick Nims. MiAP; ReMP
Traitors, The. Morton Dauwen Zabel. NP
Tramontana at Lerici. Charles Tomlinson. GTBS-P
Tramp. Richard Hughes. MoBrPo
Tramp Sings, The. Ridgely Torrence. *Fr.* Eye-Witness. PFY
Tramp! Tramp! Tramp! George Frederick Root. TreFS
Tramp, Tramp, Tramp, Keep on a-Tramping, *with music. Unknown.* AS
Tramping the right-of-way. Beaver Sign. Kenneth Porter. NePoAm
Trample! trample! went the roan. The Cavalier's Escape. George Walter Thornbury. FaBoBe; GN; HBV; OTPC
Tramplings tumultuous and a charge of sound! A Vision. "Michael Field." SyP
Tramp's Song, The. Mary Devenport O'Neill. AnIV
Trampwoman's Tragedy, A. Thomas Hardy. AtBAP; BeLS; HBMV; MoVE; OBNC
Trance, The. Stephen Spender. ChMP; CoBMV
Trance and Transformation. Goethe, *tr. fr. German by* Carol North Valhope *and* Ernst Morwitz. LiTW
Trance of Time, The. Cardinal Newman. OxBoCh
Tranquil Sea. Claire Aven Thomson. EtS
Tranquility. *Unknown, tr. fr. Sanskrit by* Joseph Nadin Rawson. *Fr.* The Upanishads. OnPM
Trans Canada. F. R. Scott. PeCV

Transaction on the Roman Exchange. Henrietta A. Burke. JKCP (1955 ed.)
Transcendence. Richard Hovey. OQP; TRV; WGRP
Transcendence of God, The. Milton. *Fr.* Samson Agonistes. OBS
Transcendent beauty though thou art. *Unknown.* SeCSL
Transcendental Blues Transcendental Blues. Yusuf Rahman. BF
Transcendentalism. *Unknown.* BOHV; NA
Transcendentalism; a Poem in Twelve Books. Robert Browning. DiPo; PoVP; PP
Transcontinent. Donald Hall. OCS
Transfiguration, The. James M. Hayes. JKCP
Transfiguration, The. Edwin Muir. BoPe; FaBoMo; MasP; OxBS
Transfiguration, The. *Unknown, tr. fr. Sanskrit by* Sir Edwin Arnold. *Fr.* Bhagavad Gita. OuHeWo
Transfiguration of Beauty, The. Michelangelo, *tr. fr. Italian by* John Addington Symonds. AWP
Transfigured. Sarah Morgan Bryan Piatt. AA
Transfigured Bird. James Merrill. MoAB
Transfigured Life. Dante Gabriel Rossetti. The House of Life, LX. MaVP; PoVP; ViPo
Transfigured Night. Ralph Gustafson. MoCV
Transfigured Swan. Louis Untermeyer. MAP
Transformation. Lewis Alexander. CDC; PoNe
Transformation. Catullus, *tr. fr. Latin by* Horace Gregory. LiTW
Transformation. Jessie B. Rittenhouse. HBMV
Transformation. Lon Woodrum. SoP
Transformation of a Texas Girl, The. James Barton Adams. SCC
Transformation Scene. Constance Carrier. GoYe
Transformations. Thomas Hardy. PIA; PoIE
Transformed. Henry W. Frost. SoP
Transformed. D. Weston Gates. STF
Transforming Friendship. *Unknown.* SoP
Transience. Sarojini Naidu. MCCG
Transient as a Rose. John Lydgate. *See* Lat Noman Booste of Konnyng nor Vertu.
Transient Beauty. Basho, *tr. fr. Japanese by* H. G. Henderson. OnPM
Transient city, marvellously fair, A. Buffalo. Florence Earle Coates. PAH
Transition. Emerson. MWA-1
Transition. May Sarton. NePoAm
Transitional Poem, *sel.* C. Day Lewis.
"When nature plays hedge-schoolmaster." EnLit
Translat. ex Martial. Martial, *tr. fr. Latin by* John Weever. TuPP
Translated out of Horace, Which Begins Rectius Vives. Horace, *See* To Licinius. *tr. by* Sir Philip Sidney.
Translated Way, The. Franklin P. Adams. BOHV; FiBHP
Translated, won't the operatic word. Opera in English? Benjamin M. Steigman. WhC
Translation. Roy Fuller. ChMP
Translation. Anne Spencer. BANP
Translation from Du Bellay ("Happy, who like Ulysses or that lord"). G. K. Chesterton. *See* Heureux qui, comme Ulysse . . .
Translation from Petrarch, A ("What a grudge I am bearing. ."). *Pr. tr. fr. Italian by* J. M. Synge. Sonnets to Laura: To Laura in Death, XXXII. MoBrPo; NeMA
Translation from Villon, A ("Mother of God that's Lady of the Heavens"). *See* Two Translations from Villon. *Pr. tr. fr. French by* J. M. Synge.
Translation from Vergil's Aeneid. *See* Certain Books of Vergil's Aeneis. *Tr. by* the Earl of Surrey.
Translation from Walther von der Vogelweide ("I never set my two eyes. . ."). *Tr. fr. German by* J. M. Synge. MoBrPo
Translation is man's deep, continual task. Required Course. Frances Stoakley Lankford. GoYe
Translation of Lines by Benserade. Samuel Johnson. *See* In Bed We Laugh.
Translations from the Chinese, *sels.* Christopher Morley. EvOK
He Comforts Himself.
Human Instinct, A.
Man with the Rake, The.
Secret Thoughts.
Transmigration. Seth D. Cudjoe. ACV
Transmutation, The. Edwin Muir. FaBoEn
Transplanting. Theodore Roethke. WIRo
Transport. Stefan George. *See* Rapture.
Transport. William Meredith. WaP
Transport *Dorchester* set forth upon her dangerous mission north, The. Four Men of God. Edgar A. Guest. OHFP (1958 ed.)
Transportation Problem. Richard Armour. WhC
Transvaal Morning, A. William Plomer. BoSA
Trap. A. R. Ammons. NYTB
Trap. Walter H. Kerr. FiSC
Trapezists. Daisy Aldan. NYTB
Trapped. Adelaide Crapsey. MCCG
Trapped. Vernoy E. Hite. TNV
Trapped Dingo. Judith Wright. NeLNL
Trapped Fly, A. Robert Herrick. WiR
(Amber Bead, The.) ChTr; PoeP
Trapped me in ice. No, not one chink is gaping. Ennui. Peter Viereck. NYBP
Trappist Abbey, The: Matins. Thomas Merton. PoPl
Traps. Mary Carolyn Davies. HBMV
Trastevere. Edwin Denby. ANYP
Traubel, Traubel, boil and bubble. I Like to Sing Also. John Updike. FiBHP
Traümerei at Ostendorff's. "William Laird." HBMV
Travel. Marvin Bell. TDP
Travel. Leonard Cohen. MeWo
Travel. Edna St. Vincent Millay. FaPON; LaNeLa; MoShBr; MoSiPe; MPB; NP; PDV; PFY; RePo; StVeCh; TiPo
Travel. Robert Louis Stevenson. BrPo; FaBoCh; FaPON; GoTP; HT; LoGBV; MoShBr; MPB; PoVP; StVeCh (1940 ed.); TiPo; WaKn
Travel Bureau, The. Ruth Comfort Mitchell. HBMV
Travel gets us through the breach. Death and the Maiden. Dick Gallup. ANYP
Travel Song. Hugo von Hofmannsthal. *See* Travelers' Song.
Travel Song. Anne Glenny Wilson. BoAu
Traveller, The. W. H. Auden. ReMP; SyP
Traveller, The. John Berryman. CBV
Traveler. Frances Frost. BoChLi
Traveller, The. Goldsmith. CEP; EiPP; EnPE; OAEP
Sels.
First, Best Country, The. GN
France. OBEC
Happiness Dependent on Ourselves. OBEC
Real Happiness. OBEC
"Remote, unfriended, melancholy, slow." ViBoPo
Traveler, The. Vachel Lindsay. MAP; MoAmPo; NeMA
Traveler, The. Allen Tate. LiTM
Traveler. Sister Mary Thérèse. JKCP (1955 ed.)
Traveller, A. *Unknown.* WGRP
Traveler Caught in a Storm, A. Kiokusui, *tr. fr. Japanese.* GaP
Traveller for many long years I have been, A. The Widow That Keeps the Cock Inn. *Unknown.* CoMu
Traveler on a dusty road, A. Little and Great. Charles Mackay. HBV; HBVY; PoLF
Traveler one, when skies were rose and gold, A. I Am the Door. *Unknown.* OQP
Traveler, pluck a stem of moly. Moly. Edith M. Thomas. HBV
Traveller take heed for journeys undertaken in the dark of the year. October Journey. Margaret Walker. AmNP; IDB; PoNe
Traveller wended the wilds among, A. The Quaker's Meeting. Samuel Lover. BOHV; CenHV; OnYI
"Traveler, what lies over the hill?" Over the Hill. George Macdonald. GaP
Traveller who crossed Les Halles at summer's end, The. Sunflower. André Breton. LiTW
Traveller who walks a temperate zone, A. Against Romanticism. Kingsley Amis. NePoEA
Travellers. Arthur S. John Adcock. BoTP
Travellers, The. Mark A. De Wolfe Howe. AA
Traveller's Curse after Misdirection, The. Robert Graves, *tr. fr. Welsh.* BrPo; CMoP; DTC; ExPo; FiBHP; HoPM; LiTM; MoAB; MoBrPo; NeMA; SiTL
Traveller's Ditty. Miriam Allen deFord. HBMV
Traveller's Guide to Antarctica. Adrien Stoutenburg. NYBP
Traveller's Hope. Charles Granville. HBV; OBVV

Traveler's Rest. Ogden Nash. InMe
Traveller's Return, The. Robert Southey. BoTP; OTPC
Traveller's Tale, A. William Plomer. BoSA
Travelers who came that day to Pisa's Baptistry. Echo. Elizabeth Stanton Hardy. GoYe
Travelling. Dorothy Gradon. BoTP
Traveling America, I am England-haunted. Traveling America. "Jan Struther." AmFN
Travelling Backward. Gene Baro. NYBP
Travelling eye has seen its many birds, The. Many Birds. Anne Welsh. PeSA
Travelling Light. Minnie Leona Upton. PCH
Traveling on My Knees. Sandra Goodwin. STF
Travelling Out, The. Lucile Adler. NYBP
Travelling south, leaves overflow the farms. The Puritan on His Honeymoon. Robert Bly. NePoEA
Traveling Storm. Mark Van Doren. MoSiPe
Traveling through the Dark. William Stafford. CoAP; FIW; LiTM (1970 ed.); NMP; PoAn
Traveling to the better land. Lead Me On. *Unknown.* SoP
Travelogue, A; Clovelly. Carolyn Wells. InMe
Travelogue for Exiles. Karl Shapiro. AnFE; CoAnAm; MoAmPo (1950 ed.); NeMA; PG (1945 ed.); TrJP; TwAmPo
Travels with a Donkey, *sel.* Robert Louis Stevenson.
Camper's Night Song. BBV
Traverse not the globe for lore! The sternest. Advice against Travel. James Clarence Mangan. OBVV
Travesty of Miss Fanshawe's Enigma. Horace Mayhew. BOHV
Tray, The. Thomas Cole. NePoAm
Tray's Epitaph. "Peter Pindar." TreFS
Treachery. Margaret Cole. MemP
Tread lightly here, for here, 'tis said. An Epitaph on a Robin Redbreast [*or* A Robin's Epitaph]. Samuel Rogers. CBEP; OTPC (1923 ed.); PRWS
Tread lightly, she is near. Requiescat. Oscar Wilde. BrPo; EnLit; GTSL; HBV; InvP; MoBrPo; NeMA; OBNC; OBVV; OnYI; OxBI; PeVV; PoVP; TreF; TrGrPo; ViPP; WePo; WHA
Tread Not the Snow. Mikata Shami, *tr. fr. Japanese by* Ishii *and* Obata. OnPM
Tread softly, for here you stand. On Ithaca Standing. Lawrence Durrell. FaBoTw
Tread softly here. The Woodpecker. Richard Church. HaMV
Treade Junos steps who list for me. *Unknown.* SeCSL
Treading a field I saw afar. Death on a Live Wire. Michael Baldwin. MoBS
Treading pigeon arcs his wings, The. The Ivory Bed. Winfield Townley Scott. ErPo
Treadmill prisoner of that century, The. Scene with Figure. Babette Deutsch. TrJP
Treason. Lora Dunetz. NePoAm
Treason. Sir John Harington. *See* Of Treason.
Treason doth never prosper [*or* Treason never prospers]—what's the reason? Of Treason [*or* Epigram]. Sir John Harington. ALV; CBEP; CBV; DiPo; ELU; ExPo; FiBHP; HBV; InvP; LiTG; OtMeF; OxBoLi; SiCE; SiTL; TuPP
Treason's Last Device. Edmund Clarence Stedman. PAH
Treasure. Elizabeth-Ellen Long. BiCB
Treasure. Lucilius, *tr. fr. Greek by* William Cowper. AWP; LiTW
Treasure, The. Dorothy Frances McCrae. BoAu
Treasure, A. Reed Whittemore. NePoEA
Treasure Boat. Seiki Fujino, *tr. fr. Japanese by* Sumake Kimizuka. HW
Treasure Hunt. Art Wilson. WSL
Treasure not so the forlorn days. Behind the Line. Edmund Blunden. ChMP
Treasure of the Haunted Rambler, The. John Sladek. HYE
Treasures, The. Job, XXXVIII: 22-32, Bible, *O.T.* BoW
Treasures. St. Matthew, Bible, *N.T.* *See* Treasures in Heaven.
Treasures. Mary Dixon Thayer. MPB; SoPo
Treasures. *Unknown.* PoToHe (new ed.)
Treasures in Heaven. St. Matthew, VI: 19-21, Bible, *N.T.* GoTP
(Treasures.) TrGrPo
Treasures of Darkness. Sarah Faris. SoP
Treasury Holiday, *sels.* William Harmon. QAH
"Animals of the forest and plants of the field are friends."
"Now/ poem and month."
"Past all calculation and belief it came so huge."
"Poem/ is/ word/ list."
"Poor Ed Sanders: no sooner had he gotten in good."
"So let the month end: the new fiscal year."
Treatie of Human Learning, A. Fulke Greville. FCP
"Chiefe use then in man, The, " *sel.* OBS; SiCE
(Man's Service, 1 *st.*) PoFr
Treatise of the Subtle Body, A. Salamis. Lawrence Durrell. NYBP
Trebetherick. John Betjeman. CMoP; EvOK; ExPo
Tree, The. Björnstjerne Björnson, *tr. fr. Norwegian.* DD; HH; FaPON; MPB; OHIP; OTPC (1946 ed.); PCH; PoSC; PRWS
Tree, The. Ilya Ehrenburg, *tr. fr. Russian by* Babette Deutsch. TrJP
Tree, The. John Freeman. BoTP
Tree, The. Alfred Kreymborg. HBMV; PoPl; TSW
Tree, The. Ezra Pound. APA; CMoP; CoAnAm; InPo; TwAmPo
Tree, A. *Unknown, wr. at. to* Christina Rossetti. RIS
("In spring I look gay.") BoTP; OxNR
Tree, The. Jones Very. AnAmPo; AnNE; DD; GN; GoTP; HBV; OHIP; PoRL; PoSC
Tree, The. Pat Wilson. AnNZ
Tree, The. Countess of Winchilsea. BWP; CEP; CoBE; EiPP; OBEC
Tree and Sky. Siegfried Sassoon. TSW
Tree and the Chaff, The. Psalms, I, Bible, *O.T.* *See* Godly and the Ungodly, The.
Tree and the Lady, The. Thomas Hardy. MoAB; MoBrPo
Tree ascending there, O pure transcension, A! Rainer Maria Rilke. Sonnets to Orpheus, Pt. I, I. UnS
Tree at Dusk, A. Winifred Welles. MPB; SP; TSW
Tree at My Window. Robert Frost. AmPP; AnNE; BoLiVe; BoNaP; FaBoBe; FaBoEn; MAP; MoAB; MoAmPo; MoVE; NePA; OxBA; PoIE; PoPo; TrGrPo
Tree at Post 4, The. Kenneth Mackenzie. MoAuPo
Tree Birthdays. Mary Carolyn Davies. BiCB; OHIP
Tree Buds, The. Kate L. Brown. TVC
Tree-building. Franklin Cable. OQP; PGD
Tree Design, A. Arna Bontemps. CDC
Tree Feelings. Charlotte Perkins Gilman. GFA; PGD
Tree Felling. George Woodcock. NeBP
Tree for Kindling, A. James Koller. FRC
Tree has entered my hands, The. A Girl. Ezra Pound. BoLP; MAP; MoAB; MoAmPo; MoPW; NeMA
Tree in December. Melville Cane. MAP; MoAmPo
Tree in Pamela's Garden, The. E. A. Robinson. MoLP
Tree in the Desert, The. Friedrich Hebbel, *tr. fr. German by* Herman Salinger *and* Marion Salinger. LiTW
Tree in the Garden, The. Christine Chaundler. BoTP
Tree in the Rain. James Applewhite. YAP
Tree is built of many things, A. Tree-building. Franklin Cable. OQP; PGD
Tree is more than a shadow, A. A Tree Design. Arna Bontemps. CDC
Tree is such a sacred thing, A. The Cross and the Tree. William L. Stidger. ChIP; PGD
Tree lay down, The. The Hurricane. William Carlos Williams. PoeP
Tree-leaves labour up and down. Nobody Comes. Thomas Hardy. MoVE; PoFS; ViPP
Tree may be laughter in the spring, A. Winter Night. Collister Hutchison. TiPo (1952 ed.)
Tree of deepest root is found, The. The Three Warnings. Hester Thrale. BeLS; HBV
Tree of Faith its bare dry boughs must shed, The. Adjustment. Whittier. WGRP
Tree of Life, The. Thomas Lovell Beddoes. ERoP-2
Tree of Life, The. *Unknown, tr. fr. Irish by* Robin Flower. BiS
Tree of Love, The. Ramon Lull. CAW
Tree of my treasure and longing, The. Two Songs in Praise of Steingerd. Cormac Ogmundarson. LiTW
Tree of Silence, The. Vassar Miller. NePoEA-2; PoDB
Tree of the Cross, The. "Angelus Silesius," *tr. fr. German.* CAW
Tree on the Hill. *Unknown.* OTPC; PPL
Tree of Time. K. D. Sethna. ACV
Tree-planting. Samuel Francis Smith. OHIP
Tree Planting. *Unknown.* OHIP
Tree Purge. George Rostrevor Hamilton. POTE

Tree rose up, A. O clear transcendency! Rainer Maria Rilke. Sonnets to Orpheus, Pt. I, I. ReMP
Tree Shadows. *Unknown, tr. fr. Japanese.* GFA
Tree, sky and star my teachers. Autumn Hour. George Chapman. JKCP (1955 ed.)
Tree-sleeping. Robert P. Tristram Coffin. LOW
Tree Stands Very Straight and Still, The. Annette Wynne. SoPo; SUS
Tree still bends over the lake. Winter. Sheila Wingfield. BoLP; EnLoPo
Tree Tag. Mary E. Caragher. GoYe
Tree that fell last year, The. Our Calvary. Constance Holm. OQP
Tree that never had to fight, The. Good Timber. Douglas Malloch. SoP
Tree, The. The summer lake, the river, the winter lake. Rain Portrait. John Unterecker. ThO
Tree the tempest with a crash of wood, The. On a Tree Fallen across the Road. Robert Frost. MWA-2; PoeP
Tree-Toad. Hilda Conkling. GBV (1922 ed.); RG
Tree-Toad, The. Orrick Johns. HBMV; NP
Tree Toad, The. Monica Shannon. FaPON; MPB; TiPo (1952 ed.)
Tree-Toad is a small gray person. Tree-Toad. Hilda Conkling. GBV (1922 ed.); RG
Tree, Tree. Federico García Lorca, *tr. fr. Spanish.* PoPl
Tree unto which you reached, The. Ancient Sorrow. Giosuè Carducci. OnPM
Tree, whereon the pitying skies. The Dying Eusebio's Address to the Cross. Calderón de la Barca, *tr. by* D. F. MacCarthy. OuHeWo
Tree, which heaven has willed to dower. The Cross. Calderón de la Barca, *tr. by* Richard Chenevix Trench. CAW
Treehouse, The. James A. Emanuel. AmNP; NNP
Trees. Harry Behn. SiSoSe; SoPo; TiPo; YeAr
Trees. Bliss Carman. DD; OHIP; PoRL
Trees. Thomas Curtis Clark. OQP; PGD
Trees, The. Samuel Valentine Cole. OHIP
Trees. Sara Coleridge. BoTP; DD; MPB; OHIP; PCH; TVC
Trees. Walter de la Mare. GTBS; OHIP
Trees. Ted Hughes. NYBP
Trees. Joyce Kilmer. BBV (1923 ed.); BLPA; DD; FaBoBe; FaFP; FaPON; HBV; HBVY; HH; InP; JKCP; MAP; MaRV; MCCG; MPB; NeHB; NeMA; NP; OHFP; OTD; OTPC (1946 ed.); PEDC; PoMa; PoPo; TreF; UnPo; WBLP; WGRP; YT
Trees, The. Lucy Larcom. OHIP
Trees, The. Christopher Morley. OHIP
Trees. Howard Nemerov. BoNaP
Trees, The. Adrienne Rich. CoAP; CoPo; WIRo
Trees. William Haskell Simpson. *Fr.* In Arizona. NP
Trees. Spenser. *Fr.* The Faerie Queene, I, 1. PoG
Trees, The. Herbert Trench. POTE
Trees. *Unknown.* SoP
Trees along our city streets, The. City Trees. Vere Dargan. OQP; PGD
Trees along this city street, The. City Trees. Edna St. Vincent Millay. FaPON; LaNeLa; OCS; PoMa; RePo
Trees & brown squares. The Clearing. LeRoi Jones. CoPo
Trees and Cattle. James Dickey. NePoEA-2
Trees and herbage, as the seasons wane, The. Flowers of the Sea. Yasuhide. OnPM
Trees and the menace of night. Rhymes and Rhythms, XXI. W. E. Henley. Po
Trees are a' ivied, the leaves they are green. The Bonnie Laddie's Lang a-Grouwin'. *Unknown.* OxBS
Trees are all wonderful yellow and red, The. Autumn. Arthur A. Knipe. GFA
Trees are bare, their branches high over the pool where we drink, The. Exile. Tu Fu. OnPM
Trees Are Down, The. Charlotte Mew. BoNaP; MoAB; MoBrPo
Trees are God's great alphabet, The. A B C's in Green. Leonora Speyer. DD; HBMV; HBVY; OHIP; OQP
Trees are humming a lazy song, The. Interlude. Holger Lundbergh. PoMa
Trees are in their autumn beauty, The. The Wild Swans at Coole. W. B. Yeats. ACV; BoLiVe; BoPe; CBV; ChTr; CMoP; DiPo; EnLi-2 (1949 ed.); FIW; GTBS-D; HT; ILP; MaPo; MBW-2; MoAB; MoBrPo; MoVE; NoP; NP; OAEP (2d ed.); OnYI; PAn; PIA; Po; PoIE; PoPo; PoVP; ReMP; StP; TDP; WePo; WHA
Trees are the kindest things I know. Trees. Harry Behn. SiSoSe; SoPo; TiPo; YeAr
Trees are tracing in the waning haze, The. Evening. Victor van Vriesland. TrJP
Tree are waving to and fro, The. Just like This. D. A. Olney. BoTP
Trees both in hills and plaines, in plenty be. William Wood. SCAP
Trees crept into church. Delius in the Cathedral. Derek Parker. MuSP
Tree's early leaf-buds [*or* buds] were bursting their brown, The. The Tree. Björnstjerne Björnson. DD; FaPON; HH; MPB; OHIP; OTPC (1946 ed.); PCH; PoSC; PRWS
Trees growing—right in front of my window. Pruning Trees. Po Chü i. FIW
Trees in groves. Saadi. Emerson. AmP; OxBA
Trees in Sherwood forest are old and good, The. Sonnet To ——. John Hamilton Reynolds. OBRV
Trees in the Garden, The. Stephen Crane. War Is Kind, XXVI. AmPP; VaPo
(Trees in the Garden Rained Flowers, The.) LiTM (1970 ed.)
Trees in the Garden. D. H. Lawrence. CMoP; MoAB; MoBrPo; Po
Trees in the Garden Rained Flowers, The. Stephen Crane. *See* Trees in the Garden.
Trees in the old days used to stand. Carentan O Carentan. Louis Simpson. CoAP; MoBS; NMP; OPoP
Trees inside are moving out into the forest, The. The Trees. Adriene Rich. CoAP; CoPo; WIRo
Trees learn music from the birds they hold, The. Wood Music. Ethel King. GoYe
Tree's leaves may be ever so good, A. Leaves Compared with Flowers. Robert Frost. MWA-2
Trees, like great jade elephants, The. John Gould Fletcher. Irradiations, VII [X]. MAP; MAPA; NeMA; NePA; TwAmPo
Trees of the elder lands, The. St. Anthony's Township. Gilbert Sheldon. CH
Trees of the Garden, The. Dante Gabriel Rossetti. The House of Life, LXXXIX. MaVP; PoVP; ViPo
Trees of the Lord are full of sap, The. The Rich Earth. *Fr.* Psalm CIV, Bible, *O.T.* GoTP
Trees on the Calais Road. Edmund Blunden. BrPo
Trees shake gentle skaters out. Cadenza. Miriam Waddington. CaP
Trees So High, The. *Unknown.* OBB; OxBoLi; SiTL
Trees That Shade a House. Katharine Worth. PoMa
Trees Used in Games and Sports. Mary Isabel Curtis. GFA
Trees were taller than the night, The. The Robber. W. J. Turner. MoBrPo
Trees, Who Are Distant. Bertram Warr. CaP
Tree-Top Road, The. May Riley Smith. HBV; MaRV
Treetops, spires and houses—all have grown. Winter Gulls. Alan Ross. POTi
Treizaine. Sir Thomas Wyatt. *See* If in the World There Be More Woe.
Trelawny. Robert Stephen Hawker. *See* Song of the Western Men, The.
Trelawny Lies by Shelley. Charles L. O'Donnell. HBMV
Tremble before your [*or* thy] chattels. Cry of the People. John G. Neihardt. MAP; PoFr
Trembling before thine awful throne. Forgiveness of Sins a Joy Unknown to Angels. Augustus Lucas Hillhouse. AA
Trembling finger of a woman, The. War. Charles Simic. YAP
Trembling I write my dream, and recollect. A Vision. Philip Freneau. *Fr.* The House of Night. AnFE; APA; CoAnAm
Trembling old men are stamm'ring. Lines on Carmen Sylva. Emma Lazarus. TrJP
Trembling train clings to the leaning wall, The. Moonrise in the Rockies. Ella Higginson. AA
Trembling with grief came Mary Magdalene. Mary Knew. Ida Norton Munson. ChIP
Tremendous, marching through smashed buildings, trees. Pieta. Guy Butler. BoSA
Tremor, like magnitude, shook the world, A. Coup d'Etat. Ruth Herschberger. LiTA
Tremulous distance, A. Stance. Theodore Enslin. CoPo
Trench Blues, *with music.* *Unknown.* OuSiCo
Trenches, The. Frederic Manning. MCCG

Trenton and Princeton. *Unknown.* PAH
Trepidation of the Druids. Wordsworth. Ecclesiastical Sonnets, Pt. I, Sonnet III. Sonn
Trespass. Robert Frost. FaBV
Tresses of thy glossy hair, The. To Harriett. John Clare. AtBAP
Tretis of the Tua Mariit Wemen and the Wedo. William Dunbar. *See* Tua Maritt Wemen and the Wedo, The.
Triad. Adelaide Crapsey. InP; MAP; MCCG; MoAmPo (1942 ed.); NeMA; NP; PFY; PoPl
Triad of Things Not Decreed, The. Alice Furlong. AnIV
Triads. Swinburne. PoVP
Triads of Ireland, The, *sels.* *Unknown, tr. fr. Old Irish.*
"Three accomplishments well regarded in Ireland: a clever/ verse," *tr. by* Thomas Kinsella. OxBI
"Three slender things that best support the world," OnYI
Trial, The. Dannie Abse. ACV
Trial, The. W. H. Auden. NePA
Trial, The. Longfellow. *Fr.* Giles Corey of the Salem Farms. PAH
Trial, The. Muriel Rukeyser. NAMP; PoNe
Trial and Error. Phyllis McGinley. SiTL
Trial by Existence, The. Robert Frost. CoBA
Trial by Jury, *sels.* W. S. Gilbert.
Judge's Song, The. PoVP
Rover's Apology, The. ALV
Trial of Treasure, The, *sels.* *Unknown.*
"Hey ho, care away, let the world pass." TuPP
My Dear Lady. ElL
("Am not I in blessed case.") TuPP
Trial Run, A. Robert Frost. WePo
Trials. Grace E. Troy. STF
Triangle. Roslyn Greer. TNV
Triangles are commands of God. The Starfish. Robert P. Tristram Coffin. ImOP
Tribe prophetic with their ardent eyes, The. Gypsies on the March. Baudelaire. OnPM
Tribes, The. Roy Fuller. BoSA; LiTM (1970 ed.); ToPo
Tributary wish, to be a part, The. Great Zimbabwe. Peter Jackson. BoSA
Tribute, The. Coventry Patmore. The Angel in the House, I, iv, 2. FaPL; HBV; OBNC
Tribute, A ("Lincoln, the man who freed the slave"). *Unknown.* PGD
Tribute of Grasses, A (to W. W.). Hamlin Garland. AA; AnAmPo
Tribute on the Passing of a Very Real Person. *Unknown.* PoToHe (new ed.)
Tribute to America. Shelley. PaA; PAL
Tribute to Dante, A ("Dante Alighieri, a dark oracle"). Boccaccio. *See* Inscription for a Portrait of Dante.
Tribute to Dante, A ("If Dante mourns, there wheresoe'er he be"). Boccaccio. *See* To One Who Had Censured His Public Exposition of Dante.
Tribute to Grass. John J. Ingalls. WBLP
Tribute to Henry Ford (1-3). Richard Kostelanetz. YAP
Tribute to Our Soldiers. Marion Kennedy. PEDC
Tribute to the Angels, *sels.* Hilda Doolittle ("H. D.").
Ah (You Say), This Is Holy Wisdom. CrMA
Hermes Trismegistus. FaBoTw
Swiftly Relight the Flame. FaBoTw
Tribute to the Founder, A. Kingsley Amis. NePoEA-2
Tribute to Washington. *Unknown.* OHIP
Tribute to Wyatt ("Wyatt resteth here"). Earl of Surrey. *See* On the Death of Sir Thomas Wyatt.
Trick, The. W. H. Davies. ChMP
Trick that everyone abhors, A. Rebecca. Hilaire Belloc. BoChLi (1939 ed.); RIS; StaSt
Tricked Again. Ridhiana. NBP
Trickling tears that falls along my cheeks, The. A Lover Rejected Complaineth. Edward de Vere, Earl of Oxford. RelE
Tricks of Imagination, The. Shakespeare. *See* Lunatic, the Lover, and the Poet, The.
Tricksters. William Rose Benét. HBMV
Tri-colored Ribbon, The. Peadar Kearney. OnYI
Trico's Song. John Lyly. *Fr.* Alexander and Campaspe, V, i. OBSC; TrGrPo
(Spring, The.) CH; MemP
(Spring's Welcome.) AnEnPo; BEL; OBEV; TOP
(What Bird So Sings.) EG; ElL; SiCE; ThWaDe; TuPP; ViBoPo
Trifle. Georgia Douglas Johnson. AmNP
Trifle, A. Henry Timrod. HBV
Trifles. *Unknown.* HBV
Trilby. Alice Brown. AA
Trilby, *sel.* George Du Maurier.
Little Work, A, *after the French of* Leon van Montenaeken, *fr.* Pt. VIII. FaBoBe; HBV; NeHB; OQP
(Little, A.) MaRV
(Little Work, a Little Play, A.) PoLF; PoToHe (new ed.); PTK; TreFS
Trilobite, Grapholite, Nautilus pie. Boston Nursery Rhymes. Joseph Cook. BOHV; InMe
Trilogy for X, *sel.* Louis MacNeice.
And Love Hung Still, II. LiTL; MoBrPo
("And love hung still as crystal over the bed.") ErPo
For X, I. EnLoPo
("When clerks and navvies fondle.") ErPo
Trimmed Lamp, The. Laura Simmons. ChIP; MaRV
Trinitas. Whittier. AmePo; SoP
Trinitie Sunday. George Herbert. *See* Trinity Sunday.
Trinity, The. Marian Osborne. CaP
Trinity, The. *Unknown.* ACP
Trinity: a Dream Sequence, *sels.* Naomi Long Madgett. Kal
"Stark day corrodes the silver of the dream."
"You would not recognize yourself if I should tell you."
Trinity [*or* Trinitee] blessed, deity coequal. A Prayer to the Trinity [*or* To the Trinity]. Richard Stanyhurst. CoBE; ElL; OxBoCh; PoEL-2; TuPP
Trinity Place. Phyllis McGinley. MoAmPo (1962 ed.); OCS
Trinity [*or* Trinitie] Sunday. George Herbert. MaMe
Trinket. Winifred Welles. NP
Triolet: "All women born are so perverse." Robert Bridges. HBV; PoVP; PV; SeCePo
Triolet: "Easy is the triolet." W. E. Henley. BOHV
Triolet: "I intended a handspring." Margaret Hoover. PCD
Triolet: "I love you, my Lord!" Paul T. Gilbert. BOHV; PV
Triolet: "Night is full of the crying, The." Alexander K. Laing. YT
Triolet: "When first we met did not guess." Robert Bridges. BrPo; PoVP
(When First We Met.) Po
Triolet on a Dark Day. Margaret Fishback. PoSC
Triolet on a Downhill Road. Margaret Fishback. WhC
Trip and go, heave and ho! A-Maying, a-Playing [*or* A Clownish Song]. Thomas Nashe. *Fr.* Summer's Last Will and Testament. ElL; OBSC
Trip down to Bangor, the Fourth of July, A. The Red Light Saloon. *Unknown.* ShS
Trip for Hell and Self, The. Joseph Cardarelli. QAH
Trip It, Gipsies [Trip It Fine]. Thomas Middleton *and* William Rowley. *Fr.* The Spanish Gipsy, III, i. OAEP; SeCL
(Song: Trip it gipsies, trip it fine.") OBS
Trip on the Erie, A. *Unknown.* ABF; IHA
Trip: San Francisco. Langston Hughes. AmFN; GoSl
Trip to Cambridge, The. *Unknown.* PAH
Trip to Four or Five Towns, A. John Logan. AmPC; CoAP
"In New York I got drunk, to tell the truth," *sel.* NMP
Trip to Louisiana, some favors to find, A. The Lily of the West. *Unknown.* BFSS
Trip to Paris and Belgium, A, *sels.* Dante Gabriel Rossetti. PeVV
Antwerp to Ghent.
Boulogne to Amiens and Paris.
London to Folkestone.
Trip to the Grand Banks, A, *with music.* *Unknown.* ShS
Trip upon trenchers, and dance upon dishes. *Unknown.* OxNR
Tripe. J. B. Morton. InMe
Triple-decker and the double-cone, The. Saturday Sundae. F. R. Scott. CaP
Triple Dream, The. Mikhail Lermontov, *tr. fr. Russian by* Vladimir Nabokov. LiTW
Triple Feature. Denise Levertov. NoP
Triple Fool[e], The. John Donne. CoBE; DiPo; MaMe; OAEP; Po; PP; SCEP-1
Triplet on the Reign of the Great Sultan, A. James Clarence Mangan. IrPN
Trippers. Sir Osbert Sitwell. HaMV
Tripping down the Field-Path. Charles Swain. HBV; VA
Tristan and Isolda. Newman Levy. InMe

Tristan da Cunha. Roy Campbell. MoBrPo; MoVE; OnHM; PeSA; RoGo
Tristram and Iseult. Matthew Arnold. PoVP; ViPo; ViPP; VP
Tristram and Iseult. Swinburne. Tristram of Lyonesse: Prelude. PoVP
(Love, That Is First and Last.) LiTL
Tristram and Isolt. Don Marquis. HBMV
Tristram lies sick to death. Tristram's End. Laurence Binyon. EnLit; OBMV
Tristram of Lyonesse, *sels.* Swinburne.
Death of Urgan, The, *fr.* The Last Pilgrimage. WHA
Sunrise at Sea, *br. sel. fr.* The Sailing of the Swallow. EtS
Swimming. GN
Tristram and Iseult. Prelude. PoVP
(Love, That Is First and Last.) LiTL
Tristram's End. Laurence Binyon. EnLit; OBMV
Tristrem and the Hunters. *At. to* Thomas of Erceldoune. *Fr.* Sir Tristrem. OxBS
Trit trot to market to buy a penny doll. *Unknown.* OxNR
Triumph, The. Ben Jonson. *See* Triumph of Charis, The.
Triumph, The. Sidney Lanier. *Fr.* The Psalm of the West. PAH
Triumph. John Crowe Ransom. HBMV
Triumph, The. William Gilmore Simms. Sonn
Triumph. L. D. Stearns. BLRP
Triumph may be of several kinds, A. Emily Dickinson. NePA
Triumph of Bacchus and Ariadne. Lorenzo de' Medici, *tr. fr. Italian by* Richard Aldington. *Fr.* Carnival Songs. CTC
Triumph of Beautie Song, The, *sel.* James Shirley.
"Heigh-ho, what shall a shepheard doe." ErPo
Triumph of Beauty, The, *sel.* James Shirley.
"Cease, warring thoughts, and let his brain." TuPP
Triumph of Charis, The. Ben Jonson. *Fr.* A Celebration of Charis. BEL; CABA; CBEP; ELP; ExPo; GoBC; LiTB; LoBV; NoP; SeCeV; TOP; WHA
(Her Triumph.) AnAnS-2; AtBAP; CaFP; CTC; EIL; FaBoEn; HBV; InPo; LiTL; MaPo; OAEP; Po; PoEL-2; SCEP-2; SeCP; SeCV-1; SeEP; TuPP; ViBoPo
("See the Chariot at hand here of Love.") InvP; SiCE
(Triumph, The.) AnFE; OBEV
"Have you seen but a bright lily grow," *sel.* EG
(Have You Seen a Bright Lily Grow.) OTPC (1923 ed.)
(So Sweet Is She.) GN
(So White, So Soft, So Sweet.) TrGrPo
(Triumph, The.) PG, 8 *ll.*
Triumph of Chastity, The. Barbara Howes. NePoAm-2
Triumph of Death, The. Barbara Howes. MoAmPo (1962 ed.); NePoAm-2
Triumph of Death, The. Shakespeare. *See* Sonnets, LXXI.
Triumph of Doubt, The. John Peale Bishop. EaLo
Triumph of Dulness, The. Pope. *Fr.* The Dunciad. OBEC
Triumph of Forgotten Things, The. Edith M. Thomas. HBV
Triumph of Freedom, The. William Lloyd Garrison. PoFr
Triumph of His Grace. Charles Wesley. BePJ; SoP
Triumph of Ignorance, The. Pope. *See* Conclusion: "In vain, in vain . . ."
Triumph of Infidelity, The, *sel.* Timothy Dwight.
Smooth Divine, The. AA; AnAmPo; PPON; WGRP
(Minister, New Style, A.) AmPP (3d ed.)
Triumph of Joseph, The. Charles Jeremiah Wells. *Fr.* Joseph and His Brethren. VA
Triumph of Life, The. Shelley. ChER; ERoP-2; MasP; PoEL-4
Triumph of Love. John Hall Wheelock. MAP; MoAmPo
(Triumph of the Singer, The.) NP
Triumph of Peace, The, *sel.* James Shirley.
"Come away, away, away." TuPP
Triumph of Sensibility. Sylvia Townsend Warner. MoAB; MoBrPo
Triumph of the Defeated. Byron. MaRV
Triumph of the Singer, The. John Hall Wheelock. *See* Triumph of Love.
Triumph of the Whale. Charles Lamb. EtS; OBRV
"Io! Paean! Io! sing," *sel.* ImOP
Triumph of Time, The. Swinburne. MaVP; PoVP; ViPo; ViPP; VP
Sels.
"I have put my days and dreams out of mind." ViBoPo
"I will go back to the great sweet mother." FaPL; GTSL
(Return, The.) EtS
(Sea, The.) BoLiVE; TrGrPo; TSW
(Stanzas.) HBV
(Triumph of Time, The.) OAEP
"There lived a singer in the France of old." GTSL
Triumphal arch, that fill'st the sky. To the Rainbow. Thomas Campbell. HBV
Triumphal Chant. Exodus, XV: 1-13, 18, Bible, *O.T.* TrGrPo
(Song of Moses, The, XV: 1-18.) LiTW
(Then Sang Moses, XV: 1-18.) TrJP
("Then sang Moses and the children of Israel this song," XV: 1-27.) PoFr
Triumphal March. T. S. Eliot. *Fr.* Coriolan. BWP; MBW-2; ShBV-4; WaaP
Triumphal Ode MCMXXXIX. George Barker. LiTB; WaP
Triumphalis. Bliss Carman. HBMV; PG
Triumphant Entry, The. Henry Vaughan. *Fr.* Palm-Sunday. MaRV; StJW
Triumphs of Owen, The. Thomas Gray, *after the Welsh of* Meilir ap Gwalchmai. CEP; EnRP; LiTW; PoEL-3; PrWP
Triumphs of Thy Conquering Power, The. William H. Bathurst. BePJ
Trivia. Beatrice M. Murphy. TNV
Trivia; or, The Art of Walking the Streets of London, *sels.* John Gay.
I: Of the Implements for Walking the Streets, and Signs of the Weather. CEP; EiCP
II: Of Walking the Streets by Day. CEP; EiPP
Dangers of Football, The. EnLi-1 (1949 ed.); SD
Great Frost, The. OBEC; SeCePo
Of Narrow Streets. EnLi-1 (1949 ed.)
On Walking the Streets by Day. TOP
(Morning, The, *shorter sel.*) EnLi-1 (1949 ed.)
Pell Mell Celebrated, The. EnLi-1 (1949 ed.)
Pleasure of Walking through an Alley, The. EnLi-1 (1949 ed.)
"Thus far the muse has traced in useful lays." EnLi-1 (1949 ed.)
III: Of Walking the Streets by Night. EiCP
"Consider, reader, what fatigues I've known." EnLi-1 (1949 ed.)
Evening, The. EnLi-1 (1949 ed.)
"O Trivia, Goddess, leave these low abodes." EnLi-1 (1949 ed.)
Of Ballad-Singers. EnLi-1 (1949 ed.)
(Ballad Singers.) MuSP
Of Crossing the Street. EnLi-1 (1949 ed.)
Of Pick-Pockets. EnLi-1 (1949 ed.)
Of Watchmen. EnLi-1 (1949 ed.)
Triviality, A. Waring Cuney. CDC
Troades. Euripides. *See* Trojan Women.
Troas, *sel.* Seneca, *tr. fr. Latin by* the Earl of Rochester.
Chorus: "After death, nothing is," *fr.* II. PeRV
Trochee trips from long to short. Metrical Feet [*or* Lessons for a Boy]. Samuel Taylor Coleridge. ExPo; HBV; PCD
Troelus a Chresyd, *sel.* *Unknown, tr. fr. Welsh by* Gwyn Williams.
Prayer of Calcas, The. PrWP
Troia Fuit. Reginald Wright Kauffman. HBV
Troilus and Cressida. Chaucer. *See* Troilus and Criseyde.
Troilus and Cressida. Aubrey Thomas De Vere. IrPN
Troilus and Cressida, *sels.* Dryden.
"Can life be a blessing." ATP (1953 ed.); SeCePo; SeCL; ViBoPo
(Song.) CEP; NoP; SeCV-2; SeEP
Prologue: "See my lov'd Britons, see your Shakespeare rise." CEP; MBW-1; SeCV-2
Troilus and Cressida, *sels.* Shakespeare.
Helen of Troy, *fr.* IV, i. TreFT
On Degree, *fr.* I, iii. ExPo
("Heavens themselves, the planets and this center.") ImOP
Portrait of Cressida, *fr.* IV, v. TrGrPo
Portrait of Helen, *fr.* II, ii, *and* IV, i. TrGrPo
Ulysses Advises Achilles [Not to Let Slip Opportunity], *fr.* III, iii. LiTB; LiTG
Troilus and Criseyde, *sels.* Chaucer.
"As proude Bayard ginneth for to skip," *fr.* I. MyFE
At the Gate. SeCePo
But Whan the Cok, *fr.* III. AtBAP
Complaint of Troilus, The, *fr.* V. DiPo; OBEV (new ed.)
Despair of Troilus, The, *fr.* IV. LoBV
"Go, litel book, go litel myn tragedie," *fr.* V. MyFE; ViBoPo

(Envoy, The.) FiP
"If no love is, O god, what fele I so?" *fr.* I. LO
(Canticus Troili.) AtBAP
(Song of Troilus.) AWP
(Troilus Soliloquizes.) EG
"O younge freshe [*or* yonge fresshe] folkes, he or [*or* and] she," *fr.* V. CAW; ExPo; LO
(Exhortation to Youth.) PoLi
(Love Unfeigned, The.) OBEV
"Owt [*or* out] of thise blake wawes for to sayle," II. EnLi-1; ILP; PP
Sorrow of Troilus, The, *fr.* V. PoEL-1
"Therewith when he was ware, and gan behold," *fr.* V. LO
"With-inne the temple he went him forth pleyinge," *fr.* I. LO
Wooing of Criseide, The, III. PoEL-1
(O Blisful Light, *shorter sel.*) AtBAP
Trojan Women, The, *sels.* Euripides, *tr. fr. Greek.*
Cassandra's Epithalamium, *tr. by* Ann Stanford. HW
Troy, *tr. by* Gilbert Murray. WoL
Trojans outside the Walls, The. Homer, *tr. fr. Greek by* George Chapman. *Fr.* The Iliad, VIII. OBS
Troll the Bowl! Thomas Dekker. *See* Cold's the Wind.
Troll's Nosegay, The. Robert Graves. PoCh; Sonn
Trompe l'Oeil. Daryl Hine. MoCV
Troop home to silent grots and caves! The Mermaidens' Vesper-Hymn [*or* Siren Chorus]. George Darley. Syren Songs, VI. ChTr; FaBoEn; LoBV; NBM; OBNC; OBRV; OxBl; PeER; PoEL-4; ViBoPo
Troop of the Guard, A. Hermann Hagedorn. HBV; OHIP
Troop Train. Karl Shapiro. OxBA; WaaP; WaP
Trooper and Maid, The. *Unknown.* BaBo
Trooper Temple Pulvermacher. William Branford. BoSA
Troops, The. Siegfried Sassoon. CMoP; POTE
(Prelude: "Dim, gradual thinning of the shapeless gloom.") GTSL
(Prelude: Troops, The.) ChMP; GTBS-D
Troops Returning from Milan. Niccolò degli Albizzi. *See* Prolonged Sonnet: When the Troops Were Returning from Milan.
Troopship in the Tropics. Alun Lewis. WaP
Tropes of One Season. Charles Edward Eaton. FiSC
Trophy, The. Edwin Muir. LiTM; POTE
Trophy case for Grail chasers, A. The Cemetery Plot of Ed Sanders Shall Consist of. Ed Sanders. ANYP
Tropic of ice. Cape Ann: a View. John Malcolm Brinnin. NYBP
Tropic Siesta. Luis Carlos López, *tr. fr. Spanish by* Donald Devenish Walsh. WoL
Tropic Storm. Walter Adolphe Roberts. *Fr.* Boyhood Etchings. PoNe
Tropic Sunset. Walter Adolphe Roberts. *Fr.* Boyhood Etchings. PoNe
Tropical Girl to Her Garden. Genevieve Taggard. NP
Tropical Morning at Sea, A. Edward Rowland Sill. EtS
Tropical Tempest. Arthur Davison Ficke. Sonnets of a Portrait Painter, XVI.
("I have seen beauty where light stabs the hills.") AnAmPo
Tropical Town. Salomón de la Selva. HBV
Tropical Weather. Epes Sargent. EtS
Tropics, The. Douglas Brooke Wheelton Sladen. VA
Tropics in New York, The. Claude McKay. AmNP; GoSl; Kal; PoNe; TTY
Tropics Vanish, and Meseems That I, The. Robert Louis Stevenson. PeVV
Trosachs, The. Wordsworth. EnLi-2; EPN; GTSL; HBV; MBW-2; OBEV; OBRV; SeCePo
Trot Along, Pony. Marion Edey. SoPo; TiPo
Trot, and a canter, a gallop, and over, A. *Unknown.* OxNR
Trot, Trot! Mary Frances Butts. HBV; HBVY
("Every evening Baby goes.") PPL
(Trot, Trot to Town.) SAS
Troth ladye Ile not court ye too't. *Unknown.* SeCSL
Troubadour Alba: "'Neath leafy hawthorn in a garden gay." *Unknown, tr. fr. French by* Frances Winwar. EnLi-1
Troubadour of God, The. Charles Wharton Stork. WGRP
Troubadour Song: "'Tis no wonder if my songs." Bernart of Ventadorn, *tr. fr. French by* Bernard D. N. Grebanier. EnLi-1
Troubadours. Arthur Davison Ficke. Sonnets of a Portrait Painter, X. HBMV
Trouble. David Keppel. FaFP; PoLF; TreF; WBLP
Trouble. Don Marquis. *Fr.* Archy and Mehitabel. TreFT
Trouble/ with the car. Letter 22. Charles Olson. FRC
Trouble at Sea. Thomas Prys, *tr. fr. Welsh by* Gwyn Williams. PrWP
Trouble at the Farm. Ivy O. Eastwick. BoTP
Trouble in the Amen Corner. T. C. Harbaugh. BLPA
Trouble Is, The, *sel.* Renée Resendez.
"Trouble is I, The." WOW
Trouble, not of clouds, or weeping rain, A. On the Departure of Sir Walter Scott from Abbotsford, for Naples. Wordsworth. EnRP
Trouble Not the Maiden's Soul. Johan Ludvig Runeberg, *tr. fr. Swedish by* Charles W. Stork. LiTW
Trouble, Trouble *with music.* *Unknown.* OuSiCo
Trouble with a kitten is, The. The Kitten. Ogden Nash. FaPON; MoShBr; WhC
Trouble with you is, The. Denunciation: or, Unfrock'd Again. Philip Whalen. NeAP
Troubled Jesus. Waring Cuney. BANP; GoSl
Troubled man turned head away, The. Country Life. Frank Kendon. POTE
Troubled Soldier, The. *See* Jack o' Diamonds; or, The Rabble Soldier.
Troubled Unquickening, The. William Baylebridge. *Fr.* Sextains. BoAV
Troubles. Dorothy Aldis. StVeCh
Troubles of a Book, The. Laura Riding. NYTB
Troubles of the Day. William Barnes. GTBS-P
Troubles, they say, are sent us to grow wise on. Dream and Image. Heinrich van Morungen. LiTW
Trousers of Wind. *Unknown, tr. fr. Amharic by* Sylvia Pankhurst *and* Ato Menghestu Lemme. PBA; TTY
Trout, The. Daryl Hine. CoAP; NYTB
Trout, The. John Montague. NMP; OPoP
Trout leaps high, A. Uejima Onitsura, *tr. fr. Japanese by* Harold G. Henderson. FIW
Trout Map, The. Allen Tate. FaBoMo
Troy ("In Salamis, filled with the foaming"). Euripides, *tr. fr. Greek by* Gilbert Murray. *Fr.* Trojan Women. WoL
Troy. Robin Flower. SeCePo
Troy. Edwin Muir. CMoP
Troy. Thomas Sackville. *Fr.* Induction to "The Mirror for Magistrates." SeCePo
Troy Depicted. Shakespeare. *Fr.* The Rape of Lucrece. OBSC
Troy rac'd, Greece wrack'd, who mourns? Ye both may boast. To the Ruins of Troy and Greece. George Chapman. ReIE
Troy Town. Dante Gabriel Rossetti. BEL; MaVP; PoVP; ViPo; ViPP; VP
Troylus and Criseyde. Chaucer. *See* Troilus and Criseyde.
Troynovant ("Troynovant is now no more a city"). Thomas Dekker. *Fr.* Entertainment to James. ChTr; LoBV; OBSC
Truant, The. E. J. Pratt. OBCV
Truants, The. Walter de la Mare. CMoP; InP; MoBrPo
Truants from love, we dream of wrath. Oliver Wendell Holmes. *Fr.* The Professor at the Breakfast Table. OQP
Truce, gentle love, a parley now I crave. Idea, LXIII. Michael Drayton. NoP; ReIE; Sonn; TuPP
Truckdriver, The. Coleman Barks. QAH
Trucker, A. Thom Gunn. TPM
Trucks. James S. Tippett. FaPON; GFA; OTD
Trudge, Body. Robert Graves. MoAB
True Account of Talking to the Sun at Fire Island, A. Frank O'Hara. ANYP
True and False. Isabella Valancy Crawford. PeCV (1967 ed.)
True and False Glory. Milton. *Fr.* Paradise Regained, III. LiTB; OBS
True and False Singing. *Unknown.* *See* Ballata: Of True and False Singing.
True Apostolate, The. Ruby T. Weyburn. BLRP
True Aristocrat, The. W. Stewart. WBLP
Aristocrats of Labor, *sel.* OQP; PGD
True as the church clock hand the hour pursues. John Clare. *Fr.* The Cottager. OBRV
True Beauty. Francis Beaumont. EIL; HBV
True Beauty, The. Thomas Carew. *See* Disdain Returned.
Trueblue Gentleman, A. Kenneth Patchen. OA
True-born Englishman, The, *sels.* Defoe.
English Race, The, *fr.* I. OBEC
Introduction. BEL

True-born (continued)
Part I. BEL; CEP
"Romans first with Julius Caesar came, The," *fr.* I. FOL
"Satire be kind, and draw a silent veil," *fr.* I. TOP
"Wherever God erects a house of prayer," *fr.* I. TreF
True Brahmin, in the morning meadows wet. ,Gardener. Emerson. *Fr.* Quatrains. MWA-1; OxBA
True Brotherhood. Ella Wheeler Wilcox. OQP; WBLP
True Christian hearts cease to lament. The Song of a Happy Rising. John Thewlis. ACP
True Confession of George Barker, The, *sels.* George Barker.
"I see the young bride move among." ErPo
"I sent a letter to my love." FaBoTw
"True culture is not for the masses." The Goldfish. William F. Kirk. LHV
True Description of Love, A. *Unknown.* TuPP
True ease in writing comes from art, not chance. The Craft of Verse [*or* Sound and Sense]. Pope. *Fr.* An Essay on Criticism. BoLiVe; ExPo; TrGrPo; UnPo
True Form and Shape of a Monsterous Child, The. William Elderton. ReIE
True Freedom. Charles MacKay. PGD
True Freedom. *Unknown, at. to* Lao-tzu, *tr. fr. Chinese by* Witter Bynner. *Fr.* Tao Teh King. OnPM
True Freedom breaks the yokes that gall. Ferdinand Freiligrath. *Fr.* Black, Red and Gold. PoFr
True Friendship. *Unknown, Fr.* The Panchatantra. *tr. fr. Sanskirt by* Arthur Ryder. AWP; JAWP; WBP
("'Tis hard to find in life.") LiTW
True friendship unfeigned. A Plain Description Of Perfect Friendship. *At. to* Henry Cheke. EIL; TuPP
True Gift, The. *Unknown.* ChIP; MaRV
True Greatness. "Owen Meredith." MaRV
True Greatness. Isaac Watts. MaRV
True Happiness. Morris Talpalar. PoToHe (new ed.)
True Heaven, The. Paul Hamilton Hayne. WGRP
True Hymn[e], A. George Herbert. InvP; MaMe; OxBoCh
True is it that Ambrosio Salerino. Epitaphs, V. Gabriello Chiabrera. AWP
True Knight, The. Stephen Hawes. *Fr.* The Pastime of Pleasure, *ch.* 27. ACP; AnEnPo; OBEV
(True Knighthood.) TrGrPo
True Knowledge. Panatattu. WGRP
True Lent, A. Robert Herrick. *See* To Keep a True Lent.
True Light, The. Charles Wesley. *See* Morning Hymn, A.
True Love. *See also* Truelove.
True Love. Phoebe Cary. PoToHe
True Love. Waring Cuney. CDC
True Love, A. Nicholas Grimald. EIL; OBEV; TuPP
(True love, A.) OBSC
True Love. James Russell Lowell. *Fr.* Love. LiTL; MaRV; OQP
True Love. Ernest Rhys. POTE
True Love. Shakespeare. *See* Sonnets, CXVI.
True Love. Shelley. *Fr.* Epipsychidion. LoBV
True Love. Sir Philip Sidney. *See* My True Love Hath My Heart.
True Love. *Unknown, tr. fr. Greek by* Louis Untermeyer. UnTE
True Love. Judith Viorst. MeWo
True Love at Length United. *Unknown.* *See* Wandering Maiden, The.
True Love Ditty, A. Thomas Middleton. *Fr.* Blurt, Master Constable. EIL
True Love in this differs from gold and clay. Shelley. *Fr.* Epipsychidion. LO; OBNC
True love is but a [*or* an] humble, low-born thing. True Love. James Russell Lowell. *Fr.* Love. LiTL; MaRV; OQP
True Love is founded in rocks of Remembrance. Love and Law. Vachel Lindsay. OQP
True Lover, The. Abbie Huston Evans. NP
True Lover, The. A. E. Housman. A Shropshire Lad, LIII. ATP; BoLiVe; LiTL; MeWo; PoVP
True Lover's Farewell, The ("Farewell, farewell, my pretty maid"). *Unknown.* *See* Lass of Lochroyan, The.
True love's own talisman, which here. A Footnote to a Famous Lyric. Louise Imogen Guiney. AA
True love's the gift which God has given. Sir Walter Scott. *Fr.* The Lay of the Last Minstrel, V. OBRV
True Maid, A. Matthew Prior. ALV; CBV; EiCL; ErPo; LiTG; MeWo; PV
True Martyr, The. Thomas Wade. EPN; OBVV
True mirth resides not in the smiling skin. Mirth. Robert Herrick. LiTB
True Need, The. Thomas Curtis Clark. OQP
True Night. René Char, *tr. fr. French by* Jackson Mathews. PoPl
True or False. Catullus, *tr. fr. Latin by* Walter Savage Landor. AWP; JAWP; OuHeWo; WBP
True, our converse a stranger is to speech. Walden. Henry David Thoreau. MAmP
True Paddy's Song, The, *with music.* *Unknown.* OuSiCo
True poesy is not in words. Pastoral Poesy. John Clare. ACV; ERoP-2
True Preacher, The. William Cowper. *Fr.* The Task, II. MaRV
True Rest. Goethe, *tr. fr. German by* John S. Dwight. MaRV; OQP; TRV; WBLP
(Rest.) SoP; TreFT
True Riches. Bessie June Martin. STF
True Riches. *Unknown.* MaRV
True Riches. Isaac Watts. OBEC
True Romance. Edwin Honig. SiTL
True Romance, The. Herbert Jones. HBMV
True Story, A. *Unknown.* *See* There Was a Little Rabbit Sprig.
True Story of Skipper Ireson, The. Charles Buxton Going. YT
True Story of Web-Spinner, The. Mary Howitt. OTPC (1923 ed.)
True Tale of Robin Hood, A. *Unknown.* ESPB
True Tar, The. Henry Carey. Two Songs, I. WaPE
True, the Good and the Beautiful, The, *abr.* Delmore Schwartz. MiAP
True Thomas. *Unknown.* *See* Thomas the Rhymer.
"True 'tis P T, and P T 'tis, 'tis true." O D V. *Unknown.* BOHV
True to a Dream. Donald Petersen. NePoEA-2
True to Poll. F. C. Burnand. *See* His Heart Was True to Poll.
True to the Best. Benjamin Keech. PoToHe
True Vine, The. St. John, XV: 1-27, Bible, *N.T.* WoL
True Vine. Elinor Wylie. AnFE; APA; CoAnAm; LiTA
True, we must tame our rebel will. Courage. Matthew Arnold. MBW-2
True Weather for Women, The. Louis Simpson. NePoAm; NoP
True Wisdom. *Unknown.* BePJ; SoP; STF
True Wisdom knows. Lest Fools Should Fail. Piet Hein. TIHL
True wit is nature to advantage dress'd. Pope. *Fr.* An Essay on Criticism. ShBV-3
True Woman. Dante Gabriel Rossetti. The House of Life, LVI-LVIII.
Her Heaven, 3. EPN; MaVP; PoVP; ViPo; VP
Her Love, 2. EPN; MaVP; PoVP; ViPo; VP
Herself, 1. EPN; MaVP; PoVP; ViPo; ViPP; VP
True Work Is Worship. Edwin Markham. *Fr.* The Angelus. MaRV
True worth is in being, not seeming. Nobility [*or* The Noble Life]. Alice Cary. MaRV; OHFP; OQP; WBLP
Truelove, A. Nicholas Grimald. *See* True Love, A.
Truelove. *Unknown, tr. fr. German by* Jethro Bithell. AWP
Truer life draws nigher, The. Every Year. Albert G. Pike. FaChP
Truest poet is not one, The. The Poet. T. A. Daly. JKCP
Truest Poetry Is the Most Feigning, The; or, Ars Poetica for Hard Times. W. H. Auden. NYBP
Truism, The. Louis MacNeice. PoIE
Truly buzzards/ Around my sky are circling! Glyph. *Unknown.* LiTA
Truly Great. W. H. Davies. HBV; OBMV; OBVV
Truly Great, The. Stephen Spender. *See* I Think Continually of Those Who Were Truly Great.
Truly, My Satan, thou art but a Dunce. To the Accuser Who Is the God of This World [*or* Epilogue]. Blake. *Fr.* The Gates of Paradise. CABA; EiCL; ERoP-1; FaBoEn; NoP; OBNC; PeER; TrGrPo; UnPo (1st ed.); ViBoPo
Truly the light is sweet. The Light Is Sweet. Ecclesiastes, Bible, *O.T.* FaPON

Truly, the light is sweet. A Man's Bread. Josephine Preston Peabody. YeAr
Truly these women are like birds; they take. Birds. "Seumas O'Sullivan." OxBI
Trumansburg Fair. William Hathaway. QAH
Trump hath blown, The. The Lonely Bugle Grieves. Grenville Mellen. *Fr.* Ode on the Celebration of the Battle of Bunker Hill, June 17, 1825. AA
Trumpet, The. Ilya Ehrenburg, *tr. fr. Russian by* Y. Hornstein. TrJP
Trumpet, The. Edward Thomas. HBMV; MMA; MoBrPo; OHIP; POTE; SiSw; TSW
Trumpet, The. *Unknown, tr. fr. Arabic by* Sir Edwin Arnold. OnPM
Trumpet, A/ A trumpet. Lewis Has a Trumpet. Karla Kuskin. PDV
Trumpet and Flute. Gunnar Hernaes, *tr. fr. Norwegian by* Martin S. Allwood. LiTW
Trumpet for Yuletide. Louis J. Sanker. JKCP (1955 ed.)
Trumpet of a prophecy, The! O wind. The West Wind. Shelley. *Fr.* Ode to the West Wind. PCH
Trumpet Player. Langston Hughes. TPM; TTY
Trumpet sounds it in my soul, De. Moanin'. *Unknown.* ABF
Trumpet-Vine Arbour, The. Amy Lowell. *Fr.* 1777. MAPA; NP
Trumpeter, The. *Unknown.* CoMu
Trumpeter of Fyvie, The. *Unknown. See* Andrew Lammie.
Trumpets. Enter a King, in the sunset glare. Stage Directions. William Rose Benét. ShBV-2
Trumpet's loud clangor, The. The Instruments [*or* Fife and Drum]. Dryden. *Fr.* Song for St. Cecilia's Day. GN; PoPo
Trumpets of the Mind, The. Victor Hugo, *tr. fr. French.* WoL
Trumpet's voice, loud and authoritative, The. Reasons for Attendance. Philip Larkin. CBV; OPoP; PoeP; ToPo
Trumpets were curled away, the drum beat no more, The. The Swan. Stephen Spender. UnS
Trundled from/ the strangeness of the sea. The Sea-Elephant. William Carlos Williams. LiTA; PoeP
Trunk of cherry-tree without bark or flowers. Materia Nupcial. "Pablo Neruda." ErPo
Trus' an' Smile. B. Y. Williams. BLRP
Trust. Avis B. Christiansen. SoP
Trust. Annie Johnson Flint. SoP
Trust. C. A. Fox. SoP
Trust. Frances Anne Kemble. *See* Faith.
Trust. Betsey Kline. SoP
Trust. Lizette Woodworth Reese. AA
Trust. Christina Rossetti. Monna Innominata, XIII. VA
("If I could trust mine own self with your fate.") ViPo
Trust, The. James Tate. YAP
Trust. Thomas à Kempis. SoP
Trust ("The clouds hang heavy around my way"). *Unknown.* SoP
Trust ("Though the rain may fall and the wind is blowing"). *Unknown.* SoP
Trust; a Song. Eben E. Rexford. BLRP
Trust and Obedience. *Unknown.* BLRP
Trust and Wait. Oswald J. Smith. SoP
Trust God. Philip Doddridge. SoP
Trust Him. *Unknown.* STF
Trust in God and Do the Right. Norman Macleod. PaPo
Trust in God, *sel.* BLRP; TreFT
Trust in Jesus. Josiah Conder. BePJ
Trust in the Lord: So shalt thou dwell. Psalm XXXVII, Bible, *O.T. Paraphrased by* Charles Frederic Sheldon. BLRP
Trust in Women. *Unknown.* BOHV; NA
("When nettles in winter bring forth roses red.") LO
Trust Is Best. *Unknown.* SoP
Trust me, I have not earned your dear rebuke. Christina Rossetti. Monna Innominata, VI. ViPo; VP
Trust not his wanton tears. Wily Cupid [*or* Aeliana's Ditty *or* Of Cupid]. Henry Chettle. *Fr.* Piers Plainness' Seven Years' Prenticeship. ALV; EG; EIL; OBSC
Trust Not the Treason. Spenser. *See* Amoretti, XLVII. CBV
Trust not too much, fair youth, unto thy feature. White Primit Falls. *Unknown.* ChTr; EG
Trust Only Yourself. *Unknown.* MeEL
Trust the Form of Airy Things. Henry Harington. LO
(Song: "Trust the form of airy things.") SeCL
Trust the Great Artist. Thomas Curtis Clark. WBLP
Trust Thou Thy Love. Ruskin. OBEV; OBVV; VA
Trusting God. Enola Chamberlin. SoP
Trusting Jesus. Grace B. Renfrow. BePJ
Trusty, Dusky, Vivid, True. Robert Louis Stevenson. *See* My Wife.
Trusty Learning A. B. C. Eliza Lee Follen. SAS
Truth. "Æ." AnIL; GTSL; MoBrPo; TOP
Truth. W. H. Auden. MaRV
Truth. Robert Browning. *Fr.* A Death in the Desert. MaRV
Truth. Chaucer. *See* Balade de Bon Conseyl.
Truth, *sel.* William Cowper.
Simple Faith. OBEC
Truth, The. W. H. Davies. FaBoTw
Truth. John Donne. *See* Satire III: "Kind pity chokes my spleen. . ."
Truth. Max Eastman. *See* Invocation: "Truth, be more precious to me than the eyes."
Truth. Donald Green. WSL
Truth, The. Ted Joans. BOLo; TTY
(Voice in the Crowd.) Kal
Truth. Ben Jonson. PG
Truth, The. Archibald Lampman. CaP
Truth. Cecil Francis Lloyd. CaP
Truth. John Masefield. WGRP
Truth. Howard Nemerov. LiTM (1970 ed.); MoVE
Truth. Jessica Nelson North. HBVY; NP
Truth. Coventry Patmore. *See* Magna Est Veritas.
Truth about B. F., The. Albert Stillman. InMe
Truth about Horace, The. Eugene Field. BOHV; InMe; InP; LHV
Truth and Falsehood. James Russell Lowell. *See* Once to Every Man and Nation.
Truth and Love Abide. James Russell Lowell. *Fr.* Elegy on the Death of Dr. Channing. MaRV
Truth, be more precious to me than the eyes. Invocation [*or* Truth]. Max Eastman. MaRV; OQP; WGRP
Truth, Beauty, Love, in these are formed a ring. The Trinity. Marian Osborne. CaP
Truth, Crushed to Earth. Bryant. *Fr.* The Battlefield. MaRV; NeHB; OQP
("Truth, crushed to earth shall rise again.") SoP; TRV
(Truth, the Invincible.) TreF
Truth Doth Truth Deserve. Sir Philip Sidney. *Fr.* Arcadia. HBV; LiTL
(Advice to the Same.) SiPS
Truth for him was like a tree, The. Exaggerator. Mark Van Doren. AnFE; CoAnAm
Truth Has Perished. Ulma Seligman, *tr. fr. Yiddish by* Joseph Leftwich. TrJP
Truth in Poetry. George Crabbe. *Fr.* The Village. OBEC; SeCePo
Truth is a golden sunset far away. Threnody. I. O. Scherzo. HoPM
Truth is a native, naked beauty; but. Roger Williams. SCAP
Truth is as old as God. Emily Dickinson. MoAmPo
Truth is enough for prose. At the Mermaid Cafeteria. Christopher Morley. PFY
Truth Is Great, The. Coventry Patmore. *See* Magna Est Veritas.
Truth is love and love is truth. Mendacity. A. E. Coppard. GTBS-W; LiTL; LiTM; OBMV
Truth Is Quite Messy, The. William J. Harris. BOLo
"Truth is simple, truth is clear." Tolstoy Seeks the Peasant Rhythm. James Schevill. FRC
Truth is that there comes a time, The. Sad Strains of a Gay Waltz. Wallace Stevens. OxBA
Truth is the trial of itself. Truth. Ben Jonson. PG
Truth Is Within. Robert Browning. *Fr.* Paracelsus, Pt. I. MaRV
Truth-loving Persians do not dwell upon. The Persian Version. Robert Graves. CMoP; LiTB; LiTM (rev. ed.); SiTL
Truth needs no champions: in the infinite deep. Truth and Love Abide. James Russell Lowell. *Fr.* Elegy on the Death of Dr. Channing. MaRV
Truth Never Dies. *Unknown.* OQP; SoP; WBLP
"Truth," said a traveller. The Black Riders, XXVIII. Stephen Crane. AP
Truth Shall Set You Free. Chaucer. *See* Balade de Bon Conseyl.

Truth, so far, in my book; the truth which draws. Elizabeth Barrett Browning. *Fr.* Aurora Leigh, VII. WGRP
Truth: So the frontlet's older legend ran. 1643 "Veritas" 1878. Oliver Wendell Holmes. *Fr.* Two Sonnets: Harvard. AP
Truth the Dead Know, The. Anne Sexton. MoAmPo (1962 ed.); NePoEA-2; ToPo
Truth, the Invincible. Bryant. *See* Truth Crushed to Earth.
Truth to your mighty winds on dusky shores. On the Death of William Edward Burghardt Du Bois. Conrad Kent Rivers. NBP
Truthful James. Bret Harte. CenHV
Truth's Complaint over England. Thomas Lodge. ACP (1952 ed.)
Truth's Integrity. *Unknown.* *See* Love Will Find Out the Way.
Truths That Never Can Be Proved, The. Tennyson. In Memoriam A. H. H., CXXIX, CXXX, CXXXI. MaRV
Truxton's Victory. *Unknown.* PAH
Try Again. Eliza Cook. *See* King Bruce and the Spider.
Try Again. *Unknown.* *See* Try, Try Again.
Try as you may to banish from your mind. The Death of Keats. Vernon Watkins. ML
Try first this figure 2. A Lesson in Handwriting. Alastair Reid. NYBP
Try Smiling. *Unknown.* BLPA; FaFP; WBLP
Try the Uplook. *Unknown.* BLRP; SoP
Try This Once. *Unknown.* WBLP
Try Tropic. Genevieve Taggard. MAP; MoAmPo
Try, Try Again. *Unknown, at. to* William Edward Hickson, *also to* T. H. Palmer. FaFP; FaPON, *st.* 1; TreF (Try Again.) PTK; RePo; TVC
Trying for Solitude. Jack Lindeman. WOW
Trying to chop mother down is like. She Went to Stay. Robert Creeley. ToPo
Trying to fall asleep. Night Thought. Gerald Jonas. NYBP
Trying to Forget. Emily Dickinson. *See* Bereaved of all I went abroad.
Trying to open locked doors with a sword, threading. Sojourn in the Whale. Marianne Moore. PoIE
Trying to Sleep. Ralph Pomeroy. ELU
Tryst, The. E. V. Knox. CenHV
Tryst, The. Christopher Morley. ALV; BOHV; HBMV
Tryst, A. Louise Chandler Moulton. HBV
Tryst, The. William Soutar. ErPo; GoTS; GTBS-D; NeBP; OxBS
Tryst, The. Lauchlan MacLean Watt. MaRV
Tryst after Death, The, *abr.* *Unknown,* *tr. fr. Old Irish by* Kuno Meyer. LiTW; OnYI
Tryst in Brobdingnag, A. Adrienne Rich. NYBP
Tryst of the Night, The. May C. G. Byron. VA
Tryste Noël. Louise Imogen Guiney. HBV; JKCP; OBVV (Five Carols for Christmastide, I.) ISi
Tryste with Morfudd true I made, A. The Mist. *Unknown, formerly at. to* Dafydd ap Gwilym. PrWP
Trysting, A. Richard Dehmel, *tr. fr. German by* Jethro Bithell. AWP
Ts'ai Chi'h. Ezra Pound. NoP
Tsar Lazar and Tsaritsa Militsa, *sel.* *Unknown, tr. fr. Serbian by* George Rapall Noyes *and* Leonard Bacon.
"And when he was himself again, she questioned him withal." PoFr
Tségihi. A Prayer of the Night Chant. *Unknown, tr. fr. Navajo Indian by* Washington Matthews. ExPo
Tsigane's Canzonet, The. Edward King. AA
"Tu Non Se' in Terra, Si Come Tu Credi. . ." Kathleen Raine. NeBP
Tu Quoque. Austin Dobson. BOHV
Tu-Whit To-Whit. Shakespeare. *See* When Icicles Hang by the Wall.
Tu-whit, tu-whit, tu-whee! *See* Te-whit! te-whit! te-whee!
"Tu-whitt, Tu-whitt, Tu-whoo, Tu-whoo." "Good Night," Says the Owl. Lady Erskine-Crum. BoTP
Tua Mariit Wemen and the Wedo, The. William Dunbar. GoTS (Tretis of the Tua Mariit Wemen and the Wedo, The.) OxBS
Widow Speaks, The, *sel.* PoEL-1
Tubal Cain. Charles Mackay. GTBS; MPB; WBLP
Tuberose. Louis James Block. AA
Tubs of . . ./ memory. Roof Garden. James Schuyler. ANYP
Tuck the earth, fold the sod. Dirge. William Alexander Percy. HBMV
Tucking in yellow curls, she poises, set. The Diver. Leonard E. Nathan. ErPo
Tucking the Baby In. Curtis May. HBV
Tudor Aspersions. R. A. Piddington. FiBHP
Tudor Church Music. Sylvia Townsend Warner. UnS
Tudor indeed is gone and every rose. Ezra Pound. *Fr.* The Pisan Cantos. FaBoTw
Tudor Rose, The. Sebastian Brant, *tr. fr. German by* Alexander Barclay. *Fr.* The Ship of Fools. ACP
Tuesday 7:00 PM. John Wieners. FRC
Tuft of Flowers, The. Robert Frost. AmP; AmPP; AnNE; AP; AtBAP; AWP; CBEP; CoBMV; GoYe; HBV; HBVY; InP; JAWP; LaNeLa; LiTA; MAP; MoAB; MoAmPo; MoPW; NeMA; NoP; OxBA; PoPo; SeCeV; TSW; WBP
Tuft of Kelp, The. Herman Melville. CBV; ChTr; MAmP; MWA-1
Tug-of-War, A. M. M. Hutchinson. BoTP
Tug pulls, tightening the steel strand, The. From Le Havre. Charles G. Bell. NePoAm
Tugged Hand, The. W. H. Davies. MoPW
Tugging at containment. I Swear to You, That Ship Never Sunk in Middle-Passage! Lawrence S. Cumberbatch. WSL
Tugs. James S. Tippett. FaPON; GFA
Tulip. William Jay Smith. RePo
Tulip. Humbert Wolfe. MoBrPo; NP; TSW
Tulip Tree. Sacheverell Sitwell. MoBrPo
Tulips. Padraic Colum. ImOP
Tulips. Sylvia Plath. NaP; NYBP; PIA
Tulips and Addresses. Edward Field. NYBP
Tulips are too excitable, it is winter here, The. Tulips. Sylvia Plath. NaP; NYBP; PIA
Tulips from Their Blood. Edwin Brooks. NBP
Tulips now are pushing up, The. April. Eunice Tietjens. SoPo; YeAr
Tullie's Love, *sels.* Robert Greene.
Mars and Venus. OBSC
(Sonnet or Dittie: "Mars in a fury . . .") LoBV
Shepherd's Ode, The. OBSC
When Gods Had Fram'd the Sweet of Women's Face. ReIE (Love and Jealousy.) EIL
Tullochgorum. John Skinner. GoTS; OBEC; OxBS
Tumadir al-Khansa for Her Brother. *Unknown, tr. fr. Arabic by* E. Powys Mathers. *Fr.* The Thousand and One Nights. AWP; JAWP; PG (1945 ed.); WBP
Tumble, The. Ann Taylor. HBVY
Tumble me down, and I will sit. To Fortune. Robert Herrick. SeCV-1
Tumbleweed. David Wagoner. BoNaP
Tumbling among its stones. The Ladder. Gene Baro. NePoEA-2
Tumbling Doggie. *Unknown.* SAS
Tumbling-Hair. E. E. Cummings. CLwM
Tumbling Jack goes clickety-clack. *Unknown.* RIS
Tumbling Mustard. Malcolm Cowley. AmFN
Tummy Ache. Aileen Fisher. SoPo
Tumult. Charles Enoch Wheeler. PoNe
Tumult Ends, The. Roland Robinson. NeLNL
Tumult in a Syrian town had place, A. The Great Physician. Sadi. *Fr.* The Bustan. AWP; OuHeWo
Tumult of death, dizziness hath seized me, The. Elegy. Moses Rimos of Majorca. TrJP
Tumult of my fretted mind, The. Self-Analysis. Anna Wickham. MoBrPo; TrGrPo (1942 ed.)
Tumult, weeping, many new ghosts. Snow Storm. Tu Fu. NaP
Tumultous sea, whose wrath and foam are spent. Eumares. Asclepiades. AWP; JAWP; WBP
Tumultuously move against my heart. Invasion. Hubert Witheford. AnNZ
Tune, A. Arthur Symons. BoLP; MuSP; OBNC
Tune beyond us as we are, A. Wallace Stevens. *Fr.* The Man with the Blue Guitar. CMoP
Tune for a Lonesome Fife. Donald Justice. NYBP (Another Song.) NePoEA-2
Tune is cowboy, the words, sentimental crap, The. D-Y Bar. James Welch. YAP
Tune me for life again, oh, quiet Musician. A Prayer after Illness. Violet Alleyn Storey. TrPWD
Tune Me, O Lord, into One Harmony. Christina Rossetti. TrPWD

Tune of [the] Seven Towers, The. William Morris. PoVP; ViPP
Tune on my pipe the praises of my Love. In Praise of His Daphnis. Sir John Wotton. EIL
Tune on my pipe the praises of my Love. Of His Mistress [*or* Melicertus' Description of His Mistress]. Robert Greene. *Fr.* Menaphon. EIL; ReIE
Tune Thou My Harp. Amy Carmichael. TRV
Tune thy music to thy heart. Heart's Music. *Unknown.* OBEV (new ed.)
Tuned in on my own frequency. Self-Portrait, from Another Direction. Philip Whalen. FRC
Tuneful Alexis, on the Thame's fair side. The Progress of Wit; a Caveat. Aaron Hill. EiCL
Tunnel, The. Hart Crane. *Fr.* The Bridge. AmP; AP; CMoP; LiTA; LiTG; MAP; MoAB; MoAmPo; MoVE; NePA; OxBA; PoFS
Tunnel, The. Mark Strand. TDP; TwCP
Tunnel Beach. James K. Baxter. AnNZ
Tunning [*or* Tunnyng] of Elynour Rummyng, The. John Skelton. *See* Elynour Rummynge.
Tuppence Coloured. Babette Deutsch. PFY
Turbine, The. Harriet Monroe. NP
Turf Carrier on Aranmore. John Hewitt. PoRA (rev. ed.)
Turf Stacks. Louis MacNeice. *See* Among These Turf-Stacks.
Turin beneath, on the green banks of the Po. At the Tombs of the House of Savoy. William Jay Smith. NePoAm-2
Turk. Sam Cornish. BF
Turk and Pope. Robert Wisdom. ReIE
Turk by the name of Haroun, A. *Unknown.* SiTL
Turk in Armenia, The. Sir William Watson. PoFr
Turkey, The. Ogden Nash. RePo
Turkey and the Ant, The. John Gay. *Fr.* Fables. OTPC (1923 ed.)
Turkey-Cock. D. H. Lawrence. AnEnPo
Turkey in the Straw. *Unknown.* AS (A *vers., with music,* B *and* C *vers.*); FaFP; TrAS, *with music*; TreFS; YaD
Turkey is my favorite bird, The. Thanksgiving. Margarete Münsterberg. GFA
Turkey Time. *Unknown.* PCH
Turkeys Observed. Seamus Heaney. FIW
Turkish Garden. C. A. Trypanis. NYTB
Turkish Lady, The. *Unknown.* *See* Young Beichan.
Turkish Legend, A. Thomas Bailey Aldrich. GN; HBV; HBVY; OTPC (1946 ed.); YT
Turko-Persian Bazaar-Boutique. Eugene Lesser. FRC
Turn Again to Life. Mary Lee Hall. MaRV; PoLF
Turn All Thy Thoughts to Eyes. Thomas Campion. LiTL; ViBoPo
Turn Back, O Man. Clifford Bax. MaRV; TRV
Turn back. Turn, young lady dear. The Robber Bridegroom. Allen Tate. TwAmPo
Turn Back, You Wanton Flyer. Thomas Campion. EnLi-1; UnTE
(Basia.) GTSL
Turn from that girl. I Shall Laugh Purely. Robinson Jeffers. CrMA; LiTA; LiTM (rev. ed.); WaP
"Turn, gentle hermit of the dale." Edwin and Angelina. Goldsmith. *Fr.* The Vicar of Wakefield. CEP; OTPC
Turn I my looks unto the skies. Rosader's Sonnet [*or* Rosader's Second Sonetto]. Thomas Lodge. *Fr.* Rosalynde; or, Euphues' Golden Legacy. OBSC; SiCE; TuPP
Turn in the road was illumined, The. Garden of Gethsemane. Boris Pasternak. MoRP
Turn inward on the brain. What the Emanation of Casey Jones Said to the Medium. A. J. M. Smith. MoCV
Turn like a top, spin on your dusty axis. Instead of a Journey. Michael Hamburger. NYBP
Turn Me to My Yellow Leaves. William Stanley Braithwaite. BANP
Turn not aside, Shepherd, to see. Help, Good Shepherd. Ruth Pitter. OxBoCh
Turn not to the prophet's page, O Son! For the Holy Family by Michelangelo. Dante Gabriel Rossetti. GoBC
Turn, now, tired mind unto your rest. Forests. Walter de la Mare. CMoP
Turn O Libertad. Walt Whitman. AmePo
Turn o' the Year. Katharine Tynan. HBV
Turn o'er thy outward man, and judge aright. The Outward Man Accused. Edward Taylor. *Fr.* God's Determinations. LiTA
Turn of the Moon. Robert Graves. BoC
Turn of the Road, The. Alice Rollit Coe. HBV
Turn of the Road, The. Fannie Stearns Davis. HBMV
Turn on and sing my happy song. A Song. Michael McClure. FRC
Turn on the prudent ant thy heedful eyes. The Ant. Samuel Johnson. CBV; EiCL
Turn on Your Side and Bear the Day to Me. George Barker. AtBAP
Turn out more ale, turn up the light. Dum Vivimus Vigilemus. Charles Henry Webb. AA
Turn over world! O monstrous world! Universe into Stone. A. J. M. Smith. PeCV
"Turn to me in the darkness." Titus and Berenice. John Heath-Stubbs. GTBS-P
Turn to the Grass. Mary Gilmore. MoAuPo
Turn to the Left. Deems Taylor, *tr. fr. French.* UnTE
Turn, turn, my wheel! Turn round and round. Kéramos. Longfellow. MAmP; PoEL-5; YT
Turn, Turn Thy Beauteous Face Away. Beaumont *and* Fletcher. *Fr.* Love's Cure. AtBAP
(Song: "Turn, turn thy beauteous face away.") PoEL-2
Turn under, plow. Plowman's Song. Raymond Knister. CaP
"Turn, Willie Macintosh [*or* Mackintosh]." Willie Macintosh [*or* Burning of Auchindown]. *Unknown.* BFSS; BuBa; CBEP; ESPB; OBB; OxBB; OxBoLi; ViBoFo
Turn with me from the city's clamorous street. Thomas a Kempis. Richard Rogers Bowker. AA
Turnaround place, The. Coleman Barks. *Fr.* Body Poems. QAH
Turncoat, The. LeRoi Jones. NeAP; NoP
Turned from the "eau-forte." Mauberley, I. Ezra Pound. *Fr.* Hugh Selwyn Mauberley. NoP
Turners Dish of Lentten Stuffe; or, A Galymaufery. William Turner. CoMu
Turning. Sophia Castro-Leon. QAH
Turning, The. Philip Booth. NePoAm-2
Turning. Robert Finch. MoCV; OBCV
Turning, The. Philip Murray. NePoAm
Turning and turning in the widening gyre. The Second Coming. W. B. Yeats. AtBAP; BWP; CABA; CBV; CMoP; CoBMV; DiPo; EaLo; EnL; ExPo; FaBoEn; FaBoMo; ForPo; GTBS-P; GTBS-W; HoPM; ILP; InPo; LiTB; LiTG; LiTM; LoBV; MaPo; MasP; MBW-2; MoAB; MoBrPo (1962 ed.); MoVE; MoRP; NoP; OAEP (2d ed.); OxBI; PAn; Po; PoAn; PoDB; PoE; PoeP; PoFS; PoIE; PoPo; ReMP; SeCePo; SeCeV; StP; TDP; UnPo (3d ed.); WaP
Turning Aside from Battles. Sextus Propertius, *tr. fr. Latin by* Ezra Pound. WaaP
Turning aside, never meeting. The Poacher. R. S. Thomas. POTi
Turning Dervish, The. Arthur Symons. MoBrPo
Turning from Plato to the rocky sergeant. Apocalypse. John Frederick Nims. MiAP
Turning from Shelley's sculptured face aside. On a Grave in Christ-Church, Hants. Oscar Fay Adams. AA
Turning it over, considering, like a madman. The Dream Songs, LXXV. John Berryman. NaP
Turning of the Babies in the Bed, The. Paul Laurence Dunbar. MAP; MoAmPo (1942 ed.); NeMA
Turning of the Leaves, The. Vernon Watkins. FaBoMo; NeBP
Turning the corner, I. Second Sight. W. S. Merwin. StP
Turning the secrets from her pack of cards. A Fortune-Teller. Witter Bynner. HBMV
Turnip Seller, The. Samuel Johnson. *See* Of the Man Who Turnips Cries.
Turnstile, The. William Barnes. CH; OBVV
Turris Eburnea. Aubrey Thomas De Vere. *Fr.* May Carols. PoVP
Turris Eburnea. *Unknown.* GoBC
Turtle, The. Ogden Nash. FaFP; FiBHP; LiTM; NePA; SiTL; WhC
(Autres Bêtes, Autres Moeurs.) NAMP; TreFS
Turtle, The. James Schevill. FiMAP
Turtle, The. *Unknown.* PAH
Turtle and Flamingo, The. James Thomas Fields. BOHV; HBV
(Song of the Turtle and Flamingo.) GN
Turtle, clam, and crab as well, The. Covering the Subject. Richard Armour. RePo; WaKn

Turtle-Dove, The. *Unknown.* OxBoLi
(“Oh, don't you see the turtle-dove.”) LO
Turtle Dove, The. Geoffrey Hill. NePoEA
Turtle-Dove's Nest, The. *Unknown, sometimes at. to* Ann Hawkshaw. HBVY, *abr.*; OTPC (1923 ed.); SAS
(“High in the pine-tree.”) BoTP
Turtle is a simple byrde, The. *Unknown.* SeCSL
Turtle lives 'twixt plated decks, The. The Turtle [*or* Autres Bêtes, Autres Moeurs]. Ogden Nash. FaFP; FiBHP; LiTM; NAMP; SiTL; TreFS; WhC
Turtle on yon withered bough, The. Song of Thyrsis. Philip Freneau. *Fr.* Female Frailty. AA; AnFE; APA; CoAnAm; HBV; LiTA; OnPM; ViBoPo
Turtle Soup. “Lewis Carroll.” *Fr.* Alice's Adventures in Wonderland, *ch.* 10. InMe
(“Beautiful soup, so rich and green.”) Par
Turtle-tortle, what dost thou there? Play-Song. *Unknown.* LiTW
Turtle Town. Helen Wing. GFA
Turvey Top. William Sawyer. BOHV; NA
Tuscan Cypress, *sels.* Agnes Mary Frances Robinson.
“Ah love, I cannot die,” XV.
(Rispetto.) HBMV
“Ah me, you well might wait,” VIII. VA
“Let us forget we loved each other,” XII.
(Rispetto.) HBMV
“Love me today and think not,” IV. VA
“What good is there, ah me,” II.
(Rispetto.) HBMV
“When I am dead,” VII. VA
Tuscan, that wanderest through the realms of gloom. Dante. Longfellow. AA; AnNE; CoBA; MAmP
Tush hang it, have at all, says Curio. Henry Parrot. SiCE
Tuskegee. Leslie Pinckney Hill. BANP; PoNe
Tusks of Blood, The. Samuel Greenberg. MoPo
Tusks that clashed in mighty brawls, The. On the Vanity of Earthly Greatness. Arthur Guiterman. HoPM; NAMP; PoPl; PoPo; PV; TrJP; WhC
Tuslag. T. A. Robertson. OxBS
Tut! Bah! We take another case. The Poets at Tea, 5. Barry Pain. Par
Tutelage, The. Robert Mowry Bell. AA
Tutivillus, the Devil. *Unknown.* MeEL
Tutor [Who Tooted the Flute], A. Carolyn Wells. *See* Limerick: “Tutor who tooted the flute, A.”
Tutto è Sciolto. James Joyce. OBMV; OxBI
Twa Books, The. Allan Ramsay. OxBS
Twa Brothers, The (*diff. versions*). *Unknown.* ATP; BaBo (A *and* B *vers.*); CH; ESPB (A *and* B *vers.*); OBB; OxBB; ViBoFo (A *and* B *vers.*)
(Two Little Boys.) BaBo
Twa Corbies, The. *Unknown.* AnFE; BoLiVe; CBEP; CH; ELP; EnL; EnLi-1; EnLit; EnSB; ESPB; ExPo; FaBoCh; FIW; FosPo; GoTS; GTBS; GTBS-D; GTBS-P; GTBS-W; GTSE; GTSL; HBV; ILP; InP; InPo; LiTL; LoGBV; NoP; OBB; OBEV; OxBS; PIA; PoAn; SeCePo; SeCeV; ShBV-2; StP; StPo; TOP
(“As I was walking all alane.”) LO
(Three Crows, The, *with music.*) BFSS
(Three Ravens, The, B *vers.*) BaBo; ViBoPo
(Two Corbies, The.) BuBa; Po
Twa Dogs, The. Burns. CABL; CEP
Twa Knights, The. *Unknown.* ESPB
Twa Magicians, The. *Unknown.* BaBo; ESPB; OxBB
Twa race doon by the Gatehope-Slack. Solway Sands. Elizabeth Craigmyle. VA
Twa Sisters, The. *Unknown.* *See* Two Sisters, The.
Twain that, in twining, before in the twine, The. A Twister. *Unknown.* SiTL
Twain that were foes, while Mary lived, are fled. His Lady's Death. Pierre de Ronsard. *Fr.* Amours de Marie. AWP
Twang. T. L. Robinson. WSL
'Twas a balmy summer evening, and a goodly crowd was there. The Face upon [*or* on] the [Barroom] Floor. H. Antoine D'Arcy. BeLS; BLPA; FaBoBe; FaFP; GSP; HBV; NeHB; PaPo; TreF; YaD
'Twas a balmy summer morning. The Dawning of the Day. James Clarence Mangan. GoBC
'Twas a busy day in the courtroom, and a curious crowd was there. The Bank Thief. J. R. Farrell. BeLS; BLPA
'Twas a calm and peaceful evening in a camp called Arapahoe. Buckskin Joe. *Unknown.* CoSo
'Twas a Christmas morning. Stagolee. *Unknown.* ABF
'Twas a dangerous cliff, as they freely confessed. A Fence or an Ambulance. Joseph Malins. BLPA
'Twas a death-bed summons, and forth I went. Her Death and After. Thomas Hardy. ViPo (1962 ed.)
'Twas a dispute 'twixt heav'n and earth. Song. Earl of Rochester. PeRV
'Twas a fierce night when old Mawgan died. Mawgan of Melhuach. Robert Stephen Hawker. EPN; VA
'Twas a Friday morn when we set sail. The Mermaid. *Unknown.* LiTG; SiTL; TreF
'Twas a grand display was the prince's ball. Baron Renfrew's Ball. Charles Graham Halpine. PAH
'Twas a Jacqueminot rose. A Rose. Arlo Bates. HBV
'Twas a jolly old pedagogue, long ago. The Jolly Old Pedagogue. George Arnold. HBV; OnPP; TreFS
'Twas a long journey lay before us. Journey to Brundusium. Horace. WoL
'Twas a new feeling—something more. Did Not [*or* Quantum Est Quod Desit]. Thomas Moore. ALV; EnLoPo; ErPo; NBM
'Twas a pleasant summer's morning. As I'd Nothing Else to Do. Herbert Fry. TreFS
'Twas a pretty little maiden. The Lost Pleiad. Arthur Reed Ropes. BOHV
'Twas a Sheep. . .Not a Lamb. *Unknown.* SoP
'Twas a stylish congregation, that of Theophrastus Brown. Trouble in the Amen Corner. T. C. Harbaugh. BLPA
'Twas a tough task, believe it, thus to tame. Upon Dr. Davies' British Grammar. James Howell. PrWP
'Twas a wonderful brave fight. The Fight at Sumter. *Unknown.* PAH
'Twas after a supper of Norfolk brawn. Turvey Top. William Sawyer. BOHV; NA
'Twas after dread Pultowa's day. Mazeppa. Byron. EnRP; MERP
'Twas all along the Binder Line. Sensitive Sydney. Wallace Irwin. FiBHP
'Twas all on a winter's night. Mary of the Wild Moor. *Unknown.* BFSS
'Twas all on board a ship down in a southern sea. The Golden Vanity. *Unknown.* BaBo
'Twas an evening in November. *Unknown.* CenHV
'Twas April when she came to town. Bessie Brown, M. D. Samuel Minturn Peck. BOHV
'Twas at thatt hour of beauty when the setting sun. Robert Bridges. *Fr.* The Testament of Beauty. MoVE; OxBoCh
'Twas at the Cimarron Crossing. Oliver Wiggins. “Stanley Vestal.” IHA
'Twas at the Pictures, Child, We Met. A. P. Herbert. WhC
'Twas at the royal feast, for Persia won. Alexander's Feast; or, The Power of Music. Dryden. ACP; AnFE; ATP; BoLiVe; CEP; CoBE; EiCL; EiPP; EnL; EnLi-1; EnLit; FiP; GN; GoBC; GTBS; GTBS-D; GTBS-P; GTBS-W; GTSE; GTSL; HBV; LiTB; LoBV; MBW-1; NoP; OAEP; OBS; OtMeF; OuHeWo; PoE; SeCeV; SeCV-2; SeEP; StP; TOP; TrGrPo; WHA; WiR; YAT
'Twas at the silent, solemn hour. William and Margaret. David Mallet. CEP; OBEC
'Twas August, and the fierce sun overhead. East London. Matthew Arnold. EPN; MaRV; OAEP; OHIP; PoVP; StJW; WGRP
'Twas autumn daybreak gold and wild. The Three Beggars. Walter de la Mare. RIS
'Twas battered and scarred, and the auctioneer. The Touch of the Master's Hand. Myra Brooks Welch. BLPA; FaChP; PoToHe (new ed.); SoP; STF; TRV
'Twas Bedford Special Assize, one daft Midsummer's Day. Ned Bratts. Robert Browning. CABL
'Twas brillig, and the slithy toves. Jabberwocky. “Lewis Carroll.” *Fr.* Through the Looking-Glass. ALV; BoChLi; CABA; CaFP; CBEP; CBV; DiPo; EnLi-2 (1949 ed.); FaBoBe; FaBV; FaFP; FaPON; FiBHP; GoJo; GoTP; HBV; HoPM; InP; LBN; LiTB; LiTG; NA; NAMP; NBM; OnSP; OTPC; PeVV; PIA; PoIE; PoPl; PoPo; PoRA; PoVP; RIS; SeCeV; ShBV-2; SiTL; TiPo; TreF; TrGrPo; VaPo; WhC
'Twas brussels, and the loos liège. Somewhere-in-Europe-Wocky. F. G. Hartswick. BOHV
'Twas but a poor little room: a farm servant's loft in a garret. Dorothy's Room. Arthur Joseph Munby. *Fr.* Dorothy; a Country Story. VA

'Twas but a single Rose. Upon a Virgin Kissing a Rose. Robert Herrick. SCEP-2; SeCP; SeCV-1
'Twas Captain Church, bescarred and brown. King Philip's Last Stand. Clinton Scollard. PAH
'Twas Christmas Eve, the snow lay deep. When the Christ Child Came. Frederic E. Weatherly. OHIP
'Twas down at Dan McDevitt's at the corner of this street. Throw Him Down M'Closkey. John W. Kelley. TreF
'Twas early in the month of May. Barbara Allen. *Unknown.* CBEP
'Twas early on a May morning. Lady Isabel. *Unknown.* BaBo; ESPB
'Twas Euclid, and the theorem pi. Plane Geometry. Emma Rounds. ImOP
'Twas eve, and Time, his vigorous course pursuing. Akinetos. Richard Henry Horne. *Fr.* Orion. VA
'Twas evening, though not sun-set, and spring-tide [*or* the tide]. Tamar and the Nymph [*or* The Shepherd and the Nymph]. Walter Savage Landor. *Fr.* Gebir. EnRP; OBNC; PeER; VA
'Twas Ever Thus. Henry S. Leigh. BOHV; HBV
'Twas ever thus from childhood's hour! Disaster. Charles Stuart Calverley. BOHV; CenHV; HBV
'Twas Friday morn: the train drew near. Through Baltimore. Bayard Taylor. PAH
'Twas Friday morn when we set sail. The Mermaid (B *vers.*). *Unknown.* ViBoFo
'Twas gilbert. The kchesterton. The Jabberwocky of Authors. Harry Persons Taber. BOHV
'Twas going to snow—'twas snowing! Curse his luck! The Drove-Road. W. W. Gibson. EnLit
'Twas good to live when all the range. Way Out West. *Unknown.* CoSo
'Twas Goosey Goosey Gander. Goosey Goosey Gander—by Various Authors (Macaulay's Version). William Percy French. CenHV
'Twas homeward bound one night on the deep. Lady Franklin's Lament, *vers.* II. *Unknown.* ShS
'Twas hurry and scurry at Monmouth town. Molly Pitcher. Kate Brownlee Sherwood. GoTP; MC; OTPC (1946 ed.); PAH
'Twas in a basement tobble d'hote. Reverie. Don Marquis. PoLF
'Twas in eighteen hundred and fifty-three. The Greenland Whale Fishery [*or* Greenland Fishery]. *Unknown.* SoAmSa; ViBoFo
'Twas in heaven pronounced, and 'twas muttered in hell. *See* 'Twas whispered in heaven. . .
'Twas in mid autumn, and the woods were still. Death as the Teacher of Love-Lore. Frank T. Marzials. VA
'Twas in the that island summer where. He Loves and He Rides Away. Sydney Dobell. OBNC
'Twas in that place o' Scotland's Isle. The Twa Dogs. Burns. CABL; CEP
'Twas in that pleasant season, when the year. Consolation. George Darley. ERoP-2
'Twas in the days of the Revolution. Emily Geiger. *Unknown.* PAL; PoLF
'Twas in the grey and dawning light. The Easter Glory. A. J. Beattie. SoP
'Twas in the lonely stable whence the Holy Babe had gone. The Murmur from the Stable. Rubén Darío. CAW
'Twas in the merry month of May. Barbara Allen. *Unknown.* TrAS
'Twas in the middle of the night. Mary's Ghost. Thomas Hood. FiBHP
'Twas in the month of August, or the middle of July. She Said the Same to Me. *Unknown.* AS
'Twas in the month of December, and in the year 1883. The Famous Tay Whale. William McGonagall. PeVV
'Twas in the month of February 'way down in the Southern Seas. Blow Ye Winds, 2. *Unknown.* SoAmSa
'Twas in the month when lilacs bloom. Dutchman's Breeches. Arthur Guiterman. YT
'Twas in the moon of winter time when all the birds had fled. Jesous Ahatonhia. Jesse Edgar Middleton, *after* Jean de Brébeuf. CaP; ChrBoLe
'Twas in the night the manna fell. Manna. Margaret E. Sangster. SoP
'Twas in the prime of summer time. The Dream of Eugene Aram. Thomas Hood. BeLS; EnRP; HBV; StPo; VA
'Twas in the reign of George the Third. A New Song Called the Gaspee. *Unknown.* PAH
'Twas in the schooner *Kandahar.* The Schooner *Kandahar. At. to* Sepley Collin. ShS
'Twas in the town of Jacksboro in the spring [*or* year] of seventy-three. The Buffalo Skinners. *Unknown.* ABF; AS; BaBo
'Twas in the year of eighty-five. A Woodsman Goes to Sea. Charles R. Knapp. IHA
'Twas in the year of forty-nine. The Whale. *Unknown.* ChTr
'Twas in the year two thousand and one. The Last Man. Thomas Hood. OBRV
'Twas in the years of long ago. My Name in Mother's Prayer. *Unknown.* SoP
'Twas Jolly, Jolly Wat. C. W. Stubbs. OHIP
'Twas Juet spoke—the *Half Moon's* mate. The Death of Colman. Thomas Frost. PAH
'Twas June on the face of the earth, June with the rose's breath. The Eve [*or* On the Eve] of Bunker Hill. Clinton Scollard. DD; MC; PAH; PEDC; PoRL
'Twas just at sunrise, and a glorious day. The Battle of Erie. *Unknown.* PAH
'Twas Just before the Hay Was Mown. Charles Swain. VA
'Twas just before the last fierce charge. The Last Fierce Charge. *Unknown.* ViBoFo
'Twas just this time, last year, I died. Emily Dickinson. DiPo
'Twas late, and the gay company was gone. The Declaration. Nathaniel Parker Willis. BOHV
'Twas late in my long journey, when I had clomb to where. Introduction. Robert Bridges. *Fr.* The Testament of Beauty. MoVE
'Twas late last night when my lord came home. The Raggle Taggle Gypsies. *Unknown.* GoTP
'Twas later when the summer went. Emily Dickenson. OnPM
'Twas like a maelstrom, with a notch. Emily Dickinson. AmePo; CABA; CMoP; ExPo; LiTA; LiTM; NePA; NoP; SeCeV
'Twas long ago—ere ever the signal gun. How He Saved St. Michael's. Mary A. P. Stansbury. BLPA
'Twas long ago I read the story sweet. Hidden Treasure. *Unknown.* FaChP
'Twas May upon the mountains, and on the airy wing. The Surprise at Ticonderoga. Mary A. P. Stansbury. MC; PAH
'Twas mercy brought me from my pagan land. On Being Brought from Africa to America. Phillis Wheatley. BALP; Kal; TTY
'Twas midnight—Donna Julia was in bed. Byron. *Fr.* Don Juan. UnTE
'Twas midnight on the ocean. The Dying Fisherman's Song. *Unknown.* TreFT
'Twas midsummer; cooling breezes all the languid forests fanned. The Death of Jefferson. Hezekiah Butterworth. PAH; ThLM
'Twas moonlight in the ripe barley. The Walking of the Moon-Woman. John Shaw Neilson. ACV
'Twas more than a million years ago. Annabel Lee. Stanley Huntley. BOHV
'Twas my Beloved spake. Canticle. John Norris. SeCL; SeEP
Twas my pleasure to walk in the river meadows. The Midnight Court. Brian Merriman, *tr. by* Frank O'Connor. AnIL
'Twas my wont to wander beside the stream. The Midnight Court. Brian Merriman, *tr. by* Arland Ussher. OnYI
'Twas Night. *Unknown.* OBS
'Twas night; the noise and bustle of the day. Bologna and Byron. Samuel Rogers. *Fr.* Italy. OBRV
'Twas night upon the Darro. The Thanksgiving for America. Hezekiah Butterworth. PAH
'Twas noontide of summer. Evening Star. Poe. AmP; AP; MAmP; MWA-1
'Twas not enough, Ben Johnson, to be thought. To His Friend Ben. Johnson, of His Horace Made English. Lord Herbert of Cherbury. AnAnS-2
'Twas not his person nor his partes. *Unknown.* SeCSL
'Twas not in him to deal with cringing touch. Roosevelt. T. E. Thomas. PEDC
'Twas not my wish. About the Shelleys. *Unknown, quoted by* Wordsworth. WhC
'Twas November the fourth, in the year of ninety-one. Sainclaire's Defeat. *Unknown.* PAH

'Twas now the hour that turneth back desire. Dante. *Fr.* Divina Commedia: Purgatorio. CAW
Twas of a gay young cavalier. Riddles Wisely Expounded. *Unknown.* BaBo (C *vers.*); ViBoFo (B *vers.*)
'Twas of a lofty ship, boys, and she put out to sea. The *Golden Vanity. Unknown.* SoAmSa
'Twas of a maiden both young and fair. The Dark-eyed Sailor. *Unknown.* ShS
'Twas on a Holy Thursday, their innocent faces clean. Holy Thursday. Blake. *Fr.* Songs of Innocence. AnFE; BoC; CBEP; CEP; CH; CoBE; DiPo; EG; EiCL; EiPP; EnL; EnPE; EnRP; ERoP-1; HBV; MemP; NoP; OAEP; OBEC; OTPC; PeER; PoE; PoeP; PoFS; PoIE; StP; YAT
'Twas on a lofty vase's side. Ode on [*or* On] the Death of a Favourite Cat, Drowned in a Tub of Goldfishes [*or* On a Favourite Cat Drowned. . .]. Thomas Gray. ATP; BEL; BeLS; BOHV; CBEP; CEP; CIV; EiCL; EiCP; EnLi-2 (1949 ed.); EnLit; ExPo; FaBoBe; GBV (1952 ed.); GN; GTBS; GTBS-D; GTBS-P; GTBS-W; GTSE; GTSL; HBV; HoPM; InMe; InvP; LiTB; LiTG; MCCG; NeHB; NoP; OAEP; OBEC; OBEV; OnSP; OTPC (1923 ed.); PAn; PoE; PoEL-3; PoLF; PoRA; SeCeV; ShBV-2; TDP; TOP; VaPo; WiR; YAT
'Twas on a Monday morning. Charlie, He's [*or* Is] My Darling. Burns. *See also* An' Charlie he's my darling. HBV; ViBoPo.
'Twas on a Monday morning. Charlie Is My Darling. James Hogg. OTPC (1946 ed.)
'Twas on a Monday morning, the first I saw my darling. Hanging Out the Linen Clothes. *Unknown.* AS
'Twas on a night, an evening bright. Proud Lady Margaret. *Unknown.* BaBo; ESPB
'Twas on a pleasant mountain. The Battle of King's Mountain. *Unknown.* PAH
'Twas on a simmer's afternoon. The Lass o' Gowrie. Lady Nairne. HBV
'Twas on a windy night. The Sabine Farmer's Serenade. Francis Sylvester Mahony. BOHV; HBV
'Twas on an evening fair I went to take the air. Willie's Fatal Visit. *Unknown.* BaBo; ESPB
'Twas on board the sloop of war *Wasp*, boys. The *Wasp's* Frolic. *Unknown.* PAH
'Twas on Lake Erie's broad expanse. John Maynard. Horatio Alger, Jr. BeLS; BLPA; FaBoBe
'Twas on one dark and cheerless night to the south-'ard of the Cape. The *Flying Dutchman. Unknown.* ShS
'Twas on the famous trotting-ground. How the Old Horse Won the Bet. Oliver Wendell Holmes. AnNE
'Twas on the first of February from Lunenburg we set sail. The *Donzella* and the *Ceylon. At. to* Daniel Smith. ShS
'Twas on the fourteenth day of April we sailed from the land. The Bold *Princess Royal, vers.* II. *Unknown.* ShS
'Twas on the glorious day. The Death of General Pike. Laughton Osborn. PAH
'Twas on the Isle of Patmos. The Heavenly Vision. Avis B. Christiansen. SoP
'Twas on the shores that round our coast. The Yarn of the *Nancy Bell.* W. S. Gilbert. ATP (1935 ed.); BBV; BeLS; BLPA; BoChLi; BOHV; CenHV; EtS; EvOK; FaBoBe; FaBoCh; FaBV; FaFP; GBV; GoTP; GSP; HBV; HoPM; InMe; LoGBV; MCCG; MoShBr; OnMSP; OTPC (1946 ed.); PCD; PoVP; PTK; ShBV-1; StVeCh; TreFS; TrGrPo; TSW
'Twas on the twelfth of April. Sumter—a Ballad of 1861. *Unknown.* PAH
'Twas once upon a time, when Jenny Wren was young. Mother Goose. MPB (1956 ed.)
'Twas one October mornin'. Bigerlow. *Unknown.* AS
'Twas one of the charmed days. The Heart of All the Scene. Emerson. *Fr.* Woodnotes, I. AA
'Twas only a cheerful, radiant smile. Life's Little Things. *Unknown.* STF
'Twas out upon mid ocean that the *San Jacinto* hailed. The Death of the Lincoln Despotism. *Unknown.* PAH
'Twas raw, and chill, and cold outside. An Old Bachelor. Tudor Jenks. BOHV; LHV
"'Twas so, I saw thy birth: that drowsy lake. The Shower [*or* Showre]. Henry Vaughan. AnAnS-1; LiTB; MemP; MeP; MePo; SeCP; ViBoPo
'Twas spring, and dawn returning breathed new-born. Idyll of the Rose. Decimus Magnus Ausonius. AWP
'Twas summer, and the spot a cool retreat. A Dream. Elizabeth Clementine Kinney. AA
'Twas summer, and the sun had mounted high. The Wanderer. Wordsworth. *Fr.* The Excursion, I. EnRP
'Twas Summer I recall. Elegies, III. Philippe Thoby-Marcelin. PoNe
'Twas summer time, the radiant world of June. John Francis O'Donnell. *Fr.* Happy Christmases. IrPN
'Twas sung of old how one Amphion. Poverty and Poetry. Thomas Tickell. WaPE
'Twas sure a luckless planet. Out of Luck. Abraham ibn Ezra. TrJP
'Twas the body of Judas Iscariot. The Ballad of Judas Iscariot. Robert Buchanan. HBV; VA
'Twas the day beside the Pyramids. The Old Grenadier's Story. George Walter Thornbury. VA
'Twas the dead of the night. By the pineknot's red light. New England's Chevy Chase. Edward Everett Hale. HBV; HBVY; PAH; PAL; PoRL; YaD
'Twas the deep mid-watch of the silent night. The Cid's Rising. Felicia Dorothea Hemans. FOL; OBRV
'Twas the dream of a God. Ireland. Dora Sigerson Shorter. OBEV; OBVV; OxBI
'Twas the end of round-up, the last day of June. Whose Old Cow? *Unknown.* CoSo
'Twas the eve before Christmas. "Good night," had been said. Annie and Willie's Prayer. Sophia P. Snow. BeLS; BLPA
'Twas the Frogge in the well. The Marriage of the Frog and the Mouse. *Unknown.* OA
'Twas the heart of the murky night, and the lowest ebb of the tide. Wayne at Stony Point. Clinton Scollard. MC; PAH
'Twas the lean coyote told me, baring his slavish soul. The Desert. Henry Herbert Knibbs. SCC
'Twas the night before Christmas, when all through the house. A Visit from St. Nicholas [*or* The Night Before Christmas]. Clement C. Moore. AA; AmePo; BeLS; BLPA; BoChLi; BOHV; ChBR; DD; FaBoBe; FaBV; FaFP; FaPON; GaP; GFA; GoTP; HBV; HBVY; HH; LHV; MPB; NeHB; OHFP; OnMSP; OTPC; PaPo; PCH; PEDC; PoPl; PoRh; PRWS; PTK; RePo; RIS; SAS; SiSoSe; StVeCh; TiPo; TreF; TVC; WBLP; YaD
'Twas the proud Sir Peter Parker came sailing in from the sea. The Boasting of Sir Peter Parker. Clinton Scollard. PAH
'Twas the soul of Judas Iscariot. Judas Iscariot. Robert Buchanan. *Fr.* The Ballad of Judas Iscariot. OBVV; OxBoCh
'Twas the spring in the air. Danny's Wooing. David McKee Wright. PoAu-1
'Twas the very verge of May. Dewey at Manila. Robert Underwood Johnson. HBV; MC; PAH
'Twas the voice of the sweet dove. The Old Sweet Dove of Wiveton. Stevie Smith. OA; PoG
'Twas the year of the famine in Plymouth of old. Five Kernels of Corn. Hezekiah Butterworth. DD; MC; PAH
'Twas then I thought I'd have some fun. Breaking in a Tenderfoot. *Unknown.* IHA
'Twas three an' thirty year ago. The Rivals. Paul Laurence Dunbar. IHA
'Twas thus the subtle love. Three Hymns, 1. Charles Wesley. WaPE
'Twas twilight, and the sunless day went down. The Shipwreck. Byron. *Fr.* Don Juan. OBRV; WHA
'Twas warm—at first—like us. Emily Dickinson. CMoP; ExPo; ForPo; LiTA; QFR
'Twas when bright Cynthia with her silver car. A Night-Piece; or Modern Philosophy. Christopher Smart. VaPo
'Twas when fleet Snowball's head was waxen gray. Sir Walter Scott. *Fr.* The Fortunes of Nigel. NBM
'Twas when the rain fell steady an' the Ark was pitched an' ready. The Legends of Evil, II. Kipling. MoShBr
'Twas when the sea's tremendous roar. My Father's at the Helm. *Unknown.* BePJ
'Twas when the seas were roaring. A Ballad. John Gay. *Fr.* The What D'Ye Call It. CEP; HBV; StP; ViBoPo
'Twas whispered in Heaven [*or* in heaven pronounced], 'twas muttered in Hell. A Riddle [*or* Enigma on the Letter H]. Catherine M. Fanshawe. BOHV; ChTr; GN; GoTP; LiTG; OTPC; RIS; SiTL
'Twas yesterday He made me and tomorrow I shall die. Song of the Gulf Stream. Francis Alan Ford. EtS
Tweed and Till. *Unknown.* *See* Two Rivers.
Tweed Visited, The. William Lisle Bowles. Sonn

Tweedledum and Tweedledee. Mother Goose. NA; OTPC; OxNR; RIS; SiTL
'Tween Earth and Sky. Augusta Webster. *See* Seeds.
"Tweet" pipes the robin as the cat creeps by. The Firetail's Nest. John Clare. EnRP; Sonn
12th Dance—Getting Leather by Language—21 Februray 1964. Jackson MacLow. CoPo
Twelfth day of Christmas, The. The Twelve Days of Christmas. *Unknown.* LiTL; OxBoLi
Twelfth Night. John Peale Bishop. UnPo (3d ed.)
Twelfth Night. Philip Booth. NePoEA
Twelfth Night. Elizabeth J. Coatsworth. *See* Song of the Camels.
Twelfth Night. Laurie Lee. BoC
Twelfth Night, *sels.* Shakespeare.
"Come away, come away, death," *fr.* II, iv. AnFE; AtBAP; CBEP; EG; ElL; EnLi-1 (1949 ed.); ExPo; ILP; InPo; MaPo; NoP; OAEP; OBSC; PAn; PoEL-2; SiCE; TOP; ViBoPo; WHA
(Clown's Song, The.) CTC
(Come Away, Death.) DiPo; ELP; PoRA; SeCeV
(Dirge.) OBEV
(Dirge of Love.) GTBS; GTBS-D; GTBS-P; GTBS-W; GTSE; GTSL
(Feste's Song.) VaPo
(Love's Despair.) TrGrPo
(Song: "Come away, come away, death.") FiP
(Two of Feste's Songs.) BoLiVe
"Come hither, boy: if ever thou shalt love," *fr.* II, iv. LO
"Give me some music.—Now, good morrow, friends," II, iv. MyFE
If Music Be the Food of Love, *fr.* I, i. PoFS; UnS
(Food of Love, The.) TrGrPo
(Music.) TreFS
Love, *fr.* II, iii. TreFT
"Make me a willow cabin at your gate," *fr.* I, v. MemP
"O Mistress mine, where are you roaming," *fr.* II, iii. AnFE; BEL; CLwM; EG; ElL; EnL; EnLi-1; EnLit; ExPo; LoBV; MaPo (1969 ed.); OAEP; OBSC; OuHeWo; PoE; SiCE; TOP; WHA
(Carpe Diem.) GTBS; GTBS-D; GTBS-P; GTBS-W; GTSE; GTSL
(Clown's Song: "O mistris mine where are you roming?") FaBoEn
(Feste's Song from Twelfth Night.) ALV
(O Mistress Mine.) BoLP; CBEP; CTC; DiPo; ELP; EnRePo; FaBV; FaFP; HH; InMe; InPo; LiTB; MCCG; MeWo; NoP; OtMeF; PAn; PoeP; PoFS; PoPo; PoRA; SeCeV; ShBV-2; TreFT; TrGrPo; ViBoPo; WePo
(Song: "O mistress mine, where are you roaming?") FiP; GoJo; HBV; MemP; PG (1945 ed.)
(Songs from the Plays.) AWP; JAWP; WBP
(Sweet-and-twenty.) LiTG; LiTL; OBEV
(Two of Feste's Songs.) BoLiVe
She Never Told Her Love, *fr.* II, iv. MemP; MeWo
(Love Concealed.) TreFS
(Patience on a Monument.) TrGrPo
"When that I was and a little tiny boy," *fr.* V, i. AnFE; AtBAP; CH; EG; ElL; EnRePo; ExPo; FaBoCh; HBV; InPo; LiTB; LoBV; LoGBV; MyFE; NoP; OAEP; OBSC; PoEL-2; PoIE; PoRA; SiCE; SiTL; ViBoPo; WaKn
(Epilogue: "When that I was and a little tiny boy.") WePo
(Feste's Final Song.) VaPo
(Feste's Song.) OxBoLi
(Rain It Raineth Every Day, The.) OTPC (1923 ed.)
(Song: "When that I was and a little tiny boy.") EP; FiP; LiTG
(Wind and the Rain, The.) CBEP; DiPo; WiR
Twelfth Night Carol. *Unknown.* PCD; PCH; PoRL
12th Raga: For John Wieners. David Meltzer. NeAP
Twelve, The. Aleksandr Aleksandrovich Blok, *tr. fr. Russian by* Babette Deutsch and Avrahm Yarmolinsky. AWP, *abr.*; LiTW; PoFr, *abr.*
Twelve Articles. Swift. BOHV; InMe
Twelve Bells/ Benny's on the ropes. The Memory of Boxer Benny (Kid) Paret. Frank Lima. PoNe (1970 ed.)
Twelve by the Clock. Jorge Guillén, *tr. fr. Spanish by* Frances Avery Pleak. WoL
Twelve Days of Christmas, The ("The first day of Christmas"). *Unknown.* FaFP; LiTL; OxBoLi; OxNR; RePo; SiTL; TreFT
(First Day of Christmas, The.) ChBR
Twelve-Elf, The. Christian Morgenstern, *ad. fr. German by* Louis Untermeyer. StaSt
Twelve Gates. Lorenzo Thomas. BF
Twelve good friends. Peter and John. Elinor Wylie. HBMV; MaC; MAP; MoAB; MoAmPo; MoBS; MoRP; StJW
Twelve Good Joys. *Unknown.* OBB
"Twelve herds of oxen, no lesse flockes of sheepe." Homer. *Fr.* The Odyssey, XIV. CTC
Twelve hundred million men are spread. Kipling. PV
Twelve little figures around me. A Clock. *Unknown.* OTPC (1946 ed.)
Twelve Months, The. "Gregory Gander." TreFT
Twelve o'clock/ Along the reaches of the street. Rhapsody on a Windy Night. T. S. Eliot. ACV; AmP; CMoP; ExPo; InPo; MAP; MoAmPo (1942 ed.)
Twelve o'clock—a misty night. The Hightwayman's Ghost. Richard Garnett. StPo
Twelve o'Clock Boat. J. A. R. McKellar. BoAV; MoAuPo
Twelve Oxen. *Unknown.* *See* I Have Twelve Oxen.
Twelve pears [*or* pairs] hanging high. Mother Goose. BoChLi; OxNR
Twelve P.M. William Dean Howells. AmePo
Twelve Properties or Conditions of a Lover, The, *sels.* Sir Thomas More.
Eleventh Property, The. EnRePo
First Property, The EnRePo
Seventh Property, The. CoBE; EnRePo
Tenth Properte, The. CoBE
Twelve snails went walking after night. The Haughty Snail-King. Vachel Lindsay. LOW
Twelve Spartan virgins, noble, young, and fair. Song of the Sleepy Bridgegroom. Theocritus. *Fr.* Idylls, XVIII. HW
Twelve stars upon the brow of her. Our Lady of the Skies. James M. Hayes. ISi
Twelve Weapons of Spiritual Battle, The, *sels.* Sir Thomas More. EnRePo
Eternal Reward, Eternal Pain.
Peace of a Good Mind, The.
This Life a Dream and Shadow.
Twelve years ago I made a mock. School and Schoolfellows. Winthrop Mackworth Praed. OBRV
Twelve years ago, when I could face. The Voice in the Wild Oak. Henry Clarence Kendall. VA
Twelve years old, my father put. Harvest Time. G. A. Watermeyer. PeSA
Twentieth-Century Blues. Kenneth Fearing. CMoP
Twentieth Century Love-Song. Richard Church. HaMV
Twentieth year is well nigh past, The. To Mary [*or* My Mary *or* To the Same]. William Cowper. BEL; CBEP; EiCP; EiPP; EnLi-2 (1949 ed.); EnLoPo; EnRP; FaPL; FiP; GTBS; GTBS-D; GTBS-P; GTBS-W; GTSE; GTSL; LiTL; LO; OAEP; OBEC; OBEV; TreFS
Twenty abreast down the Golden Street ten thousand riders marched. Riders of the Stars. Henry Herbert Knibbs. SCC
Twenty Below. R. A. D. Ford. CaP
Twenty brothers of Eynhallow, The. Our Lady of the Waves. George Mackay Brown. NePoEA-2
Twenty-eight young men bathe by the shore. Song of Myself, XI. Walt Whitman. ExPo; MaPo
25 December 1960. Ingrid Jonker, *tr. fr. Afrikaans by* Jack Cope *and* Uys Krige. PeSA
Twenty Foolish Fairies. Nancy Byrd Turner. SUS
Twenty, forty, sixty, eighty. Then. Walter de la Mare. GaP; TVC
Twenty-four Years. Dylan Thomas. CMoP; DiPo; LiTM; MoAB; PoIE; ToPo
Twenty-fourth of December, The. *Unknown.* PCH
Twenty-fourth Psalm, The [*wr.*]. Psalms, XXIX, Bible, *O.T.* PoPo
Twenty Froggies. George Cooper. *See* Frogs at School.
Twenty Golden Years Ago. James Clarence Mangan. IrPN, *abr.*; NBM, *abr.*; OnYI; PeER
Twenty lost years have stoln their hours away. Alone, in an Inn (at Southampton). Aaron Hill. EiCL
29th Dance—Having an Instrument—22 March 1964. Jackson MacLow. CoPo
Twenty-ninth Ode of the Third Book of Horace, The. Horace. *See* To Maecenas.
Twenty-one miles of boys in blue. The Last Review. Emily J. Bugbee. BLPA

Twenty-second of August, The. The Cruise of the *Fair American*. *Unknown.* PAH
Twenty-second of December, The. Bryant. GN
Twenty-second of February, The. Bryant. DD; HH; MPB; OTPC (1946 ed.); PoRL
Twenty Stars to Match His Face. William Stanley Braithwaite. HBMV
Twenty-third Psalm, The. Psalms, XXIII, Bible, *O.T.* *See* Lord Is My Shepherd, The.
Twenty-Third Psalm. Dawn Finlay. SoP
Twenty-Third Psalm ("God of love my shepherd is"). *Unknown, at. to* George Herbert. CBV; MaMe; SeCSL
Twenty-third Street Runs into Heaven. Kenneth Patchen. ErPo
Twenty white horses. *See* Thirty white horses upon a red hill.
Twenty Years After. Evan V. Shute. CaP
Twenty Years Ago. *Unknown.* *See* Forty Years Ago.
Twenty years ago. Mud. Richard Church. MoBrPo (1942 ed.)
Twenty years are gone. Palinode. Oliver St. John Gogarty. OBMV; PG (1955 ed.)
Twenty Years Hence. Walter Savage Landor. EPN; OBEV (1st ed.); PCD; TOP; TrGrPo; ViBoPo
(Poems, LVIII.) PG
'Twere a dree night, a dree night, as the squire's end drew nigh. The Dree Night. *Unknown.* ChTr
'Twere Long to Tell. Wordsworth. *Fr.* The Prelude, II. AtBAP
'Twere time that I died too, now she is dead. The Lady Venetia Digby. Ben Jonson. GoBC
Twice. M. M. Hutchinson. BoTP
Twice. Christina Rossetti. GTSL; OBEV; OBNC; OBVV; ViBoPo
Twice a week the winter thorough. A. E. Housman. A Shropshire Lad, XVII. PoVP
Twice a year,/ Chatty and blithe. Alma Mater, Forget Me. William Cole. FiBHP
Twice Fed. A. A. Bassett. HBV
Twice had Diana bent her golden bowe. Giles Fletcher. *Fr.* Christ's Victory and Triumph: Christ's Victory On Earth. SeEP
Twice happy Violets! that first had birth. Violets in Thaumanthia's Bosome. Sir Edward Sherburne. OBS
"Twice have I sought Clan-Alpine's glen." Roderick Dhu. Sir Walter Scott. *Fr.* The Lady of the Lake, V. OBRV
Twice nineteen years, dear Nancy, on this day. On Our Thirty-ninth Wedding Day. Jonathan Odell. CaP
Twice one are two. Twice. M. M. Hutchinson. BoTP
Twice or thrice had I loved thee. Air [or Aire] and Angels. John Donne. AnAnS-1; AtBAP; BoW; BWP; CBEP; EG; EnRePo; MaMe; MBW-1; MeLP; MePo; NoP; OBS; PIA; PoFS; SCEP-1; SeCP; SeCV-1; TuPP
Twice recently young girls have. Finger of Necessity. Coleman Barks. QAH
Twice Shy. Seamus Heaney. TwCP
Twice thirty centuries and more ago. The First Spousal. Coventry Patmore. *Fr.* The Unknown Eros. OBVV
Twice welcome, disrupter of stillness! Night Express. MacKnight Black. NP
Twickenham Ferry. Théophile Marzials. HBV; VA
Twicknam Garden. John Donne. AnAnS-1; EnLoPo; MaMe; MeLP; MePo; OBS; PIA; PoEL-2; PoFS; ReIE; SeCP; SeEP; TuPP
(Twickenham Garden[s].) CBEP; DiPo; LoBV; MBW-1
Twig, The, turned in her hand and the diviner said: "Water." The Water-Witch. Martha Eugenie Perry. CaP
Twigs of the birch imprint the December sky, The. The Prospect. Thomas Hardy. NeMA
Twilight. Ch'en Yün, *tr. fr. Chinese by* Henry H. Hart. LiTW
Twilight. Olive Custance. CAW; HBV; JKCP; VA
Twilight. Eileen Duggan. JKCP (1955 ed.)
Twilight. Gerald Gould. MoBrPo (1942 ed.)
Twilight. Hazel Hall. AnAmPo; HBMV
Twilight. Charles Heavysege. VA
Twilight. Heine, *tr. fr. German by* Louis Untermeyer. AWP; JAWP; WBP
Twilight. D. H. Lawrence. OBMV
Twilight. Longfellow. CH
Twilight. Virginia McCormick. HBMV
Twilight. Joaquin Arcadio Pagaza, *tr. fr. Spanish by* Alice Stone Blackwell. CAW
Twilight. Agnes Mary Frances Robinson. HBV
Twilight. Feodor Ivanovich Tyutchev, *tr. fr. Russian by* Babette Deutsch. OnPM
Twilight, a timid fawn, went glimmering by. Refuge. "Æ." HBV; OnYI; POTE
Twilight. And on a dusty ribboned way. The Road to Emmaus. Ida Norton Munson. ChIP
Twilight: and pine trees keep the blessed enclosure. Convent Cemetery, Mount Carmel. Sister Mary St. Virginia. GoBC
Twilight at Sea. Amelia B. Welby. AA; HBV; OTPC; PTK
Twilight at the Heights. Joaquin Miller. AA
Twilight Calm. Christina Rossetti. BoNaP; GTSE; OBNC
Twilight comes, The; the sun. June Twilight. John Masefield. BoPe; GoYe
Twilight deepens o'er the sleeping hills, The. The Morning Light. *Unknown.* SoP
Twilight falls on the hill. Vespers. Odell Shepard. TrPWD
Twilight Hours, like birds, flew by, The. Twilight at Sea. Amelia B. Welby. AA; HBV; OTPC; PTK
Twilight in California. Philip Dow. QAH
Twilight in Middle March, A. Francis Ledwidge. OnYI; OxBI; WHA
Twilight is sad and cloudy, The. Twilight. Longfellow. CH
Twilight is spacious, near things in it seem far. Miracles. Conrad Aiken. HBMV; MAP; MoAmPo; NeMA
Twilight leaned mirrored in a pool. The Old Angler. Walter de la Mare. GoTL (1949 ed.); OAEP (2d ed.)
Twilight of Disquietude, The, *sels.* Christopher Brennan. PoAu-1
My Heart Was Wandering [in the Sands].
Years That Go to Make Me Man, The.
Twilight of Earth. "Æ." AnIL; TOP
Twilight of the Outward Life. Hugo von Hofmannsthal. *See* Ballad of the Outer Life.
Twilight on Sumter. Richard Henry Stoddard. PAH; PAP
Twilight on Tweed. Andrew Lang. OBVV; PoVP
Twilight People, The. "Seumas O'Sullivan." OnYI
Twilight. Red in the west. The Wild Duck. John Masefield. BEL; BrPo; ShBV-2
Twilight Song. John Hunter-Duvar. *Fr.* De Roberval. VA; WHW
Twilight Song. E. A. Robinson. HBV
Twilight Turns from Amethyst, The. James Joyce. Chamber Music, II. CBV; HW
Twilight twiles in the vernal vale, The. In the Gloaming. James C. Bayles. NA
Twilight was coming on, yet through the gloom. Wordsworth. *Fr.* The Prelude, V. SyP
Twilights. James Wright. NaP
Twilit Revelation. Léonie Adams. MAP; MoAB; MoAmPo
Twin. Phyllis Haring. PeSA
Twin Epitaph. Menke Katz. NYTB
Twin Sisters, The. *Unknown.* *See* Two Sisters, The.
Twin songs there are, of joyance, or of pain. Morton Luce. *Fr.* Thysia. HBV
Twin stars through my purpling pane. Dusk. Angelina Weld Grimké. CDC
Twine laurels to lay o'er the Blue and the Gray. Memorial Day, 1889. S. E. Kiser. DD; HH; PEDC
Twine then the rays. Psycholophon. Gelett Burgess. CenHV; NA
Twined together and, as is customary. Never Such Love. Robert Graves. FaBoEn
Twining a wreath, I found, one day. Love and Wine. Julianus. OnPM
Twink Drives Back, in a Bad Mood, from a Party in Massachusetts. George Amabile. NYBP
Twinkle, twinkle, little bat! *parody.* "Lewis Carroll." *Fr.* Alice's Adventures in Wonderland, *ch.* 7. Par; WhC
Twinkle, Twinkle, Little Star. Jane Taylor. BoTP; GFA; OxNR; SAS; SiTL; TVC
(Little Star, The.) OTPC; StVeCh
(Star, The.) BoChLi; FaBoBe; FaFP; FaPON; HBV; HBVY; MPB; OxNR, *st.* 1; Par, *st.* 1; PCH, *abr.*; PPL; RIS; SoPo, 3 *sts.*; TiPo, *st.* 1; TreF
(Stars at Night, The, 3 *sts.*) ThGo
Twinkling Gown. Dorothy Vena Johnson. GoSl
Twinkum, twankum, twirlum, twitch. The Little Creature. Walter de la Mare. EvOK

Twins, The. Dorothy Aldis. BiCB
Twins. Robert Graves. PV
Twins, The. Kathryn Jackson. BiCB
Twins, The. Henry Sambrooke Leigh. BiCB; BOHV; CenHV; FaPON; GaP; GoTP; HBV; HBVY; MaC; OTPC (1946 ed.); PoMa; PoPl; ShM; StaSt; StVeCh (1940 ed.); TiPo; TSW; WaKn
Twins. "Owen Meredith." ErPo
Twins, The. Elizabeth Madox Roberts. BiCB; TiPo
Twins, The. Karl Shapiro. AnFE; CBV; CoAnAm; MiAP; MoAmPo (1950 ed.); Po; PoSa; TwAmPo
Twins, The. Judith Wright. PoAu-2
Twirl about, dance about. Dreidel Song. Efraim Rosenzweig. TiPo (1952 ed.)
Twirled down the years. Cold Waltzes. Colette Inez. QAH
Twirling your blue skirts, traveling the sward. Blue Girls. John Crowe Ransom. AmP; AnFE; APA; CBV; ChTr; CMoP; CoAnAm; HoPM; LiTA; LiTL; MAP; MoAB; MoAmPo; MoPW; MoVE; NP; PoPo; PoSa; ReMP; TreFT; TwAmPo
Twist about, turn about. *Unknown.* OxNR
Twist Me a Crown. Christina Rossetti. *Fr.* Sing-Song. VA
Twist of fresh flowers of your dark hair, A. Ballade of Muhammad Din Tilai. *Unknown.* PG (1945 ed.)
Twist-Rime on Spring. Arthur Guiterman. PoSC
Twist the tinsel. Round and Round. Dorothy Brown Thompson. BiCB; ChBR
Twist thou and twine! in light and gloom. Featherstone's Doom. Robert Stephen Hawker. OBNC; VA
Twist Ye, Twine Ye! Even So. Sir Walter Scott. *Fr.* Guy Mannering, *ch.* 3. EnRP; TOP
Twisted apple, with rain and magian fire, The. June Morning. Hugh McCrae. BoAV; PoAu-1
Twister Twisting Twine. *Unknown, at. to* John Wallis. ChTr
(Twister, A.) SiTL
("When a twister a-twisting will twist him a twist".) OTPC; OxNR
Twitched strings, the clang of metal, beaten drums. Javanese Dancers. Arthur Symons. PoVP; VA
'Twixt Carrowbrough Edge and Settlingstones. Old Skinflint. W. W. Gibson. OBMV
'Twixt clouded heights Spain hurls to doom. The *Brooklyn* at Santiago. Wallace Rice. PAH
'Twixt Cup and Lip. Mark Hollis. FiBHP
'Twixt death and doubtfulness. To His Lady, of Her Doubtful Answer. Thomas Howell. TuPP
Twixt devil and deep sea, man hacks his caves. Arachne. William Empson. InvP; MoVE; OBMV
'Twixt failure and success the point's so fine. Don't Give Up. *Unknown.* FaFP; PoToHe (new ed.)
Twixt hope & feare the best affection sits. *Unknown.* SeCSL
'Twixt kings and tyrants there's this difference known. Kings and Tyrants. Robert Herrick. PoFr
'Twixt optimist and pessimist. The Difference [*or* Optimist and Pessimist]. *Unknown, at. to* McLandburgh Wilson. GoTP; TreFT
Twixt the Girthhead and Langwood-end. The Lads of Wamphray. *Unknown.* BaBo; ESPB
'Twixt those twin worlds—the world of Sleep. Percy Bysshe shelley. Dante Gabriel Rossetti. Five English Poets, V. PoVP
Twm was a dunce at school, and was whipped and shaken. The Airy Tomb. R. S. Thomas. ToPo
Two, The. Hugo von Hofmannsthal, *tr. fr. German by* Ludwig Lewisohn. AWP; JAWP; WBP; TrJP, *tr. by* Jethro Bithell
Two/ Gorillas. Poem. Frank Lima. ANYP
Two. Winfield Townley Scott. NYBP
Two against One. *Unknown, tr. fr. Greek by* Louis Untermeyer. UnTE
Two-an'-six. Claude McKay. BANP; GoSl
Two Anchors, The. Richard Henry Stoddard. BeLS
Two and One Are a Problem. Ogden Nash. FiBHP
Two and two four. Exercise Book. Paul Dehn. WePo
Two Angels. Richard Monckton Milnes. OBRV
Two Angels, The. Whittier. AA
Two angels came through the gate of heaven. A Song of Two Angels. Laura E. Richard. AA
Two Apple-howling Songs. *Unknown. See* Apple Howling Songs.
Two apples, a book. Autumn Eve. Amelia Andriello. SiSoSe
Two April Mornings, The. Wordsworth. EnRP; ERoP-1; FosPo; GTBS-D; GTBS-P; GTBS-W; GTSE; GTSL; MBW-2; MERP; PIA; PoIE
Two Argosies. Wallace Bruce. AA
Two Armies. Stephen Spender. ChMP; CoBMV; SeCeV; WaP
Two armies covered hill and plain. Music in Camp. John R. Thompson. AA; BLPA; HBV; PaA; PAP
Two as One. Bhartrihari, *tr. fr. Sanskrit by* Paul Elmer More. OnPM
Two at a Fireside. Edwin Markham. OQP; TRV
Two at Norfolk. Wallace Stevens. FaBoMo
Two beings stood on the edge of things. Supernal Dialogue. Harriet Monroe. NP
Two bells go pealing through my age. Harald, the Agnostic Ale-loving Old Shepherd Enemy of the Whisky-drinking Ploughmen and Harvesters, Walks over the Sabbath Hill to the Shearing. George Mackay Brown. NePoEA-2
Two birds within one nest. Home. Dora Greenwell. HBV
Two Birthday Poems. Dick Lourie. ThO
Two black heifers and a red. Drinking Time. D. J. O'Sullivan. OnYI
Two Blind mice/ See how they run! Paul Dehn. *Fr.* Rhymes for a Modern Nursery. FiBHP
Two bloated bodies in rotted rags. War. Sulamith Ish-Kishor. GoYe
Two bodies have I. *Unknown.* OxNR
Two bodies lie beneath this stone. On Thomas Carew. *Unknown.* CBEP
Two bonny pilgrims of the air—a songbird and his wife. God's Ways and Mine. Grace Canfield Halladay. SoP
Two-boots in the forest walks. The Intruder. James Reeves. PDV
Two Born Brothers. *Unknown. See* Twa Brothers, The.
Two Boys, The. Mary Lamb. CBEP; OBRV
Two boys uncoached are tossing a poem together. Catch. Robert Francis. PP
Two bricklayers are setting the walls. The Bricklayer's Lunch Hour. Allen Ginsberg. CBV
Two brothers freely cast their lot. James and John. Cardinal Newman. SoP
Two brothers we are. *Unknown.* OxNR
Two brown heads with tossing curls. Katie Lee and Willie Grey. *Unknown, at. to* Josie R. Hunt *and to* J. H. Pixley. BeLS; BLPA
Two Bums Walk Out of Eden. Robert Francis. PPON
Two, by themselves, each other, love and feare. Pyramus and Thisbe. John Donne. MaMe; ReIE
Two Campers in Cloud Country. Sylvia Plath. NYBP
Two Cantos of Mutabilitie. Spenser. *Fr.* The Faerie Queene. ReEn; SiCE
("What man that sees the ever-whirling wheele.") MBW-1
Two Carols to Our Lady. *Unknown. See* I Sing of a Maiden *and* Rosa Mystica.
Two caterpillars crawling on a leaf. Immortality. Joseph Jefferson. BLPA; NeHB
Two cats/ One up a tree. Diamond Cut Diamond. Ewart Milne. FaBoCh; LoGBV; NeIP
Two Cats on the Hearth. Bernice Kenyon. CIV
Two Chalices. Edwin McNeill Poteat. ChIP
Two Children, The. Emily Brontë. PoEL-5
(A. E.) NBM
Two Children. Nicolás Guillén, *tr. fr. Spanish by* H. R. Hays. LiTW
Two Christs were at Golgotha. Early Lynching. Carl Sandburg. MAP; MoAmPo
Two Chronometers. Kenneth Slessor. *See* Five Visions of Captain Cook.
Two Coffees in the Español. Conrad Aiken. Preludes for Memnon, II. LiTA; LiTG; TwAmPo
Two Confessions. William Langland, *mod. by* Henry W. Wells. *Fr.* The Vision of Piers Plowman. WoL
Two Corbies, The. *Unknown. See* Twa Corbies, The.
Two Countries. José Martí, *tr. fr. Spanish by* Mona Hinton. TTY
Two Crosses. Addie M. Hedrick. ChIP
Two Days. T. A. Daly. LHV
Two days ago the wild-rose buds. Puzzles. John Drinkwater. WaKn
Two Dedications, *sel.* Gwendolyn Brooks.
Chicago Picasso, The. LiTM (1970 ed.)
Two Dedicatory Poems ("At th' ivory tribunall of your

Two (continued)
hand"). Richard Crashaw. MaMe
Two Dedicatory Poems ("Though now 'tis neither May nor June"). Richard Crashaw. MaMe
(Love's Nightingale.) LoBV
Two Deep Clear Eyes. Walter de la Mare. ThGo
Two Deserts, The. Coventry Patmore. The Unknown Eros, I, xviii. BoNaP; PoVP; VA
Two devills at one blow thou hast laid flat. Upon the Dumbe Devill Cast Out, and the Slanderous Jewes Put to Silence. Richard Crashaw. MaMe
Two Dogs. F. Hey. SAS
Two Dogs, The. *Unknown.* OTPC (1946 ed.); PCH
("Two little dogs.") OxNR
Two Doves, The. La Fontaine, *tr. fr. French by* Elizur Wright. OuHeWo
Two doves upon the selfsame branch. Christina Rossetti. EG
Two Dreams. Clarence Franklin. BF
Two Drinking Songs. Alcaeus, *tr. fr. Greek by* C. M. Bowra. LiTW
Two drummers sat at dinner, in a grand hotel one day. My Mother Was a Lady. Edward B. Marks. TreF; YaD
Two Easter Lilies. John Banister Tabb. StJW
Two Egrets. John Ciardi. CaFP; PoPl
Two XI. E. E. Cummings. *See* My Sweet Old Etcetera.
Two empires by the sea. International Hymn [*or* Peace Hymn for England and America]. George Huntington. MaRV; PaA; PoLF
Two Epigrams. Blake. PeER
"Her whole life is an epigram," I.
"When a man has married a wife," II.
Two Epigrams. J. V Cunningham. SiTL
"Elders at their services begin, The," I.
"You ask me how Contempt who claims to sleep," II.
Two Epigrams. James Kenneth Stephen.
Cynicus to W. Shakespeare [*or* Shakspere]. BOHV; CenHV; WhC
Senex to Matt. Prior. BOHV; CenHV; FiBHP; WhC
Two Epigrams. Sir William Watson. TrGrPo
Love.
Poet, The.
Two evils, monstrous either one apart. Winter Remembered. John Crowe Ransom. AP; CaFP; CBEP; MoAB; MoPW; OxBA; PoAn; UnPo
Two Eyes Our Souls Possess. "Angelus Silesius," *tr. fr. German by* Paul Carus. OnPM
Two Families, The. Joyce L. Brisley. BoTP
Two Festivals. Lucy Larcom. DD
Two Figures in Dense Violet Light [*or* Night]. Wallace Stevens. CLwM; MAP; MoAB; MoAmPo; OnPM
Two Fires. Meleager, *tr. fr. Greek by* Robert Guthrie MacGregor. OnPM
Two Fires, The. Judith Wright. MoBrPo (1962 ed.)
Two Fish Cosmologies. Dick Lourie. ThO
Two Fishermen. Stanley Moss. CoAP
Two Fishers. *Unknown.* BOHV
Two fleets have sailed from Spain. The one would seek. The Sailing of the Fleet. *Unknown.* PAH
Two Folk Songs. *Unknown, tr. fr. Finnish by* L. R. Lind. LiTW
"Blue and white are the heavens."
"Kukkuu, kukkuu, sounds the distant voice."
Two forms inseparable in unity. Robert Southey. *Fr.* The Curse of Kehama. OBRV
Two Foscari, The, *sel.* Byron.
Swimming. GN
Two Foxes, The. *Unknown.* FTB
Two Freedoms, The. Jon Silkin. PoDB
Two Friends, The. John Dennis. PeRV
Two Friends, The. Charles Godfrey Leland. AA; AmePo
Two friends talked of dark politics in light. Night Out. R. A. Simpson. PoAu-2
Two from the Country. R. Ernest Holmes. WSL
Two Fusiliers. Robert Graves. MMA
Two Garden Scenes. Charles Burgess. NePoAm-2
Two gates unto the road of life there are. The Road of Life. William Morris. *Fr.* The Earthly Paradise. OBNC
Two gaz'd into a pool, he gaz'd and she. An Echo from Willowwood. Christina Rossetti. VA
Two Generations. L. A. G. Strong. OBMV
Two Gentlemen of Soho, *parody, sel.* A. P. Herbert.
Recipe. WhC
Two Gentlemen of Verona, The, *sels.* Shakespeare.
My Thoughts Do Harbour, *fr.* III, i. CTC
This Spring of Love, *fr.* I, iii. ChTr
"Who is Silvia [*or* Sylvia]? What is she," *fr.* IV, ii. AnFE; ATP; BEL; BoLP; CoBE; DiPo; EG; ElL; EnL; EnLi-1; EnLit; EnRePo; FaBoBe; FaFP; GN; ILP; InPo; LiTB; NeHB; NoP; OAEP; OTPC; OuHeWo; PoIE; PTK; SeCeV; SiCE; SiTL; TOP; TreF; TrGrPo
(Silvia.) HBV; OBEV; OnPP
(Song: "Who is Silvia [*or* Sylvia]?") LiTG; ViBoPo; WHA
(Song of the Musicians.) BoLiVe
(Song to Silvia.) OBSC
(To Silvia.) MCCG; PoPo
Two gentlemen their appetite had fed. Saying Not Meaning. William Basil Wake. BOHV
Two German officers crossed the Rhine, parley voo. Mademoiselle from Armentières [*or* Hinky, Dinky Parlee-Voo]. *Unknown.* AS; SiTL; SoAmSa
Two girls discover. The Secret. Denise Levertov. NaP
Two girls of twelve or so at a table. Charles Reznikoff. OCS
Two Glasses, The. Ella Wheeler Wilcox. BLPA
Two Gods. Sam Walter Foss. MaRV
Two Gods devise the scene. Chess. John Thompson. BoAu
Two Graces. *Unknown.* FaBoCh; LoGBV
"Hurly, hurly, roon the table."
"Some hae meat that canna eat."
Two Guests from Alabama. Walt Whitman. *Fr.* Out of the Cradle Endlessly Rocking. OA
Two hands lie still, the hairy and the white. Love for a Hand. Karl Shapiro. CoAP; FiMAP; MoLP; NYBP; ToPo
Two hands upon the breast. Now and Afterwards. Dinah Maria Mulock Craik. PoLF; WGRP
Two Hangovers. James Wright. AmPC
Two Harvests, The. Francisco de Medrano, *tr. fr. Spanish by* Longfellow. OnPM
Two Heads Are Better than One. Joseph Jekyll. WhC
Two Heavens. Leigh Hunt. GN
Two heavy trestles, and a board. My Table. W. B. Yeats. Meditations in Time of Civil War, III. CABL; LiTB; PIA
Two Heroes. Harriet Monroe. *Fr.* The Commemoration Ode. OHIP
Two Highwaymen, The. Wilfrid Scawen Blunt. The Love Sonnets of Proteus, LXXI. MoBrPo (1942 ed.); OBEV (1st ed.)
Two Homes. Martha Snell Nicholson. FaChP
Two honder year ago de worl' is purty slow. Two Hundred Years Ago. William Henry Drummond. HBV
Two honest tradesmen meeting in the Strand. The Three Black Crows. John Byrom. BOHV
Two Horses. W. S. Merwin. NePA; TwAmPo
Two hours, or more, beyond the prime of a blithe April day. The Battle of Charleston Harbor. Paul Hamilton Hayne. PAH
Two householders (semi-detached) once found. The Unexploded Bomb. C. Day Lewis. TPM
Two Houses, The. Thomas Hardy. NP
Two Houses. Edward Thomas. ChMP; FaBoCh; LoGBV
Two hummingbirds as evanescent as. Vision. Richard Eberhart. NYBP
250 Willow Lane. Joseph Joel Keith. FiSC
Two Hundred Girls in Tights & Halters. Daniel Hoffman. ELU
Two Hundred Lines a Day. Martial, *tr. fr. Latin by* Rolfe Humphries. ML
224 Stoop. Victor Hernandez Cruz. BOLo
229. José Garcia Villa. PoPl
Two hundred wagons, rolling out to Oregon. The Oregon Trail. Arthur Guiterman. FaPON; MPB
Two Hundred Years Ago. William Henry Drummond. HBV
Two Illustrations That the World Is What You Make of It. Wallace Stevens. NePoAm
Two in August. John Crowe Ransom. AWP; InPo; MoPo; NePA; OxBA
Two in Bed. Abram Bunn Ross. FaPON; MPB; SoPo; TiPo
Two in the Campagna. Robert Browning. BoLiVe; ELP; EnLi-2 (1949 ed.); ExPo; FaBoEn; GTBS-D; GTBS-P; HBV; MaVP; MBW-2; MeWo; NoP; OAEP; OBNC; PoEL-5; PoVP; SeCePo; SeCeV; TOP; TrGrPo; ViPo; ViPP; WHA
"How say you? Let us, O my dove," *sel.* BoLP
Two Infinities. Edward Dowden. VA

Two Inscriptions for the Christmas Candle. Anna Hempstead Branch. MaRV
Two Invocations of the Virgin. Chaucer. *See* Invocatio ad Mariam *and* Invocation: "O mother-maid!"
Two Italian Gentlemen. Anthony Munday. *See* Fedele and Fortunio.
Two ivory women by a milky sea. The Bathers. Hart Crane. SyP
Two jays in the sumac. A. R. Ammons. *Fr.* Tape for the Turn of the Year. FRC
Two Jazz Poems. Carl Wendell Hines, Jr. AmNP; Kal
Two kinds of courage are there in the creed. Courage. Arthur Adams. BoAu
Two Kinds of People. Ella Wheeler Wilcox. *See* Lifting and Leaning.
Two Kisses. Mary Fleming. JKCP (1926 ed.)
Two Kisses. Stephen Spender. CMoP
Two Kitchen Songs. Edith Sitwell. CMoP
Two Kites, The. James Reaney. TwCaPo
Two Ladies Bidding Us "Good Morning." James P. Vaughn. NNP
Two ladies to the summit of my mind. Sonnet: Of Beauty and Duty. Dante. AWP; JAWP; WBP
Two Lean Cats. Myron O'Higgins. PoNe
Two leaps the water from its race. The [*or* A] Mill. William Allingham. ChTr; IrPN; NBM; SeCePo
Two Leaves. Jesse Stuart. FiSC
Two Legs Sat upon Three Legs. *Unknown.* OTPC; OxNR; PPL; RIS; SiTL
(Riddles.) HBV; HBVY
Two lengths has every day. Emily Dickinson. MoPo
Two Little Babes. *Unknown.* *See* Cruel Mother, The.
Two little beaks went tap! tap! tap! To Let. D. Newey-Johnson. BoTP
Two little birdies, one wintry day. The Birdies' Breakfast. *Unknown.* BoTP
Two little birds one Autumn day. *Unknown.* GFA
Two Little Blackbirds. *Unknown.* BoTP
Two little blackbirds sat upon a hill. *Unknown.* SAS
Two little blackbirds singing in the sun. Two Little Blackbirds. *Unknown.* BoTP
Two Little Boys. *Unknown.* *See* Twa Brothers, The.
Two little boys with frowsy head. Tit for Tat. Esther Antin. RIS
Two Little Children, *with music.* *Unknown.* BFSS
Two little clouds, one summer's [*or* April] day. The Rainbow Fairies. Lizzie M. Hadley. BoTP; GFA; OTPC (1946 ed.); TVC
Two little creatures. Monkeys. Padraic Colum. AnFE
Two little dicky birds/ Sitting on a wall. *Unknown.* OxNR
Two little dicky-birds/ Sitting on a twig. Dicky-Birds. Natalie Joan. BoTP
Two little dogs/ Sat by the fire. The Two Dogs. *Unknown.* OTPC (1946 ed.); OxNR; PCH
Two little elves/ Were lost one night. A Fairy Dream. Dorothy Gradon. BoTP
Two little feet, so small that both may nestle. Little Feet. Elizabeth Akers Allen. HBV
Two little girls are better than one. One and One. Mary Mapes Dodge. HBV; HBVY; PPL
Two little girls, one fair, one dark. The Lost Children. Randall Jarrell. CoAP
Two Little Kittens. *Unknown, at to* Jane Taylor. BoTP; CIV; SAS; UTS
(One Stormy Night.) PCH
Two little niggers lyin' in bed. Shortenin' Bread. *Unknown.* ABF
Two little sisters a-marching down the stream. The Twin Sisters. *Unknown.* BFSS
Two Little Skeezucks, The. Eugene Field. MPB
Two Lives, *sels.* William Ellery Leonard.
Indian Summer, *fr.* Pt. III. AnAmPo; HBMV; NP; PG (1945 ed.)
"That once the gentle mind of my dead wife," *fr.* Pt. III. AnAmPo
"Under the trees I sat, under the blue," *fr.* Pt. III. AnAmPo
Two Lives and Others. Winfield Townley Scott. PoPl
Two Long Vacations; Grasmere. Arthur Gray Butler. OBVV
Two Look at Two. Robert Frost. AnAmPo; AP; CoBA; CoBMV; CrMA; LiTL; MAP; MoAB; MoAmPo; PoeP
Two Lovers. "George Eliot." HBV
Two Lovers, The. Richard Hovey. HBV
Two lovers by a moss-grown spring. Two Lovers. "George Eliot." HBV
Two Lovers Discoursing, *with music.* *Unknown.* ShS
Two Lovers in the Toils of Honor. Corneille, *tr. fr. French by* Paul Landis. *Fr.* The Cid. LiTW
Two Loves. Richard Eberhart. CMoP; FiMAP
Two Loves, The. Laurence Housman. HBMV
Two loves had I. Now both are dead. Dead Love. Mary Mathews Adams. AA
Two loves I have of comfort and despair. Sonnets, CXLIV. Shakespeare. CABA; CBEP; InvP; LoBV; OAEP; PoEL-2; ReEn; ReIE; Sonn
Two low whistles, quaint and clear. Guild's Signal. Bret Harte. PaPo
Two Mad Songs. Emmett Jarrett. *Fr.* Designs for the City of Man. ThO
Two Magicians, The. *Unknown.* ChTr; OxBoLi
Two Magpies Sat on a Garden Rail. D'Arcy W. Thompson. MoShBr
Two magpies under the cypresses. What Birds Were There. Brother Antoninus. ToPo
Two Maidens Went Milking. *Unknown.* UnTE
Two main lines, The. Forehead. Coleman Barks. *Fr.* Body Poems. QAH
Two Married (I-IV). Helen Frazee-Bower. HBMV
Two Married Women and the Widow, The. William Dunbar. *See* Tua Mariit Wemen and the Wedo, The.
Two Masks, The. George Meredith. VA
Two Men. E. A. Robinson. BOHV; GoTP; LaNeLa; WhC
Two Men in Armour. John Heath-Stubbs. NeBP
Two men stood thigh-deep in the sea. The Fishers. Brian Vrepont. MoAuPo
Two men went up to pray; and one gave thanks. The Newer Vainglory. Alice Meynell. JKCP; MaRV; MoRP; OQP
Two men wrote a lexicon, Liddell and Scott. *Unknown.* CenHV
Two 'Mericana Men. T. A. Daly. MPB
Two minutes' rest till the next man goes in! A Cricket Bowler. Edward Craccroft Lefroy. OBVV
Two mirrors, face to face, is all I need. World beyond World. Arthur Davison Ficke. NP
"Two mites"—a simple little farthing. "More Than They All." L. M. Warner. SoP
Two mites, two drops (yet all her house and land). The Widows Mites. Richard Crashaw. MaMe; OxBoCh
Two Monologues from the Passion of M'Phail. Horace Gregory. *See* Passion of M'Phail, The.
Two Morsels of Profundity from the Minor Pre-Socratics. John Simon. SiTL
Two Mothers, The. Shane Leslie. ISi
Two Mothers. *Unknown.* SoP
Two Mountains Men Have Climbed. Pauline Starkweather. GoYe
Two Musics. Norman McCaig. NeBP
Two Mysteries, The. Mary Mapes Dodge. AA; HBV; MaRV; WGRP
Two Neighbours, The. George Campbell Hay. OxBS
Two neighbours, who were rather dense. Parable. William Soutar. HaMV
Two Nests, The. Francis Carlin. BiS; PFY
Two never-ever-will-be Lovers each. Mathematics of Encounter. Isabella Gardner. ErPo
Two noble dukes of great renown. A Song of the Banishment of Two Dukes. Thomas Deloney. SiCE
Two Noble Kinsmen, The, *sels.* Fletcher *and* Shakespeare.
Funeral Song: "Urns and odors, bring away," *fr.* I, v. AtBAP; ChTr; OBS; UnPo (1st ed.)
(Dirge of the Three Queens.) OBEV
(Song: "Urnes and odours bring away!") BoW
(Urns and Odours Bring Away!) ElL; SiCE
"Hail Sovereign Queen of secrets, who hast power," *fr.* V, i. PoEL-2
Roses, Their Sharp Spines Being Gone, *fr.* I, i. EG; HW; MyFE; NoP; SiCE; ViBoPo
(Bridal Song.) CBEP; ElL; OBEV; OBSC
Two Nocturnes. Katherine Mansfield. HBMV
Arabian Shawl, The.
Sleeping Together.
Two nudists of Dover. Third Limick. Ogden Nash. NePA
Two Nut Trees. Edith Sitwell. *See* King of China's Daughter, The.

Two of a Trade. Samuel Willoughby Duffield. AA
Two, of course there are two. Death & Co. Sylvia Plath. OPoP
Two of far nobler shape, erect and tall. Milton. *Fr.* Paradise Lost, IV. TreFS
Two of Feste's Songs. Shakespeare. *See* Come Away, Come Away Death *and* O Mistress Mine. . .
Two of Thy children one summer day worked in their garden, Lord. The Garden. Rose Parkwood. WGRP
Two of us, two of us climb the stairs. Being Twins. Kathryn Jackson. BiCB
Two of You. Mark Van Doren. UnPo (1st ed.)
Two Old Bachelors, The. Edward Lear. BeLS; BOHV; FiBHP; ShM
Two Old Crows. Vachel Lindsay. LOW; RePo
Two Old Kings, The. Lord De Tabley. OBEV (new ed.); OBVV; VA
Two Old Lenten Rhymes. *Unknown.*
"Lenten stuff is come to the town," I. ACP; WHL
"Lenton has brought us, as I understand," II. ACP
Two Old Men Look at the Sea. J. R. Hervey. AnNZ
Two Old Women of Mumbling Hill, The ("The two old trees on Mumbling Hill"). James Reeves. ShM
Two-ones is the name for it, The. The Twins. Elizabeth Madox Roberts. BiCB; TiPo
Two or three angels. The Black Riders, XXXII. Stephen Crane. AnAmPo
Two or three minutes—two or three hours. Minutes of Gold [*or* A Minute]. *Unknown.* PoToHe; SoP
Two Others, on Either Side. Edith Mirick. ChIP
Two pairs of mallards, tandem. Nearing Winter. Ernest Sandeen. NYBP
Two pale old men. Distance. Babette Deutsch. PoMa
Two Parents, The. "Hugh MacDiarmid." FaBoTw
Two Parodies. *Unknown.* CoSo
"Backward, turn backward, film guy, in your flight."
"Backward, turn backward, O Time with your wheels."
Two Pastorals. Sir Philip Sidney. FCP
("Join mates in mirth to me.") TuPP
(Upon His Meeting with His Two Worthy Friends and Fellow-Poets.) SiCE
Two Paths. Julia C. R. Dorr. AA
Two Pathways, The. Avis B. Christiansen. SoP
Two People. E. V. Rieu. BBGG
Two people. Fast. John Tagliabue. SD
Two people live in Rosamund. Two People. E. V. Rieu. BBGG
Two Pewits. Edward Thomas. CH
Two Pictures ("Two pictures hung on the dingy wall"). *Unknown.* BeLS; BLPA; FaBoBe
Two Pieces after Suetonius. Robert Penn Warren. NoP
Two Pigeons, The. *Unknown, tr. fr. Russian by* W. R. S. Ralston. OnPM
Two pilgrims on the sand espied. The Oyster and the Litigants. La Fontaine. WoL
Two Poems. Robert J. Abrams. NNP
"For my unborn son," II.
"I do not want to turn away," I.
Two Poems. Frances Cornford. EnLoPo
"I am a lamp, a lamp that is out," I.
"My love came back to me," II.
Two Poems. Edward Marshall. CoPo
Two Poems about President Harding. James Wright. AmPC; CoAP
His Death, I.
His Tomb in Ohio, II.
Two Poems against His Rival. Catullus, *tr. fr. Latin by* Jack Lindsay. LiTW
"If ever there was man who justly stank," I.
"Rufus, I trusted you. How vain that trust," II.
Two Poems Concerning the Slave Trade. Robert Southey. Sonn
"High in the air exposed the slave is hung," II.
"Hold your mad hands! for ever on your plain," I.
Two Poems on the Catholic Bavarians. Edgar Bowers. PoCh
"Fierce and brooding holocaust of faith, The," I.
"I know a wasted place high in the Alps," II.
Two Poems on the Emotions. David Shapiro. ANYP
Dust, I.
Love, II.
Two Poems to Miss Lucy Fortescue. George Lyttelton. WaPE
On Her Pleading Want of Time, II.
"To him who in an hour must die," I.
Two Poets, The. Alice Meynell. OBVV
Two Poets of Croisic, The, *sel.* Robert Browning.
Such a Starved Bank of Moss. EPN
(Apparitions.) TSW
Two Points of View. Lucian B. Watkins. BANP
Two Prayers. Andrew Gillies. BLRP; FaChP; MaRV; PoToHe; SoP; TRV
Two Prayers. Charlotte Perkins Gilman. OQP; WGRP
Two Puritans. *Unknown.* UnTE
(Off a Puritane.) CoMu
Two purple pigeons circle a London square. The Exiled Heart. Maurice Lindsay. OxBS
Two Pursuits. Christina Rossetti. EPN
Two Questions. William Stanley Braithwaite. BALP
Two Rabbins, The. Whittier. AmePo
Two Red Roses across the Moon. William Morris. CBEP; EnLit; PoIE; PoRA; PoVP
Two regiments surround the throne. Dingaan and Retief. Charles Barter. *Fr.* Stray Memories of Natal and Zululand. BoSA
Two respectable rhymes. Rhymes. Y. Y. Segal. WHW
Two Rivers. Emerson. AmePo; AmLP; AmPP; AnNE; AP; CoBA; MAmP; MWA-1; NoP; OxBA; TrGrPo
Two Rivers. *Unknown.* BuBa; CBEP; ChTr; OBEV; ShBV-1
(Rivers Till and Tweed, The.) WhC
(Tweed and Till.) BoNaP; FaBoCh; PV
Two roads diverged in a yellow wood. The Road Not Taken. Robert Frost. AmPP; AnFE; AnNE; AP; APA; ChTr; CMoP; CoAnAm; CoBA; CoBMV; DiPo; EvOK; FaBoCh; FaFP; GTBS-D; GTBS-W; ILP; InP; LiTA; LiTG; LiTM; LoGBV; MAP; MAPA; MaPo (1969 ed.); MoAB; MoAmPo; NePA; OxBA; PAn; PG; PoE; PoLF; PoPl; PoPo; ReMP; SeCeV; TIHL; TreFT; TwAmPo; TwCP
Two Robin Red-Breasts built their nest. The Robin Red-Breasts [*or* I'll Try]. Ann Hawkshaw. OTPC(1923 ed.); PPL; SAS
Two Rural Sisters. Charles Cotton. *See* Resolution in Four Sonnets. . .
Two Sayings, The. Elizabeth Barrett Browning. MaRV
Two Scenes. John Ashbery. ANYP
Two separate divided silences. Severed Selves. Dante Gabriel Rossetti. The House of Life, XL. MaVP; PoVP; SyP; ViPo; VP
Two Sewing. Hazel Hall. MoSiPe; NP
Two shall be born, the whole wide world apart. Fate. Susan Marr Spalding. AA; BBV (1951 ed.); BLPA; HBV; NeHB; PoToHe
Two Ships, The. Bret Harte. MaRV
Two Short Ballettes . . . Made for His Pastime While He Was Prisoner in the Tower of London. Sir Thomas More.
Davy, the Dicer. TuPP
Lewis, the Lost Lover. OBSC; TuPP
(Fortune.) GoBC; PoLi
Two Shots: a Love Affair. Fanny Howe. QAH
Two Sides of War. Grantland Rice. TreFT
Two [*or* Twa] Sisters, The (*diff. versions*). *Unknown.* BaBo (A, B, *and* C *vers.*); BEL; BFSS (B *vers., with music*); CBEP; CH; CoBE; EnLit; ESPB (A *and* B *vers.*); HBV; NoP; OuHeWo; OxBS; PoMa; TOP; ViBoFo (A, B, *and* D *vers.*; C *vers., with music*)
(Binnorie.) AnFE; BoLiVe; BuBa; OBB; OBEV; OnSP; ShBV-1; TrGrPo; WHA
(Cruel Sister, The.) BaBo; OxBB
(Twin Sisters, The, A *vers., with music.*) BFSS
(Two [*or* Twa] Sisters of [*or* o'] Binnorie, The.) EnSB; GBV (1952 ed.) StaSt
Two Smiles. Oliver Herford. *See* Smile of the Walrus, The.
Two Societies, The. John Hall Wheelock. PoCh
Two Solitudes. Evelyn Ames. GoYe
Two Somewhat Different Epigrams. Langston Hughes. Kal; NePoAm-2
"I look with awe upon the human race," II.
"Oh, God of dust and rainbows, help us see," I.
Two Songs. C. Day Lewis. OAEP (2d ed.)
Love Was Once Light as Air.
Oh Light Was My Head.
Two Songs. Heine, *tr. fr. German by* Sir Theodore Martin. WoL

"Immovable, unchanging," I.
"People have teased and vexed me," II.
Two Songs. Kabir. *See* Songs of Kabir.
Two Songs. Abraham Reisen, *tr. fr. Yiddish by* Marie Syrkin. LiTW
"On with another new love," II.
"Sweetest Melody, The," I.
Two Songs at the Marriage of the Lord Fauconberg and the Lady Mary Cromwell. Andrew Marvell. MaMe
Two Songs by Amiens. Shakespeare. *See* Blow, Blow, Thou Winter Wind *and* Under the Greenwood Tree.
Two Songs from a Play. W. B. Yeats. *Fr.* The Resurrection.
"I saw a staring virgin stand," I. CABA; CMoP; CoBMV; ExPo; FosPo; ILP; LiTB; MoPo; NoP; PAn; PoDB; PoFS; PoIE; SeCeV; UnPo
(Song from a Play.) FaBoTw
"In pity for man's darkening thought," II. CABA; CMoP; CoBMV; ExPo; FosPo; ILP; LiTB; MoPo; NoP; PAn; PoDB; PoFS; PoIE; SeCeV; UnPo
Two Songs in Praise of Steingerd. Cormac Ogmundarson, *tr. fr. Old Norse by* W. G. Collingwood *and* Jón Stefánsson. LiTW
"Moon of her brow, The, it is beaming," I.
"Tree of my treasure and longing, The," II.
Two Songs of a Fool. W. B. Yeats.
"I slept on my three-legged stool by the fire," II. CMoP; OA; PoG
"Speckled cat and a tame hare, A," I. CMoP; OA; PoDB; PoG
Two Songs of Advent. Yvor Winters. NP
"Coyote, on delicate mocking feet," II.
"On the desert, between pale mountains," I.
Two Songs on the Economy of Abundance. James Agee. MAP; MoAmPo
Red Sea.
Temperance Note; and Weather Prophecy.
Two Sonnet-Songs. Frank T. Marzials. VA
"Fleet, fleet and few," II.
"Hist, hist, ye winds," I.
Two Sonnets. David P. Berenberg. HBMV
"Antigone and Helen-would they laugh."
"Or is it all illusion? Do the years."
Two Sonnets, *sel.* John Crowe Ransom.
"It was beside the fire that I had lit," I. LO
Two Sonnets. Charles Hamilton Sorley.
"Saints have adored the lofty soul of you," I. HBMV; MMA; MoBrPo; NeMA; TrGrPo (1942 ed.)
"Such, such is Death: no triumph; no defeat," II. HBMV; MMA; MoBrPo; NeMA; TrGrPo (1942 ed.)
Two Sonnets. Dylan Thomas. *See* Altarwise by Owl-Light.
Two Sonnets. James Thomson. PoVP
"Striving to sing glad songs, I but attain," II.
"Why are your songs all wild and bitter sad," I.
Two Sonnets for a Lost Love. Samuel A. De Witt. GoYe
"If I were less the man, I might have kept," II.
"'There is no permanence,' you sagely said," I.
Two Sonnets from a Sequence. Edgar Holt. BoAV
"This side of madness, while the flames abate," I.
"Under the midnights' iron rain, under," II.
Two Sonnets: Harvard. Oliver Wendell Holmes. AP
"Christo et Ecclesiae" 1700.
1643 "Veritas" 1878.
Two Sonnets on Fame. Keats.
"Fame, like a wayward girl, will still be coy," I. EnRP; Sonn
(On Fame.) CABA; CBEP; EnLit
"How fevered is the man, who cannot look," II. EnL; EnRP
(On Fame.) EnLit; EPN
Two Sons. Robert Buchanan. VA
Two souls diverse out of our human sight. On the Deaths of Thomas Carlyle and George Eliot. Swinburne. BEL; HBV; PoVP; TOP; VA
Two soules move here, and mine (a third) must move. Of the Progresse of the Soule; the Second Anniversary. John Donne. MaMe
Two Spanish Gypsy Lullabies. *Unknown.* FIW
Two Spirits, The. James Benjamin Kenyon. AA
Two Spirits, The; an Allegory. Shelley. CH; EPN; ERoP-2; WiR
"Some say, when nights are dry and clear," *sel.* LO LO
Two Springs she saw—two radiant Tuscan springs. Mimma Bella, II. Eugene Lee-Hamilton. HBV
Two Stars, The. W. H. Davies. MoBrPo
Two stars alone of primal magnitude. Washington and Lincoln. Wendell Phillips Stafford. PGD
Two stars once on their lonely way. Orbits. Richard Le Gallienne. VA
Two States of Prayer. Thomas Merton. JKCP (1955 ed.)
Two statesmen met by moonlight. What the Moon Saw. Vachel Lindsay. CrMA
Two steps from my garden rail. Hayyim Nahman Bialik. Songs of the People, I. AWP; JAWP; WBP
Two Strange Worlds. Francesca Yetunde Pereira. PBA
Two Streams, The. Oliver Wendell Holmes. *Fr.* The Professor at the Breakfast Table. AP
Two Streams, The. Thomas Moore. *Fr.* Evenings in Greece. GoBC
Two stubborn beaks. Argument. Mildred Weston. PoMa; WhC
Two summers since, I saw at Lammas fair. Phoebe Dawson. George Crabbe. GoTL
Two Surprises. R. W. McAlpine. PoLF
Two Swans, The. Thomas Hood. CH
Two swans break, The. The Love of Swans. Leonard Mann. MoAuPo
Two Swede families live downstairs and an Irish policeman upstairs. House. Carl Sandburg. CMoP
Two tapsters traded on Thames's side. Ballad of the Two Tapsters. Vernon Watkins. MoBS
Two Taverns. Edwin Markham. TSW
Two that could not have lived their single lives. Two in August. John Crowe Ransom. AWP; InPo; MoPo; NePA; OxBA
Two that through windy nights kept company. The Two Neighbours. George Campbell Hay. OxBS
Two thieves, pursuing their profession. The Thieves and the Ass. La Fontaine. OnPM
Two Things. Donald C. Babcock. NePoAm
Two things have I asked of Thee. Neither Poverty nor Riches. Proverbs, Bible, *O.T.* TrJP
Two Things Have Met in Me. Solomon ibn Gabirol, *tr. fr. Hebrew by* Israel Zangwill. LiTW
Two things make woman slow, we find. Good Reasons. Keith Preston. WhC
"Two things," said Kant, "fill me with breathless awe." The Third Wonder [*or* Breathless Awe]. Edwin Markham. MAP; MaRV
Two things there are with Memory will abide. Memories. Thomas Bailey Aldrich. AA
Two things were set. Two Things. Donald C. Babcock. NePoAm
2000 A.D. Beverly Connelly. FiSC
Two thousand feet beneath our wheels. Cockpit in the Clouds. Dick Dorrance. FaPON; PoMa; TiPo
Two thousand years are far enough! It Isn't Far to Bethlehem. Arthur R. Macdougall, Jr. PGD
Two Tramps in Mud Time. Robert Frost. AmPP; AnNE; AP; BoLiVe; CMoP; CoBA; CoBMV; LiTA; LiTM; MAP; MasP; MoAB; MoAmPo; NAMP; NePA; PoFS; TrGrPo; UnPo (3d ed.)
Two Translations from Villon. *Pr. tr. fr. French by* J. M. Synge. OBMV
"Man I had a love for, The." MoBrPo
(Old Woman's Lamentations, An.) OBMV
"Mother of God that's Lady of the Heavens." MoBrPo
(Translation from Villon, A.) NeMA
Two Travelers. C. Day Lewis. EnLit
Two Trees, The. W. B. Yeats. BrPo; MaPo; POTE
Two Triolets. Harrison Robertson. HBV
What He Said.
What She Thought.
Two Variations. Denise Levertov. NaP
2 Variations: All About Love. Philip Whalen. NeAP
Two vases stood on the Shelf of Life. Vases. Nan Terrell Reed. BLPA
Two Vast Enjoyments Commemorated. John Danforth. SCAP
Two Veterans. Walt Whitman. *See* Dirge for Two Veterans.
Two Views of a Cadaver Room. Sylvia Plath. GoYe; NMP
Two Villages, The. Rose Terry Cooke. HBV
Two Voices. Alice Corbin. HBMV; NP
Two Voices, The. Tennyson. MasP; PoVP
Sels.
Dragon-Fly, The. OA

Two (continued)
Life Not Death ("Whatever crazy sorrow saith"), 2 *sts.* MaRV
Two voices are there: one is of the deep. A Sonnet [*or* Wordsworth]. James Kenneth Stephen. CenHV; EnLi-2 (1949 ed.); FiBHP; HBV; ML; Par; VA; WhC
Two voices are there; one is of the sea. Thought of a Briton on the Subjugation of Switzerland [*or* Sonnet *or* England and Switzerland, 1802]. Wordsworth. BEL; BoLiVe; ChER; EnL; EnLi-2; EnRP; EPN; GTBS; GTBS-D; GTBS-P; GTBS-W; GTSE; GTSL; MBW-2; MCCG; MERP; OBRV; PoFr; SeCeV; ShBV-3; TOP
Two Voices in a Meadow. Richard Wilbur. CaFP; CBV; NePoAm-2; UnPo (3d ed.)
Two-Volume Novel. Dorothy Parker. InMe
Two Voyages. Maurice James Craig. NeIP
Two Ways. John V. A. Weaver. HBMV; NP
Two Ways of Giving. *Unknown.* SoP
Two Ways of Visiting. Timothy Dwight. *Fr.* Greenfield Hill. AmPP (4th ed.)
Two webfoot brothers loved a fair. That Gentle Man from Boston Town. Joaquin Miller. BOHV
Two Weeks. Nicolás Guillén, *tr. fr. Spanish by* Langston Hughes. PoNe
Two weeping for beauty perished, husband. Exhortation to the Artists. Hyam Plutzik. FiMAP
Two Went Up to [*or* into] the Temple to Pray. Richard Crashaw. ALV; CAW; MaMe; MaRV; TRV
(Pharisee and Publican.) SoP
Two were silent in a sunless church, The. Her Dilemma. Thomas Hardy. BrPo; Po
Two white ducks waddle past my door. Ducks. Robert Bly. PV
Two White Horses, *with music. Unknown.* AS
Two wild duck of the upland spaces. Duck. John Lyle Donaghy. OxBI
Two winds, one calm, another fierce to see. Robert Tofte. *Fr.* Laura. ReIE
Two winged genii in the air. Love and Youth. William James Linton. VA
Two Wise Generals. Ted Hughes. MoBS
Two Witches, *sels.* Robert Frost.
Pauper Witch of Grafton, The. CMoP; CrMA; MWA-2
Witch of Coös, The. AmP; AnNE; AP; AtBAP; CMoP; CoBMV; DiPo; ExPo; LiTM (rev. ed.); MoAB; NePA; ReMP; SeCeV (1967 ed.); ViBoPo (1958 ed.)
Two Wives, The. Daniel Henderson. ShM
Two Wives, The. William Dean Howells. AA
Two Women. Tania van Zyl. PeSA
Two Women. Nathaniel Parker Willis. *See* Unseen Spirits.
Two women had these words engraved. Epitaphs; for a Fickle Man. Mark Van Doren. ViBoPo
Two women loved him, shapes of Heaven. Thomas Caulfield Irwin. *Fr.* Swift. IrPN
Two women on the lone wet strand. The Watchers. William Stanley Braithwaite. PoNe
Two words from China: "Ku li"—bitter strength. Ku Li. "Robin Hyde." AnNZ
Two worlds hast thou to dwell in, Sweet. First Skylark of Spring. Sir William Watson. VA
Two Yankee wags, one summer day. Here She Goes, and There She Goes. James Nack. BOHV
Two Years Later. John Wieners. CoPo
Two years the blank walls stared at him. A History. John Williams. NePoAm-2
Two years thus spent in gathering knowledge. Tom Brainless at College [*or* as Student and Preacher]. John Trumbull. *Fr.* The Progress of Dulness. AmPP; ATP (1935 ed.)
'Twould make our eastern people crave. California Ball. John A. Stone. SGR
'Twould ring the bells of Heaven. The Bells of Heaven. Ralph Hodgson. BoTP; BrPo; EaLo; GoJo; GTBS-W; LiTM; MemP; MoAB; MoBrPo; OBEV (new ed.); OtMeF; PoIE; PoSa; PPON; ShBV-1; SiSoSe; SP; TreFT; UTS
Tyburn and Westminster. John Heywood. ACP
Tyger, The. Blake. *See* Tiger, The.
Tying a Knot in the Devil's Tail. *Unknown.* ABF
Tying her bonnet under her chin. The Love-Knot. Nora Perry. AA; BOHV; HBV
Tyl it was noon, they stoden for to se. At the Gate. Chaucer. *Fr.* Troilus and Criseyde. SeCePo
Tymes Goe by Turnes. Robert Southwell. *See* Times Go by Turns.
Tyne Dock. Francis Scarfe. NeBP
Tyneside Widow, The. Swinburne. PoVP
Type of the antique Rome! Rich reliquary. The Coliseum. Poe. AmPP (3d ed.); AP; MWA-1
Typewriter, The. Mariana Griswold Van Rensselaer. GFA
Tyrannick [*or* Tyrannic] Love; or, The Royal Martyr, *sels.* Dryden.
Ah How Sweet It Is to Love, *fr.* IV, i. EiCL; EnLi-1; HBV; HoPM; LiTL; MaPo; OBEV (1st ed.); PoIE; ViBoPo
(Song: "Ah, how sweet it is to love.") CavP; EiPP; FaBoEn; PeRV
Epilogue: "Hold, are you mad? you damned confounded dog." BWP; MaPo (1969 ed.); MBW-1; OAEP; SeCV-2; ViBoPo
Prologue: "Self-love (which never rightly understood)". OAEP; ViBoPo
Tyrannicide. Walter Savage Landor. PoFr
Tyranny. Sidney Lanier. MAmP
Tyrant Apple Is Eaten, The. Norman McCaig. NeBP
Tyrant cat, by surname Nibblelard, A. The Council Held by the Rats. La Fontaine. CIV
Tyrant has fallen, The. Vincenzo Monti. *Fr.* Ode on Superstition. PoFr
Tyrant's Death, The. Judith, XIII: 6-15, Bible, Apocrypha. PoFr
Tyrants of the Golden City tremble, The. Shelley. *Fr.* The Revolt of Islam. PoFr
Tyrants when they come to die. King David. Heine. PoFr
Tyr'd with all these for restfull death I cry. *See* Tired with all these . . .
Tyre brought me up, who born in thee had been. Of Himself. Meleager. AWP
Tyre of the farther West! be thou too warned. United States. John Keble. CoBE
Tyre of the West, and glorying in the name. England. Cardinal Newman. ACP; CAW; GoBC; JKCP; PoVP; VA
Tyrian dye why do you wear. To His Mistress. Abraham Cowley. EG; SeCL
Tywater. Richard Wilbur. CMoP; GTBS-W; LiTA; LiTM (rev. ed.) MemP; MiAP; MoAB; NePA; PoSa; ReMP
"Tzu-yeh" Song, A: "All night I could not sleep." *Unknown, tr. fr. Chinese by* Arthur Waley. OnPM
"Tzu-yeh" Song A: "I heard my love was going to Yang-chou." *Unknown, tr. fr. Chinese by* Arthur Waley. OnPM

U

U is for Umbrellas. Phyllis McGinley. *Fr.* All Around the Town. TiPo
U Name This One. Carolyn M. Rodgers. TNV; WSL
USA. Paul Engle. SiTL
U.S. Air Force, The. Robert Crawford. PoRL
U.S. Sailor with the Japanese Skull, The. Winfield Townley Scott. FiMAP; LiTM (1970 ed.); MiAP; NMP; WaP
Ubasti. Gelett Burgess. CIV
Ubi Sunt Qui ante Nos Fuerunt? *Unknown.* CoBE; EnLi-1; EPP, *Middle and mod. Eng.*; ILP; NoP; OAEP; PIA; PoAn; SeCeV
(Contempt of the World.) MeEL
Ubique. *At. to* Joshua Sylvester. *See* Were I as Base as Is the Lowly Plain.
Uccello. Gregory Corso. NeAP
Uccello on the Heath. Geoffrey Grigson. WaP
Uffia. Harriet R. White. BOHV; NA
Ug was a hairy but painstaking artist. The Story of Ug. Edwin Meade Robinson. HBMV; YaD
Uh—go down, go down, you little red. Go Down, You Little Red Rising Sun. *Unknown.* OuSiCo
Uhuru. Ahmed Legraham Alhamisi. BF
"Ukraina is sad for that she has no place to dwell in." Fragment. *Unknown.* PoFr
Ula Masondo's Dream. William Plomer. MoBS
Ulalume. Poe. AA; AmP; AmePo; AmPP; AnAmPo; AnEnPo; AnFE; AP; APA; ATP; AWP; CoAnAm; CoBA; DiPo; JAWP; LiTA; LiTG; LO; MAmP; MWA-1; NePA; OuHeWo; OxBA; PoFS; PoIE; PoPo; TDP; TOP; TreF; UnPo; ViBoPo; WBP; WHA
Ulf in Ireland. Charles De Kay. AA

Ulric Dahlgren. Kate Brownlee Sherwood. PAH
Ulsterman, An. "Lynn Doyle." OnYI
Ultima in mortis hora. The Benedictine Ultima. *Unknown.* CAW
Ultima Ratio Regum. Stephen Spender. BBV (1951 ed.); EnLi-2 (1949 ed.); FaFP; LiTB; LiTM; MaRV; SeCePo; WaaP; WaP
Ultima Thule, *sel.* Longfellow.
Dedication: "With favoring winds, o'er sunlit seas." ViBoPo
Ultima Veritas. Washington Gladden. MaRV *abr.*; OQP
(Holding.) FaChP
(I Shall See Him.) SoP
Ultimate Atrocity, The. Siegfried Sassoon. CMoP
Ultimate Equality. Ray Durem. *See* You know, Joe.
Ultimate Exile, *sel.* R. N. Currey.
"How lovely are the waters of Babylon." BoSA; PeSA
Ultimate Joy, The. *Unknown.* BOHV
Ultimatum. Peggy Pond Church. TRV
Ultra-Germano-Criticasterism. Leigh Hunt. PP
Ulysses. Robert Graves. ChMP; CMoP; FaBoTw; OxBI
Ulysses. Tennyson. ATP; AWP; BEL; BoLiVe; BWP; CABA; CaFP; CBEP; CBV; CoBE; DiPo; EnL; EnLi-2; EnLit; EPN; ExPo; FiP; ForPo; GTSE; HBV; HoPM; ILP; InP; InPo; LiTB; LoBV; MaPo; MaVP; MBW-2; MCCG; MyFE; NoP; OAEP; OnPP; OuHeWo; PAn; Po; PoAn; PoE; PoFS; PoIE; PoPo; PoRA; PoSa; PoVP; PTK; SeCePo; SeCeV; ShBV-4; StP; TOP; TreF; TrGrPo; UnPo; VA; VaPo; ViBoPo; ViPo; ViPP; VP; WHA; YT
Sels.
Challenge of Life, The. MaRV
(Experience.) OQP
("I am a part of all that I have met.") TRV
"There lies the port; the vessel puffs her sail." EtS; MaRV; OQP; OTPC
Ulysses Advises Achilles [Not to Let Slip Opportunity]. Shakespeare. *Fr.* Troilus and Cressida, III, iii. LiTB; LiTG
Ulysses and His Dog. Homer, *tr. fr. Greek by* Pope. *Fr.* The Odyssey, XVII. FiP; OBEC
("And a dog, lying there, lifted its head," *pr. tr. by* Martin Johnson.) LO
Ulysses and the Siren. Samuel Daniel. BWP; CABA; ElL; EnRePo; LoBV; NoP; OBEV; OBSC; PoEL-2; ReEn; ReIE; SiCE; StP; TuPP; ViBoPo
Ulysses and the Sirens. Homer, *tr. fr. Greek by* George Chapman. *Fr.* The Odyssey, XII. ReEn
Ulysses has come back to me again! Ulysses Returns, I. Roselle Mercier Montgomery. HBMV
Ulysses Hears the Prophecies of Tiresias. Homer, *tr. fr. Greek by* George Chapman. *Fr.* The Odyssey, XI. LoBV
Ulysses in Autumn. Joseph Auslander. MAP; MoAmPo (1942 ed.)
Ulysses in the Waves. Homer, *tr. fr. Greek by* George Chapman. *Fr.* The Odyssey, V. OBS
Ulysses Pondering. Stanley Plumly. NYTB
Ulysses Returns, I-IV. Roselle Mercier Montgomery. HBMV
Ulysses S. Grant. Paul Southworth Bliss. StaSt
Umber slant lands under the Apennines, The. To the South. Brewster Ghiselin. LiTA; LiTM (rev. ed.); NePA
Umbrella, The. Ann Stanford. NYBP
Umbrella Brigade, The. Laura E. Richards. SoPo; SUS; TiPo
Umbrellas. Rowena Bennett. TiPo (1959 ed.)
Umpire, The. Milton Bracker. SD
Umpire, The. Walker Gibson. NePoAm; SD
Umpire is a lonely man, The. The Umpire. Milton Bracker. SD
Un, Deux, Trols, *with music. Unknown, tr. fr. French.* ABF
Una Anciana Mexicana. Alice Corbin. NP
Una Bhan. Robert Farren, *ad. fr. Gaelic.* JKCP (1955 ed.)
Unable are the loved to die. Emily Dickinson. MWA-2
Unable by Long and Hard Travel to Banish Love, Returns Her Friend. George Turberville. TuPP
Unable to breathe, I inhaled the classic Aegean. Small Perfect Manhattan. Peter Viereck. MiAP
Unable to find a wife. Dawn Song. *Unknown. Fr.* Nihon Shoki. HW
Unafraid. E. Margaret Clarkson. SoP
Unalterables. Arthur Gregor. NYBP
Unanswered. Martha Dickinson Bianchi. AA
Unanswered Prayer[s]. Oliver Huckel. MaRV
(I Thank Thee, Lord.) BLRP; WBLP
Unanswered Prayers. Ella Wheeler Wilcox. WGRP
Unanswered yet the prayer your lips have pleaded. Sometime, Somewhere [*or* Pray without Ceasing]. Ophelia Guyon Browning. BLPA; BLRP; NeHB; STF
Unarmed Combat. Henry Reed. Lessons of the War, III. LiTB
Unarmed she goeth, yet her hands. Charity. George Parsons Lathrop. CAW; JKCP
Unattainable, The. Harry Romaine. BOHV
Unaware that Avessek. Colette Inez. QAH
Unawares. Emma A. Lent. PoLF; SoP
Unawkward Singers, The. David Ferry. NePoAm-2
Unbelief. Elizabeth York Case. *See* There Is No Unbelief.
Unbelievable, The. Edwin Markham. MaRV
Unbeliever, The. Elizabeth Bishop. FiMAP; LiTA
Unbeliever, An. Anna Hempstead Branch. MaRV; PFY; WGRP
Unbeliever. Dorothy Dow. HBMV
Unbeseechable, The. Frances Cornford. MoBrPo
Unbidden Wedding Guest, The. Kurt Marti, *tr. fr. German by* Christa Wolf *and* Virginia Tufte. HW
Un-Birthday Cake. Aileen Fisher. BiCB
Unblinding, The. Laurence Lieberman. NYBP
Unborn, The. Julia Neely Finch. AA
Unborn, The. Thomas Hardy. CMoP
Unborn. Irene Rutherford McLeod. HBMV
Unborn, The. Judith Wright. MoAuPo
Unborn Eternal Self. *Unknown, tr. fr. Sanskrit by* Joseph Nadin Rawson. *Fr.* The Upanishads. OnPM
Unbridled Now. Laura Lourene LeGear. GoYe
Unbroken. A. R. Ammons. FRC
Unbroken Code, The. Robert Dana. NYTB
Uncautiously, unheeding, thinking. The Thieves of Love. R. A. D. Ford. PeCV (1967 ed.)
Uncelestial City, The, *sels.* Humbert Wolfe. BoC
"It is easier to be angry than to pity."
"She has dusted the ornaments, rubbed down the chairs."
"You cannot traffick in peace."
Uncertain State of a Lover, The. *Unknown.* ElL
Uncertainty. Henrietta C. Parks. TNV
Uncertainty of Life, The. Barnabe Googe. SiCE
Uncessant Minutes, whilst you move you tell. To His Watch, When He Could Not Sleep. Lord Herbert of Cherbury. EP; MePo; PoEL-2
Unchangeable, The. Shakespeare. *See* Sonnets, CIX.
Unchanged. Martial, *tr. fr. Latin by* Paul Nixon. WoL
Unchanging Jesus. Karl Johann Philipp Spitta, *tr. fr. German by* R. Massie. BLRP
Unchanging One, The. Frances Ridley Havergal. SoP
Uncivil sickness, hast thou no regard. Henry Constable. *Fr.* Diana. ReIE
Unclaimed. Florida Watts Smyth. StaSt
Uncle, The. Whittier. *Fr.* Snow-bound. GoTP
Uncle Ambrose. James Still. AmFN
Uncle Ananias. E. A. Robinson. AnNE; BoLiVe (1945 ed.); LaNeLa; MaPo; MoAmPo (1950 ed.); NePA; NoP
Uncle Andy and I. Leroy F. Jackson. GaP
Uncle Dog: The Poet at 9. Robert Sward. CoAP; CoPo
Uncle Eph's Banjo Song. James Edwin Campbell. BANP
Uncle Frank. Monica Shannon. GaP
Uncle Gabe's White Folks. Thomas Nelson Page. AA
Uncle Jim. Alice Corbin. *Fr.* Echoes of Childhood. PoNe
Uncle Jim. Countee Cullen. BANP
Uncle Remus and His Friends, *sel.* Joel Chandler Harris.
My Honey, My Love. AA; FaBoBe
Plantation Play-Song. MCCG
Plough-Hands' Song, The. AA; LHV
Revival Hymn. HBV; MCCG
Time Goes by Turns. IHA
Uncle Simon and Uncle Jim. "Artemus Ward". BOHV; NA
Unclose Those Eyelids. Henry Glapthorne. SeCL
Uncommon. Callimachus, *tr. fr. Greek by* Robert Guthrie MacGregor. OnPM
Unconcerned, The. Thomas Flatman. CEP; FaBoCh; PeRV
Unconquerably, men venture on the quest. The Polar Quest. Richard Burton. AA
Unconquer'd captive—close thine eye. Virginia Capta. Margaret Junkin Preston. PAH
Unconquered Air, The. Florence Earle Coates. PoMa

Unconscious Cerebration. W. E. H. Lecky. *See* Say Not That the Past Is Dead.
Unconscious of amused and tolerant eyes. Portrait of a Child. Louis Untermeyer. HBMV
Unconstant Lover, The, *with music.* *Unknown.* TrAS
Uncourtly Love. Walther von der Vogelweide, *tr. fr. German by* Jethro Bithell. LiTW
Uncouth Knight, The. Hugh Mccrae. PoAu-1
Undead, The. Richard Wilbur. CoAP
Under. J. C. Squire. FaBoTw
Under a budding hedge I hid. While April Rain Went By. Shaemas O'Sheel. HBMV
Under a daisied bank. The Milkmaid. Thomas Hardy. SiTL
Under a dung-cake. Fable. D. J. Opperman. PeSA
Under a Lady's Picture. Edmund Waller. EnLoPo
Under a lawne, than skyes more cleare. Upon Roses. Robert Herrick. SeCP
Under a lonely sky a lonely tree. On a Lonely Spray. James Stephens. AnFE; OnYI
Under a low sky. Silence. William Carlos Williams. BiS
Under a sky of azure. O, Fair New Mexico. Elizabeth Garrett. PoRL
Under a southern wind. Song. Theodore Roethke. CrMA
Under a Spell. Catullus, *tr. fr. Latin.* OnPM
Under a splintered mast. A Talisman. Marianne Moore. AnFE; APA; CoAnAm; GoJo; MAP; MoAB; MoAmPo; NP; ViBoPo
Under a spreading chestnut-tree. The Village Blacksmith. Longfellow. AA; AmePo; AnNE; CoBA; FaBoBe; FaFP; FaPL; FaPON; GoTP; HBV; HBVY; NeHB; OnPP; OTPC; PaPo; PoPl; PTK; SoP; StVeCh; TreF; WBLP
Under a spreading gooseberry bush the village burglar lies. The Village Blacksmith. *Unknown.* FiBHP
Under a stagnant sky. To James McNeill Whistler. W. E. Henley. PoVP; SyP
Under a sultry, yellow sky. Mercedes. Elizabeth Stoddard. AA
Under a Telephone Pole. Carl Sandburg. PoPo
Under a throne I saw a virgin sit. Sonnet. Fulke Greville. Caelica, LXXXI [LXXXII]. ReIE; SiCE; TuPP
Under a toadstool/ Crept a wee elf. The Elf and the Dormouse. Oliver Herford. AA; BoChLi; FaBoBe; FaPON; GFA; GoTP; HBV; HBVY; MPB; OnMSP; OTPC (1946 ed.); PCH; PoRh; PRWS; SoPo; SP; TiPo; TSW; TVC; UTS
Under a tree. Mary Is with Child. *Unknown.* MeEL
Under a tree in the shade sits a toad. The Toad. Louis Kent. WaKn
Under a wall of bronze. The Swan. John Gould Fletcher. OTPC (1946 ed.)
Under a Wiltshire Apple Tree. Anna de Bary. CH
Under All Change. Josephine W. Johnson. MoRP
Under All This Slate. James Hayford. NePoAm-2
Under an Eastern sky. For Me. *Unknown.* ChIP; OQP
Under an elm tree where the river reaches. Captured. Archibald MacLeish. HBMV
Under an undermin'd, and shot-bruis'd wall. Fall of a Wall. John Donne. MaMe; ReIE
Under Ben Bulben. W. B. Yeats. AnIV; CMoP; CoBMV; LiTM (rev. ed.); LoBV; NoP; OxBI
Sels.
For His Own Epitaph. AnFE
"Irish poets, learn your trade." ML
Under broad banners and barbarian. Against the Age. Louis Simpson. NePoEA-2
Under Cancer. John Hollander. CoAP
Under cool trees the City tombs. Bunhill's Fields. Anne Ridler. NeBP
Under enormous and cemented cliffs. The Second Iron Age (1939-1945). Michael Harrington. CaP
Under Glass. Alfred Kreymborg. AnAmPo; MAPA
Under great yellow flags and banners of the ancient Cold. The Shadow of Cain. Edith Sitwell. CoBMV
Under green apple boughs. Madonna Mia. Swinburne. HBV
Under Ground. James Reeves. RePo
Under her gentle seeing. On a Young Poetess's Grave. Robert Buchanan. VA
Under his careful crown he keeps. King Midas Has Asses' Ears. Donald Finkel. NePoEA-2
Under his helmet, up against his pack. Asleep. Wilfred Owen. MMA; POTE; WePo
Under his view the wind. The View. Howard Nemerov. NYBP
Under Investigation. John Morgan. YAP
Under Leafy Bowers. Judah Al-Harizi, *tr. fr. Hebrew.* TrJP
Under Milk Wood, *sels.* Dylan Thomas.
Every Morning When I Wake. LOW
Johnnie Crack and Flossie Snail. FaPON; GoJo; LOW; PDV (Song.) FiBHP
Under Monadnock. A New Hampshire Boy. Morris Bishop. HBMV
Under museum glass it is remote. The Wonder Shell. Barbara D. Holender. NYTB
Under my keel another boat. A Shadow Boat. Arlo Bates. HBV
Under My Window. Thomas Westwood. HBV; HBVY; OTPC (1923 ed.)
Under my window Dolores sings. Spanish Song. Charles Divine. HBMV
Under my window-ledge the waters race. Coole Park and Ballylee, 1931. W. B. Yeats. CMoP; GTBS-P; MaPo (1969 ed.); NoP; OBMV; TDP
Under night's silent canopy. The Spectre Is on the Move. G. Allana. ACV
Under no hanging heaven-rooted tree. Stony Limits. "Hugh MacDiarmid." CABL
Under Oaks. James Dickey. NYTB
Under one star, now, or under two? A Double Star. David McCord. MAP
Under our curtain of fire. The White Comrade. Robert Haven Schauffler. StJW
Under Sea. *See* Undersea.
Under Sirius. W. H. Auden. NePA
Under Song. *See* Undersong.
Under the African lintel, Table Mountain. David Wright. *Fr.* South African Broadsheets. PeSA
Under the after-sunset sky. Two Pewits. Edward Thomas. CH
Under the almond tree. In Kensington Gardens. Arthur Symons. EnLoPo
Under the apple bough. Remembrance. George Parsons Lathrop. AA
Under the Apple Boughs. Dylan Thomas. *See* Fern Hill.
Under the arch of life, where love and death. Soul's Beauty. Dante Gabriel Rossetti. The House of Life, LXXVII. CoBE; EnLit; MaVP; OAEP; OBEV (new ed.); OBVV; PAn; PoVP; ViPo; ViPP
Under the azure where the noon sun totters. Antony and Cleopatra. José Maria de Heredia, *tr. by* Henri Coulette. NePoEA
Under the bark remembers now my heart. Sonnet. Roy Daniells. PeCV
Under the bed. Saturday Towels. Lysbeth Boyd Borie. UTS
Under the big 500-watted lamps, in the huge sawdusted government inspected slaughter-house. The Slaughter-House. Alfred Hayes. LiTA; LiTM
Under the Blue. Francis Fisher Browne. AA
Under the Boughs. Gene Baro. BoNaP
Under the bronze crown. A Baroque Wall-Fountain in the Villa Sciarra. Richard Wilbur. AmPP (5th ed.); NePoEA; NoP; NYBP; PoCh; ToPo; TwCP
Under the bronze leaves a colt was foaled. Song. "St.-J. Perse." *Fr.* Anabasis. AtBAP; LiTW; PoPl
Under the Casuarina. Elizabeth Riddell. PoAu-2
Under the Cliff. Geoffrey Grigson. WaP
Under the concrete benches. Weed Puller. Theodore Roethke. AmPP (5th ed.); PoAn
Under the cover of night. Cities and Seas. Norman Jordan. PoNe (1970 ed.)
Under the crosses white on a foreign meadow. Silent Testimony. Catherine Parmenter. PGD
Under the Drooping Willow Tree. *Unknown.* CBEP; OxBoLi
Under the dying sun. The Reaper. L. H. Allen. MoAuPo; NeLNL; PoAu-1
Under the eaves, out of the wet. To a Phoebe Bird. Witter Bynner. HBMV; YT
Under the Eildon Tree. Sidney Goodsir Smith. OxBS
Under the elms, on our city street. Grandfather's Ghost. Joseph Payne Brennan. FiSC

Under the financier's. The Jersey Marsh. David Galler. NYBP
Under the flower. The Sojourners. Emmett Jarrett. *Fr.* Design for the City of Man. ThO
Under the forest, where the air is dark. The Manzanita. Yvor Winters. NYTB
Under the French horns of a November afternoon. A Man in Blue. James Schuyler. ANYP
Under the Frontier Post. Wang Chang-ling, *tr. fr. Chinese by* Rewi Alley. ChTr
Under the Goal Posts. Arthur Guiterman. BBV (1951 ed.)
Under the great hill sloping bare. The King's Missive. Whittier. PAH
Under the green hedges, after the snow. Violets. John Moultrie. BoTP
Under the green lamp-light her letter there. Letter of a Mother. Robert Penn Warren. MAP; MoAmPo
Under the Greenwood Tree. Shakespeare. *Fr.* As You Like It, II, v. AnFE; BBV (1923 ed.); BEL; BoNaP; BoTP; CBEP; CH; EG; ElL; ELP; EnLi-1; EnLit; EnRePo; ExPo; FaBoBe; FaFP; FaPON; GBV; GN; GTBS; GTBS-D; GTBS-P; GTBS-W; GTSE; GTSL; HoPM; InPo; LiTB; LiTG; MCCG; MemP; MPB; NoP; OAEP; OBEV; OBSC; OHIP; OTPC; OuHeWo; PCH; PoeP; PTK; RG; SeCeV; ShBV-2; SiCE; TiPo; TOP; TreFS; ViBoPo; WHA; WiR; WoL
(Greenwood Tree, The.) RIS
(In the Greenwood.) AnEnPo
(Song: "Under the greenwood tree.") CTC; FiP; MemP
(Songs from the Plays.) AWP; JAWP; WBP
(Songs of the Greenwood.) TrGrPo
(Two Songs by Amiens, 2.) BoLiVe
Under the Harvest Moon. Carl Sandburg. NP; OQP
Under the heather. *Unknown.* RIS
Under the high-arching bridge. Helen Hoyt. NP
Under the Hill. Daryl Hine. MoCV
Under the hive-like dome the stooping haunted readers. The British Museum Reading Room. Louis MacNeice. LiTM; MoAB; MoBrPo; SeCePo; WaP
Under the Holly Bough. Charles Mackay. DD
(Holly Bough, The.) OBVV
(Reconciliation.) MaRV
Under the killdeer cry. Our People. William Stafford. NoP
Under the Leaves. Albert Laighton. HBV; OHIP
Under the Leaves Green. *Unknown. See* Who Shall Have My Fair Lady?
Under the light, yet under. Emily Dickinson. AP; Po
Under the lily shadow. The Swan. F. S. Flint. NP
Under the lime tree. Penelope. Judy Thurman. NYTB
Under the Lime Tree. Walther von der Vogelweide. *See* Tandaradei.
Under the Linden[s]. Walther von der Vogelweide. *See* Tandaradei.
Under the linden the music is gay. A Meeting. Heine. PoMS
Under the Lindens. Walter Savage Landor. HBV
Under the lindens on [*or* linden by] the heather. Tandaradei. Walther von der Vogelweide. AWP; LiTW
Under the long dark boughs, like jewels red. Cherry Robbers. D. H. Lawrence. MoAB; MoBrPo; PoIE
Under the long fell's stony eaves. The Ploughman. Gordon Bottomley. POTE
Under the long grass. Their Thanksgiving Day. Louise Driscoll. PCH
Under the low dark sky and the sodden leaves. Wet Summer; Botanic Gardens. Nan McDonald. BoAV
Under the lucent glass. In the Egyptian Museum. Janet Lewis. NYBP; QFR
Under the Mistletoe. Countee Cullen. GoSl
Under the Mistletoe. George Francis Shults. BOHV
Under the mock-oranges the children spy. The People in the Park. Léonie Adams. MoVE
Under the Moon. W. B. Yeats. EG; HT
Under the mountain, as when I first knew. Elegy in Six Sonnets. Frederick Goddard Tuckerman. *Fr.* Sonnets. AmePo; AP; MAmP; NoP; PIA; QFR
Under the Oak. D. H. Lawrence. OnHM
Under the Old Elm, *sels.* James Russell Lowell.
Great Virginian, The, *fr.* VII. PGD
Imperial Man, *fr.* VIII. PGD
New-come Chief, *fr.* III. MC
Ours, and All Men's. PAL; PGD
Unwasted Days, *abr., fr.* VI. MCCG
Washington ("Soldier and statesman, rarest union"), *fr.* V. DD; GN; HH; MC; OHIP; OQP, *abr.*; OTPC
Washington under the Old Elm. PEDC
Whom We Revere, *fr.* III. PGD
Under the orchards, under. Rogation Days. Kenneth Rexroth. NaP
Under the pale October sun I was wandering. The Swans. Catulle Mendès. OnPM
Under the parabola of a ball. How to Kill. Keith Douglas. ChMP
Under the pent-house branches the eight swans have come. A Dark World. E. J. Scovell. MoVE
Under the Pines. Arthur S. Bourinot. OBCV
Under the pines and hemlocks. The Deer. Mary Austin. FaPON
Under the pink quilted covers. The Fortress. Anne Sexton. LiTM (1970 ed.); ToPo
Under the plane trees cool and green as rain. The Flute-Man. Mary Oliver. TDP
Under the Pondweed. *Unknown, tr. fr. Chinese by* Helen Waddell. *Fr.* Shi King. AWP
Under the Portrait of John Milton. Dryden. *See* Lines Printed under the Engraved Portrait of Milton.
Under the Pyrenees. Alfred Noyes. *Fr.* The Last Voyage. GoBC
Under the Red Cross. Chauncey Hickox. AA
Under the roof and the roof's shadow turns. The Merry-Go-Round. Rainer Maria Rilke. CAD
"Under the roots of the roses." Mors et Vita. Richard Henry Stoddard. AA
Under the Round Tower. W. B. Yeats. SiSw
Under the scarlet-licking leaves. My Many-Coated Man. Laurie Lee. NYBP; POTi
Under the sea, which is their sky, they rise. Submarine Mountains. Cale Young Rice. EtS
Under the Shade of the Trees. Margaret Junkin Preston. DD; MC; PAH
Under the shadows of a cliff. A Rise. Ernest McGaffey. AA
Under the shape of his sail, Ulysses. Presence of an External Master of Knowledge. Wallace Stevens. NePA
Under the slanting light of the yellow sun of October. The Modern Romans. Charles Frederick Johnson. AA; LHV
Under the slumber and winter of a silent night. In Lord Carpenter's Country. Barry O. Higgs. PeSA
Under the Snow. Robert Collyer. AA
Under the Snow. T. Hempstead. SoP
Under the sovereign crests of dead volcanoes. On a Bougainvillaea Vine in Haiti [*or* at the Summer Palace]. Barbara Howes. MoAmPo (1962 ed.); NYBP
Under the Stars. Wallace Rice. AA; OHIP
Under the Sun. Henry Charles Beeching. OTPC (1946 ed.); YT
Under the sun, groaned Solomon. Solomon. Hermann Hagedorn. GoBC
Under the sun on the gray hill. The Man on the Hill. Maurice Hewlett. *Fr.* The Song of the Plow. POTE
Under the surface of flux and of fear there is an underground movement. Louis MacNeice. *Fr.* The Kingdom. LiTM
Under the tall black sky you look out of your body. Endless. Muriel Rukeyser. NYBP
Under the Tent of the Sky. Rowena Bennett. UTS
Under the tree the farmer said. Cherries. Frederic E. Weatherly. SAS
Under the trees I sat, under the blue. William Ellery Leonard. *Fr.* Two Lives, Pt. III. AnAmPo
Under the viaduct, by the hot canal. Plaque. Bruce Ruddick. CaP
Under the Violets. Oliver Wendell Holmes. *Fr.* The Professor at the Breakfast Table. AA
Under the Violets. Edward Young. AA
Under the walls of Monterey. Victor Galbraith. Longfellow. PAH
Under the water tower at the edge of town. To the Evening Star: Central Minnesota. James Wright. NaP
Under the Waterfall. Thomas Hardy. CTC; LiTB; PoVP
Under the Wattle. Douglas Brook Wheelton Sladen. OBVV
Under the wide and starry sky. Requiem. Robert Louis Stevenson. AnFE; ATP; BBV; BrPo; DD; EPN; FaBV; FaPL; GoTP; GoTS; GTSL; HBV; HBVY; ILP; InP; LiTG; MaRV; MCCG; MoBrPo; MPB; NeHB; NeMA; OBEV; OBNC; OBVV; OQP; OtMeF; OTPC; PCD; PoFS; PoIE; PoLF;

Under (continued)
PoPl; PoRA; PoSa; PoVP; ShBV-2; TIHL; TOP; TreF; TrGrPo; TSW; VA; ViBoPo; WaKn; WGRP; WHA; YAT; YT
Under the willow. Issa, *tr. fr. Japanese by* Lewis Mackenzie. FIW
Under the Willow Shades. Sir William Davenant. ELP; MeWo
(Willow, The.) UnTE
Under the willow the willow. Recruiting Drive. Charles Causley. NePoEA; PPON; TPM
Under the Window: Ouro Preto. Elizabeth Bishop. NYBP
Under the winter, dear. Song. Eugene Lee-Hamilton. OBVV
Under the Woods. Edward Thomas. CH; LoBV
Under the yellow moon, when the young men and maidens pass in the lanes. The Last Fairy. Rosamund Marriott Watson. OBVV
Under the yellow sun. A White Tree in Bloom. John Richard Moreland. PGD
Under the yew-tree's heavy weight. Les Hiboux. Baudelaire. AWP; JAWP; WBP
Under these brooding skies. Reflections on the Fall of France, June, 1940. Eiluned Lewis. POTE
Under this beech why sittest thou here so sad. An Eglogue to Mr. Johnson. Thomas Randolph. SeEP
Under this crust. *Unknown.* WhC
Under this loop of honeysuckle. The Caterpillar. Robert Graves. TSW
Under this shade of crimson wings abhorred. The World in Armor. Sir William Watson. PoVP
Under this sod and beneath these trees. An Epitaph [*or* On Samuel Pease]. *Unknown.* MoShBr; ShM
Under this sod lies a great bucking hoss. To Midnight. *Unknown.* CoSo
Under this stone lies Gabriel John. Gabriel John. *Unknown.* CBEP
Under this stone, reader, survey. On [*or* Epitaph on] Sir John Vanbrugh [Architect]. Abel Evans. FiBHP; OBEC; PV; TreFT; ViBoPo
Under this stone there lieth at rest. An Epitaph of Sir Thomas Gravener Knight. Sir Thomas Wyatt. EnRePo; EP; OBSC; SiPS
Under this tree, where light and shade. Peace and Rest. W. H. Davies. BoPe
Under thy shadow may I lurk awhile. St. Peter's Shadow. Richard Crashaw. ACP; MaMe; SCEP-1
Under Which Lyre. W. H. Auden. MoAB; MoBrPo (1950 ed.)
Under white eyelids. The Sleeper. "Isobel Hume." HBMV
Under yonder beech-tree single on the green-sward. Love in the Valley. George Meredith. AnEnPo; AWP; BEL; EnL; EnLi-2; EPN; ErPo; GTBS-D; GTBS-W; GTSL; HBV; InPo; LiTB; LiTG; LiTL; OBEV; OBVV; OnPP; PoVP; ShBV-4; TreFT, 2 *sts.*; TOP; TrGrPo; UnTE; VaPo; ViBoPo; ViPo; VP; WHA
Under Your Voice, among Legends. Phyllis Harris. ThO
Underfoot on the hill the water spurts. Sunday on Hampstead Heath. George Woodcock. NeBP
Undergraduate. Merrill Moore. ErPo
Underground, The. Guy Boas. CenHV
Underground. Ian Mudie. BoAV; MoAuPo
Underground Gardens, The. Robert Mezey. NaP
Underground grower, blind and a common brown, An. Potato. Richard Wilbur. CrMA; LiTA; MoAB; TrGrPo (rev. ed.); TwAmPo
Underground Rumbling. James S. Tippett. GFA
Underneath an old [*or* a huge] oak tree. The Raven [and the Oak]. Samuel Taylor Coleridge. OTPC (1923 ed.); WiR
Underneath my belt. When I Was Lost. Dorothy Aldis. SoPo
Underneath My Window. Sir Philip Sidney. *See* Astrophel and Stella: Eleventh Song.
Underneath the abject willow. W. H. Auden. OTD, 8 *ll.*; PAn
Underneath the boardwalk, way, way back. The Secret Cavern. Margaret Widdemer. FaPON; MPB; RePo
Underneath the Clothes. Madeleine Nightingale. RIS
Underneath the growing grass. The Bourne. Christina Rossetti. CBV; ELP; FaBoEn; HBV; LoBV; OBNC
Underneath the leaves of life. The Riddle. W. H. Auden. EnLi-2 (1949 ed.)
Underneath the tree on some. Like They Say. Robert Creeley. ELU
Underneath the water-weeds. The Tadpole. Elizabeth Gould. BoTP
Underneath their eider-robe. The Poetry of a Root Crop. Charles Kingsley. LoBV
Underneath this ancient pew. *Unknown.* WhC
Underneath this greedy stone. Erotion [*or* Epitaph on Erotion]. Martial. OBRV; OnPM
Underneath this marble hearse. *See* Underneath this sable hearse.
Underneath this marble stone. Epitaph. Abraham Cowley. EnLoPo
Underneath this myrtle shade. The Epicure. Abraham Cowley. AWP; EG; OBEV; PG (1945 ed.); SeCP; SiTL
Underneath this pretty cover. With a Copy of Swift's Works. J. V. Cunningham. QFR
Underneath this sable [*or* marble] hearse [*or* herse]. On the Countess Dowager of Pembroke [*or* Epitaph on . . .]. William Browne, *wr. at. to* Ben Jonson. AWP; BEL; CABA; CavP; CBEP; EG; HBV; InP; InvP; JAWP; LoBV; MyFE; OBEV; OBS; OnPP; PoEL-2; PoRA (rev. ed.); ReEn; SeCeV; SeCL; SeEP; TOP; TreFS; UnPo (1st ed.); ViBoPo; WBP; WHA; WoL
Undersea Fever. William Cole. FiBHP
Undersong, The. Emerson. *Fr.* Woodnotes. AA
Under Song, The. *Unknown.* ACP (1926 ed.)
Undersong. Mark Van Doren. PoCh
Understand, he is naked in the sea. The Loved One. Joseph Hansen. NYBP
Understand too late? Of course we can. Poem for Gerard. E. L. Mayo. ML
Understanding. H. W. Bliss. PoToHe
Understanding. Pauline E. Soroka. PoLF
Understanding. Thomas Traherne. *See* Walking.
Understanding. *Unknown.* PoToHe (new ed.)
Understanding. Nixon Waterman. *See* "To Know All Is to Forgive All."
Understanding Heart, The. Georgia Harkness. MaRV
Understanding of a medical man, The. Sonnet. Rex Warner. ChMP
Undertaker's Advertisement, An. Ernest G. Moll. WhC
Undertaking, The. John Donne. AnFE; BoLiVe; CBEP; MaMe; MePo; ReEn; SCEP-1; SeEP; TuPP
Undertaking, The. Gerrit Lansing. CoPo
Undertone. Dorothy Quick. FiSC
Undertone. William Bedell Stanford. NeIP; OnYI
Undertow. Langston Hughes. LiTM (1970 ed.)
Underwater eyes, an eel's. An Otter. Ted Hughes. BoC; NePoEA-2; NMP; OPoP
Underway, my pockets split only with fist. My Bohemia. Arthur Rimbaud. ReMP
Underwear. Lawrence Ferlinghetti. CoPo
Underwood. Howard Moss. NePA; NePoEA-2; PP; TwCP
Undine. Irving Layton. ErPo
Undiscouraged God, The. *Unknown.* MaRV
Undiscovered Country, The. Thomas Bailey Aldrich. AA
Undiscovered Country, The. William Dean Howells. MaRV; OQP; SoP
(Prayer, A: "Lord, for the erring thought.") WGRP
(Thanksgiving, A.) HBV; TrPWD
Undiscovered Planet, The. Norman Nicholson. ChMP; FaBoMo; POTi
Undisturbed the Autumn grass grows by the deserted door. On Passing a Friend's House. Wang Wei. OnPM
Undo Your Heart. *Unknown.* MeEL
Undocumented Observations from the Letters of G. Craig Sterry. QAH
Undoubtedly the kangaroos. Nature Note. Arthur Guiterman. SUS
Undue significance a starving man attaches. Emily Dickinson. LiTA; LiTM (rev. ed.)
Undulations of precision harass the mind. Kochia. Thomas Hornsby Ferril. NePoAm-2
Undying Soul, The. Whittier. *Fr.* On a Fly-Leaf of Longfellow's Poems. MaRV; OQP
Undying Thirst. Antipater of Sidon, *tr. fr. Greek by* Robert Bland. AWP; OuHeWo
Une Idole du Nord. Francis Stuart. NeIP
Une petite pêche dans un orchard fleurit. The Little Peach. *Unknown.* NA

Une Vie. Pentti Saarikoski, *tr. fr. Finnish by* Anselm Hollo. ELU
Unearned Increment. Christopher Morley. SiTL; WhC
Unearth. Alfred Barrett. GoBC
Uneasy Peace. Edmund Blunden. BrPo
Unemployed. Ralph Cheyney. ChIP
Unemployed, The. LeVan Roberts. PGD
Unemployed, An/ machinist. I'm Tired of Being Scared. John Giorno. ANYP
"Unending Sameness of Questionable Quality." Ethel Livingston. ThO
Unending Sky, The. John Masefield. FIW
Unequal Distribution. Samuel Hoffenstein. TrJP
Unerring Guide, The. Anna Shipton. BLRP
Unexpected Visit, An. Tu Fu, *tr. fr. Chinese by* Chi Hwang Chu *and* Edna Worthley Underwood. OnPM
Unexploded Bomb, The. C. Day Lewis. TPM
Unexplored, The. Burnham Eaton. FiSC
Unexplorer, The. Edna St. Vincent Millay. LOW; MoShBr; RePo; SUS
Unexpress'd, The. Walt Whitman. NePA; PP
Unfading Beauty, The. Thomas Carew. *See* Disdain Returned.
Unfailing Friend, The. Joseph Scriven. *See* What a Friend We Have in Jesus.
Unfailing One, The. Phillips Brooks. *See* Our Burden Bearer.
Unfailing One, The. Frances Ridley Havergal. *See* Rest on Him.
Unfaith. Ted Robinson. MaRV
Unfaithful Shepherdess, The. *Unknown. See* Faithless Shepherdess, The.
Unfaithful Shepherds. Ezekiel, XXXIV: 1-28, Bible, *O.T.* WoL
Unfamiliar Quartet. Stephen Vincent Benét. WhC
Unfathomable Sea! Shelley. *See* Time.
Unfathomable sea, and time, and tears, The. To N. V. de G. S. Robert Louis Stevenson. BrPo; VA
Unfathomable sea! whose waves are years. Time. Shelley. BEL; EnLi-2; EPN; EtS; Par; PoIE (1970 ed.) PoLF; YAT
Unfinished History, An. Archibald MacLeish. NYBP
Unfinished Portrait. Elinor Wylie. CoBA
Unfinished Race, The. Norman Cameron. OxBS
Unfit die, The—the fit both live and thrive. The Survival of the Fittest. Sarah N. Cleghorn. HBMV
Unflinching Dante of a later day. To an Imperilled Traveller. Nathan Haskell Dole. AA
Unfold unfold/ Thou beaten-gold. In Grato Jubilo. David McCord. UnS
Unfold, unfold! take in His light. The Revival. Henry Vaughan. BoLiVe; ELP; MaPo; MemP; OBS; OxBoCh; PoEL-2; PrWP; SeCL; SeEP; SoP; TrGrPo
Unfolde thyne armes & let me goe. *Unknown.* SeCSL
Unforeseen, The. Conrado Nale Roxlo, *tr. fr. Spanish by* Milton Ben Davis. LiTW; MoRP
Unforgivable and Unforgiven. C. D. B. Ellis. SiTL
Unforgiven, The. E. A. Robinson. CMoP
Unfortunate admiral! Your poor America. To Columbus. Rubén Darío. TTY
Unfortunate Coincidence. Dorothy Parker. ALV; PoPl; PoPo; TreF; WhC
Unfortunate Lover, The. Andrew Marvell. MaMe; MeP
Unfortunate Lovers, The, *sels.* Sir William Davenant.
Love ("'Tis, in good truth, a most wonderful thing"). SeCL
"Roses and pinks will be strewn where you go" ViBoPo
Unfortunate Male, The. Kalonymos ben Kalonymos, *tr. fr. Hebrew by* Joseph Chotzner. TrJP
Unfortunate Man, The, *with music. Unknown.* BFSS
Unfortunate Miller, The. A. E. Coppard. FaBoTw; POTE
Unfortunate Miller, The; or, The Country Lasses Witty Invention. *Unknown.* CoMu; OxBB
Unfortunate Miss Bailey. George Colman, the Younger. BOHV; DTC; FiBHP; ViBoFo
(Miss Bailey's Ghost.) OxBoLi
Unfortunate Mole, The. Mary Kennedy. GoYe
Unfortunate Reminder, The. William Pattison. UnTE
Unfriendly Fortune. John Skelton. MeEL
(Go; Piteous Heart) NCEP
Unfriendly, friendly universe. The Child Dying. Edwin Muir. ChMP; FaBoTw; GTBS-D; GTBS-P
Unfriendly Witness. George Starbuck. CBV
Unfrocked Priest, The. Joseph Campbell. AnIL; OnYI
Unfulfilment. Frances Louisa Bushnell. AA
Unfurled gull on the tide, and over the skerry, The. December Day, Hoy Sound. George Mackay Brown. OxBS
Ungathered Apples, The. James Wright. ErPo
Ungathered Love. Philip Bourke Marston. OBNC
Ungar and Rolfe. Herman Melville. *Fr.* Clarel. OxBA
Ungentle Alice, thy sorrow is my sore. *Unknown. Fr.* Arden of Feversham. LO
Ungrateful Garden, The. Carolyn Kizer. NePoEA-2
Ungratefulnesse. George Herbert. MaMe
Unguarded. Ada Foster Murray. HBV
Unguarded Gates. Thomas Bailey Aldrich. AA; AnNE; MC; PAH
Unhappie light. *See* Unhappy light.
Unhappie verse, the witnesse of my unhappie state. *See* Unhappy verse, the witness of my unhappy state.
Unhappy about some far off things. The Stars Go over the Lonely Ocean. Robinson Jeffers. GTBS-W; LiTA; LiTM (rev. ed.); NePA; WaP
Unhappy Bella. *Unknown.* ErPo
Unhappy Boston. Paul Revere. PAH
Unhappy country, what wings you have! Even here. Eagle Valor, Chicken Mind. Robinson Jeffers. ELU; LiTA; OxBA; WaP
Unhappy dreamer, who outwinged in flight. On the Death of a Metaphysician. George Santayana. AA; AnFE; AmLP; APA; CoAnAm; MAP; MoAmPo; ViBoPo
Unhappy East (not in that awe). Reply. Sidney Godolphin. OBS
Unhappy Erin, what a lot was thine! National Presage. John Kells Ingram. OnYI
Unhappy Favourite, The, *sel.* John Banks.
Description of a Sea-Battle. PeRV
Unhappy, I observe the Ass. A Rondeau of Remorse. Burges Johnson. HBMV
Unhappy [*or* Unhappie] light. Madrigal. William Drummond of Hawthornden. AtBAP; OBS
Unhappy Lover, The. Judah al-Harizi, *tr. fr. Hebrew by* Joseph Chotzner. TrJP
Unhappy Miner, The, *with music. Unknown.* SGR
Unhappy people in a happy world, An. Wallace Stevens. *Fr.* The Auroras of Autumn. CMoP
Unhappy sight, and hath she vanisht by. Astrophel and Stella, CV. Sir Philip Sidney. FCP; SiPS
Unhappy Tongue. Barnabe Googe. NoP
Unhappy [*or* Unhappie] verse, the witness of my unhappy state. Iambicum Trimetrum [*or* Iambica]. Spenser. EIL; OBEV (new ed.); OxBoLi; PoEL-1; ReIE; SiTL
Unhappy youth betrayed by fate. Against the Love of Great Ones. Richard Lovelace. AnAnS-2
Unharvested. Robert Frost. BoNaP
Unhinged the iron gates half open hung. Thomas Hood. *Fr.* The Haunted House. NBM
Unhistoric Story, The. Allen Curnow. AnNZ
Unholy Missions. Bob Kaufman. TTY
Unhurried as a snake I saw Time glide. On Time. Richard Hughes. MoBrPo
Unhurt, untoucht did I complain. The Dissembler. Abraham Cowley. AnAnS-2
Unicorn, The. George Darley. *Fr.* Nepenthe. ChTr; ERoP-2; FaBoEn; NBM; OBNC; PoEL-4
("Lo! in the mute, mid wilderness.") OBRV
Unicorn, The. Ruth Pitter. LO; MoBrPo; MoVE
Unicorn, The. Ella Young. FaPON; SoPo; TiPo
Unicorn and the Lady, The. Jean Garrigue. NYBP
Unicorn to hand, A. Haste to the Wedding. Alex Comfort. ErPo
Unicorns at Harvard ("Unicorns are astray"). Norma Farber. FiSC
Unicorn's hoofs, The! Dance Song. *Unknown.* FaBoCh; LoGBV; OA
Unicorns move furtively among. Lemon Sherbet. Marvin Solomon. NePoAm
Unillumined Verge, The. Robert Bridges. AA
Uninfected, The. E. L. Mayo. MiAP
Uninscribed Monument on One of the Battle-Fields of the Wilderness, An. Herman Melville. AA; AmLP
Uninvited, The. William D. Mundell. NYBP
Union and Liberty. Oliver Wendell Holmes. OHIP
Union Jack, The. Jeannie Kirby. BoTP
Union of Love. Jami, *tr. fr. Persian by* F. Hadland Davis. OnPM
Unique. Frances Bent Dillingham. SoP

Unison. John Hall Wheelock. MoRP
Unison, A. William Carlos Williams. PoIE; SeCeV
Unit. Mary Fullerton. BoAV
Unite, unite, let us all unite. The Padstow Night Song. *Unknown.* ChTr
United. Paulus Silentiarius, *tr. fr. Greek by* W. H. D. Rouse. AWP
United States. John Keble. CoBE
United States and *Macedonian*, The ("The Banner of Freedom high floated unfurled"). *Unknown.* PAH
United States and *Macedonian*, The ("How glows each patriot bosom"). *Unknown.* PAH
United States are rich, they're powerful and great, The. Rubén Darío. *Fr.* To Theodore Roosevelt. PoFr
Unity. "Æ." *See* Secret, The.
Unity. Lloyd Frank Merrell. ChIP
Unity. Alfred Noyes. HBV; InP
Unity of God, The. Panatattu. *See* God Is One.
Universal Change. Sophocles, *tr. fr. Greek by* Charles Stuart Calverley. *Fr.* Ajax. LiTW
Universal Favorite, The. Carolyn Wells. InMe
Universal Fire, The. *Unknown, tr. fr. Sanskrit by* Joseph Nadin Rawson. *Fr.* The Upanishads. OnPM
Universal Heart of Man, The. Wordsworth. *Fr.* The Prelude, XIII. TOP
Universal Language, The. Ella Wheeler Wilcox. ChIP; OQP
Universal Prayer, The. Pope. BEL; BoPe; CEP; EiCL; EiPP; EnLit; FaBoBe; GoBC; HBV; MaRV; OAEP; PoIE; TOP; TreFT; VaPo; WGRP
Universal Republic, The. Victor Hugo, *tr. fr. French.* OQP; PGD
(Republic of the World.) MaRV
Universal Self, The. *Unknown, tr. fr. Sanskrit by* F. Max Müller. *Fr.* The Upanishads. WoL
Universe, The. May Swenson. TPM
Universe into Stone. A. J. M. Smith. PeCV
Universe is deathless, The. Endless Self. *Unknown, at. to* Lao-tzu. *Fr.* Tao Teh King. OnPM
Universes. Adrian Henri. HYE
University. Karl Shapiro. AmPP (4th ed.); CoBA; LiTA; OxBA
University Curriculum. William Price Turner. OxBS
University Examinations in Egypt. D. J. Enright. MoPW; TwCP
Unkept Good Fridays. Thomas Hardy. MoRP
Unkind fate sent the Porlock person. The Person from Porlock. Robert Graves. BoC; ML
Unkind was he, the first who sang. A Girl's Song. Aubrey Thomas De Vere. GTBS-D
Unkindness[e]. George Herbert. EP; HBV; MaMe
Unkindness Has Killed Me. *Unknown.* MeEL
Unknowable Power is o'er me. The Visitor Abhorred. Sir William Watson. PoVP
Unknown, The. John Davidson. MoBrPo
Unknown, The. E. O. Laughlin. BLPA
Unknown, The. Denise Levertov. FRC
Unknown. Ono no Yoshiki, *tr. fr. Japanese by* Basil Hall Chamberlain. *Fr.* Kokin Shu. OnPM
("My love/ Is like the grasses," *tr. by* Arthur Waley.) AWP
Unknown Beloved, The. John Hall Wheelock. HBMV
Unknown Bird, The. Edward Thomas. ACV; DTC; FaBoEn
Unknown Citizen, The. W. H. Auden. CABA; CBV; ChMP; LiTA; LiTM; MaPo (1969 ed.); MoAB; MoRP; NePA; NYBP; PoPo; PoRA; PPON; ShBV-4; SiTL; TreFT
Unknown City, The. Sir Charles G. D. Roberts. CaP
Unknown Color, The. Countee Cullen. FaPON; GoSl
Unknown Dead, The. Henry Timrod. AmP; AP; DD; HH; MAmP
Unknown dreamer dreamed concerning men. The Missionary. Henry W. Frost. SoP
Unknown Eros, The. Coventry Patmore. *Poems indexed separately by titles and first lines.*
Unknown Girl in the Maternity Ward. Anne Sexton. CoPo
Unknown God, The. "Æ." GTSL; MoBrPo; NeMA; TOP; WGRP
Unknown God. The. Charles G. Blanden. OQP
Unknown God, The. Henry Francis Lyte. MaRV; SoP; TRV
Unknown God, The. Alice Meynell. BoPe
Unknown God, The. Sir William Watson. WGRP
Unknown God, The—alas! His feet. The Unknown God. Charles G. Blanden. OQP
Unknown in history or in time they stand. Speakers, Columbus Circle. Raymond Souster. CaP
Unknown love/ Is as bitter a thing. The Lady of Sakanoye. *Fr.* Manyo Shu. AWP; JAWP
Unknown Man in the Morgue. Merrill Moore. MAP; MoAmPo
Unknown Master of Moulins, The. The Cardinal's Dog. John Glassco. MoCV
Unknown Sculptor, The. Stanton A. Coblentz. MaRV
Unknown, she was the form I preferred. Loss. Paul Eluard. OnPM
Unknown Shepherd's Complaint, The. Richard Barnfield. ElL; TuPP
(Shepherd's Complaint, A.) OBSC
Unknown Soldier, The. Conrad Aiken. *Fr.* The Soldier. WaaP; WaP
Unknown Soldier. Alta Booth Dunn. PGD
Unknown Soldier, The. Alun Lewis. MoBrPo (1962 ed.)
Unknown Soldier, The. Arthur B. Rhinow. OQP
Unknown Soldier, The. Billy Rose. BLPA; PAL
Unknown Soldier, The. Charles A. Wagner. AnAmPo
Unknown to all except a few. A Parable. George L. Kress. STF
Unknown Traveller, The. George Rostrevor Hamilton. MemP
Unknown Warrior Sings and Curses in the Street, The. Herbert Palmer. FaBoTw
Unknown Wind, The. "Fiona Macleod." BoTP
Unless. Ella Maria Dietz Glynes. AA
Unless I Am Careful. W. W. Gibson. NP
Unless that kitty shines again in heaven. To a Black Dog, Bereaved. Elizabeth J. Coatsworth. PCD
Unless the febrile brow be cool. Open Letter to John Doe. Edward Doro. TwAmPo
Unless there were consent 'twixt hell and heaven. Thomas Campion. LO
Unless you come of the gipsy stock. Gipsy Vans. Kipling. OtMeF
Unless you knew just where to look. The Cobbler in Willow Street. George O'Neil. HBMV
Unlike are we, unlike, O princely Heart! Sonnets from the Portuguese, III. Elizabeth Barrett Browning. AnFE; EnLi-2; GTSL; HBV; OAEP; OBEV; OBVV; TrGrPo; ViPo
Unlike Virgil's verse on the *Troiae bella.* The Bachelor's Ballade. David Fisher Parry. InMe
Unlikely Rebel, The. Franklin D. Elmer, Jr. ChIP
Unloosed, unharnessed, turned back to the wild by love. The School of Desire. May Swenson. TwAmPo
Unloved, The. Arthur Symons. PoVP
Unloved to His Beloved. William Alexander Percy. HBMV
Unlucky Boat. George Mackay Brown. NePoEA-2
Unmanifest Destiny. Richard Hovey. AA; AmePo; AnAmPo; HBV; HBVY; MAP; MaRV; MoAmPo (1942 ed.); NeMA; PaA; PAL; PFY; PoFr; TRV; WGRP
Unmarried Mother Sings, An. F. R. Higgins. POTE
Unmindful of my low desert. The Quiet Nights. Katharine Tynan. HBV
"Unmitigated England." Great Central Railway, Sheffield Victoria to Banbury. John Betjeman. NYBP
Unmoored, unmanned, unheeded on the deep. The Derelict. Lucius Harwood Foote. AA
Unmoved by what the wind does. Sleeping with One Eye Open. Mark Strand. NYBP
Unmoving core, The. Return. Adèle Naudé. ACV
Unnamed Lake, The. Frederick George Scott. CaP; PTK
Unnatural, Unusual and Unfair. James Schevill. FiMAP
Unnoted as the setting of a star. Mulford. Whittier. AA
Unnoticed by the hurrying folk who pass. Wild Carrot. John Richard Moreland. NYTB
Unnumber'd suppliants crowd Preferment's gate. The Rise and Fall. Samuel Johnson. *Fr.* The Vanity of Human Wishes. PoFr
Unpardonable Sin, The. Vachel Lindsay. CMoP; LiTM (rev. ed.); MaRV; NePA
Unpayable Debt. Barbara Drake Johnston. SoP
Unpetalled Rose, The. St. Therese of Lisieux, *tr. fr. French by* Prioress Augustine of the Mother of God. CAW
Unplait the braided dark. To the Spring Sun. Freda Laughton. NeIP

Unpossessed, The. Adèle Naudé. PeSA
Unpraised Picture, An. Richard Burton. AA
Unprofitablenes. Henry Vaughan. AnAnS-1; AtBAP; MeP; SCEP-1; SeCV-1
Unpurged images of day recede, The. Byzantium. W. B. Yeats. CABA; CBV; CMoP; CoBMV; DiPo; FaBoEn; FaBoMo; GTBS-W; ILP; LiTM; LoBV; MaPo; MoAB; MoBrPo (1962 ed.) MoPo; NoP; OAEP (2d ed.); OnYI; PAn; PoE; PoeP; PoIE; SeCePo; SeCeV; StP; VaPo
Unquestionable Questions. Hy Sobiloff. SiTL
Unquestioning. Blake. *See* Eternity.
Unquiet Grave, The. *Unknown.* AnFE; AtBAP; BaBo; CBEP; CH; DTC; ELP; EnL; EnSB, *longer vers.*; ESPB; ExPo; LoBV; NoP; OBB; OxBB; PoEL-1; PoIE; ViBoFo, *with music*; ViBoPo; WePo
("Wind doth blow to-day, my love, The.") LO
Unreal!/ Unreal are both creation. Facing Death. Chih Ming. OnPM; WoL
Unreal Silence, An. Swallows Over the Camp. Uys Krige. PeSA
Unreal tall as a myth. The Bear on Delhi Road. Earle Birney. MoCV; NYBP; PoAn; PoCh
Unrealities, The. Schiller, *tr. fr. German by* James Clarence Mangan. AWP; WoL
Unrealized Ideal, The. Frederick Locker-Lampson. TSW
Unreasoning Heart. Louis Untermeyer. MAP; MoAmPo (1942 ed.)
Unregarding. Walter de la Mare. CMoP
Unregenerate. Jacqueline Embry. HBMV
Unrelated paragraphs of morning, The. Schoolroom on a Wet Afternoon. Vernon Scannell. HaMV
Unrequited Love on the Back Piazza. Margaret Fishback. CIV
Unrest. Richard Watson Dixon. OBNC
Unrest. Don Marquis. HBMV; MaRV; OQP; PoFr, *abr.*
Unresting as the pulse of arteries. Steel Mills after Midnight. Louise Crenshaw Ray. JKCP (1955 ed.)
Unreturning, The. Wilfred Owen. MoBrPo
Unreturning, The. Clinton Scollard. DD; PAH
Unreturning. Elizabeth Stoddard. AA
Unrhymed, unrhythmical, the chatter goes. At the Party. W. H. Auden. PoIE (1970 ed.)
Unriddle me my riddle. Winter Rune. Elizabeth J. Coatsworth. SUS
Unrighteous Lord of Love, what law is this. Amoretti, X. Spenser. NoP; PIA
Unromantic Song. Anthony Brode. FiBHP
Unsatisfied. Oliver Wendell Holmes. AnNE
Unsatisfied Yearning. R. K. Munkittrick. BOHV; InMe; PoMa; YT
Unscarred Fighter Remembers France, The. Kenneth Slade Alling. HBMV
Unseasonable/ as bees in April. Vermont; Indian Summer. Philip Booth. NePoEA
Unseasonable man, statue of ice. Ecclogue, 1613 December 26. John Donne. MaMe
Unseen. Fanny Crosby. TrPWD
Unseen Bridge, The. Gilbert Thomas. FaChP; HBMV; MaRV; SoP
Unseen Playmate, The. Robert Louis Stevenson. PCH
Unseen Spirits. N. P. Willis. AA; AmePo; AnAmPo; HBV
(Two Women.) BeLS; OBVV
Unseen World, The. Craven Langstroth Betts. OQP
Unsettled again and hearing Russian spoken. Hearing Russian Spoken. Donald Davie. GTBS-P; NePoEA-2
Unsettled Motorcyclist's Vision of His Death, The. Thom Gunn. ForPo; NePoEA-2
Unsexed by the Cold Sea. Winfield Townley Scott. CBV; FiMAP
(Watch Hill). ErPo
Unshaken by the storms that rage. Jesus of Nazareth Passes By. George T. Liddell. ChIP
Unshrinking Faith. William Hiley Bathurst. BLRP
(O for a Faith That Will Not Shrink.) SoP
Unshunnable is grief; we should not fear. Grief and God. Stephen Phillips. WGRP
Unsolved Mystery. George Ryan. WhC
Unstable Dream, According to the Place. Sir Thomas Wyatt. *See* Lover Having Dreamed of Enjoying of His Love, The.
Unstable monster, formless, vast, alone. Ocean. Louis Lavater. BoAu
Unsteady in the saddle. Francis Parkman. Ernest Kroll. NYTB
Unstooping. Walter de la Mare. UTS
Unsubdued. S. E. Kiser. MaRV; PoToHe
Unsuccessful Spring Poem. Philip Whalen. FRC
Unsullied Spring, O just-about-to-begin. To Spring. Virginia Moore. AnEnPo
Unsullied temple, heavenly light enshrining. The Assumption. St. Nerses. CAW
Unsung. Nettie Palmer. BoAu
Unsung Heroes, The, *abr.* Paul Laurence Dunbar. PoFr
Unsuspected Fact, An. Edward Cannon. BOHV; NA
Untended Field, The. Robert Hillyer. AnNE
Unthrift. Coventry Patmore. The Angel in the House, I, iii, 3. FaPL; HBV
(Preludes, I.) GoBC
Until a man should/ come. Man as He Shall Be. Rochelle Owens. CoPo
Until Death. Elizabeth Akers Allen. HBV
Until Eternity. Phyllis C. Michael. SoP
Until, finally,/ after aching, laming stages. Report. A. Fleming MacLiesh. *Fr.* The Jungle. NAMP
Until He Comes. . Martha Snell Nicholson. SoP
Until I caught the rhythm of his life. The Rhythm of His Life. Mary Hallet. ChIP
Until I helped. Gethsemane, Illinois. Martin S. Allwood. LiTW
Until I learned to trust. Progress. Barbara C. Ryberg. SoP; STF
Until I lose my soul and lie. A Prayer. Sara Teasdale. HBMV; TrPWD
Until I Reach-a Ma Home, *with music. Unknown.* BoAN-1
Until I was a roustabout. Animal Fair. Philip Booth. NePoAm-2
Until Jove let it be, no colonist. Georgic I. Vergil. *Fr.* Georgics. LiTW
Until my lamp and I. Discovery. Hildegarde Flanner. HBMV
Until the birth of my thirtieth birthday. Confidential Data on the Loyalty Investigation of Herbert Ashenfoot. James Schevill. FiMAP
Until the day when thou and I are wed. The Maid in the Rice-Fields. Viola Meynell. MoBrPo (1942 ed.)
Until the desert knows. Emily Dickinson. MaPo; MoPo
Until the future blossoms on your limbs. Gardening. Dabney Stuart. NYTB
Until the Shadows Lengthen. Cardinal Newman. SoP; TRV
Until thine hands clasp girdlewise the waist of the Belov'd. Ode. Sadi. AWP
Until this poem is over, I shall not leave. Windfall. F. R. Scott. CaP
Until We Built a Cabin. Aileen Fisher. TiPo (1959 ed.)
Until yesterday I was polite and peaceful. Opinions of the New [Chinese] Student. Regino Pedroso. PoNe; TTY
Until your laughter. Tumult. Charles Enoch Wheeler. PoNe
Untimely End, The. Chidiock Tichborne. *See* Elegy: "My prime of youth is but a frost of cares."
Untimely Thought. Thomas Bailey Aldrich. AnNE
Untiring shade, and ghost of dazzling gloom. Black Are the Stars. Raymond Roseliep. FiSC
Untitle. Kuwasi Balagon. BF
Untitled. Daryl Hine. TwCP
Unto a Child in Bethlehem-town. Eugene Field. *Fr.* Bethlehem-Town. PGD
Unto a heavenly course decreed. Star Morals. Nietzsche. AWP
Unto all poets I do me excuse. The Excusation of the Auctor. Stephen Hawes. *Fr.* The Pastime of Pleasure. ReIE
Unto Each Man His Handiwork. Swinburne. *Fr.* Super Flumina Babylonis. OQP, 2 *sts.*
("Whoso Loseth His Life," 4 *sts.*) MaRV
Unto God let praise be brought. And It Came to Pass at Midnight. Yannai. TrJP
Unto my faith as to a spar, I bind. Adrift. Elizabeth Dickinson Dowden. WGRP
Unto my friends I give my thoughts. Legacies. Ethelwyn Wetherald. MaRV; OQP
Unto my thinking, thou behold'st all worth. Sonnet: To Dante

Unto (continued)
Alighieri (He Interprets Dante's Dream). Guido Cavalcanti. AWP
Unto nobody my woman saith she had rather a wife be. Out of Catullus. Catullus. FCP
Unto salvation's spring. The Holy Eclogue. Sister Francisca Josefa del Castillo. CAW
Unto the blithe and lordly Fellowship. Sonnets of the Months [*or* Of the Months]: Dedication. Folgore da San Gemignano. AWP
Unto the boundless ocean of thy beauty. To Delia, I. Samuel Daniel. LiTL; LoBV; OAEP; OBSC; ReIE; SiCE
Unto the death gois all estatis. William Dunbar. *Fr.* Lament for the Makers. ML
Unto the deep the deep heart goes. The Place of Rest. "Æ." WGRP
Unto the Hills. John Campbell, *paraphrased from* Psalm CXXI, Bible, *O.T.* MaRV
Unto the prison house of pain none willingly repair. The House of Pain. Florence Earle Coates. HBV; OQP
Unto the silver night. Revelation. Sir Edmund Gosse. OBEV; OBVV
Unto the soundles vaultes of Hell below. *Unknown.* SeCSL
Unto the temple of thy beauty. *Unknown.* OBSC
Unto the Upright Praise, *sel.* Moses Hayyim Luzzatto of Padua, *tr. fr. Hebrew by* Nina Davis Salaman.
Chorus: "All ye that handle harp and viol and pipe." TrJP
Unto the winds and waves I now commit. On Leaving My Native Land. William Lloyd Garrison. SoP
Unto thy favor, which when nature formed. Robert Tofte. *Fr.* Laura. Sonn; TuPP
Unto Us a Boy Is Born, *with music.* *Unknown.* YaCaBo
Unto Us a Son Is Given. Alice Meynell. ChIP; GTBS; JKCP; MoRP; OQP; PoRL; StJW
Unto you, most froward, this letter I write. A Grotesque Love-Letter. *Unknown.* MeEL
Untold Want, The. Walt Whitman. MoAmPo (1950 ed.)
Untouched by Adam's curse—our Mary's soul! Hymn for Second Vespers; Feast of the Apparition of Our Lady of Lourdes. *Unknown.* ISi
Untrammelled giant of the West. The Parting of the Ways. Joseph B. Gilder. AA; HBV; PAH
Untried Door, The. Edward Shillito. ChIP
Untrodden Ways. Agnes Maule Machar. CaP
Untutored Giraffe, The. Oliver Herford. PoMa
"Once on a time a young giraffe," *sel.* ShM
Untwine those ringlets! Ev'ry dainty clasp. Frangipanni. *Unknown.* NA
Unutterable Beauty, The. G. A. Studdert-Kennedy. TrPWD
Unwanted, The. C. Day Lewis. PoPl
Unwanted. Edward Field. CoPo; PPON
Unwarmed by any sunset light. The World Transformed. Whittier. *Fr.* Snow-bound. AA; GBV
Unwasted Days, *abr.* James Russell Lowell. *Fr.* Under the Old Elm, VI. MCCG
Unwatch'd, the garden bough shall sway. In Memoriam A. H. H, CI. Tennyson. ELP; EnLi-2; EPN; GTBS-D; GTBS-P; OBEV (1st ed.); OBNC; PoEL-5; SeCeV; ViPo; VP
Unwelcome. Mary Elizabeth Coleridge. CH; GTBS; GTBS-D; OBEV (new ed.); OBNC; OBVV; PoVP
Unwelcome child. The Child Compassion. Margot Ruddock. OBMV
Unwilling Guest, The; an Urban Dialogue. Horace Gregory. CrMA
Unwilling Gypsy, The. Josephine Johnson. HBMV
Unwillingly Miranda wakes. A Lady Thinks She Is Thirty. Ogden Nash. PoPl
Unwind My Riddle. Stephen Crane. MWA-2; NoP
Unwinking frog of malachite, The. Museum-Piece. Audrey Alexandra Brown. CaP
Unwound the long evolvement. A Dream. Mary Fullerton. BoAV
Unwritten Poems. William Winter. AA
Unwritten Song, The. Ford Madox Ford. BoTP
Up a river of sweet milk. *Unknown.* *Fr.* The Land of Cokaigne. CAW
Up above, a passing breeze. Fir Forest. Ethel Romig Fuller. PGD
"Up above those top leaves, what do you see." Magnolia Tree in Summer. Sacheverell Sitwell. BoC
Up aloft amid the rigging. Rolling Home. *Unknown.* AmSS
Up and away, like the dew of the morning. The Everlasting Memorial. Horatius Bonar. SoP
Up and Down. Shakespeare. *Fr.* A Midsummer Night's Dream, III.ii. CTC
Up and down/ Runs arrowy fire. How a Poet's Soul Comes into Play. Robert Browning. *Fr.* Sordello. MyFE
Up and down/ she walks. The Rose. Robert Creeley. AP; ToPo
Up and down he goes. America. Alfred Kreymborg. NP
Up and down, o'er hill and valley. Triumph. L. D. Stearns. BLRP
Up and down the air you float. The Butterfly. Clinton Scollard. GFA
Up and down the beach. The Skin Divers. George Starbuck. NYBP; TDP
Up and Down the City Road. *Unknown.* EvOK
(Pop Goes the Weasel.) OxNR
Up and down the river. River Night. Frances Frost. OCS
Up and down the village streets. The Prophecy of Samuel Sewall. Whittier. MAmP
Up and up, the Incense-burner Peak! Having Climbed to the Topmost Peak of the Incense-Burner Mountain. Po Chü-i. SD
Up at a Villa—Down in the City. Robert Browning. BEL; CBEP; EnLi-2 (1949 ed.); EnLit; EPN; GTBS-P; HBV; InP; MBW-2; PoRA; PoVP; SeCeV; TOP; ViPo; ViPP; WoL
Up at Piccadilly oh! *Unknown.* OxNR
Up boy! arise, and saddle quick. The Message. Heine. AWP; JAWP; WBP
Up, Fairy! quit thy chick-weed bower. The Second Quest. Joseph Rodman Drake. *Fr.* The Culprit Fay. AA
Up from Earth's Center through the Seventh Gate. The Master-Knot. Omar Khayyám. *tr. by* Edward Fitzgerald. *Fr.* The Rubáiyát. OnPM
Up from my belly, up from my back. Chopping Fire-Wood. Robert Pack. NePoEA-2
Up from my golden saucer in the dawn. Domine Jesu! John Duffy. JKCP (1955 ed.)
Up from the Bed of the River. James Weldon Johnson. *Fr.* The Creation. EaLo
Up from the darkness on the laughing stage. Villiers de l'Isle-Adam. Aldous Huxley. HBMV
Up from the Egg; the Confessions of a Nuthatch Avoider. Ogden Nash. FiBHP; PoRA (rev. ed.)
Up from the Jordan straight his way he took. The Wilderness. Caroline Hazard. ChIP; StJW
Up from the low-roofed dockyard warehouses. Grain Elevator. A. M. Klein. CaP; TwCaPo
Up from the meadows rich with corn. Barbara Frietchie. Whittier. AmePo; AmPP (3d ed.); AnNE; AP; BBV; BeLS; BoTP; CTC; DD; FaBoBe; FaBV; FaFP; FaPL; FaPON; GN; GoTP; GSP; HBV; HBVY; MaC; MC; NeHB; OnSP; OTD; OTPC; PaA; PAH; PAL; PAP; PaPo; PoLF; PoSC; PTK; RIS; StVeCh (1940 ed.); ThLM; TreF; TrGrPo; WBLP; YaD; YT
When First I Came Here. Edward Thomas. UnPo (3d ed.)
Up from the sea a flaky, dank. The Fishermen. Emile Verhaeren. WoL
Up from the south, at break of day. Sheridan's Ride. Thomas Buchanan Read. BBV; BeLS; CoBA; DD; FaBoBe; FaBV; FaFP; GN; HBV; HBVY; MC; OHFP; OHIP; OnSP; OTPC; PaA; PAH; PAP; TreF; WBLP; YaD
Up from the Wheelbarrow. Ogden Nash. FaBoBe
Up from Toulouse, September in the air. Le Coeur de l'Immaculée. Benjamin Francis Musser. WHL
Up, Helsum Hairt. Alexander Scott. OxBS
Up-Hill [*or* Uphill]. Christina Rossetti. BLPA; CH; CoBE; EnLi-2; FaBoBe; FaChP; FaPL; GTBS; HBV; LoBV; MaRV; MCCG; MemP; NeHB; NoP; OAEP; OBEV; OBNC; OBVV; OQP; OtMeF; OTPC (1946 ed.); PCD; Po; PoFS; PoMa; PoRA; PoVP; ShBV-2; SoP; TOP; TreFS; TrGrPo; TSW; VA; ViBoPo; ViPo; VP; WGRP; WHA; WiR
("Does the road wind up-hill all the way?") EG
Up hill and down dale. *Unknown.* OxNR
Up in his loft the shy FRCO. Seated One Day. Paul Jennings. MuSP
Up in the Air. Allan Ramsay. CEP
Up in the Air. James S. Tippett. BoChLi; SoPo; SUS; TiPo
Up in the attic, down in the cellar, and under. A Treasure. Reed Whittemore. NePoEA

Up in the barn where they keep the hay. The Hayloft. Luella Markley Mockett. BrR
Up in the Morning Early. Burns. OTPC; PCH; PoSC
Up in the morning early. The Sun Is First to Rise. Elizabeth J. Coatsworth. StVeCh (1955 ed.)
Up in the morning's no' for me. Up in the Morning Early. Burns. OTPC; PCH
Up in the mountain solitudes. An Oft-Told Tale. *Unknown.* SGR
Up in the mountains, it's lonesome all the time. The Mountain Whippoorwill. Stephen Vincent Benét. IHA; StPo; TrGrPo; YaD; YT
Up in the North. *Unknown.* LiTG; OxBoLi; SiTL
Up in the sky. Song of Tom. Kirk Hall. BF
Up in the woodland where Spring. A Ballade of Spring's Unrest. Bert Leston Taylor. PoMa; YT
Up into the cherry tree. Foreign Lands. Robert Louis Stevenson. BoTP; GFA; HBV; HBVY; MPB; OTPC; PCH; PoVP; RIS; TiPo (1952 ed.); TVC; VA
Up Johnie raise in a May morning. Johnie Cock. *Unknown.* ESPB (D *vers.*)
Up-line platform bridges a metal road, The. Ravenglass Railway Station, Cumberland. Norman Nicholson. NYBP
Up my brothers! Set all men free! Goethe. *Fr.* The Awakening of Epimenides. PoFr
Up, my dogs, merrily. The Nor'-west Courier. John E. Logan. VA
Up on de Mountain, *with music.* *Unknown.* BoAN-1
Up on the Downs. John Masefield. FaBoEn
("Up on the downs the red-eyed kestrels hover.") BrPo
Up on their brooms the Witches stream. The Ride-by-Nights. Walter de la Mare. FaPON; SiSoSe; TiPo
Up! quit thy bower! late wears the hour. Good Morning [*or* Wake, Lady]. Joanna Baillie. HBV; OTPC (1923 ed.)
Up rose [*or* Uprose] the king of men with speed. The Descent of Odin; an Ode from the Norse Tongue. Thomas Gray. CEP; EiCP; EiPP
Up rose the sun; the mists were curl'd. Byron. *Fr.* Mazeppa. OBRV
Up-Set, The. Corey Ford. WhC
Up She Goes, *with music.* *Unknown.* SoAmSa
Up Silver Stairsteps. Jesse Stuart. AmFN
Up soared the lark into the air. Saint Francis' Sermon to the Birds. Longfellow. OTPC
Up street and down street. *Unknown.* OxNR
Up-Tails All. *Unknown.* UnTE
Up tails all! Down and under! Undersea Fever. William Cole. FiBHP
Up the Airy Mountain. William Allingham. *See* Fairies, The.
Up the ash tree climbs the ivy. Upper Lambourne. John Betjeman. FaBoTw; GTBS-D; POTi
Up the Barley Rows. Sora, *tr. fr. Japanese by* Harold G. Henderson. SoPo
Up the crag/ In the screaming wind. Weapons. Anna Wickham. MoBrPo
Up the dale and down the bourne. Summer Winds. George Darley. VA
Up the dark-valleyed river stroke by stroke. The Dawn on the Lievre. Archibald Lampman. CaP
Up the dusty way from Frisco town. Walk, Damn You, Walk! Whittier. PoLF
Up the Hill, down the Hill. Eleanor Farjeon. PoSC
Up the hillside down the glen. Texas. Whittier. PAH
Up the Mountain to Pick Mawu. *Unknown, tr. fr. Chinese by* David Rafael Wang. HW
Up the Noran water. Shy Geordie. Helen B. Cruickshank. ACV; GoTS; OxBS
Up the old hill to the old house again. The Long Race. E. A. Robinson. CrMA
Up the pound path. Betty Perrin. A. E. Coppard. MoBrPo (1942 ed.)
Up the reputable walks of old established trees. The Campus on the Hill. W. D. Snodgrass. AP; LiTM (1970 ed.); ToPo; TwCP
Up the sea-sadden'd valley at evening's decline. Dirge of Rory O'More. Aubrey Thomas De Vere. IrPN
Up the Spout. Swinburne. BOHV
Up the street,/ Down the street. The Old Man's Toes. Eleanor Farjeon. PoRh
Up the wooden hill. *Unknown.* OxNR
Up, Then Down. *Unknown.* SoP
Up then, Melpomene, thou mournfulst [*or* mournefulst] Muse of nine. Dido My Dear, Alas, Is Dead. Spenser. *Fr.* The Shepheardes Calender. AtBAP; ChTr
Up There in Snow. Lewis Warsh. YAP
Up this green woodland-ride let's softly rove. The Nightingale's Nest. John Clare. PeER
Up through a cloudy sky, the sun. The Battle of Bennington. Thomas P. Rodman. MC; PAH
"Up, Timothy, up with your staff and away!" The Childless Father. Wordsworth. CH
Up to both sweet-spoken Nestor stood. Nestor's Speech to Achilles and Agamemnon. Homer. *Fr.* The Iliad, I. ReEn
Up to her chamber window. Nocturne. Thomas Bailey Aldrich. HBV
Up to his shoulder. The Bird Fancier. James Kirkup. PoPo
Up to Mount Olivet my soul ascend. William Alabaster. Sonn
Up to my lips and over my gums. Toast. *Unknown.* CoSo
Up to the bed by the window, where I be lyin'. Old Shepherd's Prayer. Charlotte Mew. EaLo; MoAB; MoBrPo
Up to the breeze of the morning I fling you. Flag o' My Land. T. A. Daly. HH
Up to the ranch rides cowboy Freddy. From the Ballad of Two-Gun Freddy. Walter R. Brooks. SoPo
Up to the top of the haunted turf. Mother Goose Up-to-Date. Louis Untermeyer. MoAmPo
Up to the wedding, formal with heirloom lace. At the Savoy Chapel. Robert Graves. HW
Up! Up! let us a voyage take. Northern Seas. William Howitt. GN; OTPC (1923 ed.)
Up, up, my drowsie Soule, where thy new eare. Our Company in the Next World. John Donne. *Fr.* Of the Progresse of the Soule. OBS
Up! Up! My Friend, and Quit Your Books. Wordsworth. *See* Tables Turned, The.
Up! Up! the sky's afloat. Song for a Camper. John Farrar. YeAr
Up! Up! the time for sleep is past! The Expensive Wife. Judah ibn Sabbatai. *Fr.* The Gift of Judah the Woman-Hater. TrJP
Up, Up! Ye Dames and Lasses Gay. Samuel Taylor Coleridge. *See* Hunting Song.
Up where the white bluffs fringe the plain. Prairie Wolves. Robert V. Carr. PoOW
Up with me! up with me into the clouds! To a Sky-Lark. Wordsworth. BEL; DD; HBV; MCCG; MERP; TOP
Up with the banner of the free! The Flag. Henry Lynden Flash. MC
Up with you, lazybones! Getting Out of Bed. Eleanor Farjeon. SiSoSe
Up Y arose in verno tempore. *Unknown.* EnPo
Up yonder on the mountain. The Shepherd's Lament. Goethe. AWP; JAWP; WBP
Up, Youths and Virgins, Up, and Praise. Ben Jonson. *Fr.* Masque of Cupid. HW
Upanishads, The, *sels.* *Unknown, tr. fr. Sanskrit.*
All, The, *tr. by* Joseph Nadin Rawson. OnPM
As Pure Water, *tr. by* Joseph Nadin Rawson. OnPM
"He, being one, rules over all and everything," *tr. by* F. Max Müller. PoFr
Inner Vision, *tr. by* Joseph Nadin Rawson. OnPM
No Peace, *tr. by* Joseph Nadin Rawson. OnPM
Omnipresent Self, *tr. by* Joseph Nadin Rawson. OnPM
Self, The, *tr. by* Joseph Nadin Rawson. OnPM
Story of Svetaketu, The, *tr. by* F. Max Müller. WoL
Tranquility, *tr. by* Joseph Nadin Rawson. OnPM
Unborn Eternal Self, *tr. by* Joseph Nadin Rawson. OnPM
Universal Fire, The, *tr. by* Joseph Nadin Rawson. OnPM
Universal Self, The, *tr. by* F. Max Müller. WoL
Yoga, *tr. by* Joseph Nadin Rawson. OnPM
Upas Tree, The. Pushkin, *tr. fr. Russian.* *LiTW, tr. by* Frances Cornford *and* E. P. Salaman
Upbroke the sun. The Poor Old Cannon. Elinor Wylie. LHV
Upended it crouches on broken limbs. Poem. Charles Tomlinson. CMoP
Upheld by His Hand. Grace B. Renfrow. BePJ
Uphill. Christina Rossetti. *See* Up-Hill
Upland of Nirvana. *Unknown, tr. fr. Japanese by* Ishii *and* Obata. OnPM

Uplifted and waved until immobilized. Elephants. Marianne Moore. FaBoMo
Upon a bed of humble clay. Riddle. Thomas Parnell. WaPE
Upon a Braid of Hair in a Heart. Henry King. EnLoPo
Upon a Child ("Here a pretty baby lies"). Robert Herrick. LoBV; NoP; SeCV-1; TrGrPo
(Another.) OBEV
Upon a Child That Died. Robert Herrick. CavP; ForPo; NoP; PoeP; SeCV-1; SeEP; StP
(Epitaph upon a Child That Died.) MaRV; OBEV
Upon a cloud among the stars we stood. The Flight. Lloyd Mifflin. AA; AnAmPo; HBV
Upon a cock-horse to market I'll trot. *Unknown.* OxNR
Upon a dark ball spun in Time. Giraffe and Tree. W. J. Turner. CH
Upon a dark, light, gloomy, sunshine day. A Messe of Nonsense. *Unknown.* OBS
Upon a darksome night. The Dark Night of the Soul. St. John of the Cross. ErPo; LiTW
Upon a Day. Spenser. OAEP
Upon a day, came sorrow in to me. Sonnet: On the 9th of June 1290. Dante. AWP
Upon a day in Ramadan. The Caliph's Draught. Sir Edwin Arnold. VA
Upon a Dead Man's Head. John Skelton. CoBE; EnRePo; PoIE; SeCePo; SiCE; UnPo (1st ed.)
(Gift of a Skull, The.) ACP
(Skelton Laureate, upon a Dead Man's Head.) ReIE
Upon a Diamond Cut in Form[e] of a Heart . . . Sent in a New Year's [*or* Yeares] Gift. Sir Robert Ayton. ElL; OBS
Upon a Dying Lady (I-VII). W. B. Yeats. LiTB; UnPo (3d ed.)
Upon a Favour Offered. William Walsh. SeCL
Upon a fool's provocation. A Fool's Tongue. John Heywood. SiCE
Upon a Gloomy Night. St. John of the Cross. *See* Obscure Night of the Soul, The,
Upon a Great Black Horse-ily. *Unknown, tr. fr. German.* OTPC; PPL; SAS
Upon a great ship's tilted deck. Harry Kemp. PFY
Upon a high, unfriendly wall. To the Portrait of an Unknown Man. Anderson M. Scruggs. NYTB
Upon a Hill. Miriam LeFevre Crouse. ChIP
Upon a Hill. Keats. *See* I Stood Tiptoe.
Upon a House Shaken by the Land Agitation. W. B. Yeats. CMoP
Upon a jolting wagonseat she rode. The Pioneer Mother. Ethel Romig Fuller. PGD
Upon a letter old I came to-day. A Faded Letter. William J. Fischer. CAW
Upon a life I have not lived. He Took My Place. Horatius Bonar. BePJ
Upon A. M. Sir John Suckling. CavP; ErPo
Upon a Maid ("Here she lies, in bed of spice"). Robert Herrick. ChTr; FaBoCh; LoGBV; OxBoLi; SeEP
Upon a Maid That Died the Day She Was Married. Meleager, *tr. fr. Greek by* Robert Herrick. AWP
Upon a Moebius strip. The Moebius Strip. Charles Olson. OPoP
Upon a Mole in Celias Bosome. Thomas Carew. AnAnS-2
Upon a mountain height, far from the sea. The Wanderer. Eugene Field. PoOW; PoPl
Upon a Needle. William Pattison. WaPE
Upon a night an aungell bright. Now the Most High Is Born. James Ryman. MeEL
Upon a night like this, long years ago. Hawicks' Crossing. Jane Stuart. FiSC
Upon a noon I pilgrimed through. Her Immortality. Thomas Hardy. ViPo (1962 ed.)
Upon a Passing Bell. Thomas Washbourne. SeCL
Upon a Patch Face. Thomas, Lord Fairfax. SeCL
Upon a poet's page I wrote. Her Initials. Thomas Hardy. InP
Upon a Rare Voice. Owen Felltham. SeCL
Upon a Ribband. Thomas Carew. AnAnS-2; SCEP-2
Upon a Ring of Bells. Bunyan. CH
Upon a rock, yet uncreate. The Cosmic Egg. *Unknown.* BOHV
Upon a Sabbath-day it fell. The Eve of Saint Mark. Keats. CH; EnRP; ERoP-2; MERP; OBRV
Upon a Second Marriage. James Merrill. *See* For a Second Marriage.
Upon a showery night and still. Dandelions. Helen Gray Cone. DD; GFA; HBV; PRWS
Upon a Sickly Lady. *At. to* Charles Burnaby *and to* William Burnaby. *Fr.* The Reformed Wife. SeCL
Upon a simmer Sunday morn. The Holy Fair. Burns. BEL; CEP; EiCL; EiCP; EiPP; EnRP; OAEP
Upon a Spider Catching a Fly. Edward Taylor. AmP; AmPP (4th ed.); AP; CBEP; GTBS-W; MAmP; NePA; NoP; OxBA; PoEL-3; SCAP
"Thou sorrow, venom elfe," *sel.* OA
Upon a sultry, yellow sky. Mercedes. Elizabeth Stoddard. AA
Upon a summer Sunday: sweet the sound. The Runaways. Mark Van Doren. PoRA
Upon a summer's time. A Pleasant New Court Song. *Unknown.* CoMu
Upon a tall piano stool. Learning to Play. Abbie Farwell Brown. HH; PPL
Upon a time a neighing steed. The Council of Horses. John Gay. *Fr.* Fables. BoChLi; GN
Upon a time, before the faery broods. Lamia. Keats. BEL; CABL; EnLi-2; EnRP; EPN; ERoP-2; MBW-2; MERP; OAEP
Upon a Virgin Kissing a Rose. Robert Herrick. SCEP-2; SeCP; SeCV-1
Upon a wall of medium height. The Opportune Overthrow of Humpty Dumpty. Guy Wetmore Carryl. BBGG
Upon a Wasp Chilled with Cold. Edward Taylor. AmPP (4th ed.); AtBAP; CBEP; FaBoEn; GTBS-W; PoEL-3
Upon a Wife That Dyed Mad with Jealousie. Robert Herrick. CavP
Upon an Easter Morning. Eleanor Farjeon. PoSC
Upon an everlasting tide. The Epicurean. Sir Francis Hastings Doyle. EPN; OBVV
Upon an Hermaphrodite. John Cleveland. AnAnS-2
Upon an Honest Man's Fortune. *sel.* John Fletcher.
Man Is His Own Star, 6 *ll.* OQP
(Destiny: "An honest and a perfect man," 7 *ll.*) MaRV
Upon an island, all alone. The Converted Cannibals. G. E. Farrow. BOHV
Upon an obscure night. The Obscure Night of the Soul. St. John of the Cross. AWP; BoC; CAW; OBMV; OuHeWo
Upon an upland orchard's sunny side. Sonnet. Thomas Caulfield Irwin. IrPN
Upon ane stormy Sunday. The Plaidie. Charles Sibley. BOHV; HBV
Upon Appleton House, to My Lord Fairfax. Andrew Marvell. MaMe; ReEn, *abr.*; SeCP; SeCV-1
Sels.
"And now to the abbyss I pass." AtBAP
Carrying Their Coracles. ChTr
Hewel, or Woodpecker, The. ChTr
(Woodpecker, The.) BiS
Kingfisher, The. AtBAP; ChTr; FaBoEn
"Oh thou, that dear and happy isle." OxBoLi
"See how the flowers, as at parade." TrGrPo
(Garden, A.) CEP; HBV; OBEV;
"Within this sober frame expect." SCEP-2
Upon Batt. Robert Herrick. AnAnS-2
Upon Being Awakened at Night by My Four Year Old Daughter. Dachine Rainer. NePoAm-2
Upon Being Obliged to Leave a Pleasant Party. Thomas Moore. BOHV
Upon Ben Jonson. Robert Herrick. BEL; NoP; OAEP; OBS; SCEP-2; SeCV-1
Upon Ben Jonson. Edmund Waller. SCEP-2; SeCV-1
Upon Bishop Andrewes His Picture Before His Sermons. Richard Crashaw. MaMe; OBS
Upon Black Eyes, and Becoming Frowns. James Howell. SeCL
Upon Blood's Attempt to Steale the Crown (1671). Andrew Marvell. PeRV
Upon Castara's Absence. William Habington. *Fr.* Castara. AnAnS-2
Upon Castara's Departure. William Habington. *Fr.* Castara. SeCL
Upon Christ His Birth. Sir John Suckling. NCEP
Upon Christmas Eve. Sir John Suckling. NCEP
Upon Christ's Saying to Mary "Why Weepest Thou?" William Alabaster. Sonn
Upon Cleora's Marriage and Retirement. Pope. EiCL

Upon Combing Her Hair. Lord Herbert of Cherbury. SeEP; StP
Upon Consideration of the State of This Life He Wisheth Death. *Unknown.* SiCE; TuPP
Upon de Mountain, *with music.* *Unknown.* TrAS
Upon Differences of Opinion. Hy Sobiloff. SiTL
Upon Discovering One's Own Intolerance. Sara Henderson Hay. MaRV
Upon Dr. Davies' British Grammar. James Howell. PrWP
Upon Drinking in a Bowl. Earl of Rochester. CEP; OBS; OxBoLi; SeCV-2
Upon Eckington Bridge, River Avon. Sir Arthur Quiller-Couch. OBVV; POTE
Upon Faireford Windowes. Richard Corbett. AnAnS-2
Upon Fone a School-Master, Epigram. Robert Herrick. AnAnS-2
Upon Ford's Two Tragedies. "Loves Sacrifice" and "The Broken Heart." Richard Crashaw. MaMe; OBS
Upon Gryll. Robert Herrick. AnAnS-2
Upon Her Feet. Robert Herrick. *See* Upon Mistress Susanna Southwell, Her Feet.
Upon her head she weares a crowne of starres. An Angel Describes Truth. Ben Jonson. *Fr.* Hymenaei. OBS
Upon Her Voice. Robert Herrick. MuSP
Upon Himself. Robert Herrick. SeEP
Upon himself a miracle he wrought. Eugenio Pacelli. Francis Neilson. GoYe
Upon His Departure Hence. Robert Herrick. PCD; QFR
Upon His Drinking [a] Bowl. Earl of Rochester. CavP; EiCL; PeRV
Upon His Grand-Children. Andrew Marvell. MaMe
Upon His House. Andrew Marvell. MaMe
Upon His Leaving His Mistress. Earl of Rochester. EnLoPo; ViBoPo
(Upon Leaving His Mistress.) TrGrPo; UnTE
Upon His M. Dancing. James Shirley. *See* Upon His Mistress Dancing.
Upon His Meeting with His Two Worthy Friends and Fellow-Poets. Sir Philip Sidney. *See* Two Pastorals.
Upon His Mistress Dancing. James Shirley. CLwM; SeCL
(Upon His M. Dancing.) SeEP
Upon His Picture. Thomas Randolph. CBEP; MePo; SeCL; SeEP
Upon His Sister in Law. Robert Herrick. SeEP
Upon His Timorous Silence in Her Presence. Francis Davison. TuPP
("Are lovers full of fire?") EG
Upon his tractor's steady seat. The Plowman of Today. Hamlin Garland. StVeCh
Upon his will he binds a radiant chain. The Peacemaker. Joyce Kilmer. CAW; MaRV; PoFr
Upon Jack and Jill, Epigram. Robert Herrick. AnAnS-2
Upon Jone and Jane. Robert Herrick. AnAnS-2
Upon Julia Weeping. Robert Herrick. ExPo
Upon Julia's Clothes. Robert Herrick. AnAnS-2; AnFE; AtBAP; AWP; BEL; BoLiVe; CABA; CaFP; CBEP; ChTr; CLwM; CoBE; EnL; EnLi-1; EnLit; EnLoPo; ExPo; FaBV; FaFP; HBV; HoPM; ILP; InPo; JAWP; LiTB; LiTG; LoBV; MaPo; MeWo; NoP; OAEP; OBEV; OBS; OuHeWo; PAn; PG (1945 ed.); PIA; Po; PoEL-3; PoeP; PoFS; PoIE; SCEP-2; SeCeV; SeCP; SeCV-1; SeEP; StP; TDP; TOP; TreF; TrGrPo; ViBoPo; WBP
(Poetry of Dress, The, II.) GTBS; GTBS-D; GTBS-W; GTSE; GTSL
(Whenas in Silks My Julia Goes.) BLPA; EG; FaPL; GTBS-P; LiTL; NeHB; ShBV-4
Upon Julia's Fall. Robert Herrick. UnTE
Upon Julia's Hair[e] Filled [*or* Fill'd] with Dew. Robert Herrick. AtBAP; EG
(Dew Sat on Julia's Hair.] ELP
Upon Julia's Petticoat. Robert Herrick. *See* Julia's Petticoat.
Upon Julia's Recovery. Robert Herrick. AtBAP
Upon Julia's Voice. Robert Herrick. AtBAP; BoW; CABA; CBV; ExPo; MyFE; PoeP; SeCePo; SeCL; SeCP
Upon Kinde and True Love. Aurelian Townshend. CavP; MeLP; MePo; OBS; SeCL
("'Tis not how witty, nor how free.") EG
Upon Kings. Robert Herrick. PoFr
Upon Lazarus His Teares. Richard Crashaw. MaMe; SeCV-1
Upon learning that the mother wrote verses. Soiree. Ezra Pound. DTC
Upon Leaving His Mistress. Earl of Rochester. *See* Upon His Leaving His Mistress.
Upon Lesbia—Arguing. Alfred Cochrane. HBV
Upon Lesbia's Abuse. Catullus. *See* Lesbia Railing.
Upon Liberty, *sel.* Abraham Cowley.
"He's no small prince who every day." PeRV
Upon Love ("Love brought me to a silent grove"). Robert Herrick. BoLiVe; TrGrPo
Upon Love ("Love scorch'd my finger, but did spare"). Robert Herrick. SeCV-1
Upon Love, by Way of Question and Answer ("I bring ye love"). Robert Herrick. NoP; Po
Upon Love Fondly Refus'd for Conscience Sake. Thomas Randolph. AnAnS-2
Upon Master Fletchers Incomparable Playes. Robert Herrick. OBS
Upon Master W. Montague. Thomas Carew. SeEP
Upon M. Ben Jonson, Epigram. Robert Herrick. HoPM; OAEP
Upon Mr. Bennet, Procurer Extraordinary. Alexander Radcliffe. PeRV
Upon Mr. Staninough's Death. Richard Crashaw. *See* Death's Lecture at the Funeral of a Young Gentleman.
Upon Mr. Thomas Coryats Crudities. John Donne. *Fr.* Satires. MaMe
Upon Mrs. Anne Bradstreet Her Poems. John Rogers. SCAP
Upon Mistress Susanna Southwell, Her Feet. Robert Herrick. EnLi-1; PoFS
(Upon Her Feet.) ViBoPo
Upon my bier no garlands lay. Now. Mary Barker Dodge. AA
Upon my breast. Once in a Lonely Hour. John Hall Wheelock. NP
Upon my darling's beaming eyes. Auf meiner Herzliebsten Augelein. Heine. AWP
Upon My Heart. Charles Wesley. FaChP
Upon My Lady Carlisle's Walking in Hampton-Court Garden. Sir John Suckling. AnAnS-2; SCEP-2
Upon My Lap My Sovereign Sits. Richard Verstegan. *See* Lullaby: "Upon my lap. . ."
Upon my mantel-piece they stand. A Moral in Sèvres. Mildred Howells. AA; HBV
Upon my ryght syde y me leye. An Evening Prayer. *Unknown.* AtBAP
Upon New Year's Eve. Sir Arthur Quiller-Couch. OBVV
Upon Nirwána's brink the ráhat stood. The Ráhat. John Jerome Rooney. AA
Upon Nothing. Earl of Rochester. AtBAP; EiCL; FosPo; MePo; OBS; PeRV; Po; PoEL-3; SeEP; TrGrPo, *abr.*; ViBoPo
Upon our eyelids, dear, the dew will lie. Before Dawn in the Woods. Marguerite Wilkinson. HBMV
Upon our fullness shines the dawning day. Sonnet. Francis Lyman Windolph. MaRV
Upon Our Late Loss of the Duke of Cambridge. Edmund Waller. Po
Upon Our Lords Last Comfortable Discourse with His Disciples. Richard Crashaw. MaMe
Upon Our Saviours Tombe Wherein Never Man Was Laid. Richard Crashaw. *See* Upon the Saviour's Tomb.
Upon our Vain Flattery of Ourselves that the Succeeding Times Will Be Better than the Former. Robert Gomersal. SeCL
Upon Pagget. Robert Herrick. FaBoCh; LoGBV
Upon Parson Beanes. Robert Herrick. AnAnS-2
Upon Paul's steeple stands a tree. *Unknown.* OxNR
Upon Phillis [*or* Phyllis] Walking in a Morning before Sun-Rising. John Cleveland. AnAnS-2; LiTL; MeLP
("Sluggish morn as yet undrest.") EG
Upon Prew [*or* Prue] His Maid. Robert Herrick. CavP; ForPo; NoP; OAEP; SeCV-1; SeEP
Upon Prudence Baldwin Her Sicknesse. Robert Herrick. OAEP; PoeP; SeCV-1
Upon Prue, His Maid. Robert Herrick. *See* Upon Prew, His Maid.
Upon Roses. Robert Herrick. SeCP
Upon St. Michael's Isle. The Burial of Robert Browning. "Michael Field." VA
Upon Scarlet and Blush-coloured Ribbands, Given by Two Ladies. James Shirley. GoBC
Upon Scobble, Epigram. Robert Herrick. AnAnS-2
Upon Sibilla. Robert Herrick. SeCePo

Upon Sir Francis Drake's Return from His Voyage about the World, and the Queen's Meeting Him. *Unknown.* CoMu; ElL; FaBoCh
(Sir Francis Drake.) FOL
Upon Some Women. Robert Herrick. AnAnS-2
Upon Sudds a Laundresse. Robert Herrick. AnAnS-2
Upon that night, when fairies light. Hallowe'en. Burns. OBEC
Upon the arid shoulder. The Broom. Giacomo Leopardi. LiTW
Upon the Asse that Bore Our Saviour. Richard Crashaw. MaMe
Upon the Author; by a Known Friend. Benjamin Woodbridge. SCAP
Upon the Author of a Play Call'd Sodom. John Oldham. PeRV
Upon the Author's First Seven Years' Service. Thomas Tusser. *See* Sonnet upon the Author's First Seven Years' Service, A.
Upon the Bankruptcy of a Physician. Henricus Selyns. SCAP
Upon the barren sand. Pocahontas. George Pope Morris. MC; PAH
Upon the Beach. Ilo Orleans. RIS; TiPo (1952 ed.)
Upon the beach are thousands of crabs. Crustaceans. Roy Fuller. NeBP; ToPo
Upon the black horse of midnight I ride. Night Musick for Thérèse. Dachine Rainer. NePoAm-2
Upon the Bleeding Crucifix. Richard Crashaw. *See* On the Bleeding Wounds of Our Crucified Lord.
Upon the Body of Our Blessed [*or Bl.*] Lord, Naked and Bloody. Richard Crashaw. ACP; EnLi-1; EP; ILP; InvP; MaMe; OAEP; OBS; Po; SeCP
(On Our Crucified Lord Naked, and Bloody.) CABA; MaMe; SeCV-1
Upon the Book and Picture of the Seraphical Saint Teresa. Richard Crashaw. *See* Flaming Heart, The.
Upon the branches of our silence hang our words. The Tree of Silence. Vassar Miller. NePoEA-2; PoDB
Upon the bridge the blind man stands alone. Pont du Carrousel. Rainer Maria Rilke. OnPM
Upon the Burning of Our House. Anne Bradstreet. AmP; AmPP (4th ed.); OxBA; TDP
(Here Followes Some Verses upon the Burning of Our House.) SCAP
(Some Verses upon the Burning of Our House.) AP
(Verses upon the Burning of Our House.) MAmP
Upon the Circumcision. Milton. MeP
Upon the Crowne of Thorns. Richard Crashaw. MaMe
Upon the Crucifix. William Alabaster. PoEL-2
("Now I have found thee, I will ever more") AnAnS-1
(Sonnet: "Now I have found thee, I will ever more.") MeP
Upon the Death of a Gentleman. Richard Crashaw. CavP; MaMe
Upon the Death of G. B. John Cotton. SCAP
Upon the Death of George Santayana. Anthony Hecht. AmLP; CoPo; NePA
Upon the Death of His Much Esteemed Friend Mr. Jno Saffin Junr. Grindall Rawson. SCAP
Upon the Death of Mr. Herrys. Richard Crashaw. MaMe
Upon the Death of My Ever Desired Friend Doctor Donne Dean of Pauls. Henry King. AnAnS-2; SeCP
Upon the Death of Sir Albert [*or* Albertus] Morton's Wife. Sir Henry Wotton. AnAnS-2; CLwM; EnLoPo; OBEV; OBS; OnPM; SeCP; SeEP; TDP; TreFT; ViBoPo; WePo; WoL
(Epitaph on Sir Albert Morton's Wife.) CBEP
(On the Death of Sir Albert Morton's Wife.) TrGrPo
Upon the Death of Sir Antony Denny. *Unknown.* EnPo
Upon the Death of the Earl of Dundee. Dryden. *See* Upon the Death of the Viscount of Dundee.
Upon the Death of the Lord Hastings. Andrew Marvell. CEP; MaMe; SeCV-2
("Must noble Hastings immaturely die.") ReEn
Upon the Death of the Most Desired Mr. Herrys. Richard Crashaw. MaMe
Upon the Death of the Viscount of [*or* Earl of] Dundee. Dryden. ACP; OBS; PoFr
(Epitaph on John Graham of Claverhouse, Viscount Dundee.) MBW-1
Upon the Decease of Mrs. Anne Griffin. John Fiske. SCAP
Upon the Downs. Sir George Etherege. ViBoPo
Upon the Dramatick Poems of Mr. John Fletcher. William Cartwright. OBS
Upon the Dumbe Devill Cast Out, and the Slanderous Jewes Put to Silence. Richard Crashaw. MaMe
Upon the earth there are so many treasures. Earth Felicities, Heavens Allowances. Richard Steere. SCAP
Upon the ecstatic diving board the diver. Lone Bather. A. M. Klein. TwCaPo
Upon the eighteenth day of June. Bonny John Seton. *Unknown.* BaBo; ESPB
Upon the Ensignes of Christes Crucifyinge. William Alabaster. MePo
("O sweete, and bitter monuments of paine.") AnAnS-1
(Sonnet.) MeP
Upon the eyes, the lips, the feet. Extreme Unction. Ernest Dowson. ACP; CAW; JKCP; MoBrPo; OBMV; PeVV
Upon the Faire Ethiopian Sent to a Gentlewoman. Richard Crashaw. MaMe
Upon the Feast of St. Simon and St. Jude. Samuel Johnson. EiCP
Upon the First Sight of New England. Thomas Tillam. *See* Uppon the First Sight of New England.
Upon the flowery forefront of the year. Thalassius. Swinburne. PoVP
Upon the gale she stooped her side. The Gallant Ship. Sir Walter Scott. BoTP
Upon the gates of the prison. Prison. *Unknown.* OnPM
Upon the Gospel's sacred page. The Sacred Page. John Bowring. SoP
Upon the H. Sepulcher. Richard Crashaw. *See* Upon the Sepulchre of Our Lord.
Upon the highest hill of all. The Apple Tree. Beatrice Curtis Brown. SiSoSe
Upon the Hill and Grove at Bill-borrow. Andrew Marvell. MaMe
Upon the Hill before Centreville. George Henry Boker. PAH
Upon the hills new grass is seen. Twist-Rime on Spring. Arthur Guiterman. PoSC
Upon the hilles of Phrygie neere a Teyle there stands a tree. Philemon and Baucis. Ovid. *Fr.* Metamorphoses. EnPo; OBSC
Upon the house a crooked sign. For Sale or Rent. *Unknown.* PoToHe (new ed.)
Upon the Image of Death. Robert Southwell. CH; CoBE; ElL; OBSC; ReEn; ReIE; SiCE; TuPP
(Before My Face the Picture Hangs.) OxBoCh; PoLi
Upon the incoming ship, with sails full set. On Tsukuda-Isle in July. Munetake. OnPM
Upon the Infant Martyrs. Richard Crashaw. MaMe; NoP
Upon the King. Shakespeare. *Fr.* King Henry V, IV, i. PPON
Upon the lake. The Gramophone. James Reaney. CaP; TwCaPo
Upon the Lark and the Fowler. Bunyan. CH
Upon the Lines and Life of the Famous Scenic Poet, Master William Shakespeare. Hugh Holland. *See* Shakespeare Dead.
Upon the Loss [*or* Losse] of His Mistresses. Robert Herrick. AnAnS-2; BEL; EnLi-1 (1949 ed.); OAEP; ReEn; SCEP-2; SeCV-1; SeEP
Upon the Losse of His Little Finger. Thomas Randolph. AnAnS-2
Upon the Losse of His Mistresses. Robert Herrick. *See* Upon the Loss of His Mistresses.
Upon the marsh mud, dank and foul. Love's Miracle. Lucy Maud Montgomery. MaRV
Upon the Midlands now th' industrious muse doth fall. The Thirteenth Song. Michael Drayton. *Fr.* Polyolbion. ReEn; ReIE; TuPP
Upon the midsummer even. *See* Apon the Midsummer evin.
Upon the Most Useful Knowledge, Craft or Cunning, Which Is More Wisdom, as 'Tis Less Wit. William Wycherley. SeCV-2
Upon the Motions of the Fiend. William Alabaster. EP
Upon the mountain's edge with light touch resting. A Sunset. Samuel Taylor Coleridge. BWP; ERoP-1
Upon the Much-to Be Lamented Desease of the Reverend Mr. John Cotton. John Fiske. SCAP
Upon the New-built House at Appleton. Thomas, Lord Fairfax. SeCL

Upon the Nipples of Julia's Breast. Robert Herrick. ErPo; LiTL; UnTE; ViBoPo
Upon the patch of earth that clings. Public Aid for Niagara Falls. Morris Bishop. InMe
Upon the poop the captain stands. The Shipwreck. E. H. Palmer. BOHV; NA
Upon the Powder Day. Richard Crashaw. MaMe
Upon the road of my life. The Black Riders, LX. Stephen Crane. AP
Upon the road to Romany. From Romany to Rome. Wallace Irwin. HBV
Upon the Same (Venus Putting on Mars His Armes). Richard Crashaw. MaMe
Upon the Savior's Tomb. Richard Crashaw. StJW
(To Our Blessed Lord upon the Choice of His Sepulchre.) ACP; MaMe
(Upon Our Saviours Tombe Wherein Never Man was Laid.) MaMe; SCEP-1
Upon the seas of crumbling servitude. Mississippi Concert. Rolland Snellings. BF
Upon the Sepulchre of Our Lord. Richard Crashaw. MaMe
Upon the Shore. Robert Bridges. EtS; VA
(After the Gale.) LoBV
(Who Has Not Walked Upon the Shore.) CMoP
Upon the skyline [glows] i' the dark. The Universal Republic [*or* Republic of the World]. Victor Hugo. MaRV; OQP; PGD
Upon the slow descending air. Rapunzel Song. Gerard Previn Meyer. NYTB
Upon the Snail. Bunyan. BoPe; ChTr
Upon the Springs Issuing out from the Foot of Plimouth Beach. Samuel Sewall. SCAP
Upon the street they lie. The Children. William Soutar. POTE
Upon the Sudden Restraint of the Earle of Somerset, [Then] Falling from Favor. Sir Henry Wotton. AnAnS-2; ELP; MePo; OBS; SeCP
Upon the sunny summer hill. Clover for Breakfast. Frances Frost. RePo; StVeCh (1955 ed.)
Upon the terrace where I play. The Fountain. Rose Fyleman. GFA
Upon the Thornes Taken Downe from Our Lords Head Bloody. Richard Crashaw. MaMe
Upon the threshold of another year. New Year. Thomas Wearing. MaRV
Upon the threshold of the year we stand. The New Year. Homera Homer-Dixon. BLRP; SoP
Upon the Tomb of the Most Reverend Mr. John Cotton. Benjamin Woodbridge. SCAP
Upon the topmost branches dies. Doubt. Fernand Gregh. WGRP
Upon the Translation of the Psalmes by Sir Philip Sydney. John Donne. MaMe
Upon the tree of time. A Harvest to Seduce. Melville Cane. NYBP; PG (1955 ed.)
Upon the utmost corners of the warld. In Orknay. William Fowler. GoTS; OxBS
Upon the walls the graceful ivy climbs. Ivy. Frank Dempster Sherman. MAP
Upon the white sea sand there sat a pilgrim band. The Greatest Loss. Frances Brown. MaRV
Upon the Works of Ben Jonson, *sel.* John Oldham.
"Let dull and ignorant pretenders art condemn." PP
Upon the wreckage of thy yesterday. Building. Ella Wheeler Wilcox. OQP
Upon this greying page you wrote. On Looking at a Copy of Alice Meynell's Poems, Given Me, Years Ago, by a Friend. Amy Lowell. NP
Upon this happy New Year night. Eugene Field. *Fr.* A New Year Idyl. PoSC
Upon this leafy bush. The Linnet. Walter de la Mare. HBMV; LiTB; LoBV; NP
Upon this marble bust that is not I. The Pioneer. Edna St. Vincent Millay. PoFr
Upon this primrose hill. The Primrose [Being at Montgomery Castle]. John Donne. MaMe; MeP; SCEP-1
Upon This Rock. James L. Duff. JKCP
Upon This Rock. Robert Whitaker. ChIP
Upon This Rock. Lon Woodrum. SoP
Upon this shore which I follow to Shibutani. Gazing at the Moon while Journeying Homewards. Otomo Yakamochi. OnPM
Upon those who defy authority. True Freedom. *Unknown.* *Fr.* Tao Teh King. OnPM
Upon Thought Castara May Die. William Habington. *Fr.* Castara, I. ACP
Upon thy bended knees, thank God for work. The Sacrament of Work [*or* Gratitude for Work]. John Oxenham. MaRV; PGD
Upon thy tomb 'tis graven "Here lies one." Keats. John Banister Tabb. AmP
Upon Thy Word. Frances Ridley Havergal. SoP
Upon Time. Robert Herrick. OBS
Upon Two Greene Apricockes Sent to Cowley by Sir Crashaw. Richard Crashaw. MaMe
Upon Venus Putting on Mars His Armes. Richard Crashaw. MaMe; SeCP
Upon Visiting His Lady by Moonlight. "A. W." CTC; OBSC; ReIE; TuPP
Upon Wedlock and Death of Children. Edward Taylor. AmPP (5th ed.); AP; NoP
Upon Westminster Bridge. Wordsworth. *See* Composed upon Westminster Bridge, Sept. 3, 1802.
Upon Which to Rejoice. "Luke." QAH
Upon your heart, which is the heart of all. Sonnets from "One Person." Elinor Wylie. NP
Upon your snow-white shoulder. Your Snow-white Shoulder. Heine. UnTE
Upone Tabacco. Sir Robert Aytoun. OxBS
Upper Air. Frank Ernest Hill. AnAmPo; MAP; MoAmPo (1942 ed.)
Upper Chamber, An. Frances Bannerman. HBV; OBEV
Upper Chamber in a Darkened House, An. Frederick Goddard Tuckerman. *Fr.* Sonnets. AmePo; AnNE; MAmP; NoP
Upper Lake, The. Francis Stuart. NeIP
Upper Lambourne. John Betjeman. FaBoTw; GTBS-D; POTi
Upper Road, The. Christina Rossetti. FaChP
Upper Room, An. Daniel Lawrence Kelleher. NeIP
Upper Room, The. Belle F. Owens. ChIP
Upper Skies, The. Robert Bridges. BoTP
Uppon the First Sight of New England. Thomas Tillam. SCAP
Upright and shrewd, more woo'd of fame. Henry Charles Beeching. *Fr.* The Masque of Balliol. CenHV
Uprising See the Fitful Lark. *Unknown.* NA
Uproar, An/ a spruce-green sky, bound in iron. The Butterfly. Margaret Avison. ExPo; OBCV
Uprose the king of men with speed. *See* Up rose the king of men with speed.
Upshore from the cloud. By a Lake in Minnesota. James Wright. AmFN; FRC
Upside-down World, The. Hamish Hendry. BoTP
Upstairs. John Stevens Wade. ThO
Upstairs Downstairs. Hervey Allen. HBMV; PoNe
Upstairs in her room. Margaret. Craig Sterry. QAH
Upstairs on the third floor. Bottled; New York. Helene Johnson. CDC; GoSl
Upstart Courtier. Samuel Rowlands. SiCE
Upstood upstaffed passing sinuously away. Poem [*or* Christophe]. Russell Atkins. PoNe
Upstream. Carl Sandburg. HBV; MAP; MoAB; MoAmPo; MoRP; NeMA; PoFr; SAS
Upstream. *Unknown.* SoP
Uptown. Allen Ginsberg. TwCP
Uptown there's not a lot of living matter. Courthouse Square. Herbert Merrill. AmFN
Upward. Horatius Bonar. SoP
Upward and back to their fountains the sacred rivers are stealing. Chorus. Euripides. *Fr.* Medea. PoFr
Upward Place, The. Helen M. Wilson. SoP
Upward through crystal in a kümmel bottle. Dreamscape in Kümmel. Harold Witt. NYBP
Upward where the stars are burning. Upward. Horatius Bonar. SoP
Ur Burial. Richard Eberhart. NePoAm
Ur ol' Hyar lib in ur house on de hill. Ol' Doc' Hyar. James Edwin Campbell. BANP
Urania. Matthew Arnold. HBV; MBW-2; VP
Urania. Aubrey Thomas De Vere. IrPN
Urania. Ruth Pitter. MoVE
Urania speaks with darken'd brow. In Memoriam A. H. H., XXXVII. Tennyson. EPN; ViPo; VP

Uranium cumulus mushrooms bursting sores. Exodus. Roy Basler. SiTL
Uranus. Arthur Hugh Clough. ViPP
Urban Convalescence, An. James Merrill. CoAP
Urban Dream. Victor Hernandez Cruz. NBP
Urban History. Chester Kallman. CrMA
Urban Roses. Ted Isaac. PoPl
"Urceus Exit." Austin Dobson. ATP (1935 ed.); BoPe; GTSL; HBV; MoBrPo (1942 ed.); PTK; TOP
(I Intended an Ode.) OBEV
Urchins' Dance, The. *Unknown.* *See* By the Moon We Sport and Play.
Urge of the seed, The: the germ. Edgar Lee Masters. *Fr.* The New Spoon River. OQP
Urgency. Sarah E. Wright. PoNe (1970 ed.)
Urging Her of a Promise. Ben Jonson. *Fr.* A Celebration of Charis. AnAnS-2; SCEP-2; SeCP
Uriel. Emerson. AmePo; AnFE; AnNE; AP; APA; BWP; CoAnAm; LiTA; MAmP; MWA-1; NePA; OBEV (1st ed.); OxBA; PFY
Uriel, *sels.* William Force Stead.
"I thought the night without a sound was falling." TrPWD
(How Infinite Are Thy Ways.) OBMV
"Praise, then, to Uriel, who in unlikely places,"*fr.* Pt. IV, iii. OxBoCh
"Reach forth Thy hand!" *fr.* Pt. V, i. OxBoCh
Urn, The. Malcolm Cowley. *Fr.* Blue Juniata. AnAmPo; MoVE; NP
Urns and Odours Bring Away! Fletcher, *and* Shakespeare. *See* Funeral Song.
Ursa Major. James Kirkup. ImOP
Ursula. Robert Underwood Johnson. HBV
Us. Julius Lester. WOW
Us Potes. Franklin P. Adams. PoPl; WhC
Us Two. A. A. Milne. TiPo
Us two was pals, the Kid and me. The Kid's Last Fight. *Unknown.* TreF
Us two wuz boys when we fell out. Our Two Opinions. Eugene Field. AA; IHA; MAP; MoAmPo (1942 ed.); PFY
Use all your hidden forces. Do not miss. Attainment. Ella Wheeler Wilcox. OQP; WGRP
Use Even Me. Frances Ridley Havergal. *See* Lord, Speak to Me that I May Speak.
Use force and chisel, be lapidary, not. Collages and Compositions. Richmond Lattimore. PP
Use me, God, in Thy great harvest field. Send Me. Christina Rossetti. FaChP; MaRV; SoP; TRV
Use three physicians still: first Doctor Quiet. Health Counsel. Sir John Harington. TreFT
Use Well the Moment. Goethe, *tr. fr. German by* John Stuart Blackie. MaRV; OQP
Use your money while you're living. Your Money and Mine. *Unknown.* STF
Useful, The. W. H. Auden. *Fr.* The Quest. CMoP
Useful Plough, The. *Unknown.* DD; HBV; OTPC (1923 ed.); RIS
Uselessness. Ella Wheeler Wilcox. TrPWD
Uses of Adversity, The. Shakespeare. *Fr.* As You Like It, II, i. LiTB; TreFS; TrGrPo
(Banished Duke Speaks to His Retainers, The.) LiTG
(Good in Everything, *much abr.*) PoToHe
(Sweet Are the Uses of Adversity, 6 *ll.*) MaRV
Uses of Ocean, The. Sir Owen Seaman. ALV; FiBHP
Using the old characters. Note on Bone. Howard McCord. YAP
Usk. T. S. Eliot. Landscapes, III. CoBE; FaBoCh; LoGBV
Usless pipe stop I have been, A. *Unknown.* SeCSL
Usual Way, The. Frederic E. Weatherly. BOHV
Usually hateful crow[s], The! They Also [*or* Beauty]. Basho. OnPM; SoPo
Usurpers, The. Edwin Muir. CMoP
Utah Carl, *with music.* *Unknown.* BFSS
Utah Carroll. *Unknown.* CoSo, *with music*
Utah, We Love Thee. Evan Stephens. PoRL
Ute Lover, The. Hamlin Garland. AA; PFY
Ute Pass. Ernest Whitney. PoOW
Utile canons, the set codes of priests, The. Love Redeemed, XXXIII. William Baylebridge. BoAV
Utilitarian View of the *Monitor's* Fight, A. Herman Melville. AmePo; AmPP (5th ed.); AP; MWA-1
Utmost, The. "Owen Meredith." VA
Utmost grace the Greeks could shew, The. Grecian Kindness. Earl of Rochester. PeRV
Utmost in Friendship, The. John E. McCann. TreFT
Utmost island of Europe, loveliest land. Ireland Weeping. William Livingston. GoTS
Utopia. Jewel C. Latimore. WSL
Utopia, Limited, *sel.* W. S. Gilbert.
Sir Bailey Barre. PCD
Utopia of Lord Mayor Howard, The. Randolph Stow. PoAu-2
Utopian Journey, A. Randall Jarrell. CBV; FiMAP
Utrillo's World. John Glassco. PeCV (1967 ed.)
Utter Silence. Jorge Guillén, *tr. fr. Spanish by* Eleanor L. Turnbull. OnPM
Utterance. Emily Dickinson. *See* I found the phrase to every thought.
Utterly abandoned to the Holy Ghost! Abandoned. *Unknown.* SoP

V

V. B. Nimble, V. B. Quick ("V. B. Wigglesworth wakes at noon"). John Updike. NYBP
V. D. F. *Unknown.* HBV
V Is for Victory, as You Can Plainly See. Marsden Hartley. LiTM
V-J Day. John Ciardi. MiAP; OTD; PoPl
V-Letter. Karl Shapiro. AP; CoBMV; FiMAP; MiAP; MoLP; ThLM; TrJP; WaP
(Love Letter.) NYBP
V-Letter to Karl Shapiro in Australia. Selden Rodman. WaP
Vacant Cage, The. Charles Tennyson Turner. VA
Vacant Chair,The. Henry Stevenson Washburn. TreFS
Vacant Farmhouse, The. Walter de la Mare. HaMV
Vacation. William Stafford. AmFN
Vacation. Nixon Waterman. *See* Far from the Madding Crowd.
Vacation Exercise. M. K. Joseph. AnNZ
"Vacation is coming, where shall we go?" Compromise. Laurence McKinney. InMe
Vacation is over. Leavetaking. Eve Merriam. PDV
Vacation on Earth, A. Thomas M. Disch. HYE
Vacation Snapshot. Melvin Walker La Follette. NYTB
Vacation Song. Edna St. Vincent Millay. YeAr
Vacation Time. Rowena Bennett. SiSoSe
Vacation Time. Frank Hutt. BoTP
Vacation Time. Margaret E. Sangster. DD
Vacation Trip. Donald C. Babcock. NePoAm
Vacation Trip. William Stafford. PV
Vacationer. Walker Gibson. SD
Vacationing at Baiae, where the Herculean Way extends. The Watering Place. Propertius. LiTW
Vacillation. W. B. Yeats. MoVE; PoDB
Sels.
"Must we part, Von Hügel." OBMV
"Seek out reality, leave things that seem." MBW-2
Vacuum, The. Howard Nemerov. NePoEA
Vade Mecum. Rolfe Humphries. CBV
Vagabond. John Masefield. OtMeF
Vagabond, The. Robert Louis Stevenson. AnFE; BBV; BrPo; GTSL; HBV; HBVY; HT; MCCG; OnPP; OTPC (1946 ed.); PoMa; PoPo; PoRL; ShBV-1; TreFT; ViBoPo
Vagabond House. Don Blanding. BLPA
Vagabond Song, A. Bliss Carman. FaPON; GBV; GN; GoTP; HBV; HBVY; MAP; MCCG; MoAmPo (1942 ed.); MPB; NeMA; OTPC (1946 ed.); PoMa; PoSC; RePo; StaSt; StVeCh (1940 ed.); YT
Vagabonds, The. E. Pauline Johnson. VA
Vagabonds, The. John Townsend Trowbridge. AA; BeLS; BLPA; OnPP; PCD; TreFS
Vagrant, A. Erik Axel Karlfeldt, *tr. fr. Swedish by* Charles Wharton Stork. PoPl
Vagrant, The. Pauline Slender. HBMV
Vague in plot but clear in style. Review of a Cook Book. Louise Dyer Harris. WhC
Vague sea thuds against the marble cliffs, The. Time. Robert Graves. AtBAP; FaBoMo; LiTM (rev. ed.)
Vague Story, A. Walter Parke. BOHV
Vague winds of sorrow blow. Wandering. Hortense Flexner. HBMV

Vaguely I hear the purple roar of the torn-down 3rd Avenue El. You Are Gorgeous and I'm Coming. Frank O'Hara. NeAP
Vaile cobwebs from the white-ned floore. Upon Christmas Eve. Sir John Suckling. NCEP
Vain Advice at the Year's End. James Wright. NYBP
Vain and Careless. Robert Graves. LOW
Vain and not to trust. Woman. Irving Layton. ErPo
Vain Britons, boast no longer with proud indignity. War and Washington. Jonathan Mitchell Sewall. *Fr.* Cato. PAH
Vain Cry; Lydian Campaign, 1941. Glauco Cambon, *tr. fr. Italian by* Glauco Cambon. OnPM
Vain, delusive world, adieu. Only Jesus Will I Know. Charles Wesley. BePJ
Vain Desire, A. Theodore Wratislaw. VA
Vain Dream for John Clare. Joan Hutton. NYTB
Vain excess of flattering fortune's gifts, The. Gascoigne's Memories, II. George Gascoigne. EnRePo
Vain Finding. Walter de la Mare. BrPo
Vain, frail, short liv'd, and miserable Man. Vanity of Vanities [*or* A Song of Emptiness to Fill up the Empty Pages Following]. Michael Wigglesworth. SCAP
Vain Gratuities. E. A. Robinson. MaPo; NePA
Vain Hope, Adieu. *Unknown.* EnRePo
Vain is the chiming of forgotten bells. Poets. Joyce Kilmer. AnAmPo; NP; WGRP
Vain is the effort to forget. On the Rhine. Matthew Arnold. LO; VP
Vain is the fleeting wealth. Of [*or* On] the Vanity of Man's Life. *Unknown.* EG; OBSC; SiCE; TuPP
Vain-Love, The, *sel.* Abraham Cowley.
"I sought not from thee a return." LO
Vain Love, why dost thou boast of wings. Jealousy. Countess of Winchilsea. SeCL
Vain man, born to no happiness. Chorus. Sidney Godolphin. LoBV
Vain Men, Whose Follies. Thomas Campion. NCEP
("Vain men, whose follies make a god of love.") LO
Vain Questioning. Walter de la Mare. MoVE
Vain the ambition of kings. Vanitas Vanitatum. John Webster. *Fr.* The Devil's Law Case. PoFr
Vain, very vain, my weary search to find. Happiness Dependent on Ourselves. Goldsmith. *Fr.* The Traveller. OBEC
Vain Virtues. Dante Gabriel Rossetti. The House of Life, LXXXV. EnLi-2; HBV; MaVP; PoVP; ViPo; ViPP
Vain Wish, A. Philip Bourke Marston. VA
Vain Wish. Otomo Yakamochi, *tr. fr. Japanese by* Ishii *and* Obata. OnPM
Vainglorious Oak and the Modest Bulrush, The. Guy Wetmore Carryl. TSW
Vainly. Nelly Sachs, *tr. fr. German by* Michael Roloff. NYBP
Vainly for us the sunbeams shine. Casa's Dirge. David Macbeth Moir. VA
Vainly I strive to make a "live" at mining. The Miner's Lament, II. *Unknown.* SGR
Vainly we crave for some divine Redeemer. In a Troubled World. Stanton A. Coblentz. ChIP
Vainly were the words of parting spoken. Hermotimus. William Edmondstoune Aytoun. OBVV
Vala: or, The Four Zoas, *sels.* Blake.
"Cities, The, send to one another. . ." *fr.* Night I. ViBoPo
Enion Replies from the Caverns of the Grave. OBNC
It Is Not So with Me. SeCePo
Lamentation of Enion, The. OBNC
Night. BoW
"O Lord wilt thou not look. . ." *fr.* Night II. ViBoPo
Price of Experience, The. EnRP
Song of Enion. ERoP-1
Song of Enitharmon. ERoP-1
(Enitharmon Revives with Los.) OBNC
(Enitharmon's Song, 6 *ll.*) ChTr
Vale. Maurice Baring. JKCP (1955 ed.)
Vale. John Ciardi. MiAP
Vale! Roden Noel. OBVV
Vale. Patrick Mary Plunkett. JKCP (1955 ed.)
Vale, Amor! "Fiona Macleod." PoVP
Vale from Carthage. Peter Vierick. LiTM (1970 ed.); MiAP; MoAmPo (1950 ed.); PoPo
Vale of Teares, A. Robert Southwell. MeP
Vale of Tempe had in vain been fair, The. Ideality. Hartley Coleridge. VA
Vale of the waterfalls! The Call of the Morning. George Darley. OnYI
Valediction, A. Elizabeth Barrett Browning. HBV
Valediction, A. William Cartwright. OBS; SeCL; SeEP
("Bid me not go where neither suns nor showers," *abr.*) EG
Valediction, A. Melvin Walker La Follette. CoPo
Valediction. Louis MacNeice. AnIL; MoVE
Valediction. John Hall Wheelock. NePoAm
Valediction Forbidding Mourning, A. John Donne. AnAnS-1; BWP; CABA; CaFP; CBV; CoBE; DiPo; EnL; EnLi-1; EnLit; EnRePo; ExPo; FaBoEn; FaPL; ForPo; HoPM; ILP; LiTB; MaMe; MaPo; MasP; MBW-1; MeLP; MeP; MePo; NoP; OAEP; OBS; PAn; PIA; Po; PoAn; PoEL-2; PoeP; PoFS; PoIE; ReEn; ReIE; SCEP-1; SeCeV; SeCP; SeCV-1; SeEP; TDP; TreFT; TuPP; UnPo; VaPo
Valediction, A; Liverpool Docks. John Masefield. FaBoTw; OBMV
Valediction, A: Of My Name in the Window. John Donne. EnRePo; MaMe; MBW-1; QFR; SCEP-1
Valediction, A; of the Booke. John Donne. MaMe; SCEP-1
Valediction, A: of Weeping. John Donne. AnAnS-1; AtBAP; ATP; BWP; CABA; CBEP; EG; EnRePo; EP; MaMe; MBW-1; MeLP; MePo; NoP; OBS; PoAn; ReIE; SCEP-1; SeCP; TuPP
Valediction to My Contemporaries. Horace Gregory. MAP; MoAmPo
Valedictory. Adam Lindsay Gordon. VA
Valedictory. Tennyson. *See* In Memoriam—W. G. Ward *and* In the Garden at Swainston.
Valedictory Sonnet to the River Duddon. Wordsworth. *See* After-Thought.
Valedictory to Standard Oil of Indiana, A. David Wagoner. NYBP
Valentine, A. Matilda Barbara Betham-Edwards. OBVV
Valentine. Charles G. Blanden. DD
Valentine, A. Eugene Field. PoRL
Valentine, A. Jeannette Bliss Gillespy. *Fr.* Cameos. AA
Valentine. Donald Hall. BoLP
Valentine, A. Eleanor Hammond. GFA; RePo; TiPo; YeAr
Valentine, A. Laura E. Richards. AA; DD; HH; MPB; YeAr
Valentine. Shelley Silverstein. PoSC
Valentine, A. Hal Summers. ChMP
Valentine. Hollis Summers. GoYe
Valentine. "C. W. T." RePo; YeAr
Valentine for a Lady, A. Lucilius, *tr. fr. Greek by* Dudley Fitts. LiTW
Valentine for My Mother. Harry Lee. MPB
Valentine Promise. *Unknown.* *See* Love's Constancy.
Valentine to a Little Girl. Cardinal Newman. GoBC
Valentine to My Mother, A (1882). Christina Rossetti. *See* Valentines to My Mother (1876-1886).
Valentine Verses. Thomas Nelson Page. DD
Valentine's Day. Aileen Fisher. YeAr
Valentine's Day. Charles Kingsley. BoTP
Valentine's Message, The. Mildred J. Hill. GFA
Valentines to My Mother (1876-1886), *sels.* Christina Rossetti.
1879 ("Mother mine"). BoChLi
1880 ("More shower than shine"). DD
1882 ("My blessed mother").
(Valentine to My Mother, A.) OHIP
1885 ("All the Robin Redbreasts"). BoChLi; DD
Valerius on Women. Thomas Heywood. *See* She That Denies Me.
Valiant-for-Truth. Corinne Roosevelt Robinson. DD; HH; PEDC
Valiant Love. Richard Lovelace. SCEP-2; SeCP
Valley, The. Stanley Moss. NYBP
Valley Forge, *sel.* Maxwell Anderson.
Lafayette to Washington. PAL
Valley Forge. Thomas Buchanan Read. *Fr.* The Wagoner of the Alleghanies. MC; PAH
Valley Harvest, The. H. L. Davis. NP
Valley lay smiling before me, The. The Song of O'Ruark, Prince of Breffni. Thomas Moore. OnYI
Valley of ancient life, how many visions died. The Other Journey. Katherine Garrison Chapin. MoVE
Valley of Decision, The. John Oxenham. PGD
Valley of mine, sweet valley! The Girl and the Cuckoo. *Unknown.* OnPM

Valley of Pale Blue Flowers, The. "Fiona Macleod." PoVP
Valley of pines unclosed its gates, The. Orphic Interior. Leonardo Sinisgalli. LiTW
Valley of Silence, The. "Fiona Macleod." PoVP
Valley of Silence, The. Abram Joseph Ryan. SoP
(Song of the Mystic.) JKCP
Valley of Sleep, The. Hendrik Marsman, *tr. fr. Dutch by* A. J. Barnouw. *Fr.* The Zodiac. LiTW
Valley of the Black Pig, The. W. B. Yeats. ChTr
Valley of the Heavens, The. Luis de León, *tr. fr. Spanish by* Thomas Walsh. CAW
Valley of the Shadow. John Galsworthy. MaRV; OHIP; TrPWD
Valley of the Shadow of Death, The. William Cowper. EiCP
Valley of Unrest, The. Poe. AmPP; AP; MWA-1; PoEL-4; TDP; ViBoPo
Valley of Vain Verses, The. Henry van Dyke. HBV
Valley of White Poppies, The. "Fiona Macleod." MoSiPe; PoVP
Valley That God Forgot, The. Henry Herbert Knibbs. PCD
Valley Wind, The. Lu Yün, *tr. fr. Chinese by* Arthur Waley. OnPM
Valley with a silver-grayish mist, The. A Vision. Hugo von Hofmannsthal. TrJP
Valley's Singing Day, The. Robert Frost. UnS
Valleys, splendid as her womb, The. Sarah. "Robin Hyde." AnNZ
Valleys that we knew in sunlit hours, The. Three Nocturns. Sir Osbert Sitwell. POTE
Valour and Innocence. The Queen's Men. Kipling. AtBAP
Valor of Ben Milam, The. Clinton Scollard. HBV; MC; PAH
Valorous Acts Performed at Gaunt by the Brave Bonny Lass, Mary Ambree, The. *Unknown. See* Mary Ambree.
Valse Jeune. Louise Imogen Guiney. AA
Values. Leslie Savage Clark. ChIP
Values in Use. Marianne Moore. NePoAm-2
Vamp Passes, The. James J. Montague. HBMV
Vampire, The. Conrad Aiken. HBMV
Vampire. Walter H. Kerr. FiSC
Vampire, The [as Suggested by the Painting by Philip Burne-Jones]. Kipling. BLPA; EnLit; HBV; NeHB
Vampire Bride. Felix Stefanile. FiSC
Van Amburgh's Menagerie. *Unknown.* BLPA
Vanbrug's House. Swift. PP
Vance Song, The, *with music.* Abner Vance. OuSiCo
Vancouver Lights. Earle Birney. CaP
Van Dieman's Land. *Unknown.* BaBo; CoMu; PeVV
Vane on Hughley steeple, The. Hughley Steeple. A. E. Housman. A Shropshire Lad, LXI. PoVP; ViPo; VP
Vane, young in years, but in sage counsel old. To Sir Henry Vane the Younger. Milton. OBS; Sonn
Van Elsen. Frederick George Scott. HBV; VA
Vanessa Vanessa. Ewart Milne. NeIP
Van Gogh Influence, The. Shel Silverstein. ELU
Vanished. Emily Dickinson. *See* She died—this was the way she died.
Vanished house that for an hour I knew, A. Souvenir. E. A. Robinson. InP
Vanished Night, The. Niall MacMurray, *tr. fr. Irish by* Frank O'Connor. KiLC
Vanishers, The. Whittier. AA; SoP, *abr.*
Vanishing Act, The. Alan Stephens. TDP
Vanitas Vanitatum. John Webster. *See* All the Flowers of the Spring.
Vanitas Vanitatum. Israel Zangwill. TrJP
Vanitie ("The fleet astronomer can bore"). George Herbert. *See* Vanity.
Vanitie ("Poore silly soul, whose hope and head lies low"). George Herbert. MaMe
Vanity. Ecclesiastes, I: 12-II: 26, Bible, *O.T.* OuHeWo
Vanity. Robert Graves. GTBS-P
Vanity [*or* Vanitie] ("The fleet astronomer can bore"). George Herbert. EP; MaMe; MePo; NoP; ReEn; SCEP-1; SeCV-1
Vanity. James Thomson. *See* Once in a Saintly Passion.
Vanity. Anna Wickham. FaBoTw
Vanity of All Worldly Things, The. Anne Bradstreet. SCAP
Vanity of Existence, The. Philip Freneau. AmPP (5th ed.); AP
Vanity of Human Learning, The. Sir John Davies. *See* Man.
Vanity of Human Wishes, The: the Tenth Satire of Juvenal Imitated. Samuel Johnson. ATP; BWP; CABA; CoBE; EiCL; EiCP; EiPP; EnPE; LaA; LoBV, *abr.*; MasP; NoP; Po; PoE; PoEL-3; PoFS; UnPo (1st ed.), *abr.*; VaPo
Sels.
"Let observation with extensive view." ATP; BEL; CEP; TOP, *abr.*
Life's Last Scene. OBEC; SeCePo
"On what foundations stands the warrior's pride." ViBoPo
(Charles XII.) FOL; OBEC
Scholar's Life, The. FaBoEn; OBEC; SeCePo
("When first the college rolls receive his name.") PoIE
"Unnumbered suppliants crowd Preferment's gate." PoFr
"Where then shall Hope and Fear their objects find?" EnLi-1 (1949 ed.)
(Prayer.) OBEC
Vanity of Kissing. Bonefonius, *tr. fr. Latin by* John Nott. OnPM
Vanity of Riches ("Non ebur neque aureum"). Horace, *tr. fr. Latin by* T. Rutherford Clark. Odes, II, 18. WoL
Vanity of Spirit. Henry Vaughan. AnAnS-1; MeP; ReEn
Vanity of the World, The. Francis Quarles. *Fr.* Emblems. PPON
(False World, Thou Ly'st.) SeCePo; SeEP
(Wilt Thou Set Thine Eyes upon That Which Is Not?) OBS
Vanity of Vanities. Ecclesiastes, Bible, *O.T. See* Words of the Preacher, The.
Vanity of Vanities. Palladas, *tr. fr. Greek by* William M. Hardinge. AWP; JAWP; TRV; WBP
Vanity of Vanities. Michael Wigglesworth. AnNE
(Song of Emptiness to Fill up the Empty Pages Following, A.) SCAP
Vanity of vanities, saith Koheleth. Vanity of Vanities. Ecclesiastes, Bible, *O.T.* TrJP
Vanity of vanities, saith the Preacher, vanity of vanities; all is vanity. The Words of the Preacher. Ecclesiastes, Bible, *O.T.* TreFS
Vanity of vanities, the Preacher saith. The One Certainty. Christina Rossetti. OBNC
"Vanity, Saith the Preacher." Josephine Preston Peabody. InP
Vanity, saith the preacher, vanity! The Bishop Orders His Tomb at Saint Praxed's Church. Robert Browning. ATP; AWP; BEL; BoLiVe; BWP; CABA; CaFP; CBV; DiPo; EnL; EnLi-2; EnLit; EPN; ExPo; FiP; ForPo; GTSE; HBV; ILP; MaPo; MaVP; MBW-2; MyFE; NoP; OAEP; OtMeF; PAn; PIA; Po; PoAn; PoE; PoIE; PoVP; SeCeV; ShBV-4; VA; VaPo; ViBoPo; ViPo; ViPP; VP
Vanquished. Francis Fisher Browne. AA; DD; HBV
Vanquished, The. Charles Eglington. BoSA; PeSA
Vanquished and weary was my soul in me. Sonnet: A Trance of Love. Cino da Pistoia. AWP
Vantage Point, The. Robert Frost. CoBMV; MAmP; MaPo; OxBA
Van Winkle. Hart Crane. *Fr.* The Bridge: Powhatan's Daughter. AmP; AmPP; CrMA; FaBV; LiTA; MAP; MoAB; MoAmPo; ReMP
Vapor Trail Reflected in the Frog Pond. Galway Kinnell. OPoP
Vapour and Blue. Wilfred Campbell. CaP
Vaquero. Edward Dorn. NeAP
Vaquero. Joaquin Miller. AA; PFY
Variation. Bill Berkson. YAP
Variation: Ode to Fear. Robert Penn Warren. FiMAP
Variation on a Line by Emerson. W. S. Merwin. NePA
Variation on a Sentence. Louise Bogan. ImOP
Variation on a Theme by Dylan Thomas. Carl Bode. ToPo
Variation on a Theme by Francis Kilvert. Rolfe Humphries. UnS
Variation on a Theme by John Lyly. Sacheverell Sitwell. ViBoPo
Variation on Ronsard. T. Sturge Moore. OBMV
Variations, *sels.* Conrad Aiken.
"Beautiful body made of ivory," XIV. PG (1945 ed.)
Queen Cleopatra, X. HBMV
"Wind, wind, wind in the old trees," XII. PG (1933 ed.)
Variations (I-IV). Randall Jarrell. MiAP
Variations and Elegy: White Stag, Black Bear. James Merrill. NoP
Variations, Calypso and Fugue on a Theme of Ella Wheeler Wilcox. John Ashbery. ANYP
Variations Done for Gerald van de Wiele. Charles Olson. NeAP

Variations for Two Pianos. Donald Justice. NYBP; TDP
Variations of an Air. G. K. Chesterton. *See* Variations on an Air.
Variations on a Line from Shakespeare's Fifty-sixth Sonnet. E. L. Mayo. PoCH
Variations on a Medieval Theme. Geoffrey Dutton. PoAu-2
Variations on a Still Morning. Thomas Cole. NePoAm
Variations on a Theme. John Hay. NePoAm
Variations on a Theme. Robert Hillyer. MAP; MoAmPo
Variations on a Theme, *parody.* Joseph G. E. Hopkins. JKCP (1955 ed.)
Variations on a Theme. Anne Wilkinson. MoCV
Variations on a Theme. Oscar Williams. LiTA; NePA
Variations on a Theme by George Herbert. Marya Zaturenska. TrPWD
Variations on a Theme by Sidney Keyes. Eithne Wilkins. NeBP
Variations on a Theme by William Carlos Williams. Kenneth Koch. PV
Variations on a Theme from James. Donald Justice. TDP
Variations on a Time Theme, *sel.*. Edwin Muir.
"At the dead centre of the boundless plain." MoVE; PIA
Variations on an Air. G. K. Chesterton. InP
(Variations of an Air.) Par
Variations on an Old Nursery Rhyme. Edith Sitwell. *See* King of China's Daughter, The.
Variations on Simonides. Gladys Ely. NYTB
Variations on *The Aeneid,* sel. John Morgan.
Woman Takes Life with Own Hand. YAP
Variations: The Air Is Sweetest That a Thistle Guards. James Merrill. NePoEA
Variety, The. John Dancer. CavP
Variety. John Donne. Elegies, XVII. MaMe
Various Ends. Ruthven Todd. NeBP; SeCePo
Various the Roads of Life. Walter Savage Landor. EnRP; OQP; TOP
Various voices are his poem now, The. Glaucus. Sidney Keyes. FaBoMo
Various Wakings. Vincent Buckley. PoAu-2
Varitalk. Weare Holbrook. NYBP; SiTL
Varium et Mutabile. Sir Thomas Wyatt. *See* Is It Possible?
Varuna, The. George Henry Boker. PAH
Varus, whom I chanced to meet. A Fib Detected. Catullus. AWP
Vasari tells that Luca Signorelli. An Episode. John Addington Symonds. PoVP; VA
V-a-s-e, The. James Jeffrey Roche. AmePo; BOHV; HBV; LHV
Vase, The. Terence Tiller. ChMP
Vase of Life, The. Dante Gabriel Rossetti. The House of Life, XCV. MaVP; PoVP; SyP; ViPo
Vase of Tears, The. Stephen Spender. AtBAP; LO; POTE
Vase which holds all fat'ning liquor, The. *Unknown.* *Fr.* Riddles. CoBE
Vases. Nan Terrell Reed. BLPA
Vashti, *sel.* Lascelles Abercrombie. *Fr.* Emblems of Love, I.
Woman's Beauty. MoBrPo; PG
Vast and immaculate; no pilgrim bands. The Sea Cathedral. E. J. Pratt. CaP
Vast and solemn company of clouds, The. After Sunset. William Allingham. IrPN
Vast bodies of philosophy. To Mr. Hobbes. Abraham Cowley. LoBV; ReEn; SCEP-2; SeCV-1
Vast Chaos, of eld, was God's dominion. He Made the Night. Lloyd Mifflin. HBV
Vast corridor through Nature's roofless halls. Ute Pass. Ernest Whitney. PoOW
Vast Light. Richard Eberhart. CMoP; NMP
Vast mild melancholy splendid. Canberra in April. J. R. Rowland. PoAu-2
Vast occasion of our time, The. War. Mary Fullerton. NeLNL
Vast Superstition! Glorious style of weakness! Chorus Quintus: Tartarorum. Fulke Greville. *Fr.* Mustapha. OBS
Vastness. Tennyson. PoVP; VA
"Spring and summer," *sel.* OQP
Vaticide. Myron O'Higgins. IDB; Kal; OnHM
Vaudeville Dancer. John Hall Wheelock. UnS
Vaudracour and Julia. Wordsworth. *See* Prelude, The: "Among that band of Officers was one."
Vault inside the Castle at Goito, A. Robert Browning. *Fr.* Sordello. MyFE
Vault on the opal carpet of the sun. To Potapovitch. Hart Crane. UnS
Vault, A, see; thick/ Black shade about the ceiling. And What Sordello Would See There. Robert Browning. *Fr.* Sordello. MyFE
Vaulting Ambition. Shakespeare. *Fr.* Macbeth, I, vii. FiP
(Murder Pact, The.) WHA
Vaunting Oak. John Crowe Ransom. NoP; OxBA
Veäiry ring so round's the zun, A. William Barnes. NBM
Vedic Hymns, *sels.* *Unknown,* *tr. fr. Vedic.*
Brahma, the World Idea. Rig-Veda. WGRP
Charm to Quell a Rival, *tr. by* R. T. H. Griffith. Rig-Veda. LiTW
Creation Hymn, The, *tr. by* R. T. H. Griffith. Rig Veda, Bk. X, Hymn 129. OuHeWo
(Hymn of Creation, *tr. by* Arthur A. Macdonnell.) LiTW
Funeral Hymn, *tr. by* Arthur A. Macdonnell. Rig-Veda. LiTW
Hymn to Night, *tr. by* R. T. H. Griffith. Rig-Veda. LiTW
Hymn to Varuna, God of Fire and Light, *tr. by* R. T. H. Griffith. Rig-Veda. LiTW
Indra, the Supreme God, *tr. by* Romesh Dutt. Rig-Veda. AWP
Pushan, God of Pasture, *tr. by* Romesh Dutt. Rig-Veda. AWP; JAWP; WBP
To Liberality, *tr. by* R. T. H. Griffith. Rig-Veda, Bk. X, Hymn 117. PoFr
To the Unknown God, *tr. by* Max Müller. Rig-Veda, Bk. X, Hymn 121. OuHeWo
Veery, The. Henry van Dyke. AA
Veery-Thrush, The. Joseph Russell Taylor. AA
Vegetable Fantasies. Helen Hoyt. RIS
Vegetable Loves. Erasmus Darwin. *Fr.* The Botanic Garden: The Loves of the Plants, I. OBEC; SeCePo
Vegetables. Eleanor Farjeon. FaPON; TiPo (1959 ed.)
(Country Vegetables.) PCH
Vegetables. Rachel Field. GFA; SoPo
Veil, The. Walter de la Mare. CMoP
Veil not thy mirror, sweet Amine. To Amine. James Clarence Mangan. OBEV (new ed.); OBVV
Veil thine eyes, O belovéd, my spouse. The Bridegroom of Cana. Marjorie Pickthall. CaP
Veil upon veil. Natura Naturans. Kathleen Raine. NYBP
Veiled are the heavens, veiled the throne. Dawn on Mid-Ocean. John Hall Wheelock. EtS
Veiled in that light amazing. The Dispraise of Absalom. *Tr.* fr. Irish by Robin Flower. OxBI
Velasquez took a pliant knife. Castilian. Elinor Wylie. AnAmPo; HBMV; NAMP
Veld Eclogue, A; the Pioneers, *sel.* Roy Campbell.
"But 'nameless somethings' and 'unbounded spaces.'" BoSA
Velvet beautiful and dark, A. Peace by Night. Sister Mary Madeleva. GoBC
Velvet Hand, The. Phyllis McGinley. TreFT
Velvet Shoes. Elinor Wylie. CH; FaPON; GoJo; MAP; MoAB; MoAmPo; MPB; NeMA; NP; OTD; OTPC (1946 ed.); PCH; PFY; PG; PoPl; PTK; SiSoSe; SoPo; SP; StVeCh; TiPo (1952 ed.); TreFS; TrGrPo; TSW; WHA
Velvet Sonneteers, The. Tom MacInnes. CaP
Venadito Song. *Unknown.* *See* Lo Que Digo.
Vendor. Raymond Roseliep. FiSC
Vendor's Song. Adelaide Crapsey. AnFE; APA; CoAnAm; HBV; MAP; MoAmPo (1942 ed.)
Venemous toung, tipt with vile adders sting. Amoretti, LXXXVI. Spenser. ReEn
Venerable Bee, The. A. M. Klein. TrJP
Venerable Mother Toothache. A Charm against the Toothache. John Heath-Stubbs. BoPe; FIW; NePoEA; TwCP
Veneration of Images. Alice Meynell. GTBS
Veneta. Mary Elizabeth Coleridge. CBEP
Venetian Epigrams, *sel.* Goethe, *tr. fr. German by* F. Melian Stawell *and* Nora Purtscher-Wydenbruck.
"All the apostles of freedom." PoFr
Venetian Night, A. Hugo von Hofmannsthal, *tr. fr. German by* Ludwig Lewisohn. AWP; JAWP; WBP
Venetian Pastoral, A. Dante Gabriel Rossetti. *See* For "A Venetian Pastoral" by Giorgione.
Venetian Scene. Anne Ridler. NMP
Venetian Serenade, The. Richard Monckton Milnes. OBRV

Vengeance of Finn, The, *sel.* Austin Clarke.
Awakening of Dermuid, The. AnIV
Vengeance was once her nation's lore and law. Watkwenies. Duncan Campbell Scott. PeCV
Vengeaunce must fall on thee, thou filthie whore. Against the Court of Rome. Petrarch. Sonnets to Laura: To Laura in Life, CVII. LiTW
Vengeful across the cold November moors. The Pity of the Leaves. E. A. Robinson. AA; MoAmPo (1950 ed.)
Vengence on Cats. John Skelton. *Fr.* Phyllyp Sparowe. *See* Cursing of the Cat, The.
Veni, Coronaberis. *Unknown.* AtBAP; BoW
Veni Creator ("Lord of my heart's elation"). Bliss Carman. *See* Lord of My Heart's Elation.
Veni Creator ("Lord of the grass and hill"). Bliss Carman. *See* Overlord.
Veni Creator Spiritus. *Unknown, at. to* St. Gregory the Great *and to* Charlemagne, *paraphrased fr. Latin by* Dryden. AWP; CAW; CEP; CoBE; GoBC; HBV; MaRV; OuHeWo; SeCV-2; WBP; WGRP; WHL, *abr., tr. unknown*
Veni, Domine Jesu! Henry Augustus Rawes. WHL
Veni Sancte Spiritus. *Unknown, at. to* Robert II, King of France, *tr. fr. Latin by* Catherine Winkworth. HBV; WHL, *tr. unknown*
Venice. Byron. *Fr.* Childe Harold's Pilgrimage, IV. BEL; HBV
("I stood in Venice on the Bridge of Sighs.") OAEP, *abr.*; OBRV, *abr.*; ViBoPo, 3 *sts.*
(Venice and Rome, *abr.*) MCCG
(Venice and Sunset, *abr.*) EPN
Venice. Longfellow. AmPP
Venice. Howard Moss. MoAB
Venice. John Addington Symonds. *Fr.* Stella Maris. HBV; VA
("Venice, thou Siren of sea-cities, wrought.") PoVP
Venice and Rome. Byron. *See* Venice.
Venice and Sunset. Byron. *See* Venice.
Venice Recalled. Bruce Boyd. NeAP
Venice, thou Siren of sea-cities, wrought. Venice. John Addington Symonds. *Fr.* Stella Maris. HBV; PoVP; VA
Venite Adoremus. Margery Cannon. GoBC
Veniunt Spectentur ut Ipsi. Henry Parrot. SiCE
Venomous thorns that are so sharp and keen. Sir Thomas Wyatt. FCP
'Vention did in Boston meet, The. Convention Song. *Unknown.* PAH
Venture of Faith, The. Francis Greenwood Peabody. MaRV
Venus. Dante Gabriel Rossetti. MaVP
Venus Abandoned. Shakespeare. *Fr.* Venus and Adonis. OBSC
("'Nay then,' quoth Adon, 'you will fall again,'" *abr.*) LO
Venus Accoutered as Mars. *Unknown, tr. fr. Greek by* Louis Untermeyer. UnTE
Venus, again thou mov'st a war. To Venus. Horace. Odes, IV, 1. AWP
Venus and Adonis. William Browne. *Fr.* Britannia's Pastorals, II. CLwM; EIL
("Venus, by Adonis' side.") SeEP
Venus and Adonis. Shakespeare. BeLS
Sels.
"But if thou needs wilt hunt, be rul'd by me." SiCE
Courser and the Jennet, The. LoBV
(Courser, The.) OBSC
Death of Adonis, The. WHA
Horse, A. ExPo
Lo! Here the Gentle Lark. ChTr
"'Nay then,' quoth Adon, 'you will fall again.'" LO
(Venus Abandoned.) OBSC
"O, what a war of looks was then between them!" UnTE
Poor Wat. OBSC; UnPo (1st ed.)
"'Sweet boy,' she says, 'this night I'll waste in sorrow.'" ErPo
Venus and Cupide. Sir Thomas More. EnRePo
Venus and young Adonis sitting by her. *See* Venus, with Young Adonis Sitting by Her.
Venus, by Adonis' side. Venus and Adonis. William Browne. *Fr.* Britannia's Pastorals. CLwM; EIL; SeEP
Venus fair did ride. The Shepherd's Song of Venus and Adonis. Henry Constable. TuPP
Venus Fly Trap, The. Readymade. John Perreault. ANYP
Venus has lit her silver lamp. The Lamp in the West. Ella Higginson. AA; HBV
Venus, if men at sea you save. Shipwrecked Heart. *Unknown.* OnPM
Venus of Bolsover Castle, The. Sacheverell Sitwell. HBMV
Venus of the Louvre. Emma Lazarus. AA; AnAmPo
Venus on a Sea Horse. Maurice Carpenter. FaBoTw
Venus' Runaway. Ben Jonson. *See* Beauties, Have Ye Seen This Toy.
Venus' Speech. Louis MacNeice. CMoP
Venus, take my votive glass. The Lady Who Offers Her Looking-Glass to Venus [*or* A Farewell *or* Lais' Mirror]. Matthew Prior, *after the Greek of* Plato. AWP; CBEP; CLwM; OBEV; OnPM; ViBoPo; WoL
Venus Transiens. Amy Lowell. NP
Venus Victrix. Dante Gabriel Rossetti. The House of Life, XXXIII. MaVP; PoVP; ViPo; VP
Venus, what mood inspires you to don. Venus Accoutered as Mars. *Unknown.* UnTE
Venus, with Young Adonis Sitting by Her. Bartholomew Griffin. *Fr.* The Passionate Pilgrim. ViBoPo
("Venus and young Adonis sitting by her," *sl. diff. vers. in* Fidessa, More Chaste than Kind.) ReIE
Ver and Hiems. Shakespeare. *See* When Daisies Pied and Violets Blue.
Veracious people, The. Dante, *tr. fr. Italian by* Longfellow. *Fr.* Divina Commedia: Purgatorio. CAW
Veracruz. Robert Hayden. AmNP
Verazzano. Hezekiah Butterworth. PAH
Verbal Critics. Pope. *Fr.* Epistle to Dr. Arbuthnot. OBEC
("Pains, reading, study, are their just pretense.") PP
Verbum Supernum. *At. to* St. Ambrose, *tr. fr. Latin by* H. T. Henry. CAW
Verdancy. *Unknown.* ShM
Verdant branch was swinging here, A. So Long Ago. Morris Rosenfeld. TrJP
Verdi at Eighty. Martin Bell. MuSP
Verdict, The. Norman Cameron. SeCePo
Vergidemiarum. Joseph Hall. *See* Virgidemiarum.
Vergissmeinnicht. Keith Douglas. ChMP; GTBS-P
(Vergissmeinicht.) NePoEA
Verily God is guard! Guardian of All. *Unknown.* OnPM
Verily I Say Unto You, Yee Shall Weep and Lament. Richard Crashaw. MaMe
Verily, verily, I say unto you, He that entereth not by the door. The Good Shepherd. St. John, Bible, *N.T.* WoL
Veritable night, The. Rigmarole. William Carlos Williams. AnAmPo
Vermin only tease and pinch, The. On Fleas. Swift. TreFS
Vermont. Sarah N. Cleghorn. HBMV
Vermont; Indian Summer. Philip Booth. NePoEA
Vern. Gwendolyn Brooks. OCS; TiPo (1959 ed.)
Vernal Equinox. Amy Lowell. MAPA
Vernal Equinox. Ruth Stone. MoAmPo (1962 ed.)
Vernal Paradox. Kim Kurt. NePoAm-2
Vernal Sentiment. Theodore Roethke. ELU; MiAP
Vernal Showers. David O'Neil. AnAmPo
Vernon Castle. Harriet Monroe. HBMV
Vers de Société. H. D. Traill. Par
Vers la Vie. Arthur Upson. HBV
Vers Nonsensiques. George Du Maurier. HBV
Versailles. Stopford Brooke. VA
Versailles. Adrienne Cecile Rich. NePoEA
Versailles!—Up the chestnut alley. The Pompadour. George Walter Thornbury. BeLS
Verse. Richmond Lattimore. PP
Verse: "Past ruined Ilion Helen lives." Walter Savage Landor. *See* Past Ruin'd Ilion . . .
Verse: "What should we know." Oliver St. John Gogarty. AnIL; FaBoCh; LO; LoGBV; OBMV; PoRA
Verse, a breeze mid blossoms straying. Youth and Age. Samuel Taylor Coleridge. BEL; EnLi-2 (1949 ed.); EnRP; ERoP-1; FiP; GTBS; GTBS-D; GTBS-P; GTBS-W; GTSE; GTSL; HBV; MERP; OBEV; OBNC; OBRV; PoLF
Verse in Praise of Lord Henry Howard, Earl of Surrey. George Turberville. ReIE; SiCE; TuPP
Verse is a chalice; place within it only. Art. José Asuncion Silva. CAW
Verse-Letter: To Sir Henry Wootton. John Donne. *See* To Sir Henry Wotton ("Here's no more news . . .").
Verse Letter to the Countess of Bedford. John Donne. *See* To the Countesse of Bedford.

Verse-Letter to the Countess of Denbigh, A. Richard Crashaw. *See* To the Noblest and Best of Ladies, the Countess of Denbigh.
Verse makes heroic[k] virtue live. To Mr. Henry Lawes, Who Had Then Newly Set a Song of Mine in the Year 1635. Edmund Waller. AnAnS-2; CLwM; CTC; PP; SCEP-2; SeCP; SeCV-1
Verse may find him who a sermon flies, A. On the Following Work and Its Author. Jonathan Mitchell. SCAP
Verse, Violence, and the Vine. James Vincent Cunningham. NYTB
Verse Written in the Album of Mademoiselle ——. Pierre Dalcour, *tr. fr. French by* Langston Hughes. PoNe; TTY
Verses: "Even such is time." Sir Walter Ralegh. *See* Conclusion, The.
Verses: "I am confirm'd a woman can." Sir John Suckling. CavP
Verses: "I am monarch of all I survey." William Cowper. *See* Verses Supposed to Be Written by Alexander Selkirk.
Verses: "Who strives to mount Parnassus hill." Richard Bentley. ViBoPo
(Reply to an Imitation of the Second Ode in the Third Book of Horace, A.) OBEC
Verses by Mr Prior. Matthew Prior. PeRV
Verses Composed on the Eve of His Execution. James Graham, Marquess of Montrose. ChTr
(His Metrical Prayer.) OxBS
(On Himself, upon Hearing What Was His Sentence.) CavP; CBEP; OBS; SeCePo
Verses Copied from the Window of an Obscure Lodging-House, in the Neighborhood of London. *Unknown.* LiTL; ViBoPo
Verses for a Centennial. Archibald MacLeish. NoP
Verses for a First Birthday. George Barker. *Fr.* Second Cycle of Love Poems. MoAB; MoBrPo (1950 ed.)
Verses for Fruitwomen, *sels.* Swift.
Apples. AnIV; OnYI
(Verses Made for Women Who Cry Apples.) NCEP
Herrings. AnIV; OnYI
Onions. AnIV; OnYI
Verses for the 60th Birthday of T. S. Eliot. George Barker. ChMP
Verses Found in His Bible in the Gate-House at Westminster. Sir Walter Ralegh. *See* Conclusion, The.
Verses Found in Thomas Dudley's Pocket after His Death. Thomas Dudley. SCAP
Verses from the Shepherds' Hymn. Richard Crashaw. *See* Hymn Sung as by the Shepherds, A.
Verses Intended to Be Written below a Noble Earl's Picture. Burns. HoPM
Verses Intended to Go with a Posset Dish to My Dear Little God-daughter, 1882. James Russell Lowell. AP
Verses Made for Women Who Cry Apples. Swift. *See* Verses for Fruitwomen.
Verses Made Sometime Since upon . . . the Indian Squa. John Josselyn. SCAP
Verses Occasioned by the Death of Dr. Aikman. James Thomson. *Fr.* On the Death of Mr. William Aikman the Painter. OBEC
(On the Death of a Particular Friend.) OBEV
Verses of Man's Mortality. *At. to* Simon Wastell. *See* Man's Mortality.
Verses on a Cat. Charles Daubeny. CIV; HBV
Verses on a Cat. Shelley. CIV
Verses on Blenheim. Swift. *See* On Blenheim.
Verses on Daniel Good. *Unknown.* CoMu; OxBB
Verses on Games, *sel.* Kipling.
Boxing. OtMeF
Verses on Sir Joshua Reynolds's Painted Window at New-College, Oxford. Thomas Warton, the Younger. CEP; EiCL; OBEC; PoEL-3
Verses on the Death of Dr. Swift. Swift. CABL; CEP, *abr.*; CoBE, *abr.*; EiCL; EiPP; LoBV; MasP; MBW-1; PoEL-3; PoFS, *abr.*
(On the Death of Dr. Swift.) EiCP
Sels.
"Dean, if we believe report, The." FaBoEn
"From Dublin soon to London spread." WHA
"Had he but spar'd his tongue and pen." FaBoEn
"He never thought an honour done him." PoFr
"My female friends, whose tender hearts." SeCePo
"Perhaps I may allow the Dean." FaBoEn; OnYI
"Time is not remote, when I, The." OBEC; OxBoLi; SiTL; ViBoPo; WoL
Verses on the Prospect of Planting Arts and Learning in America. George Berkeley. *See* On the Prospect of Planting . . .
Verses Placed over the Door at the Entrance into the Apollo Room at the Devil Tavern. Ben Jonson. HBV
(Over the Door at the Entrance into the Apollo.) ReEn
Verses Supposed to Be Written by Alexander Selkirk, During His Solitary Abode in the Island of Juan Fernandez. William Cowper. CEP; HBV; PoEL-3; PoLF
(Alexander Selkirk.) FiP; FOL, 2 *sts.*
(I Am Monarch of All I Survey.) OnPP
(Monarch, The.) TreFS
(Solitude of Alexander Selkirk, The.) GTBS; GTBS-D; GTBS-P; GTBS-W; GTSE; GTSL; LiTB; LiTG; MCCG; RoGo
(Verses: "I am monarch of all I survey." PoIE
Verses to Ianthe. Walter Savage Landor. *See* Ianthe.
Verses to Mr. Vaughan of Hengwrt. Evan Evans. PrWP
Verses to St. Cecilia. David Wright. POTE (1959 ed.)
Verses to the Memory of an Unfortunate Lady. Pope. *See* Elegy to the Memory of an Unfortunate Lady.
Verses upon the Burning of Our House. Anne Bradstreet. *See* Upon the Burning . . .
Verses versus Verses. Marvin Bell. YAP
Verses Why Burnt. Walter Savage Landor. VA
Verses Written during a Sleepless Night. Pushkin, *tr. fr. Russian by* Babette Deutsch. OnPM; PoPl
Verses Written during the War, 1756-1763. Thomas Osbert Mordaunt. CBEP; OBEC
Verses Written in a Lady's Sherlock "Upon Death." Earl of Chesterfield. CEP; OBEC
(Mistaken Fair.) CBEP
Verses Written in 1872. Robert Louis Stevenson. *See* Resurgence.
Verses Written in His Bible. Sir Walter Ralegh. *See* Conclusion, The.
Verses Wrote in a Lady's Ivory Table-Book. Swift. EiCL; NCEP
Versions of Love. Roy Fuller. LiTM (1970 ed.); ToPo
Versos de Montalgo, *with music.* *Unknown, pr. tr. fr. Spanish by* Frank L. Dobie. AS
Vert-Vert, the Parrot. Louis Gresset, *tr. fr. French by* Francis Sylvester Mahony. CAW
Vertue. George Herbert. *See* Virtue.
Vertue! thou solemn grave Impertinence. John Oldham. *Fr.* A Satyr against Vertue. PeRV
Very acme of my woe, The. Little Son. Georgia Douglas Johnson. CDC
Very afraid. The Dalliance of Leopards. *Unknown.* OnPM
Very bitter weeping that ye made, The. Dante. *Fr.* La Vita Nuova. AWP
Very dark the autumn sky. A Belated Violet. Oliver Herford. AA
Very Early. Karla Kuskin. PDV; SoPo
Very Fair My Lot. Jacob David Kamzon, *tr. fr. Hebrew by* Sholom J. Kahn. TrJP
Very grandiloquent goat, A. The Grandiloquent Goat. Carolyn Wells. MoShBr
Very Happy Family, A. Joseph G. Francis. CIV
Very high in the pine-tree. The Turtle-Dove's Nest. *Unknown, at. to* Ann Hawkshaw. HBVY; OTPC (1923 ed.); SAS
Very like a Whale. Ogden Nash. DTC; PoLF; ShBV-3; TrGrPo
Very Little Sphinx, A, *sel.* Edna St. Vincent Millay.
Wonder Where This Horseshoe Went. SUS; TiPo (1952 ed.)
(Horseshoe, The.) StVeCh
(Wonder Where.) PoRh
Very lovely. Rose Fyleman. GFA; SoPo; TiPo
Very Minor Poet Speaks, A. Isabel Valle. BLPA
Very Model of a Modern College President, The.*parody.* Harold A. Larrabee. WhC
Very Names of Things Beloved, The. Robert Bridges. The Growth of Love, IV. CMoP; PoVP
Very Nearly. Queenie Scott-Hopper. FaPON; MPB; OTPC (1946 ed.); SoPo; TVC
Very old are the woods. All That's Past. Walter de la Mare. AnFE; CoBE; GoJo; InP; MoAB; NP; OAEP (2d ed.); OBMV; PG (1945 ed.); POTE; SeCeV; ShBV-4; StP; ThWaDe; TreFT; TrGrPo; ViBoPo; WHA
Very Old Song, A. "William Laird." HBV

Very Phoenix, A. Thomas Lodge. CBEP
Very pitiful lady, very young, A. Dante. *Fr.* La Vita Nuova. AWP; CTC; JAWP; WBP
Very Pretty Maid of This Town, and the Amorous 'Squire Not One Hundred Miles from the Place, The. *Unknown.* CoMu
Very pulse of ocean now was still, The. Evening in Gloucester Harbor. Epes Sargent. EtS
Very quickly will it be over with thee here. Imitation of Christ: The Thoughts of Death. Thomas à Kempis. OuHeWo
Very Rich Man, The. Dorothy Parker. PoPo
Very ripe today. My Daily Melon. G. Bishop-Dubjinsky. ThO
Very small children in patched clothing, The. The Study in Aesthetics. Ezra Pound. CMoP; NoP; NP
Very Torch, The. Erinna, *tr. fr. Greek by* John Herman Merivale. OnPM
Very Tree. Stanley J. Kunitz. NP
Very True, the Linnets Sing. Walter Savage Landor. TrGrPo
(Autumnal Song.) ERoP-1
Very ungraceful dog is Sandy, A. Sandy—a Small Dog. Alan Anderson. PCD
"Very, very queer things have been happening to me." Queer Things. James Reeves. PoMS
Very well, you liberals. Thomas Rhodes. Edgar Lee Masters. *Fr.* Spoon River Anthology. NP
Vesi, the black one, the leaper who sprang. Praises of the King Dingana (Vesi). *Unknown.* PeSA
Vesper. Alcman, *tr. fr. Greek by* F. L. Lucas. OA
Vesper. Thomas Edward Brown. *See* Vespers.
Vesper Bells. Dwight Edwards Marvin. SoP
Vesperal. Ernest Dowson. OBMV
Vespers. Thomas Edward Brown. BoTP; EnLit; MemP; YT
(Vesper.) BoC
Vespers. Henry W. Frost. SoP
Vespers. Reginald Heber. SoP
Vespers. Ian Maxwell. MoAuPo
Vespers. Louis Mercier, *tr. fr. French by* Joseph T. Shipley. CAW
Vespers. S. Weir Mitchell. OQP; WGRP
(From Dark to Light.) MaRV
Vespers. Odell Shepard. TrPWD
Vessel that rests here at last, The. The Yacht. Walter Savage Landor. OBVV
Vessels. Francis Carlin. JKCP (1955 ed.)
Vesta. Whittier. OBEV (1st ed.); TrPWD; WHA
Vestal, The. Nathalia Crane. AnAmPo; MAP; MoAmPo (1942 ed.); TrJP
Vestal, The. Pope. *Fr.* Eloisa to Abelard. ACP; CAW
Vestal Virgin, The, *sel.* John Plummer Derwent Llwyd.
"Night is soft with summer; yon faint arch, The." CaP
Vestiges. Denis Devlin. OnHM
Vestigia. Bliss Carman. CaP; MaRV; OQP; WGRP
Vestments in your church, they say, The. To a Prince of the Church. Kenneth W. Porter. MaRV
Vesture of the Soul, The. "Æ." ACV
Veteran, The. Edmund Blunden. BrPo
Veteran, The. Louis O. Coxe. MoVE
Veteran Cowboy's Ruminations, A. John M. Kuykendall. PoOW
Veteran Greeks came home, The. The Return. Edwin Muir. CMoP; MemP
Veteran of Heaven, The. Francis Thompson. HBV; MaRV; PoLi
"O Captain of the wars, whence won Ye so great scars?" *sel.* ChIP
Veteran Sirens. E. A. Robinson. AnAmPo; AnNE; BoLiVe; OnHM; QFR
Veterans, The. Denis A. McCarthy. PEDC
Veterans, The. Donagh MacDonagh. JKCP (1955 ed.); OnYI
Vex no man's secret soul—if that can be. Help. Sadi. *Fr.* The Gulistan. AWP; JAWP; OnPM; WBP
Vex not thou the poet's mind. The Poet's Mind. Tennyson. PoG; ViPP
Vexilla Regis. Venantius Fortunatus, *tr. fr. Latin by* John Mason Neale. CAW; WHL
(Hymn to the Holy Cross.) LiTW
Vexilla Regis, the Hymn of the Holy Crosse. Richard Crashaw. *See* Hymn of the Holy Crosse, The.
Vezzosi Augelli. Thomas Watson, *tr. fr. Italian.* TuPP
Via Amoris. Sir Philip Sidney. *See* Astrophel and Stella, LXXXIV.
Via Crucis, Via Lucis. T. H. Hedge. BePJ
Via Dolorosa. Phoebe Smith. PGD
Via, et Veritas, et Vita. Alice Meynell. JKCP; MaRV; OQP; WGRP
Via Longa. Patrick McDonough. HBMV
Via Lucis. Charles G. Blanden. OQP
Via Lucis. Howard Chandler Robbins. MaRV; OQP
Vial, The. David Galler. NYTB
Viaticum. Ethna MacCarthy. NeIP
Vicar, The. George Crabbe. *Fr.* The Borough. OBNC
Vicar, The. George Crabbe. *Fr.* Inebriety. AnFE
Vicar, The. Winthrop Mackworth Praed. Every-Day Characters, I. EnRP; EPN; HBV; InMe; NBM; OBEV (new ed.); OBNC; OBRV; OBVV; PoEL-4; VA
Vicar at the table's front presides, The. The Vicar. George Crabbe. *Fr.* Inebriety. AnFE
Vicar of Bray, The. *Unknown.* ALV; CEP; EiCL; HBV; OxBoLi; ViBoPo
(In Good King Charles's Golden Days.) InvP; OBEC
Vicar of Wakefield, The, *sels.* Goldsmith.
Edwin and Angelina, *fr. ch.* 8. CEP; OTPC
Elegy [*or* Elegie] on the Death of a Mad Dog, *fr. ch.* 17. ALV; BeLS; BLPA; BOHV; CBEP; CEP; FaBoBe; FaBoCh; FaFP; GN; HBV; HBVY; LBN; LiTG; LoGBV; MaC; MCCG; NA; NeHB; OAEP; OBEC; OnSP; OTD; OTPC; PoPo; PoSa; RIS; RoGo; SiTL; ShM; TreF; WaKn
Song: "When lovely woman stoops to folly," *fr. ch.* 24. AWP; BEL; CBV; CEP; EiPP; GTBS; GTSE; GTSL; ILP; JAWP; LiTL; OBEC; PoFS; PoPl; SeCePo; TOP; TrGrPo; VaPo; ViBoPo; WBP
(Stanzas on Woman.) ELP; EnLit; ExPo; OnYI; OxBI
(When Lovely Woman Stoops [to Folly].) CBEP; EnLi-1; GTBS-D; GTBS-P; GTBS-W; HBV; InP; NoP; PoIE; StP; TreF
(Woman.) LiTB; LiTG; OBEV
Vicarious Atonement. Richard Aldington. MoBrPo; WGRP
Vice. Pope. *Fr.* Essay on Man, Epistle II. ELU; PoPl
Vice, from privation of that sacred grace. Satire IV. John Marston. *Fr.* The Scourge of Villainy. ReIE
Vice is a monster of so frightful mien. Vice. Pope. *Fr.* Essay on Man. ELU; PoPl
Vice, 1966, *sel.* James Brodey.
"Throat-to-throat surgery." ANYP
Vice Versa. Christian Morgenstern, *tr. fr. German by* R. F. C. Hull. OA
Viceroy they made him, Admiral and Don. Columbus. Florence Earle Coates. DD; MC
Vices of Women, The. Juvenal, *tr. fr. Latin by* Dryden. *Fr.* Satires, VI. PeRV
Vicious winter finally yields, The. W. D. Snodgrass. Heart's Needle, X. NePoEA; PIA
Vicissitudes of the Creator. Archibald MacLeish. NePA; VaPo
Vickery's Mountain. E. A. Robinson. MAP; MoAmPo
Vicksburg—a Ballad. Paul Hamilton Hayne. AA; MC; PAH
Vicomte is wearing a brow of gloom, The. Chez Brébant. Francis Alexander Durivage. AA
Victim, The. Barbara L. Greenberg. QAH
Victimae Paschali, *abr.* Wipo, *tr. fr.* Latin. WHL
(Victimae Paschali Laudes, *tr. by* Charles Kent.) CAW
Victor, The. Thomas Kelly. *See* The Cross and the Crown.
Victor, The. Sydney King Russell. StaSt
Victor, The. William Young. HBMV
Victor and Vanquished. Longfellow. CoBA
Victor Galbraith. Longfellow. PAH
Victor of Antietam, The. Herman Melville. MC; PAH
Victor stood beside the spoil, and by the grinning dead, The. Omar and the Persian. Sarah Williams. VA
Victor was a little baby. Song. W. H. Auden. AnFE
Victoria. Henry van Dyke. SoP; TRV
Victoria Dancing. Anne Welsh. BoSA
Victoria Falls, The. William Plomer. BoSA
Victoria Market. Francis Brabazon. BoAV
Victoria Markets Recollected in Tranquillity, The, *abr.* Frank Wilmot. BoAV; NeLNL; PoAu-2
"Winds are bleak, stars are bright," *sel.* MoAuPo
Victorian Song. John Farrar. GoYe
Victories of Love, The, *sel.* Coventry Patmore.
Fragment: "He that but once too nearly hears." NBM
Victorious beauty, though your eyes. To the Countesse of Salisbury [*or* Loves Victory]. Aurelian Townsend. AnAnS-2; MeLP; MePo; OBS; SeCP

Victorious knights without reproach or fear. To the Returning Brave. Robert Underwood Johnson. PAH
Victorious Men of Earth. James Shirley. *Fr.* Cupid and Death. CBEP; OBS; TrGrPo
(Death, the Conqueror.) GoBC
(Death's Emissaries.) LoBV
(Death's Subtle Ways.) HBV
(Last Conqueror, The.) GTBS; GTBS-D; GTBS-P; GTBS-W; GTSE; GTSL
(Song: "Victorious men of earth, no more.") FaBoEn; SeCL
("Victorious men of earth, no more.") TuPP
Victorious Wrong, with vulture scream. The Final Chorus from "Hellas." Shelley. EnLi-2
Victors, The. Denise Levertov. NoP
Victors, The, *abr.* Charles Hanson Towne. OQP
Victory. Roger Axford. PGD
Victory. Eileen Duggan. AnNZ
Victory. Aline Kilmer. MaRV
Victory. Mary Britton Miller. RePo
Victory. Alfred Noyes. BEL
Victory. Arthur B. Rhinow. MaRV
Victory. Sir Owen Seaman. OQP; WGRP
(Between Midnight and Morning.) MaRV
("Ye that have faith to look with fearless eyes.") PoToHe
Victory ("I am a youthful lady"). *Unknown.* CoMu
Victory ("Long long ago on Calvary"). *Unknown.* STF
Victory ("The strife is o'er"). *Unknown.* *See* Strife Is O'er, The.
Victory, The. John Hall Wheelock. NP
Victory. Marguerite Wilkinson. ChIP
Victory Ball, A. Alfred Noyes. EnLit
Victory Bells. Grace Hazard Conkling. HBV; MC; PaA; PAH
Victory comes. The New Victory. Margaret Widdemer. WGRP
Victory Dance, A. Alfred Noyes. PoLF
Victory in Defeat. Edwin Markham. MaRV; OQP; PoIE; PoPl; StaSt; TreFT
Victory in Hungary, The. Thomas Shadwell. *Fr.* The Squire of Alsatia. SeCL
Victory in the Cabarets. Louis Untermeyer. HBMV
Victory March. M. K. Joseph. AnNZ
Victory Parade. George Edward Hoffman. PGD
Victory Which Is Peace, The. Frederic Lawrence Knowles. *See* New Age, The.
Victus. Quentin Stevenson. POTE (1959 ed.)
Videantur Quae Non Sunt. Henry Parrot. SiCE
Vietnam #4. Clarence Major. BOLo; WOW
Vietnam Turnpike. Thomas Hanna. QAH
Vieux Carré. Walter Adolphe Roberts. PoNe
View. Josephine Miles. RePo
View, The. Howard Nemerov. NYBP
View, A. Beverly Quint. NYBP
View, all ye eyes above, this sight which flings. Meditation Twenty. Edward Taylor. *Fr.* Preparatory Meditations, First Series. AP
View at Gunderson's. Joseph Warren Beach. NP
View from a Window. Eldon Grier. PeCV (1967 ed.)
View from an American Window. Peter Fellowes. QAH
View from an Attic Window, The. Howard Nemerov. CoAP
View from Heights. Arthur Davison Ficke. *See* I Am in Love with High, Far-seeing Places.
View from Here, The. William Stafford. ELU
View from the Corner. Samuel Allen. BP
View from the Gorge. Ben Belitt. NYBP
View from the Window, The. R. S. Thomas. BoC; POTi
View Me, Lord, a Work of Thine. Thomas Campion. MaRV; OxBoCh; SiCE
(View Mee, Lord.) TrPWD
View not my tomb with pity, passer-by. A Full Life. Carphyllides. OnPM
View now the winter storm! Above—one cloud. The Winter Storm at Sea. George Crabbe. *Fr.* The Borough. EtS
View of a Pig. Ted Hughes. CBV; FIW; LiTM (1970 ed.); POTi; TwCP
View of Jersey, A. Edward Field. NeAP
View of Montreal, A, *sel.* Francis Webb.
Cartier at St. Malo. BoAV
View of Rangitoto, A. Charles Brasch. AnNZ
View of T'ai-shan, A. Tu Fu, *tr. fr. Chinese by* Witter Bynner *and* Kiang Kang-hu. OuHeWo
View of the Brooklyn Bridge, A. William Meredith. MoVE
View of the Burning, A. James Merrill. NePoEA-2
View of the Capitol from the Library of Congress. Elizabeth Bishop. AmFN; FiMAP
"View of the Present State of Ireland, A." Edmund Blunden. BrPo
View of the Sea, A. Mabuchi, *tr. fr. Japanese by* Asataro Miyamori. OnPM
Viewless thing is the wind, A. Love Is Strong. Richard Burton. AA; HBV
Viewpoints. Arthur Guiterman. UTS
Views of Boston Common and Nearby. R. P. Blackmur. MoVE
Views of the Favorite Colleges. John Malcolm Brinnin. LiTA; MoAB; OnHM
Views of the Oxford Colleges. Paris Leary. CoPo
Vigi. Katharine Lee Bates. PCD
Vigil. Faith Baldwin. MaRV
Vigil. Marjorie Freeman Campbell. CaP
Vigil. Richard Dehmel, *tr. fr. German by* Ludwig Lewisohn. AWP; JAWP; LiTW; WBP
Vigil. W. E. Henley. In Hospital, VII. LoBV
Vigil, The. Denise Levertov. NePoEA-2
Vigil, The. T. Sturge Moore. POTE
Vigil, The. Theodore Roethke. *Fr.* Four for Sir John Davies. PoDB
Vigil in Gethsemane. Ruth Margaret Gibbs. SoP
Vigil of Joseph, The. Elsa Barker. StJW
Vigil of the Assumption. Gertrude von Le Fort, *tr. fr. German by* Margaret Chanler. ISi
Vigil of the Immaculate Conception. Maurice Francis Egan. CAW; JKCP
Vigil of Venus, The. *Unknown, sometimes at. to* Catullus, *tr. fr. Latin by* Thomas Stanley. AWP; OuHeWo; UnTE
—— *Tr. by* Allen Tate. LiTW
—— *Tr. by* Thomas Parnell. WoL
Vigil Strange I Kept on the Field One Night. Walt Whitman. CoBA; LoBV; MoAmPo (1950 ed.); NoP; WaaP; WHA
Vigilantes, The. Margaret Ashmun. SCC
Vigilantius, or a Servant of the Lord Found Ready. Cotton Mather. SCAP
Vigils. Siegfried Sassoon. CMoP
Down the Glimmering Staircase, *sel.* PoLF
Vigor, vitality, vim and punch. "Pep." Grace G. Bostwick. WBLP
Viking, The. Whitley Stokes. OnYI
Viking Terror, The. *Unknown, tr. fr. Old Irish by* F. N. Robinson. AnIL; OnYI; KiLC, *tr. by* Frank O'Connor
(Vikings, The, *tr. unknown.*) ChTr
Vil for the Layman. Marge Piercy. ThO
Vilest work of vilest man, The. Nature the False Goddess. James Jeffrey Roche. JKCP
Villa Sciarra; Rome. Christine Turner Curtis. GoYe
Villafranca de Córdoba. Pedro Garfias, *tr. fr. Spanish by* Kenneth Porter. PoFr
Village, The. George Crabbe. EiCL
Sels.
"Fled are those times, when, in harmonious strains." PoSa
"No shepherds now, in smooth alternate verse." PP
Parish Poor-House, The. OBEC
Pauper's Funeral, The. FaBoEn; OBNC
"Thus groan the old, till, by disease oppress'd." PoFS
Truth in Poetry. OBEC; SeCePo
"Village life, and every care that reigns, The." BEL; CoBE; EiPP; EnLi-2; EnPE; EnRP; FosPo; Po; PoE
(Village Life.) PoEL-4
Village, The. Marina Gashe. PBA
Village, The. Goldsmith. *Fr.* The Deserted Village. TrGrPo
(Auburn.) OBEC; SeCePo
(Sweet Auburn.) LiTB
("Sweet Auburn! loveliest village of the plain.") OTPC; TreFS; ViBoPo
Village, The. R. S. Thomas. HaMV
Village and Factory. Alexander Ilyich Bezymensky, *tr. fr. Russian by* Babette Deutsch. TrJP
Village Atheist, The. Edgar Lee Masters. *Fr.* Spoon River Anthology. AmP; EaLo; LiTA; MaRV; PoPo
Village Barber, The. Luis Lopez, *tr. fr. Spanish by* Thomas Walsh. OnPM
Village before Sunset. Frances Cornford. BoNaP; LoGBV
Village Blacksmith, The. Longfellow. AA; AmePo; AnNE;

Village (continued)
CoBA; FaBoBe; FaPL; FaFP; FaPON; GoTP; HBV; HBVY; NeHB; OnPP; OTPC; PaPo; PoPl; PTK; SoP; StVeCh; TreF; WBLP
Village Blacksmith, The. *Unknown.* FiBHP
Village-Born Beauty. *Unknown.* PaPo
Village Choir. *Unknown.* BOHV
Village Christmas. Margaret Widdemer. RePo
Village church, so small it has hardly shrunk, The. The Return. L. A. G. Strong. HaMV
Village-folk told me, saying, The. Foreboding. *Unknown. Fr.* Manyo Shu. OnPM
Village, happy once, is splendid now, The. The Bailiff. Ebenezer Elliott. *Fr.* The Splendid Village. NBM
Village Inn, The. John Betjeman. POTi
Village is submerged, houses and creatures, The. Ashokan. Dachine Rainer. NePoAm
Village lies in Sabbath heat, The. Sanna. Alan Paton. BoSA
Village Life. George Crabbe. *Fr.* The Village. PoEL-4
("Village life, and every care that reigns, The.") BEL; CoBE; EiCL; EiPP; EnLi-2; EnPE; EnRP; FosPo; Po; PoE
Village maid was leaving home, with tears her eyes were wet, A. Heaven Will Protect the Working Girl. Edgar Smith. FaFP; TreF
Village Noon; Mid-Day Bells. Merrill Moore. MAP; MoAmPo
Village of Erith, The. *Unknown.* ChTr
(Erith.) CBEP
Village of Winter Carols. Laurie Lee. ChMP
Village Parson, The. Goldsmith. *See* Village Preacher, The.
Village pedagogue announced one day, A. The Snuff-Boxes. *Unknown.* StPo
Village Portrait. Thomas W. Duncan. MoSiPe
Village Preacher, The. Goldsmith. *Fr.* The Deserted Village. MaRV; TrGrPo, *shorter sel.*
(Country Parson, The.) OTPC (1923 ed.)
(Village Parson, The.) OBEC; WGRP
Village Schoolmaster, The. Goldsmith. *Fr.* The Deserted Village. OBEC; PoSa; TrGrPo
(Schoolmaster, The.) OTPC (1946 ed.); ShBV-2
Village sleeps, a name unknown, till men, The. Distinction. M. A. De Wolfe Howe. AA
Village Stork, The. Bayard Taylor. PFY
Village! thy butcher's son, the steward now. The Steward. Ebenezer Elliott. *Fr.* The Splendid Village. NBM
Village where they ring, A. Dusk. Basho. OnPM; WoL
Villagers all, this frosty tide. Carol [*or* Christmas Carol]. Kenneth Grahame. *Fr.* The Wind in the Willows. FaPON; MPB; OHIP
Villagers who gather round. Spiel of the Three Mountebanks. John Crowe Ransom. MAP; MoAB; MoAmPo
Villages Démolis ("The villages are strewn"). Sir Herbert Read. BrPo
Villain, The. W. H. Davies. CBV; MoBrPo; NeMA; POTE; WHA
Villain, The, *sel.* Thomas Porter.
Serenade, to Two Ladies. SeCL
Villain shows his indiscretion. Curtain! Paul Laurence Dunbar. CenHV
Villancico. *Unknown, tr. fr. Spanish by* Thomas Walsh. AWP; JAWP; OnPM; WBP
Villanelle. W. H. Auden. MoAB; MoBrPo
(If I Could Tell You.) TDP
(Time Will Say Nothing but I Told You So.) LiTA
Villanelle. William Empson. ChMP; CMoP; EnLoPo; PoIE
Villanelle. M. D. Feld. SD
Villanelle. W. E. Henley. InP; TOP
Villanelle. Walter H. Kerr. NePoAm-2
Villanelle. Dilys Laing. ErPo; NMP
Villanelle. Margaret Winefride Simpson. OxBS
Villanelle. W. W. Skeat. FiBHP; SiTL
Villanelle. A. M. Sullivan. OQP
Villanelle of a Villaness. Edwin Meade Robinson. HBMV
Villanelle of His Lady's Treasures. Ernest Dowson. HBV
Villanelle of Light. A. M. Sullivan. JKCP (1955 ed.)
Villanelle of Marguerites. Ernest Dowson. EnLi-2; MoBrPo
Villanelle of Sunset. Ernest Dowson. BrPo
Villanelle of the Living Pan. Walter Adolphe Roberts. PoNe
Villanelle of the Poet's Road. Ernest Dowson. OBMV; PoVP; TrGrPo; ViPP
Villanelle of Things Amusing. Gelett Burgess. BOHV
Villanelle of Washington Square. Walter Adolphe Roberts. PoNe
Villanelle; the Psychological Hour. Ezra Pound. CTC; NP
Villeins clustered round the bowl, The. Brawn of England's Lay. John Hunter-Duvar. VA
Villiers de l'Isle-Adam. Aldous Huxley. HBMV
Villkins and His Dinah (A *and* B *vers.*). *Unknown.* BaBo
Villon's Ballade. Andrew Lang, *after* Villon. HBV
Villon's Good-Night. W. E. Henley, *after* Villon. CenHV
Villon's Straight Tip to all Cross Coves. W. E. Henley, *after* Villon. AWP; BOHV; CenHV; HBV; InMe; InvP; NA; SeCePo
Vincent Corbet, farther knowne. An Elegie Upon the Death of His Owne Father. Richard Corbett. AnAnS-2
Vinco. Elliot Field. ChIP
Vindictive Staircase, The; or, The Reward of Industry. W. W. Gibson. AnFE
Vine, The. Robert Herrick. CavP; ErPo; UnTE
Vine, The. James Thomson. Sunday up River, XVIII. HBV; OBEV; OBVV
("Wine of Love is music, The.") PoVP; ViBoPo
Vine and Clarel. Herman Melville. *Fr.* Clarel. MAmP
Vine and the Goat, The. Aesop, *rhymed tr. fr. Greek by* William Ellery Leonard. AWP
Vine I see, and though 'tis time to glean, A. Overripe Fruit. Kasmuneh. TrJP
Vine, my Lord, a noble vine indeed, A. Meditation. Edward Taylor. *Fr.* Preparatory Meditations, Second Series. MeP
Vine to the Goat, The. Euenus, *tr. fr. Greek by* L. R. Lind. LiTW
Vinegar Man, The. Ruth Comfort Mitchell. MPB; SP
Vines branching stilly. A Carol [*or* Five Carols for Christmastide, II]. Louise Imogen Guiney. CAW; ISi; OBVV
Vines of Lebanon that briskly grew, The. Meditation. Edward Taylor. *Fr.* Preparatory Meditations, Second Series. MeP
Vines tougher than wrists. Forcing House. Thoedore Roethke. AtBAP
Vineyard, The. *Unknown.* STF
Vingtaine. Alice Learned Bunner. AA
Immutabilis, II.
Separation, I.
Vintage, The. Belle Cooper. GoBC
Vintage to the Dungeon, The. Richard Lovelace. SCEP-2; SeCV-1
Violence in the newspapers is pure genius, The. Survival of the Fittest Groceries. William Knott. YAP
Violence of love, The. Dear. Howard McCord. YAP
Violent order is disorder, A; and. Connoisseur of Chaos. Wallace Stevens. PoeP
Violent praise the destructive rites of the hawk, The. The Beaver's Story. Vernon Watkins. NYBP
Violent Storm. Mark Strand. NYBP
Violet, The. Sir Walter Scott. EnRP; EPN
Violet, The. William Wetmore Story. HBV
Violet, *sel.* Arthur Symons.
Declaration, III. BrPo; ViBoPo
Violet, The. Jane Taylor. BoChLi; HBV; HBVY; OTPC; PRWS; RIS; TreF; TVC
Violet, The. Wordsworth. *Fr.* She Dwelt Among the Untrodden Ways. PCH
Violet and the Rose, The. Joseph Skipsey. OBVV
Violet and the Rose, The. Augusta Webster. HBV
Violet Bank, A. Shakespeare. *Fr.* A Midsummer Night's Dream, II, i. FaPON; OTPC (1946 ed.); PRWS; RePo
("I know a bank whereon the wild thyme blows.") BoNaP
(Titania's Bower.) PCH
(Where the Wild Thyme Blows.) PTK; TrGrPo
Violet bloom of summer's end. Tropes of One Season. Charles Edward Eaton. FiSC
Violet by a mossy stone, A. The Violet. Wordsworth. *Fr.* She Dwelt among the Untrodden Ways. PCH
Violet in her greenwood bower, The. The Violet. Sir Walter Scott. EnRP; EPN
Violet in her lovely hair, A. Song. Charles Swain. HBV
Violet in the wood, that's sweet to-day, The. The Violet and the Rose. Augusta Webster. HBV
Violet invited my kiss, The. The Violet and the Rose. Joseph Skipsey. OBVV
Violet is much too shy, The. A Song the Grass Sings. Charles G. Blanden. HBV

Violets. Dinah Maria Mulock Craik. PRWS
Violets, The. Stephen Crane. War Is Kind, XXIII. AA
(War Is Kind, III: "There was a land where lived no violets.") AnAmPo
Violets. Robert Herrick. *See* To Violets.
Violets. John Moultrie. BoTP
(Dear Little Violets.) PRWS
Violets. P. A. Ropes. BoTP
Violets ("I know, blue modest violets"). *Unknown.* BoTP
Violets and Roses. *Unknown.* *See* Sweet Violets, Love's Paradise.
Violets blue of the eyes divine, The. The Withered Heart [*or* Dis blauen Veilchen der Äugelein]. Heine. AWP; OnPM
Violets, daffodils. Elizabeth J. Coatsworth. TiPo (1959 ed.)
Violets in Thaumantia's Bosome. Sir Edward Sherburne. OBS
Violets, violets, sweet March violets. Violets. Dinah Maria Mulock Craik. PRWS
Violin, The. E. N. da Costa Andrade. MuSP
Violin, The. Richard Watson Gilder. PoRL
Violin Calls, The. Florence Randal Livesay. CaP
Violin Concerto, A. James Reeves. MuSP
Violinist, A. Francis William Bourdillon. OBVV; VA
Violinist, The. Archibald Lampman. CaP
Violinist's shadow vanishes, The. Cadenza. Ted Hughes. NYBP; OPoP
Violin's Complaint, The. William Roscoe Thayer. AA
Viper, The. Hilaire Belloc. BOHV; RIS
Viper, The. Ruth Pitter. FaBoTw
Vipers bugloss beckons me, The. Song to My Love. Laurence McKinney. InMe
Virelay: "Thou cruel fair, I go." Charles Cotton. LO; SeCL
Virgidemiarum, *sels.* Joseph Hall.
"Another scorns the homespun thread of rhymes," Bk. I, Satire VI. SiCE; TuPP
"Gentle squire would gladly entertain, A," Bk. II, Satire VI. ReIE; SiCE; TuPP; ViBoPo
"Great is the folly of a feeble brain," Bk. I, Satire VII. ReIE
(Love-sicke Poet, The.) FaBoEn
"Great Osmond knows not how he shall be known," Bk. III, Satire II. ReIE
"Hence, ye profane; mell not with holy things," Bk. I, Satire VIII. SiCE
"I first adventure, with foolhardy might," Prologue, Bk. I. ReEn; ReIE; SiCE; ViBoPo
"I wot not how the world's degenerate," Bk. IV, Satire VI. ReIE
"Nor ladies wanton love, nor wandering knight," Bk. I, Satire I. SiCE; TuPP
"Satire should be like the procupine, The," Bk. V, Satire III. ReEn
"Seest thou how gayly my young master goes," Bk. III, Satire VII. SiCE
"Some say my satires over-loosely flow," Prologue, Bk. III. SiCE
"Time was, and that was termed the time of gold," Bk. III, Satire I. SiCE
(Olden Days, The.) OBSC
"Too popular is tragic poesy," Bk. I, Satire IV. ReEn; SiCE
"Whilom the sisters nine were vestal maids," Bk. I, Satire II. FosPo
"With some pot-fury, ravished from their wit," Bk. I, Satire III. ReEn; SiCE
Virgil from Homer, th' Italian from him. Of Spenser's *Faerie Queene* [*or Fairy Queen*]. Thomas Freeman. SiCE; TuPP
Virgilia, *sel.* Edwin Markham.
"What was I back in the world's first wonder?" EtS
Virgil's Farewell to Dante. Dante, *tr. fr. Italian by* Laurence Binyon. *Fr.* Divinia Commedia: Purgatorio, XXVII. FaBoTw
Virgil's Tomb. Robert Cameron Rogers. AA
Virgin. Padraic Fallon. OnYI
Virgin, The. Katherine Philips. LO
Virgin, The. Wordsworth. CAW; CoBE; GoBC
(Sonnet to the Virgin.) ISi
Virgin and Unicorn. John Heath-Stubbs. NeBP
Virgin calm and gentle, in thine eyes. To Joseph. Harriet Hoock. WHL
Virgin Country. Roy McFadden. NeIP
Virgin Declares Her Beauties, A. Francesco da Barberino, *tr. fr. Italian by* Dante Gabriel Rossetti. AWP; ErPo
Virgin Mary, The. Edgar Bowers. NePoEA; QFR
Virgin Mary cannot enter into, The. And in Her Morning. Jessica Powers. ISi
Virgin Mary to Christ on the Cross, The. Robert Southwell. ViBoPo
Virgin Mary to the Child Jesus, The, *abr.* Elizabeth Barrett Browning. ISi
Virgin Mary's Conception, The. Robert Southwell. ReIE
(Virgine Maries Conception, The.) MeP
Virgin Mother, The, *sel.* D. H. Lawrence.
"I kiss you good-bye, my darling." ViBoPo
Virgin Mother, thou hast known. Latin Hymn. Winthrop Mackworth Praed. CoBE
Virgin Truly Full of Wonder. St. Ephrem, *tr. fr. Syriac by* W. H. Kent. *Fr.* Christmas Hymn. ISi
(Christmas Hymn, The.) CAW
Virginal, A. Ezra Pound. AmPP; AP; APA; CMoP; CoAnAm; CoBMV; ILP; MAP; MeWo; MoAB; MoAmPo; NeMA; NePA; OxBA; PoAn; Sonn; TwAmPo
Virgine Maries Conception, The. Robert Southwell. *See* Virgin Mary's Conception, The.
Virginia. Hart Crane. *Fr.* The Bridge: Three Songs. LiTA
Virginia. T. S. Eliot. Landscapes, II. NoP; PoSa
Virginia. Vachel Lindsay. ATP (1935 ed.)
Virginia Britannia. Marianne Moore. MoVE
Virginia Capta. Margaret Junkin Preston. PAH
Virginia gave us this imperial man. Imperial Man. James Russell Lowell. *Fr.* Under the Old Elm. PGD
Virginia Song, The. *Unknown.* PAH
Virginian Voyage, The. Michael Drayton. *See* To the Virginian Voyage.
Virginiana. Mary Johnston. HBMV
Virginians Are Coming Again, The. Vachel Lindsay. NP
Virginians of the Valley, The. Francis Orrery Ticknor. AA; AnAmPo; DD; HBV PaA; PAH
Virgins. Francis Carlin. HBMV
Virgins as I advise forbeare. *Unknown.* SeCSL
Virgins, in vain you labour to prevent. Christopher Marlowe. *Fr.* Tamburlaine the Great, Pt. I. MyFE
Virgins promis'd when I dy'd. An Epitaph upon a Child. Robert Herrick. SeCV-1
Virgins Salutation, The. Robert Southwell. MeP
(Our Lady's Salutation.) ISi
Virgin's Slumber Song, The. Francis Carlin. ISi; YeAr
Virgin's Song, The. *Unknown.* *See* Our Lady's Song.
Virgins terrify too many men. Sonnet XII. Winfield Townley Scott. ErPo
Virile Christ, A. Rex Boundy. ChIP; MaRV; OQP; TRV
Virtue. Walter de la Mare. MMA
Virtue. George Herbert. ATP; AWP; BEL; BoLiVe; BWP; CABA; CaFP; CBEP; CBV; CH; CoBE; ELP; EnLi-1; EnLit; EP; ExPo; ForPo; FosPo; HBV; InPo; InvP; JAWP; LoBV; MaPo (1969 ed.); NoP; OBEV; OnPM; PAn; PG (1955 ed.); PIA; Po; PoAn; PoE; PoFS; PoIE; PoRA; PoSa; SeCeV; SeCL; SeEP; ShBV-4; TOP; TreFT; TrGrPo; UnPo (1st ed.); ViBoPo; WBP; WGRP; WHA
("Sweet day, so cool, so calm, so bright.") EG
(Vertue.) AnAnS-1; AtBAP; FaBoEn; MaMe; MeLP; MeP; MePo; OBS; SCEP-1; SeCP; SeCV-1
Virtue. Immanuel di Roma, *tr. fr. Hebrew by* Joseph Chotzner. *Fr.* Machberoth. TrJP
Virtue, alas, now let me take some rest. Astrophel and Stella, IV. Sir Philip Sidney. FCP; MaPo; ReEn; SiPS
Virtue, beauty, and speech did strike, wound, charm. An Excellent Sonnet of a Nymph. Sir Philip Sidney. *Fr.* Arcadia. FCP; ReIE
Virtue dwells rarely in the bright eyed and fair. Virtue. Immanuel di Roma. *Fr.* Machberoth. TrJP
Virtue may unlock hell, or even. Epilogue. Francis Thompson. *Fr.* A Judgment in Heaven. PoLi
Virtue the Best Monument. Sir Walter Ralegh. FCP
Virtue's branches wither, virtue pines. A Priest's Song [*or* Song *or* O Pittie]. Thomas Dekker. *Fr.* Old Fortunatus. AtBAP; ElL; OBSC; SiCE
Virtuosa. Mary Ashley Townsend. AA
Virtuoso, A. Austin Dobson. PeVV
Virtuous Fox and the Self-righteous Cat, The. John Cunningham. OnMSP

Virtuous Wife, The. Proverbs, Bible, *O.T.* *See* Good Wife, The.
Virtuous Wife, The, *sel.* Thomas D'Urfey.
"Sawney was tall." OAEP
Virtuous Wife, The. Süsskind von Trimberg, *tr. fr. Middle High German.* TrJP
Virtuous Woman, The. Proverbs, Bible, *O.T.* *See* Good Wife, The.
Virus, The. Christian Morgenstern, *tr. fr. German by* W. D. Snodgrass *and* Lore Segal. PV
Visage becomes armed, The: within. Armed Vision. N. P. van Wyk Louw. PeSA
Viscous air, wheres' ere she fly, The. The Kingfisher. Andrew Marvell. *Fr.* Upon Appleton House. ChTr
Visibly here the tide. Wellfleet Harbor. Paul Goodman. CoAP
Vision, The. William Stanley Braithwaite. OQP
Vision, A. William Browne. *See* Rose, The.
Vision, The ("As I stood by yon roofless tower"). Burns. PoFr
Vision, The ("The sun had clos'd the winter-day"). Robert Burns. OxBS
Vision. Giosuè Carducci, *tr. fr. Italian by* Glauco Cambon. OnPM
Vision, A. John Clare. *See* I Lost the Love of Heaven.
Vision, A, *sel.* "Barry Cornwall."
"First, I saw a landscape fair." OBRV
Vision, A. Geoffrey Dearmer. HBMV
Vision. Edward Dowden. ChIP; OQP
Vision. Richard Eberhart. NYBP
Vision, A. "Michael Field." SyP
Vision, A. Philip Freneau. *Fr.* The House of Night.
("Trembling I write my dream, and recollect.") AnFE; APA; CoAnAm
Vision, A. Henry W. Frost. SoP
Vision. Rose Fyleman. PCH
Vision, The. Walter Greenough. DD
Vision. Elizabeth N. Hauer. PoToHe
Vision, A. Lord Herbert of Cherbury. AnAnS-2; SeCP
Vision, The ("I dreamed we were both in bed"). Robert Herrick. *See* Vision to Electra, The.
Vision, The ("Methought I saw as I did dream in bed"). Robert Herrick. *See* Second Vision, The.
Vision, The ("Sitting alone as one forsook"). Robert Herrick. AnAnS-2; ErPo; SeCP
(Sitting Alone.) UnTE
Vision, A. Hugo von Hofmannsthal, *tr. fr. German by* Charles Wharton Stork. TrJP
Vison. William Dean Howells. AA; AmePo; AnAmPo; CBV
Vision, The. Lounkianos, *tr. fr. Armenian by* Thomas Walsh. CAW
Vision. Ida Norton Munson. ChIP
Vision. F. R. Scott. MoCV
Vision. Frank Sidgwick. MMA
Vision, The. Thomas Traherne. PeRV
Vision, A. Henry Vaughan. *Fr.* The World. BBV; GTSL
("I saw eternity the other night," *first* 7 *ll.*) ImOP
Vision, A. Yvor Winters. MoVE
Vision, A, *sel.* W. B. Yeats.
All Souls' Night. MoVE; ReMP
Vision. Israel Zangwill. TrJP
Vision and Prayer. Dylan Thomas. LiTG; LiTM (rev. ed.); MoPo
Vision as of crowded city streets, A. Shakespeare. Longfellow. AWP; InPo; MAmP; MWA-1; TOP
Vision by Sweetwater. John Crowe Ransom. AP; CMoP; CoBMV; CrMA; FaBoMo; MoAB; OxBA
Vision Clear, The. J. M. Westrup. BoTP
Vision Concerning Piers Plowman, The. William Langland. *See* Vision of Piers Plowman, The.
Vision in Hollywood, A. Allen Ginsberg. FRC
Vision in long filaments flows. Vision. F. R. Scott. MoCV
Vision of a Past Warrior. Peter La Farge. WOW
Vision of a Queen of Fairyland, A. The First Vision. Tadhg Dall O'Huiginn. AnIL
Vision of Athens. Milton. *See* Athens.
Vision of Belshazzar, The. Byron. FOL; GN; HBV; OnMSP; OTPC; RoGo; TOP
Vision of Beulah. Blake. *See* Nightingale and Flowers.
Vision of Children, A. Thomas Ashe. VA
Vision of Christ that thou dost see, The. Blake. *Fr.* The Everlasting Gospel. OBRV
Vision of Connaught in the Thirteenth Century, A. James Clarence Mangan. AnIL; IrPN
(King Cahal Mór of the Wine-red Hand.) AnIV; GoBC
Vision of Delight, The, Presented at Court in Christmas, 1617. Ben Jonson. PoEL-2; SeCV-1
Vision of Eternity, A. Avis B. Christiansen. SoP
Vision of God, The. Dante, *tr. fr. Italian by* Laurence Binyon. *Fr.* Divina Commedia: Paradiso, XXXIII. ExPo
Vision of Ita, The. *At. to* St. Ita. *See* Jesukin.
Vision of Jesus, The. William Langland (?). *Fr.* The Vision of Piers Plowman. ACP; CAW
Vision of Judgement, A, *sel.* Robert Southey.
Absolvers, The, Pt. VI. EnRP
Vision of Judgment, The. Byron. EnRP; ERoP-2; MasP; MBW-2; MERP; OxBoLi, *first* 15 *sts.*; StP; TOP

At the Gate of Heaven, *abr.* OBRV
(Archangel, The.) LoBV
George the Third. FiP
"He ever warred with freedom and the free." PoFr
"Saint Peter sat by the celestial gate." PIA
Vision of Lazarus, The, *sel.* Fenton Johnson.
"Another sate near him." BANP
Vision of MacConglinne, The. MacConglinne, *tr. fr. Middle Irish.* CAW, *abr., tr. by* George Sigerson; CH, *tr. by* Kuno Meyer
(Vision That Appeared to Me, A, *tr. by* Kuno Meyer.) OnYI
Vision of Nature, A. William Langland (?). *Fr.* The Vision of Piers Plowman. PoEL-1
Vision of Oxford, A, *sel.* William Alexander.
"Methought I met a Lady yester even." OBVV
Vision of peace, the blessed place Jerusalem. Epithalamium for the Dedication of a Church. *Unknown.* HW
Vision of Piers Plowman, The, *sels.* William Langland (?).
"And I bowed my body and beheld all about," 5 *ll.* CTC
Avarice, *fr.* Passus V (B *text*), *mod. by* Henry W. Wells. PoLi
Average Man, The, *fr.* Passus XIII (B *text*), *mod. by* Henry W. Wells. PoLi
Crucifixion and the Harrowing of Hell, The, *fr.* Passus XXI (C *text*), *mod.* MeEV
Descent into Hell, The, *fr.* Passus XXI (C *text*). PoEL-1
Glutton and Bat the Brewer, *fr.* Passus V (B *text*), *mod. by* Grover Cronin, Jr. CoBE
(Glutton, The.) ACP
Harrowing of Hell, The, ("After sharp showers . . ."), *fr.* Passus XXI (C *text*), *mod. by* Nevill Coghill. BoPe
Harrowing of Hell, The ("Voice, A, loud in that light . . ."), *fr.* Passus XXI (C *text*), *mod. by* Nevill Coghill. BoC
Holy Church, *fr.* Passus I (B *text*). *mod.* MeEV
(Field Full of Folk, A, *mod. by* Grover Cronin, Jr.) CoBE
Holy Church Speaks.*fr.* Passus I (B *text*). *mod. by* Henry W. Wells. PoLi
Human Soul Speaks, The, *fr.* Passus XV (B *text*), *mod. by* Henry W. Wells. PoLi
"I fonde there freris alle the foure ordres," *fr.* Prologue (B *text*). YAT
(Friars, *fr.* Prologue (B *text*), *mod. vers.*) PPON
"'I have no penny,' quoth Piers, 'pullets to buy,'" *fr.* Passus IX (C *text*). MyFE
Incarnation, The, *fr.* Passus II (C *text*). PoEL-1
("For trewthe telleth that loue is triacle of hevene," *fr.* Passus II, B *text.*) OBEV (new ed.)
"King and his knights went to church, The," *fr.* Passus V (A *text*). BEL
(Confession of the Deadly Sins, The, *mod.*) MeEV
(Confessions of the Seven Deadly Sins, The, *mod. by* W. A. Neilson *and* K. G. T. Webster.) EnLi-1 (1949 ed.)
Langland's Life, *fr.* Passus VI (C *text*), *mod.* MeEV
Love We as Brothers, *fr.* Passus XI (B *text*), *mod. by* Henry W. Wells. PoLi
Maiden Meed, The, *fr.* Passus II (A *text*), *mod. by* Grover Cronin, Jr. CoBE
(Lady Meed, *fr.* Passus II, B *text, mod. by* Albert C. Baugh.) EnLit
Palace of Truth, The, *fr.* Passus V (B *text*). ACP
Palmer, The, *fr.* Passus VI (A *text*). ACP; CAW

Poverty Not All Loss, *fr.* Passus XI (B *text*), *mod. by* Henry W. Wells. PoLi
Prayer for the Poor, *fr.* Passus XIV (B *text*), *mod. by* Henry W. Wells. PoLi
("But beggars about midsummer go breadless to supper," *mod. by* Henry W. Wells.) PoFr
(Prayer for Rich and Poor, *mod. by* Nevill Coghill.) BoC
Preaching and Not Doing, *fr.* Passus X (B *text*), *mod. by* Henry W. Wells. PoLi
Prologue: "In a somer sesun [*or* summer season]," A *text.* BEL, B *text*; CoBE, *opening ll. original, mod. by* Grover Cronin, Jr.; EnLi-1, *mod. by* W. A. Neilson *and* K. G. T. Webster; EnLit, B *text, mod. by* Albert C. Baugh
(Field Full of Folk, The, *mod.*) MeEV
(Field of Folk, The, B *text.*) PoEL-1
(Induction, The: "In a summer season," *mod. by* Henry W. Wells.) PoLi
Providence, *fr.* Passus XIV (B *text*), *mod. by* Henry W. Wells. PoLi
Search for St. Truth, The, *fr.* Passus V-VII, *mod.* MeEV
Sufferings of the Poor, The, *fr.* Passus X (C *text*), *mod. by* Henry W. Wells. PoLi
("Needy are our neighbors, The," *mod. by* Henry W. Wells.) PoFr
(Poor, The.) PoEL-1
Theology, *fr.* Passus X (B *text*), *mod. by* Henry W. Wells. PoLi
(Grace for Theology.) GoBC
"This I trow be truth — who can teach thee better," *fr.* Passus I (A *text*). EG
Two Confessions, *fr.* Passus V (B *text*), *mod. by* Henry W. Wells. WoL
Vision of Jesus, The, *fr.* Passus XIX (B *text*). ACP; CAW
Vision of Nature, A, *fr.* Passus XIV (C *text*). PoEL-1
Vision of the Holy Church, The, *fr.* Passus I, *mod. by* Nevill Coghill. BoPe
(Love.) BoC
Vision of St. Bernard, The. M. Whitcomb Hess. ISi
Vision of Sin, The. Tennyson. PoVP; ViPo; ViPP
Song at the Ruin'd Inn, *sel.* PoEL-5
Vision of Sir Launfal, The. James Russell Lowell. AmePo; AnNE; MCCG; OnMSP
Sels.
Brook in Winter, The, Prelude to Pt. II. GN; OTPC
(December.) GoTP
("Down swept the chill wind.") TreF
"'For Christ's sweet sake, I beg an alms,'" *fr.* Pt. II. WGRP
He Gives Nothing ("He gives nothing but worthless gold"), *fr.* Pt. I. MaRV
"Holy Supper is kept, indeed, The," *fr.* Pt. II. TRV
Joys, *br. sel. fr.* Prelude to Pt. I. BoTP
June ("And what is so rare"), Prelude to Pt. I. BBV; DD; FaBV; GoTP; HBVY; OHFP; PoRL; PTK; StaSt
("And what is so rare as a day in June.") AmLP; FaPL
(Day in June, A.) FaPON; StVeCh
("Earth gets its price for what Earth gives us.") TreF
("For a cap and bells our lives we pay.") AA
(June Weather.) GN
(Now Is the High-Tide of the Year.) TreFS
(What Is So Rare as a Day in June.) FaBoBe; FaFP; NePA; TIHL
"Lo, it is I, be not afraid!" *fr.* Pt. II. OQP; TreF
("And the voice that was softer [*or* calmer] than silence said," *longer sel.*) ChIP; MaRV
"Not only around our infancy," *fr.* Prelude" to Pt. I. FaFP; GTBS-W; NePA
Not What We Give, 4 *ll., fr.* Pt. II.
Over His Keys, *fr.* Prelude to Pt. I. PoRL
(June.) HBV; PoLF
(Prelude to Part First.) LiTA
(Prelude from "The Vision of Sir Launfal.") LiTG
Sir Launfal and the Leper, *fr.* Pt. I. GN; OTPC
Winter Morning, A, *fr.* Pt. II. GN
(January.) PoRL
Vision of Sorrow. Thomas Sackville. *Fr.* Induction to "The Mirror for Magistrates." LoBV
Vision of Spring in Winter, A. Swinburne. PoVP
Vision of the Day of Judgment. Isaiah, LXIII, Bible, *O.T.* (*Moulton, Modern Reader's Bible*). WGRP
Vision of the Divine Mystery. Dante. *See* St. Bernard's Prayer to Our Lady.
Vision of the Holy Church, The. William Langland, *mod. by* Nevill Coghill. *Fr.* The Vision of Piers Plowman. BoPe
(Love.) BoC
Vision of the Lamentation of Beulah, A. Blake. *See* Nightingale and Flowers.
Vision of the Mermaids, A, *sel.* Gerard Manley Hopkins.
"Rowing, I reach'd a rock — the sea was low." ChTr
Vision of the Snow, The. Margaret Junkin Preston. AA
Vision of the World's Instability, A. Richard Verstegan. ElL
Vision of Turtle (One). James Brodey. ANYP
Vision of War, A. Thomas Sackville. *Fr.* Induction to "The Mirror for Magistrates." FaBoEn
Vision of William Concerning Piers the Plowman, The. William Langland. *See* Vision of Piers Plowman, The.
Vision; Second Psalm. Clive Matson. ThO
Vision Splendid, The, *sel.* John Oxenham.
"'Mid all the traffic of the ways." MaRV
Vision That Appeared to Me, A. MacConglinne. *See* Vision of MacConglinne.
Vision to Electra, The. Robert Herrick. ALV; SCEP-2; SeCP
(Vision, The.) UnTE
Vision upon This Conceit of the Faerie [*or* Faery] Queene, A. Sir Walter Ralegh. BEL; CoBE; EnLi-1 (1949 ed.); EnLit; FCP; OBSC; PoFS; SiCE; Sonn; TuPP
(Faery Queen, The.) ViBoPo
(Methought I Saw the Grave Where Laura Lay.) ILP; ReEn
(Of Spenser's Faery Queen.) SiPS
(Vision upon the Faery Queen, A.) TOP
Visionary, The. Emily Brontë. BoC; EnLi-2; GTBS-D; LiTB; LO; LoBV; OAEP; OBNC
(Julian M. and A. G. Rochelle, *longer vers.*) PeER
(Silent Is the House.) CH; ELP
Visionary and not believed. The Frozen City. Howard Nemerov. FiMAP
Visions, *sels.* William Browne.
"Rose, as fair as ever saw the north, A," V. ViBoPo
(Rose, The.) CH; HBV; OBEV; OTPC (1923 ed.)
(Vision, A.) SeCL; SeEP
Visions, *sel.* Joachim du Bellay, *tr. fr. French by* Spenser.
"I saw the bird that can the sun endure." Sonn
"I saw the bird that dares behold the sun." Sonn
"It was the time, when rest, soft sliding downe." AWP; Sonn
(Sonnet.) OnPM
"It was the time when rest, the gift of the Gods." Sonn
Visions. Edmund Leamy. BBV; GBV (1922 ed.); JKCP
Visions. . .Leaders. Clarence Franklin. BF
Visions [of Petrarch, The]. Petrarch, *tr. fr. Italian by* Spenser. *Fr.* Sonnets to Laura: To Laura in Death, Canzone III. AWP; EnLi-1; JAWP, *abr.*; WBP, *abr.*
I Saw a Phoenix in the Wood Alone, *sel.* ChTr
Visions of the Daughters of Albion. Blake. ERoP-1
Sels.
"Father of Jealousy, he thou accursed from the earth!" ViBoPo
Marigold, The. AtBAP
Take Thy Bliss, O Man. EnRP
Visions of the World's Vanity, *sel.* Spenser.
Huge Leviathan, The. ChTr
Visit. A. R. Ammons. CoAP; TwCP
Visit, The. Robert Mezey. AmPC
Visit, The. Ogden Nash. FiBHP
Visit, The. William Carlos Williams. PoeP
Visit by Water. Floris Clark McLaren. OBCV
Visit from Abroad, A. James Stephens. LOW; PoMS
Visit from Mr. Fox, A. *Unknown.* *See* Fox, The.
Visit from St. Nicholas, A. Clement Clarke Moore. AA; AmePo; BeLS; BLPA; BoChLi; BOHV; ChBR; DD; FaBoBe; FaBV; FaFP; FaPON; GaP; GFA; GoTP; HBV; HBVY; HH; LHV; MPB; NeHB; OnMSP; OTPC; PaPo; PCH; PEDC; PoPl; PoRh; PRWS; PTK; RePo; RIS; SAS; SiSoSe; StVeCh; TreF; TiPo; TVC; YaD
(Night before Christmas, The.) OHFP; WBLP
Visit from the Sea, The. Robert Louis Stevenson. GN; YT
Visit of the Professor of Aesthetics, The. Margaret Danner. *Fr.* Far from Africa. AmNP; NNP
Visit of the Wise Men, The. St. Matthew, II: 1-12, Bible, *N.T.* ChrBoLe
Visit the Sick. James J. Metcalfe. PoToHe (new ed.)
Visit to a Hospital. Jean Valentine Chace. GoYe

Visit to a Museum. Arthur Davison Ficke. NYTB
Visit to Bethlehem in Spirit, A. James Montgomery. SoP
Visit to Bronteland, A. James Kirkup. POTi
Visit to the Lambs, A. *Unknown.* OTPC (1923 ed.) SAS
Visit to Van Gogh, A. Charles Causley. PoCh
Visitant, The. Theodore Roethke. NMP; PoIE; UnPo (3d ed.)
Visitation, The. Robert Graves. BoPe
Visitation, The. Elizabeth Jennings. MoBS
Visitation, The. Calvin Le Compte. ISi
Visitation, The. Robert Southwell. MeP
"Visitation, The." Sun-Ra. BF
Visitations. Lawrence Durrell. *Fr.* Eight Aspects of Melissa. MoBrPo (1962 ed.); NeBP
Visitations: VII, *sel.* Louis MacNeice.
And the Lord Was Not in the Whirlwind. EaLo
Visiting Poet. John Frederick Nims. PV
Visiting Sea, The. Alice Meynell. BoPe
Visiting the Ruins. Chang Ch'ien, *tr. fr. Chinese by* Arthur Christy. OnPM
Visitor, The. Patrick R. Chalmers. DD; HBV; HBVY
Visitor, The. Rachel Field. TiPo (1952 ed.)
Visitor, The. Michael Goldman. WIRo
Visitor, The. Katharine Pyle. BBGG
Visitor, The. Mary Ellen Solt. QAH
Visitor Abhorred, The. Sir William Watson. PoVP
Visitors. Harry Behn. SoPo
Visitors, The. Elizabeth Jennings. BoPe
Visits to St. Elizabeths. Elizabeth Bishop. CoAP
Vista. Alfred Kreymborg. BoLP; MAPA
Vistas. Odell Shepard. HBMV
Visual Memory. Harry Martinson, *tr. fr. Swedish by* Erik Wahlgren *and* Martin S. Allwood. LiTW
Vita Benefica. Alice Wellington Rollins. AA
Vita Brevis. *Unknown, tr. fr. German by* Louis Untermeyer. UnTE
Vita Nuova, La, *sels.* Dante, *tr. fr. Italian by* Dante Gabriel Rossetti.
"All my thoughts always speak to me of Love," VI. AWP
(Divided Thoughts.) OnPM
"All ye that pass along Love's trodden way," II. AWP; JAWP; LiTW; WBP
"At whiles (yea oftentimes) I muse over," IX. AWP; JAWP; WBP
"Beyond the sphere which spreads to widest space," XXIX. AWP; CTC; JAWP; OnPM; OuHeWo; WBP
"Canst thou indeed be he that still would sing," *fr.* XIII. AWP
"Day agone, as I rode sullenly, A," IV. AWP
"Death, always cruel, Pity's foe in chief," *fr.* III. AWP; JAWP; LiTW; WBP
"Even as the others mock, thou mockest me," VII. AWP; LiTW
"Eyes that weep for pity of the heart, The," XIX. AWP; OuHeWo; WGRP
"For certain he hath seen all perfectness," XVII. AWP
"Gentle thought there is will often start, A," XXVI. AWP; JAWP; OuHeWo; WBP
"I felt a spirit of love begin to stir," XV. AWP; JAWP; WBP
"Ladies that have intelligence in love," X. AWP; LiTW; OuHeWo; WoL
"Love and the gentle heart are one same thing," XI. AWP; OuHeWo
"Love hath so long possessed me for his own," XVIII. AWP; OuHeWo
"Love's pallor and the semblance of deep ruth," XXIV. AWP; JAWP; WBP
"Mine eyes beheld the blessed pity spring," XXIII. AWP; LiTW
(Sonnet.) PoPl
"My lady carries love within her eyes," XII. AWP; JAWP; OnPM; WBP
(Within Her Eyes.) LiTW
"My lady looks so gentle and so pure," XVI. AWP; JAWP; WBP
"Song, 'tis my will that thou do seek out love," V. AwP
Sonnet: "Beatrice is gone up into high Heaven," *fr.* XIX. GoBC
Sonnet: "With sighs my bosom always laboureth," *fr.* XIX, *sl. abr.* GoBC
Sonnet: "Wonderfully out of the beautiful form," *fr.* XIX. GoBC
"Stay now with me, and list to my sighs," XX. AWP
"That lady of all gentle memories," XXII. AWP
"That she hath gone to Heaven suddenly," III. CTC
"Thoughts are broken in my memory, The," VIII. AWP; JAWP; WBP
"To every heart which the sweet pain doth move," I. AWP; OnPM
"Very bitter weeping that ye made, The," XXV. AWP
"Very pitiful lady, very young, A," XIV. AWP; CTC; JAWP; WBP
"Weep, Lovers, sith Love's very self doth weep," *fr.* III. AWP
"Whatever while the thought comes over me," XXI. AWP; JAWP; WBP
"Woe's me! by dint of all these sighs that come," XXVII. AWP
"Ye pilgrim-folk, advancing pensively," XXVIII. AWP; CTC; JAWP; WBP
("Ye pilgrims, who with pensive aspect go," *tr. by* Louise I. Guiney.) CAW
"You that thus wear a modest countenance," *fr.* XIII. AWP
Vita Nuova. Sir William Watson. OBVV
Vitae Summa Brevis Spem Nos Vetat Incohare Longam. Ernest Dowson. AWP; BrPo; CBV; ChTr; HBV; InPo; JAWP; LoBV; NoP; OBEV (new ed.); OQP; PoVP; StP; TOP; TrGrPo; ViBoPo; ViPP; WBP; WGRP; WHA
(Envoy: "They are not long, the weeping and the laughter.") MoBrPo; NeMA
(They Are Not Long.) EnLit; PeVV; PoRA; PoSa; TreFT
Vitaï Lampada. Sir Henry Newbolt. BLPA; MaRV; NeHB; OQP; PaPo; PoMa; PTK; TreF; YT
(Play the Game.) BBV
Vital Spark of Heavenly Flame! Pope. *See* Dying Christian to His Soul, The.
Vital Statistics. Ettore Bella. WOW
Vitelli rides west toward Fano, the morning sun. The Death of Vitellozzo Vitelli. Irving Feldman. TwCP
Vivaldi. Delmore Schwartz. NYBP
Vivamus, Mea Lesbia. Catullus, *tr. fr. Latin by* Frank O. Copley. StP
Vivamus Mea Lesbia atque Amemus. Thomas Campion. *See* My Sweetest Lesbia.
Vivamus Mea Lesbia atque Amemus. Ben Jonson. *See* Come, My Celia, Let Us Prove.
Vive Noir! Mari Evans. BOLo; WSL
(Stretchin' Out.) WOW
Vivérols. David Starr Jordan. AA
Vivian Beaumont, The/ Theatre. John Giorno. *Fr.* The American Book of the Dead. ANYP
Vivid, alone, against the wide expanse. Pedro. Phoebe W. Hoffman. GoYe
Vivien's Song. Tennyson. *See* In Love, If Love Be Love.
Vixen Woman, The. Harold Monro. *Fr.* Natural History. OBMV
Vixi. *At. to* Charles Mackay. HBV
Vixi Puellis Nuper Idoneus. Sir Thomas Wyatt. *See* Lover Showeth How He Is Forsaken of Such as He Sometime Enjoyed, The.
Vobiscum Est Iope. Thomas Campion. *See* When Thou Must Home.
Vlamertinghe: Passing the Chateau. Edmund Blunden. MMA; Sonn
Vocal Miner, The, *with music.* John A. Stone. SGR
Vocation. W. H. Auden. CMoP
Vocation. Rabindranath Tagore. FaPON; GaP; OTD
Vocation of St. Francis, The. Sister Mary Eleanore. WHL
Vodka. John Ciardi. ToPo
Vogelweid the Minnesinger. Walther von der Vogelweide. Longfellow. MWA-1
Voice, The. Matthew Arnold. ViPP
Voice, A. Samuel Valentine Cole. OQP
Voice, The. Norman Gale. HBV; OHIP
Voice. Zona Gale. OQP
Voice, The. Thomas Hardy. CMoP; EnLoPo; FaBoEn; GTBS-P; MaPo (1969 ed.); MoVE; NP; OAEP (2d ed.); OBNC; PoEL-5; ViPP
Voice, The. Richard Mansfield. POTE
Voice, The. Sister Maris Stella. GoBC
Voice, The. Theodore Roethke. AmLP
Voice. Harriet Prescott Spofford. AA
Voice, The. Edmund Wilson. NYBP
Voice and the Peak, The. Tennyson. EPN; PoVP
Voice by the Cedar Tree, A. Tennyson. Maud, Pt. I, v. AtBAP; HBV

Voice from Galilee, The. Horatius Bonar. *See* I Heard the Voice of Jesus Say.
Voice from heaven was heard on earth, A. St. Andrew's Voyage to Mermedonia. *Unknown. Fr.* Andreas. AnOE
Voice from the dark is calling me, A. Divorce. Anna Wickham. MoBrPo
Voice from the Invisible World, A. Goethe, *tr. fr. German by* James Clarence Mangan. AWP; JAWP; WBP
Voice from the sea to the mountains, A. The Great Voices. Charles Timothy Brooks. HBV
Voice from the Waters, A. Thomas Lovell Beddoes. *See* Dirge: "Swallow leaves her nest, The."
Voice from the Well of Life Speaks to the Maiden, The. George Peele. *See* Song at the Well, The.
Voice from the Whirlwind, The; God's Majesty. Job, Bible, *O.T.* *See* Voice Out of the Whirlind, The.
Voice from under the Table, A. Richard Wilbur. AmPP (5th ed.); NePoEA; SeCeV (1967 ed.); ToPo
Voice from the heroic dead, A. What Is That Music High in the Air? A. J. M. Smith. NMP
Voice in a Cathedral. Thomas Curtis Clark. ChIP
Voice in Darkness. Richard Dehmel, *tr. fr. German by* Margarete Münsterberg. AWP; JAWP; WBP
Voice in the Crowd. Ted Joans. *See* Truth, The.
Voice in the Wild Oak, The. Henry Clarence Kendall. VA
Voice, loud in that light, to Lucifer crying, A. The Harrowing of Hell. William Langland. *Fr.* The Vision of Piers Plowman. BoC
Voice, Marvellous voice. Circe. Alfred Kreymborg. MAPA
Voice of Christmas, The. Harry Kemp. HBV; MaRV; OQP
Voice of D. G. R., The. Sir Edmund Gosse. VA
Voice of England is a trumpet tone, The. England. George Edgar Montgomery. AA
Voice of Experience, The. Goethe, *tr. fr. German by* Walter Kaufmann. ErPo; PV
Voice of God, The. Katherine R. Barnard. BLRP; WBLP
Voice of God, The. Louis I. Newman. OQP; PoToHe; SoP; TreF
Voice of God, The. James Stephens. WGRP
Voice of God Is Calling, The. John Haynes Holmes. MaRV
Voice of magic melody, The. My Singing Aunt. James Reeves. ShM
Voice of my beloved, The. Song of Solomon, Bible, *O.T.* EnLi-1; LiTW; OuHeWo; PoPl
Voice of Nature, The. Robert Bridges. PoVP
Voice of Spring, The. Felicia Dorothea Hemans. OTPC (1946 ed.)
Voice of Spring, The. Mary Howitt. *See* Spring Is Coming.
Voice of summer, keen and shrill. To a Cricket. William Cox Bennett. BoTP; GN; HBV; OTPC
Voice of the Announcer. Archibald MacLeish. *Fr.* The Fall of the City. HoPM
Voice of the Dove, The. Joaquin Miller. AA
Voice of the Grass, The. Sarah Roberts Boyle. AA; DD, *abr.*; HBV; HBVY, *abr.*; PCH, *abr.*; PRWS, *abr.*
(Song of the Grass, The, *abr., wr. at. to* Leigh Hunt.) BoTP
Voice of the last cricket, The. Splinter. Carl Sandburg. FaPON; RePo; SUS; TiPo; UTS
Voice of the Last Trumpet Blown by the Seventh Angel, The, *sel.* Robert Crowley.
"Ye robbed, ye spoiled, ye bought, ye sold." PoFr
Voice of the Lobster, The. "Lewis Carroll." *Fr.* Alice's Adventures in Wonderland, *ch.* 10. EvOK; SAS; SiTL
("'Tis the voice of the Lobster; I heard him declare.") Par
Voice of the Poor, The. Lady Wilde. VA
Voice of the river running through Chamonix. Chamonix. George Hookham. OBVV
Voice of the Studio Announcer. Archibald MacLeish. *Fr.* The Fall of the City. HoPM
Voice of the Void, The. George Parsons Lathrop. AA
Voice of the Western Wind. Edmund Clarence Stedman. HBV
Voice of Thought, The. Thomas Holley Chivers. AnAmPo
Voice of Toil, The. William Morris. AnFE; CoBE; EPN; HBV; PoVP
Voice of Webster, The, *sel.* Robert Underwood Johnson.
"Silence was envious of the only voice." AA
Voice of Wisdom, The. Proberbs, VIII: 22-31, Bible, *O.T.* TreFT
Voice on the winds, A. To Morfydd. Lionel Johnson. AnIV; MoBrPo; OBMV; PIA; PoVP; ThWaDe; ViPP
Voice Out of the Whirlwind, The. Job, XXXVIII-XLII, Bible, *O.T.* MaRV (*Moulton, Modern Reader's Bible*); OuHeWo
(God Replies, XXXVIII: 2-41.) TrGrPo
(Job, XXXIX: 19-XL: 2.) InP
(Out of the Whirlwind, XL: 7-24, XLI.) AWP; JAWP; WBP
(Then the Lord Answered, XXXVIII: 2-24, XXXIX.) AWP; JAWP; WBP
(Then the Lord Answered Job Out of the Whirlwind, XXXVIII: 1-16.) ShBV-4
(Voice from the Whirlwind, The; God's Majesty, XXXVIII; 1-41.) PG (1955 ed.)
("Where wast thou when I laid the foundations of the earth?" XXXVIII. ImOP, 4-38, *abr.*; PoG, 4-41, *abr.*
Voice peals in this end of night, A. A Thrush before Dawn. Alice Meynell. HBMV; MoBrPo
Voice resounds like thunder-peal, A. The Watch on the Rhine. Max Schneckenburger. HBV
Voice, A, said, "Follow, follow"; and I rose. Two Pursuits. Christina Rossetti. EPN
Voice, The, said, "Hurl her down!" The Lovely Shall Be Choosers. Robert Frost. AmP; CoBMV; MAP; MoAB; MoAmPo; OxBA
Voice Sings, A. Samuel Taylor Coleridge. *See* Invocation, An: "Hear, sweet spirit."
Voice Speaks from the Well, A. George Peele. *See* Song at the Well, The.
Voice That Beautifies the Land, The. *Tr. fr. Navajo Indian by* Washington Matthews. AWP; JAWP; WBP
Voice that breathed o'er Eden, The. Holy Matrimony. John Keble. HBV; MaRV; VA
Voice was speaking, known to many ears, A. "The Spoken Word." Christopher Morley. PoFr
Voice went over the waters, A. Cuba to Columbia. Will Carleton. MC; PAH
Voiceless, The. Oliver Wendell Holmes. *Fr.* The Autocrat of the Breakfast Table, *ch.* 12. AA; CoBA; ViBoPo
Voiceless my robe when I dwell on the earth. A Swan. *Unknown.* BEL
Voices. Witter Bynner. MAP; MoAmPo (1942 ed.); PCH; TSW
Voices. Walter de la Mare. UnPo (3d ed.)
Voices. James S. Hearst. MoSiPe
Voices, The. *Unknown.* MCCG; PoMa
Voices are crying from the dust of Tyre. No Nation Liveth unto Itself. *Unknown.* MaRV
Voices at the Window. Sir Philip Sidney. *See* Astrophel and Stella: Eleventh Song.
Voices from the Other World. James Merrill. TwCP
Voices moving about in the quiet house. Falling Asleep. Siegfried Sassoon. ILP; MCCG; MoBrPo; MoVE
Voices of Heroes. Horace Gregory. PoFr; TrGrPo (1942 ed.)
Voices of Nature, The. Thomas Edward Brown. PoVP
Voices of Pine Trees, The. Rengetsu, *tr. fr. Japanese by* Asataro Miyamori. OnPM
Voices of the Air. Katherine Mansfield. HBMV
Voices of the vengeful dead curse. Celebration. John L'Heureux. YAP
Voices ring out. Branches whip the air. The Bear. John Randell Carpenter. NYTB
Void Between, The. John Lancaster Spalding. *Fr.* God and the Soul. AA
Void, damned weed! that hell's dry sweetmeats art. On Tobacco. Thomas Pestel. EIL
Void that's highly embraceable, The. Chorus. Jack Kerouac. *Fr.* Mexico City Blues. NeAP
Vois loude in that light to Lucifer seide, A. The Descent into Hell. William Langland. *Fr.* The Vision of Piers Plowman. PoEL-1
Vo'k a-Comen into Church. William Barnes. OxBoCh
(In Church.) WePo
Volant tribe of bards on earth are found, A. Wordsworth. Sonn
Vole, The. Marvin Solomon. NePoAm-2
Volpone, *sels.* Ben Jonson.
"Come, my Celia, let us prove," *fr.* III, vii. AtBAP; EIL; EnLi-1 (1949 ed.); EnRePo; FosPo; MaPo; SiCE; WHA
(After Catullus: Song, to Celia.) CLwM
(Come, My Celia.) CABA; FaBV; MeWo; NoP; PAn; TrGrPo

Volpone (continued)
(Song to Celia.) EnL; ErPo; OBS; SCEP-2; SeCeV; SeCP; SeCV-1; SiTL; TuPP
(To Celia.) AnAnS-2; FaBoEn; LoBV; ReEn; ReIE; UnTE
(Vivamus Mea Lesbia atque Amemus.) EG
"Good morning to the day; and, next, my gold," *fr.* I, i. AtBAP
"If thou hast wisdom, hear me, Celia," *fr.* III, vii. ViBoPo
Nano's Song, *fr.* I, ii. BoLiVe; LoBV; TrGrPo
(Fools.) EIL; TuPP
(Song: "Fools, they are the only nation.") AnAnS-2; InvP
Voltaire and Gibbon. Byron. *Fr.* Childe Harold's Pilgrimage, III. OBRV
Voltaire at Ferney. W. H. Auden. GTBS-W; LiTA; LiTM; NePA; PoE
Volto Sciolto e Pensieri Stretti. James Clarence Mangan. IrPN
Volubilis, North Africa. R. N. Currey. PeSA
Volucre Ferrum. John Heath. SiCE
Volume of Chopin, A. James Picot. PoAu-2
Volume II (Kinsey). David Daiches. SiTL
Voluntaries (I-V). Emerson. AmePo
Sels.
Duty ("In an age of fops and toys"), III. AnNE
(In an Age of Fops and Toys.) CBV; LiTA; MaRV; MWA-1; PoLF; PoPo
(So Nigh Is Grandeur.) HBVY; TreFS; YT
Duty ("So nigh is grandeur"), *last* 4 *ll. of* III. FaFP; GN; HBV; TreF; YaD
(Heroism.) OQP
("So nigh is grandeur to our dust.") TRV
"Freedom all winged expands," II. PoFr
"Stainless soldier on the walls," *fr.* IV *and* V. WGRP
Voluntarily every evening of/ Ephemeral death. The Man Closes the Shutters. Lionello Fiumi. LiTW
Voluntarily walled themselves up inside the stone. The Old Age Home. Theodore Holmes. CoPo
Volunteer, The. Herbert Asquith. MMA; OtMeF
Volunteer, The. Eldridge Jefferson Cutler. AA
Volunteers, The. William Haines Lytle. MC; PAH
Volunteer's Grave, A. William Alexander Percy. HBMV
Volunteer's Reply to the Poet, The. Roy Campbell. *Fr.* Talking Bronco. ViBoPo (1958 ed.)
Volunteers, The! the Volunteers! The Volunteers. William Haines Lytle. MC; PAH
Voluptuaries and Others. Margaret Avison. MoCV
Voluspo. *Unknown. See* Beginning and the End, The.
Volvox the sea roller slithers in the spent spume. Beach Encounter. Charles A. Wagner. NYTB
Voortrekker, The. Kipling. HBV
Vor a Gauguin Picture zu Singen. Kirt M. Stein. FiBHP
Vorobyev Hills. Boris Pasternak, *tr. fr. Russian by* J. M. Cohen. OnHM
Votary to publick zeal. To the Right Honourable Robert Walpole, Esq. Ambrose Philips. CEP
Vote, A, *sel.* Abraham Cowley.
Of Myself. OAEP; OBS; SeCL
("This only grant me, that my means may lie.") SeEP; TreFT
Votive Ode. Erasmus, *tr. fr. Greek by* J. T. Walford. ISi
Votive Song. Edward Coote Pinkney. AA; AnFE; APA; CoAnAm
Vouchsafe, O Lord, to be our guide. A Prayer for Gentlewomen and Others to Use. Nicholas Breton. SiCE
Vouchsafe to grace these rude, unpolish'd rimes. To the Dear Child of the Muses and His Ever Kind Maecenas, Master Anthony Cooke, Esquire. Michael Drayton. *Fr.* Idea's Mirrour. ReIE; SiCE; TuPP
Vow, The. Anthony Hecht. NePoEA; PoCh
Vow, The. Sir Edward Sherburne. SeCL
Vow. John Updike. NYBP
Vow-Breaker, The. Henry King. OBS; SeEP
Vow Breaker, The, sel. William Sampson.
"When from the wars I do return." TuPP
Vow for New Year's, A. Mary Carolyn Davies. OTD; PoToHe
Vow of Washington, The. Whittier. DD, *abr.*; MC; PAH
Washington's Vow, *sel.* OHIP
Vow to Heavenly Venus, A. Joachim du Bellay, *tr. fr. French by* Andrew Lang. AWP
Vow to Love Faithfully [Howsoever He Be Rewarded], A. Petrarch, *tr. fr. Italian by* Earl of Surrey. Sonnets to Laura: To Laura in Life, CXIII. EIL; EnLi-1 (1949 ed.); EnLit; LiTL; PoFS; SiCE; Sonn; TrGrPo; TuPP; ViBoPo
(Love's Fidelity.) AWP; JAWP; WBP
(Set Me Whereas the Sun.) CBEP; EnPo; FCP; ForPo; ILP; OnPM; ReEn; SiPS
(To His Lady.) OBSC
Vowel Englyn to the Spider. *Unknown, tr. fr. Welsh by* George Borrow. LiTW
Vows are vain. No suppliant breath. Upon Castara's Departure. William Habington. *Fr.* Castara. SeCL
Vox Humana. Thom Gunn. NePoEA-2
Vox Oppressi, To the Lady Phipps. Richard Henchman. SCAP
Vox Populi. Dryden. *Fr.* The Medal. OBS
("Almighy crowd, thou shorten'st all dispute.") PeRV
Vox Ultima Crucis. John Lydgate. OBEV; OxBoCh; StJW
"Voy wawm" said the dustman. Hymn to the Sun. Michael Roberts. FaBoCh; LoGBV
Voyage, The. Baudelaire, *tr. fr. French by* C. F. MacIntyre. LiTW
Voyage. Hart Crane. *See* Voyages.
Voyage. John Lyle Donaghy. OxBI
Voyage, The. Henry W. Frost. SoP
Voyage, The. Heine, *tr. fr. German by* John Todhunter. AWP
Voyage, The. Vachel Lindsay. MAP; MoAmPo
Voyage. Josephine Miles. LiTM (1970 ed.)
Voyage, The. Edwin Muir. GTBS-W; LiTM (rev. ed.)
Voyage, The. Karl Shapiro. MoLP
Voyage, The. Tennyson. PoVP; ViPP
Voyage à l'Infini. Walter Conrad Arensberg. AnAmPo
Voyage of Bran, The, *sel. Unknown, tr. fr. Old Irish by* Kuno Meyer.
"Branch of the apple-tree from Emain, A." AnIL
Voyage of Discovery: 1935. Richmond Lattimore. TwAmPo
Voyage of Jimmy Poo, The. James A. Emanuel. AmNP; NNP; NYTB
Voyage of Life, The. Cynewulf, *tr. fr. Anglo-Saxon by* Charles W. Kennedy. *Fr.* Christ 2. AnOE
Voyage of Maeldune, The. Tennyson. PoEL-5
Voyage of the soul is simply, The. The Helmsman; an Ode. J. V. Cunningham. MoVE
Voyage to Africa, A, *sel.* David Wright.
"Adamastor, whom Camoens and the sea." BoSA
Voyage to Cythera, A. Baudelaire, *tr. fr. French.* LiTW, *tr. by* Hubert Creekmore; SyP, *tr. by* John Gray
Voyager upon life's sea. Paddle Your Own Canoe. Sarah K. Bolton. FaFP
Voyagers. Henry van Dyke. MaRV; TRV
(Thy Sea Is Great, Our Boats Are Small.) OQP
Voyagers' Prayer. *Unknown, tr. fr. Chippewa Indian by* Tanner. TRV; WGRP
Voyager's Song. Clement Wood. HBMV
Voyages (I-VI). Hart Crane. AP; CABL; CMoP; NoP
Sels.
"Above the fresh ruffles of the surf," I. AmPP (5th ed.); CABA; ForPo; OxBA; Po; PoIE; TDP
(Sea, The.) CrMA
"And yet this great wink of eternity," II. AmLP; AmPP (5th ed.); AnFE; BoLiVe (1939 ed.); CoAnAm; CoBMV; DTC; ExPo; FaBoEn; ForPo; GTBS-W; LiTM; MAP; MoAB; MoAmPo; MoPo; MoVE; NAMP; NePA; OxBA; Po; PoDB; PoFS; PoIE; TwAmPo; UnPo (3d ed.); VaPo; ViBoPo (1958 ed.)
(Voyage.) NP
"Infinite consanguinity it bears," III. ForPo; MoPo; MoVE; OxBA; Po; PoIE
"Meticulous, past midnight in clear rime," V. MoPo; MoVE
"Where icy and bright dungeons lift," VI. AnFE; CABA; CoAnAm; MAP; MoAB; MoAmPo; MoVE; SeCeV; TwAmPo; UnPo (3d ed.)
Voyages of Captain Cock, The. William Jay Smith. ErPo; UnTE
Voyageur. R. E. Rashley. CaP
Voyeur. John Edward Hardy. ErPo
Vuillard: "The Mother and Sister of the Artist." W. D. Snodgrass. CoAP
Vulcan begat me; Minerva me taught. Description of a Gun. Pandolphus, *tr. by* Sir Thomas Wyatt. FCP; ReIE; TuPP
Vulcan contrive me such a cup. Upon His Drinking Bowl. Earl of Rochester. CavP; CEP; EiCL; OBS; OxBoLi; PeRV; SeCV-2

Vulcan! hear your glorious task. Odes of Anacreon. *Tr. by* Thomas Moore. OuHeWo

Vulcan Oh Vulcan my deare. *Unknown.* SeCSL

Vulcan's Song. John Lyly. *See* Song in Making of the Arrows, The.

Vulgar of manner, overfed. Owed to New York. Byron Rufus Newton. BLPA; NeHB; TreFS

Vulture, The. Hilaire Belloc. HBVY; OTPC (1946 ed.); RIS; StaSt

Vulture, The. Israel Kafu Hoh. ACV

Vulture and the Husbandman, The. Arthur Clement Hilton. CenHV

Vulture eats between his meals, The. The Vulture. Hilaire Belloc. HBVY; OTPC (1946 ed.); RIS; StaSt

Vulture, The Sparrow, and Other Birds, The. John Gay. *Fr.* Fables. EiCP

Vultures, The. David Diop, *tr. fr. French by* Ulli Beier. PBA; TTY

Vusumzi's Song. L. T. Manyase, *tr. fr. Xhosa by* C. M. Mcanyangwa *and* Jack Cope. PeSA

W

W. James Reeves. ChTr

W. H. Davies Simplifies the Simplicities He Loves. Louis Untermeyer. WhC

W. resteth here, that quick could never rest. *See* Wyatt resteth here . . .

W. W. LeRoi Jones. NBP

Waal, yass, stranger, them's fine cows. The Branding Iron Herd. Ralph Rigby. PoOW

Wabanaki Song. *Unknown, tr. by* Mrs. Wallace Brown. PeCV

Wabash Cannonball, The. *Unknown.* TreFT

Wacs and Waves will win the war, The. World War II. *Unknown.* SiTL

Wade/ Through black jade. The Fish. Marianne Moore. AmPP (5th ed.); AnFE; APA; CoAnAm; MAP; MoAB; MoAmPo; MoVE; OxBA; TwAmPo

Wading at Wellfleet. Elizabeth Bishop. AmP

Waement the deid. Coronach. Alexander Scott. OxBS

Wae's me! wae's me! The Cauld Lad of Hilton [*or* The Ghost's Song *or* The Wandering Spectre]. *Unknown.* AtBAP; CBEP; CH; ChTr; FaBoCh; LoGBV; OxBoLi

Waes-hael for knight and dame. King Arthur's Waes-Hael. Robert Stephen Hawker. ISi; JKCP; OBEV; OBVV; OxBoCh

Wag a leg, wag a leg. *Unknown.* OxNR

Wager, The. Pierre de Ronsard, *tr. fr. French by* Cécile Schreiber *and* Virginia Tufte. *Fr.* Pastoral Song for the Nuptials of Charles, Duke of Lorraine, and Claude, Daughter of the King. HW

Wages, The. Don Marquis. MaRV

Wages. Tennyson. EPN; OAEP; OQP; PoVP

Waggoner, The. Edmund Blunden. AnFE

Wagner. Maurice Baring. MuSP

Wagner. Rupert Brooke. MuSP; NAMP

Wagon in the Barn, The. John Drinkwater. MoSiPe

Wagon Train. E. L. Mayo. MiAP

Wagon Wheel Gap is a place I never saw. Localities. Carl Sandburg. AmFN; Po

Wagoner of the Alleghanies, The, *sels.* Thomas Buchanan Read.
 Brave at Home, The. HBV; PAP
 Rising. PAH; TreFS
 Valley Forge. MC; PAH

Wagoner's Lad, The (A *vers.*). *Unknown.* BaBo
 (Old Smoky, B *vers.*) BaBo

Wagtail and Baby. Thomas Hardy. HBMV

Waies, through which my weary steps I guyde, The. Spenser. *Fr.* The Faerie Queene, VI, Proem. MBW-1

Waif, The. A. C. Smith. VA

Waifs and Strays. Arthur Rimbaud, *tr. fr. French by* Jethro Bithell. WoL

Wail me a sad lament, ye dells and Dorian water. A Lament for Bion. Moschus, *tr. by* J. H. Hallard. EnLi-2

Wail of a waking wind in a wide-flung wheat field, The. Sea Hunger. John Hanlon Mitchell. EtS

Wail of Archy, The, *sel.* Don Marquis. *Fr.* Archy and Mehitabel.

"Gods I am pent in a cockroach." FiBHP

Wail of Prometheus Bound, The. Aeschylus, *tr. fr. Greek by* Elizabeth Barrett Browning. *Fr.* Prometheus Bound. WGRP

Wail, wail, Ah for Adonis! He is lost to us, lovely Adonis! Lament for Adonis. Bion. AWP; JAWP; WoL

Wail! wail ye o'er the dead! Dirge. George Darley. *Fr.* Sylvia; or, The May Queen. OBRV

Waile whit ase whalles bon, A. The White Beauty. *Unknown.* MeEL

Wailful sweetness of the violin, The. Ode to the Setting Sun. Francis Thompson. GoBC

Wailing diminutive of me, be still. Diminutivus Ululans. Francis MacNamara. OxBI

Wailing Lynx. Lew Sarett. NP

Wailing, wailing, wailing, the wind over land and sea. Rizpah. Tennyson. BEL; CABL; EnLi-2; EPN; PAn; PeVV; PoEL-5; PoVP; TOP; VA

Wailing wind doth not enough despair, The. Awake. Mary Elizabeth Coleridge. OBNC

Wailings of a maiden I recite. Wednesday; or, The Dumps. John Gay. *Fr.* The Shepherd's Week. EiCP; FosPo

Waillie, Waillie! *with music. Unknown, arr. by* Daniel Read *and* Isadora Bennett Read. AS

Waist Deep in the Big Muddy. Peter Seeger. WOW

Waist high sea was rolling, The. Tunnel Beach. James K. Baxter. AnNZ

Waistcoat, The. Padraic Fallon. OxBI

Wait. John Banister Tabb. FaChP

Wait, The. Quincy Troupe. WSL

Wait a minute. The Green Bus. James S. Tippett. GFA

Wait but a little while. Song. Norman Gale. HBV; VA

Wait! Church of God! in quiet contemplation. The Charter of Salvation. George Arthur Clarke. MaRV

Wait for the Hour. William Soutar. NeBP

Wait for the Wagon. *Unknown.* PAH

Wait here, and I'll be back, though the hours divide. Three Star Final. Conrad Aiken. OxBA

Wait! It would be insane to call. Do What You Will. Dorothy Hobson. GoBC

Wait, Kate! You skate at such a rate. To Kate, Skating Better than Her Date. David Daiches. FiBHP; NYBP; SD

"Wait. Let me think a minute," you said. The Wit. Elizabeth Bishop. NePoAm-2

Wait, My Soul. *Unknown.* SoP

Wait On. Dnyanodaya. MaRV; STF

Wait Patiently for Him. Frances Ridley Havergal. SoP

Wait till the Sun Shines, Nellie. Andrew B. Sterling. TreFS

Wait until the revelation. Cowboy Song. Tom Veitch. ANYP

Waitaki Dam. Denis Glover. AnNZ

Waiting. Harry Behn. SiSoSe; TiPo

Waiting. John Burroughs. AA; AmePo; AnAmPo; AnFE; APA; BLPA; CoAnAm; DD; FaBoBe; FaPL; HBV; MaRV; NeHB; OHFP; OQP; PTK; TreF; TRV; WGRP

Waiting. Hilary Corke. ErPo

Waiting. John Davidson. ViBoPo

Waiting. John Freeman. CH

Waiting. Henry W. Frost. SoP

Waiting. W. E. Henley. In Hospital, II. NBM; PoVP

Waiting. Alan Hodge. LO

Waiting. Ruth Apprich Jacob. BiCB

Waiting. James Kirkup. FIW

Waiting. Masaoka Shiki, *tr. fr. Japanese by* H. G. Henderson. OnPM

Waiting and Peeking. V. R. Lang. NePA

Waiting at night for her where she once came. The Muse. Anna Akhmatova. ML

Waiting Both. Thomas Hardy. MoAB; MoBrPo; NeMA; OxBoLi; PoeP; PoPo; WaKn; WHA

Waiting Chords, The. Stephen Henry Thayer. AA

Waiting for Death. Mordecai Gebirtig, *tr. fr. Yiddish by* Joseph Leftwich. TrJP

Waiting for Death. Michelangelo, *tr. fr. Italian by* John Addington Symonds. OnPM

Waiting for Lunch. Joseph Cardarelli. QAH

Waiting for News. Richard Church. ChMP

Waiting for Sunrise. Zygmunt Krasinski, *tr. fr. Polish by* Watson Kirkconnell. PoFr

Waiting for the Dawning. *Unknown.* BLRP

Waiting for the end, boys, waiting for the end. Just a Smack at Auden. William Empson. FaBoTw; LiTM (rev. ed.);

Waiting (continued)
MoBrPo (1962 ed.); SiTL; ToPo; UnPo (3d ed.)
Waiting for Morning. *Unknown.* STF
Waiting for the Wind. Alex Comfort. POTE
Waiting for these dry sticks in a vase. Aspects of Some Forsythia Branches. Ralph Gustafson. PeCV (1967 ed.)
Waiting for when the sun an hour or less. In Santa Maria del Popolo. Thom Gunn. GTBS-P; NePoEA-2; NMP; NoP; OPoP; PoIE; QFR
Waiting Harp, The. Gustavo Adolfo Bécquer, *tr. fr. Spanish by* Thomas Walsh. CAW
Waiting Mothers. Anne Zuker. PEDC
Waiting to Grow. *Unknown.* PEDC
Waiting today while planes roar over the seacoast. 1944—On the Invasion Coast. Jack Beeching. WaP
Waiting Watchers, The. Henry Treece. NeBP
Waiting Yonder. "H. A. C." SoP
Waitress. Michael Brownstein. ANYP
Waitress. Karl Shapiro. FiMAP; TwAmPo
Waitress/ You bring my food, I give you money. Waitress. Michael Brownstein. ANYP
Waitress, with eyes so marvellous black. Salad: After Browning. Mortimer Collins. Par
Waits, The. Margaret Deland. DD; HH
Waits, The. John Freeman. BoTP
Waits, The. Madeleine Nightingale. SUS
Waits are whining in the cold, The. From "A Vigo-Street Eclogue." Sir Owen Seaman. WhC
Wait's Carol: "Give ye good-den." Barbara Young. MoSiPe
Waiwera. Kendrick Smithyman. AnNZ
Wake. Langston Hughes. ShM
Wake, The. Tsurayuki, *tr. fr. Japanese by* Arthur Waley. WoL
Wake All the Dead. Sir William Davenant. *Fr.* The Law against Lovers. CBEP; ELP; FaBoCh; LoGBV; SeCePo; SeCL
(Song: "Wake all the dead! What hoa! What hoa!") LoBV
Wake, Awake, for Night Is Flying, *with music.* Philip Nicolai, *tr. fr. German by* Catherine Winkworth. YaCaBo
Wake Cry. Waring Cuney. BANP
Wake for Papa Montero. Nicolás Guillén, *tr. fr. Spanish by* Langston Hughes. PoNe
Wake! for the hack can scatter into flight. Extracts from the Rubaiyat of Omar Cayenne. Gelett Burgess. BOHV
Wake! For the Sun, who scatter'd into flight. Rubáiyát of Omar Khayyám. *Tr. by* Edward Fitzgerald. AtBAP; AWP; BEL; EnL; EnLi-2; EPN; FaBoBe; FaFP; FaPL; FaPON; GTBS; GTSL; HBV; JAWP; LiTB; LiTG; MasP; NeHB; NoP; OBNC; OtMeF; OuHeWo; PoEL-5; PoIE; PoVP; SeCeV; TOP; TrGrPo; UnPo (1st ed.); VA; ViBoPo; ViPo; ViPP; WBP; WHA; WoL. *See also* Awake! for Morning in the bowl of Night.
Wake from thy slumbering, Heart of the Lion! Allenby Enters Jerusalem! Stephen Chalmers. PoMa
Wake, Israel, wake! Recall today. The Banner of the Jew. Emma Lazarus. AA; TrJP
Wake, Lady! Joanna Baillie. *See* Good Morning.
Wake not, but hear me, love! Song. Lew Wallace. *Fr.* Ben-Hur. AA
Wake Not for the World-Heard Thunder. A. E. Housman. CMoP
Wake oh my Soule awake & raise. *Unknown.* SeCSL
Wake of Tim O'Hara, The. Robert Buchanan. VA
Wake of William Orr, The. William Drennan. OnYI; OxBI
Wake, Sleepy Thyrsis. *Unknown.* EnRePo
Wake: the silver dusk returning. Reveille. A. E. Housman. A Shropshire Lad, IV. BEL; CLwM; CMoP; CoBE; EnLi-2; EnLit; EPN; FaFP; GTBS-W; LiTB; LiTM (rev. ed.); MasP; MoAB; MoBrPo; NeMA; NoP; OAEP; OuHeWo; PG; PoLF; PoMA; PoPo; PoVP; TDP; TreF; ViPo
Wake thou much afflicted man. *Unknown.* SeCSL
Wake up, Jacob, day's a-breakin'. Cowboy's Gettin'-up Holler. *Unknown.* ABF; CoSo; TrAS
Wake Up! Wake Up! Basho, *tr. fr. Japanese by* Harold G. Henderson. SoPo
Wake up, wake up, darling Corey. Darling Corey. *Unknown.* OuSiCo
"Wake up! Wake up! you bloomin' lot." Song of the Leadville Mine Boss. Don Cameron. PoOW
"Wake up, wake up, you drowsy sleeper." The Drowsy Sleeper (A *vers.*). *Unknown.* BaBo
Wake Up, You Drowsy Sleepers. *Unknown.* *See* Who's That at My Bedroom Window?
Wakeful all night I lay [*or* I lay all night] and thought of God. Renunciation. Wathen Mark Wilks Call. OBVV; WGRP
Wakeful in the Township. Elizabeth Riddell. PoAu-2
Wakeful, vagrant, restless thing. The Power of Fancy. Philip Freneau. AmPP; AP; CoBA
"Waken from your sleep." The Summons. W. W. E. Ross. CaP
Waken, lords and ladies gay. Hunting Song. Sir Walter Scott. EnLi-2; EnLit; EnRP; EPN; EvOK; GN; GTBS; GTBS-D; GTBS-P; GTBS-W; GTSE; GTSL; InP; LiTG; OAEP; OTPC; RG; SD; TOP; TrGrPo; WiR
Waken, O world, if you would glimpse the wonder. Resurrection. Angela Morgan. OQP
Wakening, The. *Unknown.* *See* On a Time the Amorous Silvy.
Wakening bugles cut the night, The. A Good-by. Ednah Proctor Clarke. AA
Wakers, The. John Freeman. HBMV; TSW
Wakeupworld, The. Countee Cullen. GoSl
Waking. Jon Anderson. NYTB
Waking. John Le Gay Brereton. BoAu
Waking. Annie Higgins. ELU
Waking. Patrick MacDonogh. NeIP
Waking, The. Theodore Roethke. AmPP (5th ed.); AP; CoAP; CoBMV; CrMA; FiMAP; LiTM (1970 ed.); MoAmPo (1962 ed.); NoP; PIA; Po; PoeP; PoPl; SeCeV (1967 ed.); TDP; ToPo; TwCP
Waking,/ I remembered summer afternoons. A Passion. James McMichael. PIA
Waking Alone. *Unknown.* MeEL
Waking [*or* Walking] alone in a multitude of loves when morning's light. The Marriage [*or* On the Marriage] of a Virgin. Dylan Thomas. EnLoPo; ErPo; HW; LiTM; NoP; PoE
Waking an Angel. Philip Levine. NaP
Waking by Night. Charles Brasch. *Fr.* The Estate. AnNZ
Waking, Child, While You Slept. Ethel Anderson. *Fr.* Bucolic Eclogues. PoAu-2
Waking from Sleep. Robert Bly. FRC
Waking from sleep we heard the Great Lakes' tide. Horace Gregory. *Fr.* Chorus for Survival. AtBAP
Waking, he found himself in a train, andante. Slow Movement. Louis MacNeice. FaBoMo
Waking I look to Jesus on the Rood. Waking Thought. Marguerite Wilkinson. ChIP; OQP
Waking in the Blue. Robert Lowell. CoAP; MoAmPo (1962 ed.)
Waking of Spring, The. Olive Custance. VA
Waking of the Lark, The. Eric Mackay. VA
Waking outside his Babylonian binge. A Thousandth Poem for Dylan Thomas. John Ciardi. ToPo
Waking Song. Thomas Heywood. *See* Pack, Clouds, Away.
Waking Time. Ivy O. Eastwick. SiSoSe; TiPo (1959 ed.)
Waking Thought. Marguerite Wilkinson. ChIP; OQP
Waking Up ("Millions of cradles up in the trees"). *Unknown.* TVC
Waking Up ("Pretty little crocus, in your cosy bed"). *Unknown.* BoTP
Waking Up in the Woods. Gregory Orr. QAH
Waking with morning, I note the empty. The Landscape of Love. Thomas Cole. NePoAm
Waking World, The. Frank Mason North. MaRV
Waking Year, The. Emily Dickinson. *See* Lady red upon the hill, A.
Wal, no! I can't tell whar he lives. *See* Wall, no! I can't tell . . .
Wal, you see, it's a queer story, Missy. The Miner's Protégée. *Unknown.* IHA
Walam Olum. *Unknown.* *See* Walum-Olum.
Wald my gude lady luve me best. The Garmont of Gude Ladies. Robert Henryson. GoTS
Waldeinsamkeit. Emerson. AmPP (3d ed.); AP; HBV; MWA-1; WGRP
Walden, *sel.* Henry David Thoreau.
Smoke, *fr. ch.* 13. AA; AmePo; AmLP; AmPP; AnAmPo; AnFE; AnNE; APA; AWP; CBV; CoAnAm; CoBA; InPo; JAWP; MWA-1; NoP; OxBA; TOP; VaPo; WBP
(Light-winged Smoke.) ViBoPo
(Light-winged Smoke, Icarian Bird.) AP; OnPM

Walden (*poem*). Henry David Thoreau. MAmP
Walden in July. Donald Junkins. NYBP
Waldere I: ". . . heard him gladly." *Unknown, tr. fr. Anglo-Saxon by* Charles W. Kennedy. AnOE
Waldere II: "Waldere addressed him, the warrior brave." *Unknown, tr. fr. Anglo-Saxon by* Charles W. Kennedy. AnOE
Wales. Norman Nicholson. ChMP
Wales England wed; so I was bred. An Autobiography. Ernest Rhys. ACV; OBEV (new ed.); OBVV; POTE; PrWP; VA
Wales Visitation. Allen Ginsberg. FRC; NYBP
Wales, which I have never seen. For My Ancestors. Rolfe Humphries. PoRA (rev. ed.)
Walk, The. Leonard Clark. AtBAP
Walk, The. Thomas Hardy. CMoP; PoEL-5; PoeP
Walk, A. Hedwig Lachmann, *tr. fr. German by* Jethro Bithell. TrJP
Walk, The. W. W. E. Ross. PeCV; SD
Walk about the Subway Station. Charles Reznikoff. CAD
Walk after Dark, A. W. H. Auden. MaPo
Walk by the Charles, A. Adrienne Cecile Rich. NePoEA; NYBP
Walk Close beside Me. Roy J. Wilkins. SoP
Walk, Damn You, Walk! William de Vere. PoLF
Walk down the street. Full Swing Circus. Clive Matson. ThO
Walk fast in snow. A Devonshire Rhyme. *Unknown.* BrR; MPB; SiSoSe
Walk in Jerusalem Jus' like John, *with music. Unknown.* BoAN-2
Walk in Kyoto, A. Earle Birney. GoYe
Walk in Late Summer, A. Theodore Roethke. PoDB
"Gull rides on the ripple of a dream, A," *sel.* OA
Walk in Spring, A. K. C. Lart. BoTP
Walk in the Country, A. Galway Kinnell. NePoAm
Walk in the Garden, The. Conrad Aiken. PoCh
Walk in the half light of rain. Monsoon. Kenneth Slade Alling. NePoAm
Walk in the Precepts. Moses ibn Ezra, *tr. fr. Hebrew by* Solomon Solis-Cohen. TrJP
Walk in Würzburg, A. William Plomer. NYBP
Walk into the prison, that domed citadel. My Lessons in Jail. Miriam Waddington. MoCV
Walk, Jaw-Bone, *with music.* S. S. Steele. TrAS
Walk, Mary, down de Lane, *with music. Unknown.* BoAN-2
Walk, mounds, enclosing corrugations. The Castle. Robert Graves. NoP
Walk on a Winter Day. Sara Van Alstyne Allen. YeAr
Walk on Snow, A. Peter Viereck. MiAP; OnHM
Walk on the Beach, The. John Gould Fletcher. BoLP; MoLP
Walk Past Those Houses on a Sunday Morning. Kendrick Smithyman. AnNZ
Walk Quietly. *Unknown.* SoP
"Walk right in, Brother Wilson—how you feelin' today?" The Rain Song. Alex Rogers. BANP
Walk Slowly. Adelaide Love. BLPA
Walk this mile in silence. Pastourelle. Donald Jeffrey Hayes. AmNP
Walk to Emmaus, The. William Cowper. SoP; StJW
Walk Together Children, *with music. Unknown.* BoAN-2
Walk-up. W. S. Merwin. CoPo
Walk with the sun. Dream Song. Lewis Alexander. PoNe
Walk with thy fellow-creatures: note the hush. Fragment. Henry Vaughan. TRV; WGRP
Walked around in a daze all morning. At Ten o'Clock in the Morning. Joseph Cardarelli. QAH
Walker, The. Arturo Giovannitti. AnAmPo
"I hear footsteps over my head all night," *sel.* PoFr
Walker, The. Yvor Winters. NP
Walker of the Snow, The. Charles Dawson Shanly. OnYI; PTK; VA
Walking. Grace Ellen Glaubitz. GFA; SoPo; TiPo
Walking. Thomas Traherne. PeRV; SD; SeCL; TrGrPo, *abr.*
(To Walk Abroad.) ELP
(Understanding.) BoPe
Walking alone, all only full of grief. The Most Pithy and Pleasant History of Glaucus and Scylla. Thomas Lodge. *Fr.* Scylla's Metamorphosis. ReIE
Walking alone in a multitude of loves when morning's light. *See* Waking alone . . .
Walking along beside the beach. The Sea Bird. Keith Douglas. ChMP
Walking along the Hudson. Donald Petersen. CoAP
Walking along the streets the other day. John Taylor. SiCE
Walking Around. "Pablo Neruda," *tr. fr. Spanish by* H. R. Hays. LiTW
Walking around in the park. Toads Revisited. Philip Larkin. PoeP
Walking at Night. Amory Hare. PoLF
Walking at Night. Henry Treece. WaP
Walking at night alone. Mozart Perhaps. John Hall Wheelock. UnS
Walking between the ruined walls. Walking in London. Wrey Gardiner. NeBP
Walking by map, I chose unwonted ground. On the Hall at Stowey. Charles Tomlinson. CMoP
Walking docile as you do down the empty street. Abasis. Christopher Middleton. *Fr.* Herman Moon's Hourbook. NePoEA-2
Walking East on 125th Street (Spring 1959). Ray Johnson. BF
Walking Home at Night. Allen Ginsberg. CBV
Walking Home on St. Cecilia's Day. Peter Porter. MuSP
Walking in a Meadowe Greene. *Unknown.* ErPo
Walking in a valley greene. The Shepherd's Ode. Robert Greene. *Fr.* Tullie's Love. OBSC
Walking in Beech Leaves. Andrew Young. MoVE
Walking in bright Phoebus' blaze. Dispraise of a Courtly Life. Sir Philip Sidney. FCP; LoBV; OAEP; SiCE
Walking in Bush. Basil Dowling. AnNZ
Walking in London. Wrey Gardiner. NeBP
Walking in the scythed churchyard. Charles Causley. *Fr.* At the Grave of John Clare. FIW
Walking into the shadows, walking alone. Lee in the Mountains. Donald Davidson. MoVE; UnPo
Walking Next Day upon the Fatal Shore. Cyril Tourneur. *Fr.* The Atheist's Tragedy, II, i. ViBoPo; WaaP
Walking of the Moon-Woman, The. John Shaw Neilson. ACV
Walking on the step of the shingle, here. Wales. Norman Nicholson. ChMP
Walking on Water. James Dickey. NePoEA-2
Walking out in morning snow. The Game. Winfield Townley Scott. AnAmPo
Walking out in the late March midnight. Thorn Leaves in March. W. S. Merwin. TwCP
Walking Road, The. Richard Hughes. OBMV
Walking Sampford Way. Paul L. Grano. BoAu
Walking Song. Charles Williams. BoTP, *abr.*
Walking, striving. Melancholy. August Straum. OnPM
Walking the town as if I owned it all. In and Out: Severance of Connections, 1946. L. E. Sissman. NYBP; TwCP
Walking the Wilderness. William Stafford. NaP
Walking through trees to cool my heat and pain. Not Dead. Robert Graves. HBMV
Walking through usual flannels and faces. Aunt Cora. Kenneth Pitchford. CoPo
Walking to Dedham. David Wright. NeBP
Walking to Sleep. Richard Wilbur. NYBP
Walking to the Museum. Bone Thoughts on a Dry Day. George Starbuck. GoYe; NYBP; TDP; TwCP
Walking to-day in your garden, O gracious lady. The Moss-Rose. Sir Henry Newbolt. HBV
Walking Tour, The. W. H. Auden. *See* Chorus: "To throw away the key and walk away."
Walking under the Tour. James I, King of Scotland. *Fr.* The Kingis Quair. SeCePo
Walking with God. William Cowper. BEL; EiCL; EiCP; EiPP; EnLi-2 (1949 ed.); EnPE; EnRP; MaRV; NoP; OAEP; OBEC; PoEL-3; TOP; TRV; VaPo
(Closer Walk with God, A.) SoP
(Oh! for a Closer Walk with God.) FiP; OxBoCh
(Olney Hymns.) CEP
(Penitence.) BoPe
Walking with God. "C. H. I." SoP
Walking with God. *Unknown.* BLRP
Walking with Him in White. Charles Wesley. BePJ
Walking with Lulu in the Wood. Naomi Lazard. NYBP
Walking Woman, The. Sidney Keyes. *Fr.* Against a Second Coming. AtBAP; POTE
Walky-talky Jenny, *with music. Unknown.* AS
Wall, The. Gwendolyn Brooks. BP; PoNe (1970 ed.)
Wall, The. Alan Brownjohn. NYTB

Wall, The. William Hawkins. MoCV
Wall, The. Louis MacNeice. PoIE
Wall, The. Eve Merriam. TrJP
Wall. Elizabeth Morrow. MaRV
Wall, The. Arthur L. Phelps. CaP
Wall, The. Henry Reed. LiTB
Wall, The. Isidor Schneider. PG
Wall, Cave, and Pillar Statements, After Asôka. Alan Dugan. CoAP
Wall-Flower, The. Walter Savage Landor. OBVV
Wall-Flower, The. Henrik Wergeland, *tr. fr. Norwegian by* Sir Edmund Gosse. AWP; JAWP; WBP
Wall [*or* Wal], no! I can't tell whar he lives. Jim Bludso [of the *Prairie Belle*]. John Hay. AA; AmePo; AmPP (3d ed.); AnAmPo; BBV; BeLS; BOHV; CoBA; FaBoBe; FaFP; HBV; IHA; MaC; MCCG; MoAmPo (1942 ed.); NeMA; PaA; PaPo; PCD; PFY; PoMa; PoPo; TIHL; TreFS; YaD
Wall of China, The. Padraic Colum. RoGo
Wall of his environment, The. Walls. Hervey Allen. HBMV
Wall of Weeping, The, *sels.* Edmond Fleg, *tr. fr. French by* Humbert Wolfe. TrJP
End of Sorrow, The.
Wandering Jew Comes to the Wall, The.
Wall should be low, as to say, The. The Wall. Arthur L. Phelps. CaP
Wallace, The, *sels.* Henry the Minstrel.
Description of Wallace, A, *fr.* IX. GoTS
Schir William Wallace. OxBS
Wallace's Lament for the Graham, *fr.* X. GoTS
(Lament for the Graham.) OxBS
Wallace statur off gretnes, and off hycht. Schir William Wallace. Henry the Minstrel. *Fr.* The Wallace. OxBS
Wallam Olum. *Unknown. See* Walum-Olum.
Walloping Window-Blind, The. Charles Edward Carryl. *See* Nautical Ballad, A.
Wallowing in this bloody sty. The Drunken Fisherman. Robert Lowell. AmP; AmPP (5th ed.); AP; CBV; CMoP; CrMA; FiMAP; LiTA; LiTM (rev. ed.); MoPo; MoVE; OxBA; SeCeV; TwAmPo
Walls. Hervey Allen. HBMV
Walls. C. P. Cavafy, *tr. fr. Modern Greek by* Rae Dalven. TrJP
Walls. Robert Francis. CrMA
Walls. Myriam Page. ChIP
Walls and Arches, The. Giacomo Leopardi, *tr. fr. Italian by* Lorna de' Lucchi. PoFr
Walls cannot save the cities from their fate. Civitas Dei. Edith Lovejoy Pierce. MaRV
Walls have been shaded for so many years, The. The Soldier Walks under the Trees of the University. Randall Jarrell. OxBA; PoPl; WaP
Walls of a house are not built of wood, brick or stone, but of truth and loyalty, The. Your House. *Unknown.* PoToHe (new ed.)
Walls of a house may be be builded of wood, The. A House or a Home. J. H. Sykes. SoP
Walls of Jericho, The. Blanche Taylor Dickinson. CDC
Walnut. Jorge Carrera Andrade, *tr. fr. Spanish by* Philip Silver. ELU
Walrus and the Carpenter, The. "Lewis Carroll." *Fr.* Through the Looking-Glass. BeLS; BoChLi; BOHV; FaBoBe; FaBV; FaFP; FaPON; FiBHP; GN; GSP; HBV; HBVY; InMe; LBN; LiTB; LiTG; MaC; MCCG; NA; NeHB; OnSP; OTPC; PoRA; PoRh; PoVP; SAS; ShBV-1; SoPo; StVeCh; TreF; TVC; YT
"'Time has come, The,' the Walrus said," *sel.* TiPo
Walsinghame. *Unknown, at. to* Sir Walter Ralegh. *See* As You Came from the Holy Land.
Walt Whitman. Edwin Honig. NePA
Walt Whitman. Harrison Smith Morris. AA; DD
Walt Whitman. E. A. Robinson. AmePo; AmP; NePA; OxBA
Walt Whitman. Walt Whitman. *See* Song of Myself.
Walt Whitman. Francis Howard Williams. AA; DD
Walt Whitman, a kosmos, of Manhattan the son. Song of Myself, XXIV. Walt Whitman. PoFr
Walt Whitman at Bear Mountain. Louis Simpson. CBV; LiTM (1970 ed.); ML; NePoEA-2; PoCh; PP
Walter and His Dog. Eliza Lee Follen. SAS
Walter de la Mare Tells the Listener about Jack and Jill, *parody.* Louis Untermeyer. MoAmPo
Walter Jenks' Bath. William Meredith. CBV
Walter Lesly. *Unknown.* BaBo; ESPB
Walter Llywarch. R. S. Thomas. OPoP
Walter Reed. Rosemary Benét *and* Stephen Vincent Benét. OTD
Walter von der Vogelweid. Longfellow. MWA-1
Walthena. Elisabeth Peck. AmFN
Waltz, The. Byron. PAn
Waltz, The. Hilary Corke. NYBP
Waltz. Ruth Forbes Sherry. FiSC
Waltz. Edith Sitwell. *Fr.* Façade. OAEP (2d ed.)
Waltz in the Afternoon, A. Beth Bentley. BoLP
Waltz in, waltz in, ye little kids, and gather round my knee. The Spelling Bee at Angels. Bret Harte. StPo
Waltz Me around Again, Willie. Will D. Cobb. TreFT
Waltzer in the House, The. Stanley Kunitz. ErPo; NYBP
Waltzing It. William Thomas Moncrieff. UnS
Waltzing Matilda. A. B. Paterson. ChTr; PoAu-1; StPo; WaKn; WhC (*orig. text and popular vers.*).
Waltzing Mice. David McCord. RIS
Walum [*or* Walam *or* Wallam]-Olum. *Unknown, tr. fr. Lenape Indian.*
(Walam Olum, The, *tr. by* Daniel G. Brinton.) WoL
Sels.
Deluge, The, *tr. by* C. S. Rafinesque. LiTA
On the Creation and Ontogony, *tr. by* C. S. Rafinesque. LiTA
Waly, Waly. *Unknown.* OBEV; OxBS; ViBoPo
(Forsaken.) GTSE; GTSL; HBV
(Forsaken Bride, The.) GTBS; GTBS-D; GTBS-P; GTBS-W
(Jamie Douglas.) BaBo; ESPB; OBB; ViBoFo; WHA
(Lord Douglas.) OxBB
(O, Waly, Waly.) ELP; EnSB; GoTS; OBS
("O, waly, waly, up the bank.") EG, *abr.*; EnLoPo; LO
(Waly, Waly, Gin Love Be Bonny.) BaBo
Wan/ Swan. The Bereaved Swan. Stevie Smith. FaBoTw
Wan, fragile faces of joy! Home-Thoughts from France. Isaac Rosenberg. MMA
Wan from the wild and woful West. A Song of Sorrow. Charles Battell Loomis. BOHV
Wan-visaged Azrael, in a darkened room. Their Victory Won. Florence Earle Coates. PEDC
Wander-Lovers, The. Richard Hovey. AA; HBV
Wander, oh, wander, maiden sweet. Goethe and Frederika. Henry Sidgwick. HBV
Wander-Thirst. Gerald Gould. HT; PoMa; StaSt; TiPo; TSW
(Wanderlust.) HBV
Wandered from the Antrim hills. Saint Patrick. Edwin Markham. HH
Wanderer, The. Zoë Akins. HBMV; NP
Wanderer, The, *sels.* Christopher Brennan.
Come Out, Come Out, Ye Souls That Serve. PoAu-1
How Old Is My Heart. BoAV; PoAu-1
I Cry to You as I Pass Your Windows. PoAu-1
"I sorrow for youth—ah, not for its wildness (would that were dead!)." ACV
Land I Came Thro' Last, The. PoAu-1
O Desolate Eves [along the Way, How Oft]. BoAV; CoBE; PoAu-1
"When window-lamps had dwindled, then I rose." MoAuPo
Wanderer, The. Austin Dobson. HBV; InP; TOP
(Rondel; the Wanderer.) MoBrPo (1942 ed.)
Wanderer, The. Eugene Field. PoOW; PoPl
Wanderer, The. Amanda Benjamin Hall. HBMV
Wanderer, The. John Masefield. BrPo; CABL; MCCG
Wanderer, The, *sel.* "Owen Meredith."
Portrait, The, *fr.* II. HBV
Wanderer, The. *Unknown, tr. fr. Anglo-Saxon by* Charles W. Kennedy. AnOE; EnL; LiTW; EnLi-1 (1949 ed.), *tr. by* Stith Thompson; PoAn, *tr. by* Burton Raffel
Wanderer, The. William Carlos Williams. MAPA; TwAmPo
Wanderer, The. Wordsworth. *Fr.* The Excursion, I. EnRP
Wanderer, The. "Yehoash," *tr. fr. Yiddish by* Isidore Goldstick. TrJP
Wanderer from the Fold, The. Emily Brontë. EnLit
Wanderer is man from his birth, A. The Future. Matthew Arnold. GTBS; OAEP; PoVP; ViPo
Wanderer moon/ smiling a. Summer Song. William Carlos Williams. WIRo
Wanderer Recalls the Past, The. Wordsworth. *Fr.* The Excursion. OBNC

Wanderer without home, my memory goes. Sea News. Eric Barker. NYTB
Wanderers, The. Robert Browning. *See* Song: "Over the sea our galleys went."
Wanderers. Charles Stuart Calverley. CenHV
Wanderers. Thomas Curtis Clark. ChIP; OQP; TrPWD
Wanderers. James Hebblethwaite. BoAu; NeLNL
Wanderers, The. Arthur Symons. PoVP
Wanderers, chosen of God. Chosen of God. Stefan Zweig. *Fr.* Jeremiah. TrJP
Wanderer's First Night-Song, The. Goethe. *See* Wanderer's Night-Songs.
Wanderer's Grave, The. Rufus B. Sage. PoOW
Wanderer's Litany. Arthur Stringer. WGRP
Wanderer's Night-Songs, *sels.* Goethe, *tr. fr. German by* Longfellow.
"O'er all the hill-tops," II. AWP; InP; JAWP; WBP; WoL
(Wanderer's Night Song.) PoPl
(Wanderer's Second Night-Song, The.) OnPM
"Thou that from the heavens art," I. AWP; InP; JAWP; WBP; WoL
(Wanderer's First Night-Song, The.) OnPM
Wanderers outside the gates [*or* gate]. The Urn. Malcolm Cowley. AnAmPo; MoVE; NP
Wanderer's Second Night-Song, The. Goethe. *See* Wanderer's Night-Songs.
Wanderer's Song. Henry W. Frost. SoP
Wanderers Song, A. John Masefield. MCCG; MoAB; MoBrPo; RePo; TSW
Wanderer's Song. Arthur Symons. MoBrPo; ViBoPo
Wanderers, wanderers we are. Emigrant Song. "S. Ansky." TrJP
Wanderin' (A *and* B *vers.*), *with music.* *Unknown.* AS
Wandering. Hortense Flexner. HBMV
Wandering above a sea of glass. Down on My Luck. A. R. D. Fairburn. AnNZ
Wandering Cowboy, The. *Unknown.* CoSo
Wandering, ever wandering. The Wanderers. Arthur Symons. PoVP
Wandering Gadling, The. Sir Thomas Wyatt. CBEP
Wandering Jack. Emile Jacot. BoTP
Wandering Jew, The. Robert Mezey. NePoEA-2
Wandering Jew, The. E. A. Robinson. MAmP; PoDB; QFR
Wandering Jew Comes to the Wall, The. Edmond Fleg, *tr. fr. French by* Humbert Wolfe. *Fr.* The Wall of Weeping. TrJP
Wandering Jew once met a man, A. The Eternal Jew. Jacob Cohen. TrJP
Wandering Knight's Song, The. *Unknown, tr. fr. Spanish by* John Gibson Lockhart. ChTr; HBV
(Knights' Song, The, *tr. by* Sir John Bowring.) OnPM
("My ornaments are arms.") EG, *tr. by* John Gibson Lockhart
Wandering lost upon the mountains of our choice. W. H. Auden. *Fr.* In Time of War. CMoP; EnLit
Wandering Lunatic Mind, The. Edward Carpenter. WGRP
Wandering Maiden, The; or, True Love at Length United. *Unknown.* CoMu
Wandering Moon, The. James Reeves. RePo
Wandering Outlaw, The. Byron. *Fr.* Childe Harold's Pilgrimage, III. FiP
Wandering Spectre, The. *Unknown.* *See* Cauld Lad of Hilton, The.
Wandering tribe called the Siouxs, A. Prevalent Poetry. Charles Follen Adams. CenHV
Wandering up and down one day. The Cobbler. *Unknown.* BoTP
Wanderings of Cain, The, *sel.* Samuel Taylor Coleridge.
Fruit Plucker, The. CH; SeCeV
(Boy in the Wilderness.) OTPC (1923 ed.)
(In a Moonlight Wilderness.) FaBoCh; LoGBV
Wanderings of Oisin, The. W. B. Yeats. BrPo
"We galloped over the glossy sea," *sel.* SeCePo
Wanderlust. Gerald Gould. *See* Wander-Thirst.
Wand'ring Minstrel, A. W. S. Gilbert. *Fr.* The Mikado. TreFS
Wang Peng's Recommendation for Improving the People. Paul Eldridge. ShM
Waning Moon, The. Shelley. *See* Moon, The ("And like a dying lady").
Waning moon looks upward, this grey night, The. Nostalgia. D. H. Lawrence. NP
Waning of the Harvest Moon, The. John Wieners. CoPo
Waning Summer. Thomas Nashe. *See* Fair Summer Droops.
Wanne mine eyhnen misten. How Death Comes. *Unknown.* MeEL
Want of You, The. Ivan Leonard Wright. BLPA; FaBoBe; NeHB
Want quickens wit: Want's pupils needs must work. The Fishermen. Theocritus. Idylls, XXI. AWP
Want to go to heab'n, when I die. To See God's Bleedin' Lam'. *Unknown.* BoAN-2
Wantage Bells. John Betjeman. WePo
Wanted. Josiah Gilbert Holland. *See* God Give Us Men.
Wanted. Shel Silverstein. PV
Wanted—a Man. Edmund Clarence Stedman. LiPo; PAH
Wanted—A Messenger. *Unknown.* SoP
Wanted, a Minister's Wife. *Unknown.* BLPA; TreFS
Wanted: Men. Ad. Kenneth Fearing. CMoP
Wanted: One Cave Man with Club. Margaret Fishback. WhC
Wanting for their young limbs praise. To the Girls of My Graduating Class. Irving Layton. ErPo
Wanting His Desire, He Complaineth. Richard Edwards. ReIE
Wanting Is—What? Robert Browning. EPN; MBW-2; PoVP
Wanton droll, whose harmless play. The Kitten. Joanna Baillie. CIV
Wanton Trick, The. *Unknown.* CoMu
('Tis but a Wanton Trick.) UnTE
Wanton troopers riding by, The. The Nymph Complaining for the Death of Her Faun [*or* Fawn]. Andrew Marvell. AnAnS-1; AtBAP; CBEP; CH; GoTL; HBV; LoBV; MaMe; MePo; NoP; OBS; PAn; PoEL-2; ReEn; SCEP-2; SeCP; SeCV-1
Wanton with long delay the gay spring leaping cometh. April, 1885. Robert Bridges. NBM
Wanton's Death, The. Norman Cameron. FaBoTw
Wants. Philip Larkin. GTBS-P
Wants of Man, The. John Quincy Adams. PoLF
Wapentake. Longfellow. AA
Wapiti, The. Ogden Nash. MoShBr
War. Guillaume Apollinaire, *tr. fr. French by* Jessie Degen *and* Richard Eberhart. WaaP
War. Michael Brownstein. ANYP
War. Grace Ellery Channing. AA
War. Dryden. *Fr.* Alexander's Feast. TreFS
War. Mary Fullerton. NeLNL
War. J. C. Hall. HaMV
War. Sulamith Ish-Kishor. GoYe
War. Chief Joseph. PGD
War. Joseph Langland. MP; NePoEA; PoCh; TPM
War. J. Gilchrist Lawson. WBLP
War. Richard Le Gallienne. *See* This Is War.
War. Li Po, *tr. fr. Chinese by* Rewi Alley. ChTr
War ("Ez fer war, I call it murder"). James Russell Lowell. *Fr.* The Biglow Papers, 1st Series, No. I. MaRV
War. William Alfred McLean, Jr. BOLo
War. E. Merrill Root. OQP
War. Charles Simic. YAP
War. Arthur Stringer. TwCaPo
War. Hedd Wyn, *tr. fr. Welsh by* Gwyn Williams. PrWP
War/ I abhor,/ And yet how sweet. This Is War [*or* War]. Richard Le Gallienne. MaRV; OQP
War, The: A—Z. John R. Edwards. BOHV
War against the Trees, The. Stanley Kunitz. PPON
War and Peace. Alexander Petofi, *tr. fr. Hungarian by* Alice Stone Blackwell. PoFr
War and Washington. Jonathan Mitchell Sewall. *Fr.* Cato. PAH
War at Home, The. Willard Wattles. OQP
War Bird's Burlesque, A *with music.* *Unknown.* AS
War Comes. Zalman Schneour, *tr. fr. Yiddish by* Joseph Leftwich. TrJP
War Cry: To Mary. Pope Leo XIII, *tr. fr. Latin by* Raymond F. Roseliep. ISi
War Dance, The. Robert V. Carr. PoOW
War drum booms, The: all roads are bare. Thinking of My Brothers. Tu Fu. OnPM
War drum is beating, prepare for the fight, The. We Conquer or Die. James Pierpont. MC; PAH
War Films, The. Sir Henry Newbolt. MaRV
War God, The. Stephen Spender. MoRP

War God wakened drowsily, The. The Awakened War God. Margaret Widdemer. WGRP
War God's Horse Song, The. *Unknown, tr. fr. Navajo by* Dane Coolidge *and* Mary Roberts Coolidge. LiTA; LoGBV
War, he sung, is toil and trouble. War. Dryden. *Fr.* Alexander's Feast. TreFS
War-Horse, The. Job, Bible, *O.T.* *See* Horse, The.
War in Camp. John A. Stone. SGR
War in Chang-An City. Wang Tsan, *tr. fr. Chinese by* Rewi Alley. PPON
War in Heaven. Milton. *Fr.* Paradise Lost, VI. DiPo; ExPo
War is done mother. GI. Raymond Roseliep. FiSC
War Is Kind, *sels.* Stephen Crane.
Candid Man, The, IX. MAP; MoAmPo
"Chatter of a death-demon from a tree-top, The," XIX. AP
I Explain, VI. AA; AmP
("I explain the silvered passing of a ship at night.") AP
"I have heard the sunset song of the birches," VII. AP; MWA-2
"In the night/ Gray, heavy clouds," XVIII. AmePo; AP; MWA-2
(Peaks, The.) AA; AmP; HBV; WGRP
"Little ink more or less, A," IV. AmPP (3d ed.); AnAmPo
Man Said to the Universe, A, XXI. AmePo; AmPP; AnAmPo; AP; CoBA; ImOP; InP; LiTM (1970 ed.); NCEP; YaD
(Man, The.) BOHV
(Man to the Universe, A.) TreFT
Newspaper Is a Collection of Half-Injustices, A, XII. AmePo; AmP; AmPP (5th ed.); AP; CoBA; NCEP; ViBoPo
"On the desert," XI. AP; LiTM (1970 ed.)
Slant of Sun [on Dull Brown Walls], A, XIV. AmePo; AmP; AmPP; LiTM (1970 ed.); VaPo
(Hymn: "Slant of sun on dull brown walls, A.") MAP; MoAmPo
"There was a land where lived no violets," XXIII. AnAmPo; AP
(Violets, The.) AA
There Was a Man with a Tongue of Wood, XVI. LiTA; MoAmPo (1950 ed.); NePA
Trees in the Garden, The, XXVI. AmPP; LiTM (1970 ed.); VaPo
War Is Kind, I (title poem). AmPP; AnAmPo; AnFE; APA; CoAnAm; DiPo; HBV; InPo; LiTM (1970 ed); PoPo; StP; ThLM; ViBoPo; WaaP
(Do Not Weep, Maiden, for War Is Kind.) AmePo; AP; CoBA; LiTA; MWA-2; PAL; PoLF
Wayfarer, The, XIII. AA; AmePo; AmPP (3d ed.); CoBA; LiTA; MAP; MoAmPo; NeMA; NePA; PoMA
What? You Define Me God, *fr.* IV. AmPP (3d ed.)
War Is the Statesman's Game. Shelley. *Fr.* Queen Mab, IV. PPON
War lords perish with the millions slain, The. "One World." Brent Dow Allinson. MaRV
War Museum at Nagasaki, The. Charles Higham. NYTB
War of the Secret Agents, The. Henri Coulette. AmPC
Sels.
Cinema, at the Lighthouse. NePoEA-2
Denise: A Letter Never Sent. NePoEA-2
Epilogue: Author to Reader. NePoEA-2
Phono, at the Boar's Head. NePoEA-2
War of time O it seizes the soul tonight. Easter Eve, 1945. Muriel Rukeyser. MiAP
War on the Periphery. George Johnston. PeCV
War-path is true and straight, The. Just One Signal. *Unknown.* PAH
War Poem. Henry Treece. MaRV
War Poem. Richard West. FOL
War Poet. Roy Fuller. PP
War Poet. Sidney Keyes. MemP
War Relief. Oliver Herford. BOHV
War screams, so peace becomes a whisper. Sunday Edition. Joseph Joel Keith. FiSC
War Ship. *See* Warship.
War shook the land where Levi dwelt. The Field of Glory. E. A. Robinson. CMoP; HBV; MAP; MoAmPo
War Song, A. Bertrand de Born. *See* Well Pleaseth Me the Sweet Time of Easter.
War Song, A. Blake. *See* War Song to Englishmen, A.
War Song. John Davidson. NBM; OBNC
War Song. *Unknown.* ABF
War-Song of Dinas Vawr, The. Thomas Love Peacock. *Fr.* The Misfortunes of Elphin. ALV; AWP; CABA; EnRP; ERoP-1; EvOK; ExPo; FaBoCh; GTBS; InvP; JAWP; LiTG; LoBV; MyFE; NBM; OBRV; OnMSP; OtMeF; PTK; ShBV-2; StP; StPo; TOP; ViBoPo, 4 *ll.*; WaaP; WBP; WhC; WiR
War Song of O'Driscol. Gerald Griffin. OnYI
War Song of the Saracens. James Elroy Flecker. *Fr.* Hassan. FaBV; FOL; MoBrPo; OBVV; OtMeF; ShBV-2; WHA
War Song to Englishmen, A. Blake. *Fr.* King Edward the Third. CH; WaaP
(War Song, A.) OHIP
War Story. Jon Stallworthy. ELU
War Story. George Starbuck. TDP
War Suite. Jim Harrison. ThO
War Swaggers. Emanuel Litvinoff. WaP
War that we have carefully for years provoked, The. Blackout. Robinson Jeffers. LiTA; LiTM (rev. ed.); NePA; WaP
War-Time. *See* Wartime.
War-Token, The. Longfellow. *Fr.* The Courtship of Miles Standish, IV. PAH
War will not always be. Prospect. Thomas Curtis Clark. PoRL
War with the Weeds, The. Keith Sinclair. AnNZ
War Year, The. Ts'ao Sung, *tr. fr. Chinese by* C. H. Kwock *and* Vincent McHugh. PPON
Waradgery Tribe, The. Mary Gilmore. BoAV; NeLNL; PoAu-1
Waratah. Roland Robinson. PoAu-2
Warblers. Marsden Hartley. AnFE; CoAnAm
Ward, and still in bonds, one day, A. Regeneration. Henry Vaughan. AnAnS-1; CABA; EP; ExPo; LoBV; MeLP; MeP; MePo; NoP; OBS; SCEP-1; SeEP
Ward has no heart, they say; but I deny it. On J. W. Ward. Samuel Rogers. ALV
Ward in the States, A. Randall Jarrell. FiMAP
Ward 130 in the passage on the right. 25 December 1960. Ingrid Jonker. PeSA
Warden at ocean's gate. Liberty Enlightening the World. Edmund Clarence Stedman. PAH
Warden of the Cinque Ports, The. Longfellow. AA; AmPP (3d ed.); HBV; WHA
Warden of the universe who flings, The. Premonition. Edith Ogutsch. FiSC
Warden spoke of him as "Ninety-four," The. Five Peas on a Barrelhead. Lew Sarett. PoMa
Warder, from his watch-tower high, The. Matin-Song. *Unknown.* WoL
Wardrobe. Sister Mary Madeleva. GoBC
Waring. Robert Browning. OtMeF; PeER; PoEL-5
Warlike prince had sever'd from the rest, The. Dryden. *Fr.* Annus Mirabilis. PeRV
Warm and buoyant in his oily mail. The Whale. Erasmus Darwin. GoTP
Warm are the still and lucky miles. Song. W. H. Auden. FaBoMo; GTBS-D; POTE
Warm as a little mouse he lay. Christ Child. Henry Treece. MaRV
Warm Babies. Keith Preston. FiBHP; HBMV; WhC
Warm hands, warm, daddy's gone [*or* the men have gone] to plough. *Unknown.* OxNR; PPL
Warm night/ morning walking. Unsuccessful Spring Poem. Philip Whalen. FRC
Warm of heart shall never lack a fire, The. Elizabeth J. Coatsworth. TiPo
Warm rain sighs and throbs upon my roses, The. Roses and Rain. Archibald T. Strong. BoAu
Warm rain whispers, A, but the earth knows best. Sonnet. Kenneth Leslie. *Fr.* By Stubborn Stars. PeCV; TwCaPo
Warm summer sun. Epitaph Placed on His Daughter's Tomb. Robert Richardson, *ad. by* "Mark Twain." MaRV; PoLF; TreF
Warm sun is failing, the bleak wind is wailing, The. Autumn; a Dirge. Shelley. CH; HBV; OTPC
Warm sunshine came down. Crocus. *Unknown.* GFA
Warm Tea. Lewis MacAdams. ANYP
Warm, wild, rainy wind, blowing fitfully. May Morning. Celia Thaxter. AA

Warm wine, warm baths, warm women, onetime ladies. The Easiest Way. *Unknown.* UnTE
Warm Winter Day, A. Julian Cooper. BoNaP
Warm your feet at the sunset. Galactic Lovepoem. Adrian Henri. HYE
Warmed by her hand and shadowed by her hair. The Love-Letter. Dante Gabriel Rossetti. The House of Life, XI. MaVP; PoVP; ViPo; VP
Warn Someone. *Unknown.* SoP
Warning. John Ciardi. PDV
Warning. Harold Lewis Cook. AnAmPo
Warning, The. Adelaide Crapsey. AnAmPo; InP; MAP; MCCG; MoAmPo (1942 ed.); NeMA; NP
Warning, The. Robert Creeley. NeAP
Warning. Jesse Douglas. WhC
Warning. Robert Frost. AmePo
Warning. Sara Henderson Hay. MaRV
Warning, A. Heine, *tr. fr. German by* Louis Untermeyer. PoFr
Warning, The. Longfellow. AmePo; CoBA
Warning, A. Coventry Patmore. EnLoPo
Warning. Sydney King Russell. FiSC
Warning, A ("Thow thou be kyng of tour and town"). *Unknown.* EnLit
Warning and Reply. Emily Brontë. OBVV; OxBI; PoVP; VA
Warning for Abraham Lincoln, A. Jacinto Fombona Pachano, *tr. fr. Spanish by* Angel Flores. PoFr; WoL
Warning to a Guest. John Holloway. NePoEA
Warning to Children. Robert Graves. FaBoCh; FaFP; FlW; GTBS-W; LoGBV; NoP; PoIE; SiTL
Warning to Conquerors, A. Donagh MacDonagh. OxBI
Warning to Cupid. *Unknown, tr. fr. Greek by* Louis Untermeyer. UnTE
Warning to My Love, A. David Wagoner. NePoEA-2
Warning to One. Merrill Moore. MAP; MoAmPo; NP; TrGrPo; YaD
Warning to Skeptics, A. Leah Bodine Drake. FiSC
Warning to Snake-Killers. Robert H. Barlow. FiSC
Warning to Those Who Serve Lords, A. *Unknown.* MeEL
Warning to Travailers Seeking Accomodations at Mr. Devills Inn. Sarah Kemble Knight. SCAP
Warnings, The. Alice Furlong. AnIV
Warp and Woof. Harry Halbisch. BLRP
Warren's Address [to the American Soldiers]. John Pierpont. AA; AmePo; AnNE; DD; GN; MC; PaA; PAH; PAP; PEDC
(General Joseph Warren's Address.) WBLP
(Warren's Address at Bunker Hill.) FaBoBe; HBV; HBVY; PAL; PoFr; TreF
(Warren's Address to the Soldiers at Bunker Hill.) PTK
Warrior at Nightfall, A. *Unknown, tr. fr. Japanese.* GaP
Warrior Bards, The. Henry Treece. ML
Warrior Maid, The. Anna Hempstead Branch. HBV; LoEn
Warrior Passes, The. Hubert Kelley. DD
Warrior to His Dead Bride, The. Adelaide Anne Procter. OBVV
Warriors and chiefs! should the shaft or the sword. Song of Saul before His Last Battle. Byron. Po
Warrior's Lament, The. Sir Owen Seaman. FiBHP
Warriors Prancing, Women Dancing. Niema Rashidd. NBP
Warrior's Prayer, A. Paul Laurence Dunbar. MaRV; OQP
Warriors, tigers, flowers of Delacroix, The. Lightning for Atmosphere. Marya Zaturenska. TwAmPo
Wars, The. Conrad Aiken. *Fr.* The Soldier. WaaP
"Wars are to be," they say, they blindly say. The Lament of the Voiceless. Laura Bell Everett. OQP; PGD
War's Clown in the Proscenium. Gene Derwood. *See* In the Proscenium.
Wars we wage, The. Robert Gould Shaw. William Vaughn Moody. *Fr.* An Ode in Time of Hesitation. AA
Wars, The: we're drawn to them. War Suite. Jim Harrison. ThO
Wars worse then civil on Thessalian plains. Lucan. *Fr.* Pharsalia. ReIE
War Ship of Peace, The. Samuel Lover. PAH
Wartime Dawn, A. David Gascoyne. LiTM (1970 ed.); MoVE
War-Time Prayer, A. Anna Bunston de Bary. MaRV
Warty Bliggens, the Toad. Don Marquis. *Fr.* Archy and Mehitabel. FiBHP
Warum sind denn die Rosen so blass. Heine, *tr. fr. German by* Richard Garnett. AWP; JAWP; WBP
Wary of time O it seizes the soul tonight. Easter Eve. Muriel Rukeyser. NePA
Was a Man. Philip Booth. NePoEA-2
Was a soule from farre away. Five Carols for Christmastide, IV. Louise Imogen Guiney. ISi
Was broken./ He bade a warrior abandon his horse. The Battle of Maldon. *Unknown.* AnOE
Was clenched on a fly's carcase like a golden. The Spider's Nest. George MacBeth. NMP
Was ever man of nature's framing. Ode. Charles Cotton. CavP; PeRV
Was Galahad hired. Folkways. Isabella Gardner. SiTL
Was he then Adam of the Burning Way? Such Is the Sickness of Many a Good Thing. Robert Duncan. NoP
Was he then human? Tolls of Tyrants! could. Portrait at Wentworth. Ebenezer Elliott. Sonn
Was hunting bigger prey and came upon her. Sarah Lorton. Mary Finnin. BoAV
Was I a Samurai renowned. Ballade of a Toyokuni Color-Print. W. E. Henley. PoVP
Was I not muskrat, water-snake, raccoon? Boy in a Pond. James Whaler. *Fr.* Runaway. OA
Was I to blame to trust thy lovelike teares. *Unknown.* SeCSL
Was I too glib about eternal things. The Sequel. Theodore Roethke. NYBP
Was, Is, and Yet-to-be. Ella Wheeler Wilcox. PoToHe
Was it a dream, or did I see it plain? Amoretti, LXXVII. Spenser. ReIE
Was it a dream? The books were men. The Wounded. Louise Louis. GoYe
Was it a dream? We sail'd, I thought we sail'd. A Dream. Arthur Hugh Clough. GTBS-P; SeCePo
Was It a Form [a Gate, a Grace]? Henry Reynolds. *See* Song: "Was it a form, a gait, a grace."
"Was it a little baby." A Tonversation with Baby. Morris Bishop. FiBHP; WhC
Was it a mirror then across a room. Mirrors. Elizabeth Jennings. NePoEA
Was it at Nazareth/ of the marvellous breath? Joy's Peak. Robert Farren. ISi
Was it because the breast had bruised the breast. Leda, the Lost. Eda Lou Walton. AnAmPo
Was it fancy, sweet nurse. Don Marquis. Grotesques, I. FiBHP
Was It for This? Rene Verlon. ChIP
Was it for this I braved a pathless, dark. A Mother before a Soldier's Monument. Winnie Lynch Rockett. PGD
Was it his face that so unsettled him? Narcissus. Donald Petersen. NePoEA-2
Was it I, was it I who dallied there. Ulysses Returns, III. Roselle Mercier Montgomery. HBMV
Was it the proud full sail of this great verse. Sonnets, LXXXVI. Shakespeare. CBEP; InvP; ML; OAEP; ReEn; ReIE; SiCE; Sonn
Was it the wind they followed? The Mountain in the Sky. Howard McKinley Corning. NP
Was it the worke of Nature or of Art. Amoretti, XXI. Spenser. LiTL
Was it worth while to paint so fair. The Morning-Glory. Florence Earle Coates. HBV
Was It You? Stewart I. Long. WBLP
Was Jesus chaste? Blake. *Fr.* The Everlasting Gospel. OBRV
Was Jesus just a boy like me. Christmas "Good Night." Ethel Robb. GFA
Was never aught by Nature's art. That All Things Are as They Are Used. George Turberville. EnRePo
Was never day came on my head. George Turberville. *Fr.* The Lover Abused Renounceth Love. ElL
Was never file yet half so well yfiled. The Abused Lover Seeth His Folly and Entendeth to Trust No More. Sir Thomas Wyatt. ReIE
Was never form and never face. Beauty. Emerson. MWA-1
Was never in Scotland hard nor sene. Christ's Kirk on the Green. *At. to* James V, King of Scotland. OxBS
Was never none other. Carol Naïve. John McClure. HBMV
Was She a Witch? Laura E. Richards. MPB; PDV; SoPo

Was sorrow ever like unto our sorrow? The Voice of the Poor. Lady Wilde. VA
Was that the cuckoo's song? The Cuckoo's Song. Josui. MPB
Was that the landmark? What,—the foolish well. The Landmark. Dante Gabriel Rossetti. The House of Life, LXVII. EPN; MaVP; NBM; PoVP; ViPo
Was the arrangement made between the two couples legal? Some Litanies. Michael Benedikt. CoAP; TwCP; YAP
Was There Another Spring? Helen Hay Whitney. AA
Was there ever message sweeter. A Message. Elizabeth Stuart Phelps Ward. PAH
Was there love once? I have forgotten her. Fulfilment. Robert Nichols. HBMV
Was this His coming! I had hoped to see. Ave Maria Gratia Plena. Oscar Wilde. ACP (1926 ed.); CAW; ChIP; ISi; JKCP (1926 ed.); StJW
Was this his face, and these the finding eyes. On a Portrait of Columbus. George Edward Woodberry. AA
Was This the Face. Christopher Marlowe. *Fr.* Dr. Faustus. LiTL; PTK; TrGrPo
(Face of Helen, The.) FaBV
(Faustus to Helen.) NeHB
(Helen.) FaFP; GTBS-W; LiTB; LiTG; WHA
("Was this the face that launched [*or* lancht] a thousand ships [*or* shippes]?") AtBAP; InP; TreF; ViBoPo
Was Worm. May Swenson. GoTP
Was you ever down in Mobile bay? Mobile Bay. *Unknown.* SoAmSa
Was you ever in Quebec? Highland Laddie. *Unknown.* SoAmSa
Wash-Day. *See* Washday.
Wash, hands, wash. A Rhyme for Washing Hands. *Unknown.* BoTP
Wash is hanging on the line, The. Windy Wash Day. Dorothy Aldis. TiPo
Wash Me Whiter than Snow. Charles Wesley. BePJ
Wash the dishes, wipe the dishes. Mother Goose. BrR; OxNR
Wash your hands, or else the fire. Christmas Eve—Another to the Maids. Robert Herrick. OHIP
Wash your hands, War. On War. Crystal Kilgore. TPM
Wash-Day. Lilian McCrea. BoTP
Washday. Elizabeth F. Upson. GFA
Washed in Silver. James Stephens. ELU
Washed in the blood of the brave and the blooming. God Save the Flag. Oliver Wendell Holmes. FaFP; OHFP
Washed into the doorway. The Guest. Wendell Berry. AP; TPM
Washer of the Ford, The. "Fiona Macleod." PoVP
Washers of the Shroud, The. James Russell Lowell. AP; CoBA; HBV; PAH; PAP
Washer-Woman, The. Otto Leland Bohanan. BANP
Washerwoman's Song. L. A. G. Strong. YT
Washing. John Drinkwater. FaPON; StVeCh
Washing. Randall Jarrell. TDP
Washing and Dressing. Ann Taylor. SAS
Washing between the buildings. Larry Eigner. CoPo
Washing Day. *Unknown.* CoMu
Washing hanging from the lemon tree, The. The Five-Day Rain. Denise Levertov. NeAP
Washing hangs upon the line, A. Songs for a Colored Singer. Elizabeth Bishop. MiAP; PoNe
Washing the Dishes. Christopher Morley. PoLF
Washing-up Song, The. Elizabeth Gould. BoTP
Washing up the dishes and hold your clattering tongue. Lolly Trudom. *Unknown.* BFSS
Washington. Byron. *Fr.* Ode to Napoleon Buonaparte, *st.* 19. DD; MC; OHIP; PaA; PAH; PAL
(Cincinnatus of the West, The.) PoRL
Washington. Mae Winkler Goodman. PGD
Washington ("Soldier and statesman, rarest union"). James Russell Lowell. *Fr.* Under the Old Elm, V. DD; GN; HH; MC; OHIP; OQP, *abr.*; OTPC; RePo
(Ours, and All Men's.) PAL; PGD
(Washington under the Old Elm.) PEDC
Washington. Geraldine Meyrich. OHIP
Washington. Harriet Monroe. *Fr.* Commemoration Ode. AA; FaBoBe; MaRV; OQP; PoRL
Washington. Denis O'Crowley. OHIP; PoRL
Washington. John A. Prentice. OHIP
Washington. James Jeffrey Roche. MC; PAH
Sels.
First Citizen. PGD
"No angel led our Chieftain's steps aright." DD
Washington. Robert Haven Schauffler. PaA
Washington. Nancy Byrd Turner. FaPON; MPB; SoPo; TiPo; YeAr
Washington. B. Y. Williams. OQP; PGD
Washington. Mary Wingate. HH; OHIP
(When Shall We See Thy Like Again?) PGD
Washington and Lincoln. Wendell Phillips Stafford. PGD
Washington Cathedral. Karl Shapiro. MiAP
Washington led armies. Footnote to History. Elizabeth J. Coatsworth. SiSoSe
Washington, man of mystery. *Unknown.* RIS
Washington Monument, The. Alma Adams Wiley. PEDC
Washington Monument by Night. Carl Sandburg. CMoP; FaPON; OHIP; PoSC
Washington Sequoia, The, *sel.* Millicent Washburn Shinn.
Yosemite. AA
Washington Square. Francesco Bianco. CLwM
Washington, the brave, the wise the good. Inscription at Mount Vernon. *Unknown.* PoRL
Washington under the Old Elm. James Russell Lowell. *See* Washington ("Soldier and statesman, rarest union").
Washington's Birthday. Arthur J. Burdick. OHIP
Washington's Birthday. Charles S. Davis. HH
Washington's Birthday. Oliver Wendell Holmes. *See* Ode for Washington's Birthday.
Washington's Birthday. Margaret E. Sangster. HH; PEDC
Washington's Last Birthday. Alfred Noyes. PoMa
Washington's Monument. *Unknown.* OHIP; PAH
Washington's Song. Edmond S. Meany. PoRL
Washington's Statue. Henry T. Tuckerman. AA
Washington's Tomb. Ruth Lawrence. OHIP
Washington's Vow. Whittier. *See* Vow of Washington, The.
Washiri (Poet). Kattie M. Cumbo. BOLo
Wasn't it pleasant, O brother mine. Out to Old Aunt Mary's. James Whitcomb Riley. FaFP; OHFP
Wasn't this the site, asked the historian. House and Land. Allen Curnow. ACV; AnNZ
Wasp, The. Daryl Hine. NYBP
Wasp, The. "Fiona Macleod." BoTP; FaPON; PCH; TSW
Wasp Bite Nobi on Her Conch-Eye, A, *with music.* *Unknown.* OuSiCo
Wasp nests and yaller jackets. Cowboy Boasting Chants. *Unknown.* ABF
Wasps, The, *sel.* Aristophanes, *tr. fr. Greek. by* F, A. Wright.
"Amateur, driving too fast, An." LiBL
Wasps between my bare toes crawl and tickle; black. Sant'Angelo D'Ischia. Edwin Denby. ANYP
Wasp's Frolic, The. *Unknown.* PAH
Wasps' Nest, The. George MacBeth. FIW
Wassail Chorus at the Mermaid Tavern. Theodore Watts-Dunton. OBEV (1st ed.)
Wassail Song, The ("Here we come a-wassailing"). *Unknown.* *See* Here We Come a-Wassailing.
Wassail Song ("Wassail! Wassail! All round the town"). *Unknown.* *See* Wassail, Wassail, All over the Town.
Wassail, Wassail. John Bale. *Fr.* King John. ChTr
("Wassail, wassail, out of the milk-pail.") TuPP
Wassail, Wassail, All over the Town. *Unknown.* YaCaBo, *with music.*
(Wassail Song, *diff. vers.*) OHIP
Wassail! wassail! all over the town. Wassailer's Song. Robert Southwell. OHIP
Wassail! wassail! all round the town. Wassail Song. *Unknown.* OHIP
Wassail, wassail, out of the milk pail. Wassail, Wassail. John Bale. *Fr.* King John. ChTr; TuPP
Wassailer's Song. Robert Southwell. OHIP
Wassell wassell wassell wassell. *Unknown.* SeCSL
Waste. Harry Graham. LiTG; SiTL
(Aunt Maud.) MoShBr; ShM
Waste Land, The. T. S. Eliot. AmPP; AP; AtBAP; ATP (1953 ed.); CABA; CMoP; CoBMV; EnLit; FaBoMo; LiTA; LiTM; MasP; MBW-2; MoAB; MoAmPo (1950 ed.); MoPo; MoVE; MWA-2; NePA; NoP; OAEP (2d ed.); OxBA; ReMP; UnPo (3d ed.)
Waste Not Your Hour. Omar Khayyám, *tr. fr. Persian by* Edward Fitzgerald. *Fr.* The Rubáiyát. OnPM

Waste of War, The. William L. Stidger. PGD
Waste Places, The. James Stephens. *See* In Waste Places.
Wasted Ammunition. Stoddard King. InMe
Wasted Day, A. Frances Cornford. HBMV; MoBrPo; NeMA; TSW
Wasted Night. *Unknown, tr. fr. Greek by* Louis Untermeyer. UnTE
Wasted Sympathy, A. Winifred Howells. AA
Wasted, wasted minutes that couldn't be worse. While Someone Telephones. Elizabeth Bishop. NMP
Wasted, Weary, Wherefore Stay. Sir Walter Scott. *Fr.* Guy Mannering, *ch.* 27. EnRP
Wasting thistle whitens on my crest, The. The Wild Knight. G. K. Chesterton. WGRP
Wastrel, The. Reginald Wright Kauffman. HBV
Watch, The. Frances Cornford. DTC; HBMV; LiTM; MoBrPo
Watch, The. May Swenson. CBV
Watch, America. Robert Nathan. WaKn
Watch and Pray. Charlotte Elliott. SoP; STF
Watch and Pray. Martin Luther, *tr. fr. German.* SoP
Watch Any Day. W. H. Auden. FaBoMo
(We All Make Mistakes.) CMoP
Watch her an' catch her an' jump her juberju. Ten Thousand Miles from Home. *Unknown.* AS
Watch Hill. Winfield Townley Scott. *See* Unsexed by the Cold Sea.
Watch Long Enough, and You Will See the Leaf. Conrad Aiken. Preludes for Memnon, XIX. CMoP; NePA; OxBA
Watch, My Soul, and Pray. Johan Olof Wallin. SoP
Watch of a Swan, The. Sarah Morgan Bryan Piatt. AA
Watch on the Rhine, The. Max Schneckenburger, *tr. fr. German.* HBV
Watch on the Rhine, The. Gertrude Stein. *Fr.* Accents in Alsace. AtBAP
Watch, please, this painted ballet of the fed. Uccello on the Heath. Geoffrey Grigson. WaP
Watch that near my midriff ticks, The. Pocket and Steeple. Mark Antony De Wolfe Howe. WhC
Watch the Lights Fade. Robinson Jeffers. CMoP
Watch the net drift. Grey tides. How to Catch Tiddlers. Brian Jones. FIW
Watch thou and fear; tomorrow thou shalt die. The Choice, 2. Dante Gabriel Rossetti. The House of Life, LXXII. ATP; EnL; EnLi-2; HBV; MaVP; MyFE; OBVV; PoVP; TOP; ViPo
Watch was up on the topsail-yard a-making fast the sail, The. One of Wally's Yarns. John Masefield. BrPo
Watch well the poor in this late hour. Temperance Note; and Weather Prophecy. James Agee. *Fr.* Two Songs on the Economy of Abundance. MAP; MoAmPo
Watch will tell the time of day, A. Mr. Coggs [Watchmaker]. E. V. Lucas. BoTP; FaPON; GaP; GFA; HBV; HBVY; MPB
Watch Yourself Go By. Strickland Gillilan. BLPA; PoToHe
(Cure for Fault-finding, A, *abr.*) WBLP
Watched and well-known to the police, he walks. Variations on a Line from Shakespeare's Fifty-sixth Sonnet. E. L. Mayo. PoCh
Watcher, The. Stanton A. Coblentz. FiSC
Watcher, The. Sarah Josepha Hale. AA
Watcher, The. James Stephens. HBV; MoBrPo; OBEV (new ed.); OBVV; PoDB
Watcher, The. Ruth Stone. NYBP
Watcher, The. Margaret Widdemer. DD; HBMV; MaRV; OHIP; SoP; TSW
(Mother.) STF
(Watcher, The—Mother.) OQP
Watcher stood on the brink of time, A. The Watcher. Stanton A. Coblentz. FiSC
Watcher, who watchest by the bed of pain. Jesus of Nazareth Passeth By. Lydia Huntley Sigourney. BePJ; StJW
Watchers, The. Arlo Bates. AA NMP; NYBP
Watchers, The. W. S. Braithwaite. PoNe
Watchers. W. S. Merwin. NaP
Watchers, The. Muriel Rukeyser. NMP
Watchers, The. Charles Spear. AnNZ
Watchers of the Sky, *sels.* Alfred Noyes. The Torch Bearers, I.
"Fools have said/ That knowledge drives out wonder." MaRV
"This music leads us far." MaRV; OQP
Watchful Servant, The. Philip Doddridge. SoP
Watching. "Fanny Forester." AA
Watching. *Unknown.* SoP
Watching Angels. Christina Rossetti. *Fr.* Sing-Song. PPL
Watching by a Sick-Bed. John Masefield. NP
Watching Clouds. John Farrar. SoPo; StVeCh
Watching hands transplanting. Transplanting. Theodore Roethke. WIRo
Watching oneself. Poem without a Main Verb. John Wain. NePoEA-2; NMP
Watching Television. Robert Bly. CoAP; FRC; TPM
Watching Tennis. John Heath-Stubbs. Sonn
Watching the horses stand. At Amberley Wild Brooks. Andrew Young. OA
Watching the Moon. David McCord. RePo; YeAr
Watching the night contract the viridian fields. O Rose, O Rainbow. Nicholas Moore. NeBP
Watching the Old Man Die. A. J. M. Smith. MoCV
Watching the shied core. As Bad as a Mile. Philip Larkin. ELU
Watching this dawn's mnemonic of old dawning. Sestina in a Cantina. Malcolm Lowry. MoCV; TDP
Watching TV. To a Man in a Picture Window Watching Television. Mildred Weston. ELU
Watching You Walk. Ruthven Todd. LiTL; NeBP
Watchmaker's Shop, The. *Unknown.* BoTP
Watchman, The. Abraham Reisen, *tr. fr. Yiddish by* Joseph Leftwich. TrJP
Watchman, Tell Us of the Night. Sir John Bowring. SoP; TreFS
(What of the Night?) VA
Watchman, watchman on your height. The Watchman. Abraham Reisen. TrJP
Watchman, What of the Night? Isaiah, XXI: 11-15, Bible, *O.T.* AWP
Watchman, What of the Night? Swinburne. WiR
Watchman, what of the night? Prologue to Morning. Hermann Hagedorn. MaRV
Watchmen have waited on Capitol Hill, The. Signal Fires. Edward Everett Hale. From Potomac to Merrimac, II. PAH
Water. Hilda Conkling. ExPo; NP; PDV; TiPo
Water. John R. Crossland. BoTP
Water. Emerson. AmPP (5th ed.); PoEL-4
Water. Philip Larkin. PoeP
Water. Robert Lowell. OPoP; TDP
Water, *sel.* Kathleen Raine.
"There is a stream that flowed before the first beginning." ImOP
Water. Anne Sexton. CoPo
Water and Air. Robert Browning. *Fr.* Pauline. OBRV
Water and Shadow. Marya Zaturenska. SiSw
Water Babies, The, *sels.* Charles Kingsley.
Lost Doll, The. FaPON; MoShBr; MPB; OTPC; PRWS; SoPo; TVC
("I once had a sweet little doll, dears.") TiPo
(Song: "I once had a sweet little doll, dears.") PaPo
Tide River, The. BoNaP; HBV; PoVP; PTK
(Clear and Cool.) GN
Young and Old. BiCB; FaBoBe; FaFP; GTBS; GTBS-W; GTSL; HBV; InP; LiTG; MCCG; OTPC; PoMa; PoLF; PoVP; SiTL; TreF; TSW
(Old, Old Song, The.) MaRV
(Old Song, The.) CBEP; NeHB; OBVV; PG; TOP; WaKn
(Song: "When all the world is young, lad.") YAT
(When All the World Is Young.) BBV (1923 ed.); BoTP; LiTL; ViBoPo
Water-Boy. *Unknown.* TrGrPo
Water brimmed against the shore. Lake, Mountain, Tree. Dennis Glover. AnNZ
Water Color. Stephen Mooney. NYBP
Water Color of Grantchester Meadows. Sylvia Plath. NYBP
Water-Colour of Venice, A. Lawrence Durrell. FaBoMo; MoBrPo (1962 ed.)
Water-Course, The. George Herbert. MaMe
Water down the rocky wall, The. The Bunyip. Douglas Stewart. MoAuPo; OA
Water, for anguish of the solstice—nay. For "A Venetian Pastoral" by Giorgione. Dante Gabriel Rossetti. PoVP; VA; ViBoPo
Waterfront. Oliver Jenkins. EtS
Water-Front. Cecil ffrench Salkeld. OnYI
Water-Front Streets. Langston Hughes. OCS

Water Glass of Whisky, A. X. J. Kennedy. CoPo
Water has no color. Ilo Orleans. RIS
Water has no taste at all. Water. John R. Crossland. BoTP
Water hen is hopping, A. May Evening. Eileen Brennan. NeIP
Water-Images. Mary Elizabeth Osborn. NePoAm-2
Water in the creek glides by, The. Friction. Esther Pinch. PoMa
Water Is Burred with Rain, The. Allen Curnow. *Fr.* Not in Narrow Seas. AnNZ
Water is cool, there is a faint smile, The. A Bather in a Painting. Ashton Greene. NePoAm
Water Island. Howard Moss. CoAP; NePoEA-2; NYBP; TDP
Water Jewels. Mary Frances Butts. *See* Million Little Diamonds, A.
Water Lady, The. Thomas Hood. CH; HBV; VA; ViBoPo
Water-Lilies. Felicia Dorothea Hemans. OTPC
Water-Lilies. Sara Teasdale. MAP; MoAmPo; NeMA
Water-lilies in myriads rocked on the slight undulations. On the Atchafalaya. Longfellow. *Fr.* Evangeline. AA
Water Lily. John Farrar. GFA
Water-Lily, The. John Banister Tabb. AA; ACP; GoBC
Waterlily Fire. Muriel Rukeyser. OPoP
Water-Lion is the God verray, The. King Arthur's Dream. *Unknown.* ACP
Water makes many beds. Emily Dickinson. MWA-2
Water Mill, The. Sarah Doudney. *See* Lesson of the Water Mill, The.
Water Mill, The. Ann Hawkshaw. OTPC (1923 ed.)
Water Music. Lawrence Durrell. TPM
Water Music. Alun Lewis. ChMP; GTBS-D; MemP
Water Music. "Hugh MacDiarmid." GoTS
Water my prison shatters in a prism, The. The Trout. Daryl Hine. CoAP; NYTB
Water Noises. Elizabeth Madox Roberts. BoNaP; GFA; NP; SP
Water-Nymph and the Boy, The, *sel.* Roden Noel.
I Flung Me Round Him. HBV
("I flung me round him.") OBEV (1st ed.); OBVV
Water of life no prophet could divine. A Christening Remembered. Vernon Watkins. FaBoMo
Water of the Mirror Lake, The. A Woman of Yueh. Li Po. OnPM
Water-Ousel, The. Mary Webb. CH
Water Ouzel. William H. Matchett. CoAP; NePoEA; NYBP; PoCh
Water Ouzel, The. Harriet Monroe. NP; OTPC (1946 ed.)
Water Picture. May Swenson. BoNaP; OCS
Water plunges to devour us. Travel Song. Hugo von Hofmannsthal. TrJP
Water pulls nervously whispering satin across cool roots, cold stones. Interval. Joseph Auslander. MAP; MoAmPo (1942 ed.)
Water sings along our keel, The. Armistice. Sophie Jewett. AA
Water Snake. Ethel Jacobson. NYTB
Water Song. Solomon ibn Gabirol, *tr. fr. Hebrew by* Israel Abrahams. TrJP
Water Sprite. Donald Wandrei. FiSC
Water still flows. Illegitimate Things. William Carlos Williams. MoAB; MoAmPo
Water-still is the shade of old Coppelius. Dr. Coppelius. Wrey Gardiner. NeBP
Water strider skates upon the brook, A. Plane Geometer. David McCord. NYBP
Water stumbles after its own level. Rain. Louis Coxe. NYTB
Water the first of elements we hold. To Hiero the Syracusan. Pindar. Olympian Odes, I. EnLi-2; OuHeWo
Water the ground with his tears. The Light. John Holloway. NePoEA
Water, The! the Water! William Motherwell. OTPC; PRWS
Water ticks in the flowerbed, The. The Power. Stan Rice. QAH
Water understands, The. Water. Emerson. AmPP (5th ed.); PoEL-4
Water Wants All Sea, The. Lloyd Frankenberg. NYTB
Water, water, wild-flower. *Unknown.* RIS
Water-Wheel, The. Jack R. Clemo. ChMP
Water Witch, The, *sel.* James Fenimore Cooper.
My Brigantine, *fr. ch.* 15. AA; EtS
Water-Witch, The. Martha Eugenie Perry. CaP
Water, with lidless stare. Narcissus. Charles Gullans. NePoEA
Waterbirds sailing upon the darkness. Petron, the Desert Father. Lawrence Durrell. *Fr.* Eight Aspects of Melissa. NeBP
Watered Lilies, The. Unknown. *See* For the Master's Use.
Waterfall, A. Hugh McMillan. SoP
Waterfall, The. Frank Dempster Sherman. BoChLi; OTPC (1946 ed.); PRWS
Waterfall [*or* Water-Fall], The. Henry Vaughan. AnAnS-1; BWP; CoBE; ILP; MaPo; MeLP; MeP; MePo; NoP; OAEP; OBS; PoAn; PoE; PoEL-2; PoFS; SCEP-1; SeCV-1; StP; ViBoPo, *st.* 1; WiR
Waterfall. Anne Welsh. PeSA
Waterfall and the Eglantine, The. Wordsworth. OTPC
Waterfalls of Stone. Louis Ginsberg. PoMa
Waterfront. *See* Water Front.
Watergaw, The. "Hugh MacDiarmid." GoTS; NeBP; PoIE
Watering Place, The. Propertius, *tr. fr. Latin by* Frances Fletcher. LiTW
Watering Rhyme, A. P. A. Ropes. BoTP
Watering the Horse. Robert Bly. NaP
Waterloo ("There was a sound of revelry by night"). Byron. *Fr.* Childe Harold's Pilgrimage, III. FiP; MCCG; OBRV; PTK; TrGrPo; WaaP; WHA
(Battle of Waterloo, The.) FaFP; TreF
(Eve of the Battle of Waterloo, The.) OTPC
(Eve of Waterloo, The.) BBV, *abr.*; BeLS, *abr.*; FaBoBe; FaBoCh; FaBoEn; FaBV; HBV; OBNC; OnSP; OtMeF; PoG; ShBV-3
(Night before the Battle of Waterloo, The, *abr.*) WBLP
(Night before Waterloo.) GN, *abr.*
("There was a sound of revelry by night.") AnFE; ViBoPo
(Waterloo Eve.) FOL
Waterloo. Sir Aubrey De Vere. HBV
Waterloo Bridge. Christopher Middleton. *Fr.* Herman Moon's Hourbook. NePoEA-2
Waters. Elder Olson. NP
Waters. Kenneth Slessor. NeLNL
Waters above! Eternal springs! The Shower. Henry Vaughan. AtBAP; BoNaP; ChTr; FlW; OBS
Waters are flashing, The. The Fugitives. Shelley. PCH
Waters chased him as he fled, The. Emily Dickinson. MWA-2; PoEL-5
Waters dance on the ocean crest, The. The Conger Eel. Patrick MacGill. OnYI
Waters of Babylon. Louis Untermeyer. AnAmPo
Waters of church windows vaulted in silence. Cathedral by Sea. Norman Levine. PeCV
Waters of Life, The. Humbert Wolfe. MoBrPo; NP
Waters of the Sea. Cecil Goldbeck. EtS
Waters of the world in their cold chasm, The. Waters. Elder Olson. NP
Waters were Thy path, The. The Ship in the Midst of the Sea. Christopher Wordsworth. BePJ
Watershed. Margaret Avison. OBCV
Watershed, The. Alice Meynell. POTE
Waterspout. Luís de Camoes, *tr. fr. Portuguese.* EtS
Waterspout, The. William Hart-Smith. *Fr.* Christopher Columbus. PoAu-2
Waterwall Blues. Howard Moss. MoPo; NePA
Waterwitch, The. *Unknown.* PoAu-1
Watkwenies. Duncan Campbell Scott. PeCV
Watson and the Shark. Paul Petrie. NYTB
Wattle and Myrtle. James Lister Cuthbertson. BoAu
Wattles were sweet with September's rain, The. Beneath the Wattle Boughs. Frances Gill. VA
Watts. Shirley Kaufman. QAH
Watts. Conrad Kent Rivers. BOLo
Wave. Barbara Guest. AmPC
Wave, The. W. S. Merwin. FRC
Wave, The. John Curtis Underwood. EtS
Wave of Cliona, The. James Stephens. CMoP
Wave plunges and the sea-birds cry, The. Power. Duncan Campbell Scott. TwCaPo
Wave that is dark piles white and slips to its death, The. Fishing Season. Val Vallis. PoAu-2
Wave, wave your glorious battle-flags, brave soldier of the North. Gettysburg. Edmund Clarence Stedman. PAH

Wave withdrawing, The. "Dover Beach"—a Note to That Poem. Archibald MacLeish. CBV; NoP
"Wave ye, dark tresses! clust'ring, or apart." Not Gone Yet. John Swanwick Drennan. IrPN
Waverley, *sels.* Sir Walter Scott.
False Love, *fr. ch.* 9. ViBoPo
Hie Away! *fr. ch.* 12. BoTP; MoShBr; MPB; OTPC; PCD; PCH; PRWS; ViBoPo
(Gellatley's Song to the Deerhounds.) OBRV
(Hie Away, Hie Away.) EnRP; TiPo
To an Oak Tree, *fr. ch.* 29. OBNC
Waves. Emerson. *See* Nahant.
Waves. Mary Britton Miller. RePo
Waves. John Perreault. YAP
Waves about Iona dirge, The. To William Sharp. Clinton Scollard. HBV
Waves come rolling, and the billowes rore, The. Sea-Monsters. Spenser. *Fr.* The Faerie Queene, II, 12. AtBAP; FaBoEn
Waves forever move, The. The Sisters. John Banister Tabb. AA; MaRV
Waves Gleam in the Sunshine, The. Heine, *tr. fr. German by* Emma Lazarus. *Fr.* Songs to Seraphine. TrJP
Waves lap lap. Sampan. *Unknown.* WePo
Waves lay down their trail, The. Evening Scene. E. J. Scovell. FaBoMo
Waves of Breffny, The. Eva Gore-Booth. *See* Little Waves of Breffny, The.
Waves on the Sea-Shore, The. Ann Hawkshaw. OTPC (1923 ed.)
Waves rattling pebbles rocked me asleep. Recitative. Ronald McCuaig. PoAu-2
Waves that danced about the rock have gone, The. Grandmother and Child. Ruth Dallas. AnNZ
Waves unbuild the wasting shore, The. Faith Shall Build a Fairer Throne [*or* Heaven]. Oliver Wendell Holmes. MaRV; SoP
Waving a Bough. Boris Pasternak, *tr. fr. Russian by* Babette Deutsch. TrJP
Waving of the Corn, The. Sidney Lanier. AP
Wax. Winfield Townley Scott. ErPo
Waxen and the false grace of tulips, The. Elegy. G. S. Fraser. NeBP
Way, The. William Stanley Braithwaite. Sandy Star and Willie Gee, IV. BANP
Way, The. Leslie Savage Clark. PGD
Way, The. Robert Creeley. AP; LiTM (1970 ed.); NeAP
Way, The. Sidney Henry Morse. HBV
Way, The. Edwin Muir. LOW; SiSw
Way, The. Laura Simmons. ChIP
Way, The. Henry Van Dyke. MaRV; OQP; TRV
Way a child's hands stare through glass, The. The Sickness. Frederick Seidel. CoPo
Way a crow, The. Dust of Snow. Robert Frost. AmPP; BiS; CMoP; InP; MaPo (1969 ed.); MoShBr; MoSiPe; OxBA; PDV; TiPo; UnPo; WePo
Way-ah, we'll pay Paddy Doyle for his boots! Paddy Doyle. *Unknown.* ShS
'Way Down in Cuba. *Unknown.* AmSS
Way Down in Mexico. *Unknown.* CoSo
Way Down South. *Unknown.* EvOK; SoPo
Way down South in Dixie. Song for a Dark Girl. Langston Hughes. AmPP (5th ed.); CDC; IDB; PoNe
Way Down South in Mississippi. Verne Barnes. PoRL
Way down South in the land of cotton, I wrote this song. Crazy Song to the Air of "Dixie." "Andy Lee." AS
Way down South where bananas grow. The Elephant and the Flea. *Unknown.* TrAS
Way down South where I was born. Roll the Cotton Down, *vers.* III. *Unknown.* ShS
Way Down the Ohio, *with music. Unknown.* TrAS
Way down upon de Swanee [*or* Suwanee] Ribber [*or* River]. Old Folks at Home [*or* Swanee River]. Stephen Collins Foster. AA; FaBoBe; FaFP; HBV; InP; PoRL; TreF; WBLP
Way down upon the Wabash. El-a-noy. *Unknown.* AS; TrAS
Way down yonder in the maple swamp. *Unknown.* GoTP
Way feare with thy projectes, noe false fyre, A. Sonnet. William Alabaster. MeP
Way, hay, there she rises. Early in the Morning. *Unknown.* AmSS
Way her breasts meet is hidden from me, The. Old Fellow. Ernest Walsh. ErPo
'Way high up in the Mokiones, among the mountain tops. High Chin Bob. *Unknown.* SCC
Way high up in the Syree Peaks. Tying a Knot in the Devil's Tail. *Unknown.* ABF
'Way high up the Mogollons. The Glory Trail. Badger Clark. IHA; SCC; StPo
Way I Pray, The. Whitney Montgomery. SoP
Way I read a letter's—this, The. Emily Dickinson. AmePo; CoBA; DiPo
Way I would look at the world, the houses, The. Statute. Josephine Miles. FiMAP
Way is dark, my child, The! but leads to light. I Will Take Thy Hand. *Unknown.* SoP
Way is long and dreary, The. The Pilgrims. Adelaide Anne Procter. UnPo
Way My Ideas Think Me, The. José Garcia Villa. AnFE; CoAnAm; EaLo; TwAmPo
Way O Christ Thou Art, The. Ernest De Witt Burton. MaRV
Way of a Cat, The. Margaret E. Bruner. CIV
Way of Cape Race, The. E. J. Pratt. CoBE; EtS; WHW
Way of It, The. John Vance Cheney. HBV
Way of Judging Politics, A. Lou Lipsitz. YAP
Way of Life, The. Joseph V. B. Danquah. ACV
Way of Looking, A. Elizabeth Jennings. NePoEA; PP
Way of many way's A: a god. Doctor Faustus. Geoffrey Hill. NePo-2; NMP
Way of Perfect Love, The, *sel.* Georgiana Goddard King.
Song: "Something calls and whispers, along the city street." HBV
Way of the Air, The. Laura Riding. *Fr.* Three Sermons to the Dead. LiTA
Way of the Cross, The. Joseph I. C. Clarke. CAW
Way of the Cross, The. Leonard Feeney. WHL
Way of the World, The, *sel.* Congreve.
Song: "Love's but the frailty of the mind," *fr.*III. EnLi-1; SeCL; SeEP
Way of the World, The. James Jeffrey Roche. CAW; ChIP; JKCP; WBLP
Way of the World, The. Ryota, *tr. fr. Japanese by* H. G. Henderson. OnPM
Way of the World, The. Ella Wheeler Wilcox. *See* Solitude.
Way out in Californy. Stewball. *Unknown.* ABF
Way Out in Idaho ("Come all you jolly railroad men"), *with music, Unknown.* OuSiCo
Way Out in Idyho ("Remember what I promised you"), *with music. Unknown.* CoSo
'Way out in the land of the setting sun. Home Means Nevada. Bertha Raffetto. PoRL
Way out in western Texas, where the Clear Fork's waters flow. The Cowboy's Christmas Ball. Larry Chittenden. CoSo; SCC
Way-Out Morgan. Gwendolyn Brooks. BP
Way out upon the Platte, near Pike's Peak we were told. A Hit at the Times. A. O. Mcgrew. PoOW
Way Out West. LeRoi Jones. NeAP; NMP
Way Out West. *Unknown.* CoSo
Way Over in the Blooming Garden, *with music. Unknown.* ABF
Way Over in the New Buryin' Groun', *with music. Unknown.* AS
Way ran under boughs of checkered green, The. Wood Witchery. Richard Burton. AnAmPo
Way the Baby Slept, The. James Whitcomb Riley. AA
Way the Baby Woke, The. James Whitcomb Riley. AA
Way the ball, The. The Jump Shooter. Dennis Trudell. QAH
Way, the Truth, and the Life, The. Theodore Parker. ChIP; HBV; MaRV; OQP; TrPWD; WGRP
Way, the Truth, and the Life, The. *Unknown.* BePJ
Way, the Truth, the Life. The. George Washington Doane. *See* Christ, the Way.
Way, The; the Truth; the Life Samuel Judson Porter. BLRP
Way they scrub, The. An Indignant Male. A. B. Ross. BrR; MPB
Way Through, The. Denise Levertov. NeAP
Way through the Woods, The. Kipling. CH; FaBoCh; FaPON; GTBS-D; LoGBV; MCCG; MoVE; OBEV (new ed.); OBNC;

Way (continued)
OBVV; Po; PoSa; POTE; SeCeV; ShBV-2; StP; TDP; ThWaDe; WePo
Way to a Happy New Year, A. Robert Brewster Beattie. OQP
Way to Arcady, The. H. C. Bunner. AA; BOHV; InMe; PFY
Way to Bethlehem, The. Clinton Scollard. OQP
Way to Fairyland, The. Eunice Close. BoTP
Way to Heaven, The. Charles Goodrich Whiting. AA
Way to Hump a Cow, The. E. E. Cummings. AmP; OxBA
Way to Know a Father, The. Robert P. Tristram Coffin. PoRL
Way to Peace, The. Unknown, *tr. fr. Chinese.* SoP
Way to Power, The. Tennyson. *Fr.* Oenone. MaRV; OQP
Way to the River, The. W. S. Merwin. CoAP; NYBP
Way to the Sea, The. Laurence Lerner. NePoEA-2
Way Up on Clinch Mountain. *Unknown. See* Rye Whisky.
Way up on de mountain, Lord! Up on de Mountain. *Unknown.* BoAN-1
Way Up on Old Smoky, *with music. Unknown.* TrAS
Way was long, the wind was cold, The. The Last Minstrel. Sir Walter Scott. *Fr.* The Lay of the Last Minstrel. OTPC; TreFS
Way was rocky, rough, and steep, The. Upheld by His Hand. Grace B. Renfrow. BePJ
Way We Wonder, The. Robert Pack. NePoEA
Wayfarer, The. Stephen Crane. War Is Kind, XIII. AA; AmePo; AmPP (3d ed.); CoBA; LiTA; MAP; MoAmPo; NeMA; NePA; PoMa; WaKn
Wayfarer, The. Padraic Pearse. OxBI
Wayfarer, The/ Perceiving the pathway to truth. The Wayfarer. Stephen Crane. War Is Kind, XIII. AA; AmePo; AmPP (3d ed.); CoBA; LiTA; MAP; MoAmPo; NeMA; PoMa; WaKn
Wayfarers, The. Rupert Brooke. MoLP
Wayfarers. Dana Burnet. EtS
Wayfarers on the dusty road. By Shaded Wells. Bhartrihari. OnPM
Wayfarer's Song. Henry W. Frost. SoP
Wayland learned bitterly banishment's Ways. Deor's Lament. *Unknown.* BEL
Wayne at Stony Point. Clinton Scollard. MC; PAH
Ways, The. John Oxenham. HBMV; MaRV; PoLF; PoMa; TIHL; TRV
(High Way and a Low, A.) OQP
Ways and Means. "Lewis Carroll." *See* White Knight's Song, The.
Ways o' Men, The. Angelina Weld Grimké. CDC
Ways of Death, The. W. E. Henley. OQP
Ways of God to Men, The. Milton. *Fr.* Samson Agonistes. OBS
(Choruses from "Samson Agonistes.") SeCeV
Ways of Love, The. Jami, *tr. fr. Persian by* F. Hadland Davis. OnPM
Ways of the Gods, The. Stanton A. Coblentz. OQP
Ways of Trains, The. Elizabeth J. Coatsworth. BoChLi (1950 ed.); SoPo; TiPo
Ways of Traveling. Alice Wilkins. GFA
Ways of War. Lionel Johnson. AnIV
Ways to learn to be. On Re-Reading the Complete Works of an Elder Poet. Winfield Townley Scott. ML
Wayside, The. James Herbert Morse. AA
Wayside cherry tree, A. Hokku. Basho. InP
Wayside Inn, The. Longfellow. Tales of a Wayside Inn: Prelude, Pt. I. CoBA
Wayside Shrine. Gertrude Ryder Bennett. ChIP
Wayside Station, The. Edwin Muir. FaBoTw; MoVE
Wayside Virgin, The. Langdon Elwyn Mitchell. AA
Way-Side Well, The. Joseph Seamon Cotter, Sr. CDC; PoNe
Wayward Child. David Llorens. TNV
Wayworn and weary. The Good Companion. Belle F. Owens. ChIP
Wayworn pilgrim from a distant shore, A. Knowest Thou Isaac Jogues? Francis W. Grey. CAW
Wayzgoose, The, *sel.* Roy Campbell.
"Attend my fable if your ears be clean." BoSA
Wazir Dandan for Prince Sharken, The. *Unknown, tr. fr. Arabic by* E. Powys Mathers. *Fr.* The Thousand and One Nights. AWP; JAWP; WBP
We. Mary Carolyn Davies. GaP
We. Vladimir Kirillov, *tr. fr. Russian by* Alexander Kaun. LiTW
We. Phyllis C. Michael. SoP
We?/ whee! The Next Next Shortest Poem in the World. Martha Salemme. SiTL
We Achieve Our Joy. *Unknown, tr. fr. Chinese by* Bernhard Karlgren. *Fr.* Shi King. ChLP
We ain't no saints on the Bar-Z ranch. Bar-Z on a Sunday Night. Percival Combes. SCC
We all/ came screaming into the world. Equality. Herman L. McMillan. TNV
We all are [*or* are all] blind, until we see. Man-making. Edwin Markham. MaRV; OQP; PGD
We all gonna stop sliding stuff, tighten. Nittygritty. Joseph Bevans Bush. WSL
We all look on with anxious eyes. When Father Carves the Duck. Ernest Vincent Wright. FaBV; FaFP; PoLF; PoSC; TreF
We All Make Mistakes. W. H. Auden. *See* Watch Any Day.
We all were lonely and bereft. The Spirit of Victory. William H. Hudnut, Sr. SoP
We already and first of all discern him making this thing. Rite and Fore-Time. David Jones. *Fr.* The Anathemata. AtBAP
We always drive along until. The Harper's Farm. Dorothy Aldis. RIS
We always had to do our work at night. Before Action. Leon Gellert. BoAV
We always like a rainy day. A Rainy Day. Emily Blackmore Stapp. GFA
We Am Clim'in' Jacob's Ladder, *with music. Unknown.* BoAN-1
We and the little cheerful goldfinch. Two Angels. Richard Monckton Milnes. OBRV
We Are. Robert Hershon. ThO
We are a band of shanty boys. The Merry Shanty Boys. *Unknown.* IHA
We are a meadow where the bees hum. Bedtime. Denise Levertov. FRC; NaP; TwCP
We are a part of this rough land. Our Heritage. Jesse Stuart. AmFN
We are a people living in shells and moving. The British. A. S. J. Tessimond. ChMP
We Are All a Panning, *with music.* Mart Taylor. SGR
We are all blind until we see. *See* We all are blind. . .
We are all here. The Family Meeting. Charles Sprague. HBV
We are all in the dumps. *Unknown.* OxNR; SiTL
We are all near to death. But in my friends. One Who Watches. Siegfried Sassoon. TrJP
We Are All Nodding, *with music. Unknown.* FTB
We are all of us dreamers of dreams. Dreamer[s] of Dreams. William Herbert Carruth. MaRV; OQP; PoLF
We are all rushing through the world. Rushing Panic in San Francisco. *Unknown.* SGR
We Are All Workmen. Rainer Maria Rilke, *tr. fr. German by* Babette Deutsch. EaLo
We Are Alone. Anna Bunston de Bary. MemP
We are approaching sleep: the chestnut blossoms in the mind. Awakening. Robert Bly. NaP
We are as [*or* the] clouds that veil the midnight moon. Mutability. Shelley. BEL; BoLiVe; CBEP; CoBE; EPN; ERoP-2; HBV; ToP
We are as mendicants who wait. The Mendicants. Bliss Carman. HBV; VA
We are assembled here today. Song of the Argonauts. Sam C. Upham. SGR
We are at the hauling then hoping for it. W. S. Graham. *Fr.* The Night-fishing. FIW
We are born and pass on so quickly! Man. Marvin Stevens. MaRV
We are born, then cry. Life. "N. C." SeCL
We are born; we laugh; we weep. Life. "Barry Cornwall." VA
We Are Brethren A'. Robert Nicoll. HBV
We are bringing back some canceled notes. Dividends. Hubert Creekmore. WaP
We are budding, Master, budding. The Master and the Leaves. Thomas Hardy. PoIE
We are building in sorrow or joy. Building for Eternity. N. B. Sargent. BLPA
We are but a bleary blink. Recessional for the Class of 1959 of a School for Delinquent Negro Girls. Joseph R. Cowen. PoNe (1970 ed.)

"We are but clay," the preacher saith. Clay. E. V. Lucas. HBV
We are but two—the others sleep. The Brothers. Charles Sprague. AA
We Are Children. Robert Buchanan. VA
We are children of the sun. Children of the Sun. Fenton Johnson. BANP
We are climbing Jacob's ladder. Jacob's Ladder. *Unknown.* MaRV
We are coming, Cuba, coming; our starry banner shines, The Gathering. Herbert Swett. PAH
We are coming, Father Abraham, three hundred thousand more. Three Hundred Thousand More. James Sloan Gibbons. PaA; PAH; PoFr
We are done with little thinking. The Bigger Day. G. E. Bishop. WBLP
We are fishermen in a flat scene. Water. Anne Sexton. CoPo
We Are Four Bums, *with music.* *Unknown.* AS
We are friends. My Mind and I. Hilda Conkling. NP
We are gazing now on old Tom Moore. *See* You are gazing now. . .
We are ghost-ridden. The Dead Moon. Danske Bedinger Dandridge. AA
We are glad to have birds in our roof. Against Death. Peter Redgrove. NMP; OPoP
We Are God's Chosen Few. Swift. TRV
We are going on a journey. The Journey. Aidan Clarke. BoTP
We are here in a wood of little beeches. The Sign. Frederic Manning. NP
We are here on the central plaza. Voice of the Announcer. Archibald MacLeish. *Fr.* The Fall of the City. HoPM
We are in love's land today. Love at Sea. Swinburne, *after* Gautier. AWP; HBV; SiSw; TOP; VA
We are large with pity, slow and awkward. False Country of the Zoo. Jean Garrigue. LiTM (1970 ed.)
We are led on. Juvenal. *Fr.* The Satires. PoPl
We are light. Laughter. Miriam Waddington. WHW
We are little airy creatures. A Riddle [*or* The Five]. Swift. GN; OnYI; OTPC; RIS
We Are Living, We Are Dwelling. Arthur Cleveland Coxe. *See* Present Age, The.
We are na fou, we're nae that fou. Willie Brewed a Peck o' Maut. Burns. AWP; BEL; CEP; EnLit; JAWP; TOP; WBP
We Are Never Old. Emerson. *Fr.* The World-Soul. OQP; PoRL
We are no other than a moving row. Fatalism. Omar Khayyám, *tr. by* Edward Fitzgerald. *Fr.* The Rubáiyát. MaRV
We Are Not Cast Away. Plotinus, *tr. fr. Greek.* MaRV
We are not come to wage a strife. The Daybreakers [*or* Day-Breakers]. Arna Bontemps. AmNP; BP; CDC; GoSl; IDB; PoNe
We are not here to play, to dream, to drift. Speak Out. Maltbie D. Babcock. SoP
We Are Not Mantan. Herschell Johnson. WSL
We are not sure of sorrow. Swan Song. Swinburne. OtMeF
We are not told his name—this "rich young ruler." The Rich Young Ruler. *Unknown.* SoP
We are not wholly blest who use the earth. Charles Mair. *Fr.* Dreamland. CaP
We are nude beneath our costumes. The Metaphysical Paintings. John Perreault. ANYP
We are old. Sons of Belial. Lola Ridge. PFY
We are our fathers' sons: let those who lead us know! No Hint of Stain. William Vaughn Moody. *Fr.* An Ode in Time of Hesitation. AA
We are poor and lowly born. The Child's Hymn. Mary Howitt. GoTP
We are quite sure. He Will Give Them Back. "George Klingle." BLRP; SoP
We are resting here in the twilight. Compline. Duncan Campbell Scott. GoBC
We are secret things on the sky. We Are. Robert Hershon. ThO
We Are Seven. Wordsworth. BLPA; EnLi-2; EnRP; EPN; FaPL; GN; HBV; MBW-2; MERP; NeHB; OnPP; PoE; TreF; WBLP
We are sighing for you, far land. The Far Land. John Hall Wheelock. WGRP
We are so lonely—all of us. Each in His Inmost Heart. John D. Sheridan. JKCP (1955 ed.)
We are sons of mighty Manitou. The Red Ghosts Chant. Lilian White Spencer. PoOW
We are souls in hell, who hear no gradual music. A Prayer from 1936. Siegfried Sassoon. TrPWD
We are standing in the great dawn of a day they did not know. Odell Shepard. *Fr.* In the Dawn. MaRV
We are such little men when the stars come out. Starry Night. Hermann Hagedorn. MaRV
We Are Such Stuff as Dreams. Petronius Arbiter, *tr. fr. Latin by* Howard Mumford Jones. AWP
We are such stuff as dreams are made of, and these. Poem. Hugo von Hofmannsthal. LiTW
We are the age predestined to lie fallow. The Young Dead Speak. Sister Mary Irma. JKCP (1955 ed.)
We are the Ancient People. The Song of the Ancient People. Edna Dean Proctor. AA
We Are the Burden-Bearers! *abr.* William L. Stidger. PGD
We are the clouds that veil the midnight moon. *See* We are as clouds. . .
We are the fallen, who, with helpless faces. The Prayer of Beaten Men. William Hervey Woods. *Fr.* The House of Broken Swords. HBV
We are the frogs who will not turn to princes. Rebels from Fairy Tales. Hyacinthe Hill. WOW
We are the hollow men. The Hollow Men. T. S. Eliot. AP; APA; BoLiVe (1945 ed.); CoAnAm; CoBE; CoBMV; DiPo; EnL; ForPo; LiTA; LiTM; MAP; MAPA; MBW-2; MoAB; MoAmPo; NAMP; NeMA; OBMV; PAn; PIA; Po; PoPl; POTE; TwAmPo
We are the homeless, even as you. To Poets. Charles Hamilton Sorley. LO
We are the lovers of Local 1. Theme Song for a Songwriters' Union. Al Graham. WhC
We Are the Music-Makers. Arthur O'Shaughnessy. *See* Ode: "We are the music-makers."
We are the one for which all light. A Single Candle as the Presence of God. Gregory Orr. QAH
We are the only ones who will remember. Secret. Catherine Haydon Jacobs. GoYe
We are the partly real ones. The Moon Worshippers. Eric Robertson Dodds. POTE
We are the Pilgrims, master; we shall go. The Golden Road. James Elroy Flecker. *Fr.* Hassan. OtMeF
We are the roadside flowers. Roadside Flowers. Bliss Carman. HBMV
We are the singing shadows beauty casts. Eagle Sonnets, XX. Clement Wood. HBMV
We are the toilers whom God hath barred. The Song of the Unsuccessful. Richard Burton. OQP; WGRP
We are the trees. Song of the Trees. Mary Colborne-Veel. BoAu
We are the whirlwinds that winnow the West. The Vigilantes. Margaret Ashmun. SCC
We are they that go, that go. The Fugitives. Florence Wilkinson Evans. OQP
We are they who come faster than fate. War Song of the Saracens. James Elroy Flecker. *Fr.* Hassan. FaBV; FOL; MoBrPo; OBVV; OtMeF; ShBV-2; WHA
We are thine, O Love, being in thee and made of thee. Hymn to Love. Lascelles Abercrombie. *Fr.* Emblems of Love. OBEV (new ed.); OBVV
We are things of dry hours and the involuntary plan. Kitchenette Building. Gwendolyn Brooks. BALP; NoP; PoNe
We are those same children who amazed. Prelude XXIII. Stefan George. WaaP
We are three brethren come from [*or* out of] Spain. Three Knights from Spain. *Unknown.* AtBAP; CH; OxNR; RIS
We are tired who follow after. Natural Magic. "Æ." BEL
We are trained and quiet intellectuals. On Being Invited to a Testimonial Dinner. William Stafford. NePoAm-2
We are travelling west of Alice Springs, and Sam is at the wheel. West of Alice. W. E. Harney. NeLNL; PoAu-1
We are true lovers without hope. By Moonlight. May Sarton. MoLP
We are trying to carry this timber to the building. Timber. *Unknown.* AS
We are two countries girded for the war. Foreign Affairs. Stanley Kunitz. LiTM (1970 ed.); NYBP; TwAmPo

We are two eagles. The Flight. Sara Teasdale. HBMV; MAP; MoAmPo; NP; WHA
We are two people. Refrain. Joseph Cardarelli. QAH
We are two travellers, Roger and I. The Vagabonds. John Townsend Trowbridge. AA; BeLS; BLPA; OnPP; PCD; TreFS
We are unfair. We Own the Night. LeRoi Jones. BOLo
We are upon the Scheldt. We know we•move. Antwerp to Ghent. Dante Gabriel Rossetti. *Fr.* A Trip to Paris and Belgium. MeVV
We are used to the murmur. Engine Failure. Timothy Corsellis. WaP
We are very little creatures. A E I O U. Swift. *See also* We are little airy creatures. BoTP.
We are very slightly changed. A General Summary. Kipling. HBV
We are watching for someplace to eat. After Dinner We Take a Drive into the Night. Tony Towle. ANYP
We are what suns and winds and waters make us. Regeneration [*or* Invocation]. Walter Savage Landor. VA; ViBoPo
We are what we are made; each following day. Written in Naples. Emerson. CoBA
We arrived at Sok To. Guerrilla Camp. Keith Wilson. TPM
We ask and are answered not. God Knows. *Unknown.* SoP
We ask for peace. We, at the bound. Surrender. Angelina Weld Grimké. CDC
We ask not that the slave should lie. Abolitionist Hymn. *Unknown.* TrAS
We ate our breakfast lying on our backs. Breakfast. W. W. Gibson. OBMV
We ate with steeps of sky about our shoulders. The Terrace. Richard Wilbur. MiAP
We be simple shepherds. Shepherds' Song. Norah M. Holland. ChrBoLe
We Be Soldiers Three. *Unknown.* ChTr
We be the King's men, hale and harty. Men Who March Away. Thomas Hardy. *Fr.* The Dynasts, Pt. I. CH
We Be Three Poor Mariners, *with music. Unknown.* AmSS
We Bear About No Cats' Skins. *Unknown.* NCEP
We bear sealed orders o'er life's weltered sea. Sealed Orders. Richard Burton. HBV; OQP
We Bear the Strain of Earthly Care. Ozora Stearns Davis. TRV (Our Brother Christ.) MaRV
We being so hidden from those who. The Children Look at the Parents. A. S. J. Tessimond. ChMP
We ben chapman lyght of fote. *Unknown.* EnPo
We bern abowtyn non cattes skynnys. We Bear About No Cats' Skins. *Unknown.* NCEP
We bless Thee for Thy peace, O God. Thy Peace, O God. *Unknown.* SoP
We both were five and we both were wild. The Chronicle of Meola Creek. Keith Sinclair. AnNZ
We Break New Seas Today. John Oxenham. OQP
We break the glass, whose sacred wine. Song. Edward Coote Pinkney. AmLP; HBV
We brought a rug for sitting on. The Picnic. Dorothy Aldis. TiPo (1952 ed.)
We brought him home, I was so pleased. My New Rabbit. Elizabeth Gould. BoTP
We brush the other, invisible moon. Sleep. William Knott. YAP
We build an altar here, and pray. Home Dedication. *Unknown.* FaChP
We built/ a pregnant dead hermaphrodite snowman. Child at Sand. Robert Hershon. ThO
We built a hut, my brother and I. The Hut. Hilda Van Stockum. BrR
We built a ship upon the stairs. A Good Play. Robert Louis Stevenson. FaPON; GFA; MoShBr; MPB; OTPC; StVeCh (1940 ed.); TiPo
We built our love up like a work of art. Dirge. Louis Johnson. AnNZ
We buried him darkly at dead of night. Paul Dehn. PV
We by no shining Galilean lake. Vision. Edward Dowden. ChIP; OQP
We call him "Lord" and believe his word. Disagreeing with God. Beverly Haglund. SoP
We call up the green to hide us. Summer Wish. Louise Bogan. AnFE; CoAnAm; TwAmPo
We call you Mother of our Lord and Savior. Hymn for Laudes; Feast of Our Lady, Help of Christians. *Unknown.* ISi
We called him "Rags," he was just a cur. Rags. Edmund Vance Cooke. BLPA
We came by boat in the late arctic twilight. Visit by Water. Floris Clark McLaren. OBCV
We came from the hills where the hot winds blow. In Town. David McKee Wright. ACV
We came that way by choice. A Traveller's Tale. William Plomer. BoSA
We came to Tamichi in 1880. Song. Scott Judy *and* "Doc" Hammond. PoOW
We came to the church that was left to wind and rain. Church of the Holy Innocents, Dunedin. "Robin Hyde." ACV
We came to the high cliffs of Bonaventure. Long-billed Gannets. Frances D. Emery. GoYe
We came to the islands. We came saying. The Quest. Harold Vinal. GoYe
We came to visit the cow. Freedom, New Hampshire. Galway Kinnell. NaP
We came upon the village of the dead. Sleeping Village. Harold Vinal. FiSC
We can no longer stay on shore. The Greenland Whale Fishery. *Unknown.* BaBo
We can only see a little of the ocean. God's Love. *Unknown.* BLRP
We can slide. Sliding. Myra Cohn. SiSoSe
We cannot all be Washingtons. Like Washington. *Unknown.* DD; HH
We cannot go to the country. Raleigh Was Right. William Carlos Williams. AmPP (5th ed.); CBV; PP
We cannot kindle when we will. Morality. Matthew Arnold. EPN; GTBS; GTSL; HBV; MaRV; OQP; PoVP; SoP; TOP; TRV; ViPo; ViPP
We cannot look beyond. Light. Grace Wilkinson. OQP
We cannot rest, whose hearts are like the breakers. Architects of Dreams. Lucia Trent. PGD
We cannot retrace our steps. Gertrude Stein. *Fr.* The Mother of Us All. CrMA
We cannot tell how often as we pray. Let Us Pray. Ralph Spaulding Cushman. FaChP
We cannot trap them in our zoos, oh, no! Dinosaurs. Carolyn Stoloff. NYBP
We can't afford to win the gain. Things We Can't Afford. *Unknown.* SoP
We can't give them up, though. Avant Garde. Louis Dudek. *Fr.* Provincetown. MoCV
We can't tonight! We're overworked and busy. Tonight. Franklin P. Adams. FiBHP
We care not for money, riches or wealth. Drinking Song. Thomas Randolph. *Fr.* Aristippus. SeCL
We Cared for Each Other. Heine, *tr. fr. German by* John Todhunter. AWP
We caught the tread of dancing feet. The Harlot's House. Oscar Wilde. MoBrPo; PoVP; StP; SyP; ViPP
We chanced in passing by that afternoon. The Black Cottage. Robert Frost. AmPP; CoBA; MWA-2
We climb'd the steep where headless Edwin lies. The Old Parish Church, Whitby. Hardwicke Drummond Rawnsley. OBVV
We climbed the height by the zigzag path. The Zigzag Path. *Unknown.* SoP
We climbed to it by secret flights. The Enchanted Castle. Jeanne D'Orge. AnAmPo
We climbed to the top of Goat Point hill. Forty Years After. H. H. Porter. BOHV
We cobblers lead a merry life. The Cobblers' Song [*or* Strumbo, Dorothy, Trumpart, Cobbling Shoes]. *At. to* George Peele, *also at. to* Charles Tilney. *Fr.* Locrine. OBSC; TuPP
We come by a terrible gate. Eden; or One View of It. Theodore Spencer. LiTM; NePA
We come to another place. Mathematics. Joel Oppenheimer. CoPo
We come to music for defense. Night Concert. Virginia Earle. JKCP (1955 ed.)
We come to your doorstep. A Carol for Christmas Eve. Eleanor Farjeon. BoChLi
We come together once more, we four, in the center. Head Couples. William H. Matchett. NYBP
We come, we come, we come. A Hymn of Unity. Robert Freeman. OQP

We Conquer or Die. James Pierpont. MC; PAH
We could be going home. The Second Angel. Philip Levine. NaP
We could get the whole town out on a Tuesday night. Summer Concert. Reed Whittemore. AmFN
We could have crossed the road but hesitated. The Interrogation. Edwin Muir. CMoP; LiTB; SeCePo
We could not pause, while yet the noontide air. Obsequies of Stuart. John Reuben Thompson. PAH
We couldn't even keep the furnace lit! To Delmore Schwartz. Robert Lowell. NMP; OPoP
We count the broken lyres that rest. The Voiceless. Oliver Wendell Holmes. *Fr.* The Autocrat of the Breakfast Table. AA; CoBA; ViBoPo
We crawled and cried and laughed. Autobiography. Mbella Sonne Dipoko. TTY
We crazed for you, aspired and fell for you. The Knights to Chrysola. Rachel Annand Taylor. OBVV
We cried: Good luck! and watched them go. The Last Ascent. John Lehmann. ChMP
We cross a stream and my horse. Under the Frontier Post. Wang Chang-ling. ChTr
We cross the prairie as of old. The Kansas Emigrants. Whittier. CoBA; MC; PaA; PAH
We crossed Brook Cedron to Gethsemane. Malchus. Ida Norton Munson. ChIP
We crossed by ferry to the bare island. By Ferry to the Island. Iain Crichton Smith. BoPe
We crown'd the hard-won heights at length. After the Battle. Richard Chenevix Trench. VA
We curl into your eyes. The Female God. Isaac Rosenberg. FaBoTw
We Dance Like Ella Riffs. Carolyn M. Rodgers. TNV
We dance round in a ring and suppose. The Secret Sits. Robert Frost. LOW; SoPo
. . . We danced/ Shyly, not speaking, more as partial friends. Christopher Hassall. *Fr.* Soliloquy to Imogen. LO
We dedicate a church today. Dedication. Ethel Arnold Tilden. MaRV; OQP; SoP
We Delighted, My Friend. Léopold Sédar Senghor, *tr. fr. French by* Miriam Koshland. PBA; TTY
We descended the first night from Europe riding the ship's sling. Coming Back to America. James Dickey. NYBP
We did not dare to breathe a prayer. Hope. Oscar Wilde. *Fr.* The Ballad of Reading Gaol. MaRV
We did not know his unfamiliar head. Archaic Torso of Apollo. Rainer Maria Rilke. LiTW; PIA
We Didn't Know. Tom Paxton. PPON
We digged our trenches on the down. Song of the Dark Ages. Francis Brett Young. HBMV
We do accept thee, heavenly Peace! Acceptation. Margaret Junkin Preston. MC; PAH
We do assemble that a funeral. An Elegy in Memory of the Worshipful Major Thomas Leonard Esq. Samuel Danforth, Jr. SCAP
We Do Lie beneath the Grass. Thomas Lovell Beddoes. *See* Dirge: "We do lie beneath the grass."
We do not find Him on the difficult earth. Christmas Night. Alice Meynell. StJW
We do not know the ports from which we sail. The Stars Are True. *Unknown.* MaRV
We do not know this thing. Vale, Amor! "Fiona Macleod." PoVP
We do not know—we can but deem. The Hero. Ambrose Bierce. OQP; PoRL
We do not know who made them. Negro Spirituals. Rosemary Benét *and* Stephen Vincent Benét. AmFN; FaPON
We do not like to look out of the same window. Chorus. T. S. Eliot. *Fr.* The Family Reunion. MWA-2
We do not play on graves. Emily Dickinson. MoVE; PoEL-5; StP
We do not see them come. Scala Coeli. Kathleen Raine. NYBP
We Don't Get No Justice Here in Atlanta, *with music.* *Unknown.* OuSiCo
We don't know. Land of the Free. Archibald MacLeish. AmFN
We don't like your white cottage. Strangers. R. S. Thomas. NMP
We Don't Need No Music. Janice Marie Gadsden. WSL
We doubted our God in secret. Resurgam. Theodosia Garrison. MaRV
We drank Thunderbird all night. Poem. James T. Stewart. BF
We dream—it is good we are dreaming. Emily Dickinson. MWA-2
We drive this Sunday south into the country. Baptism. Charles G. Bell. AmFN
We drove—our autoload gang—through the growing season. Rogue Pearunners. R. G. Everson. PeCV (1967 ed.)
"We dwell in Him,"—Oh, everlasting Home. In Him. Annie Johnson Flint. BLRP; SoP; TRV
We eat and drink and laugh and energize. Death's Transfiguration. Israel Zangwill. TrJP
We eat and hear, as your kiss descends. Elegy. Tony Towle. ANYP; YAP
We enter the dismal wood where boughs black. The Wood of the Self-Destroyers. Samuel Yellen. NePoAm-2
We entered the city at noon! High bells. The radio on. One Night Stand. LeRoi Jones. NeAP
We Exist Living Dead. Jacques Wakefield. BF
We face the nations with one hand outstretched. Armistice. Eunice Mitchell Lehmer. PGD
We fancied he'd share in our cause. What's in It for Me? Edgar A. Guest. PoToHe (new ed.)
We fear to judge a watermelon. A Comparison. *Unknown.* STF
We feared the incubus, the hex. The Woods Grow Darker. Leah Bodine Drake. FiSC
We feed the birds in winter. Joe. David Mccord. TiPo (1959 ed.)
We feed the chickens every day. Off We Go to Market. Gwen A. Smith. BoTP
We fell in Dirphys' straits. At public cost. Sacrifice of Youth. Simonides. OnPM
We fight. I am clubbed from behind. Terminal Theater. Robert Sward. CoPo
We finished clearing the last. Above Pate Valley. Gary Snyder. CoAP; NaP
We Fish. Herman Melville. *Fr.* Mardi. GoTP
We follow where the Swamp Fox guides. The Swamp Fox. William Gilmore Simms. AA; AmePo; BeLS; DD; FaBoBe; MC; PaA; PAH
We followed them into the west. The West. Edwin Muir. MoVE
We fought you once—but that was long ago! Britons and Guests. Edith M. Thomas. PaA
We galloped over the glossy sea. W. B. Yeats. *Fr.* The Wanderings of Oisin. SeCePo
We gave her a discardment. The Discardment. Alan Paton. BoSA
We gazed on Corryvrekin's whirl. Iona. Arthur Cleveland Coxe. AA
We get no good/ By being ungenerous. Reading [*or* "Good from a Book"]. Elizabeth Barrett Browning. *Fr.* Aurora Leigh, I. GN; HH; PoRL
We git up in de mornin' so dog-gone soon. Levee Camp "Holler." *Unknown.* ABF
We Give Thee but Thine Own. William Walsham How. FaChP; MaRV; STF
We give Thee thanks, O Lord! Thanksgiving Day. Robert Bridges. MaRV; OHIP
We glibly talk. The Miracle of Spring. Piet Hein. TIHL
We Go. Karl Wolfskehl, *tr. fr. German by* Carol North Valhope *and* Ernst Morwitz. TrJP
We go from God to God—then though. Journey's End. Evelyn H. Healey. MaRV
We Go No More to the Forest. Mary Colborne-Veel. BoAu
We Go Out Together. Kenneth Patchen. MoAmPo (1950 ed.)
We go wading in the winter. Four Kinds of Wading. Mildred D. Shacklett. GFA
"We grasp our battle spears: we don our breast-plates of hide." The Battle. Chu Yuan, *tr. by* Arthur Waley. WaaP
We Grow Out of Iron. Aleksey Kapitonovich Gastev, *tr. fr. Russian by* Babette Deutsch *and* Avrahm Yarmolinsky. WoL
We grow to the sound of the wind. Dates. *Unknown. Fr.* The Thousand and One Nights. AWP; FaPON; JAWP; LiTW; WBP
We had a circus in our shed. Our Circus. Laura Lee Randall. GFA; TiPo (1952 ed.); UTS

We had a Goblin party on the night of Hallowe'en. Hallowe'en. Helen Wing. GFA
We had a parade for the lady near Livorno. Snapshot: Ambassadress. George Garrett. NePoAm-2
We had a pearl, a jewel that was ours. Sunrise on the Sunset. Wally Ford. WSL
We had a picnic. A Picnic. Aileen Fisher. SoPo
We had a pleasant walk to-day. The Spring Walk. Thomas Miller. OTPC (1923 ed.)
We had, at midnight, flicked the outside light. The Total Calm. Philip Booth. WIRo
We had battered their weakening rush line till it gave like a wisp of grass. Under the Goal Posts. Arthur Guiterman. BBV (1951 ed.)
We had been long in mountain snow. The Greeting of the Roses. Hamlin Garland. AA
We had climbed the last steep flight of stairs. The Bead Mat. Walter de la Mare. CBEP; MoPW
We had expected everything but revolt. Nightmare Number Three. Stephen Vincent Benét. MaC; MoAmPo (1950 ed.)
We had ridden long and were still far from the inn. Sleeping on Horseback. Po Chü-i. LiTW
We had to wait for the heat to pass. August Night. Elizabeth Madox Roberts. YeAr
We had waffles-with-syrup for breakfast. Birthdays. Marchette Chute. BiCB; SiSoSe; StVeCh
We hang the holly up once more. Christmas Singing. Elsie Williams Chandler. ChBR; SiSoSe
We have a bed, and a baby too. The Laborer. Richard Dehmel. AWP; JAWP; WBP; WoL
We Have a Day. Marion Strobel. NP
We have a flash packet, she's a packet of fame. The Clipper Ship *Dreadnaught*. *Unknown.* IHA
We have a lawn of moss. For Doreen. Donald Davie. NMP
We have a little garden. The Garden. Esther Antin. *Fr.* On Our Farm. RiS
We have a mountain at the end of our street. In a Desert Town. Lionel Stevenson. AmFN; StVeCh
We have a past in common now. Second Year in a Seminary. Peter Levi. MemP
We have a pretty witty King. Impromptu on Charles II. Earl of Rochester. ChTr
We have a secret, just we three. The Secret. *Unknown.* BoChLi; MPB (1956 ed.); OTPC (1946 ed.); SoPo; StVeCh (1940 ed.); TiPo; UTS
We have all, one time or another, met a famous figure. Back Room Joys. Justin Richardson. FiBHP
We have an old mother that peevish is grown. The Mother Country. Benjamin Franklin. PAH
We have ascended to this paradise. The Attic. Henri Coulette. NePoEA-2; PoPl; PoRA (rev. ed.)
We have bags and bags of whitest down. Keeping Store. Mary Frances Butts. GFA; OTPC (1946 ed.); PCH; PPL
We have bathed where none have seen us. Bridal Song to Amala [*or* Epithalamia *or* Song at Amala's Wedding]. Thomas Lovell Beddoes. *Fr.* Death's Jest Book. ChER; FaBoEn; LoBV; OBNC; OBVV; PoE; PoEL-4
We Have Been Believers. Margaret Walker. PoNe
We have been cruel in thought. Life's not so sweet. Frank Wilmot. *Fr.* To God; from the Warring Nations. BoAV
We have been dead, our shroud enfolds the sea. To God, from the Warring Nations. Frank Wilmot. BoAu
We have been deeply interested in the words of the song. Alsace or Alsatians. Gertrude Stein. *Fr.* Accents in Alsace. AtBAP
We Have Been Friends Together. Caroline Elizabeth Sarah Norton. VA
We Have Been Happy. Max Eastman. AnEnPo
We have been helping with the cake. Day before Christmas. Marchette Chute. ChBR
We Have Been Here Before. Morris Bishop. EvOK; FiBHP; InMe; NYBP; WhC
We have been shown. Six Variations. Denise Levertov. AmPP (5th ed.); CoPo
We have borne good sons to broken men. Miners' Wives. Joe Corrie. OxBS
We have climbed the mountain. Here in Katmandu. Donald Justice. CoAP
We have come to the jungle. Jungle. Phyllis Haring. PeSA
We have come to your shrine to worship. A Plea for Mercy. Kwesi Brew. PBA
We have come very safely—hitherto. Hitherto. Mary Gorges. SoP
We have cried in our despair. When Helen Lived. W. B. Yeats. CMoP; ViBoPo
We have faith in old proverbs full surely. Where There's a Will There's a Way. Eliza Cook. BLPA; FaFP; TreF
We have fallen on the mattress. Spring Afternoon. John Morgan. YAP
We have fed you all for a thousand years. Labor. *Unknown.* OQP; PGD
We have forgotten Paris, and his fate. Helen Grown Old. Janet Lewis. QFR
We have found our peace, and move with the turning globe. Epithalamium. A. R. D. Fairburn. AnNZ
We have found you out. Arson and Cold Lace. Worth Long. NBP
We have fulfilled our apprehension, hope. Flight into Darkness. Ralph Gustafson. PeCV
We have gone around the field. Charm to Save Cattle. *Unknown.* OnPM
We have heard no nightingales singing. Working Class. Bertram Warr. OBCV; WaP
We have heard the trumpets calling Youth. Youth. Katharine Lee Bates. PGD
We have kept faith, ye Flanders' dead. In Flanders Now. Edna Jaques. CaP; MaRV
We have known sins and evils every day and death we have known. Rabindranath Tagore. *Fr.* The Oarsmen. MaRV
We Have Lived and Loved Together. Charles Jefferys. FaBoBe; NeHB; PoToHe; TreFT
We have lived in that room larger than the world. "The Lyf So Short." John Berryman. ML
We have lived long enough to know. Storm over Rockefeller Center. Raymond Holden. AnAmPo
We have loitered and laughed in the flowery croft. A Garden Lyric. Frederick Locker-Lampson. HBV
We Have Lost Our Little Hanner. "Max Adeler." FiBHP
We have loved each other in this time twenty years. An Unfinished History. Archibald MacLeish. NYBP
We have made hawks. Shaman Song 12. Gene Fowler. ThO
"We have made them fools and weak!" said the Strong Ones. God and the Strong Ones. Margaret Widdemer. HBMV; PoFr; SoP
We have met late—it is too late to meet. A Denial. Elizabeth Barrett Browning. OBNC
We have minted her beauty in multiple golden medallions. Ox-Bone Madonna. John Duffy. ISi
We have much sand along our beach. Fun on the Beach. Alice Wilkins. GFA
We have neither summer nor winter. Nature. H. D. Carberry. PoNe
We have no heart for the fishing, we have no hand for the oar. The Dykes. Kipling. ChMo
We have no time for bridges. Seagulls. Patricia Hubbell. PDV
We have opened the door. The Dead Feast of the Kol-Folk. Whittier. PoEL-4
We have our hopes and fears that flout us. A New Heaven. John Gould Fletcher. MAP; MoAmPo
We Have Paid Enough Long Since in Our Own Blood. Vergil, *tr. fr. Latin by* Richmond Lattimore. *Fr.* Georgics. WaaP
We have sailed many months, we have sailed many weeks. "Lewis Carroll." *Fr.* The Hunting of the Snark. NA
We have saved the soul of the man who killed. What Our Lord Wrote in the Dust. *Unknown.* ChIP; OQP
We have scarcely time to tell thee. Shelly. James McIntyre. FiBHP
We have scotch'd the snake, not kill'd it. Shakespeare. *Fr.* Macbeth, III, ii. AtBAP
We Have Seen His Star in the East. Molly Anderson Haley. ChIP; PGD
We Have Seen Thee, O Love. Swinburne. *Fr.* Atalanta in Calydon. BEL; PoVP
(Chorus: "We have seen thee, O Love.") MaVP; VA
(Choruses from "Atalanta in Calydon.") EnLi-2
We have seen thee, queen of cheese. Queen of Cheese. James McIntyre. FiBHP
We have sent him seeds of the melon's core. Ku-Klux.

Madison Cawein. AA; PAH; ThLM
We have shared beauty and have shared grief, too. A Prayer for a Marriage. Mary Carolyn Davies. TrPWD
We have shot the last whiskey cup from the trapper's head. The Last Whiskey Cup. Paul Engle. ATP; YaD
We have spent the whole day until dusk. The Love Cave. Seami Motokiyo. LiTW
We have struck the regions wherein we are keel or reef. Zone. Louise Bogan. PoCh
We have sweat our share. Stable-Talk. Raymond Knister. CaP
We had taken the long way home, a mile. A Storm in Childhood. T. H. Jones. FlW
We have talent. People call us. To Pi Ssu Yao. Tu Fu. ML
We have the smallest house of all. We. Mary Carolyn Davies. GaP
We have tomorrow. Youth. Langston Hughes. AmFN; BiCB; GoSl
We have tried words before—always in vain. The Knife. Milton Kaplan. TrJP
We have ventur'd our estates. The Cavalier. Alexander Brome. PeRV
We have walked in Love's land a little way. April Love. Ernest Dowson. PG
We have walked, looking at the actual trees. Leaves before the Wind. May Sarton. MoLP; NePoAm
We heard her speaking of Chinese musicians. The Woman Who Disapproved of Music at the Bar. Horace Gregory. MoPo
We heard it calling, clear and low. The Cuckoo. Frederick Locker-Lampson. HBV
We heard the corncrake's call from close at hand. First Corncrake. John Hewitt. NeIP
We heard the phoebe calling in the wood. What We Listened for in Music. Gray Burr. HW
We heard the thrushes by the shore and sea. In Kerry. J. M. Synge. AWP; JAWP; MoBrPo; WBP
We heard them like besiegers down the street. Subway Builders. Lawrence Lee. PoMa
We, Hermia. Helena and Hermia. Shakespeare. *Fr.* A Midsummer Night's Dream, III, ii. GN
We hold these truths to be self-evident. Decoy. John Ashbery. ANYP
We hurry on, nor passing note. Digby Mackworth Dolben. OBNC
We in our wandering. A Song of the Open Road. John Addington Symonds. AWP; JAWP; WBP; WHA
We, innumerable dread legions of labor. We. Vladimir Kirillov. LiTW
We introduce ourselves. Emily Dickinson. CBV
We invoke holy Patrick, Ireland's chief apostle. Prayer to St. Patrick. Ninine. OnYI
We is gathered [*or* gathahed] hyeah, my brothahs. An Ante-Bellum Sermon. Paul Laurence Dunbar. BALP; YT
We issue from the meat of Pineapple Street. On the Island. L. E. Sissman. NYBP
We journey to Eleusis, you and I. The Greater Mystery. John Myers O'Hara. HT
We journeyed through broad woodland ways. A Spring Journey. Alice Freeman Palmer. HBV
We Keep Memorial Day. Kate Brownlee Sherwood. HH
We killed a bat last night. A Bat in the Monastery. John L'Heureux. YAP
We Kiss'd Again with Tears. Tennyson. *See* As thro' the Land at Eve We Went.
We kissed at the barrier; and passing through. On the Departure Platform. Thomas Hardy. BWP; LO; OBNC
We kneel down to pray. Like Orphans. Opal Leonore Gibbs. SoP
We knew it would rain, for all the morn. Before the Rain. Thomas Bailey Aldrich. GN
We knew not that we were to live. Emily Dickinson. MWA-2
We knew so much; when her beautiful eyes could lighten. Sagacity. William Rose Benét. MAP; MoAmPo; NeMA
We knew that he was not a model cat. Elegy. Margaret E. Bruner. CIV
We know as we grow older. Whatever Is—Is Best. Ella Wheeler Wilcox. PoToHe
We know not through what trackless space of night. The Star. Ida Norton Munson. ChIP
We know not what it is, dear, this sleep so deep and still. The Two Mysteries. Mary Mapes Dodge. AA; HBV; MaRV; WGRP
We know not yet what life shall be. Mors et Vita. Samuel Waddington. HBV
We know she lives upon that thorny hill. Jezebel. Scudder Middleton. HBMV
We know the paths wherein our feet should press. Purpose [*or* A Prayer]. John Drinkwater. OQP; SoP
We know the winter earth upon the body of the young President. November 26, 1963. Wendell Berry. AP; LiTM (1970 ed.)
We know Thee, each in part. All in All. John Banister Tabb. OQP
We labor and are heavy-laden. Come unto Me. Katharine Lee Bates. ChIP
We lack, yet cannot fix upon the lack. Later Life,VI. Christina Rossetti. VA
We laugh and we are troubled. The Beating Heart. Heine. UnTE
We lay in the trenches we'd dug in the ground. The Ballad of Bunker Hill. Edward Everett Hale. MC; PAH
We lay together in the sultry night. Summer Storm. Louis Untermeyer. UnTE
We Lay Us Down to Sleep. Louise Chandler Moulton. AA
We learned, and slowly, only. Aviators. Jon Anderson. YAP
We learned to laugh. Although the flying bombs. Rackheath. Coman Leavenworth. *Fr.* Norfolk Memorials. LiTA
We leave the well-beloved place. In Memoriam A. H. H., CII. Tennyson. EnLi-2; EPN; PoEL-5; ViPo; VP
We left/ The silent forest. Charles Mair. *Fr.* Tecumseh. OBCV
We left behind the painted buoy. The Voyage. Tennyson. PoVP; ViPP
We left the city, street and square. John Francis O'Donnell. *Fr.* A July Dawn. IrPN
We left the city when the summer day. Indolence. Robert Bridges. BrPo
We left the homestead at break of day. In the Day's Work. Jessie Litchfield. MoAuPo
We lie by towering hollyhocks. August Night, 1953. Elizabeth B. Harrod. NePoEA
We lift our glad hearts, Lord, in thankfulness. Youth's Thankfulness. Edgar Daniel Kramer. PEDC; PGD
We lift our standard to the mountain top. Manuel María Flores. *Fr.* Ode to the Fatherland. PoFr
We like to go to Granny's house. Taking Turns. Emilie Blackmore Stapp. GFA
We like you, Glorious Dead. The Glorious Survivors. A. E. Coppard. FaBoTw
We listen, wind from where. The Runner with the Lots. Léonie Adams. MoPo; NePA
We Live by Faith. Whittier. OQP
We Live in a Rickety House. Alexander McLachlan. OBCV
We Live in Deeds. Philip James Bailey. *See* Aim of Life, The.
We live in our own world. Children's Song. R. S. Thomas. BoC
We live oblivious of our transformations. Our Movement. Paul Eluard, *tr. by* Stephen Spender *and* Frances Cornford. LiTW
We live, while we see the sun. Pedro Calderón de la Barca. *Fr.* Life Is a Dream. AWP; JAWP; LiTW; PoFr; WBP
We Long to See Jesus. Anna E. Hamilton. BePJ
We look before and after. Our Sweetest Songs. Shelley. *Fr.* To a Skylark. MaRV
We looked, we loved, and therewith instantly. Pure Death. Robert Graves. CoBMV; GTBS-P; MoAB; MoPo
We Love the Name of Texas, *with music.* *Unknown.* BFSS
We Love the Venerable House. Emerson. MaRV
We love thee, Ann Maria Smith. The Editor's Wooing. "Orpheus C. Kerr." BOHV
We love to spread our branches. Deep Living. *Unknown.* SoP
We loved the wild clamor of battle. The Song of the Flags. S. Weir Mitchell. PAH
We loved thee, Swordy Well, and love thee still. Swordy Well. John Clare. WHA
We loved: we vowed our love should never die. Memoir. R. G. Howarth. PV
We Lying by Seasand. Dylan Thomas. BoPe; SyP

We made castles of grass, green halls, enormous stem-lined rooms. The Riders. Ann Stanford. TPM
We made ourselves a castle. September. Katharine Pyle. PCH
We make both mead and garden gay. Daffodils. P. A. Ropes. BoTP
We make our meek adjustments. Chaplinesque. Hart Crane. AP; CMoP; CrMA; LiTG; LiTM (rev. ed.); OxBA; ReMP
We make ourselves a place apart. Revelation. Robert Frost. InPo; PoDB
We make that lovely sighing sound. The Name. Eileen Duggan. ISi
We make the world in which we live. The World We Make. Alfred Grant Walton. PoToHe (new ed.)
We may go through the world, but it will be slow. People Will Talk. *Unknown.* TreFS
We may live without poetry, music and art. What We May Live Without. "Owen Meredith." *Fr.* Lucile. PoToHe (new ed.); TreF
We may no longer stay: go, waken Eve. Milton. *Fr.* Paradise Lost, XII. FosPo
We may not climb the heavenly steeps. Whittier. *Fr.* Our Master. BePJ; ChIP; OQP
We May Not Know. Cecil F. Alexander. TRV
We May Not Understand. Thomas Kimber. SoP
We may not work a miracle. The Higher Calling. W. M. Czamanske. STF
We may raise our voices even in this still glade. The Glade. Edward Shanks. LO
We may shut our eyes. Joys. James Russell Lowell. *Fr.* The Vision of Sir Launfal: Prelude to Pt. I. BoTP
We may well wonder at those froward hermits. The Eremites. Robert Graves. LiTB
We meet and part now over all the world. The Company of Lovers. Judith Wright. BoAV; MoAuPo
We meet 'neath the sounding rafter. The Revel [*or* Revelry for the Dying *or* Stand to Your Glasses *or* Our Last Toast]. Bartholomew Dowling. AnIV; BLPA; HBV; OnYI; TreF; VA; YaD
We meet upon the Level and we part upon the Square. The Level and the Square. Robert Morris. BLPA
We Men Are of Two Worlds. Mary Elizabeth Colman. CaP
We men of Earth have here the stuff. Earth Is Enough. Edwin Markham. MaRV; OQP; SoP; TreFS; TRV
We met but in one giddy dance. To ——. Winthrop Mackworth Praed. HBV
We met in a bushel of paradise birds. A Night Full of Nothing. Keith Sinclair. AnNZ
We Met on Roads of Laughter. Charles Divine. FaBoBe; HBMV
We met the *Flying Dutchman.* The *Flying Dutchman.* Charles Godfrey Leland. PoMS
We Met Them on the Common Way. Elizabeth C. Cardozo. MaRV
We met upon a crowded street one day. Casual Meeting. Margaret E. Bruner. PoToHe
We more than others have the perfect right. Song of the Moderns. John Gould Fletcher. AWP; InPo
We move, the wheel must always move. Politics. Tennyson. CoBE; PoRL
We move thru rooms & down the middle of freeways. Dancing All Alone. Al Young. WSL
We muse on miracles who look. Miracle. Edith Daley. MaRV
We must admire her perfect aim. The Colder the Air. Elizabeth Bishop. MiAP
We must be free or die, who speak the tongue. Faith and Freedom. Wordsworth. *Fr.* It Is Not to Be Thought Of. GN
We must be nobler for our dead, be sure. The Watchers. Arlo Bates. AA
We must have silence where we go. There Must Be Silence. Anne Tansey. JKCP (1955 ed.)
We Must Lead. Herbert Lee Pitts. WSL
We must leave the handrails and the Ariadne-threads. A l'Ange Avantgardien. F. R. Scott. MoCV
We must not hope to be mowers. As a Man Soweth. Goethe. FaChP; MaRV
We must not, in our hurried lives. His Life Is Ours. Dorothy Conant Stroud. STF
We Must Not Part. *Unknown.* DiPo; SeCL
We must pass like smoke or live within the spirit's fire. Immortality. "Æ." AnIV; AWP; JAWP; OBMV; VA; WBP; WGRP
We mustered at midnight, in darkness we formed. Bethel. A. J. H. Duganne. PAH
We mustn't get discouraged at the things which people say. Discouraged. Lucille Stanaback. STF
We Need a King. Arthur R. Macdougall, Jr. PGD
We need a new patriotism. A New Patriotism. Chauncey R. Piety. PGD
We need him now—his rugged faith that held. Abraham Lincoln, the Master [*or* The Master]. Thomas Curtis Clark. OHIP; OQP; PEDC
We Need Not Bid, for Cloistered Cell. John Keble. HBV
We need you now, strong guardians of our hearts. The Poets. Scudder Middleton. HBMV
We Needs Must Be Divided. George Santayana. Sonnets, XXXV. ViBoPo
We Needs Must Love the Highest. Tennyson. *Fr.* Idylls of the King: Guinevere. MaRV
James Wetherell. E. A. Robinson. MoAmPo
We never knew the touch of fur and feather. Timber Line Trees. Jamie Sexton Holme. PoOW
We never know how high we are. Emily Dickinson. AmP; AmPP; AnFE; AP; APA; CoAnAm; CoBA; TRV; WaKn
We never meet, yet we meet day by day. Thoughts in Separation. Alice Meynell. ACP; GoBC
We Never Speak as We Pass By. *Unknown.* TreFS
We never spent time in the mountains. Interlude. Welton Smith. BF
We, not content with naming distant views. Country Walk. Geoffrey Taylor. OxBI
We now mid hope vor better cheer. Jeane. William Barnes. LO
We often read with new delight. Sir Orfeo. *Unknown.* MeEV
We old men. The Old Men. Ernest Rhys. POTE
We only ask for sunshine. Song. Helen Hay Whitney. HBV
We only see a little of the ocean. There's More. *Unknown.* FaChP
We open here our treasures and our gifts. A Christmas Prayer. Herbert H. Hines. ChIP; MaRV; OQP; PGD
We overstate the ills of life, and take. Exaggeration. Elizabeth Barrett Browning. SoP
We Own the Night. LeRoi Jones. BOLo
We park and stare. A full sky of the stars. The Death of the Sheriff [*or* Noli Me Tangere]. Robert Lowell. FiMAP; MoAB; MoAmPo (1950 ed.)
We Pass. Beatrice M. Murphy. TNV
We passed the ice of pain. The Moment. Theodore Roethke. NYBP
We pause beside this door. January. Lucy Larcom. OQP
We pity; we should dread. The Terrible Dead. Mary Carolyn Davies. HBMV
We place Thy sacred name upon our brows. Still Thou Art Question. *Unknown.* ChIP; PGD; StJW
We planted a garden. Flowers. Harry Behn. FaPON
We play at paste. Emily Dickinson. CBEP
We play now very lightly, on the strings. Rondel for Middle Age. Louise Townsend Nicholl. NePoAm
We pledge ourselves. Facing the New Year. *Unknown.* PGD
We pledged our hearts, my love and I. The Exchange. Samuel Taylor Coleridge. FiBHP; HBV; OAEP; WhC
We plough and sow—we're so very, very low. The Song of the Lower Classes. Ernest Charles Jones. CoMu; OBVV
We Plow the Fields. Matthias Claudius, *tr. fr. German by* Jane M. Campbell. MaRV; SoP
(We Plough the Fields.) OTPC (1946 ed.)
We poets pride ourselves on what. On Hearing Mrs. Woodhouse Play the Harpsichord. W. H. Davies. BrPo; MuSP
We Poets Speak. Francis Thompson. *Fr.* Sister Songs. FaBV
We pointed it out to his bed-ridden eyes. Hospital. G. C. Millard. PeSA
We poor Agawams. Mr. Ward of Anagrams Thus. Nathaniel Ward. SCAP
We praise not now the poet's art. Bryant on His Seventieth Birthday. Whittier. DD

We praise thee, O God; we acknowledge thee to be the Lord. Te Deum Laudamus. *Unknown.* MaRV; WGRP; WHL
We pray for pity, Lord, not justice, we. Frank Wilmot. *Fr.* To God, from the Warring Nations. BoAV; NeLNL
We pray Thee, have mercy on Zion! Prayer for Redemption. *Unknown.* TrJP
We prayed for miracles: the prairie dry. Epilogue to the Outrider. Dorothy Livesay. CaP
We pulled for you when the wind was against us. Song of the Galley-Slaves. Kipling. *Fr.* Many Inventions. ChTr; GTBS-P; PoEL-5; PoFr
We pursued but to capture and destroy. The Stricken Colts. Louise D. Peck. NYTB
We put him to bed in his little nightgown. After the Fourth of July. M. Phelps Dawson. DD
We put more coal on the big red fire. Father's Story. Elizabeth Madox Roberts. FaPON; MPB; PoSC
We Put on the Buffalo. Robert P. Tristram Coffin. RePo
We put our heads here, and see nothing but beautiful yellow flowers. George Towle. Tony Towle. ANYP
We quarreled that morning. Julia Miller. Edgar Lee Masters. *Fr.* Spoon River Anthology. MoVE
We ranging down this lower track. In Memoriam A. H. H., XLVI. Tennyson. EnLi-2; EPN; ViPo; VP
We reach the utmost limit of the earth. Prometheus Bound. Aeschylus, *tr. by* Elizabeth Barrett Browning. EnLi-2 (1939 ed.)
We Reached Out Far. Peretz Markish, *tr. fr. Yiddish by* Jacob Sonntag. TrJP
We Real Cool. Gwendolyn Brooks. IDB; NoP; OCS; TTY; WOW
(Pool Players, Seven at the Golden Shovel, The.) TPM
We Reason of These Things. Wallace Stevens. *Fr.* Notes toward a Supreme Fiction. CrMA
We rejoin our hero at the edge of a vast impenetrable morass. Homer. Dick Gallup. ANYP
We remember, we do not forget, O Trail Breakers. Trail Breakers. James Daugherty. AmFN; RePo
We rode at a trot. Grenada. Mikhail Svetlov. WaaP
We rode hard, and brought the cattle from brushy springs. Proud Riders. H. L. Davis. AnAmPo; NP
We rode out with the pealing day before us. N. H. Brettell. *Fr.* Wind and an Eagle Owl. BoSA
We rode the tawny Texan hills. That Texan Cattle Man. Joaquin Miller. BOHV
We rode together. Winter Weather. William Morris. EPN; TOP
We said: there will surely be hawthorn out. Spring Snow and Tui. Mary Ursula Bethell. AnNZ
We said *We understand,* and for a while. Urban History. Chester Kallman. CrMA
We sail at dusk. The red moon. Night Patrol. Alan Ross. POTi
We sail toward evening's lonely star. Song. Celia Thaxter. AA
We sailed and sailed upon the desert sea. Hope. William Dean Howells. AA
We sailed by the old world's tideways, down through the long sea-lanes. The Secret of the Deeps. Sidney Royse Lysaght. EtS
We sailed to and fro in Erie's broad lake. Perry's Victory. *Unknown.* PAH
We sat and talked. . . .It was June, and the summer light. Horse in a Field [*or* To K. M.]. Walter de la Mare. BoC; HBMV
We sat at the hut of the fisher. Twilight. Heine. AWP; JAWP; WBP
We sat in the garden together. She said. The Conversation. Alex Raybin. ThO
We sat together at one summer's end. Adam's Curse. W. B. Yeats. CMoP; CoBMV; DiPo; Po; PP; ViPo (1962 ed.)
We sat together close and warm. The Young Mystic. Louis Untermeyer. TSW
We sat, two children, warm against the wall. The Gate. Edwin Muir. CMoP; LiTM (rev. ed.)
We sat within the farm-house old. The Fire of Drift-Wood. Longfellow. AmPP (4th ed.); AP; HBV; MAmP; MWA-1; NoP; OxBA
We saw a bloody sunset over Courtland. Remembering Nat Turner. Sterling A. Brown. PoNe
We saw and woo'd each other's eyes. To Castara: The Reward of Innocent Love. William Habington. *Fr.* Castara. ACP; CavP; LoBV
We saw him go, rifles on either side. The Crime Took Place at Granada. Antonio Machado. PoFr
We saw one first and thought it was the only one. Bloody Cranesbill on the Dunes. E. J. Scovell. ChMP
"We saw reindeer/ browsing." Rigorists. Marianne Moore. PoIE
We saw that city on the inland sea. Archibald MacLeish. *Fr.* Conquistador: Bernal Diaz' Preface. AtBAP
We saw the bare feet and the quiet hands sprawled on the street stones. In This Hour. Josephine W. Johnson. MoRP
We saw the light shine out a-far. The Golden Carol. *Unknown.* OHIP; YT
We saw the swallows gathering in the sky. Modern Love, XLVII. George Meredith. AnFE; BEL; BoLiVe; ELP; EnLi-2; EnLoPo; FaBoEn; GTBS-D; GTBS-P; GTSL; MemP; OBNC; PoAn; SeCeV; VA; ViBoPo; ViPo; VP; WHA
We saw thee come in, a wee naked babe. Farewell to the Old Year. Eleanor Farjeon. SiSoSe
We saw Thee in Thy balmy nest. Shepherds' Hymn [*or* A Hymn Sung as by the Shepherds]. Richard Crashaw. *Fr.* In the Holy Nativity of Our Lord God. ACP; BoC; CAW; EG; GoBC; OBEV; TrGrPo
We saw truth shining through the shabby compromise. Rededication. Emanuel Litvinoff. WaP
We say it for an hour, or for years. Good-by. Grace Denio Litchfield. PoToHe
We say the sea is lonely; better say. The Open Sea. William Meredith. CoAP; NePoEA; UnPo (3d ed.)
We scatter seeds with careless hand. The Effect of Example. John Keble. HBV; HBVY; MaRV
We search the world for truth. The Bible [*or* The Book Our Mothers Read *or* Knowledge]. Whittier. *Fr.* Miriam. BLRP; FaChP; MaRV; NeHB; OQP; PoToHe (new ed.); SoP; TreFT; TRV
We see Him come, and know Him ours. Robert Herrick. *Fr.* A Christmas Carol: "What Sweeter Music Can We Bring." MyFE
We See Jesus. Annie Johnson Flint. BLRP
We see them not—we cannot hear. Are They Not All Ministering Spirits? Robert Stephen Hawker. CoBE; EPN; GoBC; HBV; OBEV (1st ed.)
We see us as we truly behave. Two Scenes. John Ashbery. ANYP
We seek the saloons and the wenches. The Sailors. Karel van de Woestijne. OnPM
We seek to know, and knowing seek. In Immemoriam [*or* In Memoriam]. "Cuthbert Bede." BOHV; NA
We seek to know the moving of each sphere. Sir John Davies. *Fr.* Nosce Teipsum. MyFE
We seem to tread the self-same street. Florence MacCarthy's Farewell to His English Love. Aubrey Thomas De Vere. IrPN; NBM
We serve no weak and timid Christ. The Christ Militant. Thomas Curtis Clark. ChIP
We set out yesterday upon a winter's drive. Alexandre Dumas. *Fr.* The Lady of the Pearls. TTY
We Settled by the Lake. F. D. Reeve. NYBP
We Shall Attain. James B. Kenyon. OQP
We shall build it again though it caves in. Lost City. Marion Strobel. NP
We Shall Build On! G. A. Studdert-Kennedy. MaRV; OQP
"We shall cede with a brotherly embrace." The Rise of Shivaji. Zulfikar Ghose. MoBS
We shall come to-morrow morning, who were not to have her love. Emily Hardcastle, Spinster. John Crowe Ransom. CMoP; NoP
We shall do so much in the years to come. What Have We Done Today? [*or* Today]. Nixon Waterman. OQP; WBLP
We shall have everything we want and there'll be no more dying on the pretty plains or in the supper clubs. Ode to Joy. Frank O'Hara. NeAP
We Shall Have Far to Go. James Wreford Watson. CaP
We shall have music. Love in Age. Charles G. Bell. NePoAm-2
We shall live, maybe, till our world turns grey. Love Looks to the Future. Gerald Gould. POTE

We shall meet, but we shall miss him. The Vacant Chair. Henry Stevenson Washburn. TreFS
We Shall Meet Them. Oswald J. Smith. SoP
We shall not always plant while others reap. From the Dark Tower. Countee Cullen. BALP; BANP; CDC; IDB; Kal; LiTM (1970 ed.); NeMA; PoNe
We shall not cease from exploration. T. S. Eliot. *Fr.* Four Quartets: Little Gidding. ImOP
We Shall Not Dwell Forever in These Yellow Lands. "St.-J. Perse," *tr. fr. French by* T. S. Eliot. *Fr.* Anabasis. AtBAP
We shall not ever meet them bearded in heaven. On the Death of Friends in Childhood. Donald Justice. CBV
We shall not go up against you. This Be Our Revenge. Saul Tchernichowsky. TrJP
We shall not travel by the road we make. Road Makers. V. H. Friedlaender. MaRV
We shall not wholly die. To Poets All. Thomas Curtis Clark. MaRV
We Shall Overcome. *Unknown.* EaLo; ThLM
We shall remember him. John Butler Yeats. Jeanne Robert Foster. GoYe
We Shall Remember Them. James Terry White. PEDC
We Shall Say. Miriam Allen deFord. GoYe
We shall see her no more. The Rejected Member's Wife. Thomas Hardy. NoP
We shape ourselves the joy or fear. Destiny. Whittier. *Fr.* Raphael. MaRV
We shift and bedeck and bedrape us. Swinburne. *Fr.* Dolores. UnTE
We should not mind so small a flower. Emily Dickinson. MWA-2
We should stay longer if we durst. *See* Ye should stay longer if we durst.
We shouldered like pigs along the rail to try. Returned to Frisco, 1946. W. D. Snodgrass. AP
We shut them out, the houses. Time Out. Oliver Jenkins. GoYe
We sighed and said, The world's high purpose falters. The Lyric Deed. John G. Neihardt. DD
We, sighing, said, "Our Pan is dead." Thoreau's Flute. Louisa May Alcott. AA; DD; HBV
We sing the song that Israel sang in the desert long ago. Spring Up, O Well! *Unknown.* SoP
We sink within this earth's dark waters: we. To Him Who Walks the Water. E. Merrill Root. ChIP
We sit and talk, and kiss away the hours. James Randolph. LO
We sit, crookbacked, at the bar. At the Telephone Club. Henri Coulette. CoAP
We sit indoors and talk of the cold outside. There Are Roughly Zones. Robert Frost. CMoP
We sit late, watching the dark slowly unfold. September. Ted Hughes. SiSw
We Sit Solitary. *Unknown.* TrJP
We smile at astrological hopes. For the Conjunction of Two Planets. Adrienne Cecile Rich. ImOP
We sow the glebe, we reap the corn. Mystery. Elizabeth Barrett Browning. OBVV; UnPo
We sow the fertile seed and then we reap it. Evening Hymn in the Hovels. Francis Lauderdale Adams. OxBS
We stand apart. The Priesthood. Yvor Winters. NP
We stand talking in the cave whose walls are. On Meeting a Stranger in a Bookshop. Oscar Williams. NePA
We stand unbroken in our places. The Song of the Siberian Exiles. Nikolai Alekseyevich Nekrasov. PoFr
We stand upon, the moorish mountain side. The Pine Woods. John, Lord Hanmer. VA
We stay/ as the leaves. The Soldiers. Giuseppe Ungaretti. OnPM
We steamed into New York harbor the other day. The Statue of Liberty. Sheila Jane Crooke. YaD
We stood beside an opening grave. "I Am the Resurrection and the Life" Saith the Lord! Robert Stephen Hawker. GoBC
We stood by a pond that winter day. Neutral Tones. Thomas Hardy. BrPo; BWP; CABA; CMoP; CoBMV; FosPo; ILP; LiTL; MaPo; MeWo; MoBrPo; PAn; PoeP; PoFS; PoVP; SyP; ViPo (1962 ed.); ViPP; VP
We stood on the haunted island. The Phantom Ship. J. W. De Forest. EtS
We stood so steady. Crossing the Blackwater. Robert Dwyer Joyce. VA
We stood still in the bright sunlight. The Parade. Marjorie Seymour Watts. PCH
We stood up before day. In the Dordogne. John Peale Bishop. AnAmPo
We stood where the wooden piers. Dora Markus. Eugenio Montale. OnHM
We stopped by the seashore. Sunday Again. David Hilton. QAH
We strain toward Heaven and lay hold on Hell. Battle-Song of Failure. Amelia Josephine Burr. HBMV
We stumble down the pocked and cratered road. Madonna of the Exiles. James Edward Tobin. ISi
We summoned not the Silent Guest. The Skeleton at the Feast. James Jeffrey Roche. AA
We Sunday strode—I in leather. The Rented Garden. Bink Noll. ToPo
We Survive! Hirsch Glick, *tr. fr. Yiddish by* Ruth Rubin. TrJP
We swing ungirded hips. The Song of the Ungirt Runners. Charles Hamilton Sorley. EnLit; HBMV; MoBrPo; NeMA; OBEV (new ed.); ShBV-2; TreFT; TrGrPo (1942 ed.); TSW
We talk'd with open heart, and tongue. *See* We talked with open heart. . .
We talked all morning, she said. A Walk in the Country. Galway Kinnell. NePoAm
We talked of things but all the time we wanted each other. And What with the Blunders. Kenneth Patchen. NaP
We talked together in the Yung-shou Temple. The Letter. Po Chü i, *tr. by* Arthur Waley. LoBV
We talked [*or* Talk'd] with open heart, and tongue. The Fountain. Wordsworth. EnRP; FosPo; GTBS; GTBS-D; GTBS-P; GTBS-W; GTSE; GTSL; MBW-2; OBRV; SeCePo
We tap the sugar bush and tap a world. Sap Bucket Song. Louis Stoddard. NYTB
We Thank Thee ("For glowing autumn's brimming yield"). Thomas Curtis Clark. PGD
We Thank Thee ("Not for our lands"). Thomas Curtis Clark. OQP; PEDC; PGD, *abr.*; PoToHe (1941 ed.), *abr.*
We Thank Thee. Phyllis C. Michael. SoP
We Thank Thee ("For all life's beauties"). John Oxenham. *See* For Beauty, We Thank Thee.
We Thank Thee ("For all thy ministries"). John Oxenham. *See* We Thank Thee, Lord ("For all thy ministries").
We Thank Thee ("We thank Thee, Lord,/ That of Thy tender grace"). John Oxenham. SoP
We Thank Thee. Mattie M. Renwick. HH; OTPC (1946 ed.); PEDC
We Thank Thee ("For flowers that bloom about our feet"). *Unknown, at. to* Emerson. HH, *abr.*
(Father in Heaven,) TreFT
(Father, We Thank Thee.) SoP
(Spring Prayer.) BoTP
(Thanksgiving.) SoPo
We Thank Thee ("For mother-love and father-care"). *Unknown.* FaPON; MPB; OTPC (1946 ed.)
We thank Thee for the joy of common things. A Prayer for Thanksgiving. Joseph Auslander. TrPWD
We thank Thee for the morning light. *Unknown.* BLRP
We thank Thee, Heavenly Father. Thanks to Spring. Mary Anderson. BoTP
We Thank Thee, Lord ("For all thy ministries"). John Oxenham. WBLP
(We Thank Thee.) PGD
We Thank Thee, Lord ("We thank Thee, Lord,/ For all Thy golden silences"). John Oxenham. OQP
We thank Thee, Lord/ That of Thy tender grace. We Thank Thee. John Oxenham. SoP
We thank Thee, Lord, for quiet upland lawns. Grace and Thanksgiving. Elizabeth Gould. BoTP
We thank Thee, Lord, for this our food. *Unknown.* BLRP
We thank Thee, now, O Father. The Most Acceptable Gift. Matthias Claudius. BLRP
We Thank You! L. E. Cox. BoTP
We, that did nothing study but the way. A Renunciation. Henry King. OBEV
We that with like hearts love, we lovers twain. A Vow to Heavenly Venus. Joachim du Bellay. AWP
We, the fairies, blithe and antic. Fairies' [*or* Fairy] Song [*or* Song of Fairies Robbing an Orchard]. Thomas Ran-

dolph, *tr. by* Leigh Hunt. *Fr.* Amyntas. ALV; HBV; OBRV; PoMS
We, the Few Who Believe. Harold Vinal. FiSC
We, the symmetrians, seek justice here. N.B., Symmetrians. Gene Derwood. LiTA; NePA
We, the unborn. Chorus of the Unborn. Nelly Sachs. NYBP
We think to create festivals. Poems, 4. Antonio Machado. AWP; LiTW
We thirst at first—'tis nature's act. Emily Dickinson. WGRP
We thought at first, this man is a king for sure. Blue Blood. James Stephens, *after* O'Bruaidar. MoAB; MoBrPo; OBMV; OxBI
We thought it was a joke. Nightmare Number Four. Robert Bloch. FiSC
We three are on the cedar-shadowed lawn. Modern Love, XXI. George Meredith. OAEP; ViPo; VP
We Three Kings of Orient Are. John Henry Hopkins, Jr. OHIP; YaCaBo, *with music*
(Three Kings of Orient.) ChrBoLe
We till to sow, we sow to reap. Means and Ends. Humfrey Gifford. SoP
We told of him as one who should have soared. Discovery. E. A. Robinson. CMoP
We told them the myths about others. The Port. Bernadette Mayer. ANYP
We too (one cried), we too. To the Mother of Christ, the Son of Man. Alice Meynell. ISi
We too take ship, O soul. Be Not Afraid. Walt Whitman. *Fr.* Song of the Open Road. MaRV
We too, we too, descending once again. The Too-late Born [*or* The Silent Slain]. Archibald MacLeish. AmP; AnFE; APA; CABA; CMoP; CoAnAm; CoBMV; ExPo; GoJo; GTBS-W; LiTM; MAP; MoAB; MoAmPo; MoVE; NAMP; NePA; OxBA; SeCeV; TwAmPo; WaP
We took it to the woods, we two. Emerson. Mary Mapes Dodge. AA; DD; PoRL
We took no notes of contemplated light. To My Friends. Peter Levi. NePoEA-2
We took our work, and went, you see. Recreation. Jane Taylor. NBM; OBRV; OxBoLi
We Two. Dan Crawford. *See* Jesus and I.
We two lying on sand. Child with Shell. R. G. Everson. PeCV (1967 ed.)
We trees were chopping down the monsters in the/ Street to count their rings. The Slacker Apologizes. Peter Viereck. MiAP
We trekked into a far country. Translation. Anne Spencer. BANP
We used to be ten brothers. Ten Brothers. *Unknown.* MaC; RePo
We used to float the paper boats in spring. Poem. Donald D. Olsen. PoPl
We used to gather at the high window. When Mahalia Sings. Quandra Prettyman. IDB
We used to picnic where the thrift. Trebetherick. John Betjeman. CMoP; EvOK; ExPo
We used to shadow-box on the shining grass. Dimidium Animae Meae. Charles A. Brady. GoYe
We used to talk of so many things. Before and after Marriage. Anne Campbell. PoToHe (new ed.)
We waged a war within a war. Recapitulations, XI. Karl Shapiro. PoNe
We wait our turn, as still as mice. The Hospital Waiting-Room. W. H. Davies. BrPo; CBEP
We waited out the lion weeks. Vernal Paradox. Kim Kurt. NePoAm-2
We Waiting on You. Edward S. Spriggs. BF
We wake to hear the storm come down. The Storm. Edward Shanks. BoNaP
We walk back from the movies. Frightened Flower. William J Harris. BOLo
We walked along, while bright and red. The Two April Mornings. Wordsworth. EnRP; ERoP-1; FosPo; GTBS; GTBS-D; GTBS-P; GTBS-W; GTSE; GTSL; MBW-2; MERP; PIA; PoIE
We Walked among the Whispering Pines. John Henry Boner. AA
We walked in that green field. Fossil. Paul Engle. ReMP
We walked in the sun on Joralemon Street. Joralemon Street. Patricia Hubbell. OCS
We wander now who marched before. Old Soldier. Padraic Colum. OBMV; POTE
We wandered to the pine Forest. Shelley. *Fr.* The Recollection. CH
We, wandering to death. Marching Song. Ernst Toller. MaRV
We wanted Li Wing. Lapsus Linguae. Keith Preston. WhC
We was camped on the plains at the head of the Cimarron. Zebra Dun. *Unknown.* ViBoFo
We watch for the light of the morn to break. Song of the Bees. Hannah Flagg Gould. OTPC
We watch the only eagles in the world. At a Parade. F. T. Prince. NeBP; WaP
We watch through the shop-front while. "Blackie, The Electric Rembrandt." Thom Gunn. FIW
We watched/a red rooster. Calypso. William Carlos Williams. NePoAm-2
We watched [*or* watch'd] her breathing thro' [*or* through] the night. The Death-Bed. Thomas Hood. BEL; CBV; ELP; EnRP; GTBS; GTBS-D; GTBS-W; GTSE; GTSL; HBV; MaRV; MCCG; OBEV; OBRV; OBVV; PG; TreFS; VA
We watched our love burn with the lumberyard. The Lumberyard. Ruth Herschberger. LiTA; LiTL; LiTM (rev. ed.)
We watched the Condors winging towards the Moon. Condors. Padraic Colum. GoJo
We watched the rain come pouring down. Rainbows. Dixie Willson. GFA
We watched thy spirit flickering in the dark. In Memoriam; John Davidson. Ronald Campbell Macfie. GoTS
We Wear the Mask. Paul Laurence Dunbar. AmePo; AmNP; CDC; IDB; NoP; TTY
We went down to the river's brink. Explanation, on Coming Home Late. Richard Hughes. ELU; ThWaDe
We went to a circus in the town. Magic Lariat. Glenn Ward Dresbach. BrR
We were a noisy crew; the sun in heaven. Fishing. Wordsworth. *Fr.* The Prelude. SD
We were a people taut for war; the hills. Welsh History. R. S. Thomas. POTi
We were a tribe, a family, a people. Scotland 1941. Edwin Muir. OxBS
We were all passengers in that motorcade. Channel U.S.A.—Live. Adrien Stoutenburg. AmFN; ThLM
We were antagonists; we knew that. Reflections on Water. Kenneth Pitchford. CoPo
We were apart; yet, day by day. Isolation; to Marguerite. Matthew Arnold. Switzerland, IV. CBEP; MBW-2; PoVP; TreFT; ViPP; VP
We were born grooms, in stable-straw we sleep still. A Dream of Horses. Ted Hughes. NePoEA-2
We Were Boys Together. George Pope Morris. AA
We were camped on the plains at the head of the Cimarron. The Zebra Dun. *Unknown.* CoSo; RePo; StPo; StVeCh
We were closed, each to each, yet dear. Each to Each. Melville Cane. GoYe
We were crowded in the cabin. Ballad of the Canal. Phoebe Cary. BOHV
We were crowded in the cabin. Ballad of the Tempest [*or* The Captain's Daughter *or* The Tempest]. James Thomas Fields. BeLS; EtS; FaBoBe; FaFP; HBV; HBVY; PoLF; TreF; YaD
We were driving the down express. The Engine Driver's Story. William Wilkins. BeLS
We were forty miles from Albany. The Erie. *Unknown.* ABF; AS
We were glad together in gladsome meads. Adam Lindsay Gordon. *Fr.* The Rhyme of Joyous Garde. PoAu-1
We were hangin' "Rustler" Murphy for the stealin' of a horse. The Salvation of Texas Peters. J. W. Foley. ShM
We were leaving on a journey by slow aeroplane. Ah the Poetry of Miss Parrot's Feet Demonstrating the Tango. Tom Raworth. HYE
We were lying on a prairie on Slaughter's ranch one night. Home, Sweet Home. *Unknown.* CoSo
We were not by when Jesus came. St. Thomas the Apostle. John Keble. SoP
We were not many, we who stood. Monterey. Charles Fenno Hoffman. AA; FaBoBe; HBV; MC; OTPC (1923 ed.); PaA; PAH; PAP; PTK; ThLM

We were not wrong, believing that it cared. The Empty House. Harold Monro. BrPo
We were ordered to samoa from the coast of Panama. An International Episode. Caroline Duer. AA; PAH
We were playing on the green together. "Is It Nothing to You?" May Probyn. GoBC; JKCP; OBEV (new ed.); OBVV; VA
We were schooner-rigged and rakish, with a long and lissome hull. A Ballad of John Silver. John Masefield. BoChLi (1939 ed.); EvOK; MPB; TSW
We were shut off from the street. Crossroads. Miguel Otero Silva. WoL
We were spawned in lava mountains, from the surf line of the sea. The Strong. John Curtis Underwood. MaRV
We were taken. Arms & Exit. James W. Thompson. WSL
We were taken from the ore-bed and the mine. The Secret of the Machines. Kipling. PoMa; StVeCh
We were three women, three men. The Sorrow of Kodio. *Unknown.* PBA
We were together. Otomo no Yakamochi, *tr. fr. Japanese by* Kenneth Rexroth. LiTW
We were together since the War began. A Servant. Kipling. *Fr.* Epitaphs of the War. PoVP
We were twin brothers, tall and hale. A Flight Shot. Maurice Thompson. AA; AnAmPo
We were two daughters of one race. The Sisters. Tennyson. InvP
We were two pretty babes, the youngest she. Childhood Fled. Charles Lamb. EnRP; Sonn
We were very tired, we were very merry. Recuerdo. Edna St. Vincent Millay. AmFN; BoLP; EvOK; FaFP; LiTA; LiTL; LiTM; NP; OxBA; PTK; ThLM
We were waiting for the storm. The Storm. "Robin Christopher." RIS
We were walking and talking on the roof of the world. End of the Seers' Convention. Kenneth Fearing. LiTA
We were walking down a narrow street. Sadness. Barbara Guest. AmPC
We were young, we were merry, we were very very wise. Unwelcome. Mary Elizabeth Coleridge. CH; GTBS; GTBS-D; OBEV (new ed.); OBNC; OBVV; PoVP
We Who Are about to Die ("We who are about to die salute each other in the old way"). Harold E. Fey. PGD
We Who Are Dead. Paul L. Benjamin. PGD
We who Are Left. George Whalley. CaP
We who are left, how shall we look again. A Lament. W.W. Gibson. MMA
We, who are men, how shall we know? Song. R. S. Thomas. ToPo
We who are old, old and gay. A Faery Song. W. B. Yeats. POTE; ViBoPo
We Who Build Visions. Stanton A. Coblentz. PGD
We who have come all ways into the city. The Trail. Edward Weismiller. WaP
We who have no perfection but to die. And Only Our Shadow Walks with Us. Eithne Wilkins. NeBP
We who love music are not pretty. Facing the Music. Virginia Graham. MuSP
We who play under the pines. Song of the Rabbits [*or* The Rabbits' Song] outside the Tavern. Elizabeth J. Coatsworth. AnNE; PoMa; RIS; SUS; TiPo
We Who Were Born. Eiluned Lewis. BiCB; FaPON; TiPo (1959 ed.)
We who with songs beguile your pilgrimage. Prologue to "The Golden Journey to Samarkand." James Elroy Flecker. BrPo; GoJo; GTBS; HT; OBMV
We Whom the Dead Have Not Forgiven. Sara Bard Field. PGD
We will go no more to Shaemus, at the Nip. Shaemus. Conrad Aiken. OxBA
We will go to the wood, says Robin to Bobbin. *Unknown.* OxNR
We will have to go away, said the girls in the circus. The Circus. Kenneth Koch. ANYP; FRC
We will not die for nothing. Revolution!! Richard W. Thomas. BF
We will not whisper, we have found the place. Sonnets, XIX. Hilaire Belloc. MoBrPo
We Will Speak Out. James Russell Lowell. PoFr; TreFT
We will wait by the chestnut and the ilex tree. Orion Seeks the Goddess Diana. Sacheverell Sitwell. *Fr.* Landscape with the Giant Orion. MoVE
We wind wreaths of holly. For Randolph Bourne. James Oppenheim. AnAmPo
We wish to declare how the birds of the air. The Trail of the Bird. William John Courthope. HBVY
We wish to the new child. For C. K. at His Christening. Daniel Lawrence Kelleher. NeIP
We with our Fair pitched among the feathery clover. The Individualist Speaks. Louis MacNeice. MoVE; OBMV
We Woke Together. Christopher Brennan. BoAV
We wonder whether the dream of American liberty. Archibald MacLeish. *Fr.* Land of the Free. MoAB; MoAmPo; NeMA
We wondered, Shakespeare, that thou went'st so soon. To the Memory of Master W. Shakespeare. I. M., *at. to* John Milton. CLwM
We wondered what might change. The Survivors. S. S. Gardons. AmPC
We wondered why he always turned aside. Inheritance. Mary Potter Thatcher Higginson. AA
We won't favor you. Five Songs. David Shapiro. ANYP
We worship Thee, O Son of God. The Perfect Gift. Julia Benson Parker. BePJ
We would be building; temples still undone. Builders. Purd E. Dietz. MaRV; SoP; TRV
We would miss the fleecy vapor. The Secrets of Life. N. P. Nielson. FaChP
We Would See Jesus. John Edgar Park. MaRV
We Would See Jesus. W. J. Suckow. ChIP; MaRV; OQP
We Would See Jesus. *Unknown.* STF
We Would See Jesus ("We would see Jesus—for the shadows lengthen") Anna B. Warner. BePJ
(Let Us See Jesus.) MaRV; SoP
We would see Jesus; lo! His star is shining. We Would See Jesus. John Edgar Park. MaRV
We would see Jesus! we have longed to see Him. We Long to See Jesus. Anna E. Hamilton. BePJ
We would see Jesus! We would look upon. We Would See Jesus. W. J. Suckow. ChIP; MaRV; OQP
We wreathed about our darling's head. The Morning-Glory. Maria White Lowell. AA; HBV
We, Wystan Hugh Auden and Louis MacNeice. Their Last Will and Testament. Louis MacNeice. NAMP
Weak and irresolute is man. Human Frailty. William Cowper. HBV
Weak is the assurance that weak flesh reposeth. By Her That Is Most Assured to Her Self. Spenser. Amoretti, LVIII. EnRePo
Weak Is the Will of Man, His Judgment Blind. Wordsworth. EnRP; MBW-2
Weak Monk, The. Stevie Smith. FaBoTw
Weak-winged is song. Ode Recited at the Harvard Commemoration, July 21, 1865 [*or* The Commemoration Ode]. James Russell Lowell. AA; AmPP; AnAmPo; AP; CoBA; HBV; MAmP; PaA; TOP
Weakest Thing, The. Elizabeth Barrett Browning. HBV
Weakling, The. Arthur Adams. BoAu
Weakness of Nature. Richard Hurrell Froude. OBRV
Wealth. Emerson. ImOP; MWA-1
Wealth. Sadi, *tr. fr. Persian by* Sir Edwin Arnold. *Fr.* The Gulistan. AWP; OuHeWo
Wealth came by water to this farmless island. Delos. Bernard Spencer. FaBoMo
Wealth, my lad, was made to wander. Samuel Johnson. *Fr.* One-and-twenty. OtMeF; ViBoPo
Wealthy dromedar, A. The Boar and the Dromedar. Henry Beissel. WHW
Wealthy Man, A. William Allingham. IrPN
Wealthy young squire of Tamworth we hear, A. The Golden Glove. *Unknown.* MaC
Weapon, The. Mary Elizabeth Coleridge. *See* "He Knoweth Not That the Dead Are Thine."
Weapon shapely, naked, wan. Song of the Broad-Axe. Walt Whitman. MAP; MoAmPo; WoL
Weapon that comes down as still, A. The Ballot. John Pierpont. AA; AmePo; InP; PoRL
Weapon that you fought with was a word, The. "He Knoweth Not That the Dead Are Thine" [*or* The Weapon]. Mary Elizabeth Coleridge. ELU; MemP; OBNC; PoVP
Weapons. Anna Wickham. MoBrPo

Weapons of Evil. *Unknown, at. to* Lao-tzu, *tr. fr. Chinese by* Lin Yutang. *Fr.* Tao Teh King. MaRV
Wear it/ Like a banner. Color. Langston Hughes. BOLo
Wear it as a bangle on your arm. Fame. Eleanor Hollister Cantus. GoYe
Wear modest armour; and walk quietly. Advice to a Knight. T. H. Jones. FlW
Wearie Wayfarer, Ye, *sels.* Adam Lindsay Gordon.
Chase and the Race, The, *fr.* Fytte VII. OtMeF
Question Not, *fr.* Fytte VIII. PoToHe
(Man's Testament.) OtMeF
Risks of the Game, The, *fr.* Fytte II. OtMeF
Wearied arm and broken sword. Pocahontas. Thackeray. AmFN; DD; FaPON; GN; GoTP; MC; MPB; OnMSP; OTPC; PAH; PAL; ThLM
Wearily, drearily. In Prison. William Morris. AtBAP; CBEP; NBM; PeVV; PoVP
Wearily, still in her dressing gown. Eliza Telefair. Jocelyn Macy Sloan. GoYe
Wearin' o' [*or* of] the Green, The. *Unknown, add. words by* Dion Boucicault. AnIL; AnIV; AWP; DD; HBV; HH; JAWP; OnYI; PoFr; PoSC; TreF; WBP
(Wearing of the Green, The.) FaFP; FOL; OxBoLi; SiTL
Weariness of life that has no will, The. Everyman.. Siegfried Sassoon. BoLiVe; MoBrPo
Weariness of the bones. Lament. "Pablo de Rokha." OnPM
Weariness of this dirt and labour, The. Fatigues. Richard Aldington. BrPo
Wearing his equality like a too-small shoe. The Citizen. Vilma Howard. NNP
Wearing of the Green. Aileen Fisher. YeAr
Wearing of the Green, The. *Unknown. See* Wearin' o' the Green, The.
Wearing worry about money like a hair shirt. Worry about Money. Kathleen Raine. FaBoTw
Wearisome Sonnetteer, feeble and querulous. The Soldier's Wife. George Canning *and* John Hookham Frere. Par
Weary. Sir Henry Parkes. BoAu
Weary already, weary miles to-night. A Match with the Moon. Dante Gabriel Rossetti. NCEP
Weary and wet-shod I went forth afterwards. The Crucifixion and the Harrowing of Hell. William Langland. *Fr.* The Vision of Piers Plowman. MeEV
Weary are the hours of a sailor boy. The Sailor Boy. *Unknown.* BaBo
Weary at heart with winter yesterday. April. Obadiah Cyrus Auringer. AA
Weary Blues, The. Langston Hughes. BALP; FaBV; NoP; PoNe; UnS
Weary day rins down and dies, The. A Jacobite's Exile, 1746. Swinburne. OBVV; OtMeF
Weary form, that rested not, The. Abraham Lincoln. Whittier. *Fr.* The Emancipation Group. SoP
Weary hearts! weary hearts! by cares of life oppressed. Weary, Lonely, Restless, Homeless. Abram Joseph Ryan. SoP
Weary in Well-doing. Christina Rossetti. SeCePo; SoP; TrPWD; ViPo; VP
Weary, Lonely, Restless, Homeless. Abram Joseph Ryan. SoP
Weary Lot Is Thine, A. Sir Walter Scott. *Fr.* Rokeby, III. CH; EG
(Rover, The.) GTBS-D; GTBS-P; GTBS-W; GTSE; GTSL
(Rover's Adieu, The.) HBV; OBEV
(Rover's Farewell, The.) PoE
(Song; "Weary lot is thine, fair maid, A.") EnLoPo; OBNC; OBRV; ViBoPo
Weary men, what reap ye?—"Golden corn for the stranger." The Famine Year. Lady Wilde. OnYI; PoFr
Weary of earth and laden with my sin. Forgiveness of Sins. Samuel John Stone. SoP
Weary of erring in this Desert Life. To Our Ladies of Death. James Thomson. GoTS
Weary of myself, and sick of asking. Self-Dependence. Matthew Arnold. BBV; BEL; EnLi-2; EnLit; EPN; HBV; MaVP; MBW-2; MCCG; OAEP; OQP; Po; PoIE; PoVP; TreFS; ViPP; WGRP
Weary of the ceaseless war. Weary. Sir Henry Parkes. BoAu
Weary one had rest, the sad had joy, The. Because We Do Not See. *Unknown.* BLRP
Weary Ploughman, The. *Unknown. See* Little Farm, The.
Weary souls, that wander wide. Fly to Jesus. Charles Wesley. BePJ
Weary teacher sat alone, The. The Teacher's Dream. William Henry Venable. BeLS
Weary the cry of the wind is, weary the sea. Sorrow of Mydath. John Masefield. MoBrPo
Weary Traveler, *with music. Unknown.* BoAN-1
Weary way-wanderer, languid and sick at heart. The Soldier's Wife. Robert Southey. OBEC
Weary, weary, desolate. Yuma. Charles Henry Phelps. AA
Weary weed, tossed to and fro, A. Gulf-Weed. Cornelius George Fenner. EtS
Weary wind is slumbering on the wing, The. Sunset. Arthur Bayldon. PoAu-1
Weary with serving where I nought could get. Diella, XXVIII. Richard Lynche. Sonn; TuPP
Weary with toil, I haste me to my bed. Sonnets, XXVII. Shakespeare. DiPo; OBSC; PoFS; ReEn; SiCE
Weary year[e] his race now having run, The. Amoretti, LXII. Spenser. OBSC; ReIE; SiCE
Wearyin' for You. Frank L. Stanton. HBV
(Just a Wearyin' for You.) TreF
Weasel, The. Robert Pack. CoPo
Weasel, The. *Unknown.* ChTr
Weasel and the wren consort, The. Mole Talk. Leo Kennedy. PeCV
Weasel, by a person caught, A. The Man and the Weasel. Phaedrus. AWP; OnPM
Weather. Mary Ursula Bethell. AnNZ
Weather. Hilda Conkling. TiPo
Weather. Thomas Hardy. *See* Weathers.
Weather. Archibald MacLeish. *See* Cook County.
Weather. William Meredith. NYBP
Weather bothered him, and the delicate muscular. Mr. Pollington Remembers a Poet. Hyam Plutzik. FiMAP
Weather Factory, The. Nancy Byrd Turner. SUS
Weather Forecast. David Kilburn. HYE
Weather in London and Stratford-on-Avon was so, The. Shakespeare, Possibly, in California. Reed Whittemore. MoVE
Weather is mild, The. The Death of a Zulu. William Plomer. BoSA
Weather is the answer. Weather. Hilda Conkling. TiPo
Weather-leech of the topsail shivers, The. Tacking Ship off Shore. Walter Mitchell. AA; EtS; FaBoBe; GN; HBV; PFY
Weather-man has promised snow and sleet, The. The Humble Bumble Bee. Vachel Lindsay. UTS
Weather of Six Mornings, The. Jane Cooper. NYBP
Weather Report. Charles Wright. PIA
Weather Signs. *Unknown.* OTPC (1946 ed.)
(Rhymes about the Weather.) FaBoBe
(Weather Rule, A.) MPB (1956 ed.); OTPC (1923 ed.)
(Weather Wisdom.) HBV; HBVY; TreF
Weather Vanes. Frances Frost. SiSoSe
Weather wept, and all the trees bent down; The. "The Shimmer of Evil." Theodore Roethke. NePoAm-2
Weather Wisdom. *Unknown. See* Weather Signs.
Weather Words. David Mccord. ImOP
Weathercock, The. Rose Fyleman. BoTP
Weathercock. Elizabeth Jennings. NePoEA
Weathers. Thomas Hardy. ALV; AnEnPo; BoLiVe; BoTP; CH; EvOK; FaBoCh; FaBV; GTSL; LoGBV; MemP; MoAB; MoBrPo; OBMV; OtMeF; PoIE; PoTE; ReMP; RePo; SeCePo; ShBV-1; WePo; YT
(Weather.) WHA
Weave no more silks, ye Lyons looms. Our Orders. Julia Ward Howe. AA
Weave the warp, and weave the woof. Curse upon Edward. Thomas Gray. *Fr.* The Bard. OBEV
Weaver, The. William H. Burleigh. BLPA
Weaver, The. "Fanny Forester." BLPA
Weaver, The ("I sat at my loom in silence"). *Unknown.* BLRP
Weaver, The ("I was a bachelor, I lived by myself"). *Unknown. See* Foggy, Foggy Dew.
Weaver, The ("My life is but a weaving"). *Unknown.* SoP
Weaver of Snow, The. "Fiona Macleod." PoVP
Weaver sat by the side of his loom, A. The Weaver. "Fanny Forester." BLPA
Weavers, The. Heine, *tr. fr. German.* PoFr, *tr. by* Louis Untermeyer; TrJP

Weavers, Song, The. Thomas Deloney. *Fr.* Jack of Newbury. SiCE
Weaving, The. Harold Lewis Cook. MoSiPe
Weaving of the Wing, The. Ralph Hodgson. BrPo
Web, The. Witter Bynner. *Fr.* Chapala Poems. NP
Web, The. Theodore Weiss. CoAP
Web flew out and floated wide, The. For All Ladies of Shalott. Aline Murray Kilmer. NP
Web of Eros, The. Edith Sitwell. HBMV
Web-spinner was a miser old. The True Story of Web-Spinner. Mary Howitt. OTPC (1923 ed.)
Webster, an Ode,*sel.* William Cleaver Wilkinson.
At Marshfield. AA
Webster Ford. Edgar Lee Masters. *Fr.* Spoon River Anthology. NP
Webster was much possessed by death. Whispers of Immortality. T. S. Eliot. APA; ATP (1953 ed.); CMoP; CoAnAm; CTC; LiTA; LiTG; MAPA; MemP; MWA-2; NePA; NP OBMV; PoIE; TwAmPo
We'd ever so many kinds of cake. The Pirates' Tea-Party. Dorothy Una Ratcliffe. BoTP
We'd face, I'm sure, with more aplomb. Unsolved Mystery. George Ryan. WhC
We'd found an old Boche dug-out, and he knew. The Sentry. Wilfred Owen. AnEnPo; MMA
We'd gained our first objective hours before. Counter-Attack. Siegfried Sassoon. BrPo; EnLit; MoBrPo; WaP
We'd rather have the iceberg than the ship. The Imaginary Iceberg. Elizabeth Bishop. LiTM; MoAB; MoAmPo (1950 ed.); MoVE; ReMP
Weddase Maryam. *Unknown, tr. fr.* Ethiopian MS. *by* Sir E. A. Wallis Budge. ISi
Wedded. Isaac Rosenberg. FaBoEn; LO
Wedded Bliss. Charlotte Perkins Gilman. HBV
Wedded light and heat, The. Wind and Wave. Coventry Patmore. NBM
Wedded Love. Milton. *Fr.* Paradise Lost, IV. OBS; PoFS
(Epithalamion: "Haile wedded love, mysterious law, true sourse.") MaPo (1969 ed.)
(Hail, Wedded Love.) HW
(Their Wedded Love.) SeCePo
Wedding, The. Conrad Aiken. AnAmPo; CMoP; NoP
Wedding, The. Robert Graves. HW
Wedding, The. Tom Hood. BOHV; InMe
Wedding, The. Boris Pasternak, *tr. fr. Russian by* Michael Daly. HW
Wedding, A. Sir John Suckling. *See* Ballad upon a Wedding, A.
Wedding, A ("Rosy apple"). *Unknown. See* Rosy Apple, Lemon or Pear.
Wedding ("Since Jesus freely did appear"). *Unknown.* SoP
Wedding, The ("Thus sang she: / One, two, three"). *Unknown, tr. fr. German.* SAS
Wedding and Hanging. John Heywood. SiCE
Wedding Anniversary. Margaret E. Bruner. PoToHe
Wedding bells were ringing on a moonlight winter's night, The. The Fatal Wedding. W. H. Windom. TreFS
Wedding Celebration. Tenrai Kono, *tr. fr. Japanese by* Sumake Kimizuka. HW
Wedding Gift, The. Minna Irving. BLPA
Wedding-Hymn. Sidney Lanier. *See* Wedding Prayer.
Wedding Hymn, A, *sel.* Thomas Tiplady.
"O Thou, Who love in mercy hast created." MaRV
Wedding Hymn, A ("Jesus, stand beside them"). Thomas Tiplady. MaRV
Wedding Is Great Juno's Crown. Shakespeare. *Fr.* As You Like It, V, iv. ViBoPo
Wedding Morn. D. H. Lawrence. MoAB; MoBrPo
Wedding Night, The. Johannes Secundus, *tr. fr. Latin by* George Ogle. *Fr.* Epithalamium. UnTE
Wedding of Alcmane and Mya, The. George Chapman. *See* Epithalamion Teratos.
Wedding of the Clans, The. Aubrey Thomas De Vere. AnIL; IrPN
Wedding Prayer. Sidney Lanier. SoP
(Wedding-Hymn.) TrPWD
Wedding Procession [from a Window]. James A. Emanuel. Kal; NNP
Wedding Sermon, The. Coventry Patmore. The Angel in the House, II, xi, 3. PoVP
Wedding Signs. *Unknown.* TreFT
Wedding-Song, A. John White Chadwick. AA
Wedding Song. Goethe, *tr. fr. German by* Christa Wolf *and* Virginia Tufte. HW
Wedding Song. Conrad Ferdinand Meyer, *tr. fr. German by* Christa Wolf *and* Virginia Tufte. HW
Wedding Song ("My lord is all a-glow"). *Unknown, tr. fr. Chinese by* Arthur Waley. *Fr.* Shi King. LiTW
Wedding Song. Nancy Willard. ThO
Wedding Wind. Philip Larkin. HW; ToPo
Wedgwood Bowl, A. Frances Beatrice Taylor. CaP
Wedlock. Jenny Grahame. LiTL
Wedlock. Barbara L. Greenberg. QAH
Wedlock. *Unknown. See* When Adam Was Created.
Wednesbury Cocking. *Unknown.* EnSB
Wednesday. "Elspeth." WhC
Wednesday in Holy Week. Christina Rossetti. ChIP; PGD
Wednesday, January 1, 1701. Samuel Sewall. SCAP
Wednesday; or, The Dumps. John Gay. *Fr.* The Shepherd's Week. EiCP; FosPo, *abr.*
Wee doe account that musique good. *Unknown.* SeCSL
Wee folk will be tripping, The. When a Ring's around the Moon. Mary Jane Carr. BrR; TiPo
Wee, glossy, cowering, timorous beastie. To a Mouse. Burns, *ad. by* William Kean Seymour. WaKn
Wee Hughie. Elizabeth Shane. HBMV
Wee little nut lay deep in its nest, A. Among the Nuts. *Unknown.* BoTP; TVC
Wee Little Worm, A. James Whitcomb Riley. *Fr.* A Session with Uncle Sidney. PDV
Wee man o' leather. Riddle. *Unknown.* ChTr
Wee May o' Caledon, The. Lewis Spence. ACV
Wee, modest, crimson-tippèd flow'r. To a Mountain Daisy [*or* The Daisy]. Burns. AnEnPo; ATP; BEL; BoNaP; CEP; EiCL; EiPP; EnLi-2; EnLit; EnRP; GN; HBV; MPB; OAEP; OTPC (1923 ed.); PoLF; UnPo (1st ed.); WBLP
Wee read in profane and sacred records. A Dialogue between the Two Horses. Andrew Marvell. MaMe
Wee read of kings and gods that kindly tooke. A Cruell Mistris. Thomas Carew. AnAnS-2
Wee Sandy in the corner. The Still Small Voice. Alexander Smart. PRWS
Wee sing, wee feast, wee daunce, wee play. *Unknown.* SeCSL
Wee, sleekit, cow'rin', tim'rous beastie. To a Mouse [*or* To a Field Mouse]. Burns. AnEnPo; AnFE; ATP; BBV (1923 ed.); BEL; BoLiVe; CBEP; CBV; CEP; CoBE; DiPo; EiCL; EiCP; EiPP; EnL; EnLi-2; EnLit; EnRP; FaFP; FosPo; GoTS; GTBS; GTBS-D; GTBS-P; GTBS-W; GTSE; GTSL; HBV; HBVY; ILP; LiTG; LoBV; MCCG; MPB; NoP; OA; OAEP; OBEC; OTPC; OuHeWo; OxBS; PAn; PoAn; PoFS; PoIE; PoLF; PoMa; RG; SeCeV; ShBV-2; TIHL; TOP; TreFS; TrGrPo; WHA
Wee sprites have followed mistletoe. Mistletoe Sprites. Solveig Paulson Russell. ChBR
Wee Tammy Tyrie. *Unknown.* OxNR
Wee Wee Man, The. *Unknown.* BaBo; CH; ELP; ESPB; FaBoCh; OBB; OTPC (1946 ed.); OxBB
(Little Wee Man, The.) BuBa
Wee, wee tailor. The Oviparous Tailor [*or* The Tailor]. Thomas Lovell Beddoes. NBM; WiR
Wee Willie Gray. Burns. EiCL
Wee Willie Winkie rins [*or* runs] through the town. Willie Winkie. William Miller. BoChLi; FaFP; GaP; HBV; HBVY; OxNR; PCH; RIS; SAS; SiSoSe; SoPo; StVeCh; TiPo; VA
Wee Willy Winkie,/ Runs through the town. Willy Winkie. Daniel Henry Holmes. TSW
Weed, The. Elizabeth Bishop. MoPo
Weed Month. V. Sackville-West. *Fr.* The Land. MoBrPo (1942 ed.)
Weed Puller. Theodore Roethke. AmPP (5th ed.); PoAn
Weeds in summer. Messages. Sophia Castro-Leon. QAH
Week ago to-day, when red-haired Sally, A. Done For. Rose Terry Cooke. AA
Week is dealt out like a hand, The. Hope. Randall Jarrell. MoAB; MoAmPo (1950 ed.)
Week of Doodle, A. Reed Whittemore. NePoEA
Week on the Concord and Merrimack Rivers, A, *sels.* Henry David Thoreau.
All Things Are Current Found. AnNE; OnPM; ViBoPo; WoL
Atlantides, The. BWP; ViBoPo

Conscience. AnNE; BWP; HBV
Haze. AmePo; AmPP (3d ed.) BWP; CoBA; InPo; NoP; PoPl
(Woof of the Sun [Ethereal Gauze].) AnNE; AP; OnPM; ViBoPo
Mist. AA; AmePo; AmPP (4th ed.); AmLP; AWP; HBMV; InPo; JAWP; MWA-1; OxBA; WBP
(Low-anchored Cloud.) ImOP; NoP; ViBoPo
Weekday, A. Larry Eigner. CoPo
Week-End, *sels.* Harold Monro.
"Be staid; be careful; and be not too free," IX. SeCePo
"Contented evening; comfortable joys," III. YT
"Key will stammer, and the door reply, The," II. MoBrPo (1950 ed.); YT
"Morning! Wake up!" VI. YT
"Train, The! The twelve o'clock for paradise," I. MemP; MoBrPo (1950 ed.); YT
Week-End by the Sea. Edgar Lee Masters. MoAmPo
Weekend Stroll. Frances Cornford. BoNaP
Weel, gin ye speir, I'm no inclined. The Poets at Tea, 9. Barry Pain. Par
Weeng; an Indian Slumber Song. Lew Sarett. GaP
Weep, ah weep love's losing. Weep Love's Losing [*or* Ode]. Imr el Kais. *Fr.* The Mu'allaqát. AWP; LiTW
Weep balm and myrrh, you sweet Arabian trees. Stanzas from "Saint Peter's Complaint." Robert Southwell. ACP; CAW
Weep eyes, break heart! Parting. Thomas Middleton. *Fr.* A Chaste Maid in Cheapside. ElL; TuPP
Weep for me, friends, for now that I am hence. Tears of the World. Mu'tamid, King of Seville. AWP
Weep for the one so strong to slay, whom One has taken at last! Saul. George Sterling. HBMV
Weep him dead and mourn as you may. Keen. Edna St. Vincent Millay. HBMV
Weep, Israel! your tardy meed outpour. Bar Kochba. Emma Lazarus. TrJP
Weep, lovers, sith Love's very self doth weep. Dante. *Fr.* La Vita Nuova. AWP
Weep Love's Losing. Imr el Kais, *tr. fr. Arabic by* Lady Anne Blunt *and* Wilfrid Scawen Blunt. *Fr.* The Mu'allaqát. LiTW
(Ode: "Weep, ah weep love's losing.") AWP
Weep No More. John Fletcher, *and others. Fr.* The Queen of Corinth, III, ii. AtBAP; BEL; CH; ElL; LiTG; OBEV; OnPM; TOP; ViBoPo
(Mourn No More.) TrGrPo
("Weep no more, nor sigh, nor groan.") TuPP
Weep no more for what is past. What Is Past. Sir William Davenant. *Fr.* The Cruel Brother. TrGrPo
Weep no more, nor sigh nor groan. Weep [*or* Mourn] No More. John Fletcher, *and others. Fr.* The Queen of Corinth, III, ii. AtBAP; BEL; CH; ElL; LiTG; OBEV; OnPM; TOP; TrGrPo; TuPP; ViBoPo
Weep no more, woful Shepherds, weep no more. Immortality. Milton. *Fr.* Lycidas. BoC; MaRV
Weep not,/ You who love her. Burial of the Young Love. Waring Cuney. PoNe
Weep not, beloved friends! nor let the air. Epitaphs, I [*or* Francesco Ceni]. Gabriello Chiabrera. AWP; JAWP; OnPM; WBP
Weep not beside his tomb. Arthur Hugh Clough. *Fr.* Easter Day. PGD
Weep Not, My Wanton. Robert Greene. *See* Sephestia's Song to Her Child.
Weep not, nor backward turn your beams. The Lover Consults with Reason. Thomas Carew. TrGrPo
Weep Not! Sigh Not! William James Linton. VA
Weep not that you no longer feel the tide. Lost Youth. Roger Casement. CAW; JKCP (1926 ed.)
Weep not the Brave Dead! Cean-Salla. James Clarence Mangan. OnYI
Weep Not To-Day. Robert Bridges. OBMV; OBVV
Weep not, weep not. Go Down Death. James Weldon Johnson. AnAmPo; AmNP; MaRV; TRV
Weep not, you who love her. Burial of the Young Love. Waring Cuney. BANP
Weep, sorrowing one, for God would have thee weep. Weeping. Henry W. Frost. SoP
Weep! Weep! Weep! Tumadir al-Khansa for Her Brother. *Unknown. Fr.* The Thousand and One Nights. AWP; JAWP; PG (1945 ed.); WBP
Weep weep weep. Transcendental Blues Transcendental Blues. Yusuf Rahman. BF
Weep, weep, weep and weep. Alton Locke's Song, 1848. Charles Kingsley. *Fr.* Alton Locke. PoFr
Weep, weep, ye woodmen, wail. Dirge for Robin Hood [*or* Robin Hood's Funeral]. Anthony Munday *and* Henry Chettle. *Fr.* Death of Robert, Earl of Huntingdon. CBEP; CH; CTC; ElL; OBSC; ThWaDe; WiR
Weep [*or* Weepe] with me, all you that read. [An] Epitaph on S. P. [Salamon *or* Salomon *or* Slathiel Pavy], a Child of Q. El.'s [Queen Elizabeth's] Chappel. Ben Jonson. AnAnS-2; BEL; BWP; CABA; CBV; CoBE; ElL; EnRePo; FaBoEn; GoBC; HBV; InP; LoBV; MaPo; MePo; NoP; OAEP; OBEV; OBS; PAn; PoE; PoEL-2; PoFS; PoSa; PTK; ReEn; ReIE; SCEP-2; SeCP; SeCV-1; SeEP; TrGrPo; TuPP; UnPo (1st ed.); VaPo; ViBoPo
Weep You No More, Sad Fountains. *Unknown.* CH; EG; ElL; ELP; EnLoPo; ExPo; ForPo; LoBV; NoP; OAEP; ReEn; ReIE; ShBV-4; SiCE; TrGrPo; TuPP; ViBoPo
(Sleep Is a Reconciling.) ChTr
(Song for Music, A.) GTSL; TOP
(Tears.) BoPe; MemP; OBEV; PG
(Weepe You No More, Sad Fountaines.) AtBAP; PoEL-2
Weepe living thinges, of life the mother dyes. The Death of Our Ladie. Robert Southwell. MeP
Weepe O Mine Eyes. *Unknown.* AtBAP; PoEL-2
Weepe with me all you that read. *See* Weep with me. . .
Weepe You No More, Sad Fountaines. *Unknown. See* Weep You No More. . .
Weeper, The. Richard Crashaw. AnAnS-1; EP; MaMe; MeP; MePo; OBEV, *abr.*; SeCP; ViBoPo, *abr.*
(Saint Mary Magdalene.) AtBAP; MeLP; PoFS; ReEn; SCEP-1; SeCV-1; SeEP
"And now where're he strayes *sel.*" LiTG; Par
Weeping. Henry W. Frost. SoP
Weeping, The. Federico García Lorca, *tr. fr. Spanish by* Eleanor L. Turnbull. OnPM
Weeping and Kissing. Sir Edward Sherburne. SeCL; SeEP
Weeping and Singing. César Tiempo, *tr. fr. Spanish by* Donald Devenish Walsh. MoRP
Weeping and wakeful all the night I lie. Rhodanthe. Agathias Scholasticus. AWP
Weeping Cherry, The. Robert Herrick. AtBAP; WePo
Weeping rose in her dark night of leaves, The. A Song at Morning. Edith Sitwell. CMoP
Weeping, Sad and Lonely. Charles Carroll Sawyer. TrAS, *with music*
Weeping sorely as he journeyed. The Canadian Exile. Antoine Gerin-Lajoie. CaP
Weeping Water. Ruth Pitter. POTE
Weeping Willow. Richard Aldridge. NePoAm-2
Weeps out of Kansas [*or* western] country something new. The Birth in a Narrow Room. Gwendolyn Brooks. PoNe; TPM
Weevily Wheat, *with music. Unknown.* ABF, 2 *vers.*; AS; TrAS
'Weh Down Souf. Daniel Webster Davis. BANP
Wei Wind, *sel.* Confucius, *tr. fr. Chinese by* Ezra Pound.
Pedlar. CTC
Weighing the Baby. Ethel Lynn Beers. HBV; PoToHe (new ed.)
Weighing the steadfastness and state. Man. Henry Vaughan. AnAnS-1 AnEnPo; BWP; CBEP; FaBoEn; ForPo; HBV; MeLP; MeP; MePo; OBEV (new ed.); OBS; PoEL-2; PoFS; SCEP-1; SeCV-1
Weight distributed. One Down. Richard Armour. SD; WhC
Weightless Element, A. Gottfried Benn, *tr. fr. German by* Christopher Middleton. PoPl
Weird wife of Bein-y-Vreich! horo! horo! Cailleach Bein-y-Vreich. John Campbell Shairp. VA
Wel mended tinker! sans dispute. Of John Bunyans Life. John James. SCAP
"Wel seyd, by *corpus dominus*," quod our hoste. The Prioress's Prologue. Chaucer. *Fr.* The Canterbury Tales. OAEP
Weland experienced exile in Wermland. Deor's Lament. *Unknown, tr. by* Harold S. Stine. EnLit
Weland knew fully affliction and woe. Deor's Lament. *Unknown, tr. by* Charles W. Kennedy. AnOE
Welcome, A. William Browne. HBV; LiTL; OBEV
(Welcome, Welcome, Do I Sing.) CavP; ViBoPo

Welcome, The. Abraham Cowley. *Fr.* The Mistress. SeCV-1
Welcome! Richard Crashaw. FaChP
(Coming Child, The.) MaRV; TRV
Welcome, The. Thomas Osborne Davis. HBV; TreFT, 4 *ll.*; VA
"Come in the evening, or come in the morning," *sel.* IrPN
Welcome, The. Leonard Feeney. WHL
Welcome, A. Charles Kingsley. *See* Ode to the North-east Wind.
Welcome, The. Freda Laughton. NeIP
Welcome, The. Nettie Palmer. BoAu
Welcome, The. Arthur Powell. OQP
Welcome. R. S. Thomas. NMP
Welcome. Rose Waldo. MPB; SoPo
Welcome all who lead or follow. Verses Placed over the Door at the Entrance into the Apollo Room at Devil Tavern [*or* Over the Door at the Entrance into the Apollo]. Ben Jonson. HBV; ReEn
Welcome, all wonders in one sight! Welcome! [*or* The Coming Child]. Richard Crashaw. FaChP; MaRV; TRV
Welcome, baby, to the world of swords. News of a Baby. Elizabeth Riddell. BoAV
Welcome [*or* Wolcum] be Thou, Heavenly King [*or* thou, hevene kyng]. Welcome Yule. *Unknown.* CAW; CH
Welcome Bonny Brid! Samuel Laycock. VA
Welcome, boy, to these green fields. Alma Mater. Mary Elizabeth Osborn. NePoAm
Welcome! but yet no entrance, till we bless. The Entertainment; or, Porch-Verse at the Marriage of Master Henry Northly and the Most Witty Mistress Lettice Yard. Robert Herrick. HW
Welcome, Christmas! heel and toe. Stocking Song on Christmas Eve. Mary Mapes Dodge. ChBR; OHIP
Welcome dear book, soules joy, and food! The feast. H. Scriptures. Henry Vaughan. AnAnS-1; MeP
Welcome, dear dawn of summer's rising sway. May-Day. Aaron Hill. WaPE
Welcome deare feast of Lent: who loves not thee. Lent. George Herbert. MaMe
Welcome Death. Juan Escrivá, *tr. fr. Spanish by* Sir John Bowring. OnPM
(Song to Death, *tr. by* E. Allison Peers.) LiTW
Welcome Eild. *Unknown.* GoTS
Welcome Every Guest, *with music. Unknown.* TrAS
Welcome, fayre chylde, what is thy name? *Unknown.* Dalyaunce. AtBAP; CH
Welcome freshness over the garden lay, A. Suspended Moment. Mariana B. Davenport. GoYe
Welcome, friend. Newton to Einstein. Jeannette Chappell. GoYe
Welcome, great Cesar, welcome now you are. To the King, upon His Welcome to Hampton-Court. Robert Herrick. AnAnS-2
Welcome, happy Easter day! Easter Praise. Rodney Bennett. BoTP
Welcome, little Robin. *Unknown.* BoTP
Welcome, maids of honour [*or* honor]. To Violets [*or* Violets]. Robert Herrick. EG; HBV; MyFE; OBEV; OBS; OTPC (1923 ed.); PoeP; RG; SeCP; TrGrPo; ViBoPo
Welcome me, if you will. For James Dean. Frank O'Hara. NeAP
Welcome, most welcome to our vowes and us. To the King, Upon His Comming with His Army into the West. Robert Herrick. AnAnS-2
Welcome my griefe, my ioy; how deare's. Verily I Say Unto You, Yee Shall Weep and Lament. Richard Crashaw. MaMe
Welcome, my old friend. To an Old Danish Song-Book. Longfellow. OBVV
Welcome My World. Denis Devlin. AnIV
Welcome now, Victoria! Queen Victoria. *Unknown.* CoMu; FOL
Welcome, old friend! These many years. To Age. Walter Savage Landor. BEL; EnRP; EPN; FaPL; HBV; OQP; TreFS; VA
Welcome! Our Messiah. *Unknown.* MeEL
Welcome over the Door of an Old Inn. *Unknown. See* America Greets an Alien.
Welcome, pale primrose! starting up between. To a Primrose. John Clare. FIW; GTSE; OTPC (1923 ed.)
Welcome, precious stone of the night. Welcome to the Moon. *Unknown.* BoNaP; ChTr
Welcome, Queen Sabbath. Zalman Schneour, *tr. fr. Hebrew by* Harry H. Fein. TrJP
Welcome, red and roundy sun. The Wood-Cutter's Night Song. John Clare. EnRP; GTSE; OBRV
Welcome, Summer. Chaucer. *See* Roundel, A: "Now welcom, somer. . ."
Welcome sweet and sacred cheer. The Banquet. George Herbert. AnAnS-1; MaMe; MeP
Welcome sweet, and sacred feast; welcome life! The Holy Communion. Henry Vaughan. AnAnS-1; MeP
Welcome the lord of light, and lamp of day. Welcome to the Sun. Vergil, *tr. by* Gawin Douglas. *Fr.* The Aeneid. ACP
Welcome, Thou Safe Retreat! William Habington. OxBoCh; PoLi
Welcome, thrice welcome to this shady green. The Forest's Queen. Philip Massinger. GoBC
Welcome to Alexandra, A. Tennyson. PoVP
Welcome to Dr. Benjamin Apthorp Gould, A. Oliver Wendell Holmes. ImOP
Welcome to My Heart. *Unknown.* BePJ; SoP
Welcome to our wondering sight. A Hymn of the Nativity. Richard Crashaw. *Fr.* In the Holy Nativity of Our Lord God. ChIP
Welcome to Sack, The. Robert Herrick. AnAnS-2; SCEP-2; SeCP; SeCV-1
Welcome to Spring. Irene Thompson. BoTP
Welcome to the day returning. Ode for Washington's Birthday. Oliver Wendell Holmes. DD; PEDC
Welcome to the Moon. *Unknown, tr. fr. Gaelic.* BoNaP; ChTr
Welcome to the Nations. Oliver Wendell Holmes. PAH
Welcome to the New Year. Eleanor Farjeon. MoSiPe; YeAr
Welcome to the Prince of Ossory. William Heffernan the Blind, *tr. fr. Irish by* James Clarence Mangan. IrPN
Welcome to the Sun. Vergil, *tr. fr. Latin by* Gawin Douglas. *Fr.* The Aeneid, XII. ACP
Welcome to this flowery place. Thomas Campion. *Fr.* A Relation of the Late Royal Entertainment Given by the Lord Knowles. SiCE
Welcome to us Holy Child. Christmas Night. Hugh MacCawell. KiLC
Welcome to Venice, gentle courteous Knight. A Dialogue between the Lovelorn Sir Hugh and Certain Ladies of Venice. Thomas Deloney. UnTE
Welcome to you rich autumn days. Rich Days. W. H. Davies. BoNaP; BoTP
Welcome Visitors. Emilie Blackmore Stapp. GFA
Welcome, Welcome, Do I Sing. William Browne. *See* Welcome, A.
Welcome, welcome, ev'ry guest. Welcome Every Guest. *Unknown.* TrAS
Welcome, wild North-easter! Ode to the North-east Wind. Charles Kingsley. GN; GTBS; OTPC
Welcome Yule. *Unknown.* CAW; CH
Welder, The. Frank Lima. ANYP
Wele, herying and worshipe be to Christ that dere ous boughte. A Palm-Sunday Hymn. William Herebert. MeEL
Well, The. Denise Levertov. AP
Well, A. Aleksey Konstantinovich Tolstoy, *tr. fr. Russian by* Babette Deutsch. OnPM
We'll A' Go Pu' the Heather. Robert Nicoll. VA
"We'll all be rooned," said Hanrahan. Said Hanrahan. P. J. Hartigan. PoAu-1
We'll All Be Spacemen before We Die. Mike Evans. HYE
We'll All Feel Gay. Winfield Townley Scott. MiAP
Well, *alter ego,* Time has trudged. Why Do We Live? Israel Zangwill. TrJP
Well and/ If day on day. Trapped. Adelaide Crapsey. MCCG
Well Babe I'd die almost. Against Jealousy. Clive Matson. ThO
Well begun. Well-packed Wisdom. Benjamin Franklin. *Fr.* Poor Richard's Almanac. StaSt
Well-beloved, The. Thomas Hardy. ViPo (1962 ed.)
Well boiled in acid and then laid on glass. Description of a View. William Empson. ACV
Well boss did it ever strike you. The Hen and the Oriole. Don

Marquis. *Fr.* Archy and Mehitabel. EvOK; FiBHP
Well boss I met. Cherrio my Deario. Don Marquis. *Fr.* Archy and Mehitabel. ShBV-4
Well boss mehitabel the cat. Mehitabel Sings a Song. Don Marquis. *Fr.* Archy and Mehitabel. InMe
Well, come along boys, and listen to my tale. The [Old] Chisholm Trail. *Unknown.* CoSo (D *vers.*); TrAS
Well; come to me to-morrow. Shakespeare. *Fr.* Measure for Measure, II, ii. LO
Well Done. James Montgomery. MaRV
Well dost thou, Love, thy solemn feast to hold. Saint Valentine's Day. Coventry Patmore. *Fr.* The Unknown Eros. FaBoEn; GoBC; OBNC; PoLi
Well-drest woman in the costly car, The. Toronto Crossing. Robert Finch. TwCaPo
Well dy'd the world, that we might live to see. An Anatomie of the World. John Donne. MaMe. *See also* "When that rich Soule. . ."
Well, ev'ry Monday mornin'. John Henry. *Unknown.* OuSiCo
Well-Finder, The. Harold Vinal. FiSC
We'll Fling the Starry Banner Out. William F. Knott. HH
"Well, General Grant, have you heard the news?" Lee's Parole. Marion Manville. PAH
We'll Go No More a-Roving. Byron. *See* So We'll Go No More a-Roving.
We'll Go No More a-Roving. W. E. Henley. Echoes, VIII. MoBrPo
We'll Go to Sea No More. *Unknown.* ChTr; EtS
We'll go to the meadows, where cowslips do grow. The Meadows. Ann *or* Jane Taylor. BoTP
Well, God don't like it, no, no. God Don't Like It. *Unknown.* OuSiCo
Well, God is/ love. Puerto Rico Song. William Carlos Williams. NYBP
Well hath the powerful hand of majesty. To Sir Thomas Egerton. Samuel Daniel. OBSC
We'll Have Another Drink before the Boat Shoves Off, *with music. Unknown.* ShS
"We'll have the sun now." Confidence. Marsden Hartley. AnFE; CoAnAm
We'll heave him up from down below. Susiana. *Unknown.* ShS
Well, Heaven's hard to understand. Dick Said. Louis Untermeyer. TSW
Well, he's come home, this younger son of mine. The Father. Sara Henderson Hay. StaSt
Well, Honest John. John Clare. NCEP
(To John Clare.) Sonn
Well, honour is the subject of my story. Cassius Poisons Brutus' Mind. Shakespeare. *Fr.* Julius Caesar, I, ii. TreFS
Well, I am thinking this may be my last. Canoe. Keith Douglas. NeBP
Well, I confess, I did not guess. I'm Not a Single Man [*or* Lines in a Young Lady's Album]. Thomas Hood. ALV; HBV
Well, I have thought on't, and I find. The Retirement. John Norris. CavP; OBS
Well, I looked at the camel. At the Zoo. Anne May Smith. PCH
Well I looked upon each face. Guillamede Lorris *and* Jeande Meun. *Fr.* The Romance of the Rose. EnLi-1
Well; I may now receive, and die; my sin[ne]. John Donne. Satires, IV. MaMe; MBW-1; SeEP
Well I never, did you ever. *Unknown.* FaBoCh; LoGBV
Well I recall how first I met. Mark Twain; a Pipe Dream. Oliver Herford. BOHV
Well I Remember How You Smiled. Walter Savage Landor. *Fr.* Ianthe. CBEP; FaBoEn; GTBS; LoBV; OBNC; TrGrPo; ViBoPo
(Her Name.) OBVV
Well, I went down in Hell-Town. Johnny, Won't You Ramble? *Unknown.* OuSiCo
"Well, I would have it so. I should have known." André Chénier. *Fr.* Elegies. AWP
Well; if ever I saw such another Man since my Mother bound my head. Mary the Cook-Maid's Letter to Dr. Sheridan. Swift. LoBV; OnYI; OxBoLi
Well, if it be my time to quit the stage. The Fourth Satire of Dr. John Donne, Dean of St. Paul's, Versified. Pope. *Fr.* Imitations of Donne. MBW-1
Well! If the Bard was weather-wise, who made. Dejection; an Ode [*or* A letter to Sara Hutchinson]. Samuel Taylor Coleridge. AnEnPo; BEL; CABA; CBEP; EnL; EnLi-2; EnLit; EnRP; EPN; ERoP-1; FaBoEn; FiP; ForPo; HBV; LiTB; LoBV; MaPo; MasP; MBW-2; MERP; NCEP; NoP; OAEP; OBNC; OBRV; PAn; PeER, *longer vers.*; PIA; PoE; PoEL-4; PoFS; PoIE; SeCePo; StP
Well, if the thing is over, better it is for me. Mary, Helper of Heartbreak. Margaret Widdemer. HBMV
Well, I'm a wild cowboy, I've roved the West o'er. Wild Bronc Peeler. *Unknown.* CoSo
Well! in my many walks I've rarely found. The Pettichap's Nest. John Clare. BoPe
Well, it makes no difference. Hard to Be a Nigger. *Unknown.* ABF
Well, it's Mamma, Mamma, O Lawd, you don't know. Mamma, Mamma. *Unknown.* OuSiCo
Well, it's partly the shape of the thing. Limerick. *Unknown.* WhC
Well, las' Monday mornin'. De Grey Goose. *Unknown.* ABF
Well, mates, I don't like stories. California Joe. "Captain Jack" Crawford. CoSo
Well may'st thou halt—and gaze with brightening eye! Admonition to a Traveller. Wordsworth. GTBS; GTSE; GTSL
Well meaning readers! you that come as friends. The Flaming Heart. Richard Crashaw. AnAnS-1; CAW; GoBC; LiTB; LoBV; MaMe; MeP; OxBoCh; PoEL-2; SCEP-1; SeCePo; SeCL; SeCV-1
We'll Meet Again. J. Danson Smith. STF
We'll meet beside the dusky glen, on yon burn side. By Yon Burn Side. Robert Tannahill. HBV
We'll Meet Them. Ms. Donald A. Day. FaChP
Well met, pretty nymph, says a jolly young swain. The Country Wedding. *Unknown.* HBV
"Well met, well met, my own true love." The Demon Lover [*or* The House Carpenter]. *Unknown.* BaBo (B *and* D *vers.*); BFSS
"Well met, well met," said an old true love. James Harris (B *vers.*). *Unknown.* ViBoFo
Well mightst thou scorn thy readers to allure. Andrew Marvell. *Fr.* On Mr. Milton's *Paradise Lost.* PP
Well, Mrs. Rogers,/ I hear you're taking lodgers. Coals of Fire. A. P. Herbert. ALV
Well named "A Man of Sorrow." The Daysman. William J. Barnes. SoP
We'll Never Know. Alma Hoellein. STF
We'll not weep for summer over. After Summer. Philip Bourke Marston. HBV; VA
Well now, the virgin and the unicorn. Roy Fuller. *Fr.* Mythological Sonnets. Sonn
We'll o'er the water and o'er the sea. O'er the Water to Charlie. Burns. FaBoCh
Well of freshness, A. Juxta. Grover Jacoby. GoYe
Well of Living Water, The. Charles Wesley. BePJ
Well of Pity, The. Chaucer. *Fr.* An *A. B. C.* PoLi
Well of St. Keyne, The. Robert Southey. BeLS; BoChLi (1939 ed.); BOHV; FaBoBe; HBV; NeHB; OTPC; PTK
Well of Vertew and Flour of Womanheid, The. *Unknown.* OxBS
Well, old spy. Award. Ray Durem. BP; IDB; NNP; PPON; TTY; WOW
Well-packed Wisdom. Benjamin Franklin. *Fr.* Poor Richard's Almanac. StaSt
Well Peter dost thou wield thy active sword. Malchus' Ear [*or* On St. Peter Cutting of Malchus His Eare]. Richard Crashaw. MaMe; StJW
We'll plant a corn-flower on his grave. The Lark's Grave. Thomas Westwood. TVC
Well Pleaseth Me the Sweet Time of Easter. Bertrand de Born, *tr. fr. Provençal by* Ezra Pound. InvP
(Song of Battle.) AWP; WaaP
(War Song, A.) CTC
Well Rising, The. William Stafford. NaP
We'll Roll the Golden Chariot Along, *with music* *Unknown.* ShS
(Roll the Chariot: "We'll roll, we'll roll the chariot along," *diff. vers., with music.*) AS
We'll run all night till the morning. Run with the Bullgine. *Unknown.* SoAmSa
We'll sail from hence to Greece, to lovely Greece. The Song

We'll (continued)
of Ithamore. Christopher Marlowe. *Fr.* The Jew of Malta. WHA
Well! since it must be so, so let it be. On Dr. Woodford's Paraphrase on the Canticles. Thomas Flatman. PeRV
We'll sing a song, a soldier's song. The Soldier's Song. Peadar Kearney. OnYI
Well Sir, 'tis granted, I said D[ryden's] rhymes. An Allusion to Horace; The Tenth Satire of the First Book. Earl of Rochester. OBS; PeRV; SeEP
Well, So That Is That. W. H. Auden. *See* After Christmas.
Well, some may hate, and some may scorn. Stanzas to ——. Emily Brontë. LoBV
Well, son, I'll tell you. Mother to Son. Langston Hughes. AmNP; BiCB; BoChLi (1950 ed.); CDC; GoSl; IHA; OCS; OTD; PoNe; StVeCh; TTY
Well, that was silly; too near the edge. On Catching a Dog-Daisy in the Mower. Peter Redgrove. NePoEA-2
Well the prophets were dancing in the end much. In Sobieski's Shield. Edwin Morgan. HYE
Well, then, gourds. You can call them gourds. The Gourd-Heads. William D. Barney. FiSC
Well, then, I hate Thee, unrighteous picture. The Black Riders, XII. Stephen Crane. AP
Well then! I now do plainly see. The Wish. Abraham Cowley. *Fr.* The Mistress. BEL; BoC; CavP; CoBE; EnLi-1; EnLit; FaPL; GTBS-W; HBV; LiTB; LiTG; NoP; OAEP; OBEV; OBS; SeCL; SeCV-1; SeEP; TOP; TrGrPo; ViBoPo; WHA
Well, then, the last day the sharks appeared. The Sharks. Denise Levertov. NeAP
Well then, the promised hour is come at last. To My Dear Friend, Mr. Congreve, on His Comedy Called "The Double-Dealer." Dryden. CEP; EiCL; EiPP; FiP; MBW-1; OBS; PoE; PoEL-3; SeCV-2; SeEP
Well there is in the west country, A. The Well of St. Keyne. Robert Southey. BeLS; BoChLi (1939 ed.); BOHV; FaBoBe; HBV; NeHB; OTPC; PTK
Well, they are gone, and here must I remain. This Lime-Tree Bower My Prison. Samuel Taylor Coleridge. BWP; CBEP; EnRP; ERoP-1; LoBV; MBW-2; MERP; PeER; PoEL-4; PoIE; ShBV-4
"Well, this is where I go down to the river." Heat. Kenneth Mackenzie. PoAu-2
"Well, though it seems." Liddell and Scott; on the Completion of Their Lexicon. Thomas Hardy. OxBoLi
We'll to the woods and gather may. Alons au bois le may cueillir. Charles de'Orléans. AWP; JAWP; WBP
We'll to the Woods No More. A. E. Housman. LOW; PoRA
We'll wander to the woods no more. The Woods No More. Jay Macpherson. PeCV
Well was dry beside the door, The. Going for Water. Robert Frost. HBMV; NP
Well Water. Randall Jarrell. NoP
Well water. Eight Sandbars on the Takano River. Gary Snyder. CoPo
Well well/ mah ace boo coo. Jacques Wakefield. WSL
Well, well, my dear! So you thought you could cheat me! To Heliodora; a Fretful Monody. Meleager. LiTW
Well, well, 'tis true. Plain Dealing. Alexander Brome. OBS
Well, when all is said and done. Epilogue. "Æ." MoBrPo
Well, when I first infested this retreat. First Settler's Story. Will Carleton. IHA
Well, white man, are you confused? To the White Man. Valerie Tarver. TNV
Well-wishing to a Place of Pleasure, A. *Unknown.* SeCL
Well, World, you have kept faith with me. On His 86th Birthday. Thomas Hardy. ACV
Well worthy to be magnified are they. The Pilgrim Fathers. Wordsworth. PAH; PoRL
Well, yes, I calkerlate it is a little quiet here. When the Train Comes In. Nixon Waterman. IHA
Well, yes, I've lived in Texas, since the spring of '61. A Spool of Thread. Sophie E. Eastman. PAH
Well, yes, sir, dat am a comical name. Ashcake. Thomas Nelson Page. AA
Well, you wake up in de mornin'. De Midnight Special. *Unknown.* ABF
Well-a, jumpin', Jumpin' Judy. Drive It On. *Unknown.* OuSiCo
Well-a, Shorty George he ain' no friend of mine. Shorty George. *Unknown.* ABF
Welladay, welladay, poor Colin, thou art going to the ground. Dirge [*or* The Shepherd's Dirge]. George Peele. *Fr.* The Arraignment of Paris. EIL; OBSC
Wellcome, to the Caves of Arta! Robert Graves. NYBP
Wellfleet Harbor. Paul Goodman. CoAP
Wellington. Byron. *Fr.* Don Juan, IX. OBRV
("Oh Wellington or 'Villainton' — for fame.") OxBoLi; PeER
(On Wellington, *abr.*) FiP
Wellington. Benjamin Disraeli. EPN; FOL; OBVV; VA
Wells. Donald Hall. NMP
Wells of air pour down, The. Pour Down. John Holmes. NePoAm
Wells of Jesus Wounds, The. *Unknown.* *See* Jesus' Wounds So Wide.
Welsh harp has no silver string, The. Variation on a Theme by Francis Kilvert. Rolfe Humphries. UnS
Welsh History. R. S. Thomas. POTi
Welsh Incident. Robert Graves. BoC; CMoP; ShBV-3; WePo
Welsh Landscape. R. S. Thomas. POTi
Welsh Lullaby. *Unknown.* *See* All through the Night ("Sleep, my babe, lie still and slumber").
Welsh Marches, The. A. E. Housman. A Shropshire Lad, XXVIII. FaBoTw; PoVP; ViPo
Welsh Sea, The. James Elroy Flecker. BrPo
Welsh Testament, A. R. S. Thomas. POTi; ToPo
Welshman by the pit whose Sabbath voice, The. Orpheus. E. W. Mandel. *Fr.* Minotaur Poems. OBCV
Welshmen of Tirawley, The. Sir Samuel Ferguson. OBVV; OnYI; PoVP
Welt. Georgia Douglas Johnson. BANP
Welt ist dumm, die Welt ist blind, Die. Heine, *tr. fr. German by* James Thompson. AWP
(World Is Dull, The.) OnPM
Welter upon the waters, mighty one. Sonnet to the Sea Serpent. John G. C. Brainard. EtS
Weltering London ways where children weep, The. John Keats. Dante Gabriel Rossetti. Five English Poets, 4. EPN; PoVP
Weltschmerz. Frank Yerby. AmNP
Women's Wather. T. S. Law. OxBS
W'en de colo'ed ban' comes ma'chin' down de street. The Colored Band. Paul Laurence Dunbar. MPB
"Wen Gott Betrügt, Ist Wohl Betrogen." Arthur Hugh Clough. PoVP
(Is It True, Ye Gods, Who Treat Us.) ViPP
W'en I was young boy on de farm, dat's twenty year ago. How Bateese Came Home. William Henry Drummond. IHA
W'en us fellers stomp around, makin' lots o' noise. When a Feller's Itchin' to be Spanked. Paul Laurence Dunbar. BALP
W'en you see a man in woe. "Hullo!" S. W. Foss. CenHV; PaPo
Wench in the Street, The. *Unknown.* CBEP
("Have you observed the wench in the street.") OBS
Wendell Phillips. Amos Bronson Alcott. AA; PoFr
Wendell Phillips, *sel.* John Boyle O'Reilly.
"What shall we mourn? For the prostrate tree?" AA; DD
Wendling. Coman Leavenworth. *Fr.* Norfolk Memorials. LiTA
Wenlock. A. E. Housman. A Shropshire Lad, XXXIX. SeCePo
('Tis Time, I Think, by Wenlock Town.) NoP; PoVP
Wenlock Edge. A. E. Housman. *See* On Wenlock Edge.
Wenn ich in deine Augen seh'. Heine. *See* I Love but Thee.
Went down to New Orleans, got on a fence, Tom Turkey in de buckwheat straw. Turkey in the Straw (B *vers.*). *Unknown.* AS
Went down to St. Joe's infirmary. Those Gambler's Blues (B *vers.*) *Unknown.* AS
Went into a shoestore to buy a pair of shoes. Sale. Josephine Miles. FiMAP
Went to sleep, babe, last night in a snow-white feather bed. I'm Worried Now but I Won't Be Worried Long. *Unknown.* OuSiCo
Went to the river, couldn't get across. *Unknown.* GoTP
Went weeping little bones. But where? I Cry, Love! Love! Theodore Roethke. MoVE

Went you to conquer? and have so much lost. H: W: in Hiber: Belligeranti. John Donne. MaMe
"*Werden* and *Sein,* the old dichotomy!" Faustus. Hyam Plutzik. Horatio, III. FiMAP
We're A' [*or* All] Dry wi' the Drinkin' O't. *Unknown.* ELU; ErPo; OxNR; SiTL
We're all Americans, except the Doc. A Mad Negro Soldier Confined at Munich. Robert Lowell. NMP; PoeP
We're All Bound to Go. *Unknown. See* Heave Away.
We're all in the dumps. In the Dumps. *Unknown.* NA; SiTL
We're all inclined to bore our friends. Ballade of a Summer Hotel. "Junia." WhC
Were all the tributes of Scotia. The Praise of Derry. St. Columcille. CAW
We're alone, Doney Gal, in the rain [*or* wind] and hail. Doney Gal. *Unknown.* CoSo; OuSiCo
Were [*or* Where] beth they that biforen us weren. Ubi Sunt Qui ante Nos Fuerunt? [*or* Contempt of the World]. *Unknown.* CoBE; EnLi-1; ILP; MeEL; NoP; OAEP; PIA; PoAn; SeCeV
We're bound for blue water where the great winds blow. A Valediction. John Masefield. OBMV
Were But My Spirit Loosed upon the Air. Louise Chandler Moulton. AA HBV
Were but that sign a penitential breath. Melancholy. William Habington. *Fr.* Castara. LoBV
We're crossing the bar of another year. "I Am with Thee." Ernest Bourner Allen. BLRP
Were Flowers There? George William Allison. ChIP
We're foot — slog — slog — slog — sloggin' over Africa! Boots. Kipling. BLPA; MoBrPo; PoVP; ShBV-2; WHA
We're going down to Dixie, to Dixie, to Dixie. Hold On, Abraham. *Unknown.* ABF
We're going to have a party. The Christmas Party. Adeline White. BoTP
We're going to the fair at Holstenwall. Holstenwall. Sidney Keyes. FaBoTw
Were half the power that fills the world with terror. When War Shall Be No More [*or* Message of Peace *or* Peace]. Longfellow. *Fr.* The Arsenal at Springfield. MaRV; OQP; PEDC; PGD; WBLP
We're having a lovely time to-day! Fun in a Garret. Emma C. Dowd. GFA; SUS; TiPo
Were he and the singing two songs, or one? Questions for the Candidate. John Holmes. PP
Were he composer, he would surely write. Portrait of the Boy as Artist. Barbara Howes. MoAmPo (1962 ed.)
"We're homeward bound," I hear them say. Homeward Bound, *vers.* II. *Unknown.* ShS
"We're homeward bound," I heard our captain say. Homeward Bound, *vers.* III. *Unknown.* ShS
"We're homeward bound!" I've heard them say. Homeward Bound, *vers.* I. *Unknown.* ShS
Were I a happy bird. Faith Trembling. "Madeline Bridges." AA
Were I a King. Edward de Vere, Earl of Oxford, *at. to* William Gager. CBV; DiPo
(Choice, A.) OBSC
(Doubtful Choice, A.) ElL
(Epigram.) PoE; TuPP
Were I a painter I'd paint only skies. Heaven Tree. Henry Morton Robinson. JKCP (1955 ed.)
Were I a real poet, I would sing. Sunday up the River, X. James Thomson. OAEP
Were I a rose, and did you dare. The Amorist. *Unknown.* UnTE
Were I as Base as Is the Lowly Plain. *At. to* Joshua Sylvester. HBV; Sonn; TOP
(Constancy.) PG
(Love's Omnipresence.) GTBS; GTBS-D; GTBS-P; GTBS-W; GTSE; GTSL
(Sonnet: "Were I as base as is the lowly plain.") ElL; OBSC; TuPP; ViBoPo
(Ubique.) OBEV
Were I But His Own Wife. Ellen Mary Patrick Downing. VA
Were I immortal only I would proffer. October Birthday. Sister Mary Madeleva. JKCP(1955 ed.)
Were I Laid on Greenland's Coast. John Gay. *See* Song: "Were I laid. . ."
Were I so tall to reach the pole. True Greatness. Isaac Watts. MaRV
Were I the red-brushed fox, I should go warier. December [*or* November] Fugitive. Henry Morton Robinson. AnEnPo; GoYe
Were I To Choose. Gabriel Okara. PBA
Were I to hate the one who injures me. The Scales of Love. Hartmann von Aue. LiTW
Were I to leave no more than a good friend. The Departure; an Elegy. Henry King. SeCP
Were I to Mount beyond the Field. Sidney Keyes. The Foreign Gate, V. MoPo
Were I to name, out of the times gone by. Dearest Poets [*or* The Poets]. Leigh Hunt. HBV; OTPC (1923 ed.); Sonn
Were I to Take Wife. John Wilson. *Fr.* Belphegor; or, The Marriage of the Devil. SeCL
Were I transported to some distant star. A Plain Man's Dream. Frederick Keppel. AA
Were I west in green Arran. The Cup of O'Hara [*or* When Kian O'Hara's Cup Was Passed to Turlough O'Carolan]. Turlough Carolan. AnIV; OnYI
Were I who to my cost already am. A Satire [*or* Satyr] against Mankind. Earl of Rochester. CABL; CEP; EiCL; EiPP; FaBoEn; FosPo; LiTB; LiTG; MasP; NoP; OBS; PeRV; PIA; PoEL-3; SeCV-2; SiTL
Were it mine to repose for one night on thy bosom. Reproach. Firdausi. LiTW
Were it table, trunk or stool. The Carpenter of Nazareth. Walter Smith. ChIP
Were it undo that is y-do. A Forsaken Maiden's Lament. *Unknown.* EnPo; SeCePo
"We're married," said Eddie. The Newlyweds. John Updike. PV
Were My Heart as Some Men's Are. Thomas Campion. HBV
Were not the eye itself a sun. Godlike Heart. Goethe. OnPM
Were Not the Gael Fallen. Peadar O'Mulconry, *tr. fr. Early Modern Irish by* Robin Flower. AnIL
Were Not the Sinful Mary's Tears. Thomas Moore. StJW (Penitence.) SoP
Were pain a simple stab. Strange Guest. Gertrude Jane Codd. JKCP (1955 ed.)
We're queer folks here. Just Folks. Edgar A. Guest. FaFP; TreFS
We're sailing down the river from Liverpool. Santy Anno. *Unknown.* OuSiCo
We're still dancing. Death Motion. Paula Giddings. WSL
We're Tenting Tonight. Walter Kittredge. *See* Tenting on the Old Camp Ground.
Were thanks with every gift expressed. Thankslivinq. Chauncey R. Piety. OQP; PGD
Were the bright day no more to visit us. *Unknown.* LO
We're the children of the open and we hate the haunts o' men. Ridin' up the Rocky Trail from Town. *Unknown.* SCC
Were the whole world good as you—not an atom better. The Question. *Unknown.* WBLP
Were there lovers in the lanes of Atlantis. Song at Santa Cruz. Francis Brett Young. HBMV
Were there no crowns on earth. The Dead President. Edward Rowland Sill. LiPo; PAH
Were this impossible, I know full well. A House and Grounds. Leigh Hunt. CBEP; OBRV
We're up in the morning ere breaking of day. The Railroad Corral. *Unknown.* TrAS
We're very small, we're very small. Song of the Snowflakes. Annette Wynne. GFA
Were we now to fall. The Mechanic. Robert Creeley. NaP
Were you a leper bathed in wounds. Proving. Georgia Douglas Johnson. CDC
Were you and I to play this fugue again. Fugue. Harold Lewis Cook. NP
Were You Ever in Dumbarton? *with music. Unknown.* ShS
Were you ever in Quebec. Donkey Riding. *Unknown.* WHW
Were you ever in sweet Tipperary, where the fields are so sunny and green. Tipperary. Mary Kelly. VA
Were You on the Mountain? *Unknown, tr. fr. Irish by* Douglas Hyde. BoLP; PV
Were You There When They Crucified My Lord? *Unknown.* BoAN-2, *with music*
Werena My Heart's Licht I Wad Dee. Lady Grizel Baillie. OBEV

Were-Wolf. Julian Hawthorne. AA
Were-Wolves, The. Wilfred Campbell. VA
Werfel dead? Hark. The forest is empty. The Shooting of Werfel. Vernon Watkins. WaP
Wermland was misery's home for Wayland. Deor. *Unknown.* CaFP
Wersh an drumlie are the lees. Sang: Recoll o Skaith. Sidney Goodsir Smith. NeBP
Wert thou a king, yet not command content. Answered Thus by Sir P. S. Sir Philip Sidney. TuPP
Wert thou but blind, O Fortune, then perhaps. Poems, XCVIII. Walter Savage Landor. PG
Werther had a love for Charlotte. The Sorrows of Werther. Thackeray. ALV; BLPA; BOHV; CenHV; EnLi-2; FiBHP; HBV; InMe; InP; LiTL; NA; NBM; NeHB; OnSP; PoVP; ShM; SiTL; TOP; TreF; VA; WePo
Wesley in Heaven. Thomas Edward Brown. *See* Organist in Heaven, The.
Wessex Guidebook. Louis MacNeice. HaMV; PoIE
Wessex Heights. Thomas Hardy. CMoP; FaBoEn; OBNC; PoEL-5; UnPo
West, The. Edwin Muir. MoVE
West and away the wheels of darkness roll. Revolution. A. E. Housman. BrPo; ImOP; NoP; VP
West-Country Damosel's Complaint, The. *Unknown.* ESPB
West-Country Lover, A. Alice Brown. HBV
West Forties, The: Morning, Noon, and Night. L. E. Sissman. CoAP; NYBP
West Indies, The, *sels.* James Montgomery.
Columbus. PEDC
(Inspiration, The.) PAH
Lust of Gold, The, *abr.* PAH
West is purple, and a golden globe, The. Harvest. John Addington Symonds. PoVP
West Lake. Kenneth O. Hanson. CoAP
West London. Matthew Arnold. EPN; MCCG; OAEP; PoFr; PoPo; PoVP; Sonn
West of Alice. W. E. Harney. NeLNL; PoAu-1
West of Your City. William Stafford. LiTM (1970 ed.)
West Ridge is Menthol-Cool, The ("The West ridge is an old ridge"). D. L. Graham. BF
West road for my father, A. Legacy. Gladys McKee. JKCP
West-running Brook. Robert Frost. AmP; AP; DiPo; MAP; MoAB; MoAmPo; NoP
West Sussex Drinking Song. Hilaire Belloc. MoBrPo
West Texas. *At. to* Leona Mae Austin. CoSo
West Virginia Hills, The. Ellen King *and* H. E. Engle. PoRL
West was getting out of gold, The. Looking for a Sunset Bird in Winter. Robert Frost. BiS
West Wind, The. John Masefield. BEL; EnLi-2 (1949 ed.); EnLit; FaFP; GTBS-W; GTSL; InP; LiTB; LiTM; MemP; MoAB; MoBrPo; PG; PoPl; TOP; TreF; TSW
West Wind, The. Shelley. *Fr.* Ode to the West Wind, 2 *ll.* PCH
West wind, blow from your prairie nest. The Song My Paddle Sings. E. Pauline Johnson. CaP; FaPON; HBV; OTPC; PoRL; PTK; VA
West wind dances down the lane and sets the robins winging, The. Spring Wind. Nancy Byrd Turner. SiSoSe
West Wind's Secret, The. Mary Jane Carr. BrR
Westering. Douglas V. Kane. GoYe
Western Emigration. David Humphreys. AnAmPo
Western Formula. *Unknown.* PoOW
Western Magic. Mary Austin. AmFN
Western Star, *sel.* Stephen Vincent Benét.
"Americans are always moving on." AmFN
Western Sun withdraws the shorten'd Day, The. Moonlight in Autumn. James Thomson. *Fr.* The Seasons; Autumn. OBEC
Western Town. David Wadsworth Cannon, Jr. PoNe
Western Town. Karl Shapiro. NYBP
Western Trail, The. Robert V. Carr. PoOW
Western Wagons. Stephen Vincent Benét. WaKn
Western Waves of Ebbing Day, The. Sir Walter Scott. *Fr.* The Lady of the Lake, I. OTPC; PoEL-4
Western Wind. *Unknown. See* Western Wind, When Wilt Thou Blow?
Western wind has blown but a few days, The. The Cranes. Po Chü-i. MoBrPo (1942 ed.)
Western wind is blowing fair, The. Serenade. Oscar Wilde. HBV
Western Wind, When Wilt [*or* Will] Thou Blow? *Unknown.* AnFE; CaFP; CLwM; EG; EnLoPo; ExPo; FaBoCh; ForPo; FosPo; LiTL; LO; LoGBV; Po; PoAn; SeCeV; StP; ViBoPo
(Absence.) OBSC
(Lover in Winter Plaineth for the Spring, The.) EnLi-1 (1949 ed.); LiTG; OBEV
(O Western Wind.) GTBS-W; HoPM; LiTB; MeWo; SiTL; TrGrPo; UnTE
(Song: "Westron wynde when wyll thou blow.") SeCePo
(Western Wind.) CABA; CBEP; CBV; CTC; DiPo; ILP; MeEL; NoP; OnPM; TuPP; UnPo (3d ed.)
(Westron Winde, When Will Thou Blow?) AtBAP; EnPo; InvP; PoEL-1; PoIE
Westgate-on-Sea. John Betjeman. OxBoLi
Westland Row. James Stephens. HBMV
Westminster Abbey. Matthew Arnold. ViPo
Westminster Bridge. Wordsworth. *See* Composed upon Westminster Bridge, Sept. 3, 1802.
Westminster Wedding, A, or Like unto Like, Quoth the Devil to the Collier. *Unknown.* CoMu
Westphalian Song. *Unknown, tr. fr. German by* Samuel Taylor Coleridge. AWP; JAWP; LiTW; WBP
Westron Winde, When Will Thou Blow? *Unknown. See* Western Wind, When Wilt Thou Blow?
West's Asleep, The. Thomas Osborne Davis. OnYI
Westward at even. . .yet never, never to die! The Birds Go By. Shaw Neilson. MoAuPo
Westward Ho! Joaquin Miller. AA; FaBoBe
Westward Ho. *Unknown.* CoSo
Westward I watch the low green hills of Wales. Clevedon Church. Andrew Lang. GoTS
Westward on the high-hilled plains. A. E. Housman. A Shropshire Lad, LV. MCCG; PoVP
Wet almond-trees, in the rain. Bare Almond Trees. D. H. Lawrence. FIW
Wet day on the road, A: the slim blades cutting. Windshield. Robert Fitzgerald. CrMA
Wet gray day—rain falling slowly, mist over the, A. Morels. William Jay Smith. BoNaP; NYBP; TDP
Wet leaves fall in a pattern of rusty yellows, The. Rainy Morning. Jessica Nelson North. NP
Wet Litany, The. Kipling. SiSw
Wet or Fine. Amory Hare. HBMV
Wet Sheet and a Flowing Sea, A. Allan Cunningham. EG; EnRP; EtS; GoTS; GTBS; GTBS-D; GTBS-P; GTBS-W; GTSE; GTSL; HBV; HBVY; MCCG; NeHB; OBRV; OTPC; PaPo; PoMa; RoGo; TiPo; TreFS; WaKn
(At Sea.) GBV (1922 ed.)
(Sea Song, A.) BBV; BoTP; FaBoBe; GN; NeHB; RG; RIS
(Wet Sheet and a Flowing Sail, A.) PCH
Wet Summer. May Williams Ward. GoYe
Wet Summer; Botanic Gardens. Nan McDonald. BoAV
Wet Through. Hal Summers. HaMV
Wet Thursday. Weldon Kees. NaP; NYBP
Wet trees hang above the walks, The. The Empty House. William Dean Howells. AmePo
Wet, wayward fingers of the west wind wave the wheat. Corn Cañon. Patric Stevenson. NeIP
Wet Windy Night on a Pavement. A. S. J. Tessimond. WePo
Wet your feet, wet your feet. To an Irish Blackbird. James MacAlpine. HBMV; HBVY
We've been to the wars together. To Lou Gehrig. John Kieran. SD
We've come initil a gey queer time. Epistle to John Guthrie. Sydney Goodsir Smith. OxBS
We've despatched, *pour la guerre.* Message to General Montgomery. H. F. Ellis. WhC
We've Done Our Hitch in Hell. *Unknown.* ABF
We've formed our band and are well mann'd. Ho! for California [*or* Sacramento]. Jesse Hutchinson. SGR; TrAS
We've fought with many men acrost the seas. Fuzzy-Wuzzy. Kipling. BEL; BrPo; EnLi-2 (1949 ed.) EnLit; HBV; MCCG; MoBrPo; PoVP; StaSt; TrGrPo; VA; ViPP; YT
We've foxgloves in our garden. Foolish Flowers. Rupert Sargent Holland. GFA; OTPC
We've kept the faith. Our souls' high dreams. To Our Friends. Lucian B. Watkins. BANP
We've lived for forty years, dear wife. The Ideal Husband to His Wife. Sam Walter Foss. BOHV; InMe

We've lived owre lang, my jar and I. The Empty Jar. William Stenhouse. AnNZ
We've put a fine addition on the good old church at home. The Ladies' Aid. *Unknown.* PoLF
We've reached the land of desert sweet. Dakota Land. *Unknown.* AS; CoSo
We've smashed the tablets and the songs, forsworn. Frank Wilmot. *Fr.* To God, from the Warring Nations. BoAV
We've taken the dog for his walk. To a Child. S. S. Gardons. NePoEA-2
We've traveled together. My Bible and I. Charles Sandford. FaChP; SoP; STF
We've trod the maze of error round. Late Wisdom. George Crabbe. *Fr.* Reflections. HBV; OBEV; OBRV; TrGrPo
Wexford Girl, The. *Unknown.* ShS (2 *vers, with music*); ViBoFo
Wha Is Perfyte. Alexander Scott. GoTS
(Quha Is Perfyte.) OxBS
Wha Is That at My Bower-Door? Burns. ErPo; InvP; UnTE
Wha kens on whatna Bethlehems. The Innumerable Christ. "Hugh MacDiarmid." EaLo; OxBS
Wha lies here? Johnny Dow. *Unknown.* FiBHP; PV; SiTL; WhC
Wha wadna be in love. Maggie Lauder. *Unknown.* OBS; OxBS
Whack Fol the Diddle. Peadar Kearney. FiBHP; OnYI
Whaddaya Do for Action in This Place? George Starbuck. NePoEA-2
Whalan of Waitin' a While. J. W. Gordon. PoAu-1
Whale. William Rose Benét. EtS; MAP; MoAmPo
Whale, The. Buson, *tr. fr. Japanese by* Harold G. Henderson. SoPo
Whale, The. Erasmus Darwin. GoTP
Whale. Geoffrey Dearmer. BoTP
Whale, The. John Donne. *Fr.* The Progress of the Soul. ChTr; PoSa
Whale, The. Herman Melville. *See* Father Mapples's Hymn.
Whale, The ("It was in the year of. . ."). *Unknown.* *See* Greenland Fishery, The.
Whale, The ("Now I will fashion the tale of a fish") *Unknown, tr. fr. Anglo-Saxon by* Charles W. Kennedy. *Fr.* Physiologus. AnOE; OA
Whale, The ("Tis a hundred years"). *Unknown.* EtS
Whale and Johan, The. Viola Meynell. MemP
Whale and the *Essex,* The. A. M. Sullivan. EtS
Whale and the Tiger, The. John W. Simons. JKCP (1955 ed.)
Whale butting through scarps of moving marble, The. Explorations. Louis MacNeice. ChMP; CoBMV; ILP
Whale, His Bulwark, The. Derek Walcott. TTY
Whale, improbable as lust, The. A Tall Tale; or, A Moral Song. Phyllis Webb. OBCV
Whale of great porosity, A. A Fish Story. Henry A. Beers. BOHV
Whaleman's Song, The. *Unknown.* EtS
Whalen's Fate, *with music.* *Unknown.* ShS
Whales, The. Marguerite Young. ReMP
Whales have calves. The Guppy. Ogden Nash. WePo
Whale's Nature, The. *Unknown, tr. fr. Middle English.* *Fr.* The Bestiary. MeEV
Whales Weep Not! D. H. Lawrence. CMoP; PoIE
Whalin' up the Lachlan. Louis Esson. NeLNL
Whaling backdoor of Texarkana, The. Blue Texarkana. Glenn Stokes. WSL
Whaling for continents suspected deep in the south. The Unhistoric Story. Allen Curnow. AnNZ
Wha'll buy [my] caller herrin'? Caller Harrin'. Lady Nairne. HBV; MCCG; OBRV; OxBS
Whan bells war rung, an mass was sung. Sweet William's Ghost (B *vers.*). *Unknown.* ESPB
Whan gloamin' grey out-owre the welkin keeks. The Farmer's Ingle. Robert Fergusson. CEP
Whan my faither's faither was a bairn. The Star. William Soutar. NeBP
Whan netilles in winter [*or* wynter] bere roses rede. Impossible to Trust Women. *Unknown.* EnPo; MeEL
Whan Phoebus ent'red was in Gemine. How Grand Amour Walked in a Meadow and Met with Fame. . Stephen Hawes. *Fr.* The Pastime of Pleasure. ReIE
Whan seyd was al this miracle, every man. Sir Thopas [*or* Prologue to Sir Thopas]. Chaucer. *Fr.* The Canterbury Tales. BEL; Par
Whan that Aprille with his shoures sote [*or* soote]. Prologue. Chaucer. *Fr.* The Canterbury Tales. ATP; BEL; BoLiVe; CaFP; ChTr; CoBE; CTC; DiPo; EnL; EnLi-1; EnLit; FiP; FlW; GoBC; ILP; InP; MaPo; MBW-1; NoP; OAEP; PoIE; SeCeV; TOP; TrGrPo; ViBoPo; YAT, *abr.*
Whan That the Month of May. Chaucer. *Fr.* The Legend of Good Women: Prologue. AtBAP
Whan the Hert Is Laich. Sidney Goodsir Smith. NeBP
Whan ye see a dragon. Signs. William Soutar. ACV
Whango Tree, The. *Unknown.* BOHV; NA
Whanne I this Supplicacioun. The Parting of Venus and Old Age. John Gower. *Fr.* Confessio Amantis. PoEL-1
Whanne ic se on Rode. I Ought to Weep. *Unknown.* MeEL
"Whar hae ye been a'day—my boy Tammy?" My Boy Tammy. Hector MacNeill. CH; LO
Whar y'u from, little stranger, little boy? A Cowboy's Son. *Unknown.* SCC
Whare the braid planes in dowy murmurs wave. The Ghaists: A Kirk-yard Eclogue. Robert Fergusson. OxBS
"Wharefore sou'd ye talk o' love." Willie and Helen. Hew Ainslie. HBV; OBEV (1st ed.)
Wharf of Dreams, The. Edwin Markham. HBV
Wharton ("Wharton! the scorn and wonder of our days"). Pope. AWP; JAWP; WBP
(Characters from the Satires: Wharton.) InPo
What/ is it about? The Universe. May Swenson. TPM
What/ will make/ me think. If She Bees. Arthur Pfister. WSL
What?/ You define me God with these trinkets. What? You Define Me God. Stephen Crane. *Fr.* War Is Kind, IV. AmPP (3d ed.)
What a big nose Mrs. Mother has. Mrs. Mother Has a Nose. James Broughton. SiTL
What a calamity! What dreadful loss! Honesty at a Fire. J. C. Squire. FiBHP
What a commanding power. Prayer. Thomas Washbourne. WGRP
What a Court Hath Old England, *with music.* *Unknown.* TrAS, *incl.* You Simple Bostonians
What a dainty life the milkmaid leads! Song. Thomas Nabbes. *Fr.* Tottenham Court. EG; SeCL
What a delight it is. Tachibana Akemi. *Fr.* Poems of Solitary Delights. FlW
What a fearful battle. The Chickens. Rose Fyleman. TiPo (1952 ed.)
What a fine cow your predecessor was! To a Sacred Cow. *Unknown.* WGRP
What a Friend We Have in Jesus. Joseph Scriven. SoP; TreFT
(Unfailing Friend, The.) BLRP
What a gay/ September day! School Begins. Nell Goodale Price. BrR
What a girl called "the dailiness of life" Well Water. Randall Jarrell. NoP
What a grudge I am bearing the earth. A Translation from Petrarch. Petrarch, *tr. by* J. M. Synge. Sonnets to Laura: To Laura in Death, XXXII. MoBrPo; NeMA
What a liar/ Was the tinker woman. Outside Dunsandle. Sacheverell Sitwell. ChMP
"What a lovely world," said the baby chick. An Easter Chick. Thirza Wakley. BoTP
What a man may do for love. All for Love. *Unknown.* UnTE
What a moment, what a doubt! Sneezing. Leigh Hunt. HBV
What a night! The wind howls, hisses, and but stops. Snowstorm. John Clare. BoNaP; FiW; WiR
What a piece of work is [a] man! Man. Shakespeare. *Fr.* Hamlet, II, ii. InP; TreF
What a plague is this o' mine. Jenny wi' the Airn Teeth. Alexander Anderson. HBV
What a Proud Dreamhorse. E. E. Cummings. InvP
What a sharp little fellow is Mister Fly. Mister Fly. Thomas Miller. OTPC (1923 ed.)
What a sorrowful sunset we had tonight! Winter Sunset. Jules Laforgue. SyP
What a stir in the harbor! Palos, Spain, 1492. Annette Wynne. HH
What a sweet smell rises. Laying the Dust. Denise Levertov. ToPo
"What a waste of a beautiful girl!" Last Letter to the Western

'What (continued)
Civilization. D. T. Ogilvie. NBP
What a wild room. A Man-made World. Stephen Spender. MoRP
What a wonderful bird the frog are. The Frog. *Unknown.* MoShBr; SiTL; TreFT; WhC; YaD
What a word and I thought it would be. Alone. Richard Shelton. NYBP
What a world that was you planned us. John o' Dreams. Theodosia Garrison. HBMV
What about measure, I learnt. Peri Poietikes. Louis Zukofsky. CoPo
What! After your six-month drowsing and indolent sleeping. At the Edge of the Bay. Thomas Caldecot Chubb. EtS
What ailes Pigmalion? Is it lunacy. The Poem. Thomas Morton. SCAP
What ails this heathenish rage? Psalm II. *Paraphrased by* Sir Philip Sidney. FCP
What! alive and so bold, O Earth? Lines Written on Hearing the News of the Death of Napoleon. Shelley. ChER; ERoP-2
What Am I? Dorothy Aldis. OTPC (1946 ed.); RIS; StVeCh (1955 ed.)
(Riddle: What Am I?) SoPo
What Am I, Life? John Masefield. *Fr.* Sonnets ("Long long ago"). ImOP; NP
What am I? Nosing here, turning leaves over. Wodwo. Ted Hughes. PoIE (1970 ed.); ToPo
What, am I not thy grandchild? thou that bought'st me. Queen Eleanor and Her Dwarf. George Darley. PeER
"What am I to do with my Sister?" Prince Yuhara. *Fr.* Manyo Shu. AWP; JAWP; WBP
What Am I Who Dare to Call Thee, God! William Habington. OxBoCh
(What Am I Who Dare.) PoLi; TrPWD
What an elusive target. The Fights. Milton Acorn. MoCV
What an enchanted world is this. F Is for Fiddler. W. H. Davies. MuSP
What? an English sparrow sing? Did You Ever Hear an English Sparrow Sing? Bertha Johnston. BLPA
What answer could she give. Innocence. Norman MacCaig. NMP; OPoP
What answer shall we make to them that seek. Lincoln. Florence Kiper Frank. PGD
What are earthly honors. Henry Shirley. *Fr.* The Martyred Soldier. TuPP
What are heavy? Sea-sand and sorrow. Sea-Sand and Sorrow. Christina Rossetti. ChTr; OTD
What are little boys made of, made of? Mother Goose. ABF; BoChLi; FaFP; LiTG; OTPC; OxNR; PPL; RiS; SAS; SiTL; TreF
What are men's lives, but labyrinths of error. An Inquisition upon Fame and Honor. Fulke Greville. SiCE
What are our light afflictions here. Our Light Afflictions. *Unknown.* BLRP
What Are Outward Forms? Isaac Bickerstaffe. OnYI
What are poets? Are they only drums commanding? No Armistice in Love's War. Ralph Cheyney. PGD
"What are the bugles blowin' for?" said Files-on-Parade. Danny Deever. Kipling. AnFE; BBV (1923 ed.) BEL; BrPo; CaFP; DiPo; EnLi-2 (1949 ed.); ExPo; GTBS-P; HBC; InP; LiTB; LiTM (rev. ed.); MaC; MCCG; MoBrPo; NeMA; NoP; OAEP (2d ed.); OxBoLi; PeVV; PoE; PoFS; PoLF; PoPo; PoVP; SeCePo; ShBV-3; TOP; TreFS; TrGrPo; TSW; UnPo (3d ed.); VA; VaPo; WaaP
What are the islands to me. The Islands. Hilda Doolittle ("H. D."). MAP; MoAmPo; PG
What are the lays of artful Addison. The Charms of Nature. Joseph Warton. SeCePo
What are the long waves singing so mournfully evermore? Olivia. Edward Pollock. AA
"What are the signs of thy coming." Be Ye Also Ready. Annie Johnson Flint. FaChP
What are the simples the witches want? Herbs and Simples. Martha Keller. FiSC
What are the thoughts that are stirring his breast? Under the Shade of the Trees. Margaret Junkin Preston. DD; MC; PAH
What are the Vision and the Cry. The Confused Dawn. William Douw Lighthall. VA
What are the voices that harass their dreaming? Last Cargo. Silence Buck Bellows. EtS
What are these words that beat their wings in vain. The Gaelic. Blanche Mary Kelly. CAW
What Are They Thinking. Bryan Guinness. OxBI
"What are those Golden Builders doing?" Blake. *Fr.* Jerusalem, I. OBRV
What are to me those honours or renown. Last Words on Greece. Byron. ERoP-2
What Are We First? George Meredith. Modern Love, XXX. AnEnPo; LiTL; NBM; PoEL-5; Sonn; ViBoPo; ViPo; VP
What Are Years? Marianne Moore. AmP; AP; BWP; CMoP; CoBMV; EaLo; ForPo; LiTA; MoAB; MoAmPo (1950 ed.); MoPo; OxBA; PoDB; ReMP; TPM; TrGrPo (rev. ed.)
What are you able to build with your blocks? Block City. Robert Louis Stevenson. FaPON; MPB; PCH; SoPo; TiPo
What Are You Building? Helen W. Richardson. SoP
What are you carrying, Pilgrims, Pilgrims? Atlantic Charter, A. D. 1620-1942. Francis Brett Young. AmFN; TiPo (1952 ed.)
What Are You Doing for Jesus? Martha Snell Nicholson. BePJ
"What are you doing, friend?" I asked of one. What Are You Building? Helen W. Richardson. SoP
What are you doing like a naughty child. To a Poet. Walter Conrad Arensberg. AnAmPo
What are you doing, my lady, my lady. *Unknown.* OxNR
What are you doing out here in the snow. Welcome Visitors. Emilie Blackmore Stapp. GFA
"What are you doing there, Robin a Bobbin." "Talents Differ." Laura E. Richards. TiPo
What, are you drop't? John Webster. *Fr.* The White Devil, V, vi. PoEL-2
What, are you hurt, Sweet? So am I. To a Hurt Child. Grace Denio Litchfield. AA
What are you, Lady?—naught is here. Portrait of a Lady in the Exhibition of the Royal Academy. Winthrop Mackworth Praed. *Fr.* Every-Day Characters. CLwM; NBM; PoEL-4
What are you, rose?—lips that lean back to meet. The Rose and God. Charles Wharton Stork. HBMV
What are you singing of, soft and mild. The Song of the Wood. Frederic Edward Weatherly. OTPC (1946 ed.)
What are you, then, my love, my friend, my father. The Quarry. Vassar Miller. NePoEA-2
What are you. . .? they ask, in wonder. Cold Colloquy. Patrick Anderson. *Fr.* Poem on Canada. CaP; PeCV; TwCaPo
What are you waiting for, George, I pray? Tardy George. *Unknown.* PAH
What art thou, frost? and whence are thy keen stores. James Thomson. *Fr.* The Seasons: Winter. OxBS
What art thou, Life? The shadow of a dream. Sonnet on Life. Sir Brooke Boothby. ViBoPo
What Art Thou, Love? Jacob Allestry. SeCL; SeEP
What art Thou saying, Lord, to me. Thanksgiving. Gene H. Osborne. PGD
What art thou what wouldst thou have? *Unknown.* SeCSL
What Artifice. George Dillon. NP
What asks the Bard? He prays for nought. After Horace. A. D. Godley. BOHV
What avails it, dear Tom, to be honest and true. Written in 1740. Thomas Catesby Paget. WaPE
"What bait do you use," said a Saint to the Devil. The Lure. John Boyle O'Reilly. HBV
What bark impelled by autumn's freshening gale. Geese in Autumn. *Unknown.* OnPM
"What be you a-lookin' at, Emily Ann?" The Pear Tree. Mary Gilmore. PoAu-1
What beauty would have lovely styled. An Epitaph: On Elizabeth Chute. Ben Jonson. EnRePo; NoP
What Became of Them? *Unknown.* *See* Old Rat's Tale, An.
What beckoning [*or* beck'ning] ghost, along the moonlight shade. Elegy [*or* Verses] to the Memory of an Unfortunate Lady. Pope. ACP; CBEP; CEP; EiPP; FiP; HBV; LO; MBW-1; NoP; OBEC; OBEV; PeER; PoE; SeCeV
What Becomes of a Strain of Music. Juan Ramón Jiménez, *tr. fr. Spanish by* John Crow. WoL
What becomes of the girl who lives always alone? The Sorceress. Eugene Marais. PeSA
What began that bustle in the village. The Birth of Moshesh. D. G. T. Bereng. PeSA; TTY
What Bids Me Leave. Herbert Trench. HBMV

What bird are you in the grass-tops? Grass-Tops. Witter Bynner. MAP; MoAmPo (1942 ed.); NP
What bird is that, with voice so sweet. A Creole Slave-Song. Maurice Thompson. AA
What Bird So Sings. John Lyly. *See* Trico's Song.
What Birds Were There. Brother Antoninus. ToPo
"What bluid's that on thy coat lap." Edward (A *vers.*). *Unknown.* BaBo; ESPB
What body can be ploughed. Chanson un Peu Naïve. Louise Bogan. HBMV
What Booker can prognosticate. When the King Enjoys His Own Again. Martin Parker. FaBoCh; OBS; OxBoLi; TuPP
What; breathles nimphs? bright virgins let me know. Tenth Nimphall, The. Michael Drayton. *Fr.* The Muses Elizium. AnAnS-2
What Bright Pushbutton? Samuel Allen. PoNe (1970 ed.)
What bright soft thing is this? The Tear. Richard Crashaw. EnLi-1; GTBS-W; MaMe; LiTB; MasP; OAEP; SeCP; UnPo
What bring ye me, O camels, across the southern desert. Caravans. Josephine Preston Peabody. AA
What bring[s] you, sailor, home from the sea. Luck. W. W. Gibson. EtS; MoShBr; OBMV
What bullet killed him? Dead Soldier. Nicolás Guilleén. PoNe; TTY
What business have I here. Autumn Burial: A Meditation. Charles Gullans. QFR
What can a mother give her children. The Beautiful Gift. Grace Noll Crowell. PEDC
What can be the matter. The Wind. Dorothy Gradon. BoTP
What can be the mistery why Charing Cross. The Statue at Charing Cross. Andrew Marvell. MaMe
What can console for a dead world? Believe and Take Heart. John Lancaster Spalding. AA; JKCP
What can forgive us for. Failure. Eithne Wilkins. NeBP
What Can He Do with You? *Unknown.* SoP
What Can I Do? Horace Traubel. *Fr.* Chants Communal. TrJP
What Can I Give Him? Christina Rossetti. *See* Christmas Carol, A: "In the bleak mid-winter."
What can I give my dear. Doubt. Elinor Chipp. HBMV
What can I give thee back, O liberal. Elizabeth Barrett Browning. Sonnets from the Portuguese, VIII. GTBS; GTSL; HBV; OBVV; ViPo
What can I give you? Fifth Birthday Gift. Marjorie Lederer. BiCB
What Can I Tell My Bones? Theodore Roethke. AmPP (5th ed.)
What can I write in thee, O dainty book. In a Lady's Album. Marcus Clarke. BoAu
What can it avail. John Skelton. *Fr.* Colin Clout. SiCE TuPP
What can it mean? Is it aught to Him. God Cares [*or* He Careth]. "Marianne Farningham." BLRP; SoP; WBLP
What can lambkins do. A Chill. Christina Rossetti. BoTP; PRWS
What can strip the seeming glory. The Face of Christ. J. Stuart Holden. SoP
What can the cause be, when the K. hath given. An Epigram, to the Household, 1630. Ben Jonson. Sonn
What, can these dead bones live, whose sap is dried. The New Ezekiel. Emma Lazarus. AA; AnAmPo
What can we give in return. Australia. Dowell O'Reilly. BoAu
What Can We Poor Females Do. *Unknown.* SeCL
(Song for Two Voices, A.) SeEP
What can you do, sir, pray let me see? Two Dogs. F. Hey. SAS
What can't be cured. *Unknown.* FaFP; SiTL
What cant, oh, what hypocrisy. Cant. W. H. Davies. MoRP
What Care I. George Wither. *See* Shall I, Wasting in Despair.
What care I for caste or creed. Creed and Deed. Robert Loveman. MaRV; OQP
What care I for the leagues o' sand. The Mither's Lament. Sydney Goodsir Smith. ACV; OxBS
What care I how black I be? *Unknown.* OxNR
What care I, so they stand the same. Merops. Emerson. AmePo; AnFE; APA; CoAnAm; FaBoEn; MWA-1; OxBA
What care I tho' beauty fading. Spiritual Love. William Caldwell Roscoe. OBVV
What care I though she be fair. The Choice [*or* Choyce]. Thomas Beedome. CavP; SeCL
"What care I, what cares he." The Cowboy. John Antrobus. AA; FaBoBe; FaPON; OTPC (1946 ed.); PoRL
What care I who gets the credit? Credit. *Unknown.* STF
What care if the day. The Good Inn. Herman Knickerbocker Viele. *Fr.* The Inn of the Silver Moon. HBV
What cave are you in, hiding, rained on? A Man Writes to a Part of Himself. Robert Bly. PoIE (1970 ed.)
What celebration should there be? Holiday. Horace. AWP; JAWP; WBP
What changes here, O hair. Jorge de Montemayor, *tr. by* Sir Philip Sidney. *Fr.* Diana. FCP
What charlatans in this later day. The Deathless. Ednah Proctor Clarke. AA
What cher? Gud cher, gud cher, gud cher. A Cheerful Welcome. *Unknown.* MeEL
What Child Is This? William Chatterton Dix. MaRV
(What Child Is This, Who, Laid to Rest, *with music.*) YaCaBo
What Christ Is to Us. *Unknown.* BLRP; SoP
What Christ Said. George Macdonald. *See* Obedience.
What color [*or* colour] are they now, thy quiet waters? Evening on the Moselle. Decimus Magnus Ausonius. AnEnPo; LiTW
What color is the hole in your socks? A Meditation: What Is a Stocking in Eternity? Lewis MacAdams. ANYP; YAP
"What come that blood on your shirt sleeve?" My Son, Come Tell It to Me. *Unknown.* BFSS
What cometh here from west to east a-wending? A Death Song. William Morris. PoVP; VA
What comfort by Him do we win. By Him. Ben Jonson. TRV
What comfort! through conditioned air. Parlor Car. Dorothy Brown Thompson. PoMa
What, comrade of a night. Life. Alice Brown. AA
What conscience, say, is it in thee. To Aenone [*or* Oenone]. Robert Herrick. HBV; OBEV
What Constitutes a State? Sir William Jones. BLPA; MCCG, *abr.*; NeHB; PEDC, *abr.*; PGD
(Ode in Imitation of Alcaeus, An.) HBV; PoFV
What could be dafter. John Skelton. Robert Graves. BrPo
What could be done? The inn was full of folks! The Inn That Missed Its Chance. Amos Russell Wells. ChrBoLe
What Could Be Lovelier than to Hear. Elizabeth J. Coatsworth. BrR; SiSoSe
(Summer Rain.) RePo
What could be nicer than the spring. A Walk in Spring. K. C. Lart. BoTP
What could be viler. Malcolm Bryler. *Unknown.* SiTL
What could he know of sky and stars, or heaven's all-hidden life. The Sooth-Sayer. Sadi. *Fr.* The Gulistan. AWP
"What could I make," Socrates might have asked. The Makers. David Galler. NYBP
What could make me more morose. The Ovibos. Robert Hale. FiBHP
What could thus high thy rash ambition raise? Honest Fame. Pope. *Fr.* The Temple of Fame. OBEC
What counsel has the hooded moon? James Joyce. Chamber Music, XII. HW; OnYI; OxBI
What cry—from out the moonlit blue of wood. Wailing Lynx. Lew Sarett. NP
What Cunning Can Express. Edward de Vere, Earl of Oxford. EIL; ReEn; SiCE; TuPP
(White and Red.) OBSC
What Curious Dresses All Men Wear. Delmore Schwartz. ELU
What curious things we said. Intra Sepulchrum. Thomas Hardy. MaPo
What curled and scented sun-girls, almond-eyed. On a Lute Found in a Sarcophagus. Sir Edmund Gosse. GTSL; VA
What danger is the pilgrim in? Bunyan. *Fr.* The Pilgrim's Progress. PeRV
What dawn-pulse at the heart of heaven, or last. Beauty's Pageant. Dante Gabriel Rossetti. The House of Life, XVII. MaVP; PoVP; ViPo; VP
What days await this woman, whose strange feet. A Forecast. Archibald Lampman. VA
What death is worse than this. Sir Thomas Wyatt. FCP; SiPS
What death means is not this. Canticle. Wendell Berry. AP
What delightful hosts are they. A Parting Guest. James Whit-

What (continued)
comb Riley. HBV; MAP; MoAmPo (1942 ed.); NeMA; PoMa; TreFT; VA
What desperate nightmare rapts me to this land. Legacy: My South. Dudley Randall. NNP; PoNe (1970 ed.)
What did he have in his wagon? Little Black Man with a Rose in His Hat. Audrey Wurdemann. YaD
What did Hiamovi, the red man, Chief of the Cheyennes have? All One People. Carl Sandburg. AmFN
What did I do on my blooming vacation? The Jokesmith's Vacation. Don Marquis. ALV; FiBHP
What did she see—oh, what did she see. The Cats Have Come to Tea [*or* All the Cats]. Kate Greenaway. OTPC (1946 ed.); PCH; SAS
What did the captain say to the cook. A Capstan Chantey. Edwin James Brady. HBMV
What did the day bring? Letter from a Coward to a Hero. Robert Penn Warren. MAP; MoAmPo
What did the Indians call you? To the Avon River above Stratford Canada. James Reaney. MoCV
What did thy song boad lady? Shakespeare. *Fr.* Othello, V, ii. AtBAP
What did you build the trophy of, soldier, soldier? Victory March. M. K. Joseph. AnNZ
What did you do with the world that you bade us to bow to anew? William Rose Benét. *Fr.* Arraignment. MaRV
What did you see, Soldier? What did you see at war? Soldier, What Did You See? Don Blanding. BBV (1951 ed.); MaRV
What different dooms our birthdays bring! Miss Kilmansegg's Birth. Thomas Hood. OxBoLi
What Dim Arcadian Pastures. Alice Corbin. HBMV; NP
What dire offense from amorous causes springs. The Rape of the Lock. Pope. AtBAP; ATP; BEL; BoLiVe; BWP; CABA; CABL; CEP; CoBE; DiPo; EiCL; EiPP; EnL; EnLi-1; EnLit; ForPo; FosPo; ILP; MaPo; MasP; MBW-1; NoP; OAEP; OuHeWo; PAn; PIA; Po; PoAn; PoE; PoEL-3; PoFS; SeCeV; StP; TOP; TrGrPo; VaPo
What distant thunders rend the skies. On the Death of Captain Nicholas Biddle. Philip Freneau. PAH
What Do I Care? Sara Teasdale. NP
What Do I Care for Morning. Helene Johnson. CDC
What do I care for sorrow. Flail. Power Dalton. HBMV
What do I here! what's beauty? 'las. John Hall. *Fr.* Of Beauty LO
What Do I Know? Christopher Brennan. BoAV; NeLNL
What do I owe to you. Debt. Sara Teasdale. NP
What do I see and hear of an April morning? Shore Roads of April. Bill Adams. EtS
What Do the Birds Think? Alfred Purdy. MoCV
What do the robins whisper about. Three o'Clock in the Morning. R. S. Palfrey. DD; MPB
What do the stars do. The Stars. Christina Rossetti. *Fr.* Sing-Song. OTPC (1946 ed.)
What Do They Do? Christina Rossetti. *See* What Does the Bee Do?
What do they know of penitence. Praise. Edith Daley. SoP; TRV
What do they mean—the stripes of red? The Flag We Fly. Aileen Fisher. YeAr
What do they see. Plymouth Rock. Olive Driver. RePo
What do we hear? What majesty, what force. Vittorio Alfieri. *Fr.* The First Brutus. PoFr
What do we need for love—a midnight fire. Need. Babette Deutsch. MoLP
What Do We Plant? Henry Abbey. DD; FaPON; HBV; HBVY; MPB; OHIP; PGD; TiPo; WBLP
(What Do We Plant when We Plant the Tree?) HH; OTPC (1946 ed.)
What do you call it, bobsled champion. Twentieth-Century Blues. Kenneth Fearing. CMoP
What do you care for Caesar, who yourself. Peter at Fourteen. Constance Carrier. NePoAm
What do you carry that cannot be borne. For Karen. Daniel Hughes. NYTB
"What do you have for breakfast?" A Little Bird. Aileen Fisher. SoPo
What do you look for, what do you seek? Wishes. Norman Ault. HBMV; HBVY
"What do you paint, when you paint on a wall?" I Paint What I See. E. B. White. LiTM; NAMP; NYBP; PoFr
What do you remember thinking back? Ever Since. Archibald MacLeish. NePA
What do you see in a tired old water-logged crackers face? If You Love Them, Wouldn't You Like to See Them Better Off? Kuwasi Balagon. BF
What do you see in the fire tonight? Pictures in the Fire. Patience Strong. RePo
What do you seek within, O Soul, my Brother? Introversion. Evelyn Underhill. MaRV; WGRP
What do you sell, O ye merchants? In the Bazaars of Hyderabad. Sarojini Naidu. FaPON; GaP; MoSiPe; RePo
What do you think endures? The Greatest City. Walt Whitman. OCS; RePo
What do you think I saw to-day. The Fairy Cobbler. A. Neil Lyons. BoTP
What do you think? Last night I saw. The Dragon. Mary Mullineaux. BoTP
What Does a Man Think About. John Holmes. CrMA
What Does Easter Mean to You? May Ricker Conrad. OQP; PGD; SoP
What does he plant who plants a tree? The Heart of the Tree. Henry Cuyler Bunner. DD; HH; OHFP; OHIP; OQP; OTD; PGD
What Does It Avail Me? Louise Labé, *tr. fr. French by* Frederic Prokosch. LiTW
What does it mean? I look across the years. What Does It Mean to Be American? Roselle Mercier Montgomery. MC
What does it mean? Tired, angry, and ill at ease. Beauty. Edward Thomas. NP
What Does It Mean to Be American? Roselle Mercier Montgomery. MC
What does it take to make a day? A Day. William L. Stidger. PoToHe
What Does Little Birdie Say? Tennyson. *Fr.* Sea Dreams. GFA; HBV; HBVY; HH; MPB; OTPC
(Cradle Song: "What does little birdie say?") BoTP; PPL; TVC
(Little Birdie.) SAS
What does not change/ is the will to change. The Kingfishers. Charles Olson. NeAP; OPoP
What Does the Bee Do? Christina Rossetti. *Fr.* Sing-Song. BoTP; RIS; SUS; TiPo
(What Do They Do?) FaPON
What does the farmer in the spring? Spring Work at the Farm. Thirza Wakley. BoTP
What does the hangman think about. The Hangman at Home. Carl Sandburg. CMoP
What does the train say? The Baby Goes to Boston. Laura E. Richards. SAS; TiPo
What Does This Mean? Sir Thomas Wyatt. MeEL
("What meaneth this? When I lie alone.") FCP; SiPS
("What menythe thys when I lye alone?") EnPo
What domes and pinnacles of mist and fire. Evening in Tyringham Valley. Richard Watson Gilder. AA
What domination of what darkness dies this hour. The City. "*A* E." WGRP
What dost thou here. Moth Song. Ellen Mackay Hutchinson Cortissoz. AA
What dost thou here, thou shining, sinless thing. A Butterfly in Church. George Marion McClellan. BANP
What! dost thou pray that the outgone tide be rolled back on the strand. A Far Cry to Heaven. Edith M. Thomas. AA; PFY; WGRP
What doth it serve to see sun's burning face. Sonnet. William Drummond of Hawthornden. EIL; Sonn
What Doth the Lord Require? Micah, Bible, *O.T.* *See* Wherewith Shall I Come before the Lord?
What Doth the Lord Require of Thee. Allen Eastman Cross. MaRV
What doth this noise of thoughts within my heart. The Familie. George Herbert. AnAnS-1; MaMe; MeP
What draws you here at night, gray-headed man. Night School. Elias Lieberman. NYTB
What Dreamed I? *Unknown.* *See* Benedicite, What Dreamed I This Night?
What drinks the dragon fly, that dart of blue light. Dragon Flies. W. J. Turner. GTBS-D
What Ducks Require. John Crowe Ransom. FaBoMo
What D'Ye Call It, The, *sel.* John Gay.
Ballad, A: "'Twas when the seas were roaring," *fr.*. II, viii. CeP; HBV;StP; ViBoPo

What eagle can behold her sunbright eye. Gulling Sonnets, III. Sir John Davies. Sonn
What ecstasies her bosom fire! To a Lady on Her Passion for Old China. John Gay. EiPP; FaFP; LiTB; LoBV; OBEC; PoE; SiTL
"What else/ Is love, but the most noble, pure affection." Ben Jonson. *Fr.* The New Inn. LO
What end the gods may have ordained for me. To Leuconöe. Horace. AA
What essences from Idumean palm. Mimma Bella, XX. Eugene Lee-Hamilton. HBV
What ever 'tis, whose beauty here below. The Starre. Henry Vaughan. MePo
What Every Gardener Knows. *Ad. by* Louis Untermeyer. StaSt
What Faire Pompe Have I Spide of Glittering Ladies. Thomas Campion. *See* Love's Pilgrims.
"What fairings will ye that I bring?" The Singing Leaves. James Russell Lowell. GN; LoEn; MPB; OnSP; OTPC; StVeCh
What Far Kingdom. Arthur S. Bourinot. CaP
What faut had he done that was hang'd yesterday? Of One Hanged. John Heywood. ReIE
What fettle, mate? to me he said. The Greeting. W. W. Gibson. POTE
What fills this house. It Stays. Shirley Kaufman. QAH
What fingers plucked these long untroubled strings? The Mandoline. Jean Kenward. MuSP
"What Five Books Would You Pick to Be Marooned with on a Desert Island?" Paris Leary. CoPo
What flecks the outer gray beyond. The Dead Ship of Harpswell. Whittier. EtS
What flocks of critics hover here to-day. Prologue. Dryden. *Fr.* All for Love. DiPo
What flower is my lady like? Of His Lady. *Unknown.* ElL
What flower is this that greets the morn. The Flower of Liberty. Oliver Wendell Holmes. DD; HBVY; MC; PoRL
What Followed. Josephine Miles. FiMAP
What! for a term so scant. Westminster Abbey. Matthew Arnold. ViPo
What fragrant-footed comer. The Little Knight in Green. Katharine Lee Bates. AA
What frenzy has of late possess'd the brain! Sir Samuel Garth. SiTL
What from the founder Aesop fell. The Purpose of Fable-writing. Phaedrus. AWP
What fun to be a baby swan. A Swan Boat. Robert Palfrey Utter. PCH
What gentle ghost, besprent with April deaw. An Elegie on the Lady Jane Pawlet, Marchion: of Winton. Ben Jonson. SeCP
What gifts of speech a man may own. The Sincere Man. Alfred Grant Walton. PoToHe (new ed.)
What girl but, having gathered flowers. Humility. Robert Browning. PoVP
What gives us that fantastic fit. Natura Naturata. Sir John Denham. CEP; NCEP; PeRV
What glory's this, my Lord? Should one small point. Meditation XXI. Edward Taylor. *Fr.* Preparatory Meditions, First Series. MAmP
What God gives, and what we take. Grace for Children. Robert Herrick. OxBoCh
What God Hath [*or* Has] Promised. Annie Johnson Flint. BLRP; FaChP; MaRV; SoP; STF; TRV; WBLP
What God never sees. *Unknown.* OxNR
What god will choose me from this labouring nation. Odes, I. George Santayana. AmePo; AnFE; APA; CoAnAm
What gods are these? Bright red, or white and green. The Fox-/Hunters. Ebenezer Elliott. PeER
What gods or heroes, whose brave deeds none can dispute. At the Ball Game. Roswell Martin Field. InMe
What goes into a birthday cake. · The Birthday Cake. Victoria Chase. BiCB
What golden gaine made Higginson remove. The Reverend Mr. Higginson. Edward Johnson. SCAP
What Good Are Words? Linwood D. Smith. TNV
What good is there, ah me, what good in love? Rispetto. Agnes Mary Frances Robinson. Tuscan Cypress, II. HBMV
What Grandma Knew. Edward Field. CoPo; FRC
What Grandpa Mouse Said. Vachel Lindsay. UTS
What great yoked brutes with briskets low. Crossing the Plains. Joaquin Miller. AA; AmePo; AmLP; AmPP (3d ed.); AnAmPo; GN; MAP; MoAmPo (1942 ed.); PaA
What greater torment ever could have been. Lonely Beauty. Samuel Daniel. *Fr.* The Complaint of Rosamond. CTC; OBSC
What Greece, when learning flourished, only knew. Prologue to the University of Oxford. Dryden. OBS; PP
What grieves my bones and makes my body faint? In His Extreme Sickness. Thomas, Lord Vaux. ReIE
What Guardian Counsels? Auzias March, *tr. fr. Spanish by* Thomas Walsh. CAW
What guile [*or* guyle] is this, that those her golden tresses. Amoretti, XXXVII. Spenser. ForPo; InP; LiTL; NoP; OBSC; ReEn; SiCE; Sonn; StP; TrGrPo
What Habacuck once spake, mine eyes. Roger Williams. SCAP
What had become of the young shark? The Birth of a Shark. David Wevill. TwCP
What had you been thinking about. The Tennis Court Oath. John Ashbery. FRC
What hand trimmed these strident feathers for flight. Night Flight. George Whalley. CaP
What Happened. Margaret D. Armstrong. FaChP
What happened to Joey on our block. Of Kings and Things. Lillian Morrison. CAD
What happens to a dream deferred? Harlem [*or* Dream Deferred *or* Lenox Avenue Mural]. Langston Hughes. AmNP; AmPP (5th ed.); LiTM (1970 ed.); NoP; OCS; PoNe (1970 ed.); TPM
What happier fortune can one find. Exile. *Unknown.* KiLC
What happiness you gave to me. The Yew-Tree. *Unknown.* ChTr
What happy mortal sees that mountain now. The White Cascade. W. H. Davies. NeMA
What happy secret fountain. The Dwelling Place. Henry Vaughan. MaRV; MeLP; OBS; OxBoCh; SeEP; TrPWD; WGRP
What harm have I done to the stars? Without My Friends the Day Is Dark. Moses ibn Ezra. TrJP
What Harvest Half So Sweet Is. Thomas Campion. EG; UnTE
What has become of our astonishment. The Way We Wonder. Robert Pack. NePoEA
What has become of the good ship *Kite?* Of the Lost Ship. Eugene Richard White. AA
What has bent you. The Pine at Timber-/Line. Harriet Monroe. NP
What has that woman done to you, my dear! Tea. Jacqueline Embry. HBMV; YaD
What Has This Bugbear Death. Lucretius, *See* Against the Fear of Death. *tr. by* Dryden.
What has this bugbear Death that's worth our care? Sonnet on Death [*or* Death; a Sonnet]. William Walsh. CBEP; SeCL; SeEP; ViBoPo
What hast thou learnt today? After a Retreat. Robert Hugh Benson. JKCP
What, hast thou run thy race? Art going down? Of the Going Down of the Sun. Bunyan. CH
What Hath Man Wrought Exclamation Point. Morris Bishop. NYBP
What have I done for you. England, My England. W. E. Henley. EnLi-2 (1949 ed.); MoBrPo; OBEV; OBVV; OTPC (1923 ed.); PoLF; PoVP; TreF; YT
"What have I earned for all that work," I said. The People. W. B. Yeats. CMoP
What have I gained by the toil of the trail? The Toil of the Trail. Hamlin Garland. HBV
What, have I 'scaped love-letters. Shakespeare. *Fr.* The Merry Wives of Windsor, II, ii. LO
What, have I thus betrayed my liberty [*or* libertie]? The Yoke of Tyranny. Sir Philip Sidney. Astrophel and Stella, XLVII. AtBAP; FCP; PoEL-1; ReEn; SiPS; TrGrPo
What have I to bring them, in their stillness? The Streets of San Miguel. Keith Wilson. ThO
What have I to give? In the Far Years. Wilson MacDonald. CaP
What have I to say to you. Love Song. William Carlos Williams. NP
What, have the gods their consort sent from heaven. The Gods, Consort. *Unknown.* MuSP
What have the years left us? Song. Charles G. Blanden. OQP

What (continued)
What Have We Done Today? Nixon Waterman. WBLP
(Today.) OQP
What, have ye kithéd you a knight, Sir Douglas the Doughty. Against Garnesche. John Skelton. ViBoPo
"What have you looked at, Moon." To the Moon. Thomas Hardy. BoNaP; ChTr; CoBE
"What have you there?" the great Panjandrum said. The Truant. E. J. Pratt. OBCV
What, he on whom our voices unanimously ran. The Pope and the Net. Robert Browning. BOHV
What He Said. Harrison Robertson. *See* Two Triolets.
What He Took. Tom Hood. *See* Takings.
What heart could have thought of you. To a Snowflake. Francis Thompson. BoLiVe; BoNaP; FaBV; GoTP; HBV; ImOP; InP; LoBV; MoAB; MoBrPo; NeMA; PoPl; SeCePo; ThWaDe; TrGrPo; TSW
What heartache—ne'er a hill! From the Flats. Sidney Lanier. AmP; CoBA; NePA; OxBA
What heartbeats, lisping like a lizard in a broken cistern. Ode to the Present Century. Thomas Merton. JKCP (1955 ed.)
What heave of grapnels will resurrect the fabric. S.S.R., Lost at Sea—*The Times*. Ralph Gustafson. OBCV; PeCV
What heaven-entreated [*or* heaven-besiegèd] heart is this. To the Noblest and Best of Ladies, the Countess of Denbigh [*or* Against Irresolution]. Richard Crashaw. EP; MaMe; MeLP; MePo; OxBoCh; ReEn; SeCP
What heavy-hoofed coursers the wilderness roam. The Fall of Tecumseh. *Unknown.* PAH
What Hee Suffered. Ben Jonson. *Fr.* A Celebration of Charis. AnAnS-2; SCEP-2; SeCP
What held the bones together? Not belief. No Faith. Mark Van Doren. AnFE; CoAnAm
What helps it those,/ Who skill in song have found. For [*or* To] a Musician. George Wither. *Fr.* Hallelujah. MuSP; OBS; OxBoCh [*wr. at. to* William Austin]
What heroes from the woodland sprung. Seventy-six. Bryant. DD; HBV; MC; PAH
What hideous noyse was that? John Webster. *Fr.* The Duchess of Malfi, IV, ii. AtBAP; PoEL-2
What Highway? George N. Shuster. JKCP (1955 ed.)
What ho! my shepherds, sweet it were. A Sylvan Revel. Edward Cracroft Lefroy. Echoes from Theocritus, XXV. AWP; JAWP; WBP
What holds her fixed far eyes nor lets them range? On Dürer's "Melencolia." Sir William Watson. VA
What hope is here for modern rhyme. In Memoriam A. H. H., LXXVII. Tennyson. CoBE; EnLi-2; EPN; PP; ViPo; VP
What Horace says is. Eheu Fugaces. "Thomas Ingoldsby." NBM; OxBoLi
What hours I spent of precious time. Poetical Economy. Harry Graham. CenHV; SiTL; TreFS
What how? How now? Hath how such hearing found. On How the Cobler. *Unknown.* SCAP
What hubbub rocks the nest? What panic-freighted. Some Lines in Three Parts, III. Peter Viereck. MoAmPo (1950 ed.)
"What hundred books are best, think you?" I said. John Kendrick Bangs. CenHV
What I Do Is Me. Gerard Manley Hopkins. *See* As Kingfishers Catch Fire, Dragonflies Draw Flame.
What I Expected. Stephen Spender. CoBMV; MoAB; MoBrPo; MoPo; OAEP (2d ed.); PIA; PoIE; ReMP
What I fancy I approve. No Loathsomeness in Love. Robert Herrick. AnAnS-2; PoeP
What I gave, I have. On a Gravestone. *Unknown.* PCD
What I Have. Robert Farren. JKCP (1955 ed.)
What I have made. The Children. Constance Urdang. CoAP
What I have written, I cannot unwrite. Ending. Norman Jordan. PoNe (1970 ed.)
What I Have Wrote. Julia Moore. SiTL
("And now, Kind friends, what I have wrote.") FiBHP
What I Know. Morton Marcus. YAP
What I know. The Wind Shrieked Loud. Elizabeth J. Coatsworth. FiSC
What I know outlasts a tooth. What I Know. Morton Marcus. YAP
What I like about Clive. Lord Clive. E. C. Bentley. *Fr.* Clerihews. BOHV; CenHV; MoShBr; OxBoLi; ShBV-3; WhC
What I liked best in Sicily. Goats. Charles Erskine Scott Wood. AnEnPo
What I Live For. George Linnaeus Banks. BLPA; FaBoBe; MaRV; NeHB; TreFS
(My Aim.) WBLP
(Why Do I Live? 1 *st., wr. at. to* Thomas Guthrie.) PoToHe (new ed.)
What I need is lots of money. Take I, 4: II: 58. Philip Whalen. NeAP
What I saw was just one eye. The Bird at Dawn. Harold Monro. BoTP; GoTP; MoBrPo (1950 ed.)
What I See in Me. *Unknown.* STF
What I shall leave thee none can tell. To His Son, Vincent [Corbet]. Richard Corbet. AnAnS-2; BoC; BWP; CBEP; FaBoCh; LoGBV; SeCL; SeEP; TrGrPo
What I think in February is there for April. Collaboration. Tony Towle. ANYP
What I Think of Hiawatha. J. W. Morris. Par
What I thought was love. The Liar. LeRoi Jones. AmPP (5th ed.)
What I was would not work. Encounter in the Cage Country. James Dickey. TPM
What I will ask, if one free wish comes down. A Boon. William Meredith. NePoEA
What I will say today. Lo Que Digo. *Unknown.* AS
What If. Gertrude B. Gunderson. OQP
"What If." *Unknown.* SoP
What if:/ In a moment of pure terror I refused the call of beauty? Rune for the Disenchanted. William Wantling. WOW
What If a Day. Thomas Campion. EIL; EnRePo; NoP; PoIE; ReEn; TuPP
(Chance and Change.) BEL; SoP
What If a Much of a Which of a Wind. E. E. Cummings. AP; FaFP; GTBS-W; LiTA; LiTM; MasP; MemP; MoAmPo (1962 ed.); MoPo; MoPW; MoVE; NePA; NoP; OxBA; PoRA; ReMP; ViBoPo (1958 ed.); WaP
What if I bade you leave. Those Images. W. B. Yeats. CMoP; POTE; PP
What if I coasted near the shore. Voyager's Song. Clement Wood. HBMV
What if I cry in midnight gloom. Heard. Henry W. Frost. SoP
What if I dye for love of thee. *Unknown.* SeCSL
What if I say—/ "The Bible is God's Holy Word." Faith. Maud Frazer Jackson. MaRV; SoP
What if Orpheus. Orpheus in Greenwich Village. Jack Gilbert. PP
What If Remembrance? Richard Eberhart. FiMAP
What if small birds are peppering the sky. It Is Winter, I Know. Merrill Moore. MAP; MoAmPo
What If Some Little Paine the Passage Have. Spenser. *Fr.* The Faerie Queene, I. CH
(Death.) MaRV
(Port after Stormie Seas.) EtS
What if the air has a nipping tooth! A Skater's Valentine. Arthur Guiterman. SiSoSe
What if the back be stooped and the skin be dried. Farmers. Helene Mullins. WGRP
What if the soul her real life elsewhere holds. The Soul in the Body. Edith M. Thomas. AA
What if the sun comes out. Boy Remembers in the Field. Raymond Knister. CaP
What if the ways be stone. City Songs. Mark Van Doren. NYBP
What if the winds sang softly the whole night long. The Poet Tells about Nature. Merrill Moore. NP
What if these long races go on repeating themselves. Written in Dejection near Rome. Robert Bly. NaP
What if this present were the world's last night? Holy Sonnets, XIII. John Donne. AnAnS-1; ExPo; GTBS-W; LiTB; MaMe; MaPo (1969 ed.); MasP; MBW-1; MeLP; MeP; OAEP; OBS; SCEP-1; SeCeV; SeEP; Sonn; TuPP
What if we carved truth in the graveyards? What If. Gertrude B. Gunderson. OQP
What if your way is stormy? "What If." *Unknown.* SoP
What I'm Doing Here. Leonard Cohen. PeCV (1967 ed.)
What inn is this? Emily Dickinson. MasP; NePA
What instinct forces man to journey on. The Poet. Amy Lowell. WGRP
What Invisible Rat. Jean-Joseph Rebéarivelo, *tr. fr. French by* Alan Ryder. TTY

What! Irving? thrice welcome, warm heart and fine brain. Irving. James Russell Lowell. *Fr.* A Fable for Critics. AnNE; CoBA; MWA-1

What Is a Brook? Lucy Sprague Mitchell. PCH

What is a day, what is a year of vain delight and pleasure? *Unknown.* OBSC

What is a friend? I'll tell you. A Friend. *Unknown.* PoToHe (new ed.)

What is a [*or* the] modern poet's fate. The Poet's Fate. Thomas Hood. ELU; FiBHP; PV

What is a poet's love? The Poet's Lot. Oliver Wendell Holmes. PoEL-5

What is a sonnet? 'Tis the pearly shell. The Sonnet. Richard Watson Gilder. AA; HBV

What Is a Woman Like? *Unknown.* BOHV

What is a woman that you forsake her. Harp Song of the Dane Women. Kipling. *Fr.* Puck of Pook's Hill. AtBAP; FaBoEn; OAEP (2d ed.); OBNC; OtMeF; PoRA; POTE; SeCePo; ShBV-3

What is a yielded life? The Yielded Life. "W. A. G." BLRP

What is Africa to me. Heritage. Countee Cullen. AmNP; BALP; BANP; FaBV; MAP; MoAmPo; NoP; PoNe; TTY

What is all this washing about. Washing. John Drinkwater. FaPON; StVeCh

What Is an Epigram? Samuel Taylor Coleridge. *See* Epigram: "What is an epigram?"

What is beauty, saith my sufferings, then? Tamburlaine on Poetry. Christopher Marlowe. *Fr.* Tamburlaine the Great, Pt. I. MyFE

What Is Charm? Louisa Carroll Thomas. BLPA; NeHB

"What Is Christmas?" What Makes Christmas? *Unknown.* SoP

What Is Death? César Malan. *See* It Is Not Death to Die.

What Is Death? *Unknown.* SoP

What is death? 'Tis to be free. The Genius of Death. George Croly. HBV

What is earth, sexton? A place to dig graves. Questions with Answers. *Unknown.* BOHV

What is Freedom?—ye can tell. Shelley. *Fr.* The Masque of Anarchy. PoG

What is freinshipp? but a pleasure. *Unknown.* SeCSL

"What is funny?" you ask, my child. The Anatomy of Humor. Morris Bishop. InMe; WhC

What Is Going on inside His Head. Jonathan Cott. YAP

What is gold worth, say. Child's Song. Swinburne. GTSL; OBVV; PoVP

What Is Good? John Boyle O'Reilly. HBV; HBVY; OQP; OTPC (1946 ed.); PoToHe; TreF; WBLP

What is Greece to us now? Salute to Greece. "Clemence Dane." PoFr

What is he buzzing in my ears? Confessions. Robert Browning. ELP; EPN; GTBS-D; GTBS-P; MBW-2; PoVP; ViBoPo; ViPo

What is he, this lordling that cometh from the fight? The Knight Stained from Battle. William Herebert. MeEL

What is home without a Bible? A Home without a Bible. Charles D. Meigs. WBLP

What Is Home without a Mother? Septimus Winner. PEDC

What is hope? a smiling rainbow. Cui Bono? Thomas Carlyle. HBV; OBRV; WGRP

What is house and what is home. House and Home [*or* Home]. Joseph Beaumont. GoTL; OBS

What Is It? Marie Louise Allen. TiPo

What Is It? H. E. Wilkinson. BoTP

What Is It Jesus Saith? Christina Rossetti. ChIP; EPN

What is it like, this dying? Dying. Martha Snell Nicholson. FaChP

What is it men in women do require? Several Questions Answered [*or* The Question Answered]. Blake. EiCL; ELU; ERoP-1; ErPo; PeER; ViBoPo

What is it, O dear country of our pride. For Remembrance. Basil Ebers. DD; HH

What is it so transforms the boulevard? Another Spirit Advances. Jules Romains. AWP; JAWP; WBP

What is it that a-billowing there. First Fruits in 1812. Wallace Rice. MC; PAH

"What is it to be dead?" O Life. A Child's Question. Emma Huntington Nason. AA

What is it to grow old? Growing Old. Matthew Arnold.

EnLi-2; EnLit; FaFP; FiP; HBV; MaVP; MBW-2; OuHeWo; PoEL-5; PoVP

What is it to remember? Bliss Carman. *Fr.* Songs of the Sea-Children. OBCV

What is it you remember?—the summer mornings. To Any Member of My Generation. George Barker. WaP

"What is it you're mumbling, old Father, my Dad?" By the Exeter River. Donald Hall. MoBS

What is left at the end? Fore Thought. May Sarton. MoLP

What Is Life? Samuel Taylor Coleridge. ERoP-1; FiP

What is life if, full of care. *See* What is this life. . .

What is life or worldly pleasure? What Is Life? *Unknown.* EnRePo

What Is Love? Beaumont *and* Fletcher. *See* Tell Me, Dearest, What Is Love?

What is Love? John Clare. NCEP

What Is Love? *sel.* A. P. Herbert.

"'What is Love?' the poets question." BoLP

What Is Love? *Unknown.* SoP

What is love besides the name. *Unknown.* SeCSL

What is love but the desire. Batte's Song. Michael Drayton. *Fr.* The Shepherd's Garland. LoBV

What is love of one's land. Footsloggers. Ford Madox Ford. NP

What is love? 'tis not hereafter. Love. Shakespeare. *Fr.* Twelfth Night, II, iii. TreFT

What is lovelier than the gold. Casual Gold. Maud E. Uschold. SoPo; YeAr

What Is Man? Psalms, VIII, Bible, *O.T.* MaRV; TrGrPo

(How Glorious Is Thy Name.) TrJP

(O Lord, How Excellent Is Thy Name.) TreFS

(Psalm VIII.) AWP; JAWP; OnPM; OuHeWo; PG (1955 ed.)

(Psalm of David, A.) OTPC (1946 ed.)

(Song of Praise, A.) EnLi-1

What is more gentle than a wind in summer? Sleep and Poetry. Keats. AtBAP; ATP; EnRP; ERoP-2; MERP; PP

What is my mast? A pen. The Voyage. Vachel Lindsay. MAP; MoAmPo

What is our innocence. What Are Years? Marianne Moore. AmP; AP; BWP; CMoP; CoBMV; EaLo; ForPo; LiTA; MoAB; MoAmPo (1950 ed.); MoPo; OxBA; PoDB; ReMP; TPM; TrGrPo (rev. ed.)

What Is Our Life? Sir Walter Ralegh. *See* On the Life of Man.

What is "paradise." Emily Dickinson. CMoP; DiPo

What Is Past. Sir William Davenant. *Fr.* The Cruel Brother, V, i. TrGrPo

What Is Pink? Christina Rossetti. *Fr.* Sing-Song. GoJo; SUS; TiPo

(Color.) SoPo

What Is Poetry? Eleanor Farjeon. YeAr

What is poetry? Is it a mosaic. Fragment. Amy Lowell. WGRP

What Is Prayer? James Montgomery. BLRP; FaChP; MaRV; SoP; STF, 4 *sts.*; TRV; WGRP

What is required of us is the recognition of the frontiers between the centuries. Geography of This Time. Archibald MacLeish. PG (1945 ed.)

"What is she making?" asked the mate. The Ballad of the *Ivanhoe.* Bill Adams. BBV

What is she now? My dreams are bad. Tennyson. *Fr.* Maud. SyP

What is so nice in the dining room. Eunice in the Evening. Gwendolyn Brooks. TiPo (1959 ed.)

What Is So Rare as a Day in June? ("No price is set on the lavish summer"). James Russell Lowell. *Fr.* The Vision of Sir Launfal. NePA; TIHL

What is so rare as a day in June? *See* And what is so rare as a day in June.

What is so rare as a day in June? Question and Answer. Samuel Hoffenstein. FiBHP; PV

What is song's eternity? Song's Eternity. John Clare. CBEP; FaBoCh; LoGBV; NCEP; PG; WaKn

What Is Terrible. Roy Fuller. WaP

What Is That in Thine Hand? Eva Gray. STF

What Is That Music High in the Air? A. J. M. Smith. NMP

What is the boy now, who has lost his ball. The Ball Poem. John Berryman. CoAP; MoAmPo (1950 ed.); OCS

What Is the Church? Sam Walter Foss. OQP

What is the course of the life. Matthew Arnold. *Fr.* Rugby Chapel. MaRV
What is the cross on Golgotha to me. Golgotha's Cross. Raymond Kresensky. ChIP; OQP
What is the crown, but something set above? Prayer for the Royal Wedding. John Masefield. HW
What is the Eternal? What is the highest Self? The Eternal Self. *Unknown.* *Fr.* Bhagavad-Gita. WoL
What is the fair to whom so long I plead? Coelia, XV. William Percy. ReIE
What is the gold of all this world but dross. Nicholas Breton. *Fr.* The Soul's Harmony. SiCE
What Is the Grass? Walt Whitman. *See* Grass, The.
What is the hardest thing of all? Waiting! Waiting. Ruth Apprich Jacob. BiCB
What is the heart of a girl? The Heart of a Girl Is a Wonderful Thing. *Unknown.* BLPA
What is the horn that the dawn holds. The Horn. James Reaney. OBCV; PeCV
What is the little one thinking about? Cradle Song. Josiah Gilbert Holland. *Fr.* Bitter-sweet. AA; HBV; PCD
What is the matter with Grandpapa? Poor Dear Grandpapa. D'Arcy W. Thompson. BOHV; NA
What is the matter with Mary Jane? Rice Pudding. A. A. Milne. BBGG
What is the matter with Mary Jane? After Reading Milne. Ruth Powell. PCD
What is the meaning of the song. I Love My Love. Charles Mackay. NeHB
What is the metre of the dictionary? Altarwise by Owl-Light, IV. Dylan Thomas. CMoP; CoBMV; LiTM; MasP
What is the mirror saying with its O? A Room in the Villa. William Jay Smith. NYBP
What is the modern poet's fate? *See* What is a modern poet's fate?
What is the moral? Who rides may read. L'Envoi [*or* The Winners]. Kipling. *Fr.* The Story of the Gadsbys. BLPA; MoBrPo; NeMA; TrGrPo
What is the name of King Ringang's daughter? Beauty Rohtraut. Edward Mörike. AWP; JAWP; WBP; WoL
What is the Old Year? 'Tis a book. The Old Year. Clarence Urmy. OQP; PGD; PoToHe
"What is the real good?" What Is Good? John Boyle O'Reilly. HBV; HBVY; OQP; OTPC (1946 ed.); PoToHe; TreF; WBLP
What is the rhyme for porringer? Mother Goose. OxNR; RIS; SiTL
"What is the song I am singing?" The Founts of Song. "Fiona Macleod." WGRP
What is the sorriest thing that enters Hell? Vain Virtues. Dante Gabriel Rossetti. The House of Life, LXXXV. EnLi-2; HBV; MaVP; PoVP; ViPo; ViPP
What is the sound of the earth spinning? The Natural History of Pliny. Vincent McHugh. NePoAm-2
What is the thing of greatest price. The Soul. *Unknown.* STF
"What is the thing your eyes hold loveliest?" The Newlyweds. Cloyd Mann Criswell. PoLF
What Is the Use? *sel.* Erastus Wolcott Ellsworth.
"I saw a man, by some accounted wise." AA
What is the voice I hear. To America. Alfred Austin. GN; HBV; PAH
What is the word for "death". Flowers for Luis Bunuel. Stuart Z. Perkoff. NeAP
What Is the World? Dryden. *Fr.* To My Honor'd Friend Sir Robert Howard. TRV
(Design.) MaRV
"What is the [*or* this] world, O soldiers?" Napoleon. Walter de la Mare. FaBoCh; FaBoTw; LoGBV; MoVE; OtMeF
What is there hid in the heart of a rose. Song. Alfred Noyes. CH
What is there left to be said? A Farewell. A. R. D. Fairburn. AnNZ
What is there wanting in the Spring? The Wistful Days. Robert Underwood Johnson. AA
What is there we do not know about death. A Child, a Wasp, and an Apricot Tree. Diane Wakoski. YAP
What is this?/ The white and crumbling clouds. Rapture; an Ode. Richard Watson Dixon. OxBoCh
"What is this golden bowl, mother." Ballad of the Golden Bowl. Sara Henderson Hay. OnMSP
What is this grandeur I see up in heaven. The Grandeurs of Mary. Frederick William Faber. JKCP
What is this image in the clouded mirror. Image in a Mirror. Mae Winkler Goodman. GoYe
What is this knowledge but the sky-stolen fire. Much Knowledge, Little Reason [*or* Knowledge and Reason]. Sir John Davies. *Fr.* Nosce Teipsum. ChTr; OBSC
What is this life, if, full of care. Leisure. W. H. Davies. AnFE; AWP; BoNaP; BoTP; CH; EnLit; FaBoBe; FaFP; FaPON; GTSE; HBV; JAWP; LiTB; LiTM; MoShBr; OBEV (new ed.); OBMV; OBVV; OtMeF; PoRA (rev. ed.); PTK; RePo; SeCePo; ShBV-1; TIHL; TiPo; TOP; TrGrPo; TSW; WaKn; WBP; WePo; WHA; WoL
What is this mystery that men call death? Mystery. Jerome B. Bell. MaRV
What is this recompense you'd have from me? From a Woman to a Greedy Lover. Norman Cameron. Three Love Poems, I. ELU; FaBoTw; GTBS-P
What is this reverence in extreme delight. Ecstasy. Arthur Symons. UnTE
What is this strange and uncouth thing? The Crosse. George Herbert. AnAnS-1; MaMe; MeP
What is this that I can see. O Death. *Unknown.* TrAS
What is this that I have heard? Dawn Has Yet to Ripple In. Melville Cane. MAP; MoAmPo
What is this that roareth thus? The Motor Bus. A. D. Godley. OtMeF
What is this thing called life? Life and Death for the Christian. Avis B. Christiansen. SoP
What is this whisper of homelessness, good my heart. If the Heart Be Homeless. Annemarie Ewing. NePoAm-2
"What is this world, O soldiers?" *See* "What is the world. . ."
What Is to Be Given. Delmore Schwartz. FiMAP
What Is to Come [We Know Not]. W. E. Henley. HBV; NeMA; PoIE; PoVP; TreFT
What Is Truth? *sel.* James Harold Manning.
"I have been,/ Three separate times, in war." CaP
What Is Unwoven. Arthur Freeman. NYTB
What Is Veal? Mary Elliott. OTPC (1923 ed.)
What Is White? Thomas MacDonagh. CAW; JKCP
What Is Winter? Edmund Blunden. ChMP; GTBS-D
What Is Young Passion. Hartley Coleridge. NCEP
What is your substance, whereof are you made. Sonnets, LIII. Shakespeare. AtBAP; BWP; CTC; EIL; EnRePo; FaFP; GTBS-W; LiTB; LiTG; LiTL; MasP; OAEP; OBEV; OBSC; ViBoPo
"What is your tragedy, brother of mine?" A Ballad of Despair. Wade Wellman. FiSC
What? Is't not folly for to dread. That Death Is Not So Much to Be Feared as Daily Diseases Are. George Turberville. ReIE
What Is't to Us? Charles Churchill. *Fr.* Night. SeCePo
What it is, the literal size. The Riddle. Robert Creeley. OPoP
What it showed was always the same. The Night Mirror. John Hollander. NYBP
What It Was. Robert Sward. CoPo
What joy attends the fisher's life. The Fisher's Life. *Unknown.* ChTr; EtS
What joy hath yon glad wreath of flowers that is. The Garland and the Girdle. Michelangelo. AWP
What! kill a partridge in the month of May! On Mr. Partridge. *Unknown.* WhC
What Kin' o' Pants Does the Gambler Wear, *with music.* *Unknown.* AS
What Kind of Mistress He Would Have. Robert Herrick. TrGrPo; UnTE
What Kind of Music? James Reeves. RePo
What kind of trees. Lamp Posts. Helen Hovy. YT
What know I. The Song of the Arrow. Isabella Valancy Crawford. *Fr.* Gisli, the Chieftain. OBCV; PeCV (1967 ed.)
What Know We Greater than the Soul? Tennyson. *Fr.* Ode on the Death of the Duke of Wellington. MaRV
What Lack I Yet? Pearl Burnside McKinney. SoP
What land of Silence. Beata Solitudo. Ernest Dowson. PoVP
What large, dark hands are those at the window. Love on the Farm. D. H. Lawrence. CMoP; ErPo; FaBV; MeWo; MoAB; MoBrPo; TrGrPo
"What length of verse can serve brave Mopsa's good to show." Sir Philip Sidney. *Fr.* Arcadia. ReIE

What lewd, naked and revolting shape is this? Shopping for Meat in Winter. Oscar Williams. GTBS-W; LiTA; LiTM; NePA
What life can compare with the jolly town-rakes. The Town-Rakes. *At. to* P. A. Motteux. CoMu
What lightning shall light it? What thunder shall tell it? Martin Luther at Potsdam. Barry Pain. ALV; BOHV; NA
What links are ours with orbs that are. Meditation under Stars. George Meredith. OAEP; VP
What Lips My Lips Have Kissed. Edna St. Vincent Millay. AnFE; APA; CoAnAm; GTBS-W; LiTA; MAP; MasP; MeWo; MoAB; MoAmPo; Sonn; TwAmPo
(Sonnet: "What lips my lips have kissed, and where, and why.") HBMV; LiTG; ViBoPo
What Literature Needs. John Holmes. InMe
What little throat. The Blackbird by Belfast Lough. *Unknown.* BiS; KiLC
What lively lad most pleasured me. A Last Confession. W. B. Yeats. CMoP; ELP; ErPo; LiTL; LO
What longer need hath she of loveliness. Dirge. Sarojini Naidu. ACV
What lookest thou herein to have? A Preface to the Buyer of This Book. Thomas Tusser. SiCE; TuPP
What? Lost your temper, did you say? Lost. *Unknown.* SoP
What loud wave-motioned hooves awaken. The Blue Horses. J. P. McAuley. BoAV
What love do these men give their women. Structural Iron Workers. MacKnight Black. NP
What love is this of thine, that cannot bee. Meditation One. Edward Taylor. *Fr.* Preparatory Meditations, First Series. AmPP (4th ed.); AnNE; AP; ForPo; MeP; PoEL-3; SCAP
What lovelier home could gentle Fancy choose? Between Namur and Liège. Wordsworth. EPN; MCCG
What lovely names for girls there are! Girls' Names. Eleanor Farjeon. BiCB; SUS; TiPo
What lovely things. The Scribe. Walter de la Mare. AnFE; AtBAP; CMoP; FaBoCh; LoGBV; MoRP; TrPWD
What luck had Peter! For he took a fish. The Shekel in the Fish's Mouth. Francis Quarles. StJW
What made thee then so keen to look on Rome? Vergil. *Fr.* Eclogues, I. PoFr
What magic halo rings thy head. Aucassin and Nicolete. Francis William Bourdillon. HBV
What Makes a City. *Unknown.* MaRV
What makes a city great? Huge piles of stone. The City's Crown. William Dudley Foulke. HBMV MaRV; OQP; WGRP
What makes a garden? The Garden. Caroline Giltinan. HBMV
What Makes a Happy Life. Martial. *See* Means to Attain Happy Life, The.
What makes a hero? not success, not fame. The Hero. Sir Henry Taylor. VA
What Makes a Home. Arthur Guiterman. SoP
What Makes a Home ("A man can build a mansion"). *Unknown.* SoP
What Makes a Home ("What makes a home?"). *Unknown.* PoToHe (new ed.)
What Makes a Nation Great? Alexander Blackburn. OQP; WBLP
What makes a nation's pillars high. A Nation's Strength. *Unknown.* MaRV; PAL; PGD; SoP; TRV
What makes a plenteous harvest, when to turn. Vergil, *tr. by* Dryden. *Fr.* Georgics. AWP; EiCP
What Makes Christmas? *Unknown.* SoP
What Makes Life Interesting. Marion Montgomery. NYTB
What makes life worth the living. Giving and Forgiving. Thomas Grant Springer. PoToHe
What makes me disinclined. Pretences. Ibn Rashiq. TTY
What makes my bed seem hard, seeing it is soft? A Captive of Love. Ovid. AWP
What makes permeable the ghost? The Ghost. Hilary Corke. NYBP
What makes the crickets "crick" all night. Crickets. Helen Wing. GFA
What makes the ducks in the pond, I wonder, go. Regent's Park. Rose Fyleman. SoPo; StVeCh (1955 ed.)
What makes thee, fool, so fat? fool, thee so bare? Epigram. Francis Quarles. *Fr.* Emblems. EP
What makes us rove that starlit corridor. Science Fiction. Kingsley Amis. NePoEA-2
What makes you come here fer, mister. Prior to Miss Belle's Appearance. James Whitcomb Riley. BOHV
What makes you write at this odd rate? Epigram on Miltonicks. Samuel Wesley. EiCL; OBEC
What makes your lip so strange? Thomas Middleton. *Fr.* The Changeling, III, vi. AtBAP; PoEL-2
What Man Has Made of Man. Wordsworth. *See* Lines Written in Early Spring.
What man is he that yearneth. Chorus [*or* Old Age]. Sophocles. *Fr.* Oedipus at Colonus. AWP; JAWP; LiTW; WBP
What man is so clever, so crafty of mind. A Storm, I. *Unknown.* *Fr.* Riddles. OuHeWo
What man is so wise as to explain? Storm Riddles. *Unknown,* *Tr. fr. Anglo-Saxon by* William H. Matchett. *Fr.* Riddles. FosPo
What man is there so bold that he should say. Liberty. John Hay. AA; PoFr
What Man May Choose. Priscilla Leonard. MaRV
What man of ignorance undefiled. Oh Come, Little Children. Phyllis McGinley. FaBV
What man of you, having an hundred sheep. The Lost Sheep. St. Luke, Bible, *N.T.* TreF
What man so wise, what earthly wit so ware. Spenser. The Faerie Queene, I, 7. CoBE
What man that sees the ever-whirling wheele. Two Cantos of Mutabilitie. Spenser. *Fr.* The Faerie Queene. MBW-1; ReEn; SiCE
What man would sojourne heer. *Unknown.* SeCSL
What manner of man's flower-viewing! Satirical Poems on Daimyos, III. Issa. PoFr
What? Mars his sword? faire Cytherea say. Upon Venus Putting on Mars His Armes. Richard Crashaw. MaMe; SeCP
What matter if my words will be. To My Mother. Louis Ginsberg. PoSC
What matter if the sun be lost? Daffodil's Return. Bliss Carman. CaP
What matter it though life uncertain be. Victor Hugo. OTD
What matter makes my spade for tears or mirth. Digging. Edward Thomas. BrPo
What matter where the apple grows. The Journey. Scudder Middleton. HBMV
What matters all his love for me? A Sailor's Wife. Clara Bernhardt. CaP
What Matters It? George Frederick Cameron. VA
What matters it to us who are immortal. Immortality. *Unknown.* SoP
What May Happen to a Thimble. "B." PRWS
What may the woman labour to confess? Modern Love, XXII. George Meredith. ViPo; VP
What may we take into the vast Forever? The Future. Edward Rowland Sill. AnNE; HBV
What may words say, or what may words not say. Astrophel and Stella, XXXV. Sir Philip Sidney. CABA; FCP; ReIE; SiCE; SiPS; TuPP
What mean these peals from every tower. The Fall of Richmond. Herman Melville. MC; PAH
What meane these mortall children of mine owne. Chorus Tertius: Of Time: Eternitie. Fulke Greville. *Fr.* Mustapha. OBS
What meanes this silence of Harvardine quils. A Supplement. Benjamin Tompson. SCAP
What meanest thou, my fortune. *Unknown.* EnLoPo
What meaneth this, that Christ an hymne did singe. Sonnet. William Alabaster. AnAnS-1; MeP
What meaneth this? When [*or* What menythe thys when] I lie alone. What Does This Mean? Sir Thomas Wyatt. EnPo; FCP; MeEL; SiPS
"What means this glory 'round our feet." A Christmas Carol. James Russell Lowell. ChIP
What mean'st thou bride, this companie to keep? The Brides Going to Bed. John Donne. MaMe
What meant the poets in invective verse. Robert Greene. *Fr.* A Groatsworth of Wit Bought with a Million of Repentance. LO
What measure Fate to him shall mete. Love Serviceable. Coventry Patmore. *Fr.* The Angel in the House. EnLoPo; MaRV
What menythe thys when I lye alone? *See* What meaneth this? When I lie alone.
What Might Be Done. Charles Mackay. VA
What mist hath dimmed that glorious face! The Virgin Mary

What (continued)
to Christ on the Cross. Robert Southwell. ViBoPo
What Mr. Robinson Thinks. James Russell Lowell. The Biglow Papers, 1st Series, No. III. AA; AmPP; AnNE; BOHV; HBV; IHA; InMe; LHV; PAH; TOP; YaD
("Guvener B. is a sensible man.") AmePo
What More Can You Ask. Helen Steiner Rice. FaChP
What more? Where is the third Calixt. Ballad of the Lords of Old Time. Villon. AWP; JAWP; PeVV; WBP
What mortal, when he saw. Human Life. Matthew Arnold. EPN; MBW-2; VP
What motley cares Corilla's mind perplex. The Literary Lady. Sheridan. BOHV
What mournful metamorphosis. Variation on a Theme by John Lyly. Sacheverell Sitwell. ViBoPo
What moved me, was the way your hand. Lament. Dorothy Livesay. CaP
What moved you Martin? Epitaph to a Man. Robert Reedburg. TNV
What moves that lonely man is not the boom. The Hermit. W. H. Davies. BrPo; MoBrPo
What musical numbers float over the breeze. Petrillo. "Gilbertulus." WhC
What Must, *sel.* Archibald MacLeish.
"Lovers who must say farewell." MoLP
What Must I Do to Be Saved? *Unknown.* STF
What, must my lord be gone? Lord Vyet. A. C. Benson. OBVV
What My Child Learns of the Sea. Audre Lorde. NBP
What My Lover Said. Homer Greene. AA; HBV; TreFS
What mystery pervades a well! Emily Dickinson. MAmP; MWA-2
What Need Have I for Memory? Georgia Douglas Johnson. CDC
What need I say how it doth wound my breast. Sonnet VII: Of His Lady's Weeping. Walter Davison. ReIE
What need I travel, since I may. John Hall. EG
What need of clamourous bells, or ribands gay? Composed on the Even of the Marriage of a Friend in the Vale of Grasmere. Wordsworth. HW
What Need of Fear? *Unknown.* SoP
What need you, being come to sense. September, 1913. W. B. Yeats. BrPo; CMoP; CoBMV; GTBS-P; MoPW; PoIE; PoRA
What needest thou?—a few brief hours of rest. Vain Questioning. Walter de la Mare. MoVE
What Needeth All This Travail. *Unknown.* EIL
What needeth these threat'ning words and wasted wind? Sir Thomas Wyatt. FCP
What needs complaints. Comfort to a Youth That Had Lost His Love. Robert Herrick. OBEV
What needs my Shakespeare for his honored bones. On Shakespeare [*or* An Epitaph on the Admirable Dramatic Poet, William Shakespeare]. Milton. BEL; BoLiVe; CLwM; CoBE; DiPo; EnLit; GTBS-W; HBV; InvP; LoBV; MeLP; MePo; NoP; OAEP; PG (1945 and 1955 eds.); PoRA; SeCePo; SeCL; SeEP; TOP; TrGrPo; ViBoPo; WHA
What, never seen Nieuw Amsterdam? Peter Stuyvesant. Rosemary Benét *and* Stephen Vincent Benét. OTD
"What new mob disturbs the days?" These Are the Young. Vachel Lindsay. ATP (1935 ed.)
What news from the bottle? Mosaic Harlem. Henry Dumas. BF
What nibbles at the window. Inbound. Burnham Eaton. FiSC
What Night Would It Be? John Ciardi. PDV
What no human eye hath seen. Here and There. Johann Peter Lange. SoP
What No Man Knoweth. Hugh Francis Blunt. CAW
What No, Perdy. Sir Thomas Wyatt. *See* Rondeau: "What? No perdie!"
What noble courage must their hearts have fired. Oliver Goldsmith, the Younger. *Fr.* The Rising Village. FOL; OBCV; PeCV
What noise of viols is so sweet. Beggars. Francis Davidson. CH
What noise up there? Music in the Air. George Johnston. PeCV (1967 ed.)
What! not know our Clean Clara? Clean Clara. William Brighty Rands. BOHV; HBV; HBVY
What now avails the pageant verse. Camoens in the Hospital. Herman Melville. ViBoPo
What now, my soul, and hast thou sinned again! Conflict and Victory. Henry W. Frost. SoP
What now? Thou look'st surprised. Charles Heavysege. *Fr.* Saul. PeCV
What nudity is beautiful as this. Portrait of a Machine. Louis Untermeyer. MoAmPo (1962 ed.); ShBV-3
What nymph should I admire or trust. The Question to Lisetta. Matthew Prior. OBEV
What of all the will to do? Sung on a By-Way. "Æ." TOP
What of her glass without her? The black grey. Without Her. Dante Gabriel Rossetti. The House of Life, LIII. CBEP; CoBE; GTBS-W; MaVP; NCEP; OBNC; PIA; PoEL-5; PoVP; Sonn; VA; ViBoPo; ViPo; VP
What of it, that the realms of this epoch. The Animal Howl. "M. J." TrJP
What of lords and dukes with whom you have supped. Addressed to a Gentleman at Table, Who Kept Boasting of the Company He Kept. Burns. PV
What of radishes lettuce peas. Poem. John Gill. ThO
What of That? Emily Dickinson. *See* I reason, earth is short.
What of That? *Unknown.* SoP
What of the bow? The Song of the Bow. Sir Arthur Conan Doyle. *Fr.* The White Company. HBV; MCCG
What of the Darkness? Richard Le Gallienne. HBV; OQP
What of the faith and fire within us. Men Who March Away. Thomas Hardy. BEL; MMA; PoFr
What of the Night? Sir John Bowring. *See* Watchman, Tell Us of the Night.
What of the Night? *sel.* John Richard Moreland.
"Arrogant Kings, with envious lust." ChIP
(Coins of Love, The.) MaRV
What of this fabulous country. Canoe-Trip. Douglas Le Pan. CaP; OBCV; PeCV; TwCaPo
What of this loving. Chameleon. Susan Axelrod. QAH
"What of vile dust?" the preacher said. The Praise of Dust. G. K. Chesterton. MemP; MoBrPo; OtMeF; POTE
What Once I Was. Sir Thomas Wyatt. MeEL
("Ons in your grace I knowe I was.") EnPo
What one art thou, thus in torn weed[s] yclad? Description of Virtue. Theodore Beza, *tr. by* Nicholas Grimald. OBSC; SiCE; TuPP
What one discovers other men will use. Under Investigation. John Morgan. YAP
What One May and May Not Call a Woman. *Unknown.* TreF
What ordinary gallant now but goes. Quot Bipedes Aurum. Thomas Freeman. SiCE
What other form were worthy of your praise. Foreword. Muna Lee. *Fr.* Sonnets. HBMV
"What other men have dared, I dare." The Kiss. Tom Masson. BOHV
What other woman could be loved like you. Soul-Light. Dante Gabriel Rossetti. The House of Life, XXVIII. CoBE; MaVP; PoVP; ViPo; VP
What Our Lord Wrote in the Dust. *Unknown.* ChIP; OQP
What Pablo Picasso Did in "Les Demoiselles d'Avignon." John Robert Colombo. PeCV (1967 ed.)
What padded feet rustle the dead leaves? Druidic Gums. T. I. Moore. MoAuPo
What pain, to wake and miss you! Quite Forsaken. D. H. Lawrence. BrPo
What painter has not with a careless smutch. Accident in Art. Richard Hovey. HBV
What palace-temple of the mystic East. Turris Eburnea. *Unknown.* GoBC
What pale, Victorian invalid, obsessed. The Musical Box. Jean Kenward. MuSP
What passing-bells for these who die as cattle? Anthem for Doomed Youth. Wilfred Owen. AnFE; BoLiVe; BrPo; ChTr; CMoP; CoBMV; EnLi-2 (1949 ed.); EvOK; FaBoMo; FaFP; FlW; FosPo; GTBS-D; GTBS-P; GTBS-W; GTSL; HBMV; LiTM; MaRV; MoAB; MoBrPo; MoPW; MoVE; NeMA; NoP; NP; OAEP (2d ed.); OBEV (new ed.); PoE; PoPo; POTE; SeCePo; ShBV-4; Sonn; TreFT; TrGrPo; ViBoPo; WaP; WHA
What path list you to tread? What trade will you assay? Man's Life, after Posidonius or Crates. Nicholas Grimald. ReIE; SiCE; TuPP
What phantom is this that appears. Helen of Tyre. Longfellow. SiSw
What Piggy-Wig Found. Enid Blyton. BoTP

What place so strange,—through unrevealèd snow. Memorial Thresholds. Dante Gabriel Rossetti. The House of Life, LXXXI. MaVP; PoVP; ViPo
What pleasure can this gaudy world afford? Consideratus Considerandus. John Saffin. SCAP
What Pleasure Have Great Princes. *Unknown. See* Quiet Life, The.
What poet wrote these lovely lines? Intermission, Please! Irwin Edman. SiTL; WhC
What Poetry Is for Me. Johnie Scott. WSL
What poets feel not, when they make. A Caution to Poets. Matthew Arnold. CBEP; PoVP; PV
What poets mean by what they mean. The Reader Writes. Carl Crane. PoPl; WhC
What poets sang in Atlantis? Who can tell. Atlantis. Gordon Bottomley. POTE
What Poor Astronomers Are They. *Unknown.* OBSC; ReIE
What poor short-sighted worms we be. K. K. Can't Calculate. Frances Miriam Whitcher. BOHV
What potions have I drunk of Siren tears. Sonnets, CXIX. Shakespeare. CBEP; ReIE; WHA
What power is this released in man's dark night. Earth Bows to the New Bomb. Aline Badger Carter. ChIP
What power is this? What witchery wins my feet. Natura Benigna. Theodore Watts-Dunton. Sonn
What precious thing are you making fast. Art, I. James Thomson. EnLi-2; OBVV; PoVP
What presses about here in the evening. Waters of Babylon. Louis Untermeyer. AnAmPo
What Price. Lulu Minerva Schultz. GoYe
What Profit? Immanuel di Roma, *tr. fr. Hebrew by* Joseph Chotzner. TrJP
What profits it, O England, to prevail. The Turk in Armenia. Sir William Watson. PoFr
What race of life run you? what trade will you assay? Metrodorus' Mind to the Contrary. Metrodorus, *tr. by* Nicholas Grimald. SiCE; TuPP
What rage is this? what furor [*or* furour] of what kind? Sir Thomas Wyatt. EnLoPo; FCP; SiPS
What ran under the rosebush? Could It Have Been a Shadow? Monica Shannon. FaPON; GaP; SoPo; StVeCh (1955 ed.); TiPo
What reason first imposed thee, gentle name. The Family Name. Charles Lamb. Sonn
What Remains but Only Dying? *Unknown.* EIL
What Riches Have You? George Santayana. Sonnets, XXIX. HBV; TrGrPo
What Riddle Asked the Sphinx. Archibald MacLeish. HoPM
What? rise again with all one's bones. Giles's Hope [*or* Epigrams]. Samuel Taylor Coleridge. BOHV; HBV
What roar the seas would make that lie. Elemental. George Dillon. AnAmPo
What Robin Told. George Cooper. FaPON; GFA; MPB; TiPo
What room is there for troubled fear? What Need of Fear? *Unknown.* SoP
What! Roses growing in a meadow. Wild Roses. Mary Effie Lee Newsome. CDC
What! Roses on thy tomb; and was there then. Ave! Nero Imperator. Duffield Osborne. AA
What ruined shapes of feudal pomp are there. Kilmallock. Sir Aubrey De Vere. IrPN
What Rules the World. William Ross Wallace. *See* Hand That Rocks the Cradle, The.
What rumoured heavens are these. To the Unknown Eros. Coventry Patmore. LO; OxBoCh; PoEL-5
What said John Paul Jones on the brave *Bon Homme Richard.* The Countersigns. *Unknown.* SoAmSa
What saintly features do abound in the Vatican Museum and Church. The Church of the Sacred Heart. Ashton Greene. NePoAm
What saith the river to the rushes grey. Aeolian Harp. William Allingham. OnYI
What Sanguine Beast? LeRoy Smith, Jr. NePoAm
What saw you in your flight to-day. The Vagabonds. E. Pauline Johnson. VA
"What sawest thou, Orion, thou hunter of the starlands." Singing Stars. Katharine Tynan. VA
What say the Bells of San Blas. The Bells of San Blas. Longfellow. AmP; AmPP (3d ed.); OxBA
What says my brother?/ Death is a fearful thing. On Death. Shakespeare. *Fr.* Measure for Measure, III, i. FiP
What scenes appear where-e'er I turn my view. Eloisa. Pope. *Fr.* Eloisa to Abelard. SeCePo
What scope/ is there where. The Rope. Tania van Zyl. PeSA
What scrap is this, you thrust upon me now? The Count of Senlis at His Toilet. Lord De Tabley. PeVV
What sculptor carved the arches of a tree. The Unknown Sculptor. Stanton A. Coblentz. MaRV
What seas what shores what grey rocks and what islands. Marina. T. S. Eliot. AmP; BWP; ChMP; CMoP; EnLit; FaBoMo; GTBS-D; GTBS-P; InPo; LiTA; MBW-2; NoP; NP; PoE; PoFS; PoIE; TwAmPo
What seek'st thou at this madman's pace? His Quest. Lewis Frank Tooker. AA
What sees our mailie in the lily-pool. The Lily-Pool and the Cow. T. E. Brown. MemP
What Semiramis Said. Vachel Lindsay. TwAmPo
(Poems about the Moon.) MAPA
What shall be added to your praises? Lines for a Feast of Our Lady. Sister Maris Stella. ISi
What shall be said between us here. Félise. Swinburne. BeLS
What shall be said of this embattled day. Parted Love. Dante Gabriel Rossetti. The House of Life, XLVI. MaVP; PoVP; ViPo; VP
What shall become of the ancient race. Ancient Race. Michael Tormey. JKCP (1926 ed.)
What Shall Endure? Ethelyn M. Hartwich. OQP
What Shall He Have That Kill'd the Deer? Shakespeare. *Fr.* As You Like It, IV. OBSC; ViBoPo
(Song: "What shall he have that killed the deer?") CTC
What shall her silence Keep. Dirge. Madison Cawein. AA
What shall I call? The Christening. A. A. Milne. BiCB
What Shall I Do? *At. to* Dryden *and to* Thomas Betterton. *Fr.* The Prophetess; or, The History of Dioclesian. SeCL
What Shall I Do? Frances Anne Kemble. *Fr.* Absence. PoToHe (new ed.)
What shall I do this afternoon? Half Holiday. Olive Enoch. BoTP
What shall I do to be for ever known. The Motto. Abraham Cowley. AnAnS-2; CLwM; SCEP-2; SeCP
What shall I do to be just? The Cry of the Age. Hamlin Garland. OQP; WGRP
What shall I do to show how much I love her? What Shall I Do? *At. to* Dryden *and to* Thomas Betterton. *Fr.* The Prophetess; or, The History of Dioclesian. SeCL
What shall I do when the Summer troubles? Emily Dickinson. MWA-2
What shall I do with all the days and hours. Absence [*or* What Shall I Do?]. Frances Anne Kemble. NeHB; PoToHe (new ed.)
What shall I do with this absurdity. The Tower. W. B. Yeats. CMoP; CoBMV; FaBoMo; HoPM; LiTB; LiTM (rev ed.); MoPo; OAEP (2d ed.); SeCeV
What shall I doe I've lost my hart. *Unknown.* SeCSL
What Shall I Give? Edward Thomas. FaBoCh; LoGBV
What shall I give my children? who are poor. Gwendolyn Brooks. *Fr.* The Womanhood. BALP; PoCh
What shall I leave my son. Testament. Langston Hughes. NePoAm-2
What? Shall I ne'er more see those halcyon days. *Unknown.* *Fr.* Zepheria. Sonn; TuPP
"What shall I render thee, Father supreme." The Mother's Sacrifice. Lydia Huntley Sigourney. PaPo
What shall I render to thy Name. In Thankfull Remembrance for My Dear Husband's Safe Arrivall Sept. 3, 1662. Anne Bradstreet. TrPWD
What shall I say but, having written for use. Answering a Letter from a Younger Poet. Brewster Ghiselin. PoCh
What shall I say more than I have inferred? The Address of Richard III to His Army. Shakespeare. King Richard III, *fr.* V, iii. UnPo (1st ed.)
What shall I say, my deare deare Lord? My Dove Is One the Onely One of Her Mother. Edward Taylor. *Fr.* Preparatory Meditations, Second Series. MWA-1
What shall I say of the Great Peak? A View of T'ai-shan. Tu Fu. OuHeWo
What shall I say to you, Old Flag? Old Flag. Hubbard Parker. DD; HH; OTPC (1946 ed.); PoRL
What shall I send my love to-day. A Valentine. Matilda

What (continued)
Barbara Betham-Edwards. OBVV
What shall I sing when all is sung. All Sung. Richard Le Gallienne. OBVV
What shall I teach in the vivid afternoon. Going to School. Karl Shapiro. TrJP
What shall I wish thee? New Year's Wishes. Frances Ridley Havergal. BLRP; STF
What shall I wish thee this new year. A New Year Wish. Mary J. Lewis. BLRP; SoP
What shall I your true-love tell. Messages. Francis Thompson. CH; OtMeF
What Shall It Profit? William Dean Howells. *See* Faith.
What shall it profit a man. Anastasis. Albert E. S. Smythe. CaP
What shall my gift be to the dead one lying. Lilian Adelaide Nelson. Clement Scott. VA
What! shall that sudden blade. Custer. Edmund Clarence Stedman. PAH
What shall the world do with its children? Romans Angry about the Inner World. Robert Bly. CBV; OPoP; PoIE (1970 ed.)
What shall we be like when. Seeds. John Oxenham. WGRP
What shall we count to cool our angry pride? Count Ten. Bonaro Overstreet. PoToHe(new ed.)
What shall we do for Love these days? Epilogue. Lascelles Abercrombie. *Fr.* Emblems of Love. AnFE; HBV; MoBrPo; OBVV
What Shall We Do for the Striking Seamen? *Unknown.* ThLM
What shall we do for timber? Kilcash. *Tr. by* Frank O'Connor. KiLC; OBMV; OxBI; ThWaDe; WePo
What shall we do, my soul, to please the King. The City of the Soul. Lord Alfred Douglas. HBV
What shall we do now, Mary being dead. Mary Booth. Thomas William Parsons. AA
What shall we do—what shall we think—what shall we say? Prelude. Conrad Aiken. Preludes for Memnon, XXIX. FaBoMo
"What shall we do when the trees are bare." November. Douglas Malloch. OTD
What shall we do with the drunken sailor. The Drunken Sailor. *Unknown.* SoAmSa
What shall we fear, son, now that the stars go down. Psalm against the Darkness. A. M. Sullivan. MaRV
What shall we mourn? For the prostrate tree that sheltered the green wood? John Boyle O'Reilly. *Fr.* Wendell Phillips. AA; DD
What Shall We Render. *Unknown.* BLRP
What shall we say it is to be forgiven? Forgiveness. Elizabeth Sewell. EaLo
What shall we say of her. An Old Tale. Marya Zaturenska. NP
What shall we sing? sings Harry. Themes. Denis Glover. AnNZ
What Shame Forbids to Speak. Robert Herrick. *See* To Anthea ("Ah, my Anthea. . .").
What she collects is men. The Collector. Raymond Souster. ErPo; OBCV
What she fears in her child is what. Mother of a Daughter. Louis Johnson. AnNZ
What She Thought. Harrison Robertson. *See* Two Triolets.
What should a man desire to leave? Pro Mortuis. Francis Turner Palgrave. VA
What Should a Man Want? Wang Chi. *See* Tell Me Now.
What should be said of him cannot be said. Dante. Michelangelo. AWP; JAWP; WBP
What should I be but a prophet and a liar. The Singing-Woman from the Wood's Edge. Edna St. Vincent Millay. HBMV
What Should I Say. Sir Thomas Wyatt. *See* Farewell: "What should I say."
What should I speak in praise of Surrey's skill. Verse in Praise of Lord Henry Howard, Earl of Surrey. George Turberville. ReIE; SiCE; TuPP
What should one. The Picture of J. T. in a Prospect of Stone. Charles Tomlinson. PoCh
What should we be without the sexual myth. Men Made Out of Words. Wallace Stevens. MoAB; PoeP
What should we know. Verse. Oliver St. John Gogarty. AnIL; FaBoCh; LO; LoGBV; OBMV; PoRA
What should we name our baby? The Baby's Name. Tudor Jenks. BiCB
What should you know at last. Elegy. Robert Fitzgerald. AnAmPo
What Shulde I Saye. Sir Thomas Wyatt. *See* Farewell: "What Should I Say."
What! shut the gardens! lock the latticed gate! An Open Question. Thomas Hood. NBM
What sight so lured him through the fields he knew. Far—Far—Away. Tennyson. PoVP; ViPo
What silences we keep, year after year. Too Late. Nora Perry. PoToHe
What sin was mine, sweet, silent boy-god, Sleep. Sleep. Statius. AWP
What sky more lovely than this azure night! Night of the Immaculate Conception. Juan Maragall. CAW
What slender youth bedewed with liquid odors. Horace, *tr. by* Milton. AWP; CLwM; EnLoPo; JAWP; LiTW; MaPo (1969 ed.); PoEL-3; WiR
What slender youth, with perfumed locks. To Pyrrha. Horace, *tr. by* Goldwyn Smith. *Fr.* Odes. EnLi-1; OuHeWo
What Smouldering Senses. Dante Gabriel Rossetti. *See* Kiss, The.
What! soar'd the old eagle to die at the sun! The Death of Harrison. Nathaniel Parker Willis. PAH
What soft—cherubic creatures. Emily Dickinson. AmePo; AmPP (5th ed.); AnNE; AP; CABA; CoBA; MoAB; MoAmPo; NoP; PPON
What some believe, and would enforce. Belief and Unbelief. Philip Freneau. AmePo
What song of mine will live? Song from Old Spain. Alice Corbin. NP
What song sang the twelve with the Savior. The Last Supper. Joaquin Miller. StJW
What songs found voice upon those lips. Helen Hunt Jackson. Ina Donna Coolbrith. AA
What sort of a church would our church be. Just like Me. P. W. Sinks. BLRP
What soul would bargain for a cure that brings. Modern Love, XIV. George Meredith. ViPo; VP
"What sound awakened me, I wonder." The Deserter. A. E. Housman. OBMV; SeCeV
What sounds are those, Helvellyn, that are heard? Retrospect—Love of Nature Leading to Love of Man. Wordsworth. *Fr.* The Prelude, VIII. MBW-2
What spendthrifts are we of the day. The Casket. Nathaniel Wanley. SeCL
What sphinx of cement and aluminum bashed open their skulls and ate up their brains and imagination? Allen Ginsberg. *Fr.* Howl. NeAP; PoCh
What spirit touched the faded lambrequin? The Ilex Tree. Agnes Lee. NP
What splendid names for boys there are! Boys' Names. Eleanor Farjeon. BiCB; SUS; TiPo
What stands 'tween me and her that I adore? Echo Poem. M. Allan. FiBHP
What Star is This? *Unknown, tr. fr. Latin by* J. Chandler. MaRV
What Stillness around a God! Rainer Maria Rilke, *tr. fr. German by* Jessie Lemont. OnPM
What strength! what strife! what rude unrest! Westward Ho! Joaquin Miller. AA; FaBoBe
What stronger breastplate than a heart untainted! Thrice Armed. Shakespeare. King Henry VI, Pt. II *fr.* III, ii. MaRV
What succour can I hope the Muse will send. To the Morning. Satisfaction for Sleepe. Richard Crashaw. MaMe
What sudden bugle calls us in the night. Reveille. Louis Untermeyer. HBV; PaA
What sugared terms, what all-persuading art. Diella, IV. Richard Lynche. ReEn; Sonn; TuPP
What sweet relief the showers to thirsty plants we see. A True Love. Nicholas Grimald. EIL; OBEV; TuPP
What sweeter musick can we bring. A Christmas Caroll, Sung to the King in the Presence at White-Hall. Robert Herrick. GoJo; MPB
What swords and spears, what daggers bright. Frost. W. H. Davies. BoNaP
What tears, dear prince, can serve to water all. Sir Walter Ralegh. FCP
What tell you me of such a peasant groom. Henry Parrot. SiCE

What th' English bed, the Welch call sepulcher. The Bed. John Owen. *Fr.* Four Epigrams. PrWP
What the Birds Do. Harriet McEwen Kimball. FaChP
What the Bones Know. Carolyn Kizer. NePoAm-2
What the Bullet Sang. Bret Harte. AA; CBEP; MAP; MoAmPo (1942 ed.); OBEV; OBVV; PFY
What the cats do. The Cats. Weldon Kees. NaP
What the Chimney Sang. Bret Harte. OTD
What the Choir Sang about the New Bonnet. M. T. Morrison. BLPA
What the Christmas Tree Thinks. Mary Carolyn Davies. PCH
What the Devil Said. James Stephens. CMoP
What the Earth Asked Me. James Wright. NYBP
What the Emanation of Casey Jones Said to the Medium. A. J. M. Smith. MoCV
What the eyes do not admire. Well-Packed Wisdom. Benjamin Franklin. *Fr.* Poor Richard's Almanac. StaSt
What the Gray Cat Sings. Arthur Guiterman. MoShBr; MPB; PoMS; PoRL
What the Grecian Earns. Kenneth Patchen. ToPo
What the King Has. Ethel Romig Fuller. PoToHe (new ed.)
What the Lord High Chamberlain Said. Virginia Woodward Cloud. BBGG
What the Moon Saw. Vachel Lindsay. CrMA
What the Old Man Said. Cicely Fox Smith. EtS
What the Old Women Say. Archibald MacLeish. TPM
What the Orderly Dog Saw. Ford Madox Ford. CTC
What the Prince of I Dreamt. Henry Cholmondeley-Pennell. NA
What the Railroad to Me? Henry David Thoreau. ELU
What the Rattlesnake Said. Vachel Lindsay. TSW
What the Red-haired Bo'sun Said. Charles H. Souter. PoAu-1
What the Serpent Said to Adam. Archibald MacLeish. NePA
What the Sonnet Is. Eugene Lee-Hamilton. HoPM; OBVV; Sonn; VA
What the Thrush Said. Keats. DiPo; MBW-2; PeER
What the Thrush Says. Queenie Scott-Hopper. BoTP
What the Toys Are Thinking. ffrida Wolfe. TiPo
What the Trumpeter Said. Sebastian Evans. VA
What the Weather Does. Hamish Hendry. BoTP, *st.* 1
What the wind harried, the fire worried. Deadfall. Martha Keller. GoYe
What the Wind Said. John Press. NYTB
What the Winds Bring. Edmund Clarence Stedman. DD; PRWS
What Then? ("After the joys of earth"). *Unknown.* SoP
What Then? ("When the great busy plants of our cities"). *Unknown.* SoP; STF
What Then? W. B. Yeats. CMoP; POTE
What Then, Dancer? Kay Smith. CaP
What Then Is Love but Mourning. Thomas Campion. EnRePo; FaBoEn
What then is Merlyn's message, his word to thee weary of pain. The Wisdom of Merlyn. Wilfrid Scawen Blunt. ViBoPo
"What then, what if my lips do burn." Ulf in Ireland. Charles De Kay. AA
What there is once may not be twice. No Laws. Brian Allwood. WaP
What They Are For. Dorothy Aldis. SoPo
What They Do. Eleanor Farjeon. ThGo
What thing insistent urges me away. Star-Fear. Leonora Speyer. AnEnPo
What Thing Is Love. George Peele. *Fr.* The Hunting of Cupid. ElL; ELP; EnRePo; OAEP; SeCePo; UnTE
(Love.) OBSC
("What thing is love? for, well I wot, love is a thing.") ReEn; TuPP
What thing shall be held up to woman's beauty? Woman's Beauty. Lascelles Abercrombie. *Fr.* Emblems of Love: Vashti. MoBrPo; PG
What things have we seen. Francis Beaumont. *Fr.* Master Francis Beaumont's Letter to Ben Jonson. EnLit
"What Think Ye of Christ?" Geraldine Farrar. StJW
What this mountain meaneth [*or* betokens] and the murky [*or* and what this dark] dale. Holy Church [*or* A Field Full of Folk]. William Langland. *Fr.* The Vision of Piers Plowman. CoBE; MeEV
What tho' thy home. True Riches. Bessie June Martin. STF
What tho', Valclusa, the fond bard be fled. Sonnet to Valclusa. Thomas Russell. CEP; OBEC
What Thomas an Buile Said in a Pub. James Stephens. *See* What Tomas an Buile Said in a Pub.
What thou art, if thou wouldst know. These Stones. Menander. LiTW
What thou hast done, thou hast done; for the heavenly horses are swift. Irrevocable. Mary Wright Plummer. WGRP
What thou lovest well remains. Ezra Pound. *Fr.* Canto LXXXI. FaBoTw; GTBS-D; MoAB; NePA; OxBA; SeCeV; UnPo (3d ed.); ViBoPo (1958 ed.)
What though, for showing truth to flatter'd state. Sonnet: Written on the Day that Mr. Leigh Hunt Left Prison. Keats. ChER; MERP; PoFr; Sonn
What though my harp, and viol be. To God, on His Sickness. Robert Herrick. OxBoCh
What though my joys and comforts die? Robert Lowry. *Fr.* How Can I Keep from Singing? TRV
What though my lot is a lonely place. Let Me Grow. Mary Mapes Dodge. FaChP
What though my mistress frowne one me. *Unknown.* SeCSL
What Though the Dark! Archie Edwards. BePJ
What Though the Field Be Lost? Milton. *Fr.* Paradise Lost. EaLo; FaBoEn
What though the flowers in Joseph's garden grew. The Sepulcher in the Garden. John Finley. ChIP
What Though the Green Leaf Grow? Maybury Fleming. AA
What though the moon should come. Dilemma. Orrick Johns. MAP
What though the shades of night. St. Augustine, Bishop of Hippo. Gerard Moultrie. SoP
What though the vulgar and received praise. Elegy for Doctor Dunn. Lord Herbert of Cherbury. AnAnS-2
What though thy Muse the singer's art essay. To America. Richard Garnett. VA
What though unmarked the happy workman toil. Honors. Jean Ingelow. OQP
What though with figures I should raise. On a Mistress of Whose Affections He Was Doubtful. Thomas Nabbes. *Fr.* The Spring's Glory. EG; SeCL
What thought ye to burn, when ye kindled the pyre. Epigram IV. *Unknown.* *Fr.* Duel with Verses over a Great Man. TrJP
What thoughts I have of you tonight, Walt Whitman. A Supermarket in California. Allen Ginsberg. AmPP (5th ed.); CBV; CoAP; LiTM (1970 ed.); NaP; NeAP; PIA; TwCP
What tidings of reverent gladness are voiced by the bells that ring. On Easter Morning. Eben E Rexford. BLRP
What time I hear the storming sea. Thrustararorum. Henry Nehemiah Dodge. EtS
What time I see you passing by. Popular Songs of Tuscany. *Unknown.* AWP
"What time is it?" said the one. The Chronometer. A. M. Sullivan. WaKn
What time soft night had silently begun. Fame and Fortune. Michael Drayton. *Fr.* The Legend of Robert, Duke of Normandy. OBSC
What time the earth takes on the garb of Spring. Incipit Vita Nova. William Morton Payne. AA
What time the gifted lady took. George Sand. Dorothy Parker. FiBHP
What time the Lord drew back the sea. Panama. Amanda Theodosia Jones. PAH
What time the noble Lovewell came. Lovewell's Fight. *Unknown.* PAH
What time the poet hath hymned. "Oh, Hollow! Hollow! Hollow!" W. S. Gilbert. *Fr.* Patience. PoVP
What time the rose of dawn is laid across the lips of night. The Angler's Reveille. Henry van Dyke. *Fr.* The Toiling of Felix. BBV; GN; StVeCh
What time the weatherbeaten flocks. The Ninth Eglog. Michael Drayton. *Fr.* The Shepherd's Garland. ReIE
What time this world's great Workmaster did cast. Beauty [*or* Soul Is Form]. Spenser. *Fr.* An Hymne in Honour of Beautie. GoBC; OBSC
What time with brow the loveliest gins to scowl. Robert Tofte. *Fr.* Laura. ReIE
What Timon does old age begin t'approach. Satyr. *At. to* the Earl of Rochester *and to* Sir Charles Sedley. PeRV
What to a man who loves the air. Riches. Robert Loveman. OQP

What to do. William Wise. TiPo (1959 ed.)

What to Think Of. Mark Strand. YAP

What Tomas [or Thomas] an Buile Said in a Pub. James Stephens. AnFE; CBV; LiTM
(What Tomas Said in a Pub.) CMoP; GTSL; ILP; MemP; MoAB; MoBrPo; NeMA; NP; PoRA (rev. ed.); TrGrPo; WGRP

What Tongue Can Her Perfections Tell? Sir Philip Sidney. *Fr.* Arcadia. EnRePo; SiPS
(Her Perfections.) CLwM

What travellers of matchlesse Venice say. An Elegie Made by Mr. Aurelian Townshend in Remembrance of the Ladie Venetia Digby. Aurelian Townshend. AnAnS-2; SeCP

What treasure greater than a friend. A Friend. Santob de Carrion. TrJP

What trees were in Gethsemane. Song. Charles G. Blanden. ChIP; OQP

What Trinkets? Thomas Hornsby Ferril. NePoAm-2

What Ulysses Said to Circe on the Beach of Aeaea. Irving Layton. ErPo

What utter loneliness he knew. Before Pilate. Leslie Savage Clark. ChIP

What vaileth troth [or truth] or by it to take pain? Complaint for True Love Unrequited. Sir Thomas Wyatt. FCP; ReIE

What various hindrances we meet. Exhortation to Prayer. William Cowper. SoP

What voice did on my spirit fall. Peschera. Arthur Hugh Clough. HBV; PoVP; VA; ViPo

What voice, what harp, are those we hear. The Minstrel. Goethe. AWP

What wad na be in love. Maggie Lauder. Francis Sempill. OBS

What wants thee, that thou art in this sad taking? London Sad London. *Unknown.* OBS

What Was a Cure for Love? Thomas Godfrey. AnAmPo

What was he doing, the great god Pan. A Musical Instrument [or The Great God Pan]. Elizabeth Barrett Browning. BEL; EnLi-2; FaBoBe; FaPON; FosPo; GBV; GoTP; GTBS; GTSL; HBV; HBVY; MCCG; MemP; MuSP; OAEP; OBEV; OBVV; OnMSP; OTPC (1946 ed.); PoRL; PoVP; ShBV-3; ToP; VA; ViPo; WiR; YT

What was her beauty in our first estate. She. Richard Wilbur. AmPP (5th ed.); CoPo; ToPo

What was his creed? He Lived a Life. H. N. Fifer. PoToHe (new ed.)

What was his name? I do not know his name. The Nameless Saints. Edward Everett Hale. MaRV; OQP; WGRP

What was I back in the world's first wonder? Edwin Markham. *Fr.* Virgilia. EtS

What was it Colin gave to thee? I Lay My Lute beside Thy Door. Clarence Urmy. HBMV

What was it like to. Great Man. B. S. Johnson. ELU

What was it you remember?—the summer mornings. To Any Member of My Generation. George Barker. LiTM (rev. ed.); Sonn; ViBoPo (1958 ed.)

What Was Lost. W. B. Yeats. POTE

What Was My Dream? Joseph O'Connor. AA

What was our trust, we trust not. Morris Bishop. ImOP

What Was Solomon's Mind. Geoffrey Scott. OBMV

"What was that sound we heard." Why Must You Know? John Wheelwright. CrMA

What was the blond child building. The Builder of Houses. Jane Cooper. AmPC

What was the first prophetic word that rang. Peace. Edwin Markham. WBLP

"What was the hardest hour," you ask. The *Mary Ross.* Blanche Edith Baughan. BoAu

What was the name you called me? Evening Waterfall. Carl Sandburg. NP; OTPC (1946 ed.); TSW

What Was Your Dream, Doctor Murricombe? Sir Osbert Sitwell. AtBAP

What Was Your Name in the States? *with music Unknown.* AS

What was your war record, Prytherch? For the Record. R. S. Thomas. BoPe

What waspish whim of Fate. To a Portrait of Whistler in the Brooklyn Art Museum. Eleanor Rogers Cox. HBMV

What watch, what woe, what want, what wrack. No Pains Comparable to His Attempt [or The Shipmen]. William Hunnis. EnPo; OBSC; TuPP

What way does the Wind come? What way does he go? The

Wind. Dorothy Wordsworth. *Fr.* Address to a Child during a Boisterous Winter Evening. BoTP; OTPC (1923 ed.)

What we do not know of ourselves. A B C s (2). Charles Olson. PoAn

What we know to be not possible. Nones. W. H. Auden. CoBMV

What We Listened for in Music. Gray Burr. HW

What we looked for always remained. The Friendship. Robert Mezey. NaP

What We May Live Without. "Owen Meredith." *Fr.* Lucile, Pt. I, Canto 2. TreF
("We may live without poetry, music and art.") PoToHe (new ed.)

What we need is a great big vegetable farm! Leave Cancelled. Bill Berkson. ANYP

What! We of Spear-Danes in spent days. *Unknown. Fr.* Beowulf. ViBoPo

What We Remember. Rochelle Ratner. QAH

What We See Is What We Think. Wallace Stevens. SyP

What We, When Face to Face We See. Arthur Hugh Clough. *See* Through a Glass Darkly.

What weight of ancient witness can prevail. Private Judgment Condemned [or A Prayer]. Dryden. *Fr.* The Hind and the Panther. FiP; OBS

What went out. Force of Snow. Colette Inez. QAH

"What Went Ye Out for to See?" Arthur Hugh Clough. PoVP; StJW

What went you forth to find? Everest. Horace Shipp. HaMV

What Were They Like? Denise Levertov. PPON; WOW

What were we playing? Was it prisoner's base? Running. Richard Wilbur. CoAP

What were you carrying, Pilgrims, Pilgrims? Atlantic Charter; 1942. Francis Brett Young. *Fr.* The Island. BBV (1951 ed.); PAL

What, what, is virtue, but repose of mind? A Witching Song. James Thomson. *Fr.* The Castle of Indolence. OBEC

What, what, what,/ What's the news from Swat. A Threnody [or The Ahkoond of Swat]. George Thomas Lanigan. AA; BOHV; CaP; CBEP; CenHV; FiBHP; HBV; InMe; LHV; NA; PeCV; TreFS; WHW

What will be will. Future Simple. I. A. Richards. NYTB

What, will he come for me. Microcosmos, XVI. Nigel Heseltine. NeBP

What will it matter in a little while? Little Things. *Unknown.* SoP

What will it please you, my darling, hereafter to be? A Child's Future. Swinburne. EnLi-2

What will it profit when life here is o'er? Profit or Loss. Grace E. Troy. SoP

What Will the Stars Remember? Lilith Lorraine. ChIP

What will they give me, when journey's done? Journey's End. Humbert Wolfe. TrJP; YT

What Will We Do? Robert J. Burdette. BOHV

What will you do. What Then, Dancer? Kay Smith. CaP

What Will You Do, God, When I Die? Rainer Maria Rilke, *tr. fr. German by* Babette Deutsch. EaLo; LiTW

What Will You Do, Love? Samuel Lover. OnYI

What will you give to a barefoot lass. A Song of Riches. Katharine Lee Bates. AA

"What will you have for your birthday?" Birthday Gifts. Herbert Asquith. BiCB; SiSoSe

What will you ride on? Hey! My Pony! Eleanor Farjeon. FaPON

What winter holiday is this? The Man of Peace. Bliss Carman. DD; HH; OHIP

What wisdom have I that I surely know. Certainty. Evelyn Hardy. HBMV

What wisdom more, what better life, than pleaseth God to send? Posies for Thine Own Bedchamber. Thomas Tusser. SiCE

What wish you, immortality? Florence Wilkinson Evans. *Fr.* The Things That Endure. OQP

What with peacocks and perambulators, ripe gripes. Shorthand. Julia Vinograd. YAP

What! without feeling? Don't we make pretense. Two Vast Enjoyments Commemorated. John Danforth. SCAP

What without speech we knew and could not say. Preludes to Definition, IV. Conrad Aiken. TwAmPo

What Women Are Not. *Unknown.* MeEL

What wonder, Percy, that with jealous rage. To Percy Shelley. Leigh Hunt. Sonn
What wonders now I have to pen, sir. The Female Husband, Who Had Been Married to Another Female for Twenty-one Years. *Unknown.* CoMu
What wondrous life is this I lead! Andrew Marvell. *Fr.* The Garden. BoNaP; CH; ChTr
What wondrous love is this, Oh! my soul, oh, my soul! Wondrous Love. *Unknown.* TrAS
What wondrous sermons these seas preach to men! Along Shore. Herbert Bashford. AA
What word have you, interpreters, of men. Of Heaven Considered as a Tomb. Wallace Stevens. AnFE; AnNE; APA; CoAnAm; QFR
What word is that that changeth not. Sir Thomas Wyatt. FCP; ReIE; TuPP
What words are these have fall'n from me? In Memoriam A. H. H., XVI. Tennyson. CoBE; EnLi-2; EPN; FosPo; ViPo; VP
What work of honour and eternal name. De Guiana, Carmen Epicum. George Chapman. OBSC
What worlds of wonder are our books! Books. Eleanor Farjeon. YeAr
What would a man. The Hanging of Billy Budd. Keith Wilson. ThO
What Would He Say? Stanton A. Coblentz. ChIP
What Would He Say? Grace E. Troy. *See* If He Should Come Today.
What Would I Give! Christina Rossetti. VP
What would it be. Query. Lucie McKee. NYTB
What would it mean for you and me. The Miracle of the Dawn. Madison Cawein. HBV
What would the world be, once bereft. Wildness. Gerard Manley Hopkins. *Fr.* Inversnaid. OtMeF
What would we do in this world of ours. The Dreams Ahead. Edwin Carlile Litsey. PoToHe
What would you do here, you seekers of signs. Inscription on an Altar of the Dead. Victor Contoski. ThO
What Would You See? George Macdonald. PRWS
What would'st thou have for easement after grief. Comfort of the Fields. Archibald Lampman. CaP
What wouldst thou have, O soul. The Sacred Heart. Adelaide Anne Procter. JKCP
What wrote he on the parched and dusty ground. Contrast. Aubert Edgar Bruce. ChIP
What Yo' Gwine to Do When Yo' Lamp Burn Down? *with music.* *Unknown.* BoAN-1
"What, you are stepping westward?" Stepping Westward. Wordsworth. BEL; CH; EnLi-2; EnRP; ERoP-1; ExPo; HBV; MaPo (1969 ed.); MERP; OBRV; PoEL-4; SeCeV; ShBV-4
What You Can Get from the Body. William Hunt. YAP
What! You Define Me God. Stephen Crane. *Fr.* War Is Kind, IV. AmPP (3d ed.)
What you desire not starlight nor tearose. In the Web. E. L. Mayo. MiAP
What you give me I cheerfully accept. To Rich Givers. Walt Whitman. AnAmPo
What you gonna do when the liquor gives out, sweet thing? Sweet Thing. *Unknown.* OuSiCo
What you gwain to do when the meat gives out, my Baby? What Kin' o' Pants Does the Gambler Wear. *Unknown.* AS
"What You See Is Me." Barbara Gibbs. NYBP
What You Will Learn about the Brobinyak. John Ciardi. EvOK
Whate'er God Will. Albrecht of Brandenburg, *tr fr. German by* Nathaniel Langdon Frothingham. SoP
Whate'er has been, is, shall be—rind, pulp, core. Sidney Lanier. Sonn
Whate'er I be, old England is my dam! The Old Chartist. George Meredith. FOL; NBM; PoFr
Whate'er is born of mortal birth. To Tirzah. Blake. *Fr.* Songs of Experience. EiPP; EnRP; ERoP-1; LO; OxBoCh
Whate'er my God ordains is right. My Trust. Samuel Rodigast. SoP
Whate'er of woe the Dark may hide in womb. The Breath of Avon. Theodore Watts-Dunton. VA
Whate'er the passion — knowledge, fame, or pelf. Human Folly [*or* Man]. Pope. *Fr.* An Essay on Man, Epistle, II. BoLiVe; FiP; TrGrPo
Whate'er thou art, where'er thy footsteps stray. This, Too, Shall Pass Away. *Ad. By* A. L. Alexander. PoToHe
Whate'er thy countrymen have done. Written in the Beginning of Mézeray's History of France. Matthew Prior. BWP; CEP; EiCP; OBEC; PoE; PoEL-3; PoFS
Whate'er we leave to God, God does. Inspiration. Henry David Thoreau. AP; MWA-1; OxBA
Whate'er You Dream with Doubt Possest. Arthur Hugh Clough. *See* All Is Well.
Whatever Aunt Eliza wants to hear. Aunt Eliza's Slow Ear. Winifred Welles. GaP
Whatever blessing you my life deny. A Wish. John Norris. PeRV
Whatever crazy sorrow saith. Life Not Death. Tennyson. *Fr.* The Two Voices. MaRV
Whatever doubt the eye might have imposed. E. J. Pratt. *Fr.* Behind the Log. TwCaPo
Whatever Edens. Phyllis Harris. ThO
Whatever else be lost among the years. Let Us Keep Christmas [*or* Eternal Values]. Grace Noll Crowell. MaRV; PoToHe (new ed.); SoP; TRV
Whatever else withheld, withhold not from us. Belief in Plan of Thee. Walt Whitman. TRV
Whatever good is naturally done. Sonnet: Of Love, in Honor of His Mistress Becchina [*or* In Honor of His Mistress]. Cecco Angiolieri da Siena. AWP; OnPM
Whatever Happened? Philip Larkin. Sonn
Whatever I do, and whatever I say. Aunt Tabitha. Oliver Wendell Holmes. CenHV
Whatever I have said or sung. In Memoriam A. H. H., CXXV. Tennyson. EPN; OAEP; ViPo; VP
Whatever I said and whatever you said. Husband and Wife. Arthur Guiterman. PoToHe (new ed.)
Whatever intentions. The Meadow Brook Runs Over. Howard McKinley Corning. MAP; MoAmPo (1942 ed.)
Whatever Is — Is Best. Ella Wheeler Wilcox. BLPA; PoToHe; TreFS
Whatever Is, Is Right. Laman Blanchard. BOHV
Whatever Is, Is Right. Pope. *Fr.* An Essay on Man, Epistle I. OBEC
Whatever is to be come of me. The Wind. Robert Creeley. AmPC
Whatever it is, it must have. American Poetry. Louis Simpson. ELU; PP
Whatever it was she had so fiercely fought. The Recognition of Eve. Karl Shapiro. *Fr.* Adam and Eve. MoAB; ToPo
Whatever its function. The Purist to Her Love. Margaret Fishback. WhC
Whatever ripened in these lines. Prelude. Clemens Brentano. LiTW
What ever story of their crueltie. On the Still Surviving Markes of Our Saviours Wounds. Richard Crashaw. MaMe
Whatever the books may say, or the plausible. December: Of Aphrodite. W. S. Merwin. NePoEA
What ever 'tis, whose beauty here below. The Starre. Henry Vaughan. AnAnS-1; MeP
Whatever while the thought comes over me. Dante. *Fr.* La Vita Nuova. AWP; JAWP; WBP
Whatever you do, whatever you say. Old German Mottos. *Unknown.* StaSt
"Whatever you want is yours." The Lay of the Battle of Tombland. Dunstan Thompson. LiTA; NePA
Whatever's lost, it first was won. Elizabeth Barrett Browning. *Fr.* De Profundis. TrPWD
What'll Be the Title? Justin Richardson. *See* Titles.
What're you gonna do with the pretty Bessie Larkin. Callahan. *Unknown.* OuSiCo
What's a cuckold learne of me. *Unknown.* SeCSL
"What's all this rich land," said I to the Meath man. The Boyne Walk. F. R. Higgins. OxBI
What's become of Waring. Waring. Robert Browning. OtMeF; PeER; PoEL-5
What's Fame? a fancied life in others' breath. Fame. Pope. *Fr.* An Essay on Man. ViBoPo
What's hallowed ground? Has earth a clod. Hallowed Ground. Thomas Campbell. BLPA; HBV; MaRV
What's Hard. Laurence Lerner. NePoEA-2
What's he that wishes so? King Henry V Before the Battle of Agincourt. Shakespeare. *Fr.* King Henry V, IV, iii. PTK
What's in a Name? Helen F. More. PAH

What's in a Name? R. K. Munkittrick. BOHV; InMe
What's in It for Me? Edgar A. Guest. PoToHe (new ed.)
What's in the Cupboard? *Unknown.* ChTr; OxNR
What's in the larder? But What's in the Larder? Tennyson. ThGo
What's in There? *Unknown.* CH; OxNR
What's life but full of care and doubt. Domestic Didactics by an Old Servant. Thomas Hood. OBRV
What's love, when the most is said? When the Most Is Said. "Madeline Bridges." AA; HBV
What's my sweetheart? A laundress is she. Jeannette. Otto Julius Bierbaum. AWP
What's My Thought Like? Thomas Moore. BOHV; CBEP; OBRV
"What's new?"—What's old? what's anything. S. T. Coleridge Dismisses a Caller from Porlock. Gerard Previn Meyer. GoYe
What's she, so late from Penshurst come. On Her Coming to London. Edmund Waller. HBV
What's silver and a house to me. Her First Song. James K. Baxter. Cressida, V. AnNZ
What's that shining in the leaves. Songs for a Colored Singer, IV. Elizabeth Bishop. PoNe
"What's that stain on your shirt sleeve?" Edward (C *vers.*). *Unknown.* BaBo
"What's that that hirples ar my side?" Heriot's Ford. Kipling. PoRA
What's that we see from far? the spring of day? A Nuptial Song, or Epithalamie, on Sir Clipseby Crew and His Lady. Robert Herrick. AtBAP; HW; PoEL-3; SCEP-2; SeCP; SeCV-1
What's the best thing in the world? The Best. Elizabeth Barrett Browning. OBVV
What's the brightness of a brow? Evanescence. Harriet Prescott Spofford. AA
What's the good of a wagon. The Gold-tinted Dragon. Karla Kuskin. SoPo
What's the good [*or* use] of breathing. The Frost Pane. David McCord. BrR; RePo; RIS; StaSt; StVeCh
What's the greeting for a rajah riding on an elephant? Some Questions to Be Asked of a Rajah, Perhaps by the Associated Press. Preston Newman. FiBHP
What's the Matter, Haven't You Got Any Sense of Humor? Ogden Nash. SiTL
What's the news of the day. *Unknown.* OxNR
What's the point of having your radio set set. Sonnet on a Somewhat Inferior Radio Outfit. Cary Ross. AnAmPo
What's the Railroad to Me? Henry David Thoreau. MAmP; PoEL-4; ThLM
(Railroad, The.) FaBV
What's the Use. Ogden Nash. PoPl
What's this? A dish for fat lips. The Shape of the Fire. Theodore Roethke. AmP; LiTA; MiAP; MoAB
What's this dull town to me? Robin Adair. Caroline Keppel. FaBoBe; HBV
What's this morn's bright eye to me. Morning Hymn. Joseph Beaumont. OxBoCh; TrPWD
What's This of Death. Edna St. Vincent Millay. BoLiVe
What's this vain world to me? Rest Is Not Here. Lady Nairne. HBV
What's up, today, with our lovers? The Lovers Go Fly a Kite. W. D. Snodgrass. NYBP
"What's your age?" Mother's Party. Aileen Fisher. BiCB
What's Your Fancy. *Unknown.* UnTE
What's your name? Pudden Tame. *Unknown.* ChTr; GoTP
Whatso men sayn. Men Only Pretend. *Unknown.* MeEL
Whatsoe'er/ The form of building or the creed professed. The Sovereign Emblem. James Russell Lowell. *Fr.* The Cathedral. ChIP; MaRV
"Whatsoe'er He bids you—do it!" Leave the Miracle to Him. Thomas H. Allan. BLRP
Whatsoever I Do. Mary Louise Hector. GoBC
Whatsoever thing I see. Love Dislikes Nothing. Robert Herrick. AnAnS-2; CavP; CBEP
Whatsoever things are true. Philippians, IV: 8, Bible, *N.T.* TiPo (1952 ed.)
Whaup o' the Rede, *sel.* Will H. Ogilvie.
Blades of Harden, The. GoTS
Whaups, The. Robert Louis Stevenson. *See* To S. R. Crockett.
"Whaur are ye gaun?" said the fause knicht. The Fause Knicht on the Road. *Unknown.* BFSS
Whaur green abune the banks the links stretch oot. The Planticru. Robert Rendall. OxBS
Whaur yon broken brig hings owre. Song. William Soutar. GoTS; OxBS
Wheatlet Son of Milklet. MacConglinne, *tr. fr. Middle Irish by* Kuno Meyer. OnYI
Whee hee lo, whee hee. Evening on Howth Head. Eileen Brennan. NeIP
Whee—oop! Whoop—eee! In Town. *Unknown.* ABF
Wheel, The. Richard Brautigan. FRC
Wheel, The. Sully-Prudhomme, *tr. fr. French by* William Dock. ImOP
Wheel, The. W. B. Yeats. GTBS-P; MoVE; PoPo
Wheel Change, The. Bertolt Brecht, *tr. fr. German by* Eric Bentley. ELU
Wheel: it's a thing like pears, The. The Wheel. Richard Brautigan. FRC
Wheel, oh, wheel,/ Wheel in de middle of a wheel. 'Zekiel Saw de Wheel. *Unknown.* BoAN-2
Wheel of the quivering meat, The. Chorus. Jack Kerouac. *Fr.* Mexico City Blues. NeAP
Wheel Ruts. James Daugherty. RePo
Wheelbarrow. Eleanor Farjeon. FiBHP
Wheeler at Santiago. James Lindsay Gordon. PAH
Wheeler's Brigade at Santiago. Wallace Rice. MC
Wheelgoround, The. Robert Clairmont. PoMS
Wheels flee on silky steel. We are seated. To the Shore. May Swenson. NePoAm-2
Wheel's inventor, nameless demigod, The. The Wheel. Sully-Prudhomme. ImOP
Wheer 'asta beän saw long and meä liggin' 'ere aloän? Northern Farmer; Old Style. Tennyson. BEL; EPN; MBW-2; OAEP; PoVP; VA; ViPo
Wheesht, Wheesht. "Hugh MacDiarmid." ELU; ErPo
("Wheesht, wheesht, my foolish hert.") LO
Whelming the dwellings of men, and the toils of the slow-footed oxen. Charles Kingsley. *Fr.* Andromeda. PeVV
Whelp that nipped its mother's dug in turning from her breast, The. The Lion's Cub. Maurice Thompson. AA
When. "Æ." ATP; BEL; OnYI; POTE; TOP
When. Dorothy Aldis. RePo; SiSoSe
When. "Susan Coolidge." HBV
(Last Hour, The.) SoP
When/ Dr./ Edith. A Thin Façade for Edith Sitwell. John Malcolm Brinnin. FiBHP; NYBP
When,/ Halting in front of it. Hitomaro. *Fr.* Shui Shu. AWP; JAWP; WBP
When/ I/ Rap. A Sister Speaks of Rapping. Shirley Staples. WSL
When/ Sir/ Beelzebub. Sir Beelzebub. Edith Sitwell. *Fr.* Façade. CoBMV; FaBoMo; HoPM; MoAB; MoBrPo
When/ spit, bombs. Fake-Out. Lawrence S. Cumberbatch. WSL
When a bare hundred thousand was all that you had. Sealed Bags of Ducats. Martial. LiTW
When a Beau Goes In. Gavin Ewart. WaP
When a brass sun staggers above the sky. Tramp. Richard Hughes. MoBrPo
When a certain great king, whose initial is G. An Ancient Prophecy. Philip Freneau. OTD; PAH
When a daffadill [*or* daffodil] I see. Divination by a Daffadill [*or* Daffodil]. Robert Herrick. CavP; OBS; PoeP; SeCV-1; SeEP
When a deed is done for Freedom, through the broad earth's aching breast. The Present Crisis. James Russell Lowell. AmePo; CoBA; MaRV; OHFP; OQP
When a dream is born in you. A Pinch of Salt. Robert Graves. BoPe; HBMV; MoBrPo
When a feller hasn't got a cent. Fellowship. *Unknown.* BLPA
When a Feller's Itchin' to be Spanked. Paul Laurence Dunbar. BALP
When a fellow loves a maiden. La Cucaracha. *Unknown.* AS; TrAS
When a Fellow's Four. Mary Jane Carr. BiCB
When a felon's not engaged in his employment. The Policeman's Lot. W. S. Gilbert. *Fr.* The Pirates of Penzance. ALV; NeHB; PoVP; TreFT; TrGrPo
When a friend calls to me from the road. A Time to Talk. Robert Frost. CoBA; LaNeLa
When a friend starts on a journey of a thousand miles. The

End of the Year. Su T'ung-po. PoPl
When a Girl Looks Down. Kay Smith. CaP; OBCV; PeCV
When a goose meets a moose. Zhenya Gay. TiPo (1959 ed.)
When a great tree falls. To Be Answered in Our Next Issue. *Unknown.* WaKn
When a jolly young fisher named Fisher. Limerick. *Unknown.* LiBL
When a maid is sweet and fair. If a Maid Be Fair. Laura Goodman Salverson. CaP
When a man has cast out fear. The End of Fear. Ruth Pitter. POTE
When a Man Has Married a Wife. Blake. *See* Marriage.
When a Man Hath No Freedom [to Fight for at Home]. Byron. EnLi-2 (1949 ed.); EnRP; EPN; PoFS; PoLF; PoSa; TrGrPo
(Stanzas: "When a man hath no freedom to fight for at home.") EroP-2; NoP; PoFr
When a Man Turns Homeward. Daniel Whitehead Hicky. PoToHe
When a Man's Busy. Robert Browning. WhC
When a mounting skylark sings. Skylark and Nightingale [*or* Heaven Is Heaven]. Christina Rossetti. *Fr.* Sing-Song. RIS; YeAr
When a' other bairnies are hushed to their hame. The Mitherless Bairn. William Thom. HBV; VA
When a People Reach the Top of a Hill. Stephen Crane. *See* Blue Battalions, The.
When a Ring's around the Moon. Mary Jane Carr. BrR; TiPo
When a sighing begins/ In the violins. Chansons d'automne [*or* Song of Autumn]. Paul Verlaine. AWP; JAWP; OnPM; WBP; WoL
When a twister a-twisting will twist him a twist. Twister Twisting Twine. *Unknown, at. to* John Wallis. ChTr; OTPC; OxNR
When a Warlock Dies. Isabella Gardner. NePA
When a Woman Blue, *with music.* *Unknown.* AS
When a young man, passion-laden. A Poem of Privacy. *Unknown.* ALV
When Abraham Lincoln was shoveled into the tombs. Cool Tombs. Carl Sandburg. AmP; AmPP; AnFE; AP; AtBAP; BoLiVe; CMoP; CoAnAm; CoBA; HBMV; MAP; MoAB; MoAmPo; MoVE; NeMA; PAL; PoLF; PoPo; TrGrPo; TwAmPo; ViBoPo; WHA; WOW
When Adam broke the stone. Were I To Choose. Gabriel Okara. PBA
When Adam Day by Day. A. E. Housman. ELU; FiBHP; PoPl; WhC
When Adam delf. The Pointless Pride of Man. *Unknown.* MeEL
When Adam found his rib was gone. The Lady's-Maid's [*or* Lady's-Maid] Song. John Hollander. ErPo; LiTM (1970 ed.); NePoEA; TwCP
When Adam named in days of old. The Burro. J. J. Gibbons. PoOW
When Adam Was Created, *with music.* *Unknown.* TrAS
(Wedlock, *sl. diff., with music.*) ABF
When after many battles past. After Battle. *Unknown.* MaRV
When, after storms that woodlands rue. A Requiem for Soldiers Lost in Ocean Transports. Herman Melville. GTBS-D; PoEL-5
When against earth a wooden heel. Winter Sleep. Elinor Wylie. NePA
When age hath made me what I am not now. Upon His Picture. Thomas Randolph. CBEP; MePo; SeCL; SeEP
When Ahab saw his white leviathan. The Whale and the Tiger. John W. Simons. JKCP (1955 ed.)
When Alcuin taught the sons of Charlemagne. Emma and Eginhard [*or* The Student's Tale]. Longfellow. *Fr.* Tales of a Wayside Inn. AmPP (5th ed.); MWA-1
When Alexander Our King Was Dead. *Unknown.* GoTS
(Death of Alexander, The.) OxBS
(Quhen Alysandyr Our King Was Dede.) AtBAP
(When Alysandyr Our King Was Dede.) FaBoCh
When Alexander Pope. E. C. Bentley. FiBHP
When Alexander Pope strolled in the city. Mr. Pope. Allen Tate. AP; CABA; MAP; ML; MoAB; MoAmPo; TwCP
When all besides a vigil keep. The West's Asleep. Thomas Osborne Davis. OnYI
When All Is Done. Paul Laurence Dunbar. MaRV; SoP; TRV
When all is done and said, in the end thus shall you find. Of [*or* On] a Contented Mind [*or* Content]. Thomas, Lord Vaux. CoBE; EIL; EnRePo; GoBC; HBV; MaRV; OBSC; QFR; ReIE; SiCE; TuPP
When all his seas with serpents were aflame. Case History. Lilith Lorraine. FiSC
When all is over and you march for home. Spoils. Robert Graves. MoLP; NYBP; Sonn
When all is said and done, I urge again. Put Grief Away. Robert K. Ekvall. *Fr.* Tibetan Comforter. MaRV
When all is still within these walls. The Man's Prayer. T. A. Daly. TrPWD
When all is written and sung. Food. Ruby Weyburn Tobias. OQP
When All My Five and Country Senses See. Dylan Thomas. MaPo; MoAB; MoBrPo; SeCePo; Sonn; ToPo
When All My Heavy Heart. Bilhana, *formerly at. to* Chauras, *tr. fr. Sanskrit by* E. Powys Mathers. *Fr.* Black Marigolds. OnPM
When all night long a chap remains. The Contemplative Sentry. W. S. Gilbert. *Fr.* Iolanthe. ALV; EnLi-2; FiBHP; PoVP
When All of Them Ran Off. John Hollander. AmPC
When all of us wore smaller shoes. Ancient Lights. Austin Clarke. NMP; OPoP; OxBI
When all our hopes are sown on stony ground. A Note of Humility. Arna Bontemps. PoNe
When all our lovely words are blown away. Arbor Una Nobilis. Sister Thomas Aquinas. JKCP (1955 ed.)
When all that matters shall be written down. All That Matters. Edgar A. Guest. ATP
When all the days are hot and long. Swimming. Clinton Scollard. FaPON; GFA; MPB; UTS
When all the ground with snow is white. The Snow-Bird. Frank Dempster Sherman. SiSoSe; SoPo; TiPo; UTS
When all the haunting shadows of the night. Why Didst Thou Doubt? Lucy Guiness Kumm. SoP
When all the leaves are off the boughs. Thanksgiving Time. *Unknown.* OTPC (1946 ed.); PCH; SoPo
When all the night is horrible with clamour. All in All. Edith Nesbit. PoFr
When all the other leaves are gone. Oak Leaves. Elizabeth J. Coatsworth. StVeCh
When all the powers have fallen. Eclogue. Hal Summers. POTE
When All the World Is Young, Lad. Charles Kingsley. *See* Young and Old.
When all the world would keep a matter hid. The Fabulists. Kipling. ChMP
When All the Young Were Dying. Edmund Wilson. AnAmPo
When all these million cells that are slaves. John Masefield. Sonn
When all this All doth pass from age to age. Caelica, LXIX. Fulke Greville. EnRePo; EP
When All Thy Mercies. Addison. OxBoCh
(Hymn: "When all thy mercies, O my God.") OBEC
(Thy Mercies.) SoP
When all were dreaming but Pastheen Power. The Song of the Ghost. Alfred Perceval Graves. AnIV
When all within is dark. From Thee to Thee. Solomon ibn Gabirol. EaLo; TrJP
When all works that have. The Fool by the Roadside. W. B. Yeats. MoVE
When all your bitter grief is gone. The Mourner. W. H. Davies. POTE
When Almonds Bloom. Milicent Washburn Shinn. AA
When along the light ripple the far serenade. The Venetian Serenade. Richard Monckton Milnes. OBRV
When Alysandyr Our King Was Dede. *Unknown.* *See* When Alexander Our King Was Dead.
When an elf is as old as a year and a minute. The Seven Ages of Elf-Hood. Rachel Field. BiCB
When and how shall I earliest meet her? My Queen. *Unknown.* HBV
When André rode to Pont-du-lac. André's Ride. Augustus Henry Beesly. HBV
When Angel Death comes knocking at my door. Resignation. Mother Francis d'Assisi. WHL
When Any Mortal (Even the Most Odd). E. E. Cummings. PoDB; PoPl
When April, one day, was asked whether. April Weather. Jessie McDermott. OTPC (1946 ed.); PCH

When April pours the colours of a shell. Wild Peaches, III. Elinor Wylie. LiTA; NAMP; OxBA
When April rains make the flowers bloom. The Shamrock. Maurice Francis Egan. AA; DD; HBV; HH
When April skies are bright with sun. The Spectre Ship. Thomas Stephens Collier. EtS
When April with his showers sweet with fruit. The Prologue to The Canterbury Tales, *mod.* Chaucer. OuHeWo
When arms and numbers both have failed. Aguinaldo. Bertrand Shadwell. PAH
When Art goes bounding, lean. Art and Life. Lola Ridge. HBMV
When as. *See also* Whenas.
When as a Lad. Isabel Ecclestone Mackay. HBV
When as a young and budding pote. De Senectute. Franklin P. Adams. HBMV
When as black night, her vaile displayes. *Unknown.* SeCSL
When as in Silks My Julia Goes. Robert Herrick. *See* Upon Julia's Clothes.
When as man's life, the light of human lust. *See* Whenas man's life. . .
When as the chill Charokko blows. *See* Whenas the chill sirocco blows.
When, as the garish day is done. The New Moon. Bryant. OTPC
When as the nightingale chanted her vespers. *See* Whenas the nightingale. . .
When as the nightingale sang Pluto's mattins. The Author's Mock-Song to Mark Anthony. John Cleveland. AnAnS-2
When as the Rye Reach to the Chin. George Peele. *See* Whenas the Rye Reach. . .
When as the sheriff of Nottingham. Robin Hood and the Golden Arrow. *Unknown.* ESPB
When at break of day at a riverside. Piano and Drums. Gabriel Okara. PBA; TTY
When at close of winter's night. Birdcatcher's Song. William John Courthope. *Fr.* The Paradise of Birds. VA
When at home alone I sit. The Little Land. Robert Louis Stevenson. PoVP; PRWS; SoPo; StVeCh (1955 ed.); TVC
When at last he was well enough to take the sun. A Leg in a Plaster Cast. Muriel Rukeyser. MoAmPo
When, at the end of it all. Henry Spaulding. Donald Burnie. PaA
When at Thy footstool, Lord, I bend. Forgiveness. Henry Francis Lyte. BePJ; SoP
When, Atlas-born, the Pleiad stars arise. Works and Days. Hesiod. WoL
When Aunt Selina comes to tea. Aunt Selina. Carol Haynes. HBMV; HBVY; MPB
When Aurelia First I Courted. *Unknown.* OBS
When autumn wounds the bough. Autumnal Spring Song. Vassar Miller. NePoEA; PoSa
When awful darkness and silence reign. The Dong with a Luminous Nose. Edward Lear. CBEP; CenHV; ChTr; FaBV; LBN; NBM; PoEL-5; PoMS; SiTL; TOP; WiR
When Baby Hurts Her Hand. *Unknown, tr. fr. German.* SAS ("Pat it, kiss it.") PPL
When baby woke in woolly spread. Where Is My Butterfly Net? David McCord. FiBHP
When Banners Are Waving. *Unknown.* GN; HBV
When battle roused each warlike band. The Drummer Boy of Waterloo. *Unknown.* BFSS
When bears are seen. B Stands for Bear. Hilaire Belloc. *Fr.* A Moral Alphabet. ShM
When beasts could speak (the learned say). The Beasts' Confession. Swift. ATP (1935 ed.); CEP; EiCL; EiPP; TOP
When beauty breaks and falls asunder. Juan's Song. Louise Bogan. NYBP
When beechen [*or* Birchen] buds begin to swell. The Yellow Violet [*or* The Violet]. Bryant. AmPP; AnNE; AP; CoBA; MAmP; MWA-1; PoLF
When before the cloud-white throne. The Judgment. Katharine Lee Bates. OQP
When Bethlehem's manger first cradled the King. The Cradle and the Cross. A. S. Reitz. STF
When Beulah Did the Hula in Missoula. William Hathaway. QAH
When Bill gives me a book, I know. The Christmas Exchange. Arthur Guiterman. BrR; ChBR
When Bill was a lad he was terribly bad. Those Two Boys. Franklin P. Adams. ALV; FiBHP; MAP; MoAmPo (1942 ed.); TrJP
When birchen buds begin to swell. *See* When beechen buds. . .
When birds came to set the leaves in motion. The High Sailboat. Salvatore Quasimodo. LiTW
When biting Boreas, fell and doure. Burns. *Fr.* A Winter Night. MCCG
When blessed Marie Wip'd her Saviours feet. Marie Magdalene. George Herbert. AnAnS-1; MaMe; MeP
When Bob Got Throwed. *Unknown.* SCC
When both hands of the town clock stood at twelve. Village Noon; Mid-Day Bells. Merrill Moore. MAP; MoAmPo
When both side lights you see ahead. Rules of the Road. *Unknown.* SoAmSa
When Boys Go a-Courting, *with music. Unknown.* TrAS
When brambles vex me sore and anguish me. The Fellowship. Katharine Lee. OQP
When brave Van Rensselaer cross'd the stream. The Battle of Queenstown. William Banker, Jr. PAH
When breezes are soft and skies are fair. Green River. Bryant. AmPP (4th ed.); AP; CoBA; OxBA
When Britain first, at heaven's command. Rule, Britannia! James Thomson. *Fr.* Alfred, a Masque (*by* Thomson *and* David Mallet). BEL; CEP; EiCP; EiPP; EnLi-2 (1949 ed.); EnLit; GTBS; GTBS-D; GTBS-P; GTBS-W; GTSE; GTSL; HBV; NoP; OAEP; OBEC; PoFr; TreF; WBLP; YAT
When Britain *really* ruled the waves. The House of Peers [*or* The House of Lords *or* Song]. W. S. Gilbert. *Fr.* Iolanthe. InMe; InP; TrGrPo
When Britain, with envy and malice inflamed. Capture of Little York. *Unknown.* PAH
When British troops first landed here. Cornwallis's Surrender. *Unknown.* PAH
When Brother Francis, rich in birds, arose. Saint Stephen in San Francisco. Melvin Walker La Follette. CoPo
When brother takes me walking. The Ordinary Dog. Nancy Byrd Turner. TiPo
When brother teaches her to skate. Learning to Skate. Emilie Blackmore Stapp. GFA
When Bunyan swung his whopping axe. Folk Tune. Richard Wilbur. AmFN; OnHM
When Burbadge Played. Austin Dobson. InP; PoVP
When by me in the dusk my child sits down. John Berryman. *Fr.* Homage to Mistress Bradstreet. CrMA; ReMP
When by the marbled lake I lie and listen. Hymn. Wathen Mark Wilks Call. OBVV
When by thy scorn[e], O murd'ress [*or* murderess *or* murdresse] I am dead. The Apparition. John Donne. AnAnS-1; AtBAP; BWP; CABA; CBEP; EnLoPo; EP; ExPo; LoBV; MaMe; MePo; OBEV (new ed.); OBS; PoeP; ReEn; SCEP-1; SeCP; SeCV-1; SeEP; ViBoPo
When by Zeus relenting the mandate was revoked. Phoebus with Admetus. George Meredith. EnLi-2; OBEV; OBVV
When C. J. G. Arden goes out in the garden. To His Godson Gerald C. A. Jackson. A. E. Housman. WhC
When Cain killed Abel to end a perfect day. A Curse for the Saxaphone. Vachel Lindsay. ATP (1935 ed.)
When calm is the night, and the stars shine bright. Sleighing Song. John Shaw. AA
When came the priest thy father to recapture. Chryseis. Walter Conrad Arensberg. AnAmPo
When Captain O'Bruadir shook a sword across the sea. The Ballad of O'Bruadir. F. R. Higgins. EtS
When captains [*or* captain] courageous, whom death could not daunt. Mary Ambree [*or* The Valorous Acts Performed at Gaunt. . .]. *Unknown.* OBB; OTPC (1923 ed.); TuPP
When Carolina's hope grew pale. Sumter's Band. James Wright Simmons. PAH
When Cats Run Home. Tennyson. *See* Owl, The.
When, Celia, I Intend. *Unknown.* TuPP
(To Celia.) CBEP; SeCL
("When Celia I intend to flatter you.") SeEP
When, Celia [*or* Coelia], must my old day set. To Celia [*or* To Coelia]. Charles Cotton. HBV; OBEV
When chapman [*or* chapmen] billies leave the street. Tam o' Shanter. Burns. BEL; BeLS; BOHV; BoLiVe; CABL; CEP; EiCL; EiPP; EnL; EnLi-2; EnLit; EnRP; GoTL; GoTS; HBV; NoP; OAEP; OBEC; OnSP; OuHeWo; OxBS; PeER; PoE; SeCePo; ShBV-3; TOP; TrGrPo; UnPo (1st ed.); ViBoPo; WHA

When cherry flowers begin to blow. Yuki. Mary McNeil Fenollosa. AA
When children are playing alone on the green. The Unseen Playmate. Robert Louis Stevenson. PCH
When children, blundering on their fathers' guns. Prayer for Light. Stanton A. Coblentz. TrPWD
When chill November's surly blast. Man Was Made to Mourn; a Dirge. Burns. CEP; PoIE
When, Chloe, I your charms survey. To Chloe. Thomas Cheek. SeCL
When Christ the Babe was born. The Lamb-Child [*or* When Christ Was Born]. John Banister Tabb. ChBR; ThGo
When Christ was born in Bethlehem. Christman Carol. *Unknown, tr. by* Longfellow. ChrBoLe; OHIP
When Christ was born in Bethlehem, Pan left his Sussex-Downs. Ballad of the Epiphany. Charles Dalmon. HBMV; OnMSP; TSW
When Christ [*or* Crist] Was Born of Mary Free. *Unknown.* MeEV; YAT
When Christ was taken from the rood. Robin Redbreast. John Banister Tabb. StJW
When Christ went up to Calvary. Recognition. John Banister Tabb. ChIP; JKCP; OQP
When Christ with care and pangs of death opprest. Christs Sleeping Friends. Robert Southwell. AnAnS-1; MeP
When Christmas trees at last are burned. Ashes of the Christmas Tree. Yetza Gillespie. ChBR
When civil dudgeon [*or* fury] first grew high. Description of Hudibras and His Equipments. Samuel Butler. *Fr.* Hudibras. CEP; EiPP; FosPo; SeCV-2; SeEP; TOP; ViBoPo
When Clarindon had discern'd beforehand. Clarindon's House-Warming. Andrew Marvell. MaMe
When Claudius was emperor and grandeur still was Roman. Rise and Fall of Valentines. Fairfax Downey. InMe
When clear October suns unfold. Mallee in October. Flexmore Hudson. PoAu-2
When clerks and navvies fondle. For X. Louis MacNeice. *Fr.* Trilogy for X. EnLoPo; ErPo
When clouds appear like rocks and towers. Weather Wisdom. *Unknown.* GoTP; HBVY; OxNR; TreF
When cockle shells turn silver bells. Waillie, Waillie. *Unknown.* AS
When, Coelia, must my old day set. *See* When, Celia, must. . .
When coldness wraps this suffering clay. The Immortal Mind. Byron. WGRP
When colds and frosts and snows were wont to reign. De Mense Januarii Quae Fuit An. Do. 1595. Thomas Bastard. SiCE
When coltsfoot withers and begins to wear. Cuckoos. Andrew Young. ChTr; MoPW
When comes the Spring? The Seasons. John Vance Cheney. DD
When Congress sent great Washington. The Trip to Cambridge. *Unknown.* PAH
When conquering love did first my heart assail. To the Senses. Michael Drayton. Idea, XXIX. OAEP
When consciousness came back he found he lay. Between the Lines. W. W. Gibson. MCCG
When consummate the day hangs before you. Three Variations, I. Boris Pasternak. TrJP;
When Contemplation, like the night-calm felt. Books [*or* The Stone and the Shell]. Wordsworth. *Fr.* The Prelude, V. ERoP-1; MBW-2
When country hills are soft with snow. Les Chasse-Neige. Ralph A. Lewin. FiBHP
When cousin Sam come down vrom Lon'on. Sam'el Down vrom Lon'on. William Barnes. PeVV
When Crassus died, his friends, to grace his hearse. In Epitaphium Pingui Minerva Compositum. Thomas Freeman. TuPP
When Crist Was Born of Mary Free. *Unknown. See* When Christ Was Born of Mary Free.
When, cruel fair one, I am slain. The Tombe. Thomas Stanley. OBS
When Cupid did his grandsire Jove intreat. On Mrs. Biddy Floyd. Swift. CEP
When Cupid first instructs his darts to fly. The Prophecy of Famine; a Scots Pastoral. Charles Churchill. EiPP
When Cupid sees how thickly now. Thou'st Had Thy Day. Anacreon. OnPM
When curfew-bells begin. The Two Loves. Laurence Housman. HBMV
When Daddy/ Walks. Walking. Grace Ellen Glaubitz. GFA; SoPo; TiPo
When Daddy shaves and lets me stand and look. Daddy. Rose Fyleman. SiSoSe
When Daffodils Begin to Peer. Shakespeare. *Fr.* The Winter's Tale, IV, ii. CBEP; ChTr; EIL; ExPo; FaBoBe; FaBoCh; HBV; InPo; LoBV; LoGBV; NoP; OBSC; PoeP; SiCE; UnTE; ViBoPo; WhC
(Autolicus's Song.) FaBoEn
(Autolycus.) EG
(Pedlar's Song, The.) OxBoLi
(Song: "When daffodils [*or* daffadils] begin to peer[e].") FiP; PoEL-2
(Songs of Autolycus.) OTPC (1923 ed.)
When Daisies Pied and Violets Blue. Shakespeare. *Fr.* Love's Labour's Lost, V, ii. AnFE; CBEP; EG; EnRePo; MyFE; NoP; OBEV; OBSC; PoEL-2; PoRA; SeCeV; SiCE
(Dialogue in Praise of the Owl and the Cuckoo.) DiPo
(Song: "When daisies pied and violets blue.") CBV; FiP; HBV; VaPo
(Song[s]: Spring and Winter.) ExPo; LoBV
(Spring.) BoC; BoTP; EIL; ILP; InPo; MaPo; PAn; PoAn; PoeP; PoFS; PoIE; SeCePo; SiTL; TrGrPo; UnPo; ViBoPo
(Spring and Winter.) OBEV; ThWaDe
(Spring Song.) TreFT
(Ver and Hiems.) ALV
When Damon First Began to Love. Aphra Behn. *Fr.* The Rover, Pt. I, Act II, sc. i. UnTE
When Dandy Dandelion wakes. Dandy Dandelion. Christopher Morley. GFA
When dangers press, a mind sustain. To Quintus Dellius. Horace. OuHeWo
When Daniel Boone goes by, at night. Daniel Boone. Stephen Vincent Benét. AmFN; NAMP; PoPl
When Darby saw the setting sun. Darby and Joan. St. John Honeywood. AA; LHV
When daring Blood, his rents to have regain'd. Upon Blood's Attempt to Steale the Crown (1671). Andrew Marvell. PeRV
When dark December glooms the day. Sir Walter Scott. *Fr.* Marmion, *Introd. to* V. OBRV
When, darkly brooding on this Modern Age. Standardization. A. D. Hope. BoAV
When darkness long has veiled my mind. Peace after a Storm. William Cowper. SoP
When darkness prevail'd and aloud on the air. The Tomb of the Brave. Joseph Hutton. PAH
When Dawn Comes to the City; New York. Claude McKay. GoSl
"Tired cars go grumbling by, The," *sel.* OCS
When day follows inarticulate day. Wait for the Hour. William Soutar. NeBP
When daylight was yet sleeping under the billow. Ill Omens. Thomas Moore. PoEL-4
When days were vaster and the dark more tragic. Tuppence Coloured. Babette Deutsch. PFY
When de Co'n Pone's Hot. Paul Laurence Dunbar. BANP
When de fiddle gits to singin' out a ol' Vahginny reel. Angelina. Paul Laurence Dunbar. HBV
When de golden trumpets sound. A Group of Negro Songs. *Unknown.* NAMP
When de Good Lord Sets You Free, *with music. Unknown.* ABF
When de Saints Go Ma'chin' Home. Sterling A. Brown. AmNP
When de Whale Get Strike, *with music. Unknown.* OuSiCo
When de whippo' will cry. Whippoorwill. John Richard Moreland. IHA
When, Dearest, I but Think of [*or* on] Thee. *At. to* Sir John Suckling, *and to* Owen Felltham. CavP; HBV; OBEV; OBS; SeCL; SeEP
(Song: "When, dearest, I but think of [*or* on] thee.") LO; MePo; SeCeV
When death and hell their right in Herod claime. Christs Returne out of Egypt. Robert Southwell. MeP
When Death Came April Twelve 1945. Carl Sandburg. AP
When Death Comes. *Unknown.* MeEL
When Death comes near to grimly claim his toll. May God Give Strength. Peter van Wynen. BLRP
When Death Shall Come. Helen Frazee-Bower. *See* Who Goeth Hence.

When death, shall part us from these kids. A Dialogue between Thyrsis and Dorinda. Andrew Marvell. MaMe; SCEP-2; SeCP
When Death, the angel of our higher dreams. The Journey. Thomas Curtis Clark. MaRV
When Death to Either Shall Come. Robert Bridges. HBV; OBEV; PoPl
When Death was young and bleaching bones were few. Edna St. Vincent Millay. Epitaph for the Race of Man, II. AmP
When deep within our swelling hearts. Childhood's Trials. Mrs. C. F. Alexander. ThGo
When Delia on the Plain Appears. George Lyttelton. *See* Song: "When Delia on the plain appears."
When descends on the Atlantic. Seaweed [*or* The Equinox]. Longfellow. AmePo; AP; CoBA; EtS; HBV; MWA-1; OxBA; PCD
When despair for the world grows in me. The Peace of Wild Things. Wendell Berry. NYTB
When Diamonds, Nibbling in My Ears. W. H. Davies. BrPo
When Did the World Begin. Robert Clairmont. *See* Answers, The.
When did these gray ones. Duel in the Park. Lisa Grenelle. GoYe
When did you start your tricks. The Mosquito. D. H. Lawrence. SiTL
When Dido found Aeneas would not come. Dido [*or* Note On the Latin Gerunds]. Richard Porson. BOHV; SiTL
When disappointment saddens you. Trusting Jesus. Grace B. Renfrow. BePJ
When do I see thee most, beloved one? Lovesight. Dante Gabriel Rosetti. The House of Life, IV. BEL; BoLiVe; CoBE; EnLi-2; EnLit; EPN; FaBoEn; GTBS-D; GTBS-P; GTSL; HBV; MaVP; OAEP; OBNC; OBVV; PoVP; TOP; TrGrPo; VA; ViBoPo; ViPo; ViPP; VP; WHA
When Dobbin and Robin, unharnessed from the plow. The Circus-postered Barn. Elizabeth J. Coatsworth. MAP; MoAmPo
When doctrines meet with general approbation. Epigram. David Garrick. HBV
When Doris Danced. Richard Eberhart. CaFP; CMoP; ErPo; NoP
When Dorothy and I took tea, we sat upon the floor. Small and Early. Tudor Jenks. AA; PCD
When down I went to the rust-red quarry. The Wedding. Robert Graves. HW
When down the stair at morning. My April Lady. Henry van Dyke. HBV
When down the windy vistas of the years. Clement Wood. Eagle Sonnets, XI. HBMV
When dreaming kings, at odds with swift-paced time. Washington. Harriet Monroe. *Fr.* Commemoration Ode. AA; FaBoBe; MaRV; OQP
When droning summer earth had slewed the shadows. Woodcut. V. Sackville-West. ChMP
When Dutchy Plays the Mouth Harp. Robert V. Carr. PoOW
When Duty comes a-knocking at your gate. Duty. Edwin Markham. HBMV; HBVY; OQP; TSW
When Each Bright Star Is Clouded. Jeremiah Joseph Callanan. IrPN
When earth was finished and fashioned well. The Choristers. Bliss Carman. ACV
When Earth's Last Picture Is Painted. Kipling. *See* L'Envoi' "When Earth's last picture. . ."
When Eastern lovers feed the funeral fire. On Two Lovers Struck Dead by Lightning. Pope. PoAn
When Eire first rose from the dark-swelling flood. Eire. William Drennan. OnYI
When Eubolus the Greek learned. Dionysus. Irving Layton. ErPo
When Europe and romanticism. Blackout. Arthur Gregor. SiSw
When Eve first saw the glistering day. Song with Words. James Agee. MAP; MoAmPo
When Eve had led her lord away. Album Verses. Oliver Wendell Holmes. *Fr.* The Autocrat of the Breakfast-Table. AmPP
When Eve upon the first of Men. A Reflection [*or* Epigram]. Thomas Hood. HBV; NBM; PV
When Eve walked in her garden. First Rain. Zoïe Akins. HBMV
When Evelyn Ann/ Moved down our way. Rich. Aileen Fisher. GaP; MPB
When Even Cometh On. Lucy Evangeline Tilley. AA
When evening came and the warm glow grew deeper. The Buzzards. Martin Armstrong. HBMV; POTE
When evening comes. Yakamochi, *tr. fr. Japanese by* Arthur Waley. *Fr.* Manyo Shu. AWP; JAWP; LiTW; WBP
When every least commander's will best soldiers had obeyed. Homer. *Fr.* The Iliad, III. ReEn
When every lip invokes young loveliness. To L. C. Lucy Hawkins. HBMV
When eyeless fish meet her on. The Goddess. Thom Gunn. ToPo
When Fabre took his children locust hunting. The Locust Hunt. Philip Murray. NePoAm-2
When face to face we stand. Paradox. Angelina W. Grimké. CDC
When faces called flowers float out of the ground. E. E. Cummings. BoNaP
When Faction in league with the treacherous Gaul. The Lords of the Main. Joseph Stanbury. PAH
When fair Columbia was a child. The Daughter's Rebellion. Francis Hopkinson. PAH
When faith and love, which parted from thee never. On the Religious Memory of Mrs. Catherine Thomson [*or* Sonnet]. Milton. OBS; Sonn
When faith in friends bear fruit and foolish fancies fade. Davy Dicar's Dream. Thomas Churchyard. ReIE
When faith in God goes, man, the thinker, loses his greatest thought. Have You Lost Faith? *Unknown.* WBLP
When falls the snow, lo! every herb and tree. Flowers of Snow. Tsurayuki. OnPM
When falls the soldier brave. Sentinel Songs. Abram J. Ryan. DD; HBV
When far-spent night persuades each mortal eye. Astrophel and Stella, XCIX. Sir Philip Sidney. CABA; FCP; FosPo; MaPo; OBSC; ReEn; SiPS; Sonn
When Father Carves the Duck. Ernest V. Wright. FaBV; FaFP; PoLF; PoSC; TreF
When Father goes to town with me to buy my Sunday hat. When Polly Buys a Hat. E. Hill. BoTP
When Father Played Baseball. Edgar A. Guest. PEDC
When Father Prays. *Unknown.* SoP
When father takes his spade to dig. The Robin. Laurence Alma-Tadema. BoTP; GFA; OTPC (1946 ed.)
When Father's birthday comes around. Father's Birthday Cake. Ada Lorraine Jex. GFA
When February sun shines cold. Late Winter. Philip Henry Savage. PCH
When fell thy dreadful shadow and it seemed. Sorrow. Reginald C. Eva. OQP
When fiddlers play their tunes, you may sometimes hear. Fairy-Music. Rose Fyleman. HH; TSW
When fields here lose their colour, when the wood. The Hedge-Row Story. Lilian Bowes-Lyon. POTE
When fierce political debate. Jolly Jack. Thackeray. HBV
When first a gentle kiss. A Sum of Kisses. Juan Meléndez Valdés. OnPM
When first Apollo got my brain with childe. The Author to His Book. George Alsop. SCAP
When First by Force of Fatal Destiny. *Unknown.* ReIE
When first descending from the moorlands. Extempore Effusion upon the Death of James Hogg. Wordsworth. CBEP; ERoP-1; FiP; MBW-2; MyFE; NoP; OBRV; PeER
When first Diana leaves her bed. The Progress of Beauty. Swift. BWP; CABA; EiCL; ForPo; FosPo; NCEP; PAn
When first I came to Frisco, boys, I went upon a spree. Off to Sea Once More, *vers.* II. *Unknown.* ShS
When first I ended, then I first began. Michael Drayton. Idea, LXII, *also in* Idea's Mirrour, L. TrGrPo
When first I heard of Jesus. The Conclusion. *Unknown.* SoP
When first I heard the people tell. That Is Even So! John A. Stone. SGR
When first I looked into thy glorious eyes. To Edgar A[llan] Poe. Sarah Helen Whitman. Sonnets from the Series Relating to Edgar Allan Poe, II. AA; DD
When first I made. Summer Vacation. Wordsworth. *Fr.* The Prelude, IV. OBRV
When First I Saw Her. George Edward Woodberry. Wild Eden, V. AA; HBV

When first I saw our banner wave. Astraea at the Capitol. Whittier. PAH
When first I saw sweet Peggy. The Low-backed Car. Samuel Lover. HBV
When first I saw true beauty, and thy joys. Mount of Olives. Henry Vaughan. AnAnS-1; MeP
When first I saw you at my door. The Way of a Cat. Margaret E. Bruner. CiV
When first I saw you in the curious street. German Prisoners. Joseph Johnston Lee. MaRV
When first I started out cow-driving, I drove them on the square. The Rustler. *Unknown.* CoSo
When first I thee beheld, in colors black and white. The Lover Declareth His Affection, Together with the Cause Thereof. George Gascoigne. TuPP
When first I took to cutlass, blunderbuss and gun. The Ballad of O'Bruadir. F. R. Higgins. OBMV
When first I went to mining, I was uncommon green. An Honest Miner. John A. Stone. SGR
When first man's heart was overcast. The Glory of Christmas. V. P. Drake. SoP
When first mine eyes did view and mark. Sir Thomas Wyatt. FCP; SiPS
When first mine infant-ear. Christendom. Thomas Traherne. PoEL-2
When first my brave Johnnie lad. Johnnie, Cock Up Your Beaver. Burns. AtBAP
When first my verse [or lines] of heavenly joys made mention. Jordan. George Herbert. AnAnS-1; ATP; MaMe; MeP; MePo; OBS; PoFS; PP; SCEP-1; SeCP; SeEP; VaPo
When First My Way [to Fair I Took]. A. E. Housman. EnLi-2 (1949 ed.); EnLit; MoPW
When first that horse, within whose populous womb. Death's Songsters. Dante Gabriel Rossetti. The House of Life, LXXXVI. MaVP; PoVP; ViPo
When first the bride and bridegroom wed. At Last. Richard Henry Stoddard. HBV
When first the busy, clumsy tongue is stilled. Supersensual. Evelyn Underhill. WGRP
When first the college rolls receive his name. The Scholar's Life. Samuel Johnson. *Fr.* The Vanity of Human Wishes. FaBoEn; OBEC; PoIE; SeCePo
When first the fiery-mantled Sun. Ode to Winter. Thomas Campbell. GTBS; GTBS-D; GTBS-P; GTBS-W; GTSE; GTSL
When first the magic [or magick] of thine eye. The Vow-Breaker. Henry King. OBS; SeEP
When first the peasant, long inclined to roam. The Young Author. Samuel Johnson. EiCP
When first the post arrived at my tent. Henry to Rosamond. Michael Drayton. *Fr.* England's Heroical Epistles. AnAnS-2; OBSC
When first the sun dispels the cloudy night. Hidden in Light. Frances Ridley Havergal. SoP
When first the unflowering fern-forest. Darwinism. Agnes Mary Frances Robinson. VA
When first these eyes beheld with great delight. Thomas Watson. *Fr.* Hecatompathia. ReIE
When first thine eyes unveil, give thy soul leave. *See* When first thy eies. . .
When first thou didst entice to thee my heart. Affliction. George Herbert. AnAnS-1; BWP; CABA; EP; LiTB; MaMe; MaPo; MeLP; MeP; MePo; NoP; OBS; OxBoCh; SCEP-1; SeCP
When first Thou on me, Lord, wroughtest Thy sweet print. The Ebb and Flow. Edward Taylor. AmP; AmPP; AnNE; AP; SCAP
When first thy eies [or thine eyes] unveil, give thy soul leave. Rules and Lessons. Henry Vaughan. AnAnS-1; MeP; SoP
When first thy sweet and gracious eye. The Glance. George Herbert. AnAnS-1; MaMe; MeP
When First to This Country a Stranger I Came, *with music.* *Unknown.* OuSiCo
When first we hear the shy-come nightingales. John Clare. EG
When first we met we did not guess. Triolet. Robert Bridges. BrPo; PoVP
When first you learn to read a clock. Clock. Harold Monro. BrPo
When first you look upon her face. Leila. George Hill. AmLP
When first you sang a song to me. Your Songs. Gwendolyn B. Bennett. CDC
When first you glory shone upon my face. Commemoration. Claude McKay. BANP
When fishes flew and forests walked. The Donkey. G. K. Chesterton. ACP (1952 ed.) BoC; FaBV; GoBC; GTBS-D; MaRV; MeMP; MoBrPo; NeHB; NeMA; OBEV (new ed.); PoLF; PoMa; PoPo; PoRL; POTE; ShBV-1; StaSt; StJW; TOP; TreFT; WGRP
When flighting-time is on I go. The Birdcatcher. Ralph Hodgson. AtBAP; MoBrPo; NeMA; PoIE
When Flora Had O'erfret the Firth. *Unknown.* OBEV
(May Poem: "Quhen Flora had ourfret the firth.") OxBS
When Flora Proud. Robert Greene. FosPo
When flowers thrust their heads above the ground. Bloom. Alfred Kreymborg. HBMV; TSW
When foes insult, and prudent friends dispense. Night; an Epistle to Robert Lloyd. Charles Churchill. NCEP
When foolish kings, at odds with swift-paced Time. Two Heroes. Harriet Monroe. *Fr.* Commemoration Ode. OHIP
When for the thorns with which I long, too long. The Coronet. Andrew Marvell. AnAnS-1; FosPo; LoBV; MaMe; MaPo (1969 ed.); MeLP; MeP; MePo; NCEP; OBS; OxBoCh; PIA; PP; SCEP-2; SeCV-1
When forced to wait and wait for luncheon. Assorted Relishes. Richard Armour. WhC
When, forehead full of torments hot and red. Les Chercheuses de Poux. Arthur Rimbaud. AWP; SyP
When formed our band, we are all well manned. California. *Unknown.* AS
When fortune's blind goddess. Bonnie Black Bess. *Unknown.* CoSo
When Fortune's shield protects thee, then beware. Fortune's Treachery. Judah Halevi. TrJP
When forty winters shall besiege thy brow. Sonnets, II. Shakespeare. EG; LiTB; OBSC; ReEn; ReIE; SiCE; Sonn
When foxes eat the last gold grape. Escape. Elinor Wylie. AnFE; APA; CoAnAm; GBV (1952 ed.); LiTA; MAP; MoAmPo; PFY; RePo; ThWaDe
When Francis preached love to the birds. Saint Francis and the Birds. Seamus Heaney. FIW
When Freedom, dressed in bloodstained vest. Freedom's War Song [or Ode to Liberty]. Thomas Chatterton. *Fr.* Goddwyn. PoFr; TrGrPo
When Freedom, fair Freedom, her banner display'd. Truxton's Victory. *Unknown.* PAH
When freedom from her home was driven. The Hills Were Made for Freedom. William Goldsmith Brown. PoFr
When Freedom, from her mountain height. The American Flag. Joseph Rodman Drake. AA; AmePo; AmLP; DD; FaBoBe; FaFP; GN; HBV; HBVY; HH; MaRV; MC; OTPC; PaA; PAH; PAL; PAP; PaPo; PGD; PoFr; PTK; TreF; WBLP
When Freedom, on her natal day. The Moral Warfare. Whittier. AnNE; PAL; PoFr
When fresh grass-blades and leaves appear. Canzo. Bernard de Ventadour. LiTW
When fresshe Phebus, day of Seynt Valentyne. Ballade. Charles duc d'Orléans. EnPo
When Friendship or Love our sympathies move. The Tear [or Hours of Idleness]. Byron. EvOK; Par
When from a world of tumult we retreat. Casting All Your Care upon Him. *Unknown.* STF
When from afar these mountain tops I view. Sonnet of the Mountain. Mellin de Saint-Gelais. AWP
When from Eternity were separate. Ceremonial Ode Intended for a University. Lascelles Abercrombie. OBVV
When from her beauty long I've strove. Song: Wit and Beauty. Robert Gould. CavP
When from her winter-prison. Spring. *Unknown.* SUS
When from my fumbling hand the tired pen falls. The Scribe's Prayer. Robert Service. TrPWD
When from my lips the last faint sigh is blown. An Epicurean's Epitaph. Aubrey Thomas De Vere. VA
When from the Calyx-Canopy of Night. Freda Laughton. NeIP
When from the chrysalis of the tomb. On John Grubb. *Unknown.* WhC
When from the gloom of earth we see the sky. The Void

When (continued)
Between. John Lancaster Spalding. *Fr.* God and the Soul. AA
When from the hush of this cool wood. The Cell. George Rostrevor Hamilton. SoP; TrPWD
When from the pallid sky the sun descends. James Thomson. *Fr.* The Seasons: Winter. OxBS
When, from the tower whence I derive love's heaven. Sonnet. *Unknown.* *Fr.* Zepheria. ElL
When from the vaulted wonder of the sky. Faith's Vista. Henry Abbey. AA
When from the wars I do return. William Sampson. *Fr.* The Vow Breaker. TuPP
When from the world I shall be ta'en. *Unknown.* LO
When from this good world I depart. The Epitaph. John Alexander Bouquet. MaRV
When frost is shining on the trees. At Mrs. Appleby's. Elizabeth Upham McWebb. BrR; SiSoSe; StVeCh (1955 ed.); TiPo
When, full of warm and eager love. Snowdrop. William Wetmore Story. HBV
When furrowed fields of shaded brown. The Canadian Rossignol. Edward William Thomson. CaP
When fury sings like nothing, like a war. Variations on a Theme. John Hay. NePoAm
When gadding snow makes hill-sides white. Winter. Charles Mair. OBCV; PeCV; PoSC
When Gathering Clouds. Sir Robert Grant. MaRV
When George the King would punish folk. How We Became a Nation. Harriet Prescott Spofford. MC; PAH
When George's Grandmamma was told. George. Hilaire Belloc. FiBHP; GoTP; YT
When gladness gilds our prosperous day. Good in Ill. William Henry Burleigh. SoP
When God at first made man. The Pulley [*or* The Gifts of God]. George Herbert. AnFE; AtBAP; ATP; AWP; BEL; BoLiVe; CBEP; CBV; CoBE; DiPo; EaLo; EnL; EnLi-1; ExPo; FaBoEn; GTBS; GTBS-D; GTBS-P; GTBS-W; GTSE; GTSL; HBV; ILP; InPo; LiTB; LiTG; MaMe; MaRV; MemP; MePo; NoP; OAEP; OBEV; OBS; OtMeF; OuHeWo; OxBoCh; PAn; PoAn; PoFS; PoIE; PoSa; ReEn; SCEP-1; SeCeV; SeCL; SeCP; SeCV-1; SeEP; StP; TIHL; TreFT; TrGrPo; TRV; UnPo (1st ed.); ViBoPo; WHA
When God had finished Master Messerin. Sonnet: of the Making of Master Messerin [*or* The Making of Master Messerin]. Rustico di Filippo. AWP; JAWP; LiTW; OnPM; WBP
When God had finished the stars and whirl of coloured suns. Frederick W. Harvey. Ducks, III. YT
When God invented beauty. Loveliness. Martha Snell Nicholson. FaChP
When God Lets My Body Be. E. E. Cummings. CMoP; MAP; MoAB; MoAmPo; PoDB
When God of old came down from Heaven. Whitsunday. John Keble. OBRV
When God ordained the restless life of man. The First Chorus. George Gascoigne. *Fr.* The Glass of Government. Po
"When God put man in a garden." King Alfred Answers the Danes. G.K. Chesterton. *Fr.* The Ballad of the White Horse. HBV; OxBoCh
When God set about to create heaven and earth. Genesis, Bible, *O.T.* *tr. by* Ephraim Avigdor Speiser. FIW
When God wants to drill a man. The Shaping of a Disciple. Dale Martin Stone. SoP; STF
When God was making the world. The World in Making. Sir Gilbert Parker. CaP
When God, who is forever free. Liberty. Michael Chazarian Nalbandian. PoFr
When Gods Had Fram'd the Sweet of Women's Face. Robert Greene. *Fr.* Tullie's Love. ReIE
(Love and Jealousy.) ElL
When gold was first discovered. The National Miner. John A. Stone. SGR
When gold was found in forty-nine [*or* forty-eight] the people thought 'twas gas. The Fools of Forty-nine. John A. Stone. CoSo; SGR
When Golden Flies upon My Carcass Come. Richard Eberhart. FiMAP
When golden Phoebus moved from the Ram. Anno Domini. John Bellenden. ACP (1926 ed.)
When golden ritual and scarlet rite. Akhnaton. Thomas S. Jones, Jr. AnAmPo
When good King Arthur ruled this land. Mother Goose. BOHV; BoTP; HBV; HBVY; NA; OTPC; OxNR; PCH; PPL; RIS; SAS
When good-nights have been prattled, and prayers have been said. The Dance. Rudolph Chambers Lehmann. HBMV
When good St. David, as old writs record. In Honour of St. David's Day. *Unknown.* PrWP
When Goody O'Grumpity baked a cake. Goody O'Grumpity. Carol Ryrie Brink. FaPON; GaP; RePo
When gooseberries grow on the stem of a daisy. To Mollidusta. James Robinson Planché. NA
When gourds are mellow-yellow on the vine. All Souls. Liboria E. Romano. FiSC
When Grandmother comes to our house. The Grandmother. Elizabeth Madox Roberts. GaP; MPB
When Grandmother Polly had married and gone. The Wolves. Elizabeth Madox Roberts. UTS
When Grasshopper, chirping late. Fall of the Year. Henry Ellison. OBVV
When gray threads mar life's pattern. The Master Weaver. *Unknown.* STF
When great-grandmother was ten years old. The Sampler. Nancy Byrd Turner. BiCB
When green as a river was the barley. Daphne. Edith Sitwell. HBMV
When Green Buds Hang. A. E. Housman. ACV; BoPe
When gripping grief the heart doth wound. Music's Silver Sound. Shakespeare. *Fr.* Romeo and Juliet, IV, v. GN; HH
When groping farms are lanterned up. A Country God. Edmund Blunden. MoBrPo
When guests were present, dear little Mabel. Our Polite Parents. Carolyn Wells. BBGG
When Hannibal Crossed the Alps. Eleanor Farjeon. FOL
When hard luck overtakes you. Hard Luck. Langston Hughes. NP
When, hardly moving, you decorate night's hush. The Waters of Life. Humbert Wolfe. MoBrPo; NP
When have I last looked on? Lines Written in Dejection. W. B. Yeats. MBW-2
When, having watched for a long time the trees. Grove and Building. Edgar Bowers. NePoEA
When He appoints to meet thee, go thou forth. Specula. Thomas Edward Brown. OQP
When he brings home a whale. Naughty Boy. Robert Creeley. AmPC
When He Goes to Play with the Boys. Strickland W. Gillilan. PEDC
When he had left the mountains and received. Childhood. Wordsworth. *Fr.* The Prelude, I. CoBE
When he killed the Mudjokivis. The Modern Hiawatha. George A. Strong. *See also* He killed the noble Mudjokivis. *Fr.* The Song of Milkanwatha. BBV (1951 ed.); FaFP; LiTG; Par; ShBV-1; SiTL.
When he lies in the night away from her. The Jealous Lovers. Donald Hall. NYBP
When he married her he said. Thalamos. Peter Kane Dufault. ErPo
When he pushed his bush of black hair off his brow. Sicilian Cyclamens. D. H. Lawrence. ChMP; MoVE
When He returns, and finds the world so drear. When We Are All Asleep. Robert Buchanan. VA
When he runs hunting the chipmunk stretches. Chipmunk. Marie de L. Welch. RePo
When he saw the multitude [*or* people] he went up into a mountain. St. Matthew, Bible, *N.T.* ReIE
When He Spoke to Me of Love. M. A. Mokhomo, *tr. fr. Sotho by* Dan Kunene *and* Jack Cope. PeSA
When he takes a bath, the Antelope. Antelope. William Jay Smith. TiPo (1959 ed.)
When He Thought Himself Contemned. Thomas Howell. ElL, 3 *sts.*; ReIE; TuPP
When He was entering Jerusalem. Evil Days. Boris Pasternak. MoRP
When he was shot he toppled to the ground. Shot Who? Jim Lane. Merrill Moore. MAP; MoAmPo
When he was young and beautiful and bold. Peer Gynt. Charles Hamilton Sorley. HBMV

When he went blundering back to God. Of One Self-slain. Charles Hanson Towne. WGRP
When He Who Adores Thee. Thomas Moore. *See* Pro Patria Mori.
When he, who, from the scourge of wrong. Moses—No Man Knoweth His Sepulchure. Bryant. SoP
When he, who is the unforgiven. The Unforgiven. E. A. Robinson. CMoP
When He Would Have His Verses Read. Robert Herrick. EnL; OAEP; OBS; SCEP-2; SeCV-1; SeEP
When, head high in corn, I walked with my mother the long, golden meadows. The Walk. Leonard Clark. AtBAP
When heaven would strive to do the best she can. Michael Drayton. LO
When heavy, dark, continued, a'-day rains. Burns. *Fr.* The Brigs of Ayr. MCCG
When Helen first saw wrinkles in her face. Wrinkles. Walter Savage Landor. EnLoPo; VA
When Helen Lived. W. B. Yeats. CMoP; ViBoPo
When her soul flies to the predestined dancing-place. Her Courage. W. B. Yeats. Upon a Dying Lady, VI. LiTB
When Hercules did use to spin. The Weavers' Song. Thomas Deloney. *Fr.* Jack of Newbury. SiCE
When here, Lucinda, first we came. Arno's Vale. Charles Sackville. WaPE
When his bones are as seaweed, when his sweet tongue is parched. The White Rainbow. Starr Nelson. GoYe
When his head split open like a rotten. Three Awful Picnics. John L'Heureux. YAP
When Hitler was the Devil. The Silent Generation. Louis Simpson. NePoAm-2; ThLM
When Human Folk put out the light. Kitten's Night Thoughts. Oliver Herford. BoChLi; MPB
When Hymen once the mutual bands has wove. Epithalamium on a Late Happy Marriage. Christopher Smart. HW
When I/ die. The Rebel. Mari E. Evans. AmNP; IDB
When I/ took my/ watch to the watchfixer I. The Watch. May Swenson. CBV
When I a Lover Pale Do See. *Unknown.* SeCL
When I a verse shall make. His Prayer to Ben. Johnson. Robert Herrick. AnAnS-2; BoLiVe; CavP; EnL; EnLit; ILP; MaPo (1969 ed.); ML; NoP; OAEP; OBS; OxBoLi; PoSa; PP; ReEn; SCEP-2; SeCeV; SeCV-1; SeEP; TrGrPo; UnPo
When I admire the rose. The Rose [*or* A Fancy]. Thomas Lodge. *Fr.* The Life and Death of William Longbeard. ElL; OBSC
When I adore thee. *Unknown.* SeCSL
When I adore you and you have me in scorne. *Unknown.* SeCSL
When I am a man and can do as I wish. The Conjuror. E. V. Lucas. BiCB; BoChLi; PoMS
When I am alone, and quite alone. Hide and Seek. "Robin Christopher." RIS; StaSt
When I Am Big, I Mean to Buy. Mary Mapes Dodge. BiCB
When I Am Dead. Owen Dodson. Kal
When I Am Dead. Georgia Douglas Johnson. CDC
When I Am Dead. John G. Neihardt. HBMV; MAP
When I Am Dead. Sir Rennell Rodd. VA
When I Am Dead. Christina Rossetti. *See* Song: "When I am dead, my dearest."
When I Am Dead. Albert Stillman. InMe
When I Am Dead. *Unknown.* OxBoLi
When I Am Dead. James Edward Wilson. PoLF
When I am dead, ah, shall I then remember. If a Man Die. Florence Hamilton. MaRV
When I am dead and deep in dust. Reconciliation. J. U. Nicolson. HBMV
When I am dead, and doctors know not why. The Dampe. John Donne. MaMe; SCEP-1; SeCP
When I am dead and gone to dust. When I Am Dead. Albert Stillman. InMe
When I am dead and I am quite forgot. Tuscan Cypress, VII. Agnes Mary Frances Robinson. VA
When I am dead and nervous hands have thrust. When I Am Dead. John G. Neihardt. HBMV; MAP
When I am dead and over me bright April. I Shall Not Care. Sara Teasdale. AnEnPo; HBV; MAP; MoAmPo; NeMA; PFY; PoPl; TrGrPo
When I Am Dead and Sister to the Dust. Elsa Barker. HBV
When I am dead & thou would'st try. *Unknown.* SeCSL
When I am dead, I hope it may be said. On His Books [*or* Epigram]. Hilaire Belloc. ACP (1952 ed.); MoBrPo; OtMeF; OxBoLi; PoPl; SiTL; TreFT; WhC
When I am dead I want you to dress me. When I Am Dead. *Unknown.* OxBoLi
When I Am Dead, My Dearest. Christina Rossetti. *See* Song: "When I am dead, my dearest."
When I am dead, my spirit. When I Am Dead. Sir Rennell Rodd. VA
When I am dead, no pageant train. Dirge of Alaric the Visigoth. Edward Everett. BeLS
When I am dead unto myself, and let. De Profundis. George Macdonald. EPN
When I am dead, withhold, I pray, your blooming legacy. When I Am Dead. Georgia Douglas Johnson. CDC
When I am dead you'll find it hard. He and She. Eugene Fitch Ware. BOHV; PoLF; YaD
When I am gone and all my songs are still. Here Lies. . . Michael Lewis. YT
When I am gone and green. Lyric. Gil Orlovitz. ToPo
When I am gone, brook no complaining. Last Words. Annette von Droste-Hülshoff. CAW
When I am grown an *hombre.* Ambition. Edith Agnew. GaP; TiPo
When I am grown to man's estate. Looking Forward. Robert Louis Stevenson. BrPo; CenHV; InP; OTPC (1946 ed.); PoVP
When I am in a great city, I know that I despair. City-Life. D. H. Lawrence. CAD; OAEP (2d ed.); PoIE (1970 ed.)
When I am in my grave. Grave. Waring Cuney. PoNe
When I am listening to the sweet, tuneful airs of my country. I'r hen Iaith a'i Chanedon. Walter Dowding. ACV
When I am living in the Midlands. The South Country. Hilaire Belloc. ACP (1952 ed.); GoBC; HBV; HT; JKCP; MoBrPo; OBVV; POTE; ShBV-3
When I am lost in the deep body of the mist on a hill. Lines. Yone Noguchi. NP
When I am lying cold and dead. What No Man Knoweth. Hugh Francis Blunt. CAW
When I am lying under. What If Remembrance? Richard Eberhart. FiMAP
When I Am Not with You. Sara Teasdale. BoLP; MoLP
When I Am Old. Caroline Atherton Briggs Mason. BLPA; NeHB
When I am old—and O, how soon. When I Am Old. Caroline Atherton Briggs Mason. BLPA; NeHB
When I am old, and think of the old days. The Last Memory. Arthur Symons. HBV
When I am old and tutored by. A Franciscan Prayer. Enid Dinnis. CAW
When I am overmatched by petty cares. The Comfort of the Stars. Richard Burton. AnAmPo
When I am playing by myself. Water Noises. Elizabeth Madox Roberts. BoNaP; GFA; NP; SP
When I am sore beset I seek some quiet place. Meditation. Antoinette Goetschius. MaRV
When I am standing on a mountain crest. Love in the Winds. Richard Hovey. AA; BoLP; HBV; MAP; MoAmPo (1942 ed.); PoMa
When I am tempted to repine. Mine Were the Streets of Nazareth. Nettie Rooker. SoP
When I am the President. *Unknown.* GoTP
When I am tired of earnest men. Martin. Joyce Kilmer. MAP; NeMA; OnPP; PFY
When I am tired, the Bible is my bed. The Bible. *Unknown.* OQP; SoP
When I am very earnestly digging. Pause. Mary Ursula Bethell. AnNZ
When I am walking down the street. New Shoes. Marjorie Seymour Watts. PCH; SoPo
When I am walking sadly or triumphantly. The Shadow. Arthur Symons. OBVV
When I am walking with the children, and a girl. The Father. Donald Finkel. CoPo; PIA
When I am weary, throng'd with the cares of the vain day. Day's End. Laurence Binyon. OBVV
When I arrived last night. Note. Frank Lima. ANYP
When I ask for Lao Tzu. The Frontier. Jon Anderson. YAP
When I Awake, I Am Still with Thee. Harriet Beecher Stowe. *See* Still, Still with Thee.
When I Awoke. Raymond Patterson. NNP

When I awoke with cold. Coffee. J. V. Cunningham. MoAmPo (1962 ed.)
When I became myself I had. Ticktacktoe. John Stevens Wade. ThO
When I began my love to sow. Husbandry. William Hammond. SeCL
When I began this poem about our directions. The Yearbook. Tom Clark. ANYP
When I began to enquire. The Universal Heart of Man. Wordsworth. *Fr.* The Prelude. TOP
When I beheld the poet blind, yet bold. On [Mr. Milton's] "Paradise lost." Andrew Marvell. MaMe; OAEP; PeRV; SeEP
When I behold a forrest spread. Art above Nature, to Julia. Robert Herrick. AnAnS-2
When I behold Becchina in a rage. Sonnet: Of Becchina in a Rage. Cecco Angiolieri da Siena. AWP; JAWP; WBP
When I behold how black, immortal ink. Silet. Ezra Pound. MAP; MoAB; MoAmPo; Sonn
When I behold my mistress' face. Song. *Unknown.* SeCL
When I behold that beauty's [*or* beauties] wonderment. Amoretti, XXIV. Spenser. BEL; HBV
When I behold the bier, my last and posting horse. The Latter Day [*or* Bethinking Himself of His End, Writeth Thus]. Thomas, Lord Vaux. EnPo; PoLi; SiCE
When I behold the heavens as in their prime. Anne Bradstreet. *Fr.* Contemplations. AmLP; MaRV
When I behold thee, blameless Williamson. Sonnet: True Ambition. Benjamin Stillingfleet. OBEC
When I beneath the cold red earth am sleeping. Last Verses. William Motherwell. HBV
When I bethink[e] me on that speech whilere. Mutability. Spenser. *Fr.* The Faerie Queene, VII. MBW-1; OxBoCh; ReEn
When I burned our leaves, a wind from the dark. Looking West. William Stafford. NYBP
When I but hear her sing, I fare. Upon a Rare Voice. Owen Felltham. SeCL
When I but think upon the great dead days. Piere Vidal Old. Ezra Pound. MoAB
When I buy a bun. Buns for Tea. Dorothy M. Richardson. YT
When I Buy Pictures. Marianne Moore. OxBA
When I came forth this morn I saw. The Likeness. William Henry Davies. MemP
When I Came from Colchis. W. S. Merwin. AP; NePoEA
When I came home at evening. The Chaplet. Witter Bynner. PFY
When I came last to Ludlow. Friends. A. E. Housman. A Shropshire Lad, LVIII. PoVP; SeCePo
When I can hold a stone within my hand. Rumination. Richard Eberhart. CBV; FiMAP; LiTA; LiTM (rev. ed.)
When I can read my title clear/ to mansions in the skies. The Saint's Delight. *Unknown.* TrAS
When I carefully consider the curious habits of dogs. Meditatio [*or* Meditation]. Ezra Pound. FaBoCh; LoGBV; LOW; WePo
When I climb up. Drinking Fountain. Marchette Chute. TiPo (1959 ed.)
When I come down to sleep death's endless night. My City. James Weldon Johnson. BANP; CDC; PoNe; TIHL
When I come groping back through mists of sleep. Mortal Combat. Alice Fay di Castagnola. GoYe
When I come in f'om de co'n-fiel' aftah wo'kin' ha'd all day. At Candle-lightin' Time. Paul Laurence Dunbar. IHA
When I come to die. Memento. Federico García Lorca. OnPM
When I Consider. Milton. *See* On His Blindness.
When I consider every thing that grows. Sonnets, XV. Shakespeare. AWP; BEL; BWP; CoBE; DiPo; EnLi-1; MasP; OAEP; OBSC; OuHeWo; PoFS; ReEn; RelE; SiCE; Sonn; TrGrPo
When I Consider How My Light Is Spent. Milton. *See* On His Blindness.
When I consider how proud nations fall. One Who Dared to Die. Thomas Curtis Clark. ChIP
When I Consider Life. Dryden. *Fr.* Aureng-Zebe, IV, i. FiP
When I consider life and its few years. Tears. Lizette Woodworth Reese. AA; HBV; HBVY; InP; MAP; MaRV; MCCG; MoAmPo; NeMA; OQP; PFY; TreFS; WGRP; WHA
When I consider life, 'tis all a cheat. When I Consider Life. Dryden. *Fr.* Aureng-Zebe. FiP
When I consider men of golden talents. So That's Who I Remind Me Of. Ogden Nash. PoLF
When I consider, Thérèse. Upon Being Awakened at Night by My Four Year Old Daughter. Dachine Rainer. NePoAm-2
When I consider thy heavens, the work of thy fingers. *Fr.* Psalm VIII, Bible, *O.T.* FaPON; ImOP; InP
When I consider Time and Space. Fences. Rebecca McCann. PoMa
When I considered it too closely, when I wore it like an element. Meditation on Saviours. Robinson Jeffers. CMoP
When I contemplate all alone. In Memoriam A. H. H., LXXXIV. Tennyson. EPN; ViPo; VP
When I contemplate o'er me. The Night Serene. Luis de Leon. CAW; TrJP; WoL
When I crept over the hill, broken with tears. The Comforters. Dora Sigerson Shorter. CH; HBMV
When I decide I shall assemble you. Identity. Elizabeth Jennings. NePoEA
When I did part from thee the other night. Robert Tofte. *Fr.* Laura. RelE
When I did wake this morn from sleep. Early Morn. W. H. Davies. CH
When I Die. Fenton Johnson. CDC; PoNe
When I died, the circulating library. Seth Compton. Edgar Lee Masters. *Fr.* Spoon River Anthology. LiTA; NP
When I do count the clock that tells the time. Sonnets, XII. Shakespeare. AWP; BEL; CBEP; DiPo; EG; ElL; EnLi-1; EnRePo; EP; FaFP; InPo; JAWP; MasP; NoP; OBSC; Po; PoeP; ReEn; RelE; SiCE; Sonn; TOP; ViBoPo; WBP
When I do it, faith is lacking. He Must Do It. Oswald J. Smith. SoP
When I dragged the rotten log. Kenneth Rexroth. *Fr.* The Signature of All Things. BoNaP
When I dream of reading alone on the highest terrace. The Composition of Distances. Pien Chih-lin. LiTW
When I drift out on the Silver Sea. The Great Divide. Lew Sarett. HBMV
When I drive cab. After Anacreon. Lew Welch. NeAP
When I dyed last [*or* When last I died] and, Dear[e], I dye. The Legacy. John Donne. AtBAP; MaMe; SeCP; TrGrPo
When I eat pork, it's solemn business. To All Hog-Raisers, My Ancestors. Charles Simic. YAP
When I entreat, either thou wilt not hear. Sonnet. Henry King. AnAnS-2
When I face north a lost Cree. Returned to Say. William Stafford. NaP
When I fall asleep, and even during sleep. Baudelaire. Delmore Schwartz. ML; TwCP
When I Fall on My Knees, *with music. Unknown.* BoAN-2
When I first put this uniform on. Song: Colonel. W. S. Gilbert. *Fr.* Patience. PoVP
When I first went a-wagoning, a-wagoning did go. The Jolly Wagoner. *Unknown.* TrAS
When I forsook my homely town. The Prodigal Son. A. E. Coppard. MoBrPo (1942 ed.)
When I forth fare beyond this narrow earth. After Death. Charles Francis Richardson. AA
When I from schools came to the city first. Misacmos of Himself, Who Loves to Be Worst in the Company. Sir John Harington. SiCE
When I gaze at the sun. A Moment Please. Samuel Allen. AmNP; IDB; Kal
"When I get rich" the children dream. Horizons. Rebecca McCann. PoMa
When I Get Time. Thomas L. Masson. BLPA
When I get to be a composer. Daybreak in Alabama. Langston Hughes. AmFN
When I get up in the morning. Getting Up. Lilian McCrea. BoTP
When I go a-courtin'. Liza Jane. *Unknown.* ABF
When I go away from you. The Taxi. Amy Lowell. MAP; MoAmPo
When I go back of my head. Landscape with Figures. A. R. Ammons. FRC
When I go back to earth. The Answer. Sara Teasdale. NP
When I go free. The Little Salamander. Walter de la Mare. NP
When I go from hence let this be my parting word. Let This Be My Parting Word. Rabindranath Tagore. *Fr.* Gitanjali. MoRP

When I Go Home. Milton Lee. OQP
When I go home to the South the river lakes. The Gar. Charles G. Bell. AmFN
When I go [*or* goe] musing all alone. The Author's Abstract of Melancholy. Robert Burton. *Fr.* The Anatomy of Melancholy. OBS; SeCL
When I go riding. Dahlias. Edith Agnew. GaP
When I go to bed at night. At Night. Anne Blackwell Payne. GFA; UTS
When I goe musing all alone. *See* When I go musing all alone.
When I go walking down the street. Food. Marchette Chute. BrR; OCS
When I, good friends, was called to the Bar. The Judge's Song. W. S. Gilbert. *Fr.* Trial by Jury. PoVP
When I Grow Old. *Unknown.* SoP
When I grow old I hope to be. Growing Old. Rose Henderson. BiCB; BoChLi (1950 ed.)
When I grow old, if I should live till then. The Contented Bachelor. John Kendall. InMe
When I Grow Up. Rupert Sargent Holland. BiCB; OTPC
When I Grow Up. William Wise. BiCB
When I grow up. Plans. Dorothy Brown Thompson. BiCB
When I grow up I mean to go. When I Grow Up. Rupert Sargent Holland. BiCB
When I had firmly answered "No." The Last Ride Together (from Her Point of View.) James Kenneth Stephen. BOHV; CenHV; Par
When I had met my love the twentieth time. Her Merriment. W. H. Davies. EnLoPo
When I had money, money, O! Money. W. H. Davies. OBEV (new ed.); OBMV; OBVV
When I Had Need of Him. S. E. Kiser. BLRP
When I had turned Catullus into rhyme. Sonnet. Thomas Caulfield Irwin. IrPN
When I had wings, my brother. To a Seamew. Swinburne. EtS
When I ha'e a saxpence under my thoom. Todlin' Hame. *Unknown.* HBV
When I have a flask well laden. A Nota Bene. Karl Mikael Bellman. OnPM
When I have a house—as I sometime may. Vagabond House. Don Blanding. BLPA
When I Have Borne in Memory [What Has Tamed]. Wordsworth. EnLit; EnRP; GTBS; GTBS-D; GTBS-P; GTBS-W; GTSE; GTSL; MaPo; OBRV; PoFr
(England, 1802, V.) OBEV; HBV
When I have ceased to break my wings. Wisdom. Sara Teasdale. *Fr.* Interlude: Songs Out of Sorrow. InP
When I have ended, then I see. Dedication. Laurence Housman. TrPWD
When I Have Fears [That I May Cease to Be]. Keats. ATP; AWP; BEL; BoLiVe; BoPe; BWP; CABA; CBEP; CBV; CLwM; CoBE; DiPo; EnL; EnLi-2 (1949 ed.); EnLit; EnRP; EPN; ERoP-2; GoTP; HBV; HoPM; ILP; InP; InPo; JAWP; LiTB; MaPo; MaRV; MBW-2; MCCG; MERP; NoP; OAEP; OBEV; OBRV; OnPM; OuHeWo; PAn; Po; PoAn; PoE; PoeP; PoFS; PoIE; PoPo; PoRA; PoSa; SeCeV; Sonn; StP; TOP; TreFS; TrGrPo; WBP; WHA; YAT
(Sonnet: "When I have fears that I may cease to be.") FiP; OBNC
(Sonnet: Written in January, 1818.) ChER
(Terror of Death, The.) GTBS; GTBS-D; GTBS-P; GTBS-W; GTSE; GTSL
When I have finished with this episode. When I Have Gone Weird Ways. John G. Neihardt. HBV
When I have folded up this tent. The Last Word. Frederic Lawrence Knowles. HBV
When I have forgotten your lips. The Desolate Lover. Eileen Shanahan. NeIP
When I have gone away. Sugawara Michizane, *tr. fr. Japanese by* I. W. Furukami. LiTW
When I Have Gone Weird Ways. John G. Neihardt. HBV
When I have grown foolish. Peregrine's Sunday Song. Elinor Wylie. NYBP
When I have heard small talk about great men. Grandeur of Ghosts. Siegfried Sassoon. AnFE; HaMV; MoBrPo; OBMV
When I have lain an hour watching the skies. Clouds. John Jay Chapman. EtS
When I have lost my temper I have lost my reason, too. Temper. *Unknown.* PoToHe (new ed.); SoP
When I have lost the power to feel the pang. Strangeness of Heart. Siegfried Sassoon. MoRP; TrJP
When I have seen by Time's fell hand defaced. Sonnets, LXIV. Shakespeare. AWP; BEL; BWP; CABA; CLwM; EIL; EnL; EnLi-1 (1949 ed.); EnLit; EnLoPo; EnRePo; EP; FaFP; GTBS; GTBS-D; GTBS-P; GTBS-W; GTSE; GTSL; ILP; InP; InPo; JAWP; LiTB; LiTL; LO; MCCG; NoP; OBSC; OuHeWo; PoAn; PoeP; PoFS; PoIE; PoPo; PoRA; ReEn; ReIE; SeCeV; SiCE; Sonn; TOP; ViBoPo; WBP
When I have seen the sun emerge. Emily Dickinson. AP
When I have touched the end of days. The Gift of Work. Edwin Markham. DD
When I Hear Laughter. Wilfrid Scawen Blunt. Fr. Esther; a Young Man's Tragedy. MoBrPo (1942 ed.); NBM; OBEV; OBMV; OBVV; TrGrPo; ViBoPo
When I hear the old men. A Song of Greatness. *Unknown, tr. by* Mary Austin. AmFN; BiCB; BoChLi; FaPON; RePo; TiPo
When I Heard at the Close of the Day. Walt Whitman. AmPP (4th ed.); AnEnPo; AP; NePA; OxBA; TDP
When I Heard the Learn'd [*or* Learned] Astronomer. Walt Whitman. AmePo; AmPP; ATP (1935 ed.); BoLiVe; CABA; CaFP; CBEP; CBV; DiPo; InP; LoGBV; MAP; MaRV; MCCG; MoAmPo; NeMA; NoP; OnPM; OQP; OuHeWo; OxBA; PG (1955 ed.); PoMa; TDP; TreFT; TRV; VaPo; TrGrPo; WHA; WoL; YT
When I hold you in the night. Turn to the Left. Deems Taylor. UnTE
When I hoped I feared. Emily Dickinson. MWA-2
When I hug you you are light as a grasshopper. For Jeriann's Hands. Marge Piercy. ThO
When I in wild defiance fled. In Tribute. Vernal House. CaP
When I kneel down. Saying a Prayer. Rowena Bennett. MPB (1956 ed.)
When I kneel down my prayers to say. Prayers. Flora Hastings. OTPC (1923 ed.)
When I Knew a Little Bit. Bhartrihari, *tr. fr. Sanskrit by* Arthur W. Ryder. OnPM
When I leaned over a pool of black water. The King o' Spain's Daughter. Jeanne Robert Foster. HBMV
When I left Missouri River. A Forty-Niner Tells His Story. *Unknown.* IHA
When I left old New York, to go hunting after gold. Hunting after Gold. John A. Stone. SGR
When I left the States for gold. Seeing the Elephant. David G. Robinson. SGR
When I lie burning in thine eye. Song. Thomas Stanley. CavP; ViBoPo
When I lie where shades of darkness. Fare Well. Walter de la Mare. CoBMV; GTBS-D; GTBS-P; MoVE; OBEV (new ed.); POTE
When I lift up my eyes on high. Testimony. Mark Bullock. SoP
When I lived down in Devonshire. Autobiographical Fragment. Kingsley Amis. NePoEA-2
When I lived in Singapore. In Foreign Parts. Laura E. Richards. HBV; HBVY
When I look back across the waste of years. The Poet. Anita Grannis. HBMV
When I look back and in myself behold. On the Instability of Youth. Thomas, Lord Vaux. EnRePo
When I look back and say, of all our hours. A Prairie Ride. William Vaughn Moody. AnEnPo
When I look back upon my early days. Sonnets; a Sequence on Profane Love, XVII [XLV]. George Henry Boker. AmePo
When I look back upon my life nigh spent. A Prayer. George Macdonald. TrPWD
When I look forth at dawning, pool. Nature's Questioning. Thomas Hardy. BEL; CoBMV; EPN; InPo; MoPo; NoP; PoDB; PoFS; PoIE; ViPo
When I look in the mirror. Hysteria. Chu Shu Chen. NaP
When I look into a glass. A Thought [*or* The Mirror]. W. H. Davies. GTSL; MoShBr; MoSiPe; POTE
When I look into the mountain air. Chiliasm. Richard Eberhart. EaLo
When I looked at my poverty. Poverty. Charles Simic. YAP
When I looked into your eyes. Reflections. Amy Lowell. *Fr.* Chinoiseries. AnAmPo; NP; PoRA (rev. ed.)
When I Loved Thee. Thomas Stanley. *See* Deposition from Beauty, A.

When I Loved You. Thomas Moore. ALV; HBV
(To——.) BoLP; EnLoPo
When I Loved You. Charles A. Wagner. InMe
When I loved you, I can't but allow. When I Loved You [*or* To ——]. Thomas Moore. ALV; BoLP; EnLoPo; HBV
When I made answer, I began: "Alas!" Francesca da Rimini. Dante, *tr. by* Dante Gabriel Rossetti. *Fr.* Divina Commedia: Inferno. EPN
When I marched away to war. Colleen Oge Asthore. *Unknown.* OnYI
When I meet the morning beam. The Immortal Part. A. E. Housman. A Shropshire Lad, XLIII. MasP; MoBrPo; Po; PoVP; StP; UnPo (3d ed.)
When I meet you, I greet you with a stare. Silence. Anna Wickham. BoLP; NP
When I Met Him. Sybil Leonard Armes. FaChP
When I more large thy praises forth shall show. Chloris, XLIV. William Smith. Sonn; TuPP
When I must come to you, O my God, I pray. A Prayer to Go to Paradise with the Donkeys. Francis Jammes. EaLo; MoRP; OA
When I no more as now can find. Laughter and Tears. Tertius van Dyke. MaRV
When I opened your letter. A Thought of Marigolds. Janice Farrar. GoYe
When I pause before my mirror. Kakinomoto no Asomi Hitomaro, *tr. fr. Japanese by* I. W. Furukami. LiTW
When I perceive the sable of your hair. Sonnet. Elinor Wylie. *Fr.* One Person. NP
When I Peruse the Conquer'd Fame. Walt Whitman. ELU; GTBS-W; MCCG; PoEL-5; PoMa; PoPo
When I pictured you. Ollie, Answer Me. Stephen Berg. NaP
When I play on my fiddle in Dooney. The Fiddler of Dooney. W. B. Yeats. BEL; DiPo; FaBoCh; HBV; InP; LoGBV; NeMA; OBVV; PoMa; PoPo; TiPo; UnS; YT
When I pulled the cork. The Bottle of Chianti. Raymond Souster. ELU
When I put her out, once, by the garbage pail. The Geranium. Theodore Roethke. CoAP; PoeP
When I put on my Mother's clothes. Pretending. Myra Cohn Livingston. BiCB
When I put out to sail the sea. Across the Great Divide. Phyllis C. Michael. SoP
When I Read Shakespeare. D. H. Lawrence. NoP
When I Read the Bible Through. Amos R. Wells. SoP
When I remark her golden hair. Jessie. Eugene Field. InMe
When I remember again. The Sparrow's Dirge. John Skelton. *Fr.* Phyllyp Sparowe. FaBoCh; LoGBV; SeCePo
When I remember them, those friends of mine. Three Friends of Mine. Longfellow. MAmP
When I return I search for myself. On Going Home. Marjorie L. Agnew. GoYe
When I returned at sunset. Great City. Harold Monro. NP
When I returned from school I found we'd moved. London. John Betjeman. POTi
When I returned with drinks and nuts, my friend. The Friend of the Fourth Decade. James Merrill. NYBP
When I ride into the mountains on my little broncho bird. Cowboy Alone with His Conscience. James Barton Adams. SCC
When I ride my bicycle. Different Bicycles. Dorothy W. Baruch. FaPON; SUS; TiPo
When I rode the zebra past your door. Apparitions Are Not Singular Occurrences. Diane Wakoski. CoPo; YAP
When I run about all day. Night and Day. Mary Mapes Dodge. PRWS
When I Sail Away. Elizabeth Clark Hardy. *See* Some Time at Eve.
When I sailed out of Baltimore. A Child's Pet. W. H. Davies. CH
When I saw my mother's head on the cold pillow. Keine Lazarovitch. Irving Layton. ACV
When I saw that clumsy crow. Night Crow. Theodore Roethke. AmP; BiS; ELU; MoVE
When I saw the fox, it was kneeling. The Fox. Charles Tomlinson. OPoP
When I saw the grapefruit drying, cherries in each center lying. Arrogance Repressed. John Betjeman. FiBHP
When I saw the woman's leg on the floor of the subway train. The Leg in the Subway. Oscar Williams. AnFE; CoAnAm; LiTM; NePA; TwAmPo
When I Saw You Last, Rose. Austin Dobson. HBV; InP; YT
When I See Another's Pain. Mani Leib, *tr. fr. Yiddish by* Joseph Leftwich. TrJP
When I see birches bend to left and right. Birches. Robert Frost. AmPP; AnNE; CMoP; CoBA; DiPo; FaBV; HaMV; HBMV; ILP; LiTA; LiTM; LoGBV; MAP; MAPA; MaPo (1969 ed.); MCCG; MoAB; MoAmPo; MoVE; NeMA; NoP; OxBA; PAn; PFY; PoFS; PoIE; PoLF; PoPl; PoRA; StP; TOP; TreF; TrGrPo; TwAmPo; UnPo (3d ed.)
When I see blood pouring down the valleys. The Damage You Have Done. Ellis Ayitey Komey. PBA
When I see buildings in a town together. Mr. Frost Goes South to Boston. Firman Houghton. Par
When I see carved so clearly on your face. Two Solitudes. Evelyn Ames. GoYe
When I see her walk before me. Sidewalk Orgy. Richard O'-Connell. PV
When I See Old Men. Raymond Souster. CaP
When I see the falling bombs. Conflict. F. R. Scott. CaP; PeCV
When I see the first. Otomo no Yakamochi, *tr. fr. Japanese by* Kenneth Rexroth. LiTW
When I see the lark a-moving. The Lark. Bernart de Ventadorn. CTC
When I Set Out for Lyonnesse. Thomas Hardy. BrPo; CLwM; GTSE; HT; MoBrPo; NeMA; Po; PoeP; PoVP; SeCePo; ShBV-2; ViPo
When I shall be divorced, some ten years hence. Youth's Agitations. Matthew Arnold. CBEP
When I shall be without regret. Epitaph. J. V. Cunningham. ELU; PoCh
When I shall come before Thy gate and stand. The Password. Reginald C. Eva. ChIP
When I sit up to bread and milk. At Breakfast. I. M. Mills. BoTP
When I solidly do ponder. Francis Daniel Pastorius. SCAP
When I some antique jar behold. To a Lady. John Gay. OBEV (new ed.)
When I spin round without a stop. Spinning Top. Frank Dempster Sherman. GFA
When I stand at the judgment seat of Christ. His Plan for Me. Martha Snell Nicholson. STF
When I stand in the center of that man's madness. Reflection by a Mailbox. Stanley Kunitz. TrJP; WaP
When I stepped homeward to my hill. Home-coming. Léonie Adams. HBMV; MAP; MoAmPo; NeMA; TSW
When I Survey the Bright. William Habington. *See* Nox Nocti Indicat Scientiam.
When I Survey the Wondrous Cross. Isaac Watts. BePJ; MaRV; SoP; WGRP
(Crucifixion to the World by the Cross of Christ.) EiCL; EiPP; OBEC
When I Think More of My Own Future Than of Myself. Ron Padgett. YAP
When I think of all you've got. A Father's Heart Is Touched. Samuel Hoffenstein. FiBHP
When I Think of His Love. Louis Paul Lehman, Jr. SoP
When I think of it all I am so sad. Choucoune. Oswald Durand. PoNe
When I think of my fear. The Unblinding. Laurence Lieberman. NYBP
When I think of my kindness which is tentative and quiet. Kind. Josephine Miles. FiMAP
When I think of the cross where my Saviour died. When I Think of His Love. Louis Paul Lehman, Jr. SoP
When I Think of the Hungry People. O-Shi-O, *tr. fr. Japanese.* MaRV; TRV
When I think of the last great round-up. The Cowboy's Dream [*or* The Great Round-up]. *Unknown.* ABF; CoSo
When I think of things denied me. Oh, No Cross That I May Carry! Alice Mortenson. BePJ
When I think on the happy days. Absence. *Unknown.* GTSL
When I think upon things three. Three Sorrowful Things. *Unknown.* MeEV
When I Thy Parts Run O'er. Robert Herrick. UnTE
When I thy singing next shall heare. Againe. Robert Herrick. SeCP
When I to you sometimes make friendly motion. To the Lady Rogers, of Her Unprofitable Sparing. Sir John Harington. SiCE
When I try to skate. Skating. Herbert Asquith. BoChLi;

BrR; FaPON; SoPo; StVeCh; SUS; TiPo
When I verse shall make. *See* When I a verse shall make.
When I visited America. He Comforts Himself. Christopher Morley. *Fr.* Translations from the Chinese. EvOK
When I wake in the early mist. Very Early. Karla Kuskin. PDV; SoPo
When I wake up again, when I wake up. The Report. Jon Swan. NYBP
When I walk forth into the woods. Ode. Barnabe Barnes. *Fr.* Parthenophil and Parthenophe. TuPP
When I walk home through snow or slush. Winter Song. David Daiches. NYBP
When I was a bachelor [*or* little boy],/ I lived by myself,/ And all the bread and cheese I got. Mother Goose. BoTP; GFA; HBV; OTPC; OxNR; Po; PPL; RIS; SAS
When I was a bachelor, brisk and young. Blue Bottle. *Unknown.* OuSiCo
When I was a bachelor, I lived by myself [*or* all alone *or* batchelor early and young]. Foggy, Foggy Dew [*or* The Foggy Dew]. *Unknown.* AS; CoMu; DTC; ELP; LiTB; LiTG; OxBoLi; SiTL; UnTE (2 *vers.*)
When I was a beggarly boy. Aladdin. James Russell Lowell. AnNE; BBV (1951 ed.); HBV; NeHB; OTD; PoMS; RoGo; StVeCh (1940 ed.); TreFT; WaKn
When I was a boy. The Piper's Progress. Francis Sylvester Mahony. FiBHP
When I was a boy, and saw bright rows of icicles. Conrad Aiken. *Fr.* Improvisations: Light and Snow. BoNaP
When I was a boy desiring the title of man. George. Dudley Randall. BP; Kal
When I was a boy I heard the sea upstairs in a shell. Old Men Are Facts. Vivian Smith. NeLNL
When I was a boy, I used to go to bed. The Remorse for Time. Howard Nemerov. Sonn
When I was a boy my mother often said to me. I Want a Girl. Will Dillon. TreFS
When I Was a Brave Cowboy, *with music.* *Unknown.* CoSo
When I was a burst of thunder. Memnon. Leslie Holdsworth Allen. BoAu
When I was a child and thought as a child, I put. The Wandering Jew. Robert Mezey. NePoEA-2
When I was a child I knew red miners. Childhood. Margaret Walker. BOLo; Kal; TDP
When I was a child I saw. To a Child. Judith Wright. BoAV
When I Was a Cowboy, *with music.* *Unknown.* ABF
(Leadbelly's Chisholm Trail, *longer vers., with music.*) CoSo
When I was a cowboy I learned to throw the line. The Sporting Cowboy. *Unknown.* OuSiCo
When I was a cowboy way out on de western plains. When I Was a Cowboy [*or* Leadbelly's Chisholm Trail]. *Unknown.* ABF; CoSo
When I Was a Greenhorn and Young. Charles Kingsley. *See* Song: "When I was a greenhorn. . ."
When I was a kid. Growing Clean. Donald Green. WSL
When I Was a King in Babylon. W. E. Henley. *See* To W. A.
When I Was a Lad. W. S. Gilbert. *Fr.* H.M.S. Pinafore. PoPo
(First Lord's Song, The.) TreFS
(Ruler of the Queen's Navee, The.) DiPo
(Sir Joseph's Song.) CoBE; LiTB; SiTL
When I was a lad and so was my dad. *Unknown.* OxNR
When I was a lad of twenty. I Was a Bustle-Maker Once, Girls. Patrick Barrington. WhC
When I was a lad there were hansoms in London. Hansom Cabbies. Wilfrid Thorley. HBMV
When I was a little boy as fat as I could roll. Toll-a-Winker. *Unknown.* OuSiCo
When I was a little boy, I followed hope. Hope. Gamaliel Bradford. HBMV
When I was a little boy I had but little wit. *Unknown.* OxNR; RIS
When I was a little boy I lived by myself. Mother Goose. *See* When I was a bachelor.
When I was a little boy I washed my mammy's dishes. *Unknown.* OxNR
When I was a little boy my mammy kept me in. *Unknown.* OxNR
When I Was a Little Girl. Alice Milligan. OnYI; OxBI
When I was a little girl,/ About seven years old. *Unknown.* OxNR
When I was a little lad. Duna. Marjorie Pickthall. HBV; MCCG; PoTo
When I was a live man. Matter. Louis Untermeyer. YT
When I was a maid. The Old Story Over Again. James Kenney. OnYI
When I was a passenger in the barque *Windrush.* The Sun's over the Foreyard. Christopher Morley. EtS
When I was a serving maid, down in Drury Lane. Bell-Bottom Trousers. *Unknown.* AmSS
When I Was a Tree. Vachel Lindsay. ATP (1935 ed.)
When I was a windy boy and a bit. Lament. Dylan Thomas. ErPo; MasP
When I was a young man/ coming up. Art Berger. *Fr.* No Generation Gap. WOW
When I was a young man I lived upon the square. The Bad Boy. *Unknown.* CoSo
When I was as high as that. A Memory. L. A. G. Strong. PoPl; SiTL; WhC
When I was a-stealin' cross the deep blue sea. Trench Blues. *Unknown.* OuSiCo
When I was at the funeral. Snapshot: Politician. George Garrett. NePoAm-2
"When I was at the party." Betty at the Party. *Unknown, at to* Mary E. Bradley. BiCB; BoTP
When I was born a happy child. Epitaph for a Timid Lady. Frances Cornford. ELU
When I was born, my mother taped my ears. Youth's Progress. John Updike. FiBHP
When I was born on Amman hill. The Collier. Vernon Watkins. DTC; FaBoTw; FIW; MoVE
When I was bound apprentice, in famous Lincolnshire. The Lincolnshire Poacher [*or* The Poacher]. *Unknown.* CH; OnMSP; OxBoLi; SD; WiR
When I was but thirteen or so. Romance. Walter James Turner. BiCB; CH; CLwM; GoJo; HBMV; HBVY; HT; ILP; LiTM; MemP, *abr.*; MoBrPo; OBMV; PoMS; PoRA; POTE; PTK; ShBV-1; ThWaDe; TrGrPo; WePo; WHA
When I Was Christened. David McCord. Perambulator Poems, V. BiCB; RIS; WhC
When I was coming down from the country. The Forgotten City. William Carlos Williams. LiTA; NePA; PoPl
When I was dead, my spirit turned. At Home. Christina Rossetti. PoVP; VA
When I was down beside the sea. At the Seaside. Robert Louis Stevenson. FaPON; GFA; MPB (1956 ed.); OTPC; StVeCh (1940 ed.); SUS; TiPo
When I Was Fair and Young. Elizabeth I, Queen of England. CBEP; CTC; EnLi-1; PoRA; ReEn; TuPP
(Importune Me No More.) ElL; FOL; UnTE
(Youth and Cupid.) OBSC
When I was far from the sea's voice and vastness. Providence. Cale Young Rice. WGRP
When I was forced from Stella ever dear. Astrophel and Stella, LXXXVII. Sir Philip Sidney. FCP; SiPS
When I was happy in my youth. I Stand Corrected. Margaret Fishback. PoPl; WhC
When I was home de. Po' Boy Blues. Langston Hughes. BANP
When I was ill in the long ago. The Market Town. Frances Carlin. HBMV
When I was in the garden. The Queen Bee. Mary K. Robinson. BoTP
When I was introduced to Grief. Grief. Victor Contoski. ThO
When I was just a little boy. The Ships of Yule. Bliss Carman. BiCB; CaP; HBVY; RePo; WHW
When I was just a tiny chap. The Gypsy Heart. Harry Noyes Pratt. PoMa
When I was just as far as I could walk. The Telephone. Robert Frost. AnFE; APA; CLwM; CoAnAm; HBV
When I was little, oh a very small boy. So Long Folks, Off to the War. Anthony Ostroff. NePoAm-2; PoPl
When I was little, when. The Poplar's Shadow. May Swenson. NYBP
When I Was Lost. Dorothy Aldis. SoPo
When I was making myself a game. Little Rain. Elizabeth Madox Roberts. PoRh; SoPo; SUS; TiPo (1952 ed.)
When I was marked for suffering, Love forswore. Sonnet. Cervantes. AWP; PoFr
When I was on Night Line. Ego. Philip Booth. TwCP
When I was once in Baltimore. Sheep. W. H. Davies. LiTM; MoBrPo; OA; PrWP; StPo

When I was one. The End. A. A. Milne. SiSoSe; ThGo
(End, The.) BiCB
When I was one. Sophisticate. Barbara Young. BiCB; SiSoSe
When I Was One-and-twenty. A. E. Housman. A Shropshire Lad, XIII. AnFE; BBV; BiCB; BoLiVe; BoLP; CMoP; CoBE; DiPo; ELP; EnLi-2; EnLit; FaBV; FaFP; GTBS-W; GTSL; HBV; LiTB; LiTL; LiTM; MasP; MeWo; MoAB; MoBrPo; NeMA; OAEP; OtMeF; OuHeWo; PG; PoLF; PoPl; PoPo; PoVP; TreF; TrGrPo; ViBoPo; VP; WHA; YAT
When I was only six years old. When I Was Six. Zora Cross. BiCB; BoAu; FaPON; HBVY
When I Was Otherwise Than Now I Am. *Unknown.* NCEP
When I was seven. Growing Up. Harry Behn. BiCB; PDV; SiSoSe; SoPo
When I was seventeen I heard. To Critics. Walter Learned. AA; AnAmPo; HBV
When I was sick and lay a-bed. The Land of Counterpane. Robert Louis Stevenson. BoChLi; BrPo; EvOK; FaBoBe; FaFP; FaPON; HBV; HBVY; ILP; MPB; NeHB; OTPC; PCH; PoPl; PoVP; RIS; SoPo; StVeCh; TreF; VA
When I Was Single (A *and* B *vers.*), *with music.* *Unknown.* ABF
(I Wish I Was Single Again, *with music.*) AS; BFSS
(Single Girl, The.) TrAS
When I Was Six. Zora Cross. BiCB; BoAu; FaPON; HBVY
When I Was Small. André de Chénier, *tr. fr. French by* Elizabeth Gerteiny. ErPo
When I was small, a woman died. Emily Dickinson. OnPM
When I was small and trees were high. Tree-sleeping. Robert P. Tristram Coffin. LOW
When I was small I hated rain. For April Showers. Emily Rose Burt. GFA
When I was ten and she fifteen. Time's Revenge. Walter Learned. HBV
When I was told of your death, Heraclitus. Callimachus to Heraclitus. Callimachus. OnPM
When I was very small indeed. Palm Leaves of Childhood. G. Adali-Mortti. PBA
When I was very young. Dimple Diggers. "Robin Christopher." RIS
When I was wandering far from home. The Bust. W. H. Davies. MoPW
When I Was Young. Alun Llywelyn-Williams, *tr. fr. Welsh by* Gwyn Williams. PrWP
When I was young. Jimmy's Father. John Stevens Wade. ThO
When I was young/ I dared to sing. The Pit of Bliss. James Stephens. AnFE
When I Was Young and Foolish, *with music.* *Unknown.* AS
When I was young and full o' pride. Blow Me Eyes! Wallace Irwin. BOHV; BoLP; GSP; HBMV; InMe; StPo
When I was young and in my prime. A Long Time Ago, *vers.* III. *Unknown.* ShS
When I was young and slender, a spender, a lender. Song for a Cracked Voice. Wallace Irwin. InMe
When I was young—and very young. Wisdom. Daniel Whitehead Hicky. BiCB
When I was young, I had a bed. The Ship o' Bed. Robert P. Tristram Coffin. TSW
When I was young I had a care. Soliloquy. Francis Ledwidge. EnLit
When I was young, I had no sense. The Fiddle. Neil Munro. BoTP
When I was young I heard a tune. For the Eightieth Birthday of a Great Singer. Edward Shanks. UnS
When I was young, I put on rouge. The Onion Skin. Kenneth Pitchford. *Fr.* Good for Nothing Man. CoPo
When I was young I said. Experience. J. V. Cunningham. CBV
When I was young, I said to Sorrow. Song [*or* Sorrow]. Aubrey Thomas De Vere. GTBS-D; WiR
When I was young I scribbled, boasting, on my wall. The Summing-Up. Stanley Kunitz. ELU
When I was young I used to wait. The Blue-Tail Fly. *Unknown.* FaFP; SiTL; TreFT; ViBoFo
When I was young, I was out of tune with the herd. Returning to the Fields. T'ao Ch'ien [Tao Yuan-ming]. LiTW; PoFr
When I was young I'd little sense. The Mysteries. L. A. G. Strong. HaMV
When I was young the days were long. The Flying Wheel. Katharine Tynan. WGRP
When I was young the twilight seemed too long. Twilight. Agnes Mary Frances Robinson. HBV
When I was young, throughout the hot season. Satire on Paying Calls. Ch'eng Hsaiao. WoL
When I was young unapt for use of man. *Unknown.* SeCSL
When I was young, when I was young! Lament for Prytherch. R. S. Thomas. POTi
When I was young, with sharper sense. A Summer Commentary Yvor Winters. LiTM; QFR; UnPo (3d ed.)
When I was younger. Pastoral. William Carlos Williams. AmPP (5th ed.); OxBA
When I Watch the Living Meet. A. E. Housman. A Shropshire Lad, XII. AnFE; CBV; CMoP; MasP; MoBrPo; OAEP; PoVP; TrGrPo; ViPo; WHA
When I watch you. Miss Rosie. Lucille Clifton. TwCP
When I went down past Charing Cross. The Poet. W. H. Davies. DTC
When I Went Off to Prospect, *with music.* John A. Stone. SGR
When I went out to kill myself, I caught. Saint Judas. James Wright. CBV; NMP
When I went to bed at night. Through the Porthole. Marjorie Wilson. BoTP
When I went to the Bar as a very young man. Said I to Myself, Said I. W. S. Gilbert. *Fr.* Iolanthe. PoVP
When I Went to the Circus. D. H. Lawrence. CMoP; LiTB
When I went up the minster tower. At Lincoln. Oscar Fay Adams. AA
When I went up to Nazareth. The Lilies of the Field. Daniel Henderson. MaRV; StJW
When I woke, the lake-lights were quivering on the wall. Coming Awake. D. H. Lawrence. BrPo
When I wooed Carinda first. Of His Mistress Grown Old. William Hicks. SeCL
When I would send you rimes that could relate. The Effigy. Guido Cavalcanti. LiTW
When I would sing of crooked streams and fields. The Song. Jones Very. MAmP
When I would think of you, my mind holds only. The Kestrels. Sidney Keyes. FaBoMo; POTE
When Icicles Hang by the Wall. Shakespeare. *Fr.* Love's Labour's Lost, V, ii. AnFE; ATP; BBV (1923 ed.); BEL; CaFP; CBEP; CoBE; EG; EnLi-1; EnLit; FaPON; GN; GoJo; LiTB; MyFE; OBSC; OTPC; OuHeWo; PIA; PoEL-2; PoRA; PoSa; PoSC; RoGo; SeCeV; SiCE; TOP
(Hiems.) FaBoCh; LoGBV
(Merry Note, A.) WiR
(Song: "When icicles hang by the wall.") CBV; FiP; HBV; YAT
(Songs: Spring and Winter.) ExPo
(Songs from the Plays.) AWP; JAWP; WBP
(Spring and Winter, 2.) OBEV
(To-Whit To-Who.) PoG
(Tu-Whit To-Who.) CH
(Winter.) BoC; BoNaP; ChTr; EIL; EnL; GBV (1952 ed.); GTBS; GTBS-D; GTBS-P; GTBS-W; GTSE; GTSL; ILP; InPo; LiTG; MaPo; MCCG; MPB; PAn; PCD; PCH; PoAn; PoE; PoeP; PoFS; PoIE; PoPo; PTK; RG; SeCePo; ShBV-1; TreFS; TrGrPo; UnPo; ViBoPo; WaKn; WHA
(Winter Song.) BoLiVe
(Winter's Song.) FaBoEn
When I'm a big man, then I'll buy me a gun. A Plan. John Alden Carpenter. RIS
When I'm a little older. My Plan. Marchette Chute. BiCB; BrR; FaPON
"When I'm alone"—the words tripped off his tongue. Alone [*or* When I'm Alone]. Siegfried Sassoon. BoLiVe; MoBrPo; OBMV; POTE; ShBV-3; TrGrPo (1942 ed.); WePo; YT
When I'm an aviator. Trails of Smoke. Rowena Bennett. MPB (1956 ed.)
When I'm asleep, dreaming and lulled and warm. Sick Leave. Siegfried Sassoon. NP
When I'm big I want to be. Space. Inez Hogan. RePo
When I'm discharged in Liverpool 'n' draws my bit o' pay. Hell's Pavement. John Masefield. BrPo
When I'm Going Well. R. G. Everson. PeCV (1967 ed.)
When I'm in bed at night. Night Watchmen. Jimmy Garthwaite. BrR

When I'm in bed at night. Noises in the Night. Lilian McCrea. BoTP
When I'm in health and asked to choose between the This and That, alas! Carpe Diem. Ridgely Torrence. *Fr.* The House of a Hundred Lights. AA
When in death I shall calm recline. Legacy. Thomas Moore. AS
When in dim dreams I trace the tangled maze. To Olive. Lord Alfred Douglas. OBVV
When in disgrace with fortune and men's eyes. Sonnets, XXIX. Shakespeare. AnFE; AtBAP; ATP; AWP; BEL; BoLiVe; BoLP; BWP; CBEP; CBV; CoBE; CTC; DiPo; EIL; EnL; EnLi-1; EnLit; ExPo; FaBoEn; FaBV; GTBS; GTBS-D; GTBS-P; GTBS-W; GTSE; GTSL; HBV; ILP; InP; InPo; InvP; JAWP; LiTB; LiTG; LiTL; LoBV; MaPo; MaRV; MasP; MemP; MeWo; NoP; OAEP; OBEV; OBSC; OuHeWo; PAn; PG; Po; PoAn; PoE; PoEL-2; PoFS; PoIE; PoMa; PoPl; PoPo; PoRA; PoSa; ReEn; ReIE; SeCeV; SiCE; Sonn; TIHL; TOP; TreF; TrGrPo; TRV; ViBoPo; WBP; WHA
When in her face mine eyes I fix. Madrigal. Earl of Stirling. Aurora, Madrigal I. EIL
When in mid-air, the Golden Trump shall sound. Poet's Resurrection. Dryden. *Fr.* To the Pious Memory of the Accomplished Young Lady, Mrs. Anne Killigrew. WHA
When in My Arms. Pushkin, *tr. fr. Russian by* Babette Deutsch. ErPo
When in my dreams thy lovely face. Dream Land. Frances Ann Kemble. OBVV
When, in my effervescent youth. Who'd Be a Hero (Fictional)? Morris Bishop. FiBHP
When in my walks I meet some ruddy lad. A Proem. Samuel Ward. AA; AmLP
When in my youth I travellèd. The Grey Squirrels. William Howitt. TVC
When in Rome. Mari E. Evans. AmNP
When in some sudden hush of earth. The Retreat. Sir Herbert Read. BrPo
When in summer thou walkest. Thou Flower of Spring. John Clare. LO
When in that gold/ Of fires, quietly sitting. Listening to Foxhounds. James Dickey. WIRo
When in the bedded dark of night. Marriage [To K.]. Donald Hall. MoLP; NePoEA
When in the chronicle of wasted time. Sonnets, CVI. Shakespeare. AnFE; AWP; BEL; BoLiVe; CBEP; CBV; CLwM; CoBE; CTC; DiPo; EG; EIL; EnL; EnLi-1; EnLit; EnLoPo; EnRePo; ExPo; FaBoCh; FaBoEn; FaBV; FiP; GTBS; GTBS-D; GTBS-P; GTBS-W; GTSE; GTSL; HBV; InPo; JAWP; LiTB; LiTG; LiTL; LoBV; LoGBV; MaPo; MasP; MCCG; NoP; OAEP; OBEV; OBSC; OuHeWo; PAn; PIA; Po; PoE; PoeP; PoFS; PoIE; PoPo; PoRA; ReEn; ReIE; SeCeV; ShBV-3; SiCE; Sonn; StP; TOP; TreFT; TrGrPo; ViBoPo; WBP; WHA
When in the Crowd I Suddenly Behold. Robert Nathan. MAP; MoLP
When, in the dawn of love and my desire. The Miracle. Allan Dowling. ErPo
When in the dim beginning of the years. The Testing [*or* Man-Test]. Edwin Markham. MaRV; MoRP; OQP
When in the down I sink my head. In Memoriam A. H. H., LXVIII. Tennyson. EPN; OAEP; ViPo; VP
When in the festival of August heat. Horas Tempestatis Quoque Enumero; the Sundial. John Hollander. NePoEA
When in the First Great Hour. Edith M. Thomas. *Fr.* The Inverted Torch. AA
When in the glass I see the heavy clay. A Chorister in Avalon. Humbert Wolfe. BoPe
When, in the gold October dusk, I saw you near to setting. Arcturus in Autumn. Sara Teasdale. NP
When, in the hour of lonely woe. Trust in Jesus. Josiah Conder. BePJ
When in the mirror of a permanent tear. Elegy on Gordon Barber, Lamentably Drowned in His Eighteenth Year. Gene Derwood. FaFP; GTBS-W; LiTA; LiTG; LiTM; NePA; TwAmPo
When, in the morning, fresh from sleep. In the Morning. Cecilia Loftus. GFA
When, in the sky, my Star of Hope. Then God Bends Low. Dorothy Conant Stroud. SoP
When in the spring the swallows all return. Sappho, XCIII. Bliss Carman. PeCV
When in the starry gloom. Easter. Richard Watson Gilder. DD
When in the sun the hot red acres smoulder. The Zulu Girl. Roy Campbell. AtBAP; BoSA; ChMP; JKCP (1955 ed.); MoPW; MoVE; OBMV; PoPl; POTE
When in the Woods I Wander All Alone. Edward Hovell-Thurlow. HBV; HBVY
When in thy glass thou studiest thy face. Afternoon. Wendell Phillips Garrison. *Fr.* Post-Meridian. AA
When inclined to be discouraged. Have Faith in God. Joe Budzynski. STF
When Indians heare that some there are. Roger Williams. SCAP
When indoor young ones club their wicked wits. The First of April. William Hone. PoRL
When is He nearest to all of us. Gethsemane's Gift. Katherine Brégy. MaRV; StJW
When is the Muse most lustily acclaimed? Song's Apostasy. Sir William Watson. EPN
When Isaac watched his father strain back. Abraham's Madness. Bink Noll. ToPo
When Israel Came Forth Out of Egypt. Psalms, CXIV, Bible, *O.T.* TrJP
(Psalm CXIV.) LiTW
When Israel, of the Lord beloved. Rebecca's Hymn. Sir Walter Scott. *Fr.* Ivanhoe. EnRP; ViBoPo
When Israel Out of Egypt Came. A. E. Housman. LiTB
When Israel was in Egypt's land. Go Down, Moses. *Unknown.* AmPP; EaLo
When it behoves me to go to you, O my God, let. Prayer to Go to Paradise with the Donkeys. Francis Jammes. LiTW
When it comes. Feelings of a Very Light Negro as the Confrontation Approaches. Pearl Cleage. WSL
When it comes to a question of trusting. The Average Man. Margaret E. Sangster. WBLP
When it comes to saddle hawses, there's a difference in steeds. The Ol' Cow Hawse. Earl Alonzo Brininstool. SCC
When it is finally ours, this freedom, this liberty. Frederick Douglass. Robert Hayden. AmNP; IDB; Kal; NoP; PoNe; TTY; WOW
When it is not yet day. Looking for Mushrooms at Sunrise. W. S. Merwin. NaP
When it is not yet twilight. Benedetta Barzini. Gerard Malanga. YAP
When it is the winter time. Ice. Dorothy Aldis. GFA; SUS; TiPo
When it rained in Devon. London Rain. Nancy Byrd Turner. MoSiPe
When it sank it thundered. Ivesiana. Bill Berkson. ANYP
When it was dark in Martin Place. Cenotaph. Brian Fitzpatrick. MoAuPo
When it was said that she was dead. A Conversational Neighbor. Richard R. Kirk. PoMa
When It's Iris Time in Tennessee. Willa Mae Waid. PoRL
When it's just past April. The Flower-Cart Man. Rachel Field. OCS; SiSoSe; SoPo
When its rays fall on its cheeks the cat licks them, thinking them milk. The Moon. Bhasa. LiTW
When I've a saxpence under my thumb. Todlen Butt, and Todlen Ben. *Unknown.* OBS
When I've hoed and dug my garden. My Garden. Frederic E. Weatherly. OTPC (1946 ed.)
When Jack Frost comes—oh! the fun. Jack Frost. *Unknown.* GFA
When Jack the King's commander. The Fate of John Burgoyne. *Unknown.* PAH
When Jacky's a [very] good boy. Mother Goose. BrR; EvOK; OxNR; PPL
When Jacob from the land of Canaan down. The Exodus from Egypt. Ezekielos of Alexandria. TrJP
When Januar' wind war blawin cauld. The Lass That Made the Bed for Me. Burns. InvP; UnTE
When Jemmy the Second, not Jemmy the First. A New Song Entitled the Warming Pan. *Unknown.* CoMu
When Jessie comes with her soft breast. Jessie. Thomas Edward Brown. HBV; OBEV
When Jesus came to Golgotha they hanged Him on a Tree. Indifference [*or* The Crucifixion]. G. A. Studdert-Kennedy. ChIP; MaRV; OQP; PGD; SoP; StJW; TRV

When Jesus Christ was four years old. The Birds. Hilaire Belloc. JKCP
When Jesus hung upon the tree. The Other Mother. F. M. Roger. SoP
When Jesus lay on Mary's knee. The Winds at Bethlehem. Winifred M. Letts. StJW
When Jesus walked upon the earth. The Greatest. Marion Brown Shelton. MaRV
When Jesus was a little Child. Mother and Child. Ivy O. Eastwick. SiSoSe
When Jesus was a little thing. His Mother in Her Hood of Blue. Lizette Woodworth Reese. ISi; OHIP
When Jesus Wept, *with music.* William Billings. TrAS
When Jill complaines to Jack for want of meate. Upon Jack and Jill, Epigram. Robert Herrick. AnAnS-2
When Jim and Bill and I were boys a many years ago. Ashes on the Slide. Eugene Field. BBV (1923 ed.)
When John Henry was little boy. John Henry. *Unknown.* BaBo (A *vers.*); ThLM
When John Henry was about three days old. John Henry. *Unknown.* AmFN; TiPo (1959 ed.)
When John Henry was nothin' but a baby. John Henry. *Unknown.* FaBoBe
When John the Baptist was so young. Apocrypha. Babette Deutsch. HBMV
When John was christened, up he reached. It Really Happened. Elizabeth Henley. BiCB
When Johnny Comes Marching Home. Patrick Sarsfield Gilmore. PaA; PAH; PAL; PoSC; ThLM; TrAS, *with music*; TreF
When Johnson sought (as Shakespear says) that bourn. Introduction and Anecdotes. "Peter Pindar." *Fr.* Bozzy and Piozzi. PoEL-3
When Johnson's Ale Was New, *with music.* *Unknown.* ShS
When Jonathan Bing was young, they say. Jonathan Bing Does Arithmetic. Beatrice Curtis Brown. GaP; RIS
When Joseph was an old man. The Cherry-Tree Carol [*or* Joseph and Mary]. *Unknown.* BaBo; BFSS
When Jove lay blest in his Alcmena's charms. To a Friend on His Nuptials. Matthew Prior. HW
When Juan woke he found some good things ready. Byron. *Fr.* Don Juan, II. EnLit
When Julius Caesar went to town. The Same Old Story. James J. Montague. HBMV
When Julius Fabricius, Sub-Prefect of the Weald. The Land. Kipling. MoBrPo; OnMSP; ViPP
When Kian O'Hara's Cup Was Passed to Turlough O'Carolan. Turlough Carolan. *See* Cup of O'Hara, The.
When king Kynghill in his hand. Songe of Seyncte Warburghe. Thomas Chatterton. PeER
When Klopstock England Defied. Blake. PeER; ERoP-1
When lads have done with labor. A. E. Housman and a Few Friends. Humbert Wolfe. FiBHP; Par; WhC
When lads were home from labour. Fancy's Knell. A. E. Housman. AnFE; EG; FaBoCh; MoPW; PoRA; ShBV-4
When Lady Jane refused to be. Save the Tiger! A. P. Herbert. OnSP
When land is gone and money spent. *Unknown.* OxNR
When languor and disease invade. Rejoicing in Hope. Augustus Montague Toplady. BePJ
When last I died, and, dear, I die. *See* When I dyed last, and, dear, I dye.
When last I heard your nimble fingers play. To Lucia Playing on Her Lute. Samuel Pordage. SeCL
When last I walked there. To Rimbaud in Hell. Joseph Cardarelli. QAH
When late I attempted your pity to move. An Expostulation. Isaac Bickerstaffe. BoLP; FiBHP; PV
When late I heard the trembling cello play. The Cello. Richard Watson Gilder. AA
When late in summer the streams run yellow. A Song of Early Autumn. Richard Watson Gilder. DD; HBV
When lately Pym descended into hell. On the Death of Pym. William Drummond of Hawthornden. ALV
When laughing Ann trips down the street. Laughing Ann. A. P. Herbert. OnPP
When Lazarus left his charnel-cave. In Memoriam A. H. H., XXXI. Tennyson. EPN; MemP; ViPo; VP
When Learning's triumph o'er her barbarous [*or* barb'rous] foes. Prologue Spoken by Mr. Garrick at the Opening of the Theatre [Royal] in Drury-Lane, 1747. Samuel Johnson. CEP; EiCL; EiCP; EiPP; MBW-1; NoP; OBEC; PoFS; SeCeV
When leaves are dressed in red and brown. Autumn Races. Emilie Blackmore Stapp. GFA
When leaves of April glisten. The Concert. Phyllis McGinley. YeAr
When leaves turn outward to the light. Poet and Lark. "Madeline Bridges." AA HBV
When leaving with your loving in my veins. Late Light. Barbara Bellow Watson. NYBP
When legislators keep the law. Latter-Day Warnings. Oliver Wendell Holmes. *Fr.* The Autocrat of the Breakfast-Table. PCD
When legs beneath kilts grow sturdy and strong. Childhood. *Unknown.* FIW
When Let by Rain. Edward Taylor. *See* Address to the Soul . . .
When Letty had scarce pass'd her third glad year. Letty's Globe. Charles Tennyson Turner. CBEP; EPN; HBV; OBEV; OBVV; PeVV; VA
When Life has borne its harvest from my heart. A Prayer in Late Autumn. Violet Alleyn Storey. TrPWD
When life hath run its largest round. Birthday of Daniel Webster. Oliver Wendell Holmes. DD
When Life Is Done. Edgar A. Guest. MaRV
When Life Is Quite Through With. E. E. Cummings. NoP; CrMA
When life's cares around you gather. Keep Looking Up. Carlton Buck. SoP
When Life's Day Closes. Thomas Tiplady. MaRV
When like a bud my Julia blows. To Julia under Lock and Key. Sir Owen Seamean. BOHV
When, like the early rose. Eileen [*or* Aileen] Aroon. Gerald Griffin. AnIV; GoBC; HBV IrPN; OBVV; OnYI; PCD
When like the rising day. Gerald Griffin. *Fr.* Eileen Aroon. OBEV (new ed.)
When like wistaria against this wall. A Weightless Element. Gottfried Benn. PoPl
When Lilacs Last in the Dooryard Bloom'd. Walt Whitman. *Fr.* Memories of President Lincoln. AmePo; AmP; AmPP (3d ed.); AnAmPo; AnEnPo; AP; ATP; AWP; BoLiVe; CABA; CoBA; DiPo; ExPo; FaBoEn, *abr.*; ForPo; GTBS-D, *sts.* 1-6; HBV; InPo; JAWP; LiPo; LiTA; LoBV; MAmP; MAP; MaPo; MasP; MoAmPo; MWA-1; NeMA, *sts.* 1-6; NoP; OuHeWo; OxBA; PaA; PAL; PAn; PIA; Po; PoAn; PoE; PoEL-5; PoFS; PoIE; PoPo; PoRA; PTK, *abr.*; SeCeV; StP; TDP; TOP; TreF; TrGrPo; VaPo; ViBoPo; WHA; WoL; YT
Death Carol: "Come lovely and soothing Death," XIV. AnFE; APA; CoAnAm; MaRV; MoRP
When Lincoln Came to Springfield. Vachel Lindsay. LiPo; MAP; MoAmPo; NeMA
When Little Birdie Bye-bye Goes. *Unknown.* OTPC; PPL (Bye-bye.) SAS
When little boys grow patient at last, weary. Death of Little Boys. Allen Tate. CBV; LiTA; MAP; MoAB; MoAmPo; TwCP
When little boys with merry noise. Reinforcements. Thomas Toke Lynch. OBVV
When little Calathine was brought to bed. Little Calathine. *Unknown.* OnPM
When little daily winds have died away. Winter; Two Sonnets, II. Malcolm Cowley. *Fr.* Blue Juniata. MAP; MoAmPo (1942 ed.)
When little Dickie Swope's a man. An Impetuous Resolve. James Whitcomb Riley. BiCB
When little Fred/ Was called to bed. Mother Goose. HBV; HBVY
When little heads weary have gone to their bed. The Plumpuppets. Christopher Morley. FaPON; GaP; MPB; TiPo
When little John Hardy was four years old. John Hardy (A *vers.*). *Unknown.* ViBoFo
When little things would irk me, and I grow. Morning Prayer. *Unknown.* PoToHe
When lo! a harlot form soft sliding by. Dunces' Opera. Pope. *Fr.* The Dunciad, IV. MuSP
When Londons fatal bills were blown abroad. Marlburyes Fate. Benjamin Tompson. SCAP
When long the shadows of the wind had rolled. The Sheaves. E. A. Robinson. ReMP
When, looking on the present face of things. October 1803. Wordsworth. EnRP

When lordly Saturn in a sable robe. Eurymachus's Fancy. Robert Greene. *Fr.* Francesco's Fortunes. OBSC
When Louis came home to the flat. Meet Me in St. Louis. Andrew B. Sterling. TreFT
When, lov'd by poet and painter. The Ivory Gate. Mortimer Collins. VA
When Love arose in heart and deed. The Flowers. William Brighty Rands. OBEV; OBVV
When love at first did move. Song. Ben Jonson. *Fr.* The Masque of Beauty. GoBC
When love begins with Ganymede, he gathers. Ganymede. Witter Bynner. AnFE; CoAnAm
When Love, born first of thought and will. Divorce. Charles Williams. POTE
When Love Comes Knocking. William Henry Gardner. AA
When Love ensnares my mind unbidden. Composition in Late Spring. Irving Layton. PeCV
When Love had strove us to subdue. Love. Joseph Beaumont. OBS
When love has passed its limits. Chorus. Euripides. *Fr.* Medea. LiTW
When love in the faint heart trembles. Song of Eros. George Edward Woodberry. *Fr.* Agathon. AA; HBV
When Love Meets Love. Thomas Edward Brown. OBVV; UnPo
When love of us called Him to see. Richard Crashaw. BoC
When love on time and measure makes his ground. Song [*or* False Love]. *At. to* John Lilliat. EIL; LO; OBSC
When Love, our great Immortal. The Rose of Stars. George Edward Woodberry. *Fr.* Wild Eden. AA; HBV
When love, puffed up with rage of high disdain. Sir Philip Sidney. FCP
When love was false and I was full of care. The Constant One. George Dillon. AmLP
When love with unconfinèd wings. To Althea, from Prison. Richard Lovelace. AnAnS-2; AnEnPo; AnFE; ATP; AWP; BEL; BLPA; CABA; CavP; CBEP; CBV; CoBE; EnL; EnLi-1; EnLit; FaBoBe; FaBoEn; FaPL; GTBS; GTBS-D; GTBS-P; GTBS-W; GTSE; GTSL; HBV; ILP; InPo; JAWP; LiTB; LiTG; LiTL; LoBV; MCCG; MeLP; MemP; MePo; MeWo; NeHB; NoP; OAEP; OBEV; OBS; OuHeWo; PoAn; PCD; PG (1945 ed.); PoE; PoFS; PoIE; PoPo; PoRA; PoSa; ReEn; SCEP-2; SeCeV; SeCL; SeCP; SeCV-1; SeEP; TOP; TreF; TrGrPo; ViBoPo; WBP; WHA; YAT
When Lovely Woman, *parody.* Phoebe Cary. ALV; BOHV; FaBoBe; HBV; TreFS
(When Lovely Woman Wants a Favor.) InP
When Lovely Woman [Stoops to Folly]. Goldsmith. *See* Song: "When lovely woman stoops to folly."
When Lovely Woman Wants a Favor. Phoebe Cary. *See* When Lovely Woman.
When love's brief dream is done. Remember. Georgia Douglas Johnson. PoNe
When Lucinda's blooming beauty. Lucinda. *Unknown.* SeCL
When Lucy McLockett. Lucy McLockett. Phyllis McGinley. BiCB
When lyart leaves bestrow the yird. The Jolly Beggars; a Cantata. Burns. BEL; CEP; EiCL; EiCP; EiPP; EnRP; NoP; OAEP; PoEL-4
When Lynus meets me, after salutations. Of Lynus, Borrowing. Sir John Harington. SiCE
When Mahalia Sings. Quandra Prettyman. IDB
When maidens are young, and in their spring. Serenade. Aphra Behn. *Fr.* The Emperor of the Moon. SeCL
When maidens such as Hester die. Hester. Charles Lamb. EnRP; GTBS; GTBS-D; GTBS-P; GTBS-W; GTSE; GTSL; HBV; LoBV; OBEV; OBRV; OTPC (1923 ed.); PoE
When making for the brook, the falconer doth espy. Hawking. Michael Drayton. *Fr.* Polyolbion. SD
When Malindy Sings. Paul Laurence Dunbar. MCCG; NoP; PoNe
When man and woman die, as poets sung. The Difference. Benjamin Franklin. PoPo; WhC
When man has conquered space. Earth's Bondman. Betty Page Dabney. GoYe
When Man rose up out of the red mountains. The Return of Eve. G. K. Chesterton. ISi; PoLi
When many a day had come and fled. Kilmeny. James Hogg. *Fr.* The Queen's Wake. OtMeF
When many years we'd been apart. Reminiscence. Wallace Irwin. FiBHP
When March doth into April merge. Alisoun. *Unknown.* MeEV
When Mary Ann Dollinger got the skule daown thar on Injun Bay. Courting in Kentucky. Florence E. Pratt. BOHV
When Mary bids Thee sleep, Thou sleepest. Jesus, Child and Lord. Frederick William Faber. BePJ
When Mary came to Bethlehem. Mary of Bethlehem. Mary King. ISi
When Mary Goes Walking. Patrick R. Chalmers. BoTP; HBVY
When Mary thro' the Garden Went. Mary Elizabeth Coleridge. BoTP
When May bedecks the naked trees. The Maryland Yellow-Throat. Henry van Dyke. HBV
When May has come, and all around. The Archer. Clinton Scollard. FaPON; GaP
When May is here, and every morn. Fairy Music. Francis Ledwidge. YeAr
When May is in his prime, then may each heart rejoice. May [*or* M. Edwards' May]. Richard Edwards. OBSC; SiCE; TuPP
When May-time comes I love to feel. May-Time. Margaret Gant. PCH
When Me an' my Ma an' Pa went to the Fair. Going to the Fair. James Whitcomb Riley. IHA
When men a dangerous disease did 'scape. To Doctor Empiric [k]. Ben Jonson. BOHV; NoP; SeCP; TuPP
When men discovered freedom first. The Ash and the Oak. Louis Simpson. NePoAm
When men go down to the sea in ships. Beyond the Horizon. Robert Freeman. MaRV; OQP
When men must labor that the wheels may grind. History of the Modern World. Stanton A. Coblentz. PGD
When men shall find thy flower [*or* flow'r], thy glory, pass. To Delia, XXXVI [XXXVIII]. Samuel Daniel. EG; EIL; HBV; LiTL; MeWo; LO; NoP; OBEV; OBSC; PoE; ReEn; SiCE; Sonn; TrGrPo; TuPP
When men turn mob. Music and Drum. Archibald MacLeish. MoRP
When [*or* While] men were all asleep the snow came flying. London Snow. Robert Bridges. AnFE; BoNaP; BrPo; CBV; CH; ChTr; CMoP; CoBMV; GTBS-P; GTBS-W; GTSE; LiTB; LiTG; LiTM (rev. ed.); LoBV; MoAB; MoBrPo; NBM; NoP; OBNC; Po; PoE; PoEL-5; PoIE; PoMa; PoSa; PoVP; ReMP; SeCePo; SeCeV; ShBV-3; StP; TrGrPo; WePo; WiR; YAT
When Midgit was a puppy. A Puppy's Problem. Emilie Poulsson. PPL
When midnight comes a host of dogs [*or* boys] and men. Badger. John Clare. EnRP; ERoP-2; ExPo; LiTB; NBM; NCEP; NoP; PoE; PoEL-4; UnPo (3d ed.); WiR
When mighty roast beef was the Englishman's food. Song in Praise of Old English Roast Beef. Richard Leveridge. OBEC
When mighty Rome was conqueror. On the Bad Government of Toledo. Gómez Manrique. WoL
When mighty rost beef was the Englishman's food. The Roast Beef of Old England. Henry Fielding. *Fr.* Don Quixote in England, I. CEP; OBEC
When mild Favonius breathes, with warbling throat. Hoc Cygno Vinces. Henry Hawkins. ACP
When milder autumn summer's heat succeeds. Field Sports. Pope. *Fr.* Windsor Forest. OBEC; SeCePo
When milkweed blows in the pasture. Horse-Chestnut Time. Kaye Starbird. PDV
When mine hour is come. When. "Æ." ATP; BEL; OnYI; POTE; TOP
When miners get into a row about their mining ground. A Miners' Meeting. John A. Stone. SGR
When Miriam Tazewell heard the tempest bursting. Miriam Tazewell. John Crowe Ransom. TDP
When mirth is full and free. Reverses. Cardinal Newman. VA
When Mr. Apollinax visited the United States. Mr. Apollinax. T. S. Eliot. OnHM
When Mrs. Gorm (Aunt Eloise). Opportunity. Harry Graham. DTC
When moiling seems at cease. "According to the Mighty Working." Thomas Hardy. CMoP; OnPM; ReMP
When Molly Smiles. *Unknown.* HBV

"When moonlight/ Near midnight." The Fairies in New Ross. *Unknown.* OnYI
When Moonlight Falls. Hilda Conkling. BoChLi; YT
When Moonlike ore [*or* o'er] the Hazure Seas. Thackeray. BOHV; InMe; NA; WhC
When Morgan crossed the Murray to Peechelba and doom. Morgan. Edward Harrington. PoAu-1
When Morning Gilds the Skies. *Unknown. tr. fr. German by* Edward Caswall. MaRV
When morning moves in slow processional. The Hills Keep Holy Ground. Hellene Seaman. MaRV
When Moses an' his soldiers, f'om Egypt's lan' did flee. He's Jus' de Same Today. *Unknown.* BoAN-1
When Moses and his people. Just the Same To-Day. *Unknown.* BLRP; WBLP
When Moses came down from the mountain and the cloud. John Holmes. *Fr.* The Eleventh Commandment. MoRP
When Moses, musing in the desert, found. The Burning Bush. Norman Nicholson. EaLo; NeBP; SeCePo
When most I wink, then do mine eyes best see. Sonnets, XLIII. Shakespeare. CBEP
When mother comes each morning. Mother. Rose Fyleman. DD; HH; MPB; SiSoSe
When Mother Reads Aloud. *Unknown.* FaPON; HH; MPB; OTPC (1946 ed.)
When Mother Scrubs. *Unknown.* PEDC
When Mother takes me calling. The Extraordinary Dog. Nancy Byrd Turner. TiPo
When mother takes the Fairy Book. The Fairy Book. Abbie Farwell Brown. HBV; HBVY; MPB
When mothers weep and fathers richly proud. The Confirmation. Karl Shapiro. ErPo
When mountain rocks and leafy trees. Nature's Lineaments. Robert Graves. FaBoTw
When mountains crumble and rivers all run dry. The Line of Beauty. Edward Dowden. OnYI
When music, heav'nly maid, was young. The Passions; an Ode for Music. William Collins. BEL; CEP; CoBE; EiCL; EiCP; EiPP; EnLi-2 (1949 ed.); GoTL; GTBS; GTBS-D; GTBS-P; GTBS-W; GTSE; GTSL; HBV; LoBV; OBEC
When music sounds, gone is the earth I know. Music. Walter de la Mare. HH; MuSP; PoRL
When my abodes prefixed time is spent. Amoretti, XLVI. Spenser. PoFS
When my arms wrap you round I press. Michael Robartes [*or* He] Remembers Forgotten Beauty. W. B. Yeats. BrPo; CTC; PoVP; ViPo (1962 ed.)
When My Beloved Sleeping Lies. Irene Rutherford McLeod. HBV
When my birthday was coming. Little Brother's Secret. Katherine Mansfield. FaPON; MoSiPe; OTD; TiPo
When My Blood Runs Chilly and Col', *with music. Unknown.* ABF
When my brother Tommy. Two in Bed. Abram Bunn Ross. FaPON; MPB; SoPo; TiPo
When my Clorinda walks in white. Her Confirmation. Selwyn Image. VA
When my devotions could not pierce. Denial [*or* Deniall]. George Herbert. AnAnS-1; EnL; EP; FaBoEn; InPo; LoBV (1949 ed.); MaMe; MeP; MePo; NoP; PoEL-2; SCEP-1
When my father/ Needs water. Irrigation. Ann Nolan Clark. StVeCh (1955 ed.)
When my feet have wander'd. Litany. John S. B. Monsell. VA
When my gloomy hour comes on me. Alexander McLachlan. *Fr.* Woman. CaP
When my good angel guides me to the place. Astrophel and Stella, LX. Sir Philip Sidney. FCP; SiPS
When my grave is broke up again[e]. The Relic [*or* Relique]. John Donne. AnAnS-1; AnFE; AtBAP; CABA; CBEP; ElL; EnRePo; EP; ILP; LiTB; LiTG; LoBV; MaMe; MaPo; MBW-1; MeLP; MePo; MyFE; NoP; OAEP; OBS; PoEL-2; PoeP; ReEn; RelE; SCEP-1; SeCeV; SeCP; SeCV-1; SeEP; StP; TuPP; ViBoPo; WHA
When my gray city wavers from her sleep. City Asleep. Maurice Lesemann. NP
When my heart was the amorous worms' meat. The Amorous Worms' Meat. Petrarch. Sonnets to Laura: To Laura in Death, XXXVI. LiTW
When my house is full of flowers the brightness. Ann's House. Dick Lourie. ThO
When my house is raped. Forty Years Ago. John Perreault. ANYP
When my last song is sung and I am dead. Requiem. Theodore Maynard. GoBC
When my life has enough of love, and my spirit enough of mirth. A Wanderer's Litany. Arthur Stringer. WGRP
When my love swears that she is made of truth. Sonnets, CXXXVIII. Shakespeare. AWP; CABA; InPo; JAWP; MeWo; NoP; OAEP; PoEL-2; PoeP; ReEn; TrGrPo; ViBoPo; WBP
When my love was away. Absence. Robert Bridges. BoPe; BrPo; EG; LO; OBEV (1st ed.)
When my mother died I was very young. The Chimney Sweeper. Blake. *Fr.* Songs of Innocence. AtBAP; BoW; BWP; CaFP; CBEP; CEP; CH; DiPo; EiCL; EiPP; EnPE; EnRP; ERoP-1; FosPo; ILP; PAn; PoeP; PoIE
When my sensational moments are no more. E. E. Cummings. Sonn
When My Ship Comes In ("Somewhere, out on the blue sea sailing"). Robert Jones Burdette. FaFP
When my sun of life is low. Sundown. Bert Leston Taylor. OQP
When my time came. The Eagle's Song. Mary Austin. NP
When my uncle came to visit us. Wouldn't You after a Jaunt of 964,000,000,000,000 Million Miles? Kenneth Patchen. HYE
When My Uncle Willie Saw. Carol Freeman. BF
When my young brother was killed. War. Joseph Langland. NePoEA; PoCh; TPM
When nations are to perish in their sins. Where the Leprosy Begins. William Cowper. *Fr.* Expostulation. SoP
When Nature bids us leave to live, 'tis late. To William Roe. Ben Jonson. SeCV-1
When Nature had made all her birds. The Bobolinks. Christopher Pearse Cranch. AA; GN; OTPC
When Nature Hath Betrayed the Heart That Loved Her. Sophie Jewett. AA
When nature made her chief work, Stella's eyes. Astrophel and Stella, VII. Sir Philip Sidney. CABA; FCP; ReEn; RelE; SiCE; SiPS; Sonn; TuPP
When Nature once in lustful hot undress. Giantess. Baudelaire. ErPo
When nature plays hedge-schoolmaster. C. Day Lewis. *Fr.* Transitional Poem. EnLit
When navies are forgotten. The New Age [*or* The Victory Which Is Peace]. Frederic Lawrence Knowles. MaRV; OQP
When Neptune from his billows London spied. Of London Bridge, and the Stupendous Sight, and Structure Thereof. James Howell. ChTr
When nettles in winter bring forth roses red. Trust in Women. *Unknown.* BOHV; LO; NA
When next we met, she bade me turn. Apostasy. Aus of Kuraiza. TrJP
When Night Comes. Henry Vaughan. OQP
When night comes down on the children's eyes. At [*or* A] Night in the Wood. Nancy M. Hayes. BoTP; TVC
When night comes, list thy deed; make plain the way. When Night Comes. Henry Vaughan. OQP
When night comes on and the chills creep in. Autumn Healing. Jean Ward. LaNeLa
When night drifts along the streets of the city. Solitaire. Amy Lowell. LaNeLa; MAP; MAPA; MoAmPo; NeMA; NP
When night falls. Japan That Sank under the Sea. Satoru Sato. PoPl
When night first bids the twinkling stars appear. The Evening. John Gay. *Fr.* Trivia; or, The Art of Walking the Streets of London, III. EnLi-1 (1949 ed.)
When Night has been announced as theme, will it not cause surprise. David Gascoyne. *Fr.* Megalometropolitan Carnival. ACV
When night is almost done. Emily Dickinson. TRV
When night is come, and all around is still. Safe in His Keeping. Edgar Cooper Mason. BLRP
When night is o'er the wood. The White Owl. F. J. Patmore. PoMS
When night plows the meadows of darkness. Lonely Are the Fields of Sleep. Mary Newton Baldwin. GoYe
When night stirred at sea. The Planter's Daughter. Austin Clarke. OxBI

When night unfoldeth her dusky veil. Freya's Spinning Wheel. Adam Oehlenschläger. LiTW
When no one listens. Stranger. Thomas Merton. EaLo
When Noah, perceiving 'twas time to embark. The Dog's Cold Nose. Arthur Guiterman. StPo; TiPo (1959 ed.)
When Nobody Prays. Merl A. Clapper. STF
When None Shall Rail. David Lewis. CBEP; OBEC
When noon is warm, old Pensioners. Out of Soundings. Padraic Fallon. NeIP
When North first began. Lord North's Recantation. *Unknown.* PAH
When nothing whereon to lean remains. The Time to Trust. *Unknown.* BLRP
When November's night comes down. Hearth Song. Robert Underwood Johnson. YeAr
When now the end of agony was come. Apostrophe to Death. Caelius Sedulius. *Fr.* Carmen Paschale [*or* Easter Song]. OnYI
When nuns were spitted and poets fell. Karl Shapiro. Recapitulations, XIII. FiMAP
When ocean-clouds over inland hills. Misgivings. Herman Melville. AmePo; AmP; AP; CBEP; GTBS-D; MAmP; MWA-1; NePA; OxBA
When October horns are blowing. October. Nancy Birckhead. StaSt
When o'er the hill the eastern star. My Ain Kind Dearie, O. Burns. GoTS
When, o'er the silent seas alone. The Meeting of the Ships. Thomas Moore. EtS
When Ol' Sis' Judy Pray. James Edwin Campbell. BANP
When old cars get retired, they go to Maine. Maine. Philip Booth. AmFN
"When Old Corruption First Begun." Blake. *Fr.* An Island in the Moon. ERoP-1
When old heads felt to-day. On Hearing a Broadcast of Ceremonies in Connection with Conferring of Cardinals' Hats. Denis Wrafter. NeIP
When Old John Bax drove the mail to Coonabarabran. Old John Bax. Charles H. Souter. PoAu-1
When 'Omer Smote 'Is Bloomin' Lyre. Kipling. OtMeF; Par
When on a razor's edge all Hellas stood. The Saviors. *Unknown.* OnPM
When on my bed the moonlight falls. In Memoriam, A. H. H., LXVII. Tennyson. EnL; EPN; LoBV; NeHB; OAEP; PoE; SeCePo; SeCeV; TOP; ViPo; VP
When on my country walks I go. Amico Suo. Herbert P. Horne. VA
When on my day of life the night is falling. At Last [*or* To Paths Unknown]. Whittier. AP; MaRV; NeHB; OQP; SoP; TreFS; TrPWD; TRV; WGRP
When on my day the evening shadows fall. When Life's Day Closes. Thomas Tiplady. MaRV
When on my sick bed I languish. A Thought of Death. Thomas Flatman. CEP; OBS
When on my soul in nakedness. The Quiet Pilgrim. Edith M. Thomas. AA
When on my time of living I reflect. My Thirty Years. Juan Fransico Manzano. TTY
When, on our casual way. The Shakespearean Bear. Arthur Guiterman. BOHV; CenHV; EvOK
When, on Ramillies' bloody field. Clare's Dragoons. Thomas Osborne Davis. OnYI
When on the barn's thatch'd roof is seen. Signs of Christmas. Edwin Lees. OHIP
When, on the bearing mother, death's. Childbirth. Ted Hughes. ToPo
When on the breath of autumn [*or* autumn's] breeze. Mary Howitt. *Fr.* Cornfields. PRWS; VA
When on the green the rag-tag game had stopt. Sheet Lightning. Edmund Blunden. HaMV
When on the level summer seas. Nature's Key-Notes. Thomas Caulfield Irwin. IrPN
When on the primal peaceful blank profound. Uranus. Arthur Hugh Clough. ViPP
When once a chic busts through a egg. Gettin' Born. Anthony Euwer. PoPl; WhC
When once I knew the Lord. Hymn of Sivaite Puritans. *Unknown.* WGRP
When once I rose at morning. Lament for the Woodlands. *Unknown.* KiLC
When once the scourging prophet, with his cry. The Disused Temple. Norman Cameron. ChMP; OxBS
When once the sun sinks in the west. Evening Primrose. John Clare, *wr. at. to* Emily Brontë. CH; EG; TrGrPo
When once the sunset dyes the west with red. Lunae Custodiens. Lin Carter. FiSC
When once thy foot enters the Church, be bare. On Worship. George Herbert. *Fr.* The Church Porch. MaRV
When one calls on the Quinks they always say. The Quinks. Don Marquis. YaD
When One Knows Thee. Rabindranath Tagore. *Fr.* Gitanjali. OQP
("Thou hast made me known to friends.") NP
When Ones Loves Tensely. Don Marquis. BoLP; FiBHP
When one or other rambles. Francis Daniel Pastorius. SCAP
When one starts crying. The Twins. Dorothy Aldis. BiCB
When Orpheus died, some Muse the lyre still fingered. Plato, a Musician. Leontius. UnS
When Orpheus Went Down. Samuel Lisle. ALV
When Oscar came to join his God. Oscar Wilde. *At. to* Swinburne. PeVV; SiTL
When other ladies to the shades go down. Epigram. Pope. PoEL-3
When Other Lips and Other Hearts. Alfred Bunn. *Fr.* Bohemian Girl. TreF
When other lovers in arms across. Earl of Surrey. *Fr.* Complaint of the Absence of Her Lover Being upon the Sea. LO
When our babe he goeth walking in his garden. Garden and Cradle. Eugene Field. AA
When our brother Fire was having his dog's day. Brother Fire. Louis MacNeice. AtBAP; FaBoMo; FOL; MoAB; MoPW; OAEP (2d ed.); TPM; WaaP
When our children cried in the shadow of the gallows. Nathan Alterman. *Fr.* From All Peoples. TrJP
When our ducks waddle to the pond. The Ducks. Alice Wilkins. GFA; TiPo
When our hands are alone. Poem. William Knott. YAP
When our heads are bow'd with woe. Hymn for the Sixteenth Sunday after Trinity. Henry Hart Milman. VA
When Our Lady sings the heavens. Madonna's Lullaby. St. Alphonsus Liguori. ISi
When our rude & unfashion'd words, that long. To a Lady Who Did Sing Excellently. Lord Herbert of Cherbury. AnAnS-2; OBS; SeCP
When our tears are dry on the shore. Rediscovery. George Awoonor-Williams. TTY
When our two souls stand up erect and strong. Sonnets from the Portuguese, XXII. Elizabeth Barrett Browning. AnFE; BEL; EnLi-2; EnLit; EPN; GTSE; GTSL; HBV; LiTL; MeWo; OAEP; OBEV; TreFT; TrGrPo; ViBoPo; ViPo; WHA
When out by Shellbrook, round by stile and tree. Shellbrook. William Barnes. OBNC
When, out of an intact sea rose terrible. Cataclysm. Louis Johnson. AnNZ
When, over-arched by gorgeous night. The Unknown God. Sir William Watson. WGRP
When, over-burdened with its cares. Lincoln's Birthday—1918. John Kendrick Bangs. DD; HH
When over the fair fame of friend or foe. Let Something Good Be Said. James Whitcomb Riley. MaRV
When over the flowery, sharp pasture's. Flowers by the Sea. William Carlos Williams. AmLP; AnEnPo; CMoP; ExPo; GoJo; MoAB; MoAmPo; Po; PoeP; SeCeV (1967 ed.)
When paint or steel or wood are wearing thin. Docks. Dorothy Wellesley. ShBV-3
When partners with each other don't agree. The Wan, the Pike, and the Crab. Ivan Andreievich Krylov. BoChLi
When passion's trance is overpast. To ——. Shelley. EnRP
When pavements were blown up, exposing nerves. Epilogue to a Human Drama. Stephen Spender. EnLit; PIA
When pensive on that portraiture I gaze. Sonnet on a Family Picture. Thomas Edwards. CEP; EiCL; OBEC; Sonn
When people aren't asking questions. More about People. Ogden Nash. Po
When people call this beast to mind. The Elephant. Hilaire Belloc. BoTP; SoPo; TiPo; UTS
When people's ill they come[s] to I. On Dr. [*or* a Doctor Named] Isaac Letsome [*or* Self-composed Epitaph on a Doctor by the Name of I. Letsome *or* The Candid Physician]. *Unknown.* GoTP; LiTG; PV; TreFT; WhC
When Pershing's men go marching into Picardy. Marching

When (continued)
Song. Dana Burnet. MC; PAH
When Peter Wanderwide was young. The Death and Last Confession of Wandering Peter. Hilaire Belloc. MemP; OtMeF; TIHL
When Phoebe form'd a wanton smile. Sonnet. William Collins. EnLoPo
When Phoebus had melted the sickles of ice. Robin Hood and the Ranger. *Unknown.* ESPB; StVeCh
When Phoebus in the rainy cloud. Welcome Eild. *Unknown.* GoTS
When Phoebus lifts his head out of the Winter's wave. Michael Drayton. *Fr.* Polyolbion, Thirteenth Song. OBS
When Planes Outsoar the Spirit. Lilith Lorraine. MaRV
When poetry walked the live, spring wood. Kingcups. Sacheverell Sitwell. MoBrPo
When poets wrote and painters drew. Protogenes and Apelles. Matthew Prior. GoTL
When Polly Buys a Hat. E. Hill. BoTP
When Polly lived back in the old deep woods. Stranger. Elizabeth Madox Roberts. MAP; MoAmPo
When Pontius wished an edict might be passed. Epigram. Matthew Prior. ALV
When Poor Mary Came Wandering Home. *Unknown. See* Mary of the Wild Moor.
When poppies in the garden bleed. The End of Summer. Edna St. Vincent Millay. BoNaP
When President John Quincy. John Quincy Adams. Stephen Vincent Benét. NAMP; PoPl
When Priests Are More in Word. Shakespeare. *Fr.* King Lear, III, ii. ViBoPo
When primroses are out in spring. Days Too Short. W. H. Davies. MoBrPo; NeMA; POTE
When Psyche's friend becomes her lover. Friend and Lover. "Madeline Bridges." AA; HBV
When quacks with pills political would dope us. Canopus. Bert Leston Taylor. ALV; FiBHP; HBMV; InMe; WhC
When quiet in my room I sit. My Companion. Charles Wesley. STF
When Raging Love. Earl of Surrey. *See* Lover Comforteth Himself with the Worthiness of His Love, The.
When rain falls, I say. Chanty. Ronald McCuaig. MoAuPo
When reckless youth in an unquiet breast. Introduction to Psalm LXXXVIII. Earl of Surrey. FCP
When red hath set the beamless sun. The Shepherd in Winter. Sir Walter Scott. *Fr.* Marmion, *Introd. to* IV. OTPC (1923 ed.)
When Reedisdale and Wise William. Redesdale and Wise William. *Unknown.* ESPB
When rhymes were yet but rude, thy pen endeavored. An Epitaph in Commendation of George Turberville, a Learned Gentleman. Sir John Harington. SiCE
When Richard Cory went down town. *See* Whenever Richard Cory went down town.
"When rites and melodies begin." The Trial. W. H. Auden. NePA
When Robin Hood, and his merry men all. Robin Hood and the Valiant Knight. *Unknown.* ESPB
When Robin Hood and Little John. Robin Hood's Death [*or* The Death of Robin Hood]. *Unknown.* BuBa; ESPB; FlW; OnSP; TrGrPo; ViBoFo
When Robin Hood in the green-wood livd. Robin Hood Rescuing Will Stutly. *Unknown.* BaBo; ESPB
When Robin Hood was about twenty [*or* eighteen *or* was twenty] years old. Robin Hood and Little John. *Unknown.* BaBo (A *vers.*); ESPB; OTPC (1946 ed.); StaSt; StVeCh; ViBoFo
When Roland saw that life had fled. *Unknown. Fr.* The Song of Roland. EnLi-1; OuHeWo
When rosy plumelets tuft the larch. In Memoriam A. H. H., XCI. Tennyson. EPN; FaBoEn; OBNC; ViBoPo; ViPo; VP
When russet beech-leaves drift in air. Autumn Memories. George Francis Savage-Armstrong. VA
When Ruth was left half desolate. Ruth; or, The influences of Nature. Wordsworth. ChER; EnRP; ERoP-1; GTBS; GTBS-D; GTBS-P; GTBS-W; GTSE; GTSL; MERP; PoEL-4
When Ruth was old. The Immigrant. Frank Kendon. MemP; MoBrPo (1942 ed.); POTE
When ruthful time the South's memorial places. The Stricken South to the North. Paul Hamilton Hayne. PAH
When Sadness Fills a Journey. John Waller. NeBP
When sage Ulysses sailed by. Beware of Sirens. —— Bewe. RelE; SiCE
When Sam goes back in memory. Sam. Walter de la Mare. FaBV; MoAB; MoBrPo; NeMA; OnMSP; PoMS; PoPo; TiPo; WePo
When sane men gather in to talk of Love. Irene Rutherford McLeod. *Fr.* Sonnets. HBMV
When Santa Claus Comes. *Unknown.* ChBR
When Santa Claus has trimmed our Christmas tree. At Christmas Time. Mary Brennan Clapp. GFA
When sap ebbed low and your green days were over. To My Blackthorn Stick. F. R. Higgins. POTE
When Sarah Pierrepont let her spirit rage. Address to the Scholars of New England. John Crowe Ransom. AmPP; LiTM (rev. ed.); NePA
When Sarah's papa was from home a great way. The Letter. Elizabeth Turner. *Fr.* Mrs. Turner's Object-Lessons. OTPC (1923 ed.)
When Satan Fell. D. H. Lawrence. MoRP
When school is out, we love to follow. Sniff. Frances Frost. BrR; SiSoSe; TiPo (1959 ed.)
When scribblers of the Saxon brood. Verses to Mr. Vaughan of Hengwrt. Evan Evans. PrWP
When Senses Fled. John Woods. CoPo
When Serpents Bargain for the Right to Squirm. E. E. Cummings. TwCP
When seven years were come and gane. Sweet William's Ghost (F *vers.*). *Unknown.* ESPB
When shades of night have come. Domestic Scenes. Miguel de Unamuno. WoL
When Shakespeare leads the mind a dance. The Critic's Rules. Robert Lloyd. *Fr.* Shakespeare; an Epistle to Mr. Garrick. OBEC
When shall disunion and estrangement end? The Mock Caliph. *Unknown.* EnLi-1
When shall I expel you from my blood? The Knife. "J. R." MoAuPo
When shall I, Lord, this mortal load untied. To Our Saviour. Agostinho de Cruz. CAW
When shall I make a song for you, my love? Unsung. Nettie Palmer. BoAu
When shall I see the half-moon sink again. End of Another Home Holiday. D. H. Lawrence. DTC; FaBoMo; MoVE
When shall I see the white-thorn leaves agen. The Yellowhammer. John Clare. BoPe
When shall the Island Queen of Ocean lay. The Bower of Peace. Robert Southey. *Fr.* Ode Written during the War with America, 1814. MC; PAH
When shall we be married. *Unknown.* OxNR; SiTL, *st.* 1
When shall we learn, what should be clear as day. Canzone. W. H. Auden. LiTA; LiTM; MoVE
When Shall We See Thy Like Again? Mary Wingate. *See* Washington.
When shaven crown, and hallow'd girdle's power. Satyr III. John Oldham. *Fr.* Satires upon the Jesuits. SeCV-2
When shawes beene sheene, and shradds full fayre. Robin Hood and Guy of Gisborne. *Unknown.* ATP (1935 ed.); BaBo; BEL; CoBE; ESPB; OAEP; OBB; TOP
When She a Maiden Slim. Maurice Hewlett. OHIP
When she came suddenly in. The Door. Robert Graves. LiTB
When she carries food to the table and stoops down. Part of Plenty. Bernard Spencer. ErPo; LiTB; LiTL; LiTM; MoLP
When She Comes Home. James Whitcomb Riley. AA; FaBoBe; HBV
When she fed the/ child. The Feeding. Joel Oppenheimer. NeAP
When she gives a "psychic reading." Crepe de Chine. Tennessee Williams. NYBP
When she is far, I only want to see her. Love Grows by What It Feeds On. Bhartrihari. OnPM
When She Plays upon the Harp or Lute. Moses ibn Ezra, *tr. fr. Hebrew by* Solomon Solis-Cohen. TrJP
When she rises in the morning. Gloire de Dijon. D. H. Lawrence. BrPo; CMoP; ELP; EnLoPo; ErPo; OAEP (2d ed.)
When she sleeps, her soul, I know. Doubts. Rupert Brooke. CH; SiSw
When she, that soul of fire, appears. Portrait. Pushkin. OnPM
When she threatened to leave me. The Peacemaker. W. H. Davies. BoPe

When she walks in the field of long grass. Field of Long Grass. A. J. M. Smith. BoLP
When she was born she came with smiling eye. Robert Tofte. *Fr.* Laura. ReIE; Sonn; TuPP
When she was in her garden. Ann and the Fairy Song. Walter de la Mare. *Fr.* A Child's Day. FaBV
When shepherds pipe on oaten straws Spring, 2. Shakespeare. *Fr.* Love's Labour's Lost, V, ii. UnPo
When Sherman Marched Down to the Sea, *with music.* Samuel H. M. Byers. BFSS
When Silence Divests Me. Henry Birnbaum. GoYe
When silver Diane full of beames bright. A Starscape. John Bellenden. ACP
When silver snow decks Susan's clothes. Blind-Man's Buff. Blake. WiR
When, sin-stricken, burdened, and weary. "My Grace Is Sufficient for Thee." *Unknown.* BLRP; SoP
When Sir Beelzebub. Edith Sitwell. *See* Sir Beelzebub.
When Sir Joshua Reynolds died. Sir Joshua Reynolds [*or* Epigram]. Blake. ELU; FiBHP; LiTG; OxBoLi; SiTL
When Sir Ulrich's widow in church knelt to pray. The Fair Agnete. Agnes Miegel. CAW
When Sisyphus was pushing the stone up the mountain. Sisyphus. Josephine Miles. NYBP
When ski-ing in the Engadine. Patience. Harry Graham. FiBHP; MoShBR; WhC
When Slavery Seems Sweet. Ed Bullins. NBP
When sleep, the supposed guardian. Dead Morning. Raymond Holden. MAP; MoAmPo (1942 ed.)
When slumbering in my convict cell my childhood days I see. The Convict. *Unknown.* CoSo
When Smoke Stood Up from Ludlow. A. E. Housman. A Shropshire Lad, VII. AnFE; EnLit; MoBrPo; OuHeWo; PoPo; PoVP; VP
(Blackbird, The.) HBV
When snow-balls pack on the horses' hoofs. Sugar Weather. Peter McArthur. CaP
When snow like sheep lay in the fold. In Memory of Jane Frazer. Geoffrey Hill. NePoEA
When snows are gone and skies are clear. The Robin. *Unknown.* PoPo
When Sol did cast no light. The Seaman's Happy Return. *Unknown.* ChTr
When Solomon was reigning in his glory. Solomon and the Bees. John Godfrey Saxe. GN; GoTP; OTPC
When some belovèd voice that was to you. Substitution. Elizabeth Barrett Browning. MaRV; WGRP
When some great sorrow, like a mighty river. This, Too, Shall [*or* Will] Pass Away. Lanta Wilson Smith. BLPA; NeHB; STF
When some grim sorceress, whose skill. To Helen. Winthrop Mackworth Praed. LoBV
When sorrow (using mine owne fier's might). Astrophel and Stella, CVIII. Sir Philip Sidney. FCP; MaPo (1969 ed.); SiPS; Sonn
When sorrowe singes a litle a litles enough. *Unknown.* SeCSL
When souls that have put off their mortal gear. Recognition. John White Chadwick. AA
When sporgles spanned the floreate mead. Uffia. Harriet R. White. BOHV; NA
When spring begins, the maids in flocks. Spring. Edith Sitwell. OAEP (2d ed.)
When spring came tiptoe up the hill. The Dress of Spring. May Justus. YeAr
When Spring Came to Nazareth. Mary Sinton Leitch. ChIP
When Spring Comes Back to England. Alfred Noyes. HBV
(World's May-Queen, The.) OBVV
When Spring comes laughing. A Song of the Four Seasons. Austin Dobson. BoC; HBV
When spring comes on with freshness of new leaves. To Men Unborn. David Osborne Hamilton. HH; PEDC
When spring is in the fields that stained your wing. To a Linnet in a Cage. Francis Ledwidge. OnYI; RoGo
When spring revives in Arun's veins. Kingscups. Eleanor Farjeon. GBV (1952 ed.)
When spring, to woods and wastes around. The Murdered Traveller. Bryant. CoBA
When spring unbound comes o'er us like a flood. In April. Ethelwyn Wetherald. CaP
When spring-time flushes the desert grass. The Ballad of the King's Jest. Kipling. GBV
When spurred by tasks unceasing or undone. Rest Where You Are. *Unknown. at. to* Charles Poole Cleaves. OQP; SoP
When Stars Are in the Quiet Skies. Sir Edward Bulwer-Lytton. *Fr.* Ernest Maltravers. VA
(Night and Love.) HBV
When Stars Are Shrouded. "I. T." EIL
When stars begin softly to spatter. Milking Kraal. F. C. Slater. BoSA; TDP
When stars pursue their solemn flight. Music in the Night. Harriet Prescott Spofford. AA
When stars ride in on the wings of dusk. Refuge. Lew Sarett. HBMV; MaRV
When statesmen gravely say "We must be realistic." W. H. Auden. PV
When stealthy age creeps on me unaware. A Litany for Old Age. Una W. Harsen. TrPWD
When Stella strikes the tuneful string. To Miss ——. Samuel Johnson. CABA
When stone-hewn storms knock against our cottage. Third and Fourth. Keidrych Rhys. NeBP
When storms arise. Hymn. Paul Laurence Dunbar. FaChP; SoP; TrPWD; TRV
When storms blow loud, 'tis sweet to watch at ease. Suave Mari Magno. Lucretius. *Fr.* De Rerum Natura. AWP
When storms go growling off to lonely places. The Whale and the *Essex.* A. M. Sullivan. EtS
When storms of life are round me beating. Alone with God. *Unknown.* SoP
When, stricken by the freezing blast. Daniel Webster. Oliver Wendell Holmes. PAH
When Structure Fails Rhyme Attempts to Come to the Rescue. William Carlos Williams. PP
When stubble-lands were greening, you came among the stooks. The Green Autumn Stubble. *Tr. fr. Irish by* Patrick Browne. OxBI
When Sue Wears Red. Langston Hughes. GoSl; TTY
When summer came, we locked up our lives and fled. The Gentle Snorer. Mona Van Duyn. NePA
When summer comes I like to stay. On the Beach. Emilie Blackmore Stapp. GFA
When summer took in hand the winter to assail. Love's Rebel [*or* Complaint of a Lover That Defied Love and Was by Love After the More Tormented]. Earl of Surrey. FCP; OBSC; ReIE; SiCE; SiPS
When Summer's End Is Nighing. A. E. Housman. MoVE
When summer's in the city. The Ice-Cream Man. Rachel Field. BoChLi; FaPON; GaP; SiSoSe; SoPo
When sun, light-handed, sows this Indian water. Aubade: Lake Erie. Thomas James Merton. NYBP
When suns are low, and nights are long. The Queen of the Year. Edna Dean Proctor. DD
When sunset falls upon your day. Measure of Success. *Unknown.* STF
When sunset flows into golden glows. Star Song. Robert Underwood Johnson. HBV
When sunshine met the wave. In the Beginning. Harriet Monroe. AA
When supper time is almost come. Milking Time. Elizabeth Madox Roberts. BoChLi; FaPON; GoJo; OTPC (1946 ed.); RIS; SUS; UTS
When Susanna Jones wears red. When Sue Wears Red. Langston Hughes. GoSl; TTY
When Susan's work was done, she'd [*or* she would] sit. Old Susan. Walter de la Mare. CMoP; InP; MoBrPo; NeMA; OnPP; PoRL; TreFS
When swallows Northward flew. Lord Guy. George F. Warren. BOHV
When sycamore leaves wer a-spreaden. Woak Hill. William Barnes. GTSL
When tempest winnowed grain from bran. The Victor of Antietam. Herman Melville. MC; PAH
When temptations fierce assail me. A Prayer for Help. *Unknown.* SoP
When that Abe Lincoln was a boy. Prairie. K. N. Lewellyn. YeAr
When that April with his showers sweet. *See* Whan that Aprille with his shoures sote.
When that brave honor of the Latin name. Ruins of Rome, V. Joachim du Bellay. OnPM
When that day comes, whose evening sayes I'm gone. His

When (continued)
Sailing from Julia. Robert Herrick. PoEL-3
"When that dead face, bowered in the furthest years." The Love-Moon. Dante Gabriel Rossetti. The House of Life, XXXVII. MaVP; PoVP; ViPo; VP
When that everybody's legal twin Mrs. Trio. Circus Nerves and Worries. Kenward Elmslie. ANYP
When that great Kings return to clay. The Burial. Kipling. BoSA
When that I call unto my mind. Sir Thomas Wyatt. FCP
When that I, poor soul, was born. The Nymph Diana's Song. Jorge de Montemayor, *tr. by* Bartholomew Young. *Fr.* Diana. ReIE
When That I Was and a Little Tiny Boy. Shakespeare. *Fr.* Twelfth Night, V, i. AnFE; AtBAP; CH; EG; EIL; EnRePo; ExPo; FaBoCh; HBV; InPo; LiTB; LoBV; LoGBV; MyFE; NoP; OAEP; OBSC; PoIE; PoRA; SiCE; SiTL; ViBoPo; WaKn
(Epilogue: "When that I was and a little tiny boy.") WePo
(Feste's Final Song.) VaPo
(Feste's Song.) OxBoLi
(Rain It Raineth Every Day, The.) OTPC (1923 ed.)
(Song: "When that I was and a little tiny boy.") EP; FiP; LiTG; PoEL-2
(Wind and the Rain, The.) CBEP; DiPo; WiR
When that my days were fewer. Middle Age. Rudolph Chambers Lehmann. HBV
When that old joke was new. Old Fashioned Fun. Thackeray. BOHV; InMe
When that our English tongue. "That Did in Luve So Lively Write." Georgine M. Adams. InMe
When that our gentle Lord was born. A Ballad of Wise Men. George M. P. Baird. ChrBoLe
When that rich Soul[e] which to her heaven is gone. An Anatomie [*or* Anatomy] of the World; the First Anniversary. John Donne. *See also* "Well dy'd the world . . ." AnAnS-1; MasP; MBW-1; MeP; SCEP-1; SeCV-1; SeEP.
When That St. George Had Slain His Dragon. *Unknown.* SiTL
(Limerick: "When that Seint George hadde sleyne ye dragone.") NA
When that sweet April showers with downward shoot. Chaucer. Prologue to "The Canterbury Tales." WoL
When that the chill Charocco blows. *See* Whenas the Chill sirocco blows.
When that the Eternal deigned to look. Ballade of Illegal Ornaments. Hilaire Belloc. ACP (1952 ed.)
When that the fields put on their gay attire. To the Redbreast. John Bampfylde. Sonn
When that which is divine in us doth try. The Model and the Statue. Michelangelo. OnPM
When the air is wine and the wind is free. Song of the Queen Bee. E. B. White. NYBP
When the *Alabama's* keel was laid. The *Alabama.* *Unknown.* ShS, *vers.* I; SoAmSa
When the allegorical man came calling. The Inflatable Globe. Theodore Spencer. LiTA; LiTM; NePA; WaP
When the anchors that faith has cast. Ultima Veritas. Washington Gladden. MaRV
When the anchor's weigh'd and the ship's unmoored. Jack the Guinea Pig. *Unknown.* AmSS
When the angry passion gathering in my mother's face I see. The Patter of the Shingle. *Unknown.* BLPA
When the anxious hearts say "Where?" Missing. *Unknown.* WGRP
When the *Ark* and *Dove* within the glassy wave. The *Ark* and the *Dove.* Daniel Sargent. EtS
When the Arts in their infancy were. The Magpie's Nest. Charles *and* Mary Lamb. OTPC (1923 ed.); PRWS
When the Assault Was Intended to the City. Milton. GTBS; GTBS-D; GTBS-P; GTBS-W; GTSE; GTSL; MBW-1; NoP; OuHeWo; RoGo; Sonn
(Sonnet: "Captain or Colonel, or Knight in Arms.") SeEP
When the Atlantic upsloped itself. Winter Tryst. Mark Van Doren. LiTA; LiTM (1946 ed.)
When the autumn winds go wailing. Ungathered Love. Philip Bourke Marston. OBNC
When the band comes along the street. The Band. —— John. GFA
When the bat's on the wing and the bird's in the tree. The Starlighter. Arthur Guiterman. GaP; MoSiPe; SiSoSe
When the bird flew from the Columbus hull. Jeremiad. Oscar Williams. LiTA
When the black car came thundering from its pale. Proserpine at Enna. Ronald Bottrall. SeCePo
When the black herds of the rain were grazing. The Lost Heifer. Austin Clarke. OxBI
When the blessed Saviour calls you. You Will Find a Joy in Service. Dorothy Conant Stroud. STF
When the breath of twilight blows to flame the misty skies. By the Margin of the Great Deep. "Æ." HBMV; OBEV; OBVV; PoVP
When the breeze from the bluebottle's blustering blim. To Marie. John Bennett. BOHV; NA
When the breeze of a joyful dawn blew free. Recollections of the Arabian Nights. Tennyson. PoVP
When the bright eyes of the day. Day and Night. James Stephens. BoTP
When the British warrior queen. Boadicea. William Cowper. BeLS; FOL; HBV; OTPC
When the bubble moon is young. June. Harrison S. Morris. HBV
When the buds began to burst. The Three Roses. Walter Savage Landor. CLwM
When the burnt flesh is finally at rest. Annotations of Auschwitz. Peter Porter. FOL; NMP
When the Cannon Booms No More. William Herbert Carruth. PEDC
When the cat's away. Well-packed Wisdom. Benjamin Franklin. *Fr.* Poor Richard's Almanac. StaSt
When the Century Dragged. Robert Penn Warren. MoAmPo (1962 ed.)
When the child's brow, with torment flushing red. The Louse-Catchers. Arthur Rimbaud, *tr. by* Roy Campbell. LiTW
When the chill Charoko blows. *See* Whenas the chill sirocco blows.
When the Christ Child Came. Frederic E. Weatherly. OHIP
When the Church Is No Longer Regarded. T. S. Eliot. *Fr.* The Rock. MaRV
When the church seeks a pastor. Some Bird. *Unknown.* STF
When the city cast out the best. Ibycus. John Heath-Stubbs. PoCh
When the clouds are upon the hills. *Unknown.* OxNR
When the clouds' swoln bosoms echo back the shouts. In Tenebris, II. Thomas Hardy. BrPo; CMoP; LiTM (rev. ed.); ViPo
When the Cock Crows, *sel.* Arturo Giovannitti.
"Six men drove up to his house at midnight." WOW
When the cock in the dish. The Innocents. Elinor Wylie. StJW
When the cold comes. Where? When? Which? Langston Hughes. Kal; NePoAm-2
When the corn stands yellow in September. Harvest. Carl Sandburg. WIRo
When the Cows Come Home. Christina Rossetti. *Fr.* Sing-Song. OTPC (1946 ed.); UTS
(Do You Know?) StVeCh (1940 ed.)
(Milking Time.) GFA; MPB; PRWS
When the crop is fair in the olive-yard. The Cocooning. Frédéric Mistral. *Fr.* The Mirèio. AWP; JAWP; PoPl; WBP; WoL
When the curtain of night, 'tween the dark and the light. Whistling Boy. Nixon Waterman. PoLF
When the curtains of night are pinned back by the stars. I'll Remember You, Love, in My Prayers. *Unknown.* AS; BLPA; FaBoBe; NeHB
When the dark-eyed lad, Columbus. Dark-eyed Lad Columbus. Nancy Byrd Turner. SiSoSe
When the daughter. *Unknown.* HW
When the dawn at last is breaking. Consecration. Loma Ried Lauden. SoP
When the dawn comes. *Unknown.* *Fr.* Kokin Shu. AWP
When the day and the night do meete. Cobbe's Prophecies. *Unknown.* NA
When the day darkens. The Unknown Wind. "Fiona Macleod." BoTP
When the day is stormy, and no sun shines through. Trust; a Song. Eben E. Rexford. BLRP
When the Daylight Wanes. Thomas Tiplady. MaRV
When the days are dark and dreary. Do Your Best. *Unknown.* SoP
When the days begin to lengthen. *Unknown.* GoTP; RIS

When the Days Shall Grow Long. Hayyim Nahman Bialik, *tr. fr. Hebrew by* A. M. Klein. TrJP
When the Dead Men Die. Rose O'Neill. HBMV
When the dentist adjusts his drill. Variation: Ode to Fear. Robert Penn Warren. FiMAP
When the devil was sick, the devil a monk would be. Epigram. *Unknown.* ALV
When the dew is on the grass. *Unknown.* OxNR
When the Dews Are Earliest Falling. Arthur Hugh Clough. OAEP
When the Drive Goes Down. Douglas Malloch. AmFN; StVeCh
When the Duke of Leeds shall have made his choice. *Unknown.* LO
When the dull dire sky weighs a heavy cover. Spleen. Baudelaire. SyP
When the dumb Hour, clothed in black. The Silent Voices. Tennyson. MaRV; OQP; VA
When the Dumb Speak. Robert Bly. FRC
When the dying flame of day. Hymn of the Moravian Nuns of Bethlehem. Longfellow. PAH
When the Earth is turned in spring. The Worm. Ralph Bergengren. FaPON; SiSoSe; UTS
When the earth was sick and the skies were grey. Kipling. *Fr.* The Other Man. PoG
When the echo of the last footstep dies. Song. E. W. Mandel. MoCV; OBCV
When the Ecstatic Body Grips. Eric Robertson Dodds. POTE; ViBoPo
When the enemy surrounds you. The Precious Blood. *Unknown.* STF
When the evening came my love said to me. Prothalamion. Francis Brett Young. HBMV
When the fair year. The Jews. Henry Vaughan. OBS
When the Fairies. Edward Dorn. NeAP
When the fairies are all for their dances drest. The Nightingale and the Lark. Ernest Whitney. ATP (1935 ed.)
When the fairies come back to Santa Fe. When the Fairies. Edward Dorn. NeAP
When the far south glittered. Pilgrimage. Austin Clarke. OxBI
When the farmer comes to town with his wagon broken down. The Farmer Comes to Town [*or* The Farmer]. *Unknown.* AS; TrAS
When the farmer's day is done. The Barnyard. Maud Burnham. PCH; PPL; TiPo
When the fiddlers play their tunes, you may sometimes hear. Fairy-Music. Rose Fyleman. HH; TSW
When the fields catch flower. April. Vidame de Chartres. AWP
When the fierce North-wind with his airy forces. The Day of Judg[e]ment. Isaac Watts. CEP; EiPP; LoBV; NoP; OBEV; SeCePo
When the fight begins within himself. Robert Browning. *Fr.* Bishop Blougram's Apology. MaRV; TRV
When the first broad sids were giv'n. Description of of a Sea-Battle. John Banks. *Fr.* The Unhappy Favourite. PeRV
When the first man who wasn't quite an ape. The Ultimate Atrocity. Siegfried Sassoon. CMoP
When the first silent frost has trod. The Ghost-Yard of the Goldenrod. Bliss Carman. TwCaPo
When the first traitor Cain. Satire II. John Oldham. *Fr.* Satires upon the Jesuits. PeRV
When the flesh of summer piecemeal mars the lawn. Sonnet in Autumn. Donald Petersen. NePoEA-2
When the flowers turn to husks. Cells Breathe in the Emptiness. Galway Kinnell. NaP
When the flush of a newborn sun fell first on Eden's green and gold. The Conundrum of the Workshops. Kipling. HBV; MoBrPo; PoVP; VA
When the folk of my household. Lament. *Tr. by* Edward Walsh. OBVV
When the forests have been destroyed their darkness remains. The Asians Dying. W. S. Merwin. CoAP; NaP; NYBP
When the foundations quaked and the pillars shook. Rejoice in the Abyss. Stephen Spender. OnHM
When the fox talks about peace. Country Proverbs. *Unknown.* StaSt
When the French fleet lay. Running the Blockade. Nora Perry. PAH
When the frost did so long a time persevere. De Gelu Diutino, Anno Dom. 1607. John Heath. SiCE
When the Frost Is on the Punkin. James Whitcomb Riley. AmePo; BOHV; BoNaP; DD; FaBoBe; FaBV; FaFP; HBV; HBVY; MAP; MCCG; MoAmPo (1942 ed.); MPB; NeMA; OTPC; PFY; PoLF; PoMa; PTK; TIHL; TreF
When the frost is white on the fodder-stack. In the Barn-Yard's Southerly Corner. Sir Charles G. D. Roberts. TwCaPo
When the full fields begin to smell of sunrise. The Trappist Abbey: Matins. Thomas Merton. PoPl
When the Full-Grown Poet Came. Walt Whitman. MaPo (1969 ed.)
When the game began between them for a jest. Stage Love. Swinburne. NoP; PoEL-5; ViPP
When the glow of fading sunlight. The Man of the Open West. Arthur W. Monroe. PoOW
When the God of Merry Love. Thomas Campion. ReIE
When the gold fever raged, I was doing very well. The Miner's Lament, I. John A. Stone. SGR
When the golden sun he knelt. The Good Day. Henry Howarth Bashford. HBV
When the gong sounds ten in the morning. Vocation. Rabindranath Tagore. FaPON; GaP; OTD
When the good woman who raised me. Moses Miles. Bob Maxey. WSL
When the Grass Shall Cover Me. Ina Donna Coolbrith. AA; HBV
When the grass was closely mown. The Dumb Soldier. Robert Louis Stevenson. GoTP
When the great busy plants of our cities. What Then? *Unknown.* SoP; STF
When the great founder of this vast pile began. A Congratulatory Poem to the Honoured Edmund Morris, Esq., on His Happy Marriage. Elkanah Settle. HW
When the great golden eagle of the West. Salt Lake City. Hayden Carruth. AmFN
When the Great Gray Ships Come In. Guy Wetmore Carryl. AA; EtS; FaBoBe; HBV; MC; PAH
When the great hero, adding to the charms. The Damnation of Byron. A. D. Hope. MoAuPo
When the Green Lies over the Earth. Angelina Weld Grimké. CDC; PoNe
When the Green Woods Laugh. Blake. *See* Laughing Song.
When the grey lake-water rushes. The Solitary Woodsman. Sir Charles G. D. Roberts. CaP; OBCV
When the gunner spoke in his sleep the hut was still. The Gunner. Francis Webb. BoAV
When the Heart Is Full of Love. *Unknown.* MaRV
When the heat of the summer. A Dragon Fly. Eleanor Farjeon. FaPON; PDV
When the heathen trumpet's clang. The Monks of Bangor's March. Sir Walter Scott. CAW
When the herds [*or* herd] were watching. Carol [*or* Bethlehem]. William Canton. BoTP; DD; HBVY; OHIP; YeAr
"When the hermit made an end." Tennyson. *Fr.* Idylls of the King: The Holy Grail. PeVV
When the heron's in the high wood and the last long furrow's sown. Mary Shepherdess. Marjorie Pickthall. ISi; WHL
When the hero's task was done. The Hero. Roy Fuller. FaBoMo
When the high heart we magnify. Greatness Passing By. John Drinkwater. MaRV
When the hills collapsed, we went inside. Landscape. John L'Heureux. YAP
When the hills of spring. Girls in Spring. Owari. OnPM
When the Himalayan peasant meets the he-bear in his pride. The Female of the Species. Kipling. BLPA; HBV; OtMeF; TreFS
When the horse has been unharnessed and we've flushed the old machine. Cleaning Up. Edward Dyson. PoAu-1
When the hot sun smiles on the endless miles. The Stampede. *Unknown.* CoSo
When the Hounds of Spring [Are on Winter's Traces]. Swinburne. *Fr.* Atalanta in Calydon. BoLiVe; CoBE; EnL; FaBoBe; HBV; LiTB; MasP; NoP; PoFS; PoVP; TreF; TrGrPo; ViPP; VP
(Chorus: "When the hounds of spring are on winter's

When (continued)
traces") AnFE; AWP; CTC; EnLit; EPN; EvOK; ExPo; FaBoEn; GTBS-P; GTSL; ILP; InPo; JAWP; OBEV; OuHeWo; Po; PoIE; PoSa; RG, *abr.*; SeCeV; ShBV-4; TOP; VA; WBP; YAT
(Choruses from "Atalanta in Calydon.") EnLi-2; ViBoPo
(Hounds of Spring, The.) BEL; FaBV; YT
When the house is silent. Song for a Little Cuckoo Clock. Elizabeth J. Coatsworth. SiSoSe
When the humid shadows hover. Rain on the Roof. Coates Kinney. HBV
When the hunter-star Orion. Retrospection. Sir Arthur Quiller-Couch. CenHV
When the hurricane unfolds. The Hurricane. Luis Palés Matos. FaPON
When the King Enjoys His Own Again. Martin Parker. FaBoCh; OxBoLi; TuPP
(King Enjoys His Own Again, The.) OBS
When the King of Siam disliked a courtier. In Dispraise of Poetry. Jack Gilbert. PP
When the Kye Comes Hame. James Hogg. HBV; OxBS
When the Lad for Longing Sighs. A. E. Housman. A Shropshire Lad, VI. MoBrPo; PoVP; ViPo
When the Lamp Is Shattered. Shelley. *See* Lines: "When the lamp is shattered."
When the landfolk of Galway converse with a stranger. Undertone. William Bedell Stanford. NeIP; OnYI
When the landlord wants the rent. Pensées de Noël. A. D. Godley. BOHV; InMe
When the last bitterness was past, she bore. Actea. Sir Rennell Rodd. VA
When the last day is ended. The Survivor. Frederic L. Knowles. OQP
When the last dread hour is o'er us. The Benedictine Ultima. *Unknown.* CAW
When the last H-bomb blast has done its stuff. Brave Old World. Elisabeth Lambert. FaFP; SiTL
When the last hope of trampled France had failed. Shelley. *Fr.* The Revolt of Islam. MyFE
When the last note is played and void the hall. Music. W. J. Turner. MuSP
When the last of gloaming's gone. The Shadow. Walter de la Mare. BoChLi (1950 ed.)
When the last pullman of the day pulls into the Grand Canyon station. View. Josephine Miles. RePo
When the last sea is sailed and [*or* when] the last shallow [*or* shallow's] charted. Prayer [*or* D'Avalos' Prayer]. John Masefield. GTSL; TrPWD
When the last star breathes like a rose. Sailors. Louis Simpson. NYBP
When the last voyage is ended. Requiem. Joseph Lee. DD; OHIP
When the leaf is tight and gray. Look to the Leaf. *Unknown.* UnTE
When the lean, gray grasses. Give Love To-Day. Ethel Talbot. HBV
When the lean recruit threw a shaky salute. The Man in the Manmade Moon. X. J. Kennedy. StP
When the least whistling wind begins to sing. Her Hair. Sir Robert Chester. *Fr.* Love's Martyr. EIL
When the leaves in autumn wither. Autumnus. Joshua Sylvester. EIL; LO; OBS; SeEP; StP; UnPo (1st ed.)
When the lessons and tasks are all ended. The Children. Charles Monroe Dickinson. AA; HBV
When the Light Falls. Stanley Kunitz. MoAmPo (1962 ed.)
When the lights come on at five o'clock on street corners. For Futures. Josephine Miles. FiMAP
When the little armadillo. Mexican Serenade. Arthur Guiterman. BOHV; BoLP; FiBHP
When the little children die. Notre Dame des Petits. Louis Mercier. ISi
When the little Grecian cities went a-warring each with each. Little Songs. Marjorie Pickthall. CaP
When the little spent winds are at rest in the tamarack tree. In the Night Watches. Sir Charles G. D. Roberts. PeCV
When the Lord brought back those that returned to Zion. Like unto Them That Dream. Psalm CXXVI, Bible, *O.T.* TrJP
When the Lord fashioned man, the Lord his God. The Mother. Catulle Mendès. TrJP
When the Lord turned again the captivity of Zion. Psalm CXXVI, Bible, *O.T.* BoPe; OnPM
When the man arrives tomorrow, bearing a token. The Husband. Donald Finkel. ELU
When the Martian Maid knocked on my door. The Martian Maid. Brian Lazarus. SiTL
When the master sits at ease. Friend Cato. Anna Wickham. MoBrPo
When the May has culled her flowers for the summer waiting long. We Keep Memorial Day. Kate Brownlee Sherwood. HH
When the merry lark doth gild. A Song for the Seasons. "Barry Cornwall." HBV
When the mice awaken. The Vigil. Denise Levertov. NePoEA-2
When the mighty Maccabean led the armies of the Lord. The Snarlers. Arthur Guiterman. PaA
When the mild weather came. Sunrise at Sea. Epes Sargent. EtS
When the miner returns from his labor. The Vocal Miner. John A. Stone. SGR
When the Mint Is in the Liquor. Clarence Ousley. PoLF
When the Mississippi Flowed in Indiana. Vachel Lindsay. Three Poems about Mark Twain, II. CMoP
When the mole goes digging. The Mole. E. L. Mayo. WaKn
When the monkey in his madness. The Monkey's Glue. Goldwin Goldsmith. NA
When the moon comes over Brooklyn. The Moon of Brooklyn. Nathalia Crane. AnAmPo
When the moon comes peeping through my windowpane at night. My Wish. Patience Strong. RePo
When the moon is on the wave. An Incantation. Byron. *Fr.* Manfred. OBRV
When the moon lights up. The Moon's Orchestra. John Gould Fletcher. Down the Mississippi, IV. HT; LaNeLa; LiTA; NP
When the moon shines o'er the corn. The Field Mouse. "Fiona Macleod." FaPON; GBV; MoShBr
When the moon was full they came to the water. Moon Fishing. Lisel Mueller. CoAP
When the moon's splendour shines in naked heaven. To His Friend in Absence. Walafrid Strabo. LiTW
When the morning was waking over the war. Among Those Killed in the Dawn Raid Was a Man Aged One Hundred. Dylan Thomas. InPo; MoPo; Sonn
When the Most Is Said. "Madeline Bridges." AA; HBV
When the mouse died at night. The Mouse. Jean Garrigue. TwCP
When the mouse died, there was a sort of pity. Death of a Whale. John Blight. PoAu-2
When the night her visions is weaving. The Harp of David. "Yehoash." TrJP
When the night is cloudy. In the Hours of Darkness. James Flexner. FaPON; MPB
When the night is still and far. The Highway. William Channing Gannett. WGRP
When the night kneels down by your bed. Faith. Preston Clark. HBMV; MaRV
When the night shall lift from Erin's hills, 'twere shame if we forget. The Hedge Schoolmasters. Seumas MacManus. CAW
When the night wind howls in the chimney cowls, and the bat in the moonlight flies. Sir Roderic's Song. W. S. Gilbert. *Fr.* Ruddigore. GBV (1952 ed.); PoMS; ShM; WhC
When the nightingale chanted her vespers. Mark Anthony. John Cleveland. SeEP
When the Nightingale Sings. *Unknown.* CBEP; EnLit
(Fairest between Lincoln and Lindsay.) MeEL
When the nightingale to his mate. Alba. Ezra Pound. *Fr.* Langue d'Oc. PoIE
When the nights are long and the dust is deep. Thistledown. Lizette Woodworth Reese. YeAr
When the Norn Mother saw the whirlwind hour. Lincoln, the Man of the People. Edwin Markham. BoChLi; GN; HBV; HH; LiPo; MAP; MC; MCCG; MoAmPo; NeMA; OHFP; OHIP; OnPP; PaA; PAH; PAL; PFY; PoMa; PTK; TreFS; TrGrPo; YT
When the north wind moans thro' the blind creek courses. A Gallop of Fire. Marie E. J. Pitt. PoAu-1
When the nursery corners are creepy dim. The Muffin-Man. Madeleine Nightingale. GaP
When the old flaming prophet climbed the sky. On a Virtuous

Young Gentlewoman That Died Suddenly. William Cartwright. CBEP; OBEV
When the old, long-preserved wine stands at the repast. Five Arabic Verses in Praise of Wine, II. *Unknown.* TrJP
When the one o'clock cock begins to crow. The Milkman. Leonard J. Feeney. MoSiPe
When the other children go. The Invisible Playmate. Margaret Widdemer. FaPON; MPB
When the "Our Father" I have said. Afterwards. Mary Dixon Thayer. GFA
When the outlook is dark, try the uplook. Try the Uplook. *Unknown.* BLRP; SoP
When the pale moon hides and the wild wind wails. The Wolf. Georgia R. Durston. GFA; UTS
When the picnic was over. Beach Fire. Frances M. Frost. TiPo
When the pine tosses its cones. Woodnotes, I. Emerson. *See also* For this present, hard. AmPP (4th ed.); CoBA; NePA; OxBA.
When the place was green with the shaky grass. Where the Lilies Used to Spring. David Gray. OxBS
When the pods went pop on the broom, green broom. A Runnable Stag. John Davidson. AnFE; BrPo; EvOK; GoTS; GTSL; HBV; LiTG; OA; OBEV (new ed.); OBVV; OnSP; PoVP; SD; ShBV-2; WiR
When the prairie schooner sailed. We Put on the Buffalo. Robert P. Tristram Coffin. RePo
When the present has latched its postern behind my tremulous stay. Afterwards. Thomas Hardy. AnFE; BEL; BoNaP; CBEP; CBV; CH; ChMP; ChTr; CMoP; EG; EnLi-2 (1949 ed.); FaBoEn; ForPo; GTBS-P; LiTB; LiTG; LiTM (rev. ed.); MoAB; MoBrPo; MoVE; NAMP; NoP; OBNC; PoAn; PoEL-5; PoeP; PoIE; POTE; QFR; SeCeV; ShBV-3; TreFT; TrGrPo; ViBoPo; ViPP; YT
When the prime mover of my many sighs. To Vittoria Colonna. Michelangelo. AWP; JAWP; WBP
When the proud World does most my world despise. Sonnets to Aurelia, I. Robert Nichols. OBMV
"When the Pulitzers showered on some dope." Words for Hart Crane. Robert Lowell. AP; CABA; CMoP; NMP
When the rain comes tumbling down. The Story of Flying Robert. Heinrich Hoffmann. RIS
When the rain is raining. Umbrellas. Rowena Bennett. TiPo (1959 ed.)
When the rains began. The Prophetess. Dorothy Livesay. MoCV
When the rattlesnake bit, I lay. The Poisoned Man. James Dickey. ToPo
When the reaper's task was ended, and the summer wearing late. The Swan Song of Parson Avery. Whittier. AA; AmePo
When the Regime ordered that books with dangerous teachings. The Burning of Books. Bertolt Brecht. PoPl
When the rigors of the world assail you. To Laughter, to Leering. Richard Eberhart. ToPo
When the ring gleamed white and your chair hugged the edge of it. Change of Address. Kathleen Fraser. NYBP; YAP
When the Ripe Fruit Falls. D. H. Lawrence. CMoP
When the ripe pears droop heavily. The Wasp. "Fiona Macleod." BoTP; FaPON; TSW
When the Roll Is Called up Yonder. James M. Black. TreFT
When the ropes droop and loosen, and the gust. For My Grandfather. Francis Webb. BoAV
When the rose came I loved the rose. Song. Arthur O'Shaughnessy. PoVP
When the rose is brightest. To Giulia Grisi. Nathaniel Parker Willis. AA; AmLP
When the Rose Is Faded. Walter de la Mare. NP
When the rose of morn through the dawn was breaking. The Dream of Ængus Og. Eleanor Rogers Cox. HBMV
When the runner's whistle lights the last miles of darkness. Soldier (T. P.). Randall Jarrell. WaP
When the Saints Go Marchin' In. *Unknown.* EaLo
When the sap runs up the tree. A-Roving. Victor Daley. BoAu
When the Saviour has given you a blessing, by paper or a book. Pass It On! *Unknown.* STF
When the scarlet cardinal tells. July [*or* It Is July]. Susan Hartley Swett. GN; OTD; OTPC (1946 ed.); PoRL; StVeCh (1940 ed.); YeAr
When the sea has devoured the ships. My Light with Yours. Edgar Lee Masters. NP
When the shades of night are falling, and the sun goes down. The Dustman. *Unknown.* BoTP
When the Shades of Night Have Come. Miguel de Unamuno, *tr. fr. Spanish by* Thomas Walsh. OnPM
When the sheen on tall summer grass is pale. The Gazelles. T. Sturge Moore. BrPo; OBMV
When the sheep are in the fauld, and the kye [*or* cows] at hame. Auld Robin Gray. Lady Anne Lindsay. BeLS; CH; GoTS; GTBS; GTBS-D; GTBS-P; GTBS-W; GTSE; GTSL; HBV; OBEC; OBEV; OnPP; ViBoPo
When the ship drives on through the tumbling sea. The Clinker. *Unknown.* PEDC; StVeCh (1940 ed.)
When the shy, slender thrush. Spring Doggerel. Rhoda Coghill. NeIP
When the shy star goes forth in heaven. James Joyce. Chamber Music, IV. HW
When the siege and assault ceased at Troy. Sir Gawain and the Green Knight. *Unknown, tr. fr. Middle English.* EnLi-1; MeEV; OuHeWo
When the sky starts in a-rainin'. Let Be. *Unknown.* WBLP
When the Sleepy Man Comes. Sir Charles G. D. Roberts. *Fr.* The Book of the Native. HBV; HBVY; MPB
When the snail crawls over the bare flag-stone. Omens. James H. Cousins. OnYI
When the snow has gone away. The Procession. Margaret Widdemer. YeAr
When the snow is on the ground. *Unknown.* SAS
When the soft winds did blow. The Goddesses' Glory. *Unknown.* SeCL
When the Son of Man Shall Come in His Glory. St. Matthew, XXV: 31-46, Bible, *N.T.* TreF
When the soul sought refuge in the place of rest. Self-Discipline. "Æ." MoBrPo; VA
When the southern gale is blowing hard. At Sea. D. H. Rogers. AnNZ
When the Spent Day Begins to Frail. E. E. Cummings. ErPo
When the spent sun throws up its rays on cloud. Acceptance. Robert Frost. CMoP; MoRP; OxBA
When the spinning-room was here. The Maids of Elfin-Mere. William Allingham. IrPN; OnYI
When the Spring comes laughing. A Song of the Four Seasons. Austin Dobson. HBV
When the springtime does come. Hallelujah, Bum Again. *Unknown.* ABF
When the Stars Are Gone. Robert Louis Stevenson. SoP
When the stars are shining bright. Look and See. Tom Robinson. BoChLi (1950 ed.)
When the storm was fiercely raging. It Is I, Be Not Afraid. A. B. Simpson. BePJ; SoP; STF
When the storm was in the sky. The Beloved. May Probyn. GoBC
"When the Students Resisted, a Minor Clash Ensued." David Knight. MoCV
When the Sultan Goes to Ispahan. Thomas Bailey Aldrich. AA; BeLS; FaBoBe; HBV
When the summer fields are mown. Aftermath. Longfellow. AP; MAmP
When the sun begins to throw. Skimmers. Ted Walker. NYBP
When the sun gets low, in winter. Human Things. Howard Nemerov. BoNaP; STP; ToPo
When the sun goes down and the world is still. Jock o'Dreams. Rose Fyleman. BoTP
When the sun has left the hill-top. A Blessing for the Blessed [*or* Sunset]. Laurence Alma-Tadema. BoTP; GFA; PRWS
When the sun has slipped away. The Skunk. Robert P. Tristram Coffin. FaPON; TiPo
When the sun is shining overhead. Shady Woods. E. M. Adams. BoTP
When the sun rises I go to work. Creativity. *Tr. by* Y. S. Han. OQP
When the sun rises on another day. Litany. Charles Angoff. TrPWD
When the sun rose I was still lying in bed. Hearing the Early Oriole. Po Chü-i. UnS
When the sun sets behind a cloud. Rules of the Road. *Unknown.* SoAmSa
When the sun shone hot the girl's arm was detected. Temperature. Gerard Malanga. NYBP
When the sun shouts and people abound. Summer Holiday. Robinson Jeffers. CrMA; MAP; MoAmPo; MoVE; OxBA

When the sun whitens. Hang On. David Hilton. QAH
When the sun's perpendicular rays. Beginning of an Undergraduate Poem. *Unknown.* SiTL
When the sun's red fiery ball. Seasong. Stefan George. LiTW
When the swans turned my sister into a swan. The Black Swan. Randall Jarrell. CMoP; FiMAP; NMP
When the sweet showers of April follow March [*or* fall and shoot]. The Prologue to The Canterbury Tales, mod. Chaucer. FlW; TrGrPo
When the tall bamboos are clicking to the restless little breeze. In a Southern Garden. Dorothea Mackellar. BoAu
When the tea is brought at five o'clock. Milk for the Cat. Harold Monro. BoPe; BoTP; FaBoBe; FaFP; GoTP; HBVY; MemP; MoBrPo; OBMV; ShBV-1; SiTL; ThWaDe; YT
When the teacher asks you to bound Texas. Texas. James Daugherty. TiPo (1959 ed.)
When the thin fountains are again. Quan lo ruis de la fontana. Jaufré Raudel. LiTW
When the third summer freed us from restraint. Cambridge and the Alps. Wordsworth. *Fr.* The Prelude, VI. MBW-2
When the tide was out. A Ship Burning and a Comet All in One Day. Richard Eberhart. NYBP; ToPo
When the Tigers claw the Bulldogs. College Song. Ed Anthony. InMe
When the time comes for me to die. Night. Thomas William Rolleston. HBV
When the timeless, daily, tedious affair. The Poet at Seven. Robert Lovell, *ad. fr. the French of* Arthur Rimbaud. NaP
When the Tom-Tom Beats. Jacques Roumain, *tr. fr. French by* Langston Hughes. PoNe
When the torch is taken. Seneca. Thomas Merton. CoPo
When the toys are growing weary. The Dustman. Frederic Edward Weatherly. HBV; OTPC
When the Train Comes In. Nixon Waterman. IHA
When the Tree Bares. Conrad Aiken. MAP; MoAmPo
When the Troops Were Returning from Milan. Niccolò degli Albizzi. *See* Prolonged Sonnet.
When the trumpet of the Lord shall sound. When the Roll Is Called up Yonder. James M. Black. TreFT
When the trumpet shall sound. The Trumpet. *Unknown.* OnPM
When the Turf Is Thy Tower. *Unknown, tr. fr. Middle English by* Mabel Van Duzee. MeEV
(Grave, The.) ChTr
(When the Turuf Is Thi Tuur.) SeCePo
When the unknown shall be known. To the Soul. Sir Frederick Napier Broome. ACV
When the Unnatural Warm Fair October. Chad Walsh. StP
When the Vacation Is Over for Good. Mark Strand. NYBP
When the vast universal night shall cover. Epithalamium. Edith Sitwell. HW
When the veil from the eyes is lifted. Si Jeunesse Savait. Edmund Clarence Stedman. AA
When the vengeance wakes, when the battle breaks. Battle Song. Robert Burns Wilson. MC; PAH
When the voice of the Master is calling. You Told Me of Jesus. *Unknown.* SoP
When the voices of children are heard on the green/ And laughing. Nurse's Song. Blake. *Fr.* Songs of Innocence. AWP; BoChLi; CBEP; CEP; CH; EiCL; EiPP; EnRP; FaBoBe; FaPON; GaP; GoTP; HBV; HBVY; InPo; MPB; OBEC; OnPM; OTPC (1923 ed.); RG; ThWaDe; TiPo (1952 ed.); WoL
When the voices of children are heard on the green/ And whisp'rings. Nurse's Song. Blake. *Fr.* Songs of Experience. CEP; EiPP; EnLi-2 (1949 ed.); EnRP; PoFS; TOP
When the volcano with stone lips drawn back. Silent. Iwan Goll. OnPM
When the war-cry of Liberty rang through the land. The Death of Warren. Epes Sargent. MC; PAH
When the War Will End. Reginald Arkell. *See* Rumors.
When the warl's couped roun' as a peerie. Munestruck. "Hugh MacDiarmid." NeBP
When the waters' countenance. The Wet Litany. Kipling. SiSw
When the waves of trouble roll. Show Me Thyself. Margaret E. Sangster. TrPWD
When the ways are heavy with mire and rut. The Ballade of Prose and Rhyme. Austin Dobson. MoBrPo (1942 ed.)
When the wayside tangles blaze. Goldenrod. Elaine Goodale Eastman. HBV
When the weather is rough, said the anxious child. Contemporary Song. Theodore Spencer. LiTA
When the weather suits you not. Try Smiling. *Unknown.* BLPA; FaFP; WBLP
When the white feet of the baby beat across the grass. Baby Running Barefoot. D. H. Lawrence. MoPW; NoP
When the white flame in us is gone. Dust. Rupert Brooke. ALV; HBV; MoBrPo; OBVV
When the white fog burns off. The Depths. Denise Levertov. NaP
When the white wave of a glory that is hardly I. Sinfonia Domestica. Jean Starr Untermeyer. HBMV; MAP; MoAmPo; NP
When the Wild Geese were flying to Flanders away. The Sailor Girl. Alfred Perceval Graves. RIS
When the wind blows. *Unknown.* OxNR
When the wind blows, walk not abroad. To the Maids Not to Walk in the Wind. Oliver St. John Gogarty. AnIL; ErPo
When the wind is in the east. Weather Signs [*or* Country Proverbs *or* The Wind and the Fisherman *or* Fishermen's Weather]. *Unknown.* BoTP; GoTP; OTPC; OxNR; PCH; PPL; RIS; StaSt
When the wind is in the thrift. By the Saltings. Ted Walker. NYBP; WIRo
When, the wind stirring the Carpathian main. A Little Garment. Diodorus. OnPM
When the wind swells the canvas and the anchor's a-trip. Believe Me, Dearest Susan. *Unknown.* SoAmSa
When the wind works against us in the dark. Storm Fear. Robert Frost. CMoP; HBV; NP; OxBA; ViBoPo
When the woods are green again. Midsummer Moon. "E. M. G. R." BoTP
When the words rustle no more. Stillness. James Elroy Flecker. BrPo; CH; GoJo; GTBS-D; MoBrPo; SyP
When the Work's All Done This Fall. *Unknown, at. to* D. J. O'Malley *or* D. J. White. AS, *with music*; BFSS, *with music*; CoSo, *with music*; IHA
When the World Ends. Mark Van Doren. GoYe
When the world goes voodoo. Creed. Walter Lowenfels. PoNe (1970 ed.)
When the world is all against you. The Optimist. *Unknown.* PV
When the World Is Burning. Ebenezer Jones. ACV; OBEV; OBVV; PrWP
When the world turns completely upside down. Wild Peaches, I. Elinor Wylie. AmP; HT; LiTA; LiTM (rev. ed.); NAMP; OxBA
"When the World Was in Building. . ." Ford Madox Ford. CTC
When the worn spirit wants repose. Sunday. James Edmeston. SoP
When the wounded seaman heard the ocean daughters. Legend. Ridgely Torrence. EtS
When the Year Grows Old. Edna St. Vincent Millay. YT
When the yellow bird's note was almost stopped. Rejoicing at the Arrival of Ch'en Hsiung. Po Chü-i. AWP
When the young Augustus Edward. On the Beach. Charles Stuart Calverley. ALV; FiBHP
When the young Dawn spread in the eastern sky. The Boar Hunt. Homer. *Fr.* The Odyssey, XIX. FlW
When the young hand of Darnley locked in hers. Mary Queen of Scots. Charles Tennyson Turner. HBV
When Thee (O holy sacrificed Lamb). To the Blessed Sacrament. Henry Constable. ACP; CAW
When Theo: Roos: unfurled his bann. The Conversational Reformer. Harry Graham. InMe; YaD
When there are no distances in music. Desolate Scythia. Edgar Lee Masters. NP
When there are so many we shall have to mourn. In Memory of Sigmund Freud. W. H. Auden. AtBAP; CoBMV; FaBoMo; LiTB; OxBA
When there are whitecaps on the ocean. Stormy Sea. Janet Vaughn. PCD
When There Is Music. David Morton. HBMV
When there is nothing left but darkness. Any Woman. Hazel Hall. MAP; MoAmPo (1942 ed.)
"When There Is Peace." Austin Dobson. PAH
When there was heard no more the war's loud sound. The Death of Ailill. Francis Ledwidge. OnYI

When there was not one moment left to us. By Return Mail. Richard Aldridge. NePoAm-2
When these graven lines you see. A Happy Man. E. A. Robinson, *after* Carphyllides. AWP; JAWP; LiTW; WBP
When these inland gulls. Desert Gulls. Dan Gillespie. QAH
When these old woods were young. Under the Woods. Edward Thomas. CH; LoBV
When these things following be done to our intent. Trust in Women. *Unknown.* BOHV; NA
When these were past, thus gan the Titanesse. Mutability. Spenser. *Fr.* The Faerie Queene, VII. PoEL-1
When they come, we begin to go. The Ancestors. Christopher Middleton. NMP; OPoP
When they found Giotto. Allan M. Laing. FiBHP
When They Grow Old. Nathan Ralph. CaP
When they had passed all those troubled ways. Tasso, *tr. by* Edward Fairfax. *Fr.* Jerusalem Delivered, XVI. TuPP
When they had pitched their smoked tepees. Indian Dance. Frederick Niven. CaP
When They Had Sung an Hymn. Edward Taylor. *See* Preparatory Meditations: "Angells sung a carole. . ."
When They Have Lost. C. Day Lewis. EnLit; MoAB; MoBrPo (1950 ed.); NeMA
When they heard Sigmund the Saviour in these coasts. The Return from the Freudian Islands. A. D. Hope. MoAuPo
When they heard the Captain humming and beheld the dancing crew. The Post Captain. Charles Edward Carryl. BOHV; PCD
When they [*or* Quhen thai] him fand, and gude Wallace him saw. Wallace's Lament for the Graham. Henry the Minstrel. *Fr.* The Wallace, X. GoTS; OxBS
When they killed my mother it made me nervous. The State. Randall Jarrell. LiTM (1970 ed.); MiAP
When they mow the fields, I see the world reformed. Ghazals. Adrienne Rich. NoP
When they pull my clock tower down. The Clock Tower. Colleen Thibaudeau. WHW
When they said the time to hide was mine. The Rabbit. Elizabeth Madox Roberts. BoChLi; GoTP; MPB; SoPo; TiPo; TSW; UTS
When they shot Malcolm Little down. At That Moment. Raymond Patterson. WOW
When they stop poems. Today Is a Day of Great Joy. Victor Hernandez Cruz. TTY
When they threw him overboard. Historical Incidents. Clarence Day. InMe
When they write an end to war, when they blot away the battle. If We Break Faith. Joseph Auslander. TRV
When thin-strewn memory I look through. Miss Loo [*or* Miss Lou]. Walter de la Mare. CMoP; HBV
When things began to happen to our favorite spot. To T. S. Eliot on His Sixtieth Birthday. W. H. Auden. ML
When Things Go Wrong. *Unknown.* SoP; STF
When things go wrong, as they sometimes will. Don't Quit [*or* You Mustn't Quit]. *Unknown.* BLPA; PoToHe; SoP; STF
When think you comes the Wind. The Rose and the Wind. Philip Bourke Marston. OBVV; VA
When This American Woman. Leonard Cohen. PeCV
When this ancient, wallpapered melody. "The Day a Dancer Learned to Sing of Dreamless Escapades." L. Goodwin. BF
When This Cruel War Is Over. Charles Carroll Sawyer. *See* Weeping, Sad and Lonely.
When this crystal shall present. The Looking Glass. James Shirley. LiTL; LO
When this flye liv'd, she us'd to play. A Flye That Flew into My Mistris Her Eye. Thomas Carew. AnAnS-2
When this is the thing you put on. Armor. James Dickey. CoAP
When this, our rose, is faded. Amantium Irae. Ernest Dowson. HBV; NoP
When this passing world is done. How Much I Owe. Robert Murray McCheyne. SoP
When This Tide Ebbs. Verna Loveday Harden. CaP
When this yokel comes maundering. The Plot against the Giant. Wallace Stevens. CaFP; CMoP; OxBA
When this young *objet trouvé* improvises sleep. Laura Age Eight. Ramon Guthrie. OPoP
When thistle-blows do lightly float. November. C. L. Cleaveland. DD; HBV
When those renownèd [*or* renoumed] noble peers of Greece. Amoretti, XLIV. Spenser. CABA; ReIE
When those we love die. Death in the Home. T. Sturge Moore. BrPo
When thou art dead, and thinkst to com. *Unknown.* SeCSL
When thou art near to me, it seems. To Anne. Clément Marot. OnPM; WoL
When Thou Did Thinke I Did Not Love. Sir Robert Ayton. *See* When Thou Didst Think I Did Not Love.
When thou didst give thy love to me. Robert Bridges. EG
When Thou Didst Think I Did Not Love. Sir Robert Ayton. ElL
(When Thou Did Thinke I Did Not Love.) OBS
When Thou Dost Dance. *Unknown.* SeCL
When thou dost eat from off this plate. Inscription for My Little Son's Silver Plate. Eugene Field. PPL
When thou faire Celia like the settinge sunn. *Unknown.* SeCSL
When thou goest into thy church. Cluttered Temples. George Herbert. SoP
When Thou hast mastered me. Paradox. E. Margaret Clarkson. SoP
When Thou Hast Shut Thy Door. "L. S. P." SoP
When thou hast spent the lingering day in pleasure and delight. Gascoigne's Good-Night. George Gascoigne. ReEn; ReIE; SiCE
When thou hast taken thy last applause, and when. Sonnet. E. E. Cummings. NP
When Thou Must Home [to Shades of Underground]. Thomas Campion, *after the Latin of* Propertius. AtBAP; AWP; BEL; BWP; CABA; CBEP; CBV; ElL; EnL; EnLi-1; EnLoPo; EnRePo; FaBoEn; InPo; JAWP; LO; LoBV; NoP; OBSC; OnPM; PoAn; PoE; PoEL-2; PoRA; PoSa; ReEn; ReIE; SeCeV; SiCE; TuPP; VaPo; ViBoPo; WBP
(O Crudelis Amor.) GTSL
(Tell, O Tell.) TrGrPo
(To Shades of Underground.) ChTr
(Vobiscum Est Iope.) HBV; OBEV
When Thou Passest through the Waters. Henry Crowell. BLRP
"When thou passest through the waters." Passing Through. Annie Johnson Flint. BLRP; SoP; STF
When thou, poor[e] excommunicate. To My Inconstant Mistress [*or* Song: To My Inconstant Mistris]. Thomas Carew. AnAnS-2; BWP; CavP; EG; EnLit; EnLoPo; HBV; LO; LoBV; MeLP; MePo; OBEV; OBS; SCEP-2; SeCePo; SeCL; SeCP; SeCV-1; SeEP; TrGrPo
When thou shalt be dispos'd to set me light. Sonnets, LXXXVIII. Shakespeare. CLwM
When thou shalt sleep, my fair Tenebrous. Remorse after Death. Baudelaire. OnPM
When thou to my true-love com'st. Westphalian Song. *Unknown.* AWP; JAWP; LiTW; WBP
When thou turn'st away from ill. Approaches. George Macdonald. MaRV; OQP; TRV
When thou wakest in the morning. Tell Jesus. *Unknown.* BePJ; STF
When three, he fished these lakes. Fishermen. James A. Emanuel. BP
When thro' life unblest we rove. On Music. Thomas Moore. MuSP
When through the Whirl of Wheels. G. A. Studdert Kennedy. MaRV
When through the winding cobbled streets of time. The Noonday April Sun. George Love. IDB; NNP
When Thy Beauty Appears. Thomas Parnell. *See* Song: "When thy beauty appears."
When thy bright beams, my Lord, do strike mine eye. Meditation XXIII. Edward Taylor. *Fr.* Preparatory Meditations, First Series. MAmP
When thy heart, with joy o'erflowing. Thy Brother. Theodore Chickering Williams. MaRV
When Tim and I stumbled/ On the rough Tarras track. Tarras Moon. James K. Baxter. AnNZ
When time has rocked the present age to sleep. To William Stanley Braithwaite. Georgia Douglas Johnson. BALP
When time seems short, and death is near. He Died for Me. George Washington Bethune. BePJ
When Time, who steals our years away. Song. Thomas Moore. TreFS

When, to a cheap and tawdry tune, the orchestra cried out. Vaudeville Dancer. John Hall Wheelock. UnS
When to a nation's loss, the virtuous die. To My Old, and Most Worthy Friend, Mr Izaak Walton. Charles Cotton. SeEP
When to any saint I pray. Saint Peray. Thomas William Parsons. HBV
When to Be Born. *Unknown.* *Fr.* Old Wives' Sayings. StaSt
When to Cut Your Nails. *Unknown.* *Fr.* Old Wives' Sayings. StaSt
When to Her Lute Corinna Sings. Thomas Campion. AtBAP; CABA; EG; EnLi-1; EnRePo; EP; ExPo; ILP; NoP; OBSC; ReEn; ReIE; SeCeV; SiCE; TuPP
(Corinna.) ElL; TrGrPo; UnS
(Of Corinna's Singing.) BEL; EnLit; HBV
When to his class the surgeon's skilful blade. Sonnet. George Henry Boker. *Fr.* Sonnets: a Sequence on Profane Love. AmePo
When to My Deadly [*or* Deadlie] Pleasure. Sir Philip Sidney. AtBAP; EnLoPo; FCP; MaPo; PoEL-1
When to my eyes. Midnight. Henry Vaughan. AnAnS-1; MeP; OAEP
When to my lone soft bed at eve returning. Povre Ame Amoureuse. Louise Labé. AWP
When to My Serene Body. Freda Laughton. NeIP
When to New Zealand first I cam. New Zealand Comforts. John Barr of Craigielee. AnNZ
When to Sneeze. *Unknown.* *Fr.* Old Wives' Sayings. StaSt
When to soft sleep we give ourselves away. Sleep. Thomas Bailey Aldrich. AA
When to the flowers so beautiful. The Forget-Me-Not. *Unknown.* BoTP
When to the garden of untroubled thought. The Child in the Garden. Henry van Dyke. HBV; MaRV
When to the music of Byrd or Tallis. King's College Chapel. Charles Causley. BoC; MuSP; POTi
When to the sessions of sweet silent thought. Sonnets, XXX. Shakespeare. AnFE; ATP; BEL; BoLiVe; CABA; CaFP; CBEP; CBV; CoBE; CTC; DiPo; EG; ElL; EnL; EnLi-1; EnLit; EnRePo; EP; ExPo; FaBoEn; FaBV; FaFP; GTBS; GTBS-D; GTBS-P; GTBS-W; GTSE; GTSL; HBV; ILP; InPo; JAWP; LiTB; LiTG; LoBV; MaPo; MasP; MemP; NeHB; NoP; OAEP; OBEV; OBSC; OuHeWo; PAn; PIA; PoE; PoEL-2; PoFS; PoIE; PoLF; PoPo; PoRA; PTK; ReEn; ReIE; SeCeV; ShBV-4; SiCE; Sonn; StP; TDP; TOP; TreFS; TrGrPo; TRV; ViBoPo; WBP; WHA; WoL
When Tom and Elizabeth took the farm. The Magpies. Denis Glover. AnNZ; TDP
When tongues will tax me in the public ear. William Baylebridge. *Fr.* A Wreath. BoAV
When trees are haggard and winter-bare. The Windmill. Geoffrey Johnson. HaMV
When trees have lost remembrance of the leaves. Crocus. Alfred Kreymborg. HBMV; MAP
When, tremulous on the sand and on the seas. Morgana. Gabriele d'Annunzio. LiTW
When trials press and foes increase. Trials. Grace E. Troy. STF
When tribes are broke and holdings gone. Wolf Song, the Rain. James Welch. YAP
When trouble comes your soul to try. The Friend Who Just Stands By. B. Y. Williams. PoLF; PoToHe
When trouble haunts me, need I sigh? The Stranger. John Clare. OxBoCh
When Trout Swim down Great Ormond Street. Conrad Aiken. Priapus and the Pool, III [IV]. AmLP; AnAmPo; CaFP; InPo; MAPA; PFY
(Whim.) TSW
When tunes jigged nimbler than the blood. Song from a Country Fair. Léonie Adams. GoJo
When Twilight comes to Prairie Street. The Winning of the TV West. John T. Alexander. AmFN; WaKn
When Two Are Parted. Heine, *tr. fr. German by* Louis Untermeyer. AWP; JAWP; WBP
When two lovers love each other well. Young Bearwell. *Unknown.* ESPB
When two men meet for the first time in all. Law in the Country of the Cats. Ted Hughes. ToPo
When Two Suns Do Appear. Sir Philip Sidney. *Fr.* Arcadia. EnRePo; SiPS
When two who love are parted. When Two Are Parted. Heine. AWP; JAWP; WBP
When tyranny's pampered and purple-clad minions. Extermination. Richard D'Alton Williams. OnYI
When under Edward or Henry the English armies. Now as Then. Anne Ridler. WaP
When unto heaven the souls elect take flight. The Vision. Lounkianos. CAW
When vain desire at last and vain regret. The One Hope. Dante Gabriel Rossetti. The House of Life, CI. BEL; EnLi-2; EnLit; EPN; HBV; MaVP; PoVP; ViPo; ViPP
When Very was a celibate. Varitalk. Weare Holbrook. NYBP; SiTL
When wake-robin is white in shady dells. It is Spring and All Is Well. Charles Erskine Scott Wood. PFY
When walking in a tiny rain. Vern. Gwendolyn Brooks. OCS; TiPo (1959 ed.)
When walking through the woods. Four-Leaf Clover. Wesley Curtright. GoSl
When, wanton fair, the snowy orb you throw. On a Lady Throwing Snowballs at Her Lover. Christopher Smart. VaPo
When War Shall Be No More. Longfellow. *Fr.* The Arsenal at Springfield. MaRV; OQP
(Message of Peace.) WBLP
(Peace.) PEDC
("Were half the power that fills the world with terror.") PGD
When warfare blusters at high Lucifer's command. War Cry: To Mary. Pope Leo XIII. ISi
When wars and ruined men shall cease. Prayer against Indifference. Joy Davidman. AnAmPo; AnEnPo; TrPWD
When waves invade the yellowing wheat. Composed While under Arrest. Mikhail Yurevich Lermontov. AWP
When We Are All Asleep. Robert Buchanan. VA
When we are dead, some Hunting-boy will pass. The Statue. Hilaire Belloc. ACP (1952 ed.); MoVE
When we are gone, love. Wood-Song. Eugene Lee-Hamilton. OBVV
When we are in love, we love the grass. Love Poem. Robert Bly. BoLP
When We Are Men. E. Stella Mead. BoTP
When we are old and these rejoicing veins. Sonnet. Edna St. Vincent Millay. ErPo
When we are older and the hidden fires. Vera Wainwright. LO
When We Are Parted. Hamilton Aïdé. HBV; VA
When We Are upon the Seas. George Wither. *Fr.* Hallelujah. BEL
When we as strangers sought. At an Inn. Thomas Hardy. VP
When we behold. Dahlias. Padraic Colum. GoJo; NePoAm
When we come to that dark house. Edith Sitwell. *Fr.* The Sleeping Beauty. MoVE
When we count out our gold at the end of the day. Service. Georgia Douglas Johnson. CDC
When We Court and Kiss. Thomas Campion. *See* I Care Not for These Ladies.
When we entered into the eastern gate. The Second Walk in the Garden. John Gould Fletcher. MAPA
When we for age could neither read nor write. Of the Last Verses in the Book [*or* Of His Divine Poems]. Edmund Waller. AnAnS-2; BEL; CEP; CoBE; FaBoEn; HBV; LoBV; MePo; NoP; OAEP; OBS; PeRV; PoE; PoFS; SCEP-2; SeCL; SeCP; SeCV-1; SeEP; ViBoPo
When we have thrown off this old suit. The Question Whither. George Meredith. EPN; HBV; OQP; WGRP
When we, in kind embracements, had agreed. *Unknown.* *Fr.* Zepheria. ReEn; ReIE; Sonn; TuPP
When we lay where Budmouth Beach is. Budmouth Dears. Thomas Hardy. *Fr.* The Dynasts. CH; LO; MoVE; PoVP
When we lived in a city. Until We Built a Cabin. Aileen Fisher. TiPo (1959 ed.)
When We Looked Back. William Stafford. NYBP
When we meet God every morning. God's Provident Love. Horace C. Carlisle. SoP
When we moved here, pulled. An Oregon Message. William Stafford. CoAP
When we, my love, are gone to dust. A Song of Dust. Lord De Tabley. EnLoPo
When we on simple rations sup. Washing the Dishes. Christopher Morley. PoLF
When We Plant a Tree. Warren P. Landers. GFA

When We See. *Unknown.* SoP
When we told you minus twenty. A Correction. Robert Frost. WhC
When we travel back in summer to the old house by the sea. Little Girl That Mother Used to Be. Nancy Byrd Turner. HH
When we two, friends from childhood, wanderers are. The Madonna's Lamp. Wilhelm, Prince of Sweden. CAW
When We Two Parted. Byron. AnFE; BEL; BoLiVe; CBEP; CBV; ChER; DiPo; EnLi-2; EnLit; EnRP; EPN; FaPL; FiP; ForPo; GTBS; GTBS-D; GTBS-P; GTBS-W; GTSE; GTSL; HBV; HoPM; LiTL; LoBV; MERP; MeWo; OAEP; OBEV; OBNC; OBRV; PG; PoFS; PoLF; TOP; TreFS; TrGrPo; ViBoPo; WePo; WHA
When We Went Gathering Cat-Tails. Rachel Field. GFA
When we were building Skua Light. The Dancing Seal. W. W. Gibson. HBMV; OnMSP; PoMS
When we were girl and boy together. Ballad of Human Life. Thomas Lovell Beddoes. BeLS; VA
When we were idlers with the loitering rills. To a Friend [*or* Friendship *or* Sonnet]. Hartley Coleridge. CBEP; ERoP-2; HBV; NBM; OBEV; OBNC; OBRV; PoLF
When we were little childer we had a quare wee house. Grace for Light. "Moira O'Neill." PoRh; SP; WHL
When we were little, wandering boys. Fratri Dilectissimo. John Buchan. OtMeF
When we were silly sisters seven. Fair Mary of Wallington. *Unknown.* ESPB; OBB
When we would reach the anguish of the dead. Near an Old Prison. Frances Cornford. OBMV
When weakness now do strive wi' might. Withstanders. William Barnes. OxBoCh
When wee were parted. *Unknown.* SeCSL
When weight of all garnered years. Love's Lord. Edward Dowden. HBV
"When we're walking in the garden." The Scottish Merchant's Daughter. *Unknown.* BFSS
When wert thou born, Desire? Of the Birth and Bringing Up of Desire. Edward de Vere, Earl of Oxford. OBSC; ReIE; SiCE; TuPP
When Wesley died, the Angelic orders. The Organist in Heaven [*or* Heaven]. Thomas Edward Brown. LoBV (1949 ed.); MuSP; OBNC; OBVV
When West Comes East. Corey Ford. InMe
When Westwall Downes [*or* Westwell Downs] I 'gan to tread. On Westwall Downes. William Strode. CBEP; FaBoEn; PoEL-2; SeCL; SeEP
When whelmed are altar, priest and creed. Epigram. Sir William Watson. WGRP
When, when, and whenever death closes our eyelids. Ezra Pound. *Fr.* Homage to Sextus Propertius. MoAB; OBMV
When whispering strains do softly steal [*or* with creeping wind]. In [*or* The] Commendation of Music. William Strode. CLwM; ELP; MuSP; OBEV (new ed.); SeCL
When Whistler's Mother's Picture's frame. Don Marquis. *Fr.* To a Lost Sweetheart. FiBHP
When Whistler's strongest colors fade. The Durable Bon Mot. Keith Preston. HBMV
When white man git to worryin'. Farmers of the South. *Unknown.* OuSiCo
When Will He Come? *Unknown.* SoP; STF
When Will Love Come? Pakenham Beatty. HBV
When will men again. The Leaping Laughers. George Barker. OBMV
When will the fountain of my tears by dry? Petition to Have Her Leave to Die [*or* Give Me Leave]. "A. W." EG; OBSC; TrGrPo
When will violence shake, when break me. The House. Winfield Townley Scott. MiAP
When will you dream,/ You Germans. Giovanni Battista Niccolini. *Fr.* Barbarossa. PoFr
When will you ever, Peace, wild wooddove, shy wings shut. Peace. Gerard Manley Hopkins. AtBAP; BoC; ELP; GTBS-D; GTBS-P; OAEP (2d ed.)
"When will you marry me, William." The West-Country Damosel's Complaint. *Unknown.* ESPB
When William asked, how veal was made. What Is Veal? Mary Elliott. OTPC (1923 ed.)
When William went from home (a trader styled). The Ear-Maker and the Mould-Mender. La Fontaine. UnTE
When Wilt Thou Save the People? Ebenezer Elliott. BLPA; EaLo; MaRV; NeHB; WePo
(God Save the People.) WBLP
(People's Anthem, The.) PoFr
When window-lamps had dwindled, then I rose. Christopher Brennan. *Fr.* The Wanderer. MoAuPo
When winds are locked along the tropic shore. The *Flying Dutchman.* A. M. Sullivan. EtS
When winds are raging o'er the upper ocean. Hymn [*or* Peace]. Harriet Beecher Stowe. FaChP; PoToHe
When winds go organing through the pines. The Wind in the Pines. Madison Cawein. AA
When winds that move not its calm surface sweep. The Ocean. Moschus. AWP; JAWP; WBP
When Windsor walls [*or* Windesor walles] sustained my wearied arm. How Each Thing save the Lover in Spring Reviveth to Pleasure. Earl of Surrey. EnPo; FCP; ReIE; SiPS; Sonn
When winter closed upon the countryside. Six Silver Handles. Sydney King Russell. FiSC
When Winter Fringes every Bough. Henry David Thoreau. MAmP
When winter hoar no longer holds. The Lover's Song. Alfred Austin. OBVV
When winter is gone and spring comes. Goodness of Age. *Unknown.* OnPM
When winter scourged the meadow and the hill. Ice. Charles G. D. Roberts. BoNaP; ExPo; OBCV; TDP; WHW
When winter snows upon thy sable [*or* golden] hairs. To Delia, XXXIX. Samuel Daniel. CTC; EnRePo; OBSC; ReIE; Sonn; TuPP
When winter winds are piercing chill. Woods in Winter. Longfellow. CBEP; MAmP
When winter's cold tempests and snows are no more. The Blue-Bird. Alexander Wilson. AA
When winter-time grows wearying, I lift my eyes on high. Winter Branches. Margaret Widdemer. RePo
When wintry days are dark and drear. The Light'ood Fire. John Henry Boner. AA
When wintry weather's all a-done. The Spring. William Barnes. BoNaP
When wise Minerva still was young. The Origin of Didactic Poetry. James Russell Lowell. PoEL-5
When with a serious musing I behold. The Marigold. George Wither. CBEP; OBS; SeCL
When with eyes closed as in an opium dream. Exotic Perfume [*or* Parfum exotique]. Baudelaire. AWP; MeWo; OnPM
When with fingers all uncertain, tiny stars have torn the curtain. Moon-Children. Michael Lewis. TSW
When with May the air is sweet. Love, Whose Month Was Ever May. Ulrich von Lichtenstein. AWP; JAWP; WBP
When, with my little daughter Blanche. Presence of Mind. Harry Graham. WhC
When with the cannon's mighty voice. The Girondins. Alexandre Dumas. *Fr.* Le Chevalier de maison rouge. PoFr
When with the thorns with which I long, too long. The Coronet. Andrew Marvell. OBS; StJW
When within my arms I hold you. Aurelia. Robert Nichols. OBMV; POTE
When without tears I looke on Christ, I see. William Alabaster. AnAnS-1; MeP
When woman is in rags, and poor. Suggestions by Steam. Thomas Hood. NBM
When women first Dame Nature wrought. Of Women. Richard Edwards. ElL
When working blackguards come to blows. Song. Ebenezer Elliott. NBM
When world is water and all is flood, God said. Noah's Ark. Marguerite Young. MoPo
When, wounded sore, the stricken heart. The Helper. Cecil Frances Alexander. SoP
When Yon Full Moon. W. H. Davies. LiTM (1946 ed.); MoBrPo
When you and I. When You and I Grow Up. Kate Greenaway. MPB; PCH
When you and I behind the Veil are past. The Long While. Omar Khayyám, *tr. by* Edward Fitzgerald. *Fr.* The Rubáiyát. OnPM
When you and I go down. Midnight Lamentation. Harold Monro. BrPo; ChMP; LO; ViBoPo
When You and I Grow Up. Kate Greenaway. MPB; PCH
When you and I have play'd the [*or* this] little hour. Reunited

When (continued)
[*or* Envoy]. Sir Gilbert Parker. *Fr.* A Lover's Diary. OBVV; OQP; VA
When you and I have wandered beyond the reach of call. Sat est Scripsisse. Austin Dobson. BoPe
When You and I Were Young, Maggie. George W. Johnson. TreF
When you and my true lover meet. The Lady's Third Song. W. B. Yeats. *Fr.* The Three Bushes. FaBoTw
When you are caught breathless in an empty station. This Is the Place to Wait. Horace Gregory. The Passion of M'Phail, V. CMoP; MoAmPo
When you are dead some day, my dear. In Pace. Arthur Reed Ropes. VA
When you are discouraged. Try This Once. *Unknown.* WBLP
When you are gone, I lie upon your bed. Suburban Wife's Song. Robert Hutchinson. NYBP
When you are late and have not let me know. Not Late Enough. Hazel Townson. PV
When you are mistresse of the song. To the Queen: An Apologie for the Length of the Following Panegyrick. Richard Crashaw. MaMe
When You Are Old. W. E. Henley. PoVP
When You Are Old. W. B. Yeats. AWP; BoLiVe; BoLP; BoPe; CMoP; CTC; DiPo; EnL; EnLi-2 (1949 ed.); FaBV; FaFP; FlW; GoJo; GTSE; GTSL; HBV; InP; InvP; JAWP; LiTG; LiTL; LiTM (rev. ed.); MaRV; MemP; MeWo; MoAB; MoBrPo; MoLP; NeMA; OBEV; OBVV; OtMeF; PoE; PoIE; PoLF; PoPl; PoPo; PoSa; PoVP; PP; TIHL; TreFS; ViPo (1962 ed.); WBP; WePo
When you are old and beautiful. At Majority. Adrienne Rich. NePoEA-2
When you are old, and I am passed away. When You Are Old. W. E. Henley. PoVP
When you are old, and I—if that should be. After Ronsard. Charles Williams. GTBS
When you are old, at evening candle-lit. Four Sonnets to Helen, 4. Pierre de Ronsard, *tr. by* Humbert Wolfe. *Fr.* Sonnets pour Hélène. LiTW
When you are very old, at evening. Of His Lady's Old Age [*or* to Helen]. Pierre de Ronsard, *tr. by* Andrew Lang. *Fr.* Sonnets pour Hélène. AWP; CTC; JAWP; OuHeWo; WBP
When you are walking by yourself. Kick a Little Stone. Dorothy Aldis. SoPo
When you ask God in the morning. Be Thankful. Mark Bullock. STF
When you awake. The Sleeper. Sydney Clouts. BoSA; PeSA
When you buy clothes on easy terms. Cotton-Mill Colic. *Unknown.* OuSiCo
When you came and you talked and you read. To William Carlos Williams. Galway Kinnell. NePoAm
When you came out of your house. Remembering Althea. William Stafford. NYBP
When you came, you were like red wine and honey. A Decade. Amy Lowell. BoLP; MAP; MoAmPo; NeMA; PoPl
When you can catch. Then. Dorothy Aldis. BiCB
When you chart your course. Request. Barbara Marshall. TNV
When You Come. Mary Aldis. NP
When you come, as you soon must, to the streets of our city. Advice to a Prophet. Richard Wilbur. AmPP (5th ed.); CoPo; MoAmPo (1962 ed.); MoRP; NMP; NYBP; OPoP; TDP; ToPo; TwCP
When you come to the end of a perfect day. A Perfect Day. Carrie Jacobs Bond. TreF; WBLP
When you come tonight. When You Come. Mary Aldis. NP
When you dance. Creole Girl. Leslie M. Collins. PoNe
When you destroy a blade of grass. To Iron-Founders and Others. Gordon Bottomley. GTSL; OBEV (new ed.); OBMV; OBVV
When You elect to call me, God, O call. Prayer to Go to Paradise with the Asses. Francis Jammes. LO
When you enter. Al Fitnah Muhajir. Nazzam Al Sudan. NBP
When you feel like saying something. The Most Vital Thing in Life. Grenville Kleiser. OTD; PoToHe (new ed.)
When you find you're a broken-down critter. Out of Sorts. W. S. Gilbert. *Fr.* The Grand Duke. ALV
When you first rub up against God's own skin. Ars Poetica about Ultimates. Tram Combs. TwCP
When you get hard knocks and buffets. Keep the Glad Flag Flying. *Unknown.* FaFP
When you get to heaven. Surprises. *Unknown.* STF
When you go to a store in Ascutney. Limerick. Richard H. Field. WhC
When You Go to Fairyland. *Unknown.* PCD
When you ground the lenses and the moons swam free. The Emancipators. Randall Jarrell. WaP
When you had played with life a space. To a Young Poet Who Killed Himself. Joyce Kilmer. YT
When you hark to the voice of the knocker. The Quarrelsome Trio. "L. G." WBLP
When you have bathed in the river. Submission. *Unknown.* ErPo
When you have come, the house is emptied quite. Evening. Mary Matheson. CaP
When you have tidied all things for the night. Solitude. Harold Monro. MoBrPo; StaSt; TrGrPo; TSW
When you hear dat Ise a-dyin'. Tone de Bell Easy. *Unknown.* ABF
When you imagine trumpet-faced musicians. Homage to Literature. Muriel Rukeyser. NAMP
When you kneel below me. Celebration. Leonard Cohen. ErPo
When you look/ into a mirror. Mirror. John Updike. WaKn
When you look down from the airplane you see lines. Field and Forest. Randall Jarrell. NoP
When you look way 'cross dat lonesome stream. Dat Lonesome Stream. *Unknown.* ABF
When you perceive these stones are wet. Epitaph. Sir William Davenant. ACP
When You Reach the Hilltop the Sky Is on Top of You. Etta Blum. GoYe
When you read what he said. The Words of Jesus. William Rose Benét. MoRP
When you ride on a train, a passenger train. Passenger Train. Edith Newlin Chase. SoPo
When you see me walkin'. After Depression Came Soul. Tommy Whitaker. TNV
When You See Millions of the Mouthless Dead. Charles Sorley. MMA
When You Send a Valentine. Mildred J. Hill. GFA
When you set forth on the voyage to Ithaca. Ithaca. C. P. Cavafy. LiTW
When you shake loose your hair from all controlling. On Lisa's Golden Hair. Francisco de Quevedo. AtBAP
When you shall see me in the toils of Time. She, to Him. Thomas Hardy. BEL; OBVV; TOP
When you sing. Shakespeare. *Fr.* The Winter's Tale, IV, iii. UnS
When you slice a Georgy melon you mus' know what you is at. How to Eat Watermelons. Frank L. Stanton. BOHV
When you speak of dauntless deeds. Ballad [*or* Deed] of Lieutenant Miles. Clinton Scollard. MC; PAH
When you start for San Francisco. Humbug Steamship Companies. *Unknown.* IHA
When you take off your clothes. In Nakedness. Marnie Pomeroy. ErPo
When you the sunburnt pilgrim see. Good Counsel to a Young Maid. Thomas Carew. ErPo
When you think of the hosts without No. Limerick. *Unknown.* SiTL
When You Touch. William Hart-Smith. BoAV
When You Walk. James Stephens. PDV; WaKn
When you watch for. Feather or Fur. John Becker. FaPON; RePo; TiPo (1959 ed.)
When you were a tadpole and I was a fish. Evolution. Langdon Smith. BeLS; BLPA; FaBoBe; FaFP; HBV; TreF; YaD
When you were alive, my Leukothea. Leukothea. Keith Douglas. NeBP
When you were there, and you, and you. Dining-Room Tea. Rupert Brooke. BrPo; MoBrPo; POTE
When you were weary, roaming the wide world over. The Betrayal. Alice Furlong. AnIV
When You Will Walk in the Field. Leah Goldberg, *tr. fr. Hebrew by* Simon Halkin. TrJP
When you wreck a shock, the spot below. The Snake. Robert Penn Warren. CBV
When young-ey'd Spring profusely throws. Invocation to

Fancy. Joseph Warton. *Fr.* Ode to Fancy. OBEC
When Young Hearts Break. Heine, *tr. fr. German by* Louis Untermeyer. AWP
(Stars Look at Love, The.) LiTW
When young I scribbled, boasting, on my wall. The Summing-up. Stanley Kunitz. PoPl
When Young Melissa Sweeps. Nancy Byrd Turner. FaPON; GaP; OTPC (1946 ed.)
When Young Rogero goes to see a play. Veniunt Spectentur ut Ipsi. Henry Parrot. SiCE
When Younglings First. *Unknown.* EnRePo
When your belly. The Peaches. Joel Oppenheimer. CoPo
When your Christian duty calls you. God Is There. Walter E. Isenhour. STF
When your client's hopping mad. The Advertising Agency Song. *Unknown.* PV
When your feet are like lead. Consolatory! St. John Emile Clavering Hankin. CenHV
When your grapes formed, you swore to save them. Hoarded Grapes. *Unknown.* UnTE
When your heart is heavy laden. Prescription. A. L. Guerard. SoP
When your lips have turned to dust, and your hands. You Need Not Fear. Frances Frieseke. JKCP (1955 ed.)
When your perfections to my thoughts appear. Henry Constable. *Fr.* Diana. SiCE
When You're Away. Samuel Hoffenstein. BoLP; FiBHP
("When you're away, I'm restless, lonely.") InP
When you're looking for a Christian. You Can Be One! Edith C. Lilly. SoP
When you're lying awake with a dismal headache. The Lord Chancellor's Song [*or* Nightmare]. W. S. Gilbert. *Fr.* Iolanthe. CoBE; LiTM; NBM; OxBoLi; PCD; PoRA (rev. ed.); ShBV-3; SiTL; YT
When You're Throwed. *Unknown.* SCC
When you're tired and worn at the close of day. Confide in a Friend. *Unknown.* PoToHe (new ed.)
"When you're together with her, and you have a good excuse." Juan Ruiz, Archpriest of Hita. *Fr.* The Book of True Love. ErPo
When Youth and Beauty Meet Togither. *Unknown.* EIL
When youth had led me half the race. Earl of Surrey. EnRePo; SiPS
When Youth observes with pitying smile. In Praise of Commonplace. Sir Owen Seaman. InMe
When youth was lord of my unchallenged fate. On a Boy's First Reading of "King Henry V." S. Weir Mitchell. AA; PFY
When you've got a thing to say. Advice to Writers for the Daily Press. Joel Chandler Harris. OTD
When-a my blood runs chilly and col', Ise got to go. When My Blood Runs Chilly and Col'. *Unknown.* ABF
Whenas. *See also* When as.
Whenas her lute is tuned to her voice. Licia, XXXI. Giles Fletcher. TuPP
Whenas in Jeans. Paul Dehn. FiBHP
Whenas in Silks My Julia Goes. Robert Herrick. *See* Upon Julia's Clothes.
Whenas [*or* When as] man's life, the light of human lust. Caelica, LXXXVII [LXXVIII]). Fulke Greville. EP; GTBS-W; LiTB; MePo; OBS; OxBoCh; PoEL-1; PoIE
Whenas—methinks that is a pretty way. To His Ever-worshipped Will from W. H. "Francis." ErPo; FiBHP
Whenas [*or* When as *or* When that] the chill sirocco [*or* charocco] blows. In Praise of Ale [*or* Give Me Ale *or* Pipe and Can]. *Unknown.* ALV; FaBoCh; HBV; OBEV; OBS; SeCL; SeEP; ViBoPo
Whenas the mildest month. The Rose [*or* The Red Rose]. Thomas Howell. EIL; OBSC; PrWP; ReIE; TuPP
Whenas [*or* When as] the nightingale chanted [*or* chaunted] her vespers. Mark Antony. John Cleveland. ALV; AnAnS-2; EG; InvP; LiTL; SeCL; SeCP; UnTE; ViBoPo
Whenas [*or* When as] the Rye [Reach to the Chin]. George Peele. *Fr.* The Old Wives' Tale. CBEP; ELP; EnLoPo; FaBoCh; InvP; LO; LoGBV; NoP; SeCePo; SiTL; TuPP; ViBoPo
(Song: "Whenas [*or* When as] the rye reach to the chin.") ALV; AtBAP; EIL; FaBoEn; LoBV; OBSC; OxBoLi; PoEL-2
(Summer Song, A.) OBEV (new ed.)
Whenas to shoot my Julia goes. To Julia in Shooting Togs. Sir Owen Seaman. BOHV
Whence and Whither. Hayyim Nahman Bialik, *tr. fr. Hebrew by* Helena Frank. TrJP
Whence are ye, vague desires. Sehnsucht. Arthur Hugh Clough. EPN
"Whence are you, learning's son?" The End of Clonmacnois. *Unknown.* KiLC
Whence came his feet into my field, and why? He and I. Dante Gabriel Rossetti. The House of Life, XCVIII. MaVP; NBM; PoVP; ViPo
Whence came this man? As if on the wings. Abraham Lincoln. Samuel Valentine Cole. OHIP; PEDC
Whence came ye; and the people of the groves. The Light of Life. *Unknown.* OnPM
Whence come ye, Cherubs? from the moon? The Chanting Cherubs—a Group by Greenough. Richard Henry Dana. AA
Whence come you, all of you so sorrowful? Sonnet: To Certain Ladies. Dante. AWP
Whence comes my love? A Sonnet Made [*or* Lines] on Isabella Markham. John Harington. EIL; OBEC; TuPP
Whence Comes This Rush of Wings? *Unknown.* *See* Carol of the Birds.
Whence comest thou, Gehazi. Gehazi. Kipling. OtMeF
Whence Cometh My Help. P. L. Montgomery. OQP
Whence Cometh War? Robert Whitaker. OQP
Whence deathless Kit-Cat took its name. Epigram on the Toasts of the Kit-Kat Club, Anno 1716. Pope. CEP
Whence is it, that amazed I hear. To the Nightingale. William Cowper. PeER
Whence, O fragrant form of light. The Water-Lily. John Banister Tabb. AA; ACP; GoBC
Whence the sudden stir that roars through my vitals? Epithalamium for Mary Stuart and the Dauphin of France. George Buchanan. GoTS
Whence thou returnst, and whither wentst, I know. Leave Taking. Milton. *Fr.* Paradise Lost, XII. FaBoEn
Whenceness of the Which. *Unknown.* BOHV
Whene'er [*or* Where'er] a noble deed is wrought. Santa Filomena. Longfellow. PEDC; PoRL
Whene'er across this sinful flesh of mine. The Sign of the Cross. Cardinal Newman. GoBC; JKCP; PoVP; VA
Whene'er bitter foe attack thee. Advice to Hotheads. Samuel ben Elhanan Isaac Archevolti of Padua. TrJP
Whene'er I come where ladies are. Love at Large. Coventry Patmore. *Fr.* The Angel in the House. HoPM; PoVP; StP
Whene'er I look into thine eyes. Wenn Ich in Deine Augen Seh'. Heine. OuHeWo
Whene'er I quote I seldom take. The Bards We Quote. Bert Leston Taylor. HBMV; WhC
Whene'er I see soft hazel eyes. The Lapful of Nuts. *Unknown.* IrPN
Whene'er I take my walks abroad. More Walks. "Thomas Ingoldsby." BOHV
Whene'er there comes a little child. "That They All May Be One." Roden Noel. VA
Whene'er with haggard eyes I view. Song [*or* Song of One Eleven Years in Prison]. George Canning, George Ellis, *and* John Hookham Frere. *Fr.* The Rovers. ALV; BOHV; CEP; EiCL; FiBHP; OBEC; TOP
Whenever a Little Child Is Born. Agnes Louisa Carter Mason. AA; BiCB
Whenever a snowflake leaves the sky. Snowflakes [*or* The Snowflake *or* Winter]. Mary Mapes Dodge. AA; GFA; HBV; OTPC (1946 ed.); PRWS
Whenever Auntie moves around. Auntie's Skirts. Robert Louis Stevenson. MPB (1956 ed.); PoVP
Whenever he observes me purchasing. Sextus the Usurer. Martial. AWP
Whenever I am prone to doubt and wonder. God and Man. S. A. Nagel. MaRV
Whenever I come on kelp-stained nets. Beacon Light. Leslie Savage Clark. ChIP; PGD
Whenever I Go There. W. S. Merwin. NaP
Whenever I look in her kind eyes. Mother. *Unknown.* DD
"Whenever I plunge my arm, like this." Under the Waterfall. Thomas Hardy. CTC; LiTB; PoVP
Whenever I ride on the Texas plains. Texas Trains and Trails. Mary Austin. SoPo; TiPo

Whenever I Say "America." Nancy Byrd Turner. YeAr
Whenever I walk to Suffern along the Erie track. The House with Nobody in It. Joyce Kilmer. BLPA; MPB; SP; StVeCh
Whenever I'm walking in a wood. Which? Joyce L. Brisley. GFA
Whenever Mr. Edwards spake. The Theology of Jonathan Edwards. Phyllis McGinley. MoAmPo (1962 ed.)
Whenever Richard Cory went down town. Richard Cory. E. A. Robinson. AmePo; AmP; AmPP; AnNE; CaFP; CBV; CMoP; CoBA; DiPo; DTC; ExPo; FaFP; ForPo; GTBS-W; ILP; LiTA; LiTG; LiTM; LoGBV; MAP; MasP; MoAB; MoAmPo; MoVE; NeMA; NePA; NP; OnPP; OxBA; PAn; PFY; PoLF; PoMa; PoPo; PoRA; StPo; TDP; TOP; TreF; TrGrPo
Whenever the bright blue nails would drop. Nails. Leonard Feeney. WHL
Whenever the days are cool and clear. The Sandhill Crane. Mary Austin. TiPo
Whenever the heart is aching. Sweet Old Chapters. *Unknown.* SoP
Whenever the moon and stars are set. Windy Nights. Robert Louis Stevenson. BoChLi; BoTP; GoJo; PoRA; PoRh; PRWS; RIS; ShBV-1; SiSoSe; StaSt; TiPo
Whenever the Presbyterian bell. J. Milton Miles. Edgar Lee Masters. *Fr.* Spoon River Anthology. CrMA
Whenever the rain comes gently down. The Leaves Drink. Alice Wilkins. GFA
Whenever there is music, it is you. When There Is Music. David Morton. HBMV
Whenever there is silence around me. There Is a Man on the Cross. Elizabeth Cheney. ChIP; MaRV; OQP; PGD; SoP; TRV
Whenever troublous hours I find. Happiness amidst Troubles. Immanuel di Roma. TrJP
Whenever war, with its red woes. The Red Cross Spirit Speaks. John Huston Finley. PEDC
Whenever We Happen to Kiss. Heine, *ad. fr. German by* Louis Untermeyer. MeWo
Whenever we touched, I thought of the Lying-in Hospital. Elegy. Robert Layzer. NePoEA; PoPl
WhenIwas, The. Dick Lourie. *Fr.* Calls on the Dream Telephone. ThO
Wher One Would Be. Sir Edward Dyer. PoEL-1
Wher shall a man an object finde. *Unknown.* SeCSL
Where. Walter de La Mare. NYBP
Where? Kenneth Patchen. LiTM (1970 ed.); ToPo
Where/ you had only. To Celebrate My Body. Diane Wakoski. YAP
Where a Dogwood Stood. Earle J. Grant. SoP
Where a Roman Villa Stood, above Freiburg. Mary Elizabeth Coleridge. OBNC; PoMa
Where a twisted tree. The Possum and the Moon. David Campbell. MoAuPo; NeLNL
Where all the winds are tranquil. A Pine-Tree Buoy. Harrison Smith Morris. AA
Where all things grow according to their own design. The Meadow. John Wieners. CoPo
"Where am I from?" From the green hills of Erin. A Broken Song. "Moira O'Neill." OBVV; PG (1945 ed.)
Where am I, O awesome friend? Yitzhak Lamdan. *Fr.* For the Sun Declined. TrJP
Where ancient forests round us spread. Hymn for the Dedication of a Church. Andrews Norton. AA
Where angel trumpets hail a brighter sun. My Own Hereafter. Eugene Lee-Hamilton. WGRP
Where are Elmer, Herman, Bert, Tom and Charley. The Hill. Edgar Lee Masters. *Fr.* Spoon River Anthology. AmLP; AmP; CMoP; ExPo; LiTA; LiTM; NePA; NP; OxBA; ReMP; SeCeV; ViBoPo
Where are my friends? I am alone. School-fellows. Winthrop Mackworth Praed. *Fr.* School and Schoolfellows. NBM
Where are my people? To Egypt. Gloria Davis. NBP
Where are now, in coign or crack. Ballade of England. Louis MacNeice. NYBP
Where are now the Captains. A Ballad of the Captains. E. J. Brady. EtS
Where are the bay-leaves, Thestylis, and the charms. The Incantation. Theocritus, *tr. by* Charles Stuart Calverley. Idylls, II. AWP; JAWP; WBP
Where are the bay-leaves, Thestylis? where are the love-charms? The Second Idyll. Theocritus, *tr. by* Jack Lindsay. *Fr.* Idylls. LiTW
Where are the brass islands? The Relics. Harry Mathews. ANYP
Where are the braves, the faces like autumn fruit. Indian Reservation: Caughnawaga. Abraham Klein. LiTM (1970 ed.); OBCV
Where are the cats? Rain. Elizabeth J. Coatsworth. CIV
Where are the dear domestics, white and black. Familiar Faces, Long Departed. Robert Hillyer. NYBP
Where are the fields of dew? The Alphabet. James Reaney. ACV
Where are the friends that I knew in my Maying. Comrades. George Edward Woodberry. HBV; PFY
Where are the gods? Tell me, where is Aegir? We, the Few Who Believe. Harold Vinal. FiSC
Where are the great, whom thou would'st wish to praise thee? Isolation. Arthur Hugh Clough. *Fr.* Dipsychus. EPN; OBVV
Where are the heroes of yesteryear? Where, O Where? Milton Bracker. SD
Where are the loves that we have loved before. L'Envoi. Willa Cather. HBV
Where are the lumberjacks who came from the woods for Christmas. River Song. Elizabeth Brewster. CaP
Where Are the Men Seized in This Wind of Madness? Aldo do Espirito Santo, *tr. fr. Portuguese by* Alan Ryder. TTY
Where are the old side-wheelers now. The River Boats. Daniel Whitehead Hicky. AmFN
Where are the opium ships—gulls of the Indian seas? Opium Clippers. Daniel Henderson. EtS
Where are the passions they essayed. Ballade of Dead Actors. W. E. Henley. ALV; InP; OBMV; PoVP
Where are the people as beautiful as poems. The Black Angel. Henri Coulette. CoAP
Where are the ribbons I tie my hair with? Ballade of Lost Objects. Phyllis McGinley. PoCh; PoRA (rev. ed.)
Where are the ships I used to know. The Ships of Saint John. Bliss Carman. EtS
Where are the swallows fled? A Doubting Heart. Adelaide Anne Procter. HBV; VA
Where are the warriors, the young men? Earth. Rolland Snellings. BF
Where are they gone, and do you know. The Little Ghosts. Thomas S. Jones, Jr. HBV
Where are they gone, the old familiar faces? The Old Familiar Faces. Charles Lamb. *See also* I have had playmates, I have had companions. EnRP.
Where are they now, the lovely dust. The Dust of Love. Chad Walsh. NYTB
Where are they now, the softly blooming flowers. Irises. Padraic Colum. BoNaP
Where Are Those High and Haunting Skies. Richard Eberhart. TDP
Where are those legs with which you run. Johnny, I Hardly Knew Ye: In Dublinese. *Unknown.* OnYI
Where are we. Bahamas. George Oppen. NYBP
Where are we going? where are we going? Song of [the] Slaves in the Desert. Whittier. AmPP; AnAmPo; OBVV; OxBA; PFY
Where are we to go when this is done? Sonnet. Alfred A. Duckett. AmNP; PoNe
"Where are you [*or* Where you] coming from, Lomey Carter." Old Christmas [Morning]. Roy Helton. MaC; MAP; MoAmPo; NeMA; PoMS
Where are you, ever-youthful, that day by day. The Blind Singer. Friedrich Hölderlin. LiTW
"Where are you from?" A Broken Song. "Moira O'Neill." OBVV
Where Are You Going. Eliza Lee Follen. SoPo
Where are you going. Holiday. Ella Young. TiPo (1952 ed.)
Where are you going,/ My little cat? Eliza Lee Follen. *Fr.* The Little Kittens. BoTP
Where are you going,/ My little kittens? The Little Kittens. Eliza Lee Follen. BoTP; GFA; TiPo; UTS
Where Are You Going, Greatheart? John Oxenham. BLPA; PAL; PGD
(Great Heart.) MaRV
"Where are you going, Master mine?" Whither Away? Mary Elizabeth Coleridge. CH

"Where are you going, Mrs. Cat." Country Cat. Elizabeth J. Coatsworth. GoTP
"Where are you going, my good old man." My Good Old Man. *Unknown.* BFSS
"Where are you going, my little cat?" Where Are You Going. Eliza Lee Follen. SoPo
"Where are you going, my pretty little dear." Dabbling in the Dew. *Unknown.* UnTE
"Where are you going, my pretty little maid?" I said. Mary Jane, the Milkmaid. *Unknown.* BFSS
"Where are you going, my pretty little miss." My Pretty Little Miss. *Unknown.* BFSS
"Where are you going [to], my pretty maid?" The Milkmaid [*or* The Pretty Maid]. Mother Goose. BFSS; GaP; HBVY; OTPC; OxNR; RIS; SiTL
Where are you going, shepherdess? Song for the Divine Bride and Mother. Lope de Vega. HW
Where are you going? To Scarborough Fair? Scarborough Fair. *Unknown.* LO; OxBoLi
"Where are you going to-night, to-night." John Evereldown. E. A. Robinson. AmPP (4th ed.); NePA; OxBA
Where are you going, winsome maid. Arrows of Love. Bhartrihari. OnPM
Where are you going, you little pig? Little Piggy [*or* Piggies]. Thomas Hood. BoTP; SoPo
Where are you hid from me, belovèd one. Legend. John Hall Wheelock. LiTL; MoLP
Where are your ancient waves, O river. Home-coming. Albert Ehrenstein. TrJP
Where are your oranges? The Children's Bells. Eleanor Farjeon. BoTP; CH
Where art thou, belovèd To-Morrow? To-Morrow. Shelley. EPN
Where art thou gone, light-ankled youth? To Youth. Walter Savage Landor. BEL; EnRP; EPN; HBV; VA
Where art thou, Muse, that thou forget'st so long. Sonnets, C. Shakespeare. OBSC
Where art thou, my beloved son. The Affliction of Margaret. Wordsworth. EnRP; GTBS; GTBS-D; GTBS-P; GTBS-W; GTSE; GTSL; OBRV; PeER; PoEL-4
Where art thou Sol, while thus the blind-fold day. On a Foule Morning, Being Then to Take a Journey. Richard Crashaw. MaMe
"Where art thou wandering, little child?" The Little Maid and the Cowslips. John Clare. BoTP
Where Athanase once hankered for a star. Letter to Karl Shapiro. E. L. Mayo. MiAP
Where Ausonian summers glowing. To the Nautilus. Hartley Coleridge. VA
Where Avalanches Wail. *Unknown.* NA
Where balsams droop their fragrant boughs. Little Ponds. Arthur Guiterman. HBMV
Where be those roses gone which sweetened so our eyes? Astrophel and Stella, CII. Sir Philip Sidney. FCP; SiPS
Where Be You [*or* Ye] Going, You Devon Maid? Keats. ErPo; HBV; LiTL; PoeP; UnTE
Where beth they that biforen us weren. *See* Were beth they that . . .
Where broods the Absolute. Quest. Edmund Clarence Stedman. *Fr.* Corda Concordia. AA
Where Cadmus, old Agenor's son, did rest and plant his reign. The Fate of Narcissus. William Warner. *Fr.* Albion's England, IX. OBSC
Where can he be going. Issa, *tr. fr. Japanese by* R. H. Blyth. FIW
Where can the good, the beautiful, the great. The Freedom of the Press. Henrik Wergeland. PoFr
Where Cape Delgado strikes the sea. E. J. Pratt. *Fr.* The Cachalot. CaP; MoCV
Where Claribel low-lieth. Claribel. Tennyson. AtBAP; PeER; PoVP; ViPo
Where close the curving mountains drew. Untrodden Ways. Agnes Maule Machar. CaP
Where [*or* Whence] comes this rush of wings afar. Carol of the Birds. *Unknown.* ChrBoLe; OHIP
Where Covent Garden's famous temple stands. The Dangers of Football. John Gay. *Fr.* Trivia; or, The Art of Walking the Streets of London, II. EnLi-1 (1949 ed.); SD
Where cross the crowded ways of life. Christ in the City [*or* The City]. Frank Mason North. MaRV; SoP; WGRP
"Where did I come from, Mother, and why?" Christmas Lullaby for a New-born Child. Yvonne Gregory. AmNP
Where did Momotara go. Momotara. Rose Fyleman. TiPo
Where did the little boy go, you say. The Runaway. Daniel Whitehead Hicky. BrR
Where did the voice come from? Bedtime Story for My Son. Peter Redgrave. BoPe; NePoEA-2
Where Did You Borrow That Last Sigh? Sir William Berkeley. *Fr.* The Lost Lady. SeCL; TuPP
Where Did You Come From? George Macdonald. *See* Baby, The.
Where did you come from. Cotton Eye Joe. *Unknown.* OuSiCo
Where Did You Get That Hat? Joseph J. Sullivan. TreF
Where Didst Thou Find, Young Bard. Keats. CBEP
Where dips the rocky highland. The Stolen Child. W. B. Yeats. BEL; CMoP; EnLi-2 (1949 ed.); MPB; OnYI; OxBI; PoMS; POTE; PoVP; ViPo (1962 ed.)
Where Do All the Daisies Go? *Unknown.* PPL
Where Do I Love You, Lovely Maid? Raymond F. Roseliep. ISi
Where do people go when they go to sleep? Nightgown, Wife's Gown. Robert Sward. ELU
Where Do the Gipsies Come From? Henry Howarth Bashford. ALV; CH
"Where do the stars grow, little Garaine?" Little Garaine. Sir Gilbert Parker. FaPON; OTPC (1946 ed.); PRWS
Where do these voices stray. The Eccho. Richard Leigh. MePo
Where do we go, my love, who have been led. The Bed. James Merrill. NePoEA
Where do you come from. *See* Oh, where do you come from.
Where do you come from, Mr. Jay? Strange Lands. Laurence Alma-Tadema. DD; HBVY; OTPC; PRWS
Where do you sing your hymns. Lament for Richard Rolston. Sir Osbert Sitwell. ChMP
Where do you think I've been to-day? The Pigeon's Story. Jeannie Kirby. BoTP
Where do you think the Fairies go. The Fairies Shopping. Margaret Deland. HBVY; PRWS
Where do you walk this moment that I fall? Next of Kin. H. B. Mallalieu. WaP
Where does Pinafore Palace stand? Lilliput Levee. William Brighty Rands. CenHV; TSW
Where dost [*or* do'st] thou careless[e] lie. An Ode to Himself. Ben Jonson. AnAnS-2; AtBAP; EnRePo; ExPo; FaBoEn; LiTB; NoP; OAEP; OBS; PoEL-2; PoFr; QFR; SCEP-2; SeCePo; SeCeV; SeCL; SeCP; SeCV-1; SeEP; TuPP
Where Englands Damon us'd to keep. The Pastoral on the King's Death. Written in 1648. Alexander Brome. OBS
Where ere thy navy spreads her canvas wings. To the King on His Navy. Edmund Waller. CEP; EiCL
Where Europe and America build their arches. The Third Continent. Mary Erulkar. ACV
Where every female delights to give her maiden to her husband. Male & Female Loves in Beulah. Blake. *Fr.* Jerusalem. OBNC
Where finds philosophy her eagle eye. City and Country Life. William Cowper. *Fr.* The Task. CoBE
Where five old graves lay circled on a hill. The Graveyard. Jane Cooper. NePoEA-2
Where Fled. John Wieners. CoPo
Where folds the central lotus. William Yeats in Limbo. Sidney Keyes. MoBrPo (1962 ed.)
Where Forlorn Sunsets Flare and Fade. W. E. Henley. *See* Over the Hills and Far Away.
Where Foyle his swelling waters rolls northward to the main. The Maiden City. Elizabeth Tonna. HBV
Where girt with orchard and with olive-yard. An Etruscan Ring. John William Mackail. VA
Where glows the Irish hearth with peat. Cois na Teineadh. T. W. Rolleston. AnIV
Where Go the Boats? Robert Louis Stevenson. BoChLi; FaBoBe; FaBoCh; GoJo; LoGBV; MPB; PRWS; PTK; SoPo; StVeCh (1940 ed.); SUS; TiPo; TreFT
Where God had walked. The First Autumn. Marshall Schacht. MoRP; YT
Where Goest Thou? Victor Hugo. *See* Poet's Simple Faith, A.
Where great Pike's Peak his summit rears. Old Balaam. *Unknown.* PoOW
Where griping griefs the heart would wound. A Song to the Lute in Music. Richard Edwards. MuSP

Where had I heard this wind before. Bereft. Robert Frost. AnFE; AtBAP; CoAnAm; FaPL; LiTM; MAP; MoAB; MoAmPo; OxBA; PoDB; TwAmPo
Where hae ye been a' the day. *Unknown.* OxNR
Where has he of race divine. Chorus of Satyrs Driving Their Goats. Euripedes. *Fr.* The Cyclops. AWP; JAWP; WBP
Where hast been toiling all day, sweetheart. The Child on the Judgment Seat. Elizabeth Rundle Charles. BLPA
Where hast thou floated? In what seas pursued. To the Immortal Memory of the Halibut on which I Dined This Day, Monday, April 26, 1784. William Cowper. SeCePo
Where have all the colours gone? The Darkening Garden. *Unknown.* BoTP
Where have these hands been. Musician. Louise Bogan. GoJo; NYBP; UnS
Where have they gone. The Saint John. George Frederick Clarke. CaP
Where have they led you, into what disguise. The Kingdom. Jon Swan. NYBP
Where have we laid him now. The Lost Christ. Franklin E. Elmer, Jr. ChIP
Where have ye [*or* you] been all the day, Billy Boy, Billy Boy? Billy Boy. *Unknown.* LO; OxNR; SiTL
"Where have you been,/ Miss Marjorie Keen?" Banbury Fair. Edith G. Millard. BoTP
"Where have you been all the day." The Young Thing. *Unknown.* RIS
Where have you been all the day, Billy boy, Billy boy? *See* Where have ye been . . .
"Where have you been all the day, Randall, my son?" Lord Randall. *Unknown.* MaC
"Where have you been Billy boy, Billy boy." Billy Boy. *Unknown.* ABF, *with music*; BLPA; IHA
Where Have You Been, My Good Old Man? *with music.* *Unknown.* OuSiCo
Where have you been, South Wind, this May-day morning? South Wind. Siegfried Sassoon. BoTP
Where Have You Gone? Mari Evans. NNP; PoNe (1970 ed.); TTY
Where have you gone to, Yesterday. Yesterday. Hugh Chesterman. BoTP; SiSoSe
"Where have you hidden them?" I asked the sea. Lost Ships. Thomas Hornsby Ferril. EtS
Where Helen Comes. John Jerome Rooney. AA
Where Helen Sits. Laura E. Richards. AA
Where hills are hard and bare. Abraham's Knife. George Garrett. PoPl
Where hints of racy sap and gum. Wild Honey. Maurice Thompson. AnFE; APA; CoAnAm; HBV
Where His Lady Keeps His Heart. "A. W." CTC; ElL; OBSC
Where Hudson's Wave. George Pope Morris. AA
Where I go are flowers blooming. Les Planches-en-Montagne. Michael Roberts. OBMV
Where I Live in This Honorable House of the Laurel Tree. Anne Sexton. TwAmPo
Where I lived the river. Eclogues. Dennis Schmitz. YAP
Where I spat in the harbor the oranges were bobbing. The Metamorphoses. Randall Jarrell. FiMAP; TPM
Where I Took Hold of Life. Robert P. Tristram Coffin. BiCB
Where I was born, near Stepney Green. Stepney Green. John Singer. WaP
Where icy and bright dungeons lift. Voyages, VI. Hart Crane. AnFE; CABA; CoAnAm; MAP; MoAB; MoAmPo; MoVE; SeCeV; TwAmPo; UnPo (3d ed.)
Where Ignorance Is Bliss. Thomas Gray. *Fr.* Ode on a Distant Prospect of Eton College. TreF
Where in its old historic splendor stands. The Hudson. George Sidney Hellman. AA
Where in the attic the dust encumbers. Mournful Numbers. Morris Bishop. WhC
Where in the summer-warm woodlands with the sweet wind. Iphione. Thomas Caulfield Irwin. EnLoPo; IrPN
Where in the valley the summer rain. Summer Rain. Laurie Lee. MoVE
Where innocent bright-eyed daisies are. Daisies. Christina Rossetti. *Fr.* Sing-Song. RIS
Where is a golden goblet fill'd so deep. The Golden Elegy. Leopold Staff. LiTW
Where is Australia, singer, do you know? Last Stanzas of "The Bush." Bernard O'Dowd. *Fr.* The Bush. BoAu; PoFr
Where Is Dominga? Francisco de Sá de Miranda, *tr. fr. Spanish by* Sir John Bowring. OnPM
Where is every piping lad. Dawn of Day. William Browne. *Fr.* The Shepherd's Pipe. ElL
Where Is Fancy Bred. Shakespeare. *See* Tell Me Where Is Fancy Bred.
Where Is God? Minot J. Savage. OQP
"Where is God!" inquired the mind. Evidence. Thomas Curtis Clark. MaRV
Where is he gone, the queer little man. Bill Manning. Joseph I. C. Clarke. JKCP (1926 ed.)
Where Is Heaven? Bliss Carman. *Fr.* Here and Now. GoTP; MaRV; OQP; TRV
Where is it now? Look, there it flies in merry sport. The Swallow's Flight. Louis Levy. TrJP
Where Is My Butterfly Net? David McCord. FiBHP
Where is my chief, my master, this bleak night, mavrone? O'Hussey's Ode to the Maguire [*or* Ode to the Maguire]. *Unknown, at. to* Eochadh O'Hussey. AnIV; IrPN; OnYI; OxBI; SeCePo
Where is my kingdom? I would be king. Kingdoms. Charles Oluf Olsen. OQP
"Where is my little basket gone?" Kitty in the Basket. Eliza Lee Follen. SAS
Where is my mother? Bothering Me at Last. David Ignatow. WOW
Where is my ruined life, and where the fame. Odes. Hafiz. AWP
Where Is My Wandering Boy Tonight? *Unknown.* FaFP; TreF
"Where is now Elijah's God?" A Martyr's Death. Menahem ben Jacob. TrJP
Where is one that, born of woman, altogether can escape. The Making of Man. Tennyson. EPN
Where Is Paris and Heleyne? Thomas of Hales. *Fr.* A Love-Song. ChTr
Where is poor Jesus gone? Jesus. Francis Lauderdale Adams. OxBS
Where is she now? Where all must be. *Unknown.* LO
Where is that holy fire, which verse is said Heroicall Epistle. John Donne. MaMe
Where is that sugar, Hammond? Early Evening Quarrel. Langston Hughes. HoPM
Where is the beauteous majesty of Denmark? Shakespeare. *Fr.* Hamlet, IV, v. AtBAP
Where is the forest, through whose echoing glade. Schubert's Ninth Symphony. Margaret Stanley-Wrench. MuSP
Where is the gallant race that rose. Thomas Mercer. *Fr.* Arthur's Seat. OxBS
Where is the Grand Duke Ruffanuff, who stole the Czar's first wife? And When They Fall. James J. Montague. HBMV
Where is the grave of Sir Arthur O'Kellyn? The Knight's Tomb. Samuel Taylor Coleridge. CBEP; EnRP; EPN; ERoP-1; FaBoCh; GN; InP; LoGBV; ShBV-1
Where is the hand to trace. With a Coin from Syracuse. Oliver St. John Gogarty. OBMV
Where is the home for me? The Home of Aphrodite. Euripedes. *Fr.* Bacchae. AWP
Where is the Jim Crow section. Merry-go-round. Langston Hughes. PoNe
"Where is the Kingdom?" asked the solemn [*or* pompous] priest. The Kingdom. Thomas Curtis Clark. ChIP; MaRV
Where is the man who has been tried and found strong and sound? A Degenerate Age. Solomon ibn Gabirol. TrJP
Where is the nightingale. Song [*or* Songs] from Cyprus. Hilda Doolittle ("H. D."). MAP; MoAmPo; NeMA
Where is the nymph, whose azure eye. Song. Thomas Moore. EnLoPo
Where Is the Real Non-Resistant? Vachel Lindsay. OQP; StJW
Where Is the Sea? Felicia Dorothea Hemans. EtS
Where is the star of Bethlehem? Christmas 1959 et Cetera. Gerald William Barrax. Kal
Where is the true man's fatherland? The Fatherland. James Russell Lowell. GN; HBV; HBVY; MaRV; OTPC; PGD; PoPl; PoRL; PTK
Where is the word of Your youth and beauty. To the Young Man Jesus. Annie Charlotte Dalton. CaP
Where is the world we roved, Ned Bunn? To Ned. Herman Melville. MWA-1; PoEL-5; ViBoPo
Where is there an end of it, the soundless wailing. T. S. Eli-

ot. *Fr.* Four Quartets: The Dry Salvages. FaBoTw
Where is this stupendous stranger. The Nativity of Our Lord. Christopher Smart. *Fr.* Hymns and Spiritual Songs. EiCP; LoBV; PoEL-3
Where Is Thy Brother? *Unknown.* MaRV
Where Is Thy God? J. Lewis Milligan, *paraphrased fr.* Psalm XLII, Bible, *O.T.* MaRV
Where Is Thy God, My Soul? Thomas T. Lynch. MaRV
Where is thy lovely perilous abode? To the Leanán Shee. Thomas Boyd. OnYI
Where Is Your Boy Tonight? *Unknown.* PaPo
Where It Is Winter. George O'Neil. HBMV
Where It's At: A Melody for Breath. Lenore Kandel. FRC
Where Lackawanna's tracks graze our backyards. 'Laine. Robert Bagg. TwAmPo
Where Late the Sweet Birds Sang. Shakespeare. *See* Sonnets, LXXIII.
Where leap the long Atlantic swells. The Cod-Fisher. Joseph C. Lincoln. EtS
Where leaves are glassy green. The Air in Spring. Basil Dowling. AnNZ
Where Lies the Land [to Which the Ship Would Go]? Arthur Hugh Clough. Songs in Absence, VII. AWP; BEL; BoTP; ChTr; EtS; FaBoBe; FaBoCh; GN; HBV; ILP; JAWP; LoGBV; MCCG; OBVV; OTPC (1946 ed.); PoIE; TOP; TreFT; VA; ViPo; ViPP; WBP; WGRP
(Songs in Absence.) OQP
("Where lies the land to which the ship would go.") EPN; GTBS; GTBS-D; GTSL
Where Lies the Land to Which Yon Ship Must Go? Wordsworth. EnRP; EtS; MBW-2; OBNC; PoEL-4; Sonn
(Sonnet: "Where lies the land to which yon ship must go?") ChER
Where, like a pillow on a bed. The Ecstasy [*or* The Extasie]. John Donne. AnAnS-1; AnFE; ATP; CABA; CBEP; DiPo; EnLoPo; EnRePo; ExPo; FaBoEn; LiTB; LiTG; LO; LoBV; MaMe; MaPo; MasP; MBW-1; MeLP; MemP; MeP; MePo; NoP; OBEV; OBS; PIA; PoEL-2; PoFS; PoIE; ReEn; ReIE; SCEP-1; SeCePo; SeCeV; SeCP; SeCV-1; SeEP; StP; TDP; TrGrPo; TuPP; UnTE; ViBoPo
Where lives the man that never yet did hear. Orchestra [*or* Of Homer's Odyssey]. Sir John Davies. EG; OBSC; ReIE; SiPS; TuPP
Where long the shadows of the wind had rolled. The Sheaves. E. A. Robinson. AP; AWP; CMoP; CoBMV; DiPo; FaBV; ForPo; InPo; JAWP; MAmP; MAP; MaPo; MoAB; MoAmPo; NePA; OxBA; PoSa; PTK; TOP; WBP; WHA; YT
Where Love Is. Amelia Josephine Burr. HBV
Where Love Is King. Hilda Doolittle ("H. D."). *Fr.* Hymen. HBMV
Where Love, There's Heaven. Mary Jacobs. STF
Where many an eagle builds her nest. On Mount Tsukuba. Mushimaro. OnPM
Where may the wearied eye repose. Washington [*or* The Cincinnatus of the West]. Byron. *Fr.* Ode to Napoleon Buonaparte. DD; MC; OHIP; PaA; PAH; PAL; PoRL
Where men have held the vision clear. The Seekers. Lucia Trevitt Auryansen. OQP
Where might there be a refuge for me. Tell Me, Tell Me. Marianne Moore. LiTM (1970 ed.); NYBP
Where More Is Meant. Christopher Morley. RePo
Where mountains round a lonely dale. The Mowers. William Allingham. IrPN
Where murdered Mumford lies. Mumford. Ina M. Porter. PAH
Where My Books Go. W. B. Yeats. OBEV; OBVV
Where my fathers stood. Devon to Me. John Galsworthy. HBMV
Where my grandmother lived. Doughtry Long, Jr. TNV
Where my kindred dwell, there I wander. Dawn Boy's Song. *Unknown, tr. by* Washington Matthews. FaBV
Where My Step Falters. Marjorie Meeker. NP
Where My Word is unspoken. T. S. Eliot. *Fr.* The Rock. TRV
Where neither king nor shepheard want comes neare. Homer. *Fr.* The Odyssey, IV. CTC
Where no one was was where my world was stilled. Isle of Arran. Alastair Reid. WIRo
Where none but Nature is the guide, Minerva hath no part. To the Reader. Thomas Howell. SiCE
Where nothing is, a little thing doth ease. Of Nothing and Althing. John Heywood. SiCE
Where now are all my flattering dreams of joy. Love Elegy. Tobias George Smollett. WaPE
Where now he roves, by wood or swamp whatever. Proem to "The Kid." Conrad Aiken. *Fr.* The Kid. MoAB
Where now lies Mustolphus? Everywhere. Why? Against Mustolphus His Lying. John Davies of Hereford. SiCE
Where now these mingled ruins lie. Stanzas Occasioned by the Ruins of a Country Inn [*or* On the Ruins of a Country Inn]. Philip Freneau. AA; OxBA
Where nowadays the Battery lies. Peter Stuyvesant's New Year's Call. Edmund Clarence Stedman. PaA; PAH
Where O America are you. After Dead Souls. Allen Ginsberg. CBV
Where, O Where? Milton Bracker. SD
Where, Oh Where Are the Hebrew Children. *Unknown.* BLPA
Where O Where Is Old Elijah? *with music.* *Unknown.* AS
Where old-time ships came, canvas seagull-white. Sea-Chronicles. Rex Ingamells. BoAV
Where, on the mountain peaks high up. On the Mountains. Alcman. LiTW
Where on the wrinkled stream the willows lean. The Water-Ousel. Mary Webb. CH
Where once the grey scrub's finches cried with thin. The Tank. Roland Robinson. PoAu-2
Where once the sun had dragged its humid breath. Homage. George O'Neil. AnAmPo
Where once we danced, where once we sang. An Ancient to Ancients. Thomas Hardy. ChMP; CMoP; CoBMV; GTBS-P; LiTM (rev. ed.); MoPo; MoVE; PoVP; TOP
Where once we hunted, white men have built many long-houses. Speech of the Salish Chief. Earle Birney. *Fr.* Damnation of Vancouver. OBCV
Where only flowers fret. Aegean. Louis Simpson. NYBP
Where ought youth to be. Winged Heels. Harry Lee. BBV (1923 ed.)
Where oxen do low. Second Dialogue between Crab and Gilluan. Thomas Durfey. *Fr.* The Bath; or, The Western Lass. PeRV
Where prophets' word, and martyrs' blood. Samuel Longfellow. *Fr.* Behold, the Fields Are White. FaChP
Where racial memories, like snakes. Landscape of Violence. R. N. Currey. PeSA
Where rain-wet crosses know the dawn that gleams. Songs above the Dust. Grantland Rice. PaA
Where Roots Tangle. Raymond Roseliep. FiSC
Where Runs the River. Francis William Bourdillon. HBV; WGRP
Where Shall a Sorrow Great. *Unknown.* EnRePo
Where shall Celia fly for shelter. Song. Christopher Smart. EnLoPo
Where Shall I Be When de Firs' Trumpet Soun'? *with music.* *Unknown.* BoAN-1
Where shall I find you. Sub Terra. William Carlos Williams. NP
"Where shall I gang, my ain true love?" The Duke of Athole's Nurse. *Unknown.* ESPB
Where shall I go then. R. P. Blackmur. Sea Island Miscellany, XIV. MoVE
Where shall I have at mine own will. Sir Thomas Wyatt. FCP; SiPS
Where shall I hide my head and my face? Breaking. J. Alex Allan. PoAu-2
Where shall I learn to get my peace again? Keats. *Fr.* Lines to Fanny. ChER
Where shall my troubled soul, at large. Echo in a Church. Lord Herbert of Cherbury. AnAnS-2; SeCSL
Where shall once the wanderer weary. Exile. Heine. OnPM
Where Shall the Baby's Dimple Be? Josiah Gilbert Holland. BLPA
Where Shall the Lover Rest. Sir Walter Scott. *Fr.* Marmion, III. CH, *abr.*; EnRP; GTBS; GTBS-D; GTBS-P; GTBS-W; GTSE, 4 *sts.*; GTSL
(Song: "Where shall the lover rest.") NBM; OBRV; PoEL-4; ViBoPo
Where Shall We Dance? "Gabriela Mistral," *tr. fr. Spanish by* Alice Stone Blackwell. OnPM
Where shall we find a perfect life whereby. The Perfect Life. Charles Francis Richardson. BePJ
Where shall we find Thee—where art Thou, O God? Search. Margaret Widdemer. TrPWD

Where shall we get religion? Beneath the open sky. Nature and Religion. Sam Walter Foss. *Fr.* The Higher Catechism. OQP
Where shall we go? August Afternoon. Marion Edey. YeAr
Where shall we go? The Hounded Lovers. William Carlos Williams. MoLP; NYBP; TrGrPo
"Where shall we go for our garlands glad." A Song of Autumn. Adam Lindsay Gordon. BoAu
Where shall we learn to die? Teach Us to Die. Arthur Penrhyn Stanley. VA
Where shall we our great professor inter. A Serio-Comic Elegy. Richard Whately. ShM
Where shall we seek for a hero, and where shall we find a story? Crispus Attucks. John Boyle O'Reilly. PAH
Where Shall Wisdom Be Found? Job, XXVIII: 12-20, 28, Bible, *O.T.* TreFT
Where Shall Wisdom Be Found? Euripides, *tr. fr. Greek by* Gilbert Murray. *Fr.* Bacchae. UnS
Where She Her Sacred Bower Adorns. Thomas Campion. LoBV
(Her Sacred Bower.) HBV
Where ships of purple gently toss. Emily Dickinson. AmP; AmPP
Where should he seek, to go away. The Mark. Louise Bogan. MoPo; MoVE; NP
Where should this music be? I' the air, or the earth? Shakespeare. *Fr.* The Tempest, I, ii. UnS
Where skies are thunderous, by a cypress walk. Some Negatives: X. at the Chateau. James Merrill. NePoEA-2
Where southern suns and winds prevail. The Nautilus. Charlotte Smith. OTPC (1923 ed.)
Where sunless rivers weep. Dream Land. Christina Rossetti. EnLi-2; PoVP; ViPo; VP
Where swallows and wheatfields are. Refuge. Archibald Lampman. PeCV (1967 ed.)
Where swell the songs thou shouldst have sung. A Soldier Poet. Rossiter Johnson. AA
Where tender Love had laid him down to sleep. Thomas Watson. *Fr.* Hecatompathia. ReIE
Where the air in this room warms by the fire like a cat. Protest. Vassar Miller. ToPo
Where the bee sucks, there suck I. Shakespeare. *Fr.* The Tempest, V, i. AnEnPo; AnFE; AWP; BEL; BoTP; CABA; CBEP; CH; CTC; DiPo; EG; EIL; EnLi-1; EnLit; EnRePo; FaBV; GN; GTSL; HBV; HBVY; ILP; InPo; JAWP; MaPo (1969 ed.); MCCG; MPB; NoP; OBEV; OBSC; OTPC; PCD; PCH; PDV; PoPl; PoRh; PTK; RIS; SeCeV; SiCE; ThWaDe; TiPo; TOP; TreFT; UTS; ViBoPo; WBP; WHA; YAT
Where the Blessed Feet Have Trod. "Michael Field." OxBoCh; StJW
Where the Blue Horses. Raymond Souster. PeCV (1967 ed.)
Where the bluebells and the wind are. Bluebells. Walter de la Mare. MPB
Where the buttercups so sweet. The Little Herd-Boy's Song. Robert Buchanan. BoTP
Where the Canyon spreads on either hand. Hangman's Tree. Lillian Zellhoefer White. AmFN
Where the cedar leaf divides the sky. Passage. Hart Crane. CMoP; ExPo; MoVE
Where the Cedars. Jacob Glatstein, *tr. fr. Yiddish by* Joseph Leftwich. TrJP
Where the cement-lined bowels of the city. The Hunt. Babette Deutsch. AnAmPo
Where the cities end, the. Transcontinent. Donald Hall. OCS
Where the city's ceaseless crowd moves on the livelong day. Sparkles from the Wheel. Walt Whitman. AP; DiPo; FaBoEn; MWA-1
Where the cowboys roost on the green rolling prairie. A Kansas Cowboy. *Unknown.* CoSo
Where the dark green hollows lift. Sea-Gulls. Norah M. Holland. MCCG
Where the Dead Men Lie. Barcroft Henry Boake. BoAu; BoAV; NeLNL; PoAu-1
Where the decay begins, the sun. The Smell on the Landing. Peter Porter. NMP
Where the dews and the rains of heaven have their fountain. The Battle in the Clouds. William Dean Howells. PAH
Where the dreaming Tiber wanders by the haunted Appian Way. The Magpie's Song. Frank S. Williamson. BoAu
Where the drift went the waters answered it. "Final Status Never Ascertained." Lloyds Registry. Merrill Moore. MAP; MoAmPo (1942 ed.)
Where the Dropwort Springs Up Lithe and Tall. John Lyle Donaghy. NeIP
Where the flowers lean to their shadows on the wall. Shadows of Chrysanthemums. E. J. Scovell. MoVE
Where the fountain murmurs in the shade. Love in Age. Ethel Anderson. MoAuPo
Where the graves were many, we looked for one. In Clonmel Parish Churchyard. Sarah Morgan Bryan Piatt. AA
Where the Grizzly Dwells. James Fox. SCC
Where the hare-bells are ringing. The Lily of the Valley. Thomas Lovell Beddoes. EG
Where the Hayfields Were. Archibald MacLeish. LOW
Where the ironbarks are hanging leaves disconsolate and pale. The Lonely Woman. M. Forrest. BoAu
Where the lazy wall is down. Sierran Vigil. Ewart Milne. NeIP
Where the Leprosy Begins. William Cowper. *Fr.* Expostulation. SoP
Where the Lilies Used to Spring. David Gray. OxBS
Where the Manatee Plays and the Manta Ray Flutters. Harold Witt. NYTB
Where the Mind Is without Fear. Rabindranath Tagore. Gitanjali, XXXV. PoFr
Where the mob gathers, swiftly shoot along. Of Pick-Pockets. John Gay. *Fr.* Trivia; or, The Art of Walking the Streets of London, III. EnLi-1 (1949 ed.)
Where the Moosatockmaguntic. Hiram Hover. Bayard Taylor. BOHV
Where the northern ocean darkens. Watch, America. Robert Nathan. WaKn
Where the Northern Ocean in vast whirls. Sea-Birds. James Thomson. EtS
Where the orange-branches mingle on the sunny garden-side. The Demon of the Mirror. Bayard Taylor. BeLS
Where the Pelican Builds. Mary Hannay Foott. PoAu-1
Where the Picnic Was. Thomas Hardy. MoPW
Where the pools are bright and deep. A Boy's Song. James Hogg. BoChLi; BoTP; CH; FaPON; GaP; HBV; HBVY; LiTG; MoShBr; OBEV; OTPC (1946 ed.); PCH; PoRh; PRWS; RIS; StVeCh (1940 ed.); TVC; WaKn; WiR
Where the quiet-colored end of evening smiles. Love among the Ruins. Robert Browning. BEL; BoLiVe; CoBE; EnL; EnLi-2 (1949 ed.); EnLit; EPN; FaBV; GTSE; HBV; MaPo; MBW-2; MCCG; OAEP; OBEV (new ed.); OBVV; PoAn; PoEL-5; PoVP; TOP; UnPo (1st ed.); ViPo; ViPP; VP
Where the Rainbow Ends. Robert Lowell. AmP; AnNE; AP; CoBMV; FiMAP; MoAB; MoAmPo (1950 ed.); NePoEA; OnHM; PoeP; TrGrPo (rev. ed.)
Where the Rainbow Ends. Richard Rive. PBA; TTY
Where the ramparts tower in flame or shadow. Epitaph in Anticipation. Leonard Bacon. WhC
Where the remote Bermudas ride. Bermudas [*or* Song of the Emigrants in Bermuda]. Andrew Marvell. AnAnS-1; AtBAP; AWP; CABA; CBEP; CEP; CH; ChTr; CoBE; EnL; ExPo; FaBoCh; FaBoEn; GN; GTBS; GTBS-D; GTBS-P; GTBS-W; GTSE; GTSL; HBV; ILP; InPo; LoBV; LoGBV; MaMe; MeP; MePo; NoP; OAEP; OBEV; OBS; OTPC (1923 ed.); OxBoCh; PAH; PoE; PoFS; ReEn; SCEP-2; SeCeV; SeCL; SeCP; SeCV-1; SeEP; ShBV-3; ThLM; ViBoPo
Where the ripe pears droop heavily. The Wasp. "Fiona Macleod." PCH; TSW
Where the road came, no longer bearing men. The Supplanting. Wendell Berry. NYTB
Where the salt creek broadens to a brown lagoon. The Hermit. James K. Baxter. AnNZ
Where the sea gulls sleep or indeed where they fly. The Ballet of the Fifth Year. Delmore Schwartz. MoAB; OxBA; TwCP
Where the seas are open moor. The Harpooning. Ted Walker. WIRo
Where the short-legged Esquimaux. An Arctic Vision. Bret Harte. PAH; MC
Where the Single Men Go in Summer. Nina Bourne. FiBHP
Where the slanting forest eves. To Nature Seekers. Robert W. Chambers. MoShBr
Where the slow river. Leda. Hilda Doolittle ("H. D.") HBMV; InPo
Where the small eels that left the deeper way. Thoughts by the Shore. George Crabbe. PoG
Where the snowy peaks gleam in the moonlight. Land Where

the Columbines Grow. Arthur J. Fynn. PoOW
Where the streams wind and the wind is always sighing. Jade Flower Palace. Tu Fu. LiTW
Where the sun shines in the street. Seeking [*or* Feet]. Mary Carolyn Davies. OQP; WGRP
Where the thistle lifts a purple crown. Daisy. Francis Thompson. AnEnPo; AWP; BeLS; BrPo; EnLit; FaBV; GoBC; GTBS-D; HBV; MoAB; MoBrPo; NeMA; OBEV (new ed.); OBNC; OBVV; VA; WHA
Where the waves of burning cloud are rolled. Ballade of the Dreamland Rose. Brian Hooker. HBMV
Where the western zun, unclouded. Zun-zet. William Barnes. PoEL-4
Where the wheel of light is turned. Pole Star for This Year. Archibald MacLeish. AmPP; AP; CoBMV; NAMP; NePA; OxBA
Where the white bridge rears up its stamping arches. In Memory of the Spanish Poet Federico García Lorca. Thomas Merton. ML
Where the Wild Thyme Blows. Shakespeare. *See* Violet Bank, A.
Where the wild wave, from ocean proudly swelling. Fort Bowyer. Charles L. S. Jones. PAH
Where the wings of a sunny dome expand. America. Herman Melville. MAmP
Where the Wood-Thrush Calls. Jessie Wallace Hughan. TSW
Where the world is grey and lone. The Ice King. A. B. Demille. WHW
Where then shall Hope and Fear their objects find? Prayer. Samuel Johnson. *Fr.* The Vanity of Human Wishes. EnLi-1 (1949 ed.); OBEC
"Where There Is No Vision," *abr.* Elizabeth Barrett Browning. *Fr.* Aurora Leigh, II. MaRV
Where there is nothing more to see. The Secret Wood. Andrew Young. POTE
Where there is personal liking we go. The Hero. Marianne Moore. *Fr.* Part of a Novel, Part of a Poem, Part of a Play. CMoP; OnHM; OxBA; TwAmPo
Where There's a Will There's a Way. Eliza Cook. BLPA; FaFP; TreF
Where There's a Will There's a Way. John Godfrey Saxe. (Find a Way.) PEDC
(On Fort Sumter, *ad., with add. st. by unknown author.*) MC; PAH
"Where There's Drink." *Unknown.* SoP
Where they once dug for money. The Old Marlborough Road. Henry David Thoreau. PoEL-4
Where They Were. *Unknown. See* If You Want to Know Where the Privates. Are.
Where thou dwellest, in what grove. The Birds. Blake. CH; OBRV
Where through entangling bays. Freedom the Goddess. Arthur Wilberforce Jose. BoAu; PoFr
Where to Seek Love. Blake. *Fr.* William Bond. TRV
("I thought love lived in the hot sunshine.") LO
Where tomahawks flash in the powwow. Late Late. George Starbuck. PPON
Where tom-tom drummed. The Inheritors. Dorothy Livesay. CaP
Where troops of virgins follow the lamb. O Glory of Virgins. Fortunatus. ISi
Where Truest Pleasure Is. *Unknown. See* Fain Would I Change That Note.
Where Unimaginably Bright. Oliver Hale. GoYe
Where Venta's Norman castle still uprears. Sonnet: On King Arthur's Round Table at Winchester. Thomas Warton, the Younger. Sonnets, VIII. EiPP; Sonn
Where voices vanish into dream. Elected Silence. Siegfried Sassoon. MoBrPo
Where wards are weak[e], and foes encountring strong. Scorn Not the Least. Robert Southwell. NCEP; SiCE
"Where was you last night, my ramboling son." My Ramboling Son. *Unknown.* BFSS
Where wast thou when I laid the foundations of the earth? Job, Bible, *O.T.* ImOP; PoG
Where water folds across the stones. Heritage. A. M. Sullivan. JKCP (1955 ed.)
Where we made the fire. Where the Picnic Was. Thomas Hardy. MoPW
Where We Must Look for Help. Robert Bly. NePoEA
Where we walk to school each day. Indian Children. Annette Wynne. BoChLi; GaP; GFA; MPB; OTPC (1946 ed.); PCH; SoPo; StVeCh; SUS; TiPo
Where we went in the boat was a long bay. The Mediterranean. Allen Tate. AmP; AP; ExPo; FaBoMo; InPo; LiTA; LiTG; LiTM; MAP; MoAB; MoAmPo; MoVE; NePA; PoCh; PoFS; ReMP; SeCeV; TwAmPo; VaPo
Where were the greenhouses going. Big Wind. Theodore Roethke. AmPP (5th ed.); GoJo; InvP; NoP; ViBoPo (1958 ed.)
Where were the pathways that your childhood knew? First Pathways. Sidney Royse Lysaght. OBVV
Where were we in that afternoon? Anniversary. Richmond Lattimore. NYBP; PoCh
Where were ye, birds, that bless His name? The Child, II. John Banister Tabb. AA
Where Were You? *Unknown.* SoP
Where were you then? A Story. Margaret Avison. MoCV
Where wert thou, Soul, ere yet my body born. Soul and Body. Samuel Waddington. OBVV; VA
Where? When? Which? Langston Hughes. Kal; NePoAm-2
Where, where but here have Pride and Truth. On Hearing That the Students of Our New University Have Joined the Agitation against Immoral Literature. W. B. Yeats. FaBoTw
Where, where will be the birds that sing. A Hundred Years to Come. Hiram Ladd Spencer, *wr. at. to* William Goldsmith Brown. HBV
Where white, stares, smokes or breaks. Aegean Islands 1940-41. Bernard Spencer. NeBP
Where will they stop, those breathing powers. Devotional Incitements. Wordsworth. OxBoCh
Where will your training lead. The Boy Washington. Dorothy Brown Thompson. SiSoSe
Where wilt thou go my harassed heart? Emily Brontë. *Fr.* Little While, a Little While, A. LO
Where wit is over-ruled by will. Desire's Government. "A. W." ElL
Where, without bloodshed, can there be. Long Feud. Louis Untermeyer. AnAmPo; AnFE; APA; CoAnAm; MAP; MoAmPo; NeMA
Where yonder ancient willow weeps. Alexander McLachlan. *Fr.* A Backwoods Hero. CaP
Where you can go farther and see less. West Texas. *At. to* Leona Mae Austin. CoSo
"Where you coming from, Lomey Carter?" *See* "Where are you coming from, Lomey Carter?"
Where you (in this saying) lag in the waving woods. Love Poem. W. S. Graham. FaBoMo
Where You Passed. Amelia Josephine Burr. HBMV
Where You've Put Me. *Unknown.* SoP
Whereas Aongus, the philosophic. On a Cock Which Was Stolen from a Good Priest. Egan O'Rahilly. OnYI
Whereas, on certain boughs and sprays. The Lawyer's Invocation to Spring. Henry Howard Brownell. BOHV; PoLF
Whereas the rebels hereabout. Tom Gage's Proclamation. Thomas Flucker. PAH
Whereas we twain, who still are bound for life. A Separation Deed. Sir Lewis Morris. OBVV
Whereat Erewhile I Wept, I Laugh. Robert Greene. *Fr.* Arbasto. ElL
Where-e'er My Flatt'ring Passions Rove. Isaac Watts. *See* Hazard of Loving the Creatures, The.
Where'er a noble deed is wrought. *See* Whene'er a noble deed is wrought.
Where'er have trod Thy sacred feet. With Thee to Soar to the Skies. *Unknown.* BePJ
Where'er there's a thistle to feed a linnet. Poets and Linnets. Tom Hood. CenHV; HBV
Where'er thy navy spreads her canvas wings. To the King, on His Navy. Edmund Waller. NoP; SCEP-2
Wherefore Hidest Thou Face, and Holdest Me for Thine Enemy? Francis Quarles. *See* Why Dost Thou Shade Thy Lovely Face?
Wherefore I ask that ye faint not at my tribulations for you. Ephesians, Bible, *N.T.* BoC
Wherefore, O fair one, dost withhold thy messengers. Parted Lovers. Judah Halevi. LiTW
Wherefore sou'd ye talk o' love. Willie and Helen. Hew Ainslie. HBV; LO; OBEV
"Wherefore starts my bosom's lord?" Comfort in Affliction. William E. Aytoun. BOHV; InMe

Wherefore these revels that my dull eyes greet? The Royal Mummy to Bohemia. Charles Warren Stoddard. AA
Wherefore this busy labor without rest? Tuskegee. Leslie Pinckney Hill. BANP; PoNe
Wherefore tonight so full of care. Dejection. Robert Bridges. QFR
Wherefore, Unlaurelled Boy. George Darley. *See* Solitary Lyre, The.
Wherefore was that cry? She Should Have Died Hereafter. Shakespeare. *Fr.* Macbeth V, v. FiP
Where's an old woman to go when the years. The Riddle. "H. E. H." PoToHe
Where's Commander All-a-Tanto? Herman Melville. *Fr.* Bridegroom Dick. OnAP; PoEL-5, *longer sel.*
Where's he that died o' Wednesday? Falstaff's Song. Edmund Clarence Stedman. AA; HBV
Where's Mary? Ivy O. Eastwick. TiPo
Where's now the object of thy fears. Resolution. Henry More. OxBoCh
Where's Peace? I start, some clear-blown night. Mr. Hosea Biglow to the Editor of the Atlantic Monthly. James Russell Lowell. *Fr.* The Biglow Papers, 2d Series, No. X. AA
"Where's the need of singing now?" Momus. E. A. Robinson. ViBoPo
Where's the Poet? Keats. DiPo; MBW-2
(Poet, The.) PeER; PP
Where's the Queen of Sheba? Gone. Walter de la Mare. GoJo
Wheresoe'er I turn mine eyes. God Everywhere. Abraham ibn Ezra. TrJP
Wheresoe'er I turn my view. Lines Written in Ridicule of Certain Poems Published in 1777. Samuel Johnson. EiPP
Whereto Should I Express. Henry VIII, King of England. TuPP
(To His Lady.) CTC; OBSC
Whereupon I told,/ That once in the stillness of a summer's noon. Books. Wordsworth. *Fr.* The Prelude, V. PoEL-4
Wherever Beauty Has Been Quick in Clay. John Masefield. MoRP
Wherever earth is home for men. Let There Be Law. Mark Van Doren. MoRP
Wherever God erects a house of prayer. Daniel Defoe. *Fr.* The True-born Englishman, I. TreF
Wherever I Am [and Whatever I Do]. Dryden. *Fr.* The Conquest of Granada. DiPo; MaPo
(Phyllis.) SeCL
(Song: "Wherever I am, and whatever I doe.") YAT
Wherever I am, there's always Pooh. Us Two. A. A. Milne. TiPo
Wherever I go, I do no wrong. William Baylebridge. *Fr.* Moreton Miles. BoAV
Wherever I walk there are only little deaths. The Deaths. Solveig von Schoultz. LiTW
Wherever may the mollusk roam. The Mollusk. James J. Montague. PoMa
Wherever on Italian ground. Italian Poppies. Joel Elias Spingarn. HBMV
Wherever she is moving now, an air. Carmina. Robert Mezey. ToPo
Wherever she may turn her ravished eyes. A Girl. Viola Meynell. MoBrPo (1942 ed.)
Wherever smoke wreaths. Home. Stephen Chalmers. HBMV
Wherever souls of men have worshiped, there. Holy Places. Herbert D. Gallaudet. MaRV
Wherever the wind's head walks. The Wind's Head. John L. Sweeney. JKCP (1955 ed.); TwAmPo
Wherever we are found. All. Antoni Slonimski. PoFr
Wherewith Shall I Come before the Lord? Micah, VI: 6-8, Bible, *O.T.* TRV
(What Doth the Lord Require?) MaRV
Whethen is it yourself, Mister Hagan? an' lookin' right hearty you are. A Curlew's Call. Jane Barlow. VA
Whether a cheerful air does rise. On Mary, Duchess of Richmond. Richard Flecknoe. SeCL
"Whether all towns and all who live in them." Tasker Norcross. E. A. Robinson. CMoP
Whether amid the gloom of night I stray. A Contemplation on Night. John Gay. CEP
Whether away my sweetest deerest. *Unknown.* SeCSL
Whether conditioned by God, or their neural structure, still. Truth. W. H. Auden. MaRV
Whether day my spirit's yearning. The Thought Eternal. Goethe. AWP; JAWP; WBP
Whether dinner was pleasant, with the windows lit by gunfire. No Credit. Kenneth Fearing. CMoP
Whether for rope to hang my love. Night-Labour. Quentin Stevenson. POTE (1959 ed.)
Whether his loves were many or but two. Before Rereading Shakespeare's Sonnets. T. Sturge Moore. BrPo
Whether I find thee bright with fair. Changeful Beauty. *Unknown, tr. by* Andrew Lang. EnLoPo
"Whether is her beauty by her words divine?" *Unknown. Fr.* Edward the Third. LO
Whether it's sunny or not, it's sure. Poem About Morning. William Meredith. NYBP
Whether Men Do Laugh or Weep. *At. to* Thomas Campion *and to* Philip Rosseter. *See* All Is Vanity.
Whether on earth, in air, or main. The Man and the Flea. John Gay. *Fr.* Fables. EiCL
Whether on Ida's shady brow. To the Muses. Blake. AnFE; BoLiVe; CBEP; CEP; ChER; ChTr; CoBE; EiCL; EiPP; EnLi-2; EnLit; EnRP; ERoP-1; GTBS-W; GTSL; HBV; LiTB; LiTG; LoBV; NoP; OAEP; OBEC; OBEV; OnPM; OuHeWo; PeER; PoFS; SeCeV; TrGrPo; ViBoPo; WHA
Whether or Not. D. H. Lawrence. MoBrPo
Whether Paul or Apollos, or Cephas. Edward Taylor. *Fr.* Preparatory Meditations. MWA-1
Whether some great, supreme, o'er-ruling pow'r. Canto First. George Canning. *Fr.* The Progress of Man. EiCL
Whether that soule which now comes up to you. An Hymne to the Saints, and to Marquesse Hamylton. John Donne. MaMe
Whether the bees have thoughts, we cannot say. The Long Waters. Theodore Roethke. NaP NYBP
Whether the moorings are invisible. Conversation. John Berryman. LiTA; LiTM; NePA; WaP
Whether the Turkish new moon minded be. Astrophel and Stella, XXX. Sir Philip Sidney. CLwM; FCP; ReEn; ReIE; SiPS; Sonn; TuPP
Whether the weather be fine, or whether the weather be not. *Unknown.* BoTP
Whether There Is Sorrow in the Demons. John Berryman. LiTM (1970 ed.)
Whether they delve in the buried coal, or plow the upland soil. The Glory of Toil. Edna Dean Proctor. PGD
Whether to Ceaser he was friend or foe? Upon the Death of G. B. John Cotton. SCAP
Whether to sally and see thee, girl of my dreams. To Meet, or Otherwise. Thomas Hardy. OBNC
Whether two-backed beast or many-splendoured-thing. Onan. Paris Leary. CoPo
Whether we climb, whether we plod. Heroism. Lizette Woodworth Reese. MaRV
Whether we flee or pursue, we are the same. Leviathan; a Poem in Four Movements. Kenneth Pitchford. CoPo
Whether we mutter a Thank you or not. *Unknown.* ThGo
Whether white or black be best. Verses Made Sometime Since upon . . . the Indian Squa. John Josselyn. SCAP
Whether you live by hut or throne. Certainties. Margaret Widdemer. HBMV
Which? Joyce L. Brisley. GFA
Which are the living? We who stride unyielding earth in engine fumes. Three City Cantos. Charles A. Wagner. GoYe
Which Are You? *Unknown.* PoLF
Which Do You Choose? Harry A. Ironside. SoP
Which I wish to remark. The Heathen Pass-ee. A. C. Hilton. CenHV
Which I wish to remark. Plain Language [*or* Talk] from Truthful James [*or* That Heathen Chinee]. Bret Harte. AmePo; AmPP; AnAmPo; BeLS; BLPA; BOHV; CenHV; CoBA; CTC; DD; FaBoBe; HBV; InMe; LHV; MAP; MoAmPo (1942 ed.); OnSP; PFY; PoE; TreF; WhC; YaD
Which Is a Proud, and Yet a Wretched Thing. Sir John Davies. *See* Man.
Which Is Me? Edward Sandford Martin. *See* My Name Is Legion.
Which is more sweet—the slow mysterious stream. Izaak Walton to River and Brook. Eugene Lee-Hamilton. VA

Which is of greater value, prythee, say. A Conjugal Conundrum. *Unknown.* BOHV
Which is the best to hit your taste. Epigram on Two Ladies. Sophia Burrell. ErPo
Which Is the Favourite? Charles *and* Mary Lamb. OTPC (1923 ed.)
Which is the German's fatherland. The German Fatherland. Ernst Moritz Arndt. HBV
"Which is the way to Baby-land?" Baby-Land. George Cooper. BoTP; HBV; HBVY; OTPC; PPL
Which is the way to Fairyland. The Way to Fairyland. Eunice Close. BoTP
"Which is the way to London Town,/ To see the King." Mother Goose. BoTP
Which is the way to London Town?/ Over the hills. *Unknown.* BoTP
"Which is the way to the nearest town." Conversation with an April Fool. Rowena Bennett. SiSoSe
Which is the weakest thing of all. The Weakest Thing. Elizabeth Barrett Browning. HBV
Which is the wind that brings the cold? What the Winds Bring. Edmund Clarence Stedman. DD; PRWS
Which Is Which? John Byrom. *See* Jacobite Toast, A.
Which is you, old two-in-one? What the Serpent Said to Adam. Archibald MacLeish. NePA
Which Loved Best? "Joy Allison." WBLP
(Which Loved Her Best?) HH; OHIP; PEDC
Which of the Angels sang so well in Heaven. On the Death of Mrs. Browning. Sydney Dobell. VA
Which of those rebell Spirits adjudg'd to Hell. Gabriel Meets Satan. Milton. *Fr.* Paradise Lost, IV. LoBV
Which road, which road did you take. Exaltation. Franz Werfel. TrJP
Which Shall It Be? Ethel Lynn Beers. BLPA; TreF
Which Side Am I Supposed to Be On? W. H. Auden. CoBMV
(Ode: To My Pupils.) MoBrPo
Which Side Are You On? Mrs. Sam Reece. WOW
Which Sword? Jason Noble Pierce. PGD
Which the best way of life? The forum rings. No Way Is Good. Poseidippus. OnPM
Which things being so, as we said when we studied. Good-bye Now, Plato and Hegel. Louis MacNeice. *Fr.* Autumn Journal. OnHM
Which way, and whence the lightning flew. Apollo's Song. Ben Jonson. *Fr.* The Masque of Augurs. LoBV
Which Way Does the Wind Blow? Lucy Aikin. OTPC
Which will you have, a ball or a cake? Choosing. Eleanor Farjeon. TiPo
Whichever harbours poison between cotton, or goes from breathing to a common form. 29th Dance—Having an Instrument—22 March 1964. Jackson MacLow. CoPo
Whichever Way the Wind Doth Blow. Caroline Atherton Brices Mason. *See* En Voyage.
Whiffaree an' a-whiffo'rye. Honey Take a Whiff on Me. *Unknown.* ABF
Whigmaleerie, A. William Soutar. OxBS
While Adam slept, from him his Eve arose. Epigram. *Unknown.* *See also* Whilst Adam slept, Eve from his side arose. ALV.
While all to this auspicious day. To Mrs. Leigh upon Her Wedding-Day. George Canning. ALV
While an intrinsic ardor prompts to write. To the University of Cambridge, in New-England. Phillis Wheatley. AmPP (5th ed.); BALP
While Anna's peers and early playmates tread. The Stuffed Owl. Wordsworth. Par
While April Rain Went By. Shaemas O'Sheel. HBMV
While at her bedroom window once. The Keys of Morning. Walter de la Mare. AtBAP; MoVE; NoP
While at the stook the shearers cow'r. To the Rev. John M'Math. Burns. EiPP
While Beast instructs his fair, and innocent wife. On Sir Voluptuous Beast. Ben Jonson. EP
While blooming youth, and gay delight. An Ode. Matthew Prior. EiCL
While blue-eyed children, goggle-faced and giggling. An Old-World Effect. Siegfried Sassoon. CMoP
While briers an' woodbines budding green. Epistle to John Lapraik, an Old Scottish [*or* Scotch] Bard. Burns. BEL; CEP; EiCL; EiPP; EnL; EnLi-2; EnPE; EnRP; MCCG; NoP; OAEP
While Butler, needy wretch! was yet alive. On the Setting Up [of] Mr. Butler's Monument in Westminster Abbey. Samuel Wesley. ALV; BOHV; CBEP; InvP; OBEC; PPON; WhC
While cleaning my old six-branched candelabrum. Cleaning the Candelabrum. Siegfried Sassoon. HaMV
While crabapple now is a windfall. The Wilding. Philip Booth. NePoEA
While crouds of princes your deserts proclaim. The Campaign. Addison. CEP
While cruel Nero only drains. Picture of Seneca Dying in a Bath. Matthew Prior. CEP
While deepening shades obscure the face of day. Gilbert White. *Fr.* The Natural History of Selborne. LO
While Delia shines at Hurlothrumbo. The Widow and Virgin Sisters. Thomas Tickell. WaPE
While duns were knocking at my door. The Ramble. Alexander Radcliffe. PeRV
While explosives blow to dust. Epithalamion. W. H. Auden. HW
While far along the eastern sky. After the Fire. Oliver Wendell Holmes. MC; PAH
While favor fed my hope, delight with hope was brought. Sir Philip Sidney. Astrophel and Stella: Fifth Song. FCP
While Fell was reposing himself on the hay. On Fell. Gotthold Lessing. ShM
While gentlefolks strut in their silver and satins. Bartleme Fair. George Alexander Stevens. ELP
While going the road to sweet Athy. Johnny, I Hardly Knew Ye. *Unknown.* AnIV; EiCL; ELP; OnYI; OxBoLi; WaaP
While he says Mass, Carmelo's sins. Fra Carmelo's Morning Sacrifice. Gervase Toelle. JKCP (1955 ed.)
While he to whom her vexing thoughts still clung. Seven Sad Sonnets, III. Mary Aldis. HBMV
While here on earth it may not be. Yes, I Have Been to Calvary. Avis B. Christiansen STF
While homeward bound across the deep. Franklin's Crew. *Unknown.* SoAmSa
"While I am quick in the body," quoth he, "I am called Anima." The Human Soul Speaks. William Langland. *Fr.* The Vision of Piers Plowman. PoLi
While I Have Vision. Peter Quennell. ChMP
While, I here in this rented room, under. The Imitation of Faust. Alfred Hayes. LiTM (1946 ed.)
While I of summum bonum was disputing. Of Summum Bonum. Sir John Harington. SiCE
While I recline. The Cotton Boll. Henry Timrod. AA; AmPP; MAmP
"While I sit at the door." Eve. Christina Rossetti. CH; GTBS-P; NBM; OxBoCh; PoEL-5; SeCeV
While I stood here, in the open, lost in myself. Milkweed. James Wright. NaP
While I stood listening, discreetly dumb. The Growth of Lorraine. E. A. Robinson. NP
While I touch the string. Common Sense and Genius. Thomas Moore. NBM
While I walked in the moonlight. Lady Murasaki Shikibu, *tr. fr. Japanese by* I. W. Furukami. LiTW
While I was all absorbed in seeing him. Dante. *Fr.* Divina Commedia: Inferno. CAW
While I watch the Christmas blaze. The Reminder. Thomas Hardy. CMoP
While I wrought out these fitful Danaan rhymes. To Some I Have Talked With by the Fire. W. B. Yeats. PoDB
While I'm gone, white mother, kill the fattened oxen. The White and the Black. N. M. Khaketla. PeSA
While Immortality Endures. Ernest Briggs. NeLNL
While in the bower, with beauty blessed. A Song. Joseph Warton. WaPE
While in the park I sing, the listning deer. At Penshurst. Edmund Waller. AnAnS-2; OAEP
While joy gave clouds the light of stars. The Villain. W. H. Davies. CBV; MoBrPo; NeMA; POTE; WHA
While life is vigorous and bright. In the Days of Thy Youth. Bhartrihari. OnPM
While life was mine, the little hour. Epigram. Thomas Moore. ALV
While long I did with patient constancy. Psalm XL. *Paraphrased by* Sir Philip Sidney. FCP

While Loveliness Goes By. Anna Hempstead Branch. MAP; MoAmPo (1942 ed.)
While lying in a north room. Light for the North Room. Alice Hansche Mortenson. SoP
While mad Ophelia we lament. On a Pretty Madwoman. Matthew Prior. CEP; EiCL
While malice, Pope, denies thy page. When None Shall Rail. David Lewis. CBEP; OBEC
While Mary and the Christ-Child. The Windflowers and the Sage. Laura Spencer Portor. StJW
While men were all asleep the snow came flying. *See* When men were all asleep . . .
While midnight clung to every shore. Natura in Urbe. E. B. White. WaKn
While Mr. Charleston, the maître d'hôtel. Table D'Hote. Richard Curry Esler. NYTB
While Morpheus thus doth gently lay. Song. Henry Killigrew. CH
While my hair was still cut straight across my forehead. The River-Merchant's Wife; a Letter. Li Po, *tr. by* Ezra Pound. AmP; AmPP; AnAmPo; AWP; BoLP; CABA; CoAnAm; DTC; InPo; LiTA; LiTL; LiTW; MoAB; MoAmPo (1950 ed.); MoPo; NAMP; NoP; NP; OBMV; OxBA; PG (1945 ed.); PIA; PoIE; PoSa; TwAmPo; TwCP; VaPo; WBP
While my lady sleepeth. Serenade. John Gibson Lockhart. OBRV
While my young cheek retains its healthful hues. Lines to William Linley while he Sang a Song to Purcell's Music. Samuel Taylor Coleridge. MuSP
While nations, howling like Lucifer, fall from the hallowed height. Remember Thy Covenant. Edith Lovejoy Pierce. MoRP
While nations rage, while empires rock and fall. Loyalty Hymn. Edith Lovejoy Pierce. ChIP; MaRV
While Northward the hot sun was sinking o'er the trees. The Psalm. Robert Bridges. FaBoTw; LiTB
While not a leaf seems faded, while the fields. Sonnet: September, 1815. Wordsworth. ChER
While now the Pole Star sinks from sight. Crossing the Tropics. Herman Melville. AA
While now the Rising Village claims a name. Oliver Goldsmith, the Younger. *Fr.* The Rising Village. CaP
While now, to serve the pilgrim train. Vine and Clarel. Herman Melville. *Fr.* Clarel. MAmP
While o'er the deep Thy servants sail. The Heavenly Breeze. George Burgess. BePJ
While o'er the globe, fair nymph! your searches run. To Lady Jane Wharton, on Her Studying the Globe. Nicholas Rowe. LO
While on Those Lovely Looks I Gaze. Earl of Rochester. CBEP; SeCL
(Song: "While on those lovely looks I gaze.") PeRV
While Passing Through This Valley. Alice Hansche Mortenson. SoP
While people hunt for what can satisfy their wants. Shelter. Gene Derwood. NePA
While rain, with eve in partnership. Beyond the Last Lamp. Thomas Hardy. MoVE; OBNC; PoVP
While riding down that greenwood road. John of Hazelgreen (C *vers.*) *Unknown.* BaBo
While riding toward Jerusalem. The Syrian's Tale. Leslie Savage Clark. ChIP
While round the armed bands. The Execution of King Charles. Andrew Marvell. *Fr.* An Horatian Ode upon Cromwell's Return from Ireland. AnEnPo; PoRA
While sauntering through the crowded street. Pre-Existence. Paul Hamilton Hayne. HBV
While she darns her children's socks, The. Prayer Time. Ruby Weyburn Tobias. SoP
While she was talking a bear happened along, violating. The Woman at Banff. William Stafford. TPM
While Shepherds Watched Their Flocks by Night. Margaret Deland. DD; GN; HBVY; StJW
While Shepherds Watched Their Flocks by Night. Nahum Tate. DD; GN; HBV; HBVY; HH; MaRV; OnYI; OTPC; OxBI; PCH; TreFS; YaCaBo, *with music*
(Christmas.) OHIP; PEDC
(Song of the Angels.) BePJ; SoP
(While Shepherds Watched.) PTK
While Sherman stood beneath the hottest fire. Before Vicksburg. George Henry Boker. PAH
While sleeping in your clothes. This Needle. Kurahashibe Otome. OnPM
While snowy nightwinds, blowing bleak. Burncombe Hollow. William Barnes. OBNC
While [*or* Whilst] some affect the sun, and some the shade. The Grave. Robert Blair. CoBE; EiPP; EnPE; EnRP
While some are being flies. 37th Dance—Banding—22 March 1964. Jackson MacLow. CoPo
While some go dancing reels. Three Old Brothers. Frank O'Connor. OnYI
While Someone Telephones. Elizabeth Bishop. NMP
While standing on the brink of woe. He Gave Himself for Me. *Unknown.* STF
While Stars of Christmas Shine. Emilie Poulsson. OHIP
While strolling down the street one eve upon mere pleasure bent. Just Tell Them That You Saw Me. Paul Dresser. TreFS
While strolling out one evening. The Banks of the Pamanaw. *Unknown.* ABF
While sways the restless sea. Sleep. "Fiona Macleod." GBV; TSW
While tenderly around me cast. Neaera's Kisses. Johannes Secundus. *Fr.* Basia. UnTE
While that my soul repairs to her devotion. Church Monuments. George Herbert. AnAnS-1; CABA; EP; ForPo; MaMe; MaPo; MeP; NoP; PIA; PoIE; QFR
While [*or* Whyle] that the sun with his beams hot. The Faithless [*or* Unfaithful] Shepherdess [*or* Philon *or* Adieu Love, Untrue Love]. *Unknown.* ALV; EIL; GTBS; GTBS-D; GTBS-P; GTBS-W; GTSE; GTSL; OBEV; OBSC; SiCE
While the Bells Ring. Lora Dunetz. NePoAm
While the Billy Boils. David McKee Wright. AnNZ
While the blue is richest. Fairies' Recall. Felicia Dorothea Hemans. OTPC
While the blue noon above us arches. Annihilation. Conrad Aiken. CrMA; LO; MAP; MoAB; MoAmPo
While the cobbler mused, there passed his pane. How the Great Guest Came [*or* The Great Guest Comes]. Edwin Markham. BeLS; BLPA; WBLP
While the Days Are Going By. George Cooper. BLRP; STF; WBLP
While the earth remaineth. After the Flood Went Down, God Said. Genesis, Bible, *O.T.* ThGo
While the evening here is approaching the mountain paths. Overnight in the Apartment by the River. Tu Fu. ChTr
While the far farewell music thins and falls. Thomas Hardy. Sonn
While the king and his ministers keep such a pother. A Wicked Treasonable Libel. Swift. UnTE
While the King Sitteth at His Table. Edward Taylor. *See* Preparatory Meditations: "Oh! thou, my Lord . . ."
While the shot and shell were screaming on the battlefield. Break the News to Mother. Charles Kassell Harris. TreFS
While the storm clouds gather. God Bless America. Irving Berlin. TreFT
While the Summer Trees Were Crying. Valentin Iremonger. *See* Evening in Summer.
While the Tragedy's afoot. Colophon. Oliver St. John Goarty. OBMV
While the two contraries of black and white. The Brown Beauty. Lord Herbert of Cherbury. AnAnS-2
While the unturned stone. Exaction. John L. Sweeney. TwAmPo
While the water-wagon's ringing showers. In the Isle of Dogs. John Davidson. OBNC
While thir hearts were jocund and sublime. Samson Hath Quit Himself. Milton. *Fr.* Samson Agonistes. LoBV
While this America settles in the mold of its vulgarity, heavily thickening to empire. Shine, Perishing Republic. Robinson Jeffers. AmLP; AmP; AmPP; AnAmPo; CBV; CMoP; InP; LiTA; LiTM; MAP; MoAB; MoAmPo; MoVE; NAMP; NePA; NoP; NP; OTD; OxBA; PoIE; UnPo (3d ed.); ViBoPo
While this night I read, I'm battleground. Invalid. Audrey McGaffin. NePoAm-2
While thus, of power and fancy'd empire vain. Crusty Critics. George Crabbe. *Fr.* The Library. OBEC
While to Bethlehem We Are Going. Sister Violante do Ceo, *tr. fr. Portuguese by* Sir John Bowring. CAW
While walking down [*or* whilst walking] a crowded city street the other day. If I Only Was the Fellow [*or* Just Try to Be the Fellow. . .]. Will S. Adkin. BLPA; WBLP

While we sail and laugh, joke and fight, comes death. In Memoriam; Ingvald Bjorndal and His Comrade. Malcolm Lowry. OBCV
While We Slept. David Wolff. AnAmPo; TrJP
While we slumber and sleep. A Song of Flight. Christina Rossetti. CAW
While we wandered, A (thus it is I dream!). Gray Nights. Ernest Dowson. PoVP; Sonn
While we were fearing it, it came. Emily Dickinson. NCEP
While winds frae off Ben Lomond blaw. Epistle to Davie, a Brother Poet. Burns. OBEC
While wise men, long beset by doubt. The Victor. Sydney King Russell. StaSt
While with a strong and yet a gentle hand. Edmund Waller. *Fr.* A Panegyric to My Lord Protector. SCEP-2; SeCV-1
While with false pride, and narrow jealousy. On the Use of New and Old Words in Poetry. Anna Seward. Sonn
While with labor assiduous due pleasure I mix. The Secretary [*or* Written at the Hague]. Matthew Prior. BWP; CEP; EiCL; PoE; PoFS
While with the living I remain. What Lack I Yet? Pearl Burnside McKinney. SoP
While words of learned strength and thundering sound. Still the Wonder Grew. Goldsmith. *Fr.* The Deserted Village. TreF
While working sadly by my window. Prose Poem: The Red Flower. Judith Gautier. OnPM
While yet I speak the winged galley flies. The Sirens, Scylla and Charybdis. Homer. *Fr.* The Odyssey, XII. LiTW
While yet the grapes were green, thou didst refuse me. Grapes. *Unknown.* AWP
While yet the Morning Star. The Unicorn. Ella Young. FaPON; SoPo; TiPo
While you, great patron of mankind! sustain. The First Epistle of the Second Book of Horace [*or* To Augustus]. Pope. CEP; EiCL; EiPP; MBW-1
While you, my Lord, bid stately piles ascend. A Journey to Exeter. John Gay. WoL
While you, my lord, the rural shades admire. A Letter from Italy. Addison. CEP
While you that in your sorrow disavow. A Christmas Sonnet. E. A. Robinson. EaLo; MaRV; PoDB
While young John runs to greet. Lines on the Celebrated Picture by Leonardo da Vinci, Called the Virgin of the Rocks. Charles Lamb. ISi
While your great-grandmother and her sons. Separate Parties. Dabney Stuart. NYBP
While your veil lay floating still around me. To Nature. Friedrich Hölderlin. LiTW
While you're all so frisky I'll sing a little song. Top Hand. *Unknown.* CoSo
While some one did chant this lovely lay, The. Gather the Rose. Spenser. *Fr.* The Faerie Queene, II. EIL
Whilom [*or* Whylom], as olde stories tellen us. The Knight's Tale. Chaucer. *Fr.* The Canterbury Tales. BEL; GoTL; TOP
Whilom in the winter's rage. The Penitent Palmer's Ode. Robert Greene. *Fr.* Francesco's Fortunes. LoBV; OBSC
Whilom the sisters nine were vestal maids. Joseph Hall. *Fr.* Virgidemiarum. FosPo
Whilom [*or* Whylom] ther was dwellynge at [*or* in] Oxenford. The Carpenter's Young Wife. Chaucer. *Fr.* The Canterbury Tales: The Miller's Tale. ExPo; MBW-1; OxBoLi
Whilom ther was dwellynge in my contree. The Friar's Tale. Chaucer. *Fr.* The Canterbury Tales. PoAn
Whilst Adam slept, Eve from his side arose. Epigram. *Unknown.* *See also* While Adam slept, from him his Eve arose. HBV.
Whilst Alexis Lay Prest. Dryden. *Fr.* Marriage a-la-Mode. ErPo; UnTE
(Song, A: "Whil'st Alexis lay prest.") CavP
Whilst beauty, youth, and gay delight. Verses by Mr. Prior. Matthew Prior. PeRV
Whilst echo cries, "What shall become of me?" Henry Constable. *Fr.* Diana. OBSC; ReEn; ReIE; SiCE; Sonn; TuPP
Whilst human kind/ Throughout the lands lay miserably crushed. Lucretius. *Fr.* De Rerum Natura: Beyond Religion. AWP; PoFr
Whilst I alone did call upon thy aid. Sonnets, LXXIX. Shakespeare. Sonn.
Whilst I beheld the neck o' the dove. Hymn. Patrick Carey. SeCL
Whil'st I, the sun's bright face may view. The Marigold. George Wither. SeEP
Whilst I was dear and thou wert kind. The Reconciliation. Horace. *Fr.* Odes. OuHeWo
Whilst in peaceful quarters lying. The Battle of Monmouth. "R. H." PAH
Whilst in this cold and blust'ring clime. To My Dear and Most Worthy Friend, Mr. Isaac Walton. Charles Cotton. FaBoEn
Whilst my souls eye beheld no light. A Dialogue betwixt God and the Soul. *At. to* Sir Henry Wotton. MeLP; OBS; OxBoCh
Whilst on Septimius' panting breast. Acme and Septimius. Catullus. AWP; UnTE
Whilst on thy head I lay my hand. A Spell of Invisibility. *At. to* Christopher Marlowe. ChTr
Whilst some affect the sun and some the shade. *See* While some affect the sun . . .
Whilst th' iron hand. John Crowne. *Fr.* The Ambitious Statesman. PeRV
Whilst the red spittle of the grape-shot sings. Evil. Arthur Rimbaud. WaaP
Whilst thus his wrath with threats the Tyrant fed. Abraham Cowley. *Fr.* Davideis. SeEP
Whilst thus my pen strives to eternize thee. Idea, XLIV. Michael Drayton. BEL; OBSC; ReEn; SiCE; Sonn; TuPP; ViBoPo
Whil'st thy weigh'd judgements, Egerton, I heare. To Thomas Lord Chancellor. Ben Jonson. OBS
Whilst walking a crowded city street the other day. *See* While walking down a crowded city street . . .
Whilst we sing the doleful knell. Ding Dong. *Unknown.* *Fr.* Swetnam, the Woman-Hater. EIL
Whilst what I write I do not see. Written in Juice of Lemmon. Abraham Cowley. AnAnS-2; SeCP; SeCV-1
Whilst yet to prove. Farewell to Love. John Donne. MaMe; ReEn
Whim. Conrad Aiken. *See* When Trout Swim down Great Ormond Street.
Whim Alley. Hervey Allen. AnAmPo; MAP
Whim of Time, A. Stephen Spender. MoAB; MoBrPo
Whimper of Sympathy. George Meredith. EPN
Whins are blythesome on the knowe, The. A New Spring. A. D. Mackie. OxBS
Whip, The. Robert Creeley. NaP; NeAP; ToPo
Whip-crack of a Union Jack, The. The Boer War. William Plomer. BoSA
Whip of Anger, The. Mary Ross. ChIP
Whipping, The. Robert Hayden. BP; IDB
Whippoorwill. John Richard Moreland. IHA
Whipp'will's sing'in to de moon. Go Sleep, Ma Honey. Edward D. Barker. AA
Whirl-Blast. Wordsworth. OTPC
Whirl, snow, on the blackbird's chatter. Eager Spring. Gordon Bottomley. MoBrPo; POTE
Whirl up, sea. Oread. Hilda Doolittle ("H. D."). AP; AWP; CMoP; ExPo; GoJo; InP; JAWP; MAP; MoAmPo; MoVE; NeMA; OxBA; RePo; TSW; WBP
Whirligig Beetle. C. Lindsay McCoy. GFA
Whirlpool, The ("He was caught in the whirlpool of dismay"). *Unknown.* PoToHe (new ed.)
Whirlpool. *Unknown,* *tr. fr. Japanese by* Arthur Waley. WoL
("They say there is.") LiTW
Whirlwind has not walked, The. Suspense. Adrien Stoutenburg. WIRo
Whirlwind Road, The. Edwin Markham. AA
Whirring Wheels. John Oxenham. *See* Prayer: "Lord, when on my bed I lie."
Whiskey Bill; a Fragment. *Unknown.* SCC
Whiskey for My Johnny. *Unknown.* *See* Whisky Johnny.
Whiskey here and whiskey there. Whiskey, Johnny, *vers.* I. *Unknown.* ShS
Whiskey is the life of man. Whiskey Johnny. *Unknown.* ShS, *vers.* III; SoAmSa
Whiskey Johnny. *Unknown.* *See* Whisky Johnny.
Whiskey on your breath, The. My Papa's Waltz. Theodore Roethke. AmP; CaFP; CBV; CrMA; FIW; HoPM; ILP; LiTM (1970 ed.); MiAP; MoAB; NoP; PoeP; PoIE; PoSa; TDP
Whisky, Drink Divine. Joseph O'Leary. OnYI

Whisky Frisky. *Unknown. See* Squirrel, The.
Whisky [*or* Whiskey] Johnny, *with music. Unknown.* ABF; AS; ShS, 3 *vers.*; SoAmSa
(Whiskey for My Johnny.) AmSS
Whisky Song, A. *Unknown.* STF
Whisper on the heath I hear, A. Spring. Robert Loveman. AA
Whisper woke the air, A. Calumny. Frances Sargent Osgood. AA; HBV
Whispered to the Afternoon. Georg Trakl, *tr. fr. German by* Glauco Cambon. OnPM
Whisperer, The. Arthur Bullen. HBMV
Whisperer, The. James Stephens. WGRP
Whisperer, The. Mark Van Doren. AnFE; CoAnAm; MAP; MoAmPo; UnTE
Whisperers, The. W. W. Gibson. HBV
Whisperin' Bill. Irving Bacheller. PoLF
Whispering Pine Tree, The. Mariana Griswold Van Rensselaer. PCH
Whisperings in Wattle-Boughs. Adam Lindsay Gordon. BoAu; OBVV
Whispers. Myra Cohn Livingston. PDV
Whispers of Heavenly Death. Walt Whitman. AnFE; APA; CoAnAm; LiTA; NePA; TOP
Whispers of Immortality. T. S. Eliot. APA; ATP (1953 ed.); CMoP; CoAnAm; CTC; LiTA; LiTG; MAPA; MemP; MWA-2; NePA; NP; OBMV; PoIE; TwAmPo
Whispers of the wheatfields. What We Remember. Rochelle Ratner. QAH
Whist. Eugene Fitch Ware. PoLF
Whistle. Dorothy Aldis. *See* Whistles.
Whistle, The. Charles Murray. GoTS; OxBS; ShBV-1
Whistle Aloud, Too Weedy Wren. Wallace Stevens. LiTA
Whistle an' I'll Come to Ye [*or* You], My Lad. Burns. BoLiVe; LiTL; MeWo; OtMeF; OxBoLi; UnTE; ViBoPo; WePo
(O Whistle, and I'll Come to You [*or* Ye], My Lad.) BoLP; EiCL; ErPo; GoTS; PoEL-4
Whistle and Wheels. Alfred G. Bailey. PeCV
Whistle Daughter Whistle ("Mother I longs to get married"). *Unknown.* ErPo
Whistle, daughter, whistle/ And you shall have a sheep. *Unknown.* BFSS, *with music*; OxNR
Whistle, Laddie, whistle. To Laddie. Anne Robinson. SUS
Whistle o'er the Lave o't. Burns. CEP; OxBS
Whistle under the water. Amy Lowell. *Fr.* Flute-Priest Song for Rain. UnS
Whistler, The. Robert Story. BOHV
Whistles. Dorothy Aldis. GFA; TiPo (1952 ed.)
(Whistle.) BoChLi (1950 ed.)
Whistles. Rachel Field. GFA; StVeCh (1955 ed.); TiPo
Whistling Boy, The. George Crabbe. PoFS; TrGrPo
Whistling Boy. John Robert Quinn. BiCB
Whistling Boy. Nixon Waterman. PoLF
Whistling in the street a car turning in the room ticking. Aram Saroyan. ANYP
Whistling Jack, The. John Shaw Neilson. NeLNL
Whistling postman swings along, The. The Postman. *Unknown.* FaPON
Whistling strangely, whistling sadly, whistling sweet and clear. The Seven Whistlers. Alice E. Gillington. VA
Whit Sunday. *See* Whitsunday.
White. George Woodcock. NeBP
White, a shingled path. Icos. Charles Tomlinson. GTBS-P; OPoP
White an' Blue. William Barnes. GTBS-P
White and crimson, cheek and breast. Cantiga. Gil Vicente. CAW; ISi
White and Red. Edward de Vere, Earl of Oxford. *See* What Cunning Can Express.
White and ruddy is my Beloved. A Song of White and Red. Sister Mary Benvenuta. JKCP (1926 ed.)
White and the Black, The. N. M. Khaketla, *tr. fr. Sotho by* Dan Kunene *and* Jack Cope. PeSA
White Anemone, The, *sel.* "Owen Meredith."
"'Tis the white anemone, fashioned so." GN; OTPC
White-arched in loops of silence, the bodega. Stork in Jerez. Laurie Lee. BoPe; POTi
White are the far-off plains, and white. Snow. Archibald Lampman. PeCV
White arms, Love, you have, and thin fingers with glittering nails. She-Devil. Douglas Goldring. HBMV
White as her hand fair Julia threw. The Snow Ball. Petronius Arbiter. LiTW
White as Snow. *Unknown. See* Blanche comme la neige.
White as the great white dusk through which he moves. The Hunter. Eleanor Glenn Wallis. NePoAm-2
White as this paper was my lady's mind. Sonnet. George Henry Boker. *Fr.* Sonnets: A Sequence on Profane Love. AmePo
White Attic. Kenward Elmslie. ANYP
White Azaleas. Harriet McEwen Kimball. AA; HBV
White Beauty, The. *Unknown.* MeEL
White Bird, The. "Anna Akhmatova," *tr. fr. Russian by* Frances Cornford *and* E. P. Salaman. LiTW
White Bird, The. Roy McFadden. ACV; NeIP
White Bird, The. Wilfred Watson. MoCV
White bird featherless. Riddle [*or* Snow *or* Riddle of Snow and Sun]. *Unknown.* CBEP; ChTr; NCEP; OxNR; RIS
White bird floats down through the air, A. Riddle. *Unknown.* ChTr
White bird of the tempest! oh, beautiful thing. Lines Addressed to a Seagull. Gerald Griffin. OnYI
White Birds, The. W. B. Yeats. EnL; VA; ViPo (1962 ed.)
White Blossom, A. D. H. Lawrence. MoBrPo; NeMA
White blossom, white, white shell; the Nazarene. Music of Colours—White Blossom. Vernon Watkins. FaBoMo; LiTM; WaP
White Blossoms. Robert Mezey. NaP
White Blossom's off the Bog, The. Alfred Perceval Graves. VA
White bone clinging to white bone. What the Wind Said. John Press. NYTB
White Butterflies. Swinburne. FaPON; MPB; OTPC; PCD; PCH; PDV; StaSt; UTS
(Envoi: "Fly, white butterflies, out to sea.") GoJo; SUS
White Butterfly, A. The Graceful Bastion. William Carlos Williams. NYBP
White Canoe, The. Alan Sullivan. CaP
White-capped Waves. James Freeman Clarke. EtS
White Captain of my soul, lead on. Prayer [*or* A Soldier's Prayer]. Robert Freeman. ChIP; MaRV; OQP; TrPWD
White Carnation, The. Margaret E. Sangster. PEDC
White Cascade, The. W. H. Davies. NeMA
White Cat. Raymond Knister. WHW
White cat, The. Cat Ballerina Assoluta. Emilie Glen. GoYe
White Cat and the Student, The. *Unknown. See* Monk and His Pet Cat, The.
White Chimes. Alfred Starr Hamilton. QAH
White chocolate jar full of petals, The. Chez Jane. Frank O'-Hara. CoAP; NeAP
White Christmas. W. R. Rodgers. ChMP; GTBS-W; LiTM; MoAB; MoBrPo (1950 ed.); PPON; SeCePo
White Christs, The. Guy Fitch Phelps. OQP
White chrysanthemum, The. Oshikochi no Mitsune, *tr. fr. Japanese by* Kenneth Rexroth. LiTW
White Chrysanthemum, The. Ryota, *tr. fr. Japanese by* H. G. Henderson. OnPM
White church on the hill, The. A New England Church. Wilton Agnew Barrett. SoP; WGRP
"White City, The." Richard Watson Gilder. PAH
White City, A. James Schuyler. ANYP
White Cliffs, The, *sels.* Alice Duer Miller.
English Are Frosty, The. PoLF
I Have Loved England. PoLF
"I have seen much to hate here," 3 *ll.* OtMeF
"Young and in love—how magical the phrase!" MaRV
White cloud drifts to meet a sail at sea, A. The Old Sailor. Glenn Ward Dresbach. EtS
White clouds/ (White stallions, white horses tethered). Centaurs and Lapithae. Sacheverell Sitwell. *Fr.* Battles of the Centaurs. AtBAP
White clouds are in the sky. A Chinese Poem Written B.C. 1121. *Unknown.* WePo
White Cockade, The ("King Charles he is King James's son"). *Unknown, tr. fr. Modern Irish by* James Joseph Callanan. OnYI
White cock's tail, The. Ploughing on Sunday. Wallace Stevens. AmLP; FaPON; GoJo; PoPl; ThWaDe
White columns of towering masonry. Monserrat. William Edwin Collin. CaP

White Company, The, *sel.* Sir Arthur Conan Doyle.
Song of the Bow, The. HBV; MCCG
White Comrade, The. Robert Haven Schauffler. StJW
White coral bells upon a slender stalk. *Unknown.* PDV
White Country. Peter Schjeldahl. ANYP
White crow flies from the fairyland, A. An Enjoyable Evening in the Village near the Lake. Lin Ho Ching. FlW
White daisies are down in the meadows. Alone. John Farrar. BoChLi; GaP; GFA; MPB; YeAr
White delightful swan, The. The Dying Swan. *Unknown.* ChTr
White Devil [*or* Divel], The, *sels.* John Webster.
"Banisht!/ It greev'd me much to heare the sentence," *fr.* I, i. AtBAP
Call for the Robin Redbreast [and the Wren], *fr.* V, iv. AtBAP; CaFP; CBEP; ChTr; ExPo; FaBoCh; LoGBV; NoP; OAEP; PoE; PoEL-2; PoRA; ReEn; SeCePo; SeCeV; SiCE; StP; TuPP; ViBoPo
(Cornelia's Song.) OBS; PoIE; TrGrPo
(Dirge, A: "Call for the robin-redbreast and the wren.") BEL; ElL; EnLi-1; FaBoEn; GTBS; GTSE; GTSL; HBV; LiTB; OBEV; ThWaDe; UnPo; WHA
(Funeral Dirge for Marcello.) AnFE
(Land Dirge, A.) CH; GTBS-D; GTBS-P; GTBS-W; LoBV
(Song: "Call for the robin-redbreast and the wren.") CBV; ShBV-3
"How now my noble cossin—what in blacke!" *fr.* III, ii. AtBAP
"Indeede I am studying alcumye," *fr.* I, ii. AtBAP
"O thou soft naturall death, thou art joint-twin," *fr.* V, iii. AtBAP
"Then here's an end of me: fare-well day-light," *fr.* V, vi. AtBAP
"What, are you drop't?" *fr.* V, vi. PoEL-2
White Dou o Truth. The Ineffable Dou. Sydney Goodsir Smith. OxBS
White Dove of the Wild Dark Eyes. Joseph Mary Plunkett. HBMV
White doves of Cytherea, by your quest. The Pledge. Adelaide Crapsey. NP; TOP
White Drake, The. *Unknown, tr. fr. French by* John Glassco. WHW
White Dream, The. May Doney. HBMV
White Dress, The. Humbert Wolfe. NP
White Dress, The. Marya Zaturenska. MoAmPo; TwAmPo
White Dusk. Marion Margaret Boyd. HBMV
White Dust, The. W. W. Gibson. MoBrPo; NeMA
White Eagle, The. Nan McDonald. PoAu-2
White England shouldering from the sea. Fair England. Helen Gray Cone. AA
White Fear. Winifred Welles. HBMV
White Fields. James Stephens. BoNaP; BoTP; FaPON; MoShBr; PoSC; SiSoSe; SoPo; SUS
White Fisher, The. *Unknown.* ESPB
White Flag, The. John Hay. HBV
White flame of a candle, The. Blue Larkspur. Sister Mariella. JKCP (1955 ed.)
White, flipping. Trap. A. R. Ammons. NYTB
White fog lifting & falling on mountain-brow. Wales Visitation. Allen Ginsberg. FRC; NYBP
"White folks is white," says Uncle Jim. Uncle Jim. Countee Cullen. BANP
White-footed Deer, The. Bryant. AnNE
White founts falling in the courts of the sun. Lepanto. G. K. Chesterton. AnFE; BEL; CAW; CoBE; FaBV; FOL; GoBC; GoTL (1949 ed.); HBMV; HBVY; InP; JKCP (1955 ed.); MoBrPo; NeMA; OBMV; OnSP; OtMeF; PoRA; POTE; ShBV-3; TIHL; TreFS; WHA
White Fox. Elizabeth Alsop Shepard. GoYe
White frost comes. October Night. Agnes Louise Dean. YeAr
White full moon like a great beautiful whore, The. Walter Benton. *Fr.* This Is My Beloved. UnTE
White Fury of the Spring, The. Lizette Woodworth Reese. SiSw
White gleam the gulls across the darkling tide. In Absence. Tu Fu. OuHeWo
White goat Amaryllis, The. The Visitor. Patrick R. Chalmers. DD; HBV; HBVY
White Goat, White Ram. W. S. Merwin. NePoEA; PoDB; TwAmPo
White Goddess, The. Robert Graves. MoBrPo (1962 ed.); PoIE
White Guardians of the Universe of Sleep. E. E. Cummings. NYBP
White gulls that sit and float. The Echoing Cliff. Andrew Young. BiS
White gum showing, The. Pine Gum. W. W. E. Ross. OBCV
White-habited, the mystic Swan. The Swan. Jay Macpherson. PeCV
White-haired Man, The. May Sarton. MoRP
White hands of languorous grace. He Praises His Wife When She Has Left Him [*or* Had Gone from Him]. *Unknown.* AnIL; OxBI
White Heliotrope. Arthur Symons. PeVV
White hen sitting, A. Christina Rossetti. *Fr.* Sing-Song. SAS
White Horse, The. Mary Mills. NePoAm
White Horse, The. Tu Fu, *tr. fr. Chinese by* Rewi Alley. ChTr
White Horse of Westbury, The. Charles Tennyson Turner. PeVV
White Horses. Eleanor Farjeon. PDV; PoRh
White Horses. Winifred Howard. BrR; SoPo; SUS; UTS
White Horses. Irene F. Pawsey. BoTP
White-hot midday in the Snake Park, A. In the Snake Park. William Plomer. NYBP
White House, The. Claude McKay. AmNP; AmPP (5th ed.)
White House Blues, The, *with music.* *Unknown.* OuSiCo
White-housed village, The. Inquisitive Barn. Frances Frost. BrR
White Houses. Claude McKay. PoNe
White I saw the swallows winging. Augury. Stefan George. SiSw
White in the Moon the Long Road Lies. A. E. Housman. A Shropshire Lad, XXXVI. AWP; BEL; CMoP; ELP; EnLi-2; JAWP; LiTB; MeWo; NoP; PoVP; TOP; VP; WBP
(Long Road, The.) TSW
White Iris, A. Pauline B. Barrington. PoLF
White is the evening nature of my thought. White. George Woodcock. NeBP
White is the sail and lonely. A Sail. Mikhail Yurevich Lermontov. AWP; JAWP; WBP
White Island, The; or Place of the Blest. Robert Herrick. AnAnS-2; ChTr; HBV; NoP; OBS; OxBoCh; SeCL; SeEP; WiR
White Isle of Leuce, The. Sir Herbert Read. FaBoTw
White Jessamine, The. John Banister Tabb. HBV
White Kite, The. *Unknown, tr. fr. Aztec by* John Hubert Cornyn. *Fr.* Song of Quetzalcoatl. LiTW
White Kitten, The. "Marian Douglas." SAS
White Knight's Song, The. "Lewis Carroll." *Fr.* Through the Looking-Glass, *ch.* 8. EnLi-2; FaBoCh; GoTP; LoGBV
(Aged, Aged Man, The.) OnPP
(A-Sitting on a Gate.) PoE; PoRA (rev. ed.)
(I'll Tell Thee Everything I Can.) InvP; Par
(Ways and Means.) BOHV; FiBHP; NA
(White Knight's Ballad, The.) PoRh
(White Knight's Tale, The.) RIS; ShBV-4
White lambs leap. Through miles of snow. The Fire in the Snow. Vernon Watkins. GTBS-W; LiTM (rev. ed.); MoVE
White little hands! Mother-Song. Alfred Austin. *Fr.* Prince Lucifer. HBV; VA
White Magic; an Ode. William Stanley Braithwaite. PoNe
White man drew a small circle in the sand, The. Circles. Carl Sandburg. AmFN; FlW
"White, man, pause and gaze around, for we tread on haunted ground." The Legend of Grand Lake. Joseph L. Westcott. PoOW
White-maned, wide-throated, the heavy-shouldered children of the wind. Granite and Cypress. Robinson Jeffers. AmPP (5th ed.); AnAmPo
White Man's Burden, The. Kipling. EnLi-2 (1949 ed.); InP; PoVP; StP
White Man's Road, The. Arthur Chapman. PoMa
White mares of the moon rush along the sky, The. Night Clouds. Amy Lowell. MAP; MoAmPo; MoSiPe; NeMA; NP; PoPl; PoPo; RePo; WHA
White mist drifts across the shrouds, A. La Mer. Oscar Wilde. SyP
White Monster, The. W. H. Davies. LiTB
White Moth, The. Sir Arthur Quiller-Couch. VA

White moth to the closing bine [*or* vine], The. The Gipsy Trail. Kipling. HBV; HT; InP; PoRA
White nymph wandering in the woods by night, A. Elegies, 2. André Chénier. AWP; JAWP; WBP
White ocean birds that seek the land. Gulls and Dreams. Lionel Stevenson. CaP
White on his back remains the snow. The Old Horse in the Field. Viola Meynell. MemP
White Owl, The. F. J. Patmore. PoMS
White Paper. Sydney Jephcott. BoAu
White Paternoster, The. *Unknown.* *See* Matthew, Mark, Luke, and John.
White Peace, The. "Fiona Macleod." EPN; FaBoBe; HBV; OQP; PoVP
White Peacock, The. "Fiona Macleod." *Fr.* Sospiri di Roma. PoVP; VA
White Peacock, The. Mary Mills. NePoAm
White pinnace on lactic waves, The. Birth by Anesthesia. George Scarbrough. GoYe
White poems. The Black Narrator. Ahmed Alhamisi. BP
White Powder! Victor Hernandez Cruz. BF
White Presence, The. Joseph Fort Newton. ChIP; MaRV ("Follow Me.") OQP
White Primit Falls. *Unknown, after the Latin of* Vergil. ChTr ("Trust not too much, fair youth, unto thy feature.") EG
White Princess, The, *sel.* William Brighty Rands.
Kitty: What She Thinks of Herself. MoShBr
(Cat of Cats, The.) CIV
(Kitten Speaks, The.) RIS
White Queen. John Fuller. NePoEA-2
White Rainbow, The. Starr Nelson. GoYe
White ram rears against a wall, A. The Ram. Robert P. Tristram Coffin. AnAmPo
White Rat, The. Marguerite Young. MoPo
White Rose, A. John Boyle O'Reilly. AA; ACP; AnAmPo; HBV; OBEV; OBVV; OnYI; PoPl
White Rose. Sacheverell Sitwell. *See* Ballad: White Rose.
White-rose garland at her feet, The. E. B. B. James Thomson. HBV
White rose had a sorrow, A. The Betrayal of the Rose. Edith M. Thomas. AA
White rose in red rose-garden. Before the Mirror. Swinburne. OBVV
White Rose over the Water, The. George Walter Thornbury. VA
White rose tree that spent its musk, The. Old Gardens. Arthur Upson. HBV
White Roses. Cora Randall Fabbri. AA
White Roses. Ernest Rhys. VA
White, said Worsley, and glistening, the ridgy plain. Douglas Stewart. *Fr.* Worsley Enchanted, II. NeLNL
White sail upon the ocean verge. Arthur. William Winter. AA
White Sand, The. Edmund Wilson. NePoAm
White sand and cedars; cedars, sand. Sandy Hook. George Houghton. AA
White Sand and Grey Sand. *Unknown.* CBEP
White Season. Frances Frost. FaPON; TiPo
White sheep, white sheep. Clouds [*or* White Sheep]. *Unknown, wr. at. to* Christina Rossetti *and to* W. H. Davies. BoTP; BrR; OTPC (1946 ed.); PCH; SoPo; StVeCh; TiPo
White sheet of paper, A. James Brodey. *Fr.* Identikit. ANYP
White sheet on the tail-gate of a truck, A. Elegy for a Dead Soldier. Karl Shapiro. AmPP (4th ed.); AP; CoBMV; FaPL; MiAP; OxBA; ThLM; ToPo; WaaP; WaP
White shields they carry in their hands. The Hosts of Faery. *Unknown.* OnYI
White Ship, The. Dante Gabriel Rossetti. OnSP; PoVP
White Ships and the Red, The. Joyce Kilmer. MC; PAH
White sky, over the hemlocks bowed with snow. The Buck in the Snow. Edna St. Vincent Millay. AmLP; CrMA; NP; OTD
White soul of England's glory, sovereign star! Nelson. Archibald T. Strong. *Fr.* Sonnets of the Empire. BoAu
White Splendor. Leslie Savage Clark. ChIP
White Squall, The, *sel.* Thackeray.
After the Storm. PRWS
White Stag, The. Ezra Pound. LOW
White, stamen-shadowed petals of wild rose. Dogrose. Patric Stevenson. NeIP
White stars falling gently. Winter Joys. Dorothy Gradon. BoTP
White Steed of the Prairies, The. *Unknown.* CoSo
White swan of cities, slumbering in thy nest. Venice. Longfellow. AmPP
White Symphony. John Gould Fletcher. AnFE; APA; CoAnAm; MAPA
White-tailed Hornet, The. Robert Frost. NoP; OxBA
White the October air, no snow, easy to breathe. How to Get There. Frank O'Hara. FRC
White though ye be; yet, lillies, know. How Lillies Came White. Robert Herrick. AnAnS-2; EG; PoeP; SCEP-2
White-Throat Sings, A. Walter Prichard Eaton. DD; HBMV
White through the azure. The Swimmer of Nemi. "Fiona Macleod." SyP
White Tintoretto clouds beneath my naked feet. The Strand. Louis MacNeice. AnIV
White Tree in Bloom, A. John Richard Moreland. PGD
White Violet. Marian Osborne. CaP
White Violets. Benjamin R. C. Low. HBMV
White violets I'll bring. Flowers: For Heliodora. Meleager. SiSw
White way is the wind's way, A. The Wind's Way. Grace Hazard Conkling. HBV
White Weekend. Quincy Troupe. NBP
White wide wonder of a cloud, The. Assuagement. Sister Claude of Jesus. JKCP (1955 ed.)
White wind whispers of the woes, The. The Four Winds. Shane Leslie. OnYI
White Window, The. James Stephens. StVeCh; SUS; TiPo
White wings of commerce sailing far. In Memory of General Grant. Henry Abbey. AA
White Witch, The. James Weldon Johnson. BANP; CDC
Whitely, while benzine. Lachrymae Christi. Hart Crane. ReMP
Whiteness. "Isobel Hume." HBMV
Whiteness of the lily once was thine, The. The Maid. Katherine Brégy. CAW; GoBC
Whiteness, or Chastity. Joseph Beaumont. LiTL; LoBV
Whiter than White. Swift. RIS
Whiter there is not nor rosier. Peggy. Blanaid Salkeld. OnYI
Whitewinged circus/ of kittiewaking. Spring, St. Stephen's Green. Leslie Daiken. OnYI
Whither. John Vance Cheney. AA
Whither? Hartley Coleridge. *See* Whither Is Gone.
Whither. Philip Becker Goetz. AA
Whither? Wilhelm Müller, *tr. fr. German by* Longfellow. AWP
Whither Away? Mary Elizabeth Coleridge. CH
Whither away delight? The Glimpse. George Herbert. MaMe
Whither away is the Spring to-day? The World's May-Queen [*or* When Spring Comes to England]. Alfred Noyes. HBV; OBVV
Whither away, O Sailor! say? Outward. John G. Neihardt. HBV
Whither away, Robin. The Flight of the Birds. Edmund Clarence Stedman. GN
Whither depart the souls of the brave that die in the battle. Arthur Hugh Clough. *Fr.* Amours de Voyage, V. OAEP
Whither doth now this fellow flee. March. Robert Loveman. AA
Whither hast vanishèd. The Search. St. John of the Cross. BoC
Whither Is Gone [the Wisdom and the Power]. Hartley Coleridge. EPN; HBV; OBRV
(Whither.) VA
Whither leads this pathway, little one? Whither. John Vance Cheney. AA
Whither, mad maiden, wilt thou roame? To His Muse. Robert Herrick. OAEP
Whither, midst falling dew. To a Waterfowl. Bryant. AA; AmePo; AmLP; AmP; AmPP; AnAmPo; AnFE; AnNE; AP; APA; AWP; BoLiVe; CBEP; CH; CoAnAm; CoBA; DD; DiPo; ExPo; FaBoBe; FaBoEn; FaFP; FaPL; ForPo; GN; GTBS; GTBS-D; HBV; HBVY; HoPM; InP; LiTA; LiTG; MAmP; MaRV; MCCG; MWA-1; NeHB; NePA; NoP; OBRV; OHFP; OQP; OTPC; OxBA; PG (1945 ed.); Po; PoE; PoEL-4; PoLF; PoPo; PTK; SeCeV; SoP; TDP; TOP; TreF; TrGrPo; TRV; UnPo (1st ed.); WBLP; WGRP
Whither, O splendid ship, thy white sails crowding. A Passer-

by [*or* Passer By]. Robert Bridges. BoC; BrPo; CaFP; CMoP; CoBMV; EnLit; EtS; ForPo; GTBS-W; GTSE; GTSL; HBV; LiTB; LiTM; MoAB; MoBrPo; NBM; OAEP; OBNC; OBVV; PoVP; SeCeV; ShBV-3; VA; WiR
Whither, O, whither art thou fled. The Search. George Herbert. AnAnS-1; MaMe; MeP
Whither, O whither didst Thou fly? The Eclipse. Henry Vaughan. HBV; MemP; SoP
Whither, oh! whither wilt thou wing thy way? Flight of the Spirit. Felicia Dorothea Hemans. Sonn
Whither shall I, the fair maiden, flee from Sorrow? Sorrow. *Unknown.* AWP
Whither So Fast? *Unknown.* ElL
"Whither thus hastes my little book so fast?" The Writer to His Book. Thomas Campion. OAEP
Whiting and the Snail, The. "Lewis Carroll." *See* Lobster Quadrille, The.
Whitman's Ride for Oregon. Hezekiah Butterworth. PAH
Whitmonday. Louise MacNeice. NYBP
Whitsun Weddings, The. Philip Larkin. NePoEA-2; PoeP; TDP
Whit Sunday. Joseph Beaumont. OxBoCh
Whitsunday. George Herbert. AtBAP; MaMe
Whitsunday. John Keble. OBRV
Whittier. James Russell Lowell. *Fr.* A Fable for Critics. AmPP (4th ed.); AnNE; AP; OxBA
("There is Whittier, whose swelling and vehement heart.") CoBA
Whittier. Margaret E. Sangster. AA; DD
Whittington and His Cat. *Unknown.* CIV
Whittling. John Pierpont. GN
Who. Moishe-Leib Halpern, *tr. fr. Yiddish by* Joseph Leftwich. TrJP
Who? Florence Hoatson. BoTP
Who/ am I. Intervals. Robert Creeley. TPM
Who/ Are you/ Who is born. Vision and Prayer. Dylan Thomas. LiTG; LiTM (rev. ed.); MoPo
Who am I? Imitation of Walt Whitman. "Judy." BOHV
Who Are My People? Rosa Zagnoni Marinoni. BLPA; PoToHe
Who Are the Dead? Euripides, *tr. fr. Greek by* James Adam. MaRV
Who are the nobles of the earth, the true aristocrats. The True Aristocrat. W. Stewart. WBLP
"Who are the winds? Who are the winds?" The Winds. "John Eglinton." OnYI
Who Are the Wise Men? B. Y. Williams. ChIP; MaRV
Who are these among you. The Decision. Owen Dodson. PoNe
Who are these? Why sit they here in twilight? Mental Cases. Wilfred Owen. BrPo; CMoP; FaBoMo; LiTM (rev. ed.); MMA; WaP
Who are they. The Passengers. David Antin. NYBP
Who are we here? Intra-Political. Margaret Avison. MoCV
"Who are we waiting for?" "Soup burnt?" . . . Eight. The Feckless Dinner Party. Walter de la Mare. FaBoTw; MoPW
Who are we? Who? Towards a Walk in the Sun. K. William Kgositsile. BF
Who are ye, spirits that stand. The Blazing Heart. Alice Williams Brotherton. AA
"Who are ye with clustered light." The Pleiads. John Banister Tabb. UTS
"Who are you and whence do you come?" A Vagrant. Erik Axel Karlfeldt. PoPl
"Who are you?" asked the cat of the bear. Elizabeth J. Coatsworth. TiPo
Who are you dusky woman, so ancient hardly human. Ethiopia Saluting the Colors. Walt Whitman. AmP; GTBS-D; PAH; PoNe
Who are you, gray mysterious visitors. Cats. William Wallace Whitelock. CIV
Who Are You, Little I. E. E. Cummings. NYBP
"Who are you, Sea Lady." Santorin. James Elroy Flecker. CLwM; FaBoTw; GoJo; OBMV
Who are you that can fly? Questions for a Flying Squirrel to Answer. Rachel Field. RePo
"Who are you that so strangely woke." The Princess of Scotland. Rachel Annand Taylor. GoTS; SiSw
Who are you there that, from your icy tower. The Astronomers of Mont Blanc. Edgar Bowers. QFR
Who art thou, girl, in such mean garb arrayed? Religion. Vauquelin de la Fresnaye, *tr. by* Wilfrid Thorley. CAW
Who beckons the green ivy up. The Miracle. Walter de la Mare. CoBE; LiTB; UnPo (3d ed.)
Who Bids Us Sing? Rhys Carpenter. WGRP
Who borrows all your ready cash. A Friend. Marguerite Power. FaFP; SiTL
Who braves it now as doth young Histrio. Ortus Novus Urbe Britannus. Henry Parrot. TuPP
Who builds a church within his heart. The Church in the Heart [*or* The Church Within]. Morris Abel Beer. MaRV; PoToHe; SoP; TRV
Who builds a home has made a wondrous thing. Altars Raised to God. Martha Snell Nicholson. FaChP
Who builds him a house of stone or brick. Builders. Hortense Flexner. HBMV
Who builds of stone a shrine to bear his name. The Glory of Lincoln. Thomas Curtis Clark. PGD
Who builds the state? Builders of the State. Richard Watson Gilder. PoRL
"Who burst the barriers of my peaceful grave?" The Lament of the Damned in Hell. Edward Young. OxBoCh
Who bury the dead. The Heavenly Tree Grows Downward. Gerrit Lansing. CoPo
Who but the wind. The Wind. Betty Miller. BrR
Who by Searching Can Find Out God? Eliza Scudder. *See* Quest, The.
"Who called?" I said, and the words. Echo. Walter de la Mare. MoVE; OBMV; SeCeV; ShBV-4
Who Calls? Frances Clarke. HH; PoRh; SiSoSe; StaSt; TSW
Who calls me bold because I won my love. Song. Cosmo Monkhouse. VA
Who Calls the English Cold? Carl Bode. *Fr.* London Sonnets. ToPo
Who calls? Who calls? Who? For a Mocking Voice. Eleanor Farjeon. CH; PoMS; TiPo (1959 ed.)
Who came in the quiet night. The Little Fox. Marion Edey. TiPo
Who can bear/ The wail of a young orphan? Rabbi Yussel Luksh of Chelm. Jacob Glatstein. TrJP
Who can find a virtuous woman? The Virtuous Wife [*or* The Good Wife *or* A Virtuous Woman]. Proverbs, Bible, *O.T.* MaRV; TrGrPo; TRV
Who Can Forget? Leslie Savage Clark. ChIP
Who can give answer to your questioning. Interrogative. Sister M. Thérèse. MoRP
Who can live in heart so glad. The Merry Country Lad [*or* Pastoral]. Nicholas Breton. *Fr.* The Passionate Shepherd. CBEP; CH; ElL; ELP; LoBV; OA; OBSC; PoE; ReEn; SiCE; TuPP; ViBoPo
Who can make a delicate adventure. Advice to a Blue-Bird. Maxwell Bodenheim. HBMV; MAP; MoAmPo (1942 ed.)
Who can make a poem of the depths of weariness. Carl Sandburg. *Fr.* The People, Yes. MaRV; NAMP
Who Can Say. Alastair Reid. NePoEA
Who can say. Song. Tennyson. FaBoCh; LoGBV
Who can scape his bow? George Herbert. EG
Who can support the anguish of love? Ode. Ibn al-Arabi. AWP; LiTW
Who can surrender to Christ, dividing his best with the stranger. Where Is the Real Non-Resistant? Vachel Lindsay. OQP; StJW
Who can tell his years, for the winds have stretched? A Labourer. R. S. Thomas. ToPo
Who can tell how the lobster got. The Lobster Pot. John Arden. ELU
Who comes dancing over the snow. The New Year. Dinah Maria Mulock Craik. BrR; DD; HH; MPB; OTPC (1946 ed.); PCH; YeAr
Who Comes Here? *Unknown.* OTPC (1923 ed.)
("Who comes here?/ A grenadier.") OxNR
Who comes to England not to learn. England. Grace Ellery Channing. AA
Who comes to-night? We ope the doors in vain. Henry James. Robert Louis Stevenson. OBNC
Who copies Yours or Oxford's better part. The Man of Ross. Pope. *Fr.* Moral Essays, Epistle III. CoBE
Who could be sad in April. One April Day. John Richard Moreland. ChIP
Who could believe an ant in theory? Credibility. John Ciardi. ToPo
Who could have thought that men and women would feel. Old

Who (continued)
Paintings on Italian Walls. Kathleen Raine. NYBP
Who cries that the days of daring are those that are faded far. Deeds of Valor at Santiago. Clinton Scollard. HBV; PAH
Who crieth: "Woe"? who: "Alas"? The Drunkard. Proverbs, Bible, *O.T.* TrJP
Who danced Saturday mornings. Roots. Harold Telemaque. PoNe
Who dare complain or be ashamed. Celebrations. Austin Clarke. OxBI
Who Dat a-Comin' ovah Yondah? *with music.* *Unknown.* BoAN-1
Who dat knockin' at de do'? Encouragement. Paul Laurence Dunbar. YT
Who did sing, whose voice. The Singer. Keith Wilson. ThO
Who died on the wires, and hung there, one of two. The Silent One. Ivor Gurney. MMA
Who Dies If England Live? Kipling. PTK
Who does God's work will get God's pay. God's Pay. *Unknown.* STF
Who does not love the juniper tree? Juniper. Eileen Duggan. CAW; ChBR; MoSiPe
Who Does Not Love True Poetry. Henry Clay Hall. PoToHe (new ed.)
Who Does Not Love Wine, Women and Song. J. H. Voss. FaFP; SiTL
Who doth behold my mistress' face. The Fairest of Her Days. *Unknown.* EIL
Who doth desire that chaste his wife should be. Truth Doth Truth Deserve [*or* Advice to the Same]. Sir Philip Sidney. *Fr.* Arcadia. HBV; LiTL; SiPS
Who doubts has met defeat ere blows can fall. Columbus the World-Giver. Maurice Francis Egan. OQP; PGD
Who dreamed that beauty passes like a dream? The Rose of the World. W. B. Yeats. BoLiVe; BrPo; CMoP; EnLi-2 (1949 ed.); EnLit; FaBoEn; HBV; MoAB; MoBrPo; OBVV; PoAn; PoeP; PoVP; VA; ViPo (1962 ed.)
Who drives the horses of the sun. The Happiest Heart. John Vance Cheney. AA; AnAmPo; AnFE; APA; CoAnAm; HBV; HBVY; MaRV; OQP; PoMa; TreFS; WGRP
Who e'er. *See* Whoe'er.
Who ere shee bee. *See* Whoe'er she be.
Who even dead, yet hath his mind entire! Canto XLVII. Ezra Pound. CrMA; MoPo
Who ever. *See* Whoever.
Who fears to speak of Easter Week. Easter Week. *Unknown.* OnYI
Who fears to speak of Ninety-Eight? The Memory of the Dead. John Kelly Ingram. AnIV; HBV; OnYI; OxBI; PoFr; VA
Who feasts tonight? The Fairies Feast. Charles M. Doughty. CH
Who fed me from her gentle breast. My Mother. Ann Taylor. BLPA; DD; MaRV; OHIP; PaPo; PEDC; TreF
Who feels not, when the Spring once more. Aubrey Thomas De Vere. *Fr.* May Carols. IrPN
Who findeth comfort in the stars and flowers. L'Envoi [*or* Dedicatory Stanzas]. Thomas Lovell Beddoes. *Fr.* Death's Jest Book. ERoP-2; LO; OBNC
Who finds for Figaro's sake. Mozart at Zell-am-See. Vernon Watkins. MuSP
Who first reform'd our stage with justest laws. An Elegy on Ben Jonson. *At. to* John Cleveland, *also at. to* James Cleyton. MeLP; OBS; SeEP
Who first said "false as dreams"? Not one who saw. Dreams. Henry Timrod. AmePo
Who Follows in His Train? Reginald Heber. *See* Son of God Goes Forth to War, The.
Who forced the Muse to this alliance? On Professor Drennan's Verse. Roy Campbell. GTBS-P; WhC
Who gallops so late through wind and wild? The Elf-King. Goethe. PoPo
Who gave thee, O Beauty. Ode to Beauty. Emerson. AmPP (5th ed.); AP; ForPo; MWA-1; PoEL-4
Who goes amid the green wood? James Joyce. Chamber Music, VIII. HW
Who Goes By Lightly. Gertrude Callaghan. JKCP (1955 ed.)
Who Goes Home, *br. sel.* G. K. Chesterton.
"Men that are men again; who goes home." OtMeF
Who Goes There? Grace Duffie Boylan. HH
Who goes there? God knows. I'm nobody. How should I answer? 'Ετώσιον ἄχθος ἀρούρης. Robert Bridges. FaBoTw; QFR
Who goes there? hankering, gross, mystical, nude. Song of Myself, XX. Walt Whitman. TrGrPo
Who goes there, in the night. Apparitions [*or* It Shall Not Be Again]. Thomas Curtis Clark. MaRV; OQP; PEDC; PGD; PoRL; TRV
Who Goes with Fergus? W. B. Yeats. CMoP; FaBoCh; GoJo; LoGBV; MBW-2; PeVV; PoIE; PoRA (rev. ed.)
Who Goeth Hence. Helen Frazee-Bower. OQP
(When Death Shall Come.) MaRV
Who governs his own course with steady hand. Portrait of a Freeman. Abraham Cowley. *Fr.* Of Liberty; an Essay. PoFr
Who grace, for zenith had, from which no shadowes grow. Despair. Fulke Greville. Caelica, LXXXIII [LXXXIV]. OBSC; PoEL-1
Who grafted quince on Western may. The Avengers. Robert Graves. HBMV
Who Guessed Amiss the Riddle of the Sphinx. James Merrill. TwAmPo
Who hail us from the hill. Homage to Mürren. Morton Dauwen Zabel. NP
Who half asleep, or waking, does not hear it. The Furnace of Colors. Vernon Watkins. NYBP
Who harbors Hatred, sees a small. Horizons. Clinton Scollard. OQP
Who, harnessed in his mail of Self, demands. Self-Mastery. Bayard Taylor. MaRV
Who has a feeling she will come one day. White Queen. John Fuller. NePoEA-2
Who has a thing to bring. L'Ancien Régime. James Thomson. PoVP
Who has but dighted his tricks in a bed. This Is What the Watchbird Sings, Who Perches in the Lovetree. Bruce Boyd. NeAP
Who has described the wave. Thoughts in the Gulf Stream. Christopher Morley. EtS
Who has ever stopped to think of the divinity of Lamont Cranston? In Memory of Radio. LeRoi Jones. NeAP; NoP
Who Has Known Heights. Mary Brent Whiteside. BLPA; MaRV; NeHB
Who has not ceased from evil ways. No Peace. *Unknown.* *Fr.* The Upanishads. OnPM
Who has not found the heaven below. Emily Dickinson. TRV
Who has not heard of the dauntless *Varuna?* *Varuna.* George Henry Boker. PAH
Who has not heard of the Vale of Cashmere. The Light of the Haram. Thomas Moore. *Fr.* Lalla Rookh. EnRP
Who has not marveled at the might of kings. Kings. John Richard Moreland. ChIP; MaRV
Who has not thought, when scuffing shells. Lower Forms of Life. Mary Winter. GoYe
Who Has Not Walked upon the Shore. Robert Bridges. *See* Upon the Shore.
Who has robbed the ocean cave [*or* wave]. Song. John Shaw. AA; AmLP; HBV
Who has seen the pageant. Argumentum ad Hominem. Hyam Plutzik. FiMAP
Who Has Seen the Wind? Bob Kaufman. Kal
Who Has Seen the Wind? Christina Rossetti. *Fr.* Sing-Song. BoTP; BrR; CoBE; FaPON; GoJo; HBV; HBVY; MPB; OTD; OTPC; OuHeWo; PCH; PDV; PoPl; PoRh; PoVP; PPL; StVeCh; SUS; TiPo; TreFT; TSW
(Wind, The.) BoChLi; FaBoBe; GFA; MaRV; NeHB; RIS
Who has strangled the tired voice. Appeal. Noemia de Sousa. TTY
Who hasn't heard of London Bridge? Hay's Wharf. Richard Church. HaMV
Who Hath a Book. Wilbur D. Nesbit. BLPA; NeHB; OTD; SiSoSe; TiPo (1959 ed.); TreFS
Who hath believed that which we have heard. Behold, My Servant. Isaiah, Bible, *O.T.* OuHeWo
Who hath desired the sea?—the sight of salt water unbounded. The Sea and the Hills. Kipling. FaBV; OtMeF
Who hath ever felt the change of love. Sir Philip Sidney. FCP
Who hath gathered the wind in his fists? The Words of Agur. Proverbs, Bible, *O.T.* TrGrPo
Who hath given man speech? or who hath set therein. Chorus. Swinburne. *Fr.* Atalanta in Calydon. MaVP; ViBoPo

Who hath heard of such cruelty before. Epigram. Sir Thomas Wyatt. CBEP; FCP; SiPS
Who Hath His Fancy [*or* Fancie] Pleasèd. Sir Philip Sidney. AtBAP; EnRePo; ElL; FCP; OAEP; PoEL-1; QFR; SiCE
(Immortality.) OBSC
(Song: "Who hath his fancy pleasèd.") OBEV; SiPS
Who hath restored my sense, given me new breath. John Fletcher. *Fr.* The Faithful Shepherdess, III, i. LO
Who hath woe?/ Who hath sorrow? Wine and Woe. Proverbs, Bible, *O.T.* MaRV
Who have been lonely once. Careless Love. Stanley Kunitz. WaP
Who have no heaven come. String Quartet. Babette Deutsch. UnS
Who hears in the night. The Train in the Night. Elizabeth Riddell. NeLNL
Who I Am. Luis Gonzaga Pinto da Gama, *tr. fr. Portugese by* Anna Lomax. TTY
Who in One Lifetime. Muriel Rukeyser. Po
Who, in the brief, incredible northern spring. Let Him Return. Leona Ames Hill. PoToHe (new ed.)
Who, in the dark, has cast the harbor-chain? Putting to Sea. Louise Bogan. LiTM
Who, in the garden-pony carrying skeps. Horses. Dorothy Wellesley. ChMP; OBMV; ShBV-4
Who invited him in? What was he doing here. The Dirty Little Accuser. Norman Cameron. OxBS
Who Is at My Window? *Unknown.* GTBS-W; LiTG; TrGrPo
("Quho is at my windou, quho, quho?") EG
Who Is Drunk? Thomas Love Peacock. *See* Not Drunk Is He.
Who is in love with loveliness. Miracle. Lizette Woodworth Reese. MAP; MoAmPo
Who is it calling by the darkened river. Voices. Walter de la Mare. UnPo (3d ed.)
"Who is it knocking in the night." The Ballad of the Angel. Theodosia Garrison. HBV
Who is it runs through the many-storied mansion of myth. Dwarf of Disintegration. Oscar Williams. LiTM (rev. ed.); MoPo; NePA; PoCh; TwAmPo
Who is it stands trembling. The Cocktail Party. Harriet Zinnes. NYTB
Who Is It Talks of Ebony? Manmohan Ghose. OBMV
Who is it that this dark [*or* darke] night. Eleventh Song [*or* A Dialogue *or* Lovers' Dialogue]). Sir Philip Sidney. *Fr.* Astrophel and Stella. AtBAP; CLwM; EG; ElL; EnLi-1; EnRePo; FCP; FosPo; NoP; OBEV; OBSC; PoEL-1; ReEn; ReIE; SeCePo; SiCE; SiPS; TuPP; ViBoPo; WoL
Who is like unto thee who teachest knowledge. Hymn of Unity. *Unknown.* TrJP
Who is lord of lordly fate. Song. Charles Heavysege. *Fr.* Count Filippo. PeCV
Who Is on the Lord's Side? Frances Ridley Havergal. MaRV
Who Is on the Lord's Side? Grace B. Renfrow. SoP
Who is quick, quick, quick. The Swallow. Carmen Bernos de Gasztold. BiS
Who is she coming, whom all gaze upon. Sonnet: A Rapture concerning His Lady. Guido Cavalcanti. AWP
Who is she here that now I see. To Little Renee on First Seeing Her Lying in Her Cradle. William Aspenwall Bradley. HBV
Who is she that ascends so high. The Assumption. Sir John Beaumont. ACP (1952 ed.); CAW; GoBC
Who is she that comes, makyng turn every man's eye. Sonetto VII [*or* Chi è questa]. Guido Cavalcanti. CTC; ReMP
Who Is She That Looks Forth. Edward Taylor. *See* Preparatory Meditations: "Wonders amazed . . ."
Who Is Silvia [*or* Sylvia]? Shakespeare. *Fr.* The Two Gentlemen of Verona, IV, ii. ATP; BoLP; DiPo; ElL; EnL; EnRePo; FaBoBe; FaFP; GN; ILP; InPo; LiTB; NeHB; NoP; OAEP; OTPC; PoIE; PTK; SeCeV; SiTL; TreF; TrGrPo
(Silvia.) HBV; OBEV; OnPP
(Song: "Who is Silvia? what is she.") LiTG; ViBoPo; WHA
(Song of the Musicians.) BoLiVe
(Song to Silvia.) OBSC
(To Silvia.) MCCG; PoPo
("Who is Silvia? what is she?") AnFE; BEL; CoBE; EG; EnLi-1; EnLit; OuHeWo; SiCE; TOP
Who Is So Low. S. Ralph Harlow. MaRV
Who is so proud. The Performing Seal. Rachel Field. *Fr.* A Circus Garland. SoPo; StVeCh; TiPo (1959 ed.); UTS
Who Is Tapping at My Window. A. G. Deming. SoPo
Who Is That a-Walking in the Corn? Fenton Johnson. GoSl; NP; PoNe
Who is that calling through the night. Christmas at Indian Point. Edgar Lee Masters. NP
Who is that in the tall grasses singing. Song for Naomi. Irving Layton. WHW
Who is that pretty fellow. Work and Play. Martial. UnTE
Who is that school-girl? The Italian Air. Lewis MacAdams. ANYP
Who Is the Angel That Cometh? Adelaide Anne Procter. MaRV
Who is the baby, that doth lie. Song by Two Voices. Thomas Lovell Beddoes. PeER
Who is the happy warrior? Who is he. Character of the Happy Warrior [*or* The Happy Warrior]. Wordsworth. BEL; BoLiVe; EnLit; EnRP; EPN; FaBoBe; FaFP; HBV; HBVY; LiTB; LiTG; LoBV; MaRV; MBW-2; MERP; OBRV; OHFP; OQP; TIHL; TOP; TreF
Who is the honest man? Constancie. George Herbert. MaMe
Who Is the Man? *with music. Unknown.* TrAS
Who Is the Ratman? Stuart Peterfreund. QAH
Who is the runner in the skies. The Runner in the Skies. James Oppenheim. AnEnPo; MAP; MoAmPo (1942 ed.); NP; PFY; TrJP
Who is the sleeping giant. Giant's Tomb in Georgian Bay. "Katherine Hale." CaP
Who is this I hear?—Lo, this is I, thine heart. The Dispute of the Heart and Body of François Villon. Villon. AWP
Who is this that cometh from Edom. Vision of the Day of Judgment. Isaiah, Bible, *O.T.* WGRP
Who is this that cometh up not alone. The Bride Song. Christina Rossetti. *Fr.* The Prince's Progress. OBEV; OBVV; TOP
Who is this that darkeneth counsel by words without knowledge? The Voice Out of the Whirlwind [*or* God Replies]. Job, Bible, *O.T.* AWP; JAWP; MaRV; OuHeWo; TrGrPo; WBP
Who is this whose feet. The Swan's Feet. E. J. Scovell. FaBoMo
Who is this ye say is slain? Ellsworth. *Unknown.* PAH
Who is thy neighbor? He whom thou. Thy Neighbor. *Unknown.* OQP; SoP
Who is waiting at the doorstep now? Threshold. Charles David Webb. NePoAm-2
Who is, who is the rider there. Who. Moishe-Leib Halpern. TrJP
Who is wise?/ He who learns from everyone. The Good Man. *Fr.* The Talmud. TrJP
Who is your lady of love, O ye that pass. The Pilgrims. Swinburne. PoVP
Who Is't Now We Hear? John Lyly. *Fr.* Alexander and Campaspe. BiS
Who journeying when the days grow shorter, stops. Historic Time. Walter Savage Landor. *Fr.* The Impious Feast. OBRV
Who keeps Saint Angel gates? A Letter to Rome. Steven Peele. ReIE
Who Kill'd [*or* Killed] John Keats? Byron. EnRP; SiTL
Who killed Cock Robin? The Death and Burial of Cock Robin. Mother Goose. GoTP; HBV; HBVY; OTPC; OxNR; PPL; RIS. *See also* Here lies Cock Robbin . . .
Who Killed John Keats? Byron. *See* Who Kill'd John Keats.
Who killed Kildare? Who dared Kildare to kill? Epigram. Swift. HBV; TreFS
Who knocks at the Geraldine's door to-night. Ballad of the Little Black Hound. Dora Sigerson Shorter. OnYI; StPo
"Who knocks?" "I, who was beautiful." The Ghost. Walter de la Mare. BrPo; ChMP; CLwM; CMoP; ELP; EnLoPo; HaMV; HBMV; LiTM (1970 ed.); MoAB; MoBrPo; MoVE
Who Know Thee Best ("Who know her but as children do"). Sister Mary Catherine. JKCP (1955 ed.)
Who Knows? A. L. Milner-Brown. PBA; TTY
Who Knows? Nora Perry. AA
Who Knows a Mountain? Ethel Romig Fuller. OQP
Who knows his will? Meditation on a Memoir. J. V. Cunningham. QFR
Who knows if in the world beneath the ground. Who Are the Dead? Euripides. MaRV

Who Knows If the Moon's. E. E. Cummings. LOW; PoMS
Who knows it not, who loves it not. A Racing Eight. James L. Cuthbertson. PoAu-1
Who knows the name and country now. Mangers. W. H. Davies. MoRP
Who knows the thoughts of a child. Who Knows? Nora Perry. AA
Who knows? This Africa so richly blest. Who Knows? A.L.Milner-Brown. PBA; TTY
Who knows this or that? Limits. Emerson. MWA-1; OA; PoEL-4
Who knows through what mysterious tensions these. The Ivory Tower. Robert Hillyer. NYBP
Who knows what days I answer for to-day? The Young Neophyte. Alice Meynell. ACP; CAW; GoBC
Who knows, when raindrops are descending. Rain. Einar Benediktsson. LiTW
Who knows when the tiger passes. Color. Rowena Bennett. MPB (1956 ed.)
Who Knows Where. Detley von Liliencron, *tr. fr. German by* Ludwig Lewisohn. AWP
Who knows whether the sea heals or corrodes? Plague of Dead Sharks. Alan Dugan. AP; LiTM (1970 ed.)
Who knows who stands there, ghost. Conducted Tour. Emma Swan. NYTB
Who Learns My Lesson Complete? Walt Whitman. AmPP (3d ed.)
Who Likes the Rain? Clara Doty Bates. BoTP; GFA; OTPC (1946 ed.); PCH; PPL; TiPo
Who Likes to Love, Let Him Take Heed. *Unknown.* ReIE
Who list the Roman greatness forth to figure. Ruins of Rome, VI. Joachim du Bellay. OnPM
Who lists to see whatever nature, art. Ruins of Rome, II. Joachim du Bellay. OnPM
Who lit the furnace of the mammoth's heart. The Sun. Francis Thompson. *Fr.* Ode to the Setting Sun. MoAB; MoBrPo
Who lived at the top end of our street. The Retired Colonel. Ted Hughes. CBV; NePoEA-2; PoIE (1970 ed.)
Who lives in suit of armor pent. Chant Royal of High Virtue. Sir Arthur Quiller-Couch. HBV
Who Liveth Well. Horatius Bonar. *See* He Liveth Long Who Liveth Well.
Who living but daily discern it he may. A Description of Life and Riches. Thomas Tusser. SiCE
Who, long before she left her teens. An Old Song Resung. Charles Larcom Graves. CenHV
Who looking back upon his troubled years. Disillusion. Bessie B. Decker. PoToHe (new ed.)
Who Love the Rain. Frances Wells Shaw. *See* Who Loves the Rain.
Who love would seek. Silent Love. *Unknown.* LiTW
Who Loves a Garden. Louise Seymour Jones. BLPA; NeHB
Who loves a garden, loves a greenhouse too. William Cowper. *Fr.* The Task, III. BoPe
Who loves not knowledge? Who shall rail. In Memoriam A. H. H., CXIV. Tennyson. OAEP; ViPo; VP
Who Loves [*or* Love] the Rain. Frances Shaw. BrR; HBMV; MPB; NP; OQP; PoToHe (new ed.); SP; TreFT
Who loves the sea has found its waters blue. Chameleon. Gordon LeClaire. EtS
Who lyst his welthe and eas retayne. Sir Thomas Wyatt. EnPo
Who made the world, sir? Ants. Alfred Kreymborg. MAPA
Who makes the Past, a patterne for next yeare. To Sir Henry Goodyere. John Donne. MaMe; SeEP
Who Maketh the Grass to Grow. Psalms, CXLVII, Bible, *O.T.* FaPON
(Psalm CXVII.) TiPo (1952 ed.)
Who masquerades behind the winds? Moods. Leib Kwitko. TrJP
Who may praise her? Olive. Swinburne. GTBS
Who may quench the god-born fire. Isabella Valancy Crawford. *Fr.* The Helot. PeCV
Who—Me? Joan Suisted. SoP
Who, mid the grasses of the field. Dante. Bryant. ViBoPo
Who minds if the wind whistles and howls. Windy Morning. Harry Behn. TiPo (1959 ed.)
Who Minds to Bring His Ship to Happy Shore. Jasper Heywood. SiCE
Who, minter of medallions. Reading a Medal. Terence Tiller. GTBS-P
Who Misses or Who Wins. Thackeray. SD
Who money has, well wages the campaign. Money. Jehan du Pontalais. BOHV
Who must be blamed for the young head. The Landscape of the Heart. Geoffrey Grigson. LiTB; LiTM; WaP
Who nearer Nature's life would truly come. Thoreau. Amos Bronson Alcott. AA
Who needs words in autumn woods. Gloria Mundi. Siegfried Sassoon. MoPW
Who Never Ate with Tears His Bread. Goethe. *See* Sorrow.
Who never wept knows laughter but a jest. Compensation. E. M. Brainard. PoToHe
Who, not to trifle with his days or blood. The Ampler Circumscription. William Baylebridge. BoAV
Who Not with Others Bides. "Angelus Silesius," *tr. fr. German by* Paul Carus. OnPM
Who now dare longer trust thy mother hand? San Francisco. John Vance Cheney. PAH
Who now remembers Almack's balls. Reminiscences of a Dancing Man. Thomas Hardy. MoVE
Who now remembers General Galliéni. General Galliéni. Robert Hillyer. PG (1955 ed.)
Who Now Shall Sneer? James Russell Lowell. PAP
Who often found their way to pleasant meadows. Elegy for Minor Poets. Louis MacNeice. HaMV; ML; PP
Who on your breast pillows his head now. The Lost Jewel. Robert Graves. EnLoPo; NYBP
Who or why, or which, or what. The Akond [*or* Ahkond] of Swat. Edward Lear. ALV; BOHV; CenHV; FaBoCh; FiBHP; GoTP; NA; OnPP; RIS; SiTL
Who owns the moonlit skies, the purple dawn. Owning. Wilmot B. Lane. CaP
Who owns these cattle, Corydon? Philondas? Prythee say. The Herdsmen. Theocritus. Idylls, IV. AWP
"Who owns these lands?" the Pilgrim said. The Staff and Scrip. Dante Gabriel Rossetti. OAEP; PoVP
Who pads through the wood. The Cat. Joseph Payne Brennan. ShM
Who paid his way in flesh sticks. Hero and Holy Man. Peter Fellowes. QAH
Who Pilots Ships. Daniel Whitehead Hicky. BrR; MoSiPe
Who plays with fire. Primer of Consequences. Virginia Brasier. ShM
Who pleasure follows pleasure slays. Sensuality. Coventry Patmore. *Fr.* The Angel in the House. OBVV
Who plots, then, the lines. Le Fou. Robert Creeley. FRC
Who Ponders National Events Shall Find. Wordsworth. EPN
Who praises God the most, what says he more than he. Richard Chenevix Trench. *Fr.* A Century of Couplets. OBRV
Who Prayed? *Unknown.* STF
Who Profits Most? *Unknown.* SoP
Who prop, thou ask'st, in these bad days, my mind? To a Friend. Matthew Arnold. EnLi-2; EPN; MBW-2; OAEP; PoVP; Sonn; ViPo; ViPP; VP
Who put that crease in your soul. Chapel Deacon. R. S. Thomas. ACV; ToPo
Who puts back into place a fallen bar. The Father's Business. Edwin Markham. TRV
Who puts off shift. My Naked Aunt. Archibald MacLeish. NePA
Who questions if the punctual sun unbars. Love Redeemed, LXXXII. William Baylebridge. BoAV; PoAu-1
Who raps at my window? Halloween. Marnie Pomeroy. PoSC
Who reach their threescore years and ten. Threescore and Ten. Richard Henry Stoddard. HBV
Who reade a chapter when they rise. George Herbert. MaMe
Who reaps the grain and plows the sod. Countryman's God. Roger Winship Stuart. MaRV
Who refuses to die is tormented. To Die. Paul Eluard. OnPM
Who Reigns? Shelley. *Fr.* Prometheus Unbound. SeCePo
Who remains in London. Spring Song in the City. Robert Buchanan. HBV; OTPC (1923 ed.); VA
Who represents my body in Pentagon? Pentagon Exorcism. Allen Ginsberg. WOW
Who ride by night through the woodland so wild? The Erl-King. Goethe, *tr. by* Sir Walter Scott. MaC
Who rideth so fast as a fleet Navajo? Song of the Navajo. Albert Pike. PoOW

Who rideth through the driving rain. The King's Son. Thomas Boyd. AnIV; OBMV; OxBI
Who rose up like a goddess from the sea. The Museum. William Abrahams. WaP
Who Runs May Read. John Keble. *Fr.* The Christian Year. SoP; VA
"There is a book, who runs may read," 1 *st.* FaChP
Who said, "Peacock Pie"? The Song of the Mad Prince. Walter de la Mare. AtBAP; FaBoCh; GoJo; LoGBV; MoVE; OAEP (2d ed.); ShBV-4
Who said to the trout? Pisces. R. S. Thomas. POTi
Who saw the petals. The Secret Song. Margaret Wise Brown. PDV
Who say[e]s that fictions on[e]ly and false hair. Jordan. George Herbert. CABA; EP; FaBoEn; LiTB; MaMe; MeLP; MePo; NoP; OBS; PAn; PIA; Po; PoAn; PoEL-2; PoFS; PP; PrWP; ReEn; SCEP-1; SeCP; SeEP; VaPo
Who says that it's by my desire. People Hide Their Love. Wu Ti. LiTW
"Who says that the Irish are fighters be birth?" The Peaceable Race. T. A. Daly. HBV
Who seeks for heaven alone to save his soul. The Way. Henry van Dyke. MaRV; OQP; TRV
Who seeks perfection in the art. Perfection. Francis Carlin. FaFP; HBMV
Who Seeks to Please All Men. Lord Holland. MaRV
Who sees my face so pale & sad with greife. *Unknown.* SeCSL
Who sees the first marsh marigold. A Charm for Spring Flowers. Rachel Field. TiPo (1959 ed.)
Who sees with equal eye, as God of all. Pope. *Fr.* An Essay on Man. FaBoEn
Who serves his country best? The Better Way. "Susan Coolidge." PaA
Who shall decide, when doctors disagree. Of the Use of Riches. Pope. *Fr.* Moral Essays, Epistle III. MBW-1
Who Shall Deliver Me? Christina Rossetti. *See* Battle Within, The.
Who shall doubt, Donne, where I a poet bee. To John Donne. Ben Jonson. AnAnS-2; MaPo; NoP; ReIE; SeCP; SeCV-1; TuPP
Who Shall Have My Fair[e] Lady? *Unknown.* AtBAP; CBEP; EG; EnLoPo; LO; OxBoLi; PoEL-1
(My Fair Lady.) UnTE
(Under the Leaves Green.) OxBoLi
Who shall invoke when we are gone. Tragic Love. Walter James Turner. LO; OBMV
Who shall know the way. Flight. Harold Vinal. FiSC
Who shall separate us from the love of Christ? Romans, Bible, *N.T.* BoC
Who Shall Speak for the People? Carl Sandburg. The People, Yes, Sec. 24. OxBA
Who shall tell the lady's grief. On the Death of a Cat, a Friend of Mine Aged Ten Years and a Half. Christina Rossetti. CIV
Who shall tell what did befall. Wealth. Emerson. ImOP; MWA-1
Who shall thy gay buffoonery describe? To the Mocking-Bird. Richard Henry Wilde. *See also* Winged mimic of the woods! AnAmPo.
Who shall understand the mysteries of Thy creations? The Royal Crown, XXIV. Solomon ibn Gabirol. AWP
Who shall welcome home. The Hosts. George M. Brady. NeIP
Who shot the snake? beat it to death on the road? In Memoriam S. L. Akintola. David Knight. MoCV
Who Sleeps by Day and Walks by Night. Henry David Thoreau. PoEL-4
Who smoke-snorts toasts o' My Lady Nicotine. Variations on an Air: After Robert Browning. G. K. Chesterton. InP; Par
Who so late. At the Garden Gate. David McCord. FaPON; RIS; StaSt
Who So List to Hount. Sir Thomas Wyatt. *See* Hind, The.
Who so valiant to decide? Young Woman at a Window. Mark Van Doren. LiTA; MoPo; MoVE
Who sows the seas, or ploughs the easy shore? Woman's Inconstancy. Phineas Fletcher. *Fr.* Sicelides. EIL
Who spurs his horse against the mountain-side. Fond Youth. Samuel Rogers. *Fr.* Human Life. OBRV
Who stands before me on the stairs. Body and Spirit. W. H. Davies. AtBAP
Who Stole the Bird's Nest? Lydia Maria Child. OTPC; PRWS; SAS
Who storms the moss-grown walls of eld. The Wages. Don Marquis. MaRV
Who strives to mount Parnassus hill. Verses [*or* Reply to an Imitation . . . of Horace]. Richard Bentley. EiCL; OBEC; ViBoPo
Who strolls so late, for mugs a bait. French Lisette; a Ballad of Maida Vale. William Plomer. ErPo; LiTM (rev. ed.); SiTL
"Who stuffed that white owl?" No one spoke in the shop. The Owl-Critic. James Thomas Fields. BLPA; BOHV; CenHV; EvOK; GoTP; GSP; HBV; RIS; StPo; TreFS; WBLP; YaD
Who tamed your lawless Tartar blood? To Russia. Joaquin Miller. AA; AmePo; AnAmPo
Who tames the lion now? Song. Thomas Lovell Beddoes. PoE; ViBoPo; WiR
Who tarried in Jericho. In Jericho. *Unknown.* SiTL
Who Taught Thee First to Sigh? Edward de Vere, Earl of Oxford. CoBE; TuPP
Who taught this pleading to unpractised eyes? To a Gipsy Child by the Sea-Shore. Matthew Arnold. PAn; ViPP
Who, then, was Cestius. Rome. Thomas Hardy. CLwM; EnLi-2; MoAB
Who thinks love is a prize to put away. For Eros II. Audrey Wurdemann. MoLP
Who Thou art I know not. God the Architect [*or* To God, the Architect]. Harry Kemp. HBMV; MaRV; TrPWD; TRV; WGRP
Who thought of the lilac? The Lilac. Humbert Wolfe. FaPON; HBVY; MoBrPo; NeMA; OTPC (1946 ed.); YT
Who Translates a Poet Badly. Gonzalez Prada, *tr. fr. Spanish by* William M. Davis. ELU
Who travels by the weary wandering way. Despair. Spenser. *Fr.* The Faerie Queene, I. PoG; SeCePo
Who Walks by the Dockside. R. G. G. Price. SiTL
Who Walks There? Kenneth Patchen. WIRo
Who Walks with Beauty. David Morton. BLPA; FaBoBe; GBV (1952 ed.); HBMV; NeHB; TreFT
Who walks with God must take His way. His Way. *Unknown.* FaChP
Who Wants a Birthday? David McCord. BiCB
Who wants my jellyfish? The Jellyfish. Ogden Nash. FaPON
Who Wants the Boys and Girls? *Unknown.* SoP
Who Wants to Travel All Over Europe and See Nothing but a Lot of American Tourists? I Do. Ogden Nash. SiTL
Who wants Wednesday? Who wants thay day? Auction. John Holmes. WaKn
Who Was It Came. Daniel Hoffman. CoAP
Who Was It, Tell Me. Heine. *See* Sag' mir wer einst die Uhren erfund.
Who was it then that lately took me in the wood? Faun-taken. Rose O'Neill. AnAmPo; HBMV
Who was there had seen us. The Dark Girl's Rhyme. Dorothy Parker. InMe
Who weeps now anywhere in the world? Solemn Hour. Rainer Maria Rilke. PoPl; TrJP
Who Were before Me. John Drinkwater. OBMV
Who were the builders? Question not the silence. The Nameless Doon [*or* Dun]. William Larminie. AnIL; IrPN; NBM; OnYI; OxBI
Who were the Wise Men in the long ago? Who Are the Wise Men? B. Y. Williams. ChIP; MaRV
Who were they, what lonely men. Jodrell Bank. Patric Dickinson. POTi
"Who Wert and Art and Evermore Shalt Be." William Channing Gannett. TrPWD
Who? Who? *Unknown.* CH
Who, who will be the next man to entrust his girl to a friend? Ezra Pound. *Fr.* Homage to Sextus Propertius. FaBoMo
Who will belive my verse in time to come. Sonnets, XVII. Shakespeare. DiPo; EnLi-1; SiCE; Sonn
Who Will Buy a Poem? Mahon O'Heffernan, *tr. fr. Early Modern Irish by* Kenneth Jackson. AnIL
Who will feed the dicky-birds on the garden wall? Who? Florence Hoatson. BoTP
Who will go drive with Fergus now. Who Goes with Fergus? W. B. Yeats. CMoP; FaBoCh; GoJo; LoGBV; MBW-2; PeVV; PoIE; PoRA (rev. ed.)
Who will in fairest book of nature know. Sir Philip Sidney.

Who (continued)
Fr. Astrophel and Stella. BWP; CABA; FCP; MaPo; NoP; PAn; ReEn; ReIE; SiCE; SiPS
Who Will Mend Them? *Unknown, tr. fr. Japanese by* Ishii *and* Obata. OnPM
Who will protect you from the thrust of wings. To My Friend, behind Walls. Carolyn Kizer. NePoAm-2
Who will remember, passing through this Gate. On Passing the New Menin Gate. Siegfried Sassoon. AnEnPo; OBMV; Sonn
Who will say a word for a country town of a sultry summer night? Not without Beauty. John A. B. McLeish. CaP
Who will say that music is all we've heard? For Marian Anderson. Frederick Bock. NYTB
Who Will Shoe Your Feet? *with music. Unknown.* BFSS
Who Will Shoe Your Pretty Little Foot? *Unknown. See* Lass of Lochroyan, The.
Who will show us where. At the Doors. "Der Nistor." TrJP
Who will watch thee, little mound. The Long Night. Harry Bache Smith. AA
Who winds the clumsy flower clock now, I wonder. Heavy, Heavy, Heavy. John Malcolm Brinnin. NYBP
Who wins his Love shall lose her. Lost Love. Andrew Lang. HBV
Who Wishes to Behold. Petrarch, *tr. fr. Italian by* Lord Charlemont. WoL
Who with the soldiers was stanch danger-sharer. The Daughter of the Regiment. Clinton Scollard. PAH
Who with thy leaves shall wipe (at need). Another. Robert Herrick. AnAnS-2
Who would be/ A mermaid fair. The Mermaid. Tennyson. BoTP; FaPON; GN; GoTP; MPB; OTPC (1946 ed.); PCH; PoMS; TSW
Who would be/ A merman bold. The Merman. Tennyson. BoTP; FaPON; GN; GoTP; OTPC (1946 ed.); PCD; PCH; PoMS
Who Would Have Thought? George Herbert. PG (1955 ed.) ("Who would have thought my shrivelled heart.") EG; LO
Who Would Have Thought. Thomas Howell. *Fr.* The Lover Deceived Writes to His Lady. EIL
Who would linger idle. The Swimmer. Roden Noel. OBVV
Who Would List. *Unknown, tr. fr. French by* Andrew Lang. *Fr.* Aucassin and Nicolette. CTC
Who would not be/ The Laureate bold. The Laureate. William Aytoun. Par
Who would please all, and himself, too. Well-packed Wisdom. Benjamin Franklin. *Fr.* Poor Richard's Almanac. StaSt
Who would true valour see. The Pilgrim [*or* The Pilgrim Song]. Bunyan. *Fr.* The Pilgrim's Progress. BoTP; CBEP; CoMu; ELP; EvOK; GN; HBV; MaRV; MemP; OBS; OtMeF; OTPC; PCH; PeRV; RG; TiPo (1952 ed.); WaKn; WiR
Who would wish back the saints upon our rough. At the Goal. Christina Rossetti. OQP
Who wrote *Who wrote Icon Basilike?* On "Who Wrote Icon Basilike" by Dr. Christopher Wordsworth, Master of Trinity. Benjamin Hall Kennedy. PV
Who'd Be a Hero (Fictional)? Morris Bishop. FiBHP
Who'd belive me if. The Third Dimension. Denise Levertov. CBV; NeAP
Who'd love again on this old rambling star. Wisdom. Padraic Fallon. OnYI
Whoe'er she be [*or* Who ere shee bee]. Wishes to His [*or* for the] Supposed Mistress. Richard Crashaw. AnFE; ATP; BEL; CoBE; EnLit; GoBC; GTBS; GTBS-D; GTBS-P; GTBS-W; GTSE; GTSL; HBV; LiTG; LiTL; MaMe; MeLP; MemP; MePo; OAEP; OBEV; OBS; PoEL-2; ReEn; SCEP-1; SeCL; SeCP; SeCV-1; SeEP; TreFT; ViBoPo; WHA
Whoe'er you are, your master see. Inscription for a Statue of Love. Voltaire. LiTW
Whoever [*or* Who ever] comes to shroud me, do not harm[e]. The Funeral[l]. John Donne. AnAnS-1; ATP; AWP; BWP; CABA; CBEP; CoBE; DiPo; EnLi-1 (1949 ed.); EnLoPo; EnRePo; InPo; JAWP; LiTL; LO; MaMe; MBW-1; MeLP; MeP; NoP; OBEV; OBS; PoE; PoEL-2; PoRA; ReEn; SCEP-1; SeCP; SeCV-1; SeEP; TOP; TuPP; WBP
Whoever [*or* Who ever] guesses, thinks, or dream[e]s he know[e]s. The Curse. John Donne. CBEP; MaMe; NoP; OAEP
Who ever had/ Such a whale of a plan. The Wall of China. Padraic Colum. RoGo
Whoever has heard of St. Gingo. The New Cecilia. Thomas Lovell Beddoes. ERoP-2; PeER
Whoever hath her wish thou hast thy Will. Sonnets, CXXXV. Shakespeare. PAn; ReEn
Whoever hath washed his hands of living. Courage. Sadi. *Fr.* The Gulistan. AWP; JAWP; OnPM; WBP
Whoever is washed ashore at that place. Legend. Ralph Gustafson. CaP; PeCV (1967 ed.)
Whoever it was who brought the first wood and coal. Banking Coal. Jean Toomer. PoNe (1970 ed.)
Whoever lives true life, will love true love. England. Elizabeth Barrett Browning. *Fr.* Aurora Leigh, I. VA
Who Ever Loved, That Not at First Sight? Christopher Marlowe. *See* It Lies Not in Our Power to Love or Hate.
Whoever loves, if he do not propose. Love's Progress. John Donne. Elegies, XVIII. LiTB; LiTG; MaMe; ViBoPo
Who ever sailes neere to Bermuda coast. Caelica, LXI. Fulke Greville. NCEP
Who ever saw so fair a sight. Samuel Daniel. *Fr.* Hymen's Triumph. OBSC
Whoever weeps somewhere out in the world. Silent Hour. Rainer Maria Rilke. AWP; OnPM; WoL
Whoever with the compasses of his eyes. Waitress. Karl Shapiro. FiMAP; TwAmPo
Whoever without money is in love. Sonnet: Of Why He Is Unhanged. Cecco Angiolieri da Siena. AWP
Whoever you are: at evening step forth. Eingang (Prelude). Rainer Maria Rilke, *tr. by* M. D. Herter Norton. Po
Whoever you are, go out into the evening. Initiation. Rainer Maria Rilke, *tr. by* C. F. MacIntyre. TrJP
Whoever You Are Holding Me Now in Hand. Walt Whitman. InvP; MWA-1; PoEL-5; PoSa
Whoever you are, I fear you are walking the walks of dreams. To You. Walt Whitman. MWA-1
Whoever you are! motion and reflection are especially for you. The Divine Ship Sails the Divine Sea for You. Walt Whitman. MoRP
Whole Armor, The. Charles Wesley. SoP
Whole day have I followed in the rocks, The. Fergus and the Druid. W. B. Yeats. CoBE
Whole day long, under the walking sun, The. The Sleeping Giant. Donald Hall. CaFP; NePoEA; NYBP; TwCP
Whole Duty of a Poem, The. Arthur Guiterman. PoToHe (new ed.)
Whole Duty of Berkshire Brooks, The. Grace Hazard Conkling. HBMV; HBVY
Whole Duty of Children. Robert Louis Stevenson. EvOK; HBV; HBVY; NeHB; OTPC; PoVP; SAS; ThGo; TreFS
Whole Duty of Man, The. Henry Vaughan. OQP
Whole gulfs of red and fleets of red. Emily Dickinson. AmLP
Whole health resides with peace. Description of Elysium. James Agee. CrMA
Whole landscape drifted away to the north, The. A Window on the North. R. A. D. Ford. MoCV
Whole process is a lie, The. The Ivy Crown. William Carlos Williams. NoP
Whole showers of tears to Chloris I will pour. Chloris, IV. William Smith. Sonn; TuPP
Whole towns shut down. The Late Snow & Lumber Strike of the Summer of Fifty-Four. Gary Snyder. NaP; NMP
Whole weight of the ocean smashes on rock, The. An Address to the Vacationers at Cape Lookout. William Stafford. NYBP
Whole, wide world, turned selfless for a day, The. Alchemy. Adelaide Love. PGD
Whole world now is but the minister, The. The Growth of Love, III. Robert Bridges. Sonn
Whole Year Christmas, The. Angela Morgan. SoP; TRV
Who'll Be a Witness for My Lord?, *with music. Unknown.* BoAN-1
Who'll buy my laces? I've laces to sell! The Lace Pedlar. Catherine A. Morin. BoTP
Who'll Buy My Valley Lilies? Eleanor Farjeon. BrR
Who'll come and play with me here under the tree. Employment. Jane Taylor. OTPC (1923 ed.); PPL
Who'll have the crumpled pieces of a heart? Laurana's Song. Richard Hovey. AA
Who'll Help a Fairy? *Unknown.* BoTP
"Who'll rage against all government." The Lion and O'Reilly. Richard Weber. PPON

Who'll That Be. Kenneth Patchen. WaKn
Who'll walk the fields with us to town. Market Day. Mary Webb. CH
Wholly the Lord's. Richard Baxter. SoP
Whom bold Cymochles traveiling to finde. Spenser. *Fr.* The Faerie Queene, II, 6. MBW-1
Whom can I confess to? In the Interest of Black Salvation. Don L. Lee. BP; WSL
Whom does He love the most? The Hungry. Caroline Giltinan. OQP; SoP
Whom first we love, you know, we seldom wed. Changes. "Owen Meredith." PoLF
Whom Having Not Seen We Love. Isaac Watts. SoP
Whom I lay down for dead rises up in blood. In All the Argosy of Your Bright Hair. Dunstan Thompson. WaP
"Whom I shall kiss," I heard a Sunbeam say. Betrayal. John Banister Tabb. ACP
Whom Lesbia Loved. Catullus, *tr. fr. Latin by* Horace Gregory. LiTW
"Whom lovest thou the best, enigmatical man." Prose Poem: The Stranger. Baudelaire. OnPM
Whom Shall One Teach. Isaiah, XXVIII: 9-13, Bible, *O.T.* TrJP
Whom the Gods Love. Margaret E. Bruner. PoLF
"Whom the Gods Love." Mark A. De Wolfe Howe. AA
"Whom the gods love die young," I used to quote. Whom the Gods Love. Margaret E. Bruner. PoLF
"Whom the gods love die young;"—if gods ye be. Mark A. De Wolfe Howe. AA
"Whom the gods love die young." The thought is old. I Die, Being Young. David Gray. *Fr.* In the Shadows. VA
"Whom the gods love die young" was said of yore. Byron. *Fr.* Don Juan, IV. EnLit
Whom the Lord loveth He chasteneth often. That's All. *Unknown.* SoP
Whom the untaught Shepherds call. Songs of the Pixies. Samuel Taylor Coleridge. OBEC
Whom thus answered the Arch Fiend now undisguised. Satan's Guile. Milton. *Fr.* Paradise Regained, I. LiTB; OBS
Whom We Revere. James Russell Lowell. *Fr.* Under the Old Elm, III. PGD
Whomsoever there are. Stout Affirmation. Kenneth Burke. TwAmPo
Whon men beth muriest at her mele. All Turns into Yesterday. *Unknown.* MeEL
Who-o-o-o-o! Harry Silleck Grannatt. StaSt
Whoop! the Doodles have broken loose. "Call All." *Unknown.* PAH
Whoopee, Ti Yi Yo, Git Along, Little Dogies. *Unknown.* AmPP; AS, *sl. abr., with music*; CoSo, *incl.* Owen Wister's *vers., with music*; FaPON; IHA; InP; MPB; StVeCh (1940 ed.); TiPo; TreF; TSW, *abr.*; WaKn
(Git Along, Little Dogies.) ABF, *with music*; MoShBr; StVeCh (1955 ed.)
(Run Along, You Little Dogies, *diff. vers., with music.*) OuSiCo
(Whoopee Hi Ogie, *with music.*) BFSS
(Whoopie Ti Yi Yo, Git Along Little Dogies.) OTPC (1946 ed.)
Whoopin' up cattle. Clear Rock's Chisholm Trail. *Unknown.* CoSo
Whooping Crane, The. Vassar Miller. ToPo
Whoppers. John A. Lomax, Jr. OuSiCo
Whore. Gene Fowler. ThO
Whore that rides in us abides, The. *Unknown.* SCAP
Who's In? Elizabeth Fleming. BoTP; BrR; MoSiPe
Who's in the Next Room? Thomas Hardy. PoEL-5; QFR
Who's Most Afraid of Death? [Thou]. E. E. Cummings. CMoP; NoP; SeCeV
Who's That a-Knocking? Emile Jacot. BoTP
Who's that a-knocking at my door? Rollicking Bill the Sailor. *Unknown.* AmSS
Who's That at My Bedroom Window? *with music.* *Unknown.* ShS
(Drowsy Sleeper, The.) BaBo (A *and* B *vers.*)
(Wake Up, You Drowsy Sleepers, *with music.*) BFSS
Who's that beggar-man? Come and see. Caw, Caw. F. Hey. SAS
Who's That Calling So Sweet? —— Deveen. SCC
Who's that dusty stranger? What's he doing here? City Sparrow. Alfred Kreymborg. OCS
Who's that knocking at my door? Abram Brown. *Unknown.* SoAmSa
Who's that knocking on the window? Innocent's Song. Charles Causley. GTBS-P; POTi
Who's that ringing at my door bell? *Unknown.* FaBoCh; LoGBV; OxNR
"Who's that ringing at the front door bell?" *Unknown.* BoTP
"Who's that tickling my back?" said the wall. The Tickle Rhyme. Ian Serraillier. SoPo
Who's that with roses and with laurels crowned. Sonata. Hal Summers. MuSP
Who's the Fool Now? *Unknown.* *See* Martin to His Man.
Who's the Pretty Girl Milkin' the Cow? *with music.* *Unknown.* AS
Who's There? Frances Frost. RePo
Who's there? Shakespeare. *Fr.* Hamlet, I, i, iv, *and* v. ExPo
Who's Who. W. H. Auden. CABA; CoBMV; MoAB; MoBrPo (1950 ed.); MoPW; NeMA; PoPo; ReMP; Sonn
Whose absolute dumbness circumscribed by sound. On First Hearing Beethoven. George Barker. UnS
Whose candles light the tulip tree? Tulip Tree. Sacheverell Sitwell. MoBrPo
Whose dog am I? A Good Day's Work. Naomi Replansky. WOW
Whose doorway was it, in the sordid street. The Rainbow. Vine Colby. HBMV
Whose eye has marked his gendering? On his throne. The Tornado. Charles de Kay. EtS
Whose freedom is by suff'rance, and at will. William Cowper. *Fr.* The Task, V. EnRP; PoFr
Whose furthest footsep never strayed. Envoy. Richard Hovey. AA; HBV
Whose Hand. *Unknown, tr. fr. Hebrew by* Arthur Davis. TrJP
"Whose I Am." Frances Ridley Havergal. SoP
Whose is that noble dauntless brow? Verses Intended to Be Written below a Noble Earl's Picture. Burns. HoPM
Whose is the love that, gleaming through the world. To Harriet ——. Shelley. Queen Mab: Dedication. EPN
Whose is the river, Excellency, whose the fish. The Geographers. Karl Shapiro. OxBA
Whose is the speech. The Two Poets. Alice Meynell. OBVV
Whose is this horrifying face. Ecce Homo. David Gascoyne. *Fr.* Miserere. ChMP; FaBoMo; FaBoTw; LiTM (rev. ed.); NeBP; OnHM
Whose little beast? Donkey. Mark Van Doren. EaLo
Whose little pigs are these, these, these? *Unknown.* OxNR
Whose love's a broad highway. The Cul-de-Sac. "Jan Struther." LO
Whose minds like horse or ox. The Learned Men. Archibald MacLeish. MoAB; MoAmPo (1950 ed.)
Whose Old Cow? *Unknown.* CoSo
Whose senses in so evil consort their stepdame Nature lays. Sir Philip Sidney. Astrophel and Stella: Seventh Song. FCP
Whose were they those voices? What footsteps came near me? Dirge. Aubrey Thomas De Vere. IrPN
Whose whips are those cracking up the river? The Last Night of Winter. Winifred Welles. NP
Whose woods these are I think I know. Stopping by Woods on a Snowy Evening. Robert Frost. AmLP; AmP; AmPP; AnFE; AnNE; AP; APA; BoLiVe; BoNaP; CABA; CaFP; CBV; CMoP; CoAnAm; CoBA; CoBMV; DiPo; ExPo; FaBoCh; FaBV; FaFP; FaPON; FlW; ForPo; GBV (1952 ed.); GoJo; GTBS-W; HBMV; HoPM; ILP; InP; InPo; LiTA; LiTG; LiTM; LoGBV; MAP; MaPo; MasP; MoAB; MoAmPo; MoShBr; MoVE; MWA-2; NeMA; NePA; NoP; NP; OTPC (1942 ed.); OxBA; OTPC (1946 ed.); PCD; PDV; PG (1955 ed.); PoAn; PoE; PoeP; PoFS; PoPo; PoRA; PoSa; PoSC; PTK; ReMP; RePo; ShBV-1; SiSoSe; StaSt; StVeCh; SUS; TDP; ThWaDe; TiPo; TreFS; TrGrPo; TSW; TwAmPo; TwCP; UnPo (3d ed.); UTS; ViBoPo (1958 ed.); WAKn; WHA
Whoso delighteth to proven and assay. Thomas More to Them That Seek Fortune. Sir Thomas More. EnRePo
Whoso Draws Nigh to God. *Unknown.* MaRV; TRV
Whoso has felt the Spirit of the highest? Knowledge. Frederic W. H. Myers. *Fr.* St. Paul. FaChP; OQP; TRV
Whoso in love would bear the bell. Ballad[e] of Ladies' Love. Villon. ErPo; UnTE
Whoso list to hunt. Sir Thomas Wyatt. *See* Hind, The.

"Whoso Loseth His Life." Swinburne. *See* Unto Each His Handiwork.
Whoso ne knoweth the strength, power, and might. Venus and Cupide. Sir Thomas More. EnRePo
Whoso That Will. Henry VIII, King of England. TuPP
Whoso the path of law would tread. The Inflamed Disciple. Arthur Kramer. InMe
Whoso thou art that passest by this place. An Epitaph of Maister Win Drowned in the Sea. George Turberville. EnPo
Whoso thy witty writings thoroughly knows. In Senecam. John Heath. SiCE
Whoso to marry a minion wife. A Minion Wife. Nicholas Udall. *Fr.* Ralph Roister Doister. EIL
Whoso walks in solitude. Emerson. *Fr.* Woodnotes, II. OBVV
Whosoe'er had look'd upon the glory of that day. Palermo. Harriet Eleanor Hamilton King. *Fr.* The Disciples. VA
Whosoever Shall Loose His Life. Richard Crashaw. MaMe
"Who've ye got there?"—Only a dying brother. "The Brigade Must Not Know, Sir!" *Unknown.* MC; OTD; PAH; ThLM
Whummil Bore, The. *Unknown.* CH; ESPB
Why. Bliss Carman. OBEV (1st ed.); OBVV
Why? Stephen Crane. The Black Riders, XXV. AA
Why. Adelaide Crapsey, *fr. the French.* MaRV
Why? Walter de la Mare. FiBHP
Why? Emily Dickinson. *See* Murmur of a bee, The.
Why. Robert Freeman. PGD
Why? Robert Norwood. OQP
Why? Christina Rossetti. Sonn
Why. H. P. Stevens. BOHV
Why? *Fr.* The Talmud. TrJP
Why? *Unknown.* FaChP
Why/ Is the sky? Questions at Night. Louis Untermeyer. FaPON; GoTP; OTPC (1946 ed.); RIS
Why Adam Sinned. Alex Rogers. BANP
Why, all the Saints and Sages who discuss'd. Omar Khayyám, *tr. by* Edward Fitzgerald. *Fr.* The Rubáiyát. TRV
Why all these fears and feigned alarms. Catalogue. Louis Untermeyer. HBMV
Why all this toil for triumphs of an hour? Life. *Unknown.* BOHV
Why am I not an epigrammatist? Me Quoque Vatem. Thomas Freeman. SiCE; TuPP
Why and Wherefore set out one day. Metaphysics. Oliver Herford. NA
Why are doors brass. Unquestionable Questions. Hy Sobiloff. SiTL
Why are her eyes so bright, so bright. Any Lover, Any Lass. Richard Middleton. HBV; OBVV
Why are not women fair. Peter Parasol. Wallace Stevens. NP
Why Are Our Summer Sports so Brittle? *Unknown.* NCEP
Why are the things that have no death. Irony. Louis Untermeyer. NP; TrJP
Why are these pipples taking their hets off? ? E. E. Cummings. FiBHP
Why are those hours, which Heaven in pity lent. To Cynthia Weeping and Not Speaking. Congreve. LiTL; LO
Why are thy looks so blank, grey friar? The Grey Friar. Thomas Love Peacock. ALV
Why are we [*or* wee] by all creatures waited on? John Donne. Holy Sonnets, XII. AnAnS-1; CABA; MaMe; MaPo; MasP; MeP; OBS; PoEL-2; SCEP-1; Sonn; TuPP
Why Are Yee Afraid, O Yee of Little Faith? Richard Crashaw. MaMe
Why are you always glad to me? A Guilty Father to His Daughter. James Schevill. FiMAP; Po
Why are you dragged to be stoned? Why? *Fr.* The Talmud. TrJP
"Why are you sad, my darling daughter?" The Ripe Fruit. *Unknown.* UnTE
Why are your eyes like dry brown flower-pods. Factory Girl. Maxwell Bodenheim. MAP; MoAmPo (1942 ed.)
Why Are Your Songs All Wild and Bitter Sad. James Thomson. Two Sonnets, I. PoVP
Why art thou bound and mayst go free? Shall reason yield to raging will? He Persuadeth His Friend from the Fond Affects of Love. Thomas Churchyard. ReIE
Why art thou not awake, my son? The Call. Jones Very. MAmP
Why Art Thou Silent! Wordsworth. CBEP; HBV; MBW-2; OBRV
(Speak!) OBEV
(To a Distant Friend.) GTBS; GTBS-D; GTBS-P; GTBS-W; GTSE; GTSL
("Why art thou silent? Is thy love a plant.") LO
Why art thou silent & invisible. To Nobodaddy. Blake. DiPo; ERoP-1
Why art thou slow, thou rest of trouble, Death. Song [*or* A Sad Song *or* Death Invoked]. Philip Massinger. *Fr.* The Emperor of the East. ACP (1952 ed.); OBS; SeCL; SeEP; TuPP; ViBoPo
Why art thou troubled, Herod? what vain fear. Herod's Suspicions. Richard Crashaw. StJW
Why, as to that, said the engineer. The Ghost That Jim Saw. Bret Harte. PoMS; ShM
Why ask to know what date, what clime? Last Lines. Emily Jane Brontë. PeER
Why be afraid of death, as though your life were breath? Death [*or* Emancipation]. Maltbie D. Babcock. BLRP; FaChP; MaRV; OQP; SoP; WBLP; WGRP
"Why?" Because all I haply can and do. Why I Am a Liberal. Robert Browning. EnLi-2; EnLit; EPN; PoFr; PoVP; Sonn
Why blush, dear girl, pray tell me why? On Seeing a Lady's Garter. *Unknown.* ErPo
Why bowest thou, O soul of mine. Heredity. Lydia Avery Coonley Ward. HBV
Why, Caelia [*or* Celia], is your spreading waist. The Poet and His Patron. Edward Moore. Fables for the Female Sex, V. CEP; EiCL; WaPE
Why came I so untimely forth. To a Very Young Lady [*or* To a Girl *or* Lady Lucy Sydney]. Edmund Waller. AnAnS-2; CBEP; EG; LO; MePo; OAEP; OBS; PoFS; SeCL; SeCP; SeEP; TrGrPo; ViBoPo; WiR
Why cannot the Ear be closed to its own destruction? Blake. *Fr.* The Book of Thel. FaBoEn
Why cannot the one good. The War God. Stephen Spender. MoRP
Why Canst Thou Not. *Unknown.* EG; EIL
(Song: "Why canst thou not, as others do.") LiTL
(Why Canst Thou Not, as Others Do.) OnPM
Why Chidest Thou the Tardy Spring? Emerson. *Fr.* May-Day. BiS
Why, Chloe, thus squander your prime. A Logical Song. *Unknown.* ErPo
Why come ye hither, stranger? The Rifleman's Song at Bennington. *Unknown.* PAH
Why Come Ye Nat to Courte? *sel.* John Skelton.
"He is set so hye." FOL
Why, cruel Herod, dost thou fear? The Magi Visit Herod. Caelius Sedulius. *Fr.* Carmen Paschale. CAW
Why, Damon, with the forward day. The Dying Man in His Garden. George Sewell. GTBS; GTBS-D; GTBS-P; GTBS-W; GTSE
Why, dear Cousin,/ why. Monks. Cardinal Newman. GoBC
Why, Death, what does thou here. On One Who Died in May. Clarence Chatham Cook. AA
Why did He choose a garden fair. Thy Will Be Done. Albert Simpson Reitz. STF
Why Did I Laugh [To-Night]? Keats. CBEP; DiPo; ERoP-2; MBW-2
("Why did I laugh tonight? No voice will tell.") Sonn
Why Did I Write ("Of all mad creatures"). Pope. *Fr.* Epistle to Dr. Arbuthnot. OBEC
Why did I write? what sin to me unknown. Pope. *Fr.* Epistle to Dr. Arbuthnot. ChTr; FiP; ViBoPo
Why did my parents send me to the schools. Of Human Knowledge. Sir John Davies. *Fr.* Nosce Teipsum. ReIE; SiCE; SiPS; TuPP
Why Did They Dig Ma's Grave So Deep? George Cooper. TreFS
Why did you give no hint that night. The Going. Thomas Hardy. ELP; FaPL; LiTB; MaPo; PoeP; StP; UnPo (3d ed.); ViPP
Why did you hate to be by yourself. As to Being Alone. James Oppenheim. PoMa; TrJP
Why did you kiss the girl who cried. What the Earth Asked Me. James Wright. NYBP
Why did you lay there asleep. Fragment from "Clemo Uti—the Water Lilies." Ring Lardner. FiBHP

Why did you lure us on like this? An Expostulation. C. S. Lewis. HYE
"Why did you melt your waxen man." Sister Helen. Dante Gabriel Rossetti. BEL; BeLS; EnL; EnLi-2; EnLit; EPN; MaVP; OAEP; PoE; PoVP; ShBV-2; TOP; ViPo; ViPP
Why Didst Thou Doubt? Lucy Guiness Kumm. SoP
Why didst thou promise such a beauteous day. Sonnets, XXXIV. Shakespeare. CBEP; OBSC; PoE
"Why do/ You thus devise." Susanna and the Elders. Adelaide Crapsey. AnAmPo; MAP; MoAmPo (1942 ed.); NP
Why do bells for Christmas ring? *See* Why do the bells of Christmas ring?
Why do I curse the jazz of this hotel? The Jazz of This Hotel. Vachel Lindsay. ATP; PoPl
Why do I deny manna to another? Sather Gate Illumination. Allen Ginsberg. NeAP
Why do I drift on a storm-tossed sea. Drifting. James McConkey. SoP
Why do I languish thus, drooping and dull? Dulnesse. George Herbert. AnAnS-1; MaMe; MeP; SCEP-1
Why Do I Live? George Linnaeus Banks, *See* What I Live For. *wr. at. to* Thomas Guthrie.
Why do I love our flag? The Flag. Edward A. Horton. HH
Why do I love thee, Sir? Emily Dickinson. CoBA
Why Do I Love You? *At. to* Roy Croft. *See* Love.
Why do I sigh to find? Declining Days. Henry Francis Lyte. SoP
Why do I sing in the morning. Secret of Song. Christine White. STF
Why do I sleep amid the snows. Roger Williams. Hezekiah Butterworth. PAH
Why Do I Use My Paper, Ink, and Pen. *Unknown.* ReIE
Why do I write today? Apology. William Carlos Williams. PoeP
Why do men smile when I speak. Is It Because I Am Black? Joseph Seamon Cotter, Jr. BANP
Why do poets like to die. More Letters Found near a Suicide. Frank Horne. BANP
Why do the bells of [*or* do bells for] Christmas ring? Song [*or* Christmas Song]. Eugene Field, *wr. at. to* Lydia Avery Coonley Ward. BoTP; DD; GaP; GFA; HH; OHIP; PCH; PRWS; SoPo; TiPo (1952 ed.); YeAr
Why do the houses stand. Song. George Macdonald. OBVV
Why do the wheels go whirring round. The Shadow Child. Harriet Monroe. HBV
Why do they come? What do they seek. On a Replica of the Parthenon. Donald Davidson. MoVE
Why do they whistle so loud, when they walk past the graveyard late at night? Thirteen o'Clock. Kenneth Fearing. ExPo
Why do we follow, like a flock of sheep. Why? Robert Norwood. OQP
Why do we greet thee, O blithe New Year. A New Year. Margaret E. Sangster. DD; PEDC
Why do we labor at the poem. Reasons for Music. Archibald MacLeish. NePA
Why Do We Lie. B. S. Johnson. ELU
Why Do We Live? . Israel Zangwill. TrJP
Why Do We Love. Sir Benjamin Rudyerd. EIL
Why do we make these journeys. Roethke. Howard Healy. NYTB
Why do we worry about the nest? Why Worry? *Unknown.* SoP
Why do [*or* doe] ye weep, sweet babes? To Primroses [Filled with Morning Dew]. Robert Herrick. AnAnS-2; EG; HBV; OBS; PoPl; SCEP-2; SeCL; SeCV-1; SeEP; ViBoPo
Why do you always stand there shivering. The Poplar. Richard Aldington. HBMV; NP
Why do you cry out, why do I like to hear you. Sound of Breaking. Conrad Aiken. AnAmPo; AWP; InPo; MAPA; PoDB
Why Do You Dally So? Statius, *tr. fr. Latin by* D. A. Slater *and* Virginia Tufte. *Fr.* Epithalamium for Stella and Violentilla. HW
Why do you flutter in my arms and scream. Clipped Wings. Lew Sarett. PoMa
Why do you hide, O dryads! when we seek. Chant for Reapers. Wilfrid Thorley. OBEV (new ed.); OBVV
Why do you lean beside the window, Will? Schoolroom: 158. James E. Warren, Jr. GoYe
Why do you lie with legs ungainly huddled. The Dug-Out. Siegfried Sassoon. AtBAP; CH; FIW; MCCG; MoBrPo; MoVE; NeMA; OHIP; POTE; WaaP; WaP
"Why do you look so pale, my son William?" The Image. Sylvia Townsend Warner. BoLiVe (1939 ed.); InP
Why do you tear from me my darling son. The Mothers' Lament at the Slaughter of the Innocents. *Unknown.* OnYI
"Why do you wear your hair like a man." After Dilettante Concetti. Henry Duff Traill. BOHV; CenHV; HBV; Par
Why doe ye weep, sweet babes? *See* Why do ye weep, sweet babes?
Why does a fire eat big sticks of wood? A Fire. Rachel Field. GFA
Why does he call. Testimony. Beverly Connelly. FiSC
Why Does It Snow? Laura E. Richards. BrR; SiSoSe
Why does my husband beat me? Poor Me. *Unknown.* ErPo
Why does the crocodile weep, Mamma? The Crocodile. Laura E. Richards. UTS
Why does the fire burn so bright? The Nursery. Mrs. Motherly. SAS
Why does the horse-faced lady of just the unmentionable age. Simulacra. Ezra Pound. NoP
Why does the raven cry aloud and no eye pities her? The Lamentation of Enion. Blake. *Fr.* Vala; or, The Four Zoas. OBNC
Why does the sea moan evermore? By the Sea. Christina Rossetti. BoNaP
Why does the thin grey strand. Sorrow. D. H. Lawrence. CMoP; GTBS-P; OBMV
Why does the wind so want to be. The Wind. Elizabeth Rendall. BoTP; HBVY
Why does this seedy lady look. The Jilted Funeral. Gelett Burgess. ShM
"Why [*or* Quhy] does [*or* dois] your brand sae [*or* sword so] drap wi[th] bluid [*or* blude *or* blood]." Edward [*or* Edward, Edward]. *Unknown.* AnFE; AtBAP; ATP; BaBo (B *vers.*); BBV; BEL; BoLiVe; BuBa; CABA; CaFP; CBEP; CBV; CH; ELP; EnLi-1; EnLit; EnRP; ESPB; ExPo; FosPo; GoTS; HBV; HoPM (A *vers.*); ILP; LiTB; LiTG; MaC; NoP; OAEP; OBB; OBEV; OnSP; OuHeWo; OxBB; OxBS; PAn; PG (1955 ed.); PoEL-1; PoIE; PoPo; PoRA; PoSa; SeCeV; ShBV-3; StP; TOP; TreFS; TrGrPo; UnPo (1st ed.); ViBoFo (A *vers.*); WHA
Why Don't I Send My Books to You? Martial, *tr. fr. Latin by* Rolfe Humphries. ML
Why Don't the Men Propose? Thomas Haynes Bayly. BOHV
Why don't we rock the casket here in the moonlight? The Pale Blue Casket. Oliver Pitcher. NNP; TTY
Why don't you go back to the sea, my dear? Light Lover. Aline Kilmer. HBMV
Why dost thou grieve, as rises from the sea. The Cloud. Salvador Díaz Mirón. PoFr
Why dost thou hail with songful lips no more. Memnon. Clinton Scollard. AA
Why dost thou haste away. Madrigal. Sir Philip Sidney. *Fr.* Arcadia. EG; OBSC; SiPS
Why dost thou like a Roman vestal make. Sonnets—Ad Innuptam, V. Patrick Moloney. BoAu
Why Dost Thou Shade Thy Lovely Face? Francis Quarles. *Fr.* Emblems. MeLP; OxBoCh; SeCL; SeEP; TrPWD
(God Who Hides, The.) MaRV
(Wherefore Hidest Thou Thy Face, and Holdest Me for Thine Enemy?) MePo; OBS
Why dost thou shade thy lovely face? O, why. To His Mistress. Earl of Rochester. LO; OBEV
Why dost thou sound, my deare Aurelian? In Answer of an Elegiacall Letter upon the Death of the King of Sweden. Thomas Carew. AnAnS-2
Why dost thou wound my wounds, O thou that passest by. And a Certain Priest Comming That Way Looked on Him and Passed By. Richard Crashaw. MaMe
Why Doth a Pussy Cat? Burges Johnson. BOHV
Why doth heaven bear a sun. An Ode. Barnabe Barnes. *Fr.* Parthenophil and Parthenophe. EIL; OBSC
Why doth the eare so tempt the voyce? To Castara, of True Delight. William Habington. AnAnS-2
Why Doubt God's Word? A. B. Simpson. BLRP
Why each is striving, from of old. Destiny. Matthew Arnold. MBW-2; VP
Why East Wind Chills. Dylan Thomas. AtBAP; MaPo
Why, everyone speaks Welsh; the stipple sheen. Variation on

Why (continued)
a Theme by Dylan Thomas. Carl Bode. ToPo
Why fadest thou in death. Song. Richard Watson Dixon. ChTr
Why Fear? *Unknown.* SoP
Why Fear to Die? Sir Philip Sidney. *Fr.* Arcadia. SiPS
Why fear to-morrow, timid heart? To-Day. Lydia Avery Coonley Ward. HBV; MaRV
Why fearest thou thy outward foe. That Each Thing Is Hurt of Itself. *Unknown.* EIL
Why flyest thou away with fear? Ballade: To a Fish of the Brooke. John Wolcot. CBEP
"Why for your spouse this pompous fuss?" On Seeing a Pompous Funeral for a Bad Husband. *Unknown.* ShM
Why from the danger did mine eyes not start. Sonnet: Of His Pain from a New Love. Guido Cavalcanti. AWP
Why groaning so, thou solid earth. Earth's Burdens. Ernest Charles Jones. VA
Why, Grubbinol, dost thou so wistful seem? Friday; or the Dirge. John Gay. *Fr.* The Shepherd's Week. BWP; CEP; EiCP; EiPP
Why has our poetry eschewed. Food and Drink. Louis Untermeyer. MAP; MoAmPo
Why hast thou breathed, O God, upon my thoughts. The Poet. Angela Morgan. SoP; TrPWD; WGRP
Why hast thou nothing in thy face? Ἔρως (Eros). Robert Bridges. CMoP; ExPo; ILP; LiTB; LO; NBM; PoEL-5; PoIE; QFR; SeCeV
Why have/ I thought the dew. Why. Adelaide Crapsey. MaRV
Why have the mighty lived—why have they died? Waterloo. Sir Aubrey De Vere. HBV
Why have they stripped the grass from the sides of the road. The Interpreters. D. J. Enright. PP
Why have ye no reuthe on my child? Mary Suffers with Her Son. *Unknown.* MeEL
Why have you come to the shining cliffs. The Knight without a Name. *Unknown.* WiR
Why have you lit so bright a fire. The Last Guest. Frances Shaw. HBMV; NP
Why have you risen, to stand with naked feet. With the Dawn. Thomas Caulfield Irwin. EnLoPo; IrPN
Why, having won her, do I woo? The Married Lover. Coventry Patmore. *Fr.* The Angel in the House. EG; EPN; FaPL; GoBC; GTBS; HBV; LiTL; MeWo; OBEV; PoVP; TreFT; TrGrPo; VA
Why He Was There. E. A. Robinson. CMoP
Why here, on this third planet from the Sun. Tellus. William Reed Huntington. AA
Why how now, Babel? Whither wilt thou build? Quo Ruis ab Demens? London's Progress. Thomas Freeman. SiCE
Why how now, Cupid, grown so wild? Cupid Ungodded. James Shirley. GoBC
Why I Am a Liberal. Robert Browning. EnLi-2; EnLit; EPN; PoFr; PoVP; Sonn
Why I Am Not a Painter. Frank O'Hara. ANYP; NeAP
Why I Drink. Henry Aldrich. ALV
("If on my theme I rightly think.") WhC
Why, I know of a bronze lock and key. Bronze. Alfred Starr Hamilton. QAH
Why I love Her. Alexander Brome. HBV; LO
Why I No Longer Travel. Laura E. Richards. MPB
Why I Rebel. Robert J. Sye. TNV
Why I tie about thy wrist. The Bracelet: To Julia. Robert Herrick. EG; HBV; MeWo; OBEV; TrGrPo
Why I Voted the Socialist Ticket. Vachel Lindsay. MoAmPo (1962 ed.)
Why I Will Not Get Out of Bed. James Tate. YAP
Why I Write Not of Love. Ben Jonson. EnLit; FosPo; OAEP; TuPP
Why, if Becchina's heart were diamond. Sonnet: Of Becchina, The Shoemaker's Daughter. Cecco Angiolieri da Siena. AWP
Why if 'tis dancing you would be. The Power of Malt. A. E. Housman. *Fr.* A Shropshire Lad, LXII. HBV
Why is a pump like Viscount Castlereagh. What's My Thought Like? Thomas Moore. BOHV; CBEP; OBRV
Why is everything I do in my life like a boomerang? Boomerang. John Perreault. ANYP
"Why is it," Queen Edain said. Deirdre. W. B. Yeats. ViBoPo
Why is it that the poets tell. Smells. Christopher Morley. PoMa; ShBV-1; YT
Why is it the children don't love me. Little Mamma. Charles Henry Webb. BOHV
Why is it, when I am in Rome. On Being a Woman. Dorothy Parker. BOHV; PoLF
Why is my daughter standing thus to-day? The Mystic Union. *Unknown.* OnPM
"Why is my district death-rate low?" Municipal. Kipling. BrPo; WhC
Why is my verse so barren of new pride. Sonnets, LXXVI. Shakespeare. CLwM; EnLi-1 (1949 ed.); InvP; PP; ReEn; ReIE; SiCE
Why Is Pussy in Bed? *Unknown.* OTPC (1923 ed.)
(Pussy in Bed.) CIV
Why is the world beloved, that fals is and vein. Despise the World. *Unknown.* MeEL
Why is there in the least touch of her hands. Quid Non Speremus, Amantes? Ernest Dowson. HBV
Why is your forehead deep-furrowed with care? Call Me Not Back from the Echoless Shore. *Unknown.* BLPA
Way It Is, The. Joe Goncalves. BF
Why It Was Cold in May. Henrietta Robins Eliot. AA
Why, let it run! who bids it stay? Clepsydra. Charles Cotton. CavP; PeRV
Why, let the stricken deer go weep. Shakespeare. *Fr.* Hamlet, III, ii. CoBE
Why, let them rail! God's full anointed ones. Invincible. Sir Gilbert Parker. *Fr.* A Lover's Diary. VA
Why, Liquor of Life? Turlough Carolan, *tr. fr. Modern Irish by* John D'Alton. OnYI
Why listen, even the water is sobbing for something. The Maid's Thought. Robinson Jeffers. BoLP; ErPo
Why, little charmer of the air. To the Nightingale. Philip Ayres. CEP
Why, Lord. Mark Van Doren. TrPWD
Why, Love, beneath the fields of asphodel. George Edward Woodberry. Ideal Passion, XXXIII. HBMV
Why, lovely charmer, tell me why. Song. Sir Richard Steele. *Fr.* The Tender Husband. HBV; LiTL; ViBoPo
Why lovest thou so this brittle worlde's joy? The Peace of a Good Mind. Sir Thomas More. *Fr.* The Twelve Weapons of Spiritual Battle. EnRePo
Why make your lodging here in this spent lane. Wild Cherry. Lizette Woodworth Reese. AnAmPo; MAP; MoAmPo
Why, man, he doth bestride the narrow world. Portrait of Caesar [*or* A Shakespeare Gallery: Caesar]. Shakespeare. *Fr.* Julius Caesar, I, ii. MaC; TrGrPo
Why mourns my beauteous friend, bereft? To Urania. Benjamin Colman. SCAP
Why muse wee thus to see the wheeles run cross. The Town Called Providence, Its Fate. Benjamin Tompson. SCAP
Why must I be hurt? Pain. Elsie Robinson. PoToHe (new ed.)
Why must my life be as obvious as an elbow? Letters: To Barbara. Kathleen Fraser. YAP
Why Must You Know? John Wheelwright. CrMA
Why My Poems Died. Bhartrihari, *tr. fr. Sanskrit by* Arthur W. Ryder. OnPM
Why, no, Sir! If a barren rascal cries. Doctor Major. Lionel Johnson. BrPo
Why Nobody Pets the Lion at the Zoo. John Ciardi. RePo
Why Not? *Unknown.* WhC
Why not come and see. An Invitation. Basho. OnPM
"Why not open your eyes." Foolish Emily and Her Kitten. Adelaide O'Keeffe. OTPC (1923 ed.)
"Why of the sheep do you not learn peace?" An Answer to the Parson [*or* Epigram]. Blake. OxBoLi; SiTL
Why pay more for your funeral when. An Undertaker's Advertisement. Ernest G. Moll. WhC
"Why, Phoebe, are you come so soon." The Blackberry Girl. Nancy Dennis Sproat. BLPA
Why practise, love, this small economy. To One on Her Waste of Time. Wilfrid Scawen Blunt. The Love Sonnets of Proteus, LVIII. ViBoPo
Why pray, of late, do Europe's kings. The Kings of Europe; a Jest. Robert Dodsley. CEP
Why puts our Grandame Nature on. On the Unusual Cold and Rainie Weather in the Summer, 1648. Robert Heath. OBS

Why Read a Book? Colette M. Burns. UTS
Why rouse from thy long winter sleep? A Queen Wasp. Walter de la Mare. AtBAP
Why say "death"? Death is neither harsh nor kind. The Presence. Robert Graves. ChMP
Why seraphim like lutanists arranged. Evening without Angels. Wallace Stevens. MoPo
Why shadow the beauty of sea or of land. Don't Worry. Elizabeth Porter Gould. FaChP
Why shou'd I thus employ my time. An Ode on Miss Harriet Hanbury at Six Years Old. Sir Charles Hanbury Williams. OBEC
Why Should a Foolish Marriage Vow. Dryden. *Fr.* Marriage-a-la-Mode, I, i. CBEP; InPo; LiTL; ViBoPo
(Song: "Why should a foolish marriage vow.") AWP; CEP; EiPP; HW; ILP; MBW-1; PeRV; SeCV-2
(Songs from the Plays.) OAEP
Why should a man. The Rose. Humbert Wolfe. MoBrPo; NP
Why should I blame her that she filled my days. No Second Troy. W. B. Yeats. BrPo; BWP; CBV; CMoP; EnLoPo; GTBS-P; MaPo; MBW-2; NP; PoE; PoEL-5; PoeP; PoIE; PoSa; SeCePo
Why Should I Care for the Men of Thames? Blake. CBEP; ChTr; PoFr
Why should I doubt. "Believe Ye That I Am Able to Do This?" Dawn Finlay. SoP
Why Should I Fear? Annie Johnson Flint. SoP
Why Should I Fear? John Newton. SoP
Why should I find Him here. Christ in the Clay-Pit. Jack Clemo. GTBS-P
Why Should I Grieve? Moses ibn Ezra, *tr. fr. Hebrew by* Solomon Solis-Cohen. TrJP
Why should I hate you, love, or why despise. In Answer to a Question. Wilfrid Scawen Blunt. The Love Sonnets of Proteus, XXVIII. ViBoPo
Why should I have returned? Noah's Raven. W. S. Merwin. AmPC; NoP
Why should I keep holiday. Compensation. Emerson. AnFE; AnNE; APA; CoAnAm; LiTA
Why should I know or care what month it is? Calendar. Witter Bynner. *Fr.* Chapala Poems. NP
Why should I let the toad work. Toads. Philip Larkin. CMoP; ForPo; NePoEA; NMP; PoeP
Why should I long for what I know. Prayer for Courage. Louis Untermeyer. OQP
Why should I longer long to live. Being Forsaken of His Friend He Complaineth. "E. S." EiL; SiCE
Why should I murmur at my lot forlorn? Hartley Coleridge. Sonn
Why should I sing in verse, why should I frame. To Delia, XVII. Samuel Daniel. Sonn; TuPP
Why should I sing of women. Song against Women. Willard Huntington Wright. HBV
Why should I stay? Nor seed nor fruit have I. The Bubble. John Banister Tabb. AA
Why Should I Wander Sadly. Süsskind von Trimberg, *tr. fr. Middle High German.* TrJP
Why should I wish to see God better than this day? Encountering God. Walt Whitman. *Fr.* Song of Myself, XLVIII. TreFT
Why Should Men Love the Church? T. S. Eliot. *Fr.* The Rock. MoRP
Why should my anxious breast repine. Friendship Is Love without His Wings. Byron. TreFT
Why should my sleepy heart be taught. The Falcon. Elinor Wylie. LOW
"Why should not Wattle do." Under the Wattle. Douglas Brook Wheelton Sladen. OBVV
Why should not we all be merry. *Unknown.* OBS
Why Should This a Desert Be. Shakespeare. *See* Orlando's Rhymes.
Why should this flower delay so long. The Last Chrysanthemum. Thomas Hardy. CMoP; LiTB; PG (1955 ed.); PoVP; ViPo (1962 ed.)
Why should this Negro insolently stride? August. Elinor Wylie. AnEnPo; FosPo; MAP; MoAB; MoAmPo; NeMA
Why should those birds disturb us as they walk. The Night Walkers. Kendrick Smithyman. AnNZ
Why should thy look requite so ill. A Paradox. William Herbert, Earl of Pembroke. EIL
Why should vain mortals tremble at the sight of. The American Hero [*or* Bunker Hill]. Nathaniel Niles. PoFr; TrAS; WaaP
Why Should We Delay? Edmund Waller. *See* To Phyllis.
Why should we murmur, why repine. Love's Bravo. Thomas Flatman. PeRV
Why should we praise them, or revere. Against Seasons. Robert Mezey. AmPC; NYBP
Why should we waste and weep? Fledglings. Thomas Lake Harris. AA
Why Should We Weep? R. E. Neighbour. SoP
Why Should We Weep for Those Who Die. Charles Tennyson Turner. MaRV
Why should we weep for those who sleep? Why Should We Weep? R. E. Neighbour. SoP
Why should you be so full of spight. *Unknown.* SeCSL
Why Should You Swear? Richard Lovelace. *See* Scrutiny, The.
Why should you thinke me so unwise. *Unknown.* SeCSL
Why should you wake, my darling, at this hour. A Fairy Tale. Kenneth Mackenzie. PoAu-2
Why should your face so please me. Song. Edwin Muir. BoPe
Why should your fair eyes with such sovereign grace. Michael Drayton. Idea, XLIII. OBSC
Why shouldst thou cease thy plaintive song. To an Obscure Poet Who Lives on My Hearth. Charles Lotin Hildreth. AA
Why Shouldst Thou Swear? Richard Lovelace. *See* Scrutiny, The.
Why, silly Man! so much admirest thou. George Wither. *Fr.* A Collection of Emblemes, Ancient and Moderne. SeCV-1
Why Sit'st [*or* Sitt'st] Thou by That Ruined Hall. Sir Walter Scott. *Fr.* The Antiquary, *ch.* 10. EnRP; EPN
(Aged Carle, The.) OAEP
Why slander we the times? Bad Times. Joseph Beaumont. MaRV
Why sleeps the future, as a snake enrolled. Wordsworth. Ecclesiastical Sonnets, Conclusion. MERP
Why so coy, my lovely maid? Anacreon, *tr. fr. Greek by* Ambrose Philips. EiCL
Why so impatient, my heart? He Cares. Kabir. MaRV
"Why so often, silent one." The Musing Maiden. Thomas Hardy. BEL
Why So Pale and Wan [Fond Lover]? Sir John Suckling. *Fr.* Aglaura, IV, ii. ALV; AnFE; AWP; BBV (1923 ed.); BEL; BoLP; CaFP; CBEP; CBV; CoBE; DiPo; EG; ELP; EnL; EnLi-1; EnLit; EvOK; FaBV; HoPM; InPo; JAWP; LiTG; LiTL; MCCG; MemP; MeWo; OBEV; OBS; OnPM; OtMeF; OuHeWo; PoFS; PoMa; PoRA; SeCePo; SeCL; ShBV-4; TOP; TreFS; TrGrPo; ViBoPo; WBP; WHA
(Constant Lover, The.) NeHB; PG
(Encouragements to a Lover.) FaFP; GTBS; GTBS-D; GTBS-P; GTBS-W; GTSE; GTSL
(Orsames' Song.) AnEnPo
(Song: "Why so pale and wan fond lover?") AnAnS-2; CABA; EnLoPo; EP; ForPo; HBV; InP; LoBV; MePo; NoP; PoE; PoEL-3; PoIE; PoPl; ReEn; SCEP-2; SeCP; SeCV-1; SeEP; YAT
Why so triumphs the world in pomp and glory vain. Saint Bernard's Verses. *At. to* St. Bernard of Clairvaux. SiCE
Why speak of those whom age is crowning? Crown of Age. M. H. SoP
"Why stand you, gentle mother." Premonition. Laura Goodman Salverson. CaP
Why standest Thou so far. Psalm X. *Paraphrased by* Sir Philip Sidney. FCP
Why stayes my Floramell where love. *Unknown.* SeCSL
Why stays my fair?—See the thick shades descend. Menalcas and Enosia. Philip Wharton. WaPE
Why the British Girls Give In So Easily. Nicholas Moore. WaP
Why the hell do you use all that black. The Nocturne. Carl Bode. ToPo
Why the Moon Is Like a Fashionable Wife. James White. EiCL
Why the prophet is dancing the sculptor knew. The Isaiah of Souillac. W. S. Merwin. PoDB
Why the Robin's Breast Was Red. James Ryder Randall. AA; CAW; JKCP
Why the Soup Tastes Like the Daily News. Marge Piercy. ThO
Why the unbroken spiral, Virtuoso. Apple Peeler. Robert Francis. CrMA; NePoAm
Why then (quod I) old proverbs never fail. George Gascoigne. LO

Why Then So Fearful? *Unknown.* SoP
Why, then thou canst not break her to the lute? Shakespeare. *Fr.* The Taming of the Shrew, II, i. UnS
Why, then, 'tis time to arm and give direction. Shakespeare. King Richard III, *fr.* V, iii. PoFr
Why then, why there. Elegy for J. F. K. W. H. Auden. FlW
Why They Waged War. John Peale Bishop. NYBP
Why think'st thou, fool, thy beautie's rayes. The Sun and Wind. Owen Felltham. CavP
Why this delay? Why waste the time in kissing? A Plea for Haste. Petronius. UnTE
Why this girl has no fear. Carmen. Victor Hernandez Cruz. CAD
Why this man gelded Martiall I muse. Raderus. John Donne. MaMe
"Why those deep sighs?" I ask her. Suspicious Sweetheart. Heine. MeWo
Why those knit brows, ye Catos of the age? All the Heaven. Petronius. OnPM
Why Thus Longing? Harriet Winslow Sewall. AA
Why thy Round Table dost to a Square prefer? King Arthur's Round Table. John Owen. *Fr.* Four Epigrams. PrWP
Why Tomas Cam Was Grumpy. James Stephens. CMoP; WhC
Why wait we for the torches' lights? Let Us Drink. Alcaeus. AWP
Why was a radio sinful? Lord knows. But it was. The Radio Under the Bed. Reed Whittemore. NYBP
Why was Cupid a boy. Cupid. Blake. BOHV
Why was I born into this dismal age. War. Hedd Wyn. PrWP
Why was it that the thunder voice of Fate? Robert Gould Shaw. Paul Laurence Dunbar. Kal
Why was my breeding order'd and prescrib'd. Milton. *Fr.* Samson Agonistes. PoFr
"Why was she lost?" my darling said aloud. Anecdote of 2 A.M. John Wain. NMP
"Why weep ye by the tide, ladie?" Jock of [*or* o'] Hazeldean. Sir Walter Scott. BEL; BeLS; CoBE; EnLi-2; EnLit; EnRP; EPN; GN; GTBS; GTBS-D; GTBS-P; GTBS-W; GTSE; GTSL; HBV; ILP; MCCG; OAEP; OBRV; OTPC; OxBS; PoPo; StP; TOP
"Why weep ye [*or* 'e] by the tide, ladye." John of Haselgreen [*or* Jock o' Hazeldean]. *Unknown.* BaBo; BFSS; ESPB (E *vers.*)
Why were the saints, saints? That Was All! *Unknown.* SoP
Why were you born when the snow was falling? A Dirge. Christina Rossetti. ChTr; LoBV; ViPo
"Why, when the world's great mind." The World and the Quietest. Matthew Arnold. VA
Why, when we were dressed for darker weather. Another Return. Winfield Townley Scott. ELU
Why, whenever she can spy me. To Chloe [*or* Time to Choose a Lover]. Horace. Odes, I, 23. LiTW; OnPM; UnTE
Why, who makes much of a miracle? Miracles. Walt Whitman. AmePo; BBV (1951 ed.); CoBA; FlW; GoTP; HBVY; LaNeLa; MoRP; NeMA; OQP; OTD; PoMa; RePo; StVeCh; WaKn; YT
Why, Why Repine. Walter Savage Landor. EPN (Resignation.) HBV; OBEV (1st ed.); TreFT
Why will they never sleep. Ode. John Peale Bishop. LiTA; LiTM; MoPo; MoVE; NePA; TwAmPo
Why will they never speak. After a Line by John Peale Bishop. Donald Justice. PoCh
Why Will Ye Die? Charles Wesley. SoP
Why will you haunt me unawares. Mathilde Blind. *Fr.* Love in Exile. VA
"Why, William, on that old gray [*or* grey] stone." Expostulation and Reply. Wordsworth. BEL; CBEP; EnL; EnLi-2; EnLit; EnRP; EPN; ERoP-1; HBV; MBW-2; MERP; OAEP; OBRV; PoE; UnPo
"Why wilt thou cast the roses from thine hair?" Mary Magdalene at the Door of Simon the Pharisee. Dante Gabriel Rossetti. GoBC; MaVP; PoVP; VA
Why Worry? *Unknown.* SoP
Why ye Blossome Cometh before ye Leafe. Oliver Herford. AA
Whyle that the sunne with his beames hot. *See* While that the sun with his beams hot.
Whylom, as olde stories tellen us. *See* Whilom, as olde stories tellen us.
Whylom ther was dwellinge at Oxenford. *See* Whilom ther was dwellynge at Oxenford.
Why's my friend so melancholy? The Counsel. Alexander Brome. CavP
Wi da lentenin days ida first o da Voar. Tuslag. T. A. Robertson. OxBS
Wichita Vortex Sutra, *sel.* Allen Ginsberg. NaP
Wicked barons laid the landscape waste, The. The Middle Ages: Two Views. Leah Bodine Drake. NePoAm-2
Wicked Polly. *Unknown.* ABF; BFSS, *with music*
Wicked Treasonable Libel, A. Swift. UnTE
Wicked witch, A. Poison Ivy! Katharine Gallagher. SiSoSe
Wickedest Man in Memphis, The. Alex J. Brown. BeLS
Wickedness of Peter Shannon, The. Alden Nowlan. MoCV
Wicker Basket, A. Robert Creeley. AmPC; ToPo
Wid his di'mond blade. Long Gone. *Unknown.* ABF
Wid Thady's Pipe beside the Door. "Madeline Bridges." JKCP (1926 ed.)
Widdicombe [*or* Widdecombe] Fair. *Unknown.* BBV (1951 ed.); CH; MoShBr; OBB; OnSP; PoMS
Widdy-widdy-wurkey. The Family. *Unknown.* TiPo (1959 ed.)
Wide across the plains. . .burning grass; the buffalo of Omaha. The Opening Session of Congress Rock and Roll. Gail Dusenbery. ThO
Wide amorphous sea, The. Form. Polly Chase Boyden. NP
Wide and curling ocean, The. By the Sea. Marchette Chute. StVeCh (1955 ed.)
Wide and shallow, in the cowslip marshes. Vermont. Sarah N. Cleghorn. HBMV
Wide as this night, old as this night is old and young as it is young. Lullaby. Kenneth Fearing. CMoP
Wide door into sorrow, The. The Narrow Doors. Fannie Stearns Davis. HBMV
Wide-eyed all night in the weatherworn inn. Mountain Hamlet. Lew Sarett. PoMa
Wide fields of corn along the valleys spread. Lo, I Am with You Always. John Charles Earle. ChIP; MaRV; OQP
Wide flocks of narrow birds have fled. Light the Lamp Early. Raymond Holden. MAP; MoAmPo (1942 ed.)
Wide-flung, the rosy banners of the dawn. His Coming. Ivy M. Fordham. SoP
Wide green earth is mine in which to wander, The. The Unwilling Gypsy. Josephine Johnson. HBMV
Wide is the world and wide its open seas. The Keeper. Arthur Stringer. MaRV
Wide Land, The. A. R. Ammons. TwCP
Wide Missouri [*or* Mizzoura], The. *Unknown.* *See* Shenandoah ("Oh, Shenandoah . . .).
Wide mouth, no ears nor eyes, A. *Unknown.* *Fr.* Riddles. CoBE
Wide o'er the valley the pennons are fluttering. The Siege of Chapultepec. William Haines Lytle. MC; PAH
Wide open and unguarded stand our gates. Unguarded Gates. Thomas Bailey Aldrich. AA; AnNE; MC; PAH
Wide Open Are Thy Loving Hands. Bernard of Clairvaux, *tr. fr. Latin by* C. P. Krauth. SoP; TRV
Wide Open Spaces, The. Oscar H. Lear. InMe
Wide sleeves sway. Dancing. Yang Kuei-fei. FaPON
Wide sun stares without a cloud, The. Written in Australia. Arthur Adams. BoAu
Wide Walls. *Unknown.* PoToHe (new ed.)
Wide was his parish, with houses far asunder. Ten of Chaucer's People: A Parson. Chaucer. *Fr.* The Canterbury Tales. PoSa
Wide was the land. The Coming of the White Man. Patrick Anderson. *Fr.* Poem on Canada. CaP
Wide waters in the waste; or, out of reach. "Rivers Unknown to Song." Alice Meynell. HBMV; NP
Wide, Wide World, The. Kipling. *Fr.* In the Neolithic Age. OtMeF
Widely is flung, warning of slaughter. The Song of the Valkyries. *Unknown.* LiTW; WaaP
Widest prairies have electric fences, The. Wires. Philip Larkin. ToPo
Widow, The. W. S. Merwin. NYBP
Widow, The, *sel.* Thomas Middleton.

"Give me fortune, give me health." TuPP
Widow, The. Allan Ramsay. HBV
Widow, The. Robert Southey. OBEV
Widow and Virgin Sisters, The. Thomas Tickell. WaPE
Widow at Windsor, The. Kipling. BrPo; FOL; OAEP (2d ed.)
Widow Bedott Papers, The, *sel.* Frances Miriam Whitcher.
Widow Bedott to Elder Sniffles. BOHV
Widow Bird [Sate Mourning for Her Love], A. Shelley. *Fr.* Charles the First, sc. V. AtBAP; BoTP; CBEP; CH; ELP; EPN; FaPON; MemP; MPB; OBRV; OTPC (1946 ed.); PoG; SeCeV; WePo
(Song, A: "Widow bird sate mourning for her love, A.") FaBoEn; LoBV; OBNC; PoEL-4; ShBV-1; ThWaDe
("Widow bird sate [*or* sat] mourning for her love, A.") GTBS; GTBS-D; GTBS-P; GTBS-W; GTSE; LO
(Winter.) StaSt
Widow Brown's Christmas. John Townsend Trowbridge. BeLS
Widow can bake and the widow can brew, The. The Widow. Allan Ramsay. HBV
Widow in Wintertime, A. Carolyn Kizer. NMP
Widow Machree. Samuel Lover. *Fr.* Handy Andy. HBV; VA
Widow Malone, The. Charles Lever. *Fr.* Charles O'Malley, the Irish Dragoon. BOHV; HBV; TreFS
Widow of Drynam, The. Patrick MacDonogh. NeIP; OnYI; OxBI
Widow poor, somewhat advanced in age, A. The Nun's Priest's Tale, *mod.* Chaucer. *Fr.* The Canterbury Tales. OuHeWo
Widow, A — she had only one! The Widow's Mite. Frederick Locker-Lampson. HBV; VA
Widow Speaks, The. William Dunbar. *Fr.* The Tua Mariit Wemen and the Wedo. PoEL-1
Widow That Keeps the Cock Inn, The. *Unknown.* CoMu
Widow, well met; whither go you today? A Contention betwixt a Wife, a Widow, and a Maid. Sir John Davies. OBSC; SiPS
Widowed Heart, The. Albert Pike. AA
Widows. Edgar Lee Masters. MoAmPo
Widows be woeful whose husbands be taken, The. A Ballad of the Rising in the North. *Unknown.* ACP
Widow's Hymn, A. George Wither. LO; OBEV
Widow's Lament in Springtime, The. William Carlos Williams. AP; CMoP; CoBMV; ForPo; LiTM (1970 ed.); MoLP; NP; PIA; PoIE
Widow's Mite, The. St. Luke, XXI: 1-4, Bible, *N.T.* TreFT
Widow's Mite, The. Frederick Locker-Lampson. HBV; VA
Widow's [*or* Widowes] Mites, The. Richard Crashaw. MaMe; OxBoCh
Widow's Solace, The. Thomas Deloney. SiCE
Widow's Weeds, A. Walter de la Mare. AtBAP; FaBV
Widsith, *sels.* *Unknown,* *tr. fr. Anglo-Saxon.*
Lone Man, The. PoLi
Widsith, the Minstrel, *tr. by* Charles W. Kennedy. AnOE
Wie langsam kriechet sie dahin. Heine, *tr. fr. German by* Richard Monckton Milnes. AWP
Wife, A. Alexander Brome. PeRV
Wife, The. Phoebe Cary. BOHV
Wife, The. Robert Creeley. AmPC; AP; CBV; ToPo
Wife, The. Anna Peyre Dinnies. AA
Wife, The. Denise Levertov. ErPo; MeWo
Wife, A. Matthew Gregory Lewis, *also at. to* Sheridan. BOHV; PV
Wife, The. *Unknown,* *tr. fr. Chinese by* Henry H. Hart. OnPM; WoL
Wife a-Lost, The. William Barnes. ELP; EnLoPo; GTBS; GTBS-D; OBEV; OBVV
Wife—at daybreak I shall be, A. Emily Dickinson. AmePo; AmPP (5th ed.); CoBA; PoeP
Wife at Usher's Well, The. *Unknown.* *See* Wife of Usher's Well, The.
Wife for a Month, A, *sel.* John Fletcher.
To the Blest Evanthe. SeCL; SeEP
Wife from Fairyland, The. Richard Le Gallienne. HBV
Wife-Hater, The. *Unknown.* CoMu
Wife I Do Hate, A. William Wycherley. SeCL
Wife of Aed mac Ainmirech, King of Ireland, Laments Her Husband, The. *Unknown,* *tr. fr. Old Irish by* Myles Dillon. AnIL
Wife of Auchtermuchty, The. *Unknown.* GoTS
Wife of Bath, The. Chaucer. *See* Canterbury Tales, The: Prologue.
Wife of Bath's Prologue, The. Chaucer. *Fr.* The Canterbury Tales. EnL, *mod. by* Theodore Morrison; EnLi-1 (1949 ed.); MBW-1; OxBoLi, *abr.*; PoEL-1
"My fifthe housbonde, god his soule blesse," *sel., abr.* FiP
Wife of Bath's Tale, The. Chaucer. *Fr.* The Canterbury Tales. EnL, *mod. by* Theodore Morrison; EnLit; MBW-1
"In days of old, when Arthur filled the throne," *mod. by* Dryden, 45 *ll.* MBW-1
"In th'olde dayes of the Kyng Arthour," 25 *ll.* ViBoPo
Wife of Judas Iscariot, The. Cale Young Rice. StJW
Wife of Kelso, The, *with music.* *Unknown.* ShS
Wife of Llew, The. Francis Ledwidge. CLwM; PoMS
Wife of Loki, The. Lady Charlotte Elliot. VA
Wife of the clown, The. The Thirty-three Ring Circus. John Logan. FRC
Wife of Usher's Well, The. *Unknown.* AnFE; AtBAP; AWP; BaBo (A *and* B *vers.*); BEL, *abr.*; BoLiVe; BuBa; CBEP; CH; ChTr; DiPo; EnLi-1; EnRP; EnSB; ESPB (A, B, C, *and* D *vers.*); ExPo; GoTS; HBV; ILP; InP, *sl. abr.*; InPo; JAWP; LiTB; LoBV, *sl. abr.*; NoP; OAEP; OBB; OBEV; OnMSP; OuHeWo; OxBB; OxBS; PIA; PoAn; PoEL-1; PoIE; SeCeV; ShBV-2; StP; TiPo (1952 ed.); TOP; TreF; TrGrPo; UnPo; ViBoFo (A, B, *and* C *vers.*); WBP
(Wife at Usher's Well, The.) EnL
Wife Speaks, The. Mary Stanley. AnNZ
Wife Talks to Herself, A. Stephen Berg. NaP
Wife to a Husband, A. Elizabeth Barrett Browning. *See* Sonnets from the Portuguese: "How do I love thee?"
Wife to Her Husband, The. *Unknown.* HBV
Wife to Husband. Christina Rossetti. VA; ViPo
Wife Waits, A. Thomas Hardy. At Casterbridge Fair, VI. BEL; EnLi-2 (1949 ed.); EnLit; PoVP
Wife was sitting at her reel ae night, A. The Strange Visitor. *Unknown.* ChTr; FaBoCh
Wife-Woman, The. Anna Spencer. BANP
Wife Wrapt [*or* Wrapped] in Wether's Skin. *Unknown.* BaBo (A, B, *and* C *vers.*); ESPB (A, B, D, *and* F *vers.*); ViBoFo (A *and* B *vers.*)
(Dandoo.) TrAS, *with music*
Wife's Lament, The. *Unknown,* *tr. fr. Anglo-Saxon by* Charles W. Kennedy. AnOE; FosPo, *tr. by* John F. Adams; LiTW
Wife's Song, A. William Cox Bennett. HBV
Wig. Kirk Hall. BF
Wil the Merry Weaver, and Charity the Chamber-Maid; or, A Brisk Encounter between a Youngman and His Love. *Unknown.* CoMu
Wilbur Wright and Orville Wright. Rosemary Benét *and* Stephen Vincent Benét. PoMa
Wilbur's Garden. Walter Clark. NYTB
Wild air, world-mothering air. The Blessed Virgin Compared to the Air We Breathe. Gerard Manley Hopkins. BrPo; ISi; MoPo; OxBoCh; PeVV; PoLi
Wild and plunging seas have smote our sides, The. Columbus. Percy Hutchison. EtS
Wild and wet, and windy wet falls the night on Hamilton. Hamilton. Marie E. J. Pitt. BoAu
Wild Animals. Elizabeth Fleming. StVeCh
Wild Ass. Padraic Colum. MoBrPo; NP
Wild (at Our First) Beasts Uttered Human Words. E. E. Cummings. NYBP
Wild Beasts. Evaleen Stein. MPB (1956 ed.); SoPo; UTS
Wild Bees. James K. Baxter. AnNZ
Wild Bees. John Clare. BoPe
Wild bird filled the morning air, A. The Fowler. W. W. Gibson. HBMV
Wild bird, whose warble, liquid sweet. In Memoriam A. H. H., LXXXVIII. Tennyson. BEL; EPN; OAEP; ViPo; VP
Wild Boar and the Ram, The. John Gay. *Fr.* Fables. EiCP; PPON
Wild boars and all. The Autumn Storm. Basho. RePo
Wild Bronc Peeler. *Unknown.* CoSo
Wild Carthage held her, Rome. A Puritan Lady. Lizette Woodworth Reese. AnAmPo; InP; MAP; MoAmPo; NP
Wild Carrot. John Richard Moreland. NYTB
Wild Cats. Vachel Lindsay. MAP; MoAmPo
Wild Cherry. Louise Townsend Nicholl. NePoAm
Wild Cherry. Lizette Woodworth Reese. AnAmPo; MAP; MoAmPo
Wild Cherry Tree. Edmund Blunden. BrPo

Wild Colonial Boy, The. *Unknown.* NeLNL; OuSiCo, *with music*; PoAu-1; ViBoFo
(Wild Montana Boy, The, *diff. vers.*) CoSo
Wild Common, The. D. H. Lawrence. CoBMV
Wild Duck, The. John Masefield. BEL; BrPo; ShBV-2
Wild duck startles like a sudden thought, The. Autumn Birds. John Clare. OA
Wild duck, stringing through the sky, The. The Madman's Song. John Masefield. *Fr.* Good Friday. ACV; BoC
Wild Eden, *sels.* George Edward Woodberry.
Child, The, XXX. AA
Divine Awe, XVI. AA
Homeward Bound, XXV. AA
O, Inexpressible as Sweet, VII. AA; HBV; PFY
(Song: "O, inexpressible as sweet.") InMe
O, Struck beneath the Laurel, XXXIII. AA; PFY
Rose of Stars, The, IX. AA; HBV
Seaward, XLI. AA
Secret, The, VI. AA; HBV
So Slow to Die, XXXVIII. AA
When First I Saw Her, V. AA; HBV
Wild Eden, III. HBV
Wild eyes—and faces ashen grey. Stars. Dowell O'Reilly. BoAu
Wild Flower Man, The. Lu Yu, *tr. fr. Chinese by* Kenneth Rexroth. NaP
Wild Flowers. Peter Newell. NA
Wild Flower's Song. Blake. BoTP; CBEP
Wild gander leads his flock through the cool night, The. The Same Old Law. Walt Whitman. *Fr.* Song of Myself. OA
Wild Geese. Elinor Chipp. FaPON; HBMV; MPB; RePo; TiPo
Wild Geese. Lady Ise, *tr. fr. Japanese by* Basil Hall Chamberlain. OnPM
Wild Geese, The. James Herbert Morse. AA
Wild Geese. Frederick Peterson. HBV; HBVY; OTPC (1923 ed.)
Wild Geese. Celia Thaxter. PRWS; UTS
Wild Geese. Katharine Tynan. GoTP
Wild geese, flying in the night, behold, The. The Wild Geese. James Herbert Morse. AA
Wild geese returning, The. Tsumori Kunimoto. PDV
Wild Goat, The. Claude McKay. CDC
Wild goose, wild goose. Haiku. Issa. LiTW
Wild heart in me that frets and grieves. Primrose Hill. Olive Custance. JKCP
Wild Home-Pussy, The. Emma Rounds. RIS
Wild Honey. Maurice Thompson. AnFE; APA; CoAnAm; HBV
Wild Honeysuckle [*or* Honey Suckle], The. Philip Freneau. AA; AmLP; AmP; AmPP; AnAmPo; AP; CBEP; CoBA; HBV; LiTA; MAmP; OxBA; PoEL-4; PoIE (1970 ed.); PoLF; TrGrPo
Wild Horse Jerry's Story. Sarah Elizabeth Howard. PoOW
Wild Horses. Carl Sandburg. RePo
Wild Huntsmen, The. Philip Gilbert Hamerton. VA
Wild Iron. Allen Curnow. AnNZ
Wild is its nature, as it were a token. Song of the Palm. Tracy Robinson. AA
Wild Knight, The. G. K. Chesterton. WGRP
"So, with the wan waste grasses on my spear," *br. sel.* MaRV
Wild March. Constance Fenimore Woolson. YeAr
Wild Marjorie. "Jean Lorrain," *tr. fr. French by* Wilfrid Thorley. CAW
Wild Miz-zou-rye, The. *Unknown.* *See* Shenandoah ("Oh, Shenandoah . . .).
Wild Montana Boy, The. *Unknown.* *See* Wild Colonial Boy, The.
Wild nights—Wild nights! Emily Dickinson. AmP; AmPP (4th ed.); AP; FaPL; MeWo; MWA-2; OxBA; PoIE; UnTE
Wild Oats. W. H. Davies. ACV
Wild Oats. Philip Larkin. PoeP
Wild Old Wicked Man, The. W. B. Yeats. AnIL; AtBAP; CMoP; MBW-2
Wild Peaches (I-IV). Elinor Wylie. AmP; HT; LiTA; LiTM (rev. ed.); NAMP; OxBA
"Down to the Puritan marrow of my bones," *sel.* InP
(Puritan Sonnet.) MAP; MoAB; MoAmPo; NeMA; TrGrPo
Wild Philomela. William Rose Benét. NP
Wild pigeon of the leaves. Birds. *Unknown.* *Fr.* The Thousand and One Nights. AWP; LiTW
Wild pleasure for Saint John, A. Saint John. Elizabeth J. Coatsworth. MoRP
Wild Plum. Orrick Johns. HBMV; MAP; NP; PG (1945 ed.)
Wild Provoke of the Endurance Sky. Joseph Ceravolo. ANYP
Wild Rattling Cowboy, A. *Unknown.* CoSo
Wild Ride, The. Louise Imogen Guiney. AA, *abr.*; CAW; HBV; JKCP; MAP; MoAmPo (1942 ed.); PFY
Wild Rippling Water, The, *with music.* *Unknown.* CoSo
Wild Romantic Dell, A. William Julius Mickle. *Fr.* The Concubine, II. OBEC
Wild Rose. William Allingham. GN, *abr.*; OTPC
Wild Rose, The. Hermann Hagedorn. PFY
Will Rose of Alloway! my thanks. Burns. Fitz-Greene Halleck. AA
Wild Roses. Edgar Fawcett. HBV
Wild Roses. Mary Effie Lee Newsome. CDC
Wild roses have reclaimed the field. Where I Took Hold of Life. Robert P. Tristram Coffin. BiCB
Wild Strawberries. Robert Graves. FaBoCh; LoGBV
Wild strawberries, gooseberries, trampled. Ave Eva. John Wheelwright. MoPo
Wild stream the clouds, and the fresh wind is singing. The Hunt. Harriet Prescott Spofford. AA
Wild Swan, The. D. S. Savage. NeBP
Wild Swan. *Unknown, tr. fr. Anglo-Saxon by* Charles W. Kennedy. *Fr.* Riddles. AnOE
Wild Swans. Edna St. Vincent Millay. CMoP; MAP; MoAmPo
Wild Swans at Coole, The. W. B. Yeats. ACV; BoLiVe; BoPe; CBV; ChTr; CMoP; DiPo; EnLi-2 (1949 ed.); FIW; GTBS-D; HT; ILP; MaPo; MBW-2; MoAB; MoBrPo; MoVE; NoP; NP; OAEP (2d ed.); OnYI; PAn; PIA; Po; PoIE; PoPo; PoVP; ReMP; StP; TDP; WePo; WHA
Wild the sea clamors from its echoing caves. All Souls' Eve. Mary E. Mannix. GoBC
Wild Thyme, The. Blake. *Fr.* Milton. WiR
Wild Thyme. Eleanor Farjeon. SiSoSe
Wild Thyme. Joyce Sambrook. BoTP
Wild Trees, The. Laurie Lee. BoPe; GTBS-D
Wild was the day; the wintry sea. The Twenty-second of December. Bryant. DD; HH; MPB
Wild was Vingthor when he awoke. The Lay of Thrym. *Unknown.* *Fr.* The Elder Edda. LiTW; OuHeWo
Wild Weather. Katharine Lee Bates. PGD
Wild Weather. Dryden. *Fr.* All for Love, I, i. BoW
("Portents and Prodigies are grown so frequent.") AtBAP
Wild white camel, camel wild, what behind. Camel. Gene Derwood. NePA
Wild, wild the storm, and the sea high running. Patrolling Barnegat. Walt Whitman. CBEP; GTSE; LoBV; NePA; NoP
Wild, wild wind, wilt thou never cease thy sighing? The Dead Church. Charles Kingsley. VA
Wild Willow. James Wreford Watson. TwCaPo
Wild wind blows, the sun shines, the birds sing loud, The. *See* Wind blows, the sun shines . . ., The.
Wild Winds. Mary Frances Butts. OTPC; PRWS
Wild winds weep, The. Mad Song. Blake. BEL; CBEP; CEP; EiPP; EnLi-2; EnLit; EnRP; ERoP-1; FosPo; ILP; MaPo (1969 ed.); PoE; PoEL-4; PoRA; TrGrPo
Wild Wishes. Ethel M. Hewitt. HBV
Wild with passion, sorrow-beladen. Song on the Water. Thomas Lovell Beddoes. EG
Wild Wreath, The. *Unknown.* OTPC (1923 ed.)
Wildebeest, The. June Daly. FaPON
Wilderness, The. Caroline Hazard. ChIP; StJW
Wilderness, The. Gyula Juhasz, *tr. fr. Hungarian by* Watson Kirkconnell. LiTW
Wilderness, The. Sidney Keyes. LiTB; LiTM (rev. ed.); NeBP
Wilderness. Carl Sandburg. AnAmPo; AP
Wilderness a secret keeps, The. Ecce in Deserto. Henry Augustin Beers. AA; AnFE; APA; CoAnAm
Wilderness and the solitary place shall be glad for them, The. Isaiah, Bible, *O.T.* BoPe
Wilderness Gothic. Alfred Purdy. MoCV; PeCV (1967 ed.)
Wilderness Is Tamed, The. Elizabeth J. Coatsworth. *See* Axe Has Cut the Forest Down, The.
Wilderness Rivers. Elizabeth J. Coatsworth. AmFN
Wilderness Road. Martha Keller. FiSC
Wilderness Theme. Ian Mudie. PoAu-2
Wilding, The. Philip Booth. NePoEA

Wildly round our woodland quarters. The Lumbermen. Whittier. WoL
Wildness. Gerard Manley Hopkins. *Fr.* Inversnaid. OtMeF
Wildness. Blanche Shoemaker Wagstaff. HBMV
Wildness of haggard flights. Nocturne. Roussan Camille. TTY
Wildtrack, *sel.* John Wain.
Sestina for Khasan Israelov. ToPo
Wildwest. Archibald MacLeish. Frescoes for Mr. Rockefeller's City, II. ReMP; UnPo
Wilful waste brings woeful want. *Unknown.* OxNR
Wilhelm Meister, *sels.* Goethe, *tr. fr. German.*
Mignon, *fr.* Wilhelm Meister's Apprenticeship, *Bk.* III, *ch.* 1. LiTW, *tr. by* Anthony Hecht; PoPl, *tr. by* Edgar A. Bowring
(Mignon's Song, *tr. by* James Elroy Flecker.) • AWP; JAWP; WBP
Sorrow, *fr.* Wilhelm Meister's Apprenticeship, *Bk.* II, *ch.* 13, *tr. by* Gretchen Warren. MaRV
(Who Never Ate with Tears His Bread, *tr. by* Farnsworth Wright.) WGRP
Wilhelmina Mergenthaler. Harry P. Taber. BBGG
Will, The. John Donne. ATP (1935 ed.); LiTB; LiTG; MaMe; MePo; SCEP-1; SeEP; TOP; TuPP
Will. Tennyson. EPN
Will. Ella Wheeler Wilcox. BLPA; NeHB; PoToHe
Will Beauty Come. Robert Nathan. HBMV
Will came back from school that day. Dunkirk. Robert Nathan. MaC; OnSP
Will days, indeed, yet come in forgiveness and grace. When You Will Walk in the Field. Leah Goldberg. TrJP
Will dissolves, the heart becomes excited, The. Soliloquy in an Air-Raid. Roy Fuller. LiTM
Will Ever? Walter de la Mare. GBV
Will God's Patience Hold Out for You? Edythe Johnson. STF
Will he ever be weary of wandering. Will Ever? Walter de la Mare. GBV
Will he love me forever? Lady Horikawa, *tr. fr. Japanese by* I. W. Furukami. LiTW
Will He No Come Back Again? *Unknown.* MemP; OBEC; OBEV (new ed.), *abr.*
Will it be like this, Charlie? A Black Stick with a Ball of Cotton for a Head and a Running Machine for a Mouth. Calvin C. Hernton. BF
Will it be remembered? April 29th. Alexander Bergman. WOW
Will It Be So? Edith M. Thomas. *Fr.* The Inverted Torch. AA
Will it last? he says. The Snowflake Which Is Now and Hence Forever. Archibald MacLeish. NoP
Will lightning strike me if I take. Thoughts of Loved Ones. Margaret Fishback. FiBHP
Will Love again awake. Muse and Poet. Robert Bridges. OBMV
Will never sell. Get that script out of my face. Poetry. Eric Priestley. WSL
Will night already spread her wings and weave. Night-Thoughts. Solomon ibn Gabirol. TrJP
Will not our hearts within us burn. The White Presence [*or* "Follow Me"]. Joseph Fort Newton. ChIP; MaRV; OQP
Will not the Local Party Secretary? On Reading a Soviet Novel. Roy Fuller. ToPo
Will of God, The. Frederick William Faber. MaRV; SoP; VA
Will of God, The. Gerhardt Tersteegen, *tr. fr. German by* Emma Frances Bevan. SoP
Will of God be done by us, The. Blessed Be the Holy Will of God. *Unknown.* OnYI
Will of Good we must obey, The. The Death of King Edward VII. *Unknown.* OxBoLi
Will of Writing, The. James Schevill. FiMAP
Will seeing Concan make a dog a lion? Ritual Not Religion. *Unknown.* WGRP
Will sprawl, now that the heat of day is best. Caliban upon Setebos. Robert Browning. AWP; EPN; MaVP; NoP; OAEP; PeVV; PoVP; ViPo; VP; WGRP
Will Stewart and John. *Unknown.* ESPB
Will the Real Black People Please Stand. Desirée A. Barnwell. WSL
Will the wolves lie down with the lambs and feed them? The End of Sorrow. Edmond Fleg. *Fr.* The Wall of Weeping. TrJP
Will there never come a season. The Pedestrian's Plaint. E. V. Lucas. CenHV
Will there never come a season. To R. K. [*or* Lapsus Calami *or* The Millennium]. James Kenneth Stephen. BOHV; CenHV; EnLi-2 (1949 ed.); NBM; OtMeF; Par; VA; WhC
Will there really be morning? Emily Dickinson. AA; BoChLi; FaPON; SiSoSe; SoPo; WGRP
Wll they ever come to me, ever again. Where Shall Wisdom Be Found? Euripides. *Fr.* Baachae. UnS
Will they never fade or pass! The Farmer Remembers the Somme. Vance Palmer. MoAuPo; PoAu-1
Will they stop. Requiem. Kenneth Fearing. CMoP
Will to Serve, The. Joseph B. Gilder, *wr. at. to* Jeannette L. Gilder. *Fr.* The Parting of the Ways. OQP
("Be thou guardian of the weak.") MaRV
Will to Win. F. R. Scott. OBCV
Will winter never be over? February. Adeline D. Whitney. OTD; YeAr
"Will ye gang to the Hielands, Leezie Lindsay." Leezie Lindsay. *Unknown.* BFSS
Will ye gang wi' me and fare. The Bush aboon Traquair. John Campbell Shairp. OBVV
Will Ye No Come Back Again? Lady Caroline Nairne. ShBV-1
Will ye see what wonders love hath wrought? Sir Thomas Wyatt. FCP; SiPS
Will ye that I should sing. A Lady of High Degree. *Unknown.* AWP
Will You. Kate Greenaway. *See* Will You Be My Little Wife.
Will You Be as Hard? Douglas Hyde, *tr. fr. Irish by* Lady Gregory. OBMV
Will You Be My Little Wife. Kate Greenaway. MoShBr
(Will You?) SiSoSe
Will You Buy Any Tape? Shakespeare. *Fr.* The Winter's Tale, IV, iii. GaP; OBSC; SiCE; ViBoPo
(Songs of Autolycus, The, 3.) OTPC (1923 ed.)
Will You Come? Edward Thomas. CH; GoJo; LoBV; MemP
Will you come a boating, my gay old hag. The Gay Old Hag. *Unknown.* IrPN
Will you come to the bower I have shaded for you? Walter Savage Landor. *Fr.* A Reply to Lines by Thomas Moore. ChTr
Will you come to Turvy Land. Topsy-turvy Land. Phyllis M. Stone. BoTP
"Will you gang wi' me, Leezie Lindsay." Leezie Lindsay. *Unknown.* FaBoCh; LoGBV
Will you glimmer on the sea? Moonrise. Hilda Doolittle ("H. D.") NP
Will you hear a Spanish lady. The Spanish Lady's Love. *Unknown.* OBB
Will you hear of a bloody battle? The Downfall of Piracy. *At. to* Benjamin Franklin. PAH
Will you heare a tale of Robin Hood. Robin Hood and the Pedlars. *Unknown.* ESPB
Will you know. *Unknown.* SeCSL
Will you knowe my mistris face. *Unknown.* SeCSL
Will you lend me your mare to ride but a mile? *Unknown.* OxNR
Will you lend your eyes to Christ. Operation—Souls. *Unknown.* STF
Will you, like other men. Impulsive Dialogue. Maxwell Bodenheim. NP
Will you love. Two Shots: a Love Affair. Fanny Howe. QAH
Will You Love Me in December as You Do in May? James J. Walker. TreFT
Will You Love Me When I'm Old? *Unknown.* BLPA; FaBoBe; NeHB
Will you never be quiet, you mournfullest voice in Nature. Peewits on the Hills. Alice V. Stuart. ACV
Will You, One Day. Marian Ramie. HBMV
Will You Perhaps. Delmore Schwartz. *See* "Mentrechè il Vento, Come Fa, Si Tace."
Will you, sometime, who have sought so long and seek. The Question. Edwin Muir. BoPe
Will you take a sprig of hornbeam? Forester's Song. A. E. Coppard. FaPON; MPB

"Will you take a walk with me." The Clucking [*or* Clocking] Hen. Ann Hawkshaw. BoTP; HBVY; OTPC; PPL; SAS
"Will you walk a little faster?" said a whiting to a snail. The Lobster Quadrille [*or* The Mock Turtle's Song *or* The Whiting and the Snail]. "Lewis Carroll." *Fr.* Alice's Adventures in Wonderland. BoChLi; BoTP; ChTr; EnLi-2; FaPON; HBV; HBVY; MoShBr; MPB (1956 ed.); OTPC (1946 ed.); Par; PCD; PCH; PoVP; PRWS; RIS; SAS; StVeCh; TiPo (1952 ed.); UTS
"Will you walk into my parlor?" said the Spider to the Fly. The Spider and the Fly. Mary Howitt. BeLS; FaFP; FaPON; GFA; HBV; HBVY; OHFP; OnSP; OTPC; Par; RIS; TreFS; TVC; WBLP
Will you wear white, O my dear, O my dear? Jennie Jenkins. *Unknown.* OuSiCo
Willard Wirtz, secretary of labor. Evening News: St. Louis. "Luke." QAH
William and Helen. Sir Walter Scott, *imitated fr.* Lenore (*by* Gottfried August Bürger). EnRP; OAEP
William and Margaret. David Mallet. CEP; OBEC
William and Mary. *Unknown.* OxNR
William Blake. Dante Gabriel Rossetti. Five English Poets, 2. PoVP
William Blake. James Thomson. CBEP; HBV; OAEP; OBVV; PoVP
William Blake Sees God. Roy McFadden. NeIP
William Bond. Blake. MyFE; NCEP; OxBB; PeER
"I thought love lived in the hot sunshine," *sel.* LO
(Where to Seek Love.) TRV
William Brown of Oregon. Joaquin Miller. BOHV
William Byrd. Sidney Keyes. MuSP
William Dewy, Tranter Reuben, Farmer Ledlow late at plough. Friends Beyond. Thomas Hardy. CoBMV; GTBS-P; MaPo; OBEV (new ed.); OBVV; PoVP
William I—1066. Eleanor Farjeon. BBV (1951 ed.)
William Gifford. Walter Savage Landor. GTBS-P
William Glen. *Unknown.* BaBo
William H. Herndon. Edgar Lee Masters. *Fr.* Spoon River Anthology. LiPo; NP; TOP
William Hall, *with music.* *Unknown.* BFSS
William Jake Hall. Campfire and Bunkhouse. *Unknown.* CoSo
William Jones. Edgar Lee Masters. *Fr.* Spoon River Anthology. ImOP
William Lisle Bowles. Byron. *Fr.* English Bards and Scotch Reviewers. OBNC
William McTrimbletoe. *Unknown.* OxNR
William of Nassau, scion. Ballad to William of Nassau. *Unknown.* PoFr
William of Orange; or, The Battle of Boyne (A *vers., with music*). *Unknown.* BFSS
(King William and King James, B *vers., with music.*) BFSS
William P. Frye, The. Jeanne Robert Foster. MC; PAH
William Penn/ Was the most level-headed of men. William Jay Smith. PV
William Shakespeare. Swinburne. *Fr.* Sonnets on English Dramatic Poets. PoVP; TrGrPo
William Shakespeare to Mrs. Anne, Regular Servant to Rev. Mr. Precentor of York. Thomas Gray. CEP; ILP
William Tell, *sel.* James Sheridan Knowles.
Switzerland. PoFr
William Tell, *poem.* Schiller, *tr. fr. German by* Sir Edward Bulwer-Lytton. PoFr
William the Bastard. "Lakon." FiBHP
William the Conqueror long did reign. England's Sovereigns in Verse. *Unknown.* BLPA
William the Conqueror, ten sixty-six. *Unknown.* OxNR
William the First was the first of our kings. William I—1066. Eleanor Farjeon. BBV (1951 ed.)
William Wallace. Francis Lauderdale Adams. OxBS
William Wilson. Malcolm Cowley. *Fr.* Blue Juniata. AnAmPo; MoVE
William Wordsworth. Sidney Keyes. ChMP; GTBS-D; POTE; SeCePo
William Wordsworth. Francis Turner Palgrave. VA
William Yeats in Limbo. Sidney Keyes. MoBrPo (1962 ed.)
Williams died two years ago yesterday. Kora for March 5th. Lewis MacAdams. ANYP
Willie. "Max Adeler." BBGG
(In Memoriam.) DTC
Willie and Earl Richard's Daughter. *Unknown.* *See* Birth of Robin Hood, The.
Willie and Helen. Hew Ainslie. HBV; OBEV (1st ed.)
("Wherefore sou'd ye talk o' love.") LO
Willie and Johnny, *with music.* *Unknown.* BFSS
Willie and Lady Maisry (A *and* B *vers.*). *Unknown.* ESPB
(Willie and Lady Margerie.) OxBB
Willie and Nellie, one evening sat. Willie's and Nellie's Wish. Julia A. Moore. FiBHP
Willie [*or* Willy] boy, Willie boy, where are you going? Mother Goose. BoTP; OxNR; RIS; SAS; StVeCh
Willie Brew'd [*or* Brewed] a Peck o' Maut. Burns. AWP; BEL; CEP; EiCL; EnLi-2; EnLit; EnRP; InPo; JAWP; OxBS; TOP; ViBoPo; WBP
(O, Willie Brew'd a Peck o' Maut.) EnL
(Willie Brewed.) OAEP
Willie Fitzgibbons who used to sell ribbons. Waltz Me around Again, Willie. Will D. Cobb. TreFT
Willie had a purple monkey climbing on a yellow stick. Willie [*or* In Memoriam]. "Max Adeler." BBGG; DTC
"Willie has taen him o'er the fame." Willie's [*or* Willy's] Lady. *Unknown.* BaBo; ESPB; OBB
Willie in his roguish way. *Unknown.* WhC
"Willie is fair, and Wille's rair." Rare Willie Drowned in Yarrow (D *vers.*). *Unknown.* ESPB
Willie Leonard; or, The Lake of Cold Finn. *Unknown.* BaBo
Willie Macintosh. *Unknown.* BFSS; CBEP; ESPB (A *and* B *vers.*); OBB; OxBoLi; ViBoFo
(Burning of Auchindown.) OxBB
(Willie Mackintosh.) BuBa
Willie o Douglas Dale. *Unknown.* BaBo; ESPB
Willie o Winsbury. *Unknown.* BaBo; ESPB (A *and* D *vers.*)
Willie pushed his Aunt Eliza. Aunt Eliza. *Unknown.* ShM
Willie Reilly. *Unknown.* *See* Willy Reilly.
Willie saw some dynamite. Little Willie. *Unknown.* FaPON
Willie stands in his stable-door. The Mother's Malison; or, Clyde's Water. *Unknown.* BaBo
Willie, take your little drum. Burgundian Carol [*or* Patapan]. Bernard de la Monnoye. ChBR; UnS
Willie Taylor was a youthful sailor. The False Lover. *Unknown.* BFSS
Willie the Weeper. *Unknown.* ABF, *with music*; BeLS; BLPA; TrAS, *diff. vers., with music*; YaD
(Willy the Weeper, *diff. vers., with music.*) AS
Willie was a widow's son. Willie and Lady Maisry. *Unknown.* ESPB
Willie was an onion. Vegetable Fantasies. Helen Hoyt. RIS
Willie Wastle dwalt on Tweed. Sic a Wife as Willie Had. Burns. GoTS
"Willie, Willie, I'll learn you a wile." Willie's Lyke-Wake. *Unknown.* ESPB
"Willie, Willie, what makes you sae sad?" Willie's Lyke-Wake. *Unknown.* OBB
Willie Winkie. William Miller. FaFP; HBV; HBVY; VA
(Wee Willie Winkie.) BoChLi, *st.* 1; GaP, *st.* 1; PCH; RIS, *st.* 1; SAS; SiSoSe, *st.* 1; StVeCh, *st.* 1
("Wee Willie Winkie runs through the town," *st.* 1.) OxNR; TiPo
Willie, with a thirst for gore. Careless Willie. *Unknown.* BBGG; FaPON
Willie Wolf. Helen Cowles LeCron. GFA
Willie's and Nellie's Wish. Julia A. Moore. FiBHP
"Willie's fair, an Willie's rare." Rare Willie Drowned in Yarrow; or, The Water o Gamrie. *Unknown.* BaBo
Willie's Fatal Visit. *Unknown.* BaBo; ESPB
Willie's Gane to Melville Castle, *with music.* *Unknown.* SaSa
Willie's Lady. *Unknown.* BaBo; ESPB; ViBoFo
(Sweet Willie.) OxBB
(Willy's Lady.) OBB
Willie's Lyke-Wake. *Unknown.* BaBo; ESPB; OBB, *diff. vers.*
Willie's pa and ma were kind. Silly Willy. "R. L. B." ShM
Willie's taen him o'er the fame. Willie's Lady. *Unknown.* ViBoFo
Willing Couple, The. *Unknown.* *See* Jovial Tinker, The.
Willing Mistress, The. Aphra Behn. *See* Amyntas Led Me to a Grove.
Willing Suspension, A. John Holmes. PoCh
Willis, The. David Law Proudfit. AA
Willobie His Avisa, *sel.* *At. to* Henry Willoby.
To Avisa. EIL
Willoughby liked being Willoughby. The Contentment of Willoughby. Frances Alexander. GoYe

Willow, The. Sir William Davenant. *See* Under the Willow Shades.

Willow. Richard Watson Dixon. *See* Song: "Feathers of the willow, The."

Willow, The. Tu Fu, *tr. fr. Chinese by* Kenneth Rexroth. NaP

Willow and Water. Edward Davison. *See* Lovers, The.

Willow Bend and Weep. Herbert Clark Johnson. PoNe

Willow-Boughs, The. Aleksandr Blok. *See* Little Catkins.

Willow Cats, The. Margaret Widdemer. BrR; OTPC (1946 ed.); RIS

Willow Garland, The. Robert Herrick. OAEP

Willow-Man, The. Juliana Horatia Ewing. TVC

Willow Poem. William Carlos William. NP

Willow shining, The. The Knowlege of Light. Henry Rago. PoCh

Willow Switch, The. Douglas Gibson. NYTB

Willow, Titwillow. W. S. Gilbert. *See* Suicide's Grave, The.

Willow-Tree, *parody.* Thackeray. BOHV; CenHV; HBV; InMe

Willow tree leans far over the brook, A. Pastorale. Robert A. Davis. GoSl

Willow: Why do you bend so low. Springtime. Alfred Kreymborg. MAPA

Willow, willow, willow, sing all of green willow. A Lover Approving His Lady Unkind Is Forced Unwilling to Utter His Mind. *Unknown.* ReIE

Willows, The. Walter Prichard Eaton. DD; FaPON; HBMV; MPB; OHIP

Willows, The, *parody.* Bret Harte. BOHV; InMe

Willows. Joseph Langland. NePoEA

Willows are taking the old river road, The. Old River Road. Blanche Whiting Keysner. GoYe

Willows are trees of life. They ride. Willows. Joseph Langland. NePoEA

Willows carried a slow sound, The. Repose of Rivers. Hart Crane. AP; AWP; CMoP; CoBMV; ExPo; ForPo; FosPo; InPo; LiTM (rev. ed.); MoAB; MoAmPo (1950 ed.); NP; OxBA; PIA; PoIE; SeCeV; TDP

Willows in the Snow. Tsuru, *tr. fr. Japanese by* William N. Porter. MPB; SUS

Willows of Massachusetts, The. Denise Levertov. WIRo

Willowwood. Dante Gabriel Rossetti. The House of Life, XLIX-LII. MaVP; OAEP; PoVP; ViPo; VP

"I sat with Love," XLIX. HBV; PoEL-5; Sonn; WHA

"O ye, all ye that walk in Willowwood," LI. ViPP

Wills. John Godfrey Saxe. *See* Woman's Will.

Will's at the dance in the Club-room below. A Wife Waits. Thomas Hardy. At Casterbridge Fair, VI. BEL; EnLi-2 (1949 ed.); EnLit; PoVP

Wills Dies in Solitude. Colin Thiele. *Fr.* Burke and Wills. NeLNL

Will's Love, The. Besmilr Brigham. ThO

Willy and the Lady. Gelett Burgess. HBMV

Willy boy, Willy boy, where are you going? *See* Willie boy, Willie boy . . .

Willy Drowned in Yarrow. *Unknown.* GTBS; GTBS-D; GTBS-P; GTBS-W

(Rare Willy.) GTSE; GTSL; HBV; OxBB, *with music*

(Rare Willy Drowned in Yarrow.) BaBo; ESPB (A, B, *and* D *vers.*); GoTS; OBB

Willy nilly, he comes or goes, with the clown's logic. Comes Away Death. E. J. Pratt. PeCV

Willy Reilly. *Unknown.* HBV; OnYI; OuSiCo, *with music*

(Sweet Riley, B *vers.*) BaBo

(Willie Riley, A *vers.*) BaBo

Willy the Weeper. *Unknown. See* Willie the Weeper.

Willy Wet-Leg. D. H. Lawrence. CMoP

Willy, Willy Wilkin. *Unknown.* OxNR

Willy Winkie. Daniel Henry Holmes. TSW

Willy's Lady. *Unknown. See* Willie's Lady.

"Willy's rare, and Willy's fair." Rare Willy [Drowned in Yarrow]. *Unknown.* ESPB; GoTS; OBB; OxBB

Wilson and Pilcer and Snack stood before the zoo elephant. Elephants Are Different to Different People. Carl Sandburg. MAP; MoAmPo

Wilt thou accept not. Worship. Shelley. *Fr.* One Word Is Too Often Profaned. MaRV

Wilt thou be gone? it is not yet near day. Romeo and Juliet in the Orchard. Shakespeare. *Fr.* Romeo and Juliet, III, v. TreFT

Wilt thou bee gon thou hartless man? *Unknown.* SeCSL

Wilt Thou Follow Me? *Unknown.* SoP

Wilt thou forgive that sin [*or* sinne] where I begun [*or* begunne]. A Hymn [*or* Hymne] to God the Father [*or* To Christ *or* For Forgiveness]. John Donne. AnAnS-1; AnFE; AtBAP; AWP; BEL; BoC; CaFP; CoBE; DiPo; EaLo; EG; EnLi-1; EnLit; EnRePo; EP; ForPo; FosPo; GoBC; GTSE; HBV; InPo; JAWP; LiTB; LiTG; LoBV; MaMe; MaRV; MBW-1; MeLP; MeP; MePo; OBEV (1st ed.); OBS; OxBoCh; PAn; PG (1945 ed.); Po; PoAn; PoE; PoEL-2; PoeP; PoFS; PoIE; PoPo; PoRA; ReEn; SCEP-1; SeCeV; SeCL; SeCP; SeCV-1; SeEP; ShBV-4; TDP; TOP; TreFT; TrGrPo; TrPWD; TuPP; ViBoPo;

"Wilt thou forsake me? and wilt thou leave me." *Unknown. Fr.* "My dear, adieu! my sweet love, farewell!" LO

Wilt thou go with me, sweet maid. An Invite to Eternity. John Clare. ERoP-2; OBNC; PeER

Wilt thou hear, O sailor, what this people say? *Unknown. Fr.* The Battle of Maldon. PoFr

Wilt Thou Lend Me Thy Mare? *Unknown.* CBEP; ELU; OBS

Wilt thou love God, as he thee! then digest. Holy Sonnets, XV. John Donne. AnAnS-1; MaMe; MasP; MeP; OBS; SCEP-1; Sonn

Wilt thou not ope thy heart to know. Emerson. *Fr.* Threnody. MaRV

Wilt thou not visit me? The Prayer. Jones Very. MaRV; OxBA; TrPWD

Wilt Thou Set Thine Eyes upon That Which Is Not? Francis Quarles. *See* Vanity of the World, The.

Wilt Thou steer my frail black bark. The Heavenly Pilot. Cormac. *Fr.* Book of Leinster. CAW; OnYI

Wilt Thou Yet Take All. Swinburne. *Fr.* Hymn to Proserpine. UnPo (1st ed.)

Wiltshire Downs. Andrew Young. ChMP; GTBS-D; GTBS-P

Wily Beguiled, *sel. Unknown.*

"Old Tithon must forsake his dear." TuPP

Wily Cupid. Henry Chettle. *Fr.* Piers Plainness' Seven Years' Prenticeship. EG

(Aeliana's Ditty.) ALV; OBSC

(Of Cupid.) EIL

Win at First and Lose at Last; or a New Game at Cards. Laurence Price. OxBoLi

Winander Lake. Wordsworth. *See* There Was a Boy.

Winchester. Lionel Johnson. OBVV

Winchester Wedding, The. Thomas D'Urfey. CavP

Wind, The. Padraic Colum. *See* I Saw the Wind Today.

Wind, The. Robert Creeley. AmPC

Wind, The. W. H. Davies. SeCePo

Wind, The. Emily Dickinson. *See* Of all the sounds despatched abroad *and* Wind tapped like a tired man, The.

Wind. Leonard Feeney. GoTP

Wind. Aileen Fisher. RePo

Wind, The. Louis Ginsberg. RIS

Wind, The. Dorothy Gradon. BoTP

Wind. Langston Hughes. *Fr.* A House in Taos. CDC

Wind. Ted Hughes. FlW

Wind, The. Letitia Elizabeth Landon. OTPC; PRWS

Wind, The. Betty Miller. BrR

Wind, The. Harold Monro. *See* Wind in the Dusk.

Wind, The. William Morris. NBM; PoVP

Wind, The. Elizabeth Rendall. BoTP; HBVY

Wind, The. Christina Rossetti. *See* Who Has Seen the Wind?

Wind, The. Charles Simic. YAP

Wind, The. James Stephens. AnIL; BoNaP; ELU

Wind, The. Robert Louis Stevenson. BoTP; GBV (1922 ed.); GFA; GN; HBVY; MPB; OTPC; PCH; PoIE (1970 ed.); PoVP; SoPo; StVeCh; SUS; TiPo; YT

Wind, The. John Banister Tabb. AnAmPo

Wind, The. *Unknown.* FaBoCh; LoGBV

("Arthur O'Bower has broken his band.") OxNR

(High Wind, The.) ChTr

Wind, The. Dorothy Wordsworth. *Fr.* Address to a Child during a Boisterous Winter Evening. BoTP

Wind/ flattening its gaunt furious self. The Wind Our Enemy. Anne Marriott. CaP

Wind, The/ skims down the path. A Letter. Sophia Castro-Leon. QAH

Wind and an Eagle Owl, *sel.* N. H. Brettell.

"We rode out with the pealing day before us." BoSA

Wind and Lyre. Edwin Markham. SoP; TRV

Wind and Mist. Edward Thomas. BrPo
Wind and Rain. *Unknown, tr. fr. Chinese by* Arthur Waley. *Fr.* The Book of Songs. HW
Wind and Silver. Amy Lowell. MAP; MoAmPo; NeMA
Wind and the beam loved the Rose, The. Nydia's Song. Sir Edward Bulwer-Lytton. *Fr.* The Last Days of Pompeii. OBVV
Wind and the Bird, The. *Unknown, tr. fr. Bushman by* W. H. I. Bleek. PeSA
Wind and the Fisherman, The. *Unknown. See* When the Wind is in the east.
Wind and the Leaves, The. George Cooper. *See* Come, Little Leaves.
Wind and the Moon, The. George Macdonald. GoJo; GoTP; HBV; HBVY; MoShBr; OnMSP; OTPC; StVeCh (1940 ed.); SUS; TreFS; TVC
Wind and the Rain, The. Robert Frost. MWA-2
Wind and the Rain, The. Shakespeare. *See* When That I Was and a Little Tiny Boy.
Wind and waters ring the bells. Veneta. Mary Elizabeth Coleridge. CBEP
Wind and Wave. Coventry Patmore. The Unknown Eros, I, ii. NBM
Wind and Wave. Charles Warren Stoddard. AA
Wind and Window-Flower. Robert Frost. YT
Wind at Penistone, The. Donald Davie. LiTM (1970 ed.); NMP; NePoEA-2
Wind at the Door, The. William Barnes. AtBAP; CBEP; ELP; GTBS-P; LO; NBM; PoEL-4
Wind at Your Door, The. Robert D. Fitzgerald. PoAu-2
Wind began to rock the grass, The. Emily Dickinson. BoNaP
Wind billowing out the seat of my britches, The. Child on Top of a Greenhouse. Theodore Roethke. AtBAP; ELU; LOW; MiAP; PoPl; StP; WePo
Wind blew all my wedding-day, The. Wedding Wind. Philip Larkin. HW; ToPo
Wind blew fresh and seaward made, The. Danaë. Simonides. LiTW
Wind, The, blew out from Bergen from the dawning to the day. The Last Hero. G. K. Chesterton. OtMeF
Wind blew strongly like the voice of fate, The. Christoph. Charles Spear. AnNZ
Wind Blew Words, The. Thomas Hardy. EPN
Wind Blow East, The, *with music. Unknown.* OuSiCo
Wind Bloweth Where It Listeth, The. Countee Cullen. NP
Wind Bloweth Where It Listeth, The. Susan L. Mitchell. AnIV
Wind Blows, The. Donagh MacDonagh. NeIP
Wind blows cold from a storm, The. The Dead City. Clinch Calkins. AnAmPo
Wind blows east, the wind blows storm, The. A Bee Sets Sail. Katharine Morse. UTS
Wind blows east, The—the wind blows west. A Salem Witch. Ednah Proctor Clarke. PAH
Wind blows from the north, The. A Complaint. Chwang Këang. OuHeWo
Wind blows, grey, The. Naito Meisetsu, *tr. fr. Japanese by* Geoffrey Bownas *and* Anthony Thwaite. FIW
Wind blows hot, The. English and foreign birds. Christmas Eve: Australia. Karl Shapiro. NYBP; PoAn; ReMP
Wind blows out of the gates of the day, The. Fairy Song [*or* Song]. W. B. Yeats. *Fr.* The Land of Heart's Desire. BEL; FIW; GBV; GTSL; HT; InP; MoBrPo; OnYI; TSW; ViBoPo
Wind blows the rain into our faces, The. Charles Reznikoff. OCS
Wind [*or* Wild wind] blows, the sun shines, the birds sing loud, The. Wild Geese. Celia Thaxter. PRWS; UTS
Wind blows wild on Bos'n Hill, The. Bos'n Hill. John Albee. AA
Wind blows, The. Winds blow the. Landscape. Robert Wells. MemP
Wind break on the beach. Legend of the Waving Lady. Ethel Livingston. ThO
Wind came in for several thousand miles all night, The. On an East Wind from the Wars. Alan Dugan. AP
Wind came up out of the sea, A. Daybreak. Longfellow. AmePo; AnNE; BoTP; HBV; PoLF; TreFT; WaKn
Wind-Clouds and Star-Drifts, *sel.* Oliver Wendell Holmes. Manhood. AP
Wind, cold, rain. History of France. Kenward Elmslie. ANYP
Wind comes from opposite poles, The. The Marriage. Mark Strand. YAP
Wind comes from the north, The. Suspense. D. H. Lawrence. MoBrPo
Wind comes, singing, The. Glad Earth. Ella C. Forbes. YeAr
Wind cracked his whip, The. Under the Tent of the Sky. Rowena Bennett. UTS
"Wind doth blow today, my love, The." The Unquiet Grave. *Unknown.* AnFE; AtBAP; BaBo; CH; CBEP; DTC; ELP; EnL; ExPo; LO; LoBV; NoP; OBB; OxBB; PoEL-1; PoIE; ViBoPo; WePo
Wind doth wander up and down, The. Destiny. Nathalia Crane. GoTP; MAP; NeMA
Wind exultant swept, The. A Mood. Winifred Howells. AA
Wind flapped loose, the wind was still, The. The Woodspurge. Dante Gabriel Rossetti. AnFE; AtBAP; BoLiVe; CaFP; CBEP; ELP; EPN; FaBoEn; GTBS-D; GTBS-P; LoBV; MemP; NBM; NoP; OAEP; OBEV (new ed.); OBNC; PoEL-5; PoIE; PoVP; TreFT; UnPo (3d ed.); VA; ViPP; WHA
Wind Force. Bernadette Mayer. ANYP
Wind from off the sea says nothing new, The. The Marrow. Theodore Roethke. NYBP
Wind from the east, oh, lapwing of the day. Odes. Hafiz. AWP
Wind from the north: the young spring day. The Song of the Four Winds. Thomas Love Peacock. *Fr.* The Misfortunes of Elphin. ERoP-1; OBRV; WiR
Wind from the south, hook in the mouth. How They Bite. *Unknown.* SD
Wind, Gentle Evergreen. Simmias. *See* On the Tomb of Sophocles.
Wind Harbour, The. Norman Levine. PeCV
Wind, hark! the wind in the angry woods, The. Summer Storm. Lionel Johnson. BrPo
Wind has a language I would I could learn, The. The Wind. Letitia Elizabeth Landon. OTPC; PRWS
"Wind has a tongue tonight, The," he said. The Chestnut Roasters. Joseph Payne Brennan. FiSC
Wind has at last got into the clock, The. The Wind, the Clock, the We. Laura Riding. LiTA
Wind has blown that searchlight out, The. Autumn Squall—Lake Erie. Lola Ingres Russo. AmFN
Wind has blown the rain away and blown, A. Sonnet. E. E. Cummings. AmPP; AnNE; MAP; MoAB; MoAmPo
Wind has lots of noises, The. Wind. Aileen Fisher. RePo
Wind has scattered my city to the sheep, The. Ruins of the City of Hay. Randolph Stow. PoAu-2
Wind Has Such a Rainy Sound, The. Christina Rossetti. *Fr.* Sing-Song. BrR; PoVP; TiPo
(Sound of the Wind, The.) BoTP
Wind Has Wings, The. *Unknown, tr. fr. Eskimo by* Raymond De Coccola *and* Paul King. WHW
Wind hits and returns, The, it is easy to personify. Sophia Nichols. Robin Blaser. CoPo
Wind in a Frolic, The. William Howitt. MoShBr; OTPC; PRWS; StVeCh (1940 ed.)
Wind in the Alleys. Lola Ridge. MAP; MoAmPo (1942 ed.); OnYI
Wind in the Dusk. Harold Monro. NeMA
(Wind, The.) OBVV
Wind in the Elms, The. J. Corson Miller. HBMV
Wind in the Grass, The. Emerson. *Fr.* To Ellen at the South. BoTP
Wind in the Grass. Mark Van Doren. FaBV
Wind in the Pine. Lew Sarett. MaRV; OTPC (1946 ed.); TRV; TrPWD
Wind in the Pines, The. Madison Cawein. AA
Wind in the Fines, The. Sir Henry Taylor. *Fr.* Edwin the Fair. VA
Wind in the street, and sadness of unknown walkers. Epithalamion. Terence Tiller. POTE
Wind in the Willows, The, *sels.* Kenneth Grahame.
Carol: "Villagers all, this frosty tide." OHIP
(Christmas Carol.) MPB
Duck's [*or* Ducks'] Ditty. BoTP; FaPON; GoJo; MoShBr; MPB; OTPC (1946 ed.); PCH; PDV; PoRh; SoPo; SUS; TiPo; UTS; WaKn

World Has Held Great Heroes, The. RePo
(Song of Mr. Toad, The.) FaPON; FiBHP; GoJo
Wind in the Wood. Paul Verlaine, *tr. fr. French by* Alan Conder. LO
Wind Is a Cat. Ethel Romig Fuller. MoSiPe; MPB; SoPo; UTS
Wind is a man and goes out from his hut, The. The Wind and the Bird. *Unknown.* PeSA
Wind is a teasing hunger, The. Captive. John Richard Moreland. PoMa
Wind is awake, pretty leaves, pretty leaves, The. The Way of It. John Vance Cheney. HBV
Wind is Blind, The. Alice Meynell. MemP; MoBrPo; SeCePo
Wind is blowing from the hill, The. Nocturne. H. A. Vaughan. PoNe
Wind is blowing, A. The book being written. The Novel. Denise Levertov. AP
Wind Is Blowing West, The. Joseph Ceravolo. ANYP
Wind is east but the hot weather continues, The. American Letter. Archibald MacLeish. AmPP; ILP; NoP; OxBA
Wind Is Ill, The. John Malcolm Brinnin. LiTA
Wind is in the cane. Come along. Jean Toomer. *Fr.* Carma. Kal
Wind is piercing chill, The. Battlefield. Richard Aldington. MMA
Wind is playing round the curtains, The. Nerves. Elizabeth Jennings. NYTB
Wind is pushing against the trees, The. March Wind. Helen Wing. GFA
Wind is rising on the sea, The. Before the Squall. Arthur Symons. PoVP
Wind Is Round, The. Howard Moss. WIRo
Wind is ruffling the tawny pelt, A. A Far Cry from Africa. Derek Walcott. ToPo; TTY
Wind is sewing with needles of rain, The. Two Sewing. Hazel Hall. MoSiPe; NP
Wind is such an optimist, The. The Wind. Louis Ginsberg. RIS
Wind is to show. Wind. Leonard Feeney. GoTP
Wind it blew, and the ship it flew, The. The Earl o' Quarterdeck. George Macdonald. BeLS; EtS; LoEn
Wind it blew from sou' sou'-east, it blew a pleasant breeze, The. The Light on Cape May. *Unknown.* ShS
Wint It Blew up the Railroad Track, The, *with music. Unknown.* AS
Wind it wailed, the wind it moaned, The. Alec Yeaton's Son. Thomas Bailey Aldrich. EtS
Wind like this tonight, A. Exile. Audrey Beecham. NeBP
Wind Me a Summer Crown. Menella Bute Smedley. HBV; OBVV
Wind meets me at Penistone, The. The Wind at Penistone. Donald Davie. LiTM (1970 ed.); NePoEA-2; NMP
Wind mutters thinly on the sagging wire. Prairie Graveyard. Anne Marriott. CaP; OBCV; PeCV
Wind o' the East dark with rain. The Efficient Wife's Complaint. Confucius. *Fr.* Airs of Pei. CTC
Wind of Death, The. Ethelwyn Wetherald. VA
Wind of Fall, A. Léonie Adams. YT
Wind of Hampstead Heath still burns my cheek, The. Breath of Hampstead Heath. Edith M. Thomas. AA
Wind of January, The. Christina Rossetti. *See* Year's Windfalls, A.
Wind of Summer. "Michael Field." VA
Wind of the city streets. To a June Breeze. H. C. Bunner. AA
Wind of the North. The Four Winds. Charles Henry Luders. AA; HBV
Wind of the Prairie. Grace Clementine Howes. GoYe
Wind of the West, that fans with fragrant wing. To the Western Wind. Judah Halevi. TrJP
Wind of the winter, drive the ships home. To the Winter Wind. John Gould Fletcher. TSW
Wind of Time, The. Joseph Payne Brennan. FiSC
Wind on the Hills, The. Dora Sigerson Shorter. HBMV; JKCP
Wind on the Lyre. George Meredith. CaFP; NBM
("That was the chirp of Ariel.") EG
Wind one morning sprang up from sleep, The. The Wind in a Frolic. William Howitt. MoShBr; OTPC; PRWS; StVeCh (1940 ed.)
Wind Our Enemy, The, *sel.* Anne Marriott.
"Wind/ flattening its gaunt furious self against.") CaP
Wind roars and the river roars, The. The Sounding Portage. Annie Charlotte Dalton. CaP
Wind rocks the car. Like This Together. Adrienne Rich. CoPo
Wind Rose in the Night, A. Aline Kilmer. HBMV
Wind sang to the cornfields, The. August. Eunice Fallon. BoTP
Wind shall lull us yet, The. From the Antique. Christina Rossetti. EnLoPo
Wind Shrieked Loud, The. Elizabeth J. Coatsworth. FiSC
Wind sings of a breed of men who taught the wind to sing, The. Men of America, Answering the Call. Hal Borland. PoFr
Wind slammed shut the door and he remembered, The. A Prisoner Freed. Geoffrey Dutton. BoAV
Wind—snow—ice—and sleet. Cold. Margaret Parton. PCD
Wind-Song. *Tr. fr. Pima Indian Song by* Natalie Curtis. RePo; SUS
Wind Song. Carl Sandburg. GBV (1952 ed.); MAP; MoAB; MoAmPo; MoShBr; NeMA; TwAmPo; YT
Wind Song. *Unknown.* GFA
Wind Sprang Up at Four o'Clock, The. T. S. Eliot. LiTB; NePA
Wind, stirring in the dark foliage, brings, The. God's Harp. Gustav Falke. AWP; JAWP; WBP
Wind stood up, and gave a shout, The. The Wind. James Stephens. AnIL; BoNaP; ELU
Wind Suffers, The. Laura Riding. AnAmPo; FaBoMo
Wind sways the pines, A. Dirge in (the) Woods. George Meredith. BoLiVe; EG; EPN; LoBV; OAEP; OBEV (new ed.); OBNC; OBVV; PoVP; SeCeV; TDP; TOP; VP; WHA; WiR
Wind-Swept Wheat, The. "Madeline Bridges." AA
Wind tapped like a tired man, The. Emily Dickinson. MoAB; MoAmPo (1950 ed.); NeMA; NePA
Wind tears at the water where I fish, The. Fishing. Keith Wright. NYTB
Wind That Shakes the Rushes, The. John Clare. PoRA (rev. ed.)
Wind that speeds the bee and plucks the bee-line. Awake! W. R. Rodgers. LiTM (rev. ed.); WaP
Wind that went through the head left it plural, The. Reading Reverdy. Ron Padgett. YAP
Wind, the Clock, the We, The. Laura Riding. LiTA
Wind the other evening overthrew, The. Love Fallen to Earth. Paul Verlaine. SyP
Wind took up the northern things, The. Emily Dickinson. AmLP
Wind voice calls and calls you, The. The Summons. Elizabeth Roberts MacDonald. CaP
Wind was a torrent of darkness among the gusty trees, The. The Highwayman. Alfred Noyes. ATP; BBV; BEL; BeLS; BoLP; EnLit; FaBV; FaFP; FaPON; GoTP; GSP; GTSL; HBV; HBVY; InP; LoEn; MaC; MCCG; OHFP; OnSP; PCD; PoLF; PoMa; PoPo; ShBV-2; TIHL; TOP; TreFS; TSW; YT
Wind was in another country, The. Mirage. R. P. Blackmur. *Fr.* Sea Island Miscellany. GTBS-W; LiTM; MoVE
Wind Was Out of the North, The. James Koller. FRC
Wind Weather. Virginia Brasier. StVeCh (1955 ed.)
Wind went forth a little after dawn, A. A Wind of Fall. Léonie Adams. . YT
Wind went wooing the rose, The. A Summer Wooing. Louise Chandler Moulton. HBV
Wind whines and whines the shingle. On the Beach at Fontana. James Joyce. AnEnPo; LO; MoBrPo; NP; OBMV
Wind whistled loud at the window-pane, The. Lullaby. William Brighty Rands. BoTP
Wind: why do you play. Improvisations. Alfred Kreymborg. MAP
Wind, wind, wind in the old trees. Variations, XII. Conrad Aiken. PG (1933 ed.)
Wind with foetid muzzle sniffed its feast, The. African Moonrise. Roy Campbell. CoBE
Wind-Wolves. William D. Sargent. MPB; TiPo; UTS
Windfall. F. R. Scott. CaP
Windflower, A. Bliss Carman. VA
Wind-Flower, The. Jones Very. AnNE

Windflowers and the Sage, The. Laura Spencer Porter. StJW
Windhover, The. Gerard Manley Hopkins. ACP; AnFE; AtBAP; ATP (1953 ed.); BoC; BrPo; BWP; CABA; CaFP; CAW; CBV; CMoP; CoBE; CoBMV; DiPo; EaLo; EnL; EnLi-2 (1949 ed.); EnLit; ExPo; FaBoEn; FaBoMo; ForPo; FosPo; GTBS-P; ILP; InvP; LiTB; LiTM; LoBV; MaPo; MoAB; MoBrPo; MoPo; MoPW; MoVE; NoP; OAEP; OBNC; PAn; PIA; Po; PoAn; PoDB; PoE; PoEL-5; PoeP; PoIE; PoPl; PoRA; PoVP; ReMP; SeCeV; ShBV-4; StP; SyP; TDP; TreFT; UnPo (3d ed.); VaPo; ViPo; ViPP; VP
Winding Banks of Erne, The. William Allingham. AnIV; IrPN; NBM
(Adieu to Belashanny.) OxBI
Winding road lies white and bare, The. The Footpath Way. Katharine Tynan. HBV
Winding way the serpent takes, The. Norembega. Whittier. PAH
Windlass Song. William Allingham. BBV (1923 ed.); GN; OTPC
Windle-Straws. Edward Dowden. HBV
Windless northern surge, the sea-gull's scream, The. The Incarnate One. Edwin Muir. PoDB; PoIE
Windmill, The. Robert Bridges. NoP
Windmill, The. Lord De Tabley. NBM
Windmill, The. John Farrar. GFA
Windmill, The. Geoffrey Johnson. HaMV
Windmill, The. Longfellow. MoShBr
Windmill, The. E. V. Lucas. BoTP
Windmill, The. Allen Upward. *Fr.* Scented Leaves from a Chinese Jar. NP
Windmill on the Cape. William Vincent Sieller. GoYe
Windmill stands up like a flower on the hill, The. The Windmill. John Farrar. GFA
Windmills, The. John Gould Fletcher. Arizona Poems, IV. CrMA; PoMa
Windmills of Holland are turning again, The. The Battle of Peace. Wilson MacDonald. MaRV
Window, The. Conrad Aiken. CMoP
Window, The. Robert Creeley. OPoP
Window, The. Edwin Muir. LiTM (rev. ed.)
Window, The. Francis Scarfe. NeBP
Window, The. Iain Crichton Smith. NePoEA-2
Window, a Table, on the North, A. Ralph Gustafson. PeCV
Window Boxes. Eleanor Farjeon. FaPON
Window Cleaner, The. Elizabeth Fleming. BoTP
Window gives onto the white trees, The. Schoolmaster. Yevgeny Yevtushenko. FIW
Window-Glance, The. Heine, *tr. fr. German by* John Todhunter. AWP
Window has four little panes, The. Nonsense Verses [*or* Rhymes]. Gelett Burgess. HBV; HBVY; TSW
Window is wide and lo! beyond its bars, The. Interlude: The Casement. Christopher Brennan. PoAu-1
Window on the North, A. R. A. D. Ford. MoCV
Window, Painted Shut. Phillip Hey. YAP
Window-screen sifts the blue cumulus, The. Garden Puzzle. Gray Burr. CoPo
Window showed a willow in the west, The. Elegy in a Firelit Room. James Wright. TwAmPo
Window Sill, The. Robert Graves. AtBAP; EnLoPo
Windowed Habitations. Charles G. Bell. NePoAm-2
Windows, The. George Herbert. AnAnS-1; BWP; CABA; CoBE; ILP; MaMe; MaPo; MeLP; MeP; NoP; OAEP; PAn; SeCP; SeCV-1
(Church Windows, The.) CBEP; OBS
Windows. Randall Jarrell. OPoP
Windows for My Soul. Angela Morgan. OQP
Windows of heaven were open wide, The. A Ballad of the Conemaugh Flood. Hardwicke Drummond Rawnsley. PAH
Windows of the Soul. Ella Wheeler Wilcox. *Fr.* Progress. OQP
Windows of Waltham, The. John Wieners. CoPo
Winds, The. Madison Cawein. MAP
Winds, The. "John Eglinton." OnYI
Winds, The. Swinburne. TOP
Winds, The. Thomas Tusser. *See* Description of the Properties of Winds, A.
Winds, The. William Carlos Williams. AnAmPo
Winds a-Blowing. May Justus. BrR
Wind's an old woman in front of the rain, The. Wind Weather. Virginia Brasier. StVeCh (1955 ed.)
Winds are bleak, stars are bright. The Victoria Markets Recollected in Tranquillity. Frank Wilmot. BoAV; MoAuPo; NeLNL; PoAu-2
Winds are high on Helle's wave, The. Byron. *Fr.* The Bride of Abydos. OBRV
Winds are roaring out of the West, The. Inisgallun. Darrell Figgis. OnYI
Winds at Bethlehem, The. Winifred M. Letts. StJW
Winds gathered deep in the winter night, The. City Birds. "Spud" Johnson. PoMa
Winds have talked with him confidingly, The. Longfellow. James Whitcomb Riley. AA; DD; PoRL
Wind's Head, The. John L. Sweeney. JKCP (1955 ed.); TwAmPo
Wind's in the heart of me, a fire's in my heels, A. A Wanderer's Song. John Masefield. MCCG; MoAB; MoBrPo; RePo; TSW
Winds of autumn, winters dipped in mud. Mists and Rain. Baudelaire. OnPM; SyP
Winds of Eros. "Æ." HBMV
Winds of Fate, The. Ella Wheeler Wilcox. BLPA; MaRV; SoP; TRV; WBLP
(One Ship Drives East.) OQP
Winds of God, The. Clinton Scollard. PoRL
Winds of March, come sweeping through the long, brown valley. March Dreams. Rose Henderson. MoSiPe
Winds of May, that dance on the sea. James Joyce. Chamber Music, IX. HW
Winds of the morning. Nobody Knows. Helen Coale Crew. GFA
Winds of the People. Miguel Hernández, *tr. fr. Spanish by* Willard Maas. PoFr
Winds of the West, Arise. George Darley. AtBAP
Winds of the world for a little season, The. The Wind's Way. Richard Le Gallienne. HBMV
Wind's on the wold, The. Inscription for an Old Bed [*or* For the Bed at Kelmscott *or* Lines for a Bed at Kelmscott Manor]. William Morris. CH; NBM; OBEV (new ed.); OBVV; PoEL-5; PoVP; WiR
Winds out of the west land blow, The. A. E. Housman. A Shropshire Lad, XXXVIII. PoVP
Winds ride bareback, The. Bareback. William Haskell Simpson. *Fr.* In Arizona. NP
Wind's Song, The. "Gabriel Setoun." HBV; HBVY; OTPC; PPL
Winds that change against the sun. Rules of the Road. *Unknown.* SoAmSa
Winds that once the Argo bore, The. Heroes. Edna Dean Proctor. HBV
Winds that sweep the southern mountains. Allatoona. *Unknown.* PAH
Winds they did blow, The. The Squirrel. *Unknown.* BoTP; OxNR
Winds through [*or* Thro'] the olive trees. Long, Long Ago [*or* A Christmas Song]. *Unknown.* BoTP; BrR; ChBR; DD; FaPON; GFA; MPB; OHIP; OTPC (1946 ed.); PDV; PEDC; PoSC; TiPo (1952 ed.)
Wind's Way, The. Grace Hazard Conkling. HBV
Wind's Way, The. Richard Le Gallienne. HBMV
Winds were yelling, the waves were swelling, The. The Last Buccaneer. Macaulay. EtS; HBV
Winds, whisper gently whilst she sleeps. Laura Sleeping. Charles Cotton. CavP; ELP; FaBoEn; LoBV; OBS; SeCL; ViBoPo
Wind's word, the Hebrew Hallelujah, A. Hallelujah; a Sestina. Robert Francis. PoCh
Wind's Work. T. Sturge Moore. BrPo; HBMV; HBVY
Windscale. Norman Nicholson. POTi
Windshield. Robert Fitzgerald. CrMA
Windsor Forest. Pope. EiCL; FosPo, *abr.*; MBW-1
Sels.
Field Sports. OBEC; SeCePo
"Groves of Eden, The, vanish'd now so long." BEL; OBEC
"See! from the brake the whirring pheasant springs." FaBoEn; FIW; PoEL-3
(Pheasant, The.) GoTP
"Time shall come, when, free as seas or wind, The." PoFr
Windy Bill. *Unknown.* CoSo, *with music*
Windy Bishop, The. Wilfred Watson. OBCV
Windy City, The, *sel.* Carl Sandburg.

Night. OCS
Windy Day, A. Winifred Howard. FaPON
Windy Day, A. Andrew Young. GoTP; MoPW; ThWaDe
Windy Morning. Harry Behn. TiPo (1959 ed.)
Windy Night, The. Thomas Buchanan Read. GN
Windy night was blowing on Rome, A. The Rider at the Gate. John Masefield. BrPo; ShBV-2
Windy Nights. Robert Louis Stevenson. BoChLi; BoTP; GoJo; PoRA; PoRh; PRWS; RIS; ShBV-1; SiSoSe; StaSt; TiPo
Windy Wash Day. Dorothy Aldis. TiPo
Wine. Francis Carlin. JKCP (1926 ed.)
Wine. Dakiki, *tr. fr. Persian by* R. A. Nicholson. LiTW
Wine. Micah Joseph Lebensohn, *tr. fr. Hebrew by* A. M. Klein. LiTW; TrJP
Wine and cakes for gentlemen. *Unknown.* OxNR
Wine and Dew. Richard Henry Stoddard. AA
Wine and Grief. Solomon ibn Gabirol, *tr. fr. Hebrew by* Emma Lazarus. LiTW; TrJP
Wine and Love and Lyre. *Unknown, tr. fr. Latin by* John Addington Symonds. UnTE
Wine and the Moon. *Unknown, tr. fr. Japanese by* Ishii *and* Obata. *Fr.* Manyo Shu. OnPM
Wine and Water. G. K. Chesterton. *Fr.* The Flying Inn. ACP (1952 ed.); CenHV; FiBHP; GoBC; HBMV; InMe; LiTM; MoBrPo; ShBV-4; ViBoPo
Wine and Woe. Proverbs, XXIII: 29-35, Bible *O.T.* [*Moulton, Modern Reader's Bible*]. MaRV
Wine and woman and song. Villanelle of the Poet's Road. Ernest Dowson. OBMV; PoVP; TrGrPo; ViPP
Wine comes in at the mouth. A Drinking Song. W. B. Yeats. CLwM
Wine-cup is glad, The: dear Zenophile's lip. The Draught of Love. Meleager. OnPM
Wine Jelly. *Unknown.* WhC
Wine Menagerie, The. Hart Crane. AP; OxBA
Wine of Love Is Music, The. James Thomson. *See* Vine, The.
Wine of the new vintage they brought us. The New Vintage. Douglas Le Pan. OBCV
Wine Press, The, *sel.* Alfred Noyes.
  Dawn of Peace, The, *fr.* Epilogue. MaRV
Wine-Press of Los, The. Blake. *Fr.* Milton. EnRP
Wine-Songs, *sels.* Moses ibn Ezra, *tr. fr. Hebrew by* Solomon Solis-Cohen. TrJP
  Awake, My Soul.
  Bring Me the Cup. TrJP
  Drink, Friends. TrJP
  Rosy Days Are Numbered, The. TrJP
Wine taken with excess. Temperance. *Unknown.* ACP; CAW
Wine to the weak and to those unsound. Wine. Francis Carlin. JKCP (1926 ed.)
Winemaker's Beat-étude, The. Alfred Purdy. MoCV
Wing by wing the wild geese fly. *Unknown, tr. fr. Japanese by* Kenneth Rexroth. LiTW
Wing of Separation,The. Ibn Darraj al Andalusi, *tr. fr. Arabic by* J. B. Trend. AWP; JAWP; WBP
Wing Tee Wee. J. P. Denison. BOHV
Wing'd seeds with decaying wings, The. Fragment. William Allingham. IrPN
Winged fancies of the learned quill, The. In Praise of Country Life. Robert Chamberlain. CavP
Winged Heels. Harry Lee. BBV (1923 ed.)
Winged horses descend to drink, The. On a Bas-Relief. Wesley Trimpi. NePoEA
Winged Hours. Dante Gabriel Rossetti. The House of Life, XXV. EPN; MaVP; PoVP; ViPo; VP
Winged lion on top of that column, The. Notes Made in the Piazza San Marco. May Swenson. CoAP
Winged Man. Stephen Vincent Benét. MAP; MoAmPo
Winged Mariner. Grace Clementine Howes. EtS
Winged mimic of the woods! thou motley fool! To the Mocking Bird. Richard Henry Wilde. *See also* Who shall thy gay buffoonery describe? AA.
Winged wonder of motion. The Dragonfly. Theodore Harding Rand. CaP
Winged Words. Robert Crawford. BoAu
Winged Worshipers, The. Charles Sprague. AA; HBV
Wings. William Rose Benét. PoMa
Wings. Victor Hugo. *See* Be like the Bird.
Wings, The. Denise Levertov. FRC
Wings. Psalms, LV: 6-7, Bible, *O.T.* FaPON; PCD; PCH
Wings. Blanche W. Schoonmaker. DD
Wings. *Unknown.* SoP
Wings and Wheels. Nancy Byrd Turner. SoPo; StVeCh (1955 ed.); SUS; TiPo
Wings at Dawn. Joseph Auslander. HBMV
Wings filmed, the threads of knowledge thicken. The Jam Trap. Charles Tomlinson. MoBrPo (1962 ed.
Wings of Love, The. James H. Cousins. AnIV
Wings of the Morning. Mabel Curtis. SoP
Wings of Time are black and white, The. Compensation. Emerson. AmPP (5th ed.); AP; ForPo; MWA-1
Winifred White. Nonsense Verses, III. Laura E. Richards. RIS
Winifreda. *Unknown.* HBV; OBEV (new ed.)
 (Translation from the Ancient British.) OBEC
Winked too much and were afraid of snakes. The Monkeys [*or* My Apish Cousins]. Marianne Moore. AnFE; APA; CMoP; CoAnAm; LiTA; NAMP; OxBA; SeCeV; TwAmPo
Winky, Blinky. *Unknown.* PCH
Winners, The. Kipling. *See* L'Envoi: "What is the moral?"
Winning of Cales, The. Thomas Deloney. CoMu
Winning of the TV West. John T. Alexander. AmFN; WaKn
Winning way, a pleasant smile, A. Little Annie Rooney. Michael Nolan. TreF
Winnipeg at Christmas. Rose Fyleman. ChBR
Winnowers, The. Robert Bridges. OAEP
Winny, *abr.* William Allingham. OTPC (1923 ed.)
Winslade, thy beech-capped hills, with waving grain. Written at Winslade, in Hampshire. Thomas Warton, the Younger. *Fr.* Sonnets. Sonn
Winsome Torment rose from slumber, rubbed his eyes, and went his way. The Hammam Name. James Elroy Flecker. BrPo; FaBoTw
Winter. Enid Blyton. BoTP
Winter. Burns. *See* Winter; a Dirge.
Winter. Thomas Campion. *See* Now Winter Nights Enlarge.
Winter. John Clare. ATP
Winter, *sel.* Charles Cotton.
  Winter's Troops. ChTr
Winter ("Oh Winter, ruler of th' inverted year). William Cowper. *Fr.* The Task, IV. OBEC
Winter. Maurice James Craig. OnYI
Winter. Walter de la Mare. ChTr; MoVE; OBMV; YeAr
Winter. Aubrey Thomas De Vere. *Fr.* The Year of Sorrow: Ireland—1849. IrPN
 (Year of Sorrow, A, *abr.*) ACP
Winter. Mary Mapes Dodge. *See* Snowflakes ("Whenever a snowflake.")
Winter. Gawin Douglas. *Fr.* Prologues to the Aeneid, Prologue to Bk. VII. SeCePo
Winter. Richard Hughes. OBMV; ThWaDe
Winter. James Hurnard. PoSC
Winter. Issa, *tr. fr. Japanese by* H. G. Henderson. OnPM
Winter. Jean Jaszi. SoPo
Winter. Joso, *tr. fr. Japanese by* H. G. Henderson. OnPM; WoL
Winter. Kalidasa, *tr. fr. Sanskrit by* Arthur W. Ryder. *Fr.* The Seasons. AWP
Winter. W. D. Landor. BoTP
Winter. Dorothy Livesay. TwCaPo
Winter. Charles Mair. OBCV; PeCV; PoSC, *abr.*
Winter. Coventry Patmore. The Unknown Eros, I, iii. OBNC
 ("I, singularly moved.") LO
Winter. Pope. *Fr.* Pastorals. EiCL
Winter ("Bread and milk . . ."). Christina Rossetti. *See* Bread and Milk.
Winter ("Sweet blackbird . . ."). Christina Rossetti. BoTP
Winter. Dante Gabriel Rossetti. CBEP; FosPo
Winter. Thomas Sackville. *Fr.* Induction to "The Mirror for Magistrates." EIL; SeCePo
Winter. Shakespeare. *See* When Icicles Hang by the Wall.
Winter. Shelley. *See* Widow Bird, A.
Winter. Robert Southey. Sonn
Winter. Spenser. *Fr.* The Faerie Queene, VII, 7. GN; OTPC
Winter. Robert Louis Stevenson. ACV; WePo
Winter. J. M. Synge. OBMV
Winter. Tennyson. PCH
Winter ("See Winter comes, to rule the varied year"). James Thomson. *Fr.* The Seasons. BEL, *sl. abr.*; CABL; CEP;

Winter (continued)
EiCL (*1st and final versions*); EiPP; EnL, *shorter sel.*; EnLi-2, *shorter sel.*; EnLit, *shorter sel.*; OAEP, *abr.*; PeER, *brief sel.*; Po, *abr.*; YAT *br. sel.*
Sels.
Approach of Winter. OBEC
"Clear frost succeds, and thro' the blew serene." FaBoEn
Frost at Night. OBEC
"Late, in the louring sky, red, fiery, streaks." FaBoEn
"Lo! from the livid East, or piercing North." AtBAP; FaBoEn; PeER, 26 *ll.*
("From all the livid east or piercing north.") YAT
"Now, solitary, and in pensive guise." FaBoEn
Storm, The. CoBE
Winter ("As thus the snows arise, and, foul and fierce"). SeCePo
(Lost Shepherd, The.) CoBE
Winter ("Now, when the cheerless empire of the sky"). OxBS
Winter ("The keener tempests come: and, fuming dun"). EnRP; NoP; ViBoPo
(Winter Storm, A.) TOP
Winter ("What art thou, frost? and whence are thy keen stores"). OxBS
Winter ("When from the pallid sky the sun descends"). OxBS
Winter Scene, A. OBEC
Winter Winds. UnPo (1st ed.)
Winter ("Chill, chill!"). *Unknown, tr. fr. Irish by* Frank O'Connor. KiLC
Winter ("Keen is the wind, bare the hill, it is difficult to find shelter"). *Unknown, tr. fr. Welsh by* Kenneth Jackson. *Fr.* The Black Book of Carmarthen. PrWP
Winter ("Old Winter is a sturdy one.") *Unknown.* DD
Winter ("Winter is a dreary season"). *Unknown, tr. fr. Irish by* Frank O'Connor. KiLC
Winter. Sheila Wingfield. BoLP; EnLoPo
Winter/ the cockroach. Gerald Butler. *Fr.* This Side of Orion. QAH
Winter; a Dirge. Burns. HBV
(Winter.) EiCP
Winter again and it is snowing. W. D. Snodgrass. Heart's Needle, V. AP; NoP
Winter Aconites. Robert Gittings. MemP
Winter afternoon, The. A Moment. L. A. G. Strong. NeMA
Winter among the Days. Raymond Holden. MAP; MoAmPo (1942 ed.)
Winter: An Ode. Samuel Johnson. CLwM
Winter and night, the white frost and the darkness. Urania. Ruth Pitter. MoVE
Winter and Red Berries. Nicholas Moore. NeBP
Winter and Spring. *Unknown.* BoTP
Winter and Summer. Stephen Spender. MoAB; MoBrPo (1950 ed.); MoPo
Winter, and the sky is a land of gray fiords. Grisaille with a Spot of Red. Samuel Yellen. NePoAm-2
Winter Apples. Winifred Welles. AnAmPo
Winter at Tomi. Ovid, *tr. fr. Latin by* F. A. Wright. AWP; JAWP; WBP
Winter be greeted by lads and lasses. A Dance Song. Burkhard von Hohenfels. LiTW
Winter blows on my eaves. Solstitium Saeculare. Robert Fitzgerald. MoVE
Winter Boats at Brighton. Alan Ross. POTi
Winter Branches. Margaret Widdemer. RePo
Winter Breath. Edward Weismiller. PoMa
Winter, by whom our stumbling feet were caught. Winter. Dorothy Livesay. TwCaPo
Winter Circus. Aileen Fisher. YeAr
Winter clenched its fist, The. The Redwing. Patric Dickinson. BoPe; HaMV; POTi
Winter Coats. Dorothy Aldis. RIS
Winter comes; I walk alone, The. The Winter's Spring. John Clare. AtBAP; PoIE
Winter crisp and the brittleness of snow. Words for Love. Ted Berrigan. ANYP
Winter Dawn. D. H. Lawrence. BrPo
Winter Day. Whittier. *Fr.* Snow-bound. TrGrPo
(Lines from "Snowbound.") BBV
(Snow, The, *longer sel.*) StVeCh
Winter Days. Henry Abbey. AA
Winter days are drawin' nigh, De. Winter Is Coming. Waverly Turner Carmichael. BANP
Winter deepening, the hay all in, The. Sonnet. Richard Wilbur. PoPl; Sonn; TDP
Winter Dusk. Walter de la Mare. AnEnPo
Winter Dusk. Richard Kendall Munkittrick. BOHV
Winter Encounters. Charles Tomlinson. LiTM (1970 ed.)
Winter Evening ("Come, Evening"). William Cowper. *Fr.* The Task, IV. CoBE
(Evening.) OBEC
Winter Evening, The ("Hark! 'tis the twanging horn"). William Cowper. The Task, IV. EiPP; EnLi-2; EnLit; OAEP; SeCePo; TOP, *sel.*
(Post-Boy, The.) FiP
(Postman, The.) CoBE
Winter Evening. Archibald Lampman. OBCV; PeCV
Winter Evening. Pushkin, *tr. fr. Russian by* C. Fillingham Coxwell. WoL
Winter evening settles down, The. Preludes, I. T. S. Eliot. AmP; AmPP; AnAmPo; BoLiVe (1945 ed.); CoBA; DiPo; ExPo; GBV (1952 ed.); GTBS-W; InP; LiTA; LiTM; MAP; MoAmPo (1942 ed.); MoShBr; MoVE; NeMA; NoP; OBMV; OCS; PoFS; PoPl; PoPo; ReMP; SeCePo; ShBV-3; TDP; TiPo (1952 ed.); TwCP; UnPo; WePo
Winter Feast. Frances Frost. YeAr
Winter Feathers. Mildred D. Shacklett. GFA
Winter Field. A. E. Coppard. BiS; MoBrPo (1942 ed.)
Winter Fire, The. Mary Howitt. OTPC (1923 ed.)
Winter flood is out, dully glasing the weald, The. The Flood. Andrew Young. ChMP
Winter for a Moment Takes the Mind. Conrad Aiken. Preludes for Memnon, I. LiTA; LiTM; MoPo; MoVE; NP; OxBA; StP; TwAmPo
Winter Galaxy, The. Charles Heavysege. OBCV
(Stars Are Glittering in the Frosty Sky, The.) CaP; PeCV
(Winter Night.) ACV
Winter Garden. David Gascoyne. ChMP; GTBS-D; GTBS-P
Winter Glass, The. Charles Cotton. HBV
Winter Gulls. Alan Ross. POTi
Winter has a joy for me. I Will Praise the Lord at All Times. William Cowper. CEP; EiCP; NoP
Winter has a pencil. Pencil and Paint. Eleanor Farjeon. PDV
Winter has at last come. Minamoto no Shigeyuki. *Fr.* Shui Shu. AWP
Winter Has Come ("Winter has come with scarcity"). *Unknown, tr. fr. Old Irish by* Kenneth Jackson. AnIL
Winter has come; fierce is the cold. Hot Cake. Shu Hsi. AtBAP; BoW; FlW; MoBrPo (1942 ed.)
Winter has come with scarcity. Winter Has Come. *Unknown.* AnIL
Winter has no cold teeth to crumble these. Rainbow Lands. Howard McKinley Corning. NP
Winter has reached thee once again at last. To Hampstead. Leigh Hunt. OBRV
Winter has wrecked the legend of your wings. To the Ghost of a Kite. James Wright. NePoEA
Winter Heavens. George Meredith. BoLiVe; CABA; Po
Winter Homily on the Calton Hill. Douglas Young. OxBS
Winter House, The. Norman Cameron. CBEP
Winter Hymn, A—to the Snow. Ebenezer Jones. OBNC
Winter in Dunbarton. Robert Lowell. ToPo
Winter in Durnover Field. Thomas Hardy. MoBrPo
Winter in East Anglia. Edmund Blunden. WePo
Winter in Étienburgh. Stephen Parker. NYBP
Winter in Lower Canada. Standish O'Grady. *Fr.* The Emigrant. OBCV
Winter in the Fens. John Clare. BoNaP; FlW
Winter in the Wood. Ivy O. Eastwick. YeAr
Winter in the world it is. Meeting in Winter. William Morris. EnLi-2 (1949 ed.)
Winter Indian. James Welch. YAP
Winter is a dreary season. Winter. *Unknown.* KiLC
Winter is cold-hearted. Summer [*or* Summer Days]. Christina Rossetti. BoNaP; CBEP; ELP; MCCG; NBM; OTPC; PRWS
Winter is fallen early. The Children of Stare. Walter de la Mare. BrPo
Winter Is Gone. Alfred Austin. LiTG; SiTL
Winter is icumen [*or* icummen] in. Ancient Music. Ezra Pound. FlW; LiTM; NePA; OxBA; Par; PIA; PoE; PPON; SiTL

Winter Is Icumen in. Bradford Smith. PoSC
Winter is passing, and the bells. Spring in the Students' Quarter. Henry Murger. AWP
Winter Is Past, The. Song of Solomon, Bible, *O.T.* *See* For, Lo, the Winter Is Past.
Winter is past, The. My Love Is like the Sun. *Unknown.* AnIV
Winter is too cold fer work. Nothin' Done. Sam S. Stinson. LHV
Winter Joys. Dorothy Gradon. BoTP
Winter Juniper. Joseph Langland. NePoEA
Winter Lakes, The. Wilfred Campbell. BoNaP; OBCV
Winter Landscape. John Berryman. AP; LiTA; LiTG; LiTM (1970 ed.); MoAmPo (1950 ed.); PoPl; TwCP
Winter Legend, A. Geoffrey Johnson. FiSC
Winter Life and Scenery. Thomas Caulfield Irwin. IrPN
Winter Lightning [for Paul], The. Howard Nemerov. FiMAP; MoVE
Winter Love. Elizabeth Jennings. NePoEA
Winter Love Song. *Unknown, tr. fr. Latin by* Helen Waddell. LiTW
Winter Madrigal, A. Morris Bishop. InMe
Winter Mask. Allen Tate. AmLP; NePA; OxBA
Winter Memories. Henry David Thoreau. AmLP; AmPP (4th ed.); MWA-1; NePA; OxBA
(Within the Circuit of this Plodding Life.) AP; MAmP
Winter midnight. Otsuji, *tr. fr. Japanese by* Kenneth Rexroth. LiTW
Winter Morning, A. James Russell Lowell. *Fr.* The Vision of Sir Launfal, Pt. II. GN
(January.) PoRL
Winter Morning. William Jay Smith. BoNaP
Winter Morning Walk, The ("'Tis morning"). William Cowper. The Task, V. EiCP; PoEL-3, 192 *ll.*
Winter Morning Walk, The ("Whose freedom is by suff'rance, and at will"). EnRP
Winter Night, A. William Barnes. ChTr; OBNC; PoG
Winter Night, A, *sel.* Burns.
"When biting Boreas, fell and doure." MCCG
Winter Night. Mary Frances Butts. OTPC; PRWS; TiPo (1952 ed.)
Winter Night. Emperor Ch'ien Wen-ti, *tr. fr. Chinese by* Arthur Waley. AtBAP; BoW; OnPM; WePo
Winter Night. Louis O. Coxe. NYBP
Winter Night. A. R. D. Fairburn. AnNZ
Winter Night. Robert Fitzgerald. PoPl
Winter Night. Roy Fuller. NeBP
Winter Night. Charles Heavysege. *See* Winter Galaxy.
Winter Night. Collister Hutchison. TiPo (1952 ed.)
Winter Night. Edna St. Vincent Millay. PoRL
Winter Night. Boris Pasternak, *tr. fr. Russian by* Eugene M. Kayden. PoPl
Winter Landscape. Stephen Spender. MoAB; MoBrPo
Winter Night, The. Whittier. *Fr.* Snow-Bound. PTK; TrGrPo
("As night drew on.") YT
Winter night is cold and drear, The. Across the Delaware. Will Carleton. MC; PAH
Winter night is round me like a skull, The. The Crocus. Norman Nicholson. BoPe; POTi
Winter-Night Song. Ford Madox Ford. NP
Winter Nightfall. Robert Bridges. GTBS-D; MoAB; MoBrPo; NeMA; OBEV; PoVP
Winter Nightfall. J. C. Squire. ShBV-3
Winter Nights. Thomas Campion. *See* Now Winter Nights Enlarge.
Winter Noon. Sara Teasdale. RePo; YeAr
Winter Noon in the Woods, *sel.* Thomas Caulfield Irwin.
"With witchlike branches, barren, bleak, and drear." IrPN
Winter Ocean. John Updike. ELU
Winter of '73, The, *with music.* Larry Gorman. ShS
Winter Offering. D. S. Savage. LiTB; LiTM; NeBP
Winter on Black Mingo, *sel.* *Unknown.*
"Cold, deserted and silent." FiBHP
Winter owl banked just in time to pass, The. Questioning Faces. Robert Frost. ELU; TDP
Winter owl skirts hemlock tree. Winter Sketch. Arthur S. Bourinot. CaP
Winter Piece, A. Bryant. AmPP (4th ed.); AP; CoBA; OxBA
Winter Piece, A. Ambrose Philips. CEP; OBEC; SeCePo
Winter Pond. Ben Belitt. NYBP
Winter Portrait. Robert Southey. BoNaP
Winter Rain. Christina Rossetti. BoNaP; WiR
Winter Rains: Cataluña. Philip Levine. NaP
Winter Remembered. John Crowe Ransom. AP; CaFP; CBEP; MoAB; MoPW; OxBA; PoAn; UnPo
Winter Rune. Elizabeth J. Coatsworth. SUS
Winter Saturday. Earle Birney. TwCaPo
Winter Scene. William Cowper. *Fr.* The Task, VI. OBEC
("Night was winter in his roughest mood, The") EnRP
Winter Scene. James Thomson. *See* Winter.
Winter Shore, The. Thomas Wade. ERoP-2; NBM
Winter Shower, A. Harumi, *tr. fr. Japanese by* Asataro Miyamori. OnPM
Winter Sketch. Arthur S. Bourinot. CaP
Winter Sleep. Edith M. Thomas. AA
Winter Sleep. Elinor Wylie. NePA
Winter snowes, all covered is the ground, The. Alexander Barclay. *Fr.* Certain Egloges. EnPo
Winter-Solitude. Archibald Lampman. PeCV (1967 ed.)
Winter Solstice, *sel.* Gerald Bullett.
So Still the World. POTE
Winter Solstice. Sara Teasdale. *See* December Day, A.
Winter Song, A. William Cox Bennett. PCH
Winter Song. David Daiches. NYBP
Winter Song. V. Sackville-West. *Fr.* The Land. MoBrPo (1942 ed.)
Winter Song. Shakespeare. *See* When Icicles Hang by the Wall.
Winter Song ("Drop down, drop down, white snowflakes!"). *Unknown, tr. fr. Czech.* PCH
(Winter's Song.) BoTP
Winter Spring. Richard Wilbur. FiMAP
Winter Stalks. Bertram J. Warr. TwCaPo
Winter Storm, A. James Thomson. *See* Winter.
Winter Storm at Sea, The. George Crabbe. *Fr.* The Borough, Letter I. EtS
Winter Storms, The. Sir William Davenant. SeCL
(Storm at Sea.) RoGo
Winter Streams. Bliss Carman. YeAr
Winter Sunrise, *sel.* Laurence Binyon.
"It is early morning within this room; without." ChMP
Winter Sunset. Jules Laforgue, *tr. fr. French by* Kate Flores. SyP
Winter Swan. Louise Bogan. AnAmPo
Winter Sweetness. Langston Hughes. GoSl
Winter Talent, A. Donald Davie. NePoEA-2
Winter, that coils in the thickets now. Deciduous Branch. Stanley Kunitz. HoPM; TwAmPo
Winter the Huntsman. Sir Osbert Sitwell. AtBAP; BoW; POTE; ShBV-2; WePo
Winter, thy cruelty extend. Song on a Young Lady Who Sung Finely. Earl of Roscommon. CavP
Winter-Time. *See* Wintertime.
Winter to Spring. Horace, *tr. fr. Latin by* Louis MacNeice. Odes, I, 4. LiTW
Winter Treats. Mildred D. Shacklett. GFA
Winter Trees. Conrad Diekmann. SD
Winter Trees, The. Clifford Dyment. POTi
Winter Trees. William Carlos Williams. NP
Winter Tryst. Ormonde de Kay, Jr. MeWo
Winter Tryst. Mark Van Doren. LiTA; LiTM (1946 ed.)
Winter Twilight. Jack Anderson. ThO
Winter Twilight, A. Arlo Bates. AA
Winter Twilight. George Tracy Elliot. AA
Winter Twilight, A. Angelina W. Grimké. CDC; PoNe
Winter; Two Sonnets. Malcolm Cowley. *Fr.* Blue Juniata. MAP; MoAmPo (1942 ed.)
Winter Verse for My Sister. William Meredith. NYBP
Winter Views Serene. George Crabbe. *Fr.* The Borough. OBNC
Winter was not unkind because uncouth. The Growth of Love, X. Robert Bridges. Sonn
Winter was so late in coming. The Discouraged Cherry Tree. Kathleen Millay. PEDC
Winter, we are by thy might. Winter-Time. Neidhart von Reuental. WoL
Winter Weather. William Morris. EPN; TOP
Winter Westerlies. James Devaney. BoAV; MoAuPo
Winter: When Icicles Hang by the Wall. Shakespeare. *See* When Icicles Hang by the Wall.
Winter will be feasts and fires in the shut houses. Fall in

Winter (continued)
Corrales. Richard Wilbur. CoPo; NoP; PIA; VaPo
Winter Will Follow. Richard Watson Dixon. *See* Heaving Roses of the Hedge Are Stirred, The.
Winter will not let go of earth. In Defense of Felons. Robert Mezey. NePoEA; ToPo
Winter Winds. James Thomson. *See* Winter.
Winter winds howled and the great barn creaked. The Barn in Winter. Claire Harris MacIntosh. CaP
Winter: winter in the woods. The King of the Wood. Clifford Dyment. POTi
Winter Wish, A. Robert Hinckley Messinger. AA; ViBoPo (Give Me the Old.) HBV
Winter with the Gulf Stream. Gerard Manley Hopkins. CMoP; ExPo; SyP
Winter withering. Tan Taigi, *tr. fr. Japanese by* Geoffrey Bownas *and* Anthony Thwaite. FIW
Wintering in the Heartlands. William Hunt. YAP
Winter's Cold. W. R. Rodgers. EnLoPo
Winter's Come, The. John Clare. ERoP-2
Winter's Dregs. George Bowering. PeCV (1967 ed.)
Winter's End. Howard Moss. NePoEA
Winter's house is cold and white. Just a Mile Beyond. Aileen Fisher. RePo
Winters know. Nature. Emerson. GBV (1952 ed.)
Winter's Morning Muse, A. Thomas Howell. SiCE
Winter's Song. Shakespeare. *See* When Icicles Hang by the Wall.
Winter's Song. *Unknown.* *See* Winter Song ("Drop down, drop down . . .").
Winter's Spring, The. John Clare. AtBAP; PoIE
Winter's Tale, A. Robert Patrick Dana. NYBP
Winter's Tale, A. D. H. Lawrence. MoAB; MoBrPo
Winter's Tale, A. Ruth Lechlitner. HYE
Winter's Tale, The, *sels.* Shakespeare.
Flowers ("Out, alas!"), *fr.* IV, iii. UnPo (1st ed.)
Flowers of Perdita, The ("Here's flowers for you"), *fr.* IV, iii. FiP
(Flowers of Middle Summer.) YeAr
("Here's flowers for you"). PoG
Jog On, Jog On [the Footpath Way], *fr.* IV, ii. CBEP; EG; FaBoCh; GN; HBV; HBVY; LoGBV; OBSC; PoG; SiCE; TiPo (1952 ed.); ViBoPo
(Autolycus' Song.) WhC
(Footpath Way, The.) RIS
(Merry Heart, The.) BoTP; EIL; PCH; SiTL; TrGrPo
(Songs of Autolycus, The.) OTPC (1923 ed.)
"Lawn as white as driven snow," *fr.* IV, iii. OAEP; OBSC; SiCE; ViBoPo
(Autolycus' Song.) LoBV
(Come Buy! [Come Buy!]) EIL; GaP
(Pedlar, The.) WiR
(Pedlar's Song.) CH
(Songs of Autolycus, The.) OTPC (1923 ed.)
Perdita's Garden, *fr.* IV, iii. WHA
"Sir, welcome," *fr.* IV, iii. AtBAP
Some Flowers o' the Spring, *fr.* IV, iii. ChTr
When Daffodils [*or* Daffadils] Begin to Peer, *fr.* IV, ii. CBEP; ChTr; EIL; ExPo; FaBoBe; FaBoCh; HBV; InPo; LoBV; LoGBV; NoP; OBSC; PoEL-2; PoeP; SiCE; UnTE; ViBoPo; WhC
(Autolicus's Song.) FaBoEn
(Autolycus.) EG
(Pedlar's Song, The.) OxBoLi
(Song: "When daffodils begin to peer.") FiP
(Songs of Autolycus, The.) OTPC (1923 ed.)
"When you sing," *fr.* IV, iii. UnS
Will You Buy Any Tape?, *fr.* IV, iii. GaP; OBSC; SiCE; ViBoPo
(Songs of Autolycus, The.) OTPC (1923 ed.)
Winter's Tale, A. Dylan Thomas. AtBAP; CMoP; FaBoMo; LiTB; SeCeV
Winter's thunder. *Unknown.* GoTP; RIS
Winter's Troops. Charles Cotton. *Fr.* Winter. ChTr
Winter s Walk, The. Samuel Johnson. CBEP; EiCP
Winterset, *sel.* Maxwell Anderson.
In All These Turning Lights I Find No Clue. TreFT
Winter-Time. Neidhart von Reuental, *tr. fr. German by* Jethro Bithell. WoL
Winter-Time. Robert Louis Stevenson. GFA; GoTP; MoBrPo; StVeCh
Winter time is bleak, the wind. Caoilte. *Unknown.* KiLC
Wintertime nighs. In Tenebris, I. Thomas Hardy. FaBoEn; LiTB; NoP; OAEP (2d ed.); PoDB; SeCePo; TreFS; UnPo; ViPo
Wintry blast goes wailing by, The. Christmas Night of '62. William Gordon McCabe. AA
Wintry Day. *Unknown.* PCH
Wintry west extends his blast, The. Winter [a Dirge]. Burns. EiCP; HBV
Wintry winds have ceased to blow, The. Resurrection. George Crabbe. OxBoCh
Wire, briar, limber-lock. *Unknown.* RIS
Wireless. Rodney Bennett. BoTP
Wires. Philip Larkin. ToPo
Wires Are So Still and High, The. Annette Wynne. GFA; PCH
Wires spread out far and wide, The. The Telegraph. Annette Wynne. GFA
Wires strung with diamonds. Snowfall. "I. V. S. W." InMe
Wisdom. Bible, Apocrypha. *See* Wisdom of Solomon, The.
Wisdom. William Cowper. *Fr.* The Task, VI. MaRV
Wisdom. Padraic Fallon. OnYI
Wisdom. Ford Madox Ford. HBV
Wisdom. Phyllis Hanson. GoYe
Wisdom. Daniel Whitehead Hicky. BiCB; OQP
Wisdom? "Laurence Hope." *See* For This Is Wisdom.
Wisdom. Langston Hughes. TiPo
Wisdom. Scudder Middleton. HBMV
Wisdom. Christina Rossetti. OBVV; TOP
Wisdom ("It was a night"). Sara Teasdale. AmLP; MAP; MoAmPo
Wisdom ("When I have ceased"). Sara Teasdale. Interlude; Songs Out of Sorrow, IV. InP
Wisdom. Frank Yerby. AmNP
Wisdom and Spirit of the universe! Influence of Natural Objects [*or* Boyhood]. Wordsworth. *Fr.* The Prelude, I. AtBAP; AWP; InPo; JAWP; LoBV; MCCG; OBRV; PeER; WBP; WHA
Wisdom be Thou. A Prayer for St. Innocent's Day. Helen Parry Eden. CAW
Wisdom Cometh with the Years. Countee Cullen. Kal
Wisdom found no place where she might dwell. Wisdom's Plight. Enoch, Bible, Pseudepigrapha. TrJP
Wisdom has no end and folly no ornament. Poem. Nathan Alterman. LiTW
Wisdom hath builded her house. The House of Wisdom. Proverbs, Bible, *O.T.* TrGrPo
Wisdom in Winter. *Unknown, tr. fr. Welsh by* Gwyn Williams. *Fr.* The Black Book of Carmarthen. PrWP
Wisdom is better than bread. Nevertheless. Gustav Davidson. GoYe
Wisdom of Folly. Ellen Thorneycroft Fowler. HBV
Wisdom of God, we would by Thee be taught. Learning. Bob Jones, Jr. SoP
Wisdom of Insecurity, The. Richard Eberhart. NePA
Wisdom of Merlyn, The, *sels.* Wilfrid Scawen Blunt.
"What then is Merlyn's message." ViBoPo
"Wouldst thou be wise, O Man?" OBMV
Wisdom of Old Jelly Roll, The. A. J. M. Smith. PeCV (1967 ed.)
Wisdom of Solomon, The, *sels.* Bible, Apocrypha.
"For the whole world before thee is as a little grain of the balance," XI: 23-27. BoC
"Souls of the righteous are in the hand of God, and there shall be no torment touch them, The." III: 1-9. BoC
Wisdom ("For she is a vapour"), VII: 25-26 (*Douay vers.*). ISi
Wisdom ("For wisdom, which is the worker"), VII: 21-29. BoC
Wisdom of the Abbot Macarius I. John Beecher. WOW
Wisdom of the Gazelle. George P. Solomos. GoYe
Wisdom of the World, The. Siegfried Sassoon. MoBrPo; NeMA
Wisdom of the world said unto me, The. Sapientia Lunae. Ernest Dowson. EnLi-2; HBV
Wisdom, out of Anguish by Denial. Pedigree. Mary Mills. NePoAm
Wisdom 'tis and courtesy. The Highest Wisdom. Jacopone da Todi. CAW
Wisdom warns me to shun that once I sought for. Phaleuciacs II. *Unknown.* SiCE
Wisdom with better thoughts prevailed; aloof. The Jew's Home. Robert Eyres. *Fr.* The Impious Feast. OBRV
Wisdom's Plight. Enoch, XLII: 1-3, Bible, Pseudepigrapha. TrJP

Wise, The. Countee Cullen. PoNe
Wise. Lizette Woodworth Reese. HBV
Wise, The. *Unknown, tr. fr. Sanskrit by* Sir Edwin Arnold. *Fr.* Bhagavad-Gita. OQP
Wise and Foolish Virgins, The. St. Matthew, XXV: 1-13, Bible, *N.T.* TreF
Wise Child, The. Edward Lucie-Smith. NYTB
Wise counsel is not always wise. The Boy and the Schoolmaster. La Fontaine. WoL
Wise emblem of our politick world. The Snayl. Richard Lovelace. AtBAP; PoEL-3; SCEP-2
Wise forget, dear heart, The. A Valentine. Jeannette Bliss Gillespy. *Fr.* Cameos. AA
Wise guys, The/ tell me. Kid Stuff. Frank Horne. AmNP; Kal; PoNe
Wise Johnny. Edwina Fallis. SiSoSe; SUS; TiPo
Wise king crowned [*or* dowered] with blessings on his throne, The. The Trophy. Edwin Muir. LiTM; POTE
Wise man holds himself in check, A. Wisdom. Scudder Middleton. HBMV
Wise Man, Wise Man. Louis Ginsberg. YT
Wise may bring their learning, The. A Child's Offering. *Unknown.* MaRV
Wise Men, The. Edgar Bowers. NePoEA
Wise Men and Shepherds. Sidney Godolphin. *See* Lord, When the Wise Men Came from Far.
Wise men, The, ask, "What language did Christ speak?" The Universal Language. Ella Wheeler Wilcox. ChIP; OQP
Wise Men in Their Bad Hours. Robinson Jeffers. AnAmPo
Wise men, indeed, to know a new-born star. A Different Way. Esther Lloyd Hagg. ChIP
Wise men love the cats for their perversity, The. The Cats. Baudelaire. OnPM
Wise Men of Gotham, The ("Seamen three! What men be ye?"). Thomas Love Peacock. *See* Three Men of Gotham.
Wise men patience never want. Thomas Campion. SiCE
Wise Men Seeking Jesus. James East. MaRV
Wisemen to glossators unknown. Apocryphal Apocalypse. John Wheelwright. MoVE
Wise men [*or* Wisemen] were but seven, ne'er more shall be for me, The. A Catch [*or* We Are Three]. *Unknown.* SeCL; SeEP
Wise Men, Wise Men. The Gifts. Odell Shepard. ChrBoLe
Wise Misogynist, The. Bhartrihari, *tr. fr. Sanskrit by* Arthur W. Ryder. OnPM
Wise old apple tree in spring, The. Pastoral, A. Robert Hillyer. BoNaP; OTD
Wise Old Owl, The. Edward Hersey Richards. BLPA; FaBoBe; FaFP; NeHB; SiTL; TreF; YaD
(Question & Answer, *with add. st.*) LiTG
("Wise old owl sat in an oak, A.") OxNR
Wise Rochefoucauld a maxim writ. The Life and Genuine Character of Dean Swift. Swift. EiPP
Wise Sarah and the Elf. Elizabeth J. Coatsworth. PoMS
Wise self is not born and does not die, The. Unborn Eternal Self. *Unknown. Fr.* The Upanishads. OnPM
Wise to have gone so early to reward. The Wazir Dandan for Prince Sharkan. *Unknown. Fr.* The Thousand and One Nights. AWP; JAWP; WBP
Wise with the wisdom of ages. Lincoln. Thomas Curtis Clark. HH
Wise Woman, The. Louis Untermeyer. ALV; HBMV
Wisely a woman prefers to a lover a man who neglects her. Distichs. John Hay. BOHV
Wisemen. *See* Wise men.
Wisest men are glad to die, The; no fear. Death. Thomas May. *Fr.* Continuation of Lucan. MaRV
Wisest of dogs was Vigi, a tawny-coated hound. Vigi. Katharine Lee Bates. PCD
Wisest of sparrows that sparrow which sitteth alone. Wisdom. Christina Rossetti. OBVV; TOP
Wisest of the wise, The. One White Hair. Walter Savage Landor. HBV; VA
Wisest scholar of the wight most wise, The. Astrophel and Stella, XXV. Sir Philip Sidney. FCP; NoP; ReEn; SiPS
Wish, A. Matthew Arnold. EPN; HBV; PoVP
Wish, The. Abraham Cowley. *Fr.* The Mistress. BEL; BoC; CavP; EnLi-1; EnLit; FaPL; GTBS-W; LiTB; LiTG; NoP; OAEP; OBEV; OBS; SeCL; SeCV-1; SeEP; TOP; TrGrPo; ViBoPo; WHA
Wish, The. John Dancer. SeCL
Wish, A. Earl of Essex. *See* Happy Were He.
Wish, The. Thomas Flatman. SeCL
Wish, A. Hamlin Garland. AA
Wish, A. Elizabeth Gould. BoTP
Wish, A. Ben Jonson. *See* Gipsy Song ("The faery beam upon you").
Wish, A. Omar Khayyám, *tr. fr. Persian by* Edward Fitzgerald. *Fr.* The Rubáiyát. OnPM
Wish, A. Vidal de Nicolas, *tr. fr. Spanish by* Chloe Vulliamy *and* Stephen Sedley. BoC
Wish, A. John Norris. PeRV
Wish, The. Walter Pope. *See* Old Man's Wish, The.
Wish, A. Samuel Rogers. BoTP; EPN; GTBS; GTBS-D; GTBS-P; GTBS-W; GTSE; GTSL; HBV; MCCG; OBEC; OBEV (new ed.); OBVV; OTPC (1923 ed.); RIS; TreFS
Wish, A. Frank Dempster Sherman. TVC
(Kite, A.) BoChLi (1950 ed.); PCH
Wish, The. Thomas Stanley, *after the Greek of* Anacreon. AWP; JAWP; WBP
Wish, A ("Now, Jesus, Mary's Son, be unto Thee"). *Unknown.* CAW
Wish, The. Rowland Watkyns. CavP
Wish at Meal-Time. John Farrar. BoChLi
Wish for the New Year, A. Phillips Brooks. STF
Wish Is Quite a Tiny Thing, A. Annette Wynne. SP
Wish of Manchin of Liath, The. *Unknown, tr. fr. Old Irish by* Kenneth Jackson. AnIL
(Hermit's Song, The.) KiLC, *tr. by* Frank O'Connor; OnYI, *tr. by* Kuno Meyer
Wish, that of the living whole, The. In Memoriam A. H. H., LV. Tennyson. AnFE; AtBAP; BEL; DiPo; EnL; EnLi-2; EnLit; EPN; FosPo; HBV; LoBV; MaPo; OAEP; OBEV (1st ed.); OBNC; OQP; OuHeWo; PoFS; SeCeV; TOP; UnPo; ViPo; VP
Wishes. Norman Ault. HBMV; HBVY
Wishes. Callistratus, *tr. fr. Greek by* John Herman Merivale. OnPM
Wishes. A. C. Child. PoToHe
Wishes. Richard Crashaw. *See* Wishes to His (Supposed) Mistress.
Wishes. Kate Greenaway. BoChLi (1950 ed.)
Wishes. F. Rogers. BoTP
Wishes. Robert Louis Stevenson. *See* Go, Little Book.
Wishes ("Said the first little chicken"). *Unknown. See* Five Little Chickens.
Wishes. Edna Kingsley Wallace. MoSiPe
Wishes at a Garden Party. Sir Walter Raleigh. *See* Wishes of an Elderly Man.
Wishes for a Bridal Couple and Their Unborn Child. Statius, *tr. fr. Latin by* D. A. Slater *and* Virginia Tufte. *Fr.* Epithalamium for Stella and Violentilla. HW
Wishes for My Son. Thomas MacDonagh. AnIV; GoBC; HBMV; JKCP; TSW
Wishes for the Supposed Mistress. Richard Crashaw. *See* Wishes to His (Supposed) Mistress.
Wishes for William. Winifred M. Letts. OnYI
Wishes of an Elderly Man, The. Sir Walter Raleigh. FaBoCh; FiBHP; LoGBV; PV; SiTL; WhC
("I wish I loved the human race.") CenHV
(Wishes at a Garden Party.) MemP
(Wishes of an Elderly Man at a Garden Party.) ShBV-4
Wishes on this child's mouth, The. Helga. Carl Sandburg. NP; TSW
Wishes to His (Supposed) Mistress. Richard Crashaw. AnFE, *sl. abr.*; ATP, *sl. abr.*; BEL; CoBE; EnLit; HBV; LiTL, *sl. abr.*; MaMe; MeLP; MePo; OBEV, *sl. abr.*; OBS; PoEL-2; SCEP-1; SeCL; SeCP; SeCV-1; SeEP; TreFT; ViBoPo, *abr.*; WHA
(Wishes.) OAEP; ReEn
(Wishes for the Supposed Mistress.) GoBC, *abr.*; GTBS; GTBS-D; GTBS-P; GTBS-W; GTSE; GTSE; GTSL, *abr.*; LiTG, *abr.*
"Whoe'er she be," *sel.* MemP
Wishful to add to my mental power. Ballade of Schopenhauer's Philosophy. Franklin P. Adams. HBMV
Wishing. William Allingham. BoChLi (1939 ed.); BoTP; DD, *abr.*; FaPON; GFA; HBV; HBVY; MPB; OHIP; OTPC; PCH; PRWS; TVC
Wishing. Henry W. Frost. SoP
Wishing-Caps, The. Kipling. OtMeF
Wishing My Death. *Unknown. See* Alone Walking.

Wishmakers' Town, *sels.* William Young.
Bells, The. AA
Bridal Pair, The. AA
Conscience-Keeper, The. AA
Flower-Seller, The. AA
Pawns, The. AA
(Losers, The.) HBMV
Wispy cuttings lie in rows, The. July in Indiana. Robert Fitzgerald. NYBP
Wistaria Blossoms. Charles Dalmon. *Fr.* Three Pictures. TSW
Wistful Days, The. Robert Underwood Johnson. AA
Wistfully shimmering, shamelessly wise and weak. Epicede. Donald Evans. NP
Wit, The. Elizabeth Bishop. NePoAm-2
Wit Predominant. Thomas Rymer. *Fr.* Edgar. SeCL
Wit, Whither Wilt Thou? *Unknown.* EIL
Wit Wonders. *Unknown.* *See* God and Yet a Man, A.
Witch, A. William Barnes. PoMS
(Country Witch, A.) GoTP
Witch, The. Mary Elizabeth Coleridge. GTBS-D; NCEP; PoVP
Witch, The. Lord Alfred Douglas. HBMV
Witch, The. Robert Herrick. *See* Hag, The.
Witch, The. Percy H. Ilott. BoTP
Witch, The. Stanley McNail. FiSC
Witch, The. Robert Southey. *See* Old Woman of Berkeley, The.
Witch, The. Katharine Tynan. OnYI
Witch, The. W. B. Yeats. ELU; FaBoTw
Witch Cat. Rowena Bennett. SiSoSe
Witch Doctor. Robert Hayden. AmNP
Witch doctor. We Waiting on You. Edward S. Spriggs. BF
Witch-elms that counterchange the floor. In Memoriam A. H. H., LXXXIX. Tennyson. OBNC; EPN; ViPo; VP
Witch Hazel. Theodore Enslin. CoPo
Witch in every closet. Party Bid. Aletha Humphreys. FiSC
Witch in the Glass, The. Sarah Morgan Bryan Platt. AA
Witch-Mother, The. Swinburne. TOP
Witch of Atlas, The. Shelley. ERoP-2
"And every beast of beating heart grew bold," *sel.* MyFE
Witch of Coös, The. Robert Frost. *Fr.* Two Witches. AmP; AnNE; AP; AtBAP; CMoP; CoBMV; DiPo; ExPo; LiTM (rev. ed.); MoAB; NePA; ReMP; SeCeV (1967 ed.); ViBoPo (1958 ed.)
Witch of East Seventy-second Street, The. Morris Bishop. NYBP
Witch of Willowby Wood, The. Rowena Bennett. PoMS; RePo
Witch that came, The (the withered hag). Provide, Provide. Robert Frost. AmP; AmPP (5th ed.); AtBAP; CABA; CBV; CMoP; MoAB; MWA-2; PoeP; TDP; TwCP
Witchcraft by a Picture. John Donne. PoFS; MaMe
Witchcraft; New Style. Lascelles Abercrombie. MoBrPo
Witches, The. Leah Bodine Drake. FiSC
Witches. Ted Hughes. GoYe
Witches, The. *Unknown.* *See* Hallowe'en.
Witches' Brew, The. Shakespeare. *See* Witches' Spell.
Witches' Charm. Shakespeare. *See* Witches' Spell.
Witches' Charms, The. Ben Jonson. *Fr.* The Masque of Queens. EIL; PoMS, *abr.*; ThWaDe
Witches' Charm, III: "Owl is abroad, The." FaBoCh; LoBV; LoGBV; ReEn
Witches' Ride, The. Karla Kuskin. PDV
Witches' Song. Elizabeth J. Coatsworth. PoMS
Witches' Song, The. Ben Jonson. CH
Witches' Spell, The. Shakespeare. *Fr.* Macbeth, IV, i. PoMS
(Charm, The) EIL
("Thrice the brinded cat hath mewed.") InvP; MyFE
(Witches' Brew.) TreFT
(Witches' Charm.) SITL
Witching Hour. Norma Farber. FiSC
Witching Song, A. James Thomsom. *Fr.* The Castle of Indolence, I. OBEC
Witching Time of Night, The. Shakespeare. *Fr.* Hamlet, III, ii. TreFT
Witch's Ballad, The. William Bell Scott. AnFE; CH; EvOK; NBM; OBEV; OBVV; PeVV
Witch's Broomstick Spell, The. *Unknown.* ChTr
Witch's Ride, The. Adelheid Wette, *tr. fr. German.* *Fr.* Hansel and Gretel. PCH
Witch's Spell, A. *Unknown.* ChTr
Witch's Whelp, The. Richard Henry Stoddard. AA; AnAmPo
Witchwood. May Justus. SiSoSe
With a brilliant sun causing his tears. John Giorno. *Fr.* The American Book of the Dead. ANYP
With a Coin from Syracuse. Oliver St. John Gogarty. OBMV
With a conscience we're able to see. The Conscience. Anthony Euwer. *Fr.* The Limeratomy. HBMV
With a Copy of Herrick. Sir Edmund Gosse. VA
With a Copy of Swift's Works. J. V. Cunningham. QFR
With a Daisy. Emily Dickinson. *See* Science—so sweet the savants say, A.
With a First Reader. Rupert Hughes. HBMV
With a Flower. Emily Dickinson. *See* I hide myself with in a flower.
With a fork drive Nature out. Marigolds. Robert Graves. BrPo
With a garlande of thornes kene. Christ Complains to Sinners. *Unknown.* MeEL
With a gentle hand. The Irish. Francis Carlin. JKCP (1926 ed.)
With a Guitar, to Jane. Shelley. BEL; EnRP; EPN; ERoP-2; HBV; MERP
(To a Lady, with a Guitar.) GTBS; GTBS-D; GTBS-P; GTBS-W; GTSE; GTSL
With a gull's beak I cry. The Bright Hillside. Rhoda Coghill. NeIP; OxBI
With a half-glance upon the sky. A Character. Tennyson. PeER
With a jack plane in his hands. The Carpenter. Clifford Dyment. POTi
With a jar of wine I sit by the flowering trees. Three with the Moon and His Shadow. Li Po. WoL
With a Kiss I Die. Shakespeare. *Fr.* Romeo and Juliet, V, iii. LiTL
With a lantern that wouldn't burn. The Draft Horse. Robert Frost. CaFP
With a Lifting of the Head. "Hugh MacDiarmid." MoBrPo
With a Little Bit of Luck. Alan Jay Lerner. FaFP
With a long heavy heave, my very famous men. Old Anchor Chanty. Herbert Trench. AnFE
With a love a madness for Shelley. I Am 25. Gregory Corso. CoPo
With a Nantucket Shell. Charles Henry Webb. AA
With a pert moustache and a ready candid smile. The Mixer. Louis MacNeice. FaBoTw
With a pick and with a shovel, and with a hoe. Words for Army Bugle Calls: Fatigue Call. *Unknown.* TreF
With a Picture Sent to a Friend. Richard Crashaw. MaMe
With a rocking. Prince Yuke, *tr. fr. Japanese by* Arthur Waley. LiTW
With a Rod No Man Alive. Walther von den Vogelweide, *tr. fr. German by* Jethro Bithell. AWP; JAWP; WBP
With A Rose from Conway Castle. Julia C. R. Dorr. AA
With a sadness curtained. The Maiden. Rochelle Ratner. QAH
With a skill that knows no measure. Old New Hampshire. John F. Holmes. PoRL
With a Spray of Apple Blossoms. Walter Savage Landor. AA
With a stronger wind. True Night. René Char. PoPl
With a sudden sweet surprise. Ship Rock. Jones Very. PoIE
With a very big yawn. Mr. Beetle. Emily Hover. BoTP
With a wall and a ditch between us, I watched the gate-legged dromedary. The Fruit of the Tree. David Wagoner. NYBP
With a wet slap the red road hit the plain. Senchi Ferry; Gold Coast. L. D. Lerner. BoSA
With a whirl of thought oppressed. The Day of Judgment [*or* On the World]. Swift. AnIV; BWP; CEP; EiCL; FaBoEn; NoP
With a yellow lantern. Glow-Worms. P. A. Ropes. BoTP
With all her eyes the goddess Night looks forth approaching many a spot. Hymn to Night. *Unknown.* *Fr.* The Rigveda. LiTW
With all its sinful doings, I must say. Italy. Byron. *Fr.* Beppo. OBRV; SeCePo
With all my heart, in truth, and passion strong. The Pride of a Jew. Judah Halevi. TrJP

With all my heart, O Lord, I will praise Thee. Psalm IX. *Paraphrased by* Sir Philip Sidney. FCP
With all my will, but much against my heart. A Farewell. Coventry Patmore. The Unknown Eros, I, xvi. ACP; AnFE; EnLoPo; FaBoEn; GTBS-P; HBV; LiTL; LO; MemP; MeWo; OBEV; OBNC; OBVV; PoEL-5; PoVP; TrGrPo
With all our mirth, I doubt if we shall be. A Chant. W. H. Davies. BoPe
With all that's ours, together let us rise. Western Emigration. David Humphreys. AnAmPo
With all the drifting race of men. Léonie Adams. *Fr.* April Mortality. TrGrPo
With all the powres my poor heart hath. The Hymn of Sainte Thomas [*or* Hymn] in Adoration of the Blessed Sacrament. Richard Crashaw. MaMe; MeLP; OBS; PoLi
With an heavy heart Envy asked pardon. Two Confessions. William Langland. *Fr.* The Vision of Piers Plowman. WoL
With an honest old friend and a merry old song. Harry Carey's General Reply, to the Libelling Gentry, Who Are Angry at His Welfare. Henry Carey. HBV
With Annie gone. For Anne. Leonard Cohen. BoLP; ELU; PoCh
With back to stars that patch. Dark House in Autumn. Conrad Pendleton. FiSC
With banked fire to mark the occasion. Family Evening. Dan Huws. NYBP
With banners furled, the clarions mute. The Night-March. Herman Melville. AnFE; CoAnAm; LiTA
With blackest moss the flower-plots [-pots; *wr.*]. Mariana. Tennyson. AWP; CABA; CBEP; CBV; CH; ChER; GTSL; HBV; InPo; JAWP; LiTL; MaPo; MaVP; MBW-2; MyFE; OAEP; OBEV; OBNC; OBRV; OBVV; OnPP; PeVV; Po; PoE; PoEL-5; PoFS; PoVP; ShBV-4; TOP; TrGrPo; UnPo (3d ed.); VaPo; ViBoPo; ViPo; ViPP; VP; WBP; WiR
With breath indrawn and every nerve alert. To a Pet Cobra. Roy Campbell. AtBAP
With breath of thyme and bees that hum. To a Greek Girl. Austin Dobson. HBV; VA
With buds embalmed alive in ice. A Mile from Eden. Anne Ridler. MoPo
With burning fervour. The Crystal. George Barker. LiTM; OBMV; POTE
With button eyes and cotton skin. The Cotton Cat. Mary Effie Lee Newsome. GoSl
With camel's hair I clothed my skin. Dream. Richard Watson Dixon. LoBV; PeVV
With careful tread, through dim green-pillared halls. Beetle Bemused. R. P. Lister. PV
With caverned bole and twisted limb they bide. Olive Trees. Padraic Colum. NePoAm
With Child. Genevieve Taggard. AnAmPo; AnEnPo; MAP; MoAmPo
With chocolate-cream that you buy in the cake. Chocolate-Cream. E. V. Lucas. *Fr.* Counsel to Those That Eat. BOHV
With cicada's nymphal skin. The Largess. Richard Eberhart. LiTA; LiTM (rev. ed.)
With coat like any mole's, as soft and black. Mole Catcher. Edmund Blunden. OBMV
With collars be they yoked, to prove the arm at length. Wrestlers. Michael Drayton. *Fr.* Polyolbion. SD
With Corse at Allatoona. Samuel H. M. Byers. PAH
With Cortez in Mexico. Wilfred Campbell. PAH
With courage seek the kingdom of the dead. The Last Journey. Leonidas of Tarentum. AWP; JAWP; WBP
With crafty brooding life turned to Jack Rose. Jack Rose. Maxwell Bodenheim. HBMV
With deadly drive Your grim advance. To a Revolutionist. Harold E. Fey. ChIP
With death, doomed to grapple. Epigram. Byron. HBV
With deep affection/ And recollection. The Bells of Shandon [*or* The Shandon Bells]. Francis Sylvester Mahony. ACP; AnIV; CAW; CH; ChTr; GoBC; GTBS; HBV; HT; IrPN; OBEV; OBRV; OBVV; OnYI; RoGo; ShBV-2; TreFS; UnPo; VA
With delicate mad hands behind his sordid bars. To One in Bedlam. Ernest Dowson. ACP; BrPo; EnLi-2; MoBrPo; NeMA; OBMV; PoVP; Sonn; ViPP; WHA
With difficulty the ship was built. The Critics. Theodore Spencer. NYBP
With Donne, whose muse on dromedary trots. On Donne's Poetry. Samuel Taylor Coleridge. CABA; CaFP; CBEP; ERoP-1; InvP; NoP; OAEP; PP; SeCePo
With doubt and dismay you are smitten. Opportunity. Berton Braley. WBLP
With Dreams of Wealth and Fame. Giuseppe Parini, *tr. fr. Italian by* Lorna de' Lucchi. WoL
With drooping sail and pennant. The White Ships and the Red. Joyce Kilmer. MC; PAH
With due condescension, I'd call your attention. The Origin of Ireland. *Unknown.* BOHV
With dying fire and light. Immortal. Richard Church. MoBrPo (1942 ed.)
With eager heart and will on fire. Peace. Henry van Dyke. MaRV
With earth's first clay they did the last man knead. Predestination. Omar Khayyám, *tr. by* Edward Fitzgerald. *Fr.* The Rubáiyát. OnPM
With Easter banners flaunting in the breeze. Marlowe. Arthur Bayldon. PoAu-1
With echoing step the worshippers. Give Me Thy Heart. Adelaide Anne Procter. ACP; CAW; GoBC; SoP
With elbow buried in the downy pillow. Clarimonde. Théophile Gautier. AWP; JAWP; WBP
With endles teares, that never cease. *Unknown.* SeCSL
With Esther. Wilfrid Scawen Blunt. *See* Esther; a Young Man's Tragedy.
With every movement, the soft particles. The Dusting of the Books. Dorothy Hughes. GoYe
With Every Rising of the Sun. Ella Wheeler Wilcox. *See* You and Today.
With every rolling stone place me in the breach. Place Me in the Breach. Yehuda Karni. TrJP
With every wife he can, and you know why. Epigram. J. V. Cunningham. PIA
With solemn benediction at the end. The Secret. José Joaquin Casas. CAW
With expectation faint & blind; yett still. *Unknown.* SeCSL
With eyes a dying candle. The Aunt. Daniel Berrigan. TwAmPo
With Eyes at the Back of Our Heads. Denise Levertov. AmPP (5th ed.); ToPo
With eyes hand-arched he looks into. Comradery. Madison Cawein. AA
With fair Ceres, Queen of grain. Song [*or* Praise of Ceres]. Thomas Heywood. *Fr.* The Silver Age. CLwM; ElL
With favoring winds o'er sunlit seas. Dedication. Longfellow. *Fr.* Ultima Thule. ViBoPo
With favoure in hir face far passyng my reason. Sodenly Afraide. *Unknown.* EnLit
With fawning wordes he courted her a while. Spenser. *Fr.* The Faerie Queene, I. MBW-1
With fifteen-ninety or sixteen-sixteen. On an Anniversary. J. M. Synge. OBMV
With fingers weary and worn. The Song of the Shirt. Thomas Hood. CABL; BEL; CoBE; EnLi-2; EnLit; EnRP; EPN; FaPL; FOL; HBV; MaC; MCCG; OBVV; OHFP; OTD; OTPC (1946 ed.); PaPo; PCD; PoFr; PoPo; PPON; StaSt; TreF; VA; WBLP; YAT
With fish, which always is served first. Red Wine. Justin Richardson. PV
With flintlock[ed] guns and polished stocks. In Hardin County, [1809]. Lulu E. Thompson. GSP; PoMa; PoSC; StPo
With floods and storms thus we be tossed. God Our Help. *Unknown.* OxBoCh
With Flowers. Emily Dickinson. *See* If recollecting were forgetting.
With focus sharp as Flemish-painted face. The [*or* A] Dome of Sunday. Karl Shapiro. AP; CMoP; CoAP; CoBMV; LiTM; MoAB; MoAmPo (1950 ed.); MoPo; NePA; OxBA; WaP
With folded claws, with eyes unblinking. Blue Ribbon Cats. Lalia Mitchell Thornton. CIV
With fore-cloth smoothed by careful hands. Allah's Tent. Arthur Colton. HBV
With Fragrant Flowers We Strew the Way. Thomas Watson. *Fr.* The Honourable Entertainment Given to the Queen's Majesty in Progress at Elvetham, 1591. ElL
(Ditty of the Six Virgins, The.) OBSC
(Ditty of the Six Virgins' Song, The.) SiCE
With Freedom's Seed. Pushkin, *tr. fr. Russian by* Babette Deutsch. OnPM, *rev. tr.*; PoFr; TTY; WoL, *rev. tr.*

With frost again the thought is clear and wise. Frost. John Hewitt. NeIP
With full-leav'd lillies I will stick. Michael Drayton. *Fr.* The Muses' Elysium: The Second Nimphall. AtBAP
With gallant pomp, and beauteous pride. Ode on a Storm. *Unknown.* EiCL
With ganial foire. The Crystal Palace [*or* Mr. Molony's Account of the Crystal Palace]. Thackeray. BOHV; InMe; PeVV
With gentle step I came at last. Afterward. Mary Matheson. CaP
With gladness hail the dawning year. The New Year. *Unknown.* PEDC
With glass like a bull's eye. Mrs. MacQueen. Walter de la Mare. BoTP
With God Conversing. Gene Derwood. LiTA; LiTM; MoRP; NePA
With grave/ Aspect he rose. Milton. *Fr.* Paradise Lost, II. ATP
With great good cheer the bells ring out. Bells of New Year. Arthur Gordon Field. PGD
With grief and mourning I sit to spin. The Girl's Lamentation. William Allingham. IrPN; SeCePo
With hairs, which for the wind to play with, hung. On Lydia Distracted. Philip Ayres. EnLoPo; SiSw; Sonn
With half a heart I wander here. In the States. Robert Louis Stevenson. BrPo; PoVP; VA
With half a hundred sudden loops and coils. The Hurrying Brook. Edmund Blunden. BoNaP
With half the Western world at stake. Sea and Land Victories. *Unknown.* PAH
With Happiness Stretch[e]d across the Hills. Blake. EnRP; NoP
With heart at rest I climbed the citadel's steep height. Epilogue [*or* Epilogue to Prose Poems]. Baudelaire. AWP; OnPM
With hearts of poor men it is so. The Poor. Emile Verhaeren. AWP; JAWP; WBP; WoL
With hearts responsive. John Oxenham. *Fr.* A Little Te Deum of the Commonplace. TrPWD
With heat and cold I feel the spiteful fiend. Upon the Motions of the Fiend. William Alabaster. EP
With heavy groans did I approach my friends. Wine and Grief. Solomon ibn Gabirol. LiTW; TrJP
With Her Beauty. Tu Fu, *tr. fr. Chinese by* Witter Bynner *and* Kiang Kang-hu. OuHeWo
With her latest roses happily encumbered. Eunice. John Betjeman. CMoP
With her two brothers this fair lady dwelt. Keats. *Fr.* Isabella. PoG
With hey, ho, the wind and the rain. Shakespeare. *Fr.* King Lear, III, ii. TiPo (1952 ed.)
With Him. Julia E. Martin. STF
With Him. Christina Rossetti FaChP
With him there was his son, a youthful Squire. Seven Pilgrims [*or* Three Canterbury Pilgrims: A Squire *or* A Squire]. Chaucer. *Fr.* The Canterbury Tales: Prologue. GoTP; MaC; TrGrPo
With his apology. *Unknown, tr. fr. Japanese by* Geoffrey Bownas *and* Anthony Thwaite. FIW
With His healing hand on a broken heart. Broken Hearts. M. P. Ferguson. SoP
With his kinde [*or* kind] mother who partakes thy woe. Temple [*or* Jesus in the Temple]. John Donne. AnAnS-1; MaMe; MeP; OBS; Sonn; StJW
With his two-fist sword, enscintillant, he cut an apple down. The Uncouth Knight. Hugh McCrae. PoAu-1
With his unspent youth. Bargain. Louise Driscoll. HBMV
With his weapon a shovel. Arawata Bill. Denis Glover. ACV
With honeysuckle, over-sweet, festooned. Arbor Vitae. Coventry Patmore. The Unknown Eros, II, iii. GoBC; LoBV; NBM; OBNC; PeVV; SeCePo
With Hopeless Love. Moses ibn Ezra, *tr. fr. Hebrew by* Solomon Solis-Cohen. TrJP
With horns and [with] hounds I waken the day. Diana's Hunting-Song. Dryden. *Fr.* The Secular Masque. InPo; SeCePo; SeCL
With How Sad Steps [O Moon]. Sir Philip Sidney. Astrophel and Stella, XXXI. AnEnPo; CaFP; BoLiVe; CH; ChTr; DiPo; EnRePo; EP; FCP; ForPo; ILP; InvP; LiTL; MeWo; PoE; PoIE; PoRA; SeCeV; StP; WHA
(His Lady's Cruelty.) OBEV
(Languishing Moon, The.) BoNaP
(Moon, The.) LoBV
(Sonnet: "With how sad steps, O moon. . .") AtBAP; ElL
(To the Moon.) LiTG
("With how sad steps, O Moon, thou climb'st the skies!") AnFE; AWP; BEL; BWP; CoBE; EG; EnL; EnLi-1; EnLit; EnLoPo; FaBoEn; ForPo; GTSL; HBV; JAWP; MaPo; NoP; OAEP; OBSC; PoAn; PoEL-1; ReEn; ReIE; SiCE; SiPS; Sonn; TOP; TrGrPo; TuPP; ViBoPo; WBP
"With How Sad Steps, O Moon, Thou Climb'st the Sky." Wordsworth. MBW-2; Sonn
(To the Moon.) CBEP
With humble and discouraged mien. Alessandro Manzoni. *Fr.* Soffermati sull' arida sponda. PoFr
With hyphens, clip off endings that don't fit. Sonneteering Made Easy. S. B. Botsford. NYBP
With Inky Sails. Heine, *tr. fr. German by* Sir Theodore Martin. WoL
With innocent wide penguin eyes, three. Bird-Witted. Marianne Moore. CMoP
With instruments in ill-accord a hundred men. The Symphony. Herman W. Stillman. PEDC
With its baby rivers and little towns, each with its abbey or its cathedral. England. Marianne Moore. CrMA; LiTA; MAP; MoAB; MoAmPo; TwAmPo
With its cloud of skirmishers in advance. An Army Corps on the March. Walt Whitman. CoBA; NoP; PAL; PoLF
With its fog-shroud the. Poems. Julius Lester. Kal
With its foot in the door of your head. Forced Entry. Jack Marshall. YAP
With Its Quiet Tongue. Kamala Das. ACV
With its rat's tooth the clock. The Alarum. Sylvia Townsend Warner. MoBrPo
With joy all relics of the past I hail. Old Ruralities. Charles Tennyson Turner. Sonn
With joy erst while, (when knotty doubts arose). Upon the Much-to Be Lamented Desease of the Reverend Mr. John Cotton. John Fiske. SCAP
With kisses my lips were wounded by you. Healing the Wound. Heine. UnTE
With leaden foot Time creeps along. Absence. Richard Jago. HBV; OBEV
With leering look [*or* looks], bull faced and freckled fair. Epigram on Tonson [*or* Jacob Tonson, His Publisher]. Dryden. ChTr; MBW-1
With Life and Death I walked when Love appeared. Hymn to Colour [*or* Color]. George Meredith. OBNC; PoVP
With lifted feet, hands still. Going down Hill on a Bicycle. Henry Charles Beeching. BBV (1951 ed.); GN; HBV; HBVY; OBEV; OBVV; OTPC (1923 ed.)
With light of magic India shines afar. India the Magic. H. A. Jules-Bois. CAW
With lights for eyes, our city turns. Lullaby. Dom Moraes. NePoEA-2
With Lilacs. Charles Henry Crandall. AA
With Lilacs in My Eye. Lucile Coleman. GoYe
With little here to do or see. To the Daisy. Wordsworth. GTBS-P; GTBS-W; GTSE; GTSL; HBV; HBVY
With little white leaves in the grasses. The Daisy. Sir Rennell Rodd. VA
With loitering step and quiet eye. In November. Archibald Lampman. OBCV
With Long Black Wings. Trumbull Stickney. NCEP
With Love among the haycocks. A Song. Ralph Hodgson. GoJo
With love exceeding a simple love of the things. Melampus. George Meredith. BoC; EnLi-2; OBVV; PoEL-5
With love he shaped the limbs, her breasts arose. Pygmalion. Louis Johnson. AnNZ
With Love I garnered mirth and dreams, and shame. Retractions, VI. James Branch Cabell. HBMV
With love that counted not the cost. Mary. Thomas Curtis Clark. ChIP
With Lullay, Lullay, like a Child. John Skelton. *See* Lullay, Lullay.
With maidenly and modest sips. The Kiss and the Cup. *Unknown.* UnTE
With manly purpose do what's right. Courage. Lowell Mason. OTD
With many a weary step at length I gain. On Bala Hill.

Samuel Taylor Coleridge. Sonn
With many a weary step, at length I gain. Robert Southey. Sonn
With margerain [*or* marjoram *or* margeran] gentle. To Mistress Margery Wentworth. John Skelton. *Fr.* The Garlande of Laurell. BoPe; CBEP; EG; EnLoPo; EnRePo; LoBV; OBEV; OBSC; TrGrPo; ViBoPo
With mask well fitted for your chosen role. Denouement. Sister Mary Eulalia. JKCP (1955 ed.)
With Me in Paradise. Alexander Harvey. ChIP
With Me My Lover Makes. C. Day Lewis. OBMV
With merry lark this maiden rose. Old-Time Service. Thomas Churchyard. *Fr.* A Fayned Fancye between the Spider and the Gowte. OBSC
With Metaphor. Sarah Wingate Taylor. GoYe
With mighty hand the Holy Lord. The Temptation and Fall of Man. *Unknown. Fr.* Genesis. AnOE
With much ado you fail to tell. A Critic. Walter Savage Landor. ChTr
With Music Strong I Come. Walt Whitman. Song of Myself, XVIII. AtBAP; TrGrPo
With my love my life was nesled. *Unknown.* SeCSL
With Myriad Voices Grass Was Filled. Conrad Aiken. *Fr.* John Deth. OA
With nets and kitchen sieves they raid the pond. The Pond. Anthony Thwaite. NYBP
With nought to hide or to betray. L'Amitié et l'Amour. John Swanwick Drennan. IrPN
With oh such peculiar branching and over-reaching of wire. St. Saviour's, Aberdeen Park, Highbury, London, N. John Betjeman. MoVE
With oaken staff and swinging lantern bright. The Andalusian Sereno. Francis Saltus Saltus. AA
With older eyes than any Roman had. Thomas Hardy, Poet. Mark Van Doren. ML
With one black shadow at its feet. Mariana in the South. Tennyson. MaVP; PoVP
With one consent, on no man's bidding. London. Maurice Hewlett. *Fr.* The Song of the Plow. PoFr
With One Swift Thought. Sister Maryanna. JKCP (1955 ed.)
With other women I beheld my love. Ballata [*or* Ballata: Of His Lady among Other Ladies]. Guido Cavalcanti. AWP; OnPM
With our late vicar, and his age the same. Poor of the Borough, The; the Parish-Clerk. George Crabbe. *Fr.* The Borough. EiCL
With paciens thou hast us fed. Farewell! Advent. James Ryman. MeEL
With pain pressing so close about your heart. Dethronement. Robert Graves. PIA
With pale green nails of polished jade. Impression Japonais. Oscar Wilde. SyP
With paste of almonds, Syb her hands doth scoure. Upon Sibilla. Robert Herrick. SeCePo
With paws in firelight dipped, and drowsy ears. Old Hound. Florence Ripley Mastin. PoMa
With Pegasus upon a day. To John Taylor. Burns. WhC
With pensive eyes the little room I view. The Garret. Pierre Jean de Béranger, *tr. by* Thackeray. HBV
With Persian cat beside my cheek. My Cat and I. Edna Gearhart. CIV
With Peter I refuse to dine. Unforgivable and Unforgiven. C. D. B. Ellis. SiTL
With Petrarch's Sonnets. Walter Savage Landor. InP
With Pipe and Flute. Austin Dobson. EPN; VA
With porcupine locks. The Katzenjammer Kids. James Reaney. MoCV; OBCV; PeCV; TwCaPo
With primal void and cosmic night. Earth's Story. Thomas Curtis Clark. OQP
With proud thanksgiving, a mother for her children. For the Fallen. Laurence Binyon. AnFE; GTBS; InP; MaRV; OBEV (new ed.); PoFr; POTE; ShBV-3; WePo
With prune-dark eyes, thick lips, jostling each other. Refugees. Louis MacNeice. LiTB; WaP
With pure nails brightly flashing their onyx. Pure Nails Brightly Flashing. Stéphane Mallarmé. LiTW
With purple glow at even. To the Lakes. Wilfred Campbell. VA
With rakish eye and 'plenished crop. The Crow. William Canton. GoTP; HBV
With reeds and bird-lime from the desert air. On a Fowler. Isidorus. AWP
With restless step of discontent! Balboa. Nora Perry. PAH
With Roses. Beatrix Demarest Lloyd. AA
With Rosy Hand. Walter Savage Landor. EPN
(Cowslips.) VA
With Rue My Heart Is Laden. A. E. Housman. A Shropshire Lad, LIV. AnFE; AWP; BEL; CBV; CMoP; EnL; EnLi-2; EnLit; EPN; FaFP; GTBS-W; GTSL; HoPM; JAWP; LiTB; LiTL; LiTM; MasP; MoAB; MoBrPo; NoP; OAEP; OuHeWo; PG; PoE; PoMa; PoVP; TOP; TreFT; TrGrPo; ViPo; VP; WBP; WoL
"With sacrifice before the rising morn." Laodamia. Wordsworth. BEL; EnRP; EPN; ERoP-1; MBW-2; OAEP
With Sa'di in the Garden, *sels.* Sir Edwin Arnold. VA
Mahmud and Ayaz; a Paraphrase on Sa'di.
Song without a Sound.
With sails full set, the ship her anchor weighs. Emigravit. Helen Hunt Jackson. AA; AnFE; APA; CoAnAm
With saintly grace and reverend tread. Presentiment. Ambrose Bierce. AA
With secrets in their eyes the blue-winged Hours. A Tree at Dusk. Winifred Welles. MPB; SP; TSW
With Seed the Sowers Scatter. A. E. Housman. *See* Stinging Nettle, The.
With Self Dissatisfied. Frederick L. Hosmer. TrPWD
With Serving Still. Sir Thomas Wyatt. EG; EIL; FCP; LoBV; SiPS; WHA
(His Reward.) OBSC
With seven matching calfskin cases for his new suits. Home Leaves. Barbara Howes. TwCP
With Shakeapeare's [*or* Shakspeare's] manhood at a boy's wild heart. Thomas Chatterton. Dante Gabriel Rossetti. Five English Poets, 1. PoVP
With sharpened pen and wit, one tunes his lays. The Praise of New Netherland. Jacob Steendam. PAH
With Ships the Sea Was Sprinkled [Far and Nigh]. Wordsworth. EnRP; HBV; MBW-2
With shot and shell, like a lossened hell. The Charge at Santiago. William Hamilton Hayne. MC; PAH
With sick and famisht eyes. Longing. George Herbert. AnAnS-1; MaMe; MeP; SeCV-1
With sighs my bosom always laboureth. Sonnet. Dante. GoBC
With silver soundes derived from deepest skill. *Unknown.* SeCSL
With six small diamonds for his eyes. The Spider. Robert P. Tristram Coffin. ImOP; OTPC (1946 ed.)
With slower pen men used to write. On the Hurry of This Time. Austin Dobson. HBV; PoVP
With snakes of rubber and glass thorax. Filling Station. A. M. Klein. TwCaPo
With snort and pant the engine dragged. The Song of the Engine. H. Worsley-Benison. BoTP
With snow-white veil and garments as of flame. Divina Commedia, IV. Longfellow. AmePo; AmP; AmPP; AnAmPo; AnFE; AP; APA; CoAnAm; CoBA; ILP; MWA-1; NePA; NoP; OxBA; TOP; TreFT
With sobbing sighs and trickling tears. The Lamentation of Beckles. Thomas Deloney. SiCE
With sober pace an heav'enly maid walks in. Abraham Cowley. *Fr.* Davideis. SeCV-1
With some pot-fury, ravished from their wit. Joseph Hall. *Fr.* Virgidemiarum. ReEn; SiCE
With song and sun-burst comes the Easter morn. Easter. Robert Whitaker. ChIP; PGD
With song I seek my fate to cheer. Love's Longing. *Unknown.* UnTE
With spangles gay and candle light. The Christmas Tree. Isabel de Savitzsky. BoTP
With steadfast heart and true. "Go Forward." "A. R. G." BLRP
With stedfast and unwavering faith, with hard and patient toil. Thanksgiving Day. James J. Montague. HH; PEDC
With Strawberries. W. E. Henley. HBV
With such a throb does blood. Joy of Knowledge. Isidor Schneider. TrJP
With such compelling cause to grieve. In Memoriam A. H. H., XXIX. Tennyson. EnLi-2; EPN; OAEP; ViPo; VP
With such unseemly caution have I taken heed. St. Francis and the Cloud. Marie de L. Welch. MoRP
With sweetest milk and sugar first. The Girl and Her Fawn. Andrew Marvell. *Fr.* The Nymph Complaining for the Death

With (continued)
of Her Fawn. BoTP; FaBoCh; GTSL; LoGBV; OA; OTPC
With tambourines of amber, queens. The Small Man Orders His Wedding. C. S. Lewis. HW
"With tears thy grief thou dost bemoan." Stanzas. Solomon ibn Gabirol. TrJP
With tentive list'ning each wight was settled in hark'ning. Vergil. *Fr.* The Aeneid, II. RelE·
With that a thundring noise seem'd shake the skie. The Overthrow of Lucifer. Phineas Fletcher. *Fr.* The Purple Island. OBS.
With that I saw two swannes of goodly hewe. Spenser. *Fr.* Prothalamion. BoC
With that low cunning, which in fools supplies. A Critical Fribble [*or* A Criticaster]. Charles Churchill. *Fr.* The Rosciad. FaBoEn; OBEC
With that pathetic impudence of youth. The Family of Nations. Willard Wattles. PAH
With that (such power was given him then), he took. Milton. *Fr.* Paradise Regained, III *and* IV. StJW
With the apples and the plums. The Dessert. Charles *and* Mary Lamb. OTPC (1923 ed.)
With the blue-dark dome old-starred at night. Galilee Shore. Allen Ginsberg. FRC
With the Dawn. Thomas Caulfield Irwin. EnLoPo; IrPN
With the effect as of carving, almost, the hillside. For an Age of Plastics. Plymouth. Donald Davie. NePoEA-2
With the fall of the first leaf that winds rend. Of Margaret. John Crowe Ransom. NoP
With the fierce range of winter deep suffus'd. Frost at Night. James Thomson. *Fr.* The Seasons: Winter. OBEC
With the green lamp of the spirit. Into the Glacier. John Haines. CoAP
With the gulls' hysteria above me. Galway Bay. George Baker. FaBoMo
With the Herring Fishers. "Hugh MacDiarmid." LiTM (1970 ed.)
With the hooves of a doe. Lenox Avenue. Sidney Alexander. PoNe
With the mist miles out on the Pacific Ocean. Wrapped Up in an Indian Blanket. John Wieners. FRC
With the Most Susceptible Element, the Mind, Already Turned under the Toxic Action. Walter Benton. WaP
With the old kindness, the old distinguished grace. Upon a Dying Lady. W. B. Yeats. LiTB; UnPo (3d ed.)
With the other geese within the goosehouse. January. James Reaney. *Fr.* A Suit of Nettles. OBCV; PIA
With the ship burning in their eyes. Survivors. Alan Ross. POTi
With the shrewd and upright man. Fool and False. *Unknown. Fr.* Panchatantra. AWP JAWP; WBP
With the spring moon's first beams. Spring Night. "Ranan Mukerji." UnTE
With the Tide. Edith Wharton. PEDC
With the treason of mingled love and wine. Girl Betrayed. Hedylos. LiTW
With the wanderer's staff in hand. Exile Song. Morris Jacob Rosenfeld. LiTW
With Thee. Cora M. Pinkham. STF
With Thee a moment! Then what dreams have play! Desire. "*A* E." OBMV; TrPWD
With thee conversing I forget all time. Eve to Adam [*or* Eve Speaks to Adam]. Milton. *Fr.* Paradise Lost, IV. ChTr; FaBoEn; TreFS; TrGrPo; WiR
With thee, O Christ, I fain would walk. The Way O Christ Thou Art. Ernest De Witt Burton. MaRV
With Thee, O God! Saint Columcille. SoP
With Thee to Soar to the Skies. *Unknown.* BePJ
With their feet in the earth. Tall Trees. Eileen Mathias. BoTP
With their harsh leaves old rhododendrons fill. The Mountain Cemetery. Edgar Bowers. NePoEA
With their lithe, long, strong legs. Bullfrog. Ted Hughes. NYBP
With their trunks the elephants. The Elephants. Dorothy Aldis. *Fr.* At the Circus. UTS
With these heaven-assailing spires. New York. "Æ." OBMV
With this ambiguous earth. Christ in the Universe [*or* Or His Bestowals There]. Alice Meynell. ACP; BoC; CAW; GoBC; HBMV; JKCP; MemP; MoBrPo; StJW
With those proud birds that feed not. The Snares. Nahab Koutchak. CAW
With tiger pace and swinging head. The Known World. Brewster Ghiselin. MoVE
". . .With Timbrels." Judith, XVI:2-17, Bible, Apocrypha. TrJP
With treble vivas and limp hedgerow flags. The Vanquished. Charles Eglington. BoSA; PeSA
With trembling fingers did we weave. In Memoriam A. H. H., XXX. Tennyson. CoBE; EnL; EnLi-2; EnLit; EPN; OAEP; ViPo; VP
With Two Fair Girls. *Unknown, tr. fr. Greek by* Robert Guthrie MacGregor. ALV; ErPo
With two 60's stuck on the scoreboard. Foul Shot. Edwin A. Hoey. OTD
With two strange fires of equal heat possest. Love and Jealousy. Sir Philip Sidney. *Fr.* Arcadia. SiPS
With two white roses on her breasts. A Brown Girl Dead. Countee Cullen. BP; Kal
With Usura/ With usura hath no man a house of good stone. Canto XLV. Ezra Pound. CMoP; LiTM (rev. ed.); MoPo; NePA; PoIE; ReMP
With virtue such as yours had Eve been arm'd. Written in a Lady's Milton. Matthew Prior. InP
With visionary care. Summer Noon, 1941. Yvor Winters. CrMA
With Walker in Nicaragua, *sel.* Joaquin Miller.
Monkeys ("How ran live monkeys"). OA; PCH
With weary steps I loiter on. In Memoriam A. H. H., XXXVIII. Tennyson. EPN; ViPo; VP
With weed and with sea-barley crowned. The Drowned Wife. Robert Horan. OnHM
With what a childish and short-sighted sense. Danger. Helen Hunt Jackson. AnFE; APA; CoAnAm
With what anguish of mind I remember my childhood. The Old Oaken Bucket, *parody. Unknown.* BLPA; FaFP; WBLP
With what attentive courtesy he bent. The Guitarist Tunes Up. Frances Cornford. ELU; MuSP
With what attractive charms this goodly frame. Mark Akenside. The Pleasures of Imagination, I. EiPP; EnPE; EnRP
With what contentment in its ordered ways. Mathematical. Jessie Nelson North. NP
With what conviction the young man spoke. W. H. Auden. PV
With what sharp checks I in myself am shent. Astrophel and Stella, XVIII. Sir Philip Sidney. FCP; ReEn; SiPS; Sonn
With what thou gavest me, O Master. Equipment. Paul Laurence Dunbar. TrPWD
"With Whom Is No Shadow of Turning." Martha Snell Nicholson. SoF
"With Whom Is No Variableness, neither Shadow of Turning." Arthur Hugh Clough. EnLi-2; EnLit; EPN; MaRV; PoVP; TOP; TreFS; TRV; ViPo; WGRP
(It Fortifies My Soul to Know.) OAEP
(Steadfast.) OQP
With whom shall I find perfect ease. "Thou Shalt Purge Me with Hyssop and I Shall Be Clean." Anna Bunston de Bary. MaRV
With whomsoever I share the spring. Song. Jan Burroway. NePoAm-2
With wide unblinking stare. Cats and Kings. Alfred Noyes. MemP
With wild surprise/ four great eyes. The Christmas Tree in the Nursery [*or* Sery]. Richard Watson Gilder. DD; HBVY; OHIP
With willing arms I row and row. The Barcarole of James Smith. Herbert S. Gorman. HBMV
With wine and words of love and every [*or* fervent *or* fervid] vow. Seduced Girl [*or* To Venus]. Hedylos. ErPo; MeWo; UnTE
With witchlike branches, barren, bleak, and drear. Thomas Caulfield Irwin. *Fr.* Winter Noon in the Woods. IrPN
With women and apples both Paris and Adam. Epigram. Thomas Moore. ALV
With Wordsworth at Rydal. James Thomas Fields. AA
With wrath-flushed cheeks, and eyelids red. Ahmed. James Berry Bensel. AA
With wrinkled hide and great frayed ears. A Circus Garland: The Elephant. Rachel Field. SoPo; StVeCh

With yellow pears. Life Half Lived. Friedrich Hölderlin. ChTr
With you. Hippocrene. Amy Lowell. MoLP
With You a Part of Me. George Santayana. To W. P., II. TrGrPo
With you first shown to me. William Barnes. EnLoPo
With your fair eyes a charming light I see. Love, the Light-Giver. Michelangelo. AWP; LiTW
With your head-cloth knotted and your shawl pinned tight. Mary Salome, Widow. Anne Ryan. JKCP (1926 ed.)
With your kind attention, a song I will trill. Down, Down, Down. William Keating. OuSiCo
With your sun-white hair and your smile. Out of the Sea. Witter Bynner. MoLP
With youth, is deade the hopes of loves returne. Sir Walter Ralegh. *Fr.* The Last Book of the Ocean to Scinthia. FaBoEn
Withal a meagre man was Aaron Stark. Aaron Stark. E. A. Robinson. MoAB; MoAmPo (1950 ed.); Sonn
Withdraw thee, soul, from strife. Sleep. Alice Brown. AA
Withdraw thy foot from thy neighbor's house. Proverbs, Bible, *O.T.* PoG
Withdrawing from the amorous grasses. The Snake. Kenneth Mackenzie. BoAV
Withdrawn from layers of upper air, ice blue and clear. Suburb Hilltop. Richard Moore. NYBP
Withdrawn on this warm ledge I lie. Summer Afternoon. Elizabeth B. Harrod. NePoEA
Wither'd pansies faint and sweet. Requiem. Sir Joseph Noel Paton. VA
Withered flowers hold the seeds of promise, The. He Will Not Fail. *Unknown.* SoP
Withered Heart, The. Heine, *tr. fr. German by* James Thomson. OnPM
(Blauen Veilchen der Äugelein, Die.) AWP
Withered leaves that drift in Russell Square, The. Drilling in Russell Square. Edward Shanks. OBMV
Withered Rose, A. "Yehoash," *tr. fr. Yiddish by* Isidore Goldstick. TrJP
Withering grass knows not its needs, The. After the Rain. Edward A. Collier. BLRP
Withhold all eulogies when I am dead. Today and Tomorrow. Edward N. Pomeroy. MaRV; OQP
Withhold your breath! Tropical Girl to Her Garden. Genevieve Taggard. NP
Within. Sydney Clouts. BoSA
Within a budding grove. The Lover and Birds [*or* Spring: The Lover and the Birds]. William Allingham. OBNC; OBVV
Within a chamber of a tower. Quia Amore Langueo. *Unknown.* ISi
Within a copse I met a shepherd-maid. Ballata: Concerning a Shepherd-Maid. Guido Cavalcanti. AWP
Within a gloomy dimble she doth dwell. Mother Maudlin the Witch. Ben Jonson. *Fr.* The Sad Shepherd. ChTr
Within a low-thatch'd hut, built in a lane. The Net-Braiders. Thomas Wade. VA
Within a narrow span of time. Shelley's Centenary. Sir William Watson. PoVP
Within a native hut, ere stirred the dawn. Nativity. Aquah Laluah. CDC; PBA; PoNe; TTY
Within a poor man's squalid home I stood. Vision. William Dean Howells. AA; AmePo; AnAmPo; CBV
Within a thick and spreading hawthorn bush. The Thrush's Nest. John Clare. BoTP; FIW; GoJo; GoTP; MemP; PoRL; PoSa; ThWaDe
Within an English village yesterday. Nora. Dora Sigerson Shorter. HBMV
Within an open curled sea of gold. A Vision. Lord Herbert of Cherbury. AnAnS-2; SeCP
Within and Without, *sels.* George Macdonald.
"Lord of Thyself and me, through the sore grief." TRV
"My soul leans toward Him." WGRP
Within Heaven's circle I had not guessed at this. The Flight into Egypt. Peter Quennell. LiTB; LiTM
Within Her Eyes. Dante. *See* My Lady Carries Love.
Within her hair Venus and Cupid sport them. Emaricdulfe, VI. "E. C." EIL; Sonn; TuPP
Within his [*or* the] sober realm of leafless trees. The Closing Scene. Thomas Buchanan Read. AA; HBV
Within King's College Chapel, Cambridge. Wordsworth. *See* Inside of King's College Chapel, Cambridge.
Within mankind's duration, so they say. The Birds. J. C. Squire. HBMV
Within me are two souls that pity each. Duality. Arthur Sherburne Hardy. AA
Within my bosom stirs once more tonight. Lament. Princess Zeb-un-Nissa. LiTW
Within My Breast. Sir Thomas Wyatt. EnRePo; FCP
Within my earthly temple there's a crowd. My Name Is Legion [*or* Which Is Me?]. Edward Sandford Martin. MaRV; OQP
Within my garden, rides a bird. Emily Dickinson. AmPP (5th ed.); TiPo (1952 ed.)
Within my head, aches the perpetual winter. Winter and Summer. Stephen Spender. MoAB; MoBrPo (1950 ed.); MoPo
Within My Heart. Judah al-Harizi, *tr. fr. Hebrew.* TrJP
Within my heart I long have kept. Blondel. Clarence Urmy. AA; HBMV; PFY
Within my house of patterned horn. The Tortoise in Eternity. Elinor Wylie. FaPON; ImOP; OA
Within my mind. The Prophecy of Taliesin. Taliesin. PoFr
Within my twenty yer of age. The Dream of the Romaunt of the Rose. Guillaume de Lorris, *tr. by* Chaucer. *Fr.* The Romance of the Rose. LoBV
Within our happy Castle there dwelt one. Stanzas Written in My Pocket Copy of Thomson's "Castle of Indolence." Wordsworth. EnRP
Within that awful [*or* this ample] volume lies. The Book of Books [*or* The Bible *or* The Divine Volume]. Sir Walter Scott. *Fr.* The Monastery, *ch.* 12. BLRP; FaChP; MaRV; NeHB; OQP; SoP; TreFT; TRV; WBLP
Within that semi-circle formed by mounds. Old Earth-works. Thomas Sweeney. OQP
Within the Bush. Burns. *Fr.* A Rose-Bud, by my Early Walk. BiS
Within the cage he ramped and raged! The Caged Mongoose. Constance Hollar. PoNe
Within the casket of thy coelick breast. An Acrostick on Mrs. Winifret Griffin. John Saffin. SCAP
Within the Circuit of This Plodding Life. Henry David Thoreau. *See* Winter Memories.
Within the city of my death. José Garcia Villa. Divine Poems, 74. MoRP
Within the cloister blissful of thy sides. Two Invocations of the Virgin, I. Chaucer. *Fr.* The Canterbury Tales: The Second Nun's Tale. ACP
Within the covert of a shady grove. Love Sleeping. Plato. AWP; OnPM; WoL
Within the flower there lies a seed. Spell of Creation. Kathleen Raine. FaBoCh; LoGBV; OxBS; PoIE; WaKn
Within the garden of Beaucaire. Provençal Lovers; Aucassin and Nicolette. Edmund Clarence Stedman. HBV
Within the garden-plot of thy fair face. To a Fair Gentlewoman, False to Her Friend. George Turberville. TuPP
Within the Gates. David W. Foley. MaRV
Within the gentle heart Love shelters him. Canzone: Of the Gentle Heart. Guido Guinicelli. AWP; CTC; GoBC; LiTW; WoL
Within the great grey flapping tent. The Auction Sale. Henry Reed. MoBrPo (1962 ed.)
Within the great wall's perfect round. The Window. Edwin Muir. LiTM (rev. ed.)
Within the house of mirrors. The Hunchback. Robert Friend. NYTB
Within the introspection of my dying. Parable. Robert Pack. NePoEA-2
Within the iron cities. The Garden of God. "Æ." WGRP
Within the isle, far from the walks of men. In Forest Depths. Richard Henry Horne. *Fr.* Orion. VA
Within the letter's rustling fold. Spring Flowers from Ireland. Denis Florence MacCarthy. ACP; GoBC
Within the mind strong fancies work. The Pass of Kirkstone. Wordsworth. HBV
Within the night, above the dark. Mary Gilmore. *Fr.* Swans at Night. MoAuPo; PoAu-1
Within the oak a throb of pigeon wings. A Twilight in Middle March. Francis Ledwidge. OnYI; OxBI; WHA
Within the pale blue haze above. The Storm. Coventry Patmore. EnLoPo
Within the precincts of this yard. The Beasts in the Tower. Charles *and* Mary Lamb. OTPC (1923 ed.)

Within the sand of what far river lies. Shadows of His Lady. Jacques Tahureau. AWP
Within the sober realm of leafless trees. Within his sober realm. . .
Within the Soul a Faculty Abides. Wordsworth. *Fr.* The Excursion, IV. OBRV
Within the still, white room that gave me birth. Alien. Helen Frazee-Bower. HBMV
Within the streams, Pausanias saith. The Last Chance. Andrew Lang. SD
Within the thin. The Madman. S. J. Pretorius. PeSA
"Within the town, of whose huge walls so monstrous high and thick." Pyramus and Thisbe. Ovid. *Fr.* Metamorphoses. LiTW; ReIE
Within the unchanging twilight. The Norns Watering Yggdrasill. William Bell Scott. VA
Within the Veil. Margaret E. Sangster. BLRP
Within the wires of the post, unloading the cans of garbage. Prisoners. Randall Jarrell. OxBA; WaP
Within the wood behind the hill. The Satyrs and the Moon. Herbert S. Gorman. HBV; PFY; TSW
Within the world a second world. The Hidden Tide. Roderic Quinn. BoAu
Within the year of Christ our Lord. Queen Elizabeth at Tilbury. Thomas Deloney. SiCE
Within these walls, Pity will war with Death. A Hospital. Alfred Noyes. PoPl
Within this ample volume lies. *See* Within that awful volume lies.
Within this black hive to-night. Beehive. Jean Toomer. IDB; PoNe; TTY
Within This Grave Do Lie. *Unknown.* ShM; WhC
(Epitaph: "Within this grave. . .") TreFT
Within this lowly grave a Conqueror lies. The Conqueror's Grave. Bryant. AA
Within This Mindless Vault. J. V. Cunningham. CBV
Within this nation-hallowed tomb. Epitaph for the Unknown Soldier. Annette Kohn. DD
Within this place lies Abraham the Civil. In Tumulum Abrahami Simple. John Weever. SiCE; TuPP
Within this restless, hurried, modern world. My Voice. Oscar Wilde. BrPo
Within this silent palace of the Night. Moonrise. Frank Dempster Sherman. AA
Within this sober frame expect. Upon Appleton House, to my Lord Fairfax. Andrew Marvell. MaMe; ReEn; SCEP-2; SeCP; SeCV-1
Within this stumbling ground for bulls. Conflict. Lincoln Fitzell. AnAmPo
Within this termitary. By an Ant-Heap. Terence Heywood. BoSA
Within this windless covert silence drops. Scarabs for the Living, IV. R. P. Blackmur. TwAmPo
Within this wood, out of a rocke did rise. The Visions of Petrarch. *Tr. by* Spenser. Sonnets to Laura: To Laura in Death, Canzone III. EnLi-1
Within those halls where student zeal. The College Cat. Alfred Denis Godley. CenHV
Within Thy Heart. Digby M. Dolben. *See* I Asked for Peace.
Within unfriendly walls. Waiting. John Davidson. ViBoPo
Within what weeks the melilot. Sweet Clover. Wallace Rice. HBV
Within your heart. Hold Fast Your Dreams. Louise Driscoll. TiPo
Within your magic web of hair lies furled. The Web of Eros. Edith Sitwell. HBMV
With-inne the temple he went him forth pleyinge. Chaucer. *Fr.* Troilus and Criseyde, I. LO
Without a Speaking Tongue. Walter Sorell. NYTB
Without and Within. Norman Ault. MaRV; StJW
Without and Within. James Russell Lowell. BOHV; HBV; TOP
Without avail the flocks of sparrows try. Eagles and Sparrows. José Santos Chocano. PoFr
Without Benefit of Declaration. Langston Hughes. AmNP; TTY
Without Ceremony. Vassar Miller. CoPo; MoAmPo (1962 ed.); TDP
Without dressmakers to connect. Because of Clothes. Laura Riding. LiTA
Without haste! Without rest! Haste Not, Rest Not. Goethe. MaRV; OQP
Without Her. Dante Gabriel Rossetti. The House of Life, LIII. CBEP; CoBE; GTBS-W; MaVP; NCEP; OBNC; PIA; PoEL-5; PoVP; Sonn; VA; ViBoPo; ViPo; VP
Without him still this whirling earth. Egotism. Edward Sandford Martin. AA
Without invention nothing is well spaced. William Carlos Williams. *Fr.* Paterson. PP
Without love's charm, both wild and rude. Boredom. Ramón de Campoamor. OnPM
Without More Weight. Giuseppe Ungaretti, *tr. fr. Italian by* Allen Mandelbaum. PoPl
Without My Friends the Day Is Dark. Moses ibn Ezra, *tr. fr. Hebrew by* Soloman Solis-Cohen. TrJP
Without Name. Pauli Murray. AmNP; PoNe
Without other cost than breath. The Quality of Heaven. William Carlos Williams. PoeP
Without Regret. Lilith Lorraine. PGD
Without Sleep. Glenway Wescott. NP
Without surprise, on that not distant shore. Delusions, VI. Charles Madge. NeBP
Without That Once Clear Aim. Stephen Spender. CMoP; Sonn
Without the evening dew and showers. Ode. Charles Cotton. ViBoPo
Without the Herdsman. Diotimus, *tr. fr. Greek by* John William Burgon. AWP
Without, the lonely night is sweet with stars. Martyrdom. "Rufus Learsi." TrJP
Without the Moon. Jules Laforgue, *tr. fr. French by* Hart Crane. LiTW
Without the slightest basis. How Jack Found That Beans May Go Back on a Chap. Guy Wetmore Carryl. ALV; HoPM; MAP; MoAmPo (1942 ed.)
Without, the sullen noises of the street! Benedictio Domini. Ernest Dowson. CAW; JKCP
Without the Way, there can be no going. The Way; the Truth; the Life. Samuel Judson Porter. BLRP
Without thought, without remorse, without shame. Walls. C. P. Cavafy. TrJP
"Withouten time is no erthely thinge." Time and Eternity. Stephen Hawes. *Fr.* The Pastime of Pleasure. PoEL-1
Withouten you. Little Elegy. Elinor Wylie. LOW
Withstanders. William Barnes. OxBoCh
Witlaf, a king of the Saxon's. King Witlaf's Drinking-Horn. Longfellow. CoBA; MWA-1
Witless gallant, a young wench that wooed, A. Idea, XXI. Michael Drayton. SICE; TUPP
Witness, The. Sri Ananda Acharya. ACV
Witness how it comes to pass. Epitaph in Sirmio. David Morton. PoLF
Witness of God. James Russell Lowell. *Fr.* The Cathedral. OQP
Witnesses, The. W. H. Auden. ShBV-4
Witnesses. Cecil Hemley. PoDB
Witnesses, The. Longfellow. AtBAP
Witnesses. W. S. Merwin. AmPC
Witnesses, The, *sel.* Clive Sansom.
"It was a night in winter." FlW
Wit's a feather and a chief a rod, A. An Honest Man. Pope. *Fr.* An Essay on Man, Epistle IV. TreF
Wit's-End Corner. Antoinette Wilson. BLRP; SoP; STF
Wit's perfection, beauty's wonder. Three Epitaphs upon the Death of a Rare Child of Six Years Old, 1. Francis Davison. OBSC; ReIE
Witty Fair One, The, *sel.* James Shirley.
Love a Thousand Sweets Distilling. SeCL
(Song: "Love a thousand sweets distilling.") SeEP
Wives, The. Donald Hall. CoAP
Wives in the Sere. Thomas Hardy. BrPo
Wizard, from your misty censer, brew. Evocation. Herman Stowell King. FiSC
Wizard Frost. Frank Dempster Sherman. YeAr
Wizard of the Nile, The, *sel.* Harry B. Smith.
My Angeline. BOHV; InMe
Wizard of the woods is he, The. The Woodpecker. John Banister Tabb. UTS
Wizard Oil, *with music. Unknown.* AS
Wizard's Funeral, The. Richard Watson Dixon. ELP; GTBS-D; LoBV; PeVV
Wizard's New Meeting, The. Peter Redgrove. HYE
Wmffre the Sweep. Rolfe Humphries. EaLo

Wo, his purple an' linen, too. Dives and Laz'us. *Unknown.* ABF; TTY
Wo worth the days! The days I spent. A Few Lines to Fill up a Vacant Page. John Danforth. SCAP
Wo worth the man, who in ill hour assayed. On the Cantos of Spenser's *Faerie Queene,* Lost in the Passage from Ireland. Thomas Edwards. Sonn
Woak Hill. William Barnes. GTSL
Wodwo. Ted Hughes. PoIE (1970 ed.); ToPo
Woe Be unto You, *with music. Unknown.* ABF
Woe for the brave ship *Orient!* The Brave Old Ship, the *Orient.* Robert Traill Spence Lowell. AA; FaBoBe
Woe having made, with many fights, his own. Astrophel and Stella, LVII. Sir Philip Sidney. FCP; ReEn; SiPS
Woe Is Me! Micah, VII; 1-6, Bible, *O.T.* TrJP
Woe is me that I from Israell. *Unknown.* SeCSL
Woe is me! what am I like? The Lament of Saint Ann. *Unknown. Fr.* The Protevangelium of James. CAW
Woe to Him ("Woe to him that has not known the woe of man"). Laurence Binyon. MaRV
Woe to thee that spoilest. Isaiah, Bible, *O.T.* PoFr
Woe unto them/ That rise up early. Intemperance. Isaiah, Bible, *O.T.* (*Moulton, Modern, Reader's Bible*). MaRV
Woe, woe to me, on me return the smart. Sir Philip Sidney. FCP
Woe worth thee, woe worth thee, false Scottlande! Earl Bothwell. *Unknown.* ESPB
Woeful spirit in my heart may not, The. Arcite's Farewell. Chaucer. *Fr.* The Canterbury Tales: The Knight's Tale. LiTL
Woefully Arrayed. *At. to* John Skelton. CABA; CBEP; ChTr; EnRePo; LoBV; OxBoCh
(Wofully Araide.) MeEL
Woes me alas unblest unhappy I. *Unknown.* SeCSL
Woe's me! by dint of all those sighs that come. Dante. *Fr.* La Vita Nuova. AWP
Woe's me, woe's me. The Ghost's Lament. *Unknown.* BuBa
Wofle New Ballad of Jane Roney and Mary Brown, The. Thackeray. BOHV
Wofully Araide. John Skelton. *See* Woefully Arrayed.
Woggly bird sat on the whango tree. The Whango Tree. *Unknown.* BOHV; NA
Woke this A.M. Poem. James Brodey. ANYP
Woke up crying the blues. A Day in the Life of a Poet. Quincy Troupe. WSL
Woken, I lay in the arms of my own warmth and listened. First Things First. W. H. Auden. NePoAm-2; NYBP
Wol ze here a wonder thynge. Riddles Wisely Expounded. *Unknown.* BaBo (A *vers.*); ESPB
Wolcum be thu, hevene kyng. *See* Welcome be Thou, Heavenly King.
Wolf, The. Donald Davidson. AnAmPo
Wolf, The. Georgia R. Durston. GFA; UTS
Wolf also shall dwell with the lamb, The. Isaiah, Bible, *O.T.* BoPe; FaPON; LiTW; PDV
Wolf and the Dog, The. La Fontaine, *tr. fr. French by* Elizur Wright. LiTW; PoFr
Wolf and the Dog, The. John Oldham. *Fr.* A Satyr Address'd to a Friend, That Is About to Leave the University, and Come Abroad in the World. PeRV
Wolf and the Lamb, The. La Fontaine, *tr. fr. French by* Elizur Wright. OuHeWo
Wolf and the Lambs, The. Ivy O. Eastwick. BoTP
Wolf and Tiger Dining, A. B. Joseph Joel Keith. FiSC
Wolf Cry, The. Lew Sarett. FaPON; PoMa
Wolf in the Kennels, The. Ivan Andreyevich Krylov, *tr. fr. Russian by* Frances Cornford *and* E. P. Salaman. LiTW
Wolf Song, the Rain. James Welch. YAP
Wolf, with hunger fierce and bold, A. The Shepherd's Dog and the Wolf. John Gay. *Fr.* Fables. OA
Wolfram's Dirge. Thomas Lovell Beddoes. *See* Dirge: "If thou wilt ease thine heart."
Wolfram's Song. Thomas Lovell Beddoes. *See* Song: "Old Adam, the carrion crow."
Wolsey. Shakespeare, *and probably* John Fletcher. King Henry VIII, *fr.* III, ii. OTPC (1923 ed.)
("Cromwell, I did not think to shed a tear.") InP
(Wolsey's Regrets.) TreFS
Wolsey's Farewell to His Greatness. Shakespeare, *and probably* John Fletcher. King Henry VIII, *fr.* III, ii. OHFP; TIHL
(Cardinal Wolsey's Farewell.) LiTB; MaRV; TreF
(Farewell to All My Greatness.) LiTG
(Farewell to Greatness.) PTK; TrGrPo
Wolves, The. Galway Kinnell. NePoEA-2
Wolves, The. Elizabeth Madox Roberts. UTS
Wolves, The. Allen Tate. LiTA; LiTG; LiTM; OxBA
Wolves of evening will be much abroad, The. Runes for an Old Believer. Rolfe Humphries. NYBP
Woman. Eaton Stannard Barrett. HBV; OnYI; OxBI; SoP
Woman. Zora Cross. BoAu
Woman. C. D. B. Ellis. SiTL
Woman. Fu Hsüan, *tr. fr. Chinese by* Arthur Waley. WoL
Woman. Goldsmith. *See* Song: "When lovely woman stoops to folly."
Woman. Kalidasa, *tr. fr. Sanskrit by* Horace H. Wilson. HBV
Woman. Irving Layton. ErPo
Woman, The. Frank Lima. ANYP
Woman, *sel.* Alexander McLachlan.
("When my gloomy hour comes on me." CaP
Woman. Valente Goenha Malangatana, *tr. fr. Portuguese by* Dorothy Guedes *and* Philippa Rumsey. PBA; TTY
Woman. Milton. *Fr.* Samson Agonistes. OBS
Woman. Thomas O'Hagan. CAW
Woman. Coventry Patmore. *See* Foreign Land, The.
Woman, A. Mary Dixon Thayer. HBMV
Woman ("A clever man builds a city"). *Unknown, tr. fr. Chinese by* H. A. Giles. *Fr.* Shi King. AWP; LiTW
Woman ("A comfort but a queer companion"). *Unknown, tr. fr. German by* Louis Untermeyer. UnTE
Woman and Cat. Paul Verlaine. *See* Femme at chatte.
Woman and Her Dead Husband, A. D. H. Lawrence. NP
Woman and Man, *abr.* Tennyson. *Fr.* The Princess, Pt. VII. OQP
Woman and the Aloe, The. Perseus Adams. PeSA
Woman and Tree. Robert Graves. CBV; ErPo
Woman at Banff, The. William Stafford. TPM
Woman at the Piano. Marya Zaturenska. MoAmPo
Woman at the Washington Zoo, The. Randall Jarrell. AP; CoAP; LiTM (1970 ed.); NMP; TwCP; UnPo (3d ed.)
Woman at the Window, The. Donald Wandrei. FiSC
Woman, bathe this head of mine. The Bathing of Oisin's Head. *Unknown.* AnIL
Woman, beguiling man, herself beguiles. Woman. C. D. B. Ellis. SiTL
Woman Blue, *with music. Unknown.* ABF
Woman-Captain, The, *sel.* Thomas Shadwell.
Let Some Great Joys Pretend to Find. OAEP
Woman Clothed with the Sun, A. Apocalypse (Revelation) XII: 1,2,5,10, Bible, *N.T.* (*Douay vers.*). ISi
Woman! experience might have told me. To Woman. Byron. HBV; ViBoPo
Woman full of wile. Growing Old [*or* Autumn]. *Unknown, tr. by* Frank O'Connor. ErPo; LiLC; OBMV
Woman, Gallup, N.M. Karen Swenson. NYBP
Woman grew, with waiting, over-quiet, A. Narrative. Elisabeth Eybers. PeSA
Woman had I seen, as I rode by, A. Bogac Bán. Darrell Figgis. AnIV
Woman-Hater, The, *sels.* Beaumont *and* Fletcher.
"Come, Sleep, and with thy sweet deceiving," *fr.* III, i. EG; EIL; ELP; SiCE
(Lullaby.) FaBoEn
(Sleep.) HBV; OBEV (1st ed.)
Woman Homer Sung, A. W. B. Yeats. CLwM
Woman I Am, The. Glen Allen. BLPA
Woman I Met, The. Thomas Hardy. AtBAP
Woman in Sunshine, The. Wallace Stevens. MoVE
Woman in the garden. Duo. Olive Tilford Dargan. HBMV
Woman in the Wagon, The. Clyde Robertson. PoOW
Woman Is a Branchy Tree, A. James Stephens. ErPo; POTE
Woman is a foreign land, A. The Foreign Land [*or* Woman]. Coventry Patmore. The Angel in the House, II, ix, 2. HBV; OBVV
Woman Looking at a Vase of Flowers. Wallace Stevens. CrMA; TDP
Woman, meanwhile, from strawberry lips, The. The Metamorphoses of a Vampire. Baudelaire. ReMP
Woman much missed, how you call to me, call to me. The

Woman (continued)
Voice. Thomas Hardy. CMoP EnLoPo; FaBoEn; GTBS-P; MaPo (1969 ed.); MoVE; NP; OAEP (2d ed.); OBNC; PoEL-5; ViPP
Woman named Tomorrow, The. Four Preludes on Playthings of the Wind, I. Carl Sandburg. AmLP; AnAmPo; AnFE; AP; BoLiVe; CMoP; CoAnAm; CoBA; InP; MAP; MoAB; MoAmPo; NePA; NP; SeCeV
Woman of Beare, The. *Unknown, tr. fr. Middle Irish by* Stephen Gwynn. AnIV
(Old Woman of Beare, The, *tr. by* Frank O'Connor.) AnIL; KiLC; OnYI, *abr., tr. by* Kuno Meyer
(Old Woman of Beare Regrets Lost Youth, The, *tr. by* Frank O'Connor.) OBMV
Woman of Llyn y Fan's Call to Her Cattle, The. *Unknown, tr. fr. Welsh by* Gwyn Jones. PrWP
Woman of Samaria, The, *sel.* Edmond Rostand, *tr. fr. French by* Henderson Daingerfield Norman.
"Curses upon this land; till plague devours," Pt. I, iv. StJW
Woman of This Earth, *sels.* Frances Frost. AnAmPo
"Before sheep came."
"History of earth is a moving of leaves in the sun, The."
Woman of Three Cows, The. *Unknown, tr. fr. Late Middle Irish or fr. Modern Irish by* James Clarence Mangan. AnIL; EnRP; IrPN; OnYI; OxBI
Woman of Words, A. Amanda B. Hall. HBMV
Woman of Yueh, A. Li Po, *tr. fr. Chinese by* Shigeyoshi Obata. OnPM
Woman one wonderful morning, A. Europa. William Plomer. MoBS
Woman par Excellence. Rochelle Owens. CoPo
Woman Passes the Door, A. George O'Neil. NP
Woman, rest on my brow your balsam hands. Night of Sine. Léopold Sédar Senghor. PBA
Woman supremely blest. Mulier Amicta Sole. Fray Angelico Chavez. ISi
"Woman, take away my tunic." Goll's Parting with His Wife. *Unknown.* AnIL
Woman Taken in Adultery, The. St. John, VIII: 2-11, Bible, *N.T.* TreFT
Woman Takes Life with Own Hand. John Morgan. *Fr.* Variations on *The Aeneid.* YAP
Woman Telephoning. Joseph Joel Keith. FiSC
Woman That Had More Babies than That, The. Wallace Stevens. LiTA
Woman: that is to say. Of Women. *Unknown. Fr.* The Thousand and One Nights. ErPo; PV
Woman, though undependable. Experts on Woman. Arthur Guiterman. InMe
Woman to Man. Judith Wright. BoAV; MoAuPo; PoAu-2
Woman Too Well Remembered, A. Louis Simpson. NoP
Woman Unconscious, A. Ted Hughes. StP
Woman Waits for Me, A. Walt Whitman. ErPo
Woman was old and ragged and gray, The. Somebody's Mother. Mary Dow Brine. BeLS; BLPA; FaFP; OTPC (1946 ed.); TreF; WBLP
Woman watches her husband rubbing his nose, The. Twenty Below. R. A. D. Ford. CaP
Woman weak and woman mortal. Streets of Baltimore. *Unknown.* BLPA
Woman Who Came behind Him in the Crowd. George Macdonald. StJW
Woman Who Disapproved of Music at the Bar, The. Horace Gregory. MoPo
Woman who has borne a child, The. The Mothers of the Earth. Grace Noll Crowell. PEDC
Woman who has grown old, The. The Crows. Louise Bogan. YT
Woman who lived in Holland, of old, A. Going Too Far. Mildred Howells. OnMSP; TiPo
Woman Who Loved Worms, The. Colette Inez. QAH
Woman Who Understands, The. Everard Jack Appleton. PoLF
Woman who walked home on the arm of John. Chant of Departure; a Missionary's Prayer. Alfred Barrett. GoBC; ISi
"Woman with a past, A." What happier omen. The Love Sonnets of Proteus, XLIX. Wilfrid Scawen Blunt. Sonn
Woman with Child, The. Freda Laughton. OnYI
Woman with Flower. Naomi Long Madgett. BP
Woman with Girdle. Anne Sexton. ErPo
Woman with her forests, moons, flowers, waters. Robert Graves. MemP
Woman with hoe in hand, and baby on your back. For Sapphire, My Sister. Alice H. Jones. WSL
Woman with no face walked into the light, A. Homage to Hieronymus Bosch. Thomas McGreevy. OnYI
Woman with the Baby to the Philosopher, The. Frances Cornford. PoMa
Woman with the caught fox. Plea for a Captive. W. S. Merwin. NePoEA-2; NYBP
Woman with the Serpent's Tongue, The. Sir William Watson. HBV
Woman withour Fear. George Dillon. AnEnPo
Woman, woman, let us say these things to each other. Prelude. Conrad Aiken. NYBP
Woman wrapped her coat, A. Isador and Ida Strauss. E. J. Pratt. *Fr.* The *Titanic.* TwCaPo
Woman Wrapped in Silence, A, *sel.* John W. Lynch.
"Little girl, A/ Had wandered," V. ISi
Woman, you'll never credit what. The Shepherd's Tale. James Kirkup. POTi
Womanhood, The, *sel.* Gwendolyn Brooks.
"Men of careful turns, haters of forks in the road." BALP
"What shall I give my children? who are poor." BALP
Womanhood, Wanton, ye Want. John Skelton. NCEP
Womanisers. John Press. ErPo
Woman's Answer, A. *At. to* The Earl of Surrey. SiPS
("Girt in my guiltless gown, as I sit here and sew.") FCP
Woman's Answer to "The Vampire," A. Felicia Blake. BLPA; NeHB
Woman's Arms. Anacreon, *tr. fr. Greek by* Abraham Cowley. UnTE
Woman's Beauty. Lascelles Abercrombie. *Fr.* Emblems of Love: Vashti. MoBrPo; PG
Woman's beauty is like a white, A. Song from "The Only Jealousy of Emer." W. B. Yeats. MoAB
Woman's Beloved, A. Marguerite Wilkinson. NP
Woman's cause is man's, The: they rise or sink. Woman and Man. Tennyson. *Fr.* The Princess, Pt. VII. OQP
Womans Constancy. John Donne. AnAnS-1; EnLit; LiTL; MaMe; MBW-1; NoP; PoE; PoeP; PoFS; ReIE; SCEP-1; SeCV-1; SeEP; TuPP
Woman's Execution, A. Edward King. AA
Woman's face is full of wiles, A. Song. Humphrey Gifford. *Fr.* A Delectable Dream. ElL; SiCE; TuPP
Woman's face, with Nature's own hand painted. Sonnets, XX. Shakespeare. CBEP; ErPo; InvP; MasP; ReEn
Woman's Faith ("Woman's faith and woman's trust"). Sir Walter Scott. *Fr.* The Betrothed, *ch.* 20. CBV; ViBoPo
Woman's Hand, A. Sir Gilbert Parker. *Fr.* A Lover's Diary. VA
Woman's hands with polished finger-nail, A. Hands on a Card-Table. Polly Chase Boyden. NP
Woman's Inconstancy. Phineas Fletcher. *Fr.* Sicelides, II, ii. ElL
Woman's Jealousy. Baltasar del Alcázar, *tr. fr. Spanish by* Sir John Bowring. OnPM
Woman's Last Word, A. Robert Browning. BEL; BLPA; BoLiVe; CBEP; EPN; FaBoBe; FaFP; GTBS; GTBS-D; HBV; InPo; LiTL; LO; MeWo; OAEP; PoVP; TreFS; TrGrPo; UnTE; ViBoPo; ViPo
Woman's Looks, A. *Unknown.* OBSC; ReEn; SiCE; TrGrPo
Woman's Love, A. John Hay. HBV
Woman's Love. *Unknown.* WBLP
Woman's love, April weather. Constancies. *Unknown.* UnTE
Woman's Prayer, A. *Unknown.* SoP
Woman's Pride, A. Helen Hay Whitney. AA
Woman's Question, A. Lena Lathrop, *wr. at. to* Elizabeth Barrett Browning. BLPA; PoToHe; WBLP
Woman's Question[s], A. Adelaide Anne Procter. HBV; LiTL; LO; VA
Woman's Ruling Passions. Pope. *Fr.* Moral Essays, Epistle II. OBEC
Woman's sho' a cur'ous critter, an' dey ain't no doubtin' dat. The Turning of the Babies in the Bed. Paul Laurence Dunbar. MAP; MoAmPo (1942 ed.); NeMA
Woman's Shortcomings, A. Elizabeth Barrett Browning. BLPA; HBV; NeHB
Woman's Song, A. Muna Lee. NP
Woman's Song. Edward Shanks. LO
Woman's Song. Judith Wright. BoAV

Woman's Thought, A. Richard Watson Gilder. HBV
Woman's Tongue Tree, The. Arthur Guiterman. PoMS
Woman's white body is a song. The Song of Songs. Heine. UnTE
Woman's Will. John Godfrey Saxe. BOHV; FaFP; HBV; SiTL; TreFT
(“Men, dying, make their wills; but wives.”) InP
(Wills.) ShM
Woman's Will. *Unknown.* HBV
Woman's Wit, *sel.* Colley Cibber.
Celia and Belinda. SeCL
Wombat, The. Ogden Nash. CenHV
Women. Louise Bogan. HBMV; LiTA; LiTL; MAP; MoAB; MoAmPo; TwCP; WHA
Women. William Cartwright. ELU;ErPo
Women. —Heath. *See* These Women All.
Women. Lizette Woodworth Reese. MAP; MoAmPo; NP
Women,/What fools we are. Two Strange Worlds. Francesca Yetunde Pereira. PBA
Women and poets see the truth arrive. Letter to the Front. Muriel Rukeyser. WaP
Women and Roses. Robert Browning. EPN; ViBoPo
Women are dancing around a fire. A Message Hidden in an Empty Wine Bottle. James Wright. AmPC
Women are door-mats and have been. Door-Mats. Mary Carolyn Davies. HBMV; YaD
Women are timid, cower and shrink. Betty Zane. Thomas Dunn. PAH
Women Are Worthy. *Unknown.* *See* I Am as Light as Any Roe.
Women at the Corners Stand, The. Louis Golding. TrJP
Women ben full of ragerie. Imitation of Chaucer. Pope. Par
Women Beware of Women, *sel.* Thomas Middleton.
“How near am I now to a happiness.” LO
Women, flashing razor blades. For the Dancer, Fred Herko. Jack Marshall. YAP
Women Folk, The. James Hogg. HBV
Women have loved before as I love now. Edna St. Vincent Millay. CMoP
Women have no wilderness in them. Women. Louise Bogan. HBMV; LiTA; LiTL; MAP; MoAB; MoAmPo; TwCP; WHA
Women He Liked. Edward Thomas. HaMV
Women, if we held the oxhide shield. Lament for a Warrior. *Unknown.* PeSA
Women Men's Shadows. Ben Jonson. *See* Song: That Women Are but Men's Shadows.
Women, of kinde, have conditions three. John Lydgate. *Fr.* A Ballad Warning Men to Beware of Deceitful Women. LO
Women of the Better Class, The. Oliver Herford. HBMV
Women of the West, The. G. Essex Evans. PoAu-1
Women of Trachis, *sel.* Sophocles, *tr. fr. Greek by* Ezra Pound.
“Kupris bears trophies away.” CTC
Women Pleased, *sels.* John Fletcher.
Song: “O fair[e] sweet face, O eyes celestial[l] bright,” *fr.* III, iv. OBS; PoEL-2
Women's Longing, *fr.* V, i. HBV
Women Singing. Sir Henry Taylor. OBVV
Women Speak out in Defense of Themselves, The. Aristophanes, *tr. fr. Greek by* Benjamin Bickley Rogers. *Fr.* The Thesmophoriazusae. TreFT
(Chorus of Women, *tr. by* W. L. Collins.) BOHV
Women tell me every day, The. Odes of Anacreon. *Tr. by* Thomas Moore. LoBV; OuHeWo
Women that are loved are more than lovable. The Colours of Love. Denis Devlin. OxBI
Women there are on earth, most sweet and high. Of Those Who Walk Alone. Richard Burton. HBV
Women through the years have stood. The Fire Tenders. Grace Noll Crowell. PEDC
Women Toilers, The. Grace Bowen Evans. OQP
Women who do not love are free. The Free Woman. Theodosia Garrison. HBMV
Women, women/ women, women. A Fixture. May Swenson. NYBP
Women's Complaint to Venus, The. *Unknown.* PeRV
Women's Eyes. Bhartrihari, *tr. fr. Sanskrit by* Arthur W. Ryder. OnPM
Women's Longing. John Fletcher. *Fr.* Women Pleased, V, i. HBV
Wonder. Dawn Finlay. SoP
Wonder, The. Kipling. *Fr.* Epitaphs of the War. PoVP
Wonder. Thomas Traherne. AnAnS-1; AtBAP; CBEP; CH; LiTB; LiTG; LoBV; MeP; NoP; PoE; PoIE; SCEP-1; SeCePo; SeCeV; SeCL; SeCP; SeCV-2; SeEP; StP; TrGrPo; WHA
Wonder and a Thousand Springs. William Alexander Percy. HBMV
Wonder-Child, The. Richard Le Gallienne. VA
Wonder—is not precisely knowing. Emily Dickinson. AmePo; MoPo
Wonder of It. Harriet Monroe. NP
Wonder of the world is o'er, The. The Twilight of Earth. “*A E.*” AnIL; TOP
Wonder of these, glory of other times. To the Right Honorable, the Lady Mary, Countess of Pembroke. Samuel Daniel. *Fr.* Delia. SiCE; TuPP
Wonder Shell, The. Barbara D. Holender. NYTB
Wonder stranger ne'r was known, A. The Suffolk Miracle. *Unknown.* BaBo (A *vers.*); ESPB; OBB
Wonder was on me in Curraghmacall, The. The Two Nests. Francis Carlin. BiS; PFY
Wonder Where This Horseshoe Went. Edna St. Vincent Millay. *Fr.* A Very Little Sphinx. SUS; TiPo (1952 ed.)
(Horseshoe, The.) StVeCh
(Wonder Where.) PoRh
Wonderer, The. Robert W. Service. BBV
Wonderful are thy works, as my soul overwhelmingly knoweth. Solomon ibn Gabirol. *Fr.* The Royal Crown. AWP
Wonderful bears that walked my room all night. Bears. Adrienne Cecile Rich. NePoEA; NYBP; TPM
Wonderful bird is the pelican, A. Limerick. Dixon Lanier Merritt. CenHV; LiBL; LiTG
Wonderful Country. Miriam Waddington. PeCV
Wonderful Crocodile, The, *with music.* *Unknown.* ABF
Wonderful Day, A. A. H. Dixon. SoP
Wonderful Derby Ram, The. *Unknown.* *See* Derby Ram, The.
Wonderful family is Stein, A. Limerick. *Unknown.* *See also* There is a wonderful family called Stein. LiBL.
Wonderful Is My Saviour. Avis B. Christiansen. SoP
Wonderful lass was Marie, petite, A. An Old Song by New Singers: How Andrew Lang Sings It. A. C. Wilkie. BOHV; NA
Wonderful Man, A. Aileen Fisher. SiSoSe
Wonderful Meadow, The. “Olive A. Wadsworth.” *See* Over in the Meadow.
Wonderful Old Man, The. *Unknown.* NA
Wonderful “One-Hoss Shay,” The. Oliver Wendell Holmes. *See* Deacon's Masterpiece, The.
Wonderful scarcity will shortly ensue, A. Thomas Bastard. SiCE
Wonderful Things. Ron Padgett. YAP
Wonderful way is the King's Highway, A. The King's Highway. John Masefield. BLRP; TRV
Wonderful Weaver, The. George Cooper. BoChLi; OTPC (1946 ed.); StVeCh (1940 ed.)
Wonderful Word, The. John Newton. SoP
Wonderful World, The. William Brighty Rands. BoChLi; DD; FaPON; GFA; HBV; HBVY; MPB; PRWS; StVeCh (1940 ed.); TIHL; TiPo (1959 ed.); TVC
(Child's World, The.) OHIP; TreFT
(World, The.) BoTP; OTPC; PCH, *abr.*
(World, The; a Child's Song.) OBVV
Wonderfully out of the beautiful form. Sonnet. Dante. GoBC
Wondering How. William Brown. QAH
Wondering I gaze upon each lineament. Sonnet: The Corpse. George Moore. SyP
Wonderland. Harry Thurston Peck. AA
Wonders. *Unknown.* EIL
(Thule, the Period of Cosmography.) NCEP
“Andalusian merchant, that returns, The,” *sel.* FaBoCh
Wonders amazed! Am I espoused to thee? Who Is She That Looks Forth. Edward Taylor. *Fr.* Preparatory Meditations, Second Series. MWA-1
Wonders of Nature (“Ah! who has seen the mailèd lobster rise”). *Unknown.* BOHV
Wonders of Nature (“My grandmother said, 'Now isn't it queer' ”). *Unknown.* ThGo
Wonders of the Peak, The, *sel.* Charles Cotton.

Wonders (continued)
Elden-Hole. PeRV
Wondrous Apple Tree, The, *with music.* *Unknown,* *tr. fr. French by* Alice M. G. White. SaSa
Wondrous is the wall-stone, by Wyrd broken [*or* broken by Fate]. The Ruin. *Unknown.* EnLit *tr. by* Harold S. Stine; YAT, *tr. by* Richard L. Hoffman
"Wondrous life!" cried Marvell at Appleton House. Round. Weldon Kees. CoAP; NaP
Wondrous Love. Countess of Pembroke. BePJ
Wondrous Love, *with music.* *Unknown.* TrAS
Wondrous Motherhood. *Unknown.* PGD
Wondrous Show, A. James Thomson. *Fr.* The Castle of Indolence, I. OBEC
Wondrous Son of God. Berniece Goertz. STF
Wondrous things have come to pass. Wizard Frost. Frank Dempster Sherman. YeAr
Wondrous this masonry wasted by Fate! The Ruin. *Unknown,* *tr. by* Charles W. Kennedy. AnOE
Wonga Vine. Judith Wright. PoAu-2
"Won't you look out of your window, Mrs. Gill?" The Mocking Fairy. Walter de la Mare. GBV; MoBrPo; MoShBr
Woo Not the World. Mu'tamid, King of Seville, *tr. fr. Arabic by* Dulcie L. Smith. AWP; JAWP; LiTW; WBP
Wood. Thomas Hornsby Ferril. PoRA
Wood and Hill. Andrew Young. HaMV
Woo'd and Married and A' ("Wooed and married and a' "). Alexander Ross. *See also* Wooed and Married and A'. OxBS.
Wood-Dove's Note, The. Emily Huntington Miller. HBV
Wood Flower. Richard Le Gallienne. HBMV
Wood Frog, The. John Hay. NYTB
Wood-Gatherers, The. F. C. Slater. BoSA
Wood is a good place to find, The. Walking with Lulu in the Wood. Naomi Lazard. NYBP
Wood is bare, The: a river-mist is steeping. Elegy. Robert Bridges. CMoP; OAEP; PoVP
Wood is full of rooks, The. The Farmer's Gun. Andrew Young. MemP; OA
Wood is one blue flame of love, The. Derbyshire Bluebells. Sacheverell Sitwell. ChMP
Wood louse sits on a splinter, The. Archygrams. Don Marquis. *Fr.* Archys Life of Mehitabel. WhC
Wood-Mouse, The. Mary Howitt. TVC
Wood Music. Ethel King. GoYe
Wood of Flowers, The. James Stephens. BoTP; MemP; PDV
Wood of the Cross. Violet Alleyn Storey. StJW
Wood of the Self-Destroyers, The. Samuel Yellen. NePoAm-2
Wood-Pigeons. John Masefield. ChMP
Wood shakes in the breeze, The. The Old Tree. Andrew Young. GoJo
Wood So Wild, The. *Unknown.* *See* I Must Go Walk the Wood.
Wood Song, A. Ralph Hodgson. GoJo; HBV
Wood-Song. Eugene Lee-Hamilton. OBVV
Wood-Song. Josephine Preston Peabody. AA
Wood, swollen with mushrooms, The. The Circle. Jean Garrigue. LiTA; MoPo
Wood, the Weed, the Wag, The. Sir Walter Ralegh. CBEP; Po; SiPS; TrGrPo
(Sir Walter Ralegh to His Son.) EnRePo; Sonn
(Sir Walter Raleigh to His Son.) ReIE; Sonn
(Three Thing[e]s There Be[e] That Prosper Up Apace.) FosPo; NoP; PoEL-2
(To His Son.) BWP; EnL; EP; FCP; PoE; PoIE; TuPP
Wood-Thrush. John Hall Wheelock. NePoAm; PoDB
Wood was rather old and dark, The. The Little Boy Lost. Stevie Smith. FaBoTw
Wood-Weasel, The. Marianne Moore. CMoP; OA; Po
Wood wind warbled wisely, The. A Beethoven Andante. Grace Hazard Conkling. PFY
Wood Witchery. Richard Burton. AnAmPo
Woodbines in October. Charlotte Fiske Bates. AA
Woodbird. Charles G. Bell. NePoAm
Woodchuck told it all about, The. On Knowing When to Stop. L. J. Bridgman. BOHV
Woodchuck's very very fat, The. The Jolly Woodchuck. Marion Edey. FaPON; PDV; TiPo
Woodcock of the Ivory Beak. Elizabeth Madox Roberts. MAP; MoAmPo
Wood-cut. V. Sackville-West. ChMP
Woodcut. R. N. D. Wilson. OxBI
Woodcutter and the Fisherman Turn Home, The. Bilhana, *formerly at. to* Chauras, *tr. fr. Sanskrit by* E. Powys Mathers. *Fr.* Black Marigolds. OnPM
Wood-Cutter's Night Song, The. John Clare. EnRP; GTSE; OBRV
Woodcutter's Wife, The. William Rose Benét. AnAmPo; AWP; InPo
Wooden Christ, The. Martha Foote Crow. ChIP; StJW
Wooden Christ within a wayside shrine, A. Wayside Shrine. Gertrude Ryder Bennett. ChIP
Wooden Fence, The. Christian Morgenstern, *tr. fr. German by* Babette Deutsch *and* Avrahm Yarmolinsky. LiTW
Wooden Mirror, The. John Logan. FRC
Wooden Ships. David Morton. EtS
Wooden Tiger, The. Samuel Yellen. NePoAm
Woodland. Sister Margaret Teresa. JKCP (1926 ed.)
Woodland Choir, The. James Thomson. *Fr.* The Seasons: Spring. CoBE
Woodland Grave, A. Lord De Tabley. VA
Woodland Mass, The. Dafydd ap Gwilym, *tr. fr. Welsh by* Gwyn Williams. PrWP
Woodland Revel, A. Clarence Urmy. HBMV
Woodland Singer, The. John Jerome Rooney. MaRV
Woodland sprite of the rakish kind, A. A Scandal among the Flowers. Charles S. Taylor. BLPA
Woodland Worship. Ethelwyn Wetherald. CaP
Woodlanders, The, *sel.* Thomas Hardy.
In a Wood. InP; OAEP; OBNC; PoPl; ViPo (1962 ed.)
Woodlands, The. William Barnes. BoNaP; GTBS-D; OBVV; PoVP
Woodlands. Sir Herbert Read. BrPo
Woodlore. Kim Kurt. NePoAm-2
Woodman, Spare That Tree. George Pope Morris. AA; BLPA; DD; FaBoBe; FaFP; FaPON, *abr.*; HBV; HH; MPB (1956 ed.); NeHB; OHIP; OTD; OTPC; PaPo; PTK; TreF; WBLP
(Oak, The.) AmePo
Woodman's axe renews its hollow stroke, The. Summer. John Clare. CBEP
Woodman's Dog, The. William Cowper. *Fr.* The Task. BoTP; ELU; OTPC (1946 ed.); PCD; PCH
Woodnotes, I ("When the pine tosses its cones"). Emerson. AmPP (4th ed.); AnNE; CoBA; NePA; OxBA
Heart of All the Scene, The, *sel.* AA
Woodnotes, II ("As sunbeams stream through liberal space"). Emerson.
Sels.
"All the forms are fugitive." WGRP
"As the sunbeams stream through liberal space." OHIP
God ("As the bee through the garden ranges"). OQP
God Hide the Whole World in Thy Heart, *br. sel.* OQP
Immanent God, The. MaRV
Mighty Heart, The. AA
Undersong, The. AA
"Whoso walks in solitude." OBVV
Woodpecker, The. Richard Church. HaMV
Woodpecker, The. Andrew Marvell. *See* Hewel, or Woodpecker, The. *Fr.* Upon Appleton House.
Woodpecker, The. Elizabeth Madox Roberts. BoChLi; FaPON; GFA; MPB; StVeCh; TiPo; UTS
Woodpecker, The. Joyce Sambrook. BoTP
Woodpecker, The. John Banister Tabb. UTS
Woodpecker and a horned owl call on me, A. Country Pastor. Mitsuko Inoue. LiTW
Woodpecker goes beating a little drum, The. Sleep. Charles Simic. CoAP
Woodpecker pecked out a little round hole, The. The Woodpecker. Elizabeth Madox Roberts. BoChLi; FaPON; GFA; MPB; StVeCh; TiPo; UTS
Woodpeckers here are redheaded, The. Ornithology in Florida. Arthur Guiterman. InMe
Woodpigeons at Raheny. Donald Davie. PP
Wood-Pile [*or* Woodpile], The. Robert Frost. AmP; CABA; CoBMV; FosPo; LiTA; MAmP; MAPA; NoP; SeCeV; TwAmPo; VaPo; YT
Woodrow Wilson. S. Omar Barker. DD
Woodrow Wilson. Donald Gillies. DD
Woodrow Wilson. Robert Underwood Johnson. DD
Woodruffe, The. Isa Craig Knox. VA
Woods. W. H. Auden. NePA; NePoAm
Woods and coppice by tempests lashed. Epping Forest. John Davidson. *Fr.* November. GTSL

Woods and downs have caught the mid-December, The. Stanzas Written on Battersea Bridge during a Southwesterly Gale. Hilaire Belloc. GoBC
Woods and Kestrel. Julian Bell. ChMP
Woods are full of fairies, The. The Child and the Fairies. *Unknown.* OTPC (1946 ed.); PCH; PRWS; StVeCh (1940 ed.)
Woods are lovely, dark and deep, The. Robert Frost. *Fr.* Stopping by Woods on a Snowy Evening. TRV
Woods are purple with the haze, The. Autumn Color. Tom Robinson. YeAr
Woods Are Still, The. "Michael Field." OBVV
Woods decay, the woods decay and fall, The. Tithonus. Tennyson. BWP; CABA; CABL; CBEP; CBV; DiPo; EnL; EPN; FaBoEn; ForPo; FosPo; GTBS-D; ILP; LiTB; LoBV; MaPo (1969 ed.); MBW-2; NoP; OAEP; OBNC; PAn; PoAn; PoE; PoEL-5; PoFS; PoVP; TOP; ViPo; ViPP; VP; WHA
Woods Grow Darker, The. Leah Bodine Drake. FiSC
Woods have stored the rain, and slow comes the smoke, The. My Lodge at Wang-ch'uan after a Long Rain. Wang Wei. LiTW
Woods in Winter. Longfellow. CBEP; MAmP
Woods No More, The. Jay Macpherson. PeCV
Woods of Arcady are dead, The. The Song of the Happy Shepherd. W. B. Yeats. PoFS; ViPo (1962 ed.)
Woods of my fathers, sovereign deity. Sylvan Ode. José Santos Chocano. WoL
Woods of Westermain, The. George Meredith. BEL; ViPo; ViPP; VP
"Enter these enchanted woods," *first 2 sts.* ShBV-3; WaKn
Woods, rocks, & mountaynes, & ye desart places. *Unknown.* SeCSL
Woods shall not decry the murderous stroke, The. On Some Trees Needlessly Slain. Stanton A. Coblentz. TRV
Woods stretch wild [*or* deep] to the mountain side, The. The Man Hunt. Madison Cawein. AnAmPo; MAP
Woods were dark and the night was black, The. The Path in the Sky. Amos R. Wells. SoP
Woods we're lost in aren't real, The. Villanelle. Walter H. Kerr. NePoAm-2
Woods were still and the snow was deep, The. Christmas Eve Legend. Frances Frost. BiCB
Woodsman Goes to Sea, A. Charles R. Knapp. IHA
Woodspurge, The. Dante Gabriel Rossetti. AnFE; AtBAP; BoLiVe; CaFP; CBEP; ELP; EPN; FaBoEn; GTBS-D; GTBS-P; LoBV; MemP; NBM; NoP; OAEP; OBEV (new ed.); OBNC; PoEL-5; PoIE; PoVP; TreFT; UnPo (3d ed.); VA; ViPP; WHA
Woodstock, *sel.* Sir Walter Scott.
Glee for King Charles, *fr. ch.* 20. CoBE; EPN
Woodworkers' Ballad. Herbert Edward Palmer. HaMV; OBEV (new ed.)
Woodyards in the Rain. Anne Marriott. CaP; TwCaPo
Wooe then the heavens (gentle love). *Unknown.* SeCSL
Wooed and Married and A' ("The bride cam' out of the byre"). *Unknown, wr. at. to* Alexander Ross. *See also* Woo'd and Married and A'. HBV.
Woof of the Sun [Ethereal Gauze]. Henry David Thoreau. *See* Haze.
Woof! Woof! Woof! Little Brown Bear. Alice Wilkins. GFA
Wooing, The. *Unknown, tr. fr. Latin by* John Addington Symonds. UnTE
Wooing Lady, The. William Jay Smith. NePoEA
Wooing Maid, The. Martin Parker. CoMu
Wooing of Criseide, The. Chaucer. Troilus and Criseyde, III. PoEL-1
(O Blisful Light.) AtBAP
Wooing Rogue, The. *Unknown.* CoMu
Wooing Song. Giles Fletcher. *Fr.* Christ's Victory and Triumph: Christ's Victory on Earth. EIL; HBV; OBEV
("Love is the blossom where there blows.") LO; ViBoPo
Wool Trade, The. John Dyer. *Fr.* The Fleece, III. OBEC; SeCePo
Woolly Lambkins. Christina Rossetti. *See* On the Grassy Banks.
Woolworth Philodendron, The. Stephen Sandy. CoPo
Woone Smile Mwore. William Barnes. VA
Woosel cock so black of hue, The. Bottom's Song. Shakespeare. *Fr.* A Midsummer Night's Dream, III,i. CTC
Wops came down to the port, The. The City of Beggars. Alfred Hayes. WaP
Word, The. Margaret Avison. MoCV
Word, The. St. John, Bible, *N.T.* *See* In the Beginning Was the Word.
Word, The. John Masefield. MaRV
Word, The. Richard Realf. *Fr.* Symbolisms. AA; AmLP; TRV; WGRP
(O Earth!) AnEnPo
(World, The.) MaRV
Word. Stephen Spender. FaBoTw; NYBP; PoPo; PP
Word, The. Tennyson. *See* In Memoriam A. H. H. "Tho' truths in manhood darkly join."
Word, The. Edward Thomas. NP
Word, The. Allen Upward. *Fr.* Scented Leaves from a Chinese Jar. NP
Word, The. Neil Weiss. NYBP
Word, The/ Is in the hand. Shaman Song 2. Gene Fowler. ThO
Word, a Word, A. Dialogue. Sister Mary Madeleva. CAW
Word about Woodpiles, A. Nancy Byrd Turner. BrR
Word bites like a fish, The. Word. Stephen Spender. FaBoTw; NYBP; PoPo; PP
Word Fitly Spoken, A. Proverbs, XXV: ii, Bible, *O.T.* FaPON
Word for the Innkeeper, A. Paul Grano. MoAuPo
Word forms, The. A B C s (1). Charles Olson. PoAn
Word has been abroad, The; is back, with a tanned look. Annunciations. Geoffrey Hill. NePoEA-2
Word has come to May Marjorie. Jellon Grame (B *vers.*). *Unknown.* ESPB
Word has gane thro a' this land. The Bonny Lass of Anglesey (B *vers.*). *Unknown.* ESPB
Word Incarnate, The. Tennyson. *See* In Memoriam A. H. H.: "Tho' truths in manhood darkly join."
Word is such a potent thing, A. Only a Word. Lois Elizabeth Ridenour. SoP
Word Made Flesh, The. W. J. Turner. OBMV
Word made flesh is seldom, A. Emily Dickinson. MAmP; MWA-2; NoP
Word of Encouragement, A. J. R. Pope. ELU; FiBHP; PV; SiTL
Word of God, The. Annie Johnson Flint. BLRP
Word of God, The. J. Harold Gwynne. STF
Word of God, The. John Huss. SoP
Word of God, The. Einar Skjaeraasen. *tr. fr. Norwegian by* Martin S. Allwood *and* Inga Wilhelmsen Allwood. HW
Word of God came unto me, The. In the Garden of the Lord. Helen Keller. MaRV; OQP; SoP; TRV; WGRP
Word of God is she whom you love, The. The Word of God. Einar Skjaeraasen. HW
Word of God to Leyden Came, The. Jeremiah Eames Rankin. AA; DD, *abr.*; HBV; MC; OTPC; PAL; PoRL
Word of God which ne'er shall cease, The. The Word of God. John Huss. SoP
Word of mystery is told, A. A Rime of the Rood. Charles L. O'Donnell. GoBC
Word of the Lord by night, The. Boston Hymn. Emerson. AnNE; LaNeLa; MC; MWA-1; PaA; PAH; PAL; TOP; TRV; WGRP
Word of the Lord came unto me, saying, The. Chorus from "The Rock"—III. T. S. Eliot. *Fr.* The Rock. LiTB
Word of the Lord from Havana, The. Richard Hovey. HBV; PAH
Word of the sun to the sky, The. Triads. Swinburne. PoVP
Word of Warning, A. *Unknown.* *See* Pilgrim at Rome, The.
Word of Willow, The. Leah Bodine Drake. FiSC
Word over All. C. Day Lewis. OAEP (2d ed.)
Word over all, beautiful as the sky. Reconciliation. Walt Whitman. AmePo; AnAmPo; AnEnPo; BoLiVe; CoBA; FaBoEn; GTBS-D; MAP; MaRV; MoAmPo; MWA-1; NeMA; NoP; OxBA; PoE; TrGrPo; WaaP
Word Poem (Perhaps Worth Considering). Nikki Giovanni. BOLo
Word shines still, The. For a Christening. Vernon Watkins. MoRP
Word sticks in the wind's throat, A. Apology. Richard Wilbur. NePoAm
Word, The, that came to Jeremiah from the Lord, saying, Stand in the gate of the Lord's house. A Call for True Repentance. Jeremiah, Bible, *O.T.* WoL
Word to a Dictator. Adelaide Love. MaRV
Word to New England, A. William Bradford. SCAP
Word to the Wise, A. Caroline Duer. AA
Word was brought to the Danish king. The King of Denmark's

Word (continued)
Ride. Caroline E. S. Norton. BBV; BeLS; GN; HBV; VA
Word, The, which came to Jeremiah from the Lord, saying, Arise, and go down to the potter's house. The Potter and the Clay. Jeremiah, Bible, *O.T.* WoL
Word with a Skylark, A. Sarah M. B. Piatt. JKCP (1926 ed.)
Words. Stella Benson. MoBrPo (1942 ed.)
Words. Helen Morgan Brooks. NNP; PoNe (1970 ed.)
Words. Will Carleton. OQP
Words. Richard Eberhart. NePA
Words, The. Gene Fowler. ThO
Words. Bernette Golden. TNV
Words. Charles Harpur. BoAu; PoAu-1
Words. Sir Thomas Herbert Parry-Williams, *tr. fr. Welsh by* Gwyn Williams. PrWP
Words. Ernest Rhys. HBMV
Words. Robert Louis Stevenson. *See* Bright Is the Ring of Words.
Words. Edward Thomas. NoP; WePo
Words. Nancy Byrd Turner. TSW
Words ("Boys flying kites haul in. . ."). *Unknown.* PoLF
Words ("Words are things of little cost"). *Unknown.* SoP
Words, The. Opal Whiteley. TSW
Words are deeds. Words. Charles Harpur. BoAu; PoAu-1
Words Are Never Enough. Charles Bruce. CaP; OBCV
Words are things of little cost. Words. *Unknown.* SoP
Words cannot utter. Easter Day. Christina Rossetti. VP
Words curl like fragrant smoke wreaths in the room. Interior. Marjorie Allen Seiffert. NP
Words, "eye," The. Lip Service. Helen G. Quigless. TNV
Words fail me. The ocean travelling stone. The Inlet. Louise Glück. YAP
Words for a Picture of Newlyweds. T'ang Yin, *tr. fr. Chinese by* David Rafael Wang. HW
Words for a Resurrection. Leo Kennedy. OBCV; PeCV
Words, for alas my trade is words, a barren burst of rhyme. To M. E. W. G. K. Chesterton. HBV
Words for Army Bugle Calls. *Unknown.* TreF
Words for Artificers. Claude F. Koch. JKCP (1955 ed.)
Words for Hart Crane. Robert Lowell. AP; CABA; CMoP; NMP
Words for Love. Ted Berrigan. ANYP
Words for the Raker of Leaves. Léonie Adams. PoCh
Words for the Wind. Theodore Roethke. AP; CoAP; FiMAP; PoCh
Words from an Old Spanish Carol. *Unknown, tr. fr. Spanish by* Ruth Sawyer. BrR; ChBR; ChrBoLe
(On Christmas Morn.) FaPON; PDV
Word's gane to the kitchen. Mary Hamilton. *Unknown.* BaBo; ESPB; LO; NoP; OAEP; OuHeWo; PoFS; ViBoFo
Words have grown old inside men, The. The Words Will Resurrect. Jorge de Lima. TTY
Words in the Wilderness. Sister Claude of Jesus. JKCP (1955 ed.)
Words in Time. Archibald MacLeish. CrMA; NePA; PoCh; PoRA
Words, like fine flowers, have their colors too. Words. Ernest Rhys. HBMV
Words Made of Water. Burns Singer. NePoEA-2
Words may well want, both ink and paper fail. Henry Lok. *Fr.* Sonnets of Christian Passions. ReEn; SiCE; Sonn; TuPP
Words move, music moves. T. S. Eliot. *Fr.* Four Quartets: Burnt Norton. UnS; ViBoPo (1958 ed.)
Words of a poem should be glass. Glass. Robert Francis. PP
Words of Agur, The. Proverbs, XXX: 4, 15-16, 18-19, 24-28, Bible, *O.T.* TrGrPo
Words of Finn, The. *Unknown, tr. fr. Old Irish.* ChTr
Words of hymns abruptly plod, The. Hymn. Louise Townsend Nicholl. EaLo
Words of Jesus, The. William Rose Benét. MoRP
Words of the Gods, The. Emerson. *Fr.* My Garden. OQP
Words of the Last Inca. José Eusebio Caro, *tr. fr. Spanish by* Alice Stone Blackwell. PoFr
Words of the Preacher, The. Ecclesiastes, I: 2-11, Bible, *O.T.* TreFS
(Ecclesiastes, I: 1-XII: 14.) WoL
(Vanity of Vanities, I: 2-9.) TrJP
Words on the Windowpane. Dante Gabriel Rossetti. SyP
Words Spoken Alone. Dannie Abse. NYBP
Words that I speak, The. Words. Bernette Golden. TNV
Words, the Words, the Words, The. William Carlos Williams. PoeP
Words to Sleep Upon. Leonora Speyer. NP
Words were meant. Poet's Protest. Doris Hedges. CaP
Words Wherein Stinging Bees Lurk. Judah Halevi, *tr. fr. Hebrew by* Nina Davis Salaman. TrJP
Words Will Resurrect, The. Jorge de Lima, *tr. fr. Portuguese by* John Nist. TTY
Words without Music. Irving Layton. CaP
Words without Music. *Unknown.* WhC
Words! Words! Jessie Fauset. CDC
Words, words and words! What else, when men are dead. Correspondent. Witter Bynner. AnFE; CoAnAm
Words, words, ye are like birds. Prelude. Josephine Preston Peabody. AA
Wordspinning. Olga Kirsch, *tr. fr. Afrikaans by* Jack Cope. PeSA
Wordsworth. William Wilberforce Lord. *Fr.* Ode to England. AA
Wordsworth. James Kenneth Stephen. *See* Sonnet, A: "Two voices are there: one is of the deep."
Wordsworth and the Woman. Reed Whittemore. CBV
Wordsworth I love, his books are like the fields. To Wordsworth. John Clare. ERoP-2; Sonn
Wordsworth to the contrary notwithstanding. In Magic Words. Merrill Moore. Sonn
Wordsworthian Reminiscence. *Unknown.* BOHV; TOP
Wordsworth's Grave. Sir William Watson. EnLit; GoTL; HBV; OBNC; PoVP
Work. Louis James Block. AA
Work. Horatius Bonar. SoP
Work. Abbie Farwell Brown. MaRV
Work. Kenyon Cox. OQP; PGD; PoRL
Work. D. H. Lawrence. OBMV; ShBV-3
(World of Work, as a Poet Would Like It to Be, The.) BoC
Work. James Russell Lowell. *See* Labor.
Work. Pushkin, *tr. fr. Russian by* Babette Deutsch *and* Avrahm Yarmolinsky. AWP; JAWP; WBP
Work. Edwin L. Sabin. DD
Work. J. W. Thompson. PoToHe (new ed.)
Work. Henry van Dyke. *Fr.* The Three Best Things. MaRV; OQP; OTD; PoMa; PoRL; SoP; SP; TIHL; TRV; YT
Work!/ Thank God for the might of it. Work—A Song of Triumph. Angela Morgan. SoP
Work; a Song of Triumph. Angela Morgan. HH; PEDC; PoLF; SoP; YaD
Work all week an' don't make enough. It's Hard on We Po' Farmers. *Unknown.* OuSiCo
Work and Play. Martial, *tr. fr. Latin by* Louis Untermeyer. UnTE
Work-basket made of an old armadillo, A. The Caledonian Market. William Plomer. ChMP; HaMV
Work for Small Men, *sel.* Sam Walter Foss.
"Despise not any man that lives." PoToHe
Work, for the Night Is Coming. Annie L. Coghill. SoP
Work, for the night is coming. Night Cometh. Sidney Dyer. HH
Work Gangs. Carl Sandburg. CoBA
Work Horses. Edith Newlin Chase. SoPo
Work is devout, and service is divine. Worship. Roy Campbell MacFie. OQP
Work Motive. Carlton Buck. SoP
Work of Happiness, The. May Sarton. MoRP
Work of Love, The. Margaret E. Sangster. BLRP
Work Room. Kenward Elmslie. ANYP
Work! That makes the red blood glow. Work. Abbie Farwell Brown. MaRV
Work That Saves, The! Horatius Bonar. BePJ
Work thou for pleasure. Work. Kenyon Cox. OQP; PGD; PoRL
Work while the sun climbeth high in the heaven. A Song of Work. Mary Blake. HH
Work while you work. One Thing at a Time. M. A. Stodart. PoToHe (new ed.)
Work with might and main. For Hire. Morris Jacob Rosenfeld. LiTW
Work Without Hope. Samuel Taylor Coleridge. BEL; BoNaP; CABA; EnLi-2; EnRP; EPN; ERoP-1; FiP; HBV; ILP; LoBV;

MaPo (1969 ed.); MBW-2; NoP; OBEV; OBRV; OQP; PG; Sonn
Sels.
"All Nature seems at work. Slugs leave their lair." YAT, 6 *ll.*
In Springtime. BoTP, 10 *ll.*
Workbox, The. Thomas Hardy. PoeP
Worke is done The: young men, and maidens set. On Himselfe. Robert Herrick. SeCP
Work, work apace, you blessed sisters three. Fidessa, More Chaste than Kind, LI. Bartholomew Griffin. SiCE; TuPP
Worked-out Mine, The. Edward Dyson. BoAu; WoL
Worker, The. Richard W. Thomas. BF; PoNe (1970 ed.)
Workers, The. Mary Blake Woodson. PEDC
Workers earn it. Money. Richard Armour. FaFP; PoPl; PoPo; TreFS; WaKn; WhC
Workers of Ireland, why crouch ye like cravens. New Words to the Tune of "O'Donnel Abu." Jim Connell. OnYI
Workers with Him. A. A. Rees. FaChP
Working Class. Bertram Warr. OBCV; WaP
Working in the Vineyard. Thomas MacKellar. SoP
Working Man's Song, The. John Stuart Blackie. VA
Working Party, A. Siegfried Sassoon. CMoP; MMA
Working people long ago, The. Labor Day. Marnie Pomeroy. PoSC
Working with God. "George Eliot." *Fr.* Stradivarius. MaRV; TRV
Workman. *Unknown. See* From Break of Day.
Workman plied his clumsy spade, A. Two Surprises. R. W. McAlpine. PoLF
Workman with a spade in half a day, A. Pompeian Quatrain: New Excavations. Leonora Speyer. InP
Workmen. Herbert Morris. NePoAm-2
Works and Days, *much abr.* Hesiod, *tr. fr. Greek by* Charles A. Elton. WoL
Works of God, The. Moses ibn Ezra, *tr. fr. Hebrew by* Solomon Solis-Cohen. TrJP
Works of human artifice soon tire, The. Art and Nature. Francisco de Medrano. OnPM
Workshop, The. Aileen Fisher. SoPo
World, The. Francis Bacon. *See* Life.
World, The. Robert Creeley. NaP
World, The. William Drummond of Hawthornden. OBS
World, The. George Herbert. BEL; MaMe; OBS; SCEP-1; SeCL; SeCV-1; SeEP; StJW; TOP
World, The. Thomas Love Peacock. PV
World, The. William Brighty Rands. *See* Wonderful World, The.
World, The. Richard Realf. *See* Word, The.
World, The. Christina Rossetti. Sonn; VP
World, The ("This is the best world"). *Unknown.* ALV
(Best and the Worst, The.) TreFT
World, The. Henry Vaughan. AnAnS-1; AtBAP; ATP; AWP; BEL; BoLiVe; BWP; CABA; CBEP; CBV; CoBE; DiPo; EnL; EnLi-1; EnLit; EP; ExPo; FaBoEn; FaBV; FaPL; FosPo; GoTL; GTBS-W; HBV; ILP; InPo; LiTB; LiTG; LoBV; MaPo; MaRV; MasP; MemP; MeP; MePo; NoP; OAEP; OBS; OuHeWo; OxBoCh; Po; PoAn; PoE; PoEL-2; PoFr, 3 *sts.*; PoFS; PoIE; ReEn; SCEP-1; SeCeV; SeCP; SeCV-1; SeEP; SoP; StP; TOP; TreFS; TrGrPo; ViBoPo; WGRP; WoL
(Eternity, *abr.*) OBEV (new ed.)
"I saw eternity the other night," *first* 7 *ll.* ImOP
(Vision, A.) BBV; GTSL
World, The. Wordsworth. *See* World Is Too Much with Us, The.
World, The; a Child's Song. William Brighty Rands. *See* Wonderful World, The.
World, The; a Ghazel. James Clarence Mangan. OBVV
World a Hunt, The. William Drummond of Hawthornden. *See* This World a Hunting Is.
World an Illusion, The. *Unknown.* MeEL
World and Soul. George MacDonald. *See* This Infant World.
World and the Quietist, The. Matthew Arnold. VA
World as Meditation, The. Wallace Stevens. AP; BWP; MaPo (1969 ed.); MoAB; PoeP
World Beautiful, The. Milton. *Fr.* Paradise Lost, IV. GN
World below the Brine, The. Walt Whitman. AmLP; BoNaP; CBV; NePA; NoP; PoE
World-besieging storm, from horizon heaped and menacing. Laurence Binyon. The Sirens, III, 4. GoTL (1949 ed.)
World Beyond, A. Nathaniel Ingersoll Bowditch. AA
World beyond World. Arthur Davison Ficke. NP
World-Brotherhood. *Unknown. See* My Country Is the World.
World Can Neither Give Nor Take, The. Selina, Countess of Huntingdon. SoP
World Comes Galloping, The; a True Story. Robert Penn Warren. Mexico Is a Foreign Country, III. FiMAP
World Comes Not to an End, The. Robert Bridges. CMoP; Sonn
World Conqueror. Laura Simmons. *See* I Have Overcome the World.
World, Defined. Edward Weismiller. AnAmPo
World did say to me, The. The Crazy World. William Gay. BoAu; BoAV; PoAu-1
World doesn't crumble apart, The. Watershed. Margaret Avison. OBCV
World-dwellers all give heed to what I say. Psalm XLIX. Countess of Pembroke. EP
World feels dusty, The. Emily Dickinson. MAP; MoAmPo
World for Love, A. John Clare. PG
World Goes None the Lamer, The. A. E. Housman. PeVV
World Goes Turning, The. George Dillon. AmLP
World goes up and the world goes down, The. Dolcino to Margaret. Charles Kingsley. PoVP
World had grown too complicated, so, The. Retort to the Anti-Abstractionists. Elizabeth Jennings. BoPe
World Has Held Great Heroes, The. Kenneth Grahame. *Fr.* The Wind in the Willows. RePo
(Song of Mr. Toad, The.) FaPON; FiBHP; GoJo
World has room for the manly man, with the spirit of manly cheer, The. The Manly Man. *Unknown.* BLPA; WBLP
World hath conquered, the wind hath scattered like dust, The. Tara Is Grass. *Unknown, tr. by* Padraic Pearse. AnIL; AnIV
World hath its own dead, The; great motions start. Edith Cavell. George Edward Woodberry. HBMV
World Hymn, The. J. Gilchrist Lawson. WBLP
World I Am Passing Through, The. Lydia Maria Child. AA; HBV
World I Have Not Made. Elizabeth Jennings. ACV
World I See, The. Mari Evans. Kal
World in Armor, The. Sir William Watson. PoVP
World in Making, The. Sir Gilbert Parker. CaP
World Is a Bundle of Hay, The. Byron. EnRP
World is a gift again, The. Spring Workman. Alan Creighton. CaP; TwCaPo
World Is a Mighty Ogre, The. Fenton Johnson. AmNP
World is a well-furnished table, The. The World. Thomas Love Peacock. PV
World is all orange-round, The. The Walking Road. Richard Hughes. OBMV
World is an inn, if you please so to term it, The. Neighbors. Arthur Guiterman. OTD
World is born ahead of me, The. O mine own twin! The First Born. Oscar Williams. GTBS-W
World is charged with the grandeur of God, The. God's Grandeur. Gerard Manley Hopkins. AnFE; AWP; BBV (1951 ed.); BoC; BrPo; BWP; CABA; CaFP; CBV; CMoP; CoBE; DiPo; EnLi-2; EnLit; ExPo; FaChP; FaFP; ForPo; FosPo; GTBS-D; GTBS-W; ILP; InPo; InvP; LiTB; LiTG; LiTM; LoBV; MaPo; MoAB; MoBrPo; MoPo; MoRP; MoVE; NoP; OBNC; OxBoCh; PAn; PeVV; PG (1955 ed.); Po; PoDB; PoE; PoeP; PoIE; PoLi; PoPo; PoVP; ReMP; SeCeV; Sonn; SoP; StP; TDP; TIHL; TrGrPo; TreFT; ViPP; VP
World is cold and gray and wet, The. Young Love. Sara Teasdale. BoLP
World is dull, the world is blind, The. Die Welt ist dumm, die Welt ist blind. Heine. AWP; OnPM
World is fleeting; all things pass away, The. Passing Away. Lucian. WoL
World is full of colour, The! Colour. Adeline White. BoTP
World , is full of loss The; bring, wind, my love. Song. Muriel Rukeyser. MiAP
World Is Full of Remarkable Things, The. LeRoi Jones. BF; BP
World is full of wistful ones who hoard their souvenirs, The. Ballad of Culinary Frustration. Phyllis McGinley. FiBHP

World (continued)
World is full of women's eyes, The. Women's Eyes. Bhartrihari. OnPM
World is full of wonderful smells, The. Zhenya Gay. TiPo (1959 ed.)
World is great, The: the birds all fly from me. I Am Lonely. "George Eliot." *Fr.* The Spanish Gypsy. GN; HBV
World is grown old, and her pleasures are past, The. The Judgment Is Near. Reginald Heber. SoP
World is heated seven times, The. A Night in June. Duncan Campbell Scott. OBCV
World is hollow like a pumpkin shell, The. Truth. Jessica Nelson North. HBVY; NP
World is in a mess today, The. Song about Whiskers. P. G. Wodehouse. FiBHP
World is in the Valley of Decision, The. The Valley of Decision. John Oxenham. PGD
World is intricate, and we are nothing, The. Preludes for Memnon, L. Conrad Aiken. NoP
World Is like a Woman of Folly, The. Moses ibn Ezra, *tr. fr. Hebrew by* Solomon Solis-Cohen. *Fr.* The World's Illusion. TrJP
World Is Mine, The. Florence Earle Coates. *See* Song: "For me the jasmine buds unfold."
World is no longer good, The. Chorus from a Tragedy. Leonard Bacon. ViBoPo
World Is One, The. Hinton White. MaRV; OQP
World is Rome, The; Carnuntum, on the Danube. Marcus Antoninus Cui Cognoment Erat Aurelius. Burns Singer. OxBS
World is sick, The. Sick. Haldor Lillenas. SoP
World is sick, and we sick men, The. Hospital Ward (of This Generation). George Rostrevor Hamilton. POTE
World is so full of a number of things, The. Happy Thought. Robert Louis Stevenson. BoTP; FaBoBe; HBV; HBVY; InP; OTPC; PoVP; RIS; SAS; TiPo; TreFS
World is something I must try, The. Tragedy. Mark Van Doren. NePoAm-2
"World is such a funny place, The." Relativity. Kathleen Millay. PoMa
World is the Inn at Bethlehem, The. Query. Lucia Trent. ChIP
World Is Too Much with Us, The. Wordsworth. AnFE; AWP; BEL; BoLiVe; CABA; CaFP; CBEP; CBV; ChTr; CoBE; DD; DiPo; EG; EnL; EnLi-2; EnLit; EnRP; EPN; ERoP-1; ExPo; FaBoEn; FaFP; FiP; GTBS; GTBS-D; GTBS-P; GTBS-W; GTSE; GTSL; HBV; HBVY; HoPM; ILP; InP; InPo; JAWP; LiTB; LiTG; MaPo; MaRV; MBW-2; MCCG; MERP; NoP; OAEP; OBNC; OBRV; OQP; OTD; OTPC (1923 ed.); OuHeWo; PAn; PoAn; PoE; PoEL-4; PoeP; PoFS; PoIE; PoLF; PoMa; PoRA; PPON; SeCeV; StP; TIHL; TOP; TreF; TrGrPo; ViBoPo; WBP; WGRP; WHA; YAT
(Sonnet.) ChER; GBV; LoBV; OHFP; ShBV-4; Sonn
(World, The.) BBV (1923 ed.); OBEV
World Narrowed to a Point, The. William Carlos Williams. MoLP
World is very evil, The. The Celestial Country. Bernard of Cluny, *tr. by* John Mason Neale. *Fr.* De Contemptu Mundi. GoBC
World is very flat, The. Night Thought of a Tortoise Suffering from Insomnia on a Lawn. E. V. Rieu. FiBHP
World Is Waiting for You, The. S. S. Calkins. PEDC
World is weaned from this one dead by the thread of a shawl, The. The Spoils of War. Vernon Watkins. WaP
World is well amended with Sir Hugh, The. Asperius Nihil Est Humili Cum Surgat in Altum. Henry Parrot. SiCE
World is white with cherry-trees, The. June. Wilson MacDonald. CaP
World is wide, The. On Life's Way [*or* Worry]. Charles F. Deems. MaRV; OQP
World is with me, and its many cares, The. Thomas Hood. Sonn
World is young to-day, The. Song. Digby Mackworth Dolben. LoBV; OBNC
World Looks On, The. Louis Newman. PoNe (1970 ed.)
World Man, The. Henry Victor Morgan. OQP
World Morose, The. Frederick William Faber. *See* Mundus Morosus.
World Music. Frances Louisa Bushnell. AA
World-Nation, A. Earl B. Marlatt. MaRV
World Needs, The. *Unknown.* PoToHe (new ed.)
World, not hush'd, lay as in a trance, The. Old Souls. Thomas Gordon Hake. VA
World of dew, The. Haiku. Issa. CaFP
World of Dream, The. Walter de la Mare. GaP
World of Dreams, The, *sel.* George Crabbe.
"I sail the sea, I walk the land." PeER
World of fools has such a store, The. Epigram. *Unknown.* ALV
World of Light, A. Elizabeth Jennings. NePoEA-2
World of Light, The. Henry Vaughan. *See* They Are All Gone.
World of mightie kings and princes I could name, A. Michael Drayton. *Fr.* Polyolbion: Twentieth Song. OBS
World of Sleep, The. Keats. *See* To Sleep.
World of stars and space being His bauble, The. Receiving Communion. Vassar Miller. NePoEA-2
World of the Lord came unto me saying, The. T. S. Eliot. *Fr.* The Rock. TRV
World of Work, as a Poet Would Like It to Be, The. D. H. Lawrence. *See* Work.
World Planners. Arvel Steece. PGD
World-Ruin. Hugh Wilgus Ramsaur. MaRV
World Secret. Hugo von Hofmannsthal, *tr. fr. German.* LiTW, *tr. by* Werner Heider; TrJP, *tr. by* Charles Wharton Stork
World shines bright for inexperienced eyes, The. A Thought from Cardinal Newman. Matthew Russell. CAW; JKCP
World Sits at the Feet of Christ, The. Whittier. *Fr.* The Over-Heart. ChIP; MaRV; TRV
World-Soul, The. Emerson. AmePo; MWA-1
We Are Never Old, *sel.* OQP; PoRL
World stands out on either side, The. Edna St. Vincent Millay. *Fr.* Renascence. MaRV
World State, The. G. K. Chesterton. CoBE; PoPo
World still goeth about to show and hide, The. Robert Bridges. *Fr.* The Growth of Love. PoVP
World Still Young, A. W. E. Henley. MeWo
(Birds in April.) YT
World-Strangeness. Sir William Watson. MoBrPo (1942 ed.); PoVP
World, that all contains, is ever moving, The. Caelica, VII. Fulke Greville. EnRePo; OBSC; ReIE; SiCE; TuPP
World, that cannot deem of worthy things, The. Amoretti, LXXXIV. Spenser. ReEn
World to Do, A. Theodore Weiss. SiSw
World Transformed, The. Whittier. *Fr.* Snow-bound. AA
("Unwarmed by any sunset light.") BBV; GBV
World Turned Upside Down, The. *Unknown.* PAH
World turns and its turning wheels, The. The Epistemological Rag. Gray Burr. CoPo
World turns and the world changes, The. T. S. Eliot. *Fr.* The Rock. TiPo
World turns softly, The. Water. Hilda Conkling. ExPo; NP; PDV; TiPo
World under the sky, The. A Gone. Larry Eigner. NeAP
World uprose as a man to find Him, The. At the End of Things. Arthur Edward Waite. WGRP
World Wants Men, The. *Unknown.* PEDC
World War. Richard Eberhart. WaP
World War I. *Unknown.* FaFP; SiTL
World War III. *Unknown.* SiTL
World War II. *Unknown.* SiTL
World Wars. *Unknown.* TreFT
World was first a private park, The. The Fisherman. Jay Macpherson. PeCV
World was flat, lawn without end, The. Out of Bounds. Jon Stallworthy. TPM
World was made when a man was born, The. Experience. John Boyle O'Reilly. ACP; OBVV
World was wide when I was young, The. Troia Fuit. Reginald Wright Kauffman. HBV
World We Make, The. Alfred Grant Walton. PoToHe (new ed.)
World Well Lost, The. Dryden. *See* Conversion ("Be vengeance wholly left . . .").
World Well Lost, The. Edmund Clarence Stedman. AA
World will find no pity in your pages, The. Siegfried Sassoon. *Fr.* On Reading the War Diary of a Defunct Ambassador. PoFr
World will not be understood, The. Comedy. Mark Van Doren. NePoAm-2

World within a War, A. Sir Herbert Read. MoPo
World without End. Catullus, *tr. fr. Latin by* E. A. Havelock. LiTW
World without Objects Is a Sensible Emptiness, A. Richard Wilbur. FiMAP; LiTM (1970 ed.); MoAmPo (1962 ed.); Po
World without Pain, A. Emily May Young. SoP
Worldly Hope, The. ("The worldly hope men set their hearts upon"). Omar Khayyám, *tr. fr. Persian by* Edward Fitzgerald. *Fr.* The Rubáiyát. MaRV
(Like Snow.) OnPM
Worldly matters again draw my steps [*or* body]. To Li Chien. Po Chü-i. LiTW
Worldly Place. Matthew Arnold. EPN; PoVP
Worldly possessions? 'twas easy to find them. Tora's Song. Knut Hamsun. PoPl
Worldly prince doth in his scepter hold, The. Nicholas Breton. *Fr.* The Soul's Harmony. SiCE
Worldly Vanity. Dryden. *See* Conversion ("Be vengeance wholly left . . .").
Worldly Wisdom. Omar Khayyám, *tr. fr. Persian by* Edward Fitzgerald. *Fr.* The Rubáiyát. MaRV
(Great Argument.) OnPM
("Myself when young did eagerly frequent.") EaLo; EG; WGRP
World's a bubble, and the Life of Man, The. Life [*or* The World *or* In Vitam Humanam.] Francis Bacon. ElL; GTBS; GTBS-D; GTBS-P; GTBS-W; GTSE; HBV; OBSC; PoIE; TreFT; WHA
World's a floore, whose swelling heapes retaine, The. Francis Quarles. *Fr.* Emblems. AnAnS-1; MeP
World's a garden, The; pleasures are the flowers. The Garden. Joshua Sylvester. CBEP
World's a Sea, The. Francis Quarles. ChTr
World's a sorry wench, akin, The. The Jester's Plea. Frederick Locker-Lampson. CenHV
World's a theater, the earth a stage, which God, The. The Author to His Booke. Thomas Heywood. *Fr.* An Apology for Actors. OBS
World's a very happy place, The. The World's Music. "Gabriel Setoun." FaBoBe; HBV; HBVY; HH; MPB; OTPC; PRWS; TVC
World's a weary place, The. All thro' the Year. *Unknown.* BLRP
World's a well strung fiddle, mans tongue the quill, The. Nathaniel Ward. SCAP
World's Advance, The. George Meredith. EPN
World's Bible, The. Annie Johnson Flint. FaChP; SoP; STF; TRV
(Christ—and We.) MaRV
(Jesus Christ—and We.) OQP
World's Bright Comforter, The. Barnabe Barnes. *Fr.* A Divine Century of Spiritual Sonnets. OxBoCh
(God's Virtue.) BoPe; OBSC
(Sonnet: "World's bright comforter, whose beamsome light, The.") ElL
("World's bright comforter, whose beamsome light, The.") SiCE
World's Centre, The. Ruth Dallas. AnNZ
World's Death-Night, The. James Chapman Woods. VA
World's Desire, The. William Rose Benét. TrPWD
World's End. G. K. Chettur. ACV
World's End, The. William Empson. CoBMV; MoVE; ToPo
World's End, The. Michael Roberts. FaBoMo
World's gone forward to its latest fair, The. The Moor. Ralph Hodgson. MoBrPo
World's Great Age Begins Anew, The. Shelley. *See* Chorus: "World's great age begins anew, The."
World's great heart, whence all things strange and rare, The. The Death of Richard Wagner. Swinburne. LoBV
World's Greatest Tricycle Rider, The. C. K. Williams. NYBP
World's Illusion, The. Moses ibn Ezra, *tr. fr. Hebrew by* Solomon Solis-Cohen. TrJP
All Ye That Go Astray, II.
He That Regards the Precious Things of Earth, IV.
In Vain Earth Decks Herself, VI.
Promises of the World, The, III.
World Is like a Woman of Folly, The, I.
Ye Anger Earth, V.
World's Justice, The. Emma Lazarus. HBV
Worlds light shines, shine as it will, The. But Men Loved Darknesse Rather Then Light. Richard Crashaw. MaMe
World's Lone Lover, The. J. R. Perkins. ChIP
World's May Queen, The. Alfred Noyes. *See* When Spring Comes Back to England.
World's Miser, The. Theodore Maynard. CAW; JKCP; MoBrPo (1942 ed.)
World's Music, The. "Gabriel Setoun." FaBoBe; HBV; HBVY; HH; MPB; OTPC; PRWS; TVC
Worlds on Worlds Are Rolling Ever. Shelley. *See* Chorus: "Worlds on worlds are rolling ever."
World's So Big, The. Aileen Fisher. SoPo
World's so wide I cannot cross it, The. Fond Affection. *Unknown.* AS
World's Wanderers, The. Shelley. BEL; EnLit; EPN; ViBoPo
World's Way, The. Thomas Bailey Aldrich. HBV; LHV
World's Way, The. Shakespeare. *See* Sonnets, LXVI.
World's Wonders, The. Robinson Jeffers. NePA; PoDB
World's Worst Boxer, The. Lucilius, *tr. fr. Greek by* Humbert Wolfe. SD
World's Worth. Dante Gabriel Rossetti. GoBC; PoVP
Worlds, you must tell me. Round. Louis Untermeyer. WhC
Worm, The. Ralph Bergengren. FaPON; SiSoSe; UTS
Worm, The. Blake. *Fr.* The Book of Thel. FIW
Worm, The. Elizabeth Madox Roberts. BoChLi; GFA; UTS; YT
Worm, The. Raymond Souster. WHW
Worm, The. Ann Taylor. PCH; PPL; SAS
Worm cries not against the storm, The. Microcosmos, XVII. Nigel Heseltine. NeBP
Worm Fed on the Heart of Corinth, A. Isaac Rosenberg. AtBAP; BrPo; MoPo
Worm in the Whirling Cross, The. John Malcolm Brinnin. MoPo
Worm unto his love, The: lo, here's fresh store. The Coffin-Worm. Ruth Pitter. MoBrPo; TrGrPo (1942 ed.)
Worm within the Rose, A. Tennyson. *Fr.* Idylls of the King: Pelleas and Etarre. PAn
("Rose, A, but one, none other rose had I.") PoEL-5
Worms and the Wind. Carl Sandburg. OA; WaKn
Worms at Heaven's Gate, The. Wallace Stevens. NP
Worms begin to drop unceasingly. The Flesh. Tiroux Yamanaka. LiTW
Worms of History, The. Robert Graves. MoPo
Worms would rather be worms. Worms and the Wind. Carl Sandburg. OA; WaKn
Wormwood. Sappho, *tr. fr. Greek by* Randolph Shaffer, Jr. WoL
Worn with the battle, by Stamford town. Saxon Grit. Robert Collyer. HBV; OTPC (1923 ed.)
Worried Skipper, The. Wallace Irwin. BLPA
Worries. Jules Supervielle, *tr. fr. French by* Glauco Cambon. OnPM
Worries. *Unknown.* PoToHe (new ed.)
Worry. Charles F. Deems. *See* On Life's Way.
Worry. George W. Swarberg. STF
Worry. *Unknown.* PoToHe (new ed.)
Worry about Money. Kathleen Raine. FaBoTw
Worry—is like a distant hill. Worry. *Unknown.* PoToHe (new ed.)
Worschippe ye that loveris bene this May. *See* Worshipe, ye that lovers been, this May.
"Worse than the sunflower," she had said. The Ecclesiast. John Ashbery. ANYP
Worship. Emerson. MWA-1
Worship. Henry W. Frost. SoP
Worship. Ruth Furbee. MaRV
Worship. Bob Jones, Jr. BePJ
Worship, *sel.* William Wilberforce Lord.
"For them, O God who only worship." AA
Worship. Roy Campbell MacFie. OQP
Worship. Shelley. *Fr.* One Word Is Too Often Profaned. MaRV
Worship. Robert Whitaker. TrPWD
Worship and Thanks to Him Belong. Robert A. West. SoP
Worship of virtu is the mede. A Carol of St. George. *Unknown.* MeEL
Worship the Lord in the Beauty of Holiness. John S. B. Monsell. MaRV
Worship the Lord, the God of wild cold kind. The Lord in the Wind. James Picot. PoAu-2

Worship the summer sun. Solstices. Richard Church. POTE
Worshipe [*or* Worschippe], ye that lovers been [*or* loveris bene], this May. Spring Song of the Birds. James I, King of Scotland. *Fr.* The Kingis Quair. OBEV; TrGrPo
Worshiper, The. Vassar Miller. NePoEA-2
Worsley Enchanted, *sels.* Douglas Stewart.
"It's cold, says Crean at the tiller," VI. NeLNL
"White, said Worsley, and glistening, the ridgy plain," II. NeLNL
Worst, The. *Unknown, tr. fr. Spanish by* Havelock Ellis. OnPM
Worst burn is to come, The. Post-War. Eileen Duggan. AnNZ
Worst camp-life man ever lived, The. Monsieur Pipereau. James Whaler. MAP; MoAmPo (1942 ed.)
Worst of all diseases, The. Sin and Its Cure. *Unknown.* STF
Worst Treason, The. Victor Hugo, *tr. fr. French by* Henry Carrington. PoFr
Worth Makes the Man. Pope. *Fr.* An Essay on Man, Epistle IV. MaRV
("Honor [*or* Honour] and shame from no condition rise.") PoFr; TrGrPo
(Man.) BoLiVe
Worth of Prayer, The. Benjamin Beddome. SoP
Worthington, *with music.* *Unknown.* AS
Worthless Heart, The. Immanuel di Roma, *tr. fr. Hebrew.* TrJP
Worth While. Ella Wheeler Wilcox. BLPA; PoToHe; TreF
Worthwhile Things Are Free. Charles R. Glazer. SoP
Worthy Fool, A. Shakespeare. *See* Motley's the Only Wear.
Worthy kyng, quhen he has seyn, The. Before Bannockburn. John Barbour. *Fr.* The Bruce. OxBS
Worthy London prentice, A. The London Prentice. *Unknown.* CoMu; UnTE
Worthy of adoration, The. The Angelic Vilancete. Gil Vicente. *Fr.* The Auto of the Four Seasons. CAW
Worthy woman from beside Bath city, A. The Wife of Bath. Chaucer. *Fr.* The Canterbury Tales. WePo
Wot a marf 'e'd got. Epitaph on a Marf. *Unknown.* PV
"Wot's in a name?" she sez . . . An' then she sighs. The Play. C. J. Dennis. *Fr.* The Sentimental Bloke. PoAu-1
Wotton, my little bere dwells on a hill. Ad Henricum Wottonem. Thomas Bastard. SiCE
Wotton, the country and the country swain. Ad Henricum Wottonum. Thomas Bastard. SiCE
Woud ye hear of William Wallace. Gude Wallace (G *vers.*) *Unknown.* ESPB
Wou'd you in love succeed, be brisk, be gay. The Advice. Charles Sackville. PeRV
"Would a man 'scape the rod?" Ben Karshook's Wisdom. Robert Browning. PoVP
Would any deem Dacus were now the man. Henry Parrot. SiCE
Would any one the true cause find. Out of the Italian. Richard Crashaw. MaMe
Would bounteous Heaven one more indulge, I'd choose. John Pomfret. *Fr.* The Choice. LO
Would God I in that Golden City were. Meditation XXIII. Edward Taylor. *Fr.* Preparatory Meditations, First Series. MAmP
Would God my heart were greater; but God wot. Chastelard and Mary Stuart. Swinburne. *Fr.* Chastelard. VA
Would God my pen might be your trump of fame. The Praise of Our Soldiers. Thomas Churchyard. TuPP
Would God That It Were Holiday! Thomas Deloney. *Fr.* The Gentle Craft. ElL
Would God the route would come for home. The Frontier. John Masefield. NP
Would I again were with you!—O ye dales. That Delightful Time. Mark Akenside. *Fr.* The Pleasure of the Imagination. SeCePo
Would I Be Called a Christian? Mrs. J. F. Moser. STF
Would I Be Shrived? Villon, *tr. fr. French by* John Swain. BLPA
Would I could cast a sail on the water. The Collar-Bone of a Hare. W. B. Yeats. AtBAP; EnL; NP
Would I describe a preacher, such as Paul. Preachers: The True vs. the Insincere. William Cowper. *Fr.* The Task, II. MaRV; TRV
Would I for All That Were. Sun-Ra. BF
Would I had met you in my days of strength. Y Is for Youth. W. H. Davies. BoPe
Would I Had Stayed. Princess Oku, *tr. fr. Japanese by* Ishii *and* Obata. OnPM
Would I Might Go Far over Sea. Marie de France, *tr. fr. French by* Arthur O'Shaughnessy. AWP; JAWP; OuHeWo; PoRA; WBP
Would I might mend the fabric of my youth. Welt. Georgia Douglas Johnson. BANP
Would I Might Rouse the Lincoln in You All. Lincoln. Vachel Lindsay. *Fr.* Litany of the Heroes. LiPo; OHIP; PoSC
Would I might wake Saint Francis in you all. St. Francis [*or* Franciscan Aspiration]. Vachel Lindsay. *Fr.* Litany of the Heroes. CAW; MoRP; OQP
Would I were a king of children. The Child-King. Morris Wintchevsky. TrJP
Would I were on the sea-lands. The Sea-Lands. Orrick Johns. HBV
Would it not be a foolish thing. Bible Study. Martha Snell Nicholson. FaChP
Would my love were a bracelet! Love's Fancy. Tamuke. OnPM
Would some little joy today. A Song of Sighing. James Thomson. EnLit
Would that I had stayed. Would I Had Stayed. Princess Oku. OnPM
Would that I streamed like water. Like Water down a Slope. Zalman Schneour. TrJP
Would That I Were. Arthur Hugh Clough. TrPWD
Would that my father had taught me the craft of a keeper of sheep. The Craft of a Keeper of Sheep. Moschus. AWP
Would that swift ships had never been; for so. Loss at Sea. Callimachus. OnPM
Would that the structure brave, the manifold music I build. Abt Vogler. Robert Browning. BEL; CoBE; DiPo; EPN; GoTL; HBV; MBW-2; NoP; OAEP; PoVP; TOP; VA; ViPo; ViPP; VP; WGRP
Would the lark sing the sweeter if he knew. An Open Secret. Caroline Atherton Briggs Mason. AA
Would we could coin for thee new words of praise. Washington's Tomb. Ruth Lawrence. OHIP
Would Wisdom for herself be wooed. The Joyful Wisdom. Coventry Patmore. The Angel in the House, I, x, 1. HBV
Would ye have fresh cheese and cream? Fresh Cheese and Cream. Robert Herrick. UnTE
Would You Be a Man of [*or* in] Fashion? *Unknown.* ALV; SeCL; SeEP
Would you be young again? Heavenward. Lady Nairne. HBV
Would You Believe? Tuli Kupferberg. WOW
Would you believe, when you this monsieur see. On English Monsieur. Ben Jonson. NoP
Would you end war? Create Great Peace. James Oppenheim. *Fr.* 1914—and After. MaRV
Would you have a young virgin of fifteen years. What's Your Fancy. *Unknown.* UnTE
Would you have freedom from wage-slavery? There Is Power in a Union. *Unknown, at. to* Joe Hill. ThLM
Would you hear of an old-time sea-fight? An Old-Time Sea-Fight [*or* John Paul Jones]. Walt Whitman. Song of Myself, XXXV. CoBA; MaC; OnMSP; PAL; SeCeV; TrGrPo; UnPo (3d ed.)
Would you hear of the River-Fight? Henry Howard Brownell *Fr.* The River Fight. AA; EtS
Would You in Venus' Wars Succeed. *Unknown.* ErPo
Would you know what's soft? I dare. Song. Thomas Carew. BEL; EG; EnLi-1; TOP
Would you like to see a city given over. The City of Golf. Robert Fuller Murray. SD
Would you like to sin. *Unknown.* PV
Would you make blazes. Ultra-Germano-Criticasterism. Leigh Hunt. PP
Would you resembled the metal you work with. Reflections in an Iron Works. "Hugh MacDiarmid." NAMP
Would you see the little men. The Little Men. Flora Fearne. BoTP
Would you see the marks of the Roman Scourge. Jesus of Nazareth. Ernest Cadman Colwell. ChIP; MaRV
Would you tell me the way to Somewhere? Somewhere. Walter de la Mare. BrR

Would you win all the world for Christ? To Win the World. John Oxenham. MaRV
Wouldn't it be lovely if the rain came down. Very Lovely. Rose Fyleman. GFA; SoPo; TiPo
Wouldn't it be wonderful to come across in cabaret. Unromantic Song. Anthony Brode. FiBHP
Wouldn't this old world be better. I Know Something Good about You. *Unknown.* BLPA; PoToHe
Wouldn't we have the nicest pets. Our Pets. Esther Antin. *Fr.* On Our Farm. RIS
Wouldn't You after a Jaunt of 964,000,000,000,000 Million Miles? Kenneth Patchen. HYE
Wouldn't you like to be a whale. Whale. Geoffrey Dearmer. BoTP
Wouldn't You Like to Know. John Godfrey Saxe. HBV
Wouldn't you say,/ Wouldn't you say: one day. One Almost Might. A. S. J. Tessimond. ChMP
Wouldst know the artist? Then go seek. Art. Lilla Cabot Perry. AA
Wouldst know the lark? A Listener's Guide to the Birds. E. B. White. NYBP
Wouldst thou be wise, O Man? At the knees of a woman begin. Wilfrid Scawen Blunt. *Fr.* The Wisdom of Merlyn. OBMV
Wouldst thou fashion for thyself a seemly life? Live Each Day. Goethe. OQP
Wouldst thou find my ashes? The Immortal Residue. Adelaide Crapsey. MaRV; MoAmPo (1942 ed.)
Would'st thou hear [*or* heare], what man can say. Epitaph on Elizabeth, L. H. Ben Jonson. AnAnS-2; CABA; EIL; ELP; EnL; EnLi-1 (1949 ed.); EnRePo; ForPo; HBV; InPo; NoP; OBEV; OBS; PoE; PoIE; ReEn; ReIE; SCEP-2; SeCP; SeCV-1; SeEP; TreFT; TuPP; ViBoPo; WHA
Would'st thou know nature in her better part. Eclogue, III. Thomas Chatterton. PeER
Wouldst thou live long? The only means are these. He Lives Long Who Lives Well. Thomas Randolph. WBLP
Wound, The. Thom Gunn. NePoEA
Wound-Dresser, The. Walt Whitman. AmePo; AmPP (5th ed.); AP; CoBA; MWA-1; ViBoPo
Wound Love gave me th'other day, The. *Unknown.* SeCSL
Wound which the dragon had dealt him began, The. Beowulf's Death. *Unknown.* *Fr.* Beowulf. AnOE
Wounded, The. Louise Louis. GoYe
Wounded Cupid, The. Robert Herrick, *after the Greek of* Anacreon. AWP
Wounded deer leaps highest, A. Emily Dickinson. AP; AWP; InPo; JAWP; NoP; WBP
Wounded Hare, The. Burns. OTPC
Wounded Hawk, The. Herbert Palmer. FaBoTw; HaMV
Wounded I sing, tormented I indite. Josephs Coat. George Herbert. MaMe; SCEP-1
Wounded Person, The. Walt Whitman. *Fr.* Song of Myself, XXXIII. PoNe
Wounded wilderness of Morris Graves, The. A Coney Island of the Mind, 11. Lawrence Ferlinghetti. NeAP
Wounded with love and piercing deep desire. Unable by Long and Hard Travel to Banish Love, Returns Her Friend. George Turberville. TuPP
Wounds of Jesus, The. Cecil J. Allen. SoP
Wow, but your letter made me vauntie! Epistle to Dr. Blacklock, Ellisland, Oct., 1789. Burns. OBEC
Wrack. Irving Feldman. AmPC
Wrack was dark an' shiny where it floated in the sea, The. Sea Wrack. "Moira O'Neill." OnYI
Wraggle Taggle Gipsies, The (*diff. versions*). *Unknown.* BoTP; CH; LiTL; OnSP; OtMeF; PCD; ThWaDe
(Black Jack Davy [*or* Davie].) BaBo; BFSS, *with music;* OuSiCo, *with music*
("Gipsies came to the good Squire's gate, The.") LO
(Gipsy [*or* Gypsy] Laddie, The.) BaBo (A, B, *and* C *vers.*); ESPB; FaBoCh; LoGBV; OxBoLi; SiTL; ViBoFo (A *and* B *vers.*)
(Gypsy Davy, 2 *sts., with music.*) AS
(Jackie Faa.) ChTr
(Johnie Faa.) BuBa
(Johnny Faa, the Gypsy Laddie.) AtBAP
(Johnny Faa, the Lord of Little Egypt.) EnSB
(Johny Faa.) *Unknown.* OxBB
(Raggle, Taggle Gypsies, The.) CBEP; FaPON; GoTP; MPB; StVeCh; TiPo (1952 ed.)
(Wraggle Taggle Gipsies, O!, The.) EvOK; SaSa *with music;* ShBV-1; WiR
Wraith-Friend, The. George Barker. OBMV
Wrangle up your mouth-harps, drag your banjo out. The Bunk-House Orchestra. Badger Clark. SCC
Wrap her hair in golden cloths. Of One Dead. Leo Kennedy. PeCV
Wrap Me Up in My Tarpaulin Jacket, *with music. Unknown.* AS
(Sailors.) OuSiCo
Wrap up in a blanket in cold weather and just read. Things to Do around a Lookout. Gary Snyder. NaP
Wrap your sulky beauty up. Water Music. Lawrence Durrell. TPM
Wrapped in a cloak. Fog, the Magician. Melville Cane. MoSiPe
Wrapped in a yielding air, beside. As He Is. W. H. Auden. MoPo
Wrapped in his shroud of wax, his swoon of wounds. Poem for Easter. Laurie Lee. BoC
Wrapped Up in an Indian Blanket. John Wieners. FRC
Wrapped [*or* Wrapt] up, O Lord, in man's degeneration. Caelica, XCVIII. Fulke Greville. EnRePo; EP; ForPo; OxBoCh; QFR; SiCE
Wrapt in my careless cloak, as I walk to and fro. Earl of Surrey. FCP; SiPS
Wrath. John Hollander. PV
Wrath of Achilles, The, *abr.* Homer, *tr. fr. Greek by* Bryant. *Fr.* The Iliad, XIX. BBV (1923 ed.)
Wrath of Lester Lame Bull, The. James Welch. YAP
Wrathful winter, 'proaching on apace, The. Induction to "The Mirror for Magistrates" [*or* The Complaint of Henrie Duke of Buckinghame *or* Winter *or* The Approach of Winter]. Thomas Sackville. BEL; EIL; OBSC; Po; PoEL-1; ReEn; ReIE; SeCePo; SiCE; TuPP
Wreath, A, *sel.* William Baylebridge.
"When tongues will tax me in the public ear." BoAV
Wreath, A. George Herbert. MaMe; SCEP-1; SeCP
Wreath, The. Henry Vaughan. SCEP-1
Wreath for Heliodora. Meleager. *See* Garland for Heliodora, A.
Wreath for One Lost, A. Harold Vinal. FiSC
Wreath of flowers as cold as snow, A. The Birth. Rosemary Dobson. PoAu-2
Wreath that star-crowned Shelley gave, The. After a Lecture on Keats. Oliver Wendell Holmes. AA; ViBoPo
Wreathe no more lilies in my hair. The Summer Is Ended. Christina Rossetti. HBV
Wreathe the Bowl. Thomas Moore. HBV
Wreathed garland of deserved praise, A. A Wreath. George Herbert. MaMe SCEP-1; SeCP
Wreck, The. John Ruskin. VA
Wreck of Number Nine, The, *with music. Unknown.* BFSS
Wreck of the *Deutschland,* The. Gerard Manley Hopkins. AtBAP; BrPo; CABL; CMoP; CoBMV; DiPo; FaBoMo; LiTB; LiTM (rev. ed.); MasP; MoVE; OAEP (2d ed.); OBNC; PAn; PoEL-5; PoVP; ReMP; SeCeV; ViPP; VP
Sels.
"On Saturday sailed from Bremen." SeCePo
"Thou mastering me," Pt. I. BoC; OxBoCh
Wreck of the *Hesperus,* The. Longfellow. AmePo; AnNE; ATP (1935 ed.); BeLS; BoChLi (1939 ed.); CoBA; EtS; FaBoBe; FaFP; FaPL; FaPON; GN; GSP; HBV; HBVY; NeHB; OnSP; OTPC; PAH; PaPo; TreF; WBLP
Wreck of the *Julie Plante,* The. William Henry Drummond. BOHV; CaP; FaPON; HBV; IHA; InMe; NA; OBCV; PeCV; StaSt; TreFS; WhC
(*Julie Plante,* The.) BeLS; BLPA; FaBoBe
Wreck of the Old 97, The. *Unknown.* ViBoFo
Wreck of the Six-Wheel Driver, The. *Unknown.* ABF
(Joseph Mica.) ViBoFo
Wreck of Walsingham, The. *Unknown.* *See* Lament for Our Lady's Shrine at Walsingham, A.
Wreck on the C. & O., The; or, The Death of Jack Hinton, *with music. Unknown.* ABF
Wreck on the Somerset Road, The, *with music. Unknown.* OuSiCo
Wreckers' Prayer, The. Theodore Goodridge Roberts. OBCV; PeCV
Wren that rages when I sit, The. No Communication. Mark Van Doren. BiS

Wrens, The. Kenneth Burke. TwAmPo
Wrens and Robins [in the Hedge]. Christina Rossetti. *Fr.* Sing-Song. GFA; SUS; TiPo
(Nesting-Time.) PCH
Wrens are back, The. The Wrens. Kenneth Burke. TwAmPo
Wrens of the Lake. *Unknown, tr. fr. Irish by* Robin Flower. BiS
Wrestler, The. Sadi, *pr. tr. fr. Persian by* Sir Edwin Arnold. *Fr.* The Gulistan. OuHeWo
Wrestlers. Michael Drayton. *Fr.* Polyolbion, First Song. SD
Wrestling Jacob. Charles Wesley. CEP; EiCL; EiPP; OBEC; OBEV (new ed.); PeER; PoEL-3; SeCePo; SoP
("Come, O thou traveller unknown.") OxBoCh
Wrestling Match, The. Robert Penn Warren. AnAmPo
Wretched Amintor with a flame. The Greater Trial. Countess of Winchilsea. TrGrPo
Wretched and foolish jealousy. Ben Jonson. LO
Wretched Catullus, play the fool no more. To Himself. Catullus. AWP; LiTW
Wretched life I live, The. Madrigal V: Allusion to the Confusion of Babel. Francis Davison. ReIE
Wretched Man. Earl of Rochester. *Fr.* A Satire against Mankind. SeCePo
Wretched of the earth, The. I Arrive in Madrid. Al Young. WSL
Wretched thing it were, to have our heart, A. Retirement [*or* Sonnet]. Richard Chenevix Trench. EPN; OBVV; OQP
Wrinkled, crabbed man they picture thee, A. Winter. Robert Southey. BoNaP; Sonn
"Wrinkled ostler, grim and thin!" Song at the Ruin'd Inn. Tennyson. *Fr.* The Vision of Sin. PoEL-5
Wrinkles ("When Helen first saw wrinkles in her face"). Walter Savage Landor. VA
("When Helen first saw wrinkles. . .") EnLoPo
Wrinkling with laughter that made no sound. At a Country Fair. John Holmes. MoShBr
Writ in Water. Meleager, *tr. fr. Greek by* John Herman Merivale. OuHeWo
Writ of Loving Well, The. Love Suffereth Long. Sara Henderson Hay. ChIP; OQP
Write a contract with the grass. Song for Government. Raymond Holden. PoFr
Write it in gold—a spirit of the sun. Lines Written in a Blank Leaf of the Prometheus Unbound. Thomas Lovell Beddoes. ERoP-2
Write it on the schoolhouse door. "Where There's Drink." *Unknown.* SoP
Write on my grave when I am dead. The Epitaph. Katharine Tynan. WGRP
Write! write! help! help, sweet Muse! and never cease! Parthenophil and Parthenophe, XVIII. Barnabe Barnes. Sonn
Writer, The. Hildebrand Jacob. SiTL
Writer, attend no schools. The Teacher. Virginia Brady Young. GoYe
Writer tenebrously moles away, The. Literary Zodiac. R. A. Piddington. PV
Writer to His Book, The. Thomas Campion. OAEP
Writing. Howard Nemerov. NYBP
Writing inside. Vision of Turtle (One). James Brodey. ANYP
Writing Letters. Rodney Bennett. BoTP
Writing on the Wall. Padraic Fallon. NeIP
Written after Swimming from Sestos to Abydos. Byron. ALV; BOHV; ERoP-2; InMe; MBW-2; NoP; OBRV; PoE
Written after the Death of Charles Lamb, *sel.* Wordsworth.
"To a good man of most dear memory." CoBE
Written among the Euganean Hills, North Italy. Shelley. *See* Lines Written among the Euganean Hills.
Written at an Inn at Henley. William Shenstone. AWP; CEP; EiCL EiPP; HBV; JAWP; OBEC; OBEV (new ed.); OTPC (1923 ed.); PoE; TOP; ViBoPo; WBP
(Written in an Inn at Henley.) LoBV
Written at Cambridge. Charles Lamb. EnRP; OBRV
Written at Florence. Wilfrid Scawen Blunt. OBEV (1st ed.); OBVV
Written at Mr. Pope's House at Twickenham. George Lyttelton. CEP
Written at Oxford: On Stealing the Body of a Girl for Dissection. *Unknown.* StP
Written at Sea, in the First Dutch War. Charles Sackville. *See* Song: "To all you ladies now at land."
Written at Stonehenge. Thomas Warton, the Younger. *See* Sonnet: Written at Stonehenge.
Written at the End of a Book. Langdon Elwyn Mitchell. AA
Written at The Hague, in the Year 1696. Matthew Prior. *See* Secretary, The.
Written at Winslade, in Hampshire. Thomas Warton, the Younger. Sonnets, I. Sonn
Written December 1790. Anna Seward. Sonn
Written 1811. Blake. *Fr.* Jerusalem, *ch.* 4. MaRV; StJW
Written in a Blank Leaf of Dugdale's "Monasticon." Thomas Warton, the Younger. *See* Sonnet: Written in a Blank Leaf. . .
Written in a Lady's Milton. Matthew Prior. InP
Written in a Little Lady's Little Album. Frederick William Faber. HBV; HBVY
Written in a Northampton County Asylum. John Clare. *See* I Am.
Written in a Song Book. Lizette Woodworth Reese. NP
Written in a Thunderstorm. John Clare. ERoP-2
Written in a Time of Crisis. Stephen Vincent Benet. PAL
Written in a Volume of Shakespeare. Thomas Hood. Sonn
Written in an Inn at Henley. William Shenstone. *See* Written at an Inn at Henley.
Written in an Ovid. Matthew Prior. EiCL
Written in Australia. Arthur Adams. BoAu
Written in Butler's Sermons. Matthew Arnold. MBW-2
Written in Dejection near Rome. Robert Bly. NaP
Written in Early Spring. Wordsworth. *See* Lines Written in Early Spring.
Written in Edinburgh. Arthur Henry Hallam. VA
Written in Emerson's Essays. Matthew Arnold. ILP; Sonn; VA
Written in Flight from His Royal Patron. Al Mutanabbi, *tr. fr. Arabic by* Herbert Howarth *and* Ibrahim Shukrallah.
Written in Juice of Lemmon. Abraham Cowley. *Fr.* The Mistress. AnAnS-2; SeCP; SeCV-1
Written in July, 1824. Mary Russell Mitford. OBRV
Written in London, September, 1802. Wordsworth. BoLiVe; EnLi-2; EPN; MERP; PAn; TrGrPo
(England, 1802.) HBV; OBEV; PPON
(In London, September, 1802.) EnRP; MaRV; MBW-2; PoPo
(London, 1802.) GTBS; GTBS-D: GTBS-P; GTBS-W; GTSL
(Sonnet: Written in London, September, 1802.) ChER
Written in March. Wordsworth. BoNaP; BoTP; DD; EnRP; FaPON; GoJo; GoTP; HBV; HBVY; LiTG; MPB; OTD; OTPC; PCH; PoG; PoRL; PTK; RG; RIS; SUS; ThWaDe; TiPo; UnPo (3d ed.); WaKn; YeAr
(Cock Is Crowing, The.) ShBV-1
(In March.) StaSt
(March.) BoChLi; PRWS
(Merry Month of March, The.) EvOK; MoShBr; SoPo
Written in My Lady Speke's Singing-Book. Edmund Waller. CavP
Written in Naples. Emerson. CoBA
Written in Prison. John Clare. ERoP-2
Written in 1740. Thomas Catesby Paget. WaPE
Written in the Album of a Child. Wordsworth. *See* To a Child.
Written in the Beginning of Mézeray's History of France. Matthew Prior. BWP; CEP; EiCP; OBEC; PoE; PoEL-3; PoFS
Written in the Euganean Hills, North Italy. Shelley. *See* Lines Written among the Euganean Hills.
Written in the Leaves of a Fan. Francis Atterbury. *See* Written on the Leaves of a White Fan.
Written in the Spring of 1785 on the Death of the Poet Laureate. Anna Seward. Sonn
Written in the Visitors' Book at the Birthplace of Robert Burns. George Washington Cable. AA
Written in Very Early Youth. Wordsworth. EnRP
Written on a Blank Page in Shakespeare's Poems, Facing "A Lover's Complaint." Keats. *See* Bright Star, Would I Were Steadfast as Thou Art.
Written on a Fly-Leaf of Theocritus. Maurice Thompson. AA
Written on a Looking-Glass. *Unknown.* HBV
Written on a Sunday Morning. Robert Southey. OBEC
Written on the Anniversary of Our Father's Death. Hartley Coleridge. Sonn

Written on the Banks of Wastwater during a Calm. "Christopher North." OBRV
Written on the Day that Mr. Leigh Hunt Left Prison. Keats. *See* Sonnet: Written on the Day. . .
Written on the Eve of Execution. Chidiock Tichborne. *See* Elegy: "My prime of youth is but a frost of cares."
Written on the Leaves of a White Fan. Francis Atterbury. SeCL
(Written in the Leaves of a Fan.) SeEP
Written on the Night before His Execution. Sir Walter Ralegh. *See* Conclusion, The.
Written on the Road. Mary Mapes Dodge. BiCB
Written on the Sense of Isolation in Contemporary Ireland. Robert Greacen. NeIP
Written on the Stub of the First Paycheck. William Stafford. *Fr.* The Move to California. PoAn
Written on the Wall at Chang's Hermitage. Tu Fu, *tr. fr. Chinese by* Kenneth Rexroth. HoPM; NaP
Written on the Walls of His Dungeon. Luis de León, *tr. fr. Spanish by* Thomas Walsh. OnPM; TrJP
(Lines on the Wall of His Prison Cell.) CAW
Written the Night before His Execution. Chidiock Tichborne. *See* Elegy: "My prime of youth is but a frost of cares."
Written to a Young Lady. Jeremiah Joseph Callanan. IrPN
Written under Capricorn, a land. Love Poem. Chris Wallace-Crabbe. PoAu-2
Written upon the Top of Ben Nevis. Keats. ERoP-2
Wrong about birds. I cannot call. Paradox: The Birds. Karl Shapiro. CrMA
Wrong is made and measured by, The. Shame. Coventry Patmore. *Fr.* The Angel in the House, I, ix, 2. OBVV
Wrong me no more. Chang'd, Yet Constant. Thomas Stanley. AnAnS-2
Wrong not, sweet [*or* dear] empress of my heart. The Silent Lover, II *or* [To the Queen]. Sir Walter Ralegh. ElL; HBV; LiTB; OAEP; OBEV; OBS, *sl. diff., at. to* Sir Robert Ayton; OBSC; PG; SiPS; ViBoPo
Wrong Road, The. Richard Church. POTE
Wronged Lover, The. Sir Philip Sidney. *Fr.* Arcadia. SiPS
("Fire to see my wrongs for anger burneth, The.") FCP
Wrote in the Banquetting-House in Grayes-Inn-Walks. Alexander Radcliffe. PeRV
Wrung Heart, The. Jack Lindsay. MemP
Wry Rowan, The. *Unknown, tr. fr. Late Middle Irish by* Eoin MacNeill. OnYI
Wry Smile, A. Roy Fuller. WaaP; WaP
W's for Windows. Phyllis McGinley. *Fr.* All Around the Town. TiPo
Wulf and Eadwacer. *Unknown, tr. fr. Anglo-Saxon.* TrGrPo
Wull ye come in early spring. Come! William Barnes. CH
Wunst I Had an Old Gray Mare, *with music. Unknown.* OuSiCo
Wunst I sassed my pa an' he. The Runaway Boy. James Whitcomb Riley. MPB
Wyatt Being in Prison, to Bryan. Sir Thomas Wyatt. SiCE; TuPP
(Epigram: "Sighs are my food, drink are my tears.") SiPS
("Sighs are my food, drink are my tears.") FCP
("Syghes ar my foode, drynke are my teares.") EnPo
Wyatt resteth here, that quick could never rest. On [*or* Of] the Death of Sir Thomas Wyatt [*or* A Tribute to Wyatt]. Earl of Surrey. BEL; CBEP; EnLi-1 (1949 ed.); EnLit; EnPo; FaBoEn; FCP; FosPo; GoTL; NCEP; NoP; ReEn; ReIE; SiCE; SiPS; TuPP
Wye and the Severn are offspring, The. The Playmates. Sir William Watson. PoVP
Wynken, Blynken, and Nod. Eugene Field. AA; AmePo; AnAmPo; BeLS; BoChLi; BoTP; FaBoBe; FaFP; FaPON; GoTP; HBV; HBVY; MPB; OTPC; PCH; PoRA; PoRh; PRWS; SoPo; StVeCh; TSW; TVC
(Dutch Lullaby, A.) AmLP; BLPA; BOHV; LiTG; NeHB; PoPl; TreF
Wynter Wakeneth Al My Care. *Unknown.* SeCePo
(This World's Joy.) OBEV
(Wynter Wakeneth.) OxBoCh
Wyoming. Charles E. Winter. PoRL
Wyoming Massacre, The. Uriah Terry. PAH

X

X marks the spot where the body lies in time. USA. Paul Engle. SiTL
X Minus X. Kenneth Fearing. AmLP; WOW
X-Ray. David Ray. NePoEA-2
X-Ray. Leonora Speyer. ImOP
X shall stand for playmates Ten. *Unknown.* OxNR
Xenokrates fell over a kettle. "Ecce Quomodo Moritur Justus." Diogenes Laertius. LiTW
Xenophanes. Emerson. AnNE; MWA-1
Xkoagu, give me your heart. Prayer to the Hunting Star, Canopus. *Unknown.* PeSA
Xmas Time. Walta Karsner. ELU
Xochitepec. Malcolm Lowry. *See* Lupus in Fabula.
Xylographer started to cross the sea, A. The Zealless Xylographer. Mary Mapes Dodge. BOHV

Y

Y Is for Youth. W. H. Davies. BoPe
Y.M.C.A. Writing Room. Roy Fuller. ToPo
Yacht, The. Catullus, *tr. fr. Latin by* John Hookham Frere. AWP; JAWP; WBP
Yacht, The. Walter Savage Landor. OBVV
Yachts, The. William Carlos Williams. AmPP; AP; CMoP; CoBMV; ExPo; FlW; ILP; InPo; LiTA; LiTM; MasP; MoAB; MoAmPo (1950 ed.); MoPo; MoVE; NAMP; NePA; NoP; OxBA; Po; PoeP; PoFS; ReMP; SeCeV; TwAmPo; VaPo; ViBoPo (1958 ed.)
Yachts on the Nile. Bernard Spencer. ChMP
Yak, The. Hilaire Belloc. ALV; BOHV; FaBV; FaPON; HBVY; InMe; MoBrPo; MPB; NA; PCH; PoRh; StaSt; TDP; TreFS; TSW; UTS
Yak, The. Nathalia Crane. StaSt
Yak, The. Oliver Herford. *Fr.* Child's Natural History. HBV; HBVY
Yak, The. Theodore Roethke. TDP
Yak, The. Virna Sheard. CaP; PeCV; WHW
Yak. William Jay Smith. GoTP; RePo; TiPo (1959 ed.)
Yang-se-fu. "Yehoash," *tr. fr. Yiddish by* Isidore Goldstick. TrJP
Yankee boy, before he's sent to school, The. Whittling. John Pierpont. GN
Yankee captains and their wives. The Captains of Small Farms. Robert P. Tristram Coffin. RePo
Yankee country churchyard holds, A. He Laughed Last. Francis Whiting Hatch. WhC
Yankee Cradle. Robert P. Tristram Coffin. EvOK
Yankee Doodle ("Once on a time old Johnny Bull"). George Pope Morris. PaA, *with orig. vers.*
Yankee Doodle (*diff. vers.*). *Unknown, at. to* Richard Shuckburg *and to* Edward Bangs. ABF, *with music;* ChTr; ExPo; FaFP; FaPON; OTPC (1946 ed.), 4 *ll.*; OxNR, 4 *ll.*; PaA; PAL; PoFr; PoRL, *sl. abr.*; SiTL; StVeCh (1955 ed.); TrAS, *with music*; TreF; YaD
(Yankee's [*or* Yankeys'] Return from Camp, The.) MC; OxBoLi; PAH
Yankee Doodle sent to Town. The Last Appendix to "Yankee Doodle." *Unknown.* PAH
Yankee Doodle went to war. The Run from Manassas Junction. *Unknown.* PAH
Yankee Doodle's Expedition to Rhode Island. *Unknown.* PAH
Yankee Man-of-War, The ("'Tis of a gallant Yankee ship"). *Unknown.* AA; AmSS, *with music*; EtS; FaBoBe; PAH; PaPo
(Stately Southerner, The, *with music.*) ShS; SoAmSa
("'Tis of a gallant Yankee ship.") LaNeLa
Yankee Privateer [The]. Arthur Hale. PaA; PAH
Yankee Ship and a Yankee Crew, A. *Unknown.* IHA
Yankee ship and a Yankee crew, A. The *Constitution's* Last Fight. James Jeffrey Roche. MC; PAH
Yankee ship came [*or* comes] down the river, A. Blow, Boys, Blow [*or* Blow, Bullies, Blow]. *Unknown.* AmSS; SoAmSa; TrAS

Yankee Thunders. *Unknown.* PAH
Yankee's [*or* Yankeys'] Return from Camp, The. *Unknown.* *See* Yankee Doodle.
Yanks. James W. Foley. PaA
Yardbird's Skull. Owen Dodson. AmNP; IDB
Yardley-Oak. William Cowper. LaA; NCEP; PeER
Yarn of the *Loch Achray,* The. John Masefield. InP; SeCeV; StPo
Yarn of the *Nancy Bell,* The. W. S. Gilbert. ATP (1935 ed.); BBV; BeLS; BLPA; BoChLi; BOHV; CenHV; EvOK; FaBoBe; FaBoCh; EtS; FaBV; FaFP; GBV; GoTP; GSP; HBV; HoPM; InMe; LoGBV; MCCG; MoShBr; OnMSP; OTPC (1946 ed.); PCD; PoVP; PTK; ShBV-1; StVeCh; TreFS; TrGrPo; TSW
Yarns of the People. Carl Sandburg. *See* They Have Yarns.
Yarrow Revisited. Wordsworth. EnLi-2; EnRP; MERP
Yarrow Unvisited. Wordsworth. BEL; EnLi-2; EnRP; GTBS; GTBS-D; GTBS-P; GTBS-W; GTSE; GTSL; HBV; MERP; PoRA
Yarrow Visited. Wordsworth. BEL; EnLi-2; EnRP; GTBS; GTBS-D; GTBS-P; GTBS-W; GTSL; HBV; MERP
Yase: September. Gary Snyder. FRC
Yattendon. Sir Henry Newbolt. HBMV
"Yaup, yaup, yaup!" The Chorus of Frogs. Ann Hawkshaw. OTPC
Yaw, Dot Is So! Charles Follen Adams. HBV
Yawcob Strauss. Charles F. Adams. PaPo
Yawn, The. Paul Blackburn. ELU
Ye Alps audacious, through the heavens that rise. The Hasty Pudding. Joel Barlow. AmPP; AP; CoBA; OxBA
Ye Ancient Divine Ones. Arthur Hugh Clough. *Fr.* Amours de Voyage. OBNC
Ye Ancient Yuba Miner, of the Days of '49, *with music.* Sam C. Upham. SGR
Ye angells bright, pluck from your wings a quill. Meditation Sixty. Edward Taylor. *Fr.* Preparatory Meditations, Second Series. PoEL-3
Ye Anger Earth. Moses ibn Ezra, *tr. fr. Hebrew by* Solomon Solis-Cohen. *Fr.* The World's Illusion. TrJP
Ye are the light of the world. Poems by the Roadside. St. Matthew, Bible, *N.T.* CAW
"Ye are the Duke of Athol's nurse." The Duke of Athole's Nurse (B *vers.*). *Unknown.* ESPB
Ye Are the Temple of God. First Corinthians, III: 16-17, Bible, *N.T.* TreFT
Ye are too young to bring me in. An Old Lover to a Young Gentlewoman. *Unknown.* TuPP
Ye are young, ye are young. An Old Man's Song. Richard Le Gallienne. HBV; VA
Ye Banks and Braes. Burns. *See* Banks o' Doon, The.
Ye banks and braes and streams around. Highland Mary. Burns. AnFE; ATP (1935 ed.); AWP; BEL; BoLiVe; CEP; EiCL; EiPP; EnLi-2; EnLit; EnRP; FaPL; GTBS; GTBS-D; GTBS-P; GTBS-W; GTSE; GTSL; HBV; InP; InPo; JAWP; OAEP; OBEC; OBEV; OuHeWo; TOP; TreFS; TrGrPo; ViBoPo; WBLP; WBP
Ye Banks and Braes o' Bonnie Doon. Burns. *See* Banks o' Doon, The.
Ye barren hearts and bitter, steep'd in brine. Lyttelton Harbour, XXXVIII. D'Arcy Cresswell. AnNZ
Ye barren peaks, so mightily outlined. Altars. Bernard Freeman Trotter. MaRV
Ye beauties! O how great the sum. On a Bed of Guernsey Lilies. Christopher Smart. *Fr.* Ode to the Earl of Northumberland. BWP; OBEC
Ye [*or* Yee] blushing virgins happy are. To Roses in the Bosom of Castara. William Habington. *Fr.* Castara. AnAnS-2; CavP; CLwM; EnLoPo; GoBC; HBV; LoBV; MeLP; OBEV; PoAn; SeCL; SeCP; SeEP; UnTE; ViBoPo
Ye brave Columbian bands! a long farewell! On Disbanding the Army. David Humphreys. PAH
Ye brave sons of Freedom, come join in the chorus. The Times. *Unknown.* PAH
Ye bubbling springs that gentle music makes. Love's Limit. *Unknown.* EG; MeWo; TrGrPo
Ye buds of Brutus' land, courageous youths, now play your parts! For Soldiers. Humphrey Gifford. CH; ElL; SiCE; TuPP
Ye call Me Master and obey Me not. Thus Speaketh Christ Our Lord. *Unknown.* ChIP; PGD
"Ye Cannot Serve God and Mammon." Robert Herrick. *See* Neutrality Loathsome.
Ye cannot shut the trees in. They All Belong to Me. Eliza Cook. PGD
Ye captive souls of blindfold Cyprian's boat. My Love Is Past. Thomas Watson. *Fr.* Hecatompathia. ReIE
Ye cats that at midnight spit love at each other. An Appeal to Cats in the Business of Love. Thomas Flatman. EnLoPo
Ye Christian heralds, go proclaim. The Christian Herald. Bourne H. Draper. SoP
Ye clerks that on your shoulders bear the shield. Preachment for Preachers. Sebastian Brant, *tr. by* Alexander Barclay. *Fr.* The Ship of Fools. ACP; CAW
Ye Clouds! that far above me float and pause. France; an Ode. Samuel Taylor Coleridge. ATP; BEL; EnLi-2 (1949 ed.); EnRP; EPN; ERoP-1; MBW-2; MERP; OAEP; PoFr; PoG; StP; TOP
Ye Columbians so bold, attend while I sing. Hull's Surrender. *Unknown.* PAH
Ye Commons and Peers. Jack Frenchman's Lamentation. *Unknown.* CoMu
Ye companies of governor-spirits grave. The Crystal. Sidney Lanier. AmePo
Ye congregated powers of heaven, who share. Shelley. *Fr.* Prometheus Unbound. EnLit
Ye coopers and hoopers, attend to my ditty. The Cooper o' Dundee. *Unknown.* CoMu
Ye Cupids, droop each little head. The Dead Sparrow. Catullus, *tr. by* Byron. EnLi-1; OuHeWo
Ye dainty [*or* dayntye] nymphs, that in this blessed brook[e]. Elisa [*or* Hobbinol's Lay of Fair Elisa]. Spenser. *Fr.* The Shepheardes Calender: April. AtBAP; OBSC
Ye dead and gone great armies of the world. The Ancient Sacrifice. Mahlon Leonard Fisher. AnAmPo
Ye distant spires, ye antique towers. Ode on a Distant Prospect of Eton College. Thomas Gray. ATP (1935 ed.); BEL; CABA; CEP; CoBE; EiCL; EiCP; EiPP; EnLi-2 (1949 ed.); EnLit; EnPE; ExPo; FosPo; GTBS; GTBS-D; GTBS-P; GTBS-W; GTSE; GTSL; HBV; LiTB; LiTG; NoP; OAEP; OBEC; OuHeWo; PAn; PoE; PoEL-3; SeCeV; StP; TOP; ViBoPo
Ye dreary plains, that round me lie. Summer on the Great American Desert. Rufus B. Sage. PoOW
Ye elms that wave on Malvern Hill. Malvern Hill. Herman Melville. AmPP; AP; MAmP; MC; MWA-1; PAH; TDP
Ye elves of hills, brooks, standing lakes, and groves. Magic. Shakespeare. *Fr.* The Tempest, V, i. AWP; JAWP; WBP
Ye famed physicians of this place. A Lamentable Case. Sir Charles Hanbury Williams. ErPo; UnTE; WaPE
Ye field flowers! the gardens eclipse you, 'tis true. Field Flowers. Thomas Campbell. OTPC (1923 ed.)
Ye Flags of Piccadilly. Arthur Hugh Clough. Songs in Absence, II. PoVP
Ye flaming powers, and winged warriours bright. Upon the Circumcision. Milton. MeP
Ye flippering soule. An Address to the Soul Occasioned by a Rain [*or* When Let by Rain]. Edward Taylor. AP; MAmP; OxBA; Po; PoEL-3
Ye Flowery Banks [o' Bonnie Doon]. Burns. *See* Banks o' Doon, The.
Ye genii who in secret state. Limitations of Human Art. William Collins. Three Fragments, 2. WaPE
Ye gentlemen and ladies fair who grace this famous city. The Hunters of Kentucky. Samuel Woodworth. AS; PAH; TrAS
"Ye gie corn to [*or* unto] my hors[e]." Mother's Malison [*or* Clyde's Water]. *Unknown.* ESPB
Ye [*or* You] goat-herd [*or* gote-heard] gods, that love the grassy mountains [*or* grassie mountaines]. Double Sestine [*or* Sestina]. Sir Philip Sidney. *Fr.* Arcadia. AtBAP; BWP; FCP; LiTB; LiTG; NoP; PoEL-1; SiCE; StP
Ye gods of love, look from above on a broken hearted maid. Young Billy Crane. Larry Gorman. ShS
Ye Gods! the raptures of that night! The Enjoyment. *Unknown.* ErPo
Ye Gods, You Gave to Me a Wife. *Unknown.* SeCL
Ye Golden Lamps of Heaven. Philip Doddridge. *See* Hymn: "Ye golden Lamps of Heav'n, farewel."
Ye good distressed!/ Ye noble few. Bear Up Awhile. James Thomson. MaRV
Ye graceful peasant-girls and mountain-maids. Ballata: His

Talk with Certain Peasant Girls. Franco Sacchetti. AWP
Ye green-hair'd nymphs! Whom Pan allows. Ode to a Water Nymph. William Mason. Po
Ye green-rob'd Dryads, oft at dusky eve. The Enthusiast; or, The Lover of Nature. Joseph Warton. CEP; EiPP; EnPE; EnRP; FaBoEn; Po; PoEL-3
Ye groves (the statesman at his desk exclaims). The Statesman in Retirement. William Cowper. *Fr.* Retirement. OBEC
Ye happy swains, whose hearts are free. Song. Sir George Etherege. HBV; LiTL; ViBoPo
Ye have been fresh and green. To Meadows [*or* Meddowes]. Robert Herrick. AtBAP; AWP; BWP; CBEP; CH; EG; FaBoEn; HBV; InPo; LoBV; MyFE; OBEV; OTPC (1923 ed.); PoEL-3; PoeP; QFR; SeCL; SeCP; SeCV-1
"Ye have not chosen me," He said. Chosen. Catherine Baird. SoP
"Ye have robbed," said he, "ye have slaughtered and made an end." He Fell among Thieves. Sir Henry Newbolt. BBV; HBV; HBVY; OBEV; OBVV; OnMSP; PoMa; ShBV-3
Ye have seen a marvel in this town. The Lament for Yellow-haired Donough. *Unknown.* KiLC
Ye have sung me your songs, ye have chanted your rimes. The Song of the Derelict. John McCrae. EtS
Ye Heavens, Uplift Your Voices. *Unknown.* OHIP
Ye Highlands [*or* hielands] and ye Lawlands [*or* Lowlands]. The Bonny [*or* Bonnie] Earl of [*or* o'] Murray [*or* Moray]. *Unknown.* AnFE; BaBo (A *vers.*) BEL; BuBa; CBEP; ELP; EnLit; ESPB; FaBoCh; GoTS; HBV; LoGBV; OBB; OBEV; OBS; OxBB; OxBS; ViBoFo
Ye hours, then, but as minutes be. William Browne. *Fr.* Britannia's Pastorals, III, Song 1. LO
Ye jolly Yankee gentlemen, who live at home in ease. The C. S. A. Commissioners. *Unknown.* PAH
Ye jovial throng, come join the song. The Battle of Muskingum. William Harrison Safford. PAH
Ye Know My Heart. Sir Thomas Wyatt. LoBV
("Ye know my heart, my lady dear.") FCP; SiPS
Ye know the ant that creeps upon the fig. The Dharra and the Date-Stone. *Unknown.* OnPM
Ye ladies that live in the city or town. The Link. Robert Lowth. WaPE
Ye ladies, walking past me piteous-eyed. Sonnet: To the Same Ladies. Dante. AWP
Ye learnèd sisters, which have oftentimes. Epithalamion. Spenser. AtBAP; BEL; BWP; CABL; EIL; EnL; EnLi-1 (1949 ed.); EnRePo; HBV; HW; ILP; LiTL; MaPo (1969 ed.); MasP; MBW-1; NoP; OAEP; OBEV; OBSC; Po; PoAn; PoEL-1; PoFS; ReEn; ReIE; SeCeV; SiCE; TOP; ViBoPo; WoL
Ye Little Birds That Sit and Sing. *At. to* Thomas Heywood. *Fr.* The Fair Maid of the Exchange. EIL; ViBoPo (Message, The.) HBV; OBEV (1st ed.)
Ye living lamps, by whose dear light. The Mower to the Glow-Worms. Andrew Marvell. ALV; AnAnS-1; AtBAP; AWP; BoC; BWP; CBEP; EG; ELP; EnLoPo; FosPo; InPo; InvP; MaMe; MemP; MePo; OBS; OnPM; OxBoLi; PoEL-2; ReEn; RIS; SCEP-2; SeCL; SeCP; TrGrPo
Ye lords of creation, men you are called. The Lords of Creation. *Unknown.* PoLF
Ye mariners, by sea and land be yours a happy doom. A Seaman's Tomb. Plato. OnPM
Ye Mariners of England. Thomas Campbell. BEL; BLPA; CBEP; CoBE; EnRP; EPN; EtS; GN; GTBS; GTBS-D; GTBS-P; GTBS-W; GTSE; GTSL; HBV; OBEV; OBRV; OTPC (1923 ed.); PTK; TreF
Ye mariners of Spain. The Song of the Galley. *Unknown.* AWP; PoFr
Ye marshes, how candid and simple and nothing-withholding and free. Sidney Lanier. *Fr.* The Marshes of Glynn. PG; TRV
Ye martial pow'rs, and all ye tuneful nine. Goliath of Gath. Phillis Wheatley. BALP
"Ye maun gang to your father, Janet." Fair Janet. *Unknown.* BaBo; ESPB; OBB; OxBB
Ye may simper, blush, and smile. To Cherry-Blossoms. Robert Herrick. SeCV-1
Ye may tramp the world over. Ould Doctor Mack. Alfred Perceval Graves. BOHV
Ye men who are dimly existing below. Chorus of Birds. Aristophanes. *Fr.* The Birds. WoL
Ye merry hearts that love to play. Win at First and Lose at Last; or, a New Game at Cards. Laurence Price. OxBoLi
"Ye midwives and women-kind, do one thing for me." The Death of Queen Jane (B *vers.*). *Unknown.* BaBo
Ye modern laureates, famous'd for your writ. Alli Veri Figlidi Delle Muse. *Unknown.* *Fr.* Zepheria. ReIE; TuPP
Ye Mongers Aye Need Masks for Cheatrie. Sidney Goodsir Smith. OxBS
Ye morning-glories, ring in the gale your bells. The New God. James Oppenheim. WGRP
Ye motions of delight, that haunt the sides. Nature's Healing. Wordsworth. *Fr.* The Prelude, XII. EPN
Ye motions of delight, that through the fields. Imagination, How Impaired and Restored. Wordsworth. *Fr.* The Prelude. OBNC
Ye mountain valleys, pitifully groan. Lament for Bion. Moschus. AWP; JAWP; WBP
Ye Muses! dames of dignified renown. Two Ways of Visiting. Timothy Dwight. *Fr.* Greenfield Hill. AmPP (4th ed.)
Ye muses, pour the pitying tear. A Great Man. Goldsmith. NA
Ye nymphs and ye swains that trip over the plains. Black Thing. *Unknown.* CoMu
Ye nymphs, if e'er your eyes were red. On the Death of Mrs. (Now Lady) Throckmorton's Bullfinch. William Cowper. HBV
Ye nymphs of Solyma! begin the song. Messiah. Pope. EiCL; OxBoCh
Ye Parliament of England. *Unknown.* AmSS, *with music;* PAH; SoAmSa
Ye people of great Murrough's band. Murrough Defeats the Danes, 994. *Unknown,* *tr. by* Frank O'Connor. KiLC
Ye people of great Murrough. On the Defeat of Ragnall by Murrough King of Leinster A.D. 994. *Unknown,* *tr. by* Kuno Meyer. OnYI
Ye people of Ireland, both country and city. A New Song of Wood's Halfpence. Swift. OxBoLi
Ye people that labour the world to measure. Geographers. Sebastian Brant, *tr. by* Alexander Barclay. *Fr.* The Ship of Fools. ACP
Ye pilgrim-folk, advancing pensively. Dante, *tr. by* Dante Gabriel Rossetti. *Fr.* La Vita Nuova. AWP; CTC; JAWP; WBP
Ye pilgrims, who with pensive aspect go. Dante, *tr. by* Louise Imogen Guiney. *Fr.* La Vita Nuova. CAW
Ye poets ragged and forlorn. Advice to the Grub-Street Verse-Writers. Swift. EiCL
Ye poor little sheep, ah well may ye stray. The Enquiry. John Dyer. EiCL; OBEC
Ye powers unseen, to whom the bards of Greece. Inscription. Mark Akenside. CBEP; OBEC
Ye pure inhabitants of light. Three Hymns, 3. Elizabeth Rowe. WaPE
Ye rascals of ringers, ye merciless foes. On Bell-Ringers. Voltaire. ShM
Ye robbed, ye spoiled, ye bought, ye sold. Robert Crowley. *Fr.* The Voice of the Last Trumpet Blown by the Seventh Angel. PoFr
Ye Sacred Muses. *Unknown.* MuSP
Ye sacred ruins and ye tragic sights. Ruins of Rome, IV. Joachim du Bellay. OnPM
Ye saw 't floueran in my breist. The Mandrake Hert. Sidney Goodsir Smith. AtBAP; OxBS
Ye say they all have passed away. Indian Names. Lydia Huntley Sigourney. AmFN; FaPON; HBV; MC; MPB; OTPC; PAH; PoLF; PoRL; RePo
Ye Servants of God. Charles Wesley. SoP
Ye servants of the Lord. The Watchful Servant. Philip Doddridge. SoP
Ye Shall Live Also. Christian F. Gellert. *See* Jesus Lives, and So Shall I.
Ye shepherd so chearful and gay. Absence. William Shenstone. Pastoral Ballad in Four Parts, I. OBEC
Ye [*or* You *or* We] should stay longer if we durst. Francis Beaumont. *Fr.* The Masque of the Inner-Temple and Gray's Inne. GoBC; OBS; TrGrPo; ViBoPo
Ye smooth-faced sons of Jacob, hug close your ingleside. The Song of the Sons of Esau. Bertha Runkle. AA
Ye Sons of Columbia. Thomas Green Fessenden. PAH
Ye Sons of Columbia. *Unknown.* *See* Fuller and Warren.

Ye sons of Columbia, unite in the cause. Ye Sons of Columbia. Thomas Green Fessenden. PAH
Ye sons of Columbia, who bravely have fought. Adams and Liberty. Robert Treat Paine. MC; PAH
Ye sons of Columbia, your attention I do crave [*or* attention now I pray]. Fuller and Warren. *Unknown.* BeLS; BFSS; CoSo; ViBoFo
Ye sons of freedom [*or* toil], wake to glory! The Marseillaise. Claude Joseph Rouget de Lisle. HBV; PoFr; PTK; TreFS; WBLP
Ye sons of Massachusetts, all who love that honored name. The Sudbury Fight. Wallace Rice. PAH
Ye sons of men, with just regard attend. Matthew Prior. *Fr.* Solomon on the Vanity of the World. EiCP
Ye sons of Sedition, how comes it to pass. On the Snake. *Unknown.* PAH
Ye sons of toil awake to glory! *See* Ye sons of freedom, wake to glory!
Ye Sorrowers. Franz Werfel, *tr. fr. German by* Ludwig Lewisohn. *Fr.* The Eternal Road. TrJP
Ye sorrowing people! who from bondage fly. The Fugitive Slaves. Jones Very. AP
Ye Spier Me. Sidney Goodsir Smith. AtBAP
Ye stately dames, whose beauties far excel. Thomas Watson. *Fr.* Hecatompathia. ReIE
Ye storm-winds of Autumn! Parting. Matthew Arnold. Switzerland, II. OAEP; ViPP; VP
Ye swains who roam from fair to fair. Would You in Venus' Wars Succeed. *Unknown.* ErPo
Ye Sylphs and Sylphids, to your chief give ear! Pope. *Fr.* The Rape of the Lock. ViBoPo
Ye sylvan muses, loftier strains recite. The Birth of the Squire; an Eclogue. John Gay. EiCL; EiCP; PoEL-3
Ye that amonge lordis and barouns. John Lydgate. *Fr.* The Dance of Death. EnPo
Ye That Do Live in Pleasures. *Unknown.* TuPP
Ye that do your Master's will. The Lord of Joy. Charles Wesley. BoPe; FaChP
Ye [*or* you] that have faith to look with fearless eyes. Victory. Sir Owen Seaman. MaRV; OQP; PoToHe; WGRP
Ye that have hearts vexed with unquiet thought. To Spenser. John Hamilton Reynolds. Sonn
Ye that in love delight. On Clarastella Singing. Robert Heath. OBS
Ye that pasen by the weiye. Jesus to Those Who Pass By. *Unknown.* MeEL
Ye that with me have fought and fail'd and fought. Sacramentum Supremum. Sir Henry Newbolt. GTSL
Ye, too, marvellous twain, that erect on the Monte Cavallo. Ye Ancient Divine Ones. Arthur Hugh Clough. *Fr.* Amours de Voyage. OBNC
Ye tradeful merchants that, with weary toil. Amoretti, XV. Spenser. BoLiVe; LiTB; LiTG; LiTL; ReEn; ReIE; SiCE; Sonn; TrGrPo
Ye two fair trees that I so long have known. Sonnet. Thomas Caulfield Irwin. IrPN
Ye walls! sole witnesses of happy sighs. Walter Savage Landor. EnLoPo
Ye wandering winds that from your threshing floor. Hubert Church. *Fr.* New Zealand. AnNZ
Ye Watchers and Ye Holy Ones, *with music.* Athelstan Riley. YaCaBo
Ye Wearie Wayfarer, *sel.* Adam Lindsay Gordon.
Sun and Rain and Dew from Heaven. PoLF
Ye wha are fain to hae your name. Braid Claith. CEP; GoTS; OBEC; OxBS
Ye white Sicilian goats, who wander. Little Theocritus. Caroline Wilder Paradise. AA
Ye Who Fear Death Remember April. John Richard Moreland. MaRV
Ye who have passed Death's haggard hills; and ye. The Trees of the Garden. Dante Gabriel Rossetti. The House of Life, LXXXIX. MaVP; PoVP; ViPo
Ye who have scorned each other. Under the Holly Bough [*or* Reconciliation]. Charles Mackay. DD; MaRV; OBVV
Ye who pass by and would raise your hand. To the Wayfarer. *Unknown.* SiSoSe
Ye Who Taste That Love Is Sweet. William Michael Rossetti. OQP
Ye wild-eyed Muses, sing the twins of Jove. Hymn to Castor and Pollux. *Unknown.* *Fr.* Homeric Hymns. AWP
Ye winds, that in your hasty flight. To the Winds. Philip Ayres. CEP
Ye winds that sweep the grove's green tops. The Mariner. Allan Cunningham. EtS
Ye wise, instruct me to endure. On Censure. Swift. CBEP
Ye young debaters over the doctrine. The Village Atheist. Edgar Lee Masters. *Fr.* Spoon River Anthology. AmP; EaLo; LiTA; MaRV; PoPo
Yea. John Crowe Ransom. Two Sonnets, I.
("It was beside the fire that I had lit.") LO
Yea, and a good cause why thus should I plain. A Funeral Song upon the Decease of Annes, His Mother. Nicholas Grimald. ReIE; TuPP
Yea, gold is son of Zeus: no rust. Gold Is the Son of Zeus: Neither Moth nor Worm May Gnaw It. "Michael Field." OBMV
Yea, Jubal?/ Nothing, mother. William Vaughn Moody. *Fr.* The Death of Eve. WoL
Yea, let me praise my lady whom I love. Sonnet: He Will Praise His Lady [*or* Praise]. Guido Guinicelli. AWP; OnPM
Yea, Lord, I too. "I Thirst." Katherine Brégy. CAW
Yea, love, I know, and I would have it thus. Love's Poor. Richard Le Gallienne. VA
Yea, Love is strong as Life; he casts out fear. Sonnet. Lady Blanche Elizabeth Lindsay. VA
"Yea, my King." Robert Browning. *Fr.* Saul. WGRP
Yea, she hath passed hereby and blessed the sheaves. Kore. Frederic Manning, *wr. at to* Ezra Pound. HBV; LoBV
Yea [*or* Yes], the coneys are scared by the thud of hoofs. Before Waterloo [*or* Chorus *or* The Field of Waterloo]. Thomas Hardy. *Fr.* The Dynasts. CMoP; FaBoCh; LoBV; LoGBV; WaaP
Yeah here am I. Two Jazz Poems. Carl Wendell Hines, Jr. AmNP; Kal
Yea, through life, death, through sorrow and through sinning. Alpha and Omega. Frederic William Henry Myers. *Fr.* Saint Paul. OQP
Yea, we have toiled all night. The Fishers. Josephine Preston Peabody. StJW
Year, The. Coventry Patmore. GTSE; ThWaDe
(Round the Year.) BoTP
(Year's Round, The.) OTPC (1946 ed.); PoRL
Year, The. *Unknown.* OTPC (1946 ed.)
Year a bird flies against the drum, The. For Now. W. S. Merwin. CoPo; NaP
Year after year before my life began. The Tomb of Honey Snaps Its Marble Chains. Derek Stanford. NeBP
Year after year I sit for them. A Model. Dollie Radford. VA
Year after year the leaf and the shoot. The Mystery. George Francis Savage-Armstrong. VA
Year ago how often did I meet, A. Samuel Hoar. Franklin Benjamin Sanborn. AA
Year ago I asked you for your soul, A. The Caged Bird. Arthur Symons. BrPo
Year ago today, A. Birthday Garden. Ivy O. Eastwick. BiCB
Year ago you came, A. Pietà. James McAuley. PoAu-2
Year Ahead, The. Horatio Nelson Powers. WBLP
"Year and I are dying out together, The." Lament in Autumn. Harold Stewart. PoAu-2
Year grows darker, but each day more lamps, The. Autumnal Consummation. Patric Stevenson. NeIP
Year had all the Days in charge, The. Why I Was Cold in May. Henrietta Robins Eliot. AA
Year had gloomily begun, The. One Week. Carolyn Wells. LBN
Year has changed his mantle cold, The. Spring. Charles d'Orléans, *tr. by* Andrew Lang. AWP; CTC; JAWP; WBP
Year his winter cloak lets fall, The. Rondeau. Charles d'Orléans, *tr. by* J. G. Legge. LiTW
Year is dead, for Death slays even time, The. Year's End. Nathaniel A. Benson. CaP
Year is done, the last act of the vaudeville, The. Midnight Show. Karl Shapiro. OxBA
Year is gone, beyond all recall, The. The Opening Year. *Unknown.* BLRP
Year is round around me now, The. Green Song. Philip Booth. BoNaP
Year is slowly, sadly dying, The. Compensation. Henry W. Frost. SoP
Year just past, The. Rest. Annie Clarke. SoP
Year of Jubilo, *with music.* Henry Clay Work. TrAS

(Year of Jubilee, The.) PAH
Year of Our Lord two thousand one hundred and seven, The. From an Ecclesiastical Chronicle. John Heath-Stubbs. HYE
Year of Seeds, The, *sels.* Ebenezer Elliott. Sonn
"Give not our blankets, tax-fed Squire, to him."
"I dreamed that God was Silence. Air was dead."
"Ralph Leech believes (and he can read and write".)
"Toy of the Titans! Tiny harp! again."
Year of Sorrow, The; Ireland—1849, *sels.* Aubrey Thomas De Vere.
Spring. IrPN; OBNC
Winter. IrPN
(Year of Sorrow, A, *abr.*) ACP
Year opens with frozen pipes, The. Omens. Michael Hamburger. NMP
Year stood at its equinox, The. The Milking-Maid. Christina Rossetti. BeLS
Year swings over slowly, like a pilot, The. Winter; Two Sonnets. Malcolm Cowley. *Fr.* Blue Juniata. MAP; MoAmPo (1942 ed.)
Year That's Awa', The. John Dunlop. HBV
Year turns, The. Summer blown from Europe. Waiting for the Wind. Alex Comfort. POTE
Year was the sixth of Constantine's sway, The. Constantine's Vision of the Cross. Cynewulf. *Fr.* Elene. AnOE
Year, with all its days, has come and gone, A. Autumn along the Beaches. John Hall Wheelock. AnAmPo
Year without Seasons, A. Mance Williams. NNP
Yearbook, The. Tom Clark. ANYP
Yearning. Alfred Kreymborg. MAPA
Years. Walter Savage Landor. *See* Years, Many Parti-coloured Years.
Years, The. John Hall Wheelock. CrMA
Years ago, at a private school. An Ever-fixed Mark. Kingsley Amis. ErPo
Years ago, when I. Following Father Home. John Talman. SoP
Years ago when I was at Balliol. To the Balliol Men Still in Africa. Hilaire Belloc. JKCP
Years and years and man's thoughtful foot. The Lane. Andrew Young. HaMV
Years are but half a score, The. On the Big Horn. Whittier. PAH
Years Are Coming. *Unknown.* OQP
Years are flowers and bloom within, The. God's Garden. Richard Burton. OQP; TRV
Year's at the Spring, The. Robert Browning. *Fr.* Pippa Passes. BEL; BLPA; BoChLi; DD; EPN; FaBoBe; FaBV; GTBS; GTSL; InP; NeHB; PoRL; PoToHe (new ed.); StVeCh; TSW; YeAr
(Good Morning.) PRWS
(Pippa's Song.) BBV (1923 ed.); BoTP; BrR; CBEP; EnLi-2; FaFP; FaPON; GoJo; GTBS-W; LiTB; LiTG; OBEV; OBVV; OHIP; OQP; OTPC; PCH; PDV; PoPo; ShBV-1; SiTL; SoP; TreF; TRV; UnPo (3d ed.)
(Song: "Year's at the spring, The.") EnLit; HBV; HBVY; MaRV; MCCG; PoPl; PTK; RG; TOP; TrGrPo; VA; WGRP; YAT
(Song from "Pippa Passes.") ATP; GBV
(Spring Song.) GoTP
Year's at the spring, and the birds do sing, The. Corinna Goes a-Singing. Frank Sidgwick. WhC
Year's Awakening, The. Thomas Hardy. CMoP
Year's Burden, A, 1870, *sel.* Swinburne.
"Are ye so strong, O Kings, O strong men? Nay." PoFr
Years creep slowly by, Lorena, The. Lorena. H. D. L. Webster. BFSS; BLPA
Year's End. Nathaniel A. Benson. CaP
Year's End, The. Timothy Cole. HBV
Years-End. Richard Wilbur. *See* At Year's-End.
Year's Ending, The. St. J. Page Yako, *tr. fr. Xhosa by* C. M. Mcanyangwa *and* Jack Cope. PeSA
Years go by, old friend! Each, as it fleets, The. To R. H. S. James Bayard Taylor. Sonn
Years had elapsed; the long room was the same. A Vision. Yvor Winters. MoVE
Years have flown since I knew thee first. Song. Richard Watson Gilder. *Fr.* The New Day. AA
Years Later. Laurence Lerner. PeSA
Years, Many Parti-coloured Years. Walter Savage Landor. ViBoPo
(Years.) CBEP; HBV; OBEV
Years of frustration, of futility. Frustration, a Heritage. Thelma Parker Cox. TNV
Years of the Modern. Walt Whitman. AmePo; AmPP (3d ed.); MaRV
Years race by on padded feet, The. Invincible. Winnie Lynch Rockett. OQP
Year's Round, The. Coventry Patmore. *See* Year, The.
Years sped onward, The. He who forever sought. Mary Aldis. Seven Sad Sonnets, VI. HBMV
Years That Go to Make Me Man, The. Christopher Brennan. *Fr.* The Twilight of Disquietude. BoAV; PoAu-1
Years they come and go, The. Ad Finem. Heine. AWP; JAWP; WBP
Year's Windfalls, A. Christina Rossetti. OTPC (1923 ed.); PRWS
"On the wind of January," 4 *ll.* BoTP
(Wind of January, The.) YeAr
Years, years ago, ere yet my dreams. The Belle of the Ball-Room. Winthrop Mackworth Praed. Every-Day Characters, III. ALV; BOHV; EnRP; HBV; InMe
Yeats in Dublin, *sel.* Vernon Watkins.
"'Young poet's The,' he murmured." PP
Yeats' Tower. Vernon Watkins. NeBP
Yee blushing virgins happy are. *See* Ye blushing virgins. . .
Yee Build the Sepulchres of the Prophets. Richard Crashaw. MaMe
Yee powr's that guard loves silken throne. *Unknown.* SeCSL
Yee Shall Not Misse of a Few Lines in Remembrance of Thomas Hooker. Edward Johnson. SCAP
Yell'ham-Wood's Story. Thomas Hardy. TOP
Yellow. Kenton Kilmer. GoYe
Yellow Apples. Rochelle Ratner. QAH
Yellow as flowers as dead fingers. Leave Train. Alan Ross. ChMP
Yellow-belly, yellow-belly, come and take a swim. Nursery Rhymes, IV [*or* Yes, by Golly]. *Unknown.* OxBoLi; SD
Yellow Bird, The. *Unknown, tr. fr. Chinese by* Robert Payne. BiS
Yellow Bird Sings, The. Rabindranath Tagore. The Gardener, XVII. OBMV
Yellow Bittern, The. Cathal Buidhe MacElgun, *tr. fr. Modern Irish by* Thomas MacDonagh. OnYI; OxBI
Yellow butterflies. Korosta Katzina Song. *Unknown.* AWP; JAWP
Yellow canary trilled, A. Jealous Adam. Itzig Manger. TrJP
Yellow Cat, The. Leslie Nelson Jennings. FiSC
Yellow chrysanthemum with furious hair, A. Dionysus. Winthrop Palmer. SiTL
Yellow Daffodil, A. Alice Hansche Mortenson. SoP
Yellow Fairy, The. Charlotte Druitt Cole. BoTP
Yellow Fog. T. S. Eliot. *Fr.* The Love Song of J. Alfred Prufrock. LOW
("Yellow fog that rubs its back upon the window-panes, The.") PoPo
Yellow goldenrod is dressed, The. August. Helen Maria Winslow. YeAr
Yellow Jessamine. Constance Fenimore Woolson. AA; HBV
Yellow leaf from the darkness, A. Brooding Grief. D. H. Lawrence. CMoP; LoBV
Yellow-lit Budweiser signs over oaken bars. Uptown. Allen Ginsberg. TwCP
Yellow Meal. *Unknown.* ShS
Yellow moon is a dancing phantom, The. On a Nightingale in April. "Fiona Macleod." HBV; OBV; PoVP
Yellow Pansy, A. Helen Gray Cone. DD; GFA; HBMV
Yellow Rose of Texas, The. *Unknown.* TreFT
Yellow Season, The. William Carlos Williams. MoAB; MoAmPo (1950 ed.)
Yellow sun yellow. The Ballad of Red Fox. Melvin Walker La Follette. LOW; NePoEA
Yellow the bracken. Autumn. Florence Hoatson. BoTP
Yellow Violet, The. Bryant. AmPP; AnNE; AP; CoBA; MAmP; MWA-1; PoLF
Yellow Witch of Caribou, The. Clyde Robertson. PoOW
Yellowhammer, The. John Clare. BoPe
Yellowhammer in her mouth, the cat came mewing, A. Carrion. Clifford Dyment. POTi

Yellowpink butterflies, The. Now. G. Bishop-Dubjinsky. ThO
Yeoman of the Guard, *sel.* W. S. Gilbert.
Family Fool. ALV; InMe; SiTL
Yep, gold's where you find it. You betcha that's true. The Ol' Jinny Mine. Daisy L. Detrick. PoOW
Yep, that's me. Stranger, ain't yew? Wal, step in. The Brothers. Amy Groesbeck. FiSC
"Yer know me little nipper." The Little Nipper an' 'Is Ma. George Fauvel Gouraud. AA
Yere yernes ful yerne, and yeldes never like, A. The Passage of a Year. *Unknown. Fr.* Sir Gawain and the Green Knight. PoEL-1
Yes. Richard Doddridge Blackmore. HBV
Yes? H. C. Bunner. HBV
Yes, all your dutiful goodness I remember. Sick Room. Francis D. Clare. JKCP (1955 ed.)
Yes and No. Clément Marot, *tr. fr. French by* Leigh Hunt. OnPM
(Love Lesson, A.) AWP; JAWP; WBP
Yes and No. Ogden Nash. MaRV
Yes and when the warm unseasonable weather. Memory Green. Archibald MacLeish. Po
Yes as alike as entirely. To My Father. W. S. Graham. FaBoTw
Yes, as I walk, I behold, in a luminous, large intuition. Arthur Hugh Clough. *Fr.* Amours de Voyage. GTBS-D
Yes! Beauty still rebels! Art. Alfred Noyes. OBEV (new ed.)
Yes, by and by. But first a larger matter. God's Speech to Job. Robert Frost. *Fr.* A Masque of Reason. OnHM
Yes, by Golly. *Unknown. See* Yellow-belly, yellow-belly. .
Yes, Cara mine, I know that I shall stand. The Island of Shadows. Richard Garnett. VA
Yes, Dear, lay bare thy lovely soul, nor fear. Confession. Elsa Barker. *Fr.* The Spirit and the Bride. HBMV
Yes, death is at the bottom of the cup. If. William Dean Howells. AA
Yes, ducks are valiant things. F. W. Harvey. *Fr.* Ducks. BoTP
Yes, every Poet is a Fool. Another [*or* Epigram]. Matthew Prior. CEP; EiCL; ML
Yes, faith is a goodly anchor. After the Burial. James Russell Lowell. AA; CoBA; MWA-1; TOP; UnPo
Yes, farewell, farewell forever. Lady Byron's Reply to Lord Byron's "Fare Thee Well." *Unknown.* BLPA
Yes! from mine eyes the tears unbidden start. Distant View of England from the Sea. William Lisle Bowles. EnRP
Yes, he was that, or that, as you prefer. T. A. H. Ambrose Bierce. AA; AnAmPo; YaD
Yes! hope may with my strong desire keep pace. Love's Justification [*or* A Deathless Flower]. Michelangelo, *tr. by* Wordsworth. AWP; CTC; JAWP; WBP; WoL
Yes, I admit I've made a book. Ballade of a Conspicuous Omission from "The Book of Humorous Verse." Carolyn Wells. BOHV
Yes, I admit that Proust is rather good. A Ballade of Diminishing Control. J. C. Squire. WhC
"Yes," I answered you last night. The Lady's "Yes." Elizabeth Barrett Browning. HBV; LiTL
Yes, I Could Love If I Could Find. *Unknown.* ALV; ErPo
Yes, I got another Johnny; but he was to Number One. My Other Chinee Cook. Brunton Stephens. PoAu-1
Yes, I Have Been to Calvary. Avis B. Christiansen. STF
Yes, I have heard the nightingale. Hast Thou Heard the Nightingale? Richard Watson Gilder. AA
Yes! I have seen the ancient oak. Felicia Dorothea Hemans. *Fr.* The Brereton Omen. CTC
Yes, I have slain, and taken moving life. The Husband. Leon Gellert. BoAu
Yes, I have walked in California. Vachel Lindsay. *Fr.* The Golden Whales of California. AtBAP
Yes, I know. They are like primroses. Looking at Sheep. R. S. Thomas. POTi
Yes, I know what you say. Tempted. Edward Rowland Sill. AA
Yes, I love cats, I don't deny. Betsey Trotwood's Cat. Louella C. Poole. CIV
Yes. I remember Adlestrop. Adlestrop. Edward Thomas. BrPo; CH; CLwM; FlW; GoJo; GTBS; GTBS-W; HT; LiTB; LiTM; NP; OBEV (new ed.); PoG; ShBV-2
Yes, I want God's heab'n to be mine. I Want God's Heab'n to Be Mine. *Unknown.* BoAN-2
"Yes, I was only sidesman here when last." Bristol and Clifton. John Betjeman. CMoP; POTi
Yes, I went down to the depot. Jesse James (A *vers.*). *Unknown.* BaBo
Yes, I will love thee when the sun. A Love Song. W. F. Hawley. OBCV
Yes, I will love then, I will love. The Duel. Abraham Cowley. AnAnS-2
Yes, I will spend the livelong day. In May. W. H. Davies. OBVV
Yes; I Write Verses. Walter Savage Landor. EnLi-2; EnRP; EPN
(I Write Verses.) TOP
(Time to Be Wise.) HBV; InMe; VA
Yes, I'm in love, I feel it now. The Je Ne Sais [*or* Sçay] quoi. William Whitehead. EiCL; LO; OBEC
Yes! in the sea of life enisled [*or* enisl'd]. To Marguerite. Matthew Arnold. *Fr.* Switzerland. BWP; CABA; CaFP; CBV; ELP; EnL; EnLi-2; EPN; FaBoEn; FiP; GTBS-D; GTBS-P; HBV; ILP; MaPo; MBW-2; NoP; OAEP; OBEV; OBNC; OBVV; PAn; PoAn; PoEL-5; PoVP; SeCeV; TOP; VaPo; ViPo; ViPP; VP
Yes, it is true: I can remember now. Apology. Edith Henrich. NYTB
Yes, It Was the Mountain Echo. Wordsworth. EnRP
Yes! it's true all my visions. General Custer versus the Titanic. Richard Brautigan. FRC
Yes, I've sev'ral kivers you can see. Kivers. Ann Cobb. AmFN
Yes, leave it with Him; the lilies all do. Leave It with Him. *Unknown.* BLRP; SoP
Yes, "Let the tent be struck:" Victorious morning. Gone Forward. Margaret Junkin Preston. DD
Yes, love, the Spring shall come again. Love's Autumn. John Payne. VA
Yes, magic lyre! now all complete. Ode to an Æolus's Harp. William Mason. WaPE
Yes, muster them out, the valiant band. Muster Out the Ranger[s]. *Unknown.* CoSo
Yes, my ha't's ez ha'd ez stone. A Coquette Conquered. Paul Laurence Dunbar. MAP; MoAmPo (1942 ed.); NeMA
Yes, Nancy Hanks. A Reply to Nancy Hanks. Julius Silberger. TiPo
Yes, nothing seems changeless, but Change. Don Marquis. *Fr.* The God-Maker, Man. MaRV
Yes, o'cose it's interestin' to a feller from the range. A Cowboy at the Carnival. *Unknown.* SCC
Yes—"on our brows we feel the breath." The Dawn of Peace. Alfred Noyes. *Fr.* The Wine Press: Epilogue. MaRV
Yes Please Gentlemen. A. R. D. Fairburn. ACV
Yes, Poet, I am coming down to earth. To a Poet. Carolyn Wells. PoMa
Yes, quietly; drumbeat nor trumpet's peal. Cleveland. William Goldsmith Brown. DD
Yes sir, it was a big surprise. The Day Euterpe Died. Thomas M. Disch. HYE
Yes, so be it, though we already knew. The Sinking of the Mendi. S. E. K. Mqhayi. PeSA
Yes! Steeple-chasing is stirring sport—and the most exciting events of all. Juniper Jim. "F. Anstey." YT
Yes, still I love thee! Time, who sets. Love Unchangeable. Rufus Dawes. AA
"Yes, stranger, them was red-hot times." Cow-Boy Fun. Wallace D. Coburn. PoOW
Yes, stranger! you well may say so. The Wickedest Man in Memphis. Alex J. Brown. BeLS
Yes; thank my stars! as early as I knew. Satire II. Pope. *Fr.* The Satires of Dr. John Donne, Versified. PoFS
Yes, that fair neck, too beautiful by half. Madame d'Albert's Laugh [*or* On Her Laugh]. Clément Marot. ALV; AWP; JAWP; OnPM; WBP
"Yes the book of Revelations will be brought forth dat day." A Group of Negro Songs. *Unknown.* NAMP
Yes, the candidate's a dodger, yes, a well known dodger. The Dodger. *Unknown.* OuSiCo
Yes, the coneys are scared by the thud of hoofs. *See* Yea, the coneys are scared by the thud of hoofs.
"Yes, the Town Clerk will see you." In I went. The Town

Clerk's Views. John Betjeman. CMoP
Yes, The will decided. But how can the heart decide. A Separation. Stephen Spender. MoLP
Yes, the Year is growing old. Midnight Mass for the Dying Year. Longfellow. GoBC; PoRL
Yes, theirs was a love that was tidal. Limerick. Paul Kieffer. LiBL
Yes, there is holy pleasure in thine eye! Admonition to a Traveller. Wordsworth. GTBS; GTBS-D; GTBS-P; GTBS-W; GTSE; GTSL
Yes, these are the dog-days, Fortunatus. Under Sirius. W. H. Auden. NePA
Yes, they are alive, and can have those colors. A Blessing in Disguise. John Ashbery. ANYP
Yes, they are changed. They Have Been with Jesus. *Unknown.* SoP
Yes! thou art fair, and I had lov'd. Too Late. William James Linton. VA
Yes—'tis decreed my Sword no more. A Runic Ode. Thomas Warton, the Elder. CEP
Yes, true, children will take advantage of. The Little Girl. Nicholas Moore. ErPo; NeBP
Yes, utterly he loves his Nazareth. Young Man in a Galilean Doorway. Herbert D. Gallaudet. ChIP
Yes, we are fighting at last, it appears. Arthur Hugh Clough. *Fr.* Amours de Voyage, II. PeVV
Yes, we did a heap o' riggin'. Old Ship Riggers. H. A. Cody. EtS
Yes, we do differ when we most agree. Religious Unity. Hartley Coleridge. MaRV
Yes, we have lost our way. No guiding star. Desert Wanderings. Thomas Curtis Clark. ChIP
Yes, we love this land together. Fatherland Song (Norwegian National Hymn). Björnstjerne Björnson. AWP
Yes, we'll come to the table. Cowboy Grace. *Unknown.* CoSo
Yes, we'll rally round the flag, boys, we'll rally once again. The Battle Cry of Freedom. George F. Root. FaBoBe; PaA; PAH; PoFr; TreFS; YaD
Yes; we'll wed, my little fay. The Conformers. Thomas Hardy. EnLi-2 (1949 ed.); ViBoPo
Yes when the dark withdrew I suffered light. A World of Light. Elizabeth Jennings. NePoEA-2
Yes, when the toilsome day is gone. Private Devotions. Phoebe H. Brown. AmePo
Yes; when the ways oppose. Ars Victrix. Austin Dobson. HBV; HBVY; MoBrPo (1942 ed.); PoVP; SyP; VA
Yes, who shall tell the value of our tears. Esther; Young Man's Tragedy, II. Wilfrid Scawen Blunt. Sonn
Yes. Why do we all, seeing of a soldier, bless him? The Soldier. Gerard Manley Hopkins. WaaP
Yes, wonderful are dreams: and I have known. Charles Harpur. *Fr.* The Tower of the Dream. PoAu-1
Yes, write if you want to—there's nothing like trying. A Familiar Letter to Several Correspondents. Oliver Wendell Holmes. BOHV; InMe
"Yes, write it in the rock," Saint Bernard said. Divinity. Matthew Arnold. EPN
Yes, yes, my boy, there's no mistake. McIlrath of Malate. John Jerome Rooney. PAH
Yes, you are always everywhere. But I. No Beauty We Could Desire. C. S. Lewis. BoPe
Yes, you despise the man to books confin'd. Moral Essays, Epistle I. Pope. CEP
"Yes, you did, too!" Little Words. Benjamin Keech. PoToHe
Yes, yours, my love, is the right human face. The Confirmation. Edwin Muir. OxBS; POTE; WePo
Yesterday. Ethel Anderson. NeLNL
Yesterday. Hugh Chesterman. BoTP; SiSoSe
Yesterday. Frank Crane. OQP
Yesterday!/ Betrayed, forsaken, crucified. The Conqueror. Ruth M. Williams. BePJ
Yesterday/ out the window. Learning to Dance. Rudy Bee Graham. BF
Yesterday a world was born. In Between Time (Transcience). Marsha Ann Jackson. TNV
Yesterday all the past. The language of size. Spain 1937. W. H. Auden. CABL; EnLit; LiTB; LiTG; WaP
Yesterday as I lay nigh dead with toil. Isaac Rosenberg. *Fr.* Moses; a Play. FaBoMo
Yesterday, at dip of dusk. Old Man Long Ago. Nancy Byrd Turner. GaP
Yesterday Dr. Marcus went to see the statue of Zeus. On Marcus the Physician. Nicarchus. LiTW
Yesterday ended when the shadows. This Is Today. Phyllis C. Michael. SoP
Yesterday has slipped the perimeter of perfection. Meditation on Time. Sister Mary Athanasius. JKCP (1955 ed.)
Yesterday, I dreamed of tomorrow. Opportunity. W. Audrey P. Good. SoP
Yesterday I skipped all day. Tiptoe. Karla Kuskin. PDV
Yesterday in Oxford Street. Rose Fyleman. OTPC (1946 ed.); PCH; PDV; RIS; TiPo
Yesterday it blew alway. To Petronilla Who Has Put Up Her Hair. Henry Howarth Bashford. HBV
Yesterday it seems you were acting on a stage. Legend. John Waller. NeBP
Yesterday my cross seemed heavy. Hours of Prayer. Julia Biebesheimer. SoP
Yesterday my gun exploded. The Perils of Obesity. Harry Graham. FiBHP
Yesterday rain fell in torrents. You Could Say. Robert Mezey. AmPC; NaP; ToPo
Yesterday, Rebecca Mason. Rebecca's After-Thought [*or* I Almost Did—Very Nigh]. Elizabeth Turner. HBV; HBVY; ThGo
Yesterday the fields were only gray with scattered snow. A Winter's Tale. D. H. Lawrence. MoAB; MoBrPo
Yesterday the twig was brown and bare. Miracle. Liberty Hyde Bailey. OHIP; OQP; YeAr
Yesterday's Child. Robert Reedburg. TNV
Yestreen I had a pint o' wine. Anna [*or* The Gowden Locks of Anna]. Burns. CBEP; TrGrPo; UnTE
Yestreen the queen had four Marys [*or* Maries]. The Four Marys [*or* Mary Hamilton's Last Goodnight]. *Unknown.* BFSS; ViBoFo
Yet/ Ere the Season died a-cold. Ezra Pound. *Fr.* Canto LXXXI. MoVE
Yet Ah, that Spring should vanish with the Rose. Omar Khayyám, *tr. by* Edward Fitzgerald. *Fr.* The Rubáiyát. SeCeV
Yet another great truth I record in my verse. The Viper. Hilaire Belloc. BOHV; RIS
Yet but Three? Shakespeare. *Fr.* A Midsummer Night's Dream, III,ii. CTC
"Yet Chloe [*or* Cloe] sure was form'd without a spot." Chloe [*or* Characters from the Satires: Chloe]. Pope. *Fr.* Moral Essays, Epistle II. AWP; ErPo; InPo; JAWP; WBP
Yet Do I Marvel. Countee Cullen. AmNP; AnAmPo; BANP; BP; CDC; IDB; NP; PoNe; TTY
Yet Each Man Kills the Thing He Loves. Oscar Wilde. *Fr.* The Ballad of Reading Gaol, I. LO, 3 *sts.*; TrGrPo, 14 *sts. fr.* I *and* II; WHA, *br. sel.*
Yet even mid merry boyhood's tricks and scapes. Frederick Goddard Tuckerman. *Fr.* Sonnets. MAmP
Yet Gentle Will the Griffin Be. Vachel Lindsay. PDV; SP; StVeCh; TSW
(Poems about the Moon, 2.) MAPA; TwAmPo
Yet goodly court he made still to his Dame. Spenser. *Fr.* The Faerie Queene, I. MBW-1
Yet had his sun not risen; from his lips. The Final Struggle. Louis James Block. *Fr.* The New World. PAH
Yet, hail to you/ Moors, mountains, headlands, and ye hollow vales. The Shepherd. Wordsworth. The Prelude, VIII. ERoP-1
Yet howsoever changed or tost. The Undying Soul. Whittier. *Fr.* On a Fly-Leaf of Longfellow's Poems. MaRV; OQP
Yet I could think, indeed, the perfect call. Arthur Hugh Clough. *Fr.* Dipsychus. OBNC
Yet I knelt on my knees and begged her for grace. Passus II: Lady Meed. William Langland. *Fr.* The Vision of Piers Plowman. EnLit
Yet If His Majesty, Our Sovereign Lord. *Unknown.* FaBoCh; LoGBV; NoP; SeEP; ViBoPo
(Coming of the King, The.) TrGrPo
(Guest, The) BoC; EaLo; GoBC; MaRV; OBS; OxBoCh; SeCL
(Guests.) EvOK; OtMeF; StJW
(Heavenlie Vistor, A.) CAW
(Preparations.) CBEP; OBEV; WePo
(Royal Guest, A.) CH
(Yet If His Majesty.) PoRA; TuPP
Yet if once we efface the joys of the chase. The Chase and the

Yet (continued)
Race. Adam Lindsay Gordon. *Fr.* Ye Wearie Wayfarer. OtMeF
Yet if some voice that man could trust. Tennyson. In Memoriam A. H. H., XXXV. EPN; MaPo; OAEP; ViBoPo; ViPo; VP
Yet in spite / Of pleasure won, and knowledge not withheld. Summer Vacation [*or* The Rededication to Nature]. Wordsworth. *Fr.* The Prelude, IV. ERoP-1; PoEL-4
Yet it is not all immaculate death. Not All Immaculate. Laura Riding. *Fr.* Three Sermons to the Dead. LiTA
Yet it was plain she struggled, and that salt. Modern Love, VIII. George Meredith. EnLit; GTBS-D; Sonn; ViPo; VP
Yet let me flap this bug with gilded wings. Pope. *Fr.* Epistle to Dr. Arbuthnot. ExPo
Yet Listen Now. Amy Carmichael. TRV
Yet London, empress of the northern clime. Dryden. *Fr.* Annus Mirabilis. ViBoPo
Yet, love, mere love, is beautiful indeed. Sonnets from the Portuguese, X. Elizabeth Barrett Browning. CTC; HBV; GTBS
Yet Love Was Born. Charles Hannibal Voss. BePJ
Yet Love Will Dream. Whittier. *See* Life and Love.
Yet Love will dream and Faith will trust. Life and Love. Whittier. TRV
Yet never fam'd was he, nor foremost found. Robert Bloomfield. *Fr.* The Farmer's Boy. PeER
Yet not in solitude if Christ anear me. Not in Solitude. Frederic William Henry Myers. *Fr.* Saint Paul. OQP
Yet not to thine eternal resting-place. Bryant. *Fr.* Thanatopsis. PTK
Yet, O my friend—pale conjuror, I call. Bring Them Not Back. James Benjamin Kenyon. AA
Yet, O stricken heart, remember, O remember. In Memoriam F. A. S. Robert Louis Stevenson. BrPo; GTBS
Yet often I think the king of that country. The Gospel of Labor. Henry van Dyke. TRV
Yet on fresh billows seaward wilt thou ride. Seek a Haven. Horace. *Fr.* Odes. OnPM
Yet, once again, Antinous did reply. Sir John Davies. *Fr.* Orchestra. LO
Yet once more, O ye laurels, and once more. Lycidas. Milton. AnEnPo; AnFE; AtBAP; ATP; AWP; BEL; BoLiVe; BWP; CABA; CaFP; CBV; ChTr; DiPo; EnL; EnLi-1; EnLit; ExPo; FaBoEn; FiP; FosPo; GTBS; GTBS-D; GTBS-P; GTBS-W; GTSL; HBV; ILP; InPo; JAWP; LiTB; LiTG; LoBV; MaPo; MasP; MBW-1; MCCG; MemP; MyFE; NoP; OAEP; OBEV; OBS; OuHeWo; PAn; PIA; Po; PoAn; PoE; PoEL-3; PoFS; PoIE; SeCeV; SeEP; StP; TOP; TrGrPo; UnPo; VaPo; ViBoPo; WBP; WGRP; WHA; WoL
Yet one more hour, then comes the night. My Drinking Song. Richard Dehmel. AWP
Yet one smile more, departing, distant sun. November. Bryant. Sonn
Yet pity for a horse o'er-driven. In Memoriam A. H. H., LXIII. Tennyson. EPN; ViPo; VP
Yet sighs, dear sighs, indeed true friends you are. Astrophel and Stella, XCV. Sir Philip Sidney. FCP; SiPS
Yet still there whispers the small voice within. Conscience. Byron. MaRV
Yet there are watchmen, who with friendly light. Of Watchmen. John Gay. *Fr.* Trivia; or, The Art of Walking the Streets of London, III. EnLi-1 (1949 ed.)
"Yet there's one scruple with which I am much." Philip Massinger. *Fr.* The Renegado. ACP (1952 ed.)
Yet thou, they say, for marriage dost provide. Against Women: Satire VI. Juvenal. *Fr.* The Satires. LiTW; UnTE
Yet through the turmoil comfortless and loud. The Albatross. William Pember Reeves. AnNZ
Yet to the wondrous St. Peter's, and yet to the solemn Rotonda. Ah, That I Were Far Away. Arthur Hugh Clough. *Fr.* Amours de Voyage. OBNC
Yet Vain, Perhaps, the Fruits. Frederick Goddard Tuckerman. *Fr.* Sonnets. AnNE
Yet wear we on; the deep light disallowed. Frederick Goddard Tuckerman. *Fr.* Sonnets. AmePo
Yet, when I muse on what life is, I seem. To a Republican Friend, 1848, Continued [*or* Continued]. Matthew Arnold. EPN; MBW-2; PoVP; Sonn; ViPP
Yet while my Hector still survives, I see. Hector and Andromache. Homer, *tr. by* Pope. *Fr.* The Iliad, VI. OBEC
Yet wulde I nat the causer fared amisse. Subject to All Pain. *Unknown.* MeEL
Yet, yet a moment, one dim ray of light. Pope. *Fr.* The Dunciad. AtBAP; EiCL; EiPP; MBW-1; PoEL-3
Yeux Glauques. Ezra Pound. *Fr.* Hugh Selwyn Mauberley. CMoP; MoAmPo (1962 ed.)
Ye've left the sun an' the can'le licht and the starlicht. The Licht Nichts. Violet Jacob. ACV
Yew in the Graveyard, The. Tennyson. *See.* In Memoriam A. H. H.: "Old yew, which graspest at the stones."
Yew-Tree, The. *Unknown, tr. fr. Welsh.* ChTr
Yew-Tree, The. Vernon Watkins. EaLo; LiTB
Yew-Trees. Wordsworth. BEL; CABA; EnLi-2; EnRP; ERoP-1; UnPo (3d ed.)
Y'heave ho! my lads, the wind blows free. Sailing. Godfrey Marks. TreFS
Yield all, my love; but be withal as coy. Upon A. M. Sir John Suckling. CavP; ErPo
Yielded. Cardinal Newman. *See* Sensitiveness.
Yielded Instrument, A. Avis B. Christiansen. SoP
Yielded Life. "W. A. G." BLRP
Yielded to Him. Connie Calenberg. SoP
Yip! Yip! Yip! Yip! tunin' up the fiddle. The Cowboys' [*or* Cowboy's] Ball. Henry Herbert Knibbs. PoOW; SCC
Yippee! she is shooting in the harbor! he is jumping. Blocks. Frank O'Hara. ANYP
Ylen's Song. Richard Hovey. *Fr.* The Birth of Galahad. AA
Yo ho, ma hahties, da's a hurricane a-brewin'. Black Sailor's Chanty. Charles Keeler. EtS
Yoga. *Unknown, tr. fr. Sanskrit by* Joseph Nadin Rawson. *Fr.* The Upanishads. OnPM
Yoke, The. Kalonymos ben Kalonymos, *tr. fr. Hebrew by* Joseph Chotzner. *Fr.* The Touchstone. TrJP
Yoke of Tyranny, The. Sir Philip Sidney. *See* Astrophel and Stella. XLVII.
Yokes he made were true, The. My Yoke Is Easy. Gladys Latchaw. ChIP; MaRV
Yolp, Yolp, Yolp, Yolp. *Unknown.* ElL; OA
Yom Kippur. Israel Zangwill. TrJP
Yon clouds that roam the deserts of the air. The Bedouins of the Skies. James Benjamin Kenyon. AA
Yon cottager who weaves at her own door. Simple Faith. William Cowper. *Fr.* Truth. OBEC
Yon Far Country. A. E. Housman. *See* Into My Heart an Air That Kills.
Yon flakes that fret the eastern sky. More Poems, XXV. A. E. Housman. VP
Yon goes a gallant which will get repute. In Rudionem. John Weever. SiCE; TuPP
Yon is the laddie lo'ed to daunder far. Lintie in a Cage. Alice V. Stuart. OxBS
Yon laddie wi' the gowdan pow. A Riddle. William Soutar. OxBS
Yon silvery billows breaking on the beach. The Sonnet's Voice. Theodore Watts-Dunton. EtS; HBV; InP; TOP; VA
Yon whey-faced brother, who delights to wear. The Moral Bully. Oliver Wendell Holmes. AmePo; AnAmPo; AnNE
Yonder come Roberta! Tell me how do you know? Midnight Special. *Unknown.* AS
Yonder comes a courteous knight. The Baffled [*or* Courteous] Knight. *Unknown.* BaBo; ESPB; OxBB
Yonder comes dat ole Joe Brown. Walky-talky Jennie. *Unknown.* AS
Yonder Comes My Pretty Little Girl. *Unknown.* *See* Roving Gambler, The.
Yonder comes my woman! It's how do you know? The Midnight Special. *Unknown.* BFSS
Yonder Comes the High Sheriff, *with music.* *Unknown.* AS
Yonder great shadow—that blot on the passionate glare of the desert. The Dead of the Wilderness. Hayyim Nahman Bialik. AWP; JAWP; WBP
Yonder in the heather there's a bed for sleeping. In City Streets. Ada Smith. HBV; OTPC (1923 ed.)
Yonder is an old crow sitting on an oak. The Old Crow. *Unknown.* FTB
Yonder, lo! the tide is flowing. The Swimmer. Roden Noel. OBVV
Yonder School, *with music.* *Unknown.* BFSS
Yonder See the Morning Blink. A. E. Housman. CMoP;

EnLit; MaRV; MoShBr; PoE; WePo
Yonder, that swarm of things insectual. A Sequelula to "The Dynasts." Max Beerbohm. Par
"Yonder there behold! a soul that stationed." Political Chaos in Italy. Dante. *Fr.* Divina Commedia: Purgatorio. WoL
Yonder, yonder see the fair rainbow. Corn-grinding Song. *Tr. by* Natalie Curtis. RePo; SUS
Yonder's the man with his life in his hand. "Atkins." George Meredith. PoVP
Yond's the Cardinall's window: This fortification. John Webster. *Fr.* The Duchess of Malfi, V, iii. PoEL-2
Yonghy-Bonghy-Bo, The. Edward Lear. *See* Courtship of the Yonghy-Bonghy-Bo, The. . .
Yonnondio. Walt Whitman. MCCG
Yorkshire Bite, The. *Unknown.* BaBo
Yorkshire Moors, The. Hal Summers. HaMV
Yorktown Centennial Lyric. Paul Hamilton Hayne. PAH
Yosemite. Milicent Washburn Shinn. *Fr.* Washington Sequoia. AA
You. Tom Clark. ANYP
"Chords knotted together like insane nouns, The," IV.
"Door behind me was you, The," I. YAP
"O Earth Mother, who consents to everything, who forgives," V.
"Today I get this letter from you and the sun," III.
"You are bright, tremendous, wow," II.
You. Edgar A. Guest. ATP
You. John Masefield. MoRP
You. Kenneth Rexroth. *Fr.* A Bestiary. HoPM
You. *Unknown.* MeWo
You/ Who leap among words. Demosthenes to the Radio Announcer. David Ross. PG (1945 ed.)
You/ Over there/ Beyond the hill. Echo. Mildred Weston. BoNaP; PoMa
You/ Boo! The Next Shortest Poem in the World. *Unknown.* SiTL
You!/ the great America. One Way. Tommy Whitaker. TNV
You abandon me, woman, because I am very poor. El Abandonado. *Unknown.* ABF; AS
You, after all, were good. Afterthoughts of Donna Elvira. Carolyn Kizer. NePoAm-2
You All Are Static; I Alone Am Moving. Peter Viereck. LiTA
You also, laughing one. A Girl. Babette Deutsch. HBMV
You an' me, bister, been giraffes. To and on Other Intellectual Poets on Reading That the U.S.A.F. Had Sent a Team of Scientists to Africa. Ramon Guthrie. NMP
You and I. Henry Alford. BLPA; FaBoBe; NeHB
You and I and Amyas. William Cornish. CBEP
Latet Anguis, 4 // OBEV (new ed.)
You and I by this lamp with these. Together. Ludwig Lewisohn. HBMV; PoToHe; TrJP
You and I have found the secret way. The Secret Love. "Æ." HBV
You and It. Mark Strand. NYBP
You and Today. Ella Wheeler Wilcox. OQP
(With Every Rising of the Sun.) TreFT
You, Andrew Marvell. Archibald MacLeish. AmLP; AmP; AmPP; AnAmPo; AnEnPo; AnFE; AP; APA; AWP; BoLiVe; CaFP; CBV; CMoP; CoAnAm; CoBA; CoBMV; FaBV; FosPo; GTBS-W; HoPM; InP; InPo; LiTA; LiTM; MAP; MoAB; MoAmPo; MoVE; NeMA; OxBA; NoP; NP; PoAn; PoIE; PoMa; PoRA; StP; TDP; TreFT; TrGrPo; TwAmPo; TwCP; VaPo; ViBoPo; WoL
You approach me carrying a book. Superballs. Tom Clark. ANYP
You are a [*or* the] friend then, as I make it out. Ben Jonson Entertains a Man from Stratford. E. A. Robinson. AmPP; APA; ATP; CoAnAm; InP; MAP; MAPA; MoAB; MoAmPo; MoPo; TwAmPo
You Are a Jew! Delmore Schwartz. *Fr.* Genesis. TrJP
You Are a Part of Me. Frank Yerby. AmNP
You are a riddle I would not unravel. Riddle. Josephine Miles. FiMAP
You are a sunrise. To a Golden-haired Girl in a Louisiana Town. Vachel Lindsay. MAP; MoAmPo; MoLP; NeMA
You are a Treasure, Lord, beyond all price. Against Despair. Sister Mary Ada. JKCP (1955 ed.)
You are a tried and loyal friend. To My Setter, Scout. Frank H. Seldon. BLPA
You are a tulip seen to-day. A Meditation for His Mistress[e] Robert Herrick. OBEV; OBS; SeCP
You are all these people. To a Single Shadow without Pity. Sam Cornish. NBP
You Are Always New. "Anna Akhmatova," *tr. fr. Russian by* C. M. Bowra. LiTW
You are as gold. Song. Hilda Doolittle ("H. D."). AnFE; APA; CoAnAm; CoBA; LiTA; LiTM; MAP; MAPA; MoAmPo; TwAmPo
You are beautiful. What Ulysses Said to Circe on the Beach of Aeaea. Irving Layton. ErPo
You are beautiful and faded. A Lady. Amy Lowell. MAP; MAPA; MoAmPo; NeMA; NP
You are blind like us. To Germany. Charles Hamilton Sorley. MoBrPo
You are bright, tremendous, wow. You (II). Tom Clark. ANYP
You are but these to me: a freckled face. Sonnet Sequence. Darwin T. Turner. BALP
You are carried in a basket. Operation. W. E. Henley. *Fr.* In Hospital. PoVP
You are clear,/ O rose, cut in rock. The Garden. Hilda Doolittle ("H. D."). AnFE; APA; AtBAP; CoAnAm; CoBA; LiTA; MAPA; NP; TwAmPo
You are coming home at night. Coming Home. Rolfe Humphries. MoRP
You are coming to woo me, but not as of yore. Lips That Touch Liquor. George W. Young. TreFT
You are disdainful and magnificent. Sonnet to a Negro in Harlem. Helene Johnson. AmNP; BANP; CDC
You are earth, loam, actual fields. A Poet's Eye-View. Anne Wilkinson. TwCaPo
You are falling asleep and I sit looking at you. After Dark. Adrienne Rich. LiTM (1970 ed.)
You are famous in my mind. Before the Storm. William Stafford. NaP
You are fayre and lovely too. *Unknown.* SeCSL
You [*or* We] are gazing [*or* looking] now on old Tom Moore. The Days of Forty-nine. *Unknown.* CoSo; IHA; PAH
You are going far away, far away from poor Jeannette. Jeannette and Jeannot. Charles Jeffries. BLPA
You Are Gorgeous and I'm Coming. Frank O'Hara. NeAP
You are here now,/ Who were so loud and feared. The Sleeping Fury. Louise Bogan. LiTM
You are lighting yourself. Jonathan Cott. YAP
You are like startled song-wings against my heart. Songs to a Woman. Maxwell Bodenheim. NP
You are like the lightning. Love's Terror. *Unknown.* WoL
You Are like the Snow Only. E. E. Cummings. AtBAP
You are looking now on old Tom Moore. *See* You are gazing now. . .
You are loveliness and all desire. Living and Dying. "Michael Lewis." *Fr.* Cherry Blossoms. UnTE
You are more beautiful than light. Marriage Song. William Thomas Walsh. JKCP (1955 ed.)
You are my companion. To F. W. Edith Wyatt. NP
You Are My Sisters. Georges Rodenbach, *tr. fr. French by* Thomas Walsh. CAW
You are my song come true. Reparation. Helen Hoyt. HBMV
You are no more, but sunken in a sea. Sea-Change. Genevieve Taggard. EtS; NP
You are not, Cynthia, better pleased than I. To the Unconstant Cynthia. Sir Robert Howard. SeCL
You are not dead—Life has but set you free! On the Death of an Aged Friend. Roselle Mercier Montgomery. MaRV
You are not merry, brother. Why not laugh. The Prodigal Son. E. A. Robinson. MAP; MoAmPo
You are now/ In London, that great sea, whose ebb and flow. Shelley. *Fr.* Letter to Maria Gisborne. ChER; OBRV; PeER
You are, O Life, the strangest friend I know. Prometheus Unbound. Sister Miriam. JKCP (1955 ed.)
"You are old, Father William," the young man cried. The Old Man's Comforts [*or* The Old Man's Comforts and How He Gained Them *or* Father William]. Robert Southey. HBV; HoPM; OTPC; PaPo; Par; YAT
"You are old, Father William," the young man said. Father William. "Lewis Carroll." *Fr.* Alice's Adventures in

'You (continued)
Wonderland. ALV; BiCB; BoChLi; BOHV; FaPL; FaPON; FiBHP; GoJo; GoTP; HBV; HoPM; InMe; LBN; LiTB; LiTG; OnPP; OTPC (1946 ed.); Par; PCD; PDV; PoLF; PoRA; PoVP; RePo; RIS; ShBV-2; SiTL; StaSt; TiPo; TOP; TreF; TrGrPo; TSW; WaKn; WhC; YAT
"You are old, Father William," the young man said,/ "And your nose has a look of surprise." Father William. *Unknown.* BOHV; NA; SiTL
You are on an expedition for a museum. She. Edward Field. FRC
You Are on U.S. 40 Headed West. Vera White. AmFN
You are over there, Father Malloy. Father Malloy. Edgar Lee Masters. *Fr.* Spoon River Anthology. NP; OxBA; PoPo
You are Power. More Letters Found by a Suicide. Frank Horne. BANP
You are so beautiful I don't know where to look. The Rising. Julia Vinograd. YAP
You are so fond of law, I hear. Disputes. Alonso Jerónimo de Salas Barbadillo. OnPM
You are still the one with the stone and the sling. Man of My Time. Salvatore Quasimodo. PoPl
You are such a well-rounded sponge. Sediment. David Ignatow. NYBP
You are so witty, profligate, and thin. Extempore to Voltaire Criticising Milton. Edward Young. ViBoPo
You are that legendary figure, never seen. Homage to Vaslav Nijinsky. James Kirkup. UnS
You Are the Brave. Ray Patterson. NBP
(In Time of Crisis.) IDB
You are the fellow that has to decide. You. Edgar A. Guest. ATP
You Are the Future. Rainer Maria Rilke, *tr. fr. German by* Babette Deutsch. MaRV
You are the lice. Special Section for the Niggas on the Lower Eastside or: Invert the Divisor and Multiply. Welton Smith. BF
You are the millions, we are multitude. The Scythians. Aleksandr Aleksandrovich Blok. AWP; WaaP
You are the old, the violent and melancholy master of that final land. For the 90th Birthday of Sibelius. James Kirkup. MuSP; POTi
You are the priest tonight. To Mary; at the Thirteenth Station. Raymond F. Roseliep. ISi
You are the problem I propose. The Metaphysical Amorist. J. V. Cunningham. TwAmPo
You are the stately sunset. Metaphor. Clark Ashton Smith. FiSC
You are the vision, you are the image of the dream. The Vision. William Stanley Braithwaite. OQP
You Are Unhappy. Heine, *tr. fr. German by* Ralph Marcus. OnPM
You are where the dauntless wind in rebellion. Madrigal to a Streetcar Token. Rafael Alberti. LiTW
You are writing a Gospel. Your Own Version. Paul Gilbert. BLRP; MaRV
You ask a sonnet? Well, it is your right. James Branch Cabell. *Fr.* Retractions. HBMV
You ask a verse, to sing (ah, laughing face!). To a Lady. John James Piatt. AA
You ask for fame or power? The Golden Text. George Frederick Cameron. VA
You ask from whence proceed these monstrous crimes. The Vices of Women. Juvenal. *Fr.* Satires, VI. PeRV
You ask me, Fresher, who it is. Ballade of Andrew Lang. Dugald Sutherland MacColl. CenHV
You ask me how Contempt who claims to sleep. Epigram [*or* Two Epigrams, II]. J. V. Cunningham. ELU; ErPo; NePoAm; SiTL; StP
You ask me how I know it's true. The Heavens Declare the Glory of God. Helen Steiner Rice. FaChP
You ask me, Lydia, "whether I." To "Lydia Languish." Austin Dobson. NBM; PoVP
You ask me why I have no verses sent. To a Poetic Lover. Martial, *tr. by* W. Hay. ALV
You ask me "why I like him." Nay. Friends. E. V. Lucas. HBV
You Ask Me, Why, tho' [*or* though] Ill at Ease. Tennyson. CABA; BEL; CoBE; EnLit; MBW-2; OAEP; PoVP; ViPo; ViPP
You ask me why, upon my breast. A Knot of Blue and Gray. *Unknown.* PEDC
You ask my love. What shall my love then be? On the Nature of Love. Wilfrid Scawen Blunt. The Love Sonnets of Proteus, XXII. ViBoPo
You ask what I have found, and far and wide I go. The Curse of Cromwell. W. B. Yeats. SeCePo
You ask what land I love the best. The Song of Iowa. S. H. M. Byers. PoRL
You ask what place I like the best. The Kinkaiders [*or* The Kinkaider's Song]. *Unknown.* AS; CoSo
You ask why Mary was called contrary? Contrary Mary. Nancy Byrd Turner. HBMV; HBVY; TSW
You asked me, "What is courage?" And I took. Courage. Helen Frazee-Bower. OTD
You at the Pump (History of North and South). Frank O'Hara. ANYP
You, Atalanta, were so fleet. To Atalanta. Dorothy Dow. HBMV
You ax about dat music made. The Banjo of the Past. Howard Weeden. AA
You bad-eyed, tough-mouthed son-of-a-gun. Pardners. Berton Braley. SCC
You bad leetle boy, not moche you care. Leetle Bateese. William Henry Drummond. CaP
You Beat Your Pate. Pope. *See* To a Blockhead.
You beauteous [*or* beautious] ladies, great and small. The Lady Turned Serving-Man [*or* The Famous Flower of Serving-Men]. *Unknown.* ESPB; OBB; OxBB
You became. My Company. Sir Herbert Read. BrPo; FaBoMo; MMA
You, being less than either dew or frost. Love Song Out of Nothing. Vassar Miller. NePoEA
You believe in a live city. News of My Friends. Grant Code. FiSC
You bells in the steeple, ring, ring out your changes. Songs of Seven: Seven Times Two. Jean Ingelow. GBV (1922 ed.); GN; HBV; OTPC (1923 ed.)
You better sure shall live not evermore. Translated Out of Horace Which Begins Rectius Vives. Horace. *Fr.* Odes. FCP; ReIE
You bible-sharps that thump on tubs. Villon's Good-Night. W. E. Henley. CenHV
You bid me hold my peace. Poet to the Birds. Alice Meynell. NP
You Bid Me Try. Austin Dobson. *See* Rondeau, The: "You bid me try, Blue Eyes to write."
You Black Bright Stars. *Unknown.* EnRePo
You Blessed Bowers. *Unknown.* EIL
You boast about your ancient line. Family Trees. Douglas Malloch. OHIP; PEDC
You brave heroic [*or* heroique] minds. To [*or* Ode to] the Virginian Voyage. Michael Drayton. AtBAP; CBEP; CoBE; EnLi-1 (1949 ed.); EnRePo; HBV; LoBV; MC; NoP; OAEP; OBEV; OBS; PaA; PAH; PoEL-2; PoFr; ReEn; ReIE; SeCePo; SeEP; StP; ThLM; TuPP; ViBoPo
You bring no joy, but strange regret. Sosei Hoshi, *tr. fr. Japanese by* I. W. Furukami. LiTW
You bring the only changes to this season. For Nicholas, Born in September. Tod Perry. NYBP
You broke your teeth upon the question Why. The Resolution. Vassar Miller. CoPo
You burned the dawn. Wake for Papa Montero. Nicolás Guillén. PoNe
You buy some flowers for your table. Poems in Praise of Practically Nothing, I. Samuel Hoffenstein. BOHV; FiBHP; InMe; SiTL; TrJP
You buy yourself a new suit of clothes. Poems in Praise of Practically Nothing, IV. Samuel Hoffenstein. BOHV; InMe; SiTL
You called me a name on such and such a day. For T. S. E. Only. Hyam Plutzik. FiMAP
You came back to us in a dream and we were not here. Come Back. W. S. Merwin. NaP
You came like the dawn. On the Death of a Child. Edward Silvera. PoNe
You came to it through wild country, there the sea's voice. The House in the Green Well. John Hall Wheelock. MoAmPo (1962 ed.)
You came to me bearing bright roses. Crowned. Amy Lowell. HBV

You Can Be One! Edith C. Lilly. SoP
You can come in. Welcome. R. S. Thomas. NMP
You can find it only in attics or in ads. The Spinning Wheel. A. M. Klein. CaP
You can fool the hapless public. You Can't Fool God. Grenville Kleiser. STF
You can get all of the soul out of the body. What You Can Get from the Body. William Hunt. YAP
You can go in the stall. Unclaimed. Florida Watts Smyth. StaSt
You can push. Fourteen Ways of Touching the Peter. George MacBeth. FIW
You can say anything. The Art of Poetry. Dennis Trudell. QAH
You can stop me. There's Somethin'. Adam Small. PeSA
"You can talk about yer sheep dorgs," said the man from Allan's Creek. Daley's Dorg Wattle. W. T. Goodge. PoAu-1
You cannot build again what you have broken. The Witch. Lord Alfred Douglas. HBMV
You cannot cage a field. Lives. Henry Reed. BoNaP; LiTB
You cannot choose but love, lad. To an Old Tune. William Alexander Percy. HBMV
You cannot choose your battlefields. The Colors [*or* Standards]. Nathalia Crane. GoTP; MAP; NeMA; StaSt
You cannot dream. Things Lovelier. Humbert Wolfe. MoBrPo; TrJP
You cannot hope. The British Journalist. Humbert Wolfe. BoC; FiBHP; PV
You cannot justly of the Court complain. To a Witty Man of Wealth and Quality; Who, after His Dismissal from Court, Said, He Might Justly Complain of It. William Wycherley. SeCV-2
You cannot rest behind the plate. Villanelle. M. D. Feld. SD
You cannot traffick in peace. Humbert Wolfe. *Fr.* The Uncelestial City. BoC
You cannot will to men your health. Some Things You Cannot Will to Men. Walter E. Isenhour. STF
You Can't Be Wise. Paul Engle. PoPl
You can't beat English lawns. Our final hope. Rolling the Lawn. William Empson. MoBrPo (1962 ed.)
You can't believe in mother much. God's Mothers. Douglas Malloch. PEDC
You can't expect a cowboy to agitate his shanks. The Cowboy's Dance Song. James Barton Adams. CoSo; SCC
You Can't Fool God. Grenville Kleiser. STF
You Can't Go Home Again, *sel.* Thomas Wolfe.
"Something has spoken to me in the night." TRV
You can't keep it, I say. Civilizing the Child. Lisel Mueller. TPM
You can't live in the city. Beggar. Nicanor Parra. CAD
You Can't Please Everybody. Edward Verrall Lucas. MemP
You can't see fairies unless you're good. Fairies. Marchette Chute. MoSiPe
You can't spend all day staring into the sea, however. War. Michael Brownstein. ANYP
You can't tell me God would have Heaven. A Malemute Dog. Pat O'Cotter. BLPA
You captains bold and brave, hear our cries, hear our cries. Captain Kidd [*or* Captain Robert Kidd]. *Unknown.* ABF; SoAmSa
You Charm'd Me Not. Dryden. *See* Song: "You charm'd me not with that fair face.".
You child, how can you dare complain. Equals. Louis Untermeyer. MeWo; UnTE
You climb three "golden steps." Always Another Viewpoint. Kenneth Patchen. TPM
You close your book and put it down. Love. Louis Untermeyer. HBMV
You come along. . .tearing your shirt. To a Contemporary Bunkshooter. Carl Sandburg. CoBA; WGRP
You come and say that it is restful here. From an Old Maid. Vassar Miller. ToPo
You come not, as aforetime, to the headstone every day. Remember. William Johnson Cory. OBVV; TOP
You come to fetch me from my work tonight. Putting in the Seed. Robert Frost. ErPo; FaBoEn; OxBA
You Could Say. Robert Mezey. AmPC; NaP; ToPo
You couldn't pack a Broadwood half a mile. The Song of the Banjo. Kipling. FaBoCh; OtMeF; PoVP
You courtiers scorn us country clowns. A Contest between Court and Country [*or* Court and Country Love]. *Unknown.* SeCL; UnTE
You crash over the trees. Storm. Hilda Doolittle ("H. D."). TiPo; TSW
You cry as the gull cries. The Contrary Experience. Sir Herbert Read. FaBoMo
You cut your hair and it made me very shy. Reaching-Out Poem. Kathleen Fraser. YAP
You, Damon, covet to possess. Lover's Choice. Thomas Bedingfield. HBV
You dare to say with perjured lips. Mare Liberum. Henry van Dyke. PaA; PAH
You did late review my lays. To Christopher North. Tennyson. EvOK; FiBHP
You did not come. Broken Appointment. Thomas Hardy. BWP; CBEP; DTC; MoPW; NoP; OAEP (2d ed.); ViPo; ViPP
You did not leave this fruited land. Evangeline. Norma E. Smith. CaP
You did not walk with me. The Walk. Thomas Hardy. CMoP; PoEL-5; PoeP
You did right, injured husband, to ruin the face. Insufficient Vengeance. Martial. UnTE
You didn't have to travel to become an airplane. Communication on His Thirtieth Birthday. Marvin Bell. CoAP
You died two thousand years ago, Catullus. To a Roman. J. C. Squire. HBMV
You dig instant revolution against. Down Wind against the Highest Peaks. Clarence Major. NBP
You disappoint no creditor, you say? To Sextus. Martial, *tr. by* J. A. Pott *and* F. A. Wright. ALV
You do look, my son, in a moved sort. Prospero [*or* Clouds]. Shakespeare. *Fr.* The Tempest, IV, i. BoC; FiP
You do not do, you do not do. Daddy. Sylvia Plath. CoAP; LiTM (1970 ed.); NaP; NMP; OPoP; TwCP
You do not seem to realize that beauty is a liability. Roses Only. Marianne Moore. AnFE; CoAnAm; LiTM
You, Doctor Martin. Anne Sexton. MoAmPo (1962 ed.); OPoP
You don't have to go to heaven. Which Do You Choose? Harry A. Ironside. SoP
You don't have to tell how you live each day. It's in [*or* God Shows in] Your Face. *Unknown.* PoLF; SoP
You don't see buffalo skulls very much any more. Something Starting Over. Thomas Hornsby Ferril. AnAmPo
You dowagers with Roman noses. The Witnesses. W. H. Auden. ShBV-4
You Drive in a Circle. Ted Hughes. NYBP
You drop a tear for those that die. Lines. Aubrey Thomas De Vere. IrPN
You drove the nails in his white, white feet. Good Friday. Edgar Daniel Kramer. OQP
You earthly Souls that court a wanton flame. La Belle Confidente. Thomas Stanley. FaBoEn; MeLP; MePo; OBS
You entered my life in a casual way. To a Friend. Grace Strickler Dawson. BLPA; NeHB
You Eyes, you large and all-inquiring Eyes. For Arvia. E. A. Robinson. BiCB; TSW
You Felons on Trial in Courts. Walt Whitman. CBEP
You Fight On, *with music.* *Unknown.* AS
You fish for people. Aged Fisherman. Witter Bynner. GoYe
You fools behind the panes who peer. Challenge. John Drinkwater. PoMa
You found the green before the Spring was sweet. Ave atque Vale. Thomas S. Jones, Jr. HBV
You from Givenchy, since no years can harden. V. D. F. *Unknown.* HBV
You gallants all, that love good wine. A Ballad to the Tune of Bateman. Sir Charles Sedley. CoMu; PeRV
You gave me roses, love, last night. The Mystery. Lilian Whiting. AA
"You gave me the key of your heart, my love." Constancy. John Boyle O'Reilly. BOHV; OnYI
You gave them all the dances, but came home with me. The Technique of Laughter. Jascha Kessler. AmPC
You gave us the bumble bee who has a soul. Letters to Dead Imagists. Carl Sandburg. AmPP (3d ed.)
You Gentlemen of England, *with music.* *Unknown.* SoAmSa
You get a girl; and you say you love her. Poems in Praise of Practically Nothing, III. Samuel Hoffenstein. BOHV; InMe; SiTL

You get that end of the road feeling, you know? A Poem for Everybody. Eugene Lesser. FRC
You give but little when you give of your possessions. On Giving. Kahlil Gibran. *Fr.* The Prophet. MaRV; PoPl
You Give Me Sappho. Sister M. Therese. NYTB
You give your cheeks a rosy stain. Artificial Beauty. Lucian. AWP; JAWP; OnPM; WBP
You go aboard [of] a leaky boat and sail for San Francisco. A Ripping Trip. *Unknown.* CoSo; SGR
You Go, I'll Go wid You, *with music.* *Unknown.* BoAN-2
You go singing through my garden on little dancing feet. To Felicity Who Calls Me Mary. Frances Chesterton. HBMV
You go to your church, and I'll go to mine. Your Church and Mine. Phillips H. Lord. BLPA; MaRV
You goat-herd gods, that love the grassy mountains. *See* Ye goat-herd gods. . .
You good folks of Nottingham I would have you draw near. The Red Wig. *Unknown.* CoMu
You goodman Glutton, bellied like a butt. Glutton. Samuel Rowlands. SiCE
You Got a Right, *with music.* *Unknown.* BoAn-1
You Got to Cross It foh Yohself, *with music.* *Unknown.* AS
You gote-heard gods, that love the grassie mountaines. *See* Ye goat-herd gods. . .
You graves of grisly ghosts. The Lover Complaineth of His Lady's Unconstancy. *Unknown.* ReIE
You guard your maidenhood, my girl; but why? To a Recalcitrant Virgin. Asclepiades. LiTW
You had expected more. Now that I leave. The Departure. Robert Pack. NePoEA
You had no little maid, so I remember. A Nun Speaks to Mary. Sister Mary Madeleva. ISi
You had two girls—Baptiste. At the Cedars. Duncan Campbell Scott. CaP; VA
You have a most attractive pan. Poems of Passion, Carefully Restrained So as to Offend Nobody. Samuel Hoffenstein. InMe
You have asked me, "What am I?" Dick Diespecker. *Fr.* Between Two Furious Oceans. TwCaPo
You have asked, my little friend, why I'm so sad and still. Utah Carl. *Unknown.* BFSS
You have been good to me, I give you this. Idolatry. Arna Bontemps. AmNP; PoNe
You have beheld a smiling rose. The Lilly [*or* Lily] in a Christal [*or* Crystal]. Robert Herrick. AnAnS-2; AtBAP; PoEL-3; PoeP; SCEP-2; SeCePo; SeCP
You have black eyes. Algerian Refugee Camp, Aïn-Khemouda. Alan Ross. POTi
You have coats and robes. You Will Die. *Unknown.* *Fr.* Shi King. AWP; JAWP; WBP
You have come along with me. Dora. Howard McCord. YAP
You have come from very far, but what is distance. To the International Brigade. Rafael Alberti. PoFr
You have heaped my hands with rubies. Odysseus' Song to Calypso. Peter Kane Dufault. ErPo
"You have heard," said a youth to his sweetheart, who stood. The Whistler. Robert Story. BOHV
You have here no otherness. J. V. Cunningham. *Fr.* To What Strangers, What Welcome? TDP
You have loved forty women, but you have only one thumb. Personality. Carl Sandburg. CrMA
You have netted this dawn. The Archaeology of Love. Richard Murphy. EnLoPo
You have never hear de story of de young Napoleon Doré? 'Poleon Doré. William Henry Drummond. BBV (1923 ed.)
You have no enemies, you say? No Enemies. Charles Mackay. GoTP; MaRV
You have no mortal lineaments this day. Ordination. Sister Mary Immaculate. GoBC
You have not conquered me—it is the surge. Infidelity. Louis Untermeyer. NP; TrJP
You have not heard my love's dark throat. A Song of Praise. Countee Cullen. NP
You have not left me usurer's black blood. Lines to My Father. Leslie Daiken. NeIP; OxBI
You have refin'd me, and to worthyest things. To the Countesse of Bedford. John Donne. MaMe
You have replaced Beethoven. Sometimes Even My Knees Smile. Diane Wakoski. YAP
You have said, for certain. Confession. D. S. Savage. NeBP
You have seen the house built, you have seen it adorned. Chorus X. T. S. Eliot. *Fr.* The Rock. PoDB
You have stopped short of love, your May is over. The Old Saint. Muriel Stuart. HBMV
You have taken back the promise. Fidelis. Adelaide Anne Procter. BLPA; FaBoBe; NeHB
You have taught me laughter. The Masters. Margaret Widdemer. HBMV
You have thrust Nature out, to make. To Some Builders of Cities. Stanley Snaith. HaMV
You have your hat and coat on and she says she will be right down. The Evening Out. Ogden Nash. MoAmPo (1950 ed.)
You have your water and your grain. My Little Birds. *Unknown.* FaPON
You haven't got so very far. Spring. Orrick Johns. InMe
You hear Youth laughing down green, budding aisles. Theresa Helburn. PFY
You (Her Eyes, Solstice). G. Bishop-Dubjinsky. ThO
You Hire a Cook. Samuel Hoffenstein. WhC
(Poems in Praise of Practically Nothing, V.) InMe
You hold a silver ship/ Upon your arm. Our Lady of Good Voyage. Lucy A. K. Adee. ISi
You hollow-cheeked son. Baboon 2. *Unknown.* PeSA
You hungry birds, I bring my crumbs. Crumbs. Walter de la Mare. SoPo
You husbandmen and ploughmen, of every degree. The Little Farm; or, The Weary Ploughman. *Unknown.* CoMu
You hypocrite! To a Weeping Willow. Louis Untermeyer. MeWo
You I dare not love. To One. Gustaf Munch-Petersen. LiTW
You I love, by all that's true. To Silvia. *Unknown.* SeCL
You, I presume, could adroitly and gingerly. How the Women Will Stop War. Aristophanes. *Fr.* Lysistrata. WaaP
You, if you were sensible. Under the Oak. D. H. Lawrence. OnHM
You in whose veins runs the fire of loving. Voice. Zona Gale. OQP
You in your school forever flog and flay us. On a Schoolmaster. *Unknown.* OnPM
You Kicked and Stomped and Beat Me, *with music.* *Unknown.* OuSiCo
You Kissed Me. Josephine Slocum Hunt. BLPA; FaBoBe
You kissed me in June. September. Dorothy Frances McCrae. BoAu
You kissed me! My head dropped low on your breast. You Kissed Me. Josephine Slocum Hunt. BLPA; FaBoBe
You knew her?—Mary the small. As Mr. Browning Has It. A. C. Wilkie. *Fr.* An Old Song by New Singers. BOHV
You knew the Master. Come and talk about him. Knew the Master. James Reeves. MuSP
You knew—who knew not Astrophil? On Sir Philip Sidney. Matthew Royden. *Fr.* An Elegy, or Friend's Passion for His Astrophil. EIL
You Know. Jean Garrigue. NYBP
You know it's April by the falling-off. B Negative. X. J. Kennedy. NePoEA-2
You Know, Joe. Ray Durem. BOLo
(Ultimate Equality.) PoNe (1970 ed.)
"You know, my friends with what a brave carouse." The Bride. Ambrose Bierce. AA; LHV
"You know Orion always comes up sideways." The Star-Splitter. Robert Frost. ImOP
You know Saint Wigbald's,—yonder nunnery cell. How the Abbey of Saint Werewulf Juxta Slingsby Came by Brother Fabian's Manuscript. Sebastian Evans. PeVV
You know that day at Peach Tree Creek. Logan at Peach Tree Creek. Hamlin Garland. MC; PAH
You know the answer to the last surmise. Sonnet for My Son. Melanie Gordon Barber. GoYe
You know the bloom, unearthly white. The Evening Primrose. Dorothy Parker. ALV; InMe
You know the fellow. A Public Nuisance. Reginald Arkell. SD
You know the old woman. The Old Woman. Beatrix Potter. GoJo; PDV
You know the password, then. Meeting of a Poetry Society. Henry Rago. AnAmPo

You know the school; you call it old. Country School. Allen Curnow. AnNZ
You know the way. Lemuel's Blessing. W. S. Merwin. CoPo
You know there goes a tale. The Modern Jonas. *Unknown.* PAH
You know those rose sherbets. You Know. Jean Garrigue. NYBP
You know those windless summer evenings, swollen to stasis. Cicadas [*or* Cigales]. Richard Wilbur. FiMAP; NePoEA
You know w'at for ees school keep out. Leetla Giorgio Washeenton. T. A. Daly. FaPON; MPB; OTPC (1946 ed.); PoSC; TSW
You know we French Stormed [*or* storm'd] Ratisbon. Incident of the French Camp. Robert Browning. BBV; BEL; BeLS; EnLi-2 (1949 ed.); EPN; GN; GoTP; HBV; HBVY; MaC; MaVP; MBW-2; MCCG; NeHB; OnSP; OTPC; PoPo; PoVP; PTK; RoGo; TreF; TrGrPo; TSW; VA
You know we must be lonely, you and I. Souls. Paul Wertheimer. TrJP
You know what it is to be born alone. Baby Tortoise. D. H. Lawrence. BoPe; CMoP
You know you'll play the wedding theme. Irregular Sonnet for a Marriage. A. K. Ramanujan. NYTB
You ladies all that are in fashion. A New Song Called The Curling of the Hair. *Unknown.* CoMu
You Laughed and Laughed and Laughed. Gabriel Okara. PBA
You lay a wreath on murdered Lincoln's bier. Abraham Lincoln. Tom Taylor. MCCG; PaA; PAH; VA
You leap out of bed; you start to get ready. Poems in Praise of Practically Nothing, VI. Samuel Hoffenstein. BOHV; InMe; SiTL
You learn new things every week. Fourteenth Street. Tony Towle. YAP
You learned Lear's *Nonsense Rhymes* by heart, not rote. A Plea to Girls and Boys. Robert Graves. GTBS-P
You leave us: you will see the Rhine. In Memoriam A. H. H., XCVIII. Tennyson. EPN; ViPo; VP
You left me, sweet, two legacies. Emily Dickinson. FaPL
You left me when the weary weight of sorrow. Forgiven. Margaret E. Sangster. PoToHe
You left the field and no one heard. The Decision. E. J. Pratt. CBV
You like it under the trees in autumn. The Motive for Metaphor. Wallace Stevens. AP; MoAB; MoAmPo (1950 ed.)
You like not that French novel? Modern Love, XXV. George Meredith. ViPo; VP
You like the country better than the town. To a Friend in the Country. Oliver St. John Gogarty. OnYI
You Lingering Sparse Leaves of Me. Walt Whitman. CBEP
You little, eager, peeping thing. The Awakening. Angela Morgan. OHIP
You little know the heart that you advise. In Answer to a Lady Who Advised Retirement. Lady Mary Wortley Montagu. OBEC
You Little Stars [*or* Starres] That Live in Skies [*or* Skyes]. Caelica, IV. Fulke Greville. CBEP; ElL; NCEP; SiCE; TuPP
(His Lady's Eyes.) OBSC
(Sonnet.) ReIE
You look/ like a classic geisha. Samisen. James Kirkup. NYTB
You look at me. A Drop of Dew. Schmuel Halkin. TrJP
You look long about you. Within. Sydney Clouts. BoSA
You looked at me with eyes grown bright with pain. Parting after a Quarrel. Eunice Tietjens. BoLP; HBMV; NP
You, love, and I. Counting the Beats. Robert Graves. CBV; DTC; ELP; GTBS-P; Po; PoIE; ViBoPo (1958 ed.)
You love? that's high as you shall go. Attainment [*or* Preludes, II]. Coventry Patmore. *Fr.* The Angel in the House. GoBC; OBVV
You love the roses—so do I. Roses. "George Eliot." BoTP
You love us when we're heroes, home on leave. Glory of Women. Siegfried Sassoon. MMA
You loved me for a little. Midsummer. Sydney King Russell. BLPA; FaBoBe; NeHB
You loved the hay in the meadow. Her Way. William Rose Benét. HBMV
You lovely fisher-maiden. The Fisher Maiden. Heine. OnPM
You lucky man, you. Congratulations. Sappho. HW
You, Madam, may with safety go. The Fortune-Teller. Matthew Prior. CEP
You made me a slave and kept me a slave. Etc. etc. etc. Dorothy C. Parrish. TNV
You made your little lover kind. Little Lover. Leonora Speyer. HBMV
You married men, whom Fate hath assign'd. The Merry Cuckold. *Unknown.* CoMu
You Masks of the Masquerade. Gustave Kahn, *tr. fr. French by* Jethro Bithell. TrJP
You, master of delays. Killing No Murder. Sylvia Townsend Warner. MoBrPo
You may be very ugly and freckledy and small. Consolation. Rose Fyleman. GaP
You May Bury Me in de Eas', *with music. Unknown.* BoAN-1
You may call a woman a kitten. What One May and May Not Call a Woman. *Unknown.* TreF
You may call, you may call. The Bad Kittens. Elizabeth J. Coatsworth. FaPON; MoSiPe; MPB; PoRL; RePo; YT
You may drink to your leman in gold. Wine and Dew. Richard Henry Stoddard. AA
You may get through the world, but 'twill be very slow. People Will Talk. Samuel Dodge. WBLP
You may give over plough, boys. Tommy's Dead. Sydney Dobell. HBV; PeVV; VA
You may hear a pygmy talking. No Doubt. Helen Baker Adams. STF
You may lift me up in your arms, lad, and turn my face to the sun. The Famous Ballad of the Jubilee Cup. Sir Arthur Quiller-Couch. InMe; NA; OnSP; WhC; YT
You may never see rain, unless you see. A Dance for Rain. Witter Bynner. HT
You may not believe it, for hardly could I. The Pumpkin. Robert Graves. PDV; PoMS
You may not stand in the halls of fame. Be Friendly. Walter E. Isenhour. STF
You may notch it on de palin's as a mighty resky plan. Rev. Gabe Tucker's Remarks. *Unknown.* BOHV
You may sing of your heroes of war and of peace. The Minister's Wife. *Unknown.* SoP
You may smile if you're a mind to, but perhaps you'll lend an ear. The Ghostly Crew, 2 *vers. Unknown.* ShS
You may talk about pleasures. A Trip on the Erie. *Unknown.* ABF; IHA
You may talk o' gin and beer. Gunga Din. Kipling. BBV; BEL; BoPe; BrPo; EnLi-2 (1949 ed.); EnLit; FaFP; FaPL; HBV; LiTB; LiTM (rev. ed.); MCCG; MoBrPo; NeMA; OnMSP; PoMa; PoPl; PoPo; PoVP; ShBV-2; TreF; WePo; YAT
You may tempt the upper classes. Edgar Smith. *Fr.* Heaven Will Protect the Working-Girl. FiBHP
You may think it quite an easy task. The Preacher's Wife. *Unknown.* SoP; STF
You Mean My Mother. *Unknown.* PEDC
You meaner beauties of the night. On His Mistress [*or* Mistris], the Queen of Bohemia [*or* Elizabeth of Bohemia]. Sir Henry Wotton. AnAnS-2; CBEP; EG; ElL; ELP; EnLoPo; FaBoCh; GTBS; GTBS-D; GTBS-P; GTBS-W; GTSE; GTSL; HBV; LoBV; MeLP; MePo; MyFE; OBEV; OBS; OtMeF; ReEn; SeCP; SeEP; TrGrPo; ViBoPo
You meet a girl and you surrender. Poems in Praise of Practically Nothing, III. Samuel Hoffenstein. InMe
You—Mermaid! Your sea-green hair and sin-sweet singing. Fisherman's Blunder off New Bedford, Massachusetts. Annemarie Ewing. NePoAm-2
You messenger that cómes from Rome. To an Anti-poetical Priest. Giolla Brighde MacNamee. AnIV
You might climb up to heaven. After. Robert Hershon. ThO
You might come here Sunday on a whim. Degrees of Gray in Philipsburg. Richard Hugo. CoAP
You might suppose it easy. The Boatman. Jay Macpherson. MoCV; OBCV; PIA
You Mus' Hab Dat True Religion, *with music. Unknown.* BoAN-2
You muses nurses of delights. *Unknown.* SeCSL
You must agree that Rubens was a fool. To English Connoisseurs [*or* Epigram]. Blake. OxBoLi; SiTL
You must be sad; for though it is to Heaven. To Two Bereaved. Thomas Ashe. OBEV

You must be troubled, Asthore. De Profundis. Katharine Tynan. VA
"You must be very old, Sir Giles." Old Love. William Morris. GTBS; ViPP
"You must give back," her mother said. Gifts Returned. Walter Savage Landor. BOHV; OBVV
You must have been still sleeping, your wife there. The Sacred Hearth. David Gascoyne. FaBoTw
You must know that my uncle is a farmer. Down by the Old Mill Stream. John Read. TreFS
You must live through the time when everything hurts. The Double Shame. Stephen Spender. GTBS-W; LiTB; LiTL; LiTM (rev. ed.)
You must not wonder, though you think it strange. For That He Looked Not upon Her. George Gascoigne. EIL
You must remember this, the cold turning year. Note from an Intimate Diary. Emanuel Litvinov. NeBP
You must wake and call me early, mother dear. The May Queen. Tennyson. DD; MPB; OTPC; PoRL
You Mustn't Quit. *Unknown.* *See* Don't Quit.
You, my son,/ Have shown me God. The Open Door. Grace Coolidge. MaRV; TRV
You, Nebuchadnezzar, whoa, sah! Nebuchadnezzar. Irwin Russell. HBV; IHA
You need a place much more than time. The Invitation. Tom Buchan. ACV
You need no other death than this. Slow Death. Hazel Hall. MAP; MoAmPo (1942 ed.)
You Need Not Fear. Frances Frieseke. JKCP (1955 ed.)
You need not pity me. I shall not die. Treachery. Margaret Cole. MemP
You need not see what someone is doing. Sext. W. H. Auden. *Fr.* Horae Canonicae. PoDB
You, Neighbor God. Rainer Maria Rilke, *tr. fr. German by* Babette Deutsch. MoRP
"You never attained to Him?" "If to attain." Via, et Veritas, et Vita. Alice Meynell. JKCP; MaRV; OQP; WGRP
You never bade me hope, 'tis true. Maiden Eyes. Gerald Griffin. HBV
You Never Can Be Old. Shakespeare. *See* Sonnets, CIV.
You Never Can Tell. Ella Wheeler Wilcox. BLPA; NeHB; PoToHe; TreFS; TreFT
You never got to recline. For Mother on Father's Day. James Tate. YAP
You never know what life means till you die. Robert Browning. *Fr.* The Ring and the Book, XI: Guido. OAEP
You never know with a doorbell. Doorbells. Rachel Field. FaPON; GaP; StVeCh (1955 ed.); TiPo
You noble Diggers all, stand up now, stand up now. The Digger's Song. Gerrard Winstanley. PoFr
You not alone, when you are still alone. Idea, XI. Michael Drayton. PoEL-2
You Nymphs, Call'd Naiads. Shakespeare. *Fr.* The Tempest, IV, i. ViBoPo
You, O Tsui-Xgoa. Hymn to Tsui-Xgoa. *Unknown.* PeSA
You of the covered breasts, the lovely head. Epitaph of a Faithful Man. Robert Mezey. ELU
You of the painted wagons, folk of the shimmering eye. Beggars. Rhys Carpenter. HBMV
You oft have heard of that dark night. The Easter Robin. Geraldine Farrar. StJW
You often have in dreams, I know. Joy and Dream. Goethe. LiTW
You on the quay, or you who watch at the station. The Unknown Traveller. George Rostrevor Hamilton. MemP
You open your timeless eyes. To Liane-Neila. Iwan Goll. OnPM
You opened my eyes. Malcolm. Kattie M. Cumbo. BOLo
You oughta see my Uncla Joe. Da Greata Stronga Man. T. A. Daly. YT
You over there, young man with the guide-book. Home, Sweet Home, with Variations, V [VI]. H. C. Bunner. BOHV; CenHV; InMe
You painted no Madonnas. To Mother. Thomas W. Fessenden. MaRV; SoP
You plant like Paul, you water like Apollos. The Rev. Nicholas Noyes to the Rev. Cotton Mather. Nicholas Noyes. SCAP
You play a fife. Elizabeth J. Coatsworth. RIS
You practice every possible virtue. Poems in Praise of Practically Nothing, V. Samuel Hoffenstein. BOHV; InMe
You praise the firm restraint with which they write. On Some South African Novelists. Roy Campbell. AnFE; BoSA; ChMP; CoBE; GTBS-P; MoBrPo; MoPW; MoVE; PoPl; SiTL; WhC
You Preach to Me of Laws. Iris Tree. HBMV
You prefer a buffoon to a scholar. Cynical Ode to an Ultra-cynical Public. Charles Mackay. BOHV
You probably could put their names to them. "As When Emotion Too Far Exceeds Its Cause." G. C. Oden. AmNP; Kal
You promise heavens free from strife. Mimnermus in Church. William Johnson Cory. EPN; GTBS; GTSE; HBV; LO; OBEV; TreFT; VA
You promised to send me some violets. Did you forget? Letter from Town; the Almond Tree. D. H. Lawrence. MoPW
You pure and nimble boy, like candle flame. David. Guy Butler. BoSA
You rambling [or ramblin'] boys of Liverpool, I'd [*or* I'll] you [*or* ye's] to beware. The Banks of Newfoundland. *Unknown.* ShS; SoAmSa
You ramping girls which rage with wanton lust. Cressid's Complaint. George Whetstone. ReIE
You reached in to pull my mind out of the mire. Rebirth. Paula Giddings. WSL
You read the *New York Times.* Alfred Corning Clark. Robert Lowell. PoeP
You remember Davies? He died, you know. Death of a Peasant. R. S. Thomas. FIW; PoIE
You remember that pastoral frolic. Limerick. "R. K. B." LiBL
You remember the big Gaston. Monsieur Gaston. A. M. Klein. MoCV
You Repocrat squires in the Farm Bureau. Farmhands' Refrain. H. H. Lewis. LiTM
You ride dat horse, you call him Macadoni. Jesus, Won't You Come B'm-by. *Unknown.* AS
You Rise Up. Paul Eluard, *tr. fr. French by* Wallace Fowlie. PoPl
You root deep. Trees. William Haskell Simpson. *Fr.* In Arizona. NP
You roving young heroes of Prince Edward's Island. The Boys of the Island. *Unknown.* IHA
You ruffled black blossom. Turkey-Cock. D. H. Lawrence. AnEnPo
You rural goddesses. The Milkmaid's Life. Martin Parker. TuPP
You ruthless flea, who desecrate my couch. Song of the Flea. Judah Al-Harizi. TrJP
You, sad Captain, big-knobbed staff of life. The Voyages of Captain Cock. William Jay Smith. ErPo; UnTE
You said, "A sound can never die, you know." Summer Evening. Sara Henderson Hay. PoMa
You said, "How strange! Among all who have come by." Following the Sun. Jascha Kessler. AmPC
You said that your people. To Richard Wright. Conrad Kent Rivers. AmNP; IDB
You said the lodestar of the mind. St. Thomas Aquinas. J. Corson Miller. JKCP (1955 ed.)
You said to me:/ I shall become your comrade. Nudities. André Spire, *tr. by* Stanley Burnshaw. TrJP
You said to me: But I will be your comrade. Nudities. André Spire, *tr. by* Jethro Bithell. AWP; ErPo
You said to me, "My father did not weep." Inheritance. Alfonsina Storni. OnPM
You sail and you seek for the Fortunate Isles. The Fortunate Isles. Joaquin Miller. WGRP
You sang me a song. Sing Again. Marie van Vorst. AA
You saved the golden seeds of holy mirth. Saint Francis of Assisi. "Joan Ramsay." MaRV
You saw me staring at the girl. Songs of the Plains, II. Glenn Ward Dresbach. NP
You say, as I have often given tongue. To a Poet, Who Would Have Me Praise Certain Bad Poets, Imitators of His and Mine. W. B. Yeats. CTC; ML; PV
You say, but with no touch of scorn. In Memoriam A. H. H., XCVI. Tennyson. BEL; EnL; EnLi-2; EnLit; EPN; OAEP; OQP; TOP; ViPo; VP; WGRP
You Say I Love Not. Robert Herrick. LiTL
(To His Mistress Objecting to Him neither Toying or Talking.) EnLit; FaBV
("You say I love not, 'cause I do not play.") EG

You say I touch the barberries. Barberries. Mary Aldis. HBMV
You say, "I will come." Lady Otomo no Sakanoye, *tr. fr. Japanese by* Kenneth Rexroth. LiTW
You say it will cost much to follow. The Cost. Flora L. Osgood. STF
You say it's made of silver. The Moon. Robert Beverly Hale. SiTL
You say my Love no marvel is to you. Sonnet. George Henry Boker. *Fr.* Sonnets. AmLP
You say, sir, once a wit allow'd. Why the Moon Is Like a Fashionable Wife. James White. EiCL
You say that I forget you, and you lie. To Celio. Sister Juana Inés de la Cruz. LiTW
You say that in your eyes alone is all the world. Love Poem. Jiri Wolker. LiTW
You say, "Where goest thou?" I cannot tell. The Poet's Simple Faith [*or* Where Goest Thou?]. Victor Hugo. MaRV; OQP; TRV; WGRP
You say yes and I say yes. Point of No Return. Mari Evans. NNP
You say you heard King Borborigmi laugh? King Borborigmi. Conrad Aiken. MAPA
You say you know me. I am the one. The Menagerie. Harold Bond. YAP
You Say You Love. William King. SeCL
You say you love me, nay, can swear it too. Clarastella Distrusting. Robert Heath. SeCL
You say you love! Repeat again. You Say You Love. William King. SeCL
You secret vales, you solitary fields. Henry Constable. *Fr.* Diana. OBSC
You see/ Nestled into a hollow of the downs. Fragment. William Allingham. *Fr.* By the Way. IrPN
You see me here, you gods, a poor old man. King Lear Pledges Revenge. Shakespeare. *Fr.* King Lear, II, iv. TreFT
You see, merry Phyllis, that dear little maid. A Tea-Party. Kate Greenaway. MPB; OTPC; PPL
You see the goodly hair that Galla wears. Of Galla's Goodly Periwig. Sir John Harington. SiCE
You see the ways the fisherman doth take. Neither Hook nor Line. Bunyan. SD
You see this dog. It was but yesterday. Flush or Faunus. Elizabeth Barrett Browning. BoC; NBM
You see this pebble-stone? It's a thing I bought. The Cock and the Bull. Charles Stuart Calverley. ALV; BOHV; InMe; NA; Par
"You see those mothers squabbling there?" In the Cemetery. Thomas Hardy. Sonn
You see, we three. Chums. Arthur Guiterman. GaP; MPB
You seem to have lived, my lady. On Again Meeting a Lady. Otomo Miyori. OnPM
You seemed a caryatid melting. Love. Maxwell Bodenheim. NP
You send me your love in a letter. Child and Poet. Swinburne. EnLit; EPN; PoVP
You served me well, Prytherch. Servant. R. S. Thomas. POTi
You Shall above All Things Be Glad and Young. E. E. Cummings. MoPW; NePA; OxBA
You shall hear how Pau-Puk-Keewis. Pau-Puk-Keewis. Longfellow. *Fr.* The Song of Hiawatha. CoBA
You shall not be overbold. The Titmouse. Emerson. PrWS
You shall not vanish into dust today. Funeral. Murray Bennett. GoYe
You should have seen it, Father, the day. The Barren Fig Tree. Elizabeth Bartlett. WOW
You should hear/ our brook in Spring! Rambunctious Brook. Frances Frost. BrR
You should see these musical mice. New Strain. George Starbuck. TwCP
You should stay longer if we durst. *See* Ye should stay longer if we durst.
You shun me, Chloe, wild and shy. To Chloe. Horace. AWP; JAWP; WBP
You simple-minded African bird. Autumn Song. Noel Harry Brettell. ACV
You sit at your high windows, old men. The Old Men. Alexander Javitz. TrJP
You sit there, sissified. Die Black Pervert. Reginald Lockett. BF
You sleep at the top of streets. To Waken a Small Person. Donald Justice. NYBP
You sleep upon your mother's breast. A Rhyme of One. Frederick Locker-Lampson. HBV
You sleeping child asleep, away. To Ping-ku, Asleep. Lawrence Durrell. ChMP; NeBP
You smile at the granite of Milton. The Street of Named Houses. Robert David Cohen. NYBP
You Smile upon Your Friend To-Day. A. E. Housman. A Shropshire Lad, LVII. PoVP
You smiled, you spoke, and I believed. To Ianthe. Walter Savage Landor. OAEP; PV; VA
You speak; and my spirit to the soft breathing. Fantasy. Giosuè Carducci. LiTW
You speak. You say: Today's character is not. As You Leave the Room. Wallace Stevens. AP
You splice together two broomsticks, then reef. Sonnet at Easter. Howard Nemerov. FiMAP
You spoke keys and looked. The Tyrant Apple Is Eaten. Norman MacCaig. NeBP
You Spotted Snakes [with Double Tongue]. Shakespeare. *Fr.* A Midsummer Night's Dream, II, ii. AnFE; BoTP; EG; InvP; LiTB; LiTG; OBSC; OTPC (1923 ed.); PoeP; PoRA; ShBV-1; SiCE; ViBoPo
(Fairies' Lullaby The.) ElL; WHA
(Fairies' Song, The.) LoBV
(Fairy Land, 2.) OBEV
(Fairy Lullaby.) FaPON; GoTP; RIS
(Fairy Songs: "You spotted snakes with double tongue.") HBV; TrGrPo
(Lullaby for Titania.) GN; RG
(Song: "You spotted snakes with double tongue.") FiP; MemP
(Song of the Fairies.) BoLiVe
You sprouted from sand. Navajo Children, Canyon de Chelly, Arizona. Christopher Middleton. FIW
You squires o' th' shade, that love to tread. New Prison. Charles Cotton. PeRV
You stand atop your hill. New Hampshire Farm Woman. Rachel Graham. GoYe
You stand near the window as lights wink. Twenty-third Street Runs into Heaven. Kenneth Patchen. ErPo
You stared out of the window on the emptiness. To a Spanish Poet. Stephen Spender. CMoP; OAEP (2d ed.)
You start with yourself. The Trust. James Tate. YAP
You strange, astonish'd-looking, angel-faced. The Fish, the Man, and the Spirit [*or* To a Fish]. Leigh Hunt. ATP; BoC; CBV; ChTr; EPN; EnRP; FiBHP; NBM; OA; OBEV (new ed.); PoEL-4; RoGo; SeCePo; ViBoPo
You suffered starvation in deserted villages. For Tu Fu. Feng Chih. LiTW
You take a bath, and sit there bathing. Samuel Hoffenstein. *Fr.* Poems in Praise of Practically Nothing. EvOK; InMe
You take a town you cannot keep. Love's Spite. Aubrey Thomas De Vere. HBV; VA
You take the dollar. For One Moment. David Ignatow. TPM
You talk about your business. Speak Out for Jesus. *Unknown.* STF
You talk about your harbor girls. Haul Away, My Rosy. *Unknown.* OuSiCo
You talk of gayety and innocence! Sir Walter Scott. *Fr.* The Talisman. NBM
You Talk of Going but Don't Even Have a Suitcase. John Wieners. FRC
You talk of the deeds of the old pioneers. A Cleary Pioneer. Fred Crewe. PaA
You talk too much. Now All at Once It Is Colder. Marge Piercy. ThO
You taught me ways of gracefulness and fashions of address. To a Little Girl. Helen Parry Eden. HBV; OTPC (1923 ed.)
You tell me I'm handsome, I know not how true. Song the Ninth. Edward Moore. CEP
You tell me that the day is fine. To My Hairdresser. Warham St. Leger. CenHV
You tell me they only do to us. My Brother. James Danner. BF
You Tell Me to Sit Quiet. A. C. Jordan. PBA
You tell me you're promised a lover. A Letter of Advice. Winthrop Mackworth Praed. HBV; OBRV; OxBoLi; TOP; WhC

You Tell on Yourself. *Unknown.* PoToHe (new ed.)
You tender hearted Christians, I pray you lend an ear. The Millman Song. *Unknown.* ShS
You that are she and you, that's double shee. To the Lady Bedford. John Donne. MaMe
You that but seek your modest rolls and coffee. Rue Bonaparte. Joseph Warren Beach. NP
You that crossed the ocean old. Ponce De León. Edith M. Thomas. OTD; PAH
You, that decipher out the fate. Mourning. Andrew Marvell. CABA; MaMe; SeCP
You that delight in concord liston all. *Unknown.* SeCSL
You that do search for every purling spring. Astrophel and Stella, XV. Sir Philip Sidney. CoBE; FCP; ILP; MaPo (1969 ed.); OBSC; ReEn; ReIE; SiCE; SiPS; Sonn; TuPP
You that do see this child disfigured here. The True Form and Shape of a Monsterous Child. William Elderton. ReIE
You that extol the bliss of this our nation. Against an Extreme Flatterer That Preached at Bath on the Queen's Day the Fortieth Year of Her Reign. Sir John Harington. SiCE
You that have been this evenings light. Sir R. Hatton. SeCSL
You that have faith to look with fearless eyes. *See* Ye that have faith. . .
You that have spent the silent night. Gascoigne's Good Morrow. George Gascoigne. EnRePo; SiCE; TuPP
You that have that daintie eare. *Unknown.* SeCSL
You That in Love Find Luck [and Abundance]. Sir Thomas Wyatt. *See* Sonnet: "You that in love find luck. . ."
You that in music do delight. The Printer to the Reader. *At. to* Richard Jones. EIL; ReIE
You that know the way. Lemuel's Blessing. W. S. Merwin. NYBP
You That Love England. C. Day Lewis. FaBoMo
You that nightly cross the straits. Crossing the Straits. Charles Brasch. AnNZ
You that prophane our windows with a tongue. Beauty in Worship. *Unknown. Fr.* A Poem, in Defence of the Decent Ornaments of Christ-Church, Oxon. OBS
You that seek what life is in death. Time and Eternity. Fulke Greville. Caelica, LXXXII. EnRePo; OBSC
You That Sing in the Blackthorn. Alfred Noyes. *Fr.* The Last Voyage, II. GoBC
You that the city life embrace. To My Friend Mr. John Anderson. Charles Cotton. PeRV
You that think Love can convey. Celia Singing. Thomas Carew. EG; EnLit; LiTL; LO; SeCL; SeEP
You that thus wear a modest countenance. Dante. *Fr.* La Vita Nuova. AWP
You that uphold the world. Pagan Prayer. Alice Brown. WGRP
You that with allegory's curious frame. Astrophel and Stella, XXVIII. Sir Philip Sidney. FCP; ILP; ReEn; ReIE; SiCE; SiPS; TuPP
You, the choice minions of the proud-lipped Nine. To Poets. George Darley. Sonn
You, the woman; I, the man; this, the world. The Character of Love Seen as a Search for the Lost. Kenneth Patchen. NaP
You, the Young Rainbow. Edith Sitwell. MoVE
You there, and you, and you. Bacchanal. Irving Layton. OBCV
You think Fuseli is not a great painter. I'm glad. To Hunt [*or* Epigram]. Blake. OxBoLi; SiTL
"You think I am dead." Talking in Their Sleep. Edith M. Thomas. BoNaP; DD; OHIP; PEDC; PTK
You think it horrible that lust and rage. The Spur. W. B. Yeats. ELU
You think it's only a garden. The Secrets of Our Garden. Rupert Sargent Holland. OTPC
You think love can convey. Celia Singing. Thomas Carew. CLwM
You think of everything. To Francis Sauf Que. Ron Padgett. YAP
You think of him as one who fails. I Think of Him as One Who Fights. Anna Hempstead Branch. HBMV
You think that when a woman yields. In Your Arrogance. Lynne Lawner. ErPo
You thought it was a falling leaf we heard. Rondel for September. Karle Wilson Baker. HBMV
You thought my heart too far diseased. In Memoriam A. H. H., LXVI. Tennyson. EPN; ViPo; VP
You tiptoed/ Naked. Spring in the Jungle. Eugene Redmond. TNV
You to the left and I to the right. At the Crossroads. Richard Hovey. BBV (1951 ed.); HBV; MAP; MoAmPo (1942 ed.); NeMA; PFY; PoMa
You to whose soul a death propitious brings. An Elegy, for Father Anselm, of the Order of Reformed Cistercians. Helen Parry Eden. JKCP
You told me Age was a black wolf that lay. Comfort. Margaret Widdemer. GoYe
You told me, Maro, whilst you live. A Hinted Wish [*or* A Legacy]. Martial. AWP; JAWP; LiTW; OnPM; OuHeWo; WBP
You Told Me of Jesus. *Unknown.* SoP
You too listless to examine. Lines to Our Elders. Countee Cullen. CDC
You too, of course, have counted sheep. Sheep Herders. Maurice Lesemann. NP
You tossed a blanket from the bed. Preludes, III. T. S. Eliot. AnAmPo; BoLiVe (1945 ed.); CoBA; InP; LiTA; LiTM; NoP; OBMV; ReMP; UnPo
You Turn for Sugar an' Tea, *with music.* *Unknown.* OuSiCo
You undergo before your time, my son. For My Son. Antoni Boguslawski. PoFr
You Understand. *Unknown.* SeCL
("You understand no tender vows.") SeEP
You understand it? How they returned from Culloden. Culloden and After. Iain Crichton Smith. OxBS
You Virgins. James Shirley. *See* Piping Peace.
You, Voyager, with exile-heart that yearns. Speak to the Sun. Dedie Huffman Wilson. GoYe
You wait, expecting one alone. Remembrance. Rainer Maria Rilke. ReMP
You waken slowly. In your dream you're straying. Sonnet. William Bell. NePoEA
You walk the floor of autumn where her corpse. Autumnall. Joseph Bennett. NePA
You walk the hills, blind in your dreaming. Warning. Harold Lewis Cook. AnAmPo
You walk unaware. Maeve. Mervyn Peake. LO
You walk up a deep roadbed to a hilltop. Variations on a Theme. Robert Hillyer. MAP; MoAmPo
You walk up there in the light. Song of Fate. Friedrich Hölderlin, *tr. by* Emery Neff. WoL
You want clear spectacles: your eyes are dim. The Accusation of the Inward Man. Edward Taylor. *Fr.* God's Determinations. LiTA
You want to integrate me into your anonymity. Black Narcissus. Gerald William Barrax. Kal
You wear the morning like your dress. Song [*or* Song: Inviting the Influence of a Young Lady]. Hilaire Belloc. OBEV (new ed.); OBVV
You, weeping wide at war, weep with me now. The Coward. Eve Merriam. TrJP
You Went to the Verge, You Say, and Came Back Safely? Conrad Aiken. Preludes for Memnon, XIV. LiTA; LiTG; TwAmPo; TwCP
You were a foolish, though an amorous fellow. Foolish Leander. Mateo Vázquez de Leca. OnPM
You were a sophist. Advice. Gwendolyn B. Bennett. CDC
You were a witness, lamp, you saw him kneel. All-knowing Lamp. *Unknown.* UnTE
You were always a dreamer, Rose—red Rose. A Rose Will Fade. Dora Sigerson Shorter. HBV
You were always a one to. Foibles. Harold Bond. YAP
You were amused to find you too could fear. Letter I. William Empson. ChMP; LiTB
You Were at the Dead River. George Abbe. FiSC
You were born; must die; were loved; must love. Sonnet: You Were Born; Must Die. Stephen Spender. EnLit; MoAB; MoBrPo (1950 ed.); Sonn
You were dawn on the Cuillin and benign day on the Clarach. Dain do Eimhir, LIV. Sorley Maclean. NeBP
You were no more to me than many others. The Masquerader. Aline Kilmer. HBMV
You were praised, my books. Salutation the Second. Ezra Pound. OxBA
You Were Wearing. Kenneth Koch. ANYP; NoP
You were with me and it wasn't flying, exactly. A Dream as Reported. Virginia Earle. GoYe

"You! What d'you mean by this?" I rapped. Inspection. Wilfred Owen. WaP
You whispered, "Still the stars shine cold above me." Sonnet. William Bell. FaBoTw
You who are born of the hills. The Hill-born. Struthers Burt. MaRV
You who are earth, and cannot rise. To the World, the Perfection of Love. William Habington. AnAnS-2
You who are given to me to Time are given. Love in Time's Despite. Edwin Muir. LiTL
You who are inland born know not the pain. Sea Longing. Harold Vinal. PoMa
You who descend river by river. Giraffe. *Unknown.* PeSA
You who desired so much—in vain to ask. To Emily Dickinson. Hart Crane. CMoP; ForPo; ML; Sonn
You Who Dog My Footsteps. Leib Kwitko, *tr. fr. Yiddish by* Joseph Leftwich. TrJP
You Who Don't Believe It, *with music.* John A. Stone. SGR
You who dread the cares and labors. The Last Landlord. Elizabeth Akers Allen. AA
You who go out on schedule. Two Variations. Densie Levertov. NaP
You who have felt the sting of dire defeat. Challenge. Harry W. Falconer. PoToHe (1941 ed.)
You who have grown so intimate with stars. To an Aviator. Daniel Whitehead Hicky. MoSiPe
You who have raised. Last Hill. Edith Mirick. ChIP
You who have spoken words in the earth. Reproach to Dead Poets. Archibald MacLeish. CMoP
You, who in April laughed, a green god in the sun. Poem. Brenda Chamberlain. NeBP
You, who in sultry weather. A Plea for a Plural. Rudolf Chambers Lehmann. CenHV
You who know unrequited love. Daphne and Apollo. George Macy. InMe
You who like a boulder stand. The Wildebeest. June Daly. FaPON
You who make your escape from the tumult. Hyena. *Unknown.* PeSA
You who practise the four elegant occupations. Scroll Section. Robert Finch. PeCV
You who seek the knightly order. The Knightly Code. Eustache Deschamps. CAW
You, who sought the great adventure. On an American Soldier of Fortune Slain in France. Clinton Scollard. MC
You Who Were Made for This Music. Louis Zukofsky. CoPo
You who were the snake hidden under my house. Fire at Murdering Hut. Judith Wright. ACV
You who with birch or laurel. To the Harpies. Arthur Davison Ficke. HBV
You who would sorrow even for a token. Reciprocity. Vassar Miller. NePoEA
You, Whoever You Are. Walt Whitman. AmFN
You whom I never knew. "The Sad Years." Eva Gore-Booth. HBMV
You! whom the aged brandy does not burn. The Nightmare. Jascha Kessler. AmPC
You whom the kings saluted; who refused not. To the Unknown Soldier. G. K. Chesterton. MMA
You whom the waters make fierce and the moon quiets. A Sestina for Cynthia. David Lougée. NePA
You whose flesh, now dust and planet. To a Saxon Poet. Jorge Luis Borges. ML
You will ask how I came to be eavesdropping, in the first place. Confession Overheard in a Subway. Kenneth Fearing. LiTA; LiTM (rev ed.); WaP
You will be enough for me. Little Serenade. Kenton Kilmer. WHL
You will be the color of water. Prophecy. Marjorie Meeker. NP
You will be what you will be. Will. Ella Wheeler Wilcox. BLPA
You will come back to me. Barren Stone. Nicholás Guillén. PoNe
You will come, my bird, Bonita? Juanita. Joaquin Miller. AA
You will come one day in a waver of love. Dream Girl. Carl Sandburg. MoLP
You Will Die. *Unknown.* *Fr.* Shi King. AWP; JAWP; WBP
You will die and your friends with you and be forgotten. To the Rulers. John Frederick Nims. JKCP (1955 ed.)
You Will Find a Joy in Service. Dorothy Conant Stroud. STF
You will find me drinking rum. The Logical Vegetarian. G. K. Chesterton. CenHV; LiTG; SiTL
You Will Grieve. Guillaume Apollinaire, *tr. fr. French by* Patricia Terry. OnPM
You will like their upstairs. A Reunion. James Schuyler. ANYP
You will not be like those who turn their faces away. The Pipes. Lou Lipsitz. YAP
You will not hear it as the sea. Hart Crane. *Fr.* The Bridge: The River. ViBoPo (1941 ed.)
You will not see the sorrow of no time. No Time. Terence Tiller. NeBP
You will print such books as these! A Warning. Heine. PoFr
You will remember that the Twelfth was always dry. The Glorious Twelfth. Robert Greacen. NeIP
You will remember the kisses, real or imagined. Resurrection. Kenneth Fearing. CMoP
You with shooting-sticks and cases for field-glasses. W. H. Auden. *Fr.* The Dog beneath the Skin. NAMP
You within Love. Norman McCaig. NeBP
You Wi'yam, come 'ere, sah, dis instance. Kentucky Philosophy. Harrison Robertson. BOHV; HBV; IHA
You wonder why Drab sells her love for gold? Epigram. J. V. Cunningham. NePoAm
You won't even die like a dog. Postscript. Raymond Souster. PeCV
You Work and Work. Samuel Hoffenstein. WhC
You work in the factory all of your life. Too Old to Work. Joe Glazer. ThLM
You would give your red lips to press. A Woman. Mary Dixon Thayer. HBMV
You would have scoffed if we had told you yesterday. To a Child in Death. Charlotte Mew. MoAB; MoBrPo; POTE
You Would Have Understood Me. Ernest Dowson. EnLit; MoBrPo; PeVV; PoVP
(Lyric: "You would have understood me.") HBV
You would not recognize me. The Tourist from Syracuse. Donald Justice. TwCP
You would not recognize yourself if I should tell you. Naomi Long Madgett. *Fr.* Trinity: a Dream Sequence. Kal
You would think the fury of aerial bombardment. The Fury of Aerial Bombardment. Richard Eberhart. AmP; CMoP; ExPo; HoPM; ILP; LiTA; LiTM (1970 ed.); MiAP; NMP; Po; PoIE; PoPo; ToPo; TwCP; UnPo (3d ed.); WaP
You wouldn't believe. All Hallow Eve. Carolyn Wells. DD
You wrong me, Strephon, when you say. Song. "Ephelia." CavP; LiTL
You wrote a line too much, my sage. Cynicus to W. Shakspere. James Kenneth Stephen. *Fr.* Two Epigrams. BOHV; CenHV; WhC
You X-ari bush. Zebra. *Unknown.* PeSA
You yacht on the Hudson. The Erie Canal Ballad. *Unknown.* ABF
You—you/ Your shadow is sunlight. In Excelsis. Amy Lowell. MAP; MoAmPo
You, you are all unloving, loveless, you. The Sea. D. H. Lawrence. BoNaP; NAMP; POTE
You young friskies who to-day. The Next War. Robert Graves. BrPo
"You'd be better off dead!" they said. Ghost. R. H. Grenville. FiSC
You'd be surprised, I'm sure, to know. A Little Word. *Unknown.* STF
You'd better be. The Skunk. Dorothy Baruch. SoPo
You'd have men's hearts up from the dust. Near Perigord. Ezra Pound. CABL; FaBoMo; LiTA; LiTM (rev. ed.)
You'd Say It Was a Funeral. James Reeves. ShM
You'd scarce expect one of my age. Tall Oaks from Little Acorns Grow [*or* The Boy Reciter]. David Everett. AmePo; BLPA; FaFP; OTD; TreF
You'd think I'd hate the hills?—well, this life brings. A Hill-Woman. John Farrar. OnPP
Youghall Harbor. *Unknown,* *tr. fr. Modern Irish by* Sir Samuel Ferguson. OnYI
You'l marvel when I tell ye o. Loudon Hill, or, Drumclog. *Unknown.* ESPB
You'le aske perhaps wherefore I stay. An Excuse of Absence. Thomas Carew. SeCP

You'll come to our ball;—since we parted. Our Ball. Winthrop Mackworth Praed. *Fr.* Letters from Teignmouth. EnRP
You'll find the road is long and rough, with soft spots far apart. Grantland Rice. *Fr.* Alumnus Football. TreFS
You'll Know Love. F. T. Macartney. MoAuPo
You'll lose your meäster soon, then, I do vind. Eclogue: Two Farms in Woone. William Barnes. NBM
You'll Love Me Yet! Robert Browning. *Fr.* Pippa Passes, sc. iii. EPN; HoPM; MeWo; OBEV (1st ed.)
(Song: "You'll love me yet!") HBV
You'll not forget these rocks and what I told you? Dialogue on the Headland. Robert Graves. ACV
You'll see sometime—half. Memorandum. William Stafford. NYBP
You'll wait a long, long time for anything much. On Looking Up by Chance at the Constellations. Robert Frost. CMoP; NePA; NP
Young Acacia, The. Hayyim Nahman Bialik, *tr. fr. Hebrew by* Helena Frank. TrJP
Young Africa's Resolve. Dennis Osadebay. ACV
Young Allan. *Unknown.* BaBo; ESPB
Young America. Carolyn Wells. DD
Young American, The. Alexander H. Everett. PaPo
Young and in love—how magical the phrase! Alice Duer Miller. *Fr.* The White Cliffs. MaRV
Young and Old. Charles Kingsley. *Fr.* The Water Babies, *ch.* 2. BiCB; FaBoBe; FaFP; GTBS; GTBS-W; GTSL; HBV; InP; LITG; MCCG; OTPC; PoLF; PoMa; PoVP; SiTL; TreF; TSW
(Old, Old Song, The.) MaRV
(Old Song, The.) CBEP; NeHB; OBVV; PG; TOP; WaKn
(Song: "When all the world is young, lad.") YAT
(When All the World Is Young, Lad.) BBV (1923 ed.); BoTP; LiTL; ViBoPo
Young and Simple though I Am. Thomas Campion. EnL; FaBoEn; PAn; SeCeV; TuPP
Young and trusting, blithe and fair. Surrender. Ruth Guthrie Harding. HBMV
Young Andrew. *Unknown.* ESPB; OBB, *sl. diff.*
(Younge Andrew.) OxBB
Young Apollo, golden-haired, A. Youth [*or* Quatrain]. Frances Cornford. ELU; WhC
Young Argonauts. Sheila Wingfield. SD
Young at his father's fire. Fathers and Sons. *Unknown.* KiLC
Young Author, The. Samuel Johnson. EiCP
Young Bather, The. *Unknown, tr. fr. Greek by* Louis Untermeyer. UnTE
Young Bearwell. *Unknown.* ESPB
Young Beichan (*diff. versions*). *Unknown.* BaBo (A *and* B *vers.*); EnSB; ESPB (A *and* C *vers.*); FlW; LoEn; OBB; ViBoFo
(Lord Bateman, *with music.*) BFSS
(Lord Beichan and Susie Pye.) GN
(Loving Ballad of Lord Bateman, The.) BeLS; BLPA; CoBE; OBB
(Turkish Lady, The.) BaBo; MaC
(Young Beichan and Susie Pye.) HBV; OnMSP
(Young Bekie.) BuBa; FaBoCh; OBB; OxBB
Young Ben he was a nice young man. Faithless Sally Brown. Thomas Hood. BEL; BOHV; HBV; TreFS
Young Benjie. *Unknown.* BaBo; OBB, *abr.*; OxBB
Young Billy Crane, *with music.* Larry Gorman. ShS
Young Birch, A. Robert Frost. BoNaP; LiTA
Young Blondes. Gavin Ewart. ErPo
Young Boy, A. Jessica Nelson North. NP
Young boys are stealing my loquats, The. Thieves. Perseus Adams. ACV
Young Bride, A. Sappho. *See* One Girl.
Young Bride's Dream, The. Rhoda Coghill. OxBI
Young bride's present, The. *Unknown.* HW
Young Buck's Sunday Blue. Kenneth Pitchford. *Fr.* Good for Nothing Man. CoPo
Young Calves, The. Robert P. Tristram Coffin. StVeCh (1955 ed.); TiPo
Young cannot look back and say, The. Looking Backward. Martha Snell Nicholson. SoP
Young Charlotte. Seba Smith, *wr. at. to* William Lorenzo Carter. BaBo; LoEn
(Frozen Girl, The.) AS, *with music*; IHA
(Young Charlottie.) BeLS; BLPA; CoSo, *with music*
Young child, Christ, is straight and wise, The. Child. Carl Sandburg. OQP; SoP; StJW; TRV
Young Colin Clout, a lad of peerless meed. The Ditty. John Gay. *Fr.* The Shepherd's Week. LoBV
Young Companions, *with music. Unknown.* CoSo
Young Cordwainer, The. Robert Graves. MoBS
Young Coridon and Phillis. *At. to* Sir Charles Sedley. CoMu; ErPo
Young Dandelion, The ("I am a bold fellow"). Dinah Maria Mulock Craik. DD; GoTP; RePo
Young Dandelion ("Young Dandelion / On a hedge-side"). Dinah Maria Mulock Craik. PRWS
Young David, A: Birmingham. Helen Morgan Brooks. PoNe (1970 ed.)
Young Dead Soldiers, The. Archibald MacLeish. MaRV; WaP
Young Dead Speak, The. Sister Mary Irma. JKCP (1955 ed.)
Young Democracy. Bernard O'Dowd. BoAu
"Hark! Young Democracy from sleep," *sel.* PoAu-1
Young Dove, The. Moses ibn Ezra, *tr. fr. Hebrew by* Solomon Solis-Cohen. TrJP
Young Earl of Essex's Victory over the Emperor of Germany, The. *Unknown.* ESPB
Young Edmondale, *with music. Unknown.* BFSS
Young Edwin in the Lowlands Low (A *and* B *vers.*). *Unknown.* BaBo
Young Endymion sleeps Endymion's sleep, The. Keats. Longfellow. AmP; AP; MAmP; Sonn
Young eyes leave the volume and stray out, The. History Lesson. Mark Van Doren. NYBP
Young Fellow Named Sydney, A. *Unknown. See* Limerick: "There was a young fellow named Sydney."
Young Firwood, A. Dante Gabriel Rossetti. GN; PoRL
Young Flash the Deer. Thornton Burgess. RePo
Young folks, old folks, everybody come. Bible Stories. *Unknown.* LiTG
Young Forbest, *with music. Unknown.* ShS
"Young friend," 'e sez. . . Young friend! Well, spare me days! Pilot Cove. C. J. Dennis. WhC
Young Gazelle, The. Walter Parke. BOHV
Young Girl: Annam. Padraic Colum. LOW
Young girl dancing lifts her face, The. The Dancer. W. J. Turner. OBMV; POTE
Young girl of thirteen, A. The Cloak. Violet Anderson. CaP
Young girl stood beside me, The. The Orange Tree. John Shaw Neilson. BoAV; MoAuPo; NeLNL; PoAu-1
Young girl, The, questions: "Whether were it better." Wisdom. Ford Madox Ford. HBV
Young girls have gone, The. By the River. Stuart Merrill. SiSw
Young girls have gone down to the river, The. Prose Poem: By the River. Judith Gautier. OnPM
Young girls, if you'll listen. Pearl Bryan. *Unknown.* ViBoFo
Young Girl's Song, A. Paul Heyse, *tr. fr. German by* E. H. Mueller. PoPl
Young Girl's Song. *Unknown. See* Maidens Came, The.
Young Glass-Stainer, The. Thomas Hardy. CTC
Young grass burnt up, so hot the air was, The. In the Field. Harold Lenoir Davis. NP
Young Gray Head, The. Caroline Anne Bowles. BeLS
Young, having risen early, had gone, The. The Guardians. Geoffrey Hill. NePoEA-2
Young head in sunlight! Not a woman born. No Woman Born. Robert Farren. OxBI
Young Highland Girl Studying Poetry, A. Iain Crichton Smith. NePoEA-2; PP
Young homosexuals and hot girls, The. Lone Gentleman. "Pablo Neruda." ErPo
Young Hodge met Mog the miller's maid. Don't Be Foolish Pray. *Unknown.* CoMu
Young Housewife, The. William Carlos Williams. BWP; NoP
Young Hunting (*diff. versions*). *Unknown.* BaBo; BFSS, *with music*; ESPB, (3 *vers.*); OBB; OxBB; OxBoLi; ViBoFo
(Love Henry, *with music.*) BFSS
(Loving Henry.) BaBo
Young I am, and yet unskill'd. Song for a Girl [*or* Sung by a Young Girl]. Dryden. ELP; ErPo; UnTE
Young I was who now am old. On Himself. Robert Herrick. UnTE

Young is she, and slight to view. Dorothea. Sarah N. Cleghorn. HBMV
Young Janie was a strappin' lass. The Thocht. William Soutar. NeBP
Young Japanese son was in love with a servant boy, The. Dream Data. Robert Duncan. NeAP
Young Jemmy is a lad. England's Darling; or, Great Britain's Joy and Hope on That Noble Prince James, Duke of Monmouth. *Unknown.* CoMu
Young Jesus. Leslie Savage Clark. ChIP
Young Jockey he courted sweet Mog the brunette. Mog the Brunette. *Unknown.* CoMu
Young John. *Unknown. See* False Lover Won Back, The.
Young Johnny, *with music. Unknown.* BFSS
Young Johnny Scott, *with music. Unknown.* BFSS
Young Johnstone. *Unknown.* BaBo; ESPB; OxBB
Young Lady Named Bright, A. *Unknown, See* Limerick: "There was a young lady named Bright." *at. to* Arthur Buller.
Young lady of fair Mytilene, A. Limerick. *Unknown.* CenHV
Young Lady of Lynn, The. *Unknown. See* Limerick; "There was a young lady of Lynn/ Who was so exceedingly thin."
Young Lady of Niger, The. *Unknown. See* Limerick: "There was a young lady of Niger."
Young Man and the Young Nun, The. Albert D. Mackie. OxBS
Young Lady of Norway, A. Edward Lear. *See* Limerick: "There was a young lady of Norway."
Young man growing old, and old man aging, A. Cuban Voyage. Paul Engle. ReMP
Young Lady of Spain, A. *Unknown. See* Limerick: "There was a young lady of Spain."
Young Laird and Edinburgh Katy, The. Allan Ramsay. CEP; EiPP
Young Lambs. John Clare. GoTP; TrGrPo
("Spring is coming by a many signs, The.") EG
Young lambs to sell! Mother Goose. OTPC
Young Lincoln. Edwin Markham. DD; LiPo; OHIP; OQP; PEDC
Young Linnets, The. Ann Hawkshaw. OTPC
Young Lochinvar. Sir Walter Scott. *See* Lochinvar.
Young Lochinvar: the True Story in Blank Verse. *Unknown, at. to* J. J. Fay. BOHV; FiBHP; InMe
Young lords o the north country, The. Lady Maisry. *Unknown.* BaBo (A *vers.*); ESPB; OBB; OxBB; ViBoFo
Young Love. Andrew Marvell. EP; MaMe
Young Love. Gerald Massey. OBVV
Young Love. Shakespeare. *See* Tell Me Where Is Fancy Bred.
Young Love. Sara Teasdale. BoLP
Young Love lies sleeping. Dream-Love. Christina Rossetti. CH; GTBS-D; GTSL; NBM; PoEL-5
Young Love Storms like New Wine. "Angelus Silesius," *tr. fr. German by* Paul Carus. OnPM
Young Lovers, The. Ridgely Torrence. *Fr.* The House of a Hundred Lights. AA
Young Man, The. Lewis Macadams. ANYP
Young man—/ Young man. The Prodigal Son. James Weldon Johnson. StJW
Young man, alone, on the high bridge over the Tagus, A. The High Bridge above the Tagus River at Toledo. William Carlos Williams. CTC
Young Man in a Galilean Doorway. Herbert D. Gallaudet. ChIP
Young Man in April, The. Rupert Brooke. BoLP
Young man lately in our town, A. The Maids Conjuring Book. *Unknown.* CoMu
Young man left his native shores, A. Look Out Below! Charles R. Thatcher. PoAu-1
Young Man of Nazareth, The. *Unknown.* SoP
Young man on a journey had met her, A. Limerick. *Unknown.* LiBL
Young man once was sitting, A. Popular Ballad: "Never Forget Your Parents." Franklin P. Adams. BOHV
Young man out of Nazareth, The. The Young Man of Nazareth. *Unknown.* SoP
Young man that once I was, come talk with me. Sentimental Monologue. John Hall Wheelock. NYTB
Young Man Thinks of Sons, The. R. A. K. Mason. AnNZ
Young Man to an Old Woman Courting Him, A. John Cleveland. AnAnS-2
Young Man Who Wouldn't Plow Corn, The, *with music. Unknown.* BFSS
Young Man's Epigram on Existence, A. Thomas Hardy. BrPo
Young Man's Exhortation, A. Thomas Hardy. ViPP
Young Man's Fancy. Ray Mathew. BoAV
Young Man's Song, A. William Bell. FaBoTw; NePoEA
Young Mary, loitering once her garden way. Mary and Gabriel. Rupert Brooke. ISi
Young May Moon, The. Thomas Moore. ELP; EnRP; HBV; OAEP; OBEV
Young men and maids, pray lend attention. The Silver Dagger. *Unknown.* BaBo
Young men and maids, pray tell your age. Locks and Bolts. *Unknown.* TrAS
Young Men Come Less Often, The —Isn't It So? Horace, *tr. fr. Latin by* Robert Fitzgerald. Odes, I, 25. ErPo
Young men dancing, and the old. Youthful Age. Thomas Stanley. AWP; JAWP; WBP
Young men die in battle, The. Scapegoats. Eleanor D. Breed. MaRV; PGD
Young men give ear to me a while. The Maid's Complaint for Want of a Dil Doul. *Unknown.* CoMu
Young men go walking in the woods. The Pediment of Appearance. Wallace Stevens. Po
Young men leave the country for the town, The. The Way to the Sea. Laurence Lerner. NePoEA-2
Young men riding in the street. Image from D'Orleans. Ezra Pound. FIW; LOW
Young men walking the open streets. Remember Your Lovers. Sidney Keyes. WaP
Young Mistah Rooster Man planted him a gyarden. Miss Hen. Booth Lowrey. IHA
Young Molly Bawn. *Unknown.* OnYI
Young Monroe at Gerry's Rock. *Unknown. See* Jam on Gerry's Rock, The.
Young moon is white, The. A Japanese Love-Song. Alfred Noyes. OBVV
Young moon, take my face up yonder. Re-Birth. *Unknown.* PeSA
Young Mouse, The. Jefferys Taylor. OTPC (1923 ed.)
Young mouse, small and innocent, A. The Old Cat and the Young Mouse. La Fontaine. CIV
Young Mystic, The. Louis Untermeyer. TSW
Young Negro Poet. Calvin C. Hernton. Kal
Young Neophyte, The. Alice Meynell. ACP; CAW; GoBC
Young Night Thought. Robert Louis Stevenson. GaP; NeHB; RIS
Young Ones, Flip Side, The. James A. Emanuel. Kal
Young Paris. George Crabbe. *Fr.* Posthumous Tales. OBRV
Young Peggy. *Unknown.* BaBo; ESPB
Young people, all attention give and hear what I do say. The Blind Man's Regret. *Unknown.* BFSS
Young people in the bus began to sing. Girls and Soldiers Singing. Leonard Mann. BoAu
Young people who delight in sin [*or* hear, and I will tell]. Wicked Polly. *Unknown.* ABF; BFSS
Young Philander woo'd me long. Song. *Unknown.* ErPo
Young Pithy, from your Djetis bed. Lines to Homo Somejerktensis. Earnest A. Hooton. WhC
Young Poet. Myron O'Higgins. PoNe
"Young poets, The, " he murmured. Vernon Watkins. *Fr.* Yeats in Dublin. PP
Young Priest to His Hands, The. Edward F. Garesché. CAW
Young Prince, The. Horatio Colony. TwAmPo
Young Prince Peter suddenly, once. Prince Peter. Nancy Byrd Turner. GaP; RIS
Young prince violent in wrath, The. The Young Prince. Horatio Colony. TwAmPo
Young Reaper, The. Aleksey Koltsov, *tr. fr. Russian by* C. Fillingham Coxwell. WoL
Young Recruit, The. Arthur Davison Ficke. ELU
Young Reynard. George Meredith. HoPM
Young Roger came tapping at Dolly's window. Roger and Dolly. Henry Carey. CoMu; OxNR, *st.* 1
Young Romilly through Barden Woods. The Founding of Bolton Priory. Wordsworth. OTPC
Young Ronald. *Unknown.* ESPB
Young Rory O'More courted Kathleen Bawn. Rory O'More. Samuel Lover. BOHV; HBV; VA
Young Sammy Watkins. *Unknown.* BBGG

Young Sea. Carl Sandburg. RePo
Young Shepherd Bathing His Feet. Peter Clarke. PBA
Young shepherd, turn aside and move. Melisea, Her Song in Scorn of Her Shepherd Narcissus. Jorge de Montemayor, *tr. by* Bartholomew Young. *Fr.* Diana. TuPP
Young Silvia. —— De la Sale. SeCL
Young Sir Guyon proudly said. Queen's Song. Stopford Brooke. *Fr.* Riquet of the Tuft. VA
Young skull which the wind scrapes, which the sand. On the Relative Merit of Friend and Foe, Being Dead. Donald Thompson. WaP
Young squirrel's mother, The, said, "Come out!" Squirrel in the Rain. Frances Frost. RePo
Young Strephon and Phillis. *Unknown.* UnTE
Young Thing, The. *Unknown.* RIS
Young things who frequent picture-palaces, The. The Jung Idea. "P. H." SiTL
Young to the end through sympathy with youth. James McCosh. Robert Bridges. AA
Young, waiting for the draft to war. A Dream of Apricots. James Schevill. NYTB
Young Warrior. George Edward Hoffman. ChIP
Young was the woman. A Maiden Ring-adorned. Cynewulf. *Fr.* Christ. ISi
Young Washington. Arthur Guiterman. FaPON; MPB; OHIP; PoSC
Young Waters. *Unknown.* EnLit; ESPB; OBB; OxBB; TOP
Young Wife, A. D. H. Lawrence. BrPo; ChMP; ELP; MoBrPo; StP
Young wife's dreams, The. *Unknown.* HW
Young Willie stands in his stable door. Clyde's Waters. *Unknown.* OxBB
Young Windebank. Margaret L. Woods. HBV; HBVY; VA
Young Woman. Chaucer. *Fr.* The Canterbury Tales: The Miller's Tale. BoW
Young Woman. Howard Nemerov. CBV; ErPo; FiMAP
Young Woman at a Window. Mark Van Doren. LiTA; MoPo; MoVE
Young Woman at a Window. William Carlos Williams. OCS
Young women in their April moodiness. The True Weather for Women. Louis Simpson. NePoAm; NoP
Young women they [*or* they'll] run like hares on the mountain. Hares on the Mountain. *Unknown.* ErPo; UnTE
Younge Andrew. *Unknown.* *See* Young Andrew.
Younger Van Eyck, The. E. C. Bentley. *Fr.* Clerihews. FiBHP
Youngest of all three took her white hand, The. Blanche comme la neige. *Unknown.* OuSiCo
Youpe! Youpe! River Along. *Unknown.* IHA
Your abdomen still twitches, probing the air. Dead Wasp. Gregory Orr. QAH
Your absence has gone through me. Separation. W. S. Merwin. AmPC
Your arms will clasp the gathered grain. The Island. Edwin Muir. PoIE
Your Attention Please. Peter Porter. HYE
Your Beauty and My Reason. *Unknown.* TrGrPo
("Like two proud armies marching in the field.") OBSC
Your beauty is as timeless as the earth. Her Pedigree. Arthur Davison Ficke. Sonnets of a Portrait Painter, IX. HBMV
Your beauty, ripe and calm and fresh. The Philosopher and the Lover [*or* To a Mistress Dying]. Sir William Davenant. ACP; BWP; FaBoEn; GoBC; LO; MePo; OBEV
Your beauty, which I lost sight of once. Love Song. Denise Levertov. PoIE (1970 ed.)
Your body derns. Scunner. "Hugh MacDiarmid." FaBoTw
Your Body Drifting. Iwan Goll, *tr. fr. French by* Iwan Goll. OnPM
Your body gleams like copper on the veld. The Fallen Zulu Commander. C. M. van Den Heever. PeSA
Your body has narrow slits instead of windows. In Memory of Your Body. David Shapiro. ANYP
Your Body Is Stars. Stephen Spender. CMoP; FaBoTw; MoLP
Your body to hold, your perfect breasts. Undine. Irving Layton. ErPo
Your body's motion is like music. Like Music. John Hall Wheelock. NP
Your bow swept over a string, and a long low note quivered to the air. Jan Kubelik. Carl Sandburg. NP
Your boy and my boy. Your Cross and My Cross. Emma Finty Cox. PEDC
Your boy's-ambition was to be a Horseman. Stud Groom. John Glassco. OBCV
Your brother is dead. Dreaming with a Friend. Stephen Berg. NaP
Your buttonholes for eyes, your solemn face. The Statue. John Fuller. NePoEA-2
Your Chase Had a Beast in View. John Peale Bishop. LiTA
Your children are not your children. On Children. Kahlil Gibran. *Fr.* The Prophet. PoPl; PoToHe (new ed.)
Your Church and Mine. Phillips H. Lord. BLPA; MaRV
Your clear and living voice among the ruins. The Temple. Josephine W. Johnson. MoRP
Your clear eye is the one absolutely beautiful thing. Child. Sylvia Plath. FIW
Your clothes of snow and satin and pure blood. The Bed. Karl Shapiro. NYBP
Your comedy I've read, my friend. To a Living Author. *Unknown.* SiTL
Your Corner. Mary Harrington. SoP
Your courtiers scorn we country clowns. A Ballad of the Courtier and the Country Clown. *Unknown.* CoMu
Your Cross and My Cross. Emma Finty Cox. PEDC
Your doctor, Lord. For Dr. and Mrs. Dresser. Margaret Avison. MoCV; PeCV (1967 ed.)
Your door is shut against my tightened face. The White House[s]. Claude McKay. AmNP;AmPP(5th ed.);PoNe
Your downcast, harlequin, defenceless face. Lynched Negro. Maxwell Bodenheim. PoNe
Your dream had left me numb and cold. Salutation. "Æ." OnYI
Your dusky shadow at the window lingers. Morning and Evening. Antoni Slonimski. TrJP
Your Excellency. Giuseppe Giusti, *tr. fr. Italian by* Lorna de' Lucchi. WoL
Your eyen [*or* yen] two wol slee me sodenly [*or* will slay me suddenly]. Merciles Beaute. Chaucer. ACP; AtBAP; CBEP; CLwM; CTC; EnLi-1 (1949 ed.); EnLoPo; MeEL; NoP; OBEV (1st ed.); OnPM; PAn; StP; TrGrPo
Your eyes are tonight so unusually thoughtful and sad. The Giraffe. Nikolai Gumilev. LiTW
Your eyes drink of me. The Mystery. Sara Teasdale. HBMV
Your Eyes Have Their Silence. Gerald William Barrax. YAP
Your eyes open. Nothing. Barrie Reid. BoAV
"Your eyes that once were never weary of mine." Ephemera. W. B. Yeats. BrPo
Your eyes were made for laughter. Don't. James Jeffrey Roche. HBV
Your eyes, your flowing hair. Auburn. Paul Verlaine. ErPo
Your face did not rot. The Lost Pilot. James Tate. CoAP; TwCP; YAP
Your face is an Eastern garden of response and gladness. Summa contra Gentiles. Paris Leary. CoPo
Your face is the face of all the others. The Face of Love. Ingrid Jonker. PeSA
Your face was lifted to the golden sky. Rupert Brooke, I. W. W. Gibson. HBMV
Your Fair Looks Inflame My Desire. Thomas Campion. UnTE
Your fair looks urge my desire. Be Wise, and Fly Not. Thomas Campion. UnTE
Your Father Knoweth. *Unknown.* *See* God Knoweth Best.
"Your father's gone," my bald headmaster said. The Lesson. Edward Lucie-Smith. TwCP
Your Field of Labor. Ellen M. Huntington Gates. *See* Your Mission.
Your Flag and My Flag. Wilbur D. Nesbit. FaFP; OQP; PEDC; PoRL; WBLP
Your flute/ you carved from the shinbone of a mighty bull. Flute Players. Jean-Joseph Rabéarivelo. PBA
Your Friend. *Unknown.* TreFT
Your friends shall be the tall wind. For a Child. Fannie Stearns Davis. FaPON; MPB
Your ghost will walk, you lover of trees. "De Gustibus." Robert Browning. EPN; HBV; MaVP; MBW-2; OAEP; PoVP; VA; ViPo; VP
Your Glory, Lincoln. Mae Winkler Goodman. PGD
Your grieving moonlight face looks down. Reproach. Robert Graves. GTSL

Your hair has turned white. Hitomaro, *tr. fr. Japanese by* Kenneth Rexroth. LiTW
Your hair is growing long, Uncle Ambrose. Uncle Ambrose. James Still. AmFN
Your hair that makes the most of vines. Grand Canal. Alan Ross. POTi
Your hand in mine, we walk out. A Sword in a Cloud of Light. Kenneth Rexroth. NMP
Your Hands. Ernest Dowson. UnTE
Your Hands. Angelina Weld Grimké. CDC
Your hands lie open in the long fresh grass. Silent Noon. Dante Gabriel Rossetti. The House of Life, XIX. BEL; BoLiVe; ELP; EnLi-2; EnLit; EPN; GTBS-D; HBV; ILP; LiTL; LO; MaVP; MeWo; NoP; OAEP; OBNC; PAn; PoEL-5; PoVP; Sonn; TrGrPo; ViPo; ViPP; VP; WHA; YAT
Your hands, my dear, adorable. The Chilterns. Rupert Brooke. MoBrPo
Your hay it is mow'd, and your corn is reap'd. Harvest Song [*or* Song]. Dryden. *Fr.* King Arthur. CEP; SeCV-2
Your heart,/ a sponge lying in the vinegar bowl. George Washington Absent from His Country. Diane Wakoski. YAP
Your heart is a music-box, dearest! Song. Frances Sargent Osgood. AA
Your heart trembles in the shadows, like a face. When the Tom-Tom Beats. Jacques Roumain. PoNe
Your heifer's pretty neck is not yet broke. Too Young for Love. Horace. *Fr.* Odes. UnTE
Your hooves have stamped at the black margin of the wood. On a Picture of a Black Centaur by Edmund Dulac. W. B. Yeats. SyP
Your House. *Unknown.* PoToHe (new ed.)
Your House of Happiness. B. Y. Williams. MaRV
Your husband will be with us at the treat. To His Mistress. Ovid. ErPo
Your Irish wit made you bequeath. Heartbreak House. Patric Dickinson. POTi
Your kindness is no kindness now. Kindness. Catherine Davis. NYBP
Your Kisses ("Sweet, can I sing you the song of your kisses"). Arthur Symons. MeWo
Your Kisses ("Your kisses, and the way you curl"). Arthur Symons. *See* Leves Amores.
Your Lad, and My Lad. Randall Parrish. MC; PAH
Your Last Drive. Thomas Hardy. OBNC
Your learning, James, in classics and romance. Letter to a Teacher of English. Robert Hillyer. AnFE; CoAnAm
Your leaves bound up compact and fair. To an Author. Philip Freneau. AmPP; CoBA; MAmP; OxBA
Your letter does not move me. Der Brief, den du geschrieben. Heine, *tr. by* Louis Untermeyer. ALV
Your letter, fat with snapshots, came today. Vacation Snapshot. Melvin Walker la Follette. NYTB
Your Looks So Often Cast. Sir Thomas Wyatt. EnRePo; FCP; SiPS
Your love is dead, lady, your love is dead. Madrigal. R. S. Thomas. ELU; EnLoPo
Your loveliness was like a wave. Spent Wave. John Hall Wheelock. LiTM (1946 ed.)
Your lovely fair did first invite. The Excuse. Robert Heath. SeCL
Your lovely hands. William Carlos Williams. *Fr.* Paterson. MoLP
Your majesty shall shortly have your wish. And Ride in Triumph [*or* Persepolis]. Christopher Marlowe. *Fr.* Tamburlaine the Great, Pt. I, Act II, sc. v. CLwM; WHA
Your midriff sags toward your knees. Woman with Girdle. Anne Sexton. ErPo
Your milk-white maiden gown. The Maiden Gown. William Cavendish, Duke of Newcastle. SeCL
Your mind and you are our Sargasso Sea. Portrait d'une Femme. Ezra Pound. AnAmPo; AP; APA; CABA; CLwM; CMoP; CoAnAm; ForPo; HBMV; MAP; MoAB; MoAmPo; MoVE; NoP; PoAn; PoFS; TwAmPo; TwCP
Your mind lies open like the map of rivers. Five Birds Rise. William Hayward. NYBP
Your Mission. Ellen M. Huntington Gates. BLPA; BLRP; NeHB; TreFT
(Your Field of Labor, *abr.*) SoP
Your mistris, that you follow whores, still taxeth you. A Selfe Accuser. John Donne. MaMe
Your Money and Mine. *Unknown.* STF
Your Mouth. Jenab Shehabuddin, *tr. fr. Turkish by* E. Powys Mathers. LiTW
"Your name is Achilles Deatheridge?" Achilles Deatheridge. Edgar Lee Masters. AmFN; MaC; PoMa
"Your Need Is Greater than Mine." Theodore Enslin. CoPo
Your Neighbor. H. Howard Biggar. PoToHe
Your neighbor, sir, whose roses you admire. My Neighbor's Reply. *Unknown.* PoToHe
Your northern grasses are as blue as jade. In Spring. Li Po. LiTW
Your Own Version. Paul Gilbert. BLRP; MaRV
Your park's like a gothic cathedral to me. To Madame la Duchesse de Bauffremont. Louis Morpeau. PoNe
Your peevish voice remarked "Oh, rats." To an Unknown Neighbor at the Circus. Rosemary Benét. InMe
Your piano is the better instrument. More Letters Found near a Suicide. Frank Horne. BANP
Your Place. John Oxenham. BLRP; FaChP; MaRV; OQP; SoP; TRV
Your plan I love not; with a number you. George Crabbe. *Fr.* The Borough. LO
Your Pleasures Spring like Daisies. Walter Savage Landor. *See* Ianthe: "From you, Ianthe, little troubles pass."
Your pocket-handkerchief is large enough. Metaphysical Poem. Maxwell Bodenheim. AnAmPo
Your poem must eternal be. An Eternal Poem. Samuel Taylor Coleridge. BOHV
Your Presence. David Diop, *tr. fr. French by* Ulli Beier. PBA
Your quiet and eager eyes wander about. Harbour. Harold Monro. BoPe
Your recollection burns in my lantern. Nickajack Cave. Coleman Barks. QAH
Your Sanctuary. Walter Lyman French. MaRV
Your shadow I have seen you play with often. The Child and the Shadow. Elizabeth Jennings. NePoEA-2
Your Shining Eyes. *Unknown.* TuPP
Your shrunken head was bent. The Murder Trial. Perseus Adams. PeSA
Your skill has fashioned stately creeds. The Lost Christ. Thomas Curtis Clark. ChIP; OQP
Your sky is a hard and a dazzling blue. In Spain. Emily Lawless. AnIV
Your smiles are not, as other women's be [*or* bee]. To the Lady May. Aurelian Townsend. MePo; SeCL; SeEP
Your smiling, or the hope, the thought of it. A Simile for Her Smile. Richard Wilbur. CBV; FiMAP; HoPM; MiAP; MoLP
Your Snow-white Shoulder. Heine, *tr. fr. German by* Louis Untermeyer. UnTE
Your Songs. Gwendolyn B. Bennett. CDC
Your soul is a sealed garden. Clair de lune. Paul Verlaine, *tr. by* Arthur Symons. AWP
Your soul is like a landscape choice and fair. A Pastel. Paul Verlaine. SyP
Your steps, children of my still hours. The Steps. Paul Valéry. ReMP
Your tall French legs, my V for victory. Will to Win. F. R. Scott. OBCV
Your Tears. Edwin Markham. HBMV
Your Teeth Are Ivory Towers. William Empson. ToPo
Your thighs are appletrees. Portrait of a Lady. William Carlos Williams. AmPP (5th ed.); CMoP; NoP; OxBA; PoIE; TwAmPo
Your thoughts dont have words every day. Emily Dickinson. DiPo; MAmP
Your threats how vain, Corregidor. A Ballad of Manila Bay. Sir Charles G. D. Roberts. PAH
Your tiny picture makes me yearn. Christie's Portrait. Gerald Massey. VA
Your trail runs to the Westward. To James Whitcomb Riley. Kipling. YT
Your train leaves at eleven forty-five and it is now but eleven thirty-nine and a half. Dr. Fell and Points West. Ogden Nash. RePo
Your two great eyes will slay me suddenly. A Rondel of Merciless Beauty. Chaucer, *mod. by* Louis Untermeyer. MeWo; TrGrPo
Your ugly token. Upon a Dead Man's Head [*or* The Gift of a Skull]. John Skelton. ACP; CoBE; EnRePo; PoIE; ReIE; SeCePo; SiCE; UnPo (1st ed.)

Your verses, dear friend, I surmise. Limerick. *Unknown.* LiBL
Your villa, Furius, is not placed. Cold Blast of Debt. Catullus. OnPM
Your voice is the color of a robin's breast. To O. E. A. Claude McKay. BANP; PoNe
Your voice speaks:/ Little child out of Eternity. Christmas. Gertrude von Le Fort. ISi
Your voice speaks:/ The angel of the Lord came in unto Mary. Vigil of the Assumption. Gertrude von Le Fort. ISi
Your voice was the rugged. The Meeting of Sighs. Blanche Edith Baughan. BoAu
Your voice, with clear location of June days. June Light. Richard Wilbur. CaFP
Your walk sacerdotal and slow, undulant. A Black Girl Goes By. Emile Roumer. TTY
Your white raincoat hangs. Things You Left Behind. Gregory Orr. QAH
Your will is done. Its promise, that I fled. Oedipus to the Oracle. Wesley Trimpi. NePoEA
Your wistful eyes searched each one as he passed. Stray Dog. Charlotte Mish. PoLF
Your words came just when needed. Accept My Full Heart's Thanks. Ella Wheeler Wilcox. PoToHe
Your words dropped into my heart like pebbles into a pool. Absence. Claude McKay. CDC
Your words, my friend (right healthful caustics), blame. Astrophel and Stella, XXI. Sir Philip Sidney. CABA; FCP; ReEn; ReIE; SiCE; SiPS; TuPP
Your World. Georgia Douglas Johnson. AmNP
Your world is unimportant to me. The Invisible Man. Conrad Kent Rivers. Kal
Your yen two wol slee me sodenly. *See* Your eyen two wol slee me sodenly.
Your youth is like a water-wetted stone. Susan to Diana. Frances Cornford. MoVE
You're a good girl; you're gray with virtue. Poems in Praise of Practically Nothing, IV. Samuel Hoffenstein. InMe
You're a poet. *Unknown.* FaFP; SiTL
You're a traitor convicted, you know very well! Jefferson D. H. S. Cornwell. PAH
You're in my mind. To My Wife. James Forsyth. WaP
You're kind to women, children, worms. Poems in Praise of Practically Nothing. Samuel Hoffenstein. InMe
Youre love if vertuous will shew forth some fruitts of devotion. *Unknown.* SeCSL
You're not alone when you are still alone. Idea, XI [*or* Give Me My Self]. Michael Drayton. LiTL; LO; TrGrPo
You're ravishing and, plain to see. To His Girl. Martial. UnTE
You're So Kind. Groucho Marx. SiTL
You're starting, my boy, on life's journey. Have Courage, My Boy, to Say, No. *Unknown.* STF
You're the cook's understudy. Slip-Shoe Lovey. Edgar Lee Masters. NP
You're the Top. Cole Porter. Po
You're through—now walking up and down. The Ageing Athlete. Neil Weiss. SD
You're very well polished, I'm free to confess. The Cowboy to His Friend in Need. Burke Jenkins. SCC
Yours. Rabindranath Tagore. MoRP
Yours is an . . .up. Name. Ron Padgett. YAP
Yours is the face that the earth turns to me. Love Poem. Kathleen Raine. LiTB; MoAB; MoBrPo (1962 ed.); MoPo; NeBP
Yours is the sullen sorrow. Last Words to Miriam. D. H. Lawrence. CoBMV
Yours was a wondrous story. To the Flag of Stars. Thomas Curtis Clark. PEDC
Yourself. Jones Very. AA; AmLP; MAmP; NePA; OxBA; PoEL-4; Sonn
You's as stiff an' as cold as a stone. The Dead Pussy Cat. *Unknown.* CIV
Youth. Katharine Lee Bates. PGD
Youth. Robert Browning. *See* David's Song.
Youth. Preston Clark. HBMV
Youth. Virginia Woodward Cloud. AA
Youth. Frances Cornford. ELU
(Quatrain: "Young Apollo, golden-haired, A.") WhC
Youth, A. Stephen Crane. *See* Youth in Apparel That Glittered, A.
Youth. Bartholomew Griffin. *See* Sonnet: "I have not spent the April of my time."
Youth. Theresa Helburn. PFY
Youth. Langston Hughes. AmFN; BiCB; GoSl
Youth. Georgia Douglas Johnson. BANP; GoSl; PoNe
Youth. Thomas S. Jones, Jr. OQP
Youth. George Cabot Lodge. AA
Youth. Jessie B. Rittenhouse. HBMV
Youth. Blanaid Salkeld. OxBI
Youth. Barend Toerien, *tr. fr. Afrikaans by* Barend Toerien. PeSA
Youth. *Unknown.* OBSC
Youth. R. Wever. *See* In Youth Is Pleasure.
Youth. James Wright. NaP
Youth and Age. George Arnold. EPN; HBV
Youth and Age. Ecclesiastes, Bible, *O.T.* *See* Remember Now Thy Creator.
Youth and Age. Byron. *See* Stanzas for Music: "There's not a joy . . ."
Youth and Age. Thomas Campion. *See* Though You Are Young.
Youth and Age. Samuel Taylor Coleridge. BEL; EnLi-2 (1949 ed.); EnRP; ERoP-1; FiP; GTBS; GTBS-D; GTBS-P; GTBS-W; GTSE; GTSL; HBV; MERP; OBEV; OBNC; OBRV; PoLF
Youth and Age. Mimnermus, *tr. fr. Greek by* John Addington Symonds. AWP; OnPM
Youth and Age. Vance Palmer. BoAu; NeLNL
Youth and Age. William Bell Scott. VA
Youth and Age. Shakespeare. *See* Crabbed Age and Youth.
Youth and Age. Earl of Surrey. *See* How No Age Is Content.
Youth and Age. Ridgely Torrence. *Fr.* The House of a Hundred Lights. AA
Youth and Age. W. B. Yeats. ELU
Youth and Age on Beaulieu River, Hants. John Betjeman. ChMP; FaBoTw; TwCP
Youth and Art. Robert Browning. BOHV; BoLiVe; CTC; HBV; MaPo; MBW-2; PoVP; VA; ViBoPo; ViPo
Youth and Beauty. Aurelian Townsend. AnAnS-2; EP; MePo; SeCP
Youth and Calm. Matthew Arnold. MBW-2; PoVP
Youth and Cupid. Elizabeth I, Queen of England. *See* When I Was Fair and Young.
Youth and Death. Edward Merril Root. OQP
Youth and Maidenhood. Sarah Williams. OBVV
Youth and Maturity. Fulke Greville. *See* Nurse-Life Wheat within His Green Husk Growing, The.
Youth and the Northwind, The. John Godfrey Saxe. StPo
Youth and Truth. Walter E. Isenhour. SoP
Youth Autumnal. Raymond Roseliep. JKCP (1955 ed.)
Youth cocks his hat and rides up the street. Points of View. Amy Lowell. LOW
Youth, Day, Old Age, and Night. Walt Whitman. AnAmPo
Youth Dreams, The. Rainer Maria Rilke, *tr. fr. German by* Ludwig Lewisohn. AWP; JAWP; TrJP; WBP
Youth gone, and beauty gone if ever there. Monna Innominata, XIV. Christina Rossetti. OBNC; Sonn; ViBoPo; ViPo; VP
Youth had a man's heart, The; he was a man in the din of battle. The Lovely Youth. Aneirin. LiTW
Youth hath many charms. Youth and Age. George Arnold. EPN; HBV
Youth in Age. George Meredith. PoVP
Youth in Apparel That Glittered, A. Stephen Crane. The Black Riders, XXVII. AmePo; AnAmPo; LiTA; NePA
(Content.) AA
(Youth, A.) MoAmPo (1950 ed.)
Youth in Arms, *sels.* Harold Monro. Carrion. MMA
"Happy boy, happy boy." NP
Youth is conservative. A Human Instinct. Christopher Morley. *Fr.* Translations from the Chinese. EvOK
Youth Is Sweet and Well. Lorenzo de' Medici, *tr. fr. Italian by* Lorna de' Lucchi. WoL
Youth is the time when hearts are large. On the Slain Collegians. Herman Melville. MAmP; MWA-1
Youth, large, lusty, loving—youth full of grace, force, fascination. Youth, Day, Old Age, and Night. Walt Whitman. AnAmPo
Youth, Love, and Death. Philip James Bailey. *Fr.* Festus. VA

Youth Mowing, A. D. H. Lawrence. MoAB; MoBrPo; TrGrPo
Youth of Jesus, The. Clement of Alexandria. *See* Shepherd of Eager Youth.
Youth of Nature, The. Matthew Arnold. PoVP
Youth of the Mountain. Walter Hard. AnNE
Youth rambles on life's arid mount. The Progress of Poesy. Matthew Arnold. EnL; MBW-2; PoVP;
Youth Sings a Song of Rosebuds. Countee Cullen. BANP; NoP; PoLF; PoNe
Youth that rides the wildest horse. Youth and Age. Vance Palmer. BoAu; NeLNL
Youth with [the] Red-gold Hair, The. Edith Sitwell. FaBoTw; MoVE
Youthful Age. Thomas Stanley, *after the Greek of* Anacreon. AWP; JAWP; WBP
Youthful mouse, not up to trap, A. The Cockerel, the Cat, and the Young Mouse. La Fontaine. WoL
Youth's Agitations. Matthew Arnold. CBEP
Youth's Antiphony. Dante Gabriel Rossetti. The House of Life, XIII. MaVP; PoVP; TOP; ViPo; VP
Youth's bright palace. A Lament. Denis Florence MacCarthy. JKCP (1926 ed.); OBVV
Youth's Prayer, A. Mary S. Edgar. *See* God, Who Touchest Earth. . .
Youth's Progress. John Updike. FiBHP
Youth's Spring Tribute. Dante Gabriel Rossetti. The House of Life, XIV. MaVP; PoVP; ViPo; VP
Youth's Thankfulness. Edgar Daniel Kramer. PEDC; PGD
Youth's the season made for joys. Song. John Gay. *Fr.* The Beggar's Opera. CEP; OBEC; WiR
You've all heard of Larry O'Toole. Larry O'Toole. Thackeray. ALV
You've been a wanderer, you! The Quest. Cladys Cromwell. HBMV
You've come early to see us this year. John Frost. William Miller. PCH
You've Got to Be Taught. Oscar Hammerstein, II. AmFN
You've heard of Slattery's light dragoons. O'Duffy's Ironsides. "Tom Moore, Jr." OnYI
You've heard of the Turks and the Greeks. The Battle of Navarino. *Unknown.* CoMu
You've lost your religion, the Rabbi said. Debate with the Rabbi. Howard Nemerov. PoPl
You've never heard of the voice of God? The Voice of God. Katherine R. Barnard. BLRP; WBLP
You've plucked a curlew, drawn a hen. On an Island. J. M. Synge. MoBrPo; OBVV; PeVV
You've read of several kinds of Cat. The Ad-dressing of Cats. T. S. Eliot. GoTP
You've seen a pair of faithful lovers die. Epilogue to "Mithridates, King of Pontus." Dryden. OAEP
You've seen a strawberry. Nevertheless. Marianne Moore. BWP; CMoP; ForPo; MoAB; OxBA; SeCeV
You've time to build houses, and in them to dwell. No Time for God. *Unknown.* SoP
Ypres. Laurence Binyon. MMA
Ypres. Ivor Gurney. FOL
Yr "pure" Miles a. New Miles Poem. Alden Van Buskirk. YAP
Ys Yt Possyble. Sir Thomas Wyatt. *See* Is It Possible.
Ystrad Fflur. T. Gwynn Jones, *tr. fr. Welsh by* Alun Llywelyn-Williams. PrWP
Yt fell abowght the Lamasse tyde. *See* It fell about. . .
Yuki. Mary McNeil Fenollosa. AA
Yukon, The, *sel.* Joaquin Miller.
Arctic Moon, The. MAP; MoAmPo (1942 ed.)
Yule Days, The. *Unknown.* ChTr
Yule Log, The. William Hamilton Hayne. AA
Yule-log sparkled keen with frost, The. Tennyson. *Fr.* In Memoriam A. H. H., LXXVIII. TRV
Yuletide. Alice Furlong. JKCP
Yule-Tide Fires. *Unknown.* PCD; PCH; PoRL
Yuma. Charles Henry Phelps. AA
Yung Wind, *sels.* Confucius, *tr. fr. Chinese by* Ezra Pound. CTC
Baroness Mu Impeded in Her Wish to Help Famine Victims in Wei.
Sans Equity and sans Poise.
Yussouf. James Russell Lowell. BBV (1951 ed.); BeLS; BLPA; BoTP; FaBoBe; MPB; NeHB; OTPC (1946 ed.)
Yvonne of Brittany. Ernest Dowson. PoVP

Z

Z, Y, X, and W, V. *Unknown.* OxNR
Zacchaeus in the Leaves. Vernon Watkins. FaBoTw
Zaccheus. Sister Julie. JKCP (1955 ed.)
Zachary Taylor. Rosemary Benét *and* Stephen Vincent Benét. OTD
Zack Bumstead useter flosserfize. A Philosopher. Sam Walter Foss. BOHV
Zagonyi. George Henry Boker. PAH
Zalinka. Tom MacInnes. PeCV
Zalka Peetruza. Ray Garfield Dandridge. BANP
Zambra Dance, The. Dryden. *See* Song of the Zambra Dance.
Zapata & the Landlord. Alfred B. Spellman. NNP
Zaph Describes the Haunts of Malzah. Charles Heavysege. *Fr.* Saul. OBCV
Zapolya, *sels.* Samuel Taylor Coleridge.
Glycine's Song, *fr.* Pt. II, Act II, sc.i. OBEV; OTPC (1946 ed.)
(Song: "Sunny shaft did I behold, A.) BOTP; LO
(Sunny Shaft, A.) CEP
Hunting Song, *fr.* Pt. II, Act IV, sc.i. OTD; PRWS; ThWaDe
(Up, Up! Ye Dames and Lasses Gay!) BoTP; OTPC (1923 ed.)
Zarathustra. Thomas S. Jones, Jr. AnAmPo
Zarian was saying: Florence is youth. A Water-Colour of Venice. Lawrence Durrell. FaBoMo; MoBrPo (1962 ed.)
Zeal in Labor. Horatius Bonar. SoP
Zeal of Jehu, The. Cardinal Newman. OBRV
Zealless Xylographer, The. Mary Mapes Dodge. BOHV
Zealots of Yearning. David Rokeah, *tr. fr. Hebrew by* I. M. Lask. TrJP
Zealous lock-smith dyed of late, A. On a Puritanicall Lock-Smith. William Camden. ShM; WhC
Zealous Puritan, The. *Unknown.* OBS; SeEP
Zealously my Muse doth salute all thee. To Mr. R. W. John Donne. MaMe
Zebaoth. Else Lasker-Schüler, *tr. fr. German by* Jethro Bithell. TrJP
Zebra. "Isak Dinesen." GoJo
Zebra. William Jay Smith. TiPo (1959 ed.)
Zebra. *Unknown, tr. fr. Hottentot.* PeSA
Zebra, The. Roland Young. StaSt
(Miscegeneous Zebra, The.) BOHV
Zebra Dun, The. *Unknown.* CoSo (A *and* B *vers., with music*); RePo; StPo; StVeCh; ViBoFo
Zebra Stallion. *Unknown, tr. fr. Hottentot.* PeSA
Zebras, The. Roy Campbell. AnFE; BoSA; GTBS-D; LiTB; LiTM; MoBrPo; MoPW; ReMP; ShBV-4; ViBoPo
Zechariah, *sels.* Bible, *O.T.*
I Return unto Zion, VIII: 3-5. TrJP
Open Thy Doors, O Lebanon, XI: 1-14. AWP
Zechariah. Earl Marlatt. MoRP
Zeenty, peenty, heathery, mithery. Counting-out Rhyme. *Unknown.* ChTr
Zeke. L. A. G. Strong. MoBrPo
Zekiel Saw de Wheel, *with music. Unknown.* BoAN-2
Zek'l Weep, *with music. Unknown.* AS
Zelanto, the Fountain of Fame,*sel.* Anthony Munday. Love. OBSC
Zen Archer, The. James Kirkup. EaLo
Zenith/ All these regrets. Towards the South. Guillaume Apollinaire. OnPM
Zennor. Anne Ridler. MoVE
Zeno desirous of the idle fame. Of Zeno. Everard Guilpin. *Fr.* Skialetheia. SiCE
Zenocrate, lovelier than the Love of Jove. Tamburlaine to Zenocrate. Christopher Marlowe. *Fr.* Tamburlaine the Great, Pt. I. WHA
Zepheria, *sels. Unknown.*
Alli veri figlioli delle Muse, introd. ReIE; TuPP
"Illuminating lamps, ye orbs crystallite." ReIE
"Proud in thy love, how many have I cited." ReIE; Sonn; TuPP
Sonnet: "When, from the tower whence I derive love's heaven." EIL
"Thy coral-colored lips, how should I portray." ReIE
"What? Shall I ne'er more see those halcyon days." Sonn; TuPP

Zepheria (continued)
"When we, in kind embracements, had agreed." ReEN; ReIE; Sonn; TuPP
Zephyr. Eugene Fitch Ware. PoLF
Zeppelin, The. Rowena Bastin Bennett. GFA
Zermatt: To the Matterhorn. Thomas Hardy. OBNC
Zest of Life, The. Henry van Dyke. OQP; WBLP
Zeus,/ Brazen-thunder-hurler. The Faun Sees Snow for the First Time. Richard Aldington. MoBrPo
Zeus—by what name soe'er. Hymn to Zeus. Aeschylus. *Fr.* Agamemnon. WGRP
Zeus rains; a storm comes in its might. Two Drinking Songs. Alcaeus, *tr. fr. Greek by* C. M. Bowra. LiTW
Zeuxis, the painter, strove in vain. Jean de Meun. *Fr.* The Romance of the Rose. WoL
Zig-zag bee, *zzz* and *zzz*-ing, came, A. The Bee. John Fandel. GoYe
Zigzag Boy and Girl, The. *Unknown.* GFA
Zigzag Path, The. *Unknown.* SoP
Zig-zagging it went. The Old Line Fence. A. W. Bellaw. BOHV
Zillebeke Brook. Edmund Blunden. MMA
Zimbabwe. F. D. Sinclair. PeSA
Zimri. Dryden. *Fr.* Absalom and Achitophel, Pt.I. AnFE; AWP; JAWP; SeCePo; ShBV-4; WBP
(Characters from the Satires: Zimri.) InPo
(George Villiers, Duke of Buckingham.) PoSa
("In the first rank of these did Zimri stand.") PoFS; ViBoPo
(Malcontents, The.) OBS
Zinc afternoon, A. The barges black. Embankment before Snow. Alan Ross. POTi
Zinnias, ochre, orange, chrome and amber, The. Transition. May Sarton. NePoAm
Zion, City of Our God. John Newton. SoP
Zion, wilt thou not ask if peace's wing. Ode to Zion. Judah Halevi. TrJP
Zionist Marching Song. Naphtali Herz Imber, *tr. fr. Hebrew by* Israel Zangwill. TrJP
Zip Coon. *Unknown, at. to* Bob Farrell. YaD
(Old Zip Coon, *with music.*) TrAS
Zizi's Lament. Gregory Corso. NeAP
Zobo Bird, The. Frank A. Collymore. GoJo
Zodiac, The, *sel.* Hendrik Marsman, *tr. fr. Dutch by* A. J. Barnouw.
Valley of Sleep, The. LiTW
Zola. E. A. Robinson. AmePo; FOL; MoVE; NePA; OxBA
Zollicoffer. Henry Lynden Flash. PAH
Zollverein was hardly neutral, The. One recalls. Philatelic Lessons: the German Collection. Lawrence P. Spingarn. NYBP
Zombie. Joseph Cardarelli. QAH
Zone. Guillaume Apollinaire, *tr. fr. French by* Selden Rodman. OnHM
Zone. Louise Bogan. PoCh
Zones of warmth around his heart, The. Sculptured Worship. William Stanley Braithwaite. Sandy Star and Willie Gee, I. BANP
Zonnebeke Road, The. Edmund Blunden. MMA
Zoo, The. Boris Pasternak, *tr. fr. Russian by* Lydia Pasternak. FIW
Zoo, The. Gilbert Sorrentino. NeAP
Zoo, The. Humbert Wolfe. GBV (1952 ed.); MoShBr; WaKn
Zoo Club, The. Robert Hershon. ThO
Zoo in the City, The. Sara Van Alstyne Allen. GoYe
Zoo is full of cages and it lies, The. Picture Postcard of a Zoo. Oscar Williams. Sonn
Zoo lies in the parkland thickets, The. The Zoo. Boris Pasternak. FIW
Zoo Manners. Eileen Mathias. BoTP
Zoo of You, The. Arthur Freeman. ErPo
Zoo, with Lamp and Chairs. David Hilton. QAH
Zooming across the sky. Up in the Air. James S. Tippett. BoChLi; SoPo; TiPo
Zooming overhead. . .and steel-framed birds, A. Aladdin Throws Away His Lamp. Elias Lieberman. PoMa
Zophiel; or, The Bride of Seven, *sels.* Maria Gowen Brooks. AA
Palace of the Gnomes.
Respite, The.
Zoroaster Devoutly Questions Ormazd. *At. to* Zoroaster, *tr. fr. Persian by* A. V. Williams Jackson. *Fr.* Gathas. WGRP
(Sacred Book, The.) AWP
Zounds! how the price went flashing through. Israel Freyer's Bid for Gold. Edmund Clarence Stedman. PAH
Zu fragmentarisch ist Welt und Leben. Heine. *See* Philosophy.
Zucca, The, *sel.* Shelley.
"Summer was dead and autumn was expiring." ERoP-2
Zuleika. Arthur O'Shaughnessy. PoVP
Zulia. Arthur Symons. CIV
Zulu Girl, The. Roy Campbell. AtBAP; BoSA; ChMP; JKCP (1955 ed.); MoPW; MoVE; OBMV; PoPl; POTE
Zulu King, The; New Orleans. Josephine Copeland. GoSl
Zummer Stream. William Barnes. BoNaP
Zun-zet. William Barnes. PoEL-4
"Zut!" cried the Princess, with a breezy smile. Romantic Episode. Vincent Starrett. FiSC

AUTHOR INDEX

"A."
Child's Fancy, A.
Deaf and Dumb.
My Pony.
New Fern, A.
Spring and Summer.
"A., F. P. *See* **Adams, Franklin Pierce**
"A. K." *See* **"K., A"**
"A. L. C." *See* **"C., A. L"**
"A. R. G." *See* **"G., A. R"**
"A. W." *See* **"W., A"**
"A. W. C." *See* **"C., A. W"**
"A. W. S." *See* **"S., A. W"**
Aaron, Madeleine
God Is Here.
Aaronson, Leonard [*or* Lazarus]
Baptism, The.
Homeward Journey, The.
Pesci Misti.
Abba Arika *See* **Rab**
Abbe, George
Clean Gentleman, The.
Conversation with a Friend.
Death Is a Little Thing.
Horizon Thong.
New York City.
Passer, The.
You Were at the Dead River.
Abbey, Henry
Donald.
Faith's Vista.
In Memory of General Grant.
What Do We Plant?
Winter Days.
Abbott, Clifton
Just Keep On.
Abbott, Lyman
I want to walk by the side of the man.
Man Who Has Won, The, *sel.*
Abbott, Wenonah Stevens
Soul's Soliloquy, A.
Abd-ar-Rahman I
Palm-Tree, The.
A Beckett, Gilbert Abbott
Holiday Task, A.
Polka Lyric, A.
Abeel, Neilson
Gay Head.
Abeita, Louise *See* **E-Yeh-Shure'**
Abelard, Peter
David's Lament for Jonathan.
Good Friday; the Third Nocturn.
To Gabriel of the Annunciation.
Abenatar Melo, David
Thanksgiving.
Abercrombie, Lascelles
All Last Night.
Balkis.
Ceremonial Ode Intended for a University.
Emblems of Love, *sels.*
Epilogue: "What shall we do for Love these days?"
Epitaph: "Sir, you should [*or* shall] notice me: I am the Man."
Fear, The.
Fool's Adventure, The, *sel.*
Hope and Despair.
Hymn to Love.
Judith, *sel.*
Margaret's Song.
Mary and the Bramble.
New God, The; a Miracle, *sel.*
Sale of Saint Thomas, The, *sel.*
Seeker, The.
Small Fountains.
Song: "Balkis was in her marble town."
Stream's Song, The.
Tormented by the World.
Vashti, *sel.*
Witchcraft; New Style.
Woman's Beauty.
Abrahams, Peter
Lonely Road.
Me, Colored.
Tell Freedom, *sel.*
Abrahams, William
In the Henry James Country.
Museum, The.
Poem in Time of War.
Séance.
Abrams, Robert J.
Two Poems.
Abse, Dannie
After the Release of Ezra Pound.
Game, The.
Inscription on the Flyleaf of a Bible.
Letter to Alex Comfort.
Mountaineers, The.
Second Coming, The.
Trial, The.
Words Spoken Alone.
Abu Bakr (of Marrakesh)
Sword, The.
Abu Dharr
Oranges, The.
Abu-l-Ala al-Maarri
Aweary Am I.
Cryptic Streets, The.
Draught of Life, The.
Man's Natural Element.
Summum Bonum.
This World.
Abu'l-Atahija
Atheist Buries His Son, The.
For Haroun Al Raschid.
Abulfadhel Ahmed
Blessed Spot, A.
Abu Nuwas
Escape, An.
Great Offence, The.
Abu Said ibn Abi-l-Khair
Six Rubaiyat.
Abu Zakariya
Bubbling Wine.
Acconci, Vito Hannibal
Kay Price and Stella Pajunas.
Re.
Tic.
Acharya, Ananda
My Faith.
Realization.
Witness, The.
Ackerley, J. R.
Ghosts.
Ackerly, W. C.
Prayer of an Unemployed Man.
Ackerson, John
Ecce Homo.
Acorn, Milton
Fights, The.
I've Tasted My Blood.
Poem in June.
Acton, Ellen M. V.
Exodus from a Renaissance Gallery.
Ada, Sister Mary
Against Despair.
Adair, Ivan
Real Presence.
Adali-Mortti, G.
Palm Leaves of Childhood.
Adam, Helen
Fair Young Wife, The.
I Love My Love.
Step Mother, The.
Adam of St. Victor
Eagle Swift, The.
Hail, Mother of the Savior.
Lux Advenit Veneranda.
Adams, Amy Belle
Annie McConkus.
Adams, Arthur Henry
Australian, The.
Courage.
Fleet Street.
Pair of Lovers in the Street, A.
Pleiades, The.
Weakling, The.
Written in Australia.
Adams, Bill (Bertram Martin Adams)
Ballad of the *Ivanhoe,* The.
Homeward Bound, The.
Peg-Leg's Fiddle.
Shore Roads of April.
Stowaway.
Adams, Charles Follen ("Yawcob Strauss")
Leedle Yawcob Strauss.
Prevalent Poetry.
Yaw, Dot Is So!
Yawcob Strauss.
Adams, E. M.
Action Rhyme.
Haymaking.
Paddling Pool, The.
Sea, The.
Shady Woods.
Snowman, The.
Adams, Francis Lauderdale
Evening Hymn in the Hovels.
Hagar.
Jesus.
To the Christians.
William Wallace.
Adams, Franklin Pierce ("F.P.A.")
Ad Leuconoen.
Ad Persephonen.
Ad Xanthium Phoceum.
Ballade of Lawn Tennis, A.
Ballade of Schopenhauer's Philosophy.
Baseball Note.
Baseball's Sad Lexicon.
Christopher Columbus.
De Senectute.
Erring in Company.
February 14, 22 B.C.
Garland of Recital Programs, A.
Georgie Porgie.
Happy Lifetime to You.
Jim and Bill.
Life.
Maud Muller Mutatur.
Metaphysics.

Adams (continued)
Persicos Odi.
Poetry and Thoughts on Same.
Popular Ballad: "Never Forget Your Parents."
Rarae Aves.
Regarding (1) the U.S. and (2) New York.
Rich Man, The.
Song: "Don't Tell Me What You Dreamt Last Night."
"Such Stuff as Dreams."
Those Two Boys.
Thoughts on the Cosmos.
To a Lady.
To a Lady Troubled by Insomnia.
To a Thesaurus.
To a Young Woman on the *World* Staff.
To His Lyre.
To the Polyandrous Lydia.
Tonight.
Translated Way, The.
Us Potes.
Adams, Georgia B.
Family Altar, The.
He Giveth Peace!
Helping Hand, A.
Hour of Prayer, The.
Secret Place of Prayer, The.
Thank Thee, Lord.
Thoughts of Him.
Adams, Georgine M.
"That Did in Luve So Lively Write."
Adams, H. M.
Johnny's Farm.
Adams, Helen Baker
No Doubt.
Adams, Henry
Prayer to the Dynamo.
Prayer to the Virgin of Chartres.
Adams, James Barton
At a Cowboy Dance.
Billy, He's in Trouble.
Cowboy Alone with His Conscience, A.
Cowboy Toast, A.
Cowboy versus Broncho.
Cowboy's Hopeless Love, A.
Cowboy's Worrying Love, A.
Dust of the Overland Trail, The.
Idaho Cowboy Dance, An.
Ruin of Bobtail Bend, The.
Tough Cuss from Bitter Creek, A.
Transformation of a Texas Girl, The.
Adams, John Quincy
Lip and the Heart, The.
Send Forth, O God, Thy Light and Truth.
To Sally.
Wants of Man, The.
Adams, Léonie (Mrs. William Troy)
Alas, Kind Element.
April Mortality.
Bell Tower.
Caryatid.
Country Summer.
Death and the Lady.
Early Waking.
Figurehead, The.
Font in the Forest, The.
Ghostly Tree.
Grapes Making.
Gull Goes Up, A.
Home-coming.
Horn, The.
Kingdom of Heaven.
Lament of Quarry, The.
Light at Equinox.
Lullaby: "Hush, lullay,/ Your treasures all."
Mount, The.
Night-Piece.
People in the Park, The.
Reminder, The.
River in the Meadows, The.
Runner with the Lots, The.
Send Forth the High Falcon.
Song from a Country Fair.
Sundown.
This Measure.
Those Not Elect.
Thought's End.
Twilit Revelation.
Wind of Fall, A.
With all the drifting race of men.
Words for the Raker of Leaves.
Adams, Marguerite Janvrin
American History.
They Who Possess the Sea.
Adams, Mary Mathews (Mrs. Charles Kendall Adams)
Dead Love.
Adams, Oscar Fay
At Lincoln.
On a Grave in Christ-Church, Hants.
Adams, Perseus
Murder Trial, The.
My Grandmother.
Thieves.
Woman and the Aloe, The.
Adams, Samuel Hopkins
Centipede, The.
Adams, Sarah Flower (Mrs. William Bridges Adams)
Hymn: "He sendeth sun, he sendeth shower."
Love.
Mourners Came at Break of Day, The.
Nearer, My God, to Thee.
Adams, William Henry Davenport
Last Voyage of the Fairies, The.
Adcock, Arthur St. John
By Deputy.
Sam.
Travellers.
Adcock, Fleur
Christmas Dawn.
Addaeus [*or* Addoeus]
Draught-Ox, The.
Addison, Joseph
Blenheim.
Campaign, The.
Cato, *sels.*
Cato's Soliloquy.
Heavens, The.
How Are Thy Servants Blest.
Hymn: "Spacious firmament on high, The."
Hymn: "When all thy mercies, O my God."
Hymn to the Creation.
Immortality.
Italy and Britain.
Letter from Italy, A.
My voice is still for war.
O Liberty, thou goddess heavenly bright.
Ode: "How are thy servants blest, O Lord!"
Ode: "Spacious firmament on high, The."
Pastoral Hymn.
Psalm XIX: "Spacious firmament on high, The."
Sempronius, why, why wilt thou urge the fate.
Song: "Echo, tell me, while I wander."
Spacious Firmament on High, The.
Thy Mercies.
To a Rogue.
When All Thy Mercies.
Addison, Medora (Mrs. Charles Read Nutter)
Some Day.
Spell, The.
Addleshaw, Percy ("Percy Hemingway")
Happy Wanderer, The.
Ade, George
R-e-m-o-r-s-e.
Adeane, Louis
Four Poems for April.
Night Loves Us, The.
Poem on Hampstead Heath.
Adee, Lucy A. K.
Let All the Earth Keep Silence.
Our Lady of Good Voyage.
"Adelar, Max" (Charles Heber Clark)
In Memoriam.
Obituary.
Our Fathers.
Out of the Hurly-Burly.
We Have Lost Our Little Hanner.
Willie.
Adkin, Will S.
If I Only Was the Fellow.
Just Try to Be the Fellow That Your Mother Thinks You Are.
Adler, Felix
City of Our Hopes, The.
Hail! the Glorious Golden City.
Adler, Frederick Herbert
Song for May Day, A.
Adler, Friedrich
By the Waterfall.
Adler, Lucile
Mural of Borodino.
Travelling Out, The.
Adoff, Arnold
Dry July.
Today Is Sun.
Adrian, Vonna Hicks
For My Shakespeare Class.
Ady, Endre
Grape Hill, The.
Last Boats, The.
"Æ" (George William Russell)
Ancient.
Babylon.
By the Margin of the Great Deep.
Carrowmore.
Chivalry.
Cities, The.
City, The.
Continuity.
Dark Rapture.
Dawn.
Desire.
Dust.
Earth Breath, The.
Epilogue: "Well, when all is said and done."
Exiles.
Farewell, A: "I go down from the hill in gladness."
Farewell, A: "Only in my deep heart I love you, sweetest heart."
Frolic.
Garden of God, The.
Gates of Dreamland, The.
Gay, The.
Germinal.
Gift, The.
Gods of War.
Great Breath, The.
Hermit, The.
Holy Hill, A.
Immortality.
Inheritance.
Krishna.
Leader, A.
Lonely, The.
Man to the Angel, The.
Memory of Earth, The.
Mountain Wind, A.
Natural Magic.
New York.
Om.

On Behalf of Some Irishmen Not Followers of Tradition.
Outcast, The.
Oversoul.
Pain.
Parting.
Place of Rest, The.
Prisoner, A.
Promise.
Reconciliation.
Refuge.
Rest.
Salutation.
Secret, The.
Secret Love, The.
Self-Discipline.
Sung on a By-Way.
Terence MacSwiney.
Tragedy.
Truth.
Twilight of Earth.
Unity.
Unknown God, The.
Vesture of the Soul, The.
When.
Winds of Eros.

Aeschylus
Achaians Have Got Troy, upon This Very Day, The.
Aeschylus.
Agamemnon, *sels.*
Battle of Salamis, The.
Cassandra's Lament.
Chorus: "Great fortune is an hungry thing."
Chorus: "O Zeus our king and Night our friend."
Chorus of the Furies ("Look, sisters, look!").
Dead, The, are not to rise; their roll our grief.
Eumenides, *sel.*
Furies, The.
God of War, The.
God of War, Money Changer of Dead Bodies, The.
Hymn to Zeus.
If I Were to Tell of Our Labours, Our Hard Lodging.
Lament for the Two Brothers Slain by Each Other's Hand.
Persians, *sel.*
Prometheus Bound.
Salamis.
Septem contra Thebas.
Seven against Thebes, The, *sel.*
Signal Fire, The.
Wail of Prometheus Bound, The.

Aesop (6th century B.C.)
Ass in the Lion's Skin, The. ("An ass put on a lion's skin and went).
Boy and the Wolf, The.
Frogs Who Wanted a King, The ("The frogs were living happy as could be").
Greedy Fox and the Elusive Grapes, The.
Mountain in Labor, The.
Shepherd-Boy and the Wolf, The.
Swan and the Goose, The.
Vine and the Goat, The.

Agathias Scholasticus
Epigram on Plutarch.
Happy Woman, A.
Leave a Kiss within the Cup.
Not Such Your Burden.
Plutarch.
Rhodanthe.
Swallows, The.

Agee, James
Description of Elysium.
Happy Hen, The.
In Heavy Mind.
Lullaby, A: "Sleep, child, lie quiet, let be."
Lyrics, *sels.*
Millions Are Learning How.
No doubt left. Enough deceiving.
Not met and marred with the year's whole turn of grief.
Permit Me Voyage.
Rapid Transit.
Red Sea.
So It Begins.
Song with Words.
Sonnet: "Now stands our love on that still verge of day."
Sonnet: "Our doom is in our being."
Sonnet: "So it begins. Adam is in his earth."
Sonnet: "Those former loves wherein our lives have run."
Sonnets, *sels.*
Sunday: Outskirts of Knoxville, Tennessee.
Temperance Note; and Weather Prophecy.
Two Songs on the Economy of Abundance.

Agnes, Sister
Our Lady's Assumption.

Agnew, Edith
Ambition.
Dahlias.
"Los Pastores."
Progress.
Summer Comes.

Agnew, Joan
Freedom.
Sons of the King[s].

Agnew, Marjorie L.
On Going Home.

Agostinho da Cruz
To Our Saviour.

"Ahmatova, Anna." *See "Akhmatova, Anna"*

Aicard, Jean
In Provence.

Aïdé, Hamilton
Danube River, The.
Forsaken, The.
Remember or Forget.
When We Are Parted.

Aig-Imoukhuede, Frank
One Wife for One Man.

Aikin, Anna Letitia *See* **Barbauld, Anna Letitia**

Aiken, Conrad
A Is for Alpha: Alpha Is for A.
All Lovely Things.
And Already the Minutes.
And in the Hanging Gardens.
And you who love, you who attach yourselves.
Annihilation.
Argument, The, *sel.*
At a Concert of Music.
Atlantis.
Awakening, The.
"Beautiful body made of ivory."
Beloved, Let Us Once More Praise the Rain.
Bend as the Bow Bends.
Birdcage, The.
Blind Date.
Bread and Music.
Build a house of gold for Punch.
But How It Came from Earth.
But no, the familiar symbol, as that the/ curtain.
Calyx of the Oboe Breaks, The.
Carver, The.
Chiaroscuro: Rose.
Cloister.
Coming Forth by Day of Osiris Jones, The, *sel.*
Dead Cleopatra Lies in a Crystal Casket.
Discordants.
Do Not Believe Your Shakespeare's Grief.
Doctors' Row.
Elder Tree.
Evensong.
Fade, then,—die, depart, and come no more.
Farewell Voyaging World!
First Note, Simple, The; the Second Note, Distinct.
Frostbite.
Goya.
Green, green, and green again, and greener still.
Habeas Corpus Blues, The.
Hatteras Calling.
House of Dust, The, *sels.*
If Man, That Angel of Bright Consciousness.
Improvisations: Light and Snow, *sels.*
John Deth, *sel.*
Keep in the Heart the Journal [Nature Keeps].
Kid, The, *sels.*
King Borborigmi.
Like a tower of brass is Punch.
Limberick.
Look he comes! how tall he is!
Lovers, The.
Miracles.
Morning Song of Senlin.
Music.
Music I Heard [with You].
Nameless Ones, The.
Nocturne of Remembered Spring.
North Infinity Street.
Nothing to Say, You Say?
Nuit Blanche; North End.
Nursery, The.
One Star Fell and Another.
Pave the sky with stars for Punch.
Poem: "And this digester, this digester of food."
Portrait of a Girl.
Portrait of One Dead.
Prelude: "Rimbaud and Verlaine, precious pair of poets."
Prelude: "Stood, at the closed door, and remembered."
Prelude: "This is not you?"
Prelude: "What shall we do—what shall we think—what shall we say?"
Prelude: "Winter for a moment takes the mind."
Prelude: "Woman, woman, let us say these things to each other."
Prelude: "You went to the verge, you say, and come back safely."
Preludes for Memnon; or, Preludes to Attitude, *sels.*
Preludes to Attitude.
Preludes to Definition.
Priapus and the Pool, *sels.*
Proem to "The Kid."
Punch, the Immortal Liar, *sels.*
Puppet Dreams, The.
Quarrel, The.
Queen Cleopatra.
Return, The.
Rimbaud and Verlaine, Precious Pair of Poets.
Road, The.
Room, The.
Samadhi.
Sea Holly.
See, as the Carver Carves a Rose.
Senlin, a Biography, *sels.*

Aiken (continued)
Shaemus.
Sleep: and between the Closed Eyelids of Sleep.
Snowflake on Asphodel.
So, in the Evening, to the Simple Cloister.
Soldier, The, *sels.*
Solomon, Clown, put by your crown.
Sonnet, A: "Think, when a starry night of bitter frost."
Sound of Breaking.
Sounding, The.
South End.
Stepping Stones, The.
Stone Too Can Pray.
Sursum Corda.
Systole and Diastole.
Tetélestai.
Then Came I to the Shoreless Shore of Silence.
There is nothing moving there, in that desert of silence.
This girl gave her heart to me.
This Is the Shape of the Leaf.
Three Star Final.
Time Has Come, the Clock Says Time Has Come, The.
Time in the Rock, *sels.*
Two Coffees in the Españl.
Unknown Soldier, The.
Vampire, The.
Variations, *sels.*
Walk in the Garden, The.
Wars, The.
Watch Long Enough, and You Will See the Leaf.
Wedding, The.
When I was a boy, and saw bright rows of icicles.
When the Tree Bares.
When Trout Swim down Great Ormond Street.
Whim.
Window, The.
Winter for a Moment Takes the Mind.
With Myriad Voices Grass Was Filled.
You Went to the Verge, You Say, and Came Back Safely?
Aikin, Lucy
Which Way Does the Wind Blow?
Ainger, A. C.
God Is Working His Purpose Out.
Ainger, Alfred
On Taine.
Ainslie, Douglas
Stirrup Cup, The.
Ainslie, Hew
Ingle-Side, The.
Willie and Helen.
Ainsworth, Percy Clough
"And the Life Everlasting."
Kingdom Within, The.
Ainsworth, Ruth
Good Night.
Aird, Thomas
Swallow, The.
Airey, Peter
Song of the Dial, The.
Ai Shih-te
Human Mind, The.
Akahito (Yamabe no Akahito)
I wish I could lend a coat.
Love, that dwarfs our life.
Tanka: "Men of valor, The."
Akenside, Mark
Against Suspicion, *sel.*
Amoret.
Benevolence.
Complaint, The.
Created Universe, The.
Early Influences.
England, Unprepared for War.
For a Grotto.
For a Statue of Chaucer at Woodstock.
Hymn to Science.
Inscription: "Ye powers unseen, to whom the bards of Greece."
Inscription for a Grotto.
Invocation to the Genius of Greece.
Nature.
Nature's Influence on Man.
Nightingale, The.
Ode: Allusion to Horace.
Ode on a Sermon Against Glory.
Ode to the Country Gentlemen of England, An, *sel.*
Ode to the Evening Star.
Pleasures of Imagination, The, *sels.*
Poet, The; a Rhapsody.
Poets.
Song: "Shape alone let others prize, The."
That Delightful Time.
To the Evening Star.
With what attractive charms this goodly frame.
Akerman, John Young
Harnet and the Bittle, a Wiltshire Tale, The ("A harnet zet in a hollur tree").
Akers, Elizabeth *See* **Allen, Elizabeth Akers**
Akhenaton *See* **Ikhnaton**
"Akhmatova, Anna" (Anna Andreyevna Gorenko)
All Is Sold ("All is sold, all is lost, all is plundered").
Broad Gold.
Like a White Stone.
Muse, The.
Prayer: "Make me feverish, sleepless, and breathless."
White Bird, The.
You Are Always New.
Akins, Zoë
Conquered.
First Rain.
I Am the Wind.
Norah.
Rain, Rain.
This Is My Hour.
Tragedienne, The.
Wanderer, The.
Alabaster, William
Away feare with thy projectes, noe false fyre.
Incarnatio Est Maximum Donum Dei.
Morning Meditation, A: I.
My soul within the bed of heaven doth grow.
O Starry Temple of Unvalted Space.
On the Reed of Our Lord's Passion.
Sonnet: "Beehould a cluster to itt selfe a vine."
Sonnet: "Haile gracefull morning of eternall daye."
Sonnet: "Holy, holy, holy Lord unnamed."
Sonnet: "Jesu thie love within mee is soe maine."
Sonnet: "My soule a world is by contraccion."
Sonnet: "Night, the starlesse night of passion, The."
Sonnet: "Now I have found thee, I will ever more."
Sonnet: "Now that the midd day heate doth scorch my shame."
Sonnet: "O starry temple of unvalted space."
Sonnet: "O sweete, and bitter monuments of paine."
Sonnet: "Sunne begins uppon my heart to shine, The."
Sonnet: "Three sortes of teares doe from myne eies distraine."
Sonnet: "Way feare with thy projectes, noe false fyre, A."
Sonnet: "What meaneth this, that Christ an hymne did singe."
Sonnet: "When without tears I looke on Christ, I see."
Sunne begins uppon my heart to shine, The.
Up to Mount Olivet my soul ascend.
Upon Christ's Saying to Mary "Why Weepest Thou?"
Upon the Crucifix.
Upon the Ensignes of Christes Crucifyinge.
Upon the Motions of the Fiend.
When without tears I looke on Christ, I see.
Alasdair, Alasdair MacMhaighstir *See* **MacDonald, Alexander**
Al-Aswad, Son of Ya'fur
Old Age.
Alba, Nanina
Be Daedalus.
Albee, John
At the Grave of Champernowne.
Bos'n Hill.
Dandelions.
Landor.
Music and Memory.
Soldier's Grave, A.
Albert, Samuel L.
After a Game of Squash.
All of Her.
Honeymoon.
Near the Base Line.
One, Two, Three.
Rebuff.
Street-Walker in March.
Alberti, Rafael
Chaplin's Sad Speech.
Collegiate Angels, The.
Madrigal to a Streetcar Token.
Sea, the Sea, The.
To the International Brigade.
Albertson, Charles Carroll
Holy Child, The.
Prayer at a Wedding.
Albertson, Cyrus E.
Reflections.
Albertus Magnus, Sister (Marion McGrath)
Prayer, A: "O Thou great Author of the World."
Albinovanus
Plants and trees made poor and old, The.
Albrecht of Brandenburg
Whate'er God Will.
Albrecht von Johannsdorf
Pilgrimage, The.
Albright, Mary E.
Let Me Go Back.
Alcaeus
Armoury, An.
Let Us Drink.
Storm, The.
Two Drinking Songs.
Alcázar Baltasar del
Woman's Jealousy.
Alcman
Asleep.
Fragment: "Mountain summits sleep, The.
No More, O Maidens.
On the Mountains.
Sleep upon the World.
Vesper.
Alcott, Amos Bronson
Bartol.
Channing.

Emerson.
Garrison.
Hawthorne.
Margaret Fuller.
Thoreau.
Wendell Phillips.
Alcott, Louisa May
My Kingdom.
Thoreau's Flute.
Aldan, Daisy
Trapezists.
Aldana, Francisco
Image of God, The.
Alden, Ada *See* **Murray, Ada Foster**
Alden, Henry Mills
Magic Mirror, The.
Aldington, Hilda Doolittle *See* **Doolittle, Hilda ("H. D.")**
Aldington, Richard
After Two Years.
All Lovely Things.
At the British Museum.
Barrage.
Battlefield.
Bombardment.
Choricos.
Epilogue: "Have I spoken too much or not enough of love?"
Evening.
Fatigues.
Faun Sees Snow for the First Time, The.
Her Mouth.
Images.
In the Trenches.
In the Tube.
Lesbia.
Loss.
Moment's Interlude, A.
On the March.
Poplar, The.
Possession.
Prelude: "How could I love you more?"
Reserve.
Ruined House, A.
Soliloquy I.
Soliloquy II.
Three Little Girls.
Vicarious Atonement.
Aldis, Dorothy
About Buttons.
Alike.
At the Circus.
Balloon Man, The.
Bare-Back Rider.
Blum.
Brooms.
Clouds.
Clown, The.
Elephants, The.
Emma's Store.
Everybody Says.
Feet.
First Winter's Day.
Flies.
For Christmas.
Fourth of July Night.
Grasshoppers, The.
Hands.
Harpers' Farm, The.
Hiding.
Hot Weather.
Hungry Waves, The.
I Have to Have It.
Ice.
In Spring in Warm Weather.
In the Barnyard.
Kick a Little Stone.
Little.
Lucky Thing, A.
Mister Carrot.
My Brother.
Names.
Night and Morning.
Not Any More.
On a Snowy Day.
Our Little Calf.
Our Silly Little Sister.
Picnic, The.
Radiator Lions.
Reason, The.
Riddle: What Am I?
Seals, The.
Setting the Table.
Singing.
Skipping Ropes.
Snow.
Somersault.
Story of the Baby Squirrel, The.
Then.
Troubles.
Twins, The.
What Am I?
What They Are For.
When.
When I Was Lost.
Whistle.
Whistles.
Windy Wash Day.
Winter Coats.
Aldis, Mary
Barberries.
Flash-Lights.
Seven Sad Sonnets.
When You Come.
Years sped onward, The. He who forever sought.
Aldiss, Brian W.
Progression of the Species.
Aldrich, Anne Reeve
April—and Dying.
Crowned Poet, A.
Death at Daybreak.
Eternal Justice, The.
Fanny.
Fraternity.
In November.
Little Parable, A.
Love's Change.
Music of Hungary.
Recollection.
Song about Singing, A.
Suppose.
Aldrich, Henry
Catch, A: "If all be true that I do think."
Five Reasons [for Drinking], The.
If All Be True That I Do Think.
Reasons for Drinking.
Why I Drink.
Aldrich, James
Death-Bed, A.
Aldrich, Thomas Bailey
Act V (Midnight).
Alec Yeaton's Son.
Andromeda.
Appreciation.
Baby Bell.
Before the Rain.
Bells at Midnight, The.
By the Potomac.
Circumstance.
Difference.
Enamored [*or* Enamoured] Architect of Airy Rhyme.
Euterpe.
Face against the Pane, The.
Flight of the Goddess, The.
Forever and a Day.
Fredericksburg.
Guilielmus Rex.
Heredity.
Hint from Herrick, A.
Identity.
Kriss Kringle.
Lady of Castlenoire.
L'Eau Dormante.
Maple Leaves.
Marjorie's Almanac.
Masks.
Memories.
Memory.
Menu, The.
Nocturne: "Up to her chamber window."
October.
Ode, An: On the Unveiling of the Shaw Memorial on Boston Common.
On an Intaglio Head of Minerva.
On Reading.
Originality.
Outward Bound.
Palabras Cariñsas.
Pessimist and Optimist.
Petition, A.
Prescience.
Quits.
Realism.
Reminiscence.
Sargent's Portrait of Edwin Booth at "The Players."
Shadow of the Night, A.
Sleep.
Sleepy Song.
Tennyson.
Thalia.
Tiger-Lilies.
To Hafiz.
Turkish Legend, A.
Undiscovered Country, The.
Unguarded Gates.
Untimely Thought.
When the Sultan Goes to Ispahan.
World's Way, The.
Aldridge, Richard
By Return Mail.
In Early Spring.
Matter of Life and Death, A.
Oxford.
Pine Bough, The.
Serendipity of Love, A.
Spring Night.
To Himself.
Weeping Willow.
Aleichem, Sholom
Epitaph: "Here lies a simple Jew."
Sleep, My Child.
Alepoudelis, Odysseus *See* **"Elytis, Odysseus"**
Alexander, Mrs.
Crow, The.
Alexander, Albert Lewis
Church Within, The.
Alexander, Cecil Frances
Adoration of the Wise Men, The.
All Things Bright and Beautiful.
Burial of Moses.
Childhood's Trials.
Christmas Hymn, A.
Creation, The.
Dreams.
Evening Hymn.
Evening Song.
Good Tidings of Great Joy!
Helper, The.
His Are the Thousand Sparkling Rills.
Jesus Calls Us o'er the Tumult.
Little Sister Left in Charge, The.
Morning Hymn, *abr.*
Once in Royal David's City.
St. Simon and St. Jude's Day.
Saw Ye Never in the Meadows, *abr.*
There Is a Green Hill Far Away.
We May Not Know.
Alexander, Floyce
Aphrodite.

Alexander (continued)
Guerilla.
Li Po.
Lotus Eaters, The.
Nowhere.
Poem for a Painter.
Alexander, Frances
Contentment of Willoughby, The.
Alexander, John T.
Winning of the TV West.
Alexander, Joseph Addison
Doomed Man, The.
Hidden Line, The.
Alexander, Lewis
Africa.
Dark Brother, The.
Day and Night.
Dream Song.
Japanese Hokku.
Negro Woman.
Nocturne Varial.
Tanka (I-VIII).
Transformation.
Alexander, S. J.
To San Francisco.
Alexander, Sidney
Castle, The.
Lenox Avenue.
Tonight the Pacifist Moon.
Alexander, W. L.
I Will Guide Thee.
Alexander, Sir William *See* **Stirling, William Alexander, Earl of**
Alexander, William, Archbishop of Armagh
Alone?
Birthday Crown, The.
Frost-Morning.
Methought I met a Lady yester even.
Vision of Oxford, A, *sel.*
Alexander, Mrs. William *See* **Alexander, Cecil Frances**
Alfieri, Vittorio
First Brutus, The, *sel.*
To Dante.
What do we hear? What majesty, what force.
Al-Fituri, Muhammad
I Am a Negro.
Knell, The.
Alford, Henry
Bride, The.
Colonos.
Gypsy Girl, The.
Harvest Home.
Hymn for Family Worship, A.
Lady Mary.
Master's Call, The.
You and I.
Alford, Janie
Mother Love.
Thanks Be to God.
Alford, John
Glory, Glory to the Sun.
Alger, Horatio, Jr.
John Maynard.
Alhamisi, Ahmed Legraham
Black Narrator, The.
Pome. For Weird. Hearts. & All You Mothers.
Uhuru.
Al-Harizi, Judah
Heavy-hearted.
Love Song.
Song of the Flea.
Song of the Pen, The.
Under Leafy Bowers.
Unhappy Lover, The.
Within My Heart.
Alighieri, Dante *See* **Dante Alighieri**
Alishan, Leo
Easter Song.
Allan, Edwin
Ass, The.
Allan, James Alexander
Breaking.
Allan, M.
Echo Poem.
Allan, Thomas H.
Leave the Miracle to Him.
Allana, Gulam Ali
Spectre Is on the Move, The.
Allen, Alice E.
Life's Common Things.
My Mother's Garden.
Allen, Bob
Musical Vietnams.
Allen, Cecil J.
Wounds of Jesus, The.
Allen, Elizabeth Akers
Bringing Our Sheaves.
Endurance.
In a Garret.
In April.
Last Landlord, The.
Left Behind.
Little Feet.
Lost Light.
"My Dearling."
Rock Me to Sleep.
Sea-Birds.
Snow.
Until Death.
Allen, Ernest Bourner
Hymn of Peace, A.
"I Am with Thee."
Allen, Freda Hanbury
Blessed.
Teach Me.
Allen, George Leonard
Portrait.
To Melody.
Allen, Glen
Woman I Am, The.
Allen, Grace Elisabeth
Pinkletinks.
Allen, Grant
Ballade of Evolution, A.
Allen, Hervey
Carolina Spring Song.
Gargantua.
Leif was a man's name.
Moments.
Refuge.
Saga of Leif the Lucky, *sel.*
Shadow to Shadow.
Southward Sidonian Hanno.
Tower of Genghis Khan, The.
Upstairs Downstairs.
Walls.
Whim Alley.
Allen, John Alexander
Admiral.
Allen, Leslie Holdsworth
Memnon.
Reaper, The.
Allen, Lyman Whitney
Coming of His Feet, The.
People's King, The.
Star of Sangamon, The.
Allen, Marie Louise
First Snow.
Five Years Old.
Mitten Song, The.
My Zipper Suit.
Sneezing.
What Is It?
Allen, Marjorie *See* **Seiffert, Marjorie Allen**
Allen, Samuel ("Paul Vesey")
American Gothic.
If the Stars Should Fall.
Love Song.
Moment Please, A.
To Satch.
View from the Corner.
What Bright Pushbutton?
Allen, Sara Van Alstyne
Marble Statuette Harpist.
Walk on a Winter Day.
Zoo in the City, The.
Allen, William S.
Erie Canal, The ("I've got a mule, her name is Sal").
Low Bridge, Everbody Down.
Allen, Willis Boyd
Thalatta.
Aller, Katharine L.
God of a Universe within Whose Bounds.
Allerton, Ellen Palmer
Beautiful Things.
Allestry, Jacob
What Art Thou, Love?
Alline, Henry
Amazing sight, the Savior stands.
Christ Inviting Sinners to His Grace, *sel.*
Alling, Kenneth Slade
Beauty.
Dead Wasp.
Dr. Donne.
Duality.
First World War.
Monsoon.
On the Park Bench.
Onion Skin in Barn.
Rain.
Unscarred Fighter Remembers France, The.
Allingham, William
Abbey Asaroe.
Abbot of Inisfalen, The.
Aeolian Harp.
After Sunset.
Among the Heather.
Amy Margaret.
Ballytullagh.
Bird, The.
Blowing Bubbles.
Boy.
Bubble, The.
By the Way, *sel.*
Child's Song, A.
Day and Night Songs.
Death Deposed.
Dirty Old Man, The.
Dream A.
Earth's Night.
Elf Singing, The.
Evening, An.
Fairies, The.
Fairy Folk, The.
Fairy King, The.
Four Ducks on a Pond.
Fragment: "Near where the riotous Atlantic surge."
Fragment: "Wing'd seeds with decaying wings, The."
Fragment: "You see/ Nestled into a hollow of the downs."
George Levison.
Girls Going to the Fair.
Girl's Lamentation, The.
Half-waking.
Homeward Bound.
I Love You Dear.
In a Spring Grove.
In Snow.
Irish History.
Kate o' Belashanny.
Late Autumn.
Laurence Bloomfield In Ireland, *sel.*
Laurence Bloomfield in Ireland, *sel.*
Leprecaun [*or* Fairy Shoemaker], The.

Little Men, The.
Lough, The.
Lovely Mary Donnelly.
Lover and Birds, The.
Lupracaun, or Fairy Shoemaker, The.
Maids of Elfin-Mere, The.
Meadowsweet.
Memory, A.
Midsummer.
Milkmaid, The.
Mill, A [*or* The].
Mowers, The.
Nanny's Sailor Lad.
No Funeral Gloom.
Nobleman's Wedding, The.
Robin Redbreast.
Ruined Chapel, The.
Ruins at Sunset.
Sailor, The.
Song: "Across the Sea."
Song: "I walk'd in the lonesome evening."
Song: "O spirit of the Summertime!"
Spring.
Spring: The Lover and the Birds.
Sunday Bells.
Swing Song, A.
Three Fragments.
Up the Airy Mountain.
Wealthy Man, A.
Wild Rose.
Winding Banks of Erne, The.
Windlass Song.
Winny, *abr.*
Wishing.

Allinson, Brent Dow
"One World."

Allison, Drummond
Brass Horse, The.
Dedication: "Had there been peace there never had been riven."
My Sister Helen.

Allison, George William
Were Flowers There?

"Allison, Joy" (Mary A. Cragin)
Which Loved Best?

Allison, William Talbot
O Amber Day, amid the Autumn Gloom.

Allison, Young Ewing
Buccaneers, The.
Dead Men's Song, The.
Derelict.

Allonby, Margaret
Book for Christmas, A.
Eurydice.
For Sheila.
In this savage place the sun stands still.
Lustration of the Winter Tree, *sel.*
O Theophilus.
Reflection.

Allott, Kenneth
Cheshire Cat.
Departure Platform.
Fête Champêtre.

Allston, Washington
America to Great Britain.
On the Late S. T. Coleridge.
Rosalie.
To Benjamin West.

Allwood, Brian
No Laws.

Allwood, Martin Samuel
Gethsemane, Illinois.

Al-Mahdi
Preacher, The.

Alma-Tadema, Laurence
Bed-Time.
Blessing for the Blessed, A.
Gravel Path, The.
If No One Ever Marries Me.
Lambs in the Meadow.
Playgrounds.
Robin, The.
Snowdrops.
Strange Lands.
Sunset.

Al-Mu'tamid *See* **Mu'tamid, King of Seville**

Al Mutanabbi
Shame Hitherto.
Written in Flight from His Royal Patron.

Almy, Amy Bruner
Carpenter, The.

Alphaeus
Mycenae.

Alpheus of Mitylene
Life through Verse.

Alphonsa, Mother Mary *See* **Lathrop, Rose Hawthorne**

Alphonsus Liguori, Saint
Madonna's Lullaby.

Alqamah
His Camel.

Alsop, George
Author to His Book, The.
Be just (domestick monarchs) unto them.
Could'st thou (O Earth) live thus obscure.
Heavens bright lamp, shine forth some of thy light.
Lines on a Purple Cap Received as a Present from My Brother.
Poor vaunting earth, gloss'd with uncertain pride.
'Tis said the Gods lower down that chain above.
To My Cosen Mrs. Ellinor Evins.
Trafique is earth's great Atlas, that supports.

Alston, Joseph Blynth
"Stack Arms!"

Altenburg, Michael
Battle Hymn.

Alterman, Nathan
From All Peoples, *sel.*
Poem: "Wisdom has no end and folly no ornament."
Saul.
When our children cried in the shadow of the gallows.

Altgood, Laurence
Song of the Brave.

Altolaguirre, Manuel
To a Cloud.

Altrocchi, Julia Cooley
Pigeon-Feeders in Battery Park, The.

Altrocchi, Rudolph
Insect Wives.

Alvarez, Alfred
Lost.
Operation.

Alvarez Quintero, Serafín *and* **Joaquín Alrez Quintero**
Fan, The.

Alyea, Dorothy
Keepsake from Quinault.

Amabile, George
Flowers: Calabria.
Period.
Snowfall: Four Variations.
Sun-Shower, The.
Twink Drives Back, in a Bad Mood, from a Party in Massachusetts.

Amarou
Drunken Rose, The.

Ameer Baraka, Imamu *See* **Jones, LeRoi**

Amen, Grover
Cot, The.

Amenhotep IV *See* **Ikhnaton**

Ames, A. S.
Abraham Lincoln.

Ames, Evelyn
Because I Live.
Two Solitudes.

Ames, Mary Clemmer *See* **Clemmer, Mary**

Amichai, Yehuda
My Mother Once Told Me.
Song of Resignation.

Amini, Johari *See* **Latimore, Jewel C**

Amis, Kingsley
After Goliath.
Against Romanticism.
Autobiographical Fragment.
Bookshop Idyll, A.
Departure.
Dream of Fair Women, A.
Ever-fixed Mark, An.
Masters.
New Approach Needed.
Nothing to Fear.
On a Portrait of Mme·Rimsky-Korsakov.
Science Fiction.
Sight Unseen.
Terrible Beauty.
Tribute to the Founder, A.

Amittai ben Shefatiah
Hymn of Weeping.

Ammonides
Secret Weapon.

Ammons, Archie Randolph
Bridge.
Corsons Inlet.
Dinah.
Gravelly Run.
Landscape with Figures.
Spindle.
Tape for the Turn of the Year, *sel.*
Trap.
Two jays in the sumac.
Unbroken.
Visit.
Wide Land, The.

Amon-Re
Hymn of Victory: Thutmose III.

Amoss, Harry
Pedagogical Principles.
Riding.

Ana, Marcos
Prisoner, The.
To the Faithful.

Anacreon
Design for a Bowl.
Heat.
Ode: "As late I sought the spangled bowers."
Ode: "Give me the harp of epic song."
Ode: "I care not for the idle state."
Ode: "I saw the smiling bard of pleasure."
Ode: "Listen to the Muse's lyre."
Ode: "Sculptor, wouldst thou glad my soul."
Ode: "Vulcan! hear your glorious task."
Ode: "Women tell me every day, The."
Odes, *sels.*
Temperate Drinking.
Thou'st Had Thy Day.
To Dionysus.
To Eros.
To Himself.
To His Young Mistress.
Why so coy, my lovely maid?
Woman's Arms.

Anatolius
Christ in the Tempest.
Fierce Was the Wild Billow.
Jesus, Deliverer.
Peace on Earth.

"Ande" (Angela Milne)
Coconut, The.

Andersen, Hans Christian
Pearl, The.

Andersen, Johannes Carl
Summer.

Anderson, Bishop
Bible, The.
Anderson, Alan
Lower Animals.
Sandy—A Small Dog.
Anderson, Alexander "Surfaceman "
Cuddle Doon.
Jenny wi' the Airn Teeth.
Langsyne, When Life Was Bonnie.
Anderson, Charles
Finger Pop'in.
Prayer to the White Man's God.
Anderson, Ethel Louisa Mason
Bucolic Eclogues, *sel.*
Flood.
Kunai-mai-pa Mo.
Love in Age.
Migrants.
Waking, Child, While You Slept.
Yesterday.
Anderson, Jack
Dream of Metals, A.
Habitat.
Invention of New Jersey.
Night, Window, Wind.
Rendezvous, The.
Winter Twilight.
Anderson, John
Clipper Ships.
Shadows of Sails.
Anderson, John Redwood
Mary O'Brian.
Anderson, Jon
Aviators.
Christ, I was twelve.
Death's Only Son.
Entrance to a Mirror.
Frontier, The.
Giving-In, The.
History of Psychotherapy, The.
Looking for Jonathan.
Monument to Resignation, The.
Parachutist, The.
Summer Deaths, The, *sel.*
Totem.
Waking.
Anderson, Margaret Steele
Breaking, The.
Somebody's Garden.
Anderson, Mary
In the April Rain.
Praise.
Thanks to Spring.
Anderson, Mary Louisa
Now, Lord, upon Thy Sea of Air.
Anderson, Maxwell
In All These Turning Lights I Find No Clue.
Judith of Minnewaulken, *sel.*
Lafayette to Washington.
Lucifer.
Parallax.
Toll the Bell for Damon.
Valley Forge, *sel.*
Winterset, *sel.*
Anderson, Molly *See* **Haley, Molly Anderson**
Anderson, Patrick
Camp.
Canoe.
Capital Square.
Cold Colloquy.
Coming of the White Man, The.
Drinker.
My Bird-wrung Youth.
Poem on Canada, *sels.*
Ski Train.
Sleighride.
Anderson, Persis Greely
Lengthy Symphony.
Melodie Grotesque.
Question Mark, The.
Anderson, S. E.
Junglegrave.
New Dance, A.
Soul-Smiles.
Sound of Afroamerican History Chapt I, The.
Sound of Afroamerican History Chapt II, The.
Anderson, Sherwood
American Spring Song.
Chicago.
Evening Song.
Lame One, The.
Song of Industrial America.
Anderson, Violet
Cloak, The.
Through the Barber Shop Window.
Andrade, Edward Neville da Costa
Song: "Nothing I have is worth a tear."
Violin, The.
Andrade, Jorge Carrera
Stroke of One.
Andrade, Mário de
Aspiration.
Rondeau for You.
André, John
Cow-Chace, The.
Andrew, Father
Love's Argument.
Andrew, Harold
Poem for the Living.
Andrew of Crete, Saint
Christian, Dost Thou See Them?
Andrew of Wyntown
Macbeth.
Andrewes, Francis
I Bear, in Sign of Love.
Phyllis Inamorata.
Shepherdess' Valentine, *sel.*
Andrews, Arnold
Master Blacksmith, The.
Andrews, Charlton
Our Modest Doughboys.
Andrews, H. G.
Give me of love my love to prove.
Take heed, my love.
Andrews, John
Anatomy of Baseness, The, *sel.*
To the Detracted.
Andrews, John Williams
La Madonna di Lorenzetti.
Andrews, Mary Raymond Shipman
Call to Arms, A.
Andriello, Amelia
Autumn Eve.
Aneirin [*or* Aneurin]
Gododdin, *sel.*
Lovely Youth, The.
Month of January—smoky is the vale.
Odes of the Months, *sel.*
To Cattraeth's vale in glittering row.
Angelita, Sister Mary
Dust.
Signum Cui Contradicetur.
Spinning Top, The.
To a Poet.
Angell, Walter Foster
To New Haven and Boston.
"Angelus Silesius" (Johannes Scheffler)
Cherubic Pilgrim, The.
Death Is a Blessed Thing.
In Spirit Senses Are.
In Thine Own Heart.
Man Beholdeth God, A.
Nearest Way to God, The.
Not After nor Before.
Nothing Fair on Earth I See.
Rose, The.
Song of Praise to Mary.
Soul Wherein God Dwells, The.
They Say That Time Is Swift.
Thou Art Not in a Place.
Tree of the Cross, The.
Two Eyes Our Souls Possess.
Who Not with Others Bides.
Young Love Storms like New Wine.
Angermayer, Frances
Conversion.
Last Thoughts of a Fighting Man.
Angiolieri, Cecco, da Siena *See* **Cecco Angiolieri da Siena**
Angoff, Charles
Litany: "When the sun rises on another day."
Little Girl, A.
Angus, Marion
Alas! Poor Queen.
Mary's Song.
"Anise." *See* **Strong, Anna Louise**
Annan, Annie Rankin
Dandelion.
Annand, J. K.
Arctic Convoy.
Annand, Rachel *See* **Taylor, Rachel Annand**
Anselm, Saint
To Our Lord in the Sacrament.
Ansen, Alan
Fatness.
Fit of Something against Something, A.
Tennyson.
"Ansky, S." (Solomon Rappoport)
Emigrant Song.
Tailor, The.
Anstadt, Henry
Little Rhyme and a Little Reason, A.
Anster, John
If I Might Choose.
Sonnet: "If I might choose where my tired limbs shall lie."
Anstey, Christopher
Letter Containing a Panegyric on Bath, *abr.*
New Bath Guide, The, *sels.*
Taste and Spirit.
"Anstey,F." (Thomas Anstey Guthrie)
Burglar Bill.
Conscience-Curst, The.
Juniper Jim.
Limerick: "There was an old man of Bengal."
Ordinary valour only works, The.
Select Passages from a Coming Poet.
Ant, Howard
Bucket of Sea-Serpents.
Antar [*or* Antara]
Abla.
Antella, Simone dall'
Prolonged Sonnet.
Anthony, Ed
College Song.
Anthony, Edward ("A. C. Gate', "
Advice to Small Children.
Bloodhound, The.
Character Building.
Collies, The.
Dachshund, The.
Duty of the Student.
I know a barber.
I know seven mice.
Let Others Share.
Oddity Land, *sels.*
Anthony of Padua, Saint
Death-Bed Hymn of Saint Anthony of Padua.
Antin, David
Passengers, The.
Antin, Esther
Corn.
Garden, The.
Making Mushrooms.

On Our Farm.
Our Pets.
Peter and Polly.
Tit for Tat.
Antipater of Sidon
Aristeides.
Eagle on a Tombstone.
Erinna.
Man at Peace.
Mournful Nut-Tree, The.
Pindar.
Terrifying Tell-Tale, The.
Undying Thirst.
Antiphilus of Byzantium
Freshet, A.
Antistius
Small Cleodemus.
Antokolsky, Pavel
Hate!
Antoninus, Brother (William Everson)
Advent.
August.
Canticle to the Christ in the Holy Eucharist,A.
Canticle to the Waterbirds, A.
Hospice of the Word.
I Am Long Weaned.
In All These Acts.
Jacob and the Angel.
March.
Presence, The.
Raid, The.
Siege of Silence, A.
Song the Body Dreamed in the Spirit's Mad Behest, The.
South Coast, The.
Stranger, The.
What Birds Were There.
Antrobus, John
Cowboy, The.
Anyte [*or* Anytes]
By the Fountain.
Dolphin's Tomb, The.
Maid Antibia, The.
Shepherd's Gift, A.
Aplon, Roger
After a Lobster Dinner and Playing like Kids on a King-Sized Bed.
New Sound, The.
Three.
Apollinaire, Guillaume
Departure.
Goodbye, The.
Poem to Lou.
Porpoise.
Shadow.
Towards the South.
War.
You Will Grieve.
Zone.
Apollinaris, Sidonius
Invitation to the Dance.
Appel, Benjamin
Talker, The.
Appleman, Philip
Crystal Anniversary.
Appleton, Everard Jack
Fighting Failure, The.
One, The.
Woman Who Understands, The.
Applewhite, James
Birthday, with Leaves.
Church and Clouds.
January.
Lawn and Light.
Leaf Mirrors.
My Grandfather's Funeral.
Steps from the Stream, *sels.*
Tree in the Rain.
Apuleius, Lucius
Eros and Psyche, *sel.*
His skin is brilliant with the nimble flood.
Aquinas, Saint Thomas *See* **Thomas Aquinas, Saint**
Aragon, Louis
Dirge for the Barrel-Organ of the New Barbarism.
Archer, Kate Rennie
Lairdless Place, The.
Archevolti Samuel ben Elhanan Isaac, of Padua
Advice to Hotheads.
Archias
Best Not to Be Born.
Archias of Byzantium
Sea Dirge.
Archibald, Esther
Hast Thou Considered Job's Wife?
In My Place.
Archilochus
Poet's Shield, The.
Tossed on a Sea of Trouble.
"Archpoet of Cologne, The"
Confession of Golias, The.
Arden, John
Lobster Pot, The.
Arensberg, Walter Conrad
About an Allegory.
Chryseis.
Inner Significance of the Statues Seated outside the Boston Public Library, The.
Masterpiece, The.
Out of Doors.
To a Poet.
To Hasekawa.
Voyage à l'Infini.
Aretino, Pietro
Stragglers.
Arey, John
To Becky in France.
Argensola, Bartolomé Leonardo de
Not of This World.
To Mary Magdalen.
Argentarius, Marcus
Blackbird, A.
Epigram: "Thou art in danger, Cincius, on my word."
Love's Tyranny.
Reading Hesiod.
Rumoresque Senum Severiorum.
Argyll, 9th Duke of *See* **Campbell, John Douglas Sutherland**
Ariosto, Ludovico [*or* Lodovico]
Angelica and the Ork.
Can I Believe.
Lover's Prison, The.
Lunar Valley of Lost Things, The.
Of dames, of knights, of arms, of love's delight.
Orlando Furioso, *sels.*
Rise up! the flute sounds in the distance.
Song for the Third Marriage of Lucrezia Borgia, *sel.*
Though an ill mind appear in simulation.
Aristaenetus
Pleasing Constraint, The.
Aristophanes
Amateur, driving too fast, An.
Birds, *sels.*
Chorus of Birds.
Chorus of the Clouds.
Chorus of Women.
Clouds, The, *sel.*
Frogs, The, *sel.*
Grand Chorus of Birds.
How the Women Will Stop War.
Let us hasten—let us fly.
Limerick: "Amateur, driving too fast, An."
Lysistrata, *sel.*
Midst the Free Green Fields.
Peace, The, *sel.*
Song of the Clouds.
Take My Wings and Dance with Me.
Thesmophoriazusae, The, *sel.*
Wasps, The, *sel.*
Women Speak out in Defense of Themselves, The.
Arkell, Reginald
New Garden, The.
Public Nuisance, A.
Rumors.
When the War Will End.
Arkwright, John Stanhope
Supreme Sacrifice, The.
"Arkwright, Peleg." *See* **Proudfit, David Law**
Armattoe, R. E. G.
Deep down the Blackman's Mind.
Armes, Sybil Leonard
Altars.
Home.
Path, The.
Service.
Tell Me, Mother.
When I Met Him.
Armknecht, Richard F.
Crow's Nest.
Armour, Richard
Ant, The.
Assorted Relishes.
Blurb, The.
Covering the Subject.
Epitaph: "Insured for every accident."
Horses.
Money.
New Technique.
Not a Cloud in the Sky.
One Down.
Pillow Cases.
Three Links of Light Armour.
To a Human Skeleton.
Transportation Problem.
Armstrong, George Francis Savage *See* **Savage-Armstrong, George Francis**
Armstrong, Hamilton Fish
Lines for the Hour.
Armstrong, John
Art of Preserving Health, The, *sels.*
Blest Winter Nights.
Home of the Naiads, The.
Imitation of Spenser, An.
Armstrong, Margaret D.
Invocation for the New Year.
What Happened.
Armstrong, Martin
Bird's Epitaph, A.
Buzzards, The.
Cage, The.
Gold.
Miss Thompson Goes Shopping.
Mrs. Reece Laughs.
On a Little Bird.
Armstrong, Phyllis Eleanor
Form 1040A.
"Armytage, R." *See* **Watson, Rosamund Marriott**
Arndt, Ernst Moritz
German Fatherland, The.
Arnold, Sir Edwin
After Death in Arabia, *abr.*
Almond Blossom.
Caliph's Draught, The.
Darien.
Destiny.
End Which Comes, The.
Farewell, friends! yet not farewell.
He and She.
Light of Asia, The, *sels.*
Mahmud and Ayaz; a Paraphrase on Sa'di.
Musmee, The.
Nirvana.

Arnold (continued)
Pearls of the Faith, *sel.*
Raglan.
She and He.
Somewhere.
Song without a Sound.
Swallows, The.
Swallow's Nest, The.
To a Pair of Egyptian Slippers.
With Sa'di in the Garden, *sels.*
Arnold, Emily Gail
In April.
Arnold, George
Alone by the Hearth.
Beer.
Farewell to Summer.
Golden Fish, The.
In the Dark.
Jolly Old Pedagogue, The.
Jubilate.
September.
Sweet September.
Youth and Age.
Arnold, Irene (Mrs. Major Arnold)
Pray!
Thank God for the Country.
Arnold, Matthew
Absence.
Ah, Love, Let Us Be True.
And near me on the grass lies Glanvil's book.
And you, ye stars.
Apollo.
Austerity of Poetry.
Bacchanalia; or, The New Age.
Balder Dead, *sels.*
Better Part, The.
Buried Life, The.
But when the Gods and Heroes heard, they brought.
Cadmus and Harmonia.
Calais Sands.
Callicles' Song.
Calm Soul of All Things.
Caution to Poets, A.
Children dear, was it yesterday.
Church of Brou, The, *sel.*
Combat, The.
Consolation.
Contagion of Courage.
Continued.
Courage.
Death of Sohrab, The.
Desire.
Despondency.
Destiny.
Divinity, The.
Dover Beach.
Dream, A.
Early Death and Fame.
East, The.
East London.
Empedocles on Etna.
Euphrosyne.
Farewell, A: "My horse's feet beside the lake."
For rigorous teachers seized my youth.
Forsaken Merman, The.
Forth from the east, up the ascent of Heaven.
Fragment of Chorus of a "Dejaneira."
Fulness of life and power of feeling.
Future, The.
Geist's Grave.
Good Shepherd with the Kid, The.
Growing Old.
Heine's Grave.
Human Life.
Immortality.
In Harmony with Nature.
In Utrumque Paratus.
Incremation, The.
Inward Peace.
Is it so small a thing.
Iseult of Brittany.
Isolation: To Marguerite.
Jacopone da Todi.
Lake, The.
Last Word, The.
Life and Thought.
Lines Written in Kensington Gardens.
Longing.
Meeting.
Memorial Verses.
Morality.
Mycerinus.
Neckan, The.
Noon is hot, The. When we have crossed the stream.
Obermann Once More.
On the Rhine.
Oxus.
Palladium.
Parting.
Persistency of Poetry.
Philomela.
Pis-Aller.
Poor Matthias.
Progress.
Progress of Poesy, The.
Quiet Work.
Religious Isolation.
Requiescat.
Resignation.
Revolutions.
River, The.
Rugby Chapel [November, 1857].
S.S. *Lusitania.*
Saint Brandan.
Scholar-Gipsy, The.
Second Asgard, The.
Second Best, The.
Self-Deception.
Self-Dependence.
Separation.
Shakespeare.
Sick King in Bokhara, The.
So, on the bloody sand, Sohrab lay dead.
Sohrab and Rustum.
Song for Apollo.
Song of Callicles, The ("Far, far from here").
Song of Callicles, The ("Through the black, rushing smoke-bursts").
Song of the Muses, The.
Stanzas from the Grande Chartreuse.
Stanzas in Memory of the Author of "Obermann."
Strayed Reveller, The.
Summer Night, A.
Switzerland.
Terrace at Berne, The.
Then, at the point of death, Sohrab replied.
These things, Ulysses.
Thyrsis.
To a Friend.
To a Gipsy Child by the Sea-Shore.
To a Republican Friend, 1848.
To a Republican Friend, 1848, Continued.
To an Independent Preacher.
To Fausta.
To Marguerite ("We were apart").
To Marguerite ("Yes! in the sea of life enisled").
Tomb, The.
Too Late.
Tristram and Iseult.
Urania.
Voice, The.
West London.
Westminster Abbey.
What is the course of the life.
Wish, A.
World and the Quietist, The.
Worldly Place.
Written in Butler's Sermons.
Written in Emerson's Essays.
Youth and Calm.
Youth of Nature, The.
Youth's Agitations.
Arnold, Sarah Louise
Mother, The.
Arnstein, Flora J.
Timers.
Arrieta, Rafael Alberto
January Night.
Arthur, Ruth M.
Snowflakes.
Arundel, Philip Howard, 1st Earl of
See **Howard, Philip, 1st Earl of Arundel**
Asayasu (Bunya no Asayasu)
Across clear drops of dew.
Jewels.
Asbaje, Juana de *See* **Juana Inés de la Cruz, Sister**
Asbury, Alban
If This Is All.
Asclepiades
Better Eros, The.
Desire Knows.
Epitaph of a Courtesan.
Eumares.
Rain, Night, and Wine.
To a Recalcitrant Virgin.
Asgrímsson, Eysteinn
Author's Entreaty for His Lay.
Lilya, *sel.*
Ash, Sarah Leeds
Changeless Shore.
Ashbery, John
Blessing in Disguise, A.
Boy, A.
Bungalows, The.
Civilization and Its Discontents.
Decoy.
Ecclesiast, The.
Europe.
Farm Implements and Rutabagas in a Landscape.
Faust.
Grapevine, The.
How Much Longer Will I Be Able to Inhabit the Divine Sepulcher.
Idaho.
Instruction Manual, The.
Last Month.
Last World, A.
Le Livre Est sur la Table.
Leaving the Atocha Station.
Rivers and Mountains.
Tennis Court Oath, The.
These Lacustrine Cities.
They Dream Only of America.
Ticket, The.
Two Scenes.
Variations, Calypso and Fugue on a Theme of Ella Wheeler Wilcox.
Ashby-Sterry, Joseph
King of the Cradle, The.
Little Rebel, The.
Marlow Madrigal, A.
Portrait, A.
Spring's Delights.
Ashe, Thomas
By the Salpétrière.
City Clerk, The.
Machine Hand, A.
Marian.
Meet We No Angels, Pansie?
No and Yes.
Phantoms.

Poeta Nascitur.
To Two Bereaved.
Vision of Children, A.
Ashmole, Elias
Hermatic Poems.
Ashmore, John
M. Antonio Flaminio: To His Farm.
Ashmun, Margaret
Vigilantes, The.
"Asmus." *See* **Claudius, Matthias**
Aspinwall, Alicia
Patrick Goes to School.
Asquith, Herbert
Aunt Jane.
Birthday Gifts.
Eggs.
Elephant, The.
Frowning Cliff, The.
Hairy Dog, The.
Ship Sails Up to Bideford, A.
Skating.
Tortoise, The.
Volunteer, The.
Asquith, Raymond
In Praise of Young Girls.
Astley, Thea
Droving Man.
Asturias, Miguel Angel
Indians Come down from Mixco, The.
Atamian, David
Iguanas.
Athanasius, Sister Mary
Meditation on Time.
Atherstone, Edwin
Sunrise at Sea.
Atherton, John
Tank Town.
Atherton, William
Modern Miracle.
Atkins, Russell
At War.
Christophe.
Editorial Poem on an Incident of Effects Far-Reaching.
Irritable Song.
It's Here in The.
Poem: "Upstood upstaffed passing sinuously away."
Atkinson, T. Moore
In the Quiet.
Search.
Ato Tobira
Once Only.
Atterbury, Francis
Impromptu.
Song: "Fair Sylvia, cease to blame my youth."
Written in the Leaves of a Fan.
Written on the Leaves of a White Fan.
Attowell, George
Francis' New Jig.
Attwood, A. A.
Farmyard, The.
Atwell, Roy
Some Little Bug.
Atwood, Margaret
Against Still Life.
Being with you.
Circle Game, The, *sels.*
Eventual Proteus.
Explorers, The.
Returning to the room.
Settlers, The.
Summer again.
Auber, Harriet
Holy Spirit, The.
Auchterlonie, Dorothy (Mrs. H. M. Green)
Apopemptic Hymn.
Audelay, John
Be True to Your Condition in Life.
In His Utter Wretchedness.
Auden, Wystan Hugh
Advent.
After Christmas.
After Reading a Child's Guide to Modern Physics.
Airman's Alphabet, The.
Alonso to Ferdinand.
Always the Following Wind.
And the age ended, and the last deliverer died.
Another Time.
Anthem for St. Cecilia's Day.
As a young child the wisest could adore him.
As He Is.
As I Walked Out One Evening.
As Well As Can Be Expected.
At lucky moments we seem on the brink.
At the Grave of Henry James.
At the Party.
Atlantis.
August for the People.
Autumn 1940.
Ballad: O What Is That Sound?
Base words are uttered only by the base.
Bride in the '30's, A.
But in the evening the oppression lifted.
Canzone: "When shall we learn, what should be clear as day."
Capital, The.
Carry Her over the Water.
Casino.
Chorus: "Doom is dark and deeper than any sea-dingle."
Chorus: "He is the Way."
Chorus: "To throw away the key and walk away."
City, The.
City without Walls.
Come to our well-run desert.
Commentary, *sel.*
Composer, The.
Consider This and in Our Time.
Crisis.
Cultural Presupposition, The.
Dear, though the Night Is Gone.
Decoys, The.
Deep in earth's opaque mirror.
Dialogue between Mary and Gabriel.
Diaspora, The.
Dog beneath the Skin, The, *sel.*
Doom is Dark [and Deeper Than Any Sea-Dingle].
Door, The.
Earth, receive an honoured guest.
Edward Lear.
Elegy for J. F. K.
Epilogue: "'O where are you going?' said reader to rider."
Epitaph on a Tyrant.
Epithalamion: "While explosives blow to dust."
Fairground.
Fall of Rome, The.
Family Ghosts.
Far from the Heart of Culture.
1st September 1939.
First Things First.
Fish in the Unruffled Lakes.
Five Songs, *sel.*
Flight into Egypt, The.
Follow, poet, follow right.
For the Time Being; a Christmas Oratorio, *sels.*
Foxtrot from a Play.
Fugal-Chorus from "For the Time Being" ("Great is Caesar").
Get There If You Can and See the Land You Once Were Proud to Own.
Hammerfest.
He Is the Way.
He stayed: and was imprisoned in possession.
He turned his field into a meeting-place.
He was their servant—some say he was blind.
He watched the stars and noted birds in flight.
Healthy Spot, A.
Hearing of Harvests Rotting in the Valleys.
Here war is simple like a monument.
Herman Melville.
Herod.
His generous bearing was a new invention.
Horae Canonicae, *sels.*
Horatians, The.
Hunting Season.
If I Could Tell You.
If, on Account of the Political Situation.
I'm beginning to lose patience.
In Memoriam: Ernst Toller.
In Memory of Ernst Toller.
In Memory of Sigmund Freud.
In Memory of W. B. Yeats.
In Praise of Limestone.
In Schrafft's.
In the nightmare of the dark.
In Time of War, *sels.*
Island Cemetery, The.
It's No Use Raising a Shout.
James Honeyman.
Jew Wrecked in the German Cell, The.
Judge enforcing the obsolete law, The.
Jumbled in the Common Box.
Kingdom of Number is all boundaries, The.
Labyrinth, The.
Lady, Weeping at the Crossroads.
Lakes.
Law like Love.
Law, Say the Gardeners, Is the Sun.
Lay Your Sleeping Head, [My Love].
Leaning out over.
Leap Before You Look.
Lesson, The.
Let the Florid Music Praise.
Life of man is never quite completed, The.
Look, Stranger, on This Island Now.
Love Feast, The.
Lullaby: "Lay your sleeping head, my love."
Managers, The.
Matthew Arnold.
Miranda's Song.
Mundus et Infans.
Munitions Expert.
Musée des Beaux Arts.
New Year Letter, *sel.*
Night Falls on China.
Night Mail, The.
Nones.
Note on Intellectuals.
Nothing Is Given: We Must Find Our Law.
Now the Leaves Are Falling Fast.
Now Through Night's Caressing Grip.
Numbers and Faces, *sel.*
Nursery Rhyme.
O for Doors to Be Open and an Invite with Gilded Edges.
O Love, the interest itself in thoughtless heaven.
O unicorn among the cedars.
O What Is That Sound [Which so Thrills the Ear].
O Where Are You Going?
Objects.
Ode: To My Pupils.

Auden (continued)
On Installing an American Kitchen in Lower Austria.
On This Island.
Once for candy cook had stolen.
One Evening.
Orators, The, *sel.*
Our Bias.
Our Father, whose creative Will.
Our Hunting Fathers Told the Story.
Over the Heather [the Wet Wind Blows].
Paid on Both Sides, *sel.*
Paysage Moralisé.
Perhaps.
Petition.
Pick a quarrel, go to war.
Plains.
Postscript.
Powers and Times Are Not Gods.
Preface.
Presumptuous, The.
Prime.
Private faces in public places.
Prologue: "O love, the interest itself in thoughtless Heaven."
Quarry, The.
Quest, The. *sel.*
Refugee Blues.
Riddle, The: "Underneath the leaves of life."
Rimbaud.
Roman Soldier on the Wall, A.
Roman Wall Blues.
Runner.
Sea and the Mirror, The, *sels.*
Seascape.
September 1, 1939.
Sext.
Shield of Achilles, The.
Silly Fool, The.
Sir, No Man's Enemy [Forgiving All].
So from the years the gifts were showered.
Sob, Heavy World.
Some of our dead are famous, but they would not care.
Something Is Bound to Happen.
Song: As I Walked Out One Evening.
Song: "Deftly, admiral, cast your fly."
Song: Fish in the Unruffled Lakes.
Song: "Lay your sleeping head, my love."
Song: "'O where are you going?' said reader to rider."
Song: "Say this city has ten million souls."
Song: "So large a morning, so itself, to lean."
Song: "Stop all the clocks."
Song: "Victor was a little baby."
Song: "Warm are the still and lucky miles."
Song for St. Cecilia's Day.
Song for the New Year.
Song of the Master and Boatswain.
Spain.
Spain 1937.
Spring 1940.
Stop All the Clocks.
Strings' Excitement, The.
Symmetries and Asymmetries, *sel.*
Taller Today, We Remember.
Thanksgiving for a Habitat.
That Night When Joy Began.
Their Lonely Betters.
There Will Be No Peace.
They wondered why the fruit had been forbidden.
This Lunar Beauty.
Three Companions, The.
Time Will Say Nothing but I Told You So.
To T. S. Eliot on His Sixtieth Birthday.
Traveller, The.
Trial, The.
Truest Poetry Is the Most Feigning, The; or, Ars Poetica for Hard Times.
Truth.
Under Sirius.
Under Which Lyre.
Underneath the abject willow.
Unknown Citizen, The.
Useful, The.
Villanelle.
Vocation.
Voltaire at Ferney.
Walk after Dark, A.
Walking Tour, The.
Wandering lost upon the mountains of our choice.
Watch Any Day.
We All Make Mistakes.
Well, So That Is That.
When statesmen gravely say "We must be realistic."
Which Side Am I Supposed to Be On?
Who's Who.
With what conviction the young man spoke.
Witnesses, The.
Woods.
You with shooting-sticks and cases for field-glasses.

Auden, Wystan Hugh *and* Christopher $I-sherwoo
Ascent of F 6, The, *sel.*
At Last the Secret Is Out.

Augustine, Saint
Delay.
Great Art Thou, O Lord.
Joys of Paradise.
Take My Heart.
Thou Hast Made Us for Thyself.

Auler, Virginia
My Christ.

Ault, Norman
Clouds.
Ducks.
Father Time.
Pig's Tail, The.
Wishes.
Without and Within.

"Aunt Effie." *See* **Hawkshaw, Ann**

"Aunt Mary [*or* May]." *See* **Lathbury, Mary Artemisia**

Auringer, Obadiah Cyrus
April.
Ballad of Oriskany, The.
Flight of the War-Eagle, The.

Auryansen, Lucia Trevitt
Seekers, The.

Aus of Kuraiza
Apostasy.

Auslander, Joseph
Abraham Lincoln.
Blackbird Suddenly, A.
César Franck.
Dawn at the Rain's Edge.
Derricks and Rainbows.
Elegy: "Fled is the swiftness of all the white-footed ones."
Enigma.
Gifts without Season.
He is not dead,/ Your son, your dear beloved son.
He Is Risen, *sel.*
If We Break Faith.
Interval.
Near Dusk.
Prayer for Thanksgiving, A.
Remember Me, Gulls!
Revenants.
Snow Advent.
Sunrise Trumpets.
Three Things.
Touch.
Ulysses in Autumn.
Wings at Dawn.

Ausonius, Decimus Magnus
Evening on the Moselle.
Idyll of the Rose.
To His Wife.
To My Wife.

Austin, Albert Gordon
Chez-Nous.

Austin, Alfred
Agatha.
At His Grave.
Britannia to Columbia.
Grave-Digger's Song.
Haymakers' Song, The.
Is Life Worth Living?
Last Night, The.
Last Redoubt, The.
Lover's Song, The.
Love's Trinity.
Mother-Song.
Primroses.
Prince Lucifer, *sels.*
To America.
Winter Is Gone.

Austin, John
Fain Would My Thoughts.
Hark, My Soul.

Austin, Mary
At Carmel.
Beggar Wind, The.
Brown Bear, The.
Charm for Going a-Hunting.
Deer, The.
Drouth.
Eagle's Song, The.
Feller I Know, A.
First I am frosted.
Grizzly Bear.
I come more softly than a bird.
I have no wings, but yet I fly.
I never speak a word.
Little Song of Spring, A.
O the shepherds in Judea.
Prairie-Dog Town.
Rathers.
Rhyming Riddles, *sels.*
Rocky Mountain Sheep, The.
Sandhill Crane, The.
Shepherds in Judea, The.
Sounds.
Texas Trains and Trails.
Western Magic.

Austin, William
Carol: "All this night shrill chanticler."
Chanticleer.

Auxier, Sylvia Trent
Breaking Point.

Avison, Margaret
Butterfly, The.
Butterfly Bones; or Sonnet against Sonnets.
Christmas.
For Dr. and Mrs. Dresser.
In a Season of Unemployment.
Intra-Political.
Janitor Working on Threshold.
Knowledge of Age.
Meeting Together of Poles & Latitudes; in Prospect.
Mordent for a Melody.
New Year's Poem.
Person, or a Hymn on and to the Holy Ghost.
Perspective.
Rigor Viris.
Snow.
Story, A.
Stray Dog, near Ecully, Valley of the Rhône.
Tennis.

Voluptuaries and Others.
Watershed.
Word, The.
"Avond, Jan van." *See* **Slater, Francis Carey**
Avrett, Robert
Renaissance.
Awooner, Kofi (George Williams)
Rediscovery.
Sea Eats the Land at Home, The.
Axelrod, Susan
Chameleon.
Home, The.
Snips and Snails.
Axford, Roger
Victory.
Ayer, Ethan
Exceeding Great Army, An.
Like a Whisper.
Ayer, Jean
Everyday Things.
Ayer, William Ward
Be Still.
Ayers, Vivian
Instantaneous ("Instantaneously!").
Ayre, Anna Chandler
Jack o'Lantern.
Ayres, Philip
Complains, Being Hindered the Sight of His Nymph.
Cynthia on Horseback.
Emblems of Love, *sel.*
Fly, The.
Her name is at my tongue whene'er I speak.
Invites His Nymph to His Cottage.
Invites Poets and Historians to Write in Cynthia's Praise.
On a Fair Beggar.
On Lydia Distracted.
Platonic Love.
To Love; a Sonnet.
To the Nightingale.
To the Winds.
Ayton [*or* Aytoun], Sir Robert
I Lov'd Thee Once.
On a Woman's Inconstancy.
To an Inconstant One.
Upon a Diamond Cut in Form[e] of a Heart . . . Sent in a New Year's [*or* Yeares] Gift.
Upone Tabacco.
When Thou Did Thinke I Did Not Love.
Aytoun, William Edmonstoune
Battle of Killiekrankie, The.
Biter Bit, The.
Broken Pitcher, The.
Comfort in Affliction.
Execution of Montrose, The.
Hermotimus.
Husband's Petition, The.
Laureate, The.
Lay of the Levite, The.
Lay of the Lover's Friend, The.
Massacre of the Macpherson, The.
Old Scottish Cavalier, The.
Aytoun, William E., *and* Sir Theodore Martin
Cry of the Lovelorn, The.
Eastern Serenade.
Lay of the Love-lorn, The.
Azumamaro
Moon, The.

B

"B. "
What May Happen to a Thimble.
"B., C. B. "
Because You Prayed.
"B., E. G. "
To Betty.
"B., E. R. "
Popcorn Party, The.
"B., M. E. "
Deliverance.
God Will Answer.
"B., M. K. "
Four Sunbeams, The.
"B., N. M. "
New Year Thoughts.
"B., R."
This story's strange, but altogether true.
"B., R. K. "
Limerick: "Should a plan we suggest just that minute."
Limerick: "You remember that pastoral frolic."
"B., R. L. "
Silly Willy.
"B., W. "
Mary.
"B. H." *See* **"H., B"**
"B. L. T." *See* **Taylor, Bert Leston**
"B. V." ("Bysshe Vanolis") *See* **Thomson, James (1834-1882)**
Babcock, Donald Campbell
Adios.
America.
Anthill, The ("The anthill lay unsheltered in the sun").
Chartres Cathedral.
". . . Discourse Heard One Day. . ."
In a Garden.
Meditation by Mascoma Lake.
Migrant, The.
Neoplatonic Soliloquy.
Program Note on Sibelius.
Two Things.
Vacation Trip.
Babcock, Edwina Stanton
Told in the Market-Place.
Babcock, Maltbie Davenport
Be Strong!
Companionship.
Courage.
Death.
Emancipation.
"Give Us This Day Our Daily Bread."
My Father's World.
No Distant Lord.
Our Daily Bread.
Pain.
School Days.
Speak Out.
This Is My Father's World.
Today, O Lord.
Babcock, William Henry
Bennington.
Bacchylides
Peace on Earth.
Song and Wine.
Bachelder, Phoebe Smith
Communion.
Holy Week.
Bacheller, Irving
Whisperin' Bill.
Bachmann, Ingeborg
More beautiful than the remarkable moon and her noble light.
To the Sun.
Backus, Bertha Adams
Then Laugh.
Bacmeister, Rhoda Warner
Bridges.
Galoshes.
Stars.
Bacon, Eleanor Kenly
Luminous Hands of God, The.
Bacon, Francis
In Vitam Humanam.
Life.
Life of Man, The.
World, The.
Bacon, Helen C.
Song for Decoration Day.
Bacon, Josephine Dodge Daskam
Brother, Lift Your Flag with Mine.
Motherhood.
Omar for Ladies, An.
Sleepy Song, The.
Bacon, Leonard
Afternoon in Artillery Walk, An; Mary Milton Loquitur.
Archaeologist of the Future, The.
Chorus from a Tragedy.
Day of the Slaves, The.
Epitaph in Anticipation.
Horatian Variation.
Pilgrim Fathers, The.
Reason, The.
Richard Tolman's Universe.
Tower of Ivory.
Bacon, Peggy
Cobbler.
Darkness.
Fatigue.
Hearth.
Token.
Baden-Powell, Sir Robert
Man, matron, maiden.
Badley, Mary Esther
Parade, The.
Bagg, Robert
Ballad in Blonde Hair Foretold.
For Her on the First Day Out.
'Laine.
Oracle at Delphi.
Ronald Wyn.
See That One?
Soft Answers.
Speak This Kindly to Her.
Baggesen, Jens
Childhood.
"Bagritsky, Eduard" (Eduard Dzyubin)
He Tries Out the Concords Gently.
My Honeyed Languor.
Piece of Black Bread, A.
Baha Ad-din Zuhayr
On a Blind Girl.
Bailey, Alfred Goldsworthy
Algonkian Burial.
Border River.
Colonial Set.
Miramichi Lightning.
Off Saguenay.
Shrouds and Away.
Tao.
Whistle and Wheels.
Bailey, Anthony
Green and the Black, The.
Bailey, Carolyn Sherwin
After Winter.
Christmas Party, A.
If.
Spider Silverlegs.
Bailey, H. Sewall
Sailor Man.
Bailey, Lansing C.
Eight Volunteers.
Bailey, Liberty Hyde
Farmer.
Miracle.
Bailey, Margaret
Prayer, A: "God, give me sympathy and sense."
Bailey, Philip James
Aim of Life, The.
Country Town, A.
Festus, *sels.*
Great Black Crow, The.

Bailey (continued)
Helen's Song.
Lucifer and Elissa.
My Lady.
Poet, The.
Thanks, thanks! With the Muse is always love and light.
We Live in Deeds.
Youth, Love, and Death.
Baillie, Lady Grizel
Werena My Heart's Licht I Wad Dee.
Baillie, Joanna
Country Inn, The, *sel.*
Good Morning.
Good-Night.
Kitten, The.
Orra, *sel.*
Outlaw's Song, The.
Song: "Though richer swains thy love pursue."
Song of the Outlaws.
Wake, Lady!
Bairam at Tunisie
Autobiography, An.
Baird, Catherine
Blind Man Prays, A.
Chosen.
Baird, George M. P.
Ballad of Wise Men, A.
Baird, Martha
Effortlessly Democratic Santa Fe Trail.
Bajza, Joseph
Apotheosis, *abr.*
Baker, Anna R.
In His Sight.
Baker, Barbara Anne
Grow in Hope and Grace.
Baker, Dorothy
Castles in the Sand.
In the Woods.
Baker, George Augustus
Thoughts on the Commandments.
Baker, Glen
Simon the Cyrenian Speaks.
Baker, Harry
Christmas Hymn, A.
Baker, Sir Henry William
Christ the Consoler.
Heaven.
King of Love, The.
Lord Is My Shepherd, The.
Baker, Howard
Letter from the Country, A.
Ode to the Sea.
Baker, Isaac W.
Arrival of the San Francisco, *with music.*
O! California, *with music.*
Baker, J. G.
My Trundle Bed.
Baker, Julia Aldrich
Mizpah.
Baker, Karle Wilson 'Charlotte Wilson'
Beauty's Hands Are Cool.
Box-Car Letters.
Burning Bush.
Child's Game, A.
City Lights.
Courage.
Creeds.
Days.
Friendly Faces of Old Sorrows, The.
Good Company.
Growing Old.
I Shall Be Loved as Quiet Things.
I shall not get my poem done.
Let Me Grow Lovely.
Morning Song.
Ploughman, The.
Poet Songs (I-III).
Pronouns.
Rondel for September.
She Is Wise, Our Ancient Mother.
Silver Lantern, A,
Baker, Olaf
Little Saling.
Baker, Ray Stannard *See* **"Grayson, David"**
Bakewell, John
Hail, Thou Once Despised Jesus!
Balagon, Kuwasi
Children of the Cosmos.
If You Love Them, Wouldn't You Like to See Them Better Off?
Untitle.
Balbulus, Notker *See* **Notker Balbulus**
Balch, Emily Greene
Flag Speaks, The.
Baldwin, A. W. I.
Ten Little Dicky-Birds.
Baldwin, Augustus Henry
New Year, The.
On the Threshold.
Baldwin, Eleanor
Old Falcon, The.
Baldwin, Faith
Vigil.
Baldwin, Mary Newton
Lonely Are the Fields of Sleep.
Baldwin, Michael
Death on a Live Wire.
Baldwin, William
Beloved to the Spouse, The.
Christ, My Beloved.
Christ to His Spouse.
How Collingbourne was Cruelly Executed for Making a Foolish Rhyme.
Spouse to the Beloved, The.
Baldwin, William, *and others.*
Mirror for Magistrates, A [*or* The], *sels.*
Bale, John
King John, *sel.*
Wassail, Wassail.
Bales, C. O.
Discipleship.
Balfour, Mary
Dew Each Trembling Leaf Inwreath'd, The.
In Ringlets Curl'd Thy Tresses Flow.
Ball, John
Sermon to the Rebels at Blackheath.
Ball, William
Praise to Jesus!
Ballantine, James
Castles in the Air.
Creep afore Ye Gang.
Its Ain Drap o' Dew.
Muckle-mou'd Meg.
Ballantyne, Gina
Daffodils.
Native Land.
Ballard, Colin Robert
Pacific Railway, The.
Ballard, Dorothy Scott
Father, The.
Ballard, Harlan Hoge
In the Catacombs.
Balmont, Konstantin Dmitreyevich
Psalm of Silence, The.
Balsdon, Dacre
Endurance Test.
Bamberger, Augustus Wright
Each a Part of All.
Out of the Vast.
Bampfylde, John
On Hearing That Torture Was Suppressed Throughout the Austrian Dominions.
To the Redbreast.
Bancroft, Charles
Tadoussac.
Bancroft, Charles W. H.
Three Children, The.
Bancroft, Thomas
Cross, The.
Bangham, Mary Dickerson
Come, Holy Babe!
Bangs, Janet Norris
Design for Peace.
Reply.
Bangs, John Kendrick
Blind.
"Don't Care" and "Never Mind" ("'Don't care' is no friend of mine").
I Never Knew a Night So Black.
Lincoln's Birthday.
Little Elf, The.
May 30, 1893.
Mona Lisa.
My Dog.
On File.
On Lincoln's Birthday.
Philosopher, A.
Philosophy.
Teddy's Wonderings.
Thanksgiving, A.
Thanksgiving Day.
To a Withered Rose.
Today.
"What hundred books are best, think you?" I said.
Banim, John
He Said That He Was Not Our Brother.
Irish Mother in the Penal Days, The.
Soggarth Aroon.
Banker, William, Jr
Battle of Queenstown, The.
Banko
Cattle.
Banks, George Linnaeus
My Aim.
What I Live For.
Why Do I Live?
Banks, John
Description of a Sea-Battle.
Description of London, A.
Explanatory Epistle, An.
Innocent Usurper, The, *sel.*
On Fame.
Sweet harmony of life, just musick flows.
Unhappy Favourite, The, *sel.*
Bannerman, Frances
Upper Chamber, An.
Banning, Kendall
Heart's Haven.
Once on a Time.
Banning, Lex
Captain Arthur Phillip and the Birds.
Banville, Théodore Faullain de
Goddess, The.
Prose Poem: Angels, The.
Prose Poem: Harlequin.
Baraka, Imamu Ameer *See* **Jones, LeRoi**
Barbould, Anna Letitia (Anna Letitia Aikin)
Come, Says Jesus' Voice.
Doll's House, The.
Home.
How Blest the Righteous.
Life.
Life! I Know Not What Thou Art.
Love to God.
Ode to Life.
Barber, Frances
Play-acting.
Barber, Melanie Gordon
Sonnet for My Son.
Barberino [*or* Barberini], Francesco da
Of Caution.
Virgin Declares Her Beauties, A.
Barbour, John
Before Bannockburn.
Bruce, The, *sels.*

Bruce Consults His Men.
Buik of Alexander, The, *sel.*
Freedom.
Prologue to the Avowis of Alexander.
Storys to rede ar delitabill.
Barclay, Alexander
Certain Eclogues [*or* Egloges], *sels.*
Fourth Egloge of Alexander Barclay, The,
Entituled Codrus and Minalcas, Treat-
ing of the Behavior of Rich Men against
Poets.
Prologue, The: "Famous poets with the
muses nine, The."
Winter snowes, all covered is the ground,
The.
Barclay, Edwin
Human Greatness.
Bardeen, Charles William
Birds' Ball, The.
Barham, Richard Harris *See* "Ingolds-
by, Thomas"
Baring, Maurice
Ballad: "Roses in my garden, The."
Diffugere Nives, 1917.
Dying Reservist, The.
God, who had made you valiant, strong
and swift.
I Dare Not Pray to Thee.
I. M. H.
I Too Have Travelled.
In Memoriam, A. H., *sel.*
Julian Grenfell.
Moan in the Form of a Ballade.
Mozart.
Vale.
Wagner.
Baring-Gould, Sabine
Child's Evening Hymn.
City God Hath Made, The.
For Evening.
Hymn: "Now the day is over."
Night.
Now the Day Is Over.
Olive Tree, The.
Onward!
Onward, Christain Soldiers.
Barker, Edna L. S.
Child of the World.
Barker, Edward D.
Go Sleep, Ma Honey.
Barker, Elsa
Caresses.
Confession.
Consummation.
Fulfilment.
I Know.
Inscription, The: "Sealed with the seal of
Life, thy soul and mine."
Love's Immortality.
Prayer for Love, A.
Spirit and the Bride, The, *sels.*
Vigil of Joseph, The.
When I Am Dead and Sister to the Dust.
Barker, Eric
In Memory of Robinson Jeffers.
Sea News.
Barker, George
Allegory of the Adolescent and the Adult.
And Now There Is Nothing Left.
Channel Crossing.
Crystal, The.
Cutty Sark, The.
Death of Yeats, The.
Dog, Dog in My Manger.
Dreams of a Summer Night, *sel.*
Elegy: Separation of Man from God.
Elegy: "These errors loved no less than
the saint loves arrows."
Elegy on the Eve.
Epistle: "Meeting a monster of mourning
wherever I go."

Epistle to Dylan Thomas.
Epitaph for the Poet.
Evening Star.
Everywhere is our wilderness every-
where.
First Cycle of Love Poems (I-V).
Fourth Cycle of Love Poems, *sel.*
Galway Bay.
He Comes Among.
Holy Poems (I-III).
I see the young bride move among.
I sent a letter to my love.
Just a Fishing Smack at Empson.
Leaping Laughers, The.
Letter to a Young Poet.
Little Song in Assisi, A.
Love Poem: "Less the dog begged to die
in the sky."
Love Poem: "My joy, my jockey, my Ga-
briel."
Love Poem: "O Golden Fleece she is
where she lies tonight."
Love Poem: "O tender under her right
breast."
Love Poem: "Then like the ship at rest in
the bay."
Memorial (For Two Young Seamen Lost
Overboard in a Storm in Mid-Pacific,
January, 1940).
Monarch who wears a shrieking crown,
The.
Munich Elegy No. 1.
My darkling child the stars have obeyed.
My Joy, My Jockey, My Gabriel.
News of the World I ("Cold shuttered
loveless star, skulker in clouds").
News of the World II ("In the first year of
the last disgrace").
News of the World III ("Let her lie naked
here, my hand resting").
O Golden Fleece.
O Tender under Her Right Breast.
On First Hearing Beethoven.
Pacific Sonnets, *sel.*
Resolution of Dependence.
Sacred Elegy V: "These errors loved no
less than the saint loves arrows."
Satan Is on Your Tongue.
Second Cycle of Love Poems, *sels.*
Secular Elegies.
Shut the Seven Seas against Us.
So in a one man Europe I sit here.
Sonnet: "And now there is nothing left to
celebrate."
Sonnet of Fishes.
Sonnet to My Mother.
Sparrow's Feather, A.
Stanzas on a Visit to Longleat House in
Wiltshire, October 1953.
Summer Idyll.
Summer Song I ("I looked into my heart
to write").
Summer Song II ("Soft is the collied
night, and cool").
Third Cycle of Love Poems, *sels.*
This is that month, Elizabeth.
Three Dead and the Three Living, The.
Three Memorial Sonnets.
To Any Member of My Generation.
To Father Gerard Manley Hopkins, S.J.
To My Mother.
To My Son, *sel.*
Triumphal Ode MCMXXXIX.
True Confession of George Barker, The,
sels.
Turn on Your Side and Bear the Day to
Me.
Verses for a First Birthday.
Verses for the 60th Birthday of T. S. Eliot.
Wraith-Friend, The.
Barker, Shirley

Clipper Captain.
Sonnets from a Sequence, *sels.*
Barker, Squire Omar
Batchin'.
Code of the Cow Country.
Hot Ir'n!
Law West of the Pecos, The.
Rodeo Days.
Sheep Beezness, The.
To a Jack Rabbit.
Woodrow Wilson.
Barks, Coleman
Appendix.
Bags Under the Eyes.
Body Poems, *sels.*
Brain.
Choosing.
Downy Hair in the Shape of a Flame.
Ear Lobe.
Elbow.
Feather River Valley, 1956.
Finger of Necessity.
Forehead.
Goosepimples.
Heart.
Inner Ear.
Navel.
Nickajack Cave.
Oracle, The.
Scar.
Semen.
Skull.
Stomach.
Truckdriver, The.
Turnaround place, The.
Barlow, George
Dead Child, The.
If Only Thou Art True.
Old Maid, The.
Soul, The.
Spiritual Passion.
Barlow, Jane
Christmas Rede.
Curlew's Call, A.
Out of Hearing.
Barlow, Joel
Advice to a Raven in Russia, December,
1812.
Columbiad, The, *sel.*
First American Congress, The.
Freedom.
Hasty Pudding, The.
League of Nations, A.
Let the green Succatash with thee con-
tend.
On the Discoveries of Captain Lewis.
One Centred System.
Praise of the Pudding.
Pudding Prepared and Eaten, The.
Song, A: "Fame let thy trumpet sound."
To Freedom.
Barlow, Robert Hayward
Edgar Allan Poe.
Mythological Episode.
Shub-Ad.
Warning to Snake-Killers.
Barnard, Lady Anne *See* **Lindsay, Lady
Anne**
Barnard, Charlotte Allington 'Claribel'

Come Back to Erin.
I Cannot Sing the Old Songs.
Take Back the Heart.
Barnard, Katherine R.
Voice of God, The.
Barnard, Mary
Pleiades, The.
Barnefield, Richard *See* **Barnfield, Rich-
ard**
Barnes, Barnabe
Content.

Barnes (continued)
Divine Century of Spiritual Sonnets, A, *sels.*
Fortress of hope, anchor of faithful zeal.
God's Virtue.
Gracious, Divine, and most omnipotent.
I burn, yet am I cold; I am a-cold, yet burn.
Life of Man, The.
Madrigal: "Once in an arbor was my mistress sleeping."
Mistress, behold in this true-speaking glass.
No more lewd lays of lighter loves I sing.
O Powers Celestial, with what sophistry.
Ode: "When I walk forth into the woods."
Ode, An: "Why doth heaven bear a sun."
Parthenophil and Parthenophe, *sels.*
Soft, lovely, rose-like lips, conjoined with mine.
Sonnet: "Ah, sweet Content, where is thy mild abode?"
Sonnet: "Blast of wind, A, a momentary breath."
Sonnet: "World's bright comforter, whose beamsome light, The."
To the Most Beautiful Lady, the Lady Bridget Manners.
World's Bright Comforter, The.
Barnes, Kate
Mare, A.
Barnes, Verne
Way Down South in Mississippi.
Barnes, William
Bachelor, The.
Best Man in the Vield, The.
Blackbird, The.
Blackmwore Maidens.
Brisk Wind, A.
Broken Jug, The.
Burncombe Hollow.
Castle Ruins The.
Clote, The (Water-Lily).
Come!
Country Witch, A.
Dove, The.
Easter Monday.
Easter Zunday.
Eclogue: Two Farms in Woone.
Englyn on a Yellow Greyhound, An.
Evenen in the Village.
Evening, and Maidens.
Fall, The.
Girt Woak Tree That's in the Dell, The.
Head-Stone, The.
Heäre, The.
In Church.
Jeane.
Jeane's Wedden Day in Mornen.
Leaves.
Liady-Day an' Ridden House.
Linden Lea.
Lost Little Sister, The.
Mater Dolorosa.
May.
May Tree, The.
Melhill Feast.
Mirth and Music.
Mother o' blossoms, and ov all.
Mother's Dream, The.
Musings.
My Love's Guardian Angel.
Oak Tree, The.
Old House, The.
Readen ov a Head-Stwone.
Rings.
Rustic Childhood.
Rwose in the Dark, The.
Sam'el Down vrom Lon'on.
Shellbrook.
Sonnet: Leaves.
Spring, The.
Surprise, The.
Times o' Year.
To Me.
Tokens.
Troubles of the Day.
Turnstile, The.
Veäiry ring so round's the zun, A.
Vo'k a-Comen into Church.
White an' Blue.
Wife a-Lost, The.
Wind at the Door, The.
Winter Night, A.
Witch, A.
With you first shown to me.
Withstanders.
Woak Hill.
Woodlands, The.
Woone Smile Mwore.
Zummer Stream.
Zun-zet.
Barnes, William J.
Daysman, The.
Barnett, Mavis Clare
Silence.
Barnett, Stella
Evening in the Subrubs.
Barney, William D.
Gourd-Heads, The.
In the Beginninging.
Panther Possible, The.
Barnfield [*or* Barnefield], Richard
Affectionate Shepherd, The, *sel.*
Against the Dispraisers of Poetry.
As It Fell upon a Day.
Cherry-lipped Adonis in his snowy shape.
Comparison of the Life of Man, A.
Cynthia, *sels.*
Daphnis to Ganymede.
Epitaph upon the Death of Sir Philip Sidney, Knight, Lord-Governor of Vlissing, An.
I sing not of Angelica the fair.
If Music and Sweet Poetry.
Lady Pecunia; or, The Praise of Money, *sel.*
Nightingale, The.
Ode, An: "As it fell upon a day."
Philomel.
Remembrance of Some English Poets, A.
Shepherd's Complaint, A.
Sighing, and sadly sitting by my love.
Sonnet: "But now my muse, toil'd with continual care."
Sonnet: "Sometimes I wish that I his pillow were."
Sonnet: "Stoics think, The (and they come near the truth)."
To a Friend in Praise of Music and Poetry.
To His Friend Master [*or* Maister] R. L., in Praise of Music and Poetry.
To His Mistress.
To the Learned and Accomplish'd Gentleman Maister Nicholas Blackleech of Gray's Inn.
To the Nightingale.
Unknown Shepherd's Complaint, The.
Barnwell, Desirée A.
Will the Real Black People Please Stand.
Baro, Gene
Cherry.
For Hani, Aged Fine, That She Be Better Able to Distinguish a Villain.
Horsemen, The.
Judges, Judges.
Ladder, The.
Lament for Better or Worse.
Northwind.
Northern Spring, A.
Sebastian.
Street, The.
Travelling Backward.
Under the Boughs.
Baron, Robert
To Eliza, upon May Day Morning, 1649.
"Baron Ireland." *See* **Salsbury, Nate**
Barozai, Gui
Christmas Carols.
Barr, Alice M.
Guard Thy Tongue.
Barr, Amelia Edith Huddleston
Thanksgiving.
Barr, Isabel Harriss
Dialogue, without End.
Madaket Beach.
Morning Concert—Nantucket.
Barr, John, of Craigielee
Bonny Harvest Moon, The.
New Zealand Comforts.
Rise Oot Your Bed.
There's Nae Place like Otago Yet.
To My Auld Dog Dash.
Barr, Matthias
Moon So Round and Yellow.
Only a Baby Small.
Barr, Nancy *See* **Mavity, Nancy Barr**
Barratt, Ken
Burke and Wills.
Barrax, Gerald William
Black Narcissus.
Christmas 1959 et Cetera.
Death of a Squirrel in McKinley Park, The.
I Called Them Trees.
Patroness.
Sacrifice, The.
Second Dance Poem.
Your Eyes Have Their Silence.
Barret, Pringle
Hint to the Wise, A.
Old Woman Who Lives in the Town, The.
Perhaps.
Barrett, Alfred Joseph
Chant of Departure; a Missionary's Prayer.
Martyr's Mass, A.
Mary's Assumption.
Mint by Night.
Rosebush and the Trinity, The.
Unearth.
Barrett, Diana
Beer and Skittles.
Barrett, Eaton Stannard
Woman.
Barrett, Wilton Agnew
New England Church, A.
Barrington, Patrick
Air Sentry, The.
Diplomatic Platypus, The.
Here a Nit-Wit Lies.
I Had a Duck-billed Platypus.
I Had a Hippopotamus.
I Was a Bustle-Maker Once, Girls.
Take Me in Your Arms, Miss Moneypenny-Wilson.
Barrington, Pauline B.
White Iris, A.
Barrios, Miguel de
Epitaph: "Daniel and Abigail."
Barris, Amanda
Pumpkin Speaks, A.
Barrow, Raymond
There Is a Mystic Splendor.
Barrows, Marjorie
Cricket, The.
Enchanted Garden, The.
May Morning.
Barry, Beatrice
Medical Corps, The.
Barstow, Henry H.
If Easter Be Not True.
Barter, Charles

Changes.
Dingaan and Retief.
Stray Memories of Natal and Zululand, *sels.*
Barter-Snow, Dorothy M.
Old Violin, The.
Bartleson, F. A.
New Year's Eve.
Bartlett, Elizabeth
After the Storm.
Barren Fig Tree, The.
Behold This Dreamer.
Cage, The.
Dark Angel.
Question Is Proof, The.
Bartlett, I. J.
Town of Don't-You-Worry, The.
Bartlett, Ruth Fitch
Belief.
Bartole, Genevieve
Canadian Farmer.
Bartolomeo di Sant' Angelo *See* **Sant' Angelo, Bartolomeo di**
Barton, Bernard
Bible, The.
Bruce and the Spider.
Despise Not Thou the Chastening of the Almighty.
Not Ours the Vows.
Squirrel, The.
Barton, Marie
There Was a Garden.
Baruch, Dorothy Walter
Automobile Mechanics.
Barber's Clippers.
Cat.
Different Bicycles.
Funny the Way Different Cars Start.
I Would Like to Be—a Bee.
Lawn-Mower.
Merry-go-round.
On a Steamer.
Popcorn-Popper, The.
Rabbits.
Riding in a Motor Boat.
Riding in an Airplane.
Skunk, The.
Stop—Go.
Baruch of Worms
Elegy: "Those reckless hosts rush to the wells."
Bashford, Sir Henry Howarth
Good Day, The.
Lullaby in Bethlehem.
Parliament Hill.
To Petronilla Who Has Put Up Her Hair.
Where Do the Gipsies Come From?
Bashford, Herbert
Alice.
Along Shore.
Arid Lands, The.
By the Pacific.
Morning in Camp.
Mount Rainier.
Night in Camp.
Song of the Forest Ranger, The.
Sunset.
Basho (Matsuo Basho)
Afterglow, The.
All That Is Left.
Autumn Storm, The.
Beauty.
Camellia, The.
Cicada-Shell.
Crescent Moon.
Crow, A.
Dusk.
End of Summer, The.
Friend sparrow, do not eat, I pray.
Haiku: "Ancient pond, The."
Haiku: "New moon in the sky."
Haiku: "Old Pond, An."
Haiku: "On this road."
Hail on the Pine Trees.
Harbingers.
Hokku: "Cry of the cicada, The."
Hokku: "Wayside cherry tree, A."
In My New Clothing.
Into the Darkness.
Invitation, An.
Leaving the House of a Friend.
Lonely pond in age-old stillness sleeps, A.
Monkey's Raincoat, The.
Morning-Glories.
Nothing in the voice of the cicada.
O cricket, from your cheery cry.
Old men, white-haired, beside the ancestral graves.
Old Pond, The.
On a bare branch.
On a Journey.
On Izumo Cliff.
On the Heights.
Plum Blossoms ("Far across hill and dale").
Quick-falling dew.
Rice Fields.
Roadside thistle, eager, The.
Spring Days.
Stillness, The.
They Also.
Transient Beauty.
Wake Up! Wake Up!
Basler, Roy
Exodus.
Basse, William
Angler's Song, The (*in* Izaak Walton's The Compleat Angler).
Elegy on Shakespeare.
Hunter's Song, The.
On Mr. Wm. Shakespeare.
Bassett, A. A.
Twice Fed.
Bastard, Thomas
Ad Curiosum Lectorem.
Ad Eandem.
Ad Henricum Wottonem ("Wotton my little Bere dwells on a hill").
Ad Henricum Wottonum ("Wotton, the country and the country swain").
Ad Lectorem ("How quickly doth the reader pass away").
Ad Lectorem ("If my books easy of digestion be").
Ad Lectorem ("Reader, my book flies low, and comes not near").
Ad Lectorem ("Reader, there is no biting in my verse").
Ad Reginam Elizabetham ("Live long Elisa, that the wolf of Spain").
Ad Reginam Elizabetham ("Mother of England, and sweet nurse of all").
Ad Samuelem Danielem.
De Mense Ianuarii Quae Fuit An. Do. 1595.
De Microcosmo.
De Naevo in Facie Faustinae.
De Piscatione.
De Poeta Martiali.
De Subiecto Operis Sui.
First and riper world of men and skill, The.
Heywood goes down, saith Davie, sickerly.
In Cacum.
In Caium.
In Philonem.
Laetus did in his mistress' quarrel die.
Methinks 'Tis pretty Sport [to Hear a Child].
Nisus writes epigrams and so do I.
On a Child Beginning to Talk.
Our fathers did but use the world before.
They which read Horace, Virgil, and the rest.
Wonderful scarcity will shortly ensue, A.
Bate, John
Cologne.
Bates, Arlo
America.
America, last hope of man and truth.
Conceits.
Cyclamen, The.
In Paradise.
Kitty's Laugh.
Kitty's "No."
Like to a Coin.
On the Road to Chorrera.
Rose, A.
Shadow Boat, A.
Torch-Bearers, *sel.*
Watchers, The.
Winter Twilight, A.
Bates, Brainard L. *See* **Bates, Esther Willard,** *and* **Brainard L. Bates**
Bates, Charlotte Fiske
André.
Character, A.
Clue, The.
Delay.
Living Book, The.
Woodbines in October.
Bates, Clara Doty
Spring Questions.
Thistle-Down.
Who Likes the Rain?
Bates, David
Speak Gently.
Bates, Esther Willard, ***and*** **Brainard L. Bates**
Ipswich Bar.
Bates, G. E.
Pentagonia.
Bates, Herbert
Heavens Are Our Riddle.
Prairie.
Bates, Katharine Lee
All the Road to Egypt.
Alone into the Mountain.
America the Beautiful.
At Nazareth.
By the Sea of Galilee.
Changing Road, The.
Christmas Island.
Come unto Me.
Debt, The.
Despised and Rejected.
Dogs of Bethlehem, The.
Earth Listens.
Fellowship, The.
First Voyage of John Cabot, The.
For Deeper Life.
Gypsy-Heart.
In His Steps.
Judgment, The.
Kings of the East, The.
Little Knight in Green, The.
Love Planted a Rose.
New Crusade, The.
Robin's Secret.
Sarah Threeneedles.
Somebody's Boy.
Song of Riches, A.
Song of Waking, A.
Splendid Isolation.
Stranger in Scythopolis, A.
Tempted.
Thou Knowest.
Three Steps.
Vigi.
Wild Weather.
Youth.
Bathurst, William Hiley

Bathurst (continued)
O for a Faith That Will Not Shrink.
O Thou Whose Compassionate Care.
Triumphs of Thy Conquering Power, The.
Unshrinking Faith.
Batterham, Eric N.
Once.
Baudelaire, Charles
Abyss, The.
Accursed, The.
Albatross, The.
All, All.
Balcon, Le.
Beauté, La.
Beauty.
Blind, The.
Carrion, A.
Cat, The.
Cats, The.
Clock, The.
Correspondences.
Cracked Bell, The.
Dawn.
De Profundis Clamavi.
Despair of the Old Woman, The.
Don Juan in Hell.
Elevation.
Enemy, The.
Epilogue: "With heart at rest I climbed the citadel's steep height."
Epilogue to Prose Poems.
Exotic Perfume.
Giantess.
Gypsies on the March.
Harmonie du soir.
Hiboux, Les.
Ideal, The.
Ill Luck.
Jewels, The.
King of the Rainy Country, The.
Litanies of Satan, The.
Litany to Satan.
Lovers' Death, The.
Metamorphoses of the [*or* a] Vampire.
Mists and Rain.
Music, The.
My Cat.
Parfum exotique.
Prose Poem: Dog and the Flask, The.
Prose Poem: Stranger, The.
Prose Poem: Window, The.
Ransom, The.
Remorse after Death.
Sed Non Satiata.
Sois sage, o ma douleur.
Spleen ("Old Pluvius, month of rains, in peevish mood").
Spleen ("When the dull dire sky weighs a heavy cover").
Spleen LXXV: "January, angry at the whole damned town."
Swan, The.
Thee I Adore.
To a Passer-by.
To Beauty.
To the Reader.
Voyage, The.
Voyage to Cythera, A.
Baughan, Blanche Edith
Five Prayers.
God's Acre.
Greatest Gift, The.
In Exile.
Mary Ross, The.
Meeting of Sighs, The.
Old Place, The (New Zealand).
On the Just and the Unjust.
Ship and the Sea, The.
Baum, Peter
Horror.
Psalms of Love.
Bax, Sir Arnold *See* **"O'Byrne, Dermot"**
Bax, Clifford
Full Moon.
In the Train.
Town Maid.
Turn Back, O Man.
Baxter, Elizabeth
In Your Absence.
Baxter, J. Sidlow
Another Christmas.
Baxter, James Keir
Antelopes, The.
Cressida, *sels.*
Elegy for an Unknown Soldier.
Her Decision.
Her First Song.
Her Second Song.
Hermit, The.
High Country Weather.
Homecoming, The.
In the Lecture Room.
Lounge Bar.
Mill Girl.
Never No More.
Parting, The.
Poem by the Clock Tower, Sumner.
Poem in the Matukituki Valley.
Rocket Show.
Rope for Harry Fat, A.
Seraphion.
Sestina.
Tarras Moon.
To My Father.
Tunnel Beach.
Wild Bees.
Baxter, Richard
Death.
Death of Dives, The.
Entering by His Door.
Happy Any Way.
Lord, It Belongs Not to My Care.
Love Breathing Thanks and Praise, *sel.*
Madness, *sel.*
Preacher's Urgency, A.
Wholly the Lord's.
Baybars, Taner
Emigrant's Iconoclasm.
Bayldon, Arthur Albert Dawson
Marlowe.
Sunset.
Baylebridge, William (*originally* Charles Wiliam Blocksidge)
Ampler Circumscription, The.
As fire, unfound ere pole approaches pole.
Choir of spirits on a cloud, A.
God, to get the clay that stayed me.
Life's Testament, *sels.*
Love feeds, like Intellect, his lamp with truth.
Love Redeemed, *sels.*
Master-Foe, The.
Moreton Miles, *sel.*
Sextains, *sels.*
This miracle in me I scan.
Troubled Unquickening, The.
When tongues will tax me in the public ear.
Wherever I go, I do no wrong.
Wreath, A, *sel.*
Bayles, James C.
In the Gloaming.
Bayley, Charles E.
Grace Sufficient.
Morning Challenge.
Penman's Prayer.
Bayliss, John Clifford
October.
To My Wife.
Bayly, Thomas Haynes
Do You Remember.
I'd Be a Butterfly.
Long, Long Ago.
Mistletoe Bough, The.
Oh, No! We Never Mention Her.
Oh! Where Do Fairies Hide Their Heads.
She Wore a Wreath of Roses.
Why Don't the Men Propose?
Beach, Joseph Warren
Dropping Your Aitches.
Rue Bonaparte.
View at Gunderson's.
"Beachcomber." *See* **Morton, John Bingham**
Beaconsfield, Earl of *See* **Disraeli, Benjamin**
Beaglehole, John Cawte
Considerations on Certain Music of J. S. Bach, *sel.*
Meditating in silence after the last note.
Beard, Daniel Carter
Behind the Looking Glass.
Beardsley, Aubrey
Ballad of a Barber, The.
Three Musicians, The.
Beatriz de Dia
Estat ai en greu cossirier.
Beattie, A. J.
Easter Glory, The.
Beattie, James
But Who the Melodies of Morn Can Tell?
Epitaph, An: "Like thee I once have stemm'd the sea of life."
Epitaph, Intended for Himself.
Minstrel, The, *sels.*
Nature and the Poets.
Nature's Charms.
Retirement, *sel.*
Solitude.
To Mr. Alexander Ross.
Beattie, Robert Brewster
Way to a Happy New Year, A.
Beattie, William
Evening Hymn of the Alpine Shepherds.
Beatty, Pakenham
Charles Lamb.
Death of Hampden, The.
When Will Love Come?
Beaumont, Francis
Examination of His Mistress' Perfections, The.
Fie on Love.
Fit Only for Apollo.
Francis Beaumont's Letter from the Country to Jonson.
Indifferent, The.
Letter to Ben Jonson.
Masque of the Inner-Temple and Gray's Inne, The, *sels.*
Master Francis Beaumont's Letter to Ben Jonson.
More pleasing were these sweet delights.
On blessed youths, for Jove doth pause.
On the Marriage of a Beauteous Young Gentlewoman with an Ancient Man.
Peace and silence be the guide.
Pining for Love.
Shake Off Your Heavy Trance.
Song for a Dance.
Songs from a Masque.
Superlative Dance and Song.
True Beauty.
What things have we seen.
Ye [*or* You *or* We] should stay longer if we durst.
Beaumont, Francis *and* John Fletcher
Aspatia's Song.
Away, Delights!
Better music ne'er was known.
Bridal Song ("Cynthia, to thy power").
Bridal Song ("Hold back thy hours").
Captain, The, *sels.*

Come, Sleep.
Come, You Whose Loves Are Dead.
Cupid's Revenge, *sel.*
Hold Back Thy Hours Dark Night.
I could never have the power.
I Died True.
Jillian of Berry.
Knight of the Burning Pestle, The, *sels.*
Laugh and Sing ("'Tis mirth that fills the veins with blood").
Lay a Garland on My Hearse.
Lovers, Rejoice [*or* Rejoyce]!
Love's Cure, *sel.*
Lullaby: "Come sleep, and with the sweet deceiving."
Maid's Tragedy, The, *sels.*
Merrythought's Song ("For Jillian of Berry").
Merrythought's Song ("I would not be a servingman").
Mirth ("'Tis mirth that fills the veins with blood").
Month of May, The.
Sad Song, The.
Sleep ("Come, Sleep, and with thy sweet deceiving").
Song: "Turn, turn thy beauteous face away.
Tell Me, Dearest, What Is Love?
To Bed, to Bed.
Turn, Turn Thy Beauteous Face Away.
What Is Love?
Woman-Hater, The, *sels.*

Beaumont, Sir John
Assumption, The.
He makes sweet music who, in serious lines.
O Thou Who Art Our Author and Our End.
Of His Dear Son, Gervase.
Of My Dear Son [*or* Sonne], Gervase Beaumont.
Of Sir Philip Sidney.
Of True Liberty.
On the Coincidence of the Feasts of the Annunciation and the Resurrection in 1627.
To His Late Majesty, Concerning the True Form of English Poetry.

Beaumont, Joseph
Ascension, The.
Bad Times.
Garden, The.
Gentle Check, The.
Gnat, The.
Home.
House and Home.
Love.
Morning Hymn.
O vile ingrateful me.
Purification of the Blessed Virgin.
Snow, The.
Whiteness, or Chastity.
Whit Sunday.

Beaumont, Thomas
His Despair.
To His Mistress.
To His Mistress, Sending Her the Arcadia.

Beaver, Bruce
Cow Dance.

Bechtel, Louise Seaman
Grandfather Frog.

Beck, Thomas
Bless, Dear Saviour, This Child.

Beck, Victor Emanuel
Sifting.

Becker, Charlotte
Door-Bell, The.

Becker, Edna
Reflections.

Becker, John
Are You a Marsupial?
Feather or Fur.
For Maria at Four.
Tale of the Skunk and Poor Jez, The.
Things to Learn About.

Beckett, Gilbert Abbott à. *See* **À Beckett, Gilbert Abbott**

Bécquer, Gustavo Adolfo
Love Passing By.
Rimas, *sels.*
Shadowy Swallows.
Song: "I am a passion; I am a flame."
They Closed Her Eyes.
Three Rimas.
Waiting Harp, The.

Beddoes, Thomas Lovell
Alpine Spirit's Song.
Another [Fantastic Simile].
Athulf's Death Song.
Ballad of Human Life.
Beautiful Night, A.
"Bona de Mortuis".
Bridal Song to Amala.
Bride's Tragedy, The, *sels.*
Carrion Crow, The.
Crocodile, A.
Dear, I could weep, but that my brain is dry.
Death's Jest Book, *sels.*
Dedicatory Stanzas.
Dirge: "If thou wilt ease thine heart."
Dirge: "Sorrow, lie still and wear."
Dirge: "Swallow leaves her nest, The"
Dirge: "We do lie beneath the grass."
Dirge for Wolfram.
Dirge Written for a Drama.
Do Not Minute.
Dream, A.
Dream-Pedlary.
Dreams to Sell.
Durst thou again say life and soul has lifted.
Early Fragments, *sels.*
Epithalamia.
Fair and bright assembly, A: never strode.
Fantastic Simile, A.
Fragment: "Bury him deep. So damned a work should lie."
Fragments Intended for the Dramas, *sel.*
Ghosts' Moonshine, The.
Grief-in-Idleness.
Has no one seen my heart of you?
Her Kisses.
Hesperus Sings.
Hist, oh hist.
How Many Times?
How Many Times Do I Love Thee, Dear?
I never knew before/ The meaning of this love.
I should not say.
If Thou Wilt Ease Thine Heart.
I'll Be as True.
In a Garden by Moonlight.
Isbrand's Song.
Ivory Gate, The, *sel.*
Lady, Was It Fair of Thee.
Last Man, The, *sel.*
L'Envoi: "Who findeth comfort in the stars and flowers."
Lily of the Valley, The.
Lines: "How lovely is the heaven of this night."
Lines Written at Geneva; July 16, 1824.
Lines Written in a Blank Leaf of the Prometheus Unbound.
Lord Alcohol.
Love Goes a-Hawking.
Love-in-Idleness.
Mandrake's Song.
Man's Anxious, but Ineffectual Guard against Death.
Mariners' Song.
Mighty Thoughts of an Old World, The.
My will lies there, my hope, and all my life.
New Cecilia, The.
Old Adam.
Old Adam, the Carrion Crow.
Old Ghost, The.
Oviparous Tailor, The.
Phantom-Lover, The.
Phantom-Wooer, The.
Poor Old Pilgrim Misery.
Reason Why, The.
Resurrection Song.
Sailors' Song.
Sea Song.
Second Brother, The, *sels.*
Second Dirge.
Sibylla's Dirge.
Silenus in Proteus.
Song: "A ho! A ho!/ Love's horn doth blow.
Song: "Hither haste, and gently strew."
Song: "How many times do I love thee, dear?"
Song: "Mighty thoughts of an old world, The."
Song: "Old Adam, the carrion crow."
Song: "Strew not earth with empty stars."
Song: "We have bathed, where none have seen us."
Song: "Who tames the lion now?"
Song at Amala's Wedding.
Song by Isbrand.
Song by the Deaths.
Song by Two Voices.
Song from the Ship.
Song of Thanatos, The.
Song of the Stygian Naiades.
Song on the Water.
Song That Wolfram Heard in Hell, The.
Songs at Amala's Wedding.
Sonnet: To Tartar, a Terrier Beauty.
Squats on a Toad-Stool under a Tree.
Stanzas: "Mighty thought of an old world, The."
Stanzas from "The Ivory Gate."
Subterranean City, A.
Swallow Leaves Her Nest, The.
Tailor, The.
Then all the minutes of my life to come.
Then listen, as I listened unto you.
Threnody: "Far away."
Threnody: "No sunny ray, no silver night."
To Night.
To Sea, to Sea!
To Silence.
Torrismond, *sels.*
Tree of Life, The.
Voice from the Waters, A.
We Do Lie beneath the Grass.
Wolfram's Dirge.
Wolfram's Song.

Beddome, Benjamin
Communion of Saints.
Glorious Gift of God, The.
Worth of Prayer, The.

Bede, The Venerable
Ascension Hymn.
Hymn, A: "Hymn of glory let us sing, A."
Hymn of Glory Let Us Sing, A.
Hymnum Canentes Martyrum.
O God that art the sole hope of the world.

"Bede, Cuthbert" (Edward Bradley)
In Immemoriam.
In Memoriam.
Limerick: "There was a queer fellow named Woodin."

Bedford-Jones, Henry James O'Brien
How Do You Do?
Bedingfield, Thomas
Lover's Choice, The.
Beecham, Audrey
Exile.
Beecham, Sir Thomas
Hark the herald angels sing, *parody.*
Beecher, John
Wisdom of the Abbot Macarius I.
Beeching, Henry Charles
Accidian.
Bicycling Song.
Blackbird, The.
Boy's Prayer, A.
Going down Hill on a Bicycle.
I am a most superior person.
I am featly-tripping Lee.
Knowledge after Death.
Masque of Balliol, The, *sels.*
Prayer: "God who created me."
Prayers.
Summer Day, A.
To My Totem.
Under the Sun.
Upright and shrewd, more woo'd of fame.
Beeching, Jack
1944—on the Invasion Coast.
Beedome, Thomas
Broken Heart, The.
Choice, The.
Epitaph on Drake.
To His Mistresse on Her Scorne.
To the Noble Sir Francis Drake.
Beer, Henry
Babe of Bethlehem, The.
Beer, Morris Abel
Achievement.
Book Is an Enchanted Gate, A.
Boy of Old Manhattan, A.
Church in the Heart, The.
Manhattan.
Beer, Patricia
Fifth Sense, The.
Beerbohm, Max
Brave Rover.
Lines on a Certain Friend's Remarkable Faculty for Swift Generalization.
On the Imprint of the First English Edition of the Works of Max Beerbohm.
Sequelula to "The Dynasts," A.
Beer-Hofmann, Richard
"Evil Man, An!"
Graf von Charolais, Der, *sel.*
Jacob's Dream, *sel.*
Beers, Ethel Lynn
All Quiet along [*or* on] the Potomac.
Picket-Guard, The.
Weighing the Baby.
Which Shall It Be?
Beers, Henry Augustin
Biftek aux Champignons.
Ecce in Deserto.
Fish Story, A.
Laye of ye Woodpeckore, Ye.
On a Miniature.
Posthumous.
Singer of One Song, The.
Beers, Lorna
"Soft Sell."
Top Hat and Tales.
Beesly, Augustus Henry
André's Ride.
Beeton, Douglas Ridley
Autumn.
Behemb, Martin
I Shall Be Satisfied.
Behn, Aphra
Abdelazer, *sel.*
Amyntas Led Me to a Grove.
"And Forgive Us Our Trespasses."
Beneath a Cool Shade.
Coquette, The.
Defiance, The.
Dutch Lover, The, *sel.*
Emperor of the Moon, The, *sel.*
Libertine, The.
Love Armed.
Love in Fantastic Triumph.
Lucky Chance, The, *sel.*
Lycidus, *sel.*
O What Pleasure 'Tis to Find.
Rover, The, *sel.*
Serenade: "When maidens are young, and in their spring."
Song: Love Arm'd [*or* Armed].
Song: "Love in fantastic [*or* fantastique] triumph sate [*or* satt]."
That Beauty I Ador'd Before.
Thousand Martyrs I Have Made, A.
When Damon First Began to Love.
Willing Mistress, The.
Behn, Harry
Adventure.
Christmas Carol, A: "Angel told Mary, An."
Curiosity.
Easter Snowfall.
Evening.
Flowers.
Follow the Leader.
Gnome, The.
Growing Up.
Hallowe'en.
Invitation.
Kite, The.
Last Leaf, The.
Lesson.
Make Believe.
Mr. Pyme.
Others.
Spring.
Spring Rain.
Surprise.
This Happy Day.
Trees.
Visitors.
Waiting.
Windy Morning.
Behrend, Alice
Snowflakes.
Beissel, Henry
Boar and the Dromedar, The.
In the one-two domestic goose one-two one-two step.
New Wings for Icarus, *sel.*
Belfrage, Sally
Progress.
Belitt, Ben
Late Dandelions.
Papermill Graveyard.
View from the Gorge.
Winter Pond.
"Bell, Acton." *See* **Brontë, Anne**
Bell, Arthur W.
Case History.
Streamlined Stream-Knowledge.
Bell, Birdie
I Have Always Found It So.
Bell, Charles Dent
Solemn Rondeau.
Bell, Charles G.
Banana.
Baptism.
Barn Swallow.
Diretro al Sol.
Fire, The.
From Le Havre.
Gar, The.
Girl Walking.
Heraclitus in the West.
Island Dogs ("The island crawls with dogs").
Love in Age.
On a Baltimore Bus.
Termites.
This Little Vigil.
Windowed Habitations.
Woodbird.
"Bell, Currer." *See* **Brontë, Charlotte**
"Bell, Ellis." *See* **Brontë, Emily**
Bell, Henry Glassford
Mary, Queen of Scots.
Bell, Jerome B.
Mystery.
Bell, John Joy
Lights, The.
On the Quay.
Ships, The.
Bell, Julian
Moths, The.
Pluviose.
Redshanks, The.
Woods and Kestrel.
Bell, Mackenzie
At Stratford-on-Avon.
At the Grave of Dante Gabriel Rossetti.
Spring's Immortality.
Bell, Martin
Benefit Night at the Opera, A.
Songs, The ("Continuous, a medley of old pop numbers").
Verdi at Eighty.
Bell, Marvin
Address to the Parents, The.
Afterword to My Father, An.
All Girls Drill Team, The.
Communication on His Thirtieth Birthday.
Danger at Funny Junction, The.
Delicate Bird Who Is Flying Up Our Asses, The.
For My Sister, Contemplating Divorce.
Giving In, The.
Growth, The.
Hole in the Sea, The.
How I Came to Rule the World.
Israeli Navy, The.
My Hate.
On Returning to Teach.
Perfection of Dentistry, The.
Things We Dreamt We Died For.
Three Corners of Reality, The.
Travel.
Verses versus Verses.
Bell, Maurice
Alabama, The.
Bell, Robert Mowry
Second Volume, The.
Tutelage, The.
Bell, Walker Meriwether
Jefferson Davis.
Bell, William
Elegy IX: "My dear, observe the rose! though she desire it."
Elegy: "Now Christendom bids her cathedrals call."
Elegy: "Tonight the moon is high, to summon all."
On a Dying Boy.
Sonnet: "You waken slowly. In your dream you're straying."
Sonnet: "You whispered, 'still the stars shine cold above me.'"
To a Lady on Her Marriage.
Young Man's Song, A.
Bella, Ettore
Vital Statistics.
Bellamann, Henry
Charleston Garden, A.
Cups of Illusion.
Deeper Seas, The.

Gulf Stream, The.
Bellaw, Americus Wellington
Conjugal Conjugations.
Old Line Fence, The.
Bellay, Joachim du *See* **Du Bellay, Joachim**
Belle, John Cross
Secret Prayer.
Belleau, Remy
April.
Bellenden, John
Anno Domini.
Starscape, A.
Bellerby, Frances
It Is Not Likely Now.
Belli, Giuseppe Gioacchino
Confessor, The.
Bellman, Karl Mikael
Cradle Song: "Lullaby, my little one."
Belloc, Elizabeth
Nightingale, The.
Belloc, Hilaire
Almighty God, Whose Justice Like a Sun.
Auvergnat.
B Stands for Bear.
Ballade of Hell and of Mrs. Roebeck.
Ballade of Illegal Ornaments.
Ballade of the Heresiarchs.
Ballade to Our Lady of Czestochowa.
Because My Faltering Feet.
Big Baboon, The.
Birds, The.
Bison, The.
Charles Augustus Fortescue.
Courtesy.
Crusade.
Cuckoo!
Death and Last Confession of Wandering Peter, The.
Dedication on the Gift of a Book to a Child.
Dedicatory Ode, *sel.*
Discovery.
Dodo, The.
Dromedary, The.
Duncton Hill.
Early Dawn.
Early Morning, The.
Elephant, The.
Epigram: "When I am dead, I hope it may be said."
Epitaph on the Favourite Dog of a Politician.
Epitaph on the Politician.
False Heart, The.
Fatigue.
For False Heart.
Foreword, A: "Child! do not throw this book about."
Frog, The.
G.
Game of Cricket, The.
Garden Party, The.
George Who Played with a Dangerous Toy, and Suffered a Catastrophe of Considerable Dimensions.
Godolphin Horne.
Grandmamma's Birthday.
Greetings of the Season.
Habitations.
Ha'nacker Mill.
Henry King.
Her Faith.
Heretics All.
Hippopotamus, The.
In a Boat.
Jim, Who Ran Away from His Nurse, and Was Eaten by a Lion.
Juliet.
Leader, The.
Lines to a Don.
Lion, The.
Llama, The.
Lord Finchley.
Lord Heygate.
Lord High-Bo.
Lord Lundy.
Matilda.
Microbe, The.
Moon's Funeral, The.
Moral Alphabet, A, *sel.*
Night, The.
Noel.
On a Dead Hostess.
On a General Election.
On a Great Election.
On a Hand.
On a Politician.
On a Sleeping Friend.
On a Sundial.
On His Books.
On Hygiene.
On Lady Poltagrue, a Public Peril.
On Mundane Acquaintances.
On Noman, a Guest.
On Two Ministers of State.
Our Lord and Our Lady.
Pacifist, The.
Prophet Lost in the Hills at Evening, The.
Python, The.
Rebecca.
Rebel, The.
Rhinoceros, The ("Rhinoceros, your hide looks all undone").
Sarah Byng.
Song: Inviting the Influence of a Young Lady upon the Opening Year.
Song: "You wear the morning like your dress."
Sonnet: "Because my faltering feet may fail to dare."
Sonnet: "We will not whisper, we have found the place."
Sonnets, *sels.*
South Country, The.
Stanzas Written on Battersea Bridge during a Southwesterly Gale.
Statue, The.
Tarantella.
Telephone, The.
They Say, and I Am Glad They Say.
They Say That In The Unchanging Place.
Tiger, The.
To Dives.
To the Balliol Men Still in Africa.
Viper, The.
Vulture, The.
West Sussex Drinking Song.
Yak, The.
Bellows, Silence Buck
Last Cargo.
Beloof, Robert
Spring Night, A.
Belsham, R. A.
Christ for Everything ("Christ for life, and Christ for living").
Belting, Natalia M.
Dark gray clouds, The.
Some say the sun is a golden earring.
Belvin, William
Palermo, Mother's Day, 1943.
Bemis, Arthur Roszelle, Jr
Decoration Day Prayer.
Benaya, Margaret
Exile, The.
Benedict, Hester A.
Good-Night.
Benedikt, Michael
Beloved Head, A.
Divine Love.
European Shoe, The.
Eye, The.
Joy.
Some Litanies.
Benediktsson, Einar
Rain.
Benét, Laura
Adventure.
Babylon.
Bird of Paradise, The.
Cushy Cow.
Mountain Convent.
Penny, The.
Peter.
Rowers, The.
"She Wandered after Strange Gods."
Thrush, The.
Benét, Rosemary (Mrs. Stephen Vincent Benét)
To an Unknown Neighbor at the Circus.
Benét, Rosemary, *and* Stephen Vincent Ben,
Abraham Lincoln.
Benjamin Franklin [1706-1790].
Christopher Columbus.
Clipper Ships and Captains.
Crawford Long and William Morton.
George Washington.
James Monroe.
John Adams.
Johnny Appleseed.
Nancy Hanks.
Negro Spirituals.
Peregrine White and Virginia Dare.
Peter Stuyvesant.
Walter Reed.
Wilbur Wright and Orville Wright.
Zachary Taylor.
Benét, Stephen Vincent
Aaron Burr.
American Names.
Americans are always moving on.
Americans, Who Whistle As You Go!
Andrew Jackson.
Ballad of William Sycamore, The.
Battle of Gettysburg, The.
Captain Kidd.
Cotton Mather.
Daniel Boone.
Dulce Ridentem.
Enlistments, The.
Flood Tide.
For All Blasphemers.
For City Spring.
Gaunt man, Abraham Lincoln, woke one morning, The.
General Public, The.
Going Back to School.
Invocation: "American muse, whose strong and diverse heart."
It was noon when the company marched to the railroad-station.
Jack Ellyat Heard the Guns.
John Brown.
John Brown's Body, *sels.*
John Brown's Prayer.
John James Audubon.
John Quincy Adams.
King David.
Lewis and Clark.
Lincoln Calls for Volunteers.
Listen to the People: Independence Day, 1941, *sel.*
Litany for Dicatorships.
Love Came By from the Riversmoke.
Metropolitan Nightmare.
Mountain Whippoorwill, The.
Nightmare at Noon.
Nightmare Number Three.
1935.
Now That I Am Clean Again.
Out of John Brown's Strong Sinews.
Portrait of a Boy.

Benét (continued)
Rain after a Vaudeville Show.
Retort Discourteous, The.
Robert E. Lee.
Significance of John Brown, The.
Slaver, The.
Soliloquy of Lincoln before Manassas.
Song of the Breath, The.
Song of the Riders.
Southern Ships and Settlers.
Stonewall Jackson.
There Was a Girl I Used to Go With.
Thirteen Sisters, The.
This is Independence Day.
This is the hidden place that hiders know.
Thomas Jefferson.
Three Elements.
To Rosemary.
Unfamiliar Quartet.
Western Star, *sel.*
Western Wagons.
Winged Man.
Written in a Time of Crisis.

Benét, William Rose
Arraignment, *sel.*
At Warm Springs.
Bast.
Bestiary, The *sel.*
Brazen Tongue.
Contemplate Pliny's crocodile.
Death of Robin Hood, The.
Debutantrum.
Eternal Masculine.
Falconer of God, The.
Fancy, The.
Fawn in the Snow, The.
Gaspara Stampa.
Her Way.
Horse Thief, The.
How to Catch Unicorns.
Inscription for a Mirror in a Deserted Dwelling.
Jesse James.
Judgment.
Light in the Temple, The.
Lullaby of the Catfish and the Crab.
Mad Blake.
Merchants from Cathay.
Moon Rider.
Night.
Old Adam, The.
Old Bill's Memory Book.
On Sunday in the Sunlight.
Oregon Trail, The.
Pearl Diver.
Roundhouse, The.
Sagacity.
Skater of Ghost Lake, The.
Song under Shadow.
Stage Directions.
Strong Swimmer, The.
Subversive.
There Lived a Lady in Milan.
Third Row, Centre.
To My Wife.
Tricksters.
Whale.
What did you do with the world that you bade us to bow to anew?
Wild Philomela.
Wings.
Woodcutter's Wife, The.
Words of Jesus, The.
World's Desire, The.

Benevieni, Girolamo
Lauda.

Benford, Lawrence
Beginning of a Long Poem on Why I Burned the City, The.

Benison, H. Worsley- *See* **Worsley-Benison, H.**

Benjacob, Isaac
Epitaph, An: "Here lies Nachshon, a man of great renown."

Benjamin, Park
Old Sexton, The.
To Arms.

Benjamin, Paul L.
We Who Are Dead.

Benjamin, Virginia Sarah
Puzzling Example, A.

Ben Kalir, Eleazar
O Hark to the Herald.
Palms and Myrtles.
Prayer for Dew.
Terrible Sons, The.
To Him Who Is Feared.

Benlowes, Edward
Evening Prayer.
Life and Death.
Theophila; or, Love's Sacrifice, *sels.*
To His Muse.

Benn, Gottfried
Poplar.
Weightless Element, A.

Bennett, Anna Elizabeth
Candle Song.

Bennett, Arnold
It Pays.
Limerick: "There was a young man of Montrose."

Bennett, Bob
Girl with the Afro, The.
"It Is Time for Action."

Bennett, Gertrude Ryder
Diary of a Raccoon.
These Times.
Wayside Shrine.

Bennett, Gwendolyn B.
Advice.
Fantasy.
Hatred.
Heritage.
Lines Written at the Grave of Alexandre [*or* Alexander] Dumas.
Nocturne: "This cool night is strange."
Quatrains.
Secret.
Sonnet I: "He came in silvern armor, trimmed with black."
Sonnet II: "Some things are very dear to me."
Sonnets, *sels.*
To a Dark Girl.
Your Songs.

Bennett, Henry
Saint Patrick.
St. Patrick Was a Gentleman.

Bennett, Henry Holcomb
Flag Goes By, The.

Bennett, John
Abbot of Derry, The.
God Bless You, Dear, To-Day!
Her Answer.
In a Rose Garden.
Ingenious Little Old Man, The.
Master Sky-Lark, *sels.*
Seven Themes from the Zoo, No.2
Sky Lark's Song, The.
Song of the Hunt, The.
Song of the Spanish Main, The.
Tiger's Tale, A.
To Marie.

Bennett, Joseph Deericks
Autumnall.
Complaint.
Earthly Love.
Headsong.
On the Nativity of Christ Our Lord.
Pointillism.
Quatrina.
To C. T. C.
To Eliza, Duchess of Dorset.

Bennett, Lerone, Jr
Blues and Bitterness.

Bennett, Murray
Funeral.

Bennett, Peggy
Mother Is a Sun, A.
Parable.
Shut Up, I Said.
Snap Judgement on the Llama, A.

Bennett, Rodney
Christmas-Tree Song, A.
Easter Praise.
Fluttering Leaves.
Growing River, The.
Little Brown Seed.
Little Old Lady, The.
Merry Birds.
Mr. Brown.
Mrs. Jenny Wren.
My Dog, Spot.
Pigeons, The.
Postman's Knock.
Robin's Song.
Ten Little Christmas Trees.
Thank You for Friends, A.
There—and Back.
Three Little Men in a Boat.
Wireless.
Writing Letters.

Bennett, Rowena Bastin
Airplane, The.
April Puddle.
Boats.
Christmas Brownie.
Color.
Come, Ride with Me to Toyland.
Conversation between Mr. and Mrs. Santa Claus.
Conversation with an April Fool.
Elfin Plane, The.
End-of-Summer Poem.
Fire on the Hearth.
Four Seasons.
Freight Train, The.
Golden Cobwebs.
Grumbling Truck, The.
If I Were a Pilgrim Child.
Jack-in-the-Pulpit.
Lady Sleep.
Meeting the Easter Bunny.
Mrs. C. (Or Any Other Too Practical Person).
Modern Dragon, A.
Motor Cars.
Necks.
Picture People.
Pockets.
Pussy Willows.
Remembering the Winter.
Rubber Boots.
Saying a Prayer.
Shell Castles.
Smoke Animals.
Sunrise.
Tails.
Thanksgiving Magic.
Trails of Smoke.
Umbrellas.
Under the Tent of the Sky.
Vacation Time.
Witch Cat.
Witch of Willowby Wood, The.
Zeppelin, The.

Bennett, S. F.
In the Sweet By and By.

Bennett, William Cox
Baby May.
Be Mine, and I Will Give Thy Name.
Christmas Song, A.
Invocation to Rain in Summer.

Lullaby, O Lullaby.
Right above the Wrong, The, 1857.
Summer Invocation.
To a Cricket.
Wife's Song, A.
Winter Song, A.
Benoit, Pierre
Diaduminius.
Bensel, James Berry
Ahmed.
February.
Benson, Arthur Christopher
After Construing.
Amen.
English Shell, An.
Knapweed.
Land of Hope and Glory.
Lord Vyet.
Phoenix, The.
Prelude: "Hush'd is each busy shout."
Realism.
Benson, Louis FitzGerald
Dedication: "O thou whose gracious presence blest," *abr.*
Dedication for a Home.
Far Trumpets Blowing.
Light of God is Falling, The.
O Thou Whose Feet Have Climbed Life's Hill.
O Thou Whose Gracious Presence Blest.
Songs of Jesus.
Benson, Margaret
Once on a Time.
Benson, Mary Josephine
Smoking Flax.
Benson, Nathaniel Anketell
Holy Night.
Year's End.
Benson, Robert Hugh
After a Retreat.
At High Mass.
Priest's Lament, The.
Teresian Contemplative, The.
Benson, Stella
Five Smooth Stones.
Words.
Bent, O. M.
Robin, The.
Bentley, Beth
Waltz in the Afternoon, A.
Bentley, Edmund Clerihew
After dinner Erasmus.
Art of Biography, The.
Biography for Beginners.
Cervantes.
Clerihews, *sels.*
Clive.
"Dear me!" exclaimed Homer.
Dr. Clifford.
Geoffrey Chaucer.
George the Third.
Great Duke of Wellington, The.
Great Emperor Otto, The.
If only Mr. Roosevelt.
Intrepid Ricardo, The.
J. S. Mill.
Liszt.
Lord Clive.
Mr. Bernard Shaw.
Mr. Hilaire Belloc.
Savonarola.
Sir Christopher Wren.
Sir Humphry Davy.
Sir Walter Raleigh.
When Alexander Pope.
Younger Van Eyck, The.
Bentley, Nicolas
On Mrs. W——.
Bentley, Richard
Reply to an Imitation of the Second Ode in the Third Book of Horace, A.

Verses: "Who strives to mount Parnassus hill."
Benton, Frank
Old Buck's Ghost.
Benton, Joel
Abraham Lincoln.
At Chappaqua.
Grover Cleveland.
Hallowe'en.
Poet, The.
Scarlet Tanager, The.
Benton, Myron B.
Mowers, The.
Benton, Patricia
Desert River.
Benton, Walter
I saw autumn today. . .incipiently, on the sunset.
It was like something done in fever, when nothing fits.
Summary of the Distance between the Bomber and the Objective.
This Is My Beloved, *sels.*
White full moon like a great beautiful whore, The.
With the Most Susceptible Element, the Mind, Already Turned under the Toxic Action.
Benveniste, Asa
Gardeners, The.
Benvenuta, Sister Mary
Hawkesyard.
Mater Incognita.
Song of White and Red, A.
Béranger, Pierre Jean de
Garret, The.
King of Yvetot, The.
Berceo, Gonzalo de
He walked those mountains wild, and lived within that nook.
Life of San Millan, *sel.*
Miracles of Our Lady, The, *sel.*
San Miguel de la Tumba.
Berenberg, David Paul
Or is it all illusion? Do the years.
Two Sonnets.
Bereng, David Granmer T.
Birth of Moshesh, The.
Berg, Stephen
Animals, The.
Between Us.
Dreaming with a Friend.
Entering the Body, *sel.*
Glimpse of the Body Shop, A.
Gooseberries.
Holes, The.
Ollie, Answer Me.
People Trying to Love.
Survivor, The.
To My Friends.
Wife Talks to Herself, A.
Bergé, Carole
Chiaroscuro.
Bergengren, Ralph Wilhelm
Apple Blossoms.
Dirigible, The.
Worm, The.
Berger, Art
No Generation Gap, *sel.*
When I was a young man/ coming up.
Bergman, Alexander
April 29th.
Chronicler, The.
Letter.
Bergonzi, Bernard
Anemones for Miss Austen.
Bergquist, Beatrice
Song of the Robin, The.
Berkeley, George
On the Prospect of Planting Arts and Learning in America.

Verses on the Prospect of Planting Arts and Learning in America.
Berkeley [*or* Berkley], Sir William
Lost Lady, The, *sel.*
Where Did You Borrow That Last Sigh?
Berkson, Bill
Blind Geronimo.
"Blue Is the Hero."
Call It Goofus.
Christmas Eve.
East End.
February.
Ivesiana.
Leave Cancelled.
October.
Oscar.
Out There.
Russian New Year.
Sound from Leopardi.
Stanky.
Strawberry Blond.
Surabaja [*or* Surabaya].
Variation.
Berlin, Irving
God Bless America.
Bernard [*or* Bernart] de Ventadour [*orentadorn*],
Canzo: "When fresh grass-blades and leaves appear."
Lark, The.
No Marvel Is It.
Troubadour Song: "'Tis no wonder if my songs."
Bernard of Clairvaux, Saint
Conqueror Renowned, The.
Hail, Thou Head!
His Salvation.
In Thine hour of holy sadness.
Jesu Dulcis.
King in His Beauty, The.
Of Our Lord's Passion, *sel.*
Passion Hymn.
Thy Kingdom Come.
Wide Open Are Thy Loving Hands.
Bernard of Cluny [*or* of Morlaix],
Celestial Country, The.
De Contemptu Mundi, *sels.*
Jerusalem.
Jerusalem, the Golden.
Mariale, *sel.*
Morning Shall Awaken, The.
Bernart of Ventadorn *See* **Bernard de Ventadour**
Bernetta, Sister Mary
One Day at Rouen.
Bernhardt, Clara
Sailor's Wife, A.
Berrigan, Daniel
Aunt, The.
Everything That Is.
Haydn: The Horn.
Here the Stem Rises.
If Stones Can Dream.
News Stand, The.
Poet Prays Her, The.
Somewhere the Equation Breaks Down.
To a Dead Poet, His Book.
To Wallace Stevens.
Berrigan, Ted
Bean Spasms.
For You.
Grace to be born and live as variously as possible.
I wake up back aching from soft bed Pat.
It is a human universe: and I.
It's 8:54 A.M. in Brooklyn it's the 28th of July and.
Many Happy Returns.
Personal Poem #8.
Personal Poem #7.
Poem upon the page is as massive as, The.

Berrigan (continued)
Resolution.
Sonnet: "Academy of the future is opening its doors, The."
Sonnet: "Dear Marge, hello. It is 5:15 a.m."
Sonnet: "Each tree stands alone in stillness."
Sonnet: "In Joe Brainard's collage its white arrow."
Sonnet: "Into the closed air of the slow."
Sonnet for Dick Gallup, A.
Summer so histrionic, marvelous dirty days.
Sweeter than sour apples flesh to boys.
Words for Love.
Berry, H. W.
To an Egyptian Boy.
Berry, Wendell
Ascent.
Canticle.
Guest, The.
Man Walking and Singing, A.
May Song.
November Twenty-sixth Nineteen Hundred and Sixty-three.
Peace of Wild Things, The.
Supplanting, The.
Berryman, John
April Fool's Day, or, St. Mary of Egypt.
Ball Poem, The.
Canto Amor.
Cloud and Flame.
Conversation.
Desires of Men and Women.
Dispossessed, The.
Dream Songs, The, *sels.*
Governor your husband lived so long, The.
Henry's Confession.
Homage to Mistress Bradstreet.
Moon and the Night and the Men, The.
New Year's Eve.
Note to Wang Wei.
Parting as Descent.
Snow Line.
Song of the Tortured Girl, The.
Spinning Heart, The.
Statue, The.
Sympathy, a Welcome, A.
That dark brown rabbit, lightness in his ears.
Three around the Old Gentleman.
Traveller, The.
When by me in the dusk my child sits down.
Whether There Is Sorrow in the Demons.
Winter Landscape.
Bersohn, Robert
Dignity of Labor, The.
Bertram, James
Epitaph for an American Bomber.
Rondeau in Wartime.
Bertrand, Sister Mary
Our Lady of Mercy.
Our Lady of the Apocalypse.
Bertrand [*or* Bertran *or* Bertrans]
A Perigord pres del muralh.
Planh for the Young English King.
Protestation.
Song of Battle.
War Song, A.
Well Pleaseth Me the Sweet Time of Easter.
Berwick, Thurso
Idleset: "Ill's the airt o the word the day."
Besant, Sir Walter
Day Is Coming, The.
To Daphne.
Best, Charles
Looke How the Pale Queene.
Moon, The.
Of the Moon.
Sonnet of the Moon, A.
Best, Susie Montgomery
Ich Dien.
Thanksgiving.
Betham-Edwards, Matilda Barbara
Child's Hymn, A.
Child's Prayer, A.
Gethsemane.
Pansy and the Prayer-Book, The.
Valentine, A.
Bethell, Mary Ursula ("Evelyn Hayes")
Detail.
Garden-Lion.
Long Harbour, The.
Looking Down on Mesopotamia.
Pause.
Small Hours, The.
Spring Snow and Tui.
Weather.
Bethune, George Washington
Blessed Name, The.
He Died for Me.
It Is Not Death to Die.
O Jesus! When I Think of Thee.
Bethune, Lebert
Blue Tanganyika.
Bwagamoyo.
Harlem Freeze Frame.
Juju of My Own, A.
To Strike for Night.
Betjeman, John
Archaeological Picnic, The.
Arrest of Oscar Wilde at the Cadogan Hotel, The.
Arrogance Repressed.
Before Invasion, 1940.
Before the Anaesthetic; or, A Real Fright.
Blackfriars.
Bristol and Clifton.
Business Girls.
Child Ill, A.
Christmas.
Cottage Hospital, The.
Deal out again the dog-eared poetry books.
Dear Old Village, The.
Death in Leamington.
Diary of a Church Mouse.
East Anglian Bathe.
Eunice.
False Security.
Great Central Railway, Sheffield Victoria to Banbury.
Greenaway.
Hunter Trials.
In a Bath Teashop.
In Memoriam: A. C., R. J. O., K. S.
In the Public Gardens.
In Westminster Abbey.
Incident in the Early Life of Ebenezer Jones, Poet, 1828, An.
Indoor Games near Newbury.
Ireland with Emily.
Late-Flowering Lust.
Licorice Fields at Pontefract, The.
Lincolnshire Tale, A.
London.
Margate, 1940.
Matlock Bath.
"New King Arrives in His Capital by Air . . ."—Daily Newspaper.
Norfolk.
North Coast Recollections.
Old Liberals, The.
Olympic Girl, The.
Parliament Hill Fields.
Planster's Vision, The.
Potpourri from a Surrey Garden.
Remorse.
St. Saviour's, Aberdeen Park, Highbury, London, N.
Seaside Golf.
Senex.
Shropshire Lad, A.
Slough.
Subaltern's Love-Song, A.
Summoned by Bells, *sel.*
Sunday Afternoon Service in St. Enodoc Church, Cornwall.
Sunday Morning, King's Cambridge.
Town Clerk's Views, The.
Trebetherick.
Upper Lambourne.
Village Inn, The.
Wantage Bells.
Westgate-on-Sea.
Youth and Age on Beaulieu River, Hants.
Betts, Craven Langstroth
Don Quixote.
Hollyhocks, The.
Longfellow.
To the Moonflower.
Unseen World, The.
Betts, Frank
Pawns, The.
Bevington, Helen Smith
Bowl of October, A.
Honeybee, The.
It's a debatable land. The winds are variable.
Man from Porlock, The.
Nature Study, After Dufy.
Report from the Carolinas, *sel.*
Summer Fable, from Montaigne, A.
Bewe, —— Beware of Sirens
Bey, Yillie (William Manns, II)
Making of a Militant.
Beyer, Evelyn
Jump or Jiggle.
Beza, Theodore
Description of Vertue.
Marcus Tullius Cicero's Death.
Now have I lived, O Rome, enough for me.
Bezruc, Petr
Ostrava.
Bezymensky, Alexander Ilyich
Village and Factory.
Bhai Vir Singh
Dream of Love.
Bhanot, V.
I Am Alone ("I am alive to loneliness").
Bhartrihari
Angler, The.
Arrows of Love.
Better in the Wild.
Better Part, The.
By Shaded Wells.
Dignity.
Dilemma.
Flaming Banners.
Friend or Stranger.
Half-Way Knowledge.
Heart in Brahma, The.
In the Days of Thy Youth.
Loaded Ass, The.
Love Grows by What It Feeds On.
Love in Moonlight.
Love, the Fisher.
Nothing and the Soul.
Peace.
Round Robin.
Sign, The.
Snake and the Mouse, The.
Struggling Fancies.
Stubborn Fool, The.
Sweet and Bitter.
Time.
Two as One.
When I Knew a Little Bit.

Why My Poems Died.
Wise Misogynist, The.
Women's Eyes.
Bhasa
Dialogue from "The Dream Queen."
Dream Queen, The, *sel.*
Moon, The.
Bhushan, V. N.
Creation.
Bialik, Hayyim Nahman [*or* Chaim Nachman]
Alone.
Beneath Thy Wing.
Blessing over Food.
City of Slaughter, The.
Dance of Despair, The.
Dead of the Wilderness, The.
Death of David, The.
For Hanukkah.
Grasshopper's Song, The.
Graveyard, The.
I Know on a Night Overcast.
If Thou Wouldst Know.
Mathmid, The.
Midnight Prayer.
Night.
On a hill there blooms a palm.
Queen Sabbath.
Should I Be a Rabbi?
Songs of the People, *sels.*
Stars Are Lit, The.
Sunset.
Talmud Student, The.
Throbs the Night with Mystic Silence.
Two steps from my garden rail.
When the Days Shall Grow Long.
Whence and Whither.
Young Acacia, The.
Bianchi, Martha Gilbert Dickinson
Forgiveness Lane.
Heaven.
Her Music.
Priest's Prayer, A.
Reality.
Separation.
Unanswered.
Bianco, Francesco
Cry, A.
Feather.
Lakes.
Washington Square.
Bianor
Loss after Loss.
Bibbs, Hart Leroi
Dirge for J. A. Rogers.
"Liberalissimo."
Six Sunday.
Split Standard.
Bible, Apocrypha
Baruch, *sel.*
Blessed Is God ("Blessed is God that liveth forever").
Dirge: "Her house is become like a man dishonored."
Ecclesiasticus, *sels.*
First Maccabees, *sels.*
Great Mourning.
Judas Maccabeus.
Judith, *sels.*
Let Us Now Praise Famous Men.
Music.
On Death—a Sonnet.
Path of Wisdom, The.
Praise of Famous Men.
Snow.
Sun, Moon and Stars.
Test of Men, The.
Tobit, *sel.*
Tyrant's Death, The.
Wisdom.
Wisdom of Solomon, The, *sels.*
". . .With Timbrels."
Bible, New Testament
Acts, The, *sels.*
Adoration of the Shepherds, The.
Angels of Bethlehem, The.
Apocalypse.
Be of Good Cheer.
Beatitudes, The.
Benedictus.
Brotherhood.
Charity.
Child of Nazareth, The.
Children of the Light.
Christmas Eve.
Christmas Story, The.
Come unto Me.
Death of Jesus, The.
Death's Conqueror.
Duties of Man, The.
Easter Morning.
Effective Prayer.
Ephesians, *sel.*
Evidence, The.
First Christmas, The.
First Corinthians, *sels.*
First John, *sel.*
Glory of God Revealed in Jesus, The.
God Provides.
God Was in Christ.
Good Samaritan, The.
Good Shepherd, The.
Good Tidings.
Gospel of Love, The.
Great Commandment, The.
Greater Love Hath No Man.
Greatest of These, The.
Greatness of Love, The.
Hebrews, *sel.*
Hymn of the Blessed Virgin, The.
I Am the Bread of Life.
In the Beginning Was the Word.
Inscription on the Cross.
Jesus and the Children.
Jesus and the Woman at the Well.
Jesus Answers the Pharisees.
Jesus Eats with Sinners.
Jesus' Parable of the Sower.
Last Judgment, The.
Last Supper, The.
Light of the World, The.
Lord's Prayer, The.
Lost Sheep, The.
Love.
Love Is Patient.
Love One Another.
Love the Indispensable and Crowning Grace.
Magnificat, The.
Mary and Elizabeth.
Mary and Gabriel.
Mary and Simeon.
My Peace I Give unto You.
My Yoke Is Easy.
Mystery of Death, The.
New Jerusalem, The.
Nunc Dimittis, The.
On Taking up One's Cross.
On the Road to Emmaus.
Parable of the Talents, The.
Paul on the Road to Damascus.
Peace of Christ, The.
Pharisee and the Publican, The.
Philippians, *sel.*
Poem of the Our Father, The.
Poems by the Roadside.
Prelude of the New Testament ("Hail Mary full of grace!").
Prodigal Son, The.
Revelation, *sels.*
Rich Man and the Kingdom of Heaven, The.
Romans, *sels.*
St. John, *sels.*
St. Luke, *sels.*
St. Mark, *sels.*
St. Matthew, *sels.*
St. Paul on Charity.
Second Corinthians, *sels.*
Second Timothy, *sel.*
Sermon on the Mount, The.
Sparrow, The.
Spiritual Gifts.
There Shall Be No Night.
Things That Are Caesar's, The.
Think on These Things.
Tidings of Great Joy.
To Him Be Glory.
To His Disciples.
Treasures.
Treasures in Heaven.
True Vine, The.
Visit of the Wise Men, The.
When the Son of Man Shall Come in His Glory.
Widow's Mite, The.
Wise and Foolish Virgins, The.
Woman Clothed with the Sun, A.
Woman Taken in Adultery, The.
Word, The.
Ye Are the Temple of God.
Bible, Old Testament
Abraham and Isaac.
Adam and Eve.
Address of Ruth to Naomi.
Affliction.
After the Flood Went Down, God Said.
All Flesh Is Grass.
All Is Vanity.
Amos, *sel.*
And There Shall Come Forth.
And They Shall Beat Their Swords into Plowshares.
Apocrypha.
Arise, My Love, My Fair One.
As a Seal upon Thy Heart.
As Fowlers Lie in Wait.
Awake!
Balaam's Blessing.
Be Thankful unto Him.
Beati Omnes.
Beatus Vir.
Behold, My Servant.
Behold, Thou Art Fair.
Belshazzar's Feast.
Benediction.
Better Path, The.
Blessed of the Lord Be His Land.
Blessing, A.
Blessing of the Priests.
But Fear Thou Not, O Jacob.
Call for True Repentance, A.
Canticle of Canticles.
Cast Thy Bread Upon the Waters.
Child Moses, The.
Choose Life.
Closing Doxology, The.
Comfort When Work Seems Difficult.
Comfort Ye, Comfort Ye My People.
Creation, The.
Cry in Distress, A ("My God, my God, why hast thou forsaken me?").
Cry of the Daughter of My People, The.
Cum Invocarem.
Cursed Be the Day.
Daniel, *sel.*
David and Bathsheba.
David and Goliath.
David's Lament.
De Profundis.
Deliverance of Jehovah, The.
Desolation in Zion.
Deuteronomy, *sels.*

Bible (continued)
Domine Quid Multiplicati Sunt.
Downfall of the Tyrant.
Drunkard, The.
Earth Abideth Forever, The.
Ecclesiastes.
End of the World, The.
Enjoy the Good.
Entreat Me Not to Leave Thee.
Eternal Quest, The.
Everlasting Arms, The.
Except the Lord Build the House.
Exodus, *sels.*
Ezekiel, *sels.*
Fear of the Lord, The.
First Kings, *sel.*
First Samuel, *sels.*
Floods Clap Their Hands, The.
Fool Hath Said in His Heart, The.
Foolish Woman, A.
For, Lo, the Winter Is Past.
For Ye Shall Go out with Joy.
Four Things.
Garden of Eden, The.
Genesis, *sels.*
Give Ear, O Ye Heavens.
Give Ear, Ye Heavens.
Glory of God, The.
Go to the Ant.
God, Our Dwelling Place.
God Our Refuge.
God Replies.
Godly and the Ungodly, The.
God's Glory.
God's Precepts Perfect.
Good Wife, The.
Habakkuk, *sel.*
Hallelujah.
Hallelujah Chorus, A.
Hannah's Song of Thanksgiving.
Happy Is the Man.
Happy Is the Man That Findeth Wisdom.
Hark! My Beloved!
Hay Appeareth, The.
He That Is Slow to Anger.
Hear the Word of the Lord.
Heathen Are Come into Thine Inheritance, The.
Heavens, The.
Heavens Above and the Law Within, The.
Heavens Declare the Glory of God, The.
Ho, Everyone That Thirsteth.
Horse, The.
House of Wisdom, The (" Wisdom hath builded her house").
How Are the Mighty Fallen.
How Beautiful upon the Mountains.
How Glorious Is Thy Name.
How Is the Gold Become Dim.
How Lovely Are Thy Tabernacles.
Hymn of the World Within, The.
Hymn of the World Without.
Hymns of Praise.
I Am My Beloved's.
I Am the Rose of Sharon.
I Have a Goodly Heritage.
I Return unto Zion.
I Sleep, but My Heart Waketh.
I Waste Away.
I Will Lift Up Mine Eyes unto the Hills.
I Will Sing Praise.
Immortality.
In Darkness and Aridity.
In the End of Days.
Intemperance.
Intreat [*or* Entreat] Me Not to Leave Thee.
Isaiah, *sels.*
Isaiah's Angels.
Isaias.
Israel, My Servant.
It Is Better . . .
Jehovah's Immovable Throne.
Jephthah's Daughter.
Jeremiah, *sels.*
Job, *sels.*
Jonah, *sels.*
Jonah's Prayer.
Joseph and His Brethen.
Judges, *sels.*
Keep Not Thou Silence.
Lamentation.
Lamentation for the Fall of Jerusalem.
Lamentations, *sels.*
Lauda Anima Mea.
Laudate Dominum.
Law Within, The.
Leader, The.
Leave It All Quietly to God.
Legacy, The.
Let Me Alone.
Let Me Sing of My Well-Beloved.
Let the Day Perish.
Let the Nations Be Glad.
Leviathan.
Life's Uncertainty.
Lift up Your Heads.
Lift Up Your Heads, O Ye Gates.
Light Is Sweet, The.
Like unto Them That Dream.
Lips of the Wise, The.
Live Joyfully.
Lo, the Winter Is Past.
Lord Gave, The.
Lord Is a Man of War, The.
Lord Is Good to All, The.
Lord Is My Shepherd, The.
Lord, Make Me to Know Mine End.
Lord's My Shepherd, The.
Love.
Love Lyrics.
Merry Heart, A.
Messiah, The.
Micah, *sels.*
Mighty Fortress, A.
Misery of Jerusalem, The.
Mother of the House, The.
My Light and My Salvation.
My Soul Is Weary of My Life.
My Soul Thirsteth for God.
My Thoughts Are Not Your Thoughts.
Naomi and Ruth.
Neither Poverty nor Riches.
Neither Shall They Learn War Any More.
Nineteenth Psalm, The.
Noah and the Flood.
Not Flesh of Brass.
Numbers, *sels.*
O Lord, How Excellent Is Thy Name.
O Lord, How Long Shall I Cry?
O Lord, Thou Hast Enticed Me.
Oh That I Knew Where I Might Find Him.
Oh That I Were in the Wilderness.
O Ye That Would Swallow the Needy.
Ocean, The.
Of God's Great power in the Leviathan.
On My Bed I Sought Him.
Open Thy Doors, O Lebanon.
Our Help.
Our Refuge.
Out of the Whirlwind.
Peace! and There Is No Peace.
Peaceable Kingdom, The.
Perfect Peace.
Pilgrim's Song.
Potter and the Clay, The.
Power from God.
Praise the Lord, O My Soul!
Price of Wisdom, The.
Prince of Peace.
Prince of Peace, The.
Protection of Jehovah, The.
Proverbs, *sels.*
Psalm of David, A.
Psalm of David, A.
Psalm of Praise.
Psalms, *sels.*
Rainbow, The.
Refuge, The.
Remember Also Thy Creator.
Remember Now Thy Creator.
Remember Then Thy Creator.
Reproof, A.
Return, Return, O Shulammite.
Rich Earth, The.
Rod of Jesse, The.
Ruth.
Ruth to Naomi.
Samuel, Book I.
Samuel, Book II.
Search, The.
Searcher of Hearts Is Thy Maker, The.
Second Samuel, *sels.*
Serenity of Faith, The.
Set Me as a Seal.
Seven Evils.
She of the Impudent Face.
Shepherd's Psalm, The.
Sing unto Jehovah [*or* the Lord].
Sluggard, The—a Sonnet.
Solomon Judges between Two Women Disputing over a Child.
Song of Deborah [and Barak], The.
Song of Exile, A.
Song of Hannah, The.
Song of Moses, The.
Song of Praise, A.
Song of Praise, A.
Song of Safety, A.
Song of Solomon, The.
Song of Songs, The.
Song of Supplication, A.
Song of the Harlot.
Song of the Well.
Song of Trust, A.
Sower of Discord, A.
Sparrow, The.
Spring.
Story of Ruth, The.
Ten Commandments, The.
Thanksgiving.
Thanksgiving.
Then Sang Deborah and Barak.
Then Sang Moses.
Then the Lord Answered.
They That Go Down to the Sea in Ships.
They That Wait upon the Lord.
Thou Wilt Revive Me.
Though the Earth Be Removed.
Thy Mother Was like a Vine.
Time for Everything, A.
Time of the Singing of Birds, The.
To Dwell Together in Unity.
Too Wonderful.
Treasures, The.
Tree and the Chaff, The.
Triumphal Chant.
Twenty-fourth Psalm, The [*wr.*].
Twenty-third Psalm, The.
Vanity.
Vanity of Vanities.
Virtuous Wife, The.
Virtuous Woman, The.
Vision of the Day of Judgment.
Voice from the Whirlwind, The; God's Majesty.
Voice of Wisdom, The.
Voice Out of the Whirlwind, The.
War-Horse, The.
Watchman, What of the Night?
What Doth the Lord Require?
What Is Man?

When Israel Came Forth Out of Egypt.
Where Shall Wisdom Be Found?
Wherewith Shall I Come before the Lord?
Who Maketh the Grass to Grow.
Whom Shall One Teach.
Wine and Woe.
Wings.
Winter Is Past, The.
Woe Is Me!
Word Fitly Spoken, A.
Words of Agur, The.
Words of the Preacher, The.
Youth and Age.
Zechariah, *sels.*
Bible, Pseudepigrapha
Enoch, *sels.*
Seven Metal Mountains, The.
Wisdom's Plight.
Bickerstaffe, Isaac
Expostulation, An.
Jolly Miller, The.
Love in a Village, *sels.*
Song: "How happy were my days."
Song: "There was a jolly miller once."
There Was a Jolly Miller.
What Are Outward Forms?
Bickersteth, Edward Henry, Bishop of Exeter
Give Us Men!
O God, the Rock of Ages.
Peace, Perfect Peace.
Prince of Peace, The.
Biebesheimer, Julia
Hours of Prayer.
Bierbaum, Otto Julius
Blacksmith Pain.
Jeannette.
Kindly Vision.
Oft in the Silent Night.
Bierce, Ambrose
Another Way.
Bride, The.
Creation.
Death of Grant, The.
Hero, The.
Montefiore.
My country 'tis of thee./ Sweet land of felony.
Presentiment.
T. A. H.
Bigelow, Marguerite Ogden *See* **Wilkinson, Marguerite Ogden Bigelow**
Biggar, H. Howard
Your Neighbor.
Biggs, Maurice
Spring Offensive, 1941.
Bilal
Muhammedan Call to Prayer.
Bilderdijk, Willem
Prayer: "Merciful God, who readst my inmost mind."
Bilhana
Black Marigolds.
Death Sends Me the Flickering of Powdery Lids.
Her Mouth Carelessly Scented.
I Have a Need.
I Have No Surety.
I Know My Princess.
I know That I Have Savoured.
I Love Long Black Eyes.
I Mind That I Went Round with Men and Women.
I Mind the Coming.
I Mind the Time of the Falling of Blossoms.
I See Her.
I See the Heavy Startled Hair.
I Seem to See My Prison Walls.
If I See in My Soul.
If My Girl with Lotus Eyes.
Love Is a God.
My Eyes That Hurry to See.
Pleased Intimacy, The.
She Swims Back in the Crowning Hour.
She with Young Limbs.
Spread We Our Nets.
Stainless Fair Appearance, The.
When All My Heavy Heart.
Woodcutter and the Fisherman Turn Home, The.
Biller, Matthew
American Freedom, The.
"Billings, Josh" (Henry Wheeler Shaw)
Explanation.
Billings, William
Chester.
David's Lamentation.
When Jesus Wept.
Bingham, G. Clifton
Love's Old Sweet Song.
Binney, Thomas
Eternal Light!
Binns, Elsie
Christmas Is Remembering.
Smallest Angel, The.
Binyon, Laurence
Amasis.
August.
Bab-Lock-Hythe.
Beauty.
Belfry, The.
Burning of the Leaves, The.
Day's End.
Dray, The.
Eleonora Duse as Magda.
Ezekiel.
Ferry Hinksey.
Fetching the Wounded.
Fog.
For the Fallen.
Glimpse of Time, A.
History.
House That Was, The.
Hunger.
In Misty Blue.
Invocation to Youth.
It is early morning within this room; without.
Lament: "Fall now, my cold thoughts, frozen fall."
Little Dancers, The.
Little Hands.
Magnets.
My Boat Swings Out and Back.
Mystery of Dawn, ere yet the glory streams.
New Idol, A.
Nothing Is Enough.
November.
O World, Be Nobler.
Sirens, The, *sels.*
Song, A: "For Mercy, Courage, Kindness, Mirth."
Sower, The.
Sowing Seed.
Statues, The.
They went with songs to the battle.
This Is England.
Tristram's End.
Winter Sunrise, *sel.*
Woe to Him ("Woe to him that has not known the woe of man").
World-besieging storm, from horizon heaped and menacing.
Ypres.
Bion
Bion's Lament for Adonis.
Dream of Venus, A.
For Adonis I am crying, for Adonis' beauty dead.
I Dreamt I Saw Great Venus.
Lament for Adonis.
Biondi, Clemente
For a Blind Beggar's Sign.
Biram, John
Albatross, The.
Birche, William
Song between the Queen's Majesty and England, A.
Birckhead, Nancy
Everywhere.
Here I Am.
October.
Strange Teeth, The.
Bird, Robert Montgomery
Fairy Folk, The.
Bird, Stephan Moylan
May.
Silent Ranges, The.
Birdseye, George
Paradise.
Paradise; a Hindoo Legend.
Birkenhead, Sir John
Four-legg'd Elder, The; or, A Horrible Relation of a Dog and an Elder's Maid.
Birnbaum, Henry
Room I Once Knew, A.
When Silence Divests Me.
Birney, Earle
Bear on the Delhi Road, The.
Bushed.
Canada; Case History.
Cartagena de Indias.
Christmas Comes.
Climbers.
Damnation of Vancouver, *sel.*
David.
El Greco: Espolio.
For Steve.
Irapuato.
Man Is a Snow.
Mappemounde.
Monody on a Century.
North Star West.
On Going to the Wars.
Pacific Door.
Québec May.
Road to Nijmegen, The.
Sinalóa.
Slug in Woods.
Speech of the Salish Chief.
This Page My Pigeon.
Time-Bomb.
Vancouver Lights.
Walk in Kyoto, A.
Winter Saturday.
Birnie, Patrick
Auld Man's Mear's Dead, The.
Bishop, Annette
Rufflecumtuffle.
Bishop, Elizabeth
Armadillo, The—Brazil.
Arrival at Santos.
At the Fishhouses.
Bight, The.
Burglar of Babylon, The.
Casabianca.
Cirque d'Hiver.
Cold Spring, A.
Colder the Air, The.
Electrical Storm.
Filling Station.
First Death in Nova Scotia.
Fish, The.
Florida.
From the Country to the City.
House Guest.
Imaginary Iceberg, The.
Invitation to Miss Marianne Moore.
Jeronimo's House.
Large Bad Picture.
Late Air.

Bishop (continued)
Letter to N.Y.
Little Exercise.
Man-Moth, The.
Manuelzinho.
Map, The.
Miracle for Breakfast, A.
Monument, The.
Over 2000 Illustrations and a Complete Concordance.
Prodigal, The.
Riverman, The.
Roosters.
Sandpiper.
Seascape.
Sleeping on the Ceiling.
Songs for a Colored Singer.
Squatter's Children.
Unbeliever, The.
Under the Window: Ouro Preto.
View of the Capitol from the Library of Congress.
Visits to St. Elizabeths.
Wading at Wellfleet.
Weed, The.
While Someone Telephones.
Wit, The.
Bishop, G. E.
Bigger Day, The.
Bishop, John Peale
Admonition.
Apparition.
Birds of Paradise, The.
Boys, by Girls Held in Their Thighs.
Colloquy with a King-Crab.
Dream, The.
Fiametta.
Frieze, A.
Green and Pleasant Land, A.
Hours, The.
In the Dordogne.
Interlude, An.
Metamorphoses of M.
Ode: "Why will they never sleep."
Percy Shelley.
Perspectives Are Precipices.
Recollection, A.
Return, The.
Saint Francis.
Sleep brought me vision of my lady dead.
Speaking of Poetry.
Statue of Shadow, The.
Submarine Bed, The.
This Dim and Ptolemaic Man.
Triumph of Doubt, The.
Twelfth Night.
Why They Waged War.
Your Chase Had a Beast in View.
Bishop, Morris
Ambition.
Anatomy of Humor, The.
Complete Misanthropist, The.
Drinking Song for Present-Day Gatherings
$E = MC^2$
Early Morning.
Ecclesiastes.
Epitaph for a Funny Fellow.
Eschatology.
Ghoulish Old Fellow in Kent, A.
How to Treat Elves.
I Hear America Griping.
Immoral Arctic, The.
It Rolls On.
Limerick: "Clergyman out in Dumont, A."
Limerick: "Said a girl from beyond Pompton Lakes."
Limerick: "Said old Peeping Tom of Fort Lee."
Limerick: "There's a vaporish maiden in Harrison."
Lines Written in a Moment of Vibrant Ill-Health.
Merry Old Souls.
Mournful Numbers.
Naughty Preposition, The.
New Hampshire Boy, A.
Ozymandias Revisited.
Perforated Spirit, The.
Public Aid for Niagara Falls.
Salute to the Modern Language Association, A, Convening in the Hotel Pennsylvania, December 28th-30th.
Settling Some Old Football Scores.
Sing a Song of the Cities.
Song of the Pop-Bottlers.
Sonnet and Limerick.
Tales the Barbers Tell, The.
There's Money in Mother and Father.
Tonversation with Baby, A.
We Have Been Here Before.
What Hath Man Wrought Exclamation Point.
What was our trust, we trust not.
Who'd Be a Hero (Fictional)?
Winter Madrigal, A.
Witch of East Seventy-second Street, The.
Bishop, Roy
Inefficacious Egg, The.
Bishop, Samuel
At Newmarket.
Epigram: "Fool and knave with different views, A."
To His Wife, on the Fourteenth Anniversary of Her Wedding-Day, with a Ring.
To Mary.
Touchstone, The.
Bishop, Verna
Choose.
Bishop-Dubjinsky, G.
Alice 1963.
Is Here, As If.
My Daily Melon.
Now.
Pissarro's One Pure Note.
Quellisma, Seven Variations.
You (Her Eyes, Solstice).
Bitton, W. Nelson
Resurgam.
Bixler, William Allen
Beautiful.
Björnson, Björnstjerne
Boy and the Flute, The.
Child in Our Soul, The.
Fatherland Song (Norwegian National Hymn).
Synnöve's Song.
Tree, The.
Black, Austin
Soul.
Black, D. M.
Basilisk, The.
My Species.
Black, James M.
When the Roll Is Called up Yonder.
Black, MacKnight
Beside a Balance Wheel.
Corliss Engine-Wheel.
Express Trains.
Heart.
Night Express.
Rock, Be My Dream.
Structural Iron Workers.
"Black Bart."
I've labored long and hard for bread.
Blackburn, Alexander
What Makes a Nation Great?
Blackburn, Paul
Assistance, The.
Bañlbufar, a Brazier, Relativity, Cloud Formations & the Kindness & Relentlessness of Time.
Continuity, The.
Crossing, The.
El Camino Verde.
Encounter, The.
Good Morning Love!
Letter, The.
Málaga: Port.
Meditation on the BMT.
Night Song for Two Mystics.
Once-over, The.
One-Night Stand, The: An Approach to the Bridge.
Park Poem.
Problem, The.
Proposition, The.
Purse-Seine, The.
Routine, The.
Sirventes: "I have made a sirventes against the city of Toulouse."
Song of the Hesitations.
Stone, The.
Three Part Invention.
Yawn, The.
Blackburn, Thomas
Aftermath, An.
Easter Hymn.
Ganga.
Hospital for Defectives.
Lucky Marriage, The.
Not a Tree.
Oedipus.
Blackie, John Stuart
Emigrant Lassie, The.
My Bath.
My Loves.
Working Man's Song, The.
Blackmore, Sir Richard
Description of Chaos.
Prince Arthur, *sel.*
Blackmore, Richard Doddridge
Dominus Illuminatio Mea.
In the Hour of Death.
Yes.
Blackmur, Richard P.
All Things Are a Flowing.
Before Sentence Is Passed.
Dead Ride Fast, The.
Half-Tide Ledge.
In the Wind's Eye.
Mirage.
Missa Vocis.
On Common Ground.
One grey and foaming day.
Rape of Europa, The.
Scarabs for the Living.
Sea Island Miscellany, *sels.*
Too Much for One: Not Enough to Go Around.
Views of Boston Common and Nearby.
Where shall I go then.
Blackstock, Walter
Old Voyager.
Blackwell, Harriet Gray
Forest.
Hill People.
Blackwood, Algernon
Jack o' the Inkpot.
Blackwood, Helen Selina Sheridan *See* **Sheridan, Helen Selina**
Bladen, Peter
Coronation Day at Melrose.
Blaikie, John Arthur
Absence.
Love's Secret Name.
Song: "In thy white bosom Love is laid."
Blair, George
Carpenter of Nazareth, The.
Blair, Robert

Church and Church-yard at Night.
Friendship.
Grave, The.
Blaisdell, James Arnold
Beneath the Forms of Outward Rite.
Blake, Felicia
Woman's Answer to "The Vampire," A.
Blake, James Vila
In Him.
Blake, James W.
Sidewalks of New York, The.
Blake, Marie
Barter.
Blake, Mary
Song of Work, A.
Blake, Mary Elizabeth McGrath
Dawning o' the Year, The.
Blake, William
Abstinence and Desire.
Ah! Sunflower [Weary of Time].
Ah! weak and wide astray!
America, *sels.*
America; a Prophecy.
Ancient Proverb, An.
And Did Those Feet in Ancient Time.
Angel, The ("I asked a thief...").
Angel, The ("I dreamt a dream!").
Angel Singing, An.
Answer to the Parson, An.
Apparition, The.
Are not the joys of morning sweeter?
Auguries of Innocence.
Bard, The.
Birdsong.
Birds, The.
Blind-Man's Buff.
Blossom, The.
Book of Los, The, *sel.*
Book of Thel, The.
Book of Urizen, The.
But still the thunder of Los peals loud, and thus the thunders cry.
Caverns of the Grave I've Seen, The.
Character, A.
Chariot of Fire.
Children of a Future Age.
Chimney Sweeper, The ("A little black thing among the snow").
Chimney Sweeper, The ("When my mother died I was very young").
Choir of Day, The.
Clod and the Pebble, The.
Clod of Clay heard the Worm's voice and raised her pitying head, The.
Cradle Song, A: "Sleep! sleep! beauty bright."
Cradle Song, A: "Sweet dreams, form a shade."
Cromek ("A pretty sneaking knave").
Crystal Cabinet, The.
Cupid.
Dead brood over Europe, the cloud and vision descends over cheerful France, The.
Dedication of the Illustrations to Blair's "Grave," *sel.*
Divine Image, A ("Cruelty has a human heart").
Divine Image, The ("To Mercy, Pity, Peace, and Love").
Door of Death, The.
Dream, A.
Earth's Answer.
Echoing [*or* Ecchoing] Green, The.
Empire Is No More.
England! Awake! Awake! Awake!
Enion Replies from the Caverns of the Grave.
Enitharmon Revives with Los.
Epigram: Answer to the Parson, An.
Epigram: Character, A.
Epigram: Sir Joshua Reynolds.
Epigram: To English Connoisseurs.
Epigram: To Flaxman.
Epigram: To Hunt.
Epigraph: "I give you the end of a golden string."
Epilogue: "I am sure this Jesus will not do."
Epilogue: "Truly, My Satan, thou art but a Dunce."
Eternity ("He who bends [*or* binds] to himself a joy")
Ethinthus, Queen of Waters.
Europe, *sel.*
Everlasting Gospel, The, *sels.*
Every night and every morn.
Fields from Islington to Marybone, The.
Fly, The.
For the Sexes.
Four Zoas, The.
French Revolution, The, *sels.*
Garden of Love, The.
Gates of Paradise, The.
Ghost of Abel, The.
Gnomic Verses.
God appears, and God is Light.
Golden Net, The.
Good English Hospitality.
Great Things.
Grown Old in Love from Seven till Seven Times Seven.
Guardian Angels of the Creatures.
Hail Matrimony, made of love.
Happy Songs.
He has observ'd the golden rule.
Hear the Voice of the Bard (*Introd. to* Songs of Experience).
He's a blockhead who wants a proof of what he can't perceive.
Holy Thursday ("Is this a holy thing to see").
Holy Thursday (" 'Twas on a Holy Thursday").
How Sweet I Roamed from Field to Field.
Human Abstract, The.
Human Image, The, *sel.*
I ask'd my dear friend, Orator Prig.
I Asked a Thief [to Steal Me a Peach].
I Give You the End of a Golden String.
I Heard an Angel Singing.
I Laid Me Down upon a Bank.
I Saw a Chapel All of Gold.
I Saw a Monk of Charlemain [*or* Charlemaine].
I see the four-fold man, the humanity in deadly sleep.
Will Give You.
If You Trap the Moment.
Immortal, The.
In a wife I would desire.
In Deadly Fear.
Infant Joy.
Infant Sorrow.
Injunction.
Innocence.
Introduction: "Hear the voice of the Bard!"
Introduction: "Piping down the valleys wild."
Introduction to "Songs of Experience."
Introduction to "Songs of Innocence."
Island in the Moon, An, *sels.*
It Is Not So with Me.
Jerusalem, *sels.*
Jerusalem.
King Edward the Third, *sels.*
Lacedemonian Instruction.
Lamb, The.
Lamentation of Enion, The.
Land of Dreams, The.
Lark's Song, The.
Laughing Song.
Let liberty, the charter'd right of Englishmen.
Let the Brothels of Paris Be Opened.
Liberty.
Little Black Boy, The.
Little Boy Found, The.
Little Boy Lost ("Father! father! where are you going?").
Little Boy Lost, A ("Nought loves another as itself").
Little Girl Found, The.
Little Girl Lost, A ("Children of the future age").
Little Girl Lost, The ("In futurity/ I prophetic see").
Little Lamb.
Little Vagabond, The.
London ("I wander thro' each charter'd street").
London ("There souls of men are bought and sold").
Long John Brown and Little Mary Bell.
Los is by mortals nam'd Time, Enitharmon is nam'd Space.
Love to faults is always blind.
Love's Secret.
Mad Song.
Male & Female Loves in Beulah.
Many Birds.
Marigold, The.
Marriage.
Marriage of Heaven and Hell, The.
Marriage Ring, The.
Mayors, The.
Mental Traveller, The.
Merlin's Prophecy.
Milton, *sels.*
Mr. Cromek.
Mock On, Mock On, Voltaire, Rousseau.
Mockery.
Monk, The.
Morning.
Motto to the Songs of Innocence & of Experience.
My Pretty Rose Tree.
My Silks and Fine Array.
My Spectre around Me [Night and Day].
Never pain to tell thy love.
Never Seek to Tell Thy Love.
New Jerusalem, A [*or* The].
New Law, The.
Night ("Still the Faint harps").
Night ("The sun descending in the west").
Nightingale and Flowers.
Noise of trampling, the wind of trumpets, The.
Nurse's Song ("When the voices of children are heard on the green/ And laughing").
Nurse's Song ("When the voices of children are heard on the green/ And whisp'rings").
O Lapwing.
O Lord, wilt thou not look upon our sore afflictions.
On Another's Sorrow.
Only man that e'er I knew.
Piper, The.
"Piper, sit thee down and write."
Piping down the Valleys Wild (*Introd. to* Songs of Innocence).
Play Time.
Poet's Voice, The.
Poison Tree, A.
Popular Rhymes.
Preface: "And did those feet in ancient time."
Preface to "Milton."
Prelude: "And did those feet in ancient time."

Blake (continued)
Prelude: "England! awake! awake! awake!"
Prelude: "Fields from Islington to Marybone, The."
Price of Experience, The.
Proverbs of Hell.
Question Answer'd, The.
Reason and Imagination.
Reeds of Innocence.
Rhine was red with human blood, The.
Riches.
Robin Redbreast, A, *much abr.*
Schoolboy [*or* School Boy], The.
Scoffers, The.
Several Questions Answered.
Shepherd, The.
Sick Rose, The.
Silent, Silent, Night.
Sir Joshua praises Michael Angelo.
Sir Joshua Reynolds.
Sleep, Sleep, Beauty Bright.
Smile, The.
Soft deceit & idleness.
Soft Snow.
Song: "And did those feet in ancient time."
Song: "Fresh from the dewy hill, the merry year."
Song: "How sweet I roamed [*or* roam'd] from field to field."
Song: "I love the jocund dance."
Song: "Love and harmony combine."
Song: "Memory, hither come."
Song: "My silks and fine array."
Song: "Never seek to tell thy love."
Song of Enion.
Song of Enitharmon.
Song of Liberty, A.
Songs of Experience, *sels.*
Songs of Innocence, *sels.*
Sonnet: "Thou fair-haired angel of the evening."
Spring.
Stanzas from "Milton."
Sunflower, The.
Sweet Dreams Form a Shade.
Sword and the Sickle, The.
Take Thy Bliss, O Man.
Thel's Motto.
They said this mystery shall never cease.
Things to Remember.
Thou hast a lap full of seed.
Three Things to Remember.
Tiger, The.
Till We Have Built Jerusalem.
To Autumn.
To English Connoisseurs.
To Flaxman.
To God.
To Hayley.
To Hunt.
To Mrs. Ann Flaxman.
To Morning.
To My Friend Butts I Write.
To My Mirtle.
To Nobodaddy.
To Spring.
To Summer.
To the Accuser Who Is the God of This World.
To the Christians.
To the Evening Star.
To the Jews.
To the Muses.
To the Queen.
To Tirzah.
To Winter.
Two Epigrams.
Tyger, The.
Unquestioning.
Vala; or, The Four Zoas, *sels.*
Vision of Beulah.
Vision of Christ that thou dost see, The.
Vision of the Lamentation of Beulah, A.
Visions of the Daughters of Albion.
War Song, A.
War Song to Englishmen, A.
Was Jesus chaste?
"What are those Golden Builders doing?"
When a Man Has Married a Wife.
When Klopstock England Defied.
"When Old Corruption First Begun."
When the Green Woods Laugh.
Where to Seek Love.
Why cannot the Ear be closed to its own destruction?
Why Should I Care for the Men of Thames?
Wild Flower's Song.
Wild Thyme, The.
William Bond.
Wine-Press of Los, The.
With Happiness Stretch[e]d across the Hills.
Worm, The.
Written 1811.

Blamire, Susanna
Siller Croun, The.

Blanchard, Edith Richmond
Cats.

Blanchard, Laman
Art of Book-keeping, The.
False Love and True Logic.
Hidden Joys.
Nell Gwynne's Looking-Glass.
Ode to the Human Heart.
Whatever Is, Is Right.

Bland, Edith Nesbit *See* **Nesbit, Edith**

Bland, Henry Meade
Contrasts.

Bland, James A.
Carry Me Back to Old Virginny.
In the Evening by the Moonlight.
Oh! Dem Golden Slippers.
Old Virginny.

Blanden, Charles Granger
Ascent.
Enough.
"John Anderson, My Jo."
Paradise.
Passion Flower, The.
Quatrain: "Christ bears a thousand crosses now."
Rose Is a Royal Lady, The.
Song: "Life, in one semester."
Song: "What have the years left us?"
Song: "What trees were in Gethsemane."
Song the Grass Sings, A.
Songs I Sing, The.
Unknown God. The.
Valentine.
Via Lucis.

Blanding, Don
Aloha Oe.
Hollywood.
Journey Ends, A.
Soldier, What Did You See?
Vagabond House.

Blane, William
He Shall Bear the Glory.
Thirty Pieces of Silver.

Blankner, Frederika
Remainder.

Blaser, Robin
Faerie Queene, The, *sel.*
4 Part Geometry Lesson, A.
Herons.
Okay a nightingale.
Park, The.
Poem: "And when I pay death's duty."
Poem: "For years I've heard."
Poem by the Charles River.
Sophia Nichols.

Blasing, Randy
Book of Shells, A.
Dreams of the Accuser.
Dynasties, the Sky Overhead, The.
Oklahoma Plates.

Blazek, Douglas
Chicago Kid Winters.

Blenkhorn, Ada
Heavenly Stranger, The.

Blew, William John
O Lord, Thy Wing Outspread.

Blewett, Jean
At Quebec.
Song of the Golden Sea.

Blicher, Steen Steensen
Heather, The.

Blight, John
Becalmed.
Cat-o'-Nine-Tails, The.
Cormorants.
Crab.
Death of a Whale.
Stonefish and Starfish.

"Blind Harry." *See* **Henry The Minstrel**

Blind, Mathilde
After-Glow, The.
April Rain.
Dare Quam Accipere.
Dead, The.
Dost thou remember ever, for my sake.
Hymn to Horus.
I charge you, O winds of the West.
Love in Exile, *sels.*
Why will you haunt me unawares.

Bliss, H. W.
Understanding.

Bliss, Paul Southworth
Ulysses S. Grant.

Bliss, Philip Paul
More Holiness.

Bliss, P. P. *and* **Mary G. Brainard** *See* **Brainard, Mary Gardiner,** *and* **P. P. Bliss**

Blitzstein, Marc
Art for Art's Sake.
Cradle Will Rock, The, *sel.*

Blixen, Karen *See* **"Dinesen, Isak"**

Bloch, Jean-Richard
Idea of a Swimmer.

Bloch, Robert
Nightmare Number Four.

Block, Alexander Alexandrovich *See* **Blok, Aleksandr Aleksandrovich**

Block, Louis James
Fate.
Final Struggle, The.
Garden Where There Is No Winter, The.
New World, The, *sel.*
Tuberose.
Work.

Blocksidge, Charles William *See* **Baylebridge,William**

Bloede, Gertrude *See* **"Sterne, Stuart"**

Blok, Aleksandr Aleksandrovich
Aviator, The.
I Planted My Bright Paradise.
Little Catkins.
Russia.
Scythians, The.
She Came Out of the Frost.
Twelve, The.
Willow-Boughs, The.

Blood, Henry Ames
Comrades.
Shakespeare.

Bloomfield, Robert
Again, the year's decline, midst storms and floods.
Banks of Wye, The, *sels.*

Coracle Fishers, The.
Farmer's Boy, The, *sels.*
Health! I seek thee;—dost thou love.
Live, trifling incidents, and grace my songs.
Meandering Wye.
Moonlight . . . Scattered Clouds.
Shooter's Hill, *sel.*
Yet never fam'd was he, nor foremost found.
Bloomgarden [*or* Blumgarten], Solomon
See **"Yehoash"**
Blossom, Henry
Kiss Me Again.
Blount, Edward Augustus, Jr
Crew Poem, A.
Blouz, Hovhannes
Caravan, The.
Blum, Etta
When You Reach the Hilltop the Sky Is on Top of You.
Blumenthal, Walter Hart
Da Silva Gives the Cue.
Blundell of Crosby, William
England's Prayer.
Blunden, Edmund
Almswomen.
And mathematics, fresh as May.
And nigh this toppling reed, still as the dead.
Another Altar.
At the Great Wall of China.
Barn, The.
Behind the Line.
Bleue Maison.
Country God, A.
Eastern Tempest.
Festubert: The Old German Line.
Forefathers.
Giant Puffball, The.
Gods of the Earth Beneath, The.
Hurrying Brook, The.
Idlers, The.
In Festubert.
In My Time.
In Wiltshire.
Infantryman, An.
Into the Salient.
Late Light.
Les Halles d'Ypres.
May Day Garland, The.
Memory of Kent, The.
Midnight Skaters, The.
Mole Catcher.
Muffled.
New Moon,
1916 Seen from 1921.
November Morning.
Old Homes.
Pike, The.
Poor Man's Pig, The.
Psalm, A: "O God, in whom my deepest being dwells."
Recovery, The.
Reliques, *sel.*
Report on Experience.
Sheepbells.
Sheet Lightning.
Shepherd.
Sighing Time, The.
Silver Bird of Herndyke Mill, The.
Solutions.
Spell of France, The.
Sunlit Vale, The.
Survival, The.
Thiepval Wood.
Thoughts of Thomas Hardy.
Threshold.
To Our Catchment Board.
Trees on the Calais Road.
Uneasy Peace.
Veteran, The.
"View of the Present State of Ireland, A."
Vlamertinghe: Passing the Chateau.
Waggoner, The.
What Is Winter?
Wild Cherry Tree.
Winter in East Anglia.
Zillebeke Brook.
Zonnebeke Road, The.
Blunt, Hugh Francis
Candlemas.
What No Man Knoweth.
Blunt, Wilfrid Scawen
As to His Choice of Her.
Deeds That Might Have Been, The.
Depreciating Her Beauty.
Esther; a Young Man's Tragedy, *sels.*
Falcon, The.
Farewell: "Farewell, then. It is finished."
Farewell: "Juliet, farewell, I would not be forgiven."
Farewell to Juliet ("I see you, Juliet, still, with your straw hat").
Farewell to Juliet ("Juliet, farewell. I would not be forgiven").
Farewell to Juliet ("Lame, impotent conclusion to youth's dreams").
Gibraltar.
He Has Fallen from the Height of His Love.
Honour Dishonoured.
How Shall I Build.
In Answer to a Question.
In Vinculis, *sels.*
Laughter and Death.
Liberty, Equality, Fraternity.
Love Lyrics of Proteus, The, *sel.*
Love Sonnets of Proteus, The, *sels.*
Nocturne, A: "Moon has gone to her rest, The."
Old Squire, The.
On the Nature of Love.
Pleasures of Love, The.
Prison Sonnet.
St. Valentine's Day.
Sinner-Saint, The.
Song: "O fly not, Pleasure, pleasant-hearted Pleasure."
Sonnet: "Lame, impotent conclusion to youth's dreams."
Sonnet: "Love, how ignobly hast thou met thy doom!"
Sonnet: "Oh! leave the Past to bury its own dead."
Sonnet: "Why practise, love, this small economy?"
Sonnet: "Why should I hate you, love, or why despise."
Sonnet: "You ask my love. What shall my love then be?"
To a Happy Warrior.
To Manon, as to His Choice of Her.
To Manon, Comparing Her to a Falcon.
To Manon on Her Lightheartedness.
To Manon, on His Fortune in Loving Her.
To One on Her Waste of Time.
To One Who Would Make a Confession.
Two Highwaymen, The.
When I Hear Laughter.
Wisdom of Merlyn, The, *sels.*
With Esther.
Wouldst thou be wise, O Man? At the knees of a woman begin.
Written at Florence.
Bly, Robert
After Drinking All Night with a Friend, We Go Out in a Boat at Dawn to See Who Can Write the Best Poem.
After the Industrial Revolution.
After Working.
Afternoon Sleep.
Asian Peace Offers Rejected without Publication.
Awakening.
Barnfire during Church.
Clear Air of October, The.
Counting Small-Boned Bodies.
Depression.
Dream of Suffocation, A.
Driving to Town Late to Mail a Letter.
Driving toward the Lac Qui Parle River.
Ducks.
Executive's Death, The.
Getting Up Early.
Great Society, The.
Hatred of Men with Black Hair.
Hearing Men Shout at Night on MacDougal Street.
Hurrying Away from the Earth.
In a Train.
Looking at New-Fallen Snow from a Train.
Looking at Some Flowers.
Love Poem: "When we are in love, we love the grass."
Man Whom the Sea Kept Awake, The.
Man Writes to a Part of Himself, A.
Missouri Traveller Writes Home, A; 1830.
Night.
Old Boards.
Poem against the Rich.
Poem in Three Parts.
Puritan on His Honeymoon, The.
Romans Angry about the Inner World.
Silence.
Sleet Storm on the Merritt Parkway.
Snowfall in the Afternoon.
Surprised by Evening.
Taking the Hands.
Those Being Eaten by America.
Three Kinds of Pleasures.
Waking from Sleep.
Watching Television.
Watering the Horse.
When the Dumb Speak.
Where We Must Look for Help.
Written in Dejection near Rome.
Blyton, Enid
Fairy Music.
Field-Mouse, The.
What Piggy-Wig Found.
Winter.
Boake, Barcroft Henry
Where the Dead Men Lie.
Boas, Guy
Underground, The.
Bobston, Charles A.
Lovesick Cowboy, The.
Boccaccio, Giovanni
Apology for Love.
Fiammetta.
Inscription for a Portrait of Dante.
Of Fiammetta Singing.
Of His Last Sight of Fiammetta.
Of Three Girls and [of] Their Talk.
Olympia.
Queen of the Angels, The.
Sonnets, *sels.*
To Dante in Paradise, after Fiammetta's Death.
To One Who Had Censured His Public Exposition of Dante.
Tribute to Dante, A ("Dante Alighieri, a dark oracle").
Tribute to Dante, A ("If Dante mourns, there wheresoe'er he be").
Bock, Frederick
Big, Fat Summer—and the Lean and Hard.
For Marian Anderson.
Bode, Carl

Bode (continued)
Bad Children, The.
Burial of Terror, The.
City considered as a Tulip Tree, The.
Covent Garden Market.
Eastertide.
Feast of Saint Andrew the Apostle.
London Sonnets, *sels.*
Nocturne, The: "Why the hell do you use all that black."
Personal Letter to the Ephesians.
Planet, The.
Requiem.
Sacred Seasons, The, *sels.*
Sonnet: Head Next to Mine.
Sonnet: Window, The.
Variation on a Theme by Dylan Thomas.
Who Calls the English Cold?

Bode, John E.
O Jesus, I Have Promised.
To the End.

Bodenheim, Maxwell
Advice to a Blue-Bird.
Advice to a Forest.
City Girl.
Death.
Factory Girl.
Forgetfulness.
Here Is Your Realism.
Hill-Side Tree.
Impulsive Dialogue.
Interlude.
Interne, The.
Jack Rose.
Love.
Lynched Negro.
Metaphysical Poem.
Miner, The.
Minna.
Negroes.
New York City.
Old Age.
Old Jew, The.
Poem: "O men, walk on the hills."
Poem to Negro and Whites.
Poet to His Love.
Rear Porches of an Apartment Building.
Soldiers.
Songs to a Woman.
To a Discarded Steel Rail.
To an Enemy.

Boesch, Raymond
Life Is Leaving One Strange Port.

Boethius (Anicius Manlius Severinus Boethius)
Consolation of Philosophy, *sel.*
Happy Too Much.
O Stelliferi Conditor Orbis.
O Thou Whose Pow'r.
This Discord in the Pact of Things.

Bogan, Louise
After the Persian.
Alchemist, The.
Baroque Comment.
Cartography.
Cassandra.
Changed Woman, The.
Chanson un Peu Naïve.
Come, Break with Time.
Crossed Apple, The.
Crows, The.
Daemon, The.
Decoration.
Dream, The.
Evening in the Sanitarium.
Exhortation.
Fiend's Weather.
Henceforth, from the Mind.
I Saw Eternity.
Juan's Song.
July Dawn.
Knowledge.
M., Singing.
Man Alone.
March Twilight.
Mark, The.
Medusa.
Meeting, The.
Men Loved Wholly beyond Wisdom.
Musician.
Old Countryside.
Packet of Letters.
Portrait.
Putting to Sea.
Question in a Field.
Romantic, The.
Several Voices Out of a Cloud.
Simple Autumnal.
Single Sonnet.
Sleeping Fury, The.
Song: "Love me because I am lost."
Song for a Lyre.
Song for a Slight Voice.
Song for the Last Act.
Spirit's Song.
Statue and Birds.
Summer Wish.
To an Artist, to Take Heart.
To Be Sung on the Water.
To My Brother.
Train Tune.
Variation on a Sentence.
Winter Swan.
Women.
Zone.

Bogart, Elizabeth ("Estelle")
He Came Too Late.

Bogle, Donald E.
Aristotelian Elegy, An.
Now.

Boguslawski, Antoni
For My Son.

Bohanan, Otto Leland
Dawn's Awake, The.
Washer-Woman, The.

Boileau-Despréaux, Nicholas
Art of Poetry, The.
Art poétique, L', *sels.*
Rash author, 'tis a vain presumptuous crime.

Boilleau, Joan
I Saw a Ghost.

Boker, George Henry
Absence from thee is something worse than death.
Awaking of the Poetic Faculty, The.
Ballad of New Orleans, The.
Ballad of Sir John Franklin, A.
Battle of Lookout Mountain, The.
Before Vicksburg.
Black Regiment, The.
Countess Laura.
Crossing at Fredericksburg, The.
Cruise of the *Monitor,* The.
Dirge for a Soldier.
Ferry, The.
Flag, The.
Hooker's Across.
Lincoln.
Love is that orbit of the restless soul.
On Board the *Cumberland* (March 7, 1862).
Our Heroic Times, *sel.*
Sonnet: "Ah, could I grow in some remote degree."
Sonnet: "I am ashamed through this thick husk of clay."
Sonnet: "I cannot tell what charms my lady finds."
Sonnet: "I know that every note and chord of woe."
Sonnet: "I strive to live my life in whitest truth."
Sonnet: "If she should give me all I ask of her."
Sonnet: "If thou art sinful, there are thousands then."
Sonnet: "My darling, now the slumber of the night."
Sonnet: "My lady's senses are so pure and fine."
Sonnet: "Oh! sigh no more, no longer paint the air."
Sonnet: "Oh spring, that hides the wrinkled earth in green."
Sonnet: "Satyr nature riots in my blood, The."
Sonnet: "Some one within my hearing said tonight."
Sonnet: "This fellow calls me sordid, that one poor."
Sonnet: "Three seasons only in his calendar."
Sonnet: "Thus in her absence is my fancy cool."
Sonnet: "Tonight I walked with the grim Florentine."
Sonnet: "When I look back upon my early days."
Sonnet: "When to his class the surgeon's skilful blade."
Sonnet: "White as this paper was my lady's mind."
Sonnet: "You say my love no marvel is to you."
Sonnets, *sels.*
Sonnets; a Sequence on Profane Love, *sels.*
To England.
To My Lady.
Upon the Hill before Centreville.
Varuna, The.
Zagonyi.

Bold, Henry
Chloris, Forbear Awhile.

Boleyn, Anne
Defiled Is My Name.

Bolton, Edmund
Canzon Pastoral in Honor of Her Majesty, A.
Carol, A: "Sweet Music, sweeter far."
Palinode, A.
To Favonius.

Bolton, Sarah Knowles
Inevitable, The.
Live in the Present.
Live Today.
Paddle Your Own Canoe.

Bomke, Mary Cockburn
Roving Alley-Cat, A.

Bonar, Horatius
Abide with Us.
Be True.
Be True Thyself.
Begin the Day With God.
Begin with God.
Beyond the Smiling and the Weeping.
Bless the Blessed Morn.
Blessing and Honor.
Book of God, The.
Calm Me, My God.
Choose Thou for Me.
Christ Is All.
Cross and Throne.
Day, The.
Dropping Down the River.
Everlasting Memorial, The.
Fairest He, The.
Few More Years Shall Roll, A.
First and the Last, The.
God's Way.
Harvest.

He Is Near!
He Liveth Long Who Liveth Well.
He Took My Place.
Here, O my Lord, I see Thee face to face.
His Glory Tell.
Honesty.
How We Learn.
I Heard the Voice of Jesus Say.
I Lay My Sins on Jesus.
I Was a Wandering Sheep.
It Is Finished.
Life.
Linger Not!
Little While, A.
Lost but Found.
Love Is of God.
Master's Touch, The.
More of Thee.
My All.
My Prayer.
No, Not Despairingly.
O Love of God.
Our Share in Calvary.
Same Forever, The.
Take Him.
This Do in Remembrance of Me, *sel.*
Thou Must Be True.
Thy Love Alone.
Thy Way, Not Mine.
Touch of His Hand, The.
Upward.
Voice from Galilee, The.
Who Liveth Well.
Work.
Work That Saves, The!
Zeal in Labor.
Bonaventure, Saint
Blessed is the man, O Virgin Mary.
Psalter of the Blessed Virgin Mary, *sels.*
Boncho
Haiku: "Long, long river, The."
Bond, Carrie Jacobs
I Love You Truly.
Perfect Day, A.
Bond, Harold
Dreamside Bestiary.
Foibles.
Glove, The.
Him: the Roach.
Menagerie, The.
Bond, Horace Julian
Bishop of Atlanta, The: Ray Charles.
Habana.
Look at That Gal.
Rotation.
Bone, Florence
Prayer for a Little Home, A.
Bonefonius
Vanity of Kissing.
Boner, John Henry
Light'ood Fire, The.
Poe's Cottage at Fordham.
Remembrance.
We Walked among the Whispering Pines.
Bonhoeffer, Dietrich
Dietrich Bonhoeffer, Awaiting Execution in a Concentration Camp, Prays for His Fellow Prisoners.
Bonn, John Louis
Admonition.
Madonna; 1936.
Resurgence.
Bontemps, Arna
Black Man Talks of Reaping, A.
Blight.
Close Your Eyes!
Dark Girl.
Day-Breakers, The.
Gethsemane.
God Give to Men ("God give the yellow man").
Golgotha Is a Mountain.
Homing.
Idolatry.
Lancelot.
Length of Moon.
Miracles.
Nocturne at Bethesda.
Nocturne of the Wharves.
Note of Humility, A.
Reconnaissance.
Return, The.
Southern Mansion.
To a Young Girl Leaving the Hill Country.
Tree Design, A.
Boodson, Alison
Carol: "Fire is what's precious now."
Night Alert.
Poem: "He lying spilt like water from a bowl."
Poem: "I do not want to be your weeping woman."
Booth, Barton
Song: "Sweet are the charms of her I love."
Booth, Eva Gore- *See* **Gore-Booth, Eva**
Booth, Philip
Adam.
Animal Fair.
Barred Islands.
Catwise.
Choosing a Homesite.
Cider.
Cold Water Flat.
Countershadow, The.
Crossing.
Day the Tide, The.
Ego.
First Lesson.
Great Farm.
Green Song.
Hard Country.
Heron.
Instruction in the Art.
Jake's Wharf.
Maine.
Marin.
Nightsong.
North.
Offshore.
Round, The.
Siasconset Song.
Total Calm, The.
Tower, The.
Turning, The.
Twelfth Night.
Vermont; Indian Summer.
Was a Man.
Wilding, The.
Boothby, Sir Brooke
Sonnet on Life.
Boothroyd, John Basil
"And Now. . ."
Holy Order.
Please Excuse Typing.
Sanctuary.
Borges, Jorge Luis
Afterglow.
Butcher Shop.
Dagger, The
Hengest Cyning.
Plainness.
To a Saxon Poet.
Borgese, Giuseppe Antonio
Dream of a Decent Death.
Easter Sunday, 1945.
Borie, Lysbeth Boyd
Five-in-June.
Five Years Old.
Grace Ananne [*or* GraceAnAnne].
Greaty-great Grannie.
Just for Jesus.
Saturday Towels.
Borland, Hal
Caravans.
Men of America, Answering the Call.
Borregaard, Ebbe
Each Found Himself at the End of. . .
Some Stories of the Beauty Wapiti.
Borrow, George
Lavengro, *sel.*
Life is sweet, brother.
Borthwick, Jane
Light Shining Out of Darkness.
Boscán, Juan
Quarry, The.
Bose, Buddhadeva
Burden of Everyday, The.
Bosman, Herman Charles
At the safari's end a porter.
Learning Destiny.
Luck in the Square Stone, The, *sel.*
Old I Am.
Poet, The.
Recovery from Mental Illness.
Seed.
Bossidy, John Collins
Boston ("And this is good old Boston").
Boston Toast, A ("And this is [*or* is to *or* Here's to] good old Boston").
On the Aristocracy of Harvard ("Here's to good old Boston").
To Boston.
Bostelmann, Carl John
Christ in the Andes.
Bostwick, Grace G.
"Pep."
Reward, The.
Bostwick, Helen Louise Barron
Little Dandelion.
Boswell, Arthur
Roughchin, the Pirate.
Bosworth, William
Chaste and Lost Lovers, The, *sel.*
See'st Not My Love.
Botrel, Theodore
Little Gregory.
Botsford, S. B.
Sonneteering Made Easy.
Bottomley, Gordon
Atlantis.
Blanid's Song.
Crier by Night, The, *sel.*
Dawn.
Eager Spring.
Eagle Song.
Elegiac Mood.
End of the World, The.
Hymn of Form, A.
Hymn of Touch, A.
I Am Tired of the Wind.
"L'Apparition" of Gustave Moreau.
L'Oiseau Bleu.
Louse Crept Out of My Lady's Shift, A.
Maid of Arc, The.
My Moon.
Netted Strawberries.
Night and Morning Songs, *sels.*
Ploughman, The.
Suilven and the Eagle, *sel.*
To Iron-Founders and Others.
Bottrall, Ronald
Icarus.
Proserpine at Enna.
Rondeau: "Homage to change that scatters the poppy seed."
Botwood, Edward
Hot Stuff.
Boufflers, Stanislas Jean, Marquis de
Paying a Debt.
Boufiers, Marie-Francoise-Catherine de Beauveau, Marquise de

Bouflers (continued)
Air: Sentir avec Ardeur.
Boulton, Harold
All through the Night ("Sleep, my love, and peace attend thee").
Boundy, Rex
Virile Christ, A.
Boundzekei-Dongala, Emmanuel
Fantasy under the Moon.
Bouquet, John Alexander
Epitaph, The: "When from this good world I depart."
Sorrow Turned into Joy.
Bourdillon, Francis William
Ah, happy who have seen Him, whom the world.
Aucassin and Nicolete.
Eurydice.
Light.
Light and Love.
Lost God, A, *sel.*
Night Has a Thousand Eyes, The.
Old and Young.
Violinist, A.
Where Runs the River.
Bourignon, Antoinette
Come, Saviour!
Bourinot, Arthur Stanley
Dark Flows the River.
Johnny Appleseed.
Legend of Paul Bunyan, A.
Nicolas Gatineau.
Only Silence.
Paul Bunyan.
Snow Anthology.
Sonnets to My Mother.
Tom Thomson.
Under the Pines.
What Far Kingdom.
Winter Sketch.
Bourman, Nicholas
Epitaph, An, Upon the Death of the Right Reverent Father in God J. Jewel, Doctor of Divinity and Bishop of Sarisbury, Who Deceased the Twenty-second of September, 1571.
Bourne, David
Parachute Descent.
Bourne, Nina
Where the Single Men Go in Summer.
Bourne, Vincent
Cricket, The.
Housekeeper, The.
Jackdaw, The.
Snail, The ("The frugal snail with forecast of repose").
Snail, The ("To grass, or leaf, or fruit, or wall").
Bouvé, Thomas Tracy
Shannon and the *Chesapeake,* The.
Bovshover, Joseph
To the Laggards.
Bowditch, Nathaniel Ingersoll
World Beyond, A.
Bowen, Arnold Vincent
Only Pretty Ringtime, The.
Bowen, Charles Synge Christopher Bowen, Baron
Just & Unjust.
Rain, The.
Rain It Raineth, The.
Bowen, Edward Ernest
Forty Years On.
Shemuel.
Bowen, Euros
Birds of Rhiannon, The.
Bowen, John Eliot
Man Who Rode to Conemaugh, The.
Bowen, Robert Adger
Gloaming.
Bower, Helen Frazee- *See* **Frazee-Bower, Helen**
Bowering, George
Circus Maximus.
Está Muy Caliente.
Grass, The.
Inside the Tulip.
Moon Shadow.
Winter's Dregs.
Bowers, Edgar
Adam's Song to Heaven.
Aix-la-Chappelle, 1945.
Astronomers of Mont Blanc, The.
Centaur Overheard, The.
Dark Earth and Summer.
From William Tyndale to John Frith.
Grove and Building.
Mirror, The.
Mountain Cemetery, The.
Stoic, The; for Laura von Courten.
To the Contemporary Muse.
Two Poems on the Catholic Bavarians.
Virgin Mary, The.
Wise Men, The.
Bowes-Lyon, Lilian
Duchess.
Feather, The.
Hedge-Row Story, The.
Shepherd's Coat, A.
Stars Go By, The.
Bowie, Beverly
To My New Mistress.
Bowie, Walter Russell
Continuing Christ, The.
Empty Soul, The.
God of the Nations.
Holy City, The.
O Love That Triumphs over Loss.
Bowker, Richard Rogers
Thomas à Kempis.
Bowles, Caroline Anne (Mrs. Robert Southey)
Lady-Bird.
To Death.
To the Ladybird.
Young Gray Head, The.
Bowles, Fred G.
Song of the Road, A.
Bowles, William Lisle
At Dover Cliffs.
At Ostend.
At Tynemouth Priory, after a Tempestuous Voyage.
Bells of Ostend, The.
Bird in a Cage, The.
Butterfly and the Bee, The.
Distant View of England from the Sea.
Dover Cliffs.
Hope.
Influence of Time on Grief.
Milton: On the Busts of Milton, in Youth and Age ("Milton, our noblest poet").
Netley Abbey.
On a Beautiful Landscape.
River Cherwell, The.
Sonnet: At Dover Cliffs, July 20, 1787.
Sonnet: At Ostend, July 22, 1787.
Sonnet: "Evening, as slow thy placid shades descend."
Sonnet: "Languid, and sad, and slow, from day to day."
Sonnet: Netley Abbey.
Sonnet: "O Time! who know'st a lenient hand to lay."
Sonnet: On a Distant View of England.
Sonnet, July 18th, 1787.
Time and Grief.
To a Friend.
To the River Itchin, near Winton.
Tweed Visited, The.
Bowman, Gladys M.
Only One Life.
Bowman, Louise Hollingsworth
Quiet Hour, The.
Bowman, Louise Morey
Sea Lavender.
She Plans Her Funeral.
Bowring, Sir John
Cross, The.
From the Recesses.
God Is Love.
In the Cross of Christ I Glory.
Sacred Page, The.
Soul Eternal, The.
Towering o'er the Wrecks of Time.
Watchman, Tell Us of the Night.
What of the Night?
Bowsher, Kathryn T.
My Hiding Place.
Thy Nail-pierced Hands.
Boyars, Arthur
Initial.
Boyd, Baird
Cowboy ("I'm wild and wooly").
Drunken Desperado, The.
Boyd, Bruce
Sanctuary.
This Is What the Watchbird Sings, Who Perches in the Lovetree.
Venice Recalled.
Boyd, James
Long Distance, 1944.
Boyd, Marion Margaret
To One Older.
White Dusk.
Boyd, Mark Alexander
Cupid and Venus.
Fra Bank to Bank.
Sonnet [*or* Sonet]: "Fra bank to bank [*or* banc to banc], fra wood to wood [*or* wod to wod], I rin."
"Boyd, Nancy." *See* **Millay, Edna St. Vincent**
Boyd, Thomas
Heath, The.
King's Son, The.
Love on the Mountain.
To the Leanán Shee.
Boyden, Polly Chase
Form.
Hands on a Card-Table.
Mud.
New Mexico.
Self-Control.
Boyesen, Hjalmar Hjorth
Thoralf and Synnov.
Boylan, Grace Duffie
Who Goes There?
Boyle, Kay
Communication to Nancy Cunard, A.
Flying Foxes and Others.
Funeral in Hungary.
Poem of Love, A.
Boyle, Roger, Earl of Orrery *See* **Orrery, Roger Boyle, Baron Broghill, 1st Earl of**
Boyle, Rosalie
Old Women Remember.
Boyle, Sarah Roberts
Song of the Grass, The.
Voice of the Grass, The.
Boyle, Virginia Frazer
I Kilt er Cat.
I Know that My Redeemer Liveth.
Tennessee.
Brabazon, Francis
Victoria Market.
Brabham, Mouzon W.
Father's Prayer, A.
Bracker, Milton
Fish-eye.
P Is for Paleontology.

Umpire, The.
Where, O Where?
Brackett, Anna Callender
Benedicite.
In Hades.
Bradbury, Bianca
Nor'easter.
Bradbury, Ray
Dublin Limerick, A.
Bradby, Godfrey Fox
April.
"Could Ye Not Watch One Hour?"
In Hoc Signo.
Kingdoms.
Bradby, H. C.
Comfort for the Sleepless.
Braddock, Emily A.
Corn and the Lilies, The.
Braden, Charles S.
Cross, The.
Bradford, Gamaliel
Ardor.
Exit God.
God.
Hope.
Judas.
My Delight.
Bradford, William
Epitaphium Meum.
New England's Growth.
Of Boston in New England.
Plymouth Harvest, The.
Word to New England, A.
Bradley, Christine E.
Skippets, the Bad One.
Bradley, Dwight
Disciple, The.
Bradley, Edward *See* **"Bede, Cuthbert"**
Bradley, Katherine, *and* **Edith Cooper** *See* **"Field, Michael"**
Bradley, Mary Emily Neely
Betty at the Party.
Beyond Recall.
Chrysalis, A.
In Death.
Spray of Honeysuckle, A.
Bradley, Samuel M.
Roc's Brood.
This Here Is Hell.
Bradley, William Aspenwall
To Little Renée on First Seeing Her Lying in Her Cradle.
Bradstreet, Anne
Another Letter to Her Husband, Absent upon Publick Employment.
As Weary Pilgrim, Now at Rest.
Author to Her Book, The.
Before the Birth of One of Her Children.
Contemplations.
Epitaph on My Dear and Ever Honoured Mother, An.
Flesh and the Spirit, The.
Four Seasons of the Year, The.
Here Followes Some Verses upon the Burning of Our House.
In Memory of My Dear Grandchild Elizabeth Bradstreet.
In Thankful Remembrance for My Dear Husband's Safe Arrivall Sept. 3, 1662.
Letter to Her Husband, A ("Phoebus, make haste").
Letter to Her Husband, Absent upon Public[k] Employment, A ("My head, my heart, mine eyes, my life—nay more").
Longing for Heaven.
On My Dear Grand-Child Simon Bradstreet.
Prologue, The: "To sing of wars, of captains, and of kings."
Some Verses upon the Burning of Our House, July 10th, 1666.
Spring.
To My Dear and Loving Husband.
Upon the Burning of Our House.
Vanity of All Worldly Things, The.
Verses upon the Burning of Our House.
When I behold the heavens as in their prime.
Bradstreet, Samuel
Almanack for the Year of Our Lord, 1657, An.
Brady, Charles A.
Ballad of St. Thomas, A.
Dimidium Animae Meae.
Brady, Edwin James
Ballad of the Captains, A.
Capstan Chantey, A.
Coachman's Yarn, The.
Great Grey Water, The.
Lost and Given Over.
Southerly.
Brady, George M.
Autumn House, The.
Day, The.
Garden, The.
Generations, The.
Hosts, The.
Land-Fall.
Old Michael.
Settled Men, The.
Bragança, Nadejda de
Prayer: "O God, I love Thee in the stars at Night."
Bragdon, Claude
Beautiful Necessity, The, *sel.*
Point, the Line, the Surface and Sphere, The.
Brainard, E. M.
Compensation.
Brainard, John Gardiner Calkins
Captain, The, *abr.*
Deep, The.
Epithalamium: "I saw two clouds at morning."
Fall of Niagara, The.
I Saw Two Clouds at Morning.
Mr. Merry's Lament for "Long Tom."
On the Death of Commodore Oliver H. Perry.
Sonnet to the Sea Serpent.
Stanzas: "Dead leaves strew the forest walk, The."
Brainard, Mary Gardiner
Faith and Sight.
I know not what shall befall me: God hangs a mist o'er my eyes.
Not Knowing.
Brainard, Mary Gardiner ***and*** **P. P. Bliss**
God Knoweth.
Braine, Sheila E.
Apple-Elf, The.
Mr. Scarecrow.
Braithwaite, William Charles
Christ Our Contemporary.
Braithwaite, William Stanley
Arsenal of the Lord, The.
Del Cascar.
Exit.
House of Falling Leaves, The.
Hymn for the Slain in Battle.
I Am Glad Daylong.
If I Could Touch.
Ironic: LL.D.
It's a Long Way.
Laughing It Out.
October XXIX, 1795 (Keats' Birthday).
Rhapsody.
Rye Bread.
Sandy Star and Willie Gee (*Complete,* I-V).
Scintilla.
Sculptured Worship.
Sea Lyric.
Sic Vita.
Sorrow Is the Only Faithful One.
To ——: "Half in the dim light from the hall."
Turn Me to My Yellow Leaves.
Twenty Stars to Match His Face.
Two Questions.
Vision, The.
Watchers, The.
Way, The.
White Magic; an Ode.
Braley, Berton
At Your Service; the Panama Gang.
Business Is Business.
Do It Now.
Hills, The.
Loyalty.
Opportunity.
Pan in Pandemonium.
Pardners.
Prayer, A: "Lord, let me live like a regular man."
Song of Power, A.
Start Where You Stand.
Success ("It's doing your job. . .").
That's Success!
Thinker, The.
Braley, Ephraim
Canaday I. O.
Bramston, James
Art of Politicks, The, *sel.*
Time's Changes.
Bramwich, John
Hymn: "Britannia's sons, though slaves ye be."
Branch, Anna Hempstead
Connecticut Road Song.
Ere the Golden Bowl Is Broken.
Grieve Not, Ladies.
Her Hands.
Her Words.
I Think of Him as One Who Fights.
Mathematics or the Gift of Tongues.
Monk in the Kitchen, The.
My Mother's Hands.
Song for My Mother, A: Her Hands.
Song for My Mother, A: Her Stories.
Song for My Mother, A: Her Words.
Songs for My Mother, *sels.*
There is no small work unto God.
To a Dog.
To a New York Shop Girl Dressed for Sunday.
Two Inscriptions for the Christmas Candle.
Unbeliever, An.
Warrior Maid, The.
While Loveliness Goes By.
Branch, M. W.
Schmaltztenor.
Branch, Mary Lydia Bolles
Petrified Fern, The.
Brand, Millen
Chipmunk, The.
Local Light.
Lost.
Brandt, Sebastian *See* **Brant, Sebastian**
Branford, William
Trooper Temple Pulvermacher.
Brant [*or* Brandt], Sebastian
Ballade to Our Lady.
Geographers.
Preachment for Preachers.
Ship of Fools, The, *sels.*
Star of the Sea.
Tudor Rose, The.
Brasch, Charles
Crossing the Straits.
Discovery, The.
Estate, The, *sel.*

Brasch (continued)
Genesis, *sel.*
Henley on Taieri.
I Think of Your Generation.
In Memory of Robin Hyde, 1906-39.
Nineteen Thirty-nine, *sel.*
On Mt. Iron.
Poland, October.
View of Rangitoto, A.
Waking by Night.
Brasier, Virginia
Generosity.
Heartbeat of Democracy.
Primer of Consequences.
Psychological Prediction.
Wind Weather.
Brathwaite, Edward
Owl.
Brathwaite, Richard
English Gentlewoman, The, *sel.*
My Mistress.
Nature's Embassy, *sel.*
Nightingale, The.
Of Maids' Inconstancy.
Strappado for the Devil, A, *sels.*
To the Precision.
Brautigan, Richard
Fever Monument, The.
General Custer Versus the Titanic.
Horse Race.
In a Cafe.
Our Beautiful West Coast Thing.
Pomegranate Circus, The.
Sidney Greenstreet Blues, The.
Wheel, The.
Bravo, Mario
Song of the General Strike.
Brawley, Benjamin
Chaucer.
My Hero: to Robert Gould Shaw.
Brayton, Teresa
Christmas Song, A.
Brazelton, Ethel M. C.
Poor Lil' Brack Sheep.
Breathnach, Michael
Man-Child.
Brecht, Bertolt
Burning of Books, The.
Children's Crusade 1939.
Coal for Mike.
Difficult Times.
In Memory of Marie A.
Of Swimming in Lakes and Rivers.
Time's Mutability.
To Posterity.
Wheel Change, The.
Breck, Carrie Ellis
Christmas Thought, A.
They Two.
Breed, Eleanor D.
Scapegoats.
Breeser, Bettye
Nature at Three.
Brégy, Katherine Marie Cornelia
April Fools.
Gethsemane's Gift.
"I Thirst . . ."
Japanese Cherries.
Maid, The.
Breining, June
Inexperience.
"Breitmann, Hans." *See* **Leland, Charles Godfrey**
Bremser, Ray
Blood.
Poem of Holy Madness, *sel.*
Brenan, Gerald
My Sailor of Seven.
Brenan, Joseph
Come to Me, Dearest.
Brennan, Christopher John
Adam to Lilith.
Anguish'd Doubt Broods over Eden, The.
Burden of Tyre, The, *sel.*
Come Out, Come Out, Ye Souls That Serve.
Fire in the Heavens [and Fire Along the Hills].
Grand Cortège, The.
How Old Is My Heart.
I Cry to You as I Pass Your Windows.
I Said, This Misery Must End.
I Saw My Life as Whitest Flame.
I sorrow for youth—ah, not for its wildness (would that were dead!).
Interlude: The Casement.
Land I Came thro' Last, The.
Let them devour and be devour'd!
Let Us Go Down [the Long Dead Night Is Done].
Lilith, *sels.*
Lilith on the Fate of Man.
My Heart Was Wandering [in the Sands].
O Desolate Eves [along the Way, How Oft].
O White Wind.
Pangs That Guard the Gates of Joy, The.
Pauca Mea, *sel.*
Point of Noon, The.
Quest of Silence, The, *sel.*
Sweet Silence after Bells.
Towards the Source, *sels.*
Twilight of Disquietude, The, *sels.*
Wanderer, The, *sels.*
We Woke Together.
What Do I Know?
When window-lamps had dwindled, then I rose.
Years That Go to Make Me Man. The.
Brennan, Eileen
Eveing on Howth Head.
May Evening.
One Kingfisher and One Yellow Rose.
Thoughts at the Museum.
Brennan, Gerald
Mornin's Mornin', The.
Brennan, Joseph Payne
Avery Anameer.
Cat, The.
Chestnut Roasters, The.
Ghost-Town Saloon: Winter.
Grandfather's Ghost.
Humming Stair, The.
Last Pagan Mourns for Dark Rosaleen, The.
Man I Met, The.
Nightmare.
One Day of Rain.
Ossian.
Raccoon on the Road.
Recognition of Death.
Scythe of Dreams, The.
Serpent Waits, The.
Wind of Time, The.
Brent, Hally Carrington
I Think I Know No Finer Things than Dogs.
Brentano, Clemens Maria
Bridal Song.
Prelude: "Whatever ripened in these lines."
Brereton, Ethel C.
Three Dogs.
Brereton, Jane
On Beau Nash's Picture, Which Once Stood between the Busts of Newton and Pope.
On Mr. Nash's Picture.
Brereton, John Le Gay
Buffalo Creek.
Dead, The.
Robe of Grass, The.
Waking.
Bretherton, C. H.
In Winter.
Breton, André
Sunflower.
Breton, Nicholas
Aglaia.
Assurance, An.
Coridon's Supplication to Phillis.
Country Lad, The.
Country Song.
Cradle Song, A: "Come little babe, come silly soul."
Displeasure against Love, A.
Go, Muse, unto the Bower.
Happy Countryman, The.
His Complaint against Love and Fortune.
His Wisdom.
I have neither plums nor cherries.
I Would Thou Wert Not Fair.
In the Merry Month of May.
Invective against the Wicked of the World, An, *sel.*
Ipsa Quae.
Merry Country Lad, The.
Odd Conceit, An.
Olden Love-making.
Passionate Shepherd, The, *sels.*
Pastoral I: "Flora hath been all about."
Pastoral, A: "In the merry month of May."
Pastoral, A: "On a hill there grows a flower."
Pastoral, A: "Sweet birds, that sit and sing amid the shady valleys."
Pastoral: "Who can live in heart so glad."
Pastoral of Phillis and Corydon, A.
Phyllida and Corydon ("In the merry month of May").
Phyllida and Corydon ("On a hill there grows a flower").
Phyllis.
Ploughman's Song, The.
Plowman's Song, The.
Prayer for Gentlewomen and Others to Use, A.
Preamble to N[icholas] B[reton] His Garden-Plot, The.
Pretty Twinkling Starry Eyes.
Rare News.
Report Song, A.
Say That I Should Say [I Love Ye].
Shepherd and Shepherdess.
Shepherd's Dream, A.
Solemn Conceit, A.
Sonet to the Tune of A Hone a Hone, A.
Song: "Lovely kind and kindly loving."
Song of Phillida and Coridon.
Sonnet, A: "Those eyes that hold the hand of every heart."
Soul's Harmony, The, *sels.*
Strange Description of a Rare Garden-Plot, A.
Strange Fortunes of Two Excellent Princes, The, *sel.*
Supplication, A.
Sweet Lullaby, A.
Sweet Pastoral, A.
To His Muse.
What is the gold of all this world but dross.
Worldly prince doth in his scepter hold, The.
Breton, Nicholas *and others*,
Honourable Entertainment Given to the Queen's Majesty in Progress at Elvetham, 1591, *sels.*
Brettell, Noel Harry
Autumn Song.
Cataclysm.
Elephant.

Giraffes.
Outside Kimberley.
We rode out with the pealing day before us.
Wind and an Eagle Owl, *sel.*
Brew, Kwesi
Ancestral Faces.
Lonely Traveller, The.
Plea for Mercy, A.
Search, The.
Brewster, Elizabeth
East Coast—Canada.
Egoist Dead, The.
Eviction.
In the Library.
River Song.
Brewster, Townsend T.
Black Is Beautiful.
Brick, Norman
Of Snow.
"Bridges, Madeline" (Mary Ainge De Vere)
Breath, A ("A breath can fan love's flame to burning").
Faith Trembling.
Farewell, A: "I put thy hand aside."
Friend and Lover.
Give.
God Keep You.
Life's Mirror.
Poet and Lark.
Spinner, The.
Third Proposition, The.
When the Most Is Said.
Wid Thady's Pipe beside the Door.
Wind-Swept Wheat, The.
Bridges [*or* Brydges], Matthew
And Jesus Wept.
Crown Him with Many Crowns.
Rise, Glorious Conqueror! Rise.
Seraphs' Song, The.
Bridges, Robert (1844-1930)
Absence.
Affliction of Richard, The.
After the Gale.
All earthly beauty hath one cause and proof.
Angel Spirits of Sleep.
April, 1885.
Asian Birds.
Awake, My Heart to Be Loved.
But love's true passion is of immortal happiness.
Cheddar Pinks.
Cliff-Top, The.
Clouds Have Left the Sky, The.
Dear Lady, When Thou Frownest.
Dejection.
Elegy: "Clear and gentle stream!"
Elegy: "I have lov'd flowers that fade."
Elegy: Summer House on the Mound, The.
Elegy: "Wood is bare, The: a river-mist is steeping."
Elegy on a Lady, Whom Grief for the Death of Her Betrothed Killed.
Ἔρως (Eros).
Ἐτώσιον ἄχθος ἀρούρης.
Evening Darkens Over, The.
First Spring Morning.
Flycatchers.
Fortunatus Nimium.
Founder's day.
Friendship.
Gay Robin Is Seen No More.
Gheluvelt.
Ghosts.
Gird on Thy Sword.
Growth of Love, The, *sels.*
Hill Pines Were Sighing, The.
How was November's melancholy endear'd to me.
Hymn of Nature, A.
I Have Loved Flowers That Fade.
I Heard a Linnet Courting.
I Love All Beauteous Things.
I Never Shall Love the Snow Again.
I Praise the Tender Flower.
I will be what God made me, nor protest.
I Will Not Let Thee Go.
Idle Flowers, The.
Idle Life I Lead, The.
In higher natures, poetic or mystical.
Indolence.
Introduction: "'Twas late in my long journey, when I had clomb to where."
James McCosh.
Jesus.
Johannes Milton, Senex.
Linnet, The.
London Snow.
Long Are the Hours the Sun Is Above.
Low Barometer.
Melancholia.
Muse and Poet.
My Delight and Thy Delight.
Nightingales.
Nimium Fortunatus.
Noel; Christmas Eve, 1913.
North Wind Came Up Yesternight, The.
November.
O Weary Pilgrims, Chanting of Your Woe.
O Youth Whose Hope Is High.
On a Dead Child.
Our happiest earthly comradeships hold a foretaste.
Our Lady.
Passer-by, A.
Pater Filio.
Philosopher to His Mistress, The.
Poor Poll.
Poor Withered Rose.
Poppy Grows upon the Shore, A.
Psalm, The: "While Northward the hot sun was sinking o'er the trees."
Screaming Tarn.
Since to be loved endures.
Sky's unresting cloudland, that with varying play, The.
Snow Lies Sprinkled on the Beach, The.
So Sweet Love Seemed [That April Morn].
Song of My Heart, A.
South Wind, The.
Spirits.
Spring Goeth All the White.
Storm Is Over, The.
Testament of Beauty, The, *sels.*
Thanksgiving Day.
There Is a Hill Beside the Silver Thames.
This world is unto God a work of art.
Thou Didst Delight My Eyes.
To L. B. C. L. M.
To the United States of America.
Triolet: "All women born are so perverse."
Triolet: "When first we met did not guess."
'Twas at thatt hour of beauty when the setting sun.
Unillumined Verge, The.
Upon the Shore.
Upper Skies, The.
Very Names of Things Beloved, The.
Voice of Nature, The.
Weep Not To-Day.
When Death to Either Shall Come.
When thou didst give thy love to me.
Who Has Not Walked upon the Shore.
Windmill, The.
Winnowers, The.
Winter Nightfall.
World Comes Not to an End, The.
World still goeth about to show and hide, The.
Bridges, Robert ("Droch" 1858-1941)
Toast to our Native Land, A.
Bridges, Shirley
Imaginary Figures of the Virtues.
Bridgman, Lewis Jesse
On Knowing When to Stop.
Brien, Neva
Thanksgiving and Praise.
Brierre, Jean
Harlem.
Briggs, C.
Framework-Knitters Petition, The.
Briggs, Caroline Atherton *See* **Mason, Caroline Atherton Briggs**
Briggs, Ernest
Lonely Child, The.
While Immortality Endures.
Briggs, George Wallace
Knowledge through Suffering.
Briggs, Greta
London under Bombardment.
Briggs, Olga Hampel
Brief History.
Brigham, Besmilr
Carver and the Rock Are One, The.
Crosses, The.
Ghosts of the Dead.
Tell Our Daughters.
Tomb.
Will's Love, The.
Bright, Verne
Comrade Christ.
Revelation.
Brinckman, Rosemary
Fish and Bird.
Brine, Mary Dow
Somebody's Mother.
Brininstool, Earl Alonzo
Disappointed Tenderfoot, The.
Ol' Cow Hawse, The.
Range Rider's Soliloquy, The.
Stampede, The.
Brink, Carol Ryrie
Crèche, The.
Goody O'Grumpity.
Brinnin, John Malcolm
At the Airport.
Cape Ann: a View.
Double Crucifixion, The.
Every Earthly Creature.
Fêtes, Fates.
Heavy Heavy Heavy.
Hotel Paradiso e Commerciale.
Islands; a Song.
La Creazione Degli Animali.
My Father, My Son.
Nuns at Eve.
Skin Diving in the Virgins.
Thin Facade for Edith Sitwell, A.
Views of the Favorite Colleges.
Wind Is Ill, The.
Worm in the Whirling Cross, The.
Brisley, Joyce L.
Two Families, The.
Which?
Bristol, Augusta Cooper
Pyxidanthera, The.
Bristol, George Digby, 2d Earl of
Elvira, *sel.*
Bristol, John Digby, 1st Earl of
Grieve Not, Dear Love.
Briussov, Valerii Yacovlevich *See* **Bryusov, Valery Yakovlevich**
Bro, Marguerite Harmon
Prayer: "God, listen through my words to the beating of my heart."

Brock, David
Natural Selection.
Brock, Edwin
Catastrophe.
Curtain Poem, The.
To My Mother.
Brock, Henry Irving
Limerick: "In this book every line has been clean."
Brock, Van K.
Sea Birds, The.
Brockman, Zoe Kincaid
Grapevine, The.
In an Editor's Office.
Brocks, Maria Gowen
Song of Egla.
Brod, Max
Goldfish on the Writing Desk.
Brode, Anthony
Breakfast with Gerard Manley Hopkins.
Calypsomania.
Obituary.
Unromantic Song.
Brodey, James
All these numbers, several are possibly aghast.
Expansion to Aveline's.
First range through.
Homeward Bound.
Ideantikit, *sels.*
Poem: "Back at San Francisco Greyhound, leaning."
Poem: "Woke this A.M."
Poem, to Jane Wilson on Television.
Rosewood Vision.
Steamshovel, seen from afar, The.
"The: the"/ matter-of-factness, plural.
Throat-to throat surgery.
Vice, 1966, *sel.*
Vision of Turtle (One).
White sheet of paper, A.
Brodie, Hugh R.
Airman's Prayer, An.
Sergeant's Prayer, A.
Brody, Alter
City Park, A.
Cry of the Peoples, The.
Lamentations.
Brome, Alexander
Anti-Politician, The.
Cavalier, The.
Contrary, The.
Counsel, The.
Courtship.
Love, Drink and Debt.
Love's without Reason.
Mad Lover, The.
Mock Song, A.
Now I'm Resolved to Love No More.
Pastoral on the King's Death, The. Written in 1648.
Plain Dealing.
Resolve, The.
Riddle, The: "No more, no more."
Royalist, The.
To a Painted Lady.
To His Friend J. H.
Why I love Her.
Wife, A.
Brome, Richard
Bonny, bonny bird I had, A.
Come, Come Away!
Jovial Crew, A; or, The Merry Beggars, *sels.*
Merry Beggars, The, *sel.*
Northern Lass, The, *sels.*
Round, a round, a round, boys, a round, A.
Song: "Peace, wayward barne! O cease thy moan!"
Song of the Beggars.
Bromley, Beatrice Marion
Camp Fire.
Bromley, Isaac H.
Passenjare, The.
Bronowski, Jacob
Take Your Gun.
Brontë, Anne ("Acton Bell")
Doubter's Prayer, The.
He Doeth All Things Well.
Hope, A.
If This Be All.
Prayer, A: "My God (oh, let me call Thee mine)."
Brontë, Charlotte ("Currer Bell")
Christ in Introspect.
Life.
On the Death of Anne Brontë.
Brontë, Emily ("Ellis Bell")
A. E.
All Hushed and Still within the House.
And when thy heart is resting.
Anticipation.
Appeal, The.
At Castle Wood.
Ay—There It Is.
Bluebell, The.
Come, the wind may never again.
Death.
Dream, A.
Enough of Thought, Philosopher.
Evening Sun, The.
Fall, Leaves, Fall.
God of Visions.
He comes with western winds, with evening's wandering airs.
Her Last Lines.
Holyday.
How still, how happy! These are words.
I Am the Only Being [Whose Doom].
I Gazed upon the Cloudless Moon.
I Gazed Within.
I'm Happiest When Most Away.
Julian M. and A. G. Rochelle.
Last Lines.
Lines: "Shall earth no more inspire thee."
Linnet in the Rocky Dells, The.
Little While, A.
Little While, a Little While, A.
Love and Friendship.
Love Is like the Wild Rose-Briar.
Morning Star, The.
My Lady's Grave.
Night is darkening round me, The.
Night Wind, The.
No Coward Soul Is Mine.
Oh, for the Time When I Shall Sleep.
Old Stoic, The.
Philosopher, The, *sel.*
Plead for Me.
Prisoner, The.
Prisoner, The; a Fragment.
R. Alcona to J. Brenzaida.
Redbreast, Early in the Morning.
Remembrance.
Shall Earth No More Inspire Thee?
Silent Is the House.
Sleep Brings No Joy.
Sleep Not, Dream Not, *sel.*
Song: "Fall, leaves, fall; die, flowers, away."
Song: "Linnet in the rocky dells, The."
Song: "Night is darkening round me, The."
Stanzas: "I'll not weep that thou art going to leave me."
Stanzas to——("Well, some may hate").
"Still let my tyrants know, I am not doom'd to wear."
Sun Has Set, The.
Sympathy.
Tell Me, Tell Me, Smiling Child.
That Wind.
There Let Thy Bleeding Branch Atone.
Though earth and man were gone.
To a Wreath of Snow.
To Imagination.
Two Children, The.
Visionary, The.
Wanderer from the Fold, The.
Warning and Reply.
Where wilt thou go my harassed heart?
Brontë, Patrick
Cottager's Hymn, The.
His Presence.
Brook, Frances
God's Aftermath.
Brooke, Fulke Greville, 1st Baron *See* **Greville, Fulke, 1st Baron Brooke**
Brooke, Brian
Smoke of the Camp Fire.
Brooke, Jocelyn
Three Barrows Down.
Brooke, Rupert
Ah, God! to see the branches stir.
Busy Heart, The.
Channel Passage, A.
Chilterns, The.
Clouds.
Colloquial.
Day That I Have Loved.
Dead, The ("Blow out, you bugles").
Dead, The ("These hearts were woven").
Dear, They Have Poached the Eyes You Loved So Well.
Dining-Room Tea.
Doubts.
Dust.
Fish, The.
Fishes' Heaven.
Fragment: "I strayed about the deck, an hour, to-night."
Funeral of Youth, The: Threnody.
Great Lover, The.
Heaven.
Hill, The.
Letter to a Live Poet, A.
Little Dog's Day, The.
Love.
Mary and Gabriel.
Memory, A.
Menelaus and Helen.
Mummia.
Mutability.
Night Journey, The.
1914.
Oh! Death Will Find Me.
O Thou/ God of all long desirous roaming.
Old Vicarage, Grantchester, The.
One before the Last, The.
One Day.
Peace.
Pine Trees and the Sky; Evening.
Retrospect.
Safety.
Second Best.
Soldier, The.
Song: "'Oh! Love,' they said, 'is King of Kings.'"
Song of the Pilgrims, The, *sel.*
Sonnet: "I said I splendidly loved you; it's not true."
Sonnet: "Not with vain tears, when we're beyond the sun."
Sonnet: "Oh! Death will find me, long before I tire."
There's Wisdom in Women.
These I have loved.
Thoughts on the Shape of the Human Body.
Tiara Tahiti.
Wagner.

Wayfarers, The.
Young Man in April, The.
Brooke, Stopford Augustus
Courage.
Earth and Man, The.
Jungfrau's Cry, The.
Lines: "In the day the sun is darkened."
Moment, A.
Prince Riquet's Song.
Queen's Song.
Riquet of the Tuft, *sels.*
Versailles.
Brookhouse, Christopher
Man in the Ocelot Suit, The.
Brooks, Charles Timothy
Great Voices, The.
Plea for Flood Ireson, A.
Brooks, Edwin
Tulips from Their Blood.
Brooks, Elbridge Streeter
Rodney's Ride.
Brooks, Eugene
De Gaulle Nods Once.
Brooks, Francis
Down the Little Big Horn.
Intaglios.
On the Plains.
Tennessee.
Brooks, Gwendolyn
Andre.
Ballad of Late Annie, The.
Bean Eaters, The.
Birth in a Narrow Room, The.
Blackstone Rangers, The.
Bronzeville Man with a Belt in the Back.
But Can See Better There, and Laughing There.
Certainty We Two Shall Meet, The.
Chicago *Defender* Sends a Man to Little Rock, Fall, 1957, The.
Chicago Picasso, The.
Children of the Poor, The, *sel.*
Cynthia in the Snow.
Eunice in the Evening.
First Fight. Then Fiddle.
Flags.
Hunchback Girl: She Thinks of Heaven.
Jack.
Kitchenette Building.
Loam Norton.
Love Note II: Flags.
Malcolm X.
Martin Luther King Jr.
Medgar Evers.
Men of careful turns, haters of forks in the road.
Mentors.
My Dreams, My Works, Must Wait Till after Hell.
Negro Hero.
Of DeWitt Williams on His Way to Lincoln Cemetery.
Old Marrieds, The.
Old Mary.
Old Tennis Player.
Otto.
Parents, The; People Like Our Marriage.
Pete at the Zoo.
Piano after War.
Pool Players, Seven at the Golden Shovel.
"Pygmies Are Pygmies Still, Though Percht on Alps."
Riot.
Rudolph Is Tired of the City.
Sermon on the Warpland, The.
Song in the Front Yard, A.
Strong Men, Riding Horses.
Two Dedications, *sel.*
Vern.
Wall, The.
Way-Out Morgan.
We Real Cool.
What shall I give my children? who are poor.
Womanhood, The, *sel.*
Brooks, Helen Morgan
Plans.
Words.
Young David, A: Birmingham.
Brooks, Jonathan Henderson
And One Shall Live in Two.
Last Quarter Moon of the Dying Year, The.
Muse in Late November.
My Angel.
Paean.
Resurrection, The.
She Said . . .
Brooks, Louise Upham
Crowns.
Brooks, Maria Gowen
Farewell to Cuba.
Palace of the Gnomes.
Respite, The.
Zophiel; or, The Bride of Seven, *sels.*
Brooks, Phillips
Be Such a Man.
Christmas Carol: "Earth has grown old with its burden of care, The."
Christmas Carol, A: "Everywhere, everywhere Christmas tonight."
Christmas Everywhere.
Easter Morning.
Everywhere, Everywhere, Christmas Tonight.
Helper, The.
His Birth.
If I Knew.
O Little Town of Bethlehem.
Our Burden Bearer.
Unfailing One, The.
Wish for the New Year, A.
Brooks, Shirley
For A' That and A' That, *parody.*
I paints and paints.
Philosopher and Her Father, The.
Practical Answer, A.
Brooks, Walter Rollin
From the Ballad of Two-Gun Freddy.
Brooks, William E.
At the Lincoln Memorial.
Inasmuch!
Memorial Day.
Three Wise Kings.
Broome, Sir Frederick Napier
Leave-taking, A.
To the Soul.
Broome, William
Belinda's Recovery from Sickness.
Rose-Bud, The.
Broomell, Myron Henry
Lightning, The.
Prayer for the Age.
Brophy, Liam
Assumpta Est Maria.
Brotherton, Alice Williams
Blazing Heart, The.
First Thanksgiving Day, The.
My Enemy.
Thanksgiving.
Brough, Robert Barnabas
Early Christian, An.
Look at this skin—at fourscore years.
Marquis of Carabas, The.
My Lord Tomnoddy.
Broughton, James Richard
Birds of America, The.
Feathers or Lead?
Fruits of Experience.
Genesis of Vowels.
Lighthouse Keeper's Offspring, The.
Mrs. Mother Has a Nose.
Psalm of St. Priapus, The.
Psyche to Cupid: Her Ditty.
Brown, Abbie Farwell
All Wool.
Clothes.
Fairy Book, The.
Fisherman, The.
Friends.
Grandser.
Learning to Play.
Lizard, The.
Lost Playmate, The.
Music Box, A.
Nicest Story, The.
On Opening a New Book.
Peach, The.
Pirate Treasure.
Somebody's Birthday.
Work.
Brown, Alan
Street.
Brown, Alex J.
Wickedest Man in Memphis, The.
Brown, Alice
Artisan, The.
Benedictine Garden, A.
Candlemas.
Cloistered.
Edwin Booth.
Farewell, A: "Thou wilt not look on me?"
Hora Christi.
Life.
Pagan Prayer.
Revelation.
Road to Castaly, The, *sel.*
Seaward Bound.
Sleep.
Sunrise on Mansfield Mountain.
To an Enchantress.
Trilby.
West-Country Lover, A.
Brown, Alison
If Ever Time Shall Come.
Brown, Audrey Alexandra
Amber Beads.
Dark Cat, The.
Goldfish, The.
Museum-Piece.
Night Boat.
Reveillé.
Strangers, The.
Brown, Beatrice Curtis
Anniversary in September.
Apple Tree, The.
Jonathan Bing.
Jonathan Bing Dances for Spring.
Jonathan Bing Does Arithmetic.
Jonathan Bing's Tea.
My Kite.
New Song to Sing about Jonathan Bing, A.
Brown, Catherine Bernard
Prayer for Pentecost, A.
Brown, Earl Bigelow
Daily Cross.
New Crucifixion.
Brown, Edith Shaw
Little Child, A.
Brown, Fannie
Reflected Glory.
Brown, Ford Madox
For the Picture, "The Last of England."
O. M. B.
Brown, Frances
Greatest Loss, The.
Brown, Frank London
Jazz.
Brown, George Mackay
Death of Peter Esson, The.
December Day, Hoy Sound.
Five Voyages of Arnor, The.

Brown (continued)
Harald, the Agnostic Ale-loving Old Shepherd Enemy of the Whisky-drinking Ploughmen and Harvesters, Walks over the Sabbath Hill to the Shearing.
Old Women, The.
Our Lady of the Waves.
Stars.
Unlucky Boat.
Brown, Harry
Drill, The.
Incident on a Front Not Far from Castel de Sangro.
Poem of Bunker Hill, The, *sel.*
Then once more men's ears were full of "Yankee Doodle."
Brown, Irene Fowler
Rear Guard, The.
Brown, Isabella Maria
Another Day.
Prayer: "I had thought of putting an/ altar."
Brown, John
Night.
Brown, Joseph ("Luke")
Evening News: St. Louis.
Haiku: "Pine trees explode, The."
Some Few, Some Very Few.
Upon Which to Rejoice.
Brown, Joseph Brownlee
Thalatta! Thalatta!
Brown, Julian
Mr. Ripley Parodies Mr. Nash—or Vice Versa.
Brown, Kate Louise
Apple Blossom.
Christ Candle, The.
Christmas Candle, The.
Dandelion.
Five-fingered Maple, The.
In the Heart of a Seed.
Lady Moon, The.
Little Plant, The.
Pine Music.
Pussy Willow.
Tree Buds, The.
Brown, Mabel E.
My Father Cares.
Brown, Margaret Wise
Bumble Bee.
Dear Father/ hear and bless.
Fish with the Deep Sea Smile, The.
Little Black Bug.
Little Donkey Close Your Eyes ("Little Donkey on the hill").
Secret Song, The.
Brown, Oliver Madox
Before and After.
Laura's Song.
Brown, Palmer
Spangled Pandemonium, The.
Brown, Phoebe Hinsdale
I Love to Steal Awhile Away.
Private Devotion.
Brown, Robert Carlton
I Am Aladdin.
Brown, Spencer
In an Old House.
Brown, Sterling Allen
After Winter.
Challenge.
Effie.
Foreclosure.
Long Gone.
Maumee Ruth.
Memphis Blues.
Mose ("Mose is black and evil").
Odyssey of Big Boy.
Old Lem.
Remembering Nat Turner.
Return.
Revelations.
Salutamus.
Sister Lou.
Slim Greer.
Southern Road.
Sporting Beasley.
Strange Legacies.
Strong Men.
To a Certain Lady, in Her Garden.
When de Saints Go Ma'chin' Home.
Brown, T. Clarke
Rhode Island.
Brown, Theron
His Majesty.
Brown, Thomas (Tom)
Doctor Fell.
I do not like thee, Doctor Fell.
I Do Not Love Thee, Doctor Fell.
No Reason Why.
Non Amo Te.
Brown, Thomas Edward
Catherine Kinrade.
Chalse a Killey.
Conjergal Rights.
Disguises.
Dora.
Garden, A.
I Bended unto Me.
Ibant Obscurae.
In the Coach, *sel.*
Jessie.
Lily-Pool and the Cow, The.
My Garden.
O Englishwoman on the Pincian.
O God to Thee I Yield.
Opifex.
Organist in Heaven, The.
Oxford Idyll, An.
Peggy's Wedding.
Praesto.
Preparation.
Risus Dei.
Roman Women, *sel.*
Salve!
Specula.
To E. M. O.
To K. H.
Vesper.
Vespers.
Voices of Nature, The.
Wesley in Heaven.
When Love Meets Love.
Brown, Tom (1663-1704) *See* **Brown, Thomas**
Brown, William
American Patrol.
Exchange of Letters On Suicide Porpoises, An.
Man in the Street.
Minding Our Own Business.
Wondering How.
Brown, William Adams
Prayer for Peace, A.
Brown, William Goldsmith
Cleveland.
Hills Were Made for Freedom, The.
Mother, Home, Heaven.
Brown, William Laird *See* **"Laird, William"**
Browne, Cecil
Reply, A.
Browne, Charles Farrar *See* **"Ward, Artemus"**
Browne, Felicia Dorothea *See* **Hemans, Felicia Dorothea**
Browne, Francis Fisher
Santa Barbara.
Under the Blue.
Vanquished.
Browne, Irving
At Shakespeare's Grave.
Man's Pillow.
My New World.
Browne, Isaac Hawkins
Boy! bring an ounce of Freeman's best.
Fire Side, The; a Pastoral Soliloquy.
Foundling Hospital for Wit, The, *sel.*
In Imitation of Pope.
In Imitation of Young.
Pipe of Tobacco, A, *sels.*
"Browne, Matthew." *See* **Rands, William Brighty**
Browne, Michael Dennis
Delta, The.
Iowa.
King in May, The.
News from the House.
Peter.
Browne, Moses
Barber, The.
Musing by a River.
Shrimp, The.
Browne, Simon
Lesson of Love.
Browne, Sir Thomas
Colloquy with God, A.
Evening Hymn.
Religio Medici, *sel.*
Browne, William
Britannia's Pastorals, *sels.*
Caelia, *sels.*
Celadyne's Song.
Celia Is Gone.
Complete Lover, The.
Dawn of Day.
Epigram: "King to Oxford sent a troop of horse, The."
Epitaph: "May, be thou never graced with birds that sing."
Epitaph: "Underneath this sable hearse."
Epitaph in Obitum M. S., Xo Maij, 1614.
Epitaph on the Countess [Dowager] of Pembroke.
Frolic Mariners of Devon, The.
Gentle Nymphs, Be Not Refusing.
Glide Soft, Ye Silver Floods.
I oft have heard men say there be.
In Obitum M. S., X Maii, 1614.
Inner Temple Masque, The, *sels.*
Love Who Will, for I'll Love None.
Lydford Journey.
Memory ("Marina's gone, and now sit I").
Memory ("So shuts the marigold her leaves").
Ode, An: "Awake fair Muse for I intend."
On a Rope Maker Hanged.
On the Countess Dowager of Pembroke.
On the Death of Marie, Countess of Pembroke.
On the Dowager Countess of Pembroke.
Practising the Virginals.
Praise of Poets.
Rose, The.
Round, A: "Now that the spring hath filled our veins."
Shall I Love Again.
Shall I Tell You Whom I Love?
Shepherd's Pipe, The, *sel.*
Since She Is Gone.
Sirens' Song, The.
So Shuts the Marigold Her Leaves ("Marina's gone. . .").
Son of Erebus and Night.
Song: "For her gait, if she be walking."
Song: "Love, that looks still on your eyes."
Song: "Shall I tell you whom I love?"
Song of the Sirens.
Thyrsis' Praise of His Mistress.
Venus and Adonis.
Vision, A.

Visions, *sels.*
Welcome, A.
Welcome, Welcome, Do I Sing.
Ye hours, then, but as minutes be.
Browne, Sir William
Oxford & Cambridge.
Brownell, Amanda Benjamin Hall *See* **Hall, Amanda Benjamin**
Brownell, Florence Kerr
Coin in the Fist.
Brownell, Henry Howard
Abraham Lincoln.
Battle of Charlestown, The.
Bay Fight, The.
Burial of the Dane, The.
Bury Them.
Eagle of Corinth, The.
Lawyer's Invocation to Spring, The.
Night Quarters.
Old Cove, The.
River Fight, The.
Sphinx, The.
Sumter.
Would you hear of the River-Fight?
Browning, Elizabeth Barrett
Adequacy.
Aurora Leigh, *sels.*
Because thou hast the power and own'st the grace.
Belovèd.
Best, The.
Bianca among the Nightingales.
Books.
By Solitary Fires.
Casa Guidi Windows, *sels.*
Catarina to Camoens, *sel.*
Cheerfulness Taught by Reason.
Child's Thought of God, A.
Comfort.
Complaints.
Confessions ("Face to face in my chamber").
Consolation.
Content.
Convinced by Sorrow.
Court Lady, A.
Cowper's Grave.
Critics say that epics have died out, The.
Cry is up in England, which doth ring, A.
Cry of the Children, The.
Cry of the Human, The.
Curse, The.
Curse for a Nation, A., *sels.*
De Profundis, *sel.*
Dead Pan, The.
Denial, A.
Deserted Garden, The.
Drama of Exile, A, *sel.*
England.
Exaggeration.
Farewells from Paradise.
Ferment of New Wine, The.
Flush or Faunus.
For Love's Sake Only.
Forced Recruit, The.
Glory in the Commonplace.
Go from Me [Yet I feel That I Shall Stand].
"Good from a Book."
Great God Pan, The.
Grief.
Hymn: "Since without Thee we do no good."
I just knew it when we swept.
I never gave a lock of hair away.
Inclusions.
Juliet of Nations.
Keep my riband, take and keep it.
Lady Geraldine's Courtship.
Lady's "Yes," The.
Lessons from the Gorse.
Life and Love.
Live and Love.
Look, The.
Lord Turned, and Looked upon Peter, The.
Lord Walter's Wife.
Mask, The.
Meaning of the Look, The.
Mediator, The.
Mother and Poet.
Motherless.
Musical Instrument, A.
My Doves.
My Heart and I.
My Kate.
Mystery.
Nevermore Alone.
North and the South, The.
Patience Taught by Nature.
Pet Name, The.
Poet, The.
Poets, The.
Poet's Vow, The, *sel.*
Portrait, A.
Praise of Earth.
Prologue: "I heard an angel speak last night."
Reading.
Reed, A, *sel.*
Rhyme of the Duchess May, The, *sel.*
Romance of the Swan's Nest, The.
Romney and Aurora.
Rosalind's Scroll.
Round Our Restlessness.
Runaway Slave at Pilgrim's Point, The.
Sea-Mew, The.
Sleep, The.
Sonnet: "Accuse me not, beseech thee, that I wear."
Sonnet: "And wilt thou have me fashion into speech."
Sonnet: "And yet, because thou overcomest so."
Sonnet: "Because thou hast the power and own'st the grace."
Sonnet: "Belovèd, my Belovèd, when I think."
Sonnet: "Belovèd, thou hast brought me many flowers."
Sonnet: "But only three in all God's universe."
Sonnet: "Can it be right to give what I can give?"
Sonnet: "Face of all the world is changed, I think, The."
Sonnet: "First time he kissed me, he but only kissed."
Sonnet: "First time that the sun rose on thine oath, The."
Sonnet: "Go from me. Yet I feel that I shall stand."
Sonnet: "How do I love thee? Let me count the ways."
Sonnet: "I lift my heavy heart up solemnly."
Sonnet: "I lived with visions for my company."
Sonnet: "I never gave a lock of hair away."
Sonnet: "I thank all who have loved me in their hearts."
Sonnet: "I thought once how Theocritus had sung."
Sonnet: "If I leave all for thee, wilt thou exchange."
Sonnet: "If thou must love me, let it be for nought."
Sonnet: "Indeed this very love which is my boast."
Sonnet: "Is it indeed so? If I lay here dead."
Sonnet: "Let the world's sharpness, like a clasping knife."
Sonnet: "My future will not copy fair my past."
Sonnet: "My letters all dead paper, mute and white!"
Sonnet: "My own Belovèd, who hast lifted me."
Sonnet: "My poet, thou canst touch on all the notes."
Sonnet: "Say over again, and yet once over again."
Sonnet: "Soul's Rialto hath its merchandise, The."
Sonnet: "Thou comest! all is said without a word."
Sonnet: "Thou hast thy calling to some palace floor."
Sonnet: "Unlike are we, unlike, O princely Heart."
Sonnet: "What can I give thee back."
Sonnet: "When our two souls stand up erect and strong."
Sonnet: "When we met first and loved, I did not build."
Sonnet: "Yet love, mere love, is beautiful indeed."
Sonnets from the Portuguese (*Complete,* I-XLIV).
Substitution.
Sursum Corda.
Sympathy.
Tears.
They look up with their pale and sunken faces.
Thought for a Lonely Death-Bed, A.
Truth, so far, in my book; the truth which draws.
Two Sayings, The.
Valediction, A.
Virgin Mary to the Child Jesus, The, *abr.*
Weakest Thing, The.
What can I give thee back, O liberal.
Whatever's lost, it first was won.
"Where There Is No Vision," *abr.*
Wife to a Husband, A.
Woman's Shortcomings, A.
Browning, Frederick G.
Amen.
Browning, Ophelia Guyon
Pray without Ceasing.
Sometime, Somewhere.
Browning, Robert
Abt Vogler.
Adam, Lilith, and Eve.
After.
All-loving, The.
All Service Ranks the Same with God.
Among the Rocks.
Ancient Doctrine, The.
And so I somehow-nohow played.
And What Sordello Would See There.
Andrea del Sarto.
Andromeda.
Another Way of Love.
Any Wife to Any Husband.
Apparent Failure.
Apparitions.
Appearances.
April in England.
Artemis Prologizes.
Asolando, *sels.*
At Ecelin.
At the Mermaid, *sel.*
Avenger Speaks, The.
Awakening of Man, The.
Bad Dreams.
Before, *sel.*
Belief and Unbelief.
Ben Karshook's Wisdom.
Bishop Blougram's Apology.

Browning (continued)
Bishop Orders His Tomb at Saint Praxed's Church, The.
Blot in the 'Scutcheon, A, *sel.*
Boot and Saddle ("Boot, saddle, to horse, and away!").
Boy and the Angel, The.
Builder and maker Thou, of houses not made with hands!
By the Fireside.
Caliban upon Setebos.
Cavalier Tunes.
"Childe Roland to the Dark Tower Came."
Christmas-Eve and Easter-Day, *sels.*
Cleon.
Common Problem, The.
Confessional, The.
Confessions ("What is he buzzing in my ears?").
Count Gismond.
Cristina.
David's Song.
"De Gustibus."
Deaf and Dumb.
Death in the Desert, A.
Dedication: "O lyric Love, half angel and half bird."
Dedication of the Ring and the Book.
Development.
Development of Man, The.
Dis Aliter Visum; or, Le Byron de Nos Jours.
Dramatic Idyls, *sel.*
Dramatis Personae, *sel.*
Dubiety.
Earl Mertoun's Song.
Earth breaks up, time drops away.
Earth's Immortalities.
Echetlos.
Englishman in Italy, The.
Epilogue: "At the midnight in the silence of the sleep-time."
Epilogue: "Oh, Love—no, Love! All the noise below, Love."
Epilogue: "On the first of the Feast of Feasts."
Epilogue: "Touch him ne'er so lightly, into song he broke."
Epistle, An: "Karshish, the picker-up of learning's crumbs."
Epistle, An, Containing the Strange Medical Experience of Karshish, the Arab Physician.
Epistle of Karshish, An.
Epitaph: "Thou whom these eyes saw never."
Escape Me?—Never.
Eurydice to Orpheus.
Evelyn Hope.
Eyes, calm beside thee (Lady, could'st thou know!).
Face, A.
Faith.
Fame.
Ferishtah's Fancies, *sel.*
Fifine at the Fair, *sels.*
Flight of the Duchess, The, *sels.*
Flower's Name, The.
Fra Lippo Lippi.
Garden Fancies, *sels.*
Giuseppe Caponsacchi.
Give a Rouse.
Glove, The.
God's View of Service.
Good Morning.
Grammarian's Funeral, A.
Greece.
Guardian Angel, The.
Guido.
Gypsies.
He who did most, shall bear most; the strongest shall stand the most weak.
Heap Cassia, Sandal-Buds and Stripes.
Here's to Nelson's Memory.
Hervé Riel.
Holy-Cross Day.
Home Thoughts from Abroad.
Home Thoughts, from the Sea.
House.
House: A Reply.
Householder, The.
How a Poet's Soul Comes into Play.
How It Strikes a Contemporary.
How say you? Let us, O my dove.
How They Brought the Good News from Ghent to Aix.
Humility.
I believe it! 'Tis thou, God, that givest, 'tis I who receive.
I Go to Prove My Soul.
I have done with being judged.
I know not too well how I found my way home in the night.
I never realized God's birth before.
I say, the acknowledgment of God in Christ.
Illimitable God, The.
In a Balcony.
In a Gondola.
In a Year.
In Doubt of Doubt.
In His Good Time.
In the Doorway.
In Three Days.
Incident of the French Camp.
Instans Tyrannus.
Into the street the Piper stept.
Italian in England, The.
It's wiser being good than bad.
James Lee's Wife.
Johannes Agricola in Meditation.
Joy of Living, The.
Karshish and Lazarus.
Karshish, the Arab Physician ("Karshish, the picker-up of learning's crumbs").
La Saisiaz, *sel.*
Laboratory, The; Ancien Régime.
Last Ride Together, The.
Life.
Life in a Love.
Light Woman, A.
Likeness, A.
Live in a Love.
Lost Leader, The.
Lost Mistress, The.
Love.
Love among the Ruins.
Love in a Life.
Love's Pursuit.
Lyric Love.
Magical Nature.
Man's Destiny.
Marching Along.
Master Hugues of Saxe-Gotha.
May and Death.
Meeting at Night.
Memorabilia.
Misconceptions.
Mr. Sludge, "The Medium," *br. sel.*
Moment Eternal, The.
Moon Rainbow, A.
Moth's Kiss, First, The.
Muckle-Mouth Meg.
My God, my God, let me for once look on thee.
My Last Duchess.
My Lode-Star.
My Star.
My Sun Sets to Rise Again.
Nationality in Drinks, *sel.*
Natural Magic.
Ned Bratts.
Never the Time and the Place.
New Year's Hymn.
Night and Morning.
No one ever plucked.
North Country, The.
Now.
O God, where do they tend—these struggling aims?
Oh, good gigantic smile o' the brown old earth.
O Lyric Love.
O Never Star Was Lost.
Oh, the Wild Joy of Living.
O thou pale form.
Oft Have I Stood by Thee.
Old Pictures in Florence.
Old Pope Is Comforted by the Thought of the Young Pompilia, The.
Old Whom God Loves, The.
One Way of Love.
One Word More.
Orpheus and Eurydice.
Our Known Unknown.
Our Wars Are Wars of Life.
Over the Sea Our Galleys Went.
Paracelsus, *sels.*
Parting at Morning.
Patriot, The.
Pauline, *sels.*
Pearl, a Girl, A.
Phases of the Moon.
Pheidippides.
Pictor Ignotus.
Pied Piper of Hamelin, The.
Pippa Passes.
Pisgah-Sights.
Poetics.
Pompilia.
Pope, The.
Pope and the Net, The.
Popularity.
Porphyria's Lover.
Prologue: "'Poet's age is sad, The: for why?'"
Prologue to "Asolando."
Prologue to "La Saisiaz."
Prospice.
Protus.
"Quis pro Domino?"
Rabbi Ben Ezra.
Religion.
Respectability.
Rest Remaineth.
Ring and the Book, The, *sels.*
Rudel to the Lady of Tripoli.
Saul.
Saul. . .sat out my singing,—one arm round the tent-prop to raise.
Scene in a Garden.
Service.
Shelley.
Shop.
Sibrandus Schafnaburgensis.
Soliloquy of the Spanish Cloister.
Song: "All service ranks the same with God."
Song: "Give her but a least excuse to love me."
Song: "Heap cassia, sandal-buds and stripes."
Song: "Moth's kiss, first! The."
Song: "Nay but you, who do not love her."
Song: "Over the sea our galleys went."
Song: This Tress.
Song: "Thus the Mayne glideth."
Song: "Year's at the spring, The."
Song: "You'll love me yet! and I can tarry."
Song from "Pippa Passes."

Sordello, *sels.*
Speculative.
Spring Song.
Statue and the Bust, The.
Stay we here/ With the wild hawks?
Such a Starved Bank of Moss.
Summum Bonum.
Sunrise.
That One Face.
Then I turned my harp—took off the lilies we twine round its chords.
Therefore to whom turn I but to thee, the ineffable Name?
There's a blessing on the hearth.
Through the Metidja to Abd-el-Kadr.
Thus the Mayne Glideth.
Time's Revenges.
Toccata of Galuppi's, A.
Too Late.
Transcendentalism; a Poem in Twelve Books.
Truth.
Truth Is Within.
Two in the Campagna.
Two Poets of Croisic, The, *sel.*
Up at a Villa—Down in the City.
Vault inside the Castle at Goito, A.
Wanderers, The.
Wanting Is—What?
Waring.
Water and Air.
When a Man's Busy.
When the fight begins within himself.
Why I Am a Liberal.
Woman's Last Word, A.
Women and Roses.
"Yea, my King."
Year's at the Spring, The.
You never know what life means till you die.
You'll Love Me Yet!
Youth.
Youth and Art.

Brownjohn, Alan
In This City.
Man Watching.
Wall, The.

Brownstein, Michael
Against the Grain.
Behind the Wheel.
Big City.
Children, It's Time.
Clean and Clear.
Diamond.
Driving through Belgium.
I Am Not the Constant Reader.
Kites.
Lily Flower.
Lost in a Corridor of Power.
Nations.
No Empty Hands.
Plains of Abraham, The.
Pounds and Ounces.
Something Else.
Spiral Landscape.
Waitress.
War.

Bruce, Aubert Edgar
Contrast.

Bruce, Charles
Attic, The.
Back Road Farm.
Biography.
Dreaming Trout, The.
Eastern Shore.
Fisherman's Son.
Flowing Summer, The, *sels.*
Hayfield, The.
Words Are Never Enough.

Bruce, George
Death Mask of a Fisherman.
Kinnaird Head.
My House.
Singers, The.
Sumburgh Heid.

Bruce, John
Pike, The.

Bruce, Michael
Ode to the Cuckoo.
To the Cuckoo.

Bruce, Richard
Cavalier.
Shadow.

Bruce, Wallace
Our Nation Forever.
Parson Allen's Ride.
Two Argosies.

Bruechert, Betty
Drought.

Bruhn, Carl F.
"Land of Beginning Again, The."

Bruner, Margaret E.
Angry Word, An.
Atonement.
Beggar, The.
Beyond the Grave.
Casual Meeting.
Christmas Eve Meditation.
Clown, The.
Cruelty.
Dog's Vigil, A.
Dreaded Task, The.
Elegy: "We knew that he was not a model cat."
Epitaph for a Cat.
For One Lately Bereft.
For One Who Is Serene.
Gift, The.
God's Ways Are Strange.
Good-by.
Greater Gift, The.
Grocery Store Cat, The.
If Lincoln Should Return.
Lonely Dog, The.
Midwinter.
Monk and the Peasant, The.
Old Cat Meditates, An.
On City Streets.
Plea for Tolerance.
Prayer for Strength.
Rebirth.
Remembrance.
Retaliation.
Selfishness.
Sinner, The.
Sonnet: "There have been many cats I loved and lost."
Souvenirs.
There have been times when on a city street.
There Is a Loneliness.
Time's Hand Is Kind.
Way of a Cat, The.
Wedding Anniversary.
Whom the Gods Love.

Brunini, John Gilland
Assumption, The.
Descent of the Holy Ghost.
For a Young Idealist: "Godspeed!"
Repeated Pilgrimage.
Resurrection, The.
Silent Sufferer.
To Mary at Christmas.

Brunner, John
Citizen Bacillus.
To Myself on the Occasion of My Twenty-first Century.

Bruno, Eric
Libera Nos a Malo.

Bruno, Giordano
Spurning the Earth.

Bruns, John Dickson
Foe at the Gates, The.

Bryan, Elizabeth Mabel
Father of the Man.

Bryant, Frederick J., Jr.
Black Orpheus.
Languages We Are, The.
Nothing Lovely as a Tree.

Bryant, John H.
At the Lincoln Tomb.

Bryant, William Cullen
Abraham Lincoln.
African Chief, The.
Ah mother of a mighty race.
America ("O mother of a mighty race").
Antiquity of Freedom, The.
Autumn Woods.
Battlefield, The.
Be Ye Also Ready.
Blessed Are They That Mourn.
But quit thy meaner game, indignant Muse.
Centennial Hymn.
Christmas.
Communion Hymn.
Conjunction of Jupiter and Venus, The, *sel.*
Conqueror's Grave, The.
Dante.
Death of Lincoln, The.
Death of Slavery, The.
Death of the Flowers, The.
Dedication: "Thou, whose unmeasured temple stands."
Earth.
Earth, that nourished thee, shall claim.
Embargo, The, *sel.*
Evening Revery, An, *sel.*
Evening Wind, The.
Father, thy hand.
Flood of Years, The.
Forest Hymn.
Forest Maid, The.
Green Mountain Boys, The.
Green River.
Holy Star, The.
How Amiable Are Thy Tabernacles!
Hunter of the Prairies, The.
Hymn of the City.
Hymn of the Waldenses.
Hymn to the North Star.
I Broke the Spell that Held Me Long.
I Cannot Forget with What Fervid Devotion.
"I Will Send Them Prophets and Apostles."
I Would Not Always Reason.
In Memory of John Lothrop Motley.
Indian at the Burial-Place of His Fathers, An.
Inscription for the Entrance to a Wood.
June.
March.
May Sun Sheds an Amber Light, The.
Monument Mountain.
Moses—No Man Knoweth His Sepulchre.
Mother's Hymn, The.
Murdered Traveller, The.
Mutation.
Mutual Kindness.
My Autumn Walk.
New Moon, The.
November.
O Fairest of the Rural Maids.
Oh Freedom! thou art not, as poets dream.
Oh Mother of a Mighty Race.
O thou great movement of the universe.
Other Sheep I Have, Which Are Not of This Fold.
Our Country's Call.

Bryant (continued)
Past, The.
Path, The, *sel.*
Path we planned beneath October's sky, The.
Planting of the Apple Tree, The.
Poet, The.
Prairies, The.
Prayer to Make Your Own, A.
Robert of Lincoln.
Seventy-six.
Snow-Shower, The.
So Live.
Song for New Year's Eve, A.
Song of Marion's Men.
Stream of Life, The.
Summer Wind.
Thanatopsis.
Thou Hast Put All Things under His Feet.
To ——: "Ay, thou art for the grave; thy glances shine."
To a Mosquito.
To a Waterfowl.
To Cole, the Painter, Departing for Europe.
To the Evening Wind.
To the Fringed Gentian.
To the Memory of Abraham Lincoln.
Truth, Crushed to Earth.
Truth, the Invincible.
Twenty-second of December, The.
Twenty-second of February, The.
White-footed Deer, The.
Winter Piece, A.
Yellow Violet, The.
Yet not to thine eternal resting-place.
Brydges, Matthew *See* **Bridges, Matthew**
Brydges, Sir Samuel Egerton
On Dreams.
To Miss M——, Written by Moonlight.
Bryusov, Valery Yakovlevich
Radiant Ranks of Seraphim.
Buchan, John, 1st Baron Tweedsmuir
Fratri Dilectissimo.
Buchan, Tom
Invitation, The.
Buchanan, Dugald
Day of Judgment, The.
Omnia Vanitas.
Buchanan, George
Epithalamium for Mary Stuart and the Dauphin of France, *abr.*
Of the Sad Lot of the Humanists in Paris.
Buchanan, J. A.
Oregon State Song.
Buchanan, Robert Williams
Ballad of Judas Iscariot, The.
Book of Orm, The, *sel.*
Churchyard, The.
Dawn, The.
Dream of the World without Death, The.
Faery Foster-Mother, The.
Faery Reaper, The.
Green Gnome, The.
Image in the Forum, The.
Judas Iscariot.
Langley Lane.
Little Herd-Boy's Song, The.
Little Milliner, The.
On a Young Poetess's Grave.
Pilgrim and the Herdboy, The.
Spring Song in the City.
Summer Pool, The.
Tom Dunstan; or, The Politician.
Two Sons.
Wake of Tim O'Hara, The.
We Are Children.
When We Are All Asleep.
Bucher, Helen Hall
Pennsylvania.
Buck, Byron
Song from a Two-Desk Office.
Buck, Carlton
Above Myself.
Cheer the New Year.
Christ Supreme.
Discovery.
Forward with Christ.
Grace to Share.
Keep Looking Up.
Light after Darkness.
My God Is Near.
Place of Prayer, The.
Rejoice, Be Glad.
Resolution.
Solitary Place, The.
Symphony of the Soul.
Take a Man.
Work Motive.
Buck, Richard Henry
Kentucky Babe.
Buckham, James
Child of To-Day, A.
Hearts Proof, The.
Buckingham, George Villiers, 2d Duke of
I have made, too, one of the most delicate, dainty similes.
On the London Fire's Monument.
Part of an Ode of Horace Paraphras'd by the Duke of Buckingham, 1680.
Prayer: "Lord God of the oak and the elm."
Rehearsal, The, *sel.*
Buckingham and Normanby, Duke of *See* **Sheffield, John, Duke of Buckingham and Normanby**
Buckley, Vincent
Korea.
Late Tutorial.
Various Wakings.
Buckner, Samuel O.
Do It Right.
Bucks, W. H.
Let Me Go.
Buckton, Alice M.
At the Garden Rail.
At Welbedacht.
Budbill, David
New York in the Spring.
Budzynski, Joe
Have Faith in God.
Bukowski, Charles
Day I Kicked a Bankroll Out the Window, The.
Bulcke, Karl
There is an Old City.
Bullen, Arthur Henry
Whisperer, The.
Bullett, Gerald
Because I love her.
Carol: "We saw Him sleeping in His manger bed."
Exile, The.
Footnote to Tennyson.
So Still the World.
Winter Solstice, *sel.*
Bullins, Ed
When Slavery Seems Sweet.
Bulloch, John Malcolm
To Homer.
Bullock, J.
Fear Not.
Bullock, Mark
Be Thankful.
Testimony.
Bullock, Mary
Blessed Nearness.
Bullwinkle, Christine Wood
Night.
Bulwer-Lytton, Edward, Baron Lytton
Absent Yet Present.
Cardinal's Soliloquy, The.
Christ's Sympathy.
Ernest Maltravers, *sel.*
Last Days of Pompeii, The, *sel.*
Night and Love.
Nydia's Song.
Richelieu; or, The Conspiracy, *sel.*
When Stars Are in the Quiet Skies.
Bulwer-Lytton, Edward Robert, 1st Earl of Lytton *See* **"Meredith, Owen"**
Bumstead, Eudora S.
Little Red Hen, The.
Summer Lullaby, A.
Bunin, Ivan Alekseyevich
Flax.
Bunker, John
Old Woman, The.
Petition of Youth before Battle.
Remembrance.
Serenade: "Sometimes you seem a star."
Bunn, Alfred
Bohemian Girl, The, *sels.*
I Dreamt I Dwelt in Marble Halls.
Light of Other Days, The.
Then You'll Remember Me.
When Other Lips and Other Hearts.
Bunner, Alice Learned (Mrs. Henry Cuyler Bunner)
Immutabilis.
Separation.
Vingtaine.
Bunner, Henry Cuyler
Appeal to Harold, The.
Behold the Deeds!
Candor.
Chaperon, The.
Da Capo.
Deaf.
Feminine.
Grandfather Watts's Private Fourth ("Grandfather Watts used to tell us boys").
Heart of the Tree, The.
Home, Sweet Home, with Variations, *parody.*
J. B.
Les Morts Vont Vite.
Old Flag, The.
On Reading a Poet's First Book.
One, Two, Three!
Pitcher of Mignonette, A.
Shake, Mulleary, and Go-ethe.
She Was a Beauty.
Strong as Death.
To a June Breeze.
Way to Arcady, The.
Yes?
Bunston, Anna *See* **De Bary, Anna Bunston**
Bunting, Basil
Complaint of the Morepethshire Farmer, The.
Gin the Goodwife Stint.
Bunyan, John
Enough.
He That Is Down.
Lanthorn is to keep the candle Light, The.
My Little Bird.
Neither Hook nor Line.
Of the Child with the Bird at the Bush.
Of the Going Down of the Sun.
Pilgrim, The.
Pilgrim Song, The.
Pilgrim's Progress, The, *sels.*
Pilgrim's Song.
Shepherd Boy Sings [in the Valley of Humiliation], The.
Shepherd Boy's Song, The.
Shepherd's Song, The.
Song in the Valley of Humiliation.
Song of Low Degree, A.

Song of the Shepherd in the Valley of Humiliation, The.
Time and Eternity.
Upon a Ring of Bells.
Upon the Lark and the Fowler.
Upon the Snail.
What danger is the pilgrim in?

Buonarroti *See* **Michelangelo Buonarroti**

Burbidge, Thomas
Eventide.
If I Desire.
Mother's Love.
She Bewitched Me.
To Imperia.

Burch, Loren W.
Communion.
Into Thy Hands.

Burden, Jean
Absence.
Evangel.

Burdette, Robert Jones
Christ.
Limerick: "There was a young man of Cohoes."
My Guide.
Orphan Born.
Romance of the Carpet, The.
Russian and Turk.
"Soldier, Rest!"
"Songs without Words."
What Will We Do?
When My Ship Comes In ("Somewhere, out on the blue sea sailing").

Burdick, Arthur J.
Washington's Birthday.

Burdick, Loraine
My Prayer.

Burford, William
Christmas Tree, A.
Fire, The.
Rider, The.
Tomboy, The.

Burgess, Bangs
Life's Finest Things.

Burgess, Charles
Albatross.
Five Serpents.
Lady and Crocodile.
Two Garden Scenes.

Burgess, Gelett
Abstemia.
Abstrosophy.
Adolphus Elfinstone.
Ah, Yes, I Wrote It.
Ah, Yes, I Wrote the "Purple Cow."
Alphabet of Famous Goops, An, *sel.*
Bohunkus would take off his hat, and bow and smile, and things like that.
Cinq Ans Après.
Dighton Is Engaged!
Ego Sum.
Extracts from the Rubaiyat of Omar Cayenne.
Felicia Ropps.
Floorless Room, The.
Hair.
I seen a dunce of a poet once, a-writin' a little book.
I Wish That My Room Had a Floor.
I'd Rather Have Fingers than Toes.
Invisible Bridge, The.
Jilted Funeral, The.
Kitty Wants to Write.
Lament: "Ban of Time there is no disobeying, The."
Lazy Roof, The.
Limerick: "I wish that my room had a floor!"
Limerick: "I'd rather have fingers than toes."
Limerick: "I'd rather have habits than clothes."
Limerick: "Remarkable truly, is art!"
My Feet.
My Legs Are So Weary.
My Room.
Nonsense Quatrains: "Ah, yes! I wrote the 'Purple Cow'."
Nonsense Quatrains: "I never saw a Purple Cow."
Nonsense Quatrains: "I sent my Collie to the wash."
Nonsense Quatrains: "Many people seem to think."
Nonsense Quatrains: "Proper way to leave a room, The."
Nonsense Rhymes.
Nonsense Verses.
On Digital Extremities.
Over the Hills with Nancy, *abr.*
Protest of the Illiterate, The, *sel.*
Psycholophon.
Purple Cow, The.
Queer Quatrains.
Roof, The.
Sunset, The.
Table Manners.
Tardiness.
Ubasti.
Villanelle of Things Amusing.
Willy and the Lady.

Burgess, George
Heavenly Breeze, The.

Burgess, Helen M.
Mother's Petition, in Wartime.

Burgess, Stella Fisher
One There Was.

Burgess, Thornton
Paddy the Beaver.
Young Flash the Deer.

Burgh, Hugh de
Punchinello.

Burghley, William Cecil, 1st Baron
To Mistress Anne Cecil, upon Making Her a New Year's Gift, January 1, 1567-8.

Burgon, John William
Pedra.
Petra.

Burgoyne, Arthur G.
"Everybody Works but Father" as W. S. Gilbert Would Have Written It.

Burgunder, Rose
Boys's Place, A.

Burke, Francis
Mediatrix of Grace, The.
Sequence, with Strophes in Paraphrase Thereof, A.

Burke, Henrietta A.
Transaction on the Roman Exchange.

Burke, Henry
Schooner 8Blizzard,9 The.

Burke, Kenneth
Conspirators, The.
Enigma.
Mercy Killing.
Stout Affirmation.
Wrens, The.

Burke, Thomas
Piccadilly.

Burket, Gail Brooks
Christian Home, The.
Columbus Never Knew.
February 12, 1809.
House in Springfield.
Noel.
Thought for a New Year.

Burkhard von Hohenfels
Dance Song, A.

Burkholder, Clarence M.
Easter Beatitudes.
Prayer, A: "Lord, let not my religion be."

Burleigh, Harry Thacker
Little Child of Mary.

Burleigh, William Henry
Good in Ill.
Weaver, The.

Burnand, Sir Francis Cowley
Fisherman's Chant, The.
Fishing for sticklebacks, with rod and line.
His Heart Was True to Poll.
Oh, My Geraldine.
True to Poll.

Burnell, Fritz S.
Isle of Apple-Trees, The.
Pool, The.

Burnet, Dana
Marching Song.
Road to Vagabondia, The.
Sack of Old Panama, The, *abr.*
Song: "Love's on the highroad."
Song for Youth.
They sat in a tavern in wicked Port Royal.
Wayfarers.

Burnet, W. Hodgson
Autumn Leaves.

Burnett, Olive H.
Best for Us, The.

Burnham, Maud
Barnyard, The.
Five Little Fairies, The.
Pigeons, The.

Burnham, Richard
Friend of Sinners.

Burnie, Donald
Eliza Spaulding.
Henry Spaulding.

Burns, Colette M.
Why Read a Book?

Burns, J. D.
For England.

Burns, Richard
Alum.

Burns, Robert
Address to a Haggis.
Address to a Lady.
Address to the Deil.
Address to the Toothache.
Address to the Unco Guid, or the Rigidly Righteous.
Addressed to a Gentleman at Table, Who Kept Boasting of the Company He Kept.
Ae Fond Kiss.
Afton Water.
Anna.
As I came O'er Cairney Mount.
As Others See Us.
Auld Lang Syne.
Banks o' Doon, The.
Bannockburn.
Bard's Epitaph, A.
Before Bannockburn.
Birks of Aberfeldy, The.
Blooming Nelly.
Bonie Doon.
Bonnie Doon.
Bonnie Lesley [*or* Leslie].
Bonnie Wee Thing.
Book-Worms, The.
Brigs of Ayr, The, *sel.*
Bruce [*or* Bruce's Address] to His Army [*or* Men] at Bannockburn.
Bruce's March to Bannockburn.
Ca' the Yowes to the Knowes.
Charlie, He's My Darling.
Cheerfu' supper done, wi' serious face, The.
Child's Grace, A.
Chloe.
Comin' thro' [*or* through] the Rye (*diff. versions*).

Burns (continued)
Composed in Spring.
Contented wi' Little and Cantie wi' Mair.
Corn Rigs Are Bonny.
Cotter's Saturday Night, The.
Could You Do That?
Daisy, The.
Day Returns, The.
Death and Doctor Hornbook.
De'il's Awa wi' the Exciseman, The.
Drinking Song.
Duncan Gray.
Epigram: "No more of your titled acquaintances boast."
Epistle to a Young Friend.
Epistle to Davie, a Brother Poet.
Epistle to Dr. Blacklock, Ellisland, 21st Oct. 1789, *abr.*
Epistle to James Smith.
Epistle to John Lapraik [an Old Scottish Bard].
Epitaph for James Smith.
Epitaph on a Friend.
Epitaph on John Dove.
Epitaph on My Father.
Exciseman, The.
False Love.
Farewell, A: "Go fetch to me a pint o' wine."
Farewell, The: "It was a' for our rightfu' king."
Farewell to Nancy.
Flow Gently, Sweet Afton.
For A' That and A' That ("Is there for honest poverty").
For the Sake of [*or* o'] Somebody.
Gie the Lass Her Fairin'.
Gloomy Night Is Gathering Fast, The.
Go Fetch to Me a Pint o' Wine.
Godly Girzie.
Gowden Locks of Anna, The.
Green Grow the Rashes.
Hallowe'en.
Hark! the Mavis.
Here's a Health to Them That's Awa'.
Highland Mary.
Holy Fair, The.
Holy Willie's Prayer.
How Can I Keep My Maidenhead.
Hymn of Marriage.
I am nae poet, in a sense.
I Do Confess Thou Art Sae Fair.
I Hae a Wife o' My Ain.
I Love My Jean.
I Murder Hate by Field or Flood.
I Once Was a Maid.
I'm O'er [*or* Owre] Young to Marry Yet.
Inventory, The.
Is There for Honest Poverty.
It Was A' for Our Rightfu' King.
Jean.
John Anderson.
John Anderson, My Jo ("John Anderson, my jo, John,/When we were first acquent").
John Barleycorn.
Johnnie, Cock Up Your Beaver.
Jolly Beggars, The.
Jolly Mortals, Fill Your Glasses.
Kirk's Alarm, The.
Lament for Culloden.
Lass and the Friar, The.
Lass That Made the Bed to Me, The.
Last May a Braw Wooer.
Letter to a Young Friend.
Lines on the Author's Death.
Lines on War.
Lord Galloway.
Lovely Lass o' Inverness, The.
Lovely Lass to a Friar Came, A.
Macpherson's [*or* M'Pherson's] Farewell.
Man Was Made to Mourn; a Dirge.
Man's a Man for A' That, A.
Man's Inhumanity to Man.
Mary Morison.
Mary Queen of Scots.
Merry Hae I Been Teethin a Heckle.
Mother's Lament for the Death of Her Son, A.
Muirland Meg.
My Ain Kind Dearie, O.
My Bonnie Highland Laddie.
My Bonnie [*or* Bonie] Mary.
My Heart's in the Highlands.
My Jean.
My Love Is like a Red Red Rose.
My Love, She's But a Lassie Yet.
My Luve's like a Red, Red Rose.
My Nanie, O.
My Nannie's Awa'.
My Wife's a Winsome Wee Thing.
Nine Inch Will Please a Lady.
Nobody.
November Evening.
Nut-gathering Lass, The.
O Mally's Meek, Mally's Sweet.
O My Luve's like a Red, Red Rose.
O, Open the Door to Me, O!
O Saw Ye Bonnie Lesley.
O, Were My Love.
Oh Wert Thou in the Cauld Blast.
O Whistle an' I'll Come to Ye [*or* You], My Lad.
O, Willie Brew'd a Peck o' Maut.
O'er the Water to Charlie.
Of A' the Airts [the Wind Can Blow].
On a Wag in Mauchline.
On Andrew Turner.
On the Author.
Open the Door to Me, O.
Parson's Looks, The.
Patriarch, The.
Plowman, The.
Poet's Grace, A.
Poet's Welcome to His Love-begotten Daughter, A.
Prayer for My Native Land.
Prayer in the Prospect of Death, A.
Prayer under the Pressure of Violent Anguish.
Rantin' Dog the Daddie o't, The.
Rantin, Rovin Robin.
Red, Red Rose, A.
Rigs o' Barley, The.
Robert Bruce to His Men at Bannockburn.
Robert Bruce's Address to His Army, before the Battle of Bannockburn.
Rose-Bud, A, [by my Early Walk].
Sacred lowe of weel-placed love, The.
Saw Ye Bonny Lesley?
Scots Wha Hae [wi' Wallace Bled].
See the Smoking Bowl before Us.
She is a winsome wee thing.
She'll Do It.
Sic a Wife as Willie Had.
Silver Tassie, The.
Simmer's a Pleasant Time.
Sketch.
Song: "Again rejoicing Nature sees."
Song: Green Grow the Rashes.
Song: "It was upon a Lammas night."
Song: Mary Morison.
Song: "My luve is like a red, red rose."
Song: My Nanie, O.
Sonnet on the Death of Robert Riddell of Glenriddell.
Sonnet to Robert Graham, Esq.
Sonnet upon Sonnets, A.
Such a Parcel of Rogues in a Nation.
Supper time.
Sweet Afton.
Tam Glen.
Tam o' Shanter.
Tam Samson's Elegy.
Then gently scan your brother man.
There'll Never Be Peace.
Thou Lingering Star.
Thrusting of It, The.
To a Field Mouse.
To a Louse [On Seeing One on a Lady's Bonnet at Church].
To a Mountain Daisy [On Turning One Down, with the Plow, in April, 1786].
To a Mouse [on Turning Her Up in Her Nest with the Plough, November, 1785].
To James Smith.
To John Taylor.
To Mary in Heaven.
To Miss Ferrier.
To Ruin.
To the Rev. John M'Math.
To William Simpson of Ochiltree.
Tommie Makes My Tail Toddle.
Twa Dogs, The.
Up in the Morning Early.
Verses Intended to Be Written below a Noble Earl's Picture.
Vision, The ("As I stood by yon roofless tower").
Vision, The ("The sun had clos'd the winter-day").
Wee Willie Gray.
Wha Is That at My Bower-Door?
When biting Boreas, fell and doure.
When heavy, dark, continued, a'-day rains.
Whistle an' I'll Come to Ye [*or* You], My Lad.
Whistle o'er the Lave o't.
Willie Brew'd [*or* Brewed] a Peck o' Maut.
Winter.
Winter; a Dirge.
Winter Night, A, *sel.*
Within the Bush.
Wounded Hare, The.
Ye Banks and Braes o' Bonnie Doon.
Ye Flowery Banks [o' Bonnie Doon].

Burns, Vincent Godfrey
If Jesus Came Back Today, *sel.*
Sonnet for Christmas.

Burnshaw, Stanley
Bread.
End of the Flower-World (A.D. 2300).
House in St. Petersburg.
Strange.

Burnside, Helen
"Tired."

Burr, Amelia Josephine
Battle-Song of Failure.
Certainty Enough.
Deliver Us From. . . .
Gorgio Lad.
Joyce Kilmer.
Mother Moon.
Mother of Judas, The.
Mothers of Men.
My Mother.
New Life.
Night Magic.
Nocturne: "All the earth a hush of white."
Pershing at the Tomb of Lafayette.
Perugia.
Rain in the Night.
Reality.
Romany Gold.
Song of Living, A.
Surrender.
To Her—Unspoken.
Where Love Is.
Where You Passed.

Burr, Gray

Butterfly, The.
Epistemological Rag, The.
Garden Puzzle.
Glance at the Album, A.
Play of Opposites, A.
Sailing, Sailing.
Skater's Waltz, A.
What We Listened for in Music.
Burr, William Norris
God's Dream.
Burr, Winifred Adams
Ghosts.
Opening Door.
Burrell, Sophia
Epigram on Two Ladies.
Burroughs, Alethea S.
Savannah.
"Burroughs, Ellen." *See* **Jewett, Sophie**
Burroughs, John
My Own Shall Come to Me.
Return, The.
Song of the Toad, The.
Waiting.
Burroway, Jan
Owed to Dickens, 1956.
Song: "With whomsoever I share the spring."
Bursk, Christopher
Adjust, Adjust.
Burstein, Abraham
Love of Hell, The.
Burt, Emily Rose
Escape, The.
For April Showers.
Burt, Nathaniel
Out.
Burt, Struthers
Be not afraid, O Dead, be not afraid.
Fifty Years Spent.
Free Men.
Hill-born, The.
I Know a Lovely Lady Who Is Dead.
Land, The, *sel.*
Resurgam.
Burton, Ernest De Witt
Way O Christ Thou Art, The.
Burton, Henry
Jesus Himself.
Light upon the Mountains, A.
Pass It On.
There's a Light upon the Mountains.
Burton, John
Do I Really Pray?
Holy Bible, Book Divine.
Prayer: "I often say my prayers."
Burton, John, Jr.
Savior, While My Heart Is Tender.
Burton, Katherine
Exile, The.
November Eleventh.
Burton, Richard
Across the Fields to Anne.
Black Sheep.
City of the Dead, The.
Comfort of the Stars, The.
Deserted Farms.
Extras.
Factory Children.
First Song, The.
Forefather, The.
Glorious Game, The.
God's Garden.
Human Touch, The.
Idols.
In Sleep.
Love Is Strong.
Mary Magdalene.
Modern Saint, The.
Of Those Who Walk Alone.
Old Santa Fé Trail, The.
On a Ferry Boat.
On Syrian Hills.
Polar Quest, The.
Rhyme for Remembrance of May.
Sealed Orders.
Song of the Sea.
Song of the Unsuccessful, The.
Strength in Weakness.
Unpraised Picture, An.
Wood Witchery.
Burton, Sir Richard Francis
Do What Thy Manhood Bids Thee Do.
In these drear wastes of sea-born land, these wilds where none may dwell but He.
Kasidah, The, *sel.*
Burton, Robert
Anatomy of Melancholy, The, *sels.*
Author's Abstract of Melancholy, The.
Dost ask (my dear) what service I will have?
Bush, Jocelyn
Little Red Sled, The.
Bush, Joseph Bevans
Nittygritty.
Bushnell, Frances Louisa
In the Dark.
Unfulfilment.
World Music.
Buson, (Taniguchi Buson)
Chums.
Haze.
Mists of Daybreak.
Red Peony, The.
Spring Breeze.
Spring rain! And as yet.
Spring Scene.
Whale, The.
Busse, Carl
In the Night of the Full Moon.
Quiet Kingdom, The.
Buster, Marjorie Lorene
My Friend.
Butchart, Isabel
Dawn.
Butler, Arthur Gray
Edith and Harold.
Two Long Vacations; Grasmere.
Butler, Ellis Parker
Secret Combination, The.
Butler, Frances Anne Kemble *See* **Kemble, Frances Anne**
Butler, Gerald
But usually, words fill our heads, which we bring.
Morphine combined with scopolamine is called.
Reason why all colors look deeper, The.
Take a walk in my head.
This Side of Orion, *sels.*
Winter/ the cockroach.
Butler, Guy
Cape Coloured Batman.
Common Dawn.
David.
Giotto's Campanile.
Home Thoughts.
Myths.
Pieta.
Stranger to Europe.
Surveyor.
Butler, Henry Montague
Lift Up Your Hearts!
Butler, Samuel (1612-80)
Art of Love, The.
Character of Sydrophel, The.
Egyptians say, The, The Sun has twice.
For All Fanatics.
Godly Casuistry.
Hudibras, *sels.*
Hypocrisy.
In mathematicks he was greater.
Inventions.
Law, The.
Love ("All love at first, like generous wine").
Love ("Lovers like wrestlers").
Marriage is but a beast, some say.
Martial Mouse, A.
Metaphysical Sectarian, The.
Miscellaneous Thoughts, *sel.*
Portrait of Hudibras.
Portrait of Sidrophel.
Presbyterian Church Government.
Presbyterian Knight and Independent Squire, *abr.*
Religion of Hudibras, The.
Sidrophel, the Rosicrucian Conjurer.
Sir Hudibras.
Sir Hudibras his passing worth.
Sir Hudibras's Religion.
Sir Sidrophel, the Conjuror.
Smatterers.
This sturdy squire, he had, as well.
To His Mistress.
Butler, Samuel (1835-1902)
O God! O Montreal!
Psalm of Montreal, A.
Butler, William Allen
"All's Well!"
Incognita of Raphael.
Nothing to Wear.
Tom Twist.
Butler, William T.
Gathering on the Plains, The.
Butterfield, Frances Westgate
Time Out.
Butterfield, Mary
My Load.
Butterworth, Hezekiah
Bird with a Broken Wing, The.
Broken Pinion, The.
Church of the Revolution.
Crown Our Washington.
Death of Jefferson, The.
Five Kernals of Corn.
Fountain of Youth, The.
Garfield's Ride at Chickamauga.
"Go bring the captive, he shall die."
Immortal Morn.
In the morning light trills the gay swallow.
Legend of Waukulla, The.
Ortiz.
Roger Williams.
Snow-Bird, The.
Thanksgiving for America, The.
Thanksgiving in Boston Harbor, The.
Verazzano.
Whitman's Ride for Oregon.
"Buttle, Myra" (Victor William Williams Saunders Purcell)
Sweeney in Articulo.
Butts, Antony
Massenet/Never Wrote a Mass in A.
Butts, Mary Frances
Build a Fence of Trust.
Christmas Trees, The.
Happy Hour, The.
In Galilee.
Keeping Store.
King, The.
Million Little Diamonds, A.
Night.
Sweetest Place, The.
That's July.
That's June.
Today.
Trot, Trot!
Water Jewels.
Wild Winds.
Winter Night.
Buxton, Esther W.

Buxton (continued)
Putting the World to Bed.
Byer, B. L.
Ageless Christ, The.
Byers, Samuel H. M.
Sherman's March to the Sea.
Song of Iowa, The.
Song of Sherman's March to the Sea.
When Sherman Marched Down to the Sea.
With Corse at Allatoona.
Bynner, Witter ("Emanuel Morgan")
Against the Cold.
Aged Fisherman.
Asleep.
Autumn Walk, An.
Beforehand.
Calendar.
Captain's Table.
Chapala Poems, *sels.*
Chaplet, The.
Charioteer.
Chariots.
Consummation.
Correspondent.
Dance for Rain, A.
Day, The.
Defeat.
Dream.
During a Chorale by César Franck.
Ecce Homo.
Farmer Remembers Lincoln, A.
Fortune-Teller, A.
Ganymede.
Ghost.
God's Acre.
Golden Heart, The.
Grass-Tops.
Grenstone River.
Grieve Not for Beauty ("Almost the body leads the laggard soul").
I Change.
I Need No Sky.
If I were only dafter.
Jeremiah.
Kids.
Lightning.
Lotuses.
Masque of Life and Death, A.
Montezuma.
Mystic, The.
New God, The.
New World, The, *sels.*
Night.
Out of the Sea.
Pittsburgh.
Poet, The.
Poet Lived in Galilee, A.
Prayer: "Let us not look upon."
Prepare.
Republic to Republic.
Sandpiper, The.
Sentence.
Singing Huntsman, The.
Somebody called Walt Whitman.
Songs Ascending.
Spectra, *sel.*
Spouse.
Squanderings.
Tamazunchali.
To A. E. Housman.
To a Phoebe Bird.
To Celia, *sels.*
Train-Mates.
Voices.
Web, The.
Bynum, Daisy Moore
If.
Byrne, William A.
Bog Lands, The.
Byrom, John
Careless Content.
Contentment; or, The Happy Workman's Song.
Desponding Soul's Wish, The.
Epigram: "God bless the King—I mean the faith's defender!"
Epigram on Handel and Bononcini.
Epigram on the Feuds between Handel and Bononcini.
Extempore Verses Intended to Allay the Violence of Party-Spirit.
Extempore Verses upon a Trial of Skill between the Two Great Masters of the Noble Science of Defence, Messrs. Figg and Sutton.
Hymn for Christmas Day.
Hymn on the Omnipresence, An.
In Thy Love.
Jacobite Toast, A.
My Dog Tray.
My Spirit Longeth for Thee.
On Clergymen Preaching Politics.
Pastoral, A: "My time, O ye Muses, was happily spent."
Salutation of the Blessed Virgin, The.
Self-Righteousness.
Soul's Tendency towards Its True Centre, The.
Three Black Crows, The.
Toast, A.
Tom the Porter.
Which Is Which?
Byron, George Gordon Noel Byron, 6th Baron
Address to the Ocean.
Alas! the love of women! it is known.
All for Love.
And Angling, Too.
And now they were diverted by their suite.
And Thou Art Dead, as Young and Fair.
Another epic! Who inflicts again.
Apostrophe to the Ocean.
Archangel, The.
At the Gate of Heaven.
At Thirty Years.
Author's Purpose, The.
Ave Maria.
Away, away, my steed and I.
Battle of Waterloo.
Behold! in various throngs the scribbling crew.
Beppo.
Bride of Abydos, The.
Bright Be the Place of Thy Soul!
But quiet to quick bosoms is a hell.
By the Deep Sea.
Can tyrants but by tyrants conquer'd be.
Canto the Third.
Castled crag of Drachenfels, The.
Childe Harold's Farewell to England.
Childe Harold's Good Night.
Cincinnatus of the West, The.
Clime of the unforgotten brave!
Coliseum, The ("Arches on arches").
Coliseum, The ("The stars are forth").
Conscience.
Contemporary Poets.
Corsair, The, *sels.*
Darkness.
Death of Haidée, The.
Dedication: "Bob Southey! You're a poet—Poet-laureate."
Dedication to the Poet Laureate.
Deep and Dark Blue Ocean.
Desire and Disillusion.
Destruction of Sennacherib, The.
Don Juan, *sels.*
Don Juan and Haidee.
Don Juan's Education.
Donna Julia.
Dream, The.
Egeria, sweet creation of some heart.
Elegy: "O snatch'd away in beauty's bloom!"
Elegy on Thyrza.
English Bards and Scotch Reviewers, *sels.*
Epigram: "With death doomed to grapple."
Epigrams on Castlereagh.
Epilogue: "There's something in a stupid ass."
Epistle to Augusta.
Epitaph to a Dog.
Epitaph to a Newfoundland Dog.
Eve of [the Battle of] Waterloo, The.
Evening.
Fair Greece! sad relic of departed worth!
Fame ("From mighty wrongs to petty perfidy").
Fare Thee Well.
Farewell: "Farewell! if ever fondest prayer."
Farewell! If Ever Fondest Prayer.
Fatal Spell, The.
First Kiss of Love, The.
First Love.
For me, I know nought; nothing I deny.
For Music.
Fourth day came, but not a breath of air, The.
Fragment, A: "Could I remount the river of my years."
Fragment: "I would to heaven that I were so much clay."
Freedom's Hero.
Friendship.
Friendship Is Love without His Wings.
From the Turkish ("The chain I gave was fair to view").
George the Fourth in Ireland.
George the Third.
Giaour, The, *sel.*
Girl of Cadiz, The.
Greece.
Gulbeyaz.
Haidee ("It was the cooling hour").
Haidee ("One of the two, according to your choice").
He ever warred with freedom and the free.
He Who Ascends to Mountain-Tops.
Hesperus.
Hesperus the Bringer.
Highlands' Swelling Blue, The.
Hours of Idleness.
Hymn to Hesperus.
I Loved, I Love You.
I made a footing in the wall.
I Speak Not, I Trace Not, I Breathe Not Thy Name.
I want a hero: an uncommon want.
I Would I Were a Careless Child.
Illustrious Holland! hard would be his lot.
Immortal Mind, The.
In her first passion woman loves her lover.
In the great world—which, being interpreted.
Incantation, An.
Invocation: "Bob Southey! You're a poet—Poet laureate."
Is thy face like thy mother's, my fair child!
Island, The, *sel.*
Isles of Greece, The.
Isolation of Genius, The.
It Is the Hush of Night.
Italy.
Juan and Haidee.
Juan in England.
Juan was taught from out the best edition.
Lachin y Gair.
Lady Adeline Amundeville.

Lake Leman ("Clear, placid Leman!").
Lake Leman ("Lake Leman woos me").
Lake Leman lies by Chillon's walls.
Lake Poets, The.
Lambro's Return.
Lara, *sel.*
Last Words on Greece.
Light broke in upon my brain, A.
Lines Inscribed upon a Cup Formed from a Skull.
Lines to Mr. Hodgson.
Lines Written in an Album at Malta.
Lovers, The.
Maid of Athens [Ere We Part].
Manfred; a Dramatic Poem.
Many are poets who have never penn'd.
Mazeppa.
Moon is up, and yet it is not night, The.
My Boat Is on the Shore.
My Days of Love Are Over.
Name of commonwealth is past and gone, The.
Napoleon.
Nature.
Newstead Abbey.
Next comes the dull disciple of thy school.
Night ("It is the hush of night").
Night and Storm in the Alps.
Night before the Battle of Waterloo, The.
Night before Waterloo.
Norman Abbey.
Oh! Snatch'd Away in Beauty's Bloom.
O Talk Not to Me.
Oh, thou! in Hellas deemed of heavenly birth.
Oh! Weep for Those.
Ocean, The ("Roll on thou deep and dark blue ocean, rol").
Ode on Venice.
Ode to a Lady Whose Lover Was Killed by a Ball.
Ode to Napoleon Buonaparte, *sel.*
Ode to the Framers of the Frame Bill, An.
Of all the barbarous middle ages, that.
Old Lambro pass'd unseen a private gate.
On John Adams, of Southwell.
On Jordan's Bank.
On My Thirty-third Birthday.
On the Castle of Chillon.
On This Day I Complete My Thirty-sixth Year.
On Wellington.
Pleasant Things.
Poet and the World, The.
Poetical Commandments.
Poet's Credo.
Prisoner of Chillon, The.
Prometheus.
Remember Thee! Remember Thee!
Remorse.
Romantic to Burlesque.
Rome.
Rome and Freedom.
Sea, The.
Sennacherib.
She Walks in Beauty.
Shipwreck, The.
Siege of Corinth, The.
Siege of Ismail, The.
Sketch, A.
Sketch from Private Life, A.
Sky, Mountains, River ("The sky is changed").
So Late into the Night.
So We'll Go No More a-Roving.
Song: "So, we'll go no more a-roving."
Song for the Luddites.
Song of Saul before His Last Battle.
Song of the Corsairs.
Sonnet on Chillon.
Sonnet to Lake Leman.
Sonnet to the Prince Regent.
Southey and Wordsworth.
Stanzas: "Could love for ever."
Stanzas: "When a man hath no freedom to fight for at home."
Stanzas for Music ("I speak not, I trace not").
Stanzas for Music ("There be none of beauty's daughters").
Stanzas for Music ("There's not a joy").
Stanzas for Music ("They say that hope is happiness").
Stanzas to Augusta ("Though the day of my destiny's over").
Stanzas to the Po.
Stanzas Written on the Road between Florence and Pisa.
Still must I hear?—shall hoarse Fitzgerald bawl.
Stop!—for thy tread is on an empire's dust!
Summer.
Sun of the Sleepless!
Sunset over the Aegean.
Swimming.
Tear, The.
There Be None of Beauty's Daughters.
There Is Pleasure in the Pathless Woods.
There was in him a vital scorn of all.
They Accuse Me.
They tell me 'tis decided; you depart.
Thus, usually, when he was asked to sing.
'Tis pleasing to be schooled in a strange tongue.
'Tis Sweet [to Hear].
To England.
To Ianthe.
To Inez.
To the Ocean.
To Thomas Moore ("My boat is on the shore").
To Woman.
Triumph of the Defeated.
'Twas midnight—Donna Julia was in bed.
Two Foscari, The, *sel.*
Up rose the sun; the mists were curl'd.
Venice.
Venice and Rome.
Venice and Sunset.
Vision of Belshazzar, The.
Vision of Judgment, The.
Voltaire and Gibbon.
Waltz, The.
Wandering Outlaw, The.
Washington.
Waterloo ("There was a sound of revelry by night").
We'll Go No More a-Roving.
Wellington.
When a Man Hath No Freedom [to Fight for at Home].
When Juan woke he found some good things ready.
When We Two Parted.
Who Kill'd [*or* Killed] John Keats?
"Whom the gods love die young" was said of yore.
William Lisle Bowles.
Winds are high on Helle's wave, The.
World Is a Bundle of Hay, The.
Written after Swimming from Sestos to Abydos.
Youth and Age.

Byron, May Clarissa Gillington
Adventurers, The.
Dead March, A.
Fairy Th[illegible]ll, The.
My Little House.
Pageant of Seamen, The.
Storm-Child, The.
Tryst of the Night, The.

C

"C., A. L."
To Him All Life Was Beauty.

"C., E."
Emaricdulfe, *sel.*
Sonnet: "Within her hair Venus and Cupid sport them."

"C., H. A."
Waiting Yonder.

"C., J."
Alcilia, *sel.*
Frailty of Beauty, The.

"C., N."
Life.

"C., W. C."
God of the Gallant Trees.

"C. B. B." *See* **"B., C. B"**
"C. G. L." *See* **"L., C. G"**
"C. H. I." *See* **"I., C. H"**
"C. N. S." *See* **"S., C. N"**
"C. W. T." *See* **"T., C. W"**

Cabell, James Branch
Alone in April.
And therefore praise I even the most high.
Easter Eve.
Garden-Song.
Retractions, *sels.*
Story of the Flowery Kingdom.
You ask a sonnet? Well, it is your right.

Cable, Franklin
Tree-building.

Cable, George Washington
New Arrival, The.
Written in the Visitors' Book at the Birthplace of Robert Burns.

Cabral, Olga
Another Late Edition, *sel.*
Electronic Tape Found in a Bottle.
This Morning the Sun.

Cædmon
Approach of Pharaoh, The.
Christ and Satan, *sels.*
Coming of Pharaoh, The.
Creation, The.
Exodus, *sels.*
Far and Wide She Went.
Genesis, *sels.*
Here the Eternal Lord, protector of all creatures.
Hymn: "Now let us praise the Keeper of the Heavenly Kingdom."
Hymn of the World's Creator, The.
Lamentations of the Fallen Angels.
Murky waves / Covered over the children of evil.
Then spoke the Lord.

Cahoon, Herbert
Angleworm.

Calderón de la Barca, Pedro
Cross, The.
Demon Speaks, The.
Devocion de la Cruz, La, *sel.*
Dream Called Life, The.
Dying Eusebio's Address to the Cross, The.
Holy Eucharist, The.
Life Is a Dream, *sel.*
Life's a Dream.
Magico prodigioso, El, *sel.*
Thou Art of All Created Things.
We live, while we see the sun.

Caldwell, William W.
Robin's Come.

Calenberg, Connie
I Love Thee, Lord.
Prayer: "How prone we are."

Calenberg (continued)
Take My Hand, O Blessed Master.
Yielded to Him.
Calhoun, George
McKinley Brook.
Rufus's Mare.
Calhoun, John
Peter Emberley.
Calkins, Clinch
Dead City, The.
Mourning Dove.
Calkins, S. S.
World Is Waiting for You, The.
Call, Frank Oliver
Blue Homespun.
Old Habitant, An.
Sonnet Series of French Canada, A, *sels.*
Call, Virginia
Diamonds.
Call, Wathen Mark Wilks
Hymn: "When by the marbled lake I lie and listen."
People's Petition, The.
Renunciation.
Summer Days.
Callaghan, Gertrude
Award.
Native Son.
New England Fog.
Sorrow's Ladder.
Who Goes By Lightly.
Callanan, Jeremiah [*or* James] Joseph
Dirge of O'Sullivan Bear.
Lines to the Blessed Sacrament.
Pure Is the Dewy Gem.
Serenade: "Blue waves are sleeping, The."
Song: "Awake thee, my Bessy, the morning is fair."
To ——: "Lady — the lyre thou bid'st me take."
When Each Bright Star Is Clouded.
Written to a Young Lady.
Callimachus
Callimachus to Heraclitus.
Crethis.
Dead Boy.
Elegy on Herakleitos.
His Son.
Loss at Sea.
Saon of Acanthus.
Sinister Dialogue.
Sopolis.
Timon's Epitaph.
To Archinus.
Uncommon.
Callinus
Call to Action, A.
Rallying Song.
Callistratus
Patriotic Song ("I'll wreathe my sword in myrtle bough").
Wishes.
Calverley, Charles Stuart
A, B, C.
Alphabet, The.
And, if you asked of him to say.
Auld Wife [Sat at Her Ivied Door], The.
Ballad: "Auld wife sat at her ivied door," The.
Beer.
But hark! a sound is stealing on my ear.
Cat, The.
Changed.
Cock and the Bull, The.
Companions.
Contentment.
Disaster.
First Love.
"Forever."
Gemini and Virgo.
"Hic Vir, Hic Est."
In the Gloaming ("In the gloaming to be roaming"), *parody.*
Lines on Hearing the Organ.
Lines Suggested by the Fourteenth of February ("Darkness succeeds to twilight").
Lines Suggested by the Fourteenth of February ("Ere the morn the East has crimsoned").
Love.
Lovers, and a Reflection.
Morning.
Ode to Tobacco.
On the Beach.
On the Brink.
Peace.
Play.
Precious Stones.
Sad Memories.
Schoolmaster Abroad with His Son, The.
Shelter.
Striking.
Wanderers.
Calverley, Sybil Horatia
Midsummer.
Calvert, George Henry
Bunker Hill.
Calvin, John
Salutation to Jesus Christ.
Cambon, Glauco
Vain Cry; Lydian Campaign, 1941.
Cambridge, Ada (Mrs. George Frederick Cross)
Faith.
Honour.
Oh, to be there to-night!
On Australian Hills, *sel.*
Camden, Harriet Parker
Oklahoma.
Camden, William
On a Puritanicall Lock-Smith.
On a Thieving Locksmith.
Cameron, C. C.
Success.
Cameron, Don
Drilling Missed Holes.
Song of the Leadville Mine Boss.
Cameron, George Frederick
Ah Me! The Mighty Love.
Future, The.
Golden Text, The.
In After Days.
My Political Faith.
Relics.
Standing on Tiptoe.
What Matters It?
Cameron, Norman
Bear in Mind, O Ye Recording Angels.
Central Europe.
Compassionate Fool, The.
Dirty Little Accuser, The.
Disused Temple, The.
El Aghir.
Fight with a Water-Spirit.
Firm of Happiness Limited, The.
For the Fly-Leaf of a School-Book.
Forgive Me, Sire.
From a Woman to a Greedy Lover.
Green, Green Is El Aghir.
Hook for Leviathan, A.
In the Queen's Room.
Invader, The.
Lucifer.
Shepherdess.
Steep, Stone Steps.
Thespians at Thermopylae, The.
Three Love Poems.
Unfinished Race, The.
Verdict, The.
Wanton's Death, The.
Winter House, The.
Cametas
On the Lawn.
Camille, Roussan
Nedjé.
Nocturne: "Wildness of haggard flights."
Cammaerts, Emile
Homeland, The.
Camoes [*or* Camoens], Luís
Babylon and Sion (Goa and Lisbon).
Cape of Tempests, The.
Lusiads, The (*or* Lusiadas), *sels.*
On Revisiting Cintra after the Death of Catarina.
On the Death of Catarina de Attayda.
Passage to India, *abr.*
Sonnet: "Leave me, all sweet refrains my lip hath made."
Sonnet: "Time and the mortal will stand never fast."
Waterspout.
Camp, James
Female Dancer.
Campana, Dino
Old Lines; a Fragment.
Campanella, Tommaso
People, The.
Campbell, A. Y.
Animula Vagula.
Campbell, Alice B.
Sally and Manda.
Campbell, Alistair
At the Fishing Settlement.
Hut near Desolated Pines.
Lie on the Sand.
Narcissus.
Now He is Dead.
Now Sleeps the Gorge.
O Catch Miss Daisy Pinks.
Campbell, Anne
Before and after Marriage.
Shabby Old Dad.
There Is Always a Place for You.
To My Friend.
Campbell, Archibald Y.
Dromedary, The.
Campbell, Calder
Burman Lover, The.
Ossian's Serenade.
Campbell, David
Ariel.
Beach Queen.
Bird Cage, *sel.*
End of Exploring, The.
Harry Pearce.
Heart of Light.
Magpie Singing His Delight, The.
Men in Green.
Monaro, The.
Night Sowing.
Pallid Cuckoo.
Possum and the Moon, The.
Soldier's Song.
Speak with the Sun.
Stockman, The.
Campbell, Elizabeth K.
Psychology Class.
Campbell, George
Litany: "I hold the splendid daylight in my hands."
Campbell, James Edwin
Compensation.
Conjuh Man, De.
Negro Serenade.
Ol' Doc' Hyar.
Uncle Eph's Banjo Song.
When Ol' Sis' Judy Pray.
Campbell, Joseph ("Seasamh MacCathmhaoil")
As I Came Over the Grey, Grey Hills.
At Harvest.
Besom-Man, The.

Blanaid's Song ("Blanaid loves roses").
Blind Man at the Fair, The.
Chesspieces.
Ciaran, the Master of Horses and Lands.
Dancer, The.
Fighting-Man, A.
Go, Ploughman, Plough.
Herb-Leech, The.
Hills of Cualann, The.
I Am the Gilly of Christ.
I Am the Mountainy Singer.
I Will Go with My Father a-Ploughing.
Ninepenny Fidil, The.
O Glorious Childbearer.
Old Age Pensioner, The.
Old Woman, The.
On Waking.
Poet Loosed a Wingèd Song, The.
Shining Spaces of the South, The.
Three Colts Exercising in a Six-Acre.
Tinkers, The.
Unfrocked Priest, The.

Campbell, Marion Susan
Riding through Jerusalem.

Campbell, Marjorie Freeman
Only the Heart.
Vigil.

Campbell, Nancy (Mrs. Joseph Campbell)
Apple-Tree, The.
Like One I Know.
Monkey, The.

Campbell, Robert Bhain
Final Poem.
Task, The.

Campbell, Roy
African Moonrise.
Attend my fable if your ears by clean.
Autumn.
Ballad of Don Juan Tenorio and the Statue of the Comendador.
Buffel's Kop.
But "nameless somethings" and "unbounded spaces."
Choosing a Mast.
Christ in the Hospital.
Death of Polybius Jubb, The.
Death of the Bull.
Dreaming Spires.
Driving Cattle to Casas Buenas.
Fall of Satan, The.
Familiar Daemon.
Fishing Boats in Martigues.
Flaming Terrapin, The, *sels.*
Georgiad, The, *sel.*
Good Resolution, A.
Hail, Mediocrity, beneath whose spell.
Hialmar.
Horses on the Camargue.
Invocation to the African Muse.
Limerick: "He died in attempting to swallow."
Luis de Camoes.
Mass at Dawn.
Mazeppa.
Mithraic Emblems, *sel.*
Noah.
On Professor Drennan's Verse.
On Some South African Novelists.
On the Death of a Journalist.
On the Same.
Out of the Ark's Grim Hold.
Palm, The.
Poets in Africa.
Pomegranates.
Rounding the Cape.
Secret Muse, The.
Serf, The.
Sisters, The.
Sling, The.
Snake, The.
Talking Bronco, *sel.*
Theology of Bongwi, the Baboon, The.
To a Pet Cobra.
To the Sun.
Toledo, July 1936.
Tristan da Cunha.
Veld Eclogue, A; the Pioneers, *sel.*
Volunteer's Reply to the Poet, The.
Wayzgoose, The, *sel.*
Zebras, The.
Zulu Girl, The.

Campbell, Thomas
At summer eve, when Heaven's ethereal bow.
Battle of Hohenlinden, The.
Battle of the Baltic, The.
Beatific Sea, The.
Beech Tree's Petition, The.
Caroline, II: To the Evening Star.
Dead Eagle, The.
Exile of Erin, The.
Field Flowers.
Freedom and Love.
Glenara.
Hallowed Ground.
Harper, The.
Hohenlinden.
Irish Harper and His Dog, The.
Jilted Nymph, The.
Last Man, The.
Lines on Leaving a Scene in Bavaria.
Lochiel's Warning.
Lord Ullin's Daughter.
Maid of Neidpath, The.
Margaret and Dora.
Men of England.
Mighty Sea! Cameleon-like Thou Changest.
My Dog Tray.
Napoleon and the British Sailor.
Ode to the Germans.
Ode to Winter.
Parrot, The.
Pilgrim of a Day, The.
Pleasures of Hope, The, *sel.*
River of Life, The.
Soldier's Dream, The.
Song: "Earl March looked on his dying child."
Song: "How delicious is the winning."
Song: "Oh, how hard it is to find."
Song to the Evening Star ("Gem of the crimson-colour'd even").
Song to the Evening Star ("Star that bringest . . .").
Thought Suggested by the New Year, A.
To a Young Lady, Who Asked Me to Write Something Original for Her Album.
To the Evening Star ("Gem of the crimson-colour'd even").
To the Evening Star ("Star that bringest home the bee").
To the Rainbow.
Ye Mariners of England.

Campbell, Walter Stanley *See* **"Vestal, Stanley"**

Campbell, Wilfred (William Wilfred Campbell)
Bereavement of the Fields.
Canadian Folk Song.
Hills and the Sea, The.
How One Winter Came in the Lake Region.
Indian Summer.
Lake Memory, A.
Lines on a Re-reading of Parts of the Old Testament, *sel.*
Stella Flammarum.
Sublimity! Sublimity! I lay thee down.
To the Lakes.
Vapour and Blue.
Were-Wolves, The.
Winter Lakes, The.
With Cortez in Mexico.

Campion [*or* Campian], Thomas
Advice to a Girl.
Amarillis [*or* Amaryllis].
Author of Light.
Awake, Awake!
Bar Not the Door.
Basia.
Be Wise, and Fly Not.
Beauty Is but a Painted Hell.
Beauty Is Not Bound.
Beauty, Since You So Much Desire.
Blame Not My Cheeks.
Can you the author of our joy.
Chance and Change.
Cherry-ripe.
Come, Cheerful Day!
Come, Follow Me.
Come, Let Us Sound with Melody [the Praises].
Come, O Come.
Come, Oh, Come, My Life's Delight.
Come, You Pretty False-eyed Wanton.
Content.
Corinna.
Cypress Curtain of the Night [Is Spread], The.
Dear If I with Guile.
Devotion ("Follow thy fair sun, unhappy shadow").
Devotion ("Follow your saint, follow with accents sweet!").
Dido ("Dido was the Carthage Queen").
Dismissal.
Effect of Love, The.
Fain Would I Wed [a Fair Young Man].
Fire, Fire, Fire, Fire.
First Love.
Follow.
Follow, follow.
Follow Thy Fair Sun [Unhappy Shadow].
Follow Your Saint [Follow with Accents Sweet].
Fortunati Nimium.
Give Beauty All Her Right.
Harden Now Thy Tired Heart.
Hark, All You Ladies That Do Sleep!
Her Fair Inflaming Eyes.
Her Sacred Bower.
Hours of Sleepy Night, The.
Hymn in Praise of Neptune, A.
I Care Not for These Ladies.
In Imagine Pertransit Homo.
In Praise of Neptune.
In the Dark What the Day Doth Forbid.
Integer Vitae.
It Fell on a Summer's Day.
Jack and Joan.
Just Beguiler.
Kind Are Her Answers.
Lamentation, A.
Laura.
Let Us Live and Love.
Life Upright, The.
Lo, when back mine eye.
Lord Hay's Mask, *sel.*
Lords' Mask, The, *sel.*
Love Me or Not.
Love's Pilgrims.
Maids Are Simple.
Maid's Complaint, A.
Man of life upright, The.
Mountebank's Mask, The, *sel.*
My Life's Delight.
My Love Hath Vowed He Will Forsake Me.
My Sweetest Lesbia [Let Us Live and Love].

Campion (continued)
Neptune.
Never Love [Unless You Can].
Never Weather-beaten Sail.
Night as Well as Brightest Day.
Now Winter Nights Enlarge.
O Come Quickly!
O Crudelis Amor.
O Sweet Delight.
Of Corinna's Singing.
Oft have I sigh'd for him that heares me not.
Out of My Soul's Depth.
Peaceful Western Wind, The.
Phoebus and Pan.
Pilgrimage towards Loves Holy Land, A.
Place of Cupid's Fire, The.
Proserpina.
Relation of the Late Royal Entertainment Given by the Lord Knowles, A, *sels.*
Renunciation, A.
Respect My Faith.
Rose-cheeked [*or* cheek'd *or* cheekt] Laura [Come].
Roses.
Secret Love or Two I Must Confess, A.
Seek the Lord.
Shall I come, if I swim? wide are the waves, you see.
Shall I Come, Sweet Love, to Thee.
Sic Transit.
Sing a Song of Joy, *sel.*
Sleep, Angry Beauty.
So Quick, So Hot [So Mad Is Thy Fond Sute].
So sweet is thy discourse to me.
So Tir'd Are All My Thoughts.
Some hot, some cold.
Song: "O sweet delight, O more than human bliss."
Song: To the Masquers Representing Stars.
Song from a Booke of Ayres, A.
Stars Dance, The.
Tell, O Tell.
There Is a Garden in Her Face.
There Is None, O None but You.
Think'st Thou to Seduce Me Then.
Thou Art Not Fair.
Thou Joy'st, Fond Boy.
Though You Are Young.
Thrice Toss These Oaken Ashes [in the Air].
To Lesbia ("My sweetest Lesbia").
To Music Bent Is My Retired Mind.
To Shades of Underground.
Turn All Thy Thoughts to Eyes.
Turn Back, You Wanton Flyer.
Unless there were consent 'twixt hell and heaven.
Vain Men, Whose Follies.
View Me, Lord, a Work of Thine.
Vivamus Mea Lesbia atque Amemus.
Vobiscum Est Iope.
Welcome to this flowery place.
Were My Heart as Some Men's Are.
What Faire Pompe Have I Spide of Glittering Ladies.
What Harvest Half So Sweet Is.
What If a Day.
What Then Is Love but Mourning.
When the God of Merry Love.
When Thou Must Home [to Shades of Underground].
When to Her Lute Corinna Sings.
When We Court and Kiss.
Where She Her Sacred Bower Adorns.
Winter.
Winter Nights.
Wise men patience never want.
Writer to His Book, The.
Young and Simple though I Am.
Your Fair Looks Inflame My Desire.
Youth and Age.

Campoamor, Ramón de
Boredom.
Traditions.

Cane, Edward
Future, The.

Cane, Melville
After Reading the Reviews of "Finnegans Wake."
Alpine View.
Bed-Time Story.
By One, Unsure.
Color.
Dawn Has Yet to Ripple In.
Each to Each.
Fog, the Magician.
Harvest to Seduce, A.
Honey.
Hymn to Night.
Operatic Note.
Park Pigeons.
Peepers.
Phosphorescence.
Presence of Snow.
Rural Dumpheap.
Snow toward Evening.
Sun and Cloud.
Tree in December.

Canfield, Harry Clifford
Elegy on the Loss of U.S. Submarine S4, *sel.*
Entrapped inside a submarine.

Canning, George
Candid Friend, The.
Canto First.
Cat and the Bird, The.
Dutch, The.
Elderly Gentlemen, The.
Ipecacuanha.
To Mrs. Leigh upon Her Wedding-Day.

Canning, George, George Ellis, *and* John Hookham Frere
Rovers, The, *sel.*
Song: "Whene'er with haggard eyes I view."
Song by Rogero [the Captive].
Song of One Eleven Years in Prison.

Canning, George *and* John Hookham Frere
Friend of Humanity and the Knife-Grinder, The.
InscriptioFor the Door of the Cell in Newgate Where Mrs.
Knife-Grinder, The.
Sapphics.
Soldier's Friend, The.
Soldier's Wife, The.

Canning, George, John Hookham Frere, *and others*
New Morality.

Cannon, David Wadsworth, Jr.
Freedom in Mah Soul.
Western Town.

Cannon, Edward
Unsuspected Fact, An.

Cannon, Margery
Venite Adoremus.

Canterbury, George
New Mexico and Arizona.

Canton, William
Bethlehem.
Carol: "When the herds were watching."
Child's Prayer, A.
Crow, The.
Hold Thou My Hands.
Karma.
Laus Infantium.
New Poet, A.
Rhymes about a Little Woman.
She Was a Treasure.
Thank-You, A.

Cantus, Eleanor Hollister
Fame.

Capell, William
I Saw Death Slain.

Capes, Molly
Hallowe'en.

Capetanakis, Demetrios
Abel.
Isles of Greece, The.

Capp, Joseph
Generalization.
Man Is a Fool.

Caragher, Mary E.
Tree Tag.

Carbell, E. T.
Frogs' Singing-School, The.

Carberry, H. D.
I Shall Remember.
Nature.
Return.

"Carbery, Ethna" (Anna Johnston MacManus)
Hills o' My Heart.
In Tir-na'n-Og.
Love-Talker, The.
Mea Culpa.
Shadow House of Lugh, The.

Cardarelli, Joseph
At Ten o'Clock in the Morning.
Marlborough Poems, The, *sel.*
On Blindness.
Refrain.
Rose do you know.
To Rimbaud in Hell.
Trip for Hell and Self, The.
Waiting for Lunch.
Zombie.

Cardozo, Elizabeth C.
We Met Them on the Common Way.

Cardozo, Nancy
Day Dream.

Carducci, Giosuè
Ancient Sorrow.
Fantasy.
Hymn to Satan, *abr.*
Ox, The.
Petrarch.
Primo Vere.
Snowfall.
Vision.

Carew, Lady Elizabeth
Chorus: "Tis not enough for one that is a wife."
Mariam, *sel.*

Carew, Thomas
Ask Me No More.
Ask Me No More Where Jove Bestows.
Beautiful Mistress, A.
Boldness[e] in Love.
Celia Bleeding, to the Surgeon.
Celia Singing ("Hark, how my Celia").
Celia Singing ("You that think Love can convey").
Comparison, The.
Complement, The.
Cruell Mistris, A.
Deposition from Love, A.
Disdain [*or* Disdaine] Returned.
Divine Mistris, A.
Elegie upon the Death of the Deane of Pauls, Dr. John Donne, An.
Elegy upon the Death of Doctor Donne, Dean of Paul's, An.
Elegy upon the Death of the Dean of Paul's, Dr. John Donne, An.
Epitaph, An: "This little vault, this narrow room."
Epitaph on Maria, Lady Wentworth.
Epitaph on the Lady Mary Villers [*or* Vil-

liers] ("The Lady Mary Villers lyes").
Epitaph on the Lady Villiers ("This little vault. . .").
Eternity of Love Protested.
Excuse of Absence, An.
Fear Not, Dear Love.
Flye That Flew into My Mistris Her Eye, A.
Give Me More Love, or More Disdain.
Good Advice.
Good Counsel to a Young Maid.
He That Loves a Rosy Cheek.
Her Sweet Voice.
Hymeneall Dialogue, An.
I will enjoy thee now.
In Answer of an Elegiacall Letter upon the Death of the King of Sweden.
Ingrateful[l] Beauty Threatened.
Inscription on the Tomb of the Lady Mary Wentworth, The.
Lover Consults with Reason, The.
Love's Courtship.
Maria Wentworth.
Mark How the Bashful Morn [in Vain].
Mediocrity [*or* Mediocritie] in Love Rejected.
More Love or More Disdain.
Murdering Beauty.
New-Yeares Gift, A.
Now That the Winter's Gone.
Obsequies to the Lady Anne Hay.
On a Damaske Rose Sticking upon a Ladies Breast.
On Sight of a Gentlewomans Face in the Water.
Other, An ("The purest soule that e're was sent").
Other, An ("This little vault, this narrow room").
Pastorall Dialogue, A ("As Celia rested in the shade").
Pastorall Dialogue, A ("This Mossie Bank They Prest").
Persuasions to Enjoy; a Song.
Persuasions to Love.
Prayer to the Wind, A.
Protestation, The.
Rapture, A.
Red, and White Roses.
Second Rapture, The.
Secrecy [*or* Secresie] Protested.
Song, A: "Ask me no more where Jove bestows."
Song: "Beautiful Mistress, A.
Song: Celia Singing.
Song: Eternity of Love Protested.
Song: "Give me more love or more disdain."
Song, A: "In her fair cheeks two pits do lie."
Song: Murdring Beautie.
Song: Perswasions to Enjoy.
Song: To Her Againe, She Burning in a Feaver.
Song: To My Inconstant Mistress.
Song: To My Mistris, I Burning in Love.
Song: To One That Desired to Know My Mistris.
Song: "Would you know what's soft? I dare."
Spring, The.
Steadfast Mind, The.
To A. L.: Perswasions to Love.
To a Lady That Desired I Would Love Her.
To Ben Johnson.
To Celia, upon Love's Ubiquity.
To His Inconstant Mistress.
To My Cousin (C. R.) Marrying My Lady (A.).
To My Friend G. N. from Wrest.
To My Inconstant Mistress [*or* Mistris].
To My Mistresse in Absence.
To My Mistris Sitting by a Rivers Side.
To My Worthy Friend Master Geo. [*or* George] Sands [On His Translation of the Psalmes].
To Saxham.
To T. H. a Lady Resembling My Mistresse.
True Beauty, The.
Unfading Beauty, The.
Upon a Mole in Celias Bosome.
Upon a Ribband.
Upon Master W. Montague.

Carey, Henry
Ballad of Sally in Our Alley, The.
Contrivances, The, *sel.*
Drinking-Song, A.
Happy Myrtillo.
Harry Carey's General Reply, to the Libelling Gentry, Who Are Angry at His Welfare.
Huntsman's Rouse, The.
Love for Love's Sake.
Maiden's Ideal of a Husband, A.
Maid's Husband, The.
Namby-Pamby.
Polly Peachum.
Roger and Dolly.
Sally in Our Alley.
Sally Sweetbread.
True Tar, The.

Carey, Patrick
Chains.
Crucifixus pro Nobis.
Hymn: Crucifixus pro Nobis.
Hymn: "Whilst I beheld the neck o' the dove."
Nulla Fides.

Carleton, Emma
Faith.

Carleton, Sara King
Grand Finale.
Late October.

Carleton, Will
Across the Delaware.
Betsey and I Are Out.
Country Doctor, The.
Cuba to Columbia.
Death-Doomed.
Doctor's Story, The.
First Settler's Story, The.
Flash—The Fireman's Story.
Little Black-eyed Rebel, The.
New Church Organ, The.
Out of the Old House, Nancy.
Over the Hill to the Poor-House.
Prize of the Margaretta, The.
Schoolmaster's Guests, The.
Second Settler's Story, The.
Words.

Carleton, William
Sir Turlough; or, The Churchyard Bride.

Carlin, Francis (James Francis Carlin MacDonnell)
Alchemy.
Ballad of Douglas Bridge.
Before I Stumbled.
Beyond Rathkelly.
Gray Plume, The.
Hope's Song.
Irish, The.
Joy to You.
MacDiarmod's Daughter.
Market Town, The.
Perfection.
Plea for Hope.
Solar Road, The.
Two Nests, The.
Vessels.
Virgins.
Virgin's Slumber Song, The.
Wine.

Carlin, George W.
In Palestine.

Carlisle, Horace C.
God's Provident Love.

Carlyle, Jane Welsh (Mrs. Thomas Carlyle)
To a Swallow Building under Our Eaves.

Carlyle, Thomas
Adieu.
Corn Must Be Sown.
Cui Bono?
Music.
Sower's Song, The.
Today.

Carman, Bliss
April Morning, An.
Arnold, Master of the *Scud.*
Autumn Garden, An.
Choristers, The.
Christmas Eve Choral, A.
Christmas Song.
Daffodil's Return.
Daisies, The.
Daphne.
Deserted Pasture, The.
Envoy: "Have little care that life is brief."
Ghost-Yard of the Goldenrod, The.
Gift, The.
Golden Rowan.
Grave-Tree, The.
Gravedigger, The.
Hack and Hew.
Hem and Haw.
Here and Now, *sel.*
Heretic, The.
I Loved Thee, Atthis, in the Long Ago.
I see the golden hunter go.
In a Copy of Browning.
In October.
In Philistia.
In the House of Idiedaily.
Joys of the Road, The.
Lord of My Heart's Elation.
Lord of the Far Horizons.
Low Tide on Grand-Pré.
Man of Peace, The.
Marian Drury.
Mendicants, The.
Mr. Moon.
Moment Musicale.
More Ancient Mariner, A.
Northern Vigil, A.
Old Grey Wall, The.
On the Tomb of Bliss Carman.
Over the Wintry Threshold.
Overlord.
Roadside Flowers.
Sappho, *sel.*
Sea Child, A.
Seamark, A.
Sending of the Magi, The.
Ships of Saint John, The.
Ships of Yule, The.
Son of the Sea, A.
Song: "Love, by that loosened hair."
Songs of the Sea-Children, *sels.*
Spring Song.
Tecumseh and the Eagles.
Threnody for a Poet.
Trees.
Triumphalis.
Vagabond Song, A.
Veni Creator ("Lord of my heart's elation").
Veni Creator ("Lord of the grass and hill").
Vestigia.
What is it to remember?
Where Is Heaven?

Carman (continued)
Why.
Windflower, A.
Winter Streams.
Carmer, Carl
Antique Shop.
Black Boy.
Cathedral of St. Louis, The.
Slave Quarter.
Carmichael, Amy
Autumn.
Come, Lord Jesus.
Comforted.
Content with Thee.
Deliver Me.
Do We Not Hear Thy Footfall?
Evening Star, The.
Flame of God.
Footfall, The.
For All in Pain.
For Our Children.
Fret Not Thyself.
God of the Nebulae.
Have We Not Seen Thy Shining Garment's Hem?
Hope.
I Promise Thee.
In Acceptance Lieth Peace.
In Any Office.
Last Defile, The.
Lord, Thou Hast Suffered.
Love of God.
Make Me Thy Fuel.
Make Me Thy Mountaineer.
One Thing Have I Desired.
Out of the Heat.
Prayer, A: "Dear Lord, for all in pain."
Sunset.
Think It Not Strange.
Toward Jerusalem.
Tune Thou My Harp.
Yet Listen Now.
Carmichael, Waverly Turner
Keep Me, Jesus. Keep Me.
Carnegie, James, Earl of Southesk
Flitch of Dunmow, The.
Carnevali, Emanuel
His Majesty the Letter-Carrier.
In This Hotel.
Invocation to Death.
Serenade: "Come on, don't be afraid you'll spoil me."
Sermon.
Carney, Julia A. Fletcher
Kind Deeds.
Little Things.
Caro, José Eusebio
Words of the Last Inca.
Carolan [*or* O'Carolan], Turlough
Cup of O'Hara, The.
When Kian O'Hara's Cup Was Passed to Turlough O'Carolan.
Why, Liquor of Life?
Carossa, Hans
Mysterious Landscape.
Carpenter, Amelia Walstien Jolls
Old Flemish Lace.
Recollection.
Ride to Cherokee, The.
Carpenter, Edward
Among the Ferns.
Beethoven.
England, Arise!
Have Faith.
I lay among the ferns.
Love's Vision.
Over the Great City.
Songs of the Birds, The.
Stupid Old Body, The.
Wandering Lunatic Mind, The.
Carpenter, Henry Bernard
Mightier Church, A.
Reed, The.
Carpenter, J. C.
Her Bright Smile.
Carpenter, John Alden
Contemplation.
Plan, A.
Spring.
Carpenter, John Randell
Bear, The.
Carpenter, Joseph Edward
Do They Think of Me at Home.
Carpenter, Lois R.
At His Feet.
Carpenter, Margaret Haley
September Afternoon.
Carpenter, Maurice
To S.T.C. on His 179th Birthday, October 12th, 1951.
Venus on a Sea Horse.
Carpenter, Rhys
Beggars.
Master Singers, The.
Who Bids Us Sing?
Carpenter, Rue
Liar, The.
Stout.
Carpenter, William Boyd
Before Thy Throne.
Three Days.
Carphyllides
Full Life, A.
Carr, Elias F.
Ode to New Jersey.
Carr, Mary Jane
Big Swing-Tree Is Green Again, The.
Birthday of the Lord, The.
Castle in the Fire, The.
Once I Nearly Touched a Bird.
Pirate Wind.
Shop of Dreams.
Six Birthday Candles Shining.
West Wind's Secret, The.
When a Fellow's Four.
When a Ring's around the Moon.
Carr, Robert Van
Bill Haller's Dance.
Cowboy's Salvation Song.
Love Lyrics of a Cowboy.
Old Cowboy's Lament, The.
Prairie Wolves.
Rattlesnake, The.
Remember the Promise, Dakotah.
Romance of the Range.
Roundup Cook, The.
Silhouette in Sepia.
War Dance, The.
Western Trail, The.
When Dutchy Plays the Mouth Harp.
Carrera Andrade, Jorge
Perfect Life, The.
Reaping the Barley.
Walnut.
Carrier, Constance
Black Water and Bright Air.
Colonel B.
Fugue.
Party.
Peter at Fourteen.
Pro Patria.
Seminary.
Transformation Scene.
Carrington, James B.
I Planted Little Trees To-day.
"Carroll, Lewis" (Charles Lutwidge Dodgson)
Aged Aged Man, The.
Alice's Adventures in Wonderland, *sels.*
A-Sitting on a Gate.
Atalanta in Camden-Town.
Baker's Tale, The.
Brother and Sister.
Crocodile, The.
Disillusioned.
Doll Song.
Doll's Song.
Dutchess' Lullaby, The.
Evidence Read at the Trial of the Knave of Hearts.
Father William, *parody.*
Gardener's Song, The.
Hiawatha's Photographing.
How Doth the Little Crocodile, *parody.*
How to Recognize a Snark.
Humpty Dumpty's Recitation.
Hunting of the Snark, The.
I'll Tell Thee Everything I Can.
Jabberwocky.
King-Fisher Song, The.
Landing, The.
Limerick: "There was a young lady of station."
Little Birds.
Little Birds Are Playing.
Lobster Quadrille, The.
Mad Gardener's Song, The.
Maggie's Visit to Oxford, *sel.*
Manlet, The.
Melancholetta, *sel.*
Melancholy Pig, The.
Mock Turtle's Song, The.
My dismal sister! Couldst thou know.
Of Alice in Wonderland.
Pig-Tale, The.
Poeta Fit, Non Nascitur.
Quadrille, A.
Rules and Regulations.
Sea Dirge, A.
She's All My Fancy Painted Him.
Snark, The.
Some Hallucinations.
Song of Love, A.
Speak Roughly to Your Little Boy.
Strange Wild Song, A.
Sylvie and Bruno, *sels.*
Sylvie and Bruno Concluded, *sels.*
Through the Looking-Glass, *sels.*
"Time has come, The," the walrus said.
To the Looking Glass world it was Alice that said.
Turtle Soup.
Twinkle, twinkle, little bat! *parody.*
Voice of the Lobster, The.
Walrus and the Carpenter, The.
Ways and Means.
We have sailed many months, we have sailed many weeks.
White Knight's Song, The.
Whiting and the Snail, The.
Carroll, Patrick Joseph
Johneen.
Lady Day in Ireland.
St. Patrick's Treasure.
Carroll, Paul
Father.
Carruth, Hayden
Event Itself, The.
I Could Take.
Keraunograph.
New Orleans.
On a Certain Engagement South of Seoul.
Salt Lake City.
Seasons.
Summer's Early End at Hudson Bay.
Carruth, Lucy
My Prayer.
Carruth, William Herbert
Autumn.
Dreamer of Dreams.
Dreamers of Dreams.
Each in His Own Tongue.
When the Cannon Booms No More.

Carryl, Charles Edward
Admiral's Caravan, The, *sel.*
Alphabet, An.
Camel's Complaint, The.
Camel's Lament, The.
Davy and the Goblin, *sels.*
My Recollectest Thoughts.
Nautical Ballad, A.
Plaint of the Camel, The.
Post Captain, The.
Robinson Crusoe.
Robinson Crusoe's Story.
Song in the Dell, The.
Walloping Window-Blind, The.
Carryl, Guy Wetmore
Arrogant Frog and the Superior Bull, The.
Ballad, A: "As I was walkin' the jungle round, a-killin' of tigers an' time."
Ballad, A, in the Manner of R-dy-rd K-pl-ng, *parody.*
Embarrassing Episode of Little Miss Muffet, The.
Gastronomic Guile of Simple Simon, The.
Harmonious Heedlessness of Little Boy Blue, The.
How a Cat Was Annoyed and a Poet Was Booted.
How a Fisherman Corked Up His Foe in a Jar.
How a Girl Was Too Reckless of Grammar by Far.
How Jack Found That Beans May go Back on a Chap.
How the Babes in the Wood Showed They Couldn't Be Beaten.
How the Helpmate of Blue-Beard Made Free with a Door.
Inhuman Wolf and the Lamb Sans Gene The.
Little Boy Blue.
Little Red Riding Hood.
Microscopic Trout and the Machiavellan Fisherman, The.
Opportune Overthrow of Humpty Dumpty, The.
Red Riding Hood.
Singular Sangfroid of Baby Bunting, The.
Sycophantic Fox and the Gullible Raven.
Vainglorious Oak and the Modest Bulrush, The.
When the Great Gray Ships Come In.
Carsley, Sara E.
Little Boats of Britain, The.
Portrait of a Very Old Man.
Carson, Mary Newland
My "Patch of Blue."
Carter, Aline Badger
Earth Bows to the New Bomb.
Give Our Conscience Light.
Immortal Words.
Carter, Ann A. G.
Nursery Song, A.
Robin to His Mate, The.
Carter, D.
Mrs. Indiarubber Duck.
Carter, Elizabeth
Ode to Wisdom.
Carter, Emily
Baby in the Basket, The.
Carter, Hodding
Slave Story.
Carter, Lin
Carcosa.
Dark Yuggoth.
Dream-Daemon, The.
Lunae Custodiens.
Sabbat, The.
Cartwright, William
Come, my sweet, whiles every strain.
Dead Sparrow, The.
Drinking Song.
Falsehood.
Good Eating Song, A.
House Blessing, A.
Lesbia on Her Sparrow.
New Year's Gift to Brian Lord Bishop of Sarum, A.
No Platonic Love.
On a Virtuous Young Gentlewoman That Died Suddenly.
On the Queen's Return from the Low Countries.
Ordinary, The, *sel.*
Royal Slave, The, *sel.*
Seal Up Her Eyes, O Sleep.
Siege, The, *sel.*
Song of Dalliance, A.
There are two births; the one when light.
To Chloe.
To Chloë Who Wished Herself Young Enough for Me.
Upon the Dramatick Poems of Mr. John Fletcher.
Valediction, A.
Women.
Caruthers, Mazie V.
Fish-Day.
Matilda, Matriarch.
Matilda's Manners.
Mothering.
Prayer of Any Husband.
Threnody for a Pet Cat.
Carvalho, Ronald de
Brazil.
Per Amica Silentia Lunae.
Carver, Mabel MacDonald
Addict.
Codicil.
Semi-private.
Cary, Alice
Among the Beautiful Pictures.
Balder's Wife.
Dying Hymn, A.
Elihu.
Gray Swan, The.
Her Mother.
Leaves, The.
Make Believe.
My Creed.
Nobility.
Noble Life, The.
Order for a Picture, An.
To Mother Fairie.
Cary, Phoebe
Ballad of the Canal.
Compensation,
Day Is Done, The, *parody.*
Don't Give Up.
Dreams and Realities, *sel.*
Jacob.
John Greenleaf Whittier.
John Thompson's Daughter.
Keep a Stiff Upper Lip.
Leak in the Dike [*or* Dyke], The.
Legend of the Northland, A.
Little Gottlieb.
Lovers, The.
Love's Moods and Tenses.
Nearer Home.
Obedience.
Our Heroes.
Peace.
Ready.
Reuben.
Sometimes, I think, the things we see.
Suppose.
Thaddeus Stevens.
There's a Bower of Bean-Vines.
True Love.
When Lovely Woman, *parody.*
When Lovely Woman Wants a Favor.
Wife, The.
Cary, Thomas
On His Mistress Crossing the Sea.
On His Mistresse Going to Sea.
Casa, Giovanni della
To Sleep.
Casal, Julian del
Friar, The.
Casas, José Joaquin
Secret, The.
Case, Elizabeth York
Faith.
There Is No Unbelief.
Unbelief.
Case, Phila H.
Nobody's Child.
Casement, Roger
Hamilcar Barca.
In the Streets of Catania.
Lost Youth.
Casey, D. A.
Spouse of Christ, The.
Casey, John Keegan
Maire My Girl.
Rising of the Moon, The, A.D. 1798.
Cassidy, Alice Caroline Coates *See* **Coates, Carol**
Cassin, Maxine
Annals.
Casterline, Helen Annis
God Cares.
Castiello, Jaime
Partners.
Castilla, Ethel
Australian Girl, An.
Castillejo, Cristóbal de
Some Day, Some Day (Alguna Vez).
Castro de Murguía, Rosalia
Carillon, The.
Castro-Leon, Sophia
Again Beginning.
Eye, The.
Letter, A.
Messages.
Paces.
Soft Rain.
Turning.
Caswall, Edward
Come, Wandering Sheep.
Sleep, Holy Babe.
Cater, Catherine
Here and Now.
Cather, Willa Sibert
Grandmither, Think Not I Forget.
Hawthorn Tree, The.
L'Envoi: "Where are the loves that we loved before."
Likeness, A.
Palatine, The.
Spanish Johnny.
Catherine, Sister Mary
Who Know Thee Best ("Who know her but as children do").
Catlin, Ellen Weston
Childlike Heart.
Cato, Nancy
Independence.
Catton, Bruce
Names from the War.
Catullus, Caius [*or* Gaius] Valerius
Acme and Septimius.
Ad Lesbiam.
Bridal Hymn.
Cataclysm.
Catullus Talks to Himself (Catullus, you're a fool. I said).
Cold Blast of Debt.
Comparison, The.
Complaint, The.
Counting Kisses.
Dead Sparrow, The.
Dead Starling, The.

Catullus (continued)
Death of Lesbia's Bird, The.
Debate on Marriage versus Virginity, A.
Dialogue with a Door.
Farewell to Bithynia.
Farewell to Lesbia.
Fib Detected, A.
Flavius, If Your Girl Friend.
Home to Sermio.
Hymn to Diana.
Hymn to Marriage, for Manlius and Junia.
I Must, Varus, Tell You.
Inconsistency of Women's Love.
Invitation to an Invitation, An.
Lesbia Railing.
Lesbia's Disgrace.
Lesbia's Vow.
Letter to Manlius Torquatus.
Love and Death.
Love and Hate.
Love Is All.
Love's Unreason.
My Woman.
Odi et Amo.
On an Unpleasant Woman.
On the Burial of His Brother.
On the Inconstancy of Women.
Out of Catullus.
Out of Catullus ("Unto nobody my woman saith she had rather a wife be").
Prayer against Love.
Quarrel with Juventius.
Quintilia Dead.
Rendezvous, The.
Return to Sirmio.
Rite at a Brother's Grave.
Sappho.
Sirmio.
Spring.
Spring Holidays.
To Himself.
To His Cup Bearer.
To Lesbia ("I hate, and yet I love thee too").
To Lesbia ("Let us, my Lesbia! live and love").
To Lesbia ("Thy kisses dost thou bid me count").
To Naso.
To Quintius.
To the Garden God.
To Varus.
Transformation.
True or False.
Two Poems against His Rival.
Under a Spell.
Upon Lesbia's Abuse.
Vivamus, Mea Lesbia.
Whom Lesbia Loved.
World without End.
Yacht, The.

"Caudwell, Christopher" (Christopher St. John Sprigge)
Classic Encounter.
Though Rulers Fall.

Causley, Charles
At Grantchester.
At the British War Cemetery, Bayeux.
At the Grave of John Clare, *sel.*
Autobiography.
Ballad for Katharine of Aragon, A.
Ballad of Charlotte Dymond, The.
Chief Petty Officer.
Convoy.
Cowboy Song ("I come from Salem County").
Death of an Aircraft.
Fauré.
For an Ex-Far East Prisoner of War.
Innocent's Song.
Keats at Teignmouth: 1818.
King's College Chapel.
My Friend Maloney.
Nursery Rhyme of Innocence and Experience.
On Seeing a Poet of the First World War on the Station at Abbeville.
Ou Phrontis.
Recruiting Drive.
Sailor's Carol.
Seasons in North Cornwall, The.
Song of the Dying Gunner A.A.1.
Timothy Winters.
To a Poet Who Has Never Travelled.
Visit to Van Gogh, A.
Walking in the scythed churchyard.

Cavafy, Constantine P.
Alexander Jannai.
First Step, The.
Ithaca.
One of the Jews (50 A.D.).
Return.
To Remain.
Walls.

Cavalcanti, Guido
Ballata: Concerning a Shepherd-Maid.
Ballata: He Reveals His Increasing Love for Mandetta.
Ballata: In Exile at Sarzana.
Ballata V: "Light do I see within my Lady's eyes."
Ballata: Of a Continual Death in Love.
Ballata: Of His Lady among Other Ladies.
Ballata: "With other women I beheld my love."
Ballata of Love's Power.
Canzone: Donna Mi Priegha.
Canzone: "Lady asks me, A/ I speak in season."
Chi è questa.
Effigy, The.
Love's Assize.
Sonetto XXXV: To Guido Orlando.
Sonetto VII: "Who is she that comes, makyng turn every man's eye."
Sonnet: He Compares All Things with His Lady.
Sonnet: He Speaks of a Third Love.
Sonnet: Of an Ill-favored Lady.
Sonnet: Of His Pain from a New Love.
Sonnet: Of the Eyes of a Certain Mandetta.
Sonnet: On the Detection of a False Friend.
Sonnet: Rapture Concerning His Lady, A.
Sonnet: To a Friend Who Does Not Pity His Love.
Sonnet: To Dante Alighieri (He Interprets Dante's Dream).
Sonnet: To Dante Alighieri (He Mistrusts the Love of Lapo Gianni).
Sonnet: To Dante Alighieri (He Reports the Successful Issue of Lapo Gianni's Love).
Sonnet: To His Lady Joan, of Florence.
To Dante.

Cavazza, Elisabeth Jones *See* **Pullen, Elizabeth Jones Cavazza**

Cavendish, Margaret, Duchess of Newcastle. *See* **Newcastle, Margaret Cavendish, Duchess of**

Cavendish, William, Duke of Newcastle *See* **Newcastle, William Cavendish, Duke of**

Cawein, Madison
Abandoned.
Attainment.
Ballad of Low-lie-down.
Comradery.
Covered Bridge, The.
Creek-Road, The.
Death.
Deserted.
Dirge: "What shall her silence keep."
Enchantment.
Flight.
Here Is the Place Where Loveliness Keeps House.
I Hear the Woodlands Calling.
Ku Klux.
Man Hunt, The.
"Mene, Mene, Tekel, Upharsin."
Miracle of the Dawn, The.
Morning Serenade.
Mosby at Hamilton.
Old Bayou, The.
Old Home, The.
Old Man Rain.
Opportunity.
Proem: "There is no rhyme that is half so sweet."
Rain-Crow, The.
Snow.
Soul, The.
To a Wind Flower.
Wind in the Pines, The.
Winds, The.

Cayley, George John
Epitaph, An: "Lovely young lady I mourn in my rhymes, A."

Cecco Angiolieri da Siena
In Honor of His Mistress.
Love in Men and Devils.
Of All He Would Do.
Past Help.
Sonnet: He Argues His Case with Death.
Sonnet: He Is Past All Help.
Sonnet: He Rails against Dante.
Sonnet: He Will Not Be Too Deeply in Love.
Sonnet: In Absence from Becchina.
Sonnet: Of All He Would Do.
Sonnet: Of Becchina in a Rage.
Sonnet: Of Becchina, the Shoemaker's Daughter.
Sonnet: Of Love, in Honor of His Mistress Becchina.
Sonnet: Of Love in Men and Devils.
Sonnet: Of the 20th June 1291.
Sonnet: Of Why He Is Unhanged.
Sonnet: Of Why He Would Be a Scullion.
Sonnet: To Dante Alighieri (He Writes to Dante, Defying Him).
Sonnet: To Dante Alighieri (On the Last Sonnet of the "Vita Nuova").

Cech, Svatopluk
Here and there, Freedom is an empty name.
Songs of the Slave, *sel.*

Cecil, William, 1st Baron Burghley *See* **Burghley, William Cecil, 1st Baron**

"Ceiriog." *See* **Hughes, John Ceiriog**

Celan, Paul
Death Fugue.

Celano, Tommáso di *See* **Thomas of Celano**

Cennick, John
Children of the Heavenly King.
Thou Dear Redeemer.

Ceravolo, Joseph
Book of Wild Flowers, The
Dangers of the Journey to the Happy Land.
Don't Break It.
Drunken Winter.
Fill and Illumined.
Happiness in the Trees.
Ho Ho Ho Caribou.
In My Crib.
Route.
Song of Autumn, A.
Spring of Work Storm.

Story from the Bushmen, A.
Wild Provoke of the Endurance Sky.
Wind Is Blowing West, The.
Cervantes Saavedra, Miguel de
Friendship.
Sonnet: "When I was marked for suffering, Love forswore."
Césaire, Aimé
I shall not regard my swelled head as a sign of real glory.
Memorandum on My Martinique, *sel.*
Neither the teacher of the class nor the priest with his catechism.
Return to My Native Land, *sel.*
Cestrian, W.
Because of You.
Cetina, Gutierre de
Madrigal: "Eyes that are clear, serene."
Chace, Jean Valentine
Visit to a Hospital.
Chadwick, John White
Abiding Love, The.
Auld Lang Syne.
Full Cycle.
Golden-Robin's Nest, The.
His Mother's Joy.
Hymn: "Eternal Ruler of the ceaseless round."
Hymn: "Father, we come not as of old."
King Edwin's Feast.
Kingdom of God on Earth, The.
Making of Man, The.
Mugford's Victory.
O Love, That Dost with Goodness Crown.
Recognition.
Rise of Man, The.
Starlight.
Wedding-Song, A.
Chaffee, Eleanor Alletta
Cobbler, The.
Cricket.
Difference, The.
Cha Liang-cheng
Hungry China, *sel.*
I see Hunger watching at every house door.
There Is No Nearer Nearness.
Chalkhill, John
Angler, The (*in* Izaak Walton's The Compleat Angler).
Coridon's Song.
Rhotus on Arcadia.
Thealma and Clearchus, *sel.*
Chalmers, Allan Knight
Oh, Haunting Spirit of the Ever True.
Chalmers, Patrick Reginald
Badger, The.
Cuckoo, The.
Gardener's Cat, The.
Hay Harvest.
"Hold."
If I Had a Broomstick.
In an Old Nursery.
Lavender's for Ladies.
Little Young Lambs, The.
My Woodcock.
Pan-Pipes.
Puk-Wudjies.
Road, The.
Tortoiseshell Cat, The.
Visitor, The.
When Mary Goes Walking.
Chalmers, Stephen
Allenby Enters Jerusalem.
Home.
New Physican, The.
Chamberlain, Brenda
Dead Ponies.
First Woman's Lament.
Fisherman Husband.
Give No White Flower.
In Old Age.
Lament: "My man is a bone ringèd with weed."
Poem: "You, who in April laughed, a green god in the sun."
Second Woman's Lament.
Song: "Bone-aged is my white horse."
Song: "Heron is harsh with despair."
Song-Talysarn.
Chamberlain, C. H.
Illinois.
Chamberlain [*or* Chamberlin], Enola
After the Dark.
God's Gift.
Heart Prayer.
Trusting God.
Chamberlain, Richard
To the Much Honoured R. F. Esq.
Chamberlain, Robert
Farewell this company.
In Praise of Country Life.
Swaggering Damsel, The, *sel.*
Chamberlayne, Sir James
Dedication: "This little book, my God and King."
Chambers, ——
To Mistress Sarah Hickford.
Chambers, Robert William
"Grey Horse Troop," The.
Officer Brady.
Recruit, The.
The Recruit.
To Nature Seekers.
Chamisso, Adelbert von
Tragic Story, A.
Chandler, Ellen Louise *See* **Moulton,Louise Chandler**
Chandler, Elsie Williams
Christmas Singing.
Chandler, Len
I Would Be a Painter Most of All.
Chandler, Mary
To Mrs. Boteler.
Chan Fang-sheng
Sailing Homeward.
Chang Chi
Old Temple in Mountains.
Chang Ch'ien
Visiting the Ruins.
Chang Chung-sur
Spring, The.
Chang Heng
Bones of Chuang Tzu, The.
Channing, Grace Ellery (Mrs. Charles Walter Stetson)
England.
Judgment.
Song of Arno, A.
War.
Channing, William Ellery
Barren Moors, The.
Earth-Spirit, The.
Edith.
Flight of the Wild Geese.
Hymn of the Earth.
In this sweet solitude, the mountain sits.
Lady, there is a hope that all men have.
Mountain, The, *sel.*
Poet's Hope, A.
Prayer, A: "To Thy continual Presence, in me wrought."
Flight of the Wild Geese.
Sleepy Hollow.
Tears in Spring.
Channing-Stetson, Grace Ellery *See* **Channing , Grace Ellery**
Chao Ying-tou
Decrees of God, The.
Chapin, Edwin H.
Ocean Burial, The.
Chapin, Katherine Garrison (Mrs. Francis Biddle)
In Cycle Repeated.
Love Beleaguered.
Other Journey, The.
Plain-Chant for America.
Portrait in Winter.
This the last refuge I can give you.
Chaplin, Kathleen M.
Merry Little Men.
Chaplin, Ralph
Mourn Not the Dead.
To France.
Chapman, Arthur
Beecher Island.
Out Where the West Begins.
White Man's Road, The.
Chapman, George (1559?-1634)
Ad Deum.
And, now gives Time, her states description.
And so, farewell for ever.
As cedars beaten with continual storms.
As when the moon hath comforted the night.
Bridal Song ("Now, sleep, bind fast the flood of air").
Bridal Song ("O come, soft rest of cares! come, Night!").
Bussy d'Ambois, *sels.*
Come, Night.
Conspiracy of Charles, Duke of Byron, The, *sels.*
Corinna Bathes.
Coronet for His Mistress Philosophy, A, *sels.*
De Guiana, Carmen Epicum.
Descend, Fair Sun!
Earth from heavenly light conceived heat, The.
Epistle Dedicatory to Chapman's Translation of the Iliad, The, *sels.*
Epithalamion Teratos [*or* Teratus].
Eugenia, *sel.*
Euthymiae Raptus; or, The Teares of Peace, *sels.*
Hymne to Our Saviour on the Crosse, A.
Hymnus in Noctem.
I long to know/ How my dear mistress fares.
Ile sooth his plots: and strow my hate with smiles.
Ile weare those golden spurres upon my heeles.
Learning.
Love and Philosophy.
Masque of the Middle Temple and Lincoln's Inn, The, *sels.*
Master Spirit, The.
Natures Naked Jem.
Night.
Now all ye [*or* the] peacefull regents of the night.
Now shall we see, that nature hath no end.
Now, Sleep, Bind Fast.
Ovid's Banquet of Sense, *sels.*
Pilot, The.
Poetry and Learning.
Poor slaves, how terrible this Death is to them!
Praise of Homer.
Presage of Storme.
Princes statue, A, or in marble carv'd.
Repentance.
Rich Mine of Knowledge.
Shadow of Night, The.
Since I am free,/ Offending no just law, let no law make.
Since perfect happiness, by princes sought.

Chapman (continued)
Song: "O come soft rest of cares! come, Night!"
Sonnet: "Muses that sing love's sensual empery."
Such love is like a smoky fire.
Tears of Peace, The.
Thus, by the way, to human loves interring.
To fear a violent good, abuseth goodness.
To the High-born Prince of Men, Henry.
To the Ruins of Troy and Greece.
Tragedy of Caesar and Pompey, The, *sel.*
Tragedy of Charles, Duke of Byron, The, *sels.*
Wedding of Alcmane and Mya, The.
Chapman, George (20th century)
Autumn Hour.
Knell.
Chapman, John Alexander
Gipsy Queen.
Chapman, John Jay
Clouds.
Lines on the Death of Bismarck.
Song: "Old Farmer Oats and his son Ned."
Toil Away.
Chapman, Mary Berri *See* **Hansbrough, Mary Berri Chapman**
Chapone, Hester
To Stella.
Chappell, George S.
Innocence.
Chappell, Jeannette
Newton to Einstein.
Chapple, Bennett
Great Oak.
Char, René
Contravention.
True Night.
Charasson, Henriette (Mme Rene Johannet)
Ave Maria.
Charles I, King of England
On a Quiet Conscience.
Charles, Elizabeth Rundle
Child on the Judgment Seat, The.
Compensation.
Nature No Self-Acting Instrument.
Charles, Jack
To Chuck—Concerning a Rendezvous in Siam.
Charles, Mabel Munns
Living Tithe, The.
Charles, Mary Grant
Flood.
Charles, Robert E.
Roundabout Turn, A.
Charles d'Orléans *See* **Orléans, Charles, Duc d'**
Chartres, Vidame de
April.
Chase, Edith Newlin
New Baby Calf, The.
Passenger Train.
Tiger-Cat Tim.
Work Horses.
Chase, Frank
Tale of the Dixie-Belle, The.
Chase, Polly *See* **Boyden, Polly Chase**
Chase, Victoria
Birthday Cake, The.
Chatterton, Thomas
Accounte of W. Canynge's Feast, The.
Aella; a Tragycal Enterlude, *sels.*
African Song, An.
Bristowe Tragedie; or the Dethe of Syr Charles Bawdin.
Eclogue: "Would'st thou know nature in her better part?"
Eclogues, *sel.*
Excelente Balade of Charitie, An.
Freedom's War Song.
Goddwyn, *sel.*
Hymn for Christmas Day, A.
Last Verses.
Minstrel's Song.
My Love Is Dead.
Mynstrelles Songe: "Angelles bee wrogte to bee of neidher kynde."
Mynstrelles Songe: "Boddynge flourettes bloshes atte the lyghte, The."
Mynstrelles Songe: "O! synge untoe mie roundelaie."
O, Sing unto My Roundelay.
Ode to Liberty.
Song: "O sing unto my roundelay."
Song from "Aella."
Song of the Three Minstrels.
Songe of Seyncte Warburghe.
Songs of the Three Minstrels.
Chattopadhyaya, Harindranth
Imagery.
Chaucer, Geoffrey
A. B. C., An [*or* The].
Against Women Unconstant.
Allas the Wo! Allas, the peynes stronge.
And as for me, though that my wit be lite [*or* thogh that I can but lyte].
Arcite's Farewell.
As proude Bayard ginneth for to skip.
At the Gate.
Balade: "Hyd[e], Absolon [*or* Absalon], thy gilte tresses clere."
Balade de [*or* of] Bon Conseyl [*or* Conseil *or* Conseill].
Ballad of Good Counsel.
Ballade against Woman Inconstant, A.
Ballade of Good Counsel.
Ballade to Rosamund.
Birds' Rondel, The.
Book of the Duchesse, The, *sels.*
But Whan the Cok.
Canterbury Tales, The, *sels.*
Canticus Troili.
Carpenter's Young Wife, The.
Chaucer's Complaint to His Empty Purse.
Chaucer's Envoy to the Story of Patient Griselda.
Chaucers Word[e]s unto Adam, His Owne Scriveyn.
Clerk of Oxenford, The.
Clerk's [*or* Clerkes] Tale, The.
Complaint of Chaucer to His Empty Purse, The.
Complaint of Troilus, The.
Complaint to His Purse.
Compleint [*or* Compleinte *or* Compleynt] of Chaucer to His Empty Purse [*or* Purs], The.
Compleynt of Chaucer to His Purse, The.
Counsel upon Marriage.
Croesus.
Daisy, The.
Despair of Troilus, The.
Dream, The.
Emily's Prayer to Diana.
Envoy, The: "Go, litel book, go litel myn tragedie."
Exhortation to Youth.
Franklin's Tale, The.
Friar's Tale, The.
General Prologue, The.
Gentilesse.
Good Parson, The.
Hide, Absolon.
I am, thow woost, yet of thy compaignye.
In days of old, when Arthur filled the throne.
Introduction: "'Thou beel amy, thou Pardoner,' he sayde."
Invocatio ad Mariam.
Invocation: "O mother-maid! O maiden-mother free!"
Knight, A.
Knight's [*or* Knightes] Tale, The.
La Prière de Nostre Dame.
Lack of Steadfastness.
Lady without Paragon, A.
Lak of Stedfastnesse.
Lat Take a Cat.
Legend of Good Women, The: Prologue, *sels.*
Love Unfeigned, The.
Man of Law's Prologue, Introduction to the.
Manciple's Tale, The, *sel.*
May Morning.
Merchant's Tale, The, *abr.*
Merciles[s] Beaute [*or* Beauty].
Miller, A.
Miller was a chap of sixteen stone, The.
Miller's Tale, The.
Monk's Tale, The, *sels.*
Murder Will Out.
My fifthe housbonde, god his soule blesse!
Nonne Preestes Tale, The.
Now Welcome Summer.
Nun's Priest's Tale, The.
O Blisful Light.
O Mooder Mayde.
Of His Lady.
Out [*or* Owt] of thise blake wawes for to saile [*or* saylle].
Pardoner's Tale, The.
Parish Priest, The.
Parlement of Foules, The, *sels.*
Parliament of Fowls, The.
Patient Griselda.
Poor Parson, The.
Poor Widow's Cock, The.
Portrait of the Prioress, The.
Poure Persoun, The.
Prayer to the Blessed Virgin, A.
Prayer to Venus.
Prioress's Tale, The.
Proem to "The Parlement of Foules."
Prologue: "'Lordynges,' quod he, 'in chirches whan I preche.'"
Prologue: "This worthy limitour, this noble frere."
Prologue of the Prioress's Tale, The.
Prologue of the Pardoner's Tale, The.
Prologue to Sir Thopas.
Prologue to "The Canterbury Tales."
Prologue to the Man of Law's Tale.
Prologue to the Prioress's Tale.
Prologue to the Pardoner's Tale.
Prologue to the Wife of Bath's Tale, The.
Qui Bien Aime a Tard Oublie.
Reeve's Tale, The.
Rondel of Merciless Beauty.
Roundel, A: "Now welcom somer, with thy sonne softe."
Roundel: "Your eyen two will slay me suddenly."
Second Nun's Tale, The, *sel.*
She is the clernesse and the verray light.
Shipman, The.
Sir Thopas.
Sometime [*or* Somtyme *or* Sometimes] this [*or* the] world was so steadfast [*or* stedfast] and stable.
Song of Troilus.
Song to His Purse for the King, A.
Sorrow of Troilus, The.
Squire, A.
Take Any Bird.
Tale of Hugelin, Count of Pisa, The.
Ten of Chaucer's People.
That thee is sent, receyve in buxumnesse.
Ther is at the west syde of Ytaille.

Therewith when he was ware, and gan behold.
These rioters, of whom I make my rime.
This Chauntecleer stood hye up-on his toos.
This Fresshe Flour.
Three Canterbury Pilgrims.
Three Roundels of Love Unreturned.
To My Empty Purse.
To Rosamond [*or* Rosemounde].
To Rosemounde.
Troilus and Cressida.
Troilus and Criseyde, *sels.*
Troylus and Criseyde.
Truth.
Truth Shall Set You Free.
Two Invocations of the Virgin.
Welcome, Summer.
Well of Pity, The.
Whan That the Month of May.
When that sweet April showers with downward shoot.
Wife of Bath, The.
Wife of Bath's Prologue, The.
Wife of Bath's Tale, The.
With-inne the temple he went him forth pleyinge.
Wooing of Criseide, The.
Young Woman.

Chaundler, Christine
Child's Christmas Carol, A.
Tree in the Garden, The.

Chavez, Fray Angelico
Esther.
In Extremis.
Lady of Lidice.
Lady of Peace.
Mary.
Mulier Amicta Sole.
Sea-Birds.
Southwestern Night.

Chawner, George F.
Prayer, A: "Those who love Thee may they find."

Chaya, Prem
On My Short-Sightedness.

Chazeau, Eunice de
Only a Gambler Loves Peace.

Cheek, Thomas
To Chloe.

Ch'en Tzu-ang
Business Men.
Evening.

Ch'en Tzu-lung
Little Cart, The.

Ch'en Yün
Twilight.

Cheney, Ednah Dow
Larger Prayer, The.
Prayer—Answer.

Cheney, Elizabeth
Faith's Expulsive Power.
Feathered Faith.
There Is a Man on the Cross.
Overheard in an Orchard.

Cheney, John Vance
"Birds have hid, the winds are low, The."
Evening Songs.
Every One to His Own Way.
Happiest Heart, The.
Kitchen Clock, The.
Lincoln.
Man with the Hoe, The; a Reply.
On a Picture of Lincoln.
Rainbow, The.
San Francisco.
Seasons, The.
Skilful Listener, The.
Strong, The.
Way of It, The.
Whither.

Ch'eng Hsiao
Satire on Paying Calls.

Chénier, André Marie de
Elegies, *sels.*
"Well, I would have it so. I should have known."
When I Was Small.

Cherbury, Edward Herbert, 1st Baron *See* **Herbert of Cherbury**

Chernick, Hank
Situation Normal.

Cherry, Andrew
Green Little Shamrock of Ireland, The.
Shamrock, The.

Cherry, Edith E.
Kept for Jesus.

Cherry, Edith Gilling
Into the Dark.

Cherwinski, Joseph
Manhattan Menagerie.
Still Day, A.

Chesley, Elizabeth
Of Natural Forces.

Chesson, Nora Hopper *See* **Hopper, Nora**

Chester, Anson G.
Tapestry Weavers, The.

Chester, Sir Robert
Ditty: "O holy Love, religious saint!"
Her Hair.
Love's Martyr, *sels.*

Chester, Thomas
Sir Launfal.

Chesterfield Philip Dormer Stanhope, 4th Earl of
Advice to a Lady in Autumn.
Immortal Newton Never Spoke.
On a Full-Length Portrait of Beau Marsh, *wr.* [Nash].
To Miss Eleanor Ambrose on the Occasion of Her Wearing an Orange Lily at a Ball in Dublin Castle on July the 12th.
Verses Written in a Lady's Sherlock "Upon Death."

Chesterman, Hugh
Coal Man, The.
Noah and the Rabbit.
Outside.
Rhyme Sheet of Other Lands, A.
Sir Nicketty Nox.
Yesterday.

Chesterton, Frances
Alle Vögel Sind Schon Da.
How Far Is It to Bethlehem?
To Felicity Who Calls Me Mary.

Chesterton, Gilbert Keith
Antichrist, or the Reunion of Christendom; an Ode.
Ballad of the Battle of Gibeon, The.
Ballad of the White Horse, The, *sels.*
Ballade d'une Grande Dame.
Ballade of an Anti-Puritan, A.
Ballade of Suicide, A.
Beatific Vision, The.
Before the gods that made the gods.
Before the Roman Came to Rye.
Black Virgin, The.
Building.
Christ-Child, The.
Christmas Carol, A: "Christ-child lay on Mary's lap, The."
Citizenship; Form 8889512, Sub-section Q.
Commercial Candour.
Convert, The.
Dedication A: "He was, through boyhood's storm and shower."
Donkey, The.
Ecclesiastes.
Elegy in a Country Churchyard.
Englishman, The.
Fantasia.
Feast of the Snow, The.
Feast on Wine or Fast on Water.
Femina contra Mundum.
Flying Inn, The, *sel.*
For a War Memorial.
Geography.
Good Rich Man, The.
Grave of Arthur, The.
Harp of Alfred, The.
Holy of Holies, The.
Home at Last.
House of Christmas, The.
Hymn, A: "From all that terror teaches," *abr. sel.*
Hymn, A: "O God of earth and altar."
Hymn for the Church Militant.
King Alfred Answers the Danes.
Kingdom of Heaven, The.
Last Hero, The.
Lepanto.
Litany: "From all that terror teaches".
Logical Vegetarian, The.
Me Heart.
Men that are men again; who goes home?
Music.
Myth of Arthur, The.
O God of Earth and Altar.
Old Song, The.
On a Prohibitionist Poem.
Praise of Dust, The.
Prayer: "O God of earth and altar."
Prayer in Darkness, A.
Regina Angelorum.
Return of Eve, The.
Rolling English Road, The.
Secret People, The.
Skeleton, The.
So, with the wan waste grasses on my spear.
Song against Grocers, The.
Song against Songs, The.
Song of Quoodle, The.
Song of Right and Wrong, The.
Song of the Strange Ascetic, The.
Songs of Education, *sel.*
Songs of Guthrum and Alfred, The.
Strange Music, The.
Sword of Surprise, The.
To F. C. in Memoriam Palestine.
To M. E. W.
To sweat a slave to a race of slaves.
To the Unknown Warrior.
Translation from Du Bellay ("Happy, who like Ulysses or that lord").
Variations on an Air.
Who Goes Home, *br. sel.*
Wild Knight, The.
Wine and Water.
World State, The.

Chettle, Henry
Aeliana's Ditty.
Of Cupid.
Piers Plainness' Seven Years' Prenticeship, *sel.*
Wily Cupid.

Chettle, Henry *and* **Anthony Munday** *See* **Munday, Anthony,** *and* **Henry Chettle**

Chettur, Govinda Krishna
World's End.

Chew, Beverly
Old Books Are Best.

Cheyne, Irene
Old Mr. Tatterlock.

Cheyney, Ralph
Comrade Jesus.
No Armistice in Love's War.
Unemployed.

Cheyney, Ralph, *and* **Lucia Trent** *See* **Trent, Lucia,** *and* **Ralph Cheyney**

Chiabrera, Gabriello
Epitaphs.
Francesco Ceni.
There never breathed a man, who, when his life.
Chichester, Bishop of *See* **King, Henry**
Chien Liang Tse
Glimpse of Beauty, A.
Ch'ien Wen-ti, Emperor
Lo-yang.
Winter Night.
Chih Ming
Facing Death.
Child, A. C.
Wishes.
Child, Lydia Maria
Apple-Seed John.
Thanksgiving Day.
Who Stole the Bird's Nest?
World I Am Passing Through, The.
Child, O. C. A.
Battle-Plane in France, A.
Child, Philip
Basilisk, The.
Dancing Partners.
Descent for the Lost.
Lyric: "I touched a shining mote of sand."
Macrocosm.
Oak.
Childe, Wilfred Rowland
Last Abbot of Gloucester, The.
Our Lady with Two Angels.
Shepherd of Meriador, The.
Childress, W. Lomax
Beautiful World, The.
Childress, William
Korea Bound, 1952.
Ch'in Chia
To His Wife.
Chipp, Elinor
Before Dawn.
Doubt.
Lullaby: "Sleep, little baby, sleep and rest."
Wild Geese.
Chisato
Autumn Moon.
Chisoku
Dragonfly, The.
Face of the dragonfly, The.
Chittenden, Larry
Cowboy's Christmas Ball, *with music.*
Texas Types—"The Bad Man."
Chivers, Thomas Holley
Avalon.
Voice of Thought, The.
Chocano, José Santos
Eagles and Sparrows.
Sylvan Ode.
Cholmondeley, Hester H.
Betrayal.
Still as of Old.
Cholmondeley-Pennell, Henry
Bloated Biggaboon, The.
Ghostries.
How the Daughters Come Down at Dunoon.
I've Lost My ——.
Lay of the Deserted Influenzaed.
Our Traveller.
What the Prince of I Dreamt.
Chora
Storm, The.
Chorley, Henry Fothergill
Brave Old Oak, The.
Choe, Henry Fothergill ***and*** **John Lodge Ellerton**
God, the Omnipotent.
Choyce, A. Newberry
Come Michaelmas.
Let Me Love Bright Things.
Oblation.
Christesen, Clement B.
Dawn at Flying-Fish Point.
Reef Wrack.
Regent-Bird and Girl.
Christian, Marcus B.
Craftsman, The.
Dialect Quatrain.
Drums of Haiti.
McDonogh Day in New Orleans.
Song of Hannibal; Rome.
Christiansen, Avis B.
Careful for Nothing.
Choice, The.
Confidence.
Emmaus Road, The.
Faith ("Faith is not in understanding").
Faith ("Only believe! How sweet that tender message").
Fill All My Vision.
Forbearance.
Glorious Mystery.
God's Best.
God's Way Is Perfect.
Guidance ("How wonderful to lay my hand").
Guidance ("There is a tender hand that guides me").
Hast Thou Spoken, Blessed Master?
Heavenly Vision, The.
Himself He Could Not Save.
How We Need the Secret Place.
Life and Death for the Christian.
O Blessed Moment.
Peace.
Satisfaction.
Silence My Heart.
Sufficiency.
Thou Art My Victory.
Too Busy.
Trust.
Two Pathways, The.
Vision of Eternity, A.
Wonderful Is My Saviour.
Yes, I Have Been to Calvary.
Yielded Instrument, A.
Christine de Pisan *See* **Pisan, Christine de**
Christman, William Weaver
Snow Lies Light, The, *sel.*
"Christopher Robin" (Abraham B. Shiffrin)
Dimple Diggers.
Hide and Seek.
One, Two, Three.
Rain.
Storm, The.
Chubb, Thomas Caldecot
At the Edge of the Bay.
Praise of New England.
Chu Ching-Yü,
Toilette, The.
Chudleigh, Mary, Lady
Resolve, The.
Chu Hsi
Boats Are Afloat, The.
Chu Miao Tuan
Butterflies.
Church, Benjamin
To the Heirs of the Pilgrims.
Church, Edward A.
Cornerstone, The.
Church, Hubert
Favonius.
Fugue, A, *sel.*
New Zealand, *sel.*
Retrospection.
Rosalind.
Spring in New Zealand.
There was a music throbbed athwart the street.
Ye wandering winds that from your threshing floor.
Church, Peggy Pond
Ultimatum.
Church, Richard
Edward Millington.
From an Upland Valley.
Hay's Wharf.
House in Wartime, A.
Immortal.
In a Woman's Face.
Lantern, The.
Londoner in the Country, The.
Man without Faith, The.
Mountain Lake, The.
Mud.
Nocturne: "See how the dying west puts forth her song."
On Hearing the First Cuckoo.
Pigeon, The.
Portent.
Preface to a Musician.
Purification, The.
Road in the Weald, A.
Solstices.
Something in Common.
Thinking of a Master.
To all Musicians.
Twentieth Century Love-Song.
Waiting for News.
Woodpecker, The.
Wrong Road, The.
Churchill, Charles
Conference, The, *sel.*
Conscience.
Critical Fribble, A.
Dedication to the Sermons, The.
Duellist, The, *sel.*
Farewell, The: "Farewell to Europe, and at once farewell."
Gotham, *sel.*
Hail, Liberty! a glorious word.
Happy, thrice happy now the savage race.
Night.
Night; an Epistle to Robert Lloyd.
On Himself.
Pains of Education, The.
Prophecy of Famine, The; a Scots Pastoral.
Rosciad, The, *sel.*
What Is't to Us?
Churchyard, Thomas
Davy Dicar's Dream.
Farewell to a Fondling, A.
Fayned Fancye betweene the Spider and the Gowte, A, *sel.*
He Persuadeth His Friend from the Fond Affects of Love.
How Thomas Wolsey Did Arise unto Great Authority and Government, His Maner of Life, Pompe, and Dignity, and How Hee Fell Downe into Great Disgrace, and Was Arrested of High Treason.
Lover Deceived by His Lady's Unconstancy Writeth unto Her as Followeth, The.
Old-Time Service.
Praise of Our Soldiers, The.
Sorrowful Verses Made on the Death of Our Most Sovereign Lady Queen Elizabeth My Gracious Mistress.
Chu Shu Chen
Hysteria.
Chute, Marchette
Bees.
Birthdays.
By the Sea.
Cats.
Christmas.
Dandelions.

Day before Christmas.
Drinking Fountain.
Easter Parade.
Fairies.
Food.
Fourth of July.
Going to Bed.
My Dog.
My Plan.
One Night.
Presents.
Secret, The.
Sliding.
Snowflakes.
Spring.
Spring Rain.
Tracks in the Snow.
Chu Yuan
Battle, The.
Great Summons, The.
Lord of the East, The.
Chwang Këang, Lady
Complaint, A.
Chworowsky, Karl M.
Motherhood.
Ciardi, John
After Sunday Dinner We Uncles Snooze.
Aunt Mary ("Aunt Mary died of eating twelve red peppers").
Camptown.
Children When They're Very Sweet.
Composition for a Nativity.
Counting on Flowers.
Credibility.
Dan Dunder.
Dolls, The.
Elegy: "My father was born with a spade in his hand and traded it."
Elegy Just in Case.
English A.
Evil Eye, The.
For My Twenty-fifth Birthday in Nineteen Forty-one.
Fragments from Italy, *sel.*
Gift, The.
Goodmorning with Light.
Homecoming—Massachusetts.
Home Revisited: Midnight.
How to Tell the Top of a Hill.
I Took a Bow and Arrow.
In Ego with Us All.
In Place of a Curse.
In the Stoneworks.
In the Year of Many Conversions and the Private Soul.
Island Galaxy, An.
Light-House-Keeper's White-Mouse, The.
Magus, A.
Men Marry What They Need. I Marry You.
Morning in the Park.
Most like an Arch This Marriage.
Mummy Slept Late and Daddy Fixed Breakfast.
My Father's Watch.
Mystic River.
Nona Domenica Garnaro sits in the sun.
Ode for the Burial of a Citizen.
On a Photo of Sgt. Ciardi a Year Later.
Palaver's No Prayer.
Pilot in the Jungle, The.
Pinwheel's Song, The.
Poem for My Thirty-second Birthday.
Prattle.
Rain Sizes.
Reason for the Pelican, The.
River Is a Piece of Sky, The.
Some Cook!
Someone.
Song: "Bells of Sunday rang us down, The."
Song for an Allegorical Play.
Suburban Homecoming.
Thanks That Flesh Is Sad, A.
That Summer's Shore.
Thousandth Poem for Dylan Thomas, A.
To Judith Asleep.
Two Egrets.
V-J Day.
Vale.
Vodka.
Warning.
What Night Would It Be?
What You Will Learn about the Brobinyak.
Why Nobody Pets the Lion at the Zoo.
Cibber, Colley
Blind Boy, The.
Celia and Belinda.
Woman's Wit, *sel.*.
Cino da Pistoia
At the Grave of Selvaggia.
Canzone: His Lament for Selvaggia.
In Great Bitterness.
Madrigal: To His Lady Selvaggia Vergiolesi.
Sonnet: Death Is Not without but within Him.
Sonnet: Of the Grave of Selvaggia.
Sonnet: To Dante Alighieri (He Conceives of Some Compensation in Death).
Sonnet: To Dante Alighieri (He Interprets Dante's Dream).
Sonnet: To Love, in Great Bitterness.
Sonnet: Trance of Love, A.
Ciullo [*or* Cielo] d'Alcamo
Dialogue: Lover and Lady.
Clairmont, Robert
Answers, The.
Hero in the Land of Dough, A.
Wheelgoround, The.
When Did the World Begin.
Clancy, Joseph P.
Boxer.
Clancy, Liam P.
Christmas Eve.
Gaelic Christmas, A.
Clanvowe, Thomas
Cuckoo and the Nightingale, The.
Clapp, Frederick Mortimer
Cancelled Itinerary.
Cattle.
Clapp, Mary Brennan
At Christmas Time.
Gilead.
Clapp, Ross B.
Mother's Love.
Clapper, Merl A.
When Nobody Prays.
Clar, Clarence E.
In His Service.
Clare, Francis D.
Sick Room.
Clare, John
Address to a Lark, *sel.*
Address to Plenty, *sel.*
"Adieu."
After Reading in a Letter Proposals for Building a Cottage.
And even silence found a tongue.
Autumn ("I love the fitful gust.")
Autumn ("The thistledown's flying").
Autumn Birds.
Autumn Evening.
Autumn Robin, The.
Autumn Wind, The.
Badger.
Bat.
Beanfield, The.
Birds' Lament.
Birds' Nests.
Bits of Straw.
Blackbird startles from the homestead hedge, The.
Bonny Lassie O.
Break of Day.
Child Harold, *sels.*
Childhood, *sel.*
Clock-a-Clay.
Clock-o'-Clay.
Come Hither.
Come Hither, My Dear One.
Cottager, The, *sel.*
Country Letter.
Cowper.
Crow, The.
Crows in Spring.
Death.
Deluge.
Dewdrops.
Dying Child, The.
Emmonsail's Heath in Winter.
Enclosure.
Eternity of Nature.
Evening Primrose.
Evening Star, The.
Fairy Things.
Farewell: "Farewell to the bushy clump close to the river."
Fear of Flowers, The.
February.
February: a Thaw.
Firetail's Nest, The.
First Love.
Firwood.
Flitting, The, *sel.*
Fragment: "Cataract, whirling to the precipice, The."
Fragment: "Language has not the power to speak what love indites."
Frightened Ploughman, The.
Giddy Maid, The.
Gipsies ("The gipsies seek wide sheltering woods again").
Gipsies ("The snow falls deep; the forest lies alone").
Gipsy Camp, The.
Graves of Infants.
Green lane now I traverse, where it goes, The.
Gypsies.
Hares at Play.
Hedgehog, The.
Hen's Nest.
Hesperus.
Honey Dew Falls from the Tree.
I Am.
I Feel I Am.
I Hid My Love [When Young].
I Lost the Love of Heaven.
I love at early morn, from new-mown swath.
I Love the Blue Violet.
I Ne'er Was Struck.
I Pass in Silence.
I Peeled Bits of Straw.
I saw her crop a rose.
Invitation to Eternity.
Invite to Eternity, An.
I've left my own old home of homes.
Joys of Childhood, *sel.*
July, *sel.*
Landscape sleeps in mist from morn till noon, The.
Let Ye Then My Birds Alone.
Little Maid and the Cowslips, The.
Little Trotty Wagtail.
Lord, Hear My Prayer.
Lout, The.
Love.

Clare (continued)
Love and Solitude.
Love Lies Beyond the Tomb.
Love Lives beyond the Tomb.
Love, Meet Me in the Green Glen.
Love's Story.
Maid o' the West, The.
Maple Hangs Its Green Bee Flowers, The.
March.
Mary.
Meet Me in the Green Glen.
Meet Me in the Primrose Lane.
Milkmaid singing leaves her bed, The.
Mole, The.
Mouse's Nest.
My Early Home.
My life hath been one love—no blot it out.
Nature.
Nightingale's Nest, The.
No single hour can stand for naught.
Noon.
November.
Now is Past.
Old Cottagers, The.
Old Year, The.
One Careless Look.
Pale Sun, The ("Pale sunbeams gleam").
Pastoral Poesy.
Peace.
Peasant Poet, The.
Peggy Said Good Morning.
Pettichap's Nest, The.
Pleasant Sounds.
Ploughboy, The.
Ploughman Singing.
Poets Love Nature.
Ragwort, The.
Red Robin, The.
Remembrance, *sel.*
Remembrances.
Schoolboys in Winter.
Secret Love.
Sheep in Winter.
Shepherd-boy, that hastens now and then, The.
Shepherd's Calendar, The, *sel.*
Signs of Winter.
Silent Love.
Sleep of Spring, The.
Snowstorm.
Solitude.
Song: "Floods come o'er the meadow leas, The."
Song: "Go with your tauntings, go."
Song: Love Lives beyond the Tomb.
Song: "One gloomy eve I roam'd about."
Song's Eternity.
Stanzas: "Black absence hides upon the past."
Stanzas: "How beautiful this hill of fun swells on!"
Stranger, The.
Sudden Shower.
Summer.
Summer Evening.
Summer Images.
Summer Moods.
Summer Morning.
Swordy Well.
Thou Flower of Spring.
Thrush's Nest, The.
To a Primrose.
To Harriett.
To John Clare.
To Mary ("I sleep with thee and wake with thee").
To Mary: It Is the Evening Hour.
To the Ivy.
To the Snipe.
To Wordsworth.
True as the church clock hand the hour pursues.
Vision, A.
Well, Honest John.
What is Love?
When first we hear the shy-come nightingales.
Wild Bees.
Wind That Shakes the Rushes, The.
Winter.
Winter in the Fens.
Winter's Come, The.
Winter's Spring, The.
Wood-Cutter's Night Song, The.
World for Love, A.
Written in a Northampton County Asylum.
Written in a Thunderstorm.
Written in Prison.
Yellowhammer, The.
Young Lambs.

"Claribel." *See* **Barnard, Charlotte Alington**

Clark, Ann Nolan
Irrigation.
Mountains.

Clark, Arthur H.
A-Working on the Railway.
Poor Reuben Ranzo.

Clark, Badger
Border Affair, A.
Bunk-House Orchestra, The.
Cottonwood Leaves.
Cowboy's Prayer, A.
Glory Trail, The.
God Meets Me in the Mountains.
Just a-Ridin'.
Legend of Boastful Bill, The.
Old Cowman, The.
Outlaw, The.
Pioneers.
Ranger, A.
Ridin'.
Sheep-Herder, The.
Smoke-blue Plains, The.

Clark, Charles Heber *See* **Adeler, Max**

Clark, David R.
Asylum.

Clark, Eunice (Mrs. John Knox Jessup)
Fallow Land.
People Has No Obituary, The.

Clark, Henry W.
Far Distances.
Host and Guest.

Clark, J. K.
Retreat.

Clark, John Pepper
Agbor Dancer.
Fulani Cattle.
Ibadan.

Clark, Leonard
Charles.
Peace, like a Lamb.
Walk, The.

Clark, Leslie Savage
Beacon Light.
Before Pilate.
Bread.
Carpenter.
Conquest.
Hands of Christ, The.
Hilltops.
Holier Night.
In Nazareth.
In the Time of Trouble.
Incense.
Litany for Peace.
Magi.
Of Things Not Seen.
Offering.
Remembrance.
Son of Man.
Sovereignty.
Syrian's Tale, The.
Temple Offering.
This Little Earth.
Values.
Way, The.
White Splendor.
Who Can Forget?
Young Jesus.

Clark, Lewis Gaylord
Flamingo, The.

Clark, Martha Haskell
Hurdy-Gurdy Days.
Red Geraniums.
To a Kitten.

Clark, Preston
Faith.
Youth.

Clark, Robert
Generations.

Clark, Thomas Curtis
Abraham Lincoln, the Master.
Apparitions.
At Mount Vernon.
Blow, Bugle!
Bugle Song of Peace.
By an Ancient Sea.
Call, The.
Carry On!
Challenge.
Christ Militant, The.
Christ of Today, The.
Come, Follow Me!
Common Blessings.
Day Breaks, The.
Desert Wanderings.
Disillusioned.
Earth's Story.
Easter.
Evidence.
Faith and Science.
Faith for Tomorrow.
Faith of Christ's Freemen, The.
Farewell and Hail!
For Those Who Died.
Forgotten Star, The.
Friends.
Glory of Lincoln, The.
God Give Me Joy.
God's Dreams.
He Shall Speak Peace.
His Is the Way.
How Shall We Honor Lincoln.
I Am Still Rich.
In an Age of Science.
It Shall Not Be Again!
Journey, The.
Keep Love in Your Life.
Kingdom, The.
Knowledge.
Lincoln.
Lincoln, Come Back.
Lost Christ, The.
Mary.
Master, The.
Message of the Bells, The.
Mother.
My America.
My Country, Right!
Nazareth.
New Crucifxion.
New Dreams for Old.
O Sun of Life.
On a World War Battlefield.
One Who Dared to Die.
Our faith is in the Christ who walks.
Poet's Call, The.
Prophet, The.
Prospect.
Redemption.

Repentance.
Requiem.
Search, The.
Song of Christian Workingmen.
Sons of Promise.
Take Time to Live.
There Lived a Man.
There Was a Man.
This Is America.
Thy Kingdom Come!
To Poets All.
To the Flag of Stars.
To the Master Poet.
Today.
Touch of Human Hands, The.
Tragedy, The.
Trees.
True Need, The.
Trust the Great Artist.
Voice in a Cathedral.
Wanderers.
We Thank Thee ("For glowing autumn's brimming yield").
We Thank Thee ("Not for our lands").
Clark, Tom
Baseball.
Comanche.
Daily News.
I'm on an Island.
Lake, The: Coda.
Penmanship.
Poem: "Like musical instruments."
Poem: "My heart in pieces like the bits."
Sonnet: "Orgasm completely, The."
Stationery Motion.
Sunglasses.
Superballs.
Yearbook, The.
You.
Clark, Walter
Wilbur's Garden.
Clark, Willis Gaylord
Remembrance, A.
Clarke, Aidan
Journey, The.
Clarke, Andrew Stuart Currie
Prayer: "Bless Thou this year, O Lord!"
Prayer for a
Clarke, Annie
Rest.
Soul's Response, The.
Clarke, Austin
Aisling.
Ancient Lights.
Awakening of Dermuid, The.
Blackbird of Derrycairn, The.
Celebrations.
Celibacy.
Early Unfinished Sketch.
Envy of Poor Lovers, The.
Fair at Windgap, The.
Intercessors.
Jewels, The.
Living in Sin.
Lost Heifer, The.
Lucky Coin, The.
Marriage.
Mnemosyne Lay in Dust, *sels.*
Mount Parnassus.
Night and Morning.
One night he heard heart-breaking sound.
Past the house where he was got.
Penal Law.
Pilgrimage.
Planter's Daughter, The.
Rememorised, Maurice Devane.
Respectable People.
Straight-jacketing sprang to every lock.
Straying Student, The.
Strong Wind, A.
Tenebrae.
Vengeance of Finn, The, *sel.*
Clarke, C. R.
Song of the Mariner's Needle.
Clarke, Ednah Proctor
Dancer, The.
Deathless, The.
Good-by, A.
Mocking-Bird, The.
Salem Witch, A.
To a Wild Rose Found in October.
Clarke, F. W.
Rhyme of the Rain Machine, The.
Clarke, Frances (Frances Clarke Sayers)
Who Calls?
Clarke, George Arthur
Charter of Salvation, The.
Clarke, George Frederick
Saint John, The.
Clarke, George Herbert
Christ before Pilate.
Fog-Horn.
Halt and Parley.
Over Salève.
Santa Maria del Fiore.
Clarke, Herbert Edwin
Age, The.
Cry, A.
In the Wood.
Lady Mine.
Clarke, James Freeman
Come Visit Us.
White-capped Waves.
Clarke, Joseph I. C.
Bill Manning.
Fighting Race, The.
Fret of Father Carty, The.
Pro Libra Mea.
Way of the Cross, The.
Clarke, Marcus
In a Lady's Album.
Clarke, Peter
In Air.
Play Song.
Young Shepherd Bathing His Feet.
Clarkson, E. Margaret
Adoration—A Carol.
Best for Me, The.
By Faith ("By faith and not by sight").
He Knows.
Homemaker, The.
Let Us Come Boldly.
Paradox.
Prayer by the Open Book.
Prayer to the Holy Spirit.
Song: "Life with its weariness."
This I Know.
To a Mute Musician.
Unafraid.
Clarkson, M. F.
Potter's Hand, The.
Clarkson, M. J.
Secret of the Cross, The.
Claude of Jesus, Sister
Assuagement.
More than the Moment.
Words in the Wilderness.
Claudel, Paul
Blessed be your name, my God.
Five Grand Odes, *sel.*
Fourth Station.
Our Lady, Help of Christians.
Seventh Station.
Shadows.
Claudian (Claudius Claudianus)
Epitaph: "Fate to beauty still must give."
Epithalamium for Honorius and Maria, *sels.*
Fescennine Verses in Honor of the Marriage of the Emperor Honorius, *sel.*
Hairdresser's Art, The.
Lonely Isle, The.
Old Man of Verona, The.
Palm Tree Mates with Palm.
Preparing for the Wedding.
Sing, Woods and Rivers All.
Thorns Arm the Rose.
Claudius, Matthias ("Asmus")
At My Father's Grave.
Hen, The.
Most Acceptable Gift, The.
We Plow the Fields.
Clayburn, M. D.
Holy Book, The.
Clayre, Alasdair
Professor Drinking Wine.
Claytor, Gertrude
Grant at Appomattox.
Sorceress.
Stair, The ("The stair is curved, the railing high").
Cleage, Pearl
Confession.
Feelings of a Very Light Negro as the Confrontation Approaches.
For Death by Choice.
Glimpse.
My feet/ are rooted in a/ poison lake.
Responsive Reading.
Retrospect.
Cleanthes
God Leads the Way.
Hymn of Cleanthes, The.
Hymn to Zeus.
Cleaveland, C. L.
November.
Cleaveland, Elizabeth Hannah Jocelyn
No Sects [*or* Sect] in Heaven.
Cleaves, Charles Poole
His Name.
Cleghorn, Sarah Norcliffe
Anodyne, The.
Come, Captain Age.
Comrade Jesus.
Contented at Forty.
Dorothea.
Emilia.
For Sleep When Overtired.
Golf Links, The.
Hemlock Mountain.
Incentive, The.
Judge Me, O Lord!
Quatrain: "Golf links lie so near the mill, The."
Saint R. L. S.
Survival of the Fittest, The.
Vermont.
Cleland, William
Hallo My Fancy.
Hollo, My Fancy!
Clemens, Samuel Langhorne *See* **"Twain, Mark"**
Clement of Alexandria (Titus Flavius Clemens)
Earliest Christian Hymn ("Curb for stubborn steed").
Earliest Christian Hymn, The ("Shepherd of tender youth").
Hymn to Christ the Saviour.
Shepherd of Eager [*or* Tender] Youth.
Youth of Jesus, The.
Clements, John R.
God's Trails Lead Home.
Clemmer, Mary
Something Beyond.
Clemo, Jack R.
Calvinist in Love, A.
Christ in the Clay-Pit.
Water-Wheel, The.
Clephane, Elizabeth Cecilia
Beneath the Cross.
Ninety and Nine, The.
There Were Ninety and Nine.

Clerk, Sir John, of Penicuik
Miller, The.
O Merry May the Maid Be.
Clerk-Maxwell, James *See* **Maxwell, James Clerk**
Clerke, William
So, So.
Song: "So, so,/ Lo, lilies fade, before the roses show."
Cleveland, C. L. *See* **Cleaveland, C.L.**
Cleveland, John
Antiplatonick, The.
Author's Mock-Song to Mark Anthony, The.
Come, keen iambics, with your badger's feet.
Epitaph on the Earl of Strafford.
Fair Nymph Scorning a Black Boy Courting Her, A.
Fuscara or the Bee Errant.
General Eclipse, The.
Gravestones, II ("Here lies wise and valiant dust").
Hecatomb to His Mistress, The.
Mark Antony [*or* Anthony].
Mystical grammar of amorous glances.
On Scotland.
On the Memory of Mr. Edward King [Drown'd in the Irish Seas].
Rebel Scot, The, *sel.*
Senses Festival, The.
Square-Cap.
To the State of Love; or, The Senses Festival.
Upon an Hermaphrodite.
Upon Phillis [*or* Phyllis] Walking in a Morning before Sun-Rising.
Young Man to an Old Woman Courting Him, A.
Cleveland, Philip Jerome
By Night.
I Yield Thee Praise.
There Is a Love.
Clifford, Ethel
Dark Road, The.
Harp of Sorrow, The.
Last Hour, The.
Clifford, George, 3d Earl of Cumberland
My Thoughts Are Winged with Hopes.
To Cynthia.
Clifford, John
Anvil, The—God's Word.
Anvil of God's Word, The.
God's Word.
Hammers and Anvil.
Clifford, Margaret Rowe
Arizona.
Clifton, Lucille
For de Lawd.
Good Times.
Miss Rosie.
Clive, Caroline
Conflict.
Close, Eunice
Here We Come a-Haying.
Way to Fairyland, The.
Cloud, Frederick
Hands.
Cloud, Virginia Woodward
Ballad of Sweet P, The.
Care.
Mother's Song, The.
Old Street, An.
What the Lord High Chamberlain Said.
Youth.
Clough, Arthur Hugh
Afloat; We Move. Delicious!
Ah, That I Were Far Away.
Ah! Yet Consider It Again!
All Is Well.
Amours de Voyage.
At Venice.
Autumn in the Highlands.
Bathers, The.
Bethesda.
"Blank Misgivings of a Creature Moving About in Worlds Not Realized," *sel.*
Bothie of Tober-na-Vuolich, The, *sels.*
But That from Slow Dissolving Pomps of Dawn.
Columbus.
Come Back.
Currente Calamo.
Dipsychus, *sels.*
Duty—That's to Say Complying.
Easter Day.
Engagement, The.
Epi-Strauss-ium.
Go from the east to the west, as the sun and the stars direct thee.
Green Fields of England!
Hope Evermore and Believe.
How Often Sit I.
"Tuvos "Auuvos (Hymnos Ahymnos).
I cannot but ask, in the park and the streets.
I dreamt a dream; till morning light.
I had a vision; was it in my sleep?
I Have Seen Higher, Holier Things than These.
In a Lecture-Room.
In a London Square.
In Controversial Foul Impureness.
In Stratis Viarum.
In the Depths.
In the Great Metropolis.
In the Piazza at Night.
Is It True, Ye Gods, Who Treat Us.
Isolation.
It Fortifies My Soul to Know.
Ite Domum Saturae, Venit Hesperus.
Jacob.
Juxtaposition.
Keeping On.
Last Words; Napoleon and Wellington, *sel.*
Latest Decalogue, The.
Les Vaches.
Letter from Rome, A.
Life Is Struggle.
Light words they were, and lightly falsely said.
Look!
Mari Magno, *sel.*
My Wind Is Turned to Bitter North.
New Sinai, The.
Noli Aemulari.
O Let Me Love unto Myself Alone.
O Ship, Ship, Ship.
O Thou Whose Image.
Old Things Need Not Be Therefore True.
On the Lido.
Our gaieties, our luxuries.
Parvenant.
"Perchè Pensa? Pensando S'Invecchia."
Peschiera.
Protest, A.
Put Forth Thy Leaf, Thou Lofty Plane.
Qua Cursum Ventus.
Questioning Spirit, The.
Qui Laborat, Orat.
Rome Is Fallen, I Hear.
Say Not.
Say Not the Struggle [Nought Availeth].
Scene is different, and the place, The; the air.
Sehnsucht.
Serve in Thy Post.
Seven Sonnets, *sel.*
Sic Itur.
Sleeping Child, A.
So, I have seen a man killed!
So Not Seeing I Sung.
So Pleasant It Is to Have Money.
Some Future Day When What Is Now Is Not.
Somewhere—but where I cannot guess.
Songs in Absence, *sels.*
Sonnet: "But whether in the uncoloured light of truth."
Spectator ab Extra.
Spirit from Perfecter Ages, A.
Spirit's Song, The.
Steadfast.
That There Are Powers above Us I Admit.
There are two different kinds, I believe, of human attraction.
There Is No God.
"There Is No God," the Wicked Saith.
Thesis and Antithesis.
Through a Glass Darkly.
Τὸ Καλόν.
To Spend Uncounted Years of Pain.
Uranus.
Weep not beside his tomb.
"Wen Gott Betrügt, Ist Wohl Betrogen."
What We, When Face to Face We See.
"What Went Ye Out for to See?"
Whate'er You Dream with Doubt Possest.
When the Dews Are Earliest Falling.
Where Lies the Land [to Which the Ship Would Go]?
Whither depart the souls of the brave that die in the battle.
"With Whom Is No Variableness, neither Shadow of Turning."
Would That I Were.
Ye Ancient Divine Ones.
Ye Flags of Piccadilly.
Yes, as I walk, I behold, in a luminous, large intuition.
Yes, we are fighting at last, it appears.
Yet I could think, indeed, the perfect call.
Clouts, Sydney
Animal Kingdom.
Dawn Hippo.
Earth, Sky.
Grave's Cherub, The.
Hawk, The.
Of Thomas Traherne and the Pebble Outside.
Poetry Is Death Cast Out.
Prince Henry the Navigator.
Roy Kloof.
Roy Kloof Went Riding.
Sea and the Eagle, The.
Situation, The.
Sleeper, The.
Within.
Clute, Oscar
O Love of God Most Full.
Cluysenaar, Anne
Epithalamium: "Rings of the sun rise, The."
Coan, Titus Munson
Crystal, The.
Dream of Flowers, A.
Nihil Humani Alienum.
Coates, Carol
Choral Symphony Conductor.
Circle, The.
Country Reverie.
Light.
Coates, Florence Earle
America.
Angelus, The.
Be Thou My Guide.
Buffalo.
By the Conemaugh.
Christ of the Andes, The.
Columbus.
Death.
Dream the Great Dream.

Hero, A.
His Face.
House of Pain, The.
Immortal.
India.
Morning-Glory, The.
Narrow Window, A.
New Mars, The.
Per Aspera.
Perdita.
Pilgrim Song.
Requiem for a Young Soldier.
Seeker in the Night, A.
Song: "For me the jasmine buds unfold."
Song: "If love were but a little thing."
Suppliant.
Survival.
Tennyson.
Thanksgiving.
Their Victory Won.
To-Morrow.
Unconquered Air, The.
World Is Mine, The.
Coates, Grace Stone
Prairie Birth.
Coats, Adelbert Sumpter
Common Lot, The.
Pentecost.
Coatsworth, Elizabeth Jane (Mrs. Henry Beston)
After Christmas a Landlord Remembers.
All Goats.
Announcement.
April Fool.
August Smiles.
Bad Kittens, The.
Barn, The.
Bedtime.
Blue on White.
Bread the Holy.
By the Fire.
Calling in the Cat.
Candle and Star.
Cat and Northern Lights. The.
Circus-postered Barn, The.
Cold winter now is in the wood.
Complete Hen, The.
Conquest.
Conquistador.
Counters.
Country Cat.
Daniel Webster's Horses.
Down the Rain Falls.
Easter.
Eerily Sweet.
Empty House.
Ever Since.
Fields Are Spread, The.
Fireside Kitten, The.
Footnote to History.
Green Woods.
Hard from the southeast blows the wind.
He who has never known hunger.
Horse would tire, A.
How Gray the Rain.
It's Pleasant to Think.
January.
Kangaroo, The.
Labor of Fields.
Lady, The.
Lady Comes to an Inn, A.
Lullaby: "Sleep, mouseling, sleep."
March.
Mary's Lullaby.
Moon, The.
Mouse, The.
Murder House.
Navajo, The.
Nile, The.
No shop does the bird use.
No Snake in Springtime.
November.
Oak Leaves.
Old Mare, The.
On a Night of Snow.
Pirates.
Plant cut down to the root, The.
Pleiades, The.
Pretty Futility.
Rabbits' Song outside the Tavern, The.
Rain.
Reminiscences of a Landlord.
Saint John.
Sea gull curves his wings, The.
Sitting Here.
Sleigh Bells at Night.
Snow.
Sometimes a Little House Will Please.
Song for a Hot Day.
Song for a Little Cuckoo Clock.
Song for Midsummer Night.
Song of the Camels.
Song of the Parrot.
Song to Night.
Storm Snapped Its Fingers, The.
Straws.
Summer Rain.
Sun Is First to Rise, The.
Sunday.
Swift Things Are Beautiful.
Syracuse.
This Air That Blows In from the Sea.
This Is the Hay That No Man Planted.
To a Black Dog, Bereaved.
To Think.
Tracks in the Snow.
Twelfth Night.
Violets, daffodils.
Warm of heart shall never lack a fire, The.
Ways of Trains, The.
What Could Be Lovelier than to Hear.
"Who are you?" asked the cat of the bear.
Wilderness Is Tamed, The.
Wilderness Rivers.
Wind Shrieked Loud, The.
Winter Rune.
Wise Sarah and the Elf.
Witches' Song.
You play a fife.
Cobb, Ann
Kivers.
Cobb, Will D.
School Days.
Waltz Me around Again, Willie.
Cobbes, John
To Chloris.
Coblentz, Catherine Cate
Boundaries.
Earth Worshiped, The!
God.
Housewife, The.
Nature's Sorrow Cure.
Our History.
Coblentz, Stanton Arthur
Atlantis.
Bringers of the Hemlock.
Calm.
Civilization.
Flesh Is Weak, The.
History of the Modern World.
In a Troubled World.
In the Storm.
Land's End (Point Lobos, California).
Last Judgment.
O Prophets and Redeemers!
Omnipresence.
On Some Trees Needlessly Slain.
Pageant of Man, The, *sel.*
Patient Is Time.
Prayer for Light.
Second Coming, The.
Unknown Sculptor, The.
Watcher, The.
Ways of the Gods, The.
We Who Build Visions.
What Would He Say?
Coburn, Wallace D.
Cow-Boy Fun.
Cowboy's Fate, The.
Stampede, The.
Cochrane, Alfred
Eight-Day Clock, The.
Omnia Vincit.
To Anthea, Who May Command Him Anything (New Style).
Upon Lesbia—Arguing.
Cochrane, Frances
Face to Face.
Cochrane, J. C.
Somewhere.
"Cockatoo Jack."
Numerella Shore, The.
Cockburn, Alison
Flowers of the Forest, The.
Cocke, Zitella
Miss Nancy's Gown.
My Cross.
Cocteau, Jean
I have sung, to deceive the evil-sounding clock of time.
Plain-Song.
Poem of Circumstance.
Codd, Gertrude Jane
Song against Servants.
Strange Guest.
Code, Grant
Ballad of Two Kings.
Building of Sand.
Foreboding.
High Place at Marib, The.
Highway to Nowhere.
News of My Friends.
Night Refuses a Dreamer, The.
Nursery Rhymes for Surrealists.
Playground of the Pixie.
Cody, Hiram Alfred
Old Figurehead Carver, The.
Old Ship Riggers.
Coe, Alice Rollit
Turn of the Road, The.
Coffin, Charles
Glad Tidings from the King of Kings.
Coffin, Robert Barry ("Barry Gray")
Ships at Sea.
Coffin, Robert Peter Tristram
Alexander Graham Bell Did Not Invent the Telephone.
America Is Corn.
America Was Schoolmasters.
Captains of Small Farms, The.
Christening-Day Wishes for My God-Child, Grace Lane Berkley II.
Citizens in the Round.
Country Church.
Covered Bridge.
Cripple, The.
First Flight.
Fog, The.
Getting Through.
Golden Falcon.
Gracious and the Gentle Thing, The.
Graveyard.
Hen Overboard.
Jelly Fish, The.
John Popham.
Joy Meets Boy.
Little Boys of Texas.
Lonely Lover.
Lullaby for Peregrine.
My Father Loved the Jumping-off Place.
New Englanders Are Maples.
Old Blue.
Old Farmer Alone.
Pheasant, The.
Ram, The.
Satin Mice Creaking Last Summer's Grass, The.

Coffin (continued)
Secret Heart, The.
Ship o' Bed, The.
Skunk, The.
Spider, The.
Square-Toed Princes.
Star-Pudding.
Starfish, The.
Stone Crop, The.
Tall Axe-Man, The.
This Is My Country.
Thunder Pools.
Tree-sleeping.
Way to Know a Father, The.
We Put on the Buffalo.
Where I Took Hold of Life.
Yankee Cradle.
Young Calves, The.
Coghill, Annie L.
Work, for the Night Is Coming.
Coghill, Rhoda
Bright Hillside, The.
Dead.
In Wicklow.
Plough-Horse, The.
Poem: "Is to love, this—to nurse a name."
Runaway.
Spring Doggerel.
Young Bride's Dream, The.
Cogswell, Fred
Christmas Carol, A: "Holly wreath that now, The."
Cohan, Charles C.
Montana.
Cohan, George M.
Life's a Funny Proposition after All.
Mary's a Grand Old Name.
Cohen, Jacob
Eternal Jew, The.
Harp of David, The.
Surely My Soul.
Cohen, Leonard
Another Night with Telescope.
Ballad: "He pulled a flower."
Ballad: "My lady was found mutilated."
Bus, The.
Celebration.
Credo.
For Anne.
Genius, The.
I Wonder How Many People in This City.
If It Were Spring.
Kite Is a Victim, A.
Only Tourist in Havana Turns His Thoughts Homeward, The.
Out of the Land of Heaven.
Poem: "I heard of a man."
Poem for Marc Chagall.
Prayer for Messiah.
Travel.
What I'm Doing Here.
When This American Woman.
Cohen, Robert David
Bones of Incontention, The.
Day on Kind Continent.
Storm, The.
Street of Named Houses, The.
Cohen, Solomon Solis- *See* **Solis-Cohen, Solomon**
Cohn, Myra
Sliding.
Cokayne, Sir Aston
Funeral Elegy on the Death of His Very Good Friend, Mr. Michael Drayton.
Know all to whom these few sad lines shall come.
Of a Mistress.
To Plautia.
Colborne-Veel, Mary
Blessing, The.
Empty Houses.
Song of the Trees.
We Go No More to the Forest.
Colby, Vine
Rainbow, The.
Colcord, Lincoln
Fishing Fleet, The.
"Col. D. Streamer." *See* **Graham, Harry**
Cole, Barry
End to Complacency, An.
Men Are Coming Back, The.
Cole, Charlotte Druitt
Christmas Eve.
Clothes-Line, The.
Dormouse, The.
Garden Path, The.
Green Lady, The.
Pimpernel.
Pudding Charms.
Spider's Web, The.
Sun and Moon.
Three Mice.
Yellow Fairy, The.
Cole, Elsie
Song of the Foot-Track.
Cole, Eugene Roger
Oh, You Wholly Rectangular.
Cole, Harriet
End of the Way, The.
Cole, Helen Wieand
Gifts.
Peace on Earth.
Cole, Mamie Gene
Child's Appeal, The.
Cole, Margaret
Treachery.
Cole, Samuel Valentine
Abraham Lincoln.
Hammer and Anvil.
Roosevelt.
Satisfied.
Trees, The.
Voice, A.
Cole, Thomas
By the Beautiful Sea.
La Grande Jatte; Sunday Afternoon.
Landscape of Love, The.
My Lady Takes the Sunlight for Her Gown.
Old Woman's Song.
Praise to Light.
Tray, The.
Variations on a Still Morning.
Cole, Timothy
Year's End, The.
Cole, William
Alma Mater, Forget Me.
Back Yard, July Night.
Epitaph on a Career Woman.
Geeandess.
Just Dropped In.
Poor Kid.
Saturday Review, The.
Time Piece.
Undersea Fever.
Coleman, Helena
As Day Begins to Wane.
More Lovely Grows the Earth.
Coleman, Herbert T. J.
Cockle-Shell and Sandal-Shoon.
Poet Confides, The.
Coleman, Lucile
Echoes of Jesus.
With Lilacs in My Eye.
Coleridge, Derwent
And So Men Say, I Love Thee!
Coleridge, Hartley
Birth of Speech, The.
Dedicatory Sonnet to S. T. Coleridge.
Early Death.
Friendship.
From Country to Town.
Full Well I Know.
Hast Thou Not Seen an Aged Rifted Tower.
He Lived amidst th' Untrodden Ways.
How long I sailed, and never took a thought.
Ideality.
If I Have Sinn'd in Act.
Imitation of Wordsworth, An.
Jesus Praying.
Lark and the Nightingale, The.
Lines: "I have been cherish'd and forgiven."
Long Time a Child.
May, 1840.
"Multum Dilexit."
Night.
November.
On Wordsworth.
Poietes Apoietes.
Prayer: "Be not afraid to pray—to pray is right."
Religious Unity.
Reply.
She Is Not Fair [to Outward View].
Solitary-hearted, The.
Song: "She is not fair to outward view."
Song: "'Tis sweet to hear the merry lark."
Sonnet: "Long time a child, and still a child, when years."
Sonnet: November.
Sonnet: To a Friend.
Sonnets on the Seasons, *sel.*
Soul, The.
Think upon death, 'tis good to think of death.
Three Sonnets, *sels.*
Time was when I could weep; but now all care.
'Tis Strange to Me.
To a Deaf and Dumb Little Girl.
To a Friend.
To a Lofty Beauty, from Her Poor Kinsman.
To Lilly.
To Shakespeare.
To the Nautilus.
To Wordsworth.
What Is Young Passion.
Whither?
Whither Is Gone [the Wisdom and the Power].
Why should I murmur at my lot forlorn?
Written on the Anniversary of Our Father's Death.
Coleridge, Mary Elizabeth
After Reading Certain Books.
After St. Augustine.
As I Went Singing over the Earth.
Awake.
Bid me remember, O my gracious Lord.
Blue and White.
Blue Bird, The.
Change.
Chillingham.
Companionship.
Cut It Down.
Death, *sel.*
Dedication, A: "Life of my learning, fire of all my Art."
Depart from Me.
Deserted House, The.
Egypt's Might Is Tumbled Down.
From My Window.
Gibberish.
Gifts.
Gone.
Good Friday in My Heart.
"He Knoweth Not That the Dead Are Thine."
Huguenot, A.
I Saw a Stable.
In a Volume of Austin Dobson.
In Dispraise of the Moon.
Jealousy.

King, The.
L' Oiseau Bleu.
Lord of the Winds.
Moment, A.
Mortal Combat.
Night Is Fallen.
On Such a Day.
Other Side of a Mirror, The.
Our Lady.
Punctilio.
Shadow.
Street Lanterns.
There Was No Place Found.
Three Helpers in Battle.
To Memory.
Train, The.
Unwelcome.
Veneta.
Weapon, The.
When Mary thro' the Garden Went.
Where a Roman Villa Stood, above Freiburg.
Whither Away?
Witch, The.

Coleridge, Samuel Taylor
All impulses of soul and sense.
All Seasons Shall Be Sweet.
Ancient Mariner, The.
And haply, bason'd in some unsunn'd cleft.
Answer to a Child's Question.
Apologia pro Vita Sua.
Ballad of the Dark Ladie, The.
Beyond the shadow of the ship.
Birds, The.
Boy in the Wilderness.
Broken Friendship.
Catullan Hendecasyllables.
Charity in Thought.
Child's Evening Prayer, A.
Christabel.
Christmas Carol, A: "Shepherds went their hasty way, The."
Cologne.
Complaint.
Composed on a Journey Homeward.
Constancy to an Ideal Object.
Dejection; an Ode.
Desired Swan-Song, The.
Destiny of Nations, The, *sels.*
Desultory Poem, A, Written on the Christmas Eve of 1794, *sel.*
Dungeon, The.
Eolian Harp, The.
Epigram: "In Köln, a town of monks and bones."
Epigram: "What is an epigram? a dwarfish whole."
Epigram: "'What? rise again with all one's bones.'"
Epitaph: "Stop, Christian passer by!—Stop, child of God."
Epitaph on Himself.
Eternal Poem, An.
"Even so" (the exulting Maiden said).
Exchange, The.
Fair breeze blew, the white foam flew, The.
Farewell to Love.
Fears in Solitude.
For what is freedom, but the unfettered use.
For when it dawn'd—they dropp'd their arms.
Fragment: "Encinctur'd with a twine of leaves."
France; an Ode.
Friendship.
Frost at Midnight.
Fruit Plucker, The.
Garden of Boccaccio, The.
Giles's Hope.
Glycine's Song.
Good, Great Man, The.
He Prayeth Best.
He Prayeth Well.
Hear, Sweet Spirit.
House That Jack Built, The.
Human Life; on the Denial of Immortality.
Hunting Song.
Hymn before Sunrise, in the Vale of Chamouni.
I Mix in Life.
If I Had but Two Little Wings.
In a Moonlight Wilderness.
In Springtime.
Inscription for a Fountain on a Heath.
Invocation, An: "Hear, sweet spirit."
Job.
Knight's Tomb, The.
Koskiusko.
Kubla Khan; or, A Vision in a Dream.
La Fayette.
La Fayette.
Lessons for a Boy.
Letter to Sara Hutchinson, A.
Lewti; or, The Circassian Love-Chaunt.
Life.
Limbo.
Lines Composed in a Concert-Room.
Lines to William Linley while He Sang a Song to Purcell's Music.
Lines Written in the Album at Elbingerode.
Little Child, a Limber Elf, A.
Love.
Lovely lady, Christabel, The.
Love's Apparition and Evanishment.
Metrical Feet.
Moving moon went up the sky, The.
Ne Plus Ultra.
Nightingale, The.
Nightingales.
O, Lift One Thought.
Ode to the Departing Year.
On a Bad Singer.
On a Discovery Made Too Late.
On a Lord.
On a Ruined House in a Romantic Country.
On Bala Hill.
On Donne's Poetry.
On His Baptismal Birthday.
On My Joyful Departure from the City of Cologne.
On the green sheep-track, up the heathy hill.
Osorio.
Pains of Sleep, The.
Pantisocracy.
Phantom.
Phantom or Fact.
Psyche.
Raven, The.
Recollections of Love.
Reflections on Having Left a Place of Retirement.
Religious Musings, *sels.*
Remorse, (Osorio), *sel.*
Rhyme of the Ancient Mariner, The.
Rhymester, A.
Rime of the Ancient Mariner, The.
Scars Remaining, The.
Self-Knowledge.
Shepherds, The.
"Ship was cheered, the harbour cleared, The."
Sickness, 'tis true.
So gentle Ellen now no more.
Something Childish, but Very Natural.
Song: "Hear, sweet spirit."
Song: "Sunny shaft did I behold, A."
Song from "Osorio."
Sonnet: Oft o'er My Brain.
Sonnet: To the River Otter.
Sonnet to a Friend Who Asked How I Felt When the Nurse First Presented My Infant to Me.
Sonnets Attempted in the Manner of Contemporary Writers.
Sunset, A.
Swan Song.
Swans Sing.
There is one Mind, one omnipresent Mind.
This Lime-Tree Bower My Prison.
Three Graves, The, *sel.*
Time, Real and Imaginary.
To a Young Ass.
To a Young Friend, *br. sel.*
To Nature.
To Simplicity.
To the Reverend W. L. Bowles.
To the River Otter.
To William Wordsworth.
Tombless Epitaph, A, *sel.*
Toy-bewitched.
Up, Up! Ye Dames and Lasses Gay.
Voice Sings, A.
Wanderings of Cain, The, *sel.*
What Is an Epigram?
What Is Life?
Work Without Hope.
Youth and Age.
Zapolya, *sels.*

Coleridge, Samuel Taylor, *and* **Robert Southey** *See* **Southey, Robert,** *and* **Samuel Taylor Coleridge**

Coleridge, Sara
Calendar, A.
Child, The.
Garden Year, The.
He Came Unlook'd For.
I Was a Brook.
Months, The.
Mother, The.
O sleep, my babe, hear not the rippling wave.
One Face Alone.
Phantasmion, *sels.*
Song: "He came unlook'd for, undersir'd."
Trees.

Collenette, Peter
Precision.

Collier, Edward A.
After the Rain.

Collier, Thomas Stephens
Cleopatra Dying.
Compensation.
Disappointment.
Infallibility.
Power.
Spectre Ship, The.
Time.

Collin, William Edwin
Monserrat.
Sancho.

Collins, Helen Johnson
To an Avenue Sport.

Collins, John
To-Morrow.

Collins, Leslie M.
Creole Girl.
Stevedore.

Collins, Mortimer
Ad Chloen, M. A.
Chloe, M.A.
Greek Idyl, A.
If.
Ivory Gate, The.
Kate Temple's Song.

Collins (continued)
Martial in London.
My Aunt's Spectre.
My Thrush.
Positivists, The.
Queen and Slave.
Salad.
Salad—after Tennyson.
Sky-making.
To F. C.
Collins, W. F.
Lincoln Statue, The.
Collins, William
Captain Molly.
Molly Maguire at Monmouth.
Dirge in "Cymbeline."
Eclogue the Second.
Fidele.
How Sleep the Brave.
Lament for Tintoretta.
Limitations of Human Art.
Lookout, The.
Luckless Collings.
Ode: "How sleep the brave, who sink to rest."
Ode: Written in the Beginning of the Year 1746.
Ode Occasion'd by the Death of Mr. Thomson.
Ode on the Death of Mr. Thomson.
Ode on the Poetical Character.
Ode, An, on the Popular Superstitions of the Highlands of Scotland [Considered as the Subject of Poetry].
Ode to Evening.
Ode to Fear.
Ode to Mercy.
Ode to Pity.
Ode to Simplicity.
Ode Written in the Beginning of the Year [*or* Ode Written in] 1746.
Passions, The; an Ode to [*or* for] Music.
Persian Eclogues, *sel.*
St. Kilda.
Sleep of the Brave, The.
Song from Shakespeare's "Cymbeline," A ("To fair Fidele's grassy tomb").
Sonnet: "When Phoebe form'd a wanton smile."
Three Fragments,
To Evening.
Collinson, Laurence
Sea and the Tiger, The.
Collop, John
Leper Cleansed, The.
To the Soul.
Collyer, Robert
Saxon Grit.
Under the Snow.
Collymore, Frank A.
In Memoriam.
Zobo Bird, The.
Colman, Benjamin
Another to Urania.
Hymn of Praise, on a Recovery from Sickness, A.
Poem on Elijahs Translation, A.
Quarrel with Fortune, A.
To Philomela.
To Urania.
Colman, George, the Younger
Gluggity Glug.
Miss Bailey's Ghost.
My Muse and I, Ere Yough and Spirits Fled.
Myrtle and the Vine, The, *sel.*
Sir Marmaduke.
Unfortunate Miss Bailey.
Colman, Mary Elizabeth
We Men Are of Two Worlds.
Colombo, John Robert
How They Made the Golem.
Ideal Angels.
Riverdale Lion.
What Pablo Picasso Did in "Les Demoiselles d'Avignon."
Colonne, Guido delle *See* **Guido delle Colonne**
Colony, Horatio
Autumnal.
Ghost Pet.
Gold That Fell on Danae, The.
Summer Lightning.
Thunder over Earth.
Young Prince, The.
Colton, Arthur Willis
Allah's Tent.
Harps Hung Up in Babylon.
Phillis and Corydon.
Sometime It May Be.
Song with a Discord, A.
To Faustine.
Colum, Mary M.
Dirge of the Lone Woman.
Colum, Padraic
Across the Door.
After Speaking of One Dead a Long Time.
Asses, *sel.*
At Ferns Castle.
Ballad of Downal Baun.
Belfast; High Street.
Burial of Saint Brendan, The.
Catalpa Trees.
Christ the Comrade.
Condors.
Cradle Song: "Christ by Thine own darkened hour."
Cradle Song, A: "O men from the fields."
Dahlias.
David ap Gwillam's Mass of the Birds.
Deer of Ireland, The.
Drover, A.
Dublin; the Old Squares.
Fourth Station.
Fuchsia Hedges in Connacht.
Garadh.
Garland Sunday.
Her skin is so white as a lily, an' each.
"I know where I'd get."
I Saw the Wind Today.
Interior.
Irises.
Lilies.
Monkeys.
No Child.
Old Man Said, An.
Old Soldier.
Old Woman of the Roads, An [*or* The].
Olive Trees.
On Not Hearing the Birds Sing in Ireland.
On the Death of Roger Casement.
Otters.
Peach Tree with Fruit.
Plougher, The.
Plower, The.
Polonius and the Ballad-Singers.
Poor Scholar of the 'Forties, A.
Poplar Tree.
Puppet Play, The.
Reminiscence, *sel.*
River-Mates.
Sea Bird to the Wave, The.
Shall I Go Bound and You Go Free?
She Moved through the Fair.
Spider.
Stations of the Cross, The.
Terrible Robber Men, The.
Tin-Whistle Player, The.
Tulips.
Wall of China, The.
Wild Ass.
Wind, The.
Young Girl: Annam.
Columba, Saint *See* **Columcille, Saint**
Columba, Mother M.
From My Window.
Columcille [*or* Columba], Saint
Day of Wrath, The.
Lon's away/ Cill Garad is sad today.
On a Dead Scholar, *sel.*
On His Exile to Iona.
Praise of Derry, The.
With Thee, O God!
Colwell, Ernest Cadman
Jesus of Nazareth.
Combe, William
Dr. Syntax in Search of the Picturesque, *sel.*
In Search of the Picturesque.
Combes, Percival
Bar-Z on a Sunday Night.
Combs, Alonzo W.
Ol' Man, De.
Combs, Tram
Ars Poetica about Ultimates.
Aware Aware.
Just after Noon with Fierce Shears.
Cometas
Country Gods.
Comfort, Alex
After Shakespeare.
After You, Madam.
Atoll in the Mind, The.
Bullocks, The.
Epitaph: "One whom I knew, a student and a poet."
Fear of the Earth.
Fifth Elegy.
Haste to the Wedding.
Hoc Est Corpus.
Love Poem: "There is a white mare that my love keeps."
Lovers, The.
Notes for My Son.
Pick upon Pick.
Poem: "One whom I knew, a student and a poet."
Postures of Love, The.
Song for the Heroes.
Sublimation.
Waiting for the Wind.
Comfort, Florence Crocker
Make Way!
Comstock, Mary Edgar
Gifts.
Comyn, Michael
Oisin in the Land of Youth.
Conant, Isabel Fiske
Blue Persian.
Carpenter.
Emergency.
Many Wings.
Concanen, Matthew
Heaps on Heaps.
Match at Football, A, *sel.*
Conder, Josiah
Day by Day.
Following.
Trust in Jesus.
"Condol, F. Kevin." *See* **Miriam, Sister**
Cone, Helen Gray ("Coroebus Green")
Arraignment.
Ballad of Cassandra Brown, The.
Common Street, The.
Contrast, The.
Dandelions, The.
Fair England.
Heartbreak Road.
Last Cup of Canary, The.
Ride to the Lady, The.
Spring Beauties, The.
Thisbe.
Yellow Pansy, A.

Confucius
Airs of Pei, *sel.*
Alba ("Creeper grows over thorn").
Aliter.
Baroness Mu Impeded in Her Wish to Help Famine Victims in Wei.
Be kind, good sir, and I'll lift my sark.
"Chkk! chkk!" hopper-grass.
Chou and the South, *sel.*
Deer Sing, *sel.*
Efficient Wife's Complaint, The.
Fraternitas.
Hep-Cat Chung, 'ware my town.
In chariot like an hibiscus flower at his side.
In the South be drooping trees.
Marsh bank, lotus rank.
Pedlar.
Sans Equity and sans Poise.
Shao and the South, *sels.*
So he won't talk to me when we meet?
Songs of Ch'en, *sels.*
Songs of Cheng, *sels.*
Songs of T'ang, *sel.*
Three stars, five stars rise over the hill.
Wei Wind, *sel.*
Yung Wind, *sels.*
Congdon, A. Kirby
Blow Fish.
Ego.
Television-Movie.
Conger, Katharine Janeway
This Is America.
Conger, Marion
Fall Days.
Congreve, William
All or Nothing.
Amoret.
Ancient Phyllis.
Better Bargain, The.
Buxom Joan.
Double-Dealer, The, *sel.*
False! or Inconstancy.
False Though She Be [to Me].
Heaven hath no rage like love to hatred turned.
Hue and Cry after Fair Amoret, A.
Letter to Viscount Cobham.
Love for Love, *sels.*
Love's but the Frailty of the Mind.
Mourning Bride, The, *sels.*
Music has charms to soothe a savage breast.
Nil Admirari.
Nymph and a Swain, A.
Ode in Imitation of Horace, An.
Of Improving the Present Time, *sel.*
Old Bachelor, The, *sel.*
Pious Celinda.
Pious Selinda.
Soldier and a Sailor, A.
Song: "Ah stay! ah turn! ah whither would you fly."
Song: "False though she be to me and love."
Song: "Love's but the frailty of the mind."
Song: "Pious Selinda goes to prayers."
Song: "See, see, she wakes! Sabina wakes."
Song: "Soldier and a sailor, A."
Song: "Tell me no more I am deceived."
Song; Set by Mr. John Eccles.
Thus grief still treads upon the heels of pleasure.
To Cynthia Weeping and Not Speaking.
Way of the World, The, *sel.*
Conkling, Grace Hazard
After Sunset.
Beethoven Andante, A.
Goatherd, The.
Guadalupe.
I Have Cared for You, Moon.
Letter to Elsa, A.
Little Rose Is Dust, My Dear, The.
Nightingales.
Pablo.
Python.
Refugees.
Road to the Pool, The.
Snail, The.
Star, The.
Tampico.
To a New-born Baby Girl.
Victory Bells.
Whole Duty of Berkshire Brooks, The.
Wind's Way, The.
Conkling, Hilda
About Animals.
Blue Jay.
Bluebird.
Books.
Butterfly ("As I walked through my garden").
Butterfly ("Butterfly,/ I like the way you wear your wings").
Cellar, The.
Chickadee, The.
Dandelion.
Easter.
Fairies.
For You, Mother.
Hills.
I Am.
I Keep Wondering.
Lilacs.
Little Girl's Songs, A.
Little Papoose.
Little Snail.
Loveliness.
Moon Song.
Moonbeam.
Morning.
Mouse.
Music.
My Mind and I.
Old Bridge, The.
Pigeons Just Awake.
Poems.
Poplars.
Red Rooster, The.
Snow-flake Song.
Spring Song.
Thunder Shower.
Tired.
Tree-Toad.
Water.
Weather.
When Moonlight Falls.
Connell, Hugh
Dream, A.
Erris Coast, 1943.
Mountain Tree, The.
Connell, Jim
New Words to the Tune of "O'Donnel Abu."
"Connell, Norreys." *See* **O'Riordan,Conal**
Connellan, Leo
This Scenery.
Connelly, Beverly
Testimony.
2000 A.D.
Conner, J. W.
John Chinaman, My Jo, *with music.*
Connolly, Francis X.
For Having Thee.
No More Destructive Flame.
Connolly, Myles E.
Lament for a Poor Poet.
Quo Vadis?
Said the Innkeeper.
Connor, Tony
Poet's Reflection, The.
Conolly, Luke Aylmer
Enchanted Island, The.
Conquest, Robert
Adriatic.
Aids to Composition.
Far Out.
Golden Age, The.
Motives of Rhythm, The.
On the Danube.
Performance of "Boris Godunov," A.
Seal Rocks: San Francisco.
Conrad, May Ricker
What Does Easter Mean to You?
Constable, Henry
Diana, *sels.*
Fair grace of graces, muse of muses all.
Fair sun, if you would have me praise your light.
Grace full of grace, though in these verses here.
Hope, like the hyena [*or* hyaena], coming to be old.
If This Be Love.
Love's Franciscan.
Mine eye with all the deadly sins is fraught.
My tears are true, though others be divine.
Needs Must I Leave, and Yet Needs Must I Love.
Not that thy hand is soft, is sweet, is white.
O Gracious Shepherd.
Of the Nativity of the Lady Rich's Daughter.
On Sir Philip Sidney.
On the Death of Sir Philip Sidney.
Ready to seek out death in my disgrace.
Resolved to love, unworthy to obtain.
Shepherd's Song of Venus and Adonis, The.
Sonnet: "Dear to my soul! then leave me not forsaken!"
Sonnet: "If ever Sorrow spoke from soul that loves."
Sonnet: "My lady's presence makes the roses red."
Sun, his journey ending in the west, The.
To God the Father.
To God the Son.
To His Mistress.
To Our Blessed Lady.
To Our Lady.
To Saint Catherine.
To Saint Margaret.
To St. Mary Magdalen.
To St. Peter and St. Paul.
To Sir Philip Sidney's Soul.
To the Blessed Sacrament.
Uncivil sickness, hast thou no regard.
When your perfections to my thoughts appear.
Whilst echo cries, "What shall become of me?"
You secret vales, you solitary fields.
Constable, Thomas
Old October.
Constantine of Rhodes
Before the Ikon of the Mother of God.
Constantine of Russia, Grand Duke
Teach Me, O Lord.
Contardo, Luis Felipe
Calling, The.
Contoski, Victor
Autumn.
Dirty Thoughts.
Fallen Tree Elegy.
First Animal, The.
Grief.
Inscription on an Altar of the Dead.

Contoski (continued)
Invitation.
Keepsake.
Money.
Morning Moon.
Perspective.
Summer Night.
Converse, Florence
Liberté, Egalité, Fraternité.
Rune of Riches, A.
Conway, Katherine Eleanor
Annunciation Night.
Christ and the Mourners.
Heaviest Cross of All, The.
Saturninus.
Conway, Margaret Devereaux
Annunciation, The.
Coogler, J. Gordon
Poor South! Her books get fewer and fewer.
Cook, —— So nigh is grandeur to man
Cook, Albert Jay
There's About Two Million Fellows.
Cook, Clarence Chatham
On One Who Died in May.
Cook, Eliza
A B C.
Christmas Holly, The.
Death of Master Tommy Rook, The.
Englishman, The.
Indian Hunter, The.
King Bruce and the Spider.
Mouse and the Cake, The.
No!
Old Arm-Chair, The.
Quiet Eye, The.
Sailor's Grave.
Sea-Child, The.
Song of the Seaweed, *sel.*
Star in the West, The.
They All Belong to Me.
Try Again.
Where There's a Will There's a Way.
Cook, Harold Lewis
Coward.
Fugue.
Man.
Starlight.
Warning.
Weaving, The.
Cook, Joseph
Boston Nursery Rhymes.
Cook, Warren F.
Revelation.
Cooke, Donald E.
My Penguin Playmate.
New Year, The.
Cooke, Edmund Vance
Born without a Chance.
Fin de Siècle.
How Did You Die?
Moo-Cow-Moo, The.
Off Manilly.
Rags.
Three Crosses, The.
Cooke, John Esten
Band in the Pines, The.
Cooke, Philip Pendleton
Florence Vane.
Cooke, Rose Terry
Arachne.
Bluebeard's Closet.
Death of Goody Nurse, The.
Done For.
In Vain.
Lise.
Our Dead Heroes.
Segovia and Madrid.
Then.
Two Villages, The.
Cooksley, Sidney
Puzzle.
Coolbrith, Ina Donna
Fruitionless.
Helen Hunt Jackson.
Mariposa Lily, The.
When the Grass Shall Cover Me.
Cooley, Julia *See* **Altrocchi, Julia Cooley**
Coolidge, Clark
Blue Kinds.
Fed Drapes.
Ghost.
Hammer, The.
High Pitched Whale.
Lark bender hair air.
Listene/ secting.
Mangrove in Crome.
Moon silent mike breasts.
Movies.
Ounce code orange.
Prune acrylic whose.
Scrip Ant.
Styro.
Coolidge, Grace Goodhue (Mrs. Calvin Coolidge)
Open Door, The.
Quest, The.
"Coolidge, Susan" (Sarah Chauncey Woolsey)
Begin Again.
Better Way, The.
Bind-Weed.
Calvary and Easter.
Child's Thought of Harvest, A.
Christ Has Risen.
Commonplace.
Commonplaces.
Easter Song.
God's Plan.
Gulf Stream.
He Cares.
Helen.
Hodge the Cat.
How Does the Soul Grow?
How the Leaves Came Down.
Last Hour, The.
Little Christmas Tree, The.
New Every Morning.
Patriotism.
Single Stitch, A.
Time to Go.
When.
Coon, Jeanette Saxton
Mother's Prayer, A.
Coon, Zula Evelyn
Easter.
Coonley, Lydia Avery *See* **Ward, Lydia Avery Coonley**
Cooper, Alice Cecilia
San Juan Capistrano.
Cooper, Belle
Street Melody, A.
Vintage, The.
Cooper, Charles
Idle Chatter.
Cooper, Edith, *and* **Katherine Bradley** *See* **"Field, Michael"**
Cooper, George
Babyland [*or* Baby-Land].
Bob White.
Christmas Bells.
Come, Little Leaves.
Frogs at School.
Mother.
New Year, The.
October's Party.
Only One.
Only One Mother.
Our Mother.
Sweet Genevieve.
Twenty Froggies.
What Robin Told.
While the Days Are Going By.
Why Did They Dig Ma's Grave So Deep?
Wind and the Leaves, The.
Wonderful Weaver, The.
Cooper, James Fenimore (1789-1851)
My Brigantine.
Water Witch, The, *sel.*
Fate.
Cooper, James Fenimore (1892-1918)
Fate.
Cooper, Jane
Builder of Houses, The.
Faithful, The.
For a Very Old Man, on the Death of His Wife.
For Thomas Hardy.
Graveyard, The.
Morning on the St. John's.
Obligations.
Sundial, The.
Weather of Six Mornings, The.
Cooper, Julian
Basie Band, The.
Sitar Player, The.
Stravinsky.
Warm Winter Day, A.
Cooper, Junius
Jabberwocky (as the Author of "The Faerie Queene" Might Have Written It).
Cooper, Robert
In Youth, in Age.
Cooper, Thomas
Chartist Song.
Cooperman, Hasye
Mists Are Rising Now, The.
Cope, Jack
Flying Fish, The.
If You Come Back.
Rock Painting.
Sappho.
Sons.
Copeland, Josephine
Zulu King, The; New Orleans.
Copenhaver, Laura S.
Missions.
Copland, Aaron
Lincoln Portrait, *abr.*
Coplen, Grace Wilson
Fireflies.
My Swinging Shadow.
Coppard, Alfred Edgar
Apostate, The.
Betty Perrin.
Epitaph: "Like silver dew."
Forester's Song.
Glorious Survivors, The.
Mendacity.
Night Piece.
Oracle, The.
Prodigal Son, The.
Sluggard, The.
Stay, O Stay.
Unfortunate Miller, The.
Winter Field.
Coppée, François
Promenades and Interiors, *sel.*
Coppinger, Matthew
Song, A: "I will not tell her that she's fair."
To Clelia.
Corbet, Richard
Certain True Woords Spoken Concerning One Benet Corbett after Her Death.
Distracted Puritan, The.
Elegie Upon the Death of His Owne Father, An.
Epitaph on Doctor Donne, Deane of Pauls, An.
Fairies' Farewell, The.
Farewell, Rewards and Fairies.

Farewell to the Fairies.
Great Tom.
Like to the Thundering Tone.
On Mr. Francis Beaumont (Then Newly Dead).
Proper New Ballad, A, Intituled The Fairies' Farewell or God-a-Mercy Will.
To His Son.
To His Son, Vincent Corbet [on His Birth-Day, November 10, 1630, Being Then Three Years Old].
Upon Faireford Windowes.
Corbett, Mrs. E. T.
Inventor's Wife, The.
Three Wise Couples, The.
Three Wise Women, The.
Corbière, Tristan (Edouard Joachim Corbière)
Cries Out of Blindness.
Epitaph; for Himself.
Epitaph for Tristan-Joachim-Edouard Corbière, Philosopher, Stray, Stillborn.
Paris at Night.
Rhapsody of the Deaf Man.
To My Mouse-colored Mare.
To the Eternal Feminine.
Toad, The.
Corbin, Alice (Alice Corbin Henderson)
Apparitions.
Delphy.
Echoes of Childhood, *sels.*
Harvest, The.
Humoresque.
If War Is Right.
In the Desert.
Juan Quintana.
Love Me at Last.
Mandy's Religion.
Music.
Nodes.
O World.
On the Acequia Madre.
One City Only.
Pool, The.
Sand Paintings.
Song from Old Spain, A.
Star of Bethlehem
Two Voices.
Una Anciana Mexicana.
Uncle Jim.
What Dim Arcadian Pastures.
Corbin, Lloyd M., Jr. (Djangatolum)
Ali.
Corder, W.
Murder of Maria Marten, The.
"Corinna."
Sehnsucht; or, What You Will.
Corke, Hilary
Any Man to His Secretary.
Calm Winter Sleep.
Chair, Dog, and Clock.
Choice, The.
Destroying Angel.
Ghost, The.
November Poppies.
Poem at Equinox.
Snake, The.
Storm of Love, A.
Waiting.
Waltz, The.
Corkery, Daniel
Call, The.
No Miracle.
Cormac Mac Cuilenan
Book of Leinster, *sel.*
Heavenly Pilot, The.
Cormack, Barbara Villy
Reprieve.
Corneille, Pierre
Cid, The, *sel.*
Epitaph for Elizabeth Ranquet.
Stanzas: "If, Marchioness, you can descry."
Two Lovers in the Toils of Honor.
Cornell, Annette Patton
Sailor's Woman.
Cornet, Barbara E.
Lord, I Love Thy Morning.
Success.
Cornford, Frances (Darwin)
After the Party.
All Souls' Night.
At Night ("My brain is like the ravaged shores").
At Night ("On moony nights the dogs bark shrill").
Autumn Morning at Cambridge.
Corner of the Field, The.
Country Bedroom, The.
Dogs.
Epitaph for a Timid Lady.
Feri's Dream.
Flowers in a Meadow, The.
For M. S. Singing Frühlingsglaube in 1945.
For Nijinsky's Tomb.
Glimpse, A.
Guitarist Tunes Up, The.
Hills, The.
In France.
Lincolnshire Remembered.
Little Dog, The.
London Despair.
Near an Old Prison.
Old Nurse, The.
Pre-Existence.
Princess and the Gypsies, The.
Quatrain: "Young Apollo, golden-haired, A."
Recollection, A.
Rhyme for a Phonetician.
She Warns Him.
Single Woman, The.
Spring Morning.
Summer Beach.
Susan to Diana.
To a Fat Lady Seen from the Train.
Two Poems.
Unbeseechable, The.
Village before Sunset.
Wasted Day, A.
Watch, The.
Weekend Stroll.
Woman with the Baby to the Philosopher, The.
Youth.
Cornford, John
Huesca.
Poem: "Heart of the heartless world."
Corning, Howard McKinley
Autumn Bird.
Farewell to Fields.
Green Councillors.
Judas.
Meadow Brook Runs Over, The.
Mountain in the Sky, The.
Pruning Vines.
Question.
Rainbow Lands.
Song to Say a Farewell.
These People.
Cornish, Sam
Promenade.
To a Single Shadow without Pity.
Turk.
Cornish, William
Ah! the Sighs.
Desire.
Gratitude.
Pleasure It Is.
Rutterkin.
Spring.
You and I and Amyas.
"Cornwall, Barry" (Bryan Waller Procter)
Blood Horse, The.
Fate of the Oak, The.
First I saw a landscape fair.
For a Fountain.
Golden-tressed Adelaide.
Hermione.
Horned Owl, The.
Hunter's Song, The.
Inscription for a Fountain.
Is My Lover on the Sea?
Life.
Peace! What Do Tears Avail?
Petition to Time, A.
Poet's Song to His Wife, The.
Poet's Thought, A.
Sea, The.
Sea, The—in Calm.
Sit Down, Sad Soul.
Softly Woo Away Her Breath.
Song for the Seasons, A.
Stars, The.
Stormy Petrel, The.
Vision, A, *sel.*
Cornwall, Ursula
Sowing Seeds.
Cornwallis, Kinahan
Battle of Murfreesboro, The.
Cornwell, Henry Sylvester
Jefferson D.
May.
Sunset City, The.
Corridan, Frances O'Connell
First Born.
Strong Arms.
Corrie, Joe
Image o' God, The.
Miners' Wives.
Corrigan, Winifred
I Turn the Key.
Corrothers, James David
At the Closed Gate of Justice.
Black Cat Crossed His Luck, De.
Dream and the Song.
In the Matter of Two Men.
Indignation Dinner, An.
Negro Singer, The.
Paul Laurence Dunbar.
Road to the Bow, The.
Corsellis, Timothy
Engine Failure.
Repression.
They Have Taken It from Me.
Thrush, The.
To Stephen Spender.
Corso, Gregory
Birthplace Revisited.
But I Do Not Need Kindness.
Dialogue—2 Dollmakers.
Dream of a Baseball Star.
Dreamed Realization, A.
From Another Room.
Hello.
I Am 25.
Italian Extravaganza.
Last Warmth of Arnold, The.
Looking at the Map of the World.
Mad Yak, The.
Marriage.
Notes after Blacking Out.
Owl.
Paranoia in Crete.
Poets Hitchhiking on the Highway.
Requiem for "Bird" Parker.
Uccello.
Zizi's Lament.
Cortez, Jayne
Bull Shit.
For Real.

Cortez (continued)
How Long Has Trane Been Gone?
Cortissoz, Ellen Mackay Hutchinson
April Fantasie.
Bride's Toilette, The.
Cry from the Shore, A.
Harvest.
Her Picture.
Moth-Song.
On Kingston Bridge.
Pamela in Town.
Praise-God Barebones.
Quaker Ladies.
Quest, The.
Sea-Way.
So Wags the World.
Corwin, Norman
Man unto His Fellow Man.
On a Note of Triumph, *sel.*
Cory, William Johnson
Amaturus.
Anteros.
Dirge, A: "Naiad, hid beneath the bank."
Eton Boating Song.
Europa.
Heraclitus.
Invocation, An: "I never prayed for Dryads, to haunt the woods again."
Mimnermus in Church.
Mortem, Quae Violat Suavia, Pellit Amor.
Notes of an Interview.
Oh, Earlier Shall the Rosebuds Blow.
Poor French Sailor's Scottish Sweetheart, A.
Remember.
Separation, A.
Cosins, John
Come, Holy Ghost, our souls inspire.
Cosmas, Saint
Menaion, *sel.*
Nativity Ode.
Purification, The.
Cota de Maguaque, Rodrigo
Such Is Love.
Cott, Jonathan
Angels Adoring.
Forsaking the Course.
He Spends Time in Southern California.
There are words that slip out of you.
What Is Going on inside His Head.
You are lighting yourself.
Cotter, James F.
Autumn Is a Season.
Cotter, Joseph Seamon, Sr.
Tragedy of Pete, The.
Way-Side Well, The.
Cotter, Joseph Seamon Jr.
And What Shall You Say?
April Day, An.
Band of Gideon, The.
Deserter, The.
Is It Because I Am Black?
Prayer, A: "As I lie in bed."
Rain Music.
Supplication.
Cotterell, George
Autumn Flitting, An.
In the Twilight.
Cotterill, Thomas
God Speaks Through the Bible.
Cotton, Charles
Alice.
Amongst the mourners that attend his hearse.
Anacreontick.
Angler's Ballad, The.
Bee, the Ant, and the Sparrow, The.
Celia, my fairest Celia, fell.
Clepsydra.
Elden-Hole.
Epistle to John Bradshaw Esq., *sel.*
Epitaph on M. H., An.
Epitaph on Mr. Robert Port.
Epitaph on Mistress Mary Draper.
Evening.
Evening Quatrains.
Forbidden Fruit.
Invitation to Phyllis, An.
Joys of Marriage, The.
Know then with horses twain, one sound, one lame.
Laura Sleeping.
Les Amours.
Margaret.
Montross.
Morning Quatrains, The.
New Prison.
New Year, The.
Noon Quatrains.
Ode: "Come, let us drink away the time."
Ode: "Good night, my Love."
Ode: "Was ever man of nature's framing."
Ode: "Without the evening dew and showers," 6 *sts.*
Ode to Chloris.
Ode to Cupid.
Old Tityrus to Eugenia, *sel.*
On Rutt the Judge.
Resolution in Four Sonnets, of a Poetical Question Put to Me by a Friend, Concerning Four Rural Sisters.
Retirement, The.
Retreat, The.
Rondeau: "Thou fool! if madness be so rife."
Song: "Join once again, my Celia."
Song: "See, how like twilight slumber falls."
Song; Set by Mr. Coleman.
Sonnet: "Chloris, whilst thou and I were free."
Summer Evening.
Tempest, The.
To Calista.
To Celia.
To Chloris.
To Mr. Izaak Walton.
To My Dear and Most Worthy Friend, Mr Isaac Walton.
To My Friend Mr. John Anderson.
To My Old, and Most Worthy Friend, Mr. Izaak Walton.
Two Rural Sisters.
Virelay: "Thou cruel fair, I go."
Winter, *sel.*
Winter Glass, The.
Winter's Troops.
Wonders of the Peak, The, *sel.*
Cotton, Henry
Fly, fly! The foe advances fast.
Cotton, John
In Saram.
Thankful Acknowledgment of God's Providence, A.
To My Reverend Dear Brother M. Samuel Stone.
Upon the Death of G. B.
Pumpkins.
Report Back.
Coulby, Margaret
Sudden Spring.
Coulette, Henri
At the Telephone Club.
Attic, The.
Black Angel, The.
Cinema, at the Lighthouse.
Denise: A Letter Never Sent.
Epilogue: Author to Reader.
Family Goldschmitt, The.
Intaglio.
Junk Shop, The.
Phono, at the Boar's Head.
Sickness of Friends, The.
War of the Secret Agents, The.
Coulter, John
Morning Bus.
Counselman, Mary Elizabeth
Room in Darkness.
Coupey, Pierre
Study No. X.
Cournos, John
Catherine Takes a Stroll.
Courthope, William John
Birdcatcher's Song.
Dodoism.
In Praise of Gilbert White.
Ode: To the Roc.
Paradise of Birds, The, *sels.*
Trail of the Bird, The.
Courtney, Margaret
Be Kind.
Cousens, Mildred
American Vineyard.
Cousins, James H.
Behind the Plough.
Corn Crake, The.
Curse on a Closed Gate, A.
High and Low.
Omens.
Starling's Spring Rondel, A.
Wings of Love, The.
Coutts, Francis Burdett Money *See* **Money-Coutts, Francis Burdett**
Covey, Leona
Easter Surprise, An.
Coward, Noel
Mad Dogs and Englishmen.
Cowen, Joseph R.
Recessional for the Class of 1959 of a School for Delinquent Negro Girls.
Cowgill, Frank B.
Final Armistice, The.
Cowherd, Ella Conrad
Sleep.
Cowley, Abraham
Against Hope.
Age.
All-over Love.
Anacreontic on Drinking.
Annunciation, The.
Another.
Awake, Awake, My Lyre!
Beauty.
But since I know thy falsehood and thy pride.
Change, The.
Chronicle, The; a Ballad.
Clad All in White.
Country Mouse, The.
Coy nature (which remain'd though [*or* tho] aged grown).
Creation, The.
Davideis, *sels.*
Dissembler, The.
Drinking.
Duel, The.
Ecstasy, The.
Epicure, The ("Fill the bowl with rosy wine").
Epicure, The ("Underneath this myrtle shade").
Epitaph: "Underneath this marble stone."
Essay on Solitude.
Extasie, The.
Frailty, The.
Garden, The, *sel.*
Great Diocletian.
Hell.
He's no small prince who every day.
Hope.
Hymn to Light.

I sing the Man who Judah's Scepter bore.
I sought not from thee a return.
If learned in other things you be.
Leaving Me, and Then Loving Many.
Life and Fame.
Love ("Five years ago").
Love ("I'll sing of heroes and of kings.").
Love and Life.
Love's Absence in the Spring.
Love's Riddle, *sel.*
Mistress, The, *sels.*
Motto, The.
Muse, The.
My Diet.
Ode: Of Wit.
Ode upon Doctor Harvey.
Ode upon Liberty, *sel.*
Of Drinking.
Of Liberty; an Essay, *sel.*
Of Myself.
Of Solitude.
Of Wit.
On Drinking.
On the Death of Crashaw.
On the Death of Mr. Crashaw.
On the Death of Mr. William Hervey.
On the Praise of Poetry.
Platonick Love.
Portrait of a Freeman.
Power of Numbers, The.
Praise of Pindar, The.
Profane, The.
Prophet, The.
Reason, the Use of It in Divine Matters.
Request, The.
Resolved to Love, *sel.*
Sleep, *sel.*
Sleep is a god too proud to wait in palaces.
Soul, The.
Spring, The.
Supplication, A.
Swallow, The.
Thief, The.
Thraldome, The.
'Tis morning; well; I fain would yet sleep on.
To His Mistress.
To Mr. Hobbes [*or* Hobs].
To Sir William Davenant upon His Two First Books of Gondibert.
To the Royal Society.
Today Is Ours.
Upon Liberty, *sel.*
Vain-Love, The, *sel.*
Vote, A, *sel.*
Welcome, The.
Whilst thus his wrath with threats the Tyrant fed.
Wish, The.
With sober pace an heav'enly maid walks in.
Written in Juice of Lemmon.

Cowley, Abraham *and* Richard Crashaw
On Hope, by Way of Question and Answer, betweene A. Cowley, and R. Crashaw.

Cowley, Malcolm
Blue Juniata, *sels.*
Eight Melons.
Farm Died, The.
Flower in the Sea, The.
For St. Bartholomew's Eve.
Hill above the Mine, The.
Lady from Harlem, The.
Long Voyage, The.
Mine No. 6.
Piney Woods.
Stone Horse Shoals.
Towers of Song.
Tumbling Mustard.
Urn, The.
William Wilson.
Winter; Two Sonnets.

Cowper, William
Absence of Occupation ("Lucrative offices are seldom lost").
Addressed to a Young Lady.
Alexander Selkirk during His Solitary Abode in the Island of Juan Fernandez.
Beau's Reply.
Boadicea.
Castaway, The.
Chaffinch's Nest at Sea, The.
City and Country Life.
Closer Walk with God, A.
Colubriad, The.
Contentment.
Contrite Heart, The.
Conversation.
Could Time, his night reversed, restore the hours.
Cross, The.
Discipline in Education.
Dispute between Nose and Eyes.
Diverting History of John Gilpin, The.
Dog and the Water-Lily, The.
England.
Epistle to Robert Lloyd, Esq., An.
Epitaph, An: "Here lies one who never drew."
Epitaph on a Hare.
Epitaph on Johnson.
Evening.
Exhortation to Prayer.
Expostulation, *sel.*
Forbearance.
Fountain Opened, The.
Fragment: "Pity, Religion has so seldom found."
Freedom has a thousand charms to show.
Garden, The.
God Made the Country.
God Moves in a Mysterious Way.
Happy Change, The.
Hark, My Soul! It Is the Lord.
Hope, *sel.*
Human Frailty.
Humanity.
I Am Monarch of All I Survey.
I know the mind that feels indeed the fire.
I praise the Frenchman, his remark was shrewd.
I say the pulpit (in the sober use).
I Will Praise the Lord at All Times.
In Him Confiding.
In His Mental Illness, William Cowper Finds He Is Not Alone.
Jehovah-Rophi.
Jehovah-Shammah.
John Gilpin.
Joy and Peace in Believing.
Landscape.
Learned to Trust.
Light and Glory of the World, [The].
Light Shining Out of Darkness.
Lines on a Bill of Mortality, 1790.
Lines on Receiving His Mother's Picture.
Lines Written during a Period of Insanity.
Lines Written on a Window-Shutter at Weston.
Lines Written under the Influence of Delirium.
Lord it is my chief complaint.
Lord Will Happiness Divine, The.
Loss of the *Royal George,* The.
Love of England.
Love of the World Reproved, The; or, Hypocrisy Detected.
Lovest Thou Me?
Man that hails you Tom or Jack, The.
Monarch, The.
My Former Hopes Are Fled.
My Mary.
Mysterious Way, The.
Narcissus.
Nature and God.
Night was winter in his roughest mood, The.
Nightingale and [the] Glow-Worm, The.
Nose and the Eyes, The.
Oh! for a Closer Walk with God.
O Lord, My Best Desire Fulfil.
Ode, An: Secundum Artem.
Of Preachers.
On a Hare.
On a Spaniel, Called Beau, Killing a Young Bird.
On Friendship, *sel.*
On the Death of Mrs. (now Lady) Throckmorton's Bullfinch.
On the Loss of the *Royal George.*
On the Receipt of My Mother's Picture Out of Norfolk.
Pairing-Time Anticipated.
Peace after a Storm.
Penitence.
Pernicious Weed.
Place of Prayer, The.
Playthings.
Poetic Pains.
Poetry; Satire and Pulpit.
Poplar-Field, The.
Post-Boy, The.
Postman, The.
Praise for the Fountain Opened.
Preachers; the True vs. the Insincere.
Providence.
Report of an Adjudged Case; Not to Be Found in Any of the Books.
Retired Cat, The.
Retirement, *sels.*
Retirement ("Far from the world, O Lord, I flee").
Riddle, A: "I am just two and two, I am warm, I am cold."
Rights of Women, The.
Rural Walk, The.
Self-Portrait.
Shrubbery, The.
Simple Faith.
Slavery.
Slaves Cannot Breathe in England.
Sofa, The.
Solitude of Alexander Selkirk, The.
Sonnet to Mrs. Unwin.
Sonnet to William Wilberforce, Esq.
Spirit's Light, The.
Squirrel, The.
Statesman in Retirement.
Stream, The.
Stricken Deer, The.
Table Talk, *sels.*
Task, The, *sels.*
Temptation.
Though clasp'd and cradled in his nurse's arms.
Thy Saints are comforted, I know.
Time-Piece, The.
'Tis my happiness below.
To a Young Lady.
To Mary ("The twentieth year is well nigh past").
To Mary Unwin ("Mary! I want a lyre with other strings").
To Mary Unwin ("The twentieth year is well-nigh past").
To the Immortal Memory of the Halibut on which I Dined This Day, Monday, April 26, 1784.
To the Nightingale.
To the Rev. Mr. Newton.
To the Same.
To William Hayley, Esq.

Cowper (continued)
To William Wilberforce.
Town and Country.
True Preacher, The.
Truth, *sel.*
Valley of the Shadow of Death, The.
Verses: "I am monarch of all I survey."
Verses Supposed to Be Written by Alexander Selkirk, During His Solitary Abode in the Island of Juan Fernandez.
Walk to Emmaus, The.
Walking with God.
Where the Leprosy Begins.
Who loves a garden, loves a greenhouse too.
Whose freedom is by suff'rance, and at will.
Winter ("Oh Winter, ruler of th' inverted year).
Winter Evening ("Come, Evening").
Winter Evening, The ("Hark! 'tis the twanging horn").
Winter Morning Walk, The ("'Tis morning").
Winter Scene.
Wisdom.
Woodman's Dog, The.
Yardley-Oak.

Cox, C. C.
I Love Thee, Gracious Lord.

Cox, Donald
Meditation.

Cox, Eleanor Rogers
At Benediction.
Death of Cuchulain.
Dream of Ængus Og, The.
Dreaming of Cities Dead.
Gods and Heroes of the Gael.
Return, The.
Three White Birds of Angus.
To a Portrait of Whistler in the Brooklyn Art Museum.

Cox, Elizabeth
Mask.

Cox, Emma Finty
Your Cross and My Cross.

Cox, Kenyon
Bumblebeaver, The.
Herringdove, The.
Kangarooster, The.
Mixed Beasts.
Octopussycat, The.
Rhinocerostrich, The.
Work.

Cox, L. E.
We Thank You!

Cox, Leo
Bells of Ste. Anne des Monts, The.
Cornfield.
Easter Thought.
Father Point in August.

Cox, Lilian
Never Night Again.

Cox, Palmer
Mouse's Lullaby, The.

Cox, Thelma Parker
Evolution.
Frustration, a Heritage.

Coxe, Arthur Cleveland
America.
Body of Jesus.
England and America, *sel.*
Hallowe'en.
He Standeth at the Door.
House Not Made with Hands, A.
Iona.
O Where Are Kings and Empires Now.
Present Age, The.
We Are Living, We Are Dwelling.

Coxe, Louis O.
Autumnal.
Daedalus to Icarus.
Dead Marine.
From the Window Down.
Hannah Dustin.
Lake, The.
Old Lecher, The.
Pin-up Girl.
Rain.
Red Right Returning.
Squaring the Circle.
Veteran, The.
Winter Night.

Coyle, Henry
She Made Home Happy.

Crabbe, Chris Wallace- *See* **Wallace-Crabbe, Chris**

Crabbe, George
Alas! for Peter not a helping hand.
Amusements.
Ancient Mansion, The, *sel.*
Ancient Virgin, An.
Behold the cot! where thrives th' industrious swain.
Books.
Borough, The, *sels.*
Burials.
Can scenes like these withdraw thee from thy wood.
Caroline, The.
Critics.
Crusty Critics.
Dean's Lady, The.
Dejected Lover, The.
Delay Has Danger, *sel.*
"Describe the Borough"—though our idle tribe.
Fled are those times, when, in harmonious strains.
Frank Courtship, The, *sel.*
George loved the cause of freedom, but reproved.
Grave Jonas Kindred, Sybil Kindred's sire.
His Mother's Wedding Ring.
His Wife's Wedding Ring.
I sail the sea, I walk the land.
I sing of news, and all those vapid sheets.
Inebriety, *sel.*
Jonas Kindred's Household.
Lady of the Manor, The.
Late Wisdom.
Library, The, *sels.*
Life.
Lover's Journey, The.
Marriage Ring, A.
Meeting.
My Record ends: But hark! e'en now I hear.
Newspaper, The, *sel.*
Next at our altar stood a luckless pair.
Next died the Widow Goe, an active dame.
No shepherds now, in smooth alternate verse.
Parish Poor-House, The.
Parish Register, The, *sels.*
Pauper's Funeral, The.
Peace, peace, my friend; these subjects fly.
Peter Grimes.
Phoebe Dawson.
Players.
Poor of the Borough, The: Peter Grimes.
Poor of the Borough, The; the Parish-Clerk.
Posthumous Tales, *sels.*
Reflections, *sel.*
Resurrection.
Sad Lover, The.
Sailing upon the River.
Schools.
Sir Eustace Grey.
Slum Dwelling, A.
Something one day occurr'd about a bill.
Spring to Winter.
Tales of the Hall, *sels.*
Then those ill-favour'd ones, whom none.
Thoughts by the Shore.
Thus groan the old, till, by disease oppress'd.
Truth in Poetry.
Vicar, The.
Village, The.
Village Life.
Whistling Boy, The.
Winter Storm at Sea, The.
Winter Views Serene.
World of Dreams, The, *sel.*
Young Paris.
Your plan I love not; with a number you.

Craddle, W.
Egoism.
Glabrous girl and hispid boy, The.
Male and Female.
On a Certain Scholar.

Cragin, Mary A. *See* **"Allison, Joy"**

Craig, Alexander
Hillside.
Misery of Man, The.
Sonnet: "Go you, O winds that blow from north to south."
To His Pandora, from England.
To Pandora.

Craig, Maurice James
Ballad to a Traditional Refrain.
Fable: "Tale is every time the same, The."
From Burton the Anatomist.
High on a ridge of tiles.
Love Poem: "Flowers upon your lips and hands."
Poem: "High on a ridge of tiles."
Two Voyages.
Winter.

Craig, Robert J.
Evening.

Craigmyle, Elizabeth
Solway Sands.

Craik, Dinah Maria Mulock
Address to the New Year.
Autumn's Processional.
Blackbird, The.
Douglas, Douglas, Tender and True.
Down the wintry mountain.
Four Years.
Friendship.
God Rest Ye Merry, Gentleman.
Green Things Growing.
Highland Cattle, *sel.*
In Our Boat.
Lettice.
New Year, The.
Now and Afterwards.
Philip My King.
Plighted.
Too Late.
Violets.
Young Dandelion, The ("I am a bold fellow").
Young Dandelion ("Young Dandelion/ On a hedge-side").

Cranch, Christopher Pearse
After the Centennial.
Bobolinks, The.
Enosis.
Gnosis.
In in Thee, and Thou in Me.
Pines and the Sea, The.
So Far, So Near.
Stanza from an Early Poem.

Crandall, Charles Henry
Human Plan, The.
Stella.

Three Trees.
With Lilacs.
Crane, Carl
Reader Writes, The.
Crane, Edward L.
Poor and Wealthy Children.
Crane, Elizabeth Green
Gentian.
Crane, Frank
Because You Care.
Yesterday.
Crane, Hart
Air Plant, The (Grand Cayman, W.I).
At Melville's Tomb.
Atlantis.
Ave Maria.
Bathers, The.
Black Tambourine.
Bridge, The.
Broken Tower, The.
Cape Hatteras.
Chaplinesque.
Cutty Sark.
Dance, The.
Down, down—born pioneers in time's despite.
Emblems of Conduct.
For the Marriage of Faustus and Helen (I-III).
Harbor Dawn, The.
Hurricane, The.
Idiot, The.
Imperator Victus.
In Shadow.
Indiana.
Island Quarry.
Key West.
Lachrymae Christi.
Legend.
March.
My Grandmother's Love Letters.
Name for All, A.
National Winter Garden.
North Labrador.
O Carib Isle!
Paraphrase.
Passage.
Phantom Bark, The.
Power.
Powhatan's Daughter.
Praise for an Urn.
Proem: To Brooklyn Bridge.
Purgatorio.
Quaker Hill.
Recitative.
Repose of Rivers.
River, The.
Royal Palm.
Sea, The.
Southern Cross.
Sunday Morning Apples.
Three Songs.
To Brooklyn Bridge.
To Emily Dickinson.
To Potapovitch.
To Shakespeare.
Tunnel, The.
Van Winkle.
Virginia.
Voyage.
Voyages (I-VI).
Wine Menagerie, The.
You will not hear it as the sea.
Crane, Nathalia
Alliances.
Blind Girl, The.
Colors, The.
Dead Bee, The.
Death of Poetry, The, *sel.*
Desire.
Destiny.
Discoverer, The.
Dust, The.
Flathouse Roof, The.
Gossips, The.
Janitor's Boy, The.
Moon of Brooklyn, The.
Requiem.
Song: "Great is the rose."
Spooks.
Standards.
Swinging Stair, The.
Tadmor, *sel.*
Vestal, The.
Yak, The.
Crane, Orin L.
Slow Me Down, Lord!
Crane, Stephen
Ancestry.
Black Riders, The, *sels.*
Blades, [*or* Blade] of Grass, The.
Blue Battalions, The.
Book of Wisdom, The.
Candid Man, The.
Charity, Thou Art a Lie.
Content.
Heart, The.
Hymn: "Slant of sun on dull brown walls, A."
I Explain.
I Saw a Man [Pursuing the Horizon].
I Stood upon a High Place.
I Walked in a Desert.
If I Should Cast Off This Tattered Coat.
If War Be Kind.
Impact of a Dollar upon the Heart, The.
In a Lonely Place.
In the Desert.
In the Night.
It Was Wrong to Do This, Said the Angel.
Learned Man, A.
Little Ink More or Less, A.
Livid Lightnings Flashed in the Clouds, The.
Man, The.
Man Adrift on a Slim Spar, A.
Man feared that he might find an assassin, A.
Man Said to the Universe, A.
Man Saw a Ball of Gold in the Sky, A.
Man to the Universe, A.
Many Workmen.
Newspaper is a Collection of Half-Injustices, A.
Ocean said to me once, The.
On the Desert ("On the desert/ A silence").
Peaks, The.
Row of Thick Pillars, A.
'Scaped.
Slant of Sun [on Dull Brown Walls], A.
Tell me not in joyous numbers.
There Was a Man.
There Was a Man with a Tongue of Wood.
There Was Crimson Clash of War.
There Was One I Met upon the Road.
There Were Many Who Went.
Three Poems.
Trees in the Garden Rained Flowers, The.
Unwind My Riddle.
Violets, The.
War Is Kind, *sels.*
Wayfarer, The.
What! You Define Me God.
When a People Reach the Top of a Hill.
Why?
Youth, A.
Youth in Apparel That Glittered, A.
Crane, Walter
Across the Fields.
Crocus, The.
Seat for Three, A; Written on a Settle.
Cranston, Claudia
In the Name of Jesus Christ.
Crapsey, Adelaide
Adventure.
Amaze.
Arbutus.
Cradle-Song: "Madonna, Madonna [*or* Madonnina]."
Dirge: "Never the nightingale."
Expenses.
Fate Defied.
For Lucas Cranach's Eve.
Guarded Wound, The.
Immortal Residue, The.
Lonely Death, The.
Moon Shadows.
Niagara.
Night Winds.
November Night.
On Seeing Weather-beaten Trees.
Pledge, The.
Roma Aeterna.
Rose-Marie of the Angels.
Snow.
Song: "I make my shroud but no one knows."
Susanna and the Elders.
To Man Who Goes Seeking Immortality.
Trapped.
Triad.
Vendor's Song.
Warning, The.
Why.
Crashaw, Richard
Against Irresolution.
Alexias, the Complaint of the Forsaken Wife of Sainte Alexis.
And a Certain Priest Comming That Way Looked on Him and Passed By.
And He Answered Them Nothing.
And now where're he strays.
Another [Upon the Death of Mr. Herrys].
Answer for Hope.
Apologie for the Precedent [*or* Fore-going] Hymne [*or* Hymnes].
Authors Motto, The.
Beginning of Heliodorus, The.
Blessed Be the Paps Which Thou Hast Sucked.
Blind Cured by the Word of Our Saviour, The.
But Men Loved Darknesse Rather Then Light.
But Now They Have Seen, and Hated.
Casting the times with their strong signes.
Charitas Nimia; or, The Dear[e] Bargain.
Christ Crucified.
Christ to Thomas.
Christ's Victory.
Close, The.
Come See the Place Where the Lord Lay.
Coming Child, The.
Dear Bargain, The.
Dear soul be strong!
Deare reliques of a dislodg'd soule, whose lacke.
Death's Lecture at the Funeral of a Young Gentleman.
Description of a Religious House and Condition of Life.
Dives Asking a Drop.
Divine Love.
Dumbe Healed, and the People Enjoyned Silence, The.
Easter Day.
Elegy upon the Death of Mr. Stanninow Fellow of Queenes Colledge, An.
Epitaph on Husband and Wife Who Died and Were Buried Together, An.
Epitaph upon Doctor Brooke, An.
Epitaph upon Husband and Wife Which

Crashaw (continued)
[*or* Who] Died and Were Buried Together, An.
Epitaph Upon Mr. Ashton a Conformable Citizen, An.
Epithalamium: "Come, virgin tapers of pure wax."
Fair hope! our earlyer heav'n by thee.
Flaming Heart, The.
For Hope.
Give to Caesar.
Herod's Suspicions.
Himn, The, O Gloriosa Domina.
Himne for the Circumcision Day of Our Lord, An.
His Epitaph.
Holy Name of Jesus, The.
Holy Nativity of Our Lord God.
Hymn in Adoration of the Blessed Sacrament.
Hymn of Saint[e] Thomas in Adoration of The Blessed Sacrament, The.
Hymn of the Holy Cross, The.
Hymn of the Nativity.
Hymn Sung as by the Shepherds, A.
Hymn to Saint Teresa.
Hymn to the Name and Honor [*or* Honour] of the Admirable Saint[e] Teresa, A.
Hymne for the Epiphanie, A.
Hymne of the Nativity, Sung as by the Shepheards, An.
I Am Not Worthy That Thou Should'st Come Under My Roofe.
I Am Ready Not Onely to Be Bound But to Dye.
I Am the Door.
In Amorem Divinum (Hermannus Hugo).
In Cicatrices Domini Jesu.
In Memory of the Vertuous and Learned Lady Madre de Teresa.
In Praise of Lessius His Rule of Health.
In the Glorious Assumption of Our Blessed Lady.
In the Glorious Epiphanie of Our Lord God.
In the Holy Nativity of Our Lord God.
It Is Better to Go into Heaven with One Eye.
Lauda Sion Salvatorem.
Letter to the Countess of Denbigh against Irresolution and Delay in Matters of Religion, A.
Loves Horoscope.
Love's Nightingale.
Luke 11.
M. Crashaw's Answer for Hope.
Malchus' Ear.
Mongst all the palaces in Hells command.
Music's Duel.
Nativity, The.
Neither Durst Any Man from That Day Aske Him Any More Questions.
New Year's Day.
O heart, the equal poise of love's both parts.
O how oft shalt thou complain.
O sweet incendiary! show here thy art.
Ode Which Was Prefixed to a Prayer Booke Given to a Young Gentlewoman, An.
Office of the Holy Cross[e], The.
On a Foule Morning, Being Then to Take a Journey.
On a Prayer Booke Sent to Mrs. M. R.
On a Treatise of Charity.
On a Young Married Couple.
On Dives.
On Marriage.
On Mr. G. Herberts Booke Intituled the Temple.
On Nanus Mounted Upon an Ant.
On Our Crucified Lord, Naked and Bloody.
On St. Peter Casting Away His Nets at Our Saviours Call.
On St. Peter Cutting of Malchus His Eare.
On the Assumption [of the Virgin Mary].
On the Baptized Ethiopian [*or* Aethiopian].
On the Bleeding Wounds of Our Crucified Lord.
On the Blessed Virgin's Bashfulness.
On the Frontispiece of Isaacsons Chronologie Explained.
On the Glorious Assumption of Our Blessed Lady.
On the Miracle of Loaves.
On the Miracle of Multiplyed Loaves.
On the Name of Jesus.
On the Prodigall.
On the Still Surviving Markes of Our Saviours Wounds.
On the Water of Our Lords Baptisme.
On the Wounds of Our Crucified Lord.
Our Lord in His Circumcision to His Father.
Out of Barclay's Euphormion.
Out of Grotius His Tragedy of Christes Sufferinges.
Out of Horace.
Out of Martiall.
Out of Petronius.
Out of the Greeke, Cupid's Cryer.
Out of the Italian ("Love now no fire hath left him").
Out of the Italian ("To thy lover").
Out of the Italian ("Would any one the true cause find").
Out of Virgil, In the Praise of the Spring.
Pharisee and Publican.
Prayer: "Lo here a little volume, but great book!"
Prayer; an Ode.
Quaerit Jesum Suum Maria.
Qui Perdiderit Animam Suam.
Recommendation, The.
Richard Crashaw's Answer; for Hope.
Saint Mary Magdalene.
St. Peter's Shadow.
Sainte Mary Magdalene.
Samson to His Delilah.
Sancta Maria Dolorum or The Mother of Sorrows.
She Began to Wash His Feet with Teares.
Shepherd's Hymn, The.
Shepherds Hymn Their Saviour.
Sicke Implore St. Peter's Shadow, The.
Song: "Lord, when the sense of thy sweet grace."
Song of Divine Love, A.
Sospetto d'Herode, sels.
Tear [*or* Teare], The.
Temperance, or the Cheap Physitian.
To a Young Gentle-Woman, Councel Concerning Her Choice.
To Our Blessed Lord upon the Choice of His Sepulchre.
To Our Lord, upon the Water Made Wine.
To Pontius Washing His Hands.
To Pontius Washing His Blood-Stained Hands.
To the Infant Martyrs ("Goe, smiling soules, your new built Cages break").
To the Morning. Satisfaction for Sleepe.
To the Name above Every Name, the Name of Jesus, [a Hymn].
To the Noblest and Best of Ladies [*or* Ladyes], the Countess[e] of Denbigh.
To the Queen: an Apologie for the Length of the Following Panegyrick.
To the Queen: Upon the Duke of Yorke His Birth A Panegyricke.
To the Queen's Majesty.
To the Same Party, Councel Concerning Her Choise.
Two Dedicatory Poems ("At th' ivory tribunall of your hand").
Two Dedicatory Poems ("Though now 'tis neither May nor June").
Two Went Up to [*or* into] the Temple to Pray.
Upon Bishop Andrewes His Picture Before His Sermons.
Upon Ford's Two Tragedies. "Loves Sacrifice" and "The Broken Heart."
Upon Lazarus His Teares.
Upon Mr. Staninough's Death.
Upon Our Lords Last Comfortable Discourse with His Disciples.
Upon Our Saviours Tombe Wherein Never Man Was Laid.
Upon the Asse that Bore Our Saviour.
Upon the Bleeding Crucifix.
Upon the Body of Our Blessed [*or Bl.*] Lord, Naked and Bloody.
Upon the Book and Picture of the Seraphical Saint Teresa.
Upon the Crowne of Thorns.
Upon the Death of a Gentleman.
Upon the Death of Mr. Herrys.
Upon the Death of the Most Desired Mr. Herrys.
Upon the Dumbe Devill Cast Out, and the Slanderous Jewes Put to Silence.
Upon the Faire Ethiopian Sent to a Gentlewoman.
Upon the H. Sepulcher.
Upon the Infant Martyrs.
Upon the Powder Day.
Upon the Same (Venus Putting on Mars His Armes).
Upon the Savior's Tomb.
Upon the Sepulchre of Our Lord.
Upon the Thornes Taken Downe from Our Lords Head Bloody.
Upon Two Greene Apricockes Sent to Cowley by Sir Crashaw.
Upon Venus Putting on Mars His Armes.
Verily I Say Unto You, Yee Shall Weep and Lament.
Verse-Letter to the Countess of Denbigh, A.
Verses from the Shepherds' Hymn.
Vexilla Regis, the Hymn of the Holy Crosse.
Weeper, The.
Welcome!
When love of us called Him to see.
Whosoever Shall Loose His Life.
Why Are Yee Afraid, O Yee of Little Faith?
Widow's [*or* Widowes] Mites, The.
Wishes.
Wishes for the Supposed Mistress.
Wishes to His (Supposed) Mistress.
With a Picture Sent to a Friend.
Yee Build the Sepulchres of the Prophets.

Crashaw, Richard *and* Abraham Cowley
On Hope, by Way of Question and Answer, betweene A. Cowley, and R. Crashaw.

Craster, Mrs. Edward
Centipede, A [*or* The].
Centipede Was Happy Quite, A.
Puzzled Centipede, The.
Quandary.

Craveirinha, José
Poem of the Future Citizen.

"Crawford, Captain Jack"
California Joe.
Death of Custer, The.

Crawford, Dan
Jesus and I.
We Two.
Crawford, F. Marion
New National Hymn, A.
Crawford, Isabella Valancy
Axe, The.
Axe of the Pioneer, The.
"Bite deep and wide, O Axe, the tree."
Canoe, The.
City Tree, The.
Dark Stag, The.
Gisli, the Chieftain, *sel.*
Helot, The, *sel.*
In this shrill moon the scouts of winter ran.
Laughter.
Lily Bed, The.
Love Me, Love My Dog.
Love's Land.
Malcolm's Katie, *sels.*
"O love, art thou a silver fish?"
Song of the Arrow, The.
South Wind laid his moccasins aside, The.
True and False.
Who may quench the god-born fire.
Crawford, John Wallace *See* **Crawford, "Captain Jack"**
Crawford, Louisa Macartney
Kathleen Mavourneen.
Crawford, Raymond H.
Christian Mother's Love, A.
Crawford, Robert MacArthur
Song: "Love, love me only."
U.S. Air Force, The.
Winged Words.
Crawford, Vesta Pierce
Pioneer Woman.
Creekmore, Hubert
Concert at Sea.
Dividends.
Music in the Rec Hut.
Pocket Guide for Servicemen.
Creeley, Robert
After Lorca.
All That Is Lovely in Men.
Anger.
Awakening, The.
Ballad of the Despairing Husband.
Bed, The.
Chance, The.
Counterpoint, A.
Death of Venus, The.
Distance.
Door, The.
End of the Day, The.
For the New Year.
Form of Adaptation, A.
Form of Women, A.
Gift of Great Value, A.
Hart Crane.
House, The.
I Know a Man.
If You.
Immoral Proposition, The.
Innocence, The.
Intervals.
Invoice, The.
Jack's Blues.
Just Friends.
Kind of Act of, The.
Kore.
Language, The.
Le Fou.
Like They Say.
Loves Comes Quietly.
Marriage, A.
Mechanic, The.
Mountains in the Desert, The ("The mountains blue now").
Name, The.
Naughty Boy.
Night Sky, A.
Oh No.
Operation, The.
Pattern, The.
Please.
Pool, The.
Rain, The.
Reason, A.
Rhyme, The.
Rhythm, The.
Riddle, The: "What it is, the literal size."
Rose, The.
Saints, The.
She Went to Stay.
Sight, A.
Sing Song.
Snow, The.
Something.
Souvenir, The.
Three Ladies, The.
Warning, The.
Way, The.
Whip, The.
Wicker Basket, A.
Wife, The.
Wind, The.
Window, The.
World, The.
Creeley, Thomas
I.
Creelman, Josephine Rice
My Mother.
Creighton, Alan
Pastoral: "Farmhouse skyline, draped with trees, The."
Return of a Reaper.
Spring Workman.
Crellin, Charles C.
Ode to the Flag.
Crespo, Manuel
Song to the Soviet Union.
Cressman, H. E.
Coxswain's Line, The.
Cresson, Abigail
Cloak of Laughter.
Little Gods, The.
Market Day.
Cresswell, D'Arcy
Impatient Poet, The.
Lyttelton Harbour, *sels.*
Time Lags Abed.
To L——.
Crew, Helen Coale
Bedtime.
In a Low Rocking-Chair.
Nobody Knows.
Crewdson, Jane
Gratitude.
Crewe, Fred
Cleary Pioneer, A.
Crewe, Robert Offley Ashburton Crewe-Milnes, Marquess of
Harrow Grave in Flanders, A.
Seven Years.
Crews, Judson
Declaration at Forty.
Love Poem: "Oh your thighs."
Oh Beach Love Blossom.
"Crichton, John" (Norman Gregor Guthrie)
Bed of Campanula, A.
Crinagoras
Epitaph on an Infant.
Sepulchral Imprecation.
This torch, still burning in my hand.
Cripps, Arthur Shearly
Black Christ, The.
Lazarus.
Les Belles Roses sans Mercie.
Pagan's Baptism, A.
Resurgat.
To the Veld.
Criswell, Cloyd Mann
Newlyweds, The.
Crites, Lucile
Folks and Me.
"Croakers, The." *See* **Halleck, Fitz-Greene,** *and* **Joseph Rodman Drake**
Croasdell, Anne
Muffin Man, The.
Croffut, William Augustus
Dirge, Concerning the Late Lamented King of the Cannibal Islands, A.
Living Memory, A.
Croker, Henry
Evangelize!
Croly, George
A Fauxbourg.
Aestuary, An.
Approach of Evening.
Death and Resurection.
Death of Leonidas, The.
Genius of Death, The.
Leonidas.
Paris in 1815, *sel.*
Prayer in the Spirit.
Spirit of God, Descend Upon My Heart.
Cromwell, Gladys
Crowning Gift, The.
Folded Power.
Mould, The.
Quest, The.
Renewal.
Cromwell, Henry
No, No! I Ne'er Shall Love Thee Less.
Crooke, Sheila Jane
Statue of Liberty, The.
Crosby, Ernest H.
Choir Practice.
How Did He Live?
In the Garden.
Life and Death.
Loves Comes.
Rebels.
Search, The.
Soul of the World, The.
Tournament of Man, The.
Crosby, Fanny (Frances Jane Crosby)
All the Way My Saviour Leads Me.
Best of All, The.
Blind.
Blind but Happy.
Contentment.
Keep Thou My Way, O Lord.
Little While, A.
Music in the Air.
Saved By Grace.
Secret Prayer.
State We Honor, The.
Thy Will Be Done in Me.
Unseen.
Cross, Allen Eastman
Hidden Years, The.
More Light Shall Break from Out Thy Word.
Pass On the Torch.
What Doth the Lord Require of Thee.
Cross, Mrs. George Frederick *See* **Cambridge, Ada**
Cross, Zora
Elegy on an Australian Schoolboy, *sel.*
O brother in the restless rest of God!
When I Was Six.
Woman.
Crossland, John R.
Water.
Crossman, Samuel
Hope in Death.
I Said Sometimes with Tears.
Love Unknown.
Croswell, William

Croswell (continued)
Clouds, The.
Song of Faith.
Crot, Robert J.
Dead, The.
Crouch, Pearl Riggs
Snowstorm, The.
Story in the Snow, A.
Crouch, Stanley
After the Rain.
All Praise.
Blackie Speaks on Campus: a Valentine for Vachel Lindsay.
Blackie Thinks of His Brothers.
Blues, for Sallie.
Chops Are Flyin.
Revelation, The.
Riding across John Lee's Finger.
Sallie Jewel.
Crouse, Miriam LeFevre
Dawn.
Lent.
Upon a Hill.
Crow, Martha Foote
Wooden Christ, The.
Crowell, Albert
Joy of Incompleteness, The.
Crowell, Grace Noll (Mrs. Norman H. Crowell)
Assurance.
Beautiful Gift, The.
Because of Thy Great Bounty.
Common Tasks, The.
Courage to Live.
Day Will Bring Some Lovely Thing, The.
Definition.
Eternal Values.
Fire Tenders, The.
I Have Found Such Joy.
I Think That God Is Proud.
Let Us Keep Christmas.
Mothers of the Earth, The.
New Houses.
Poet, The.
Poet Prays, The.
Power.
Prayer for a Day's Walk.
Questioning.
Quiet Things.
Recompense.
Shooting Stars.
So Long As There Are Homes.
Crowell, Henry
When Thou Passest through the Waters.
Crowell, Norman H.
My Candidate.
Crowley, Robert
Voice of the Last Trumpet Blown by the Seventh Angel, The, *sel.*
Ye robbed, ye spoiled, ye bought, ye sold.
Crowne, John
Ambitious Statesman, The, *sel.*
Calisto, *sel.*
I hate those potent madmen, who keep all.
Kind Lovers, Love On.
Regulus, *sel.*
Song: "Kind lovers, love on."
To Many Deaths Decreed.
Whilst th' iron hand.
"Crowquill, Alfred." *See* **Forrester,Alfred A**
"Cruger, Percy." *See* **Winner, Septimus**
Cruickshank, Helen B.
Comfort in Puirtith.
Shy Geordie.
Cruz, Juana Inés de la *See* **Juana Inés de la Cruz**
Cruz, Victor Hernandez
Bring the Soul Blocks.
Carmen.
Cities #8, *sel.*
Little cousins/ play on your.
Man I Thought You Was Talking Another Language That Day.
O.K. ("O.K./ you scat taking.")
Sometimes on My Way back down to the Block.
Today Is a Day of Great Joy.
224 Stoop.
Urban Dream.
White Powder!
Cudjoe, Seth D.
Transmigration.
Cullen, Cornelius C.
Battle of Somerset.
Cullen, Countee
Any Human to Another.
Black Magdalens.
Brown Girl Dead, A.
For a Lady I Know.
For a Mouthy Woman.
For a Pessimist.
For a Poet.
For a Virgin Lady.
For John Keats [Apostle of Beauty].
For My Grandmother.
For Paul Laurence Dunbar.
Four Epitaphs.
From the Dark Tower.
Fruit of the Flower.
Heritage.
I Have a Rendezvous with Life.
I Have Wrapped My Dreams in a Silken Cloth.
Incident.
Judas Iscariot.
Lady I Know, A.
Lines to Our Elders.
Litany of the Dark People, The.
Loss of Love, The.
Magnets.
Protest.
Red.
Saturday's Child.
Simon the Cyrenian Speaks.
Song in Spite of Myself.
Song of Praise, A.
Tableau.
That Bright Chimeric Beast.
Timid Lover.
To John Keats, Poet. At Springtime.
To Lovers of Earth: Fair Warning.
Uncle Jim.
Under the Mistletoe.
Unknown Color, The.
Wakeupworld, The.
Wind Bloweth Where It Listeth, The.
Wisdom Cometh with the Years.
Wise, The.
Yet Do I Marvel.
Youth Sings a Song of Rosebuds.
Cumberbatch, Lawrence S.
Again the Summoning.
Fake-out.
I Swear to You, That Ship Never Sunk in Middle-Passage!
In the Early Morning Breeze.
Cumberland, Earl of *See* **Clifford, George, Earl of Cumberland**
Cumbo, Kattie M.
Dark People.
Malcolm.
Washiri (Poet).
Cummings, Alison Elizabeth
To a Little Sister, Aged Ten.
Cummings, Edward Estlin
All Ignorance Toboggans into Know.
All in Green Went My Love Riding.
Along the Brittle Treacherous Bright Streets.
Always before Your Voice [My Soul].
Annie Died the Other Day.
Anyone Lived in a Pretty How Town.
As Freedom Is a Breakfastfood.
As Joe Gould says.
Because You Take Life in Your Stride.
Being to Timelessness as It's to Time.
Buffalo Bill's.
Buy Me an Ounce and I'll Sell You a Pound.
Cambridge Ladies [Who Live in Furnished Souls], The.
Chansons Innocentes, *sels.*
Come, Gaze with Me upon This Dome.
Cruelly, Love.
Darling! Because My Blood Can Sing.
Dive for Dreams.
Dominic Has a Doll.
Enter No (Silence Is the Blood Whose Flesh).
Fair Ladies Tall Lovers.
Faithfully Tinying at Twilight Voice.
First of All My Dreams, The.
Four III.
From Spiralling Ecstatically This.
Gee I Like to Think of Dead.
Great, A.
Hate blows a bubble of despair into.
Her Careful Distinct Sex Whose Sharp Lips Comb.
Honour Corruption Villainy Holiness.
Hours Rise Up Putting Off Stars and It Is, The.
I.
I Am a Little Church (No Great Cathedral).
I Am So Glad and Very.
I Go to This Window.
I Like My Body [When It Is with Your].
I Sing of Olaf [Glad and Big].
I Thank You God.
I Thank You God for Most This Amazing.
If I Have Made, My Lady, Intricate.
If in Beginning Twilight.
If There Are Any Heavens.
If You Can't Eat You Got To.
Impossibility Motivated by Midnight.
Impression ("Stinging/ gold swarms").
Impression ("The hours rise up putting off stars and it is").
In Just-/ Spring When the World Is Mud.
In Time of Daffodils.
Is 5, *sels.*
It Is at Moments after I Have Dreamed.
It Is So Long Since My Heart Has Been with Yours.
It May Not Always Be So.
It really must.
It Was a Goodly Co.
Item.
It's jolly/ Odd what pops into.
It's Over a (See Just).
Jehovah Buried, Satan Dead.
La Guerre.
Lady Will You Come with Me into.
Life Is More True.
Listen.
Little Tree.
Love Is More Thicker than Forget.
Love Is the Every Only God.
Maggie and Milly and Molly and May.
Man Who Had Fallen among Thieves, A.
May I Feel Said He.
May my heart always be open to little.
Me Up at Does.
Memorabilia.
Might these be thrushes climbing through almost.
Mr. U Will Not Be Missed.
Moon Is Hiding In, The.
My Father Moved through Dooms of Love.
My girl's tall with hard long eyes.

My Love.
My Specialty Is Living Said.
My Sweet Old Etcetera.
Next to of Course God America I.
No Man, If Men Are Gods.
Noone and a Star Stand, Am to Am.
"Noone" autumnal this great lady's gaze.
Nobody Loses All the Time.
Nonsun Blob A.
Now Does Our World Descend.
Now That Fierce Few.
O By the By.
O Sweet Spontaneous.
O Thou to Whom the Musical White Spring.
Of Nicolette.
One!
111.
147.
One X.
Orientale.
Paris: This April Sunset Completely Utters.
Pity This Busy Monster, Manunkind.
Plato Told [Him].
Poem: "Maggie and Milly and Molly and May."
Poem, or Beauty Hurts Mr. Vinal.
Poets yeggs and thirsties.
Politician, A.
Ponder, Darling, These Busted Statues.
Portrait ("Buffalo Bill's.")
Portrait ("Here is little Effie's head").
Pretty a Day, A.
Puella Mea.
R-P-O-P-H-E-S-S-A-G-R.
Salesman Is an It That Stinks Excuse, A.
Season 'Tis, My Lovely Lambs, The.
Serene Immediate Silliest and Whose.
She Being Brand.
Since Feeling Is First.
So Shy Shy Shy (and with a).
Somebody Knew Lincoln Somebody Xerxes.
Somewhere I Have Never Travelled [Gladly Beyond].
Song: "All in green went my love riding."
Song: "Always before your voice my soul."
Song: "Thy fingers make early flowers of all things."
Sonnet: "And what were roses."
Sonnet: "O Thou to whom the musical white springs."
Sonnet: "This is the garden: colours come and go."
Sonnet: "When thou hast taken thy last applause."
Sonnet: "Wind has blown the rain away and blown, A."
Sonnet Entitled How to Run the World.
Sonnets—Actualities, sels.
Sonnets—Realties, sels.
Sonnets — Unrealities, sel.
Spring.
Spring Is Like a Perhaps Hand.
Spring Omnipotent Goddess.
Sunset.
These Children Singing in Stone a.
This Is the Garden.
This Little Bride & Groom Are.
306.
Tumbling-Hair.
Two XI.
Way to Hump a Cow, The.
What a Proud Dreamhorse.
What If a Much of a Which of a Wind.
When Any Mortal (Even the Most Odd).
When faces called flowers float out of the ground.
When God Lets My Body Be.

When Life Is Quite Through With.
When my sensational moments are no more.
When Serpents Bargain for the Right to Squirm.
When the Spent Day Begins to Frail.
White Guardians of the Universe of Sleep.
Who Are You, Little I.
Who Knows If the Moon's.
Who's Most Afraid of Death? [Thou].
Wild (at Our First) Beasts Uttered Human Words.
You Are like the Snow Only.
You Shall above All Things Be Glad and Young.

Cummins, P. D.
Hearing, I Saw.

Cuney, Waring
Burial of the Young Love.
Conception.
Crucifixion.
Death Bed, The.
Dust.
Finis.
Grave.
I Think I See Him There.
Lame Man and the Blind Man.
My Lord, What a Morning.
No Images.
Radical, The.
Threnody: "Only quiet death."
Triviality, A.
Troubled Jesus.
True Love.
Wake Cry.

Cunningham, Allan
At Sea.
Gone Were But the Winter Cold.
Hame, Hame, Hame.
John Grumlie.
Loyalty.
Mariner, The.
Sea Song, A.
Song of the Elfin Miller.
Spring of the Year, The.
Sun Rises Bright in France, The.
Wet Sheet and a Flowing Sea, A.

Cunningham, James Vincent
Agnosco Veteris Vestigia Flammae.
Ars Amoris.
August Hail.
Coffee.
Dark thoughts are my companions. I have wined.
Elders at Their Services Begin, The.
Epigram: "And now you're ready who while she was here."
Epigram: "And what is love? Misunderstanding, pain."
Epigram: "Arms and the man I sing, and sing for joy."
Epigram: "Dear, my familiar hand in love's own gesture."
Epigram: "Elders at their services begin, The."
Epigram: "Friend, on this scaffold Thomas More lies dead."
Epigram: "Good Fortune, when I hailed her recently."
Epigram: "Here lies my wife. Eternal peace."
Epigram: "Here lies New Critic who would fox us."
Epigram: "I had gone broke, and got set to come back."
Epigram: "I married in my youth a wife."
Epigram: "Man who goes for Christian resignation, The."
Epigram: "My name is Ebenezer Brown."
Epigram: "This is my curse, Pompous, I pray."

Epigram: "With every wife he can, and you know why."
Epigram: "You ask me how Contempt who claims to sleep."
Epigram: "You wonder why Drab sells her love for gold?"
Epigraph from *The Judge Is Fury.*
Epitaph: "When I shall be without regret."
Experience.
Five Epigrams.
For a College Yearbook.
For My Contemporaries.
Hang up your weaponed wit.
Helmsman, The; an Ode.
Here lies New Critic who would fox us.
Horoscope.
I was in Vegas. Celibate and able.
If wisdom, as it seems it is.
In Whose Will Is Our Peace?
Interview with Doctor Drink.
It Was in Vegas.
Lector Aere Perennior.
Lip.
Meditation on a Memoir.
Meditation on Statistical Method.
Metaphysical Amorist, The.
Montana Pastoral.
Nescit Vox Missa Reverti.
On a Cold Night.
On the Calculus.
Phoenix, The.
Pick-up, The.
This humanist whom no beliefs constrained.
To a Friend, on Her Examination for the Doctorate in English.
To the Reader.
To What Strangers, What Welcome, sel.
Two Epigrams.
Verse, Violence, and the Vine.
With a Copy of Swift's Works.
Within This Mindless Vault.
You have here no otherness.

Cunningham, John
Day; a Pastoral.
Kate of Aberdeen.
Landscape, A.
Miller, The.
Virtuous Fox and the Self-righteous Cat, The.

Cunningham, John William
Calvary's Cry.

Cunningham, Nora B.
Feast, The.

Cunninghame-Graham, Robert *See* Graham, Robert

Curchod, Mary M.
I Would Go Back.

Curnow, Allen
At Dead Low Water.
Attitudes for a New Zealand Poet, III.
Bishop Boundary-rides His Diocese, The.
Country School.
Crash at Leithfield.
Elegy on My Father.
House and Land.
Landfall in Unknown Seas.
Magellan.
Not in Narrow Seas, sels.
Out of Sleep.
Stratagem.
Time.
Unhistoric Story, The.
Water Is Burred with Rain, The.
Wild Iron.

Curran, Edwin
Autumn.
Clod, The.
First Frost.
Painted Hills of Arizona, The.

Curran, John Philpot
Cusha-Ma-Chree.
Deserter, The.
Deserter's Lamentation, The.
Let Us Be Merry before We Go.
Currey, Ralph Nixon
Children Waking: Indian Hill Station.
Cock-Crow.
Durban Revisited.
Halo.
How lovely are the waters of Babylon.
In Memoriam; Roy Campbell.
Landscape.
Landscape of Violence.
Man's Roots, *sel.*
Marrakech.
Marshal Lyautey.
Morocco.
Remembering Snow.
Song: "There is no joy in water apart from the sun."
Ultimate Exile, *sel.*
Volubilis, North Africa.
Currie, Mary Montgomerie Currie, Baroness *See* **"Fane, Violet"**
Curtis, Christine Turner
Villa Sciarra; Rome.
Curtis, George William
Ebb and Flow.
Egyptian Serenade.
Curtis, Mabel
Wings of the Morning.
Curtis, Mary Isabel
Trees Used in Games and Sports.
Curtis, Thelma
God's Will Is Best.
Curtwright [*or* Curtright], Wesley
Close of Day, The.
Four-Leaf Clover.
Heart of the Woods.
Curzon, George Nathaniel, Marquis Curzon
On an Insignificant Fellow.
Cusack, Cyril
Cross Talk.
Cushman, Charlotte
God's Work.
Cushman, Ralph Spaulding
Christmas Prayer.
His Presence Came like Sunrise.
I Love a Tree.
I Will Not Hurry.
Let Us Pray.
Parson's Prayer, The.
Preacher's Prayer, A.
Secret, The.
Sheer Joy.
Too Busy?
Cussons, Sheila
1945.
Cust, Henry
Non Nobis.
Custance, Olive (Lady Alfred Douglas)
Parting Hour, The.
Primrose Hill.
Twilight.
Waking of Spring, The.
Cuthbertson, James Lister
Bush, The.
Corona Inutilis.
Racing Eight, A.
Wattle and Myrtle.
Cuthriell, J. F.
My Mother.
Cutler, Eldridge Jefferson
Volunteer, The.
Cutler, Julian S.
Through the Year.
Cutter, Walter A.
Loyalties.
Cutts, John, Baron Cutts
Innocent Gazer, The.
Only Tell Her That I Love.
Song: "Only tell her that I love."
Cynewulf
Battle-fear mounted.
Christ, *sels.*
Christ Tells of His Passion.
Constantine's Vision of the Cross.
Death of Saint Guthlac.
Elene, *sels.*
Fates of the Apostles, *sel.*
Guthlac, *sel.*
Heaven.
Helena Embarks for Palestine.
Human Race Comes to Be Judged, The.
I have great need that the Saint grant help.
Juliana, *sel.*
King was frightened, The.
Last Judgment, The.
Maiden Ring-adorned, A.
Now I pray the man who may love this lay.
Prayer to Christ Our Lord, *mod.*
Ruler of warriors then called the wisest, The.
Then had passed by, in the course of years.
Then the glorious King, Constantine.
Then the wisest, before the assembly.
Thus wisely they taught the victorious King.
"To thee, Constantine, the King of Angels."
Voyage of Life, The.
Czamanske, W. M.
Higher Calling, The.

D

"D., D. "
Boston Boy Went out to Yuma, A.
"D., H." *See* **Doolittle, Hilda**
"D., J. "
Essay on the Fleet Riding in the Downes, An.
"D., M. P. "
Little Mother.
"D. N. R." *See* **"R., D. N"**
Dabney, Betty Page
Earth's Bondman.
Dacre, Harry
Daisy Bell.
Dadié, Bernard
Dry Your Tears, Africa!
I Give You Thanks My God.
Daeubler, Theodore
Beech, The.
Dafydd ap [*or* ab] Gwilym
Garland of Peacock Feathers, A.
Mass of the Grove, The.
Reproach to Morvyth, A.
Stars, The.
Woodland Mass, The.
"Dagonet." *See* **Sims, George Robert**
"Dahl, Basil" (Joseph Ovshover)
Revolution.
Daiches, David
Cosmogony.
Final Thoughts on the Weather in England during 1953.
Thoughts on Progress.
To Kate, Skating Better than Her Date.
Volume II (Kinsey).
Winter Song.
Daigaku, Horiguchi
Muddy Rat, The.
Daihaku, Princess
Crossing the Mountain Alone.
Daiken, Leslie
Bohernabreena.
June Song of a Man Who Looks Two Ways.
Larch Hill.
Lines to My Father.
Lines Written in a Country Parson's Orchard.
Nostalgie d'Automne.
Spring, St. Stephen's Green.
Dainty, Evelyn
Birds on the School Windowsill, The.
Dakiki [*or* Daqiqi]
On His Love.
Wine.
Dakin, Laurence
All night I raced the moon.
How gently sings my soul and whets its wings.
How sweetly sings this stream.
Peasant sun went crushing grapes, The.
Pyramus and Thisbe, *sel.*
Song: "Peasant sun went crushing grapes, The."
Tancred, *sels.*
Dalcour, Pierre
Verse Written in the Album of Mademoiselle ——.
Dale, Arthur B.
Torch, The.
Daley, Edith
Miracle.
Praise.
Daley, Victor James
A-Roving.
Ascetic, The.
Day and Night.
Dreams.
Faith.
In a Wine Cellar.
Muses of Australia, The.
Narcissus and Some Tadpoles.
Night, *sel.*
Suns, planets, stars, in glorious array.
Tamerlane.
Dallas, Fred
Smithfield Market Fire, The.
Dallas, Mary Kyle
He'd Nothing but His Violin.
Dallas, Ruth
Farmyard.
Grandmother and Child.
Milking before Dawn.
Roads.
World's Centre, The.
Dalmon, Charles
Almond Blossoms.
Ballad of the Epiphany.
Caterpillar's Apology for Eating a Favorite Gladiolus, A.
Cow at Sullington, A.
Early Morning Meadow Song.
Elegy for Edward Thomas, *sel.*
Legend of Cherries, A.
O What If the Fowler?
Snowfall on Plum Trees After They Had Bloomed, A.
Stanzas from "Elegy for Edward Thomas."
Sussex Legend, A.
Three Pictures.
Wistaria Blossoms.
Dalton, Annie Charlotte
For an Eskimo.
Neighing North, The.
Praying-Mantis, The.
Robin's Egg, The.
Sounding Portage, The.
To the Young Man Jesus.
"Dalton, Power" (Harold Caleb Dalton)
Finite.
Flail.

Dalven, Rae
My Father.
Daly, Eugene Howell
Alpheus and Arethusa.
Daly, James
Eagle, The.
Daly, James Jeremiah
In Coventry.
Latin Tongue, The.
Nox Ignatiana.
October of the Angels.
Daly, John
Toast to the Flag, A.
Daly, June
Wildebeest, The.
Daly, Thomas Augustin
Between Two Loves.
Blossomy Barrow, The.
Boy from Rome, Da.
Child's Christmas Song, A.
Comica Man, Da.
Day of the Circus Horse, The.
Een Napoli.
Flag o' My Land.
Greata Stronga Man, Da.
Leetla Boy, Da.
Leetla Giorgio Washeenton.
Man's Prayer, The.
Mia Carlotta.
October.
On the Road to Arden.
Peaceable Race, The.
Poet, The.
Pup een da Snow, Da.
Sanctum, The.
Song of the Thrush, The.
Song to One, A.
Tides of Love, The.
To a Plain Sweetheart.
To a Robin.
To a Thrush.
To th' Minstrel Girl.
Two Days.
Two 'Mericana Men.
Dalziel, Kathleen
He Could Have Found His Way.
Damadian, Mihran
Imprisoned Revolutionist, The, *abr.*
Damas, Léon
Poems.
Put Down.
They Came This Evening.
Damascene, Saint John *See* **John of Damascus, Saint**
Damon, Samuel Foster
Bridge.
Dana, Katherine Floyd *See* **"Wadsworth, Olive A."**
Dana, Richard Henry
Buccaneer, The, *sel.*
Chanting Cherubs, The—A Group by Greenough.
Immortality.
Island, The.
Little Beach Bird, The.
Moss Supplicateth for the Poet, The.
Dana, Robert Patrick
Notes on a Child's Coloring Book.
On the Expressway.
Unbroken Code, The.
Winter's Tale, A.
Dancer, John
Ha! now you think you've cheated me. Oh, no!
Variety, The.
Wish, The.
Dancy, Walter K.
Jazz Coltrane Sings.
Dandridge, Danske Bedlinger
Dead Moon, The.
On the Eve of War.
Spirit of the Fall, The.
Dandridge, Ray Garfield
Drum Majah, De.
'Ittle Touzle Head.
Sprin' Fevah.
Time to Die.
Zalka Peetruza.
"Dane, Barry." *See* **Logan, John Edward**
"Dane, Clemence" (Winifred Ashton)
Salute to Greece.
Danforth, John
Few Lines to Fill up a Vacant Page, A.
Mercies of the Year, The.
On My Lord Bacon.
Poem upon the Triumphant Translation of . . . Mrs. Anne Eliot, A.
Profit and Loss: An Elegy upon the Decease of Mrs. Mary Gerrish.
Two Vast Enjoyments Commemorated.
Danforth, Samuel (1626-1674)
Almanac Verse.
Danforth, Samuel (1666-1727)
Ad Librum.
Elegy in Memory of the Worshipful Major Thomas Leonard Esq., An.
Dangerfield, George
To Ultima Thule.
Daniel, Arnaut
Aura amara, L'.
Autet e bas.
Bel m'es quan lo vens m'alena.
Canzo of Bird-Songs and Love.
Mot eran dous miei cossir.
Daniel, George
Anti-Platonicke.
Pure Platonicke.
Robin, The.
Daniel, Samuel
And forth h' is brought unto th' accomplishment.
Are They Shadow[e]s [That We See]?
Beauty, Time, and Love (7 *sonnets*).
Beauty's Glass.
But love whilst that thou may'st [*or* maist] be loved again[e].
Care-Charmer Sleep [Son of the Sable Night.].
Chorus: "Behold what furies still."
Chorus: "How dost thou wear and weary out thy days."
Chorus: "Then thus we have beheld."
Civil Wars, The, *sels.*
Cleopatra, *sels.*
Complaint of Rosamund, The, *abr.*
Constancy.
Delia.
Description of Beauty, A.
Early Love.
Eidola.
English Poetry.
Enjoy Thy April Now.
Epistle to Henry Wriothesley, Earl of Southampton.
Eyes, Hide My Love.
Fading Beauty.
Fair Is My Love.
First Flame.
Had Sorrow Ever Fitter Place.
Half-blown Rose, The.
Henry's Lament.
High Mind, The.
How many thousands never heard the name.
Hymen's Triumph, *sels.*
I sing the civil wars, tumultuous broils.
Knowing the heart of man is set to be.
Lonely Beauty.
Love.
Love Is a Sickness[e].
Most Unloving One, The.
Musophilus, or Defence of All Learning, *abr.*
O Fearfull, Frowning Nemesis.
Ode, An: "Now each creature joys the other."
Philotas.
Poet and Critic.
Poetry of England, The.
Richard II as Captive.
Rosamond's Appeal.
Secrecy.
Shadows.
Song: "Are they shadowes that we see?"
Song: "Love is a sickness full of woes."
Sonnet: "And yet I cannot reprehend the flight."
Sonnet: "Beauty, sweet love, is like the morning dew."
Sonnet: "But love whilst that thou may'st [*or* maist] be loved again."
Sonnet: "Care-charmer Sleep, son of the sable Night."
Sonnet: "Drawn with th' attractive virtue of her eyes."
Sonnet: "Fair and lovely maid, look from the shore."
Sonnet: "Fair is my Love, and cruel as she's fair."
Sonnet: "I must not grieve my Love, whose eyes would read."
Sonnet: "I once may see when years shall wreck my wrong."
Sonnet: "Let others sing of knights and paladins."
Sonnet: "Look, Delia, how we esteem the half-blown rose."
Sonnet: "My spotless love hovers, with purest wings."
Sonnet: "O had she not been fair and thus unkind."
Sonnet: "Reign in my thoughts, fair hand, sweet eye, rare voice!"
Sonnet: "Star of my mishap impos'd this paining, The."
Sonnet: "Unto the boundless ocean of thy beauty."
Sonnet: "When men shall find thy flower, thy glory, pass."
Sonnet: "When winter snows upon thy sable hairs [*or* golden hears]."
Sonnets.
Sonnets to Delia.
Sorrow.
Tethys' Festival, *sel.*
To Delia, *sels.*
To His Reader.
To Sir Thomas Egerton.
To the Lady Lucy, Countess of Bedford.
To the Lady Margaret, Countess of Cumberland.
To the Reader.
To the Right Honorable, the Lady Mary, Countess of Pembroke.
To the Right Worthy and Judicious Favorer of Virtue, Master [*or* Maister] Fulke Greville.
To the Right Worthy Knight Sir Fulke Greville.
Tragedie of Philotas, The, *sels.*
Tragedy of Cleopatra, The.
Ulysses and the Siren.
Who ever saw so fair a sight.
Daniel ben Judah
Living God, The.
Daniell, Edith
Inspect Us.
Daniell, Eric H.
Silent Stars, The.
Daniells, Roy
Buffalo.
Deeper into the Forest.

Daniells (continued)
Ducks.
Farewell to Winnipeg.
Mole, The.
Noah.
Sonnet: "I never swung a staff and deep, oh deep."
Sonnet: "See the white stillness of the unicorn."
Sonnet: "Under the bark remembers now my heart."
Summer Days.
Daniels, Roy
Journey.
Dannecker, Hazel I.
Balloon Man.
Danner, James
My Brother.
Singer, The.
Danner, Margaret
Dance of the Abakweta.
Elevator Man Adheres to Form, The.
Etta Moten's Attic.
Far from Africa: Four Poems.
Garnishing the Aviary.
I'll Walk the Tightrope.
Sadie's Playhouse.
Slave and the Iron Lace, The.
These Beasts and the Benin Bronze.
Through the Varied Patterned Lace.
Visit of the Professor of Aesthetics, The.
D'Annunzio, Gabriele
Evening in May.
Morgana.
September.
Danquah, Joseph V. B.
Way of Life, The.
Dansui
Even before His Majesty.
Dante da Maiano *See* **Maiano, Dante da**
Dante Alighieri
All Ye That Pass.
Already was Tithonus' mistress fair.
At whiles (yea oftentimes) I muse over.
Ballata: He Will Gaze upon Beatrice.
Being Underived.
"Canst thou indeed be he that still would sing."
Canzone: He Beseeches Death for the Life of Beatrice.
Canzone: To the Lady Pietra, of Sienna.
Celestial Pilot, The.
Dante and Beatrice in the Earthly Paradise.
Dante's Angels.
Dante's Heaven.
Day agone, as I rode sullenly, A.
Death, Always Cruel.
Divided Thoughts.
Divina Commedia, *sels.*
Even as the Others Mock.
Eyes that weep for pity of the heart, The.
For certain he hath seen all perfectness.
Francesca da Rimini.
How haughty was thy mien.
I Felt a Spirit of Love Begin to Stir.
In the midway of this our mortal life.
Inferno.
Into the justice of eternity.
Ladies That Have Intelligence in Love.
Love's pallor and the semblance of deep ruth.
Midway the Journey.
Mine Eyes Beheld the Blessed Pity.
My Lady Carries Love.
New Life, The.
"Now say," he said, "were it not worse indeed."
O petty blood-nobility of ours!
One World.
Paolo and Francesca.
Paradise.
Paradiso, *sels.*
Pier delle Vigne.
Political Chaos in Italy.
Primal Cause, The.
Purgatorio, *sels.*
Saint Bernard's Prayer to Our Lady.
Saints in Glory, The.
Sestina; of the Lady Pietra degli Scrovigni.
Song, 'tis my will that thou do seek out Love.
Sonnet: "Beatrice is gone up into high Heaven."
Sonnet: "Because mine eyes can never have their fill."
Sonnet: "Beyond the sphere which spreads to widest space."
Sonnet: "Last All Saints' holy-day, even now gone by."
Sonnet: "Mine eyes beheld the blessed pity spring."
Sonnet: "My lady looks so gentle and so pure."
Sonnet: Of Beatrice de Portinari on All Saints' Day.
Sonnet: Of Beauty and Duty.
Sonnet: On the 9th of June 1290.
Sonnet: To Brunetto Latini.
Sonnet: To Certain Ladies.
Sonnet: To Guido Cavalcanti.
Sonnet: To the Lady Pietra degli Scrovigni.
Sonnet: To the Same Ladies.
Sonnet: "With sighs my bosom always laboureth."
Sonnet: "Wonderfully out of the beautiful form."
Stay now with me, and list to my sighs.
That lady of all gentle memories.
That she hath gone to Heaven suddenly.
"Thou Virgin Mother, daughter of thy Son."
Thoughts are broken in my memory, The.
To Beatrice on All Saints' Day.
To Every Heart.
'Twas now the hour that turneth back desire.
Veracious people, The.
Very bitter weeping that ye made, The.
Very pitiful lady, very young, A.
Virgil's Farewell to Dante.
Vision of God, The.
Vision of the Divine Mystery.
Vita Nuova, La, *sels.*
Weep, lovers, sith Love's very self doth weep.
Whatever while the thought comes over me.
While I was all absorbed in seeing him.
Within Her Eyes.
Woe's me! by dint of all those sighs that come.
Ye pilgrim-folk, advancing pensively.
Ye pilgrims, who with pensive aspect go.
You that thus wear a modest countenance.
Danyel, John
Can Doleful Notes to Mesur'd Accents Set.
Chromatic Tunes.
Da Ponte, Lorenzo
Capriccio Dramatico, Il, *sel.*
Don Giovanni, *sel.*
Giovinette, che fate all' amore.
To an Artful Theatre Manager.
Darby, Charles
Bacchanalia; or, A Description of a Drunken Club, *sel.*
But by this time tongues 'gan to rest.
Darby, John Nelson
Egypt Left Behind.
D'Arcy, Hugh Antoine
Face on the Floor, The.
D'Arcy, Jack
Conservative Shepherd to His Love, The, *parody.*
Darcy, Louise
To a Mole.
Dargan, Olive Tilford
Duo.
New Freedom, The.
Path Flower.
Rescue.
To William Blake.
Dargan, Vere
City Trees.
Darío, Rubén (Félix Rubén García Sarmiento)
Afternoon in the Tropics.
Alleluya.
Murmur from the Stable, The.
Portico.
Slings.
Sonatina.
Symphony in Gray Major.
To Columbus.
To Roosevelt.
United States are rich, they're powerful and great, The.
Darley, George
As from the moist and gelid sleep.
Call of the Morning, The.
Chorus of Sirens.
Chorus of Spirits.
Consolation.
Deadman's Dirge.
Dirge: "Wail! wail ye o'er the dead!"
Dove's Loneliness, The.
Ecstasie, rash production of the thoughts.
Elfin Pedlar, The.
Enchanted Lyre, The.
Enchanted Spring, The.
Errors of Ecstasie, *sel.*
Ethelstan, *sel.*
Fallen Star, The.
Flower of Beauty, The.
Hoopoe.
Hundred-sunned Phenix.
Hurry Me Nymphs.
In Dreamy Swoon.
It Is Not Beauty I Demand.
Last Night.
Lay of the Forlorn.
Lilian's Song.
Lines: "Hurry me Nymphs! O, hurry me."
List no more the ominous din.
Loveliness of Love, The.
Love's Likeness.
Lyre, The.
Mermaidens' Vesper-Hymn, The.
Morning-Song.
Nepenthe, *sels.*
Nephon's Song.
O Blest Unfabled Incense Tree.
O'er the Wild Gannet's Bath.
On the Death of a Recluse.
Onward to Far Ida.
Phoenix, The ("O blest unfabled incense tree").
Phoenix, The ("O fast her amber blood doth flow").
Queen Eleanor and Her Dwarf.
Robin's Cross.
Romanzo to Sylvia.
Runilda's Chant.
Sea-Ritual, The.
Serenade: "Awake thee, my Lady-love."

Serenade of a Loyal Martyr.
Siren Chorus.
Solitary Lyre, The.
Song: "Down the dimpled green-sward dancing."
Song, A: "It is not beauty I demand."
Song: "I've taught thee love's sweet lesson o'er."
Song: "Streams that wind among the hills, The."
Song: "Sweet in her green dell the flower of beauty slumbers."
Song of the Mermaids.
Summer Winds.
Sylvia; or, The May Queen, *sels.*
Syren Songs, *sels.*
Thomas à Becket, *sel.*
Thou whose thrilling hand in mine.
To ——: "Thou whom of all the beings I have seen."
To Helene.
To Mie Tirante.
To Poets.
To the Moon.
Unicorn, The.
Wherefore, Unlaurelled Boy.
Winds of the West, Arise.

Darling, Margaret Stanion
Country Lane.

Darmesteter, Agnes Mary Frances Robinson *See* **Robinson, Agnes Mary Frances**

Darnley, Henry Stuart [*or* Stewart], Lord
Gife Langour.
To the Queen.

Darring, Walter
Surprised by Me.

Darrough, Rose
Only Heaven Is Given Away.

Darwin, Erasmus
Botanic Garden, The, *sels.*
Economy of Vegetation, The.
Eliza.
French Revolution, The.
Immortal Nature.
Loves of the Plants, The.
Stay thy Soft Murmuring.
Steam Power.
Vegetable Loves.
Whale, The.

Darwin, Frances *See* **Cornford, Frances**

Daryush, Elizabeth
Autumn, Dark Wanderer.
Eyes That Queenly Sit.
Farewell for a While.
Fresh Spring.
Frustration.
November.
O Strong to Bless.
Still-Life.

Das, Kamala
With Its Quiet Tongue.

Daswani, Tilottama
I, Pluto.

Daubeny, Charles
Verses on a Cat.

Daugherty, James Henry
Gates of the Rockies.
Missouri Rhapsody.
Texas.
Trail Breakers.
Wheel Ruts.

D'Auria, Gemma
Subject for Prophecy.

Davenant [*or* D'Avenant], Sir William
Aubade.
Awake! Awake!
By what bold passion am I rudely led.
Christians Reply to the Phylosopher, The.
Cruel Brother, The, *sel.*
Dying Lover, The.
Endimion Porter and Olivia.
Epitaph: "When you perceive these stones are wet."
For the Lady Olivia Porter; a Present upon a New-Years Day.
From Brescia swiftly o're the bord'ring plain.
Gondibert, *sels.*
Jealousy.
Lark Now Leaves His Wat'ry [*or* Watery] Nest, The.
Law against Lovers, The, *sel.*
Life and Death.
Love.
Lover and Philosopher.
Morning.
Morning Song.
News from Plymouth, *sel.*
O Thou That Sleep'st like Pig in Straw.
Of all the Lombards, by their trophies knowne.
Philosopher and the Lover, The; to a Mistress Dying.
Philosopher's Disquisition Directed to the Dying Christian, The, *sel.*
Praise and Prayer.
Rivals, The, *sel.*
Siege of Rhodes, The, *sel.*
Song: "Before we shall again behold."
Song: Endimion Porter and Olivia.
Song: "Lark now leaves his wat'ry nest, The."
Song: "My lodging it is on the cold ground."
Song: "O thou that sleep'st like pig in straw."
Song: "Roses and pinks will be strewn where you go."
Song: Souldier Going to the Field The.
Song: "Wake all the dead! What hoa! What hoa!"
Souldier Going to the Field, The.
Storm at Sea.
Tell me, why Heav'n at first did suffer sin?
To a Mistress Dying.
To streets (the people's region) early fame.
To the Queen.
To the Queen, Entertain'd at Night by the Countess of Anglesey.
Tomorrow and Tomorrow.
Under the Willow Shades.
Unfortunate Lovers, The, *sels.*
Wake All the Dead.
What Is Past.
Willow, The.
Winter Storms, The.

Davenport, Mariana B.
Suspended Moment.

Davenport, R. A.
Serious Danger, A.

Davenport, Robert
King John and Matilda, *sel.*
Requiem.

David, Beatrix Demarest
Night-Wind.

David, Sister Mary
Plain Chant of the Hill Country.

David ben Meshullam
Be Not Silent.

Davida, Sister
In Gusts of Music.

Davidman, Joy
Prayer against Indifference.

Davidson, Donald
Apple and Mole.
Cross Section of a Landscape.
Fire on Belmont Street.
John Darrow.
Lee in the Mountains.
On a Replica of the Parthenon.
Spoken at a Castle Gate.
Tall Men, The *sel.*
Wolf, The.

Davidson, Edward
In This Dark House.

Davidson, Francis
Beggars.

Davidson, Gustav
Ambushed by Angels.
Downgoing.
From Nothing Strange.
Nevertheless.
Ritual.
Somewhere I Chanced to Read.

Davidson, John
Ballad of a Nun, A.
Ballad of Heaven, A.
Ballad of Hell, A.
Butterflies.
Christmas Eve.
Cinque Port, A.
Crystal Palace, The.
Dedication to the Generation Knocking at the Door.
Eclogue: Merchantman, The.
Eclogue: Queen Elizabeth's Day.
Epping Forest.
Harvest-Home Song.
Holiday.
I step into my heart and there I meet.
Imagination.
In Romney Marsh.
In the Isle of Dogs.
Last Journey, The.
Last Rose, The.
London.
Merchantman, The.
New Year's Eve, *sel.*
Northern Suburb, A.
November, *sel.*
On Entering a Chapel.
Outcast, The.
Piper, Play.
Runnable Stag, A.
St. Michael's Mount.
Song: "Boat is chafing at our long delay, The."
Song: "Closes and courts and lanes."
Song of a Train.
Summer.
Testament of John Davidson, The, *sel.*
Thirty Bob a Week.
To the New Men.
To the New Women.
Unknown, The.
Waiting.
War Song.

Davidson, Margaret Gilman
Moritura.

Davie, Donald
After an Accident.
At Knaresborough.
Bolyai, the Geometer.
Corrib: An Emblem.
Evangelist, The.
For an Age of Plastics. Plymouth.
For Doreen.
Fountain, The.
Garden Party, The.
Gardens No Emblems.
Hearing Russian Spoken.
Heigh-ho on a Winter Afternoon.
Homage to William Cowper.
Life of Service, The.
Mushroom Gatherers, The.
New York in August.
Rain on South-East England.
Remembering the 'Thirties.
River, The.
Time Passing, Beloved ("Time passing,

Davie (continued)
and the memories of love").
Wind at Penistone, The.
Winter Talent, A.
Woodpigeons at Raheny.
Davieau, Robert Stiles
Arizona Village.
Davies, Idris
Gwalia Deserta, *sel.*
Lay Preacher Ponders, The.
Davies, John, of Hereford
Against Gaudy, Bragging, Undoughty Daccus.
Against Mustolphus His Lying.
Against the Fantastical Attire That Many Ladies Wear Nowadays.
Although we do not all the good we love.
Author Loving These Homely Meats [Specially], The.
Homely Meats.
In Rainy-gloomy Weather.
Lies have short wings. He lies that so sings.
Little or nothing said soon mended is.
Of a Flatterer.
Of the Small Respect Had of Learned Men in General.
Some blaze the precious beauties of their loves.
Sonnet: "It is as true as strange, else trial feigns."
Sonnet: "So shoots a star as doth my mistress glide."
Spend and God will send, but wot ye what follow.
To Old John Heywood the Epigrammatist, Wheresoever.
To Our English Terence, Master William Shakespeare.
Davies, Sir John
Dauncing (bright Lady) then began to be[e].
For why should we the busy soul believe.
If you would know the love which I you bear.
Oft did I hear our eyes the passage were.
Once did my Philomel reflect on me.
"Or from what spring doth your opinion rise."
Sickness, intending my love to betray.
To Envy.
We seek to know the moving of each sphere.
Yet, once again, Antinous did reply.
Acclamation, An.
Ad Musam.
Affliction.
Contention between Four Maids Concerning That which Addeth Most Perfection to That Sex.
Contention betwixt a Wife, a Widow, and a Maid, A.
Dance of Love, The.
Dancing Sea, The.
Dedication: "Strongest and the noblest argument, The."
Dedication: "To that clear majesty which in the north."
Dedications [*of* Orchestra].
Elizabethan Week-End.
Gulling Sonnets, *sels.*
Hymns of [*or* to] Astraea, *sels.*
I Know Myself a Man.
Immortality of the Soul, The ("For why should we the busy soul believe").
In Ciprium.
In Dacum.
In Decium.
In Flaccum.
In Gerontem.
In Haywodum.
In Rufum.
In Severum.
In Titum.
In What Manner the Soul Is United to the Body.
Knowledge and Reason.
Man.
Mariner's Song, The.
Meditations of a Gull.
Much Knowledge, Little Reason.
Muse Reviving, The.
Nosce Teipsum.
Of a Gull.
Of Astraea.
Of Homer's Odyssey.
Of Human Knowledge.
Of Tabacco.
Of the Soul of Man and the Immortality Thereof.
On a Pair of Garters.
Orchestra; or, A Poem of [*or* on] Dancing.
Sea Danceth, The.
Sight.
Sonnets to Philomel, *sels.*
Soul and the Body, The.
That the Soul Is Immortal, and Cannot Die.
To Astraea.
To His Good Friend, Sir Anthony Cooke.
To His Lady.
To His Very Friend, Master Richard Martin.
To My Most Gracious Dread Sovereign.
To Queen Elizabeth.
To the Lark.
To the Nightingale.
To the Prince.
To the Rose.
To the Spring.
Vanity of Human Learning, The.
Which Is a Proud, and Yet a Wretched Thing.
Davies, Mary Carolyn
After All and After All.
Be Different to Trees.
David.
Day before April, The.
Dead Make Rules, The.
Door, The.
Door-Mats.
Easter.
Feet.
Fishing Pole, The.
Gown, The.
Gymnastic Clock, The.
Hunger.
If I Had Known.
If I Were Santa's Little Boy.
I'll Wear a Shamrock.
June.
Leading.
Left Out.
Let Me Be a Giver.
Let's Have a Picnic Out-of-Doors.
Man's Woman, A.
Men Are the Devil.
New Year, A.
Out of the Earth.
Prayer for a Marriage, A.
Prayer for a Sleeping Child, A.
Prayer for Every Day, A.
Rust.
Saturday's Party in Fairyland, The.
Seeking.
Six in June.
Stars, The.
Terrible Dead, The.
To Give One's Life.
Traps.
Tree Birthdays.
Vow for New Year's, A.
We.
What the Christmas Tree Thinks.
Davies, Sneyd
At Seeing Archbishop Williams's Monument at Carnarvonshire.
On Dr. Crank's Victory over the Gout.
Rhapsody to Milton.
To a Gentleman in Love with a Negro Woman.
Davies, William Henry
Ambition.
Battle, The.
Beautiful, The.
Best Friend, The.
Bird of Paradise, The.
Body and Spirit.
Born of Tears.
Bust, The.
Butterflies.
Cant.
Chant, A.
Chase, The.
Child and the Mariner, The.
Child's Pet, A.
Christ the Man.
Come, Let Us Find.
Days That Have Been.
Days Too Short.
Dog, The.
Dragonfly, The.
Dreams of the Sea.
Elements, The.
Epitaph, An: "Beneath this stone lies one good man; and when."
Example, The.
Eyes.
F is for Fiddler.
Facts.
Fancy's Home.
Flirt, The.
Flying Blossoms.
Fog, The.
Foliage, *sel.*
Frost.
Ghost, The.
Great Time, A.
Greeting, A.
Happy Child, The.
Happy Wind.
Heap of Rags, The.
Her Merriment.
Hermit, The.
Hospital Waiting-Room, The.
Hour of Magic, The.
I Am the Poet Davies, William.
In May.
In the Snow.
Inquest, The.
Jenny Wren.
Joy and Pleasure.
Kingfisher, The.
Lamorna Cove.
Leaves.
Lesiure.
Likeness, The.
Little Ones, The.
Love Lights His Fire.
Lovely Dames.
Lovely Woman, A.
Love's Caution.
Loyalty.
Maiden and Her Hair, A.
Mangers.
Mind's Liberty, The.
Mirror, The.
Money.
Moon, The.
Mourner, The.
Muse, The.
Music's Tragedy.
My Garden.

My love could walk in richer hues.
Nature's Friend.
No Master.
Oh, Sweet Content.
On a Cold Day.
On Hearing Mrs. Woodhouse Play the Harpsichord.
One Poet Visits Another.
One Token.
Peace and Rest.
Peacemaker, The.
Poet, The.
Pond, The.
Poor Kings.
Power of Silence, The.
Rabbit, The.
Rain, The.
Rainbow, The.
Rat, The.
Rich Days.
Sailor to His Parrot, The.
School's Out.
Sheep.
Sleepers, The.
Sluggard, The.
Songs of Joy.
Speed.
Sweet Stay-at-Home.
Thought, A.
Thunderstorms.
To a Lady Friend.
To Sparrows Fighting.
To the Wind at Morn.
Trick, The.
Truly Great.
Truth, The.
Tugged Hand, The.
Two Stars, The.
Villain, The.
When Diamonds, Nibbling in My Ears.
When Yon Full Moon.
White Cascade, The.
White Monster, The.
Wild Oats.
Wind, The.
Y Is for Youth.

Davies-Woodrow, Constance *See* **Woodrow, Constance Davies**

Davis, Catherine
After a Time.
Insights.
Kindness.
Nausea.

Davis, Charles S.
Washington's Birthday.

Davis, Chester M.
Easter Prayer, An.

Davis, Daniel Webster
Hog Meat.
'Weh Down Souf.

Davis, Edna Ethel
Lore.

Davis, Emily *See* **Pfeiffer, Emily**

Davis, F. W.
Thankful Heart.

Davis, Fannie Stearns
Circus, The.
Evening Song.
For a Child.
Forbidden Lure, The.
Moods, The.
Moon Folly.
Narrow Doors, The.
Pupil to His Master, The.
Songs of Conn the Fool, The, *sel.*
Souls.
Turn of the Road, The.

Davis, Florence Boyce
Legend of the Christmas Rose, The.
Sunsets.
This and That.
Three Wise Monkeys, The.

Davis, Francis
Nanny.

Davis, Frank Marshall
Arthur Ridgewood, M.D.
Flowers of Darkness.
Four Glimpses of Night.
Giles Johnson, Ph.D.
I Sing No New Songs.
Midsummer Morn.
Rain.
Robert Whitmore.
Tenement Room; Chicago.

Davis, Gloria
To Egypt.

Davis, Gussie L.
In the Baggage Coach Ahead.

Davis, Harold Lenoir
By the River.
In the Field.
My Step-Grandfather.
Old Are Sleepy, The.
Proud Riders.
Running Vines [in a Field].
Spirit, The.
Valley Harvest, The.

Davis, Helen Bayley
Jack Frost.
Song for a Child.

Davis, J. C.
Cowboy Race, A.

Davis, John
Sun, The.

Davis, Julia Johnson
Loss.
She Sews Fine Linen.
To My Little Son.

Davis, Katherine
Act II.

Davis, Leland
Ballad of Adam's First, The.

Davis, Mary [*or* Mollie] Evelyn Moore
Counsel.

Davis, Norma L.
Daydreamers.
Dry Time.
This Is My Song.

Davis, Ozora Stearns
Brotherhood.
Courage.
Our Brother Christ.
Pathway to Paradise, The.
Today.
We Bear the Strain of Earthly Care.

Davis, Robert
I Thank Thee, Lord, for Strength of Arm.

Davis, Robert A.
Dust Bowl.
Pastorale: "Willow tree leans, A."

Davis, Robert H.
Roosevelt.

Davis, Roy
Retrospect.
Thoughts.

Davis, Thomas Osborne
Battle Eve of the [Irish] Brigade, The.
Boatman of Kinsale, The.
Clare's Dragoons.
Fate of King Dathi, The.
Fontenoy.
Geraldines, The, *sel.*
Geraldines, The! the Geraldines!—'tis full a thousand years.
Girl I Left behind Me, The ("The dames of France").
Irish Hurrah, The.
Lament for the Death of Eoghan Ruadh O'Neill.
My Grave.
My Land.
Oh! for a Steed.
O, the Marriage!
Sack of Baltimore, The.
This Native Land.
Tone's Grave.
Welcome, The.
West's Asleep, The.

Davison, Edward
Enchanted Heart, The.
Lovers, The.
Nocturne: "Be thou at peace this night."
Novice, The.
Snare, The.
Sonnet: "She is so young, and never never before."
Willow and Water.

Davison, Francis
Ah Cupid, I mistook thee.
Commendation of Her Beauty, Stature, Behavior, and Wit.
Her Commendation.
His Farewell to His Unkind and Unconstant Mistress.
In health and ease am I.
Like to the seely fly.
Madrigal V: Allusion to the Confusion of Babel.
Madrigal: "Some there are as fair to see to."
Madrigal: "Sound of thy sweet name, my dearest treasure, The."
Madrigal: To Cupid.
My Only Star.
Ode V: His Farewell to His Unkind and Unconstant Mistress.
Ode VIII: That All Other Creatures Have Their Abiding in Heaven, Hell, Earth, Air, Water, or Fire; but He in All of Them.
Song: "Lady, you are with beauties so enriched."
Sonnet I: Dedication of These Rimes to His First Love.
Sonnet III: Upon His Absence from Her.
"Sorrow seldom killeth any."
Sound of Thy Sweet Name, The.
Three Epitaphs upon the Death of a Rare Child of Six Years Old.
To Cupid.
To Samuel Daniel, Prince of English Poets.
Upon His Timorous Silence in Her Presence.

Davison, Francis Douglas
Bought.

Davison, Peter
Artemis.
Breaking of the Day, The.
Finale: Presto.
Lunch at the Coq D'or.
North Shore.
Peeper, The.
Pleaders, The.
Star Watcher, The.

Davison, Walter
At Her Fair Hands.
How Can the Heart Forget Her.
Ode: "At her fair hands."
Ode II: Dialogue between Him and His Heart, A.
Sonnet I: He Demands Pardon for Looking, Loving, and Writing.
Sonnet: Of His Lady's Weeping.
To His Lady, Who Had Vowed Virginity.

Dawe, Bruce
City, The: Midnight.
Only the Beards Are Different.

Dawes, Rufus
Love Unchangeable.

Dawson, Daniel Lewis
Seeker in the Marshes, The.

Dawson, Grace Strickler

Dawson (continued)
To a Friend.
Dawson, M. Phelps
After the Fourth of July.
Dawson, William James
Angel at the Ford, The.
Bird's Song at Morning.
Child's Portrait, A.
Deliverance.
Ideal Memory.
Inspirations.
To a Desolate Friend.
Day, Beth
Three Gates.
Day, Clarence
And/Or.
Historical Incidents.
Man Is but a Castaway.
Marco Polo.
Menelaus.
Might and Right ("Might and right are always fighting").
Our Friend the Egg.
Sad Story.
Day, Mrs. Donald A.
We'll Meet Them.
Day, Dorothea
Captain, The.
My Captain.
Day, George Edward
Brothers.
Master of Laborers, The.
Day, Holman F.
Grampy Sings a Song.
Day, John
Ditty, A: "Peace, peace, peace, make no noise."
High steward of thy vines.
Humour Out of Breath, *sel.*
I will have one built/ Like Pompey's theatre.
Parliament of Bees, The, *sels.*
This baseness follows your profession.
Day, John, Thomas Dekker, *and* Samuel Rowley *See* **Dekker, Thomas, Samuel Rowley, *and* John Day**
Day, Richard Edwin
England.
To Shakespeare.
Day, Sarah J.
Crocus.
Day, Thomas Fleming
Clipper, The.
Coasters, The.
Main-Sheet Song, The.
Making Land.
Day, William
Mount Vernon, the Home of Washington.
Day Lewis, Cecil
Album, The.
All Gone.
Almost Human.
As One Who Wanders into Old Workings.
Birthday Poem for Thomas Hardy.
Bombers.
But Two There Are. . .
Can the Mole Take.
Chiefly to Mind Appears.
Children look down upon the morning-grey.
Chorus: "Since you have come thus far."
Christmas Eve.
Christmas Tree, The.
Chrysanthemum Show, The.
Come, Live with Me and Be My Love.
Come Up, Methuselah.
Committee, The.
Conflict, The.
Consider These, for We Have Condemned [Them].
Cornet Solo.
Dead, The.
Departure in the Dark.
Desire Is a Witch.
Do Not Expect Again a Phoenix Hour.
Double Vision, The.
Edward Elgar.
Emily Brontë.
Few Things Can More Inflame.
Flight, The.
Flight to Australia.
For those who had the power.
From Feathers to Iron, *sels.*
Great Magicians, The.
Happy View, A.
Hard Frost, A.
I walk these many rooms, wishing to trace.
In Heaven, I Suppose, Lie Down [Together].
In Me Two Worlds.
In the Chaotic Age.
In the Heart of Contemplation.
In the Shelter.
In These Our Winter Days.
Is It Far to Go?
It Is Becoming Now to Declare My Allegiance.
I've Heard Them Lilting at Loom and Belting.
Jig.
Let Us Be Off!
"Let Us Now Praise Famous Men."
Live you by love confined.
Love Was Once Light as Air.
Magnetic Mountain, The, *sels.*
Maple and Sumach.
Marriage of Two.
Meeting, A.
Misfit, The—1939-1945.
My Love Is a Tower.
Nabara, The.
Naked, he sags across her cumbered knees.
Nearing Again the Legendary Isle.
Neurotic, The.
Newsreel.
Noah and the Waters, *sel.*
Now I Have Come to Reason.
Now She Is Like the White Tree-Rose.
O Dreams, O Destinations.
Oh Light Was My Head.
On the Sea Wall.
One and One.
Overtures to Death.
Pegasus.
Pieta, *sel.*
Poet, The.
Reconciliation.
Rest from Loving and Be Living.
Room, The.
Saint Anthony's Shirt, *sel.*
Saints and heroes, you dare say.
Seen from the Train.
Singing Children: Luca Della Robbia (T. H.).
Sitting, The.
Sky-wide an Estuary.
Son and Father.
Sonnet: "To travel like a bird, lightly to view."
Statuette; Late Minoan.
Sun Came Out in April, The.
Symbols of gross experience!—our grief.
Tempt Me No More.
Third Enemy Speaks.
This man was strong, and like a seacape parted.
This Young Girl.
Though Bodies Are Apart.
Though Winter's Barricade Delays.
Time to Dance, A, *sels.*
Transitional Poem, *sel.*
Two Songs.
Two Travelers.
Unexploded Bomb, The.
Unwanted, The.
When nature plays hedge-schoolmaster.
When They Have Lost.
With Me My Lover Makes.
Word over All.
You That Love England.
Dayre, Sydney
Remorse.
Dayton, Irene
Ear Is Not Deaf.
Deamer, Dulcie
Artemis.
Dean, Agnes Louise
October Night.
Dean, Elma
Elder Brother, The (Poem for All Good and Loyal Dogs).
Old Men's Ward.
Dean, J. E.
Dwell in the Depths.
Deane, Anthony C.
Ballad of Jack and Jill, The.
Ballad of [*or* to] the *Billycock,* The.
Ballad to the *Billycock,* The.
Here Is the Tale, *parody.*
Imitation.
Jack and Jill—as Kipling Might Have Written It.
Rural Bliss.
Rustic Song, A.
Dearmer, Geoffrey
Giraffe, The.
Vision, A.
Whale.
Dearmer, Percy
Servants of the Great Adventure.
De Bary, Anna Bunston
As Rivers of Water in a Dry Place.
Bargain, The.
In the Heart.
Primrose by the Wayside, A.
Snowdrop.
"Thou Shalt Purge Me with Hyssop and I Shall Be Clean."
Under a Wiltshire Apple Tree.
War-Time Prayer, A.
We Are Alone.
De Béranger, Pierre Jean *See* **Béranger, Pierre Jean de**
De Bragança, Nadejda *See* **Bragança, Nadejda de**
De Bruché, Countess *See* **Stoner, Winifred Sackville**
DeBurgh, H. J.
Half Hours with the Classics.
De Casseres, Benjamin
Moth-Terror.
De Cheney, Mrs. C. L.
Storm Thrush, The.
Decimus Magnus Ausonius *See* **Ausonius, Decimus Magnus**
Deck, James G.
King in His Beauty, The.
Decker, Bessie B.
Disillusion.
Dederick, Robert
Karoo Town.
Robben Island.
Deems, Charles F.
On Life's Way.
Worry.
Defoe, Daniel
English Race, The.
Hail hi'roglyphick state machin.

Hymn to the Pillory, A, *sel.*
Kentish Petition, The, 1701, *sel.*
Satire, be kind and draw a silent veil.
'Tis fatal to tyrannic power, when they.
True-born Englishman, The, *sels.*
Wherever God erects a house of prayer.
DeFord, Miriam Allen
Ronsard.
Traveller's Ditty.
We Shall Say.
De Forest, John William
Miss Ravenel's Conversion, *sel.*
National Hymn, A.
Phantom Ship, The.
Sea-Maiden, The.
De Genestet, Petrus Augustus *See* **Genestet, Petrus Augustus de**
De Hearn, Nellie
Shut-in, The.
Dehmel, Richard
Before the Storm.
Harvest Song.
Laborer, The.
My Drinking Song.
Silent Town, The.
Song before Night.
To ——? "I have baptized thee Withy, because of thy slender limbs."
Trysting, A.
Vigil.
Voice in Darkness.
Dehn, Paul
Alternative Endings to an Unwritten Ballad.
At the Dark Hour.
Exercise Book.
Fern House at Kew.
Flight-Sergeant Foster flattened Gloucester.
Game of Consequences, A.
Government Official.
Hark, the herald angels sing, *parody.*
Hey diddle diddle,/ The physicists fiddle.
In a cavern, in a canyon.
Jack and Jill went up the hill/ To fetch some heavy water.
Jenny kiss'd me when we met.
Lament for a Sailor.
Leaden Treasury of English Verse, A, *sels.*
Little Miss Muffet/ Crouched on a tuffet.
Nuclear wind, when wilt thou blow.
O nuclear wind, when wilt thou blow.
Reunion.
Rhymes for a Modern Nursery, *sels.*
Two Blind mice/ See how they run!
We buried him darkly at dead of night.
Whenas in Jeans.
Dei-Anang, Michael
Africa Speaks.
My Africa.
Deissler, Mary Louise
Man of Galilee.
Deitz, Purd Eugene
Builders.
DeJong, David Cornel
On the Twenty-fifth of July.
De Kay, Charles
Arcana Sylvarum.
Draft Riot, The.
Tornado, The.
Ulf in Ireland.
De Kay, Ormande, Jr
Winter Tryst.
Dekker, Thomas
Basket Maker's Song.
Behold you not this globe, this golden bowl.
Bridal Song.
Christ's Coming to Judgment.
Cold's the Wind.
Content.
Drinking Song.
Entertainment to James, *sel.*
Fortune.
Fortune and Virtue.
Fortune Smiles.
Hey Derry Derry.
Honest Whore, The, *sels.*
King's Entertainment, The, *sel.*
Like an ill husband, though I knew the same.
London's Tempe; *or,* The Field of Happiness, *sel.*
May.
Maytime.
O Pittie.
O Sweet Content.
Oh, the Month of May!
Oh, whither am I rapt beyond myself?
Old Fortunatus, *sels.*
Patience, my lord! why, 'tis the soul of peace.
Patient Grissill.
Pleasant Comedie of Old Fortunatus, The.
Priest's Song, A.
Saint Hugh.
Shoemaker's Holiday, The, *sels.*
Song: "Virtue's branches wither, virtue pines."
Song of the Basket Maker.
Song of the Cyclops, The.
Stay, Fortunatus, once more hear me speak.
Sweet Content.
Troll the Bowl!
Troynovant ("Troynovant is now no more a city").
Dekker, Thomas, *and* John Ford
Cast away care, he that loves sorrow.
Country Glee.
Live with Me Still.
Sun's Darling, The, *sels.*
Dekker, Thomas *and others.*
Cradle Song: "Golden slumbers kiss your eyes."
Golden Slumbers [Kiss Your Eyes].
Happy Heart, The.
Lullaby: "Golden slumbers kiss your eyes."
Pleasant Comedy of Patient Grissell [*or* Grissill], *sels.*
Dekker, Thomas, Samuel Rowley, *and* John Day
Noble Soldier, The, *sel.*
O Sorrow, Sorrow.
Delafield, Harriet L.
No Escape.
De la Mare, Walter ("Walter Ramal")
Afraid.
Alas.
Alas, Alack.
All but Blind.
All Gone.
All That's Past.
Alone.
Alulvan.
Ann and the Fairy Song.
Arabia.
As Lucy Went a-Walking.
As Soon as Ever Twilight Comes.
At Ease.
At Home, Alone with the Cat.
At the Keyhole.
Autumn.
Away.
Ballad of Christmas, A.
Bandog, The.
Barber's, The.
Bards, The.
Bead Mat, The.
Bees' Song, The.
Before Dawn.
Berries.
Bewitched.
Bindweed, The.
Bluebells.
Bones.
Bookworm, The.
Bottle, The.
Breughel's Winter.
Broken Kaleidoscope, The
Buckle, The.
Bunches of Grapes.
Burning-Glass, The.
Buttons.
Catechism, The.
Chart, The.
Chicken.
Child Asleep, A.
Children of Stare, The.
Child's Day, A, *sels.*
Christening, The.
Clear Eyes ("Clear eyes do dim at last").
Corner, The.
Corner Stone, The.
Crumbs.
Cupboard, The.
Dark Château, The.
Dove, The.
Dream-Song.
Dreamer, The.
Drugged.
Dunce, The.
Dust to Dust.
Echo.
Echoes.
Eeka, Neeka.
Eel, The.
Empty House, The.
End, The.
England.
Epitaph, An: "Here lies a most beautiful lady."
Estranged.
Exile, The.
Eyes.
Faint Music.
False Gods.
Fare Well.
Feckless Dinner Party, The.
Fiddler, A.
Five Eyes.
Fly, The.
Forests.
Full Moon.
Funeral, The.
Galliass, The.
Ghost, The.
Go Far; Come Near.
Goldfinch, A.
Gone.
Good-bye.
Grace.
Hare, The.
"Hawthorn Hath a Deathly Smell, The."
Hidden Mermaids, The.
Holly, The.
Horse in a Field.
Horseman, The.
"How Sleep the Brave."
Huntsmen, The.
Hyssop.
I Met at Eve.
I Sit Alone.
In Memory of G. K. Chesterton.
In the Dock.
In the Dying of Daylight.
Jenny Wren.
Jim Jay.
Journey, The.
Keys of Morning, The.

De (continued)
King David.
Kiph.
Last Chapter, The.
Last Coachload, The.
Linnet, The.
Listeners, The.
Little Bird, The.
Little Creature, The.
Little Green Orchard, The.
Little Salamander, The.
Lord of Tartary.
Lost Playmate, The.
Lost Shoe, The.
Lovelocks.
Lucy.
Lullaby: "Sleep, sleep, lovely white soul."
Maerchen.
Many a Mickle.
Marionettes, The.
Market Place, The.
Martha.
Me.
Mermaids, The.
Mima.
Miracle, The.
Miss Loo.
Miss T.
Mrs. MacQueen.
Mocking Fairy, The.
Moonlight.
Moonshine.
Moth, The.
Motley.
Mountains, The.
Music.
Napoleon.
Never More, Sailor.
Nicholas Nye.
Nod.
Nostalgia.
Now Silent Falls.
O Dear Me!
O for a Moon to Light Me Home.
O heart, hold thee secure.
Off the Ground.
Old Angler, The.
Old Men, The.
Old Shellover.
Old Summerhouse, The.
Old Susan.
Once.
Peace.
Polonius.
Ponjoo.
Pooh!
Poor Bird.
Poor Henry.
Quack!
Quartette, The.
Queen Wasp, A.
Quiet Enemy, The.
Railway Junction, The.
Rainbow, The.
Recluse, A.
Remembrance.
Reserved.
Ride-by-Nights, The.
Robin, A.
Sam.
Scarecrow, The.
Scribe, The.
Seeds.
Shadow, The.
She Said.
Ship of Rio, The.
Silver.
Silver Penny, The.
Sleeper, The.
Sleepyhead.
Slim Cunning Hands.
Softly, drowsily.
Solitude.
Someone [*or* Some One].
Somewhere.
Song of Enchantment, A.
Song of Finis, The.
Song of Shadows, The.
Song of the Mad Prince, The.
"Sooeep!"
Spectacle, The.
Spectre, The.
Stranger, The.
Strangers.
Summer Evening.
Sunday, A.
Sunk Lyonesse.
Sunken Garden, The.
Supper.
Suppose.
Tartary.
Then.
Then as Now.
Theologians.
There Blooms No Bud in May.
Three Beggars, The.
Three Cherry Trees, The.
Thunder.
Tillie.
Tired Tim.
Tit for Tat.
Titmouse.
To a Candle.
To K. M.
Tom's Angel.
Tom's Little Dog.
Trees.
Truants, The.
Two Deep Clear Eyes.
Unregarding.
Unstooping.
Vacant Farmhouse, The.
Vain Finding.
Vain Questioning.
Veil, The.
Virtue.
Voices.
When the Rose Is Faded.
Where.
Why?
Widow's Weeds, A.
Will Ever?
Winter.
Winter Dusk.
World of Dream, The.

Deland, Margaret Wade
Affaire d'Amour.
Bossy and the Daisy.
By One Great Heart.
Christmas Silence, The.
Clover, The.
Doubt.
Easter Music.
Fairies' Shopping, The.
Life.
Love and Death.
Love's Wisdom.
Sent with a Rose to a Young Lady.
Waits, The.
While Shepherds Watched Their Flocks by Night.

Delaney, W. W. *See* **"Lee, Andy"**

Delany, Clarissa Scott
Interim.
Joy.
Mask, The.
Solace.

De la Sale, ——
Young Silvia.

De Leeuw, Adele
Auction Sale—Household Furnishings.

Delegall, Walt
Elegy for a Lady.
Psalm for Sonny Rollins.

De Lisle, Rouget *See* **Rouget de Lisle, Claude Joseph**

Delius, Anthony
And round these men spread the sub-tropic latitudes.
Brief Farewell.
But stricken with the high cafard, the town.
Cetewayo, chief of the Zulus.
Chameleon.
Coming, The.
Deaf-and-Dumb School.
Distance.
Ethnic Anthem, The ("Ethnasia will last a thousand years").
Explorer, The.
Footnote.
Gamblers, The.
Great Divide, The, *sels.*
Intuition.
Lady Anne Bathing.
Let's say, the opposition knows the ring.
Oh, Jack St. James can always cut a dash.
Ocean, with a calm sardonic titter, The.
Pilgrims, The.
Shadow.
Thinker, The.

Del Medigo, Joseph Solomon
Epigram: "If men be judged wise by their beards and their girth."

Deloney, Thomas
Dialogue between the Lovelorn Sir Hugh and Certain Ladies of Venice, A.
Gentle Craft, The, *sels.*
Jack of Newbury, *sels.*
Joyful [*or* Joyfull] New Ballad, A.
Lamentation of Beckles, The.
"Maiden fair I dare not wed, A."
My masters, I thank you, it's time to pack home.
Princely Ditty in Praise of the English Rose, A.
Queen Elizabeth at Tilbury.
Song: "Primrose in the green forest, The."
Song of the Banishment of the Two Dukes, A.
Weavers, Song, The.
Widow's Solace, The.
Winning of Cales, The.
Would God That It Were Holiday!

De Long, Juanita
My Hereafter.

De Longchamps, Joanne
Blind, I Speak to the Cigarette.
Ceremony.
Temple Fever: Sounion.

Demarest, Mary Augusta
My Ain Countree.

De' Medici, Lorenzo *See* **Medici, Lorenzo de**

Demille, A. B.
Ice King, The.

De Mille, James
Gallant Highwayman, The.

Deming, A. G.
Who Is Tapping at My Window.

Demorest, William Curtis "Will Seedy"
Little Flag on Our House, The.

De Morgan, Augustus
Fleas, The.
Great Fleas ("Great fleas have little fleas").
On Fleas.

Demosthenes
Epitaph on Those Who Fell at the Battle of Chaeronea.

Dempster, Roland Tombekai
Africa's Plea.

Is This Africa?
Denby, Edwin
Aaron.
Air.
Ciampino.
Climate, The.
Dishonor.
Domestic Cat, A.
Drenched saw Doris home, midnight gale.
First Warm Days.
Forza D'Agrò.
Girl, A.
Grand republic's poet is, The.
Heavy bus slows, New York my ride.
New Year's near, glass autumn long gone.
Northern Boulevard.
People on Sunday.
Postcard, A.
Roar drowns the reproach, facing him.
Sant 'Angelo d'Ischia.
Shoulder, The ("The shoulder of a man is shaped like a baby pig").
Silence at Night, The.
Size balls are saddens Lamarck, The.
Standing on the Streetcorner.
Summer.
Suppose there's a cranky woman inside me who.
Trastevere.
Denham, Sir John
Against Love.
Cooper's Hill.
Elegie upon the Death of the Lord Hastings, An.
Natura Naturata.
News from Colchester.
On Mr. Abraham Cowley, His Death and Burial amongst the Ancient Poets.
On the Earl of Strafford's Trial and Death.
Somnus.
Sophy, The, *sel.*
Thames, The.
Thames from Cooper's Hill, The.
To the Five Members of the Honourable House of Commons.
Deniehy, Daniel Henry
To His Wife.
Denison, J. P.
Wing Tee Wee.
Denison, Mabel Brown
Omnipotence.
Denman, Annie
For His Sake.
Dennen, Grace Atherton
Gold-of-Ophir Roses.
Denney, Reuel
Connecticut River, The.
Laboratory Midnight, The.
McSorley's Bar.
Tennis in San Juan.
To the Roman Bridge on Michigan Avenue.
Dennis, C. J.
Ant Explorer, The.
Growth of Sym, The.
Intro, The.
Joi, the Glug.
Pilot Cove.
Play, The.
Sentimental Bloke, The, *sel.*
Stoush o' Day, The.
Dennis, John
Two Friends, The.
Denny, Sir Edward
Hope of Our Hearts.
Dennys, John
Angler's Song, The.
Secrets of Angling, The, *sel.*
Dent, Thomas C.
Come Visit My Garden.
Love.
Denton, Clara Janetta
Something to Be Thankful For.
Denwood, Jonathan
Bleeberrying.
Denza, Luigi
Funiculi, Funicula.
De Regniers, Beatrice Schenk
I Looked in the Mirror.
Keep a Poem in Your Pocket.
Derham, Enid
Farewell: "I leave the world to-morrow."
Mountain Road, The.
O City, Look the Eastward Way.
Suburbs, The.
Derleth, August
Moon and Fog.
Place-Ghost.
Planetary Arc-Light, The.
Dermody, Thomas
Decayed Monastery, A.
John Baynham's Epitaph.
Ode to Myself, An.
Petition of Tom Dermody to the Three Fates in Council Sitting, The.
Shepherd's Despair, The.
"Der Nistor " (Pinhas Kahanovitch)
At the Doors.
Derosier, Lola
Last Day, The.
Derwood, Gene
After Reading St. John the Divine.
Bird, Bird.
Camel.
Elegy: "When in the mirror of a permanent tear."
Elegy on Gordon Barber, Lamentably Drowned in His Eighteenth Year.
In Autumn.
In Common.
In the Proscenium.
Innocent, The.
Mailed to G. B.
N. B., Symmetrians.
Rides.
Shelter.
So, Man?
Spring Air.
Star.
Third Madrigal.
To George Barker.
War's Clown in the Proscenium.
With God Conversing.
Derzhavin, Gavril Romanovich
O Thou Eternal One!
De Savitzsky Isabel
Christmas Tree, The.
Desbordes-Valmore, Marceline
Roses of Sa'adi, The.
Deschamps, Eustache
Knightly Code, The.
De Selincourt, Mrs. Aubrey *See* **McLeod, Irene Rutherford**
Deshoulières, Antoinette
Grisette Dines.
Desmond, Gerald, Earl of
Against Blame of Women.
Desportes, Philippe
Conquest.
His Lady's Might.
Those Eyes Which Set My Fancy on Afire.
Desprez, Frank
Lasca.
De Suze, Carl
Guitar Lament for a Mountain Boy.
De Tabley, John Byrne Leicester Warren, 3d Baron
Anticipation.
Chorus: "In wonder and time-mists."
Chorus: "Sweet are the ways of death to weary feet.
Chorus: "Throned are the gods and in.
Churchyard on the Sands, The.
Circe.
Conclusion.
Count of Senlis at His Toilet, The.
Fortune's Wheel.
Frosty Day, A.
Knight in the Wood, The.
Medea, *sel.*
Nuptial Song.
Ocean Wood, The.
Ode, An: "Sire of the rising day."
Philoctetes, *sels.*
Simple Maid, A.
Song of Dust, A.
Song of Faith Forsworn, A.
Song of the fields and a song of the woods, A.
Song of the Rolling Wind, A, *sel.*
Two Old Kings, The.
Windmill, The.
Woodland Grave, A.
Detrick, Daisy L.
Little Johnny Mine, The.
Ol' Jinny Mine, The.
Dett, Robert Nathaniel
Rubinstein Staccato Etude, The.
Staccato! Staccato! The Rubinstein Staccato Etude.
Deutsch, Babette
Apocrypha.
Capriccio.
Dancers, The.
Destruction of Letters.
Distance.
Dogma.
Earliness at the Cape.
Fireworks.
Girl, A.
Homage to the Philosopher.
Hound, The.
Hunt, The.
In a Museum.
July in Dutchess County.
Late Reflections.
Morning Workout.
Natural Law.
Need.
New Words for an Old Song.
New York—December, 1931.
No Moon, No Star.
Old Women.
Ombres Chinoises.
Paradigm.
Piano Recital.
Pity.
Reflections in a Little Park.
Scene with Figure.
Small Colored Boy in the Subway.
Solitude.
Songs ("I would make songs for you").
String Quartet.
They Came to the Wedding.
Tuppence Coloured.
Devaney, James
Evening Gleam, The.
Mortality.
Song of the Captured Woman.
Winter Westerlies.
Deveen,
Who's That Calling So Sweet?
De Vega, Lope *See* **Lope de Vega Carpio, Félix**
Dever, Joseph
Queen of Horizons.
De Vere, Sir Aubrey
Castleconnell.
Children Band, The.
Kilmallock.

De (continued)
Landrail, The.
Liberty of the Press.
Opening of the Tomb of Charlemagne, The.
Reality.
Right Use of Prayer, The.
Rock of Cashel, The.
Waterloo.
De Vere, Aubrey Thomas
Autumnal Ode.
Ballad of Sarsfield, A.
Cardinal Manning.
Coleridge.
Correggio's Cupolas at Parma.
Dei Genitrix.
Dirge: "Whose were they those voices? What footsteps came near me?"
Dirge of Kildare, The.
Dirge of Rory O'More.
Divine Presence, The.
Epicurean's Epitaph, An.
Epilogue: "At my casement I sat by night, while the wind remote in dark valleys."
Epitaph: "He roamed half-round the world of woe."
Evening Melody.
Fest. Puritatis.
Festum Nativitatis.
Florence MacCarthy's Farewell to His English Love [*or* Lover].
Flowers I Would Bring.
Friendly Blight, The.
Girl's Song, A.
Glauce.
Human Life.
Hymn for the Feast of the Annunciation.
Implicit Faith.
In Ruin Reconciled.
Incompatibility.
Ione ("Ione, fifteen years have o'er you passed.").
Joy and Sorrow.
Lines: "You drop a tear for those that die."
Little Black Rose, The.
Love's Spite.
Mater Amabilis.
Mater Christi.
May Carols, *sels.*
Mighty Mountain Plains, The.
Night through yonder cloudy cleft, The.
Parvuli Ejus.
Poet to a Painter, A.
Queen's Vespers, The.
Religio Novissima.
Roisin Dubh.
Sacraments of Nature, The.
Sad Is Our Youth.
Scene in a Madhouse.
Sea-Watcher, The.
Serenade: "Softly, O midnight hours!"
Song: "He found me sitting among flowers."
Song: "Little Black Rose shall be red at last, The!"
Song: "Seek not the tree of silkiest bark."
Song: "Sing the old song, amid the sounds dispersing."
Song: "Softly, O midnight hours!"
Song: "When I was young, I said to Sorrow."
Sorrow ("Count each affliction, whether light or grave").
Sorrow ("When I was young, I said to Sorrow").
Spring.
Spring Song.
Sun God, The.
Three Woes, The.
Troilus and Cressida.
Turris Eburnea.
Urania.
Wedding of the Clans, The.
Who feels not, when the Spring once more.
Winter.
Year of Sorrow, The; Ireland—1849, *sels.*
De Vere, Edward, 17th Earl of Oxford *See* **Vere, Edward de**
De Vere, Mary Ainge *See* **"Bridges, Madeline"**
De Vere, William
Walk, Damn You, Walk!
Devereux, Robert *See* **Essex, Robert Devereux, Earl of**
De Vito, Ethel Barnett
Birthday Gift.
Devlin, Denis
Ballad of Mistress Death.
Colours of Love, The.
Encounter.
Statue and the Perturbed Burghers, The.
Tomb of Michael Collins, The.
Vestiges.
Welcome My World.
De Vries, Peter
Theme and Variation.
To My Friends.
Dewar, A. W.
Life and the Weaver.
Dewey, Berenice C.
Conversation.
Dewey, George Washington
Blind Louise.
De Witt, Samuel A.
Quatrains for a Bank Cashier.
Two Sonnets for a Lost Love.
Dhingra, Baldoon
Day and Night.
Diamond, Lucy
Eskimo Baby, An.
Fairy Umbrellas.
Greenland Winter, A.
Kayak Song, A.
Diaper, William
Eclogue: "Lycon begin—begin the mournful tale."
Frost at Sea.
Nereides; or, Sea-Eclogues, *sels.*
Sea Eclogue: "Otys, begin."
Díaz Loyola, Carlos *See 'Rokha, Pablo de"*
Diaz Mirón, Salvador
Cloud, The.
Nox.
Dibdin, Charles
Blow High, Blow Low.
Captain Wattle and Miss Roe.
Jack's Fidelity.
Nongtongpaw.
Poor Jack.
Poor Tom, or the Sailor's Epitaph.
Tar for All Weathers, The.
Tom Bowling.
Dibdin, Thomas
Child That Has a Cold, A.
Di Castagnola, Countess Alice Fay
Mortal Combat.
Dickens, Charles
Fine Old English Gentleman, The; New Version.
Ivy Green, The.
Merry Autumn Days.
Pickwick Papers, *sel.*
Things That Never Die.
Dickenson, John
Shepherd's Complaint, The, *sel.*
Tityrus to His Fair Phyllis.
Dickey, James
Armor.
At Darien Bridge.
Beholders, The.
Being, The.
Between Two Prisoners.
Birth, A.
Bread.
Buckdancer's Choice.
Bums, on Waking.
By Canoe through the Fir Forest.
Call, The.
Cherrylog Road.
Coming Back to America.
Common Grave, The.
Dog Sleeping on My Feet, A.
Drowning with Others.
Dusk of Horses, The.
Encounter in the Cage Country.
Falling.
Fence Wire.
Firebombing, The.
Flash, The.
For the Nightly Ascent of the Hunter Orion over a Forest Clearing.
Goodbye to Serpents.
Heaven of Animals, The.
Hospital Window, The.
Ice Skin, The.
In the Lupanar at Pompeii.
In the Marble Quarry.
In the Mountain Tent.
In the Tree House at Night.
Jewel, The.
Leap, The.
Lifeguard, The.
Listening to Foxhounds.
Madness.
Movement of Fish, The.
On the Hill below the Lighthouse.
Owl King, The.
Performance, The.
Poisoned Man, The.
Salt Marsh, The.
Scarred Girl, The.
Scratch, The.
Shark's Parlor, The.
Slave Quarters.
Sun.
To Landrum Guy, Beginning to Write at Sixty.
Trees and Cattle.
Under Oaks.
Walking on Water.
Dickey, William
Canonical Hours.
Love among the Manichees.
On Setting Out.
Resolving Doubts.
Spectrum.
Things Kept.
Dickie, E. P.
"And I, if I Be Lifted Up, Shall Draw All Men."
"If I Be Lifted Up".
Dickinson, Blanche Taylor
Four Walls.
Poem: "Ah I know what happiness is!"
Revelation.
That Hill.
To an Icicle.
Walls of Jericho, The.
Dickinson, Charles Monroe
Children, The.
Dickinson, Dorothy
There's a hole in the fence.
Dickinson, Emily
Abraham to kill him.
Adrift! A little boat adrift!
Afraid? Of whom am I afraid?
After a hundred years.
After great pain, a formal feeling comes.
Alter! When the hills do.
Altered look about the hills, An.

Although I put away his life.
Ample make this bed.
And this of all my hopes.
Apparently with no surprise.
Arcturus is his other name.
As by the dead we love to sit.
As imperceptibly as grief.
As the starved maelstrom laps the navies.
At half-past three a single bird.
At last to be identified!
At least—to pray—is left—is left.
Auctioneer of parting, The.
Awful tempest mashed the air, An.
Back from the cordial grave I drag thee.
Beauty is not caused—it is.
Because I could not stop for Death.
Because my brook is fluent.
Because that you are going.
Bee his burnished carriage, A.
Bee is not afraid of me, The.
Bees are black, with gilt surcingles.
Before I got my eye put out.
Behind me dips eternity.
Behold this little bane.
Belshazzar had a letter.
Bereaved of all, I went abroad.
Besides the autumn poets sing.
Bible is an antique volume, The.
Bird came down the walk, A.
Bliss is the plaything of the child.
Body grows without, The.
Bone that has no marrow, The.
Brain is wider than the sky, The.
Brain within it's groove, The.
Bring me the sunset in a cup.
Bustle in a house, The.
By chivalries as tiny.
Clock stopped, A.
Clover's simple fame, The.
Color—caste—denomination.
Come slowly, Eden!
Could mortal lip divine.
Cricket sang, The.
Crisis is a hair.
Crumblin is not an instant's act.
Dare you see a soul at the white heat?
Day came slow, till five o'clock, The.
Dear March, come in!
Death-blow is a life-blow to some, A.
Death is a dialogue between.
Death is the supple suitor.
Delayed till she had ceased to know.
Departed—to the judgment.
Did life's penurious length?
Did the harebell loose her girdle.
Did we abolish frost.
Did you ever stand in a cavern's mouth?
Difference between despair, The.
Ditch is dear to the drunken man, The.
Doubt me, my dim companion!
Drop fell on the apple tree, A.
Drowning is not so pitiful.
Drunkard cannot meet a cork, A.
Dying! To be afraid of thee.
Each life converges to some centre.
Elysium is as far as to.
Essential oils are wrung.
Estranged from beauty—none can be.
Except the smaller size.
Expanse cannot be lost.
Exultation is the going.
Faded boy in sallow clothes, A.
Faith is a fine invention.
Faith—is the pierless bridge.
Fame is the one that does not stay.
Far from love the Heavenly Father.
Fascinating chill that music leaves, The.
Finding is the first act.
Fingers of the light, The.
First day's night had come, The.
Floss won't save you from an abyss.
Forbidden fruit a flavor has.
Forever at his side to walk.
Four trees upon a solitary acre.
Frost was never seen, The.
Further [*or* Farther] in summer than the birds.
Gentian weaves her fringes, The.
Given in marriage unto thee.
Glass was the street, in tinsel peril.
Glee—the great storm is over.
God is a distant—stately lover.
God made a little gentian.
Going to him! Happy letter! Tell him.
Good to hide, and hear 'em hunt.
Great streets of silence led away.
Grief is a mouse.
Have you got a brook in your little heart?
He ate and drank the precious words.
He fumbles at your soul.
He preached upon "breadth" till it argued him narrow.
He scanned it, staggered, dropped the loop.
Heart asks pleasure first, The.
Heart, we will forget him!
Heaven has different signs to me.
Heaven is what I cannot reach!
"Heavenly Father," take to thee.
Hope is a subtle glutton.
Hope is the thing with feathers.
How happy is the little stone.
How many times these low feet staggered.
How the waters closed above him.
I am afraid to own a body.
I asked no other thing.
I breathed enough to take the trick.
I bring an unaccustomed wine.
I cannot dance upon my toes.
I cannot live with you.
I died for beauty—but was scarce.
I dreaded that first robin, so.
I dwell in Possibility.
I felt a cleavage [*or* cleaving] in my mind.
I felt a funeral, in my brain.
I found the phrase [*or* words] to every thought.
I gave myself to him.
I got so I could hear his name.
I had been hungry, all the years.
I had no time to hate, because.
I had not minded walls.
I have a king who does not speak.
I have never seen volcanoes.
I have no life but this.
I have not told my garden yet.
I heard a fly buzz—when I died.
I heard, as if I had no ear.
I held a jewel in my fingers.
I hide myself within a flower.
I know a place where summer strives.
I know some lonely houses off the road.
I know that He exists.
I like a look of agony.
I like to see it lap the miles.
I lost a World—the other day!
I make his crescent fill or lack.
I many times thought peace had come.
I measure every grief I meet.
I never hear that one is dead.
I never hear the word "escape."
I never lost as much but twice.
I never saw a moor.
I read my sentence steadily.
I reason, earth is short.
I reckon—when I count at all.
I saw no way—the heavens were stitched.
I should not dare to be so sad.
I started early, took my dog.
I stepped from plank to plank.
I taste a liquor never brewed.
I think the hemlock likes to stand.
I thought that nature was enough.
I took my power in my hand.
I took one draught of life.
I was a phoebe—nothing more.
I went to heaven.
I would not paint—a picture.
I years had been from home.
Ideals are the fairy oil.
If any sink, assure that this, now standing.
If he were living—dare I ask?
If I can stop one heart from breaking.
If I could tell how glad I was.
If I should die.
If I shouldn't be alive.
If my bark sink.
If you were coming in the fall.
If your nerve, deny you.
I'll tell you how the sun rose.
I'm ceded, I've stopped being theirs.
I'm nobody! Who are you?
I'm "wife"; I've finished that.
Immortality she gave, The.
In lands I never saw, they say.
In winter in my room.
It dropped so low in my regard.
It is [*or* 'Tis] an honorable thought.
It makes no difference abroad.
It sifts from leaden sieves.
It sounded as if the streets were running.
It troubled me as once I was.
It was a quiet way.
It was not death, for I stood up.
It would have starved a gnat.
It's easy to invent a life.
It's such a little thing to weep.
I've dropped my brain—my soul is numb.
I've known a Heaven like a tent.
I've seen a dying eye.
Jesus! thy Crucifix.
Just lost, when I was saved.
Lady red upon the hill, A.
Lamp burns sure, within, The.
Last night that she lived, The.
Lay this laurel on the one.
Leaves like women, interchange, The.
Light exists in spring, A.
Lightly stepped a yellow star.
Like trains of cars on tracks of plush.
Little madness in the spring, A.
Lives he in any other world.
Loneliness one dare not sound, The.
Long, long sleep, a famous sleep, A.
Loss of something ever felt I, A.
Love can do all but raise the dead.
Love is that later thing than death.
Love's stricken "why."
Me prove it now—whoever doubt.
Mine by the right of the white election!
Missing all, prevented me, The.
Mob within the heart, The.
Moon is distant from the sea, The.
Moon upon her fluent route, The.
Moon was but a chin of gold, The.
Morns are meeker than they were, The.
Most she touched me by her muteness.
Mountain sat upon the plain, The.
Mountains grow unnoticed, The.
Much madness is divinest sense.
Murmur of a bee, The.
Mushroom is the elf of plants, The.
Musicians wrestle everywhere.
My country need not change her gown.
My life closed twice before its close.
My life had stood—a loaded gun.
My period had come for prayer.
My truimph lasted till the drums.
Name—of it—is "Autumn," The.
Narrow fellow in the grass, A.
Nature and God—I neither knew.
"Nature" is what we see.
New feet within my garden go.

Dickinson (continued)
No passenger was known to flee.
No rack can torture me.
None can experience stint.
Not any more to be lacked.
Not any sunny tone.
Not probable—the barest chance.
Not what we did shall be the test.
Not with a club, the heart is broken.
Oh Future! thou secreted peace.
Of all the souls that stand create.
Of all the sounds despatched abroad.
Of bronze and blaze.
Of course I prayed.
Of God we ask one favor.
On this wondrous sea.
One and one—Are one.
One blessing had I, than the rest.
One crown not any seek.
One crucifixion is recorded only.
One dignity delays for all.
One need not be a chamber—to be haunted.
Only ghost I ever saw, The.
Only news I know, The.
Our journey had advanced.
Our little kinsmen after rain.
Our lives are Swiss.
Our share of night to bear.
Outer, The—from the inner.
Overtakelessness of those, The.
Pain has an element of blank.
Papa above!
Pedigree of honey, The.
Perception of an object costs.
Pink, small and punctual.
Pit, A—but Heaven over it.
Poets light but lamps, The.
Popular heart is a cannon first, The.
Prayer is the little implement.
Precious—mouldering pleasure—'tis, A.
Presentiment—is that long shadow—on the lawn.
Prison gets to be a friend, A.
Props assist the house, The.
Proud of my broken heart, since thou didst break it.
Publication—is the auction.
Rat is the concisest tenant, The.
Rather arid delight.
Rearrange a wife's affection?
Remorse is memory awake.
Revolution is the pod.
Road was lit with moon and star, The.
Robin is a Gabriel, The.
Robin is the one, The.
Route of evanescence, A.
Saddest noise, the sweetest noise, The.
Safe despair it is that raves.
Safe in their alabaster chambers.
Said Death to Passion.
Savior! I've no one else to tell.
Saviour must have been, The.
Science—so the savants say, A.
Secret told, A.
Shady friend for torrid days, A.
Shall I take thee, the Poet said.
She dealt her pretty words like blades.
She died—this was the way she died.
She lay as if at play.
She rose to his requirement, dropped.
She sights a bird, she chuckles.
Show is not the show, The.
Skies cant keep their secret, The!
Sky is low, the clouds are mean, The.
Sleep is supposed to be.
So the eyes accost and sunder.
So well that I can live without.
Solemn thing—it was—I said, A.
Solemn thing within the soul, A.
Some keep the Sabbath [*or* Sunday] going to church.
Some things that fly there be.
Some, too fragile for winter winds.
Some we see nor more, tenements of wonder.
Some wretched creature, savior take.
Soul has bandaged moments, The.
Soul selects her own society, The.
Soul unto itself, The.
Soul's superior instants, The.
Spider as an artist, The.
Split the lark—and you'll find the music.
Spurn the temerity.
Step lightly on this narrow spot!
Struck was I, nor yet by lightning.
Success is counted sweetest.
Summer has two beginnings.
Sun and moon must make their haste, The.
Surgeons must be very careful.
Sweet is the swamp with its secrets.
Sweet—safe—houses.
Talk with prudence to a beggar.
Tell all the truth but tell it slant.
That after horror that was Us.
That I did always love.
That it will never come again.
That such have died enables us.
Their height in heaven comforts not.
There came a day at summer's full.
There came a wind like a bugle.
There is a flower that bees prefer.
There is a morn by men unseen.
There is a shame of nobleness.
There is a solitude of space.
There is a strength in knowing that it can be borne.
There is no frigate like a book.
There's a certain slant of light.
There's been a death in the opposite house.
These are the days when birds come back.
They called me to the window, for.
They dropped like flakes, they dropped like stars.
They might not need me; but they might.
They put us far apart.
They say that "Time assuages."
They shut me up in prose.
They talk as slow as legends grow.
This consciousness that is aware.
This dirty little heart.
This is a blossom of the brain.
This is my letter to the World.
This—is the land—the sunset washes.
This quiet dust was gentlemen and ladies.
This was a poet—it is that.
This world is not conclusion.
Those—dying then.
Those not live yet.
Though I get home how late, how late!
Though the great waters sleep.
Thought beneath so slight a film, The.
Thought went up my mind today, A.
Through lane it lay—thro' bramble.
Through the straight pass of suffering.
"Till death" is narrow loving.
Tint I cannot take is best, The.
'Tis an honorable thought.
'Tis little I could care for pearls.
'Tis not that dying hurts us so.
'Tis so appalling-it exhilirates.
Title divine—is mine!
To die—without the dying.
To fight aloud is very brave.
To flee from memory.
To hear an oriole sing.
To know just how He suffered—would be dear.
To make a prairie it takes a clover and one bee.
To my quick ear the leaves conferred.
To pile like thunder to its close.
Triumph may be of several kinds, A.
Truth is as old as God.
'Twas just this time, last year, I died.
'Twas later when the summer went.
'Twas like a maelstrom, with a notch.
'Twas warm—at first—like us.
Two lengths has every day.
Unable are the loved to die.
Under the light, yet under.
Undue significance a starving man attaches.
Until the desert knows.
Water makes many beds.
Waters chased him as he fled, The.
Way I read a letter's—this, The.
We do not play on graves.
We dream—it is good we are dreaming.
We introduce ourselves.
We knew not that we were to live.
We never know how high we are.
We play at paste.
We should not mind so small a flower.
We thirst at first—'tis nature's act.
What inn is this?
What is "paradise."
What mystery pervades a well!
What shall I do when the Summer troubles?
What soft—cherubic creatures.
When I have seen the sun emerge.
When I hoped I feared.
When I was small, a woman died.
When night is almost done.
Where ships of purple gently toss.
While we were fearing it, it came.
Who has not found the heaven below.
Whole gulfs of red and fleets of red.
Why do I love thee, Sir?
Wife—at daybreak I shall be, A.
Wild nights—Wild nights!
Will there really be morning?
Wind began to rock the grass, The.
Wind tapped like a tired man, The.
Wind took up the northern things, The.
Within my garden, rides a bird.
Wonder—is not precisely knowing.
Word made flesh is seldom, A.
World feels dusty, The.
Wounded deer leaps highest, A.
You left me, sweet, two legacies.
Your thoughts dont have words every day.
Dickinson, John
Liberty Song, The.
Song of American Freedom, A.
Dickinson, Martha Gilbert *See* **Bianchi, Martha Dickinson**
Dickinson, Patric
Bluebells.
Common Terns.
Dam, The.
Geologic.
Heartbreak House.
Hounds, The.
I am no poet who can set.
Jodrell Bank.
Lament for the Great Yachts.
Lines for an Eminent Poet and Critic.
On Dow Crag.
Onset, The.
Redwing, The.
Roman Wall, The.
Royal Military Canal, The.
Scale of Things, The.
Swallows, The.
Dickinson, Peter
By-Election Idyll.

Dickson, Aimor R.
Company One Keeps, The.
Diego, Gerardo
Seesaw.
Diekmann, Conrad
Winter Trees.
Dienstag, Alan
Three Women.
Diers, Theodore C.
My Nebraska.
Diespecker, Dick
All these are your essence, you are their flesh and their force.
Between Two Furious Oceans, *sels.*
You have asked me, "What am I?"
Dietmar von Aist
Bird Was Singing, A.
Lady Stood, A.
Linden Tree, The.
Parting at Morning.
Dietz, Howard
On the Rising Generation.
Digby, Sir Kenelm
On His Late Espoused Saint.
Digby, George, Earl of Bristol
Song: "See, O see!/ How every tree."
Digby, George, 2d Earl of Bristol *See* **Bristol, George Digby, 2d Earl of**
Digby, Kenelm Henry
Catholic Faith, The.
Erin.
Digges, Leonard
Sonnet: "If, of a wretched state and all forlorn."
To the Memory of the Deceased Author Master W. Shakespeare.
Dillard, R. H. W.
Alice for Annie, An.
Desert Fox.
Dillenback, John D.
Colorado.
Diller, John Irving
Lullaby Town.
Dillingham, Elizabeth T.
Fairy Song, A.
Dillingham, Frances Bent
Unique.
Dillon, Dan
Testing, Testing.
Dillon, George
Address to the Doomed, *sel.*
April's Amazing Meaning.
Boy in the Wind.
Constant One, The.
Elemental.
En Route.
Fall of Stars.
Hard Lovers, The.
Hours of the Day, The.
In Two Months Now.
Kind Inn, A.
Memory of Lake Superior.
No Question.
One Beauty Still.
Remember, though the Telescope Extend.
Serenader.
To Losers.
What Artifice.
Woman withour Fear.
World Goes Turning, The.
Dillon, Wentworth *See* **Roscommon, Wentworth Dillon, Earl of**
Dillon, Will
I Want a Girl (Just Like the Girl That Married Dear Old Dad).
Dimmette, Celia
Apology of the Young Scientists.
Dimond, William
Mariner's Dream, The.
"Dinesen, Isak" (Karen Blixen)
Zebra.
Dinis, King of Portugal
Song: "Friend and lover mine."
Dinnies, Anna Peyre
Wife, The.
Dinnis, Enid
Cherub-Folk, The.
Franciscan Dream, A.
Diodorus
Little Garment, A.
Diogenes Laertius
"Ecce Quomodo Mortiur Justus."
Diop, Birago
Breaths.
Omen.
Diop, David
Africa.
He Who Has Lost All.
Suffer, Poor Negro.
Those Who Lost Everything.
Vultures, The.
Your Presence.
Diotimus
Without the Herdsman.
Dipalma, Raymond *and* Stephen Shrader
Andalusian Lute, The: Another Baedeker.
Busted Lute, The: a Baedeker.
Dipoko, Mbella Sonne
Autobiography.
Disch, Thomas M.
Day Euterpe Died, The.
Narcissus.
Vacation on Earth, A.
Dismond, Binga
At Early Morn.
Status Quo.
Disraeli, Benjamin
Wellington.
Ditlevsen, Tove
Man's Love, A.
Ditmars, Rembrandt William B.
Lincoln.
Divall, Edith Hickman
Changeless.
In Whom Is No Variableness.
Divine, Charles
At the Lavendar Lantern.
Little Senorita.
Look Not to Me for Wisdom.
Never Will You Hold Me.
Paris; the Seine at Night.
Spanish Song.
We Met on Roads of Laughter.
Dix, William Chatterton
As with Gladness Men of Old.
Come Unto Me, Ye Weary.
Pearl of Great Price, The.
Silver Lamps.
What Child Is This?
Dixon, A. H.
Wonderful Day, A.
Dixon, Alan
Cat in the Long Grass.
Dixon, Richard Watson
All who have loved, be sure of this from me.
Both Less and More.
By the Sea.
Dream.
Fallen Rain.
Feathers of the Willow, The.
Heaving Roses of the Hedge Are Stirred, The.
Humanity.
Judgment of the May, The.
Love hath great store of sweetness, and 'tis well.
Love's Consolation, *sels.*
Mano; a Poetical History, *sels.*
November.
O Ubi? Nusquam.
Ode: Spirit Wooed, The.
Ode on Advancing Age.
Ode on Conflicting Claims.
Of a Vision of Hell, Which a Monk Had.
Of Temperance in Fortune.
Rapture; an Ode.
Skylark, The.
Song: "Feathers of the willow, The."
Song: "Why fadest thou in death."
Sonnet: "Give me the darkest corner of a cloud."
Unrest.
Willow.
Winter Will Follow.
Wizard's Funeral, The.
Djangatolum *See* **Corbin, Lloyd M., Jr**
Djellaladin Pasha, Mahmud
Song: "If you love God, take your mirror between your hands and look."
D'Lettuso, Homer
Old Houses.
Dnyanodaya
Wait On.
Doak, H. L.
Beggar, The.
Scarecrow, The.
Doane, George Washington
Banner of the Cross, The.
Christ, the Way.
Evening.
Evening Contemplation.
Life Sculpture.
Robin Redbreast.
Sculptors of Life.
Softly Now the Light of Day.
Way, the Truth, the Life. The.
"Doane, Jerry." *See* **Morse, Katharine Duncan**
Doane, William Croswell
Ancient of Days.
Bishop Doane on His Dog ["Cluny"].
Modern Baby, The.
Dobbs, Kildare
Exequy: To Peter Allt.
Dobell, Bertram
Microcosm.
Dobell, Sydney Thompson
America.
Balder, *sels.*
Ballad of Keith of Ravelston, The.
Chanted Calendar, A.
Dante, Shakespeare, Milton.
Desolate.
Eden-Gate.
Epigram on the Death of Edward Forbes.
Even-Song, An.
Fragment of a Sleep-Song.
He Loves and He Rides Away.
Home, in War-Time.
"How's My Boy?"
Isabel.
Keith of Ravelston.
Laus Deo.
Nuptial Eve, A.
On the Death of Mrs. Browning.
Orphan's Song, The.
Procession of the Flowers, The.
Ravelston, Ravelston.
Return!
Sea Ballad.
Sonnet: Army Surgeon, The.
Sonnet: Common Grave, The.
Tommy's Dead.
Dobson, Austin
Ars Victrix.
Ballad of Heroes, A.
Ballad of Imitation, The.
Ballad to Queen Elizabeth, A.
Ballade of Prose and Rhyme, The.
Before Sedan.
Cap That Fits.
Child Musician, The.

Dobson (continued)
City Flower, A.
Clean Hands.
Cradle, The.
Curé's Progress, The.
Dance of Death, The.
Dead Letter, A.
Dialogue, A.
Dialogue from Plato, A.
Don Quixote.
Dora versus Rose.
Fame.
Fame and Friendship.
Fame Is a Food That Dead Men Eat.
Familiar Epistle, A.
Fancy from Fontenelle, A.
Farewell, Renown!
For a Copy of Theocritus.
Forgotten Grave, The.
Gage d'Amour, A.
Garden Song, A.
Gentleman of the Old School, A.
Good-Night, Babette!
Greek Gift, A.
Growing Gray.
Henry Wadsworth Longfellow.
In After Days.
In Town.
In Vain Today.
Incognita.
Jocosa Lyra.
Kiss, A.
Ladies of St. James's, The.
Little Blue-Ribbons.
Maltworm's Madrigal, The.
Milkmaid, The.
O Navis.
O Poet, then, forbear.
On a Fan That Belonged to the Marquise de Pompadour.
On a Nankin Plate.
On the Future of Poetry.
On the Hurry of This Time.
Paradox of Time, The.
Postscript to "Retaliation," A.
Prodigals, The.
Rank and File.
Rondeau, The: "You bid me try, Blue-Eyes, to write."
Rondeau to Ethel, A.
Rondel; the Wanderer.
Rose and the Gardener, The.
Rose-Leaves.
Sat est Scripsisse.
Song of Angiola in Heaven, A.
Song of the Four Seasons, A.
Sonnet in Dialogue, A.
To a Greek Girl.
To Brander Matthews.
To Daffodils.
To "Lydia Languish."
Tu Quoque.
"Urceus Exit."
Virtuoso, A.
Wanderer, The.
When Burbadge Played.
When I Saw You Last, Rose.
"When There Is Peace."
With Pipe and Flute.
You Bid Me Try.
Dobson, Rosemary
Across the Straits.
Birth, The.
Chance Met.
Cockerel Sun.
Detail from an Annunciation by Crivelli.
Devil and the Angel, The, *sels.*
In a Convex Mirror.
In My End Is My Beginning.
Methuselah.
Missal, The.
Raising of the Dead, The.
"Doc Long." *See* **Long, Doughtry, Jr**
Dodd, Lee Wilson
Comrade, The.
Flower, The.
Dodd, Leonard
Compel Them to Come In.
Dodd, P.
Epigram: "Joe hates a sycophant. It shows."
On Joe.
Doddridge, Philip
Amazing, Beauteous Change!
Awake, My Soul.
Dum Vivimus, Vivamus.
Evening Hymn.
Finest English Epigram, The.
Happy Day.
Hear Us, in This Thy House.
Hymn: "Ye golden Lamps of Heav'n, farewel."
Jesus, I Love Thy Charming Name.
Live While You Live.
Lovest Thou Me? Feed My Lambs.
Prince of Peace, The.
Saviour Comes, The.
Trust God.
Watchful Servant, The.
Ye Golden Lamps of Heaven.
Dodds, Eric Robertson
Moon Worshippers, The.
When the Ecstatic Body Grips.
Dodge, H. C.
If.
Splendid Fellow, A.
Dodge, Henry Nehemiah
Spirit of Freedom, Thou Dost Love the Sea.
Thrustararorum.
Dodge, Josephine Daskam *See* **Bacon, Josephine Dodge Daskam**
Dodge Mary Abigail ("Gail Hamilton")
Both Sides.
Dodge, Mary Barker
Now.
Dodge, Mary Mapes
Birdies with Broken Wings.
Christmas.
Courtesy.
Emerson.
Frost-King, The.
Home and Mother.
In Trust.
Lazy Lou.
Let Me Grow.
Life in Laconics.
Little Dutchman, The.
Mayor of Scuttleton, The.
Melons.
Minuet, The.
Mother.
Nearly Ready.
Night and Day.
Not Only in the Christmas-Tide.
Now the Noisy Winds are Still.
Oh, No!
Offertory.
Once Before.
One and One.
Over the Way.
Shadow-Evidence.
Snowflake, The.
Snowflakes ("Little white feathers").
Snowflakes ("Whenever a snowflake").
Stars, The.
Stocking Song on Christmas Eve.
Sweet Red Rose, The.
Two Mysteries, The.
When I Am Big, I Mean to Buy.
Winter.
Written on the Road.
Zealless Xylographer, The.
Dodge, Samuel
People Will Talk.
Dodgson, Charles Lutwidge *See* **"Carroll, Lewis"**
Dodington, George Bubb, Baron Melcombe
Ode: "Love thy country, wish it well."
Shorten Sail.
Dodsley, Robert
Epigram: "Cries Sylvia to a reverend Dean."
Kings of Europe, The; a Jest.
Man's a Bubble.
Song: "Man's a poor deluded bubble."
Dodson, Owen
Bring me those needles, Martha.
Circle One.
Confession Stone, The.
Conversation on V.
Decision, The.
Drunken Lover.
Epitaph for a Negro Woman.
For My Brother.
Hymn Written after Jeremiah Preached to Me in a Dream.
Open Letter.
Poems for My Brother Kenneth.
Rag Doll and Summer Birds.
Sailors on Leave.
Sickle Pears.
Six o'Clock.
Sorrow Is the Only Faithful One.
When I Am Dead.
Yardbird's Skull.
Doherty, Kevin F.
Astronomer, The.
Doherty, Lillian
Stella Matutina.
Dolama, Abu
Humorous Verse.
Dolben, Digby Mackworth
April of the Ages, The.
Come to Me, Beloved.
Flowers for the Altar.
Garden, The.
He Would Have His Lady Sing.
Heaven.
Homo Factus Est.
I Asked for Peace.
Prayer, A: "From falsehood and error."
Requests.
Shrine, The.
Song, A: "World is young today, The."
Strange, All-absorbing Love.
We hurry on, nor passing note.
Within Thy Heart.
Dole, Nathan Haskell
Our Native Birds.
Patriot Hymn, The.
Russia.
Russian Fantasy, A.
To an Imperilled Traveller.
Dollard James B. ("Silav-Na-Mon")
Fairy Harpers, The.
Song of the Little Villages.
Sons of Patrick, The.
Soul of Karnaghan Buidhe, The.
Dolliver, Clara
No Baby in the House.
Domett, Alfred
About the heights, soft clouds, a few.
And near some river-mouth—shoal—marshy-wide.
And Tangi and his tribe thus much had gained.
But evening now.
Captain Cook.
Christmas Hymn, A.
Christmas Hymn, 1837.
Christmas Hymn, A: New Style, *sel.*

Christmas Hymn, A: Old Style, 1837.
Glee for Winter, A.
In deep blue sky the sun is bright.
It is the calm and solemn night!
It was a wondrous realm beguiled.
Maori Girl's Song, A.
Or to the beach descending, with joined hands.
Ranolf and Amohia, *sels.*
So Ranolf felt when over wood and wild.
To murder one so young!

Dominici, Giovanni
Mother Most Powerful.

Dominis, Lilia K.
Hawaiian National Hymn.

Donaghy, Emily
God Knoweth Best.

Donaghy, John Lyle
At My Whisper.
Duck.
Ebb.
Fossil, The.
Glenarm.
Grave, The.
Heron, The.
Leitrim Woman, A.
Linota Rufescens.
Seeing.
Voyage.
Where the Dropwort Springs Up Lithe and Tall.

Donaghy, William A.
Ancestry.
Fourth Station.
He Falls.
He Is Buried.
Stations of the Cross, The, *sels.*
Thirteenth Station.

Donahoe, D. J.
Angelic Chorus, The.

Doney, May
Comfort.
White Dream, The.

Donian, Mitchell
If someone asks you.

Donne, John
Air [or Aire] and Angels.
Aire and Angels.
Anagram, The, II.
Anatomie [*or* Anatomy] of the World, An; the First Anniversary.
Anatomy of the World, An.
Anniversary [*or* Anniversarie], The.
Annunciation.
Annuntiation and Passion, The.
Antiquary.
Apparition, The.
Ascension.
Ascention.
Autumnal, The.
Autumnall, The.
Bait [*or* Baite], The.
Batter my heart, three person'd God; for, you.
Benediction, The.
Blossom, The.
Blossome, The.
Blow Your Trumpets, Angels.
Bracelet, The.
Break [*or* Breake] of Day.
Bridegroomes Comming, The.
Brides Going to Bed, The.
Broken Heart, The.
Burnt Ship, A.
But thou which lov'st to be.
But we by a love, so much refined.
Cales and Guyana.
Calm, The.
Calme, The.
Canonization, The.
Change.
Community.
Comparison, The.
Computation, The.
Confined Love.
Contemplation of Our State in Our Deathbed.
Crosse, The.
Crucifying.
Curse, The.
Dampe, The.
Daybreak.
Death.
Death, Be Not Proud.
Devout Fits.
Disinherited.
Dissolution, The.
Doth Not a Tenarif, or Higher Hill.
Dream [*or* Dreame], The ("Deare love, for nothing lesse then thee").
Dreame, The ("Image of her whom I love").
Ecclogue 1613. December 26.
Ecstasy, The.
Elegie: Autumnall, The.
Elegie: Death.
Elegie: Going to Bed.
Elegie: His Picture.
Elegie: "Natures lay ideot, I taught thee to love."
Elegie: On His Mistris.
Elegie: Perfume, The.
Elegie: To His Mistris Going to Bed.
Elegie on His Mistris.
Elegie on Mrs. Boulstred.
Elegie on the L. C.
Elegie on the Lady Marckham.
Elegie upon the Untimely Death of the Incomparable Prince Henry.
Elegies, *sels.*
Elegy: Autumnal[l], The.
Elegy: Going to Bed.
Elegy V: His Picture.
Elegy: "Image of her whom I love, move then she."
Elegy: "Nature's lay idiot, I taught thee to love."
Elegy: "No spring nor summer beauty hath such grace."
Elegy on His Mistress.
Elegy on the L. C.
Epigram: Burnt Ship, A.
Epitaph on Himselfe.
Epithalamion, An: "Haile [*or* Hail] Bishop Valentine, whose day this is."
Epithalamion: Time of the Mariage, The.
Epithalamion Made at Lincolnes [*or* Lincoln's] Inn[e].
Epithalamium on the Lady Elizabeth and Count Palatine Being Married on St. Valentine's Day, An.
Equality of Persons.
Expiration, The.
Expostulation, The.
Extasy [*or* Extasie], The.
Fall of a Wall.
Farewell to Love.
Feasts and Revells.
Feaver, A.
Fever, A.
First Anniversary, The.
First Song.
Flea, The.
For Forgiveness.
Forget.
Forget this rotten world; and unto thee.
From being anxious or secure.
Funeral[l], The.
Funerall, The.
Go and Catch a Falling Star.
God grant thee thine own wish, and grant thee mine.
Goe, and catche a falling starre.
Going to Bed.
Going to the Chappell.
Good Friday [*or* Goodfriday], 1613. Riding Westward.
Good-Morrow, The.
Good-Night, The.
Goodfriday, 1613. Riding Westward.
H: W: in Hiber: Belligeranti.
Her Apparrelling.
Hero and Leander.
Heroicall Epistle.
His Parting from Her.
His Picture.
Holy Sonnets.
How witty's ruin! how importunate.
Hymn [*or* Hymne] to Christ, at the Authors Last Going into Germany, A.
Hymn [*or* Hymne] to God My God, in My Sickness[e].
Hymn [*or* Hymne] to God the Father, A.
Hymne to Christ, at the Authors Last Going into Germany, A.
Hymne to God My God, in My Sicknesse.
Hymne to God the Father, A.
Hymne to the Saints, and to Marquesse Hamylton, An.
Inconstancy.
Indifferent, The.
Infinitati Sacrum, *sel.*
It quickned next a toyfull Ape, and so.
Jealosie.
Jeat Ring Sent, A.
Jesus in the Temple.
Julia.
Klockius.
La Corona.
Lame Beggar [*or* Begger], A.
Lamentations of Jeremy, The.
Lecture upon the Shadow, A.
Legacie, The.
Legacy, The.
Letter to Sir H. Wotton at His Going Ambassador to Venice.
Letter to the Lady Carey, and Mrs. Essex Riche, from Amyens, A.
Licentious Person, A.
Lier, The.
Litanie, The.
Litany [*or* Litanie], The.
Lovers' Infiniteness[e].
Loves Alchemy [*or* Alchymie].
Love's Deity [*or* Deitie].
Love's Diet.
Love's Exchange.
Love's Growth.
Love's Infiniteness.
Love's Progress.
Loves Usury.
Loves Warre.
Manliness.
Mercurius Gallo-Belgicus.
Message, The.
Nativitie [*or* Nativity].
Nativity.
Negative Love.
New Philosophy, The.
Niobe.
Nocturnal upon Saint Lucy's Day [Being the Shortest Day], A.
O Fortune, thou'rt not worth my least exclaim.
O how feeble is man's power.
Obscure Writer, An.
Obsequies of [*or* to] the Lord Harrington.
Of a Death in Winter ("The ravenous earth that now wooes her").
Of the Progress[e] of the Soul[e]; the Second Anniversary.
Omnibus.

Donne (continued)
On Going to Bed.
On His Mistris.
Only our love hath no decay.
Our Companie in the Next World.
Paradox, The.
Perfume, The.
Phryne.
Primrose, The [Being at Montgomery Castle].
Progress of the Soul, The ("I sing the progress of a deathless soul"), *sels.*
Progress of the Soul, The ("Nothing could make me sooner to confess").
Prohibition, The.
Pyramus and Thisbe.
Raderus.
Raising of the Bride.
Ralphius.
Raysing of the Bridegroome.
Relic, The.
Religion.
Relique, The.
Resurrection.
Resurrection Imperfect.
Sacrament, The.
Satire: "Away, thou fondling motley humorist."
Satire III: "Kind pity [*or* Kinde pitty] chokes my spleen; brave scorn forbids."
Satire: "Sir though (I thank God for it) I do hate."
Satire IV: "Well I may now receive, and die. My sin."
Satires, *sels.*
Satyre III: "Kinde pitty chokes my spleene; brave scorn forbids."
Satyre: Of [*or* On] Religion.
Second Anniversary, The.
Selfe Accuser, A.
Selfe Love.
She of whose soul, if we may say 'twas gold.
She, she is dead; she's dead: when thou knowst this.
Sir John Wingefield.
So did the world from the first hour decay.
Song: Catch a Falling Star.
Song: "Goe, and catche a falling starre."
Song: "Sweetest love, I do not go[e]."
Sonnet: "As due by many titles I resigne."
Sonnet: "At the round earths imagin'd [*or* imagined] corners, blow."
Sonnet: "Batter my heart, three person'd God; for, you."
Sonnet: "Death, be not proud, though some have called thee."
Sonnet: "Father, part of his double interest."
Sonnet: "I am a little world made cunningly."
Sonnet: "If faithfull soules be alike glorifi'd."
Sonnet: "If poisonous minerals, and if that tree."
Sonnet: "O might those sighs and tears return again."
Sonnet: "Oh my black soul! now thou art summoned."
Sonnet: "Oh, to vex me, contraries [*or* contraryes] meet in one."
Sonnet: "Show me deare Christ, thy spouse, so bright and clear."
Sonnet: "Since she whom I lov'd [*or* loved] hath payd [*or* paid] her last debt."
Sonnet: "Spit in my face you Jewes, and pierce my side."
Sonnet: "This is my play's [*or* playes] last scene, here heavens appoint."
Sonnet: "Thou hast made me, and shall thy work decay?"
Sonnet: Token, The.
Sonnet: "What if this present were the world's last night?"
Sonnet: "Why are wee by all creatures waited on?"
Sonnet: "Wilt thou love God, as he thee! then digest."
Soules Ignorance in This Life and Knowledge in the Next, The.
South and west winds joined, and, as they blew, The.
Storm, The.
Storme, The.
Sun [*or* Sunne] Rising, The.
Sunne Rising, The.
Sweetest Love, I Do Not Go.
Tale of a Citizen and His Wife, A.
Temple.
Think [*or* Thinke] then, my soul, that death is but a groom.
This Is My Body.
Thou seest me here at midnight, now all rest.
Thou shalt not laugh in this leafe, Muse, nor they.
To Christ.
To E. of D. with Six Holy Sonnets.
To His Mistress Going to Bed.
To Mr. B. B.
To Mr. C. B.
To Mr. E. G.
To Mr. George Herbert.
To Mr. I. L. ("Blest are your North parts").
To Mr. I. L. ("Of that short roll of friends").
To Mr. R. W. ("If, as mine is, thy life a slumber be").
To Mr. R. W. ("Kindly I envy thy songs perfection").
To Mr. R. W. ("Muse not that by thy mind").
To Mr. R. W. ("Zealously my Muse").
To Mr. Rowland Woodward ("Like one who'in her third widdowhood doth professe").
To Mr. S. B.
To Mr. T. W. ("All haile sweet poet").
To Mr. T. W. ("At once, from hence . . .").
To Mr. T. W. ("Hast thee harsh verse").
To Mr. T. W. ("Pregnant again with th'old twins").
To Mr. Tilman after He Had Taken Orders.
To Mrs. M. H.
To Sir Edward Herbert, at Julyers.
To Sir H. W. at His Going Ambassador to Venice.
To Sir Henry Goodyere.
To Sir Henry Wotton ("Here's no more news than virtue").
To Sir Henry Wotton ("Sir, more than kisses, letters mingle souls").
To the Countesse of Bedford ("Honour is so sublime perfection").
To the Countesse of Bedford ("Reason is our soul's left hand").
To the Countesse of Bedford ("T'have written then, when you writ").
To the Countesse of Bedford ("Though I be dead").
To the Countesse of Bedford ("You have refin'd mee").
To the Countesse of Bedford on New-Yeares Day.
To the Countesse of Huntingdon ("Man to Gods image").
To the Countesse of Huntington ("That unripe side of earth").
To the Countesse of Salisbury.
To the Lady Bedford.
To the Lady Magdalen Herbert.
Triple Fool[e], The.
Truth.
Twicknam Garden.
Undertaking, The.
Upon Mr. Thomas Coryats Crudities.
Upon the Translation of the Psalmes by Sir Philip Sydney.
Valediction Forbidding Mourning, A.
Valediction, A: Of My Name in the Window.
Valediction, A; of the Booke.
Valediction, A: of Weeping.
Variety.
Verse-Letter: To Sir Henry Wootton.
Verse Letter to the Countess of Bedford.
Well; I may now receive, and die; my sin [ne].
Whale, The.
Why are we [*or* wee] by all creatures waited on?
Will, The.
Witchcraft by a Picture.
Womans Constancy.

Donnelly, Dorothy
Blue Flag.
Girandole.

Donnelly, Eleanor Cecilia
Ladye Chapel at Eden Hall.
Mary Immaculate.

Donohue, James J.
God Said: Let There Be Sky.
Hymn: "Eternal Founder of the sky."
Last Antiphon: To Mary.
Praise of Engineers.

Dooher, Muredach J.
Renascence.

Dooley, Ebon
To Our First Born.

Doolittle, Esther Hull
Secret.

Doolittle, Hilda "H.D."
Adonis.
Ah (You Say), This Is Holy Wisdom.
At Baia.
At Ithaca.
Choros: "Give me your poppies."
Circe.
Cities.
Egypt.
Erige Cor Tuum ad Me in Caelum.
Evadne.
Evening.
Fragment 113: "Not honey."
Fragment Thirty-Six.
Garden, The.
Gather for festival.
Halcyon, *sel.*
Heat.
Helen.
Helmsman, The.
Hermes of the Ways.
Hermes Trismegistus.
Hesperides—Fragment Thirty-six.
Holy Satyr.
Hymen, *sel.*
I Would Forgo.
Incident Here and There, An.
Islands, The.
Lais.
Leda.
Let Zeus Record, *sel.*
Lethe.
Mid-Day.
Moon in Your Hands, The.
Moonrise.
Morpheus, *sel.*
Never More Will the Wind.
Not Honey.

O Heart, Small Urn.
Orchard.
Oread.
Pear Tree.
Pool, The.
Pygmalion.
Sea Gods.
Sea Rose.
Sheltered Garden.
Shrine, The.
Simaetha.
Sitalkas.
Socratic.
Song: "You are as gold."
Song from Cyprus, A.
Songs from Cyprus, *sels.*
Storm.
Swiftly Relight the Flame.
There Is a Spell, for Instance.
Tribute to the Angels, *sels.*
Where Love Is King.
Doran, —— Quietness
Doran, Louise A.
Ship, The.
Dorgan, John Aylmer
Beautiful, The.
Dead Solomon, The.
D'Orge, Jeanne
Convent, The.
Enchanted Castle, The.
Portrait.
Dorn, Alfred
Challengers.
Dark Hotel.
Invisible Painter.
Reversions.
Dorn, Edward
Air of June Sings, The.
Are They Dancing.
Biggest Killing, The.
From Gloucester Out.
Hide of My Mother, The.
Rick of Green Wood, The.
Song, The: "So light no one noticed."
Sousa.
Vaquero.
When the Fairies.
Dorney, Elizabeth
Chemistry of Character, The.
Doro, Edward
Open Letter to John Doe.
To a Lad Who Would Wed Himself with Music.
Dorothy Ann, Sister Mary
Exchange.
Dorr, Henry R.
Comrades.
Dorr, Julia C. R.
Fallow Field, The.
Legend of the Organ-Builder, The.
No More the Thunder of Cannon.
Not Mine.
O Earth! Art Thou Not Weary?
Outgrown.
Prayer for One Dead.
Two Paths.
With A Rose from Conway Castle.
Dorrance, Dick
Cockpit in the Clouds.
Dorset, Charles Sackville, 6th Earl of *See* **Sackville, Charles, 6th Earl of Dorset**
Dorset, Thomas Sackville, 1st Earl of e Sackville, Thomas, 1st Earl of Dorset
Dos Passos, John
Phases of the Moon.
Doten, Elizabeth
In a Hundred Years.
Prayer, A: "God of the Granite and the Rose!"
Reconciliation, *sel.*
Doty, Walter G.
Best Firm, The.
Doudney, Sarah
Christian's "Good-Night," The.
Lesson of the Water Mill, The.
Man o' Airlie, The, *sel.*
Sweet Surprises.
Water Mill, The.
Doughty, Charles Montague
Bladyn's Song of Cloten.
Dawn in Britain, The, *sels.*
Druids' Hymn to the Sun.
Fairies Feast, The.
Gauls Sacrifice Their Prisoners, The.
Roman Officer Writes Home, A.
Douglas, Lord Alfred Bruce
City of the Soul, The.
Dead Poet, The.
Each New Hour's Passage Is the Acolyte.
Green River, The.
Impression de Nuit; London.
Lighten Our Darkness.
Night Coming Out of a Garden.
Of a Dead Poet.
Plainte Eternelle.
Prayer, A: "Often the western wind has sung to me."
Rejected.
Song, A: "Steal from the meadows, rob the tall green hills."
Sonnet on the Sonnet.
Summer Storm, A.
To Olive.
Witch, The.
Douglas, Gawin [*or* Gavin]
Difficulties of Translation, The, *abr.*
Frend, farly nocht; an caus is to complene.
Hart's Castle.
King Hart, *sel.*
Nightmare.
Palace of Honor, The, *sel.*
Prologues to the Aeneid, *sels.*
Quhill schortly, with the blesand torch of day.
Winter.
Douglas, Gilean
Children of Martha.
Douglas, Jesse
Warning.
Douglas, Keith
Aristocrats.
Cairo Jag.
Canoe.
Deceased, The.
Desert Flowers.
Enfidaville.
Haydn—Military Symphony.
How to Kill.
Landscape with Figures.
Leukothea.
Mersa.
Offensive, The.
On a Return from Egypt.
Oxford.
Poem: "These grasses, ancient enemies."
Remember Me.
Round Number, A.
Sea Bird, The.
Simplify Me When I'm Dead.
Snakeskin and Stone.
Song: "Do I venture away too far."
Time Eating.
Vergissmeinnicht.
"Douglas, Marian" (Annie Douglas Green Robinso
Good Thanksgiving, A.
Little Sorrow.
One Saturday.
White Kitten, The.
Douglas, Olive, Lady *See* **Custance, Olive**
Douglas, William
Annie Laurie.
Dover, Cedric
In a Girl's Album.
Dow, Dorothy (Mrs. James Edward Fitzgerald)
Song: "I could make you songs."
Things.
To Atalanta.
Unbeliever.
Dow, Philip
Bats.
Death.
Drunk Last Night with Poets, I Go to Work Anyway.
Early Morning.
For a Happy Girl.
Life of the Poet, The.
Morning, in the Pastures Near Suisun.
Our Garden.
Twilight in California.
Dowd, Emma C.
Fun in a Garret.
Dowden, Edward
Autumn Song, An.
Communion.
I found Thee in my heart, O Lord.
In the Cathedral Close.
Leonardo's "Monna Lisa."
Line of Beauty, The.
Love's Lord.
Mona Lisa.
New Hymns for Solitude, *sel.*
Oasis.
Renunciants.
Seeking God.
Singer, The.
Two Infinities.
Vision.
Windle-Straws.
Dowden, Elizabeth Dickinson (Mrs. Edward Dowden)
Adrift.
Dowding, Walter
I'r hen Iaith a'i Chanedon.
Dowling, Allan
I Sought with Eager Hand.
Joy of Love, The.
Miracle, The.
Dowling, Bartholomew
Revel, The.
Revelry for the Dying.
Stand to Your Glasses.
Dowling, Basil
Air in Spring, The.
Autumn Scene.
Canterbury.
Early Days, The.
Mortal Love.
Naseby; Late Autumn.
Shunting.
Summer Afternoon.
Walking in Bush.
Downey, Fairfax
Rise and Fall of Valentines.
Downing, Eleanor
Mary.
On the Feast of the Assumption.
Pilgrim, The.
Downing, Ellen Mary Patrick
My Owen.
Were I But His Own Wife.
"Downing, Major Jack." *See* **Smith, Seba**
Dowson, Ernest Christopher
Ad Domnulam Suam.
Amantium Irae.
Amor Profanus.
April Love.
Autumnal.
Beata Solitudo.

Dowson (continued)
Benedictio Domini.
Breton Afternoon.
Carthusians.
Chanson sans Paroles.
Cynara.
De Amore.
Dead Child, The.
Dregs.
Envoy: "They are not long, the weeping and the laughter."
Epigram: "Because I am idolatrous and have besought."
Exchanges.
Exile.
Extreme Unction.
Faithful in My Fashion.
Flos Lunae.
Garden of Shadow, The.
Gray Nights.
Impenitentia Ultima.
Last Word, A.
Let Be at Last.
Lord over life and all the ways of breath.
Lyric: "You would have understood me, had you waited."
Non Sum Qualis Eram Bonae sub Regno Cynarae.
Nuns of the Perpetual Adoration.
O Mors! Quam Amara Est Memoria Tua Homini Pacem Habenti in Substantiis Suis.
Quid Non Speremus, Amantes?
Royal Love Scene, The,
Saint Germain-en-Laye.
Sapientia Lunae.
Spleen.
To Cynara.
To His Mistress.
To One in Bedlam.
Vesperal.
Villanelle of His Lady's Treasures.
Villanelle of Marguerites.
Villanelle of Sunset.
Villanelle of the Poet's Road.
Vitae Summa Brevis Spem Nos Vetat Incohare Longam.
You Would Have Understood Me.
Your Hands.
Yvonne of Brittany.
Doyle, Sir Arthur Conan
Cremona.
Song of the Bow, The.
White Company, The, *sel.*
Doyle, Camilla
Prettiest Things, The.
Rabbit, The.
Doyle, Sir Francis Hastings
The Red Thread of Honor.
Epicurean, The.
Loss of the *Birkenhead,* The.
Old Cavalier, The.
Private of the Buffs, The.
Red Thread of Honour, The.
Doyle, Kirby
Strange.
"Doyle, Lynn" (Leslie Alexander Montgomery)
Ulsterman, An.
Doyle, Marion
Golden Month, The.
Month of the Thunder Moon, The.
Drachmann, Holger
Amber.
Dracontius, Blossius Aemilius
Birds, The.
Drag, Ian
House-Weary.
Drake, Francis
To the Memory of the Learned and Reverend, Mr. Jonathan Mitchell.
Drake, Gaston V.
Contrary Boy, The.
Drake, Joseph Rodman
American Flag, The.
Assembling of the Fays, The.
Bronx.
Culprit Fay, The, *sels.*
Elfin Knight, An.
Elfin Song.
Fairy Dawn.
Fairy in Armor, A.
Fay's Crime, The.
Fay's Departure, The.
Fay's Sentence, The ("Thou shalt seek the beach of sand").
First Quest, The.
Second Quest, The.
Soft and pale is the moony beam.
Throne of the Lily-King, The.
To the Defenders of New Orleans.
Drake, Joseph Rodman, *and* **Fitz-Greene Halleck** *See* **Halleck, Fitz-Greene,** *and* **Joseph Rodman Drake**
Drake, Leah Bodine
Changeling.
Final Green, The.
Gods of the Dana, The.
Green Door, The.
Honey from the Lion.
Middle Ages, The; Two Views.
Pool, The.
Precarious Ground.
Rider, The.
Warning to Skeptics, A.
Witches, The.
Woods Grow Darker, The.
Word of Willow, The.
Drake, V. P.
Glory of Christmas, The.
Drane, Augusta Theodosia *See* **Francis Raphael, Mother**
Drannan, William F.
Old Scout's Lament, The.
Draper, A. S.
Indian Summer.
Draper, Bourne H.
Christian Herald, The.
Draper, Jane
I look into the Stars.
Draper, William H.
Hush, All Ye Sounds of War.
Dratt, Florence Evelyn
Christmas Song, A.
Drayson, Phyllis
Blackbird, The.
Hide and Seek.
Drayton, Michael
Adventures of Oberon, King of the Fairies, While Searching for Queen Mab, The.
Agincourt.
Arming of Pigwiggen, The
Away yee barb'rous woods; how ever yee be plac't.
Ballad of Agincourt, The.
Ballad of Dowsabell, The.
Baron's War, The, *sel.*
Batte's Song: "What is love but the desire."
Battle of Agincourt.
Birds in the Fens.
Cassamen and Dowsabell.
Christopher Marlowe.
Clear Anker, on whose silver-sanded shore.
Cloris and Mertilla.
Come, Let Us Kiss and Part.
Crier, The.
Cryer, The.
Death of Edward, The.
Description of Elysium [*or* Elizium], The.
Dowsabel.
Dying Crane, The.
Earl of Surrey to Geraldine, The.
Earle Douglasse for this day doth with the Percies stand, The.
Eclogues.
Eighth Eclogue, The.
Endimion and Phoebe, *sels.*
Endymion's Convoy.
England's Heroical Epistles, *sels.*
English Musical Instruments.
Epistle of Rosamond to King Henry the Second.
Eternall and all-working God, which wast.
Fame and Fortune.
Fine Day, A.
Fools Gaze at Painted Courts.
For from my cradle you must know that I.
Forest of Arden, The.
Fourth Song, The, *sel.*
Give Me My Self.
Gorbo and Batte.
Harmony of the Church, The, *sels.*
Hawking.
Heart, The.
Henry Howard, Earl of Surrey, to [the Lady] Geraldine.
Henry to Rosamond.
His Ballad of Agincourt.
His Defense against the Idle Critic.
How Many Foolish Things.
I Hear Some Say.
I Pray Thee Leave, Love Me No More.
Idea; or, The Shepherd's Garland.
Idea's Mirrour, *sels.*
It was not long e're he perceiv'd the skies.
Jovial Shepheard's Song, The.
King Henry to Rosamond.
Last Verses.
Late 'twas in June, the fleece when fully grown.
Legend of Robert, Duke of Normandy, The, *sel.*
Lines: "Clear had the day been from the dawn."
Looking-Glass, The.
Love is the heaven's fair aspèct.
Love's Farewell.
Low'ring heaven had mask'd her in a cloud, The.
Many there be excelling in this kind.
Moone-Calfe, The, *sel.*
Mortimeriados, *sels.*
Most Excellent Song Which Was Salomon's, The.
Muses' Elysium, The, *sels.*
Musical Love.
My fair, look from those turrets of thine eyes.
My heart, imprisoned in a hopeless isle.
Night and Day.
Nimphidia.
Ninth Ecologue, The ("Gorbo, as thou camest this way").
Ninth Eglog, The ("What time the weatherbeaten flocks").
Noah's Floud, *sel.*
Nymphidia; or, The Court of Fairy.
Nymphs' Song, The.
Ode to the Cambro-Britains and Their Harp, His Ballad of Agincourt.
Ode to the Virginian Voyage.
Ode Written in the Peak[e], An.
Of all the beasts which we for our veneriall name.
Palace of the Fairies, The.
Parting, The.
Phoebe on Latmus.

Pigwiggen.
Pigwiggen was this fairy knight.
Poets' Paradise, The.
Polyolbion, *sels.*
Prothalamion.
Queen Mab's Chariot.
Queen's Chariot, The.
Roundelay, A: "Tell me, thou skilful shepherd's swain."
Rowland's Rhyme.
Sacrifice to Apollo, The.
Second Nimphall, The.
Seventh Nimphall, The.
Severn, The.
Sheepheards Daffadill, The.
Shepheards Sirena, The.
Shepherd's Anthem, The.
Shepherd's Daffodil, The.
Shepherd's Garland, The, *sels.*
Shepherd's [*or* Shepheards] Sirena, The, *sel.*
Sirena.
Sixth Nymphal, The.
Skeltoniad, A.
So Well I Love Thee.
Song: "Now are the Tritons heard, to Loving-land to call."
Song of Jonah in the Whale's Belly, The.
Song to Beta ("O thou fair silver Thames").
Song to Sirena.
Sonnet: "Black pitchy night, companion of my woe."
Sonnet: "Bright star of beauty, on whose eyelids sit."
Sonnet: "Dear [*or* Deare], why should you command me to my rest."
Sonnet: "Evil spirit, your beauty haunts me still, An."
Sonnet: "How many paltry, foolish, painted things."
Sonnet: "Into these loves, who but for passion looks."
Sonnet: "My heart the anvil where my thoughts do beat."
Sonnet: "Since there's no help, come let us kiss and part."
Sonnet: "To nothing fitter can I thee compare."
Sonnet: "Witless gallant, a young wench that wooed, A."
Sonnet: "You're [*or* You] not alone when you are still alone."
Sonnet from "Idea."
Sonnets.
Sonnets to "Idea."
Stay, stay, sweet Time! Behold, or ere thou pass.
Stay, Thames, to heare my song, thou great and famous flood.
Sylvia.
Tenth Nimphall, The.
Third Eclogue, The,
Thirteenth Song, The, *abr.*
To Cupid.
To Henry Reynolds, of Poets and Poesy, *sel.*
To Himselfe and the Harpe, *abr.*
To His Coy Love.
To His Rival.
To His Valentine.
To Miracle.
To My Most Dearly-Loved [Friend] Henry Reynolds, Esquire, of Poets and Poesie.
To the Cambro-Britons [*or* Britains] and Their Harp, His Ballad of Agincourt.
To the Critic.
To the Dear Child of the Muses and His Ever Kind Maecenas, Master Anthony Cooke, Esquire.
To the Excellent and Most Accomplish'd Lady, Lucy, Countess of Bedford.
To the New Yeere.
To the Reader of These Sonnets.
To the River Anker.
To the Senses.
To the Virginian Voyage.
To these, the gentle South, with kisses smooth and soft.
To Time.
Virginian Voyage, The.
When first I ended, then I first began.
When heaven would strive to do the best she can.
When Phoebus lifts his head out of the Winter's wave.
Why should your fair eyes with such sovereign grace.
With full-leav'd lillies I will stick.
World of mightie kings and princes I could name, A.
Wrestlers.

Drennan, John Swanwick
Avaro ("Avaro sick is seen to shiver").
Epigram: "Avaro sick is seen to shiver."
Epigram: "For love is like a plant that clings."
Epigram: "Golden casket I designed, A."
Epigram: "Love signed the contract blithe and leal."
Epigram: "Metaphysic Sphynx that preys on us, The."
Epigram: "Of the divine and human thought."
Epigram: "With nought to hide or to betray."
Epigrams (I-VIII).
L'Amitié et L'Amour.
Love.
Not Gone Yet.
On the Telescopic Moon.
Perdita.
Spinozaism, A.

Drennan, Marie
Peace Must Come As a Troubadour.

Drennan, William
Aspiration.
Branch of the Sweet and Early Rose.
Eire.
Wake of William Orr, The.

Dresbach, Glenn Ward
Autumn Road, An.
Early Morning in a Glade.
I saw a grown girl coming down.
In Western Mountains, *sel.*
Last Corn Shock, The.
Life or Death.
Little Spring Flows Clear Again, The.
Magic Lariat.
Old Sailor, The.
Ship's Bell.
Since Youth Is All for Gladness.
Songs of the Plains, I-IV.
Through the Blowing Leaves.

Dresser, Paul
Just Tell Them That You Saw Me.
My Gal Sal.
On the Banks of the Wabash, Far Away.

Drewry, Carleton
Evensong.
In This Strange House.
Invocation: "O world watched over by the cold moon and the mindless stars."
I Said to the Leaf.
Rings in a Roundness.
Song in Humility, A.

"Drinan, Adam." *See* **Macleod, Joseph Gordon**

Drinkwater, John
Bird's Nest, The.
Birthright.
Bobby Blue.
Challenge.
Christmas Eve.
Christmas Night, A.
Crowning of Dreaming John, The.
Deer.
Feckenham Men, The.
Foundation of Faith.
Greatness Passing By.
I Want to Know.
Invocation: "As pools beneath stone arches take."
Mamble.
May Garden.
Moonlit Apples.
Morning Thanksgiving.
My Estate.
Petition.
Plea, The.
Prayer, A: "Lord, not for light in darkness do we pray."
Prayer, A: "We know the paths wherein our feet should press."
Purpose.
Puzzles.
Reciprocity.
Snail.
Sun, The.
Sunrise on Rydal Water.
Tiptoe Night.
To and Fro about the City.
Town Window, A.
Wagon in the Barn, The.
Washing.
Who Were before Me.

Driscoll, Louise
Banquet, The.
Bargain.
Epitaph: "Here lies the flesh that tried."
God's Pity.
Good Hour, The.
Grace for Gardens.
Highway, The.
Hold Fast Your Dreams.
Idol, The.
Indifference.
July Meadow.
Marigolds.
Metal Checks, The.
Mid-August.
My Garden Is a Pleasant Place.
November Garden.
Spring Market.
Thanksgiving.
Their Thanksgiving Day.

Driver, C. J.
Birthdays.
In Solitary Confinement, Sea Point Police Cells.
To Jann, in Her Absence.

Driver, Olive
Lake Winnipesaukee.
May Moon.
Plymouth Rock.

"Droch." *See* **Bridges, Robert (1858-1941)**

Dromgoole, Will Allen
Bridge Builder, The.
Building the Bridge for Him.

Droste-Hülshoff, Annette von
Gethsemane.
Last Words.

Drummond William, of Hawthornden
Angels, The.
Angels for the Nativity of Our Lord, The.
As in a Dusky and Tempestuous Night.
Baptist, The.
Book, The.

Drummond (continued)
Book of the World, The.
Change Should Breed Change.
Doth Then the World Go Thus.
Flowers of Sion, *sels.*
For the Baptist[e].
For the Magdalene.
For the Nativity of Our Lord ("O than the fairest day").
Good that never satisfies the mind, A.
Her Passing.
Hymne of the Ascension, An.
I fear not henceforth death.
I know that all beneath the moon decays.
If Crossed with All Mishaps.
In This World's Raging Sea.
Inexorable.
Invocation: "Phoebus, arise!"
Iölas' Epitaph.
Ivory, Coral, Gold, The.
Kiss, A.
Kisses Desired.
Lament: "Chaste maids which haunt fair Aganippe's well."
Lament, A: "My thoughts hold mortal strife."
Lessons of Nature, The.
Life, a Bubble.
Like the Idalian Queen.
Love Which Is Here a Care.
Madrigal: "Beautie [*or* Beauty], and the life, The."
Madrigal: "I fear not henceforth death."
Madrigal: "Ivory, coral, gold, The."
Madrigal: "Like the Idalian queen."
Madrigal: Love Vagabonding.
Madrigal: "My thoughts hold mortal strife."
Madrigal: "This life, which seems so fair."
Madrigal: "Unhappy [*or* Unhappie] light."
My Thoughts Hold Mortal Strife.
Nativitie, The.
No Trust in Time.
Now while the night her sable veil hath spread.
Of Phyllis.
On the Death of Pym.
On the Margin Wrought.
Phoebus, Arise!
Phyllis.
Regret [*or* Regrat].
Saint John Baptist.
Sleep, Silence' Child.
Sleeping Beauty.
Solitary Life, A.
Sonet to Sleepe.
Song: "It autumne was, and on our hemispheare."
Song: "Phoebus, arise."
Song of the Ascension.
Sonnet: "Alexis, here she stayed; among these pines."
Sonnet: "As in a duskie and tempestuous night."
Sonnet: "Dear quirister, who from those shadows sends."
Sonnet: "How that vast heaven intitled First is rolled."
Sonnet: "I fear to me such fortune be assign'd."
Sonnet: "In minds pure glasse when I my selfe behold."
Sonnet: "Look how the flower which lingeringly doth fade."
Sonnet: "My lute, be as thou wast when thou didst grow."
Sonnet: "Of this fair volume which we World do name."
Sonnet: "Passing glance, a lightning long the skies, A."
Sonnet: "Sleep, Silence' child, sweet father of soft rest."
Sonnet: "Sweet Spring, thou turn'st with all thy goodly train."
Sonnet: "That learned Grecian (who did so excel)."
Sonnet: "What doth it serve to see sun's burning face."
Spring Bereaved ("Alexis, here she stayed").
Spring Bereaved ("Sweet Spring, thou turn'st with all thy goodly train").
Spring Bereaved ("That zephyr every year").
Stolen Pleasure.
Summons to Love.
Tears on the Death of Meliades, *sel.*
Tell Me No More.
That I so slenderly set forth my mind.
This Life [a Bubble].
This Life Which Seems So Fair.
This World a Hunting Is.
Thrice Happy He.
Thy Sun Posts Westward.
To a Nightingale.
To Chloris.
To His Lute.
To Sir William Alexander.
To the Nightingale ("Dear quirister, who from those shadows sends").
Too long I followed have my fond desire.
World, The.
World a Hunt, The.

Drummond, William Henry
How Bateese Came Home.
Johnnie Courteau.
Julie Plante, The.
Leetle Bateese.
Madeleine Verchères.
Ole Tam on Bord-a Plouffe.
'Poleon Dore.
Stove Pipe Hole, De.
Two Hundred Years Ago.
Wreck of the *Julie Plante,* The.

Dryden John
Absalom and Achitophel, Pt. I.
Achitophel.
After the Pangs of a Desparate Lover.
Ah, Fading Joy.
Ah How Sweet It Is to Love.
Albion and Albanius, *sel.*
Alexander's Feast; or, The Power of Music [*or* Musique].
All, All of a Piece [Throughout].
All For Love, *sels.*
Amboyna, *sel.*
Amphitryon, *sels.*
And welcom now (Great Monarch) to your own.
Annus Mirabilis, *sels.*
Assignation, The, *sel.*
Astraea Redux.
Aureng-Zebe, *sels.*
Ave atque Vale.
Calm Was the Even [and Clear Was the Sky].
Can Life Be a Blessing.
Catholic Church, The.
Characters from the Satires: Achitophel.
Characters from the Satires: Og and Doeg.
Characters from the Satires: Zimri.
Charm, A.
Chorus: "All, all of a piece throughout."
Church of England, The.
Churches of Rome and of England, The.
Church's Testimony, The.
Cleomenes, *sel.*
Cleopatra and Antony.
Confession of Faith.
Conquest of Granada, The, *sels.*
Conversion ("Be vengeance wholly left to powers divine").
Conversion ("But, gracious God, how well dost Thou provide").
Cymon and Iphigenia, *sel.*
Dame, said the Panther, times are mended well.
Damon and Celimena.
Design.
Diana's Hunting-Song.
Doeg, though without knowing how or why.
Duke of Buckingham, The ("A numerous host").
Earl of Shaftesbury, The.
Enemies of David, The.
Epigram: "Here lies my wife: here let her lie!"
Epigram on Milton.
Epigram on Tonson.
Epilogue: "Poets, like disputants, when reasons fail."
Epilogue: "Pretty task, A; and so I told the Fool."
Epilogue: "They who have best succeeded on the stage."
Epilogue Spoken at Oxford by Mrs. Marshall.
Epilogue Spoken to the King at the Opening the Play-House at Oxford, The.
Epilogue to "Mithridates, King of Pontus."
Epilogue to the University of Oxford, 1674.
Epilogue to "Tyrannic Love."
Epitaph Intended for His Wife.
Epitaph on His Wife.
Epitaph on John Graham of Claverhouse, Viscount Dundee.
Evening's Love, An, *sels.*
Fair Iris and Her Swain.
Fair Iris I Love.
Fairest Isle.
False Achitophel, The.
False and Fickle.
Farewell, Ungrateful Traitor.
Fife and Drum.
Finite Reason.
Fire of London, The, *sels.*
First Prologue to "Secret Love; or, The Maiden Queen."
Fourth Day's Battle, The.
From hence began that plot; the nation's curse.
George Villiers, Duke of Buckingham.
Great Fire, The.
Here Lies My Wife.
Heroic [*or* Heroique] Stanzas, Consecrated to the Glorious Memory of His Most Serene and Renowned Highnesse, Oliver, Late Lord Protector of This Common-Wealth.
Hidden Flame, The.
Hind and the Panther, The, *sels.*
Hourly I Die.
How Happy the Lover.
How I loved/ Witness, ye days and nights.
How Unhappy a Lover Am I.
Human Happiness.
I Feed a Flame Within [Which So Torments Me].
Incantation to Oedipus.
Indian Emperor, The, *sels.*
Instruments, The.
Jacob Tonson, His Publisher.
Kind Keeper, The.
King Arthur, *sels.*
King James II.
Kiss Me, Dear.
Lady's Song, The.
Levi, thou art a load, I'll lay thee down.

Limberham; or, The Kind Keeper, *sel.*
Lines beneath the Portrait of Milton.
Lines on Milton.
Lines Printed under the Engraved Portrait of Milton.
London.
Long betwixt Love and Fear.
Lord Shaftesbury.
Love.
Love Triumphant, *sel.*
Love's Despair.
Love's Fancy.
MacFlecknoe; or, A Satire upon the True-Blue Protestant Poet T. S.
Maiden Queen, The.
Malcontents, The.
Marriage à la Mode, *sels.*
Medal, The; a Satire against Sedition.
Mercury's Song to Phaedra.
Midnight.
New London, The.
Next these, a troop of buisy spirits press.
No, No, Poor Suffering [*or* Suff'ring] Heart.
Now with a general peace the world was blest.
Oak, The.
Ode in Honor of St. Cecilia's Day, An.
Ode to the Pious Memory of the Accomplished Young Lady, Mrs. Anne Killigrew.
Oedipus, *sels.*
Of all the tyrannies of human kind.
Og and Doeg.
On the Death of Mr. Purcell.
One evening, while the cooler shade she sought.
One Happy Moment.
Phyllis.
Poet Shadwell, The.
Poet's Resurrection.
Popish Plot, The.
Portrait of Milton, The.
Power of Love, The.
Power of Music, The.
Prayer, A: "What weight of ancient witness can prevail."
Presbyterians, The.
Priestcraft and Private Judgement.
Primacy of Dullness, The.
Private Judgment Condemned.
Prologue: "He who writ this, not without pains and thought."
Prologue: "If yet there be a few that take delight."
Prologue: "Lord, how reformed and quiet are we grown."
Prologue: "Our author, by experience, finds it true."
Prologue: "See, my loved Britons, see your Shakespeare rise."
Prologue: "What flocks of critics hover here to-day."
Prologue and Epilogue to "Tyrannick Love; or, The Royal Martyr."
Prologue to "Aureng-Zebe."
Prologue to "Love Triumphant."
Prologue to "Secret Love; or, The Maiden-Queen."
Prologue to "The Tempest."
Prologue to the University of Oxford, 1673.
Prologue to the University of Oxford, 1674.
Prologue to the University of Oxford, 1676.
Reason and Revelation.
Rebirth of London, The.
Religio Laici.
Rondelay: "Chloe found Amyntas lying."
Scriptures, The.
Sea Battle, The.
Second Part of Absalom and Achitophel, The.
Secret Love; or, The Maiden Queen, *sels.*
Secular Masque, The.
Shadwell.
Shaftesbury.
She comes. She's here.
Sigismonda and Guiscardo, *sel.*
Sir Fopling Flutter.
Some in my speedy pace I must outrun.
Song: "After the pangs of a desperate lover."
Song: "Ah, fading joy! how quickly art thou past!"
Song: "Ah, how sweet it is to love."
Song: "Calm was the even, and cleer was the sky."
Song: "Can life be a blessing."
Song, A: "Celia, that I once was blest."
Song, A: "Celimena, of my heart."
Song: "Day is come, I see it rise, The."
Song: "Fair Iris I love, and hourly I die."
Song: "Fair, sweet and young, receive a prize."
Song: "Farewell, ungrateful traitor!"
Song, A: "Go tell Amynta gentle swain."
Song: "How happy the lover."
Song: "I feed a flame within, which so torments me."
Song: "Long betwixt love and fear Phillis tormented."
Song: "No, no, poor suff'ring heart no change endeavour."
Song: "Sylvia the fair, in the bloom of fifteen."
Song: "Wherever I am, and whatever I doe."
Song, A: "Whil'st Alexis lay prest."
Song: "Why should a foolish marriage vow."
Song, A: "You charm'd me not with that fair face."
Song: Your hay it is mow'd and your corn is reap'd.
Song for a Girl.
Song for St. Cecilia's Day, A, 1687.
Song from the Italian, A.
Song of Momus to Mars, The.
Song of the River Thames, A.
Song of the Zambra Dance.
Song of Venus.
Song to a Fair, Young Lady, Going Out of [the] Town in the Spring.
Song to a Minuet.
Songs from "The Secular Masque."
Spanish Friar, The, *sel.*
Spell, A.
Sung by a Young Girl.
Sylvoe, *sel.*
Tears of Amynta, The, for the Death of Damon.
Theodore and Honoria.
This plot, which failed for want of common sense.
Thomas Shadwell the Poet.
Thus man by his own strength to Heaven would soar.
Time seems not now beneath his years to stoop.
To a Fair Young Lady, Going Out of [the] Town in the Spring.
To His Sacred Majesty, a Panegyrick on His Coronation, 1661, *sel.*
To My Dear Friend Mr. Congreve [on His Comedy Call'd "The Double-Dealer"].
To My Friend, Dr. Charleton.
To My Friend Mr. Motteux.
To My Honor'd Friend, Dr. Charleton.
To My Honor'd Friend Sir Robert Howard, on His Excellent Poems.
To My Honored Kinsman, John Dryden [*or* Driden], of Chesterton [in the County of Huntingdon, Esquire].
To the Memory of Mr. Oldham.
To the Pious Memory of the Accomplished [*or* Accomplisht] Young Lady, Mrs. Anne Killigrew.
To the University of Oxford, 1674.
To this the Panther, with a scornful[l] smile.
Tradition.
Troilus and Cressida, *sels.*
Tyrannick [*or* Tyrannic] Love; or, The Royal Martyr, *sels.*
Under the Portrait of John Milton.
Upon the Death of the Viscount of [*or* Earl of] Dundee.
Vox Populi.
War.
Warlike prince had sever'd from the rest, The.
What Is the World?
When I Consider Life.
Wherever I Am [and Whatever I Do].
Whilst Alexis Lay Prest.
Why Should a Foolish Marriage Vow.
Wild Weather.
World Well Lost, The.
Worldly Vanity.
Yet London, empress of the northern clime.
You Charm'd Me Not.
Zambra Dance, The.
Zimri.

Dryden, John, *and* **Sir Robert Howard** *See* **Howard, Sir Robert,** *and* **John Dryden**

Dryden, John, *and* **Nahum Tate** *See* **Tate, Nahum,** *and* **John Dryden**

Dryden, Myrtle May
Just Forget.

Dschellaleddin Rumi *See* **Rumi, Jalaled-Din**

Du Autermont, Harriet
Some Faith at Any Cost.

Du Bellay, Joachim
Happy Ulysses, The.
Heureux qui, comme Ulysse, a fait un beau voyage.
Hymn to the Winds.
I saw the bird that can the sun endure [*or* that dares behold the sun].
Olive, *sel.*
Pale Is Death.
Regrets, *sels.*
Returning Home.
Rome.
Ruins of Rome.
Sonnet: "If life on earth be less than is a day."
Sonnet: "If of our life the span be not a day."
Sonnet: "It was the time, when rest, soft sliding downe."
Sonnet to Heavenly Beauty, A.
To His Friend in Elysium.
Visions, *sel.*
Vow to Heavenly Venus, A.

Du Bois, Gertrude
Meditation in St. Mary's.

DuBois, William Edward Burghardt
Litany at [*or* of] Atlanta, A.
Litany of Atlanta, A.

Ducic, Jovan
Clock, The.

Duck, Stephen
On Mites.

Duckett, Alfred A.
Portrait Philippines.

Duckett (continued)
Sonnet: "Where are we to go when this is done?"
Duclaux, Agnes Mary Frances *See* **Robinson, Agnes Mary Frances**
Dudek, Louis
Air by Sammartini, An.
Atlantis, *sel.*
Avant Garde.
Commotion of these waves, however strong, cannot disturb.
Dawn.
Europe, *sels.*
Fishing Village.
García Lorca.
I Have Seen the Robins Fall.
Ignorant present has scribbled over the past, The.
Jungle, The.
Marine Aquarium, The.
Mountains, The.
Mouths.
Narrative.
News.
O Contemporaries.
Ocean, The.
Old Song.
Pomegranate, The.
Provincetown, *sels.*
Puerto Rican Side-Street.
Sea retains such images, The.
Store-House, A.
Street in April, A.
Dudley, Dorothy
La Rue de la Montagne Sainte-Geneviève.
Dudley, Helen
Song: "Few more windy days, A."
To One Unknown.
Dudley, Thomas
Verses Found in Thomas Dudley's Pocket after His Death.
Duer, Alice *See* **Miller, Alice Duer**
Duer, Caroline
International Episode, An.
Portrait, A.
Word to the Wise, A.
Duerden, Richard
Dance with Banderillas.
Moon Is to Blood.
Musica No. 3.
Duewel, Wesley
On with the Message! [On, On, and On]!
Dufault, Peter Kane
Black Jess.
In an Old Orchard.
Letter for Allhallows, A.
Lines for a Night Driver.
Notes on a Girl.
Odysseus' Song to Calypso.
On Aesthetics, More or Less.
Owl.
Possibilities.
Thalamos.
Tour de Force.
Duff Esther Lilian
Black and White.
Lad's Love.
Of a Certain Green-Eyed Monster.
Duff, James L.
Cradle Song: "Sleep enfold thee,/ Jesukin."
Dies Irae.
Loan of a Stall, The.
Upon This Rock.
Dufferin, Lady *See* **Sheridan, Helen Selina**
Duffett, Thomas
Celia.
To Francelia.
Duffield, George, Jr.
Stand Up for Jesus.
Duffield, Lois
Forgiveness.
He Was Alone.
Mother Sings, A.
"One of the Least of These."
Duffield, Samuel Willoughby
Two of a Trade.
Duffin, Celia
Old Dog, An.
Duffy, Sir Charles Gavan
Irish Rapparees, The.
Duffy, John
Annunciation, The.
Domine Jesu!
Our Lady's Labor.
Ox-Bone Madonna.
Thrush, The.
Duffy, Nona Keen
Above the Stable.
Spring Is in the Making.
Dugan, Alan
Dedication for a Building.
Elegy: "I know but will not tell."
Funeral Oration for a Mouse.
How We Heard the Name.
Love Song: I and Thou.
Memorial Service for the Invasion Beach.
Mirror Perilous, The.
Morning Song.
On an East Wind from the Wars.
On Don Juan del Norte, Not Don Juan Tenorio del Sur.
On Hurricane Jackson.
Plague of Dead Sharks.
Poem: "Always prudent but unprepared."
Poem: "Person who can do, The."
Portrait.
Stutterer.
There He Was.
Thesis, Antithesis, and Nostalgia.
Wall, Cave, and Pillar Statements, After Asôka.
Dugan, Mrs. D. H.
Christ Is Risen!
Dugan, Maurice *See* **O'Dugan, Maurice**
Duganne, A. J. H.
Bethel.
Duggan, Eileen
After the Annunciation.
Aspiration.
Ballad of the Bushman.
Bushfeller, The.
Contrast.
Didymus.
Discipline of Consequences, The.
Epiphany.
Interlude.
Juniper.
Last Song, The.
Milker, The.
Musterer, The.
Name, The.
Peasantry.
Pilgrimage.
Plea.
Post-War.
Presumption.
St. Peter.
Tides Run up the Wairau, The.
Twilight.
Victory.
Dugmore, H. H.
And this is now their home.
Reminiscence of 1820, A, *sel.*
Duke, Daryl
It Was My June.
Duke, Richard
Caelia.
Epistle from Mr. Duke to Mr. Otway, An.
Dumas, Alexandre
Chevalier de maison rouge, Le, *sel.*
Girondins, The.
Lady of the Pearls, The, *sel.*
We set out yesterday upon a winter's drive.
Dumas, Henry
America.
Cuttin Down to Size.
Image.
Knock on Wood.
Mosaic Harlem.
Du Maurier, George
Legend of Camelot, A.
Little, A.
Little Work, A.
Lost Illusion, A.
Music.
Trilby, *sel.*
Vers Nonsensiques.
"Dum-Dum." *See* **Kendall, John Kaye**
Dunbar, Jennie
A-Hunting.
Dunbar, Paul Laurence
Accountability.
After the Quarrel.
Angelina.
Ante-Bellum Sermon, An.
At Candle-lightin' Time.
Boy's Summer Song, A.
Chrismus on the Plantation.
Colored Band, The.
Columbian Ode.
Compensation.
Conquerors, The.
Conscience and Remorse.
Coquette Conquered, A.
Corn-Song, A.
Curtain!
Dawn.
Death Song, A.
Debt, The.
Deserted Plantation, The.
Differences.
Discovered.
Encouraged.
Encouragement.
Equipment.
Ere Sleep Comes Down to Soothe the Weary Eyes.
Frederick Douglass.
Harriet Beecher Stowe.
Haunted Oak, The.
He Had His Dream.
Howdy, Honey, Howdy!
Hymn, A: "Lead gently, Lord, and slow."
Hymn: "O li'l' lamb out in de col'."
Hymn: "When storms arise."
Hymn, A, after Reading "Lead, Kindly Light."
In the Morning.
Keep a-Pluggin' Away.
Life.
Li'l' Gal.
Lincoln.
Little Brown Baby.
Lonesome.
Lover's Lane.
Lullaby: "Bedtime's come fu' little boys."
Master-Player, The.
My Sort o' Man.
Negro Love Song, A.
Ode to Ethiopia.
Old Cabin, The.
On the Road.
Paradox.
Party, The.
Poet, The.
Poet and His Song, The.
Prayer, A: "O Lord, the hard-won miles."
Precedent.
Promise.

Retort.
Rivals, The.
Robert Gould Shaw.
Ships That Pass in the Night.
Song, A: "Thou art the soul of a summer's day."
Song of Summer.
Sympathy.
Theology.
To a Captious Critic.
Turning of the Babies in the Bed, The.
Unsung Heroes, The, *abr.*
Warrior's Prayer, A.
We Wear the Mask.
When a Feller's Itchin' to be Spanked.
When All Is Done.
When de Co'n Pone's Hot.
When Malindy Sings.

Dunbar, William
Amends to the Tailors and Soutars.
Ane Ballat of Our Lady.
Ballad of Kynd Kittok, The.
Ballad of Our Lady.
Book of the Two Married Women and the Widow, The.
Dance of the Sevin Deidly Synnis, The.
Fear of Death Confounds Me, The.
Flyting of Dumbar and Kennedie, The, *sel.*
Followis How Dumbar Wes Desyr to Be ane Freir.
Golden Targe, The.
Goldyn [*or* Golden] Targe, The.
Hymn of the Resurrection, A.
Hymn to Mary, A.
Iersch brybour baird, vyle beggar with thy brattis.
In Honour of the City of London.
Lament for the Makaris [*or* Makars].
Man of Valour to His Fair Lady, The.
Manere of the Crying of ane Playe, The.
Meditation in Winter.
Meditatioun in Wyntir.
O reverend Chaucere, rose of rethoris all.
Of the Resurrection of Christ.
On the Nativity of Christ.
On the Resurrection of Christ.
Petition of the Gray Horse, Auld Dunbar, The.
Poet's Dream, The.
Quehn Merche wes with variiand windis past.
Quod Dunbar to Kennedy.
Remonstrance to the King.
Testament of Mr. Andro Kennedy, The.
Thrissil and the Rois, The, *sel.*
To a Lady.
To a Ladye.
To the City of London.
To the Merchantis of Edinburgh.
To the Princess Margaret Tudor.
Tretis of the Tua Mariit Wemen and the Wedo.
Tua Mariit Wemen and the Wedo, The.
Two Married Women and the Widow, The.
Unto the death gois all estatis.
Widow Speaks, The.

Duncan, Mary Lundie
Child's Evening Prayer, A.
Child's Morning Prayer, A.
Jesus, Tender Shepherd [Hear Me].
My Little Brother.
Shadows, The.

Duncan, Rea Lubar
Juncture.

Duncan, Robert
After a Passage in Baudelaire.
Dance, The.
Dream Data.
Earth's Winter Song.
Food for Fire, Food for Thought.
Hero Song.
In the Place of a Passage 22.
Ingmar Bergman's Seventh Seal.
Interlude, An.
Multiversity, The.
My Mother Would Be a Falconress.
Often I Am Permitted to Return to a Meadow.
Owl Is an Only Bird of Poetry, An.
Parsifal.
Poem Beginning with a Line by Pindar, A.
Question, The.
Reaper, The.
Shelley's *Arethusa* Set to New Measures.
Song of the Borderguard, The.
Strains of Sight.
Structure of Rime XXIII.
This Place Rumord to Have Been Sodom.

Duncan, Thomas W.
Village Portrait.

Dunetz, Lora
Ailing Parent, The.
All That Summer.
"And All the While the Sky Is Falling. . ."
Black Cat.
Treason.
While the Bells Ring.

Dunkin, L. E.
I'm Not Alone.

Dunlop, John
Dinna Ask Me.
Year That's Awa', The.

Dunn, Alta Booth
Unknown Soldier.

Dunn, Max
Flower of Exile.
I Danced before I Had Two Feet.

Dunn, Stephen P.
Prayer of the Young Stoic.

Dunnam, Ouida Smith
Prayer of a Beginning Teacher.

Dunning, Emerette H.
Memorial Day.

Dunsany, Edward John Moreton Drax Plunkett, 18th Baron
Bringing Him Up.
Call to the Wild, A.
Deserted Kingdom, The.
Heterodoxy, A.
I met with Death in his country.
Memory, The.
On the Safe Side.
Snow on the East Wind.
Somewhere lost in the haze.
Songs from an Evil Wood.

Dunster, Mark
They Say on Leaving Eden.

Dupree, Edgar
Light of Faith, The.

Dupuy, J.
Michael Met a White Duck.

Durack, Mary (Mrs. H. C. Miller)
Red Jack.

Durand, Oswald
Black Man's Son, The.
Choucoune.
If.

Durbin, Eliza W.
Our Washington.

Durbin, Harriet Whitney
Little Dutch Garden, A.

Durell, Ann
Cornish Magic.

Durem, Ray
Award.
Basic.
Problem in Social Geometry—the Inverted Square!
Ultimate Equality.
You Know, Joe.

D'Urfey [*or* Durfey *or* D'Urfé] Thomas
Ballad of Andrew and Maudlin, A.
Bath, The; or, The Western Lass, *sel.*
Born with the Vices.
Bright Was the Morning.
Brother Solon's Hunting Song.
Campaigners, The; or, The Pleasant Adventures at Brussels, *sel.*
Chloe Divine.
Fisherman's Song, The.
Fool's Preferment, A, *sel.*
Hunting Song.
I'll [*or* I'le] Sail upon the Dog-Star.
Kingston Church.
Maid's Longing, The.
Marriage-Hater Match'd, The, *sel.*
Musick Commended, and Scraping Ridiculed, etc.
Pills to Purge Melancholy, *sel.*
Sawney Was Tall.
Scotch Song.
Second Dialogue between Crab and Gillian.
Shepherd Kept Sheep on a Hill So High, A.
Solon's Song.
Song, A: "Boast no more fond love, thy power."
Song, A: "Night her blackest sables wore, The."
To Cynthia: a Song.
Virtuous Wife, The, *sel.*
Winchester Wedding, The.

D'Urfey, Thomas *and others*
All Hail to the Days That Merit More Praise, *with music.*

Durham, Richard V.
Dawn Patrol; Chicago.

Durivage, Francis Alexander
Chez Brébant.

Durrell, Lawrence
Adepts, The.
Alexandria.
At Epidaurus.
Ballad of the Good Lord Nelson, A.
By the Lake.
Carol on Corfu.
Conon in Alexandria.
Conon in Exile.
Coptic Poem ("A Coptic deputation, going to Ethiopia").
Critics, The.
Delos.
Eight Aspects of Melissa.
Encounter, The.
Green Coconuts.
In a Time of Crisis.
In Arcadia.
In the Garden; Villa Cleobolus.
Lost Cities, The.
Mythology.
Nemea.
Night, The.
On First Looking into Loeb's Horace.
On Ithaca Standing.
On Seeming to Presume.
Paphos.
Petron, the Desert Father.
Prospect of Children, A.
Rising Sun, The.
Salamis.
Sarajevo.
Song for Zarathustra.
Stoic.
Swans.
This Unimportant Morning.
To Argos.
To Ping-ku, Asleep.
Visitations.
Water-Colour of Venice, A.
Water Music.

Durston Georgia Roberts ("George Durston")
Hippopotamus, The.
Rabbit, The.
Wolf, The.
Durward, Bernard Isaac
Good Night.
Durward, John T.
Missed Again.
Duryee, Mary Ballard
Homestead—Winter Morning.
Dusenbery, Gail
Backyard on Fulton Street, The.
Guitar, The.
I Carried with Me Poems.
Letter to Duncan.
Midnight on March 27th.
New Year's.
Opening Session of Congress Rock and Roll, The.
Saturday Night.
Shadow, The.
Du Toit, J. D. *See* **"Totius"**
Dutt, Aru
Still Barred Thy Doors.
Dutt, Michael Madhusudan
Satan.
Dutt, Toru
Our Casuarina Tree.
Dutton, Geoffrey
January.
Mountain, The.
Nightflight and Sunrise.
Prisoner Freed, A.
Temple by the Sea, The.
Variations on a Medieval Theme.
Duval, Paul *See* **"Lorrain, Jean"**
Duvar, John Hunter *See* **Hunter-Duvar, John**
Dwight, Thomas
To the Federal Convention.
Dwight, Timothy
And when new regions prompt their feet to roam.
Assault on the Fortess, The.
Church and School.
Columbia.
Greenfield Hill, *sels.*
I Love Thy Kingdom, Lord.
Love to the Church.
Minister, New Style, A.
Psalm CXXXVII: "I love thy kingdom, Lord."
Smooth Divine, The.
Star of Columbia, *with music.*
Sweet Simplicity.
Triumph of Infidelity, The, *sel.*
Two Ways of Visiting.
Dyer, Lady Catherine
Epitaph on the Monument of Sir William Dyer at Colmworth, 1641.
Dyer, Sir Edward
Contentment.
Corydon to His Phyllis.
Cynthia.
Fancy, Farewell.
Kingdom.
Love Is Love.
Lowest Trees Have Tops [*or* Topps], The.
Man Whose Thoughts, The.
Modest Love, A.
My Mind to Me a Kingdom Is.
My Mynde to Me a Kingdome Is.
Prometheus When First from Heaven.
Wher One Would Be.
Dyer, John
Ah gentle shepherd, thine the lot to tend.
Below me trees unnumber'd rise.
British Commerce.
Country Walk, The.
English Fog, The.
English Weather.
Enquiry, The.
Ever charming, ever new.
Fall'n, fall'n, a silent heap; her heroes all.
Fleece, The, *sels.*
Grongar Hill.
Nation's Wealth, A.
O may I with myself agree.
Old castles on the cliff arise.
Ruins of Rome, The. *sel.*
To Clio.
To His Son.
Wool Trade, The.
Dyment, Clifford
As a Boy with a Richness of Needs I Wandered.
Axe in the Wood, The.
Bahnhofstrasse.
Carpenter, The.
Carrion.
Children, The.
Coming of the Fog.
Dark City, The.
Desert, The.
Fox.
From Many a Mangled Truth a War Is Won.
Holidays in Childhood.
King of the Wood, The.
Man and Beast.
Pastoral: "In the old days the white gates swung."
Raven, The.
Savage the Daylight and Annihilate Night.
Snow, The.
Swans, The.
Switch Cut in April, A.
Temple, The.
To London the Train Gallops, Its Shrill Steel Hooves.
Winter Trees, The.
Dyson, Edward
Cleaning Up.
Peter Simson's Farm.
Worked-out Mine, The.
Dyson, Will
Death Is but Death.
Planet Moon, *sel.*
Dzyubin, Eduard *See* **"Bagritsky, Eduard"**

E

"E." *See* **Fullerton, mary Elizabeth**
"E. C." *See* **"C., E"**
"E. G. B." *See* **"B., E. G"**
"E. H. K." *See* **"K., E. H"**
"E. H. R." *See* **"R., E. H"**
"E. M. G. R." *See* **"R., E. M. G"**
"E. O. G." *See* **"G., E. O."**
"E. R. B." *See* **"B., E. R"**
"E. S." *See* **"S., E"**
"E. W." *See* **"W., E"**
"Eagle, Solomon." *See* **Squire, Sir John Collins**
Eakman, Florence
Our Clock.
Earhart, Amelia
Courage.
Earle, John Charles
Lo, I Am with You Always.
Onward and Upward.
Seeking and Finding God.
Earle, Virginia
Dream as Reported, A.
Night Concert.
Receive, Beloved.
Earley, Jackie
To Be a Woman.
Earls, Michael
Autumn Rose-Tree, An.
To a Carmelite Postulant.
Earp, Thomas Wade
Adventure.
East, James
Wise Men Seeking Jesus.
"Eastaway, Edward." *See* **Thomas, Edward**
Easter, Marguerite Elizabeth
My Laddie's Hounds.
Eastman, Barrett
How We Burned the *Philadelphia.*
Joy Enough.
Richard Somers.
Eastman, Charles Gamage
Dirge: "Softly! She is lying with her lips apart."
Eastman, Elaine Goodale
Ashes of Roses.
Baby.
Countrywoman of Mine, A.
Goldenrod.
Eastman, Max
April Earth, The.
At the Aquarium.
Diogenes.
Egrets.
Hymn to God in Time of Stress, A.
Invocation: "Truth, be more precious to me than the eyes."
Rainy Song.
Truth.
We Have Been Happy.
Eastman, Sophie E.
Spool of Thread, A.
Eastwick, Ivy O.
And Dancing.
At Sunset.
Birthday Cake.
Birthday Garden.
Cherry Tree.
Dark Danny.
Elizabeth Ann Peabody.
Feather for My Cap, A.
First Snow.
Hurry Tomorrow.
I'm Glad My Birthday Comes in May!
Jack-in-the-Pulpit.
Jolly Days.
Larch Wood Secrets.
Lucy Lavender.
Mary's Lullaby.
May Mornings.
Mickleham Way.
Midsummer Magic.
Miller, Miller.
Morning.
Mother and Child.
My True Love.
Pretty Maid Marion.
Robber, The.
Scarf, The.
Seven Today.
Shadow Dance.
Sing a Song of Moonlight.
Sing a Song of Sunshine.
Snow in Spring.
Stay, Christmas!
Timothy Boon.
Trouble at the Farm.
Waking Time.
Where's Mary?
Winter in the Wood.
Wolf and the Lambs, The.
Eastwood, Earle V.
Barter.
Eaton, Anthony

Dove Apologizes to His God for Being Caught by a Cat, The.
Eaton, Arthur Wentworth Hamilton
Egyptian Lotus, The.
Phantom Light of the Baie des Chaleurs, The.
Pray for the Dead.
Eaton, Burnham
Inbound.
Lost Voice on This Hill.
Shadowed.
Technique.
Unexplored, The.
Eaton, Charles Edward
Peony for Apollo, A.
Tropes of One Season.
Eaton, Evelyn Sibyl Mary
Gardener, The.
Eaton, Walter Prichard
Birches, The.
White-Throat Sings, A.
Willows, The.
Eberhart, Richard
Advantage of the Outside, The.
Am I My Neighbor's Keeper?
At Lake Geneva.
Attic, The.
Attitudes.
Book of Nature, The.
Broken bones were left to brokenness.
Brother of Men, *sel.*
Burr Oaks, *sel.*
Cancer Cells, The.
Chiliasm.
Cold Fall.
Cousin Florence.
Cover Me Over.
Dam Neck, Virginia.
Day-Bed, The.
Enigma, The.
For a Lamb.
Forgotten Rock, The.
Forms of the Human.
From Four Lakes' Days.
From "Suite in Prison."
Full of Joy Do Not Know, The; They Need Not.
Fury of Aerial Bombardment, The.
Go to the Shine That's on a Tree.
Goal of Intellectual Man, The.
Grave Piece.
Groundhog, The.
Half-Bent Man.
Hardening into Print.
Hark Back.
Horse Chestnut Tree, The.
Human Being Is a Lonely Creature, The.
I Walked Out to the Graveyard to See the Dead.
Idols of Imagination.
If I Could Only Live at the Pitch That Is Near Madness.
If This Be Love.
Imagining How It Would Be to Be Dead.
In a Hard Intellectual Light.
In After Time.
In the Garden.
Incomparable Light, The.
Indian Pipe.
It Is That Bane of Self in Love.
La Crosse at Ninety Miles an Hour.
Largess, The.
Legend of Viable Women, A.
Lost Children, The.
Maine Roustabout, A.
Man Is God's Nature.
Man of Sense, A.
Marrakech.
Matador.
Matin Pandemoniums, The.
Maze.
Meditation, A.
Moment of Vision, The.
"Mysticism Has Not the Patience to Wait for God's Revelation."
New England Bachelor, A.
New Hampshire, February.
1934.
Now Is the Air Made of Chiming Balls.
Ode to the Chinese Paper Snake.
Off Spectacle Island.
On a Squirrel Crossing the Road in Autumn, in New England.
On Shooting Particles beyond the World.
Order and Disorder.
Preacher Sought to Find Out Acceptable Words, The.
R. G. E.
Rainscapes, Hydrangeas, Roses, and Singing Birds.
Reality! Reality! What Is It?
Recapitulation, The.
Remember the Source.
Rich Interior Life, The.
Roc, The.
Rumination.
Sainte Anne de Beaupre.
Sea Burial from the Cruiser "Reve."
Sea-Hawk.
Seals, Terns, Time.
Sea Scape with Parable.
Sestina.
Ship Burning and a Comet All in One Day, A.
Soul Longs to Return Whence It Came, The.
Spider, The.
Spring Mountain Climb.
Stone, A.
This Fevers Me.
To a Poet Who Has Had a Heart Attack.
To Auden on His Fiftieth.
To Laughter, to Leering.
Tobacconist of Eighth Street, The.
Two Loves.
Ur Burial.
Vast Light.
Vision.
What If Remembrance?
When Doris Danced.
When Golden Flies upon My Carcass Come.
Where Are Those High and Haunting Skies.
Wisdom of Insecurity, The.
Words.
World War.
Eberling, Georgia Moore
Centuries Are His, The.
Ebers, Basil
For Remembrance.
Ebon *See* **Dooley, Ebon**
Ebright, Frederick
Benediction.
Memorial to the Great Big Beautiful Self-sacrificing Advertisers.
Echeruo, Michael
Melting Pot.
Edelman, Katherine
Irish Grandmother.
Saturday Shopping.
Edelstein, Hyman
Indian Night Tableau.
Last Mathematician.
Palimpsest.
Eden, Helen Parry
Confessional, The.
Elegy, for Father Anselm, of the Order of Reformed Cistercians, An.
Four-Paws.
Phoenix Liberty, The.
Poet and the Wood-Louse, The.
Prayer for St. Innocent's Day, A.
Purpose of Amendment, A.
Put Up Again Thy Sword into Its Place.
Sorrow.
To a Little Girl.
To Betsey-Jane, on Her Desiring to Go Incontinently to Heaven.
Edes, Richard *See* **Eedes, Richard**
Edey, Marion
Ant Village, The.
August Afternoon.
Christmas Eve.
Jolly Woodchuck, The.
Little Fox, The.
Midsummer Night.
Open the Door.
Our Birthday.
So Many Monkeys.
Trot Along, Pony.
Edfelt, Johannes
Life of Life.
Edgar, Mary S.
Camp Hymn, The.
God, Who Touchest Earth With Beauty.
Prayer-Poem, A.
Youth's Prayer, A.
Edgerton, James Arthur
Tell Him So.
Edman, Irwin
Advice to a Young Man (of Letters) Who Doesn't Know How to Take Care of Himself.
Curse of Faint Praise, The.
Flower for a Professor's Garden of Verses.
Intermission, Please!
Kiss-Fest, The.
La Donna E Perpetuum Mobile.
Little Bow to Books on How To, A.
New Hellas, The.
Peace.
Prayer for All Poets at This Time.
To Harold Jacoby.
To Henry David Thoreau.
Edmeston, James
Evening Blessing, An.
Hymn: "Lead us, heavenly Father, lead us."
Prayer to the Trinity.
Saviour, Breathe an Evening Blessing.
Sunday.
Edminson, V. L.
Temper in October.
Edmonds, Paul
Little Tommy Tiddler.
Edmund, Father *See* **Hill, Benjamin Dionysius**
Edsall, Florence Small
Stars.
To a Cat Purring.
Edsall, Richard Linn
Resurgent.
Edwardes, Richard *See* **Edwards, Richard**
Edwardine, Sister Mary
Ad Mariam.
At Palomar.
Disillusion.
Madonna Remembers.
Edwards, Amelia Blanford
Give Me Three Grains of Corn, Mother.
Edwards, Archie
What Though the Dark!
Edwards, Donald Earl
Cross, The.
Faith.
Edwards, Harry
How to Change the U. S. A.
Edwards, Jeannette Slocomb
Hester MacDonagh.
Edwards, John R.
War, The: A—Z.

Edwards, Louise Betts
Christian Soul.
Edwards, Mathilda C.
Church Walking with the World.
Edwards, Matilda Barbara Betham
See **Betham-Edwards, Matilda Barbara**
Edwards [*or* Edwardes], Richard
Amantium Irae [Amoris Redintegratio Est].
Being Importunate, at the Length He Obtaineth.
Fortitude; a Young Man of Egypt and Valerian.
M. Edwards' May.
Master Edwards' May.
May.
Of Fortune's Power.
Of Women.
Song to the Lute in Music, A.
Wanting His Desire, He Complaineth.
Edwards, Solomon
Brothers.
Dream.
Shoplifter.
Edwards, Thomas
On a Family Picture.
On the Cantos of Spenser's *Faerie Queene,* Lost in the Passage from Ireland.
On the Edition of Mr. Pope's Works with a Commentary and Notes.
Sonnet: "Matthew, whose skilful hand and well-worn spade."
Sonnet on a Family Picture.
To Shakespeare.
To the Author of *Clarissa.*
To the Editor of Mr. Pope's Works.
Tongue-doughty pedant; whose ambitious mind.
Eedes [*or* Edes], Richard
No Love, to Love of Man and Wife.
Of Man and Wife.
Egan, Maurice Francis
Columbus the World-Giver.
He Made Us Free.
Madonna of the Empty Arms.
Maurice de Guerin.
Old Violin, The.
Shamrock, The.
Vigil of the Immaculate Conception.
Egar, J. H.
Sing, Sing for Christmas.
Egbert, Ella Elizabeth
Days like These.
Egerton, Helen Merrill
Sandpipers.
Eglington, Charles
Arrival and Departure.
Buffalo.
Cheetah.
Lourenç Marques.
Lowveld, The.
Meeting.
Vanquished, The.
"Eglinton, John" (William Kirkpatrick Magee)
Winds, The.
Eguren, José Mará
Abbey, The.
Ehrenburg, Ilya Grigoryevich
Our Children's Children Will Marvel.
Sons of Our Sons, The.
Tree, The.
Trumpet, The.
Ehrenstein, Albert
Ares.
Grief.
Home-coming.
Homer.
Suffering.
Ehrmann, Max
Away.
Hate and the Love of the World, The.
I Ponder on Life.
If You Have Made Gentler the Churlish World.
If You Made Gentler the Churlish World.
Mother.
Prayer, A: "Let me do my work each day."
Eichendorff, Baron Joseph von
Old Garden, The.
Poet-Hearts.
Returning Spring.
Eigner, Larry
B.
Bird shadows mounting.
Do It Yrself.
Dog yelped, skunk let fly, The.
Environs.
Fete, A.
Gone, A.
I will have an image.
Keep Me Still, for I Do Not Want to Dream.
Noise Grimaced.
Open.
Passages.
Shock, The.
Sleep, A.
Washing between the buildings.
Weekday, A.
Eisenberg, Emanuel
Reflections in a Hospital.
Ekvall, Robert K.
Put Grief Away.
Tibetan Comforter, *sel.*
Elam, William C.
Mecklenburg Declaration, The.
Elderton, William
True Form and Shape of a Monsterous Child, The.
Eldridge, Jessie Cannon
Have I?
Eldridge, Paul
Wang Peng's Recommendation for Improving the People.
Eldridge, Richard Burdick
Soul Remembers, The.
Eleanore, Sister Mary
Candles.
Lesson, The.
Missionary, The.
Vocation of St. Francis, The.
Eleazar
Thy Faithful Sons.
Elijah ben Menahem Hazaken of Le Mans
Precepts He Gave His Folk.
"Eliot, George" (Mary Ann [*or* Marian] Eva Lewes Ross)
At Set of Sun.
Brother and Sister, *abr.*
Choir Invisible, The.
Count That Day Lost.
Dark, The.
Day Well Spent, A.
I Am Lonely.
Jerusalem.
Life's Purpose.
Making Life Worth While.
Minor Prophet, A, *sels.*
O May I Join the Choir Invisible.
Roses.
Song of the Zincali.
Spanish Gypsy, The, *sels.*
Spring Song.
Stradivarius, *sel.*
Tide of Faith, The.
Two Lovers.
Working with God.
Eliot, Henrietta Robins
Why It Was Cold in May.
Eliot, Thomas Stearns
Ad-dressing of Cats, The.
Although I do not hope to turn again.
And now you live dispersed on ribbon roads.
Animula.
Ash on an Old Man's Sleeve.
Ash Wednesday.
Aunt Helen.
Boston Evening Transcript, The.
Burbank with a Baedeker; Bleistein with a Cigar ("Burbank crossed a little bridge").
Burnt Norton.
Cape Ann.
Chorus: "In an old house there is always listening."
Chorus: "It is hard for those who have never known persecution."
Chorus: "Son of Man, behold with thine eyes, and hear with thine ears."
Chorus: "We do not like to look out of the same window."
Chorus: "Word of the Lord came unto me, The."
Chorus: "You have seen the house built, you have seen it adorned."
Conversation Galante.
Coriolan, *sel.*
Cousin Nancy.
Dove, The.
Dry Salvages, The.
Eagle Soars in the Summit of Heaven, The.
East Coker.
Endless cycle of idea and action.
Eyes I dare not meet in dreams.
Eyes That Last I Saw in Tears.
Family Reunion, The, *sels.*
Forgive Us, O Lord.
Four Quartets, *sels.*
Fragment of an Agon.
Garlic and sapphires in the mud.
Gerontion.
Growltiger's Last Stand.
Gus; the Theatre Cat.
Hippopotamus, The.
Hollow Men, The.
I have known two worlds.
If humility and purity be not in the heart.
If the lost word is lost, if the spent word is spent.
In the beginning God created the world.
In the land of lobelias and tennis flannels.
Journey of the Magi.
Knowledge without Wisdom.
La Figlia Che Piange.
Lady, Three White Leopards.
Lady, whose shrine stands on the promontory.
Landscapes (I-V).
Last Temptation, The.
Lines for an Old Man.
Lines for Cuscuscaraway and Mirza Murad Ali Beg.
Lines to Ralph Hodgson Esqre.
Little Gidding.
Love Song of J. Alfred Prufrock, The.
Macavity; the Mystery Cat.
Marina.
Men have left God not for other gods, they say.
Men Who Turn from God.
Mr. Apollinax.
Mr. Eliot's Sunday Morning Service.
Morning at the Window.
Murder in the Cathedral, *sels.*
Naming of Cats, The.
New Hampshire.

O Light Invisible, We Praise Thee.
Old Gumbie Cat, The.
Portrait of a Lady.
Prelude: "Winter evening settles down, The."
Preludes (I-IV).
Rannoch by Glencoe.
Rhapsody on a Windy Night.
Rock, The, *sels.*
Rum Tum Tugger, The.
Salutation.
Skimbleshanks; the Railway Cat.
Song for Simeon, A.
Song of the Jellicles, The.
Sweeney among the Nightingales.
There Shall Always Be the Church.
Triumphal March.
Usk.
Virginia.
Waste Land, The.
We shall not cease from exploration.
When the Church Is No Longer Regarded.
Where is there an end of it, the soundless wailing.
Where My Word is unspoken.
Whispers of Immortality.
Why Should Men Love the Church?
Wind Sprang Up at Four o'Clock, The.
Words move, music moves.
World of the Lord came unto me saying, The.
World turns and the world changes, The.
Yellow Fog.

Elizabeth, Empress of Austria-Hungary
Inscription on a Shrine near Ischl.

Elizabeth I, Queen of England
Daughter of Debate, The.
Doubt of Future Foes, The.
I grieve, and dare not show my discontent.
Importune Me No More.
When I Was Fair and Young.

Ellerton, John Lodge
God of the Living, The.
Living unto Thee.
Now the Laborer's Task Is O'er.

Ellerton, John Lodge, *and* Henry Fothergill Chorley *See* **Chorley, Henry Fothergill, *and* John Lodge Ellerton**

Elliot, Lady Charlotte
Wife of Loki, The.

Elliot, George Tracy
Winter Twilight.

Elliot, Sir Gilbert
Amynta.
My Sheep I Neglected.

Elliot, Henry Rutherford
Laugh It Off.

Elliot, Jane [*or* Jean] (1727-1805)
Flowers of the Forest, The.
Lament for Flodden.

Elliot, Jean (*contemporary*)
Exercise in a Meadow.

Elliott, Charlotte
Hour of Prayer, The.
Just As I Am.
Let Me Be with Thee.
My Soul Shall Cling to Thee.
Sunday Evening.
Thy Will be Done!
Watch and Pray.

Elliott, Ebenezer
Bailiff, The.
Battle Song.
Builders, The.
Drone *v.* Worker.
Elegy on William Çobbett.
Epigram: "'Prepare to meet the King of Terrors,' cried."
Fox-Hunters, The.
Give not our blankets, tax-fed Squire, to him.
God Save the People.
I dreamed that God was Silence. Air was dead.
I sing of men and angels, and the days.
In these days, every mother's son or daughter.
John. In the sound of that rebellious word.
Land Which No One Knows, The.
People's Anthem, The.
Plaint.
Poet *vs.* Parson.
Poet's Epitaph, A.
Portrait at Wentworth.
Ralph Leech believes (and he can read and write).
Song: "When working blackguards come to blows."
Spirits and Men, *sel.*
Splendid Village, The, *sels.*
Steward, The.
Toy of the Titans! Tiny harp! again.
When Wilt Thou Save the People?
Year of Seeds, The, *sels.*

Elliott, Ellen Coit
Choice.

Elliott, F. Ann
Pictures.
Snow, The.

Elliott, Mary
Crocus, The.
Nest, The.
Oak, The.
Silkworms.
Think before You Act.
What Is Veal?

Ellis, C. D. B.
Head and Heart.
Unforgivable and Unforgiven.
Woman.

Ellis, Colin
Against Publishing Satires.
Bishop Spaniel's Sermons.
Spaniel's Sermon.

Ellis, Edwin John
At Golgotha I stood alone.
Himself, *sel.*

Ellis, George *See* **"Gander, Sir Gregory"**

Ellis, George, George Canning, *and* John Hookham Frere *See* **Canning, George, George Ellis, *and* John Hookham Frere**

Ellis, H. F.
Message to General Montgomery.

Ellis, Vivian Locke
At Common Dawn.

Ellison, Henry
Fall of the Year.

Ellsworth, Erastus Wolcott
I saw a man, by some accounted wise.
Mayflower, The.
What Is the Use? *sel.*

Ellwanger, William De Lancey
To Jessie's Dancing Feet.

Ellwood, Thomas
Prayer, A: "O, that mine eyes might closèd be."

Elmer, Franklin D., Jr
Christmas Blessing.
Lost Christ, The.
Tale of One Hill.
Unlikely Rebel, The.

Elmslie, Kenward
Another Island Groupage.
Circus Nerves and Worries.
Duo-tang.
Dustbowl, The.
Experts at Veneers.
Feathered Dancers.
Flaming Creatures.
Florida Hillocks.
History of France.
Japanese City.
Shirley Temple Surrounded by Lions.
White Attic.
Work Room.

Elmslie, W. G.
Hand That Held It, The.

"Elspeth. (Elspeth MacDuffie O'Halloran)"
It's a Fib.
Sentimental Journey.
Wednesday.

Eluard, Paul
All Life.
Death Is Dead.
Fish, The.
From Solitude to Solitude towards Life.
Loss.
Our Movement.
Through an Embrace.
To Die.
You Rise Up.

Elwes, Richard
These Faithful Verses.

Ely, Gladys
Variations on Simonides.

Elys, Edmund
My Mind Keeps Out the Host of Sin.

"Elytis, Odysseus" (Odysseus Alepoudelis)
Body of Summer, The.

Emans, Elaine V.
Birthday.
For a Birthday.

Emanuel, James A.
After the Record Is Broken.
Fishermen.
Get Up, Blues.
Negro, The.
Treehouse, The.
Voyage of Jimmy Poo, The.
Wedding Procession [from a Window].
Young Ones, Flip Side, The.

Embry, Jacqueline
Tea.
Unregenerate.

Embury, Emma Catharine
Love Unsought.

Embury, Lucy
Christmas Prayer, A.

Emerson, Caroline D.
Modern Ballad, A; the Ups and Downs of the Elevator Car.

Emerson, Chester B.
Quest, The.

Emerson, Ralph Waldo
Adakrue Nemontai Aiona.
All the forms are fugitive.
Alphonso of Castile.
America, My Country.
And When I Am Entombèd.
Anxiety, *sel.*
Apology, The.
April.
April and May.
Art.
As the sunbeams stream through liberal space.
Astraea.
Atom from Atom.
Bacchus.
Beauty.
Berrying.
Blight.
Bohemian Hymn, The.
Borrowing.
Boston.
Boston Hymn.
Brahma.
Celestial Love, *sel.*

Emerson (continued)
Character.
Chickadee, The.
Climacteric.
Compensation ("The wings of Time").
Compensation ("Why should I keep holiday").
Concord Hymn.
Culture.
Days.
Duty ("In an age of fops and toys").
Each and All.
Earth, The.
Eros.
Experience.
Fable: "Mountain and the squirrel, The."
Faith.
Fate.
Forbearance.
Forerunners.
Fragments.
Fragments on Nature and Life.
Fragments on the Poet and the Poetic Gift, *sels.*
Freedom.
Freedom all winged expands.
Friendship ("A ruddy drop of manly blood").
Gardener.
Give All to Love.
God.
God Hide the Whole World in Thy Heart.
God's Altar.
Good-bye.
Good-bye, Proud World.
Good Hope.
Grace.
Hamatreya.
Heart of All the Scene, The.
Heroism ("Ruby wine is drunk").
Heroism ("So nigh is grandeur to our dust").
History.
Humble-Bee, The.
Hush!
Hymn: "By the rude bridge that arched the flood."
Hymn Sung at the Completion of the Concord Monument.
I have an arrow that will find its mark.
I Know the Trusty Almanac.
If bright the sun, he tarries.
Immanent God, The.
In the Woods.
Informing Spirit, The.
Intellect.
Journals, *sel.*
Letter, A.
Limits.
Love's Nobility.
May-Day, *sels.*
Merlin.
Merops.
Mighty Heart, The.
Mithridates.
Mountain and the Squirrel, The.
Music.
Musketaquid.
My Garden, *sel.*
Nahant.
Nature ("The rounded world is fair to see").
Nature ("A subtle chain of countless rings").
Nature ("Winters know").
Needless Worry.
Nemesis.
No Great, No Small.
Ode: "O tenderly the haughty day."
Ode: Sung in the Town Hall, Concord, July 4, 1857.
Ode Inscribed to W. H. Channing.
Ode Sung in the Town Hall, Concord, July 4, 1857.
Ode to Beauty.
Orator.
Pale genius roves alone.
Pan.
Parks and Ponds.
Past, The.
Poet, The, *sel.*
Poet, The ("Thy trivial harp").
Poet ("To clothe the fiery thought").
Politics.
Problem, The.
Quatrain: "Though love repine."
Quatrains, *sels.*
Rhodora, The [On Being Asked, Whence Is the Flower].
Rhythm.
Right upward on the road of fame.
River, The.
Romany Girl, The.
Saadi.
Sacrifice.
Seashore [*or* Sea-Shore].
Shakespeare.
Shun Passion.
Snow-Storm, The.
So Nigh Is Grandeur.
Song of Nature.
Sphinx, The.
Stainless soldier on the walls.
Subtle chain of countless rings, A.
Terminus.
Test, The.
Thanksgiving.
Thought.
Threnody: "South-wind brings, The."
Titmouse, The.
To Ellen.
To Ellen at the South.
To Eva.
Transition.
Two Rivers.
Undersong, The.
Uriel.
Voluntaries (I-V).
Waldeinsamkeit.
Water.
Waves.
We Are Never Old.
We Love the Venerable House.
Wealth.
Whoso walks in solitude.
Why Chidest Thou the Tardy Spring?
Wilt thou not ope thy heart to know.
Wind in the Grass, The.
Woodnotes, I ("When the pine tosses its cones").
Woodnotes, II ("As sunbeams stream through liberal space").
Words of the Gods, The.
World-Soul, The.
Worship.
Written in Naples.
Xenophanes.
Emery, Frances D.
Long-billed Gannets.
Emery, Gilbert
Soldier-Dead.
Emilio, Marguerite
Prayer for Teachers, A.
Emmett, Daniel Decatur
Dixie ("I wish I was in de land ob cotton").
Old Dan Tucker.
Emmons, Dick
Cold Fact.
Emory, Susan L.
Old Woman's Answer to a Letter from Her Girlhood, An.
Emory, William Closson
Be Still.
Empson, William
Arachne.
Aubade.
Bacchus.
Beautiful Train, The.
Camping Out.
Chinese Ballad.
Courage Means Running.
Description of a View.
Dissatisfaction with Metaphysics.
Doctrinal Point.
Earth Has Shrunk in the Wash.
Flighting for Duck.
Four Legs, Two Legs, Three Legs.
High Dive.
Homage to the British Museum.
Ignorance of Death.
Invitation to Juno.
Just a Smack at Auden.
Last Pain, The.
Legal Fiction.
Let It Go.
Letter I ("You were amused to find you too could fear").
Letter IV ("Hatched in a rasping darkness of dry sand").
Manchouli.
Missing Dates.
Note on Local Flora.
Part of Mandevil's Travels.
Reflection from Rochester.
Rolling the Lawn.
Scales, The.
Sea Voyage.
Sonnet: "Not wrongly moved by this dismaying scene."
Success.
This Last Pain.
To an Old Lady.
Villanelle.
World's End, The.
Your Teeth Are Ivory Towers.
Encina, Juan del
Come, Let Us Eat and Drink Today.
Endicoff, Max
Excavation, The.
Engels, Norbert
Ex Maria Virgine.
For an Old Man.
One Immortality.
Engels, Vincent David
At the Last.
Engle, H. E. *and* Ellen King
West Virginia Hills, The.
Engle, Paul
America Remembers, *sel.*
Beasts.
Break the Heart's Anger, *sel.*
Cat's Eye.
Chameleon.
Cuban Voyage.
Ending, The.
Fossil.
Here by this midland lake, the sand-shored water.
I will make a new song of the word.
If Everything.
In a Bar near Shibuya Station, Tokyo.
Last Whiskey Cup, The.
Modern Romance, A.
New World, The.
No Gull's Wings.
Only the Moonlight.
Orion.
USA.
You Can't Be Wise.
English, Maurice
Form Was the World.
English, Thomas Dunn

Arnold at Stillwater.
Assunpink and Princeton.
Battle of Monmouth, The.
Battle of New Orleans, The.
Battle of the Cowpens, The.
Battle of the King's Mill.
Ben Bolt.
Betty Zane.
Burning of Jamestown, The.
Charge by the Ford, The.
Fall of Maubila, The.
Old Mill, The.
Sack of Deerfield, The.
Engonopoulos, Nikos
Hydra of Birds, The.
Ennius, Quintus
Annales, *sel.*
Like a Shower of Rain.
Ennodius, Saint (Magnus Felix Ennodius)
How of the Virgin Mother Shall I Sing?
Hymnus Sanctae Mariae, *sel.*
Enoch, Olive
Bluebells.
Half Holiday.
Laughter.
Enright, Dennis Joseph
Apocalypse.
Arab Music.
"Black" Country, The.
Interpreters, The.
Last Democrat, The.
Laughing Hyena, by Hokusai, The.
Parliament of Cats.
To a War Poet, on Teaching Him in a New Country.
University Examinations in Egypt.
Enriqueta, María
Thoughts of a Little Girl.
Enslin, Theodore
Belongings, The.
Forms, *sel.*
Landscape with Figures.
Stance.
Tangere.
Tansy for August.
Things being what they are do not imply necessity.
Witch Hazel.
"Your Need Is Greater thân Mine."
Enzo, King of Sardinia
On the Fitness of Seasons.
"Ephelia. (Joan Philips?) "
Song: "Know, Celadon, in vain you use."
Song: "You wrong me, Strephon, when you say."
Ephrem, Saint
Christmas Hymn, *sel.*
Virgin Truly Full of Wonder.
Erasmus, Desiderius
Votive Ode.
Ercilla y Zúñga, Alonso de
Araucana, La.
Erinna
Baucis.
Erinna to Her Friend.
Very Torch, The.
Erskine, Francis Robert St. Clair, Earl of Rosslyn
Bedtime.
Memory.
Erskine, John
Apparition.
At the Front.
Childhood.
Dialogue.
Modern Ode to the Modern School.
Shepherd Speaks, The.
Song, The: "Song lay silent in my pen, A.
Erskine, Thomas Erskine,1st Baron
On Scott's [Poem] "The Field of Waterloo."
Erskine, William
Epigram: "This house, where once a lawyer dwelt."
This House Where Once a Lawyer Dwelt.
Erskine-Crum, Lady
"Good Night," Says the Owl.
Erulkar, Mary
Third Continent, The.
Eschenbach, Wolfram von *See* **Wolfram von Eschenbach**
Escrivá, Juan
Song to Death.
Welcome Death.
Esler, Richard Curry
Table D'Hote.
Espaillat, Rhina P.
From the Rain Down.
Espinel, Vicente Martínez
Faint Heart Never Won Fair Lady.
Espirito Santo, Aldo do
Where Are the Men Seized in This Wind of Madness?
Essex, Edwin
Loneliness.
Essex, Robert Devereux, 2d Earl of
Change.
Change Thy Mind [since She Doth Change].
Content.
Happy Were He.
Passion, A.
To Plead My Faith.
Wish, A.
Esson, Louis (Thomas Louis Buvelot Esson)
Brogan's Lane.
Cradle Song: "Baby, O baby, fain you are for bed."
Old Black Billy an' Me, The.
Shearer's Wife, The.
Whalin' up the Lachlan.
"Estelle." *See* **Bogart, Elizabeth**
Estelle, Sister Mary
From Desert to Metropolis.
Estrello, Francisco E.
Hands of Christ.
Etherege, Sir George
Chloris, 'Tis Not in Your Power.
Comical Revenge, The; or, Love in a Tub, *sels.*
If She Be Not as Kind as Fair.
Letter to Lord Middleton, A.
Lines to a Lady, Who Asked of Him How Long He Would Love Her.
Love in a Tub.
Man of Mode, The; or, Sir Fopling Flutter, *sels.*
Rival, The.
She Would if She Could, *sel.*
Silvia.
Song: "If she be not as kind as fair."
Song: "Ladies, though to your conquering eyes."
Song: "Pleasures of love, and the joys of good wine, The."
Song: "Tell me no more I am deceived."
Song: "Ye happy swains, whose hearts are free."
To a Lady.
To a Lady Asking [Him] How Long He Would Love Her.
To a Very Young Lady.
To Little or No Purpose [I Spent Many Days].
Upon the Downs.
Etter, Dave
Country Graveyard.
Evangelist.
Firewood Hill.
Old Dubuque.
Prairie Summer.
Red Nude, The.
St. Dexter's Fire.
Snow Country.
Euenus, [*or* Evenus]
Swallow, A.
Vine to the Goat, The.
Eugenius III, Pope
Dedication: "Eugenius, thy son, who guards the Rock."
Eulalia, Sister Mary
Denouement.
Mother.
Question of Sacrifice, A.
To Archbishop Stepinac.
Euripides
Aftermath, The.
Alcestis, *sels.*
Andromache, *sel.*
Bacchae, *sels.*
Bellerophon, *sel.*
Breed of Athletes, The.
Cassandra's Epithalamium.
Children.
Chorus: "And Pergamos."
Chorus: "Could I take me to some cavern for mine hiding."
Chorus: Kings of Troy, The.
Chorus: Love Song.
Chorus: "Upward and back to their fountains the sacred rivers are stealing."
Chorus: "When love has passed its limits."
Chorus of Satyrs, Driving Their Goats.
Cresophontes, *sel.*
Cyclops, *sels.*
Daughters of Troy, The.
Earth and Sky.
Eloquent herald this, a speech-crammed babbler! An.
Had I, my father, the persuasive voice.
Hear then what to my mind/ Deliberate thought presents.
Helen, *sel.*
Hippolytus, *sels.*
Home of Aphrodite.
Iphigenia [*or* Iphigeneia] in Aulis.
It Is a Gracious House and Ever Was.
Longing.
Love.
Medea, *sels.*
No More, O My Spirit.
O for the Wings of a Dove.
Prayer to Peace.
Soul of the deceased, although it live, The.
Strength of Fate, The.
Suppliants, *sel.*
Supplices.
There Are No Gods.
Troades.
Trojan Women, The, *sels.*
Troy ("In Salamis, filled with the foaming").
Where Shall Wisdom Be Found?
Who Are the Dead?
Euwer, Anthony
Face, The.
Gettin' Born.
Hands, The.
Limeratomy, The.
Limerick: "Ankle's chief end is exposiery, The."
Limerick: "As a [*or* For] beauty I'm not a great star."
Limerick: "For beauty I am not a star."
Limerick: "Hands they were made to assist, The."
Limerick: "In the wax works of Nature they strike."
Limerick: "No matter how grouchy you're feeling."

Euwer (continued)
Limerick: "Now the ears, so I always had thunk."
Limerick: "Now the sneeze is a joy-vent, I s'pose."
Limerick: "With a conscience we're able to see."
My Face.
Smile, The.
Eva, Reginald C.
Password, The.
Sorrow.
Evald, Johannes *See* **Ewald, Johannes**
Evans, Abbie Huston
All Those Hymnings up to God.
By the Salt Margin.
Come to Birth.
Country Miracle.
Euroclydon.
First Concerns.
Fundament Is Shifted, The.
In Conclusion.
Jones's Pasture.
Mineral Collection.
Moonrise.
On the Curve-Edge.
Return to Life.
Sun-up in March.
This World.
True Lover, The.
Evans, Abel
Epitaph on Sir John Vanbrugh [Architect].
For Sir John Vanbrugh, Architect.
On Blenheim House.
On Sir John Vanbrugh.
Evans, Donald
Body of the Queen.
Bonfire of Kings.
Dinner at the Hotel de la Tigresse Verte.
En Monocle.
Epicede.
In the Gentlemanly Interest.
In the Vices.
Evans, Evan
Verses to Mr. Vaughan of Hengwrt.
Evans, F. Gwynne
Little Thomas.
Matilda.
Evans, Florence Wilkinson
At the Salon.
Fugitives, The.
Illuminated Canticle, The.
Students.
Things That Endure, The, *sel.*
Heart's Country, The.
What wish you, immortality?
Evans, George Essex
Australian Symphony, An.
Women of the West, The.
Evans, Grace Bowen
Women Toilers, The.
Evans, Helen Kitchell
Kind of Dad I'd Buy, The.
Evans, Jonathan
It Is Finished.
Evans, Mari E.
Alarm Clock, The.
And the Old Women Gathered.
Emancipation of George Hector (a colored Turtle), The.
I Am Not Lazy.
If There Be Sorrow.
Langston.
Point of No Return.
Rebel, The.
Shrine to What Should Be.
Speak the Truth to the People.
Status Symbol.
Stretchin' Out.
Vive Noir!
When in Rome.
Where Have You Gone?
World I See, The.
Evans, Mary Ann [*or* Marian] *See* **"Eliot, George"**
Evans, Mike
Mushrooms.
We'll All Be Spacemen before We Die.
Evans, Patrick
At Morning an Iris.
Green Grass Growing.
Evans, Sebastian
Dirge for Summer, A.
Fifteen Days of Judgement, The.
How the Abbey of Saint Werewulf Juxta Slingsby Came by Brother Fabian's Manuscript.
Seven Fiddlers, The.
Shadows.
What the Trumpeter Said.
Everaerts, Jan Nicolai *See* **Johannes Secundus**
Everett, Alexander Hill
Young American, The.
Everett, David
Boy Reciter, The.
Lines Spoken by a Boy of Seven Years.
Tall Oaks from Little Acorns Grow.
Everett, Edward
Dirge of Alaric the Visigoth.
Everett, Laura Bell
Death-Grapple.
Lament of the Voiceless, The.
Miser, The.
Resurgence.
Eversley, Mary
Just to Be Needed.
Everson, Ronald G.
Child with Shell.
Cold-Weather Love.
Laprairie Hunger Strike.
Letter from Underground.
Loaves, The.
Old Snapshot.
Rogue Pearunners.
When I'm Going Well.
Everson, William *See* **Antoninus, Brother**
Everts, Lillian
Playmates.
"Evoe." *See* **Knox, Edmund George Valpy**
Ewald [*or* Evald], Johannes
King Christian.
Ewart, Gavin
Bofors A.A. Gun, The.
Cigarette for the Bambino.
Crossing the Bar.
"For Whom the Bell Tolls."
Hymn to Proust.
Nymphs and Satyrs.
Poem: "To go, to leave the classics and the buildings."
Psychoanalysis.
Sonnet: "Point where beauty and intelligence meet, The."
When a Beau Goes In.
Young Blondes.
Ewer, W. N.
Chosen People, The.
Epigram: "How odd/ of God."
Five Souls.
Ewing, Annemarie
Ballad: "Mother mine, Mother mine, what do you see?"
Fisherman's Blunder Off New Bedford, Massachusetts.
If the Heart Be Homeless.
Man Within, The.
Rhyme from Grandma Goose.
Sleep, Madame, Sleep.
Ewing, Juliana Horatia
Big Smith.
Bluebells.
Burial of the Linnet.
For Good Luck.
Friend in the Garden, A.
Kit's Cradle.
Little Kings and Queens of the May.
Willow-Man, The.
Excell, Patricia
Forgotten Objects on a Beach.
Exeley, Frank J.
Child of My Love.
Exeter, Bishop of
"Till He Come!"
Eybers, Elisabeth
Hagar.
Narrative.
Röntgen Photograph.
Sleep-Walking Child.
Snail.
"E Yeh Shure" (Louise Abeita)
Beauty.
Ezekiel, Nissim
Enterprise.
Morning Prayer.
Ezekielos [*or* Ezechiel] of Alexandria
Exodus from Egypt, The.
Ezobi, Joseph
Barren Soul, A.
Silver Bowl, The, *sel.*

F

"F. L. H." *See* **"H., F. L"**
"F. McK." *See* **"McK., F"**
"F. P. A." *See* **Adams, Franklin Pierce**
Fabbri, Cora Randall
White Roses.
Faber, Frederick William
All-Embracing, The.
Cherwell Water Lily [*or Waterlily], The.*
Expectation, The.
Faith of Our Fathers.
God Our Father.
God's Mercy.
God's Presence.
Grandeurs of Mary, The.
He Satisfies.
Heart of the Eternal, The.
Hymn: "There's a wideness in God's mercy."
Jesus, Child and Lord.
Jesus, My God and My All.
Mundus Morosus.
My God, How Wonderful Thou Art.
Nearest Friend, The.
O Paradise! O Paradise!
Our Heavenly Father, *sel.*
Our Lady in the Middle Ages.
Our Lady's Expectation, *sel.*
Paradise.
Right Is Right.
Right Must Win.
Shadow of the Rock, The.
There's a Wideness in God's Mercy.
Will of God, The.
World Morose, The.
Written in a Little Lady's Little Album.
Fabio, Sarah Webster
Black Man's Feast.
Fabyan, Robert
Dedication of the Chronicles of England and France.
Fadiman, Clifton
Alimentary.
Jacobean.
Theological.

Faerstein, Chana
Homage to Aesop.
Fahy, Francis A.
Little Mary Cassidy.
Ould Plaid Shawl, The.
Fainlight, Ruth
Report, A.
"Fair. C. A. "
Chinese Poems: Arthur Waley.
Fairbridge, Kingsley Ogilvie
Song-Maker, The.
Fairbridge, Wolfe Seymour
Consecration of the House.
Fairburn, Arthur Rex Dugard
Beggar to Burgher.
Disquisition on Death, *sel.*
Down on My luck.
Epithalamium: "We have found our peace."
Farewell, A: "What is there left to be said?"
Full Fathom Five.
I went through the market-place crying, There is no death.
Impetuous Lover, The.
La Belle Dame sans Merci.
Landscape with Figures.
Night Song.
Old friend, dear friend.
One Race, One Flag.
Song: "O lovers, this song I give to you."
Song at Summer's End.
To a Friend in the Wilderness, *sel.*
To Daphnis and Chloe in the Park, *sel.*
Winter Night.
Yes Please Gentlemen.
Fairfax, John
Beyond Astronaut.
Fairfax, Robert
That Was My Woe.
Fairfax, Thomas, 3d Baron
Upon a Patch Face.
Upon the New-built House at Appleton.
Falconer, E. J.
Cradle Song at Bethlehem.
Doves.
Elephant, The.
Little Finger Game, A.
Marketing.
Falconer, Edmund (Edmund O'Rourke)
Killarney.
Falconer, Harry W.
Challenge.
Falconer, William
All Hands Unmoor!
But now Athenian mountains they descry.
High o'er the Poop the Audacious Seas Aspire.
In vain the cords and axes were prepared.
Shipwreck, The, *sels.*
Shortening Sail.
Faleti, Adebayo
Independence.
Falke, Gustav
God's Harp.
Strand-Thistle.
Falkenbury, Francis E.
South Street.
Fallis, Edwina
Prairie Spring.
September.
Wise Johnny.
Fallon, Eunice
August.
Fallon, Padraic
Elegy for a Countryman.
Farmer.
Lady Day.
Long John.
Mary Hynes.
Out of Soundings.
Raftery's Dialogue with the Whiskey.
River Walk, The.
Virgin.
Waistcoat, The.
Wisdom.
Writing on the Wall.
"Falstaff, Jake" (Herman Fetzer)
Beautiful Sunday.
Day in Spring, A.
Dick Johnson Reel, The.
Elfin Wife, The.
Fandel, John
Bee, The.
Indians.
Pulse of Darkness, The.
Synonym for God, A.
Thrush for Hawk.
Fandel, Peter
Roosevelt.
Fane, Sir Francis
Cupid, I Scorn to Beg the Art.
Love in the Dark, *sel.*
To a Perjur'd Mistress.
Fane, Julian
Ad Matrem.
Fane, Mildmay, Earl of Westmorland
See **Westmorland, Mildmay Fane, 2d Earl of**
"Fane. Violet "
In Green Old Gardens.
May Song, A.
Fang Che Chai
Kite, The.
Fanning, Ella Augusta
Summer Cat, The.
Fanning, William Henry
Resurrection.
Fanshawe, Catherine Maria
Enigma.
Enigma on the Letter H.
Fragment: "There is a river clear and fair."
Fragment in Imitation of Wordsworth.
Imitation of Wordsworth, An.
Letter for You, A.
Riddle, A: Letter "H," The.
Riddle, A: "'Twas whispered in heaven [*or* in heaven pronounced], 'twas muttered in hell."
Fanshawe, Sir Richard
But, our Winter come, in vain.
Fall, The.
Hope.
Il Pastor Fido, *sels.*
Now War Is All the World About.
Ode, An, upon Occasion of His Majesties Proclamation in the Year 1630.
Of Beauty.
Of Time.
Only the island which we sow.
Rose, A.
Rose of Life, The.
Farallon, Cerise
Pride and Hesitation.
Serpent of God, The.
Farber, Norma
Beyond the Tapestries.
Night Before America, The.
Parkinson and the Octopus ["Parkinson broached the octopus").
Song of the Withy Greatcoat.
Unicorns at Harvard ("Unicorns are astray").
Witching Hour.
Farbstein, W. E.
Double Duty.
Fardd, Beddyn
Fall of Llywelyn, the Last Welsh Prince, The.
Fargo, Ruth Scofield
Perfection.
Faris, Sarah
Treasures of Darkness.
Farjeon, Eleanor
After Rain.
Annar-Mariar's Christmas Shopping.
Argus ("Argus was a puppy").
Bedtime.
Blow the Stars Home.
Books.
Boys' Names.
Carol for Christmas Eve, A.
Carol Singers, The.
Cats.
Children's Bells, The.
Child's Carol.
Choosing.
Circus.
City Show, The.
City Streets and Country Roads.
Coach.
Cock, The.
Country Vegetables.
Dancing.
Down! Down!
Dragon-Fly, A.
Earth and Sky.
Farewell to the Old Year.
Farm Cart.
Flower-Seller, The.
For a Cock.
For a Dewdrop.
For a Mocking Voice.
For Autumn.
For Christmas Day.
For Snow.
For Them.
Fred.
Geography.
Getting Out of Bed.
Girls' Names.
Good Bishop Valentine.
Good Night!
Great Discovery, The.
Griselda ("Griselda is greedy, I'm sorry to say").
Gypsy, The.
Heigh-ho, April!
Hey! My Pony!
In the Week When Christmas Comes.
Jenny White and Johnny Black.
Jill Came from the Fair.
Jim at the Corner.
Joan's Door.
Kingcups.
Kitten, A.
Light the Lamps Up, Lamplighter.
Mary's Song.
Meeting Mary.
Milk-Cart Pony, The.
Minnie.
Mrs. Malone.
Mrs. Peck-Pigeon.
Moon-Come-Out.
Morning Song, A.
Mother's Tale, The.
Music.
News! News!
Night Will Never Stay, The.
Now Every Child.
October's Song.
Old Man's Toes, The.
Old Wife's Song.
On the Staircase.
Our Brother Is Born.
Our Mother's Tunes.
Over the Garden Wall.
Pencil and Paint.
People, Look East
Picking Up Sticks.
Prayer for Little Things, A.
Quarrel, The.

Farjeon (continued)
Riding of the Kings, The.
Sailor.
St. Valentine's Way.
School-Bell.
Shepherd and the King, The.
Shopman, The.
Sisters.
Sounds in the Morning, The.
Sun and Wind.
There Are Big Waves.
There Isn't Time.
This Holy Night.
Three Little Puffins.
Through a Shop Window.
Tide in the river, The.
Up the Hill, down the Hill.
Upon an Easter Morning.
Vegetables.
Welcome to the New Year.
What Is Poetry?
What They Do.
Wheelbarrow.
When Hannibal Crossed the Alps.
White Horses.
Who'll Buy My Valley Lilies?
Wild Thyme.
William I—1066.
Window Boxes.
Farjeon, Eleanor *and* Herbert
Henry VIII.
Rob Roy.
Sir Philip Sidney.
Farjeon, Herbert
Apologia.
Farley, Corinne
Soul-feeding Hyacinths.
Farley, Henry
Bounty of Our Age, The.
St. Paul's Church, Her Bill for the Parliament, *sel.*
To See a Quaint Outlandish Fowl.
Farley, Robert E.
Thinking Happiness.
Farmer, Edward
Little Jim.
Farmingham, Marianne
Old, Old Bible, The.
Farnaby, Giles
Among the Daffadillies.
Farnham, Jessie
Garland for a Storyteller.
"Farningham, Marianne" (Mary Anne Hearne)
Burden, The.
Consecration.
God Cares.
He Careth.
Last Hymn, The.
Let Us Give Thanks.
Farquhar, George
Love and a Bottle, *sel.*
Song: "How blest are lovers in disguise!"
Farrar, Geraldine
Easter Robin, The.
Legend of the Dogwood Tree, The.
Little Christmas Donkey, The.
Shepherd's Madrigal, The.
"What Think Ye of Christ?"
Farrar, Janice
Thought of Marigolds, A.
Farrar, John Chipman
Alone.
Ambitious Mouse, The.
Brest Left Behind.
Broom.
Bundles.
Catfish.
Chanticleer.
Choice.
Comparison, A.
Critic, The.
Cuckoo Clock, The.
Days of the Week, The.
Drum, The.
Hill-Woman, A.
Hillside Farmer, A.
Moral Song.
Morning at the Beach.
Parenthood.
Penny Problem.
Prayer: "Last night I crept across the snow."
Preference, A.
Roller Skates.
Serious Omission.
Shops.
Song for a Camper.
Spring Wish.
Summer Wish.
Threnody: "Red leaves fall upon the lake, The."
Time Is Today, The.
Tracks.
Victorian Song.
Watching Clouds.
Water Lily.
Windmill, The.
Wish at Meal-Time.
Farrell, J. R.
Bank Thief, The.
Farren, Robert (Roibeárd O'Faracháin)
All That Is, and Can Delight.
Beset Wife, The.
Cool Gold Wines of Paradise, The.
Finding of the Táin, The.
Immolation.
Island Boatman's Love-Croon, The.
Joy's Peak.
Lineage.
Mary.
Mason, The.
No Woman Born.
Pets, The.
To the Bell-Ringer.
Una Bhan.
What I Have.
Farrington, Harry Webb
Airmen's Hymn, The.
As He Walked with Us.
Bethlehem.
Dear Lord, Who Sought at Dawn.
Our Christ.
Farrow, G. E.
Converted Cannibals, The.
Retired Pork-Butcher and the Spook, The.
Faubion, Dorothy
Hump, the Escalator.
Faulds, Lena E.
American Flag, The.
Fauset, Jessie Redmond (Mrs. Herbert Harris)
Christmas Eve in France.
Dead Fires.
Enigma.
Fragment: "Breath of life imbued those few dim days, The."
I Think I See Her.
La Vie C'est la Vie.
Noblesse Oblige.
Oblivion.
Oriflamme.
Rencontre.
Return, The.
Touché.
Words! Words!
Fawcett, Edgar
Fireflies.
January Is Here.
My Little One.
Oriole.
To an Oriole.
Wild Roses.
Fawcett, John
Blest Be the Tie That Binds.
Brotherly Love.
Lord, Dismiss Us.
Fawkes, Francis
Brown Jug, The.
Nosegay for Laura, A.
Fay, W. M. L.
Harvest Home.
Faydi
On the Death of His Child.
Fazio degli Uberti
Canzone: His Portrait of His Lady.
Of England and of Its Marvels.
Fearing, Kenneth
A la Carte.
Ad.
American Rhapsody.
Any Man's Advice to His Son.
Aphrodite Metropolis.
C Stands for Civilization.
Confession Overheard in a Subway.
Cultural Notes.
Denouement.
Devil's Dream.
Dirge: "1-2-3 was the number he played."
Elegy in a Theatrical Warehouse.
End of the Seers' Convention.
Evening Song.
Homage.
John Standish, Artist.
King Juke.
Love 20! the First Quarter Mile.
Lullaby: "Wide as this night, old as this night is old and young as it is young."
Memo.
Minnie and Mrs. Hoyne.
No Credit.
Operative No. 174 Resigns.
Pact.
Pay-Off.
People vs. the People, The.
Portrait.
Readings, Forecasts, Personal Guidance.
Requiem.
Resurrection.
SOS.
These are the live!
Thirteen o'Clock.
Tomorrow.
Twentieth-Century Blues.
X Minus X.
Fearne, Flora
Little Men, The.
Fearon, Paul
Night Piece to Another Julia.
Serenade: "High in the dark the moon rides white."
Feeney, Leonard
Altar Boy, The.
Because of Her Who Flowered So Fair.
Family Portrait.
Fledgling Robin, A.
Geranium, The.
Gift of Flowers, A.
Lonely Crib, The.
Milkman, The.
Nails.
Song for a Listener, *sel.*
Though art be on vacation.
Way of the Cross, The.
Welcome, The.
Wind.
Feeney, Thomas Butler
Captain Kelly Lets His Daughter Go to Be a Nun.
Feinman, Alvin
November Sunday Morning.
Feinstein, Martin

Burning Bush.
Feld, M. D.
Villanelle.
Feldman, Irving
Ark, The.
Assimilation.
Death of Vitellozzo Vitelli, The.
Double, The.
Greenwich Village Saturday Night.
Hand, The.
Little Lullaby.
Lost Language, The.
Marionette, The.
Old Men, The.
Picasso's "Portrait de Femme."
Scene of a Summer Morning.
Wrack.
Feldman, Ruth
Sarcophagus Cover.
Fellowes, Peter
Change of Heart, A.
Hero and Holy Man.
In the Garden.
Predator.
View from an American Window.
Felltham, Owen
Sun and Wind, The.
Sympathy, The.
Upon a Rare Voice.
Felsinki, Aloizy
Polish National Hymn, *abr.*
Feng Chih
For Tu Fu.
On a Puppy.
Room and the Windows, The.
Fenner, Cornelius George
Gulf-Weed.
Fenner, Lanon A., Jr.
Sweet Thing, A/ Last Thoughts.
Fenollosa, Ernest Francisco
Golden Age, The.
Fenollosa, Mary McNeil ("Sidney McCall")
Birth of the Flowers, The.
Blossoms.
Drifting Petal, A.
Flying Fish.
Miyoko San.
Morning Fancy.
Proud Vegetables, The.
Sunrise in the Hills of Satsuma.
Yuki.
Fenton, Elijah
Olivia.
So smooth and clear the Fountain was.
To a Lady Sitting before Her Glass.
Ferber, Edna
To William Allen White.
Ferguson, James
Auld Daddy Darkness.
Old Daddy Darkness.
Ferguson, M. P.
Broken Hearts.
Ferguson, Mary
Second Benefit!
Ferguson, Sir Samuel
Abdication of Fergus Mac Roy, The.
Bird and Brook, *sel.*
Bird that pipest on the bough.
Burial of King Cormac, The.
Congal, *sels.*
Death of Dermid, The.
Deirdre, *sel.*
Fairy Thorn, The.
Forging of the Anchor, The.
Lament for the Death of Thomas Davis.
Lament for Thomas Davis.
"Land Is Ours, The."
Paul Veronese: Three Sonnets.
Pretty Girl of Loch Dan, The.
Simile.
Welshmen of Tirawley, The.
Fergusson, Robert
Auld Reikie.
Braid Claith.
Daft Days, The.
Epigram on a Lawyer's Desiring One of the Tribe to Look with Respect to a Gibbet.
Farmer's Ingle, The.
Ghaists, The: a Kirk-yard Eclogue.
Hallow-Fair.
Leith Races, *sel.*
My Winsome Dear.
Rising of the Session, The.
Ferid ed-Din Attar
Then from a Ruin.
Ferlinghetti, Lawrence
Away above a Harborful.
Christ Climbed Down.
Coney Island of the Mind, A, *sels.*
Constantly risking absurdity.
Crazy.
Dog.
Dove sta amore.
Fortune.
Funny Fantasies Are Never so Real as Oldstyle.
Great Chinese Dragon, The.
He.
I Am Waiting, *sel.*
I am waiting for my case to come up.
In a Surrealist Year.
In Golden Gate Park that day.
Moscow in the Wilderness, Segovia in the Snow.
New York-Albany.
One Thousand Fearful Words for Fidel Castro.
Oral Messages, *sel.*
Pennycandystore Beyond the El, The.
Pictures of the Gone World, *sels.*
Poet's eye obscenely seeing, The.
Reading Yeats I Do Not Think.
Sarolla's women in their picture hats.
Sweet and Various the Woodlark.
Tentative Description of a Dinner to Promote the Impeachment of President Eisenhower.
Terrible.
Underwear.
Fernández de Lizardi, José Joaquín
Epitaph to the Liberty of America.
Ferne, Doris
Nijinsky.
Sounding.
Fero, Gracia L.
Sharing His Cross.
Ferril, Thomas Hornsby
Basic Communication.
House in Denver.
Kochia.
Lost Ships.
Man Who Thought He Was a Horse, The.
Old Men on the Blue.
Something Starting Over.
Train Butcher, The.
What Trinkets?
Wood.
Ferriter, Pierce
He Charges Her To Lay Aside Her Weapons.
Lamentation for the Death of Sir Maurice Fitzgerald, Knight of Kerry, A.
Ferry, David
Antagonist, The.
Johnson on Pope.
Lines for a Dead Poet.
On the Way to the Island.
Out of That Sea.
Poem about Waking.
Unawkward Singers, The.
Fessenden, Thomas Green
Ye Sons of Columbia.
Fessenden, Thomas Whittemore
Mother.
To Mother.
Fet [*or* Foeth], Afanasi Afanasievich
I Come Again.
Morning Song.
Swallows.
Fetter, George Griffith
Name of Mother, The.
Fetzer, Herman *See* **"Falstaff, Jake"**
Fewster, Ernest
Cliff Rose, The.
Pearly Everlasting, The.
Fey, Harold E.
To a Revolutionist.
We Who Are about to Die ("We who are about to die salute each other in the old way").
French Salkeld, Cecil
Water-Front.
Fiacc, Padraic
Boy and the Geese, The.
Deranged.
Poet, The.
Stolen Fifer, The.
Fiawoo, F. K.
Soliloquy on Death.
Fichman, Jacob [*or* Yaakov]
Abishag.
In the Old City.
Samarian Nights.
Ficke, Arthur Davison
Alcibiades to a Jealous Girl.
Among Shadows.
April Moment.
Chrysanthemum Legend, The.
Don Quixote.
Elegy: "O fortunate man! who tilled the stubborn soil."
Epitaph for the Poet V., *sels.*
Fate with Devoted . . .
Father.
Her Pedigree.
I Am in Love with High Far-seeing Places.
I Am Weary of Being Bitter.
Immortals in Exile.
In That Dim Monument Where Tybalt Lies.
Leaf-Movement.
Like Him Whose Spirit.
Meeting.
Oracle, The.
Perspective of Co-ordination.
Portrait of an Old Woman.
Sonnet: "Across the shaken bastions of the year."
Sonnet: "I have seen beauty where light stabs the hills."
Sonnet: "Last night I kissed you with a brutal might."
Sonnet: "Out of the dusk into whose gloom you went."
Sonnet: "So you go back—because they bid you come."
Sonnet: "There are strange shadows fostered of the moon."
Sonnets of a Portrait Painter, *sels.*
Spring Landscape.
Summons.
Three Sisters, The.
To the Harpies.
Tropical Tempest.
Troubadours.
View from Heights.
Visit to a Museum.
World beyond World.
Young Recruit, The.
Fiedler, Leslie A.

Fiedler (continued)
Dumb Dick.
Field, Arthur Gordon
America Prays.
Bells of New Year.
Discoverer, The.
Name of Washington, The.
New Song, The.
Perpetual Christmas.
Field, Edward
Bride of Frankenstein, The.
Dirty Floor, The.
Event, An.
Floor Is Dirty, The.
Graffiti.
Notes from a Slave Ship.
Ode to Fidel Castro.
Plant Poems.
She.
Telephone, The.
Tulips and Addresses.
Unwanted.
View of Jersey, A.
What Grandma Knew.
Field, Elliot
Vinco.
Field, Eugene
Apple-Pie and Cheese.
Ashes on the Slide.
Bachelor Hall.
Bethlehem-Town ("As I was going to Bethlehem-town").
Bibliomaniac's Prayer, The.
Boy, The.
Casey's Table d'Hote.
Child and Mother.
Chipeta.
Christmas Eve.
Christmas Song.
Christmas Wish, A.
Clink of the Ice, The.
Colorado Sand Storm, A.
Death of Robin Hood, The.
Dibdin's Ghost.
Dinkey-Bird, The.
Doll's Wooing, The.
Duel, The.
Dutch Lullaby, A.
Epigram: "He is not drunk who, from the floor."
Father's Letter.
Fly-away Horse, The.
Garden and Cradle.
In the Firelight.
Inscription for My Little Son's Silver Plate.
Jessie.
Jest 'fore Christmas.
Little Blue Pigeon.
Little Boy Blue.
Little Peach, The.
Lyttel Boy, The.
My Sabine Farm.
New Year Idyl, A, *sel.*
Night Wind, The.
Nightfall in Dordrecht.
Norse Lullaby.
Orkney Lullaby.
Our Two Opinions.
Piazza Tragedy, A.
Pioneer, The.
Play on Words, A.
Rock-a-by Lady, The.
Seein' Things.
Shuffle-Shoon and Amber-Locks.
Sioux, The.
Song: "Why do the bells of [*or* do bells for] Christmas ring?"
Song of the All-Wool Shirt.
Star of the East.
Sugar-Plum Tree, The.
Three Kings, The.
Three Kings of Cologne, The.
Truth about Horace, The.
Two Little Skeezucks, The.
Unto a Child in Bethlehem-town.
Upon this happy New Year night.
Valentine, A.
Wanderer, The.
Wynken, Blynken, and Nod.
"Field, Michael" (Katherine Bradley *and* E. Cooper)
Aeolian Harp, An.
And on My Eyes Dark Sleep by Night.
Aridity.
Burial of Robert Browning, The.
Bury Her at Even.
Canute the Great, *sel.*
Dancers, The.
Depression.
Dream, The.
Earth to Earth.
Ebbtide at Sundown.
Gold Is the Son of Zeus: Neither Moth nor Worm May Gnaw It.
If They Honoured Me, Giving Me Their Gifts.
Iris.
La Gioconda, by Leonardo Da Vinci, in the Louvre.
Lettice.
Renewal.
Sweeter Far than the Harp, More Gold than Gold.
To the Lord Love.
Tragic Mary Queen of Scots, The.
Vision, A.
Where the Blessed Feet Have Trod.
Wind of Summer.
Woods Are Still, The.
Field, Mildred Fowler
Carpenter Christ.
Field, Nathaniel
Amends for Ladies, *sel.*
Matin Song.
Rise, Lady Mistress, Rise!
Song: "Rise Lady Mistresse, rise."
Field, Rachel Lyman (Mrs. Arthur Pederson)
Acrobat.
Almost.
Animal Store, The.
At the Theater.
Barefoot Days.
Birthday, A.
Busy Body, The.
Charm for Spring Flowers, A.
Chestnut Stands.
Circus Garland, A, *sels.*
City Lights.
City Rain.
Cranberry Road.
Dog Day, A.
Doorbells.
Eighth Street West.
Elephant, The.
Fire, A.
Flower-Cart Man, The.
For Christmas.
For My Father.
Fourth of July.
General Store.
Girl on the Milk-white Horse, The.
Good Green Bus.
Green Fiddler, The.
Gypsies.
Gypsy Children.
Hills, The.
I Want a Pasture.
Ice-Cream Man, The.
I'd Like to Be a Lighthouse.
If Once You Have Slept on an Island.
In Praise of Dust.
Islands.
Little Rose Tree, The.
Manhattan Lullaby.
Marooned.
Merry-go-round.
My Inside-Self.
New Year's Day.
Next Day.
Old Coach Road, The.
Old Gardener Time.
Old Music Box, The.
Old Wharves, The.
Parade.
Performing Seal, The.
Picnic Day.
Piper, The.
Playhouse Key, The.
Pointed People, The.
Pretzel Man, The.
Pushcart Row.
Questions for a Flying Squirrel to Answer.
Roads.
Sampler, The.
Seven Ages of Elf-Hood, The.
Skyscrapers.
Some People.
Something Told the Wild Geese.
Song for a Blue Roadster.
Spring Signs.
Summer Morning, A.
Taxis.
Ticking Clocks.
Vegetables.
Visitor, The.
When We Went Gathering Cat-Tails.
Whistles.
Field, Richard H.
Limerick: "When you go to a store in Ascutney."
Field, Roswell Martin
At the Ball Game.
Field, Sara Bard (Mrs. Charles Erskine Scott Wood)
Aslant the shoulder of each prisoner.
Barabbas, *sels.*
Contemporary.
In secret mountain fastnesses we stored.
November 2 A.M. Conspiracy.
We Whom the Dead Have Not Forgiven.
Field, Walter Taylor
Flag of the Free.
Fielding, Henry
A-Hunting We Will Go.
Don Quixote in England, *sels.*
Hunting Song.
Letter to Sir Robert Walpole, A.
On a Halfpenny which a Young Lady Gave a Beggar, and which the Author Redeemed for Half-a-Crown.
Roast Beef of Old England, The.
Tragedy of Tragedies, The.
Fields, Annie
Cedar Mountain.
Little Guinever.
On Waking from a Dreamless Sleep.
Return, The.
"Song, to the Gods, Is Sweetest Sacrifice."
Theocritus.
Fields, James Thomas
Alarmed Skipper, The.
Ballad of the Tempest.
Captain's Daughter, The.
Common Sense.
Mabel, in New Hampshire.
Nantucket Skipper, The.
On a Watchman Asleep at Midnight.
Owl-Critic, The.
Song of the Turtle and Flamingo.

Stars and Stripes, The.
Tempest, The.
Turtle and Flamingo, The.
With Wordsworth at Rydal.
Fields, Julia
Aardvark.
Alabama.
Birmingham.
Black Students.
Harlem in January.
I Heard a Young Man Saying.
Madness One Monday Evening.
Moths.
No Time for Poetry.
Fields, Maurice C.
How Long till April?
Fife, Austin *and* Alta Fife
Early This Spring We'll Leave Nauvoo.
Fifer, H. N.
He Lived a Life, *sel.*
Figgis, Darrell ("Michael Ireland")
Bogac Bán.
Inisgallun.
Figueroa, Francisco de
Mortal Grief.
Filicaja, Vincenzo da
Italy.
Providence.
Sonnet: "Italia, O Italia, upon whom."
Finch, Anne, Countess of Winchilsea
See **Winchilsea, Anne Finch, Countess of**
Finch, Francis Miles
Blue and the Gray, The.
Nathan Hale.
Finch, Julia Neely
Unborn, The.
Finch, Robert
Alone.
Aria Senza da Capo.
Campers.
Collective Portrait, The.
Effect of Snow, The.
Egg-and-Dart.
History Class.
Jardin de la Chapelle Expiatoire.
Lost Tribe, The.
Mountain, The.
Network, The.
Nowell, Nowell.
Peacock and Nightingale.
Report.
Room.
Scroll-Section.
Shadows, The.
Statue, The.
Time's Bright Sand.
Toronto Crossing.
Train Window.
Turning.
Finerty, John F.
May-Day at Sea.
Finger, Charles Joseph
Cowboy's Dream, The ("Last night as I lay on the prairie").
Fink, William W.
Larrie O'Dee.
Finkel, Donald
Bush on Mount Venus, The.
Clothing's New Emperor, The.
Cocteau's *Opium*: 1.
Cocteau's *Opium*: 2.
Esthetic of Imitation, An.
Father, The.
Flagpole Sitter, The.
Give Way.
Great Wave, The: Hokusai.
Hands.
Hunting Song.
Husband, The.
Imbecile, The.
Joyful Noise, A.
Juan Belmonte, Torero.
King Midas Has Asses' Ears.
Letter to My Daughter.
Oedipus at San Francisco.
Sirens, The.
Solo for Bent Spoon.
Spring Song.
Target Practice.
Finlay, Dawn
Anemone.
"Believe Ye That I Am Able to Do This?"
Guide, The.
In the Early Hours.
Twenty-Third Psalm.
Wonder.
Finlay, Ian Hamilton
Island Moment.
Orkney Interior.
Finley, John
Bachelor's Hall.
Birthday Prayer, A.
Sepulcher in the Garden, The.
Finley John Huston
Red Cross Spirit Speaks, The.
Road to Dieppe, The.
Three Wise Men, The.
Finn, A. E.
See God in Everything.
Finnin, Olive Mary
Farm near Norman's Lane, The.
Sarah Lorton.
Three Trees at Solstice.
Firdausi [*or* Firdusi] (Abul Kasim Mansur)
Alas for Youth.
Dream of Dakiki, The.
On the Sultan Mahmúd.
Reproach.
Firkins, Chester
On a Subway Express.
"Firth. "
Britannia Rules of Orthography.
Firth, Peter
To My Wife.
Fischer, Helen Field
Mystic Borderland, The.
There Is a Mystic Borderland.
Fischer, William J.
Faded Letter, A.
Fishback, Margaret
Brooklynese Champion.
Christmas Pageant.
Complacent Cliff-Dweller, The.
Hallowe'en Indignation Meeting.
Hell's Bells.
I Stand Corrected.
I Take 'Em and Like 'Em.
In Extremis.
Kerchoo!
Lie of the Land, The.
Midsummer Melancholy.
On Viewing a Florist's Whimsy at Fifty-ninth and Madison.
Poem for Mother's Day.
Purist to Her Love, The.
Sentimental Lines to a Young Man Who Favors Pink Wallpaper, While I Personally Lean to the Blue.
Sitting Pretty.
Sprig Fever.
Strange Interlude, A.
This Way Out.
Thoughts of Loved Ones.
Triolet on a Dark Day.
Triolet on a Downhill Road.
Unrequited Love on the Back Piazza.
Wanted: One Cave Man with Club.
Fisher, A. G.
Day by Day.
Fisher, A. Hugh
Ceylon.
Fisher, Aileen
All Dressed Up for Easter.
Autumn Rain.
Away We Go.
Bells of Peace, The.
Birthday Cake.
But That Was Yesterday.
Christmas Shoppers.
Christmas Tree.
Coffeepot Face, A.
Counting Sheep.
December.
Down in the Hollow.
Early, Early Easter Day.
Fall.
Fireflies.
Flag We Fly, The.
Halloween Concert.
Hayfield.
Holly Fairies.
Hoppity Toads.
Houses ("Houses are faces").
I Like It When It's Mizzly.
January Snow.
June.
Just a Mile Beyond.
Legends of Christmas.
Light in the Darkness.
Little Bird, A.
Little Brother.
Little Talk.
Moth Miller.
Mother's Party.
Newspaper.
November.
Otherwise.
Outdoor Christmas Tree, The.
Package, The.
Picnic, A.
Puppy.
Pussy-Willows.
Raccoons.
Race, The.
Rich.
Richer.
Snoring.
Snowman's Resolution, The.
Something Very Elegant.
Taking Down the Tree.
Tummy Ache.
Un-Birthday Cake.
Until We Built a Cabin.
Valentine's Day.
Wearing of the Green.
Wind.
Winter Circus.
Wonderful Man, A.
Workshop, The.
World's So Big, The.
Fisher, Ed
Talk of the Town, The.
Fisher, I. H. *See* **"Hume, Isobel"**
Fisher, Jasper
Fuimus Troes, *sels.*
Morisco, A.
Song; a Morisko.
Song to a Viol.
Fisher, K.
Story of the Corn.
Fisher, Mahlon Leonard
Ancient Sacrifice, The.
As an Old Mercer.
November.
On a Sculptured Head of the Christ.
Per Contra.
Realization.

Fisher (continued)
To Nature.
Fisher, Philip John
"I Die Daily."
Fisher, William C.
Eternal Light, The.
My Boy and His Saviour.
My Saviour's Love for Me.
Fiske, John
Upon the Decease of Mrs. Anne Griffin.
Upon the Much-to Be Lamented Desease of the Reverend Mr. John Cotton.
Fitch, Robert
High Brow.
Fitger, Arthur
Evening Prayer.
Fitts, Dudley
Priam.
Fitzell, Lincoln
Conflict.
Fitzgeffrey, OR Fitzgeffry Charles
Bee, The.
Holy Transportations, *sel.*
Sir Francis Drake, *sels.*
Take Frankincense, O God.
Fitzgerald, Edward
Because.
Chivalry at a Discount.
Meadows in Spring, The.
Old Song.
Song of the Fire.
Three Arrows, The.
Fitzgerald, F. Scott
Epitaph from "The Great Gatsby."
Obit on Parnassus.
There'd Be an Orchestra.
Thousand-and-First Ship, *sel.*
Fitzgerald, Mary Scott
Rendezvous.
Fitzgerald, Robert
Adulescentia, *sel.*
Before Harvest.
Celestine.
Cobb Would Have Caught It.
Colorado.
Elegy: "What should you know at last when spirit's."
Errantry.
History.
Imprisoned, The.
Jesu, Joy of Man's Desiring.
July in Indiana.
Miraculously, through prayer to Saint Anthony.
Mise en Scène.
Painter, The.
Portraits.
Queens, The.
Sea Pieces.
Solstitium Saeculare.
Souls Lake.
Windshield.
Winter Night.
Fitzgerald, Robert David
Back from the Paved Way.
Cock that crowed this dawn up, heard, The.
Copernicus, *sel.*
Envy Goes Groping.
Essay on Memory.
Face of the Waters, The.
Fifth Day.
Glad World.
Macquarie Place.
1918-1941.
Traditional Tune.
Wind at Your Door, The.
Fitzpatrick, Brian
Cenotaph.
Fitzpatrick, John
Mater Dolorosa.
Fitzsimon, Henry
Swearing.
Fiumi, Lionello
Man Closes the Shutters, The.
Flaccus, Aulus Persius *See* **Persius**
Flaccus, Kimball
Dance of Death.
Flaccus, Quintus Horatius *See* **Horace**
Flagg, Hannah *See* **Gould, Hannah Flagg**
Flagg, James Montgomery
Limerick: "Said the Reverend Jabez McCotton."
Flagg, Wilson
O'Lincoln Family, The.
Flaischlen, Cäsar
Most Quietly at Times.
Flanner, Hildegarde (Mrs. Frederick Monhoff)
Birds.
Communion.
Daphne.
Discovery.
Flowers of Apollo, The.
Memo.
Noon on Alameda Street.
Of Old Sat Freedom on the Heights.
Pacific Winter.
Prayer for This Day.
Sonnets in Quaker Language.
Spring's on the Curb.
This Morning.
To One of Little Faith.
Flash, Henry Lynden
Flag, The.
Gallant Fifty-one, The.
Stonewall Jackson.
Zollicoffer.
Flatman, Thomas
Advice, The.
Appeal to Cats in the Business of Love, An.
Bachelor's Song, The.
Death.
Defiance, The.
Doomsday Thought, A.
Love's Bravo.
On Dr. Woodford's Paraphrase on the Canticles.
On Marriage.
Pastoral Dialogue, Castara and Parthenia.
Retirement, The.
Sad Day, The.
Slight, The.
Song: "Oh the sad day."
Thought of Death, A.
Unconcerned, The.
Wish, The.
Flecker, James Elroy
Ballad of Camden Town, The.
Ballad of Hampstead Heath, The.
Ballad of the Londoner.
Brumana.
Don Juan Declaims.
Dying Patriot, The.
Epilogue: "Away, for we are ready to a man!"
Epilogue to Hassan.
Epithalamion: "Smile then, children, hand in hand."
Gates of Damascus.
Golden Journey to Samarkand, The.
Golden Road, The.
Hammam Name, The.
Hassan, *sels.*
In Phaeacia.
Inscription for Arthur Rackham's Rip Van Winkle.
Lord Arnaldos.
November Eves (November evenings! Damp and still).
Oak and Olive.
Old Ships, The.
Painter's Mistress, The.
Parrot, The.
Prayer: "Let me not know how sins and sorrows glide."
Prologue: "We who with songs beguile your pilgrimage."
Prologue to "The Golden Journey to Samarkand."
Queen's Song, The.
Rioupéroux.
Saadabad.
Santorin.
Ship, an Isle, a Sickle Moon, A.
Stillness.
Tenebris Interlucentem.
Thy dawn, O Master of the world, thy dawn.
To a Poet a Thousand Years Hence.
Town without a Market, The.
War Song of the Saracens.
Welsh Sea, The.
Flecknoe, Richard
Invocation of Silence.
Noble Love.
On Mary, Duchess of Richmond.
Silence Invoked.
Fleg, Edmond
End of Sorrow, The.
Wall of Weeping, The, *sels.*
Wandering Jew Comes to the Wall, The.
"Fleming, Archibald." *See* **MacLiesh, Archibald Fleming**
Fleming, Elizabeth
Balloon Seller, The.
Chain of Princes Street, The.
Fires.
Hedgehog and His Coat, The.
Hurdy-Gurdy Man, The.
If I Were a Pig.
In the Mirror.
Lavender Bush, The.
My Barrow.
Old Mrs. Jarvis.
Patchwork Quilt, The.
Secret, The.
Toadstools.
Who's In?
Wild Animals.
Window Cleaner, The.
Fleming, Marjory [*or* Marjorie]
Melancholy Lay, A.
Six-Year-Old Marjory Fleming Pens a Poem.
Sonnet on a Monkey, A.
Sonnet to a Monkey.
To a Monkey.
Fleming, Mary
Two Kisses.
Fleming, Maybury
To Demeter.
To Sleep.
What Though the Green Leaf Grow?
Fletcher, Bob
Love Dirge to the Whitehouse, A.
Fletcher, Frank
O Son of Man.
Fletcher, Giles, the Elder
Elegy, An: "Down in a bed, and on a bed of down."
If sad complaint would show a lover's pain.
Licia, *sels.*
So down the silver streams of Eridan.
Sonnet: "Like Memnon's rock, touched [*or* touch'd] with the rising sun."
Time.
Twice had Diana bent her golden bowe.

Fletcher, Giles, the Younger
Had I a voice of steel to tune my song.
Celestial City, The.
Christ.
Christ's Triumph after Death.
Christ's Triumph over Death.
Christ's Victory and Triumph, *sels.*
Christ's Victory in Heaven.
Christ's Victory on Earth.
Easter Morn.
Excellency of Christ.
He Is a Path.
Heavenly Jerusalem, The.
In Gethsemane.
Incarnation, The.
On the Crucifixion.
Wooing Song.
Fletcher, Iain
Adolescents in the Dusk.
Fletcher, John
Arm, Arm, Arm, Arm.
Beauty Clear and Fair.
Beggars' Bush, *sel.*
Bonduca, *sel.*
Care-charming Sleep, [Thou Easer of All Woes].
Cast our caps and cares away.
Come Hither, You That Love.
Come, Shepherds, Come!
Dead Host's Welcome, The.
Destiny.
Elder Brother, The, *sel.*
Evening Knell, The.
Evening Song.
Faithful Shepherdess, The, *sels.*
Folding the Flocks.
God Lyaeus.
God of Sheep, The.
Had we a difference with some petty isle.
Hail, holy earth, whose cold arms do embrace.
Hear, Ye Ladies [That Despise].
Hence All You Vain Delights.
Here be woods as green.
Honest Man's Fortune, The.
Hymn to Pan.
I cast my cloud off, and appear myself.
Into Slumbers.
Invocation to Sleep.
I've walked through all the lodgings.
Little French Lawyer, The, *sel.*
Love Song ("Now the lusty spring is seen").
Love Song ("Take, oh take those lips away").
Lover's Progress, The, *sel.*
Love's Emblems.
Mad Lover, The, *sels.*
Man Is His Own Star.
Mighty Love.
My man Thomas.
Night-Walker, The; or, The Little Thief, *sel.*
Now the Lusty Spring.
Passionate Man's Song, The.
Power of Love, The.
Prayer to Venus.
Priest's Chant, The.
River God, The.
River God to Amoret, The.
River-God's Song, The.
Rule a Wife and Have a Wife, *sel.*
Satyr's Farewell, The.
Satyr's Song ("See, the day begins to break").
Shall I stray/ In the middle air.
Sing His Praises.
Song: "Beauty clear and fair."
Song: "Care charming Sleep, thou easer of all woes."
Song: "Do not fear to put thy feet."
Song: "Drink today, and drown all sorrow."
Song: "Heare ye Ladies that despise."
Song: "Let the bells ring, and let the boys sing."
Song: "Now the lusty spring is seen."
Song: "O fair[e] sweet face, O eyes celestial[l] bright."
Song: "Sing his praises that doth keep."
Song for the Sick Emperor.
Song in the Wood.
Song to Bacchus.
Song to Sleep.
Spanish Curate, The, *sels.*
Sweetest Melancholy.
Thou Easer of All Woes.
'Tis Late and Cold.
To Pan.
To Sleep.
To the Blest Evanthe.
To the fair fields where loves eternal dwell.
Tragedy of Valentinian, The, *sels.*
Upon an Honest Man's Fortune. *sel.*
Who hath restored my sense, given me new breath.
Wife for a Month, A, *sel.*
Women Pleased, *sels.*
Women's Longing.
Fletcher, John *and* Philip Massinger
Double Marriage, The, *sel.*
'Tis a substantial thing, and not a word.
Fletcher, John *and* (*at.*) Thomas Middleton
Melancholy.
Nice Valour, The, *sel.*
O Sweetest Melancholy.
Song: "Hence, all you vain delights."
Fletcher, John, *and* William Rowley
Come Follow Me, You Country Lasses.
Maid in the Mill, The, *sel.*
Fletcher, John *and* William Shakespeare *See* **Shakespeare, William *and* John Fletcher**
Fletcher, John, *and others,*
Bloody Brother, The, *sels.*
Drink To-Day [and Drown All Sorrow].
Drinking Song.
Hide, Oh, Hide Those Hills.
Mourn No More.
Queen of Corinth, The, *sel.*
Tragedy of Rollo, Duke of Normandy, The.
Weep No More.
Fletcher, John Gould
Ad Majorem Hominis Gloriam.
Advent.
Arizona Poems, *sels.*
Autumnal Clouds.
Before Olympus.
Birth of Lucifer, The.
Blake.
Blue Symphony, The.
Broadway's Canyon.
Clouds across the Canyon.
Down the Mississippi.
Elegy on a Nordic White Protestant.
Elegy on an Empty Skyscraper.
Embarkation.
Enduring, The.
Exit.
Full Moon.
Grand Canyon of the Colorado, *sel.*
Green Symphony.
Heat.
Hoopskirt, The.
Irradiations, *sels.*
Last Frontier, The.
Last Judgment.
Lincoln.
Lofty House, The.
London Nightfall.
Mexican Quarter.
Moon's Orchestra, The.
New Heaven, A.
Night Landing.
Rain in the Street.
Rebel, A.
Reunion.
Road, The.
Second Walk in the Garden, The.
Silence, The.
Skaters, The.
Song of the Midnight Rain.
Song of the Moderns.
Spring.
Stevedores, The.
Swan, The.
There Was a Darkness in this Man.
To a Survivor of the Flood.
To Columbus.
To the Winter Wind.
Towards the North Star.
Trees, like great jade elephants, The.
Walk on the Beach, The.
White Symphony.
Windmills, The.
Fletcher, Julia A. *See* **Carney, Julia A. Fletcher**
Fletcher, Phineas
Apollyonists, The.
Brittain's Ida, *sel.*
But ah! let me under some Kentish hill.
Canto I: "Of Men, nay Beasts; worse, Monsters; worst of all."
Chromis.
Desiderium.
Divine Wooer, The, *sel.*
Eclog. III: "Fisher-lad, A (no higher dares he look)."
Elisa, or an Elegy upon the Unripe Decease of Sir Antony Irby, *sel.*
Hymn, A: "Drop, drop, slow tears."
Lines Written at Cambridge, to W. R., Esquire.
Litany, A: "Drop, drop, slow tears."
Locusts, or Apollyonists, The, *sels.*
Me Lord? can'st Thou mispend.
Of men, nay beasts; worse, monsters; worst of all.
Overthrow of Lucifer, The.
Piscatorie Eclogues, *sels.*
Purple Island, The, *sels.*
Sicelides, *sel.*
Sin, Despair, and Lucifer.
Song: "Fond men! whose wretched care the life soon ending."
To My Soul.
Woman's Inconstancy.
Fletcher, Robert
Epitaph on His Deceased Friend, An.
Flexner, Hortense (Mrs. Wyncie King)
Builders.
Faith.
French Clock.
Poets.
Wandering.
Flexner, James
In the Hours of Darkness.
Flint, Annie Johnson
Answered Prayer, The.
At the Place of the Sea.
Be Ye Also Ready.
Behold, I Come!
Blessings That Remain, The.
But God.
Carpenter's Son.
Christ—and We.
Cross and the Tomb, The.
Daily with You.
Everlasting Love, The.
He Giveth More [Grace].

Flint (continued)
He Is Risen.
His Will Be Done.
Hitherto and Henceforth.
I Look Not Back.
In a Small Place.
In Him.
Jesus Christ—and We.
Mary and Martha.
My Prayer.
Name of Jesus, The.
Not I, but God.
Old Year and the New, The.
One Day at a Time.
Our Father's Hand.
Passing Through.
Pray—Give—Go.
Red Sea Place in Your Life, The.
Sepulcher, The.
Sometimes.
Thanksgiving, A.
This Moment.
Thou Remainest.
Thread and the Cable, The.
Three Prayers, The.
Threefold Work, The.
Through the Waters.
Thy Will Be Done.
Trust.
We See Jesus.
What God Hath [*or* Has] Promised.
Why Should I Fear?
Word of God, The.
World's Bible, The.

Flint, F. Barrie
Immanence.

Flint, Francis Stewart
Beggar.
Chrysanthemums.
In the Garden.
Lilac.
London.
Plane-Tree.
Prayer: "As I walk through the streets."
Sadness.
Swan, The.

Flint, Roland
August from My Desk.

Flohr, Natalie
Martyr, The.

Flores, Manuel María
Ode to the Fatherland, *sel.*
We lift our standard to the mountain top.

Florio, John
Of Books.

Florit, Eugenio
Signal, The.

Flower, Newman
Creed in a Garden, A.

Flower, Robin
Say Not that Beauty.
Troy.

Flower, Sarah *See* **Adams, Sarah Flower**

Flucker, Thomas
Tom Gage's Proclamation.

Flynn, Claire Wallace
Glory of the Grass, The.

Flynn, Clarence Edwin
Appreciation.
Clock of God, The.

Flynn, Joseph
Down Went McGinty.

Focht, Mildred
David, Aged Four.

Foeth, Afanasi *See* **Fet, Afanasi Afanasievich**

Fogazzaro, Antonio
Bells, The.

Fogel, Ephim G.
Shipment to Maidenek.

Folcachiero de' Folcachieri
Canzone: He Speaks of His Condition through Love.

Foley, David W.
Within the Gates.

Foley, Helen
Gorse.

Foley, James William
Drop a Pebble in the Water.
Echo of a Song, The.
Greetings for Two.
Nemesis.
North Dakota Hymn.
Passamquoddy's Apple Toddy.
Salvation of Texas Peters, The.
Scientific Proof.
Song of Summer Days.
Yanks.

Folgore da San Geminiano *See* **San Geminiano, Folgore da**

Follain, Jean
Comings and Goings, *sels.*

Follansbee, Mitchell D.
I Like to Quote.

Follen, Eliza Lee (Cabot)
Annie's Garden.
Baby's Birthday, The.
Birdie.
Cock and Hens.
Ding Dong! Ding Dong!
Do You Guess It Is I?
Dog and the Cat, and the Duck and the Rat, The.
Farm Yard, The.
Fiddlededee.
Follow Me!
Good Moolly Cow, The.
Kitty in the Basket.
Little Boy's Good-Night, The.
Little Kittens, The.
Moon, The.
New Moon, The.
Oh! Look at the Moon.
Ringely, Ringely.
Runaway Brook.
Trusty Learning A. B. C.
Walter and His Dog.
Where Are You Going.
Where are you going,/ My little cat?

Fontaine, Jean de la *See* **La Fontaine, Jean de**
Warning for Abraham Lincoln, A.

Fontenelle, Bernard le Bovier de
To Apollo Making Love.

Foote, Agnes C.
Annunciation to All Women.

Foote, Lucius Harwood
Derelict, The.
Don Juan.
El Vaquero.
On the Heights.
Poetry.

Foote, Samuel
Great Panjandrum [Himself], The.

Foott, Mary Hannay
Where the Pelican Builds.

Forbes, Ella C.
Glad Earth.

Ford, Charles Henri
Baby's in Jail; the Animal Day Plays Alone.
Plaint.

Ford, Charles L.
Sacrament, The.

Ford, Corey
Up-Set, The.
When West Comes East.

Ford, Edsel
Fox, The.

Ford Ford Madox (*formerly* Ford Madox Hueffer)
A Solis Ortus Cardine.
And my dear one sat in the shadows; very softly she wept.
Children's Song.
Footsloggers.
Gray Matter.
House, A, *sel.*
I am the house!
Iron Music, The.
Old Houses of Flanders, The.
On Heaven.
"There Shall Be More Joy."
Unwritten Song, The.
What the Orderly Dog Saw.
"When the World Was in Building. . ."
Winter-Night Song.
Wisdom.

Ford, Francis Alan
Song of the Gulf Stream.

Ford, Gregory J.
Bits and Pieces.

Ford, John
Beasts onely capable of sense, enjoy.
Broken Heart, The, *sels.*
Can You Paint a Thought?
Cunning arts man, The/ Faltered not in a line.
Dawn.
Dirge: "Glories, pleasures, pomps, delights, and ease."
Fly Hence Shadows.
Glories, Pleasures.
If thou canst wake with me, forget to eate.
Lady's Trial, The, *sel.*
Lover's Melancholy, The, *sels.*
Minutes are numbered by the fall of sands.
Now Love Dies.
Oh No More, No More, Too Late.
Pleasures, Beauty, Youth Attend Ye.
Song: "Fly hence, shadows, that do keep."
Song: "Glories, pleasures, pomps, delights, and ease."
Song: "Oh, no more, no more, too late."

Ford, John, *and* Thomas Dekker *See* **Dekker, Thomas, *and* John Ford**

Ford, Mary A.
Hundred Years from Now, A.

Ford, R. A. D.
Back to Dublin.
Delusion of Reference, A.
Lynx.
Revenge of the Hunted.
Roadside near Moscow.
Thieves of Love, The.
Twenty Below.
Window on the North, A.

Ford, Richard Clyde
Forest Boat Song.

Ford, Robert
Bonniest Bairn in A' the Warl', The.

Ford, Wally
Dry Wishing Well.
Sunrise on the Sunset.

Forde, Thomas
Fond Love, No More.
Love's Labyrinth, *sel.*

Fordham, Ivy M.
His Coming.

Foresman, Rebecca
How to Forget.
If.

"Forester, Fanny" (Emily Chubbuck Judson)
My Bird.
Watching.
Weaver, The.

Forrest, M.
Lonely Woman, The.

Forrest, William
Marigold, The ("The God above, for man's delight").

Marigold, The ("To Mary our Queen").
New Ballade of the Marigolde, A.
Forrester, Alfred A. ("Alfred Crowquill")
To My Nose.
Forster, William
Devil and the Governor, The, *sel.*
In New South Wales, as I plainly see.
Forsyth, James
Artillery Shoot.
Soldier's Dove.
To My Wife.
Forsyth, P. T.
Question, A.
Fort, Janetta *See* **Denton, Clara Janetta**
Fort, Paul
Ah! what joy, the bagpipe and the flute.
Ballad of the Bells, *sel.*
Ballade: "Pretty maid she died, she died, in love-bed as she lay, The."
Pan and the Cherries.
Pretty Maid, The.
Sailor and the Shark, The.
Fortunatus (Venantius Honorius Clementianus Fortatus)
Hail, Day of Days! In Peals of Praise.
Hymn to the Holy Cross.
O Glory of Virgins.
Vexilla Regis.
Foscolo, Ugo
To His Dead Brother.
Fosdick, Harry Emerson
God of Grace and God of Glory.
Prince of Peace, The.
Foss, Sam Walter
And what is faith? The anchored trust that at the core of things.
Bring Me Men.
Calf-Path, The.
Coming American, The, *sel.*
Cosmopolitan Woman, A.
Country Summer Pastoral, A, *sl. abr.*
Creedless Love, The.
Cyrus Brown's Prayer.
Despise not any man that lives.
Higher Catechism, The.
House by the Side of the Road, The.
"Hullo!"
Husband and Heathen.
Ideal Husband to His Wife, The.
Man from the Crowd, The.
Meeting of the Clabberhuses, The.
Nature and Religion.
Philosopher, A.
Prayer of Cyrus Brown, The.
Then Ag'in.
Town of Hay, The.
Two Gods.
What Is the Church?
Work for Small Men, *sel.*
Foster, Jeanne Robert
John Butler Yeats.
King o' Spain's Daughter, The.
Pair of Lovers, A.
William P. Frye, The.
Foster, Stephen Collins
Camptown Races, De, *with music.*
Come Where My Love Lies Dreaming.
Jeanie with the Light Brown Hair.
Massa's in de Cold, Cold Ground.
My Old Kentucky Home.
Oh! Susanna.
Old Black Joe.
Old Folks at Home.
Swanee River.
Foster, William Prescott
Icebergs.
Sea's Voice, The.
Foulke, William Dudley
Ad Patriam, *sel.*
City's Crown, The.
Land of My Heart.
Life's Evening.
Fowler, Ellen Thorneycroft
Wisdom of Folly.
Fowler, Elsie Melchert
Christmas Morning.
If You Never Talked with Fairies.
If You've Never.
Little Christ Child.
Miracle, The.
Secrets.
Fowler, Gene
Shaman Songs, *sels.*
305 Honda.
3 Meditations.
Whore.
Words, The.
Fowler, Hazel J.
Prayer: "Take from the earth its tragic hunger, Lord."
Fowler, Lona M.
Middle-Time, The.
Fowler, Mary B.
Promise, The.
Fowler, Wilbur Humphrey
Prayer, A: "Purge me, O God."
Fowler, William
In Orknay.
Ship-broken Men Whom Stormy Seas Sore Toss.
Fox, C. A.
Trust.
Fox, James
Where the Grizzly Dwells.
Fox, Moireen
Fairy Lover, The.
Liadain to Curither.
Fox, Ruth
Another Kind of Burning.
Fox, William Johnson
Barons Bold, The.
Life Is Love.
Fox-Smith, Cicely *See* **Smith, Cicely Fox**
"Foxton, E." (Sarah Hammond Palfrey)
Pilgrim, The.
France, Judson
Aristocratic Trio, An.
Frances, Emmanuel ben David
Price of Begging, The.
Frances, Jacob ben David
Song of Hate.
"Francis."
They Answer Back; to His Ever-worshipped Will from W. H.
To His Ever-worshipped Will from W. H.
Francis, Saint *See* **Francis of Assisi, Saint**
Francis, Colin
Tony O!
Francis, Joseph G.
Elephant, An.
Lion, A.
Musical Evening, A.
Very Happy Family, A.
Francis, Marilyn
Neighbors.
Francis, Robert
Apple Peeler.
Base Stealer, The.
Beyond Biology.
Blue Jay.
Boy Riding Forward Backward.
Catch: "Two boys uncoached are tossing a poem together."
Cold.
Come Out into the Sun.
Eagle Plain.
Epitaph: "Believer he and unbeliever both."
Farm Boy after Summer.
Fate of Elms, The.
Glass.
Hallelujah; a Sestina.
Hide-and-Seek.
High Diver.
Hogwash.
Mr. Eliot's Day.
Mouse Whose Name Is Time, The.
Night Train.
Orb Weaver, The.
Picasso and Matisse.
Pitcher.
Sailboat, Your Secret.
Salt.
Seed-Eaters, The.
Sing a Song of Juniper.
Skier.
Swimmer.
That Dark Other Mountain.
Two Bums Walk Out of Eden.
Walls.
Francis d'Assisi, Mother
Resignation.
Samaritan Woman.
Francis Raphael, Mother (Augusta Theodosia Drane
Maris Stella.
Francis of Assisi Saint
Cantica: Our Lord Christ.
Canticle of the Sun.
Cantico del Sole.
Lord, Make Me an Instrument of Your Peace.
Praise of Created Things.
Prayer: "Lord, make me an instrument of Thy Peace."
St. Francis' Prayer.
Sermon to the Birds.
Song of the Creatures, The.
Francis Xavier, Saint
Hymn: "My God, I love thee, not because."
Hymn of Love.
My God, I Love Thee.
Francisca Josefa del Castillo, Sister
Christmas Carol: "Land grew bright in a single flower, The."
Holy Eclogue, The.
Franck, Johann
Jesus, Priceless Treasure.
Peace and Joy in Jesus Christ.
Frank, Edgar
Goshen!
Frank, Florence Kiper
Baby.
Jew to Jesus, The.
Jewish Conscript, The.
Lincoln.
Movies, The.
Now in the Bloom.
Sleep the Mother.
Frank, John Frederick
One No. 7.
Frankel, Doris
Song of the Truck.
Frankenberg, Lloyd
Existentialism.
Hide in the Heart.
Letter to the Night.
Night of the Full Moon, The.
Return, The.
Roots Go Down.
Sea, The.
Water Wants All Sea, The.
Franklin, Benjamin
Difference, The.
Enough Not One.
Epitaph: "Body of, The."
Epitaph on a Talkative Old Maid.
Epitaph on a Worthy Clergyman.
Here Skugg Lies Snug.
Jack and Roger.

Franklin (continued)
Mother Country, The.
On Skugg.
Paper.
Poor Richard's Almanac, *sels.*
Quatrain: "Jack eating rotten cheese, did say."
Well-packed Wisdom.
What the eyes do not admire.
Franklin, Clarence
Death of Days and Nights of Life.
Two Dreams.
Visions. . .Leaders.
Franklin, Michael
Scarecrow, The.
Fraser, Al
To the "JFK" Quintet.
Fraser, Alexander Louis
By Cobequid Bay.
Life's Illusion.
Fraser, George S.
Bought Embrace, A.
Crisis.
Elegy: "Waxen and the false grace of tulips, The."
Lean Street.
Letter to Anne Ridler.
Meditation of a Patriot.
Nilotic Elegy.
On a Memory of Beauty.
Poem about Love, A.
Rostov.
Song for Music.
Sonnet: "My simple heart, bred in provincial tenderness."
Summer and Winter.
Time, The.
Fraser, Hermia Harris
Copper Song, The.
Rousing Canoe Song, The.
Song of Welcome.
Fraser, James Anderson
Apprehension.
Fraser, John
Maiden and the Lily, The.
Fraser, Kathleen
Change of Address.
Child Drowns in the Sea of Its Own Imagining, A.
Grass.
How Tuesday Began.
Letters: To Barbara.
Poem in Which My Legs Are Accepted.
Reaching-Out Poem.
Song for a Man in Doubt.
Soundings.
Frazee-Bower, Helen
Alien.
Book, The.
Courage.
I Bid You Keep Some Few Small Dreams.
Song of Diligence, A.
Stranger, The.
Stranger came to Bethlehem, A.
Take Time to Talk with God.
This Is the Tragedy.
Three Crosses.
Two Married (I-IV).
Who Goeth Hence.
Fredericks, Joseph Paget- *See* **Paget-Fredericks, Joseph**
Fredericks, Leo
Rain and the Rainbow, The.
Free, Spencer Michael
Human Touch, The.
Freeman, Arthur
Cell of Himself, The.
Conversation Piece.
Naples Again.
Roadside: Spleen.
What Is Unwoven.
Zoo of You, The.
Freeman, Carol
Christmas Morning, I.
Gift.
I Saw Them Lynch.
When My Uncle Willie Saw.
Freeman, Carolyn R.
Easter Airplane, The.
Freeman, Hollis
Birds of the Air, The.
Freeman, John
Armistice Day.
Asylum.
Black Poplar-Boughs.
Caterpillars.
Crowns, The.
Happy Death.
Hounds, The.
It Was the Lovely Moon.
Knocking at the Door.
Music Comes.
Stone Trees.
To End Her Fear.
Tree, The.
Waiting.
Waits, The.
Wakers, The.
Freeman, Mary Eleanor Wilkins
Christmas Tree, The.
Now Is the Cherry in Blossom.
Ostrich Is a Silly Bird, The.
Freeman, Robert
Beyond the Horizon.
Evening Prayer.
God Bless Our Home.
Hymn of Unity, A.
In My Father's House.
Prayer: "White Captain of my soul, lead on."
Soldier's Prayer, A.
Why.
Freeman, Thomas
Aliud.
In Christophorum.
In Epitaphium Pingui Minerva Compositum.
In Marcellum.
In Owenni Epigrammata.
In Phaedram.
In Superbum.
Lectori Quomodo Legat.
Me Quoque Vatem.
O Tempora! O Mores!
Of Spenser's Faerie Queene [*or* Fairy Queen].
Pity, oh pity! death had power.
Quo Ruis ab Demens? Londons Progress.
Quot Bipedes Aurum.
To George Chapman.
To Master W. Shakespeare.
To the Stationer.
Freeze, Mary D.
Our Times Are in His Hands.
Freiligrath, Ferdinand
Black, Red, and Gold, *sel.*
True Freedom breaks the yokes that gall.
Frémont, John Charles
On Recrossing the Rocky Mountains after Many Years.
French, Walter Lyman
Your Sanctuary.
French, William Percy
Fighting McGuire.
Goosey Goosey Gander—by Various Authors.
"Me loving subjects," sez she.
Musician to His Love, The.
Queen's Afterdinner Speech, The, *sel.*
Freneau, Philip
Adventures of Simon Swaugum, a Village Merchant, The.
Amanda's Complaint.
Americans!
Ancient Prophecy, An.
Barney's Invitation.
Battle of Lake Champlain, The.
Battle of Stonington on the Seaboard of Connecticut, The.
Beauties of Santa Cruz, The.
Belief and Unbelief.
Bonhomme Richard and *Serapis*, The.
British Prison Ship, The, *sel.*
By some sad means, when Reason holds no sway.
Columbus in Chains.
Columbus to Ferdinand.
Death.
Death's Epitaph.
Discovery.
Emancipation from British Dependence.
Epitaph: "Here—for they could not help but die."
Eutaw Springs.
Fading Rose, The, *sel.*
Female Frailty, *sel.*
From the vast caverns of old ocean's bed.
Hospital Prison Ship, The.
House of Night, The, *sels.*
Human Frailty.
Hurricane, The.
Indian Burying Ground, The.
Indian Student, The; or, Force of Nature.
Northern Soldier, The.
Occasioned by General Washington's Arrival in Philadelphia, on His Way to His Residence in Virginia.
Ode: "God save the Rights of Man!"
On a Honey Bee [Drinking from a Glass of Wine and Drowned Therein].
On a Travelling Speculator.
On Mr. Paine's "Rights of Man."
On the Anniversary of the Storming of the Bastille, at Paris, July 14th, 1789.
On the British Invasion.
On the British King's Speech.
On the Capture of the *Guerrière*.
On the Death of Benjamin Franklin.
On the Death of Captain Nicholas Biddle.
On the Departure of the British from Charleston.
On the Emigration to America.
On the Religion of Nature.
On the Ruins of a Country Inn.
On the Uniformity and Perfection of Nature.
On the Universality and Other Attributes of the God of Nature.
Parting Glass, The.
Plato to Theon.
Power of Fancy, The.
Reflections, *sel.*
Republican Genius of Europe, The.
Royal Adventurer, The.
Sabbath-Day Chace.
Scurrilous Scribe, The.
Sick of thy Northern glooms, come, shepherd, seek.
Sir Henry Clinton's Invitation to the Refugees.
Song: On Captain Barney's Victory over the Ship *General Monk*.
Song of Thyrsis.
Stanzas: "No tongue can tell, no pen describe."
Stanzas Occasioned by the Ruins of a Country Inn, Unroofed and Blown Down in a Storm.
To a Caty-did.
To a Honey Bee.
To a Republican.
To an Author.
To Sir Toby.

To the Memory of the Brave Americans.
Vanity of Existence, The.
Vision, A.
Wild Honeysuckle [*or* Honey Suckle], The.
Frere, John Hookham
Bees and Monks.
Boy and His Top, The.
Boy and the Parrot, The.
Boy and the Wolf, The.
Cavern and the Hut, The.
King Arthur and His Round Table, *sel.*
Piece of Glass, and the Piece of Ice, The.
Showing How the Cavern Followed the Hut's Advice.
Frere, John Hookham, *and* **George Canning** *See* **Canning, George,** *and* **John Hookham Frere**
Frere, John Hookham, George Canning, *and* **Geo. Ellis** *See* **Canning, George, George Ellis,** *and* **John Hookham Frere**
Friedlaender, Violet Helen
Planting Trees.
Road Makers.
Friend, Robert
Doll, The.
Hunchback, The.
Letter to P.
Fries, Annerika
Soul Growth.
Frieseke, Frances
Armor the Bud.
You Need Not Fear.
Frink, A. L.
Rose Still Grows beyond the Wall.
Frisch, Anthony
Convict, The.
Joan of Arc to the Tribunal.
Skiers, The.
Frishman, David
Messiah, The.
Fröding, Gustaf
Dance by the Roadside, The.
Froissart, Jean
Rondel: To His Mistress, to Succor His Heart.
Frolicher, John C.
Pearl Harbor.
Frost, Frances Mary
Apple Season.
Apple Song.
Autumn Morning.
Beach Fire.
Before sheep came, before my fathers drove.
Blue Smoke.
Christmas Eve Legend.
Christmas in the Woods.
Clothes.
Clover for Breakfast.
Counting-out Rhyme for March.
Cover.
Dandelions.
Easter in the Woods.
Father.
First Departure.
Growing.
Hallowe'en.
Hydrographic Report.
Inquisitive Barn.
Kentucky Birthday; February 12, 1815.
Little Whistler, The.
Long Night Moon, The: December.
Maple Feast.
Night of Wind.
Night Plane.
Nocturne: "Over New England now, the snow."
Park Avenue Cat.
Potato Digger.
Proud, The.
Rambunctious Brook.
River Night.
School Is Out.
Sea Town.
Small Song.
Sniff.
Song for December Thirty-first.
Spring Families.
Spring in Hiding.
Squirrel.
Squirrel in the Rain.
Trains at Night.
Traveler.
Weather Vanes.
White Season.
Who's There?
Winter Feast.
Woman of This Earth, *sels.*
Frost, Henry W.
Abundant Life.
Adoration.
At Rest.
Bethlehem's Babe.
Bible, The.
Call of the East, The.
Calvary.
Comforted.
Commissioned.
Communion Hymn.
Compensation.
Confession, A.
Conflict and Victory.
Death.
Derelict, The.
Devotion.
Discipleship.
Earth-bound.
Easter.
Easter Day.
Evening Prayer, An.
Fears.
Following.
Friendship.
Gloaming, The.
Good-Night.
Heard.
Heart Wish.
Heart-Break.
Highlands, The.
Home-Bound.
In Memoriam.
Longing.
Lord's Day, The.
Man's Life.
Missionary, The.
Misunderstanding.
My Creed.
Name, The.
Nativity, The.
Peace.
Peacefulness.
Pilgrimage.
Praise.
Prayer: "To worship Him who is my Father-God."
Prayer for Guidance.
Prayer for Missionaries, A.
Quietness.
Resurrection.
Sacrifice.
Save Me.
Shadows.
Shut In ("Shut in; a prisoner").
Sovereignty.
Spiritual Conflict.
Surrender.
Transformed.
Vespers.
Vision, A.
Voyage, The.
Waiting.
Wanderer's Song.
Wayfarer's Song.
Weeping.
Wishing.
Worship.
Frost, Robert
Acceptance.
Acquainted with the Night.
After Apple-picking.
Aim Was Song, The.
All Revelation.
Armful, The.
At Woodward's Gardens.
Axe-Helve, The.
Bear, The.
Bearer of Evil Things, The.
Bereft.
Birches.
Birds Do Thus, The.
Birthplace, The.
Black Cottage, The.
Blue-Butterfly Day.
Blue Ribbon at Amesbury, A.
Bonfire, The.
Brook in the City, A.
Brown's Descent.
But God's Own Descent.
By Myself.
Cabin in the Clearing, A.
Caesar's Lost Transport Ships.
Canis Major.
Choose Something like a Star.
Closed for Good.
Cocoon, The.
Code, The.
Come In.
Considerable Speck, A.
Correction, A.
Cow in Apple Time, The.
Death of the Hired Man, The.
Demiurge's Laugh, The.
Departmental.
Desert Places.
Design.
Directive.
Draft Horse, The.
Drumlin Woodchuck, A.
Dust of Snow.
Early April.
Egg and the Machine, The.
Ends.
Evening in a Sugar Orchard.
Fear, The.
Fear of God, The.
Fire and Ice.
Fireflies in the Garden.
For Once, Then, Something.
Forgive, O Lord, My Little Jokes on Thee.
From Plane to Plane.
Gathering Leaves.
Gift Outright, The.
God's Speech to Job.
God's Thanks to Job.
Going for Water.
Good-by and Keep Cold.
Good Hours.
Grindstone, The.
Gum-Gatherer, The.
Haec Fabula Docet.
Happiness Makes Up in Height for What It Lacks in Length.
Hardship of Accounting, The.
Hill Wife, The.
Hillside Thaw, A.
Home.
Home Burial.
Home Defined.
House Fear.
Hundred Collars, A.

Frost (continued)
Hyla Brook.
I Could Give All to Time.
Impulse, The.
In a Poem.
In Dives' Dive.
In Hardwood Groves.
In Winter in the Woods Alone.
Ingenuities of Debt, The.
Innate Helium.
Investment, The.
It Bids Pretty Fair.
Kitty Hawk, *sel.*
Last Mowing, The.
Last Word of a Bluebird, The.
Leaf-Treader, A.
Leaves Compared with Flowers.
Lesson for Today, The.
Line-Gang, The.
Lodged.
Lone Striker, A.
Loneliness.
Looking for a Sunset Bird in Winter.
Lost in Heaven.
Love and a Question.
Lovely Shall Be Choosers, The.
Masque of Reason, A, *sels.*
Meeting and Passing.
Mending Wall.
Middleness of the Road, The.
Minor Bird, A.
Moon Compasses.
Most of It, The.
Mountain, The.
Mowing.
My Butterfly.
My November Guest.
My What-is-it.
Need of Being Versed in Country Things, The.
Neither Out Far nor in Deep.
Never again Would Birds' Song Be the Same.
New Hampshire.
Nothing Gold Can Stay.
Now Close the Windows.
October.
Oft-repeated Dream, The.
Old Dog, The.
Old Man's Winter Night, An.
On a Tree Fallen across the Road.
On Being Chosen Poet of Vermont.
On Looking up by Chance at the Constellations.
On the Heart's Beginning to Cloud the Mind.
Once by the Pacific.
One Step Backward Taken.
Onset, The.
Our Singing Strength.
Out, Out.
Oven Bird, The.
Pan with Us.
Passing Glimpse, A.
Pasture, The.
Patch of Old Snow, A.
Paul's Wife.
Pauper Witch of Grafton, The.
Peaceful Shepherd, The.
Peck of Gold, A.
Pod of the Milkweed.
Prayer in Spring, A.
Provide, Provide.
Putting in the Seed.
Quest of the Orchis, The.
Questioning Faces.
Range-finding.
Record Stride, A.
Reluctance.
Revelation.
Road Not Taken, The.
Rose Family, The.
Rose Pogonias.
Runaway, The.
Sand Dunes.
Secret Sits, The.
Semi-Revolution, A.
Servant to Servants, A.
Silken Tent, The.
Sky Pair, A.
Smile, The.
Soldier, A.
Sound of the Trees [*or* of Trees], The.
Span of Life, The.
Spring Pools.
Star-Splitter, The.
Stars.
Stopping by Woods on a Snowy Evening.
Storm Fear.
Strong Are Saying Nothing, The.
Subverted Flower, The.
Telephone, The.
There Are Roughly Zones.
There Is a Nook Among the Alders.
They Were Welcome to Their Belief.
Thine emulous, fond flowers are dead too.
Time to Talk, A.
To a Young Wretch.
To E. T.
To Earthward.
To the Thawing Wind.
Too Anxious for Rivers.
Tree at My Window.
Trespass.
Trial by Existence, The.
Trial Run, A.
Tuft of Flowers, The.
Two Look at Two.
Two Tramps in Mud Time.
Two Witches, *sels.*
Unharvested.
Valley's Singing Day, The.
Vantage Point, The.
Warning.
West-running Brook.
White-tailed Hornet, The.
Wind and the Rain, The.
Wind and Window-Flower.
Witch of Coös, The.
Wood-Pile [*or* Woodpile], The.
Woods are lovely, dark and deep, The.
Young Birch, A.
Frost, Thomas
Death of Colman, The.
Guns in the Grass, The.
Frothingham, Nathaniel Langdon
Bible, The.
Crossed Swords, The.
Froude, Richard Hurrell
Weakness of Nature.
Frug, Simeon Grigoryevich
Sail Peacefully Home.
Song: "Night is an ancient sorceress, The."
Talmud, The.
Fry, Christopher
Boy with a Cart, The, *sel.*
In our fields, fallow and burdened, in grass and furrow.
Rain.
Fry, Herbert
As I'd Nothing Else to Do.
Fuguet, Dollett
Blithe Mask, The.
Fu Hsüan
Gentle Wind, A.
Woman.
Fujino, Seiki
Treasure Boat.
Fujiwara Ietaka
Old Scent of the Plum Tree.
Fujiwara no Kamatari
I have got her.
Fujiwara no Michinobu
Day will soon be gone, The.
Fujiwara no Toshiyuki
Although it is not plainly visible to the eye.
Autumn Leaves.
Fuller, Ethel Romig
Diary, *sel.*
Fir Forest.
Frost.
God Hears Prayer.
Hope's Forecast.
Mother—a Portrait.
Old Year is a diary where is set, The.
Pioneer Mother, The.
Proof.
Today.
What the King Has.
Who Knows a Mountain?
Wind Is a Cat.
Fuller, John
Band Music.
In a Railway Compartment.
Morvin.
Snapshot.
Statue, The.
White Queen.
Fuller, Margaret Witter
Dryad Song.
Passion-Flower, The.
Fuller, Roy
Ballad: "Father, through the dark that parts us."
Brahms Peruses the Score of "Siegfried."
Crustaceans.
Day, The.
During a Bombardment by V-Weapons.
Emotion of Fiction, The.
End of a Leave, The.
Epitaph on a Bombing Victim.
Giraffes, The.
Good-bye for a Long Time.
Green Hills of Africa, The.
Hero, The.
Homage to Arthur Waley.
Ides of March, The.
Image, The.
In Africa.
January 1940.
Letter to My Wife.
Meditation.
Mythological Sonnets, *sels.*
Native Working on the Aerodrome.
Nino, the Wonder Dog.
November, 1941.
October, 1942.
On Reading a Soviet Novel.
Perturbations of Uranus, The.
Petty Officers' Mess, The.
Plains, The.
Poem: "Pity, repulsion, love and anger."
Pure Poet, The.
Rhetoric of a Journey.
Sadness, Glass, Theory.
Soliloquy in an Air-Raid.
Spring 1943.
Spring 1942.
Suns in a skein, the uncut stones of night.
That the dread happenings of myths reveal.
There actually stood the fabled riders.
They See Dark Skies.
Translation.
Tribes, The.
Versions of Love.
War Poet.
Well now, the virgin and the unicorn.
What Is Terrible.
Winter Night.
Wry Smile, A.

Y.M.C.A. Writing Room.
Fuller, Violet
Ring, Joyful Bells!
Fullerton, Mary Elizabeth ("E.")
Adventure.
Comet.
Communal.
Cubes.
Dream, A.
Emus.
Flesh.
Heart's Not Yet a Neighbour, The.
Independence.
Inspiration.
Learning.
Lichen.
Lion.
Lovers.
Passivity.
Selector's Wife, The.
Skull, The.
Unit.
War.
Funaroff, Sol
Bellbuoy.
Dusk of the Gods, *sel.*
Of my deep hunger.
Funk, Wilfred John
Hospital.
Rest in Peace.
Surgeon, The.
Furbee, Ruth
Worship.
Furlong, Alice
Betrayal, The.
My Share of the World.
Triad of Things Not Decreed, The.
Warnings, The.
Yuletide.
Furness, William Henry
Evening Hymn.
Light of Stars, The.
Furse, Margaret Cecilia
Lamp Flower, The.
Fyleman, Rose
Alms in Autumn.
At Dawn.
Attic, The.
Balloon Man, The.
Barge, The.
Best Game the Fairies Play, The.
Bingo Has an Enemy ("Bingo is kind and friendly").
Birthday Child, The.
Boat, The.
Chickens, The.
Child Next Door, The.
Christmas Wish, A.
Christmas-Time.
Cock, The.
Consolation.
Conversation.
Cuckoo, The.
Daddy.
Dentist, The.
Differences.
Donkey, The.
Fairies, The.
Fairies Have Never a Penny to Spend, The.
Fairy Flute, The.
Fairy Music.
Fairy Tailor, The.
Fairy Went a-Marketing, A.
Fountain, The.
Frog, The.
Goblin, The.
Good Morning.
Grown-ups.
Have You Watched the Fairies?
Husky Hi.
If Only. . .
In the Park.
Jock o' Dreams.
Jonathan.
Mary Middling.
Mice.
Mr. Minnitt.
Mrs. Barks.
Mrs. Brown.
Momotara.
Mother.
My Donkey.
My Policeman.
New Neighbor, The.
October.
Please.
Pretty Lady.
Primrose Hill.
Regent's Park.
Richard Has Something to Say.
Shop Windows.
Singing Fairy, The.
Singing-Time.
Sometimes.
Spring, The.
Temple Bar.
There Are No Wolves in England Now.
Timothy.
Trafalgar Square.
Very lovely.
Vision.
Weathercock, The.
Winnipeg at Christmas.
Yesterday in Oxford Street.
Fynn, Arthur J.
Land Where the Columbines Grow.

G

"G., A. R."
"Go Forward."
"G., E. O."
My Church ("My church has but one temple").
"G., L."
Quarrelsome Trio, The.
"G., W. A."
Yielded Life.
"G. S. O." *See* **"O., G. S"**
"G. T. S." *See* **"S., G. T"**
"G. W. S." *See* **"S., G. W"**
Gabriel, Charles
Help Me to Live!
Gabriel y Galán, José María
Lord, The.
Gadbury, John
Ballad upon the Popish Plot, A.
Gadsden, Janice Marie
Everything.
We Don't Need No Music.
Gaffney, Francis A.
Our Lady of the Rosary.
Gág, Wanda
A B C Bunny, The.
Galai, Benyamin
To My Generation.
Galbreath, C. B.
Another Reply to "In Flanders Fields."
Gale, Norman
Bartholomew.
Bartholomew is very sweet.
Bobby's First Poem.
Child of Loneliness.
Content.
Country Faith, The.
Dawn and Dark.
Dead Friend, A.
Dinah.
Fairy Book, The.
First Kiss, The.
Mustard and Cress.
Pastoral, A: "Along the lane beside the mead."
Prayer, A: "Tend me my birds, and bring again."
Priest, A.
Question, The.
Second Coming, The.
Shaded Pool, The.
Song: "This peach is pink with such a pink."
Song: "Wait but a little while."
Thanks.
To My Brothers.
Voice, The.
Gale, Vi
Shore Birds.
Gale, Zona
Children of Tomorrow.
Credo.
Voice.
Gal'ed, Zerubavel
Chickory.
Galindez, Bartolomé
In the Azure Night.
Gallagher, Dorothy Hamilton
Morning.
Gallagher, F. O'Neil
All Alone Tree, The.
Gallagher, James F.
As Always.
Love's Growing Pains.
Gallagher, Katharine
Chant for Skippers.
Poison Ivy!
Gallagher, Margaret Miriam *See* **Miriam, Sister**
Gallagher, William Davis
Autumn in the West.
Cardinal Bird, The.
Mothers of the West, The.
Gallaudet, Herbert D.
Holy Places.
Young Man in a Galilean Doorway.
Galler, David
Ballade of the Session after Camarillo.
Daphne
Execrators, The.
Jersey Marsh, The.
Makers, The.
Vial, The.
Gallup, Dick
After Alcman.
Building a House.
Death and the Maiden.
Door to the Future, The.
Ember Grease.
Eskimoes Again.
Fits of Candor.
From the Beaumont Series.
Furniture Man, The.
Homer.
Hygiene Sonnet.
La Bohème.
Out-dated Poem.
Pretty Beads.
Relaxation.
Return of Philista, The.
Some Feathers.
Galsworthy, John
Courage.
Devon to Me.
Limerick: "Angry young husband called Bicket, An."
Mountain Air.
Never Get Out!
Past.
Peace in the World.
Prayer for Gentleness to All Creatures.
Reminder.

Galsworthy (continued)
So Might It Be.
Valley of the Shadow.
Galvam, Francisco
To Our Lord.
Galvin, James J.
Lady of O.
Morning Star.
Ox-Bone Madonna.
Photograph.
Spanish Alleluja.
Gama, Luis Gonzaga Pinto da
Who I Am.
Gamble, William M. T.
Medieval Appreciations.
"Gander, Sir Gregory" (George Ellis)
Twelve Months, The.
Gannett, William Channing
Consider the Lilies.
God Ploughed.
Highway, The.
Stream of Faith, The.
"Who Wert and Art and Evermore Shalt Be."
Gant, Margaret
May-Time.
Garabrant, Nellie M.
Dandelion.
Fairy Artist, The.
García Lorca, Federico
Arrest of Antoñito el Camborio in the Streets of Seville, The.
Ballad of the Spanish Civil Guard.
Cazador (Hunter).
Cry, The.
Faithless Wife, The.
Lament for Ignacio Sanchez Mejias.
Lament for the Death of a Bullfighter.
Little Town.
Madrigal de Verano.
Madrigal to the City of Santiago.
Memento.
Odyssey of a Snail, The.
Somnambulistic Ballad.
Tree, Tree.
Weeping, The.
Gard, Lillian Gilchrist
New Year, The.
Gard, Wayne
Life.
Gardiner, Wrey
Dr. Coppelius.
Our True Beginnings.
Poetry Is Happiness.
Walking in London.
Gardner, Carl
Reflections.
Gardner, Isabella
Folkways.
Gimboling.
In the Museum.
Letter from Slough Pond.
Masked Shrew, The.
Mathematics of Encounter.
Milkman, The.
Nightmare.
That "Craning of the Neck."
When a Warlock Dies.
Gardner, Jo
Let Me Lift Jesus, Lord.
Lilies of the Valley.
Only One, The.
Gardner, William Henry
When Love Comes Knocking.
Gardons, S. S.
Fourth of July.
Mother, The.
Survivors, The.
To a Child.
Garesché, Edward F.
At the Leap of the Waters.
Niagara.
Young Priest to His Hands, The.
Garfias, Pedro
Villafranca de Córdoba.
Garioch, Robert
At Robert Fergusson's Grave, October 1962.
Elegy: "They are lang deid, folk that I used to ken."
Embro to the Ploy.
Ghaisties.
On Seein an Aik-Tree Sprent wi Galls.
Garland, Hamlin
Cry of the Age, The.
Do You Fear the Wind?
Gift of Water, The.
Gold-Seekers, The.
Greeting of the Roses, The.
Herald Crane, The.
Horses Chawin' Hay.
In the Days When the Cattle Ran.
Logan at Peach Tree Creek.
Magic.
Massasauga, The.
Meadow Lark, The.
Mountains Are a Lonely Folk, The.
My Prairies.
Passing of the Buffalo, The.
Pioneers.
Plowing; a Memory.
Plowman of Today, The.
Toil of the Trail, The.
Tribute of Grasses, A (to W. W.).
Ute Lover, The.
Wish, A.
Garlick, Phyllis L.
Christ with me, Christ before me, Christ behind me.
Fairy Feet.
Fairy Shoemaker, The.
Lullaby: "Lullaby, lullaby,/ Shadows creep across the sky."
St. Patrick, *sel.*
Garnett, Louise Ayres
Hello!
Jorridge and Porridge.
Lead on, lead on, America.
Moon, The.
Song of Liberty, *sel.*
Garnett, Richard
Age.
Ballad of the Boat, The.
Didactic Poem, The.
Epigram: "Amid all triads let it be confest."
Epigram: "'I hardly ever open my lips,' one cries."
Epigram: "Philosopher, whom dost thou most affect."
Epigram: "'Tis highly rational, we can't dispute."
Fading-Leaf and Fallen-Leaf.
Fair Circassian, The.
Highwayman's Ghost, The.
Island of Shadows, The.
Lyrical Poem, The.
Marigold.
Nocturne: "Keen winds of cloud and vaporous drift."
On an Urn.
Silence and Speech.
Sonnet: Age.
To America.
Garnier, Robert
Antonius, *sel.*
Chorus: "Alas, with what tormenting fire."
Of Death.
Garrett, Elizabeth
O, Fair New Mexico.
Garrett, George
Abraham's Knife.
Cædmon.
On Reading the *Metamorphoses.*
Saints.
Snapshot: Ambassadress.
Snapshot of a Pedant.
Snapshot: Politician.
Tiresias.
Garrick, David
David Garrick, the Actor, to Sir John Hill, a Physician Who Wrote Plays.
Epigram: "When doctrines meet with general approbation."
Heart of Oak.
Here lies Nolly Goldsmith.
On a Certain Lord Giving Some Thousand Pounds for a House.
To Mr. Gray.
Garrigue, Jean
Amsterdam Letter.
Apologia.
Circle, The.
Clovers, The.
Cortege for Colette.
False Country of the Zoo.
Forest.
From This There's No Returning.
From Venice Was That Afternoon.
Homage to Ghosts.
Lightly like Music Running.
Morality.
Mouse, The.
Of History More Like Myth.
Poem: "Something, so great a sweetness, came."
Primer of Plato.
Rain Song.
Stranger, The.
Unicorn and the Lady, The.
You Know.
Garrison Theodosia Pickering (Mrs. Frederic J. Faulks)
April.
Ballad of the Angel, The.
Ballad of the Cross, The.
Closed Door, The.
Cynic, The.
Days, The.
Debt, The.
Dreamers, The.
Free Woman, The.
Great Cross of Mercy, The.
Green Inn, The.
Ilicet.
John o' Dreams.
Kerry Lads, The.
Memorial Day.
Monseigneur Plays.
Neighbors, The.
One Fight More.
Poplars, The.
Prayer, A: "Let me work and be glad."
Red Cross Christmas Seal, The.
Resurgam.
Road's End, The.
Saint Jeanne.
Sainte Jeanne.
Shade.
Shepherd Who Stayed, The.
Sing Thou, My Soul.
Stains.
Torch, The.
Garrison, Wendell Phillips
Afternoon.
Evening.
Post-Meridian.
Garrison, William Lloyd
Freedom for the Mind.
Liberty for All.
On Leaving My Native Land.
Triumph of Freedom, The.

Garrison, Winfred Ernest
At Carcassonne.
Book, The.
Easter Morning.
For an Hour.
Love and Life.
Temptation.
Thy Sea So Great.
Garrod, Heathcote William
Thou should'st be living at this hour.
Garstin, Crosbie
Figure-Head, The.
Nocturne: "Red flame flowers bloom and die, The."
On the Back Veld.
Garth, Sir Samuel
Dispensary, The, *sels.*
Nor far from that most famous theatre.
Portrait of a Physician.
What frenzy has of late possess'd the brain!
Garthwaite, Jimmy (Wymond Bradbury Garthwaite)
Being Sick.
Engineers.
Night Watchmen.
Organ-Grinder, The.
Run, Kitty, Run!
Salt and Pepper Dance.
School after Christmas.
'Spress!
Garvin, Amelia Beers (Warnock) *See* **"Hale, Katherine."**
Garvin, Margaret Root
To Each His Own.
Gascoigne, George
Adventures of Master F. I. [*or* F. J.], The, *sels.*
Anatomy of a Lover, The.
And If I Did, What Then?
Arraignment of a Lover, The.
As some men say there is a kind of seed.
Behold him, priests, and though he stink of sweat.
But that my lord may plainly understand.
Constancy of a Lover, The.
Dan Bartholmew's Dolorous Discourses.
Deep Desire Sung This Song.
Discourse of the Adventures Passed by Master F. J., A.
Fair Bersabe the bright, once bathing in a well.
Farewell, A: "And if I did, what then?"
Fie, Pleasure, Fie!
First Chorus, The.
For that He Looked Not upon Her.
For whiles I mark this weak and wretched world.
Fruits of War, The.
Gascoigne's Arraignment.
Gascoigne's De Profundis.
Gascoigne's Good Morrow.
Gascoigne's Good-Night.
Gascoigne's Lullaby [*or* Lullabie].
Gascoigne's Memories, *sels.*
Gascoigne's Passion.
Gascoigne's Praise of His Mistress.
Gascoigne's Woodmanship.
Glass of Government, The, *sel.*
Green Knight's Farewell to Fancy, The.
Grief of Joy, The, *sel.*
He Wrote to the Same Friend from Excester This Sonnet Following.
He Wrote unto a Scottish Dame Whom He Chose for His Mistress in the French Court as Followeth.
I Could Not though I Would.
In Praise of a Gentlewoman [Who, though She Were Not Very Fair, Yet Was She as Hard-favored as Might Be].
Inscription in a Garden.
Libel of Divorce, A.
Looks of a Lover Enamoured, The.
Lover Declareth His Affection, Together with the Cause Thereof, The.
Lover's Lullaby, A.
Lullabie of a Lover, The.
Lullaby: "Sing lullaby, as women do."
Lullaby of a Lover, The.
Magnum Vectigal Parcimonia.
My Worthy Lord, I Pray You.
Of All the Birds That I Do Know.
Passion of a Lover, The.
Praise of Philip Sparrow, The.
Sing Lullaby, as Women Do.
Sonet Written in Prayse of the Browne Beautie, A.
Steel Glass, The, *sels.*
Strange Passion of a Lover, A.
Why then (quod I) old proverbs never fail.
Gascoyne, David
Apologia.
Autumn Park, An.
De Profundis.
Ecce Homo.
Elegy, An: "Friend, whose unnatural early death."
Eve.
Ex Nihilo.
Gravel-Pit Field, The.
In Defence of Humanism.
Jardin du Palais Royal.
Kyrie.
Lachrymae.
Megalometropolitan Carnival, *sel.*
Miserere.
On the Grand Canal.
Orpheus in the Underworld.
Pieta.
Rex Mundi.
Sacred Hearth, The.
Sanctus.
September Sun: 1947.
Snow in Europe.
Spring MCMXL.
Tenebrae.
Three Stars of Prophecy, The.
Tough Generation, A.
Wartime Dawn, A.
When Night has been announced as theme, will it not cause surprise.
Winter Garden.
Gaselee, Sir Stephen
On China Blue.
Gasetsu
Iris, The.
Gashe, Marina
Village, The.
Gass, Irene
Little King, The.
Gastev, Aleksey Kapitonovich
We Grow Out of Iron.
Gaston, William
Old North State, The.
Gasztold, Carmen Bernos de
Camel, The.
Prayer of the Cat, The.
Prayer of the Cock, The.
Prayer of the Cricket, The.
Prayer of the Dog, The.
Prayer of the Goldfish, The.
Prayer of the Little Ducks [Who Went into the Ark], The.
Prayer of the Mouse, The.
Prayer of the Old Horse, The.
Swallow, The.
"Gate, A. C." *See* **Anthony, Edward**
Gates, D. Weston
Transformed.
Gates, Ellen M. Huntington
Beautiful Hands.
Home of the Soul.
I Shall Not Cry Return.
Sleep Sweet.
Your Field of Labor.
Your Mission.
Gates, Jessie Rose
Peace.
Peace after Sorrow.
Gatto, Alfonso
Grass and Milk.
Midnight at Mestre.
Gautier, Judith
By the River.
Prose Poem: By the River.
Prose Poem: House in the Heart.
Prose Poem: Indifference.
Prose Poem: Mysterious Flute.
Prose Poem: Red Flower, The.
Prose Poem: Sadness of the Husbandman.
Prose Poem: Sages' Dance.
Gautier, Théophile
Art.
Clarimonde.
Posthumous Coquetry.
Gay, John
Achilles, *sel.*
Acis and Galatea, *sels.*
Air: "O ruddier than the cherry."
Ballad: "Of all the girls that e'er were seen."
Ballad: "'Twas when the seas were roaring."
Ballad Singers.
Before the Barn-Door Crowing.
Beggar's Opera, The, *sels.*
Birth of the Squire, The; an Eclogue.
Black-eyed Susan.
Blouzelinda's Funeral.
Consider, reader, what fatigues I've known.
Contemplation on Night, A.
Council of Horses, The.
Damon and Cupid.
Dangers of Football, The.
Ditty, The: "Young Colin Clout."
Eagle, and the Assembly of Animals, The.
Elegy on a Lap Dog, An.
Elephant and the Bookseller, The.
Employments of Life, The.
Epigram: "Life is a jest, and all things show it."
Epistle: "Pult'ney, methinks you blame my breach of word."
Epitaph, An: "Life is a jest, and all things show it."
Evening, The.
Fables, *sels.*
Fair Maid of the Inn, The.
Fan, The, *sel.*
Father and Jupiter, The.
Fly-fishing.
Fox at the Point of Death, The.
Fox may steal your hens, Sir, A.
Friday; or, The Dirge.
Go, Rose.
Great Frost, The.
Hare and Many Friends, The.
Hare with Many Friends, The.
Highwaymen, The.
His Epitaph.
His Own Epitaph.
How happy could I be with either.
If the Heart of a Man.
I'm like a skiff on the ocean tost.
Journey to Exeter, A, *abr.*
Let Us Take the Road.
Lion and the Cub, The.
Lion, the Fox, and the Geese, The.
Love in Her Eyes Sits Playing.
Macheath and Polly.
Man and the Flea, The.
Man may escape from rope and gun.

Gay (continued)
Mr. Pope's Welcome from Greece.
Modes of the court so common are grown, The.
Molly Mog; or, The Fair Maid of the Inn.
Morning, The.
My Own Epitaph.
New Song, A.
New Song of New Similes, A.
"O Polly, you might have toy'd and kist."
O Ruddier than the Cherry.
Of Ballad-Singers.
Of Crossing the Street.
Of Narrow Streets.
Of Pick-Pockets.
Of the Implements for Walking the Streets, and Signs of the Weather.
Of Walking the Streets by Day.
Of Walking the Streets by Night.
Old Hen and the Cock, The.
On a Miscellany of Poems [to Bernard Lintott].
On His Dog.
On Walking the Streets by Day.
Over the Hills and Far Away.
Painter Who Pleased Nobody and Everybody, The.
Pell Mell Celebrated, The.
Pleasure of Walking through an Alley, The.
Plutus, Cupid, and Time.
Poet and the Rose, The.
Polly, *sel.*
Ratcatcher and Cats, The.
Recitativo: "I rage, I melt, I burn."
Rise, happy youth, this bright machine survey.
Rural Sports, *sel.*
Saturday; or, The Flights.
She who hath felt a real pain.
Shepherd and the Philosopher, The.
Shepherd's Dog and the Wolf, The.
Shepherd's Week, The.
Sick Man and the Angel, The.
Song: "Before the barn-door crowing."
Song: "Can love be controll'd by advice?"
Song: "If any wench Venus's girdle wear."
Song: "Love in her eyes sits playing."
Song: "O ruddier than the cherry."
Song: "Sleep, O sleep."
Song: "Think of dress in ev'ry light."
Song: "Thus when the swallow, seeking prey."
Song: "Were I laid on Greenland's coast."
Song: "Youth's the season made for joys."
Spell, The.
Sweet William's Farewell to Black-eyed Susan.
Tame Stag, The.
Think of Dress in Every Light.
Through All the Employments of Life.
Thursday; or, The Spell.
To a Lady.
To a Lady on Her Passion for Old China.
Toilette, The; a Town Eclogue.
Trivia; or, The Art of Walking the Streets of London, *sels.*
Turkey and the Ant, The.
Vulture, The Sparrow, and Other Birds, The.
Wednesday; or, The Dumps.
Were I Laid on Greenland's Coast.
What D'Ye Call It, The, *sel.*
Wild Boar and the Ram, The.

Gay, William
Australia, 1894.
Australian Federation.
Communion Hymn.
Crazy World, The.
To M.

Gay, Zhenya
Elephant Is an Odd Affair, An.
I was lying still in a field one day.
I'd like to be a worm.
My Birthday's in Winter.
Night Things Are Soft and Loud.
On a Windy Day.
When a goose meets a moose.
World is full of wonderful smells, The.

Gearhart, Edna
My Cat and I.

Gearhart, Gladys M.
He Is Coming.

Gebirtig, Mordecai
Waiting for Death.

Geddes, Alexander
Epistle to the President of the Scottish Society of Antiquaries: On Being Chosen a Correspondent Member, *sel.*
Nor will the search be hard or long.
Satire: "Satire, my friend ('twixt me and you).

Gee, Lethonia
Black Music Man.
By Glistening, Dancing Seas.

Geijer, Erik Gustaf
Charcoal-Burner's Son, The.

Gellert, Christian Fürchtegott
A Jesus Lives, and Shall I.
Ye Shall Live Also.

Gellert, Lawrence
Ah'm Broke an' Hungry
Ku Kluck Klan
Look over Yonder

Gellert, Leon
Anzac Cove.
Before Action.
Cross, The.
House-Mates.
Husband, The.
In the Trench.
Jester in the Trench, The.
These Men.
Through a Porthole.

Gelsted, Otto
Ninth of April, The.

Genestet, Petrus Augustus de
Such Is Holland!

Genoveva, Sister Mary
Archers of the King.

Geoghegan, Arthur Gerald
After Aughrim.

Geoghegan, J. B.
Down in a Coal Mine.

Georgakas, Dan
Acrobat from Xanadu Disdained All Nets, The.
As Soon As He Learned.
Consider These Greek Widows of America.
Empire City.
Harvest Song.
Hiroshima Crewman.
Lament: "It is we, it is we."
Scene Pope John Wouldn't Let Fellini Film, The.

George, Daniel
Ode to the Fourth of July, *with music.*

George, Marguerite
Brief Biography.
Here I Lie.
I, Too, Have Known.
Paneled in Pine.
Prisoner.

George, Stefan
After the Festival.
Augury.
From Nether Dark the Seed.
From out the Glow the Wrath of Heaven Spoke.
Invocation and Prelude.
Jahr der Seele, Das, *sel.*
Lord of the Isle, The.
My Child Came Home.
No way too long—no path too steep.
Prelude XXIII: "We are those same children who amazed."
Rapture.
Seasong.
Stanzas concerning Love.
Tapestry, The.
To a Young Leader of the First World War.
Transport.

Géraldy, Paul
Meditation.

Gerard Edwin ("Trooper Gerardy")
Lofty Lane.

Gerard, Richard H.
Sweet Adeline.

Gerhardt, Paul
All My Heart This Night Rejoices.
Commit Thy Way.
Commitment.
Courage.
Give to the Winds Thy Fears.
Holy Ghost, Dispel Our Sadness.
My Friend.
Song of the Sojourner.

Gerin-Lajoie, Antoine
Canadian Exile, The.

Germanus, St.
Great and Mighty Wonder, A,

Gerondi, Abraham
Hymn for the Eve of the New Year.

Gershwin, Ira
Babbitt and the Bromide.
Embraceable You.
Funny Face, *sel.*

Gessner, Muriel M.
For February Twelfth.

Gething, Peter
Prayer: "I do not ask a truce."

Gezelle, Guido
To the Sun.

Ghiraldo, Alberto
My Clarion Call.

Ghiselin, Brewster
Answering a Letter from a Younger Poet.
Crotalus Rex.
Her Mood around Me.
Known World, The.
New World.
Of the New Prosody.
To the South.

Ghose, Sri Aurobindo
Dream of Surreal Science, A.

Ghose, Kashiprosad
Moon in September, The.

Ghose, Manmohan
London.
Who Is It Talks of Ebony?

Ghose, Zulfikar
Egypt.
Geranium Man, The.
Pheasant ("Pheasant sat by a bush").
Rise of Shivaji, The.
This Landscape, These People.

Gibbon, John Murray
October.

Gibbon, Monk
Babe, The.
Bees, The.
Devil's Cauldron.
Discovery, The.
Dispossessed Poet.
Forebears.
French Peasants.
From Disciple to Master.
Salt.
Shawls, The.
Song: "Singer within the little streets."

Gibbon, Perceval
Jim.
Gibbons, J. J.
Burro, The.
Gibbons, James Sloan
Three Hundred Thousand More.
Gibbs, Barbara
"What You See Is Me."
Gibbs, Elise
Four.
Not Self-denial.
Gibbs, Jessie Wiseman
If We Believed in God.
Gibbs, Margaret E.
On the Banisters.
Song of the Bath, The.
Gibbs, Opal Leonore
Interceding.
Like Orphans.
Gibbs, Ruth Margaret
Because You Prayed.
Rift, The.
Vigil in Gethsemane.
Gibran, Kahlil
Crime and Punishment.
Of Love.
On Children.
On Giving.
On Work.
Prophet, The, *sels.*
Gibson, Barbara
Thinking about the Unthinkable.
Gibson, Douglas
Dead Branch, The.
Willow Switch, The.
Gibson, Evelyn K.
Heartsearch.
Gibson George Herbert ("Ironbark")
Ballad of Queens
My Mate Bill.
Gibson, M. Allen
Cry of Faith, A.
Gibson, Walker
Advice to Travelers.
Allergy.
Athletes.
Billiards.
Blues for an Old Blue.
Circus Ship *Euzkera*, The.
David.
Epistle to the Reader.
Essay in Defense of the Movies.
Essay on Lunch.
Game, The.
In Memory of the Circus Ship *Euzkera*, Wrecked in the Caribbean Sea, 1 September 1948.
Love.
Mountains, The.
Thaw.
Umpire, The.
Vacationer.
Gibson, Wilfred Wilson
Back.
Battle: Hit.
Before Action.
Between the Lines.
Breakfast.
By the Weir.
Catch for Singing, A.
Color.
Comrades.
Conscript, The.
Dancers, The.
Dancing Seal, The.
Drove-Road, The.
Fear, The.
Fisherman's Luck.
Flannan Isle.
For G.
Fowler, The.
Going, The.
Golden Room, The.
Gorse, The.
Greeting, The.
Hands.
Henry Turnbull.
Hill-born.
Hit.
Home.
Housewife, The.
I dreamt not that love's way.
Ice, The.
Ice-Cart, The.
Inspiration.
Lament, A: "We who are left, how shall we look again."
Luck.
Mark Anderson.
Marriage.
Messages, The.
Michael's Song.
Oblivion.
Old Skinflint.
On Hampstead Heath.
On the Embankment.
One Night.
Parrot, The ("Long since I'd ceased to care").
Parrots, The ("Somewhere, somewhen I've seen")
Ponies, The.
Prelude: "As one, at midnight, wakened by the call."
Proem: "Snug in my easy chair."
Prometheus.
Question, The.
Quiet, The.
Ridge, The, 1919.
Rupert Brooke ("Your face was lifted to the golden sky").
Shop, The.
Sight.
Snow, The.
Snug in My Easy Chair.
Song: "If once I could gather in song."
Stone, The.
Tenants.
To Rupert Brooke.
Unless I Am Careful.
Vindictive Staircase, The; or, The Reward of Industry.
Whisperers, The.
White Dust, The.
Gibson, William
Ditty: "Heavy of heart and light of purse."
Giddings, Paula
Death Motion.
Rebirth.
Resurrection.
Gifford, Lady *See* **Sheridan, Helen Selina.**
Gifford, Fannie Stearns Davis *See* **Davis, Fannie Stearns**
Gifford, Humphrey [*or* Humfrey]
Delectable Dream, A, *sel.*
For Soldiers.
Means and Ends.
Prayer, A: "O mighty God, Which for us men."
Song: "Woman's face is full of wiles, A."
Gifford, William
Baviad, The, *sel.*
Della Cruscans, The.
Gilbert, Lady *See* **Mulholland, Rosa**
Gilbert, Ellen
Prodigal.
Gilbert, Fred
Man Who Broke the Bank at Monte Carlo, The.
Gilbert, Jack
Abnormal Is Not Courage, The.
Don Giovanni on His Way to Hell (II).
In Dispraise of Poetry.
Orpheus in Greenwich Village.
Gilbert, James Stanley
Beyond the Chagres.
Gilbert, Sister Mary
Meditation on a March Wind.
Gilbert, Mercedes
Friendless Blues, *with music.*
Gilbert, Morris
Epitaph on a Madman's Grave.
Gilbert, Nicolas Joseph Laurent
Ode—Imitated from the Psalms.
Gilbert, Paul
Your Own Version.
Gilbert, Paul T.
Triolet: "I love you, my Lord!"
Gilbert, R. V.
Great Victory, The.
Gilbert, Ruth
And There Shall Be No More Death, *sel.*
Annunciation.
Blossom of the Branches, The, *sels.*
Li Po.
Nativity.
Quickening, The.
Rachel.
That which the long scythe whispered to the grass.
Gilbert Sir William Schwenck
Aesthete, The.
Arac's Song.
Bishop of Rum-ti-Foo, The.
British Tar, The.
Bunthorne's Recitative and Song ("Am I alone").
Bunthorne's Song ("If you're anxious for to shine").
Captain and the Mermaids, The.
Captain Reece.
Come mighty Must! The Mighty Must.
Contemplative Sentry, The.
Darned Mounseer, The.
Disagreeable Man, The.
Discontented Sugar Broker, A.
Duke of Plaza-Toro, The.
Ellen McJones [*or* M'Jones] Aberdeen.
Emily, John, James, and I.
Etiquette.
Fable of the Magnet and the Churn, The.
Family Fool, The.
Ferdinando and Elvira; or, The Gentle Pieman.
First Lord's Song, The.
Folly of Brown, The.
General John.
Gentle Alice Brown.
Gondoliers, The, *sels.*
Grand Duke, The, *sel.*
Grand Inquisitor's Song, The.
H.M.S. Pinafore, *sels.*
His Excellency, *sels.*
House of Lords, The.
House of Peers, The.
Humane Mikado, The.
I Am the Captain of the Pinafore.
I Am the Monarch of the Sea.
Iolanthe, *sels.*
It Was the Cat.
Judge's Song, The.
King Goodheart.
King of Canoodle-Dum, The.
Ko-Ko's Song ("As some day it may happen that a victim must be found").
Ko-Ko's Song ("On a tree by a river a little tom-tit").
Ko-Ko's Song ("There is beauty in the bellow of the blast"), *much abr.*
Lady and an Ape, A.
Let the Punishment Fit the Crime.

Gilbert (continued)
Limerick: "There was a young [*or* an old] man of St. Bees."
Limerick: "There was an old man of St. Bees."
Limerick in Blank Verse, A.
Little Buttercup.
Lord Chancellor's Song ("When you're lying awake").
Lost Mr. Blake, The.
Mad Margaret's Song.
Major-General, The.
Major-General's Song.
Mighty Must, The.
Mikado, The, *sels.*
Mister William.
Modern Major-General, The.
My Name Is John Wellington Wells.
My Object All Sublime.
Nightmare.
"Oh, Hollow! Hollow! Hollow!"
Old Man of St. Bees.
Out of Sorts.
Patience, *sels.*
Perils of Invisibility, The.
Pinafore.
Pirates of Penzance, The, *sels.*
Played-out Humorist, The.
Policeman's Lot, The.
Practical Joker, The.
Princess Ida, *sels.*
Pygmalion and Galatea, *sel.*
Recitation and Song: "Am I alone."
Rival Curates, The.
Rover's Apology, The.
Ruddigore, *sels.*
Ruler of the Queen's Navee, The.
Said I to Myself, Said I.
Sing for the Garish Eye.
Sir Bailey Barre.
Sir Guy the Crusader.
Sir Joseph's Song.
Sir Roderic's Song.
Song: Bunthorne.
Song: Colonel.
Song: "When Britain really ruled the waves."
Sorcerer, The, *sel.*
Story of Prince Agib, The.
Suicide's Grave, The.
Susceptible Chancellor, The.
There Lived a King.
They'll None of 'em Be Missed.
"Thing is but a statue after all, The!"
Thomas Winterbottom Hance.
Three Little Maids from School.
Titwillow.
To Phoebe.
To Sit in Solemn Silence.
To the Terrestrial Globe.
Trial by Jury, *sels.*
Utopia, Limited, *sel.*
Wand'ring Minstrel, A.
When I Was a Lad.
Willow, Titwillow.
Yarn of the *Nancy Bell*, The.
Yeoman of the Guard, *sel.*
Gilbert, Zack
In Spite of All This Much Needed Thunder.
"Gilbertulus." *See* **Howe, Mark Antony De Wolfe**
Gilchrist, Marie Emilie
Apples in New Hampshire.
Gilder, Jeannette Leonard
My Creed.
Gilder, Joseph B.
Be thou guardian of the weak.
Parting of the Ways, The.
Will to Serve, The.
Gilder, Richard Watson
After-Song.
Ah, Be Not False.
Anger of Christ, The.
At the President's Grave.
Birds of Bethlehem, The.
Birthday Song, A.
Builders of the State.
Call Me Not Dead.
Celestial Passion, The.
Cello, The.
Charleston.
Child, A.
Christ of Judea, look thou in my heart!
Christ the Answer.
Christmas Hymn, A.
Christmas Tree in the Nursery, The.
Comfort of the Trees, The.
Cost.
Credo, *sel.*
Doubter, The.
Easter.
Evening in Tyringham Valley.
God of the Strong, God of the Weak.
Great Nature Is an Army Gay.
Hast Thou Heard the Nightingale?
Heroic Age, The.
Holy Land.
How to the Singer Comes the Song?
Hymn: "God of the strong, God of the weak," *abr.*
I Count My Time by Times That I Meet Thee.
I like her gentle hand that sometimes strays.
Inauguration Day.
Invisible, The.
John Paul Jones.
Land That We Love.
Memorial Day.
Midsummer Song, A.
Motto for a Tree-planting.
My Love for Thee.
Navies nor armies can exalt the state.
New Day, The, *sels.*
Noël.
O, Love Is Not a Summer Mood.
Ode: "I am the spirit of the morning sea."
Of One Who neither Sees nor Hears.
On the Life-Mask of Abraham Lincoln.
Passing Christ, The.
Passing of Christ, The, *sel.*
Prelude: "Night was dark, though sometimes a faint star, The."
Real Christ, The.
Sherman.
Song: "Because the rose must fade."
Song: "Not from the whole wide world I chose thee."
Song, A: "Years have flown since I knew thee first."
Song of a Heathen, The.
Song of Early Autumn, A.
Sonnet, The: "What is a sonnet? 'Tis the pearly shell."
Sonnets after the Italian.
Violin, The.
"White City, The."
Woman's Thought, A.
Gilfillan, Robert
Exile's Song, The.
'Tis Sair to Dream.
Gill, Eric
Mutans Nomen Evae.
Gill, Frances
Beneath the Wattle Boughs.
Gill, John
Chicago, *sel.*
Conjured.
Frances.
In Defense of Marriage.
Oh gentlemen gentlemen don't worry.
Other Garden, The.
Poem: "What of radishes lettuce peas."
Scène à Faire.
Some Friends.
Spring Malediction, *sel.*
"Today Well, Tomorrow Cold in the Mouth."
Gill, Julia
Christ and the Little Ones.
Gill, T. H.
Thy Word.
Thy Word Is Like a Garden, Lord.
Gilleland, Anna M.
Give My Heart a Song.
Gillespie, Dan
Abandoned Copper Refinery.
Desert Gulls.
For a Bum Seen Walking the Rails.
Poem for the Disappearing Bear.
Strip Mining Pit.
To New Jerusalem.
Gillespie, Yetza
Ashes of the Christmas Tree.
Snow in the Caucasus.
Gillespy, Jeannette Bliss
Cameos.
Forgiven?
Valentine, A.
Gillies, Andrew
Two Prayers.
Gillies, Donald
Woodrow Wilson.
Gillilan, Strickland
Are You There?
As I Go on My Way.
Be Hopeful.
Cure for Fault-finding, A.
Dixie Lullaby, A.
Finnigan to Flannigan.
Finnigin to Flannigan.
Folks Need a Lot of Loving.
Her Great Secret.
Lines on the Antiquity of Microbes.
Line Written on the Antiquity of Microbes.
Need of Loving.
On the Antiquity of Microbes.
Other Fellow's Job, The.
Reading Mother, The.
Watch Yourself Go By.
When He Goes to Play with the Boys.
Gillington, Alice E.
Doom-Bar, The.
Rosy Musk-Mallow, The.
Seven Whistlers, The.
Gillington, May Clarissa *See* **Byron,May Clarissa Gillington**
Gillman, Frederick J.
God Send Us Men.
Gillman, Richard
Bones of a French Lady in a Museum.
Moved by Her Music.
On a Very Young, Very Dead Soldier.
Snow Fell with a Will.
Gillom, Arthur L.
I Want You.
Gilman, Charlotte Perkins Stetson
Beds of Fleur-de-Lys, The.
Common Inference, A.
Conservative, A.
Flag of Peace, The.
For Us.
Give Way!
Living God, The.
"Man Must Live, A."
Preach about the old sins, Preacher!
Resolve.
Similar Cases.
To Labor.
To the Preacher, *sel.*
Tree Feelings.

Two Prayers.
Wedded Bliss.
Gilman, Samuel
Fair Harvard.
Gilmore, Anna Neil
February.
February, Tall and Trim.
Gilmore, Joseph Henry
He Leadeth Me.
Gilmore, Mary
Baying Hounds, The.
Boolee, the Bringer of Life.
Dedicatory.
Dice Were Loaded, The.
Disinherited, The, *sel.*
Eve-Song.
I Saw the Beauty Go.
Marri'd.
Myall in Prison, The.
Nationality.
Never Admit the Pain.
Nurse No Long Grief.
Of Wonder.
Old Botany Bay.
Pear-Tree, The.
Shepherd, The.
Song of the Woman-Drawer, The.
Sudden autumn winds, like hounds, The.
Swans at Night, *sel.*
Sweethearts.
Tenancy, The.
They Called Her Sunshine.
Turn to the Grass.
Waradgery Tribe, The.
Within the night, above the dark.
Gilmore, Patrick Sarsfield (Louis Lambert)
When Johnny Comes Marching Home.
Gil Polo, Gaspar
Diana Enamorada, *sel.*
Ring Forth, Fair Nymphs, Your Joyful Songs for Gladness.
Giltinan, Caroline (Mrs. Leo P. Harlow)
Builder, The.
Communion.
Contrition across the Waves.
Garden, The.
Hungry, The.
Overnight, a Rose.
Spring.
"Ginger." *See* **Irwin, Wallace**
Ginsberg, Allen
Aether.
After Dead Souls.
America.
American Change.
Bricklayer's Lunch Hour, The.
Death to Van Gogh's Ear!
Face the Nation.
Galilee Shore.
Green Automobile, The.
Howl.
Ignu.
In Back of the Real.
In the Baggage Room at Greyhound.
Kaddish.
Love Poem on Theme by Whitman.
Malest Cornifici Tuo Catullo.
Message.
Pentagon Exorcism.
Poem Rocket.
Sather Gate Illumination.
Shrouded Stranger, The.
Song: Fie My Fum.
Sunflower Sutra.
Supermarket in California, A.
To Aunt Rose.
Uptown.
Vision in Hollywood, A.
Wales Visitation.
Walking Home at Night.
What sphinx of cement and aluminum bashed open their skulls and ate up their brains and imagination?
Wichita Vortex Sutra, *sel.*
Ginsberg, Louis
Biography of an Agnostic.
Buttercups.
Childhood.
Clocks.
Coral Islands.
Dirt and Deity.
Fog.
Hounds of the Soul, The.
Magnet Is Mistaken, The.
Morning in Spring.
Ode to Machines.
Old Ships.
Prices.
Roots.
Song: "I know that any weed can tell."
Song: "Love that is hoarded, moulds at last."
Song in Spring.
Soon at Last My Sighs and Moans.
To My Mother.
Waterfalls of Stone.
Wind, The.
Wise Man, Wise Man.
Giorno, John
American Book of the Dead, The, *sels.*
Astronaut Jim Lovell.
Easy to Grow.
Father, A/ accused of shooting.
I'm Tired of Being Scared.
Outlaw.
Paratrooper.
Pornographic Poem.
She Tasted Death.
Stray deer, A/ pursued by four Newark policemen.
Swallows, The/ returned at dawn today.
Vivian Beaumont, The/ Theatre.
With a brilliant sun causing his tears.
Giovanni, Nikki
Black Judgement.
For Saundra.
Funeral of Martin Luther King, Jr., The.
Great Pax Whitie, The.
Knoxville, Tennessee.
My Poem.
Nikki-Roasa.
Poem: "Black Revolution is passing you bye, The."
Poem (No Name No. 2).
Word Poem (Perhaps Worth Considering).
Giovannitti, Arturo
Six men drove up to his house at midnight.
Walker, The.
When the Cock Crows, *sel.*
Gittings, Robert
Emperor's Double, The.
Winter Aconites.
Giusti, Giuseppe
Your Excellency.
Gjellerup, Karl
O, Let Me Kiss.
Pair, A.
Gladden, Washington
Holding.
I Shall See Him.
Ideal City, The.
My Pilot.
O Happy Soul.
O Master, Let Me Walk with Thee.
Service.
Ultima Veritas.
Glaenzer, Richard Butler
Ballad of Redhead's Day, A.
Glanz-Leyeless, A.
Castles.
Glapthorne, Henry
Unclose Those Eyelids.
Glasgow, Ellen
Creed, A.
Glasgow, J. Scott
Pipes o' Gordon's Men, The.
Glassco, John
Brummell at Calais.
Burden of Junk, The.
Cardinal's Dog, The.
Day, The.
Deserted Buildings under Shefford Mountain.
Entailed Farm, The.
Quebec Farmhouse.
Rural Mail, The.
Stud Groom.
Utrillo's World.
Glatstein, Jacob
Back to the Ghetto.
Being.
Bratzlav Rabbi to His Scribe, The.
Rabbi Yussell Luksh of Chelm.
Where the Cedars.
Glaubitz, Grace Ellen
Christmas Birthday.
Walking.
Glaze, Andrew
Outlanders, The.
Glazebrook, Harriet A.
Lips That Touch Liquor Shall Never Touch Mine, The.
Glazer, Charles R.
Worthwhile Things Are Free.
Glazer, Joe
Too Old to Work.
Gleason, Madeline
Once and Upon.
Glen, Emilie
Cat Ballerina Assoluta.
Glick, Hirsch
We Survive!
Gloag, John
Board Meets, The.
Glover, Denis
Arawata Bill.
Arrowtown.
Casual Man, The.
Drift ("Drift drift upon the beach").
Dunedin Revisited.
For a Child.
Home Thoughts.
I Remember.
In the Township.
Lake, Mountain, Tree.
Magpies, The.
Off Banks Peninsula.
Once the Days.
Security.
Song: "If everywhere in the street."
Song: "These songs will not stand."
Songs.
Themes.
Thistledown.
Threnody: "In Plimmerton, in Plimmerton."
To a Woman.
Waitaki Dam.
Glover, Guy
Lucifer, The.
Glover, Jean
Owre the Muir amang the Heather.
Glover, R. W.
It Isn't the Town, It's You.
Glover, Richard
Admiral Hosier's Ghost.
Glück, Louise
Cottonmouth Country.
Early December in Croton-on-Hudson.
Edge, The.

Glück (continued)
Inlet, The.
Racer's Widow, The.
Glyn Cothi, Lewis
On the Death of His Son.
Saxons of Flint, The.
"Glyndon, Howard." *See* **Searing, Laura Catherine Redden**
Glynes, Ella Maria Dietz
Unless.
Goch, Llewelyn
Elegy for Lucy Lloyd.
Gode, Marguerite
Nature's Wash Day.
Godeschalk
Sequaire.
Godfrey, Thomas
Invitation, The.
Patriot, The.
What Was a Cure for Love?
Godley, Alfred Denis
After Horace.
College Cat, The.
Eureka!
Football and Rowing—an Eclogue.
Lines on a Mysterious Occurrence.
Motor Bus, The.
Pensées de Noël.
Godley, Elizabeth
Extremely Naughty Children.
Ragged Robin.
Godolphin, Sidney
Chorus: "Doth not our chiefest bliss then lie."
Chorus: "Vain man, born to no happiness."
Constancye.
Lord When the Wise Men Came from Far [r].
On Ben Jonson.
Quatrains.
Reply.
Song: "Cloris, it is not thy disdaine."
Song: "Noe more unto my thoughts appeare."
Song: "Or love me less [*or* mee lesse], or love me more."
To Chloris.
To the Tune of, In Fayth I Cannot Keepe My Fathers Sheepe.
Wise Men and Shepherds.
Godoy Alcayaga, Lucila *See* **"Mistral, Gabriela"**
Godric, Saint
Cry to Mary, A.
Godwhen [*or* Godwin], A
Song for My Lady.
Song in His Lady's Absence, A.
Goertz, Berniece
Wondrous Son of God.
Goethe, Johann Wolfgang von
All is changing now—it seems as though all must be parted.
All the apostles of freedom, I've hated them all my life.
As a Man Soweth.
Awakening of Epimenides, The, *sel.*
Easter Chorus: "Christ is arisen."
Elf-King, The.
Erl-King, The.
Faust, *sels.*
Gentle Reminders, *abr.*
Godlike Heart.
Haste Not, Rest Not.
Hermann and Dorothea, *sel.*
I'd open room for millions on the earth.
Irish Lamentation, An.
Joy and Dream.
King of Thule, The.
Lay of the Captive Count, The.
Live Each Day.
Lose This Day Loitering.
Lover Is Near, The.
Mignon.
Minstrel, The.
Nor Will These Tears Be the Last.
O Child of Beauty Rare.
On Lavater's Song of a Christian to Christ.
Prologue: "Lose this day loitering, 'twill be the same story."
Prologue in Heaven.
Prometheus.
Rest.
Rose, The.
Shepherd's Lament, The.
Soldier's Song.
Sorrow.
Thought Eternal, The.
To a Golden Heart, Worn round [*or* around] His Neck.
To the Parted One.
Trance and Transformation.
True Rest.
Up my brothers! Set all men free!
Use Well the Moment.
Venetian Epigrams, *sel.*
Voice from the Invisible World, A.
Voice of Experience, The.
Wanderer's First Night-Song, The.
Wanderer's Night-Songs, *sels.*
Wanderer's Second Night-Song, The.
Wedding Song.
Who Never Ate with Tears His Bread.
Wilhelm Meister, *sels.*
Goetschius, Antoinette
Meditation.
Goetz, Philip Becker
Whither.
Goffe, Thomas
Courageous Turk, The, *sel.*
Drop Golden Showers, Gentle Sleep.
Lullaby, lullaby baby.
Tragedy of Orestes, The, *sel.*
Gogarty, Oliver St. John
After Galen.
Between Brielle and Manasquan.
Boon Companion, The.
Colophon.
Conquest, The.
Crab Tree, The.
Death May Be . . .
Dedication: "Tall unpopular men."
Exorcism.
Forge, The.
Golden Stockings.
Good Luck.
Image-Maker, The.
Johnny, I Hardly Knew Ye: In Miltonese, *parody.*
Leda and the Swan.
Marcus Curtius.
Non Dolet.
O Boys! O Boys!
On Troy.
Our Friends Go with Us.
Palinode.
Parable for Poetasters, A.
Per Iter Tenebricosum.
Plum Tree by the House, The.
Portrait with Background.
Prayer for His Lady, A.
Ringsend.
To a Boon Companion.
To a Friend in the Country.
To an Old Tenor.
To Death.
To Petronius Arbiter.
To the Liffey with the Swans.
To the Maids Not to Walk in the Wind.
To W. B. Yeats Who Says That His Castle of Ballylee Is His Monument.
Verse: "What should we know."
With a Coin from Syracuse.
Going, Charles Buxton
Armistice.
At the Top of the Road.
Blessed Road, The.
Columbus.
Great Master Dreamer.
My Soul and I.
Sleepy Song, A.
Spring in England.
They Who Wait.
To Arcady.
True Story of Skipper Ireson, The.
Gold, Albert Reginald
Fishers.
Gold, Michael
Strange Funeral in Braddock, A.
Goldbeck, Cecil
Waters of the Sea.
Goldberg, Israel *See* **"Learsi, Rufus"**
Goldberg, Leah
Blade of Grass Sings to the River, The.
When You Will Walk in the Field.
Golden, Bernette
Morning.
There Are Seeds to Sow.
Words.
Golding, Arthur
At length my chariot wheel about the mark hath found the way.
Golding, Louis
Broken Bodies.
Doom-devoted.
"I."
Is It Because of Some Dear Grace.
Jack.
Judaeus Errans.
O Bird, So Lovely.
Ploughman at the Plough.
Prophet and Fool.
Quarries in Syracuse.
Second Seeing.
Women at the Corners Stand, The.
Goldman, Mark
On Luck.
Goldman, Michael
Crack, The.
Visitor, The.
Goldrick, O. J.
Grand Opening of the People's Theatre.
Goldring, Douglas
Newport Street, E.
She-Devil.
Streets.
Goldring, Maude
Drowned Seaman, The.
Goldsmith, Goldwin
Monkey's Glue, The.
Goldsmith, Oliver
Auburn.
Blest Retirement.
But the chaste blackbird, to its partner true.
Captivity, The; an Oratorio, *sels.*
Common Man, The.
Country Parson, The.
David Garrick.
Deserted Village, The.
Edmund Burke.
Edwin and Angelina.
Elegie on the Death of a Mad Dog, An.
Elegy on Mrs. Mary Blaize.
Elegy on That [*or* the] Glory of Her Sex, Mrs. Mary Blaize, An.
Elegy on the Death of a Mad Dog.
Emma.
Evening.
Farewell to Poetry.
First, Best Country, The.
France.

Good-natur'd Man, The, *sel.*
Great Man, A.
Happiness Dependent on Ourselves.
Haunch of Venison, The.
Hope.
Memory.
Mrs. Mary Blaize.
On a Beautiful Youth Struck Blind with Lightning.
On a Bookseller.
Parson, The.
Parson Gray.
Pitying Heart, The.
Real Happiness.
Retaliation.
Schoolmaster, The.
She Stoops to Conquer, *sel.*
Sir Joshua Reynolds.
Song: "Let schoolmasters puzzle their brains."
Song: "O memory, thou fond deceiver."
Song: "When lovely woman stoops to folly."
Stanzas on Woman.
Still the Wonder Grew.
Sweet smiling village, loveliest of the lawn.
Sweet was the sound when oft at evening's close.
Three Jolly Pigeons, The.
Three Pigeons, The.
Thus, when soft love subdues the heart.
Traveller, The.
Vicar of Wakefield, The, *sels.*
Village, The.
Village Parson, The.
Village Preacher, The.
Village Schoolmaster, The.
When Lovely Woman [Stoops to Folly].
Woman.

Goldsmith, Oliver, the Younger
How sweet it is, at first approach of morn.
Not fifty summers yet have passed thy clime.
Rising Village, The, *sels.*
What noble courage must their hearts have fired.
While now the Rising Village claims a name.

Goll, Claire
But All the Roses.
I Look Forward.
Prayer: " In the bright bay of your morning, O God."
To Sleep, to Sleep.

Goll, Iwan [*or* Yvan]
From All the Queens.
I Am the Wake.
I Am Your Brook.
John Landless beside the Road.
John Landless Leads the Caravan.
Lay Your Head.
Love Song.
Pear-Tree, The.
Silent.
Since My Birth.
Song for a Jewess.
To Liane-Neila.
Your Body Drifting.

Gomeii
Baby's Hands.

Gomersal, Robert
Upon our Vain Flattery of Ourselves that the Succeeding Times Will Be Better than the Former.

Gómez, Antonio Enríquez
Elegy: "I die for Your holy word without regret."

Gómez Restrepo, Antonio
Toledo ("Perched on its yellow peak").

Gómez Manrique *See* **Manrique, Gómez**

Goncalves, Joe
Way It Is, The.

Gonçlves Dias, Antônio
Song of Exile, *sel.*
There are palm trees in my homeland.

Góngora Y Argote, Luis de
Let Me Go Warm.
Love Song of Polyphemus, The.
Nativity of Christ, The.
Not All Sweet Nightingales.
Polifemo y Galatea.
Polyphemus and Galatea, *sel.*
Rosemary Spray, The.

Gonz. ález [*or* Gonzáles] Martéz, Enrique
Then Twist the Neck of This Delusive Swan.

Good, W. Audrey P.
Opportunity.

Goodale, Dora Read
Feast Time of the Year, The.
Flight of the Heart, The.
High and Low.
Judgment, The.
Lift Up Your Hearts.
May Basket, The.
Ripe Grain.
Soul of Man, The.

Goodchild, John Arthur
Firstborn, The.
Parable of the Spirit, A.
Schöne Rothraut.

Goode, Nellie
Alive.

Goodge, W. T.
Daley's Dorg Wattle.

Gooding, Lorie C.
By Candlelight.

Goodman, Mae Winkler
Image in a Mirror.
Memorial.
Washington.
Your Glory, Lincoln.

Goodman, Paul
April 1962.
Little Prayer, A.
Long Lines.
Lordly Hudson, The.
March, 1941.
Poems of My Lambretta.
Surfers at Santa Cruz.
Wellfleet Harbor.

Goodman, Ryah Tumarkin
Hug Your Hunger, Brother.
Silence Spoke with Your Voice.
They Know.

Goodreau, William
Island Cook.
Sea House, The.

Goodrich Samuel Griswold ("Peter Parley")
Higglety, Pigglety, Pop!
Lake Superior.

Goodwin, Hooper Reynolds
Parabola, The.

Goodwin, L.
"Day a Dancer Learned to Sing of Dreamless Escapades, The."

Goodwin, Sandra
Traveling on My Knees.

Googe, Barnabe
Coming Homeward Out of Spain.
Commynge Homewarde Out of Spayne.
Egloga Quinta: "Some doleful thing there is at hand."
Egloga Secunda: "My beasts, go feed upon the plain."
Epitaph of the Death of Nicholas Grimald, An.
Fly, The.
Going towards Spain.
Goyng towardes Spayne.
Oculi Augent Dolorem.
Of Edwards of the Chapel.
Of Mistress D. S.
Of Money.
Oftener Seen, the More I Lust, The.
Once Musing as I Sat.
Out of an Old Poet.
Out of Sight, Out of Mind.
Refusal, A.
To Alexander Neville.
To Doctor Bale.
To Master Edward Cobham.

To the Translation of Palingenius.
Uncertainty of Life, The.
Unhappy Tongue.

Gordon, A. C.
Kree.
Roses of Memory.

Gordon, A. M. R. *See* **Rose, Alexander MacGregor**

Gordon, Adam Lindsay
After the Quarrel.
By Wood and Wold.
Chase and the Race, The.
Dedication, A: "They are rhymes rudely strung with intent less."
Gone.
How We Beat the Favo[u]rite.
Last Leap, The.
Man's Testament.
Question Not.
Rhyme of Joyous Garde, The, *sel.*
Risks of the Game, The.
Sick Stockrider, The.
Song of Autumn, A.
Sun and Rain and Dew from Heaven.
Valedictory.
We were glad together in gladsome meads.
Wearie Wayfarer, Ye, *sels.*
Whisperings in Wattle-Boughs.
Ye Wearie Wayfarer, *sel.*

Gordon, Charles F.
Long Night Home, The.

Gordon, Don
Kimono, The.
Laocoon.
Sea.

Gordon, James William (Jim Grahame)

Whalan of Waitin' a While.

Gordon, James Lindsay
Wheeler at Santiago.

Gordon, Judah Leib
Simhat Torah.

Gordon, Lesley
Armadillo, The.

Gordon, Ralph
Robin and Man.

Gordon, Ruth McKee
Summer Sky.

Gordon, William Steward
Hymn for the New Age, A.

Gore-Booth, Eva
Cross, The.
Crucifixion.
Form.
Harvest.
Little Waves of Breffny, The.
Quest, The.
"Sad Years, The."
Waves of Breffny, The.

Gorenko, Anna Andreyevna *See* **"Akhmatova, Anna"**

Gorges, Mary
Hitherto.

Goring, J. H.
English, The.
Home.

Gorman, Herbert Sherman

Gorman (continued)
Barcarole of James Smith, The.
Chanson de Chateaulaire.
Lèse-Majesté.
Satyrs and the Moon, The.
Gorman Larry (Lawrence E. Gorman)
Beware of Larry Gorman, *with music.*
Boys of the Island, The, *with music.*
Byrontown, *with music.*
Gull Decoy, The, *with music.*
History of Prince Edward Island, The.
McCullam Camp.
Scow on Cowden Shore, The, 3 *vers., with music.*
Tomah Stream, *with music.*
Winter of '73, The, *with music.*
Young Billy Crane, *with music.*
Gorostiza, Jose
Pauses, II.
Gorter, Herman
Sea, The.
Gorton, Samuel
Serpent with a voyce, so slie and fine, The.
Goss, Clay
And If I Die before I Wake.
Goss, Linda
Revolution Man Black.
Gosse, Sir Edmund William
Charcoal-Burner, The.
De Rosis Hibernia.
Dream of November, A.
Epithaiamium: "High in the organ loft with lilied hair."
Hans Christian Andersen.
Illusion.
Impression.
Labor and Love.
Lying in the Grass.
Missive, The.
On a Lute Found in a Sarcophagus.
On Yes Tor.
Pipe-Player, The.
Revelation.
Sestina.
Song for Music.
Swan, The.
Theocritus.
Voice of D. G. R., The.
With a Copy of Herrick.
Gotlieb, Phyllis
How and When and Where and Why.
This One's on Me.
Gottfried von Strassburg
To Mary.
Gottlieb, Darcy
Balzac.
Goudge, Elizabeth
In the Stable.
Thanksgiving for the Earth.
Gould, Alice Lawry
Small Rain.
Gould, C. C.
Come Carol, Make Carol.
Gould, Dorothy
Armistice Day Vow.
Dreamer, The.
His Task—and Ours.
In the Name of Our Sons.
Reconsecration.
Gould, Elizabeth
Grace and Thanksgiving.
Midsummer Night.
Mincemeat.
Mistress Comfort.
My New Rabbit.
Red in Autumn.
Shining Things.
Slumber in Spring.
Such a Blustery Day!
Tadpole, The.
Washing-up Song, The.
Wish, A.
Gould, Elizabeth Porter
Don't Worry.
Gould, Gerald
Atonement, The.
Child's Song.
Compensation.
Happy Tree, The.
I Am Frightened.
Lancelot and Guinevere.
Love Looks to the Future.
Mortality.
Overworked Horse, The.
Sea-Captain, The.
Song: "She whom I love will sit apart."
Twilight.
Wander-Thirst.
Wanderlust.
Gould, Hannah Flagg
Frost, The.
Jack Frost.
Name in the Sand, A.
Song of the Bees.
Gould, Margaret R.
Leviathan.
Gould, Mona
This Was My Brother.
Gould, Robert
Rival Sisters, The, *sel.*
Song: "Fair, and soft, and gay, and young."
Song: Hopeless Comfort, The.
Song: Wit and Beauty.
To Julian.
Gould, Wallace
After Tschaikowsky.
Communion.
Drunken Heracles (Metropolitan Museum).
Moment Musicale.
Night Song.
Gouldsbury, Cullen
Councillor, The.
Gouraud, George Fauvel
Little Nipper an' 'Is Ma, The.
Gourmont, Remy de
Hair.
Govan, Donald D.
Recollection.
Gower, Jean Milne
Big Thompson Canon.
Curtain, The (Old Tabor Grand Opera House).
Gower, John
"Adieu, for now I've made an end."
Ceix and Alceone, *sel.*
Confessio Amantis, *sels.*
Flees he tok and goth to Bote, The.
Florent and the Loathly Hag.
House of Sleep, The.
Jason and Medea.
Parting of Venus and Old Age, The.
Poet Meets Venus and Her Priest, The.
Prolog: "Books composed before our day," The.
Grace, William J.
Suspense.
Grade, Chaim
Sodom.
To Life I Said Yes.
Gradon, Dorothy
Fairy Dream, A.
North Wind, The.
Travelling.
Wind, The.
Winter Joys.
Grady, Richard F.
God Wills It.
Grafflin, Margaret Johnston
Like Mother, Like Son.
To My Son.
Graham, A. M.
Aconite, The.
Graham, Al
Casey's Daughter at the Bat, *parody.*
Folks, I Give You Science!
Theme Song for a Songwriters' Union.
Graham, Charles
Picture That Is Turned toward the Wall, The.
Graham, D. L.
Clown, The.
Portrait of Johnny Doller, A.
Soul.
West Ridge is Menthol-Cool, The ("The West ridge is an old ridge").
Graham, H. Isabel
My Presence Shall Go with Thee.
Graham Harry ("Col. D. Streamer")
Aunt Eliza.
Aunt Maud.
Bath, The.
Billy.
Children's Don't, A, *sel.*
Cockney of the North, The.
Common Sense.
Conversational Reformer, The.
Don't tell Papa his nose is red.
Grandpapa.
Impetuous Samuel.
Lord Gorbals.
Misfortunes Never Come Singly.
Mr. Jones.
My First Love.
Necessity.
Nurse.
Opportunity.
Patience.
Perils of Obesity, The.
Poetical Economy.
Presence of Mind.
Quiet Fun.
Self-Sacrifice.
Stern Parent, The.
Tact.
Tenderheartedness.
Waste.
Graham, James, Marquess of Montrose
Epitaph on King Charles I.
His Metrical Prayer; on the Eve of His Own Execution.
His Metrical Vow; on the Death of King Charles I.
I'll Never Love Thee More.
Lines on the Execution of King Charles I.
Montrose to His Mistress.
My Dear and Only Love.
On Himself, upon Hearing What Was His Sentence.
On the Death of Charles I.
On the Death of King Charles I.
Proper New Ballad, A.
Touch, The.
Verses Composed on the Eve of His Execution.
Graham, Rachel
New Hampshire Farm Woman.
Graham Robert (Robert Cunninghame-Graham)
Cavalier's Song.
If Doughty Deeds [My Lady Please].
O Tell Me How to Woo Thee.
Graham, Rudy Bee
Learning to Dance.
Lynching for Skip James, A.
Memorandum.
Graham, Virginia
Facing the Music.
To the Gentleman in Row D.
Graham, William Sydney
Almost I, yes, I hear.
At Whose Sheltering Shall the Day Sea.

Baldy Bane.
Children of Greenock, The.
Dark Dialogues, The, *sels.*
Definition of My Brother.
Gigha.
Hill of Intrusion, The.
Letter II ("Burned in this element").
Letter VI ("A day the wind was hardly").
Listen. Put on Morning.
Love Poem: "Where you (in this saying) lag in the waving woods."
Many without Elegy.
Name like a River, The.
Nightfishing, The, *sel.*
Night's Fall Unlocks the Dirge of the Sea.
Now in the third voice.
Poem: "O gentle queen of the afternoon."
To My Father.
We are at the hauling then hoping for it.
Grahame, James
Sabbath, The, *sel.*
Sunday Morning.
Grahame, Jenny
Wedlock.
Grahame, Kenneth
Carol: "Villagers all, this frosty tide."
Christmas Carol: "Villagers all, this frosty tide."
Duck's [*or* Ducks'] Ditty.
Song of Mr. Toad, The.
Wind in the Willows, The, *sels.*
World Has Held Great Heroes, The.
"Grahame, Jim." *See* **Gordon, James William.**
Grainger, James
Ode to Solitude.
Solitude, *sel.*
Granich, Irwin
Little Children, The.
Grannatt, Harry Silleck
Happy Ending.
Who-o-o-o-o!
Grannis, Anita
Poet, The.
Granniss, Anna Jane
Exchange of Wills, An.
Grano, Paul Langton
"New Shirt, A!" Why?
Pray Pity for Bill Smith.
Walking Sampford Way.
Word for the Innkeeper, A.
Grant, Earle J.
Where a Dogwood Stood.
Grant, Gordon
Last Gloucesterman, The.
Old Quartermaster, The.
Grant, John Cameron
John Greenleaf Whittier.
Grant, Lillian
Lines Written in a Mausoleum.
Grant, Sir Robert
Majesty and Mercy of God, The.
When Gathering Clouds.
Granville, Charles
Traveller's Hope.
Granville [*or* Grenville], George Baron Lano
Cloe.
Happiest Mortals Once Were We, The.
I'll Tell Her.
Impatient with Desire.
Song: "I'll tell her the next time, said I."
Song: To Myra.
To Cloe.
Grass, Günter
Family Matters.
Gasco, or the Toad.
Graves, Alfred Perceval
Father O'Flynn.
Haymaking.
Irish Lullaby: "I've found my bonny babe a nest."
Little Red Lark, The.
Ould Doctor Mack.
Sailor Girl, The.
Song of the Ghost, The.
White Blossom's off the Bog, The.
Graves, Charles Larcom
Horace, Book V, Ode III.
Old Song Resung, An.
Graves, John Woodcock
John Peel.
Song: "D'ye ken John Peel with his coat so gay?"
Graves, Richard
On the Death of an Epicure.
Graves, Robert
Advice to Colonel Valentine.
Allie ("Allie, call the birds in").
Ambrosia of Dionysus and Semele, The.
Apples and Water.
At Best, Poets.
At the Savoy Chapel.
Avengers, The.
Babylon.
Bards, The.
Beauty in Trouble.
Bird of Paradise.
Birth of a Great Man.
Blue-Fly, The.
Castle, The.
Cat-Goddesses.
Caterpillar, The.
Certain Mercies.
Clearing, The.
Climate of Thought, The.
Cold Weather Proverb.
Cool Web, The.
Corner Knot, The.
Corporal Stare.
Counting the Beats.
Cruel Moon, The.
Cry Faugh!
Damocles.
Dead Cow Farm.
Death Room, The.
Defeat of the Rebels.
Despite and Still.
Dethronement.
Devil's Advice to Story-Tellers, The.
Dialogue on the Headland.
Dr. Newman with the crooked pince-nez.
Door, The.
Double Red Daisies.
Down, Wanton, Down!
1805.
English Wood, An.
Epitaph on an Unfortunate Artist.
Eremites, The.
Escape.
Face in the Mirror, The.
Fallen Tower of Siloam, The.
Finland.
Florist Rose, The.
Flying Crooked.
For the Rain It Raineth Every Day.
Forced Music, A.
Foreboding, The.
Frog and the Golden Ball, The.
From the Embassy.
Frosty Night, A.
Full Moon.
Galatea and Pygmalion.
Glutton, The.
Great-Grandmother, The.
Grotesques.
Haunted House, The.
Henry and Mary.
History of Peace, A.
Homage to Texas.
I Wonder What It Feels Like to Be Drowned?
I'd Love to Be a Fairy's Child.
In Broken Images.
In Procession.
In the Wilderness.
In Time.
Intercession in Late October.
Interruption.
It's a Queer Time.
Jealous Man, A.
John Skelton.
King Stephen.
Kit Logan and Lady Helen.
Lament for Pasiphae.
Last Post, The.
Laureate, The.
Legion, The.
Legs, The.
Like Snow.
Lollocks.
Lost Acres.
Lost Jewel, A.
Lost Love.
Lost World, A.
Love Story, A.
Love without Hope.
Lovers in Winter.
Lust in Song.
Marigolds.
Mid-Winter Waking.
Mirror, Mirror.
My Name and I.
Naked and the Nude, The.
Nature's Lineaments.
Neglectful Edward.
Never Such Love.
New Legends.
Next War, The.
Nobody.
Not Dead.
O Love in Me.
Ogres and Pygmies.
Oldest Soldier, The.
On Dwelling.
On Portents.
Outlaws.
Persian Version, The.
Person from Porlock, The.
Pier-Glass, The.
Pinch of Salt, A.
Plea to Boys and Girls, A.
Poets, The.
Portrait, The.
Pot and Kettle.
Presence, The.
Pumpkin, The.
Pure Death.
Pygmalion to Galatea.
Quayside.
Quiet Glades of Eden, The.
Read Me, Please!
Recalling War.
Reproach.
Reproach to Julia.
Richard Roe and John Doe ("Richard Roe wished himself Solomon").
Rocky Acres.
Saint.
Sea Side.
Secret Land, The.
Sergeant-Major Money.
She Is No Liar.
She Tells Her Love [While Half Asleep].
Sick Love.
Sir John addressed the Snake-god in his temple.
Sirocco at Deyá.
Six Badgers, The.
Song: Lift Boy.
Song: One Hard Look.

Graves (continued)
Spoils.
Star-Talk.
Straw, The.
Sullen Moods.
Survivor, The.
Thief.
Thieves, The.
Through Nightmare.
Time.
To an Ungentle Critic.
To Bring the Dead to Life.
To Calliope.
To Juan at the Winter Solstice.
To Sleep.
To Walk on Hills.
To Whom Else?
Traveller's Curse after Misdirection, The.
Troll's Nosegay, The.
Trudge, Body.
Turn of the Moon.
Twins.
Two Fusiliers.
Ulysses.
Vain and Careless.
Vanity.
Visitation, The.
Warning to Children.
Wedding, The.
Wellcome, to the Caves of Arta!
Welsh Incident.
White Goddess, The.
Wild Strawberries.
Window Sill, The.
Woman and Tree.
Woman with her forests, moons, flowers, waters.
Worms of History, The.
Young Cordwainer, The.

Gray, Alexander
Epitaph on a Vagabond.
Scotland.
Sir Halewyn.

"Gray, Barry." *See* **Coffin, Robert Barry.**

Gray, David
Cross of Gold, The.
Dear Old Toiling One, The.
Divided.
Golden Wedding, The.
I Die, Being Young.
In the Shadows, *sels.*
My Epitaph.
On Lebanon.
Sonnet: "If it must be; if it must be, O God!"
Where the Lilies Used to Spring.

Gray, Eva
Christ, My Salvation ("Christ, my Lord is my salvation").
Father's Place, A.
God Uses Broken Things.
How Excellent Is Thy Name!
It Was for Me.
Light and Love, Hope and Faith.
My Daily Prayer.
My Lord Knows Best for Me.
What Is That in Thine Hand?

Gray, Frances Angevine
Otherwhere.
Tapers.
Tenant.

Gray, John
Barber, The.
Condemned Women.
Crocuses in the Grass.
Flying Fish, The.
Gazelles and Unicorn.
Green.
Les Demoiselles De Sauve.
Long Road, The, *sel.*
Lord, If Thou Art Not Present.
Mishka.
Night Nurse Goes Her Round, The.
Ox, The.
Poem: "Geranium, houseleek, laid in oblong beds."
To a Madonna.

Gray, Lillian
New Year's Thoughts.

Gray, Stephen
Girl with Doves.
Girl with Long Dark Hair.

Gray, Thomas
Alliance of Education and Government, The, *abr.*
Bard, The.
Boast of heraldry, the pomp of power, The.
Cat and the Fish, The.
Curse upon Edward, The.
Descent of Odin, The; an Ode from the Norse Tongue.
Elegy Written in a Country Churchyard.
Fatal Sisters, The.
Hymn to Adversity.
Impromptu.
Ode on a Distant Prospect of Eton College.
Ode on the Death of a Favorite [*or* Favourite] Cat, Drowned in a Tub [*or* Bowl] of Goldfishes.
Ode on the Pleasure Arising from Vicissitude.
Ode on the Spring.
On a Distant Prospect of Eton College.
On a Favorite Cat, Drowned in a Tub of Goldfishes.
On a rock, whose haughty brow.
On Lord Holland's Seat near Margate, Kent.
On the Death of a Favorite Cat, Drowned in a Tub of Goldfishes.
On the Death of Mr. Richard West.
Peopled Air, The.
Progress of Poesy, The.
Sketch of His Own Character.
Song: "Thrysis, when we parted, swore."
Sonnet: "In vain to me the smiling mornings shine."
Sonnet: On the Death of Richard West.
Stanzas Cancelled from the Elegy.
Stanzas to Mr. Bentley.
Tophet; an Epigram.
Triumphs of Owen, The.
Where Ignorance Is Bliss.
William Shakespeare to Mrs. Anne, Regular Servant to Rev. Mr. Precentor of York.

Gray, William
Hunt Is Up, The.
King's Hunt Is Up, The.

Gray, William B.
She Is More to Be Pitied than Censured.

Grayer, Rosalie
Altar Smoke.

Grayson, Caroline
After.

"Grayson, David", (Ray Stannard Baker)
Argument with a Millionaire, An.
Happy Farmer, The.

Grayson, Ethel Kirk
Summer's End.

Greacen, Robert
Bird, The.
Cycling to Dublin.
Far Country, The.
Glorious Twelfth, The.
Michael Walked in the Wood.
To a Faithless Lover.
Written on the Sense of Isolation in Contemporary Ireland.

Greeff, Adele
Sonnet XI: "Is God invisible? This very room."

Green, Brenda Heloise
New England Is New England Is New England.

"Green, Coroebus." *See* **Cone, Helen Gray**

Green, Donald
Growing Clean.
Making It, or Black Corruption.
Truth.

Green, Henry Mackenzie
Bush Goblins.
Cicada, The.

Green, Joseph
Elegy by Green for Byles's Cat.

Green, Judith
Bush-Fiddle, The.

Green, L. Worthington
Bull Fight, The.

Green, Mary McBride
Aeroplane.
Taking Off.

Green, Matthew
And may my humble dwelling stand.
But now more serious let me grow.
Cure for the Spleen, A.
Epigram, An: "Gil's history appears to me."
Epigram, An, on the Reverend Mr. Laurence Echard's, and Bishop Gilbert Burnet's Histories.
On Even Keel.
Spleen, The.

Green, Roger Lancelyn
On First Looking into the Dark Future.

Greenaway, Kate
All the Cats.
Alphabet, The.
Around the World.
Ball.
Blue Shoes.
Boat Sails Away, The.
Cats Have Come to Tea, The.
Child's Song.
Daisies, The.
Five Little Sisters Walking in a Row.
Five Sisters.
Happy Child, A.
Higgledy, piggledy! see how they run!
In Go-Cart So Tiny.
Lamb, The.
Little Jumping Girls, The.
Little Phillis.
Little Wind.
Naughty Blackbird, The.
O Ring the Bells.
Older Grown.
On the Bridge.
Polly, Peg, and Poppety.
Prince Finikin.
Ring-a-Ring.
School is over.
Susan Blue.
Tea-Party, A [*or* The].
To Baby.
Tommy was a silly boy.
When You and I Grow Up.
Will You.
Will You Be My Little Wife.
Wishes.

Greenberg, Barbara L.
April Thirty-first.
"Boarding of Pan American Flight 207 Will Be Delayed Ten Minutes."
Gentleman's Garden, The.
Husband, The.
Poem for a Dead Aunt.
Victim, The.
Wedlock.

Greenberg, Samuel
Blank Book Letter, The.
Conduct.
Essence.
Essentials.
Glass Bubbles, The.
I Cannot Believe That I Am of Wind.
Immortality.
Killing.
Man.
Opponent Charm Sustained, The.
Peace.
Philosophic Apology, The.
Soul's Kiss.
Spirituality.
To Dear Daniel.
Tusks of Blood, The.
Greenberg, Uri Zvi
Jerusalem, *sel.*
Jerusalem the Dismembered.
Greene, Albert Gorton
Baron's Last Banquet, The.
Old Grimes.
Greene, Ashton
Bather in a Painting, A.
Church of the Sacred Heart, The.
Lagoon, The.
Parade, The.
Greene, Homer
My Daughter Louise.
What My Lover Said.
Greene, Kathleen Conyngham
Old Joan.
Greene, Richard L.
Autolycus' Song (in Basic English).
Song to Imogen (in Basic English).
Greene, Robert
Arbasto, *sels.*
Ciceronis Amor.
Content.
Coridon and Phillis.
Cupid Abroad Was Lated.
Description of Sir Geoffrey Chaucer, The.
Doralicia's Song.
Doron's Description of Samela.
Doron's Jig [*or* Jigge].
Eurymachus's Fancy.
Fair Is My Love.
Fair Is My Love for April in [*or* Is *or* April's in] Her Face.
Farewell to Folly, *sel.*
Fawnia.
Fickle Seat Whereon Proud Fortune Sits, The.
Fie, Fie on Blind Fancy!
Francesco's Fortunes, *sels.*
From his flock stray'd Coridon.
Greene's Groatsworth of Wit, *sels.*
Greene's Mourning Garment, *sels.*
Greene's Orpharion, *sel.*
Greene's Vision, *sel.*
Groatsworth of Wit.
Hexametra Alexis in Laudem Rosamundi.
Ideals.
In Cypres Sat Fair Venus by a Fount.
In Praise of His Loving and Best-beloved Fawnia.
In Praise of Rosamund.
In Time We See That Silver Drops.
Infida's Song.
Jig, A.
Lamilia's Song.
Love and Jealousy.
Madrigal, A: "Swans, The, whose pens as white as ivory," *sel.*
Maesia's Song.
Mars and Venus.
Melicertus' Description of His Mistress.
Menaphon, *sels.*
Mind Content, A.
Morando, the Tritameron of Love, *sel.*
Mourning Garment, The.
Never Too Late, *sels.*
Obscure and Dark Is All the Gloomy Air.
Of His Mistress.
Palinode, A.
Palmer's Ode, The.
Pandosto, *sel.*
Penitent Palmer's Ode, The.
Perimedes, *sels.*
Phillis and Corydon.
Philomela, the Lady Fitzwater's Nightingale, *sels.*
Poor Estate, The.
Samela.
Sephestia's Song to Her Child [*or* Childe].
Shepherd's Ode, The.
Shepherd's Wife's Song, The.
Sir Geoffrey Chaucer.
Song: "Sweet are the thoughts that savor of content."
Sonnet: "Fair is my love, for April in her face."
Sonnet or Dittie: "Mars in a fury gainst love's brightest queen."
"Swans, whose pens as white as ivory, The."
Sweet Adon.
Sweet Are the Thoughts That Savor of Content.
Tullie's Love, *sels.*
Weep Not, My Wanton.
What meant the poets in invective verse.
When Flora Proud.
When Gods Had Fram'd the Sweet of Women's Face.
Whereat Erewhile I Wept, I Laugh
Greene, Sarah Pratt
Lamp, The.
Massa ob de Sheepfol', De.
Sheepfol', De ("De Massa . . .").
Greenfield, Marjorie H.
Things I Like.
Greenleaf, Lawrence N.
Lodge Room over Simpkins' Store, The.
Pike's Peakers, The.
Greenough, Walter
Vision, The.
Greenwell, Dora
Battle-Flag of Sigurd, The.
Content.
His Name.
Home.
Man with Three Friends, The.
My Saviour.
Song of Farewell, A.
To Christina Rossetti.
"Greenwood, Grace" (Sara Jane Clarke Lippincot
Illumination for Victories in Mexico.
Greenwood, James
On the Ladies' Head-Dresses.
Greenwood, Roland R.
Coward, The.
Greer, Roslyn
Triangle.
Gregh, Fernand
Doubt.
Gregor, Arthur
Blackout.
Irreconcilables.
Spirits, Dancing.
Unalterables.
Gregoria Francisca, Sister
Envying a Little Bird.
Gregory, Carole
Ghetto Lovesong—Migration.
Gregory, Horace
And of Columbus.
Ask No Return.
Beggar on the Beach, The.
Chorus for Survival, *sel.*
Do I have to prove that I can sell anything?
Elizabeth at the Piano.
Emerson: Last Days at Concord.
For You, My Son.
Foreigner Comes to Earth on Boston Common, A.
Fortune for Mirabel.
Haunted Odysseus; the Last Testament.
Homage to Circe.
If It Offend Thee.
Interior; the Suburbs.
Longface Mahoney Discusses Heaven.
No Cock Crows at Morning.
O Mors Aeterna.
Passion of M'Phail, The, *sels.*
Poems for My Daughter.
Postman's Bell Is Answered Everywhere, The.
Prisoner's Song.
Salvos for Randolph Bourne.
Spyglass.
Stanzas for My Daughter.
Tell us that love/ returns.
They Found Him Sitting in a Chair.
They Were All like Geniuses.
This Is the Place to Wait.
To the Last Wedding Guest.
Tombstone with Cherubin.
Two Monologues from the Passion of M'Phail.
Unwilling Guest, The; an Urban Dialogue.
Valediction to My Contemporaries.
Voices of Heroes.
Waking from sleep we heard the Great Lakes' tide.
Woman Who Disapproved of Music at the Bar, The.
Gregory, Augusta Gregory, Lady
Army of the Sidhe, The.
Come ride and ride to the garden.
Old Woman Remembers, The.
Gregory, Padraic
Dream-Teller, The.
Gregory, Yvonne
Christmas Lullaby for a New-born Child.
Gregory of Narek [*or* Makar], Saint
Christ-Child, The.
Gregory the Great, Saint
Morning Hymn.
Greig, Desmond A.
On a Scooter.
To a Flea in a Glass of Water.
Grenelle, Lisa
Devil Doll.
Duel in the Park.
Grenfell, Julian
Into Battle.
To a Black Greyhound.
Grenville, George *See* **Granville, George, Baron Lansdowne**
Grenville, R. H.
Borderline.
Ghost.
Intuition.
Nightmare.
Pawnshop Window.
Praise.
Gresham, Walter J.
Crowded Ways of Life.
Greshoff, Jan
I Beat the Drum.
Gresset, Louis
Vert-Vert, the Parrot.
Greville Fanny Macartney
Prayer for Indifference.
Greville, Fulke, 1st Baron Brooke
Absence and Presence.
Another, of His Cynthia.
Caelica.

Greville (continued)
Caelica and Philocell.
Change.
Chorus: "Oh wearisome condition of humanity!"
Chorus Primus: Wise Counsellors.
Chorus Quintus: Tartarorum.
Chorus Sacerdotum.
Chorus Tertius: Of Time: Eternitie.
Cupid, My Little Boy, Come Home Again.
Cupid, my pretty boy, leave off thy crying.
Cynthia ("Away with these self-loving lads").
Despair.
Earth, The, with thunder torn, with fire blasted.
His Lady's Eyes.
I, with Whose Colo[u]rs, Myra Dressed [8OR9 Drest]
Inquisition upon Fame and Honor, An.
Love and Fortune.
Love and Honour.
Love, the Delight of All Well-thinking Minds.
Love's Glory.
Man, dreame no more of curious mysteries.
Man's Service.
More than Most Fair.
Mustapha, *sels.*
Myra.
O Wearisome Condition [of Humanity].
Of His Cynthia.
Of Humane Learning, *sel.*
Saving God, The.
Sion lies [*or* Syon lyes] waste, and thy Jerusalem.
Song to His Cynthia.
Sonnet: "Away with these self-loving lads."
Sonnet: "Caelica, I overnight was finely used."
Sonnet: "Cupid, thou naughty boy, when thou wert loathed."
Sonnet: "Cynthia, because your horns look divers ways."
Sonnet: "Down [*or* Downe] in the depth of mine iniquity."
Sonnet: "Earth with thunder torn, with fire blasted, The."
Sonnet: "Eternal [*or* Eternall] Truth, almighty, infinite."
Sonnet: "Farewell, sweet boy; complain not of my truth."
Sonnet: "Fle, foolish earth, think you the heaven wants glory."
Sonnet: "I, with whose colors Myra dressed her head."
Sonnet: "In night, when colors all to black are cast."
Sonnet: "Man, dreame no more of curious mysteries."
Sonnet XCIV: "Men, that delight to multiply desire."
Sonnet: "O false and treacherous Probability."
Sonnet: "Sion lies [*or* Syon lyes] waste, and thy Jerusalem."
Sonnet: "Under a throne I saw a virgin sit."
Sonnet: "When as mans life, the light of human lust."
Sonnet: "Whenas [*or* When as] man's life, the light of human lust."
Sonnet: "World, that all contains, is ever moving, The."
Sonnet: "You little stars that live in skies."
Three Things There Be.
Time and Eternity.
To His Lady.
To Myra.
Treatie of Human Learning, A.
Youth and Maturity.

Grey, Francis W.
Knowest Thou Isaac Jogues?

Grey of Fallodon, Pamela Grey, Viscountess
Echo.
Legend of the Tortoise, The.
Moon Magic.

Grier, Eldon
I Am Almost Asleep.
In Memory of García Lorca.
Minotaur, The.
More Than Most People.
On the Subject of Waves.
Quebec.
Sensible Is the Label.
View from a Window.

Gries, Walter F.
Cornish Miner, The.

Grieve, Christopher Murray *See* **"MacDiarmid, Hugh"**

Griffin, Bartholomew
Fair Is My Love.
Fair [*or* Faire] is my love that feeds among the lilies.
Faire Is My Love.
Fidessa, More Chaste than Kind, *sels.*
Her Heart.
My Love.
Sleep.
Sonnet: "Fair [*or* Faire] is my Love that feeds among the lilies."
Sonnet: "I have not spent the April of my time."
Venus, with Young Adonis Sitting by Her.
Youth.

Griffin, Gerald
Aileen Aroon.
Ancient Lullaby.
Eileen Aroon.
Gone! Gone! Forever Gone.
Hy-Brasail, the Isle of the Blest.
I Love My Love in the Morning.
Know Ye Not That Lovely River.
Lines Addressed to a Seagull.
Maiden Eyes.
Nightingale, The.
Nocturne: "Sleep that like the couched dove."
O Brazil, the Isle of the Blest.
Place in Thy Memory, A.
Sleep That like the Couchèd Dove.
Song: "Place in thy memory, dearest, A."
To the Blessed Virgin Mary.
War Song of O'Driscol.
When like the rising day.

Griffin, Howard
Suppose in Perfect Reason.

Griffin, Pamela
Elegy in a Museum.
Swan's Nest, The.

Griffin, Sin Killer
Man of Calvary, The.

Griffith, William
Aloha.
Canticle.
I, Who Fade with the Lilacs.
Loves and Losses of Pierrot, *sel.*
Pierrette in Memory.
Spring Song.

Grigg, Joseph
Ashamed of Jesus.
Christ at the Door.
Not Ashamed of Christ.

Grigson, Geoffrey
Above the High.
Four, The.
Landscape of the Heart, The.
Lecture Note: Elizabethan Period.
Meeting by the Gjulika Meadow.
New Dummy, The.
Uccello on the Heath.
Under the Cliff.

Grilikhes, Alexandra
Runner, The.

Grimald, Nicholas
Concerning Virgil's Aeneids.
Funeral Song upon the Decease of Annes, His Mother, A.
Garden, The.
Of Friendship.
To His Familiar Friend.
True Love, A.
Truelove, A.

Grimard, Luc
Amitié Amoureuse.

Grimes, John
Queen of Crete, The.

Grimes, Katharine Atherton
Farm Boy, The.

Grimes, Marie
Kitten and Firefly.

Grimes, Willard M.
Piazza di Spagna.

Grimké, Angelina Weld
Black Finger, The.
Dusk.
Eyes of My Regret, The.
For the Candle Light.
Grass Fingers.
Greenness.
Hushed by the Hands of Sleep.
I Weep.
Mona Lisa, A.
Paradox.
Puppet Player, The.
Surrender.
Tenebris.
To Clarissa Scott Delany.
Ways o' Men, The.
When the Green Lies over the Earth.
Winter Twilight, A.
Your Hands.

Grissom, Arthur
Artist, The.
Ballade of Forgotten Loves.

Griswold, Mariana *See* **Van Rensselaer, Mariana Griswold**

Groesbeck, Amy
Brothers, The.
Momist.

Grosseteste, Robert
Little Song, A.

Grossman, Reuben
Therefore, We Thank Thee, God.

Grove, Eliza
Cat to Her Kittens, A.
Dancing Lesson, The.
Greedy Piggy That Ate Too Fast, The.
Little Hobby-Horse, A.

Grove, Matthew
In Praise of His Lady.
Pelops and Hippodamia, *sel.*

Grover, Edwin Osgood
Knapsack Trail, The.

Gruber, Abraham L.
My Neighbor's Roses.

Gruber, Edmund L.
Caisson Song, The.

Grudin, Louis
Airborn.
Citizen.

Guarini, Giovanni Battista
Claim to Love.
Faithful Shepherd, The.
How I forsook/ Elias and Pisa after, and betook.
Spring.

Gudmundur Gudmundsson
Lament: "Snows cloaked/ Mountain cliffs."
Guerard, A. L.
Prescription.
Guerard, Vera E.
At Sea.
Spring of Joy.
Guérin, Charles
In My Old Verses.
Partings.
Guerzo di Montecanti
Sonnet: He Is Out of Heart with His Time.
Guest, Barbara
Belgravia.
"Everything in the Air Is a Bird."
First of May, The.
Hero Leaves His Ship, The.
Les Réalités.
Parachutes, My Love, Could Carry Us Higher.
Piazzas.
Sadness.
Santa Fé Trail.
Sunday Evening.
Wave.
Guest, Edgar Albert
All That Matters.
Becoming a Dad.
Creed, A.
Equipment.
Forgetful Pa.
Four Men of God.
Friend's Greeting, A.
Grace at Evening.
Home.
It Couldn't Be Done.
Just Folks.
Kindly Neighbor, The.
Laymen, The.
Lord, Make a Regular Man Out of Me.
Lord, this humble house we'd keep.
Mother Thought, A.
My Bible.
My Books and I, *sel.*
My Creed.
Myself.
Out Fishin'.
Prayer for the Home, *sel.*
Radio, The.
Send Her a Valentine.
Sermons We See.
Sittin' on the Porch.
Stick to It.
Success.
What's in It for Me?
When Father Played Baseball.
When Life Is Done.
You.
Guidi, Benedetto
Love Enslaved.
Guidiccioni, Giovanni
To Italy.
Guido delle Colonne
Canzone: To Love and to His Lady.
Guilhade, Joan de
For Mr. X I've Only Mischief.
Guillaume de Lorris
Briddes that han left their song, The.
Guillaume de Lorris, *and* Jean de Meun
Dream of the Romaunt of the Rose, The.
Garden of Amour, The.
Love vs. Marriage.
Romaunt of the Rose, The.
Well I looked upon each face.
Guillaume de Poitiers
Behold the Meads.
Count William's Escapade.
Guillén, Jorge
I said: All now complete! Twelve by the Clock.
Names.
Twelve by the Clock.
Utter Silence.
Guillén, Nicolás
Barren Stone.
Cane.
Dead Soldier.
Federico.
Guadalupe, W. I.
Proposition.
Sightseers in a Courtyard.
Two Children.
Two Weeks.
Wake for Papa Montero.
Guilpin, Everard
De Ignoto.
Fie on these Lydian tunes which blunt our sprights.
Of Cornelius.
Of Pansa.
Of Titus.
Of Zeno.
Proemium I: "As in the greatest of societies."
Satira Prima.
Satyra Quinta.
Skialetheia, *sels.*
To Clodius.
To Deloney.
To Licus.
To the Reader.
Guiney, Louise Imogen
Carol, A: "Vines branching stilly."
Deo Optimo Maximo.
Five Carols for Christmastide.
Footnote to a Famous Lyric, A.
Friend's Song for Simoisius, A.
In Leinster.
John Brown; a Paradox.
Kings, The.
Martyr's Memorial.
Memorial Day.
Monochrome.
Nam Semen Est Verbum Dei.
Ode for a Master Mariner Ashore.
Of Joan's Youth.
On First Entering Westminster Abbey.
Outdoor Litany, An.
Pax Paganica.
Sanctuary.
Song: "I try to knead and spin, but my life is low the while."
Song in Leinster.
To a Dog's Memory.
Tryste Noël.
Valse Jeune.
Wild Ride, The.
Guinicelli, Guido
Canzone: He Perceives His Rashness in Love.
Canzone: Of the Gentle Heart.
Of the Gentle Heart.
Praise.
Sonnet: He Will Praise His Lady.
Sonnet: Of Moderation and Tolerance.
Guinness, Bryan
Summer Is Coming, The.
What Are They Thinking.
Guiterman, Arthur
Afternoon Tea.
Ain't Nature Commonplace!
Ambiguous Dog, The.
Anthologistics.
Anthony Wayne.
Bears.
Belsnickel.
Blessing on Little Boys.
Blue Hen's Chickens, The.
Boy and a Pup, A.
Call to the Colors, The.
Christmas Exchange, The.
Chums.
Coming of the Trees, The.
Constitution for a League of Nations.
Daniel Boone.
Death and General Putnam.
Dog's Cold Nose, The.
Dreamer, A.
Dutchman's Beeches.
Edinburgh.
Education.
Eight Oars and a Coxswain ("Eight oars compel").
Elegy: "Jackals prowl, the serpents hiss, The."
Epilogue to a Book of Verse.
Experts on Woman.
First Thanksgiving, The.
Garden Song.
Growing Up.
Haarlem Heights.
Habits of the Hippopotamus.
Harvest Home.
He Leads Us Still.
Hills.
House Blessing.
How Are You?
Husband and Wife.
In Praise of Llamas.
In the Hospital.
Independence Square, Christmas 1783.
Indian Pipe and Moccasin Flower.
Indispensability.
Irreverent Brahmin, The.
Kit Carson.
Lament for the Alamo.
Legend of the First Cam-u-el, The.
Little Lost Pup.
Little Ponds.
London Bobby, The.
March.
Mavrone.
Mexican Serenade.
Nature Note.
Neighbors.
New York.
Ode to the Hayden Planetarium.
Of Certain Irish Fairies.
Of Courtesy.
Of Giving.
Of Quarrels.
Of Tact.
Offer, An.
On the Vanity of Earthly Greatness.
Oregon Trail, The.
Ornithology in Florida.
Our Colonel.
Pilgrims' Thanksgiving Feast, The.
Pioneer, The.
Poem on Spring, The.
Poet's Proverb, A.
Prologue for a Magician.
Pure Mathematician, A.
Pussy-Willows.
Quivira.
Reward of Virtue.
Rush of the *Oregon,* The.
School Days in New Amsterdam.
Scribe's Prayer, The.
Shakespearean Bear, The.
Skater's Valentine, A.
Sketch from the Life, A.
Snarlers, The.
Starlighter, The.
Storming of Stony Point, The.
Strictly Germ-proof.
Superstitious Ghost, The.
Thanksgiving Wishes.
This Is She.
Thunderstorm.
Tract for Autos, A.
Twist-Rime on Spring.

Guiterman (continued)
Under the Goal Posts.
Viewpoints.
What Makes a Home.
What the Gray Cat Sings.
Whole Duty of a Poem, The.
Woman's Tongue Tree, The.
Young Washington.
Guittone d'Arezzo
Lady of Heaven.
Gulick, Alida Carey
On Waking.
Gullans, Charles
Autumn; an Ode.
Autumn Burial: a Meditation.
First Love.
Narcissus.
Parachutes, The.
Poema Morale.
To a Friend.
Gumilev [*or* Gumilyov], Nikolai Stepanovich
Giraffe, The.
How Could We, Beforehand, Live in Quiet.
Listen:/ There roams, far away, by the waters of Clead.
Gummere, Francis Barton
John Bright.
Gunderson, Gertrude B.
Three Things.
What If.
Gunn, Louise D.
Conversation with Rain.
Gunn, Thom
Annihilation of Nothing, The.
Beach Head, The.
Before the Carnival.
Black Jackets.
Blackie, the Electric Rembrandt.
Byrnies, The.
Considering the Snail.
Corridor, The.
Liebesleben, Das
Flying above California.
From the Highest Camp.
Goddess, The.
In Santa Maria del Popolo.
In the Tank.
Incident on a Journey.
Inherited Estate, The.
Innocence.
Jesus and His Mother.
Loot.
Merlin in the Cave; He Speculates Without a Book.
Mirror for Poets, A.
My Sad Captains.
Nature of an Action, The.
On the Move.
Rastignac at 45.
St. Martin and the Beggar.
Silver Age, The.
Tamer and Hawk.
To Yvor Winters, 1955.
Trucker, A.
Unsettled Motorcyclist's Vision of His Death, The.
Vox Humana.
Wound, The.
Gunsaulus, Frank W.
Goal, The.
Guri, Haim
But We Shall Bloom.
Prayer: "Thy blessing on the boys—for time has come."
Gurley, Edith B.
His Gift and Mine.
Gurney, Dorothy Frances
God's Garden.
Lord God Planted a Garden, The.
O Perfect Love.
Gurney, Ivor
Bohemians, The.
Love Song, The.
Silent One, The.
To His Love.
Ypres.
Gurney, Lawrence
Nevada.
Gustafson, Mary
Eyes Up!
Gustafson, Ralph
Armorial.
Aspects of Some Forsythia Branches.
At the Ocean's Verge.
Carta Canadensis.
Dedication: "'They shall not die in vain,' we said."
Fish, The.
Flight into Darkness.
In the Yukon.
Legend.
Meaning, The.
My Love Eats an Apple.
Mythos.
On Such a Wet and Blustery Night.
On the Road to Vicenza.
On the *Struma* Massacre.
On This Sea-Floor.
"S.S.R., Lost at Sea."—The *Times.*
Swans of Vadstena, The.
Transfigured Night.
Window, a Table, on the North, A.
Guthrie, Charles E.
God's Will.
Guthrie, James
Last Song.
Guthrie, Norman Gregor *See* **"Crichton, John"**
Guthrie, Ramon
Clown, The: He Dances in the Clearing by Night.
Laura Age Eight.
Noël Tragique.
Postlude: for Goya.
To and on Other Intellectual Poets on Reading That the U.S.A.F. Had Sent a Team of Scientists to Africa.
Guthrie, Thomas Anstey *See* **"Anstey, F."**
Guthrie, Woody
Hard Travelin'.
Tom Joad, *with music.*
Gutiérrez Nájera, Manuel
In the Depths of Night.
Gutteridge, Bernard
Burma Hills.
Namkwin Pul.
Patrol; Buonamary.
Guyon, Jeanne Marie Bouvier de la Motte
Adoration.
By Thy Life I Live.
Little Bird I Am, A.
Prisoner's Song, A.
Since God Is There.
Gwynn, Stephen Lucious
Ireland.
Gwynne, J. Harold
For This Child I Prayed.
Good Shepherd, The.
Word of God, The.
Gyles, Althea
Sympathy.

H

"H., B."
Anacreon to the Sophist.
"H., F. L."
Father Knows, The.
"H., H." *See* **Jackson, Helen Hunt**
"H., H. E."
Riddle, The: "Where's an old woman to go when the years."
"H., J. B."
Inventin'est Man, The.
"H., J. P."
Ode to a Side Car.
"H., M."
Crown of Age.
"H., M. E."
First Things First.
"H., M. G."
He Never Will Forget.
"H., M. K."
Prayer Hymn.
"H., P."
Jung Idea, The.
"H., R."
Battle of Monmouth, The.
"H. A. C." *See* **"C., H. A"**
"H. D." *See* **Doolittle, Hilda**
"H. E. H." *See* **"H., H. E"**
Haaff, Katherine Maurine
Good Thoughts.
Haas, Rosamond
Abstract Painter in Spring.
Habington, William
Against Them Who Lay Unchastity to the Sex of Women.
Castara, *sels.*
Cogitabo pro Peccato Meo.
Compliment, The.
Description of Castara, The.
Dialogue betweene Araphill and Castara, A.
Elegie: "Goe stop the swift-wing'd moments in their flight."
Fine Young Folly.
His Muse Speakes to Him.
Melancholy.
Nox Nocti Indicat Scientiam.
Queen of Aragon, The, *sel.*
Quoniam Ego in Flagella Paratus Sum.
Recogitabo Tibi Omnes Annos Meos.
Reward of Innocent Love, The.
Song: "Fine young folly, though you were."
Time! Where Didst Thou Those Years Inter.
To a Friend, Inviting Him to a Meeting Upon Promise.
To a Wanton.
To Castara ("Doe not their prophane orgies heare").
To Castara ("Give me a heart where no impure").
To Castara, of True Delight.
To Castara: The Reward of Innocent Love.
To Castara, upon an Embrace.
To Castara, upon Beautie.
To Castara, Ventring to Walke Too Farre in the Neighbouring Wood.
To Death, Castara Being Sicke.
To Roses in the Bosome of Castara.
To the Right Honourable the Countesse of C.
To the World, the Perfection of Love.
Upon Castara's Absence.
Upon Castara's Departure.
Upon Thought Castara May Die.

Welcome, Thou Safe Retreat!
What Am I Who Dare to Call Thee, God!
When I Survey the Bright.
Hackett, Eloise
Conventionality.
Hackett, Francis
Dead Aviator, The.
Sea Dawn.
Hadden, Maude Miner
Creative Force.
Haden-Guest, Anthony
How the Consolations of Philosophy Worked Out in Actual Practice.
Hadewijch
Eighteenth Song, The: "New year hath come in sight, The."
Hadley, Lizzie M.
Rainbow Fairies, The.
Hadley, Lydia
Four Calls, The.
Hadrian Emperor (Publius Aelius Hadrianus)
Adriani Morientis ad Animam Suam.
Animula Blandula Vagula.
Emperor Hadrian's Dying Address to His Soul.
On the Soul.
To His Soul.
Haenigsen, H. W.
Listen, Pigeon, Bend an Ear.
Hafen, Ann Woodbury
Mountain Liars.
Hafiz
Comrades, the Morning Breaks.
From the Garden of Heaven.
Grievous folly shames my sixtieth year, A.
I Cease Not from Desire.
Jewel of the Secret Treasury, The.
Lady That Hast My Heart.
Odes, *sels.*
Persian Song, A.
Rose Is Not the Rose, The.
Slaves of Thy Shining Eyes.
Hagarty, Sir John H.
Funeral of Napoleon I.
Hagedorn, Hermann
Early Morning at Bargis.
Evening Prayer.
Eyes of God, The.
Hymn to the Victorious Dead.
Light.
Mother.
Mother in the House, The.
Noah.
Prayer during Battle.
Prologue to Morning.
Service.
Solomon.
Song: "Song is so old."
Starry Night.
Troop of the Guard, A.
Wild Rose, The.
Hageman, Samuel Miller
Silence.
Hagemeyer, Dora
Parable of the Mustard Weed, The.
Hagen, John Milton
Cowboy and His Love, The,
Song of the Cattle Trail.
Hagerup, Inger
Dies Irae.
Hagg, Esther Lloyd
Different Way, A.
His Garments.
It Was Not Strange.
They Saw and Believed.
Hagiwara, Sakutaro
Bar at Night, A.
Haglund, Beverly
Disagreeing with God.
Hagthorpe, John
To Time.
Haight, Dorothy
New Orleans Balcony, A.
Haines, John
Cauliflower, The.
Color, The.
Dance, The.
Great Society, The.
If the Owl Calls Again.
Into the Glacier.
"It Must All Be Done Over."
Larkspur.
Moons.
Paul Klee.
Red Atlantis.
Stone Harp, The.
To Turn Back.
Hake, Thomas Gordon
Old Souls.
Sibyl, The.
Hakutsu
O pine-tree standing.
Halas, Frantisek
Again.
And Then There.
Halbisch, Harry
Warp and Woof.
Hale, Arthur
Manila Bay.
Yankee Privateer [The].
Hale, Edward Everett
Adrian Block's Song.
Alma Mater's Roll.
Anne Hutchinson's Exile.
Ballad of Bunker Hill, The.
Columbus.
From Potomac to Merrimac.
Is There Some Desert.
Lamentable Ballad of the Bloody Brook, The.
Lend a Hand.
Look Up.
Marching Song of Stark's Man, The.
Merrimac Side, and Agiochook.
Nameless Saints, The.
New England's Chevy Chase, April 19, 1775.
Omnipresence.
One Thousandth Psalm, The.
Potomac Side.
Put It Through.
Signal Fires.
"Hale, Katherine" (Amelia Beers Warnock Garvin
Eternal Moment.
Giant's Tomb in Georgian Bay.
Lost Garden.
Portrait of a Cree.
Hale, Oliver
Where Unimaginably Bright.
Hale, Robert Beverly
Moon, The.
Ovibos, The.
Hale, Sarah Josepha Buell
Alice Ray.
Mary and Her Lamb.
Mary Had a Little Lamb.
Mary's Lamb.
Watcher, The.
Hales, Thomas *See* **Thomas of Hales**
Halevi [*or* Ha-Levi], Judah
Amid the Myrtles.
Asleep in the Bosom of Youth.
Awake, My Fair.
Dove, The.
Earth in Spring, The.
Fortune's Treachery.
God, Whom Shall I Compare to Thee?
Grey Hair, The.
He Cometh.
Hymn for Atonement Day.
Immortal Israel.
Israel's Duration.
Letter to His Friend Isaac, A.
Longing.
Longing for Jerusalem.
Lord, Where Shall I Find Thee?
Love Song, A.
Marriage Song.
Meditation on Communion with God.
Mirror, The.
My Heart Is in the East.
My Sweetheart's Dainty Lips.
Ode to Zion.
On Parting with Moses ibn Ezra.
Ophra.
Parted Lovers.
Pride of a Jew, The.
Sabbath, My Love.
Song of Loneliness.
Time-Servers.
To the Bridegroom.
To the Choice Bridegroom.
To the Western Wind.
To Zion.
Words Wherein Stinging Bees Lurk.
Haley, Molly Anderson
And Lo, the Star!
Architect, The.
Christmas Prayer, A.
Faithless Generation Asked a Sign, A.
"He Is Our Peace."
Intolerance.
Prayer for Christian Unity, A.
River of Grace, A.
Thy Blessing, Lord, on All Vacation Days!
We Have Seen His Star in the East.
"Haliburton, Hugh." *See* **Robertson, James Logie.**
Halkin, Schmuel
Drop of Dew, A.
Hall, Agnes Maxwell- *See* **Maxwell-Hall, Agnes**
Hall, Amanda Benjamin (Mrs. John Angell Brownell
I'll Build My House.
Joe Tinker.
Joy o' Living.
Too Soon the Lightest Feet.
Wanderer, The.
Woman of Words, A.
Hall, Carolyn
Child upon the Stair, The.
Fireflies.
Hall, Christopher Newman
My Times Are in Thy Hand.
Hall, Donald
Abroad Thoughts from Home.
Adventure with a Lady, An.
Airstrip in Essex, 1960, An.
Assassin, The.
Beautiful Horses, The.
Body Politic, The.
By the Exeter River.
Child, The.
Christ Church Meadows, Oxford.
Christmas Eve in Whitneyville, 1955.
Clown, The.
Detroit.
Exile.
Farm, The.
Five Epigrams.
Frontier, The.
Funeral, The.
In the Old House.
Je Suis une Table.
Jealous Lovers, The.
Kill, The.
Laocoon.
Long River, The.

Hall (continued)
Marriage.
Marriage: To K.
Morning Porches, The.
Munch's Scream.
My Son, My Executioner.
New Hampshire.
1934.
Old Pilot's Death, The.
Philander.
Second Stanza for Dr. Johnson, A.
Self-Portrait, as a Bear.
Sestina.
Shudder, The.
Six Poets in Search of a Lawyer.
Sleeping Giant, The.
Snow, The.
Three Movements, The.
Transcontinent.
Valentine.
Wells.
Wives, The.

Hall, Eugene J.
Engineer's Story, The.

Hall, Gertrude
Angels.
Dust, The.
Mrs. Golightly.
My Old Counselor.

Hall, Hazel
Admonition before Grief.
Any Woman.
Flight.
Footsteps.
Foreboding.
Here Comes the Thief.
Hunger.
Instruction.
June Night.
Late Winter.
Maker of Songs.
My Needle Says.
My Song.
On the Street.
One by One.
Slow Death.
Submergence.
Twilight.
Two Sewing.

Hall, Henry Clay
Who Does Not Love True Poetry.

Hall, J. C.
Crack, The.
Montgomery.
Responsibilities.
Telescope, The.
War.

Hall, James Norman
Eat and Walk.

Hall [*or* Halle], John (1529?-1566?)
Ditty of the Pen Inveighing against Usury and False Dealing, A.
Epicurean Ode, An.
Example of the Praise of God for His Omnipotency, An, out of the CXIII Psalm.
Song of the Lute in the Praise of God and Dispraise of Idolatry, A.

Hall, John (1627-56)
Farewell, farewell, poor joys, let not my hearse.
Look, how the daffodils arise.
This gapes for marriage, yet his fickle head.
What do I here! what's beauty? 'las.
What need I travel, since I may.
Call, The.
Lure, The, *sel.*
Morning Star, The.
Of Beauty, *sel.*
On an Hour-Glass [*or* Houre-Glasse].
Pastoral[l] Hymn[e], A: "Happy choristers of air."

To His Tutor.

Hall, John (b.1943)
Dark Shadows.

Hall, Joseph
Hence, ye profane; mell not with holy things.
Love-sicke Poet, The.
Olden Days, The.
Prologue: "I first adventure, with foolhardy might."
Satire VI: "Another scorns the homespun thread of rhymes."
Satire: "Gentle squire would gladly entertain, A."
Satire: "Great is the folly of a feeble brain."
Satire: "Great Osmond knows not how he shall be known."
Satire: "I wot not how the world's degenerate."
Satire I: "Nor lady's wanton love, nor wand'ring knight."
Satire should be like the porcupine, The.
Seest thou how gayly my young master goes.
Some say my satires over-loosely flow.
Too popular is tragic poesy.
Vergidemiarum.
Virgidemiarum, *sels.*
Whilom the sisters nine were vestal maids.
With some pot-fury, ravished from their wit.

Hall, Kay DeBard
Deer in Aspens.

Hall, Kirk
Illusions.
Impressions.
Song of Tom.
Wig.

Hall, Margaret S.
Life Is So Short.

Hall, Mary Lee
Turn Again to Life.

Hall, Rodney
Eyewitness.

Hall, Sharlot Mabridth
Arizona.
Last Camp-Fire, The.
Song of the Colorado, The.

Hall, Tim
Come Here, My Friends.

Hall-Stevenson, John
Black Bird, The.

Hallack, Cecily
Divine Office of the Kitchen, The.

Halladay, Grace Canfield
God's Ways and Mine.

Halladay, Mary Edith
Friendships.

Hallam, Arthur Henry
On the Picture of the Three Fates in the Palazzo Pitti, at Florence.
Written in Edinburgh.

Halle, John (1529?-1566?) *See* **Hall,John.**

Halleck, Fitz-Greene
Alnwick Castle.
Burns.
Fanny, *sel.*
Field of the Grounded Arms, The.
Joseph Rodman Drake.
Marco Bozzaris.
On His Friend, Joseph Rodman Drake.
On the Death of Joseph Rodman Drake.
Red Jacket.

Halleck, Fitz-Greene *and* Joseph Rodman Drake
Ode to Fortune.
Manho frets at Worldly Strife, The.
National Paintings, The.
Ode to Fortune.

Hallar, Soeran
Song of Denmark, *sel.*
This is the ironhard winter foretold.

Hallet, Mary
Calvary.
My Saviour.
Rhythm of His Life, The.

Halley, H. H.
Bible, The.

Hallock, Grace Taber
Comfortable Apple Trees, The.
Dog and the Cat, The.
Grasshopper Hop-o-the Grasses.
Mud Turtles.
Pleasant Cow, The.
Proud Toad, The.
Snakes and Snails.

Hall-Stevenson, John
Makarony Fables, *sel.*

Halpern, Moishe-Leib
Gingilee.
My Portrait.
Restless as a Wolf.
Who.

Halpine, Charles Graham
Baron Renfrew's Ball.
Feminine Arithmetic.
Irish Astronomy.
Janette's Hair.
Lecompton's Black Brigade.
Mr Johnson's Policy of Reconstruction.
Sambo's Right to be Kilt.
Song of Sherman's Army, The.
Song of the Soldier.

Halsham, John
My Last Terrier.

Ham, Marion Franklin
O Lord of Life, Thy Kingdom Is at Hand.
Prayer, A: "I pray not for the joy that knows."

Hambleton, Ronald
Comrades as We Rest Within.
Sockeye Salmon.
That Strain Again.

Hamburger, Michael
Blind Man.
Child Accepts, A.
Death of an Old Man, The.
Dual Site, The.
Epitaph for a Horseman.
Homage to the Weather.
In October.
Instead of a Journey.
Man of the World.
Mathematics of Love.
Omens.
Poet's Progress, A.
Security.
Song about Great Men, A.

Hamerton, Philip Gilbert
Sanyassi, The.
Wild Huntsmen, The.

Hamilton, Alfred Starr
Abroad.
Anything Remembered.
April Lights.
Bronze.
Didn't You Ever Search for Another Sun?
Guardian.
Liquid'll.
Moreso.
Psyche.
Town.
White Chimes.

Hamilton, Ann (Mrs. Daniel C. Sayre)
Chanson d'Or.
Inscription: "It is not hard to tell a rose."

Pause.
Hamilton, Anna E.
Christ's Giving.

Sympathy.
We Long to See Jesus.
Hamilton, Anne (1843-73)
Deserts.
Hamilton, Bobb
America.
Brother Harlem Bedford Watts Tells Mr. Charlie Where Its At.
Poem to a Nigger Cop.
Hamilton, Charles Granville
Contrast.
Hamilton, Clayton
Lines Written on November 15, 1933, by a Man Born November 14, 1881, to Another Born November 15, 1881.
Hamilton, David Osborne
To Men Unborn.
Hamilton, E. H.
Afraid? Of What?
Hamilton, Elizabeth
My Ain Fireside.
Hamilton, Eugene Lee- *See* **Lee-Hamilton, Eugene**
Hamilton, Florence
If a Man Die.
"Hamilton, Gail." *See* **Dodge, Mary Abigail.**
Hamilton George Rostrevor ("George Rostrevor")
Bodily Beauty.
Cell, The.
Choirs.
Does memory make you sad of heart?
Going to Sleep.
Hospital Ward (of this Generation).
Tears.
Three Cities.
Tree Purge.
Unknown Traveller, The.
Hamilton, Harold
School of Sorrow, The.
Hamilton, Harriet Eleanor *See* **King,Harriet Eleanor Hamilton**
Hamilton, Horace E.
Before Dawn.
Hamilton, John
Cold Blows the Wind.
Hamilton, Marion Ethel
Bird at Night.
Hamilton, Robert Browning
Along the Road.
Pleasure and Sorrow.
Hamilton, William, of Bongour
Braes of Yarrow, The.
Hamilton, Sir William Rowan
Prayer, A: "O brooding Spirit of Wisdom and of Love."
Hamlet, Frances Crosby
But When Ye Pray.
Our Flag.
Prayer: "Thou who didst multiply, by Galilee."
Hammarskjöld, Dag
Lord—Thine the Day.
Hammeiri, Avigdor
Hut, The.
Hammerstein, Oscar, II
If I Loved You.
It Might as Well Be Spring.
You've Got to Be Taught.
Hamminger, Graham Lee
Tobacco.
Hammitt, Deecort
Hail! South Dakota.
Hammon, Jupiter
Address to Miss Phillis Wheatley, An, *sel.*
Evening Thought, An.
O come you pious youth! adore.
Hammond, "Doc," and Scott Judy *See* **Judy, Scott, and "Doc" Hammond**
Hammond, Eleanor
April Fool.
From a Street Corner.
Honest Mr. Robin.
In September.
Lonely Wind.
Magic Window, The.
March.
Rain in April.
St. Patrick's Day.
Sleepy Maple Trees, The.
Valentine, A.
Hammond, James
Elegy: On Delia's Being in the Country.
Elegy: To Delia.
Love Elegies, *sels.*
Hammond, William
Cruel Mistress, The.
Husbandry.
Man's Life.
Rose, The.
Tell Me, O Love.
Hamori, Andras
For the Antigone.
Notes to the Life of Ovid.
Hampton, Christopher
Black and White Spring.
Old Woman in a Cage.
Hampton, Edgar Lloyd
Peace Call, The.
Hamsun, Knut
Tora's Song.
Hanby, Benjamin R.
Darling Nelly Gray.
Hancock, Carolyn
Ninety-nine.
Stars.
Hand, Q. R.
And I can remember still your first lies America.
I Wonder.
Handy, Mrs. M. P.
Only a Little Thing.
Handy, William Christopher
Hesitating Blues, The.
St. Louis Blues.
Hanes, Leigh
Chipmunk ("The chipmunk thinks I am a tree")
Deserts ("Deserts are more than shimmering heat and sand").
Moon Magic.
Old Fence Post.
Hankey, Donald
Lord of Us All.
Hankey, Katherine
I Love to Tell the Story.
Hankin, St. John Emile Clavering
Consolatory!
De Gustibus.
Editor's Tragedy, The.
Elegy on the Late King of Patagonia, An.
Hanmer, Lord John
Pine Woods, The.
Hanna, Edward Judson
Three Gifts.
Hanna, Thomas
Christmas, Ibiza, 1966.
Downtown Swan Thing, The.
I Make Fallout Too.
Leader, The.
Song of Casyor Brioschi, The.
Vietnam Turnpike.
Hannay, Patrick
Maid Me Loved, A.
Song: "Now do the birds in their warbling words."
Hanrahan, Agnes I.
Rosies.
Hansbrough, Mary Berri Chapman
Journey, The.
Hansen, Joseph
Dakota: Five Times Six.
Loved One, The.
Hansen-Bay, C.
Lord Christ, My Darling Is So Dear.
Hanson, Gertrude
Heart Is Bethlehem, The.
I Must Light a Candle.
This Holy Night.
Hanson, Joseph Mills
Laramie Trail.
Springfield Calibre Fifty, The.
Hanson, Kenneth O.
Before the Storm.
Take It from Me.
West Lake.
Hanson, Phyllis
Wisdom.
Han Wu
Descriptive Poem.
Harbaugh, Henry
Aloe Plant, The.
Harbaugh, T. C.
Trouble in the Amen Corner.
Harburg, E. Y.
Atheist.
Hard, Walter
Health Note, A.
Medical Aid.
Youth of the Mountain.
Harden, Verna Loveday
Post Mortem.
When This Tide Ebbs.
Hardenberg, George Friedrich Philipp von *See* **"Novalis"**
Harding, Ruth Guthrie
Call to a Scot, The.
Daffodils.
From a Car-Window.
On a Fly-Leaf of Schopenhauer's "Immortality."
Returning.
Surrender.
Threnody: "There's a grass-grown road from the valley."
Harding, Samuel
Of Death.
Sicily and Naples, *sel.*
Hardt, Ernst
Specter, The.
Hardy, Arthur Sherburne
Duality.
Immortality.
Iter Supremum.
Hardy, Elizabeth Clark
Some Time at Eve.
When I Sail Away.
Hardy, Elizabeth Stanton
Echo.
Sea Shell.
Hardy, Evelyn
Certainty.
Hardy, Jane L.
Lincoln.
Hardy, John Edward
Voyeur.
Hardy, Thomas
"According to the Mighty Working."
After a Journey.
After Jena.
After the Club-Dance.
After the Fair.
After the Visit.
Afterwards.
Ah, Are You Digging on My Grave?
Albuera.
Ancient to Ancients, An.
And if some day.

Hardy (continued)
"And There Was a Great Calm."
At a Country Fair.
At a Lunar Eclipse.
At a Watering-Place.
At an Inn.
At Casterbridge Fair.
At Castle Boterel.
At Madame Tussaud's in Victorian Years.
At Tea.
At the Alter-Rail.
At the Draper's.
At the Railway Station, Upway.
August Midnight, An.
Autumn in King's Hintock Park.
Ballad Singer, The.
Barthélémon at Vauxhall.
Beauty, The, *sel.*
Beauty's Soliloquy during Her Honeymoon, A.
Beeny Cliff.
Before Waterloo.
Beyond the Last Lamp.
Birds at Winter Nightfall.
Blinded Bird, The.
Boatman's Song, The.
Broken Appointment, A.
Budmouth Dears.
By Her Aunt's Grave.
By the Earth's Corpse.
Channel Firing.
Children and Sir Nameless, The.
Choirmaster's Burial, The.
Chorus: "Yea, the coneys are scared by the thud of hoofs."
Chorus of the Years.
Christmas Ghost Story, A.
Christmas: 1924.
Church-Builder, The.
Church Romance, A.
Clock-Winder, The.
Comet at Yell'ham, The.
Conformers, The.
Contretemps, The.
Convergence of the Twain, The; Lines on the Loss of the *Titanic.*
Curate's Kindness, The.
Curtains Now Are Drawn, The.
Dark-eyed Gentleman, The.
Darkling Thrush, The.
Dead and the Living One, The.
Dead Quire, The.
Departure.
Division, The.
Drizzling Easter Morning, A.
Drummer Hodge.
During Wind and Rain.
Dynasts, The, *sels.*
Embarcation.
End of the Episode, The.
Epitaph on a Pessimist.
Exeunt Omnes.
Faded Face, The.
Faintheart in a Railway Train.
Fallow Deer at the Lonely House, The.
Fiddler, The.
Field of Talavera, The.
Field of Waterloo, The.
First or Last.
First Sight of Her and After.
Five Students, The.
For Life I Had Never Cared Greatly.
Former Beauties.
Friends Beyond.
Garden Seat, The.
George Meredith.
God-forgotten.
God's Education.
God's Funeral.
Going, The.
Going and Staying.
Great Things.
Hap.
Harbour Bridge, The.
Haunter, The.
Haunting Fingers.
He Abjures Love.
He Fears His Good Fortune.
Heiress and Architect.
Her Apotheosis.
Her Death and After.
Her Dilemma.
Her Immortality.
Her Initials.
Heredity.
His Immortality.
House of Hospitalities, The.
How Great My Grief.
I Found Her Out There.
I hate my beauty in the glass.
I Look into My Glass.
I Looked Up from My Writing.
I Need Not Go.
I Said to Love.
I Say I'll Seek Her.
I Was the Midmost.
Impercipient, The.
In a Cathedral City.
In a Museum.
In a Wood.
In Church.
In Death Divided.
In Front of the Landscape.
In Tenebris.
In the Cemetery.
In the Days of Crinoline.
In the Evening.
In the Mind's Eye.
In the Moonlight.
In the Old Theater, Fiesole.
In the Restaurant.
In the Servants' Quarters.
In the Study.
In Time of "The Breaking of Nations."
Inquiry, The.
Intra Sepulchrum.
Jezreel.
Julie-Jane.
Lacking Sense, The.
Last Chrysanthemum, The.
Last Signal, The.
Last Words to a Dumb Friend.
Lausanne.
Let Me Enjoy ["Let me enjoy the earth no less").
Liddell and Scott; on the Completion of Their Lexicon.
Lines on the Loss of the *Titanic.*
Lines to a Movement in Mozart's E-Flat Symphony.
Man He Killed, The.
Man Was Drawing Near to Me, A.
Market-Girl, The.
Master and the Leaves, The.
Men Who March Away ("We be the King's men").
Men Who March Away ("What of the faith and fire within us").
Midnight on the Great Western.
Milkmaid, The.
Missed Train, The.
Musing Maiden, The.
Mute Opinion.
My Spirit Will Not Haunt the Mound.
Nature's Questioning.
Near Lanivet, 1872.
Neutral Tones.
New Year's Eve.
Newcomer's Wife, The.
Night of the Dance, The.
Night of Trafalgar, The.
1967.
No Buyers; a Street Scene.
Nobody Comes.
O I Won't Lead a Homely Life.
Old Furniture.
On a Midsummer['s] Eve.
On an Invitation to the United States.
On His 86th Birthday.
On Sturminster Foot-Bridge.
On the Departure Platform.
On the Doorstep.
On the Portrait of a Woman about to Be Hanged.
Overworld, The.
Oxen, The.
Pedigree, The.
Phantom Horsewoman, The.
Pity of It, The.
Placid Man's Epitaph, A.
Poet, A.
Postponement.
Prospect, The.
Proud Songsters.
Puzzled Game-Birds, The.
Rain on a Grave.
Refusal, A.
Regret Not Me.
Rejected Member's Wife, The.
Reminder, The.
Reminiscences of a Dancing Man.
Respectable Burgher, The.
Roman Road, The.
Rome.
Ruined Maid, The.
Sacrilege, The.
Satin Shoes, The.
Satire of Circumstance, A ("I stood at the back of the shop. . .").
Satires of Circumstance, I-XV.
Second Attempt, A.
Self-unseeing, The.
Selfsame Song, The.
Seventy-four and Twenty.
Shadow on the Stone, The.
She Hears the Storm.
She, to Him.
Shelley's Skylark.
Shiver, The.
Shut Out That Moon.
Singer Asleep, A.
Snow in the Suburbs.
Song of Hope.
Souls of the Slain, The.
Statue of Liberty, The.
Stranger's Song, The.
Subalterns, The.
Superseded, The.
Surview.
Tess's Lament.
Thought in Two Moods, A.
Thunderstorm in Town, A.
To a Lady Playing and Singing in the Morning.
To an Unborn Pauper Child.
To-be-forgotten, The.
To Life.
To Lizbie Browne.
To Meet, or Otherwise.
To the Moon.
Tolerance.
Trafalgar.
Trampwoman's Tragedy, A.
Transformations.
Tree and the Lady, The.
Two Houses, The.
Unborn, The.
Under the Waterfall.
Unkept Good Fridays.
Voice, The.
Wagtail and Baby.
Waiting Both.
Walk, The.

Weather.
Weathers.
Well-beloved, The.
Wessex Heights.
When I Set Out for Lyonnesse.
Where the Picnic Was.
While the far farewell music thins and falls.
Who's in the Next Room?
Wife Waits, A.
Wind Blew Words, The.
Winter in Durnover Field.
Wives in the Sere.
Woman I Met, The.
Woodlanders, The, *sel.*
Workbox, The.
Year's Awakening, The.
Yell'ham-Wood's Story.
Young Glass-Stainer, The.
Young Man's Epigram on Existence, A.
Young Man's Exhortation, A.
Your Last Drive.
Zermatt: To the Matterhorn.

Hare, Amory
Life.
Walking at Night.
Wet or Fine.

Hare, Maurice Evan
Byway in Biography.
Limerick: "There once was a man [*or* was a young man] who said: 'Damn!'"
Limerick: "There was a young man who said, 'Damn!'"

Hare, R.
Lonely?—Tired?—Afraid?

Haresnape, Geoffrey
African Tramp, The.

Harford, Lesbia
Beauty and Terror.
Day's End.
Experience.
He Had Served Eighty Masters.
I Have Golden Shoes.
Lovers Parted.
Revolution.
This Way Only.

Haring, Phyllis
Earth Asks and Receives Rain, The.
Foetus.
Forbidden, The.
Jungle.
Overture to Strangers.
Twin.

Harington [*or* Harrington], Henry
Song: "Trust the form of airy things."
Trust the Form of Airy Things.

Harington John (fl. 1550)
Comparison of Life and Death.
Elegy Wrote in the Tower, 1554.
Lines on Isabella Markham.
Sonnet Made on Isabella Markham, A.

Harington, Sir John (1561-1612)
Against an Atheist.
Against an Extreme Flatterer That Preached at Bath on the Queen's Day the Fortieth Year of Her Reign.
Against Feasting.
Against Paulus.
Against Writers That Carp at Other Men's Books.
Author to a Daughter of Nine Years Old, The.
Author to His Wife, of a Woman's Eloquence, The.
Author to Queen Elizabeth, in Praise of Her Reading, The.
Comfort for Poor Poets, A.
Comparison of the Sonnet and the Epigram.
Critics.
Critics and Cooks.
Epigram: "Readers and the hearers like my books, The."
Epigram: "Treason doth never prosper."
Epitaph in Commendation of George Turberville, a Learned Gentleman, An.
Fair, Rich, and Young.
Gratulatory Elegy of the Peaceable Entry of King James, A.
Health Counsel.
In Roman.
Lesbia's Rule of Praise.
Misacmos, of Himself, Who Loves to Be Worst in the Company.
Of a Certain [*or* Certaine] Man.
Of a Fair Shrew.
Of a Precise Tailor.
Of an Heroical Answer of a Great Roman Lady to Her Husband.
Of Cinna's Election.
Of Clergymen and Their Livings.
Of Don Pedro and His Poetry.
Of Enclosing a Common.
Of Faustus, a Stealer of Verses.
Of Friendship.
Of Galla's Goodly Periwig.
Of Good Sauce.
Of His Muse.
Of Honest Theft. To My Good Friend Master Samuel Daniel.
Of Lynus, Borrowing.
Of Summum Bonum.
Of the Pillars of the Church.
Of Treason.
Of Two Religions.
On Treason.
Rule to Play, A.
To James the VI, King of Scotland.
To Master Bastard, a Minister That Made a Pleasant Book of English Epigrams.
To Master Bastard, Taxing Him of Flattery.
To Master John Davies.
To Mr. John Davies.
To Sextus, an Ill Reader.
To the Lady Rogers, of Her Unprofitable Sparing.
Treason.

Harkness, Georgia
Agony of God, The.
For God So Loved the World.
Simon of Cyrene.
Swinging toward the Light.
Understanding Heart, The.

Harlow, S. Ralph
Church Triumphant.
O Young and Fearless Prophet.
Who Is So Low.

Harman, Elizabeth
Soldier's Dirge. A.

Harmon, William
Animals of the forest and plants of the field are friends.
Now/ poem and month.
Past all calculation and belief it came so huge.
Poem/ is/ word/ list.
Poor Ed Sanders: no sooner had he gotten in good.
So let the month end: the new fiscal year.
Treasury Holiday, *sels.*

Harney, W. E.
West of Alice.

Harney, Will Wallace
Adonais.
Stab, The.

Harper, Frances E. W.
Let the Light Enter.
Slave Auction, The.

Harpur, Charles
Aboriginal Mother's Lament, An.
But hark! What hubbub now is this that comes.
Creek of the Four Graves, The, *sel.*
Love Sonnets, VIII.
Midsummer['s] Noon in the Australian Forest, A.
Regret, A.
Settler in the olden times went forth, A.
Similitude, A.
Sonnet: "She loves me! From her own bliss-breathing lips."
Temple of Infamy, The, *sel.*
Tower of the Dream, The, *sel.*
Words.
Yes, wonderful are dreams: and I have known.

"Harriet Annie. "
Death of Gaudentis.

Harrigan, Edward
My Dad's Dinner Pail.

Harriman, Dorothy
Cat on the Porch at Dusk.

Harrington, Edward
Bushrangers, The.

Harrington, Henry *See* **Harington, Henry**

Harrington, John (fl. 1550) *See* **Harington, John**

Harrington, Sir John (1561-1612) *See*- **Harington, Sir John**

Harris, June Brown
Home.

Harris, Louise Dyer
Crossing Boston Common.
Review of a Cook Book.

Harris, Marguerite
My Sun-killed Tree.

Harris, Max
Lullaby: "Girl with eyes like dying flowers."
Mad Jasper.
Martin Buber in the Pub.
Plowman, The.
Tantanoola Tiger, The.

Harris, Norman
Fable: "There is an inevitability."

Harris, Phyllis
Furniture.
Mandylion.
Outside.
Source, The.
Under Your Voice, among Legends.
Whatever Edens.

Harris, Thomas Lake
California.
Fledglings.
God Speaks in All Religions.
Sea-Sleep.

Harris, William J.
Frightened Flower.
Historic Moment, An.
On Wearing Ears.
Truth Is Quite Messy, The.

Harrison, Eugene M.
Soul Winner's Prayer, The.

Harrison, Florence
Faerie Fair, The.
Summer Day, A.

Harrison, Henry Sydnor
Osculation.

Harrison, Jim
Cardinal.
Cold August.
Horse.
Morning.
Night in Boston.
War Suite.

Harrison, Susan Frances
At St. Jerome.
Château Papineau.
September.

Harrison, Sam
After the Show.
Chez Madame.
Journey.
Meeting.
Poem: "This room is very old and very wise."
Rain.
Harrison, T.
Shade.
Harrison, Tony
Bedbug, The.
Harrison, Virginia Bioren
Music of the Dawn.
One Gift I Ask.
Harrod, Elizabeth B.
August Night, 1953.
Calvinist Autumnal.
Sonnet against the Too-facile Mystic.
Summer Afternoon.
"Harry. "
Feet.
"Harry, Blind." *See* **Henry the Minstrel**
Harsen, Una W.
Litany for Old Age, A.
Prayer before Meat.
Sacrament.
To Mary, Mother of Christ.
Hart, Elizabeth Anna
Mother Tabbyskins.
Old Mother Tabbyskins.
Sweeping the Skies.
Hart, Joseph
Pray with Faith.
Hart, Richard
Inhibited Persian, An.
Mother with Young Kittens, A.
Hart-Smith, William
Baiamai's Never-failing Stream.
Bathymeter.
Christopher Columbus, *sels.*
Cipangu.
Columbus Goes West.
Comes Fog and Mist.
Departure.
Drama.
Holding-Paddock.
La Perouse.
Shag Rookery.
Shepherd and the Hawk, The.
Space.
Tractor.
Waterspout, The.
When You Touch.
Harte, Bret (Francis Bret Harte)
Aged Stranger, The.
Arctic Vision, An.
At the Hacienda.
Ballad of the Emeu, The.
Caldwell of Springfield.
Chicago.
Chiquita.
Crotalus.
Dickens in Camp.
Dow's Flat—1856.
Flynn of Virginia.
Ghost That Jim Saw, The.
Greyport Legend.
Grizzly.
Guild's Signal.
Heathen Chinee, The.
Her Letter.
"How Are You, Sanitary?"
Jessie.
Jim.
John Burns of Gettysburg.
Madroñ.
Mrs. Judge Jenkins, *parody.*
Mountain Heart's-Ease, The.
Personified Sentimental, The.
Plain Language from Truthful James.
Plain Talk from Truthful James.
Ramon.
Relieving Guard.
Return of Belisarius, The; Mud Flat, 1860.
Reveille, The.
Second Review of the Grand Army, A.
Serenade: "I'm a gay tra, la, la."
Society upon the Stanislaus [*or* Stanislow], The.
Spelling Bee at Angels, The.
Swiss Air.
To a Sea-Bird.
To the Pliocene Skull.
Truthful James.
Two Ships, The.
What the Bullet Sang.
What the Chimney Sang.
Willows, The, *parody.*
Harte, Walter
To Mr. Pope.
Hartigan, Patrick Joseph ("John O'Brien")
Said Hanrahan.
Tangmalangaloo.
Hartley, John
To a Daisy.
Hartley, Marsden
Confidence.
Crucifixion of Noel, The.
In Robin Hood Cove.
V Is for Victory, as You Can Plainly See.
Warblers.
Hartman, Helen M.
Moving Day.
Hartman, Mary R.
Life's Made Up of Little Things.
Hartmann von Aue
None Is Happy.
Scales of Love, The.
Hartnoll, Phyllis
Carpenter, The.
Hartswick, F. G.
Somewhere-in-Europe-Wocky.
Hartswick, Jennie Betts
To St. Valentine.
Hartwich, Ethelyn M.
What Shall Endure?
Harumi
Winter Shower, A.
Harvey, Alexander
With Me in Paradise.
Harvey, Christopher
Comfort in Extremity.
Harvey, Frederick William
Prisoners.
Sleepers, The.
When God had finished the stars and whirl of coloured suns.
Yes, ducks are valiant things.
Harvey, Gabriel
Due Commendation of the Quipping Autor, A.
Four Letters and Certain Sonnets, *sel.*
Greene's Memorial; or, Certain Funeral Sonnets, *sels.*
His Admonition to Greene's Companions.
His Apology of His Good Father.
Harvey, J. E.
Forgetting God.
Harwood, Gwen
Last Meeting.
Panther and Peacock.
Prizegiving.
Harwood, Ruth
Shoe Factory, The.
"Hashimura Togo." *See* **Irwin, Wallace**
Hashin
Loneliness.
No Sky at All.
Haskell, J.
Christian's Victory—Triumph.
Haskin, Leslie L.
Christ the Carpenter.
Haskins, Minnie Louise
Gate of the Year, The, *sel.*
Hasley, Louis
On Her Twenty-fifth Birthday.
Hasluck, Paul
Drunken Man on Highgate Hill, A.
Hass, Robert
Adhesive: for Earlene.
Black Mountain, Los Altos.
Book Buying in the Tenderloin.
Letter to a Poet.
On the Coast near Sausalito.
Hassall, Christopher Vernon
I heard a voice say "Look into your heart."
No Clock with Numbered Eyes.
Soliloquy to Imogen, *sels.*
Symphony.
. . . We danced/ Shyly, not speaking, more as partial friends.
Haste, Gwendolen
Montana Wives.
Tomorrow Is a Birthday.
Hastings, Fanny de Groot
Late Comer.
Hastings, Lady Flora
Prayers.
To a Butterfly.
Hastings, Maria
Sing Little Bird.
Hastings, Lady T.
"Exactly So."
Hastings, Thomas
Exhortation.
In Sorrow.
Latter Day, The.
Hatch, Edwin
Breathe on Me, Breath of God.
Heaven.
Hatch, Francis Whiting
He Laughed Last.
So This Is Middle Age!
Hathaway, William
Attic.
Card Burning in Central Park.
Conspiracy in Iowa.
Crazy Lady, The.
Hermit Advises a Monk When Things Are Bleak Indeed, A.
Rod Slemmon's Dream.
Trumansburg Fair.
When Beulah Did the Hula in Missoula.
Hatton, Sir R.
You that have been this evenings light.
Hauer, Elizabeth N.
Vision.
Hausgen, Mattie Lee
Her Choice.
Her Favorites.
Lovely Bed, A.
Spider Web, The.
Hausted, Peter
Have Pity, Grief.
Of His Mistress.
Rival Friends, The, *sels.*
Song, The: "Have pity (Grief) I can not pay."
Havens, Mrs.
Ask, and Ye Shall Receive.
Haver, Harvey E.
Quiet Hour, The.
Havergal, Frances Ridley
Afterwards.
Another Year.
Another Year Is Dawning.
At the Portal.
Be Quiet; Fear Not.

Behold Your King!
Bells across the Snow.
Chosen Lessons.
Confidence.
Crown the Year.
Daily Strength.
Easter Prayer.
Enough for Me.
For Easter.
For Every Day.
Gave My Life for Thee.
God Is Faithful.
Happy Christmas, A.
Hidden in Light.
Hush!
I Am Trusting Thee.
I Gave My Life for Thee.
Life-Mosaic.
Lord, Speak to Me, that I May Speak.
New Things.
New Year Wish, A.
New Year's Wishes.
Now I See.
Peace.
Perfect Peace.
Prayer, A: "Lord, in mercy pardon me."
Reality.
Rest on Him.
Secret of a Happy Day, The.
Take My Life.
Teacher's Prayer, A.
Thou Art Coming!
Thy Presence.
Unchanging One, The.
Unfailing One, The.
Upon Thy Word.
Use Even Me.
Wait Patiently for Him.
Who Is on the Lord's Side?
"Whose I Am."
Haweis, Hugh Reginald
Homeland, The.
Haweis, Thomas
Come and Welcome.
Remember Me!
Hawes, Stephen
And as Dame Fame was in laudation.
"And forasmuch that he made Nature."
And in meanewhyle the gentyll porteres.
Dame Music.
Epitaph: "O mortal folk, you may behold and see."
Epitaph of Graunde Amoure, The.
Excusation of the Auctor, The.
Here Beginneth the Pastime of Pleasure.
His Epitaph.
How Grand Amour Walked in a Meadow and Met with Fame Environed with Tongues of Fire.
Of the Great Marriage between Grand Amour and La Belle Pucelle.
Pair of Wings, A.
Pastime [*or* Passetyme] of Pleasure, The, *sels.*
Seven Deadly Sins, The.
Than forth I went into a meadow green.
Time and Eternity.
True Knight, The.
Hawker, Robert Stephen
Aishah Schechinah.
Are They Not All Ministering Spirits?
Aunt Mary; a Christmas Chant.
Christ-Cross Rhyme, A.
Datur Hora Quieti.
Death Song.
Featherstone's Doom.
First Fathers, The.
"I Am the Resurrection and the Life," Saith the Lord!
King Arthur's Waes-hael.
Mawgan of Melhuach.
Morwennae Statio.
Mystic Magi, The.
"Pater Vester Pascit Illa."
Queen Guennivar's Round.
Silent Tower of Bottreau[x], The.
Song of the Western Men, The.
Southern Cross, The.
To Alfred Tennyson.
Trelawny.
Hawkes, Clarence
Mountain to the Pine, The.
Hawkes, Henry Warburton
Amid the Din of Earthly Strife.
"Thy Kingdom Come!" O Lord.
Hawkes, William
Christmas Still Lives.
Hawkins, Henry
Bee, The.
Hoc Cygno Vinces.
Hawkins, Lucy
To L. C.
Hawkins, William
New Light, A.
Spring Rain.
Wall, The.
Hawkshaw Ann [*or* Anne] ("Aunt Effie")
Chorus of Frogs, The.
Clocking Hen, The.
Clucking Hen, The.
Common Things.
Dame Duck's First Lecture on Education.
Freddie [*or* Freddy] and the Cherry Tree ("Freddie saw some fine [*or* nice] ripe cherries").
Glow-Worms, The.
Great Brown Owl, The.
I'll Try.
Moonlight, The.
Mother Duck.
Muffin-Man's Bell, The.
Old Kitchen Clock, The.
Pussy-Cat.
Robin Redbreasts, The.
Water Mill, The.
Waves on the Sea-Shore, The.
Young Linnets, The.
Hawley, Charles B.
My Little Love.
Hawley, W. F.
Love Song, A.
Hawling, Mary S.
Futility.
Return.
"Hawthorne, Alice." *See* **Winner, Septimus**
Hawthorne, Hildegarde
My Rose.
Song, A: "Sing me a sweet, low song of night."
Hawthorne, Julian
Were-Wolf.
Hawthorne, Nathaniel
Star of Calvary, The.
Hawthorne, Rose *See* **Lathrop, Rose Hawthorne**
Hay, Clarence Leonard
Down and Out.
"Hay, Elijah." *See* **Seiffert, Marjorie Allen**
Hay, George Campbell
Flooer o the Gean.
Smoky Smirr o' Rain, The.
Song: "Day will rise and the sun from eastward."
Sonnet: "Beckie, my luve!—What is't, ye twa-faced tod?"
Two Neighbours, The.
Hay, Helen *See* **Whitney, Helen Hay**
Hay John (1838-1905)
Banty Tim.
Christine.
Distichs.
Enchanted Shirt, The.
Good and Bad Luck.
Jim Bludso [of the *Prairie Belle*].
Liberty.
Little Breeches.
Miles Keogh's Horse.
Not in Dumb Resignation.
Religion and Doctrine.
Stirrup-Cup, The.
Surrender of Spain, The.
Thy Will Be Done.
White Flag, The.
Woman's Love, A.
Hay, John (1915-)
Aboriginal Sin.
And Grow.
Bird Song.
Chickadees, The.
December Storm.
Energy of Light, The.
Life Must Burn.
Natural Architecture.
Old Man of Tennessee.
Railway Station.
Sent Ahead.
Silver Leaf, The.
Town Meeting.
Variations on a Theme.
Wood Frog, The.
Hay, Sara Henderson
Ballad of the Golden Bowl.
"Bottle Should Be Plainly Labeled 'Poison'."
Christmas, the Year One, A.D.
Daily Manna, The.
Daily Paradox.
Entrance into Heaven.
Father, The.
For a Dead Kitten.
Incident with Lions.
Love Suffereth Long.
Man Named Legion, The.
On Being Told That One's Ideas Are Victorian.
Pigeon English.
Portrait of a Certain Gentleman.
Prayer in April.
Prodigal, The.
Reflections on an Ideal Existence.
Search, The.
Shape God Wears, The.
Summer Evening.
Upon Discovering One's Own Intolerance.
Warning.
Hay, Sara Henderson, *and* Raymond Holden
Detour—Gypsy Trail Closed.
Hayden, Joe
Hot Time in the Old Town, A.
Hayden, Robert Earl
Approximations.
Ballad of Nat Turner, The.
Ballad of Remembrance, A.
Ballad of Sue Ellen Westerfield, The.
Diver, The.
Eine Kleine Nachtmusik.
Frederick Douglass.
Full Moon.
Homage to the Empress of the Blues.
Incense of the Lucky Virgin.
Kid.
Letter from the South.
Middle Passage.
Mourning Poem for the Queen of Sunday.
O Daedalus, Fly away Home.
Photograph of Isadora Duncan, A.
Runagate Runagate.
Sub Specie Aeternitatis.

Hayden (continued)
"Summertime and the Living."
Those Winter Sundays.
Veracruz.
Whipping, The.
Witch Doctor.

Hayes, Alfred
Angel, The.
City of Beggars, The.
Death of the Craneman, The.
Epistle to the Gentiles.
Imitation of Faust, The.
Nice Part of Town, A.
Slaughter-House, The.

Hayes, Donald Jeffrey
After All.
Alien.
Appoggiatura.
Auf Wiedersehen.
Benediction.
Haven.
Inscription: "He wrote upon his heart."
Night.
Nocturne: "Softly blow lightly."
Pastourelle.
Poet.
Prescience.
Threnody: "Let happy throats be mute."

Hayes, Ednah Proctor Clarke *See* **Clarke, Ednah Proctor**

"Hayes, Evelyn." *See* **Bethell, Mary Ursula.**

Hayes, J. Milton
Green Eye of the Yellow God, The.

Hayes, James M.
Mother of the Rose, The.
Old Nuns.
Our Lady of the Skies.
Transfiguration, The.

Hayes, John Russell
Old-fashioned Garden, The.

Hayes, Nancy M.
At Night in the Wood.
Night in the Wood, A.
Shiny Little House, The.

Hayford, Gladys May Casely (Aquah Laluah)
Baby Cobina.
Nativity.
Rainy Season Love Song.
Serving Girl, The.
Shadow of Darkness.
Souls of Black and White, The.

Hayford, James
Horn.
In a Closed Universe.
Overseer of the Poor.
Resident Worm, The.
Under All This Slate.

Hayley, William
Card of Invitation to Mr. Gibbon, at Brighthelmstone, A.
To Mr. William Long, on his Recovery from a Dangerous Illness.
To Mrs. Smith, Occasioned by the First of Her Sonnets.

Hayman, Jane
Murdered Girl Is Found on a Bridge, The.

Hayman, Robert
Of the Great and Famous [Ever-to-Be-Honored Knight, Sir Francis Drake].

Hayne, Paul Hamilton
Aspects of the Pines.
Battle of Charleston Harbor, The.
Between the Sunken Sun and the New Moon.
Beyond the Potomac.
Bryant Dead.
Butler's Proclamation.
Charleston (February, 1865).
In Harbor.
Little While I Fain Would Linger Yet, A ("A little while, my life is almost set!").

Mocking-Bird, The.
My Study.
Pre-Existence.
Rose and the Thorn, The.
South Carolina to the States of the North.
Storm in the Distance, A.
Stricken South to the North, The.
To O. W. Holmes.
True Heaven, The.
Vicksburg—a Ballad.
Yorktown Centennial Lyric.

Hayne, William Hamilton
Charge at Santiago, The.
Cyclone at Sea, A.
Exiles.
Moonlight Song of the Mocking-Bird.
Night Mists.
Oliver Wendell Holmes.
Pine Needles, *sel.*
Sea Lyric, A.
Sewing.
"Sleep and His Brother Death."
Southern Snow-Bird, The.
To a Cherokee Rose.
Yule Log, The.

Haynes, Albert E., Jr
Eclipse.
Law, The.

Haynes, Carol
Any Husband or Wife.
Any Wife or Husband.
Aunt Selina.

Haynes, Renée
Ingenious Raconteur.

Hays, Will S.
O'Grady's Goat ("O'Grady lived in Shanty row").

Hayward, William
Five Birds Rise.

Haywood, Carolyn
Little Clown Puppet.

Hazard, Caroline
Great Swamp Fight, The.
In Shadow.
Ninth Hour, The.
Out of Egypt Have I Called My Son.
Wilderness, The.

Hazard, Grace Walcott *See* **Conkling,Grace Hazard**

Hazeltine, Alice Isabel
Child at a Crèche, A.
Christmas Night.

Hazo, Samuel
Challenge.
God and Man.
Opposition, The.
Siesta.
To a Commencement of Scoundrels.

Hazzard, John Edward
Ain't It Awful, Mabel?

Head, Theresa Gamble
This Day That's Mine.

Healey, Evelyn H.
Journey's End.

Healy, Howard
Roethke.

Healy, Ian
Advice from a Nightwatchman.
Air Shaft.
Poems from the Coalfields.

Healy, Patrick
My Wishes.

Heaney, Seamus
Blackberry-Picking.
Digging.
Saint Francis and the Birds.
Turkeys Observed.
Twice Shy.

Heard, Lillian G.
Humble Service.

Hearn, L. M.
I Have Found It!

Hearn, Mary Anne *See* **"Farningm, Marianne"**

Hearst, James S.
Voices.

Heath,——
These Women All.
Women.

Heath, Ella
Poetry.

Heath, John
Ad Collegium Wintoniensem.
Ad Modernos Epigrammatistas.
Ad Tho. Bastardum Epigrammatistam.
Ad Zoilum.
De Gelu Diutino, Anno Dom. 1607.
Health is a jewel, true; which when we buy.
In Ariostum Orlandi Furiosi Autorem.
In Beatricem Praepropere Defunctam ("In Beatrice did all perfections grow").
In Porcum.
In Senecam.
Parson having a tithe pig or two, A.
Those which have travelled o'er the earth's round ball.
Volucre Ferrum.

Heath, Robert
Clarastella Distrusting.
Excuse, The.
On Clarastella Singing.
On Clarastella Walking in Her Garden.
On the Unusual Cold and Rainie Weather in the Summer, 1648.
Seeing Her Dancing.
Song in a Siege.
To Clarastella on St. Valentines Day Morning.

Heath-Stubbs, John
Address Not Known.
Beggar's Serenade.
Canticle of the Sun Dancing on Easter Morning.
Care in Heaven.
Charm against the Toothache, A.
Churchyard of St. Mary Magdalene, Old Milton.
Death of Digenes Akritas, The.
Don Juan Muses.
Epitaph: "Mr. Heath-Stubbs as you must understand."
For the Nativity.
From an Ecclesiastical Chronicle.
Ghost in the Cellarage, The.
History of the Flood, The.
Homage to J. S. Bach.
Ibycus.
Lady's Complaint, The.
Maria Aegyptiaca.
Mermaid at Zennor, The.
Old King, The.
Poet of Bray, The.
Prayer to St. Lucy.
Saint Cecilia.
Sonata by Scarlatti, A.
Starling, The ("The Starling is my darling, although").
"Through the Dear Might of Him That Walked the Waves."
Titus and Berenice.
Two Men in Armour.
Virgin and Unicorn.
Watching Tennis.

Heaton, John Langdon
Sea Irony.

Heavysege, Charles
Count Filippo, *sels.*

David Exorcising Malzah, the Evil Spirit from the Lord.
Flight of Malzah, The.
How Great unto the Living Seem the Dead!
Jephthah's Daughter, *sel.*
Malzah and the Angel Zelehtha.
Malzah's Song.
Night.
Now let the drums roll muffled; let the bells'.
Oh, think how hard it is to die when young!
Saul, *sels.*
Song: "Who is lord of lordly fate."
Stars Are Glittering in the Frosty Sky, The.
To hunt and to be hunted make existence.
Twilight.
What now? Thou look'st surprised.
Winter Galaxy, The.
Winter Night.
Zaph Describes the Haunts of Malzah.

Hebbel, Friedrich
Tree in the Desert, The.

Hebblethwaite, James
Perdita.
Symbol, The.
Wanderers.

Heber, Reginald
Bread of the World.
Brightest and Best of the Sons of the Morning.
By Cool Siloam's Shady Rill.
Epiphany.
From Greenland's Icy Mountains.
Holy, Holy, Holy.
Hymn: "Brightest and best of the sons of the morning."
If Thou Wert by My Side, My Love.
Judgment Is Near, The.
Lo, the Lilies of the Field.
Providence.
Son of God Goes Forth to War, The.
Sympathy.
Thrice Holy.
Vespers.
Who Follows in His Train?

Hébert, Anne
Someone Could Certainly Be Found.

Hecht, Anthony
Adam.
Behold the Lilies of the Field.
Birdwatchers of America.
Clair de Lune.
Divination by a Cat.
Dover Bitch, The.
Drinking Song.
End of the Weekend, The.
Firmness.
Gift of Song, The.
Hill, A.
"It Out-Herods Herod, Pray You Avoid It."
Japan.
Jason.
La Condition Botanique.
Letter, A.
Lizards and Snakes.
Man Who Married Magdalene, The: Variation on a Theme by Louis Simpson.
"More Light! More Light!"
Origin of Centaurs, The.
Ostia Antica.
Place of Pain in the Universe, The.
Samuel Sewall.
Song of the Beasts, The.
Tarantula or the Dance of Death.
Third Avenue in Sunlight.
Upon the Death of George Santayana.
Vow, The.

Hector, Mary Louise
Whatsoever I Do.

Hedge, Frederic Henry
Questionings.

Hedge, T. H.
Via Crucis, Via Lucis.

Hedges, Doris
Onwardness.
Poet's Protest.
Prayer: "O God of Goodness, Forwardness, and Fulness."

Hedrick, Addie M.
Two Crosses.

Hedylos
Girl Betrayed.
Seduced Girl.
To Venus.

Heermans, Mary A.
Arbor Day Song.

Heffernan the Blind, William
Welcome to the Prince of Ossory.

Heidenstam, Verner von
Fellow-Citizens.
Home.
How Easily Men's Cheeks are Hot with Wrath!

Hein, Piet
Cure for Exhaustion, The.
Lest Fools Should Fail.
Lilac Time.
Literary Gruk.
Mankind.
Miracle of Spring, The.
Road to Wisdom, The.

Heine, Heinrich
Ad Finem.
And When I Lamented.
Anno 1829.
Ashes.
Auf meiner Herzliebsten Äugelein.
Azra, The.
Beating Heart, The.
Belshazzar.
Best Religion, The.
Blauen Veilchen der Äugelein, Die.
Brief, den du geschrieben, Der.
By the Waters of Babylon.
Choir Boys, The.
Coffin, The.
Come, O Friend, to Greet the Bride.
Dear Maiden.
Dearest Friend, Thou Art in Love.
Du bist wie eine Blume.
Du schönes Fischer-Mädchen.
Enfant perdu.
Epilog: "Like the ears of the wheat."
Epilogue: "Like the stalks of wheat in the fields."
Es fällt ein Stern herunter.
Es stehen unbeweglich.
Evening Twilight.
Exile.
Farewell: "Linden blossomed, the nightingale sang, The."
Fichtenbaum steht einsam, Ein.
Firelight.
Fisher-Maiden, The.
Forlornly.
Fresco-Sonnets to Christian Sethe.
Fürchte Nichts, geliebte Seele.
Give me a mask, I'll join the masquerade.
Good Fortune.
Grenadiers, The.
Healing the Wound.
Hebrew Melodies, *sels.*
Heimkehr, Die, *sels.*
Homeward Bound, *sels.*
I, a Most Wretched Atlas.
I Close Her Eyes.
I laugh at each dull bore, taste's parasite.
I Love but Thee.
I Met by Chance.
I Wept as I Lay Dreaming.
Ich Weiss Nicht, Was Soll es Bedeuten.
"If, Jerusalem, I Ever Should Forget Thee."
I'm Black and Blue.
Im Traum sah ich ein Männchen klein und putzig.
Katharine.
King David.
Kings from the East, The.
Knight Olaf.
Lassie, What Mair Wad You Hae?
Lorelei [*or* Loreley], The.
Lost Child.
Lotosblume ängstigt, Die.
Lotus-Flower, The.
Love Dead.
Love's Résumé.
Mädchen mit dem rothen Mündchen.
Madonna, A.
Maiden Lies in Her Chamber, A.
Meeting, A.
Mein Herz, mein Herz ist traurig.
Mein Kind, wir waren Kinder.
Mein Liebchen, wir sassen zusammen.
Mermaidens, The.
Message, The.
Mir träumte von einem Königskind.
Mir träumte wieder der alte Traum.
Mond ist aufgegangen, Der.
Morning After, The.
Mortal, Sneer Not at the Devil.
My Heart, My Heart Is Mournful.
My Songs Are Poisoned!
New Jewish Hospital at Hamburg, The.
Night by the Sea, A.
Night on the Shore.
North Sea, The, *sels.*
Oh Lovely Fishermaiden.
Philosophy.
Picture, The.
Pine Tree, The.
Prayer, A: "My darling, thou art flowerlike."
Precaution.
Princess Sabbath.
Proem: "Out of my own great woe."
Quiet Night, The.
Religion.
Rose, die Lilie, die Taube, die Sonne, Die.
Sag' mir wer einst die Uhren erfund.
Sag', wo ist dein schönes Liebchen.
Sea Hath Its Pearls, The.
Shadow-Love.
Shepherd Boy, The.
Solomon.
Song: "There stands a lonely pine-tree."
Song of Songs, The.
Song of the Vivandiere.
Songs to Seraphine, *sel.*
Sonnet to a Cat.
Sonnet to My Mother, A.
Stars Look at Love, The.
Storm, The.
Superfluous Bite.
Suspicious Sweetheart.
Tannhäuser, *sel.*
Tell me where thy lovely love is.
Tendency, The.
They gave me advice and counsel in store.
This delightful young man.
This Mad Carnival of Loving.
This White and Slender Body.
Thou Hast Diamonds.
Thou Seemest like a Flower.
Three Sweethearts.
To Angélique, *sel.*
To Edom.
To His Mother.

Heine (continued)
To My Mother.
Twilight.
Two Songs.
Voyage, The.
Warning, A.
Warum sind denn die Rosen so blass.
Waves Gleam in the Sunshine, The.
We Cared for Each Other.
Weavers, The.
Welt ist dumm, die Welt ist blind, Die.
Wenn ich in deine Augen seh'.
When Two Are Parted.
When Young Hearts Break.
Whenever We Happen to Kiss.
Who Was It, Tell Me.
Wie langsam kriechet sie dahin.
Window-Glance, The.
With Inky Sails.
Withered Heart, The.
You Are Unhappy.
Your Snow-white Shoulder.
Zu fragmentarisch ist Welt und Leben.
Heinrich von Morungen
Dream and Image.
Heinrich von Rugge
He that Loves a Rosy Cheek.
Helburn, Theresa
Mother.
You hear Youth laughing down green, budding aisles.
Youth.
"Helen."
Another Cynical Variation.
Helen, Sister Mary
Idenity.
Heller, Binem
Pesach Has Come to the Ghetto Again.
Hellman, Geoffrey
Dynastic Tiff.
Hellman, George Sidney
Coleridge.
Hudson, The.
In a China Shop.
Helmer, Charles D.
Battle of Oriskany.
Helphingtine, Mary J.
Blessings of Surrender, The.
Helsley, Shel
Christ Alone.
Helton, Roy
Glimpses.
In Passing.
Lonesome Water.
Miracles.
Old Christmas.
Old Christmas Morning.
Song of Dark Waters, The.
Hemans, Felicia Dorothea (Browne)
Birds of Passage.
Brererton Omen, The, *sel.*
Casabianca.
Child's First Grief, The.
Cid's Rising, The.
Death-Hymn, A.
Dirge: "Calm on the bosom of thy God."
England's Dead.
Fairies' Recall.
Fairy Song.
First Grief, The.
Flight of the Spirit.
Foliage.
Graves of a Household, The.
He Never Smiled Again.
Homes of England, The.
Hour of Death, The.
Hymn for Christmas.
Landing of the Pilgrim Fathers [in New England], The.
Pilgrim Fathers, The.
Prayer, A: "Father in Heaven! from whom the simplest flower."
Sabbath Sonnet.
Siege of Valencia, The, *sel.*
Voice of Spring, The.
Water-Lilies.
Where Is the Sea?
Yes! I have seen the ancient oak.
Hemenway, Abby Maria ("Marie Josephine")
Annunciation Night.
Mary of Nazareth, *sel.*
"Hemingway, Percy." *See* **Addleshaw, Percy.**
Hemley, Cecil
If He Were Anywhere.
My Absent God.
Witnesses.
Hemminger, Graham Lee
This Smoking World.
Hemphrey, Malcolm
Lanes in Summer.
Hempseed, Isabell
Rufty and Tufty.
Hempstead, T.
Under the Snow.
Hemsley, Stuart
S.P.C.A. Sermon.
Henchman, Richard
In Consort to Wednesday, Jan. 1st, 1701.
Vox Oppressi, To the Lady Phipps.
Henderson, Alice Corbin *See* **Corbin, Alice**
Henderson, Daniel
Hard Rows to Hoe.
Homing Heart, The.
Hymn for a Household.
Lilies of the Field, The.
Nantucket Whalers.
Opium Clippers.
Poet of Gardens, The.
Road to France, The.
St. Swithin.
Scarlet Thread, The.
Stranger, The.
Two Wives, The.
Henderson, David
Boston Road Blues ("Boston Road is as wide as a boulevard").
Downtown-Boy Uptown.
It Is Not Enough.
Keep on Pushing.
Neon Diaspora.
Number 5—December.
Psychedelic Firemen.
Sketches of Harlem.
Henderson, Dorothy
Chinese Lullaby.
Henderson, E. H.
March Wind, The.
Henderson, Florence L.
Garden That I Love, The.
Henderson, Hamish
First Elegy [for the Dead in Cyrenaica.]
Flyting o'Life and Daith, The.
Henderson, John
Of Love and Time.
Henderson, Rose
Growing Old.
March Dreams.
Henderson, Ruth Evelyn
Boy's Day.
My Spirit Will Grow Up.
Hendry, Hamish
Silver Bells.
Silver Road, The.
Upside-down World, The.
What the Weather Does.
Hendry, J. F.
Constant North, The.
Inverberg.
Orpheus.
Ship, The.
Tir-Nan-Og.
Heney, Thomas
Boundary Rider, The.
Henley, Elizabeth
Birthday-Cake Glockenspiel, The.
It Really Happened.
Henley, William Ernest
All in a Garden Green.
Apparition.
As Like the Woman as You Can.
Ballade Made in the Hot Weather.
Ballade of a Toyokuni Color-Print.
Ballade of Dead Actors.
Ballade of Ladies' Names.
Ballade of Spring.
Ballade of Youth and Age.
Before.
Birds in April.
Blackbird, The.
Bowl of Roses, A.
Casualty.
Collige Rosas.
Culture in the Slums.
Desolate Shore, A.
Discharged.
Double Ballade of Life and Fate.
Echoes.
England, My England.
Enter Patient.
Envoy: "Do you remember."
Epilogue to Rhymes and Rhythms.
Falmouth.
Fresh from His Fastnesses.
Full Sea Rolls and Thunders, The.
Her Little Feet.
Home.
House-Surgeon.
I am the Reaper.
I. M. Margaritae Sorori.
I. M.—R. T. Hamilton Bruce.
I Took a Hansom on To-Day.
In Hospital.
In Memoriam Margaritae Sorori.
In the Dials.
Inter Sodales.
Invictus.
Largo e mesto.
Late Lark Twitters, A.
London Voluntaries.
Madam Life.
Made in the Hot Weather.
Margaritae Sorori [*or* Sororis].
Midsummer Midnight Skies.
Nightingale, The.
O Gather Me the Rose.
On the way to Kew.
Operation.
Out of the Night.
Out of the Night That Covers Me.
Out of the Poisonous East.
Out of Tune.
Over the Hills and Far Away.
Pastoral: "It's the Spring."
Prologue to "Rhymes and Rhythms."
Rain.
Rhymes and Rhythms, *sels.*
Romance.
Rondel: Beside the Idle Summer Sea.
Sands Are Alive with Sunshine, The.
Scherzando.
Scrubber.
Since Those We Love and Those We Hate.
So Be My Passing.
So Let Me Hence.
Some Late Lark Singing.
Space and Dread and the Dark.
Spirit of Wine, The.
Staff-Nurse: New Style.
Staff-Nurse: Old Style.

Stanzas: "Where forlorn sunsets flare and fade."
Street Scene.
There's a Regret.
Thrush Sings, A.
To A. D.
To James McNeill Whistler.
To K. de M.
To My Mother.
To Robert Louis Stevenson.
To W. A.
Triolet: "Easy is the triolet."
Vigil.
Villanelle.
Villon's Good-Night.
Villon's Straight Tip to all Cross Coves.
Waiting.
Ways of Death, The.
We'll Go No More a-Roving.
What Is to Come [We Know Not].
When I Was a King in Babylon.
When You Are Old.
Where Forlorn Sunsets Flare and Fade.
With Strawberries.
World Still Young, A.
Henly, Anthony
Song: "No, no, no, no, resistance is but vain."
Hennell, Thomas
Mermaiden, A.
Queen Anne's Musicians.
Shepherd and Shepherdess.
Hennequin, Emile
Prose Poem: Irremediable, The.
Prose Poem: Words.
Hennessy, Doyle
And Left Me Stranded on a Hush.
Henniker-Heaton, Peter J.
Post Early for Space.
Henri, Adrian
Galactic Lovepoem.
Universes.
Henrich, Edith
Apology.
Protagonist.
Henry VIII, King of England
Alas! What Shall I Do for Love?
As the Holly Groweth Green.
Good Company.
Green Groweth the Holly.
Holly, The.
Pastime.
Pastime with Good Company.
Song: "As the holly groweth green."
To His Lady.
Whereto Should I Express.
Whoso That Will.
"Henry, O." (William Sidney Porter)
Options.
Henry the Minstrel ("Blind Harry', "
Description of Wallace, A.
Lament for the Graham.
Schir William Wallace.
Wallace, The, *sels.*
Henryson, Robert
Assembly of the Gods, The.
Bludy Serk, The.
Cresseid's Complaint against Fortune.
Cressida's Leprosy.
Garment of Good Ladies, The.
Preiching of the Swallow, The.
Prologue: "Ane doolie season to ane careful dyte."
Robene and Makyne.
Robin and Makin [*or* Makyne].
Taill of the Foxe, That Begylit the Wolf, in the Schadow of the Mone.
Testament of cresseid, The.
To Our Lady.
Henschke, Alfred *See* **"Klabund"**
Hensley, Sophia Almon
Because of You.
Henson, Pauline
On the Edge of the Copper Pit.
Henze, Helen Rowe
Etruscan Warrior's Head.
Hepburn, Elizabeth Newport
Machines—or Men.
Hepburn, Mary F.
February Twelfth.
Hepburn, Thomas Nicoll *See* **"Setoun, Gabriel"**
Heppenstall, Rayner
Actaeon.
Consolation in July.
Fleur de Lys.
Hagiograph.
St. Stephen's Word.
Spring Song.
Tammuz.
Herbert, Sir Alan Patrick
At the Theater.
Bacon and Eggs.
Barnacle, The.
Beaucourt Revisited.
Bowline, The.
Centipede, The.
Chameleon, The.
Coals of Fire.
Come to Britain; a Humble Contribution to the Movement.
Cupid's Darts.
Farmer, The.
Finale.
Green Estaminet, The.
Hattage.
He Didn't Oughter.
I Can't Think What He Sees in Her.
I've Got the Giggles Today.
Laughing Ann.
Mullion.
Perseverance; or, Half a Coronet, *sel.*
Prodigy, The.
Queen in Parliament, 1941, The.
Racing-Man, The.
Recipe.
Save the Tiger!
Spider, The.
Stop, Science—Stop!
To a Junior Waiter.
Tomato Juice.
'Twas at the Pictures, Child, We Met.
Two Gentlemen of Soho, *parody, sel.*
What Is Love? *sel.*
Herbert, Albert, Jr
Heart for All Her Children.
Herbert, E.
Balloon Man, The.
Herbert, Edward *See* **Herbert of Cherbury, Edward Herbert, 1st Baron**
Herbert, George
Aaron.
Affliction ("Broken in pieces all asunder").
Affliction ("Kill me not ev'ry day").
Affliction ("My God, I read this day").
Affliction ("My heart did heave").
Affliction ("When first thou didst entice to thee my heart").
Agonie [*or* Agony], The.
Altar, The.
Ana(Mary Army)gram.
And Now in Age I Bud Again.
Another Version.
Answer, The.
Antiphon: "Let all the world in ev'ry corner sing."
Antiphon: "Praised be the God of love."
Artillerie [*or* Artillery].
Assurance.
Avarice.
Bag, The.
Banquet, The.
Be Useful, *abr.*
Bitter-Sweet.
British Church, The.
Bunch of Grapes, The.
Businesse.
Call, The.
Charms and Knots.
Christ Our Lord.
Christmas.
Church-Floor[e], The.
Church-Lock and Key.
Church Militant, The, *sel.*
Church-Monuments.
Church-Music [*or* Musick].
Church-Porch, The.
Church-Rents and Schismes.
Church Windows, The.
Clasping of Hands.
Cluttered Temples.
Collar, The.
Complaining.
Confession.
Conscience.
Constancie.
Content.
Courage.
Crosse, The.
Dare to Be True.
Dawning, The.
Death.
Decay.
Dedication, The: "Lord, my first fruits present themselves to thee."
Denial.
Dialogue.
Dialogue-Antheme, A.
Discharge, The.
Discipline.
Divinitie.
Dooms-Day.
Dotage.
Dulnesse.
Easter.
Easter Wings.
Elixer, The.
Employment ("He that is weary, let him sit").
Employment ("If as a flower doth spread and die").
Even-song ("Blest be the God of Love").
Even-Song ("Day is spent, and hath his will on mee, The").
Faith.
Familie, The.
Flower, The.
Foil, The.
Forerunners, The.
Frailtie.
Frailty.
Giddinesse.
Gifts of God, The.
Glance, The.
Glimpse, The.
Good Friday.
Grace.
Grief.
Grieve Not the Holy Spirit.
H. Baptisme ("Since, Lord, to thee/ A narrow way and little gate").
H. Baptisme ("As he that sees a dark and shadie grove").
H. Communion, The ("Not in rich furniture, or fine aray").
H. Communion, The ("O gratious Lord, how shall I know").
H. Scriptures, The.
Heart to Praise Thee, A.
Heaven.
Holdfast, The.

Herbert (continued)
Holy Baptism ("As he that sees a dark and shadie grove").
Holy Baptism ("Since, Lord, to thee/ A narrow way and little gate").
Holy Communion.
Holy Scriptures, The.
Home.
Hope.
Humilitie.
Humility [*or* Humilitie].
I got me flowers to straw [*or* strew] Thy way.
Iesu.
Invitation, The.
Jesu.
Jews, The.
Jordan ("When first my lines *or* verse").
Jordan ("Who sayes [*or* says] that fictions").
Josephs Coat.
Judgement.
Justice ("I cannot skill of these thy wayes").
Justice ("O Dreadfull justice").
Knell, The.
Lent.
L'Envoy: "King of glorie, king of peace."
Let vain or busy thoughts have there no part.
Life.
Longing.
Love ("Immortal Heat, O let thy greater flame").
Love ("Immortal love, authour of this great frame").
Love ("Love bade me welcome; yet my soul drew back").
Love ("Thou art too hard for me in love").
Love Bade Me Welcome.
Love-Joy.
Love Unknown.
Man.
Mans Medley.
Marie Magdalene.
Mattens.
Method, The.
Miserie.
Mortification.
Nature.
Obedience.
Odour, The.
Offering, An.
On Worship.
Our Life is Hid with Christ in God.
Our Prayer.
Paradise.
Parodie, A: "Souls joy, when thou art gone."
Peace.
Pearl, The.
Perseverance.
Philosophers Have Measured Mountains.
Pilgrimage, The.
Posie, The.
Praise ("King of Glorie, King of Peace").
Praise ("Lord, I will mean and speak thy praise").
Praise ("To write a verse or two is all the praise").
Prayer: "Of what an easie quick accesse."
Prayer: "Prayer the churches [*or* church's] banquet, angels age.
Priesthood, The.
Providence.
Psalme Twenty-three ("Happy me! O happy sheepe!").
Pulley, The.
Quidditie, The.
Quip, The.
Rain, The.
Redemption.
Repentance.
Reprisal[l], The.
Resurrection.
Rose, The.
Sacrifice, The.
Search, The.
Second Thanksgiving, The.
Self-Condemnation.
Sepulchre.
Shall I Be Silent?
Sighs and Grones.
Sin.
Sinne ("Lord, with what care hast thou begirt us round").
Sinne ("O that I could a sinne once see!").
Sinner, The.
Sinnes Round.
Sins' [*or* Sinnes] Round.
Sion.
Size, The.
Son, The.
Sonne, The.
Sonnet: "My God, where is that ancient heat towards thee."
Sonnet: "Sure Lord, there is enough in thee to dry."
Starre, The.
Storm, The.
Submission.
Sunday.
Superliminare.
Temper, The ("How should I praise thee, Lord!").
Temper, The ("It cannot be. Where is that mightie joy").
Thanksgiving, The.
Time.
To All Angels and Saints.
To His Mother.
To My Successor.
Trinity [*or* Trinitie] Sunday.
True Hymn[e], A.
Ungratefulnesse.
Unkindness[e].
Vanitie ("Poore silly soul, whose hope and head lies low").
Vanity [*or* Vanitie] ("The fleet astronomer can bore").
Virtue.
Water-Course, The.
Whitsunday.
Who can scape his bow?
Who reade a chapter when they rise.
Who Would Have Thought?
Windows, The.
World, The.
Wreath, A.
Herbert, Henry William
Come Back.
Herbert, Mary, Countess of Pembroke
See **Pembroke, Mary Sidney Herbert, Countess of**
Herbert, Moss
Gentle Park, A.
Herbert, Petrus
Faith.
Herbert, William, Earl of Pembroke
See **Pembroke, William Herbert, Earl of**
Herbert of Cherbury, Edward Herbert, 1st Baron
Another Sonnet to Black Itself.
Brown Beauty, The.
Description, A.
Ditty in Imitation of the Spanish ("Entre tanto que l'Avril").
Echo in a Church.
Echo to a Rock.
Elegy for Doctor Dunn.
Elegy Over a Tomb.
Epitaph. Cæcil. Boulstr.
Epitaph for Himself.
Epitaph on Sir Philip Sidney.
First Meeting, The.
Green-Sickness Beauty, The.
In a Glass-Window for Inconstancy.
Innumerable Beauties.
Kissing.
La Gialletta Gallante; or, The Sun-burn'd Exotique Beauty.
Long, their fixed eyes to Heaven bent.
Love Speaks at Last.
Loves End.
Madrigal: "Dear, when I did from you remove."
Madrigal: "How should I love my best?"
October 14, 1644.
Ode, An, Upon a Question Moved, Whether Love Should Continue for Ever?
Parted Souls.
Platonick Love.
Sinner's Lament, A.
Sonnet: "Innumerable Beauties, thou white haire."
Sonnet: "Thus ends my love, but this doth grieve me most."
Sonnet of Black Beauty.
Tears, Flow No More.
Thought, The.
To a Lady Who Did Sing Excellently.
To Her Eyes.
To Her Hair.
To His Friend Ben. Johnson, of His Horace Made English.
To His Mistress for Her True Picture.
To His Watch, When He Could Not Sleep.
To Mrs. Diana Cecyll.
Upon Combing Her Hair.
Vision, A.
Herbertson, Agnes Grozier
Little Betty Blue.
There was a little goblin.
Herbin, John Frederic
Diver, The.
Haying.
Herder, Johann Gottfried von
Esthonian Bridal Song.
Sir Olaf.
Herebert, William
Devout Man Prays to His Relations, The.
Knight Stained from Battle, The.
Palm-Sunday Hymn, A.
Heredia, José Maria de
Antony and Cleopatra (3 *sonnets*).
Flute, The; a Pastoral.
Laborer, The.
Herford, Beatrice
Old Man, The.
Herford, Oliver
Ant, The.
Bashful Earthquake, The, *sel.*
Belated Violet, A.
Cat, The.
Catfish.
Child's Natural History, *sels.*
Chimpanzee, The.
Christmas Legend, A.
Cloud, The.
Cow, The.
Dog, The (As Seen by the Cat).
Earth.
Elf and the Dormouse, The.
Eve.
Fall of J. W. Beane, The.
Geese.
Hen, The.
Here Lies Bill.
Hippopotamus, The.
I Heard a Bird Sing.

If This Little World To-night.
Japanesque.
Kitten's Night Thoughts.
Kitten's Thought, A.
Laughing Willow, The.
Limerick: "There once was a sculptor called [*or* named] Phidias."
Limerick: "There once were some learned M. D.'s."
Limerick: "There was a young lady of Twickenham."
Love Story, A.
Mark Twain; a Pipe Dream.
Metaphysics.
Milk Jug, The.
Missing Link, The.
Mrs. Seymour Fentolin.
Mon-goos, The.
Moon, The.
More Animals.
Music of the Future, The.
My Sense of Sight.
Once on a time a young giraffe.
Penguin, A.
Phyllis Lee.
Platypus, The.
Proem: "If this little world to-night."
Seal, A.
Silver Question, The.
Smile of the Goat, The.
Smile of the Walrus, The.
Snail's Dream, The.
Some Geese.
Stairs.
Thanksgiving Fable, A.
Two Smiles.
Untutored Giraffe, The.
War Relief.
Why ye Blossome Cometh before ye Leafe.
Women of the Better Class, The.
Yak, The.

"Hermes, Paul." *See* **Thayer, William Roscoe**

Hernaes, Gunnar
Trumpet and Flute.

Hernández, José
Departure of Martín Fierro, The, *abr.*

Hernández, Miguel
Winds of the People.

Herndon, John G.
Fairies, The.
Friendly People.

Hernton, Calvin C.
Black Stick with a Ball of Cotton for a Head and a Running Machine for a Mouth, A.
Distant Drum, The.
Elements of Grammar.
Jitterbugging in the Streets.
Madhouse.
Young Negro Poet.

Herrera, Fernando de
Disembodied Spirit, The.
Ideal Beauty.

Herrera S., Demetrio
Training.

Herrera y Reissig, Julio
Parish Church, The.

Herrick, Robert
Againe.
Age Not to Be Rejected.
Alms, *sel.*
Amber Bead, The.
Anacreontic.
Another [To His Booke].
Another Charm.
Another Grace for a Child ("Here a little child I stand").
Another New-Yeeres Gift, or Song for the Circumcision.
Apparition of His Mistresse Calling Him to Elizium, The.
Apron of Flowers, The.
Argument of His Book, The.
Argument of This Book.
Art above Nature; to Julia.
As in Silks My Julia Goes.
Bacchanalian Verse, A.
Bad Season Makes the Poet Sad, The.
Bag of the Bee, The.
Beggar, to Mab the Fairy Queen, The.
Bellman, The.
Bracelet, The: To Julia.
Ceremonies for Candlemas Day, The ("Kindle the Christmas brand").
Ceremonies for Candlemas[s] Eve ("Down with the rosemary and bays").
Ceremonies for Christmas[se] ("Come bring with a noise").
Ceremony for Candlemas Day, A ("Down with the rosemary and so").
Charm, A ("If ye fear to be affrighted").
Charm, A ("In the morning when you rise").
Charm, or an Allay for Love, A.
Cheat of Cupid, The; or, The Ungentle Guest.
A
Cherry-Pit.
Cherry-ripe.
Child's Grace, A ("Here a little child I stand").
Child's Present to His Child-Saviour, A.
Chop-Cherry.
Christ and We.
Christian Militant, The.
Christmas Carol, A: "What sweeter music can we bring."
Christmas Carol, Sung to the King in the Presence at Whitehall, A.
Christmas Eve—Another Ceremony.
Christmas Eve—Another to the Maids.
Christ's Incarnation.
Clothes Do but Cheat and Cozen Us.
Cock-Crow, *sl. abr.*
Comfort to a Youth That Had Lost His Love.
Coming [*or* Comming] of Good Luck, The.
Comming of Good Luck, The.
Conjuration, to Electra, A.
Connubii Flores; or, The Well-Wishes at Weddings.
Corinna's Going a-Maying.
Counsel to Girls.
Country Life, A; to His Brother, M. Tho: Herrick.
Cruell Maid, The.
Daffodils.
Dean-bourn, a Rude River in Devon, by Which Sometimes He Lived ("Dean-bourn, farewell; I never look to see").
Definition of Beauty, The.
Delight in Disorder.
Dew Sat on Julia's Hair.
Dirge upon the Death of the Right Valiant Lord, Bernard Stuart, A.
Discontents in Devon.
Divination by a Daffadil[l].
Dreams.
End-Piece for His Book, An.
Entertainment, The; or, Porch Verse at the Marriage of Master Henry Northly and the Most Witty Mistress Lettice Yard.
Epitaph on a Virgin.
Epitaph on the Tomb of Sir Edward Giles and His Wife.
Epitaph upon a Child, An ("Virgins promised when I died").
Epitaph upon a Child that Died ("Here she lies, a pretty bud").
Epitaph upon a Virgin, An.
Epithalamie to Sir Thomas Southwell and His Lady, An.
Eternity.
Fair Days; or, Dawns Deceitful, *br. sel.*
Fair was the dawn, and, but e'en now, the skies.
Fairies, The.
Five Wines.
Four Sweet Months, The.
Fresh Cheese and Cream.
Frozen Heart, The.
Funeral Rites of the Rose, The.
A
Gather Ye Rose-Buds [While Ye May].
Give, if thou canst, an alms; if not, afford.
Go, Pretty Child.
Going a-Maying.
Good Christians.
Good Men Afflicted Most.
Good-Night, or Blessing, The.
Grace ("Here a little child I stand").
Grace before Meat.
Grace for a Child.
Grace for Children ("What God gives, and what we take").
Hag, The.
Herrick's Cavalier.
Hesperides ("I sing of brooks, of blossoms, birds and bowers").
His Age.
His Answer to a Question.
His Cavalier.
His Charge to Julia at His Death.
His Content in the Country.
His Creed.
His Desire.
His Ejaculation to God.
His Fare-well to Sack.
His Grange, or Private Wealth.
His Lachrimae or Mirth, Turned to Mourning.
His Letanie, to the Holy Spirit.
His Litany to the Holy Spirit.
His Parting with Mrs. Dorothy Kennedy, *sel.*
His Poetry His Pillar.
His Prayer for Absolution.
His Prayer to Ben Jonson [*or* Johnson].
His Request to Julia.
His Return[e] to London.
His Sailing from Julia.
His Saviour's Words Going to the Cross.
His Tears to Thamasis.
His Winding Sheet.
His Wish to God.
Hock-Cart, or Harvest Home, The.
Holding to God.
How Lillies [*or* Lilies] Came White.
How Marigolds Came Yellow.
How Roses Came Red.
How Violets Came Blue.
Humility.
I Call and I Call.
I'll Come to Thee.
Impossibilities to His Friend.
In the Dark None Dainty.
In the Hour of My Distress.
Instead of Neat Inclosures.
Invitation, The.
Julia.
Julia's Petticoat.
July; the Succession of the Four Sweet Months.
Kings and Tyrants.
Kisse, The.
Kissing and Bussing.
Lady Dying in Childbed, A.
Lilly in a Christal, The.
Litany to the Holy Spirit.

Herrick (continued)
Little mushroom table spread, A.
Littles.
Love Dislikes Nothing.
Love Perfumes All Parts.
Love What It Is.
Lovers How They Come and Part.
Lyrick for Legacies.
Mad Maid's Song, The.
Meddow Verse, The; or, Aniversary to Mistris Bridget Lowman.
Meditation for His Mistresse, A.
Mercy and Love.
Mirth.
Neutrality Loathsome.
New Charon, The.
New-Yeeres Gift, The, or Circumcisions Song, Sung to the King in the Presence at White Hall.
A
Night-Piece, to Julia.
No Coming to God without Christ.
No Fault in Women.
No Loathsomnesse in Love.
No, no, the utmost share.
Not Every Day Fit for Verse.
Nuptial Verse to Mistress Elizabeth Lee Now Lady Tracy, A.
Nuptiall Song, or Epithalamie, on Sir Clipseby Crew and His Lady, A.
Obedience.
Oberon's Feast.
Ode for Ben Jonson, An.
Ode for Him, An.
Ode on the Birth of Our Saviour, An.
Of Her Breath.
Old Wives Prayer, The.
Olive Branch, The.
On a Dark Road.
On Himself ("Born I was to meet with age").
On Himself ("Worke is done, The: young men, and maidens set").
On Himself ("Young I was who now am old").
Parting Verse, the Feast There Ended, The.
Pillar of Fame, The.
Poet Loves a Mistress[e], But Not to Marry, The.
Poetry of Dress, The.
Prayers Must Have Poise.
Primrose, The.
Prithee (lest maids should censure thee) but say.
Resurrection Possible and Probable, The.
Rock of Rubies, The.
Rod, The.
Rosarie, The.
Rubies and Pearls.
Science in God.
Second Vision, The.
Short Hymne to Venus, A.
Show Me Thy Feet.
A
Sins Loathed, and Yet Loved.
Sitting Alone.
So Look the Mornings.
Soft Musick.
Star Song, The; a Carol to the King.
Succession of the Four Sweet Months, The.
Suspition upon His Over-much Familiarity with a Gentlewoman, The.
Temptation.
Ternarie [*or* Ternary] of Littles, upon a Pipkin of Jellie [*or* Jelly] Sent to a Lady, A.
Thankful Heart, A.
Thanksgiving.
Thanksgiving to God, for His House, A.
There's pain in parting, and a kind of hell.
This Cross-Tree Here.
'Tis Hard to Find God.
To a Child.
To a Gentlewoman Objecting to Him His Gray Hairs.
To Aenone.
To Anthea ("Ah my Anthea! Must my heart still break?").
To Anthea ("Bid me to live").
To Anthea ("If dear Anthea").
To Anthea ("Now is the time").
To Anthea Lying in Bed.
To Anthea, Who May Command Him Any Thing.
To Blossoms.
To Cherry-Blossomes.
To Critics.
To Daffodills [*or* Daffadills].
To Daisies, Not to Shut so Soon[e].
To Dean-bourn, a Rude River in Devon.
To Death.
To Dianeme.
To Dianeme, Again.
To Electra ("I dare not ask a kiss").
To Electra ("More white than whitest lilies far").
To Finde God.
To Fortune.
To God ("Come to me God; but do not come").
To God ("Lord, I am like the mistletoe").
To God, on His Sickness.
To His Book's End.
To His Conscience.
To His Dying Brother, Master William Herrick.
To His Ever-loving God.
To His Honoured Kinsman, Sir William Soame.
To His Lovely Mistresses.
To His Maid Prew.
To His Mistress.
To His Mistress Objecting to Him neither Toying or Talking.
To His Mistresses.
To His Muse.
To His Saviour, a Child; a Present by a Child.
To His Tomb-Maker.
To Keep a True Lent.
To Larr.
To Laurels.
To Live Merrily, and to Trust to Good Verses.
To Master Denham, on His Prospective Poem.
To Meadows.

To M. Henry Lawes, the Excellent Composer, of His Lyrics.
To Music [*or* Musique], to Becalm[e] His Fever.
To Musick ("Begin to charme").
To Musick ("Musick, thou Queen of Heaven, care-charming-spel").
To Oenone.
To Perilla.
A
To Phyllis [*or* Phillis], to Love and Live with Him.
To Primroses Filled [*or* Fill'd] with Morning-Dew.
To Robin Redbreast.
To the King, Upon His Comming with His Army into the West.
To the King, upon His Welcome to Hampton-Court.
To the Most Fair and Lovely Mistress [*or* Mistris], Anne Soame, Now Lady Abdie.
To the Most Learned, Wise, and Arch-Antiquary, M. John Selden.
To the Reverend Shade of His Religious Father.
To the Rose.
To the Soure Reader.
To the Virgins, to Make Much of Time.
To the Water Nymphs, Drinking at the Fountain.
To the Western Wind.
To the Willow-Tree.
To the Yew and Cypress to Grace His Funeral.
To Violets.
To Virgins ("Hear ye virgins. . .").
True Lent, A.
Upon a Child ("Here a pretty baby lies").
Upon a Child That Died.
Upon a Maid ("Here she lies, in bed of spice").
Upon a Virgin Kissing a Rose.
Upon a Wife That Dyed Mad with Jealousie.
Upon Batt.
Upon Ben Jonson.
Upon Fone a School-Master, Epigram.
Upon Gryll.
Upon Her Feet.
Upon Her Voice.
Upon Himself.
Upon His Departure Hence.
Upon His Sister in Law.
Upon Jack and Jill, Epigram.
Upon Jone and Jane.
Upon Julia Weeping.
Upon Julia's Clothes.
Upon Julia's Fall.
Upon Julia's Hair[e] Filled [*or* Fill'd] with Dew.
Upon Julia's Petticoat.
Upon Julia's Recovery.
Upon Julia's Voice.
Upon Kings.
Upon Love ("Love brought me to a silent grove").
Upon Love ("Love scorch'd my finger, but did spare").
Upon Love, by Way of Question and Answer ("I bring ye love").
Upon Master Fletchers Incomparable Playes.
Upon M. Ben Jonson, Epigram.
Upon Mistress Susanna Southwell, Her Feet.
Upon Pagget.
Upon Parson Beanes.
Upon Prew [*or* Prue] His Maid.
Upon Prudence Baldwin Her Sicknesse.
Upon Prue, His Maid.
Upon Roses.
Upon Scobble, Epigram.
Upon Sibilla.
Upon Some Women.
Upon Sudds a Laundresse.
Upon the Loss [*or* Losse] of His Mistresses.
A
Upon the Nipples of Julia's Breast.
Upon Time.
Vine, The.
Violets.
Vision, The ("I dreamed we were both in bed").
Vision, The ("Methought I saw as I did dream in bed").
Vision, The ("Sitting alone as one forsook").
Vision to Electra, The.
We see Him come, and know Him ours.
Weeping Cherry, The.
Welcome to Sack, The.

What Kind of Mistress He Would Have.
What Shame Forbids to Speak.
When as in Silks My Julia Goes.
When He Would Have His Verses Read.
When I Thy Parts Run O'er.
Whenas in Silks My Julia Goes.
White Island, The; or Place of the Blest.
Willow Garland, The.
Witch, The.
Wounded Cupid, The.
"Ye Cannot Serve God and Mammon."
You Say I Love Not.
Herschberger, Ruth
Coup d'Etat.
In Panelled Rooms.
Lumberyard, The.
Nature Poem.
Herschel, Sir William
God's Instrument.
Herschell, William
Kid Has Gone to the Colors, The.
Service Flag, The.
Soldier of the Silences, The.
Hersey, Harold
Lay of the Last Frontier.
Hershenson, Miriam
Husbands and Wives.
Love Poem-1940.
Hershon, Robert
After.
Child at Sand.
German Eyes.
How to Walk in a Crowd.
In This Forest.
Loves of the Public Servants.
Midtown Poem.
On Horror.
Paintings of Roses.
Report to the Blue Guard.
Shoemaker's Booth, The.
We Are.
Zoo Club, The.
Hervey, Christopher
Confusion.
Hervey, John Russell
Carnival.
Hydro Works.
John Donne's Defiance.
Man of Crete.
Man Who Wanted to Be a Seagull, The.
Neighbour.
Sonnet of Departure.
Threnos.
Two Old Men Look at the Sea.
Hervey, Thomas Kibble
I Think on Thee.
Herwegh, Georg
Dare to Be Free.
Herzing, Albert
Small Boy, Dreaming, A.
Heseltine, Nigel
Microcosmos, *abr.*
Hesiod
Five Ages, The.
Shield of Heracles, The, *sel.*
These were men that in harness of battle fought.
Works and Days, *much abr.*
Hesketh, Phoebe
Fox, The.
Hess, M. Whitcomb
First Grandchild.
Mirror, The.
Vision of St. Bernard, The.
Hesse, Hermann
Midsummer.
Night.
Spring Song.
Hessey, Vera
Frog and the Bird, The.
Hetherington, George
Charles at the Siege.
Palm House, Botanic Gardens.
Sonnet: "Now keep that long revolver at your side."
Sonnet: "Since I keep only what I give away."
Hetrick, Lawrence
Arrowhead Field.
Hewison, R. J. P.
Genius.
Hewitt, Ethel M.
Wild Wishes.
Hewitt, John
First Corncrake.
Frost.
Glens, The.
Leaf.
Little Lough, The.
Load.
Lyric: "Let but a thrush begin."
O Country People.
Once Alien Here.
Poem in May.
Swathe Uncut, The.
Turf Carrier on Aranmore.
Hewitt, Luisa
Plans.
Secrets.
Hewitt, Mary Elizabeth *See* **Stebbins, Mary Elizabeth Moore**
Hewlett, Maurice
He loathed his bond, but could not stir.
Man on the Hill, The.
1914 Autumn and Winter.
Old Thought, An, *abr.*
Poll Tax (1378).
Rosa Nascosa.
Song of the Plow, The, *sels.*
When She a Maiden Slim.
Hey, F.
Boy and the Squirrel, The.
Cat in the Snow, The.
Caw, Caw.
Fox and Goose.
Kittens, The.
Pug-Dog and Spitz.
Two Dogs.
Hey, Phillip
Lines Written in Objection, or, The Limpopo Express.
Möbius.
Poem That Tries to Be a Tree, The.
Popcorn.
Subject, with Apologies.
Supposition at 2 A.M.
Window, Painted Shut.
Heyduk, Adolf
Three Fields.
Heyen, William
Boys Will Be Princes.
Heym, Georg
Famine.
Heyrick, Thomas
Battle between a Cock and a Capon, The.
Martial.
On a Sunbeam.
On an Indian Tomineios, The Least of Birds.
On the Death of a Monkey.
Submarine Voyage, The, *sel.*
There lies a broken anker, on whose trust.
Heyse, Paul
Rispetti: On the Death of a Child.
Young Girl's Song, A.
Heyward, DuBose
Dusk.
Evening in the Great Smokies.
Gamesters All.
Mountain Woman, The.
New England Landscape.
Porgy, Maria, and Bess.
Heyward, Janie Screven
Autumn Leaves.
Spirit's Grace, The.
Heywood, Jasper
Easter Day.
Look or You Leap.
Lookers-on, The.
Who Minds to Bring His Ship to Happy Shore.
Heywood, John
Among other things profiting in our tongue.
Buying a Pig.
Cardinal Fisher.
Cock and the Hen, The.
Description of a Most Noble Lady, A.
Dialogue Containing the Number of the Effectual Proverbs in the English Tongue, A, *sels.*
English Schoolboy, The.
Epigram on This Book of Epigrams, An.
Fool's Tongue, A.
Four P's, The, *sel.*
Give place, ye ladies, and be gone.
"Gloria Patri," The.
Green Willow Is My Garland, A.
How God Will Not Do for Us.
If Love, for Love for Long Time Had.
Jack and His Father.
Looking and Leaping.
Love Continual.
Maister and the Man, The.
Of a Cat's Look.
Of a Husband Hang'd.
Of a Sheep's Eye.
Of Birds and Birders.
Of Clipping and Cleaning.
Of Common Meddlers.
Of Difference between Wise Men and Fools.
Of Enough and a Feast.
Of Heywood.
Of Holding of a Nose.
Of Late and Never.
Of Loving a Dog.
Of mine acquaintance a certain young man.
Of Nothing and Althing.
Of One Hanged.
Of Rebellion.
Of Taking Things Wrong.
Of the Senses.
On the Princess Mary.
One Driveth Out Another.
Palmer, The.
Play of the Four P's.
Play of the Weather, The, *sels.*
Praise of His Lady, A.
Sir, I pray you, be you not master god?
Spider and the Fly, The, *abr.*
Tyburn and Westminster.
Wedding and Hanging.
Heywood, Terence
By an Ant-Heap.
Cactus.
Flamingo's Egg, A.
Grisaille.
Mantis.
Notes for a Bestiary.
Heywood, Thomas
Apology for Actors, An, *sel.*
Author to His Booke, The.
Challenge for Beauty, A, *sel.*
Cherubim, The, *sel.*
Golden Age, The, *sel.*
Good-Morrow.
Hence with Passion, Sighs and Tears.
Hierarchie of the Blessed Angels, *sel.*
Honor Done to Poets of Old and Modern Poets, The.
Hymn to Diana.

Heywood (continued)
I have wandered like a sheep that's lost.
I remember,/ There lived a Spanish Princess of our name.
Maidenhead Well Lost, A, *sel.*
Matin Song.
Now what is love I will thee tell.
On Homer's Birthplace.
Pack, Clouds, Away.
Passing Bell, The.
Praise of Ceres.
Rape of Lucrece, The, *sels.*
Search for God, The.
She That Denies Me [I Would Have].
Silver Age, The, *sel.*
Song: "With fair Ceres, Queen of grain."
To Give My Love Good-Morrow.
Valerius on Women.
Waking Song.
Hickey, Agnes MacCarthy
Old Essex Door.
Hickey, Emily Henrietta
Belovèd, It Is Morn.
Sea Story, A.
Song: "Belovèd, it is morn!"
Hickok, Eliza M.
God Answers Prayer.
Prayer: "I know not by what methods rare."
This I Know.
Hickox, Chauncey
Under the Red Cross.
Hicks, Mabel
Crosses.
Hicks, William
Of His Mistress Grown Old.
Hicks, William Edward, *and* **Siegfried August Mahlmann** *See* **Mahlmann, Siegfried August,** *and* **William Edward Hickson**
Hicky, Daniel Whitehead
Escape.
Georgia Towns.
Machines.
No Friend like Music.
Nocturne: Georgia Coast.
Okefenokee Swamp.
Polo Player.
River Boats, The.
Runaway, The.
Say That He Loved Old Ships.
Ship for Singapore, A.
Small Song.
To an Aviator.
When a Man Turns Homeward.
Who Pilots Ships.
Wisdom.
Hiebert, Paul Gerhardt
Farmer and the Farmer's Wife, The.
Steeds.
Hiers, Lois Smith
On Laying Up Treasure.
Higgins, Annie
Waking.
Higgins, Frederick Robert
Ballad of O'Bruadir, The.
Boyne Walk, The.
Cradle Song: "Out in the dark something complains."
Father and Son.
Gallows Tree, The.
Little Clan, The.
Old Air, An.
Old Jockey, The.
Padraic O'Conaire, Gaelic Storyteller.
Scribe, The.
Song for the Clatter-Bones.
Spanish Man, The.
To My Blackthorn Stick.
Unmarried Mother Sings, An.
Higginson, Anne *See* **Spicer, Anne Higginson**
Higginson, Nesta *See* **"O'Neill, Moira"**
Higginson, Ella
Beggars.
Beside the Sea.
Four-Leaf Clover.
Grand Ronde Valley, The.
Lamp in the West, The.
Month of Falling Stars, The.
Moonrise in the Rockies.
Higginson, Mary Potter Thacher
Changelings.
Ghost-Flowers.
In the Dark.
Inheritance.
Higginson, Thomas Wentworth
Decoration.
Ode to a Butterfly.
Since Cleopatra Died.
Snowing of the Pines, The.
"Such Stuff as Dreams Are Made Of."
Thank Thee.
Things I Miss, The.
To Duty.
Higgs, Barry O.
Deaf.
In Lord Carpenter's Country.
Night Shore.
Parson's Pleasure.
Reversion.
Higham, Charles
Barnacle Geese.
Crime Story.
Mozart.
War Museum at Nagasaki, The.
Highet, Gilbert
Homage to Ezra Pound.
Higo, Aig
Hidesong.
Hilali
Flute, The.
Hilary of Aries, Saint
Thou Bounteous Giver of the Light.
Hill, Geoffrey
Genesis.
Gideon at the Well.
God's Little Mountain.
Guardians, The.
In Memory of Jane Frazer.
In Piam Memoriam.
Of Commerce and Society.
Orpheus and Eurydice.
Pastoral, A: "Mobile, immaculate and austere."
Re-Birth of Venus, The.
To the (Supposed) Patron.
Turtle Dove, The.
Hill, George
Leila.
Oak, The.
Song of the Elfin Steersman.
Hill, Hyacinthe
Old Emily.
Rebels from Fairy Tales.
Hill, Leona Ames
Let Him Return.
Hill, Leslie Pinckney
Christmas at Melrose.
My Charge.
Of Greatness in Teaching.
So Quietly.
Summer Magic.
Teacher, The.
Tuskegee.
Hiil, Marion
Lovelilts.
Hill, Mildred J.
Valentine's Message, The.
When You Send a Valentine.
Hill, Quentine
Time Poem.
Hill, Thomas
Bobolink, The.
Hille, Peter
Beauty.
Maiden, The.
Hillhouse, Augustus Lucas
Forgiveness of Sins a Joy Unknown to Angels.
Hillhouse, James Abraham
Demon-Lover, The.
Hadad, *sel.*
Hills, Elijah Clarence
To Pikes Peak.
Hillyer, Robert Silliman
As One Who Bears beneath His Neighbor's Roof.
Assassination, The.
Bats, The.
Christmas Pastoral.
Elegy on a Dead Mermaid Washed Ashore at Plymouth Rock.
Epigram: "Bring hemlock, black as Cretan cheese."
Eppur Si Muove?
Eternal Return, The.
Familiar Faces, Long Departed.
General Galliéni.
Golden spring redeems the withered year, The.
In the Shadowy Whatnot Corner.
Intermezzo.
Ivory Tower, The.
Let all men see the ruins of the shrine.
Letter to a Teacher of English.
Letter to Robert Frost, A.
Lullaby: "Long canoe, The."
Lunar Moth.
Mentis Trist.
Moo!
Night Piece.
Over Bright Summer Seas.
Over the waters but a single bough.
Pastoral X: "Grapes are ripe, the frost is near, The."
Pastoral: "So soft in the hemlock wood."
Pastoral, A: "Wise old apple tree in spring, The."
Prothalamion, *sel.*
Relic, The.
Rendezvous.
Seven Times One Are Seven.
Sonnet: "Even as love grows more, I write the less."
Sonnet: "Golden spring redeems the withered year, The."
Sonnet: "I will fling wide the windows of my soul."
Sonnet: "Let all men see the ruins of the shrine."
Sonnet: "Over the waters but a single bough."
Sonnet: "Quickly and pleasantly the seasons blow."
Sonnet: "Then judge me as thou wilt I cannot flee."
Sonnets, *sels.*
Spiritism.
Termites, The.
Thermopylae.
Thermopylae and Golgotha.
Thought in Time, A.
To a Scarlatti Passepied.
Untended Field, The.
Variations on a Theme.
Hillyer, William Hurd
My Master's Face.
Hilton, Alfarata
Busy Person, A.
Hilton, Arthur Clement
Ding Dong.

Heathen Pass-ee, The.
Limerick: "There was a young critic of King's."
Limerick: "There was a young genius of Queens'."
Limerick: "There was a young gourmand of John's."
Limerick: "There was a young man of Sid. Sussex."
Octopus.
Vulture and the Husbandman, The.

Hilton, David
Childhood Ambition.
Getting Short.
Hang On.
His day closes like a dry mouth.
In Praise of BIC Pens.
Newlyweds' Accident, The.
Poet Tries to Turn in His Jock, The.
Sunday Again.
Zoo, with Lamp and Chairs.

Hilton, John
Fair Oriana, Beauty's Queen.

Himmell, Sophie
In the Month of Green Fire.

Hinds, Samuel
Baby Sleeps.

Hine, Al (Alfred Blakelee Hine)
Christmas 1945.

Hine, Daryl
After the Agony in the Garden.
Bewilderment at the Entrance of the Fat Boy into Eden, A.
Bluebeard's Wife.
Doppelganger, The.
Double Goer, The.
In Praise of Music in Time of Pestilence.
Plain Fare (Night Thoughts on Crossing the Continent by Bus).
Survivors, The.
Trompe l'Oeil.
Trout, The.
Under the Hill.
Untitled.
Wasp, The.

Hines, Carl Wendell, Jr
Two Jazz Poems.

Hines, Herbert H.
Christmas Prayer, A.

Hines, Nellie Womack
Home.

Hinkson, Katharine Tynan *See* **Tynan, Katharine**

Hintz, Philora
Faith to Understand.

Hioki no Ko-okima
On the shore of Nawa.

Hird, Martha
Stars.

Hirshbein, Peretz
Captive.
I Shall Weep.
Stars Fade.

Hirst, Henry Beck
Fringilla Melodia, The.
Funeral of Time, The.

Hisaki
Dirge, A: "Looking on the peaceful face."

Hite, Vernoy E.
Malcolm X.
Trapped.

Hitomaro, (Kakinomoto no Hitomaro)
For my sister's sake.
Hills of autumn drop, The.
In the ocean of the sky.
Lines from an Elegy on the Death of His Wife.
May the men who are born.
May those who are born after me.
Moon's Ship, The.
O boy cutting grass.
On the moor of Kasuga.
Plovers, The.
When,/ Halting in front of it.
When I pause before my mirror.
Your hair has turned white.

Hittan of Tayyi
Hamasah, *sel.*
His Children.

Hoadly, John
Chloe Resolved.

Hoagland, Everett
Night Interpreted.

Hoare, Florence
Pedlar Jim.

Hoatson, Florence
Autumn.
Bird Bath, The.
Christmas Eve.
Fairy Frilly.
Who?

Hobbs, Valine
Change of Heart, A.
One Day When We Went Walking.

Hoberman, Mary Ann
Birthday Bus, The.
Comparison.
It's fun to go out and buy new shoes to wear.
Slushy snow splashes and sploshes, The.

Hobsbaum, Philip
Chopin in London.
Conversation Piece.
Rock Pool, The.
Study in a Minor Key, *sel.*

Hobson, Dorothy
Do What You Will.

Hobson, Katherine Thayer
Duality.

Hoccleve [*or* Occleve], Thomas
De Regimine Principum, *sels.*
Description of His Ugly Lady, A.
Hoccleve's Humorous Praise of His Lady.
Hoccleve's Lament for Chaucer and Gower, *abr.*
I dar nat telle how that the fressh repeir.
La Male Regle de T. Hoccleve, *sel.*
Lament for Chaucer.
Prologue: "Musing upon the restless bisinesse."
Regiment of Princes, The.
To Chaucer.

Ho Chih-fang
Let Me Speak of Pure Things.

Hochman, Sandra
Couple, The.
Goldfish Wife, The.

Hodes, Aubrey
Jew Walks in Westminster Abbey, A.

Hodge, Alan
Waiting.

Hodges, Leigh M.
Give Them the Flowers Now.

Hodgson, Florence B.
How Can I Smile.

Hodgson, Ralph
After.
And Every Sky Was Blue and Rain.
Babylon.
Bells of Heaven, The.
Birdcatcher, The.
Bride, The.
Bull, The.
Eve.
Ghoul Care.
Gipsy Girl, The.
Great Auk's Ghost, The.
Gypsy Girl, The.
Hammers, The.
Hymn to Moloch.
I heard the hymn of being sound.
I Love a Hill.
Journeyman, The.
Late, Last Rook, The.
Moor, The.
Mystery, The.
Peace, The.
Reason.
Reason Has Moons.
Riddle, The: "He told himself and he told his wife."
Silver Wedding.
Song, A: "With love among the haycocks."
Song of Honour [*or* Honor], The.
Stupidity Street.
Thrown.
Time.
Time, You Old Gipsy [*or* Gypsy] Man.
To Deck a Woman, *sel.*
Weaving of the Wing, The.
Wood Song, A.

Hodgson, William Noel
Before Action.

Hoellein, Alma
How Could I Face the Future?
There Is a Place.
We'll Never Know.

Hoey, Edwin A.
Foul Shot.

Hoey, George
Asleep at the Switch.

Hoff, Clayton
I Saw Two Lions.

Hoffenstein, Samuel
As the Crow Flies, *sel.*
Be gay, be merry, and don't be wary of milking the modest minute.
Bird, The.
Breathes There a Man.
Cloud.
Father's Heart Is Touched, A.
How much we pay to say, "*Je suis.*"
I Burned My Candle at Both Ends.
I'd rather listen to a flute.
If You Love Me.
Little While to Love and Rave, A.
Lullaby: "Sleep, my little baby, sleep."
Madrigal Macabre.
Mr. Walter de la Mare Makes the Little Ones Dizzy.
More Hair.
Observation.
Ocean Spills, The.
Of All the Idiots That Abound.
Poem Intended to Incite the Utmost Depression, A.
Poems in Praise of Practically Nothing, *sels.*
Poems of Passion, Carefully Restrained So as to Offend Nobody.
Primer.
Progress.
Question and Answer.
Sheep.
Some Folks I Know.
Song of Fairly Utter Despair.
Song, on Reading that the Cyclotron Has Produced Cosmic Rays, *sel.*
To a Cat.
Unequal Distribution.
When You're Away.
You Hire a Cook.
You take a bath, and sit there bathing.
You Work and Work.

Hoffman, Charles Fenno
Mint Julep, The.
Monterey.
Sparkling and Bright.

Hoffman, Daniel Gerard
Armada of Thirty Whales, An.
As I Was Going to Saint Ives.
At the Winter Solstice.

Hoffman (continued)
City of Satisfactions, The.
Exploration.
Flushing Meadows, 1939.
How We Logged Katahdin Stream.
In Humbleness.
In the Beginning.
In the Days of Rin-Tin-Tin.
Letter to Wilbur Frohock, A.
Meeting, A.
1956.
Seals in Penobscot Bay, The.
Three Jovial Gentlemen.
Two Hundred Girls in Tights & Halters.
Who Was It Came.
Hoffman, George Edward
As It Began to Dawn.
Hymn: "O world of love and beauty."
Refreshment.
Victory Parade.
Young Warrior.
Hoffman, O. S.
Five Best Doctors, The.
Hoffman, Phoebe
Cats of Baddeck, The.
Hoffman, Phoebe W.
Pedro.
Hoffman, William M.
Cloisters, The.
Holy Light Equally Lights.
Marrakech.
Mustache.
Screw Spring.
Hoffmann, Heinrich
Dreadful Story of Pauline and the Matches, The.
Harriet and the Matches.
Slovenly Peter.
Story of Augustus Who Would Not Have Any Soup, The.
Story of Flying Robert, The.
Story of Johnny Head-in-Air, The.
Story of Little Suck-a-Thumb, The.
Story of the Wild Huntsman, The.
Hofmannsthal, Hugo von
Ballad of the Outer Life.
Many Indeed Must Perish in the Keel.
Poem: "We are such stuff as dreams are made of, and these."
Ship's Cook, a Captive Sings, The.
Stanzas on Mutability.
Travel Song.
Twilight of the Outward Life.
Two, The.
Venetian Night, A.
Vision, A.
World Secret.
Hofstein, David
My Thread.
Hogan, Inez
Blanket Street.
Middle-aged Child.
Space.
Hogan, Michael ("Bard of Thomond")
O'Neill's War Song.
Hogg, James ("The Ettrick Shepherd")
Boy's Song, A.
Charlie Is My Darling.
Donald Macdonald.
Flying Tailor, The.
Isabelle.
James Rigg.
Kilmeny.
Lock the Door, Lariston.
Love Is like a Dizziness.
McLean's Welcome.
Moggy and Me.
My Love She's But a Lassie Yet.
Queen's Wake, The, *sel.*
She's But a Lassie Yet.
Skylark, The.
There's Gowd in the Breast.
When the Kye Comes Hame.
Women Folk, The.
Hogg, Robert
Little Falls.
Poem: "In its going down, the moon."
Song: "Sun is mine, The."
Hoh, Israel Kafu
Vulture, The.
Holbrook, David
Dead Metaphors.
Delivering Children.
Fingers in the Door.
Living? Our Supervisors Will Do That for Us!
Poor Old Horse.
Somewhere in Tuscany.
Holbrook, Florence
Prayer, A: "Not more of light I ask, O God."
Holbrook, Weare
Varitalk.
Holcroft, Thomas
Gaffer Gray.
Holden, J. Stuart
Face of Christ, The.
Holden, Raymond
Dead Morning.
Fawn, The.
Geese in the Running Water.
Light the Lamp Early.
Proud, Unhoped-for Light.
Song for Government.
Storm over Rockefeller Center.
Winter among the Days.
Holden, Raymond, *and* **Sara Henderson Hay** *See* **Hay, Sara Henderson,** *and* **Raymond Holden**
Holden, Stephen
In Praise of Antonioni.
Holder, C. S.
King's Wood, The.
Hölderlin, Friedrich
Ages.
Blind Singer, The.
Evening Fantasy.
Half of Life, The.
Song of Fate.
To Nature.
Holender, Barbara D.
Quality of Pain, A.
Wonder Shell, The.
Holiday, Barten *See* **Holyday, Barten**
Holland, Lord
Who Seeks to Please All Men.
Holland, Hugh
Shakespeare Dead.
Sonnet to Shakespeare.
Upon the Lines and Life of the Famous Scenic Poet, Master William Shakespeare.
Holland, Josiah Gilbert
Babyhood.
Bitter-sweet, *sels.*
Christmas Carol, A: "There's a song in the air!"
Cradle Song: "What is the little one thinking about?"
Daniel Gray.
Day's Demand, The.
Give Us Men.
God Give Us Men!
Gradatim.
Hymn: "For Summer's bloom and Autumn's blight."
Lullaby: "Rockaby, lullaby, bees in the clover!"
Mistress of the manse, The, *sel.*
Rockaby, Lullaby.
Song of Doubt, A.
Song of Faith, A.
There's a Song in the Air!
To My Dog "Blanco."
Wanted.
Where Shall the Baby's Dimple Be?
Holland, Norah M.
First Christmas, The.
Little Dog-Angel, A.
Mary Sings.
Sea-Gulls.
Sea Song.
Shepherd's Song.
Three Kings Came Riding.
Holland, Sir Richard
Buke of the Howlat, The, *sel.*
Roye Robert the Bruss the rayke he avowit, The.
Holland, Rupert Sargent
Foolish Flowers.
Jack-in-the-Pulpit.
P's and Q's.
Secrets of Our Garden, The.
Teapot Dragon, The.
When I Grow Up.
Hollander, John
Aristotle to Phyllis.
By the Sea.
Danish Wit.
Digging It Out.
Fear of Trembling, The.
Great Bear, The.
Horas Tempestatis Quoque Enumero; the Sundial.
Lady's-Maid's Song, The.
Last Words.
Lion Named Passion, A.
Lower Criticism, The.
Movie-Going.
Night Mirror, The.
Ninth of July, The.
Non Sum Qualis Eram in Bona Urbe Nordica Illa.
Paysage Moralisé.
Slepynge Long in Greet Quiete Is Eek a Greet Norice to Leccherie.
Sunday Evenings.
Under Cancer.
When All of Them Ran Off.
Wrath.
Hollar, Constance
Caged Mongoose, The.
Holley, Horace
Hill, The.
Holliday, Carl
Thus Speak the Slain.
Hollis, Mark
Careless Talk.
'Twixt Cup and Lip.
Holloway, Ariel Williams
Northboun'.
Holloway, John
Brothers, The.
Elegy for an Estrangement.
Family Poem.
Journey through the Night.
Light, The.
Warning to a Guest.
Holloway, John Wesley
Black Mammies.
Calling the Doctor.
Corn Song, The.
Miss Melerlee.
Holm, Constance
Our Calvary.
"Holm, Saxe." *See* **Jackson, Helen Hunt**
Holman, M. Carl
And on This Shore.
Letter across Doubt and Distance.
Mr. Z.
Notes for a Movie Script.
Picnic; the Liberated.

Song: "Dressed up in my melancholy."
Three Brown Girls Singing.
Holme, Jamie Sexton
Mountain Evenings.
Timber Line Trees.
Holme, Vincent
Good Friday.
Holmes, Daniel Henry
Willy Winkie.
Holmes, Edmond G. A.
Immanence.
Holmes, George S.
And Yet Fools Say.
Holmes, Georgiana *See* **"Klingle, George"**
Holmes, John
At a Country Fair.
Auction.
Broken One, The.
Bucyrus.
But Choose.
Carry Me Back.
Chance, The.
Core, The.
Eleventh Commandment, The, *sel.*
Evening Meal in the Twentieth Century.
Fear of Dying, The.
Flower, The.
Fortune Teller, The.
Good Night! Good Night!
Grass.
Having New England Fathers.
Herself.
Letter, The.
Man at Work.
Map of My Country.
Metaphor for My Son.
Misery.
New View, The.
Old Men and Young Men.
Overgrown Back Yard, The.
Poetry Defined.
Pour Down.
Prayer on the Night before Easter.
Questions for the Candidate.
Rhyme of Rain.
Somerset Dam for Supper, The.
Spiral, The.
Table for One.
Take Home This Heart.
Testament.
Thrifty Elephant, The.
What Does a Man Think About.
What Literature Needs.
When Moses came down from the mountain and the cloud.
Willing Suspension, A.
Holmes, John F.
Old New Hampshire.
Holmes, John Haynes
All Hail, the Pageant of the Years.
God of the Nations.
Hymn: "Great Spirit of the speeding spheres.]
Hymn: "Thou God of all, whose presence dwells."
Hymn of At-One-Ment.
O Father, Thou Who Givest All.
O God of Field and City.
O God Whose Love Is over All.
O God, Whose Smile Is in the Sky.
Voice of God Is Calling, The.
Holmes, Lilian
Pipes and Drums.
Holmes, Oliver Wendell
Additional Verses to "Hail Columbia."
Aestivation.
After a Lecture on Keats.
After the Fire.
Album Verses.
Army Hymn.
As on the gauzy wings of fancy flying.
At the Pantomime.
At the Saturday Club.
Aunt Tabitha.
Autocrat of the Breakfast Table, The, *sels.*
Ballad of the Boston Tea-Party, A.
Ballad of the Oysterman, The.
Bill and Joe.
Birthday of Daniel Webster.
Boys, The.
Broomstick Train, The.
Brother Jonathan's Lament for Sister Caroline.
Build thee more stately mansions, O my soul.
Cacoëthes Scribendi.
Chambered Nautilus, The.
"Christo et Ecclesiae" 1700.
Contentment.
Crooked Footpath, The.
Daily Trials.
Daniel Webster.
Deacon's Masterpiece, The; or, The Wonderful "One-Hoss Shay."
Dorchester Giant, The.
Dorothy Q.
Eggstravagance, An.
Epilogue to the Breakfast Table Series.
Faith Shall Build a Fairer Throne.
Familiar Letter to Several Correspondents, A.
Farewell to Agassiz, A.
Father of all! in Death's relentless claim.
Flower of Liberty, The.
Freedom, Our Queen.
God Save the Flag.
Grandmother's Story of Bunker Hill Battle.
Heaven.
Height of the Ridiculous, The.
How the Old Horse Won the Bet.
Hymn of Trust.
If she had—Well: She longed, and knew not wherefore.
In Memory of Abraham Lincoln.
In Thine Arms.
Intramural Aestivation, or Summer in Town, by a Teacher of Latin.
Iris, *sel.*
Iron Gate, The, *sel.*
It chanced to be our washing day.
James Russell Lowell ("Thou shouldst have sung the swan song for the choir").
La Grisette.
Last Leaf, The.
Latter-Day Warnings.
Lexington.
Living Temple, The.
Manhood.
Many Things.
Moral Bully, The.
Music Grinders, The.
My Aunt.
Ode for a Social Meeting.
Ode for Washington's Birthday.
Old Ironsides.
Old Man Dreams, The.
On Lending a Punch-Bowl.
On the Death of President Garfield.
"One-Hoss Shay" The; or, The Deacon's Masterpiece.
Our Father's Door.
Our Hymn.
Peau de Chagrin of State Street, The.
Poem, A: Dedication of the Pittsfield Cemetery, September 9, 1850, *sel.*
Poem for the Meeting of the American Medical Association, A.
Poet at the Breakfast Table, The, *sel.*
Poet's Lot, The.
Professor at the Breakfast Table, The, *sels.*
Sea Dialogue, A.
September Gale, The.
Sherman's in Savannah.
1643 "Veritas" 1878.
Strong Heroic Line, The.
Sun-Day Hymn, A.
Then As to Feasting.
To an Insect.
To My Readers.
To the Portrait of "A Gentleman."
Truants from love, we dream of wrath.
Two Sonnets: Harvard.
Two Streams, The.
Under the Violets.
Union and Liberty.
Unsatisfied.
Voiceless, The.
Washington's Birthday.
Welcome to Dr. Benjamin Apthorp Gould, A.
Welcome to the Nations.
Wind-Clouds and Star-Drifts, *sel.*
Wonderful "One-Hoss Shay," The.
Holmes, R. Ernest
Black Lady in an Afro Hairdo Cheers for Cassius.
Black Woman.
Two from the Country.
Holmes, Ruth
No Thoroughfare.
Holmes, Theodore
Buddha.
Christ.
Dysynni Valley, The.
Old Age Home, The.
Holmes, W. K.
Dream Ship, The.
Old Brown Horse, The.
Holt, Edgar
Two Sonnets from a Sequence.
Holt, Henry Dobbs
Am I Nearer Heaven To-night?
Holt, Jessie
Dying.
Hölty, Ludwig
Harvest Song.
Holub, Miroslav
Boy's Head, A.
History Lesson, A.
Holyday, Barten
Song: "O harmless feast."
Technogamia, *sels.*
Tobacco's a musician.
Holz, Arno
Buddha.
Leave-taking, A.
Phantasus ("Its roof among the stars projected").
Phantasus, I-8 ("On a mountain of sugar-candy").
Phantasus, VI-14 ("I wish you were real!").
Roses Red.
Homan, Helen Walker
Rain at Night.
Home, Anne *See* **Hunter, Anne**
"Home, Cecil." *See* **Webster, Augusta**
Home, F. Wyville
Dover Cliff.
English Girl, An.
In a September Night.
Homer
Achilles' baneful wrath resound, O goddess that impos'd.
Achilles' Shield.
Achilles Shows Himself in the Battle by the Ships.
Achilles to Lycaon.
And a dog, lying there, lifted its head and pricked its ears.
Boar Hunt, The.

Homer (continued)
But Minerva fetch'd/ The winds from sea.
Chief reply'd, The: This time forbids to rest.
Death of Hector, The.
Downe to the King's most bright-kept baths they went.
End of the Suitors, The.
Escape from Cyclop, The.
For my part, I'le not meddle with the cause.
From her bed's high and odoriferous roome.
Hector and Andromache.
Hector to Andromache.
"I myself will now go home and see."
Iliad, The, *sels.*
In mean time flew our ships, and straight we fetched.
Lamentations, The.
Last Parting of Hector and Andromache, The.
Meanwhile Achilles, plung'd.
Nausicaa ("Now when they came to the bright running river").
Nestor's Speech to Achilles and Agamemnon.
Nstor's Speech to Achilles and Agamemnon.
Night Encampment outside Troy.
Nor had great Hector and his friends the rampire overrun.
"O that I were as sure to live, immortal, and sustain."
"O tyrant, armed with insolence and pride!"
Odyssey, The, *sels.*
Our ship now pass'd the streights of th' ocean flood.
Parting of Hector and Andromache, The.
Patroclus' Body Saved.
Preparation of the Pyre for Patroclus.
Priam and Achilles.
Pyre of Patroclus, The.
Quarrel, The.
Return of Ulysses, The.
Sacrifice, The.
Sarpedon to Glaukos.
Scylla and Charybdis.
She with his sight made breathless haste to meet him.
Sirens, Scylla and Charybdis, The.
Thetis and Achilles.
Trojans outside the Walls, The.
"Twelve herds of oxen, no lesse flockes of sheepe."
Ulysses and His Dog.
Ulysses and the Sirens.
Ulysses Hears the Prophecies of Tiresias.
Ulysses in the Waves.
When every least commander's will best soldiers had obeyed.
Where neither king nor shepheard want comes neare.
Wrath of Achilles, The, *abr.*
Homer-Dixon, Homera
New Year, The.
Honan, Daniel J.
Dostoievsky to a Young Communist.
Hone, William
First of April, The.
Honestus
Requirements: "Not too old, and not too young."
Honeywood, St. John
Darby and Joan.
Radical Song of 1786, A.
Honig, Edwin
Happening.
Jane Retreat.
My Face Looks Out.
November through a Giant Copper Beech.
Tall Toms, The.
True Romance.
Walt Whitman.
Honora, Sister Mary
After Mardi Gras.
Eighteen.
Land of the Free.
Hoock, Harriet
Answer.
To Joseph.
Hood, E. P.
God, Who Hath Made the Daisies.
Hood, Thomas
Answer to Pauper.
Autumn ("I saw old Autumn in the misty morn").
Bachelor's Dream, The.
Ballad: "It was not in the winter."
Ballad: "Spring it is cheery."
Ben Bluff.
Bridge of Sighs, The.
Centipede along the threshold crept, The.
Death.
Death of Leander, The.
Death-Bed, The.
Death's Ramble.
Domestic Asides; or, Truth in Parentheses.
Domestic Didactics by an Old Servant.
Dream Fairy, The.
Dream of Eugene Aram, The.
Dust to Dust.
Epigram: "After such years of dissension and strife."
Epigram: "When Eve upon the first of men."
Fair Ines.
Fairy's Reply to Saturn, The.
Faithless Nelly [*or* Nellie] Gray.
Faithless Sally Brown.
False Poets and True.
Farewell, Life.
Fewer Books, More Salad.
Flowers.
Fragment: "Mary, I believ'd you quick."
Friendly Address, A.
Gold.
Good Night.
Green Dryad's Plea, The.
Haunted House, The.
Her Death.
Her Moral.
Hero and Leander, *sels.*
I Remember.
I Remember, I Remember.
I'm Not a Single Man.
It Is Not Death.
It Was Not in the Winter.
It Was the Time of Roses.
Lake and a Fairy Boat, A.
Last Man, The.
Lay of the Laborer.
Lear.
Lines in a Young Lady's Album.
Little Piggy [*or* Piggies].
Mary's Ghost.
Melodies of Time, The.
Miss Kilamsegg and Her Precious Leg, *sels.*
Natural Tears.
No!
No human figure stirr'd, to go or come.
Nocturnal Sketch, A.
November.
November in England.
Ode: Autumn.
Ode: "I saw old Autumn in the misty morn."
Ode on a Distant Prospect of Clapham Academy.
Ode to Autumn.
Ode to the Moon.
On a Royal Demise.
On Mistress Nicely, a Pattern for Housekeepers.
Open Question, An.
Our Village—by a Villager.
Parental Ode to My Son, [Aged Three Years and Five Months,] A.
Past and Present.
Peter's Tears.
Plain Direction, A.
Plea of the Midsummer Fairies, The, *sels.*
Please to Ring the Belle.
Poet's Fate, The.
Queen Mab.
Reflection, A.
Ruth.
Sailor's Apology for Bow-Legs, A.
Sally Simpkin's Lament.
Scylla's Lament.
Sea of Death, The.
Serenade: "Ah, sweet, thou little knowest how."
Shakespeare.
Shakespeare: The Fairies' Advocate.
She Is Far from the Land.
Silence.
Song: "Lake and a fairy boat, A."
Song: "O lady, leave thy silken thread."
Song of the Shirt, The.
Sonnet: "It is not death."
Sonnet: Silence.
Sonnet to Vauxhall.
Stanzas: "Farewell, Life! my senses swim."
Stars Are with the Voyager, The.
Suggestions by Steam.
Sun Was Slumbering in the West, The.
Sweated Labor.
Tender Babes.
Tim Turpin.
Time of Roses, The.
Titania.
To Minerva.
To My Son.
To My Son, Aged Three Years and Five Months.
Tom Tatter's Birthday Ode.
Two Swans, The.
Unhinged the iron gates half open hung.
Water Lady, The.
World is with me, and its many cares, The.
Written in a Volume of Shakespeare.
Hood, Tom (Thomas Hood, Jr.)
All in the Downs.
Catch, A: "If you were queen of bloaters."
In Memoriam Technicam.
Little tigers are at rest, The.
Muddled Metaphors.
Poets and Linnets.
Ravings.
Takings.
Wedding, The.
What He Took.
Hooft, Pieter Corneliszoon
Thus Spoke My Love.
Hook, Theodore
Cautionary Verses [to Youth of Both Sexes].
Hooker, Brian
Ballade of the Dreamland Rose.
From Life.
Ghosts.
Little Person, A.
Mother of Men.

Portrait, A.
Song: "Only a little while since first we met."
Hookes, Nicholas
To Amanda Walking in the Garden.
Hookham, George
Chamonix.
Hooley, Teresa
Christ in Woolworth's.
Legend of Gethsemane, A.
To-day I saw a butterfly.
Hooper, Ellen Sturgis
Beauty and Duty.
Duty.
Straight Road, The.
To R. W. E.
Hooper, Lucy Hamilton
Three Loves.
Hooton, Earnest Albert
Fat-buttocked Bushmen, The.
Lines to Homo Somejerktensis.
Ode to a Dental Hygienist.
To Chloe.
Hoover, Gene Boardman
Mountain Dawn.
Hoover, Margaret
Triolet: "I intended a handspring."
Hope, A. D.
Australia.
Chorale: "Often had I found her fair."
Conquistador.
Damnation of Byron, The.
Death of the Bird, The.
Elegy, The: "Madam, no more! The time has come to eat."
Epistle, An: "First, last and always dearest, closest, best."
Gateway, The.
Imperial Adam.
Pronunciation of Erse, The.
Pyramis; or, The House of Ascent.
Return from the Freudian Islands, The.
Standardization.
Hope, Francis
Peeping Tom.
Hope, Henry
Now I Have Found a Friend.
Hope, James Barron
John Smith's Approach to Jamestown.
"Hope, Laurence" (Adela Florence Cory Nicolson)
Ashore.
Bride, The.
Carpe Diem.
For This Is Wisdom.
In the Early, Pearly Morning, *sel.*
Kashmiri Song ("Pale hands I love").
Khristna and His Flute.
Less Than the Dust.
Masters, The.
Teak Forest, The, *sel.*
Wisdom?
Hope, Margaret
Through the Ages.
Hopegood, Olive
Feathers.
Hopegood, Peter
Dithyramb in Retrospect.
First Aid.
Free Martin.
Nicorn's Dower, The.
Protagonist, The.
There Sleeps in the Churchyard.
Hô P'ei Yü,
Poem of Ten "Ones," The.
Hopkins, Ellice
Life in Death.
Hopkins, Gerard Manley
Alchemist in the City, The.
Andromeda.
As Kingfishers Catch Fire, Dragonflies Draw Flame.
Ash-Boughs.
At the Wedding March.
Bad I am, but yet thy child.
Barnfloor and Winepress.
Binsey Poplars (Felled 1879).
Blessed Virgin Compared to the Air We Breathe, The.
Brothers.
Bugler's First Communion, The.
Caged Skylark, The.
Candle Indoors, The.
Carrion Comfort.
Christ Speaks.
Cuckoo, The.
Duns Scotus's Oxford.
Easter Communion.
Epithalamion: "Hark, hearer, hear what I do."
Felix Randal.
Fragment: Furl of Fresh-leaved Dog-Rose Down, The.
Fragment: "Repeat that, repeat."
Fragment: "Strike, churl; hurl, cheerless wind, then; heltering hail."
God's Grandeur.
Golden Echo, The.
Habit of Perfection, The.
Harry Ploughman.
Heaven-Haven.
Henry Purcell.
Hurrahing in Harvest.
I Wake and Feel the Fell of Dark.
In Honor of St. Alphonsus Rodriguez.
In the Valley of the Elwy.
Inversnaid.
Justus Quidem Tu Es, Domine.
Lantern out of Doors, The.
Leaden Echo and the Golden Echo, The.
Life Death Does End.
Loss of the *Eurydice,* The.
May Magnificat, The.
Moonless Darkness Stands Between.
Moonrise.
My Own Heart Let Me More Have Pity On.
No, they are come; their horn is lifted up.
No Worst, There Is None.
Nun Takes the Veil, A.
Of a Death in Winter ("Manshape, that shone").
On a Piece of Music.
On a Poetess.
On Saturday sailed from Bremen.
Patience.
Patience, Hard Thing!
Peace.
Pied Beauty.
Repeat That, Repeat.
Rosa Mystica.
Rowing, I reach'd a rock — the sea was low.
St. Alphonsus Rodriguez.
Sea and the Skylark, The.
Six Epigrams, *sel.*
Soldier, The.
Sonnet: "I wake and feel the fell of dark, not day."
Sonnet: "No worst, there is none. Pitched past pitch of grief."
Sonnet: "Not, I'll not, carrion comfort, Despair, not feast on thee."
Sonnet: "Patience, hard thing! the hard thing but to pray."
Sonnet: "Thou art indeed just, Lord."
Spelt from Sibyl's Leaves.
Spring.
Spring and Death.
Spring and Fall.
Starlight Night, The.
A
Summer Malison, The.
Terrible Sonnets, The.
That Nature Is a Heraclitean Fire and of the Comfort of the Resurrection.
Thou Art Indeed Just, Lord.
Times are nightfall, look, their light grows less, The.
To Him Who Ever Thought with Love of Me.
To His Watch.
To Oxford.
To R. B.
To Seem the Stranger Lies My Lot.
To What Serves Mortal Beauty?
Tom's Garland.
Vision of the Mermaids, A, *sel.*
What I Do Is Me.
Wildness.
Windhover, The.
Winter with the Gulf Stream.
Wreck of the *Deutschland,* The.
Hopkins, John
To Amasia, Tickling a Gentleman.
Hopkins, John Henry, Jr
Three Kings of Orient.
We Three Kings of Orient Are.
Hopkins, Joseph G. E.
For a Child Who Died.
To a Baffled Idealist.
Variations on a Theme, *parody.*
Hopkins, Minnie Case
Autumn Leaves.
Heart Is a Strange Thing, The.
Hopkinson, Francis
American Independence.
Battle of the Kegs, The.
British Valor Displayed.
Daughter's Rebellion, The.
New Roof, The.
On the Late Successful Expedition against Louisbourg.
Hopkinson, Joseph
Hail, Columbia!
Hoppe, Ann
Consecration.
Hopper, Edward
Jesus Saviour, Pilot Me.
Hopper Nora
Carol of Three Kings, The.
Dark Man, The.
Fairy Fiddler, The.
June.
King of Ireland's Son, The.
March.
Marriage Charm, A.
'Tis I Go Fiddling, Fiddling.
Hopper, Queenie Scott- *See* **Scott-Hopper, Queenie**
Horace, (Quintus Horatius Flaccus)
Again? New tumults in my breast?
Albi, Ne Doreas, *wr.* [Doleas].
Another to the Same.
Art of Poetry, The.
Ask Not Ungainly.
Bandusia, Stainless Mirror ("O fons Bandusiae").
Barine, the Incorrigible.
Bold Satirist, The, *abr.*
Bore, The.
By the Flat Cup.
Country Life.
Death of Cleopatra, The ("Nunc est bibendum").
Did any punishment attend.
Diffugere Nives.
Epodes, *sel.*
Extremum Tanain.
Fifth Ode of Horace, The ("Quis multa gracilis").
For Whom, Pyrrha?

Horace (continued)
Fountain of Bandusia, The.
Frippery.
Gift of Song, The.
Golden Mean, The.
Guardian of Hill and Woodland.
Happiness.
Happy the Man.
Happy the man whom bount'ous Gods allow.
Holiday ("Festo quid potius die").
Horace to Pyrrha.
Horat. Ode 29. Book 3. Paraphras'd in Pindarique Verse.
Horrors of Civil War, The.
I Hate Their Empty Shows.
Integer Vitae.
Invocation: "Maidens young and virgins tender."
It Always Happens.
Journey to Brundusium, *abr.*
Let the youth hardened by a sharp soldier's life.
Many by valor have deserved renown.
Martial Rage.
Mistrust To-Morrow.
Moderation.
Muses Love Me, The.
O Cruel Still.
O Fons Bandusiae.
Ode to Thaliarchus.
Odes, *sels.*
Passing of Lydia, The.
Persian Fopperies ("Persicos odi").
Persian Pomp.
Pine Tree for Diana, The ("Montium custos nemorumque").
Proud Chloe's Heart.
Questioning Lydia ("Lydia, dic, per omnes").
Reconciliation, The ("Donec gratus eram").
Returned Warrior ("O saepe mecum").
Revenge ("Audivere, Lyce")
Revery of a Business Man.
Satires, *sels.*
Seek a Haven ("O navis referent").
Ship of State, The ("O navis, referent").
Snow dissolv'd, no more is seen, The.
Teasing Lovers, The.
Tell Me, Lydia ("Cum tu, Lydia").
This Monument Will Outlast.
Time to Choose a Lover.
To a Girl.
To an Ambitious Friend ("Quid bellicosus").
To Aristius Fuscus.
To Chloe ("Vitas hinnuleo").
To Faunus ("Faune, Nympharum").
To Fuscus Aristus.
To His Cup-Bearer.
To His Servant.
To Leuconöe ("Tu ne quaesieris").
To Licinius ("Rectius vives").
To Ligurinus.
To Lucius Sestius ("Solvitur acris hiems").
To Maecenas ("Tyrrhena regum progenies").
To Phidyle ("Caelo supinas").
To Phyllis ("Est mihi").
To Postumus ("Eheu, fugaces").
To Pyrrha ("Quis multa tracilis").
To Quintus Dellius ("Aequam memento").
To Thaliarchus ("Vides ut alta").
To the Fountain of Bandusia ("O fons Bandusiae").
To the Ship in Which Virgil Sailed to Athens ("Sic te diva potens Cypri").
To Venus ("Intermissa, Venus").
Today and Tomorrow.
Too Young for Love.
Town and the Country Mouse, The, *sl. abr.*
Translated out of Horace, Which Begins Rectius Vives.
Twenty-ninth Ode of the Third Book of Horace, The.
Vanity of Riches ("Non ebur neque aureum").
What slender youth bedewed with liquid odors.
Winter to Spring.
Young Men Come Less Often, The — Isn't It So?

Horan, Robert
Drowned Wife, The.
Emblems of Evening.
Farewell to Narcissus.
Little City.

Horikawa, Lady
How can one e'er be sure.
Will he love me forever?

Horn, Edward Newman
Darling, If You Only Knew.
In the Tub We Soak Our Skin.
Pussycat Sits on a Chair.
Tiger stalking in the night, The.

Horn, Herschel
Landscape near a Steel Mill.

Horne, Cyril Morton
To My Unborn Son.

Horne, Frank
Immortality.
Kid Stuff.
Letters [*or* Notes] Found near a Suicide.
More Letters Found near a Suicide.
Nigger.
Notes Found near a Suicide.
On Seeing Two Brown Boys in a Catholic Church.
Symphony.
To a Persistent Phantom.
To James.
Toast.

Horne, Herbert P.
Amico Suo.
Formosae Puellae.
If She Be Made of White and Red.
Nancy Dawson.

Horne, Richard Henry [*or* Hengist]
Akinetos.
Distraught for Meropé.
Eos.
Genius.
In Forest Depths.
Meeting of Orion and Artemis.
Orion; an Epic Poem, *sels.*
Pelters of Pyramids.
Plough, The.
Plow, The.
Slave, The.
Solitude and the Lily.

Horner, Joyce
Public Holiday; Paris.

Horton, Edward A.
Flag The.

Horton, George
Night in Lesbos, A.

Horton, George Moses
Eye of Love, The.
George Moses Horton, Myself.
On Liberty and Slavery.
Powers of Love, The.
Setting Sun, The.
Swan, The—Vain Pleasures.
To a Departing Favorite.

Hosking, Arthur Nicholas
Land of the Free.

Hoskins, John
Absence.
Epitaph on a Bellows-Maker, An.
Epitaph on a Man for Doing Nothing, An.
John Hoskins to His Little Child Benjamin, from the Tower.
Ode: "Absence, hear thou my protestation."
Of a Cozener.
Present in Absence.
That Time and Absence Proves Rather Helps than Hurts to Loves.

Hoskins, Katherine
Bee and the Petunia, The.
Côte d'Azur.
Not Lotte.
Nuit Blanche.

Hosmer, Frederick Lucian
Father, to Thee.
Friends Beyond.
Indwelling God, The.
My Dead.
O Beautiful, My Country.
Prayer in Sorrow.
Prophecy Sublime, The.
Through Unknown Paths.

Thy Kingdom Come, O Lord.
With Self Dissatisfied.

Hosmer, William Henry Cuyler
Song of Texas.

Hoss, Margaret McBride
Land Where the Taffy Birds Grow, The.

Hough, Graham
Age of Innocence.
Dark Corner.

Houghton, Firman
Mr. Frost Goes South to Boston.
She Sees Another Door Opening.

Houghton, George Washington Wright
Handsel Ring, The.
Legend of Walbach Tower, The.
Manor Lord, The.
March Winds, The.
Sandy Hook.

Houghton, Richard Monckton Milnes, 1st Baron *See* **Milnes, Richard Monckton, 1st Baron Houghton**

Houghton, Will H.
By Life, or by Death.

House, Vernal
In Tribute.

Houselander, Caryll
Litany to Our Lady.
Mediocracy.
Reed, The.
Soeur Marie Emilie.

Housman, Alfred Edward
Along the Field as We Came By.
Alta Quies.
Amelia Mixed the Mustard.
As I Gird on for Fighting.
As through the wild green hills of Wyre.
Away with Bloodshed.
Be Still, My Soul, Be Still.
Because I Liked You Better.
Blackbird, The.
Bredon Hill.
Bring, in this timeless grave to throw.
Carpenter's Son, The.
Chestnut Casts His Flambeaux [and the Flowers], The.
Clunton and Clunbury.
Could Man Be Drunk Forever.
Crossing Alone the Nighted Ferry.
Culprit, The.
Day of Battle, The.
Dedication: "They say my verse is sad: no wonder."
Delight it is in youth and May.
Deserter, The.
Easter Hymn.
Eight o'Clock.

1887.
A
Elephant, or the Force of Habit, The.
Epilogue: "Terence, this is stupid stuff."
Epitaph, An: "Here dead lie we because we did not choose."
Epitaph on an Army of Mercenaries.
Epithalamium: "He is here, Urania's son."
Fairies Break Their Dances, The.
Fancy's Knell.
Far in a Western Brookland.
Farewell: "Farewell to barn and stack and tree."

Farms of Home Lie Lost in Even, The.
For My Funeral.
Fragment of a Greek Tragedy.
Friends.

From Far, from Eve and Morning.
Good-by, Young Man, Good-by.
Good Creatures, Do You Love Your Lives.
Grenadier.
Hallelujah!
He Would Not Stay for Me.
Hell Gate.
Her Strong Enchantments Failing.
Here Dead Lie We [Because We Did Not Choose].
Ho, Everyone That Thirsteth.
How Clear, How Lovely Bright.
Hughley Steeple.
I Did Not Lose My Heart [in Summer's Even].
I Hoed and Trenched and Weeded.
I Knew a Cappadocian.
I to My Perils.
If it chance your eye offend you.
If truth in hearts that perish.
Illic Jacet.
Immortal Part, The.
In Midnights of November.
In my own shire, if I was sad.
In the Morning.
In valleys green and still.
Infant Innocence.
Inhuman Henry; or, Cruelty to Fabulous Animals.
Into My Heart an Air That Kills.
Is My Team Plowing?
Isle of Portland, The.
It Nods and Curtseys and Recovers.
Jar of Nations, The.
Lads in Their Hundreds, The.
Lancer.
Last Poems.
Laugh, Be Jolly.
Laws of God, the Laws of Man, The.
Lent Lily, The.
Loitering with a vacant eye.
Long Road, The.
Look not in my eyes, for fear.
Loveliest of Trees [the Cherry Now].
March.
Merry Guide, The.
My Dreams Are of a Field Afar.
New Mistress, The.
Night Is Freezing Fast, The.
Now Dreary Dawns the Eastern Light.
Now Hollow Fires Burn Out to Black.
O Billows Bounding Far.
Oh Fair Enough Are Sky and Plain.
Oh Is It the Jar of Nations.
O See How Thick the Goldcup Flowers.
Oh, When I Was in Love with You.
Oh Who Is That Young Sinner.
Olive, The.
On moonlit heath and lonesome bank.
On the Idle Hill of Summer.
On Wenlock Edge [the Wood's in Trouble].
On your midnight pallet lying.
Oracles, The.
Others, I Am Not the First.
Power of Malt, The.
R. L. S.
Rain, It Streams on Stone, The.
Recruit, The.
Reveille.
Revolution.
Say, lad, have you things to do?
Shades of Night, The.
Shake Hands.
Shot? so quick, so clean an ending?
Shropshire Lad, A.
Sigh That Heaves the Grasses, The.
Sinner's Rue.
Smooth between Sea and Land.
Soldier from the Wars Returning.
Stars Have Not Dealt Me, The.
Stars, I Have Seen Them Fall.
Stinging Nettle, The.
Street Sounds to the Soldiers' Tread, The.
Strong Love.
Summer Time on Bredon.
Tell Me Not Here [It Needs Not Saying].
Terence, This Is Stupid Stuff.
Then and Now.
There Is Hallelujah Hannah.
There pass the careless people.
They Say My Verse Is Sad.
Think No More Lad [Laugh, Be Jolly].
This time of year a twelvemonth past.
'Tis Time, I Think, by Wenlock Town.
To an Athlete Dying Young.
To His Godson Gerald C. A. Jackson.
To Stand Up Straight and Tread the Turning Mill.
To Think That Two and Two Are Four.
True Lover, The.
Twice a week the winter thorough.
Wake Not for the World-Heard Thunder.
We'll to the Woods No More.
Welsh Marches, The.
Wenlock.
Wenlock Edge.
Westward on the high-hilled plains.
When Adam Day by Day.
When First My Way [to Fair I Took].
When Green Buds Hang.
When I Was One-and-twenty.
When I Watch the Living Meet.
When Israel Out of Egypt Came.
When Smoke Stood Up from Ludlow.
When Summer's End Is Nighing.
When the Lad for Longing Sighs.
White in the Moon the Long Road Lies.
Winds out of the west land blow, The.
With Rue My Heart Is Laden.
With Seed the Sowers Scatter.
World Goes None the Lamer, The.
Yon Far Country.
Yonder See the Morning Blink.
You Smile upon Your Friend To-Day.

Housman, Laurence
All Fellows, *sel.*
"And the Word Was Made Flesh."
Bonds.
Comrades.
Continuing City, The.
Dead Warrior, A.
Dear love, when with a two-fold mind.
Dedication: "When I have ended, then I see."
Deus Noster Ignis Consumens.
Farewell to Town.
Gardener, The.
God's Mother.
Help-Givers, The.
Prayer for the Healing of the Wounds of Christ, A.
Resurrection.
Rue, *sel.*
Settlers, The.
Spikenard.
To Thomas Hardy.
Two Loves, The.

Houston, Margaret Bell
Admonitions.
Cerelle.

Hovanessian, Diana der
Six Lines Unheard.

Hovell-Thurlow, Edward, 2d Baron Thurlow
Heron, The.
May.
When in the Woods I Wander All Alone.

Hover, Donald H.
Other Person's Place, The.

Hover, Emily
Mr. Beetle.

Hovey, Richard
Accident in Art.
At the Crossroads.
At the End of the Day.
Barney McGee.
Battle of Manila, The.
Birth of Galahad, The, *sel.*
Call of the Bugles, The.
Chanson de Rosemonde.
Comrades.
Contemporaries.
Dartmouth Winter-Song.
Eleazar Wheelock.
Envoy: "Whose furthest footstep never strayed."
Here falls no light of sun nor stars.
Hunting Song.
I said in my heart, "I am sick of four walls and a ceiling."
Immanence.
Kavanagh, The.
King Arthur, *sel.*
Laurana's Song.
Love in the Winds.
Mocking Bird, The.
Sea Gipsy, The.
Sea Gypsy, The.
Spring, *sels.*
Stein Song, A.
Taliesin, *sel.*
Transcendence.
Two Lovers, The.
Unmanifest Destiny.
Wander-Lovers, The.
Word of the Lord from Havana, The.
Ylen's Song.

How, William Walsham
Funeral Hymn.
Lord Jesus, When We Stand Afar.
O Word of God Incarnate.
Our Work.
Soldiers of the Cross, Arise.
We Give Thee but Thine Own.

Howard, Dorothy S.
Birkett's Eagle.

Howard, Edward
Now Having Proved Thy Fond Delays.

Howard, Frances Minturn
Heron in Swamp.
Narcissus in a Cocktail Glass.
Prophecy in Flame.

Howard, Henry *See* **Surrey, Henry Howard, Earl of**

Howard, J. Gordon
My Life.

Howard, James
English Monsieur, The, *sel.*
Ladies, Farewell!

Howard, Philip, 1st Earl of Arundel

Howard (continued)
Hymn: "O Christ, the glorious crown."
Though Here in Flesh I Be.
Through Thy Cross and Passion.
Howard, Richard
Author of *Christine*, The.
Bonnard: A Novel.
Crepuscular.
Far Cry after a Close Call, A.
Gaiety, *sel.*
Queer's Song.
Saturday Morning.
Howard, Sir Robert
To the Unconstant Cynthia.
Howard, Sir Robert, *and* John Dryden
Indian- Queen, The, *sel.*
Poor Mortals.
Song of Aerial Spirits.
Howard, Robert Ervin
Earth-Born.
Sands of Time, The.
Howard, Sarah Elizabeth
Round-up, The.
Wild Horse Jerry's Story.
Howard, Vilma
Citizen, The.
Howard, Winifred
Fairy Wings.
Squirrels' Christmas, The.
White Horses.
Windy Day, A.
Howarth, Ellen Clementine
'Tis But a Little Faded Flower.
Howarth, Robert Guy
Elegy: "Here, awaiting what hereafter."
Memoir.
On a Row of Nuns in a Cemetery.
Howe, Fanny
Corn Dance, The.
Jasmine and the Gypsies.
Two Shots: a Love Affair.
Howe, George
Sun-Witch to the Sun, The.
Howe, Joseph
Acadia, *sel.*
In ev'ry thought, in ev'ry wish I own.
Song of the Micmac, The.
Howe, Julia Ward
Battle Hymn of the American Republic.
Battle Hymn of the Republic.
Decoration Day.
J. A. G.
Lincoln.
Message of Peace, The.
Our Country.
Our Orders.
Pardon.
Parricide.
Robert E. Lee.
Howe, Mark Antony DeWolfe ("Gilbertulus', "
Ben Franklin's Head (1728).
Distinction.
Petrillo, *parody.*
Pocket and Steeple.
Travellers, The.
"Whom the Gods Love."
"Whom the gods love die young;"—if gods ye be.
Howell, Elizabeth Lloyd
Milton's Prayer of [*or* for] Patience.
Howell, James
Of London Bridge, and the Stupendous Sight, and Structure Thereof.
Stanzas for Lent.
Upon Black Eyes, and Becoming Frowns.
Upon Dr. Davies' British Grammar.
Howell, Thomas
Jack Shows His Qualities and Great Good Will to Jone.
Lover Deceived Writes to His Lady, The, *sel.*
Man's Life Likened to a Stage Play.
Of Misery.
Of the Golden World.
Reward Doth Not Always Answer Desert.
Rose, The.
To His Lady, of Her Doubtful Answer.
To One Who after Death Would Leave His Lively Picture.
To the Reader.
When He Thought Himself Contemned.
Who Would Have Thought.
Winter's Morning Muse, A.
Howells, Mildred
Down a Woodland Way.
God's Will.
Going Too Far.
Moral in Sèvres, A.
Romance.
Howells, William Dean
Battle in the Clouds, The.
Bewildered Guest, The.
Calvary.
Caprice.
Change.
Company.
Earliest Spring.
Empty House, The.
Faith.
From Generation to Generation.
Hope.
If.
In August.
In Earliest Spring.
Judgment Day.
Labor and Capital.
Living.
Lost Beliefs.
Prayer, A: "Lord, for the erring thought."
Robin and the Cows, The.
Song the Oriole Sings, The.
Thanksgiving.
This Day.
Twelve P.M.
Two Wives, The.
Undiscovered Country, The.
Vison.
What Shall It Profit?
Howells, Winifred
Forthfaring.
Mood, A.
Past.
Poet and the Child, The.
Wasted Sympathy, A.
Howes, Barbara
Cat on Couch.
Chimera.
City Afternoon.
Death of a Vermont Farm Woman.
Early Supper.
Flight.
Home Leave.
Lace Maker, The.
Landscape, Deer Season.
Letter from the Caribbean, A.
Light and Dark.
L'Ile du Levant; the Nudist Colony.
Looking Up at Leaves.
Mistral.
On a Bougainvillaea Vine in Haiti [*or* at the Summer Palace].
On Galveston Beach.
Portrait of the Boy as Artist.
Rune for C., A.
Sea School.
To W. H. Auden on His Fiftieth Birthday.
Triumph of Chastity, The.
Triumph of Death, The.
Howes, Grace Clementine
Wind of the Prairie.
Winged Mariner.
Howitt, Mary
Barley-Mowers' Song, The.
Birds in Summer.
Broom Flower, The.
Buttercups and Daisies.
Child's Hymn, The.
Cornfields, *abr.*
Fairies of the Caldon Low, The.
Father Is Coming.
Flax Flower, The.
Hawking Party in the Olden Time, A.
Humming Bird, The.
Lion, The.
Little Children.
Marien Lee.
Monkey, The.
Old Christmas.
Rose of May, The.
Sale of the Pet Lamb, The.
Sea Fowler, The.
Sea-Gull, The.
September.
Spider and the Fly, The.
Spring Is Coming.
Spring Song, A.
Squirrel, The.
Swinging Song, A.
True Story of Web-Spinner, The.
Voice of Spring, The.
When on the breath of autumn [*or* autumn's] breeze.
Winter Fire, The.
Wood-Mouse, The.
Howitt, William
Departure of the Swallow, The.
Grey Squirrels, The.
Northern Seas.
Wind in a Frolic, The.
Howland, Edward
Condemned, The.
Howland, Mary Woolsey
In the Hospital.
Rest.
Howliston, Mary H.
Our Flag.
Hoyland, John S.
Prayer for Brotherhood, A.
Prayer for Family Love, A.
Prayer for Our Home.
Hoyt, Charles Hale
Bowery, The.
Hoyt, Charles Sumner
Is This the Time to Halt?
Hoyt, Helen (Mrs. William W. Lyman)
Arches.
At Daybreak.
Ellis Park.
Golden Bough.
Happiness Betrays Me.
Homage.
In the Park.
Lamp Posts.
Lover Sings of a Garden, The.
Memory.
New-born, The.
Rain at Night.
Reparation.
Sense of Death, The.
Since I Have Felt the Sense of Death.
Stone-Age Sea, The.
Hoyt, Helen Underwood
Kate.
Vegetable Fantasies.
Hoyt, Henry Martyn
Land of Dreams, The.
1917-1919.
Spell, The.
Hoyt, Ralph
Old.

Hsin Ch'i-chi
Drinking.
Hsi P'ei Lan
Morning Bell of Fang T'a, The.
Hsü Chien
Just Sixteen.
Hsüeh Feng
Palace Poem, A.
Hsüeh T'ao
Home from the Wars.
Hsü Pên.
Hermit, The.
Huang-fu Sung
Dream of Chiangnan, A.
Hubbard, P. M.
Subjectivity at Sestos.
To Cynthia, Not to Let Him Read the Ladies' Magazines.
Hubbell, Patricia
Autumn.
Black Snake, The.
Christmas Present, The.
Concrete Mixers.
Construction.
Joralemon Street.
Night.
Prayer for Reptiles.
Seagulls.
Streetcleaner's Lament, The.
Ten O'Clock.
Huckel, Oliver
I Thank Thee, Lord.
O Mind of God, Broad as the Sky.
Unanswered Prayer[s].
Hudnut, William Herbert, Sr
In Him Ye Are Made Full.
Quit You like Men.
Spirit of Victory, The.
Hudnut, William Herbert, Jr
No Prisoner of Time.
Hudson, Deatt
Some Tips on Watching Birds.
Hudson, Flexmore
Mallee in October.
Song of an Australian.
Hueffer, Ford Madox *See* **Ford, Ford Madox**
Huerta, Efraín
Sounds of Dawn, The.
Huff, Barbara A.
Afternoon with Grandmother.
Library, The.
Huff, Robert
Course, The.
Getting Drunk with Daughter.
Rainbow.
Smoker, The.
Traditional Red.
Hughan, Jessie Wallace
Where the Wood-Thrush Calls.
Hughes, Daniel
Damascus Road, The.
For Karen.
Hughes, Dave ("Old Arkansaw")
Drifter, The.
Hughes, Dorothy
Age of Sheen, The.
Dusting of the Books, The.
Hughes, Henry
Chloris a Constant Comfort.
Hughes, James D.
My Son.
Hughes, John
Court of Neptune, The.
Hughes, John Ceiriog
Alun Mabon's Song.
Epilogue to Alun Mabon.
Liberty.
Hughes, Langston
Acceptance.
African Dance.
Afro-American Fragment.
Alabama Earth.
American Heartbreak.
Angola Question Mark.
April Rain Song.
As I Grew Older.
Ballad of the Landlord.
Birmingham Sunday.
Black Man Speaks, The.
Border Line.
Bound No'th Blues.
Brass Spittoons.
Children's Rhymes.
City.
City; San Francisco.
College Formal: Renaissance Casino.
Color.
Corner Meeting.
Could Be ("Could be Hastings Street").
Cross.
Cultural Exchange.
Cycle.
Daybreak in Alabama.
Desert.
Dive.
Dream Boogie.
Dream Deferred.
Dream Variation [*or* Variations].
Dreams.
Dressed Up.
Drum.
Early Evening Quarrel.
End.
Epilogue: "I, too, sing America."
Esthete in Harlem.
Fantasy in Purple.
Feet o' Jesus.
Fire.
Florida Road Workers.
Garment.
Go Slow.
Gone Boy.
Hard Daddy.
Hard Luck.
Harlem ("Here on the edge of hell.")
Harlem ("What happens to a dream deferred").
Harlem Night Song.
Harlem Sweeties.
Havana Dreams.
Heaven: the City Called Heaven.
Homesick Blues.
House in Taos, A.
I Am the Darker Brother.
I Dream a World.
I Thought It Was Tangiers I Wanted.
I, Too, Sing America.
Impasse.
In Time of Silver Rain.
Jazz Band in a Parisian Cabaret.
Jazzonia.
Juke Box Love Song.
Kid in the Park.
Last Call.
Late Corner.
Lenox Avenue Mural.
Let America Be America Again.
Life Is Fine.
Little Dreams.
Little Green Tree Blues.
Luck.
Ma Lord.
Madam and Her Madam.
Me and the Mule.
Merry-go-round.
Mexican Market Woman.
Midnight Raffle.
Montmartre.
Moon.
Mother to Son.
Motto.
Negro Speaks of Rivers, The.
October 16: The Raid.
Pennsylvania Station.
Personal.
Po' Boy Blues.
Poem: "Night is beautiful, The."
Prayer: "I ask you this."
Rain.
Refugee in America.
Request for Requiems.
Sailor.
Same in Blues.
Saturday Night.
Sea Calm.
Seascape.
Slave.
Snail.
Song for a Dark Girl.
Song for a Suicide.
Song to a Negro Wash-woman.
Stars.
Subway Rush Hour.
Suicide's Note.
Sun.
Testament.
Theme for English B.
To Midnight Nan at LeRoy's.
Trip: San Francisco.
Trumpet Player.
Two Somewhat Different Epigrams.
Undertow.
Wake.
Water-Front Streets.
Weary Blues, The.
When Sue Wears Red.
Where? When? Which?
Wind.
Winter Sweetness.
Wisdom.
Without Benefit of Declaration.
Youth.
Hughes, Mary D.
Blessings of God, The.
Hughes, Richard
Burial of the Spirit.
Explanation, on Coming Home Late.
Felo de Se.
Glaucopis.
Image, The.
Invocation to the Muse.
Lover's Reply to Good Advice.
Old Cat Care.
On Time.
Ruin, The.
Sermon, The.
Tramp.
Walking Road, The.
Winter.
Hughes, Rupert
1898-1899.
1861-1865.
For Decoration Day.
Martyrs of the *Maine*, The.
With a First Reader.
Hughes, Ted
Bayonet Charge.
Bullfrog.
Cadenza.
Cat and Mouse.
Childbirth.
Complaint.
Crag Jack's Apostasy.
Dark Women.
Decay of Vanity, The.
Dick Straightup.
Dream of Horses, A.
Encounter.
Esther's Tomcat.
Famous Poet.
Fern.
Foxgloves.

Hughes (continued)
Ghost Crabs.
Griefs for Dead Soldiers.
Hag, The.
Hawk in the Rain, The.
Hawk Roosting.
Horses, The.
Jaguar, The.
Lake, The.
Law in the Country of the Cats.

Martyrdom of Bishop Farrar, The.
Mayday on Holderness.
My Brother Bert.
My Sister Jane.
New Moon in January.
November.
Otter, An.
Pause for Breath, A.
Pennines in April.
Pibroch.
Pike.
Retired Colonel, The.
Roarers in a Ring.
Second Glance at a Jaguar.
Secretary.
September.
Six Young Men.
Song: "O lady, when the tipped cup of the moon blessed you."
Stealing Trout.
Still-Life.
Thought-Fox, The.
Thrushes.
To Paint a Water Lily.
Trees.
Two Wise Generals.
View of a Pig.
Wind.
Witches.
Wodwo.
Woman Unconscious, A.
You Drive in a Circle.

Hughes, Thomas
If ever you go to Dolgelly.

Hugo, Richard
Death of the Kapowsin Tavern.
Degrees of Gray in Philipsburg.
Lady in Kicking Horse Reservoir, The.

Hugo, Victor
After Six Thousand Years.
Age Is Great and Strong, The.
At Dawn.
Be like the Bird.
Children of the Poor, The.
Genesis of Butterflies, The.
Good Night.
Grave and the Rose, The.
Heard on the Mountain.
House and Home.
Indignation.
Lion at Noon, The.
More Strong than Time.
My Two Daughters.
Nocturne: "I walked beside the deep, one night of stars."
O France When Thou Art Prone and Bound.
Poet's Simple Faith, The.
Poor Children.
Republic of the World.
Sunset, A.
To Make the People Happy.
Trumpets of the Mind, The.
Universal Republic, The.
What matter it though life uncertain be.
Where Goest Thou?
Wings.
Worst Treason, The.

Huidobro, Vincente
I Am Partly Moon.

Hull, John Mervin
Gates of the Year, The.

Hulme, Thomas Ernest
Above the Dock.
Autumn.
Conversion.
Embankment, The.
Fantasia of a Fallen Gentleman on a Cold Bitter Night on the Embankment.
Mana Aboda.

Hultman, J. A.
Thanks to God.

Hume, Alexander
Of the Day Estivall.
Summer Day.
Summer's Day, A.

"Hume Isobel" (I. H. Fisher)
Home-coming.
Sleeper, The.
Whiteness.

Hume, Tobias
Soldier's Song.

Humphrey, Frances
My Book of Life.

Humphreys, Aletha
Arachnida, Female.
Party Bid.

Humphreys, David
On Disbanding the Army.
Western Emigration.

Humphries, Rolfe
Aeolus.
Anecdote in Verse.
Aria.
Autumnal.
Coming Home.
Cynneddf, The.
Dafydd ap Gwilym Resents the Winter.
Down the Field.
He Visits a Hospital.

Hunt, Helen *See* **Jackson, Helen Hunt**

Hunt, J. H.
I Look Up.

Hunt, Josephine Slocum
You Kissed Me.

Hunt, Leigh
Abou Ben Adhem.

Captain Sword.
Cupid Drowned.
Dearest Poets, The.
Fancy Concert, The.
Fish and the Man, The.
Fish Answers, A.
Fish, the Man, and the Spirit, The.
Glove and the Lions, The.
House and Grounds, A.
If You Be a Nun.
Jaffar.
Jenny Kiss'd [*or* Kissed] Me.
Jovial Priest's Confession, The.
Lover of Music to his Pianoforte, A.
Nile, The.
Nun, The.
Nymphs, The, *sel.*
On Receiving a Crown of Ivy from the Same (Keats).
On the Grasshopper and Cricket.
Places of Nestling Green.
Poets, The.
Ready she sat with one hand to turn o'er.
Rondeau: "Jenny kissed me when we met."
Sneezing.
Sonnet to Hampstead.
Story of Rimini, The, *sels.*
There are the fair-limbed nymphs o' the woods.
Thought of the Nile, A.
To ——, M.D.
To a Fish.
To Hampstead.
To John Keats.
To Mrs. L. H.
To Percy Shelley.
To the Grasshopper and the Cricket.
To the Spirit Great and Good.
Two Heavens.
Ultra-Germano-Criticasterism.

Hunt, William
Autumn in the Plains.
Dead Knock About, The.
Moving Along.
My Work with Snow.
So That Women Will Talk to Trees.
Song from the End of the Earth.
What You Can Get from the Body.
Wintering in the Heartlands.

Hunter, Anne
My Mother Bids Me Bind My Hair.

Hunter, John
Dreams and Deeds.

Hunter-Duvar, John
Adieu to France.
Brawn of England's Lay.
De Roberval; a Drama, *sels.*
Emigration of the Fairies, The, *sel.*
First halt. They heard within a sugar patch.
Gallant Fleet, The.
Here, then, we stand on the Canadian shore.
La Belle Sauvage.
Ohnawa.
Twilight Song.

Hunting, G. F.
Help One Another.

Huntington, Ellen M. *See* **Gates, Ellen M. Huntington**

Huntington, George
International Hymn.
Peace Hymn for England and America.

Huntington, Gertrude *See* **McGiffert,Gertrude Huntington**

Huntington, Selina, Countess of
World Can Neither Give Nor Take, The.

Huntington, William Reed
Authority.
Tellus.

Huntley, Lydia Howard *See* **Sigourney, Lydia Huntley**

Huntley, Stanley
Annabel Lee, *parody.*

Hurd, Harry Elmore
Black and White Shuffle.

Hurley, Mary Rita
Beach House.

Hurnard, James
Winter.

Husband, E.
I Shall See Them Again.

Huss, John
Word of God, The.

Hussey, Jennie Evelyn
Lead Me to Calvary.

Hussey, Norah E.
I Spy.
My Garden.
Toad the Tailor.

Hussey, Ruth Anne
Little Rain Men.

Hutchinson, Barney
Cold Logic.

Hutchinson, Ellen Mackay *See* **Cortissoz, Ellen Mackay Hutchinson**

Hutchinson, Jesse
Ho! for California!
Sacramento.

Hutchinson, M. M.
Dancing on the Shore.
Harvest.
Making Tens.

My New Umbrella.
Ten Little Indian Boys.
Thames, The.
Tug-of-War, A.
Twice.
Hutchinson, Robert
Suburban Wife's Song.
Hutchison, Collister
Winter Night.
Hutchison, Percy
Columbus.
Hutchison, Percy Adams
Methinks the Measure.
Hutt, Frank
Vacation Time.
Hutton, Joan
Vain Dream for John Clare.
Hutton, Joseph
Tomb of the Brave, The.
Hutton, Laurence
Doves of Venice, The.
Huws, Daniel
Family Evening.
Goodbye to Regal.
Goodbye to Regal.
Huxley, Aldous
Canal, The.
Cicadas, The.
Doors of the Temple.
Fifth Philosopher's Song.
First Philosopher's Song.
Frascati's.
Jonah.
Male and Female Created He Them.
Ninth Philosopher's Song.
Soles Occidere et Redire Possunt, *sel.*
Song of Poplars.
Sunset, A.
Villiers de l'Isle-Adam.
Huxley, Thomas Henry
Tennyson.
Hyde, Douglas
Cold, Sharp Lamentation.
Cooleen, The.
He Meditates on the Life of a Rich Man.
Will You Be as Hard?
Hyde, Fillmore
Philosophical Poem on Cats, A.
"Hyde, Robin" (Iris Guiver Wilkinson)
Beaches, The, *sels.*
Church of the Holy Innocents, Dunedin.
English Rider, The.
Houses, The, *sels.*
Journey from New Zealand.
Ku Li.
People, The, *sels.*
Sarah.
Sisters.
Hyde, William De Witt
Creation's Lord, We Give Thee Thanks.
Hynson, George B.
Our Delaware.
Hywel ab Owain Gwynedd
Ode to a Chosen Girl.

I

"I., C. H. "
Walking with God.
"I. V. S. W." *See* **"W., I. V. S"**
"I. W." *See* **"W., I"**
Ibarbourou, Juana de
Fleeting Restlessness.
Smith, The.
Ibn Adiya, Al-Samau'al
Are We Not the People, *sel.*
Now listen to boasting which leaves the heart dazed.
Oh, Would That I Knew.
Oh, Ye Censurers.
Ibn al-Arabi
Ode: "They journeyed."
Ode: "Who can Support the anguish of Love?"
Ibn al-Rumi
On a Valetudinarian.
Ibn Chasdai, Abraham
Advice to Bores.
Elusive Maid, The.
Meek and the Proud, The.
Poor Scholar, The.
Ibn Darraj al Andalusi
Wing of Separation,The.
Ibn Ezra, Abraham
Far Sweeter than Honey.
Freedom.
God Everywhere.
Law, The.
Living God, The.
Out of Luck.
Ibn Ezra, Moses
All Ye That Go Astray.
Awake, My Soul.
Beautiful Is the Loved One.
Beauty of the Stars, The.
Book of Tarshish, The, *sel.*
Bring Me the Cup.
Drink, Friends.
Dying Wife to Her Husband, A.
Elegy: "In pain she bore the son who her embrace."
Elegy: "My thoughts impelled me to the resting-place."
End of Man Is Death, The.
God That Doest Wondrously.
He That Regards the Precious Things of Earth.
Hot Flame of My Grief, The.
I Went Out into the Garden.
In Vain Earth Decks Herself.
Joy of Life.
Man Is a Weaver.
Men Are Children of this World.
My Love Is like a Myrtle.
My Love Sways, Dancing.
On My Sorrowful Life.
Promises of the World, The.
Rejoice, O Youth, in the Lovely Hind.
Rosy Days Are Numbered, The.
Sorrow Shatters My Heart.
Splendor of Thine Eyes, The.
Strange Love.
Those Beauteous Maids.
To a Plagiarist.
Walk in the Precepts.
When She Plays upon the Harp or Lute.
Why Should I Grieve?
Wine-Songs, *sels.*
With Hopeless Love.
Without My Friends the Day Is Dark.
Works of God, The.
World Is like a Woman of Folly, The.
World's Illusion, The.
Ye Anger Earth.
Young Dove, The.
Ibn Gabirol, Solomon
Almighty! What Is Man?
Defiance.
Degenerate Age, A.
From Thee to Thee.
I Have Sought Thee Daily.
In Praise of Wisdom.
Invitation.
Meditations.
Morning Song.
My God.
Night.
Night-Thoughts.
O Soul, with Storms Beset.
Royal Crown, The, *abr.*
Song of the Wind and the Rain.
Stanzas: "With tears thy grief thou dost bemoan."
Two Things Have Met in Me.
Water Song.
Wine and Grief.
Wonderful are thy works, as my soul overwhelmingly knoweth.
Ibn Kolthum
Pour Us Wine.
Ibn Maatuk
Perturbation at Dawn.
Ibn Rashiq
Pretences.
Ibn Sabbatai, Judah
Expensive Wife, The.
Gift of Judah the Woman-Hater, The, *sel.*
Ibn Tibbon, Judah
Father's Testament, A.
Ibnu'l-Farid
Remembrance.
Ibn Zaydun
Cordova.
Ibsen, Henrik
Brand, *sel.*
Brand Speaks.
In the Orchard.
Ibycus
Autumn Love.
Ichihara, Prince
Solitary Pine.
"Idas." *See* **Wayland, John Elton**
Ignatius, Sister Mary
Our Lady of the Libraries.
Ignatius Loyola, Saint
Anima Christi.
Teach Us to Serve Thee, Lord.
Ignatow, David
Bagel, The.
Bothering Me at Last.
Dream, The.
Escapade, The.
Europe and America.
For One Moment.
Gardeners, The.
How Come?
News Report.
Promenade.
Sediment.
Simultaneously.
To Nowhere.
Ikhnaton (Amenhotep IV)
Hymn to the Sun.
Ilott, Percy H.
Witch, The.
Image, Selwyn
Her Confirmation.
Meditation for Christmas, A.
Prayer, A: "Dear, let me dream of love."
Protestation, The.
Iman, Yusef
Love Your Enemy.
Show Me Lord Show Me.
Imber, Naphtali Herz
Hatikvah—a Song of Hope.
Zionist Marching Song.
Imelda, Sister Mary
Etching, An.
Immanuel di Roma
Elegy: "Floods of tears well from my deepest heart, The."
Happiness amidst Troubles.
Love.
Machberoth, *sel.*
My Sweet Gazelle!
Oh, Let Thy Teachings.
On the Wall.
Paradise.
Virtue.
What Profit?
Worthless Heart, The.

Imr el Kais
Assignation, The.
Night Long, The.
A
Storm, The.
Weep Love's Losing.
Inber, Vera
Leningrad: 1943.
Pulkovo Meridian, The, *sel.*
Inchfawn, Fay
For Martha's Kitchen.
More Than.
Inez, Colette
Cold Waltzes.
For Denise McNair.
Force of Snow.
Sauerkraut Talk Shreds in His Ear.
Slumnight.
Unaware that Avessek.
Woman Who Loved Worms, The.
Ingalls, Jeremy
Invasion of Greece, The.
My Head on My Shoulders.
Ingalls, John James
Opportunity.
Tribute to Grass.
Ingamells, Rex
Forgotten People, *sel.*
Golden Bird, The.
No more the smoke-wisp signal climbs; no more.
Noon Is on the Cattle-Track, The.
Sea-Chronicles.
Ship from Thames.
Inge, Charles Cuthbert
Limerick "Certain young gourmet of Crediton, A."
On Monsieur Coué.
Inge, William Ralph
Limerick: "There was a good canon of Durham."
Ingelow, Jean
About the Fairies.
Apprenticed.
Birthday Morning.
Calling the Cows Home.
Dappled sky, a world of meadows, A.
Divided.
For Exmoor.
Heigh Ho!
High Tide on the Coast of Lincolnshire, The (1571).
Honors.
I Will Trust.
Kinsman.
Like a Laverock in the Lift.
Long White Seam, The.
Longing for Home.
Maternity.
Noble-Tuck Man, The.
One Morning, Oh! So Early.
Playing on the virginals.
Sailing beyond Seas.
Sea-nurtured.
Seven Times Five.
Seven Times Four.
Seven Times One.
Seven Times Seven.
Seven Times Six.
Seven Times Three.
Seven Times Two.
Singing Lesson, The.
Song of the Old Love.
Songs of Seven.
Songs of the Night Watches, *sel.*
Sorrows Humanize Our Race.
Summer Morning.
Supper at the Mill, *sel.*
Sweet Is Childhood.
Ingemann, Bernhard Severin
Pilgrim's Song.
Ingham, John Hall
Genesis.
George Washington.
Summer Sanctuary, A.
Inghilfredi, Siciliano
Canzone: He Rebukes the Evil of That Time, *sel.*
"Ingoldsby, Thomas" (Richard Harris Barham)
As I Laye a-Thynkynge.
Confession, The.
Cynotaph, The, *sel.*
Eheu Fugaces.
Forlorn One, The.
Hon. Mr. Sucklethumbkin's Story.
Ingoldsby Legends, The, *sels.*
Jackdaw of Rheims, The.
Knight and the Lady, The.
Last Lines.
Lay of St. Cuthbert, The.
Misadventures at Margate.
Mr. Barney Maguire's Account of the Coronation.
More Walks.
Not a Sou Had He Got.
St. Cuthbert Intervenes.
Ingraham, Nicholas Lloyd
House Cleaning.
Ingram, John Kells
Memory of the Dead, The.
National Presage.
Social Future, The.
Ingram, K. E.
Lizard.
Inman, Mary L.
Cry for a Dead Soldier.
Old Woman Sitting in the Sun.
Innes, Guy
It's Three No Trumps.
Innocent III, Pope
Golden Sequence, The
"Innsley, Owen" (Lucy White Jennison)
Bondage.
Burden of Love, The.
Dream of Death, A.
Inoue, Mitsuko
Country Pastor.
Iqbal, Muhammad
In the sea wave tosses side by side with wave.
Invocation, An: "In the sea wave tosses side by side with wave," *sel.*
"Ireland, Michael." *See* **Figgis, Darrell**
Iremonger, Valentin
Descending.
Dog, The.
Elizabeth.
Evening in Summer.
Going down the Mountain.
Hector.
Icarus.
In New Ross.
In This River.
Recollection in Autumn.
Spring Stops Me Suddenly.
These Apple Trees.
This Houre Her Vigill.
Time, the Faithless.
While the Summer Trees Were Crying.
Iriarte, [*or* Yriarte], Tomás de
Bee and the Cuckoo, The.
Flint and the Steel, The.
Musical Ass, The.
Iris, Scharmel
After the Martyrdom.
Fisherman Speaks, A.
Friar of Genoa, The.
Irma, Sister Mary
Joy.
Young Dead Speak, The.
"Ironbark." *See* **Gibson, George Herbert**
"Ironquill." *See* **Ware, Eugene Fitch**
Ironside, Harry A.
Which Do You Choose?
Irvin, Eric
Brother Ass.
Christmas 1942.
Midnight Patrol.
Irvin, Margaret
Chanticleer.
Irving, Minna (Mrs. Harry Michener)
Americans All.
Betsy's Battle-Flag.
His Living Monument.
Lincoln Leads.
Old Year's Prayer, The.
Wedding Gift, The.
Irving, Washington
Certain Young Lady, A.
Irwin, Thomas Caulfield
Antique Glimpses, *sel.*
Autumn.
December.
Dumb are the heavens: sphere controlling sphere.
Elizabethan Days, *sel.*
Faerie's Child, The.
Ghost's Promenade, The.
Glints of the Year—from a Window.
Grey-faced Spirit! let us sit.
Hours I Remember Lonely and Lovely to Me.
Imogen—in Wales.
Iphione.
L'Angelo.
Leaving Troy.
May Sunday, A.
Minnie.
Nature's Key-Notes.
Objects of the Summer Scene, The.
Song: "My dreams were doleful and drear."
Sonnet: "Apples ripen under yellowing leaves, The."
Sonnet: "Awakened, I behold through dewy leaves."
Sonnet: "I walk of grey noons by the old canal."
Sonnet: "Into the wood at close of rainy day."
Sonnet: "Now, winter's dolorous days are o'er, and through."
Sonnet: "Rainbow o'er the sea of afternoon, The."
Sonnet: "Regions of soft clear air, of cold green leaves."
Sonnet: "Remote from smoky cities, aged and grey."
Sonnet: "Roadside inn this summer Saturday, A."
Sonnet: "Rough green wealth of wheaten fields that sway, The."
Sonnet: "Upon an upland orchard's sunny side."
Sonnet: "When I had turned Catullus into rhyme."
Sonnet: "Ye two fair trees that I so long have known."
Sonnets (I-XIV).
Spring.
Suire, The.
Swift, *sel.*
'Tis pleasant, stretched on grassy lawn.
To a Skull, *sel.*
Two women loved him, shapes of Heaven.
Winter Life and Scenery.
Winter Noon in the Woods, *sel.*
With the Dawn.
With witchlike branches, barren, bleak, and drear.
Irwin, Wallace ("Ginger"; "Hashimura Togo")

Arthur with a lighted taper.
Aunt Nerissa's Muffin.
Blow Me Eyes!
Constant Cannibal Maiden, The.
Fate of the Cabbage Rose, The.
From Romany to Rome.
Grain of Salt, A.
Nautical Extravaganza, A.
Powerful Eyes o' Jeremy Tait, The.
Reminiscence.
Rhyme of the Chivalrous Shark, The.
Science for the Young.
Sea Serpant, The.
Sensitive Sydney.
Such a Pleasant Familee.
Worried Skipper, The.
Isaac, Ted
Urban Roses.
Isaac ben Samuel of Dampière
His Hand Shall Cover Us.
Isaacs, Jorge
Nima, The.
Isbell, Hugh O.
Crucifixion.
Faith.
Ise, Lady
Rains of Spring, The.
Wild Geese.
Isenhour, Walter E.
Be Friendly.
Beside a Baby's Bed.
Dear Little Arms, The.
Down-Pullers, The.
Give Us Sober Men.
God Is There.
Going Home with Jesus.
Happiness.
House Is Not the Home, The.
If You're the Man You Ought to Be.
It Might Have Been.
It's Wonderful.
Jesus Never Fails.
Keeping Victory.
Some Things You Cannot Will to Men.
Youth and Truth.
Ishak, Abu *See* **Hill, Elton**
Isherwood, Christopher, *and* **Wystan Hugh Auden** *See* **Auden, Wystan Hugh,** *and* **Christopher Isherwood**
Ishikawa Kimiko
No Spare Time.
Ishikawa Takuboku
I picked up my mother.
Ish-Kishor, Sulamith
War.
Isidorus
On a Fowler.
Island, E. H. L.
Penny Whistle Blues.
Isler, Elizabeth
Little Things, The.
Islwyn
For everything is sacred, poetry.
Gwel uwchlaw cymylau amser.
Storm, The, *sel.*
Issa (Kobayashi Issa)
Another [Beggar Poem] ("For one copper").
Another Beggar Poem ("A bleak day!").
Contentment in Poverty.
Contrast.
Death it can bring.
Dews Disappear, The.
Dislike of a Governor.
Firefly, The.
Haikai.
Haiku: "In my life."
Haiku: "World of dew, The."
I could eat it!
Just bent on viewing cherries.
Kotatsu, from which to watch, A.
Late Snow.
Misery of the Beggars at the Gate of Zenkoji, The.
On the Eta, the Untouchables.
Red sky in the morning.
Satirical Poems on Daimyos.
Sleeping, waking.
Snow thaws, The.
Temple That Charged Admission, The.
Under the willow.
Where can he be going.
Winter.
Ivanov, Vyacheslav Ivanovich
Funeral.
Holy Rose, The.
Iwano, Homei
Sad Love and Sad Song.
Izard, Forrest
"Art of Our Necessities Is Strange, The."
Izembo
Shower, A.

J

"J., L."
Day at the Farm, A.
See "R., J. A"
"J. B. H." *See* **"H., J. B"**
"J. D." *See* **"D., J"**
"J., M."
Animal Howl, The.
Deportation.
Funeral, The.
Song of a Jewish Boy.
"J. H. S." *See* **"S., J. H"**
"J. P. H." *See* **"H., J. P"**
Jacinto, Antonio
Monangamba.
"Jack the Grumbler. "
California over the Left.
Jackmon, Marvin E.
Burn, Baby, Burn.
That Old Time Religion.
Jacks, Olive Cecilia
Offering, The.
Jackson, Ada
Again the Story Is Told.
I Have a Roof.
In Memoriam.
Mary Shakespeare.
Jackson, Byron *See* **Jackson, Kathryn,** *and* **Byron Jackson**
Jackson, Helen Hunt ("H. H."; "Saxe Holm")
Ah, well, Friend Death, good friend thou art.
Cheyenne Mountain.
Coronation.
Danger.
Doubt.
Down to Sleep.
Dream, A.
Emigravit.
Habeas Corpus.
If I Can Live.
Last Prayer, A.
Morn.
My Legacy.
Not As I Will.
October's Bright Blue Weather.
Poppies in the Wheat.
Prayer: "Father, I scarcely dare to pray."
September.
September Days Are Here.
Song of Clover, A.
Spinning.
That Things Are No Worse, Sire.
Jackson, Kathryn
Being Twins.
Brown Bear's Honey Song.
Twins, The.
Jackson, Kathryn *and* **Byron Jackson**
Noonday Sun.
Open Range.
Jackson, Leroy F.
All Aboard for Bombay.
Buzzy Brown.
Candle, A.
Columbus.
Duckle, Duckle, Daisy.
Grandpa Dropped His Glasses.
Hero, The.
Hippity Hop to Bed.
I've Got a New Book from My Grandfather Hyde.
Jelly Jake and Butter Bill.
Kitty Caught a Hornet.
Little Pig Asleep, A.
Off to Yakima.
Old Father Annum.
Polly Picklenose ("Polly, Polly, goodness gracious").
Sea Gull, The.
Simple Sam.
To China.
Uncle Andy and I.
Jackson, Mae
Blues Today, The.
For Some Poets.
I Remember.
I Used to Wrap My White Doll Up in.
Jackson, Marsha Ann
In Between Time (Transcience).
Tears and a Dream.
Jackson, Maud Frazer
Faith.
New Years and Old.
Jackson, Peter
Afrikaans Homestead.
At the Grave of Cecil Rhodes.
Dombashawa.
Great Zimbabwe.
In Loco.
Jackson, Sara
Lily McQueen.
Jacob, Hildebrand
Writer, The.
Jacob, Max
It May Be.
To Modigliani to Prove to Him That I Am a Poet.
Jacob, Ruth Apprich
Waiting.
Jacob, Violet
Last o' the Tinkler, The.
Licht Nichts, The.
Pride.
Tam i' the Kirk.
Jacobs, Catherine Haydon
Secret.
Jacobs, Elijah L.
High Wheat Country.
Saturday in the County Seat.
Jacobs, Henry
Avon, The.
Jacobs, Mary
Where Love, There's Heaven.
Jacobsen, Josephine
Animals, The.
Eyes of Children at the Brink of the Sea's Grasp, The.
For Any Member of the Security Police.
Listen, David!
Mollesse.
Sea Fog, The.
Short Short Story.
Jacobson, Ethel
Atomic Courtesy.
Limerick: "To smash the simple atom."
Lines Scratched in Wet Cement.

Jacobson (continued)
Water Snake.
Jacoby, Grover
Juxta.
Jacopo da Lentino
Canzonetta: He Will Neither Boast Nor Lament to His Lady.
Canzonetta: Of His Lady and of His Making Her Likeness.
No Jewel so Worthy.
Of His Lady's Face.
Sonnet: Of His Lady in Heaven.
Sonnet: Of His Lady's Face.
Jacopone da Todi
Christ and His Mother at the Cross.
Highest Wisdom, The.
Little Angels, The.
Nativity Song.
Of Impatience Which Brings All Our Gains to Nothing.
To Jesus.
Jacot, Emile
Jack Tar.
Wandering Jack.
Who's That a-Knocking?
Jager, Maria
O World, Be Not So Fair.
Jago, Richard
Absence.
Hamlet's Soliloquy Imitated.
Swallows, The; an Elegy.
Jahin, Salah
Quatrains.
Jalalu'd-din Rumi *See* **Rumi, Jalal ed-Din**
James, Alice Archer Sewall
Butterfly, The.
Processional.
Sinfonia Eroica.
James, John
Of John Bunyans Life.
On the Decease of the Religious and Honourable Jno Haynes Esqr.
James, Thomas
Lines on His Companions Who Died in the Northern Seas.
James I, King of England
Argument of the Book, The.
Epitaph on Sir Philip Sidney, An.
Epithalamion upon the Marquis of Huntilies Marriage, An.
Sonnet: "Azured vault, the crystal circles bright, The."
Sonnet on Sir William Alexander's Harsh Verses, A.
James I, King of Scotland
Blissit mot be the heye goddis all.
Coming of Love, The.
Good Counsel.
He Sees His Beloved.
Kingis Quair [*or Quhair*], *The, abr.*
Spring Song of the Birds.
Walking under the Tour.
James VI, King of Scotland *See* **James I, King of England**
Jameson, Anna Brownell
Take Me, Mother Earth.
Jameson, Vivien
Little Star, The.
Jami
Baharistan, *sel.*
Bewildered Arab, The.
Changing World, The.
Fragment: "Though decked the tray."
Glorious God, The.
God behind the Veil.
Great Idealist, The.
Hidden Truth, The.
Life within Our Forms, The.
Man's Prime Desire.
Night.
One Heart, One Love.
Salámán and Absál, *sel.*
Song of Mystic Unity, The.
Union of Love.
Ways of Love, The.
Jamil
Buthaina ("Buthaina, if the flower of youth could raise its head anew").
Jamison, Roscoe Conkling
Negro Soldiers, The.
Jammes, Francis
Alone.
Amsterdam.
Child Reads an Almanac, The.
Géorgiques Chrétiennes, *sel.*
Love.
Palm Sunday.
Prayer That an Infant May Not Die.
Prayer to Go to Paradise with the Asses.
Robinson Crusoe Returns to Amsterdam.
This day, O Father, give us daily bread.
Jansen, Annette
Prayer for Neighborhood Evangelism.
Janta, Alexander
Psalm of the Singing Grave.
Janvier, Francis de Haes
God Save Our President.
Janvier, Margaret Thomson *See* **"Vandegrift, Margaret"**
Janvier, Thomas A.
Santiago.
Japp, Alexander Hay
Landor.
Memories.
Music Lesson, A.
Shelley.
Jaques [*or* Jacques], Edna
In Flanders Now.
Red Cross, The.
Jaques, Florence Page
Goblinade, A.
There Once Was a Puffin.
Jarrell, Randall
Angels at Hamburg, The.
Augsburg Adoration, The.
Bats.
Bird of Night, The.
Black Swan, The.
Blind Sheep, The.
Breath of Night, The.
Burning the Letters.
Camp in the Prussian Forest, A.
Chipmunk's Song, The.
Country Life, A.
Cow Wandering in the Bare Field, The.
Dead in Melanesia, The.
Dead Wingman, The.
Death of the Ball Turret Gunner, The.
Eighth Air Force.
Emancipators, The.
Field and Forest.
For an Emigrant.
Game at Salzburg, A.
Girl in a Library, A.
Hope.
Hunt in the Black Forest, A.
In Montecito.
Jews at Haifa.
Jonah.
Knight, Death, and the Devil, The.
Lady Bates.
Lines, The.
Loss.
Losses.
Lost Children, The.
Lullaby, A: "For wars his life and half a world away."
Märchen, The.
Metamorphoses, The.
Mockingbird, The.
Nestus Gurley.
Next Day.
90 North.
Officers' Prison Camp Seen from a Troop-Train, An.
Orient Express, The.
Pilot from the Carrier, A.
Pilots, Man Your Planes.
Port of Embarkation.
Prisoners.
Refugees, The.
Say Good-Bye to Big Daddy.
Second Air Force.
Seele im Raum.
Sick Child, A.
Sick Nought, The.
Siegfried.
Sleeping Beauty, The; Variation of the Prince.
Snow-Leopard, The.
Soldier (T. P.).
Soldier Walks under the Trees of the University, The.
Soul, A.
State, The.
Utopian Journey, A.
Variations (I-IV).
Ward in the States, A.
Washing.
Well Water.
Windows.
Woman at the Washington Zoo, The.
Jarrett, Emmett
City, The ("In Homer's time").
City, The ("Set over against lust").
Design for the City of Man; a Vision, *sels.*
Invitation.
Overture.
Runes.
Sojourners, The.
Two Mad Songs.
Jaszi, Jean
Clock, The.
Clouds.
Fight.
My Horses.
Tom Ducket.
Winter.
Javitz, Alexander
Old Men, The.
Jayadeva
Gita Govinda, The, *sels.*
Hymn to Vishnu.
Sandal and garment of yellow and lotus garlands upon his body of blue.
Song: "Low whispers the wind from Malaya."
Jean de Meun *and* Guillaume de Lorris *See* **Guillaume de Lorris *and* Jean de Meun**
Jeck, Randolph
Ode of Lament.
Jeffers, Lance
Black Soul of the Land.
Man with a Furnace in His Hand.
My Blackness Is the Beauty of This Land.
Jeffers, Robinson
Age in Prospect.
All the Little Hoofprints.
And boys, be in nothing so moderate as in love of man.
Answer, The.
Ante Mortem.
Apology for Bad Dreams.
Ascent to the Sierras.
Ave Caesar.
Battle.
Birds.
Birth-Dues.
Black-out.
Bloody Sire, The.
Boats in a Fog.

But I Am Growing Old and Indolent.
Calm and Full the Ocean.
Cassandra.
Clouds of Evening.
Compensation.
Continent's End.
Credo.
Cremation.
Crumbs or the Loaf.
Divinely Superfluous Beauty.
Eagle Valor, Chicken Mind.
Edison.
Evening Ebb.
Excesses of God, The.
Eye, The.
Fawn's Foster-Mother.
Fire on the Hills.
Fourth Act.
Gale in April.
Granite and Cypress.
Gray Weather.
Haunted Country.
Hurt Hawks.
I Shall Laugh Purely.
Inquisitors, The.
Joy.
Let Them Alone.
Life from the Lifeless.
Look, How Beautiful.
Love the Wild Swan.
Maid's Thought, The.
Margrave.
May-June, 1940.
Meditation on Saviours.
My Burial Place.
Night.
Noon.
Nova.
November Surf.
Oh, Lovely Rock.
Ocean.
Ode to Hengist and Horsa.
Original Sin.
Pelicans.
People and a Heron.
Phenomena.
Post Mortem.
Practical People.
Prescription of Painful Ends.
Promise of Peace.
Purse-Seine, The.
Rearmament.
Reference to a Passage in Plutarch's Life of Sulla.
Return.
Roan Stallion.
Rock and Hawk.
Salmon-fishing.
Science.
Self-Criticism in February.
Shine, Perishing Republic.
Shine, Republic.
Shiva.
Signpost.
Stars Go over the Lonely Ocean, The.
Steelhead.
Still the Mind Smiles.
Summer Holiday.
Summit Redwood, The.
Tamar, *sel.*
That Nova was a moderate star like our good sun.
They two had unbridled the horses.
To a Young Artist.
To the Stone-Cutters.
Tor House.
Watch the Lights Fade.
Wise Men in Their Bad Hours.
World's Wonders, The.

Jefferson, Joseph
Immortality.

Jefferys, Charles
Jeannette and Jeannot.
We Have Lived and Loved Together.

Jeffrey, Francis, Lord Jeffrey
Epitaph: "Here lies the body of Richard Hind."
Epitaph; in Christ Church, Bristol, on Thomas Turner, Twice Master of the Company of Bakers.
Epitaph; in St. Olave's Church, Southwark, on Mr. Munday.
Epitaphs.
On Peter Robinson.

Jeffrey, William
Carlyle on Burns.
On Glaister's Hill, *sel.*
Stones.

Jeffries, Christie
Lone Huntsman.

Jehudah Halevi *See* **Halevi, Judah**

Jeitteles, Alois
To My Distant Beloved.

Jeitteles, Benedict
Epitaph for a Judge.

Jekyll, Joseph
Two Heads Are Better than One.

Jelal ed-Din Rumi *See* **Rumi, Jalal ed-Din**

Jellicoe, S. Charles
Advice to a Lover.

Jenkins, Burke
Cowboy to His Friends in Need.

Jenkins, Oliver
Captain's Walk; Salem.
Merry-go-round.
Ship Comes In, A.
Time Out.
Waterfront.

Jenkins, William Vaughan
O God of Love, to Thee We Bow.

Jenks, Tudor
Baby's Name, The.
Limerick: "'It's a very warm day,' observed Billy."
Old Bachelor, An.
On the Road.
Small and Early.
Spirit of the *Maine,* The.

Jenkyn, Pathericke [*or* Pattericke]
Love and Respect.
To the Sun.

Jenner, Edward
Signs of Rain.

Jennett, Sean
And the Dead.
Cycle; Seven War Poems.
I Was a Labourer.
Island, The.
Mahoney.
Merchandise.
My Subtle and Proclamant Song.
Old Joyce.
Omphalos; the Well.
Quick, The.

Jennings, Elizabeth
Answers.
Beyond Possession.
Child and the Shadow, The.
Climbers, The.
Communication.
Confidence, The.
Counterpart, The.
Death, A.
Delay.
Disguises.
Enemies, The.
Escape and Return.
Florence; Design for a City.
Fountain.
Game of Cards, A.
Ghosts.
Harvest and Consecration.
I have the shells now in a leather box.
Identity.
Idler, The.
In the Night.
Mirrors.
Music and Words.
Nerves.
Not in the Guide-Books.
Old Man.
Parting, The.
Retort to the Anti-Abstractionists.
Room, The.
Song for a Departure.
Storm, The.
Teresa of Avila.
Visitation, The.
Visitors, The.
Way of Looking, A.
Weathercock.
Winter Love.
World I Have Not Made.
World of Light, A.

Jennings, Leslie Nelson
Belden Hollow.
Keep Darkness.
Yellow Cat, The.

Jennings, Paul
Materia Musica.
Seated One Day.

Jennison, Lucy White *See* **"Innsley,Owen"**

Jensen, Johannes V.
At Memphis Station.
Bathing Girl, A.

Jenyns, Soame
Epitaph on Dr. Johnson.

Jephcott, 'Sydney
Dreamers, The.
Thredbo River.
White Paper.

Jeremy, Sister Mary
Academy.
Desdemona.
Legend.

Jewett, Eleanore Myers
Down among the Wharves.

Jewett, Ellen A.
Sermon in a Stocking.

Jewett, Sarah Orne
Discontent.

Jewett, Sophie ("Ellen Burroughs")
Armistice.
If Spirits Walk.
In the Dark.
Least of Carols, The.
Shepherds, The.
Smiling Demon of Notre Dame, A.
Song: "Thy face I have seen as one seeth."
When Nature Hath Betrayed the Heart That Loved Her.

Jex, Ada Lorraine
Father's Birthday Cake.

Jiménez, Juan Ramón
Conclusive Voyage, The.
Galante Garden, I.
New Leaves.
Nocturne: "My weeping and the starlight."
Only Rose, The.
Shepherd's Star, The.
What Becomes of a Strain of Music.

Joachim, Paulin
Burial.

Joan, Natalie
Dicky-Birds.
Kind Mousie, The.

Joans, Ted
It Is Time.
Lester Young.
My Ace of Spades.

Joans (continued)
.38, The.
Truth, The.
Voice in the Crowd.
Johannes Secundus (Jan Nicolai Everaerts)
Basia, *sels.*
Epithalamium: "Hour is come, with pleasure crowned, The."
Insatiate, The.
Neaera's Kisses.
Wedding Night, The.
John, ——
Band, The.
John, Gwen
Child's Winter Evening, A.
John Damascene, Saint *See* **John of Damascus, Saint**
John Frederick, Sister Mary
Joculator Domini.
John of Damascus, Saint [*or* St. John Damasce],
Day of Resurrection, The.
Easter Hymn.
Resurrection, The.
Risen with Healing in His Wings.
Today in Bethlehem Hear I.
John of the Cross, Saint
Dark Night of the Soul, The.
Living Flame of Love, The.
O Flame of Living Love.
Obscure Night of the Soul, The.
Romance VIII.
Search, The.
Stanzas Concerning Christ and the Soul.
Upon a Gloomy Night.
John II of Castile
Cancion: "O love, I never, never thought."
Johns, Orrick
Answer, The.
Dilemma.
Door, The.
Failure.
Home Fire, The.
Interpreter, The.
Little Things.
Mothers and Children.
Sea-Lands, The.
Shopping Day.
Spring.
Tree-Toad, The.
Wild Plum.
Johnson, Albert E.
Return of the Prodigal.
Johnson, Alicia Loy
Black Lotus.
Black Poetry Day, A.
Monologue.
Johnson, Annie Porter
Night Had Gone, The.
Johnson, B. S.
All This Sunday Long.
Great Man.
Why Do We Lie.
Johnson, Burges
Anxious Farmer, The.
Glad Young Chamois, The.
Gnu Wooing, The.
Incorrigible.
My Sore Thumb.
Rondeau of Remorse, A.
Service, The.
Soap, the Oppressor.
Why Doth a Pussy Cat?
Johnson, Charles
Crossed Legs.
Parking Lot World of Sergeant Pepper, The.
Johnson, Charles Bertram
Little Cabin, A.
Negro Poets.
Johnson, Charles Frederick
Modern Romans, The.
Then and Now.
Johnson, Denis
Checking the Traps.
In a Rented Room.
Man Among the Seals, The.
Poem About Baseballs, A.
Quickly Aging Here.
Johnson, Don Allen ("Mustafa', "
Brainwashing Dramatized.
O White Mistress.
Johnson, Dorothy Vena
Epitaph for a Bigot.
Green Valley.
Palace.
Twinkling Gown.
Johnson, Emily Pauline ("Tekahion Wake', "
At Husking Time.
Brier.
Corn Husker, The.
Lullaby of the Iroquois.
Shadow River.
Song My Paddle Sings, The.
Trail to Lillooet, The.
Train Dogs, The.
Vagabonds, The.
Johnson, Edward
Among These Troopes of Christs Souldiers, Came . . . Mr. Roger Harlackenden.
Mr. Eliot Pastor of the Church of Christ at Roxbury.
Mr. Thomas Shepheard.
Oh King of Saints, how great's thy work, say we.
Onely the Reverend Grave and Godly Mr. Buckly Remaines.
Reverend Mr. Higginson, The.
Yee Shall Not Misse of a Few Lines in Remembrance of Thomas Hooker.
Johnson, Edythe
Will God's Patience Hold Out for You?
Johnson, Esther ("Stella")
O shield me from his rage, celestial Powers!
To Dr. Swift on His Birthday.
Johnson, Fenton
Another sate near him, whose harp of gold.
Aunt Jane Allen.
Banjo Player, The.
Children of the Sun.
Counting.
Daily Grind, The.
Drunkard, The.
Lonely Mother, The.
Lost Love, The.
Marathon Runner, The.
Minister, The.
Negro Peddler's Song, A.
New Day, The.
Old Repair Man, The.
Puck Goes to Court.
Rulers.
Scarlet Woman, The.
Tired.
Vision of Lazarus, The, *sel.*
When I Die.
Who Is That a-Walking in the Corn?
World Is a Mighty Ogre, The.
Johnson, Geoffrey
All Over the World.
Appian Way, The.
Autostrada, The.
Drought.
First of April, The.
Glassblower, The.
Peat-Cutters.
Windmill, The.
Winter Legend, A.
Johnson, George W.
When You and I Were Young, Maggie.
Johnson, Georgia Douglas
Benediction.
Black Woman.
Common Dust.
Conquest.
Credo.
Dreams of the Dreamer, The.
Guardianship.
Heart of a Woman, The.
Hope.
I Closed My Shutters Fast Last Night.
I Want to Die While You Love Me.
Interracial.
I've Learned to Sing.
Lethe.
Little Son.
Lost Illusions.
Lovelight.
My Little Dreams.
Old Black Men.
Poet Speaks, The.
Prejudice.
Proving.
Recessional.
Remember.
Service.
Suppliant, The.
To William Stanley Braithwaite.
Tomorrow's Men.
Trifle.
Welt.
What Need Have I for Memory?
When I Am Dead.
Your World.
Youth.
Johnson, Helene
Bottled, New York.
Fulfillment.
Invocation: "Let me be buried in the rain."
Little Brown Boy.
Magalu.
Poem: "Little brown boy."
Remember Not.
Road, The.
Sonnet to a Negro in Harlem.
Summer Matures.
What Do I Care for Morning.
Johnson, Herbert Clark
Boy's Need, A.
Crossing a Creek.
On Calvary's Lonely Hill.
Willow Bend and Weep.
Johnson, Herschell
To Mareta.
We Are Not Mantan.
Johnson, Hilda
Ballade of Expansion.
Quest of the purple cow, The.
Johnson, James Weldon
Brothers.
Creation, The.
Envoy: "If homely virtues draw from me a tune."
Fifty Years, 1863-1913.
Glory of the Day Was in Her Face, The.
Go Down Death (A Funeral Sermon).
Lift Every Voice and Sing.
Listen, Lord.
My City.
O Black and Unknown Bards.
Prodigal Son, The.
Saint Peter Relates an Incident of the Resurrection Day.
Sence You Went Away.
Up from the Bed of the River.
White Witch, The.

Johnson, Josephine
In This Stern Hour.
Supplication.
Unwilling Gypsy, The.
Johnson, Josephine Winslow
Betrayal, The.
Final Autumn.
In This Hour.
Lightship, The.
Quiet Flower, The.
Temple, The.
Under All Change.
Johnson, Lionel Pigot
Age of a Dream, The.
Ah! fair face gone from sight.
Ardour of red flame is thine, The.
Bagley Wood.
Beyond.
By the Statue of King Charles at Charing Cross.
Cadgwith.
Christmas and Ireland.
Church of a Dream, The.
Comrades.
Dark Angel, The.
Darkness, The.
Dead.
Doctor Major.
Friend, A.
Friends.
In Memory, *sel.*
Ireland.
Last Music, The.
London Town.
Mary Star of the sea!
Mystic and Cavalier.
Our Lady of France.
Our Lady of the May.
Our Lady of the Snows.
Oxford.
Oxford Nights.
Precept of Silence, The.
Red Wind, The.
Roman Stage, The.
Sancta Silvarum.
Summer Storm.
Te Martyrum Candidatus.
To a Traveler.
To Morfydd.
To My Patrons.
To the Dead of '98.
Ways of War.
Winchester.
Johnson, Louis
Adversaries.
Cataclysm.
Comedian.
Dirge: "We built our love up like a work of art."
Elegy: "Fond, frozen, first and only lover."
Fable of a Forgotten Woman.
Mother of a Daughter.
Poem in Karori.
Pygmalion.
Sandwich Man, The.
Johnson, Margaret
Around and around a dusty little room.
Day Dreams, or Ten Years Old.
Johnson, Margaret Spencer
My Father Cares.
Johnson, Norman M.
Hob the Elf.
Johnson, Pauline *See* **Johnson, Emily Pauline**
Johnson, Ray
Walking East on 125th Street (Spring 1959).
Johnson, Ray M.
Greatest Work, The.
Johnson, Robert Underwood
As a Bell in a Chime.
Blossom of the Soul, The.
Browning at Asolo.
Dewey at Manila.
English Mother, An.
Hearth Song.
In Tesla's Laboratory.
Irish Love-Song, An.
Italian Rhapsody.
Love Once Was like an April Dawn.
Silence was envious of the only voice.
Star Song.
To My Countrymen.
To the Returning Brave.
Ursula.
Voice of Webster, The, *sel.*
Wistful Days, The.
Woodrow Wilson.
Johnson, Ronald
Emanations.
Invaders, The.
Letters to Walt Whitman.
Three Paintings by Arthur Dove.
Johnson, Rossiter
Evelyn.
Ninety-nine in the Shade.
Soldier Poet, A.
Johnson, Samuel (1709-84)
Anacreon's Dove.
Ant, The.
As with My Hat.
Burlesque of Lope de Vega.
Charles XII.
Epigram: "If a man who turnips cries."
Epitaph on Claudy Phillips, a Musician, An.
Epitaph upon the Celebrated Claudy Philips, Musician, Who Died Very Poor, An.
Hermit Hoar.
I Put My Hat upon My Head.
If the [*or* a] Man Who Turnips Cries.
Imitation in the Style of Thomas Gray.
In Bed We Laugh.
In Misery's darkest cavern known.
Life's Last Scene.
Lines on the Death of Mr. Levett.
Lines Written in Ridicule of Certain Poems Published in 1777.
London [a Poem in Imitation of the Third Satire of Juvenal].
Long-Expected One-and-twenty.
On the Coming of Age of a Rich, Extravagant Young Man.
On the Death of Dr. Robert Levet.
On the Death of Mr. Robert Levet, a Practiser in Physic.
One-and-twenty.
Poverty in London.
Prayer: "Where then shall Hope and Fear their objects find?"
Prologue: "Prest by the load of life, the weary mind."
Prologue: "When learning's triumph o'er her barb'rous foes."
Prologue Spoken by Mr. Garrick at the Opening of the Theatre Royal [*or* in Drury-Lane], 1747.
Prologue to "The Good-natur'd Man."
Scholar's Life, The.
Short Song of Congratulation, A.
To a Young Heir.
To Miss ——.
Translation of Lines by Benserade.
Turnip Seller, The.
Upon the Feast of St. Simon and St. Jude.
Vanity of Human Wishes, The; the Tenth Satire of Juvenal Imitated.
Wealth, my lad, was made to wander.
Winter: An Ode.
Winter's Walk, The.
Young Author, The.
Johnson, Samuel (1822-82)
City of God.
Inspiration.
Made Perfect Through Suffering.
Prayer for Strength.
Johnson, Spud
City Birds.
Johnson, Victoria Beaudin
Second Crucifixion.
Johnson, Victoria Saffelle
Dedication: "Holy Jesus, Thou art born."
Johnson, William *See* **Cory, William Johnson**
Johnson, William Martin
On Snow-Flakes Melting on His Lady's Breast.
Johnson, William Samuel
Chiffons!
Johnson, Willis Fletcher
Immortality.
Johnson, Yvette
Ghetto.
Reality.
Sapling.
This Is the City.
Johnson-Cory, William *See* **Cory, William Johnson**
Johnston, Anna *See* **"Carbery, Ethna"**
Johnston, Barbara Drake
Peace.
Stormy Night.
Unpayable Debt.
Johnston, Bertha
Did You Ever Hear an English Sparrow Sing?
Johnston, George
Beside the Sea.
Bulge, The.
Eating Fish.
Flight.
Frost.
Huntress, The.
Music in the Air.
Music on the Water.
Noctambule.
O Earth, Turn!
Rest Hour.
War on the Periphery.
Johnston, Mary
Virginiana.
Johnston, William
On the Downtown Side of an Uptown Street.
Johnstone, D. V.
Star of the Morning.
Johnstone, Henry, Lord Johnstone
Charm to Call Sleep, A.
Fastidious Serpent, The.
Good-Night Prayer for a Little Child.
Guessing Song.
Snake Story.
Jomei, Emperor
Cry of the Stag.
Jonas, George
Five Stanzas on Perfection.
For the Record.
Four Stanzas Written in Anxiety.
Jonas, Gerald
Love.
Night Thought.
Jonas, Samuel Alroy
Lines on the Back of a Confederate Note.
Jones, Alice H.
For Sapphire, My Sister.
Jones, Amanda Theodosia
Panama.
Jones, Annabelle
My Best.
Jones, Arthur Glyn Prys- *See* **Prys-Jones, Arthur Glyn**

Jones, Bob, Jr
Broken Things.
Learning.
Scarred.
Worship.
Jones, Brian
Garden of a London House, The.
How to Catch Tiddlers.
Jones, Charles A.
Gee, But There's Class to a Man Like That.
Jones, Charles L. S.
Fort Bowyer.
Hero of Bridgewater, The.
Jones, Cullen
Now That the Flowers.
Jones, Douglas G.
Annunciation.
Beautiful Creatures Brief as These.
Boy in the Lamont Poetry Room, Harvard.
Death of a Hornet.
I Thought There Were Limits.
Northern Water Trush.
Perishing Bird, The.
Poem for Good Friday.
Soliloquy to Absent Friends.
Jones, David
Anathemata, The, *sels.*
Englynion to His Love.
In Parenthesis, *sel.*
Rite and Fore-Time.
So they would go a long while in the solid dark.
Stands a lady/ on a mountain.
Jones, Emily B. C. (Mrs. F. L. Lucas)
Jerked Heartstrings in Town.
Middle-Age.
Jones, Ebenezer
Development of Idiotcy, A.
Face, The.
Hand, The.
Song of the Kings of Gold.
When the World Is Burning.
Winter Hymn, A—to the Snow.
Jones, Edward Smyth
Song of Thanks, A.
Jones, Elijah
How Big Was Alexander?
Jones, Ernest Charles
Earth's Burdens.
Song of the Lower Classes, The.
Song of the Wage-Slave, The.
Jones, Evan
Noah's Song.
Jones, Frederick Scheetz
On the Democracy of Yale.
To New Haven.
Jones, Glyn
Esyllt.
Gold.
Merthyr.
Night.
Perfect.
Song: "I kept neat my virginity."
Jones, Herbert
True Romance, The.
Jones, Howard
Fall To.
Jones, Jessie Orton
I Can Climb Our Apple Tree.
Jones, John
Adrasta, *sel.*
Come, Lovers, Bring Your Cares.
Jones, Joshua Henry
To a Skull.
Jones, Lawrence M.
I Am the Flag.
Jones LeRoi (Imamu Ameer Baraka)
Agony, An. As Now.
As a Possible Lover.
Audubon, Drafted.
Black Art.
Bludoo Baby, Want Money, and Alligator Got It to Give.
Clearing, The.
Dance, The.
Death of Nick Charles, The.
Each Morning.
Election Day (Newark, New Jersey).
End of Man Is His Beauty, The.
Epistrophe.
For Crow Jane.
For Hettie.
Guerrilla Handbook, A.
Hegel.
Hymn for Lanie Poo, *sel.*
In Memory of Radio.
Insidious Dr. Fu Man Chu, The.
Invention of Comics, The.
Liar, The.
Lines to Garcia Lorca.
Measure of Memory, The.
New Sheriff, The.
Notes for a Speech.
One Night Stand.
Ostriches & Grandmothers!
Poem for Black Hearts, A.
Political Poem.
Politics of Rich Painters, The.
Preface to a Twenty Volume Suicide Note.
Pressures, The.
Snake Eyes.
There Must Be a Lone Ranger!!!
Three Movements and a Coda.
To a Publisher. . .Cut-out.
Turncoat, The.
W. W.
Way Out West.
We Own the Night.
World Is Full of Remarkable Things, The.
Jones, Louise Seymour
Who Loves a Garden.
Jones, Lucy Hamilton *See* **Hooper, Lucy Hamilton**
Jones, M. Keel
Election Reflection.
Jones, Margaret Wynne
Tale from the Garden, A.
Jones, Mary
Spider, The.
Jones, Mary Hoxie
Four Deer, The.
Jones, Ralph M.
Bed-Time.
Jones, Robert
Madrigal: "O I do love, then kiss me."
O I Do Love, Then Kiss Me.
Jones, T. Gwynn
Grave, The.
Ystrad Fflur.
Jones, T. H.
Advice to a Knight.
Storm in Childhood, A.
Jones, Thomas Samuel, Jr
Akhnaton.
Cædmon.
Cathedral, The.
Clonard.
Daphne.
Empedocles.
Gautama.
In the Fall o' Year.
Lao-tse.
Little Ghosts, The.
Path of the Stars, The.
Pythagoras.
Saint Thomas Aquinas.
Sometimes.
To Song.
Youth.
Zarathustra.
Jones, W. S. Handley
He Is Not Risen.
Jones, Sir William
Baby, The.
Epigram: "On parent knees, a naked new-born child."
Moral Tetrastich, A.
Ode in Imitation of Alcaeus, An.
On Parent Knees.
What Constitutes a State?
Jones-Quartey, K. B.
Stranger, Why Do You Wonder So?
Jonker, Ingrid
Begin Summer.
Child Who Was Shot Dead by Soldiers at Nyanga, The.
Face of Love, The.
I Don't Want Any More Visitors.
I Drift in the Wind.
Lost City.
Pregnant Woman.
25 December 1960.
Jonson, Ben
Aeglamour's Lament.
After Catullus: Song, to Celia.
Alchemist, The, *sels.*
All Your Fortunes We Can Tell Ye.
Angel Describes Truth, An.
Another Birthday.
Another. In Defence of Their Inconstancie.
Another Ladyes Exception Present at the Hearing.
Answer to Master Wither's Song.
Apollo's Song.
Ask Not to Know This Man.
Beautie, I know, is good, and bloud is more.
Beauties, Have Ye Seen This Toy.
Begging Another, on Colour of Mending the Former.
Ben Jonson's [*or* Johnsons] Sociable Rules for the Apollo.
Buz, Quoth the Blue Fly.
By Him.
Case is Altered, The, *sel.*
Catch, A: "Buz, quoth the blue fly."
Celebration of Charis, A.
Ceremonies for Candlemas Day, The.
Chorus: "Spring all the Graces of the age."
Claiming [*or* Clayming] a Second Kiss by Desert.
Clerimont's Song.
Come, My Celia, Let Us Prove.
Come on, sir. Now, you set your foot on shore.
Cupid.
Cynthia's Revels, *sels.*
Dances Inspired by Love.
Do but look on her eyes, they do light.
Dream, The.
Drink to Me Only with Thine Eyes.
Echo's Lament of Narcissus.
Echo's Song.
Elegie, An: "Let me be what I am, as Virgil cold."
Elegie, An: "'Tis true, I'm broke! Vowes, oathes, and all I had."
Elegie on the Lady Jane Pawlet, Marchion: of Winton, An.
Elegy, An: "Since you must go, and I must bid farewell."
Elegy, An: "Though beauty be the mark of praise."
Elizabeth L. H.
Epicoene; or, The Silent Woman, *sel.*
Epigram: "Tonight, grave Sir, both my poor house and I."
Epigram to King Charles for an Hundred

Pounds He Sent Me in My Sickness, An.
Epigram, to the Household, An, 1630.
Epistle Answering to One That Asked to Be Sealed of the Tribe of Ben, An.
Epistle to Elizabeth, Countess of Rutland, *sels.*
Epistle, An, to Sir Edward Sackville, now Earl of Dorset.
Epitaph, An: On Elizabeth Chute.
Epitaph: "Weep with me, all you that read."
Epitaph, An: "What beauty would have lovely styled."
Epitaph on Elizabeth, L. H.
Epitaph on Master Philip Gray, An.
Epitaph on S. P. [Salamon *or* Salomon *or* Salathiel Pavy], a Child of Q. El.'s [Queen Elizabeth's] Chapel (*or* Chappel], An.
Epode.
Execration upon Vulcan, An.
Faeries' Song, The.
Fair Friend, 'Tis True.
Fair Phyllis.
Farewell to the World, A.
Fit of Rhyme [*or* Rime] Against Rhyme [*or* Rime], A.
Fools.
Fortunate Isles and Their Union, The, *sel.*
Ghyrlond of the Blessed Virgin Marie, The.
Gipsy Song ("The faery beam upon you").
Gipsy Song ("To the old, long life and treasure").
Glad Time Is at His Point Arrived.
Glove, The.
Good morning to the day; and, next, my gold.
Gypsies Metamorphosed, The, *sels.*
Had Those That Dwell in Error Foul.
Have You Seen [but] a Bright Lily Grow.
He stood a soldier to the last right end.
Her Man Described by Her Owne Dictamen.
Her Triumph.
Here She Was Wont to Go! and Here! and Here!
Hermogenes's Song.
Hesperus' Hymn [*or* Song] to Cynthia.
His Discourse with Cupid.
His Excuse for Loving.
Hour-Glass, The.
How He Saw Her.
Hue and Cry after Cupid, The, *sel.*
Humble Petition of Poor Ben to the Best of Monarchs, Masters, Men, King Charles, The.
Hymenaei, *sel.*
Hymn: "Queen and huntress chaste and fair."
Hymn for the Nativity of My Savior, A.
Hymn to Comus.
Hymn to Cynthia.
Hymn to Diana.
Hymn [*or* Hymne] to God the Father, A.
Hymn to the Belly.
Hymne, The: "Queene, and Huntresse, chaste, and faire."
Hymne on the Nativitie of My Saviour, A.
I Follow, Lo, the Footing.
I have blown, sir,/ Hard for your worship.
I therefore will begin: soule of the age!
If I Freely May Discover.
If thou hast wisdom, hear me, Celia.
In Authorem.
In Defense of Their Inconstancy.
In the Person of Woman-kind.
Inviting a Friend to Supper.
It Is Not Growing like a Tree.
It Was a Beauty That I saw.
Jackman's Song, The.
Karolin's Song.
Kiss, The ("For love's sake, kiss me once again").
Kiss, The ("Oh, that joy so soon should waste").
Lady Venetia Digby, The.
Little Shrub Growing By, A.
Love.
Love and Death.
Love Restored, *sel.*
Lovel's Song.
Love's Triumph.
Mab.
Mab the Mistress-Fairy.
Masque of Augurs, The, *sel.*
Masque of Beauty, The, *sel.*
Masque of Christmas, The.
Masque of Cupid, *sel.*
Masque of Hymen, *sel.*
Masque of Queens, The, *sel.*
Mother Maudlin the Witch.
Musicall Strife, The; in a Pastorall Dialogue.
My Picture Left in Scotland.
Nano's Song.
Neptune's Triumph, *sel.*
New Inn, The, *sels.*
New yeares, expect new gifts: Sister, your harpe.
New-Yeares-Gift Sung to King Charles, 1635, A.
No. I'll have no bawds.
Noble Balm.
Noble Nature, The.
Nymph's Passion, A.
Nymph's Secret, A.
O sacred poesie, thou spirit of artes.
Oh, That Joy So Soon Should Waste.
Oak and Lily.
Oberon, the Fairy Prince, *sel.*
Ode, An: "High-spirited friend."
Ode to Himself ("Come leave the loathed stage").
Ode to Himself, An ("Where do'st thou careless lie").
Of Life and Death.
On Court-Worme.
On Elizabeth L. H.
On English Monsieur.
On Gut.
On His First Sonne.
On Lucy, Countess[e] of Bedford.
On Margaret Ratcliffe.
On My First Daughter.
On My First Son [*or* Sonne].
On Playwright.
On Poet-Ape.
On Reformed Gamester.
On Sir Voluptuous Beast.
On Something That Walk[e]s Somewhere.
On Spies.
On the Portrait of Shakespeare Prefixed to the First Folio Edition, 1623.
Over the Door at the Entrance into the Apollo.
Pans Anniversarie; or, The Shepherds Holy-Day.
Patrico's Song.
Picture of Her Mind, The.
Pindaric Ode, A: To the Immortal Memory and Friendship of That Noble Pair, Sir Lucius Cary and Sir Henry Morison.
Pleasure Reconciled to Virtue [*or* Vertue].
Poetaster, The, *sels.*
Power of Poets, The.
Praises of a Countrie Life, The.
Proportion.
Queen and Huntress.
Queen Mab.
Queene and Huntresse.
Sad Shepherd, The, *sels.*
Satyr, The, *sel.*
Second Mask, Which Was of Beauty, The, *sel.*
Shadow, The.
Short Measures.
Silent Woman, The.
Simplex Munditiis.
Slow, Slow, Fresh Fount.
So Sweet Is She.
So White, So Soft, So Sweet.
Song: "Drink to me only with thine eyes."
Song: "Faiery beame upon you, The."
Song: "Fooles, they are the onely nation."
Song: "If I freely may discover."
Song: "Kiss me, sweet; the wary lover."
Song, A: "Oh do[e] not wanton with those eyes."
Song: "O, that joy so soon should waste."
Song: "Slow, slow, fresh fount, keep time with my salt tears."
Song: "Still to be neat, still to be dressed."
Song: That Women Are but Men's Shadows [*or* Shaddowes].
Song: "Though I am young and cannot tell."
Song: To Celia ("Come, my Celia, let us prove").
Song: To Celia ("Drink to me only with thine eyes").
Song: To Celia ("Kiss me, sweet; the wary lover").
Song: To Comus.
Song: To Cynthia.
Song: "When love at first did move."
Song of Echo.
Sonnet, to the Noble Lady, the Lady Mary Worth, A.
Spring, A, now she is dead! of what? of thorns.
Still to Be Neat, Still to Be Dressed [*or* Drest].
Such Sweet Neglect.
Sweet Swan of Avon! what a sight it were.
Swell Me a Bowl.
That Women Are but Men's Shadows.
There is no bountie to be shew'd to such.
Thou hast thy ponds, that pay thee tribute fish.
Though I Am Young [and Cannot Tell].
'Tis not to be told/ What servile villainies men will do for gold.
To Celia ("Come my Celia, let us prove").
To Celia ("Drinke to me, onely, with thine eyes").
To Celia ("Kiss me, sweet; the wary lover").
To Censorious Courtling.
To Diana.
To Doctor Empirick [*or* Empiric].
To Edward Allen (Alleyne).
To Elizabeth, Countess of Rutland.
To Fine Lady Would-Be.
To Fool or Knave.
To Francis Beaumont.
To Heaven.
To Himself.
To John Donne ("Donne, the delight of Phoebus, and each Muse").
To John Donne ("Who shall doubt, Donne, where I a poet be").
To King James.
To Lucy, Countess[e] of Bedford, with Mr. Donne's Satires [*or* Satyres].
To Mary Lady Wroth.
To My Book[e].
To My Bookseller.
To My Mere English Censurer.
To Penshurst.

Jonson (continued)
To Sir Henrie Saville [upon His Translation of Tacitus].
To Sir Henry Cary.
To Sir Henry Goodyear.
To Sir Robert Wroth.
To the Ghost of Martial.
To the Holy Trinitie.
To the Immortal[l] Memory [*or* Memorie] and Friendship of That Noble Pair[e], Sir Lucius Cary and Sir Henry Morison.
To the Learned Critic.
To the Memory of My Beloved Master William Shakespeare [and What He Hath Left Us].
To the Reader.
To the Same.
To the World: A Farewell for a Gentlewoman, Virtuous and Noble.
To Thomas Lord Chancellor.
To William Camden.
To William Earle of Pembroke.
To William Roe.
Triumph, The.
Triumph of Charis, The.
Truth.
Up, Youths and Virgins, Up, and Praise.
Urging Her of a Promise.
Venus' Runaway.
Verses Placed over the Door at the Entrance into the Apollo Room at the Devil Tavern.
Vision of Delight, The, Presented at Court in Christmas, 1617.
Vivamus Mea Lesbia atque Amemus.
Volpone, *sels.*
"What else/ Is love, but the most noble, pure affection."
What Hee Suffered.
Why I Write Not of Love.
Wish, A.
Witches' Charms, The.
Witches' Song, The.
Women Men's Shadows.
Wretched and foolish jealousy.
Jordan, A. C.
You Tell Me to Sit Quiet.
Jordan, Barbara Leslie
Desert Shipwreck.
Jordan, Charlotte Brewster
To Borglum's Seated Statue of Abraham Lincoln.
Jordan, David Starr
Altruism.
And So at Last.
Men Told Me, Lord!
To Love, at Last, the Victory.
Vivérols.
Jordan, Ethel Blair
Disarm the Hearts.
Jordan, Norman
Black Warrior.
Cities and Seas.
Ending.
Feeding the Lions.
Sacrifice, The.
Sinner.
Jordan, Thomas
Alarm in 1645, An, *sel.*
Careless Gallant, The.
Cavalier's Lullaby for His Mistress, A.
Coronemus Nos Rosis Antequam Marcescant.
Epicure, The, Sung by One in the Habit of a Town Gallant.
Epitaph: "In this marble, buried lies."
Farewell to Sorrow, A.
Jorgensen, Johannes
Plants Stand Silent Round Me, The.
Josa
Crocuses.
Jose, Arthur Wilberforce
Freedom the Goddess.
Pioneers.
Sum of Things, The.
Joseph, Chief
War.
Joseph, Michael Kennedy
Braque.
Child's castle crumbles, The; hot air shimmers.
Dancing Ploughmen, The.
Drunken Gunners.
For Any Beachhead.
Lovers and the City, The, *sel.*
Mercury Bay Eclogue, *sel.*
New Moses, The.
Old Montague.
On the Mountain.
Secular Litany.
Vacation Exercise.
Victory March.
Joseph, Rosemary
Capturing a Spring.
Joseph of the Studium, Saint
Finished Course, The.
Joso
"I've seen everything."
Little Duck, The.
Winter.
Josselyn, John
And the bitter storm augments; the wild winds wage.
Description of a New England Spring.
Verses Made Sometime Since upon . . . the Indian Squa.
Josui
Cuckoo's Song, The.
Joyce, James
All Day I Hear [the Noise of Waters].
Alone.
At that hour when all things have repose.
Ballad of Persse O'Reilly, The.
Bid Adieu to Maidenhood.
Bright Cap and Streamers.
Chamber Music.
Ecce Puer.
Finnegans Wake, *sel.*
Flood.
Flower Given to My Daughter, A.
From dewy dreams, my soul, arise.
Gentle Lady, do not sing.
Go seek her out all courteously.
Goldenhair.
Holy Office, The.
I Hear an Army [Charging upon the Land].
In the dark pine-wood.
It Was Out by Donnycarney.
Memory of the Players in a Mirror at Midnight, A.
My dove, my beautiful one.
My Love Is in a Light Attire.
Nightpiece.
Noise of Waters, The.
O cool is the valley now.
O Sweetheart, Hear You.
On the Beach at Fontana.
She Weeps over Rahoon.
Simples.
Song: "Lean out of the window."
Song: "O, it was out by Donnycarney."
Strings in the Earth and Air.
This Heart That Flutters near My Heart.
Tilly.
Tutto è Sciolto.
Twilight Turns from Amethyst, The.
What counsel has the hooded moon?
When the shy star goes forth in heaven.
Who goes amid the green wood?
Winds of May, that dance on the sea.
Joyce, Robert Dwyer
Crossing the Blackwater.
Fineen the Rover.
Leprahaun, The.
Juan de la Cruz, San *See* **John of the Cross, Saint**
Juana Ines de la Cruz Sister (*originally* Juana de Asbaje)
But Venus first.
Divine Narcissus, The.
Redondillas.
To Celio.
To Her Portrait.
Juan Chi
Fifteen Poems of My Heart, *sel.*
Once I dressed up.
"Judah,"
Fragrant Thy Memories.
Judah ha-Levi *See* **Halevi, Judah**
Judd, Sylvester
Light of the World.
Judson, Adoniram
In Spite of Sorrow.
Sowing and Reaping.
Judson, Emily Chubbuck *See* **"Forester, Fanny"**
"Judy."
Imitation of Walt Whitman.
Remember [*parody on* Christina Rossetti].
Judy, Scott, *and* "Doc" Hammond
Song: "We came to Tamichi in 1880."
Juhasz, Gyula
Wilderness, The.
Jules-Bois, H. A.
India the Magic.
Julian, V. M.
Mr. Squirrel.
Julianus [*or* Julian the Egyptian],
Love and Wine.
Old Fisherman.
Julie, Sister
Zaccheus.
Junge, Carl S.
Dinosaur, The.
"Junia."
Ballade of a Summer Hotel.
Junkins, Donald
Walden in July.
Jurica, Alice B.
Good Friday.
Justema, William
Song: "This is the song of those who live alone."
Justice, Donald
After a Line by John Peale Bishop.
Anniversaries.
Anonymous Drawing.
Another Song.
Beyond the Hunting Woods.
Birthday Candle, A.
But That Is Another Story.
Counting the Mad.
Crossing Kansas by Train.
Dream Sestina, A.
Dreams of Water.
Here in Katmandu.
In Bertram's Garden.
Ladies by Their Windows.
Love's Stratagems.
Man Closing Up, The.
Memo from the Desk of X.
Missing Person, The.
On a Painting by Patient B of the Independence State Hospital for the Insane.
On the Death of Friends in Childhood.
Poet at Seven, The.
Sestina.
Snowfall, The.
Southern Gothic.
Stray Dog by the Summerhouse, The.

Tales from a Family Album.
To the Hawks.
To Waken a Small Person.
Tourist from Syracuse, The.
Tune for a Lonesome Fife.
Variations for Two Pianos.
Variations on a Theme from James.
Justus, May
Dress of Spring, The.
Footwear.
Garden Path, A.
Remember September.
Strawberry Jam.
Winds a-Blowing.
Witchwood.
Juvenal (Decimus Junius Juvenalis)
Against Women.
Celestial Wisdom.
Hear what Claudius suffered: When his wife knew he was asleep.
In Saturn's reign, at nature's early birth.
Memorial Trees.
Satires, The, *sels.*
Tenth Satire of Juvenal, The, *abr.*
Vices of Women, The.
We are led on.

K

"K., A."
La Donna e Mobile.
"K., E. H."
City Church, The.
Kaberry, C. J.
Indian Elephant, The.
Kabir
He Cares.
Hope in Him While Thou Livest.
My Lord Hides Himself.
Songs of Kabir.
Two Songs.
Kaga no Chiyo
Haiku: "I wonder in what fields today."
On Her Child's Death.
Spring rain:/ Everything just grows.
To Her Husband, at the Wedding.
Kagawa, Toyohiko
As the Sculptor.
Burden, The.
Day's End.
Love.
Meditation.
Only a Flower.
Penniless.
Sculptor of the Soul.
Kageki
Butterflies.
Maiden, A.
Kahanovitch, Pinhas *See* **"Der Nistor"**
Kahn, Gustave
Homage.
Pilgrim from the East, The.
Song: "O lovely April, rich and bright."
You Masks of the Masquerade.
Kahn, Hannah
To Be Black, to Be Lost.
Kaikini, P. R.
Donkey, The.
Kalakaua, King of the Hawaiian Islands
Our Native Land.
Kalar, Joseph
Invocation to the Wind.
Paper Mill.
Kalidasa
Aja's Lament over His Dead Wife.
Autumn.
Cloud-Messenger, The, *sel.*
Early Spring.
Nightfall.
O cloud, the parching spirit stirs thy pity.
Rains, The.
Seasons, The, *sels.*
Spring.
Summer.
Winter.
Woman.
Kalir See Ben Kalir, Eleazar
Kallman, Chester
Little Epithalamium.
Night Music.
Nightmare of a Cook.
Urban History.
Kalmar, Bert *and* Harry Ruby
"America, I Love You."
Kalonymos ben Judah
Although Tormented.
Kalonymos ben Kalonymos
Hypocrite, The.
Touchstone, The, *sels.*
Unfortunate Male, The.
Yoke, The.
Kalonymos ben Moses of Lucca
His Sovereignty.
Kamal ud-Din of Isfahan
O Love, Thy Hair!
Kamzon, Jacob David
Very Fair My Lot.
Kanbara, Yumei
Dark-red Shadow-Spots, The.
Kandel, Lenore
First They Slaughtered the Angels, *sel.*
Songs of the Blue-Light Dakini.
Where It's At: A Melody for Breath.
Kane, Douglas V.
Westering.
Kantor, MacKinlay
Appomattox.
Kaplan, Milton
Circus, The.
Knife, The.
Kariuki, Joseph E.
New Life.
Karlfeldt, Erik Axel
Imagined Happiness.
Vagrant, A.
Karni, Yehuda
Place Me in the Breach.
Karsner, Walta
Xmas Time.
Kartack, Elsie F.
Pop-Corn Land.
Kasa, Lady
I dreamed I held/ A sword against my flesh.
Tolling Bells.
Kasmuneh
Overripe Fruit.
Timid Gazelle, The.
Kästner, Erich
Anonymous Gravestone.
Moral Taxi Ride, The.
Ragout Fin de Siècle.
Rooming-House Melancholy.
"Kate, Ricketty" (Mrs. A. J. Filson)
Affinity.
Kato Gyodai
Snow melting!
Katz, Menke
Praise to the Stutterer.
Twin Epitaph.
Katzin, Olga *See* **"Sagittarius"**
Kauffman, Reginald Wright
Call, The.
Troia Fuit.
Wastrel, The.
Kauffman, Russell E.
Christ of God, The.
Kaufman, Bob
Afterwards, They Shall Dance.
Battle Report.
Benediction.
Cincophrenicpoet.
I, Too, Know What I Am Not.
Perhaps.
Response.
To My Son Parker, Asleep in the Next Room.
Unholy Missions.
Who Has Seen the Wind?
Kaufman, George Simon
Advice to Worriers.
Lines to a Man Who Thinks that Apple Betty with Hard Sauce Is Food for a Human Being.
Kaufman, Herbert
Hell-Gate of Soissons, The.
This Is Your Hour.
Kaufman, Shirley
Beetle on the Shasta Daylight.
Hunger, The.
I Hear You.
It Stays.
Mothers, Daughters.
Room.
Watts.
Kavanagh, Patrick
Auditors In.
Canal Bank Walk.
Christmas Childhood, A.
Epic.
Father Mat.
Glut on the Market, A.
Great Hunger, The, *sel.*
Health and wealth and love he too dreamed of in May.
If Ever You Go to Dublin Town.
Important Statement.
Intimate Parnassus.
Memory of Brother Michael.
My father played the melodion.
October.
On Looking into E. V. Rieu's Homer.
One, The.
Pegasus.
Question to Life.
Sanctity.
Self-Slaved, The.
Shancoduff.
Spraying the Potatoes.
Through the Open Door.
To the Man after the Harrow.
Kavinoky, Bernice
Poet to Dancer.
"Kay."
Christmas Verse, A.
Kay, Ellen de Young
Cante Hondo.
Magnanimous, The.
Tiresias' Lament.
To a Blue Hippopotamus.
Kay, W. Lowrie
Lancaster County Tragedy.
Kaye-Smith, Sheila
Ascension Day.
Lady Day in Harvest.
Kayper-Mensah, Albert
Second Birthday, A.
Kazan, Molly
Thanksgiving, 1963.
"Kazanova, Kid." *See* **Stack, Philip**
Kazin, Vasili
Carpenter's Plane, The.
Kearney, Peadar
Down by the Glenside.
Soldier's Song, The.
Tri-colored Ribbon, The.
Whack Fol the Diddle.
Kearns, Lionel
In-Group.

Kearns (continued)
Insight.
Stuntman.
Keating, Geoffrey
From my grief on Fál's proud plain I sleep.
Keen Thyself, Poor Wight.
My Grief on Fál's Proud Plain, *sel.*
Keating, Norma
Never, Never Can Nothingness Come.
Keating, William
Down, Down, Down.
Keats, John
Addressed to Haydon ("Great spirits now on earth are sojourning").
Addressed to Haydon ("Highmindedness, a jealousy for good").
After Dark Vapours [*or* Vapors].
Ah! dearest love, sweet home of all my fears.
And, truly, I would rather be struck dumb.
Apollo then, with sudden scrutiny and gloomless eyes.
As when, upon a trancèd summer-night.
Ballad: La Belle Dame sans Merci.
Banquet, The.
Bards of Passion and of Mirth.
Beginning of Love, The.
Beneath my palm trees, by the river side.
Bright Star.
Bright Star! Would I Were Steadfast [*or* Stedfast] as Thou Art.
Bruised Titans, The.
But one of the whole mammoth-brood still kept.
Cancelled First Stanza.
Could all this be forgotten? Yes, a schism.
Daisy's Song, A.
Dawlish Fair.
Day Is Gone, The.
December.
Dedication: To Leigh Hunt.
Den of the Titans, The.
Dove, The.
Dream, A.
Dream, after Reading Dante's Episode of Paolo and Francesca, A.
Endymion [a Poetic Romance], *sels.*
Epistle to George Keats.
Epistle to John Hamilton Reynolds.
Epistle to My Brother George.
Epistle to Reynolds, *sel.*
Eve of St. Agnes, The.
Eve of Saint Mark, The.
Faery Song.
Fairy Song.
Fall of Hyperion, The.
Fancy.
Fragment of an Ode to Maia [Written on May Day, 1818].
From the Bridge.
God of the Meridian.
Goldfinches.
Grasshopper and the Cricket, The.
Happy Insensibility.
Happy Is England.
He Saw Far in the Concave Green of the Sea.
Here Is Wine.
His Last Sonnet.
Hither Hither Love.
How Many Bards Gild the Lapses of Time.
Human Seasons, The.
Hymn of Pan.
Hymn to Pan.
Hyperion; a Fragment.
Hyperion: a Vision.
Hyperion's Arrival.
I Had a Dove.
I Stood Tiptoe [upon a Little Hill].
Imitation of Spenser.
In a Drear-nighted December.
Is there so small a range.
Isabella; or, The Pot of Basil.
Keen, Fitful Gusts [Are Whispering Here and There].
La Belle Dame sans Merci.
Lamia.
Last Sonnet.
Life Again.
Lines: "This living hand, now warm and capable."
Lines on the Mermaid Tavern.
Lines Supposed to Have Been Addressed to Fanny Brawne.
Lines to Fanny, *sels.*
Love and Friendship.
Magic Casements.
Meg Merrilies [*or* Merrilees]
Mermaid Tavern, The.
Minnows.
Modern Love.
Morning.
Muse of my native land! loftiest Muse!
Nature's Enchantment.
Naughty Boy, The.
Nightingale, The.
O leave them, Muse! O leave them to their woes.
O Melancholy, linger here awhile!
O Moon! the oldest shades 'mong oldest trees.
O Solitude! If I Must with Thee Dwell.
O Sorrow!
O sovereign power of love! O grief! O balm!
O that our dreamings all, of sleep or wake.
Ode: "Bards of Passion and of Mirth."
Ode on a Grecian Urn.
Ode on Indolence.
Ode on Melancholy.
Ode on the Poets.
Ode to a Nightingale.
Ode to Apollo.
Ode to Autumn.
Ode to Fanny, *sel.*
Ode to Psyche.
Ode to the Nightingale.
Old Meg ("Old Meg she was a gipsy").
On a Dream.
On a Grecian Urn.
On a Picture of Leander.
On an Engraved Gem of Leander.
On Death.
On Fame ("Fame, like a wayward girl, will still be coy").
On Fame ("How fever'd is that man").
On First Looking into Chapman's Homer.
On Leaving Some Friends at an Early Hour.
On Looking into Chapman's Homer.
On Melancholy.
On Oxford.
On Seeing a Lock of Milton's Hair.
On Seeing the Elgin Marbles [for the First Time].
On Sitting Down to Read "King Lear" Once Again.
On the Grasshopper and Cricket.
On the Sea.
On the Sonnet.
On Visiting the Tomb of Burns.
Out went the taper as she hurried in.
Poet, The ("At Morn, at Noon, at Eve, and Middle Night").
Poet, The ("Where's the Poet? show him! show him").
Poetry of Earth Is Never Dead, The.
Portrait, A.
Proud Florentines, The.
Real Woman, A.
Realm of Fancy, The.
Robin Hood.
Saturn.
Schism, A/ Nurtured by foppery and barbarism.
Sharing Eve's Apple.
She was a gordian shape of dazzling hue.
Shell's Song, The.
Should he upon an evening ramble fare.
Sigh of Silence, The.
Sleep and Poetry.
Sleeping Youth, A.
So she was gently glad to see him laid.
Solitude.
Song: "I had a dove and the sweet dove died."
Song: "O Sorrow,/ Why dost borrow."
Song about Myself, A.
Song of Spring.
Song of the Indian Maid.
Sonnet: Addressed to Haydon.
Sonnet: "After dark vapours have oppress'd our plains."
Sonnet: "Bright star, would I were steadfast as thou art."
Sonnet: "Keen, fitful gusts are whisp'ring here and there."
Sonnet: On a Picture of Leander.
Sonnet: On First Looking into Chapman's Homer.
Sonnet: To Homer.
Sonnet: "To one who has been long in city pent."
Sonnet: To Sleep.
Sonnet: "When I have fears that I may cease to be."
Sonnet: Written at the End of "The Floure and the Lefe."
Sonnet: Written in January, 1818.
Sonnet: Written on the Day That Mr. Leigh Hunt Left Prison.
Sonnet Addressed to Haydon.
Sonnet on a Picture of Leander.
Sonnet on the Sea.
Sonnet on the Sonnet.
Sonnet to a Young Lady Who Sent Me a Laurel Crown.
Sonnet to Chatterton.
Sonnet to Mrs. Reynolds' Cat.
Sonnet to Sleep.
Sonnet Written in Disgust of Vulgar Superstition.
Spenserian Stanzas on Charles Armitage Brown.
Staffa.
Stanzas: "In a drear-nighted December."
Stol'n to this paradise, and so entranced.
Stop and consider! life is but a day.
Surely I dreamt to-day, or did I see.
Sweet Peas.
Teignmouth.
Terror of Death, The.
There Was a Naughty Boy.
Thing of Beauty, A [Is a Joy Forever].
This Living Hand.
Thou Shalt See the Field-Mouse Peep.
To ——: "Had I a man's fair form, then might my sighs."
To ——: "Time's sea hath been five years at its slow ebb."
To a Cat.
To a Nightingale.
To Ailsa Rock.
To Autumn.
To Byron.
To Charles Cowden Clarke.
To Dream of Thee.
To Fancy.
To Fanny.
To G. A. W.
To Haydon.

To Homer.
To Kosciusko.
To Leigh Hunt, Esq.
To Maia.
To Mrs. Reynolds's Cat.
To My Brother George.
To My Brothers.
To One Long in City Pent.
To One Who Has Been Long in City Pent.
To Psyche.
To Sleep.
To Sorrow, I bade good-morrow.
To Spenser.
To the Nile.
To the Poets.
Two Sonnets on Fame.
Upon a Hill.
What the Thrush Said.
When I Have Fears [That I May Cease to Be].
Where Be You [*or* Ye] Going, You Devon Maid?
Where Didst Thou Find, Young Bard.
Where shall I learn to get my peace again?
Where's the Poet?
Why Did I Laugh [To-Night]?
With her two brothers this fair lady dwelt.
World of Sleep, The.
Written on a Blank Page in Shakespeare's Poems, Facing "A Lover's Complaint."
Written on the Day that Mr. Leigh Hunt Left Prison.
Written upon the Top of Ben Nevis.

Keble, John
As We Pray.
Balaam.
Bathing.
Burial of the Dead.
Christian Year, The, *sel.*
Effect of Example, The.
Evening, *sel.*
Evening Hymn.
Fill High the Bowl.
Forest Leaves in Autumn.
Gardening.
Help Us to Live.
Holy Matrimony.
Hymn: "New every morning is thy love."
Morning.
Noontide.
November.
Oh, Timely Happy, Timely Wise, *sel.*
Purification, The, *sel.*
Purity of Heart.
Red o'er the Forest.
St. Stephen's Day.
St. Thomas the Apostle.
Seed Time Hymn.
'Tis gone, that bright and orbed blaze.
United States.
We Need Not Bid, for Cloistered Cell.
Whitsunday.
Who Runs May Read.

Keech, Benjamin
Discovery.
Little Words.
Love Is Kind.
True to the Best.

Keegan, C. Kearnie
I Stood Alone.

Keeler, Charles Augustus
Black Sailor's Chanty.
Camilla.
Cleaning Ship.
Ocean Lullaby, An.

Keeling, Mildred
God's World.

Keener, Ruth Douglas
Statue in a Blizzard.

Kees, Weldon
Aspects of Robinson.
Back.
Brief Introduction to the History of Culture, A.
Cats, The.
Colloquy.
Coming of the Plague, The.
Contours of Fixation, The.
Conversation in the Drawing Room, The.
Crime Club.
Early Winter.
For My Daughter.
Homage to Arthur Waley.
January.
1926.
Patient Is Rallying, The.
Problems of a Journalist.
Relating to Robinson.
Report of the Meeting.
River Song.
Robinson.
Robinson at Home.
Round: "'Wondrous life!' cried Marvell at Appleton House."
Saratoga Ending.
Smiles of the Bathers, The.
Wet Thursday.

Keesing, Nancy
Bread.
Old Men.
Revelation.

Keith, Joseph Joel
Bedtime Tales.
Books.
Child Wife.
Crickets and Mice.
Definitions.
Flogged Child.
Immaculate Palm.
In the First House.
Mr. Lerner.
Nightmare in Morganza.
Old Meg of Kitrann.
Party Line.
Salems of Oppression.
She Walks.
Sunday Edition.
Though She Slumbers.
250 Willow Lane.
Wolf and Tiger Dining, A. B.
Woman Telephoning.

Kell, Richard
Memorandum for Minos.

Kelleher, Daniel Lawrence
For C. K. at His Christening.
Its Name Is Known.
Mother.
Upper Room, An.

Kelleher, John
Snow.

Keller, Helen
In the Garden of the Lord.

Keller, Martha
Andrew Jackson.
Brady's Bend.
Deadfall.
Herbs and Simples.
Mountain Meadows.
Wilderness Road.

Kelley, Andrew *See* **"Mix, Parmenas"**

Kelley, Ethel M.
I've Got a Dog.

Kelley, Francis Clement
Throne of the King, The.

Kelley, Hubert
Warrior Passes, The.

Kelley, Reeve Spencer
Back Again from Yucca Flats.
Rain in the Southwest.
Sound of Morning in New Mexico, The.

Kellogg, Kate
Lady Moon.

Kelly, Blanche Mary
Brother Juniper.
Gaelic, The.
Housewife's Prayer, The.
Kingfisher, The.
Mirror, The.
Omniscience.
Silentium Altum.

Kelly, John W.
Slide, Kelly, Slide.
Throw Him Down M'Closkey.

Kelly, Mary Eva
Tipperary.

Kelly, Patrick
Light Shoes.

Kelly, Robert
Alchemist, The.
Boar, The.
Boat, The.
Exchanges II, The.
Face in the Rock Wall.
Going.
Knee Lunes.
Moon Closes, The.
Parallel Texts.
Process, The.
Round Dance, & Canticle.
Song: "Circle and wheel of. Who cares what I'll."
Spels, *sels.*
Sun of the Center.
Thor's Thrush, *sel.*
Three Organ Rituals for Erik Satie.
To Her Body, against Time.

Kelly, Thomas
Cross and the Crown, The.
Lo, He Comes!
Sacred Book, The.
Victor, The.

Kelly, Walt
Boston Charlie.
How Low Is the Lowing Herd.

Kemble, Frances Anne
Absence.
Black Wall-Flower, The.
Dream Land.
Faith.
Lament of a Mocking-Bird.
To Shakespeare.
Trust.
What Shall I Do?

Kemp, Arnold
Black Cop's Communion, A.
End of the World, The.
Guilt Redeemed.
Hello Blackness.
How to Succeed.
Love Me Black Woman.

Kemp, Harry Hibbard
Alienation.
Blind.
Chant of the Box Cars.
Conquerors, The.
Farewell: "Tell them, O Sky-born, when I die."
God the Architect.
Good Morning, America!
He Did Not Know.
Humming Bird, The.
In a Storm.
Joses, the Brother of Jesus.
Literary Love.
Love-Faith.
Nicodemus.
Passing Flower, The.
Phantasy of Heaven, A.
Prayer, A: "I kneel not now to pray that Thou."
Resurrection.
Seaman's Confession of Faith, A.
Seeker after God, The.

Kemp (continued)
Tell All the World.
To God, the Architect.
Upon a great ship's tilted deck.
Voice of Christmas, The.
Kemp, Lysander
Song: "Because he was gone, without a goodbye."
Kempis, Thomas à. *See* **Thomas à Kempis**
Ken, Thomas
Anodyne, An.
Awake, My Soul.
Direct This Day.
Evening Hymn, An.
Evening Prayer.
Glory to Thee [My God] This Night.
Morning Hymn.
Now.
Old Hundredth.
Priest of Christ, The.
Kendall, Henry Clarence
Bell-Birds.
Beyond Kerguelen.
Coogee.
Jim the Splitter.
Last of His Tribe, The.
Mooni.
Orara.
Prefatory Sonnet.
Rain Comes Sobbing to the Door, The.
September in Australia.
To a Mountain.
Voice in the Wild Oak, The.
Kendall, John Kaye ("Dum-Dum"),
Cat That Followed His Nose, The.
Circumstance without Pomp.
Contented Bachelor, The.
Hug Me Tight.
My Last Illusion.
Ode to the Nightingale.
Pipes in the Sty.
Problem of the Poles, The.
Soldier of Weight, A.
Kendall, Laura E.
Evening Prayer, An.
Kendall, May
Ballad: "He said: 'The shadows darken down.'"
Board School Pastoral A.
Lay of the Trilobite, The.
Legend, A.
Page of Lancelot, The.
Pure Hypothesis, A.
Seraph and the Snob, The.
Taking Long Views.
Kendall, Timothe
Quip to the Reader.
To the Reader.
Kendon, Frank
Country Life.
I Spend My Days Vainly.
Immigrant, The.
Kernel, The.
Looker-on, The.
Now You Are in Your Country.
So Deep Is Death.
Son in December, A.
Kendrew, Mary E.
If Thou Dost Need.
Kendrick, John
Fable, A: Mice and Felis, The.
Kendrick, Lucile
Not All the Crosses.
Kenealy, Edward
Castle Hyde.
Castlehyde.
Kenin, Millea
Can you see our way home?
Kennedy, Benjamin Hall
On "Who Wrote Icon Basilike" by Dr. Christopher Wordsworth, Master of Trinity.
Kennedy, Charles Rann
Already our kingdoms are beginning to totter.
Terrible Meek, The, *sel.*
Kennedy, Charles William
I've Worked for a Silver Shilling.
Kennedy, Edward D.
Strange, Is It Not.
Kennedy, Edwin O.
Prayer for Charity, A.
Kennedy, Geoffrey Anketell Studdert- *See* **Studdert-Kennedy, Geoffrey Anketell**
Kennedy, Gerta
Abstract Painter.
At the Nadir.
Chesapeake.
Christmas Songs.
For Keats and the Florentine Night.
Song of January.
Kennedy, Leo
Calling Eagles.
Epithalamium: "This body of my mother, pierced by me."
Mad Boy's Song.
Mole Talk.
Of One Dead.
Rite of Spring.
Words for a Resurrection.
Kennedy, Marion
Tribute to Our Soldiers.
Kennedy, Mary
Indolent Gardener, The.
Moon Door.
One of the Sidhe.
Unfortunate Mole, The.
Kennedy, Sara Beaumont
Prayer Rug, The.
Kennedy, Thomas
Night Dancers.
Kennedy, Walter
Honour with Age.
Kennedy, X. J.
Apocrypha.
Ars Poetica.
Artificer.
B Negative.
Cross Ties.
Down in Dallas.
Driving Cross-Country.
Epitaph for a Postal Clerk.
Faces from a Bestiary.
First Confession.
Golgotha.
Hearthside Story.
In a Prominent Bar in Secaucus [One Day].
Lilith.
Little Elegy [for a Child Who Skipped Rope].
Man in the Manmade Moon, The.
Nothing in Heaven Functions as it Ought.
Nude Descending a Staircase.
On a Child Who Lived One Minute.
One A.M.
Overheard in the Louvre.
Solitary Confinement.
Song to the Tune of "Somebody Stole My Gal."
To Someone Who Insisted I Look Up Someone.
Water Glass of Whisky, A.
Kennet of the Dene, Edward Hilton Young,1st Baron *See* **Young, Edward Hilton**
Kenney, James
Green Leaves All Turn Yellow, The.
Old Story Over Again, The.
Kenny, Herbert A.
Pleasure Is Too Surely Found.
Kenny, Nick
Patty-Poem.
Kenrick, Daniel
To Celia ("I spend my sad life in sighs and in cries").
Kenseth, Arnold
B-52's.
How They Came from the Blue Snows.
To the Ladies.
Kent, Charles
Pope at Twickenham.
Kent, Louis
Hunt, The.
Toad, The.
Kenward, Jean
Mandoline, The.
Musical Box, The.
Kenyon, Bernice Lesbia
Cat's World.
Homecoming in Storm.
Night of Rain.
Two Cats on the Hearth.
Kenyon, James Benjamin
Bedouins of the Skies, The.
Bring Them Not Back.
Challenge, A.
Come Slowly, Paradise.
Death and Night.
Play, The.
Tacita.
Two Spirits, The.
We Shall Attain.
Kenyon, John
Champagne Rosée [*or* Rosé].
Kenyon, Theda
City Bird.
Keohler, Thomas
Night's Ancient Cloud.
Keppel, Lady Caroline
Robin Adair.
Keppel, David
Trouble.
Keppel, Frederick
Plain Man's Dream, A.
Kernahan, Coulson
Cricket Triolet, A.
Kerner, Justinus
Home-Sickness.
Kerouac, Jack (John Kerouac)
Chorus: "Big Engines, The."
Chorus: "Essence of Existence, The."
Chorus: "Glenn Miller and I were heroes."
Chorus: "Got up and dressed up."
Chorus: "Love's multitudinous boneyard."
Chorus: "Nobody knows the other side."
Chorus: "Old Man Mose."
Chorus: "Only awake to Universal Mind."
Chorus: "Praised be man, he is existing in milk."
Chorus: "Saints, I give myself up to thee."
Chorus: "Void that's highly embraceable, The."
Chorus: "Wheel of the quivering meat, The."
Mexico City Blues, *sels.*
121st Chorus.
Kerr, Hazel M.
New Gethsemane.
Kerr, Hugh Thomson
Come Thou My Light.
God of Our Life through All the Circling Years.
Thy Will Be Done.
"Kerr, Orpheus C." (Robert Henry Newell)
American Traveller, The.
Editor's Wooing, The.

Great Fight, A.
National Hymns, The.
Picciola.
Rejected "National Hymns," The.
Kerr, Walter H.
Curtains for a Spinster.
Dignity of Man—Lesson #1, The.
Hanged Thing, The.
Prenatal Fantasy.
Proud Trees, The.
Stone, The.
Trap.
Vampire.
Villanelle.
Kerr, Watson
Ancient Thought, The.
Kerrigan, Anthony
Eurasian Girl.
Studio, The.
Kersh, Gerald
Soldier, A: His Prayer.
Soldier, The, 1939-1945.
Kessler, Jascha
Following the Sun.
Gardener at Thirty, The.
High Summer.
Imperial Valley, Calif.
My Grandmother's Funeral.
Nightmare, The.
October Flies.
P.S.
Requiem for an Abstract Artist.
Technique of Laughter, The.
Technique of Love, The.
Technique of Power, The.
Kessler, Milton
El-Painter's Daughter, The.
Ketcham, Howard
Limerick: "This bird is the keel-billed toucan."
Ketchum, Annie Chambers
Bonnie Blue Flag, The ("Come, brothers! rally for the right").
Ketchum, Arthur
Bethlehem.
Candle-lighting Song.
Countersign.
Legends for Trees, *sels.*
Road to Granada, The.
Spirit of the Birch, The.
Thanksgiving.
Kethe, William
Hundredth Psalm, The (Metrical Version).
Old Hundredth.
Scotch Te Deum.
Kettle, Thomas Michael
Lady of Life, The.
Parnell's Memory.
To My Daughter Betty [The Gift of God].
Key, Francis Scott
Defence of Fort M'Henry.
Hymn: "Lord, with glowing heart I'd praise thee."
On a Young Lady's Going into a Shower Bath.
Our Rock.
Star-spangled Banner, The.
Keyes, Sidney
Against a Second Coming, *sel.*
Alexander Pope at Stanton Harcourt.
Anti-Symbolist, The.
Cruel Solstice, The.
Early Spring.
Elegy: "April again and it is a year again."
Foreign Gate, The, *sel.*
Gardener, The.
Glaucus.
Grail, The.
Greenwich Observatory.
Holstenwall.
Kestrels, The.
Moonlight Night on the Port.
Neutrality.
Pheasant.
Plowman.
Remember Your Lovers.
Rome Remember.
Snow, The.
Sour Land, *sel.*
Spring Night.
Time Will Not Grant.
Walking Woman, The.
War Poet.
Were I to Mount beyond the Field.
Wilderness, The.
William Byrd.
William Wordsworth.
William Yeats in Limbo.
Keysner, Blanche Whiting
Old River Road.
Kgositsile, Keorapetse William
Awakening, The.
Ivory Masks in Orbit.
Towards a Walk in the Sun.
Khaketla, B. Makalo
Lesotho.
Khaketla, N. M.
White and the Black, The.
Khansa
Tears.
Khayyám, Omar *See* **Omar Khayyám**
Khodasevich, Vladislav Felitsyanovich
It Scarcely Seems Worth While.
Monkey, The.
Ki, Princess
Not Alone.
Kickham, Charles Joseph
Irish Peasant Girl, The.
Rory of the Hill.
"Kid Kazanova." *See* **Stack, Philip**
Kieffer, Paul
Limerick: "Yes, theirs was a love that was tidal."
Kieran, John
Advice from an Expert.
To Lou Gehrig.
Kikaku
Butterfly, The.
Cock Again, The.
Fairies.
Kikurio
Daffodils.
Kilburn, David
Weather Forecast.
Kilgore, Crystal
On War.
Killigrew, Henry
Song: "While Morpheus thus doth gently lay."
Killigrew, Sir William
Beauty Paramount.
Selindra, *sel.*
Kilmer, Aline (Mrs. Joyce Kilmer)
Ambition.
Experience.
For All Ladies of Shalott.
Heart Knoweth Its Own Bitterness, The.
I Shall Not Be Afraid.
Light Lover.
Masquerader, The.
My Mirror.
Olim Meminisse Juvabit.
One Shall Be Taken and the Other Left.
Remembrance.
Shards.
Song against Children.
Stirrup Cup, The.
Things.
To Aphrodite; with a Mirror.
Victory.
Wind Rose in the Night, A.
Kilmer, Joyce
Ballade of My Lady's Beauty.
Blue Valentine, A.
Citizen of the World.
Dave Lilly.
Daw's Dinner.
Easter.
Gates and Doors.
His Laureate.
House with Nobody in It, The.
In Fairyland.
Kings.
King's Ballad, The.
Main Street.
Martin.
Memorial Day.
Multiplication.
Peacemaker, The.
Pennies.
Poets.
Prayer of a Soldier in France.
Roofs.
Rouge Bouquet.
Servant Girl and Grocer's Boy.
Singing Girl, The.
Thanksgiving.
Theology.
To a Young Poet Who Killed Himself.
Trees.
White Ships and the Red, The.
Kilmer, Mrs. Joyce *See* **Kilmer, Aline**
Kilmer, Kenton
Dawn.
Little Serenade.
Yellow.
Kimball, Hannah Parker
Beyond.
One Way of Trusting.
Soul and Sense.
Kimball, Harriet McEwen
All's Well.
Blessed Task, The.
Guest, The.
What the Birds Do.
White Azaleas.
Kimber, Thomas
We May Not Understand.
Kindig, L. James
Is It Nothing to You?
King, Alfred Castner
Miner, The.
Ruined Cabin, The.
King, Anna M.
Faith and Sight.
King, Ben
Cultured Girl Again, The.
How Often.
If I Should Die Tonight.
Jane Jones.
Pessimist, The.
Sum of Life, The.
That Cat.
King, Dorothy
Billy Boy.
Gipsy Man.
Jenny and Johnny.
King, Edith
Acorns.
Beetle, The.
Cobwebs.
Duck, The.
Evening Song.
Hedgehog, The.
Holly, The.
Mole, The.
Pebbles.
Rabbit, The.
Robin's Song.
To the Bat.
King, Edward
Captain Loredan.

King (continued)
Tsigane's Canzonet, The.
Woman's Execution, A.
King, Ellen, *and* **H. E. Engle** *See* **Engle, H. E.,** *and* **Ellen King**
King, Ethel
Wood Music.
King, Georgiana Goddard
Man Called Dante, I Have Heard, A.
Song: "Something calls and whispers, along the city street."
Way of Perfect Love, The, *sel.*
King, Harriet Eleanor Hamilton
But yet one thought has often stayed by me.
Crocus, The.
Disciples, The, *sel.*
Garden of the Holy Souls, The.
Hours of the Passion, *sel.*
Love's Strength.
Palermo.
Sermon in the Hospital, The, *sel.*
King, Helen
Human Touch, The.
King, Henry, Bishop of Chichester
Conjectured to Be upon the Death of Sir Walter Raleigh.
Contemplation upon Flowers, A.
Dear loss! since thy untimely fate.
Departure, The; an Elegy.
Double Rock, The
Elegy, An: "I will not weep, for 'twere as great a sin."
Elegy upon My Best Friend, An.
Elegy upon the Most Incomparable King Charles the First, An, *sel.*
Even Such Is Man.
Exequy, The.
Farwell, The: "Farewell fond Love, under whose childish whipp."
Go Thou, That Vainly Dost Mine Eyes Invite.
Legacy, The.
Like to the Falling of a Star.
Madam Gabrina, or the Ill-Favourd Choice.
Of Human Life.
On His Wife's Death.
On the Life of Man.
Paradox: That Fruition Destroys Love, *sel.*
Renunciation.
Retreat, The.
Sic Vita.
Since lovers' joys then leave so sick a taste.
Sleep on my Love, in thy cold bed.
Sonnet: Double Rock, The.
Sonnet: "Tell me no more how fair she is."
Sonnet: "When I entreat, either thou wilt not hear."
Surrender, The.
Tell Me No More.
That Distant Bliss.
Thou from th' enthroned martyrs blood-stain'd line.
To a Lady Who Sent Me a Copy of Verses at My Going to Bed.
To His Unconstant Friend.
To My Dead Friend Ben: Johnson.
To My Honoured Friend Mr. George Sandys.
Upon a Braid of Hair in a Heart.
Upon the Death of My Ever Desired Friend Doctor Donne Dean of Pauls.
Vow-Breaker, The.
King, Herman Stowell
Evocation.
King, Jill
Grief Plucked Me Out of Sleep.
King, Leyland
Didn't it come like.
I could never ask you.
King, Mary (Mrs. Anthony H. White)
Mary of Bethlehem.
King, Stoddard
Çommissary Report.
Étude Géographique.
Mrs. Brown and the Famous Author.
Song of Switzerland.
Wasted Ammunition.
King, William
You Say You Love.
Kingsley, Charles
Airly Beacon.
Alton Locke, *sels.*
Andromeda, *sels.*
Andromeda and the Sea Nymphs.
Ballad: A.D. 1400.
Ballad of Earl Haldan's Daughter, The.
Crusader Chorus.
Dead Church, The.
Do the Work That's Nearest.
Dolcino to Margaret.
Drifting Away.
Easter Week.
Farewell, A: "My fairest child, I have no song to give you," 2 *sts.*
Friends! in this world of hurry.
Great Physician, The.
Hey Nonny!
Instruction sore long time I bore.
Killarney.
Knight's Leap, The.
Last Buccaneer, The.
Lorraine.
Lost Doll, The.
Margaret to Dolcino.
Myth, A.
Nereids, The.
Night Bird, The.
North-east Wind, The.
Ode to the North-east Wind.
Old Buccaneer, The.
Old, Old Song, The.
Old Song, The.
Oubit, The.
Parable from Liebig, A.
Poetry of a Root Crop, The.
Saint's Tragedy, The, *sels.*
Sands of [*or* o'] Dee, The.
Sing Heigh-ho!
Song: "I once had a sweet little doll, dears."
Song: "Oh! that we two were Maying."
Song: "When all the world is young, lad."
Song: "When I was a greenhorn and young."
There Sits a Bird.
Three Fishers, The.
Tide River, The.
To a Child.
Valentine's Day.
Water Babies, The, *sels.*
Welcome, A.
Whelming the dwellings of men, and the toils of the slow-footed oxen.
When All the World Is Young, Lad.
When I Was a Greenhorn and Young.
Young and Old.
Kingsley, Henry
At Glastonbury.
Magdalen.
Kingston, Jeremy
Distances.
Kinnell, Galway
Another Night in the Ruins.
Avenue Bearing the Initial of Christ into the New World, The.
Bear, The.
Behind the Power Station on 14th, the held breath.
Burning.
Cells Breathe in the Emptiness.
Chicago.
Children set fires in ashbarrels.
Correspondence School Instructor Says Goodbye to His Poetry Students, The.
Duck-Chasing.
First Song.
Fishmarket closed, the fishes gone into flesh, The.
Flower Herding on Mount Monadnock.
For Robert Frost, *sel.*
For the Lost Generation.
Fossils, The.
Freedom, New Hampshire.
From the Station House.
Full Moon.
Homecoming of Emma Lazarus, The.
How Many Nights.
I saw you once on the TV.
In a Parlor Containing a Table.
In Fields of Summer.
In sunlight on the avenue.
In the Farmhouse.
In the pushcart market, on Sunday.
Island of Night.
La Bagarède.
Leaping Falls.
Near Barbizon.
Passion.
Poem, The.
Poems of Night.
Porcupine, The.
Promise was broken too freely, The.
Promontory Moon.
Rain over a Continent.
Reply to the Provinces.
Ruins under the Stars.
Sometimes I see them.
Spindrift.
Spring Oak.
Supper after the Last, The.
To Christ Our Lord.
To William Carlos Williams.
Told by Seafarers.
Vapor Trail Reflected in the Frog Pond.
Walk in the Country, A.
Wolves, The.
Kinney, Coates
Rain on the Roof.
Kinney, Elizabeth Clementine
Blind Psalmist, The.
Dream, A.
Moonlight in Italy.
Quakeress Bride, The.
To the Boy.
Ki no Akimine
Beloved person must I think, The.
Kinon, Victor
Agnus Dei.
Kinoshita Yuji
Late Summer.
Ki no Tsurayuki
Most fragile of all is the cherry-bloom.
Kinsella, Thomas
Another September.
Baggot Street Deserta.
Country Walk, A.
Fifth Sunday after Easter.
First Light.
Folk Wisdom.
In the Ringwood.
King John's Castle.
Mask of Love.
Mirror in February.
Night Songs.
Old Atheist Pauses by the Sea, An.
Pause en Route.
Ritual of Departure.
Secret Garden, The.
Kintsune, (the prime minister Kintsune)

Flowers whirl away, The.
Kinwelmersh, Francis
For Christmas Day.
For Whitsunday.
Kiokusui Traveler Caught in a Storm, A.
Kiper, Florence *See* **Frank, Florence Kiper**
Kipling, Alice Macdonald
At the Dawn.
Kipling, Rudyard
All the world over, nursing their scars.
Astrologer's Song, An.
Bagheera's Song.
Ballad of East and West, The.
Ballad of Fisher's Boardinghouse, The.
Ballad of the King's Jest, The.
Barrack-Room Ballads, *sel.*
Batteries Out of Ammunition.
Beginner, The.
Betrothed, The.
Big Steamers.
Bombed in London.
Boots.
Boxing.
Bridegroom, The.
Bridge-Guard in the Karroo.
Buddha at Kamakura, The.
Burial, The.
By the Hoof of the Wild Goat.
Camel's Hump, The.
Captive, The.
Certain Maxims of Hafiz.
Chant-Pagan.
Charm, A.
Children's Song, The.
Cities and Thrones and Powers.
"Cleared."
Coastwise Lights, The.
Code of Morals, A.
Cold Iron.
Common Form.
Commonplaces.
Conundrum of the Workshops, The.
Coward, The.
Danny Deever.
Dead Statesman, A.
Dedication: "Beyond the path of the outmost sun through utter darkness hurled."
Dedication, A: "My new-cut ashlar takes the light."
Delilah.
Derelict, The.
Destroyers in Collision.
Divided Destinies.
Dove of Dacca, The.
Drifter off Tarentum, A.
Eddi's Service.
England.
Envoy: "There's a whisper down the field where the year has shot her yield."
Envoy: "When Earth's last picture is painted and the tubes are twisted and dried."
Epitaphs of the War, 1914-18.
"Equality of Sacrifice."
Et Dona Ferentes.
Evarra and His Gods.
Ex-Clerk.
Explorer, The.
Fabulists, The.
Fairies' Siege, The.
Feet of the Young Men, The.
Female of the Species, The.
First Friend, The.
Flowers, The.
"Follow Me 'Ome."
For to Admire.
Ford o' Kabul River.
Frankie's Trade.
Fuzzy-Wuzzy.
Galley-Slave, The.
Gehazi.
General Summary, A.
Gertrude's Prayer.
Gethsemane.
Gipsy Trail, The.
Gipsy Vans.
Grave near Cairo, A.
Great-Heart.
Gunga Din.
Harp Song of the Dane Women.
He drank strong waters and his speech was coarse.
Heriot's Ford.
If.
In Springtime.
In the Neolithic Age, *br. sel.*
Jam-Pot, The.
Jane Smith.
Jane's Marriage.
Job That's Crying to Be Done, The.
Jobson's Amen.
Jungle Book, The, *sels.*
King, The.
La Nuit Blanche.
Ladies, The.
Land, The.
Land of Our Birth.
Last Chantey, The.
Last Rhyme of True Thomas, The.
Law of the Jungle, The.
Legends of Evil, The.
L'Envoi: "There's a whisper down the field where the year has shot her yield."
L'Envoi: "What is the moral? Who rides may read."
L'Envoi: "When earth's last picture is painted and the tubes are twisted and dried."
Lest We Forget!
Lichtenberg.
Light That Failed, The, *sel.*
Limerick: "There was a small boy of [*or* young man from] Quebec."
Limerick: "There was a young man from Quebec."
Liner She's a Lady, The.
Long Trail, The.
Looking-Glass, The.
Love Song of Har Dyal, The.
McAndrew's Hymn.
Mandalay.
Many Inventions, *sel.*
Mary Gloster, The.
Maxim: "If he play, being young and unskilful."
Mesopotamia.
Mine Sweepers.
Mother Love.
Mother o' Mine.
Municipal.
My Boy Jack.
My New-cut Ashlar.
My Rival.
Naaman's Song.
O Mary Pierced with Sorrow.
Other Man, The, *sel.*
Our Lady of the Snows.
Pagett, M.P.
Pan in Vermont.
Pict Song, A.
Pink Dominoes.
Plain Tales from the Hills, *sels.*
Post That Fitted, The.
Power of the Dog, The.
Predestination.
Puck of Pook's Hill, *sels.*
Queen's Men, The.
Rebirth.
Recall, The.
Recessional.
Reeds of Runnymede, The.
Refined Man, The.
Return, The.
Rhyme of the Three Captains, The.
Road Song of the Bandar Log, The.
Rolling Down to Rio.
Romulus and Remus.
Runes on Weland's Sword, The.
Sacrifice of Er-Heb, The.
St. Helena Lullaby, A.
Salonikan Grave.
Screw-Guns.
Sea and the Hills, The.
Seal Lullaby.
Seal's Lullaby.
Second Jungle Book, The, *sels.*
Secret of the Machines, The.
Servant, A.
"Service Man, The."
Sestina of the Tramp-Royal.
Shillin' a Day.
Shiv and the Grasshopper ("Shiv, who poured the harvest and made the winds to blow").
Sing-Song of Old Man Kangaroo, The.
Sir Richard's Song.
Skating.
Smuggler's Song, A.
Son, A.
Song before Action, *sel.*
Song of Diego Valdez, The.
Song of the Banjo, The.
Song of the Galley-Slaves.
Song of the Little Hunter, The.
Song to Mithras, A.
Sons of Martha, The.
Storm Cone, The.
Story of Uriah, The.
Study of an Elevation, in Indian Ink.
Supplication of the Black Aberdeen.
Sussex.
There was a strife 'twixt man and maid.
To James Whitcomb Riley.
Tomlinson.
Tommy.
Twelve hundred million men are spread.
Vampire, The [as Suggested by the Painting by Philip Burne-Jones].
Verses on Games, *sel.*
Voortrekker, The.
Way through the Woods, The.
Wet Litany, The.
When Earth's Last Picture Is Painted.
When 'Omer Smote 'Is Bloomin' Lyre.
When the earth was sick and the skies were grey.
White Man's Burden, The.
Who Dies If England Live?
Wide, Wide World, The.
Widow at Windsor, The.
Winners, The.
Wishing-Caps, The.
Wonder, The.
Kirby, Jeannie
Aeroplane, The.
Child's Morning Prayer, A.
I Wonder.
Pigeon's Story, The.
Proud Little Spruce Fir.
Timid Bunnies.
Union Jack, The.
Kirby, Patrick F.
Compline.
Consecration.
Rain.
Riddles.
Sequel to Finality.
Song for These Days.
Kirillov, Vladimir Timofeevich
We.
Kirk, Richard

Kirk (continued)
Conversational Neighbor, A.
Kirk, William F.
Courtship of Miles Standish, The, *parody.*
Giving.
Goldfish, The.
Lumberyak, The.
The Lumberyak.
Sonnet on Stewed Prunes.
Kirkconnell, Watson
Ah, Flood of Life on which I am a wave.
Courting of Olga Karg, The.
Crow and the Nighthawk, The.
Road to Bethlehem, The.
Tide of Life, The, *sel.*
Kirkup James
Autumn Grove after Rain, by Wentien.
Bird Fancier, The.
Blessed Received in Paradise, The.
Bowl of Goldfish, The; a Fable.
Boy with a Mouth Organ.
Cave, A.
Charm for the Ear-Ache, A.
City of the North, A.
Correct Compassion, A.
Earth Tremor in Lugano.
Earthquake.
For the 90th Birthday of Sibelius.
Ghosts, Fire, Water.
Giving and Taking.
Homage to Vaslav Nijinsky.
Japanese Children.
La Bête Humaine.
Landscape, by Ch'eng Sui.
Liadov: "The Enchanted Lake."
Lonely Scarecrow, The.
Mortally.
Nature of Love, The.
No More Hiroshimas.
Old Gramophone Records.
Pavement Artist, The.
Pentecost.
Poem To Be Cast into the Sea in a Bottle.
Poet, The.
Prayer: "Peace, you were always there."
Rugby League Game.
Sakunami.
Samisen.
Shepherd's Tale, The.
Submerged Village, The.
Symphony Orchestra.
Tea in a Space-Ship.
To an Old Lady Asleep at a Poetry Reading.
To the Ancestral North.
Ursa Major.
Visit to Brontëland, A.
Waiting.
Zen Archer, The.
Kirsch, Olga
Blockhouse.
Wordspinning.
Kirschenbaum, Leo
Iberia.
Kirwan, M.
Look not upon me, seek no more to stay me.
These are my tears that now you see.
Kisa'i of Merv
Beauty's Queen.
Kiser, Samuel Ellsworth
Bargain Sale, A.
A Blessing of Toil.
Fighter, The.
Little Prayer, A.
Memorial Day.
Memorial Day, 1889.
My Creed.
Ridiculous Optimist, The.
Unsubdued.
When I Had Need of Him.
Kitahara, Hakushu
Impression of a Fountain.
Rain on Castle Island.
Kitasono, Katue
Green Sunday.
Kitchel, Mary Eva
So Runs Our Song.
Kittredge, Walter
Tenting on the Old Camp Ground.
We're Tenting Tonight.
Kiyowara Fukuyabu
River-Fog.
Kizer, Carolyn
Afterthoughts of Donna Elvira.
Complex Autumnal.
Great Blue Heron, The.
Intruder, The.
Lovemusic.
Summer near the River.
To My Friend, behind Walls.
Ungrateful Garden, The.
What the Bones Know.
Widow in Wintertime, A.
"Klabund" (Alfred Henschke)
Fever.
Klee, Paul
Bimbo's Pome.
Klein. Abraham Moses
Autobiographical.
Baal Shem Tov.
Ballad of the Days of the Messiah.
Bandit.
Bestiary.
Biography.
Bread.
Design for Mediaeval Tapestry.
Filling Station.
For the Sisters of the Hôtel Dieu.
Frigidaire.
Grain Elevator.
Haggadah.
Heirloom.
In re Solomon Warshawer.
Indian Reservation: Caughnawaga.
Lone Bather.
Monsieur Gaston.
Montreal.
Orders.
Political Meeting.
Psalm VI: "And on that day, upon the heavenly scarp."
Psalm XII: "These were the ones who thanked their God."
Psalm of the Fruitful Field.
Psalter of Avram Haktani, The, *sels.*
Quebec Liquor Commission Store.
Rabbi Yom-Tob of Mayence Petitions His God.
Rev Owl.
Rocking Chair, The.
Spinning Wheel, The.
Still Small Voice, The.
Sugaring, The.
Venerable Bee, The.
Kleiser, Grenville
Bridge You'll Never Cross, The.
Challenge, The.
Most Vital Thing in Life, The.
My Daily Prayer.
Thanksgiving.
You Can't Fool God.
Kline, Betsy W.
Be Still.
Trust.
"Klingle, George" (Georgiana Klingle Holmes)
As Thy Days So Shall Thy Strength Be.
At Dawn of the Year.
Be Patient.
He Will Give Them Back.
Hour by Hour.
Miracle, A.
Palm Sunday Hymn.
Knapp, Charles R.
Woodsman Goes to Sea, A.
Knibbs, Harry [*or* Henry] Herbert
Charley Lee.
Cowboys' Ball, The.
Desert, The.
Long Road West, The.
Oro Stage, The.
Out There Somewhere.
Riders of the Stars.
Roll a Rock Down.
Shallows of the Ford, The.
Valley That God Forgot, The.
Knickman, Lester
Could You Spare Some Time for Jesus?
Knight, David
Chief of the West, Darkling, The.
In Memoriam S. L. Akintola.
Palms, The.
"When the Students Resisted, a Minor Clash Ensued."
Knight, Etheridge
As You Leave Me.
For Black Poets Who Think of Suicide.
Hard Rock Returns to Prison from the Hospital for the Criminal Insane.
He Sees Through Stone.
Idea of Ancestry, The.
It Was a Funky Deal.
Nickle Bet, A.
Knight, Henry Coggswell
Lunar Stanzas.
Knight, John
Father to the Man.
Knight, Nellie
Mary.
Knight, Sarah Kemble
Pleasent Delusion of a Sumpteous Citty.
Resentments Composed because of the Clamor of Town Topers Outside My Apartment.
Thoughts on Pausing at a Cottage near the Paukataug River.
Thoughts on the Sight of the Moon.
Warning to Travailers Seeking Accomodations at Mr. Devills Inn.
Knight-Adkin, James H.
No Man's Land.
Patrol, The.
Knipe, Arthur A.
Autumn.
Discovery, A.
Thirsty Flowers.
Knister, Raymond
Boy Remembers in the Field.
Change.
Colt, The.
Feed.
Hawk, The.
Lake Harvest.
Nell.
Plowman, The.
Plowman's Song.
Row of Stalls, A, *sel.*
Stable-Talk.
White Cat.
Knobloch, M. H.
My Bible and I.
Knott, William ("Saint Geraud) "
Death.
Goodbye.
I Am the Stars' Bugging-Device.
I only keep this voice to give to anything afraid of me.
Karezzas, Cuntras, Cockturnes, Manshrieks, Carrioncries.
Late August to Early November.
November Light, Short Days Dark Fiery Sunsets.

Nuremburg, U.S.A.
Poem: "After your death."
Poem: "Alright if I have to be famous let it be for this great."
Poem: "Beach holds and sifts us through her dreaming fingers, The."
Poem: "I am one man, worshipping silk knees."
Poem: "It must be true."
Poem: "My sperm is lyre in your blood your."
Poem: "Only response, The."
Poem: "When our hands are alone."
Poem to Poetry.
Prosepoem.
Sergey Yesenin Speaking Isadora Duncan.
Sleep.
Song: "Naomi looks for her child."
Survival of the Fittest Groceries.
To American Poets.
Knott, William F.
We'll Fling the Starry Banner Out.
Knowlan, Alden A.
Marian at the Pentecostal Meeting.
Knowles, Frederic Lawrence
Golgotha.
I Thank Thee.
If Love Were Jester at the Court of Death.
Last Word, The.
Laus Mortis.
L'Envoi: "O love triumphant over guilt and sin."
Life.
Love Triumphant.
Memory, A.
My Faith.
Nature, the Artist.
New Age, The.
On a Flyleaf of Burns's Songs.
Out of the Depths.
Pasture, A.
Song of Desire, A.
Survivor, The.
Tenant, The.
To Jesus of Nazareth.
To Mother Nature.
Victory Which Is Peace, The.
Knowles, James Sheridan
Switzerland.
William Tell, *sel.*
Knox, Edmund George Valpy ("Evoe"),
Inspiration.
Limerick: "There was a young curate of Hants."
Mr. A. E. Housman on the Olympic Games.
My Own Simplified Spelling.
Nimble Stag, The.
Stately Homes of England, The.
To the God of Love.
Tryst, The.
Knox, Isa Craig
Woodruffe, The.
Knox, J. Mason
Co-operation.
Knox, John
Lord Is My Shepherd, The.
Knox, Ronald Arbuthnott
Absolute and Abitofhell.
Limerick: "Clergyman [*or* Evangelical vicar] in want, A."
Limerick: "Evangelical vicar in want."
Limerick: "There once was a man [*or* was a young man] who said, 'God.'"
Limerick: "There was a young man who said, 'God.'"
Knox, William
Mortality.
Oh! Why Should the Spirit of Mortal Be Proud?
Kobayashi Issa *See* **Issa**
Kobbé, Gustav
From the Harbor Hill.
To a Little Girl.
Kober, Arthur
Evidence.
Koch, Christopher
Half-heard.
Koch, Claude F.
Words for Artificers.
Koch, James H.
To a Young Lady Swinging Upside Down on a Birch Limb over a Winter-swollen Creek.
Koch, Kenneth
Artist, The.
Aus einer Kindheit.
Circus, The.
Departure from Hydra, The.
Fresh Air.
Geography.
Locks.
Ma Provence.
Mending Sump.
Permanently.
Railway Stationery, The.
Sleeping with Women.
Taking a Walk with You.
Thank You.
Variations on a Theme by William Carlos Williams.
You Were Wearing.
Kochanowski, Jan
To Sleep.
Kodo
Cuckoo, The.
Koehler, G. Stanley
Ground Swell.
New Construction; Bath Iron Works.
Siciliana; the Landings at Gela.
Kogyoku, Empress
Separation.
Köhler, Willibald
Bridge, The.
Kohn, Annette
Epitaph for the Unknown Soldier.
Old Soldier Dead.
Kolars, Mary
If This Old Place.
Kollar, Jan
Daughter of the Slava, The, *sel.*
He only is worthy of freedom who honors the freedom of others.
Koller, James
Cistern Dry & the Well, The.
Crossed the River.
Tree for Kindling, A.
Wind Was Out of the North, The.
Koltsov, Aleksey Vasilyevich
Young Reaper, The.
Komey, Ellis Ayitey
Damage You Have Done, The.
Oblivion.
Kono, Tenrai
Wedding Celebration.
Konrick, Vera Bishop
Erda.
Koopman, Harry Lyman
Icarus.
John Brown.
Revealed.
Satirist, The.
Sea and Shore.
Körte, Sister Mary Norbert
Among the Lions Night Is Still.
At the Edge.
8 May 1967.
"In the Most Lightsome Darkness."
"New Flower, A—Pure and Untorn."
Poets of Peace and Gladness, The.
That Is Tad.
To Dance in a Loving Ring.
Kostelanetz, Richard
Tribute to Henry Ford (1-3).
Kotomichi
Moon, The.
Koutchak, Nahab
Snares, The.
Kramer, Aaron
Cablegram.
Homecoming.
Kramer, Arthur
Adventures.
Inflamed Disciple, The.
Kramer, Edgar Daniel
Envy.
God's Book.
Good Friday.
New Year Prayer.
Sequence.
Tall Trees.
Youth's Thankfulness.
Krasinski, Zygmunt
Waiting for Sunrise.
Kraus, Karl
Express Train.
On the Threshold.
Kresensky, Raymond
Afternoon in a Church.
Christ on Madison Street.
Comrade, Remember.
Discovery.
Golgotha's Cross.
Heaven in My Hand.
Jesus Was a Humble Man.
Men Follow Simon.
Prayer of the Unemployed.
Refusal.
Suffering God, The.
To the Tomb.
Kress, George L.
Parable, A.
Kreymborg, Alfred
America.
Ants.
Arabs.
Ballad of the Common Man (for the Jefferson Memorial).
Ballad of the Lincoln Penny.
Berceuse Ariettes, *sel.*
Bloom.
Cézanne.
Circe.
City Sparrow.
Convention.
Credo.
Crocus.
Dawns.
Dirge: "She came—."
Ditty the City Sang, The.
Dorothy.
Ego's Dream.
Epigram: "Isn't it."
Festoons of Fishes.
Geometry.
Idealists.
Improvisation.
Indian Sky.
Less Lonely.
Life.
Madonna di Campagna.
Man Whom Men Deplore, A.
Manhattan Epitaphs: Lawyer.
Manikin and Minikin.
Monotone.
Nun Snow.
Old Manuscript.
Our window is stained.
Parasite.
Pasts.
Peasant.
Race Prejudice.

Kreymborg (continued)
Rain Inters Maggiore.
Ribbon Two Yards Wide, A.
Springtime.
There's a Nation.
Threnody: "I have been a snob to-day."
Tree, The.
Under Glass.
Vista.
Yearning.
Krige, Uys
Distant View.
Encounter.
Farm Gate.
Soldier, The.
Swallows Over the Camp.
Kriloff, Ivan Andreievich *See* **Krylov, Ivan Andreyevich**
Krinagoras *See* **Crinagoras**
Kroll, Ernest
Francis Parkman.
Kronthal, Joseph
Be Careful What You Say.
Krows, Jane W.
Lesson, The.
Little Satellite.
Milkman, The.
My House.
Space Travel.
Kruger, Charlotte M.
Beautiful Saviour.
Kruger, Fania
Passover Eve.
Krylov, Ivan Andreyevich
Peasant and the Sheep, The.
Swan, the Pike, and the Crab, The.
Wolf in the Kennels, The.
Kuder, Blanche Bane
Blue Bowl, The.
Kuhn, Walter J.
My Only Plea.
Kumin, Maxine W.
400-Meter Freestyle.
Fräulein Reads Instructive Rhymes.
Halfway.
May 10th.
Pawnbroker, The.
Prothalamion.
Sound of Night, The.
Kumm, Lucy Guiness
Why Didst Thou Doubt?
Kunimoto, Tsumori
Wild geese returning, The.
Kunitz, Stanley Jasspon
After the Last Dynasty.
Benediction.
Between the Acts.
Careless Love.
Change.
Choice of Weapons, A.
Dark and the Fair, The.
Daughters of the Horseleech, The.
Deciduous Branch.
End of Summer.
Father and Son.
For the Word Is Flesh.
Foreign Affairs.
He.
Hemorrhage, The.
In a Strange House.
Lovers Relentlessly.
Mens Creatrix.
Reflection by a Mailbox.
Science of the Night, The.
Scourge, The.
She Wept, She Railed.
Soul's Adventure.
Spark of Laurel.
Summing-Up, The.
Thief, The.
Very Tree.
Waltzer in the House, The.
War against the Trees, The.
When the Light Falls.
Kupferberg, Tuli
Would You Believe?
Kurahashibe Otome
This Needle.
Kuroyanagi Shoha
Heavy cart rumbles, A.
Kurt, Kim
Runaway.
Sun-Bather, The.
Vernal Paradox.
Woodlore.
Kurth, Paula
Association Copy.
Kurtz, Aaron
Behold the Sea, *sel.*
They Got You Last Night.
Kurtz, E. C.
Someone's Bible.
Kushniroff, Aaron
Die My Shriek.
Kuskin, Karla
Balloon, The.
Catherine.
Full of the Moon.
Gold-tinted Dragon, The.
Lewis Has a Trumpet.
Question, The.
Spring.
Tiptoe.
Very Early.
Witches' Ride, The.
Kuykendall, John M.
Veteran Cowboy's Ruminations, A.
Kuzma, Greg
In Love with the Bears.
Kuzmin, Mikhail Alekseyevich
Now Dry Thy Eyes.
This Summer's Love, *sel.*
Kwaso
Butterfly.
Kwitko, Leib
Moods.
You Who Dog My Footsteps.
Kyd, Thomas
Cornelia, *sel.*
Of Fortune, *abr.*
Kyei, Kojo Gyinaye
African in Louisiana.
Talking Drums, The.
Kynaston, Sir Francis
Know, 'twas well said, that spirits are too high.
To Cynthia, on Concealment of Her Beauty.
To Cynthia on Her Being an Incendiary.
To Cynthia, on Her Changing.
To Cynthia, on Her Embraces.
To Cynthia on His Love after Death.
Kyoshi, Takahama
Against the broad sky.
In the old man's eyes.
On far hills.
Snake, The.
Snake fled, The.

L

"L., C. G."
Master, The.
"L. E. L." *See* **Landon, Letitia Elizabeth**
"L. G." *See* **"G., L."**
"L. J." *See* **"J., L"**
"L. R." *See* **"R., L"**
"L. S. P." *See* **"P., L. S"**
"L. W." *See* **"W., L"**
Labé, Louise
And If at Last.
Povre Ame Amoureuse.
What Does It Avail Me?
LaBombard, Joan
Sibyl, The.
Labrunie, Gérard *See* **Nerval, Gérard de**
Lacaussade, Auguste
My lips from this day forgot how to smile.
Salaziennes, Les, *sel.*
Lacey, Florence
Promise.
La Chance, Frances Rhoads
I Am in Christ.
Lachmann, Hedwig
Home-Sickness.
Walk, A.
La Coste [*or* La Conte], Marie
Somebody's Darling.
"Lady of Sakanoye, The." *See* **Sakanoye, The Lady of**
La Farge, Christopher
Here is no tragedy.
Prayer for Living and Dying.
Prologue, Each to the Other, *sel.*
La Farge, Peter
Vision of a Past Warrior.
La Follette, Melvin Walker
Arrivals and Departures.
Ballad of Red Fox, The.
Blue Horse, The.
Didactic Sonnet.
Hunt.
I Knew a Boy with Hair like Gold.
Love for a Hare.
Saint Stephen in San Francisco.
Sleeping Saint, The.
Spring Landscape.
Summerhouse.
Vacation Snapshot.
Valediction, A.
La Fontaine, Jean de
Acorn and the Pumpkin, The.
Ape, The.
Bird Wounded by an Arrow, The.
Boy and the Schoolmaster, The.
Castle Builder, The.
Cat Changed into a Woman, The.
Cobbler and the Rich Man, The.
Cock and the Pearl, The.
Cockerel, the Cat, and the Young Mouse, The.
Council Held by e Rats, The.
Crow and the Fox, The.
Cudgelled but Contented Cuckold, The.
Ear-Maker and the Mould-Mender, The.
Earthen Pot and the Iron Pot, The.
Fair Exchange, A.
Fox and the Bust, The.
Fox and the Grapes, The.
Gascon Punished, The ("A Gascon, being heard one day to swear").
Hag and the Slavies, The.
Hen with the Golden Eggs, The.
Jay in the Feathers of the Peacock, The.
Lion Grown Old, The.
Love and Folly.
Man and the Flea, The.
Monkey and the Cat, The.
Oak and the Reed, The.
Old Cat and the Young Mouse, The.
Old Man and the Ass, The.
Oyster and the Litigants, The.
Raven and the Fox, The.
Sick Lion and the Fox, The.
Superfluous Saddle, The.
Swan and the Cook, The.
Thieves and the Ass, The.
To Promise Is One Thing, to Perform Is Another.
Two Doves, The.
Wolf and the Dog, The.

Wolf and the Lamb, The.
Laforgue, Jules
Asides from the Clowns, *sel.*
Character and Talent.
Cigarette, The.
Complaint on the Oblivion of the Dead.
End of a Day in the Provinces, The.
For the Book of Love.
Lightning of the Abyss.
My clear-cut heart, my tender soul.
Winter Sunset.
Without the Moon.
La Fresnaye, Jean de *See* **Vauquelin de la Fresnaye, Jean**
Lagerkvist, Pär
Beauty Is Most at Twilight's Close.
Lagerlöf, Selma
Child of Peace, The.
La Grone, Oliver
Bathed Is My Blood.
My America.
This Hour.
Laight, Frederick E.
Drought.
Soliloquy.
Laighton, Albert
Under the Leaves.
Laing, Alexander, of Brechin
My Ain Wife.
Laing Alexander Kinnan
Last Romantic, The.
Original Sin.
Triolet: "Night is full of the crying, The."
Laing, Allan M.
Family Life.
Instead of blushing cherry hue.
Jack the Ripper.
Samuel Pepys.
When they found Giotto.
Laing, Dilys Bennett
Aubade.
Forgive Me.
How Music's Made.
In the Hospital.
Lines on the Sea.
Pinwheel.
Villanelle.
"Laird, William" (William Laird Brown)
Prayer, A: "Lord, make my childish soul stand straight."
Traümerei at Ostendorff's.
Very Old Song, A.
"Lakon."
William the Bastard.
Lal, P.
Song for Beauty, A.
Laluah, Aquah *See* **Hayford, Gladys May Casely**
Lamantia, Philip
Man Is in Pain.
Morning Light Song.
Still Poem 9.
Terror Conduction.
Lamar, Mirabeau Buonaparte
Daughter of Mendoza, The.
Lamartine, Alphonse Marie Louis de
Cedars of Lebanon, The.
Crucifix, The.
Lake, The.
Lamb, Arthur J.
Asleep in the Deep.
Bird in a Gilded Cage, A.
Lamb, Charles
As when a child on some long winter's night.
Childhood Fled.
Family Name, The.
Farewell to Tobacco.
Free Thoughts on Several Eminent Composers.
Gypsy's Malison, The.
Hester.
In My Own Album.
John Woodvil; a Tragedy, *sel.*
Lines on the Celebrated Picture by Leonardo da Vinci, Called the Virgin of the Rocks.
Methinks how dainty sweet it were, reclined.
Names, The.
Nonsense Verses.
Old Familiar Faces, The.
On an Infant Dying as Soon as Born.
Springy motion in her gait, A.
To John Lamb, Esq. of the South-Sea House.
Triumph of the Whale.
Written at Cambridge.
Lamb, Charles *and* Mary
Anger ("Anger in its time and place").
Beasts in the Tower, The.
Cleanliness.
Crumbs to the Birds.
Dessert, The.
Envy.
Feigned Courage.
First Tooth, The.
Going into Breeches.
Magpie's Nest.
Neatness in Apparel.
Orange, The.
Peach, The.
Which Is the Favourite?
Lamb, Mary
Aspiration.
Breakfast.
Child, A.
Choosing a Name.
Helen.
In Memoriam.
Maternal Lady with the Virgin Grace.
Parental Recollections.
Reason why my brother's so severe, The.
Two Boys, The.
Lambdin, Sylvia S.
January.
Lambert, Clara
Skyscraper Is a City's House.
Summon the Workers.
Lambert, Elisabeth
Brave Old World.
"Lambert, Louis." *See* **Gilmore, Patrick Sarsfield**
Lamdan, Yitzhak
For the Sun Declined, *sel.*
Where am I, O awesome friend?
La Monnoye, Bernard de
Burgundian Carol.
Patapan.
Lampman, Archibald
After the Shower.
Among the Millet.
Among the Orchards.
Between the Rapids.
City of the End of Things, The.
Comfort of the Fields.
Dawn on the Lievre, The.
Forecast, A.
Heat.
In November.
January Morning, A.
Largest Life, The.
Life and Nature.
Loons, The.
Midnight.
Morning on the Lièvre.
Peccavi, Domine.
Personality.
Prayer, A: "O Earth, O dewy mother, breathe on us."
Refuge.
September.
Snow.
Solitude.
Summer Evening, A.
Sunset at Les Eboulements, A.
Temagami.
There Is a Beauty.
Thunderstorm, A.
Truth, The.
Violinist, The.
Winter Evening.
Winter-Solitude.
Lamprey, Louise
Days of the Leaders, 1925, *sel.*
Deaf, The.
Lampton, William James
New Version, The.
Landau, Zisha [*or* Ziche]
For All That Ever Has Been Ours.
Landels, Thomas Durley
At Eighty-three, *sel.*
Immanence.
Pilate Remembers.
Pontius Pilate, *sel.*
Thank God for life, with all its endless store.
Landers, Warren P.
When We Plant a Tree.
Landeweer, Elizabeth
Dakota Badlands.
Landon, Letitia Elizabeth ("L. E. L.)"
Little Shroud, The.
Wind, The.
Landor, Robert Eyres
Babylon.
Festival, The.
Historic Time.
Impious Feast, The, *sels.*
Jew's Home, The.
Nineveh.
Sleep.
Landor, W. D.
Winter.
Landor, Walter Savage
Absence ("Here, ever since you went abroad").
Absence ("Ianthe! you resolve to cross the sea").
According to eternal laws.
Advice.
Age.
Ah! What Avails the Sceptred Race!
Alas, How Soon the Hours Are Over.
Alas! 'tis very sad to hear.
Alciphron and Leucippe.
Appeal, The.
Around the Child.
Autumn.
Autumnal Song.
Behold, O Aspasia! I Send You Verses.
But Gebir when he heard of her approach.
Child of a Day.
Children.
Chrysolites and Rubies, The.
Citation and Examination of William Shakespeare, The, *sel.*
Commination.
Copy of Verses sent by Cleone to Aspasia, A.
Corinna, from Athens, to Tanagra.
Corinna to Tanagra from Athens.
Corythos, *sel.*
Cowslips.
Crimean Heroes, The.
Critic, A.
Daniel Defoe.
Death.
Death of Artemidora, The.
Death of the Day.
Death Stands above Me [Whispering Low].
Death Undreaded.

Landor (continued)
Defiance.
Dirce.
Do You Remember Me?
Dragon-Fly, The.
Dull Is My Verse.
Dying Speech of an Old Philosopher.
End, The.
Envoi: "I strove with none, for none was worth my strife."
Epigram: "Alas, how soon the hours are over."
Epigram: "Grateful heart for all things blesses, The."
Epigram: "I held her hand, the pledge of bliss."
Epigram: "Joy is the blossom, sorrow is the fruit."
Epigram: "No truer word, save God's, was ever spoken."
Faesulan Idyl.
Fame.
Farewell to Italy.
Fate! I have Asked.
Fault Is Not Mine, The.
Fiesolan Idyl.
Finis.
Florence.
For an Epitaph at Fiesole.
Foreign Ruler, A.
Foren Ruler, A.
Friends, whom she lookt [*or* look'd] at blandly from her couch.
From you, Ianthe, little troubles pass.
Gardener and the Mole, The.
Gebir, *sels.*
Georges, The.
Gifts Returned [*or* Return'd].
Give Me the Eyes.
God Scatters Beauty.
Graceful Acacia.
Hamadryad, The.
Heart's-Ease.
Hegemon to Praxinoe.
Helen and Corythos.
Hellenics, The, *sel.*
Her Lips.
Her Name.
His Epitaph.
Honey-Moon, The.
How Many Voices.
How to Read Me.
I Entreat You, Alfred Tennyson.
I Know Not Whether I Am Proud.
I Strove with None.
I Write Verses.
Ianthe, *sels.*
In After Time.
In Clementina's Artless Mien.
Interlude.
Introduction to "The Last Fruit off an Old Tree."
Invocation, An: "We are what suns and winds."
Iphigeneia and Agamemnon ("Iphigeneia, when she heard her doom").
Ireland.
Ireland Never Was Contented.
Izaac Walton, Cotton, and William Oldways.
Last Fruit off an Old Tree, The, *sels.*
Late Leaves.
Lately Our Poets.
Leaf after Leaf Drops Off.
Lines to a Dragon Fly.
Little Aglae.
Long awaited day, The.
Macaulay.
Maid I Love, The.
Maid's Lament, The.
Malvolio.
Man.
Margaret.
Masar.
Memory.
Mild Is the Parting Year.
Mimnermus Incert.
Mother, I Cannot Mind My Wheel.
Myrtis, *sel.*
Night Airs.
No Truer Word.
Of Clementina.
On a Child.
On Catullus.
On Death.
On Himself.
On His Ninth Decade.
On His Own Agamemnon and Iphigeneia.
On His Own Death.
On His Seventy-fifth Birthday.
On Living Too Long.
On Lucretia Borgia's Hair.
On Man.
On Music.
On One Peter and His Wife.
On Seeing a Hair of Lucretia Borgia.
On Southey's Death.
On Ternissa's Death.
On the Dead.
On the Death of M. d'Ossoli and His Wife, Margaret Fuller.
On the Death of Southey ("Not the last struggles of the Sun").
On the Hellenics.
On the Smooth Brow and Clustering Hair.
On Thomas Hood.
On Timely Death.
One White Hair, The.
One Year Ago ("One year ago my path was green.")
Overture.
Past Ruin'd Ilion Helen Lives.
Pericles and Aspasia, *sels.*
Persistence.
Plays.
Poem: "I cannot tell, not I, why she."
Proem to Hellenics.
Progress of Evening.
Prophecy, A.
Proud Word You Never Spoke [but You Will Speak].
Regeneration.
Remain, ah not in youth alone.
Reply to Lines by Thomas Moore, A, *sel.*
Resignation.
Rose Aylmer.
Rose Aylmer's Hair, Given by Her Sister.
Sea-Nymph's Parting, The.
Separation.
Shakespeare and Milton.
She I love (alas in vain!).
Shepherd and Nymph.
Shepherd and the Nymph, The.
So Late Removed from Him She Swore.
So Then, I Feel Not Deeply!
Some of Wordsworth.
Song: " Often I have heard it said."
Sweet Was the Song.
Tamar and the Nymph.
Ternissa! You Are Fled!
Test, The.
There Are Sweet Flowers.
There Are Who Say.
There Falls with Every Wedding Chime.
Thou Needst Not.
Thought, A.
Thrasymedes and Eunoe, *sel.*
Three Roses, The.
Time to Be Wise.
To a Cyclamen.
To Age.
To His Verse.
To Ianthe ("Past ruined Ilion Helen lives").
To Ianthe ("You smiled, you spoke, and I believed").
To Mary Lamb.
To Miss Arundell.
To My Child Carlino.
To My Ninth Decade.
To Our House-Dog Captain.
To Poets.
To Robert Browning.
To Shelley.
To Sleep.
To the Poet T. J. Mathias.
To the Sister of Elia.
To Wordsworth.
To Youth.
Twenty Years Hence.
Tyrannicide.
Under the Lindens.
Various the Roads of Life.
Verse: "Past ruined Ilion Helen lives."
Verses to Ianthe.
Verses Why Burnt.
Very True, the Linnets Sing.
Wall-Flower, The.
Well I Remember How You Smiled.
Why, Why Repine.
Will you come to the bower I have shaded for you?
William Gifford.
With a Spray of Apple Blossoms.
With Petrarch's Sonnets.
With Rosy Hand.
Wrinkles ("When Helen first saw wrinkles in her face").
Yacht, The.
Ye walls! sole witnesses of happy sighs.
Years.
Years, Many Parti-coloured Years.
Yes; I Write Verses.
Your Pleasures Spring like Daisies.

Lane, Bertha Palmer
Star, The.

Lane, Franklin K.
I Am What You Make Me.

Lane, Temple
Fairy Tree, The.

Lane, Wilmot B.
Owning.

Lang, Andrew
Aesop.
Almae Matres.
Ballad of the Primitive Jest.
Ballade of Blue China.
Ballade of His Choice of a Sepulcher.
Ballade of Middle Age.
Ballade of Primitive Man.
Ballade of the Primitive Jest.
Ballade of the Southern Cross.
Ballade to Theocritus, in Winter.
Brahma.
But now the dentist cannot die.
Clevedon Church.
Herodotus in Egypt.
Homeric Unity.
I'd Leave.
If the wild bowler thinks he bowls.
Last Chance, The.
Limerick: "There was a young lady of Limerick."
Limerick: "There was an auld birkie ca'ed Milton."
Lost Love.
Man and the Ascidian.
Melville and Coghill.
New Shakespeare, A.
Nightingale Weather.
Odyssey, The.
Of Blue China.
Of His Choice of a Sepulchre.

Of Life.
Of the Book-Hunter.
On Calais Sands.
Psalm of Life, A, *parody.*
Romance.
San Terenzo.
Scot to Jeanne d'Arc, A.
Scythe Song.
Spinet, The.
Telling the Bees.
Three Portraits of Prince Charles.
To Theocritus, in Winter.
Twilight on Tweed.
Villon's Ballade.

Lang, Andrew, *and* Edward Burnett Tylor
Double Ballade of Primitive Man.

Lang, Elizabeth
Honey Bear.

Lang, V. R.
Waiting and Peeking.

Langbridge, Frederick
Quite by Chance.

Langdon, Esther Davis
Grace for a Spring Morning in the Mountains.

Lange, Johann Peter
Here and There.
Lord of Life Is Risen, The.

Langford, Dorothy J.
On Top of Troubled Waters.
Son of Man, The.

Langhorn, Richard
Affections of My Soul, The.
O Father of Mercy.

Langhorne, Charles Hartley
Theocritus.

Langhorne, John
Apology for Vagrants.
Country Justice, The.
Evening Primrose, The.
Fables of Flora, The, *sel.*
Farewell Hymn to the Valley of Irwan, A.
Solyman and Almena, *sel.*

Langland, Joseph
Aria for Flute and Oboe.
Crane.
Ecclesiastes.
Hiroshima Lullaby, A.
Hunters in the Snow: Brueghel.
Orioles ("Orioles shine in blue air")
Pruners; Conca di Marini.
Sacrifice of a Rainbow Trout.
Sacrifice of a Red Squirrel.
Sea-Change, A: For Harold.
War.
Willows.
Winter Juniper.

Langland, William
And I bowed my body and beheld all about.
Avarice.
Average Man, The.
Confession of the Deadly Sins, The.
Confessions of the Seven Deadly Sins, The.
Crucifixion and the Harrowing of Hell, The.
Descent into Hell, The.
Field Full of Folk, The ("In a summer season").
Field Full of Folk, A ("What this mountain betokens").
Glutton, The.
Glutton and Bat the Brewer.
Grace for Theology.
Harrowing of Hell, The ("After sharp showers . . .").
Harrowing of Hell, The ("Voice, A, loud in that light. . .")
Holy Church.
Human Soul Speaks, The.
"I have no penny," quoth Piers, "pullets to buy."
Incarnation, The.
Induction, The: "In a summer season. . ."
Langland's Life.
Love.
Love We as Brothers.
Maiden Meed, The.
Palace of Truth, The.
Palmer, The.
Passus II: Lady Meed.
Piers Plowman.
Poor, The.
Poverty Not All Loss.
Prayer for Rich and Poor.
Prayer for the Poor.
Preaching and Not Doing.
Prologue: "In a somer sesun [*or* summer season], when softe [*or* soft] was the sonne [*or* sun *or* when the sun was softest]."
Providence.
Search for St. Truth, The.
Sufferings of the Poor, The.
Theology.
This I trow be truth—who can teach thee better.
Two Confessions.
Vision Concerning Piers Plowman, The.
Vision of Jesus, The.
Vision of Nature, A.
Vision of Piers Plowman, The, *sels.*
Vision of the Holy Church, The.
Vision of William Concerning Piers the Plowman, The.

Langley, Eve
Australia.
Native-born.
This Year, before It Ends.

Langworthy, Yolande
Drifting Sands and a Caravan.

Lanier, Clifford
Edgar Allan Poe.

Lanier, Sidney
As the marsh-hen secretly builds on the watery sod.
Ballad of Trees and the Master, A.
Barnacles.
Battle of Lexington, The.
Beautiful glooms, soft dusks in the noonday fire.
Betrayal, The.
Centennial Meditation of Columbia, The.
Cloud, The.
Corn.
Cross, The.
Crystal, The.
Crystal Christ, The.
Dear Land of All My Love.
Dying Words of Stonewall Jackson, The.
Evening Song.
For the outside leagues of liberty.
From the Crystal.
From the Flats.
Harlequin of Dreams, The.
Hound, The.
Hymns of the Marshes, *sel.*
I speak for each no-tongueéd tree.
Jacquerie, The, *sels.*
Land of the Wilful Gospel.
Laus Mariae.
Lexington.
Marsh Song—At Sunset.
Marshes of Glynn, The.
Mocking Bird, The.
My Springs.
Night and Day.
Oh, what amiss may I forgive in Thee.
Oh, what is abroad in the marsh and the terminal sea?
Opposition.
Owl against Robin, *abr.*
Psalm of the West, The, *sels.*
Raven Days, The.
Remonstrance.
Resurrection.
Revenge of Hamish, The.
Sailing.
Song: "Hound was cuffed, The."
Song for "The Jacquerie" ("The hound was cuffed").
Song of the Chattahoochee.
Stirrup-Cup, The.
Story of Vinland, The.
Struggle.
Sunrise.
Symphony, The.
Tampa Robins.
Thar's More in the Man than Thar Is in the Land.
To the edge of the wood I am drawn, I am drawn.
Triumph, The.
Tyranny.
Waving of the Corn, The.
Wedding-Hymn.
Wedding Prayer.
Whate'er has been, is, shall be—rind, pulp, core.
Ye marshes, how candid and simple and nothing-withholding and free.

Lanigan, George Thomas
Ahkoond of Swat, The.
Dirge of the Moolla of Kotal.
Quatrain: "Squeak's heard in the orchestra, A."
Threnody, A: Ahkoond of Swat, The.
Threnody, A: "What, what, what."
Threnody on the Ahkoond of Swat, A.

Lankford, Frances Stoakley
Prayer at a Nursery Window.
Required Course.

Lanning, Jane McKay
Lent.

Lansdowne, George Granville, Baron
See **Granville, George, Baron Lansdowne**

Lansing, Gerrit
Conventicle.
Ghazel of Absence, A.
Heavenly Tree Grows Downward, The.
Malefic Surgeon, The.
Tabernacles.
Undertaking, The.

Lanusse, Armand
Epigram: "'Do you not wish to renounce the Devil?'"

Lao-tzu, [*or* Lao-tse]
How can a man's life keep its course.

Lape, Fred
Midsummer Pause.

Laramore, Vivian Yeiser
Talk to Me Tenderly.

Larcom, Lucy
Apple Blossoms.
Brown Thrush, The.
Calling the Violet.
Closer to Christ.
Day of Joy, The.
Flag, The.
For the rosebud's break of beauty.
Hal's Birthday.
Hannah Binding Shoes.
Hymn Written for the Two Hundredth Anniversary of the Old South Church, Beverly, Massachusetts.
January.
March.
Mistress Hale of Beverly.
Mountains.
Nature's Easter Music.
Nineteenth of April (1861), The.

Larcom (continued)
Our Christ.
Plant a Tree.
Red-Top and Timothy.
Rivulet, The.
Sinking of the *Merrmac[k].*
Sir Robin.
Strip of Blue, A.
Thanksgiving, A.
Tolling.
Trees, The.
Two Festivals.

Lardner, Ring
Fragment from "Clemo Uti—the Water Lilies."

Larkin, Philip
Absences.
Afternoons.
Age.
Arrivals, Departures.
Arundel Tomb, An.
As Bad as a Mile.
At Grass.
Born Yesterday.
Church Going.
Coming.
Deceptions.
Dry-Point.
Essential Beauty.
Faith Healing.
First Sight.
Going.
Heaviest of Flowers, the Head.
Here.
Home Is So Sad.
I Remember, I Remember.
If, My Darling.
Lines on a Young Lady's Photograph Album.
Maiden Name.
Mr. Bleaney.
Myxomatosis.
Next, Please.
MCMXIV.
No Road.
North Ship, The.
One Man Walking a Deserted Platform.
Places, Loved Ones.
Poetry of Departures.
Reasons for Attendance.
Spring.
Sunny Prestatyn.
Take One Home for the Kiddies.
Toads.
Toads Revisited.
Wants.
Water.
Wedding Wind.
Whatever Happened?
Whitsun Weddings, The.
Wild Oats.
Wires.

Larminie, William
Fand, *sel.*
Killarney.
Moytura, *sel.*
Nameless Doon [*or* Dun], The.
Nameless Ruin, The.
Sword of Tethra, The.

Larrabee, Harold A.
Itch to Etch, The.
Professors.
Very Model of a Modern College President, The, *parody.*

Larremore, Wilbur
Blossom Time.
Madam Hickory.

Larsen, Carl
Plot to Assassinate the Chase Manhattan Bank, The.

Larsson, Raymond Ellsworth
Antique Carved Figures.
Epistle for Spring.
No city shall I call my own.
O City, Cities! *sel.*
To Our Lady, the Ark of the Covenants.

Lart, K. C.
Walk in Spring, A.

Lasker-Schüler, Else
Always in the Parting Year.
I Have a Blue Piano.
I Know That I Must Die Soon.
Love-Song.
Love's Flight.
My Love-Song.
Rock Crumbles, The.
To Gottfried Benn.
To Senna Hoy.
Zebaoth.

Lasynys, Elis Wyn o
Death the Great.

Latchaw, Gladys
My Yoke Is Easy.

Lathbury, Mary Artemisia ("Aunt Mary")
Bread of Life, The.
Break Thou the Bread of Life.
Day Is Dying in the West.
Easter Song.
Room for Him! Room!
Song of Hope.
Summer Sunshine.

Lathrop, Adele
Because He Lives.

Lathrop, George Parsons
Charity.
Child's Wish Granted, The.
Flown Soul, The.
Keenan's Charge.
Marthy Virginia's Hand.
Name of Washington, The.
Remembrance.
South Wind.
Sunshine of Thine Eyes, The.
Voice of the Void, The.

Lathrop, Lena
Woman's Question, A.

Lathrop, Mary T.
Day Dawn of the Heart.

Lathrop, Ona Freeman
Mother's Reward, A.

Lathrop, Rose Hawthorne (Mrs. George Parsons Latrop; Mother Mary Alphonsa)
Clock's Song, The.
Despair.
Dorothy.
Give Me Not Tears.
Song before Grief, A.

Lathrop, Walter
Here Is a Toast That I Want to Drink.

Latimer, Bette Darcie
For William Edward Burghardt DuBois on His Eightieth Birthday.

Latimore, Jewel C. (Johari Amini)
Masque.
Utopia.

La Trobe, John Antes
Peace of Christ, The.

Lattimore, Richmond
American Nights.
Anniversary.
Bathtubs.
Collages and Compostions.
Despair in Seascape.
Father, The.
Game Resumed.
It.
Krankenhaus of Leutkirch, The.
Max Schmitt in a Single Scull.
North Philadelphia, Trenton, and New York.
Rise and Shine.
Shadowgraphs, The.
Ship Bottom.
Siding Near Chillicothe, A.
Spider.
Verse.
Voyage of Discovery: 1935.

Laube, Clifford James
At the Battery Sea-Wall.
Ave, Vita Nostra!
Bees of Christ, The.
Dream across the Dark.
Last Rally.
To Fear.
To Lizard Head.

Lauber, Jane W.
Suffering.

Lauden, Loma Ried
Consecration.

Laufer, Calvin W.
O Master of the Loving Heart.

Laughlin Elmer Osborn
Unknown, The.

Laughlin, James
Busy Day.
Letter to Hitler, A.
Summons, The.

Laughton, Freda
At the Party.
Bull, The.
Rain on a Cottage Roof.
To the Spring Sun.
Welcome, The.
When from the Calyx-Canopy of Night.
When to My Serene Body.
Woman with Child, The.

Lauren, Joseph
Butterfly and the Caterpillar, The.
Fox and the Grapes, The.

Laurence, Elsie
Alone.

Lavater, Louis
Barrier, The.
Faithless.
Mopoke.
Ocean.

Law, Margaret Lathrop
Hands.
Those Who Soar.

Law, T. S.
Wemen's Wather.

Lawless, Emily
After Aughrim.
Clare Coast.
Dirge of the Munster Forest.
Fontenoy, 1745.
In Spain.
In Spain; Drinking Song.
Stranger's Grave, The.

Lawless, Margaret Elward
Manhattan.

Lawner, Lynne
In Your Arrogance.
Possession.

Lawrence, A. H.
To Be a Nurse.

Lawrence David Herbert
After the Opera.
Autumn Rain.
Aware.
Baby Asleep after Pain, A.
Baby Running Barefoot.
Baby Tortoise.
Ballad of Another Ophelia.
Bare Almond-Trees.
Bat.
Bavarian Gentians.
Bei Hennef.
Bombardment.
Bride, The.
Brooding Grief.

Call into Death.
Cherry Robbers.
City Life.
Collier's Wife, The.
Coming Awake.
Discord in Childhood.
Doe at Evening, A.
Don'ts.
Dreams Old and Nascent.
Elephant Is Slow to Mate, The.
End of Another Home Holiday.
Evil Is Homeless.
Fate and the Younger Generation.
Fidelity.
Fireflies in the Corn.
Flapper.
Giorno dei Morti.
Gloire de Dijon.
Glory.
God and the Holy Ghost.
Gods, The! The Gods!
Green.
Grief.
Hands of God, The.
History.
How Beastly the Bourgeois Is.
Humming-Bird.
Hymn to Priapus.
In a Boat.
In the Cities.
In Trouble and Shame.
It's No Good!
Kangaroo.
Kisses in the Train.
Last Words to Miriam.
Let Us Be Men.
Letter from Town; the Almond Tree.
Lightning.
Love on the Farm.
Lucifer.
Moonrise.
Morning Work.
Mosquito, The.
Mosquito Knows, The.
Mountain Lion.
My Way Is Not Thy Way.
New Heaven and Earth.
New Moon.
New Year's Eve.
Nonentity.
North Country, The.
Nostalgia.
On the Balcony.
Optimist, The.
Passing Visit to Helen.
Pax.
People.
Piano.
Quite Forsaken.
Rainbow.
Reading a Letter.
Red Geranium and Godly Mignonette.
Release.
Resurrection.
River Roses.
Roses on the Breakfast Table.
Sea, The.
Sea-Weed.
Service of All the Dead.
Shadows.
Ship of Death, The.
Sicilian Cyclamens.
Sinners.
Snake.
Snap-Dragon.
Snowy Day in School, A.
Song of a Man Who Has Come Through.
Sorrow.
Spray.
Spring Morning.
Street Lamps.
Suburbs on a Hazy Day.
Sunday Afternoon in Italy.
Suspense.
Swan.
Tell Me a Word.
Tommies in the Train.
Tortoise Family Connections.
Tortoise Gallantry.
Tortoise Shell.
Tortoise Shout.
Trees in the Garden.
Turkey-Cock.
Twilight.
Under the Oak.
Virgin Mother, The, *sel.*
Wedding Morn.
Whales Weep Not!
When I Read Shakespeare.
When I Went to the Circus.
When Satan Fell.
When the Ripe Fruit Falls.
Whether or Not.
White Blossom, A.
Wild Common, The.
Willy Wet-Leg.
Winter Dawn.
Winter's Tale, A.
Woman and Her Dead Husband, A.
Work.
World of Work, as a Poet Would Like It to Be, The.
Young Wife, A.
Youth Mowing, A.

Lawrence, J. B.
I Believe.

Lawrence, Ruth
Washington's Tomb.

Lawson, Henry
Andy's Gone with Cattle.
Ballad of the Drover.
Great Grey Plain, The.
Roaring Days, The.
Sliprails and the Spur, The.
Song of the Darling River.
Talbragar.
Teams, The.

Lawson, James Gilchrist
All Nature Has a Voice to Tell.
O Lord, I Come Pleading.
War.
World Hymn, The.

Lawson, Marie A.
Halloween.

Lawson, Sylvia
Trader's Return.

Lawson, Will
Bill the Whaler.

Lawton, William Cranston
My Fatherland.
Song, Youth, and Sorrow.

Lax, Robert
Kalymniad, *sel.*
Novel.

Laxness, Halldór
She Was All That You Loved.

Lay, Norma
Sea Sonnet.

Layamon Arthur's Dream
Arthur's Last Fight.
Battle of Bath, The.
Birth of Arthur, The.
Brut, The, *sels.*
Building of London, The.
Prolog, The: "There was a priest in the land."
Prophecy of Diana, The.
Round Table, The.

Laycock, Samuel
Welcome Bonny Brid!

Layton, Irving
Bacchanal.
Berry Picking.
Birth of Tragedy, The.
Boys in October.
Bull Calf, The.
Cain.
Cold Green Element, The.
Composition in Late Spring.
Day Aviva Came to Paris, The.
Dionysus.
El Gusano.
Fertile Muck, The.
For Louise, Age 17.
Golfers.
Gothic Landscape.
Hostia.
Jewish Main Street.
Keine Lazarovitch.
Misunderstanding.
Nausicäa.
Newsboy.
Overheard in a Barbershop.
Song for Naomi.
Spider Danced a Cosy Jig, A.
Swimmer, The.
Tall Man Executes a Jig, A.
To the Girls of My Graduating Class.
Undine.
What Ulysses Said to Circe on the Beach of Aeaea.
Woman.
Words without Music.

Layzer, Robert
Elegy: "Whenever we touched, I thought of the Lying-in Hospital."
Insult, The.
Lawn Roller, The.
Saint's Parade.
Sleeping Beauty, The.

Lazard, Naomi
Walking with Lulu in the Wood.

Lazarus, Brian
Martian Maid, The.

Lazarus, Emma
Banner of the Jew, The.
Bar Kochba.
Cranes of Ibycus, The.
Crowing of the Red Cock, The.
Gifts.
Inscription for the Statue of Liberty.
Inscription on the Statue of Liberty.
Lines on Carmen Sylva.
Mater Amabilis.
New Colossus, The.
New Ezekiel, The.
On the Proposal to Erect a Monument in England to Lord Byron.
Venus of the Louvre.
World's Justice, The.

Lea, Fanny Heaslip
Dead Faith, The.

Lea, John
Silver House, The.

Leahy, Jack
How We Built a Church at Ashcroft.

Leal, Maybell Whiting
Holy Matrimony.

Leamy, Edmund
Gethsemane.
Ireland.
Lullaby: "Oh, honey, li'l honey, come and lay yo' wooly head."
Music Magic.
My Lips Would Sing.
My Ship.
Three Tarry Men.
Ticket Agent, The.
Visions.

Leapor, Mary
Hymn to the Morning, An.
New Ballad, A.
Proserpine's Ragout.

Leapor (continued)
Sylvia and the Bee.
Lear, Edward
A. Apple Pie.

Akond of Swat, The.
At Dingle Bank.
Author of the "Pobble," The.
By Way of Preface.
Calico Pie.
Cold Are the Crabs.
Courtship of the Yonghy-Bonghy-Bo, The.
Cummerbund, The.
Dong with a Luminous Nose, The.
Duck and the Kangaroo, The.
Floating Old Man, The.
How Pleasant to Know Mr. Lear.
Incidents in the Life of My Uncle Arly.
Jumblies, The.
Limerick: "There is a young lady whose nose/ Continually prospers and grows."
Limerick: "There was a young girl of Majorca."
Limerick: "There was a young lady in white."
Limerick: "There was a young lady of Bute."
Limerick: "There was a young lady of Corsica."
Limerick: "There was a young lady of Firle."
Limerick: "There was a young lady of Hull."
Limerick: "There was a young lady of Norway."
Limerick: "There was a young lady of Portugal!"
Limerick: "There was a young lady of Russia."
Limerick: "There was a young lady of Ryde/ Whose shoe-strings were seldom untied."
Limerick: "There was a young lady whose bonnet."
Limerick: "There was a young lady whose chin."
Limerick: "There was a young lady whose eyes."
Limerick: "There was a young lady whose nose/ Was so long. .."
Limerick: "There was a young person of Crete."
Limerick: "There was a young person of Smyrna."
Limerick: "There was an old lady of Chertsey."
Limerick: "There was an old lady whose folly."
Limerick: "There was an old man in a barge."
Limerick: "There was an old man in a boat."
Limerick: "There was an old man in a pew."
Limerick: "There was an old man in a tree."
Limerick: "There was an old man of Berlin."
Limerick: "There was an old man of Cape Horn."
Limerick: "There was an old man of Corfu."
Limerick: "There was an old man of Dumbree."
Limerick: "There was an old man of Hong Kong."
Limerick: "There was an old man of Ibreem."
Limerick: "There was an old man of Kamschatka."
Limerick: "There was an old man of Leghorn."
Limerick: "There was an old man of Melrose."
Limerick: "There was an old man of the coast."
Limerick: "There was an old man of the Dargle."
Limerick: "There was an old man of the Dee."
Limerick: "There was an old man of The Hague."
Limerick: "There was an old man of the Isles."
Limerick: "There was an old man of the West."
Limerick: "There was an old man of Thermopylae."
Limerick: "There was an old man of Vesuvius."
Limerick: "There was an old man of Whitehaven."
Limerick: "There was an old man on the Border."
Limerick: "There was an old man on whose nose."
Limerick: "There was an old man who said: 'How.'"
Limerick: "There was an old man who said, 'Hush!'"
Limerick: "There was an old man who said, 'Well!'"
Limerick: "There was an old man who supposed."
Limerick: "There was an old man, who when little."
Limerick: "There was an old man with a beard,/ Who said, 'It is just as I feared!'"
Limerick: "There was an old man with a beard,/ Who sat on a horse when he reared."
Limerick: "There was an old man with a gong."
Limerick: "There was an old man with a poker."
Limerick: "There was an old person of Anerly."
Limerick: "There was an old person of Bromley."
Limerick: "There was an old person of Burton."
Limerick: "There was an old person of Dean."
Limerick: "There was an old person of Diss."
Limerick: "There was an old person of Gretna."
Limerick: "There was an old person of Hurst."
Limerick: "There was an old person of Ickley."
Limerick: "There was an old person of Minety."
Limerick: "There was an old person of Shoreham."
Limerick: "There was an old person of Sparta."
Limerick: "There was an old person of Stroud."
Limerick: "There was an old person of Ware."
Limerick: "There was an old person of Wick."
Limerick: "There was an old person of Woking."
Limerick: "There was an old person whose habits."
Lines to a Young Lady.
M.
Mr. and Mrs. Discobbolos.
Mr. and Mrs. Spikky Sparrow.
Mr. Lear.
Moppsikon Floppsikon Bear, The.
New Vestments, The.
Nonsense Alphabet ("A was an ape").
Nonsense Alphabet, A ("A was once an apple-pie").
Nonsense Limericks.
Nonsense Pictures in Rhyme.
Nonsense Verses.
Nutcrackers and the Sugar-Tongs, The.
Old Man with a Beard.
Owl and the Pussy-Cat, The.
Pobble Who Has No Toes, The.
Quangle Wangle's Hat, The.
Says I to Myself.
Self Portrait.
Self-Portrait of the Laureate of Nonsense.
Sonnet, A: "Cold are the crabs that crawl on yonder hills."
Table and the Chair, The.
Teapots and Quails.
There was a Young Lady of Sweden.
There Was an Old Man in a Tree.
There was an old man of Dumbree.
There was an old man of the Dargle.
There Was an Old Man, on Whose Nose.
There Was an Old Person of Bradley.
There was an old person of Skye.
Two Old Bachelors, The.
Yonghy-Bonghy-Bo, The.
Young Lady of Norway, A.
Lear, Oscar H.
Wide Open Spaces, The.
Learned, Walter
Explanation, An.
Growing Old.
In Explanation.
Last Reservation, The.
On the Fly-Leaf of a Book of Old Plays.
On the Fly-Leaf of Manon Lescaut.
Prime of Life, The.
Time's Revenge.
To Critics.
"Learsi, Rufus" (Israel Goldberg)
Martyrdom.
Leary, Paris
Elegy for Helen Trent.
First Reader.
Love Lifted Me.
Manifesto.
Onan.
September 1, 1965.
Summa contra Gentiles.
Views of the Oxford Colleges.
"What Five Books Would You Pick to Be Marooned with on a Desert Island?"
Leatham, E. Rutter
Thank you for the world so sweet.
Leavens, Emily
Death on the Rancherie.
Leavenworth, Coman
Norfolk Memorials.
North Pickenham.
Rackheath.
Wendling.
LeBar, Winifred Stoddard
And Thou Would'st Not!
Lebedev-Kumach, Vasili
Comrade, Do Not Forget!
Lebensohn, Micah Joseph
Wine.
Leca, Mateo Vázquez de
Foolish Leander.
Lechlitner, Ruth
Kansas Boy.
Second Blossoming.
Winter's Tale, A.
Lecky, William Edward Hartpole
Early Thoughts.
Of an Old Song.

On an Old Song.
Say Not That the Past Is Dead.
Unconscious Cerebration.
LeClaire, Gordon
Chameleon.
Love.
Miser.
Old Seawoman.
Le Clercq, J. G. Clemenceau *See* **"Tanaquil, Paul"**
Le Compte, Calvin
Visitation, The.
Leconte de Lisle, Charles Marie René
Hialmar Speaks to the Raven.
LeCron, Helen Cowles
Little Charlie Chipmunk.
Little Danny Donkey.
Sally Centipede.
Willie Wolf.
Lederer, Marjorie
Fifth Birthday Gift.
Ledoux, Louis V.
At Sunset.
Fulfilment.
Music of a Friend, The.
Slumber Song: "Drowsily come the sheep."
Ledward, Patricia
Evening in Camp.
Ledwidge, Francis
Ardan Mór.
August.
Behind the Closed Eye.
Death of Ailill, The.
Dream of Artemis, A, *sel.*
Evening in England, An.
Fairy Music.
Find, The.
God, whose kindly hand doth sow.
Had I a Golden Pound.
Herons, The.
Homecoming of the Sheep, The.
In September.
June.
Lament for the Poets: 1916.
Lament for Thomas MacDonagh.
Little Boy in the Morning, A.
Mother's Song, A.
My Mother.
Shadow People, The.
Ships of Arcady, The.
Soliloquy.
Thomas MacDonagh.
To a Linnet in a Cage.
To a Sparrow.
Twilight in Middle March, A.
Wife of Llew, The.
Lee, Agnes
Convention.
Enemies.
Ilex Tree, The.
Lonely Man, A.
Mrs. Malooly.
Motherhood.
Numbers.
Old Lizette on Sleep.
Old Woman with Flowers, An.
Radium.
Shakespeare.
Statue in a Garden, A.
Sweeper, The.
Tower, The.
Lee, Al
Far Side of Introspection, The.
"Lee, Andy" (W.W. Delaney)
Crazy Song to the Air of "Dixie."
Lee, Bert
Photograph: Mother and Father: 1930.
Lee, Don L.
Assassination.
Awareness.
Back Again, Home.
But He Was Cool.
Cure All, The.
Education.
In the Interest of Black Salvation.
New Integrationist, The.
Poem Looking for a Reader, A.
Re-Act for Action ("Re-act to Animals").
Taxes.
Lee, Edith M.
Fault Is Mine, The.
Lee, Harry
Madness.
My Master.
My Master Was So Very Poor.
Valentine for My Mother.
Winged Heels.
Lee, Joseph Johnston
German Prisoners.
Lee, Laurie
Apples.
April Rise.
Autumn Apples.
Bombay Arrival.
Boy in Ice.
Christmas Landscape.
Cock-Pheasant.
Day of These Days.
Deliverance.
Edge of Day, The.
Field of Autumn.
First Love.
Home from Abroad.
Juniper.
Larch Tree.
Long Summer.
Long War, The.
Milkmaid.
Music in a Spanish Town (Cordoba 1936).
My Many-Coated Man.
Poem for Easter.
Scot in the Desert.
Seafront.
Stork in Jerez.
Summer Rain.
Sunken Evening [in Trafalgar Square].
Three Winds, The.
Town Owl.
Twelfth Night.
Village of Winter Carols.
Wild Trees, The.
Lee, Lawrence
Subway Builders.
Lee, Mary *See* **Chudleigh, Lady**
Lee, Milton
When I Go Home.
Lee, Muna
After Reading Saint Teresa, Luis de Leon and Ramon Lull.
As Helen Once.
Dirge: "Though you should whisper."
I have a thousand pictures of the sea.
Melilot.
Song of Happiness, A.
Sonnets, *sels.*
Woman's Song, A.
Lee, Nathaniel
Blush Not Redder than the Morning.
Caesar Borgia, *sel.*
Song: "Now, now the fight's done, and the great god of war."
Theodosius; or, The Force of Love, *sel.*
Lee, Walter M.
Father, Teach Me.
Leech, Michael T.
Conceit with Aunties, Urn and Puss.
Lee-Hamilton, Eugene
Charles II of Spain to Approaching Death.
Death of Puck, The.
Elfin Skates.
Fairy Godmothers.
Flight from Glory, A.
Henry I to the Sea.
Idle Charon.
Ipsissimus.
Izaak Walton to River and Brook.
Lost Years.
Luca Signorelli to His Son.
Luther to a Bluebottle Fly (1540).
Mimma Bella, *sels.*
My Own Hereafter.
On His "Sonnets of the Wingless Hours."
Sea-Shell Murmurs.
Sir Walter Raleigh to a Caged Linnet.
Song: "Under the winter, dear."
Stradivarius to an Unfinished Violin (1710).
Sunken Gold.
To My Tortoise 'Ανάγκη (Ananke).
To My Tortoise Chronos.
To the Muse.
What the Sonnet Is.
Wood-Song.
Lees, Edwin
Signs of Christmas.
Leeson, Jane Eliza
Hymn, A: "Loving Shepherd of thy sheep."
Saviour Teach Me [Day by Day].
Le Fanu, Joseph Sheridan
Beatrice, *sel.*
Drunkard to His Bottle, A.
Hymn: "Hush! oh ye billows."
Legend of the Glaive, The, *sel.*
Song of the Spirits, The.
Lefevre, H. T.
This I Can Do.
Le Fort, Gertrude von
Christmas.
Vigil of the Assumption.
Lefroy, Edward Cracroft
Ageanax.
Cleonicos.
Cricket Bowler, A.
Echoes from Theocritus, *sels.*
Epitaph of Eusthenes, The.
Flute of Daphnis, The.
Football Player, A.
Grave of Hipponax, The.
Monument of Cleita, The.
On a Spring Board.
Sacred Grove, A.
Shepherd Maiden, A.
Sicilian Night, A.
Summer Day in Old Sicily, A.
Sylvan Revel, A.
Thyrsis.
Leftwich, Joseph
Tailor, The.
Le Gallienne, Richard
After the War.
All Sung.
Ballad of London, A.
Ballade Catalogue of Lovely Things, A.
Ballade of the Unchanging Beauty.
Beatus Vir.
Brooklyn Bridge at Dawn.
Called Away.
Caravan from China Comes, A.
Dream Tryst.
Eternal Way, The.
Frost Fancy, A.
I Meant to Do My Work Today.
Lady April.
London Beautiful.
Love's Poor.
May Is Building Her House.
Melton Mowbray Pork Pie, A.
Old Man's Song, An.
Orbits.
Passionate Reader to His Poet, The.

Le (continued)
Prayer, A: "Out of the deeps I cry to thee, O God!"
Regret.
Second Crucifixion, The.
She's somewhere in the sunlight strong.
Song: "She's somewhere in the sunlight strong."
Song: "Take it love!"
Song of Bread and Honey, A.
Songs for Fragoletta.
Spirit of Sadness.
This Is War.
War.
What of the Darkness?
Wife from Fairyland, The.
Wind's Way, The.
Wonder-Child, The.
Wood Flower.

Legaré, James Matthew
Ahab Mohammed.
Amy.
To a Lily.

LeGear, Laura Lourene
Unbridled Now.

Léger, Alexis Saint-Léger *See* **"Perse, St.-J"**

Legg, Bernice Hall
Forest Meditation, A.

Legler, Philip
They Make a Lovely Pretense.

Lehman, Louis Paul, Jr
Dusk for Me.
He Takes My Hand.
When I Think of His Love.

Lehmann, Geoffrey
Last Campaign, The.
Lines Based on a 1924 Advertisement.

Lehmann, John
Ballad of Banners (1944), The.
Death in Hospital, A.
In a London Terminus.
Last Ascent, The.
Sphere of Glass, The.

Lehmann, Rudolph Chambers
Bird in the Room, The.
Dance, The.
Middle Age.
Plea for a Plural, A.
Singing Water.

Lehmer, Eunice Mitchell
Armistice.

Leib, Mani (Mani Leib Brahinsky)
Door and Window Bolted Fast.
Hush, Hush.
When I See Another's Pain.

Leichliter, Jo Ann
At Thanksgiving.

Leigh, Amy E.
If I But Knew.

Leigh, Frederick, *and* **Frederick Murray** *See* **Murray, Frederick,** *and* **Frederick Leigh**

Leigh, Henry Sambrooke
Answer, An.
Cossimbazar.
Maud.
My Love and My Heart.
Not Quite Fair.
Nursery Legend, A.
Only Seven.
Romaunt of Humpty Dumpty, The.
'Twas Ever Thus.
Twins, The.

Leigh, Richard
Eccho, The.
Her Window.
Sleeping on Her Couch.
Thus Lovely Sleep.

Leighton, Louise
Earthly Illusion.

Leighton, Robert
Dried-up Fountain, The.
Duty Our Ladder.

Leipoldt, C. Louis
Banded Cobra, The.
On My Old Ramkiekie.

Leiser, Joseph
Day of Atonement, The, *sel.*
Kol Nidra.

Leisner, Dorothy Roberts *See* **Roberts, Dorothy**

Leitch, Mary Sinton
Before.
Failure.
From Bethlehem Blown.
He Who Loves the Ocean.
Poet, The.
River, The.
Sea Words.
When Spring Came to Nazareth.

Leitner, Della Adams
Forbearance.
Tomorrow.

Leitner, S. N.
That's Faith.

Leivick, Halper
Night, Stars, Glow-Worms.

Leland, Charles Godfrey ("Hans Breitmann")
Ballad: "Noble Ritter Hugo, Der."
Ballad by Hans Breitmann.
Ballad of Charity, The.
Ballad of the Mermaid.
El Capitan-General.
Flying Dutchman, The.
Hans Breitmann's Party [*or* Barty].
Legend of Heinz von Stein, The.
Out and Fight.
Story of Samuel Jackson, The.
Two Friends, The.

Lemaître, Jules
Cat, A.

Lemke, E.
Rhyme for Musicians, A.

Lemon, Mark
How to Make a Man of Consequence.

LeNart, Marie
Atonement.
Give Us Great Dreams.
Litany: "Oh, by Thy cross and passion."

Lengyel, Cornel
Fool Song.

Lennen, Elinor
Evaluation.
Fellowship.
His Last Week.
Nor House nor Heart.
On Entering a Forest.
Pilgrimage.
Praetorium Scene: Good Friday.
Prayer for a Play House.

Lennon, Florence Becker
Little White Schoolhouse Blues.

"Lennox."
Neighbors.

Lenski, Lois
Fourth of July Song.
Oh! to Have a Birthday.
Old Santa Is an Active Man.
People.

Lent, Emma A.
Memorial Day.
Unawares.

Lentino, Jacopo da *See* **Jacopo da Lentino**

Leo XIII, Pope
Return from Egypt, The.
War Cry: To Mary.

Léon, Luis Ponce de (Fray Luis de Léon)
At the Ascension.
At the Assumption.
Avarice.
Life of the Blessed, The.
Life Removed, The.
Lines on the Wall of His Prison Cell.
Love Song.
Night Scene, The.
To Reitrement.
Valley of the Heavens, The.
Written on the Walls of His Dungeon.

Leonard, Eddie
Ida, Sweet as Apple Cider.

Leonard, Priscilla
Happiness.
Lost Key, The.
Making of Man, The.
This Is the Making of Man.
Tide Will Win, The.
What Man May Choose.

Leonard, William Ellery
Image of Delight, The.
Indian Summer.
Lo, had begun again for her the time.
Lynching Bee, The.
Quaker Meeting-House.
That once the gentle mind of my dead wife.
To the Victor.
Two Lives, *sels.*
Under the trees I sat, under the blue.

Leonidas of Alexandria
Menodotis ("Menodotis's portrait here is kept").

Leonidas of Tarentum
Apelles the Painter.
Cleitagoras.
Epitaph of a Sailor.
Fisherman, The.
Last Journey, The.
Philocles.
Spinning Woman, The.
Spring Sailing.
Tomb of Crethon, The.

Leontius
Plato, a Musician.

Leopardi, Giacomo
A sè stesso.
Broom, The.
Evening of the Feast-Day, The.
Infinite, The.
Infinito, L'.
To Italy.
Walls and Arches, The.

Le Pan, Douglas
Canoe-Trip.
Country without a Mythology, A.
Coureurs de Boise.
Finale.
Incident, An.
Lion, Leopard, Lady.
New Vintage, The.
Nimbus.
One of the Regiment.

Lermontov, Mikhail Yurevich
Composed While under Arrest.
Dagger.
Demon [*or* Daemon], The, *sel.*
Gratitude.
Land of Masters.
Mountain, The.
My Country.
On the Death of Pushkin.
On the sightless seas of ether.
On the vast aerial ocean.
Reed, The.
Sail, A.
Thought, A.
Triple Dream, The.

Lerner, Alan Jay
With a Little Bit of Luck.

Lerner, Laurence David
All Day and All October.

Desert Travellers, The.
Fourteen July 1956.
In a Shoreham Garden.
Meditation upon the Toothache, A.
Poet at Fifty, The.
St. Enda.
Senchi Ferry; Gold Coast.
Way to the Sea, The.
What's Hard.
Years Later.
Lesemann, Maurice
City Asleep.
Lost.
Man Walks in the Wind, A.
Noctiflora.
Ranchers.
Sheep Herders.
Leslie, Cy
On Riots.
Leslie, Kenneth
By Stubborn Stars, *sels.*
Easter Song.
Escapade.
From Soil Somehow the Poet's Word.
Halibut Cove Harvest.
My Love Is Sleeping.
Silver Herring Throbbed Thick in My Seine, The.
Sonnet: "Silver herring throbbed thick in my seine, The."
Sonnet: "Warm rain whispers, but the earth knows best, A."
Leslie, Shane
Fleet Street.
Four Winds, The.
Ireland, Mother of Priests.
Monaghan.
Muckish Mountain (The Pig's Back.)
Priest or Poet.
Two Mothers, The.
Lesoro, E. A. S.
Muscovy Drake, The.
Lesser, Eugene
Poem for Ed's Birthday.
Poem for Everybody, A.
Sometimes Life Is Not a Literary Experience.
Turko-Persian Bazaar-Boutique.
Lessing, Gotthold Ephraim
By What Sweet Name.
I Asked My Fair, One Happy Day.
Mendax.
On Fell.
To a Slow Walker and Quick Eater.
Lester, Julius
Poems.
Us.
L'Estrange, Sir Roger
Loyalty Confin'd.
Mr. Le Strange His Verses in the Prison at Linn.
Letts, Winifred M. (Mrs. W. H. Foster Verschoyle
Boys.
Children's Ghosts, The.
Connaught Rangers, The.
Elfin People Fill the Tubes, The.
Hallows' E'en.
Harbor, The.
In Service.
Kerry Cow, The.
My Blessing Be on Waterford.
Pensioners.
Quantity and Quality.
Shops.
Soft Day, A.
Somehow, Somewhere, Sometime.
Spires of Oxford, The.
Spring, the Travelling Man.
Synge's Grave.
Tim, an Irish Terrier.
To Scott.
Winds at Bethlehem, The.
Wishes for William.
Lettsom, John Coakley
On a Doctor Named Isaac Letsome.
Self-composed Epitaph on a Doctor by the Name of I. Letsome.
Leuty, Helen
Night, The.
Poplars.
Levenson, Christopher
Prophecy, A.
Lever, Charles James
Bad Luck to This Marching.
Charles O'Malley, the Irish Dragoon, *sels.*
Harry Lorrequer, *sel.*
It's Little for Glory I Care.
Larry M'Hale.
Man for Galway, The.
Mickey Free's Song.
Pope, The.
Pope He Leads a Happy Life, The.
Widow Malone, The.
Leveridge, Lilian
Cry from the Canadian Hills, A.
First Robin, The.
Leveridge, Richard
Song in Praise of Old English Roast Beef, A.
Levertov [*or* Levertoff], Denise
Absence, The.
Anteroom, The.
Autumn Journey.
Barricades, The.
Bedtime.
Beyond the End.
Breathing, The.
Charge, The.
Christmas 1944.
Come into Animal Presence.
Common Ground, A, *sel.*
Crystal Night.
Day Begins, A.
Depths, The.
Dog of Art, The.
During the Eichmann Trial, *sel.*
"Else a Great Prince in Prison Lies."
Face to Face.
Five-Day Rain, The.
Five Poems from Mexico.
Folding a Shirt.
From the Roof.
Goddess, The.
Gypsy's Window, The.
Hands, The.
Illustrious Ancestors.
In Memory of Boris Pasternak.
Jacob's Ladder, The.
Laying the Dust.
Living.
Losing Track.
Love Song.
Man, A.
Map of the Western Part of the Country of Essex in England, A.
Matins.
Merritt Parkway.
Mutes, The.
Not "common speech."
Novel, The.
Novices, The.
Obsessions.
October.
Offender, The.
Old Adam, The.
Our Bodies.
Partial Resemblance.
Pleasures.
Poem: "Some are too much at home in the role of wanderer."
Presence, The.
Psalm Concerning the Castle.
Pulse, The.
Pure Products.
Quarry Pool, The.
Rainwalkers, The.
Resolve, The.
Resting Figure.
Scenes from the Life of the Peppertrees.
Secret, The.
Seems like We Must Be Somewhere Else.
Sharks, The.
Six Variations.
Solitude, A.
Song for Ishtar.
Springtime, The.
Third Dimension, The.
Third Generation, The.
Thirst Song.
To the Reader.
To the Snake.
Triple Feature.
Two Variations.
Unknown, The.
Victors, The.
Vigil, The.
Way Through, The.
Well, The.
What Were They Like?
Wife, The.
Willows of Massachusetts, The.
Wings, The.
With Eyes at the Back of Our Heads.
Levi, Adele
Death of Friends, The.
Levi Ben Amittai
Kibbutz Sabbath.
Levi, David
Bible, The, *sel.*
Thou, Zion, old and suffering.
Levi, Peter
He Met Her at the Green Horse.
In a Corner of Eden.
L'Aurore Grelottante.
Second Year in a Seminary.
Ship-building Emperors Commanded.
To My Friends.
Levi Yitzhok [*or* Isaac] of Berditchev
Invocation: "Good morning to you, Lord of the world!"
Kaddish.
Levien, Michael
In the Falling Deer's Mouth.
Levine, Norman
Cathedral by Sea.
Crabbing.
Wind Harbour, The.
Levine, Philip
Animals Are Passing from Our Lives.
Baby Villon.
Blasting from Heaven.
Businessman of Alicante, The.
Cemetery at Academy, California, The.
Children's Crusade, The.
Commanding Elephants.
Cutting Edge, The.
Drunkard, The.
For Fran.
Gangrene.
Heaven.
Horse, The.
Lights I Have Seen Before.
Mad Day in March.
Midget, The.
Negatives, The.
Night Thoughts over a Sick Child.
On the Edge.
Passing Out.
Second Angel, The.
Sierra Kid.
Silent in America.
Small Game.

Levine (continued)
Sunday Afternoon.
Waking an Angel.
Winter Rains: Cataluñ.
Levy, Amy
Between the Showers.
Birch-Tree at Loschwitz, The.
Epitaph: "This is the end of him, here he lies."
In the Mile End Road.
June.
London Plane-Tree, A.
London Poets.
New Love, New Life.
Plane-Tree, The.
To Vernon Lee.
Levy, D. A.
Bells of the Cherokee Ponies, The.
Levy, Louis
Swallow's Flight, The.
Levy, Newman
Ballad of Sir Brian and the Three Wishes, The.
Belle of the Balkans, The.
Carmen.
Hottentot Tot, The.
I wonder What Became of Rand, McNally.
If You Stick a Stock of Liquor.
Midsummer Fantasy.
Midsummer Jingle.
Rain.
Reporters, The.
Revolving Door, The.
Scandalous Tale of Percival and Genevieve, The.
Thais.
Tristan and Isolda.
Levy, Newman, *and* **Nate Salsbury** *See* **Salsbury, Nate,** *and* **Newman Levy**
Lewin, Ralph A.
Les Chasse-Neige.
Lewis, Alonzo
Death Song.
Lewis, Alun
All Day It Has Rained.
Bivouac.
Christmas Holiday.
Dawn on the East Coast.
Defeated, The.
In Hospital: Poona (I).
In Hospital: Poona (II).
Jason and Medea.
Jungle, The.
Mountain over Aberdare, The.
Must/ All this aching.
Peasants, The.
Postscript for Gweno.
Sacco Writes to His Son.
Sentry, The.
Song: "First month[s] of his absence, The."
Song (on Seeing Dead Bodies Floating off the Cape).
To a Comrade in Arms.
To Edward Thomas.
Troopship in the Tropics.
Unknown Soldier, The.
Water Music.
Lewis, Cecil Day *See* **Day Lewis, Cecil**
Lewis, Clifford
"Lean Hard on Me."
Lewis Clive Staples
Aridity.
Awake, My Lute!
Day with a White Mark, The.
Ecstasy, The.
Expostulation, An.
"Man Is a Lumpe Where All Beasts Kneaded Be."
No Beauty We Could Desire.
Passing today by a cottage, I shed tears.
Poem for Psychoanalysts and/ or Theologians.
Posturing.
Prelude to Space.
Small Man Orders His Wedding, The.
Lewis, David
When None Shall Rail.
Lewis, Dominic Bevan Wyndham ("Timothy Shy")
Ballade of the Harrowing of Hell.
Envoi: "I warmed both hands before the fire of Life."
Having a Wonderful Time.
I would set all things whatsoever front to back.
Jig for Sackbuts.
Lost Chord, The.
Shot at Random, A.
Lewis, Eiluned
Reflections on the Fall of France, June, 1940.
We Who Were Born.
Lewis, Gardner E.
How to Tell Juan Don from Another.
Poem, neither Hilláryous Norgay.
Lewis, H. H.
Farmhand's Refrain.
Lewis, Janet (Mrs. Yvor Winters)
Candle Flame, The.
For Elizabeth Madox Roberts.
Girl Help.
Helen Grown Old.
In the Egyptian Museum.
Lines with a Gift of Herbs.
Love Poem: "Instinctively, unwittingly."
Lewis, Judd Mortimer
Forget It.
Lewis, Mary J.
New Year Wish, A.
Lewis, Matthew Gregory
Allan Water.
Wife, A.
"Lewis, Michael" (Louis Untermeyer)
April Winds.
August.
Broken Monologue.
Chart, The.
Cherry Blossoms, *sels.*
Cursing and Blessing.
Dead Liar Speaks, A.
Finis?
Food for Thought.
Here Lies . . .
In Spring.
January.
Leaving.
Living and Dying.
Longing.
Moon-Children.
Remembering.
Skiing Song.
Spring Ring-Jingle.
Lewis, Michael Arthur
Caulker, The.
Lewis, Muriel
Pastoral: "Farmer turns for home, The; his team's glad tread."
Lewis, Percy Wyndham
One-Way Song, *sels.*
Lewis, Robert
If You Had a Friend.
Lewis, Sarah Carter
Anticipation.
Lewis, Saunders
Café Scene.
Lewis, Sinclair
Cat.
Lewisohn, John
Rabbit, The.
Lewisohn, Ludwig
Heinrich Heine.
Together.
Leybourne, George
Flying Trapeze, The.
Man on the Flying Trapeze, The.
Leyden, John
Lords of the Wilderness.
L'Heureux, John
Bat in the Monastery, A.
Celebration.
Concert, The: Oratorio for a Season of Wrath.
Discovering God Is Waking One Morning.
Encounter.
Landscape.
Three Awful Picnics.
Libaire, George
Limerick: "Half baked potato, named Sue, A."
Limerick: "These places abound in the old."
Libero, Libero de
Cicada.
Lichfield, Leon
Printer, to Her Majesty, The.
Li Chi
Chinese Ballad.
Liddell, Catherine C.
Jesus the Carpenter.
Poet in the City, The.
Liddell, George T.
Christ of Common Folks, The.
Jesus of Nazareth Passes By.
Lieber, Francis
Ship Canal from the Atlantic to the Pacific, The.
Lieberman, Elias
Aladdin Throws Away His Lamp.
Brothers.
Caravels of Columbus, The.
Classroom in October.
Heart Specialist.
I Am an American.
It Is Time to Build.
Night School.
Sholom Aleichem.
Lieberman, Laurence
Coral Reef, The.
Orange County Plague: Scenes.
Unblinding, The.
Liessin, Abraham
Spring Nocturne.
Lighthall, William Douw
Caughnawaga Beadwork Seller, The.
Confused Dawn, The.
Montreal.
Praeterita ex Instantibus.
Liguori, Alfonso Maria de' *See* **Alphonsus Liguori, Saint**
Li Ho
Ninth Moon.
Li-I
Following the Army to the North.
Li Kwang-t'ien
Over the Bridge.
Liliencron, Detlev Freiherr von
After the Hunt.
Autumn.
Death in the Corn.
Who Knows Where.
Lillard, R. W.
America's Answer.
Lillenas, Haldor
Sick.
Lillington, Kenneth
Ballade to My Psychoanalyst.
Lilly, Edith C.
You Can Be One!
Lily, John *See* **Lyly, John**

Lima, Frank
Glycerin.
Inventory—to 100th Street.
Memory of Boxer Benny (Kid) Paret, The.
Mom I'm All Screwed Up.
Mulata—to Skinny.
News.
Penicillin.
Poem: "Two/ Gorillas."
Primavera.
Pudgy.
Welder, The.
Woman, The.
Lima, Jorge de
Bird, The.
Papa John.
Paraclete.
Words Will Resurrect, The.
Lincoln, Abraham
Faith of Abraham Lincoln, The.
I Am Not Bound to Win.
Memory.
Lincoln, Joseph Crosby
Cod-Fisher, The.
November's Come.
Rainy Day, A.
Lincoln, Mary W.
Kings of France.
Lindberg, Gene
Home Winner, The.
Lindegren, Erik
Journey, IV.
Man without a Road, The, X.
Lindeman, Jack
Trying for Solitude.
Lindsay, Lady Anne (Lady Anne Lindsay Barnard)
Auld Robin Gray.
Day and Night.
Lindsay, Lady Caroline Blanche Elizabeth Fitzroy
Sonnet: "Yea, Love is strong as life; he casts out fear."
Lindsay [*or* Lyndsay], Sir David
After the Flood.
Ane Satyre [*or* Satire] of the Threi [*or* Three] Estaitis.
Ane Supplication in Contemptioum of Syde Taillis, *abr.*
Carman's Account of a Law-Suit, A.
Childhood of James V, The.
Complaint of the Common Weill of Scotland.
Complaynt of Schir David Lindesay, The, *sel.*
Compleynt of the Comoun Weill of Scotland.
Dreme, The, *sel.*
Have I nocht made ane honest shift.
Historie of Squyer William Meldrum, The, *sel.*
Monarche, The, *sel.*
Of the Realme of Scotland.
Satire of the Three Estates, The, *sel.*
So Young ane King.
Squire Meldrum at Carrickfergus.
Lindsay, Forbes
Ball and the Club, The.
Lindsay, Jack
Budding Spring.
Wrung Heart, The.
Lindsay, Maurice
Exiled Heart, The.
Hurlygush.
May Day Demonstrators.
Lindsay, Ruth Temple
Hunters, The.
Lindsay, Vachel
Above the Battle's Front.
Abraham Lincoln Walks at Midnight.
Aladdin and the Jinn.
Alexander Campbell, *sel.*
Apple-Barrel of Johnny Appleseed, The.
Babylon, Babylon, Babylon the Great.
Blacksmith's Serenade, The.
Booker Washington Trilogy, The, *sels.*
Broncho That Would Not Be Broken, The.
Bryan, Bryan, Bryan, Bryan.
Chinese Nightingale, The.
Comet of Going-to-the-Sun, The.
Congo, The.
Conscientious Deacon, The.
Curse for the Saxophone, A.
Dandelion, The.
Daniel.
Daniel Jazz, The.
Dirge for a Righteous Kitten, A.
Dove of New Snow, The.
Eagle That Is Forgotten, The.
Euclid.
Every Soul Is a Circus, *sel.*
Explanation of the Grasshopper, An.
Factory Windows Are Always Broken.
Flower-fed Buffaloes, The.
Flute of the Lonely, The.
Foreign Missions in Battle Array.
Franciscan Aspiration.
General William Booth Enters [into] Heaven.
Ghost of the Buffaloes, The.
Ghosts of the Buffaloes, The.
Golden Whales of California, The, *sel.*
Grasshopper, The.
Haughty Snail-King, The.
How Samson Bore Away the Gates of Gaza.
Humble Bumble Bee, The.
I am a tramp by the long trail's border.
I Want to Go Wandering.
I Went Down into the Desert to Meet Elijah.
In Memory of a Child.
In Praise of Johnny Appleseed.
In the Congo.
Incense.
Indian Summer Day on the Prairie, An.
Jazz of This Hotel, The.
John Brown.
Johnny Appleseed, *sel.*
Johnny Appleseed's Hymn to the Sun.
Kalamazoo.
Kallyope Yell, The.
Kansas.
Knight in Disguise, The.
Leaden-eyed, The.
Lincoln.
Lion, The.
Litany of the Heroes, *sels.*
Little Turtle, The.
Love and Law.
Moon's the North Wind's Cooky, The.
Mouse That Gnawed the Oak-Tree Down, The.
My Fathers Came from Kentucky.
Mysterious Cat, The.
Nancy Hanks, Mother of Abraham Lincoln.
Negro Sermon, A; Simon Legree.
Net to Snare the Moonlight, A.
Old Horse in the City, The.
On the Building of Springfield.
Oration, An, Entitled "Old, Old, Old, Old Andrew Jackson," *abr.*
Poems about the Moon.
Pontoon Bridge Miracle, The.
Potatoes' Dance, The.
Prologue to "Rhymes to Be Traded for Bread."
Rain.
Rhyme about an Electrical Advertising Sign, A.
St. Francis.
Santa-Fé Trail, The (A Humoresque).
Scissors-Grinder, The.
Sense of Humor, A.
Simon Legree—a Negro Sermon.
Sorceress, The.
Springfield of the Far Future, The.
Star of My Heart.
These Are the Young.
Three Hours.
Three Poems about Mark Twain, *sel.*
To a Golden-haired Girl in a Louisiana Town.
To Reformers in Despair.
Traveler, The.
Two Old Crows.
Unpardonable Sin, The.
Virginia.
Virginians Are Coming Again, The.
Voyage, The.
What Grandpa Mouse Said.
What Semiramis Said.
What the Moon Saw.
What the Rattlesnake Said.
When I Was a Tree.
When Lincoln Came to Springfield.
When the Mississippi Flowed in Indiana.
Where Is the Real Non-Resistant?
Why I Voted the Socialist Ticket.
Wild Cats.
Yes, I have walked in California.
Yet Gentle Will the Griffin Be.
Lindsey, Hazel M.
Teaching, I Am Taught.
Lindsey, Therese Kayser
Man Christ, The.
Lindsey, William
En Garde, Messieurs.
Hundred-Yard Dash, The.
Lin Ho Ching
Enjoyable Evening in the Village near the Lake, An.
Liningston, Myra Cohn
Mrs. Spider.
Link, Carolyn Wilson
Elements.
Link, Gordden
Artist and Ape.
Link, Lenore M.
Holding Hands.
Linn, Edith Willis
Be Still.
Linton, Virginia
Ramblers, The.
Linton, William James
Epicurean.
Eviction.
Faint Heart.
Heart and Will.
Love and Youth.
Love's Blindness.
Our Cause.
Patience.
Silenced Singer, The.
Spring and Autumn.
Threnody, A: In Memory of Albert Darasz, *sel.*
Too Late.
Weep Not! Sigh Not!
Li Pin
Homeward.
Lipkin, Jean
Father.
Pre Domina.
Li Po [*or* Li Tai Po *or in Japanese* Rihaku]
Answer to a Worldly One.
Bringing in the Wine.
Chang Liang.

Li (continued)
Clearing at Dawn.
Deserted Garden, The.
Drinking Alone in the Moonlight: "If Heaven did not love wine."
Drinking Alone in the Moonlight: "Pot of wine among flowers, A."
Exile's Letter.
Girls on the Yueh River.
In Spring.
In the Mountains on a Summer Day.
Lament of the Frontier Guard.
Long War, The.
Moon at the Fortified Pass, The.
My Far-off Home.
Nefarious War, The.
Night of Sorrow, The.
Nocturne: "Blue water. . . a clear moon."
On a Quiet Night.
River Merchant's Wife, The; a Letter.
Soldier's Wife, A.
Summer Day, A.
Summit Temple, The.
Taking Leave of a Friend.
Three with the Moon and His Shadow.
To Tan Ch'iu.
War.
Woman of Yueh, A.
Lippincott, Sara Jane Clark *See* **"Greenwood, Grace"**
Lippitt, Lucile
He Lives at Last.
Lippmann, Julie Mathilde
Love and Life.
Pines, The.
Stone Walls.
Lipsitz, Lou
Already Late.
City Summer.
Drunk, Two Afternoons.
Fantasy for Those Who Hate Their Work.
For Kayak Magazine.
For WGF Who Was Told He Didn't Publish Enough to Be Promoted to Associate Professor.
I Am Thinking of Chicago and of What Survives.
Pipes, The.
Skinny Poem.
Thaw in the City.
Way of Judging Politics, A.
Li Shang-yin
Cicada, A.
Lisle, Charles Marie Leconte de *See* **Leconte de Lisle, Charles Marie**
Lisle, Rouget de *See* **Rouget de Lisle, Claude Joseph**
Lisle, Samuel
When Orpheus Went Down.
Lissauer, Ernst
Chant of Hate against England, A.
Hymn of Hate against England, A.
Lister Richard Percival
At the Ship.
Beetle Bemused.
Bone China.
Gemlike Flame, The.
Human Races, The.
I Thought I Saw Stars.
Lament of an Idle Demon.
Musician, The.
On a Horse and a Goat.
On Becoming Man.
Tale of Jorkyns and Gertie, The; or, Vice Rewarded.
Time Passes.
Li Tai Po *See* **Li Po**
Litchfield, Grace Denio
Good-by.
My Letter.
My Other Me.
To a Hurt Child.
Litchfield, Jessie
In the Day's Work.
Litsey, Edwin Carlile
Dreams Ahead, The.
Little, Arthur J.
Christ Unconquered, *sel.*
Invocations: "Mother of God, mother of man reborn."
Little, Katharine Day
Hazlitt Sups.
Little, Lizzie M.
Life.
Little, Philip Francis
Three Poplars, The.
Littlefield, Hazel
Not for its Own Sake.
Littlefield, Milton S.
Come, O Lord, like Morning Sunlight.
O Son of Man, Thou Madest Known.
Littleton, Edward
On a Spider.
Littlewood, W. E.
Heart of God, The.
Littlewort, Dorothy
Prayer of a Teacher.
Litvinoff, Emanuel
All Ruin Is the Same.
Garrison Town.
If I Forget Thee.
Poem for the Atomic Age.
Rededication.
War Swaggers.
Liu Chi
Soldier to His Wife, A.
Soldier's Wife to Her Husband.
Liu Chia
Drinking Bout, A.
Liu Hsi-Chun
Song of Grief.
Liu Tsung-yuan
Ice in a Stream.
Livesay, Dorothy
Abracadabra.
Child Looks Out, The.
Colour of God's Face, The, *sels.*
Contact.
Epilogue to the Outrider.
Fantasia.
Improvisation on an Old Theme.
Inheritors, The.
Interval with Fire.
Lament: "What moved me, was the way your hand."
Land, The.
Leader, The.
Of Mourners.
On Looking into Henry Moore.
People, The.
Prelude for Spring.
Prophetess, The.
Signature.
This Arrow.
Winter.
Livesay, Florence Randal
Tim, the Fairy.
Violin Calls, The.
Livingston, Edna
Question, A.
Livingston, Ethel
Legend of the Waving Lady.
Postcard: Two Figures from an Oriental Print.
Slow Rhythm.
Somehow You Know When It Arrives.
They Are Closing In.
"Unending Sameness of Questionable Quality."
Livingston, Myra Cohn
Night, The.
October Magic.
Pretending.
Time for Building, A.
Whispers.
Livingston, William (1808-70)
Ireland Weeping.
Message to the Bard.
Livingston, William
In Cherry Lane.
Livingstone, Douglas
Evasion, An.
One Time.
Peace Delegate.
Sunstrike.
To a Dead Elephant.
Li Yi
On Hearing a Flute at Night from the Wall of Shou-hsiang.
Llewellyn, Karl Nickerson
Prairie.
Llorens, David
Resonant Silence, A.
Wayward Child.
Lloyd, Beatrix Demarest
Love and Time.
With Roses.
Lloyd, Cecil Francis
March Winds.
Truth.
Lloyd, Charles
Essay on the Genius of Pope, An, *sel.*
'Tis not so much, these men more forms survey.
Lloyd, Elizabeth *See* **Howell, Elizabeth Lloyd**
Lloyd, Robert
Critic's Rules, The.
Shakespeare; an Epistle to Mr. Garrick.
Lloyd, William, Bishop of St. Asaph
Reflection on the Course of Human Life, A.
Lloyd, William F.
Our Times Are in Thy Hand.
Lluellyn, Martin
Cock-throwing.
Llull, Ramon *See* **Lull, Ramon**
Llwyd, John Plummer Derwent
Night is soft with summer; yon faint arch, The.
Vestal Virgin, The, *sel.*
Llywarch Hen
Tercets.
Llywarch the Aged
Hearth of Urien, The.
"Llywelyn" (Beryl Llywelyn Lucas)
Birds.
Llywelyn-Williams, Alun
When I Was Young.
Locher, David A.
Discobolus.
Lochhead, Marion
Christmas Night.
Nox Est Perpetua.
Lochore, Robert
Marriage and the Care o't.
Locker-Lampson, Frederick
At Her Window.
Circumstance.
Cuckoo, The.
Garden Lyric, A.
Jester's Plea, The.
Loulou and Her Cat.
Love, Time and Death.
Mr. Placid's Flirtation.
Mrs. Smith.
My Mistress's Boots.
Nice Correspondent, A.
Old Buffer, An.
On a Sense of Humor.
On an Old Muff.
Our Photographs.
Rhyme of One, A.

Rotten Row.
St. James's Street.
Skeleton in the Cupboard, The.
Some Ladies.
Susan.
Terrible Infant, A.
To My Grandmother.
To My Mistress.
Unrealized Ideal, The.
Widow's Mite, The.

Lockett Reginald
Death of the Moonshine Supermen.
Die Black Pervert.
This Poem for Black Women.

Lockett, Tena L.
Almost Revolutionist, The.

Lockhart, John Gibson
Beyond.
Lament for Capt. Paton.
Lines: "When youthful faith hath fled."
On Peter Robertson.
Serenade: "While my lady sleepeth."

Lockman, John
Penitent Nun, The.

Lockwood, William A.
Limerick: "There was a trim maiden named Wood."

Lodge, Edith
Song of the Hill.

Lodge, George Cabot
Day and Dark.
East Wind, The.
Song of the Wave, The.
Youth.

Lodge, Thomas
Accurst Be Love!
Armistice.
Blithe [*or* Blith] and Bonny Country Lass, A.
Carpe Diem.
Contents of the Scedule Which Sir John of Bordeaux Gave to His Sons, The.
Corydon's Song.
Earth Late Choked with Showers, The.
Fancy, A ("First shall the heavens want starry light").
Fancy, A ("When I admire the rose").
Fatal Star, The.
Fidelity.
Fig for Momus, A, *sel.*
For Pity, Pretty Eyes, Surcease.
Her Rambling.
Life and Death of William Longbeard, The, *sels.*
Like Desert Woods.
Love Guards [*or* Guides] the Roses of Thy Lips.
Love in My Bosom like a Bee.
Lover's Protestation, A.
Love's Protestation.
Love's Witchery.
Margarite of America, A, *sel.*
Melancholy.
Montanus' Sonnet.
Most Pithy and Pleasant History of Glaucus and Scylla, The.
My Bonny Lass, Thine Eye.
My Frail and Earthly Bark, by Reason's Guide.
My Mistress.
My Mistress When She Goes.
O shady vales! O fair enrichèd meads!
Ode: "Now I find thy looks were feigned."
Of Ceaseless Thoughts My Mind Hath Fram'd His Wings.
Of Rosalind.
Old Damon's Pastoral.
Passion's Hounds.
Phillis.
Phoebe's Sonnet.
Phyllis, *sels.*
Pluck the Fruit and Taste the Pleasure.
Robert, Second Duke of Normandy, *sel.*
Rosader's Sonnet ("In sorrow's cell").
Rosader's Sonnet ("Turn I my looks").
Rosalind.
Rosalynde; or, Euphues' Golden Legacy, *sels.*
Rose, The.
Scillaes [*or* Scilla's *or* Scylla's] Metamorphosis, *sels.*
Solitary Shepherd's Song, The.
Sonetto: "Of all chaste birds the phoenix doth excel."
Song: "Now I see thy looks were feigned."
Song: "Pluck the fruit and taste the pleasure."
Sonnet: "Earth, late choked [*or* chok'd] with showers, The."
Sonnet: "Love guards the roses of thy lips."
Sonnet: "My Phyllis [*or* Phillis] hath the morning sun."
Sonnet: "O shady vales, O fair enriched meads."
Strive No More.
To a Dear Friend Lately Given Over to Covetousness.
To Master Everard Digby.
To Master Michael Drayton.
To Phyllis.
To Phyllis, the Fair Shepherdess.
Truth's Complaint over England.
Very Phoenix, A.

Loesser, Frank
Praise the Lord and Pass the Ammunition.

Loewinsohn, Ron
Insomniac Poem.
Mrs. Loewinsohn &c.
My Sons.
Pastoral: "Death./ The death of a million."
Stillness of the Poem, The.
Thing Made Real, The.

Lofting, Hugh
Betwixt and Between.
Mister Beers.
Oom-pah.
Picnic.

Lofton, Blanche De Good
Song of the Seasons.

Logan George B., Jr.
Dawn.

Logan, John (1748-88)
Braes of Yarrow, The.

Logan, John (b.1923)
Achilles and the King.
Concert Scene.
Honolulu and Back.
In the Morning.
Lines on His Birthday.
Lines to His Son on Reaching Adolescence.
Nude Kneeling in Sand.
Picnic, The.
Rescue, The.
Shore Scene.
Thirty-three Ring Circus, The.
Trip to Four or Five Towns, A.
Wooden Mirror, The.

Logan, John Daniel
Heliodore.

Logan, John Edward ("Barry Dane")
Blood-Red Ring Hung round the Moon, A.
Dead Singer, A.
Nor'-West Courier, The.

Logau, Friedrich von
Retribution.

Logsdon, S. F.
Our Guiding Light.

Logue, Christopher
Story of Two Gentlemen and the Gardener, The.

Loines, Russell Hilliard
On a Magazine Sonnet.

Lok, Henry
It is not, Lord, the sound of many words.
Sonnets of Christian Passions; or, Sundry Christian Passions, *sels.*
Sundry Christian Passions.
Words may well want, both ink and paper fail.

Lom, Iain (John MacDonald)
Day of Inverlochy, The.
To Mackinnon of Strath.

Lomax, John A.
Old Mackenzie Trail, The.
Whoppers.

Long, Doughtry, Jr. ("Doc Long) "
Black people/ have got to be black.
Blast of Wind, A, a Momentary Breath.
From the window.
If 'Trane had only seen.
One Time Henry Dreamed the Number.
Where my grandmother lived.

Long, Elizabeth-Ellen
After-Christmas Poem.
Autumn Song.
Christmas Song.
Discarded Christmas Tree.
Mountain Medicine.
Rain Clouds.
Treasure.

Long, Florence Duncan
Make Me Available.

Long, Frank Belknap
Adjuration.
It Is Not Only the Dead.
New Adam, The.

Long, Haniel
Butterflies.
Cause of This I Know Not, The.
Dead Men Tell No Tales.
Faun, The.
Girl Athletes.
Herd Boy, The.
His Deaths.
Poet, The.
Song: "Poppies paramour the girls."
Students, *much abr.*

Long, John D.
Prayer, A: "I would, dear Jesus, I could break."

Long, Richard Hoopell
City of God.
Poet and Peasant.
Skylark's Nest, The.
Super-Lark, The.

Long, Stewart I.
Was It You?

Long, William *See* **"Yates, Peter"**

Long, Worth
Arson and Cold Lace.
Safari.

Longfellow, Henry Wadsworth
Aceldama.
Aftermath.
All-seeing Gods, The.
All Things Must Have an End: The World Itself.
Arrow and the Song, The.
Arsenal at Springfield, The.
As Brothers Live Together.
As the bow unto the cord is.
Auf Wiedersehen, *sel.*
Autumn ("Thou comest, Autumn, heralded by the rain").
Azrael.
Ballad of the French Fleet, A.
Battle of Lovell's Pond, The.

Longfellow (continued)
Bayard Taylor.
Beleaguered City, The.
Belfry of Bruges, The.
Belisarius.
Bells of Lynn, The.
Bells of San Blas, The.
Birds of Killingworth, The.
Blind Bartimeus [*or* Bartimaeus].
Bridge, The.
Broken Oar, The.
Builders, The.
Building of the *Long Serpent*, The.
Building of the Ship, The.
Burial of the Minnisink.
By what astrology of fear or hope.
Carillon.
Castle Builder, The, *sel.*
Catawba Wine.
Challenge, The.
Challenge of Thor, The.
Challenge to Youth.
Chamber over the Gate, The.
Charlemagne.
Chaucer.
Children.
Children's Hour, The.
Christmas Bells.
Christus; a Mystery, *sels.*
Church Scene, The.
Come, read to me some poem.
Consolation.
Coplas de Manrique, *sel.*
Courtship of Miles Standish, The.
Cover the embers.
Cross of Snow, The.
Cumberland, The.
Curfew.
Dante ("Oft have I seen").
Dante ("Tuscan, that wanderest").
Dawn is not distant, The.
Day is Done, The.
Daybreak.
Death of Minnehaha, The.
Decoration Day.
Dedication: "As one who, walking in the twilight gloom."
Dedication: "Nothing that is shall perish utterly."
Dedication: "With favoring winds, o'er sunlit seas."
Discoverer of the North Cape, The.
Divina Commedia. (*poems introductory to* Longfellow's *tr. of the* Divine Comedy I-VI).
Do you ne'er think what wondrous beings these?
Dutch Picture, A.
Einar Tamberskelver.
Eliot's Oak.
Embarkation, The, *abr.*
Emma and Eginhard.
Emperor's Bird's Nest, The.
Endymion.
Equinox, The.
Eternal Word, The.
Evangeline.
Evening Star, The.
Excelsior.
Expedition to Wessagusset, The.
Fate of the Prophets, The.
Fiftieth Birthday of Agassiz, The.
Finding of Gabriel, The.
Fire of Drift-Wood, The.
Firefly Song.
Flight into Egypt, The.
Flowers.
Foe Within, The.
Follow Me.
For age is opportunity no less.
Four Winds, The.
From My Arm-Chair.
Galley of Count Arnaldos, The.
Gaspar Becerra.
Ghosts, The.
Giles Corey of the Salem Farms, *sels.*
Giotto's Tower.
Goblet of Life, The.
God's-Acre.
Golden Legend, The, *sel.*
Golden Mile-Stone, The.
Hanging of the Crane, The, *sel.*
Harvest Moon, The.
Haunted Houses.
Hawthorne.
He That Doeth the Will.
Heights, The.
Helen of Tyre.
Hiawatha.
Hiawatha and Mudjekeewis.
Hiawatha's Brothers.
Hiawatha's Canoe.
Hiawatha's Childhood.
Hiawatha's Fishing.
Hiawatha's Sailing.
Hiawatha's Wooing.
Him Evermore I Behold.
Holidays.
Home Song.
Hunting of Pau-Puk-Keewis, The.
Hymn—for My Brother's Ordination.
Hymn of the Moravian Nuns of Bethlehem.
Hymn to the Night.
I Heard the Bells on Christmas Day.
In the Acadian land, on the shores of the Basin of Minas.
In the Churchyard at Cambridge.
In the Forest.
In the market-place of Bruges stands the belfry old and brown.
It Is Too Late!
It were a double grief, if the true-hearted.
Jericho's Blind Beggar.
Jewish Cemetery at Newport, The.
John Endicott, *sels.*
Jugurtha.
Keats.
Kéramos.
Killed at the Ford.
King Olaf's Death-Drink.
King Olaf's Return.
King Olaf's War-Horns.
King Robert of Sicily.
King Witlaf's Drinking-Horn.
Ladder of Saint Augustine, The.
Lakes of the Atchafalaya, The.
Leap of Roushan Beg, The.
Legend of Rabbi Ben Levi, The.
Let War's Tempests Cease.
Life.
Light of Stars, The.
Little Moon, The.
Lives of Great Men All Remind Us.
Love and Hate.
Lullaby of Nokomis,*abr.*
Maidenhood.
Manuscripts of God, The.
Masque of Pandora, The, *sel.*
Message of Peace, A.
Mezzo Cammin.
Michael Angelo: a Fragment, *sel.*
Midnight Mass for the Dying Year.
Midnight Ride of Paul Revere, The.
Milton.
Monk of Casal-Maggiore, The.
Morituri Salutamus.
My Books.
My Lost Youth.
My work is finished; I am strong.
Nameless Grave, A.
Nature.
New Household, A.
Nuremberg.
O Ship of State.
Ocean of Life, The.
Oft Have I Seen at Some Cathedral Door.
Old Age.
Old Bridge at Florence, The.
Old Clock on the Stairs, The.
On Dante's "Divine Comedy."
On the Atchafalaya.
On Translating the "Divina Commedia."
Pau-Puk-Keewis.
Paul Revere's Ride.
Peace.
Peace-Pipe, The.
Peace through Prayer.
Phantom Ship, The.
Potter's Song, The.
Prayer, A: "My Redeemer and my Lord."
Prelude: "This is the forest primeval. The murmuring pines and the hemlocks."
President Garfield.
Primeval Forest.
Proclamation, The.
Prologue: "Delusions of the days that once have been."
Prologue: "Tonight we strive to read, as we may best."
Prologue to "Evangeline."
Prometheus.
Psalm of Life, A.
Rain in Summer, *sl. abr.*
Rainy Day, The.
Reaper and the Flowers, The.
Republic, The.
Resignation.
Revenge of Rain-in-the-Face, The.
Ropewalk, The.
Saga of King Olaf, The, *sels.*
Sail On, O Ship of State!
Saint Francis' Sermon to the Birds, *abr.*
St. John's, Cambridge.
Sandalphon.
Santa Filomena.
Scanderbeg.
Sea Memories.
Seaside and the Fireside, The, *sel.*
Seaweed [*or* Sea Weed].
Secret of the Sea, The.
Serenade: "Stars of the summer night!"
Shakespeare.
Ship of State, The.
Ships That Pass in the Night.
Sicilian's Tale, The.
Sifting of Peter, The.
Simon Danz.
Singers, The.
Sir Humphrey Gilbert.
Skeleton in Armor, The.
Slave in the Dismal Swamp, The.
Slave's Dream, The.
Snow.
Snow-Flakes.
Song: "Stay, stay at home, my heart, and rest."
Song of Hiawatha, The, *sels.*
Sonnets on the Divina Commedia.
Sound of the Sea, The.
Spanish Student, The, *sel.*
Spirit of Poetry, The.
Stars of the Summer Night.
Sunset.
Suspiria.
Tales of a Wayside Inn, *sels.*
Talk not of wasted affection! affection never was wasted.
Then the Master/ With a gesture.
There is no death! What seems so is transition.
They were approaching the region where reigns perpetual summer.

This Is Indeed the Blessed Mary's Land.
Thou, Too, Sail On!
Three Friends of Mine.
Three Kings, The.
Three Silences of Molinos, The.
Tide, The.
Tide Rises, the Tide Falls, The.
To a Child, *sel.*
To an Old Danish Song-Book.
To One alone my thoughts arise.
To the Driving Cloud.
To-Morrow.
Too Late?
Trial, The.
Twilight.
Ultima Thule, *sel.*
Venice.
Victor and Vanquished.
Victor Galbraith.
Village Blacksmith, The.
Walter von der Vogelweid.
Wapentake.
War-Token, The.
Warden of the Cinque Ports, The.
Warning, The.
Wayside Inn, The.
When War Shall Be No More.
Windmill, The.
Witnesses, The.
Woods in Winter.
Wreck of the *Hesperus,* The.

Longfellow, Samuel
Behold, the Fields Are White, *sel.*
Christian Life, The.
Church Universal, The.
God of the Earth, the Sky, the Sea.
God through All and in You All.
In Thy Hand.
Peace on Earth.
Summer Days Are Come Again.
Where prophets' word, and martyrs' blood.

Longstaff, W. D.
Take Time to Be Holy.

Longwell, E. Elizabeth
Pear Tree, The.

Lonzano, Menahem ben Judah
Gentleman, The.

Looke, John
Famous Sea-Fight, A.

Loomis, Charles Battell
Classic Ode, A.
O-u-g-h.
Propinquity Needed.
Song of Sorrow, A.
Timon of Archimedes.

Lope de Vega Carpio, Félix
Christmas Cradlesong, A.
Clover.
Good Shepherd, The.
Lullaby, The: "As through the palms ye wander."
Madonna, to Her Sleeping Child, The.
Song for the Divine Bride and Mother.
Song for the Virgin Mother, A.
Song of the Virgin Mother, A.
Tomorrow.

Lopez, Luis
Village Barber, The.

López, Luis Carlos
Country Girl, Don't Stay Away.
Tropic Siesta.

López de Ayala, Pero
Song to the Virgin Mary.

Lopez-Penha, Abraham Z.
Dusk.

López Velarde, Ramón
Ascension and the Assumption, The.

Lord, Caroline A.
Song of Street Labor, A.

Lord, Everett W.
Legend of the Admen, The.

Lord, May Carleton
Old Man with a Mowing Machine.
Prayer: "Keep me from fretting, Lord, today."

Lord, Phillips H.
Your Church and Mine.

Lord, William Wilberforce
Brook, The.
Keats.
Ode to England, *sels.*
On the Defeat of Henry Clay.
To Rosina Pico.
Wordsworth.
Worship, *sel.*

Lorde, Audre
And Fall Shall Sit in Judgment.
Pirouette.
What My Child Learns of the Sea.

Lorentz, Pare
Black spruce and Norway pine.
Down the Yellowstone, the Milk, the White and Cheyenne.
River, The, *sels.*

Loring, Frederick Wadsworth
Fair Millinger, The.
In the Old Churchyard at Fredericksburg.

"Lorrain, Jean" (Paul Duval)
Wild Marjorie.

Lorraine, Lilith
Case History.
If He Should Come.
If These Endure.
It May Be Like This.
Let Dreamers Wake.
No Escape.
Not Made with Hands.
Since We Are Property.
What Will the Stars Remember?
When Planes Outsoar the Spirit.
Without Regret.

Lorris, Guillaume de, *and* Jean de Meun
See **Guillaume de Lorris *and* Jean de Meun**

"Lothrop, Amy." *See* **Warner, Anna Bartlett**

Louchheim, Katie
Dinner at Eight.

Lougée, David
Sestina for Cynthia, A.

Louis, Louise
Wounded, The.

Lounkianos
Vision, The.

Lourie, Dick
Ann's House.
Bestfriend, The.
Calls on the Dream Telephone, *sels.*
"English."
Hitler Dwarf, The.
In the Master Bedroom of the White House.
Madman Goes to a Party, The.
Madman Looks at His Fortune, The.
Rink.
Two Birthday Poems.
Two Fish Cosmologies.
WhenIwas, The.

Louw, N. P. van Wyk
Armed Vision.
At Dawn the Light Will Come.
Ballad of the Drinker in His Pub.
From the Ballad of Evil.
Gods Are Mighty, The.
Oh the Inconstant.

Louys, Pierre
Absence.
Bilitis.
Desire.
Despairing Embrace, The.
Endearments.
Kiss, The.
Little House, The.
Remorse.
Songs of Bilitis, The, *sels.*

Love, Adelaide
Alchemy.
Beyond Electrons.
For a Materialist.
Lien, The.
No Sweeter Thing.
Poet's Prayer.
Walk Slowly.
Word to a Dictator.

Love, George
Noonday April Sun, The.

Love, John, Jr
Barber, Spare Those Hairs.

Lovecraft, Howard Phillips
Harbour Whistles.
Nyarlathotep.

Lovejoy, George Newell
Easter Carol: "O Earth! throughout thy borders."
Gift, The.
Mother, The.

Lovelace, Richard
Against the Love of Great Ones.
Anniversary, An.
Another ("As I beheld a winters evening air").
Another ("The Centaur, Syren, I fore-go").
Black Patch on Lucasta's Face, A.
Elinda's Glove.
Ellinda's Glove.
Female Glory.
Fly Caught in a Cobweb, A.
Glove, The.
Going to the Warres [*or* Wars].
Grasse-Hopper, The.
Grasshopper, The.
Gratiana Dancing [*or* Dauncing] and Singing.
La Bella Bona Roba.
Loose Saraband, A.
Love Made in the First Age: To Chloris.
Lucasta Laughing.
Lucasta Weeping ("Lucasta wept, and still the bright").
Lucasta's World.
Ode: Grasshopper, The.
Ode: Rose, The.
Paradox, A.
Rose, The.
Scrutiny [*or* Scrutinie], The.
Snayl, The.
Song: "If to be absent were to be."
Song: Scrutiny, The.
Song: To Althea, from Prison.
Song: To Lucasta, Going beyond the Seas.
Song: To Lucasta, Going to the Warres.
Song: "Why should you swear I am forsworn."
Stone Walls.
Strive Not, Vain Lover, to Be Fine.
That Fond Impossibility.
To a Lady That Desired Me I Would Bear My Part with Her in a Song.
To Althea, from Prison.
To Amarantha, That She Would Dishevell Her Haire.
To Fletcher Reviv'd.
To Lucasta ("Ah Lucasta, why so bright!").
To Lucasta ("I laugh and I sing but cannot tell").
To Lucasta ("Tell me not, sweet, I am unkind").
To Lucasta, from Prison.
To Lucasta: Her Reserved Looks.
To Lucasta, [on] Going beyond the Seas.

Lovelace (continued)
To Lucasta, [on] Going to the Wars [*or* Warres].
To Lucasta: The Rose.
To My Truly Valiant, Learned Friend, Who in His Book Resolv'd the Art Gladiatory into the Mathematics.
Valiant Love.
Vintage to the Dungeon, The.
Why Should You Swear?
Why Shouldst Thou Swear?

Loveman, Robert
April.
April Rain.
Creed and Deed.
Diamond.
Georgia.
Hobson and His Men.
March.
Rain Song.
Riches.
Spring.
Sunset, A.

Lover, Samuel
Angel's Whisper, The.
Ask and Have.
Baby Dear.
Barney O'Hea.
Birth of Saint Patrick, The.
Fairy Boy, The.
Fairy Tempter, The.
Father Land and Mother Tongue.
Father Molloy.
Handy Andy, *sel.*
How to Ask and Have.
Lanty Leary.
Low-backed Car, The.
Paddy O'Rafther.
Quaker's Meeting, The.
Rory O'More; or, Good Omens.
St. Kevin.
War Ship of Peace, The.
What Will You Do, Love?
Widow Machree.

Lovett, Robert
Forbidden Drink.

Low, Benjamin Robbins Curtis
Due North.
Little Boy to the Locomotive, The.
Locomotive to the Little Boy, The.
To-Day.
White Violets.

Lowater, Ninette M.
Song of Labor, The.

Lowbury, Edward
Swan.

Lowe, C. M.
Hay-Time.

Lowe Robert, Viscount Sherbrooke
Song of the Squatter.
Songs of the Squatters.

Lowell, Amy
Apology.
Aquarium, An.
Bombardment, The.
Book of Hours of Sister Clotilde, The.
Carrefour.
Chinoiseries.
City of Falling Leaves, The.
Crowned.
Decade, A.
Dolphins in Blue Water.
Evelyn Ray.
Falling Snow.
Flute-Priest Song for Rain, *sel.*
Four Sides to a House.
Fragment: "What is poetry? Is it a mosaic."
Free Fantasia on Japanese Themes.
Fringed Gentians.
Garden by Moonlight, The.
Gift, A.
Grievance.
Hippocrene.
Hoar-Frost.
In Excelsis.
Lady, A.
Lamp of Life, The.
Lilacs.
Listening.
Little Garden, A.
Little Ivory Figures Pulled with String.
Madonna of the Evening Flowers.
Meeting-House Hill.
Merchandise.
Music.
Night Clouds.
Ombre Chinoise.
On Looking at a Copy of Alice Meynell's Poems, Given Me, Years Ago, by a Friend.
Patterns.
Poet, The.
Points of View.
Red Slippers.
Reflections.
Roxbury Garden, A, *abr.*
Sea Shell.
1777, *sels.*
Shooting the Sun.
Sisters, The.
Solitaire.
Taxi, The.
Texas.
To a Friend.
Trades.
Trumpet-Vine Arbour, The.
Venus Transiens.
Vernal Equinox.
Whistle under the water.
Wind and Silver.

Lowell, James Russell
Abraham Lincoln.
Absence.
After the Burial.
Aladdin.
America's Gospel.
And the voice that was calmer [*or* softer] than silence said.
Auf Wiedersehen.
Auspex.
Autograph, An.
Beaver Brook, *sel.*
Beloved, in the noisy city here.
Bible of the Race, The.
Bibliolatres.
Biglow Papers, The, *sels.*
Bow Down, Dear Land.
Brook in Winter, The.
Bryant.
But stay, here comes Tityrus Griswold, and leads on.
But what's that? a mass meeting? No, there come in lots.
Candidate's Creed, The.
Candidate's Letter, The ("Dear Sir,—You wish to know my notions").
Careless Seems the Great Avenger.
Cathedral, The.
Chippewa Legend, A.
Christmas Carol, A: "What means this glory 'round our feet."
Columbus, *sel.*
Commemoration Ode, The.
Commitment.
Cooper.
Count me o'er earth's chosen heroes—they were souls that stood alone.
Courtin', The.
Darkened Mind, The.
Day in June, A.
Debate in the Sennit, The.
December.
Earth gets its price for what Earth gives us.
Elegy on the Death of Dr. Channing, *sels.*
Emerson.
Ez fer War.
Fable for Critics, A, *sels.*
Fatherland, The.
First Snowfall [*or* Snow-Fall], The.
Fitz Adam's Story.
Flawless His Heart.
For an Autograph.
"For Christ's sweet sake, I beg an alms."
Fountain, The.
Fourth of July Ode.
Freedom ("Are we, then, wholly fallen? Can it be").
Glance behind the Curtain, A, *sel.*
God Is Not Dumb.
Great Virginian, The.
Greatly begin! though thou have time.
Harvard Commemoration Ode, The.
Hawthorne.
He Gives Nothing.
Hear now this fairy legend of old Greece.
Hebe.
Heritage, The.
His Throne Is with the Outcast.
Holmes.
"Holy Supper is kept, indeed, The."
Hosea Biglow's Lament.
I with uncovered head.
Imperial Man.
In a Copy of Omar Kháyyám.
In the Twilight.
International Copyright.
Irving.
January.
Jonathan to John.
Joys.
June ("And what is so rare").
June ("Over his keys the musing organist").
June Weather.
Kossuth.
Labor.
Letter from Mr. Ezekiel Biglow of Jaalam to the Hon. Joseph T. Buckingham, A ("Thrash away, you'll hev to rattle")
Letter from Mr. Hosea Biglow to the Hon. J. T. Buckingham, A ("This kind o' sogerin'").
Life is a leaf of paper white.
Life may be given in many ways.
Life's Purpose.
Lincoln ("Nature, they say, doth dote").
Lincoln ("Such was he, our Martyr-Chief").
"Lo, it is I, be not afraid!"
Longing, *sel.*
Love, *sel.*
Lowell.
Many loved truth, and lavished life's best oil.
Martyr Chief, The ("Nature, they say, doth dote"), *abr.*
Mr. Hosea Biglow Speaks.
Mr. Hosea Biglow to the Editor of the Atlantic Monthly.
Monna Lisa.
My Love.
New Occasions Teach New Duties.
New-come Chief.
Not Only around Our Infancy.
Now Is the High-Tide of the Year.
Ode for the Fourth of July, 1876, An.
Ode Recited at the Harvard Commemoration, July 21, 1865.
On Freedom.
On Himself.
On Receiving a Copy of Mr. Austin Dob-

son's "Old World Idylls."
On the Death of a Friend's Child, *sel.*
Once to Every Man and Nation.
One day more/ These muttering shoal-brains leave the helm to me.
Oriental Apologue, An.
Origin of Didactic Poetry, The.
Our Martyr-Chief.
Ours, and All Men's.
Palinode.
Parable, A.
Pious Editor's Creed, The.
Poe and Longfellow.
Prelude: "Over his keys."
Prelude from "The Vision of Sir Launfal."
Prepared for a Soldiers' and Sailors' Monument in Boston.
Present Crisis, The.
Recall, The.
Rhoecus.
St. Michael the Weigher.
Search, The.
She Came and Went.
Shepherd of King Admetus, The.
Singing Leaves, The.
Sir Launfal and the Leper.
Sixty-eighth Birthday.
Slaves.
Sonnet: "For this true nobleness I seek in vain."
Sonnet: "I would not have this perfect love of ours."
Sovereign Emblem, The.
Spring ("I, country-born an' bred, know where to find").
Spring ("O little city-gals, don't never go it").
Stanza on Freedom, A.
Stanzas on Freedom.
Stealing.
Street, The.
Sub Pondere Crescit.
Sunthin' in the Pastoral Line.
There are truths you Americans need to be told.
Therefore I cannot think thee wholly gone.
There's Holmes, who is matchless among you for wit.
Thing We Long For, The.
'Tis Sorrow Builds the Shining Ladder Up.
To a Recruiting Sergent.
To His Countrymen.
To the Dandelion.
To the Spirit of Keats.
To Whittier.
True Love.
Truth and Falsehood.
Truth and Love Abide.
Under the Old Elm, *sels.*
Unwasted Days, *abr.*
Verses Intended to Go with a Posset Dish to My Dear Little Goddaughter, 1882.
Vision of Sir Launfal, The.
War ("Ez fer war, I call it murder").
Washers of the Shroud, The.
Washington ("Soldier and statesman, rarest union").
Washington under the Old Elm.
We Will Speak Out.
What Is So Rare as a Day in June? ("No price is set on the lavish summer").
What Mr. Robinson Thinks.
Whittier.
Who Now Shall Sneer?
Whom We Revere.
Winter Morning, A.
Without and Within.
Witness of God.
Work.
Yussouf.

Lowell, Maria White
Morning-Glory, The.
Opium Fantasy, An.
Song: "O bird, thou dartest to the sun."

Lowell, Robert Traill Spence (1816-91)
After-Comers, The.
Brave Old Ship, the *Orient*, The.
Relief of Lucknow, The.

Lowell, Robert (1917-)
After the Surprising Conversions.
Alfred Corning Clark.
As a Plane Tree by the Water.
At a Bible House.
Ballad for the Dead Ladies.
Between the Porch and the Altar.
Black Spring.
Bomber, The.
Caligula.
Central Park.
Charles the Fifth and the Peasant.
Children of Light.
Child's Song.
Christ Is Here.
Christmas Eve under Hooker's Statue.
Christmas in Black Rock.
Coastguard House, The.
Colloquy in Black Rock.
Concord.
Crucifix, The.
Dead in Europe, The.
Death from Cancer.
Death of the Sheriff, The.
Drunken Fisherman, The.
Dunbarton.
Eel, The.
Exile's Return, The.
Fall 1961.
Falling Asleep over the Aeneid.
Florence.
For George Santayana.
For the Union Dead.
Ford Madox Ford.
Ghost, The.
Grandparents.
Harvard.
Her Dead Brother.
Holy Innocents, The.
"Hot night makes us keep our bedroom windows open, The."
In Memory of Arthur Winslow.
In the Cage.
Inauguration Day: January 1953.
Jonathan Edwards in Western Massachusetts.
July in Washington.
Lady Ralegh's Lament.
Lesson, The.
Mad Negro Soldier Confined at Munich, A.
Magnolia's Shadow, The.
Man and Wife.
Mary Winslow.
Memories of West Street and Lepke.
Middle Age.
Mr. Edwards and the Spider.
Mother Marie Therese.
Mouth of the Hudson, The.
My Last Afternoon with Uncle Devereux Winslow.
Neo-Classical Urn, The.
New Year's Day.
News from Mount Amiata.
Noli Me Tangere.
North Sea Undertaker's Complaint, The.
On the Eve of the Feast of the Immaculate Conception, 1942.
Poet at Seven, The.
Public Garden, The.
Quaker Graveyard in Nantucket, The.
Salem.
Scream, The.
September.
Shako, The.
Skunk Hour.
Slough of Despond, The.
Soft Wood.
Sparrow Hills.
Such Is the Sickness of Many a Good Thing.
Sylvia.
Tenth Muse.
Terminal Days at Beverly Farms.
To Delmore Schwartz.
"To Speak of Woe That Is in Marriage."
Waking in the Blue.
Water.
Where the Rainbow Ends.
Winter in Dunbarton.
Words for Hart Crane.

Lowenfels, Walter
Creed.
For a Hemiplegic.
Speech to the Court.

Lowrey, Booth
Miss Hen.
Ole Billy William ("Ole Mistah Billy William Goat").
Projenkin' Son, De.

Lowry, Henry Dawson
Holiday.
Spring Will Come, The.

Lowry, Malcolm
Cain Shall Not Slay Abel Today on Our Good Ground.
Christ Walks in This Infernal District Too.
Drunkards, The.
Flowering Past, The.
In Memoriam; Ingvald Bjorndal and His Comrade.
Lupus in Fabula.
Queer Poem.
Salmon Drowns Eagle.
Sestina in a Cantina.
In Memoriam; Ingvald Bjorndal and His Comrade.
Xochitepec.

Lowry, Robert
How Can I Keep From Singing? *sel.*
What though my joys and comforts die?

Lowth, Robert
Link, The.

Loy, Mina
Apology of Genius.
Der Blinde Junge.
Human Cylinders.
Love Songs.

Loyola, Mother
Rabboni! Master!

Loyola, Saint Ignatius *See* **Ignatius Loyola, Saint**

Lubbock, Phyllis M.
I picked a primrose, pale as death.

Lubke, Bernice W.
All-sufficient Christ, The.

Lucan (Marcus Annaeus Lucanus)
Cato's Address to His Troops in Lybia.
Coracle, The.
Pharsalia, *sels.*
Pompey and Cornelia.
Portents, The.
Wars worse then civil on Thessalian plains.

Lucas, Alice
Prayer before Sleep.

Lucas, Beryl Llywelyn *See* **"Llywelyn"**

Lucas, Daniel Bedinger
In the Land Where We Were Dreaming, *abr.*

Lucas, Edward Verrall
Carpenter.

Lucas (continued)
Cat's Conscience, The.
Chocolate-Cream.
Clay.
Conjuror, The.
Counsel to Those That Eat, *sels.*
Friends.
In Brittany ("In Brittany the churches").
In Normandy.
Mr. Coggs.
Nature of the Cat, The, *sel.*
O England, Country of My Heart's Desire.
Pedestrian's Plaint, The.
Potatoes.
Stamp Battalion.
Windmill, The.
You Can't Please Everybody.
Lucas, Frank Laurence
Beleaguered Cities.
Modernity.
Pipe of Peace, The.
Proud Motherhood.
Spain, 1809.
Lucas, James R.
Beat, The.
Lucas, Margaret J.
Christ, My Life.
Lucas, St. John
Curate Thinks You Have No Soul, The.
Pain.
Luce, Morton
Bow down, my song, before her presence high.
I watch beside you in your silent room.
Like some lone miser, dear, behold me stand.
So sang I in the springtime of my years.
Sonnet: "Bow down, my song, before her presence high."
Sonnet: "Comes the New Year; wailing the north winds blow."
Sonnet: "Hear, O Self-Giver, infinite as good."
Sonnet: "How shall I tell the measure of my love?"
Sonnet: "I watch beside you in your silent room."
Sonnet: "Like some lone miser, dear, behold me stand."
Sonnet: "So sang I in the springtime of my years."
Sonnet: "Twin songs there are, of joyance, or of pain."
Thysia, *sels.*
Twin songs there are, of joyance, or of pain.
Lucian (Lucianus)
Artificial Beauty.
Dead Child [*or* Childe], A.
Golden Mean, The.
Passing Away.
Time as Variable.
Lucie-Smith, Edward
Afterwards.
At the Roman Baths, Bath.
Fault, The.
Hymn Tunes, The.
In the Future.
Lesson, The.
Meeting Myself.
On Looking at Stubbs's Anatomy of the Horse.
Poet in Winter.
Rabbit Cry.
Wise Child, The.
Lucillius [*or* Lucilius]
Better to Be Brave.
Boxer's Face, The.
Dead Song-Writer, A.
On an Old Woman.
Sluggard, The.
Treasure.
Valentine for a Lady, A.
World's Worst Boxer, The.
Lucius Apuleius *See* **Apuleius, Lucius**
Lucretius (Titus Lucretius Carus)
Address to Venus.
Against the Fear of Death.
Beginnings of Civilization.
Beyond Religion.
Cause of Thunder, The.
Concerning the Nature of Love.
Concerning the Nature of Things.
Darling of God and Men, beneath the gliding stars.
De Rerum Natura, *sels.*
Fear of Death, The.
Nature of Love, The.
No Single Thing Abides.
Of Human Progress.
Of the Nature of Things.
On the Nature of Things.
Origins and Savage Period of Mankind.
Origins of Vegetable and Animal Life.
Prayer to Venus.
Suave Mari Magno.
What Has This Bugbear Death.
Whilst human kind/ Throughout the lands lay miserably crushed.
Luders, Charles Henry
Corsage Bouquet, A.
Four Winds, The.
Haunts of the Halcyon, The.
Heart of Oak.
Mountebanks, The.
Old Thought, An.
Ludlow, Fitz Hugh [*or* Fitzhugh]
Socrates Snooks.
Too Late.
Ludlow, Wilma C.
Imitation of Christ.
Ludlum, William
Business Man's Prayer, A.
Stairway to the Stars, The.
That Radio Religion.
Luff, W.
I Buried the Year.
Lui Chi
Poet Thinks, A.
"Luke"
See Brown, Joseph
Luke, Jemima Thompson
I Think When I Read That Sweet Story of Old.
"Of Such Is the Kingdom of God."
Prayer for Purity.
Lulham, Habberton
Nested.
Lull [*or* Llull], Ramon
Lover and the Belovèd, The.
Tree of Love, The.
Lummis, Charles Fletcher
Cowboy's Valentine, The.
John Charles Frémont.
Poe-'em of Passion, A.
Lumumba, Patrice Emery
Dawn in the Heart of Africa.
Lunacharsky, Anatoli Vasilyevich
Faust and the City, *sel.*
Song of the Old Man in Chains.
Lund, Christie
Prayer for a Bride's House.
Lundbergh, Holger
Interlude.
Lunt, George
Requiem.
Luria, Isaac
Sabbath of Rest, A.
Lushington, Franklin
No More Words.
Luther, Martin
All Hail, Thou Noble Guest.
Away in a Manger.
Bed in My Heart, A.
Cradle Hymn.
Easter.
Feste Burg ist unser Gott, Ein.
God's Unchanging Word.
He Upholds.
Hymn: "Mighty fortress is our God, A."
Lord, Keep Us Steadfast in Thy Word.
Luther's Hymn.
Mighty Fortress Is Our God, A.
Missionary Prayer, A.
Praise to Jesus.
Watch and Pray.
Luttrell, Henry
Advice to Julia, *sels.*
After the Wedding.
Dress.
Honeymoon, The.
Lovers and Friends.
Peace, The.
Lutz, Gertrude May
Prisoner of War.
Lu Yu
Herd Boy, The.
Wild Flower Man, The.
Lu Yün
Valley Wind, The.
Luzi, Mario
Excerpts from a "Gothic Notebook."
Gothic Notebook, *sel.*
Luzzatto, Isaac
Death, Thou Hast Seized Me.
Luzzatto, Moses Hayyim of Padua
Chorus: "All ye that handle harp and viol and pipe."
Unto the Upright Praise, *sel.*
Lyall, Sir Alfred Comyn
Badminton.
Hindu Ascetic, The.
Meditations of a Hindu Prince.
Studies at Delhi, *sels.*
Lyall, J.
Songs in the Night.
Lydgate, John
Against Women's Fashions.
Ballad Warning Men to Beware of Deceitful Women, A, *sel.*
Beware of Doubleness.
Child Jesus to Mary the Rose, The.
Complaint of the Black Knight, The.
Court of Sapience, *sel.*
Dance, The.
Dance of Death, The, *sel.*
Duplicity of Women, The.
Epithalamium for Gloucester, *sel.*
Fall of Princes, The, *sel.*
Henry before Agincourt: October 25, 1415.
Howe maryages have grounde and cause be.
In May, when Flora, the fresshe lusty quene.
Lament: "Farewell Mercy, farewell thy piteous grace."
Lat Noman Booste of Konnyng nor Vertu.
Life of Our Lady, The, *sel.*
Lover's New Year's Gift, A.
O thoughtful herte, plunged in distresse.
To the Virgin.
Transient as a Rose.
Vox Ultima Crucis.
Women, of kinde, have conditions three.
Ye that amonge lordis and barouns.
Lydston, Donna R.
Family, The.
Lyly, John
Alexander and Campaspe, *sels.*
Apelles' Song.
Apollo's Song.
Cards and Kisses.

Cupid and Campaspe.
Cupid and My Campaspe.
Cupid's Indictment.
Daphne.
Endimion.
Endymion, *sel.*
Fairy Song, A.
Fools in Love's College.
Galathea [*or* Gallathea], *sel.*
Midas, *sels.*
Mother Bombie, *sel.*
Mydas.
O Cupid! Monarch over Kings.
Oh, for a Bowl of Fat Canary.
Pan's Song.
Sapho and Phao, *sels.*
Sappho and Phao.
Serving Men's Song, A.
Song: "Cupid and my Campaspe played."
Song: "It is all one in Venus' wanton school."
Song by Apelles.
Song by Fairies.
Song in Making of the Arrows, A.
Song of Accius and Silena.
Song of Apelles.
Song of Daphne to the Lute, A.
Song of Diana's Nymphs, A.
Song to Apollo.
Spring, The.
Spring's Welcome.
Syrinx.
Trico's Song.
Vulcan's Song.
What Bird So Sings.
Who Is't Now We Hear?

Lynch, J. J.
Comfort.

Lynch, John W.
Crucifixion, The.
Little girl, A/ Had wandered in the night.
Woman Wrapped in Silence, A, *sel.*

Lynch, Stanislaus
Blue Peter.

Lynch, Thomas Toke
Gracious Spirit.
Holy Spirit, Dwell with Me.
Jesus Christ the Lord.
Lift Up Your Heads, Rejoice!
Reinforcements.
Thousand Years Have Come, A.
Where Is Thy God, My Soul?

Lynche, Richard
Diella, *sel.*
Love's Despair.

Lynd, Sylvia
Cowper at Olney.
Happy Hour, The.
To Sheila Playing Haydn.

Lynde, Benjamin
Lines Descriptive of Thomson's Island.

Lyndsay, Sir David *See* **Lindsay, Sir David**

Lyne, Sandford
Dog, The.
Guest of Our Lovely Daughter, The.
Home-Made Peach Ice Cream.
Notes from an Ohio Tavern.
Poem for a Selfpitying Friend/ for Lost Loves.
Star-gaze Poem.

Lynn, Ethel *See* **Beers, Ethel Lynn**

Lyon, Lilian Bowes *See* **Bowes-Lyon,Lilian**

Lyon, P. H. B.
Envoi: "Earth puts her colours by."

Lyon, Roger H.
Keep On Praying.

Lyons, A. Neil
Fairy Cobbler, The.

Lysaght, Edward
Garnyvillo.

Lysaght, Sidney Royse
Deserted Home, A.
First Pathways.
New Horizons.
Secret of the Deeps, The.

Lyster, Mrs. Henry F.
Michigan, My Michigan!

Lyte, Henry Francis
Abide with Me.
Agnes.
Declining Days.
Delight in God's House.
Forgiveness.
Hymn: "Abide with me; fast falls the eventide."
"Lo, We Have Left All."
Lost Love, A.
Prayer for Humility.
Secret Place, The.
Unknown God, The.

Lyte, Henry Francis, *and* **John Quarles** *See* **Quarles, John,** *and* **Henry Francis Lyte**

Lytle, William Haines
Antony and Cleopatra.
Antony to Cleopatra.
Siege of Chapultepec, The.
Volunteers, The.

Lyttelton George, Baron Lyttelton
Epistle to Mr. Pope, An.
Ode, in Imitation of Pastor Fido.
On Her Pleading Want of Time.
Song: "Heavy hours are almost past, The."
Song: "When Delia on the plain appears."
Tell Me, My Heart, if This Be Love.
To the Memory of a Lady, *abr.*
Two Poems to Miss Lucy Fortescue.
When Delia on the Plain Appears.
Written at Mr. Pope's House at Twickenham.

Lyttelton, Lucy
Simon the Cyrenean.

Lytton, Edward Robert Bulwer-Lytton, 1st Earl of *See* **"Meredith, Owen"**

M

"M., F."
Another, of Another Mind ("A king, oh boon for my aspiring mind!").

"M., P. S."
Dawn.

"M., Q. B."
Old and the New, The.

"M., S. M."
Surrender.

"M. E. B." *See* **"B., M. E"**
"M. E. H." *See* **"H., M. E"**
"M. G. H." *See* **"H., M. G"**
"M. H." *See* **"H., M"**
"M. J." *See* **"J., M"**
"M. K. B." *See* **"B., M. K"**
"M. K. H." *See* **"H., M. K"**
"M. P. D." *See* **"D., M. P"**

Maas, Willard
Kind Look, The.
Letter to R.
No Season for Our Season.
On Reading Gene Derwood's "The Innocent."

Mabbe, James
Spanish Bawd, The.

Mabuchi
Tempest, The.
View of the Sea, A.

MacAdams, Lewis
Ache, The.
After G. de Nerval.
Animals, The.
Claes Oldenburg Story, The.
Clock Works, The.
Dazzling Day, The.
Have Sky.
In Memoriam.
Italian Air, The.
Kora for March 5th.
Lace Curtains, The.
Meditation, A: What Is a Stocking in Eternity?
Olive Grove.
Poem: "There is lightning on the edge of the water."
Red River.
Sonnet: "Phoebe runs in from the warm rain."
Trailer Park.
Warm Tea.
Young Man, The.

Macainsh, Noel
Kangaroo by Nightfall.

McAllister, Claire
Aeneid.
Daphne.
Dedication, A: "Lucilla, saved from shipwreck on the seas."
July in the Jardin des Plantes.
Mystery.
Petrarch for Laura.

MacAlpine, James
To an Irish Blackbird.

McAlpine, R. W.
Two Surprises.

Mac an Bhaird, Laoiseach
Civil Irish and Wild Irish.
Man of Experience, A.

MacAndrew, Rachel
Pony, The.
Robin Hood.

Macarthur, Bessie J. B.
Nocht o' Mortal Sicht.

Macarthur, Gloria
Phineas Pratt.

McArthur, Peter
Earthborn.
Sugar Weather.

Macartney, Frances *See* **Greville, Fanny**

Macartney, Frederick Thomas Bennett
Bargain Basement.
Desert Claypan.
You'll Know Love.

Macaulay, Thomas Babington Macauley, 1st Baron
Armada, The.
Battle of Ivry, The.
Battle of [the] Lake Regillus, The, *sels.*
Battle of Naseby, The.
Country Clergyman's Trip to Cambridge, The.
Death of Herminius, The.
England's Standard.
Epitaph on a Jacobite.
Fight at the Bridge, The.
Fight in the Centre, The.
From every warlike city.
Herminius's Horse.
Horatius [at the Bridge].
How Horatius Kept the Bridge.
Ivry.
Jacobite's Epitaph, A.
Last Buccaneer, The.
Lays of Ancient Rome, *sels.*
Night sank upon the dusky beach, and on the purple sea.
Sermon in a Churchyard.

McAuley, James Phillip
Art of Poetry, An.

McAuley (continued)
At Bungendore.
Blue Horses, The.
Canticle.
Celebration of Love.
Death of Chiron, The.
Incarnation of Sirius, The.
Late Winter.
Missa Papae Marcelli.
New Guinea.
New Guinea Lament.
Pietà.
She like the Moon Arises.
Sleep.
MacBeth, George
Ash.
Bedtime Story.
Circe Undersea.
Compasses, The.
Crab-Apple Crisis, The.
Drawer, The.
Fourteen Ways of Touching the Peter.
Mother Superior.
Return, The.
Scissor-Man.
Spider's Nest, The.
Star, A.
Wasps' Nest, The.
McBurney, William B (Carroll Malone)
Croppy Boy, The.
McCabe, James H.
On the Reported New Outbreak of Christianity.
McCabe, William Gordon
Christmas Night of '62.
Dreaming in the Trenches.
MacCaig, Norman
Aspects.
Birds All Singing.
By Achmelvich Bridge.
Celtic Cross.
Edinburgh Spring.
Ego.
Feeding Ducks.
Fetching Cows.
Golden Calf.
Innocence.
Near Midnight.
November Night, Edinburgh.
Nude in a Fountain.
Spate in Winter Midnight.
Summer Farm.
Too Bright a Day.
Two Musics.
Tyrant Apple Is Eaten, The.
You within Love.
McCall, James Edward
New Negro, The.
"McCall, Sidney." *See* **Fenollosa, Mary McNeil**
McCann, John E.
Utmost in Friendship, The.
McCann, Michael Joseph
O'Donnell Aboo.
McCann, Rebecca
Fences.
Horizons.
Humane Thought.
McCarn, Corneille
Queer Habits.
McCarroll, James
Grey Linnet, The.
McCarthy, Denis Aloysius
Ah, Sweet Is Tipperary.
Christmas Legends.
Land Where Hate Should Die, The.
Poor Man's Daily Bread, The.
Rosa Mystica.
Saint Brigid.
Song for the Flag, A.
Tailor That Came from Mayo, The.
Veterans, The.
MacCarthy, Denis Florence
Bell-Founder, The, *sel.*
Bless the Dear Old Verdant Land.
Dead Tribune, The.
Foray of Con O'Donnell [A.D. 1495], The, *sels.*
Ireland, *abr.*
Irish Wolf-Hound, The.
Labor Song.
Lament: "Youth's bright palace."
"Now, by Columba!" Con exclaimed.
Spring Flowers from Ireland.
Summer Longings.
MacCarthy, Donal, 1st Earl Clancarty
Body's Speech, The.
MacCarthy, Ethna
Ghosts.
Insomnia.
Viaticum.
M'Carthy, Justin Huntly
Ballad of Dead Ladies, A ("I wonder in what Isle of Bliss").
If I were King, *sels.*
McCarthy, Leonard
Breviary on the Subway.
Holy Thursday.
McCartney, Mabel E.
Refuge.
"MacCathmhaoil, Seosamh." *See* **Campbell, Joseph**
McCauliff, George A.
Quiet Place, The.
MacCawell, Hugh
Christmas Night.
McCheyne, Robert Murray
How Much I Owe.
Jehovah Tsidkenu—The Lord Our Righteousness.
McClellan, Goerge Marion
Butterfly in Church, A.
Dogwood Blossoms.
Feet of Judas, The.
Hills of Sewanee, The.
McClellan, Isaac *See* **McLellan, Isaac, Jr**
McClintock, Charles W.
Everybody Works but Father.
McClure, John
Carol: "Month can never forget the year, The."
Carol Naive.
Chanson Naïve.
Man to Man.
McClure, Michael
Aelf-scin, the Shining Scimmer the Gleam, the Shining, The.
Breech, The.
Canticle.
Flowers of Politics, The, I ("This is the huge dream of us that we are heroes").
Flowers of Politics, The, II ("Only what is heroic and courageious moves our blood").
For Artaud.
Gesture the gesture the gesture the gesture, The.
Hymn to St. Geryon, *sel.*
Mad Sonnet 11: "I love seahorses, teddybears, African violets."
Mad Sonnet 5: "Oh science, I love the touch of velvet."
Oh Bright Oh Black Singbeast Lovebeast Catkin Sleek.
Oh Ease Oh Body-Strain Oh Love Oh Ease Me Not!
Ode for Soft Voice.
Ode to the Negative Universe.
Only what is heroic and courageious moves our blood.
Peyote Poem, *sel.*
Rug, The.
Song, A: "Turn on and sing my happy song."
Thought, A.
MacColl, Dugald Sutherland
Ballade of Andrew Lang.
MacConglinne
Vision of MacConglinne, The.
Vision That Appeared to Me, A.
Wheatlet Son of Milklet.
McConkey, James
Drifting.
Mac-Con-Mara (Macnamara), Donogh
Fair Hills of Eiré, O, The!
MacConmidhe, Giollabhrighde
Childless.
McCord, David
Any Day Now.
Ascot Waistcoat.
At the Garden Gate.
Axolotl, The.
Baccalaureate.
Backstair Ballad.
Big Chief Wotapotami.
Bucket of Bees, A.
Cities and Science.
Cocoon.
Convalescence, I-VIII.
Cow has a cud, The.
Crew Cut.
Crickets.
Crows, The.
Dog in a Car.
Double Star, A.
Epitaph on a Waiter.
Euterpe; a Symmetric.
Every Time I Climb a Tree.
Fisherman, The.
Fred.
Frost Pane, The.
Go Fly a Saucer.
Hex on the Mexican X, A.
History of Education.
In Grato Jubilo.
Isabel Jones & Curabel Lee.
Joe.
Kite.
Lacquer Liquor Locker, The.
Lessons in Limericks.
Mr. Macklin's Jack o'Lantern ("Mr. Macklin takes his knife").
Monday morning back to school.
New Chitons for Old Gods, *sel.*
Newt, The.
Night in November.
Notes on a Track Meet.
Notice.
Of Red in Spring.
Ogden Nash Gets All the Cash.
On a Waiter.
Our Mr. Toad.
Out in the Woods with Father.
Out of November; Speaking for One.
Perambulator Poems (I-VII).
Pickety fence, The.
Plane Geometer.
Progress.
Rainbow, The.
Reflection in Blue.
Reservation.
Second Half.
Snail.
Song of the Train.
Spider, The.
Sportif.
Thin ice/ Free advice.
This Is My Rock.
Tiger Lily.
Tiggady Rue.
To a Child.

Waltzing Mice.
Watching the Moon.
Weather Words.
When I Was Christened.
Where Is My Butterfly Net?
Who Wants a Birthday?
McCord, Howard
Dear.
Dora.
Hope.
Months of the Tribe, The.
My Brother's Death.
Note on Bone.
Out.
Quasi-stellar Radio Sources.
Toad Man, The.
McCormick, Virginia Taylor
To One Who Died in Autumn.
Twilight.
McCormick, Washington Jay
In Montana [a Land of Contrasts].
Rigger, The.
McCoy, C. Lindsay
Caroline Cricket.
Devil's Darning Needle.
Honey Bee.
Hornets.
Katy-did.
Lady Bug.
Snail.
Whirligig Beetle.
McCoy, Samuel
Thompson Street.
McCracken, Hattie B.
I Would Be Great.
McCrae, Dorothy Frances
Homesick.
September.
Treasure, The.
McCrae, George Gordon
Day had fled, the moon arose, The.
Forby Sutherland.
Mamba the Bright-eyed, *sel.*
McCrae, Hugh Raymond
Ambuscade.
Australian Spring.
Bridal Song, A.
Camden Magpie.
Colombine.
End of Desire, The.
Enigma.
Evening.
Fantasy.
Fragment: "As if stone Caesar shook."
I Blow My Pipes.
Joan of Arc.
June Morning.
Mad Marjory.
Mimshi Maiden, The.
Morning.
Mouse, The.
Muse-haunted.
Never Again.
Song of the Rain.
Spring.
Uncouth Knight, The.
McCrae, John
Anxious Dead, The.
Harvest of the Sea, The.
In Flanders Fields.
Song of the Derelict, The.
McCrea, Lilian
Boots and Shoes.
Getting Up.
My Toys.
Noises in the Night.
Pussy-Cat and Puppy-Dog.
Rain.
Wash-Day.
McCreary, Frederick R.
Before Winter.
Since Christmas.
McCreery, John Luckey
There Is No Death.
McCuaig, Ronald
Au Tombeau de Mon Père.
Betty by the Sea.
Chanty: "When rain falls, I say."
Daily Round, The.
Is Love Not Everlasting?
L'Après Midi d'une Fille aux Cheveux de Lin.
Love Me and Never Leave Me.
Mokie's Madrigal.
Music in the Air.
Passionate Clerk to His Love, The.
Recitative.
McCulloch, Margaret
Aftermath.
McCullough, Mary E.
Presence.
Thought for Easter.
McCully, Laura E.
Canoe Song at Twilight.
McDermot, Thomas Henry *See* **"Redcam, Tom"**
McDermott, Jessie
April Weather.
MacDermott, Martin
Girl of the Red Mouth.
MacDiarmid, Belle (Mrs. J. Warren Ritchie)
I Shall Not Weep.
MacDiarmid, Ethel
Call of the Plains, The.
"MacDiarmid, Hugh" (Christopher Murray Grieve)
Antenora.
At My Father's Grave.
At the Cenotaph.
Bonnie Broukit Bairn, The.
British Leftish Poetry, 1930-1940.
Cattle Show.
Cophetua.
Crowdieknow.
Day of the Crucifixion, The.
De Profundis.
Deep-Sea Fishing.
Eemis-Stane, The.
Empty Vessel.
Fleggit Bride, The.
Glen of Silence, The.
Great Wheel, The.
I Heard Christ Sing.
If I Was Not a Soldier.
In the Hedgeback.
Innumerable Christ, The.
Love.
Man in the Moon, The.
Milk-Wort and Bog Cotton.
Munestruck.
O Wha's Been Here afore Me, Lass.
O Wha's the Bride?
Old Wife in High Spirits.
On the Oxford Book of Victorian Verse.
Parley of Beasts.
Parrot Cry, The.
Reflections in a Slum.
Reflections in an Iron Works.
Scarlet Woman, The.
Scunner.
Skeleton of the Future, The.
Spanish War, The.
Stony Limits.
To a Sea Eagle.
Two Parents, The.
Water Music.
Watergaw, The.
Wheesht, Wheesht.
With a Lifting of the Head.
With the Herring Fishers.
MacDonagh, Donagh
Childhood.
Dublin Made Me.
Galway.
Going to Mass Last Sunday.
Hungry Grass, The.
Invitation, The.
Love's Language.
On the Bridge of Athlone; a Prophecy.
Prothalamium.
Revel, A.
Veterans, The.
Warning to Conquerors, A.
Wind Blows, The.
Macdonagh, Thomas
In Paris.
John-John.
Night Hunt, The.
Of a Poet Patriot.
Offering.
On a Poet Patriot.
Our Story.
Song: "Love is cruel, Love is sweet."
What Is White?
Wishes for My Son.
Macdonald, Agnes Foley
Eternal.
MacDonald, Alexander (Alasdair MacMhaighstir Aladair)
Birlinn Chlann-Raghnaill.
McDonald, Dorothy Nell
Birthday Wish, A.
MacDonald, Elizabeth Roberts
Summons, The.
Macdonald, Frederika Richardson
New Year's Eve—Midnight.
Macdonald, George
Adela Cathcart, *sel.*
Approaches.
At the Back of the North Wind, *sels.*
Baby, The.
Carpenter, The.
Christmas Prayer, A.
Come Down.
De Profundis.
Decision.
Dorcas.
Earl o' Quarterdeck, The.
Evening Hymn, *sel.*
I Need Thee.
Light.
Little White Lily.
Lord of Thyself and me, through the sore grief.
Lost and Found.
Mammon Marriage.
May.
Memorial of Africa, A, *sel.*
My Morning Song.
My soul leans toward Him; stretches out its arms.
O God, whose daylight leadeth down.
Obedience.
Oneness with Him.
Over the Hill.
Paul Faber, Surgeon, *sel.*
Prayer, A: "When I look back upon my life nigh spent."
Preacher's Prayer, The.
Rest.
Sacrifice.
Shadows, The.
Sir Lark and King Sun.
Song: "I dream'd that I woke from a dream."
Song: "Where did you come from, baby dear?"
Song: "Why do the houses stand."
Sonnet: "This infant world has taken long to make."
Sweeper of the Floor, The.
Sweet Peril.

Macdonald (continued)
That Holy Thing.
This Infant World.
To My God.
What Christ Said.
What Would You See?
Where Did You Come From?
Wind and the Moon, The.
Within and Without, *sels.*
Woman Who Came behind Him in the Crowd.
World and Soul.
MacDonald, Goodridge
Elegy, Montreal Morgue.
Sailor, The.
MacDonald, James Edward Hervey
Gallows and Cross.
Hanging, The.
Kitchen Window.
MacDonald, John *See* **Lom, Iain**
McDonald, L. A.
It's You.
Macdonald, Lucy Maud *See* **Montgomery, Lucy Maud**
McDonald, Nancy May
Hatters, The.
Makers, The.
Quiet Street, The.
Wet Summer; Botanic Gardens.
White Eagle, The.
MacDonald, Wilson Pugsley
Armand Dussault.
As the stars go out so let me go.
Baby Show, De.
Battle of Peace, The.
Exit.
In a Wood Clearing.
In the Far Years.
John Graydon.
June.
Last Portage, The, *sel.*
Masked Ball, The.
Moonlight on Lake Sydenham.
Nineteen Twenty-six.
Pierre of Timagami in New York.
Song of the Ski, The.
Teemothy Hatch.
Toll-Gate Man, The.
McDonall, Amy
Feast Day, The.
MacDonnell, James Francis Carlin *See* **Carlin, Francis**
McDonnell, Thomas P.
Next Voice You Hear, The.
Psalm for Moderns, A.
MacDonogh, Patrick
Be Still as You Are Beautiful.
Dodona's Oaks Were Still.
Flowering Currant.
River, The.
She Walked Unaware.
Snare, The.
Song: "She spoke to me gently with words of sweet meaning."
Song for a Proud Relation.
Soon with the Lilac Fades Another Spring.
This Morning I Wakened among Loud Cries of Seagulls.
Waking.
Widow of Drynam, The.
MacDonough, Patrick
Bring Home the Poet.
Via Longa.
McDougal, Violet
Sea Wolf, The.
Macdougall, Arthur R., Jr
Bitter Question.
Captain of the Years.
Captains of the Years, The.
Death of Christ.
It Isn't Far to Bethlehem.
We Need a King.
McDougall, Jean
Quarrel.
McDougall, Joseph Easton
New House, The.
Macduff, John
Jesus, My Saviour, Look on Me!
McDuffee, Franklin
Hakluyt Unpurchased.
Mace, Frances Laughton
Alcyone.
Only Waiting.
Succession, The.
Macedonius
Dedication of a Ship.
Greet All Equally.
MacElgun [*or* Mac Giolla Ghunn), Cathal Buidhe
Yellow Bittern, The.
McElhaney, Georgia Lee
Conquistador.
Dervish.
Effigy.
MacEwen, Gwendolyn
Arcanum One.
Caravan, The.
Thing Is Violent, The.
MacEwen, Pearl Forbes
Kite, The.
My Little Dog.
McFadden, David
Elephant.
McFadden, Isobel
April.
McFadden, Roy
Address to an Absolute.
Aged Writer, An.
Elegy: "Out on the roads of sky the moon stands poised."
Epithalamium: "So you are married, girl. It makes me sad."
Independence.
Mihailovich.
Orator, The.
Saint Francis and the Birds.
Virgin Country.
White Bird, The.
William Blake Sees God.
MacFarlan, James
Scotland's Tribute to Wallace.
McFarland, John T.
Be Merciful.
Journey, The.
McFarlane, Basil
Final Man, The.
McFarlane, J. E. Clare
On National Vanity.
Macfie, Ronald Campbell
In Memoriam; John Davidson.
MacFie, Roy Campbell
Worship.
McGaffey, Ernest
As the Day Breaks.
Geronimo.
I Fear No Power a Woman Wields.
Little Big Horn.
Mark.
Rise, A.
McGaffin, Audrey
At Cambridge.
Avalon.
Cemetery Is, The.
Inertia.
Invalid.
Poor Relation, A.
McGahey, Jeanne
Oregon Winter.
McGarvey, Margaret
D-Dawn.
McGaugh, Lawrence
Glimpses #xii, *sel.*
Old man walks to me, The.
McGee, Clyde
Cross Makers.
Free Enterprise.
Gratitude.
Mary at the Cross.
McGee, Thomas D'Arcy
Celtic Cross, The.
Celts, The.
Exile's Devotion, The.
Irish Wife, The.
Jacques Cartier.
Man of the North Countrie, The.
To Ask Our Lady's Patronage for a Book on Columbus.
McGeorge, Alice Sutton
Autumn's Fete.
McGiffert, Gertrude Huntington
Maine Trail, A.
MacGill, Patrick
Conger Eel, The.
Death and the Fairies.
Dedication: "I speak with a proud tongue of the people who were."
It's a Far, Far Cry.
Slainthe!
Song of the Old Days, A.
MacGillivray, Arthur
Death.
Madonna of the Dons.
Macgillivray, Pittendrigh
Return, The.
McGinlay, James
Passing Years, The.
McGinley, Phyllis
All Around the Town, *sels.*
Ballad of Culinary Frustration.
Ballade of Lost Objects.
Ballroom Dancing Class.
B's the Bus.
C Is for the Circus.
Carol with Variations.
Certain Age, A.
Concert, The.
Conversation in Avila.
Country Club Sunday.
Day after Sunday, The.
E is the Escalator.
Enigma in Altman's.
Evening Musicale.
F Is the Fighting Firetruck.
Fourteenth Birthday.
Giveaway, The.
Good Humor Man, The.
In Praise of Diversity.
Intimations of Mortality.
Journey toward Evening.
J's the Jumping Jay-Walker.
Lament for Lost Lodgings.
Literary Landscape with Dove and Poet.
Lucy McLockett.
Midcentury Love Letter.
My Six Toothbrushes.
New Order, The.
Oh Come, Little Children.
Occupation: Housewife.
Old Feminist, The.
Portrait of a Girl with Comic Book.
P's the Proud Policeman.
Q Is for the Quietness.
R is for the Restaurant.
Recipe for a Marriage.
Recipe for an Evening Musicale.
Reflections at Dawn.
Reflections Outside of a Gymnasium.
Saint Francis Borgia; or, A Refutation for Heredity.
Spanish Lions, The.
Star-spangled Ode.
Text for Today.

Theology of Jonathan Edwards, The.
Thunderer, The.
Tirade on Tea.
Trial and Error.
Trinity Place.
U is for Umbrellas.
Velvet Hand, The.
W's for Windows.

Mac Giolla Ghunna, Cathal Buidhe *See* **MacElgun, Cathal Buidhe**

McGlennon, Felix
Love, Sweet Love.

McGonagall, William
Death of Prince Leopold, The.
Famous Tay Whale, The.
Tay Bridge Disaster, The.

McGovern, Margaret
Madeline at Jefferson Market Night Court.

MacGowan, Liam
Connolly.

MacGowran, Hugh
Description of an Irish Feast, The; or, O'-Rourk's Frolic.
O'Rourk's Frolic.

McGrath, Marion *See* **Albertus Magnus, Sister**

McGrath, Thomas
Against the False Magicians.
Gone away Blues.
Ode for the American Dead in Korea.
Odor of Blood, The.
Remembering That Island.
Repeated Journey, The.

McGreevy, Thomas
Aodh Ruadh O'Domhnaill.
Gioconda.
Homage to Hieronymus Bosch.
Homage to Jack Yeats.
Red Hugh.

MacGregor, Gertrude *See* **Moffat, MacGregor**

McGrew, A. O.
Hit at the Times, A.

McGroarty, John Steven
Blow, Bugles, Blow.
King's Highway, The.
Port o' Heart's Desire, The.

McGuire, Harry
Phantoms.

Machado, Antonio
Autumn Dawn.
Crime Took Place at Granada, The.
Four Poems.
Iberian God, *sel.*
"O master of fortunes and of poverties."
Poems.

Machado, Manuel
On the Annunciation of Fra Angelico.

Machado de Assis, Joaquim Maria
Blue Fly.

Machar, Agnes Maule
Untrodden Ways.

Machiavelli, Niccolò,
Opportunity.

McHugh, Vincent
Amphimachos the Dandy.
Crawl Blues.
Deposition by John Wilmot, A.
I am very fond of the little ribs of women.
Mantis Friend, The.
Mice at the Door, The.
Natural History of Pliny, The.
Ode in a Night of Overhanging Weather.
Suite from Catullus.
Talking to Myself, *sel.*

MacInnes, Tom
Ballade of Faith.
Chinatown Chant.
Modernists, The.
Tiger of Desire, The.
To Walt Whitman.
Velvet Sonneteers, The.
Zalinka.

McInnis, Edgar
Fire Burial.
Requiem for a Dead Warrior.

MacIntosh, Claire Harris
Barn in Winter, The.
Spirit of the *Bluenose,* The.

MacIntyre, Charlotte Grant
Symphony, The.

MacIntyre, Duncan Ban
Ben Dorain.
Last Leave of the Hills.
Praise of Ben Dorain, The.

McIntyre, James
On the High Cost of Dairy Products.
Queen of Cheese.
Shelly.

McIntyre, Robert
In the Carpenter Shop.
Missionaries, The.
Nazareth Shop, The.

"McK., F."
Strike the Blow.

Mack, Louise
Before Exile.
To Sydney.

"M'K., S. C."
Quiet from Fear of Evil.

Mackail, John William
Etruscan Ring, An.
Old tips come out as good as new.
Roughly, so to say, you know.

Mackay, Charles
Bachelor's Mono-Rhyme, A.
Cleon and I.
Climbing to the Light.
Cynical Ode to an Ultra-Cynical Public.
Earl Norman and John Truman.
Good Time Coming, The.
Holly Bough, The.
I Love My Love.
If I Were a Voice.
Little and Great.
Miller of the Dee, The.
No Enemies.
Reconciliation.
Ship, The.
Song: "Men of thought! be up and stirring."
Tell Me, Ye Wingèd Winds.
True Freedom.
Tubal Cain.
Under the Holly Bough.
What Might Be Done.

McKay, Claude
Absence.
Africa.
After the Winter.
America.
Baptism.
Barrier, The.
Commemoration.
Desolate.
Enslaved.
Exhortation: Summer, 1919.
Flame-Heart.
Flower of Love.
Harlem Dancer, The.
Harlem Shadows.
Heritage.
Home Thoughts.
Homing Swallows.
If We Must Die.
Lynching, The.
Moon Song.
My House.
My Mother.
North and South.
Outcast.
Russian Cathedral.
St. Isaac's Church, Petrograd.
Song of the Moon, A.
Spanish Needle, The.
Spring in New Hampshire.
Tired Worker, The.
To O. E. A.
To the White Fiends.
Tropics in New York, The.
Two-an'-six.
When Dawn Comes to the City; New York.
White House, The.
White Houses.
Wild Goat, The.

Mackay, Eric
Ecstasy.
In Tuscany.
Mary Arden.
Waking of the Lark, The.

MacKay, Isabel Ecclestone
Fires of Driftwood.
Helen—Old.
When as a Lad.

McKay, J. T.
Making Port.

McKay, James Thompson
Cenotaph of Lincoln, The.

Mackay, Jessie
Burial of Sir John McKenzie, The.
Dunedin in the Gloaming.
For Love of Appin.
Grey Company, The.
In Galilee.
Maisrie.
Noosing of the Sun-God, The.
October in New Zealand.
Ortygia.
Song of the Drift Weed.

McKay, Lois Weakley
Night.

MacKay, Louise Alexander (John Smalacombe)
Admonition for Spring.
Battle Hymn of the Spanish Rebellion.
Erotica Antiqua, *sel.*
I Wish My Tongue Were a Quiver.
Ill-tempered Lover, The, *sel.*
Look, I Have Thrown All Right.
Now There Is Nothing Left.
Nunc Scio, Quid Sit Amor.
Propertian.
Snow Story.

Mackay, Lydia Miller
Dewdrops, The.

Mackay, Margaret
Asleep in Jesus.

MacKaye, Percy
Automobile, The.
Goethals, the Prophet Engineer.
Hymn of the New World.
Look Inland Now.
Man went down to Panama, A.
Prayer of the Peoples, A.
To Sleep.

McKee, Gladys
First Geography.
First Reader (Fifth Reading).
Legacy.
Spring Cellar.

McKee, Lucie
Query.

McKeehan, Irene Pettit
Closing the Doors.

McKeighan, Irene
Crowd, The.

Mackellar, Dorothea
Dusk in the Domain.
Fancy Dress.
In a Southern Garden.
My Country.

Mackellar (continued)
Open Sea, The.
McKellar, John Alexander Ross
Football Field; Evening.
Fourth Napoleon, *sel.*
Love in a Cottage.
Res Publica.
Retreat from Heaven, The.
Twelve o'Clock Boat.
MacKellar, Thomas
Jesus First and Jesus Last.
Working in the Vineyard.
McKelway, St. Clair
Boogie-woogie Ballads.
Mackenzie, Compton
Lilies of the Field, The.
Song of Parting, A.
Mackenzie, Kenneth
Caesura.
Confession.
Fairy Tale, A.
Heat.
Legerdemain.
Moonlit Doorway, The.
Old Inmate, An.
Pat Young.
Snake, The.
Table-Birds.
Tree at Post 4, The.
Mackie, Albert D.
Molecatcher.
New Spring, A.
Young Man and the Young Nun, The.
McKinnell, H. J.
Risen Lord, The.
McKinney, Laurence
Compromise.
English Horn.
Hubbub in Hub.
Old School Tie-up, The.
Song to My Love.
McKinney, Pearl Burnside
What Lack I Yet?
MacKinstry, Elizabeth
Man Who Hid His Own Front Door, The.
Mackintosh, H. S.
"Il Est Cocu—le Chef de Gare!"
Mackintosh, Newton
Fin de Siècle.
Limerick: "Cleopatra, who thought they maligned her."
Lucy Lake.
Optimism.
Pessimism.
McKuen, Rod
Brownstone.
Spring Song.
McLachlan, Alexander
And art thou come to this at last.
Backwoods Hero, A, *sel.*
Emigrant, The, *sel.*
God, *sel.*
Hail, Thou great mysterious Being!
O! Come to the Greenwood Shade.
Song: "Old England is eaten by knaves."
To an Indian Skull, *sel.*
We Live in a Rickety House.
When my gloomy hour comes on me.
Where yonder ancient willow weeps.
Woman, *sel.*
McLachlan, H. D. C.
Cattle-Round-up, The.
McLaren, Floris Clark
Crusoe.
Frozen Fire.
No More the Slow Stream.
Tide Trapped.
Visit by Water.
Maclaren, Hamish
Dolphins, The.
Harp in the Rigging.
Sailor and Inland Flower.
Maclean, Sorley
Dain do Eimhir, *sels.*
Dain Eile, *sel.*
I Walked with My Reason.
Knightsbridge of Libya.
My eye is not on Calvary, nor on Bethlehem the Blessed.
Nightmare, The.
To a Depraved Lying Woman.
McLean, William Alfred, Jr
War.
MacLeish, Archibald
Aeterna Poetae Memoria.
Ah How the Throat of a Girl.
Alien.
America is West and the wind blowing.
America was always promises.
America Was Promises, *sels.*
American Letter.
. . . & Forty-second Street.
And we marched against them there in the next spring.
Argument, The.
Ars Poetica.
Bernál Díaz's Preface to His Book.
Brave New World.
Burying Ground by the Ties.
Calypso's Island.
Captured.
Conquistador, *sels.*
Cook County.
Curse God and Die, You Said to Me.
Dawn on the Wall-Head There.
Discovery of This Time.
Dr. Sigmund Freud Discovers the Sea Shell.
"Dover Beach"—A Note to That Poem.
Dusk.
Einstein.
Eleven.
Empire Builders.
End of the World, The.
Epistle to Be Left in the Earth.
Ever Since.
Ezry.
Fall of the City, The; a Verse Play for Radio.
Final Chorus: "Bellies bitter with drinking."
Frescoes for Mr. Rockefeller's City.
Geography of This Time.
Hamlet of A. MacLeish, The, *sel.*
He lies upon his bed.
Hypocrite Auteur.
Immortal Autumn.
Immortal Helix.
In My Thirtieth Year.
Invocation to the Social Muse.
J. B., *sel.*
L'an Trentiesme de Mon Eage [*or* Age].
Land of the Free.
Landscape as a Nude.
Le Secret Humain.
Learned Men, The.
Lines for an Interment.
Lovers who must say farewell.
Memorial Rain.
Memory Green.
Men.
Music and Drum.
My Naked Aunt.
Night after night I lie like this listening.
"Not Marble nor the Gilded Monuments."
Oil Painting of the Artist as the Artist.
Panic, *sels.*
Poem in Prose.
Poet Speaks from the Visitors' Gallery, A.
Pole Star for This Year.
Pony Rock.
Prologue: "These alternate nights and days, these seasons."
Psyche with the Candle.
Reasons for Music.
Reconciliation, The.
Reed-Player, The.
Reply to Mr. Wordsworth, *sel.*
Reproach to Dead Poets.
Salute.
Seafarer.
Signature for Tempo.
Silence, The.
Silent Slain, The.
Snow Fall, The.
Snowflake Which Is Now and Hence Forever, The.
Space-time, our scientists tell us, is impervious.
Speech to a Crowd.
Speech to Those Who Say Comrade.
Theory of Poetry.
Too-late Born, The.
Unfinished History, An.
Verses for a Centennial.
Vicissitudes of the Creator.
Voice of the Announcer.
Voice of the Studio Announcer.
We saw that city on the inland sea.
We wonder whether the dream of American liberty.
Weather.
What Must, *sel.*
What Riddle Asked the Sphinx.
What the Old Women Say.
What the Serpent Said to Adam.
Where the Hayfields Were.
Wildwest.
Words in Time.
You, Andrew Marvell.
Young Dead Soldiers, The.
McLellan, Isaac, Jr
New England's Dead.
MacLellan, Robert
Sang: "There's a reid lowe in yer cheek."
"Macleod, Fiona" (William Sharp)
Bells of Youth, The.
Bugles of Dreamland, The.
Cross of the Dumb, The.
Dawn amid Scotch Firs.
Dead Calm and Mist, A.
Deep peace, pure white of the moon to you.
Desire.
Dim Face of Beauty.
Dream Fantasy.
Dreams within Dreams.
Dull day darkens to its close, The.
Field Mouse, The.
Founts of Song, The.
From the Hills of Dream.
High Noon at Midsummer on the Campagna ("High noon,/ And from the purple-veiled hills").
Hushing Song.
Invocation of Peace, *sel.*
Isle of Lost Dreams.
Last Aboriginal, The.
Loch Coruisk (Skye).
Madonna Natura.
Moon-Child, The.
Mystic's Prayer, The.
On a Nightingale in April.
Paris Nocturne, A.
Red Poppies.
Redeemer, The.
Rose of Flame, The.
Shule, Agrah!
Sleep.
Song: "Love in my heart: oh, heart of me, heart of me."

Sonnet VII: "Dull day darkens to its close, The. The sheen."
Sospiri di Roma, *sels.*
Susurro.
Swimmer of Nemi, The.
Unknown Wind, The.
Vale, Amor!
Valley of Pale Blue Flowers, The.
Valley of Silence, The.
Washer of the Ford, The.
Wasp, The.
Weaver of Snow, The.
White Peace, The.
White Peacock, The.

McLeod Irene Rutherford (Mrs. Aubrey de Sélincourt)
Beyond the murk that swallows me.
Is Love, Then, So Simple?
Lone Dog.
Prayer, A: "O Love, give me a passionate heart."
Rebel.
Sea-Song.
Shall I be fearful thus to speak my mind.
So Beautiful You Are, Indeed.
Song: "How do I love you?"
Song from "April."
Sonnet: "Between my love and me there runs a thread."
Sonnet: "In heaven there is a star I call my own."
Sonnet: "Shall I be fearful thus to speak my mind."
Sonnet: "Sweet, when I think how summer's smallest bird."
Sonnet: "When sane men gather in to talk of love."
Sonnets, *sels.*
Sweet, when I think how summer's smallest bird.
Unborn.
When My Beloved Sleeping Lies.
When sane men gather in to talk of Love.

Macleod, Joseph Gordon ("Adam Drinan) "
Autumnal Evening, An.
Below the dancing larches freckled.
Ecliptic, The: Cancer, or, The Crab, *sel.*
Love Song.
Men of the Rocks, *sel.*
Moonpoison, mullock of sacrifice.
Our pastures are bitten and bare.
Sagittarius or the Archer.

Macleod, Norman (1812-72)
Creed, A.
Trust in God and Do the Right.

MacLiesh, Archibald Fleming ("Archibald Fleming)
Destroyers, The, *sel.*
Jungle, The, *sel.*
Now all things melt and shift.
Report.

MacLow, Jackson
1st Dance—Making Things New—6 February 1964.
2nd Dance—Seeing Lines—6 February 1964.
10th Dance—Coming On as a Horn—20 February 1964.
3rd Dance—Making a Structure with a Roof or under a Roof—6-7 February 1964.
13th Dance—Matching Parcels—21 February 1964.
37th Dance—Banding—22 March 1964.
12th Dance—Getting Leather by Language—21 Februray 1964.
29th Dance—Having an Instrument—22 March 1964.

"McM."
Allegro.

McMahan, Helen
October.

MacMahon, Bryan
Corner Boys.

MacMahon, M. J.
Jack Dempsey's Grave.
Nonpareil's Grave, The.

MacManus, Anna Johnston *See* **"Carbery, Ethna"**

MacManus, Francis
Pattern of Saint Brendan.

MacManus, Seumas
Hedge Schoolmasters, The.
In Dark Hour.
Lullaby: "Softly now the burn is rushing."
Resignation.
Shane O'Neill.

MacManus, Theodore F.
Cave Sedem.

McMaster, Guy Humphreys
Carmen Bellicosum.
Old Continentals, The.

McMichael, James
Passion, A.

McMillan, Herman L.
Equality.
Looking for Equality.
Lost Love.
Nocturnal.

McMillan, Hugh
Waterfall, A.

MacMurray, Niall
Vanished Night, The.

Macnab, Roy
Child of the Long Grass.
El Alamein Revisited.
India became his jasmined youth, Goa.
Majuba Hill.
Man of Grass, The, *sel.*
River, The.
Road to Bologna, The.
Settler, The.
Seven of the Clock.
Stages.

McNabb, Vincent
Spotless Maid, The.

Macnaghten, Hugh
Idyll: "In Switzerland one idle day."

McNail, Stanley
Elsie's House.
House on Maple Hill, The.
Lottie Mae ("Lottie was a skinny child").
Secrets of Cisterns, The.
Witch, The.

Macnair, J. H.
Household Gods.

MacNamara, Brinsley
On Seeing Swift in Laracor.

Macnamara, Donogh *See* **Mac-Con-Mara, Donogh**

MacNamara, Francis
Diminutivus Ululans.

MacNamee, Giolla Brighde
To an Anti-poetical Priest.

McNeal-Sweeney, Mildred Isabel *See***Sweeney, Mildred Isabel McNeal**

MacNeice, Louis
Alcohol.
Among These Turf-Stacks.
And Love Hung Still.
And man is a spirit.
And the Lord Was Not in the Whirlwind.
Aubade.
August.
August is nearly over, the people.
Autobiography.
Autumn Journal, *sels.*
Bagpipe Music.
Ballade in a Bad Temper.
Ballade of England.
Bar-Room Matins.
Birmingham.
British Museum Reading Room, The.
Brother Fire.
Burnt Bridge, The.
Carrickfergus.
Christina.
Circe.
Coda.
Conversation.
Corner Seat.
County Sligo.
Cradle Song: "Clock's untiring fingers wind the wool of darkness, The."
Cradle Song: "Sleep, my darling, sleep."
Creditor, The.
Death-Wish, The.
Didymus.
Dublin.
Eclogue for Christmas, An.
Elegy for Minor Poets.
Entered in the Minutes.
Entirely.
Explorations.
For X.
Galway.
Glacier, The.
Good-bye Now, Plato and Hegel.
Hands and Eyes.
Heated Minutes, The.
Hold-Up.
Holes in the Sky, *sel.*
Individualist Speaks, The.
Jehu.
Jigsaw III.
June Thunder.
Kingdom, The, *sels.*
Leaving Barra.
Les Sylphides.
Libertine, The.
Little dapper man but with shiny elbows, A.
London Rain.
Meeting Point.
Mixer, The.
Morning Sun.
Museums.
Nature Morte.
Neutrality.
Nightmare leaves fatigue.
Nostalgia.
Now we are back to normal, now the mind is.
Nuts in May.
Ode: "Tonight is so coarse with chocolate."
Order to View.
Perseus.
Prayer before Birth.
Prayer in Mid-Passage.
Prognosis.
Refugees.
Sense of Smell, The.
Sleep serene, avoid the backward.
Slow Movement.
Snow.
Spring Voices.
Springboard, The.
Strand, The.
Streets of Laredo, The.
Stylite.
Suicide.
Sunday Morning.
Sunlight on the Garden, The.
Their Last Will and Testament.
These days are misty, insulated, mute.
To Mary—A Dedication.
Toast, A.
Trilogy for X, *sel.*
Truism, The.
Turf Stacks.
Under the surface of flux and of fear there

MacNeice (continued)
is an underground movement.
Valediction.
Venus' Speech.
Visitations: VII, *sel.*
Wall, The.
Wessex Guidebook.
Whitmonday.
MacNeill, Hector
My Boy Tammy.
Macomber, W.
Christ Is Coming.
Macourek, Milos
Punching Clock, The.
McPeek, James A. S.
For Transient Things.
Macpherson, James ("Ossian")
Carthon, a Poem.
Cath-Loda, *sel.*
Cuthullin sat by Tura's wall.
Fingal: An Ancient Epic Poem, *sel.*
"King of Morven," Carthon said, "I fall in the midst of my course."
Night is dull and dark.
Ossian's Address to the Sun.
Six Bards, The, *sel.*
Songs of Selma, The.
Tale of the times of old, A!/ Why, thou wanderer unseen!
Macpherson, Jay
Beauty of Job's Daughters, The.
Boatman, The.
Eurynome.
Eve in Reflection.
Fisherman, The.
Go Take the World.
Hail Wedded Love!
Ill Wind, The.
Innocents, The.
Leviathan.
Marriage of Earth and Heaven, The.
Martyrs, The.
Swan, The.
Third Eye, The.
Woods No More, The.
MacVeagh, F. W.
Here Ananias lies because he lied.
McWebb, Elizabeth Upham
At Mrs. Appleby's.
Macy, Arthur
Boston Cats, The.
Peppery Man, The.
Rollicking Mastodon, The.
Macy, George
Daphne and Apollo.
Maddock, Anne Elizabeth
Spring.
Maddow, Ben
City, The.
Madeleva, Sister Mary
Apology for Youth.
As One Finding Peace.
Beech Trees.
Christmas in Provence.
Design for a Stream-lined Sunrise.
Dialogue.
Gates.
In Desert Places.
Knights Errant.
Midnight Mass.
Motif for Mary's Dolors.
New Things and Old.
November Afternoons.
Nun Speaks to Mary, A.
October Birthday.
Of Wounds.
Peace by Night.
Pepper Tree, The.
Return.
Riddles.
Snow Storm.
Madge, Charles
Adventures of my separate bark, The.
Among all the myths and masks and make-believes.
At War.
Ballad of Hope and Fear.
Birds of Tin, The.
Delusions VIII ("Placed in a country on a desert verging").
Delusions IV ("Sometimes at evening travellers have heard").
Delusions VI ("Without surprise, on that not distant shore").
First, erected ironworks in a spiry hollow.
Flesh is sad but there are books unread, The.
Fortune.
Hours of the Planets, The.
In Conjunction.
Lusty Juventus.
Monument, A.
Nightly Deed, A.
Now English eyes the cancerous sun behold!
Poem by Stages, *sels.*
Rumba of the Three Lost Souls.
Solar Creation.
Times, The.
To Make a Bridge.
To us, goddess, who are in barbary.
Madgett Naomi Long (Naomi Long Witherspoon)
Alabama Centennial.
Midway.
Mortality.
Nocturne: "See how dark the night settles on my face."
Reckoning, The.
Refugee.
Stark day corrodes the silver of the dream.
Trinity: a Dream Sequence, *sels.*
Woman with Flower.
You would not recognize yourself if I should tell you.
Madison, Dolly
La Fayette.
Mael-Isu
Deus Meus.
Maeterlinck, Maurice
Last Words, The.
Song: "Three little maidens they have slain."
Magaret, Helene
Impiety, *sel.*
Lord, I have not time to pray.
Thoroughbred, The.
Magee, John Gillespie, Jr
High Flight.
Magee, William Kirkpatrick *See* **"Eglinton, John"**
"Maggie."
Passionate Encyclopedia Britannica Reader to His Love.
Magil, A. B.
They Are Ours.
Maginn, William
I Give My Soldier Boy a Blade.
Irishman and the Lady, The.
St. Patrick of Ireland, My Dear!
Soldier-Boy, The.
Magrath, Andrew
Andrew Magrath's Reply to John O'Tuomy.
Lament of the Mangaire Sugach.
Maguire, Francis
Address to the Body.
And Rest in a Flame.
Bull, The.
People as Flowers.
Root, The.
Sin, The; a Definition.
Sweet Land.
To a Dog Barking at Night.
Maguire, Robert
Prayer: "Prayer—the fragrance of a flower."
Maguire, Tom
Bold Robert Emmet.
Mahlmann, Siegfried August
Allah.
Our Country.
Mahony, Francis Sylvester ("Father Prout")
Ad Leuconoen.
Attractions of a Fashionable Irish Watering Place, The.
Bells of Shandon, The.
In Mortem Venerabilis Andreae Prout Carmen.
L'Envoy to W. L. H. Ainsworth, Esq.
Malbrouck.
Panegyric on Geese, A.
Piper's Progress, The.
Red-Breast of Aquitania, The.
Sabine Farmer's Serenade, The.
Shandon Bells, The.
Solvitur Acris Hiems.
Maiano, Dante da
Sonnet: He Craves Interpreting of a Dream of His.
Sonnet: To Dante Alighieri (He Interprets Dante Alighieri's Dream).
Mailer, Norman
Dr. Hu/ speaks.
Eternities.
Mains, J. Riley
Good Old Days of '50, '1, and '2, The.
Mair, Alexander William
Hesiod, 1908.
Mair, Charles
Buffalo Herds, The.
Dreamland, *sel.*
Fireflies, The, *sel.*
He comes! Yohewah! the Great Spirit, comes.
How dreamy-dark it is!
Iena's Song.
Lefroy in the Forest, *abr.*
Once we were strong.
Tecumseh, *sels.*
Tell me more of those unrivalled wastes.
There was a time on this fair continent.
We are not wholly blest who use the earth.
We left/ The silent forest.
Winter.
Mais, Roger
I, Remembering.
Maisun, Lady
She Scorns Her Husband the Caliph.
Maitland, Dollie *See* **Radford, Dollie**
Maitland, Sir Richard
Aganis the Thievis of Liddisdale.
Solace in Age.
Major, Clarence
Brother Malcolm: Waste Limit.
Celebrated Return.
Down Wind against the Highest Peaks.
Vietnam #4.
Major, Joseph
Poem for Thel—the Very Tops of Trees.
Malam, Charles
Dusk in the Sugar Woods.
House Demolished.
Steam Shovel.
Malan, César
It Is Not Death to Die.
No, No, It Is Not Dying.
What Is Death?
Malanga, Gerard
Benedetta Barzini.
Temperature.
Malangatana, Valente Goenha

To the Anxious Mother.
Woman.
Maleska, Eugene T.
Assembly; Harlem School.
Countee Cullen.
To a Negro Boy Graduating.
Malet, David *See* **Mallet, David**
Malins, Joseph
Fence or an Ambulance, A.
Mallalleu, Herbert B.
Cozzo Grillo.
Look for Me on England.
New Year's Eve.
Next of Kin.
Platform Goodbye.
To Naples.
Mallarmé, Stéphane
Afternoon of a Faun, The.
Anguish.
Another Fan Belonging to Mademoiselle Mallarmé.
Apreès-Midi d'un faune, L'.
Flowers.
Funeral Toast.
Hérodiade, *sel.*
Little Air.
Proud of my music, let me often make.
Pure Nails Brightly Flashing.
Saint.
Sea Breeze.
Sea-Wind.
Sigh.
Sonnet: "This virgin, beautiful and lively day."
Swan, The.
To mine own self I am a wilderness.
Mallet [*or* Malet *or* Malloch], David
Birks of Endermay, The.
William and Margaret.
Mallet, David, *and* **James Thomson** *See* **Thomson, James,** *and* **David Mallet**
Malloch, David *See* **Mallet, David**
Malloch, Douglas
"Ain't It Fine Today!"
Be the Best.
Be the Best of Whatever You Are.
Comrade Rides Ahead, A.
Family Trees.
God's Mothers.
Good Timber.
If Easter Eggs Would Hatch.
It's Fine Today.
June.
My Son.
November.
Things of the Spirit, The.
When the Drive Goes Down.
Mallock, William Hurrell
Human Life.
Lines: "Homeless man goes, even on life's sunniest slope."
Malon de Chaide, Pedro
Conversion of the Magdalene, The, *sel.*
Encircling Thee Thy holy brides.
Sonnet: "O patience, that dost wait eternally!"
"Malone, Carroll." *See* **McBurney, William B**
Malone, Walter
Agnostic's Creed, The.
He Who Hath Loved.
Masterpiece, The.
October in Tennessee.
Opportunity.
Malouf, David
At My Grandmother's.
Manchester,——
Mister Angleworm.
Manchester, Leslie Clare
Revelation, The.
Mandel, Eli W.
David.
Estevan, Saskatchewan.
Fire Place, The.
Four Songs from the Book of Samuel.
It has been hours in these rooms.
Job.
Merits of Laughter and Lust.
Metamorphosis.
Minotaur Poems, *sels.*
Orpheus.
Phaeton.
Song: "When the echo of the last footstep dies."
Mandeville, Bernard
Fable of the Bees, The, *sel.*
Grumbling Hive, The: or, Knaves Turn'd Honest.
Mangan, James Clarence
Advice against Travel.
Cean-Salla.
Dawning of the Day, The.
Disaster.
Dying Enthusiast, The.
Enthusiasm.
Gone in the Wind.
Hymn for Pentecost.
Karamanian Exile, The.
Love.
Lover's Farewell, The.
Mariner's Bride, The.
Nameless One, The.
Night Is Falling, The.
Night Is Nearing.
St. Patrick's Hymn before Tara[h].
Saw-Mill, The.
Shapes and Signs.
Siberia.
Song: "O, strew the way with rosy flowers."
Sonnet: "Bird that discoursest from yon poplar bough."
Soul and Country.
Three Proverbs.
Time of the Barmecides, The.
To Amine.
To My Native Land.
To the Ingleezee Khafir, Calling Himself Djann Bool Djenkinzun.
Triplet on the Reign of the Great Sultan, A.
Twenty Golden Years Ago.
Vision of Connaught in the Thirteenth Century, A.
Volto Sciolto e Pensieri Stretti.
World, The; a Ghazel.
Manger, Itzig
Adam and Eve.
Autumn.
I Am the Autumn.
Jealous Adam.
Mother Sarah's Lullaby.
Mangoaela, Z. D.
Boast of Masopha.
Manifold, John Streeter
Bunyip and the Whistling Kettle, The.
Camouflage.
Defensive Position.
Deserter, The.
Fife Tune.
Griesly Wife, The.
"Heureux Qui Comme Ulysse."
Listening to a Broadcast.
Night Piece.
Ration Party.
Sirens, The.
Song: "My dark-headed Käthchen, my spit-kitten darling."
Suburban Lullaby.
Tomb of Lieutenant John Learmonth, A.I.F., The.
Manilius, Marcus
Times, The.
Mann, Leonard
At Manly.
Earth, The.
Escape.
Freedom.
Girls and Soldiers Singing.
Love of Swans, The.
Meditation in Winter.
Soldier Overseas.
Manning, Frederic
At Even.
Kore.
Sacrifice.
Sign, The.
Trenches, The.
Manning, James Harold
I have been,/ Three separate times, in war.
What Is Truth? *sel.*
Manning, Rena M.
To a Kitten.
Manning, Robert *See* **Mannyng, Robert**
Mannix, Mary E.
All Souls' Eve.
Mannyng [*or* Manning], Robert
Bishop's Harp, The.
No Thyng Ys to Man So Dere.
Praise of Women.
Round Table, The.
Manrique, Gómez
On the Bad Government of Toledo.
Manrique, Jorge
Coplas on the Death of His Father.
Ode on the Death of His Father.
Mansel, W. L.
Sun's Perpendicular Rays, The.
Mansfield, Katherine
Little Brother's Secret.
Sanary.
Sleeping Together.
To L. H. B.
Two Nocturnes.
Voices of the Air.
Mansfield, Margery Swett
Blessing Mrs. Larkin.
Mansfield, Richard
Eagle's Song, The.
Voice, The.
Mantuan, Baptista Spagnuoli
Eglogs of the Poet B. Mantuan Carmelitan, The, *sel.*
Second Egloge Entituled Fortunatus, The.
Manville, Marion (Mrs. Marion Manville Pope)
Lee's Parole.
Surrender of New Orleans, The.
Manyase, L. T.
Mother Crab and Her Family, The.
Vusumzi's Song.
Manzano, Juan Fransico
My Thirty Years.
Manzoni, Alessandro
Fifth of May, The—Napoleon.
Ode, *sel.*
Soffermati sull' arida sponda, *sel.*
With humble and discouraged mien.
Mao Tse-tung
Midstream.
Mapes, Edith L.
Oh if They Only Knew!
Shall I Pray On?
Maragall, Juan
Canto Espiritual.
Night of the Immaculate Conception.
Marais, Eugene
Dance of the Rain, The.
Desert Lark, The.
Heart-of-the-Daybreak.
Sorceress, The.

Maran, René
Human Soul.
Marcabrun
At the Fountain.
Marcela de Carpio de San Félix, Sister
Amor Mysticus.
Marcelin, Philippe Thoby- *See* **Thoby-Marcelin, Philippe**
March, Auzias
What Guardian Counsels?
March, Daniel
Hark! The Voice of Jesus Calling.
March, Joseph Moncure
City Autumn.
Marcus, Morton
Letter from the Great Society.
Look Closely.
What I Know.
Marcus Argentarius *See* **Argentarius, Marcus**
Margaret of Navarre
Recipe for a Happy Life.
Margaret Teresa, Sister
Matthew.
Woodland.
Margetson, George Reginald
Fledgling Bard and the Poetry Society, The, *much abr.*
Margolis, Silvia
Never Ask Me Why.
"Maria del Occidente." *See* **Brooks, Maria Gowan**
Maria del Rey, Sister
"Haec Est Domus Dei et Porta Coeli."
Marie de France
Chartivel, *sel.*
Sarrazine's Song to Her Dead Lover.
Song from "Chartivel."
Would I Might Go Far over Sea.
"Marie Josephine." *See* **Hemenway, Abby Maria**
Mariella, Sister
Blue Larkspur.
Jefferson Highway, The.
Sheep Herd, The.
Marinetti, Filippo Tommaso
Against the Hope of Reconstruction.
Marini, Giambattista *See* **Marino, Giovanni Battista**
Marino, Giovanni Battista
Bed, The.
Marinoni, Rosa Zagnoni
Ash Wednesday.
At Sunrise.
Crushed Fender.
For a New Home.
Pause.
Who Are My People?
Maris Stella, Sister
Afternoon in a Tree.
Bay Violets.
Cause of Our Joy.
Grapes.
I Who Had Been Afraid.
It is the Reed.
Landscape with Children.
Lines for a Feast of Our Lady.
Love Is Not Solace.
Now That Can Never Be Done.
Out of Darkness.
Ox and Donkey's Carol.
Oxford Bells.
Pelicans My Father Sees, The.
San Marco Museum, Florence.
This One Heart-shaken.
Voice, The.
Mark, Rickman
Snow in Town.
"Mark Twain." *See* **"Twain, Mark"**
Markham, Edwin
Anchored to the Infinite.
Angelus, The, *sel.*
Ascension, The.
At Little Virgil's Window.
Avengers, The.
Behold, O world, the toiling man.
Breathless Awe.
Brotherhood.
Christ of the Andes, The.
Color of the ground was in him, the red earth, The.
Conscripts of the Dream, *sel.*
Consecration of the Common Way, The.
Courage, All.
Creed, A ("Here is the truth in a little creed").
Creed, A ("There is a destiny that makes us brothers").
Day and the Work, The.
Dream, The.
Duty.
Earth Is Enough.
Epitaph, An: "Let us not think of our departed dead."
Errand Imperious, The.
Father's Business, The.
For the New Year.
Forgotten Man, The.
Free Nation, A.
Gift of Work, The.
Give thanks, O heart, for the high souls.
Great Guest Comes, The.
Guard of the Sepulcher, A.
Harvest Song, A.
How Shall We Honor Them?
How the Great Guest Came.
How to Go and Forget.
If He Should Come.
Inbrothered ("There is a destiny").
Incarnation.
Invisible Bride, The.
Joy of the Hills, The.
Joy of the Morning.
Last Furrow, The.
League of Love in Action, The.
Lincoln Slain.
Lincoln, the Man of the People.
Lincoln Triumphant.
Live and Help Live.
Look into the Gulf, A.
Lord of All, The.
Love's Vigil.
Man-making.
Man-Test.
Man With the Hoe, The.
My Comrade.
Nail-torn God, The.
Need of the Hour, The.
New Trinity, The.
Night Moths, The.
O Christ of Olivet, you hushed the wars.
Opportunity.
Our Dead.
Our Dead, Overseas.
Outwitted.
Peace.
Pilgrim, The.
Place of Peace, The.
Poet, The.
Poetry.
Prayer, A: "Teach me, Father, how to go."
Preparedness.
Quatrain: "Here is the Truth in a little creed."
Revelation.
Right Kind of People, The.
Rules for the Road.
Saint Patrick.
Shine on Me, Secret Splendor.
Song for Heroes, A.
Task That Is Given to You, The.
Testing, The.
Thanksgiving Rosary, A.
Third Wonder, The.
Toiler, The, *sel.*
True Work Is Worship.
Two at a Fireside.
Two Taverns.
Unbelievable, The.
Victory in Defeat.
Virgilia, *sel.*
Wharf of Dreams, The.
What was I back in the world's first wonder?
Whirlwind Road, The.
Wind and Lyre.
Young Lincoln.
Your Tears.
Markham, Gervase
Fragment: "I walk'd [*or* walked] along a stream for pureness rare."
Markham, Lucia Clark
Bluebells.
Markish, Peretz
We Reached Out Far.
Marks, Edward B.
Little Lost Child, The.
My Mother Was a Lady; or, If Jack Were Only Here.
Marks, Godfrey
Sailing.
Marks, Margaret
Chorus for Refusal.
Lady with Arrows.
Tactic.
Marks, S. J.
How.
Marlatt, Earl Bowman
Crucifixion.
Malachi.
Paul.
Pax Nobiscum.
Peter.
World-Nation, A.
Zechariah.
Marlowe, Christopher
Hero and Leander.
Ah Faustus,/ Now hast thou but one bare hour [*or* hower] to live.
And ride in triumph through Persepolis!
Beauty.
Bloody Conquests of Mighty Tamburlaine, The.
But, leaving these vain trifles of men's souls.
By this, Leander, being near the land.
Conquests of Tamburlaine, The.
Disdains Zenocrate to live with me?
Divine Zenocrate.
Dr. Faustus.
Edward the Second, *sels.*
Emperor of the Threefold World.
End of Dr. Faustus, The.
End of Faustus, The.
Epilogue: "Cut is the branch that might have grown full straight."
Face of Helen, The.
Fair Is Too Foul an Epithet.
Faustus.
Faustus Faces His Doom.
Faustus to Helen.
Finale.
Forward, then, ye jades!
Helen.
Her veil was artificial flowers and leaves.
Hero the Fair[e].
I must have wanton poets, pleasant wits.
If All the Pens That Ever Poets Held.
It Lies Not in Our Power to Love or Hate.
Jew of Malta, The, *sels.*
Last Hour of Faustus, The.
Look for rebellion, look to be depos'd.

Love at First Sight.
Mine Argosy from Alexandria.
Nature That Framed [*or* Fram'd] Us of Four Elements.
Now Clear the Triple Region of the Air.
O Hero, Hero, thus he cry'dc full oft.
On this feast day, O curséd day and hour.
Passionate Shepherd to His Love, The,

Perfect Bliss and Sole Felicity.
Persepolis.
She stay'd not for her robes, but straight arose.
Shepherd to His Love, The.
Shepherd's Plea, The.
Song of Ithamore, The.
Tamburlaine the Great, *sels.*
Tell me what is that Lucifer thy Lord.
"That I might have unto my paramour."
Thirst of reign and sweetness of a crown, The.
Those walléd garrisons will I subdue.
To Entertain Divine Zenocrate.
Tragedie of Edward the Second, The.
Tragical History of Dr. Faustus, The.
Virgins, in vain you labour to prevent.
Was This the Face.
Who Ever Loved, That Not at First Sight?

Marlowe, Christopher *and* Thomas Nashe
I Have an Orchard.
Tragedy of Dido, The, *sel.*

Marot, Clément
Ballade of a Friar.
Friar Lubin.
Love Lesson, A.
Madame d'Albert's [*or* d'Albret's] Laugh.
Of Himself.
On Her Laugh.
Posy Ring, The.
To Anne.
Toast to a Departing Duchess.
Yes and No.

Marquina, Eduardo
Montoro's Song against Count Alvaro de Luna, High Constable of Castile.

Marquis, Don (Donald Robert Marquis)
Another Villon-ous Variation.
Archy a Low Brow.
Archy and Mehitabel, *sels.*
Archy Confesses.
Archy Does His Part, *sel.*
Archy Experiences a Seizure.
Archy, the Cockroach, Speaks.
Archygrams.
Archys Autobiography.
Archys Last Name.
Archys Life of Mehitabel, *sels.*
Artists Shouldn't Have Offspring.
As the skull of man grows broader.
Awakening, The.
Ballade: "Outcast bones from a thousand biers."
Ballade of the Under Side.
Certain Maxims of Archy.
Chant Royal of the Dejected Dipsomaniac.
Cheerio My Deario.
Down in a Wine Vault.
Fate Is Unfair.
Flattered Lightning Bug, The.
For I Am Sad.
Freddy the Rat Perishes.
Gentleman of Fifty Soliloquizes, A.
God-Maker, Man, The.
Grotesques, *sels.*
Heir and Serf.
Hen and the Oriole, The.
Hero Cockroach, The.
Honey Bee, The.
Hot-Weather Song, A.
I Have Looked Inward, *sels.*
I oft stand in the snow at dawn.
I rose. . .I rose. . .
I sometimes think that I will.
In the Bayou.
Jokesmith's Vacation, The.
King Cophetua and the Beggar Maid.
Lilies.
Limerick: "There was a young fellow named Sydney."
Little While, A.
Mehitabel Sings a Song.
Mehitabel Tries Marriage.
Mrs. Swartz.
Name, The.
Noah an' Jonah an' Cap'n John Smith.
Only Thy Dust.
Pete the Parrot and Shakespeare.
Prohibition.
Quinks, The.
Reverie.
Savage Portraits.
Small Talk.
Song of a Thousand Years.
Song of Mehitabel, The.
There was a locked door.
Time time said old King Tut.
To a Lost Sweetheart, *sels.*
Tomcat, The.
Tragedy of the Deep, A.
Tristram and Isolt.
Trouble.
Unrest.
Wages, The.
Wail of Archy, The, *sel.*
Warty Bliggens, the Toad.
Was it fancy, sweet nurse.
When Ones Loves Tensely.
When Whistler's Mother's Picture's frame.
Yes, nothing seems changeless, but Change.

Marr, Barbara
Prayer: "Lord, make me sensitive to the sight."

Marriott, Anne
Beaver Pond.
Prairie Graveyard.
Sandstone.
Search.
Wind Our Enemy, The, *sel.*
Woodyards in the Rain.

Marriott, Sir James
Ode on Lyric Poetry.

Marriott, John
Devonshire Lane, The.
On John Donne's Book of Poems.

Marron, Os
Nocturnal.

Marryat, Frederick
Captain Stood on the Carronade, The.
Dog Fiend, The.
Old Navy, The.
Snarleyyow; or, The Dog Fiend, *sel.*

Mars, Ann (Annalita Marsigli)
Shadow.

Marsh, Daniel L.
Greatest Person in the Universe, The.

Marsh, E. L.
Magic Piper, The.

Marshall, Barbara
Colonized Mind.
Little Black Boy.
On Philosophy.
Request.

Marshall, Edward
Leave the Word Alone.
Memory as Memorial in the Last.
Sept. 1957.
Two Poems.

Marshall, Jack
Bearings.
For Kathleen, Gone on a Brief Journey.
For the Dancer, Fred Herko.
Forced Entry.
Hitchhiker.
Light Poem.
On the President's State Visit to Mexico.
Setting Out.

Marshall, James
Oregon Trail, 1851.

Marshall, Lenore G.
Invented a Person.

Marshall, Tom
Astrology.

Marshall, William E.
Brookfield.
But see this happy village festival.
To a Mayflower.

Marsman, Hendrik
Valley of Sleep, The.
Zodiac, The, *sel.*

Marson, Una
Hunted.
Nightfall.

Marston, John
Ambitious Gorgons, wide-mouthed Lamians.
Antonio and Mellida, *sel.*
Antonio's Revenge, *sel.*
Dutch Courtesan, The, *sel.*
I cannot sleepe, my eyes ill neighbouring lids.
Malcontent, The, *sel.*
My thoughts are fixed in contemplation.
O Love, How Strangely Sweet.
Proemium in Librum Primum.
Prologue: "Rawish dank of clumsy winter ramps, The."
Prologue to "Antonio's Revenge."
Satire, *sel.*
Satire VIII; "Curio, ay me! Thy mistress' monkey's dead!"
Satire X: Humors, *sel.*
Satire II: "I cannot hold, I cannot, I, indure."
Satire VII: "'Man, a man, a kingdom for a man, A!'"
Satire IV: "Vice, from privation of that sacred grace."
Scholar and His Dog, A.
Scourge of Villainy [*or* Villanie *or* Villany], The, *sels.*
Song: "O Love, how strangely sweet."
To Detraction [I Present My Poesie].
To Everlasting Oblivion.

Marston, John Westland
Marie de Meranie, *sel.*
Parting of King Philip and Marie, The.

Marston, Philip Bourke
After.
After Summer.
At Last.
At the Last.
Garden Fairies.
Greeting, A.
Her Pity.
How My Songs of Her Began.
If You Were Here.
Love and Music.
Love's Music.
No Death.
Not Thou but I.
Old Churchyard of Bonchurch, The.
Rose and the Wind, The.
Roses' Song.
To the Spirit of Poetry.
Too Late.
Ungathered Love.
Vain Wish, A.

Marston, Westland *See* **Marston, John Westland**

Martí, José

Martí (continued)
I am a sincere man.
I grow a white rose.
Simple Verses, *sels.*
Two Countries.
Marti, Kurt
Unbidden Wedding Guest, The.
Martial (Marcus Valerius Martialis)
Abnegation.
Advantages of Learning, The.
Antiquary, The.
Any Author to Any Friend.
Bad Joke, A.
Bought Locks.
Contentment.
Country Pleasures.
De Coenatione Micae.
Dinner with Ligurinus.
Dude, The.
Epigram: "They say your lady friends have no long life."
Epigram: "Things that make the happier life, are these, The."
Epitaph on Erotion.
Erotion.
Familiarity Breeds Indifference.
For a Son's Marriage.
Golden Sorrow, A.
Grammar of Love, The.
Happy Life, The.
Hinted Wish, A.
How to Raise a Son.
In All the Humors.
Incentive, The.
Insufficient Vengeance.
Legacy, A.
Lover's Play of Words.
Martial, the Things for to Attain.
Martial's Quiet Life.
Means to Attain [a] Happy Life, The.
Mistaken Resolve, The.
More than Quit.
My Friend, the Things That Do Attain.
On the Death of a Young and Favorite Slave.
Post-Obits and the Poets.
Procrastination.
Reactionary Critic.
Sealed Bags of Ducats.
Sextus the Usurer.
Temperament.
Things That Cause a Quiet Life, The.
To a Capricious Friend.
To a Married Couple That Could Not Agree.
To a Poetic Lover.
To a Schoolmaster.
To an Old Fraud.
To Fidentinus.
To His Book.
To His Cousin.
To His Girl.
To Julius.
To Sabidius.
To Sextus.
To-Morrow.
Too Literal Pupil, The.
Total Abstainer, A.
Translat. ex Martial.
Two Hundred Lines a Day.
Unchanged.
What Makes a Happy Life.
Why Don't I Send My Books to You?
Work and Play.
Martin, Ada Louise
Sleep.
Martin, Arthur Patchett
Cynic of the Woods, The.
Love and War.
Martin, Bessie June
Let Me Look at Me.
True Riches.
Martin, C. D.
God's Goodness.
Martin, David
Gordon Childe.
Martin, Edward Sandford
Christmas, 1898.
Egotism.
Girl of Pompeii, A.
Infirm.
Little Brother of the Rich, A.
My Name Is Legion.
Sea Is His, The.
Which Is Me?
Martin, I. L.
At the Tennis Clinic.
Dark Eyes at Forest Hills.
Martin, John
God's Dark.
Martin, Julia E.
With Him.
Martin, Margaret Nickerson
Judas Iscariot.
Martin, Michael C.
Electric Storm.
Guard.
Martin, Paul
Full-Hearted Men!
Martin, Philip
In March.
Martin, Sarah Catherine
Old Mother Hubbard.
Martin, Sir Theodore, *and* **William E. Aytoun** *See* **Aytoun, William Edmonstoune,** *and* **Sir Theodore Martin**
Martin, William Wesley
Apple Orchard in the Spring, The.
Martineau, Harriet
On, On, Forever.
Martinez, Maurice
Suburbia.
Martinson, Harry
Visual Memory.
Marvell, Andrew
Ametas and Thestylis Making Hay-Ropes.
And now to the abbyss I pass.
Appleton House.
Bermudas.
But who considers well will find indeed.
Carrying Their Coracles.
Character of Holland, The.
Charles II.
Clarindon's House-Warming.
Clorinda and Damon.
Coronet, The.
Cromwell Dead.
Damon the Mower.
Daphnis and Chloe.
Definition of Love, The.
Dialogue between the Resolved Soul, and Created Pleasure, A.
Dialogue between the Soul and Body, A.
Dialogue between the Two Horses, A.
Dialogue between Thyrsis and Dorinda, A.
Drop of Dew, A.
Dutch in the Thames [*or* the Medway], The.
Elegy upon the Death of my Lord Francis Villiers, An.
Epitaph, An: "Enough; and leave the rest to fame."
Epitaph upon ——, An.
Execution of King Charles, The.
Eyes and Tears.
Fair Singer, The.
First Anniversary of the Government under His Royal Highness the Lord Protector [O. C.], The.
Fleckno, an English Priest at Rome.
Further Advice to a Painter.
Gallery, The.
Garden, The ("How vainly men themselves amaze").
Garden, A ("See how the flowers, as at parade").
Girl and Her Fawn, The.
Girl Describes Her Fawn, The.
Here at the fountain's sliding foot.
Hewel, or Woodpecker, The.
Horatian Ode upon Cromwel[l]'s Return from Ireland, An.
I saw him dead, a leaden slumber lies [*or* lyes].
King Charles upon The Scaffold.
Kingfisher, The.
Last Instructions to a Painter, The.
Loyall [or Loyal] Scot, The.
Match, The.
Mourning.
Mower Against Gardens, The.
Mower to [*or* of] the Glow-Worms [*or* Glow worms], The.
Mower's Song, The.
Musicks Empire.
Music's Empire.
Nymph Complaining for the Death of Her Faun, The.
Oh thou, that dear and happy isle.
On a Drop of Dew.
On Milton's "Paradise Lost."
On Mr. Milton's Paradise lost.
On Paradise Lost.
On the Lord Mayor and Court of Aldermen, Presenting the Late King and Duke of York Each with a Copy of Their Freedoms, Anno Dom. 1674.
On the Victory Obtained by Blake over the Spaniards.
Paint last the King, and a dead shade of Night.
Picture of Little T. C. in a Prospect of Flowers, The.
Poem upon the Death of Oliver Cromwell, A.
So restless Cromwell could not cease.
Song of the Emigrants in Bermuda.
Statue at Charing Cross, The.
Statue in Stocks-Market, The.
Thoughts in a Garden.
Thoughts in a Summer Garden.
'Tis not a freedom that, where all command.
To Glow-Worms.
To His Coy Mistress.
To His Noble Friend, Mr. Richard Lovelace, upon His Poems.
To His Worthy Friend Doctor Witty upon His Translation of the Popular Errors.
To the King.
Tom May's Death.
Two Songs at the Marriage of the Lord Fauconberg and the Lady Mary Cromwell.
Unfortunate Lover, The.
Upon Appleton House, to My Lord Fairfax.
Upon Blood's Attempt to Steale the Crown (1671).
Upon His Grand-Children.
Upon His House.
Upon the Death of the Lord Hastings.
Upon the Hill and Grove at Bill-borrow.
Well mightst thou scorn thy readers to allure.
What wondrous life is this I lead!
Woodpecker, The.
Young Love.
Marvin, Dwight Edwards
Lord, Give Me Faith.
Vesper Bells.

Marx, Anne
Lacemaker, The (Vermeer).
Nightmare.
Marx, Groucho
You're So Kind.
Mary Catherine, Sister, O.S.U
Again for You.
New Testament, Revised Edition.
Beside Lilia Dead.
Mary Immaculata, Sister
Ordination.
Spring Comes to Our Garden.
Mary Madeleva, Sister
At Winter's End.
Ballad of the Happy Christmas Wind.
Ballade on Eschatology.
Serenade, The: "This age-old church."
Wardrobe.
Mary of the Visitation, Sister
As One Finding Peace.
Gifts.
In Tenebris.
Mary Queen of Scots
Prayer before [Her] Execution.
Mary Thérèse, Sister
I Send Our Lady.
Maryanna, Sister
Knight, The.
Meditations in a Museum Cloister.
With One Swift Thought.
Marzials, Frank T.
Death as the Fool.
Death as the Teacher of Love-Lore.
Two Sonnet-Songs.
Marzials, Theóphile Julius Henry
Carpe Diem.
May Margaret.
Pastoral, A: "Flower of the medlar."
Song: "There's one great bunch of stars in heaven."
Tragedy, A.
Twickenham Ferry.
Masaoka Shiki
Waiting.
Mase, Sidney Warren
It's Simply Great.
Masefield, John
Ah, we are neither heaven nor earth, but men.
All through the windless night the clipper rolled.
"All Ye That Pass By."
Another Cross.
August, 1914.
Ballad of John Silver, A.
Beauty.
Being Her Friend.
Book & Bookplate.
C. L. M.
Cape Horn Gospel—I ("'I was in a hooker once,' said Karlssen").
Cape Horn Gospel—II ("Jake was a dirty Dago lad").
Captain Stratton's Fancy.
Cargoes.
Chief Centurions, The.
Choice, The.
Clipper Loitered South, The.
Cobbler bent at his wooden foot, The.
Consecration, A.
Countrymen, The.
Creed, A.
Cry to Music, A.
Dauber, *sels.*
D'Avalo's Prayer.
Dawn.
Dead Knight, The.
Drop Me The Seed.
End, The.
Everlasting Mercy, The.
Fox Awakes, The.
Fox knew well that, before they tore him, The.
From the Gallows Hill to the Tineton Copse.
Frontier, The.
Golden City of St. Mary, The.
Good Friday, *sel.*
Hell's Pavement.
How Many Ways.
I Could Not Sleep for Thinking of the Sky.
I did not think, I did not strive.
I Never See the Red Rose.
I opened the window wide and leaned.
If I Could Come Again to That Dear Place.
If I could get within this changing I.
Ignorance.
In the Great Green Commonwealth of Thought.
It May Be So with Us.
John Fitzgerald Kennedy.
June Twilight.
King's Highway, The.
Laugh and Be Merry.
Lemmings, The.
Let that which is to come be as it may.
Lines: "By this the sun was all one glitter."
Lollingdon Downs, *sels.*
London Town.
Long, long ago, when all the glittering earth.
Madman's Song, The.
Men Are Made Human by the Mighty Fall.
Midnight.
Mother Carey.
Night on the Downland.
O God, beloved God, in pity send.
Old Song Re-sung, An.
On Eastnor Knoll.
On Growing Old.
One of Wally's Yarns.
Only a Beauty, Only a Power.
Passing Strange, The.
Past the gibbet-stock all stuck with nails.
Ploughman, The.
Port of Holy Peter.
Port of Many Ships.
Posted.
Prayer: "When the last sea is sailed."
Prayer for the Royal Marriage.
Revelation.
Reynard the Fox, *sels.*
Rider at the Gate, The.
Right Royal.
Roadways.
Rose of the World, The.
Roses Are Beauty.
Rounding the Horn.
Sea-Change.
Sea Fever.
Seekers, The.
Ship and Her Makers, The.
Ships.
Si talked with Dauber, standing by the side.
So in the empty sky the stars appear.
Sonnet: "Ah, we are neither heaven nor earth, but men."
Sonnet: "Flesh, I have knocked at many a dusty door."
Sonnet: "Here in the self is all that man can know."
Sonnet: "I could not sleep for thinking of the sky."
Sonnet: "I never see the red rose crown the year."
Sonnet: "If I could get within this changing I."
Sonnet: "Is there a great green commonwealth of Thought."
Sonnet: "Now they are gone with all their songs and sins."
Sonnet: "O little self, within whose smallness lies."
Sonnet on the Death of His Wife.
Sonnets ("Like bones the ruins of the cities stand"), *sel.*
Sonnets ("Long long ago"), *sels.*
Sorrow of Mydath.
Spanish Waters.
Tarry Buccaneer, The.
Tewkesbury Road.
There Is No God, As I Was Taught.
They were a lovely pack for looks.
To C. L. M.
To His Mother, C. L. M.
Tom Dansey was a famous whip.
Tomorrow.
Trade Winds.
Tragedy of Pompey the Great, The, *sels.*
Truth.
Unending Sky, The.
Up on the Downs.
Vagabond.
Valediction, A; Liverpool Docks.
Wanderer, The.
Wanderers Song, A.
Watching by a Sick-Bed.
West Wind, The.
What Am I, Life?
When all these million cells that are slaves.
Wherever Beauty Has Been Quick in Clay.
Wild Duck, The.
Wood-Pigeons.
Word, The.
Yarn of the *Loch Achray,* The.
You.
Mason, Agnes Louisa Carter
Whenever a Little Child Is Born.
Mason, Caroline Atherton Briggs
Do They Miss Me at Home?
En Voyage.
Eventide.
Four Winds, The.
God Knows Best.
Open Secret, An.
President Lincoln's Grave.
Reconcilation.
When I Am Old.
Whichever Way the Wind Doth Blow.
Mason, Edgar Cooper
Safe in His Keeping.
Satisfied.
Tear Down the Walls.
Mason, Guy
Adventure.
Independence.
Mason, Lowell
Courage.
Mason, Madeline
Janus.
Mason, Marie
Mary's Easter.
"Mason, Mark." *See* **Winner, Septimus**
Mason, Mary Augusta
My Little Neighbor.
Scarlet Tanager, The.
Mason, Mary J.
Saviour, Who Died for Me.
Mason, Ronald Allison Kells
After Death.
Be Swift O Sun.
Body of John.
Ecce Homunculus.
Footnote to John II: 4.
Fugue.
Judas Iscariot.

Mason (continued)
On the Swag.
Our Love Was a Grim Citadel.
Poem: "If the drink that satisfied."
Prelude: "This short straight sword."
Song of Allegiance.
Sonnet of Brotherhood.
Young Man Thinks of Sons, The.
Mason, W. L.
My Airedale Dog.
Mason, Walt
Eyes of Lincoln, The.
Football.
Little Green Tents.
Mason, William
English Garden, The, *sel.*
Landscape.
Ode to a Friend.
Ode to a Water Nymph.
Ode to an Æolus's Harp.
Ode to Morning.
Sonnet: Anniversary, February 23, 1795.
Massey, Gerald
Christie's Portrait.
Deserter from the Cause, The.
England.
His Banner over Me.
Little Willie.
Men of "Forty-eight," The.
Mother's Idol Broken The, *sel.*
O, Lay Thy Hand in Mine, Dear.
Our Wee White Rose.
Parting.
Young Love.
Massey, Reginald
Child, The.
Massinger, Philip
Death Invoked.
Emperor of the East, The, *sel.*
Forest's Queen, The.
Look on this maid of honour, now.
Maid of Honour, The, *sel.*
Picture, The, *sel.*
Renegado, The, *sel.*
Sad Song, A.
Song: "Blushing rose and purple flower, The."
Song: "Why art thou slow, thou rest of trouble, Death."
Song of Pleasure, A.
"Yet there's one scruple with which I am much."
Massinger, Philip, *and* **John Fletcher**
See **Fletcher, John,** *and* **Philip Massinger**
Massingham, Harold
Cow.
Masson, Tom (Thomas Lansing Masson)
Kiss, The.
Red Cross Nurses, The.
When I Get Time.
Master, Thomas
On Lutestrings Cat-eaten.
Masters, Edgar Lee
Aaron Hatfield.
Achilles Deatheridge.
Aldhelm.
Anne [*or* Ann] Rutledge.
Archibald Higbie.
Arlo Will.
Bert Kessler.
"Butch" Weldy.
Carl Hamblin.
Cassius Hueffer.
Chandler Nicholas.
Christmas at Indian Point.
Daisy Fraser.
Davis Matlock.
Desolate Scythia.
Doc Hill.
Dost Thou not see about our feet.
Editor Whedon.
Edmund Pollard.
Elliott Hawkins.
Elsa Wertman.
English Thornton.
Euripides Alexopoulos.
Father Malloy.
Fiddler Jones.
Garden, The.
George Gray.
Hamilton Greene.
Hannah Armstrong.
Hare Drummer.
Harry Wilmans.
Henry C. Calhoun.
Herman Altman.
Hill, The.
Howard Lamson.
J. Milton Miles.
Jack Kelso, *sel.*
Jacob Godbey.
James Garber.
Jay Hawkins.
John Hancock Otis.
John Horace Burleson.
John Wasson.
Jonathan Houghton.
Julia Miller.
Knowlt Hoheimer.
Lake Boats, The.
Lost Orchard, The.
Lucinda Matlock.
Mrs. Williams.
Mollie [*or* Ollie] McGee.
Mourner's Bench, The.
My Light with Yours.
Nathan Suffrin.
New Spoon River, The, *sels.*
New World, The, *sel.*
O You Young Eagles!
Ollie [*or* Mollie] McGee.
Over a lost orchard I have strayed.
Percy Bysshe Shelley.
Perry Zoll.
Petit, the Poet.
Portrait of a Poet.
Rutherford McDowell.
Scholfield Huxley.
Seth Compton.
Sexsmith the Dentist.
Silence.
Slip-Shoe Lovey.
Spoon River Anthology, *sels.*
Supplication.
This America is an ancient land.
Thomas Rhodes.
Thomas Trevelyan.
Urge of the seed, The: the germ.
Village Atheist, The.
Webster Ford.
Week-End by the Sea.
Widows.
William H. Herndon.
William Jones.
Masters, Marcia
Country Ways.
Impressions of My Father, *sel.*
Mastin, Florence Ripley
Eight-Cylinder Man.
Old Hound.
Return to Spring.
Matchett, William H.
Aunt Alice in April.
Cedar Waxwing.
Head Couples.
Middle-Man.
Mole, The.
Moths, The.
Old Inn on the Eastern Shore.
Packing a Photograph from Firenze.
Return to Lane's Island.
Spit-Bug, The.
Water Ouzel.
Mather, Cotton
Epitaph: "Dummer the shepherd sacrific'd."
Go then, my dove, but now no longer mine.
O Glorious Christ of God; I live.
Vigilantius, or a Servant of the Lord Found Ready.
Matheson, Annie
Love's Cosmopolitan.
Song of Handicrafts, A.
Matheson, George
Christian Freedom.
Christ's Bondservant.
Gather Us In.
O Love That Wilt Not Let Me Go.
Peace, Be Still!
Matheson, Mary
Afterward.
Evening.
Matheus, John Frederick
Requiem.
Mathew, Ray
At a Time.
For Harry and June.
Genesis.
Let Us Not Pretend.
Love and Marriage.
'Morning, Morning.
Our Father.
Picnic.
Poems Come Easier, The.
Young Man's Fancy.
Mathews, Albert
To an Autumn Leaf.
Mathews, Cornelius
Poet, The.
Mathews, Esther
Song: "I can't be talkin' of love, dear."
Mathews, Harry
Comatas.
Firing Squad, The.
Invitation to a Sabbath.
Relics, The.
Ring, The.
Sense of Responsibility, The.
Mathews, Jack
Catfish, The.
Paradigm of a Hero.
Mathias, Eileen
All in Red.
Go Out.
In the Wood.
Just Jumbo.
Little Things.
My Hut.
Sea Fairies.
Tall Trees.
Zoo Manners.
Matson, Clive
Against Jealousy.
Drink Wine in the Corner Store.
Full Swing Circus.
I Watch.
Today.
Vision; Second Psalm.
Matsuo Basho *See* **Basho**
Mattam, Donald
In a Town Garden.
Table Talk.
Matthesius, John
Morning Prayer for Day's Work.
Matthew, Sir Tobie
Answer, An.
Matthews, Alice Clear
Of the Mathematician.
Matthews, Brander
American Girl, An.
Matthews, Harley

Return of the Native, The.
Matthews, Jack
Beekeeper, The.
Thaw, The.
Matthews, Margaret
Faith, Hope, Love.
Matthews, T. S.
Song for Mother's Day.
Mattocks, Brewer
Preacher's Mistake, The.
Matusovsky, Mikhail Lvovich
Long Roads.
Maugham, Henry Neville
Husband of Poverty, The, *sel.*
Knight of Bethlehem, A.
Song: "There was a Knight of Bethlehem."
Maura, Sister
Blessing of St. Francis, The.
Deirdre's Song at Sunrise.
Rosary, The, *abr.*
Maura, Sister Mary
Data for Accreditation.
Lucifer at Leisure.
Motif from the Second Shepherd's Play.
Our Lady of the Refugees.
Professor of Medieval Balladry.
To the Queen of Dolors.
Maurer, Irving
O God, Hear Thou the Nation's Prayer.
"Maurice, Furnley." *See* **Wilmot, Frank**
Mauropus, John
Our Lady of the Passion.
Mavity, Nancy Barr
Prisoners.
Maxey, Bob
Blues.
City Enscriber, The.
Moses Miles.
Maxfield, J. J.
Eye of Faith, The.
Maxtone, Mary
Skywriting.
Maxwell, Ian
Vespers.
Maxwell, James Clerk
In Memory of Edward Wilson, *parody.*
Rigid Body Sings, *parody.*
Maxwell, Joseph R. N.
Old Bard Speaks, The.
Maxwell, William
Dance at Silver Valley, The.
Maxwell-Hall, Agnes
Jamaica Market.
Lizard.
May, Beulah
Captain of St. Kitts, The.
Deprecating Parrots.
Fishers in the Night.
May, Curtis
Tucking the Baby In.
May, Edwina
Haitches!
May, Julia Harris
Day by Day.
May, Thomas
Continuation of Lucan, *br. sel.*
Death.
Love's Prime.
Not He That Knows.
Old Couple, The, *sel.*
Song, A: "Not he, that knows how to acquire."
Tragedy of Cleopatra, The, *sel.*
Mayakovsky, Vladimir
At the Top of My Voice.
My verse will reach you.
Our March.
Spring.
Maybin, Patrick
April, 1940.
Ballykinlar, May, 1940.
Fallen Tree, The.
Monks at Ards, The.
Thoughts from Abroad.
Mayer, Bernadette
America.
Ancient Degree, An.
Corn.
Index.
It Moves Across.
Laura Cashdollars.
Painting by Chimes.
Poem: "I am beginning to alter."
Port, The.
Sea.
Sermon.
Steps.
Wind Force.
Mayer, Frank H.
At Timber Line.
Mayhall, Jane
Mozart.
Mayhew, Horace
Travesty of Miss Fanshawe's Enigma.
Maynard, Don
Athlete.
Maynard, Francis X.
Chiseler, The.
Maynard, Sara
Ox, The.
Maynard, Theodore
Apocalypse.
Cecidit, Cecidit Babylon Magna!
Certain Rich Man, A.
Desideravi.
Duel, The.
Dwell with Me, Lovely Images.
Exile.
Faith.
Faith's Difficulty.
If I Had Ridden Horses.
On the Edge of the Pacific.
Requiem.
Ships, The.
Song of Colours, A.
Song of Laughter, A.
World's Miser, The.
Mayne, Jasper
Amorous War, The, *sel.*
First Song, Sung by Two Amazons, The.
Scorne then their censure, who gave out thy wit.
Time.
To the Memory of Ben Johnson, *sel.*
Mayne, John
Hallowe'en.
Logan Braes ("By Logan's streams that rin sae deep").
Mayo, Edward Leslie
Anglo-Saxon.
D Minor, The.
Diver, The.
El Greco.
En Route.
I Saw My Father.
In the Web.
Letter to Karl Shapiro.
Mole, The.
Nausea.
Oracle.
Poem for Gerard.
Pool, The.
Uninfected, The.
Variations on a Line from Shakespeare's Fifty-sixth Sonnet.
Wagon Train.
Mayo, Herbert
Induced Current.
Mazzaro, Jerome
Between Motions.
Meacham, Harry M.
To a Young Poet.
Mead, E. Stella
Last Gate, The.
Merry Man of Paris, The.
When We Are Men.
Meany, Edmond S.
Washington's Song.
Mearns, Hughes
Alibi.
Antigonish.
Case, A.
Crime Note.
Frustrated Male.
Lady with Technique, The.
Later Antigonishes, *sels.*
Little Man, The.
Little Man Who Wasn't There, The.
Me.
Perfect Reactionary, The.
Reveille.
Medary, Anna
Hallowe'en.
Learning to Swim.
Medici, Lorenzo de'
Carnival Songs, *sel.*
Lyric, A: "How can I sing light-souled."
One general song of praise arise.
Orazione, *sel.*
Triumph of Bacchus and Ariadne.
Youth Is Sweet and Well.
Medley, Samuel
He Lives.
Medrano, Francisco de
Art and Nature.
Two Harvests, The.
Meehan, John James
Race of the *Oregon,* The.
Meeker, Marjorie
After Pain.
Memorial Sonnet.
Prophecy.
Where My Step Falters.
Meidhre, Brian MacGiolla *See* **Merriman, Brian**
Meigs, Charles D.
Home without a Bible, A.
Others.
Meigs, Mildred Plew
Abraham Lincoln.
Johnny Fife and Johnny's Wife.
Organ Grinders' Garden, The.
Pirate Don Durk of Dowdee.
Road to Raffydiddle, The.
Shepherd Left Behind, The.
Silver Ships.
To Chicago at Night.
Meiji, Emperor
Buried Fire.
Meilir ap Gwalchmai
His Delight.
Meinloh von Sevelingen
I Serve.
Mëir of Rothenburg
Burning of the Law, The.
Mei Yao Ch'en
Friend Advises Me to Stop Drinking, A.
On the Death of a New Born Child.
Melcombe, Baron *See* **Dodington, George Bubb, Baron Melcombe**
Meleager
Against Mosquitoes.
Bride, A.
Child Eros, The.
Draught of Love, The.
Flowers: For Heliodora.
Garland for Heliodora, A.
Heliodora's Garland.
Heliodore ("Pour wine").
Heliodore Dead.
In the Spring.
Little Love-God, The.

Meleager (continued)
Lost Desire.
Love at the Door.
Love, the Vagrant.
Lover's Curse, A.
Message, The.
O Gentle Ships.
Of Himself.
Of His Death.
Spring ("Now Winter's winds are banished from the sky").
To Heliodora.
To Heliodora; a Fretful Monody.
To Heilodora, Dead.
Two Fires.
Upon a Maid That Died the Day She Was Married.
Wreath for Heliodora.
Writ in Water.
Meléndez Valdés, Juan
Sum of Kisses, A.
Mellen, Grenville
Lonely Bugle Grieves, The.
Ode on the Celebration of the Battle of Bunker Hill, June 17, 1825, *sel.*
Mellichamp, Leslie
Epitaph: "Here he lies moulding."
Mello, Francisco Manuel de
Death's Apology.
On Ascending a Hill Leading to a Convent.
Meltzer, David
15th Raga: For Bela Lugosi.
Prayerwheel 2.
Revelation.
12th Raga: For John Wieners.
Melville, George John Whyte- *See* **Whyte-Melville, George John**
Melville, Herman
Aeolian Harp, The.
After the Pleasure Party.
Always with Us!—The Black Preacher.
America.
Apparition, The.
Art.
At the Cannon's Mouth.
Attic Landscape, The.
Berg, The.
Billy Budd, Foretopman, *sel.*
Billy in the Darbies.
Blue-Bird, The.
Bridegroom Dick, *sel.*
Camoens.
Camoens in the Hospital.
Clarel, *sels.*
College Colonel, The.
"Coming Storm, The."
Commemorative of a Naval Victory.
Conflict of Convictions, The.
Crossing the Tropics.
Cumberland, The.
Dirge for McPherson, A.
Dupont's Round Fight.
Eagle of the Blue, The.
Enthusiast, The.
Enviable Isles, The.
Epilogue: "If Luther's day expand to Darwin's year."
Fall of Richmond, The.
Falstaff's Lament over Prince Hal Become Henry V.
Far Off-Shore.
Father Mapple's Hymn.
"Formerly a Slave."
Fortitude of the North, The.
Fragments of a Lost Gnostic Poem of the Twelfth Century.
Gold in the Mountain.
Greek Architecture.
Healed of My Hurt.
House-Top, The.
Immolated.
In a Bye-Canal.
In a Garret.
In the Pauper's Turnip-Field.
In the Prison Pen.
John Marr, *sel.*
L'Envoi: "My towers at last! these rovings end."
L'Envoi: Return of the Sire de Nesle, The.
Lone Founts.
Maldive Shark, The.
Malvern Hill.
March into Virginia, The.
Mardi, *sel.*
Martyr, The.
Memorials on the Slain at Chickamauga.
Misgivings.
Moby Dick, *sel.*
Monody.
Nathan.
Night-March, The.
Of Rama.
Of Rome.
On Mammon.
On the Grave of a Young Cavalry Officer Killed in the Valley of Virginia.
On the Photograph of a Corps Commander.
On the Slain Collegians.
Pebbles.
Pontoosuce.
Portent, The.
Prelusive.
Ravaged Villa, The.
Requiem, A.
Requiem for Soldiers Lost in Ocean Transports, A.
Returned Volunteer to His Rifle, The.
Ribs and Terrors, The.
Running the Batteries.
Seedsmen of Old Saturn's Land.
Sheridan at Cedar Creek.
Shiloh; a Requiem.
Since as in night's deck-watch ye show.
Sodom.
Southern Cross.
Stone Fleet, The.
Stonewall Jackson.
Surrender at Appomatox, The.
Temeraire, The.
Time's Long Ago.
To Ned.
Tuft of Kelp, The.
Ungar and Rolfe.
Uninscribed Monument on One of the Battle-Fields of the Wilderness, An.
Utilitarian View of the *Monitor's* Fight, A.
Victor of Antietam, The.
Vine and Clarel.
We Fish.
Whale, The.
Where's Commander All-a-Tanto?
Ménage, Gilles
Happy Man, The.
Menahem Ben Jacob
Harvesting of the Roses, The.
Martyr's Death, A.
Menahem ben Makhir of Ratisbon
How Sweet Thy Precious Gift of Rest.
Menai, Huw (Hugh Menai Williams)
In Our Time.
Old Peasant in the Billiard Saloon, The.
Paradox.
Menander
I Hold Him Happiest.
These Stones.
Mendelssohn, Moses
Self-Portrait.
Mendès, Catulle
I Go by Road.
Mother, The.
Swans, The.
Mendes, Moses
Ass, The.
Chaplet, The, *sels.*
On the Death of a Lady's Owl.
Philanderer, The.
Mendes, Murilo
Psalm: "I proclaim Thee great and wonderful."
Mendoza, Inigo de
Chant of the Ninth Order of Seraphim.
Méndez Dorich, Rafael
She Was Carrying the Lamp.
Menéndez y Pelayo, Marcelino
Rome.
Mensah, Albert Kayper- *See* **Kayper-Mensah, Albert**
Menth, Robert
Cry from the Battlefield.
Mercantini, Luigi
Garibaldi Hymn, The.
Mercer, Ernestine
Artist.
On Looking Backward.
Mercer, Margaret
Exhortation to Prayer.
Mercer, Thomas
Arthur's Seat, *sel.*
Where is the gallant race that rose.
Mercier, Louis
Notre Dame des Petits.
Vespers.
Mercier, Roselle *See* **Montgomery, Roselle Mercier**
Meredith, George
Appeasement of Demeter, The.
Appreciation.
"Atkins."
Ballad of Past Meridian, A.
Burden of Strength The.
Coin of Pity, The.
Dirge in Woods.
Discipline of Wisdom, The.
Dream is the thought in the ghost, The.
Dusty Answer, A.
Earth and Man.
Earth's Secret.
End of Love, The.
Faith on Trial, A, *sel.*
For, Singing Till His Heaven Fills.
Garden of Epicurus, The.
Great Mother Nature! teach me, like thee.
Hard Weather.
Here Jack and Tom Are Paired with Moll and Meg.
Hiding the Skeleton.
Hymn to Colour [*or* Color].
In fellowship Religion has its founts.
Internal Harmony.
Juggling Jerry.
King Harald's Trance.
Kinship with the Stars.
Lark Ascending, The.
Last Words of Juggling Jerry, The.
Lines: "Love within the lover's breast."
Love born of knowledge, love that gains.
Love Dies.
Love in the Valley.
Love's Grave.
Lucifer in Starlight.
Manfred.
Marian.
Meditation under Stars.
Melampus.
Men and Man.
Modern Love.
Nature and Life.
Not solely that the future she destroys.
Nuptials of Attila, The, *abr.*

O briar-scents, on yon wet wing.
Ode to the Spirit of Earth in Autumn, *sel.*
On Hearing the News from Venice.
On the Danger of War.
One Twilight Hour.
Orchard and the Heath, The.
Orson of the Muse, An.
Outer and Inner.
Phoebus with Admetus.
Promise in Disturbance, The.
Seed-Time.
Sense and Spirit.
Should Thy Love Die.
Society.
Song: "No, no, the falling blossom is no sign."
Song in the Songless.
Sonnet: "All other joys of life he strove to warm."
Sonnet: "Along the garden terrace."
Sonnet: "Am I failing? For no longer can I cast."
Sonnet: "But where began the change; and what's my crime?"
Sonnet: "By this he knew she wept with waking eyes."
Sonnet: "Distraction is the panacea, Sir!"
Sonnet: "Full faith I have she holds that rarest gift."
Sonnet: "Give to imagination some pure light."
Sonnet: "He felt the wild beast in him between whiles."
Sonnet: "He found her by the ocean's moaning verge."
Sonnet: "Here Jack and Tom are paired with Moll and Meg."
Sonnet: "It is the season of the sweet wild rose."
Sonnet: "Mark where the pressing wind shoots javelin-like."
Sonnet: "Thus piteously love closed what he begat."
Sonnet: "What are we first? First, animals; and next."
Spirit of Shakespeare, The.
Star Sirius, The.
Sweet o' the Year, The.
Tardy Spring.
Test of Manhood, The. *sel.*
Thrush in February, The.
To a Skylark.
To J. M.
Two Masks, The.
What Are We First?
Whimper of Sympathy.
Wind on the Lyre.
Winter Heavens.
Woods of Westermain, The.
World's Advance, The.
Young Reynard.
Youth in Age.

"Meredith, Owen" (Edward Robert Bulwer-Lytton, 1st Earl of Lytton)
Babylonia, *sel.*
Changes.
Chess-Board, The.
Dinner Hour, The.
Forebearance.
Going Back Again.
Indian Love Song.
Last Lines, *sel.*
Last Wish, The.
Legend of the Dead Lambs, The.
Lucile, *sels.*
Night in Italy, A, *sel.*
One Thing.
Portrait, The.
Since We Parted.
Tempora Acta.
'Tis the white anemone, fashioned so like the stars of the winter snow.
True Greatness.
Twins.
Utmost, The.
Wanderer, The, *sel.*
What We May Live Without.
White Anemone, The, *sel.*

Meredith, William
Battle Problem.
Boon, A.
Chinese Banyan, The.
Do Not Embrace Your Mind's New Negro Friend.
Fear of Beasts, The.
For Guillaume Apollinaire.
Korean Woman Seated by a Wall, A.
Love Letter from an Impossible Land.
Old Field Mowed, An.
On Falling Asleep by Firelight.
On Falling Asleep to Birdsong.
On Looking into Robert Frost in Kanji.
Open Sea, The.
Perhaps the Best Time.
Picture of a Castle.
Poem About Morning.
Rainy Season, The.
Starlight.
Thoughts on One's Head.
To a Western Bard Still a Whoop and a Holler Away from English Poetry.
Transport.
View of the Brooklyn Bridge, A.
Walter Jenks' Bath.
Weather.
Winter Verse for My Sister.

Meredith, William Tuckey
Farragut.

Merezhkovsky, Dmitry Sergeyevich
Prayer for Wings.

Merilaas, Kersti
Saint.

Merington, Marguerite
Hey Nonny No.

Merivale, Herman Charles
Aetate XIX.
Darwinity.
Ready, Ay, Ready.
Thaisa's Dirge ("Thaisa fair, under the cold sea lying").
Town of Nice, The.

Merkel, Andrew
Ann stood and watched the combers race to shore.
Tallahassee, *sel.*

Merrell, Lloyd Frank
Reincarnation.
Resurrection.
Unity.

Merriam, Eve
Alligator on the Escalator.
Ballad of the Double Bed.
Bam, Bam, Bam.
Catch a Little Rhyme.
City Traffic.
Coward, The.
Direct Song.
Lazy Thought, A.
Leavetaking.
Love-making, The: His and Hers.
Moment before Conception, The.
Monogramania.
Restricted.
Summer Rain.
Wall, The.

Merriam, Lillie Fuller
At the Door.

Merrick, James
Chameleon, The.
Ignorance of Man, The.

Merrill, Bob
Promise Me a Rose.

Merrill, Charles Edmund, Jr
Persicos Odi.

Merrill, Herbert
Courthouse Square.

Merrill, James
After Greece.
Bed, The.
Black Swan, The.
Broken Home, The.
Cloud Country.
Country of a Thousand Years of Peace, The.
Current, The.
Days of 1964.
Drowning Poet, The.
Foliage of Vision.
For a Second Marriage.
Friend of the Fourth Decade, The.
Getting Through.
Greenhouse, The.
Hotel de l'Univers et Portugal.
Kite Poem.
Laboratory Poem.
Mad Scene, The.
Mirror.
Night Laundry.
Octopus, The.
Olive Grove.
Parrot Fish, The.
Renewal, A.
Scenes of Childhood.
Some Negatives: X. at the Chateau.
Swimming by Night.
Thousand and Second Night, The.
Timepiece, A.
Transfigured Bird.
Upon a Second Marriage.
Urban Convalescence, An.
Variations and Elegy: White Stag, Black Bear.
Variations: The Air Is Sweetest That a Thistle Guards.
View of the Burning, A.
Voices from the Other World.
Who Guessed Amiss the Riddle of the Sphinx.

Merrill, William Pierson
Call to the Strong, The.
Expect!
Festal Song.
Not Alone for Mighty Empire.
People's Thanksgiving, The.
Rise Up, O Men of God!

Merriman, Brian [*or* Brian MacGiolla Meidhre
Maiden's Complaint, The.
Midnight Court, The.

Merritt, Dixon Lanier
Limerick: "Wonderful bird is the pelican, A."

Merryman, Bryan *See* **Merriman, Brian**
Merryman, Mildred Plew *See* **Meigs, Mildred Plew**

Mersar
Allace! So Sobir Is the Micht.

Mertins, Louis
Indian Songs.

Merton, Thomas
Advice to a Young Prophet.
Argument, An—Of the Passion of Christ.
Aubade: Lake Erie.
Baroque Gravure, A.
Blessed Virgin Mary Compared to a Window, The.
Duns Scotus.
Elegy for the Monastery Barn.
Evening of the Visitation, The.
Figure for an Apocalypse.
For My Brother.

Merton (continued)
In Memory of the Spanish Poet Federico García Lorca.
Like Ilium.
Messias.
Ode to the Present Century.
Practical Program for Monks, A.
St. Malachy.
Seneca.
Stranger.
To a Severe Nun.
Trappist Abbey, The: Matins.
Two States of Prayer.
Merwin, William Stanley
Air: "Naturally it is night."
Animals, The.
Annunciation, The.
Another Year Come.
Asians Dying, The.
Avoiding News by the River.
Backwater Pond: The Canoeists.
Ballad of John Cable and Three Gentlemen.
Bell Buoy.
Blind Girl.
Blue Cockerel.
Bones, The.
Bucolic.
Burning Mountain.
By Day and by Night.
Caesar.
Camel.
Colloquy at Peniel.
Come Back.
December among the Vanished.
December: Of Aphrodite.
Defeated, The.
Despair.
Dictum: For a Masque of Deluge.
Dream Again, The.
Drunk in the Furnace, The.
Dusk in Winter.
Evening.
Fog-Horn.
For Now.
For the Anniversary of My Death.
Foreign Summer.
Gods, The.
Grandfather in the Old Men's Home.
Grandmother and Grandson.
Herds, The.
Iceberg, The.
In the Gorge.
In the Night Fields.
Indigestion of the Vampire, The.
Isaiah of Souillac, The.
It Is March.
John Otto.
Lemuel's Blessing.
Leviathan.
Looking for Mushrooms at Sunrise.
Lost Month.
Mariners' Carol.
Master, The.
Moths, The.
My Friends.
Native, The.
New Moon in November.
Noah's Raven.
Old Room, The.
On the Subject of Poetry.
Peasant.
Plea for a Captive.
Poem, The: "Coming late, as always."
"Portland" Going Out, The.
Resolution.
Reunion.
Room, The.
Saint of the Uplands, The.
Scale in May, A.
Second Sight.
Separation.
Sire.
Small Woman on Swallow Street.
Song of Three Smiles.
Spring.
Students of Justice, The.
Thorn Leaves in March.
Toro.
Two Horses.
Variation on a Line by Emerson.
Walk-up.
Watchers.
Wave, The.
Way to the River, The.
When I Came from Colchis.
Whenever I Go There.
White Goat, White Ram.
Widow, The.
Witnesses.
Messinger, Robert Hinckley
Give Me the Old.
Winter Wish, A.
Metastasio, Pietro
Age of Gold.
Metcalf, Nelson C.
Kid in Upper 4, The.
Metcalfe, James J.
Visit the Sick.
Metrodorus
Metrodorus' Mind to the Contrary.
Meudt, Edna
Part-Time Tenant.
Meun, Jean de
Table Manners for the Hostess.
Meun, Jean de, *and* **Guillaume de Lorris**
See **Guillaume de Lorris** *and* **Jean de Meun**
Meuttman, Margaret Moore
Survival.
Mew, Charlotte
A Quoi Bon Dire.
Absence.
Again.
Beside the Bed.
Call, The.
Cenotaph, The.
Changeling, The.
Exspecto Resurrectionem.
Farmer's Bride, The.
Here Lies a Prisoner.
How old was Mary out of whom you cast.
I Have Been through the Gates.
In Saturday Market, there's eggs a-plenty.
In the Fields.
Madeleine in Church, *sel.*
Moorland Night.
Not for That City.
Old Shepherd's Prayer.
On the Asylum Road.
Pedler, The.
Rambling Sailor, The.
Saturday Market, *sel.*
Sea Love.
Song: "Love, love today, my dear."
Spring.
To a Child in Death.
Trees Are Down, The.
Mey, Mildred T.
Quiet Days.
Meyer, Bertha
God's Eye Is on the Sparrow.
Meyer, Conrad Ferdinand
Wedding Song.
Meyer, F. B.
Faith.
Meyer, Gerard Previn
Rapunzel Song.
S. T. Coleridge Dismisses a Caller from Porlock.
Meyer, June
All the World Moved.
Meyer, Lucy R.
He Was Not Willing.
Meyers, Bert
Picture Framing.
Meyerstein, Edward Harry William
Elegy on the Death of Mme. Anna Pavlova, *sel.*
Glory and the ardour of the stage, The.
Husband and Wife.
Ivy and Holly.
Meynell, Alice (Mrs. Wilfrid Meynell)
Advent Meditation.
After a Parting.
At Night.
Changeless.
Chimes.
Christ in the Universe.
Christmas Night.
Courts, The.
Crucifixion, The.
Dead Harvest, A.
Easter Night.
General Communion, A.
"I Am the Way."
In Early Spring.
In Portugal, 1912.
Lady of the Lambs, The.
Lady Poverty, The.
Launch, The.
Letter from a Girl to Her Own Old Age, A.
Maternity.
Modern Poet, The.
Mother.
My Heart Shall Be Thy Garden.
Newer Vainglory, The.
No Sudden Thing of Glory.
November Blue.
October Redbreast, The.
One Wept Whose Only Child Was Dead.
Or His Bestowals There.
Parentage.
Parted.
Poet of One Mood, A.
Poet to the Birds, The.
Rainy Summer, The.
Renouncement.
"Rivers Unknown to Song."
San Lorenzo Giustiniani's Mother.
Shepherdess, The.
Song: "My Fair, no beauty of thine will last."
Song of Derivations, A.
Song of the Night at Daybreak.
Thoughts in Separation.
Threshing Machine, The.
Thrush before Dawn, A.
To a Daisy.
To the Body.
To the Mother of Christ, the Son of Man.
To W. M.
Two Poets, The.
Unknown God, The.
Unto Us a Son Is Given.
Veneration of Images.
Via, et Veritas, et Vita.
Visiting Sea, The.
Watershed, The.
Wind is Blind, The.
Young Neophyte, The.
Meynell, Sir Francis
In Praise of Unfamous Men.
Man and Beast.
Mirage at Mickleham.
Permanence.
Time Is Not Mocked.
Meynell, Viola (Mrs. John Dallyn)
Blind Man's Morning, The.
Dusting.
Frozen Ocean, The.
Girl, A.

Jonah and the Whale.
Maid in the Rice-Fields, The.
Old Horse in the Field, The.
Whale and Johan, The.
Meynell, Wilfrid
Folded Flock, The.
Joseph Mary Plunkett.
Meyrich, Geraldine
Washington.
Meysey-Wigley, Caroline *See* **Clive, Caroline**
Mezey, Robert
After Hours.
Against Seasons.
April Fourth.
Bedtime Story, A.
Carmina.
Coffee-House Lecture, A.
Confession, A.
End of an Outing, The.
Epitaph of a Faithful Man.
Evening, An.
Flights.
Friendship, The.
Funeral Home, The.
If I Should Die Before I Wake.
In Defense of Felons.
In the Soul Hour.
In your watercolor, Nely Silvínová.
Lovemaker, The.
My Mother.
New Year's Eve in Solitude.
Night on Clinton.
No Country You Remember.
Reaching the Horizon.
Salesman, The.
Simpler Thing, a Chair, A.
Sky Full of Dead.
Street Scene.
There.
Theresienstadt Poems, *sel.*
To Her.
To Philip Levine, on the Day of Atonement.
Touch It.
Underground Gardens, The.
Visit, The.
Wandering Jew, The.
White Blossoms.
You Could Say.
Mezquida, Anna Blake
Hope.
My House Has Windows.
Michael, James Lionel
Eye of the Beholder, The.
Michael, Phyllis C.
Across the Great Divide.
All Nature Sings.
Another New Year.
Boy Is a Boy, A.
Feet of Clay.
Girl Is a Girl, A.
God Is.
God Keeps His Word.
God Knew.
God's Garden.
God's Gardener.
God's Symphony.
He Cares.
How Can I Doubt?
I Do Not Fear Tomorrow.
If You Believe.
It's Never Easy.
"Little Child Shall Lead Them, A."
Lord, Bless Our Home.
Lord, Give Us Bread.
Lord of All.
Merry Christmas ("Merry Christmas to you, the young and the gay.")
Our Home.
Prayer Is a Power.
Rule On.
Take Thou My Hand.
This Is Today.
Until Eternity.
We.
We Thank Thee.
Michael Marie, Sister
Our Lady on Calvary.
Michael of Kildare, Friar
Sweet Jesus.
Michaelis, Aline
Lindbergh.
Michaels, Molly
Dolphins.
Perfect Child, The.
Three Peters, The.
Michaux, Henri
Impulses.
In the Land of Magic.
Michelangelo Buonarroti
Amulet of Love, The.
Artist and His Work, The.
Beauty and the Artist.
Carnal and Spiritual Love.
Celestial Love.
Dante.
Deathless Flower, A.
Defence of Night, The.
Doom of Beauty, The.
Eternal Lord! Eased of a Cumbrous Load.
Fearful Joy.
For Inspiration.
Garland and the Girdle, The.
His Great Love on High.
I know not if from uncreated spheres.
Joy May Kill.
Last Refuge.
Love, the Light-Giver.
Love's Entreaty.
Love's Justification.
Model and the Statue, The.
On Dante Alighieri.
On Rome in the Pontificate of Julius II.
On the Brink of Death.
On the Crucifix.
Prayer for Faith, A.
Prayer for Inspiration, A.
Prayer for Purification, A.
Prayer for Strength, A.
Ravished by all that to the eyes is fair.
Sacred Night.
Soul of Dante, The.
Speech of Night, The.
Thou Alone Art Good.
To the Marchesana of Pescara.
To the Supreme Being.
To Vittoria Colonna.
Transfiguration of Beauty, The.
Waiting for Death.
Michelson, Max
Bird, The.
Hymn to Night, A.
Love Lyric.
O Brother Tree.
Michie, James
Closing Time.
Dooley Is a Traitor.
Ghost of an Education, The.
Park Concert.
Three Dreams.
Michizane, Sugawara
When I have gone away.
Mickiewicz, Adam
Sages, The.
To a Polish Mother.
Mickle, William Julius
Concubine, The (Sir Martyn), *sels.*
Cumnor Hall.
Mariner's Wife, The.
Sailor's Wife, The.
Sir Martyn.
Sunset.
There's Nae Luck about the House.
Wild Romantic Dell, A.
Middleton, Christopher
Abasis.
Alba after Six Years.
Ancestors, The.
Ant Sun, The.
Dress, The.
Edward Lear in February.
For a Junior School Poetry Book.
Forenoon, The.
Herman Moon's Hourbook, *sels.*
In Some Seer's Cloud Car.
Male Torso.
Navajo Children, Canyon de Chelly, Arizona.
News from Norwood.
Ode on Contemplating Clapham Junction.
Paganini.
Pointed Boots.
Tanker.
Thinking of Hölderlin.
Thousand Things, The.
Waterloo Bridge.
Middleton, Jesse Edgar
Jesous Ahatonhia.
Middleton, Richard
Any Lover, Any Lass.
Dream Song.
For He Had Great Possessions.
Lass That Died of Love, The.
Love's Mortality.
On a Dead Child.
Pagan Epitaph.
Serenade: "By day my timid passions stand."
Song of the King's Minstrel, The.
Middleton, Scudder
Jezebel.
Journey, The.
Poets, The.
Wisdom.
Middleton, Thomas
Alas! how can I sleep? who truly loves.
Blurt, Master Constable, *sels.*
Changeling, The, *sels.*
Chaste Maid in Cheapside, A, *sel.*
Come, my dainty doxies.
Give me fortune, give me health.
Here we are, if you have any more.
How near am I now to a happiness.
Lips and Eyes.
Mad World, My Masters, A, *sel.*
Midnight.
More Dissemblers besides Women, *sel.*
Parting.
Song: "Love for such a cherry lip."
Song: Love Is like a Lamb.
True Love Ditty, A.
What makes your lip so strange?
Widow, The, *sel.*
Women Beware of Women, *sel.*
Middleton, Thomas, *and* William Rowley
Song: "Trip it gipsies, trip it fine."
Spanish Gipsy, The, *sel.*
Trip It, Gipsies [Trip It Fine].
Midlane, Albert
Little Lamb Went Straying, A.
There's a Friend for Little Children.
Miegel, Agnes
Fair Agnete, The.
Mifflin, Lloyd
Battlefield, The.
Doors, The.
Fiat Lux.
Flight, The.
Half-Mast.
Harvest Waits, The.
He Made the Night.

Mifflin (continued)
Milton.
Sesostris.
Ship, The.
Sovereigns, The.
Theseus and Ariadne.
To a Maple Seed.
To an Old Venetian Wine-Glass.
To the Milkweed.
Mihalkov, Sergei *See* **Mikhalkov, Sergel** *and* **El-Registan**
Mikata Shami
Tread Not the Snow.
Mikhalkov, Sergel ***and*** **El-Registan**
Hymn of the Soviet Union.
Miles, Alfred H.
Big and Little Things.
Miles, C. Austin
In the Garden.
Miles, George Henry
Raphael's San Sisto Madonna.
Said the Rose.
Miles, Josephine
Appointment in Doctor's Office.
Belief.
Bombay.
Care.
Confessed.
Day the Winds, The.
Driver Saying.
Education.
Enlightenment.
Entry.
For Futures.
Forecast.
Government Injunction [Restraining Harlem Cosmetic Co.].
Halt, The.
Harvest Moon.
Herald.
Housewife.
Idea of Joy.
Kind.
Lark.
Lineman Calling.
Lucifer Alone.
Meeting.
Mercury.
Monkey.
Moonrise in City Park.
Opal.
Plastic Glass, The.
Polo Match. Sunday, 2 P.M.
Preliminary to Classroom Lecture.
Pride.
Reason.
Riddle: "You are a riddle I would not unravel."
Sale.
Savages, The.
Sisyphus.
Son.
Statute.
Sympathizers, The.
Thoroughgoing, The.
View.
Voyage.
What Followed.
Miles, Sarah Elizabeth
Looking unto Jesus.
Millard, Edith G.
Banbury Fair.
Millard, Geoffrey C.
Hospital.
Millay, Edna St. Vincent "Nancy Boyd"
Afternoon on a Hill.
Anguish, The.
Ashes of Life.
Autumn Daybreak.
Ballad of the Harp-Weaver, The.
Before this coiling planet shall be cold.
Betrothal, The.
Blue-Flag in the Bog, The.
Broken dike, the levee washed away, The.
Buck in the Snow, The.
Cameo, The.
Chorus: "Give away hcr gowns."
City Trees.
Counting-out Rhyme.
Curse, The.
Departure.
Dirge without Music.
Elegy: "Let them bury your big eyes."
Elegy before Death.
End of Summer, The.
Endymion.
Epitaph: "Heap not on this mound."
Epitaph for the Race of Man, *sels.*
Euclid Alone Has Looked on Beauty.
Even in the Moment of Our Earliest Kiss.
Exiled.
Fawn, The.
Feast.
Figs from Thistles.
First Fig.
God's World.
Hearing your words, and not a word among them.
Heart, Have No Pity on This House of Bone.
Here Is a Wound That Never Will Heal.
Horseshoe, The.
Hungry Heart, The.
I, Being Born a Woman.
I do but ask that you be always fair.
I Know I Am but Summer to Your Heart.
I Like Americans.
I read with varying degrees.
I Shall Go Back.
I will put Chaos into fourteen lines.
If I Should Learn, in Some Quite Casual Way.
In the Grave No Flower.
Into the golden vessel of great song.
Journal, *sel.*
Justice Denied in Massachusetts.
Keen.
Lament: "Listen, children:/ Your father is dead."
Lethe.
Look, Edwin!
Memorial to D. C., *sels.*
Modern Declaration.
Moriturus.
My Candle Burns at Both Ends.
Never May the Fruit Be Plucked.
Not in a Silver Casket Cool with Pearls.
Not That It Matters.
Now by the path I climbed, I journey back.
O, loveliest throat of all sweet throats.
Oh, my beloved, have you thought of this.
Oh, Sleep Forever in the Latmian Cave.
Oh, Think Not I Am Faithful to a Vow.
On Hearing a Symphony of Beethoven.
On the Wide Heath.
Passer Mortuus Est.
Pastoral: "If it were only still!"
Peace Was My Earliest Love.
Pear Tree, The.
Penitent, The.
Philosopher, The.
Pioneer, The.
Pity Me Not.
Poet and His Book, The.
Portrait by a Neighbor.
Prayer to Persephone.
Recuerdo.
Renascence.
Return, The.
Say What You Will.
Second Fig.
See where Capella with her golden kids.
She Is Overheard Singing.
Shroud, The.
Singing-Woman from the Wood's Edge, The.
Song of a Second April.
Sonnet: "And you as well must die, beloved dust."
Sonnet: "Cherish you then the hope I shall forget."
Sonnet: "Euclid alone has looked on beauty bare."
Sonnet: "Here lies, and none to mourn him but the sea."
Sonnet: "Him not the golden fang of furious heaven."
Sonnet: "I, being born a woman and distressed."
Sonnet: "I know I am but summer to your heart."
Sonnet: "Into the golden vessel of great song."
Sonnet: "Love is not all: it is not meat nor drink."
Sonnet: "Not with libations but with shouts and laughter."
Sonnet: "Oh, my beloved, have you thought of this."
Sonnet: "Oh, think not I am faithful to a vow!"
Sonnet: Pity Me Not.
Sonnet: "Say what you will, and scratch my heart to find."
Sonnet: "What lips my lips have kissed, and where, and why."
Sonnet: "When we are old and these rejoicing veins."
Sonnet to Gath.
Spring.
Spring and the Fall, The.
Strawberry Shrub, The.
Tavern.
Thou Art Not Lovelier Than Lilacs.
Thursday.
Time Does Not Bring Relief.
To a Young Poet.
To Jesus on His Birthday.
Travel.
Unexplorer, The.
Vacation Song.
Very Little Sphinx, A, *sel.*
What Lips My Lips Have Kissed.
What's This of Death.
When Death was young and bleaching bones were few.
When the Year Grows Old.
Wild Swans.
Winter Night.
Women have loved before as I love now.
Wonder Where This Horseshoe Went.
World stands out on either side, The.
Millay, Kathleen (Mrs. Howard Irving Young)
Absent Minded Birch Tree, The.
Discouraged Cherry Tree, The.
Gargoyle in the Snow, The.
Relativity.
Timid Ash Tree, The.
Miller, Albert G.
Pygmalion.
Miller, Alice Duer
American to France, An.
English Are Frosty, The.
I Have Loved England.
If They Meant All They Said.
Song: "Light of spring, The."
Song in Exile.
Sonnet, A: "Dear, if you love me, hold me most your friend."
White Cliffs, The, *sels.*

Young and in love—how magical the phrase!
Miller, Betty
Wind, The.
Miller, Cincinnatus Heine [*or* Hiner] *See* **Miller, Joaquin**
Miller, Emily Huntington
Bluebird, The.
I Love to Hear the Story.
Land of Heart's Desire, The.
New Year Song.
Thy Peace.
Wood-Dove's Note, The.
Miller, Francesca Falk
Abraham Lincoln.
George Washington.
Invocation: "Help me to make this working day."
Old Face, An.
Miller, Heather Ross
Taking Steps at Thirteen Months.
Miller, Helen Janet
Only the Wind Says Spring.
Miller, J. R.
If the Lord Should Come.
Miller, James
Foreign Songsters.
Italian Opera.
Life of a Beau, The.
Miller, Jason
Blind Man.
Blossom.
Constancy, The.
Fire Song.
First Note.
Solitary, The.
Square in Savannah.
Step.
Summer Night.
Miller, Joaquin (Cincinnatus Heine [*or* HineMiller],
Adios.
Alaska.
Arctic Moon, The.
At the Grave of Walker.
Bravest Battle, The.
By the Pacific Ocean.
Byron, *sel.*
Christmas Morning.
Columbus.
Crossing the Plains.
Cuba Libre.
Dead in the Sierras.
Defense [*or* Defence] of the Alamo, The.
Exodus for Oregon.
For Those Who Fail.
Fortunate Isles, The.
Greatest Battle That Ever Was Fought, The.
In Men Whom Men Condemn [as Ill].
Juanita.
Kit Carson's Ride.
Land That Man Has Newly Trod, A.
Last Supper, The.
Lines: "In men whom men condemn as ill."
Monkeys.
Mothers of Men, The.
Peter Cooper.
Picture of a Bull.
Rejoice.
Resurge San Francisco.
Sail On!
San Francisco.
Song: "There is many a love in the land, my love."
That Gentle Man from Boston Town.
That Texan Cattle Man.
To Russia.
Twilight at the Heights.
Vaquero.
Voice of the Dove, The.
Westward Ho!
William Brown of Oregon.
With Walker in Nicaragua, *sel.*
Yukon, The, *sel.*
Miller, Joseph Corson
Epicedium.
Flying Fish.
Hymn to the Guardian Angel.
Mad Poll.
March of Humanity, The.
Roses.
St. Thomas Aquinas.
Song for Love's Coming of Age.
Wind in the Elms, The.
Miller, Joseph Dana
Hymn of Hate, The.
Miller, Katherine Wise
Stevenson's Birthday.
Miller, Madeleine Sweeny
How Far to Bethlehem?
Miller, Mary Britton
Camel.
Cat, The.
Foal.
Here She Is.
Lion.
Shore.
Son just born, A.
Victory.
Waves.
Miller, Merlin G.
Just to Be Glad.
Miller, Nellie Burget
Little Day Moon.
Mist, The.
Morning Clouds.
Our House.
Shack, The.
Shadow on the Loom, The.
Snow, The.
Sun Drops Red, The.
Miller, Olive Beaupré
Circus Parade, The.
Road to China, The.
Miller, Peter
Capture of Edwin Alonzo Boyd, The.
Prevention of Stacy Miller, The.
Miller, Ruth
Birds.
Cover my eyes with your palm.
Cycle, *sel.*
Floating Island, The.
Fruit.
Fundisi.
Honey.
It Is Better to Be Together.
Long Since Last.
Penguin on the Beach.
Plankton.
Sterkfontein.
Miller, Sadie Louise
Gain of Losses, The.
Miller, Thomas
Mister Fly.
Mother to Her Infant, The.
My Dearest Baby, Go to Sleep.
Old Baron, The.
Sea-Deeps, The.
Spring Walk, The.
Sun, The.
Miller, Vassar
Adam's Footprint.
Apology.
At a Child's Baptism.
Autumnal Spring Song.
Ballad of the Unmiraculous Miracle.
Bout with Burning.
Ceremony.
Christmas Mourning.
Defense Rests.
Epithalamium: "Crept side by side beyond the thresh."
Faintly and from Far Away.
Fantasy on the Resurrection.
Final Hunger, The.
For Instruction.
From an Old Maid.
Fulfillment.
How Far?
In Consolation.
Joyful Prophecy.
Judas.
Lesson in Detachment, A.
Love Song Out of Nothing.
Love's Eschatology.
New Icarus, The.
No Return.
One Thing Needful, The.
Paradox.
Protest.
Quarry, The.
Receiving Communion.
Reciprocity.
Resolution, The.
Resolve.
Return.
Song for a Marriage.
Though He Slay Me.
Tree of Silence, The.
Whooping Crane, The.
Without Ceremony.
Worshiper, The.
Miller, William
John Frost.
Spring, *sel.*
Spring comes linking and jinking through the woods, The.
Willie Winkie.
Millett, William
I Am Ham Melanite.
Milligan, Alice
Dark Palace, The.
Fainne Gael an Lae.
Song of Freedom, A.
When I Was a Little Girl.
Milligan, J. Lewis
Where Is Thy God?
Milligan, Spike
Thousand Hairy Savages, A.
Millikin, Richard Alfred
Groves of Blarney, The.
Mills, Elizabeth Randall- *See* **Randall-Mills, Elizabeth**
Mills, Ida M.
At Breakfast.
In Days Gone By.
Mills, Mary
Apostasy.
Fable: "Bough will bend, the leaf will sometime fall, The.
Garden Party.
Library, The.
Pedigree.
Postscript.
White Horse, The.
White Peacock, The.
Millward, Pamela
Diogenes the Trainman.
I Was Down the Field.
Just as the Small Waves Came Where No Waves Were.
Mad Willow Lover.
To C., Crossing the Park.
Milman, Henry Hart
Beacons, The.
Burial Hymn.
Crucifixion, The.
For Palm Sunday.
Holy Field, The.
Hymn for the Sixteenth Sunday after Trinity.

Milman (continued)
Ride On in Majesty.
Samor, *sel.*
Milne, Alan Alexander
At the Zoo.
Ballad of Private Chadd, The.
Binker ("Binker—what I call him—is a secret of my own").
Buckingham Palace.
Christening, The.
Dormouse and the Doctor, The.
End, The.
Engineer, The.
Forgiven.
Four Friends, The.
From a Full Heart.
Furry Bear.
Good Little Girl, The.
Growing Up.
Halfway Down.
Happiness.
Hoppity.
If I Were King.
In the Fashion.
King's Breakfast, The.
London, 1940.
Market Square.
Miss James.
Missing.
Old Sailor, The.
Politeness.
Puppy and I.
Rice Pudding.
Sand-between-the-Toes.
Thought, A.
Three Foxes, The.
Us Two.
Milne, Angela *See* **"Ande"**
Milne, Ewart
Could I Believe.
Deirdre and the Poets.
Diamond Cut Diamond.
Dublin Bay.
Evergreen.
Hills of Pomeroy, The.
In a Valley of This Restless Mind.
Sierran Vigil.
Tinker's Moon.
Vanessa Vanessa.
Milner, B. E.
Christmas Night.
Milner, E. V.
Open to Visitors.
Milner-Brown, A. L.
Who Knows?
Milnes, Richard Monckton, 1st Baron Houghton
Brookside, The.
Columbus and the *Mayflower.*
Envoy to an American Lady, An.
Good Night and Good Morning.
In Memoriam.
Lady Moon.
Men of Old, The.
Our Mother Tongue.
Palm-Tree and the Pine, The.
Shadows.
Small Things.
Two Angels.
Venetian Serenade, The.
Milns, William
Federal Constitution, The.
Milton, Brock
Night Shower.
Milton, John (c.1563-1647)
Fair Oriana in the Morn.
Milton, John (1608-1674)
And call the vales, and bid them hither cast.
And in a moment will create.
As when a vulture on Imaus bred.
By the rushy-fringèd bank.
Can this be he.
Fairfax, Whose Name in Arms through Europe Rings.
God made thee perfet, not immutable.
He, above the rest/ In shape and gesture proudly eminent.
High on a throne of royal state, which far.
I, dark in light, exposed.
Last came, and last did go.
Now too nigh/ Th' archangel stood.
O for that warning voice, which he who saw.
Occasions drew me early to this city.
. . .Others more mild,/ Retreated in a silent valley, sing.
She, as a veil down to the slender waist.
She that has that is clad in cómplete steel.
Shepherds on the lawn, The.
Silent, and in face/ Confounded, long they sat, as stricken mute.
So spake the archangel Michael; then paused.
So talked the spirted sly snake; and Eve.
Some say no evil thing that walks by night.
Southward through Eden went a river large.
Sweet bird that shunn'st the noise of folly.
There can be slain/ No sacrifice.
They err who count it glorious to subdue.
This is true liberty, when free-born men.
This only hope relieves me, that the strife.
To him she hasted; in her face excuse.
To whom the wingèd Hierarch replied.
To whom thus also th' angel last replied.
Two of far nobler shape, erect and tall.
We may no longer stay: go, waken Eve.
Why was my breeding order'd and prescrib'd.
With grave/ Aspect he rose.
With that (such power was given him then), he took.
Adam and Eve ("Birds their choir apply; airs, vernal airs, The").
Adam and Eve ("So passed they naked on, nor shunned the sight").
Adam, First Man of Men.
Adam's Morning Hymn.
All Is Best.
And God Created the Great Whales.
Another on the University Carrier.
Arcades.
Areopagitica, *sel.*
Ark, The.
At a Solemn Music [*or* Musick].
At a Vacation Exercise [in the College, Part Latin, Part English].
Athens.
Atonement, The.
Banishment, The.
Banishment from Paradise.
Beëlzebub Rises to Speak.
Blindness of Samson, The.
But to His Mother Mary.
Chastity.
Comus; a Masque Presented at Ludlow Castle.
Cottager and His Landlord, The.
Council of Satan, The.
Creation of Man, The.
Creation of the World, The.
Creation of Woman, The.
Death of Samson.
Delilah.
Deliverer, The.
Departure from Paradise, The.
Description of Chaos.
Echo.
Eden.
Epilogue: "All is best, though we oft doubt."
Epitaph, An, on the Admirable Dramatic Poet, William Shakespeare.
Epitaph on the Marchioness of Winchester, An.
Epithalamion: "Haile wedded love, mysterious law, true sourse."
Eternal Spring, The.
Eve.
Eve Penitent.
Eve to Adam ("With thee conversing, I forget all time").
Evening in Paradise.
Eve's Speech to Adam.
Eve's Temptation and Fall.
Exit from Eden.
Expulsion from Paradise.
Fall, The.
Fall of the Angels, The.
Fallen Angels, The ("Him the Almighty Power").
Fallen Angels ("Nine times the space that measures day and night").
Fallen Angels, The ("Of Man's first disobedience, and the fruit").
Farewell of the Attendant Spirit.
Final Chorus: "All is best, though we oft doubt."
First Day of Creation, The.
First Temptation, The.
Free Will and God's Foreknowledge.
Gabriel Meets Satan.
Garden, The.
Great Creator from His Work Returned, The.
Hail, Holy Light.
He That Has Light Within.
Heaven.
Hell.
Heroic Vengeance.
How Soon Hath Time.
Hymn: "It was the winter wild."
Hymn on the Morning of Christ's Nativity.
Hymn to Light.
Il Penseroso.
Immortality.
Inner Light.
Invocation: "Of Man's first disobedience, and the fruit."
Invocation of Comus, The.
Invocation to Light, The.
Invocation to the Heavenly Muse.
Invocation to Urania.
Katherine Milton: Died MDCLVIII.
Lady That in the Prime.
Lady's Song.
L'Allegro.
Last Chorus: "All is best, though we oft doubt."
Late Massacre in Piedmont, The.
Lawrence of Virtuous Father Virtuous Son.
Leave Taking.
Let Us with a Gladsome Mind, *abr.*
Light.
Lucifer.
Lycidas.
Magi, The.
Mammon.
Mask, A.
Mask Presented at Ludlow-Castle, A.
Masque Presented at Ludlow Castle, A.
May Morning.
Messiah, The.
Methought I Saw My Late Espoused Saint.
Mirth, with Thee I Mean to Live.
Moon and the Nightingale, The.
Morning Hymn of Adam and Eve.

Myself Am Hell.
Nativity, The.
New Worlds.
Night Falls on Eden.
Now Came Still Evening On.
O Dark, Dark, Dark, *abr.*
O Earth, How Like to Heav'n.
O Foolishnes of Men.
O Nightingale.
O Nightingale That on Yon Bloomy Spray.
Ode on the Morning of Christ's Nativity.
O'er the Smooth Enamelled Green.
On a May Morning.
On His Being Arrived at the Age of Twenty-three.
On His Blindness.
On His Deceased Wife.
On His Having Arrived at the Age of Twenty-three.
On His Late Wife.
On His Twenty-third Birthday.
On May Morning.
On Shakespeare.
On the Detraction Which Followed upon My Writing Certain Treatises ("A Book was writ of late called *Tetrachordon').*
On the Detraction Which Followed upon My Writing Certain Treatises ("I did but prompt the age").
On the Late Massacre in Piedmont [*or* Piemont].
On the Lord General Fairfax at the Siege of Colchester.
On the Massacre in Piedmont.
On the Morning of Christ's Nativity.
On the New Forcers of Conscience under the Long Parliament.
On the Oxford Carrier ("Here lieth one who did most truly prove").
On the Religious Memory of Mrs. Catharine Thomason.
On the Same.
On the University Carrier ("Here lieth one who did most truly prove").
On the University Carrier (Who Sickn'd in the Time of His Vacancy) ("Here lies old Hobson").
On Time.
O'er the Smooth Enamelled Green.
Over All the Face of Earth Main Ocean Flowed.
Pandemonium and Its Architect.
Panorama, The.
Paradise.
Paradise Lost, *sels.*
Paradise Regained.
Parthians, The.
Passion, The.
Peaceful Night, The.
Place of the Damned, The.
Plan of Salvation, The.
Poet-Preacher's Prayer, A.
Praise the Lord.
Prospect of Eden, The.
Psalm LXXXIV: "How lovely are thy dwellings fair!"
Retreat from Paradise, The.
Rivers Arise; a Fragment.
Rome.
Sabrina ("There is a gentle nymph").
Sabrina Fair.
Samson Agonistes.
Satan.
Satan and His Host.
Satan and the Fallen Angels.
Satan Beholds Eve.
Satan Defiant.
Satan Discovers Eden.
Satan Journeys to the Garden of Eden.
Satan Looks upon Adam and Eve in Paradise.
Satan on War.
Satan Ponders His Fallen State.
Satan Views the World.
Satan's Adjuration.
Satan's Guile.
Satan's Metamorphosis.
Satan's Pride.
Satan's Soliloquy.
Satan's Speech.
Scene in Paradise, A.
Scheme of Redemption, The.
Second Sonnet on "Tetrachordon."
Sometimes, with Secure Delight.
Song: "Nymphs and shepherds, dance no more."
Song: "O'er [*or* O're] the smooth enamel [l]ed green."
Song: On May Morning.
Song: "O're the smooth enamel'd green."
Song: "Sabrina fair."
Song: "Star that bids the shepherd fold, The."
Song: "Sweet Echo, sweetest nymph, that liv'st unseen."
Song: "To the ocean now I fly."
Song on May Morning.
Sonnet: Avenge O Lord Thy Slaughter'd Saints.
Sonnet: "Captain or Colonel, or Knight in Arms."
Sonnet: "Cyriack, this three years' day."
Sonnet: "Cyriack, whose grandsire on the royal bench."
Sonnet: "Daughter to that good Earl, once President."
Sonnet: "How soon hath Time, the subtle thief of youth."
Sonnet: "I did but prompt the age to quit their clogs."
Sonnet: "Lawrence, of virtuous father virtuous son."
Sonnet: "Methought I saw my late espouséd saint."
Sonnet: "O Nightingale, that on yon bloomy spray."
Sonnet: On His Being Arrived at the Age of Twenty-three.
Sonnet: On the Late Massacre in Piedmont.
Sonnet XIV: On the Religious Memorie of Mrs. Catherine Thomason My Christian Friend Deceased Dec. 16, 1646.
Sonnet: To Mr. H. Lawes, on His Aires.
Sonnet: "When I consider how my light is spent."
Sonnet on His Blindness.
Sonnet on His Deceased Wife.
Standing on Earth.
Star That Bids the Shepherd Fold, The.
Subject of Heroic Song, The.
Sum of Wisdom, The.
Summons, The.
Superior Fiend, The.
Sweet Echo [Sweetest Nymph, That Liv'st Unseen].
Table Richly Spread, A.
Temperance and Virginity.
Tenure of Kings and Magistrates, The, *sel.*
Their Banishment.
Their Wedded Love.
Then, When I Am Thy Captive, Talk of Chains.
Thus Eve to Adam.
To a Virtuous Young Lady.
To Cyriack Skinner ("Cyriack, this three years' day").
To Cyriack Skinner ("Cyriack, whose grandsire, on the royal bench").
To Mr. Cyriack Skinner upon his Blindness.
To Mr. H. Lawes on His Airs.
To Mr. Lawrence.
To My Friend Mr. Henry Lawes [on His Airs].
To Oliver Cromwell.
To Sir Henry Vane the Younger.
To the Lady Margaret Ley.
To the Lord General Cromwell (May, 1652).
To the Lord General Fairfax.
To the Nightingale.
To the Ocean Now I Fly.
Transcendence of God, The.
True and False Glory.
Upon the Circumcision.
Vision of Athens.
War in Heaven.
Ways of God to Men, The.
Wedded Love.
What Though the Field Be Lost?
When I Consider How My Light Is Spent.
When the Assault Was Intended to the City.
Woman.
World Beautiful, The.

"Mimi." *See* **Duryee, Mary Ballard**

Mimnermus
Elegiac.
Sun's Golden Bowl, The.
Youth and Age.

Minamoto no Shigeyuki
Winter has at last come.

Minde, Henry S.
Thou Who Taught the Thronging People.

Miner, Virginia Scott
Golden Spurs.

Minot, John Clair
Brook That Runs to France, The.
Little Flags, The.

Minot, Laurence
Burgesses of Calais, The.
Song of Laurence Minot.

"Minski, Nikolai Maksimovich" (Nikolai Maksimovich Vilenkin)
Force.

Miriam, Sister (Margaret Miriam Gallagher; "F. kevin Condol")
Give Me the Sun.
Prometheus Unbound.

Miriam Teresa, Sister
To the Most Holy Crown of Thorns.

Mirick, Edith
Last Hill.
Miracle.
Two Others, on Either Side.

Misch, Robert J.
To J. S.

Mish, Charlotte
Stray Dog.

"Miss X *and* Miss Y."
Merry Month, The.

Mistral, Frédéric
Aliscamp, The.
Cocooning, The.
Leaf-picking, The.
Mares of the Camargue, The.
Mirèio, The, *sels.*

"Mistral, Gabriela" (Lucila Godoy Alcayaga)
Close to Me.
Hymn for the Day.
Little Girl That Lost a Finger, The.
Night.
Poem of the Son.
Teacher's Prayer, The.
Where Shall We Dance?

Mitchell, Adrian
Accountant in His Bath, The ("The accountant dried his imperfect back").

Mitchell (continued)
Banana.
Lying in State.
Telegram One.
Mitchell, Anna Virginia
Sonnet: "Be secret, heart, and if your dreams have come."
Mitchell, Cyprus R.
Soul of Jesus Is Restless, The.
Mitchell, Jack
Ballad of the Sailor Ben.
Hints on Writing Verse.
Mitchell, John
Reply to "In Flanders Fields."
Mitchell, John Hanlon
City Song, A.
Farm Wife.
Sea Hunger.
Mitchell, Jonathan
On the Following Work and Its Author.
Mitchell, Elwyn Langdon ("John Philip Varley")
Carol: "Mary, the mother, sits on the hill."
Fear.
Purpose.
Song: "Mary, the mother, sits on the hill."
Sweets That Die.
Technique.
To a Writer of the Day.
To One Being Old.
Wayside Virgin, The.
Written at the End of a Book.
Mitchell, Lucy Sprague
Back and Forth.
House of the Mouse, The.
It Is Raining.
Lost Ball, The.
My Bed.
What Is a Brook?
Mitchell, Lulu W.
Toiler, Canst Thou Dream?
Mitchell, Ruth Comfort (Mrs. William Sanborn Young)
Bride, The.
Compensation.
Night Court, The.
Quièn Sabe?
Travel Bureau, The.
Vinegar Man, The.
Mitchell, Silas Weir
Decanter of Madeira, Aged 86, to George Bancroft, Aged 86.
From Dark to Light.
Good Night.
Herndon.
How the *Cumberland* Went Down.
Idleness.
Kearsarge.
Lincoln.
Of One Who Seemed to Have Failed.
On a Boy's First Reading of "King Henry V."
Quaker Graveyard, The.
Song of the Flags, The.
To a Magnolia Flower in the Garden of the Armenian Convent at Venice.
Vespers.
Mitchell, Susan L.
Heart's Low Door, The.
Immortality.
Irish Council Bill, 1907, The [*parody on the* Shan Van Vocht], *sel.*
Is it this you call Home Rule?
Living Chalice, The.
Wind Bloweth Where It Listeth, The.
Mitchell, Walter
Cheer of the *Trenton,* The.
Reefing Topsails.
Tacking Ship off Shore.
Mitchell, William
Shall We Forget.
Mitford, John
Roman Legions, The.
Mitford, Mary Russell
Joy of Life.
Rienzi, *sel.*
Written in July, 1824.
Mitsukuni
Lotus Leaves.
Mitsune (Oshikochi no Mitsune)
Since I heard/ Faintly the voice.
White chrysanthemum, The.
"Mix, Parmenas" (Andrew J. Kelley)
Accepted and Will Appear.
He Came to Pay.
Mizell, Don A.
Hope was faced alone.
I want you to hear me.
Mkalimoto, Ernie
Energy for a New Thang.
Mnasalcas
To a Dead Cricket.
Mockett, Luella Markley
Haymow, The.
Modena, Leone da
Epitaph: "Implacable angel, The."
Modisane, Bloke
Black Blues.
Blue Black.
Lonely.
One Thought for My Lady.
Moffat, Gertrude MacGregor
All Night I Heard.
Moffit, John
Closing Cadence.
Presence.
Mohammed
Koran, The, *sel.*
Teaching of Mohammed, The.
Mohr, Joseph
Heilige Nacht.
Silent Night [Holy Night].
Stille Nacht.
Moir, David Macbeth
Casa's Dirge.
Mokhomo, M. A.
When He Spoke to Me of Love.
Molière (Jean Baptiste Poquelin)
To Monsieur de la Mothe le Vayer.
Moll, Ernest.
After Reading a Book on Abnormal Psychology.
At the Grave of a Land-Shark.
Beware the Cuckoo.
Clearing for the Plough.
Dew-Plants.
Eagles over the Lambing Paddock.
Fishing in the Australian Alps.
Foxes among the Lambs.
Gnarled Riverina Gum-Tree, A.
On Having Grown Old.
Returned Soldier.
Undertaker's Advertisement, An.
Mollineux, Mary
Solitude.
Molloy, James Lyman
Bantry Bay.
Kerry Dance, The.
Moloney, Patrick
I make not my division of the hours.
Know that the age of Pyrrha is long passed.
O sweet Queen-city of the golden South.
Rude rebuffs of bay-besieging winds, The.
Sonnets—Ad Innuptam (I-VII).
Thy throne is ringed by amorous cavaliers.
Momaday, N. Scott
Angle of Geese.
Before an Old Painting of the Crucifixion.
Earth and I Gave You Turquoise.
Mombert, Alfred
Along the Strand.
Idyl: "And my young sweet heart sat at board with me."
Sleeping They Bear Me.
Moment, John J.
Best Treasure, The.
New Year.
Palm Sunday.
Moncrieff, William Thomas
Waltzing It.
Money, Sir Leo
King Cotton, *sel.*
Mills of Lancashire grind very small, The.
Money-Coutts, Francis Burdett
Any Father to Any Son.
Dream, The.
Empires.
Forgive!/ And tell me that sweet tale.
Little Sequence, A, *sels.*
Mors, Morituri Te Salutamus.
No wonder you so oft have wept.
On a Fair Woman.
On a Wife.
Monkhouse, Cosmo
Dead March, A.
In Arcady.
Limerick: "Lady there was of Antigua, A."
Limerick: "Poor benighted Hindoo, The."
Limerick: "There once was a girl of New York."
Limerick: "There once was a person of Benin."
Limerick: "There was a young girl of Lahore."
Night Express, The.
Satisfied Tiger, The.
Secret, The.
Song: "Who calls me bold because I won my love."
Song of the Seasons, A.
Spectrum, The.
To a New-born Child.
Monkman, Robina
Sea Burial.
Monod, Theodore
Christ Alone.
None of Self and All of Thee.
Monro, Harold
At a Country Dance in Provence.
At Home, Alone with the Dog.
Bird at Dawn, The.
Bitter Sanctuary.
Carrion.
Cat's Meat.
Children of Love.
City-Storm.
Clock.
Curate's Christmas Eve, The.
Dawn, *sel.*
Dawn of Womanhood.
Dog.
Dogs.
Elm Angel.
Empty House, The.
Evening.
Every Thing.
Flower Is Looking, A.
Foundered Tram, The.
Fresh Air, The.
God.
Goldfish.
Great City.
Guest, The.
Harbour.
Hearthstone.
Hurrier, The.
If Suddenly a Clod of Earth.
Living.
London Interior.

Man Carrying Bale.
Midnight Lamentation.
Milk for the Cat.
Natural History, The, *sel.*
Nightingale near the House, The.
Officers' Mess (1916).
One Blackbird.
Overheard on a Saltmarsh.
Real Property.
Rebellious Vine, The.
She Was Young and Blithe and Fair.
Silent Pool, The.
Solitude.
Strange Companion, The.
Strange Meetings, *sels.*
Street Fight.
Suburb.
Terrible Door, The.
Thistledown.
Vixen Woman, The.
Week-End, *sels.*
Wind, The.
Wind in the Dusk.
Youth in Arms, *sels.*

Monroe, Arthur W.
Cliff Dwelling, The.
Forest Fire, The.
Lost in a Blizzard.
Man of the Open West, The.
Toll of the Desert, The.

Monroe, Harriet
Blue Ridge, The.
Commemoration Ode (World's Columbian Exposition, Chicago, 1892), *sels.*
Democracy.
Farewell, A: "Good-bye [*or* Good-by]—no [*or* nay], do not grieve that it is over."
Fortunate One, The.
Hotel, The.
I Love My Life, but Not Too Well.
In the Beginning.
Inner Silence, The.
Lincoln.
Love Song.
Lullaby: "My little one, sleep softly."
Man of Science Speaks, The.
Mother Earth.
Mountain Song.
Nancy Hanks.
Night-blooming Cereus, The.
Now.
On the Porch.
Pain.
Pine at Timber-Line, The.
Romney, The.
Shadow Child, The.
Supernal Dialogue.
Thief on the Cross, The.
Turbine, The.
Two Heroes.
Vernon Castle.
Washington.
Water Ouzel, The.
Wonder of It.

Monsell, John Samuel Bewley
Fight the Good Fight.
In the Garden.
Light of the World.
Litany: "When my feet have wander'd."
O Love Divine.
Sing to the Lord of Harvest.
Worship the Lord in the Beauty of Holiness.

Mont, Pol de
Evening Landscape.

Montagne, Victor Alexis de la
Congress, 1878.

Montagu, Lady Mary Wortley
Farewell to Bath.
In Answer to a Lady Who Advised Retirement.
Lady M. M——'s Farewel to Bath.
Lover, The; a Ballad.
Restrained Passion.

Montague, James Jackson
And When They Fall.
Mollusk, The.
Same Old Story, The.
Scot's Farewell to His Golf Ball, A.
Sleepytown Express, The.
Thanksgiving Day.
Vamp Passes, The.

Montague, James L.
Mad Actor.

Montague, John
All Legendary Obstacles.
Bright Day, A.
First Invasion of Ireland, The.
Murphy in Manchester.
Poisoned Lands.
Time Out.
Trout, The.

Montale, Eugenio
Dora Markus.
Pain of Living, The.
Sunflower, The.

Montemayor, Jorge de
Diana, *sels.*
Melisea, Her Song in Scorn of Her Shepherd Narcissus.
Nymph Diana's Song, The.
Nymph Selvagia, The, Her Song.
Of this high grace with bliss conjoined.
Song: "Shepherd, who can pass such wrong."
What changes here, O hair.

Montesquiou-Fezensac, Comte Robert de
Child's Prayer, The.

Montgomerie, Alexander
About ane bank, where birdis on bewis.
Adieu, O Daisy of Delight!
Cherry and the Slae, The, *sel.*
Description of Tyme, A.
Hay! Now the Day Dawis.
Hey! Now the Day Dawns!
Nicht Is Neir Gone, The.
Night Is Near Gone, The.
Solsequium, The.
To Henry Constable and Henry Keir.
To His Maistres.
To R. Hudson.

Montgomerie, William
Author Unknown.
Elegy: "Narrowing of knowledge to one window to a door, A."
Elegy for William Soutar.
Epitaph: "My brother is skull and skeleton now."
Estuary.
Glasgow Street.
Is there no vision in a lovely place?
Kinfauns Castle, *sel.*

Montgomery, Carrie Judd
Discerning the Lord's Body.
Praise at Midnight.

Montgomery, Eleanor Elizabeth
Adieu.
New Zealand Regret, A.

Montgomery, George Edgar
At Night.
Dead Soldier, A.
England.
To a Child.

Montgomery, James
According to The Gracious Word.
Angels, from the Realms of Glory.
Arnold von Winkelried.
At Home in Heaven.
Christ Our Example in Suffering.
Columbus.
Come to Calvary's Holy Mountain.
Daisy, The.
Earth Is Full of God's Goodness, The.
Field Flower, A.
Go to Dark Gethsemane.
God Is My Strong Salvation.
Good Tidings of Great Joy to All People.
In the Hour of Trial.
Indian Mother About to Destroy Her Child, An.
Inspiration, The.
King Eternal, The.
Lord Is My Shepherd, The.
Lust of Gold, The.
Make Way for Liberty.
Mother's Love.
Nativity.
Night.
Patriot's Pass-Word, The.
Soliloquy of a Water-Wagtail.
Stranger and His Friend, The.
There Is a Land.
This Do in Remembrance of Me.
Visit to Bethlehem in Spirit, A.
Well Done.
West Indies, The, *sels.*
What Is Prayer?

Montgomery, James Stuart
Landlubber's Chantey, The.
Swashbuckler's Song, The.

Montgomery, Leslie Alexander *See* **"Doyle, Lynn"**

Montgomery, Lucy Maud (Mrs. Ewan Macdonald)
Love's Miracle.
Off to the Fishing Ground.

Montgomery, Marion
What Makes Life Interesting.

Montgomery, P. L.
Whence Cometh My Help.

Montgomery, Roselle Mercier
Armistice Day.
Counsel.
On the Death of an Aged Friend.
Ulysses Returns, I-IV.
What Does It Mean to Be American?

Montgomery, U. M.
Grey Brother.

Montgomery, Whitney
Way I Pray, The.

Monti, Vincenzo
Ode on Superstition, *sel.*
Tyrant has fallen, The.

Montoro, Antonio de
Ropero, El ("Ropero, so sad and so forlorn").

Montrose, James Graham, 5th Earl and 1st Marquess of *See* **Graham, James, Marquess of Montrose**

Montross, Lois Seyster (Mrs. Lynn Montross)
Codes.
Decent Burial.
I Wear a Crimson Cloak To-Night.

Montross, Percy
Oh, My Darling Clementine.

Moodie, Susanna Strickland
Canadian Hunter's Song.
Indian Summer.

Moody, Minnie Hite
Say This of Horses.

Moody, William Vaughn
Bracelet of Grass, The.
Counting Man, The.
Daguerreotype, The.
Death of Eve, The, *sel.*
Faded Pictures.
Fire-Bringer, The, *sels.*
Gloucester Moors.
Good Friday Night.
Grey Day, A ("Grey drizzling mists. . .").

Moody (continued)
Heart's Wild-Flower.
Jetsam, *sel.*
Menagerie, The.
No Hint of Stain.
Ode in Time of Hesitation, An.
On a Soldier Fallen in the Philippines.
Once at a simple turning of the way.
Pandora's Songs.
Prairie Ride, A.
Quarry, The.
Road-Hymn for the Start.
Robert Gould Shaw.
Serf's Secret, The.
Thammuz.
This earth is not the steadfast place.
Yea, Jubal?/ Nothing, mother.
Mooney, Stephen
Water Color.
Moore, Augustus M.
Ballade of Ballade-Mongers, A.
Moore, Bertha
Child's Thought, A.
Moore, Charles Leonard
Disenchantment.
Or Ever the Earth Was.
Soul unto Soul Glooms Darkling.
Spring Returns, The.
Then Shall We See.
Thou Livest, O Soul!
To England.
Moore, Clement Clarke
Night before Christmas, The.
Visit from St. Nicholas, A.
Moore, Edward
Fables for the Female Sex, *sel.*
Hymn to Poverty, A.
Nun, The.
Poet, and His Patron, The.
Song: "For a shape, and a bloom, and an air, and a mien."
Song the Eighth: "That Jenny's my friend."
Song the Ninth: "You tell me I'm handsome."
Moore, Esther P.
Afraid?
Moore, George
Parisian Idyl, A, *sel.*
Rondo: "Did I love thee? I only did desire."
Sapphic Dream, A.
Sonnet: Corpse, The.
Sonnet: "Idly she yawned, and threw her heavy hair."
This is the twilight of the summer dead.
Moore, John
Christmas Snow.
Moore, Sir John Henry
Duke of Benevento, The.
Song: "Indeed, my Caelia, 'tis in vain.
Moore, John Travers
Last Flower, The.
Moore, Julia A.
Ashtabula Disaster, The.
Departed Friend, A.
Little Libbie.
"Lord Byron" was an Englishman.
Sketch of Lord Byron's Life, *sel.*
What I Have Wrote.
Willie's and Nellie's Wish.
Moore, Marianne
Apparition of Splendor.
Arctic Ox, The.
Armour's Underming Modesty.
Arthur Mitchell.
At Rest in the Blast.
Bird-witted.
Carriage from Sweden, A.
Charity Overcoming Envy.
Critics and Connoisseurs.
Dock Rats.
Dream.
Elephants.
England.
Face, A.
Fish, The.
Four Quartz Crystal Clocks.
Frigate Pelican, The.
Glory.
Granite and Steel.
Grave, A.
Graveyard, A.
Harp You Play So Well, The.
He "Digesteth Harde Yron."
Hero, The.
His Shield.
I May, I Might, I Must.
Icosasphere, The.
In Distrust of Merits.
In the Public Garden.
Jerboa, The.
Keeping Their World Large.
Labors of Hercules, The.
Leonardo Da Vinci's.
Melancthon.
Melchior Vulpius.
Mind, Intractable Thing, The.
Mind Is an Enchanting Thing, The.
Monkeys, The.
My Apish Cousins.
Nevertheless.
Nine Nectarines and Other Porcelain.
No Swan So Fine.
O to Be a Dragon.
Old Amusement Park.
Pangolin, The.
Paper Nautilus, The.
Part of a Novel, Part of a Poem, Part of a Play, *sels.*
Past Is the Present, The.
Pedantic Literalist.
Peter.
Poetry.
Propriety.
Rigorists.
Roses Only.
Saint Nicholas.
St. Valentine.
See in the Midst of Fair Leaves.
Silence.
Snakes, Mongooses, Snake-Charmers and the Like.
Sojourn in the Whale.
Spenser's Ireland.
Staff of Aesculapius, The.
Steeple-Jack, The.
Student, The.
Sun!
Talisman, A.
Tell Me, Tell Me.
That Harp You Play so Well.
Then the Ermine.
Those Various Scalpels.
To a Chameleon.
To a Giraffe.
To a Snail.
To a Steam Roller.
Tom Fool at Jamaica.
Values in Use.
Virginia Britannia.
What Are Years?
When I Buy Pictures.
Wood-Weasel, The.
Moore, Maurice
Easter, Day of Christ Eternal.
Moore, Mavor
Biography.
Moore, Merrill
And Then Her Burial.
And to the Young Men.
Answer.
Bees before Winter.
Book of How, The.
Clerk in the Hospital Record Room in Summer.
Constellation.
Domestic: Climax.
"Final Status Never Ascertained." Lloyds Registry.
Flies, The.
He Said the Facts.
How She Resolved to Act.
Hymn for Water.
In Magic Words.
It Is Winter, I Know.
Joe Greene.
Just Then the Door.
Liquids.
No Envy, John Carter.
Noise That Time Makes, The.
O Mad Spring, One Waits.
Old Men and Old Women Going Home on the Street Car.
Pandora and the Moon.
Poet Tells about Nature, The.
Scientia Vincit Omnia?
Shot Who? Jim Lane!
There Is a Way of Life.
They Also Stand. . .
Undergraduate.
Unknown Man in the Morgue.
Village Noon; Mid-Day Bells.
Warning to One.
Moore, Nicholas
Act of Love.
Alcestis in Ely.
Fred Apollus at Fava's.
Hair's Breadth, The.
Incidents in Playfair House.
Little Girl, The.
Love.
O Rose, O Rainbow.
Phallic Symbol, The.
Why the British Girls Give In So Easily.
Winter and Red Berries.
Moore, Richard
Deep Discussion, A.
Suburb Hilltop.
Moore, Rosalie
Catalog.
Gnat.
Imprecation for an Aesthetic Society with Newts, Warts, Waxes and Pins.
Moore, Stephen
Second Mile, The.
Moore, Sturge *See* **Moore, Thomas Sturge**
Moore, Thomas
All That's Bright Must Fade.
Argument, An.
At the Mid Hour of Night.
Believe Me, if All Those Endearing Young Charms.
Bendemeer.
Bird, Let Loose in Eastern Skies, The.
By Bendemeer's Stream.
Canadian Boat Song, A.
Child's Song.
Come, Rest in This Bosom.
Come, Ye Disconsolate.
Common Sense and Genius.
Copy of an Intercepted Despatch.
Cupid Stung ("Cupid once upon a bed.")
Dear Fanny.
Dear Harp of My Country.
Did Not.
Duke Is the Lad, The.
Echo.
Echoes.
Epigram: "'Come, come,! said Tom's father, 'at your time of life.'"

Epigram: "While life was mine, the little hour."
Epigram: "With women and apples both Paris and Adam."
Epistle of Condolence.
Epitaph on a Well-known Poet.
Epitaph on Robert Southey.
Evenings in Greece, *sel.*
Farewell, but Whenever [You Welcome the Hour].
Fill the Bumper Fair.
French Cookery.
Fudge Family in Paris, The, *sels.*
Garden Song, A.
Glory of God in Creation, The.
Glory of Patriotism, The.
Go Where Glory Waits Thee.
Golden Hour, The.
Hark! the Vesper Hymn Is Stealing.
Harp That Once through Tara's Halls, The.
Has Sorrow Thy Young Days Shaded?
How Dear to Me the Hour.
How Oft Has the Banshee Cried.
I Pray You.
I Saw from the Beach.
I Wish I Was by That Dim Lake.
I Wish I Were by That Dim Lake.
If You Have Seen.
Ill Omens.
Irish Peasant to His Mistress, The.
Joke Versified, A.
Journey Onwards, The.
Kiss, The.
Lake of the Dismal Swamp, The.
Lalla Rookh, *sels.*
Last Rose of Summer, The.
Legacy.
Let Erin Remember the Days of Old.
Let Fate do her worst; there are relics of joy.
Light of Other Days, The.
Light of the Haram, The.
"Living Dog" and "The Dead Lion," The.
Long, Long Be My Heart with Such Memories Filled.
Love Is a Hunter Boy.
Love's Young Dream.
Lying.
Meeting of the Ships, The.
Meeting of the Waters, The.
Minstrel Boy, The.
Miriam's Song.
Miss Biddy Fudge to Miss Dorothy.
Mountain Sprite, The.
My Birthday.
Nay, tempt me not to love again.
Nonsense.
Oh Blame Not the Bard.
Oh, Breath Not His Name.
Oh, Come to Me When Daylight Sets.
Oh, Thou! Who Dry'st the Mourner's Tear.
Odes to Nea, *sels.*
Of All the Men.
Oft in the Stilly Night.
On Music.
On Taking a wife.
Paddy's Metamorphosis.
Peace Be around Thee.
Peace to the Slumberers!
Penitence.
Peri's Lament for Hinda, The.
Pro Patria Mori.
Quantum Est Quod Desit.
Recent Dialogue, A.
Row Gently Here.
Scene from a Play, Acted at Oxford, Called "Matriculation."
Scotch Air.
She Is Far from the Land.
Snake, The.
Song: "Come, rest in this bosom, my own stricken deer."
Song: "When Time, who steals our years away."
Song: "Where is the nymph, whose azure eye."
Song of Fionnuala, The.
Song of O'Ruark, Prince of Breffni, The.
Sound the Loud Timbrel.
Stricken Deer, The.
Sweet Innisfallen.
Syrian Evening, A.
Take Back the Virgin Page.
Temple to Friendship, A.
Thee, Thee, Only Thee.
They May Rail at This Life.
This Life Is All Chequer'd with Pleasures and Woes.
This World Is All a Fleeting Show.
Thoughts on Editors.
Thro' Grief and thro' Danger.
Time I've Lost in Wooing, The.
'Tis the Last Rose of Summer.
To ——: "When I loved you, I can't but allow."
To Cloe.
To Fanny.
To Ladies' Eyes.
To My Mother.
Torch of Liberty, The.
Two Streams, The.
Upon Being Obliged to Leave a Pleasant Party.
Were Not the Sinful Mary's Tears.
What's My Thought Like?
When He Who Adores Thee.
When I Loved You.
Wreathe the Bowl.
Young May Moon, The.

Moore, Thomas Sturge
Beautiful Meals.
Before Rereading Shakespeare's Sonnets.
Daughter of Admetus, A.
Days and Nights.
Death in the Home.
Duet, A.
Dying Swan, The.
Event, The.
Faun, The.
Faun Tells of the Rout of the Amazons, The.
From Sappho's Death: Three Pictures by Gustave Moreau.
From Titian's "Bacchanal" in the Prado at Madrid.
Gazelles, The.
Kindness.
Light Heart.
Lubber Breeze.
Response to Rimbaud's Later Manner.
Sent from Egypt with a Fair Robe of Tissue to a Sicilian Vinedresser.
Shells.
Silence.
Summer Lightning.
To Silence.
Tongues.
Variation on Ronsard.
Vigil, The.
Wind's Work.

"Moore, Tom, Jr. "
O'Duffy's Ironsides.

Moore, Tom Inglis
Comrade in Arms.
Druidic Gums.
Kookaburra, *sel.*
No, Not the Owl.
Over the multiple terrors of Mars.
Song for Lovers.
Star Drill.

Moore, Virginia
Good Ground, The.
Joan of Arc, 1926.
To Spring.

Moore, William H. A.
Dusk Song.
It Was Not Fate.

Moorse, George H.
Bran.

Moraes, Dom
Bells for William Wordsworth.
Cainsmorning.
Final Word, The.
Girl.
Glitter of Pebbles.
Guardians, The.
Jason.
Kanheri Caves.
Lullaby: "With lights for eyes, our city turns."
Queen.
Song: "Gross sun squats above, The."
Song: "I sowed my wild oats."

Moran, Anna-Modine
Sustaining Power, The.

Moran, Irene Shirley
Lilacs for Remembrance.

Mordaunt Charles, Earl of Peterborough
Chloe.

Mordaunt, Thomas Osbert
Answer.
Call, The.
Clarion.
One Crowded Hour.
Sound, Sound the Clarion.
Verses Written during the War, 1756-1763.

Mordecai ben Isaac
Fair Thou Art.
Rock of My Salvation.

Morden, Phyllis B.
Godmother.

More, Hannah
Bas Bleu, *sel.*
Book, A.
Conversation.
Riddle, A: Book, A.
Search after Happiness, The, *sel.*
Solitude.

More, Helen F.
What's in a Name?

More, Henry
Democritus Platonissans; or, An Essay upon the Infinity of Worlds out of Platonick Principles, *abr.*
Eternal Life.
Hymn to Charity and Humility.
Hymne in Honour of Those Two Despised Virtues, Charitie and Humilitie, An.
In Him We Live.
Philosopher's Devotion, The.
Resolution.
Resolution; the Song of Hylobaris Concerning Divine Providence.

More, Sir Thomas (Saint Thomas More)
Age.
Childhood.
Consider Well.
Davy, the Dicer.
Death.
Eleventh Property, The.
Eternal Reward, Eternal Pain.
Eternity.
Fame.
First Property, The.
Fortune.
Lewis, the Lost Lover.
Manhood.
Of Fortune.
Peace of a Good Mind, The.

More (continued)
Rueful Lamentation on the Death of Queen Elizabeth, A.
Seventh Property [*or* Properte], The.
Tenth Properte, The.
This Life a Dream and Shadow.
Thomas More to Them That Seek Fortune.
Time.
To Fortune.
Twelve Properties or Conditions of a Lover, The, *sels.*
Twelve Weapons of Spiritual Battle, The, *sels.*
Two Short Ballettes . . . Made for His Pastime While He Was Prisoner in the Tower of London.
Venus and Cupide.
Moreland, John Richard
Birch Trees.
Captive.
Christ Is Crucified Anew.
Coins of Love, The.
Faith.
Grave, A.
Greater Guilt, The.
His Hands.
If a Man Die, Shall He Live Again?
If I Could Grasp a Wave from the Great Sea.
Intolerance.
Kings.
O Years Unborn.
One April Day.
Only One King.
Promise Lan', De.
Recompense.
Resurgam.
Revealment.
Sand Dunes and Sea.
Secret, The.
Song of Thanksgiving.
Splendid Lover, The.
Stranger, The.
Symbols.
To One Who Worshipped Gods of Gold.
Tokens.
What of the Night? *sel.*
Whippoorwill.
White Tree in Bloom, A.
Wild Carrot.
Ye Who Fear Death Remember April.
Moreland, Patrick Dacus
Compensate.
Crucified.
Moreno, José Rosas *See Rosas Moreno, José*
Moreno Villa, José
Kite, The.
Longings.
Opposites.
Morford, Sybil
Fairies, The.
Morgan, Angela
And the Lord God whispered and said to me.
Awakening, The.
Choice.
Come, workers! Poets, artists, dreamers, more and more.
Gandhi.
God Does Do Such Wonderful Things.
God Prays.
Hail Man!
Humanitarian, The, *sel.*
Hymn to Labor.
In Such an Age.
June Rapture.
Let Us Declare! *sel.*
Lindbergh.
Poet, The.
Reality.
Resurrection.
Seeing how the world suffered and bled.
Song of the New World.
Stand Forth!
Thanksgiving.
Three Green Trees.
To-Day.
Whole Year Christmas, The.
Windows for My Soul.
Work; a Song of Triumph.
Morgan, Bessie
'Spacially Jim.
Morgan, Edwin
From the Domain of Arnheim.
In Sobieski's Shield.
Second Life, The.
"Morgan, Emanuel." *See* **Bynner, Witter**
Morgan, Evan
Christmas Dawn at Sea, A.
Eel, The.
Morgan, Henry Victor
World Man, The.
Morgan, James Appleton
Malum Opus.
Morgan, John
Central Park: It's About This Eden Thing.
Expedition North.
Spring Afternoon.
Under Investigation.
Variations on *The Aeneid,* sel.
Woman Takes Life with Own Hand.
Morgan, John Hunt
Similia Similibus.
Morgan, R. S.
And Other Poems.
Morgan Sydney, Lady Morgan
Kate Kearney.
Morgenstern, Christian
Cloud Fantasies, I.
Korf's Joke ("Korf invents a novel kind of joke").
Mousetrap, The.
Night Song of the Fish.
She-Goat and Glow-Worm.
Twelve-Elf, The.
Vice Versa.
Virus, The.
Wooden Fence, The.
Morgridge, Harriet S.
Jack and Jill.
Mother Goose Sonnets, *sels.*
Simple Simon.
Moriarty, Helen Louise
Convent Echoes.
Mörike, Eduard Friedrich
Beauty Rohtraut.
Prayer: "Lord, as thou wilt, bestow."
Morin, Catherine A.
High June.
Lace Pedlar, The.
Morin, Maud
Bachelors' Buttons.
Shower and Sunshine.
Moritake, Arakida
Fallen flowers seemed, The.
Haiku: "Falling flower, The."
Hokku: "I thought I saw the fallen leaves."
Morlaix, Bernard de *See* **Bernard of Cluny [*or* of Morlaix]**
Morley, Christopher
Animal Crackers.
At the Dog Show.
At the Mermaid Cafeteria.
Code, The.
Confession in Holy Week.
Crib, The.
Dandy Dandelion.
Deny Yourself.
Epitaph for Any New Yorker.
Epitaph on the Proofreader of the Encyclopedia Britannica.
Gospel of Mr. Pepys, The.
Grapes of Wrath, The.
Grub Street Recessional, A.
Hallowe'en Memory, A.
He Comforts Himself.
Human Instinct, A.
I Know a Secret.
In Honor of Taffy Topaz.
Island, The.
Man with the Rake, The.
Mandarin on the Air.
Mar Quong, Chinese Laundryman.
Milkman, The.
Moon-Sheep, The.
My Pipe.
Nursery Rhymes for the Tender-hearted, *sels.*
Of a Child That Had Fever.
Of an Ancient Spaniel in Her Fifteenth Year.
Old Swimmer, The.
Plumpuppets, The.
Poets Easily Consoled.
Power-House, The.
Pre-Raphaelite, A/ Had to have things right.
Private Enterprise.
Psychoanalysts.
Quickening.
Secret Laughter.
Secret Thoughts.
Six Weeks Old.
Skating Song.
Smells.
Smells (Junior).
Song for a Little House.
"Spoken Word, The."
Sun's over the Foreyard, The.
This is all we ever say.
Thoughts for St. Stephen.
Thoughts in the Gulf Stream.
Thoughts on Being Invited to Dinner.
To a Child.
To a Post-Office Inkwell.
To a Very Young Gentleman.
To the Little House.
Translations from the Chinese, *sels.*
Trees, The.
Tryst, The.
Unearned Increment.
Washing the Dishes.
Where More Is Meant.
Morley, Thomas
Hard by a Crystal Fountain.
Morningstar, Margaret
Teacher Sees a Boy, The.
Moronelli di Fiorenza, Pier
Canzonetta: Bitter Song to His Lady, A.
Morpeau, Louis
To Madame la Duchesse de Bauffremont.
Morpurgo, Rachel
Song: "Ah, vale of woe, of gloom and darkness moulded."
Sonnet: "My soul surcharged with grief now loud complains."
Morrill, Belle Chapman
Kindly Screen, The.
My Galilees.
To a Japanese Girl Grieved over the War on China.
Morris, Alice S.
Mrs. Santa Claus' Christmas Present.
Morris, C.
Contrast, The.
Morris, Charles
Reason Fair to Fill My Glass, A.
Morris, Francis St. Vincent
Eleventh Hour, The.

Morris, George Hornell
Sailor's Prayer, A.
Morris, George Pope
Jeannie Marsh.
Leap for Life, A.
Main-Truck, The; or, A Leap for Life.
My Mother's Bible.
Near the Lake.
Oak, The.
Pocahontas.
Retort, The.
Searcher of Hearts.
Where Hudson's Wave.
Woodman, Spare That Tree.
Yankee Doodle ("Once on a time old Johnny Bull").
Morris, Gouverneur, Jr
D'Artagnan's Ride.
Morris, Harrison Smith
Destiny.
Fickle Hope.
June.
Lonely-Bird, The.
Mohammed and Seid.
Pine-Tree Buoy, A.
Separate Peace.
Walt Whitman.
Morris, Harry
Girod Street Cemetery; New Orleans.
Morris, Herbert
Brahms, The.
North of Wales, The.
Road, The.
Spanish Blue.
This Alice.
Workmen.
Morris, Hilda
November.
November Wears a Paisley Shawl.
Morris, Ida Goldsmith
Give to the Living.
Morris, J. W.
Collusion between a Alegaiter and a Water-Snaik.
What I Think of Hiawatha.
Morris, John
Letter from a Friend, A.
Shh! The Professor Is Sleeping.
Morris, Joseph
Influence.
Morris, Sir Lewis
At Last.
Beginnings of Faith, The.
Brotherhood, *sel.*
Christmas 1898, *sel.*
God Within Yet Above.
Heathen Hymn, A.
I praise Thee not, with impious pride.
On a Thrush Singing in Autumn.
Separation Deed, A.
Song: "Love took my life and thrill'd it."
Surface and the Depths, The.
There shall come from out this noise of strife and groaning.
'Tis nigh two thousand years.
To a Child of Fancy.
Tolerance.
Morris, Robert
Level and the Square, The.
Morris, William
Ancient Castle, An.
Antiphony.
Apology, An: "Of Heaven or Hell I have no power to sing."
Atalanta's Defeat.
Atalanta's Race.
Atalanta's Victory.
Blue Closet, The.
Brooding of Sigurd, The.
Burghers' Battle, The.
Chapel in Lyoness, The.
Concerning Geffray Teste Noire.
Dawn talks to-day.
Day Is Coming, The.
Day of Days, The.
Death Song, A.
Defence [*or* Defense] of Guenevere, The.
Down Among the Dead Men.
Dream of John Ball, A, *sel.*
Earthly Paradise, The, *sels.*
Echoes of Love's House.
Eve of Crécy, The.
February, *abr.*
For the Bed at Kelmscott.
From Far Away.
Garden by the Sea, A.
Gilliflower [*or* Gillyflower] of Gold, The.
Gold Wings across the Sea.
Golden Apples, The.
Golden Wings.
Gunnar in the Pit of Adders.
Haystack in the Floods, The.
Hollow Land, The, *sel.*
I Know a Little Garden-Close.
Iceland First Seen.
In Prison.
Inscription for an Old Bed.
Introduction: "Forget six counties overhung with smoke."
Judgment [*or* Judgement] of God, The.
June.
King's Visit, The.
Lady of the Land, The.
Land across the Sea, A.
L'Envoi: "Here are we for the last time face to face."
Life and Death of Jason, The, *sels.*
Lines for a Bed at Kelmscott Manor.
Love Is Enough, *sels.*
March.
Masters, in This Hall.
Meeting in Winter.
Message of the March Wind, The.
Minstrels and Maids.
Near Avalon.
No Master.
November.
Nymph's Song to Hylas, The.
O Bitter Sea.
O Death, That Maketh Life So Sweet.
O happy seafarers are ye.
O love, this morn when the sweet nightingale.
October.
Of the Passing Away of Brynhild.
Ogier the Dane.
Old Love.
Outlanders, Whence Come Ye Last?
Pomona.
Praise of My Lady.
Prologue: "Forget six counties overhung with smoke."
Prologue: "Of Heaven or Hell I have no power to sing."
Prologue to "The Earthly Paradise."
Rapunzel.
Riding Together.
Road of Life, The.
Sailing of the *Sword*, The.
Shameful Death.
Sheriff, The.
Sigurd Rideth to the Glittering Heath.
Sigurd the Volsung.
Sigurd's Ride.
Singer's Prelude, The.
Sir Giles's War-Song.
Song: "Christ keep the Hollow Land."
Song: "Fair is the night, and fair the day."
Song: "Gold wings across the sea!"
Song: To Psyche.
Song from "Ogier the Dane."
Song from "The Hill of Venus."
Song of Jehane du Castel Beau, The.
Song of the Argonauts.
Story of Sigurd the Volsung, The, *sels.*
Summer Dawn.
Tapestry Trees.
To the Muse of the North.
Tune of [the] Seven Towers, The.
Two Red Roses across the Moon.
Voice of Toil, The.
Wind, The.
Winter Weather.
Morris-Jones, Sir John
Seagulls, The.
Morrison, Lillian
Lobster Cove Shindig.
Of Kings and Things.
Morrison, M. T.
What the Choir Sang about the New Bonnet.
Morrison, Margaret
I'm the Police Cop Man, I Am.
Morrison, Mary
Nobody Knows but Mother.
Morrissett, Ann
Here I Am.
Morrow, Elizabeth
This Pine-Tree.
Wall.
Morse, James Herbert
Brook Song.
His Statement of the Case.
Silence.
Wayside, The.
Wild Geese, The.
Morse, Katherine Duncan ("Jerry Doane)' "
Bee Sets Sail, A.
Fairy Frock, The.
To ——: "They could not shut you out of heaven."
Morse, Madeline
Christmas Prayer.
Morse, Samuel French
Children at Night.
Toward Harvest.
Track into the Swamp, The.
Morse, Sidney Henry
Way, The.
Mortenson, Alice Hansche
Another Day.
As I Go down the Sunset Hill.
Beauty of Jesus in Me, The.
Behold, My Cross Was Gone!
Bethlehem Star, The, Shines On!
Christmas Bells.
Essence of Tomorrow.
He Wore a Crown of Thorns.
He's Come! The Saviour Has Come!
His Book.
I Needed the Quiet.
It's a Beautiful Day!
Joy Is Built of Little Things.
Let Not Your Heart Be Troubled.
Light for the North Room.
O Christ of Calvary, This Lent.
O My Saviour and Redeemer.
Oh, No Cross That I May Carry!
Of what are you weaving your life today.
Spring Fever.
They've Crucified Our Lord.
This Peace He Gives.
Threads You Use, The.
To This Lilac-Scented Room.
While Passing Through This Valley.
Yellow Daffodil, A.
Morton,— Balloon Man, The
Morton, Sir Albertus
Greedy Lover, Pause Awhile.
Morton, David
Acquaintance.
Adoration.

Morton (continued)
After Storm.
Boke of Two Ladies, *sel.*
Chorus for Easter.
Daffodils over Night.
Dead, The ("Think you the dead are lonely in that place").
Epitaph in Sirmio.
Fields at Evening.
Immortalis.
In a Girls' School.
Kings Are Passing Deathward, The.
Lover to Lover.
Mariners.
Old Ships.
Petition for a Miracle.
Schoolboy [*or* School Boy] Reads His Iliad, The.
Ships in Harbour.
Symbol.
Touring.
When There Is Music.
Who Walks with Beauty.
Wooden Ships.

Morton, Frances McKinnon
Breath of Prayer, A.
Meaning of Prayer, The.

Morton John Bingham ("Beachcomber")
Ballade of Charon and the River Girl.
Bonnie Jeanie.
Dancing Cabman, The.
Epitaph for a Lighthouse-Keeper's Horse.
Epitaph on a Warthog.
Miss Multitude at the Trombone.
Now We Are Sick.
On Sir Henry Ferrett, M.P.
Song of the Ballet.
Tripe.

Morton, Sarah Wentworth
To Aaron Burr, under Trial for High Treason.

Morton, Thomas
Carmen Elegiacum.
Epitaph: "Time that bringes all things to light."
New Canaans Genius; Epilogus.
New English Canaan, *sels.*
Poem, The: "I sing th'adventures of mine worthy wights."
Poem, The: "Rise Oedipeus, and if thou canst unfould."
Poem, The: "What ailes Pigmalion? Is it lunacy."
Songe, The: "Drinke and be merry, merry, merry boyes."

Morus, Huw
In Praise of a Girl.

Moschus
Craft of a Keeper of Sheep, The.
Cupid Turned Plowman.
Epitaph of Bion.
I Dreamt I Saw Great Venus.
Love's Lesson.
Ocean, The.

Moser, Mrs. J. F.
Would I Be Called a Christian?

Moses, W. R.
American History.
Angina Pectoris.
Big Dam.
Boy at Target Practice; a Contemplation.
Surface Fishing.

Mosley, Joseph M., Jr
Black Church on Sunday.

Moss, Alice P.
God's Bank Ain't Busted Yet!

Moss, Elizabeth Patton
Sermon without Words.

Moss, Howard
Around the Fish; after Paul Klee.
Arsenic.
Balcony with Birds, A.
Burning Love Letters.
Chalk from Eden.
Crossing the Park.
Dead Leaf, A.
Elegy for My Father.
Elizabethan Tragedy; a Footnote.
Finding Them Lost.
Front Street.
Geography; A Song.
Gift to Be Simple, The.
Going to Sleep in the Country.
Great Spaces.
Hermit, The.
Horror Movie.
King Midas.
Lesson from Van Gogh, A.
Lie, The.
Local Places.
Meeting, The.
Movies for the Home.
Piano Practice.
Problem in Morals, A.
Pruned Tree, The.
Rain.
Still Pond, No More Moving.
Summer Gone, A.
Swim off the Rocks, A.
Tourists.
Traction: November 22, 1963.
Tragedy.
Underwood.
Venice.
Water Island.
Waterwall Blues.
Wind Is Round, The.
Winter's End.

Moss, Stanley
Squall.
Two Fishermen.
Valley, The.

Mother Goose
A was an apple pie;/ B bit it.
All around the mulberry bush.
As I was going along, long, long [*or* along, along].
As I was going to St. Ives.
As round as an apple, as deep as a cup.
As soft as silk, as white as milk.
As the days grow longer.
As Tommy Snooks and Bessy [*or* Bessie] Brooks.
Baa, baa, black sheep, have you any wool?
Barber, barber, shave a pig.
Bat, bat, come under my hat.
Bear went over the mountain, A.
Bessie Bell and Mary Gray.
Bessy [*or* Bessie] Bell and Mary Gray.
Black within and red without.
Blow, wind, blow! And go, mill, go!
Bobby Shaftoe's [*or* Shafto's *or* Shafto has] gone to sea.
Bryan O'Lin had no breeches to wear.
Bye [*or* By], baby bunting.
Carrion crow sat on an oak, A.
Cat came fiddling out of a barn, A.
Clap, clap handies.
Cobbler, cobbler, mend my shoe.
Cock-a-doodle-doo!/ My dame has lost her shoe.
Cock doth crow, The.
Cocks crow in the morn.
Come, butter, come.
Come, let's to bed.
Curly locks! Curly locks! wilt thou be mine?
Cushy cow bonny, let down thy milk.
Daffadowndilly/ Has come up to town.
Daffy-down-dilly is new come [*or* Daffadowndilly/ Has come up] to town.
Dance to your daddy [*or* daddie].
Dear, dear! what can the matter be?
Dickery, dickery, dare.
Diddle, diddle [*or* Deedle, deedle], dumpling, my son John.
Dillar, a dollar, A,/ A ten o'clock scholar.
Ding, dong, bell,/ Pussy's in the well!
Doctor Faustus was a good man.
Doctor Foster went to Gloucester [*or* Glos'ter].
Dog and a cat went out together, A.
Dove, The, says, "Coo, coo, what shall I do?"
Elizabeth, Lizzy [*or* Elspeth], Betsy, and Bess.
Fair maid who, [on] the first of May, The.
Farmer went trotting [*or* riding] upon [*or* on] his grey mare, A.
Flour [*or* Flower] of England, fruit of Spain.
For every evil under [*or* ill beneath] the sun.
For want of a nail, the shoe was lost.
Four and twenty tailors went to kill a snail.
Georgie Porgie [*or* Georgey Porgey], pudding and pie.
Girls and boys come out to play.
Goosey, goosey, gander, where [*or* whither] shall I [*or* we] wander?
Grand old Duke of York, The.
Great A, little a.
Handy Spandy, Jack-a-dandy.
Hark! hark! The dogs do bark.
Hector Protector was dressed all in green.
Here am I,/ Little jumping Joan.
Here comes a candle to light you to bed.
Here goes my lord.
Here sits the Lord Mayor.
Hey [*or* Hi *or* High *or* Sing hey], diddle, diddle,/ the cat and the fiddle.
Hey diddle, dinkety, poppety, pet.
Hey, my kitten, my kitten.
Hey, rub-a-dub-dub [ho! rub-a-dub], three men in a tub.
Hick-a-more, hack-a-more.
Hickory, dickory, dock.
Hie, hie, says Anthony.
Higgledy, piggledy [*or* Higgleby, piggleby *or* Hickety, pickety], my black [*or* fat] hen.
Higher than a house,/ higher than a tree.
Hill full, a hole full, A.
Hippety hop to the barber shop.
Hot-cross buns! Hot-cross buns!/ One a penny, two a penny.
How many days has my [*or* the] baby to play?
How many miles [is it] to Babylon [*or* Barley Bridge]?
Humpty Dumpty sat on a wall.
Hush-a-bye [*or* Rock-a-bye], baby, on [*or* in] the tree top.
I am a gold lock.
I had a little hen, the prettiest ever seen.
I had a little hobby horse.
I had a little husband.
I had a little nut-tree; nothing would it bear.
I had a little pony.
I have a little sister, they call her Peep, Peep.
I love sixpence, jolly [*or* pretty] little sixpence.
I saw a ship a-sailing.
I saw three ships come sailing by.
I went to the wood and got it.
If all the seas were one sea.
If all the world were [*or* was] apple pie.
If I had [*or* I'd] as much money as I could spend.
If wishes were horses, beggars would ride.

If you sneeze on [*or* Sneeze on a] Monday, you sneeze for danger.
I'll tell you a story/ About Jack a Nory.
In marble halls as white as milk.
Intery, mintery, cutery, corn.
"Is John Smith within?"
It was on a merry time/ When Jenny Wren was young.
Jack and Jill [*or* Gill] went up the hill.
Jack, be nimble.
Jack Sprat [*or* Spratt] could eat no fat.
Jack Sprat's pig.
Jennie [*or* Jeanie *or* Jenny], come tie my.
Jenny Wren fell sick.
Johnny shall have a new bonnet.
King of France, the king of France, The,/ with forty [*or* fifty] thousand men.
Ladybird, ladybird [*or* Lady-bug, lady-bug] fly away home!
Lion and the unicorn, The.
Little Betty Blue/ Lost her holiday shoe.
Little Bo-Peep has lost her sheep.
Little boy and a little girl, A.
Little Boy Blue, come blow [up] your horn.
Little cock sparrow sat on a [green] tree, A.
"Little girl, little girl."
Little green bird sat on a fence rail, A.
Little Jack Horner/ Sat in the corner.
Little Jenny Wren/ Fell sick upon a time.
Little King Boggen, he built a fine hall.
Little maid, pretty maid,/ Whither goest thou?
Little Miss Muffet/ Sat on a tuffet.
Little Nancy [*or* Nanny *or* Nan] Etticoat.
Little Polly Flinders/ sat among the cinders.
Little Robin Redbreast sat upon a tree [*or* rail].
Little Sally Waters.
Little Tommy Tucker/ Sings for his supper.
Lives in winter.
Long legs, crooked thighs.
Lucy Locket lost her pocket.
Man in the wilderness asked of [*or* said to] me, The [*or* A].
Mary had a pretty bird.
Mary, Mary [*or* Mistress Mary], quite contrary.
Mr. East gave a feast.
Monday's child is fair of [*or* in] face.
Multiplication is vexation.
My maid Mary,/ She minds her [*or* the] dairy.
Needles and pins, needles and pins.
North wind doth blow, The.
Nose, nose, jolly red nose.
O my pretty cock and my pretty crowing cock.
Old King Cole was a merry old soul.
Old Mother Goose when/ She wanted to wander.
Old Mother Twitchett has [*or* had] but one eye.
"Old woman, old woman, shall we go a-shearing?"
On Saturday night.
Once I saw a little bird going hop, hop, hop.
One for [the] money.
One misty moisty morning.
One, two,/ Buckle my shoe.
One, two, three, four,/ Mary at the cottage door.
1, 2, 3, 4, 5!/ I caught a hare alive.
Over the water and over the sea [*or* lea].
Pat-a-cake, pat-a-cake, baker's man.
Pease-porridge [*or*-pudding] hot.
Peter, Peter, pumpkin-eater.
Peter Piper picked a peck of pickled [*or* pickling] pepper[s].
Peter White will never [*or* ne'er] go right.
Polly, put the kettle on.
Poor old Robinson Crusoe!
Poor pussy-cat mew.
Pussy-cat Mew [*or* Mole] jumped over a coal.
Pussy-cat, pussy-cat, where have you been?
Queen of Hearts, The,/ She made some tarts.
Rain, rain, go away.
Riddle, a riddle, as I suppose, A.
Riddle-me riddle-me riddle-me-ree.
Ride a cock-horse to Banbury Cross, To see a fine lady upon a white horse.
Ride away, ride away,/ Johnny shall ride.
Robert Barnes, fellow fine.
Robert Rowley rolled a round roll 'round.
Robin and Richard [*or* Richard and Robin] were two pretty [*or* little] men.
Robin Hood, Robin Hood,/ In the mickle wood!
"Robin Hood, Robin Hood,"/Said Little John.
Rock-a-bye [*or* Hush-a-bye], baby, thy cradle is green.
Roses are red [*or* The rose is red].
Rub-a-dub-dub, /Three men in a tub.
Runs all day and never walks.
See saw, Margery Daw.
See-saw, sacradown.
Shoe the colt, shoe the colt.
Simple Simon met a pieman.
Sing a song of sixpence.
Sing, sing! what shall I sing?
Six [*or* Some *or* Ten] little mice sat down [*or* in a barn] to spin.
Smiling girls, rosy boys.
Solomon Grundy/ Born on a Monday.
Spring is showery, flowery, bowery.
Taffy was a Welshman, Taffy was a thief.
There was a crooked man, and he went [*or* walked] a crooked mile.
There was a little boy and a little girl.
There was a little man, and he had a little gun.
There was a little man, and he woo'd a little maid.
There was a man in [*or* of] our town [*or* of Newington],/ And he was wondrous wise.
There was a piper had [*or* he had] a cow.
There was an old woman/ Lived under a hill.
There was an old woman/ Lived up on a hill.
There was an old woman, and what do you think.
There was an old woman called Nothing-at-all.
There was an old woman in Surrey.
There was an old woman lived under a hill/ And if she's not gone.
There was an old woman lived under a hill/ She put a mouse in a bag.
There was an old [*or* a little] woman, so [*or* as] I've heard tell.
There was an old woman tossed [*or* went] up in a basket.
There was an old woman who lived in a shoe.
There were two birds sat on a stone.
There were two blackbirds sitting on a hill.
They that wash on Monday.
Thirty days hath September.
Thirty [*or* Twenty] white horses upon a red hill.
This is the house that Jack built.
This is the way the ladies ride: Tri-tre-tre-tree!
This little pig went to market.
Three blind mice, see how they run!
Three wise men of Gotham.
To market, to market, to buy a fat pig.
To market, to market, to buy a plum bun.
Tom, Tom, the piper's son/ Stole a pig and away he run.
Tommy's tears and Mary's fears.
'Twas once upon a time, when Jenny Wren was young.
Tweedledum and Tweedledee.
Twelve pears [*or* pairs] hanging high.
Wash the dishes, wipe the dishes.
What are little boys made of, made of?
What is the rhyme for porringer?
When good King Arthur ruled this land.
When I was a bachelor [*or* little boy],/ I lived by myself,/ And all the bread and cheese I got.
When I was a little boy I lived by myself.
When little Fred/ Was called to bed.
"Which is the way to London Town,/ To see the King."
Willie [*or* Willy] boy, Willie boy, where are you going?
Young lambs to sell!

Motherly, Mrs.
Cow, The.
Dickey-Bird, The.
Fishes, The.
Flying Flowers.
Nursery, The.

Motherwell, William
Cavalier's Song, The.
I plucked the berry from the bush, the brown nut from the tree.
Jeanie Morrison.
Last Verses.
Sing On, Blithe Bird!
Water, The! the Water!

Motokiyo, Seami
Love-Cave, The.

Moton, Cora Ball
Sight.

Mott, Adrian
Cloud House, The.

Motteux Peter Anthony [*or* Pierre Antoine]
London.
Love's a Jest, *sel.*
Rondelay, A: "Man Is For Woman Made."
Slaves to London.
Song, A: "Slaves to London, I'll deceive you."

Moult, Thomas
Prelude to Cricket.
Summer Days, *sel.*

Moulton, Louise Chandler (Ellen Louise Chandler)
Hic Jacet.
Last Good-by, The.
Laura Sleeping.
Laus Veneris.
Louisa May Alcott.
Love's Resurrection Day.
Painted Fan, A.
Shadow Dance, The.
Shall I Complain?
Somebody's Child.
Spring Is Late, The.
Summer Wooing, A.
To-Night.
Tryst, A.
We Lay Us Down to Sleep.
Were But My Spirit Loosed upon the Air.

Moultrie, Gerard
St. Augustine, Bishop of Hippo.

Moultrie, John

Moultrie (continued)
But here, at starting, I must just premise.
Dear Little Violets.
Fairy Maimounè, The.
Forget Thee?
Sir Launfal, *sel.*
Violets.
Mountain, George J.
Indian's Grave, The.
Mousley, James P.
Prayer: "God of light and blossom."
Mowrer, Paul Scott
Mozart's Grave.
Moxon, Edward
Moonlight.
Nightingale, The.
Similes.
Moxon, Frederick
All at Sea.
Moyles, Lois
Report from California.
Tale Told by a Head, A.
Thomas in the Fields.
Mphahlele, Ezekiel
Exile in Nigeria.
Mqhayi, S.E.K
Black Army, The.
Sinking of the Mendi, The.
Mudie, Ian
Australia Day, 1942; in Memoriam W. J. Miles.
They'll Tell You about Me.
This Land.
Underground.
Wilderness Theme.
Mueller, Lisel
Apples.
Civilizing the Child.
For a Nativity.
Lonesome Dream, The.
Moon Fishing.
Names.
People at the Party, The.
Reading the Brothers Grimm to Jenny.
Sans Souci.
Muhammadjii
Black Hair.
Muhlenberg, William Augustus
Carol, Brothers, Carol.
Fulfillment.
Heaven's Magnificence.
I Would Not Live Alway.
Muir, Alexander
Maple Leaf Forever, The.
Muir, Edwin
Abraham.
Absent, The.
Animals, The.
Annunciation, The.
Antichrist.
Ballad of the Flood.
Bird, The.
Brothers, The.
Castle, The.
Child Dying, The.
Childhood.
Church, The.
City, The.
Combat, The.
Confirmation, The.
Day, The.
Difficult Land, The.
Enchanted Knight, The.
Face, The.
Fathers, The.
For Ann Scott-Moncrieff.
For once in a dream or trance I saw the gods.
Gate, The.
Good Man in Hell, The.
Good Town, The.
Grove, The.
Horses, The ("Barely a twelvemonth after").
Horses ("Those lumbering horses in the steady plough").
Human Fold, The.
In Love for Long.
Incarnate One, The.
Interrogation, The.
Island, The.
Journey, The.
Killing, The.
Labyrinth, The.
Lost and Found.
Love in Time's Despite.
Love's Remorse.
Merlin.
Myth, The.
Mythical Journey, The.
Oedipus.
Old Gods, The.
One Foot in Eden.
Orpheus' Dream.
Question, The.
Reading in War Time.
Recurrence, The.
Return, The ("The doors flapped open in Ulysses' house").
Return, The ("The veteran Greeks came home").
Rider Victory, The.
Road, The.
Robert the Bruce.
Scotland 1941.
Scotland's Winter.
Son, The.
Song: "Why should your face so please me."
Stationary Journey, The.
Succession, The.
Sufficient Place, The.
Sunset.
Then.
Three Mirrors, The.
To Ann Scott-Moncrieff.
To Franz Kafka.
Too Much.
Town Betrayed, The.
Toy Horse, The.
Transfiguration, The.
Transmutation, The.
Trophy, The.
Troy.
Usurpers, The.
Variations on a Time Theme, *sel.*.
Voyage, The.
Way, The.
Wayside Station, The.
West, The.
Window, The.
Muir, Henry D.
Soldier's Grave. The.
Mu'izzi, Amur
To a Young Lover.
"Mukerji. Rana "
Spring Night.
Mulchinock, William Pembroke
Rose of Tralee, The.
Mulgan, Alan
Breaking a line of pines, a wide white gate.
Golden Wedding, *sel.*
Mulholland, Rosa (Lady Gilbert)
Irish Franciscan, The.
Love and Death.
Sister Mary of the Love of God.
Müller, Wilhelm
Song of the Bird, The.
Whither?
Mullineaux, Mary
Dragon, The.
Mullins, Helene (Helen Gallagher Mullins)
Boy Christ, The.
Even in the Darkness.
Farmers.
Thirty Pieces of Silver for Jesus.
Mulock, Dinah Maria *See* **Craik, Dinah Maria Mulock**
Mumford, Lewis
Consolation in War.
Munby, Arthur Joseph
Beauty at the Plough.
Country Kisses.
Doris; a Pastoral.
Dorothy; a Country Story, *sels.*
Dorothy's Room.
Flos Florum.
Susan; a Poem of Degrees, *sel.*
Sweet Nature's Voice.
Munch-Petersen, Gustaf
To One.
Munday, Anthony
Anthony Munday unto All Young Gentlemen in Commendation of this Gallery and Workmen Thereof.
Beauty Bathing.
Beauty Sat Bathing [by a Spring].
Colin.
Fedele and Fortunio, *sels.*
I Serve a Mistress.
If love be like the flower that in the night.
Love.
Primaleon of Greece, *sel.*
To Colin Clout.
Two Italian Gentlemen.
Zelanto, the Fountain of Fame,*sel.*
Munday, Anthony, *and* Henry Chettle
Death of Robert, Earl of Huntingdon, *sel*
Dirge: "Weep, weep, ye woodmen, wail.'
Dirge for Robin Hood.
Robin Hood's Funeral.
Song: "Weep, weep, ye woodmen, wail.'
Mundell, William D.
Uninvited, The.
Mundorf, Frank
Letter from a State Hospital.
Remembering Lincoln.
Mundy, Anthony
Concrete Poem, A.
Mundy, John
Lightly She Whipped o'er the Dales.
Munetake
On Tsukuda-Isle in July.
Snow.
Munger, Robert
God's Will.
Mungin, Horace
Blues.
Of Man and Nature.
Munkittrick, Richard Kendall
At the Shrine.
Autumn Haze.
Bulb, A.
Ghosts.
To Miguel de Cervantes Saavadra.
Unsatisfied Yearning.
What's in a Name?
Winter Dusk.
Muñoz Marín, Luis
Pamphlet.
Munro, Kathryn
Fallen Leaves.
Munro, Neil
Fiddle, The.
Heather, The.
Munson, Ida Norton
Assurance.
Bethlehem Road, The.
Easter Light.
Hour Is Late, The.
Launch Out into the Deep.

Malchus.
Mary Knew.
Open Door, The.
Resurrection.
Road to Emmaus, The.
Sight.
Star, The.
Surgeon's Hands, The.
Vision.
Munson, Miriam Ott
Grandmother's Garden.
Münsterberg, Margarete
My Favorite Tree.
Thanksgiving.
Murano, Shiro
Pole Vault.
Murasaki Shikibu, Lady
While I walked in the moonlight.
Murchison, Lee
In the Beginning Was the.
Sprinters, The.
Murger, Henry
Old Loves.
Spring in the Students' Quarter.
Murphy, Beatrice M.
Evicted.
Letter, The.
Signs.
Trivia.
We Pass.
Murphy, John Maher
Family History.
Murphy, R. D.
Back Lane.
Murphy, Richard
Archaeology of Love, The.
Battle of Aughrim, The, *sels.*
Country Woman and a Country Man, A.
Girl at the Seaside.
Graves at Inishbofin.
Poet on the Island, The.
Rapparees.
Sailing to an Island.
Story I Have to Tell, The.
Murray, Ada Foster (Mrs. Henry Mills Alden)
Above Salerno.
Her Dwelling-Place.
Old-fashioned Poet, An.
Prevision.
Unguarded.
Murray, Albert Leonard
Thankfulness.
There Always Will Be God.
Murray, Charles
Whistle, The.
Murray, Sir David
Caelia, *sel.*
Sonnet: "Ponder thy cares, and sum them all in one."
Murray, Ellen
Shepherd Dog of the Pyrenees, The.
Murray, Frederick, *and* Frederick Leigh
Charlie Piecan.
Murray, George
Lesson of Mercy, A.
Thin Man, a Sculpture, The.
To a Humming Bird in a Garden.
Murray, Kenton Foster
Challenge.
Murray, Mabel
Regret.
Murray, Pauli
Dark Testament.
Without Name.
Murray, Philip
Carrara.
Cloud of Unknowing, The.
Finches, The.
In the Annals of Tacitus.
Little Litany to St. Francis, A.
Locust Hunt, The.
Turning, The.
Murray, Robert Fuller
Andrew M'Crie.
City of Golf, The.
End of April, The.
Man from Inversnaid, The.
Murton, Jessie Wilmore
Song of the Builders.
Strength.
Mus, David
Against Art.
This Suite.
Mushimaro
On Mount Tsukuba.
Musser, Benjamin Francis
Der Heilige Mantel von Aachen.
Holy Land of Walsingham, The.
Le Coeur de l'Immaculée.
Musset, Alfred de
Juana.
On a Dead Lady.
Song: "Should you, of mirth and hope bereft."
Souvenir.
"Mustafa." *See* **Johnson, Don Allen**
Mustapää, P.
Folk Tale.
Mu'tamid, King of Seville
Fountain, The.
Great Poet, The.
I Traveled with Them.
Letter, A.
Tears of the World.
Thy Garden.
Woo Not the World.
Muth, Edna Tucker
Mother's Day.
Ruth Goes By.
Muth, Eleanor
Night Enchantment.
Muuse, 'Abdillaahi
Elder's Reproof to His Wife, An.
Myall, Charles
Indian Lullaby.
Myers, Ernest
Achilles.
Etsi Omnes, Ego Non.
Fiorentina.
Gordon.
Sea-Maids' Music, The.
Myers Frederic William Henry
Advent.
Alpha and Omega.
Atlandid islands, phantom-fair.
Christ All-sufficient.
Evanescence.
Experience.
Hark what a sound, and too divine for hearing.
Harold at Two Years Old.
I Saw, I Saw the Lovely Child.
Immortality.
Inner Light, The.
Knowledge.
Last Appeal, A.
Letter from Newport, A.
Not in Solitude.
O God, How Many Years Ago.
On a Grave at Grindelwald.
Prayer, A: "O for one minute hark what we are saying!"
Saint Paul, *abr.*
Saints, The (St. Paul).
Song, A: "Pouring music, soft and strong, The."
Surrender to Christ.
Teneriffe, *sel.*
Myers, Neil
Near Mons.
Myles, Glenn
Percy/ 68.

N

"N., A. M."
God's Treasure.
"N. C." *See* **"C., N."**
"N. M. B." *See* **"B., N. M"**
Nabbes, Thomas
Hannibal and Scipio, *sel.*
Love Sets Order in the Elements.
Microcosmus, *sel.*
On a Mistress of Whose Affections He Was Doubtful.
Song: "Beauty no more the subject be."
Song: "What a dainty life the milkmaid leads!"
Spring's Glory, The, *sel.*
Tottenham Court, *sel.*
Nabokov, Vladimir
Ballad of Longwood Glen, The.
Evening of Russian Poetry, An.
Lines Written in Oregon.
Literary Dinner.
Ode to a Model.
On Discovering a Butterfly.
Room, The.
Nack, James
Here She Goes and There She Goes.
Nadaud, Gustave
Carcassonne.
Naden, Constance Caroline Woodhill
Pantheist's Song of Immortality, The.
Nadir, Moishe (Yitzhok Reis)
Adjectives.
Nadson, Semyon Yakovlevich
Brother, The.
Nagayasu, Syuichi
Bored Mirror, The.
Nagel, S. A.
God and Man.
Nago Okimaro
Even in the Palace.
Nahman of Bratzlav
Annul Wars.
Heart of the World, The.
Nahum
Spring Song.
Naidu, Sarojini
Coromandel Fishers.
Cradle Song: "From groves of spice."
Dirge: "What longer need hath she of loveliness."
Hindu Cradle Song.
In the Bazaars of Hyderabad.
Palanquin Bearers.
Soul's Prayer, The.
Transience.
Nairne, Carolina Oliphant, Baroness
Auld House, The.
Caller Herrin'.
Heavenward.
Laird o' Cockpen, The.
Land o' the Leal, The.
Lass O' Gowrie.
Lullaby: "Baloo, loo, lammy, now baloo, my dear."
Rest Is Not Here.
Rowan Tree, The.
Will Ye No Come Back Again?
Naito Joso *See* **Joso**
Naito Meisetsu
Wind blows, grey, The.
Najara, Israel
God of the World.
Love of My Soul.
Nakatsukasa
If it were not for the voice.
O nightingale.

Nalbandian, Michael Chazarian
Liberty.
Nalé Roxlo, Conrado
Game, The.
Unforeseen, The.
Namdev
Before all Time, before all worlds.
Everlasting to Everlasting, *sel.*
Nance, Berta Hart
Achievement.
Moonlight.
Nanmor, Dafydd
Ode to Rhys ap Maredudd of Tywyn.
Naoyoshi
Beautiful Night, A.
Napier, Elliott
All Men Are Free!
France.
Mater Dolorosa.
Russia.
Narihira, (Ariwara no Narihira)
I am so lost.
I knew quite well that some day.
Nash, Ogden
Admiral Byrd.
Adventures of Isabel.
Anatomy of Happiness, The.
And Three Hundred and Sixty-six in Leap Year.
Ant, The.
Arthur.
Autres Bêtes, Autres Moeurs.
Bankers Are Just like Anybody Else, except Richer.
Bat, The.
Benjamin.
Big Tent under the Roof, The.
Birds, The.
Boy Who Laughed at Santa Claus, The.
Brief Lines in Not So Brief.
Camel, The.
Canary, The.
Carnival of Animals, The, *sels.*
Carol for Children, A.
Caution to Everybody, A.
Celery.
Centipede, The.
Clean Platter, The.
Cow, The.
Decline and Fall of a Roman Umpire.
Do You Plan to Speak Bantu? or Abbreviation Is the Thief of Sanity.
Dr. Fell and Points West.
Don't Guess, Let Me Tell You.
Drink with Something in It, A.
Duck, The.
Edouard.
Eel, The.
Evening Out, The.
Exit, Pursued by a Bear.
Family Court.
Firefly, The.
Fly, The.
Fragonard.
Funebrial Reflections.
Genealogical Reflection.
Gentlemen of the High Command.
Germ, The.
Golly, How Truth Will Out.
Goodbye Now; or, Pardon My Gauntlet.
Grackle, The ("Grackle's voice is less than mellow, The").
Grandpa Is Ashamed.
Guppy, The.
Hippopotamus, The.
Hunter, The.
I Can't Have a Martini, Dear, but You Take One.
I Never Even Suggested It.
I Want to Sit Next to Emily.
I Will Arise and Go Now.
Ill Met by Zenith.
Introduction: "Camille St. Saëns was racked with pains."
Introduction to Dogs, An.
Introspective Reflection.
Japanese, The.
Jellyfish, The.
Kind of an Ode to Duty.
Kindly Unhitch That Star, Buddy.
Kitten, The.
Lady Thinks She Is Thirty, A.
Lama, The.
Lather as You Go.
Limerick: "There was a young belle of Old Natchez."
Limerick: "There was an old man in a trunk."
Lines in Dispraise of Dispraise.
Line-up for Yesterday.
Lion, The.
Lucy Lake.
Max Schling, Max Schling, Lend Me Your Green Thumb.
More about People.
No Doctors Today, Thank You.
Notes for the Chart in 306.
Oh, Please Don't Get Up!
Oh, Stop Being Thankful All over the Place.
Octopus, The.
Old Men.
One, Two, Buckle My Shoe.
Oyster, The.
Panther, The.
Parsnip, The.
Peekaboo, I Almost See You.
Phoenix, The.
Piano Tuner, Untune Me That Tune.
Pig, The.
Porcupine, The.
Porpoise, The.
Portrait of the Artist as a Prematurely Old Man.
Poultries, The.
Praying Mantis, The.
Private Dining Room, The.
Purist, The.
Reflections on Ice-breaking.
Requiem.
Rhinoceros, The ("The rhino is a homely beast").
Sea-Gull, The.
Seven Spiritual Ages of Mrs. Marmaduke Moore, The.
Shrew, The.
Sniffle, The.
So That's Who I Remind Me Of.
Song of the Open Road.
Song to Be Sung by the Father of Infant Female Children.
Spring Comes to Murray Hill.
Squirrel, The.
Tableau at Twilight.
Taboo to Boot.
Tale of Custard the Dragon, The.
Tale of the Custard Dragon, The.
Termite, The.
Terrible People, The.
That Reminds Me.
Third Limick.
Thoughts Thought While Waiting for a Pronouncement from a Doctor, a Big Executive, the Department of Internal Revenue, or Any Other Momentous Pronouncer.
To a Small Boy Standing on My Shoes While I Am Wearing Them.
Traveler's Rest.
Turkey, The.
Turtle, The.
Two and One Are a Problem.
Up from the Egg; the Confessions of a Nuthatch Avoider.
Up from the Wheelbarrow.
Very like a Whale.
Visit, The.
Wapiti, The.
What's the Matter, Haven't You Got Any Sense of Humor?
What's the Use.
Who Wants to Travel All Over Europe and See Nothing but a Lot of American Tourists? I Do.
Wombat, The.
Yes and No.
Nashe [*or* Nash], Thomas
Adieu, Farewell, Earth's Bliss [*or* Blisse]!
A-Maying, a-Playing.
Autumn.
Beauty is but a flower.
Birds in Spring.
Clownish Song, A.
Death's Summons.
Dust Hath Closed Helen's Eye.
Fair Summer Droops.
Harvest.
In a Time of Pestilence.
In Plague Time.
In Time of Pestilence.
In Time of Plague.
Litany in Plague Time, A.
Litany in Time of Plague, A.
Lord, Have Mercy on Us.
Rich men, trust not in wealth.
Song: "Adieu, farewell, earth's bliss."
Song: "Spring, the sweete spring, is the year's pleasant king."
Song In Plague-Time.
Spring.
Spring, the Sweet Spring.
Summer's Farewell.
Summer's Last Will and Testament, *sels.*
Waning Summer.
Nashe, Thomas, *and* **Christopher Marlowe** *See* **Marlowe, Christopher,** *and* **Thomas Nashe**
Nason, Elias
Jesus Only.
Nason, Emma Huntington
Child's Question, A.
Cricket's Story The.
Nathan, Leonard E.
Diver, The.
Dusk.
To Somewhere.
Nathan, Robert
At the Symphony.
Be Not Afraid.
Beauty Is Ever to the Lonely Mind.
Because My Grief Seems Quiet and Apart.
Bells in the Country.
Christmas 1942.
Comes Fall.
Daughter at Evening, The.
Dunkirk.
Epistle: "Christian, be up before the end of day."
Epitaph: "Say he was sad, for there was none to love him."
I Ride the Great Black Horses of My Heart.
Mountaineer, The.
Now from the World the Light of God Is Gone.
Poet Describes His Love, The.
Sonnet: "Because my grief seems quiet and apart."
Sonnet VI: "Now from the world the light of God is gone."
There Are Four Doors Which Open on the Skies.

These Are the Chosen People.
Watch, America.
When in the Crowd I Suddenly Behold.
Will Beauty Come.
Nau, Ignace
Belle-de-nuit.
Naudé, Adèle
Africa.
From a Venetian Sequence.
Idiot, The.
Memling's Virgin with Apple.
Oracle of Delphi, The.
Portrait.
Return.
Unpossessed, The.
Nayadu, Sarojini *See* **Naidu, Sarojini**
Naylor, James Ball
King David and King Solomon.
Neal, Gaston
Personal Jihad.
Today.
Neal, John
Men of the North.
Music of the Night.
Neal, Larry
Baroness and the Black Musician, The.
For Our Women.
Malcolm X—An Autobiography.
Narrative of the Black Magicians, The.
Orishas.
Neale, John Mason
Art Thou Weary?
Light's Glittering Morn.
Nealy, Mary E.
Maul, The.
Nechayev, Georgi Efimovich
Freedom.
Neele, Henry
Moan, Moan, Ye Dying Gales.
Neidhart von Reuental
Bargain, The.
On the Mountain.
Winter-Time.
Neighbour, R. E.
Why Should We Weep?
Neihardt, John G.
Battle Cry.
Child's Heritage, The.
Cry of the People.
Easter.
Easter, 1923.
Envoi: "O seek me not within a tomb."
L'Envoi: "Seek not for me within a tomb."
Let Me Live Out My Years.
Lyric Deed, The.
Outward.
Prayer for Pain.
Shooting of the Cup, The.
Song of Three Friends, The, *sel.*
When I Am Dead.
When I Have Gone Weird Ways.
Neill, H. S.
Second Sight.
Neilson, Francis
Eugenio Pacelli.
Neilson, John Shaw
Beauty Imposes.
Birds Go By, The.
Break of Day, The.
Cool, Cool Country, The.
Crane Is My Neighbour, The.
Green Singer, The.
I Spoke to the Violet.
Land Where I Was Born, The.
Love's Coming.
May.
Native Companions Dancing.
O Heart of Spring!
Orange Tree, The.

Poor Can Feed the Birds, The.
Poor, Poor Country, The.
Schoolgirls Hastening.
Song Be Delicate.
Stony Town.
Strawberries in November.
Sundowner, The.
'Tis the White Plum Tree.
To a Blue Flower.
To a School-Girl.
Walking of the Moon-Woman, The.
Whistling Jack, The.
Nekrasov, Nikolai Alekseyevich
Capitals Are Rocked, The.
Hymn, A: "Lord, give them freedom who are weak."
On Passing through the Haymarket.
Song of the Siberian Exiles, The.
Nelson, Alice Dunbar Moore
I Sit and Sew.
Snow in October.
Sonnet: "I had no thought of violets of late."
Nelson, Frank Carleton
Human Heart, The.
Nelson, Hope
'Tis March.
Nelson, Lawrence Emerson
My Pompous Friend.
Nelson, Paula
House, The.
Nelson, Starr
White Rainbow, The.
Nemerov, Howard
Absent-Minded Professor.
Angel and Stone.
At a Country Hotel.
Book of Kells, The.
Boom!
Brainstorm.
Chromium-plated Hat, A; Inlaid with Scenes from Siegfried.
Companions, The.
Daily Globe, The.
Dandelions.
De Anima.
Debate with the Rabbi.
Dial Tone, The.
Dialogue.
Ecstasies of Dialectic, The.
Elegy for a Nature Poet.
Fable of the War, A.
First Leaf, The.
Frozen City, The.
Glass Dialectic.
Goldfish.
Goose Fish, The.
History of a Literary Movement.
Human Things.
I Only Am Escaped Alone to Tell Thee.
Iron Characters, The.
Learning by Doing.
Lie, The.
Lion & Honeycomb.
Lives of Gulls and Children, The.
Lot Later.
Marriage of Heaven and Earth, The.
May Day Dancing, The.
Moment.
Mousemeal.
Mud Turtle, The.
Murder of William Remington, The.
Phoenix, The.
Poem of Margery Kempe, A.
Political Reflection.
Pond, The.
Praising the Poets of That Country.
Presidential Address to a Party of Exiles Leaving for the Moon.
Primer of the Daily Round, A.
Redeployment.

Remorse for Time, The.
Runes.
Salt Garden, The.
Sanctuary, The.
Scales of the Eyes, The.
Sestina on Her Portrait.
Snow Globe, The.
Sonnet at Easter.
Spell before Winter, A.
Storm Windows.
Sunday at the End of Summer.
To the Mannequins.
Town Dump, The.
Trees.
Truth.
Vacuum, The.
View, The.
View from an Attic Window, The.
Winter Lightning [for Paul], The.
Writing.
Young Woman.
Nerses, Saint
Annunciation, The.
Assumption, The.
"Neruda, Pablo" (Neftalí Ricardo Reyes Basuato)
Almería.
Battle of the Jarama, The.
Death Alone.
International Brigade Arrives at Madrid, The.
Lone Gentleman.
Materia Nupcial.
November 7th.
Return of Autumn.
Walking Around.
Nerval, Gérard de (Gérard Labrunie)
Artemis.
Desdichado, El.
Fantasy.
Old Tune, An.
Nervo, Amado
Mystical Poets.
Nesbit, Edith (Edith Nesbit Bland)
All in All.
Baby Seed Song.
Ballad of a Bridal.
Bird's Song in Spring.
Child's Song in Spring.
Mr. Ody met a body.
Sleep, My Treasure.
Summer Song.
Tragedy, A.
Nesbit, Wilbur D.
Christmas Dusk.
Forever on Thanksgiving Day.
Friend or Two, A.
Hymn of Thanksgiving, A.
Let Us Smile.
Smile ("Thing that goes the farthest, The").
Thanksgiving Night.
Who Hath a Book.
Your Flag and My Flag.
Nesmith, James Ernest
Statue of Lorenzo de' Medici, The.
Netherclift, Beryl
London Trees.
Neumark, George
Leave God to Order.
Neville, Helen
Body's Freedom.
Nevin, Alice
God's Will.
Nevin, Edwin Henry
I Am with You Alway.
Newbolt, Sir Henry
Clifton Chapel.
Commemoration.
Craven.
Day's End.

Newbolt (continued)
Drake's Drum ("Drake he's in his hammock an' a thousand miles away").
Fighting *Téméraire,* The.
Final Mystery, The.
Finis.
From Generation to Generation.
Gillespie.
Hawke.
He Fell among Thieves.
Imogen.
Master and Man.
Messmates.
Moss-Rose, The.
Old *Supurb,* The.
Only Son, The.
Play the Game.
Rilloby-Rill.
Sacramentum Supremum.
Sailing at Dawn.
St. George's Day—Ypres 1915.
Song: "Flowers that in thy garden rise, The."
To a River in the South.
Toy Band, The.
Vitaï Lampada.
War Films, The.
Yattendon.

Newbury, Colin
Epilogue of the Wandering Jew, The.
Letter from Paparua.
New Wine, Old Bottles.

Newcastle, Margaret Cavendish, Duchess of
Convent of Pleasure, The, *sel.*
My Cabinets Are Oyster-Shells.
O do not grieve, Dear Heart, nor shed a tear.
O Love, how thou art [*or* Love, how thou'rt] tired out with rhyme!
Sea-Goddess, The.
Song by Lady Happy, as a Sea-Goddess.
Soul's Garment, The.

Newscastle, William Cavendish, Duke of
Fulfillment.
Heaven's Mould, The.
Love Play.
Love's Epitaph.
Love's Matrimony ("There is no happy life.").
Love's Vision ("Dear, let us two each other spy").
Love's Vision ("There is no happy life.").
Maiden Gown, The.

Newell, Catherine Parmenter
Dream House.

Newell, J. R.
Christmas Carol: "From the starry heav'ns descending."

Newell, Mary Elizabeth
For a Valentine.

Newell, Peter
Educated Love Bird, The.
Her Dairy.
Her Polka Dots.
Timid Hortense.
Wild Flowers.

Newell, Robert Henry *See* **"Kerr, Orpheus C"**

Newell, William R.
For Me.

Newey-Johnson, D.
To Let.

Newlin, Edith H. *See* **Chase, Edith Newlin**

Newlove, John
Double-Headed Snake, The.
Good Company, Fine Houses.
I Talk to You.
Pride, The.

Newman, Israel
Iron Horse, The.
Precedents.

Newman, John Henry, Cardinal
Angel ("My work is done").
Angel ("Softly and gently, dearly-ransom'd soul").
Angel of the Agony.
Angelic Guidance.
Chorus of Angels.
Chorus of the Elements.
Discovery, The.
Dream of Gerontius, The.
Elements, The.
England.
Fifth Choir of Angelicals.
Flowers without Fruit.
Greek Fathers, The.
Guardian Angel.
James and John.
Jesu, Maria—I am near to death.
Judaism.
Lead, Kindly Light.
Light in the Darkness.
Monks.
My Lady Nature and Her Daughters.
Patient Church, The.
Pillar of the Cloud, The.
Praise to the Holiest in the Height.
Progress of Unbelief.
Queen of Seasons, The.
Refrigerium.
Relics of Saints.
Rest.
Reverses.
St. Philip in Himself.
Sensitiveness.
Sign of the Cross, The.
Snapdragon.
Solitude.
Soul before God, The.
Substance and Shadow.
Thanksgiving, A.
Trance of Time, The.
Until the Shadows Lengthen.
Valentine to a Little Girl.
Yielded.
Zeal of Jehu, The.

Newman, Joseph S.
Baby Toodles.
Hero and Leander.

Newman, Louis I.
Voice of God, The.
World Looks On, The.

Newman, Preston
Some Questions to Be Asked of a Rajah, Perhaps by the Associated Press.

Newsome, Mary Effie Lee
Arctic Tern in a Museum.
Baker's Boy, The.
Bats.
Cotton Cat, The.
Cricket and the Star, The.
Little Birches.
Morning Light.
Pansy.
Quilt, The.
Quoits.
Sassafras Tea.
Sky Pictures.
Wild Roses.

Newton, Byron Rufus
Owed to New York.

Newton, Charlotte
Fulfillment.

Newton, Douglas
Gaiety of Descendants.
Invasion Weather.

Newton, Earl L.
Skippery Boo, The.

Newton, John
All Our Griefs to Tell.
Effort, The.
Friend That Sticketh Closer Than a Brother, A.
Glorious Things of Thee Are Spoken.
Greenfields.
How Sweet the Name of Jesus Sounds.
How Tedious and Tasteless the Hours.
In Evil Long I Took Delight.
In Sweet Communion.
Jesus! my Shepherd, Husband, Friend.
Joy.
Looking at the Cross.
Lord Will Provide, The.
My Prayer.
Name of Jesus, The.
Nothing to Wish or to Fear.
Now May He Who from the Dead.
Prayer Answered by Crosses.
Precious Name, The.
Thou Art Coming to a King.
Why Should I Fear?
Wonderful Word, The.
Zion, City of Our God.

Newton, Joseph Fort
"Follow Me."
White Presence, The.

Newton, Mary Leslie
Queen Anne's Lace.

Ngani, A. Z.
Praises of King George VI.

Nicarchus [*or* Nicarchos],
Fortunatus the R. A. ("Fortunatus the portrait-painter got twenty sons").
On Marcus the Physician.
Requirements: "Not for me a giantess."

Niccolini, Giovanni Battista
Barbarossa, *sel.*
When will you dream,/ You Germans.

Niccolò degli Albizzi
Prolonged Sonnet: When the Troops Were Returning from Milan.
Troops Returning from Milan.

Nichol, John
Good Night.
H. W. L.
Mare Mediterraneum.

Nicholas, A. X.
For Lee.
For Mack.
For Poki.
This Baptism with Fire.

Nicholas, Michael
Today: the Idea Market.

Nicholl, Louise Townsend
Ark of the Covenant.
Celestial Body.
Choir-Boys on Christmas Eve.
Cigar Smoke, Sunday, after Dinner.
Cleavage.
Color Alone Can Speak.
Creation.
Cruse, The.
Different Speech, A.
Different Winter.
For a Child Named Katherine.
Hymn: "Words of hymns abruptly plod, The."
Improvising.
In the motionless haze of interior heat.
Incense.
Knowing What Time It Is at Night.
Made Lake, The.
Marigold.
Ornamental Water.
Pediment: Ballet.
Physical Goegraphy.
Recital, *sel.*
Rondel for Middle Age.
Shape of the Heart, The.
Three Persons.
Time in the Sun.

Wild Cherry.
Nicholls, W. Leslie
Albert Dürer.
Nichols, Carrie May
Boomerang, The.
Nichols, John Bowyer Buchanan
I am Huxley, blond and merry.
Lines by a Person of Quality.
On the Toilet Table of Queen Marie-Antoinette.
Pastoral, A: "My love and I among the mountains strayed."
Nichols, J. W. H.
Quite Suddenly.
Soon Thou Wilt Come.
Nichols, Jeannette
All the Tree's Hands.
Nichols, John
I Came from Salem City.
Nichols, Robert
Assault, The.
Aurelia.
Battery Moving Up to a New Position from Rest Camp: Dawn.
By the Wood.
Casualty.
Catch for Spring, A.
"Come let us sigh a requiem over love."
Dawn on the Somme.
Day's March, The.
Don Juan's Address to the Sunset.
Flower of Flame, The, *sel.*
Fulfilment.
Full Heart, The.
Harlot's Catch.
I Love a Flower.
Moon behind High Tranquil Leaves, The.
Nearer.
Our Dead.
Secret Garden, The.
Sonnets to Aurelia, *sels.*
Sprig of Lime, The.
Thanksgiving.
To ——: "Asleep within the deadest hour of the night."
To D'Annunzio; Lines from the Sea.
Nicholson, J. U.
Old Maid.
Reconciliation.
String Stars of Pearls.
Nicholson, John
On a Calm Summer's Night.
Nicholson, L.
Bubbles.
Nicholson, Martha Snell
Altars Raised to God.
And His Name Shall Be Called Wonderful.
Beauty for Ashes.
Bible Study.
Cup, The.
Dominion.
Dying.
For the Blind.
His Plan for Me.
His Promises.
Home.
If I But Read.
In a Garden.
Lo, I Am with You Always.
Look Up.
Looking Backward.
Loveliness.
My Lord.
New Year's Message, A.
On a Sick Bed.
Prayer for a New House.
Steward of God.
Suppose that Christ Had Not Been Born.
This Easter Day.
To My Friend.
Two Homes.
Until He Comes.
What Are You Doing for Jesus?
"With Whom Is No Shadow of Turning."
Nicholson, Meredith
From Bethlehem to Calvary.
Nicholson, Norman
August.
Blackberry, The.
Bond Street.
Burning Bush, The.
Cædmon.
Carol: "Mary laid her Child among."
Cleator Moor.
Cockley Moor, Dockray, Penrith.
Cowper.
Crocus, The.
Expanding Universe, The.
Five Minutes.
For All Sorts and Conditions.
For the Bicentenary of Isaac Watts.
For the New Year.
Gathering Sticks on Sunday.
Innocents' Day.
Michaelmas.
Millom Old Quarry.
Motion of the Earth, The.
Now in the Time of This Mortal Life.
Old Man at a Cricket Match.
Poem for Epiphany.
Pot Geranium, The.
Preachers, The.
Ravenglass Railway Station, Cumberland.
Ride to Jerusalem, The.
Rockferns.
Song at Night.
South Cumberland, 16th May 1943 ("The sun has set").
South Cumberland, 10th May 1943 ("The fat flakes fall").
Tame Hare, The.
Thomas Gray in Patterdale.
To a Child before Birth.
To the River Duddon.
Undiscovered Planet, The.
Wales.
Windscale.
Nicias
Fountains at the Tomb, The.
Nicklaus, Frederick
Contract.
Nicol, Abioseh
African Easter.
Continent That Lies within Us, The.
Meaning of Africa, The.
Nicolai, Philip
Sleepers, Wake.
Wake, Awake, for Night Is Flying.
Nicolas, Vidal de
Wish, A.
Nicoll, Robert
Bonnie Bessie Lee.
Hero, The.
We Are Brethren A'.
We'll A' Go Pu' the Heather.
Nicolson, Adela Florence Cory *See* **"Hope, Laurence"**
Nicostratus
Prattling Swallows.
Niebuhr, Reinhold
Prayer for Serenity.
Nielson, N. P.
Secrets of Life, The.
Nietzsche, Friedrich Wilhelm
Among Foes.
Solitary, The.
Star Morals.
Nightingale, Madeleine
Apple Rhyme, The.
Caravan, The.
Muffin-Man, The.
Ring-a-Ring o' Fairies.
Scissor-Man, The.
Underneath the Clothes.
Waits, The.
Nijlen, Jan van
Master of Time, The.
Nikitin, Ivan Savich
Night in a Village, A.
Niles, Nathaniel
American Hero, The.
Bunker Hill.
Nims, John Frederick
Agamemnon before Troy.
Apocalypse.
Barrier.
Blessing.
Clock Symphony.
Dollar Bill.
Fairy Tale.
First Date.
For My Son.
La Ci Darem la Mano.
Love Poem: "My clumsiest dear, whose hands shipwreck vases."
Madrigal: "Beside the rivers of the midnight town."
Midwest.
Nature Lover.
Necromancers, The.
New Year's Eve, 1938.
Non-Euclidean Elegy.
To the Rulers.
Trainwrecked Soldiers.
Visiting Poet.
Ninine
Prayer to St. Patrick.
Niven, Frederick
Indian Dance.
Nixon, John, Jr
Spidersilk.
Through a Fog of Stars.
Nizami
Poet in His Poverty, The.
Njegos, Petar Petrovic
Mountain Wreath, The, *sel.*
Speech of Abbot Stephen.
Noble, Fay Lewis
Prayer for Song.
Nobutsuna
Flute, A.
Noel, Roden Berkeley Wriothesley
Casual Song, A.
Dying.
I Flung Me Round Him.
Lady to a Lover, A.
Lament: "I am lying in thy tomb, love."
Merry-go-round, The.
Old, The.
Sea Slumber-Song.
Secret of the Nightingale, The.
Swimmer, The.
"That They All May Be One."
Toy Cross, The.
Vale!
Water-Nymph and the Boy, The, *sel.*
Noel, Thomas
Old Winter.
Pauper's Drive, The.
"Nogar, Rui "
Poem of the Conscripted Warrior.
Noguchi, Yone
Hokku: "Bits of song—what else?"
I Have Cast the World.
Lines: "When I am lost in the deep body of the mist on a hill."
Poet, The.
Noin Hoshi
Tanka: "In the evening/ Quiet of the country town."
Nolan, Bertha

Nolan (continued)
My Mother.
Nolan, Edward
Oxford Is a Stage.
Nolan, Michael
Little Annie Rooney.
Noll, Bink
Abraham's Madness.
Afternoon for a Small Boy.
Air Tunnel, Monticello.
"All My Pretty Ones? Did You Say All?"
For Jane Kane, Whom We Knew in Our Young Marriages.
Lunch on Omaha Beach.
Picador Bit, The.
Rented Garden, The.
Song in a Winter Night.
Nomberg, David
Russian Cradle Song, A.
Norcross, Ellinor L.
Devotions.
Norman, Charles
Rockefeller Center.
Norris, Alfred
Prayer for Faith, A.
Norris, John
Aspiration, The.
Canticle.
Choice, The.
Hymn to Darkness.
Meditation, The.
Reply, The.
Retirement, The.
Second Chap. of the Cant. from the 10. Verse to the 13.
Superstition.
Wish, A.
Norris, Kathleen
Mother.
Norris, Leslie
Ballad of Billy Rose, The.
It's Somebody's Birthday.
Norse, Harold
Colosseum.
"North, Christopher" (John Wilson)
Calm as the Cloudless Heaven.
Come Forth, Come Forth.
Evening Cloud, The.
Rose and the Gauntlet, The.
Sacred Poetry.
Written on the Banks of Wastwater during a Calm.
North, E.
Out of Doors.
North, Frank Mason
Christ in the City.
City, The.
Waking World, The.
North, Jessica Nelson
Balloon Man.
Hibernalia.
Mathematical.
Rainy Morning.
To Duncan.
Truth.
Young Boy, A.
Norton, Andrews
Hymn for the Dedication of a Church.
Norton, Caroline Elizabeth Sarah Sheridan
Arab to His Favorite Steed, The.
Arab's Farewell to His Horse [*or* Steed].
I Do Not Love Thee.
King of Denmark's Ride, The.
Love Not.
Not Lost, but Gone Before.
We Have Been Friends Together.
Norton, Eleanour
Chopin Prelude.
Norton, Glenn, *and* L. F. Post *See* **Post, L. F., *and* Glenn Norton**
Norton, Grace Fallow
Adventure.
Allegra Agonistes.
Deer on the Mountain.
I Give Thanks.
Little Gray Songs from St. Joseph's, *sels.*
Love Is a Terrible Thing.
Make No Vows.
O Sleep.
This Is My Love for You.
Norton, John
Funeral Elogy, upon . . . Mrs. Anne Bradstreet, A.
Norton, Thomas
Against Women either Good or Bad.
Man May Live Thrice Nestor's Life, A.
Norwood, Eille
Limerick: "Pretty young actress, a stammerer, A."
Norwood, Robert
After the Order of Melchisedec.
But, this I found.
Man of Kerioth, The, *sel.*
Resurrection and the Life, The.
Why?
Noss, Murray
Hiroshima.
Notker Balbulus
Cantemus Cuncti Melodum.
Media Vita.
Nottage, May Hastings
My Father's Voice in Prayer.
Nott-Bower, E. E.
Haulage.
Patience.
"Novalis" (Georg Friedrich Philipp von Hardenerg)
Hymn to the Night, II.
Hymns to the Night, *sel.*
Novo, Salvador
Departed Friend, The.
Nowell, M. H.
Of Disdainful Daphne.
Nowlan, Alden
Anatomy of Angels, The.
Aunt Jane ("Aunt Jane, of whom I dreamed").
Beets.
Execution, The.
God Sour the Milk of the Knacking Wench.
Grove beyond the Barley, The.
Loneliness of the Long Distance Runner, The.
Stoney Ridge Dance Hall.
Wickedness of Peter Shannon, The.
Noyes, Alfred
Admiral's Ghost, The.
Apes and Ivory.
Art.
Assisi.
Avenue of the Allies, The.
Barrel-Organ, The.
Betsy Jane's Sixth Birthday.
Blinded Soldier to His Love, The.
Bring on the pomp and pride of old Castile.
Butterflies.
Call of the Spring, The.
Caterpillar, The.
Cats and Kings.
Creation.
Daddy Fell into the Pond.
Dawn of Peace, The.
Diplomats, The.
Double Fortress, The.
Drake, *sels.*
Edinburgh.
Epilogue: "Carol, every violet has."
Flower of Old Japan, The, sel.
Fools have said/ That knowledge drives out wonder.
Forty Singing Seamen.
Go down to Kew in Lilac-Time.
Highwayman, The.
Hospital, A.
In the Cool of the Evening.
Japanese Love-Song, A.
Kilmeny.
Last Voyage, The, *sels.*
Loom of Years, The, *sel.*
Messages.
Messenger, The.
Moon Is Up, The.
New Duckling, The.
O, woven in one wide loom thro' the throbbing weft of the whole.
Old Gray Squirrel.
Old Man Mountain.
On the Death of Francis Thompson.
Our Lady of the Sea.
Pact, The.
Pirates.
Prayer, A: "Angels, where you soar."
River of Stars, The.
Saint George and the Dragon ("Saint George he slew the dragon").
Seagulls on the Serpentine.
Seven Wise Men.
Sherwood.
Skunk, The.
Song: "Fairy band are we, A."
Song: "I came to the door of the House of Love."
Song: "What is there hid in the heart of a rose."
Song of Sherwood, A.
Strong City, The.
Tales of the Mermaid Tavern, *sel.*
Torch Bearers, The.
Touchstone on a Bus, *sel.*
Under the Pyrenees.
Unity.
Victory.
Victory Ball, A.
Victory Dance, A.
Washington's Last Birthday.
Watchers of the Sky, *sels.*
When Spring Comes Back to England.
Wine Press, The, *sel.*
World's May Queen, The.
You That Sing in the Blackthorn.
Noyes, Nicholas
Consolatory Poem Dedicated unto Mr. Cotton Mather, A.
Prefatory Poem, on. . .*Magnalia Christi Americana,* A.
Prefatory Poem to the Little Book, Entituled, *Christianus per Ignem,* A.
Rev. Nicholas Noyes to the Rev. Cotton Mather, The.
To My Worthy Friend, Mr. James Bayley.
Nugent, Gerald
Farewell to Fál, A.
Nugent, Robert, Earl Nugent
Epigram: "I loved thee beautiful and kind.
I Loved Thee.
Revenge.
Nunan, Thomas
Dreamer, The.
Núñez de Arce, Gaspar
Miserere.
Nurton, C.
My Doggie.
Nuttall, Jeff
Poem: "Ran jet self into starscum 0067 hrs."
Nutter, C. D.
On Time with God.
Nutter, Medora Addison
Mountain Creed.

Nutting, J. K.
How the Froggies Go to Sleep, *sel.*
Little, Wee Froggies, The.
Nuur, Faarah
Limits of Submission, The.
Modern Love Songs.
Nweke, Chuba
Moon Song.
Nygren, David F.
I Had a Part.

O

"O., G. S."
Engine Driver, The.
Oakes, Urian
Elegie upon that Reverend . . . Mr. Thomas Shepard, An.
To the Reader.
Oakes-Smith, Elizabeth *See* **Smith, Elizabeth Oakes**
Oakley, Ebenezer S.
Thoughts That Move the Heart of Man, The.
Oaks, Gladys
Anatole France at Eighty.
Oatman, Jr, Johnson
Higher Ground.
O'Bolger, T. D.
Counsels of O'Riordan, the Rann Maker, The.
O'Brien, —— Benny Havens, Oh!
O'Brien, Edward Joseph
Her Fairness, Wedded to a Star.
Irish.
Shepherd Boy, The.
O'Brien, Fitz-James
Demon of the Gibbet, The.
Kane.
Legend of the Easter Eggs, The.
Minot's Ledge.
Second Mate, The.
"O'Brien, John." *See* **Hartigan, Patrick Joseph**
O'Brien, Katharine
Spring Song.
O'Brien, R. C.
Poor Grandpa.
O'Brien, Seumas
Poet, The.
O'Brien, Thomas
Always Battling.
International Brigade Dead.
Terror.
"O'Byrne, Dermot" (Sir Arnold Bax)
Dublin Ballad, A; 1916.
O'Carolan, Turlough *See* **Carolan, Turlough**
"Occidente, Maria del." *See* **Brooks,Maria Gowen**
Occleve, Thomas *See* **Hoccleve, Thomas**
O'Connell, Richard
Sidewalk Orgy.
O'Connor, Frank (*originally* Michael O'-Donova
Mary Hynes.
Three Old Brothers.
O'Connor, Joseph
General's Death, The.
What Was My Dream?
O'Connor, Michael
Reveille.
O'Connor, Patrick
In Pace in Idipsum Dormiam et Requiescam.
Mantle of Mary, The.
O'Connor, Philip
Poems.
O'Conor, Norreys Jephson
Beside the Blackwater.
In Memoriam; Francis Ledwidge.
In the Monastery.
In the Moonlight.
To a Child.
O'Cotter, Pat
Malemute Dog, A.
O'Crowley, Denis
Washington.
O'Curnain, Diarmad
Love's Despair.
O'Daly, Carrol
Eileen Aroon.
Lover and Echo.
O'Daly, Murdoch
Consecration.
In the Heart of Jesus.
Odaro (Barbara Jones)
Alafia.
Odell, Jonathan
On Our Thirty-ninth Wedding Day.
Oden, Gloria Catherine
". . . As When Emotion Too Far Exceeds Its Cause."
Carousel, The.
Map, The.
Private Letter to Brazil, A.
Review from Staten Island.
O'Donnell, Charles L.
Ad Matrem, in Caelis.
Address to the Crown.
Cloister.
Dead Musician, The.
Process.
Prodigals.
Resolution.
Rime of the Rood, A.
Road of Ireland, A.
Security.
Shed, The.
Son of God, The.
Spinner, The.
To St. Joseph.
Trelawny Lies by Shelley.
O'Donnell, George Marion
Semmes in the Garden ("Semmes waited under the still trees.").
O'Donnell, John Francis
Adare, *sel.*
April.
By the Turnstile.
Down looked the moon, but looked no more.
Drifting.
From the grey wicket of the morn.
Geraldine's Garden.
Happy Christmases, *sels.*
I row in my boat in the twilight, half-purple, half-grey, overhead.
In the December weather, grey and grim.
In the Market-Place.
In the Twilight, *sel.*
July Dawn, A, *sel.*
Lilies, The.
Limerick Town, *sel.*
May, *sel.*
Morn comes freshly from the east, The.
My Jack.
O dim delicious heaven of dreams.
Open, sweet flowers, your eyes.
Ossian, *sel.*
Reminiscences of a Day, *sel.*
Spinning Song, A.
Spoke my heart in the dearth of the night.
Spring, The.
To Spring, *sel.*
'Twas summer time, the radiant world of June.
We left the city, street and square.
O'Donnell, T. C.
If I.
O'Donovan, Michael *See* **O'Connor, Frank**
O'Dowd, Bernard
Alma Venus, *sel.*
As many, Mother, are your moods and forms.
Australia.
Bush, The, *sels.*
Cow, The.
Door of existence, beacon of our haze.
Last Stanzas of "The Bush."
Love and Sacrifice.
Poet, The.
Proletaria.
Quail.
Young Democracy.
O'Dugan [*or* Dugan], Maurice
Coolun, The.
Oehlenschlaeger, Adam G.
Aspirations.
Freya's Spinning Wheel.
There Is a Charming Land.
Oesch, Mary Mae
Beatitudes for a Housewife.
Oever, Karel van den
Telephone Pole, The.
O Farachàin, Roibéard *See* **Farren, Robert**
Offaly, Gerald Fitzgerald, Baron of
Gambler's Repentance, The.
O'Flaherty, Charles
Donnybrook Jig, The.
Humours of Donnybrook Fair, The.
Ogarev, Nikolay Platonovich
Road, The.
O'Gillan, Angus
Clonmacnoise.
Dead at Clonmacnois, The.
Ogilvie, D. T.
Last Letter to the Western Civilization.
Ogilvie, Will H.
Blades of Harden, The.
Death of Ben Hall, The.
Drought.
From the Gulf.
How the Fire Queen Crossed the Swamp.
Raiders, The.
Whaup o' the Rede, *sel.*
Ogle, George
Banks of Banna, The.
Mailligh Mo Stor.
Ogletree, Carolyn J.
Formula.
Life Is the Art of Drawing.
Ogmundarson, Cormac
Two Songs in Praise of Steingerd.
O'Gnive, Fearflatha
Downfall of the Gael, The.
O'Gorman, Ned
Childhood.
L'Annunciazione.
Myth.
O'Grady, Desmond
Arrival: The Capital.
O'Grady, Standish
And first Morency, far famed water, you.
Emigrant, The, *sels.*
Old Nick in Sorel ("Old Nick took a fancy, as many men tell").
Winter in Lower Canada.
O'Grady, Standish James
Lough Bray.
Ogutsch, Edith
Musings of an Insomniac.
Premonition.
O'Hagan, Thomas
Another Year.
Giotto's Campanile.
Woman.
O'Halloran, Elspeth McDuffie *See* **"Elspeth"**

O'Hara, Frank
Ave Maria.
Biotherm.
Blocks.
Chez Jane.
Day Lady Died, The.
For James Dean.
For Janice and Kenneth to Voyage.
Getting Up Ahead of Someone (Sun).
Hotel Transylvanie.
How to Get There.
In Favor of One's Time.
In Memory of My Feelings.
Mary Desti's Ass.
Naphtha.
Ode: "Idea of justice may be precious, An."
Ode: Salute to the French Negro Poets.
Ode to Joy.
Ode to Michael Goldberg's Birth and Other Births.
On Seeing Larry Rivers' "Washington Crossing the Delaware" at the Museum of Modern Art.
Poem: "Hate is only one of many responses."
Poem: "Krushchev is coming the right day!"
Poem: "Lana Turner has collapsed!"
Poem Read at Joan Mitchell's.
Romanze, or the Music Students.
Song: "Is it dirty/ does it look dirty."
Step Away from Them, A.
Steps.
To Hell with It.
To the Harbormaster.
True Account of Talking to the Sun at Fire Island, A.
Why I Am Not a Painter.
You Are Gorgeous and I'm Coming.
You at the Pump (History of North and South).
O'Hara, John Myers
Atropos.
Greater Mystery, The.
O'Hara, Theodore
Bivouac of the Dead, The.
O'Heffernan, Mahon
Who Will Buy a Poem?
O'Higgins, Myron
Blues for Bessie.
Sunset Horn.
Two Lean Cats.
Vaticide.
Young Poet.
O'Huiginn, Tadhg Dall
First Vision, The.
Second Vision, The.
O'Huiginn, Tadhg O'g
On the Breaking-up of a School.
O'Kane, T. C.
My Mother's Prayer.
Okara, Gabriel
Call of the River Nun, The.
Mystic Drum, The.
Once upon a Time.
Piano and Drums.
To Adhiambo.
Were I To Choose.
You Laughed and Laughed and Laughed.
O'Keeffe, Adelaide
Beasts, Birds, and Fishes.
Butterfly, The.
Foolish Emily and Her Kitten.
George and the Chimney-Sweeper.
Going to Bed at Night.
Lucy's Canary.
Nimble Dick.
O'Keeffe, John
Amo Amas.
Friar of Orders Gray, The.
Jingle.
Merry Sherwood, *sel.*
Robin Hood, *wr. title.*
O'Kelly, Patrick
Blessings on Doneraile.
Curse of Doneraile, The.
Okigbo, Christopher
Death lay in ambush.
Distances, *sel.*
Lament of the Flutes.
Oku, Princess
Journeying Alone.
Would I Had Stayed.
Okura
Because he is young.
Olcott, Chauncey
My Wild Irish Rose.
"Old Arkansaw." *See* **Hughes, Dave**
Oldham, G. Ashton
America First.
Oldham, John
Careless Good Fellow, The.
Cup, The.
Dissuasive against Poetry, A.
If you for orders, and a gown design.
Let dull and ignorant pretenders art condemn.
Letter from the Country to a Friend in Town, A.
Loyola's Instructions to His Followers.
Parting, The.
Prologue: "For who can longer hold? when every press."
Quiet Soul, A.
Satire [*or* Satyr] A, *sel.*
Satire I: Garnet's Ghost Addressing to the Jesuits.
Satires [*or* Satyrs] upon the Jesuits, *sels.*
Satyr, A.
Satyr III: "When shaven crown, and hallow'd girdle's power."
Satyr Address'd to a Friend, That Is About to Leave the University, and Come Abroad in the World, A, *sel.*
Satyr against Vertue, A, *sel.*
Satyr in Imitation of the Third of Juvenal, A, *sel.*
Satyrs upon the Jesuits.
Streets of London, The.
'Tis endless, Sir, to tell the many ways.
To the Memory of Mr. Charles Morwent, *sel.*
Upon the Author of a Play Call'd Sodom.
Upon the Works of Ben Jonson, *sel.*
Vertue! thou solemn grave Impertinence.
Wolf and the Dog, The.
Oldmixon, John
I Lately Vowed [but 'Twas in Haste].
Prithee, Chloe, Not So Fast.
To Cloe.
To Corinna.
Olds, N. S.
Rivets.
Oldys, William
Anacreontick, An.
Fly, The.
On a Fly Drinking Out of [*or* from] His Cup.
To a Fly.
O'Leary, Cormac
Reflections on Cleopathera's Needle.
O'Leary, Eileen
Lament for Art O'Leary, The.
O'Leary, Ellen
To God and Ireland True.
O'Leary, Joseph
Whisky, Drink Divine.
O'Leary, Shawn
Bayonet, The.
Oleson, Helmer O.
Ballad of Johnny Appleseed, A.
Olier, Jean Jacques
O Jesu.
Oliphant, Carolina *See* **Nairne, Carolina Oliphant, Baroness**
Olitski, Leib
My Song to the Jewish People.
Olivares Figueroa, R.
Sower, The.
Oliver, Mary
Flute-Man, The.
Isabel Sparrow.
Roo.
Oliver, W. H.
Beachcomber, The.
Death and the Maiden, *sel.*
Mourn her in the valleys, you young lovers, and throughout your gloom.
Phoenix, The.
Sleep Will Come Singly.
Oliver, Wade
Christ Speaks.
Ships with Your Silver Nets.
Olney, D. A.
Just like This.
Olney, William
Prayer and Promises.
Olsen, Charles Oluf
Kingdoms.
Olsen, Donald D.
Poem: "We used to float the paper boats in spring."
Olson, Charles
A B C s ("The word forms").
A B C s ("What we do not know of ourselves").
Anecdotes of the Late War, *sel.*
As the Dead Prey upon Us.
Death of Europe, The.
Distances, The.
I, Maximus of Gloucester, to You.
Kingfishers, The.
Knowing All Ways, including the Transposition of Continents.
La Torre.
Letter for Melville 1951.
Letter 27.
Letter 22.
Librarian, The.
Lordly and Isolate Satyrs, The.
Maximus, from Dogtown, I.
Maximus, to Gloucester, Letter 19.
Maximus, to Himself.
Moebius Strip, The.
Moon Is the Number 18, The.
Move Over.
Newly Discovered "Homeric" Hymn, A.
River Map, The, and We're Done.
Songs of Maximus, The.
That (like the man sd) Booth.
Variations Done for Gerald van de Wiele.
Olson, Elder
Crucifix.
Essay on Deity.
Ice-Skaters.
In Defense of Superficiality.
Jack-in-the-Box.
Knight, with Umbrella.
Night There Was Dancing in the Streets, The.
Plot Improbable, Character Unsympathetic.
Waters.
Olson, Ted
Hawk's Way.
Starlings.
Things That Endure.
O'Malley, Charles J.
Poet's Harvesting, The.
O'Malley, D. J.
Horse Wrangler, The, *with music.*
Tenderfoot, The.

Omar B. Abi Rabi'a
Damsel, The.
Omar Khayyám
And those who husbanded the golden grain.
Awake! for Morning in the bowl of Night.
Ball, The ("The ball no question makes of ayes and noes").
Bird of Time, The.
Book of verses underneath the bough, A.
Careless Delight.
Dreaming when dawn's left hand was in the sky.
Equity with God.
Fatalism.
Fifteen Rubaiyat.
For in and out, above, about, below.
Great Argument.
Heart's Desire.
Heaven and Hell.
Iram Indeed Is Gone.
Like Snow.
Long While, The.
Master-Knot, The.
Minister of Wine, The.
Moment's halt, A—a momentary taste.
Moving Finger, The.
Myself When Young Did Eagerly Frequent.
New Year, The.
Omar and Death, *abr.*
Paradise.
Predestination.
Quatrains.
Ritual of the Grape.
Rubáiyát of Omar Khayyám of Naishápúr.
Sleep Unbroken.
So Red the Rose.
Soul Is All, The.
There Is No Sin.
Think, in this batter'd Caravanserai.
This Life Flies.
Waste Not Your Hour.
Why, all the Saints and Sages who discuss'd.
Wish, A.
Worldly Hope, The. ("The worldly hope men set their hearts upon").
Worldly Wisdom.
Yet Ah, that Spring should vanish with the Rose.
O'Mulconry, Peadar
Were Not the Gael Fallen.
Onakatomi no Yoshinobu
Deer on pine mountain, The.
Deer which lives, The.
Ondaatje, Michael
House Divided, A.
Prometheus, with Wings.
Onderdonk, Henry Ustic
How Wondrous Are Thy Works.
Spirit, in Our Hearts, The.
O'Neil, David
Modern Orchard, A.
Starvation Peak Evening.
Vernal Showers.
O'Neil, George
Adam's Wonder.
Cobbler in Willow Street, The.
Events.
Fable: "I led him on into the frosted wood."
Homage.
Socrates Prays a Day and a Night.
Where It Is Winter.
Woman Passes the Door, A.
O'Neill, D. L.
J. F. K.
O'Neill, Mary Devenport
Dead in Wars and in Revolutions.
Galway.
Old Waterford Woman, An.
Scene-Shifter Death.
Tramp's Song, The.
O'Neill, Moira (Nesta Higginson Skrine)
Birds.
Broken Song, A.
Bud in the Frost, A.
Corrymeela.
Fairy Lough, The.
Forgettin'.
Grace for Light.
Grand Match, The.
Sea Wrack.
Song of Glenann, A.
O'Neill, Rose
Eighteenth Century Lady.
Faun-taken.
When the Dead Men Die.
Onitsura
Cherry-blossoms, more.
Directions.
Ono no Komachi
Thing which fades, A.
Ono no Takamura
Did I ever think.
Ono no Yoshiki
My love/ Is like the grasses.
Unknown.
Onstott, Mary Brown
Expatriate.
Opdyke, Oliver (John Baker Opdyke)
My Road.
Spring Lay, A.
Ophel, Frederick William
His Epitaph.
Pioneers.
Opie, Amelia
Orphan Boy's Tale, The.
Opitz, Martin
Beauty of This Earth.
Opoku, Andrew Amankwa
River Afram.
Oppen, George
Bahamas.
Oppenheim, Garrett
Diary of a Nondescript.
Oppenheim, James
Action.
As to Being Alone.
Bread and Roses.
Create Great Peace.
Death.
For Randolph Bourne.
Future, The.
Handful of Dust, A.
Hebrews.
Immoral.
Lincoln Child, The.
Lonely Child, The.
Machinery is enough for a scientist.
Memories of Whitman and Lincoln.
New God, The.
New York Skyscraper, A, *sel.*
Night, *sels.*
Night Note.
1914—and After, *sel.*
Not Overlooked.
O sprawling city! worlds in a world!
Pittsburgh.
Priest, The.
Reason, The.
Report on the Planet, Earth.
Runner in the Skies, The.
Saturday Night.
Slave, The.
Tasting the Earth.
Oppenheimer, Joel
Bath, The.
Blue Funk.
Bus Trip, The.
Cartography.
Couple, The.
Feeding, The.
For the Barbers.
Leave It to Me Blues.
Love Bit, The.
Mare Nostrum.
Mathematics.
Numbers, The.
Peaches, The.
Torn Nightgown, The.
Oppenheimer, Paul
Commemoration for the Physicist X, A.
Death of Hoelderlin, The.
Opper, Emma A.
Charms, The.
Opperman, D. J.
Christmas Carol: "Three outas from the bleak Karoo."
Fable: "Under a dung-cake."
Fable of the Speckled Cow.
O'Rahilly [*or* O'Reilly], Egan
Brightness of Brightness.
Geraldine's Daughter, The.
Grey Eye Weeping, A.
I have received jewels of conspicuous beauty.
Lament for Banba.
Last Lines.
More Power to Cromwell.
On a Cock Which Was Stolen from a Good Priest.
On a Pair of Shoes Presented to Him, *sel.*
Pitiful the playing of the flood with dire destruction!
Reverie, The.
Sleepless Night, A.
Storm, The, *sel.*
Orde, Julian
Changing Wind, The.
Orden, J. Rodríguez la
To an Andalusian Fan.
O'Reilly, Dowell
Australia.
Faith, Love, and Death.
Sea-Grief.
Stars.
O'Reilly, Egan *See* **O'Rahilly, Egan**
O'Reilly, John Boyle
Art Master, An.
At Best.
At Fredericksburg (December 13, 1862).
Boston.
Builder's Lesson, A.
Chicago.
Constancy.
Crispus Attucks.
Cry of a Dreamer, The.
Cry of the Dreamer, The.
Disappointment.
Experience.
Forever.
In Bohemia.
Infinite, The.
Lure, The.
Mayflower.
Message of Peace, A.
Midnight—September 19, 1881.
Name of Mary.
Pilgrim Fathers, The.
Ride of Colin Graves, The.
Savage, A.
Song: "Love was true to me."
To-Day.
Wendell Phillips, *sel.*
What Is Good?
What shall we mourn? For the prostrate tree that sheltered the green wood?
White Rose, A.
O'Reilly, Mary A.

O'Reilly (continued)
Christmas Carol, A: "Night in the far Judean land."
Orente, Rose J.
Master City, The.
Orford, Horace Walpole, 4th Earl of *See* **Walpole, Horace, 4th Earl of Orford**
Oribe, Emilio
Ode to the Sky of the New Atlantis.
"Orinda." *See* **Philips, Katherine**
O'Riordan, Conal ("Norreys Connell")
Care Is Heavy.
Hymn to the Virgin Mary.
Requiem.
Orléans, Charles, duc d'
alons au bois le may cueillir.
Ballade: "Looking one day toward the coast of France."
Ballade: "O sely ankir, that in thi selle."
Ballade: "When fresshe Phebus, day of Seynt Valentyne."
Come, Death—My Lady Is Dead.
Confession.
Confession of a Stolen Kiss.
Dieu Qu'il la Fait.
Go, Sad Complaint.
Honor, Joy ("Honoure, joy, healthe, and pleasaunce")
Kiss, The ("My ghostly father").
My Ghostly Father.
My Gostly Fader, I Me Confess.
Oft in My Thought.
Rondeau: "Year his winter cloak lets fall, The."
Rondel: "Strengthen, my Love, this castle of my heart."
Roundel: "My ghostly fadir, Y me confesse."
Smiling Mouth, The.
So Fair, So Fresh.
Spring ("The year has changed his mantle cold").
Orleans, Ilo
Anatomy Lesson.
Any Bird.
"Give me the sky."
I offered the donkey.
I saw a dog.
I thank you God, /For a hundred things.
In the Garden.
It isn't hard/ to drive a car.
Little man/ Little man.
Shoes have tongues.
Sky came tripping, The.
Soap is green.
Soldiers fight by land and air.
Upon the Beach.
Water has no color.
Orlovitz, Gil
Art of the Sonnet, *sels.*
Bowed negress, who aghast but the light.
Homage to Charles Laughton.
If I could rise and see my father young.
Index (8).
Lyric: "Angora anger who art in heaven."
Lyric: "When I am gone and green."
Masterindex: 23.
Rooster, The.
Such folly of margins that may retaliate.
Orlovsky, Peter
Second Poem: "Morning again, nothing has to be done."
Ormsby, Stephanie
Caribbean, The.
Orner, Raymond
New Year, The.
O'Rourke, May
Stick, The.
Orr, Gregory
Being and Wind.
Dead Wasp.
I Will Give You a Purpose.
Marina.
Single Candle as the Presence of God, A.
Things You Left Behind.
Waking Up in the Woods.
Orr, Hugh Robert
Calvary.
They Softly Walk.
Orr, James
Irishman, The.
Orr, Patrick
Annie Shore and Johnnie Doon.
In the Mohave.
Orred, Meta
In the Gloaming ("In the gloaming, Oh my darling").
Orrery, Roger Boyle, Earl of
Excellency of Wine, The.
O'Ryan, Edmond
Ah! What Woes Are Mine.
Osadebay, Dennis C.
African Trader's Complaint, The.
Young Africa's Resolve.
Osborn, Frederic J.
There Is a Time.
Osborn, Laughton
Death of General Pike, The.
Osborn, Margot
Always the Melting Moon Comes.
Osborn, Mary Elizabeth
Alma Mater.
Come Not Near.
Exquisite Lady.
Mid-Century.
Old Man in the Park.
Rural Legend.
Thought for the Winter Season.
Water-Images.
Osborn, Mary I.
Every Day.
My Playmate.
Swing, The.
Osborn, Selleck
Modest Wit, A.
Osborne, Charles
So Fly by Night.
Osborne, Duffield
Ave! Nero Imperator.
Osborne, Edith D.
Path of the Padres, The.
Popcorn Man, The.
Osborne, Gene H.
Thanksgiving.
Osborne, Louis Shreve
Riding Down from Bangor.
Osborne, Marian
Trinity, The.
White Violet.
Osgood, Flora L.
Come unto Me.
Cost, The.
Rose Leaf, The.
Osgood, Frances Sargent
Calumny.
Dancing Girl, A.
Labor.
On a Dead Poet.
On Sivori's Violin.
Song: "Your heart is a music-box, dearest!"
To Sleep.
Osgood, Kate Putnam
Driving Home the Cows.
O'Shaughnessy, Arthur William Edgar
At Her Grave.
Barcarolle.
Black Marble.
Doom.
Dreamers of Dreams, The.
Enchainment.
Fair Maid and the Sun, The.
Fountain of Tears, The.
Has Summer Come without the Rose?
If She But Knew.
Love Symphony, A.
Music-Makers, The.
New Love and the Old, The.
Ode: "We are the music-makers," 3 *sts.*
Poets, The.
St. John Baptist.
Silences.
Song: "Has summer come without the rose?"
Song: "I made another garden, yea."
Song: "I went to her who loveth me no more."
Song: "When the rose came I loved the rose."
We Are the Music-Makers.
Zuleika.
O'Shea, Diarmuid
Prayer at Dawn.
O'Sheel, Shaemas
He Whom a Dream Hath Possessed.
Lover Praises His Lady's Bright Beauty, The.
Lover Thinks of His Lady in the North, The.
Mary's Baby.
Roma Mater Sempaeterna.
They Went Forth to Battle, but They Always Fell.
While April Rain Went By.
O-Shi-O
When I Think of the Hungry People.
"Ossian." *See* **Macpherson, James**
Ossian-Nilsson, K. G.
March for Youth, A.
Ostenso, Martha
Return, The.
Ostriker, Alicia
Hybris, Nemesis, One, Two, Three.
Ostroff, Anthony
Cock.
Polemic.
River Glideth in a Secret Tongue, The.
So Long Folks, Off to the War.
Sparrows at the Airport, The.
O'Sullivan, Daniel James
Dawn in Inishtrahull.
Drinking Time.
Glaucous-Gull's Death, The.
January.
Lament for Seán.
Moschatel.
Nightfall in Inishtrahull.
O'Sullivan, Owen Roe
Rodney's Glory.
"O'Sullivan, Seumas" (James Starkey)
Ballad of the Fiddler, The.
Birds.
Credo.
Half Door, The.
Lament for Sean MacDermott.
Lamplighter, The.
Land War, The.
Lullaby: "Husheen, the herons are crying."
Milkman, The.
My Sorrow.
Nelson Street.
Others, The.
Piper, A [*or* The].
Praise.
Rain.
Sedges, The.
Sheep, The.
Sketch.
Splendid and Terrible [Your Love].
Starling Lake, The.
Trains, The.

Twilight People, The.
Otero Silva, Miguel
Crossroads.
Otomo Miyori
On Again Meeting a Lady.
Otomo Oemaru
Then settle, frost!
Otomo Tabito
Grotesque!
Passing the Cape.
Otsuji
Winter midnight.
O'Tuomy, John
O'Tuomy's Drinking Song.
Otway, Thomas
Come, All Ye Youths.
Enchantment, The.
Friendship in Fashion, *sel.*
Orphan, The, *sel.*
Song: "How blest he appears."
Ousley, Clarence
When the Mint Is in the Liquor.
Outram, George
Annuity, The.
On Hearing a Lady Praise a Certain Rev. Doctor's Eyes.
Ou-ty, Emperor *See* **Wu Ti, Emperor**
Ou-yang Hsiu
Cicada, The.
Green Jade Plum Trees in Spring.
Overstreet, Bonaro W.
Count Ten.
First Day of Teaching.
Overton, A. M.
He Maketh No Mistake.
Ovid (Publius Ovidius Naso)
About my temples go triumphant bays.
Acteon.
Advice to a Fair Wanton.
Amores, *sels.*
Apology for Loose Behavior.
Art of Love, The, *sels.*
Baucis and Philemon.
Captive of Love, A.
Complaisant Swain, The.
Conclusion: "Now have I brought a woork too end which neither Joves fierce wrath."
Cyclops.
Daedalus.
Elegies, *sels.*
Elegy to His Mistress.
Envy, why carpest thou my time is spent so ill.
Envy, why twit'st thou me my time's spent ill.
Fable of Acis, Polyphemus and Galatea, The, *sel.*
Flood, The.
I Heard the Ruffian-Shepherd Rudely Blow.
If for thy self thou wilt not watch thy whore.
Impotent Lover, The.
In Cupid's school whoe'er would take degree.
In Love with Two.
In Summer's Heat.
King Midas.
Kiss, if you can: Resistance if she make.
Lente, Lente.
Long Have I Borne Much.
Love, as a Warrior Lord.
Meleager.
Metamorphoses, *sels.*
Ovid's Fifth Elegy.
Philemon and Baucis.
Phoenix Self-born, The.
Possessive Lover, The.
Pyramus and Thisbe.
Shameful Impotence.
Slowly, Slowly.
To Corinna's Chamber-maid.
To His Mistress.
To Verse Let Kings Give Place.
Winter at Tomi.
Ovshover, Joseph *See* **"Dahl, Basil"**
Owari
Girls in Spring.
Owen, Dora
Children, Children, Don't Forget.
Owen, Everard
Three Hills.
Owen, Goronwy
Invitation, The.
Owen, J. Elgar
Maturity.
Owen, John
Bed, The.
Four Epigrams.
King Arthur's Round Table.
Of Labienus.
To Polla.
Owen, Wilfred
A Terre.
Anthem for Doomed Youth.
Apologia pro Poemate Meo.
Arms and the Boy.
Asleep.
At a Calvary near the Ancre.
Calls, The.
Chances, The.
Conscious.
Disabled.
Dulce et Decorum Est.
End, The.
Exposure.
Fragment: Abyss of War, The.
From My Diary, July 1914.
Futility.
Greater Love.
Hospital Barge at Cérisy.
Insensibility.
Inspection.
Last Laugh, The.
Le Christianisme.
Mental Cases.
Miners.
Music.
Next War, The.
On Seeing a Piece of Our Artillery Brought into Action.
Parable of the Old Man and the Young.
Send-off, The.
Sentry, The.
Shadwell Stair.
Show, The.
Song of Songs.
Spring Offensive.
Strange Meeting.
To a Child.
To My Friend.
Unreturning, The.
Owens, Belle F.
Garden, The.
Good Companion, The.
Upper Room, The.
Owens, Daniel J.
Borne ("Borne across a river of grey, life forces").
Owens, Rochelle
Between the Karim Shahir.
Chugachimute I Love the Name.
Evolution.
Macrobius Mingling with Nature.
Man as He Shall Be.
Medieval Christ Speaks on a Spanish Sculpture of Himself.
Strawberries Mit Cream.
Woman par Excellence.
Owens, Vilda Sauvage
If I Ever Have Time for Things That Matter.
Passing of the Unknown Soldier, The.
Oxenham, John (*originally* William Arthur Dunrley)
A Dieu! and Au Revoir.
After Work.
All One in Christ.
Art Thou Lonely?
Be with Me, Lord!
Bide a Wee!
Break Down the Walls.
Brothers of the Faith.
Chaos—and the Way Out, *sel.*
Christ, The.
Coming Day, The.
Credo.
Cross at the Crossways, The.
Crowning Wonder, The.
Day, The—the Way.
Dies Irae—Dies Pacis.
Easter.
Face to Face with Reality.
Faith.
Follow Me.
For a maiden sweetness, and for strength of men.
For all the wonders of this wondrous world.
For all Thy ministries.
For Beauty, We Thank Thee.
Goal and the Way, The.
God's Sunshine.
Golden Cord, The.
Gratitude for Work.
Great Heart.
He Is Risen.
He—They—We.
Hearts Courageous.
High Way and a Low, A.
His Youth.
How—When—Where.
In Christ.
Influence.
Judgment Day.
Key, The.
Law of Love, The.
Life's Chequer-Board.
Little Poem of Life, The.
Little Te Deum of the Commonplace, A, *sels.*
Little Word, A.
Live Christ.
Lord, Give Me Faith.
Lord, I Would Follow.
Love.
Love's Aim.
Love's Prerogative.
Morning Breaks, The.
New Earth, A.
No East or West.
On the Road.
Paul.
Per Ardua ad Astra.
Peter.
Philosopher's Garden.
Pilgrim Way, The.
Prayer, A: "Lord, when on my bed I lie."
Prayer, A: "'Mid all the traffic of the ways."
Prayer, A: "Through every minute of this day."
Prayer for Peace, A.
Prayer for the Churches.
Prince of Life, The.
Profit and Loss ("Profit?—Loss?").
Promotion.
Props.
Sacrament of Sleep, The.
Sacrament of Work, The.
Seeds.

Oxenham (continued)
So Little and So Much.
Some Blesseds.
Te Deum of the Commonplace, A.
Thanksgiving.
To Whom Shall the World Hence forth Belong?
To Win the World.
Valley of Decision, The.
Vision Splendid, The, *sel.*
Ways, The.
We Break New Seas Today.
We Thank Thee ("For all life's beauties").
We Thank Thee ("For all thy ministries").
We Thank Thee ("We thank Thee, Lord,/ That of Thy tender grace").
We Thank Thee, Lord ("We thank Thee, Lord,/ For all Thy golden silences").
Where Are You Going, Greatheart?
Whirring Wheels.
With hearts responsive.
Your Place.
Oxford, Earl of *See* **Vere, Edward de, Earl of Oxford**

P

"P., L. S."
When Thou Hast Shut Thy Door.
"P. H." *See* **"H., P"**
"P. S. M." *See* **"M., P. S"**
Pace, Charles Nelson
Cross, The.
Prayer for Today, A.
Pack, Richardson
On Her Entering Her Room.
Pack, Robert
Adam on His Way Home.
Anecdote of the Sparrow.
Bird in Search of a Cage, A.
Boat, The.
Chopping Fire-Wood.
Departure, The.
Descending.
Don't Sit under the Apple Tree With Anyone Else but Me.
Election, The.
Faithful Lover, The.
Father.
Idyl in Idleness, An.
In a Field.
My House.
On the Seventh Anniversary of the Death of My Father.
Parable.
Poem for You.
Raking Leaves.
Resurrection.
Self-Portrait.
Shooting, The.
Way We Wonder, The.
Weasel, The.
Packard, Frederick
Balearic Idyll.
Packard, William
Haircut.
Packard, Winthrop
Shoogy-Shoo, The.
Padgett, Ron
After the Broken Arm.
Body English.
Clouds go rolling over, The.
December.
Detach, Invading.
Ems Dispatch, The.
Farmer's Head, The.
Homage to Max Jacob.
Joe Brainard's Painting "Bingo."
Man Saw a Ball of Gold, A.
Mister Horse.
Name.
Passage Charles Dallery.
Pied quarts of Chevrolets trim blent Sir her eyes on, The.
Reading Reverdy.
Sandwich Man, The.
Some Bombs, *sel.*
Statue of a Libertine, The.
Strawberries in Mexico.
To Francis Sauf Que.
Tone Arm, *sel.*
When I Think More of My Own Future Than of Myself.
Wonderful Things.
Pagan, Isobel
Ca' the Yowes to the Knowes.
Pagaza, Joaquin Arcadio
Twilight.
Page, Irene
Jane, Do Be Careful.
Page, Myriam
Walls.
Page, Patricia K.
Adolescence.
Arras.
Average.
Bands and the Beautiful Children, The.
Christmas Eve; Market Square.
Crow, The.
Cullen ("Cullen renounced his cradle at fifteen").
Element.
Images of Angels.
Landlady.
Man with One Small Hand.
Permanent Tourists, The.
Puppets.
Sailor.
See them joined by strings to history.
Stenographers, The.
Stories of Snow.
Summer.
Summer Resort.
T-Bar.
Page, Thomas Nelson
Ashcake.
Dragon of the Seas, The.
Uncle Gabe's White Folks.
Valentine Verses.
Paget, Thomas Catesby
To a Young Lady That Told Me My Fortune in the Cards.
Written in 1740.
Paget-Fredericks, Joseph
Alone.
Pipings.
Paiewonsky, Edgar
Days.
Icons.
Neighbor.
Pain, Barry
Bangkolidye.
Macaulay at Tea.
Martin Luther at Potsdam.
Oh! Weary Mother.
Poets at Tea, The.
Pain, Philip
Meditation 8.
Meditations for August 1, 1666.
Meditations for July 19, 1666.
Meditations for July 25, 1666,
Meditations for July 26, 1666.
Porch, The.
Paine, Albert Bigelow
Hills of Rest, The.
In Louisiana.
Little Child, The.
Mis' Smith.
New Memorial Day, The.
Sary "Fixes Up" Things.
Superman, The.
Paine, Carol
Color Blind.
Paine, Robert Treat
Adams and Liberty.
Paine, Theodora L.
Danger.
Paine, Thomas
Liberty Tree.
Painton, Edith Putnam
Parody, A: "Farewell! A long farewell to all our school days!"
"Pai Ta-shun." *See* **Peterson, Frederick**
Aimless.
Palen, Jennie M.
Early Dutch.
Legend of Ramapo Mountain.
Palés Matos, Luis
Elegy of the Duke of Marmalade.
Hurricane, The.
San Sabas.
Palfrey, R. S.
Three o'Clock in the Morning.
Palfrey, Sarah Hammond *See* **"Foxton, E."**
Palgrave, Francis Turner
Ancient and Modern Muses, The.
City of God, The.
Creç.
Danish Barrow, A.
Eutopia.
God Save Elizabeth.
Little Child's Hymn, A.
Pro Mortuis.
Reine d'Amour.
Take Up Thy Cross.
Trafalgar.
William Wordsworth.
Palladas [*or* Pallades],
Muse on Death.
On Maurus the Rhetor.
Praise of Women.
Vanity of Vanities.
Pallen, Condé Benoist
Babe of Bethlehem, The.
Christus Triumphans.
Maria Immaculata.
Raising of the Flag, The.
Palmer, Alice Freeman
Butterfly, The.
Communion Hymn.
Hallowed Places.
On a Gloomy Easter.
Spring Journey, A.
Palmer, Doug
Clap Hands.
High Tide, And.
In a Field.
My People.
These Poems.
Palmer, E. Harriet
Parterre, The.
Shipwreck, The.
Palmer Herbert Edward
Abélard Tells His Love to Héloïse.
Aunt Zillah Speaks.
Hate.
Ishmael.
Nature in War-Time.
Prayer for Rain.
To Some Reviewers Who Have Wilfully Abused Certain True Poets.
Unknown Warrior Sings and Curses in the Street, The.
Woodworkers' Ballad.
Wounded Hawk, The.
Palmer, John F.
Band Played On, The.
Palmer, John Williamson
Fight at San Jacinto, The.
Fight at the San Jacinto, The.

For Charlie's Sake.
Maryland Battalion, The.
Ned Braddock.
Reid at Fayal.
Stonewall Jackson's Way.
Theodosia Burr; the Wrecker's Story.
Palmer, Nettie
Barrack Yard, The.
Mother, The.
Unsung.
Welcome, The.
Palmer, Ray
Blessed Face, The.
Faith.
I Saw Thee.
Jesus.
Jesus, These Eyes Have Never Seen.
My Faith Looks Up to Thee.
O Jesus! Sweet the Tears I Shed.
Palmer, Samuel
Shoreham: Twilight Time.
Palmer, Vance
Farmer Remembers the Somme, The.
Pathfinders, The.
Youth and Age.
Palmer, William Pitt
Smack in School, The.
Palmer, Winthrop
Arlington Cemetery Looking toward the Capitol.
Dionysus.
For the Existentialists.
House Plant.
Palquera, Shem-Tob ben Joseph
Adapt Thyself.
Mouth and the Ears, The.
Paman, Clement
On Christmas Day.
On Christmas Day to My Heart.
Panatattu
God Is One.
True Knowledge.
Unity of God, The.
Pandolphus
Description of a Gun.
Pao Chao
Ruined City, The.
Paradise, Caroline Wilder Fellowes
Little Theocritus.
Paramore, Edward E., Jr
Ballad of Yukon Jake, The.
Paravicino y Arteaga, Hortensio Félix
Divine Passion, The.
Parini, Giuseppe
With Dreams of Wealth and Fame.
Park, Frances
Sad Song about Greenwich Village, A.
Park, John Edgar
We Would See Jesus.
Parke, Walter
Foam and Fangs.
His Mother-in-Law.
Limerick: "There was a princess of Bengal."
Limerick: "There was an old stupid who wrote."
My Madeline.
Vague Story, A.
Young Gazelle, The.
Parker, Derek
Delius in the Cathedral.
Parker, Dorothy
Actress, The.
Autobiography.
Autumn Valentine.
Ballade of Big Plans.
Ballade of Unfortunate Mammals.
Bohemia.
Choice, The.
Coda.
Comment.
Counselor, The.
Crusader, The.
Danger of Writing Defiant Verse, The.
Dark Girl's Rhyme, The.
De Profundis.
Dilemma.
Evening Primrose, The.
Experience.
Fable: "Oh, there once was a lady."
Fighting Words.
Gentlest Lady, The.
George Sand.
Godmother.
Inventory.
Little Old Lady in Lavender Silk, The.
Love Song.
Maid-Servant at the Inn, The.
Men.
News Item.
Observation.
On Being a Woman.
One Perfect Rose.
Philosophy.
Portrait of the Artist.
Prologue to a Saga.
Résumé.
Social Note.
Some Beautiful Letters.
Song of Perfect Propriety.
Story.
Theory.
They Part.
Thought for a Sunshiny Morning.
Threnody: "Lilacs blossom just as sweet."
Two-Volume Novel.
Unfortunate Coincidence.
Very Rich Man, The.
Parker, Edwin P.
My Offering.
Parker, Sir Gilbert
Art.
Envoy: "When you and I have played the little hour."
Invincible.
Little Garaine.
Lover's Diary, A, *sels.*
Love's Outset.
Reunited.
Woman's Hand, A.
World in Making, The.
Parker, Helen Adams
Apple Blossoms.
Parker, Henry, Baron Morley
To His Posterity.
Parker, Hubbard
Old Flag.
Parker, J.
God Holds the Key.
Parker, Julia Benson
Perfect Gift, The.
Parker, Martin
Description of a Strange (and Miraculous) Fish, A.
Keep a Good Tongue in Your Head.
King Enjoys His Own Again, The.
Maunding Soldier, The; or The Fruits of Warre Is Beggery.
Milkmaid's Life, The.
Sailors for My Money.
Saylors for My Money.
When the King Enjoys His Own Again.
Wooing Maid, The.
Parker, Stephen
Winter in Étienburgh.
Parker, Theodore
Higher Good, The.
Jesus ("Jesus, there is no dearer name than thine").
Way, the Truth, and the Life, The.
Parker, William Henry
Tell Me the Stories of Jesus.
Parkes, Francis Ernest Kobina
Apocalypse.
Blind Steersmen.
Three Phases of Africa.
Parkes, Frank
African Heaven.
Parkes, Sir Henry
Weary.
Parkhurst, John
Of Alphus.
Parks, Henrietta C.
My Life.
Uncertainty.
Parkwood, Rose
Garden, The.
Parlett, Phyllis E.
Christian Mother, A.
"Parley, Peter." *See* **Goodrich, Samuel Griswold**
Parmenter, Catherine
Christmas.
Christmas Eve.
Crossroads, The.
"Disabled"—Armistice Day.
Discovery.
Kittens.
Land of Destiny.
Pilgrimage.
Silent Testimony.
To the Memory of John Burroughs.
Parmenter, Ross
Rain.
Parnell, Fanny
After Death.
Post-Mortem.
Parnell, Thomas
Death speaks:/ When men my scythe and darts supply.
Elegy, An: To and Old Beauty.
Hermit, The.
Hymn to Contentment, A.
My Days Have Been So Wondrous Free.
Night-Piece on Death, A.
On a Lady with Foul Breath.
Riddle: "Upon a bed of humble clay."
Small Silver-coloured Bookworm, The.
Song: "My days have been so wondrous free."
Song: "When thy beauty appears."
When Thy Beauty Appears.
Parone, Edward
Morning Track, The.
Parr, Michael
Look Now, the Hawk.
Parra, Nicanor
Beggar.
Parrish, Dorothy C.
Etc. Etc. Etc.
Hush Now.
Indictment.
Soliloquy.
Parrish, Elsie
Some Things That Easter Brings.
Parrish, Randall
Your Lad, and My Lad.
Parrot, Henry
Asperius Nihil Est Humili cum Surgat in Altum.
Brutus, that brave and complete cavalier.
Country farmer had a friend at court, A.
Cutbert our cobbler can no more forbear.
Dupliciter Beatus.
Ebrius Dissimulans.
Epilogus: "Thus have I waded through a worthless task."
Faunus for feats of fencing bears the bell.
Have you not heard of Monsieur Maximus.
Heard ye not yet of Captain Ferdinand?
Humor of Tobacco and the Rest, The.

Parrot (continued)
I cry you mercy, sir, I knew you not.
Impar Impares Odit.
In Obitum Alienius.
Knot of knaves are early met together, A.
Magus would needs, forsooth, this other day.
Musco, that always kept with policy.
Nemo Nascitur Artifex.
Nil Perdunt Mendici.
Nullum Stimulum Ignavis.
Nuptiae post Nummos.
Olim Haec Meminisse Juvabit.
Ortus Novus Urbe Britannus.
Paulus a pamphlet doth in prose present.
Perdat Qui Caveat Emptor.
Peter hath lost his purse, but will conceal it.
Rufus is wondrous rich, but what of that?
Shall Simon Suckegg, simple Simkins' son.
Sic Ars Diluditur Arte.
Silus hath sold his crimson satin suite.
Sir, can you tell where my young master lives.
Such were those epigrams of elder times.
Suum Cuique Pulchrum.
Tempus Edax Rerum.
To the Ungentilized Censurer.
Tush hang it, have at all, says Curio.
Veniunt Spectentur ut Ipsi.
Videantur Quae Non Sunt.
What tell you me of such a peasant groom.
Would any deem Dacus were now the man.

Parry, David Fisher
Bachelor's Ballade, The.
Miniver Cheevy, Jr., *parody.*

Parry, Edward Abbott
I Would Like You for a Comrade.

Parry, Joseph
Friends Old and New.

Parry, R. Williams
Fox, The.

Parry-Williams, Sir Thomas Herbert
Words.

Parsons, Mary Catherine
My Valentine.
Station, The.

Parsons, Thomas William
Andrew.
Dirge: For One Who Fell in Battle.
Dirge: "Room for a soldier! lay him in the clover."
Everett.
Her Epitaph.
Into the Noiseless Country.
Like as the lark that, soaring higher and higher.
Mary Booth.
O Ye Sweet Heavens!
Obituary.
On a Bust of Dante.
Paradisi Gloria.
Saint Peray.
To a Lady.
To a Young Girl Dying.

Parton, Margaret
Cold.

Partridge, Sybil F. (Sister Mary Xavier)
Just for Today (*sl. diff. versions*).
To-Day.

Partridge, William Ordway
Creeds.
Nathan Hale.

Pascal, Paul
Tact.

Pascoli, Giovanni
Drayman, The.
Hopes and Memories.

Passerat, Jean
Love in May.

Pasternak, Boris Leonidovich
Caucasus, The ("The Caucasus lay vast in light").
Christmas Star.
Cocks, The.
Definition of the Soul.
Evil Days.
Fresh Paint.
Garden of Gethsemane.
Here the Trace.
Improvisation.
In the Breeze.
Magdalene.
May It Be.
Out of Superstition.
Poem: "So they begin. With two years gone."
Spring ("How many buds").
Star of the Nativity.
Three Variations.
Vorobyev Hills.
Waving a Bough.
Wedding, The.
Winter Night.
Zoo, The.

Pastorius, Francis Daniel
As often as some where before my feet.
Delight in Books from Evening.
Epigrams.
Extract the quint-essence.
I have a pretty little flow'r.
If Any Be Pleased to Walk into My Poor Garden.
If thou wouldst roses scent.
Learn, lads and lasses, of my garden.
Most weeds, whilst young.
On His Garden Book.
Thy garden, orchard, fields.
To God alone, the only donour.
When I solidly do ponder.
When one or other rambles.

Patchen, Kenneth
All the Roary Night.
Always Another Viewpoint.
And What with the Blunders.
As We Are So Wonderfully Done with Each Other.
At the New Year.
Because Going Nowhere Takes a Long Time.
Because He Liked to Be at Home.
Because in This Sorrowing Statue of Flesh.
Because My Hands Hear the Flowers Thinking.
Because Sometimes You Can't Always Be So.
Because They Were Very Poor That Winter.
Before the Bells of This New Year Ring.
Behold, One of Several Little Christs.
But there is no black jaw which cannot be broken by our word.
Carts of the Wee Blind Lass, The.
Character of Love Seen as a Search for the Lost, The.
Christ! Christ! Christ! That the World.
Constant Bridegrooms, The.
Deer and the Snake, The.
Do the Dead Know What Time It Is?
Easy Decision, An.
Elegy for the Silent Voices and the Joiners of Everything.
Everlasting Contenders, The.
Fog.
For Miriam.
Fox, The.
From My High Love.
Gautama in the Deer Park at Benares.
Great Sled-Makers, The.
Hunted City, The, *sel.*
I/ want you/ to listen.
I Went to the City.
In a Crumbling.
In Memory of Kathleen.
In Order To.
In the Moonlight.
Journal of Albion Moonlight, The, *sels.*
Known Soldier, The.
Land of the Never-ending Heart.
Like a Mourningless Child.
Little Green Blackbird, The.
Little hill climbs up to the village and puts its green hands, The.
Lute in the Attic, The.
Magical Mouse, The.
New Being, The.
Nice Day for a Lynching.
Now I Went Down to the Ringside and Little Henry Armstrong Was There.
O Now the Drenched Land Wakes.
O She Is as Lovely-Often.
O When I Take My Love Out Walking.
Orange Bears, The.
Origin of Baseball, The.
Pastoral: "Dove walks with sticky feet, The."
Reason for Skylarks, The.
Rest, Heart of the Tired World.
Street Corner College.
There Is Nothing False in Thee.
Trueblue Gentleman, A.
Twenty-third Street Runs into Heaven.
We Go Out Together.
What the Grecian Earns.
Where?
Who Walks There?
Who'll That Be.
Wouldn't You after a Jaunt of 964,000,-000,000,000 Million Miles?

Pater, Walter
Mona Lisa.

Paterson, Andrew Barton
Bush Christening, A.
Bushman's Song, A.
Clancy of The Overflow.
Man from Snowy River, The.
On Kiley's Run.
Song of the Artesian Water.
Waltzing Matilda.

Patmore, Coventry Kersey Dighton
Amaranth, The.
Angel in the House, The, *sels.*
Arbor Vitae.
Attainment, The.
Auras of Delight.
Azalea, The.
Child's Purchase, The.
Constancy.
Courtesy.
Dartmoor.
Dean's Consent, The.
Deliciae Sapientiae de Amore.
Departure.
Eros.
Faint Yet Pursuing.
Farewell, A: "With all my will, but much against my heart."
First Spousal, The.
Foreign Land, The.
Fragment: "He that but once too nearly hears."
Girl of All Periods, The.
Going to Church.
Honor and Desert.
Honoria's Surrender.
If I Were Dead.
Impossibility, The.
Joyful Wisdom, The.
Kiss, The.
Legem Tuam Dilexi.

London Fete, A.
Love at Large.
Love in Action.
Love Serviceable.
Love wakes men, once a life-time each.
Love, won or lost, is countless gain.
Lover, The.
Love's Reality.
Magna Est Veritas.
Married Lover, The.
My memory of Heaven awakes.
Nearest the Dearest.
Pain.
Parting.
Preludes.
Prologue, A: "Thou Speaker of all wisdom in a Word."
Prophets Who Cannot Sing.
Rainbow, The.
Regina Coeli.
Remembered Grace.
Revelation, The.
Rose of the World, The.
Rosy Bosom'd Hours, The.
Round the Year.
Saint Valentine's Day.
Sensuality.
Shadow of Night, The.
Shame.
Spirit's Epochs, The.
Storm, The.
To the Body.
To the Unknown Eros.
Toys, The.
Tribute, The.
Truth.
Truth Is Great, The.
Two Deserts, The.
Unknown Eros, The.
Unthrift.
Victories of Love, The, *sel.*
Warning, A.
Wedding Sermon, The.
Wind and Wave.
Winter.
Woman.
Year, The.
Year's Round, The.

Patmore, F. J.
White Owl, The.

Paton, Alan
Discardment, The.
I Have Approached.
Prison House, The.
Samuel.
Sanna.
To a Small Boy Who Died at Diepkloof Reformatory.

Paton, Sir Joseph Noel
Last of the *Eurydice,* The.
Requiem.

Patrick, Johnstone G.
Closing Prayer.
Grace; before Reading Emily Brontë's Poems.
Prayer for Peace.

Patrick, Luther
Sleepin' at the Foot of the Bed.

Patten, Arthur B.
Faith of Our Mothers.

Patten, Brian
Little Johnny's Confession.
Perhaps Where He Is Only Loving Rockets Can Land.
Small Dragon, A.

Patterson, Charles
Listen.

Patterson, Emily
Caravans.

Patterson, Raymond Richard
Accident, The.
At That Moment.
Black All Day.
In Time of Crisis.
Invitation.
I've Got a Home in That Rock.
Love Song, A.
Night-Piece.
When I Awoke.
You Are the Brave.

Pattison, William
On a Painted Lady.
Unfortunate Reminder, The.
Upon a Needle.

Patton, Margaret French (Mrs. Thomas Archer Jone)
Needle Travel.

Paul, Dorothy
Captive Ships at Manila, The.
Figurehead.

"Paul, John." *See* **Webb, Charles Henry**

Paul, Louis
Cynical Portraits.

Paul the Silentiary *See* **Paulus Silentiarius**

Paulding, James Kirke
Ode to Jamestown.
Old Man's Carousal, The.

Paulinus, Sister Mary
Canticle of Quietness.
Here at the Stable Door.

Paull, H. M.
Eastern Question, An.

Paulus Silentiarius *or* **Paul the Silentiary**
No Matter.
Tantalus.
United.

Pawsey, Irene F.
Bramble Jam.
Browny Bee.
Browny Hen, The.
Egg for Easter, An.
Eggs for Breakfast.
Found in the Woods.
Greedy Little Pig, The.
Haytime.
June.
Thief, The.
White Horses.

Paxton, Jean Grigsby
Preparedness.
Release.

Paxton, Tom
We Didn't Know.

Payn, James
I never had a piece of toast.

Payne, Anne Blackwell
Ambition.
At Night.
Fairy Aeroplanes.
Fairy Carpets.
Little Girl in Bloom, A.
Neighbors.
Robin.
Silver Sheep.
To a Young Priest.
Top of Day, The.

Payne, Antoinette T.
Oh! Lord.

Payne, John
Cadences.
Kyrielle.
Love's Autumn.
Merry Ballad of Vintners, A.
Of Three Damsels in a Meadow.
Rococo.
Rondeau Redoublé.
Sibyl.
Songs' End.
Thorgerda.

Payne, John Howard
Clari, the Maid of Milan, *sel.*
Home, Sweet Home.

Payne, William Morton
"Ej Blot til Lyst."
Incipit Vita Nova.
Lohengrin.
Tannhäuser.

Paz, Octavio
Street, The.

Peabody, Francis Greenwood
Of Such Is the Kingdom.
Venture of Faith, The.

Peabody, Josephine Preston
Caravans.
Changeling Grateful, A.
Concerning Love.
Cradle Song: "Lord Gabriel, wilt thou not rejoice."
Far-off Rose, A.
Fishers, The.
House and the Road, The.
Hymn: "Dear Lord, Whose serving-maiden."
Isolation.
Man's Bread, A.
Prelude: "Words, words, ye are like birds."
Rubric.
Singing Man, The.
Song of a Shepherd-Boy at Bethlehem, The.
Song of Solomon, A.
Sonnet in a Garden.
Spinning in April.
To a Dog.
"Vanity, Saith the Preacher."
Wood-Song.

Peabody, William Bourn Oliver
Lament of Anastasius.
Pussy, Pussy, Do Not Mew.

Peach, Arthur Wallace
"Cap'n".
Mosaic Worker, The.
O Youth with Blossoms Laden.
Secret, The.

Peacham, Henry
Nuptial Hymn.
Period of Mourning, The, *sel.*

Peacock, Thomas Love
After careful meditation.
Bacchus.
Beech and Oak.
Beneath the Cypress Shade.
Brilliancies of Winter, The.
Castles in the Air.
Catch, A: "Seamen three!"
Chorus: "Hail to the Headlong! the Headlong Ap-Headlong!"
Chorus: "If I drink water while this doth last."
Crotchet Castle, *sels.*
Cypress, The.
Fate of a Broom, The—an Anticipation.
For the Slender Beech and the Sapling Oak.
Friar, The.
Friar's Hunting Song.
Glee—The Ghosts.
Grave of Love, The.
Greatness ("He took castle and towns").
Greenwood Tree, The.
Gryll Grange, *sel.*
Headlong Hall, *sels.*
In the Days of Old.
Indignation of Taliesin, The.
Larissa.
Lines from Crotchet Castle.
Love and Age.
Maid Marian, *sels.*

Peacock (continued)
Margaret Love Peacock [for Her Tombstone, 1826].
Melincourt, *sels.*
Men of Gotham, The.
Merlin's Apple-Trees.
Misfortunes of Elphin, The, *sels.*
Mr. Cypress's Song.
New Order of Chivalry, A.
Newark Abbey.
Nightmare Abbey, *sels.*
Not Drunk Is He.
Oak and the Beech, The.
Priest and the Mulberry-Tree, The.
Quintetto upon the Christmas Pie, *sel.*
Rhododaphne, *sels.*
Rich and Poor; or, Saint and Sinner.
Seamen Three.
Song: "For the tender beech and the sapling oak."
Song: "In his last bin Sir Peter Lies."
Song: "It was a friar of orders free."
Song by Mr. Cypress.
Song of Gwythno.
Song of the Four Winds, The.
Sun-Dial, The.
Taliesin and Melanghel.
There Is a Fever of the Spirit.
Three Men of Gotham.
War-Song of Dinas Vawr, The.
Who Is Drunk?
Wise Men of Gotham, The ("Seamen three! What men be ye?").
World, The.
Peacocke, Isabel Maud
Happy Islands, The.
Peake, Mervyn Laurence
Cocky Walkers, The.
Maeve.
Peale, Rembrandt
Don't Be Sorrowful, Darling.
Pearce, Norman V.
Blind.
Pearce, Theodosia
God, Thou Hast Made the World Beautiful.
Pearse, Mark Guy
Don't Trouble Trouble.
Facing the New Year.
Grace for Grace.
My Prayer.
Orthodox.
Pearse, Padraic
Fool, The.
I Am Ireland.
Ideal.
Lullaby of a [*or* the] Woman of the Mountain.
Lullaby of the Woman of the Mountain.
Mother, The.
Rann I Made.
Rebel, The.
To Death.
Wayfarer, The.
Pearson, James Larkin
Here Is Wisdom.
Peavyhouse, William W.
Theodore Roosevelt.
Pechey, R. F.
Living Jesus, The.
Peck, Elisabeth
Between the Walls of the Valley.
Walthena.
Peck, Harry Thurston
Heliotrope.
Jefferson Davis.
Other One, The.
Wonderland.
Peck, Kathryn Blackburn
Carpenter's Son, The.
Lord of Heaven to Earth Came Down, The.
Rejoice! He Liveth!
Peck, Louise D.
Stricken Colts, The.
Peck, Sam
River Lea, The
Peck, Samuel Minturn
Autumn's Mirth.
Bessie Brown, M.D.
Captain's Feather, The.
Kiss in the Rain, A.
My Little Girl.
Sassafras.
Southern Girl, A.
Pedley, Katherine Greenleaf
Golgotha.
Pedroso, Regino
Opinions of the New Chinese Student.
Tomorrow.
Peel, Arthur J.
Shadows.
Peele, George
And Who Has Seen a Fair Alluring Face.
Arraignment of Paris, The, *sels.*
Bathsheba's Song.
Bethsabe's Song.
Celanta at the Well of Life.
Colin, the Enamored Shepherd, Singeth This Passion of Love.
Colin's Passion of Love.
Come, gentle Zephyr, tricked with those perfumes.
Coridon and Melampus' Song.
Cupid's Curse.
David and Bethsabe, *sels.*
Dirge: "Welladay, welladay, poor Colin."
Fair and Fair.
Fair Maiden.
Farewell to Arms, A.
Farewell to John Norris and Sir Francis Drake, A.
Harvester's Song ("All ye that lovely lovers be").
His Golden Lock[e]s [Time Hath to Silver Turned].
Hunting of Cupid, The, *sels.*
Love.
Not Iris in Her Pride.
Now comes my lover tripping like the roe.
Now for the crown and throne of Israel.
O Gentle Love.
Oenone's Complaint.
Old Knight, The.
Old Wife's Tale, The.
Old Wives' [*or* Wife's] Tale, The, *sels.*
Polyhymnia, *sel.*
Shepherd's Dirge, The.
Sonet, A: "His golden lockes, Time hath to silver turn'd."
Song: "Lo! here we come a-reaping."
Song: "When as the rye [*or* rie] reach to the chin."
Song: "Whenas the rye reach to the chin."
Song at the Well, The.
Song of Coridon and Melampus.
Song of Oenone and Paris.
Sonnet, A: "His golden locks time hath to silver turn'd."
Spell, A.
Summer Song, A.
To the Author.
Voice from the Well of Life Speaks to the Maiden, The.
Voice Speaks from the Well, A.
What Thing Is Love.
When as the Rye Reach to the Chin.
Whenas [*or* When as] the Rye [Reach to the Chin].
Peele, Steven
Letter to Rome, A.
Pegis, Jessie Corrigan
Eyes of Wonder, The.
Stay Little Always.
Péguy, Charles
Eve, *sel.*
For the past three days she had been wandering, and following.
Freedom, *sel.*
Happy Are Those Who Have Died.
I have often played with man, saith the Lord.
Mystery of the Innocent Saints, The, *sel.*
Night, *sel.*
Nights follow each other and are linked.
Passion of Our Lady, The, *sel.*
Sleep.
Such is the mystery of man's freedom, says God.
Peifer, Mrs. Roy L.
Crucifixion.
Pelham, M.
Comical Girl, The.
Pellew, George
Death.
On a Cast from an Antique.
Pellow, John Dynham Cornish
After London.
Temple of the Trees, The.
Peloubet, Maurice E.
Eternal Kinship, The.
Pembroke, Mary Sidney Herbert, Countess of
Dialogue between Two Shepherds, Thenot and Piers, in Praise of Astrea, A.
Psalm LVIII: "And call ye this to utter what is just."
Psalm LVI: "Fountain of pity now with pity flow."
Psalm CL: "O laud the Lord, the God of hosts commend."
Psalm CXXXIX: "O Lord, in me there lieth nought."
Psalm XCII: "O lovely thing."
Psalm LXXV: "Thee, God, O thee, we sing, we celebrate."
Psalm XLIX: "World-dwellers all give heed to what I say."
Wondrous Love.
Pembroke, William Herbert, Earl of
Disdain Me Still.
Paradox, A.
Pendleton, Conrad
Dark House in Autumn.
Pennant, Edmund
Lost Explorer.
Pennell, Henry Cholmondeley *See* **Cholmondeley-Pennell, Henry**
Penney, William Edward
Town of Nogood, The.
Percikow, Henri
Childhood.
Living among the Toilers.
Percival, James Gates
Apostrophe to the Island of Cuba.
Coral Grove, The.
Elegiac.
It Is Great for Our Country to Die.
May.
New England.
Perry's Victory on Lake Erie.
Seneca Lake.
To Seneca Lake.
"Percy, Florence." *See* **Allen, Elizabeth Akers**
Percy, Thomas
O Nancy, Wilt Thou Go with Me?
Song: "O Nancy, wilt thou go with me?"
Percy, William
Coelia, *sels.*
Sonnet: "It shall be said I died for Coelia!"

Sonnets to the Fairest Coelia.
Percy, William Alexander
Dirge: "Tuck the earth, fold the sod."
Epilogue: "Giver of bliss and pain, of song and prayer," *sel.*
Farmers.
Giver of bliss and pain, of song and prayer.
Hymn to the Sun.
In an Autumn Wood.
In April Once, *sel.*
Little Page's Song, A.
Little Shepherd's Song, The.
Overtones.
Page's Road Song, A.
Spring of God, The.
Stirrup Cup, The.
To an Old Tune.
To Butterfly.
Unloved to His Beloved.
Volunteer's Grave, A.
Wonder and a Thousand Springs.
Pereira, Francesca Yetunde
Burden, The.
Mother Dark.
Paradox, The.
Two Strange Worlds.
Peretz, Isaac [*or* Yitzchok] Leibush
All through the Stranger's Wood.
Believe Not.
Eternal Sabbath.
Hope and Faith.
In the Silent Night.
Little People.
Three Seamstresses, The.
Pérez de Ayala, Ramón
She Was a Pretty Little Girl.
Perkins, Fanny Elizabeth
To a Cat.
Perkins, Jacob Randolph
And the Greatness of These.
Back of God, The.
World's Lone Lover, The.
Perkins, Lucy Alice
"Laborers Together with God."
Perkins, Lucy Fitch
Gardener, The.
Honey-Bee.
Perkins, Silas H.
Common Road, The.
Perkoff, Stuart Z.
Feasts of Death, Feasts of Love.
Flowers for Luis Bunuel.
Recluses, The.
Perlberg, Mark M.
Hiroshige.
Perpetuo, Betty
Morning Prayer, A.
Perreault, John
Boomerang.
Disguised ("Disguised as my next door neighbor").
Forty Years Ago.
Friends.
High.
Hunger.
I Am the Pony in the Central Park Zoo.
Metaphysical Paintings, The.
No One in Particular.
Nude Republic, The.
Readymade.
Shoe.
Talk.
Waves.
Perronet, Edward
Coronation.
Perry, Josephine Hovey
Hail, Vermont!
Perry, Lilla Cabot (Mrs. Thomas Sergeant Perry)
Art.
As It Was.
As She Feared It Would Be.
Life and Death.
Meeting after Long Absence.
Perry, Martha Eugenie
Lonely Shell, The.
Mainspring, The.
Terror in Beauty.
Water-Witch, The.
Perry, Nora
Balboa.
Coming of Spring, The.
Coming of the Spring, The.
Cressid.
In June.
Love-Knot, The.
Next Year.
Riding Down.
Running the Blockade.
Some Day of Days.
Too Late.
Who Knows?
Perry, Ronald
Prologue for a Bestiary.
Shellpicker, The.
Still-Life.
Perry, Tod
For Nicholas, Born in September.
"Perse, St.-J." (Alexis Saint-Léger Léger)
Anabasis, *sels.*
I Have Built Myself, with Honour and Dignity.
Song: "I have halted my horse by the trees of the doves."
Song: "Under the bronze leaves a colt was foaled."
Such Is the Way of the World.
Three Sections from "Anabasis."
Thus Was the City Founded.
We Shall Not Dwell Forever in These Yellow Lands.
Persius (Aulus Persius Flaccus)
Prologue to the First Satire ("I never did").
Satires, *sel.*
Person, Amy L.
I Go Alone.
Pestel *or* Pestell, Thomas
For the Right Honorable Lucy, Countess of Huntingdon, 1649.
On Tobacco.
Psalm for Christmas Day.
Psalm for Sunday Night, A.
Relief on Easter Eve, The.
Song: "Silly boy, there is no cause."
"Peter."
Bus, The.
Saint Wears a Halo, The.
Speed Track, The.
Peter, John
Christmas on Three Continents.
Cypress.
Estrangement.
Hearts's Desire.
Reading Tolstoy.
Peterborough, Charles Mordaunt, Earl of *See* **Mordaunt, Charles, Earl of Peterborough**
Peterfreund, Stuart
American Poetry.
Miller.
Percussion, Salt and Honey.
Who Is the Ratman?
Peters, Edmund W.
Bicycalamity.
Peters, Lenrie
After They Put Down Their Overalls.
Peters, Mary
Jesus, How Much Thy Name Unfolds.
Peters, Phillis Wheatley *See* **Wheatley, Phillis**
Petersen, Donald
Narcissus.
Sonnet in Autumn.
True to a Dream.
Walking along the Hudson.
Petersen, M.
Kitchen Prayer, A.
Petersen, Nils
Hazard.
Petersham, Maud, *and* Miska Petersham
Lazy Mary, Will You Get Up?
Peterson, Arthur
Kelpius's Hymn.
Peterson, Frederick ("Pai-Ta-Shun")
Bridge, The.
Solitude.
Wild Geese.
Peterson, Henry
Death of Lyon, The.
O gallant brothers of the generous South.
Ode for Decoration Day.
Rinaldo.
Peterson, Robert
Dear America.
Peterson, Ruth Delong
Midwest Town.
Petofi, Alexander [*or* Sandor]
In the Forest.
National Song: "Rise, Magyar."
War and Peace.
Petrarch (Francesco Petrarca)
Against the Court of Rome.
Amorous Worms' Meat, The.
Canzone: "Clear, fresh, sweet waters."
Canzoniere.
Complaint of a Lover Rebuked.
Contrarious Passions in a Lover, The.
Description of the Contrarious Passions in a Lover.
Flying Lesson, The.
He Hopes That Time Will Render Her More Merciful.
He Understands the Great Cruelty of Death.
He Wishes He Might Die and Follow Laura.
Heart on the Hill, The.
I Saw a Phoenix in the Wood Alone.
If Amorous Faith.
If It Be Destined.
In Spain ("So feeble is the thread that doth the burden stay").
In Wintry Midnight, o'er a Stormy Main.
Jealous Enemy, The.
Last Trial, The.
Laura Waits for Him in Heaven.
Lover Compareth His State to a Ship in Perilous Storm Tossed on the Sea, The.
Lover for Shamefastness Hideth His Desire within His Faithful Heart, The.
Love's Fidelity.
Love's Inconsistency.
Mine old dear enemy, my froward master.
Night.
Nightingale, The.
Ode to the Virgin.
Of His Foolish Passion for Laura.
Praises of Laura Transcend His Poetic Power, The ("Ashamed at times that I am silent").
Set Me Where Phoebus' Heat.
Set Me Whereas the Sun Doth Parch the Green.
Seven Penitential Psalms, *sel.*
Signs of Love.
Sonnet: "Ashamed at times that I am silent."
Sonnet: "Father in heaven! after the days misspent."

Petrarch (continued)
Sonnet: "Fountain of sorrow, inn of cursed ire."
Sonnet: "I find no peace, and all my war is done."
Sonnet: "Lady, if grace to me so long be lent."
Sonnet: "More my own poor wishes would commend me, The."
Sonnet: "My tameless will doth recklessly pursue."
Sonnet: "Set me whereas the sun doth parch the green."
Sonnets to Laura, *sels.*
To His Lady.
To the Virgin Mary, *abr.*
To Young Imaginaries in Knowledge.
Visions [of Petrarch, The].
Vow to Love Faithfully [Howsoever He Be Rewarded], A.
Who Wishes to Behold.
Petrie, Paul
Church of San Antonio de la Florida, The.
Enigma Variations, The.
Murderer, The.
Watson and the Shark.
Petronius Arbiter (Caius Petronius Arbiter)
Against Consummation.
All the Heaven.
Doing a Filthy Pleasure Is [and Short].
Encouragement to Exile.
Foeda Est in Coitu.
Fragmentum.
Good God, What a Night That Was.
Malady of Love Is Nerves, The.
Plea for Haste, A.
Plea for Postponement, A.
Snow Ball, The.
We Are Such Stuff as Dreams.
Petrova, Olga
To a Child Who Inquires.
Pettengill, Margaret Miller
There Will Be Peace.
Pfeiffer, Edward Heyman
Soul Speaks, The.
Pfeiffer, Emily (Davis)
Song of Winter, A.
To a Moth That Drinketh of the Ripe October.
To the Herald Honeysuckle.
Pfeiffer, Eric
Centaur in the Groundlevel Apartment.
Pfingston, Roger
Saint Francis.
Pfister, Arthur
If Beer Cans Were Bullets.
If She Bees.
Ode to the Idiots.
Poet's Guilt, The.
Phaedrus
Aesop at Play.
Dog in the River, The.
Man and the Weasel, The.
Purpose of Fable-writing, The.
Phelps, Arthur Leonard
Wall, The.
Phelps, Charles Henry
Henry Ward Beecher.
Rare Moments.
Yuma.
Phelps, Elizabeth Stuart *See* **Ward, Elizabeth Stuart Phelps**
Phelps, Guy Fitch
White Christs, The.
Phelps, S. D.
Something for Jesus.
Phelps-Rider, Alice
On Hearing Jazz.
Philbrick, Charles
New England Suite.
"Philibin, An." *See* **"Pilibin, An"**
Philip, John
Subject of the Bishop's Miracle, The.
Philip, Sister Mary
Air Mail, Special.
Poet's Bread.
To-Day.
Philipa, Princess
To Holy Jesus.
Philipott, Thomas
On a Spark of Fire Fixing on a Gentlewoman's Breast.
Philippe de Thaon [*or* Thaun],
Pelican, The.
Philipps, Thomas
Peace of the Roses, The.
Philips, Ambrose
First Pastoral, The ("If We, O Dorset").
Happy Swain, The.
Ode to the Hon. Miss Carteret.
Pastoral Landscape.
Pastorals, *sels.*
Sixth Pastoral, The ("How still the sea!").
Song: "From White's and Will's."
To Charlotte Pulteney.
To Miss Charlotte Pulteney in Her Mother's Arms.
To Miss Georgiana.
To Miss Margaret Pulteney.
To Seignora Cuzzoni.
To Signora Cuzzoni.
To the Earl of Dorset.
To the Right Honourable Robert Walpole, Esq.
Winter Piece, A.
Philips, Joan *See* **"Ephelia"**
Philips, John
Splendid Shilling, The.
Thirsty Poet, The.
Philips, Katharine ("Orinda")
Answer to Another Persuading a Lady to Marriage, An.
Friendship's Mystery.
On the Fair Weather just at the Coronation.
Orinda to Lucasia.
Orinda to Lucasia Parting, October, 1661, at London.
To Mris. M[ary] A[wbrey] upon Absence.
To My Excellent Lucasia, on Our Friendship.
To My Lucasia, in Defence of Declared Friendship.
To One Persuading a Lady to Marriage.
Virgin, The.
Phillimore, John Swinnerton
Dying Thief, The.
In a Meadow.
Phillip, John
Comedy of Patient and Meek Grissell, *sel.*
Lullaby: "Lullaby baby, lullaby baby."
Patient and Meek Grissill.
Phillips, Charles
Music.
Phillips, Marie Tello
Sorrow.
Phillips, Redmond
Butchers.
Phillips, Stephen
Apparition, The.
Beautiful Lie the Dead.
Benediction.
Christ's Reign of Peace.
Dream, A.
Grief and God.
Herod, *sel.*
I in the Grayness Rose.
Poet's Prayer, The.
Right of Asylum, The.
Phillips, Susan Kelly
Rose of Eden, The.
Phillpotts, Eden
Badger, The.
The Badgers.
Man's Days.
Old Singer, The.
Puddle, The.
Philodemus of Gadara
Remonstrance.
Philpot, William
Maritae Suae.
Phocylides
Problem in Logic.
Small City on a Rock, A.
Phoenice, J.
Hawk Remembered.
Piatt, John James
Child in the Street, The.
Chrysalis, The.
Dear President, The.
Farther.
Guerdon, The.
Ireland.
Leaves at My Window.
Lost Genius, The.
Mower in Ohio, The.
October Morning.
Purpose.
Rose and Root.
Suggested Device of a New Western State.
To a Lady.
To Abraham Lincoln.
Torch-Light in Autumn.
Piatt, Sarah Morgan Bryan
After Wings.
Call on Sir Walter Raleigh, A.
Envoy: "Sweet World, if you will hear me now."
"How old is God? Has He grey hair?"
In Clonmel Parish Churchyard.
Into the World and Out.
Irish Wild-Flower, An.
My Babes in the Wood.
Questions of the Hour, *sel.*
Term of Death, The.
Tradition of Conquest.
Transfigured.
Watch of a Swan, The.
Witch in the Glass, The.
Word with a Skylark, A.
Pichette, Henri
Apoem I.
Pickard, Cynthia
Cinderella.
Pickering [*or* Pikeryng], John
Haltersick's Song.
History of Horestes, The.
Horestes, *sel.*
New Interlude of Vice, Containing the History of Horestes, A.
Song: "Farewell, adieu, that courtly [*or* court-like] life!"
Pickering, Theodosia *See* **Garrison, Theodosia Pickering**
Pickthall, Marjorie Lowry Christie
Bega.
Bridegroom of Cana, The.
Canada to England.
Child's Song of Christmas, A.
Duna.
Ebb Tide.
I Sat among the Green Leaves.
Immortal, The.
Lamp of Poor Souls, The.
Little Sister of the Prophet, The.
Little Songs.
Lovers of Marchaid, The.
Mary Shepherdess.
Mary Tired.
Mother in Egypt, A.
On Amaryllis, a Tortoyse.

Père Lalemant.
Quiet.
Resurgam.
Swallow Song.
To a Believer.

Pico della Mirandola Giovanni, Conte
Consider.
Golden Sestina, The.

Picot, James
Do You Not Hear?
Finale.
Lord in the Wind, The.
Main Range.
To the Rosella in the Poinsettia Tree.
Volume of Chopin, A.

Piddington, R. A.
Literary Zodiac.
Tudor Aspersions.

Pien Chih-lin
Composition of Distances, The.
History of Communications and a Running Account, The.

Pierce, Dorothy Mason
Good Night.
John Plans.
Sprinkling.

Pierce, Edith Lovejoy
Apocalypse.
Certain Saturday, A.
Christmas Amnesty.
Civitas Dei.
Crucifix.
Dirge: "O sad, sad world, O world that knows not Love."
Emmaus.
Great Powers Conference.
Had There Been Peace.
Hymn to the Perfect.
In the Wilderness.
Incarnation.
Let Me Not Die.
Loyalty Hymn.
O Christ Thou Art within Me like a Sea.
On Christmas Eve.
Prayer: "Bear with me, Master, when I turn from Thee."
Prayer for the Useless Days.
Remember Thy Covenant.
Song of the Wise Men.
Sons of Failure.
Supplication.
Third Day, The.

Pierce, Jason Noble
Which Sword?

Piercy, Marge
Apologies.
Embryos.
For Jeriann's Hands.
Homo Faber: the Shell Game.
Now All at Once It Is Colder.
Peaceable Kingdom, The.
Rain Falls on Ioannina.
Song of the Nudge.
Vil for the Layman.
Why the Soup Tastes Like the Daily News.

Pierpoint, Folliott Sandford
For the Beauty of the Earth.

Pierpont, James S.
Jingle Bells.
We Conquer or Die.

Pierpont, John
Ballot, The.
Centennial Hymn.
Exile at Rest, The.
Fourth of July, The.
Fugitive Slave's Apostrophe to the North Star, The.
General Joseph Warren's Address.
Kidnapping of Sims, The.
My Child.
On Laying the Cornerstone of the Bunker Hill Monument.
Pilgrim Fathers, The.
Sparkling Bowl, The.
Warren's Address [to the American Soldiers].
Whittling.

Piety, Chauncey Roscoe
Come Back, Lincoln.
Gifts.
My World.
New Patriotism, A.
Soul of Lincoln, The.
Thanksliving.

Pigott, Jean Sophia
Jesus, I Am Resting, Resting.

Pigott, Mostyn T.
Hundred Best Books, The.

Pike, Albert
Buena Vista.
Dixie ("Southrons, hear your country call you!").
Song of the Navajo.
To the Mocking-Bird.
Widowed Heart, The.

Pike, Albert G.
Every Year.

Pike, Cecily E.
Jack Frost.

Pikeryng, John *See* **Pickering, John**

Pilcher, Charles Venn
Teachers, The.

"Pilibin [*or* Philibin], An" (John Hacket-Pollock)
Retrospect.

Pilkington, Francis
O Softly Singing Lute.

Pimental Coronel, Ramón
Jesus.

Pinch, Esther
City Nature.
Friction.

Pinckney, Josephine
In the Barn.
Misses Poar Drive to Church, The.
Peggy Considers Her Grandmothers.
Phyllis and the Philosopher.

Pindar
First Olympionique: To Hiero of Syracuse.
First Pythian Ode of Pindar, The.
I Bless This Man.
Island of the Blest, The.
Isthmian Odes.
Life after Death.
Nemean Odes.
Odes, *sels.*
Olympian Odes.
Power of Music, The.
Pythian Odes.
To Hiero the Syracusan.

"Pindar, Peter" (John Wolcott)
Actor, An.
Apple Dumplings and a King.
Ballade: To a Fish of the Brooke.
Bozzy and Piozzi, *sel.*
Epigram: "Midas, they say, possessed the art of old."
Introduction and Anecdotes.
Pilgrims and the Peas, The.
Razor Seller, The.
Royal Tour, The.
To a Fly.
To a Kiss.
Tray's Epitaph.

Pineo, J. Franklin
Except Ye Repent.

"Pink."
Groaning Board, The.

Pinkerton, H. A. (Mrs. Wesley Trimpi)
Degrees of Shade.
Deprivation.
Error Pursued.
Prism, The.

Pinkerton, Helen
Indecision.

Pinkham, Cora M.
God's Ideal Mother.
With Thee.

Pinkney, Dorothy Cowles
Dame Liberty Reports from Travel.

Pinkney, Edward Coote [*or* Coate]
Health, A.
Serenade, A: "Look out upon the stars, my love."
Song: "We break the glass, whose sacred wine."
Votive Song.

Pinto, Vivian de Sola
At Piccadilly Circus.

Piozzi, Hester Thrale *See* **Thrale, Hester**

Piper, Edwin Ford
Bindlestiff.
Church, The.
Gee-up Dar, Mules.
Last Antelope, The.
Prairie Schooner, The.
Sweetgrass Range.

Pisan, Christine de
If Frequently to Mass.

Pise, Charles Constantine
American Flag, The.

Pitcher, Oliver
Pale Blue Casket, The.
Raison d'Etre.
Salute.

Pitchford, Kenneth
Aunt Cora.
Blizzard Ape, The.
Blues Ballad.
Death Swoops.
Good for Nothing Man, *sels.*
I saw in the East a sign, a sign.
Jacqueline Gray.
Leviathan; a Poem in Four Movements.
Off Viareggio.
104 Boulevard Saint-Germain.
Onion Skin, The.
Pickup in Tony's Hashhouse.
Queen, The.
Reflections on Water.
Young Buck's Sunday Blue.

Pitt, Charles
Bandit's Grave, The.

Pitt, Marie Elizabeth Josephine
Gallop of Fire, A.
Hamilton.

Pitt, William
Sailor's Consolation, The.

Pitter, Ruth
Bat, The.
Beautiful Negress, The.
Burning the Bee-Tree.
But for Lust.
But My Neighbor Is My Treasure.
Captive Bird of Paradise, The.
Close, Mortal Eyes.
Coffin-Worm, The.
Digdog.
Dream, A.
Dun-Color.
End of Fear, The.
Estuary, The.
Eternal Image, The.
Fellow-creatures.
Fishers, The.
For Sleep or Death.
Heart's Desire Is Full of Sleep, The.
Help, Good Shepherd.
In the Open.
Matron-Cat's Song, The.

Pitter (continued)
Military Harpist, The.
Missal, The.
1938.
O Come Out of the Lily.
Old Woman Speaks of the Moon, An.
Paradox, The.
Rainy Summer.
Solemn Meditation, A.
Sparrow's Skull, The.
Stockdove, The.
Storm.
Stormcock in Elder.
Strawberry Plant, The.
Swan Bathing, The.
Task, The.
Tigress, The.
Time's Fool.
To J. S. Collis.
Train Will Fight to the Pass, The.
Unicorn, The.
Urania.
Viper, The.
Weeping Water.
Pitts, Herbert Lee
Reality.
We Must Lead.
Pitts, William S.
Little Brown Church in the Vale.
"Placido" Gabriel de la Concepciòn Valdès
Farewell to My Mother.
Placido's Farewell to His Mother.
Prayer to God.
Planché, James Robinson
Literary Squabble, A.
Sea-Serpent, The.
Song: "Three score and ten by common calculation."
To Mollidusta.
Plarr, Victor
Che Sara Sara.
Epitaphium Citharistriae.
Stand Not Uttering Sedately.
Plath, Sylvia
Amnesiac.
Applicant, The.
Ariel.
Arrival of the Bee Box, The.
Balloons.
Black Rook in Rainy Weather.
Blackberrying.
Blue Moles.
Child.
Colossus, The.
Daddy.
Death & Co.
Elm.
Elm Speaks, The.
Fever 1030.
Ghost's Leavetaking, The.
Hanging Man, The.
Hardcastle Crags.
Kindness.
Lady Lazarus.
Medallion.
Mirror.
Moon and the Yew Tree, The.
Morning Song.
Munich Mannequins, The.
Mushrooms.
Mussel Hunter at Rock Harbor.
Mystic.
Nick and the Candlestick.
Night Walk.
Point Shirley.
Poppies in July.
Rival, The.
Sheep in Fog.
Snakecharmer.
Stings.
Suicide off Egg Rock.
Tulips.
Two Campers in Cloud Country.
Two Views of a Cadaver Room.
Water Color of Grantchester Meadows.
Plato
Aster.
Country Music.
Dedication of a Mirror.
Farewell: "Far from the deep roar of the Aegean main."
Farmer and Sailor.
Inner Man, The.
Irony, An.
Lais' Mirror.
Love Sleeping.
Morning and Evening Star.
My Star.
On a Seal.
On Alexis.
On Archaeanassa.
On Aristophanes.
On the Athenian Dead at Ecbatana.
One to All Men.
Seaman's Tomb, A.
Star.
To Stella.
Platt, Anna M.
Crocuses.
Playford, John
Jovial Marriner, The; or, The Sea-Man's Renown.
Sea-Man's Renown, The.
Plew, Mildred *See* **Meigs, Mildred Plew**
Plimpton, Florus B.
Fort Duquesne.
Plimpton, Harriet
Northern View.
Plomer, William
Archaic Apollo.
Bamboo.
Blind Samson.
Boer War, The.
Caledonian Market, The.
Death of a Snake, The.
Death of a Zulu, The.
Devil-Dancers, The.
Dorking Thigh, The.
Europa.
Explorer, The.
Father and Son: 1939.
Flying Bum, The: 1944.
French Lisette; a Ballad of Maida Vale.
Headline History.
In the Snake Park.
Johannesburg.
Levantine, A.
Mews Flat Mona.
Namaqualand after Rain.
Pioneers, The; or, Twenty Years After.
Playboy of the Demi-World, The, 1938.
Prisoner, The.
Right-of-Way, A: 1865.
Ruined Farm, The.
Scorpion, The.
September Evening, 1938.
Tattooed.
Transvaal Morning, A.
Traveller's Tale, A.
Ula Masondo's Dream.
Victoria Falls, The.
Walk in Würzburg, A.
Plotinus
We Are Not Cast Away.
Plowman, Max
Her Beauty.
Plumly, Stanley
Ulysses Pondering.
Plummer, Mary E.
Pussy Willows.
Plummer, Mary Wright
Irrevocable.
Plunkett, Edward John Moreton Drax
See **Dunsany**
Plunkett, Joseph Mary
Claim That Has the Canker on the Rose, The.
I See His Blood upon the Rose.
My Lady Has the Grace of Death.
O Sower of Sorrow.
Our Heritage.
See the Crocus' Golden Cup.
Sic Transit.
Spark, The.
Stars Sang in God's Garden, The.
This Heritage to the Race of Kings.
To G. K. Chesterton.
White Dove of the Wild Dark Eyes.
Plunkett, Patrick Mary
Vale.
Plutzik, Hyam
Airman Who Flew over Shakespeare's England, The.
Argumentum ad Hominem.
Begetting of Cain, The.
Divisibility.
Equation, An.
Exhortation to the Artists.
Faustus.
For T. S. E. Only.
He Inspects His Armory.
Horatio, *sels.*
Identity.
Importance of Poetry, or the Coming Forth from Eternity into Time, The.
Jim Desterland.
King of Ai, The.
Mr. Pollington Remembers a Poet.
My Sister.
Mythos of Samuel Huntsman, The.
On the Photograph of a Man I Never Saw.
Ostler, The.
Portrait.
Road, The.
Po Chü-i
After Passing the Examination.
Charcoal-Seller, The.
Cranes, The.
Flower Market, The.
Gardener, The.
Getting up Early on a Spring Morning.
Good-bye to the People of Hang-chow.
Harper of Chao, The.
Hat Given to the Poet by Li Chien, The.
Having Climbed to the Topmost Peak of the Incense-Burner Mountain.
Hearing the Early Oriole.
I Look Down.
Illness ("Sad, sad—lean with long illness").
In Early Summer Lodging in a Temple to Enjoy the Moonlight.
Lao-tzu.
Letter, The.
Lodging with the Old Man of the Stream.
Losing a Slave-Girl.
Madly Singing in the Mountains.
On Being Sixty.
On Hearing Someone Sing a Poem by Yüan Chen.
People of Tao-chou, The.
Philosophers, The.
Planting Flowers on the Eastern Embankment.
Poem on the Wall, The.
Prisoner, The.
Pruning Trees.
Red Cockatoo, The.
Rejoicing at the Arrival of Ch'en Hsiung.
Remembering Golden Bells.
Sleeping on Horseback.
Temple, The.

To Li Chien ("The province I govern is humble and remote").
To Li Chien ("Wordly matters again draw my steps").
Po Fei Huang
Himalaya.
Pocock, Isaac
Heir of Vironi, The, *sel.*
Song: "Oh! say not woman's love [*or* heart] is bought."
Poe, Edgar Allan
Al Aaraaf.
Alone.
Annabel Lee.
Bells, The.
City in the Sea, The.
Coliseum, The.
Conqueror Worm, The.
Doomed City, The.
Dream, A.
Dream-Land.
Dream within a Dream, A.
Dreams.
Eldorado.
Enigma, An.
Eulalie.
Evening Star.
Fairy-Land.
Fall of the House of Usher, The, *sel.*
For Annie.
From Childhood's Hour.
Happiest Day, the Happiest Hour, The.
Haunted Palace, The.
Hear the mellow wedding bells.
Hymn: "At morn, at noon, at twilight dim."
Hymn of the Angelus.
I have no words—alas!—to tell.
Israfel.
Lake, The.
Lake, The: To ——.
Lenore.
Ligeia, *pr. tale, sel.*
'Neath Blue-Bell or Streamer.
Raven, The.
Romance.
Simple Duty, A.
Sleeper, The.
Song: "Neath blue-bell or streamer."
Song: "Spirit! that dwellest where."
Song from "Al Aaraaf."
Sonnet: Silence.
Sonnet: To Science.
Sonnet—Silence.
Sonnet to Science.
Sonnet—To Zante.
Spirits of the Dead.
Stanzas: "In youth have I known one with whom the Earth."
Tamerlane.
To ——: "Not long ago, the writer of these lines."
To ——: "Take this kiss upon thy brow!"
To Helen ("Helen, thy beauty is to me").
To My Mother.
To One in Paradise.
To Science.
The Coliseum.
Ulalume.
Valley of Unrest, The.
Poitiers, Guillaume de *See* **Guillaume de Poitiers**
Pol, Wincenty
Song of the Mound.
Polite, Allen
Am Driven Mad.
Stopped.
Polite, Frank
Mine.
Politian *See* **Poliziano, Angelo**
Politzer, Heinz
My Language.
Poliziano [*or* Politian], Angelo
Ballata of Myrrha's Eyes.
I went a roaming, maidens, one bright day.
Three Ballate.
Pollak, Felix
Speaking: The Hero.
Pollard, Adelaide A.
Have Thine Own Way, Lord!
Secret Place, The.
Pollard, Josephine
Price of a Drink.
Pollock, Edward
Olivia.
Pollock, Sir Frederick
Six Carpenters' Case, The.
Pollock, John Hackett *See* **"Pilibin, An"**
Pollock, Thomas B.
Father, into Thy Hands.
Pollock, Walter Herries
Below the Heights.
Conquest, A.
Father Francis.
Pollok, Robert
Course of Time, The, *sel.*
Ocean.
Polonsky, Yakov Petrovich
Cosmic Fabric, The.
Polsue, Dorothy B.
Come, My Sheep.
Pombo, Rafael
Our Madonna at Home.
To Bolívar.
Pomeroy, Edward Noyes
Today and Tomorrow.
Pomeroy, Marnie
April Fool's Day.
Groundhog Day.
Halloween.
In Nakedness.
January 1.
Labor Day.
Pomeroy, Ralph
Confession.
Corner.
High Wind at the Battery.
In Hotels Public and Private.
In the Redwood Forest.
Islands.
Letter to Pasternak.
Looking at the Empire State Building.
Patrol.
To Janet.
To Words.
Trying to Sleep.
Pomfret, John
Choice, The.
Would bounteous Heaven one more indulge, I'd choose.
Ponciano, Angelo de
Empties Coming Back.
Ponsonby, A. B.
Boy's Prayer.
Pontalais, Jehan du
Money.
Ponting, Herbert George
Sleeping-Bag, The.
Poole, Louella C.
Betsey Trotwood's Cat.
Black Friday.
Metempsychosis.
Parlor Cat, A.
Poole, Tom
I/ wonder why.
Poots, Tom
Black Spirit.
Pope, Alexander
All are but parts of one stupendous whole.
Alps on Alps.
And now the Queen, to glad her sons, proclaims.
As hags hold sabbaths, not for joy but spite.
As the Twig Is Bent.
At Timon's Villa.
Atticus.
Balance of Europe, The.
Belinda's Morning.
Books and the Man I sing, the first who brings.
Bufo.
But you who seek to give and merit fame.
Challenge, The.
Chaos.
Characters from the Satires: Atticus.
Characters from the Satires: Chloe.
Characters from the Satires: Sporus.
Characters from the Satires: Wharton.
Characters of Women: Flavia, Atossa, and Cloe.
Charity.
Chloe.
Close by those meads, for ever crown'd [*or* crowned] with flowers.
Conclusion: "In vain, in vain—the all-composing hour."
Contented Man, The.
Couplet on Newton.
Court of Charles II, The.
Coxcomb Bird, The.
Craft of Verse, The.
Death of Buckingham, The.
Death of the Duke of Buckingham, The.
Descend, Ye Nine.
Dire Dilemma, A.
Dogs.
Duke of Buckingham, The.
Dunces' Opera.
Dunciad, The, *sels.*
Dying Christian to His Soul, The.
Elegy to the Memory of an Unfortunate Lady.
Eloïsa to Abelard.
Engraved on the Collar of a Dog, Which I Gave to His Royal Highness.
Engraved on the Collar of His Highness' Dog.
Epigram: Engraved on the Collar of a Dog, Which I Gave to His Royal Highness.
Epigram: "I and His Highness' dog at Kew."
Epigram: "Should D——s print, how once you robb'd your brother."
Epigram: "When other ladies to the shades go down."
Epigram: "You beat your pate, and fancy wit will come."
Epigram on the Toasts of the Kit-Kat Club, Anno 1716.
Epilogue to the Satires.
Epistle: "O Happiness! Our being's end."
Epistle from Mr. Pope, to Dr. Arbuthnot.
Epistle to a Young Lady.
Epistle to Dr. Arbuthnot (Prologue to the Satires).
Epistle to Miss [*or* Mrs.] Blount, on Her Leaving the Town, after the Coronation.
Epistle to Robert Earl of Oxford.
Epitaph: "Here rests a woman, good without pretence."
Epitaph: "Nature and Nature's laws lay hid in night."
Epitaph: "Of manners gentle, of affections mild."
Epitaph Intended for Sir Isaac Newton.
Epitaph on Mrs. Corbet, Who Died [*or* Dyed] of a Cancer in Her Breast.
Epitaph on Sir Isaac Newton.

Pope (continued)
Essay on Criticism, An.
Essay on Man, An.
Faith.
Farewell to London in the year 1715, A.
Field Sports.
First Epistle of the Second Book of Horace [Imitated], The.
First follow Nature, and your judgment frame.
First Satire of the Second Book of Horace [Imitated], The.
Fool and the Poet, The.
For lo! the board with cups and spoons is crowned.
For One Who Would Not Be Buried in Westminster Abbey.
Force first made conquest, and that conquest, law.
Fourth Satire of Dr. John Donne, Dean of St. Paul's, Versified, The.
Gem and the Flower, The.
Great Chain of Being, The.
Groves of Eden, vanish'd now so long, The.
Happy the Man.
Heaven's Last Best Work.
Heloise and Abelard.
Henry St. John, Viscount Bolingbroke.
High on a gorgeous seat, that far outshone.
Honest Fame.
Honest Man, An.
Hope ("Hope springs eternal in the human breast").
Hope humble then; with trembling pinions soar.
Hope Springs Eternal ("Heav'n from all creatures hides the book of fate").
"How oft, when pressed to marriage."
Human Folly.
Hymn: "Rise, crowned with light, imperial Salem, rise!"
Ideals of Satire, The.
If wit so much from ign'rance undergo.
Imitation of Chaucer.
Imitations of Donne, *sel.*
Immortality of Verse, The.
In Defence of Satire.
In flowed at once a gay embroidered race.
Inscribed on the Collar of a Dog.
Intended for Sir Isaac Newton.
Know Then Thyself.
Life's Poor Play.
Lines Written in Windsor Forest.
Little Learning Is a Dangerous Thing, A.
Lo, the Poor Indian.
Man.
Man of Ross, The.
Messiah.
Mighty mother, and her son, who brings, The.
Moral Essays, *sels.*
Most souls, 'tis true, but peep out once an age.
Nature and Art.
New Dunciad, The, *sel.*
Not with more glories, in th' etherial plain.
Oh Happiness! our being's end and aim!
O Sons of Earth.
Ode: Dying Christian to His Soul, The.
Ode for Music on St. Cecilia's Day.
Ode on Solitude.
Ode to Quinbus Flestrin.
Ode to Solitude.
Of all the causes which conspire to blind.
Of the Characters of Women,
Of the Use of Riches ("'Tis strange, the miser. . .").
Of the Use of Riches ("Who shall decide, when doctors disagree").
Ombre at Hampton Court.
On a Certain Lady at Court.
On her white breast a sparkling cross she wore.
On Mr. Gay; in Westminster Abbey, 1732.
On One Who Made Long Epitaphs.
On the Collar of a Dog [Presented by Mr. Pope to the Prince of Wales].
On the Hon. Simon Harcourt.
On Two Lovers Struck Dead by Lightning.
One Thousand Seven Hundred and Thirty-eight.
Paragon of Animals, The.
Paraphrase on Thomas à Kempis, A.
Pastorals, *sels.*
Pheasant, The.
Playing Cards, The.
Pleasure of Hope, The.
Poet, The.
Poetical Numbers.
Poet's Use, The.
Portrait of Atticus.
Prayer of St. Francis Xavier.
Pride, the Never-Failing Vice of Fools.
Pride, where wit fails, steps in to our defence.
Prologue to Mr. Addison's Tragedy of Cato.
Proper Study of Man [*or* Mankind], The.
Rape of the Lock, The.
Regard not then if wit be old or new.
Reign of Chaos, The.
Reply, A.
Riddle of the World.
Rise, Crowned with Light.
Ruling Passion, The.
Satire: "Ask you what provocation I have had?"
Satire II: "Yes; thank my stars! as early as I knew."
Satire on Riches.
Satires of Dr. John Donne, Versified, The, *sel.*
Science.
Second Epistle of the Essay on Man, The.
She said: then, raging to Sir Plume repairs.
Sir, I Admit Your General Rule.
Solitude.
Some to conceit alone their taste confine.
Sound and Sense ("True ease in writing. . .").
Sound must seem an echo to the sense, The.
Sporus.
Summer.
Summer; the Second Pastoral, or Alexis.
Temple of Fame, The, *sel.*
Those rules of old discover'd, not devis'd.
Time shall come, when, free as seas or wind, The.
Timon's Villa.
'Tis with our judgments as our watches.
To a Blockhead.
To a Lady.
To a Lady; of the Characters of Women.
To a Young Lady.
To a Young Lady on Her Leaving the Town after the Coronation.
To a Young Lady, with the Works of Voiture.
To Augustus.
To Dr. Arbuthnot.
To James Craggs, Esq., Secretary of State.
To Miss Blount, with the Works of Voiture.
To Mr. Jervas, with Fresnoy's "Art of Painting," Translated by Mr. Dryden.
To Mrs. M. B. on Her Birthday [*or* Birth-Day].
To Richard Boyle, Earl of Burlington.
To Robert Earl of Oxford and Earl Mortimer.
Toilet, The.
Triumph of Dulness, The.
Triumph of Ignorance, The.
True wit is nature to advantage dress'd.
Universal Prayer, The.
Upon Cleora's Marriage and Retirement.
Verbal Critics.
Verses to the Memory of an Unfortunate Lady.
Vestal, The.
Vice.
Vital Spark of Heavenly Flame!
Wharton ("Wharton! the scorn and wonder of our days").
Whatever Is, Is Right.
Who sees with equal eye, as God of all.
Why Did I Write ("Of all mad creatures").
Why did I write? what sin to me unknown.
Windsor Forest.
Winter.
Woman's Ruling Passions.
Worth Makes the Man.
Ye Sylphs and Sylphids, to your chief give ear!
Yet let me flap this bug with gilded wings.
Yet, yet a moment, one dim ray of light.
You Beat Your Pate.
Pope, J. R.
Word of Encouragement, A.
Pope, Walter
Old Man's Wish, The.
Wish, The.
Popham, Ivor
Child, The.
Poquelin, Jean Baptiste *See* **Molière**
Pordage, Samuel
Corydon's Complaint.
To Lucia Playing on Her Lute.
Porson, Richard
Academic Visit to the Continent, An.
Dido.
Epigram on an Academic Visit to the Continent.
Note on the Latin Gerunds, A.
Nothing.
On a German Tour.
On an Imaginary Journey to the Continent.
Porter, Alan
Dean, The.
Love's Fragility.
Signature of Pain, The.
Porter, Bruce
Limerick: "H was an indigent hen."
Porter, Cole
You're the Top.
Porter, Mrs. David
Thou Hast Wounded the Spirit That Loved Thee.
Porter, H. H.
Forty Years After.
Porter, Hal
Adam—the First Kiss.
Bi-focal.
Lalique.
Sheep, The.
Porter, Ina M.
Mumford.
Porter, Jenny Lind
In the Beginning.
Porter, Katherine Anne
Requiescat.
Porter, Kenneth Wiggins
Beaver Sign.
Certainties.

Epitaph for a Man from Virginia City.
Judgment.
Old Coon-Dog Dreams, The.
Old Thad Stevens.
Oration, An, *sel.*
Poem on a Slippery Sidewalk.
Simon and Judas.
Stone, The.
Street Scene—1946.
Thistle, Yarrow, Clover.
To a Prince of the Church.
To the Younger Old-Americans, *sel.*

Porter, Peter
Annotations of Auschwitz.
Made in Heaven.
Phar Lap in the Melbourne Museum.
St. Cecilia's Day Epigram, A.
Smell on the Landing, The.
To Start a Controversy.
Walking Home on St. Cecilia's Day.
Your Attention Please.

Porter, Samuel Judson
Way, The; the Truth; the Life

Porter, Thomas
Serenade, to Two Ladies.
Villain, The, *sel.*

Porter, Timothy L.
Now in the/ black.

Portor, Laura Spencer (Mrs. Francis Pope)
Christ-Child, The.
Christ Child's Christmas, The.
Gift, The.
Shepherds, The.
Windflowers and the Sage, The.

Poseidippus
Doricha.
No Way Is Good.
Too Near the Waves.

Posner, David
Birds, The.
Campus, The.
On a Recent Protest against Social Conditions.

Post, L. F., *and* Glenn Norton
Gila Monster Route, The.

Post, Marie J.
Early Summer Thought.

Potamkin, Harry Alan
Cargoes of the Radanites.

Poteat, Edwin McNeill
Barabbas Speaks.
Casualty.
Eternal God Whose Searching Eye Doth Scan.
Faith.
Focus of That Face, The.
Grace at Evening.
He, Too, Loved Beauty.
If Any Man Would Come after Me.
Jericho Road, The.
Light of the World, How Long the Quest.
Mary Pondered All These Things.
Orisons.
Palm Sunday and Monday.
Prayer at Dawn.
Prayer for Contentment.
Two Chalices.

Pothinus, St.
Epigram on Marcus the Gnostic.

Potter, Beatrix
Old Woman, The.

Potter, Miriam Clark
Cake.
Present.

Pottle, Emory
I Have a Son.

Potts, Paul
For My Father.
Jean.
Muse to an Unknown Poet, The.

Poulsson, Emilie
Baby's Breakfast.
Bed-Time Song.
Books Are Keys.
Breakfast Song, The.
First Christmas, The.
Judging by Appearances.
Lovable Child, The.
Nutting Time.
Puppy's Problem, A.
Santa Claus and the Mouse.
Story of Baby's Blanket, The.
Story of Baby's Pillow, The.
While Stars of Christmas Shine.

Pound, Ezra
Age Demanded, The ("For this agility chance found"). Mauberley, III.
Alba ("When the nightingale to his mate").
Alchemist, The.
Ancient Music.
And before hell mouth; dry plain.
And the betrayers of language.
And the Days Are Not Full Enough.
And there was grass on the floor of the temple.
And Thus in Nineveh.
Ant's a Centaur, The.
Apparuit.
April.
Ballad for Gloom.
Ballad of the Goodly Fere.
Ballad of the Mulberry Road, A.
Ballatetta.
Bath Tub, The.
Be in me as the eternal moods.
Beneath the sagging roof.
Black Slippers: Bellotti.
Brennbaum.
Canto I: "And then went down to the ship."
Canto II: "Hang it all, Robert Browning."
Canto XIII: "Kung walked/ by the dynastic temple."
Canto XIV, *sel.*
Canto XV, *sel.*
Canto XVI, *sel.*
Canto XVII: "So that the vines burst from my fingers."
Canto XX, *sel.*
Canto XXIX, *sel.*
Canto XLV: "With Usura/ With usura hath no man a house of good stone."
Canto XLVII: "Who even dead, yet hath his mind entire!"
Canto LXXIX, *sel.*
Canto LXXX, *sel.*
Canto LXXXI, *sels.*
Canto CXIII, *sel.*
Clara.
Coming of War, The: Actaeon.
Commission.
"Conservatrix of Milesien."
Dance Figure (for the Marriage in Cana of Galilee).
"Daphne with her thighs in bark."
(Doria).
E. P. Ode pour l'Election de Son Sepulchre.
Envoi: "Go, dumb-born book."
Envoi (1919).
Epilogue: "O chansons foregoing."
Erat Hora.
Faun, The.
Flame, The.
For E. McC.
Fu I.
Further Instructions.
Garden, The.
Garret, The.
Girl, A.
Greek Epigram.
Gypsy, The.
Homage to Sextus Propertius, *sels.*
House of Splendour, The.
Hugh Selwyn Mauberley (Life and Contacts).
I loved a woman. The stars fell from heaven.
I Vecchi.
If you'd have me go on loving you.
Image from D'Orleans.
Immorality, An.
Impressions of Françis-Marie Arouet (de Voltaire), *sel.*
In a Station of the Metro.
Ité.
Jungle:/ Glaze green and red feathers, jungle.
La Fraisne.
Lake Isle, The.
Langue d'Oc, *sel.*
L'Art, 1910.
Liu Ch'e.
Mauberley.
Me happy, night, night full of brightness.
Medallion.
Meditatio.
Meditation.
Mr. Nixon.
Moeurs Contemporaines.
N. Y.
Near Périgord.
O Lynx, wake Silenus and Casey.
Ode pour l'Election de Son Sepulchre.
Ortus.
Pact, A.
Phyllidula.
Piere Vidal Old.
Pisan Cantos, The.
Portrait.
Portrait d'une Femme.
Pour l'Election de Son Sepulchre.
Provincia Deserta.
Pull Down Thy Vanity.
Rest, The.
Return, The.
Ritratto.
Salutation.
Salutation the Second.
Sestina; Altaforte.
Shades of Callimachus, Coan ghosts of Philetas.
She is submarine, she is an octopus, she is/ A biological process.
"Siena Mi Fé; Disfecemi Maremma."
Silet.
Simulacra.
Skin-flakes, repetitions, erosions.
Soiree.
South-Folk in Cold Country.
Spring, The.
Study in Aesthetics, The.
Tame Cat.
Tea-rose tea gown, etc., The.
Tea Shop, The.
Temperaments, The.
Then a partridge-shaped cloud over dust storm.
There died a myriad.
These fought in any case.
Tomb at [*or* of] Akr Çar, The.
Tree, The.
Ts'ai Chi'h.
Tudor indeed is gone and every rose.
Villanelle; the Psychological Hour.
Virginal, A.
What thou lovest well remains.
When, when, and whenever death closes our eyelids.
White Stag, The.

Pound (continued)
Who, who will be the next man to entrust his girl to a friend?
Yet/ Ere the Season died a-cold.
Yeux Glauques.
Pounds, Jessie B.
Beautiful Isle of Somewhere.
Pounds, Leonard
"Rake" Windermere.
Poupo, Pierre
Prayers of a Christian Bridegroom.
Powell, Arthur
Welcome, The.
Powell, Harry A.
Here We Have Idaho.
Powell, Richard Stillman
I Go Fishin'.
Powell, Ruth
After Reading Milne.
Power, John
Thy Name We Bless and Magnify.
Power, Marguerite
Friend, A.
Powers, Horatio Nelson
Chimney Swallows.
New Year, The.
Our Sister.
Year Ahead, The.
Powers, Jessica
And in Her Morning.
Beauty, Too, Seeks Surrender.
Boundaries.
Celestial Bird.
Cloud of Carmel, The.
Doxology.
I Would Define My Love.
If You Have Nothing.
Obscurity ("Obscurity becomes the final peace").
Powers, Star
Harvest Time.
Pozzi, Antonia
Mountain Climber, The.
Rendezvous.
Prada, Gonzalez
Who Translates a Poet Badly.
Prados, Emilio
I Closed My Door to the World.
Praed, Winthrop Mackworth
Belle of the Ball-Room, The.
Charade.
County Ball, The, *sel.*
Covenanter's Lament for Bothwell Brigg, The.
Epitaph on the Late King of the Sandwich Isles.
Every-Day Characters, *sels.*
Fairy Song.
Goodnight to the Season.
Intolerance.
Latin Hymn.
Letter of Advice, A.
Letters from Teignmouth, *sel.*
Mater Desiderata.
Newly-wedded, The.
One More Quadrille.
Our Ball.
Portrait of a Lady in the Exhibition of the Royal Academy.
School and Schoolfellows.
Schoolfellows.
Song of Impossibilities, A.
Stanzas on Seeing the Speaker Asleep in His Chair.
Stanzas to the Speaker Asleep.
Talented Man, The.
Time's Song.
To ——: "We met but in one giddy dance."
To Helen.
Vicar, The.
Prather, W. H.
Indian Ghost Dance and War, The.
Prati, Giovanni
Holy Viaticum Comes to Me, The.
Pratt, Anna Maria
Early News.
Little Mistake, A.
Mortifying Mistake, A.
Pratt Edwin John
Behind the Log, *sel.*
Brébeuf and His Brethren, *sels.*
Burial at Sea.
Cachalot, The, *sels.*
Come Away, Death.
Come Not the Seasons Here.
Decision, The.
Drag-Irons, The.
Dunkirk, *sel.*
Dying Eagle, The.
Erosion.
Flood-Tide, The.
From Dover to Dunkirk.
From Stone to Steel ("From stone to bronze, from bronze to steel").
Frost.
Fury of taunt was followed by fury of blow, The.
Gathering, The.
Ground-Swell, The.
Ice-Floes, The.
Iceberg, The.
Invisible Trumpets Blowing.
Isador and Ida Strauss.
Man and the Machine, The.
Martyrdom of Brébeuf and Lalemant, 16 March 1649, The.
Newfoundland.
Out on the water was the same display.
Precambrian Shield, The.
Prize Cat, The.
Roosevelt and the *Antinoe,* The, *sel.*
Sea Cathedral, The.
Sea Gulls.
Shark, The.
Silences.
There is a language in a naval log.
Thousand years now had his breed, A.
Three miles from town to town over the snow.
Titanic, The, *sels.*
To an Enemy.
Towards the Last Spike, *sels.*
Truant, The.
Way of Cape Race, The.
Whatever doubt the eye might have imposed.
Where Cape Delgado strikes the sea.
Pratt, Evelyn Florence
Courting in Kentucky.
Pratt, Harry Noyes
Gypsy Heart, The.
Pratt, Lenore
Old Boat, The.
Pratt, Lenore Alexandra
Blizzard, The.
Pratt, William W.
Golden Wedding.
Pray, Benjamin Sturgis
Motorcycle.
Prentice, George Denison
Memories.
New England.
Ocean, The.
Prentice, John A.
Washington.
Prentiss, Elizabeth Payson (Mrs. George Lewis Prentiss)
Alone with God.
Little Kitty.
Long Time Ago.
More Love to Christ.
Mystery of Life in Christ, The.
Susy Miller.
Preradovic, Petar
But so long as/ This prison-planet.
Ode to Slavdom, *sel.*
Prescott, Mary Newmarch
In the Dark, in the Dew.
Press, John
Eleusis and Beethoven.
Farewell: "Smell of death was in the air, The."
Narcissus.
Peach Tree in the Garden of an Empty House.
What the Wind Said.
Womanisers.
Pressoir, Charles Fernand
Country Graveyard.
Mambo dans le Hounfort, La.
Preston, Keith
Awful Responsibility, An.
Deep Stuff.
Durable Bon Mot, The.
Good Reasons.
Humorist, The.
Lapsus Linguae.
Marital Tragedy.
Original Cuss, An.
Warm Babies.
Preston, Margaret Junkin
Acceptation.
Dirge for Ashby.
Dirge for Ashby.
First Proclamation of Miles Standish, The.
First Thanksgiving Day, The.
Gone Forward.
Grave in Hollywood Cemetery, Richmond, A.
Hero of the Commune, The.
Last Meeting of Pocahontas and the Great Captain, The.
Mystery of Cro-a-tàn, The.
Under the Shade of the Trees.
Virginia Capta.
Vision of the Snow, The.
Prestwich, Edmund
How to Choose a Mistress.
To Phoebus Seeing a Lady before Sunrise.
Preti, Girolamo
Describes the Place where Cynthia Is Sporting Herself.
Pretorius, S. J.
Madman, The.
Prettyman, Quandra
Birth of the Poet, The.
Blues.
Crawl into Bed.
Lullaby: "Sleep, love, sleep."
Still Life: Lady with Birds.
When Mahalia Sings.
Prévert, Jacques
Belle Saison, La.
Dunce, The.
Late Rising.
To Paint the Portrait of a Bird.
Price, Arnold
I, a Justified Sinner.
Price, Daisy Conway
Easter Joy.
Follower, A.
Price, Edith Ballinger
To Patricia on Her Christening Day.
Price, Herbert
Buffalo, The.
Price, Laurence
Win at First and Lose at Last; or a New Game at Cards.
Price, Minnie
To "His" Mother.
Price, Nancy

Look, See the Cat.
Price, Nell Goodale
School Begins.
Price, Richard Geoffrey George
Who Walks by the Dockside.
Prideaux, Tom
Broadway: Twilight.
Skip-Scoop-Anellie.
Priest, Nancy Woodbury (Nancy Amelia Woodbury Wafield)
Over the River.
Priestley, Eric
Poetry.
Recreation.
"Primus."
Far from Somewhere.
Prince Frank Templeton
At a Parade.
Babiaantje, The.
Chaka.
False Bay.
In a Province.
Old Age of Michelangelo, The.
Question, The.
Soldiers Bathing.
Tears of a Muse in America, The.
To a Friend on His Marriage.
To a Man on His Horse.
Token, The.
Pringle, Thomas
Afar in the Desert.
Caffer Commando, The, *sel.*
Desolate Valley, The, *sel.*
Hark! heard ye the signals of triumph afar?
Hottentot, The.
Then, couched at night in hunter's wattled shieling.
Prinzivalle, Doria
Canzone: Of His Love.
Prior, Matthew
Against Modesty in Love.
Alma; or, The Progress of the Mind, *sel.*
Angry Lover, The.
Answer to Chloe [*or* Cloe] Jealous.
Answer to Jealousy.
Better Answer (to Cloe Jealous), A.
Chaste Florimel.
Cloe Jealous.
"Come here, my sweet Landlady, pray, how d'ye do?"
Cupid Mistaken.
Cupid's Mistaken.
Down Hall.
Dutch Proverb, A.
English Ballad, on the Taking of Namur by the King of Great Britain, 1695, An.
English Padlock, An.
Epigram: "Frank carves very ill, yet will palm all the meats."
Epigram: "Nobles and heralds, by your leave."
Epigram: "To John I owed great obligation."
Epigram: "When Pontius wished an edict might be passed."
Epigram: "Yes, every poet is a fool."
Epitaph, An: "Interred [*or* Interr'd] beneath this marble stone."
Epitaph on Himself.
Fable, A: "In Aesop's tales an honest wretch we find."
Farewell, A: "Venus, take my votive glass."
Female Phaeton, The.
For His Own Tomb-Stone.
For My Own Monument.
Fortune-Teller, The.
Garland, The.
Helen Was Just Slipped into Bed.
I Sent for Ratcliffe.
In Imitation of Anacreon.
Incurable, an Epigram, The.
Jinny the Just.
Lady Who Offers Her Looking-Glass to Venus, The.
Letter, A.
Letter to Lady Margaret Cavendish-Holles-Harley When a Child, A.
Letter to the Hon. Lady Miss Margaret Cavendish-Holles-Harley, A.
Love and Reason.
Lover's Anger, A [*or* The].
Matthew met Richard; when or where.
Merchant, to Secure His Treasure, The.
New Year's Gift to Phyllis, The.
Nonpareil.
Ode, An: "Merchant, to secure his treasure, The."
Ode, An: "While blooming youth, and gay delight."
On a Pretty Madwoman.
On Beauty; a Riddle.
On Critics.
On Exodus III, 14, I Am That I Am.
On Fleet. Shepheard's Takeing away a Child's Bread and Butter.
On My Birthday July 21.
On the Same [Helen].
Paraphrase from the French, A.
Phyllis's Age.
Picture of Seneca Dying in a Bath.
Power, *sel.*
Prior's Epitaph.
Protogenes and Apelles.
Question to Lisetta, The.
Quits.
Reasonable Affliction, A ("Helen was just slipped into bed").
Reasonable Affliction, A ("On his deathbed poor Lubin lies").
Remedy Worse than the Disease, The.
Secretary, The.
Simile, A.
Solomon.
Solomon on the Vanity of the World, *sels.*
Song: Dissembler, The.
Song, A: "If wine and music have the power."
Song, A: "In vain you tell your parting lover."
Song: "Merchant, to secure his treasure, The."
To a Child of Noble Birth.
To a Child of Quality [of Five Years Old].
To a Friend on His Nuptials.
To a Lady; She Refusing to Continue a Dispute with Me, and Leaving Me in the Argument.
To Chloe Jealous [a Better Answer].
To Cloe Jealous [a Better Answer].
To Cloe Weeping.
To the Honorable Charles Montague, Esq.
True Maid, A.
Verses by Mr Prior.
Written at The Hague, in the Year 1696.
Written in a Lady's Milton.
Written in an Ovid.
Written in the Beginning of Mézeray's History of France.
Ye sons of men, with just regard attend.
Pritchard, Glenn
Great stone frog doorstop, The.
Stone Frog, The.
Pritchard, N. H.
Metagnomy.
Pritzkow, Louis W.
Take Back Your Gold.
Probyn, May
Bees of Middleton [*or* Myddleton] Manor, The.
Beloved, The.
Christmas Carol, A: "Lacking samite and sable."
"Is It Nothing to You?"
Procter, Adelaide Anne
Angel's Story, The.
Annunciation, The.
Be Strong.
Cleansing Fires.
Doubting Heart, A.
Fidelis.
Give Me Thy Heart.
Give Me Thy Heart.
Giving.
Lead Me.
Legend, A.
Lost Chord.
No Star Is Ever Lost.
One by One.
Our Daily Bread.
Per Pacem ad Lucem.
Pilgrims, The.
Present, The.
Repose.
Requital.
Sacred Heart, The.
Shadows of the Evening Hours, The.
Thankfulness.
Warrior to His Dead Bride, The.
Who Is the Angel That Cometh?
Woman's Question[s], A.
Procter, Bryan Waller *See* **"Cornwall Barry"**
Proctor, Edna Dean
Brooklyn Bridge, The.
Captive's Hymn, The.
Cid of the West.
Columbia's Emblem.
Columbus Dying.
Forward.
Glory of Toil, The.
Heaven, O Lord, I Cannot Lose.
Heroes.
John Brown.
Lost War-Sloop, The.
Queen of the Year, The.
Sa-Cá-Ga-We-A.
Song of the Ancient People, The, *sel.*
Take Heart.
Proctor, Thomas
Mirror of Mortality, A.
Respice Finem.
Prokosch, Frederic
Conspirators, The.
Dolls, The.
Eclogue: "No one dies cleanly now."
Fable: "O the vines were golden, the birds were loud."
Festival, The.
Ode: "O happy the huntsman . . .,"V.
Propertius, Sextus
Ah Woe Is Me.
Complaint of Tarpeia's Door, The.
Cynthia, Cynthia.
Elegies, *sels.*
Hylas.
Light, Light of My Eyes.
Prayer for His Lady's Life.
Revenge to Come.
Turning Aside from Battles.
Watering Place, The.
Prosser-Thompson, Pauline
Marked for His Own.
Proudfit, David Law ("Peleg Arkwright")
Prehistoric Smith.
Willis, The.
"Prout, Father." *See* **Mahony, Francis Sylvester**
Provost, Barbara Jane
Holland.

Prowse, William Jeffery
City of Prague, The.
Prudentius (Aurellus Clemens Prudentius)
Before Sleep.
Burial of the Dead, The.
Cathemerinon, *sel.*
Holy Innocents, The.
Know thou, O Virgin, noble-blest.
Laudate for Christmas.
O Noble Virgin.
Of the Father's Love Begotten.
Prudhomme, Sully- *See* **Sully-Prudhomme**
Prys, Thomas
Trouble at Sea.
Prys-Jones, Arthur Glyn
St. Govan.
Pudney, John
After Bombardment.
For Johnny.
Map Reference T994724.
Missing.
On Seeing My Birthplace from a Jet Aircraft.
Stiles.
To You Who Wait.
Pugliesi, Giacomino
Canzone: Of His Dead Lady.
Canzonetta: Of His Lady in Absence.
Pulci, Luigi
Appeal for Illumination.
Morgante maggiore, Il, *sels.*
Prophecy.
Pullen, Alice Muriel
Quest Eternal, The.
Pullen, Elisabeth Jones Cavazza
Alicia's Bonnet.
Derelict.
Her Shadow.
Love and Poverty.
Sea-Weed, The.
Pullman, George Conrad
His Passion.
Pulsifer, Harold Trowbridge
Duel, The.
Harvest of Time, The.
I Accept.
Immortal Living.
Of Little Faith.
Peace.
Riderless Horse, The.
Thoughts upon a Walk with Natalie, My Niece, at Houghton Farm.
Pulsifer, Susan Nichols
Sounding Fog, The.
Tall City.
Purcell, Elsie B.
Distribution.
Purcell, Henry
Come Ye Sons of Art.
Purcell, Victor William Williams Saunders *See* **"Buttle, Myra."**
Purdy, Alfred W.
At Roblin Lake.
Dead Seal.
Evergreen Cemetery.
Landscape.
Rattlesnake, The.
Sculptors, The.
What Do the Birds Think?
Wilderness Gothic.
Winemaker's Beat-étude, The.
Purohit Swami
I Know That I Am a Great Sinner.
Miracle Indeed, A.
Shall I Do This?
Pushkin, Aleksandr Sergeyevich
Autumn.
Coach of Time, The.
Crucifix, The.
Gay Feast.
Grapes.
I Loved You Once.
Message to Siberia.
No, Never Think.
Portrait.
Prophet, The.
Three Springs.
To Madame A. P. Kern.
Upas Tree, The.
Verses Written during a Sleepless Night.
When in My Arms.
Winter Evening.
With Freedom's Seed.
Work.
Putinas
Torches Have Gone Out, The.
Putnam, Edith Palmer *See* **Painton, Edith Putnam**
Putnam, Howard Phelps (Phelps Putnam)
About Women.
Ballad of a Strange Thing.
Hasbrouck and the Rose.
Hymn to Chance.
Romeo and Juliet.
To the Memory of Yale College.
Puttenham, George
Cruel You Be.
Pyke, B. K.
Blacksmith.
Pyle, Katharine
Dandelion, The.
Sea Princess, The.
September.
Sweet Tooth, The.
Visitor, The.

Q

"Q." *See* **Quiller-Couch, Sir Arthur Thomas**
"Q. B. M." *See* **"M., Q. B"**
Quarles, Francis
Argalus and Parthenia, *sels.*
Authour's Dreame, The.
Behold thy darling, which thy lustfull care.
Canticle.
Child Jesus, The.
Compass Needle, A.
Delight in God Only.
Dependence on God.
Divine Care.
Divine Rapture, A.
Draw near, brave sparks, whose spirits scorn to light.
Emblems, *sels.*
Epigram: "Nay, soft and fair, good world; post not too fast."
Epigram: "Paul's midnight voice prevail'd; his music's thunder."
Epigram: "Peace, childish Cupid, peace: thy fingered eye."
Epigram: Respice Finem.
Epigram: "What makes thee, fool, so fat? fool, thee so bare?"
Eternal God! O Thou that only art.
Even like Two Little Bank-dividing Brooks.
False World, Thou Ly'st.
Forme of Prayer, A.
God Who Hides, The.
Good-Night, A.
Great All in All, that art my rest, my home.
He Is Mine.
Hos Ego Versiculos.
How shall my tongue expresse that hallow'd fire?
Human Touch, The.
I Am My Beloved's, and His Desire Is towards Me.
Like to the Arctic Needle.
Man's Plea.
Mary and Martha.
My Beloved Is Mine, and I Am His; He Feedeth among the Lilies.
My Glass Is Half Unspent.
My soule is like a bird; my flesh, the cage.
Mystical Ecstacy, A.
O Whither Shall I Fly?
On the Infancy of Our Saviour.
On the Needle of a Sundial.
On the Plough-Man.
On Those That Deserve It.
On Zacheus.
Respice Finem.
Shekel in the Fish's Mouth, The.
Song: "Oh, the fickle state of lovers!"
Vanity of the World, The.
Wherefore Hidest Thou Face, and Holdest Me for Thine Enemy?
Why Dost Thou Shade Thy Lovely Face?
Wilt Thou Set Thine Eyes upon That Which Is Not?
World's a floore, whose swelling heapes retaine, The.
World's a Sea, The.
Quarles, John, *and* Henry Francis Lyte
Long Did I Toil.
My Beloved Is Mine, and I Am His.
Quasimodo, Salvatore
Alleyway.
Ancient Winter.
And Suddenly It's Evening.
Gentle Hill, The.
High Sailboat, The.
Man of My Time.
Rain's Already with Us, The.
Quayle, William A.
All's Well.
Quennell, Peter
Divers, The.
Flight into Egypt, The.
Hero Entombed, I.
Leviathan.
Music met Leviathan returning, A.
Procne.
Small Birds.
Sunflower, The.
While I Have Vision.
Queremel, Angel Miguel
Manifesto of the Soldier Who Went Back to War.
"Querno, Camillo." *See* **Odell, Jonathan**
Quevedo y Villegas, Francisco Gómez de
Death Warnings.
Letrilla; the Lord of Dollars.
Mighty Lord Is Money, A.
On Lisa's Golden Hair.
Sonnet: Death Warnings.
Quick, Dorothy
Forest, The.
House of Life.
Monster, The.
Undertone.
Quigless, Helen G.
At the Ebony Circle.
Circled by a Horsefly.
Concert.
Lip Service.
Quiller-Couch, Sir Arthur Thomas ("Q")
Alma Mater.
Chant Royal of High Virtue.
De Tea Fabula.
Famous Ballad of the Jubilee Cup, The.
Lady Jane (Sapphics).
Letter, A.

Retrospection.
Sage Counsel.
Splendid Spur, The.
Tim the Dragoon.
Upon Eckington Bridge, River Avon.
Upon New Year's Eve.
White Moth, The.
Quillevic
Monsters.
Quillinan, Edward
Hour Glass, The.
Quinn, John
Foxhole for the Night, A.
Quinn, John Robert
Whistling Boy.
Quinn, Roderic
By Momba Tracks.
Camp within the West, The.
Circling Hearths, The.
Fisher, The.
Hidden Tide, The.
Mid-Forest Fear.
Quint, Beverly
View, A.
Quintana, Manuel José
Ode to Spain—after the Revolution of March, *sel.*
Swear, "Rather death than tyrants in the land."
Quintero, Serafín Alvarez, *and* **Joaquín Avarez Quintero** *See* **Alvarez Quintero**
Quirino, Giovanni
Sonnet: To Dante Alighieri (He Commends the Work of Dante's Life).
To Dante Alighieri.
Quirk, Charles J.
Countersign, The.
On the Parapet of Notre Dame.

R

"R., D. N."
His Return.
"R., E. H."
Big Arm-Chair, The.
"R., E. M. G."
Midsummer Moon.
"R., J."
Knife, The.
"R., J. A."
"Can God?"
"R., L."
Till He Come.
"R. B." *See* **"B., R"**
"R. K. B." *See* **"B., R. K"**
"R. L. B." *See* **"B., R. L"**
Rab (Abba Arika)
Kingdom of God, The.
Rabéarivelo *or* **Rebéarivelo, Jean-Joseph**
Flute Players.
Here She Stands.
What Invisible Rat.
Rabelais, Francois
Inscription Set upon the Great Gate of Theleme, The, *abr.*
Rabi'a, Daughter of Kab
Curse, A.
"Rachel" (Rachel Blumstein)
Barren.
Dawn.
Jonathan.
Kinnereth.
To My Country.
Racine, Jean
Athalie, *sel.*
Chorus: "God whose goodness filleth every clime, The."
Conquest of Love, The.
Phèdre, *sels.*
Radcliffe, Alexander
As concerning Man.
Call to the Guard by a Drum, A.
Epitaph on Mr. John Sprat, Late Steward of Grayes-Inn.
Epitaph upon the Worthy and Truly Vigilant, Sam. Micoe Esq., An.
Ramble, The.
Upon Mr. Bennet, Procurer Extraordinary.
Wrote in the Banquetting-House in Grayes-Inn-Walks.
Radcliffe, Martin
Is God Dead?
Radford, Dollie (Dollie Maitland)
Ah, Bring It Not.
Buttercups.
If All the World.
Model, A.
My Little Dear.
October.
Radford, Ernest
Plymouth Harbor.
Quiet.
Radishchev, Aleksandr
Sapphic Stanzas.
Raffel, Burton
On Watching the Construction of a Skyscraper.
Raffetto, Bertha
Home Means Nevada.
Raffles, Thomas
O Lord! My Hiding Place.
Rafi of Merv
Roses of Thy Cheeks, The.
Raftery, Anthony
County Mayo, The.
I Am Raftery [*or* Raferty].
Raftery, Gerald
Apartment House.
Lineman.
New Dynamo.
On a Dead Teacher.
Rago, Henry
Coming of Dusk upon a Village in Haiti, The.
Fountains of fire, The.
Knowledge of Light, The.
Meeting of a Poetry Society.
Monster, The.
Promise Your Hand.
Sky of Late Summer, A, *sel.*
Rahman Yusuf (Ronald Stone)
Transcendental Blues Transcendental Blues.
"Raimar, Freidmund." *See* **Rückert, Friedrich**
Raine, Kathleen Jessie
Air.
Beinn Naomh, *sel.*
By the River Eden.
Crystal Skull, The.
Daisies of Florence.
Desire.
Easter Poem.
Envoi: "Take of me what is not my own."
Fall, The.
For Posterity.
Goddess, The.
Human Form Divine, The.
Images.
In the Beck.
In Time.
Invocation: "There is a poem on the way."
Invocation of Death.
Isis Wanderer.
Lachesis.
Last Things.
Let in the wind.
London Night.
Love Poem: "Yours is the face that the earth turns to me".
Lyric: "Bird sings on a matin tree, A."
Message from Home.
Moment, The.
Natura Naturans.
Night in Martindale.
Nocturne: "Night comes, an angel stands."
Northumbrian Sequence, *sels.*
Old Paintings on Italian Walls.
On Leaving Ullswater.
Parting.
Puer Aeternus.
Pure I was before the world began.
Pythoness, The.
Question and Answer.
Requiem.
Rock, *sel.*
Scala Coeli.
Seen in a Glass.
Seventh Day.
Shells.
Silver Stag, The.
Spell of Creation.
Spell of Sleep.
Statues.
Still Life.
Still Pool, The.
Summit, The.
There is a stream that flowed before the first beginning.
There is stone in me that knows stone.
To My Mountain.
"Tu Non Se' in Terra, Si Come Tu Credi. . ."
Water, *sel.*
Worry about Money.
Rainer, Dachine
Ashokan.
At Eighty-seven.
Epithalamium for Cavorting Ghosts.
Night Musick for Thérèse.
Samis Idyll.
Upon Being Awakened at Night by My Four Year Old Daughter.
Rainsford, Christina
Shadbush.
Rak, Ján
Illusion.
Ralegh, Sir Walter
Advice, The.
Affection and Desire.
All the World's a Stage.
Another of the Same ("The praise of meaner wits").
Answer to Marlowe.
Author's Epitaph, Made by Himself the Night before His Death, The.
But stay, my thoughts, make end, give fortune way.
Come to Me Soon.
Conceit Begotten by the Eyes.
Conclusion, The.
Description of Love, A.
Diana.
E'en Such Is Time.
Eleventh and Last Book of the Ocean to Cynthia, The.
Epitaph: "Even such is Time, which takes in trust."
Epitaph on the Earl of Leicester.
Even Such Is Time.
Excuse, The.
Faery Queen, The.
False Love.
Farewell to False Love, A.
Farewell to the Court.
Feed Still Thyself.
Her Reply.
His Epitaph.

Ralegh (continued)
His Petition to Queen Anne of Denmark (1618).
His Pilgrimage.
Homage to Diana.
If Cynthia Be a Queen.
In Commendation of George Gascoigne's Steel Glass.
In Commendation of The Steel Glass.
Last Lines.
Lie, The.
Lines from Catullus.
Lines Written the Night Before His Execution.
Love and Time.
Merit of True Passion, The.
Methought I Saw the Grave Where Laura Lay.
My Body in the Walls Captived.
My Pilgrimage.
My Woe Must Ever Last.
Nature, That Washed Her Hands [in Milk].
Now What Is Love.
Nymph's Reply to the Shepherd, The.
Ocean to Cynthia, The.
Ocean's Love to Cynthia, The.
Of Spenser's Faery Queen.
On the Cards and Dice.
On the Life of Man.
On the Snuff of a Candle.
Passionate Man's Pilgrimage, The.
Petition to the Queen.
Pilgrimage, The.
Poem Entreating of Sorrow, A.
Poem Put into My Lady Laiton's Pocket, A.
Poesy to Prove Affection Is Not Love, A.
Praise of meaner wits this work like profit brings, The.
Praised Be Diana's Fair and Harmless Light.
Prognostication upon Cards and Dice, A.
Reply.
Shepherd's Praise of Diana, The.
Silent Lover, The.
Sir Walter Ralegh the Night before His Death.
Sir Walter Ralegh to His Son.
Sir Walter Raleigh to the Queen.
Sir Walter Raleigh's Verses, Found in His Bible in the Gatehouse at Westminster.
Soul's Errand, The.
Sufficeth it to you, my joys interred.
Sweet are the thoughts where hope persuadeth hap.
Sweet Unsure.
Three Things There Be That Prosper Up Apace.
To His Love When He Had Obtained Her.
To His Mistress.
To His Son.
To Queen Elizabeth.
To seeke new worlds, for golde, for prayse, for glory.
To the Queen.
To the Translator of Lucan's Pharsalia (1614).
Verses: "Even such is time."
Verses Found in His Bible in the Gate-House at Westminster.
Verses Written in His Bible.
Virtue the Best Monument.
Vision upon This Conceit of the Faerie [*or* Faery] Queene, A.
What Is Our Life?
What tears, dear prince, can serve to water all.
With youth, is deade the hopes of loves returne.
Wood, the Weed, the Wag, The.
Written on the Night before His Execution.

Raleigh, Sir Walter Alexander (1861-1922)
Artist, The.
Ballade of the Goth.
Eating Song.
Ode to Himself.
Stans Puer and Mensam.
Wishes at a Garden Party.
Wishes of an Elderly Man, The.

Ralph, Nathan
When They Grow Old.

Ramage, Joyce
My Companion.

"Ramal, Walter." *See* **De la Mare, Walter**

Ramanujan, A. K.
Irregular Sonnet for a Marraige.

Ramie, Marian
Will You, One Day.

Ramos, Felix V.
Look, the Soldiers!

Ramsaur, Hugh Wilgus
Epitaph, Found Somewhere in Space.
World-Ruin.

Ramsay, Allan
An Thou Were My Ain Thing.
Carle He Came o'er the Croft, The.
Caterpillar and the Ant, The.
Dainty Sang, A.
Gentle Shepherd, The, *sels.*
Give Me a Lass [with a Lump of Land].
Katy's Answer.
Lochaber No More.
My Peggy [Is a Young Thing].
Ode to Mr. F ——, An.
Peggy.
Poet's Wish, The; an Ode.
Polwart on the Green.
Sang: "My Peggy is a young thing".
Song: "At setting day and rising morn."
Twa Books, The.
Up in the Air.
Widow, The.
Young Laird and Edinburgh Katy, The.

Ramsay, Allen Beville
No teacher I of boys or smaller fry.

"Ramsay, Joan" (Louise Wilson)
Green Branches.
Saint Francis of Assisi.

Ramsdell, Katherine L.
Harder Task.

Ramsey, Thomas Weston
Caught by Chance.
Power Station.

Ranaivo, Flavien
Love Song: "Do not love me, my friend."
Song of a Common Lover.

Ranchan, Som Parkash
Swan Song.

Rand, Kenneth
Lonely Road, The.

Rand, Theodore Harding
Dragonfly, The.
June.
Loon, The.

Randall, Dudley
Blackberry Sweet.
Booker T. and W. E. B.
George.
Legacy: My South.
Melting Pot, The.
Memorial Wreath.
Perspectives.
Primitives.
Profile on the Pillow, The.
Southern Road, The.
Souvenirs.

Randall, E.
Crossroads, The.

Randall, James Ryder
After a Little While.
John Pelham.
Magdalen.
Maryland! My Maryland!
My Maryland.
Thou wilt not cower in the dust.
Why the Robin's Breast Was Red.

Randall, Laura Lee
Our Circus.

Randall, Margaret
He says we are beggars.
Retracing Paul Blackburn's Transit, *sel.*

Randall, Virginia D.
October Winds.

Randall-Mills, Elizabeth
Crossing the County Line.

Randolph, Anson Davies Fitz
Master's Invitation, The.

Randolph, Innes
Good Old Rebel.
Rebel, The.

Randolph, James
We sit and talk, and kiss away the hours.

Randolph, Thomas
Amyntas; or, The Impossible Dowry, *sel.*
Aristippus, *sel.*
Being set, let's sport a while, my fair.
Charm, A.
Devout Lover, A.
Drinking Song.
Eclogue [*or* Eglogue] to Mr. Johnson, An.
Eglogue to Mr. Johnson, An.
Elegie, An: "Love, give me leave to serve thee, and be wise."
Fairies' Song.
Fairy Song.
Gratulatory to Mr. Ben Johnson for His Adopting of Him to Be His Son, A.
He Lives Long Who Lives Well.
Jealous Lovers, The, *sel.*
Maske for Lydia, A.
Now come, my boon companions.
Ode on Leaving the Great Town.
Ode to Mr. [*or* Master] Anthony Stafford to Hasten Him into the Country, An.
On a Maid [*or* Maide] of Honour Seen by a Scholar in Somerset Garden.
On the Death of a Nightingale.
Parley with His Empty Purse, A.
Pastoral Courtship, A, *sel.*
Poetry and Philosophy.
Song of Fairies Robbing an Orchard.
To One Admiring Herself [*or* Her Selfe] in a Looking-Glass.
Upon His Picture.
Upon Love Fondly Refus'd for Conscience Sake.
Upon the Losse of His Little Finger.

Rands, William Brighty ("Matthew Browne")
Blue Boy in London, The.
Brown Bee.
Cat of Cats, The.
Child's World, The.
Clean Clara.
Cuckoo in the Pear-Tree.
Cuckoo's Palace.
Dolladine.
Dream of a Boy Who Lived at Nine-Elms, The.
Dream of a Girl Who Lived at Seven-Oaks, The.
Dream of a Little Boy Who Lived at Nine-Elms, The.
Dream of a Little Girl Who Lived at Seven-Oaks, The.
Dressing the Doll.

Drummer-Boy and the Shepherdess, The.
Father, Now My Prayer Is Said.
First Tooth, The.
Fishing Song, A.
Flowers, The.
Gipsy Jane.
Godfrey Gordon Gustavus Gore.
Gypsy Jane.
Happy World, The.
I Saw a New World.
Kitten Speaks, The.
Kitty: What She Thinks of Herself.
Lilliput Levee.
Little Christel.
Love and the Child.
Lullaby: "Baby wants a lullaby."
Lullaby: "Wind whistled loud at the window-pane, The."
Peddler's Caravan, The.
Pedlar's [*or* Peddler's] Caravan, The.
Polly.
Polly Pansy.
Praise and Love.
Reformation of Godfrey Gore, The.
Shooting Song, A.
Stalky Jack.
Thought, The.
Topsy-turvy World.
White Princess, The, *sel.*
Wonderful World, The.
World, The.
World, The; a Child's Song.

Rankin, Jeremiah Eames
Babie, The.
Fairest of Freedom's Daughters.
God Be with You till We Meet Again.
Word of God to Leyden Came, The.

Rankins, William
Satire Septimus Contra Sollistam.

Ranko [*or* Reinko],
Fall of the Plum Blossoms, The.
Plum Blossoms ("So sweet the plum trees smell").
Plum Trees.
Summer Night.

Ransetsu
Play About, Do.

Ransom, John Crowe
Address to the Scholars of New England.
Agitato Ma Non Troppo.
Amphibious Crocodile.
Antique Harvesters.
Armageddon.
Bells for John Whiteside's [Whitesides, *wr.*] Daughter.
Blackberry Winter.
Blue Girls.
Captain Carpenter.
Conrad in Twilight.
Dead Boy.
Dog.
Emily Hardcastle, Spinster.
Equilibrists, The.
First Travels of Max.
Good Ships.
Her Eyes.
Here Lies a Lady.
Husband Betrayed.
Inland City.
Janet Waking.
Judith of Bethulia.
Lady Lost.
Little Boy Blue.
Man without Sense of Direction.
Master's in the Garden Again.
Miriam Tazewell.
Miss Euphemia.
Of Margaret.
Old Man Playing with Children.
Old Man Pondered.
Old Mansion.
Painted Head.
Painting; a Head.
Parting at Dawn.
Parting, without a Sequel.
Persistent Explorer.
Philomela.
Piazza Piece.
Prelude to an Evening.
Somewhere Is Such a Kingdom.
Spiel of the Three Mountebanks.
Survey of Literature.
Swimmer, The.
Tall Girl, The.
Tom, Tom, the Piper's Son.
Triumph.
Two in August.
Two Sonnets, *sel.*
Vaunting Oak.
Vision by Sweetwater.
What Ducks Require.
Winter Remembered.
Yea.

Rao, K. Raghavendra
Journey to Golotha, The.

Raphael, Lennox
Infants of Summer.

Raplee, Elizabeth Virginia
Poet Considers Perfection, The.

Rappoport, Solomon *See* **"Ansky, S."**

Rascas, Bernard
Love of God, The.

Rashidd, Amir
Eclipse.

Rashidd, Niema
Warriors Prancing, Women Dancing.

Rashley, R. E.
Caterpillar.
Portrait of an Indian.
Voyageur.

Raskin, Philip M.
Dreams.

Ratcliffe, Dorothy Una
February.
Pirates' Tea-Party, The.
St. Bridget's Lullaby.
Song of Nidderdale, The.

Ratner, Rochelle
Artist Paints Dawn, An.
Maiden, The.
Migrant Workers.
What We Remember.
Yellow Apples.

Ratti, John
Division.

Rauschenbusch, Walter
For This World, *sel.*
Little Gate to God, The.
Postern Gate, The, *sel.*

Ravenel, Beatrice
Intervals.

Ravenscroft, Edward
Citizen Turned Gentleman, The, *sel.*
I Sigh All the Night.
In Derision of a Country Life.
Italian Husband, The, *sel.*

Ravenscroft, Thomas
Hawking for the Partridge.
Madrigal: "My mistress is as fair as fine."

Rawes, Henry Augustus
Last Hour, The.
Veni, Domine Jesu!

Rawnsley, Hardwicke Drummond
Ballad of the Conemaugh Flood, A.
Father, Whose Will Is Life and Good.
Old Parish Church, Whitby, The.

Raworth, Tom
Ah the Poetry of Miss Parrot's Feet Demonstrating the Tango.

Rawson, Grindall
To the Learned and Reverend Mr. Cotton Mather, on His Excellent Magnalia.
Upon the Death of His Much Esteemed Friend Mr. Jno Saffin Junr.

Ray, David
On a Fifteenth-Century Flemish Angel.
On the Poet's Leer.
Problems of a Writing Teacher, The.
X-Ray.

Ray, Louise Crenshaw
Middle-aged Quixote.
Philippine Madonna.
Steel Mills after Midnight.

Ray, Maude Louise
My Task.

Rayaprol, Srinavas
On Growing Old.

Raybin, Alex
Conversation, The.
Dream.
Letter, A.
Me to You.
Poem for Martha.
Strength of Willows, The.
Sunny Day.
Titan's Lament.

Raymond, Grace (Annie Raymond Stillman)
Birth.

Raymond, Richard C.
Burial.

Raymond, Rossiter W.
Christus Consolator.
Concerning Them That Are Asleep.

Read, Henri Charles
Ghosts.

Read, Sir Herbert
Analysis of Love, The.
Beata l'Alma.
Bombing Casualties: [in] Spain.
Champ de Manoeuvres.
Childhood.
Contrary Experience, The.
Cranach.
Crucifix, The.
Day's Affirmation.
Device.
End of a War, The.
Equation.
Execution of Cornelius Vane, The.
Falcon and the Dove, The.
Garden Party.
Happy are those who can relieve.
Happy Warrior, The.
Lu Yün's Lament.
Mutations of the Phoenix, *sel.*
My Company.
Nature has perpetual tears.
Night Ride.
Northern Legion, A.
Ode: Written during the Battle of Dunkirk, May, 1940.
Ode Written during the Battle of Dunkirk, May, 1940, *sel.*
Phoenix, bird of terrible pride.
Refugees, The.
Retreat, The.
Seven Sleepers, The.
Sic et Non.
Song for the Spanish Anarchists, A.
Sorrow of Unicume, The.
Summer Rain.
Time Regained.
To a Conscript of 1940.
Tourists in a Sacred Place.
Villages Démolis ("The villages are strewn").
White Isle of Leuce, The.
Woodlands.
World within a War, A.

Read, John
Down by the Old Mill Stream.

Read, Thomas Buchanan

Read (continued)
Attack, The.
Blennerhassett's Island.
Brave at Home, The.
Closing Scene, The.
Drifting.
Eagle and Vulture, The.
Flag of the *Constellation,* The.
Lines to a Blind Girl.
New Pastoral, The, *sel.*
Rising, The.
Sheridan's Ride.
Valley Forge.
Wagoner of the Alleghanies, The, *sels.*
Windy Night, The.
Realf, Richard
Apocalypse.
"De Mortuis Nil Nisi Bonum."
Defence of Lawrence, The.
Holy Nation, A.
Indirection.
O Earth!
Of Liberty and Charity, *sel.*
Old Man's Idyl, An.
Symbolisms, *sel.*
Word, The.
World, The.
Reaney, James
Alphabet, The.
Branwell's Sestina.
Chough, The.
Clouds.
Drunken Preacher's Sermon, The.
Gramophone, The.
Great Lakes Suite, The.
Horn, The.
January.
June.
Katzenjammer Kids, The.
Klaxon.
Le Tombeau de Pierre Falcon.
November.
Now is the ox-eyed daisy out.
Oracular Portcullis, The.
Orange Lilies.
Plum Tree, The.
Red Heart, The.
Suit of Nettles, A, *sels.*
To the Avon River above Stratford, Canada.
Two Kites, The.
Reavey, George
This Age, This Faust.
Reber, Clara Smith
Freedom.
Rebolledo, Conde Bernardino de
Clora!
"Redcam, Tom" (Thomas Henry McDermot)
San Gloria.
Redden, Laura Catherine *See* **Searing, Laura Catherine**
Redgrove, Peter
Against Death.
Bedtime Story for My Son.
Corposant.
Dismissal.
Early Morning Feed.
For No Good Reason.
Ghostly Father, The.
I Stroll.
New Forms.
On Catching a Dog-Daisy in the Mower.
Required of You This Night.
Shearing Grass.
Story from Russian Author.
Wizard's New Meeting, The.
Redi, Francesco
Bacchus in Tuscany, *sels.*
Bacchus's Opinion of Wine, and Other Beverages.
Creation of My Lady, The.
Redman, Ben Ray
How Could You Know?
Redmond, Eugene
Evanescent Love.
God in Vietnam.
Rush City—the Hole.
Spring in the Jungle.
Redpath, Beatrice
But I Shall Weep.
Star, The.
Reece, Byron Herbert
Pretty Polly.
Ruthless Moon, The.
Reece, Mrs. Sam
Which Side Are You On?
Reed, Anna Nelson
Message, A.
Reed, Clarence
Harlem '67.
In a Harlem Store Front Church.
Invaders, The.
My Brother and Me.
Reed David, Jr.
Love Me, and the World Is Mine.
Reed, Edward Bliss
Despair.
Heritage, The.
O God, thy ways are dark.
Poplars.
Prayer: "She cannot tell my name."
September.
September Is Here.
Reed, Henry
Auction Sale, The.
Chard Whitlow.
Chrysothemis.
Door and the Window, The.
From the far horizon, and breaking in triumph towards him.
Judging Distances.
Lessons of the War (I-III).
Lives.
Map of Verona, A.
Morning.
Naming of Parts.
Place and the Person, The, *sel.*
Sailor's Harbor.
Unarmed Combat.
Wall, The.
Reed, Ishmael
Beware: Do Not Read This Poem.
Feral Pioneers, The.
I Am a Cowboy in the Boat of Ra.
Sermonette.
Reed, J. D.
Lost Silvertip.
Reports Come In, The.
Reed, John
Fog.
Proud New York.
Sangar.
Reed, Langford
Limerick: "Consider the lowering lynx."
Reed, Mary Davis
One Year to Live.
Reed, Nan Terrell
Forget-me-not Day.
Life.
Vases.
Reedburg, Robert
Epitaph to a Man.
Yesterday's Child.
Rees, A. A.
Workers with Him.
Reese, Lizette Woodworth
After.
Anne.
Apples.
April Weather.
At Cockcrow.
Bible Stories.
Book, A.
Carol, A: "Joseph was an old man."
Carol, A: "Mary the Mother sang to her Son."
Christmas Folk-Song, A.
Common Lot, The.
Compensation.
Crows.
Daffodils.
Daily Round.
Dust, The.
Flower of Mullein, A.
Ghost Night.
Girl's Mood, A.
Good Friday.
Good Joan, The.
Heroism.
His Mother in Her Hood of Blue.
Holiday, A.
Immortality.
In Harbor.
In Time of Grief.
Keats.
Lark, The.
Little Song of Life, A.
Love Came Back at Fall o' Dew.
Lydia.
Lydia Is Gone This Many a Year.
Miracle.
Old Saul.
Ownership.
Portrait of a Florentine Lady, The.
Possessions.
Prayer of an Unbeliever.
Puritan Lady, A.
Reserve.
Road of Remembrance, The.
Robert Louis Stevenson.
Scarcity.
Song of Life, A.
Spicewood.
Spring Ecstasy.
Street Scene, A.
Sun and the Rain, The.
Sunrise.
Surety.
Taps.
Tears.
Tell Me Some Way.
Telling the Bees.
That Day You Came.
This Very Hour.
Thistledown.
Thomas à Kempis.
Thrift.
To a Town Poet.
Trust.
White Fury of the Spring, The.
Wild Cherry.
Wise.
Women.
Written in a Song Book.
Reese, Lowell O.
Snagtooth Sal.
Reese, S. Carolyn
Letter from a Wife.
Reeve, F. D.
Alcoholic.
Falls, The.
We Settled by the Lake.
Reeve, Paul Eaton
Succumbing.
Reeves, Claude
Down on Roberts' Farm.
Reeves, James
Beech Leaves.
Black Pebble, The.
Catullus to Lesbia.
Chickamungus, The.
Cows.

De Fesch.
Doctor Emmanuel.
Doze, The.
Fireworks.
Giant Thunder.
Grand Opera.
Grim and Gloomy.
Intruder, The.
Knew the Master.
Little Brother, The.
Little Fan.
My Singing Aunt.
Old Crabbed Men.
Old Wife and the Ghost, The.
Pig Tale, A.
Queer Things.
Shiny.
Snail, The.
Spells.
Three Singing Birds, The.
Two Old Women of Mumbling Hill, The ("The two old trees on Mumbling Hill").
Under Ground.
Violin Concerto, A.
W.
Wandering Moon, The.
What Kind of Music?
You'd Say It Was a Funeral.
Reeves, Katherine
Enigma.
Reeves, William Pember
Albatross, The.
Colonist in His Garden, A.
Dutch Seamen and New Holland, The.
New Zealand.
Nox Benigna.
Passing of the Forest, The.
Régnier, Henri de
Autumn Twilight.
Je ne veux de personne auprès de ma tristesse.
Night.
Régnier, Mathurin
Epitaph on Himself.
Reich, Max Isaac
For Every Man.
One Thing Needful, The.
Reid, Alastair
Calenture.
Casa d'Amunt.
Daedalus.
Day the Weather Broke, The.
Figures on the Frieze, The.
For Her Sake.
Game of Glass, A.
Geneva.
Ghosts.
Ghosts' Stories.
Glass Town, The.
In Memory of My Uncle Timothy.
Instance, An.
Isle of Arran.
Lesson in Handwriting, A.
Me to You.
Outlook Uncertain.
Pigeons.
Poet with Sea Horse.
Question in the Cobweb, The.
Small Sad Song.
Tale the Hermit Told, The.
To a Child at the Piano.
To Lighten My House.
Who Can Say.
Reid, Alice
Ragged Robin and Bouncing Bet.
Reid, Barrie
Nothing.
St. Kilda.
Reid, Dorothy E.
Men.
Mrs. Winkelsteiner.
Reinko *See* **Ranko**
Reinmar von Hagenau
As on the Heather.
Childish Game, A.
Reinmar von Zweter
Fortitude.
I Came a-Riding.
Reinosa, Rodrigo De
Offerings.
Reis, Lindoln
North Wind, The.
Reis, Yitzhok *See* **Nadir, Moishe**
Reisen, Abraham
Burn Out Burn Quick ("Burn out, my life, burn quick").
Healing.
Two Songs.
Watchman, The.
Reitz, Albert Simpson
Blessed Secret, The.
Circumstances.
Cradle and the Cross, The.
Still Will I Trust.
Thy Will Be Done.
Reitz, Shirley Elizabeth
They Watched Him There.
"Remus, Uncle." *See* **Harris, Joel Chandler**
Rendall, Elizabeth
And of Laughter That Was a Changeling.
Buttercup Cow.
Needs.
Wind, The.
Rendall, Robert
Planticru, The.
Shore Tullye.
Renfrow, Grace B.
My Choice.
That's Jesus!
Trusting Jesus.
Upheld by His Hand.
Who Is on the Lord's Side?
Rengetsu
Voices of Pine Trees, The.
Rennell, James Rennell Rodd, 1st Baron *See* **Rodd, James Rennell, 1st Baron Rennell**
Renton, William
Fisher, The.
Pale Cold Moon, The.
Rentoul, Annie Isobel
Fairy Frolics.
Rentoul, John Laurence
Australia, *abr.*
Renwick, Mattie M.
We Thank Thee.
Repass, E. A.
My Neighbor.
Replansky, Naomi
Good Day's Work, A.
Repplier, Agnes
Le Repos en Egypte; the Sphinx.
Sphinx, The.
Resendez, Renée
Trouble Is, The, *sel.*
Reuental, Neidhart von *See* **Neidhart von Reuental**
Revere, Paul
Unhappy Boston.
Rexford, Eben Eugene
Bluebird, The.
On Easter Morning.
Sign of Spring, A.
Silver Threads among the Gold.
Trust; a Song.
Rexroth, Kenneth
About the Cool Water.
Advices from Rexroth's Bestiary.
Antipater of Thessalonica.
Bestiary, A, *sels.*
Deer.
Doubled Mirrors.
For Mary.
Herring.
Kings River Canyon.
Letter to William Carlos Williams, A.
Letter to Yvor Winters, A.
Lion.
Living Pearl, A.
Lyell's Hypothesis Again.
Marcus Argentarius.
Maximian Elegy V.
Mother Goose Rhyme.
Our Canoe Idles in the Idling Current.
Quietly.
Racoon ("The racoon wears a black mask").
Rogation Days.
Signature of All Things, The, *sel.*
Sword in a Cloud of Light, A.
They are murdering all the young men.
This Shall Be Sufficient.
Thou Shalt Not Kill, *sel.*
When I dragged the rotten log.
You.
Reyes, Alfonso
Gulf of Mexico.
Reyes Basualto, Neftalí Ricardo *See* **"Neruda, Pablo"**
Reynolds, Elizabeth Gardner
Little Black Dog, The.
Reynolds, George Nugent
Mary Le More.
Reynolds, Henry
Love above Beauty.
Song: "Was it a form, a gait, a grace."
Was It a Form [a Gate, a Grace]?
Reynolds, John
Garden's Queen, The.
Nosegay, A.
Reynolds, John Hamilton
Farewell to the Muses.
Gallantly within the Ring.
Peter Bell [a Lyrical Ballad].
Sonnet: "Sweet poets of the gentle antique line."
Sonnet to ——.
To Keats.
To Spenser.
Reynolds, Lucile Hargrove
To the New Owner.
Reznikoff, Charles
After Reading Translations of Ancient Texts on Stone and Clay.
English in Virginia, The (April, 1607).
Group of Verse, A.
In the street I have just left.
Lamps Are Burning, The.
Park is green and quiet, The.
Shopgirls leave their work, The.
Te Deum.
Two girls of twelve or so at a table.
Walk about the Subway Station.
Wind blows the rain into our faces, The.
Rhabanus Maurus
Sancte Confessor.
Rhinelander, Philip H.
Bathtub Gin.
Hangover.
It's Very Unwise to Kill the Goose.
Rhinow, Arthur B.
And Yet.
Unknown Soldier, The.
Victory.
Rhoades, James
In Whom We Live and Have Our Being.
Rhodes, Eleanor Taylor
Because You Passed My Way.
Rhodes, Hugh
Advice.
Rhodes, Margaret G.

Rhodes (continued)
Best of All, The.
Carol Singers, The.
Rhodes, Nettie
Our Largest and Smallest Cities.
Rhody, Randy
Orphans.
Rhys, Ernest
Autobiography, An.
Ballads of the Last Prince, The, *sel.*
Brechva's Harp Song.
Clio.
Dagonet's Canzonet.
Diana.
London.
London Feast.
Lost in France.
Mountain Liberty.
Old Men, The.
Song of Happiness, A.
Song of the Wulfshaw Larches.
True Love.
White Roses.
Words.
Rhys, Keidrych
Good Shepherd, The.
Letter to My Wife.
Third and Fourth.
Tragic Guilt.
Rice, Albert
Black Madonna, The.
To a Certain Woman.
Rice, Cale Young
Chanson of the Bells of Osenèy.
Kinchinjunga.
Litany for Latter-Day Mystics, A.
Mary at Nazareth.
Mystic, The.
New Dreams for Old.
Nights on the Indian Ocean.
On the Moor.
Peace Triumphant.
Providence.
Submarine Mountains.
To the Afternoon Moon, at Sea.
Wife of Judas Iscariot, The.
Rice, Elizabeth Stanton
Christmas.
Rice, Grantland
Alumnus Football.
First Division Marches, The.
For when the One Great Scorer comes.
Songs above the Dust.
Two Sides of War.
You'll find the road is long and rough, with soft spots far apart.
Rice, Harvey
Cuba.
Rice, Helen Steiner
"Heavens Declare the Glory of God, The."
In Hours of Discouragement God Is Our Encouragement.
Spring Song.
What More Can You Ask.
Rice, Sir Cecil Arthur Spring- *See-* **Spring-Rice, Sir Cecil Arthur**
Rice, Stan
Autumn.
On the Murder of Martin Luther King.
Pier in Berkeley, The.
Power, The.
Rebirth.
Rice, Wallace
Armstrong at Fayal, The.
Battle-Song of the *Oregon.*
Blood Is Thicker than Water.
Brooklyn at Santiago, The.
Defeat and Victory.
Destroyer of Destroyers, The.
Dewey and His Men.
End, The.
First American Sailors, The.
First Fruits in 1812.
Immortal Flowers.
Jackson at New Orleans.
Minute-Men of North Boro', The.
Spain's Last Armada.
Sudbury Fight, The.
Sweet Clover.
Under the Stars.
Wheeler's Brigade at Santiago.
Rich, Adrienne Cecile
After Dark.
Annotation for an Epitaph.
At a Bach Concert.
At Majority.
Aunt Jennifer's Tigers.
Autumn Sequence.
Bears.
Breakfast in a Bowling Alley in Utica, New York.
Celebration in the Plaza, The.
Change of World, A.
Charleston in the 1860s.
Corpse-Plant, The.
Double Monologue.
Epilogue for a Masque of Purcell.
Face to Face.
For the Conjunction of Two Planets.
Ghazals.
Holiday.
"I Am in Danger—Sir."
Insomniacs, The.
Knot, The.
Like This Together.
Living in Sin.
Love in the Museum.
Lucifer in the Train.
Middle-aged, The.
Mourning Picture.
New Year's Eve in Troy.
Orient Wheat.
Orion.
Parting, The.
Pictures by Vuillard.
Raven, The.
Recorders in Italy.
Revivalist in Boston, A.
Roofwalker, The.
Stranger, The.
Survivors, The.
33.
Tourist and the Town, The.
Trees, The.
Tryst in Brobdingnag, A.
Versailles.
Walk by the Charles, A.
Rich, Barnabe
Barnabe Rich, Gentleman Soldier, in Praise of the Author.
Epitaph upon the Death of Sir William Drury, An.
Rich, Hiram
Jerry and Me.
Morgan Stanwood.
Skipper-Hermit, The.
Rich, Richard
Newes from Virginia.
Richard, Edward
Pastoral Poem, *sel.*
Poet's Welcome, The.
Richard Coeur de Lion (Richard Lion-Heart)
Prison Song.
Richard of Caistre
Hymn to Jesus, A.
Richards, Edward Hersey
Question & Answer.
Wise Old Owl, The.
Richards, Ivor Armstrong
Future Simple.
Spendthrift.
Richards, Joseph Addison
Boat, The.
Master of My Boat, The.
My Boat.
Richards, Laura Elizabeth
Alice's Supper.
Antonio.
At Easter Time.
Baby Goes to Boston, The.
Ballad of China, A.
Bird Song.
Cave-Boy, The.
Crocodile, The.
Dandy Cat, The.
Difference, The.
Egg, The.
Eletelephony.
Emily Jane.
Five Little Princesses, The.
Fussy.
Giraffe and the Woman, The.
Gregory Griggs.
High Barbaree, The.
In Foreign Parts.
In Samarcand.
Jippy and Jimmy.
Johnny's By-low Song.
Jumbo Jee.
Kindness to Animals.
Legend of Lake Okeefinokee, A.
Legend of Okeefinokee, A.
Little Brown Bobby.
Little Cossack, The.
Little John Bottlejohn.
Mermaidens, The.
Mrs. Snipkin and Mrs. Wobblechin.
Molly Pitcher.
Monkeys and the Crocodile, The.
Nicholas Ned.
Nonsense Verses.
Nursery Song, A.
Owl and the Eel and the Warming-Pan, The.
Owl, the Eel and the Warming-Pan, The.
Party, A.
Ponsonby Perks.
Postman, The.
Prince Tatters.
Sleepyland.
Sleigh-Ride. A.
Some Fishy Nonsense.
Song of the Cornpopper, The.
Song of Two Angels, A.
"Talents Differ."
Umbrella Brigade, The.
Valentine, A.
Was She a Witch?
Where Helen Sits.
Why Does It Snow?
Why I No Longer Travel.
Richardson, Charles Francis
After Death.
Conjecture, A.
Hundred Noble Wishes, A.
Perfect Life, The.
Prayer: "If, when I kneel to pray."
Richardson, Dorothy M. (Mrs. Alan Odle)
Buns for Tea.
Richardson, George Lynde
Classical Criticism.
Richardson, Helen W.
What Are You Building?
Richardson, Isla Paschal
Raindrops.
Richardson, Justin
Afterthought.
All Awry.
Back Room Joys.
Garlic.

High-Life Low-Down.
La Carte.
Oocuck, The.
Red Wine.
Titles.
What'll Be the Title?
Richardson, Marion Muir
Gold Seekers, The.
Richardson, Norman E.
Prayer for Aviators, A.
Richardson, Robert
Epitaph: "Warm summer sun."
Epitaph Placed on His Daughter's Tomb [by Mark Twain].
Richardson, Sherman D.
Denver Jim.
Richardson, Thomas
Proper New Song Made by a Student in Cambridge, A.
Take Heed of Gazing Overmuch.
Richmond, Rebecca
Death is a clean bold word and has no second meaning.
Richstone, May
Naming the Baby.
Rickard, Truman E., *and* Arthur Upson
Hail! Minnesota!
"Ricketty Kate." *See* **"Kate, Ricketty"**
Rickword, Edgell
Cascade, The.
Cosmogony.
Rimbaud in Africa.
Riddell, Elizabeth
Children March, The.
Country Tune.
Forebears.
Lifesaver.
News of a Baby.
Old Sailor, The.
Train in the Night, The.
Under the Casuarina.
Wakeful in the Township.
Riddell, Henry Scott
Scotland Yet.
Ridenour, Lois Elizabeth
Only a Word.
Ridge, Lola
Altitude.
April of Our Desire.
Art and Life.
Bees, The.
Débris.
Edge, The.
Faces.
Ghetto, The, *sels.*
Iron Wine.
Legion of Iron, The.
"Lights go out."
Marie.
New Orleans.
Old Sodos no longer makes saddles.
Reveille.
Sallow dawn is in the sky, A.
Snow-Dance for the Dead.
Song, The: "That day, in the slipping of torsos and straining flanks."
Sons of Belial.
To E. A. R.
Wind in the Alleys.
Ridhiana
Tricked Again.
Riding, Laura
Auspice of Jewels.
Because of Clothes.
Dear Possible.
Flowering Urn, The.
For-ever Morning.
Lucrece and Nara.
Map of Places, The.
Nor Is It Written.
Not All Immaculate.
Respect for the Dead.
Three Sermons to the Dead.
Tiger, The.
Tillaquils, The.
Troubles of a Book, The.
Way of the Air, The.
Wind Suffers, The.
Wind, the Clock, the We, The.
Ridings, J. Willard
Thesaurus Nightmare, A.
Ridler, Anne
Bathing Song.
Beads from Blackpool.
Before Sleep.
Bring Back.
Bunhill's Fields.
Christmas and Common Birth.
Deus Absconditus.
Dream Observed, A.
Edlesborough.
For a Child Expected.
For a Christening.
In Regent's Park.
Letter, A.
Lumber of Spring.
Making Love, Killing Time.
Matter of Life and Death, A. *sel.*
Mile from Eden, A.
News of the World.
Now as Then.
Now Philippa Is Gone.
O Love, Answer.
Of the Unscathing Fire.
Phoenix Answered, The.
Piero della Francesca.
Poem for a Christmas Broadcast.
River God's Song.
Sick Boy.
Speech of the Dead, The.
Spring Equinox, The.
Stone Angel.
Venetian Scene.
Zennor.
Riedemann, Myra von
Horses.
Last Will of the Drunk.
There Are Places.
Rieu, Emile Victor
Dirge for a Bad Boy.
Flattered Flying Fish, The.
Lesser Lynx, The.
Meditations of a Tortoise Dozing under a Rosetree near a Beehive at Noon While a Dog Scampers About and a Cuckoo Calls from a Distant Wood.
Night Thought of a Tortoise Suffering from Insomnia on a Lawn.
Soliloquy of a Tortoise on Revisting the Lettuce Beds after an Interval of One Hour While Supposed to Be Sleeping in a Clump of Blue Hollyhocks.
Two People.
Rigby, Ralph
Branding Iron Herd, The.
Riggs, Katherine Dixon
Mockery.
Riggs, Lenore
Bathtub Bay.
Riggs, Lynn
Spring Morning—Sante Fé.
Rihaku *See* **Li Po**
Riley, Athelstan
Ye Watchers and Ye Holy Ones.
Riley, James Whitcomb
Away.
Back to Griggsby's Station.
Barefoot Boy, A.
Beetle, The.
Bereaved.
Boy's Mother, A.
Days Gone By, The.
Dwainie.
Elf Child, The.
Extremes.
Faith.
Flying Islands of the Night, The, *sel.*
Funniest Thing in the World, The.
Going to the Fair.
Good-by er Howdy-do.
He Is Not Dead.
Honey Dripping from the Comb.
Ike Walton's Prayer.
Impetuous Resolve, An.
Just Be Glad.
Kentucky Thoroughbred, The.
Knee-Deep in June.
Let Something Good Be Said.
Life-Lesson, A.
Like His Mother Used to Make.
Lincoln.
Lincoln—the Boy.
Little Orphant Annie.
Little Red Ribbon, The.
Liz-Town Humorist, A.
Longfellow ("The winds have talked with him confidingly").
Love's Prayer.
Lugubrious Whing-Whang, The.
Man by the Name of Bolus, A.
Man in the Moon, The.
Monument for the Soldiers, A.
Name of Old Glory, The.
Old John Henry.
Old Man and Jim, The.
Old Sweetheart of Mine, An.
Old Swimmin'-Hole, The.
Old Times Were the Best, The.
On the Death of Little Mahala Ashcraft.
Our Hired Girl.
Out of the Hitherwhere.
Out to Old Aunt Mary's.
Parting Guest, A.
Prayer Perfect, The.
Prior to Miss Belle's Appearance.
Raggedy Man, The.
Rain.
Runaway Boy, The.
Sea Song from the Shore, A.
Session with Uncle Sidney, A, *sel.*
Spirk Troll-Derisive.
Sudden Shower, A.
Three Jolly Hunters, The.
Way the Baby Slept, The.
Way the Baby Woke, The.
Wee Little Worm, A.
When She Comes Home.
When the Frost Is on the Punkin.
Riley, May Louise *See* **Smith, May Riley**
Rilke, Rainer Maria
Abishag.
Adam.
Almost a girl it was, then, issuing.
Archaic Torso of Apollo.
Autumn.
Autumn Day.
Birth of Christ.
Birth of Mary.
Book of Hours, The, *sel.*
Buddha in Glory.
Dancer: O you translation.
Duino Elegies, The, *sel.*
Eingang (Prelude).
Emmaus.
Eve.
Extinguish My Eyes.
Flamingos, The.
For, Lord, the Crowded Cities Be.
Four Sonnets to Orpheus.
From a Childhood.
Garden of Olives, The.

Rilke (continued)
Harrowing of Hell, The.
I Praise.
I Would Comprehend Thee.
Initiation.
Joseph's Suspicion.
Lament: "Oh, everything is far."
Last Evening.
Last Supper, The.
Love-Song.
Lute, The.
Many have painted her. But there was one.
Merry-Go-Round, The.
Neighbor, The.
Oh, come and go, you almost child, entrancing.
O this is the beast that does not have being!
Olive Garden, The.
On the Death of Mary.
Palm of the Hand.
Poet, The.
Pont du Carrousel.
Praise.
Prayer of the Maidens to Mary.
Presaging.
Prisoner, The.
Put Out My Eyes, and I Can See You Still.
Remembrance.
Ripe apple, the banana and the pear.
Silent Hour.
Solemn Hour.
Solitary, The.
Solitude.
Song of Love, The.
Sonnets to Orpheus, *sels.*
Strophes: "There is one who takes all men within his hand."
Third Duino Elegy, The.
Though the world is changing fast.
To the Angel.
Tree ascending there, O pure transcension, A!
Tree rose up, A. O clear transcendency!
We Are All Workmen.
What Stillness around a God!
What Will You Do, God, When I Die?
You Are the Future.
You, Neighbor God.
Youth Dreams, The.

Rimbaud, Arthur
Barbarian.
Bridges, The.
Charleville.
Chercheuses de Poux, Les.
Childhood, *sels.*
Drunken Boat, The.
Evil.
Flowers.
Hunger.
I have stretched ropes from belfry to belfry.
Illuminations, *sels.*
Lice-Finders, The.
Lice Seekers, The.
Louse-Catchers, The.
Memory.
My Bohemia.
Ophelia.
Phrases, *sel.*
Poor in Church, The.
Sensation.
Seven-year-old Poet.
Shame.
Sleeper of the Valley, The.
Song of the Highest Tower.
Sonnet: "Dead men of 'ninety-two, also of 'ninety-three."
Tear.
Waifs and Strays.

Rimos Moses, of Majorca
Elegy: "Tumult of death, dizziness hath seized me, The."

Rinaldo d'Aquino
Crusade, The.

Rinkart, Martin
Now Thank We All Our God.

Risch, Warren
Am I Running from You, Jesus?

Risley, Richard Voorhees
Dewey in Manila Bay.

Rita Agnes, Sister
Limits.
On Moving into a Skylight Room.

Rito
Tea Flowers.

Rittenhouse, Jessie Belle (Mrs. Clinton Scollard)
Debts.
My Wage.
Nightingales of Surrey, The.
Seven Times the Moon Came.
Transformation.
Youth.

Ritter, Margaret Tod
Faith, I Wish I Were a Leprechaun.
Indictment.

Ritter, Ruth
Lament for One's Self.

Rive, Richard
Where the Rainbow Ends.

Rivers, Conrad Kent
Four Sheets to the Wind and a One-Way Ticket to France.
In Defense of Black Poets.
Invisible Man, The.
On Passing Two Negroes on a Dark Country Road Somewhere in Georgia.
On the Death of William Edward Burghardt Du Bois.
Still Voice of Harlem, The.
Subway, The.
To Richard Wright.
Train Runs Late to Harlem, The.
Watts.

Rives, Amélie (Princess Troubetzkoy)
Before the Rain.
Mood, A.
My Laddie.
Sonnet, A: "Take all of me—I am thine own, heart, soul."

Rizal, José
My Last Thought.

Roads, Helen Purcell
Centurion, The.
Test.

Robb, Ethel
Child's Evensong.
Christmas "Good Night."

Robbins, Howard Chandler
Put Forth, O God, Thy Spirit's Might.
Saviour, Whose Love Is like the Sun.
Spirit from Whom Our Lives Proceed.
Via Lucis.

Robbins, Martin
Spring Is a Looping-free Time.

Robbins, S. D.
Master, The.

Roberson, Ed
Eclipse.
18,000 Feet.
Othello Jones Dresses for Dinner.

Robert II, King of France
Strength, Love, Light.

Robert, Jeanne *See* **Foster, Jeanne Robert**

Roberts, Cecil Edric Mornington
Charing Cross.
Prayer for a Pilot.
Prayer for the Pilot.
Springtime in Cookham Dean.

Roberts, Sir Charles G. D.
Afoot.
Aim, The.
April Adoration, An.
As Down the Woodland Ways.
At Tide Water.
Autochthon.
Ballad of Manila Bay, A.
Bird's Song, the Sun, and the Wind, The.
Book of the Native, The, *sel.*
Brook in February, The.
Brooklyn Bridge.
Burnt Lands.
Canada.
Deserted City, The.
Domine Cui Sunt Pleiades Curae.
Epitaph for a Sailor Buried Ashore.
Flight of the Geese, The.
Frosted Pane, The.
Going Over.
Hawkbit, The.
Herring Weir, The.
Ice.
Iceberg, The.
In Apia Bay.
In the Barn-Yard's Southerly Corner.
In the Night Watches.
In the Wide Awe and Wisdom of the Night.
Isles, The.
Keepers of the Pass, The.
Kinship.
Logs, The.
Marsyas.
Mowing, The.
Night Sky, The.
O Earth, Sufficing All Our Needs.
O Solitary of the Austere Sky.
On the Road.
Pea-Fields, The.
Potato Harvest, The.
Recessional, The.
Salt Flats, The.
Solitary Woodsman, The.
Sower, The.
Tantramar Revisited.
Unknown City, The.
When the Sleepy Man Comes.

Roberts, Daniel C.
National Hymn: "God of our fathers, whose almighty hand."

Roberts, Dick (Richard Edwin Roberts)
Duty to Death, LD.

Roberts, Dorothy
Goose Girl, The.
Sisters.

Roberts, Elizabeth Madox
August Night.
Autumn.
Autumn Fields.
Ballet Song of Mary, A.
Big Brother.
Butterbean Tent, The.
Child Asleep, A.
Christmas Morning.
Cinderella's Song.
Circus, The.
Cornfield, The.
Crescent Moon.
Dick and Will [and Charles and I].
Evening Hymn.
Father's Story.
Firefly.
Grandmother, The.
Hens, The.
Horse.
Little Rain.
Milking Time.
Mr. Wells.
Mumps.

My Heart.
Orpheus.
People, The.
People Going By.
Picnic, The.
Pilaster, The.
Rabbit, The.
Richest Woman, The.
Shells in Rock.
Sky, The.
Strange Tree.
Stranger.
Twins, The.
Water Noises.
Wolves, The.
Woodcock of the Ivory Beak.
Woodpecker, The.
Worm, The.
Roberts, Frederick T.
Cup, The.
Roberts, G. D.
Old Morgan.
Roberts, Homer
Pa's Chickens.
Roberts, Jane Elizabeth Gostwycke
In the Golden Birch.
Roberts, John
Kept Every Moment.
Roberts, LeVan
Unemployed, The.
Roberts, Lloyd
Changing Year, The.
Deep Dark River.
Fruit Rancher, The.
One Morning When the Rain-Birds Call.
Roberts, Lynette
Low Tide.
Poem from Llanybri.
Seasons, The.
Shadow Remains, The.
These Words I Write on Crinkled Tin.
Roberts, Michael
Caves, The.
Der Arme Poet.
Green Lake, The.
Hymn to the Sun.
In Our Time.
In the Strange Isle.
Les Planches-en-Montagne.
Midnight.
St. Gervais.
St. Ursanne.
Shining Dark.
World's End, The.
Roberts, Richard Edwin *See* **Roberts, Dick**
Roberts, Theodore Goodridge
Blue Heron, The.
Fiddler's Green.
Lost Shipmate, The.
Maid, The.
Reformed Pirate, The.
Wreckers' Prayer, The.
Roberts, Walter Adolphe
Boyhood Etchings.
Captains, The.
Cat, The.
Maroon Girl, The.
On a Monument to Marti.
Peacocks.
San Francisco.
Tropic Storm.
Tropic Sunset.
Vieux Carré.
Villanelle of the Living Pan.
Villanelle of Washington Square.
Roberts, William H.
I Will Believe.
Robertson, Clyde
Mistress of the Matchless Mine.
Woman in the Wagon, The.
Yellow Witch of Caribou, The.
Robertson, Edith Anne
Deean Tractorman, Clear, The.
Robertson, Harrison
Kentucky Philosophy.
Two Triolets.
What He Said.
What She Thought.
Robertson, James Logie ("Hugh Haliburton")
Spring on the Ochils.
Robertson, Lexie Dean
Gossip.
New Temples.
Robertson, T. A. ("Vagaland")
Tuslag.
Robertson, W. Graham
Glad day.
Other Side of the Sky, The.
Sand Castles.
Snowdrops.
Robey, George
Limerick: "Eccentric old person of Slough, An."
Robin, Ralph
Take Notice.
Robins, Henry Burke
Better a Day of Faith.
City of God, The.
Eternal Spirit, Evermore Creating.
Life of Our Life.
Of One Blood Hath God Created.
One Hundred Fifty-first Psalm, A.
Robinson, Agnes Mary Frances (Mme Emile Duclaux)
Ah Me, Do You Remember Still.
Ballad of Orleans, A.
Celia's Home-coming.
Cockayne Country.
Darwinism.
Dawn-Angels.
Etruscan Tombs.
Le Roi Est Mort.
Let Us Forget.
Orchard at Avignon, An.
Red May.
Retrospect.
Rispetto: "What good is there, ah me, what good is Love?"
Rosa Rosarum.
Sometimes When I Sit Musing All Alone.
Temple Garlands.
Tuscan Cypress, *sels.*
Twilight.
Robinson, Anne
April and May.
Conversation.
Drummer, The.
To Laddie.
Robinson, Annie Douglas Green *See* **"Douglas, Marian"**
Robinson, Corinne Roosevelt
Belovèd, from the Hour That You Were Born.
Forgotten Countersign, The.
Life, a Question.
Lincoln.
Path That Leads to Nowhere, The.
Sagamore.
Valiant-for-Truth.
Robinson, David G.
City Council.
Life in California.
Miner's Lament, The, II ("I've just come down from the mines").
Seeing the Elephant.
Robinson, Edwin Arlington
Aaron Stark.
Altar, The.
Another Dark Lady.
As It Looked Then.
Ballade by the Fire.
Ballade of a Ship.
Ballade of Dead Friends.
Ben Jonson Entertains a Man from Stratford.
Bewick Finzer.
Calvary.
Captain Craig, *sel.*
Caput Mortuum.
Cassandra.
Charles Carville's Eyes.
Children of the Night, The.
Christmas Sonnet, A.
Clavering.
Clerks, The.
Cliff Klingenhagen.
Credo.
Dark Hills, The.
Dear Friends.
Demos.
Discovery.
Dust of Timas, the.
Eros Turannos.
Eutychides.
Exit.
Field of Glory, The.
Firelight.
Flammonde.
For a Dead Lady.
For Arvia.
Fragment: "Faint white pillars that seem to fade."
George Crabbe.
Gift of God, The.
Glass Houses.
Growth of Lorraine, The.
Happy Man, A.
Here by the windy docks I stand alone.
Hillcrest.
House on the Hill, The.
How Annandale Went Out.
I doubt if ten men in all Tilbury Town.
Isaac and Archibald.
James Wetherell.
John Evereldown.
John Gorham.
Karma.
Klondike, The.
Leonora.
Llewellyn and the Tree.
Long Race, The.
Lost Anchors.
Luke Havergal.
Man against the Sky, The.
Many Are Called.
Master, The.
Mighty Runner, A.
Mill, The.
Miniver Cheevy.
Mr. Flood's Party.
Momus.
Monadnock through the Trees.
New England.
New Tenants, The.
Nimmo.
Oh for a Poet—for a Beacon Bright.
Octaves, *sels.*
Old King Cole.
Old Story, The ("Like many a one").
Old Story, An ("Strange that I did not know him then").
Out of Wisdom Has Come Love.
Pasa Thalassa Thalassa.
Pity of the Leaves, The.
Poem for Max Nordau, A.
Poor Relation, The.
Prodigal Son, The.
Prophet of dead words defeats himself, The.
Raven, The.
Return of Morgan and Fingal, The.

Robinson (continued)
Reuben Bright.
Revealer, The.
Richard Cory.
Sheaves, The.
Sonnet: "Master and the slave go hand in hand, The."
Sonnet: "Oh for a poet—for a beacon bright."
Souvenir.
Story of the Ashes and the Flame, The.
Tasker Norcross.
There Is One Creed, and Only One.
Thomas Hood.
Three Taverns, The, *sel.*
Too Much Coffee.
Torrent, The.
Toussaint L'Ouverture.
Town down the River, The.
Tree in Pamela's Garden, The.
Twilight Song.
Two Men.
Uncle Ananias.
Unforgiven, The.
Vain Gratuities.
Veteran Sirens.
Vickery's Mountain.
Walt Whitman.
Wandering Jew, The.
Why He Was There.
Zola.

Robinson, Edwin Meade
Annual Solution, The.
David Jazz, The.
Disagreeable Feature, A.
Fishers.
How Homer Should Have Written the Iliad.
It Happens, Often.
Limericised Classics.
Limerick: "Jug and a book [*or* Book and a jug] and a dame, A."
Ode to Eve.
Rubaiyat, The.
Sad September Sentiments.
Shakespeare Might Have Boiled Othello.
Song of the Movie Mexican, A.
Spoon River Anthology.
Story of Ug, The.
"To Lucasta, on Going to the Wars."
Villanelle of a Villaness.

Robinson, Eloise
To-Day I Saw Bright Ships.

Robinson, Elsie
Beauty as a Shield.
Help Me Today.
Pain.

Robinson, F. E.
Nothing the Blood Cannot Cover.

Robinson, Grant P.
I Fights Mit Sigel!

Robinson, Henry Morton
Chantey of Notorious Bibbers.
Cock-Crow; Woodstock.
December Fugitive.
Earth-canonized.
Heaven Tree.
November Fugitive.
Second Wisdom.

Robinson, John
More Truth and Light.

Robinson, Kenneth Allan
American Laughter.
Lines to Dr. Ditmars.

Robinson, Lucy Catlin
Ballade of Islands, A.
Fire i' the Flint. The.
"Hic Me, Pater Optime, Fessam Deseris."

Robinson, Mary K.
Brown Frog, The.
Dandelion Puff, The.
Queen Bee, The.

Robinson, R. H.
Light at Evening Time.

Robinson, Robert
Hymn of Praise.

Robinson, Roland Edward
And Each Man's Leave.
Casuarina.
Dancers, The.
I Breathed into the Ash.
Lyre-Bird, The.
Rock-lily's Pale Spray, The.
Tank, The.
Tea-Tree and the Lyrebird, The.
To a Mate.
Tumult Ends, The.
Waratah.

Robinson, Selma
Bus Ride.
Ferry Ride, *sel.*
Gentle Name.
Harvesting.
Pendulum Rhyme.
Summer Shower.

Robinson, T. L.
Twang.

Robinson, Ted
April.
Ditty: "Time was long and long ago, The."
Sure.
Unfaith.

Robinson, Tom
Autumn Color.
Hard Lines.
Little Lady Wren.
Look and See.
My Dog.
Pansies.
Rabbit.
Shoes.
Swallow Tails.

Robinson, Tracy
Song of the Palm.

Robinson, Wade
Possession.

Robinson, Wey
Horse & Rider.

Roche, James Jeffrey
"Albemarle" Cushing.
Andromeda.
Boston Lullaby, A.
Constitution's Last Fight, The.
Don't.
Fight of the *Armstrong* Privateer, The.
First Citizen.
Flag, The.
Gettysburg.
Gospel of Peace, The.
If.
Jack Creamer.
Kearsarge, The.
Lament of the Scotch-Irish Exile.
Men of the Alamo, The.
My Comrade.
Nature the False Goddess.
Net of Law, The.
No Angel Led.
Panama.
Reuben James.
Sailor's Yarn, A.
Skeleton at the Feast, The.
Three Doves.
V-a-s-e, The.
Washington.
Way of the World, The.

Roche, Paul
Brick, The.
Courage for the Pusillanimous.

Rochester, John Wilmot, 2d Earl of
Allusion to Horace, An. The 10th Satire of the 1st Book.
Charles the Second.
Chaste Arabian Bird, The.
Constancy.
Description of Maidenhead, A.
Dialogue between Strephon and Daphne, A.
Disappointment, The.
Epigram: "Here lies a great and mighty King."
Epitaph on Charles II.
Et Cetera.
Fall, The.
Farewell to the Court, *sel.*
Grecian Kindness.
His Mistress.
History of the Insipids, The, *sel.*
I Cannot Change as Others Do.
Imperfect Enjoyment, The.
Impromptu on Charles II.
Insulting Beauty.
King Charles II.
King's Epitaph, The.
Letter, A, *sel.*
Letter from Artemisa in the Town, to Cloe, in the Country, A.
Love and Life: A Song.
Love—the most generous passion of the mind.
Lycias.
Maimed [*or* Maim'd] Debauchee, The.
Mistress, The: A Song.
My Dear Mistress.
My Light Thou Art.
My Lord All-Pride.
On Charles II.
Pastoral Courtship, A.
Plain Dealing's Downfall.
Platonic Lady, The.
Return.
Satire: Maimed Debauchee, The.
Satire against Mankind, A.
Song, A: "Absent from thee I languish still."
Song, A: "As Chloris [*or* Cloris] full of harmless thoughts."
Song: "Drink about till the day find us."
Song, A: "Give me leave to rail at you."
Song: "I cannot change as others do."
Song: I Promised Sylvia.
Song: "Love a woman! y'are an ass."
Song: "My dear mistress has a heart."
Song: "Phillis, be gentler I advise [*or* advice]."
Song: "Too late, alas! I must confess."
Song: "'Twas a dispute 'twixt heav'n and earth."
Song: "While on those lovely looks I gaze."
Song of a Young Lady to Her Ancient Lover, A.
Song to Cloris, A.
Spoken Extempore.
Tired with the noisome follies of the age.
To a Lady in a Letter.
To His Mistress.
Upon His Drinking [a] Bowl.
Upon His Leaving His Mistress.
Upon Leaving His Mistress.
Upon Nothing.
While on Those Lovely Looks I Gaze.
Wretched Man.

Rock, Francis J.
"Tell Ye the Faint of Heart."

Rock, Madeleine Caron
He Is the Lonely Greatness.

Rockett, Winnie Lynch
Invincible.

Mother before a Soldier's Monument, A.
Potion, The.
Rockwell, Margaret
Hiroshima.
Rodd, James Rennell, 1st Baron Rennell
Actea.
Daisy, The.
Imperator Augustus.
Roman Mirror, A.
Song of Autumn, A.
Then and Now.
When I Am Dead.
Rodenbach, Georges
You Are My Sisters.
Roder, M. Joyce
"If I Had Prayed."
Rodger, Alexander
Behave Yoursel' before Folk.
Rodgers, Carolyn M.
Eulogy.
Jesus Was Crucified or: It Must Be Deep.
Newark, for Now (68).
Non Poem about Vietnam, A.
U Name This One.
We Dance Like Ella Riffs.
Rodgers, William Robert
Airman, The.
And There Was Mary Magdalene and the Other Mary, Sitting Over against the Sepulchre.
A
Apollo and Daphne.
Autumn.
Awake!
Beagles.
Carol: "Deep in the fading leaves of night."
Christ Walking on the Water.
Direction to a Rebel.
Express.
Fountains, The.
It was a deliberate moment, and O.
Lent.
Life's Circumnavigators.
Lovers, The.
May, and the wall was warm again.
Nativity.
Neither Here nor There.
Net, The.
Pan and Syrinx.
Raider, The.
Resurrection—an Easter Sequence, *sel.*
Sing, Brothers, Sing!
Snow.
Song for Peace.
Song for War.
Spring.
Stormy Day.
Stormy Night.
Summer Holidays.
Swan, The.
White Christmas.
Winter's Cold.
Rodigast, Samuel
My Trust.
Rodman, Frances
Lost Dog.
Spring Cricket.
Rodman, Selden
Consuelo at the Country Club.
Daphne.
Eadem Mutato Resurgo.
Harpers Ferry.
Lawrence; the Last Crusade, *sel.*
Man, Not His Arms.
Norris Dam.
On a Picture by Pippin, Called "The Den."
Out of the East the plane spun; over rolling.
V-Letter to Karl Shapiro in Australia.
Rodman, Thomas P.
Battle of Bennington, The.
Rodríguez del Padrón, Juan
Prayer to the Blessed Virgin.
To the Virgin.
Roethke, Theodore
Academic.
Adamant, The.
All Morning.
Bat, The.
Beast, The.
Big Wind.
Centaur, The.
Child on Top of a Greenhouse.
Cow, The.
Cuttings, Later.
Cycle, The.
Dance, The.
Dinky.
Dolor.
Dream, The.
Dying Man, The, *sels.*
Elegy: "Her face like a rain-beaten stone on the day she rolled off."
Elegy for Jane.
Epidermal Macabre.
Exulting, The.
Far Field, The.
Field of Light, A.
First Meditation.
Flight, The.
Forcing House.
Four for Sir John Davies.
Frau Bauman, Frau Schmidt, and Frau Schwartze.
Geranium, The.
Give Way, Ye Gates.
Gull rides on the ripples of a dream, A.
Harsh Country, The.
Heard in a Violent Ward.
Heron, The.
Highway: Michigan.
I Cry, Love! Love!
I Knew a Woman [Lovely in Her Bones].
I'm Here.
In a Dark Time.
In Evening Air.
Infirmity.
Interlude.
Journey to the Interior.
Lady and the Bear, The.
Light Breather, A.
Light Comes Brighter, The.
Light Listened.
Long Waters, The.
Longing, The.
Lost Son, The.
Love's Progress.
Marrow, The.
Meadow Mouse, The.
Meditation at Oyster River.
Meditations of an Old Woman.
Mid-country Blow.
Mistake, The.
Moment, The.
Moss-gathering.
Motion, The.
My Papa's Waltz.
Night Crow.
Night Journey.
On love's worst ugly day.
On the Road to Woodlawn.
Open House.
Orchids.
Otto.
Partner, The.
Pipling.
Poem: "I knew a woman, lovely in her bones."
Praise to the End!
Prayer: "If I must of my senses lose."
Prayer before Study.
Reply, The.
Reply to a Lady Editor.
Root Cellar.
Rose, The.
Sensualists, The.
Sententious Man, The.
Sequel, The.
Shape of the Fire, The.
She.
"Shimmer of Evil, The."
Sloth, The.
Small, The.
Snake.
Song, The: "I met a ragged man."
Song: "Under a southern wind."
Song for the Squeeze-Box.
Specialist.
Supper with Lindsay.
They Sing.
They Sing, They Sing.
Thing, The.
Transplanting.
Vernal Sentiment.
Vigil, The.
Visitant, The.
Voice, The.
Waking, The.
Walk in Late Summer, A.
Weed Puller.
What Can I Tell My Bones?
Words for the Wind.
Yak, The.
Roger, F. M.
Other Mother, The.
Rogers, Alex
Rain Song, The.
Signs of Rain.
Why Adam Sinned.
Rogers, D. H.
At Sea.
Homeward Bound.
Rogers, F.
Wishes.
Rogers, John
Upon Mrs. Anne Bradstreet Her Poems.
Rogers, Robert Cameron
Dancing Faun, The.
Doubt.
Health at the Ford, A.
Rosary, The.
Shadow Rose, The.
Sleeping Priestess of Aphrodite, A.
Virgil's Tomb.
Rogers, Samuel
Another and the Same.
Bologna, and Byron.
Byron Recollected at Bologna.
Captivity.
Epitaph on a Robin Redbreast, An.
Fond Youth.
Ginevra.
Human Life, *sels.*
Inscription on a Grot.
Interview near Florence, An.
Italy, *sels.*
Man's Going Hence.
On a Tear.
On J. W. Ward.
Pleasures of Memory, The, *sel.*
Robin's Epitaph, A.
Sleeping Beauty, The.
Wish, A.
Rogers, Thomas
Spirit of Night, The.
Rojas, Fernando de
Celestina, *sel.*
Now Sleep and Take Thy Rest.
Rokeah, David
Zealots of Yearning.

"Rokha, Pablo de" (Carlos Díaz Loyola)
Lament: "Weariness of the bones."
Roland, Patrick
Spring Burning.
Rolfe, Edwin
Definition.
Elegy for Our Dead.
No Man Knows War.
Poem to Delight My Friends Who Laugh at Science-Fiction, A.
Song: "Keep the dream alive and growing always."
Rolfe, Harvey E.
Resolutions?—New and Old.
Rolland, John
In haist ga hy thee to sum hoill.
Sevin Seages, The, *sel.*
Rolle of Hampole, Richard
For now, love thou, I rede, Christ, as I thee tell.
Love is a light burden that gladdeneth young and old.
Love Is Life, *sels.*
My Trewest Tresowre.
Song of Love for Jesus, A.
Song of the Love of Jesus, A.
Song of the Passion, A.
Rolleston, Thomas William Hazen
Cois na Teineadh.
Grave of Rury, The.
Night.
Song of Maelduin.
Rollins, Alice Wellington
Death of Azron, The.
Many Things Thou Hast Given Me, Dear Heart.
Vita Benefica.
Rolls, Eric
Little Sticks.
Sheaf-Tosser.
Rolnik, Joseph
Thank God.
Romaine, Harry
Ad Coelum.
Unattainable, The.
Romains, Jules
Another Spirit Advances.
Church, The.
Romanelli, Samuele
From Battle Clamour.
Love.
Romanes, George John
Simple Nature.
Romano, Jennie
Old Houses.
Romano, Liboria E.
All Souls.
Lyric Barber.
Romig, Ethel *See* **Fuller, Ethel Romig**
Romilu, Myrtle
If to Die.
Ronsard, Pierre de
Amours de Marie, *sels.*
And Lightly, like the Flowers.
Corinna in Vendome.
Deadly Kisses.
Four Sonnets to Helen.
Fragment of a Sonnet.
His Lady's Death.
His Lady's Tomb.
Odes, *sel.*
Of His Lady's Old Age.
On His Lady's Waking.
Pastoral Song for the Nuptials of Charles, Duke of Lorraine, *sel.*
Revenge, The.
Rose, The.
Roses.
Sonnets pour Hélène, *sels.*
Summer's Revel, The.
To Helen.
To His Young Mistress.
To the Moon.
Wager, The.
Rooker, Nettie
Mine Were the Streets of Nazareth.
Rooney, John Jerome
Ave Maria.
Beam of Light, A.
Empire Builder, The.
Homing, The.
Joined the Blues.
McIlrath of Malate.
Marquette on the Shores of the Mississippi.
Men behind the Guns, The.
Râhat, The.
Revelation.
Where Helen Comes.
Woodland Singer, The.
Rooney, William
Dear Dark Head.
Poet, The.
Root, Edward Merrill
Carpenter of Eternity.
Chicago Idyll.
Eucharist.
Even as the Bird.
Filling Station.
Flames.
Nativity, The.
Prayer for Dreadful Morning.
Pretty Polly.
Scrub Oak.
Still the Cross.
To Him Who Walks the Water.
War.
Youth and Death.
Root, George Frederick
Battle Cry of Freedom, The.
Just before the Battle, Mother.
Tramp! Tramp! Tramp!
Root, William Pitt
Circle of Struggle.
Ropes, Arthur Reed
In Pace.
Lost Pleiad, The.
On the Bridge.
Ropes, P. A.
Before Spring.
Bluebells.
Daffodils.
Disappointed Shrimper, The.
Dust.
Glow-Worms.
I Will Keep Christmas.
If.
In February.
Poppies.
Violets.
Watering Rhyme, A.
Rorie, David
Pawky Duke, The.
Rorty, James
Gray Shore.
Ros, Uilleam *See* **Ross, William**
Rosas Moreno, José
Caterpillar and the Butterfly, The.
Mocking Bird and the Donkey, The.
Roscoe, William
Butterfly's Ball, The.
Great God!
Roscoe, William Caldwell
Earth.
For Ever.
Master-Chord, The.
Parting.
Poetic Land, The.
Spiritual Love.
To La Sanscoeur.
Roscoe, William Stanley
To Spring.
To Spring; on the Banks of the Cam.
Roscommon, Wentworth Dillon, 4th Earl of
On the Death of a Lady's Dog.
Song on a Young Lady Who Sung Finely.
Rose, Alexander Macgregor ("A.M.R. Gordon")
Hoch! Der Kaiser.
Kaiser & Co.
Rose, Billy
Unknown Soldier, The.
Rose, Francis Howard
Martyr's Hymn, The, *ad.*
Rose, Greta Leora
Spring Is at Work with Beginnings of Things.
Rose, Margaret
Autumn Song.
Butterfly, The.
Little Bird's Song, A.
Little Fir Tree, The.
Magic Whistle, The.
November.
Rose, Mary Catherine
Clown, The.
Parade, A.
Rose, Maud
Little Things.
Rose, R. Selden, *and* **Leonard Bacon** *See* **Bacon, Leonard,** *and* **R. Selden Rose**
Roseliep, Raymond Francis
Alan.
Black Are the Stars.
GI.
In Time of Darkness.
Lady of Letters.
Professor Nocturnal.
Scissors Grinder, The.
Symphony in Blue.
To Mary; at the Thirteenth Station.
Tour in Rain.
Vendor.
Where Do I Love You, Lovely Maid?
Where Roots Tangle.
Youth Autumnal.
Rosenbaum, Benjamin
O Pity Our Small Size.
Rosenbaum, Nathan
Pictures at an Exhibition.
Rosenberg, Dorothy
Bim Bam.
Rosenberg, Isaac
Beauty.
Break of Day in the Trenches.
Burning of the Temple, The.
Chagrin.
Daughters of War.
Dead Heroes, The.
Dead Man's Dump.
Destruction of Jerusalem by the Babylonian Hordes, The.
Expression.
Female God, The.
Girl to Soldier on Leave.
God.
Home-Thoughts from France.
I Am the Blood.
If You Are Fire.
Immortals, The.
Jew, The.
Love and Lust.
Marching.
Midsummer Frost.
Moses; a Play, *sel.*
My Soul Is Robbed.
On a Lady Singing.
On Receiving News of the War.
One Lost, The.
Returning, We Hear the Larks.
Soldier; Twentieth Century.

Spiritual Isolation.
Spring.
Through These Pale Cold Days.
Wedded.
Worm Fed on the Heart of Corinth, A.
Yesterday as I lay nigh dead with toil.
Rosenberg, James Naumburg
Darkness.
Rosenblatt, Joe
Metamorpho I.
Saphire (Metamorpho's Chick).
Rosenfeld, Morris Jacob
Another While.
Cry from the Ghetto, A.
Exile Song.
For Hire.
I Know Not Why.
Jewish May, The.
My Camping Ground.
Simchas Torah.
So Long Ago.
Rosenhane, Gustav
Sonnet: "And then I sat me down, and gave the rein."
Sonnet: "Deep in a vale where rocks on every side."
Sonnets.
Rosenzweig, Efraim
Dreidel Song.
Song of Always, A.
Rosner, Paul
Don't Say You Like Tchaikowsky.
Ross, Abram Bunn
Indignant Male, An.
Two in Bed.
Ross, Alan
Agrigento.
Algerian Refugee Camp, Aïn-Khemouda.
Antwerp: Musée Des Beaux-Arts.
At Only That Moment.
Bantu on a Bicycle.
Cricket at Brighton.
Embankment before Snow.
Grand Canal.
Iceland in Wartime.
Leave Train.
Mess Deck Casualty.
Nelson at Palermo.
Night Patrol.
North London.
Rock Paintings, Drakensberg.
Survivors.
Winter Boats at Brighton.
Winter Gulls.
Ross, Alexander
Woo'd and Married and A' ("Wooed and married and a'").
Ross, Allison
Game Out of Hand.
Ross, Cary
Sonnet on a Somewhat Inferior Radio Outfit.
Ross, Charles Sarsfield
Dear Old Mothers.
Old Mothers.
Ross, David
Book Review.
Briton Who Shot at His King.
Broadcast to the Scholars in the Eyrie.
Demosthenes to the Radio Announcer.
Fallen Flyer Aged 19.
He Bloomed among Eagles.
Houses Should Have Homes to Live In.
I Am Your Loaf, Lord.
In My Infancy.
In the Year's Morning.
Lament of Granite.
Man's Need.
News Reel.
On Apples.
Passport beyond Tyranny.
Praised Be the Psalmist.
Ross, David MacDonald
Bloody Bill.
Ross, Gertrude Robison
I Was Made of This and This.
Ross, Mary
Whip of Anger, The.
Ross, Patience Adrian
Robin Hood.
Ross, Sir Ronald
Lines Written after the Discovery by the Author of the Germ of Yellow Fever.
Reply.
Ross, W. W. Eustace
Creek, The.
Diver, The.
Fish.
If Ice.
In the Ravine.
Medici Tombs, The.
On Angels.
Pine Gum.
Saws Were Shrieking, The.
Snake Trying, The.
Summons, The.
There's a Fire in the Forest.
Walk, The.
Ross, William [*or* Uillieam Ros]
Another Song.
Rossetti, Christina Georgina
Abnegation.
Advent.
After Death.
All Things Wait upon Thee.
Aloof.
Amor Mundi.
And timid, funny, brisk little bunny.
Animals Mourn with Eve, The.
Another Spring.
Apple Gathering, An.
At Home.
At the Goal.
Baby, Sleep.
Battle Within, The.
Before the Beginning.
Before the Paling of the Stars.
Better Resurrection, A.
Bird Raptures.
Birds of Paradise.
Birthday, A.
Birthday Gift, A.
Blue-eyed phantom far before, A.
Boatman, The.
Boats Sail on the Rivers [*or* River].
Bourne, The.
Bread and Milk.
Bride Song.
Broken Doll, The.
Brown and Furry.
Brownie, Brownie, Let Down Your Milk.
But Give Me Holly, Bold and Jolly.
But if the darkness and corruption leave.
By the Sea.
Caterpillar.
Cherry Tree.
Child's Talk in April.
Chill, A.
Christ Can Give Thee Heart.
Christ Our All in All, *sel.*
Christmas Carol, A: "Before the paling of the stars."
Christmas Carol, A: "In the bleak mid-winter."
Christmas Carol, A: "Shepherds had an Angel, The."
Christmas Daybreak.
City Mouse and the Garden Mouse, The.
Cobwebs.
Color.
Consider.
Convent Threshold, The.
Coral.
De Profundis.
December.
Descent from the Cross, The, *sel.*
Despised and Rejected.
Did Adam love his Eve from first to last?
Did any bird come flying.
Dirge, A: "Why were you born when the snow was falling?"
Do You Know?
Dream Land.
Dream-Love.
Easter Carol, An: "Flash forth, thou sun."
Easter Carol, An: "Spring bursts to-day."
Easter Day.
Echo.
Echo from Willowwood, An.
1880.
1885.
Emerald Is as Green as Grass, An.
Eve.
Face of Jesus Christ, The.
Fanny's Doves ("Fanny loves").
Ferry Me across the Water.
Ferryman, The.
First Day, The.
First Spring Day, The.
Fluttered Wings.
For what is knowledge duly weighed?
Four Pets.
Frisky Lamb, A.
From the Antique.
Goblin Market.
Golden Silences.
Good Advice.
Good-by.
Good Friday.
Good Friday Evening.
Good Shepherd, The.
Green Cornfield, A.
Growing in the Vale.
Heaven Is Heaven.
Heaven Is Not Far.
Heaven Overarches [Earth and Sea].
Herself a Rose Who Bore the Rose.
Hills are Tipped with Sunshine, The.
Hold Thou Me Fast.
Holy Innocents.
Hope I Dreamed of, The.
Hopping Frog.
Horses of the Sea, The.
House of Cards, The.
How Many Seconds in a Minute?
Hurt No Living Thing.
I Bore with Thee, Long, Weary Days.
I tell you what I dreamed last night.
I Will Accept.
If a Pig Wore Wig.
If I Were a Queen.
If Only.
If stars dropped out of heaven.
Immalee.
In an Artist's Studio.
In the Bleak Mid-Winter.
Incarnate Love.
Invitation to Sleep.
Is It Well with the Child?
Is the Moon Tired?
It Is Finished.
Italia, Io Ti Saluto!
Judge Not According to the Appearance.
"Kookoorookoo! kookoorookoo!"
Lady Moon.
Lambs at Play.
Last Prayer.
Later Life, *sels.*
Lesson, A.
Let's Be Merry.
Life's Parallels, A.
Lily has a smooth stalk, The.
Linnet in a Gilded Cage, A.

Rossetti (continued)
Lord, Carry Me.
Lord, Dost Thou Look on Me.
Lord, Grant Us Calm.
Lord, Save Us, We Perish.
Love Is Strong as Death.
Love Lies Bleeding.
Love Me—I Love You.
"Love of Christ Which Passeth Knowledge, The."
Lowest Place, The.
Lullaby: "Lullaby, oh, lullaby!"
Luscious and Sorrowful.
Marvel of Marvels.
Mary Magdalene and the Other Mary.
Maude Clare.
May.
May-Time.
Meeting ("If we shall live, we live").
Meeting ("They made the chamber sweet").
Memory ("I have a room whereinto no one enters").
Memory ("I nursed it in my bosom while it lived").
Milking-Maid, The.
Milking Time.
Minnie and Mattie.
Minnie, Mattie and May.
Mirage.
Mix a Pancake.
Monna Innominata.
Months, The ("January cold").
Months, The; a Pageant, *sel.*
Mother Country.
Motherless Soft Lambkin.
Mother's Song, A.
My Gift.
Neighboring.
Nesting-Time.
New Year Ditty.
Next of Kin.
Noble Sisters.
None but He.
None Other Lamb [None Other Name].
November.
Oh, Fair to See.
O Lady Moon.
Oh roses for the flush of youth.
O Sailor, Come Ashore.
O Wind, Where Have You Been?
O wind, why do you never rest.
October.
Old and New Year Ditties, *sel.*
On the Death of a Cat, a Friend of Mine Aged Ten Years and a Half.
On the Grassy Banks.
On the Wing.
One Certainty, The.
Out of the Deep Have I Called unto Thee, O Lord.
Pancake, The.
Paradise.
Paradise; in a Dream.
Paradoxes.
Passing and Glassing.
Passing Away [Saith the World].
Pause, A.
Pause of Thought, A.
Phases of the Moon, The.
Pin Has a Head, A.
Pocket Handkerchief to Hem, A.
Postman, The.
Prayer, A: "Clother of the lily, Feeder of the sparrow."
Prayer: "Lord, grant us eyes to see, and ears to hear."
Precious Stones.
Prince's Progress, The, *sel.*
Queen of Hearts, The.
Rainbow, The.
Remember.
Remember Me.
Requiem.
Rest.
Riddle: "First it was a pretty flower, dressed in pink and white."
Rushes in a Watery Place.
Sea-Sand and Sorrow.
Seasons.
Seldom "can't."
Send Me.
Shadows To-Day.
She listen'd like a cushat dove.
Shepherds Had an Angel, The.
Shut Out.
Sing in the Silent Sky.
Sing Me a Song.
Sing-Song; a Nursery Rime Book.
Sketch, A.
Skylark, The.
Skylark and Nightingale.
Sleep at Sea.
Sleeping at Last.
Snack, A.
Somewhere or Other.
Song: "Oh roses for the flush of youth."
Song: "When I am dead, my dearest."
Song for the Least of All Saints, A.
Song of Flight, A.
Sonnet: "Come back to me, who wait and watch for you."
Sonnet: "Remember me when I am gone away."
Soul, A.
Sound of the Wind, The.
Spring.
Spring Quiet.
Star Sirius and the Pole Star dwell afar.
Stars, The.
Stay, June, Stay!
Stitching.
Summer.
Summer Days.
Summer Is Ended, The.
Summer Wish, A.
Sun and Rain.
Swallow, The.
Sweet Daffadowndilly.
Then I cried out upon him: Cease.
There is one that has a head without an eye.
There's Nothing like the Rose.
There's Snow on the Fields.
They Toil Not neither Do They Spin.
Thou Thyself.
Thread of Life, The, *sel.*
Three Enemies, The.
Three Plum Buns.
Three Seasons.
Thy Will.
To My First Love, My Mother.
Today for Me.
Too Late for Love.
Trust.
Trust me, I have not earned your dear rebuke.
Tune Me, O Lord, into One Harmony.
Twice.
Twilight Calm.
Twist Me a Crown.
Two doves upon the selfsame branch.
Two Pursuits.
Up-Hill [*or* Uphill].
Upper Road, The.
Valentine to My Mother, A (1882).
Valentines to My Mother (1876-1886), *sels.*
Watching Angels.
Weary in Well-doing.
Wednesday in Holy Week.
What Can I Give Him?
What Do They Do?
What Does the Bee Do?
What Is It Jesus Saith?
What Is Pink?
What Would I Give!
When I Am Dead.
When I Am Dead, My Dearest.
When the Cows Come Home.
White hen sitting, A.
Who Has Seen the Wind?
Who Shall Deliver Me?
Why?
Wife to Husband.
Wind, The.
Wind Has Such a Rainy Sound, The.
Wind of January, The.
Winter ("Bread and milk . . .").
Winter ("Sweet blackbird . . .").
Winter Rain.
Wisdom.
With Him.
Woolly Lambkins.
World, The.
Wrens and Robins [in the Hedge].
Year's Windfalls, A.

Rossetti, Dante Gabriel
Alas, So Long!
Antwerp and Bruges.
Antwerp to Ghent.
Ardor [*or* Ardour] and Memory.
Aspecta Medusa.
Astarte Syriaca.
At the Sunrise in 1848.
Autumn Idleness.
Autumn Song.
Ave.
Barren Spring.
Beauty's Pageant.
Birth-Bond, The.
Blessed Damozel, The.
Body's Beauty.
Boulogne to Amiens and Paris.
Bridal Birth.
Bride's Prelude, The.
Broken Music.
Burden of Nineveh, The.
Card-Dealer, The.
Chime of the Sea, The.
Chimes.
Choice, The.
Cloud and Wind.
Cloud Confines, The.
Dante at Verona.
Dark Day, A.
Dark Glass, The.
Dawn on the Night-Journey.
Day of Love, A.
Day-Dream, The.
Death-in-Love.
Death's Songsters.
Eden Bower.
Even So.
Farewell to the Glen.
First Love Remembered.
Five English Poets.
For a Marriage of St. Catherine.
For "A Venetian Pastoral" by Giorgione.
For "Our Lady of the Rocks."
For the Holy Family by Michelangelo.
For "The Wine of Circe"; a Picture by Edward Burne-Jones.
"Found."
Fragment, A: "I saw the Sibyl at Cumae."
Friar of Orders Grey, The.
From Dawn to Noon.
Genius in Beauty.
Gracious Moonlight.
He and I.
Heart of the Night, The.
Heart's Compass.
Heart's Haven.

Heart's Hope.
Her Gifts.
Her Heaven.
Her Love.
Here nothing warns.
Hero's Lamp.
Herself.
Hill Summit, The.
Hoarded Joy.
Honeysuckle, The.
Hope Overtaken.
House of Life, The.
Husbandman, The.
Inclusiveness.
Insomnia.
Introduction: "Sonnet is a moment's monument, A."
Jenny.
John Keats.
King's Tragedy, The.
Kiss, The.
Known in Vain.
Lamp's Shrine, The.
Landmark, The.
Last Confession, A.
Last Fire.
Life-in-Love.
Life the Beloved.
Lilith.
Limerick: "There is a young artist called [*or* named] Whistler."
Limerick: "There is an old he-wolf named Gambart."
Limerick: "There once was a painter named Scott."
Limerick: "There was a poor chap called Rossetti."
Limerick: "There's a combative artist named Whistler."
Limerick: "There's a Portuguese person named Howell."
Limerick: "There's an Irishman, Arthur O'Shaughnessy."
Little While, A.
London to Folkestone.
Lost Days.
Lost on Both Sides.
Love and Hope.
Love Enthroned.
Love-Letter, The.
Love-Lily.
Love-Moon, The.
Love-Sight.
Love-Sweetness.
Lovers' Walk, The.
Love's Baubles.
Love's Fatality.
Love's Last Gift.
Love's Lovers.
Love's Testament.
Lovesight [*or* Love-Sight].
Mary Magdalene at the Door of Simon the Pharisee.
Mary's Girlhood.
Match with the Moon, A.
Memorial Thresholds.
Memory.
Michelangelo's Kiss.
Mid-Rapture.
Mirror, The.
Monochord, The.
Moonstar, The.
Morrow's Message, The.
My Sister's Sleep.
New Year's Burden, A.
Newborn Death.
Not As These.
Nuptial Sleep.
Old and New Art.
Old Song Ended, An.
On Leaving Bruges.
On Refusal of Aid between Nations.
On the Poet O'Shaughnessy.
On the Site of a Mulberry-Tree.
On the "Vita Nuova" of Dante.
One Hope, The.
Orchard-Pit, The.
Our Lady of the Rocks.
Parted Love.
Passion and Worship.
Passover in the Holy Family, The.
Penumbra.
Percy Bysshe Shelley.
Portrait, The ("O Lord of all compassionate control").
Portrait, The ("This is her picture as she was").
Pride of Youth.
"Retro Me, Sathana."
St. Luke the Painter.
Samuel Taylor Coleridge.
Sea-Limits, The.
Sea-Spell, A.
Secret Parting.
Severed Selves.
Silent Noon.
Sister Helen.
Sleepless Dreams.
Song of the Bower, The.
Song-Throe, The.
Sonnet, The ("A sonnet is a moment's monument").
Soul-Light.
Soul's Beauty.
Soul's Sphere, The.
Staff and Scrip, The.
Stillborn Love.
Stratton Water.
Sudden Light.
Sun's Shame, The.
Sunset Wings.
Superscription, A.
Supreme Surrender.
Thomas Chatterton.
Three Shadows.
Through Death to Love.
Tom Agnew, Bill Agnew.
Transfigured Life.
Trees of the Garden, The.
Trip to Paris and Belgium, A, *sels.*
Troy Town.
True Woman.
Vain Virtues.
Vase of Life, The.
Venetian Pastoral, A.
Venus.
Venus Victrix.
What Smouldering Senses.
White Ship, The.
William Blake.
Willowwood.
Winged Hours.
Winter.
Without Her.
Woodspurge, The.
Words on the Windowpane.
World's Worth.
Young Firwood, A.
Youth's Antiphony.
Youth's Spring Tribute.

Rossetti, William Michael
Ye Who Taste That Love Is Sweet.

Rossi, Azariah di
Epitaph: "From out the stormy sea unto the shore."

Rosslyn, Earl of *See* **Erskine, Francis Robert St. Clair**

Rostand, Edmond
And what is a kiss, when all is done?
Curses upon this land; till plague devours.
Cyrano de Bergerac, *sels.*
Woman of Samaria, The, *sel.*

Rosten, Norman
Black Boy.
Out of Our Shame.
This Child.
To Ariake Kambara.

"Rostrevor, George." *See* **Hamilton, George Rostrever**

Rothenberg, Jerome Dennis
Bodhisattva Undoes Hell, A.
Dark bull quartered in my eye, The.
"Little Boy Lost, A."
Seventh Hell, The.
Sightings I.
Stationmaster's Lament, The.
Three Landscapes, *sel.*

Rothenberg, Jerome G.
Cortège.

Rotherburger, Leila Avery
Three Crosses.

Rouget de Lisle, Claude Joseph
Marseillaise, The [*or* La].

Roumain, Jacques
Guinea.
Langston Hughes.
When the Tom-Tom Beats.

Roumer, Emile
Black Girl Goes By, A.
Peasant Declares His Love, The.
Three Haitian Creole Moods.

Rounds, Emma
Ballad of the Merry Ferry, The.
Fire Pictures.
Johnny.
Plane Geometry.
Wild Home-Pussy, The.

Rourke, Constance
Merry Miner, The.

Routhier, Basile
O Canada.

Rowbotham, David
Little White Fox.
Moment, The.
Mullabinda.
Town, The.

Rowe, Elizabeth
On an Unsuccessful Attempt to Draw Lord Boyle's Picture.
On the Sacrament.
Three Hymns,
To a Very Young Gentleman at a Dancing-School.

Rowe, Henry
Moon.
Sun.

Rowe, Nicholas
Colin's Complaint.
Fair Penitent, The, *sel.*
To Lady Jane Wharton, on Her Studying the Globe.

Rowe, Richard
Angel of Life, The.

Rowland, Eva
Gingerbread Man, The.

Rowland, J. R.
Canberra in April.

Rowlands, Richard *See* **Verstegan, Richard**

Rowlands, Samuel
Bid me go asleep: I scorn it with my heels.
Glutton.
Idle Housewife.
Melancholy Knight, The, *sels.*
Miserable Merchant.
Poetaster, The.
Politic Peter meets his friend ashore.
Scholar newly entered marriage life, A.
Severus is extreme in eloquence.
Sir Eglamour, *parody.*
Upstart Courtier.

Rowles, Catharine Bryant
New Snow.

Rowley, Samuel, Thomas Dekker, *and* **John Day** *See* **Dekker, Thomas, Samuel Rowley,** *and* **John Day**
Rowley, William, *and* **John Fletcher** *See* **Fletcher, John,** *and* **William Rowley**
Rowley, William, *and* **Thomas Middleton** *See* **Middleton, Thomas,** *and* **William Rowley**
Rowntree, Maurice
O Heart.
Rowse, Alfred Leslie
Death-Bed.
Listening to Handel's "Messiah".
Rowswell, Albert K.
Should You Go First.
Royden, Matthew
Elegy, or Friend's Passion for His Astrophil, An, *sel.*
On Sir Philip Sidney.
Royde-Smith, Naomi
Horse, The.
Royle, Edwin Milton
Doan't You Be What You Ain't.
Rubadiri, James D.
Stanley Meets Mutesa.
Rubin, Larry
Addict, The.
Druggist, The.
Exile, The.
For a Poetry Reading to Which No One Came.
Lesson, The.
Northbound.
Synchronized.
Ruby, Harry, *and* **Bert Kalmar** *See* **Kalmar, Bert,** *and* **Harry Ruby**
Rückert, Friedrich ("Freimund Raimar")
And Then No More.
Barbarossa.
Ride round the Parapet, The.
Ruddick, Bruce
Freighter.
Plaque.
Ruddock, Margot
Autumn, Crystal Eye.
Child Compassion. The.
I Take Thee, Life.
Love Song.
O Holy Water.
Spirit, Silken Thread.
Take Away.
Rudel, Jaufré
Quan lo ruis de la fontana.
Rudnik, Raphael
Lady in the Barbershop, The.
Penny Trumpet.
Rudyerd, Sir Benjamin
Why Do We Love.
Rufinus Domesticus
Andante, ma Non Assai.
Faint Heart.
Lover's Posy, The.
Requirements: "Not too chary, not too fast."
Requirements: "Not too lean, and not too fat."
To Melité.
Ruggeri, Agnes O'Gara
To the City in the Snow.
Ruiz, Juan, Archpriest of Hita
Book of Good Love, The, *sel.*
Book of True Love, The, *sel.*
Praise of Little Women.
Prayer to Santa Maria del Vade.
"When you're together with her, and you have a good excuse."
Rukeyser, Muriel
Ajanta.
Antagonists, The.
Are You Born?
Beast in View.
Birth, A.
Boy with His Hair Cut Short.
Ceiling Unlimited.
Chapultepec Park.
Charm for Cantinflas, A.
Children, the Sandbar, That Summer.
Children's Elegy.
Citation for Horace Gregory.
City of Monuments.
Cornfield, The, *sel.*
Easter Eve, 1945.
Effort at Speech between Two People.
Eighth Elegy, *sel.*
Endless.
Even during War.
Eyes of Night-Time.
Foghorn in Horror.
For those given to voyages: these roads.
From the Duck-Pond to the Carousel.
George Robinson; Blues.
Gibbs, *sel.*
Haying before Storm.
Holy Family.
Homage to Literature.
It was much later in his life he rose.
Ives, *sel.*
Leg in a Plaster Cast, A.
Letter to the Front
Madboy's Song.
Meeting, The.
Motive of All of It, The.
Night Feeding.
Ninth Elegy, *sel.*
Nuns in the Wind.
Reading Time: 1 Minute 26 Seconds.
Return, The.
Rotten Lake Elegy.
Salamander.
Song: "World is full of loss, The; bring, wind, my love."
Soul and Body of John Brown, The.
Study in a Late Subway.
Tenth Elegy: Elegy in Joy.
Then I Saw What the Calling Was.
This is Charles Ives.
This Place in the Ways.
To Be a Jew in the Twentieth Century.
Trial, The.
Watchers, The.
Waterlily Fire.
Who in One Lifetime.
Rumi, Jalal [*or* Jelal] ed-Din [*or* Dschellaleddin]
Beauty That All Night Long, A.
I Saw the Winter Weaving.
Resurgence.
Runeberg, Johan Ludvig
National Athem [Finnish], *abr.*
Soldier Boy, The.
Trouble Not the Maiden's Soul.
Runkle, Bertha
Song of the Sons of Esau, The.
Runyan, William M.
Falling Leaves.
Mount of Blessing, The.
Runyon, Damon (Alfred Damon Runyon)
Song of Panama, A.
Ruskin, John
Awake! Awake!
Song of the Dawn, *sel.*
Trust Thou Thy Love.
Wreck, The.
Russ, Virginia
Shape of Autumn, The.
Russell Bertrand Arthur William Russell, 3d Earl
Message for the Nations of the World, A.
Russell, Charles E.
Fleet at Santiago, The.
Russell, David
My Friend the Caterpillar.
Russell, Ethel Green
Letter from the Vieux Carre.
Russell, Francis Albert Rollo
Laborare Est Orare.
Rise!
Russell, G. J.
It Might Have Been Worse.
Russell, George William *See* **"AE"**
Russell, Irwin
Blessing the Dance.
Christmas-Night in the Quarters, *sels.*
First Banjo, The.
Fust Banjo, De.
Nebuchadnezzar.
Russell, Matthew
Thought from Cardinal Newman, A.
Russell, Percy
Birth of Australia, The.
Russell, Solveig Paulson
Mistletoe Sprites.
Russell, Sydney King
Death Was a Woman.
Dust.
For Vicki at Seven.
Forecast.
Girl in the Subway.
Midsummer.
Night Peril.
Perennial Mourner.
Phyllis.
Portrait.
Shape of Fear, The.
Six Silver Handles.
Spectre.
Victor, The.
Warning.
Russell, Thomas (1762-88)
Maniac, The.
Philoctetes.
Sick with the pangs that prompt the lover's moan.
Sonnet: "Could then the babes from yon unshelter'd cot."
Sonnet: Suppos'd to Be Written at Lemnos.
Sonnet: To Oxford.
Sonnet: To Valclusa.
Supposed to be Written at Lemnos.
To Oxford.
To the Spider.
Names and Order of the Books of the Old Testament.
New Testament, The.
Old Testament, The.
Russo, Lola Ingres
Autumn Squall—Lake Erie.
Rustico di Filippo
Making of Master Messerin, The.
Sonnet: Of the Making of Master Messerin.
Rutherford, Ruth
Far Off.
Rutilius
Roma.
Rutledge, Archibald
Come, Now!
O Mariners!
Oblique.
Rutsala, Vern
News.
Rutter, Joseph
Hymen ("Hymen, god of marriage-bed").
Shepherd's Holiday, The, *sel.*
Ryan, Abram Joseph (Father Ryan)
Better than Gold ("Better than grandeur. . .").
Child's Wish, A.
Conquered Banner, The.
Rosary of My Tears, The.
Sentinel Songs.

Song of the Mystic.
Sword of Robert Lee, The.
Valley of Silence, The.
Weary, Lonely, Restless, Homeless.
Ryan, Anne
Mary Salome, Widow.
Music.
Ryan, George
Unsolved Mystery.
Ryan, George B.
Still Undaunted.
Ryan, Kathryn White
Mother, The.
Ryan, Richard
O, Saw Ye the Lass.
Ryberg, Barbara Cornet
For God So Loved.
Hand in Hand with Jesus.
Known of Him.
Progress.
Step by Step.
Ryman, James
Farewell! Advent.
Now the Most High Is Born.
Rymer, Thomas
Edgar, *sel.*
On Her Absence.
Wit Predominant.
Ryokwan
Murmuring of Pine Trees, The.
Ryota
Haiku: "No one spoke."
Harvest Moon.
Moon in the Water, The.
Way of the World, The.
White Chrysanthemum, The.
Ryskind, Morrie ("John P. Wintergreen")
Horace the Wise.
To Natalie.
Ryuho
Moon, The.
Ryusui
Coolness in Summer.

S

"S., A. W."
Life That Counts, The.
"S., C. N."
Thenot Protests.
"S., E."
Being Forsaken of His friend He Complaineth.
"S., G. T."
One Lowly Path.
"S., G. W."
Be Still.
"S., J. H."
New Year's Wish, A.
O God of the Impossible.
"S. C. M'K." *See* **"M'K., S. C"**
"S. M. M." *See* **"M., S. M"**
Saadi *See* **Sadi**
Sá de Miranda, Francisco de
Where Is Dominga?
Saarikoski, Pentti
Guest, The.
Une Vie.
Sabin, Edwin L.
Apple-Barrel, The.
Easter.
Mothers.
My Enemy.
Work.
Sabir, Adib-i
Epitaph for a Tyrannous Governor Who Choked on Wine.
Saboly, Nicolas
Boots and Saddles.
Shepherd Boys, The.
Shepherd Folk Go to Bethlehem, The.
Sacchetti, Franco
Ballata: His Talk with Certain Peasant-Girls.
Catch: On a Wet Day.
On a Wet Day.
Sachs, Nelly
Chorus of the Unborn.
Landscape of Screams.
Sleepwalker, The.
Vainly.
Sackville, Charles, 6th Earl of Dorset
Advice, The ("Phyllis, for shame, let us improve").
Advice, The ("Wou'd you in love succeed, be brisk, be gay").
Arno's Vale.
Bonny Black Bess.
Dorinda.
Fire of Love, The.
My Opinion.
On Mr. Edward Howard upon His British Princes.
On the Countess of Dorchester.
Phillis for Shame Let Us Improve.
Song: "Dorinda's sparkling wit, and eyes."
Song: "Methinks the poor town has been troubled too long."
Song: "Oh, why did e'er my thoughts aspire."
Song: "Phillis, for shame let us improve."
Song: "Phyllis [*or* Phillis], for shame, let us improve."
Song: "To all you ladies now at land."
Song: Written at Sea, in the First Dutch War.
Written at Sea, in the First Dutch War.
Sackville, Lady Margaret
Apple, The.
Epitaph, An: "As shining sand-drift."
Resurrection.
Sermon, A.
To One Who Denies the Possibility of a Permanent Peace.
Sackville, Thomas, 1st Earl of Dorset
Complaint of Henrie Duke of Buckinghame, The.
Hydeous hole al vaste, withouten shape, An.
Induction to "The Mirror [*or* A Myrrour] for Magistrates."
Mayster Sackvilles Induction.
Midnight.
Midnight Was Come.
Sleep.
Thomas Sackville in Commendation of the Work to the Reader.
Troy.
Vision of Sorrow.
Vision of War, A.
Winter.
Sackville-West, Victoria Mary (Mrs. Harold Nicolson)
Bee-Master.
Dream, A.
Full Moon.
Greater Cats, The.
King's Daughter, *sel.*
Land, The, *sels.*
On the Lake.
Saxon Song, A.
Shepherds and stars are quiet with the hills.
Sissinghurst.
Song: "If I only had loved your flesh."
Song: "My spirit like a shepherd boy."
Spring Was Late That Year, The.
Weed Month.
Winter Song.
Wood-cut.
Sadaiye
Blossoms and Storm.
Sadi [*or* Saadi] (Muslih-ud-Din)
Adam's Race.
Alas!
Bustan, The, *sels.*
Contentment.
Courage.
Dancer, The.
Friendship.
From Slavery to Slavery.
Gift of Speech, The.
Great Physician, The.
Gulistan, The. *sels.*
He Hath No Parallel.
Help.
Hyacinths to Feed Thy Soul.
Love's Last Resource.
Mesnevi.
Ode: "Until thine hands clasp girdlewise."
On the Deception of Appearances.
On True Worth.
Purgatory May Be Paradise.
Sieve, The.
Sooth-Sayer, The.
Take the Crust.
Wealth.
Wrestler, The.
Saffin, John
Acrostick on Mrs. Elizabeth Hull, An.
Acrostick on Mrs. Winifret Griffin, An.
Brief Elegie on My Dear Son John, A.
Consideratus Considerandus.
Elegie on the Deploreable Departure of the Honered and Truely Religious Chieftain John Hull, An.
Lamentation on My Dear Son Simon, A.
March 4th Anno 1698/9; a Charracteristicall Satyre.
One Presenting a Rare Book to Madame Hull.
Satyretericall Charracter of a Proud Upstart, A.
Sweetly (my dearest) I left thee asleep.
To His Excellency Joseph Dudley.
Safford, William Harrison
Battle of Muskingum, The.
Sage, Rufus B.
Night on the Prairie.
Summer on the Great American Desert.
Wanderer's Grave, The.
"Sagittarius" (Olga Katzin)
Southdown Summer.
Saha, P. K.
Child's Power of Wonder, The.
Sa'ib of Isfahan
Cliques and Critics.
Saidy, Fred
For a Little Lady.
Saigyo Hoshi
Although I do not know.
In my boat that goes.
Like those boats which are returning.
Mingling my prayer.
Since I am convinced.
Startled/ By a single scream.
Tanka: Reflection, A.
Saint *See* **under names of individual saints.**
Saint-Gelais, Mellin de
Sonnet of the Mountain, The.
"Saint Geraud." *See* **Knott, William**
St. John, Peter
Descent on Middlesex, The.
St. Leger, Warham
False Gallop of Analogies, A.
To My Hairdresser.
St. Miriam of the Temple, Sister
Mater Misericordiae.

St. Virginia, Sister Mary
Case of Thomas More, The.
Convent Cemetery, Mount Carmel.
Edmund Campion.
Great Silence.
Nun to Mary, Virgin, A.
Shrine in Nazareth.
This Sharpening Tension.
St. Way, Frank
My Wealth.
"Sakanoye, The Lady of" (Lady Otomo no Sakanoy)
Dress that my brother has put on is thin, The.
Friends Drinking Together.
Unknown love/ Is as bitter a thing.
You say, "I will come."
Salamah, Son of Jandal
Gone Is Youth.
Salas Barbadillo, Alonso Jerónimo de
Disputes.
Saldaña, Diego de
Eyes So Tristful.
Salemme, Martha
Next Next Shortest Poem in the World, The.
Salis-Seewis, Johann Gaudenz von
Song of the Silent Land.
Salkeld, Blanaid
Anchises.
Evasion.
Leave Us Religion.
Meditation.
Men Walked To and Fro.
No Uneasy Refuge.
Now Is Farewell.
Optimism.
Peggy.
Templeogue.
Terenure.
That Corner.
Youth.
Salomon, Isidore Lawrence
Fox, The.
Song for the Greenwood Fawn.
Salsbury, Nate ("Baron Ireland")
Apex.
Krazy; Reflection No. 5.
Take Nothing for Granite.
Salsbury, Nate, *and* Newman Levy
Ballade of the Ancient Wheeze.
Saltillo, José de
Rio Bravo—a Mexican Lament.
Saltus, Francis Saltus
Andalusian Sereno, The.
Bayadere, The.
Ideal, The.
Pastel.
Sphinx Speaks, The.
Salusbury, Sir John
Buen Matina.
Salvadori, Giulio
Presence of the Spirit, The.
Salverson, Laura Goodman
If a Maid Be Fair.
Premonition.
Salway, Owen C.
He Cares.
Salz, Helen
Late.
Salzburg, J. L.
Bill.
Samain, Albert
From Summer Hours.
Pannyra of the Golden Heel.
Sambrook, Joyce
Wild Thyme.
Woodpecker, The.
Sammis, J. H.
All Needs Met.
Sampley, Arthur McCullough
Defender, The.
Sampson, William
Vow Breaker, The, sel.
When from the wars I do return.
Sampter, Jessie E.
Blessings for Chanukah.
Kadia the Young Mother Speaks.
Promised Land, The.
Psalm: "They have burned to Thee many tapers."
Summer Sabbath.
Samuel ha-Nagid
Proverbs.
San Garde, Evelina
Giant's Cake, A.
San Geminiano [*or* Gemignano], Folgore da
August.
Of the Months.
On Knighthood.
September.
Sonnet: Of Virtue.
Sonnets of the Months; or, Of the Months.
To the Guelf Faction.
San Juan de la Cruz *See* **John of the Cross, Saint**
Sanaker, James A.
Compassion.
My Heart Is Fixed.
Sanborn, Franklin Benjamin
Ariana.
Samuel Hoar.
Sánchez, Luis Aníbal
Brother Dog.
Sanchez, Sonia
Blues.
Malcolm.
Poem at Thirty.
Poem for 8th Graders.
Right On: White America.
Small Comment.
Summary.
To All Sisters.
Sandburg, Carl
A.E.F.
Accomplished Facts.
Adelaide Crapsey.
All One People.
American Yarns.
Arithmetic.
At a Window.
Auctioneer.
Autumn Movement.
Baby Toes.
Balloon Faces.
Bas-Relief.
Bee Song.
Best, The.
Between Worlds.
Blossom Themes.
Blue Island Intersection.
Boxes and Bags.
Bricklayer Love.
Bringers.
Broken-Face Gargoyles.
Buffalo Dusk.
Bundles.
Caboose Thoughts.
Calls.
Chicago.
Child.
Child Margaret.
Child of the Romans.
Children of the Wind.
Choose.
Circles.
City Number.
Clean Curtains.
Clinton South of Polk.
Clocks.
Code arrives, A; language; lingo; slang.
Cool Tombs.
Copperfaces, The ("The copperfaces, the red men, handed us tobacco").
Counting.
Couple, A.
Daybreak.
Death Snips Proud Men.
Doors.
Dream Girl.
Early Lynching.
Early Moon.
Electric Sign Goes Dark, An.
Elephants Are Different to Different People.
Even Numbers.
Evening Waterfall.
Explanations of Love.
Face.
Falltime.
Fence, A.
Finale.
Fire-Logs.
Fireborn Are at Home in Fire, The.
Fish Crier.
Five Towns on the B. and O.
Flash Crimson.
Fog ("Fog comes, The/ On little cat feet").
For You.
Four Brothers, The, *sel.*
Four Preludes on Playthings of the Wind.
From the four corners of the earth.
Gone.
Good Morning, America, *sel.*
Grass.
Graves.
Great Hunt, The.
Hammer, The.
Handfuls.
Hangman at Home, The.
Happiness.
Harbor, The.
Harvest.
Harvest Sunset.
Haze.
Helga.
Hits and Runs.
Home Thoughts.
Hoof Dusk.
Hope Is a Tattered Flag.
Horses and Men in the Rain.
House.
I Am the People, the Mob.
Ice Handler.
Jan Kubelik.
Jazz Fantasia.
Joy.
Killers ("I am put high over all others in the city today").
Killers ("I am singing to you").
Kin.
Lawyers Know Too Much, The.
Letters to Dead Imagists.
Limited.
Lincoln?/ He was a mystery in smoke and flags.
Little Candle.
Little Girl, Be Careful What You Say.
Loam.
Localities.
Long Shadow of Lincoln, The.
Look at Six Eggs.
Losers.
Lost.
Mammy Hums.
Man-Hunt, The.
Man in the Street Is Fed, The.
Man with the Broken Fingers, The.
Manual System.
Manufactured Gods.

Milk-white Moon, Put the Cows to Sleep.
Mist Forms.
Mr. Attila.
Moist Moon People.
Mysterious Biography.
New Farm Tractor.
Night.
Night Stuff.
Nocturne in a Deserted Brickyard.
O prairie mother, I am one of your boys.
Old Deep Sing-Song.
Old Flagman, The.
Old Timers.
On a Flimmering Floom You Shall Ride.
Ossawatomie.
Our Prayer of Thanks.
People Who Must.
People Will Live On, The.
People with Proud Chins.
People, Yes, The, *sels.*
Personality.
Phizzog.
Picnic Boat, The.
Places.
Plunger.
Pool.
Poor, The.
Population Drifts.
Potomac Town in February.
Prairie.
Prayer of Steel.
Prayers of Steel.
Precious Moments.
Primer Lesson.
Psalm of Those Who Go Forth before Daylight.
Rat Riddles.
Red-Headed Restaurant Cashier.
Redhaw Rain.
Repetitions.
River Moons.
Road and the End, The.
Sandhill People.
Sandpipers.
Sea-Wash.
Shenandoah.
Sketch.
Skyscraper.
Slabs of the Sunburnt West, *sel.*
Sleep Impression.
Sleep Is a Suspension.
Slippery.
Smoke and Steel, *sel.*
Smoke of the fields in spring is one.
Smoke Rose Gold.
Soup.
Special Starlight.
Splinter.
Spring Grass.
Stars, Songs, Faces.
Street Window.
Sumach and Birds.
Summer Stars.
Sunsets.
Swell People.
Teamster's Farewell, A.
Ten Definitions of Poetry.
Theme in Yellow.
These Children of the Wind.
They All Want to Play Hamlet.
They Have Yarns.
Three Spring Notations on Bipeds.
Threes.
To a Contemporary Bunkshooter.
To Beachey, 1912.
To the Ghost of John Milton.
Under a Telephone Pole.
Under the Harvest Moon.
Upstream.
Washington Monument by Night.
When Death Came April Twelve 1945.
Who can make a poem of the depths of weariness.
Who Shall Speak for the People?
Wild Horses.
Wilderness.
Wind Song.
Windy City, The, *sel.*
Work Gangs.
Worms and the Wind.
Yarns of the People.
Young Sea.

Sandeen, Ernest
Nearing Winter.

Sandell, Lina
Security.

Sanders, Ed
Cemetery Plot of Ed Sanders Shall Consist of, The.
Direct retinal flood, The.
Dragged to her cell.
For Sergeant Fetta.
Good God/ a 3 & 1/2 inch bony.
How slowly I sucked off.
"I shall return!"
I walked by the pond.
Pilgrimage, The.
Soft-Man 1.
Soft-Man 3.
Toe Queen Poems, *sels.*

Sanders, Ruth Manning
Come Wary One.
Old City, The.

Sandford, Charles
My Bible and I.

Sandford, Egbert
God Is at the Organ.

Sandford, James
Of Love.

Sands, Robert Charles
Green Isle of Lovers, The.

Sandstrom, Flora
Stately Lady, The.

Sandy, Stephen
Charley III.
Destruction of Bulfinch's House, The.
Et Quid Amabo Nisi Quod Aenigma Est.
Getting On.
Hiawatha.
Hunter's Moon.
Woolworth Philodendron, The.

Sandys, George
Deo Opt. Max.
Lines Written at the Temple of the Holy Sepulchre.
Paraphrase on the Psalms of David, A, *sels.*
Psalme CXXXVII: "As on Euphrates shady banks we lay."

Sangster, Charles
Blest Spirit of Calm that dwellest in these woods!
Evening.
Meadow-Field, The.
On, through the lovely archipelago.
Pleasant Memories, *sel.*
Rapid, The.
Red Men, The.
St. Lawrence and the Saguenay, The, *sels.*
Sonnets Written in the Orillia Woods, *sel.*
Thousand Islands, The.

Sangster, Margaret Elizabeth Munson (1838-1912)
Are the Children at Home?
Armistice
Average Man, The.
Awakening.
Bit of the Book, A.
Building of the Nest, The.
Christmas Day.
Christmas in the North.
Face to Face with Trouble, *sel.*
Faith.
From Nazareth.
If Christ Were Here To-night.
Manna.
Mary.
Midnight.
Now and Then.
Oh, face to face with trouble.
Our Father's World.
Our Missionaries.
Our Own.
Patience with the Living.
Peace.
Prayer of Thanksgiving, A.
Show Me Thyself.
Sin of Omission, The.
Song for Our Flag, A.
Sunrise.
Thanksgiving ("For all true words that have been spoken").
They Never Quite Leave Us.
Thought, A.
White Carnation, The.
Whittier.
Within the Veil.
Forgiven.
Riveter, The.

Sangster, Margaret Elizabeth (1894?-)
At Prayer Meeting.
Blind Man, The.
Commencement.
Father Speaks, A.
Gratitude.
In Gratitude for Friends.
Independence Day To-Day.
Lord of the World, The.
Mother's Prayer, A.
New Year, A.
New Year Is a Banner, The.
On the Summit.
Our Flag.
Prayer for Faith, A.
Recognition.
Road Song.
Security.
Soul of a Mother, The.
Thanksgiving ("For the days when nothing happens").
Thanksgiving ("I think God loves simplicity").
There Is No Dream.
Vacation Time.
Washington's Birthday.
Work of Love, The.

Sanker, Louis John
Boy at the Door.
Honey for the Heart.
Trumpet for Yuletide.

Sannazaro, Jacopo (Actius Sincerus Sannazarius)
Celestial Queen.
De Partu Virginis, *sel.*
Like to These Unmeasurable Mountains.
Lover's Life Compared to the Alps, The.

Sansom, Clive
Blind Youth, The.
Dustman, The.
It was a night in winter.
Matthew.
Postman, The.
Witnesses, The, *sel.*

Sant' Angelo, Bartolomeo di
Sonnet: He Jests Concerning His Poverty.

Santayana, George
After Gray Vigils, Sunshine in the Heart.
As in the Midst of Battle There Is Room.
As when the scepter dangles from the hand.
Athletic Code.
Before a Statue of Achilles.
Cape Cod.

Santayana (continued)
Deem Not [because You See Me].
Faith.
I Sought on Earth.
Minuet on Reaching the Age of Fifty, A.
O Martyred Spirit.
O World.
O World, Thou Choosest Not the Better Part.
Ode: "Gathering the echoes of forgotten wisdom."
Ode: "My heart rebels against my generation."
Ode: "Of thee the Northman by his beachèd [*or* bleachèd] galley."
Ode: "Slowly the black earth gains the yellow."
Ode: "What god will choose me from this labouring nation."
Ode to the Mediterranean.
Odes, I-V.
On a Piece of Tapestry.
On the Death of a Metaphysician.
Prosit Neujahr.
Rustic at the Play, The.
Solipsism.
Sonnet: "As in the midst of battle there is room."
Sonnet: "As when the scepter dangles from the hand."
Sonnet: "Have patience; it is fit that in this wise."
Sonnet: O World.
Sonnets, *sels.*
Sorrow.
To W. P., *sel.*
We Needs Must Be Divided.
What Riches Have You?
With You a Part of Me.

Santeuil, Jean Baptiste de
Ascension Hymn.

Santic, Aleksa
Dalmatian Nocturne.

Santob [*or* Shem-Tob] de Carrion
Friend, A.
Jewish Poet Counsels a King, A.
Resignation.
Self-Defense.

Sanuki, Lady
Like a great rock, far out at sea.

Saphier, William
Meeting.

Sappho
Achtung.
Alone.
Beauty.
Bridegroom Is So Tall, The.
Bride's Lament.
Congratulations ("Fortunate bridegroom").
Congratulations ("You lucky man, you").
Door-Keeper Has Big Feet, The.
Evening.
Evening Star.
Farewell to Anactoria.
Forever Dead.
Fragment of Sappho.
Full Moon.
Highest Fruit, The.
Immortal Aphrodite.
Lonely Night.
Love.
Night Singers.
Note to Gongyla.
Ode: "Peer of gods he seemeth to me, the blissful."
Ode to Anactoria.
Ode to Aphrodite.
On My Sweet Mother.
One Girl.
Orchard Song.
Parting, The.
Round about Me.
Silver Moon, The.
Timas.
To a Bride.
To the Bride.
To the Bridegroom.
Wormwood.
Young Bride, A.

Sarbiewski, Casimir
On the Victory of Poland and Her Allies over the Sultan Osman, 1621.
To Liberty.

Sarett, Lew
Angus McGregor.
Beat against Me No Longer.
Blacktail Deer.
Blue Duck, The.
Brittle World.
Clipped Wings.
Feather.
Feud.
Five Peas on a Barrelhead.
Four Little Foxes.
God Is at the Anvil.
Granite Mountain, The.
Great Divide, The.
Hang Me among Your Winds.
Iron-Wind Dances.
Let Me Flower as I Will.
Let Me Go Down to Dust.
Loon, The.
Mountain Hamlet.
Reflection.
Refuge.
Requiem for a Modern Croesus.
Sheepherder, The.
Thunderdrums, *sel.*
To a Wild Goose over Decoys.
Wailing Lynx.
Weeng; an Indian Slumber Song.
Wind in the Pine.
Wolf Cry, The.

Sargent, Daniel
Ark and the *Dove*, The.
Change of Subject, A.
Last Day, The.
Preference.

Sargent, Elizabeth Nancy
Break, The.
Child.
Paradise.

Sargent, Epes
Death of Warren, The.
Deeds of Kindness.
Evening in Gloucester Harbor.
Heart's Summer, The.
Life on the Ocean Wave, A.
Summer Noon at Sea, A.
Sunrise at Sea.
Suppose.
Tropical Weather.

Sargent, John Osborne
Horace.

Sargent, Louise Peabody
Thy Will Be Done.

Sargent, N. B.
Building for Eternity.

Sargent, Nettie M.
Hymn of Trust, A.

Sargent, William D.
Barn-Swallow, The.
Wind-Wolves.

Sarmèd the Yahud
Quatrain: "Sarmèd, whom they intoxicated from the cup of love."
Quatrain: "This existence has, without the azure sphere, no reality."

Saroyan, Aram
Car swerves,/ injures 11.
Crickets.
French Poets.
Had West followed up her fine opening lead.
Man stands, A.
My arms are warm.
Whistling in the street a car turning in the room ticking.

Sarson, H. M.
Lovely Things.
Road to Town, The.

Sarson, May
I Must Away.

Sarton, May
By Moonlight.
Celebration, A.
Clavichord, The.
Conversation in Black and White.
Definition.
Fore Thought.
In Time like Air.
Innumerable Friend.
Leaves before the Wind.
Light Left On, A.
Nativity.
New Year Wishes.
Prothalamium.
Sacred Order, The.
Santos: New Mexico.
Song: "Now let us honor with violin and flute."
Summer Music.
These Images Remain.
Transition.
White-haired Man, The.
Work of Happiness, The.

Sassoon, Siegfried
Absolution.
Aftermath.
All-Souls' Day.
Alone.
Asking for It.
At the Cenotaph.
At the Grave of Henry Vaughan.
Attack.
Autumn.
Babylon ("Babylon that was beautiful is Nothing now").
Base Details.
Before Day.
"Blighters."
Brevities.
Case for the Miners, The.
Child's Prayer, A,
Cleaning the Candelabrum.
Concert-Interpretation.
Concert Party, A.
Conclusion.
Counter-Attack.
Daybreak in a Garden.
Dead Musicians.
Death-Bed, The.
December Stillness.
Devotion to Duty.
Does It Matter?
Down the Glimmering Staircase.
Dreamers.
Dug-out, The.
Early Chronology.
Elected Silence.
Eulogy of My House.
Everyman.
Everyone [*or* Every One] Sang ("Everyone suddenly burst out singing").
Falling Asleep.
Fancy Dress.
Fantasia on a Wittelsbach Atmosphere.
General, The.
Gloria Mundi.
Glory of Women.
Grandeur of Ghosts.
I Lived My Days Apart.

I Stood with the Dead.
Imperfect Lover, The.
In Barracks.
In Me, Past, Present, Future Meet.
Invocation: "Come down from heaven to meet me when my breath."
It Was the Love of Life.
Kiss, The.
Leaders, New Style; the General (1917).
Limitations.
Litany of the Lost.
Local Train of Thought, A.
Make Them Forget.
Midnight Interior, A.
Monody on the Demolition of Devonshire House.
Morning Express.
Musical Critic Anticipates Eternity, A.
My Past Has Gone to Bed.
Mystic as Soldier, A.
Need, The.
Old-World Effect, An.
On Passing the New Menin Gate.
On Reading the War Diary of a Defunct Ambassador.
On Scratchbury Camp.
One Who Watches.
Phoenix, The.
Picture-Show.
Power and the Glory, The.
Prayer from 1936, A.
Prayer to Time, A.
Prehistoric Burials.
Prelude: "Dim, gradual thinning of the shapeless gloom."
Prelude: Troops, The.
Presences Perfected.
Rear-Guard, The.
Redeemer, The.
Repression of War Experience.
Road, The.
Sheldonian Soliloquy.
Sick Leave.
Slumber Song: "Sleep; and my song shall build about your bed."
Songbooks of the War.
South Wind.
Stand-to; Good Friday Morning.
Storm on Fifth Avenue.
Strangeness of Heart.
Suicide in Trenches.
"They."
To a Very Wise Man.
To an Old Lady Dead.
Together.
Tree and Sky.
Troops, The.
Ultimate Atrocity, The.
Vigils.
Wisdom of the World, The.
Working Party, A.
World will find no pity in your pages, The.

Sato, Satoru
Japan That Sank under the Sea.

Saul, George Brandon
Elizabeth.
Spring Song.

Saunders, Mary Wright
Remembering Day.

Saunders, R. Crombie
Empty Glen, The.
Ressaif My Saul.

Saunders, Ripley Dunlap
Sunshine and Music.

Saunders, Ruby C.
Auditions.
Be Natural, Baby.
Don't Pay.
Generation Gap, The.
Lawd, Dese Colored Chillum.
My Man Was Here Today.

Saunders, Thomas
End of Steel.
Horizontal World.

Sauvage, Cécile
My Little Lover.

Savage, Derek S.
Absent Creation.
Confession.
February.
Living.
Scenario.
Separation.
Wild Swan, The.
Winter Offering.

Savage, Frances Higginson
Duck in Central Park.

Savage, H. H.
He Will Never Fail.
His Word Is Powerful.

Savage, Minot Judson
Affirmation, An.
Earth's Common Things.
Life's Common Duties.
My Birth.
Where Is God?

Savage, Philip Henry
Infinity.
Late Winter.
Morning.
Silkweed.
Solitude.

Savage, Richard
Bastard, The, *sel.*
To A Young Lady.

Savage-Armstrong, George Francis
Autumn Memories.
Father, The.
My Guide.
Mystery, The.
One in the Infinite.

Savonarola, Girolamo
Good Friday.
Jesus, Refuge of the Weary.
O Star of Galilee.

Sawyer, C. P.
I Used to Love My Garden.

Sawyer, Charles Carroll
Weeping, Sad and Lonely.
When This Cruel War Is Over.

Sawyer, Frederick William *See* **Sawyer, William**

Sawyer, Mark
Kite Days.

Sawyer, Ruth (Mrs. Albert C. Durand)
Feast o' St. Stephen.

Sawyer, William
"Caudal" Lecture, A.
Cremation.
Recognition, The.
Turvey Top.

Saxe, John Godfrey
Blind Men and the Elephant, The.
Briefless Barrister, The.
Comic Miseries.
Darling, Tell Me Yes.
Do I Love Thee?
Early Rising.
Echo.
Find a Way.
Game of Life, The.
How Cyrus Laid the Cable.
How I Love You.
Justine, You Love Me Not!
Mourner à la Mode, The.
My Familiar.
Puzzled Census-Taker, The.
Pyramus and Thisbe.
Rhyme of the Rail[s].
Solomon and the Bees.
Sonnet to a Clam.
Story of Life, The.
To Lesbia.
To My Love.
Too Candid by Half.
Where There's a Will There's a Way.
Wills.
Woman's Will.
Wouldn't You Like to Know.
Youth and the Northwind, The.

Saxton, Andrew Bice
First Step, The.

Sayers, Dorothy Leigh
Choice of the Cross, The.
Devil to Pay, The, *sels.*
I have sinned; I have betrayed the innocent blood.
Judgment and Mercy.

Sayers, Frances Clarke *See* **Clarke, Frances**

Sayles, James M.
Star of the Evening.

Saylor, Henri DeWitt
Steel.

Sayres, Cortlandt W.
Bankrupt.

Scannell, Vernon
Act of Love.
Autumn, *sel.*
Gunpowder Plot.
It is the football season once more.
Jealous Wife, The.
Moods of Rain.
Schoolroom on a Wet Afternoon.

Scantlebury, Elizabeth E.
Hymn of Dedication.

Scarborough, George L.
To the Men Who Lose.

Scarbrough, George
Birth by Anesthesia.

Scarfe, Francis
Cats.
Clock, The.
Grotto, The.
Progression.
Tyne Dock.
Window, The.

Schacht, Marshall
First Autumn, The.

Schauffler, Henry Park
Easter Sacraments.

Schauffler, Robert Haven
Nonsense.
"Scum o' the Earth."
Washington.
White Comrade, The.

Schaukal, Richard
Images.

Schaumann, Ruth
Evensong.
Fourth Station.
Mary on Her Way to the Temple.

Schechter, Ruth Lisa
Bound Together.

Scheffauer, Ethel Talbot
Copper Song.
Reply from the Akond of Swat, A.

Scheffauer, Herman
Marta of Milrone.

Scheffler, Johannes *See* **"Angelus Silesius"**

Scheftel, George
Divine Rebel, The.

Scherman, Tom
Elephant!

Scherzo, I. O.
Threnody: "Truth is a golden sunset far away."

Scheuer, Marjorie Somers
Fox, The.

Schevill, James
Astonished Listener Hears the Radio Announcer Bat Out the Long Balls of

Schevill (continued)
Verbs, Nouns and Adjectives, An.
Birth of Arachne, the Spider, The.
Cheops.
Coastguardsman in the Fog, The.
Confidential Data on the Loyalty Investigation of Herbert Ashenfoot.
Crow-Marble Whores of Paris, The.
D-9.
Dancers with a Hop, The.
Death of a Cat.
Death of a Dove, The.
Dramas of the Rose.
Dream of Apricots, A.
Green Frog at Roadstead, Wisconsin.
Guilty Father to His Daughter, A.
Invisible Craft of Evil, The.
Lament for a Man Who Loved God.
Mailman and Das Ewig Weibliche, The.
Old Peasant Woman at the Monastery of Zagorsk, The.
Old Pilot Tunnels under the English Channel, The.
Perhaps a Prayer.
Plea for Alias, A.
Seurat.
Song for Old Apis, A.
Story of Soutine, A.
Tolstoy Seeks the Peasant Rhythm.
Turtle, The.
Unnatural, Unusual and Unfair.
Will of Writing, The.
Schierloh, Samuel
Bucko-Mate.
Schiller, Johann Christoph Friedrich von
Farewell, ye mountains, and ye much-loved paths.
Maid of Orleans, The (*play*), *sel.*
Maid of Orleans, The (*poem*).
Ode to Joy.
Piccolomini, The, *sel.*
Rainbow, The—a Riddle.
Rousseau.
Steer, Bold Mariner, On!
Thekla's Song.
Three Lessons.
Three Words of Strength.
Time.
To My Friends.
Unrealities, The.
William Tell, *poem.*
Schjeldahl, Peter
Alcohol.
Bonner's Ferry.
Che Guevara Is Dead.
Citizen.
Fear.
Gauge.
Life Studies.
Page of Illustrations, The.
Release.
Smiles.
Soft Letter.
To the National Arts Council.
White Country.
Schlaitzer, Ilse L.
He Is the Truth.
Schlegel, Katharina von
Be Still.
Be Still, My Soul.
Schlesinger, ——
To the Parotid Gland.
Schlichter, Norman C.
Sledding Song, A.
Schlipf, Benjamin
Contentment.
Schloerb, Rolland W.
O Church of God.
O Thou Eternal Source of Life.
Prayer for Peace.
Thou Light of Ages.
Schmid, Constance M.
Synekdechestai.
Schmitz, Dennis
Autumn Testament.
Before the Coming of Winter.
Eclogues.
If I Could Meet God.
Rabbit Leaves, The.
Summers Sun, The.
Schmolke [*or* Schmolck], Benjamin
Consecration.
Heavier the Cross.
My Jesus, as Thou Wilt.
Schmuller, Aaron
Legend of His Lyre.
Schneckenburger, Max
Watch on the Rhine, The.
Schneider, Isidor
Ambience of Love, The.
Insects.
Joy of Knowledge.
Riding Stone.
Sunday Morning.
Wall, The.
Schneour, Zalman
Besieged.
Cherries.
Forsaken.
Last Words of Don Henriquez, The.
Like Water down a Slope.
Road, The.
Star There Fell, A.
War Comes.
Welcome, Queen Sabbath.
Schoeck, Richard J.
Homage (Diptych, 2).
Scholes, J. N.
He Worked.
Scholfield, William M.
Everlasting Arms, The.
Scholten, Martin
Soliloquy by the Shore.
Schomberg, Ralph
Ay or Nay?
Courtier's a Riddle, A.
Judgment of Paris, The, *sels.*
Like Birds of a Feather.
Schoolcraft, Luke
Shine On.
Schoonmaker, Blanche W.
Wings.
Schoultz, Solveig von
Deaths, The.
Schroy, Pauline
Prayer: "Lord, forgive."
Schull, Joseph
I, Jones, Soldier, *sel.*
Legend of Ghost Lagoon, The, *sel.*
Pirates' Fight, The.
Sound smashes through the dark. It is a wall.
Schultz, Lulu Minerva
What Price.
Schulz, Dale
His Presence.
Schulz, Lillian *See* **Vanada, Lillian Schulz**
Schuyler, James
Almanac, An.
Buried at Springs.
December.
"Earth's Holocaust."
Elizabethans Called It Dying, The.
Faberge.
February.
Freely Espousing.
Going.
Ilford Rose Book.
Man in Blue, A.
Master of the Golden Glow, The.
Milk.
Poem: "How about an oak leaf."
Reunion, A.
Roof Garden.
Salute.
Stun.
3/26/66.
Today.
White City, A.
Schuyler, Montgomery
Carlyle and Emerson.
Schuyler-Lighthall, William Douw
Battle of La Prairie, The.
Schwab, Antonia Y.
Danse Macabre.
Schwager, Elaine
Tracks.
Schwartz, Delmore
All Clowns Are Masked.
All of the Fruits Had Fallen.
All of Us Always Turning Away for Solace.
Aria.
At a Solemn Musick.
At This Moment of Time.
Ballad of the Children of the Czar, The.
Ballet of the Fifth Year, The.
Baudelaire.
Beautiful American Word, Sure, The.
Being Unused to Joyous Consciousness.
Conclusion, The.
Dark and Falling Summer, The.
Darkling Summer, Ominous Dusk, Rumerous Rain.
Deceptive Present, the Phoenix Year, The.
Do They Whisper.
Dog Named Ego [the Snowflakes as Kisses], A.
During December's Death.
Father and Son.
First Morning of the Second World, The.
First Night of Fall and Falling Rain, The.
For One Who Would Not Take His Life in His Hands.
For Rhoda.
For the One Who Would Take Man's Life in His Hands.
Fulfillment, The.
Genesis, *sel.*
Heavy Bear Who Goes with Me, The.
Hölderlin.
How Strange Love Is, in Every State of Consciousness.
I Did Not Know the Truth of Growing Trees.
I Waken [*or* Wakened] to a Calling.
I Wish I Had Great Knowledge or Great Art.
In the Naked Bed, in Plato's Cave.
Is It Morning? Is It the Little Morning?
Let Us Consider Where the Great Men Are.
Lincoln.
Little Morning Music, A.
Look, in the Labyrinth of Memory.
Masters of the Heart Touched the Unknown, The.
"Mentrechè il Vento, Come Fa, Si Tace."
Morning Light for One with Too Much Luck, The.
One in a Thousand of Years of the Night.
Prothalamion.
Repetitive Heart, The, *sels.*
Saint, Revolutionist.
Self Unsatisfied Runs Everywhere, The.
Sequel, The.
She Lives with the Furies of Hope and Despair.
She Was the Girl within the Picture Frame.
Shenandoah, *sel.*

Socrates' Ghost Must Haunt Me Now.
Someone Is Harshly Coughing as Before.
Starlight like Intuition Pierced the Twelve.
Starlight's Intuitions Pierced the Twelve, The.
"There'll Be Others but Non So for Me."
Time Is the Fire.
Tired and Unhappy, [You Think of Houses].
To Helen.
Today Is Armistice, a Holiday.
True, the Good and the Beautiful, The, *abr.*
Vivaldi.
What Curious Dresses All Men Wear.
What Is to Be Given.
Will You Perhaps.
You Are a Jew!

Schwob, Marcel
Actions.
Moments.
Things Dead.

Scollard, Clinton
Ad Patriam.
Archer, The.
As I Came Down from Lebanon.
At the Tomb of Washington.
Ballad of Lieutenant Miles.
Ballad of Paco Town, The.
Ballade of the Golfer in Love.
Battle of Plattsburg Bay, The.
Be Ye in Love with April-Tide.
Bell, A.
Bethlehem.
Boasting of Sir Peter Parker, The.
Butterfly, The.
Cricket.
Daughter of the Regiment, The.
Deed of Lieutenant Miles, The.
Deeds of Valor at Santiago.
Eve of Bunker Hill, The.
First Thanksgiving, The.
First Thanksgiving Day.
First Three, The.
For Our Dead.
Great Voice, The.
High Hill, The.
Horizons.
If Only the Dreams Abide.
In the Sultan's Garden.
Khamsin.
King of Dreams, The.
King Philip's Last Stand.
Kris Kringle.
Land of Our Fathers.
Man, A.
Memnon.
Memorial Day.
Men of the *Maine*, The.
Men of the *Merrimac*, The.
Montgomery at Quebec.
Noureddin, the Son of the Shah.
On a Bust of Lincoln.
On an American Soldier of Fortune Slain in France.
On the Eve of Bunker Hill.
Out in the Wood.
Patchwork.
Peace.
Petition.
Prayer, A: "Each day I walk with wonder."
Private Blair of the Regulars.
Quest, The.
Rain Riders.
Ride of Tench Tilghman, The.
Riding with Kilpatrick.
Saint Leger.
Sanctuary.
Sea Shells.
Sidney Godolphin.
Sleeper, The.
Song for Memorial Day.
Streams.
Sunflowers.
Swimming.
Thanksgiving Song.
There Is a Pool on Garda.
To William Sharp.
Unreturning, The.
Valor of Ben Milam, The.
Way to Bethlehem, The.
Wayne at Stony Point.
Winds of God, The.

Scollard, Mrs. Clinton *See* **Rittenhouse, Jessie Belle**

Scollard, Elisabeth
He Leads.

Scoloker, Anthony
Her Praises.

Scott, Alexander (1520?-1590?)
Bequest of His Heart, A.
Lament, A; 1547, *abr.*
Of May.
Quha Is Perfyte.
Returne The, Hairt.
Rondel of Love [*or* Luve], A.
To Luve Unluvit.
Up, Helsum Hairt.
Wha Is Perfyte.

Scott, Alexander (1920-)
Calvinist Sang.
Coronach.
Letter to Robert Fergusson.

Scott, Clement William
Lilian Adelaide Neilson.
Oh Promise Me.
Rus in Urbe.
Story of a Stowaway, The.

Scott, Duncan Campbell
Above St. Irénée.
At Delos.
At Gull Lake: August, 1810.
At Les Eboulements.
At the Cedars.
Bells.
Compline.
Ecstasy.
En Route.
End of the Day, The.
Fallen, The.
Forsaken, The.
Half-Breed Girl, The.
In November.
In the Selkirks.
Life and Death.
Little Song, A.
Night and the Pines.
Night Hymns on Lake Nipigon.
Night in June, A.
O Turn Once More.
Off Rivière du Loup.
On the Way to the Mission.
Onondaga Madonna, The.
Ottawa.
Piper of Arll, The.
Power.
Prairie Water Colour, A.
Prairie Wind.
Rapids at Night.
Reed-Player, The.
Sailor's Sweetheart, The.
Song, A: "In the air there are no coral-/ Reefs."
Thoughts.
Watkwenies.

Scott, Evelyn ("Ernest Souza")
Autumn Night.

Scott, Francis Reginald
À l'Ange Avantgardien.
Bangkok.
Bonne Entente.
Calamity.
Canadian Authors Meet, The.
Caring.
Cloth of Gold.
Conflict.
Eden.
Examiner.
For Brian Priestman.
Full Valleys.
Grain of Rice, A.
Lakeshore.
Lass in Wonderland, A.
Laurentian Shield.
No Curtain.
Old Song.
Recovery.
Saturday Sundae.
To the Poets of India.
Tourist Time.
Trans Canada.
Vision.
Will to Win.
Windfall.

Scott, Fred Newton
Romeo and Juliet, *parody.*

Scott, Frederick George
Ad Majorem Dei Gloriam.
Crucifixion.
Dawn.
Easter Island.
In the Woods.
Knowledge.
Requiescat.
Samson.
Snowstorm, The.
A
"Te Judice."
Time.
Unnamed Lake, The.
Van Elsen.

Scott, Geoffrey
All Our Joy Is Enough.
Frutta di Mare.
Hector, the captain bronzed, from single fight.
I Love the Beginning of All Rain.
Skaian Gate, The, *sel.*
What Was Solomon's Mind.

Scott, John, of Amwell
Drum, The.
Ode: "I hate that drum's discordant sound."
Retort on the Foregoing.

Scott, Johnie
American Dream, The *sel.*
Poem for Joyce.
Short Poem for Frustrated Poets, A.
"Speech, or dark cities screaming."
What Poetry Is for Me.

Scott, Louise Binder, *and* J. J. Thompson
Birthday Candles.
Birthday Gifts.

Scott, Nancy Bockius
Little Gopher Man, The.

Scott, Peter Dale
Argenteuil County.
Loon's Egg, The.

Scott, Robert Balgarnie Young
Doxology for Peace.
O God of Light.
O Voice That Calls to Me.
Prayer at Eventide.

Scott, Rosco Gilmore
Be Still My Heart.

Scott, Thomas
Angels, Roll the Rock Away!

Scott, Tom
Sea Dirge.

Scott, Sir Walter
Abbess, The ("The Abbess was of noble blood").
Aged Carle, The.
Alice Brand.
Allen-a-Dale.
And What though Winter Will Pinch Severe.
Anna-Marie, Love, Up Is the Sun.
Annot Lyle's Song: "Birds of Omen."
Antiquary, The, *sels.*
Ave Maria.
Battle, The ("By this, though deep the evening fell").
Battle, The ("Not far advanc'd was morning day").
Betrothed, The, *sel.*
Bible, The.
Blue Bonnets over the Border.
Boat Song.
Bonnie Dundee.
Bonny, Bonny Owl, The.
Bonny Dundee.
Book of Books, The.
Border Ballad.
Breathes There the [*or* a] Man [with Soul So Dead].
Bride of Lammermoor, The, *sel.*
Brignall Banks.
Challenge.
Chase, The ("Harp of the North!").
Christmas.
Christmas in England.
Christmas in the Olden Time.
Claud Halcro's Invocation.
Conversation.
Coronach ("He is gone on the mountain").
County Guy.
Datur Hora Quieti.
Dies Irae.
Divine Volume, The.
Doom of Devorgoil, The, *sels.*
Dreary Change, The.
Edmund's Song.
Eve of Saint John, The.
False Love.
Farewell, Thou Minstrel Harp.
Farewell to the land where the clouds love to rest.
Father's Notes of Woe, A.
"Feast was over in Branksome tower, The."
Flodden.
Football Song.
Foray, The.
Fortunes of Nigel, The, *sel.*
Friday.
Gallant Ship, The.
Gathering, The.
Gathering Song of Donald the Black [*or* Donald Dhu *or* Donuil Dhu].
Gellatley's Song to the Deerhounds.
Gin by Pailfuls.
Glee for King Charles.
Glenfinlas; or, Lord Ronald's Coronach.
Guy Mannering, *sels.*
Hail to the Chief, Who in Triumph Advances!
Harlaw.
Harold the Dauntless, *sel.*
Harold's Song.
Harp of the North.
Harp of the North, Farewell.
He paused: the listening dames again.
Heart of Midlothian, The, *sels.*
Helvellyn.
Herring, The.
Hie Away!
Humble boon was soon obtain'd, The.
Hunter's Song.
Hunting Song.
Hunting Tribes of Air and Earth, The.
Hymn to the Virgin.
I Asked of My Harp.
In peace, Love tunes the Shepherd's reed.
Indifferent, but indifferent—pshaw! he doth it not.
Innominatus.
It Was an English Ladye Bright.
Ivanhoe, *sels.*
Jock of [*or* o'] Hazeldean.
Kenilworth, *sel.*
Lady of the Lake, The, *sels.*
Last Minstrel, The.
Lay of the Last Minstrel, *sels.*
Leaders, Old Style.
Legend of Montrose, The, *sel.*
Lighthouse, The.
Lochinvar.
Look Not, Thou.
Love of Country.
Lucy Ashton's Song.
Lullaby of an Infant Chief.
MacGregor's Gathering.
Madge Wildfire Sings.
Maid of Neidpath, The.
Man the Enemy of Man.
March, March [Ettrick and Teviotdale].
Marmion, *sels.*
Melrose Abbey.
Mermaids and Mermen.
Minstrel Responds to Flattery, The.
Monastery, The, *sels.*
Monks of Bangor's March, The.
My Native Land.
My Own, My Native Land.
Native Land.
Nativity Chant, The.
Nelson and Pitt.
Nelson, Pitt, Fox.
Nora's Vow.
November's sky is chill and drear.
"Now, yield thee, or by Him who made."
O, Woman! ("O, Woman! in our hours of ease).
Old Christmas.
Old Christmastide.
Old Mortality, *sels.*
On a Day's Stint.
On Leaving Mrs. Brown's Lodgings.
On the Setting Sun.
Outlaw, The.
Oyster, The.
Palmer, The.
Patriot, The.
Patriotism.
Peveril of the Peak, *sel.*
Pibroch of Donuil [*or* Donald] Dhu.
Pirate, The, *sels.*
Pride of Youth, The.
Proud Maisie.
Quentin Durward, *sel.*
Rebecca's Hymn.
Red Harlaw.
Rob Roy, *sel.*
Roderick Dhu.
Rokeby, *sels.*
Rosabelle.
Rose is fairest when 'tis budding new, The.
Rover, The.
Rover's Adieu, The.
Rover's Farewell, The.
Serenade, A: "Ah! County Guy, the hour is nigh."
Shepherd in Winter, The.
Sir Walter Scott's Tribute.
Sir William of Deloraine at the Wizard's Tomb.
Soldier, Rest! [Thy Warfare O'er].
Soldier's Song.
Song: "Ah! County Guy, the hour is nigh."
Song: "O Brignall banks are wild and fair."
Song: "Soldier, rest! thy warfare o'er."
Song: "Weary lot is thine, fair maid, A."
Song: "Where shall the lover rest."
Song of Albert Graeme.
Song of the Reim-Kennar, The.
Song of the Tempest.
Song of the White Lady of Avenel.
"Speak not of niceness when there's chance of wreck."
Talisman, The, *sel.*
'Tis Merry in Greenwood.
To a Lady with Flowers from the Roman Wall.
To a Lock of Hair.
To an Oak Tree.
To William Erskine, Esq.
Toils Are Pitched, The.
True love's the gift which God has given.
'Twas when fleet Snowball's head was waxen gray.
Twist Ye, Twine Ye! Even So.
Violet, The.
Wasted, Weary, Wherefore Stay.
Waverley, *sels.*
Weary Lot Is Thine, A.
Western Waves of Ebbing Day, The.
When dark December glooms the day.
Where Shall the Lover Rest.
Why Sit'st [*or* Sitt'st] Thou by That Ruined Hall.
William and Helen.
Woman's Faith ("Woman's faith and woman's trust").
Woodstock, *sel.*
You talk of gayety and innocence!
Young Lochinvar.
Scott, William Bell
Glenkindie.
Hero-Worship.
Love's Calendar.
My Mother.
Norns Watering Yggdrasill, The.
Pygmalion.
To the Dead.
Witch's Ballad, The.
Youth and Age.
Scott, Winfield Townley
Annual Legend.
Another Return.
Baldness and the Swan.
Bermuda Suite.
Biography for Traman, *sel.*
Blue Sleigh.
Broken Shell.
Codicil for Pvt. John Hogg's Will.
Come Green Again.
Confidential.
Difference, The.
Double Tree, The.
Exercise in Aesthetics.
Flared down from broken cloud the calipered light.
Game, The.
Gert Swasey.
Green and Red and Darkness.
Hour Is Late, The.
House, The.
How Shall I Ever Come to Any Good?
Indian Summer—Buffalo Summer.
Into the Wind.
Ivory Bed, The.
Landscape as Metal and Flowers.
Let us record/ The evenings when we were innocents of twenty.
Memento.
Merrill's Brook.
Mr. Whittier.

Mrs. Severin.
Natural Causes.
Old Talk.
On Re-Reading the Complete Works of an Elder Poet.
Re-run.
Sonnet: "I watched the sea for hours blind with sun."
Sonnet XIII: "Rise up, rise up, Jack Spratt. And you, his wife."
Sonnet XV: "This is the way we say it in our time."
Sonnet XII: "Virgins terrify too many men."
Swedish Angel.
Three American Women and a German Bayonet.
To L. B. S.
To Marry Strangers.
Two.
Two Lives and Others.
U.S. Sailor with the Japanese Skull, The.
Unsexed by the Cold Sea.
Watch Hill.
Wax.
We'll All Feel Gay.

Scott-Gatty, Sir Alfred
Maria Jane.
Three Little Pigs, The.

Scott-Hopper, Queenie
Amy Elizabeth Ermyntrude Annie.
My Party.
Railway Tunnel, The.
Very Nearly.
What the Thrush Says.

Scott of Amwell, John *See* **Scott, John, of Amwell**

Scovell, E. J.
Before she first had smiled or looked with calm.
Bloody Cranesbill on the Dunes.
Boy Fishing, The.
Dark World, A.
Elegy, An: "In early winter before the first snow."
Evening Scene.
First Year, The, *sel.*
Love's Immaturity.
Open Air Performance of "As You Like It", An.
Shadows of Chrysanthemums.
Swan's Feet, The.

"Scrace, Richard" (Mrs. J. B. Williamson)
At the Place of the Roman Baths.
Gipsies, The.

Scriven, Joseph
Unfailing Friend, The.
What a Friend We Have in Jesus.

Scrope, Sir Carr
As Amoret with Phyllis Sat.

Scruggs, Anderson M.
Christmas, 1930.
Christmas Today.
City Trees.
Glory to Them.
How Can They Honor Him?
Only the Dream Is Real.
Pines.
Sonnet on Turning a Radio Dial.
Street Beggar.
To the Portrait of an Unknown Man.

Scudder, Eliza
Quest, The.
Thou Life within My Life.
To a Young Child.
Who by Searching Can Find Out God?

Scudder, Vida Dutton
Thy Kingdom, Lord, We Long For.

Scully, James
Crew Practice on Lake Bled, in Jugoslavia.
Facing Up.
Fantasy of Little Waters, A.
Glass Blower, The.
Grandson, The.
Late Spring, A.
Lt. Cmdr. T. E. Sanderson.
Midsummer.
Pier.

Seager, Millicent
Birds' Nests.

Seager, Ralph W.
Taste of Prayer, The.

Seagrave, Robert
Rise, My Soul.

Seal, Brajendranath
I was one with woods; my body, the Earth.
Quest Eternal, The, *sel.*

Sealey, Mrs. Macey P.
God's Unspeakable Gift.

Seaman, E. William
Higgledy-piggledy/ Ludwig van Beethoven.

Seaman, Hellene
Hills Keep Holy Ground, The.

Seaman, Sir Owen
At the Sign of the Cock.
Ballad of a Bun, A.
Between Midnight and Morning.
Bulbul, The ("Bulbul hummeth like a book, The").
From "A Vigo-Street Eclogue."
In Praise of Commonplace.
Ode to Spring in the Metropolis, An.
Of Baiting the Lion.
Of the Stalking of the Stag.
Old Songs, The.
Penalties of Baldness, The.
Plea for Trigamy, A.
Presto Furioso.
Rhyme of the Kipperling, The.
Seamy Side of Motley, The.
Song of Renunciation, A.
To a Boy-Poet of the Decadence.
To Julia in Shooting Togs.
Uses of Ocean, The.
Victory.
Warrior's Lament, The.

Searing, Laura Catherine Redden ("Howard Glyndo)
Disarmed.

Sears, Edmund Hamilton
Angels' Song, The.
Birth Song of Christ, The.
Christmas Carol: "It came upon the midnight clear."
Christmas Hymn, A.
It Came upon the Midnight Clear.
Peace on Earth.

Seaver, Edwin
To My People.

"Sec."
News, The.

Sedgwick, Henry Dwight
Leo to His Mistress.

Sedley, Sir Charles
Advice to the Old Beaux.
Ah Cloris! that I now could sit.
Ballad to the Tune of Bateman, A.
Child and Maiden.
Constancy.
Doctor and His Patients, The.
Get You Gone.
Hears Not My Phillis, How the Birds.
Indifference, The.
Knotting Song, The.
Love Still Has Something of the Sea.
Mulberry Garden, The, *sel.*
My Heart at Rest.
Not Celia That I Juster Am.
On a Cock at Rochester.
On Fruition.
Out of French.
Phillis Is My Only Joy.
Phillis Knotting.
Phyllis.
Song: "Ah Cloris! that I now could sit."
Song: "Hears not my Phyllis how the birds."
Song: "Love still has something of the sea."
Song: "Not, Celia, that I juster am."
Song: "Phillis is my only joy."
Song: "Phillis, let's shun the common fate."
Song: "Phillis, men say that all my vows."
Song: "Phyllis [*or* Phillis] is my only joy."
Song: "See! Hymen comes; how his torch blazes."
Song: "Smooth was the water, calm the air."
Song A-la-Mode.
Song to Celia.
To Celia.
To Chloris.
To Cloris ("Cloris, I cannot say your eyes").
To Cloris ("Cloris, I justly am betray'd").
To Nysus.
To Phillis.
To Scilla.

Sedulius, Caelius
Apostrophe to Death.
Carmen Paschale [*or* Easter Song], *sels.*
Christ Quiets the Tempest.
Easter Song.
Hail, Maiden Root.
Invocation: "Eternal God omnipotent! The One."
Magi Visit Herod, The.
Miracle, The.
Slaughter of the Innocents by Order of King Herod, The.

"Seedy, Will." *See* **Demorest, William Curtis**

Seeger, Alan
I Have a Rendezvous with Death.
Ode in Memory of the American Volunteers Fallen for France.
Rendezvous, The.
To —— in Church.

Seeger, Peter
Waist Deep in the Big Muddy.

Seegmiller, Wilhelmina
Old Doll, The.

Seferis, George
Argonautica.
Now When So Much Has Passed.

Sefton, Eva Weaver
Living Bread.

Segal, Y. Y.
King Rufus.
Rhymes.

Segooa, Demetrius
Praises of the Train.

Seidel, Frederick
Dayley Island.
Negro Judge, A.
Sickness, The.

Seiffert, Marjorie Allen ("Elijah Hay")
Ballad: "Follow, follow me into the South."
Ballad of Riding, A.
Dream House, The.
Interior.
Iron Fare.
Italian Chest, An.
Japanese Vase Wrought in Metals, A.
Lorenzo's Bas-Relief for a Florentine Chest.

Seiffert (continued)
Old Woman, The.
Seitz, Don C.
Night at Gettysburg.
Sekula, Irene
Mother Goose (circa 2054).
Seldon, Frank H.
To My Setter, Scout.
Selgas y Carrasco, José
Empty Cradle, The.
Selig, Richard
Phoenix, The.
Seligman, Ulma
Truth Has Perished.
Seljouk, Mehdi Ali
Like the Prime Mover.
Rendezvous with God, *sel.*
There was one in the myriad throngs.
Sellar, Walter Carruthers, *and* Julian Yeatma
How I Brought the Good News from Aix to Ghent (or Vice Versa).
Selle, Robert E.
Stepping Ashore.
Selva, Salomón de la
Tropical Town.
Selyns, Henricus
Epitaph for Peter Stuyvesant.
Nuptial Song.
Of Scolding Wives and the Third Day Ague.
On Maids and Cats.
On Mercenary and Unjust Bailiffs.
Reasons for and against Marrying Widows.
Upon the Bankruptcy of a Physician.
Sempill, Robert
Life and Death of Habbie Simson, the Piper of Kilbarchan, The.
Life and Death of the Piper of Kilbarchan, The.
Sen, Pradip
And Then the Sun.
Seneca (Lucius Annaeus Seneca)
Chorus: "After death, nothing is."
Chorus: "Climb at Court for me that will."
End of Being, The.
Epithalamium for Murder.
Medea, *sel.*
Of the Mean and Sure Estate.
Senec. Traged. ex Thyeste Chor. 2.
Stand, Whoso List.
Stood Who So List upon the Slipper Toppe.
Thyestes, *sels.*
Troas, *sel.*
Senesh, Hannah
Blessed Match, The.
Senghor, Léopold Sédar
Black Woman.
Night of Sine.
On the Appeal from the Race of Sheba: II.
Paris in the Snow.
Prayer for Peace: II.
Songs for a Three-String Guitar.
To New York.
We Delighted, My Friend.
"Seranus." *See* **Harrison, Susan Frances**
Sergeant, Howard
Autumn again, the leopardlike and burning.
High Kingdom.
Inland Sea, The.
Inundation, The.
Leaves of Europe, The, *sels.*
Man Meeting Himself.
Morning Song for a Lover.
Serini, Vittorio
Anniversary of Antonia Pozzi's Death by Suicide.
City by Night.
Serraillier, Ian
After Ever Happily; or, The Princess and the Woodcutter.
Fox, The.
Fox Rhyme, The.
Headless Gardener, The.
Mouse in the Wainscot, The.
Piano Practice.
Tickle Rhyme, The.
Serrano Plaja, Arturo
Banished, The.
Service, Robert William
Call of the Wild, The
Carry On!
Cremation of Sam McGee, The.
Fleurette.
It's a Mighty Good World.
Jean Desprez.
Law of the Yukon, The.
Men of the High North.
Men That Don't Fit In.
My Madonna.
Rhymes of a Rolling Stone, *sel.*
Scribe's Prayer, The.
Shooting of Dan McGrew, The.
Skeptic, The.
Spell of the Yukon, The.
Thank God! there is always a Land of Beyond.
Wonderer, The.
Sethna, K. D.
Tree of Time.
Seton, Elizabeth
Mary, Virgin and Mother.
"Setoun, Gabriel" (Thomas Nicoll Hepburn)
Eyes of God, The.
Fairy Ship, The.
How the Flowers Grow.
Jack Frost.
Mystery, A.
Rain in Spring.
Romance.
Wind's Song, The.
World's Music, The.
Settle, Elkanah
Cambyses, *sel.*
Congratulatory Poem to the Honoured Edmund Morris, Esq., on His Happy Marriage, A, *abr.*
She That with Love Is Not Possessed.
Sevelingen, Meinloh von *See* **Meinloh von Sevelingen**
Sewall, Alice Archer *See* **James, Alice Archer Sewall**
Sewall, Frank
Roll Out, O Song.
Sewall, Harriet Winslow
Why Thus Longing?
Sewall, Jonathan Mitchell
Cato, *sel.*
On Independence.
War and Washington.
Sewall, Samuel
Humble Springs of Stately Sandwich Beach, The.
This Morning Tom Child, the Painter, Died.
To Be Engraven on a Dial.
To the Rev'd Mr. Jno. Sparhawk on the Birth of His Son.
Upon the Springs Issuing out from the Foot of Plimouth Beach.
Wednesday, January 1, 1701.
Seward, Anna
On Catania and Syracuse Swallowed Up by an Earthquake.
On the Use of New and Old Words in Poetry.
To Honora Sneyd, April 1773.
Written December 1790.
Written in the Spring of 1785 on the Death of the Poet Laureate.
Sewell, Elizabeth
Forgiveness.
Genesis.
Image Imagination.
Job.
Sewell, George
Dying Man in His Garden, The.
Sexton, Anne
Addict, The.
All My Pretty Ones.
December 18th.
Division of Parts, The.
Farmer's Wife, The.
Flee on Your Donkey.
For God While Sleeping.
Fortress, The.
Funnel.
Her Kind.
In the Deep Museum.
Kind Sir: These Woods ("Kind Sir: This is an old game").
Letter Written on a Ferry [While] Crossing Long Island Sound.
Little Girl, My Stringbean, My Lovely Woman.
Lost Ingredient, The.
Moss of His Skin, The.
Ringing the Bells.
Road Back, The.
Said the Poet to the Analyst.
Some Foreign Letters.
Starry Night, The.
Sun, The.
Three Green Windows.
Torn Down from Glory Daily.
Truth the Dead Know, The.
Unknown Girl in the Maternity Ward.
Water.
Where I Live in This Honorable House of the Laurel Tree.
Woman with Girdle.
You, Doctor Martin.
Seymour, A. J.
Over Guiana, Clouds, *sel.*
Seymour, Aaron Crossley Hobart
Christ, the Conqueror, *abr.*
Seymour, William Kean
Caesar Remembers.
Foiled Reaper, The.
To Music.
Seymour-Smith, Martin
Green Wall My Grave.
Shabistari, Sa'd ud-din Mahmud
In the Secret Rose Garden.
Shackleford, Theodore Henry
Big Bell in Zion, The.
Shacklett, Mildred D.
Autumn Gloves.
Autumn Train.
Belonging to Summer.
Broadcasting.
Deep in the Woods.
Four Kinds of Wading.
Golden Tacks.
Movies in the Fire.
Mud Cakes.
Sometimes Wish, A.
Swing Ship, The.
Winter Feathers.
Winter Treats.
Shadwell, Bertrand
Aguinaldo.
Cervera.
Shadwell, Thomas
Amorous Bigot, The, *sel.*
Expostulation, The.
Good-Morrow, A.
Let Some Great Joys Pretend to Find.
Love and Wine.

Song: "Fringéd vallance of your eyes advance, The."
Squire of Alsatia, The, *sels.*
Timon of Athens, *sel.*
Victory in Hungary, The.
Woman-Captain, The, *sel.*

Shairp, John Campbell
Bush aboon Traquair, The.
Caileach Bein-y-Vreich.
I Have a Life with Christ to Live.

Shakespeare, William
Absence.
Address of Richard III to His Army, The.
After Horace ("Not marble, nor the gilded").
Age and Youth.
Ah, when the means are gone that buy this praise.
All That Glisters Is Not Gold.
All the World's a Stage.
All's but naught.
All's Well That Ends Well, *sel.*
Ambition.
And let the canakin clink, [clink].
And Will He [*or* A'] Not Come Again?
Antony and Cleopatra, *sels.*
Antony's Oration.
Ariel's Dirge.
Ariel's Song: "Come unto these yellow sands."
Ariel's Song: "Full fathom five thy father lies."
Ariel's Song: "Where the bee sucks, there suck I."
As You Like It, *sels.*
Asleep, My Love?
Aubade.
Autolycus [*or* Autolycus' Songs].
Balcony Scene, The.
Balthasar's Song.
Banished Duke [Living in the Forest] Speaks to His Retainers, The.
Be True.
Beauty Is a Witch.
Before Agincourt.
Blast of War, The.
Blessings on the Bride-Bed.
Blind Love.
Blood hath been shed ere now, i' the olden time.
Blossom, The.
Blow, Blow, Thou Winter Wind.
Blow, Thou Winter Wind.
Blow, Winds.
Bottom's Song.
Boy, bristle thy courage up; for Falstaff he is dead.
Boy's Song to Mariana.
Brave New World.
Brutus.
Brutus Explains Why He Murdered Caesar.
But if thou needs will hunt, be ruled by me.
But looke where sadly the poore wretch comes reading.
But love, first learnèd in a lady's eyes.
But Man, Proud Man.
Caliban ("Be not afeard; the isle is full of noises").
Cardinal Wolsey's Farewell.
Cares of Majesty, The.
Carpe Diem.
Casket Song, A.
Cassius Poisons Brutus' Mind.
Ceres, most bounteous lady, thy rich leas.
Charm, The.
Christmas.
Cleopatra.
Cleopatra and Her Barge.
Cleopatra's Barge.
Cleopatra's Death.
Cleopatra's Lament.
Clouds.
Clown's Song, The ("Come away, come away, death").
Clown's Song ("O mistris mine where are you roming?").
Cod-Piece That Will House, The.
Come apace, good Audrey. I will fetch up your goats, Audrey.
Come Away, Come Away, Death.
Come Away, Death.
Come Buy! Come Buy!.
Come, Gentle Night.
Come hither, boy: if ever thou shalt love.
Come Night, Come Romeo.
Come, Thou Monarch of the Vine.
Commonwealth of the Bees, The.
Conscience.
Consolation, A.
Content ("My crown is in my heart").
Country Song.
Course of True Love, The.
Courser and the Jennet, The.
Cowards ("Cowards die many times before their deaths").
Crabbed Age and Youth.
Crickets sing, and mans ore-labor'd sense, The.
Crown o' the earth doth melt, The.
Cymbeline, *sels.*
. . . daffodils / That come before the swallow dares.
Death of Adonis, The.
Death of Antony.
Death of Cleopatra.
Death of Cowards, The.
Death of Death, The.
Death of Hamlet.
Death of Kings, The ("Let's talk of graves").
Death of Lear.
Death of Othello.
Desdemona's Song.
Dialogue in Praise of the Owl and the Cuckoo.
Did Not the Heavenly Rhetoric of Thine Eye.
Dirge: "Come away, come away, death."
Dirge: "Fear no more the heat o' the sun."
Dirge of Love.
Discovery of Pity.
Divine Harmony, The.
Dost thou in conscience think—tell me, Emilia.
Doubts ("Our doubts are traitors").
Dream of Wrecks, A.
Drinking Song, A.
Duet.
Dumain's Rhymes.
Dying Men.
Empty Life, The.
England ("This England never did").
England ("This royal throne of kings").
Epilogue: "Now my charms are all o'erthrown."
Epilogue: "Now the hungry lion roars."
Epilogue: "Thus far, with rough and all-unable pen."
Epilogue: "When that I was and a little tiny boy."
Epilogue to "A Midsummer Night's Dream."
Epitaph: "Done to death by slanderous tongues."
Eve of Agincourt, The.
Everlasting Rest.
Evil Designs.
Fairies' Lullaby, The.
Fairies' Song, The.
Fairy Blessing, The.
Fairy Life, The.
Fairy Lullaby ("You spotted snakes").
Fairy Queen, The.
Fairy Song, A.
Fairy Songs ("Come unto these yellow sands").
Fairy Songs ("Now the hungry lion roars").
Fairy Songs ("Now, until the break of day").
Fairy Songs ("Over hill, over dale").
Fairy Songs ("Where the bee sucks").
Fairy Songs ("You spotted snakes with double tongue").
Fairy Land.
Fairy Land.
Fairy's Life, A.
Fairy's Song [*or* Wander-Song].
Fancy.
Farewell: "Farewell! thou art too dear for my possessing."
Farewell Content.
Fear No More the Heat o' the Sun.
Fear of Death, The.
Feare No More the Heate o' the Sun.
Feste's Songs.
Fidele [*or* Fidele's Dirge].
Fie on Sinful Fantasy!
Fire Seven Times Tried This, The.
Flower of This Purple Dye.
Flowers ("Out, Alas!").
Flowers of Perdita, The.
Food of Love, The.
Footpath Way, The.
For a Patriot.
For I the Ballad Will Repeat.
For much imaginary work was there.
For Thy Sweet Love.
Fortune and Men's Eyes.
Frailty, Thy Name Is Woman.
Friar Laurence's Cell.
Friar of Orders Grey, The.
Frustra.
Give me my sword. / Who's there?
Give me some music.—Now, good morrow, friends.
Go, bear him in thine arms.
Go, gentlemen, every man unto his charge.
Good in Everything.
Good Morrow. 'Tis Saint Valentine's Day.
Good morrow to you both.
Good Name, A.
Good shepherd, tell this youth what 'tis to love.
Good Sir, Whose Powers Are These?
Gracious Time, The ("Some say that ever 'gainst that season comes").
Gratitude.
Greenwood Tree, The.
Had I plantation of this isle, my lord.
Hallowed Season, The.
Hamlet, *sels.*
Hamlet's Instructions to the Players.
Hamlet's Soliloquy.
Hark! Hark! the Lark.
Hate the Idle Pleasures.
He Jests at Scars [That Never Felt a Wound].
He That Has and a Little Tiny Wit.
Heavenly Rhetoric, The.
Heere is better then the open ayre, take it thankfully.
Helena and Hermia.
Helen of Troy.
Henry V at [*or* before] Harfleur.
Henry V to His Soldiers.
Henry Fifth's Address to His Soldiers.
Her Beauty.
Her gentlewomen, like the Nereids.

Shakespeare (continued)
Here is the place my Lord, good my Lord enter.
Here lies a wretched corse.
Here Lies Juliet.
Here's a knocking indeede.
High Wedlock Then Be Honoured.
His legs bestrid the ocean: his rear'd arm.
Honour, Riches, Marriage Blessing.
Horse, A.
Horse, The.
How all occasions do inform against me.
How came the noble Timon to this change?
How now? what noise is that?
How Should I Your True Love Know.
How Sweet the Moonlight Sleeps upon This Bank!
Howle, howle, howle, howle: O you are men of stones.
I am thy fathers spirit.
I Come to Bury Caesar.
I have laied these sheetes you bad me on the bed.
I Have Lived Long Enough.
I pray you, in your letters.
I will o'ertake thee, Cleopatra, and.
If Alcibiades kill my countrymen.
If I profane with my unworthiest hand.
If It Do Come to Pass.
If Music Be the Food of Love.
If She Be Made of White and Red.
If we shadows have offended.
If you have tears, prepare to shed them now.
I'faith, sweetheart, methinks now you are in an excellent good temporality.
I'll Live in This Poor Rime.
Imagination.
In God's name, cheerly on, courageous friends.
In Such a Night.
In the Greenwood.
In the Spring-Time.
In Tune with the Infinite.
Ingratitude.
Is she to bee buried in Christian buriall, that wilfully seekes her owne salvation?
Isabella Condemns Tyranny.
It faded on the crowing of the cock.
It is the very error of the moon.
It Was a Lover and His Lass.
Jog On, Jog On [the Foot-Path Way].
John of Gaunt's Dying Speech.
Jolly Shepherd, The.
Juliet's Yearning.
Julius Caesar, *sels.*
King Henry IV, Pt. II, *sels.*
King Henry V, *sels.*
King Henry VI, Part I, *sels.*
King Henry VI, Pt. II, *sels.*
King Henry VI, Pt. III, *sels.*
King Henry before the Field of Saint Crispian.
King Henry VI Yearns for the Simple Life.
King Is Dead, A.
King John, *sels.*
King Lear, *sels.*
King Lear Condemns His Daughter.
King Lear Pledges Revenge.
King Lear to the Storm.
King Richard II, *sels.*
King Richard III, *sels.*
Lament for Imogen.
Lament of Guiderius and Arviragus.
Lawn as White as Driven Snow.
Lear and Cordelia ("Some officers take them away").
Let four captains/ Bear Hamlet, like a soldier, to the stage.
Let Me Play the Fool.
Life and Death.
Life without Passion, The.
Limerick: "And let the canakin clink, [clink]."
Lion of Winter, The.
Living Juliet, The.
Lo! Here the Gentle Lark.
Love ("Tell me where is fancy bred").
Love ("What is love? 'tis not hereafter").
Love Concealed.
Love Forsworn.
Love-in-Idleness.
Love in Spring-Time.
Lover's Complaint, A.
Love's Despair.
Love's Harmony.
Love's Labour's Lost, *sels.*
Love's Not Time's Fool.
Love's Perjuries.
Lullaby for Titania.
Lunatic, the Lover, and the Poet, The.
Lust.
Macbeth, *sels.*
Madrigal A: "Crabbed age and youth."
Madrigal: "Take, O take those lips away."
Madrigal: "Tell me where is fancy bred."
Magic.
Make me a willow cabin at your gate.
Man ("What a piece of work is a man!").
Man New Made.
Mark Antony's Lament.
Marriage of True Minds.
Marry, if you would put me to verses or to dance.
Master, the Swabber, The.
Measure for Measure, *sels.*
Memory.
Merchant of Venice, The, *sels.*
Mercutio Describes Queen Mab.
Mercutio's Queen Mab Speech.
Mercy ("The quality of mercy is not strained").
Merry Heart, The.
Merry Note, A.
Merry Wives of Windsor, The, *sels.*
Methinks your looks are sad, your cheer appall'd.
Not Poppy, nor Mandragora.
Not Thine Own.
Now Entertain Conjecture of a Time.
Now Hamlet, where's Polonius?
Now I want/ Spirits to endorce, art to enchant.
Now the Hungry Lion Roars.
O Amiable Lovely Death.
O Charmian,/Where think'st thou he is now?
O! Full of Scorpions.
O, lest your true love may seem false in this.
O, let us pay the time but needful woe.
O Mistress Mine Where Are You Roaming?
O my worshipful lord, an't please your grace.
O, pardon me, thou bleeding piece of earth.
O Romeo, Romeo! wherefore art thou Romeo?
Oh Sunne,/ Burne the great sphere thou mov'st in.
O, what a rogue and peasant slave am I!
O, what a war of looks was then between them!
Oberon and Titania to the Fairy Train.
Of the Death of Kings.
On a Day—Alack the Day!
On Death.
On Degree.
Once More into the Breach.
Once More unto the Breach [Dear Friends, Once More].
Ophelia's Death.
Ophelia's Songs.
Opportunity.
Orlando's Rhymes.
Othello, *sels.*
Our Little Life.
Our Revels Now Are Ended.
Ousel Cock, The.
Out, Out, Brief Candle!
Outer and the Inner Man, The.
Over Hill, Over Dale.
Pages' Song, The.
Passionate Shepherd's Song, The.
Patience on a Monument.
Pedlar, The.
Pedlar's Song, The ("Lawn as white. . .").
Pedlar's Song, The ("When daffodils. . .").
Perdita's Garden.
Perdition catch my soul.
Perfect Tribute, The.
Pericles, *sel.*
Pericles, Prince of Tyre.
Perils of Darkness.
Petruchio Is Undaunted by Katharina.
Phoenix and the Turtle, The.
Polonius' Advice to Laertes.
Polonius to Laertes.
Poor Naked Wretches.
Poor Soul.
Poor Wat.
Portia's Plea for Mercy.
Portrait of Brutus.
Portrait of Caesar.
Portrait of Cressida.
Portrait of Helen.
Post Mortem.
Power of Music, The.
Pray, do not mock me.
Prithee, honey-sweet husband, let me bring thee to Staines.
Prospero [Ends the Revels].
Puck and the Fairy.
Puck Speaks.
Puck's Song ("Now the hungry lion").
Quality of Mercy, The ("The quality of mercy is not strained.").
Queen Mab.
Queene Mab.
Rain It Raineth Every Day, The.
Rape of Lucrece, The.
Remembrance.
Remembrance of Things Past.
Remorse.
Remote Bermudas, The.
Revolutions.
Richard II Banishes Bolingbroke.
Richard II's Dejection.
Ridiculous Excess.
Romeo and Juliet, *sels.*
Rose Looks Fair, The.
Rugged Pyrrhus, he whose sable arm, The.
Saint Valentine's Day.
Sea Dirge, A.
Sealed in Vain.
Seals of Love.
Seasons Alter, The.
Sessions of Sweet Silent Thought.
Seven Ages of Man, The.
She Never Told Her Love.
She Should Have Died Hereafter.
Shylock's Defense.
Silvia.
Sinful father, The/ Seem'd not to strike.
Sir, welcome.
Sleep ("Methought I heard a voice").
So Sweet a Kiss.
Soliloquy from "Hamlet."
Soliloquy on Sleep.

Some Flowers o' the Spring.
Song: "Blow, blow, thou winter wind."
Song: "Come away, come away death."
Song: "Fear no more the heat o' the sun."
Song: "Full fathom [*or* fadom] five thy father lies."
Song: "Good morrow, 'tis Saint Valentine's day."
Song: "Hark, hark, the lark at heaven's gate sings."
Song: "How should I your true love know."
Song: "If the scorn of your bright eyne."
Song: "It was a lover and his lass."
Song: "O mistress mine, where are you roaming?"
Song: "Over hill, over dale."
Song: "Pardon, goddess of the night."
Song: "Sigh no more, ladies, sigh no more."
Song: Spring and Winter.
Song: "Take, O take those lips away."
Song: "Tell me where is fancy bred."
Song: "Tomorrow is [*or* Good morrow, 'tis] Saint Valentine's day."
Song: "Under the greenwood tree."
Song: "What shall he have that kill'd the deer?"
Song: "When daffodils begin to peer."
Song: "When daisies pied and violets blue."
Song: "When icicles hang by the wall."
Song: "When that I was and a little tiny boy."
Song: "Where the bee sucks, there suck I."
Song: "Who is Silvia? what is she".
Song: "You spotted snakes with double tongue."
Song at the Moated Grange, A.
Song for Mariana.
Song of Robin Goodfellow, A.
Song of the Fairies.
Song of the Fairy ("Over hill, over dale").
Song of the Musicians.
Song of the Musicians.
Song of the Two Brothers.
Song of the Two Pages.
Song to Imogen.
Song to Silvia.
Songs: Spring and Winter.
Songs of Autolycus.
Songs of the Greenwood.
Sonnet: "Against my love shall be as I am now."
Sonnet: "Against that time, if ever that time come."
Sonnet: "Ah wherefore with infection should he live."
Sonnet: "Alack! what poverty my Muse brings forth."
Sonnet: "Alas, 'tis true I have gone here and there."
Sonnet: "As an unperfect actor on the stage."
Sonnet: "As fast as thou shalt wane, so fast thou grow'st."
Sonnet: "Being your slave, what should I do but tend."
Sonnet: "Beshrew that heart that makes my heart to groan."
Sonnet: "But be contented when that fell arrest."
Sonnet: "But wherefore do not you a mightier way."
Sonnet: "Cupid laid by his brand and fell asleep."
Sonnet: "Devouring Time, blunt thou the lion's paws."
Sonnet: "Did not the heavenly rhetoric of thine eye."
Sonnet: "Expense of spirit in a waste of shame, The."
Sonnet: "Farewell, thou art too dear for my possessing."
Sonnet: "For shame! deny that thou bear'st love to any."
Sonnet: "Forward violet thus did I chide, The."
Sonnet: "From fairest creatures we desire increase."
Sonnet: "From you have I been absent in the spring."
Sonnet: "Full many a glorious morning have I seen."
Sonnet: "How can I then return in happy plight."
Sonnet: "How can my Muse want subject to invent."
Sonnet: "How heavy do I journey on the way."
Sonnet: "How like a winter hath my absence been."
Sonnet: "How oft, when thou, my music, music play'st."
Sonnet: "How sweet and lovely dost thou make the shame.
Sonnet: "I grant thou wert not married to my Muse."
Sonnet: "If the dull substance of my flesh were thought."
Sonnet: "If there be nothing new, but that which is."
Sonnet: "If thou survive my well-contented day."
Sonnet: "If thy soul check thee that I come so near."
Sonnet: "In faith, I do [*or* doe] not love thee with mine eyes."
Sonnet: "In loving thee thou know'st I am forsworn."
Sonnet: "In the old age black was not counted fair."
Sonnet: "Is it for fear to wet a widow's eye?"
Sonnet: "Is it thy will thy image should keep open."
Sonnet: "Let me confess that we two must be twain."
Sonnet: "Let me not to the marriage of true minds."
Sonnet: "Let those who are in favor with their stars."
Sonnet: "Like as the waves make toward the pebbled shore."
Sonnet: "Like as, to make our appetites more keen."
Sonnet: "Little Love-god lying once asleep, The."
Sonnet: "Lo, as a careful housewife runs to catch."
Sonnet: "Lo, in the orient when the gracious light."
Sonnet: "Look in thy glass, and tell the face thou viewest."
Sonnet: "Lord of my love, to whom in vassalage."
Sonnet: "Love is too young to know what conscience is."
Sonnet: "Music to hear, why hear'st thou music sadly?"
Sonnet: "My glass shall not persuade me I am old."
Sonnet: "My love is as a fever, longing still."
Sonnet: "My love is strengthen'd, though more weak in seeming."
Sonnet: "My mistress' eyes are nothing like the sun."
Sonnet: "My tongue-tied Muse in manners holds her still."
Sonnet: "No longer mourn for me when I am dead."
Sonnet: "No more be grieved at that which thou hast done."
Sonnet: "No, Time, thou shalt not boast that I do change."
Sonnet: "Nor mine own fears, nor the prophetic soul."
Sonnet: "Not from the stars do I my judgment pluck."
Sonnet: "Not marble, nor the gilded monuments."
Sonnet: "Not mine own fears, nor the prophetic soul."
Sonnet: "O call not me to justify the wrong."
Sonnet: "O for my sake do you with Fortune chide."
Sonnet: "O how I faint when I of you do write."
Sonnet: O! how much more doth beauty beauteous seem."
Sonnet: "O me, what eyes hath Love put in my head."
Sonnet: "O! never say that I was false of heart."
Sonnet: "O that you were yourself! but, love, you are."
Sonnet: "O thou, my lovely boy, who in thy power."
Sonnet: "O truant Muse, what shall be thy amends."
Sonnet: "Or I shall live your epitaph to make."
Sonnet: "Poor soul, the center of my sinful earth."
Sonnet: "Say that thou didst forsake me for some fault."
Sonnet: "Shall I compare thee to a summer's day?"
Sonnet: "Sin of self-love [*or* Sinne of selfe-love] possesseth all mine eye [*or* al mine eie]."
Sonnet: "Since brass, nor stone, nor earth, nor boundless sea."
Sonnet: "Sinne of selfe-love possesseth al mine eie."
Sonnet: "So am I as the rich, whose blessed key."
Sonnet: "So are you to my thoughts as food to life."
Sonnet: "So is it not with me as with that Muse."
Sonnet: "So, now I have confest that he is thine."
Sonnet: "So shall I live, supposing thou art true."
Sonnet: "Some glory in their birth, some in their skill."
Sonnet: "Sweet love, renew thy force; be it not said."
Sonnet: "Take all my loves, my love, yea, take them all."
Sonnet: "That thou hast her, it is not all my grief."
Sonnet: "That time of year thou mayst in me behold."
Sonnet: "That you were once unkind befriends me now."
Sonnet: "Then hate me when thou wilt; if ever, now."
Sonnet: "Then let not winter's ragged hand deface."
Sonnet: "They that have power to hurt and will do none."
Sonnet: "Thine eyes I love, and they, as pitying me."
Sonnet: "Those hours that with gentle work did frame."
Sonnet: "Those lines that I before have writ do lie."

Shakespeare (continued)
Sonnet: "Those lips that Love's own hand did make."
Sonnet: "Those parts of thee that the world's eye doth view."
Sonnet: "Those pretty wrongs that liberty commits."
Sonnet: "Thus can my love excuse the slow offense."
Sonnet: "Thus is his cheek the map of days outworn."
Sonnet: "Thy bosom is endearèd with all hearts."
Sonnet: "Thy glass will show thee how thy beauties wear."
Sonnet: "Tired with all these, for restful death I cry."
Sonnet: "'Tis better to be vile than vile esteemed."
Sonnet: "To me, fair friend, you never can be old."
Sonnet: "Two loves I have of comfort and despair."
Sonnet: "Tyr'd with all these for restfull death I cry."
Sonnet: "Was it the proud full sail of his great verse."
Sonnet: "Weary with toil, I haste me to my bed."
Sonnet: "What is your substance, whereof are you made."
Sonnet: "What potions have I drunk of Siren tears."
Sonnet: "When forty winters shall besiege thy brow."
Sonnet: "When I consider everything that grows."
Sonnet: "When I do count the clock that tells the time."
Sonnet: "When I have seen by time's fell hand defaced."
Sonnet: "When, in disgrace with fortune and men's eyes."
Sonnet: "When in the chronicle of wasted time."
Sonnet: "When most I wink, then do mine eyes best see."
Sonnet: "When my love swears that she is made of truth."
Sonnet: "When thou shalt be dispos'd to set me light."
Sonnet: "When to the sessions of sweet silent thought."
Sonnet: "Where art thou, Muse, that thou forget'st so long."
Sonnet: "Whilst I alone did call upon thy aid."
Sonnet: "Who will believe my verse in time to come."
Sonnet: "Whoever hath her wish thou hast thy Will."
Sonnet: "Why didst thou promise such a beauteous day."
Sonnet: "Why is my verse so barren of new pride."
Sonnet: "Woman's face, with Nature's own hand painted, A."
Sonnets, *sels.*
Soul and Body.
Spring.
Spring and Winter ("When daisies pied. . .").
Spring and Winter ("When icicles hang. . .").
Spring Song ("When daisies pied . . .").
Staff Officer, The.
Stephano's Song.
Stuff of Dreams, The.
Such Stuff as Dreams Are Made On.
Sunrise on the Sea.
Suns and Clouds.
Sweet-and-Twenty.
Sweet Are the Uses of Adversity.
"Sweet boy," she says, "this night I'll waste in sorrow."
Sweet Harmony.
Take, O Take Those Lips Away.
Take Physic, Pomp.
Taming of the Shrew, The, *sels.*
Tell Me Where Is Fancy Bred.
Tempest, The, *sels.*
That Men Should Fear.
There Is a Tide.
There's not the smallest orb which thou behold'st.
They met me in the day of successe.
This Above All.
This Blessed Plot . . . This England.
This England ("This England never did").
This England ("This royal throne of kings").
This Royal Throne of Kings.
This Spring of Love.
Thrice Armed.
Through the Forest Have I Gone.
Through the House ("Through the house give glimmering light").
Thus with a Kiss I Die.
Time and Love.
Time to Strike, The.
Times's Glory.
Timon of Athens, *sels.*
Titania's Bower.
To Be, or Not to Be.
To Dream Again.
To Gild Refinèd Gold.
To His Love.
To Silvia.
To Thine Own Self Be True.
To-Whit To-Who.
Tomorrow.
Tomorrow and Tomorrow and Tomorrow.
Tomorrow Is [*or* Good Morrow, 'Tis] Saint Valentine's Day.
Tricks of Imagination, The.
Triumph of Death, The.
Troilus and Cressida, *sels.*
Troy Depicted.
True Love.
Tu-Whit To-Whit.
Twelfth Night, *sels.*
Two Gentlemen of Verona, The, *sels.*
Two of Feste's Songs.
Two Songs by Amiens.
Ulysses Advises Achilles [Not to Let Slip Opportunity].
Unchangeable, The.
Under the Greenwood Tree.
Up and Down.
Upon the King.
Uses of Adversity, The.
Vaulting Ambition.
Venus Abandoned.
Venus and Adonis.
Ver and Hiems.
Violet Bank, A.
We have scotch'd the snake, not kill'd it.
Wedding Is Great Juno's Crown.
Well; come to me to-morrow.
What did thy song boad lady?
What, have I 'scaped love-letters.
What Shall He Have That Kill'd the Deer?
When Daffodils Begin to Peer.
When Daisies Pied and Violets Blue.
When Icicles Hang by the Wall.
When Priests Are More in Word.
When That I Was and a Little Tiny Boy.
When you sing.
Where Is Fancy Bred.
Where is the beauteous majesty of Denmark?
Where Late the Sweet Birds Sang.
Where should this music be? I' the air, or the earth?
Where the bee sucks, there suck I.
Where the Wild Thyme Blows.
Who Is Silvia [*or* Sylvia]?
Who's there?
Why, let the stricken deer go weep.
Why Should This a Desert Be.
Why, then thou canst not break her to the lute?
Why, then, 'tis time to arm and give direction.
Will You Buy Any Tape?
Wind and the Rain, The.
Winter.
Winter Song.
Winter: When Icicles Hang by the Wall.
Winter's Song.
Winter's Tale, The, *sels.*
Witches' Brew, The.
Witches' Charm.
Witches' Spell, The.
Witching Time of Night, The.
With a Kiss I Die.
With hey, ho, the wind and the rain.
World's Way, The.
Worthy Fool, A.
Yet but Three?
You Never Can Be Old.
You Nymphs, Call'd Naiads.
You Spotted Snakes [with Double Tongue].
Young Love.
Youth and Age.

Shakespeare, William, *and* John Fletcher
Bridal Song.
Cranmer's Prophecy of Queen Elizabeth.
Dirge of the Three Queens.
Farewell to All My Greatness.
Farewell to Greatness.
Funeral Song ("Urns and odors, bring away").
Higher Loyalty, The.
King Henry VIII, *sels.*
Song: "Urnes and odours bring away!"
Two Noble Kinsmen, The, *sels.*
Urns and Odours Bring Away!
Wolsey.
Wolsey's Farewell to His Greatness.

Shakespeare, William, *and others.* Passionate Pilgrim, The, *sels.*

Shams Tabrez
Self-Love.

Shanahan, Eileen
Desolate Lover, The.
Epiphany.
Kilkenny Boy, The.
Shankill.
Three Children near Clonmel.

Shane, Elizabeth
Hush Song.
Mountainy Childer, The.
Sheskinbeg.
Wee Hughie.

Shanks, Edward
Boats at Night.
Drilling in Russell Square.
Fields Are Full, The.
For the Eightieth Birthday of a Great Singer.
Glade, The.
Glow-worm, The.
Going In to Dinner.
High Germany.
Lady Godiva.
Night Piece, A.
Other Little Boats, The.
Sleeping Heroes.

Storm, The.
To the Unknown Light.
Woman's Song.
Shanly, Charles Dawson
Civil War.
Walker of the Snow, The.
Shannon, Monica
Coaxing a Fairy Fiddler.
Could It Have Been a Shadow?
Country Trucks.
Cow Time.
Four-Leaf Clover, The.
Gallop, Gallop to a Rhyme.
How to Tell Goblins from Elves.
Ideal Age for a Man, The.
Only My Opinion.
Our Hired Man (and His Daughter, Too).
Perfect Child, The.
Raking Walnuts in the Rain.
Three Old Cattlemen.
Tree Toad, The.
Uncle Frank.
Shao Ch'ang Heng
Misery.
Shapcott, Thomas William
Finches, The.
Three Kings Came.
Shapiro, David
Bicycle Rider, The.
Contribution, The.
Elegy to Sports.
Five Songs.
For the Princess Hello.
Four Stories.
Heavenly Humor, The.
Idea of a University, The.
Master Canterel at Locas Solus.
New World of Will.
Poem from Deal.
Two Poems on the Emotions.
Shapiro, Harvey
Happiness of 6 A.M.
Heart, The.
Shapiro, Karl
Adam and Eve.
Alphabet, The.
Americans Are Afraid of Lizards.
As You Say; an Anti-Poem.
August Saturday Night on the Negro Street.
Auto Wreck.
Ballade: "Here ends this cycle of my poems for you."
Bed, The.
Bourgeois Poet, The, *sels.*
Boy-Man.
Buick.
But poets are name-proud craftsmen; Greeks and Jews.
California Winter, *sel.*
Christmas Eve: Australia.
Confirmation, The.
Conscientious Objector, The.
Cut Flower, A.
D. C.
Dirty Word, The.
Dome of Sunday, The.
Drug Store.
Elegy for a Dead Soldier.
Elegy for Two Banjos.
Elegy Written on a Frontporch.
Epitaph for John and Richard.
Essay on Rime, *sels.*
First Time, The.
Fly, The.
Full Moon; New Guinea.
Garden in Chicago, A.
Geographers, The.
Glass Poem.
Glutton, The.
Going to School.
Haircut.
Hollywood.
Homecoming.
I sing the simplest flower.
I was born downtown on a wintry day.
In India.
Intellectual, The.
Interlude, The.
Jew.
Leg, The.
Love for a Hand.
Love Letter.
Manhole Covers.
Midnight Show.
Minute, The.
Mongolian Idiot.
Murder of Moses, The.
My first small book was nourished in the dark.
Necropolis.
New Ring, The.
Nigger.
Nostalgia.
October 1.
151st Psalm, The.
Paradox: the Birds.
Phenomenon, The.
Poet.
Poets of Hell, The.
Potomac, The.
Progress of Faust, The.
Puritan, The.
Recapitulations, *sels.*
Recognition of Eve, The.
Scyros.
Sickness of Adam, The.
Six Religious Lyrics, *sel.*
Southerner, The.
Sunday: New Guinea.
Terminal.
There is a general idiom to all rime.
This land grows the oldest living things.
Tingling Back, The.
Travelogue for Exiles.
Troop Train.
Twins, The.
University.
V-Letter.
Voyage, The.
Waitress.
Washington Cathedral.
Western Town.
When nuns were spitted and poets fell.
Sharman, Lyon (Abbie Mary Lyon Sharman)
Old Man Pot.
Sharp, Saundra
Reaching Back.
Seeing Eye-Dog, A.
Sharp, William *See* **"Macleod, Fiona"**
Sharpe, R. L.
Bag of Tools, A.
Sharpless, Stanley J.
In Praise of Cocoa, Cupid's Nightcap.
Shaver, Eva Gilbert
Dear Old Dad.
Shaw, Charles Green
Dissembler.
Shaw, Cuthbert
Monody to the Memory of a Young Lady, *sel.*
Time's Balm, *abr.*
Shaw, David T.
Columbia, the Gem of the Ocean.
Red, White, and Blue.
Shaw, Frances
Child's Quest, The.
Cologne Cathedral.
Harp of the Wind, The.
Last Guest, The.
Little Pagan Rain Song.
Ragpicker, The.
Rain.
Star Thought.
Who Loves [*or* Love] the Rain.
Shaw, Henry Wheeler *See* **"Billings, Josh"**
Shaw, Isabel
Christmas Chant.
Shaw, John
Sleighing Song.
Song: "Who has robbed the ocean cave [*or* wave]."
Shaw, Knowles
Handwriting on the Wall, The.
Shaw, Neufville
Drowned Sailor.
Shaw, Winifred
Fine Clay.
Shea, Don
Her Skin Runs—White Stripes.
In the News.
Inhuman Rain Rejoiced, The.
Magic Idle Windy Spaces, The.
Never to Visit You.
Pale New Lights Cling.
Shea, John Augustus
Ocean, The.
Shea, Walter
Crusts.
Most Honored Guest.
Sheard, Virna
Exile.
Hallowe'en.
Yak, The.
Shedlofsky, Walter
House of Yesterday.
Prophecy.
Sheffield, Duke of Buckingham and Normanby, John
Happy Night, The.
Essay on Satyr, An, *sel.*
Love's Slavery.
On Mr. Hobbs, and His Writings.
On One Who Died Discovering Her Kindness.
To a Coquet Beauty.
Characters of the Wits, The.
From All Uneasy Passions Free.
Reconcilement, The.
Song: "Come, Celia, let's agree at last."
Shehabuddin, Jenab
Your Mouth.
Sheldon, Charles Frederic
Psalm XXXVII: "Trust in the Lord."
Sheldon, Charles Monroe
Jesus the Carpenter.
Sheldon, Gilbert
St. Anthony's Township.
Shelley, Percy Bysshe
Adonais; an Elegy on the Death of John Keats.
Against Oblivion.
Alas! that all we loved of him should be.
Alastor; or, The Spirit of Solitude.
Among the guests who often stayed.
And every beast of beating heart grew bold.
And they, and all, in one loud symphony.
Arethusa.
As an eagle grasped/ In folds of the green serpent.
Asia.
Asia's Song.
Autumn.
Autumn; a Dirge.
Away, Away!
Aziola, The.
Beatrice's Last Words.
Boat on the Serchio, The, *sel.*
Bridal Song, A.
Can man be free if woman be a slave?

Shelley (continued)
Cenci, The.
Charioteer, The.
Charles the First, *sel.*
Child of Twelve, A.
Chorus: "Darkness has dawned in the East."
Chorus: "Life may change, but it may fly not."
Chorus: "Life of Life! thy lips enkindle."
Chorus: "O Slavery! thou frost of the world's prime."
Chorus: "World's great age begins anew, The."
Chorus: "Worlds on worlds are rolling ever."
Chorus from "Hellas."
Chorus of Spirits: "From unrembered ages we."
Circumstance.
Cloud, The.
Cold Earth Slept Below, The.
Conversation, A.
Cross, The.
Curse, The.
Daemon of the World, The, *sel.*
Day of Liberty, The.
Day of Love, The, *abr.*
Daybreak.
Death ("Death is here, and death is there").
Demogorgon's Song.
Desire of the Moth, The.
Dirge, A: "Rough wind, that moanest loud."
Dirge for the Year.
Dream of the Unknown, A.
Elegy on the Death of John Keats, An.
End of Tyranny, The.
England in 1819.
Epipsychidion.
Epithalamium for Charlotte Corday and Francis Ravaillac.
Evening: Ponte al Mare, Pisa.
Ever as We Sailed.
Feelings of a Republican on the Fall of Bonaparte.
Final Chorus from Hellas, The: "Victorious wrong, with vulture scream."
Final Chorus from Hellas: "World's great age begins anew, The."
Final Victory, The.
Flight of Love.
Fragment: Rain.
Fragment, A: To Music.
Fragment: To the Moon.
From the Arabic; an Imitation.
Fugitives, The, *st.* 1.
Garden, A.
Ginevra, *sel.*
Go Thou to Rome.
Good-Night.
Hate-Song, A.
He has outsoared the shadow of our night.
He is a portion of the loveliness.
He is made one with Nature: there is heard.
He Is Not Dead.
Hellas, *sels.*
Here pause: these graves are all too young as yet.
How wonderful is Death.
Hymn of Apollo.
Hymn of Pan.
Hymn to Apollo.
Hymn to Intellectual Beauty.
Hymn to the Spirit of Nature.
I could not choose but gaze; a fascination.
I Fear Thy Kisses, Gentle Maiden.
I love snow and all the forms.
I met Murder on the way.
I stood within the city disinterred.
In this life / Of error, ignorance, and strife.
Indian Serenade, The.
Invitation, The.
Invitation to Jane, The.
Invocation: "Earth, ocean, air, beloved brotherhood."
Invocation: "Rarely, rarely, comest thou."
Invocation to Nature.
Islands and the mountains in the day, The.
Isle, The.
Joy, the triumph, the delight, the madness, The!
Julian and Maddalo, *sel.*
Lament, A: "O world! O life! O time!"
Laon and Cythna.
Last came Anarchy; he rode.
Letter to Maria Gisborne, *sel.*
Life May Change, but It May Fly Not.
Life of Life.
Lift Not the Painted Veil.
Lifting the thunder of their acclamation.
Lines: "Cold earth slept below, The."
Lines: "When the lamp is shattered."
Lines to a Critic.
Lines to an Indian Air.
Lines Written among the Euganean Hills.
Lines Written in the Bay of Lerici.
Lines Written on Hearing the News of the Death of Napoleon.
Longest Journey, The.
Loud deep calls me home even now to feed it, The.
Love.
Love's Philosophy.
Lumen de Lumine.
Magic Car Moved On, The.
Make me thy lyre, even as the forest is.
Mask [*or* Masque] of Anarchy, The.
Masque of Anarchy, The.
Memory.
'Mid the mountains Euganean.
Mont Blanc.
Moon, The ("And like a dying lady").
Moon, The ("Art thou pale for weariness").
Morning.
Music ("Music, when soft voices die").
Music ("Silver key of the fountain of tears.").
Music, When Soft Voices Die.
Mutability.
My faint spirit was sitting in the light.
New World, A.
Night.
O Thou Immortal Deity.
Ode to Liberty.
Ode to Naples.
Ode to the West Wind.
On a battle-trumpet's blast.
On a Painted Woman.
On a Poet's Lips I Slept.
On Fanny Godwin.
On Keats.
One with Nature.
One Word Is Too Often Profaned.
Our Sweetest Songs.
Ozymandias.
Pale stars are gone, The!
Path through which that lovely twain, The.
Peace! peace! A mighty Power, which is as darkness.
Peter Bell the Third, *sel.*
Poet's Dream, The.
Political Greatness.
Power from the unknown God, A.
Prometheus Unbound.
Queen Mab, *sels.*
Question, The ("I dreamed that, as I wandered by the way").
Radiant Sister of the Day.
Rainbow's Arch, A.
Rarely, Rarely, Comest Thou.
Recollection, The.
Remorse.
Revolt of Islam, The, *sels.*
See where she stands! a mortal shape indued.
Sensitive Plant, The.
Seraph of Heaven.
She is still, she is cold.
Ship is floating in the harbour now, A.
Similes for Two Political Characters of 1819.
Song: "Rarely, rarely, comest thou."
Song: "Widow bird sate mourning for her love, A."
Song to the Men of England.
Sonnet: England in 1819.
Sonnet: "Lift not the painted veil."
Sonnet: Ozymandias.
Sonnet to Byron.
Soon as the sound had ceased whose thunder filled.
Sphere, which is as many thousand spheres, A.
Spirit of Delight.
Spouse! Sister! Angel! Pilot of the Fate.
Stand ye calm and resolute.
Stanzas: "Away! the moor is dark beneath the moon."
Stanzas—April, 1814.
Stanzas to Edward Williams.
Stanzas Written in Dejection, near Naples.
Stars burnt out in the pale blue air, The.
Summer and Winter.
Summer was dead and autumn was expiring.
There the voluptuous nightingales.
There was a Being whom my spirit oft.
Thou huntress swifter than the Moon! thou terror.
Threnos.
Time.
Time Long Past.
To ——: "I fear thy kisses, gentle maiden."
To ——: "Music, when soft voices die."
To ——: "Oh! there are spirits of the air."
To ——: "One word is too often profaned."
To ——: "When passion's trance is overpast."
To a Lady with a Guitar.
To a Skylark.
To Coleridge.
To Constantia, Singing.
To Edward Williams.
To Ianthe.
To Jane: The Invitation.
To Jane: The Keen Stars Were Twinkling.
To Jane: The Recollection.
To Mary ("So now my summer task is ended, Mary").
To Music.
To Night.
To the Lord Chancellor, *sel.*
To the Moon.
To the Night.
To the Nile.
To William Shelley.
To Wordsworth.
To-Morrow.
Trackless Deeps, The.
Tribute to America.
Triumph of Life, The.
True Love.

True Love in this differs from gold and clay.
Two Spirits, The; an Allegory.
Tyrants of the Golden City tremble, The.
Unfathomable Sea!
Verses on a Cat.
Waning Moon, The.
War Is the Statesman's Game.
We wandered to the pine Forest.
West Wind, The.
What is Freedom?—ye can tell.
When the Lamp Is Shattered.
When the last hope of trampled France had failed.
Who Reigns?
Widow Bird [Sate Mourning for Her Love], A.
Winter.
Witch of Atlas, The.
With a Guitar, to Jane.
World's Great Age Begins Anew, The.
Worlds on Worlds Are Rolling Ever.
World's Wanderers, The.
Worship.
Written among the Euganean Hills, North Italy.
Written in the Euganean Hills, North Italy.
Ye congregated powers of heaven, who share.
You are now/ In London, that great sea, whose ebb and flow.
Zucca, The, *sel.*

Shelton, Marion Brown
Greatest, The.

Shelton, Richard
Alone.
Connais-tu le Pays?
On Lake Pend Oreille.
Prophets, The.

Shen Ch'üan
Therefore We Preserve Life.

Shenstone, William
Absence.
Elegy: He Complains How Soon the Pleasing Novelty Is Over.
Hint from Voiture.
Hope.
I Have Found Out a Gift for My Fair.
Inscription: On a Tablet against a Root-House.
Inscription: On the Back of a Gothic Seat.
Kid, The.
Landscape, The.
Landskip, The.
O Sweet Anne Page.
Ode to a Young Lady, Somewhat Too Sollicitous about Her Manner of Expression.
Ode to Memory.
Pastoral Ballad, A.
Poet and the Dun, The.
Schoolmistress, The.
Shepherd's Home, The.
Slender's Ghost.
Song: Landskip, The.
Song: "O'er desert plains, and rushy meers."
To the Virtuosos.
Written at an Inn at Henley.
Written in an Inn at Henley.

Shepard, Elizabeth Alsop
White Fox.

Shepard, Odell
Adventurer, The.
Certain American Poets.
Elm, The.
Flock of Evening, The.
Gifts, The.
Hidden Weaver, The.
Home Thoughts.
Housemates.
In the Dawn.
Thanksgiving.
Vespers.
Vistas.
We are standing in the great dawn of a day they did not know.

Shepard, Sheldon
Follow Me!
Injustice.
Interpretation.

Shepherd, Hope
Trains.

Shepherd, Nathaniel Graham
Roll-Call.

Shepherd, Thomas
Alas, My God.
For Communion with God, *sel.*

Sheppard, Muriel Earley
Coquette, The.
Episode, An.
Snake Charmer, The.

Sheppard, Samuel
Of Death.

Sherbrooke, Viscount *See* **Lowe, Robert, Viscount Sherbrooke**

Sherburne, Sir Edward
And She Washed His Feet with Her Tears, and Wiped Them with the Hairs of Her Head.
Christus Matthaeum et Discipulos Alloquitur.
Conscience.
Ice and Fire.
Love's Arithmetic.
Magdalen, The.
Sweetmeat, The.
Violets in Thaumantia's Bosome.
Vow, The.
Weeping and Kissing.

Sheridan, Caroline Elizabeth Sarah *See* **Norton, Caroline Elizabeth Sarah Sheridan**

Sheridan Helen Selina, Lady Dufferin
Charming Woman, The.
Lament of the Irish Emigrant.
Love Hath a Language.
To My Son, *sel.*

Sheridan, John D.
Each in His Inmost Heart.

Sheridan, Niall
Poem: "As rock to sun or storm."

Sheridan, Richard Brinsley
Air: "I ne'er could any luster see."
Bumper of good liquor, A.
By Coelia's Arbor.
Dry Be That Tear.
Duenna, The, *sels.*
Epigram: "'I would,' says Fox, 'a tax devise.'"
Famous Toast, A.
Geranium, The.
Here's to the Maiden.
Let the Toast Pass.
Literary Lady, The.
Months, The.
Oh Yield, Fair Lids.
School for Scandal, The, *sel.*
Song: "Had I a heart for falsehood framed."
Song: "Here's to the maiden of bashful fifteen."
Song: "If a daughter you have, she's the plague of your life."

Sherlock, Phillip M.
Dinner Party, 1940.

Sherman, Francis
Builder, The.
Deserted City, The, *sel.*
House of Colour, The.
In Memorabilia Mortis.
Let Us Rise Up and Live.

Sherman, Frank Dempster
At Midnight.
Bacchus.
Bees.
Clouds.
Daisies.
Dawn.
Dewdrop, A.
February.
Four Winds, The.
Golden Rod, The.
Hollyhock, A.
Ivy.
January.
Jester Bee.
Kite, A.
Library, The.
Mary and the Lamb.
May.
Moonrise.
On a Greek Vase.
On Some Buttercups.
Prayer, A: "It is my joy in life to find."
Quatrain, A: "Hark at the lips of the pink whorl of shell."
Real Santa Claus, A.
Rose's Cup, The.
Shadows, The.
Snow-Bird, The.
Spinning Top.
To a Rose.
Waterfall, The.
Wish, A.
Wizard Frost.

Sherry, Ruth Forbes
Promises.
Waltz.

Sherwood, Alice E.
Alone with Him.

Sherwood, Grace Buchanan
After Laughter.

Sherwood, Kate Brownlee
Albert Sidney Johnston.
Molly Pitcher.
Thomas at Chickamauga.
Ulric Dahlgren.
We Keep Memorial Day.

Sherwood, Margaret
In Memoriam—Leo, a Yellow Cat.

Sherwood, Robert Emmet
Old Hokum Buncombe, The.

Sherwood, Rupe
Me and Prunes.

Shields, Ren
In the Good Old Summer Time.

Shields, Shaemas *See* **O'Sheel, Shaemas**

Shiffert, Edith
Monk Begging, Kyoto.
Morning at the Temple of Kobai.

Shiffrin, Abraham B. *See* **"Christopher, Robin"**

Shigeji, Tsuboi
Silent, But.

Shih Ee
Ch'i Lai' (March of the Volunteers).

Shiko
Lilies.
Maple Leaves.

Shillito, Edward
Ave Crux, Spes Unica!
Christmas Tree, The.
Dereliction.
I Am the Last.
Jesus of the Scars.
Life to Come, The.
Lonely Christ, The.
One Love.
Prayer for a Preacher, A.
Prayer of a Modern Thomas.
Untried Door, The.

Shinn, Milicent Washburn
Song and Science.
Washington Sequoia, The, *sel.*
When Almonds Bloom.
Yosemite.
Shipman, Thomas
Epitaph on His Grandfather, An.
Kiss, The.
Resolute Courtier, The.
Shipp, E. Richard
Eighteen-ninety.
Shipp, Horace
Everest.
Shippey, Lee
Battle Cry, A.
If We Could Only Be!
Shipton, Anna
Unerring Guide, The.
Shirk, Jeannette C.
Clock Shop, The.
Shirk, Ottis
Resolved.
Shirley, Henry
Martyred Soldier, The, *sel.*
What are earthly honors.
Shirley, James
Ajax and Ulysses.
Bard, The.
Bard's Chant.
Cease, warring thoughts, and let his brain.
Changes; or, Love in a Maze, *sel.*
Come away, away, away,
Commonwealth of Birds, The.
Contention of Ajax and Ulysses, The, *sel.*
Cupid and Death, *sels.*
Cupid Ungodded.
Cupids Call.
Death, the Conqueror ("Victorious men of earth! no more").
Death the Leveller.
Death's Emissaries.
Death's Final Conquest.
Death's Subtle Ways.
Dirge, A: "Glories of our blood and state, The."
Epitaph Inscribed on a Small Piece of Marble.
Equality.
Garden, The.
Glories of Our Blood and State, The.
Heigh-ho, what shall a shepheard doe.
Hymn, A: "O fly, my soul! What hangs upon."
Imposture, The, *sels.*
Io.
Last Conqueror, The.
Looking Glass, The.
Love, a Thousand Sweets Distilling.
Love's Victories.
Melancholy, hence! go get.
O Fly My Soul.
Of Death.
Our Blood and State.
Passing Bell, The.
Piping Peace.
Song: "Glories of our blood and state, The."
Song: "Love a thousand sweets distilling."
Song: "Victorious men of earth, no more."
Song: "You virgins that did late despair."
Song of Nuns, A.
To His Mistress Confined.
To His Mistris Confined.
To the Excellent Pattern of Beauty and Virtue, Lady Elizabeth, Countess of Ormond.
To the Painter Preparing to Draw M. M. H.
Triumph of Beautie Song, The, *sel.*
Triumph of Beauty, The, *sel.*
Triumph of Peace, The, *sel.*
Upon His M. Dancing.
Upon His Mistress Dancing.
Upon Scarlet and Blush-coloured Ribbands, Given by Two Ladies.
Victorious Men of Earth.
Witty Fair One, The, *sel.*
You Virgins.
Shivell, Paul
In God's Eternal Studios.
Studios Photographic, The, *sel.*
Shkulev, Filip Stepanovich
Revolution, The.
Shlonsky, Abraham
Grape-gathering.
Shoemaker, Blanche *See* **Wagstaff, Blanche Shoemaker**
Shoemaker, Samuel M.
So I Stay Near the Door; an Apologia for My Life.
Shoku, Princess
I would that even now.
Shorey, George H.
Bubbles.
Short, John
Carol: "There was a Boy bedded in bracken."
Shorter, Dora Sigerson
All Souls' Night.
April.
Ballad of the Little Black Hound.
Beware.
Bird from the West, A.
Comforters, The.
Gypsies' Road, The.
Ireland.
Kine of My Father, The.
Mother's Prayer, The.
New Year, A.
Nora.
One Forgotten, The.
Patchwork Quilt, The.
Piper on the Hill, The.
Rose Will Fade, A.
Sixteen Dead Men.
Wind on the Hills, The.
Shotoku, Prince
On Seeing a Dead Man.
Shove, Fredegond
Dream in Early Spring, A.
Farmer, The.
Infant Spring.
New Ghost, The.
Song: "Spring lights her candles everywhere."
Sops of Light.
Shrader, Stephen
Campaign, The: Letters from the Front.
Shu Hsi
Hot Cake.
Shuford, Gene
Harvest.
Shuler, Chester E.
Faithful Few, The.
Shults, George Francis
Under the Mistletoe.
Shuraikh
Distich.
Shurtleff, Ernest W.
Lead On, O King Eternal.
Shuster, George Nauman
Newman.
What Highway?
Shute, Evan Vere
Luck.
Night Comes Apace.
Poor Fool.
Twenty Years After.
"Shy, Timothy." *See* **Lewis, Dominic Bevan Wyndham**
Sibley, Charles
Plaidie, The.
Sickels, David Banks
It Cannot Be.
Reincarnation.
Sidey, James A.
Irish Schoolmaster, The.
Sidgwick, Frank
Aeronaut to His Lady, The.
Christmas Legend, A.
Corinna Goes a-Singing.
"Form Fours."
Glory of Early Rising, The.
His Hirsute Suit.
Imaginary Correspondence, *parody.*
Sing a Song of Sixpence, *parody.*
Vision.
Sidgwick, Henry
Goethe and Frederika.
Sidney, Mary, Countess of Pembroke *See* **Pembroke, Mary Sidney Herbert, Countess of**
Sidney, Sir Philip
Absence.
Advice to the Same ("Who doth desire that chaste his wife should be").
All my sense thy sweetness gained.
And have I heard her say, "O cruel pain!"
Answered Thus by Sir P. S.
Arcadia, *sels.*
Arcadian Duologue.
Astrophel and Stella.
Astrophel's Love Is Dead.
Bargain, The.
Because I breathe not love to every one.
Complaint of Love.
Contentment.
Countess of Pembroke's Arcadia, The.
Country Song, A.
Cupid.
Dear [*or* Deare], why make you more of a dog then me?
Delight of Solitariness, The.
Desire.
Dialogue, A.
Dispraise [*or* Disprayse] of a Courtly Life.
Disprayse of a Courtly Life.
Ditty: Heart Exchange.
Ditty, A: "My true love hath my heart and I have his."
Dorus His Comparisons.
Dorus's Song.
Double Sestine.
Echo.
Eighth Sonnet, The.
Eleventh Song.
Epithalamium: "Let mother earth now deck herself in flowers."
Excellent Sonnet of a Nymph, An.
Fair, seek not to be feared, most lovely beloved.
Farewell, A: "Leave me O love, which reachest but to dust."
Farewell, A: "Oft have I mused, but now at length I find."
Farewell, O sun, Arcadia's clearest light.
Farewell World.
Feed on my sheep, my charge, my comfort feed.
First Song: "Doubt you to whom my Muse these notes intendeth."
Fourth Song: "Only joy, now here you are."
Geron and Histor.
Get Hence Foule Griefe.
Gifts of the Animals to Man, The.
Graven Thoughts.
He That Loves.
Heart Exchange.
Her Perfections.
His Being Was in Her Alone.
His Lady's Cruelty.

If I could think how these my thoughts to leave.
Immortality.
In Vain Mine Eyes.
In Wonted Walks, Since Wonted Fancies Change.
Just Exchange.
Languishing Moon, The.
Leave Me O Love [Which Reachest but to Dust].
Leave off my sheep, it is no time to feed.
Like as the Dove.
Litany, A: "Ring out your bells."
Look into Thy Heart.
Love and Reason.
Love Is Dead.
Loved I Am, and Yet Complaine of Love.
Lovers' Dialogue.
Madrigal: "Why dost thou haste away."
Moon, The.
My mistress lowers and saith I do not love.
My Sheep Are Thoughts.
My True Love.
My True Love Hath My Heart [and I Have His].
Night.
Nightingale, The.
Nightingale, as soon as April bringeth, The.
Nymph of the Garden Where All Beauties Be.
O Faire! O Sweete!
O Hymen, Long Their Coupled Joys Maintain!
O my thoughts' sweet food, my only owner.
O Sweet Woods (*three sonnets*).
Old Age.
Philomela.
Psalm XLIII: "Judge of all, judge me."
Psalm XII: "Lord, help, it is high time for me to call."
Psalm XXXV: "Speak thou for me, against wrong speaking foes."
Ring Out Your Bells.
Rural Poesy.
Sapphics.
Satyr once did run away for dread, A.
Scourge of life, and death's extreme disgrace, The.
Sestina.
Seven Wonders of England, The.
Shepherd Song.
Shepherd's Tale, A.
Since shunning pain, I ease can never find.
Since So Mine Eyes.
Sleep ("Come, sleep! O Sleep")
Sleep ("Lock up, fair lids").
Sleep baby mine, desire, nurse beauty singeth.
Solitariness.
Song: "My true love hath my heart, and I have his."
Song: "No, no, no, no, I cannot hate my foe."
Song: "O fair! O sweet! when I do look on thee."
Song: "Who hath his fancy pleasèd."
Song: "Who is it that, this dark night."
Sonnet: "Because I breathe not love to every one."
Sonnet: "Come, sleep, O sleep, the certain knot of peace."
Sonnet: "Envious wits, what hath been mine offence."
Sonnet: "Having this day my horse, my hand, my lance."
Sonnet: "Highway, since you my chief Parnassus be."
Sonnet: "I might—unhappy word!—oh me, I might."
Sonnet: "I never drank of Aganippe well."
Sonnet: "In highest way of heaven the sun did ride."
Sonnet: "In truth, O Love, with what a boyish kind."
Sonnet: "It is most true that eyes are formed to serve."
Sonnet: "Late tired with woe, even ready for to pine."
Sonnet: "Leave me, O Love, which reachest but to dust."
Sonnet: "Let dainty wits cry on the sisters nine."
Sonnet: "Lock up, fair lids, the treasure of my heart."
Sonnet: "Love born in Greece, of late fled from his native place."
Sonnet: "Love, by sure proof I may call thee unkind."
Sonnet: "Love still a boy, and oft a wanton is."
Sonnet: "Loving in truth, and fain in verse my love to show."
Sonnet: "My mouth doth water, and my breast doth swell."
Sonnet: "My true love hath my heart, and I have his."
Sonnet: "No more, my dear, no more these counsels try."
Sonnet: "Not at first sight, nor yet with a dribbed shot."
Sonnet: "O eyes, which do the spheres of beauty move."
Sonnet: "O happy Thames that didst my Stella bear!"
Sonnet: "O kiss which dost those ruddy gems impart."
Sonnet: "O tears, no tears, but rain from beauty's skies."
Sonnet: "Some lovers speak, when their muses entertain.
Sonnet: "Stella! since thou so right a Princess art."
Sonnet: "Stella, think not that I by verse seek fame."
Sonnet: "Thou blind man's mark, thou fool's self-chosen snare."
Sonnet: "Though dusty wits dare scorn astrology."
Sonnet: "When far spent night persuades each mortal eye."
Sonnet: "When nature made her chief work, Stella's eyes."
Sonnet: "When sorrow (using mine own fire's might)."
Sonnet: "Whether the Turkish new moon minded be."
Sonnet: "With how sad steps, O Moon, thou climb'st the skies."
Sonnet: "With what sharp checks I in myself am shent."
Sonnet: "You that do search for every purling spring."
Sonnet: "Your words, my friend (right healthful caustics), blame."
Splendidis Longum Valedico Nugis.
Stella Sleeping.
Sweet glove, the witness of my secret bliss.
Sweeter Saint I Serve, A.
Tale for Husbands, A.
Thou Blind Man's Mark.
Thou pain, the only guest of loathed constraint.
To a Sparrow.
To Sleep.
To Stella.
To the Moon.
To You! To You!
True Love.
Truth Doth Truth Deserve.
Two Pastorals.
Underneath My Window.
Upon His Meeting with His Two Worthy Friends and Fellow-Poets.
Via Amoris.
Voices at the Window.
"What length of verse can serve brave Mopsa's good to show."
What Tongue Can Her Perfections Tell?
When love, puffed up with rage of high disdain.
When to My Deadly [*or* Deadlie] Pleasure.
When Two Suns Do Appear.
While favor fed my hope, delight with hope was brought.
Who hath ever felt the change of love.
Who Hath His Fancy [*or* Fancie] Pleasèd.
Who will in fairest book of nature know.
Whose senses in so evil consort their stepdame Nature lays.
Why Fear to Die?
With How Sad Steps [O Moon].
Woe, woe to me, on me return the smart.
Wronged Lover, The.
Yoke of Tyranny, The.

Sidonius Apollinaris *See* **Apollinaris Sidonius**

Siebert, Glenn
This and More.

Siegel, Eli
Alfred-Seeable Philadelphia Sky.
All the Smoke.
Disclaimer of Prejudice.
Duke of Parma's Ear.
Shortest Poem in the World, The.

Siegrist, Mary
League of Nations, The.

Sieller, William Vincent
From a Porthole in the Ice.
Windmill on the Cape.

Sigerson, Dora *See* **Shorter, Dora Sigerson**

Sigerson, George
Calling, The.
Far-away.
My Own Cáilin Donn.
Smith's Song.

Sigerson, Hester
Mad Song.

Sigmund, Jay G.
Christ in the Street.
Grubber's Day.
Men Have Forged.

Sigourney, Lydia Huntley
Advertisement of a Lost Day.
Alpine Flowers, The.
California.
Camel's Nose, The.
Columbus.
I Must Not Tease My Mother.
Indian Names.
Indian's Welcome to the Pilgrim Fathers, The.
Jesus of Nazareth Passeth By.
Mother's Sacrifice, The.
Niagara.
Return of Napoleon from St. Helena, The.

Sikelianos, Angelos
Doric.
Listen to the roar of your liberation!
On Death, *sel.*

"Silav-Na-Mon." *See* **Dollard, James Bernard**

Silberger, Julius
Reply to Nancy Hanks, A.

Silcock, Ruth
Hermit, The.

"Silesius, Angelus." *See* **Angelus Silesius**
Silkin, Jon
And I Turned from the Inner Heart.
Death of a Bird.
Death of a Son.
Death to Us, A.
Deeply Gone.
Epilogue: "All the people in my poems walk into the dark."
First It Was Singing.
Furnished Lives.
Prologue: "All the animals in my poems go into the ark."
Respectabilities.
Return, The.
Someone I Lost.
Space in the Air, A.
To Come Out Singing.
Two Freedoms, The.
Sill, Edward Rowland
Baker's Duzzen Uv Wize Sawz, A.
Be Still and Sleep.
Before Sunrise in Winter.
Broken Sword, The.
Coup de Grace, The.
Dare You?
Dead President, The.
Evening.
Eve's Daughter.
Five Lives.
Fool's Prayer, The.
For the Gifts of the Spirit.
Force.
Future, The.
Home.
Life.
Links of Chance, The.
Lover's Song, The.
Opportunity.
Prayer, A: "O God, our Father, if we had but truth."
Prayer for Peace, A.
Solitude.
Tempted.
'Tis not by guilt the onward sweep.
Tropical Morning at Sea, A.
Sill, Louise Morgan
Faith.
Sillery, Charles Doyne
She Died in Beauty.
Silva, José Asunción
Art.
First Communion.
Nocturne III: "Night, A,/ a night all full of murmurs."
Nocturne: "One night."
Silvera, Edward S.
Forgotten Dreams.
Jungle Taste.
On the Death of a Child.
South Street.
Silverman, Harold
Improvisation III.
Silverstein, Shelley
Beware, My Child.
Flag, The.
George Washington.
I must remember.
If I Had a Firecracker.
In That Dark Cave.
Mary's eyes are blue as azure.
My Invention.
Nothing to Do?
Oh Did You Hear?
On Halloween.
Peace and Joy.
Please Tell Me Just the Fabuli.
Sarah Cynthia Sylvia Stout.
There you sit.
Think of Eight Numbers.
Valentine.
Van Gogh Influence, The.
Wanted.
Silverton, Michael
Chasm, A.
Column A.
King of Sunshine, The.
Life in the Country.
Neckwear.
So long as Time & Space are the stars.
Simeon ben Isaac ben Abun of Mainz
All the Hosts of Heaven.
I Come to Supplicate.
Simic, Charles
Hearing Steps.
Marching.
My Shoes.
Poverty.
Sleep.
Stone.
Summer Morning.
Thousand Years with Solitude, A.
To All Hog-Raisers, My Ancestors.
War.
Wind, The.
Simmias [*or* Simias],
On the Tomb of Sophocles.
To Prote.
Wind, Gentle Evergreen.
Simmons, Barbara
Soul.
Simmons, Bartholomew
Stanzas to the Memory of Thomas Hood.
Simmons, Dan
Nationalism.
Simmons, Gerald L., Jr
Take Tools Our Strength.
Simmons, Herbert A.
Ascendancy.
Simmons, J. Edgar
At the Seed and Feed.
Simmons, James Wright
Sumter's Band.
Simmons, Laura
At Christmastide.
Bartimeus.
I Have Overcome the World.
Next Time.
Noel! Noel!
Othello: Tomcat.
Pentecost.
Rich Young Man, The.
Trimmed Lamp, The.
Way, The.
World Conqueror.
Simms, William Gilmore
Battle of Eutaw, The.
Decay of a People, The.
Glory and Enduring Fame.
Grape-Vine Swing, The.
Lost Pleiad, The.
Night Storm.
Song in March.
Swamp Fox, The.
Triumph, The.
Simon, Hazel H.
Potter's Face, The.
Simon, John
Ameinias.
Two Morsels of Profundity from the Minor Pre-Socratics.
Simonides (of Ceos)
At Thermopylae.
Athenian Dead, The.
Cleobulus' Epitaph.
Danaë.
Epitaph of a Thessalian Hound.
Hound, A.
Inscription to Spartans Dead at Thermopylae.
Life's Brevity.
Lost at Sea.
On the Army of Spartans, Who Died at Thermopylae.
On the Lacedaemonian Dead at Plataea.
On Those Who Fell at Thermopylae.
On Two Brothers.
Prophetic Death.
Sacrifice of Youth.
Thermopylae ("Go tell the Spartans, thou that passest by").
Thermopylae ("Of those at famed Thermopylae who lie").
Thermopylae Ode, The.
Simonides, the Younger
On Those Who Fell.
Simons, John W.
Broadcast, The.
Simeon's Light Remembered.
Whale and the Tiger, The.
Simpson, Albert Benjamin
Abiding.
Believe the Bible.
Get Somewhere.
Glad Home-coming, The.
Glory to the Name of Jesus!
God's Best.
His Best.
I Take, He Undertakes.
It Is I, Be Not Afraid.
It Means Just What It Says.
Jesus Only.
Keep Sweet.
Missionary Cry, A.
Prayer for the New Year, A.
Resting.
Thanksgiving.
Thy Kingdom Come.
To Glorify My God.
Why Doubt God's Word?
Simpson, F. A.
Lincoln and Liberty.
Simpson, George S.
Simpson's Rest.
Simpson, Henry
In February.
Simpson, Louis
Aegean.
Against the Age.
American Poetry.
As Birds Are Fitted to the Boughs.
Ash and the Oak, The.
Battle, The.
Birch.
Bird, The.
Boarder, The.
Carentan O Carentan.
Constant Lover, The.
Dream of Governors, A.
Early in the Morning.
Frogs.
Green Shepherd, The.
Heroes, The.
Hot Night on Water Street.
I Dreamed That in a City Dark As Paris.
In the Suburbs.
It Was the Last of the Parades.
John the Baptist.
Legend of Success, The Salesman's Story, The.
Lover's Ghost, The.
Man Who Married Magdalene, The.
Memories of a Lost War.
Music in Venice.
My Father in the Night Commanding No.
Nine o'Clock.
On the Lawn at the Villa.
Outward.
Redwoods, The.
Riders Held Back, The.
Rough Winds Do Shake.
Sailors.

Silent Generation, The.
Song: "Let's sing a song together once."
Squeal.
Story about Chicken Soup, A.
Summer Storm.
To the Western World.
Tom Pringle.
True Weather for Women, The.
Walt Whitman at Bear Mountain.
Woman Too Well Remembered, A.
Simpson, Margaret Winefride
Villanelle.
Simpson, R. A.
Night Out.
Simpson, William Haskell
Bareback.
Burdens.
Hopi Ghosts.
In Arizona, *sels.*
Pity Not.
Trees.
Simrock, Karl
German Slumber Song.
Go to Sleep.
Sims, George Robert
Billy's Rose ("Billy's dead, and gone to glory").
By Parcels Post.
Christmas Day in the Workhouse.
In the Workhouse: Christmas Day.
Lifeboat, The.
'Ostler Joe.
Sims, Lefty
Angels Prayer, An.
Sinclair, Donald
Path of the Old Spells, The.
Sinclair, F. D.
Stranger walls, that shell no violent prescence.
Zimbabwe.
Sinclair, John
Breakthrough.
Homage to John Coltrane, *sel.*
John Coltrane can do this for us.
Sinclair, Keith
Ballad of Halfmoon Bay, The, *sel.*
Chronicle of Meola Creek, The.
Edward Edwards was a castaway sealer.
For a Parting.
Lord of All I Survey.
Moors, Angels, Civil Wars.
Mother.
Night Full of Nothing, A.
Poem: "I met a sad girl in our town."
War with the Weeds, The.
Sinclair, Mary Craig
Beauty.
Sinclair, Upton
Making of the Soul of Man, The.
On a Steamship.
Singer, Burns
Christ comes to mind and comes across the mind.
I promise you by the harsh funeral.
Marcus Antoninus Cui Cognomen Erat Aurelius.
Nothing.
Old man dozed, The. The hospital quietened.
Peterhead in May.
Sonnets for a Dying Man, *sels.*
Still and All.
Those flaming Christians with their hygienic rose.
To see the petrel cropping in the farmyard.
Words Made of Water.
Singer, John
Stepney Green.
Singleton, Margaret Evelyn
Christmas Rose.
Insubordination.
Master Musician.
Singleton, Mary Montgomerie *See* **"Fane, Violet"**
Sinisgalli, Leonardo
Orphic Interior.
Sinks, P. W.
Just like Me.
Sinnett, Percy F.
Song of the Wild Storm-Waves, The.
Sinton, Mary *See* **Leitch, Mary Sinton**
Sipe, Muriel
Good Morning.
Sissman, Louis Edward
Day in the City, A.
Disappearance in West Cedar Street, A.
Dying: An Introduction.
Elegy: E. W.
In and Out.
In and Out: Severance of Connections, 1946.
On the Island.
Sweeney to Mrs. Porter in the Spring.
West Forties, The: Morning, Noon, and Night.
Sitwell, Edith
Ass-Face.
Aubade.
Clowns' Houses.
Coat of Fire, The.
Colonel Fantock.
Daphne.
Dark Song.
Dirge for the New Sunrise.
Drum, The; The Narrative of the Demon of Tedworth.
Epithalamium: "When the vast universal night shall cover."
Evening.
Façde, *sels.*
Fairies all received an invitation, The.
Fan, The.
Flowering Forest, The.
Gardener Janus Catches a Naiad.
Girl and Butterfly.
Gold Coast Customs, *sel.*
Hambone and the Heart, The.
Harvest.
Heart and Mind.
Hornpipe.
How Many Heavens.
Hymn to Venus.
Interlude.
Invocation: "I who was once a golden woman like those who walk."
King of China's Daughter, The.
Lament of Edward Blastock, The.
Little Ghost Who Died for Love.
Lullaby: "Though the world has slipped and gone."
Madam Mouse Trots.
Madame Mouse Trots.
Mademoiselle Richarde.
Most Lovely Shade.
Night Piece.
Old Nurse's Song, The.
Old Woman, An.
Old Woman Laments in Springtime, An.
One fantee wave.
Panope.
Peach Tree, The.
Perpetuum Mobile.
Prothalamium.
Sailor, What of the Isles?
Satyr in the Periwig, The.
Scotch Rhapsody.
Shadow of Cain, The.
Sir Beelzebub.
Sleeping Beauty, The, *sels.*
Solo for Ear-Trumpet.
Song: "In summer when the rose-bushes."
Song: "Now that Fate is dead and gone."
Song: "Once my heart was a summer rose."
Song at Morning, A.
Spinning Song.
Spring.
Still Falls the Rain.
Street Song.
Swans, The.
Tears.
Three Poems of the Atomic Age, *sel.*
Two Kitchen Songs.
Two Nut Trees.
Variations on an Old Nursery Rhyme.
Waltz.
Web of Eros, The.
When Sir Beelzebub.
When we come to that dark house.
You, the Young Rainbow.
Youth with [the] Red-gold Hair, The.
Sitwell, Sir Osbert
Aubade: Dick, the Donkey-Boy.
Ballad of Sister Anne, The.
Blind Peddler, The.
Elegy for Mr. Goodbeare.
England Reclaimed, *sel.*
English Beach Memory: Mr. Thuddock.
Fountains ("Proud fountains, wave your plumes").
Giardino Pubblico.
How Shall We Rise to Greet the Dawn?
Lament for Richard Rolston.
Lousy Peter.
Mrs. Crudeman.
Mrs. Southern's Enemy.
Next War, The.
On the Coast of Coromandel.
Osmund Toulmin.
Silence of God, The.
Sound out, proud trumpets.
"Therefore Is the Name of It Called Babel."
Three Nocturns.
To Charlotte Corday.
Trippers.
What Was Your Dream, Doctor Murricombe?
Winter the Huntsman.
Sitwell, Sacheverell
Agamemnon's Tomb.
Ballad: White Rose.
Battles of the Centaurs, *sel.*
Belle Isis; Ballad of a Rose.
Centaurs and Lapithae.
Cherry Tree.
Dandelions.
Derbyshire Bluebells.
Farnese Hercules, The.
Fisherman.
Fountains ("This night is pure and clear as thrice refinèd silver").
Kingcups.
Landscape with the Giant Orion, *sel.*
Lime Avenue, The.
Magnolia Tree in Summer.
O Rose with Two Hearts.
One by one, as harvesters, all heavy laden.
Orange Tree by Day.
Orange Tree by Night.
Orion Seeks the Goddess Diana.
Outside Dunsandle.
"Psittacus Eois Imitatrix Ales ab Indis."
Red-Gold Rain, The, *sels.*
Rio Grande, The.
River God, The.
Rosario d'Arabeschi; Poems and Rose Portraits, *sels.*
Sandalwood Song.
Sweet clavichord.
Tulip Tree.
Variation on a Theme by John Lyly.

Sitwell (continued)
Venus of Bolsover Castle, The.
White Rose.
Skeat, Walter William
Clerk Ther Was of Cauntebrigge Also, A.
Villanelle.
Skelton, John
Against Garnesche, *sel.*
And if ye stand in doubt.
And this comely dame.
Auncient Acquaintance, Madam.
Ballade of the Scottyshe Kynge, A.
Boke of Phyllyp Sparowe.
Book of Philip Sparrow, The.
Bowge of Court, The.
Colin Clout.
Colyn Cloute [*or* Colin Clout], *sels.*
Commendations of Mistress Jane Scrope, The.
Curse on the Cat, A.
Cursing of the Cat, The.
Elynour Rummynge.
Funeral of Philip Sparrow, The.
Garlande of Laurell, The, *sels.*
Gift of a Skull, The.
Go, Piteous Heart.
Gup, Scot!
He is set so hye.
Here Folowith Divers Balettis and Dities Solacious, Devised by Master Skelton, Laureate.
In Praise of Isabel Pennell.
Knowledge, Acquaintance.
L'Envoy: To His Book.
Lullay, Lullay [like a Child].
Magnificence, *sel.*
Mistress Margaret Hussey.
My Darling Dear, My Daisy Flower.
O Cat of Carlish [*or* Churlish] Kind.
On the Death of the Noble Prince King Edward the Fourth.
Parrot, The.
Parrot's Soliloquy.
Philip Sparrow.
Phyllip Sparrow.
Phyllyp Sparowe.
Prayer to the Father of [*or* in] Heaven, A.
Prelates, The.
Skelton Laureate, upon a Dead Man's Head.
Sleeper Hood-winked, The.
So many moral matters, and so little used.
So merrily singeth the nightingale!
Sparrow's Dirge, The ("Pla ce bo").
Sparrow's Dirge, The ("When I remember again").
Speak [*or* Speke], Parrot, *sels.*
Speke, Parrot.
Tell you I chyll.
Though Ye Suppose.
To His Wife.
To Maystres Isabell Pennell.
To Mistress Anne.
To Mistress Gertrude Statham.
To Mistress [*or* Maystres] Isabel[l] Pennell.
To Mistress Margaret Hussey.
To Mistress Margaret Tilney.
To Mistress Margery Wentworth.
To My Lady Mirriel Howard.
Tunning [*or* Tunnyng] of Elynour Rummyng, The.
Unfriendly Fortune.
Upon a Dead Man's Head.
Vengence on Cats.
What can it avail.
Why Come Ye Nat to Courte? *sel.*
With Lullay, Lullay, like a Child.
Wofully Araide.
Womanhood, Wanton, ye Want.
Skelton, Philip
To God, Ye Choir Above.
Skelton, Robin
"Angel."
Ballad of a Mine, A.
Brigg, The.
Skene, Don
After Reading Twenty Years of Grantland Rice.
Skidmore, Ruth Mather
Fantasy.
Skinner, Constance Lindsay
Chief's Prayer after the Salmon Catch, The.
Song of Basket-weaving.
Song of Cradle-making.
Song of the Full Catch.
Song of Whip-plaiting.
Songs of the Coast Dwellers, *sels.*
Skinner, Cornelia Otis
Path to Shottery, The.
To the Sistine Madonna.
Skinner, John
Lizzy Liberty, *abr.*
Tullochgorum.
Skinner, Murray
Futile Sacrifice.
Skipsey, Joseph
Butterfly, The.
Dewdrop, The.
Dewdrop, Wind and Sun.
Merry Bee, A.
Mother Wept.
Violet and the Rose, The.
Skirving, Adam
Johnnie Cope.
Skjaeraasen, Einar
Word of God, The.
Skrine, Nesta Higginson *See* **"O'Neill, Moira"**
Sladek, John
Love Nest.
Treasure of the Haunted Rambler, The.
Sladen, Douglas Brooke Wheelton
Charles II, *sel.*
Christmas Letter from Australia, A.
Refrain: "Come and kiss me, Mistress Beauty."
Salopia Inhospitalis.
Sunset on the Cunimbla Valley, Blue Mountains.
Tropics, The.
Under the Wattle.
Slater, Eleanor
Ballad of Wonder, A.
Bigot.
Cradle Carol.
December Twenty-fourth.
Misdirection.
Petition.
Sight and Insight.
Slater, Francis Carey "Jan van Avond"
Drought, *sel.*
Lament for a Dead Cow.
Milking Kraal.
Sky is a blue, coiled serpent, The.
Wood-Gatherers, The.
Slater, John Rothwell
Easter Reveille, An.
Slavitt, David R.
In the Seraglio.
Slemp, John Calvin
I Sought the Living God.
O Christ, Who Died.
Slender, Pauline
Vagrant, The.
Slessor, Kenneth
Atlas, The, *sels.*
Beach Burial.
Country Towns.
Crow Country.
Dutch Seacoast.
Earth-Visitors.
Five Bells.
Five Visions of Captain Cook.
Flowers turned to stone! Not all the botany.
Gulliver.
King of Cuckooz, The.
Last Trams, *sel.*
Mermaids.
Metempsychosis.
Night-Ride, The.
Post-Roads.
Sensuality.
Sleep.
Stars.
Then, from the skeletons of trams.
Two Chronometers.
Waters.
Sloan, Errol B.
And Yet.
Sloan, Jocelyn Macy
And the Pear Trees Shiver.
Eliza Telefair.
Invaders, The.
Stranger Bride.
Sloman, Joel
At Midnight.
Blueprint.
Clay Pipe.
Poem: "Hold my breath as there's a sound on the stairs."
Power Failure.
Slonimski, Antoni
All.
He Is My Countryman.
London Spring.
Morning and Evening.
Remembrance.
Sly, Muriel
Chimpanzee, The/ Is a most embarrassing animal to see.
"Smalacombe, John." *See* **MacKay, Louis Alexander**
Small, Adam
There's Somethin'.
Small, Floyd B.
Root Hog or Die, *parody.*
Smart, Alexander
Last Day of the Year, The.
Still Small Voice, The.
Smart, Christopher
Adoration.
All the Scenes of Nature Quicken.
Beauteous, Yea Beauteous More than These.
Cat, The.
Catholic Amen, The.
Christmas Day.
Citizen and the Red Lion of Brentford, The.
Epithalamium on a Late Happy Marriage.
Flowers in a Garden.
Foot, Fin or Feather.
For adoration, David's psalms.
For I am not without authority in my jeopardy.
For I Will Consider My Cat Jeoffry.
For Saturday.
For the doubling of flowers is the improvement of the gard'ner's talent.
For the feast of trumpets should be kept up.
For the Greek & Latin are not dead languages.
For the Letter Which Signifies God.
For thirdly he works it upon stretch with the forepaws extended.
Glorious the Sun in Mid Career.
Gratitude.
Hymn for Saturday.

Hymns and Spiritual Songs, *sels.*
Hymns for the Amusement of Children, *sels.*
Instrument Rhimes.
Instruments, The.
Jubilate Agno, *sels.*
Lark's Nest, A.
Let Elizur Rejoice with the Partridge.
Let Lotan Rejoice with Sauterelle.
Let Peter Rejoice with the Moon Fish.
Let Tobias bless charity with his dog.
Long-Suffering of God.
Man of Prayer, The.
Mirth.
My Cat Jeoffry [*or* Jeoffrey].
Nativity of Our Lord, The.
Night-Piece, A; or, Modern Philosophy.
O David, highest in the list.
O servant of God's holiest charge.
Ode to the Earl of Northumberland, *sel.*
On a Bed of Guernsey Lilies.
On a Lady Throwing Snowballs at Her Lover.
On Taking a Bachelor's Degree.
Patriots of Mankind.
Psalm VIII: "O Lord, our Lord," *sel.*
Rejoice in God.
Rejoice in the Lamb.
St. Mark.
St. Matthias.
St. Philip and St. James, *sel.*
Song: "Where shall Celia fly for shelter."
Song of David, The.
Song to David, A.
Spring.
Stars, The, *sel.*
Strength.
Strong Is the Horse upon His Speed.
Sublime—invention ever young.
Sweet is the dew that falls betimes.
Tell them, I am, Jehovah said.
To Ethelinda.

Smedley, Menella Bute
Little Fair Soul, The.
Wind Me a Summer Crown.

Smeeton, John P.
Jack Frost in the Garden.

Smiley, Joseph Bert
St. Peter at the Gate.

Smith, A. C.
Waif, The.

Smith, Ada
In City Streets.

Smith, Alexander
Autumn.
Barbara.
Beauty.
Boy's Poem, A., *sel.*
Forerunners.
Life-Drama, A, *sels.*
Love.
Minor Poet, A.
Scorned.
Sea-Marge.
Steamer left the black and oozy wharves, The.
To ——: "Broken moon lay, The."

Smith, Anne May
At the Zoo.

Smith, Arabella Eugenia
If I Should Die Tonight.

Smith, Arthur James Marshall
Archer, The.
Ballade un Peu Banale.
Business as Usual 1946.
Far West.
Field of Long Grass.
Fountain, The.
Good Friday.
Hyacinth for Edith, A.
Like an Old Proud King in a Parable.
Lonely Land, The.
Mermaid, The.
My Death.
News of the Phoenix.
Ode: On the Death of William Butler Yeats.
On Knowing Nothing.
One Sort of Poet.
Plot against Proteus, The.
Prothalamium.
Resurrection of Arp.
Sonnet: "How all men wrongly death to dignify."
Sorcerer, The.
Taste of Space, The.
To Henry Vaughan.
To Hold in a Poem.
Universe into Stone.
Watching the Old Man Die.
What Is That Music High in the Air?
What the Emanation of Casey Jones Said to the Medium.
Wisdom of Old Jelly Roll, The.

Smith, Belle E. *See* **Smith, Arabella Eugenia**

Smith, Bradford
Winter Is Icumen in.

Smith, Caroline Sprague
Final Struggle, The.

Smith, Charlotte
Captive Escaped in the Wilds of America, The.
Elegiac Sonnet.
First Swallow, The.
Gossamer, The.
Nautilus, The.
Partial Muse has, from my earliest hours, The.
Sonnet Written at the Close of Spring.
To Sleep.
To the Moon.
To the River Arun.

Smith, Cicely Fox
Hastings Mill.
In Prize.
In the Trades.
Pictures.
Saint George of England.
What the Old Man Said.

Smith, Clark Ashton
Amor Aeternalis.
Horologe, The.
Incubus of Time, The.
Memorial.
Metaphor.
To the Daemon Sublimity.

Smith, Dexter
Our National Banner.

Smith, Edgar
Heaven Will Protect the Working Girl.
You may tempt the upper classes.

Smith, Edward Lucie- *See* **Lucie-Smith, Edward**

Smith, Elizabeth Oakes
Drowned Mariner, The.
Her ways were gentle while a babe.
Sinless Child, The, *sel.*

Smith, Flora Emily
My Prayer.

Smith, Florence
Song: "How pleasant it is that always."

Smith, Florence Margaret *See* **Smith, Stevie**

Smith, Gwen A.
Off We Go to Market.

Smith, Harry Bache
Armorer's Song, The.
I Didn't Like Him.
Idol's Eye, The, *sel.*
Long Night, The.
My Angeline.
Same Old Story.
Song of the Turnkey, The.
Tattooed Man, The.
Wizard of the Nile, The, *sel.*

Smith, Helen Rogers
He Lifted from the Dust.

Smith, Hilda Worthington
Carpenter of Galilee, The.

Smith, Horace (*or* Horatio)
Address to a Mummy.
Bit of Colour, A.
Gouty Merchant and the Stranger, The.
Jester Condemned to Death, The.

Smith, Horace [*or* Horatio], *and* James Smith
Baby's Debut, The.
Loyal Effusion.
Theatre, The.

Smith, Iain Crichton
By Ferry to the Island.
Culloden and After.
End of the Season on a Stormy Day—Oban.
For Angus MacLeod.
For My Mother.
For the Unknown Seamen of the 1939-45 War Buried in Iona Churchyard.
John Knox.
Old Woman.
Schoolgirl on Speech-Day in the Open Air.
Window, The.
Young Highland Girl Studying Poetry, A.

Smith, J. Danson
All Things in Jesus.
He Goes Before.
Perhaps Today.
Thorns.
We'll Meet Again.

Smith, James
Surnames.

Smith, John (1580-1631)
In the Due Honor of the Author Master Robert Norton.
John Smith of His Friend Master John Taylor.
Sea Marke, The.

Smith [*or* Smyth], John (1662-1717)
Strephon.
Somewhere around Christmas.

Smith, Joseph
Eulogium on Rum.

Smith, Kay
Child's Poem.
Eye of Humility, The.
What Then, Dancer?
When a Girl Looks Down.

Smith, Langdon
Evolution.

Smith, Lanta Wilson
This, Too, Shall [*or* Will] Pass Away.

Smith, Leroy, Jr
Olduvai.
Salvation Prospect.
Sappho Rehung ("Sappho saw three stars").
Spring Song.
What Sanguine Beast?

Smith, Lewis Worthington
News from Yorktown.

Smith, Linwood D.
Dawn Song.
Free Wine on Communion Day.
Pride and Prejudice.
What Good Are Words?

Smith, Lucy
Face of Poverty.

Smith, Margoret
Cataract.

Smith, Marion Couthouy
King of the Belgians.

Smith (continued)
Star, The; Dedicated to Theodore Roosevelt, Following His Death, January 6, 1919.
Smith, Mary Brainerd
Poor for Our Sakes.
Smith, Mary Carter
Clubwoman.
Jungle.
Smith, May Riley
Departure.
God's Plans.
If We Knew.
My Life Is a Bowl.
My Uninvited Guest.
O Bells in the Steeple.
Scatter Seeds of Kindness.
Sometime.
Tired Mothers.
Tree-Top Road, The.
Smith, Naomi Gwladys Royde- *See* **Royde-Smith, Naomi Gwladys**
Smith, Ninna May
If Some Grim Tragedy.
Smith, Nora Archibald
Feast of the Doll, The.
Haughty Aspen, The; a German Legend.
Meadow Talk.
Neighbors of the Christ Night.
Smith, Norma E.
Evangeline.
Smith, Oswald J.
After.
Another Year ("Another year has now been born").
Blessed Saviour, Thou Art Mine.
God Is Near.
God Is with Me.
God's Presence Makes My Heaven.
God's Will.
He Must Do It.
Heart That Weeps, A.
House of Many Mansions, The.
I Turn to Jesus.
In God We Trust.
Master's Call, The.
O Lonely Heart.
Prayer in the Night, A.
Saviour Can Solve Every Problem, The.
Take Thou, O Lord.
Trust and Wait.
We Shall Meet Them.
Smith, Phoebe
Via Dolorosa.
Smith, Robert Paul
Fielding Error.
Small Quiet Song.
Tie Your Tongue, Sir?
Smith, Samuel Francis
America.
Daybreak.
Flower-strewn Graves.
Memorial Day.
Morning Light Is Breaking, The.
National Hymn: "My Country, 'tis of thee."
Our Honored Heroes, *sel.*
Success of the Gospel.
Tree-planting.
Smith, Seba ("Major Jack Downing")
Frozen Girl, The.
Mother in the Snow-Storm, The.
Young Charlotte.
Smith, Mrs. Seba *See* **Smith, Elizabeth Oakes**
Smith, Sheila Kaye- *See* **Kaye-Smith, Sheila**
Smith, Sidney Goodsir
Can I Forget?
Cokkils.
Deevil's Waltz, The.
Defeat o' the Hert.
Epistle to John Guthrie.
For My Newborn Son.
Ineffable Dou, The.
Largo.
Leander Stormbound.
Mandrake Hert, The.
Mither's Lament, The.
Saagin.
Salad, A.
Sang: Recoll o Skaith.
Under the Eildon Tree.
Whan the Hert Is Laich.
Ye Mongers Aye Need Masks for Cheatrie.
Ye Spier Me.
Smith, Stevie
Advice to Young Children.
Autumn.
Bereaved Swan, The.
Frog Prince, The.
Heavenly City, The.
Hymn to the Seal.
Little Boy Lost, The.
Miss Snooks, Poetess.
Mrs. Arbuthnot.
My Muse.
Occasional Yarrow, The.
Old Sweet Dove of Wiveton, The.
Pad, Pad.
Parklands, The.
River God, The.
Singing Cat, The.
So to Fatness Come.
Thoughts on the Christian Doctrine of Eternal Hell.
To Carry the Child.
To the Tune of the Coventry Carol.
Weak Monk, The.
Smith, Sydney Goodsir *See* **Smith, Sidney Goodsir**
Smith, Vivian
Bedlam Hills.
Last Summer, The.
Old Men Are Facts.
Smith, Walter
Carpenter of Nazareth, The.
Smith, Walter Chalmers
Christian Paradox, The.
Daughters of Philistia.
Glenaradale.
Olrig Grange, *sel.*
Self-exiled, The.
Smith, Welton
Beast Section, The.
Interlude ("Screams/ screams").
Interlude ("We never spent time in the mountains").
Malcolm.
Nigga Section, The.
Special Section for the Niggas on the Lower Eastside or: Invert the Divisor and Multiply.
Strategies.
Smith, William
Chloris, *sels.*
My Love, I Cannot Thy Rare Beauties Place.
Sonnet: "My Love, I cannot thy rare beauties place."
To the Most Excellent and Learned Shepherd, Colin Clout.
Smith, William Hart- *See* **Hart-Smith, William**
Smith, William Jay
American Primitive.
Antelope.
At the Tombs of the House of Savoy.
Autumn.
Butterfly.
Closing of the Rodeo, The.
Convoy.
Cupidon.
Dachshunds.
Dead Snake.
Death of a Jazz Musician.
Dog.
Dream.
Edmund Clerihew Bentley.
Elegy: "I stood between two mirrors when you died."
Fish.
Galileo Galilei.
Green Place, A.
Gull.
Hotel Continental.
Independence Day.
Jittery Jim.
Laughing Time.
Lovebirds.
Lovers, The.
Marcel Proust.
Massacre of the Innocents, The.
Mr. Smith.
Mrs. Caribou.
Mole.
Monkey.
Moon.
Morels.
Morning at Arnheim.
Neo-classical Poem.
Opossum.
Over and Under.
Owl, The.
Panda, The.
Park in Milan, The.
Parrot.
Pavane for the Nursery, A.
Peacock of Java, The.
Persian Miniature.
Pick Me Up.
Plain Talk.
"Poet."
Processional.
Rear Vision.
Rondeau: "Lord, I'm done for: now Margot."
Room in the Villa, A.
Seal.
Tempest, The.
There Was an Old Lady Named Crockett.
Things.
3 for 25.
Toaster, The.
Today I Have Touched the Earth.
Tulip.
Voyages of Captain Cock, The.
William Penn/ Was the most level-headed of men.
Winter Morning.
Wooing Lady, The.
Yak.
Zebra.
Smithyman, Kendrick
Considerations of Norfolk Island, *sel.*
Could You Once Regain.
Cousin Emily and the Night Visitor.
Defenceless Children, Your Great Enemy.
Dirge for Two Clavichords and Bowler Hat.
Elegy against a Latter Day.
Evening Music.
High in the afternoon the dove.
Icarus.
Incident at Matauri.
Moment, The.
Night Walkers, The.
Personal Poem.
This Blonde Girl.
Waiwera.

Walk Past Those Houses on a Sunday Morning.
Smollett, Tobias George
Independence.
Love Elegy.
Ode to Independence
Ode to Leven Water.
Ode to Mirth.
Ode to Sleep.
Song: "To fix her—'twere a task as vain."
Tears of Scotland, The.
To Leven Water.
Smyth, Florida Watts
Eternal Contour.
Green Mountain Boy.
North and South.
Unclaimed.
Smyth, John *See* **Smith, John (1662-1717)**
Smythe, Albert Ernest Stafford
Anastasis.
Smythe, Daniel
From My Thought.
Snaith, Stanley
Birds in the Flax.
Blue Ghosts.
Discovery, The.
Dust.
Gulls.
Hare, The.
Parachute.
Scythe, The.
Stack, The.
To Some Builders of Cities.
Snapp, Thomas
Actor, The.
Snelling, Lois
Know It Is Christmas.
Snellings, Rolland
Earth.
Mississippi Concerto.
Song of Fire, The.
Sunrise!!
Snider, P. M.
Communion.
Snodgrass, C. A.
Poem for Christmas, A.
Snodgrass, William DeWitt
After experience taught me that all the ordinary.
April Inventory.
Campus on the Hill, The.
Cardinal, A.
Easter has come around.
Flat One, A.
Heart's Needle.
Here in the scuffled dust.
Home Town.
I get numb and go in.
Late April and you are three; today.
Leaving Ithaca.
Lobsters in the Window.
Lovers Go Fly a Kite, The.
Lying Awake.
Magic Flute, The.
Manet: The Execution of Emperor Maximilian.
Marsh, The.
Mementos, I ("Sorting out letters and piles of my old").
Mementos, II ("I found them there today").
Men's Room in the College Chapel, The.
Mntis...Outis.
Monet: "Les Nymphéas."
Operation, The.
Orpheus.
Papageno.
Powwow.
Returned to Frisco, 1946.
September in the Park.
Song: "Sweet beast, I have gone prowling."
Ten Days Leave.
These Trees Stand.
Vicious winter finally yields, The.
Vuillard: "The Mother and Sister of the Artist."
Winter again and it is snowing.
Snow, Laura A. Barter
God Is in Every Tomorrow.
Snow, Roger Vinton
State of Maine Song.
Snow, Sophia P.
Annie and Willie's Prayer.
Snow, Wilbert
Aged Ninety Years.
Snyder, Gary
Above Pate Valley.
Amitabha's Vow, X.
Bubbs Creek Haircut.
Burning, *abr.*
Eight Sandbars on the Takano River.
For a Far-out Friend.
For the West.
Foxtail Pine.
Hay for the Horses.
Hunting, *sels.*
John Muir on Mt. Ritter.
Late Snow and Lumber Strike of the Summer of Fifty-four, The.
Logging, *sels.*
Maitreya the Future Buddha.
Marin-An.
Market, The.
Mid-August at Sourdough Mountain Lookout.
Mts and Rivers, *sels.*
Myths & Texts, *sels.*
Nooksack Valley.
Piute Creek.
Praise for Sick Women.
Riprap.
Sixth-Month Song in the Foothills.
Text, The.
Things to Do around a Lookout.
Things to Do around Kyoto.
This Poem Is for Bear.
This Poem Is for Birds.
This Poem Is for Deer.
This Tokyo.
Yase: September.
Snyder, Richard
To Mary, of Sailing.
Snyder, Thurmond
Beale Street, Memphis.
Beast with Chrome Teeth, The.
Seeds.
Sobiloff, Hy
Airship.
Cubism.
Family Screams.
Hans Christian Andersen in Central Park.
Little Girl Cat.
My Mother's Table.
Painting of a Lobster by Picasso.
Pittsburgh.
Unquestionable Questions.
Upon Differences of Opinion.
Soderbeck, Eleanor Foote
Great Towers of Steel.
Söderberg, Hjalmar
Darkness Gathers, The.
Södergran, Edith
Land That Is Not, The.
Moon, The.
Sodo
Spring in My Hut.
Soin
Dewdrops.
Sokan
Fan, The.
Solis-Cohen, Solomon
Spiritual Vision.
Sollitt, Kenneth W.
God Must Be Like That.
"Sologub, Feodor" (Feodor Kuzmich Teternikov)
Amphora, The.
Austere the Music of My Songs.
In a Gay Jar.
Solomon, Marvin
Cages.
Cat and the Bird, The.
Garden, The.
Giraffe, The.
Lemon Sherbet.
Vole, The.
Solomon Ephraim ben Aaron of Lenczicz
These Things I Do Remember.
Solomos, George P.
Wisdom of the Gazelle.
Solon
Constitution of Athens, The.
Rule of Fair Play.
Solt, Mary Ellen
Visitor, The.
Somerville [*or* Somerville], William
Address to His Elbow-Chair, New Cloath'd, An.
Chace, The, *sel.*
Hare-hunting.
On Presenting to a Lady a White Rose and a Red, on the Tenth of June.
Presenting to a Lady a White Rose and a Red, on the Tenth of June.
Sonastine, Worral G.
Her Mother.
Soné, Blessed
Sophocles
Ajax *sels.*
Ajax, before His Suicide.
Antigone, *sels.*
Choral Ode: "Numberless are the world's wonders."
Choral Poem "Land beloved of horsemen, fair, The."
Chorus: "Fair Salamis, the billow's roar."
Chorus: "For this one thing above all I would be praised as a man."
Chorus: "Land of running horses, fair, The."
Chorus: "Oh, may my constant feet not fail."
Chorus: "What man is he that yearneth."
Creon.
Endure what life God gives and ask no longer span.
Grove of Colonus, The.
Higher Command, The.
Kupris bears trophies away.
Not to be born at all.
Oedipus at Colonus, *sels.*
Oedipus Rex [*or* Oedipus Tyrannus], *sels.*
Old Age.
Thebes of the Seven Gates.
Universal Change.
Women of Trachis, *sel.*
Sora
Up the Barley Rows.
Sorell, Walter
All That Matters.
Without a Speaking Tongue.
Sorley, Charles Hamilton
All the Hills and Vales Along.
Expectans Expectavi.
In Memoriam S. C. W., V. C.
Marlborough, *sel.*
Peer Gynt.
Rooks.
Route March.
Seekers, The.

Sorley (continued)
So, there, when sunset made the downs look new.
Song of the Ungirt Runners, The.
Sonnet: "Saints have adored the lofty soul of you."
Sonnet: "Such, such is Death: no triumph: no defeat."
To Germany.
To Poets.
Two Sonnets.
When You See Millions of the Mouthless Dead.
Soroka, Pauline E.
Understanding.
Sorrentino, Gilbert
Classic Case, A.
Zoo, The.
Sosei (Sosei Hoshi)
Forgetfulness.
Only because she said.
You bring no joy, but strange regret.
Soseki
Over the wintry.
Soto de Rojas, Pedro
Penitence.
Soule, Jean Conder
Surprises.
Sousa, Noemia de
Appeal.
Souster, Raymond
All Animals Like Me.
Bed without a Woman, A.
Bottle of Chianti, The.
Choosing Coffins.
Collector, The.
Day before Christmas, The.
Drunk: On Crutches.
Ersatz.
Falling of the Snow, The.
Flight of the Roller-Coaster.
Girl Asleep.
Ladybug.
Man Who Finds That His Son Has Become a Thief, The.
May 15th.
Mother, The.
Need of an Angel.
Postscript.
Reality.
Search.
Six-Quart Basket, The.
Speakers, Columbus Circle.
Summer Afternoon.
Sunday Night Walk.
This Poem Will Never Be Finished.
Ties.
When I See Old Men.
Where the Blue Horses.
Worm, The.
Soutar, William
Auld House, The.
Auld Sang.
Ballad: "O! shairly ye hae seen my love."
Children, The.
Gowk, The.
In the Mood of Blake.
Makar, The.
"Nation Shall Speak Peace . . ."
Parable.
Permanence of the Young Men, The.
Poetry.
Revelation.
Riddle, A: "Yon laddie wi' the gowdan pow."
Scotland.
Signs.
Singing Bush, The.
Song: "Whaur yon broken brig hings owre."
Star, The.
Supper.
Thocht, The.
Tryst, The.
Wait for the Hour.
Whigmaleerie, A.
Souter, Charles Henry
After Johnson's Dance.
Bound for Sourabaya!
Irish Lords.
Mallee Fire, The.
Old John Bax.
What the Red-haired Bo'sun Said.
Southerne, Thomas
Maid's Last Prayer, The, *sel.*
Rambling Lady, The.
Sir Antony Love; or, The Rambling Lady, *sel.*
Song: "Pursuing beauty, men descry."
Song in the Second Act, A.
Song, Set by H. Purcell, and Sung by Mrs. Hodgson, A.
Though You Make No Return.
Southesk, Earl of *See* **Carnegie, James, Earl of Southesk**
Southey, Caroline Anne Bowles *See* **Bowles, Caroline Anne**
Southey, Robert
Absolvers, The.
After Blenheim.
Battle of Blenheim, The.
Bishop Hatto [and the Rats].
Bower of Peace, The.
Calm Sea, A.
Cataract of Lodore, The.
Corston.
Curse of Kehama, The, *sels.*
Ebb Tide, The.
Epitaph: "Time and the World, whose magnitude and weight."
Father William.
Fountain of the Fairies, The.
Go, Valentine, and tell that lovely maid.
God's Judgment [*or* Judgement] on a Wicked Bishop.
His Books.
Holly Tree, The.
Homeward Bound.
How the Waters Come Down at Ladore.
Imitated from the Persian.
Inchcape Rock, The.
Inscription for a Tablet on the Banks of a Stream.
Inscriptions for the Caledonian Canal.
Kehama's Curse.
Love Indestructible.
March to Moscow, The.
Morning Mist, The.
My Days among the Dead Are Past [*or* Passed].
Night.
Night in the Desert.
Now tell us what 'twas all about.
O God! Have Mercy, in This Dreadful Hour.
Ode Written during the War with America, 1814, *sel.*
Old Man's Comforts [and How He Gained Them], The.
Old Woman of Berkeley, The.
On the Speech of Robert Emmet.
Pig, The.
Scholar, The.
Soldier's Wife, The.
Spring.
Stream descends on Meru mountain, A.
Thalaba the Destroyer, *sels.*
To a Bee.
To a Goose.
Traveller's Return, The.
Two forms inseparable in unity.
Two Poems Concerning the Slave Trade.
Vision of Judgement, A, *sel.*
Well of St. Keyne, The.
Widow, The.
Winter.
Winter Portrait.
Witch, The.
With many a weary step, at length I gain.
Written on a Sunday Morning.
Southey, Robert, *and* Samuel Taylor Coleridge
Devil's Walk on Earth, The.
Southey, Mrs. Robert *See* **BowlesCaroline Anne.**
Southwell, Robert
At Fotheringay.
At Home in Heaven.
Before My Face the Picture Hangs.
Burning Babe, The.
Child My Choice, A.
Christ's Bloody Sweat.
Christs Returne out of Egypt.
Christs Sleeping Friends.
Come to Your Heaven, You Heavenly Choirs!
Content and Rich.
David's Peccavi.
Death of Our Ladie, The.
Decease, Release: Dum Morior, Orior.
Elegy for Margaret Howard, Lady Buckhurst.
Ensamples of Our Saviour.
Flight into Egypt, The.
From Fortune's Reach.
Her Nativity.
Humble Pomp.
I Die Alive.
Image of Death, The, *sel.*
In Freezing Winter Night.
Lewd Love Is Loss.
Life Is but Loss.
Look Home.
Looke Home.
Loss in Delay[s].
Love's Servile Lot.
Man's Civil War.
Marie Magdalens Complaint at Christs Death.
Martyrdom of Mary, Queen of Scots, The.
Nativitie of Christ, The.
New Heaven, New War [*or* Warre].
New Prince, New Pompe.
Of the Blessèd Sacrament of the Altar.
Our Lady's Salutation.
Presentation, The.
Saint Peter's Complaint, *sel.*
Scorn Not the Least.
Seek Flowers of Heaven.
Self-pleasing souls that play with beauty's bait.
Sinnes Heavie Loade.
Stanzas from "Saint Peter's Complaint."
Times Go [*or* Goe] by Turns.
To the Christian Reader.
Tymes Goe by Turnes.
Upon the Image of Death.
Vale of Teares, A.
Virgin Mary to Christ on the Cross, The.
Virgin Mary's Conception, The.
Virgine Maries Conception, The.
Virgins Salutation, The.
Visitation, The.
Wassailer's Song.
Southwold, Stephen
Mother of Men.
"Souza, Ernest." *See* **Scott, Evelyn**
Soyinka, Wole
Abiku.
Season.
Telephone Conversation.
Spacks, Barry

Farm Couple, After Norman Rockwell.
Freshmen.
Spalding, Helen
Curtain.
Dream, The.
Spalding, John Lancaster
At the Ninth Hour.
Believe and Take Heart.
Et Mori Lucrum.
Forepledged.
God and the Soul, *sels.*
Nature and the Child.
Silence.
Starry Host, The.
Void Between, The.
Spalding, Susan Marr
Fate.
Sea's Spell, The.
Song's Worth, A.
Spargur, Jill
Tragedy.
Spark, Muriel
Canaan.
She Wolf, The.
Sparshott, Francis
Entanglement.
Improperia.
Paysage Choisi.
Spear, Charles
Christoph.
Die Pelzaffen.
1894 in London.
Karl.
Watchers, The.
Spear, John Edward
If You Keep Faith with Me.
Spears, Dorothea
Begetting.
Spears, Heather
My Love behind Walls.
Spears, Woodridge
Restoration.
Spee, Frederick (Friedrich Spee von Langenfeld)
Dialogue at the Cross.
Speidel, Margaret Knowled
Autumn Days.
Spellman, Alfred B.
Beautiful Day #9, The.
Friends I Am Like You Tied.
I Looked and Saw History Caught.
John Coltrane—an Impartial Review.
Tomorrow the Heroes.
Zapata & the Landlord.
Spence, Lewis
Prows o' Reekie, The.
Wee May o' Caledon, The.
Spencer, ——
Thy Look.
Spencer, Anne
At the Carnival.
Before the Feast of Shushan.
Creed.
Dunbar.
For Jim, Easter Eve.
I Have a Friend.
Innocence.
Letter to My Sister.
Life-long, Poor Browning.
Lines to a Nasturtium (a Lover Muses).
Neighbors.
Questing.
Substitution.
Translation.
Wife-Woman, The.
Spencer, Bernard
Aegean Islands 1940-41.
Behaviour of Money.
Cold Night, A.
Delos.
Greek Excavations.
Hand, A.
Ill.
Letters.
Olive Trees.
Part of Plenty.
Rendezvous, The.
Sarcophagi.
Spring Wind, A.
Yachts on the Nile.
Spencer, Hiram Ladd
Hundred Years to Come, A.
Spencer, Lilian White
Aut Caesar aut Nullus.
Red Ghosts Chant, The.
Spring Song of Aspens.
Spencer, Theodore
Californians, The.
Circle, A.
Contemporary Song.
Critics, The.
Day, The.
Dearest and nearest brother.
Eden: Or One View of It.
Empty my heart, Lord, of daily vices.
Entropy.
Epitaph: "She was a high-class bitch and a dandy."
Inflatable Globe, The.
Invocation: "Empty my heart, Lord of daily vices."
Narrative, A.
Phoenix, The.
Polite Song.
Reason for Writing, A.
Song: "I who love you bring."
Spring Song.
Spencer, Thomas Edward
How McDougal Topped the Score.
Spencer, William Robert
Beth Gêlert.
How D'-y'-do and Good-by.
Spender, Stephen
After They Have Tired [of the Brilliance of Cities].
Air Raid across the Bay of Plymouth.
Almond Blossom in Wartime.
Already.
Anno Santo.
Auf dem Wasser zu Singen.
Awaking.
Barn, The.
Beethoven's Death Mask.
Bombed Happiness, The.
Childhood, A.
Cries of Evening, The.
Daybreak.
Discovered in Mid-Ocean.
Double Shame, The.
Dylan Thomas.
Elegy for Margaret, *sel.*
Elementary School Classroom in a Slum, An.
Empty House, The.
Epilogue: "Time is a thing."
Epilogue to a Human Drama.
Express, The.
Farewell in a Dream.
Footnote, A.
From All These Events.
Funeral, The.
Generous Years, The.
He Will Watch the Hawk.
"I" Can Never Be a Great Man, An.
I Think Continually of Those Who Were Truly Great.
Ice.
Immortal Spirit, The.
In Railway Halls [on Pavements near the Traffic].
Judas Iscariot.
Labourer in the Vineyard, The.
Landscape near an Aerodrome, The.
Lost Days.
Man-made World, A.
Marston ("Marston, dropping it in the grate, broke his pipe").
Mask.
Memento.
Midsummer.
Missing My Daughter.
Moving through the Silent Crowd.
My Parents Kept Me from Children Who Were Rough.
Never Being, But Always at the Edge.
New Year.
North, The.
Not Palaces [an Era's Crown].
O Night O Trembling Night.
Oh Young Men Oh Young Comrades.
On the Pilots Who Destroyed Germany in the Spring of 1945.
On the Third Day.
One More New Botched Beginning.
Polar Exploration.
Poor Girl.
Port Bou.
Prisoners, The.
Pylons, The.
Rejoice in the Abyss.
Rolled Over on Europe.
Room above the Square, The.
Seascape.
Separation, A.
Shapes of Death [Haunt Life].
Song: "Stranger, you who hide my love."
Sonnet: "You were born; must die."
Statistics.
Stopwatch and an Ordnance Map, A.
Swan, The.
Thoughts during an Air Raid.
To a Spanish Poet.
To My Daughter.
To Poets and Airmen.
Trance, The.
Truly Great, The.
Two Armies.
Two Kisses.
Ultima Ratio Regum.
Vase of Tears, The.
War God, The.
What I Expected.
Whim of Time, A.
Winter and Summer.
Winter Landscape.
Without That Once Clear Aim.
Word.
Your Body Is Stars.
Spenser, Edmund
Ah! when will this long weary day have end.
All This World's Riches.
Amoretti, *sels.*
And him beside rides fierce revenging Wrath.
And nigh thereto a little Chappell stoode.
April [*or* Aprill].
Aprill.
Art of Eyes, The.
Artegall and Radigund.
Astrophel.
At Court.
At last he came unto a gloomy glade.
At last she chauncèd by good hap to meet.
August ("The sixth was August").
August ("Tell me, Perigot").
Autumn.
Balme.
Be Bold.
Beauty.
Behold I see the haven nigh at hand.
Behold, O Man.
Bower of Bliss, The.

Spenser (continued)
Bright Squadrons, The.
Britomart in the House of Busirane.
But, ah! Maecenas is yclad in clay.
But the wyld man, contrarie to her feare.
But whoso may, thrice happy man him hold.
Butterfly, The.
By this the northerne wagoner had set.
Cave of Despair, The.
Cave of Mammon, The.
Colin Clout's Come Home Again.
Contempt of Poetry, The.
Cymochles and Phaedria.
Dame Nature.
Dance, The
Dance of the Graces, The.
Daphnaida, *sel.*
Death ("What if some little paine the passage have").
Death of the Dragon, The.
Deepe in the bottome of an huge great rocke.
Despair.
Dido My Dear, Alas, Is Dead.
Ditty, A: In Praise of Eliza, Queen of the Shepherds.
Ditty, A: "See where she sits upon the grassy [*or* grassie] green[e]."
Dragon, The.
Easter.
Easter Morning.
Elisa.
Epithalamion: "Ye learned sisters, which have oftentimes."
Faerie Queene, The, *sels.*
Fight of the Red Cross Knight and the Heathen Sansjoy, The.
Forthwith he gave in charge unto his squyre.
Fresh spring, the herald of love's mighty king.
Garden of Adonis, The.
Garden of Proserpina, The.
Gather the Rose.
Great travell hath the gentle Calidore.
Guardian Angels.
Happy Isle, The.
Hark how the minstrels gin to shrill aloud.
Heavenly Aid.
Her Heards Be Thousand Fishes.
Her Name upon the Strand.
Her seem'd, as she was doing sacrifize.
High time now gan it wex for Una fayre.
House of Ate, The.
House of Morpheus, The.
House of Pride, The.
House of Richesse, The.
Huge Leviathan, The.
Hymn in Honor of Love, An.
Hymn in Honour of Beauty, An.
Hymn [*or* Hymne] of Heavenly Love, An.
Hymne [*or* Hymn] in Honour of Beautie [*or* Beauty], An.
Hymne of Heavenly Beautie [*or* Beauty], An, *sel.*
Hymne of Heavenly Love, An.
Iambicum Trimetrum.
In these wylde deserts where she now abode.
Invocation to the Faerie Queene.
It Fell upon a Holy Eve.
January.
January Eclogue.
Januarye.
July.
June.
Kinds of Trees to Plant.
Lament for Daphnaida.
Leave Lady, in Your Glass.
Legend of Sir Guyon, or of Temperance, The, *abr.*
Legend of the Knight [*or* Knyght] of the Red Cross, or of Holiness.
Like as an hynd forth singled from the heard.
Like as the tide that comes from th' ocean main.
Long they thus traveilèd in friendly wise.
Long time they thus together traveilèd.
Love.
Make Haste, Sweet Love.
Malbecco and Hellenore.
Mammon movèd was with inward wrath.
Mammon's House.
March.
March Eclogue.
Martiall Mayd stayd not him to lament, The.
Mask of Cupid, The.
Mask of Mutability, The.
Masque of Cupid, The.
May.
Mermaids, The.
Mother Hubberd's Tale.
Muiopotmos, *sel.*
Music at the Bower of Bliss, The.
Mutabilitie.
Mutability [*or* Mutabilitie].
Next unto Him Was Neptune Pictured.
Nought is there under heav'ns wide hollownesse.
November.
Now al is done; bring home the bride againe.
Now Strike Your Sailes Ye Jolly Mariners!
Now when the rosy fingered morning faire.
Oak and the Brere, The.
October.
October Eclogue.
Old January.
One day, nigh weary of the irksome way.
Pastoral, A: "From thence into the open fields he fled."
Perigot's and Cuddy's Roundelay.
Port after Stormie Seas.
Prince Arthur.
Prologue: "So oft as I with state of present time."
Prosopopoia; or, Mother Hubberd's Tale, *abr.*
Prothalamion.
Red Cross Knight.
Sea Monsters.
Seasons.
She fell away in her first ages spring.
Shepheardes [*or* Shepheards *or* Shepherd's] Calendar, The, *sels.*
Shepheards boy (best knowen by that name), The.
Shepherdes Calender, The.
Shepherd's Calendar, The.
Silly man that in the thickett lay, The.
Sleep after Toil.
So as they travellèd, the drouping night.
Song, The: "So passeth, in the passing of a day."
Sonnet: "After long storms and tempests' sad assay."
Sonnet: "Being myeself [*or* my selfe] captyved here in care."
Sonnet: "Comming to kisse her lyps (such grace I found)."
Sonnet: "Fair is my love, when her fair golden hairs [*or* heares]."
Sonnet: "Fresh spring, the herald of love's mighty king."
Sonnet: "Happy ye leaves when as those lilly hands."
Sonnet: "Joy of my life! full oft for loving you."
Sonnet: "Lacking my love, I go from place to place."
Sonnet: "Like as a huntsman after weary chase."
Sonnet: "Lyke as a huntsman after weary chace."
Sonnet: "Lyke as a ship, that through the ocean wyde."
Sonnet: "Mark when she smiles with amiable cheer."
Sonnet: "Men call you fair, and you do credit it."
Sonnet: "Merry cuckoo, messenger of spring, The."
Sonnet: "Most glorious Lord of life [*or* lyfe]! that on this day."
Sonnet: "My love is like to ice, and I to fire."
Sonnet: "Oft when my spirit doth spread her bolder wings."
Sonnet: "One day I wrote her name upon the strand."
Sonnet: "Penelope, for her Ulysses' sake."
Sonnet: "Rudely thou wrongest my dear heart's desire."
Sonnet: "So oft as I her beauty do behold."
Sonnet: "Sweet is the rose, but grows upon a brere."
Sonnet: "Weary yeare his race now having run, The."
Sonnet: "Ye tradeful merchants that, with weary toil."
Sonnets.
Soul Is Form.
Summer.
Sweet and Sour.
Tale of Calidore, The.
Temple of Venus, The.
Thames Doth the Medway Wed.
That celestial power, to whom the care.
There Atin fownd Cymochles sojourning.
To Be or Not to Be.
To His Book ("Go, little book: thyself present").
To the Right Honorable and Most Virtuous Lady, the Countess of Pembroke.
To the Right Noble and Valorous Knight, Sir Walter Ralegh.
To the Right Worshipful, My Singular Good Friend, M[aster] Gabriel Harvey, Doctor of the Laws.
Trees.
Trust Not the Treason.
Two Cantos of Mutabilitie.
Upon a Day.
Visions of the World's Vanity, *sel.*
Waies, through which my weary steps I guyde, The.
What If Some Little Paine the Passage Have.
What man so wise, what earthly wit so ware.
Whom bold Cymochles traveiling to finde.
Winter.
With fawning wordes he courted her a while.
With that I saw two swannes of goodly hewe.
Yet goodly court he made still to his Dame.
"Speranza." *See* **Wilde, Lady**
Speyer, Leonora
A B C's in Green.
Answer.
Crickets at Dawn.
Duet.
Garden under Lightning.

Heart Looks On, The.
Heart Recalcitrant, The.
I'll Be Your Epitaph.
Kleptomaniac.
Ladder, The.
Little Lover.
Mary Magdalene.
New Excavations.
Oberammergau.
Pain.
Protest in Passing.
Snow in April.
Star-Fear.
Suddenly.
Tears for Sale.
These Poems I Have So Loved.
Words to Sleep Upon.
X-Ray.

Spicer, Anne Higginson
City Priest.
Hail and Farewell.

Spicer, J. L.
Communion.

Spicer, Jack
Billy the Kid.
Book of Merlin, The.
Book of Percival, The.
Imaginary Elegies, I-IV.

Spingarn, Joel Elias
Beauty.
Helios.
Italian Poppies.
Spring Passion.

Spingarn, Lawrence Perry
Museum Piece.
Philatelic Lessons: The German Collection.

Spire, André
Abishag.
Dust.
Hear, O Israel!
It Was Not You.
Lonely.
Now You're Content.
Nudities.
Spring.

Spitta, Karl Johann Philipp
O Blessèd House, That Cheerfully Receiveth.
O Happy Home.
Unchanging Jesus.

Spitteler, Carl
Theme.

Spivack, Kathleen
Cripples.
Fatlipped, You Formless.
High.
March 1st.
Mythmaking.
Straining.

Spofford, Harriet Elizabeth Prescott
Ballad: "In the summer even."
Can't.
Evanescence.
Every Day Thanksgiving Day.
Godspeed.
Hereafter.
How We Became a Nation.
Hunt, The.
Music in the Night.
Only.
Phantoms All.
Pines, The.
Sigh, A.
Snowdrop, A, *abr.*
Voice.

Sprague, Charles
Brothers, The.
Centennial Ode, *sel.*
Curiosity, *sels.*
Family Meeting, The.
Fiction.
Indians.
News, The.
Winged Worshipers, The.

Sprat, Thomas
On His Mistress Drowned.

Sprigg, Christopher St. John *See* **"Caudwell, Christopher"**

Spriggs, Edward S.
Every Harlem Face Is Afromanism Surviving.
For Brother Malcolm.
For the Truth.
My Beige Mom.
Sassafras Memories.
We Waiting on You.

Springer, Thomas Grant
Giving and Forgiving.
Harmony.

Spring-Rice, Sir Cecil Arthur
Day.
God of all power and might.
Homeland, The.
I am Andrew Cecil Bradley.
I am the Dean of Christ Church, Sir.
I Vow to Thee, My Country.
In Memoriam, A. C. M. L., *sel.*

Sproat, Nancy Dennis
Blackberry Girl, The.

Sprod, G. N.
Request Number.

Sproull, Lyman H.
Emigrant's Child, The.
Stationed Scout, The.

Sprouse, Sarah Elizabeth
Little Song of Work, A.

Squier, George L.
O Christ, the Way.

Squire, Sir John Collings "Solomon Eagle"
Another Generation.
Approaching America.
Ballade of Any Father to Any Son, A.
Ballade of Diminishing Control, A.
Ballade of Soporific Absorption.
Ballade of the Poetic Life.
Birds, The.
Discovery, The.
Epitaph: "Shiftless and shy, gentle and kind and frail."
Exquisite Sonnet, The.
Fresh Morning, A.
Hands-across-the-Sea Poem, The.
Happy Night, The.
Honesty at a Fire.
How They Do It.
If Gray Had Had to Write His Elegy in the Cemetery of Spoon River Instead of in That of Stoke Poges.
If Pope Had Written "Break, Break, Break."
It did not last; the Devil shouting Ho!
Lines: "Mine ears have heard your distant moan."
Little Commodore, The.
March, The.
On a Lady Singing Lawes's Music to Milton's Ode on the Nativity.
On Oculists.
Pipe, The.
Poor Old Man, The.
Ship, The.
Sonnet: "There was an Indian, who had known no change."
There Was an Indian.
Three Hills, The.
To a Roman.
Under.
Winter Nightfall.

Stock, Philip "Kid-Kazanova"
Admonition.

Stadler, Ernst
Form Is Delight.

Staff, Leopold
Golden Elegy, The.
Liberty.

Stafford, Juniata
My Country's Flag.

Stafford, Wendell Phillips
America Resurgent.
Invocation: "O Thou whose equal purpose runs."
Lincoln.
On the Photograph of a Lynching.
Washington and Lincoln.

Stafford, William
Address to the Vacationers at Cape Lookout, An.
Adults Only.
After School: Room Three.
At Cove on the Crooked River.
At the Bomb Testing Site.
Baby Ten Months Old Looks at the Public Domain, A.
Before the Big Storm.
Bi-focal.
Chickens the Weasel Killed.
Concealment, The: Ishi, the Last Wild Indian.
Elegy: "Responsible sound of the lawnmower, The."
Epitaph Ending in and, The.
Fall Journey.
Farm on the Great Plains, The.
Fifteen.
Fish Counter at Bonneville, The.
For the Grave of Daniel Boone.
In Dear Detail, By Ideal Light.
In Medias Res.
In the Deep Channel.
In the Oregon Country.
Lake Chelan.
Letter from Oregon.
Listening.
Long Distance.
Looking West.
"Lyf So Short, The."
Maybe Alone on My Bike.
Memorandum.
Moles.
Monday.
Montana Eclogue.
Move to California, The, *sel.*
My Father: October 1942.
On Being Invited to a Testimonial Dinner.
One Home.
Oregon Message, An.
Our People.
Outside.
Remembering Althea.
Requiem.
Returned to Say.
Right Now.
Ritual to Read to Each Other, A.
Star in the Hills, The ("A star hit in the hills behind our house").
Stared Story, A.
Testimony to an Inquisitor.
Tornado.
Traveling through the Dark.
Vacation.
Vacation Trip.
View from Here, The.
Walking the Wilderness.
Well Rising, The.
West of Your City.
When We Looked Back.
Woman at Banff, The.
Written on the Stub of the First Paycheck.

Stagnelius, Erik Johan
Memory.

Stalker, Philip A.
Talk.
Stallworthy, Jon
Camel.
Elegy for a Mis-spent Youth.
End of a Fairy Tale.
First Blood.
Out of Bounds.
War Story.
Stam, Betty Scott
Christmas.
I'm Standing, Lord.
Open My Eyes.
Stanaback, Lucille
Discouraged.
Standish, Celia
New Year's Days.
Stanfield, Leontine
Little Cat Angel, The.
Stanford, Ann
Anniversary, An; a Country Burial.
Blackberry Thicket, The.
Ceremonies.
Riders, The.
Umbrella, The.
Stanford, Derek
Carol for His Darling on Christmas Day.
Tomb of Honey Snaps Its Marble Chains, The.
Stanford, William Bedell
Angelus-Time near Dublin.
Before Salamis.
To a Greek Ship in the Port of Dublin.
Undertone.
Stanislaus, Sister M.
J. F. K.
Stanley, Arthur Penrhyn
Teach Us to Die.
Stanley, Mary (Mrs. Kendrick Smithyman)
Per Diem et per Noctem.
Record Perpetual Loss.
Wife Speaks, The.
Stanley, Thomas
All Things Drink.
Beauty.
Bracelet, The.
Celia Singing.
Chang'd, Yet Constant.
Combat, The.
Deposition from Beauty, A.
Destiny.
Divorce, The.
Exequies, The.
Expectation.
Farewell, The: "Since fate commands me hence, and I."
Fruitful Earth Drinks Up the Rain.
Horns to Bulls Wise Nature Lends.
La Belle Confidente.
La Belle Ennemie.
Loves Heretick.
Magnet, The.
Old I Am.
On a Violet in Her Breast.
Picture, The.
Relapse, The.
Repulse, The.
Roses.
Snow-Ball, The.
Song: "Celinda, by what potent art."
Song: "Fool, take up thy shaft again."
Song: "I prithee [*or* prethee] let my heart alone."
Song: "When I lie burning in thine eye."
Spring.
Swallow, The.
To Celia Pleading Want of Merit.
To One That Pleaded Her Own Want of Merit.
Tombe, The.
When I Loved Thee.
Wish, The.
Youthful Age.
Stanley-Wrench, Margaret
Bach Cantata, A.
Mozart's "Linz" Symphony.
Schubert's Ninth Symphony.
Stansbury, Joseph
Lords of the Main, The.
New Song, A.
To Cordelia.
Stansbury, Mary Anna Phinney
How He Saved St. Michael's.
Surprise at Ticonderoga, The.
Stanton, Frank Lebby
De Good Lawd Know My Name.
Graveyard Rabbit, The.
How to Eat Watermelons.
Just a Wearyin' for You.
Keep a-Goin'.
Little Way, A.
Mocking-Bird, The.
Old Battle-Field, An.
Old Flag Forever, The.
Old Hymns, The.
One Country.
Our Flag Forever.
Plantation Ditty, A.
The Old Flag Forever [*or* Our Flag Forever].
So Many!
Sweetes' Li'l' Feller.
"Tollable Well!"
Wearyin' for You.
Stanton, Henry Thompson
Moneyless Man, The.
"Stanton, Paul." *See* **Winner, Septimus**
Stanton, Ruth Edna
Farm Life.
Stanyhurst, Richard
Nature in Her Working.
Prayer to the Holy Trinity, A.
Prayer to the Trinity, A.
Sometime Lively Gerald.
To the Trinity.
Staples, Barbara H.
Room for Jesus.
Staples, Shirley
Getting It Together.
Sister Speaks of Rapping, A.
Stapleton, David
After the Concert.
Stapp, Emilie Blackmore
Autumn Races.
Learning to Skate.
On the Beach.
Rainy Day, A.
Taking Turns.
Welcome Visitors.
Stapylton [*or* Stapleton], Sir Robert
Bard's Song, The.
Starbird, Kaye
Don't Ever Cross a Crocodile.
Eat-It-All Elaine.
Flying.
Horse-Chestnut Time.
Starbuck, George
Albany schmalbany/ Governor W.
Aspects of Spring in Greater Boston.
Becalmed in old Back Bay's dead water sulk.
Bone Thoughts on a Dry Day.
Clippety cloppity.
Cold Fire.
Communication to the City Fathers of Boston.
Cora Punctuated with Strawberries.
Fable for Blackboard.
Jiminy Whillikers/ Admiral Samuel.
Late Late.
Mine eyes have seen the glory of hard/ work at least.
New Strain.
On First Looking in on Blodgett's Keats's "Chapman's Homer."
One Man's Goose; or, Poetry Redefined.
Out in the Cold.
Pit Viper.
Poem Issued by Me to Congressmen, *sel.*
Poems from a First Year in Boston.
Said ("Agatha Christie to").
Said ("J. Alfred Prufrock to").
Said ("President Johnson to").
Skindivers, The.
Starry Night, The.
Tapestry for Bayeux, A.
Technologies.
To His Chi Mistress.
Unfriendly Witness.
War Story.
Whaddaya Do for Action in This Place?
Starbuck, Victor
Moon-Madness.
Night for Adventures.
Seekers, The.
Starck, Mary
Reign of Peace, The.
Stark, Irwin
Prisoner, The.
Starkey, James *See* **"O'Sullivan, Seumas"**
Starkweather, Pauline
Two Mountains Men Have Climbed.
Starr, Hattie
Little Alabama Coon.
Starrett, Vincent
Death of Santa Claus, The.
Femme Fatale.
My Lord's Motoring.
Romantic Episode.
Sky-Writer.
Statius, Publius Papinius
Ah, Now I Know What Day This Is.
Epithalamium for Stella and Violentilla, *sels.*
Of the Night, Let the Bridegroom Sing.
Sleep.
Why Do You Dally So?
Wishes for a Bridal Couple and Their Unborn Child.
Stauffer, Donald A.
Bulldozer, The.
Lemmings, The.
Time Zones for Forty-four.
Staunton, Frank L.
Old-Time Circus Clown, The.
Stead, William Force
Festival in Tuscany.
Her Powder Box.
How Infinite Are Thy Ways.
I Closed My Eyes To-Day and Saw.
Praise, then, to Uriel, who in unlikely places.
Reach forth Thy hand!
Sweet Wild April.
Uriel, *sels.*
Stearns, L. D.
Triumph.
Stebbins, Mary Elizabeth Hewitt
Harold the Valiant.
Sunflower to the Sun, The.
Stedman, Edmund Clarence
Aaron Burr's Wooing.
Abraham Lincoln.
Aucassin and Nicolette.
Autumn Song.
Corda Concordia, *sel.*
Cuba.
Custer.
Discoverer, The.
Doorstep, The.

Falstaff's Song.
Flight of the Birds, The.
Gettysburg.
Going a-Nutting.
Hand of Lincoln, The.
Helen Keller.
Horace Greeley.
How Old Brown Took Harper's Ferry.
Hymn of the West.
Hymn to the West.
Invocation: "Thou, whose enduring hand once laid in sooth."
Israel Freyer's Bid for Gold.
John Brown of Osawatomie.
Kearny at Seven Pines.
Liberty Enlightening the World.
Morgan.
Mors Benefica.
Mother's Picture, A.
On a Great Man Whose Mind Is Clouding.
Ordeal by Fire, The, *sel.*
Pan in Wall Street.
Peter Stuyvesant's New Year's Call.
Prelude: "I saw the constellated matin choir."
Provençal Lovers; Aucassin and Nicolette.
Quest.
Salem.
Si Jeunesse Savait!
Singer, The.
Song from a Drama.
Sumter.
Thou, who dost feel life's vessel strand.
Toujours Amour.
Treason's Last Device.
Voice of the Western Wind.
Wanted—a Man.
What the Winds Bring.
World Well Lost, The.

Stedman, Jane W.
Geologist's Epitaph, A.

Steece, Arvel
There Is Yet Time.
World Planners.

Steel, M.
Little Lucy Lester.

Steele, Anne
Compassion So Divine.
Father, Whate'er of Earthly Bliss.
Great Redeemer Lives, The.
O How Sweet Are Thy Words!
Only Name Given under Heaven, The.
Prayer: "Dear Refuge of my weary soul."
Thanksgiving for National Peace.

Steele, Sir Richard
Song: "Me Cupid made a happy slave."
Song: "Why, lovely charmer, tell me why."
Tender Husband, The, *sel.*

Steele, S. S.
Walk, Jaw-Bone, *with music.*

Steenburg, Maude
Peace, Be Still.

Steendam, Jacob
Complaint of New Amsterdam, The.
Praise of New Netherland, The.

Steere, Richard
Earth Felicities, Heavens Allowances.
Monumental Memorial of Marine Mercy, A.
On a Sea-Storm nigh the Coast.
Poem upon the Caelestial Embassy, A.

Steese, Edward
Tenth Reunion.

Stefanile, Felix
Little Night Music, A.
Praying Mantis.
So Separate and Strange.
That Familiar Stranger.
Vampire Bride.

Steigman, Benjamin Morris
Opera in English?

Stein, Evaleen
Budding-Time Too Brief.
Flood-Time on the Marshes.
In Mexico.
In Youth.
November Morning.
Wild Beasts.

Stein, Gertrude
Accents in Alsace, *sels.*
Afterwards, *sel.*
Alsace or Alsatians.
Day Lost, A.
Four Saints in Three Acts, *sel.*
Heat, The.
Here is a poem.
I Am Rose.
I like to have a home life in the house.
Land of Nations, *sel.*
Mother of Us All, The, *sel.*
Noisy pearls noisy pearl coat.
Page IX.
Pale rose is a smell that has no fountain, A.
Pigeons on the grass alas.
Prothalamium for Bobolink and His Louisa A Poem.
Sacred Emily, *sel.*
Scenes, *sel.*
Watch on the Rhine, The.
We cannot retrace our steps.

Stein, Gloria T.
Heart's Poverty.

Stein, Kurt M.
An Unserer Beach.
Mama's Advice.
Morning Song.
Reflection.
Vor a Gauguin Picture zu Singen.

Steinberg, Eliezer
Terrible Thought, A.

Steinberg, Jacob
Heart, The.

Steiner, Stan
But, the Africans Walked at Night.

Steinman, David Barnard
Blueprint.

Stella, Sister Maris *See* **Maris Stella, Sister**

Stellwagon, Russell
In Memory of Two Sons.

Stem, Thad, Jr
Sure Signs.

Stembridge, Jane
Children, The.

Stenhouse, William
Empty Jar, The.

Stennett, Samuel
Majestic Sweetness.
Promised Land, The.
'Tis Finished!

Stepanchev, Stephen
Girl Skipping Rope in Flushing, A.
Inner Brother.
No Furlough.
Strength to War.

Stephanie, Sister Mary
That Far Lone Mountain.
That Far Lone Mountain.

Stephen, Alexander Maitland
Bring Torches.
Capilano ("Capilano, in the canyon").

Stephen, James Kenneth
Cynicus to W. Shakespeare [*or* Shakspere].
Election Address, An.
England and America.
Grievance, A.
Heaven and Hell.
Imitation of Robert Browning.
Lapsus Calami.
Last Ride Together, The (from Her Point of View).
Millenium.
My Education.
Of W. W. (Americanus).
Old School List, The.
On a Parisian Boulevard.
On a Rhine Steamer.
School.
Senex to Matt. Prior.
Sincere Flattery of R. B.
Sincere Flattery of W. W. (Americanus).
Sonnet, A: "Two voices are there: one is of the deep."
Sonnet on Wordsworth, A.
Splinter, The.
Thought, A.
To R. K.
Two Epigrams.
Wordsworth.

Stephens, A. G.
Babylon.

Stephens, Alan
Prologue: Moments in a Glade.
Vanishing Act, The.

Stephens, Brunton
Dominion of Australia, The (a Forecast, 1877).
My Other Chinee Cook.

Stephens, Evan
Utah, We Love Thee.

Stephens, Harry
Night Herding Song.

Stephens, James
April Showers.
Bessie Bobtail.
Blue Blood.
Breakfast Time.
Centaurs, The.
Check.
Chill of the Eve.
Christmas at Freelands.
College of Surgeons, The.
Coolin, The.
Crackling Twig, The.
Crest Jewel, The.
Daisies, The.
Danny Murphy.
Dark Wings.
Day and Night.
Deirdre.
Evening.
Evening Falls, An.
Fifteen Acres, The.
Fossils.
Fulness of Time, The.
Glass of Beer, A.
Goat Paths, The.
Good and Bad.
Hate.
Hawks.
In the College of Surgeons.
In the Cool of the Evening.
In the Night.
In the Orchard.
In the Poppy Field.
In Waste Places.
Lake, The.
Little Things.
Main-Deep, The.
Midnight.
Night, The.
Night Was Creeping.
No pride hath he who sings of escape from love.
Nothing is easy! Pity then.
O Bruadair.
O'Bruidar.
Odell.
On a Lonely Spray.

Stephens (continued)
Peadar Og Goes Courting.
Pit of Bliss, The.
Psychometrist.
Red-haired Man's Wife, The.
Righteous Anger.
Rivals, The.
Road, The.
Satyr, The.
Seumas Beg.
Shell, The.
Snare, The.
Sweet Apple.
Tanist.
Theme.
Theme with Variations, *sel.*
To the Four Courts, Please.
Visit from Abroad, A.
Voice of God, The.
Washed in Silver.
Waste Places, The.
Watcher, The.
Wave of Cliona, The.
Westland Row.
What the Devil Said.
What Thomas an Buile Said in a Pub.
What Tomas [*or* Thomas] an Buile Said in a Pub.
When You Walk.
Whisperer, The.
White Fields.
White Window, The.
Why Tomas Cam Was Grumpy.
Wind, The.
Woman Is a Branchy Tree, A.
Wood of Flowers, The.
Stephens, James Brunton *See* **Stephens, Brunton**
Stephens, William
Eyes Have It, The.
Standard Forgings Plant.
Sterling, Andrew B.
Meet Me in St. Louis.
Wait till the Sun Shines, Nellie.
Sterling, George
Aldebaran at Dusk.
Autumn in Carmel.
Black Vulture, The.
Final Faith, The.
Gardens of the Sea, The.
Guerdon of the Sun, The.
In Extremis.
Last Days, The.
Legend of the Dove, A.
Master Mariner, The.
Music at Twilight.
Night of Gods, The.
Omnia Exeunt in Mysterium.
Omnium Exeunt in Mysterium.
Sails.
Saul.
Sonnets on the Sea's Voice.
Then and Now.
Three Sonnets on Oblivion.
To Pain.
To the Goddess of Liberty.
Sterling, John
Alfred the Harper.
From Heaven High I Come to You, *with music.*
Louis XV.
Shakespeare.
To a Child.
Sternberg, Jacob
Little Birds.
"Sterne, Stuart" (Gertrude Bloede)
My Father's Child.
Night after Night.
Soul, Wherefore Fret Thee?
Sternhold, Thomas
Majesty of God.
Sterry, Craig
Dream Poem #1.
Dream Poem #3.
Margaret.
Montana Visit.
No One Can Be Trusted, Something Tells Me.
Thinking of Our Visits.
To a Suicide.
Undocumented Observations from the Letters of G.
Sterry, Joseph Ashby *See* **Ashby-Sterry, Joseph**
Stetson, Charlotte Perkins *See* **Gilman, Charlotte Perkins Stetson**
Stetson, Grace Ellery Channing *See* **Channing, Grace Ellery**
Stevens, Frank
Alley Cat.
Stevens, George Alexander
Bartleme Fair.
Maria.
Pastoral, A: "By the side of a green stagnate pool."
Stevens, George W.
Organist, The.
Stevens, H. P.
Why.
Stevens, Marvin
Man.
Stevens, Maxine
How Can You?
Stevens, Wallace
Academic Discourse at Havana.
Anecdote of Men by the Thousand.
Anecdote of the Jar.
Anglais Mort à Florence.
Annual Gaiety.
Another Weeping Woman.
Arrival at the Waldorf.
As You Leave the Room.
Asides on the Oboe.
Auroras of Autumn, The, *sels.*
Autumn Refrain.
Banjo Boomer.
Bantams in Pine-Woods.
Beginning, The.
Bethou Me, Said Sparrow.
Bird with the Coppery, Keen Claws, The.
Bouquet of Belle Scavior.
Bowl.
Candle, The, a Saint.
Comedian as the Letter C, The.
Connoisseur of Chaos.
Continual Conversation with a Silent Man.
Contrary Theses, I.
Farewell to an idea. . .A cabin stands.
Gallant Château.
Girl in a Nightgown.
Glass of Water, The.
Great Statue of the General Du Puy, The.
Gulls.
Hibiscus on the Sleeping Shores.
High-toned Old Christian Woman, A.
Holiday in Reality.
Homunculus et la Belle Etoile.
How Red the Rose That Is the Soldier's Wound.
I cannot bring a world quite round.
Idea of Order at [*or* in] Key West, The.
Idiom of the Hero.
In Battle.
Inescapable romance, inescapable choice.
It Feels Good as It Is without the Giant.
It is the Celestial Ennui of Apartments.
Le Monocle de Mon Oncle.
Life is a bitter aspic. We are not.
Life Is Motion.
Lion roars at the Enraging Desert, The.
Load of Sugar Cane, The.
Man bent over his guitar, The.
Man Carrying Thing.
Man with the Blue Guitar, The.
Martial Cadenza.
Mechanical Optimist, The.
Men Made Out of Words.
Mrs. Alfred Uruguay.
Motive for Metaphor, The.
Mozart, 1935.
No Possum, No Sop, No Taters.
Nomad Exquisite.
Not Ideas about the Thing but the Thing Itself.
Notes toward a Supreme Fiction, *sels.*
Novel, The.
Nuances of a Theme by Williams.
Of Heaven Considered as a Tomb.
Of Mere Being.
Of Modern Poetry.
Of the Manner of Addressing Clouds.
Of the Surface of Things.
On an Old Horn.
On the Adequacy of Landscape.
On the Manner of Addressing Clouds.
Ordinary Evening in New Haven, An, *sel.*
Ordinary Women, The.
Paltry Nude Starts on a Spring Voyage, The.
Parochial Theme.
Pediment of Appearance, The.
Peter Parasol.
Peter Quince at the Clavier.
Place of the Solitaires, The.
Plain Sense of Things, The.
Planet on the Table, The.
Pleasures of Merely Circulating, The.
Plot against the Giant, The.
Ploughing on Sunday.
Poem That Took the Place of a Mountain, The.
Poems of Our Climate, The.
Poetry Is a Destructive Force.
Postcard from the Volcano, A.
Prejudice against the Past, The.
Presence of an External Master of Knowledge.
President Ordains the Bee to Be, The.
Prologues to What Is Possible.
Puella Parvula.
Rabbit as King of the Ghosts, A.
Repetitions of a Young Captain.
Restatement of Romance.
Rock, The.
Room on a Garden, A.
Sad Strains of a Gay Waltz.
Sailing after Lunch.
Sea Surface Full of Clouds.
Sense of the Sleight-of-Hand Man, The.
Snow Man, The.
So-and-So Reclining on Her Couch.
Soldier, There Is a War [between the Mind].
Soldier's Wound, The.
Song of Fixed Accord.
Study of Images, I.
Study of Two Pears.
Sun This March, The.
Sunday Morning (Complete, I-VIII).
Table Talk.
Tattoo.
Tea at the Palaz of Hoon.
Thirteen Ways of Looking at a Blackbird.
This is where the serpent lives, the bodiless.
To an Old Philosopher in Rome.
To the One of Fictive Music.
Tom-tom, c'est moi. The blue guitar.
Tune beyond us as we are, A.
Two at Norfolk.
Two Figures in Dense Violet Light [*or* Night].

Two Illustrations That the World Is What You Make of It.
Unhappy people in a happy world, An.
We Reason of These Things.
What We See Is What We Think.
Whistle Aloud, Too Weedy Wren.
Woman in Sunshine, The.
Woman Looking at a Vase of Flowers.
Woman That Had More Babies than That, The.
World as Meditation, The.
Worms at Heaven's Gate, The.
Stevenson, Alec Brock
Et Sa Pauvre Chair.
Stevenson, Burton Egbert
Henry Hudson's Quest.
Peace Message, The.
Stevenson, Candace Thurber
Public Library.
Signatures.
Stevenson, Dorothy Emily
Six and Thirty.
Stevenson, James
Gallant Fighting "Joe," The.
Stevenson, John Hall *See* **Hall-Stevenson, John**
Stevenson, Lionel
Gulls and Dreams.
In a Desert Town.
Summer Interlude.
Stevenson, Mabel Rose
Springtime in Donegal.
Stevenson, Mary B.
Angel Voices.
Stevenson, Matthew
At the Florists' Feast in Norwich.
Song: "Should I sigh out my dayes in griefe."
Stevenson, Patric
Anglo-Eire Vignette.
Autumnal Consummation.
Corn Cañn.
Dogrose.
Stevenson, Quentin
Antinous.
Lufoten.
Night-Labour.
Victus.
Stevenson, Robert Louis
Alcaics; to H. F. B.
At the Seaside.
Auntie's Skirts.
Autumn Fires.
Away with Funeral Music.
Bed in Summer.
Block City.
Blows the Wind To-Day.
Bright Is the Ring of Words.
Camper's Night Song.
Canoe Speaks, The, *sel.*
Careful Angler, The.
Celestial Surgeon, The.
Child's Thought, A.
Christmas at Sea.
Christmas Sermon, A, *sel.*
Cow, The.
Day Returns, The.
Ditty: "Cock shall crow, The."
Dumb Soldier, The.
Envoy: "Go, little book, and wish to all."
Escape at Bedtime.
Evensong.
Fairy Bread.
Far-Farers, The.
Farewell to the Farm.
Fine Song for Singing, The.
Flowers, The.
Foreign Children.
Foreign Lands.
From a Railway Carriage.
Gather Ye Roses.
Go, Little Book.
Good and Bad Children.
Good Play, A.
Happy Thought.
Hayloft, The.
He Hears with Gladdened Heart the Thunder.
Heather Ale.
Henry James.
Home No More Home to Me.
House Beautiful, The.
Husband to a Wife, A.
I Will Make You Brooches.
If This Were Faith.
If to feel, in the ink of the slough.
Ille Terrarum.
In Memoriam F. A. S.
In the Highlands.
In the Season.
In the States.
Keepsake Mill.
Lad That Is Gone, A.
Lamplighter, The.
Land of Counterpane, The.
Land of Nod, The.
Land of Story-Books, The.
Last Sight, The.
Little Land, The.
Looking Forward.
Marching Song.
Mile an' a Bittock, A.
Morning Drum-Call, The.
My Bed Is a Boat.
My House.
My Shadow.
My Ship and I.
My Task.
My Treasures.
My Valentine.
My Wife.
Not I.
O to Be Up and Doing.
On the great streams the ships may go.
Once more I saw him. In the lofty room.
Our Lady of the Snows, *sel.*
Over the Sea to Skye.
Pirate Story.
Portrait, A.
Prayer: "I ask good things that I detest."
Prayer for the Household, A.
Rain, The.
Requiem.
Resurgence.
Roadside Fire, The.
Romance.
Say Not of Me That Weakly I Declined.
Self Portrait.
Sick Child, The.
Since Thou Hast Given Me This Good Hope, O God.
Sing a Song of Seasons!
Sing Me a Song.
Singing.
Skerryvore ("For love of lovely words").
Skerryvore: The Parallel ("Here all is sunny").
Song of a Traveller, The.
Song of the Road, A.
Spaewife, The.
Stormy Nights.
Summer Sun.
Sun's Travels, The.
Swing, The.
System.
There, in the night, where none can spy.
Though He That Ever Kind and True.
Thought, A.
Time to Get Up.
Time to Rise.
To a Gardener.
To Alison Cunningham.
To Andrew Lang.
To Be Honest, to Be Kind.
To K[atharine] de M[attos].
To My Wife.
To N. V. de G. S.
To S. C.
To S. R. Crockett.
Travel.
Travels with a Donkey, *sel.*
Tropics Vanish, and Meseems That I, The.
Trusty, Dusky, Vivid, True.
Unseen Playmate, The.
Vagabond, The.
Verses Written in 1872.
Visit from the Sea, The.
Whaups, The.
When the Stars Are Gone.
Where Go the Boats?
Whole Duty of Children.
Wind, The.
Windy Nights.
Winter.
Winter-Time.
Wishes.
Words.
Young Night Thought.
Stewart, Albert C.
God's Ways.
Stewart, Charles
This Is for Freedom, My Son.
Stewart, Douglas
Brindabella.
Bunyip, The.
Dosser in Springtime, The.
Fisherman, The.
Garden of Ships, The.
Green Lions.
Helmet Orchid.
It's cold, says Crean at the tiller.
Lady Feeding the Cats, *sel.*
Lament: "Sigh, wind in the pine."
Mahony's Mountain.
Mending the Bridge.
Native Inhabitant.
Nesting Time.
Old Iron.
Rock Carving.
Shuffling along in her broken shoes from the slums.
Silkworms, The.
Snow-Gum, The.
Sun Orchids.
Sunflowers, The.
Terra Australis.
White, said Worsley, and glistening, the ridgy plain.
Worsley Enchanted, *sels.*
Stewart, Gervase
I Burn for England with a Living Flame.
Landscape Lies withing My Head, The.
Poem: "I burn for England with a living flame."
Poem: "I take four devils with me when I ride."
Red Cross Nurses.
Stewart, Harold
Dialogue of the Way.
Flight of Wild Geese, A.
Lament in Autumn.
Leaf-Makers, The.
Stewart, James T.
Announcement.
Poem: a Piece.
Poem: "We drank Thunderbird all night."
Stewart, Jane G.
June.
Stewart, John of Baldynneis
To His Darrest Freind.
Stewart, Phillips
Hope.

Stewart, W.
Aristocrats of Labor.
True Aristocrat, The.
Stickney, Helen Frith
Habitué.
Stickney, Trumbull
Age in Youth.
At Sainte-Marguerite.
Athenian Garden, An.
Be Still. The Hanging Gardens Were a Dream.
Dramatic Fragment.
Driftwood, *abr.*
Eride, *sel.*
Fidelity.
He Said: "If in His Image I Was Made."
I Hear a River.
If I Have Wronged You.
If You Should Lightly.
In Ampezzo ("In days of summer let me go").
In Ampezzo ("Only once more and not again").
In Summer.
In the Past.
Leave Him Now Quiet.
Like a Pearl Dropped.
Live Blindly.
Love, I Marvel What You Are.
Melancholy Year, The.
Mnemosyne.
Mt. [*or* Mount] Lykaion.
Near Helikon.
Not That, If You Had Known.
Now in the Palace Gardens.
On Some Shells Found Inland.
Passions That We Fought With, The.
Six o'Clock.
Sonnets from Greece, *sels.*
Soul of Time, The.
This is the Violin.
With Long Black Wings.
Stidger, William Leroy
Cross and the Tree, The.
Day, A.
God's Autographs.
Grace for the Noonday Meal.
I Am the Cross.
I Saw God.
I Saw God Wash the World.
Integrity.
Judean Hills Are Holy.
Lest Thou Forget.
Motherhood.
Outdoor Son of God, The.
Poet of Palestine, The.
Resignation.
Waste of War, The.
We Are the Burden-Bearers! *abr.*
Stiles, Nina
Thank You, God.
Still, James
Uncle Ambrose.
Stillingfleet, Benjamin
Sonnet: True Ambition.
Stillman, Albert
Ballad of the Faithful Clerk.
Truth about B. F., The.
When I Am Dead.
Stillman, Annie Raymond *See* **"Raymond, Grace"**
Stillman, Herman W.
Symphony, The.
Stinson, Sam S.
Nothin' Done.
Stirling, William Alexander, Earl of
Aurora, *sels.*
Madrigal: "When in her face mine eyes I fix."
O happy Tithon! if thou know'st thy hap.
Sonnet: "Cleare moving cristall, pure as the sunne beames."
Sonnet: "I envy not Endymion now no more."
Sonnet: "I hope, I fear, resolved, and yet I doubt."
Sonnet: "Ile give thee leave my love, in beauties field."
Sonnet: "Let others of the world's decaying tell."
Sonnet: "Oh, if thou knew'st how thou thyself dost harm."
Sonnet: "Then whilst that Latmos did contain her bliss."
To Aurora.
Stirling-Maxwell, Sir William
To Anne.
Stirling-Maxwell, Lady *See* **Norton, Caroline Elizabeth Sarah**
Stitch, Wilhelmina
Blessed Are They.
Little Roads to Happiness.
Stock, Eleanor B.
Prayer of the Quest, The.
Stockard, Henry Jerome
As Some Mysterious Wanderer of the Skies.
His Hand.
Mocking-Bird, The.
Over Their Graves.
Stocking, Jay Thomas
O Master Workman of the Race.
Stockton, Mrs. M.
Love for All.
Stodart, M. A.
One Thing at a Time.
Stodart-Walker, Archibald
Counsel to Girls.
Early Bacon.
Inflictis.
Moxford Book of English Verse, The, *sels.*
Stoddard, Charles Warren
Albatross.
Ave Maria Bells.
Bells of San Gabriel, The.
Cocoa-Tree, The.
Rhyme of Life, A.
Royal Mummy to Bohemia, The.
Stigmata.
Toast, The.
Wind and Wave.
Stoddard, Elizabeth
In the Still, Star-lit Night.
Last Days.
Mercedes.
November.
On the Campagna.
Poet's Secret, The.
Summer Night, A.
Unreturning.
Stoddard, Lavinia
Soul's Defiance, The.
Stoddard, Louis
Sap Bucket Song.
Stoddard, Richard Henry
Abraham Lincoln ("Not as when some great captain falls").
Abraham Lincoln ("This man whose homely face").
Adsum.
Arab Song.
Arrow, The.
At Last.
Birds.
Catch, A: "Once the head is gray."
Colonel Ellsworth.
Day and Night My Thoughts Incline.
Divan, The.
Dying Lover, The.
Falcon, The.
Flight of the Arrow, The.
Flight of Youth, The.
Gazelle, A.
Hymn to the Sea, A.
Jar, The.
Lincoln's Birthday.
Little Drummer, The.
Lover, The.
Men of the North and West.
Mors et Vita.
O honest face, which all men knew.
Old Song Reversed, An.
Sea, The.
Shadow, The.
Sky, The.
Songs ("How are songs begot and bred?").
There Are Gains for All Our Losses.
Threescore and Ten.
Twilight on Sumter.
Two Anchors, The.
Wine and Dew.
Witch's Whelp, The.
Stoddart, Thomas Tod
Angler's Invitation, The.
Death-Wake, The; or, Lunacy, *sel.*
Her, a Statue.
Mirthful Lunacy.
Stokes, E. R.
Fill Me Now.
Stokes, Francis G.
Blue Moonshine.
Stokes, Glenn
Blue Texarkana.
Stokes, Whitley
Viking, The.
Stokes, Will
Bugs.
Stoloff, Carolyn
Dinosaurs.
Stoltze, John
Across Illinois.
Stone, Dale Martin
God Knows What He's About.
Shaping of a Disciple, The.
Stone, Ed
How Does My Garden Grow?
Stone, Eliot Kays
Days.
Stone, John A.
And Thus He Spoke.
Arrival of the Greenhorn, The.
Australia and the Amazon.
Away Up on the Yuba, *with music.*
California as It Is and Was, *with music.*
California Ball.
California Bank Robbers.
California Bloomer.
California Legislature.
California Stage Company, The.
Coming around the Horn.
Crossing the Plains.
Emigrant from Pike.
Fools of Forty-nine, The.
Gambler, The ("A gambler's life I do admire").
Gold Lake and Gold Bluff.
Hangtown Gals.
Happy Miner, The.
He Ought to Know!
He's the Man for Me.
Honest John and William Relief.
Honest Miner, An, *with music.*
Humbug Steamship Companies.
Hunting after Gold.
I Often Think of Writing Home.
I'm Sad and Lonely Here.
Joaquin the Horse-Thief.
Last Good-bye, The.
Life by the Cabin Fire, A.
Loss of the *Central America.*
Lousy Miner, The.
Miner's Drean, The.

Miner's Lament, The, I ("When the gold fever raged, I was doing very well"), *with music.*
Miners' Meeting, A.
Mountain Cottage, The.
My Log Cabin Home.
National Miner, The.
Prospecting Dream.
Rowdy, The.
Sacramento Gals.
Sensible Miner, The.
Shady Old Camp, The.
Sonora Filibusters, The.
Steam Navigation Thieves, The.
Striking a Lead.
That Is Even So!
Then Hurrah for Home!
Vocal Miner, The.
War in Camp.
When I Went Off to Prospect.
You Who Don't Believe It.
Stone, Phyllis M.
Mr. Pennycomequick.
Topsy-turvy Land.
Stone, Ruth
In a Liberal Arts Building.
In an Iridescent Time.
In the Interstices.
Magnet, The.
Orchard.
Pear, The.
Snow.
Vernal Equinox.
Watcher, The.
Stone, Samuel John
Church's One Foundation, The.
Forgiveness of Sins.
Stone, Walter
Compelled to Love.
Couple.
Nature.
On the Welsh Marches.
Stonestreet, Margielea
Galilean.
Stopher, Vashti R.
Song of Louisiana.
Stopple, Libby
Calvary.
Storer, Agnes W.
Resurrection.
Storer, Thomas
Rivers.
Storey, Violet Alleyn
Christmas Trees.
Country Church, A.
Dawn Song—St. Patrick's Day.
Hummingbird.
Neighborly.
Prayer after Illness, A.
Prayer for a Very New Angel.
Prayer for Broken Little Families, A.
Prayer for the New Year, A.
Prayer in Affliction.
Prayer in Late Autumn, A.
Rainy Day Song.
Silhouette.
Wood of the Cross.
Stork, Charles Wharton
Bronze Statuette of Kwan-yin, A.
Flemish Madonna, A.
God, You Have Been Too Good to Me.
Nails, The.
Painter in New England, A.
Rose and God, The.
Statistician, The.
Troubadour of God, The.
Storni, Alfonsina
Inheritance.
Squares and Angles.
Story, Robert
Whistler, The.
Story, William Wetmore
Cleopatra.
English Language, The, *abr.*
Io Victis!
Praxiteles and Phryne.
Snowdrop.
Speak, History! Who are life's victors?
Violet, The.
Stoutenburg, Adrien
Ants and Others.
Avalanche.
Brobdingnag.
Channel U.S.A.—Live.
Cicada.
Companions.
Night Train.
Ocean.
Rain.
Suspense.
Traveller's Guide to Antarctica.
"Stovall, R. J." *See* **O'Malley, D. J.**
Stow, Randolph
As He Lay Dying.
Dust.
Mad Maid's Whim.
Ruins of the City of Hay.
Strange Fruit.
Utopia of Lord Mayor Howard, The.
Stowe, Harriet Beecher
Abide in Me, *sel.*
Hymn: "When winds are raging o'er the upper ocean."
Other World, The.
Peace.
Soul alone, like a neglected harp, The.
Still, Still with Thee.
Still with Thee.
When I Awake, I Am Still with Thee.
Stowell, Hugh
Mercy-Seat, The.
Spread the Word.
Strachan, Pearl
Morning Overture; Chorus of Dogs.
Strahan, Speer
Holy Communion.
Mad Lover, The.
Poor, The.
Promised Country, The.
Strand, Mark
Babies, The.
Dirty Hand, The.
Eating Poetry.
Keeping Things Whole
Kite, The.
Last Bus, The.
Man in the Mirror, The.
Man in the Tree, The.
Map, The.
Marriage, The.
Moontan.
Remains, The.
Sleeping with One Eye Open.
Tunnel, The.
Violent Storm.
What to Think Of.
When the Vacation Is Over for Good.
You and It.
Strandberg, Karl Vilhelm August
Swedish National Hymn.
Straum, August
Melancholy.
"Streamer, Col. D." *See* **Graham, Harry**
Street, Alfred Billings
American Independence.
Loon, The.
Settler, The.
Street, Julian, *and* James Montgomery Flagg
Said Opie Read.
To Be Continued.
Street, T.
Time tryeth truth convicting all that strive.
Stringer, Arthur
At the Comedy.
Celt Speaks, The.
Final Lesson, The.
Keeper, The.
Memories.
Morning in the North-West.
Sappho's Tomb.
Sod-Breaker, The.
There Is Strength in the Soil.
Wanderer's Litany.
War.
Stringer, R. E. C.
Sartorial Solecism.
Strobel, Marion (Mrs. James Herbert Mitchell)
Another Song.
Captive.
Daily Prayer.
Dog over Snow.
Eight Months Old.
Frightened Face.
God for You, A.
Little Things.
Lost City.
Pastoral: "Hill was flowing with sheep, The."
To My Children.
We Have a Day.
Strode, William
Chloris in the Snow.
Commendation of Music, The.
Floating Island, The, *sel.*
I'll tell you whence the rose did first grow red.
In Commendation of Music.
Kisses.
On a Gentlewoman Walking in the Snow [e].
On Chloris Walking in the Snow.
On Westwall Downes.
Sing aloud, harmonious spheares.
Song: "My limbs I will fling."
Strodtmann, Adolf
O Spring, Come Prettily In.
Strong, Anna Louise ("Anise) "
City of God, The.
Our Country.
Strong, Archibald T.
Australia, 1905.
Australia, 1914.
Australia to England.
Dawn at Liverpool.
Gloriana's England.
Grey.
Hawke.
Nelson.
Oxford.
Roses and Rain.
Sonnets of the Empire, *sels.*
Strong, George
Epiphany, The.
Strong, George A.
Modern Hiawatha, The, *parody.*
Song of Milkanwatha, The, *parody, sel.*
Strong, Julia Hurd
Huckster's Horse, The.
Son and Surf.
Strong, Leonard Alfred George
Brewer's Man, The.
Bride, The.
Childless.
Contrary Joe.
Departure.
Door, The.
Epitaph on a Sentry.
From the Greek Anthology ("Bill Jupp lies 'ere").
In the Lane.

Strong (continued)
Knowledgeable Child, The.
Lament, A: "I seen her last night."
Lowery Cot.
Mad Woman of Punnet's Town, The.
Man's Way.
March Evening.
Memory, A.
Moment, A.
Mysteries, The.
Northern Light.
Old Dan'l.
Old Man at the Crossing, The.
Old Woman, outside the Abbey Theater, An.
Return, The.
Rufus Prays.
"Safe for Democracy."
Seals, The.
Sheepstor.
Sunday Morning.
Two Generations.
Washerwoman's Song.
Zeke.

Strong, Patience
Business of the Day, The.
My Wish.
Pictures in the Fire.
Summer Moonlight.

Strongin, Josephine
Poem: "Child—in all the flying sky."

Strongin, Lynn
After the Japanese.
Archer.
For "Poems of Two."
Love Song.
Paschal Poem, *sel.*
Run, run, run with the rising moon!

Strongwolf, Chief Joseph
Indian Prayer.

Stroud, Dorothy Conant
Bible, The.
He Lives! He Lives to Bless!
His Life Is Ours.
I Thank Thee (A Prayer).
No Room.
Not One Is Turned Away from God.
Then God Bends Low.
You Will Find a Joy in Service.

Strout, Artemisia E.
Christian Camp, The.

"Struther, Jan" (Joyce Anstruther Maxtone Graham)
Cat.
Cul-de-Sac, The.
Freedom.
R. I. P.
To Grow Older.

Stryk, Lucien
Cannery, The.
Objet d'Art.

Stryker, Carrie W.
My Friend, the Cat.

Stryker, Melancthon Woolsey
Almighty Lord, with One Accord.

Stuart, Alaric Bertrand
Jim-Jam King of the Jou-Jous, The.

Stuart, Alice V.
Lintie in a Cage.
Peewits on the Hills.

Stuart, Dabney
Gardening.
Gull.
Rescue.
River, The.
Separate Parties.

Stuart, Francis
Coogan's Wood.
Ireland.
Southern Summer.
Une Idole du Nord.
Upper Lake, The.

Stuart, Henry Longan
Account Me Not.
In Tempestiva.
Intempestiva.
Resurrexit.

Stuart, James
Distant Prospect of the City of Armagh, A.
Morna's Hill, *sel.*

Stuart, Jane
Hawicks' Crossing.

Stuart, Jesse
By Sandy Waters.
Extended Invitation.
Gone, The.
Heart-summoned.
I Sing America Now!
Man with a Bull-Tongue Plow, *sel.*
My Land Is Fair for Any Eyes to See.
Our Heritage.
Spring Voices.
There Is Shrill Music in High Winds at Night.
Two Leaves.
Up Silver Stairsteps.

Stuart, John
Come unto Me.

Stuart, Mary [*or* **Marie**] *See* **Mary Queen of Scots**

Stuart, Muriel
In the Orchard.
Man and His Makers.
Old Saint, The.
Seed Shop, The.
Seeds.

Stuart, Roger Winship
Countryman's God.

Stuart, Ruth McEnery
Endless Song, The.
Hen Roost Man, The.
Sea of Peace, The.

Stubbs, Charles William
Conscience.
Conscience and Future Judgment.
'Twas Jolly, Jolly Wat.

Stubbs, Jane
Sim Ines.

Stubbs, John Heath- *See* **Heath-Stubbs, John**

Stubbs, William
Froude informs the Scottish youth.

Studdert-Kennedy, Geoffrey Anketell "Woodbine Willie"
Awake, Awake to Love and Work.
Carpenter, The.
Christian Soldier, The.
Crucifixion, The.
Faith.
Gambler.
"Gone West."
Great Wager, The.
Indifference.
Is It a Dream?
It Is Not Finished, Lord.
Kiss of God, The.
Mother Understands, A.
My Peace I Give unto You.
Patience.
Peace and Joy.
Rose, The.
Roses in December.
Suffering God, The.
Thy Will Be Done.
Unutterable Beauty, The.
We Shall Build On!
When through the Whirl of Wheels.

Stuits, Robert Morrison
Sweetest Story Ever Told, The.

Sturgeon, Lorena W.
Love's Tribute.

Sturges-Jones, Marion
To the Crocus—with My Love.

Sturm, Christoph Christian
Christ Is Risen!

Sturm, Frank Pearce
Still-Heart.

Styles, John H., Jr
At My Mother's Knee.
My Altar.

Suasnavar, Constantino
I Have Lost My Shoes.
I Look Up Hotels.
Numbers, *sels.*

Succorsa, Janice Appleby
My Garden.

Suckling, Sir John
Actuality.
Against Fruition.
Aglaura, *sels.*
Answer to Some Verses Made in His Praise, An.
Art of Love, The.
Ballad upon a Wedding, A.
Ballade upon a Wedding, A.
Barley-break.
Besieged Heart, The.
Bride, The.
Candle, A.
Careless Lover, The.
Constancy.
Constant Lover, The ("Out upon it").
Constant Lover, The ("Why so pale and wan").
Deformed Mistress, The.
Discontented Colonel, The, *sel.*
Doubt of Martyrdom, A.
Encouragements to a Lover.
I Prithee Send Me Back My Heart.
Love, Reason, Hate.
Love's World.
Loving and Beloved.
Lutea Allison.
Maid, The (and thereby hangs a tale).
My dearest Rival, least our love.
O for Some Honest Lover's Ghost.
Of Thee, Kind Boy.
On New-Year's Day, 1640. To the King.
Orsames' Song.
Out upon It! I Have Loved.
Poem, A: "Out upon it! I have loved."
Poem with the Answer, A.
Proffered Love Rejected.
Rejected Offer, The.
Sad One, The, *sel.*
Send Back My Heart.
Session[s] of the Poets, A ("A session was held the other day").
She's Pretty to Walk With.
Siege, The.
Sir J.S.
Soldier, A.
Song, A: "Hast thou seen the down in the air."
Song: "I prithee send me back my heart."
Song: "I prithee spare me, gentle boy."
Song: "No, no, fair heretic[k], it needs must be."
Song: "Of thee (kind boy) I ask no red and white."
Song: "Out upon it, I have loved."
Song: "Why so pale and wan, fond lover?"
Song to a Lute, A.
Sonnet: "Do'st see how unregarded now?"
Sonnet: "Oh, for some honest lover's ghost."
Sonnet: "Of thee (kind boy) I ask no red and white."
Supplement of an Imperfect Copy of Verses of Mr. Wil. Shakespeare, A.
That None Beguiled Be.

There never yet was woman made.
Thinking on thee, thy beauties then.
Tis Now Since I Sat[e] Down Before.
To Cupid.
To My Love.
Upon A. M.
Upon Christ His Birth.
Upon Christmas Eve.
Upon My Lady Carlisle's Walking in Hampton-Court Garden.
Verses: "I am confirm'd a woman can."
Wedding, A.
Why So Pale and Wan [Fond Lover]?

Suckow, Ruth
Grampa Schuler.
Odd Ones, The.

Suckow, W. J.
We Would See Jesus.

Sudan, Nazzam Al
Al Fitnah Muhajir.

Suhl, Yuri
And the Earth Rebelled.
Permanent Delegate, The.

Suisted, Joan
Secret, The.
Stock-Taking.
Who—Me?

Sullam, Sarah Copia
My Inmost Hope.

Sullivan, A. W.
Swan Curse.

Sullivan, Alan
Suppliant.
White Canoe, The.

Sullivan, Aloysius Michael
Avowal.
Chronometer, The.
Destroyer.
Flying Dutchman, The.
Genesis.
Heritage.
Jet Plane.
Late Autumn.
Measurement.
Monument.
Pilgrim.
Plenitude.
Psalm against the Darkness.
Psalm to the Holy Spirit.
Seismograph.
Sextant, The.
Smoke Stack.
Villanelle.
Villanelle of Light.
Whale and the *Essex,* The.

Sullivan, Archibald Beresford
Little Gray Lamb, The.

Sullivan, Joseph J.
Where Did You Get That Hat?

Sullivan, Nancy
History of the World as Pictures, The.

Sullivan, Richard
Stranger, The.

Sullivan, Richard Webb
Star of the Sea.

Sullivan, Timothy Daniel
God Save Ireland.

Sully-Prudhomme, René Francois Armand
Appointment, The.
Naked World, The.
Struggle, The.
Wheel, The.

Summers, Hal
Cerne Abbas.
Eclogue: "When all the powers have fallen."
O Dowland, Old John Dowland.
On the Cliff.
Sonata.
Valentine, A.
Wet Through.
Yorkshire Moors, The.

Summers, Hollis Spurgeon
Concerning Unnatural Nature: An Inverted Form.
Family Reunion.
King's X.
Kite.
Valentine.

Summers, William C.
Pastor, The.
Soft Job.

Sumner, Jezaniah
Ode on Science, *with music.*

Sun-Ra
Cosmic Age, The.
Image Reach, The.
Nothing Is.
Of the Cosmic-Blueprints.
Saga of Resistance.
To the Peoples of Earth.
"Visitation, The."
Would I for All That Were.

"Sunset Joe."
Rivers of the West.
Lines on Mountain Villages.
Rivers of the West.

Sun Yün Fêng
Riding at Daybreak.

Suo [*or* Suwo], Lady
That spring night I spent.

Supervielle, Jules
Grasp.
Worries.

"Surfaceman." *See* **Anderson, Alexander**

Surrey, Henry Howard, Earl of
Although I Had a Check.
Another Tribute to Wyatt ("In the rude age, when knowledge was not rife").
As Oft as I Behold and See.
Bonum Est Mihi Quod Humiliasti Me, *abr.*
Brittle Beauty.
Complaint by Night of the Lover Not Beloved, A.
Complaint of a Lover That Defied Love and Was by Love After the More Tormented.
Complaint of the Absence of Her Lover Being upon the Sea.
Complaint of the Lover Disdained.
Complaint That His Ladie after She Knew of His Love Kept Her Face Alway Hidden from Him.
Consolation.
Cornet, The.
Death of Wyatt, The.
Description and Praise of His Love Geraldine.
Description of Spring [Wherein Each Thing Renews, Save Only the Lover].
Description of the Spring; Wherein Each Thing Renews, Save Only the Lover.
Epitaph on Clere, An.
Epitaph on Thomas Clere.
Exhortation to Learn by Others' Trouble.
Frailty and Hurtfulness of Beauty, The.
Give Place, Ye Lovers.
Golden Gift, The.
Golden Mean, The.
His Incomparable Lady.
How Each Thing save the Lover in Spring Reviveth to Pleasure.
How No Age Is Content.
If care do cause men cry, why do not I complain?
If he that erst the form so lively drew.
In Praise of His Love.
In Praise of Wyatt's Psalms.
In Windsor Castle.
In winter's just return, when Boreas gan his reign.
Lady Again Complains, The.
Lady Complains of Her Lover's Absence, A.
Laid in My Quiet Bed.
Lines to Ratclif.
London, Hast Thou Accused Me.
Lover Comforteth Himself with the Worthiness of His Love, The.
Love's Rebel.
Noble Voyage, The.
O loathsome place, where I.
Of the Death of Sir Thomas Wyatt [the Elder].
On the Death of Sir Thomas Wyatt [the Elder].
Portrait of Henry VIII, The.
Praise of His Love, A.
Prisoned in Windsor, He Recounteth His Pleasure There Passed.
Psalm LXXXVIII: "Oh Lord, upon whose will dependeth my welfare."
Psalm LXXIII: "Though, Lord, to Israel thy graces plenteous be."
Restless Heart, The.
Restless State of a Lover, The.
Sardanapulus.
Satire on London, A.
Seafarer, The.
Since fortune's wrath envieth the wealth.
So Cruel Prison.
Spring.
Such wayward ways hath love that most part in discord.
Summer Comes.
Summer Is Come.
Though I regarded not.
Too dearly had I bought my green and youthful years.
Tribute to Wyatt ['Wyatt resteth here").
When other lovers in arms across.
When Raging Love.
When youth had led me half the race.
Wrapt in my careless cloak, as I walk to and fro.
Youth and Age.

Süsskind von Trimberg
O Thought!
Power of Thought, The.
Virtuous Wife, The.
Why Should I Wander Sadly.

Sutphen, Margaret P.
Autumn Leaves.

Sutphen, Van Tassel
Deep Waters.

Sutton, Henry Septimus
Inward Light, The.

Sutu, S. D. R.
Night.
Thaba Bosio.

Su T'ung-po
Casual Lines.
End of the Year, The.
For My Brother.
Moon, Flowers, Man.
On the Birth of His Son.
Terrace in the Snow, The.
To a Traveler.

Sutzkever, Abraham
Here I Am.
Like Groping Fingers.
Remember the sun in the autumn, its rays.
Secret Town, The, *sel.*

Su Wu
Since our hair was plaited and we became man and wife.

Svetlov, Mikhail
Grenada.

Swain, Charles

Swain (continued)
Field-Path, The.
Home Is Where There's [*or* There Is] One to Love Us.
Life.
Rose Thou Gav'st, The.
Smile and Never Heed Me.
Song: "Violet in her lovely hair, A."
Take the World as It Is.
Tripping down the Field-Path.
'Twas Just before the Hay Was Mown.

Swan, Caroline D.
Stars of Cheer.

Swan, Emma
Conducted Tour.
Connecticut Elm, The.

Swan, Jon
Father Father Son and Son.
In Her Song She Is Alone.
Kingdom, The.
March Weather.
Nebraska.
Report, The.
Their Party, Our House.

Swann, Thomas Burnett
Japanese Birthday Wish, A.

Swanson, Edwin C.
Myself.

Swarberg, George W.
Mistakes.
Worry.

Sward, Robert
Kissing the Dancer.
Mothers-in-Law.
Movies, Left to Right.
Nightown, Wife's Gown.
Pet Shop.
Proposal.
Terminal Theater.
There Is No Reason Why Not to Look at Death.
Uncle Dog: The Poet at 9.
What It Was.

Swart, Edward Vincent
Casey Jones.
Tired of Eating Kisses.

Swartz, Roberta Teale
Our Father.
Prayer by Moonlight.

Sweany, Michael
Devil's Meditation, The.

Sweeney, Francis
April.
Boy Playing an Organ.
In a Class of Moral Theology.
Tanglewood.

Sweeney, John L.
Exaction.
Separation.
Wind's Head, The.

Sweeney, Mildred Isabel McNeal
Chavez.
Simple Field That I Shall Buy, The.

Sweeney, Thomas
Old Earthworks.

Sweet, Frank Herbert
Before It Is Too Late.

Sweetman, Elinor
Orchard by the Shore, The; a Pastoral.

Sweetser, F. W.
Story of the Little Rid Hin, The.

Swenson, Karen
Symbolism.
Woman, Gallup, N.M.

Swenson, Lillian M.
Dissenter, The.

Swenson, May
Above the Arno.
Almanac.
August Night.
Beginning to Squall.
Café Tableau.
Cat and the Weather.
Cause and Effect.
Centaur, The.
Cloud-Mobile, The.
Contraption, The.
Death Great Smoothener.
Even Sea, The.
Evolution.
Feel like a Bird.
Fixture, A.
Frontispiece.
Garden at St. John's, The.
Hearing the Wind at Night.
Hurricane at Sea, A.
Key to Everything, The.
Lion.
Motherhood.
Naked in Borneo.
News from the Cabin.
Notes Made in the Piazza San Marco.
On Lighting the Fire.
Poplar's Shadow, The.
Promontory Moment, The.
Question.
Rain at Wildwood.
Red Bird Tapestry, The.
Riding the "A."
School of Desire, The.
Seeing the Frog.
Snow by Morning.
Southbound on the Freeway.
Sunday in the Country.
Three Jet Planes.
To the Shore.
Universe, The.
Was Worm.
Watch, The.
Water Picture.

Swett, Herbert B.
Gathering, The.

Swett, Susan Hartley
Blue-Jay, The.
It Is July.
July.

Swift, Hildegarde Hoyt
I Came to the New World Empty-Handed.
Man of Galilee, The.
My Name Was Legion.
Teacher, The.

Swift, Joan
Oxygen.

Swift, Jonathan
A E I O U.
Abroad and at Home.
Advice to the Grub-Street Verse-Writers.
Ah! where must needy poet seek for aid.
All human race wou'd fain be wits.
Apples.
As the World Turns.
Ballad to the Tune of "The Cut-Purse," A.
Baucis and Philemon.
Beasts' Confession, The.
Beautiful Young Nymph Going to Bed, A.
Behold the fatal day arrive!
Cadenus and Vanessa.
Catullus de Lesbia.
Character, Panegyric, and Description of the Legion Club, A.
City Shower, A.
Clever Tom Clinch Going to Be Hanged.
Critics.
Cupid tho' all his darts were lost.
Day of Judgement [*or* Judgment], The.
Dean, if we believe Report, The.
Description of a City Shower, A.
Description of the Morning, A.
Directions for a Birth-Day Song.
Epigram: "As Thomas was cudgelled one day by his wife."
Epigram: "Lord Pam in the church (cou'd you think it) kneel'd down."
Epigram: "Who killed Kildare? Who dared Kildare to kill?"
Excellent New Song on a Seditious Pamphlet, An.
Excellent New Song upon His Grace Our Good Lord Archbishop of Dublin, An.
Five, The.
Flattery.
Frances Harris's Petition.
From Dublin soon to London spread.
Furniture of a Woman's Mind, The.
Gentle Echo on Woman, A.
Had he but spar'd his tongue and pen.
Half Your Book.
"He gave the little wealth he had."
He never thought an honour done him.
Herrings.
Horace, Epistle VII, Book I, Imitated and Addressed to the Earl of Oxford.
How oft am I for rhyme to seek?
Humble Petition of Frances Harris, The.
In a Glass.
In Sickness.
Lady's Dressing Room, The.
Libel on Doctor Delaney and a Certain Great Lord, A.
Life and Genuine Character of Dean Swift, The.
Mary the Cook-Maid's Letter to Dr. Sheridan.
Maypole, A.
Mrs. Frances Harris's Petition.
Mollis Abuti.
My female friends, whose tender hearts.
Near Neighbors.
New Song of Wood's Halfpence, A.
On an Ill-managed House.
On an Upright Judge.
On Blenheim.
On Censure.
On Fleas.
On Gaulstown House.
On Himself.
On Mrs. Biddy Floyd.
On Poetry; a Rapsody.
On Stella's Birthday.
On the Collar of a Dog.
On the Death of Dr. Swift.
On the Upright Judge, Who Condemned the "Drapier's" Printer.
On the World.
Onions.
Oysters.
"Perhaps I may allow the dean."
Phillis; or, The Progress of Love.
Phyllis.
Phyllis, or the Progress of Love.
Power of Time, The.
Progress of Beauty, The.
Progress of Marriage, The.
Progress of Poetry, The.
Quiet Life and a Good Name, A.
Receipt to Restore Stella's Youth, A.
Riddle, A: "We are little airy creatures."
Riddle, A; the Vowels.
Satirical Elegy on the Death of a Late Famous General, A, 1722.
Satyrical Elegy on the Death of a Late Famous General, A, 1722.
Shall I Repine.
Should a monkey wear a crown.
Soldier and a Scholar, A, *sel.*
Stella's Birthday ("As, when a beauteous nymph decays").
Stella's Birthday; March 13, 1726/7 ("This day whate'er the fates decree").
Stella's Birthday, 1720 ("All travellers at first incline").
Stella's Birthday, Written in the Year

1718 ("Stella this day is thirty-four").
Thus spoke to my Lady the Knight full of care.
Time is not remote, when I, The.
To a Lady Who Desired I Would Write Verses in the Heroic Style, *sel.*
To Dr. Delany, *sel*
To Stella.
To Stella; March 13, MDCCXXIII-IV.
To Their Excellencies the Lords Justices of Ireland, the Humble Petition of Frances Harris [Who Must Starve and Die a Maid if It Miscarries].
Twelve Articles.
Vanbrug's House.
Verses for Fruitwomen, *sels.*
Verses Made for Women Who Cry Apples.
Verses on Blenheim.
Verses on the Death of Dr. Swift.
Verses Wrote in a Lady's Ivory Table-Book.
We Are God's Chosen Few.
Whiter than White.
Wicked Treasonable Libel, A.

Swinamer, George
Gale of August, '27, The

Swinburne, Algernon Charles
Adieux à Marie Stuart.
After Death.
After Looking into Carlyle's Reminiscences.
After Sunset, *sel.*
Anactoria, *sels.*
Are ye so strong, O kings, O strong men? Nay.
At Parting.
Atalanta in Calydon.
August.
Ave atque Vale.
Baby's Eyes, A.
Baby's Feet, A.
Ballad of Burdens, A.
Ballad of Death, A.
Ballad of Dreamland, A.
Ballad of Françis Villon, A.
Ballad of Life, A.
Beaumont and Fletcher.
Before Sunset.
Before the Beginning of Years.
Before the Mirror.
Ben Jonson.
Between the Sunset and the Sea.
Birth and Death.
Bothwell, *sel.*
By the North Sea.
Chastelard, *sels.*
Child and Poet.
Children.
Child's Future, A.
Child's Laughter, A.
Child's Song.
Chorus: "Before the Beginning of years."
Chorus: "We have seen thee, O love."
Chorus: "When the hounds of spring are on winter's traces."
Chorus: "Who hath given man speech?"
Chorus from "Atalanta in Calydon."
Choruses from "Atalanta in Calydon."
Christmas Antiphon[e], A.
Christmas Carol, A: "Three damsels in the queen's chamber."
Christopher Marlowe.
Cleopatra.
Cor Cordium.
Death and Birth.
Death of Meleager, The.
Death of Richard Wagner, The.
Death of Urgan, The.
Dedication to Christina G. Rossetti.
Dedication to Poems and Ballads [First Series].
Dialogue, A.
Dickens.
Dies Irae
Dolores.
Duriesdyke.
England; an Ode ("Sea and strand").
Envoi: "Fly, white butterflies, out to sea."
Eros.
Erotion.
Etude Réaliste.
Eve of Revolution, The, *sel.*
Evening by the Sea.
Farewell, A: "There lived a singer in France of old."
Faustine.
Félise.
First Footsteps.
For the Feast of Giordano Bruno.
For who shall change with prayers or thanksgivings.
Forsaken Garden, A.
Fragoletta.
Garden of Proserpine, The.
Glad, but not flush'd with gladness.
Hendecasyllabics.
Heptalogia, The, *sels.*
Hermaphroditus.
Hertha.
Hesperia.
Higher Pantheism in a Nutshell, The, *parody.*
Hope and Fear.
Hounds of Spring, The.
Hymn of Man.
Hymn to Proserpine.
I am the queen Herodias.
Ilicet.
In a Garden.
In Guernsey.
In Memory of "Barry Cornwall."
In Memory of Walter Savage Landor.
In the Water.
Interlude, An.
Interpreters, The.
Invocation: "Maiden, and mistress of the months and stars."
Itylus.
Jacobite's Exile, 1746, A.
Jacobite's Farewell, A.
James Shirley.
John Jones.
John Knox's Indictment of the Queen.
John Marston.
John Webster.
Lake of Gaube, The.
Laud of Saint Catherine, The.
Laus Veneris.
Leave-taking, A.
Leper, The.
Life of Man, The.
Love and Sleep.
Love at Sea.
Love That Is First and Last.
Lyke-Wake Song, A.
Lyric, A: "There's nae lark loves the lift, my dear."
Madonna Mia.
Man.
Many, The.
Mary Beaton's Song ("Between the sunset and the sea.").
Masque of Queen Bersabe, The, *sel.*
Match, A.
Messidor.
Midsummer Holiday, A, *sels.*
Neap-Tide.
Nephelidia.
Non Dolet.
Not as with Sundering of the Earth.
O soul, O God, O glory of liberty.
Oblation, The.
Olive.
On a Country Road.
On the Cliffs, *sel.*
On the Death of Robert Browning.
On the Deaths of Thomas Carlyle and George Eliot.
On the Monument Erected to Mazzini at Genoa.
On the Russian Persecution of the Jews.
On the Verge.
Peace-Giver, The.
Pilgrims, The.
Prelude: Tristram and Iseult.
Prelude to Songs before Sunrise.
Proserpine.
Return, The.
Rococo.
Rondel: "Kissing her hair, I sat against her feet."
Rondel: "These many years since we began to be."
Rosamond, *sel.*
Rose.
Roundel, The: "Roundel is wrought as a ring or a starbright sphere, A."
Salt of the Earth, The.
Sapphics.
Sappho.
Satia Te Sanguine.
Sea, The.
Sequence of Sonnets on the Death of Robert Browning, A, *sel.*
Seven Years Old.
Siena.
Singing Lesson, A.
Sisters, The, *sel.*
Song: "Love laid his sleepless head."
Song in Time of Order, A.
Song of the Standard, The.
Sonnet: "This is the golden book of spirit and sense."
Sonnet for a Picture.
Sonnets on English Dramatic Poets (1590-1650), *sels.*
Spray of song that springs in April, light of love that laughs through May.
Spring Song.
Stage Love.
Stanzas: "I will go back to the great sweet mother."
Sunbows, The.
Sundew, The.
Sunrise at Sea.
Super Flumina Babylonis.
Swan Song.
Swimming.
Thalassius.
Thomas Heywood.
Thou and I and he are not gods made men for a span.
Thou hast conquered, O pale Galilean; the world has grown gray from thy breath.
To a Cat.
To a Seamew.
To Victor Hugo.
To Walt Whitman in America.
Triads.
Tristram and Iseult.
Tristram of Lyonesse, *sels.*
Triumph of Time, The.
Tyneside Widow, The.
Unto Each Man His Handiwork.
Up the Spout.
Vision of Spring in Winter, A.
Watchman, What of the Night?
We Have Seen Thee, O Love.
We shift and bedeck and bedrape us.

Swinburne (continued)
When the Hounds of Spring [Are on Winter's Traces].
White Butterflies.
"Whoso Loseth His Life."
William Shakespeare.
Wilt Thou Yet Take All.
Winds, The.
Witch-Mother, The.
Year's Burden, A, 1870, *sel.*

Swingler, Randall
Letter I ("The midnight streets as I walk back").
Letter VIII ("On the first day of snow, my train").
Swans, The.
They Live.

Sye, Robert J.
Why I Rebel.

Sykes, J. H.
House or a Home, A.

Sylvain, Normil
Negro Sings, A.

Sylvester, Joshua
Autumnus.
Beware Fair Maid.
Contented Mind, A.
Du Bartas His Divine Weeks, *sels.*
First Day of the First Week, The.
Garden, The.
Go, Silly Worm.
I Hear the Crane.
Omnia Somnia.
Sonnet: "They say that shadows [*or* shadowes] of deceasèd ghosts."
Sweet mouth, that send'st a musky-rosed breath.

Symonds, John Addington
Christmas Lullaby, A.
Church Triumphant, The.
Episode, An.
Fall of a Soul, The.
Farewell: "It is buried and done with."
Farewell: "Thou goest; to what distant place."
Harvest.
How often have I now outwatched the night.
Human Outlook, The.
Il Fior degli Eroice Furori.
In February.
In the Small Canals.
In Venice, *sels.*
Invitation to the Gondola, The.
Invocation, An: "To God, the everlasting, who abides."
Κοινὰ τὰ τῶν φίλων (Koina ta ton Philon).
Le Jeune Homme Caressant Sa Chimère.
Loftier Race, A.
Love in Dreams.
Lux Est Umbra Dei.
Morgenlied.
Musing on Venice and the thought of thee.
Night.
Nightingale, The.
O God, unknown, invisible, secure.
On a Picture by Poussin Representing Shepherds in Arcadia.
Rebuke me not! I have nor wish nor skill.
Sonnet, The: "Sonnet is a fruit which long hath slept, The."
Stella Maris, *sels.*
These Things Shall Be.
Thyself.
To Night, the Mother of Sleep and Death.
Venice.

Symons, Arthur
Abandoned, The.
Absinthe-Drinker, The.
After Love.
After Sunset.
Amends to Nature.
Amor Triumphans, *sel.*
Amoris Exsul, *sel.*
Amoris Victima, *sel.*
And yet, there was a hunger in your eyes.
April Midnight.
Arques—Afternoon.
At Carbis Bay.
At Dawn.
At Dieppe, *sels.*
At Fontainebleau.
At Toledo.
Before the Squall.
Bianca.
Caged Bird, The.
City Nights: In Bohemia.
City Nights: In the Train.
Clair de Lune.
Credo.
Crying of Water, The.
Dance of the Daughters of Herodias, The.
Declaration.
Design for a List of Pictures.
Dream, The.
During Music.
Ecstasy.
Emmy.
Envoi: "All that remains for me."
Epilogue: Credo.
Episode of a Night of May.
Epithalamium: "Sister, the bride-bed waits."
Escalade.
Fairy Wood, The.
Fisher's Widow, The.
Gardener, The.
Grey and Green.
Grey Wolf, The.
Hallucination, I.
Impression.
In Bohemia.
In Ireland: By the Pool at the Third Rosses.
In Kensington Gardens.
In the Bay.
In the Wood of Finvara.
In Winter.
Javanese Dancers.
La Mélinite: Moulin-Rouge.
Last Memory, The.
Laus Virginitatis.
Leves Amores.
Loom of Dreams, The.
Love Song.
Magnificat.
Modern Beauty.
Nerves.
Night.
Night and Wind.
Nun, The.
Old Women, The.
On an Air of Rameau.
On the Beach.
Opals.
Pale Woman, The.
Palm Sunday: Naples.
Paris.
Pastel.
Prodigal Son, The.
Prologue: "My life is like a music-hall."
Rain on the Down.
Rat, The.
Return, The.
Roundel of Rest, A.
Scènes de la Vie de Bohème, sel.
Shadow, The.
Temptation of Saint Anthony, The.
To a Portrait.
To a Sea-Gull.
Tune, A.
Turning Dervish, The.
Unloved, The.
Violet, *sel.*
Wanderers, The.
Wanderer's Song.
White Heliotrope.
Your Kisses ("Sweet, can I sing you the song of your kisses").
Your Kisses ("Your kisses, and the way you curl").
Zulia.

Symons, Julian
And the World's Face.
For My Wife.
For the Depressed.
Gladstone.
Hart Crane.
Homage to Our Leaders.
Hospital Observation.
Mr. Symons at Richmond, Mr. Pope at Twickenham.
Pub.
Reflections in Bed.
Second Man, The.
Spring Poem.
Sunday, July 14th; a Fine Day at the Baths.

Synesius
Hymn: "Ah, what are strength and beauty?"
Lord Jesus, Think on Me.

Synge, John Millington
At Dawn.
Beg-Innish.
Conviction, The.
Curse, The.
Danny.
Dread.
Epitaph after Reading Ronsard's Lines from Rabelais.
In a Dream.
In Dream.
In Glencullen.
In Kerry.
In May.
In Rebellion.
I've Thirty Months.
Notre Dames des Champs.
On a Birthday.
On an Anniversary.
On an Island.
Passing of the Shee, The.
Patch-Shaneen.
Prelude: "Still south I went and west and south again."
Queens.
Question, A.
To the Oaks of Glencree.
Winter.

Syrian, Ajan
Syrian Lover in Exile Remembers Thee, Light of My Land, The.

Syrkin, Marie
After Seeing "Lear."
Coexistence.

T

"T., B. A."
Joe Dobson.

"T., B. L." *See* **Taylor, Bert Leston**

"T., C. W."
Valentine.

"T., I."
When Stars Are Shrouded.

"T. S. W." *See* **"W., T. S"**

Ta' Abbata Sharra
Ever Watchful.

Tabb, John Banister

All in All.
Annunciation, The.
Anonymous.
Aspiration.
Assumption, The.
At Bethlehem.
At Lanier's Grave.
Becalmed.
Betrayal.
Boy Jesus, The.
Brother Ass and St. Francis.
Bubble, The.
Bunch of Roses, A.
Butterfly.
Cats.
Child, The.
Child at Bethlehem, The.
Childhood.
Child's Prayer, A.
Child's Star, The.
Christ and the Pagan.
Christ and the Winds.
Clover.
Communion.
David and Goliath.
Departed, The.
Druid, The.
Evidence, The.
Evolution.
Faith.
Fame.
Father Damien.
Fern Song.
Fire-Fly, The.
Foot Soldiers.
Fraternity.
God.
Good Night!
High and Low.
Holy Saturday.
Hospitality.
Immaculate Conception, The.
Inconvenience, An.
Indian Summer.
Influence.
Insectarian, An.
Insomnia.
Inspiration.
"Is Thy Servant a Dog?"
Keats.
Lake, The.
Lamb-Child, The.
Leaf and Soul.
Light of Bethlehem, The.
Little Child's Prayer, A.
Lone-Land.
Mater Dolorosa.
Missing.
Mouse, a Cat, and an Irish Bull, A.
My Secret.
Nekros.
Old Pastor, The.
Out of Bounds.
Overflow.
Pleiads, The.
Precipice, The.
Reaper, The.
Recognition.
Robin Redbreast.
Shakespeare's Mourners.
Sisters, The.
Tax-Gatherer, The.
Test, The.
To a Photograph.
To a Rose.
To a Songster.
To a Wood-Violet.
To His Mother.
To Shelley.
To the Christ.
Two Easter Lilies.
Wait.
Water-Lily, The.
White Jessamine, The.
Wind, The.
Woodpecker, The.

Taber, Harry Persons
Jabberwocky of Authors, The.
Wilhelmina Mergenthaler.

Tabley, Lord De *See* **De Tabley, John Byrne Leicester Warren, 3rd Baron**

Tabrar, Joseph
Mary Ann.

Tachibana Akemi
Poems of Solitary Delights, *sel.*
What a delight it is.

Tadamine (Mibu ho Tadamine)
Cascade, The.

Tadema, Laurence Alma- *See Alma-Tadema, Laurence*

Taggard, Genevieve (Mrs. Kenneth Durant)
Dilemma of the Elm.
Doomsday Morning.
Enamel Girl, The.
First Miracle.
For Eager Lovers.
Galatea Again.
Hawaiian Hilltop.
Long View.
Millions of Strawberries.
Mood from 3000 B.C.
Poem to Explain Everything About a Certain Day in Vermont, A.
Quiet Woman, The.
Sea-Change.
Solar Myth.
Song for Unbound Hair.
To the Powers of Desolation.
To the Veterans of the Abraham Lincoln Brigade.
Tropical Girl to Her Garden.
Try Tropic.
With Child.

Taggert, George
Moth and the Flame, The.

Tagliabue, John
By a Rich Fast Moving Stream.
Fast.
Pinta, the Nina and the Santa Maria, The.

Tagore, Rabindranath
Autumn.
Baby's World.
Bird, The.
Day after Day.
For Strength.
Freedom.
Gardener, The, *sels.*
Gitanjali, *sels.*
Have you not heard his silent steps?
Here is thy footstool and there rest thy feet where live the poorest.
Home, The.
I Have Got My Leave.
I was not aware of the moment.
If It Is Not My Portion.
In the Dusky Path of a Dream.
Inalienable, The.
Krishnakali.
Let This Be My Parting Word.
My Song.
Oarsmen, The, *sel.*
On the day when the lotus bloomed.
On the Slope of the Desolate River.
Over the green and yellow rice fields.
Paper Boats.
Prayer for Courage.
Prayer for Strength.
Rainy Day, The.
Song-Offering, A.
Thou art the sky and thou art the nest as well.
Thy gifts to us mortals fulfil all our needs.
Vocation.
We have known sins and evils every day and death we have known.
When One Knows Thee.
Where the Mind Is without Fear.
Yellow Bird Sings, The.
Yours.

Tahureau, Jacques
Moonlight.
Shadows of His Lady.

Taigi
Firefly, The.

Taira no Kanemori
In spite of my efforts.

Tait, William J.
Gallow Hill.

Takamura, Kotaro
My Poetry.

Talbot, Ethel
Crab-Apple.
Give Love To-Day.

Talbott, Carlton
Ballyhoo for a Mendicant.
Day Closes, The.
Royal Pickle, A.
Sisters Kastemaloff, The.

Talfourd, Sir Thomas Noon
Friend, A.
Ion, *sel.*

Taliesin [*or* Taliessin],
Battle of Argoed Llwyfain, The.
Prophecy of Taliesin, The.
Song to the Wind, A.

Tall, Grace Cornell
Needle, The.

Tallante, Mossén Juan
Prayer to Jesus.
Prayer to the Crucifix.

Tallet, José Zacarías
Rumba.

Talman, John
Following Father Home.

Talpalar, Morris
True Happiness.

Tamuke
Love's Fancy.

"Tanaquil, Paul" (J. G. Clemenceau Le Clercq)
History.

T'ang Yin
Words for a Picture of Newlyweds.

Tankervil, George
Evensong.

Tannahill, Robert
Braes o' Gleniffer, The.
By Yon Burn Side.
Jessie, the Flower o' Dunblane.
Loudoun's Bonnie Woods and Braes.
Midges Dance aboon the Burn, The.
O! Are Ye Sleepin[g] Maggie?

Tansey, Anne
There Must Be Silence.

T'ao Ch'ien [*or* T'ao Yuan-ming],
Cozy.
I Built My Hut.
Long I Have Loved to Stroll.
Once More Fields and Gardens.
Planting Beans.
Returning to the Fields.
Shady, Shady.

Tappan, William Bingham
Gethsemane.
Hour of Peaceful Rest, The.
Jesus Prays Alone.
'Tis Midnight; and on Olive's Brow.

Tapper, Thomas
Tides, The.

Tarbat, Alan C.
In Terra Nostra.

Tarkington, Louise Fletcher

Tarkington (continued)
I wish there were some wonderful place.
Land of Beginning Again, The.
Tarn, Nathaniel
For the Death of Anton Webern Particularly.
Tarrant, William G.
Master's Man, The.
Tarver, Valerie
Differences.
Explanation.
"I Pledge Allegiance."
To the White Man.
Tassin, Algernon
Attainment.
Tassis, Juan de
To a Cloistress.
Tasso, Torquato
Aminta, *sel.*
Amyntas.
Armida, the Sorceress.
Crusaders Behold Jerusalem, The.
Crusaders Reach Jerusalem, The.
Far from My Dearest Self.
Godfrey of Bulloigne.
Golden Age, The.
Jerusalem Delivered [*or* Godfrey of Bulloigne], *sels.*
Love.
Love, the Master of True Eloquence.
O Bella Età de l'Oro.
Pastoral [*or* Pastorall], A: "Oh happy golden age."
Pastoral of Tasso, A.
Pluto's Council.
Prayer Brings Rain, A.
Sacred armies and the godly Knight, The.
To His Mistress in Absence.
To the Father of the Bride.
When they had passed all those troubled ways.
Tassoni, Alessandro
Relations.
Tate, Allen
Aeneas at Washington.
Autumn.
Buried Lake, The.
Cross, The.
Death of Little Boys.
Emblems.
Eye, The.
Gay citizen, myself, and thoughtful friend.
Give me this day a faith not personal.
Horatian Epode to the Duchess of Malfi.
Idiot ("The idiot greens the meadows with his eyes.")
Jubilo.
Last Days of Alice.
Mediterranean, The.
Mr. Pope.
More Sonnets at Christmas.
Mother and Son.
Oath, The.
Ode: "Once more the country calls."
Ode to Our Young Pro-Consuls of the Air.
Ode to the Confederate Dead.
Pastoral: "Enquiring fields, courtesies, The."
Pauper, A.
Robber Bridegroom, The.
Seasons of the Soul.
Shadow and Shade.
Sonnets at Christmas (I-II).
Subway, The.
Swimmers, The.
Traveler, The.
Trout Map, The.
Winter Mask.
Wolves, The.
Tate, James
Coda.
Coming down Cleveland Avenue.
Death on Columbus Day.
Descent, The.
Destination, The.
Flight.
For Mother on Father's Day.
How the Friends Met.
Intimidations of an Autobiography.
Late Harvest.
Lost Pilot, The.
Plea Based on a Sentence from a Letter Received by the Indiana State Welfare Department.
Rescue.
Trust, The.
Why I Will Not Get Out of Bed.
Tate, Nahum
Amorist, The.
Blessed Virgin's Expostulation, The
Choice, The.
Christmas.
History of King Richard II, *sel.*
Love's Delights.
Loyal General, The, *sel.*
Penance, The.
Song of the Angels.
While Shepherds Watched Their Flocks by Night.
Tate, Nahum, *and* John Dryden
Absalom and Achitophel, Pt. II, *sels.*
Tatham, John
Letter, The.
Ostella, *sel.*
Reason.
Seeing a Lady.
To Philomel.
Tatnall, Frances Dorr
Art Thou the Same.
Taylor, Ann
Another Plum-Cake.
Baby, The.
Boy and the Sheep, The.
Jane and Eliza.
Little Girl to Her Dolly, The.
Meddlesome Matty.
My Mother.
Pin, The.
Plum-Cake, The.
Sheep, The.
Tumble, The.
Washing and Dressing.
Worm, The.
Taylor, Ann *or* Jane
Cow, The.
Evening Hymn for a Little Family, An.
Good Dobbin.
Learning to Draw.
Little Ants, The.
Little Fish That Would Not Do as It Was Bid, The.
Meadows, The.
Of What Are Your Clothes Made?
Pretty Cow.
Sleepy Harry.
Thank You, Pretty Cow.
Taylor, Bayard
Ah, moment not to be purchased.
America.
Angelo Orders His Dinner.
Ariel in the Cloven Pine.
Bedouin Song.
Camerados.
Cantelope, The.
Demon of the Mirror, The.
Deserter, The.
Echo Club, The, *sel.*
Fight of Paso Del Mar, The.
Gettysburg Ode, The, *sel.*
God, to whom we look up blindly.
Hiram Hover.
Kilimandjaro.
Lincoln at Gettysburg.
National Ode, Read at the Celebration in Independence Hall, Philadelphia, July 4, 1876.
Night with a Wolf, A.
Nubia.
Palabras Grandiosas.
Poet's Journal, The, *sel.*
Promissory Note, The.
Quaker Widow, The.
Scott and the Veteran.
Self-Mastery.
Song: "Daughter of Egypt, veil thine eyes!"
Song in Camp, The.
Song of the Camp, The.
Storm Song.
Story for a Child, A.
Sunshine of the Gods, The, *sel.*
Three Songs, The.
Through Baltimore.
To G. H. B.
To M. T.
To R. H. S.
Village Stork, The.
Taylor, Benjamin Franklin
Isle of the [the] Long Ago, The.
Isle of the Long Ago, The.
Long Ago, The.
Taylor, Bert Leston ("B.L.T.")
Ataraxia.
Ballade of Spring's Unrest, A.
Bards We Quote, The.
Behind the Door.
Bygones.
Canopus.
Cow, The.
Dinosaur, The.
Farewell: "Farewell! Another gloomy word."
Happy Thought.
Hence These Rimes.
Lazy Writer, The.
Old Stuff.
Post-Impressionism.
Rain.
Reward.
Road to Anywhere, The.
Sundown.
To Lillian Russell.
To What Base Uses!
Taylor, Charles Edward
For Sale, a Horse.
Taylor, Charles S.
Scandal among the Flowers, A.
Taylor, Deems
Concerning Mme. Robert.
"Haec Olim Meminisse Iuvabit."
Hors d'Oeuvre.
Proof Positive.
Turn to the Left.
Taylor, Edward
Accusation of the Inward Man, The.
Address to the Soul Occasioned by a Rain, An.
Advocate with the Father, An.
Almighty, The.
Another Meditation at the Same Time.
Bright and Morning Star, The.
Christ's Reply.
Ebb and Flow, The.
Elegy upon the Death of That Holy Man of God Mr. John Allen, An, *sel.*
Experience, The.
Frowardness of the Elect in the Work of Conversion, The.
Glory of and Grace in the Church, The.
God's Determinations, *sels.*
God's Selecting Love in the Decree.

He Is a New Creature.
He Is the Propitiation for Our Sin.
He Sent a Man before Them, Even Joseph, Who Was Sold.
Housewifery.
How are our Spirituall Gamesters slipt away?
Huswifery.
I Am the Root and Offspring of David.
I Am the Rose of Sharon.
I Give unto Them Eternal Life.
I Have Eate My Hony Comb with My Hony.
Joy of Church Fellowship [Rightly Attended], The.
Let Him Kiss Me with the Kisses of His Mouth.
Like to the marigold, I blushing close.
Meditations.
My Blessed Lord, how doth thy beautious spouse.
My Dove Is One the Onely One of Her Mother.
My Father, and Your Father, to My God, and Your God.
My Gracious Lord, I would thee glory doe.
Oh! Golden rose! Oh. Glittering lilly white.
Oh leaden heeld. Lord, give, forgive I pray.
Our Insufficiency to Praise God Suitably for His Mercy.
Outward Man Accused, The.
Preface, The: "Infinity, when all things it beheld."
Preparatory Meditations, *sels.*
Prologue: "Lord, can a crumb of earth [*or* dust] the earth outweigh."
Reflection, The.
Reflexion, The.
Return, Oh Shulamite, Return Return.
Sacramental Meditations.
Souls Groan to Christ for Succour, The.
Stupendious love! All saints astonishment!
The Frowardness of the Elect in the Work of Conversion.
Upon a Spider Catching a Fly.
Upon a Wasp Chilled with Cold.
Upon Wedlock and Death of Children.
When Let by Rain.
When They Had Sung an Hymn.
Whether Paul or Apollos, or Cephas.
While the King Sitteth at His Table.
Who Is She That Looks Forth.

Taylor, Emily
Mother.

Taylor, Frances Beatrice
Husbandman, The.
Wedgwood Bowl, A.

Taylor, Geoffrey
Bluebell.
Boat-Haven, Co. Mayo.
Country Walk.
Cruel Clever Cat.
English Liberal.
From an Irish-Latin Macaronic.
Limerick: "'I think' thought Sam Butler."
Song: "Rousing to rein his pad's head back."

Taylor, George Lansing
No Slave beneath the Flag.

Taylor, Helen
Bless This House.

Taylor, Sir Henry
Aretina's Song.
Characterization, A.
Edwin the Fair, *sel.*
Elena's Song.
Hero, The.
John of Launoy.
Philip van Artevelde, *sels.*
Revolutions.
Song: "Bee to the heather, The."
Song: "Down lay in a nook my lady's brach."
Song: "Quoth tongue of neither maid nor wife."
Wind in the Pines, The.
Women Singing.

Taylor, James Bayard *See* **Taylor, Bayard**

Taylor, Jane
Child's Hymn of Praise, A.
Contented John.
Cow and the Ass, The.
Daisy, The.
Dirty Jim.
Employment.
Encouragement for Little Children, *sel.*
Farm, The.
Field Daisy, The.
God Is So Good.
Good Night.
I Like Little Pussy.
I Love Little Pussy.
Little Pussy.
Little Star.
Lord, look upon a little child.
Morning.
Now and Then.
Philosopher's Scales, The.
Pond, The.
Poppy, The.
Pussy.
Recreation.
Snow.
Spider and His Wife, The.
Star, The.
Stars at Night, The.
Thanksgiving, A.
Twinkle, Twinkle, Little Star.
Violet, The.

Taylor, Jefferys
Dog of Reflection, The
Milkmaid, The.
Young Mouse, The.

Taylor, Jeremy
Christ's Coming in Triumph.
Lord, Come Away!
My Soul Doth Pant towards Thee.
Penitent, The.
Prayer, The: "My soul doth pant towards thee."

Taylor, John
Odcomb's Complaint, *sel.*
Of Seals and Arms.
Sonnet: Mackado, Fustian and Motley.
Sonnet: "Sweet semi-circled Cynthia played at maw."
Walking along the streets the other day.

Taylor, John W.
Chipeta's Ride.

Taylor, Joseph Russell
Blow Softly, Thrush.
Breath on the Oat.
Dove's Nest.
Flute, The.
Veery-Thrush, The.

Taylor, Katherine Kelley
Flying Fish.

Taylor, Mart
California Humbugs.
Couldn't Stand the Press.
Do They Miss Me at Home? A Parody.
John Chinaman's Appeal.
Miner's Farewell, The.
Old Forty-nine.
Pike County Miner, The.
Poor Diggings.
That's the Way to Talk It.
We Are All a Panning.

Taylor, Morgan
Limerick: "Lieutenant who went out to shoot, A."

Taylor, Rachel Annand
Ecstasy.
End of the Duel, The.
Joys of Art, The.
Knights to Chrysola, The.
May-Music.
Princess of Scotland, The.
Question, The.

Taylor, Sarah Wingate
Hope.
Master-Welder, The.
With Metaphor.

Taylor, Tom
Abraham Lincoln.
Fool's Revenge, The, *sel.*
Jester and His Daughter, The.

Taylor, Viola
Babylon.

Taylor, William
Brewer's Coachman, The.
To the Fair Unknown.

Tchernichowsky, Saul
Before a Statue of Apollo.
Before the Statue of Apollo.
Credo.
Dance of Saul with the Prophets, The.
Death of Tammuz, The.
Grave in Ukraine, A.
I Believe.
This Be Our Revenge.
To Ashtaroth and Bel.

Teasdale, Sara
After Parting.
All That Was Mortal.
Answer, The.
Appraisal.
April.
Arcturus in Autumn.
August Night.
Barter.
Beautiful Proud Sea.
Blue Squills.
Calm Morning at Sea.
Child, Child.
Christmas Carol: "Kings they came from out the south, The."
Coin, The.
Crystal Gazer, The.
Dark Cup, The, *sel.*
Debt.
December Day, A.
Doubt.
Effigy of a Nun.
Faces.
Falling Star, The.
February Twilight.
Flames.
Flight, The.
Four Winds.
From the Sea.
Full Moon.
Full Moon; Santa Barbara.
Grace before Sleep.
I Shall Not Care.
I Stood upon a Star.
Immortal.
In the Carpenter's Shop.
Inn of Earth, The.
Interlude: Songs Out of Sorrow, *sels.*
It Is Not a Word.
It Is Not Far.
June Day, A.
Kiss, The.
Lamp, The.
Leaves.
Let It Be Forgotten.
Lights of New York, The.

Teasdale (continued)
Like Barley Bending.
Long Hill, The.
Look, The.
Madeira from the Sea.
Mastery.
May Day.
Morning.
My Heart Is Heavy.
Mystery, The.
Night.
Night Song at Amalfi.
Old Enemy, The.
On the Dunes.
On the South Downs.
On the Sussex Downs.
Over the Roofs.
Philosopher, The.
Pierrot.
Places.
Prayer, A: "Until I lose my soul and lie."
Since There Is No Escape.
Solitary, The.
Song: "Let it be forgotten, as a flower is forgotten."
Song Making.
Spirit's House.
Spring in War Time.
Spring Night.
Stars.
Sunset; St. Louis.
Swallow Flight.
There Will Come Soft Rains.
Those Who Love.
To Dick, on His Sixth Birthday.
To Rose.
Water-Lilies.
What Do I Care?
When I Am Not with You.
Winter Noon.
Winter Solstice.
Wisdom ("It was a night").
Wisdom ("When I have ceased").
Young Love.
Tedder, Elayne
River of Life.
Tegnér, Esaias
Eternal, The.
Frithiof's Saga, *sels.*
Teichner, Miriam
Awareness.
Tejada Juan Manuel Garcia
To Jesus on the Cross.
"Tekahionwake." *See* **Johnson, Emily Pauline**
Telemaque, Harold
Adina.
Roots.
Telfer, James
Goblin's Song, The.
Temple, Anna *See* **Whitney, Anna Temple**
Temple, Anne Hunter
King Passes, The.
Templeton, J. D.
New Year, The.
Tenchi, Emperor
Through the thatched roof.
Tennant, Edward Wyndham
Home Thoughts in Laventie.
I saw green banks of daffodil.
Tennant, Pamela *See* **Grey of Fallodon, Pamela Grey, Viscountess**
Tennant, William
Anster Fair, *sel.*
On the Road to Anster Fair.
Tennyson, Alfred Tennyson, 1st Baron
Akbar's Dream, *sel.*
All in All.
Ancient Sage, The.
And Freedom rear'd in that august sunrise.
And rise, O moon, from yonder down.
And, star and system rolling past.
Are God and Nature then at strife.
Arthur's Disillusionment.
As thro' [*or* through] the Land at Eve We Went.
As when a man, that sails in a balloon.
Ask me no more: the moon may draw the sea.
At length I saw a lady within call.
Audley Court.
Aylmer's Field, *sel.*
Balin and Balan.
Balloon, The.
Be Comforted.
Becket, *sel.*
Beggar Maid, The.
Birds in the high Hall-garden.
Blackbird, The.
Blow, Bugle, Blow.
Break, Break, Break.
Brook, The.
Brook, The; an Idyl, *sels.*
Brook's Song, The.
Bugle, The.
Bugle Song.
Buonaparte.
But I was first of all the kings who drew.
But the broad light glares and beats.
But What's in the Larder?
By an Evolutionist.
Cast Your Cares on God.
Challenge of Life, The.
Character, A.
Charge of the Light Brigade, The.
Choric Song: "There is sweet music here that softer falls."
Christmas Bells.
City Child, The.
Claribel.
Cling to Faith.
Cold and clear-cut face, why come you so cruelly meek.
Columbus Day.
Come Down, O Maid [from Yonder Mountain Height].
Come into the Garden, Maud.
Come, my friends.
Come Not, When I Am Dead.
Conclusion to the May Queen and New Year's Eve.
Cradle Song: "What does little birdie say."
Crossing the Bar.
Daisy, The.
Dash Back.
De Profundis, *sel.*
Dead, Long Dead.
Death of the Duke of Clarence and Avondale, The, *sel.*
Death of the Old Year.
Dedication, A: "Dear, near and true—no truer Time himself."
Dedication: "These to his memory—since he held them dear."
Deep Dark Night, The.
Defence of Lucknow, The.
Demeter and Persephone.
Deserted House, The.
Devil and the Lady, The, *sel.*
Doubt.
Doubt and Prayer.
Dragon-Fly, The.
Dream of Fair Women, A, *sels.*
Duet: "Is it the wind of the dawn that I hear in the pine overhead?"
Dying Swan, The.
Eagle, The.
Early Spring.
Edward Gray.
Elaine's Song.
England and America in 1782.
Enoch Arden.
Epic, The (Introduction to "Morte d'Arthur").
Experience.
Faith ("Thou canst not prove the Nameless").
Faith ("You say, but with no touch of scorn").
Far—Far—Away.
Farewell, A: "Flow down, cold rivulet, to the sea."
Fatima.
Federation of the World, The.
Fire of Heaven, The.
Flower, The.
Flower in the Crannied Wall.
Follow the Christ.
Follow the Gleam.
Foresters, The, *sel.*
Fragment: "Flower in the crannied wall."
"Frater Ave atque Vale."
Freedom ("O thou so fair in summers gone").
Freedom ("Of old sat Freedom").
Gareth and Lynette, *sel.*
Geraint and Enid.
Go By.
Go Not, Happy Day.
Godiva.
Goose, The.
Guinevere.
Hands All Round.
He taught me all the mercy, for he show'd me all the sin.
Her tears fell with the dews at even.
Hesperides, The.
Higher Pantheism, The.
Holy Grail, The.
Home They Brought Her Warrior Dead.
Horns of Elfland, The.
Hymn: "Once again thou flamest heavenward, once again we see thee rise."
I cannot see the features right.
I chatter over stony ways.
I have led her home, my love, my only friend.
I loved her, one / Not learned, save in gracious household ways.
I Shall Have Had My Day.
Idyl, An: "Come down, O maid, from yonder mountain height."
Idylls of the King, *sels.*
If I were loved, as I desire to be.
If Love Be Ours.
If my body came from brutes, tho' somewhat finer than their own.
Ilion, Ilion.
In Grief.
In Love, If Love Be Love.
In Memoriam A. H. H.
In Memoriam—W. G. Ward.
In the Children's Hospital.
In the Garden at Swainston.
In the Spring.
In the Valley of Cauteretz.
Intuition.
Iphigenia.
Is that enchanted moan only the swell.
Jephthah's Daughter.
June Bracken and Heather.
Kraken, The.
Lady Clara Vere de Vere.
Lady Clare.
Lady of Shalott, The.
Lancelot and Elaine.
Lancelot and the Grail.
Larger Hope, The.
Last Tournament, The.

Leolin and Edith.
Letters, The.
Life Not Death.
Life Shall Live for Evermore.
Lilian.
Lines: "Here often, when a child I lay reclined."
Little Birdie.
Locksley Hall.
Locksley Hall Sixty Years After.
Long have I sigh'd for a calm: God grant I may find it at last!
Lord of Burleigh, The.
Lost Love.
Lotos-Eaters, The.
Lotus Eaters, The.
Love Thou Thy Land [With Love Far-brought].
Lucretius.
Lullaby: "Sweet and low, sweet and low."
Lyric from "Maud."
Lyrics from "The Princess."
Making of Man, The.
Man, that with me trod, The.
Mariana.
Mariana in the South.
Maud.
May Queen, The.
Merlin and the Gleam.
Merlin and Vivien.
Mermaid, The.
Merman, The.
Milkmaid's Song.
Miller's Daughter, The.
Million emeralds break from the ruby-budded lime. A.
Milton.
Minnie and Winnie.
Montenegro.
Morte d'Arthur.
Move Eastward, Happy Earth.
My life has crept so long on a broken wing.
My Life is Full of Weary Days.
My Lord and King.
Mystic, The.
New Year, The.
New Year's Eve ("If you're waking, call me early").
New Year's Eve ("Ring out, wild bells").
Nobility.
Northern Farmer; New Style.
Northern Farmer: Old Style.
Now Sleeps the Crimson Petal [Now the White].
O Purblind Race.
O Swallow, Swallow, Flying, Flying South.
O That 'Twere Possible.
O you chorus of indolent reviewers.
Oak, The.
Ode on the Death of the Duke of Wellington.
Oenone.
Of Old Sat Freedom on the Heights.
Of One Dead.
Olivia.
Our Echoes Roll from Soul to Soul.
Our Enemies Have Fallen.
Our little systems have their day.
Owl, The.
Palace of Art, The.
Passing of Arthur, The.
Path by which we twain did go, The.
Pelleas and Ettarre.
People's voice, A! we are a people yet.
Poet, The.
Poets and Their Bibliographies.
Poet's Mind, The.
Poet's Song, The.
Politics.
Prayer: "And slowly answer'd Arthur from the barge."
Prayer: "More things are wrought by prayer."
Prayer, The: "O living will that shalt endure."
Prayer: "Old order changeth, yielding place to new, The."
Prayer for the Dead.
Princess, The, *sels.*
Proem: "Strong Son of God, immortal Love."
Prologue: "Strong Son of God, immortal Love."
Prophecy.
Pure Heart, The.
Queen Mary, *sel.*
Recollections of the Arabian Nights.
Reconciliation, The.
Remorse.
Revenge, The [a Ballad of the Fleet].
Ring Out, Wild Bells.
Rise, Happy Morn.
Rizpah.
St. Agnes' Eve.
Sea Dreams, *sel.*
Sea-Fairies, The.
See What a Lovely Shell.
Shell, The.
Shepherd's Song.
Silent Voices, The.
Sir Galahad.
Sir John Franklin; On the Cenotaph in Westminster Abbey.
Sir Launcelot and Queen Guinevere.
Sisters, The ("We were two daughters of one race").
Sleeping House, The.
Slowly comes a hungry people, as a lion creeping nigher.
Snowdrop.
Song: "Come down, O maid, from yonder mountain height."
Song: "Come into the garden, Maud."
Song: "Go not, happy day."
Song: "Home they brought her warrior dead."
Song: "I come from haunts of coot and hern."
Song: "It is the miller's daughter."
Song: "Now sleeps the crimson petal."
Song: "O let the solid ground."
Song: "O Swallow, Swallow flying, flying South."
Song: Owl, The.
Song: "Spirit haunts the year's last hours, A."
Song: "Splendour falls on castle walls, The."
Song: "Sweet and low, sweet and low."
Song: "Tears, idle tears."
Song: "There is no land like England."
Song: "Thy voice is heard thro rolling drums."
Song: "Who can say."
Song at the Ruin'd Inn.
Song from "Maud" ("Come into the garden, Maud").
Song from "Maud" ("Go not, happy day").
Song of the Brook.
Song of the Lotos-Eaters.
Song of the Milkmaid.
Songs from "The Princess."
Sonnet: "She took the dappled partridge flecked with blood."
Splendor [*or* Splendour] Falls [on Castle Walls], The.
Spring ("Dip down upon the northern shore").
Spring ("Now fades the last long streak of snow").
Spring and Summer.
Strange friend, past, present and to be.
Strength—Human.
Stronger Faith, A.
Summer Night.
Supposed Confessions of a Second-rate Sensitive Mind.
Sweet and Low [Sweet and Low].
Talking Oak, The, *sel.*
Tears, Idle Tears [I Know Not What They Mean].
Temple, The.
Thank him who isled us here, and roughly set.
That Which Made Us.
Their Conscience as Their King.
Then rose the King and moved his host by night.
Then saw they how there hove a dusky barge.
There Is None like Her.
There Is Sweet Music Here.
There lies the port; the vessel puffs her sail.
Third of February, The, 1852.
This world was once a fluid haze of light.
Thou canst not prove that thou art body alone.
"Thou, too, my Lancelot," ask'd the King, "my friend."
Throstle, The.
Thy Voice is Heard [thro' Rolling Drums].
Till now the doubtful dusk reveal'd.
'Tis Better to Have Loved and Lost.
Tithonus.
To ——: "All good things have not kept aloof."
To ——: With the Following Poem.
To Christopher North.
To E. FitzGerald.
To E. L., on His Travels in Greece.
To Edward Fitzgerald.
To J. M. K.
To the Queen ("O loyal to the royal in thy self").
To the Queen ("Revered, beloved—O you that hold").
To the Rev. F. D. Maurice.
To Vergil.
To Virgil.
Too Late.
Truths That Never Can Be Proved, The.
Two Voices, The.
Ulysses.
Valedictory.
Vastness.
Vision of Sin, The.
Vivien's Song.
Voice and the Peak, The.
Voice by the Cedar Tree, A.
Voyage, The.
Voyage of Maeldune, The.
Wages.
Way to Power, The.
We Kiss'd Again with Tears.
We Needs Must Love the Highest.
Welcome to Alexandra, A.
What Does Little Birdie Say?
What is she now? My dreams are bad.
What Know We Greater than the Soul?
When Cats Run Home.
"When the hermit made an end."
Will.
Winter.
Woman and Man, *abr.*
Word, The.
Word Incarnate, The.
Worm within the Rose, A.

Tennyson (continued)
Yet if some voice that man could trust.
Yew in the Graveyard, The.
You Ask Me, Why, tho' [*or* though] Ill at Ease.
Yule-log sparkled keen with frost, The.
Tennyson, Charles *See* **Turner, Charles Tennyson**
Tennyson, Frederick
Blackbird, The.
Glory of Nature, The.
Harvest Home.
Holy Tide, The.
I too remember, in the after years.
Incident, An.
Iona.
Niobe, *sel.*
Skylark, The.
Thirty-first of May.
Teresa, Saint, of Avila *See* **Theresa, Saint, of Avila**
Teresa, Santa, de Jesús. *See* **Theresa, Saint, of Avila**
Terhune, Mary Virginia
If I Had Known.
Terpander
Sparta.
Terral, Rufus
Chant Royal from a Copydesk.
Terrazas, Francisco de
To a Beautiful but Heartless Coquette.
Terrell, Myra Burnham
Theodosia Burr.
Terrell, Robert L.
For Frantz Fanon.
Terry, Edward H. S.
Kinship.
Terry, Lucy
Bars Fight.
Terry, Uriah
Wyoming Massacre, The.
Tersteegen, Gerhardt
Blessed Journey, The.
Change of Raiment.
God's Eternal Now.
Lord Jesus, all my sin and guilt.
Shadow of His Wings, The.
Will of God, The.
Teschemacher, Edward
Because.
Tessimond, Arthur Seymour John
British, The.
Cats.
Children Look at the Parents, The.
Dance Band.
Daydream.
Earthfast.
Man in the Bowler Hat, The.
Man of Culture, A.
One Almost Might.
Radio.
Sleep.
Wet Windy Night on a Pavement.
Teternikov, Feodor Kuzmich *See* **"Sologub, Feodor"**
Thacker, Mary Afton
I Found God.
Thackeray, William Makepeace
Ad Ministram.
After the Storm.
Age of Wisdom, The.
At Paris, hard by the Maine barriers.
At the Church Gate.
Ballad of Bouillabaisse, The.
Cane-bottomed Chair, The.
Chronicle of the Drum, The, *sels.*
Commanders of the Faithful.
Credo, A.
Crystal Palace, The.
Dr. Birch and His Young Friends, *sel.*
End of the Play, The.
Fairy Days.
Jolly Jack.
King Canute, *abr.*
King of Brentford, The.
Larry O'Toole.
Little Billee.
Love at Two Score.
Lucy's Birthday.
Mahogany Tree, The.
Minaret Bells, The.
Mr. Molony's Account of the Ball.
Mr. Molony's Account of the Crystal Palace.
Old Fashioned Fun.
Pen and the Album, The.
Pendennis, *sel.*
Persicos Odi.
Pocahontas.
Rebecca and Rowena, *sel.*
Ronsard to His Mistress.
Sorrows of Werther, The.
Sportsmanship.
Three Sailors, The.
When Moonlike ore [*or* o'er] the Hazure Seas.
White Squall, The, *sel.*
Who Misses or Who Wins.
Willow-Tree, *parody.*
Wofle New Ballad of Jane Roney and Mary Brown, The.
Thaon [*or* Thaun], Philippe de *See* **Phillippe de Thaon [*or* Thaun]**
Thatcher, Charles Robert
Look Out Below!
Thatcher, Thomas
Love Letter to Elizabeth Thatcher, A.
Thaxter, Celia (Laighton)
As Happy Dwellers by the Seaside Hear.
August.
Be Hopeful.
Chanticleer.
Child and the Year, The.
Compensation.
Day Shall Yet Be Fair, The.
Flowers for the Brave.
Little Gustava.
Lost.
March.
May Morning.
Nikolina.
On Easter Day.
Sandpiper, The.
Seaward.
Song: "We sail towards evening's lonely star."
Song of Easter.
Spring.
Wild Geese.
Thayer, Ernest Lawrence
Casey at the Bat.
Thayer, Julia H.
Shining Hope, A.
Thayer, Louis Edwin
Hang to Your Grit!
Keep Your Grit.
Little Child's Faith, The.
Thayer, Lucius H.
Life of Man, The.
Thayer, Mary Dixon (Mrs. Maurice Fremont Smith)
Afterwards.
Bird-Song.
Finding You.
How Nice.
Prayer, A: "God, is it sinful if I feel."
Prayer, A: "I pray for you, and yet I do not frame."
To Elizabeth.
To Our Lady.
Treasures.
Woman, A.
Thayer, Stephen Henry
Europa.
Poet of Earth.
Waiting Chords, The.
Thayer, William Roscoe ("Paul Hermes")
Last Hunt, The.
Man in Nature.
Violin's Complaint, The.
Theocritus
Countryman's Wooing, A.
Cyclops, The.
Death of Daphnis, The.
Enchantment, The.
Fishermen, The.
Harvest Home.
Herdsman, The.
Idylls, *sels.*
Incantation, The.
Second Idyll, The.
Serenade: "O beautiful Amaryllis."
Song of the Sleepy Bridegroom.
Syracusan Women, The.
Theodore of Studium, Saint
Canon for Apocreos, The.
Theodorides [*or* Theodoridas],
Pass On.
Theognis
Advice to Kyrnos.
Enjoyment.
Hope.
Immortality Conferred in Vain.
Poverty.
Theophanes
Adam's Complaint.
Theresa [*or* Teresa], Saint, of Avila
Alone God Sufficeth.
Bookmark.
God Alone Suffices.
If, Lord, Thy Love for Me Is Strong.
Let Mine Eyes See Thee.
Life Above, the Life on High, The.
Lines Written in Her Breviary.
Saint Teresa's Book-Mark.
Santa Teresa's Book-Mark.
Shepherd, Shepherd, Hark.
To-Day a Shepherd.
Thérèse, Saint, of Lisieux
My Song of Today.
Scattering Flowers.
Unpetalled Rose, The.
Thérèse, Sister Mary
Bird, The.
Contemplative, The.
For Simone Weil.
Interrogative.
Moment in Ostia.
Testament.
Traveler.
You Give Me Sappho.
Thewlis, John
Song of a Happy Rising, The.
Thibaudeau, Colleen
Clock Tower, The.
Spring Poem.
Thich Nhat Hanh
Condemnation.
Thiele, Colin
Aircraft, Landing.
Bert Schultz.
Burke and Wills, *sels.*
Final Soliloquy, The.
Tom Farley.
Wills Dies in Solitude.
Thiele, Ernest W.
Ludmilla; an Ode on the Occasion of Her Departure from These Shores.
Thoby-Marcelin, Philippe
Elegies.
Thom, William
Blind Boy's Pranks, The.

Mitherless Bairn, The.
They Speak o' Wiles.
Thomas, A. F.
Apt Prayer, An.
Thomas, Beatrice Llewellyn
To Puck.
Thomas, Charles
In Search of a God.
Ode to the Smiths.
Thomas, Charles Edward
To a Moth.
Thomas, Charles F., Jr
Cowboy up to Date, The.
Thomas, Claire Richcreek
Flesh will heal and pain will fade.
Heart Wounds.
Thomas, Cordia
Lollypops, The.
Thomas, D. M.
Head-Rape, The.
Missionary.
Tithonus.
Thomas, Dylan
After the Funeral.
Altarwise by Owl-Light (I-X).
Among Those Killed in the Dawn Raid Was a Man Aged One [*or* a] Hundred.
And Death Shall Have No Dominion.
Ballad of the Long-legged Bait.
Before I Knocked and Flesh Let Enter.
Ceremony after a Fire Raid.
Conversation of Prayer, The.
Do Not Go Gentle into That Good Night.
Do You Not Father Me.
Ears in the Turrets Hear.
Especially When the October Wind.
Every Morning When I Wake.
Fern Hill.
First there was the lamb on knocking knees.
Force That through the Green Fuse Drives the Flower, The.
Grief Ago, A.
Hand That Signed the Paper Felled a City, The.
Hold Hard, These Ancient Minutes.
Holy Spring.
Hunchback in the Park, The.
I Have Longed to Move Away.
I, in My Intricate Image.
I See the Boys of Summer.
In Country Sleep.
In Memory of Ann Jones.
In My Craft or Sullen Art.
In the Beginning.
In the White Giant's Thigh.
Incarnate Devil.
Johnnie Crack and Flossie Snail.
Lament: "When I was a windy boy and a bit."
Last time I slept with the queen, The.
Light Breaks Where No Sun Shines.
Marriage of a Virgin, The.
Not from This Anger.
October.
On No Work of Words Now.
On the Marriage of a Virgin.
Over Sir John's Hill.
Poem: "Especially when the October wind."
Poem: "Force that through the green fuse drives the flower, The."
Poem: "Process in the weather of the heart, A."
Poem in October ("It was my thirtieth year to heaven").
Poem on His Birthday.
Process in the Weather of the Heart, A.
Prologue: "This day winding down now."
Refusal to Mourn the Death, by Fire, of a Child in London, A.
Should Lanterns Shine.
Song: "Johnnie Crack and Flossie Snail."
Song of the Mischievous Dog, The.
Sonnet: "Altarwise by owl-light in the halfway-house."
Sonnet: "And from the windy West came two-gunned Gabriel."
Sonnet: "Cartoons of slashes on the tide-traced crater."
Sonnet: "Death is all metaphors, shape in one history."
Sonnet: "First there was the lamb on knocking knees."
Sonnet: "From the oracular archives and the parchment."
Sonnet: "Let the tale's sailor from a Christian voyage."
Sonnet: "Now stamp the Lord's Prayer on a grain of rice."
Sonnet: "This was the crucifixion on the mountain."
Sonnet: "What is the metre of the dictionary?"
Sonnets.
This Bread I Break [Was Once the Oat].
This Side of the Truth.
Tombstone Told When She Died, The.
Twenty-four Years.
Two Sonnets.
Under Milk Wood, *sels.*
Under the Apple Boughs.
Vision and Prayer.
We Lying by Seasand.
When All My Five and Country Senses See.
Why East Wind Chills.
Winter's Tale, A.
Thomas, Edith Matilda
Autumn Fashions.
Babushka; a Russian Legend.
Betrayal of the Rose, The.
Blooming of the White Thorn, The.
Breath of Hampstead Heath.
Britons and Guests.
Christopher of the Shenandoah, A.
Evoe!
Far Cry to Heaven, A.
Fir-Tree, The.
Frost.
Frost To-Night.
If Still They Live.
In the Lilac-Rain.
Insomnia.
Inverted Torch, The, *sels.*
Little Boy's Vain Regret, A.
Moly.
Mother England.
Mother Who Died Too, The.
Muses, The.
Music.
Patmos.
Ponce de Leon.
Quiet Pilgrim, The.
Red Cross Nurse, The.
Reply of Socrates, The.
Soul in the Body, The.
Talking in Their Sleep.
Tears of the Poplars, The.
Tell Me.
Tell me, is there sovereign cure.
Thefts of the Morning.
To Imagination.
To Spain—a Last Word.
Triumph of Forgotten Things, The.
When in the First Great Hour.
Will It Be So?
Winter Sleep.
Thomas, Edward ("Edward Eastaway) "
Adlestrop.
And sedge-warblers, clinging so light.
As the Team's Head-Brass.
Aspens.
Beauty.
Bright Clouds.
Brook, The.
Cat, A.
Chalk-Pit, The.
Clouds That Are So Light, The.
Cock Crow.
Combe, The ("The combe was ever dark").
Cuckoo, The.
Dark Forest, The.
Digging.
Early One Morning ("Early one morning in May I set out").
February Afternoon.
Fifty Faggots.
Gallows, The.
Glory, The.
Good-Night.
Green Roads, The.
Gypsy, The.
Haymaking.
Head and Bottle.
If I Should Ever by Chance.
In Memoriam; Easter 1915.
It Rains.
Liberty.
Lights Out.
Lights Out.
Like the Touch of Rain.
Lob.
Long Small Room, The.
Manor Farm, The.
Melancholy.
Mill-Pond, The.
New House, The.
No One Cares Less Than I.
No One So Much as You.
October.
Old Man.
Out in the Dark.
Owl, The.
Path, The.
Penny Whistle, The.
Private, A.
Rain.
Sedge Warblers.
Sign-Post, The.
Snow.
Sowing.
Sun Used to Shine, The.
Swedes.
Tale, A.
Tall Nettles.
Tears.
Thaw.
There Was a Time.
There's Nothing like the Sun.
Trumpet, The.
Two Houses.
Two Pewits.
Under the Woods.
Unknown Bird, The.
When First I Came Here.
What Shall I Give?
Will You Come?
Wind and Mist.
Women He Liked.
Word, The.
Words.
Thomas, Evan
To the Noble Woman of Llanarth Hall.
Thomas, Frederick William
Song: "'Tis said that absence conquers love!"
Thomas, Gilbert
Across the Fens.
Christmas Carol, A: "Star that shone on Bethlehem, shine on London city."
Cup of Happiness, The.

Thomas (continued)
Invocation: "There is no balm on earth."
Ploughman, The.
Red Sky at Morning.
Unseen Bridge, The.
Thomas, Lorenzo
Onion Bucket.
Twelve Gates.
Thomas, Louisa Carroll
What Is Charm?
Thomas, Martha Banning
Chirrupy Cricket, The.
Gentle Storm.
Thomas, Percy
Give Me a Gentle Heart.
Thomas, Philip Edward *See* **Thomas, Edward**
Thomas, Richard W.
Amen.
Index to a Black Cartharsis.
Jazzy Vanity.
Just Making It.
Revolution!!
Worker, The.
Thomas, Ronald Stuart
Affinity.
Age.
Airy Tomb, The.
Alpine.
Anniversary.
Autumn on the Land.
Belfry, The.
Blackbird Singing, A.
Bread.
Chapel Deacon.
Children's Song.
Country Clergy, The.
Cynddylan on a Tractor [in Spring].
Dance, The.
Day in Autumn, A.
Death of a Peasant.
Enigma.
Epitaph: "Poem in the rock and, The."
Farm Child.
Farm Wife.
For the Record.
Here.
Hill Farmer Speaks, The.
In a Country Church.
In Church.
January.
Job.
Labourer, The ("There he goes, tacking against the fields").
Labourer, A ("Who can tell his years, for the winds have stretched").
Lament for Prytherch.
Looking at Sheep.
Madrigal: "Your love is dead, lady, your love is dead."
Maker, The.
Moor, The.
Muck Farmer, The.
Musician, The.
On the Farm.
Peasant, A.
Person from Porlock, A.
Pisces.
Poacher, The.
Poetry for Supper.
Saint Antony.
Servant.
Song: "We, who are men, how shall we know?"
Strangers.
Too Late.
View from the Window, The.
Village, The.
Walter Llywarch.
Welcome.
Welsh History.
Welsh Landscape.
Welsh Testament, A.
Thomas, Rosemary
Between Two Worlds.
East River.
Thomas, T. E.
Roosevelt.
Thomas à Kempis
From one Word are all things, and this one all things speak.
Imitation of Christ, *sels.*
Immunity.
Joys of Heaven, The.
Man Proposes.
Of Love of Silence and of Solitude.
Royal Way of the Holy Cross, The.
Thoughts of Death, The.
Trust.
Thomas Aquinas, Saint
Adoro Te Devote.
Hymn: "Sing, my tongue, the Saviour's glory."
Lauda Sion.
O Salutaris Hostia.
Pange Lingua Gloriosa.
Thomas Aquinas, Sister
Arbor Una Nobilis.
Thomas More, Saint *See* **More, Sir Thomas**
Thomas of Celano
Dies Irae.
Thomas of Hales
Love-Song, A, *abr.*
Where Is Paris and Heleyne?
Thomas of Strengnaes
Ode to Freedom.
"Thomond, Bard of." *See* **Hogan, Michael**
Thompson, Ann Louise
Leafless Tree, A.
Thompson, D'Arcy Wentworth
Once upon a Time.
Poor Dear Grandpapa.
Two Magpies Sat on a Garden Rail.
Thompson, Donald
On the Relative Merit of Friend and Foe, Being Dead.
Thompson, Dorothy Brown
Arbor Day.
Autosonic Door.
Boy Washington, The.
City and the Trucks, The.
Continental Crossing.
Fe-Fi-Fo-Fum, *sel.*
Getting Back.
I do like ogres.
I Like House Cleaning.
Lemonade Stand.
Maps.
Our House.
Parlor Car.
Plans.
Pony Express, The.
Round and Round.
This Is Halloween.
Thompson, Dunstan
Articles of War.
In All the Argosy of Your Bright Hair.
Knight of Ghosts and Shadows, A.
Largo.
Lay of the Battle of Tombland, The.
Moment of the Rose, The.
Nor Mars His Sword.
Ovid on the Dacian Coast.
This Loneliness for You Is like the Wound.
Thompson, Edith Osborne
Monkeys, The.
Thompson, Everard V.
Diversity.
Thompson, Francis
Ad Amicam.
Ad Castitatem.
After Woman, The.
All Flesh.
All's Vast.
Any Saint, *abr.*
Arab Love-Song, An.
Assumpta Maria.
At Lord's.
Athwart the sod which is treading for God.
Before Her Portrait in Youth.
But lo! at length the day is lingered out.
Carmen Genesis.
Child's Prayer, A.
Contemplation.
Correlated Greatness.
Counsel of Moderation, A.
Daisy.
Dedication: "If the rose in meek duty."
Desiderium Indesideratum.
Dread of Height, The.
Dream-Tryst.
Echo of Victor Hugo, An, *sel.*
Envoy: "Go, songs, for ended is our brief, sweet play."
Epilogue: "Heaven, which man's generations draws."
Epilogue: "Virtue may unlock hell."
Ex Ore Infantium.
Fair Inconstant, The.
Fallen Yew, A.
Field-Flower.
From the Night of Forebeing, *abr.*
Grace of the Way.
Heart, The, *sels.*
Hound of Heaven, The.
If with exultant tread.
In No Strange Land.
Judgement in Heaven, A.
Judgment [*or* Judgement] in Heaven, A, *sels.*
Kingdom of God, The.
Life's a veil the real has.
Lilium Regis.
Lillium Regis.
Lines for a Drawing of Our Lady of the Night.
Little Jesus.
Making of Viola, The.
May Burden, A.
Messages.
Mistress of Vision, The.
Nature one hour appears a thing unsexed.
Night of Forebeing, The.
Nocturn.
Now that the red glare of thy fall is blown.
O sweet is love, and sweet is lack!
Ode to the Setting Sun.
Orient Ode.
Our God Finds Us.
Pastoral: "Pan-imbued/ Tempe wood."
Poppy, The.
River has not any care, The.
Sister Songs, *sels.*
Sun, The.
To a Poet Breaking Silence.
To a Snowflake.
To Daisies.
To My Godchild—Francis M. W. M.
To Olivia.
To the Dead Cardinal of Westminster.
To the English Martyrs.
Tokens, The.
Veteran of Heaven, The.
We Poets Speak.
Thompson, Frederic
Constant.
Heaven and Earth.
Plan for a Novel.
Thompson, Irene

Caravans.
Country Child, The.
Feet.
Holiday Train, The.
Penny Wish, A.
Rainy Nights.
Secret Places.
Swinging.
Town Child, The.
Welcome to Spring.
Thompson, J. W.
Work.
Thompson, James Maurice *See* **Thompson, Maurice**
Thompson, James W.
Arms & Exit.
Beauty Then Is Being.
Mock Pop Forsooth: A Tale of Life and Death.
Thompson, John
Adventurers, The.
Chess.
Letter to a Friend.
Lyric: "Songs of adolescence, The."
Refuge.
Thompson, John, Jr
Birthday Poem, November 4th.
Love for Patsy, A.
Thompson, John B.
Chiaroscuro.
Thompson, John Beauchamp
Passover.
Thompson, John Reuben
Ashby.
Burial of Latané, The.
Lee to the Rear.
Music in Camp.
Obsequies of Stuart.
On to Richmond.
Thompson, Larry
Black Is Best.
Thompson, Leslie
There Are So Many Ways of Going Places.
Thompson, Leslie P.
Song of Satisfaction on Completing an Overhauling of Fishing Tackle, A.
Thompson, Lewis
Black Angel.
Rose.
Thompson, Lulu E.
In Hardin County, 1809.
Thompson, Maurice
Ballad of Chickamauga, The.
Creole Slave-Song, A.
Early Bluebird, An.
Flight Shot, A.
Lincoln.
Lincoln's Grave, *sel.*
Lion's Cub, The.
Prelude, A: "Spirit that moves the sap in spring."
Prophecy, A.
Wild Honey.
Written on a Fly-Leaf of Theocritus.
Thompson, Vance
Linen Bands.
Symbols.
Thompson, Will Henry
Come Love or Death.
High Tide at Gettysburg, The.
Thompson, William
Book, a friend, a song, a glass, A.
Happy Life, The, *sel.*
Thomsen, Grímur
Iceland's Song.
Thomson, Annie Howe
After the Storm.
Thomson, Claire Aven
Tranquil Sea.
Thomson, Edward William
Aspiration.
Canadian Rossignol, The.
Thomson, James (1700-1748)
All-intellectual eye, our solar round.
Approach of Winter.
As rising from the vegetable World.
At length the finished garden to the view.
Autumn.
Birds in Spring.
Britannia, *sel.*
Britannia's Empire.
British Commerce.
Castle of Indolence, The, *sels.*
Clear frost succeeds, and thro' the blew serene.
Doors that knew no shrill alarming bell, The.
Fled is the blasted verdure of the fields.
For ever, fortune, wilt thou prove.
From all the livid east or piercing north.
Frost at Night.
Happy Britannia.
He Heard Her Sing, *sel.*
Hymn: "These, as they change, Almighty Father, these."
Hymn on Solitude.
Hymn on the Seasons, A.
Indifference to Fortune.
Land of Indolence.
Late, in the louring sky, red, fiery, streaks.
Lavinia.
Liberty, *sel.*
Lisy's Parting with Her Cat.
Lo! from the Livid East.
Lost Shepherd, The.
Love of Nature.
Melancholia.
Moonlight in Autumn.
Now, solitary, and in pensive guise.
Now, when the cheerless empire of the sky.
O mortal man, who livest here by toil.
Ode: "Tell me, thou soul of her I love."
On the Death of a Particular Friend.
On the Death of Mr. William Aikman the Painter, *sel.*
Poem Sacred to the Memory of Sir Isaac Newton, A.
Praise of Industry, The.
Sea-Birds.
Seasons, The, *sels.*
Sheep Shearing, The.
Sheep-washing, The.
Sometimes the pencil, in cool airy halls.
Song: "One day the god of fond desire."
Sons of Indolence.
Spring.
Spring Flowers.
Storm, The ("Behold, slow-settling . . .").
Storm, The ("See, winter comes . . .").
Summer, *sels.*
Summer Evening and Night.
Summer Morning.
To the Memory of Sir Isaac Newton, *sel.*
To the Reverend Mr. Murdoch.
Verses Occasioned by the Death of Dr. Aikman.
What art thou, frost? and whence are thy keen stores.
When from the pallid sky the sun descends.
Winter ("See Winter comes, to rule the varied year").
Winter Scene.
Winter Storm, A.
Winter Winds.
Witching Song, A.
Wondrous Show, A.
Woodland Choir, The.
Thomson, James (1700-1748), *and* David Mallet *or* Malet *or* Maloch
Alfred, a Masque, *sel.*
Rule, Britannia!
Thomson, James ("B.V." *or* "Bysshe Vanolis)
Art, *sels.*
As I Came through the Desert.
As We Rush, as We Rush in the Train.
Bear Up Awhile.
Because he seemed to walk with an intent.
Bridge, The.
City is of Night, The; perchance of death.
City of Dreadful Night, The.
E. B. B.
Fire That Filled My Heart of Old, The.
For I Must Sing of All I Feel and Know.
Gifts.
Give a Man a Horse He Can Ride.
He stood alone within the spacious square.
How the moon triumphs through the endless nights.
I Looked Out into the Morning.
I Sat Me Weary on a Pillar's Base.
In the Room.
In the Train.
L'Ancien Régime.
Large glooms were gathered in the mighty fane.
Life's Hebe.
Midsummer Courtship.
Of all things human which are strange and wild.
Once in a Saintly Passion.
Proem: "Lo, thus, as prostrate, 'In the dust I write.'"
Reflection.
Requiem, A.
Richard Forest's Midsummer Night, *sel.*
Song: "Let my voice ring out and over the earth."
Song: "Like violets pale i' the spring o' the year."
Song: "My love is the flaming sword."
Song of Sighing, A.
Sphinx, The.
Sunday at Hampstead, *sel.*
Sunday up the River, *sels.*
To Our Ladies of Death.
Two Sonnets.
Vanity.
Vine, The.
Why Are Your Songs All Wild and Bitter Sad.
William Blake.
Wine of Love Is Music, The.
Thoreau, Henry David
All Things Are Current Found.
Among the Worst of Men That Ever Lived.
At Midnight's Hour I Raised My Head.
Atlantides, The.
Between the Traveller and the Setting Sun.
Conscience.
Crow, The.
Epitaph on the World.
Fall of the Leaf, The.
Fisher's Boy, The.
For Though the Caves Were Rabitted.
Forever in My Dream and in My Morning Thought.
Great Adventure, The.
Great Friend.
Great God, I Ask Thee for No Meaner Pelf.
Haze.
I Am a Parcel of Vain Strivings Tied [*or* Sic Vita].
I Saw a Delicate Flower Had Grown Up 2 Feet High.
I Was Born Upon Thy Bank, River.

Thoreau (continued)
I Was Made Erect and Lone.
I will not doubt for evermore.
I'm Thankful that My Life Doth Not Deceive.
Independence.
Inspiration.
Inward Morning, The.
It is No Dream of Mine.
Lately, Alas, I Knew a Gentle Boy.
Light-winged Smoke, Icarian Bird.
Lines: "Though all the Fates should prove unkind."
Love.
Love Equals Swift and Slow.
Low-anchored Cloud.
Manhood.
Men Say They Know Many Things.
Mist.
Moon Now Rises [to Her Absolute Rule], The.
My Books I'd Fain Cast Off, I Cannot Read.
My Life Has Been the Poem.
My Prayer.
Nature.
Old Marlborough Road, The.
On the Sun Coming Out in the Afternoon.
Prayer: "Great God, I ask Thee for no meaner pelf."
Railroad, The.
Sic Vita.
Smoke.
Smoke in Winter.
Stanzas: "Nature doth have her dawn each day."
Summer Rain, The.
Sympathy.
Tall Ambrosia.
Though All the Fates Should Prove Unkind.
To a Marsh Hawk in Spring.
To the Maiden in the East.
To the Mountains.
Walden, *sel.*
Walden (*poem*).
Week on the Concord and Merrimack Rivers, A, *sels.*
What's the Railroad to Me?
When Winter Fringes every Bough.
Who Sleeps by Day and Walks by Night.
Winter Memories.
Within the Circuit of This Plodding Life.
Woof of the Sun [Ethereal Gauze].

Thorley, Wilfrid
Buttercups.
Chant for Reapers.
Child-Thought, A.
Fan, the Filly.
Grocer and the Gold-Fish, The.
Hansom Cabbies.
Happy Sheep, The.
Harvest Elves, The.
Norse Sailor's Joy.
Of a Spider.
Old Inn-Sign, The.
Roger Francis.
Song for a Ball-Game.

Thorn, John
Man's flitting life findes surest stay.

Thornbury, George Walter
Cavalier's Escape, The.
Court Historian, The.
Death of Marlborough, The.
Jacobite on Tower Hill, The.
Jester's Sermon, The.
La Tricoteuse.
Melting of the Earl's Plate.
Old Grenadier's Story, The.
Pompadour, The.
Sally from Coventry, The.
Smith of Maudlin.
Three Scars, The.
Three Troopers, The.
White Rose over the Water, The.

Thorne, Anna H.
Peace Universal.

Thornton, Eliza
Reign of Peace, The.

Thornton, Francis Beauchesne
Snow Meditation.

Thornton, Lalia Mitchell
Blue Ribbon Cats.
Change.
Forgive.

Thornton, M. B.
Limerick: "All young men should take note of the case."
Limerick: "There once was a popular crooner."

Thorp, H. M.
Finger Folk.

Thorpe, Rose Hartwick
Curfew Must Not Ring Tonight.

Thorson, Inez Clark
Progression.

Thorsteinsson, Steingrímur
Swansong on the Moorlands.

Thrale, Hester Lynch (Mme Piozzi)
Three Warnings, The.

Thring, Godfrey
Jesus Christ the Lord.
Jesus Comes on Clouds Triumphant.

Thrupp, Dorothy Ann
Good Shepherd, The.

Thurber, James
Further Fables for Our Times, *sel.*
Morals.

Thurlow, Edward Hovell-Thurlow, 2d Baron *See* **Hovell-Thurlow, Edward**

Thurman, Judy
Penelope.

Thwaite, Anthony
At Birth.
At Dunwich.
Child Crying.
Looking On.
Manhood End.
Pond, The.
Rites for a Demagogue.

Thwaites, Michael
Easter Hymn.
Prophetic Hour, The.
Thermopylae.
To J. S. Bach.

Tibullus, Albius
Elegies, *sel.*
Elegy, An: "Let others pile their yellow ingots high."
No Harm to Lovers.
Pastoral Elegy, A.
Recantation, The.
Sulpicia's Rival.

Tichborne [*or* Tichbourne), Chidiock
Elegy: "My prime of youth is but a frost of cares."
His Elegy.
Lament the Night before His Execution, A.
Lines before Execution.
On the Eve of His Execution.
Poem, Written on the Eve of Execution.
Retrospect.
Tichborne's Elegy, Written [with His Own Hand] in the Tower before His Execution.
Untimely End, The.
Written on the Eve of Execution.
Written the Night before His Execution.

Tickell, Thomas
Colin and Lucy.
Fairies.
Kensington Gardens, *sel.*
Lucy and Colin.
Ode Inscribed to the Earl of Sunderland at Windsor, An.
Poverty and Poetry.
To the Earl of Warwick on the Death of Mr. Addison.
Widow and Virgin Sisters, The.

Ticknor, Francis Orrery [*or* Orray],
Albert Sidney Johnston.
Battle Ballad, A.
Little Giffen.
Our Left.
Song for the Asking, A.
Virginians of the Valley, The.

Tieck, Johann Ludwig
Autumn Song.
Love.

Tiemer-Wille, Gertrude
Repast.

Tiempo, César (*originally* Israel Zeitlin)
Harangue on the Death of Hayyim Nahman Bialik.
I Tell of Another Young Death.
Weeping and Singing.

Tierney, Joseph Paul
Donne Redone.

Tietjens, Eunice
April.
Bacchante to Her Babe, The.
City Wall, The.
Completion.
Drug Clerk, The.
Fulfillment.
Fun with Fishing.
Great Man, The.
Imprisoned.
Most-Sacred Mountain, The.
Moving.
My Mother's House.
Old Friendship.
Old Maps.
On the Height.
Parting after a Quarrel.
Pioneer Woman, The—In the North Country.
Psalm to My Belovèd.
Steam Shovel, The.
Thaw.
To My Friend, Grown Famous.

Tighe, Mary
To a Little Girl Gathering Flowers.

Tikhonov, Nikolai
Fire, the Rope.

Tilden, Ethel Arnold
Dedication: "We dedicate a church today."

Tilden, Stephen
Braddock's Fate, with an Incitement to Revenge.
British Lyon Roused, The.

Tillam, Thomas
Uppon the First Sight of New England.

Tiller, Terence
Bathers.
End of the Story, The.
Epithalamion: "Wind in the street, and sadness of unknown walkers."
Image in a Lilac Tree.
Killed in Action.
No Time.
Perfumes.
Poem: "Grecian tulip and the gothic rose, The."
Prothalamion.
Reading a Medal.
Street Performers, 1851.
Vase, The.

Tillett, Wilbur Fisk
Incarnate Love.
My Father Knows.

Tilley, Lucy Evangeline
When Even Cometh On.
Tilton, Theodore
Coeur de Lion to Berengaria.
Even This Shall Pass Away.
Flight from the Convent, The.
Fly, The.
God Save the Nation.
Great Bell Roland, The.
King's Ring, The.
Sir Marmaduke's Musings.
Timrod, Henry
At Magnolia Cemetery.
Carolina.
Charleston.
Christmas.
Cotton Boll, The.
Cry to Arms, A.
Decoration Day at Charleston.
Dreams.
Ethnogenesis.
I Know Not Why, but All This Weary Day.
I Scarcely Grieve, O Nature!
Love and Life.
Magnolia Cemetery.
Most Men Know Love But as a Part of Life.
Ode: "Sleep sweetly in your humble graves."
Ode for Decoration Day.
Ode Sung on the Occasion of Decorating the Graves of the Confederate Dead.
Ode to the Confederate Dead.
Quatorzain.
Serenade: "Hide, happy damask, from the stars."
Sonnet: Most Men Know Love.
Spring.
Trifle, A.
Unknown Dead, The.
Tinckom-Fernandez, W. G.
Beloved Vagabond, The.
Tindley, C. A.
Nothing Between.
"Tipcuca." *See* **Wilson, T. P. Cameron**
Tiplady, Thomas
Above the Hills of Time.
Grace, A.
Hymn of the Unemployed.
O Thou, who love in mercy hast created.
Prayer for the Presence of Christ, A.
Wedding Hymn, A, *sel.*
Wedding Hymn, A ("Jesus, stand beside them").
When Life's Day Closes.
When the Daylight Wanes.
Tippett, James Sterling
Autumn Woods.
Building a Skyscraper.
Busy Carpenters.
Circus Parade.
Counting the Days.
Do Not Open until Christmas.
Ducks at Dawn.
Elevated Train, The.
Engine.
Familiar Friends.
Ferry-Boats.
First Zeppelin, The.
Freight Boats.
George Washington.
Green Bus, The.
Hang Out the Flags.
I Like Christmas.
My Taxicab.
Old Log House.
Park, The.
River Bridge, The.
"Sh."
Sleet Storm.
Spider Webs.
Squirrel.
Sunning.
Trains.
Trucks.
Tugs.
Underground Rumbling.
Up in the Air.
Tipple, E. H.
Hot Weather in the Plains—India.
Titherington, Richard Handfield
Faithful unto Death.
Titley, Walter
Reply, in the Same Measure and Number of Lines, A [Horace, 2d Ode, 3d Book].
Second Ode in the Third Book of Horace, Imitated.
Tobias, Ruby Weyburn
Cross, The.
Food.
Prayer Time.
True Apostolate, The.
Tobin, James Edward
Conversation in Clichés.
Cradle Song of a Celtic Queen.
Madonna of the Exiles.
Song above Death.
Todd, Alice
If.
Postman, The.
Todd, Barbara Euphan
Aunt Matilda.
Fairy Story.
Jeremy's Secrets ("Jeremy's six, so his sisters say").
Todd, Earl D.
Resurrection and Ascension.
Todd, Ruthven
Lonely Month, The.
Mantelpiece of Shells, A.
Personal History; for My Son.
Six Winters.
To a Very Beautiful Lady.
Various Ends.
Watching You Walk.
Todhunter, John
Aghadoe.
Banshee, The.
Black Knight, The.
Maureen.
O Mighty, Melancholy Wind.
Song: "Bring from the craggy haunts of birch and pine."
Toelle, Gervase
Fra Carmelo's Morning Sacrifice.
Toerien, Barend
Absent Daughter.
Campi Flegrei.
Firmament Displays on High, The.
Quatrain: "My bloodstream chokes on gall and spleen."
Youth.
Tofte, Robert
Alba, *sel.*
As burnish'd gold, such are my sovereign's hears.
Down from the neck unto that dainty breast.
Laura, *sels.*
Love's Labour Lost.
Rich damask roses in fair cheeks do bide.
Strange is this thing! My horse I cannot make.
Two winds, one calm, another fierce to see.
Unto thy favor, which when nature formed.
What time with brow the loveliest gins to scowl.
When I did part from thee the other night.
When she was born she came with smiling eye.
"Togo, Hashimura." *See* **Irwin, Wallace**
Toleson, M. Beaunurus *See* **Tolson, Melvin Beaunearus**
Tolkien, John Ronald Renel
Goblin Feet.
Roads Go Ever On and On.
Sing All Ye Joyful.
Toller, Ernst
Book I Held Grew Cold, The.
Corpses in the Wood.
Marching Song.
O Heavy Step of Slow Monotony.
O Master Masons.
O My Swallows!
One Who Struggles, The.
To the Dead of the Revolution.
To the Living.
To the Mothers.
Tollet, Elizabeth
On this resemblance—where we find.
Tolson, Melvin Beaunearus
African China.
Dark Symphony.
Do.
Harlem Gallery, *sels.*
John Henry in Harlem.
Lamda.
Libretto for the Republic of Liberia, *sel.*
New Negro strides upon the continent, The.
Night John Henry is born an ax, The.
Rendezvous with America, *sel.*
Sea-Turtle and the Shark, The.
Tolstoy, Aleksey Konstantinovich
Well, A.
Tomlinson, Charles
Antecedents.
At Barstow.
At Delft.
Cavern, The.
Crane, The.
Distinctions.
Farewell to Van Gogh.
Four Kantian Lyrics.
Fox, The.
Hand at Callow Hill Farm, The.
How Still the Hawk.
Icos.
In Defense of Metaphysics.
Jam Trap, The.
Las Trampas U. S. A.
Le Musée Imaginaire.
Meditation on John Constable, A.
More Foreign Cities.
Observation of Facts.
Ode to Arnold Schoenberg.
On the Hall at Stowey.
Paring the Apple.
Picture of J. T. in a Prospect of Stone, The.
Poem: "Upended, it crouches on broken limbs."
Portrait in Stone.
Ruin, The.
Tramontana at Lerici.
Winter Encounters.
Tompkins, Harriet Hartridge
Silent Stars Go By, The.
Tompson, Benjamin
Chelmsfords Fate.
Edmund Davie 1682, Annagram.
Marlburyes Fate.
New-England's Crisis.
Not ink, but bloud and tears now serve the turn.
On a Fortification at Boston Begun by Women.
Seaconk or Rehoboths Fate.
Seaconk Plain Engagement.

Tompson (continued)
Supplement, A.
To My Honoured Patron Humphery Davie.
Town Called Providence, Its Fate, The.
"Tomson, Graham R." *See* **Watson, Rosamund Marriott**
Toness, Louise H.
Is This Presumption?
Tongue, Robert Clarkson
God's Plow of Sorrow.
Tonna, Charlotte Elizabeth
Maiden City, The.
Tooker, Lewis Frank
"He Bringeth Them unto Their Desired Haven."
His Quest.
Homeward Bound.
Last Fight, The.
Old Conservative, The.
Sea-King, The.
Sleep.
Toomer, Jean
At Sea.
Banking Coal.
Beehive.
Blue Meridian, The.
Brown River, Smile.
Carma, *sel.*
Cotton Song.
Each new American.
Evening Song.
Face.
Five Vignettes.
Georgia Dusk.
Her skin is like dusk on the eastern horizon.
Karintha, *sel.*
Lost Dancer, The.
November Cotton Flower.
Reapers.
Song of the Son.
Toplady, Augustus Montague
Ah! Give Me, Lord, the Single Eye.
Compared with Christ.
Deathless Principle, Arise.
Happiness Found, *sel.*
Lord It Is Not Life to Live.
Prayer, Living and Dying, A.
Rejoicing in Hope.
Rock of Ages.
Torgersen, Eric
Aubade.
Cage, The.
I'm Married.
Jensen: a Slideshow.
Legends.
Story of White Man Leading Viet Cong Patrol, The.
Torlino
Therefore I Must Tell the Truth.
Tormey, Michael
Ancient Race, The
Torregian, Sotère
Age of Gold, The.
Eulogy of the Vain Hours.
Is It for This I Live?
On the Anniversary of the Death of Frank O'Hara.
On the Death of Frank O'Hara.
Poem: "Everyone who is anyone is moving away."
Poem Written During Sleep.
Torrence, Ridgely
Adam's Song of the Visible World, *much abr.*
Bird and the Tree, The.
Carpe Diem.
Ceremony for Birth and Naming.
Compensation.
Conclusion of the Whole Matter, The.
Evensong.
Eye-Witness.
House of a Hundred Lights. The, *sels.*
Invitation.
Legend.
Lincoln's Dream.
Santa Barbara Beach.
Singers in a Cloud, The.
Son, The.
Three o'Clock—Morning.
Tramp Sings, The.
Young Lovers, The.
Youth and Age.
"Totius" [J. D. Du Toit]
Forgive and Forget.
Toulet, Paul [*or* Pierre] Jean
Simple Things.
Touré, Askia Muhammad
Floodtide.
Tourneur, Cyril
And now methinks I could e'en chide myself.
Atheist's Tragedy, The, *sels.*
Cease that harsh musick; we are not pleas'd with it.
Epitaph on a Soldier.
Madame, his grace will not be absent long.
My study's ornament, thou shell of death.
O hour of incest!
Ravish me in thine answere; art thou rare.
Revenger's Tragedy, The, *sels.*
Soldier's Death, A.
Walking Next Day upon the Fatal Shore.
Toussaint-L'Ouverture, Isaac
Farewell: "Shores of my native land."
Tovey, Herbert G.
Sure Promise, A.
Towle, Tony
After Dinner We Take a Drive into the Night.
Allegorical Figure of Brooklyn, The.
City in the Throes of Despair, The.
Collaboration.
Daybreak.
Elegy: "We eat and hear, as your kiss descends."
Enchantment.
For Irma During April.
Fourteenth Street.
From the Spanish.
George Towle.
Music.
New York.
Poem: "Engineer pushes a button in the mountains, An."
Poem: "Sky is cut into sections and put on a frame, The."
Towne, Anthony
Dead of Winter.
Towne, Charles Hanson
Around the Corner.
At Nightfall.
Best Road of All, The.
City Roofs.
Deathless Tale, The.
Easter.
Easter Canticle, An: "In every trembling bud and bloom."
Easter Prayer, An.
In Summer.
Manhattan.
Memories.
Messed Damozel, The.
Messengers.
Nightfall.
Of One Self-slain.
Pilot and Prophet.
Prayer for the Old Courage, A.
Prayer to the Giver.
Quiet Singer, The.
Roof-Tops.
Roosevelt—Pilot and Prophet!
Silence.
Song: "I saw the day's white rapture."
Song at Easter, A.
Thanksgiving.
Time-Clock, The.
Victors, The, *abr.*
Townsend, Annie Lake
Sursum Corda.
Townsend [*or* Townshend], Aurelian
Constant Lover, The.
Kind and True.
Love's Victory.
Paradox, A.
Pure Simple Love.
Though Regions Far Divided.
To the Countesse of Salisbury.
To the Lady May.
Youth and Beauty.
Townsend, Emily
Fish.
Townsend, F. H.
State the alternative preferred.
To the Cuckoo.
Townsend, George Alfred
Army Correspondent's Last Ride.
In Rama.
Townsend, Lilburn H.
Hand of Labor.
Townsend, Mary Ashley ("Xariffa")
At Set of Sun.
Creed.
Dead Singer, The.
Down the Bayou.
Embryo.
Georgia Volunteer, A.
Her Horoscope.
Reserve.
Townshend, Aurelian *See* **Townsend, Aurelian**
Traherne, Thomas
Felicity.
For Man to Act.
From dust I rise.
Hosanna.
I do believ.
Infant-Ey, An.
Infant's Eye, An.
Innocence.
Insatiableness.
Life of Sabbaths here beneath, A.
Love.
Mankind Is Sick.
My Spirit.
News.
O Lord, I wonder at thy lov.
On Christmas-Day.
On Leaping over the Moon.
On News.
One star/ Is better far.
Poverty.
Preparative, The.
Rapture, The ("Sweet infancy!/ O Heavenly Fire!").
Recovery, The.
Return, The.
Review, The.
Right Apprehension.
Salutation, The.
Serious and a Curious Night-Meditation, A.
Shadows in the Water.
Shake off thy sloth, my drowsy soul, awake.
Sin!/ O only fatal woe.
Solitude.
Thanksgiving for the Body.
Thanksgiving for the Beauty of His Providence.
Things native sweetly grew.
Third Century, The, *sels.*

To the Same Purpos [He, Not Long Before].
To Walk Abroad.
Understanding.
Vision, The.
Walking.
Wonder.

Traill, Henry Duff
After Dilettante Concetti.
Drawing-Room Ballad, A.
Puss and the Boots, The, *sel.*
Put case I circumvent and kill him: good.
Vers de Société.

Trakl, Georg
De Profundis.
In Hellbrunn.
On the Way.
Peace and Silence.
Rats, The.
Rest and Silence.
Whispered to the Afternoon.

Traller, Mae
Man's Hand—and God's.

Tramp, Edgar
Consecration.

Trapnell, Edna Valentine
Fiddler, The.

Trask, Katrina (Kate Nichols Trask)
Aidenn.
Army of the Red Cross, The.
At Last.
Love.
New Banner, The.
Sorrow.

Trask, Willard
October.
Pastoral: "I, who have ridden the world."

Traubel, Horace Logo
Chants Communal, *sel.*
Epicedium.
How Are You, Dear World, This Morning?
I served in a Great Cause.
If All the Voices of Men.
What Can I Do?

Tree, Iris (Mrs. Curtis Moffat)
To My Father.
You Preach to Me of Laws.

Tree, Maude Holt, Lady (Mrs. Beerbohm Tree)
There is many a slipton.

Treece, Henry
Ballad: "Oh, come my joy, my soldier boy."
Birdwatcher.
Christ Child.
Crimson Cherry Tree, The.
Dyke-Builder, The.
Haunted Garden, The.
Heart's Wild Geese, The.
House, The.
In the Beginning Was the Bird.
In the Third Year of War.
Love Song.
Poem: "Death walks through the mind's dark woods."
Poem: "In the dark caverns of the night."
Poem: "Through the dark aisles of the wood."
Prayer in Time of War.
That Summer.
Waiting Watchers, The.
Walking at Night.
War Poem.
Warrior Bards, The.

Trefethen, Florence
Aquarium Dream, The.

Tremayne, Sydney
Moses.

Trench, Herbert
Ay, since beyond these walls no heavens there be.
Charge, A.
Come, Let Us Make Love Deathless.
I Heard a Soldier.
I Seek Thee in the Heart Alone.
Jean Richepin's Song.
Love.
Old Anchor Chanty.
She Comes Not When Noon Is on the Roses.
To Arolilia, *sel.*
Trees, The.
What Bids Me Leave.

Trench, Richard Chenevix
After the Battle.
Century of Couplets, A, *sel.*
Elegy: "This winter eve how soft! how mild!"
Gibraltar.
God Our Refuge.
Hour with Thee, An.
If There Had Anywhere Appeared.
In Thy Presence.
Kingdom of God, The.
Lord, Many Times I Am Aweary Quite.
Love Found Me.
Not Thou from Us!
Power of Prayer, The.
Prayer: "Lord, what a change within us one short hour."
Prevailing Prayer.
Recollections of Burgos.
Renunciation.
Retirement.
Some Murmur When Their Sky Is Clear.
Sonnet: "All beautiful things bring sadness, nor alone."
Sonnet: "I stood beside a pool, from whence ascended."
Sonnet: "Lord, what a change within us one short hour."
Sonnet: "Open wound which has been healed anew," An.
Sonnet: "Wretched thing it were, to have our heart, A."
Sonnet in a Pass of Bavaria.
This Were to Pray.
Who praises God the most, what says he more than he.

Trent, Lucia (Mrs. Ralph Cheyney)
All Too Slowly.
Architects of Dream.
Armistice Day.
Blessed Agitator, The.
Bread of Brotherhood.
Dreamers Cry Their Dream, The.
Frail Hands.
From Beyond.
It Is Not Too Late.
Mary's Son.
Master Surgeon.
Prayer: "Oh, kneel to that God force of love."
Query.
Song for Tomorrow.
These Are My People.
Thought on a News Item.
To Young Dreamers.

Trent, Lucia, *and* Ralph Cheyney
Ten Years After, *sel.*
Toward a True Peace.

Triem, Eve
Gardens Are All My Heart.

Trimmer, Ellen McKay
Inventory.

Trimpi, W. Wesley
Lines for a Wedding Gift.
Oedipus to the Oracle.
On a Bas-Relief.
To Giotto.

Trott, Harlan
Out from Gloucester.

Trott, Norman L.
No Time for God.

Trott, Perient
Negro Spiritual ("Sable is my throat").

Trotter, Bernard Freeman
Altars.
For Justice.
"Ici Repose."
Poplars, The.
Songs We Need, The.

Trotter, Mary Josephine *See* **Benson, Mary Josephine**

"Troubadour. "
Law of Averages, The.
Reversible Metaphor, The.

Troubetzkoy, Amélie Rives, Princess *See* **Rives, Amélie**

Troubetzkoy, Ulrich
Christmas Lullaby.
Out of the Wilderness.

Troupe, Quincy
Day in the Life of a Poet, A.
Dirge: "It is the endless dance."
Flies on Shit.
Splib Odyssey, A.
Wait, The.
White Weekend.

Trowbridge, John Philo
Lord, Is It I?

Trowbridge, John Townsend
At Sea.
Columbus at the Convent.
Cup, The.
Darius Green and His Flying-Machine.
Evening at the Farm.
Evening on the Farm.
Linclon.
Midsummer.
Midwinter.
Peewee, The.
Pewee [or Peewee], The.
Vagabonds, The.
Widow Brown's Christmas.

Troy, Grace E.
I Would Not Ask.
If He Should Come Today.
In Quietness.
My Need.
Profit or Loss.
Trials.
What Would He Say?

Truax, Hawley
Half.
Morning, Noon, and . . .

Trudell, Dennis
Art of Poetry, The.
Gambol.
Going to Pittsburgh.
Guest, The.
Jump Shooter, The.

Trueba y La Quintana, Antonio de
Nightfall.

Trumbull, Annie Eliot
To O. S. C.

Trumbull, John
Aging Coquette, The.
Amorous Temper, An.
At once with resolution fatal.
Country Clown, The.
Dick Hairbrain Learns the Social Graces.

Trumbull (continued)
Essay on the Fine Arts, *sel.*
Future of American Literature, The.
Harriet Simper Has Her Day.
Liberty Pole, The.
M'Fingal, *sels.*
Progress of Dulness, The, *sels.*
Prospect of the Future Glory of America.
Tom Brainless at College.
Tom Brainless Seeks a Wife.
Town Meeting, The, *abr.*
Trumbull, Rose
Mary.
Trypanis, Constantine A.
El Greco.
Four Lovely Sisters ("Four lovely spinsters, sisters to a king").
Turkish Garden.
Ts'ao Ho
Impatience.
Ts'ao Sung
Protest in the Sixth Year of Ch'ien Fu, A (A.D. 879).
War Year, The.
Tse Nan
Happy Farmer, The.
Ts'en Ts'an
Song of White Snow, A.
Tso Ssu
Scholar in the Narrow Street, The.
Tsurayuki (Ki no Tsurayuki)
Avenue of Trees, The.
Elegy, An: "So frail our life, perchance tomorrow's sun."
Flowers of Snow.
Heron cries in sorrow, The.
Tanka: Cry of the Crane, The.
Time I went to see my sister, The.
Wake, The.
Tsuru
Willows in the Snow.
Tuck, Clyde Edwin
Good Shepherd, The.
Tucker, Paul
Heavenly Friend, A.
Tucker, Robert G.
Security.
Tucker, St. George
Days of My Youth.
Tuckerman, Frederick Goddard
All men,—the preacher saith,—whate'er or whence.
And me my winter's task is drawing over.
And she, her beauty never made her cold.
And so the day drops by; the horizon draws.
As Eponina brought, to move the king.
As one who walks and weeps by alien brine.
Breeze is sharp, the sky is hard and blue, The.
But unto him came swift calamity.
By this low fire I often sit to woo.
Companions were we in the grove and glen!
Cricket, The.
Elegy in Six Sonnets.
Even as a lover, dreaming, unaware.
For Nature daily through her grand design.
His heart was in his garden; but his brain.
How most unworthy, echoing in mine ears.
How oft in schoolboy-days, from the school's sway.
Last night I dreamed we parted once again.
Morning comes, The; not slow, with reddening gold.
My Anna! though thine earthly steps are done.
My Anna! When for her my head was bowed.
Nor idle all, though naught he sees in thine.
Nor looks that backward life so bare to me.
Not proud of station, nor in worldly pelf.
Not the round natural world, not the deep mind.
Oh for the face and footstep!—Woods and shores!
One still dark night, I sat alone and wrote.
Perhaps a dream; yet surely truth has beamed.
Question, The.
Refrigerium.
Sometimes, when winding slow by brook and bower.
Sonnet: " All men,—the preacher saith,—whate'er or whence."
Sonnet: "And change with hurried hand has swept these scenes."
Sonnet: "And faces, forms and phantoms, numbered not."
Sonnet: "And me my winter's task is drawing over."
Sonnet: "And she, her beauty never made her cold."
Sonnet: "And so the day drops by; the horizon draws."
Sonnet: "As Eponina brought, to move the king."
Sonnet: "As one who walks and weeps by alien brine."
Sonnet: "Breeze is sharp, the sky is hard and blue, The."
Sonnet: "But unto him came swift calamity."
Sonnet: "By this low fire I often sit to woo."
Sonnet: "Companions were we in the grove and glen!"
Sonnet: "Even as a lover, dreaming, unaware."
Sonnet: "For Nature daily through her grand design."
Sonnet: "Gertrude and Gulielma, sister-twins."
Sonnet: "His heart was in his garden; but his brain."
Sonnet: "How most unworthy, echoing in mine ears."
Sonnet: "How oft in schoolboy-days, from the school's sway."
Sonnet: "Last night I dreamed we parted once again."
Sonnet: "Morning comes, The; not slow, with reddening gold."
Sonnet: "My Anna! though thine earthly steps are done."
Sonnet: "My Anna! When for her my head was bowed."
Sonnet: "Nor idle all, though naught he sees in thine."
Sonnet: "Nor looks that backward life so bare to me."
Sonnet: "Not proud of station, nor in worldly pelf."
Sonnet: "Not the round natural world, not the deep mind."
Sonnet: "Oh for the face and footstep!—Woods and shores!"
Sonnet: "O hard endeavor, to blend in with these."
Sonnet: "One still dark night, I sat alone and wrote."
Sonnet: "Perhaps a dream; yet surely truth has beamed."
Sonnet: "Roll on, sad world! Not Mercury or Mars."
Sonnet: "Sometimes, when winding slow by brook and bower."
Sonnet: "Still craves the spirit: never Nature solves."
Sonnet: "Still pressing through these weeping solitudes."
Sonnet: "Tall stately plants with spikes and forks of gold."
Sonnet: "That boy, the farmer said, with hazel wand."
Sonnet: "Thy baby, too, the child that was to be."
Sonnet: "Under the mountain, as when first I knew."
Sonnet: "Upper chamber in a darkened house, A."
Sonnet: "Yet even mid merry boyhood's tricks and scapes."
Sonnet: "Yet vain, perhaps, the fruits our care applaud."
Sonnet: "Yet wear we on; the deep light disallowed."
Sonnets, *sels.*
Still craves the spirit: never Nature solves.
Still pressing through these weeping solitudes.
Tall Stately Plants with Spikes and Forks of Gold.
That boy, the farmer said, with hazel wand.
Thy baby, too, the child that was to be.
Upper Chamber in a Darkened House, An.
Yet even mid merry boyhood's tricks and scapes.
Yet Vain, Perhaps, the Fruits.
Yet wear we on; the deep light disallowed.
Tuckerman, Henry Theodore
Washington's Statue.
Tu Fu
After Rain.
Arrival of a Guest, The.
Beautiful Woman, The.
Clear after Rain.
Cricket, The.
Day Comes.
Emperor, The.
Empty Purse, The.
Excursion, The.
Exile.
Farewell to Han So.
Fireflies, The.
In Absence.
Jade Flower Palace.
Little Rain, The.
Mongolian Horse, The.
Moon Festival.
Newlyweds' Separation, The.
Night in the House by the River.
Night Thoughts While Travelling.
Night Vigil in the Left Court of the Palace, A.
On Meeting Li Kuei-nien down the River.
Overnight in the Apartment by the River.
Rain.
Return, The.
Snow Storm.
Soldier-Statesman Returns, The.
Song of Dagger-Dancing, A, *sel.*
South Wind.
Temple, The.
There lived years ago the beautiful Kung-sun.
Thinking of My Brothers.
To Cheng on His Deposal.
To My Retired Friend Wei.
To Pi Ssu Yao.
Unexpected Visit, An.
View of T'ai-shan, A.
White Horse, The.
Willow, The.

With Her Beauty.
Written on the Wall at Chang's Hermitage.
Tu Hsün Hao
Man and the Sea.
Taoist Monk, The.
Taxes.
Tull, Jewell Bothwell
Plea for a Cat.
Sport for Gods.
Tullar, Grant Colfax
As Thy Days.
Tunstall, Virginia Lyne (Mrs. Robert Baylor Tunstall)
Evening on the Harbor.
Spinster Song.
Tupper, Helen Isabella
For Everything Give Thanks.
Give Thanks.
Thankful Hearts.
Thanks for Everything.
Tupper, Kathryn Munro *See* **Munro, Kathryn**
Tupper, Martin Farquhar
England's Heart.
Turberville [*or* Turbervile], George
Epitaph of Maister Win Drowned in the Sea, An.
George Turbervile in Praise of the Translator of This Book.
He Declares That Albeit He Were Imprisoned in Russia, Yet His Mind Was at Liberty and Did Daily Repair to His Friend.
Lover Abused Renounceth Love, The, *sel.*
Lover Exhorteth His Lady to Take Time, While Time Is, The.
Lover Extolleth the Singular Beauty of His Lady, The.
Lover to the Thames of London, to Favour His Lady Passing Thereon, The.
Of a Rich Miser.
Of Drunkenness.
Of the Clock and the Cock.
Pine to the Mariner, The.
That All Things Are as They Are Used.
That Death Is Not So Much to Be Feared as Daily Diseases Are.
That He Findeth [*or* Finds] Others as Fair, but Not So Faithful as His Friend.
That No Man Should Write but Such as Do Excel.
To a Fair Gentlewoman, False to Her Friend.
To an Old Gentlewoman.
To an Olde Gentlewoman, That Painted Hir Face.
To His Friend.
To His Friend, Promising That Though Her Beauty Fade, Yet His Love Shall Last.
To His Friend Riding to Londonward.
To His Love That Sent Him a Ring.
To His Ring, Given to His Lady.
To One That Had Little Wit.
To the Roving Pirate.
Unable by Long and Hard Travel to Banish Love, Returns Her Friend.
Verse in Praise of Lord Henry Howard, Earl of Surrey.
Was never day came on my head.
Turbyfill, Mark
Apollo Alone Approves.
Benediction.
Prayer for Sophistication.
Shapes.
Song for Souls under Fire, A.
Strangers.
Things Not Seen.
Turco, Lewis
Gather These Bones.
House and Shutter.
Ordinary Evening in Cleveland, An.
Seer, The.
Turner, Charles Tennyson
Artist on Penmaenmawr, The.
Buoy-Bell, The.
Calvus to a Fly.
Drowned Spaniel, The.
Forest Glade, The.
Forest Lake, A.
Great Britain through the Ice.
Her First-born.
Hydraulic Ram, The.
Julius Caesar and the Honey-Bee.
Lachrymatory, The.
Lattice at Sunrise, The.
Letty's Globe.
Lion's Skeleton, The.
Mary Queen of Scots.
Old Ruralities.
On the Eclipse of the Moon of October 1865.
Orion.
Rookery, The.
Seaside, The.
Steam Threshing-Machine, The.
Summer Twilight, A.
To a "Tenting" Boy.
To the Gossamer-Light.
Vacant Cage, The.
White Horse of Westbury, The.
Why Should We Weep for Those Who Die.
Turner, Darwin T.
Death.
Guest Lecturer.
Love.
Night Slivers.
Sit-in, The.
Sonnet Sequence.
To Vanity.
Turner, Eliza Sproat
Little Goose, A.
Turner, Elizabeth
Bird-Catcher, The.
Bird's Nest, The.
Canary, The.
Good Girl, The.
How to Write a Letter.
Letter, The.
Miss Sophia.
Mrs. Turner's Object-Lessons, *sels.*
New Book, The.
Politeness.
Rebecca's After-Thought.
Rudeness.
Turner, Esther H.
Resurrection.
Turner, Ethel
Boat on the Sea, A.
Christ-Child Day in Australia, A.
Turner, Eva Moad
Testimony.
Turner, Martha Provine Leach
Good Friday.
Turner, Nancy Byrd
Adventure.
Alley Cat, An.
Autumn!
Bagpipe Man, The.
Best Time of All, The.
Black and Gold.
Boy, Bare Your Head.
Buccaneer, The.
Careless Fairy, The.
Chairoplane Chant.
Christmas Star, The.
Click o' the Latch.
Contrary Mary.
Courage Has a Crimson Coat.
Dark-eyed Lad Columbus.
Death Is a Door.
Down a Sunny Easter Meadow.
Easter Joy.
Extraordinary Dog, The.
February Birthday.
Fellowship of Prayer, The.
First Christmas Night of All.
First Thanksgiving, The.
First Thanksgiving of All.
God with Us.
Going Up to London.
Good-Night.
I Wish.
Immigrants.
Legacy.
Let Us Have Peace.
Lincoln.
The Careless Fairy.
Little Girl That Mother Used to Be.
Little Road, The.
London Rain.
Mongrel Pup, A.
More than Flowers We Have Brought.
Old Man Long Ago.
Old Quin Queeribus.
Ordinary Dog, The.
Planting a Tree.
Pop Corn Song, A.
Prayer on Christmas Eve.
Prayer on Fourth of July.
Prince Peter.
Resolute Cat, The.
Rivers Remember, The.
Sampler, The.
Ships.
Spring Wind.
Sure Sign, A.
Teacher's Prayer, The.
They Will Look for a Few Words.
Twenty Foolish Fairies.
Washington.
Weather Factory, The.
When Young Melissa Sweeps.
Whenever I Say "America."
Wings and Wheels.
Word about Woodpiles, A.
Words.
Turner, Raymond
Buttons.
Find a Role, Define a Role.
Turner, Tom
Communion.
Turner, Walter James
Dancer, The.
Dragon Flies.
Ecstasy.
Epithalamium, *sel.*
Evening.
Forest-Bird, The.
Formal Lyric.
Giraffe and Tree.
Hunter, The.
Hymn to Her Unknown.
I had watched the ascension and decline of the moon.
In the Caves of Auvergne.
In Time like Glass.
India.
Life and Death.
Lion, The.
Love-Song, A.
Music.
Music of a Tree, The.
Navigators, The.
Poetry and Science.
Princess, The.
Reflection.
Robber, The.
Romance.
Seven Days of the Sun, The, *sels.*
Silence.

Turner (continued)
Song: "Fortunate are the feet of the swallow."
Song: "Lovely hill-torrents are."
Spirits walking everywhere.
Sun, The.
Talking with Soldiers.
Tragic Love.
Word Made Flesh, The.
Turner, William
Galymaufery, A.
Turners Dish of Lentten Stuffe; or, A Galymaufery.
Turner, William Price
Alien.
Coronary Thrombosis.
University Curriculum.
Tusiani, Joseph
Anticipation.
Rest O Sun I Cannot.
Tusser, Thomas
As True as Thy Faith, This Riddle Thus Saith.
Author's Life, The.
Christmas Husbandly Fare.
Description of an Envious and Naughty Neighbor, The.
Description of Life and Riches, A.
Description of the Properties of Winds All the [*or* at All] Times of the Year, A.
Description of Time and the Year, A.
Digression from Husbandry to a Point or Two of Huswifery, A.
Digression to Hospitality, A.
Hundreth good points of good husbandry, A.
July.
Ladder to Thrift, The.
March.
October's Husbandry.
Posies for Thine Own Bedchamber.
Praise of Husbandry, The.
Preface to the Book of Housewifery, The.
Preface to the Buyer of This Book, A.
September.
Sonnet upon the Author's First Seven Years' Service, A.
Upon the Author's First Seven Years' Service.
Winds, The.
Tuttle, Stella Weston
Quickening, The.
Tutwiler, Julia S.
Alabama.
Tuwim, Julian [*or* Juljan]
Epos.
Prayer, A: "I pray Thee O Lord."
Pursuit.
Request for a Song.
There Is No Country.
"Twain, Mark" (Samuel Langhorne Clemens)
Adventures of Huckleberry Finn, The, *sel.*
Adventures of Tom Sawyer, The, *sel.*
Don't Copy Cat.
Missouri Maiden's Farewell to Alabama, A.
Ode to Stephen Dowling Bots, Dec'd.
Tweedsmuir, John Buchan, 1st Baron *See* **Buchan, John**
Tweedy, Henry Hallam
Christmas at Babbitt's.
Eternal God, Whose Power Upholds.
Twells, Henry
At Even, when the Sun Was Set.
Twig, John
Ballade of the Nurserie, A.
Twynham, Leonard
Old Dog.
Tychborn, Chidiock *See* **Tichborne, Chidiock**
Tylee, Edward Sydney
Outward Bound.
Tyler, Inez M.
Call to Pentecost, A.
Tyler, Parker
To a Photograph.
Tyler, Royall
Epigram: "How many drag the marriage chain."
Independence Day.
Tylor, Edward Burnett, *and* Andrew Lang *See* **Lang, Andrew, *and* Edward Burnett Tylor**
Tymnes
Maltese Dog, A.
Tynan, Katharine (Katharine Tynan Hinkson)
Ass Speaks, The.
Aux Carmélites.
Beloved, The.
Chanticleer.
Childless Woman in Heaven, The.
Christmas Eve in Ireland.
Cuckoo Song.
De Profundis.
Dead Coach, The.
Desire, The.
Doves, The.
Easter.
Epitaph, The: "Write on my grave when I am dead."
Farewell: "Not soon shall I forget."
Flying Wheel, The.
Footpath Way, The.
Girl's Song, A.
God on the Hearth, The.
House of Life, The.
I was born under a kind star.
In Time of Need.
Larks.
Last Voyage, The.
Leaves.
Little Ghost, The.
Lux in Tenebris.
Making of Birds, The.
Man of the House.
Mater Dei.
Meeting, The.
Memory, A.
Michael the Archangel.
Nightingale, The.
Of an Orchard.
Old Love, The.
Passiontide Communion.
Pink Almond.
Planting Bulbs.
Prayer, A: "Now wilt me take for Jesus' sake."
Quiet Nights, The.
Sad Mother, The.
She Asks for New Earth.
Sheep and Lambs.
Singing Stars.
Slow Spring.
Ten Lepers, The.
Turn o' the Year.
Wild Geese.
Witch, The.
Tyrrell, Henry
Lincoln.
Lincoln [*or* The Masterful Man *or* Lincoln's Way].
Lincoln's Way.
Masterful Man, The.
Tyrrell, Robert Yelverton
Johnny, I Hardly Knew Ye: In Swinburnese, *parody.*
Tyrtaeus
How Can Man Die Better.
Tyrwhitt, Richard St. John
Glory of Motion, The.
Tytler, James
I Hae Laid a Herring in Saut.
Tyutchev, Feodor Ivanovich
As Ocean's Stream.
July 14, at Night.
Last Love.
Night Wind.
Nightfall.
Service of the Lutherans, The.
Silentium.
Tears.
Twilight.

U

Udall [*or* Udal], Nicholas
I Mun Be Married a Sunday.
Minion Wife, A.
Ralph Roister Doister, *sels.*
Ufford, Edward Smith
Throw Out the Lifeline.
Ugga Byan
Her Absent Lord, *sel.*
This is a colder winter than last year.
Uhland, Ludwig (Johann Ludwig Uhland)
Castle by the Sea, The.
Durand of Blonden.
Hostess' Daughter, The.
Ichabod! Thy [*or* The] Glory Has Departed.
In a Lovely Garden Walking.
King on the Tower, The.
Leaf, A.
Spirits Everywhere.
Ulrich von Lichtenstein [*or* Liechtenstein]
Love, Whose Month Was Ever May.
Umaki
At an Old Battlefield.
Unamuno, Miguel de
Brazier Coals, The.
Castile.
Domestic Scenes.
Look not upon me with such eyes, my son.
When the Shades of Night Have Come.
Underhill, Evelyn (Mrs. Stuart Moore)
Corpus Christi.
Holy Spirit, The.
Immanence.
Introversion.
Lady Poverty, The.
Supersensual.
Theophany.
Underwood, Ellen H.
I Shall Not Pass Again This Way ("The bread that bringeth strength").
Service.
Underwood, John Curtis
Central, *sel.*
Strong, The.
Though men may build their bridges high and plant their piers below the sea.
Wave, The.
Underwood, Wilbur
Cattle of His Hand, The.
To the Brave Soul.
Ungaretti, Giuseppe
Island, The.
Quiet.
San Martino del Carso.
Soldiers, The.
Without More Weight.
Unland, Ludwig
Luck of Edenhall, The.
Unterecker, John
Anemones of Collioure, The.

Dolphin.
Fish.
Rain Portrait.
Statement.
Untermeyer, Jean Starr
Altar, The.
Autumn.
Birthday.
Clay Hills.
Country of No Lack.
Dew on a Dusty Heart.
End of Summer.
False Enchantment.
From the Day-Book of a Forgotten Prince.
Glimpse in Autumn.
Gothic.
High Tide.
Lake Song.
Last Plea.
Little Dirge.
Lullaby for a Man-Child.
Old Nurse Winter.
One Kind of Humility.
Passionate Sword, The.
Sinfonia Domestica.
Sung on a Sunny Morning.
Thaw.
Untermeyer, Louis
Against Time.
Any Sunset.
Appeal to the Phoenix.
Archibald MacLeish Suspends the Five Little Pigs, *parody.*
Arise! Arise!
At the Bottom of the Well.
Boy and Tadpoles.
Burning Bush.
Caliban in the Coal Mines.
Catalogue.
Cell-Mates.
Coal Fire.
Dark Chamber, The.
Dick Said.
Disenchanted.
Dog at Night.
Dream and the Blood, The.
Edgar A. Guest Considers "The Old Woman Who Lived in a Shoe" and the Good Old Verities at the Same Time.
Einstein among the Coffee-Cups.
Equals.
Fairies.
Fantasy.
Feuerzauber.
First Words before Spring.
Folk-Song: "Back she came through the trembling dusk."
Food and Drink.
Frustrate.
Glad Day.
God's Youth.
Goliath and David.
Hair-dressing.
Hands.
Important People.
Infidelity.
Irony.
Jerusalem Delivered.
Jewish Lullaby.
John Masefield Relates the Story of Tom, Tom, the Piper's Son, *parody.*
Just Home.
Koheleth.
Landscapes.
Last Words before Winter.
Leviathan.
Long Feud.
Love.
Mandy's Lay.
Matter.
Mother Goose Up-to-Date, *parodies.*
Oh, the swift plunge into the cool, green dark.
Obituary.
On the Birth of a Child.
On the Eve of New Wars.
Only of You [*or* Thee] and Me.
Owen Seaman.
Portrait of a Child.
Portrait of a Machine.
Prayer: "God, although this life is but a wraith."
Prayer: "God, though [*or* although] this life is but a wraith."
Prayer for a New House.
Prayer for Courage.
Prayer for This House.
Questions at Night.
Reveille.
Road Song.
Robert Frost.
Rondeau: "Do you recall what I recall?"
Round: "Worlds, you must tell me."
Scarcely Spring.
Shoes.
Sleepers, The.
Song Tournement: New Style.
Spring Song of a Super-Blake.
Summer Storm.
Supplication.
Swimmers.
Ten Years Old.
Then, the quick plunge into the cool, green dark.
To a Weeping Willow.
Transfigured Swan.
Unreasoning Heart.
Victory in the Cabarets.
W. H. Davies Simplifies the Simplicities He Loves.
Walter de la Mare Tells the Listener about Jack and Jill, *parody.*
Waters of Babylon.
Wise Woman, The.
Young Mystic, The.
Untermeyer, Richard, *and* Louis Untermeyer
Storm, The.
Updike, John
Bendix.
Deities and Beasts.
Ex-Basketball Player.
Great Scarf of Birds, The.
I Like to Sing Also.
January.
Mirror.
Mosquito.
Newlyweds, The.
October.
Ode, An: "I'm going to write a novel, hey."
Party Knee.
Philological.
Quilt.
Scenic.
Seagulls.
Seven Stanzas at Easter.
Sonic Boom.
Sunflower.
Telephone Poles.
V. B. Nimble, V. B. Quick ("V. B. Wigglesworth wakes at noon").
Vow.
Winter Ocean.
Youth's Progress.
Upham, Sam C.
Song of the Argonauts.
Ye Ancient Yuba Miner, of the Days of '49.
Upham, Thomas Cogswell
Song of the Pilgrims.
Upson, Arthur
After a Dolmetsch Concert.
Ex Libris.
Failures.
Incurables, The.
Old Gardens.
Song: "Flame at the core of the world."
Vers la Vie.
Upson, Arthur, *and* Truman E. Rickard
See **Rickard, Truman E., *and* Arthur Upson**
Upton, James
Lass of Richmond Hill, The.
Upton, Minnie Leona
Tabitha Soliloquizes.
Traveling Light.
Upward, Allen
Acacia Leaves, The.
Bitter Purple Willows, The.
Estuary, The.
Intoxicated Poet, The.
Jonquils, The.
Marigold, The.
Mermaid, The.
Middle Kingdom, The.
Milky Way, The.
Scented Leaves from a Chinese Jar.
Stupid Kite, The.
Windmill, The.
Word, The.
Urdang, Constance
Children, The.
Madman, The.
Urmy, Clarence Thomas
Arrow, The.
As I Came Down Mount Tamalpais.
At the Edge of the Day.
Blondel.
I Lay My Lute beside Thy Door.
Old Year, The.
Woodland Revel, A.
Urquhart, Gertrude Boughton
Coming of Mary Louise, The.
Uschold, Maud E.
Casual Gold.
March Wind.
Moonlight.
November Rain.
Usher, Leila
I Am the Cat.
U'Tam'si, Tchicaya (Gerard Felix-Tchicaya)
Debout, *sel.*
Here is the stream again under the rainbow.
Scorner, The.
Utter, Robert Palfrey
Swan Boat, A.

V

"V., B." *See* **Thomson, James (1834-1882)**
"Vagaland." *See* **Robertson, T. A**
Valdés, Gabriel de la Concepción. *See* **"Plácido"**
Valdivielso, José de
Seguidilla.
Valencia, Consuelo
After Christmas.
Valencia, Guillermo
Sursum.
Valentine, Edward Abram Uffington
Helen.
Spirit of the Wheat, The.
Valentine, Jean
To a Friend.
Valéry, Paul
Caesar.

Valéry (continued)
Cemetery by the Sea, The.
Footsteps, The.
Helen, the Sad Queen.
Hélène.
Marine Cemetery, The.
Narcissus.
Pomegranates.
Steps, The.
Valle, Adriano del
Cradle Song of the Elephants.
Valle, Isabel
Very Minor Poet Speaks, A.
Vallejo, César
Battles? No! Agonies! And before the agonies.
Hymn to the Volunteers of the Republic, *sel.*
Vallis, Val
Fishing Season.
For This, the Tide.
Michael.
Vanada, Lillian Schulz
Fuzzy Wuzzy, Creepy Crawly.
Van Alstyne, Frances Jane Crosby *See* **Crosby, Fanny**
"Van Avond, Jan." *See* **Slater, Francis Carey**
Van Brakle, John
Easter.
Easter Message.
Vanbrugh, Sir John
Aesop, *sel.*
In the Sprightly Month of May.
Nightingale, The.
Philira.
Provoked Wife, The, *sel.*
Song: "Fly, fly, you happy shepherds, fly."
Van Buren, D. B.
Eternal Question, The.
Van Buskirk, Alden
Kitchen.
Lami Poem ("Lami, leather nightingale").
Miracle traced on a plate in, The.
New Miles Poem.
Nightletter, *sel.*
Not after but within this poem I stalk my lovers.
Tales, *sel.*
Vance, Abner
Vance Song, The, *with music.*
Vance, Thomas H.
Frozen Hero, The.
Van Cleve, Florence
Books.
Star of Bethlehem.
"Vandegrift, Margaret" (Margaret Thomson Janvier)
Clown's Baby, The.
Little Wild Baby.
Sandman, The.
Van Den Heever, C. M.
Fallen Zulu Commander, The.
Vander Ark, Bertha Prince
Soul, A.
Vanderbilt, John
Highways and Byways.
Vanderbilt, Sanderson
December.
Van de Water, Frederic F.
Last Tourney, The.
Van Doren, Mark
And Then It Rained.
April, 1942.
Autonomous.
Axle Song.
Bitten.
Burial.
Cat and the Miser, The.
City Songs.
Civil War.
Close Clan, The.
Comedy.
Crow.
Defeated Farmer.
Distant Runners, The.
Donkey.
End, The.
Epitaphs; for a Fickle Man.
Escape, The.
Eternity's Low Voice.
Exaggerator.
Fields of November, The.
Foreclosure.
Former Barn Lot.
God of Galaxies, The.
He's Coming.
His Trees.
History Lesson.
If They Spoke.
Immortal.
Inconsistent.
It Should Be Easy.
Jonathan Gentry, *sel.*
Let There Be Law.
Marriage.
Midwife Cat.
Moments He Remembers, The.
Morning Worship.
Music God.
Nap.
Never Another.
No Communication.
No Faith.
Old Hundred.
Oldest Cemetery.
Once the Wind.
Our Lady Peace.
Praise Doubt.
Private Worship.
Proper Clay.
Pulse, The.
Return to Ritual.
Runaways, The.
Sonnet VI: "Chasten your fears, I have not been destroyed."
Sonnet XIV: "I was confused; I cannot promise more."
Sonnet XXXIII: "My only need—you ask me, and I tell you."
Spring Thunder.
Story-Teller, The.
Tall Tale God.
That Day.
This Amber Sunstream.
Thomas Hardy, Poet.
To a Child with Eyes.
To the Author of Hesperides and Noble Numbers.
Tom's Sleeping Song.
Tourist.
Tower, The.
Tragedy.
Traveling Storm.
Two of You.
Undersong.
When the World Ends.
Whisperer, The.
Why, Lord.
Wind in the Grass.
Winter Tryst.
Young Woman at a Window.
Van Dusen, Ruth B.
Prayer in a Country Church.
Van Duyn, Mona
Gentle Snorer, The.
Van Dyke, Henry
Adoration.
America for Me.
America's Prosperity.
America's Welcome Home.
Ancestral Dwellings, The.
Angler's Reveille, The.
Angler's Wish, An.
Builders, The.
Burning Bush, The.
But I think the king of that country comes out from his tireless host.
Child in the Garden, The.
Children in the Market-Place.
Christ of Everywhere.
Envoy: "Legend of Felix is ended, the toiling of Felix is done, The."
Face of a Friend, The.
Foundations.
Four Things.
Four Things to Do.
God of the Open Air, *sel.*
Gospel of Labor, The.
Grant us the knowledge that we need.
Great River, The.
Home.
Hymn of Joy.
Hymn of Labor.
I know that Europe's wonderful, yet something seems to lack.
If All the Skies [Were Sunshine].
Jesus, Return.
Jesus, Thou Divine Companion.
Legend of Service, A.
Let Me Live But from Year to Year.
Life.
Light between the Trees.
Lily of Yorrow, The.
Lost Word of Jesus, A.
Lover's Envy, A.
Mare Liberum.
Maryland Yellow-Throat, The.
Matins.
Mile with Me, A.
Mother's Birthday, A.
My April Lady.
Nativity, The.
Never in a costly palace did I rest on golden bed.
Night-Watch Prayer.
One in Christ.
Pan Learns Music.
Peace.
Peace Hymn of the Republic.
Prayer: "Lord, the newness of this day."
Prayer: "These are the gifts I ask of thee."
Red Cross, The.
Reliance.
Roslin and Hawthornden.
Salute to Trees, A.
Song Sparrow, The.
Tennyson.
These Are the Gifts I Ask.
They Who Tread the Path of Labor.
Things I Prize, The.
This is the gospel of labour, ring it, ye bells of the kirk!
Three Best Things, The,
Thy Sea Is Great, Our Boats Are Small.
To the Child Jesus.
Toiling of Felix, The, *sels.*
Valley of Vain Verses, The.
Veery, The.
Victoria.
Voyagers.
Way, The.
Work.
Zest of Life, The.
Van Dyke, Tertius
Laughter and Tears.
Vandyne, Mary E.
Bald-headed Tyrant, The.
Nation's Birthday, The.
Van Fossan, Josephine
Mourning.
Vanhomrigh, Esther

Hail, blushing goddess, beauteous Spring!
Van Newkirk, Allen
Spring: "Now I know why I dream."
Spring: "Orpheus was a sadist."
Spring: "There are nothing but pipes and dripping faucets here."
Van Noppen, Leonard Charles
Man of Men, A.
"Vanolis, Bysshe." *See* **Thomson, James (1834-1882)**
Van Plattenhaus, Louisa
Love to My Lord.
Van Rensselaer, Mariana Griswold
Love's Prisoner.
Manners.
Typewriter, The.
Whispering Pine Tree, The.
Van Rensselaer, Peyton
At Twilight.
Van Rensselaer, Mrs. Schuyler *See* **Van Rensselaer, Mariana Griswold**
Van Slyke, Beren
Shepherds, The.
Van Stockum, Hilda
Hut, The.
Van Tassel, Etta May
Joy as Old as Breathing, A.
Splendid Flower, The.
Van Voorhis, Linda Lyon
Ad Matrem in Coelis.
"That Which Hath Wings Shall Tell."
To a Humble Bug.
Van Vorst, Marie (Mrs. Gaetano Cogiati)
Sing Again.
Van Winkle, Gertrude
Magic Waves.
Microphone, The.
My Radio.
Static.
Van Wyk Louw, N. P. *See* **Louw, N. P. van Wyk**
Van Wynen, Peter
May God Give Strength.
Van Zile, Edward Sims
Close up the Ranks.
Van Zyl, Tania
Horses of Marini, The.
House, The.
Man with the Hollow Breast, The.
Rope, The.
She Waited.
Two Women.
"Varley, John Philip." *See* **Mitchell, Langdon Elwyn**
Vasalis, M.
Sea Dike, The.
Vaughan, H. A.
Nocturne: "Wind is blowing from the hill, The."
Old Convict, The.
Vaughan, Henry
Admission.
After the Storm.
Anguish.
As Time One Day by Me Did Pass.
Ascension-Day.
Ascension-Hymn ("Dust and clay").
Ascension-Hymn ("They are all gone into the World of Light").
Awake! Glad Heart!
Begging.
Beyond The Veil.
Bird, The.
Book, The.
Brittish Church, The.
Burial of an Infant, The.
Buriall.
Childe-hood.
Childhood [*or* Childe-hood].
Christ's Nativity.
Cock-Crowing.
Come, Come, What Doe I Here?
Constellation, The.
Content.
Corruption.
Dawning, The.
Dear, beauteous Death! the jewel of the just.
Dear Night, This World's Defeat.
Death.
Dedication, The: "My God, thou that didst dye for me."
Departed Friends.
Distraction.
Dressing.
Dwelling Place, The.
Early Rising and Prayer.
Easter-Day.
Easter Hymn.
Eclipse, The.
Eternity.
Evening-Watch, The.
Fragment: "Walk with thy fellow-creatures: note the hush."
Friends Departed.
Friends in Paradise.
Garland, The.
God's Saints.
Good Friday.
H. Scriptures.
Holy Communion, The.
Holy Scriptures.
I Walked [*or* Walkt] the Other Day [to Spend My Hour].

Idle Verse.
Jews, The.
Joy of My Life!
Joy of My Life! While Left Me Here.
Knot, The.
Lamp [*or* Lampe], The.
Lampe, The.
Love and Discipline.
Man.
Mans Fall, and Recovery.
Match, The.
Metrum V.
Midnight.
Morning-Watch, The.
Mount of Olives ("Sweet sacred hill! on whose fair brow").
Mount of Olives ("When first I saw true beauty, and thy Joys").
Nature, Man, Eternity.
Night, The ("Dear night, this world's defeat").
Night, The ("Through that pure virgin-shrine").
O Do Not Go.
O thou art such, that I could be.
Observe God in His works: here fountains flow.
Palm-Sunday.
Palm-Tree, The.
Passion, The.
Peace.
Peace of Heaven, The.
Pilgrimage, The.
Praise.
Pursuit[e], The.
Pursuite, The.
Queer, The.
Quickness.
Regeneration.
Relapse, The.
Religion.
Resolve, The.
Resurrection and Immortality.
Retreat[e], The.
Retreate, The.
Revival, The.
Rhapsody, A.
Rom. Cap. 8. Ver. 19.
Rules and Lessons.
Sap, The.
Search, The.
Seed Growing Secretly, The.
Shall these early fragrant hours.
Shepheards, The.
Shepherds, The.
Shower, The.
Showre, The.
Silence, and Stealth of Day[e]s!
Since Thou Art Gone.
Son-Dayes.
Song to Amoret, A.
Starre, The.
Storm, The.
Sun-Days.
Sure, There's a Tie of Bodies!
Tempest, The.
They Are All Gone.
They Are All Gone into the World of Light.
Timber, The.
To a Bird after a Storm.
To Amoret [Gone from Him].
To His Books.
To His Friend ——.
To His Retired Friend, *sel.*
To the Best and Most Accomplished Couple.
Triumphant Entry, The.
Unprofitablenes.
Vanity of Spirit.
Vision, A.
Waterfall [*or* Water-Fall], The.
When Night Comes.
Whole Duty of Man, The.
World, The.
World of Light, The.
Wreath, The.
Vaughan, Thomas
Stone, The.
Vaughn, F. E.
Ballad of Chicken Bill, The.
Vaughn, James P.
Four Questions Addressed to His Excellency the Prime Minister.
Movie Queen.
So?
Three Kings.
Two Ladies Bidding Us "Good Morning."
Vaughn, Janet
Our Cat.
Our Dog.
Stormy Sea.
Vauquelin de la Fresnaye, Jean
Religion.
Vaux, Thomas, 2d Baron Vaux of Harrowden
Aged Lover Renounceth Love, The.
Bethinking Himself of His End, Writeth Thus.
Content.
Death in Life.
He Renounceth All the Effects of Love.
Image of Death, The.
In His Extreme Sickness.
Latter Day, The.
Lover, Disdained, Complaineth, A.
No Pleasure without Some Pain.
Of a Contented Mind.
Of the Mean Estate.
On a Contented Mind.
On the Instability of Youth.
Sins of Youth, The.
Vaval, Duraciné
Mangoes, The.
Vazakas, Byron
All the Farewells.
Midsummer Night's Dream.
Pavilion on the Pier, The.

Vazakas (continued)
Progress of Photography, The.
Skyscraper.
Vedder, Miriam
Epitaph for a Kitten.
Veel, Mary Colborne- *See* **Colborne-Veel, Mary**
Vega Carpio, Lope de *See* **Lope de Vega Carpio**
Veitch, John
Laird of Schelynlaw, The.
Veitch, Tom
Candy Bar.
Cats Climb Trees.
Clipping.
Cowboy Song.
Fifteen Years Past.
Final Toast, The.
Fine Thing, A.
Finest Thing, The.
Improved 4-Way.
It Is a Distinct Pleasure.
Last Time, The.
Naval Engagement.
Ordinary People on Sunday.
Poison Meat.
Principally.
Something to Eat.
Veley, Margaret
First or Last?
Japanese Fan.
Venable, William Henry
Battle Cry.
El Emplazado.
Forest Song.
Founders of Ohio, The.
John Filson.
Johnny Appleseed.
My Catbird.
National Song: "America, my own!"
School Girl, The.
Teacher's Dream, The.
Venantius Fortunatus *See* **Fortunatus**
Verdaguer, Jacinto
Five Roses.
Vere, Edward de, 17th Earl of Oxford
Choice, A.
Doubtful Choice, A.
Epigram: "Were I a king, I could command content."
His Good Name Being Blemished, He Bewaileth.
If Women Could Be Fair.
Lover Rejected Complaineth, A.
Of the Birth and Bringing Up of Desire.
Of the Mighty Power of Love.
Pains and Gains.
Renunciation, A.
Were I a King.
What Cunning Can Express.
White and Red.
Who Taught Thee First to Sigh?
Vergil [*or* Virgil] (Publius Vergilius Maro
Aeneid, The, *sels.*
Aurora now from Titan's purple bed.
Batalis and the Man, The.
Battle of Actium.
Boat Race, The.
Boxing Match, The.
Certain Books of Vergil's Aeneis, *sels.*
Chariot Race, The.
Corydon and Thyrsis.
Death of Turnus, The, *abr.*
Destiny of Rome, The.
Destruction of Troy, The.
Dido among the Shades.
Dido to Aeneas.
Dido's Hunting.
Eclogues, *sels.*
Eighth Pastoral of Virgil, The.
Entrance to Hell, The.
For thee, little boy, will the earth pour forth gifts.
Fourth Eclogue, The.
From God to God.
Full soon the Queen this crafty sleight 'gan smell.
Georgics, The, *sels.*
Golden Bough, The.
Honey-Farm, The, *abr.*
I that my slender oaten pipe in verse was wont to sound.
It was then night; the sounde and quiet slepe.
Lycidas and Moeris.
Marcellus.
Messiah, The.
Next I come to the manna, the heavenly gift of honey.
Ninth Eclogue.
Prelude: "What makes a plenteous harvest."
Rang'd on the Line Opposed, Antonius Brings.
Shepherd's Gratitude, The.
Sibylline Prophecy, The.
Sixth Book of the Aeneis, The, *sel.*
Then are the trackless copses alive with the trilling of birds.
Then Mercury 'gan bend him to obey.
Towart the evyn, amyd the symmyris heit.
We Have Paid Enough Long Since in Our Own Blood.
Welcome to the Sun.
What made thee then so keen to look on Rome?
What makes a plenteous harvest, when to turn.
With tentive list'ning each wight was settled in hark'ning.
Verhaeren, Emile
Cathedral of Rheims, The.
Fishermen, The.
I Bring to You as Offering Tonight.
Mill, The.
November.
Old Masters, The.
Poor, The.
She of the Garden.
Verlaine, Paul
A Clymène.
A la promenade.
Amour, *sels.*
Art of Poetry, The.
Art Poétique.
Auburn.
Autumn Song.
Avenue, The.
Chansons d'Automne.
Chevalier Malheur, Le.
Clair de lune.
Colloque sentimental.
Confession, A.
Cortège.
Crucifix, A.
Cythère.
Dans l'Allée.
En Bateau.
Exile.
Fairer is the sea.
Fantoches.
Femme et chatte.
God Has Spoken.
Green.
I Hate to See You Clad.
Il pleut doucement sur la ville.
Indolent, The.
Lassitude.
Lines in Order to Be Slandered.
Love Fallen to Earth.
Mandoline.
Moonlight.
My God Has Spoken.
Mystical Dialogue.
Pantomime.
Parsifal.
Pastel, A.
Piano, The.
Puppets.
Retinue.
Sagesse, *sels.*
Sentimental Colloquy.
Sentimental Conversation.
Sky Is Up above the Roof, The.
Slumber dark and deep.
Song of Autumn.
Sonnet: "And I have seen again the marvellous child."
Spleen.
Spring.
Tears and Rain.
Tears Fall within Mine Heart.
Tears in my heart that weeps.
Wind in the Wood.
Woman and Cat.
Verlon, Rene
Was It for This?
Vernède, Robert Ernest
Petition, A.
Verplanck, Gulian
Prophecy.
Verry, Isabel Williams
Alcestis.
Verstegan [*or* Verstegen], Richard (Richardowlands)
Lullaby: "Upon my lap my sovereign sits."
Our Blessed Lady's Lullaby.
Our Lady's Lullaby.
Upon My Lap My Sovereign Sits.
Vision of the World's Instability, A.
Verwey, Albert
Bridge, The.
Very, Jones
Abdolonymus the Sidonian.
April Snow, The.
Autumn Flowers.
Barberry-Bush, The.
Broken Bowl, The.
Call, The.
Clouded Morning, The.
Columbine, The.
Coming of the Lord, The.
Cottage, The.
Created, The.
Day.
Dead, The.
Earth, The.
Fugitive Slaves, The.
Garden, The.
Gifts of God, The.
Hand and Foot, The.
Health of Body, Dependent on Soul.
Idler, The.
In Him We Live.
Lament of the Flowers, The.
Latter Rain, The.
Life.
Light from Within, The.
Lost, The.
Love.
Man in Harmony with Nature.
Morning.
Nature.
New Birth, The.
New Man, The.
New World, The.
October.
Old Road, The.
On the Completion of the Pacific Telegraph.

On Visiting the Graves of Hawthorne and Thoreau.
Prayer, The: "Wilt thou not visit me?"
Presence, The.
Psyche.
Robin, The.
Ship Rock.
Silent, The.
Slave, The.
Song, The: "When I would sing of crooked streams and fields."
Soul-Sickness.
Spirit-Land, The.
Strangers, The.
Stranger's Gift, The.
Thy Beauty Fades.
Thy Brother's Blood.
To the Canary Bird.
Tree, The.
Wind-Flower, The.
Yourself.
"Vesey, Paul." *See* **Allen, Samuel**
"Vestal, Stanley" (Walter Stanley Campbell)
Fandango.
Kit Carson's Last Smoke.
Oliver Wiggins.
Viau, Théophile de
Sleep.
Vicente, Gil
Angelic Vilancete, The.
Auto of the Bark of Purgatory, The, *sel.*
Auto of the Four Seasons, The, *sel.*
Cantiga: "White and crimson, cheek and breast."
Hymn of the Angels and Sibyls.
Rose Song, The.
Song: Grace and beauty has the maid.
Song: "If thou art sleeping, maiden."
Song of the Three Angels.
Victor, Florence
Contest.
Victor, Marius
Diseases, famine, enemies, in us no change have wrought.
Vida, Marco Girolamo
De Bombycibus, *sel.*
Silkworm, The.
Vidal, Peire
Song of Breath.
Vidame de Chartres *See* **Chartres, Vidame de**
Vielé, Herman Knickerbocker
Good Inn, The.
Inn of the Silver Moon, The, *sel.*
Viereck, George Sylvester
After the Battle.
Haunted House, The.
On Broadway.
Viereck, Peter
Affirmations (I-III).
Big Crash Out West.
Blindman's Buff.
Counter-Serenade; She Invokes the Autumn Instant.
Crass Times Redeemed by Dignity of Souls.
Day's No Rounder than Its Angles Are, The.
Don't Look Now but Mary Is Everybody.
Ennui.
Fiftieth Birthday.
For Two Girls Setting Out in Life.
From Ancient Fangs.
Homecoming.
Kilroy.
Look, Hart, That Horse You Ride Is Wood.
Love Song to Eohippus.
My seven sons came back from Indonesia.
Now Kindness.
Planted Skull, The.
Poet.
Slacker Apologizes, The.
Small Perfect Manhattan.
Some Lines in Three Parts.
Some Refrains at the Charles River.
To a Sinister Potato.
To Be Sung.
Vale from Carthage.
Walk on Snow, A.
You All Are Static; I Alone Am Moving.
Vigny, Alfred de
Nature.
Sound of the Horn, The.
Vilakazi B. W.
Because.
I Heard the Old Song.
In the Gold Mines.
On the Gold Mines.
Then I'll Believe.
Vildrac, Charles
After Midnight.
Vilenkin, Nikolai Maksimovich *See* **"Minski, Nikolai Maksimovich"**
Villa, José Garcia
Be Beautiful, Noble, like the Antique Ant.
Between God's Eyelashes.
Divine Poems, *sels.*
God, Is, Like, Scissors.
God Said, "I Made a Man."
Manner of a Poet's Germination, The.
Mostly Are We Mostless.
Much, beauty, is, less, than, the, face, of.
My, Fellowship, with, God.
My Most. My Most. O My Lost!
My Mouth Is Very Quiet.
Now, If You Will Look in My Brain.
Poem: "Distinction is in fire and division, The."
Saw God Dead but Laughing.
Sir, I commend to you the spirit.
There Came You Wishing Me.
229.
Way My Ideas Think Me, The.
Within the city of my death.
Villegas, Antonio
Love's Extremes.
Villiers, George, 2d Duke of Buckingham *See* **Buckingham, George Villiers, 2d Duke of**
Villon, Françis
All Things except Myself I Know.
Arbor Amoris.
Ballad against the Enemies of France.
Ballad of Dead Ladies, The.
Ballad of Ladies' Love, Number Two.
Ballad of Poor Chimney Sweeps.
Ballad of the Gibbet.
Ballad of the Lords of Old Time.
Ballad of the Women of Paris.
Ballad Written for a Bridegroom.
Ballade of Dead Ladies.
Ballade of Ladies' Love.
Ballade of the Fair Helm-Maker.
Ballade of the Gibbet.
Ballade of the Hanged Men.
Ballade of the Women of Paris.
Ballade of Villon and Fat Margot.
Complaint of the Fair Armouress, The.
Dispute of the Heart and Body of Françis Villon, The.
Double Ballad of Good Counsel, A.
Epistle in Form of a Ballad to His Friends.
Epitaph in Form of a Ballad, The, Which Villon Made for Himself and His Comrades, Expecting to be Hanged Along with Them.
Fragment of Death.
Fragment on Death.
His Mother's Service to Our Lady.
Lament of "La Belle Heaulmière," The.
Lament of the Lovely Helmet-Dealer.
Lesser Testament, The.
Little Testament, The.
No, I Am Not as Others Are.
Old Woman's Lamentations, An.
Petit Testament, Le.
Rondel: "Good-by, the tears are in my eyes."
Roundel of Farewell.
Snows of Yester-Year, The.
To Death of His Lady.
Would I Be Shrived?
Vinal, Harold
Edict.
Enduring Music, The.
Flight.
Gentleman in Oils.
Ghostly Reaper.
Heimdall.
Hymnal: "Bringer of sun, arrower of evening, star-begetter and moon-riser."
Lesbia Sewing.
Miser.
Nights Remember, The.
Quest, The.
Sea Born.
Sea Longing.
Sleeping Village.
Toward Avernus.
We, the Few Who Believe.
Well-Finder, The.
Wreath for One Lost, A.
Vincent, Clarence A.
Heaven.
Vincente, Gil *See* **Vicente, Gil**
Vinograd, Julia
I Saw the Picture.
In the lights of this festival and my birthday.
Rising, The.
Shorthand.
Violante do Ceo, Sister
Night of Marvels, The.
While to Bethlehem We Are Going.
Viorst, Judith
True Love.
Virgil *See* **Vergil**
Virtue, Vivian L.
Atlantic Moonrise.
Gleaner, The.
To Claude McKay.
Visitation, Sister Mary of the *See* **Mary of the Visitation, Sister**
Vittorelli, Jacopo
On a Nun.
Sonnet: Addressed by a Father Mourning His Recently Deceased Married Daughter to the Father Whose Daughter Had Entered a Convent.
Vivian, Mary
Four Scarlet Berries.
Snowdrops.
Vivien, Geoffrey
Song of Self-Pity, A.
Vogelweide, Walther von der *See* **Walther von der Vogelweide**
Vogt, Anton
For a Child's Drawing.
For England, in Grateful Appreciation, *sel.*
I was five when we moved to England, and the strange voices.
Volimoeller, Karl Gustav
Nocturne in G Minor.
Voltaire (Francois Marie Arouet)
Inscription for a Statue of Love.
On Bell-Ringers.
On Jean Fréron.
On the Phrase, "To Kill Time."
Vondel, Joost van den
Adam's Hymn in Paradise.

Vondel (continued)
Chorus of Batavian Women.
Hymn of Adam, The.
Von Schlichten Henry J.
Lost, but Won.
Prayer of a Patriot.
Vories, William Merrell
Life.
Voss, Charles Hannibal
Yet Love Was Born.
Voss, J. H.
Who Does Not Love Wine, Women and Song.
Vrbovska, Anca
Dream Is a Cradle, The.
Vrepont, Brian
Apple Tree, The.
Bomber, The.
Earth.
Fishers, The.
Heron, The.
Net Menders, The.
Peace.
Song-Bird.
Vriesland, Victor van
Ars Poetica.
Evening.
Vulgarius, Eugenius
Metrum Parhemiacum Tragicum.

W

"W., A."
Desire's Government.
Dispraise of Love, and Lovers' Follies.
Fiction, A.
Give Me Leave.
Hopeless Desire Soon Withers and Dies.
In Praise of a Beggar's Life.
In Priase of the Sun.
Ladies' Eyes Serve Cupid Both for Darts and Fire.
Petition to Have Her Leave to Die.
Play, Beggars, Play!
Song, in Praise of a Beggers Life, A.
To Time.
Upon Visiting His Lady by Moonlight.
Where His Lady Keeps His Heart.
"W., E."
Folkways of Sodom, The.
"W., I"
Quiet Things.
"W., I. V. S."
Snowfall.
"W., L."
All Things Be Dear but Poor Mens Labour; or The Sad Complaint of Poor People.
"W., T. S."
Hints on Pronunciation for Foreigners.
"W. A. G." *See* **"G., W. A"**
"W. B." *See* **"B., W"**
Wabnitz, William S.
Hinds of Kerry, The.
Waddell, Elizabeth
Crusaders.
Waddell, Jean Percival
Half-Light.
Rhythm ("Rhythm in the pulse of Time").
Wadding, Luke
Christmas Day Is Come.
Waddington, Miriam
Cadenza.
Catalpa Tree.
Circles.
Drug Addict, The.
Green World Two.
Investigator.
Laughter.
Lovers.
Lullaby: "Hush dove the summer."
My Lessons in the Jail.
Restricted.
Season's Lovers, The.
Thou Didst Say Me.
Three Prison Portraits, *sel.*
Wonderful Country.
Waddington, Patrick D.
Lines to the Unborn.
Waddington, Samuel
Inn of Care, The.
Morning.
Mors et Vita.
Soul and Body.
Wade, Blanche Elizabeth
Song of the Christmas Trees.
Wade, James Palmer
Hymn to No One Body, A.
Wade, John Stevens
Antique.
Ascent, The.
Beyond the Panther.
Body Job.
Each to His Own Ground.
Goat Milkers, The.
Jigsaw.
Jimmy's Father.
"Nobody."
Ticktacktoe.
Upstairs.
Wade, Thomas
Birth and Death.
Coming of Night, The.
Copse, The.
Corporeal and Mental Vision.
Face, The.
Half-asleep, The.
Net-Braiders, The.
True Martyr, The.
Winter Shore, The.
Wadsworth, Olive A." (Katherine Floyd Dana)
Over in the Meadow.
Wonderful Meadow, The.
Waelty, Lucy M.
His Will Be Done.
Wagner, Charles Abraham
Beach Encounter.
Three City Cantos.
Unknown Soldier, The.
When I Loved You.
Wagner, Charles L. H.
Let's Forget.
Wagner, Mary Boyd
Lethal Thought, The.
Wagoner, David
Calculation, The.
Closing Time.
Diary.
Emergency Maker, The.
Feast, The.
Fruit of the Tree, The.
Gift of a Mirror to a Lady.
Hold-Up, The.
Leaving Something Behind.
Man from the Top of the Mind, The.
Murder Mystery.
Nesting Ground, The.
News from the Court.
Poets Agree to Be Quiet by the Swamp, The.
Shooting of John Dillinger outside the Biograph Theater, July 22, 1934, The.
Staying Alive.
Sudden Frost.
"Tan Ta Ra, Cries Mars . . ."
To My Friend Whose Parachute Did Not Open.
Tumbleweed.
Valedictory to Standard Oil of Indiana, A.
Warning to My Love, A.
Wagoner, Glenn E.
I Never Knew.
Wagstaff, Blanche Shoemaker
All Paths Lead to You.
Earth Trembles Waiting.
Pilgrimage.
Quiet Waters.
Wildness.
Waid, Willa Mae
When It's Iris Time in Tennessee.
Wain, John
Anecdote of 2 A.M.
Anniversary.
Apology for Understatement.
Au Jardin des Plantes.
Boisterous Poem about Poetry, A, *sel.*
Brooklyn Heights.
I have a notion that the world is round.
New Sun, The.
Poem: "Like a deaf man meshed in his endless silence."
Poem without a Main Verb.
Reason for Not Writing Orthodox Nature Poetry.
Sestina for Khasan Israelov.
Song about Major Eatherly, A.
This above All Is Precious and Remarkable.
Wildtrack, *sel.*
Wainwright, Vera
When we are older and the hidden fires.
Waite, Anne M.
My Rendezvous with God.
Waite, Arthur Edward
At the End of Things.
Cast away fear.
Waite, Shirley Dillon
Cross, The.
Wake, William Basil
Saying Not Meaning.
Wakefield, Jacques
Days Prior To.
It ain't no jive.
"Oh Shit a Riot!"
Our world is.
We Exist Living Dead.
Well well/ mah ace boo coo.
Wakefield, Nancy Amelia Woodbury
See **Priest, Nancy Woodbury**
Wakeford, Amelia
Thou Alone Canst Save.
Wakeley, Charles Russell
Gethsemane.
Love.
Wakley, Thirza
Easter Chick, An.
Mouse, The.
Spring Work at the Farm.
Wakoski, Diane
Apparitions Are Not Singular Occurrences.
Belly Dancer.
Child, a Wasp, and an Apricot Tree, A.
Coins and Coffins under My Bed.
Empress, The.
Follow That Stagecoach.
George Washington Absent from His Country.
Inside Out.
Justice Is Reason Enough.
Poem to the Man on My Fire Escape.
Six of Cups.
Sometimes Even My Knees Smile.
To Celebrate My Body.
Walafrid Strabo
To His Friend in Absence.
Walcott, Derek
Alba.
Bronze.
Far Cry from Africa, A.

In the middle of the harbour.
Letter from Brooklyn, A.
Man o'War Bird.
Nearing La Guaira.
Parang.
Polish Rider, The.
Ruins of a Great House.
Sea-Chantey, A, *sel.*
Whale, His Bulwark, The.
Waldeck, Heinrich Suso
Cleansing.
Walden, William
Flight.
Waldheim, Franklin
Help Wanted.
Waldman, Anne
About Face.
After Les Fleurs (Paul Eluard).
For You.
Sonnet for the Broken Windows.
Waldo, Rose
Camp Chums.
Kite Tales.
Sing-Time.
Take Care.
Welcome.
Waley, Arthur
Censorship.
Walford, William W.
Sweet Hour of Prayer.
Walker, Archibald Stodart- *See* **Stodart-Walker, Archibald**
Walker, Dee Lawrence
Et Cetera.
Walker, James J.
Will You Love Me in December as You Do in May?
Walker, Margaret Abigail
Childhood.
For Malcolm X.
For Mary McLeod Bethune.
For My People.
Harriet Tubman.
Iowa Farmer.
Lineage.
Molly Means.
October Journey.
We Have Been Believers.
Walker, Marion Mitchell
Chickadee.
Crocus.
Lilies of the Valley.
Meadow Lark.
Oriole.
Sleepy Tulips, The.
Walker, Paul
Leaves.
Walker, Ted
Breakwaters.
By the Bridge.
By the Saltings.
Dewdrop.
Estuary.
Harpooning, The.
Heron.
Homing Pigeons.
Lemons.
Mules.
On Scafell Pike.
Skimmers.
Walker, William Sidney
Death's Alchemy.
Too solemn for day, too sweet for night.
Wallace, Edna Kingsley
Christmas Eve.
Growing Up.
Wishes.
Wallace, James Cowden
God.
Wallace, John Aikman
Prayer Moves the Hand That Moves the World.
Wallace, Lew
Ben-Hur, *sel.*
Song: "Wake not, but hear me, love!"
Wallace, Robert
Ballad of the Mouse.
Crayfish, The.
Double Play, The.
Evening.
Fly in December.
In a Spring Still Not Written Of.
In Winter.
Snapshot for Miss Bricka Who Lost in the Semi-final Round of the Pennsylvania Lawn Tennis Tournament at Haverford, July, 1960, A.
Storm, The.
Wallace, William Ross
Hand That Rocks the Cradle Is the Hand That Rules the World, The.
Sword of Bunker Hill, The.
What Rules the World.
Wallace-Crabbe, Chris
Ancient Historian.
Love Poem: "Written under Capricorn, a land."
Waller, Edmund
Apologie for Having Loved Before, An.
Apology [*or* Apologie] for Having Loved Before, An.
At Penshurst ("Had Sacharissa liv'd when mortals made").
At Penshurst ("While in the park I sing, the listning deer.").
Battel of the Summer-Islands, The.
Battle [*or* Battel] of the Summer Islands, The.
Chloris and Hylas.
Chloris Farewell.
Dancer, The.
Go, Lovely Rose.
Last Verses.
Of a Fair Lady Playing with a Snake.
Of English Verse.
Of His Divine Poems.
Of His Majesties Receiving the News of the Duke of Buckingham's Death.
Of Loving at First Sight.
Of My Lady Isabella Playing on the Lute.
Of the Last Verses in the Book.
Old Age.
On a Girdle.
On Her Coming to London.
On My Lady Isabella Playing on the Lute.
On St. James's Park, as Lately Improved by His Majesty.
On the Head of a Stag.
Panegyrick to My Lord Protector, A [*or* Panegyrick upon O. Cromwell].
Plea for Promiscuity, A.
Poets Lose Half the Praise.
Say, Lovely Dream.
Self[e] Banished, The.
Selfe Banished, The.
Song: "Chloris! farewell. I now must go."
Song: "Go, lovely rose!"
Song: "Say, lovely dream! where couldst thou find."
Song: "Stay Phoebus, stay."
Soul's Dark Cottage, The.
Story of Phoebus and Daphne Applied, The.
To a Fair Lady Playing with a Snake.
To a Girl.
To a Lady in a Garden.
To a Lady Singing a Song of His Own Composing.
To a Very Young Lady.
To Amoret.
To Flavia.
To Mr. Henry Lawes [Who Had Then Newly Set a Song of Mine in the Year 1635].
To My Young Lady, Lucy Sidney.
To One Married to an Old Man.
To Phillis.
To Phyllis.
To the King on His Navy.
To the King, upon His Majesty's Happy Return.
To the Mutable Fair.
To the Younger Lady Lucy Sydney.
Under a Lady's Picture.
Upon Ben Jonson.
Upon Our Late Loss of the Duke of Cambridge.
While with a strong and yet a gentle hand.
Why Should We Delay?
Written in My Lady Speke's Singing-Book.
Waller, John
Enemy, The.
Legend.
Limb and Mind.
When Sadness Fills a Journey.
Waller, John Francis
Kitty Neil.
Spinning-Wheel, The.
Wallgren, A. Samuel
If Asked Whereon I Rest My Claim.
Wallin, Johan Olof
Watch, My Soul, and Pray.
Wallis, Eleanor Glenn
Deathless Ones, The.
Hunter, The.
In a City Square.
Iulus.
"Trade" Rat.
Wallis, George B.
Lovely Rivers and Lakes of Maine, The.
Walpole, Henry
Martyrdom of Father Campion, The.
Walpole, Horace, 4th Earl of Orford
Anne Grenville, Countess Temple, Appointed Poet Laureate to the King of the Fairies.
Countess Temple, Appointed Poet Laureate to the King of the Fairies.
Epitaph on Lady Ossory's Bullfinch.
To Lady Anne Fitzpatrick, When about Five Years Old [with a Present of Shells].
Walsh, Chad
Dust of Love, The.
Port Authority Terminal: 9 A.M. Monday.
When the Unnatural Warm Fair October.
Walsh, Edward
Fairy Nurse, The.
Kitty Bhan.
Mairgread ni Chealleadh.
Mo Craoibhin Cno.
Walsh, Ernest
Doctor Bill Williams.
I Played on the Grass with Mary.
Old Fellow.
Serious Poem, A.
Sonnet: "My duchess was the werst she laffed she bitte."
Walsh, J. Patrick
For the Magi.
Now That You Are Gone.
Walsh, Thomas
Coelo et in Terra.
Egidio of Coimbra (A.D. 1597).
Feast of Padre Chala, The.
Garden Prayer, A.
La Preciosa.
Russian Spring Song with Minaiev, A.
Street of Doctors, The.
Tears against the Moon.

Walsh (continued)
To an English Setter.
Walsh, William (1663-1708)
Death.
Despairing Lover, The.
Elegy: Unrewarded Lover, The.
Sonnet: Death.
Sonnet on Death.
To His Book.
Upon a Favour Offered.
Walsh, William (20th century)
Letter: The Japanese, to Her Husband at War.
Walsh, William F.
Conversation.
Walsh, William Thomas
Marriage Song.
Requiem.
Walter, Howard Arnold
I Would Be True.
My Creed.
Walter, Nehemiah
Elegiack Verse, on . . . Mr. Elijah Corlet, An.
Walter, Nina Willis
Candle and Book.
Walters, Lettice D'Oyly
Seville.
Walters, Lila V.
He Shall Speak Peace unto the Nations.
Walther von der Vogelweide
Awake!
Awake! The Day Is Coming Now.
Maria Bright.
Tandaradei ("Under der Linden").
There Is a Lady Conquering with Glances.
Uncourtly Love.
Under the Lime Tree.
Under the Linden[s].
With a Rod No Man Alive.
Walton, Alfred Grant
First Impressions.
Recipe for Living.
Sincere Man, The.
World We Make, The.
Walton, Eda Lou
Leda, the Lost.
Necessary Miracle, A.
Walton, Izaak
Angler's Wish, The.
Compleat Angler, The, *sel.*
Walworth, Clarence
Holy God, We Praise Thy Name.
Wandrei, Donald
Challenger, The.
Forest Shapes.
Lyric of Doubt.
Prehistoric Huntsman, The.
Water Sprite.
Woman at the Window, The.
Wangara, Malaika Ayo
From a Bus.
Wang Chang-ling
Under the Frontier Post.
Wang Chi
On Going to a Tavern.
Success.
Tell Me Now.
What Should a Man Want?
Wang Chien
Hearing That His Friend Was Coming Back from the War.
Newlyweds' Cuisine, The.
South, The.
Wang I
Lychee, The.
Wang Tsan
War in Chang-An City.
Wang Wei
Answering Vice-Prefect Chang.
Beautiful Hsi-shih, The.
Green Stream, A.
My Lodge at Wang-ch'uan after a Long Rain.
On Passing a Friend's House.
Parting, A.
"So Farewell."
Wanley, Nathaniel
Casket, The.
Fall, The.
Humaine Cares.
Human Cares.
Instead of incense (Blessed Lord) if wee.
Invitation, The.
Resurrection, The.
Royal Presents.
Royall Presents.
Sigh, The.
Wantling, William
Rune for the Disenchanted.
"Ward, Artemus" (Charles Farrar Browne)
Uncle Simon and Uncle Jim.
Ward, C. C.
Onion, The.
Ward, Edward
Ballad on the Taxes, A.
Ward, Elizabeth Stuart Phelps
Afterward.
Conemaugh.
Eternal Christmas.
Generous Creed, A.
Gloucester Harbor.
Little Mud-Sparrows, The; Jewish Legend.
Lost Colors, The.
Message, A.
Room's Width, The.
Ward, Jean
Autumn Healing.
Ward, Kenneth
Investor's Soliloquy.
Ward, Leo
Four Friends.
Last Communion, The.
Ward, Leo L.
Marginalia for Pentecost.
Ward, Lydia Avery Coonley
Baby Corn.
Flag Song.
Heredity.
Song for Flag Day, A.
To-Day.
Ward, Marion
I Love to Love.
Ward, May Williams
Wet Summer.
Ward, Nathaniel
Mercury shew'd Apollo, Bartas book.
Mr. Ward of Anagrams Thus.
Poetry's a gift wherein but few excell.
World's a well strung fiddle, mans tongue the quill, The.
Ward, Samuel
Proem, A: "When in my walks I meet some ruddy lad."
Ward, Terence
Kevin Barry.
Ward, William Hayes
New Castalia, The.
To John Greenleaf Whittier.
Ware, Eugene Fitch ("Ironquill") "
Aztec City, The.
Ballad in "G," A.
He and She.
Manila.
Whist.
Zephyr.
Ware, Mary Winter
Redemption.
Warfield, Catherine Anne
Beauregard.
Manassas.
Waring, Anna Laetitia
In Heavenly Love Abiding.
Surrender.
Warman, Cy
Creede.
Doing Railroads for *The Rocky Mountain News.*
Memorial Day.
Old Red Hoss Mountain.
Rise and Fall of Creede, The.
Sweet Marie.
Warner, Anna Bartlett ("Amy Lothrop', "
Daffy-down-dilly.
Let Us See Jesus.
We Would See Jesus ("We would see Jesus—for the shadows lengthen")
Warner, C. E.
Inn by the Road, The.
Warner, Charles Dudley
Bookra.
Warner, Eva
Irony of God.
Warner, L. G.
Friends.
Warner, L. M.
"More Than They All."
Warner, Rex
Chough.
Lapwing.
Sonnet: "How sweet only to delight in lambs."
Sonnet: "Understanding of a medical man, The."
Warner, Susan B.
Candle Burning in the Night, A.
Warner, Sylvia Townsend
Absence, The.
After He Had Gone.
Alarum, The.
Building in Stone.
Country Thought.
Elizabeth.
Epitaph: "Her grieving parents cradled here."
Epitaph: "I, an unwedded wandering dame."
Epitaph: "I, Richard Kent, beneath these stones."
Epitaph: "John Bird, a laborer, lies here."
Green Valley, The.
Image, The.
Killing No Murder.
Modo and Alciphron.
Nelly Trim.
Rival, The.
Sad Green.
Sailor, The.
Song: "She has left me, my pretty."
Triumph of Sensibility.
Tudor Church Music.
Warner, William
Aeneas dead, Ascanius reign'd; Ascanius dead, his brother.
Albion's England, *sels.*
Eight Henry, heir indubitate of York and Lancaster.
Fate of Narcissus, The.
My Mistress.
Now of the conqueror this isle had Brutain unto name.
Warr, Bertram J.
Death of an Elephant.
Deviator, The.
Heart to Carry On, The.
On a Child with a Wooden Leg.
Poets in Time of War.
There Are Children in the Dusk.
Trees, Who Are Distant.

Winter Stalks.
Working Class.
Warren, Gretchen O.
Peace.
Warren, George F.
Lord Guy.
Warren, Hamilton
Requiem.
Warren, James Edward, Jr
Beneath Such Rains.
Schoolroom: 158.
Warren, John Byrne Leicester, Baron de Tabley *See* **De Tabley, John Byrne Leicester Warren, Baron**
Warren, Mercy
Massachusetts Song of Liberty.
Warren, Robert Penn
Aubade for Hope.
Autumnal Equinox on Mediterranean Beach.
Ballad of a Sweet Dream of Peace.
Ballad of Billie Potts, The.
Bearded Oaks.
Cardinal, The.
Colder Fire.
Colloquy with Cockroach.
Country Burying (1919).
Crime.
Croesus in Autumn.
Dark Woods, *sel.*
Fall Comes in Back-Country Vermont.
Dogwood, The.
Eidolon.
End of Season.
Fairy Story.
Fall Comes in Back-Country Vermont.
Flower, The.
Grandfather Gabriel.
History among the Rocks.
Kentucky Mountain Farm, *sels.*
Letter from a Coward to a Hero.
Letter of a Mother.
Letter to a Friend.
Love: Two Vignettes.
Mexico Is a Foreign Country, *sels.*
Mortmain.
Notes on a Life to Be Lived.
Original Sin; a Short Story.
Owl, The.
Patriotic Tour and Postulate of Joy.
Pondy Woods.
Pro Sua Vita.
Pursuit.
Revelation.
Small Soldiers with Drum in Large Landscape.
Snake, The.
Summer Storm (circa 1916) and God's Grace.
Terror.
To a Little Girl, One Year Old, in a Ruined Fortress.
Two Pieces after Suetonius.
Variation: Ode to Fear.
When the Century Dragged.
World Comes Galloping, The; a True Story.
Wrestling Match, The.
Warren, Sir Thomas Herbert
Lines for a Sundial.
May-Day on Magdalen Tower.
Warsh, Lewis
Black Boundary, The.
Like small foreign villages whose gates have been.
Suicide Rates, The, *sel.*
Up There in Snow.
Warton, Joseph
Charms of Nature, The.
Dying Indian, The.
Enthusiast, The; or, The Lover of Nature.
Invocation to Fancy.
Ode to Evening.
Ode to Fancy.
Song, A: "While in the bower, with beauty blessed."
Warton, Thomas, the Elder
American Love-Ode, An.
Joy, rose-lipped dryad, loves to dwell.
Retirement, an Ode, *sel.*
Runic Ode, A.
Warton, Thomas, the Younger
Crusade, The.
Grave of King Arthur, The.
Inscription in a Hermitage.
Ode: Solitude, at an Inn.
Ode Written at Vale-Royal Abbey in Cheshire.
On King Arthur's Round Table, at Winchester.
On the Approach of Summer, *sel.*
Pleasures of Melancholy, The.
Solemn Noon of Night, The.
Sonnet: On King Arthur's Round Table at Winchester.
Sonnet: To the River Lodon [*or* Loddon].
Sonnet: Written after Seeing Wilton-House.
Sonnet: Written at Stonehenge.
Sonnet: Written in a Blank Leaf on Dugdale's "Monasticon."
Sonnets, *sels.*
Sunshine after a Shower.
To Mr. Gray.
To the River Lodon.
Verses on Sir Joshua Reynolds's Painted Window at New-College, Oxford.
Written at Stonehenge.
Written at Winslade, in Hampshire.
Written in a Blank Leaf of Dugdale's "Monasticon."
Washbourne, Thomas
Casting All Your Care upon God, for He Careth for You.
God's Two Dwellings, *sel.*
Humility.
Prayer: "What a commanding power."
Upon a Passing Bell.
Washburn, Henry Stevenson
Song of the Harvest.
Vacant Chair,The.
Washington, Austin D.
To Be Black Is to Suffer.
Washington, Dell
Learning Family.
Wason, Harriet L.
Slide at the Empire Mine, The.
Wassall, Irma
Singing in the Dark.
Stone from the Gods.
Wasse, Walter
Hunting of the Gods, The.
Wasson, David Atwood
Joy-Month.
Wastell, Simon
Microbiblion, *sel.*
Watanabe Suiha
Noisy cricket, The.
Waterbury, Jared Bell
Onward.
Waterhouse, Gilbert
This Is the Last.
Waterman, Nixon
Far from the Madding Crowd.
If I Knew You and You Knew Me.
If We Didn't Have to Eat.
Johnny's History Lesson.
Making a Man.
Recompense.
Rose to the Living, A.
"To Know All Is to Forgive All."
Today.
Understanding.
Vacation.
What Have We Done Today?
When the Train Comes In.
Whistling Boy.
Watermeyer, G. A.
Harvest Time.
Waterston, Robert Cassie
Jesus Is Near.
Mortal and Immortal.
Watkins, Edward
Figures of Authority.
Watkins, Grace V.
Remembrance.
This I Know.
Watkins, Lucian B.
Star of Ethiopia.
To Our Friends.
Two Points of View.
Watkins, Vernon
Ballad of the Equinox.
Ballad of the Trial of Sodom.
Ballad of the Two Tapsters.
Beaver's Story, The.
Cave-Drawing, The.
Christening Remembered, A.
Collier, The.
Compost Heap, The.
Dead Words, The.
Death of Keats, The.
Discoveries.
Earth and Fire.
Feather, The.
Fingernail Sunrise.
Fire in the Snow, The.
Foal.
For a Christening.
For a Wine Festival.
Furnace of Colors, The.
Gravestones.
Healing of the Leper, The.
Heron, The.
Hurdy-Gurdy Man in Winter.
Indolence.
Infant Noah.
Lady with the Unicorn, The.
Lover's Words, A.
Mother and Child, The.
Mozart at Zell-am-See.
Mummy, The.
Music of Colours: The Blossom Scattered.
Music of Colours—White Blossom.
Napkin and Stone.
Ophelia.
Peace in the Welsh Hills.
Poet and Goldsmith.
Prayer, A: "If I dare pray for one."
Returning from Harvest.
Revolutionary, The.
She That Is Memory's Daughter.
Shooting of Werfel, The.
Snow Curlew, The.
Song of the Good Samaritan, The.
Spoils of War, The.
Strangled Prayer, The.
Sunbather, The.
Turning of the Leaves, The.
Yeats in Dublin, *sel.*
Yeats' Tower.
Yew-Tree, The.
"Young poets, The, " he murmured.
Zacchaeus in the Leaves.
Watkyns, Rowland
Wish, The.
Watson, Albert Durrant
Breeze and Billow.
Hymn for Canada, A.
Priest and Pagan.
Soul Lifted.
Watson, Barbara Bellow
Late Light.

Watson, Edward Willard
Absolution.
Watson, Flora Willis
Calendar Rhyme.
Watson, James Wreford ("James Wreford', "
Gatineaus, The.
Our Love Shall Be the Brightness.
Sic Transit Gloria Mundi.
Stay, Time.
We Shall Have Far to Go.
Wild Willow.
Watson, John Whittaker
Beautiful Snow, The.
Watson, Minor
Constancy.
Watson, Rosamund Marriott ("Graham R. Tomson"; R. Armytage")
Arsinoë's Cats
Ave atque Vale.
Deid Folks' Ferry.
Farm on the Links, The.
Hereafter.
Le Mauvais Larron.
Omnia Somnia.
Requiescat.
South Coast Idyll, A.
To My Cat.
Watson, Sara Ruth
Bouncing Ball.
Watson, Thomas
Come, Gentle Death!
Ditty of the Six Virgins, The.
Each tree did boast the wished springtime's pride.
Go idle lines unpolished rude and base.
Hecatompathia; or, Passionate Century of Love, *sels.*
Here Lieth Love.
I curse the time, wherein these lips of mine.
If Cupid Were a Child.
In clouds she shines, and so obscurely shineth.
Love is a sour delight, a sug'red grief.
Love's Grave.
Marigold So Likes the Lovely Sun[ne], The.
My heart is set him down, twixt hope and fears.
My Love Is Past ("Resolved to dust, entombed here lieth Love").
My Love Is Past ("Ye captive souls of blindfold Cyprian's boat").
Questo di Verde.
Some That Report.
Sonnet: "I saw the object of my pining thought."
Speak, gentle heart, where is thy dwelling place?
Tears of Fancy, The, *sels.*
Time.
Vezzosi Augelli.
When first these eyes beheld with great delight.
Where tender Love had laid him down to sleep.
With Fragrant Flowers We Strew the Way.
Ye stately dames, whose beauties far excel.
Watson, Wilfred
Canticle of Darkness.
Contempt for Dylan Thomas, A.
Emily Carr.
In the Cemetery of the Sun.
Invocation: "Appear, O mother, was the perpetual cry."
Juniper Tree, The.
O My Poor Darling.
White Bird, The.
Windy Bishop, The.
Watson, Sir William
April.
At a Burial.
Autumn.
Ballad of Semmerwater, The.
Byron the Voluptuary.
Church Today, The.
Dawn on the Headland.
Domine, Quo Vadis?
England My Mother.
Epigram: "Children romp within the graveyard's pale, The."
Epigram: "Love, like a bird, hath perch'd upon a spray."
Epigram: "Momentous to himself as I to me."
Epigram: "Poet gathers fruit from every tree, The."
Epigram: "Statue, The—Buonarroti said—doth wait."
Epigram: "'Tis human fortune's happiest height, to be."
Epigram: "When whelmed are altar, priest and creed."
Estrangement.
Eternal Search, The.
Exit.
First Skylark of Spring, The.
For metaphors of man we search the skies.
God-seeking.
Great Misgiving, The.
His friends he loved. His direst earthly foes.
Hope of the World, The.
Hymn to the Sea.
Invention.
Key-Board, The.
Lachrymae Musarum.
Lacrimae Musarum.
Leavetaking ("Pass thou wild light").
Love.
Ode in May.
On Durer's "Melencolia."
Play of "King Lear," The.
Playmates, The.
Poet, The.
Poet who sleepest by this wandering wave!
Shakespeare.
Shelley's Centenary.
Song: "April, April,/ Laugh thy girlish laughter."
Song: "O, like a queen's her happy tread."
Song in Imitation of the Elizabethans.
Song's Apostasy.
Sonnet: "Daughter of her whose face, and lofty name."
Sonnet: "I cast these lyric offerings at your feet."
Sonnet: "I dare but sing of you in such a strain."
Sonnet: "I move amid your throng, I watch you hold."
Sonnet: "If I had never known your face at all."
Sonnet: "If you had lived in that more stately time."
Sonnets to Miranda, *sels.*
Sovereign Poet, The.
"Things That Are More Excellent, The."
Thomas Hood.
To a Seabird.
To Christina Rossetti.
Two Epigrams.
Unknown God, The.
Visitor Abhorred, The.
Vita Nuova.
Woman with the Serpent's Tongue, The.
Wordsworth's Grave.
World in Armor, The.
World-Strangeness.
Watt, Frederick B.
Inspection, The.
Watt, Lauchlan MacLean
I Bind My Heart.
In the Way of Peace.
Long Last Mile, The.
Reapers, The.
Tryst, The.
Watt, T. S
From My Rural Pen.
Watt, W. W.
Penny Wise and Found Poolish.
So This Is Autumn.
Summer Song.
Wattles, Willard Austin
Acceptance.
Builder, The.
Comrades of the Cross.
Creeds.
Family of Nations, The.
From the Parthenon I learn.
Gabriel.
I Thought Joy Went by Me.
Jericho.
Pisgah.
Thy Kingdom Come!
War at Home, The.
Watts, Isaac
Accept Our Tribute.
Against Idleness and Mischief.
Against Quarrelling and Fighting.
Bee, The.
Busy Bee, The.
Christ hath a garden walled around.
Come, Holy Spirit, Heavenly Dove.
Comparison and Complaint, The.
Cradle Hymn, A.
Cradle Song, A: "Hush, my dear, lie still and slumber."
Crucifixion to the World, by the Cross of Christ.
Day of Judgement [*or* Judgment], The.
Divine, The.
Emmanuel's Land.
Felicity.
From All That Dwell below the Skies.
God Praised for His Goodness and Truth.
God's Dominion and Decrees.
Hazard of Loving the Creatures, The.
Heaven.
Heavens Declare Thy Glory, Lord, The.
Holy Fortitude.
Horace Paraphrased.
Hosanna for the Lord's Day, An.
House of God, The.
How Doth the Little Busy Bee.
I Sing the Mighty Power of God.
Incomprehensible, The.
Jesus Shall Reign Where'er the Sun.
Joy to the World! The Lord Is Come, *with music.*
King Triumphant.
Let Dogs Delight [to Bark and Bite].
Little Busy Bee.
Lord Jehovah Reigns, The.
Love of God, The.
Man Frail and God Eternal.
Meditation in a Grove.
Ninetieth Psalm.
Nor Eye Has Seen.
O God, Our Help in Ages Past.
O How I Love Thy Law.
Our God, Our help in Ages Past.
Prospect of Heaven Makes Death Easy, A.
Quarrelling.
Recessional.
Refuge and Present Help, A.
Sincere Praise.
Sluggard, The.

Sweet Muse.
Thy Word.
True Greatness.
True Riches.
When I Survey the Wondrous Cross.
Where-e'er My Flatt'ring Passions Rove.
Whom Having Not Seen We Love.
Watts, Marjorie Seymour
New Shoes.
Parade, The.
Policeman, The.
Watts-Dunton, Theodore
Breath of Avon, The.
Coleridge.
Coming of Love, The, *sel.*
Dream, A.
First Kiss, The.
John the Pilgrim.
Mother Carey's Chicken.
Natura Benigna.
Ode to Mother Carey's Chicken.
Sonnet's Voice, The.
Toast to Omar Khayyám.
Wassail Chorus at the Mermaid Tavern.
Waugh, Edwin
Dule's i' This Bonnet o' Mine, The.
Owd Pinder.
Sweetheart Gate, Th'.
Wavell, Archibald Percival Wavell, 1st Earl
Sonnet for the Madonna of the Cherries.
Waxman, Percy
Mother.
Wayland, John Elton ("Idas")
Epilogue at Wallack's, An.
Weare, Meshech
Blasted Herb, The.
Wearing, Thomas
New Year.
Weatherly, Frederic Edward
Bell's Dream, *abr.*
Bird in the Hand, A.
Carol, A: "Angels to the shepherds sang, The."
Cats' Tea-Party, The.
Cherries.
Darby and Joan.
Door at the End of Our Garden, The.
Douglas Gordon.
Dustman, The.
Gray Dove's Answer, The.
Holy City, The.
Limerick: "My name's Mister Benjamin Bunny."
Lobster and the Maid, The.
London Bridge.
My Garden.
Nancy Lee.
Song of the Wood, The.
Tale of a Tart, The.
Thursday.
Usual Way, The.
When the Christ Child Came.
Weaver, Bennett
To Mother—in Heaven.
Weaver, Frank G.
Omnipresent.
Weaver, John Van Alstyn
Drug Store.
Ghost.
Legend.
Nocturne: "'Nothin' or everythin' it's got to be."
Two Ways.
Weaver, Robert *See* **Wever, R.**
Weaving, Willoughby
Star, The.
Webb, Charles David
And Dust to Dust.
Jardin des Fleurs.
Monasteries.
Orestes Pursued.
Threshold.
Webb, Charles Henry ("John Paul")
Dictum Sapienti.
Dum Vivimus Vigilemus.
Gil, the Toreador.
Little Mamma.
March.
With a Nantucket Shell.
Webb, Francis
Captain of the *Oberon*, The.
Cartier at St. Malo.
Drum for Ben Boyd, A, *sels.*
Five Days Old.
For My Grandfather.
Gunner, The.
Idyll: "At noon the sun puffed up, outsize."
Laid Off.
Leichhardt in Theatre, *sel.*
Morgan's Country.
Papuan Shepherd, A.
Pioneer of Monaro, A.
Room, The.
Sea, The.
View of Montreal, A, *sel.*
Webb, Frederick G.
Dash for the Colors, The.
Webb, Jesse F.
Not Grieved for Israel.
Webb, Marion St. John
Nugly Little Man, The.
Sunset Garden, The.
Webb, Mary
Anne's Book.
Colomen.
Fallen Poplar, The.
Foxgloves.
Green Rain.
Market Day.
Secret Joy, The.
Water-Ousel, The.
Webb, Phyllis
Making.
Marvell's Garden.
Poetics against the Angel of Death.
Propositions.
Rilke.
Sprouts the Bitter Grain.
Tall Tale, A; or, A Moral Song.
"Time of Man, The."
Webb, Tessa Sweazy
Bright Abandon.
Webb, Thomas Harry Basil
Ancient Prayer, An.
Prayer, A: "Give me [*or* us] a good digestion, Lord."
Prayer Found in Chester Cathedral, A.
Webbe, Charles
Against Indifference.
More Love or More Disdain.
Sweet, Be No Longer Sad.
Weber, Helen
Lessons.
Weber, Richard
Borderline Ballad.
In Memoriam I, Elizabeth at Twenty.
In Memoriam II, Elizabeth in Italy.
Lion and O'Reilly, The.
On an Italian Hillside.
O'Reilly's Reply.
Webster, Augusta Davies ("Cecil Home',")
Circe, *sel.*
Day Is Dead.
Deaths of Myron and Klydone, The.
In a Day, *sel.*
News to the King.
Pine, The.
Seeds.
Sun drops luridly into the west, The.
Tell Me Not of Morrows, Sweet.
'Tween Earth and Sky.
Violet and the Rose, The.
Webster, Daniel
On the Death of My Son Charles.
Webster, H. D. L.
Lorena.
Webster, John
All the Flowers of the Spring.
Banisht!/ It greev'd me much to heare the sentence.
Burial, The.
Call for the Robin Redbreast [and the Wren].
Cornelia's Song.
Devil's Law Case, The, *sels.*
Dirge: "Call for the robin redbreast and the wren."
Dirge: "Hark, now everything is still."
Duchess of Malfi, The, *sels.*
Dutchesse of Malfy, The.
Farewell Cariola!
Funeral Dirge for Marcello.
General Mist of Error, A.
Hark.
Hark [*or* Hearke], Now Everything Is Still.
Hearke, Now Everything Is Still.
How now my noble cossin—what in blacke!
I am come to make thy tomb.
Indeede I am studying Alcumye.
Is she dead?/ She is what you would have her.
It may be/ I'll join with thee in a most just revenge.
Land Dirge, A.
Madman's Song, The.
Nets to Catch the Wind.
Oh heere's my mother: I ha strange newes for you.
O, I shall run mad!
Oh, Let Us Howl Some Heavy Note.
O thou soft naturall dqath, thou art joint-twin.
Shrouding of the Duchess of Malfi, The.
Song: "All the flowers of the spring."
Song: "Call for the robin redbreast and the wren."
Speech by Romelio.
Summons to Execution.
Survey our progress from our birth.
Then here's an end of me: fare-well day-light.
Tragedy of the Duchess of Malfy, The.
Vanitas Vanitatum.
What, are you drop't?
What hideous noyse was that?
White Devil [*or* Divel], The, *sels.*
Yond's the Cardinall's window: This fortification.
Webster, Louise
Tombs.
Webster, Mrs. M. M.
Marriage of Pocahontas, The.
Webster, Mary Morison
Grass.
I Set Aside.
Illi Morituri.
Ox, The.
Quiet of the Dead, The.
Secret, The.
Wedderburn, John
Ane Sang of the Birth of Christ, with the Tune of Baw Lula Low.
In Dulci Jubilo.
Wedge, Martin

Wedge (continued)
Can This Be Death?
Wedgefarth, W. Dayton
Bum.
Mother in gladness, Mother in sorrow.
Mother's Hands.
Weeden, Howard
Banjo of the Past, The.
Borrowed Child, The.
Weeden, Lula Lowe
Dance.
Have You Seen It.
Little Dandelion, The.
Me Alone.
Robin Red Breast.
Stream, The.
Weekes, Charles
In Brittany ("In Brittany I lost my way").
Poppies.
Solstice.
Think.
Weeks, Alan
Some Brothers Cry.
Weeks, Robert Kelley
Man and Nature.
Medusa.
Song for Lexington, A.
Weeks, Robert Lewis
Appalachian Front.
Weever, John
Ad Gulielmum Shakespeare.
Ad Gulielmum Warner.
Ad Jo. [*or* Io.] Marston & [*or* et] Ben. Jonson [*or* Johnson *or* Ionson].
Ad Lectorem.
Ad Michaelem Drayton.
Ad Samuelem Daniel.
De Se.
In Ed. Allen.
In Nigellum.
In Obitum Ed. Spenser Poetae Prestaniss.
In Rudionem.
In Tumulum Abrahami Simple.
In Tumulum Avari.
Weever, Robert *See* **Wever, Robert**
Weil, James L.
About the Grass.
At a Loss.
Coney Island Life, A.
Fancy Fishing.
Wein, Jules Alan
Genesis.
Weir, Arthur
Snowshoeing Song.
Weisenthal, Morris
Genealogy of a Mermaid.
Small Elegy.
Weismiller, Edward
Epitaph: "It seemed that he would rather hear."
To the Woman in Bond Street Station.
Trail, The.
Winter Breath.
World, Defined.
Weiss, Michael
Resurrection Hymn.
Weiss, Neil
Ageing Athlete, The.
First Day, The.
Hike, The.
Word, The.
Weiss, Theodore
Barracks Apt. 14.
Dance Called David, The.
Egyptian Passage, An.
Fire at Alexandria, The.
Greater Music, The.
Hayseed.
Homecoming.
House of Fire.
In the Round.
Last Day and the First, The.
Life of . . ., The.
Out of Your Hands.
Preface.
Reapings, The.
Ruins for These Times.
To Forget Me.
Web, The.
World to Do, A.
Weisslitz, E. F.
Baldpate Pond.
Weist, Carl S.
Cross on a Hill, A.
Crucifixion.
Symbol of Hope.
Welburn, Ron
Eulogy for Populations.
First Essay on the Art of the U.S.
Regenesis.
Welby, Amelia B. Coppuck
Twilight at Sea.
Welch, James
Blackfeet, Blood and Piegan Hunters.
Christmas Comes to Moccasin Flat.
D-Y Bar.
In My First Hard Springtime.
Montana, Nothing like Boston.
Spring for All Seasons.
Winter Indian.
Wolf Song, the Rain.
Wrath of Lester Lame Bull, The.
Welch, Lew
After Anacreon.
Barbara/ Van Gogh Poem.
Chicago Poem.
Hiking Poem/ High Sierra.
Welch, Marie de L.
Chipmunk.
Harvests.
Lord of Eden.
Prelude to Commencement.
St. Francis and the Cloud.
Welch, Myra Brooks
Greater Glory, The.
I Thank Thee, Lord.
I Would Be a Channel.
Master Builder, The.
Touch of the Master's Hand, The.
Welch, Sarah
Digger's Grave, The.
Welcome, L. O.
Phantom Mail Coach, The.
Weldon, Charles
Poem of the Universe, The.
Welhaven, Johan Sebastian Cammermeyer
Like an April Day.
Welles, Winifred
Actual Willow.
Angel in the Apple Tree, The.
Aunt Eliza's Slow Ear.
Behind the Waterfall.
Boy.
Child's Song to Her Mother, A.
Climb.
Cobweb.
Cruciform.
Curious Something.
Dog Who Ate a Pond Lily.
Dogs and Weather.
From a Chinese Vase.
Gesture.
"God's First Creature Was Light."
Green Grass and White Milk.
Green Moth.
Harvest Dust.
Heart of Light, The.
Indian Pipes.
Language.
Last Night of Winter, The.
Love Song from New England.
Lucky Snail, The.
Man with a Little Pleated Piano, A.
Old Ellen Sullivan.
River Skater.
Silence.
Skipping Along Alone.
Starfish.
Stocking Fairy.
Three Lovely Holes.
Tree at Dusk, A.
Trinket.
White Fear.
Winter Apples.
Wellesley, Dorothy, Duchess of Wellington
As Lambs into the Pen.
Asian Desert.
Buried Child, The.
Deserted House, *sel*
Docks.
Fire.
A
Horses.
I Think Myself to Be Alive.
Lenin, *sel.*
Matrix, *sel.*
Morning After, The.
So I came down the steps to Lenin.
Spiritual, the carnal, are one, The.
Wellesley, Henry
Demophilus.
Wellhaven, Johan Sebastian Cammermeyer *See* **Welhaven, Johan Sebastian Cammermeyer**
Wellington, Alice *See* **Rollins, Alice Wellington**
Wellington, Dorothy Wellesley, Duchess of *See* **Wellesley, Dorothy Duchess of Wellington**
Wellman, Wade
Ballad of Despair, A.
On the Staircase.
Wells, Amos Russel
Cross a Crown, The.
Glorious Name, The.
Inn That Missed Its Chance, The.
Mothers—and Others.
"My Soul Doth Magnify the Lord."
Path in the Sky, The.
People's Prayer, The.
Pray!
Read the Bible Through.
Thanksgiving for Thanksgiving.
When I Read the Bible Through.
Wells; Anna Maria
Cow-Boy's Song, The.
Wells, Carolyn
Abbie Ben Adams, *parody.*
All Hallow Eve.
Alone.
Arch Armadillo, The.
Ballade of a Conspicuous Omission from "The Book of Humorous Verse."
Careless Niece, The.
Diversions of the Re-echo Club.
Dresscessional, A.
Grandiloquent Goat, The.
Happy Hyena, The.
How to Know the Wild Animals.
How to Tell the Wild Animals.
Limerick: "Canner, exceedingly [*or* remarkably] canny, A."
Limerick: "There once was a happy hyena."
Limerick: "There once was an arch armadillo."
Limerick: "Tutor who tooted the [*or* a] flute, A."
One Week.
Our Polite Parents.
Overworked Elocutionist, An.

No Answer.
Portrait in the Guards, A.
Shape of a Bird, The.
Whitaker, Robert
Abraham Lincoln.
Easter.
"For God So Loved the World."
Holy Week.
Live for Something.
My Country.
No Room.
O Mothers of the Human Race.
Out-of-Doors.
Rivals, The.
Starred Mother, The.
Upon This Rock.
Whence Cometh War?
Worship.
Whitaker, Tommy
After Depression Came Soul.
One Way.
Whitbread, Thomas
CCC, The.
Civilities.
Pool, A.
T. S. Eliot.
To My Fellow-Mariners, March '53.
Whitcher, Frances Miriam Berry
K. K. Can't Calculate.
Widow Bedott Papers, The, *sel.*
White, Adeline
Autumn Morning.
Christmas Party, The.
Colour.
Over the Fields.
White, Alan
Poem for Combatants.
White, Anne Catherine
Morning Cometh, The.
White, Blanco *See* **White, Joseph Blanco**
White, Christine
Secret of Song.
White, Cool
Lubly Fan.
White, D. J. *See* **O'Malley, D. J**
White, Edward Lucas
Genius.
Last Bowstrings, The.
White, Elwyn Brooks
Affidavit in Platitudes.
Apostrophe to a Pram Rider.
Apostrophic Notes from the New-World Physics.
Circus, The.
Classic Waits for Me, A.
Commuter.
Dog around the Block.
Fashions in Dogs.
Father Does His Best, A.
I Marvel at the Ways of God.
I Paint What I See.
Lady Is Cold, The.
Listener's Guide to the Birds, A.
Marble-Top.
Natura in Urbe.
Nugatory.
Red Cow Is Dead, The.
Song of the Queen Bee.
To a Lady across the Way.
White, Eugene Richard
Of the Lost Ship.
White, George
I Came to Jesus.
White, Gilbert
Natural History of Selborne, The, *sel.*
While deepening shades obscure the face of day.
White, Gleeson
Ballade of Playing Cards, A.
Primrose Dame, A.
Sufficiency.
White, Harriet R.
Uffia.
White, Henry Kirke
Clifton Grove, *sel.*
Description of a Summer's Eve.
Lo! in the West, fast fades the ling'ring light.
Man's Littleness in Presence of the Stars.
Song from Fragment of an Eccentric Drama.
To an Early Primrose.
White, Hervey
I Saw the Clouds.
White, Hinton
I've Travelled Far in Many Lands.
World Is One, The.
White, James
Why the Moon Is Like a Fashionable Wife.
White, James Terry
Consummation.
If Hearts Are Dust.
We Shall Remember Them.
White, John
Clock Time by the Geyser.
White, Jon Manchip
Captain, The.
Count Orlo in England.
Orlo's Valediction.
Rout of San Romano, The.
White, Joseph Blanco
Black Is a Soul.
Hesperus with the host of heaven came.
Mysterious Night.
Night.
Night and Death.
To Night.
White, Lillian Zellhoefer
Hangman's Tree.
White, Michyle
I prepare for night changes.
White, Raelene Newell
Rain-Talk.
White, Richard
Discovery of San Francisco Bay, The.
White, Stewart Edward
Bung Yer Eye.
White, Terence Hanbury
To Myself, after Forty Years.
White, Tyner
Night Letter.
O Please Read Backwards.
White, Vera
You Are on U.S. 40 Headed West.
White, William Allen
Intermezzo for the Fourth Act, An.
Rhyme of the Dream-Maker Man, A.
Whitefield, George
Oh, Lovely Appearance of Death, *with music.*
Whitehead, Charles
Lamp, The.
Summer Storm, A.
Whitehead, Paul
Apollo and Daphne, *sel.*
Hunting Song, A.
Whitehead, William
Enthusiast, The; an Ode.
Je Ne Sais [*or* Sçy *or* Scai] Quoi, The.
On Friendship.
On the Birthday of a Young Lady.
Whiteley, Opal
Words, The.
Whitelock, William Wallace
Cats.
Whiteside, Mary Brent
Who Has Known Heights.
Whitfield, Frederick
I Need Thee.
There Is a Name I Love to Hear.
Whiting, Charles Goodrich
Blue Hills beneath the Haze.
Eagle's Fall, The.
Way to Heaven, The.
Whiting, Lilian
Lost Cat, The.
Mystery, The.
Whiting, Nathaniel
Il Insonio Insonnado, *sel.*
Le Hore di Recreatione; or, The Pleasant Historie of Albino and Bellama, *sel.*
Office of Poetry, The.
Pleasant Historie of Albino and Bellama, The.
Tinker and the Monks, The.
Whiting, Seymour W.
Alamance.
Whiting, William
Eternal Father, Strong to Save.
For Those in Peril.
Hymn: "Eternal Father, strong to save."
Whitman, James I.
Incident of French History, An.
Whitman, Ruth
Almost Ninety.
Cutting the Jewish Bride's Hair.
Dead Center.
Sound in Cambridge, Mass., A.
Whitman, S. W.
October.
Whitman, Sarah Helen
Oft since thine earthly eyes have closed on mine.
Sonnet to Edgar Allan Poe ("On our lone pathway").
Sonnets from the Series Relating to Edgar Allan Poe, *sels.*
Sonnets Relating to Edgar Allan Poe.
To Edgar Allan Poe.
Whitman, Walt
Aboard at a Ship's Helm.
After an Interval.
After the Dazzle of Day.
After the Sea-Ship.
After the Supper and Talk.
Ages and Ages Returning at Intervals.
Ah, more than any priest, O soul, we too believe in God.
Ah, Poverties, Wincings, and Sulky Retreats.
Ah, what can ever be more stately and admirable to me than mast-hemmed Manhattan?
All, all for immortality.
All my emprises have been fill'd with Thee.
All truths wait in all things.
American Feuillage.
And thou, America,/ For the scheme's culmination.
Animals.
Are You New Person Drawn toward Me?
Army Corps on the March, An.
As Adam Early in the Morning.
As Consequent from Store of Summer Rains.
As I Ebb'd with the Ocean of Life.
As I Lay with My Head in Your Lap Camerado.
As I Pondered in Silence.
As Toilsome I Wander'd [*or* Wandered] Virginia's Woods.
Base of All Metaphysics, The.
Bathe me O God in thee, mounting to thee.
Battle of the *Bonhomme Richard* and the *Serapis.*
Be Not Afraid.
Beasts, The.
Beat! Beat! Drums!

Whitman (continued)
Beautiful world of new, superber birth, that rises to my eyes.
Beginners.
Beginning My Studies.
Belief in Plan of Thee.
Birds of Passage, *sel.*
Bivouac on a Mountain Side.
Bodies of Men and Women Engirth Me, The.
Broad-Axe [*or*-Ax], The.
Brown Bird, The.
By Blue Ontario's Shore, *sels.*
By Broad Potomac's Shore.
By the Bivouac's Fitful Flame.
Camps of Green.
Cavalry Crossing A Ford.
Centenarian's Story, The.
Chanting the Square Deific.
Child Said *What Is the Grass?* A.
City Dead-House, The.
City of Orgies.
Clear Midnight, A.
Come Up From the Fields, Father.
Commonplace, The.
Crossing Brooklyn Ferry.
Dalliance of the Eagles, The.
Darest Thou Now O Soul.
Dazzling and Tremendous How Quick the Sun-Rise Would Kill Me.
Death Carol: "Come, lovely and soothing Death."
Dirge for Two Veterans.
Dismantled Ship, The.
Divine Ship Sails the Divine Sea for You, The.
Drayman, The.
Earth, My Likeness.
Eidólons.
Encountering God.
Epitaph for Lincoln.
Ethiopia Saluting the Colours [*or* Colors].
Faces.
Facing West from California's Shores.
Farm Picture, A.
First Dandelion, The.
Flashing and golden pageant of California, The.
For You O Democracy.
From Paumanok Starting I Fly Like a Bird.
From Pent-up Aching Rivers.
Gigantic beauty of a stallion, fresh and responsive to my caresses, A.
Give Me the Splendid Silent Sun.
Glimpse, A.
Gods.
Good-bye My Fancy!
Grass.
Greatest City, The.
Had I the Choice.
Halcyon Days.
Hand-Mirror, A.
Hast Never Come to Thee an Hour.
Here the Frailest Leaves of Me.
Heroes.
Hours Continuing Long, Sore and Heavy-Hearted.
Hub for the Universe, A.
Hush'd Be the Camps To-Day.
I Am He That Walks [with the Tender and Growing Night]
I am of old and young, of the foolish as much as the wise.
I am the poet of the body and I am the poet of the soul.
I am the teacher of athletes.
I do not despise you priests, all time, the world over.
I Dote upon Myself.
I Dream'd in a Dream.
I Hear America Singing.
I Hear and Behold God in Every Object.
I hear and behold God in every object, yet understand God not in the least.
I Hear and See Not Strips of Cloth Alone.
I Hear It Was Charged against Me.
I Heard You Solemn-Sweet Pipes of the Organ.
I Know I Am Deathless.
I open my scuttle at night and see the far-sprinkled systems.
I saw in Louisiana a Live-Oak Growing.
I Saw the Vision of Armies.
I Sing the Body Electric.
I Sit and Look Out.
I swear I begin to see the meaning of these things.
I Tramp a Perpetual Journey.
Imprisoned Soul, The.
In Paths Untrodden.
In This Earth, Perfection.
Indian Woman, The.
Indications and tally of time, The.
Infinity.
It avails not, time nor place—distance avails not.
It is time to explain myself—let us stand up.
Italian Music in Dakota.
John Paul Jones.
Joy, Shipmate, Joy!
Justified Mother of Men, The.
Keep heart, O comrade, God may be delayed.
Last Invocation, The.
Leaf of Grass, A.
Leaves of Grass.
Lines: "Child, A, said, '*What is the grass?*'"
Listen! I will be honest with you.
Lo, Victress on the Peaks.
Look Down Fair Moon.
Mannahatta ("I was asking for something specific").
March in the Ranks Hard-prest, and the Road Unknown, A.
Me Imperturbe.
Memories of President Lincoln.
Miracles ("I believe a leaf of grass").
Miracles ("Why, who makes much of a miracle?").
Muse in the New World, The.
My Barbaric Yawp.
Infinity.
My spirit has pass'd in compassion and determination around the whole earth.
My terminus near,/ The clouds already closing in upon me.
Myself.
Native Moments.
Necessity of Religion, The.
Night on the Prairies.
Noiseless Patient Spider, A.
Not Heat Flames Up and Consumes.
Not Heaving from My Ribb'd Breast Only.
Not songs of loyalty alone are these.
O Captain! My Captain!
O Hymen! O Hymenee!
O I see flashing that this America is only you and me.
O Magnet-South.
O my body! I dare not desert the likes of you in other men and women.
O Star of France.
O Tan-faced Prairie-Boy.
Of the Terrible Doubt of Appearances.
Old-Time Sea-Fight, An.
On the Beach at Night.
Once I Pass'd through a Populous City.
One effort more, my altar this bleak sand.
One Hour to Madness and Joy.
One's-Self I Sing.
Open Road, The.
Others May Praise What They Like.
Out of the Cradle Endlessly Rocking.
Out of the Rolling Ocean the Crowd.
Over the Carnage Rose Prophetic a Voice.
Ox-Tamer, The.
Passage to India.
Patrol[l]ing Barnegat.
Peaceful Death.
Pioneers! O Pioneers!
Poet, The.
Poets to Come.
Prairie-Grass Dividing, The.
Prairie Sunset, A.
Prayer of Columbus.
Press Close Bare-Bosom'd Night.
Quicksand Years.
Reconciliation.
Recorders Ages Hence.
Respondez!
Roots and Leaves Themselves Alone.
Runaway Slave, The.
Runner, The.
Sail forth—steer for the deep waters only.
Salut au Monde, *sel.*
Same Old Law, The.
Scented Herbage of My Breast.
Sea of Faith, The.
Shut Not Your Doors.
Sight in Camp [in the Daybreak Gray and Dim], A.
Singer in the Prison, The.
Sleepers, The.
So Long!
Sometimes with One I Love.
Song for All Seas, All Ships.
Song for the States, A.
Song Of Myself.
Song of the Answerer, *sel.*
Song of the Broad-Axe.
Song of the Exposition, *sel.*
Song of the Open Road.
Song of the Redwood-Tree.
Song of the Universal, *sels.*
Sparkles from the Wheel.
Spider, The.
Spontaneous Me.
Starting from Paumanok.
Still Though the One I Sing.
Sum of All Known Reverence, The.
Tears.
Thanks in Old Age.
There Was a Child Went Forth.
This Compost.
This Dust Was Once the Man.
This is the female form.
This Moment Yearning and Thoughtful.
Thou born to match the gale (thou art all wings).
Thou knowest my years entire, my life.
Thou Mother with Thy Equal Brood.
Thought.
To a Certain Civilian.
To a Common Prostitute.
To a Foil'd European Revolutionaire, *sel.*
To a Locomotive in Winter.
To Foreign Lands.
To Him That Was Crucified.
To Old Age.
To One Shortly to Die.
To Rich Givers.
To the Garden the World.
To the Leaven'd Soil They Trod.
To the Man-of-War-Bird.
To the States.
To Think of Time.
To Those Who've Failed.
To You ("Stranger, if you passing meet me").

To-Day and Thee.
Turn O Libertad.
Two Guests from Alabama.
Two Veterans.
Unexpress'd, The.
Untold Want, The.
Vigil Strange I Kept on the Field One Night.
Walt Whitman.
What Is the Grass?
When I Heard at the Close of the Day.
When I Heard the Learn'd [*or* Learned] Astronomer.
When I Peruse the Conquer'd Fame.
When Lilacs Last in the Dooryard Bloom'd.
When the Full-Grown Poet Came.
Whispers of Heavenly Death.
Who Learns My Lesson Complete?
Whoever You Are Holding Me Now in Hand.
With Music Strong I Come.
Woman Waits for Me, A.
World below the Brine, The.
Wound-Dresser, The.
Wounded Person, The.
Years of the Modern.
Yonnondio.
You Felons on Trial in Courts.
You Lingering Sparse Leaves of Me.
You, Whoever You Are.
Youth, Day, Old Age, and Night.
Whitney, Adeline D. T.
Equinoctial.
February.
Humpty Dumpty.
Mother Goose for Grown Folks, *sel.*
Peace.
Whitney, Anna Temple
And So Should You.
Kneeling Camel, The.
Purpose of Prayer, The.
Rest and Work.
Submission and Rest.
Whitney, Ernest
Nightingale and the Lark, The.
Ute Pass.
Whitney, F. B.
God Knows the Answer.
Whitney, Geffrey
Content.
Song: "In crystal towers and turrets richly set."
Whitney, Helen Hay (Mrs. Payne Whitney)
Cat, The.
Does the Pearl Know?
Love's Kiss.
Sigh Not for Love.
Song: "We only ask for sunshine."
To Diane.
Was There Another Spring?
Woman's Pride, A.
Whitney, Joseph Ernest
Drop of Ink, A.
Whittaker, Frederick
Custer's Last Charge.
Whittemore, Elizabeth
My Friends Are Little Lamps to Me.
Whittemore, Reed
Abbreviated Interviews with a Few Disgruntled Literary Celebrities.
After Some Day of Decision.
Alfred Lord Tennyson.
American Takes a Walk, An.
Clamming.
Day with the Foreign Legion, A.
Line of an American Poet, The
Love Song.
Notes on a Certain Terribly Critical Piece.
On the Suicide of a Friend.
Only the Dead.
Our Ruins.
Out of My Study Window.
Party, The.
Projection, A.
Radio under the Bed, The.
Recall.
Reflections upon a Recurrent Suggestion by Civil Defense Authorities That I Build a Bombshelter in My Backyard.
Self and the Weather, The.
Shakespeare, Possibly, in California.
Spring, etc.
Still Life.
Storm from the East, A.
Summer Concert.
Tarantula, The.
Treasure, A.
Week of Doodle, A.
Wordsworth and the Woman.
Whittier, John Greenleaf
Abraham Davenport.
Abraham Lincoln.
Adjustment.
Alas for him who never sees.
All souls that struggle and aspire.
All Things Are Thine.
All's Well.
Among the Hills, *sel.*
Amy Wentworth.
And so I find it well to come.
And Thou, O Lord! by whom are seen.
And yet, dear heart! remembering thee.
Andrew Rykman's Prayer, *sels.*
Angel of Patience, The.
Angels of Buena Vista, The.
Astraea.
Astraea at the Capitol.
At Last.
At Port Royal.
At School-Close.
Autograph, An.
Barbara Frietchie.
Barefoot Boy, The.
Bartholdi Statue, The.
Battle Autumn of 1862, The.
Bayard Taylor.
Bible, The.
Book Our Mothers Read, The.
Brewing of Soma, The.
Brown Dwarf of Rügen, The.
Brown of Ossawatomie.
Bryant on His Seventieth Birthday.
Burial of Barber.
Burns.
Cable Hymn, The.
Call of the Christian, The.
Calm.
Cassandra Southwick.
Centennial Hymn.
Chicago.
Clerical Oppressors.
Conductor Bradley.
Corn Song, The.
Crisis, The.
Dead Feast of the Kol-Folk, The.
Dead Ship of Harpswell, The.
Dear Lord and Father of Mankind.
Dedication: "I would the gift I offer here."
Democracy, *abr.*
Destiny.
Disarmament, *sel.*
Divine Compassion.
Double-Headed Snake of Newbury, The.
Emancipation Group, The.
Epitaph: "Bathsheba: To whom none ever said scat."
Eternal Good ("Eternal Good which overlies").
Eternal Goodness, The ("O friends! with whom my feet have trod").
Eve of Election, *sel.*
Eventide, *sel.*
Exile's Departure, The.
Faith.
Farewell, The: "Gone, gone—sold and gone."
Firelight.
First-Day Thoughts.
Fishermen, The.
For all her quiet life flowed on.
For an Autumn Festival, *sel.*
For Righteousness' Sake.
Forgive.
Forgiveness.
Friend's Burial, The.
Frost Spirit, The.
Garrison ("The storm and peril").
Godspeed.
Harvest Hymn.
Haverhill, 1640-1890.
Healer, The.
Help.
Henchman, The.
His Strength.
Hunters of Men, The.
Huskers, The, *sel.*
Hymn from the French of Lamartine, *sel.*
I bow my forehead to the dust.
I Call the Old Time Back.
I know not what the future hath.
I see the wrong that round me lies.
Ichabod.
If there be some weaker one.
In Earthen Vessels.
In Memory of James T. Fields.
In School Days.
In the "Old South."
Indian Summer.
James Russell Lowell.
John Underhill.
Joy of Giving, The.
Kallundborg Church.
Kansas Emigrants, The.
King's Missive, The.
Knowledge.
Laus Deo!
Le Marais du Cygne.
Let man be free! The mighty word.
Lexington.
Life and Love.
Lines: "Sun that brief December day, The."
Lines: "Unwarmed by any sunset light."
Lost Occasion, The.
Lumbermen, The.
Mabel Martin; a Harvest Idyl, *sel.*
Make my mortal dreams come true.
Massachusetts to Virginia.
Maud Muller.
Meeting, The.
Memories.
Miriam, *sel.*
Moral Warfare, The.
Mother.
Mulford.
My Playmate.
My Triumph.
My Trust, *sel.*
New Challenge, The.
New Wife and the Old, The.
Norembega.
Norsemen, The.
O Brother Man.
O Thou who bidst the torrent flow.
Old Burying-Ground, The.
On a Fly-Leaf of Longfellow's Poems, *sel.*
On the Big Horn.
Our Master.
Over-Heart, The.
Pageant, The.
Palatine, The.

Whittier (continued)
Palestine.
Pardon, Lord, the lips that dare.
Pentucket.
Picture memory brings to me, A.
Pipes at Lucknow, The.
Poor Voter on Election Day, The.
Prayer: "Dear Lord and Father of mankind."
Prelude: "Along the roadside, like the flowers of gold."
Pressed Gentian, The.
Proclamation, The.
Proem: "I love the old melodious lays."
Prophecy of Samuel Sewall, The.
Prophetess.
Pumpkin, The.
Quaker of the Olden Time, The.
Raphael, *sel.*
Reformers, The ("O pure reformers!").
Riddle of the World, The.
Saddest Words, The.
St. John.
Schoolmaster, The.
Shadow and the Light, The, *sel.*
Ship Builders, The.
Shoemakers, The.
Sister.
Sisters, The.
Skipper Ireson's Ride.
Snow, The.
Snow-bound; a Winter Idyl.
Song of Slaves in the Desert.
Song of the Negro Boatman.
Song of the Slaves in the Desert.
Songs of Labor: Dedication.
Storm, The.
Swan Song of Parson Avery, The.
Telling the Bees.
Texas.
Three Bells, The.
To John C. Frémont.
To Paths Unknown.
To Ronge.
To the Thirty-ninth Congress.
To William Lloyd Garrison ("Champion of those").
Trailing Arbutus, The.
Trinitas.
Two Angels, The.
Two Rabbins, The.
Uncle, The.
Undying Soul, The.
Vanishers, The.
Vesta.
Vow of Washington, The.
Washington's Vow.
We Live by Faith.
We may not climb the heavenly steeps.
Winter Day.
Winter Night, The.
World Sits at the Feet of Christ, The.
World Transformed, The.
Yet Love Will Dream.
Whittle, Daniel W.
Moment by Moment.
Whittle, Major
Hope of the Coming of the Lord, The.
Whitworth, William Henry
Time and Death.
Whyte-Melville, George John
Goodbye!
Whythorne, Thomas
Now that the Truth Is Tried.
Wickham, Anna (Mrs. Patrick Hepburn)
Affinity, The.
After Annunciation.
Cherry-Blossom Wand, The.
Contemplative Quarry, The.
Creatrix.
Dedication of the Cook.
Divorce.
Domestic Economy.
Egoist, The.
Envoi: "God, thou great symmetry."
Fired Pot, The.
Fresh Start, The.
Friend Cato.
Gift to a Jade.
Last Round, The.
Man with a Hammer, The.
Meditation at Kew.
O heavenly fool! thy most kiss-worthy face.
Prayer for Miracle.
Recompense, The.
Sehnsucht.
Self-Analysis.
Ship near Shoals.
Silence.
Since I Saw My Love.
Singer, The.
Song: "I was so shill and overworn, and sad."
Song-Maker, The.
Soul's Liberty.
Tired Man, The.
Tired Woman, The.
To a Crucifix.
To Men.
Vanity.
Weapons.
Wickham, John
Song: To a Lady with Many Names.
Widdemer, Margaret
As I Lay Quiet.
Awakened War God, The.
Barter.
Bear Hunt, The.
Beggars, The.
Belinda's Window.
Certainties.
Comfort.
Companions.
Cyprian Woman, A; Greek Folk Song.
Dark Cavalier, The.
Factories, The.
Faithless Flowers, The.
Fiddlers' Green.
Ghost to Come.
God and the Strong Ones.
Greek Folk Song; a Cyprian Woman.
If You Should Tire of Loving Me.
Invisible Playmate, The.
Little Carved Bowl, The.
Looking-Glass Pussy, The.
Masters, The.
Modern Woman to Her Lover, The.
Mother.
Mother-Prayer.
New Victory, The.
No Words Are Lost.
Old Road to Paradise, The.
Prescience.
Procession, The.
Sea Call.
Search.
Secret Cavern, The.
Song: "Going down the old way."
Teresina's Face.
Village Christmas.
Watcher, The.
Willow Cats, The.
Winter Branches.
Wieners, John
Acts of Youth, The.
For Jan.
In the Half Light of Holding and Giving.
Meadow, The.
Poem for Museum Goers, A.
Poem for Painters, A.
Poem for the Insane, A.
Poem for the Old Man, A.
Poem for Trapped Things, A.
Series 5.8, A.
Tuesday 7:00 PM.
Two Years Later.
Waning of the Harvest Moon, The.
Where Fled.
Windows of Waltham, The.
Wrapped Up in an Indian Blanket.
You Talk of Going but Don't Even Have a Suitcase.
Wiggam, Lionel
He Climbs a Hill and Turns His Face.
Mathematics.
Wiggin, Kate Douglas
Child and the World, The.
Christmas Eve.
Cuddle Down, Dolly.
Romance of a Christmas Card, The.
Wigglesworth, Michael
Day of Doom, The.
God's Controversy with New-England.
Heathen and the Infants, The.
Infants' Petition, The.
Men of Good Works.
Prayer unto Christ the Judge of the World, A.
Song of Emptiness to Fill up the Empty Pages Following, A.
Vanity of Vanities.
Wightman, Richard
Pilgrim, The.
Servants, The.
Wilberforce, Robert
"Peace Is the Tranquillity of Order."
Wilbur, Richard
Advice to a Prophet.
After the Last Bulletins.
All These Birds.
Altitudes.
Apology.
Aspen and the Stream, The.
At Year's-End.
Ballade for the Duke of Orléans.
Baroque Wall-Fountain in the Villa Sciarra, A.
Beasts.
Beautiful Changes, The.
Bell Speech.
Beowulf.
Black November Turkey, A.
Castles and Distances.
Ceremony.
Christmas Hymn, A.
Cicadas.
Cigales.
Courtyard Thaw, A.
Death of a Toad, The.
Digging for China.
Driftwood.
Epistemology.
Event, An.
Exeunt.
Fall in Corrales.
Fire-Truck, A.
First Snow in Alsace.
Folk Tune.
For K. R. on Her Sixtieth Birthday.
For the New Railway Station in Rome.
Grace.
Grasse: The Olive Trees.
Grasshopper, A.
Howl.
In a Bird Sanctuary.
In the Elegy Season.
In the Field.
In the Smoking-Car.
Juggler.
June Light.
Junk.
Lamarck Elaborated.

Lament: "Nashe's old queens who bartered young and fair."
Lightness.
Love Calls Us to the Things of This World.
Loves of the Puppets.
Marché aux Oiseaux.
Marginalia.
Merlin Enthralled.
Mind.
Museum Piece.
Next Door.
O.
Objects.
October Maples, Portland.
On the Marginal Way.
Pangloss' Song.
Pardon, The.
Part of a Letter.
Potato.
Praise in Summer.
Proof, The.
Rillons, Rillettes.
Running.
Seed Leaves.
She.
Simile for Her Smile, A.
Simplification, A.
Sonnet: "Winter deepening, the hay all in, The."
Speech for the Repeal of the McCarran Act.
Statues.
Still, Citizen Sparrow.
Stop.
Superiorities.
Terrace, The.
Then When the Ample Season.
To an American Poet Just Dead.
Two Voices in a Meadow.
Tywater.
Undead, The.
Voice from under the Table, A.
Walking to Sleep.
Winter Spring.
World without Objects Is a Sensible Emptiness, A.
Years-End.

Wilcox, Dora
At Evening.
Liebesweh.

Wilcox, Ella Wheeler
Accept My Full Heart's Thanks.
Ad Finem.
Attainment.
Better, Wiser and Happier.
Beyond, The.
Building.
Christian's New-Year Prayer, The, *sel.*
Faith.
Five Little Brothers.
Friendship after Love.
Gethsemane.
Goal, The.
Growing Old.
I Love You.
If my vain soul needs blows and bitter losses.
Illusion.
Inspiration, An.
Interlude.
Kindness.
Leaners or Lifters.
Life, *abr.*
Life's Scars.
Lifters and Leaners.
Lifting and Leaning.
Love much. Earth has enough of bitter in it.
Love Ship.
Love Thyself Last.
Midsummer.
Mistakes.
Morning Prayer, A.
My Ships.
One of Us Two.
One Ship Drives East.
Optimism.
Pin, A.
Price He Paid, The.
Progress.
Queen's Last Ride, The.
Recrimination.
Solitude.
Talk Faith.
Talk Happiness.
Talk not of strength, till your heart has known.
They Say.
Those We Love the Best.
To know thy bent and then pursue.
True Brotherhood.
Two Glasses, The.
Two Kinds of People.
Unanswered Prayers.
Universal Language, The.
Uselessness.
Was, Is, and Yet-to-be.
Way of the World, The.
Whatever Is Is Best.
Will.
Windows of the Soul.
Winds of Fate, The.
With Every Rising of the Sun.
Worth While.
You and Today.
You Never Can Tell.

Wild [*or* Wilde], Robert
Epitaph for a Godly Man's Tomb, An.
I, he, who whileom sate and sung in cage.
Iter Boreale, *sel.*

Wilde, Lady Jane Francesca ("Speranza")
Famine Year, The.
Voice of the Poor, The.

Wilde, Oscar
Apologia.
Athanasia.
Ave Imperatrix.
Ave Maria Gratia Plena.
Ballad of Reading Gaol, The.
Capital Punishment.
E. Tenebris.
East a-Callin', The.
Endymion.
Fabien dei Franchi.
For Our Sakes.
Garden, The.
Grave of Keats, The.
Harlot's House, The.
Hélas!
Hope.
How subtle-secret is your smile!
Humanitad, *sels.*
I never saw a man who looked.
Impression de Paris.
Impression du Matin.
Impression Japonais.
Impression: Le Réveillon.
Impressions, *sels.*
In Debtor's Yard the stones are hard.
In Prison.
In Reading Gaol by Reading Town.
In the Forest.
In the Gold Room.
Joy.
La Bella Donna della Mia Mente.
La Fuite de la Lune.
La Mer.
Le Jardin ("The lily's withered chalice falls").
Le Jardin des Tuileries ("This winter air is keen").
Les Ballons.
Les Silhouettes.
Magdalen Walks.
Midwinter.
My Voice.
On the Sale by Auction of Keats' Love Letters.
Portia.
"Quia Multum Amavi."
Requiescat.
Serenade: "Western wind is blowing fair, The."
Sonnet on Hearing the *Dies Irae* Sung in the Sistine Chapel.
Sonnet on Holy Week.
Sonnet to Liberty.
Sphinx, The.
Symphony in Yellow.
Taedium Vitae.
Theocritus.
Theoretikos.
To Milton.
Yet Each Man Kills the Thing He Loves.

Wilde, Richard Henry
Farewell to America, A.
My Life Is like the Summer Rose.
Stanzas: "My life is like the summer rose."
To the Mocking-Bird.

Wilde, Robert *See* **Wild, Robert**

Wilder, Amos Niven
Alive for Evermore.
And with No Language but a Cry.
De Profundis.
If I Have Lifted Up Mine Eyes to Admire.
Prayer: "Omnipotent confederate of all good."
Thanksgiving.
To Pulpit and Tribune.

Wilder, John Nichols
Stand by the Flag.

Wilder, Viney
Prayer for Brotherhood.

Wildman, John Hazard
Feel of Fineness, The.
To Pius X at Easter.

Wile, Frances Whitmarsh
All Beautiful the March of Days.

Wiley, Alma Adams
Lincoln Memorial, The.
Memorial Day.
Nation's Shrine, The.
Washington Monument, The.

Wilhelm, Prince of Sweden
Madonna's Lamp, The.

Wilkes, John
Epitaph on the Lap-Dog of Lady Frail.

Wilkie, A. C.
Old Song by New Singers An.

Wilkin, Stanley Elster
Human Pens.

Wilkins, Alice
Ducks, The.
Elephant's Trunk, The.
Fairies' Lights.
Fun on the Beach.
Leaves Drink, The.
Little Brown Bear.
Little Frog, A.
My Funny Umbrella.
New Shoes.
Snow.
Ways of Traveling.

Wilkins, Eithne
Anabasis.
And Only Our Shadow Walks with Us.
Barbed Wire.
Cockcrow.
Dreamers and the Sea, The.

Wilkins (continued)
Eye, The.
Failure.
High Place, A.
Parzival, *sel.*
Passage of an August.
Shark's Fin.
Spoken through Glass.
Variations on a Theme by Sidney Keyes.
Wilkins, Mary E. *See* **Freeman, Mary Eleanor Wilkins**
Wilkins, Roy J.
Walk Close beside Me.
Wilkins, William
Engine Driver's Story, The.
Magazine Fort, Phoenix Park, Dublin, The.
Wilkinson, Anne
Adam and God.
Carol: "I was a lover of turkey and holly."
Cautionary Tale, A.
Falconry.
For Dinah, the Adeneys' Cat.
I took my watch beside the rose.
In June and Gentle Oven.
Leda in Stratford, Ont.
Lens.
Nature Be Damned.
Once upon a Great Holiday.
Poet's Eye-View, A.
Red and the Green, The.
Summer Acres.
Variations on a Theme.
Wilkinson, Florence *See* **Evans, Florence Wilkinson**
Wilkinson, Grace
Light.
Wilkinson, H. E.
Bread.
Topsy-turvy Land.
What Is It?
Wilkinson, Iris Guiver *See* **"Hyde, Robin"**
Wilkinson, Marguerite Ogden Bigelow
Before Dawn in the Woods.
Chant Out of Doors, A.
Christ and the Common Day.
End, The.
Guilty.
His Cross.
Incantation, An.
New City, The.
Pawnbrokers.
Proud Song, A.
Psalm to the Son, A.
Scatheless.
Song of Two Wanderers, A.
Songs of an Empty House, *sel.*
Time.
To the Lighted Lady Window.
Victory.
Waking Thought.
Woman's Beloved, A.
Wilkinson, William Cleaver
At Marshfield.
Webster, an Ode,*sel.*
Willard, Emma Hart
Cradle of the Deep.
Rocked in the Cradle of the Deep.
Willard, Nancy
Church, The.
Crewel.
First Lesson.
Freak Show, The.
Graffiti Poet, The.
I Knew a Boy Who Ran with the Dogs.
In Brittany.
Wedding Song.
Willett, Florence White
Crowded Out.
Willette, Florence Hynes
For a Girl in Love.
William of Shoreham
At Prime Jesus was y-led.
Hours of the Passion, *sel.*
Song to Mary, A.
William IX, Count of Poitiers *See* **Guillaume de Poitiers**
Williams, Anna
There Shall Be Wars.
Williams, Bertye Young
Friend Who Just Stands By, The.
Prayer, A: "Oh, not for more or longer days, dear Lord."
Prayer of Busy Hands, A.
Trus' an' Smile.
Washington.
Who Are the Wise Men?
Your House of Happiness.
Williams, Charles
After Ronsard.
At Dawn.
At the "Ye That Do Truly."
Crowning of Arthur, The.
Divorce.
Dream, A.
Mount Badon.
Night Song for a Child!
Taliessin's Return to Logres.
Taliessin's Song of the Unicorn.
Theobalds' Roads.
Walking Song.
Williams, Sir Charles Hanbury
Come, Chloe, and Give Me Sweet Kisses.
Epigram of Martial, Imitated.
Isabella, *sel.*
Lamentable Case, A.
Ode on Miss Harriet Hanbury at Six Years Old, An.
Old General, The.
Williams, Charles Kenneth
World's Greatest Tricycle Rider, The.
Williams, Eugene
Story of the Alchemist, The.
Williams, Evelyn M.
Chestnut Buds.
Williams, Francis Howard
Electra.
Song: "Bird in my bower, A."
Walt Whitman.
Williams, Harry H.
In the Shade of the Old Apple Tree.
Williams, Helen Maria
Julia, a Novel, *sel.*
To Hope.
Williams, Jessie E.
Submission.
Williams, John (1664-1729)
Some Contemplations of the Poor, and Desolate State of the Church at Deerfield.
Williams, John (b. 1922)
Dead, The.
For My Students, Returning to College.
History, A.
Leaf, The.
Meaning of Violence, The.
Skaters, The.
Williams, John A.
Safari West.
Williams, Jonathan
Distances to the Friend, The.
Everybody's Homesick Soldier Boy.
Fast Ball.
In England's Green & (a Garland and a Clyster).
Little Tumescence, A.
Ride in a Blue Chevy from Alum Cave Trail to Newfound Gap, A.
Switch Blade, The; or, John's Other Wife.
Those Troublesome Disguises.
Williams, Josephine
Tides.
Williams, Loring
Recompense.
Skeptic, The.
Williams, Lucy Ariel *See* **Holloway, Ariel Williams**
Williams, Mance
For Lover Man, and All the Other Young Men Who Failed to Return from World War II.
Year without Seasons, A.
Williams, Michael
Michael the Archangel.
Williams, Oscar
Blade of Grass, A.
Borrower of Salt, The.
By Fiat of Adoration.
Chant.
Children's Playground, The.
Dinner Guest.
Dwarf of Disintegration.
Editor's Private Cocktail Party, The.
Elements, The.
First Born, The.
Hub, The.
I Sing an Old Song.
In Postures That Call.
Jeremiad.
Last Supper, The.
Leg in the Subway, The.
Little Steamboat.
Man Coming toward You, The.
Man in That Airplane, The.
Milk at the Bottom of the Sea.
Mirage, The.
On Meeting a Stranger in a Bookshop.
On the Couch.
On the Death of an Acquaintance.
One Morning the World Woke up.
Paper in the Meadow, The.
Picture Postcard of a Zoo.
Praying Mantis Visits a Penthouse, The.
Road from Election to Christmas, The.
Seesaw, The.
Shopping for Meat in Winter.
Spring.
Spritely Dead, The.
Total Revolution, A.
Variations on a Theme.
Williams, Richard D'Alton
Dying Girl, The.
Extermination.
Williams, Roger
Adulteries, murthers, robberies, thefts.
Boast Not, Proud English.
Course bread and water's most their fare.
Courteous Pagan Shall Condemn, The.
God gives them sleep on ground, on straw.
God Makes a Path.
How busie are the sonnes of men?
I have heard ingenuous Indians say.
Indians count of men as dogs, The.
Indians prize not English gold, The.
Key into the Language of America, A; or, An Help to Language of the Natives, *sels.*
Mans restlesse soule hath restlesse eyes and ears.
One step twix't me and death, (twas Davids speech).
Our English gamesters scorne to stake.
Pagans wild confesse the bonds, The.
They see Gods wonders that are call'd.
Truth is a native, naked beauty; but.
What Habacuck once spake, mine eyes.
When Indians heare that some there are.
Williams, Ruth M.
Conqueror, The.
God Has Time.
God Incarnate.

Wyoming.
Winter, Mary
Blessing the Hounds.
Flower of "The Living Desert."
Lower Forms of Life.
Winter, William
Adelaide Neilson.
After All.
Age.
Arthur.
Asleep.
Heart's Anchor, The.
I. H. B.
My Queen.
Night Watch, The.
On the Verge.
Passing Bell at Stratford, The.
Queen, The.
Refuge.
Rubicon, The.
Unwritten Poems.
Winters, Yvor
Apollo and Daphne.
April.
At the San Francisco Airport.
Before Disaster.
By the Road to the Air-Base.
Death Goes before Me.
Fragment, A: "I cannot find my way to Nazareth."
Grave, The.
Heracles.
Immobile Wind, The.
John Day, Frontiersman.
John Sutter.
Journey, The.
Manzanita, The.
Marriage, The.
October Nocturne, An.
Ode on the Despoilers of Learning in an American University (1947), An.
On a View of Pasadena from the Hills.
Orpheus.
Prayer for My Son, A.
Priesthood, The.
Quod Tegit Omnia.
Sir Gawaine and the Green Knight.
Slow Pacific Swell, The.
Sonnet to the Moon.
Spring Serpent, A.
Summer Commentary, A.
Summer Noon, 1941.
Time and the Garden.
To a Military Rifle.
To Emily Dickinson.
To the Holy Spirit.
Two Songs of Advent.
Vision, A.
Walker, The.
Winther, Christian
Last Night.
Winthrop, Theodore
But Once.
Wintle, Walter D.
Man Who Thinks He Can, The.
Thinking.
Winton, Elizabeth
Little Valentine, A.
Special Delivery.
Summer Walk, A.
Surprise, A.
Winwar, Frances
Autumn.
Winward, Stephen F.
Day by Day.
"Wiolar."
Resolution.
Wipo
Victimae Paschali, *abr.*
Wisdome [*or* Wisdom], Robert
Turk and Pope.
Wise, William
After the Party.
Grandmother's Visit.
Grownups.
Little Miss Pitt.
Telegram.
What to Do.
When I Grow Up.
Wiseman, George W.
Easter Must Be Reclaimed.
Wister, Owen
Said Aristotle unto Plato.
Wiswall, Ichabod
Judicious Observation of That Dreadful Comet, A.
Witheford, Hubert
Alone.
At the Discharge of Cannon Rise the Drowned.
Elegy in the Orongorongo Valley.
Invasion.
Magnolia Tree, The.
Wither, George
Ah Me! Am I the Swaine.
Amaryllis I did woo.
Aspiration.
Author's Resolution [in a Sonnet], The.
Brittan's Remembrancer, *sel.*
Choice, The.
Christmas Carol, A: "So, now is [*or* has] come our joyfullest [*or* joyful] feast."
Collection of Emblemes, Ancient and Moderne, A, *sel.*
Conquered King, The, *sel.*
Divided Heart, The.
Fair Virtue, the Mistress of Philarete, *sels.*
Fidelia, *sels.*
For a Musician.
Fourth Eglogue, The, *abr.*
Haleluiah, or Britan's Second Remembrancer.
Hallelujah.
Hallelujah; or, Britain's Second Remembrancer, *sels.*
Hence, Away, You Sirens!
Hymn L: Rocking Hymn, A.
Hymne I: Generall Invitation to Praise God, A.
I know that if thou please thou canst provide.
I Loved a Lass.
I Wandered Out.
It may be 'tis observ'd, I want relations.
Kiss, The.
Love Sonnet, A.
Lover's Resolution, The.
Lullaby, A: "Sweet baby, sleep! what ails my dear."
Manly Heart, The.
Marigold, The.
Our Joyful Feast.
Philarete Praises Poetry.
Protector, The, *sel.*
Shall I, Wasting in Despair.
Shepheard's Hunting, The.
Shepherd's Hunting, The, *sels.*
Sleep, Baby, Sleep.
Sonnet: "Shall I, wasting in despair."
Sonnet upon a Stolen Kiss.
Stolen Kiss, A.
Theft, The.
This glorious title hath in it exprest.
Tired Petitioner, The, *sel.*
To a Musician.
What Care I.
When We Are upon the Seas.
Why, silly Man! so much admirest thou.
Widow's Hymn, A.
Witherby, Diana
Casualty.
Witherspoon, Naomi Long *See* **Madgett, Naomi Long**
Witherup, William
Freeway.
Gothic Tale, A.
Great White Father, The.
Hybrid Villanelle on a Line of Li Po, A.
In Minnesota the barns are black.
Marian at Tassajara Springs.
On the Death of Theodore Roethke.
Three for Robert Bly, *sel.*
Witt, Harold
Dreamscape in Kümmel.
More Nudes for Florence.
Nude.
Reluctances.
Where the Manatee Plays and the Manta Ray Flutters.
Wittenberg, Ernest
Sub-average *Time* Reader, The.
Wittlin, Jozef [*or* Joseph]
Stabat Mater.
Wodehouse, E. A.
Afforestation.
Wodehouse, Pelham Grenville
Printer's Error.
Song about Whiskers.
Time like an Ever-rolling Stream.
Woestijne, Karel van de
Elegy: "Child, your white face is chanting memories."
Sailors, The.
Wojtalewicz, Mildred
Sanctuary.
Wolcot, John *See* **"Pindar, Peter"**
Wolcott, Roger
Heart Is Deep, The.
Matthew X. 28.
Wolf, Leonard
Peasant, The.
Sonnet: "Sits by a fireplace, the seducer talks."
Wolf, Robert Leopold
Eve.
Man in the Dress Suit, The.
Pagan Reinvokes the Twenty-third Psalm, A.
Wolfe, Charles
Burial of Sir John Moore after [*or* at] Corunna, The.
Go, Forget Me.
To Mary.
Wolfe, ffrida
Choosing Shoes.
Four and Eight.
Hidden.
Poppies in the Garden, The.
What the Toys Are Thinking.
Wolfe, Florence Dolby
Bones Go to Church, The.
Wolfe, Humbert
A. E. Housman and a Few Friends.
Autumn.
Blackbird, The.
British Journalist, The.
Chorister in Avalon, A.
Dead Fiddle, The.
Endymion.
Fiddle and the Bow, The.
First Harp-Player, The.
Fishes.
G. K. Chesterton.
Gray Squirrel, The.
Green Candles.
Iliad.
In the City.
It is easier to be angry than to pity.
Journey's End.
Kensington Gardens, *sels.*
Laburnum.
Lamb.

Wolfe (continued)
Lilac, The.
Love in Jeopardy.
Love Is a Keeper of Swans.
Lupin.
Man.
My Desk.
Old Lady, The.
On Dean Inge.
Queen Victoria.
Requiem, *sels.*
Return of the Fairy, The.
Rose, The.
Saint, The, *sel.*
She has dusted the ornaments, rubbed down the chairs.
Things Lovelier.
This Is Not Death.
Thought, The.
Thrushes.
Torchbearer.
Tulip.
Uncelestial City, The, *sels.*
Waters of Life, The.
White Dress, The.
You cannot traffick in peace.
Zoo, The.

Wolfe, James
How Stands the Glass Around?

Wolfe, Thomas Clayton
Burning in the Night.
Magic.
Observe the Whole of It.
Something has spoken to me in the night.
Stone, a Leaf, a Door, A.
You Can't Go Home Again, *sel.*

Wolff, David
While We Slept.

Wolfram von Eschenbach
Fealty.
His Own True Wife.
Hope for Miracles.

Wolfskehl, Karl
And Yet We Are Here!
Shekhinah.
To Be Said at the Seder.
We Go.

Wolker, Jiri
Epitaph: "Here lies the poet Wolker, lover of the world."
Love Poem: "You say that in your eyes alone is all the world."
On This My Sick-Bed Beats the World.
Pillar-Box, The.

Wood, A. J.
Rolling John, *sel.*

Wood, Alfred E.
Fight at Dajo, The.

Wood, Anna Hamilton
Anvil of God's Mercy, The.

Wood, Charles Erskine Scott
Desert, The ("Never have I found a place").
Desert, The ("She is a nun").
Desert murmurs to the sun a strange murmur, The.
Goats.
I have come into the desert.
It is Spring and All Is Well.
Poet in the Desert, The, *sels.*
Suddenly night flung wide the sapphire gate.
Sunrise.
This is the pedigree of degradation.

Wood, Clement
Eagle Sonnets, *sels.*
Glory Road, De.
I have been sure of three things all my life.
I Pass a Lighted Window.
Prayer in Time of Blindness, A.
Singing Saviors, The.
Sonnet; "Flower of the dust am I: for dust will flower."
Sonnet: "I am a tongue for beauty. Not a day."
Sonnet: "I have been sure of three things all my life."
Sonnet: "O bitter moon, O cold and bitter moon."
Sonnet: "We are the singing shadows beauty casts."
Sonnet: "When down the windy vistas of the years."
Voyager's Song.
When down the windy vistas of the years.

Wood, Edna D.
Bumblebee.
Firefly.

Wood, Robert W.
Parrot and the carrot we may easily confound, The.

Wood, Stanley
Homes of the Cliff Dwellers.

Wood, William
A Deux.
Kinds of Shel-fish.
King of waters, the sea shouldering whale, The.
Kingly lyon, and the strong arm'd beare, The.
Princely eagle, and the soaring hawke, The.
Trees both in hills and plaines, in plenty be.

Woodberry, George Edward
Agathon, *sel.*
America to England.
At Gibraltar (*Sonnets* I *and* II).
Child, The.
Comrades.
Divine Awe.
Edith Cavell.
Essex Regiment March.
For thou art founded in the eternal fact.
Homeward Bound.
I never muse upon my lady's grace.
Ideal Passion, *sels.*
Immortal Love.
Islands of the Sea, The.
Life, A.
Love is the bread that feeds the multitudes.
Love's Rosary.
My Country, *sels.*
O destined Land, unto thy citadel.
O, Inexpressible as Sweet.
O Land Beloved.
O, Struck beneath the Laurel.
Old House, The.
On a Portrait of Columbus.
Our First Century.
Roamer, The, *sel.*
Rose of Stars, The.
Seaward.
Secret, The.
So Slow to Die.
Sodoma's Christ Scourged.
Song: "O, inexpressible as sweet."
Song of Eros.
Sonnets Written in the Fall of 1914.
To Those Who Reproved the Author for Too Sanguine Patriotism.
When First I Saw Her.
Why, Love, beneath the fields of asphodel.
Wild Eden, *sels.*

"Woodbine Willie." *See* **Studdert-Kennedy, Geoffrey Anketell**

Woodbourne, Harry
Flute of May, The.

Woodbridge, Benjamin
Upon the Author; by a Known Friend.
Upon the Tomb of the Most Reverend Mr. John Cotton.

Woodcock, George
Hero, The.
Imagine the South.
Island, The.
Merthymawr.
Poem from London, 1941.
Sonnet: "Looking into the windows that doom has broken."
Sunday on Hampstead Heath.
Tree Felling.
White.

Wooddeson, Richard
Lass of Isleworth Mill, The.

Woodgate, M. V.
Fire.

Woodrow, Constance Davies
To a Vagabond.

Woodruff, Donald M.
Night Attack.

Woodrum, Lon
Even in These Dying Leaves.
Give a Message, Pulpit!
Harvest and the Tempest, The.
He Sent Them Out.
I Wasn't There.
King of Kings, The.
Know That I Am God.
Prodigal, The.
Prophecy, The.
Spirit, The.
Take My Heart.
To Make a Home.
Transformation.
Upon This Rock.

Woods, Bertha Gerneaux
Patient Scientists, The.

Woods, James Chapman
Soul Stithy, The.
World's Death-Night, The.

Woods, John
Deaths at Paragon, Indiana, The.
Playwright.
Poem at Thirty.
When Senses Fled.

Woods, Margaret Louisa
Facing the Gulf.
Father of life, with songs of wonder.
Genius Loci.
I've heard, I've heard.
March Thoughts from England.
Mariners, The.
Now Sleeps the Lord.
Rest.
Return, The, *sels.*
To the Forgotten Dead.
Young Windebank.

Woods, William Hervey
House of Broken Swords, The, *sel.*
Prayer of Beaten Men, The.

Woodson, Mary Blake
Workers, The.

Woodward, John
Ragged Coat, The.

Woodworth, Francis Channing
Snow-Bird's Song, The.

Woodworth, Samuel
Bucket, The.
Half Horse and Half Alligator.
Hunters of Kentucky, The.
Loves She like Me?
Needle, The.
Old Oaken Bucket, The.

Wooley, Celia Parker
Refracted Lights.

Woolf, Virginia
Let Us Go, Then, Exploring.

Woolner, Thomas
Given Over.
My Beautiful Lady.

Woolsey, Sarah Chauncey *See* **"Coolidge, Susan"**
Woolsey, Theodore Dwight
Eclipse of Faith, The.
Woolson, Constance Fenimore
Kentucky Belle.
Wild March.
Yellow Jessamine.
Wooton, Sir Henry *See* **Wotton, Sir Henry**
Wordsworth, C. W. V.
Song in Praise of Paella.
Wordsworth, Christopher
Giver of All.
Giving to God.
Lord's Day, A.
O Day of Rest and Gladness.
Ship in the Midst of the Sea, The.
Wordsworth, Dorothy
Address to a Child during a Boisterous Winter Evening.
Cottager to Her Infant, The.
Cottager's Lullaby, The.
Loving and Liking.
Mother's Return, The.
Wind, The.
Wordsworth, William
Action is transitory—a step, a blow.
Address to My Infant Daughter.
Admonition to a Traveller.
Affliction of Margaret, The.
After-Thought.
Alice Fell.
Alpine Descent.
Among All Lovely Things My Love Had Been.
Among that band of Officers was one.
Among the Stars.
And many an endless, endless lake.
And now, with gleams of half-extinguished thought.
And they had fixed the wedding day.
Anecdote for Fathers.
Animal Tranquillity and Decay.
As If Awakened, Summoned.
Ascent of Mount Snowdon.
At the Grave of Burns [1803].
At This Farewell.
Band of Military Officers, A.
Beetle loves his unpretending track, The.
Beside the pleasant Mill of Trompington.
Between Namur and Liège.
Bleak season was it, turbulent and wild.
Blest Statesman He, Whose Mind's Unselfish Will.
Blest the Infant Babe.
Blind Beggar, The.
Blind Highland Boy, The.
Books.
Borderers, The, *sel.*
Boy of Winander, The.
Boyhood.
By Moscow Self-devoted to a Blaze.
By the Sea.
Calais, August, 1802.
Cambridge and the Alps.
Change in the Year, A.
Character of the Happy Warrior.
Characteristics of a Child Three Years Old.
Childhood ("When he had left the mountains and received").
Childhood and School-Time.
Childless Father, The.
Communion.
Communion with Nature ("For I would walk alone").
Complaint, A.
Composed among the Ruins of a Castle in North Wales.
Composed at Neidpath Castle, the Property of Lord Queensberry, 1803.
Composed at Rydal on May Morning, 1838.
Composed by the Sea-Side, near Calais, August, 1802.
Composed by the Side of Grasmere Lake.
Composed in the Valley near Dover.
Composed near Calais, on the Road Leading to Ardes.
Composed on the Eve of the Marriage of a Friend in the Vale of Grasmere.
Composed upon an Evening of Extraordinary Splendor and Beauty.
Composed upon Westminster Bridge, Sept. 3, 1802.
Conclusion.
Conclusion: "It was a close, warm, breezeless summer night."
Consummate Happiness.
Crescent Boat, The.
Crossing the Alps ("The only track now visible was one").
Daffodils.
Dear Brook! Tomorrow's noon again.
Dedicated Spirit, A.
Desideria.
Desire We Past Illusions to Recall.
Despondency Corrected.
Devotional Incitements.
The Pet Lamb.
Did Sabine grace adorn my living line.
Discourse of the Wanderer, and an Evening Visit to the Lake.
Diverging now (as if his quest had been).
Down the Simplon Pass.
Earth Has Not Anything to Show More Fair.
Ecclesiastical Sonnets, *sels.*
Echoes.
Education of Nature, The.
1811.
1801.
Elegiac Stanzas, Suggested by a Picture of Peele Castle, in a Storm.
Elegiac Verses.
Ellen Irwin; or, The Braes of Kirtle.
England and Switzerland, 1802.
England, 1802 ("Great men have been among us. . .").
England, 1802 ("It is not to be thought of that the flood").
England, 1802 ("Milton! thou should'st be living at this hour").
England, 1802 ("O Friend! I know not which way I must look").
England, 1802 ("When I have borne in memory what has tamed").
England! The Time Is Come When Thou Shouldst Wean.
Enough of Humble Arguments.
Evening Walk, An, *sels.*
Excursion, The, *sels.*
Expostulation and Reply.
Extempore Effusion upon the Death of James Hogg.
Fact, and an Imagination, A.
Fair Seed-Time Had My Soul.
Faith.
Faith and Freedom.
"Favourite pleasure, A."
Fidelity.
Fishing.
For nature then/ (The coarser pleasures of my boyish days).
Force of Prayer, The, *sel.*
Founding of Bolton Priory, The.
Fountain, The.
France.
French and the Spanish Guerrillas, The.
French Revolution, The.
From early childhood, even as hath been said.
Gladness of the May, The.
Glen-Almain, the Narrow Glen.
Glow-Worm, The
Goody Blake and Harry Gill.
Gracious Spirit o'er this earth presides, A.
Great Men Have Been among Us.
Green Linnet, The.
Happy Warrior, The.
Hart-Leap Well.
He was of stature tall.
Here Pause: The Poet Claims at Least This Praise.
High on a mountain's highest ridge.
Hoffer.
I Grieved for Buonaparté.
I Have Felt a Presence.
I have learned/ To look on nature.
I Saw the Figure of a Lovely Maid.
I thought of Chatterton, the marvellous boy.
I Traveled among Unknown Men.
I Wandered Lonely as a Cloud.
I watch, and long have watched, with calm regret.
If This Great World of Joy and Pain.
If Thou Indeed Derive Thy Light from Heaven.
Imagination.
Imagination and Taste, How Impaired and Restored.
Immeasurable height, The.
In a Child's Album.
In a throng, a festal company.
In London, September, 1802.
In March.
In One of Those Excursions.
In These Fair Vales.
Influence of Natural Objects.
Inner Vision, The.
Inscribed upon a Rock.
Inside of King's College Chapel, Cambridge.
Intimations of Immorality from Recollections of Early Childhood.
Intimations of Sublimity.
Introduction—Childhood and School-time.
It Is a Beauteous Evening [Calm and Free].
It Is Not to Be Thought Of.
It Was an April Morning.
Kitten and Falling Leaves, The.
Kitten at Play, The.
Kitten Playing with the Falling Leaves, The.
Laodamia.
Latimer and Ridley.
Lesson, A.
Let Nature Be Your Teacher.
Liberty, *sel.*
Lines: "Nay, traveller! rest."
Lines: "Slumber did my spirit seal, A."
Lines Composed a Few Miles above Tintern Abbey.
Lines Composed at Grasmere.
Lines Left upon a Seat in a Yew Tree.
Lines, Written [a Few Miles] above Tintern Abbey.
Lines Written in Early Spring.
Lines Written Near Richmond, upon the Thames, at Evening.
London, 1802 ("Milton! thou should'st be living. . .").
London, 1802 ("O Friend! I know not which way I must look").
Lost Love, The.
Louisa.
Lucy, *complete, in 5 parts.*
Lucy Gray; or, Solitude.

Wordsworth (continued)
March.
Margaret; or, The Ruined Cottage.
Matthew.
Merry Month of March, The.
Methought I Saw the Footsteps of a Throne.
Michael.
Milton.
Milton! Thou Shouldst Be Living at This Hour.
Moon was up, the lake was shining clear, The.
Most Sweet It Is [with Unuplifted Eyes].
Mutability.
My Heart Leaps Up [When I Behold].
Nature and the Poet.
Nature's Healing.
Near Anio's Stream I Spied a Gentle Dove.
Near Dover, September, 1802.
Newton.
Night in June, A.
Night-Piece, A.
Nightingale, The.
Noble, The.
Not in the Lucid Intervals of Life.
Not Love, Not War.
November, 1806 ("Another year!").
November 1 ("How clear, how keen").
Now, whether it were by peculiar grace.
Nuns Fret Not at Their Convent's Narrow Room.
Nutting.
Oh, Blank Confusion.
O joy! that in our embers.
Oh! Mystery of Man.
O Nightingale.
O Nightingale! Thou Surely Art.
Oh! there is never sorrow of heart.
Oh! yet a few short years of useful life.
Oak of Guernica, The.
October 1803 ("When, looking on the present face of things").
Ode: Intimations of Immortality from Recollections of Early Childhood.
Ode: On Intimations of Immortality from Recollections of Early Childhood.
Ode to Duty.
Old Cumberland Beggar, The.
Old Man, An.
On Man, on Nature, and on Human Life.
On Nature's invitation do I come.
On poetry and geometric truth.
On the Beach at Calais.
On the Departure of Sir Walter Scott from Abbotsford, for Naples.
On the Extinction of the Venetian Republic.
On the Frozen Lake.
On the Sea-Shore near Calais.
On the Subjugation of Switzerland.
On the Swiss.
Once more to distant ages of the world.
One evening (surely I was led by her).
One summer evening (led by her) I found.
Our Birth Is but a Sleep and a Forgetting.
Our steeds remounted and the summons given.
Pass of Kirkstone, The.
Perfect Woman.
Personal Talk.
Persuasion.
Pet Lamb, The.
Peter Bell, *sels.*
Pilgrim Fathers, The.
Poet and the French Revolution, The.
Poet, gentle creature as he is, The.
Poet, A!—He Hath Put His Heart to School.
Poet's Epitaph, A.
Prefatory Sonnet.
Prelude, The [or, Growth of a Poet's Mind], *much abr.*
Presences of Nature in Boyhood.
Prospectus.
Protest against the Ballot.
Rainbow, The.
Rainbow in the Sky.
Raven's Nest, The.
Reaper, The.
Recluse, The.
Redbreast Chasing a Butterfly, The.
Rededication to Nature, The.
Remembrance of Collins.
Residence at Cambridge.
Residence in France.
Residence in France (Continued).
Residence in London.
Resolution and Independence.
Retrospect—Love of Nature Leading to Love of Man.
Reverie of Poor Susan, The.
River Duddon, The, *sels.*
Ruined Cottage, The.
Ruth.
Ruth; or, The Influences of Nature.
Sailor's Mother, The, *sel.*
Same, The ("Milton! thou shouldst be living at this hour").
School-Time.
Scorn Not the Sonnet.
September, 1802; Near Dover.
Seven Sisters, The; or, The Solitude of Binnorie.
She Dwelt among the Untrodden Ways.
She Was a Phantom of Delight.
Shells.
Shepherd, The.
Simon Lee.
Simplon Pass, The.
Single tree there was, A.
Skating.
Sketch, A.
Sky after Storm.
Slumber Did My Spirit Seal, A.
Small Celandine, The.
So Fair, So Sweet, Withal So Sensitive.
Solitary, The.
Solitary Reaper, The.
Song at the Feast of Brougham Castle.
Song for the Spinning Wheel.
Song for the Wandering Jew.
Sonnet: Composed after a Journey across the Hamilton Hills, Yorkshire.
Sonnet: Composed While the Author Was Engaged in Writing a Tract Occasioned by the Convention of Cintra.
Sonnet: "England! the time is come."
Sonnet: "Fair star of evening, splendor of the west."
Sonnet: French and Spanish Guerrillas, The.
Sonnet: "I saw the figure of a lovely maid."
Sonnet: "It is a beauteous evening, calm and free."
Sonnet: "It is not to be thought of that the flood."
Sonnet: London 1802.
Sonnet: "Milton, thou shouldst be living at this hour."
Sonnet: "Nuns fret not at their convent's narrow room."
Sonnet: "O Friend! I know not which way I must look."
Sonnet, The: "Scorn not the Sonnet."
Sonnet: September, 1815.
Sonnet: September, 1802.
Sonnet: September 1, 1802.
Sonnet: "Sole listener, Duddon! to the breeze that played."
Sonnet: "Surprised by joy — impatient as the wind."
Sonnet: There Is a Bondage Worse.
Sonnet: "Thought of a Briton on the Subjugation of Switzerland.
Sonnet: To ——.
Sonnet: To the Lady Beaumont.
Sonnet: Where Lies the Land.
Sonnet: Wild Duck's Nest, The.
Sonnet, A: "World is too much with us, The; late and soon."
Sonnet: Written in London, September 1802.
Sonnet to the Virgin.
Sounding cataract, The.
Sparrow's Nest, The.
Speak!
Stanzas Written in My Pocket Copy of Thomson's "Castle of Indolence."
Stepping Westward.
Stolen Boat, The.
Stone and the Shell, The.
Strange Fits of Passion Have I Known.
Strong shock, A.
Stuffed Owl, The.
Summer Vacation.
Sun Has Long Been Set, The.
Sunset in the Lake Country.
Surprised by Joy [Impatient as the Wind].
Swans.
Swiss Peasant, The.
Tables Turned, The.
Tale of Margaret, The.
Tenour which my life, holds, The.
That best portion of a good man's life.
There Is a Little Unpretending Rill.
"There!" Said a Stripling Pointing with Meet Pride.
There Was a Boy.
There Was a Roaring in the Wind All Night.
This Prayer I Make.
Thorn, The.
Thought is with me sometimes, and I say, A.
Thought of a Briton on the Subjugation of Switzerland.
Thoughts of a Briton on the Subjugation of Switzerland.
Three Cottage Girls, The.
Three Years She Grew [in Sun and Shower].
Tintern Abbey.
'Tis Said, That Some Have Died for Love.
'Tis told by one whom stormy waters threw.
To ——, in Her Seventieth Year.
To a Butterfly ("I've watched you").
To a Butterfly ("Stay near me . . .")
To a Child.
To a Distant Friend.
To a good man of most dear memory.
To a Highland Girl.
To a lodge that stood.
To a Skylark ("Ethereal minstrel!").
To a Sky-Lark ("Up with me!").
To a Young Lady.
To Catherine Wordsworth 1808-1812.
To Coleridge in Sicily.
To H. C.
To Hartley Coleridge.
To M. H.
To Milton ("Milton! thou should'st be living . . .")
To Miss Blackett on Her First Ascent to the Summit of Helvellyn.
To My Sister.
To Sleep ("A flock of sheep that leisurely pass by").
To Sleep ("Fond words have oft been spoken to thee, Sleep").

To Sleep ("O gentle Sleep! do they belong to thee.")
To the Cuckoo.
To the Daisy ("Bright flower! whose home is everywhere").
To the Daisy ("In youth from rock to rock I went").
To the Daisy ("With little here to do or see").
To the Highland Girl of Inversneyde.
To the Moon.
To the Same Flower (Celandine).
To the Same Flower (Daisy).
To the Skylark.
To the Small Celandine.
To Toussaint L'Ouverture.
Trepidation of the Druids.
Trosachs, The.
'Twere Long to Tell.
Twilight was coming on, yet through the gloom.
Two April Mornings, The.
Universal Heart of Man, The.
Up! Up! My Friend, and Quit Your Books.
Upon Westminster Bridge.
Valedictory Sonnet to the River Duddon.
Vaudracour and Julia.
Violet, The.
Virgin, The.
Volant tribe of bards on earth are found, A.
Wanderer, The.
Wanderer Recalls the Past, The.
Waterfall and the Eglantine, The.
We Are Seven.
Weak Is the Will of Man, His Judgment Blind.
Westminster Bridge.
What Man Has Made of Man.
When I Have Borne in Memory [What Has Tamed].
Where Lies the Land to Which Yon Ship Must Go?
Whirl-Blast.
Who Ponders National Events Shall Find.
Why Art Thou Silent!
Why sleeps the future, as a snake enrolled.
Winander Lake.
"With How Sad Steps, O Moon, Thou Climb'st the Sky."
With Ships the Sea Was Sprinkled [Far and Nigh].
Within King's College Chapel, Cambridge.
Within the Soul a Faculty Abides.
World, The.
World Is Too Much with Us, The.
Written after the Death of Charles Lamb, *sel.*
Written in Early Spring.
Written in London, September, 1802.
Written in March.
Written in the Album of a Child.
Written in Very Early Youth.
Yarrow Revisited.
Yarrow Unvisited.
Yarrow Visited.
Yes, It Was the Mountain Echo.
Yew-Trees.

Work, Henry Clay
Come Home, Father.
Father, Dear Father, Come Home with Me Now.
Grandfather's Clock.
Marching through Georgia.
Ship That Never Returned, The.
Year of Jubilo, *with music.*

Worley, Mrs. J. B.
Mighty Hunter, The.

Worrell, Edna Randolph
Christmas Legend.

Worsley-Benison, H.
Song of the Engine, The.

Worth, Katharine
Trees That Shade a House.

Worth, Kathryn
Circus Elephant.
Smells.

Worthington, Kim
I Held a Lamb.

Wortman, Denis
God of the Prophets.

Wotton, Sir Henry
Character of a Happy Life, A.
"D. O. M."
Description of the Spring, A.
Elizabeth of Bohemia.
Epitaph on Sir Albert Morton's Wife.
Eternall Mover.
Happy Life, The.
Hymn to My God in a Night of My Late Sicknesse, A.
It Is Finished.
May Day, A.
On a Bank [*or* the Banck] as I Sat [*or* Sate] a-Fishing.
On His Mistress [*or* Mistris], the Queen of Bohemia.
On His Mistris, the Queen of Bohemia.
On the Bank as I Sat a-Fishing.
On the Death of Sir Albert Morton's Wife.
Poem Written by Sir Henry Wotton, in His Youth, A.
Tears at the Grave of Sir Albertus Morton.
To His Mistress, the Queen of Bohemia.
Upon the Death of Sir Albert [*or* Albertus] Morton's Wife.
Upon the Sudden Restraint of the Earle of Somerset, [Then] Falling from Favor.

Wotton, Sir John
In Praise of His Daphnis.
In Praise of His Love.

Wrafter, Denis
Braggart!
Old Man to His Scythe, The.
On Hearing a Broadcast of Ceremonies in Connection with Conferring of Cardinals' Hats.
Sabbath Reflection.

Wratislaw, Theodore
Expectation.
Music-Hall, The.
Vain Desire, A.

Wrede, Princess Gabrielle
Before the Crucifix.

Wreford, Heyman
Christ Is Coming.

"Wreford, James." *See* **Watson, James Wreford**

Wreford, John R.
Lord, While for All Mankind We Pray.

Wright, Bruce McM.
African Affair, The.
Journey to a Parallel.

Wright, Catharine Morris
Hillside Pause.

Wright, Charles
Daughters of Blum, The.
Smoke.
Weather Report.

Wright, David
Adamastor, whom Camoens and the sea.
Each time I return to Johannesburg it is summer.
Invocation to the Goddess, An.
Meditation on Identity.
Monologue of a Deaf Man.
Moral Story II.
My countryman, the poet, wears a Stetson.
My grandfather was an elegant gentleman.
On the Death of an Emperor Penguin in Regent's Park, London.
Pastoral: "Afternoon wears on, The."
Rousecastle.
Seven South African Poems.
South African Broadsheets, *sel.*
Under the African lintel, Table Mountain.
Verses to St. Cecilia.
Voyage to Africa, A, *sel.*
Walking to Dedham.

Wright, David McKee
Arlington.
Danny's Wooing.
Dark Rosaleen, *sels.*
Duff, The.
In the Moonlight.
In Town.
My Love is the voice of a song.
On a shining silver morning long ago.
Shearing.
While the Billy Boils.

Wright, Ernest V.
When Father Carves the Duck.

Wright, Frederick Adam
Letter to the City Clerk.

Wright, George T.
Aquarium.

Wright, Gladys Yoakum
Texas, Our Texas.

Wright, Hetty
Disappointed Wife, The.
Epitaph on Herself, An.
Mother's Soliloquy, A.

Wright, Ivan Leonard
Want of You, The.

Wright, James
Accusation, The.
American Twilights, 1957.
As I Step Over a Puddle at the End of Winter.
Assignation, The.
At the Executed Murderer's Grave.
At the Slackening of the Tide.
Autumn Begins in Martins Ferry, Ohio.
Autumnal.
Avenger, The.
Before the Cashier's Window in a Department Store.
Beginning.
Blessing, A [*or* The].
Breath of Air, A.
By a Lake in Minnesota.
Cold Divinities, The.
Depressed by a Book of Bad Poetry, I Walk toward an Unused Pasture and Invite the Insects to Join Me.
Dream of Burial, A.
Eisenhower's Visit to Franco, 1959.
Elegy in a Firelit Room.
Evening.
For the Marsh's Birthday.
Gesture by a Lady with an Assumed Name, A.
Ghost, The.
Girl in a Window, A.
Having Lost My Sons, I Confront the Wreckage of the Moon.
"I Am a Sioux Brave," He Said in Minneapolis.
In a Warm Chicken House.
In Memory of Leopardi.
In Response to a Rumor That the Oldest Whorehouse in Wheeling, West Virginia, Has Been Condemned.
Inscription for the Tank.
Jewel, The.
Lament for My Brother on a Hayrake.

Wright (continued)
Life, The.
Listening to the Mourners.
Living by the Red River.
Lying in a Hammock at William Duffy's Farm.
Message Hidden in an Empty Wine Bottle.
Micromutations.
Milkweed.
Morality of Poetry, The.
Mutterings over the Crib of a Deaf Child.
Note Left in Jimmy Leonard's Shack, A.
On Minding One's Own Business.
On the Skeleton of a Hound.
Paul.
Poems to a Brown Cricket.
Prayer to Escape from the Market Place, A.
Private Meeting Place, The.
Quest, The.
Rain.
Rip.
Saint Judas.
Snowstorm in the Midwest.
Stages on a Journey Westward.
Three Sentences for a Dead Swan.
To a Defeated Saviour.
To a Fugitive.
To a Salesgirl, Weary of Artificial Holiday Trees.
To Flood Stage Again.
To the Evening Star: Central Minnesota.
To the Ghost of a Kite.
Twilights.
Two Hangovers.
Two Poems about President Harding.
Ungathered Apples, The.
Vain Advice at the Year's End.
What the Earth Asked Me.
Youth.

Wright, Jay
Death as History.
End of an Ethnic Dream, The.
End of Ethnic Dream, The.
Frightened Lover's Sleep, The.
On the Block: Another Night Search.
Sense of Comedy, The: I.
This Morning.

Wright, Judith
Ancestors, The.
And Mr. Ferritt.
At Cooloolah.
Bora Ring.
Builders, The.
Bull, The.
Bullocky.
Cicadas, The.
Company of Lovers, The.
Country Dance.
Egrets.
Fire at Murdering Hut.
Hawthorn Hedge, The.
Legend.
Lyrebirds.
Night and the Child.
Old Prison, The.
South of My Days.
Storm.
To a Child.
Trapped Dingo.
Twins, The.
Two Fires, The.
Unborn, The.
Woman to Man.
Woman's Song.
Wonga Vine.

Wright, Keith
Fishing.

Wright, Richard
Between the World and Me.
Hokku: in the Falling Snow.
Hokku Poems.
I Have Seen Black Hands.

Wright, Sarah E.
Urgency.

Wright, Willard Huntington
Song against Women.

Wright, William Bull
Brook, The, *sel.*
Through his million veins are poured.

Wrighton, W. T.
Dearest Spot on Earth, The.

Wroth [*or* Wroath], Lady Mary
Countess of Montgomery's Urania, The, *sel.*
Love, What Art Thou?

Wurdemann, Audrey (Mrs. Joseph Auslander)
For Eros II.
Little Black Man with a Rose in His Hat.

Wu Ti, Emperor
Autumn Wind, The.
Liberator, The.
Li Fu-jen.
People Hide Their Love.

Wu Tsung Ai
Memories of Childhood.

Wyatt, Edith Franklin
City Afternoon, A.
On the Great Plateau.
To F. W.

Wyatt, Sir Thomas
A! My Herte, A! What Aileth The.
Absence absenting causeth me to complain.
Abused Lover Seeth His Folly and Entendeth to Trust No More, The.
Accusèd though I be without desert.
After great storms the calm returns.
"Ah Robin,/ Jolly Robin."
Alas, Madam, for Stealing of a Kiss.
Alas, poor man, what hap have I.
Alas the grief and deadly woeful smart!
All heavy minds.
And If an Eye May Save or Slay.
Answer that ye made to me, my dear, The.
Appeal, The.
As power and wit will me assist.
At last withdraw your cruelty.
At most mischief.
Behold, love, thy power how she despiseth!
Betrayal.
Blame Not My Lute.
Caesar, when that the traitor of Egypt.
Comparison of Love to a Streame Falling from the Alpes.
Complaint for True Love Unrequited.
Constancy.
Courtier's Life, The.
Deme as Ye List uppon Goode Cause.
Description of Such a One as He Would Love, A.
Desire, alas, my master and my foe.
Disdain ("If in the world").
Disdain Me Not without Desert.
Divers [*or* Dyvers] Doth Use, as I Have Heard and Know.
Driven by desire I did this deed.
Each man me telleth I change most my devise.
Earnest Suit to His Unkind Mistress Not to Forsake Him, An.
Epigram: "Enemy of life, decayer of all kind, The."
Epigram: "Face that should content me wonders well, A."
Epigram: "Fruit of all the service that I serve, The."
Epigram: "Lux my fair falcon, and your fellows all."
Epigram: "Sighs are my food, drink are my tears."
Epigram: "Who hath heard of such cruelty before?"
Epigrams.
Epistle to John Poins.
Epitaph, An, of Sir Thomas Gravener, Knight.
Farewell: "What should I say."
Farewell, all my welfare.
Farewell, Unkist.
Flaming sighs that boil within my breast, The.
For shamefast harm of great and hateful need.
For to love her for her looks lovely.
For want of will in woe I plain.
Forget Not Yet [the Tried Intent].
Forsaken Lover, The.
Fortune.
Full well it may be seen.
Galley, The.
Give place all ye that doth rejoice.
Hate Whom Ye List.
He Is Not Dead.
He Ruleth Not Though He Reign [*or* Raigne] over Realms That Is Subject to His Own Lusts.
Heart and service to you proffered, The.
Heart oppress'd with desperate thought.
Help Me to Seek.
Hind, The.
His Lady's Hand.
His Reward.
Honesty.
How Like You This?
How oft have I my dear and cruel foe.
How Should I Be So Pleasant?
How the Lover Perisheth in His Delight, As the Fly in the Fire.
I am as I am and so will I be.
I love loved [*or* lovyd] and so doth she.
I see that chance hath chosen me.
If chance assigned.
If ever man might him avant.
If fancy would favor.
If in the World There Be More Woe.
If it be so that I forsake thee.
If Thou Wilt Mighty Be.
If waker care, if sudden pale color.
If with complaint the pain might be expressed.
In Eternum [I Was Once Determed].
In faith I wot not well what to say.
In Faith Methinks It Is No Right.
In Spain ("Tagus, farewell, that westward with thy streams").
Is It Possible.
It May Be Good [Like It Who List].
It Was My Choice.
Joy so short, alas, the pain so near, The.
Knot which first my heart did strain, The.
Lament my loss, my labor, and my pain.
Liberty.
Like as the bird in the cage enclosed.
Like as the swan towards her death.
Lo! How I seek and sue to have.
Lo, what it is to love!
Long Love That in My Thought Doth Harbor, The.
Longer to muse.
Love and fortune and my mind, remember.
Love doth again.
Lover Beseecheth His Mistress Not to Forget His Steadfast Faith and True Intent, The.
Lover Compareth His Heart to the Overcharged Gun, The.

Lover Complaineth [*or* Complayneth] the Unkindness of His Love, The.
Lover Describeth His Being Striken with Sight of His Love, The.
Lover Forsaken, The.
Lover Forsaketh His Unkind Love, The.
Lover Having Dreamed of Enjoying of His Love, Complaineth That the Dream Is Not either Longer or Truer, The.
Lover Like to a Ship Tossed on the Sea, The.
Lover Rejoiceth, The.
Lover Rejoiceth the Enjoying of His Love, The.
Lover Renounceth Love, The.
Lover Sendeth Sighs to Move His Suit, The.
Lover Showeth [*or* Sheweth] How He Is Forsaken of Such as He Sometime Enjoyed, The.
Lover to His Bed, with Describing of His Unquiet State, The.
Lover's Appeal, The.
Love's Snare.
Luckes, my fair falcon, and your fellows all.
Lute Obeys, The.
Lux, My Fair Falcon.
Madam, withouten Many Words.
Madame, withouten Many Words.
Marvel No More.
May Time.
Me list no more to sing.
Mistrustful minds be moved.
Most wretched heart, most miserable.
My Galley Charged with Forgetfulness.
My hope, alas, hath me abused.
My love is like unto th' eternal fire.
My love took scorn my service to retain.
My Lute and I.
My Pen, Take Pain [a Little Space].
Nature, That Gave the Bee.
No! Indeed.
Now all of change.
Now must I learn to live at rest.
O Goodly Hand.
O Miserable sorrow withouten cure.
Of Dissembling Words.
Of His Love Called Anna.
Of His Love That Pricked Her Finger with a Needle.
Of His Return[e] from Spain[e].
Of Love.
Of purpose love chose first for to be blind.
Of Such as Had Forsaken Him.
Of the Courtier's Life.
Of the Mean and Sure Estate [Written to John Poins].
Pass forth, my wonted cries.
Patience.
Patience, for I have wrong.
Patience for my device.
Patience of all my smart.
Patience, Though I Have Not.
Penitential Psalms.
Perdy, [*or* Perdie] I Said It Not.
Pillar perished is whereto I leant, The.
Process of time worketh such wonder.
Promise, A.
Protest, A.
Psalm CXXX: "From depth of sin and from a deep despair."
Psalm CXLIII: "Hear my prayer, O Lord, hear my request."
Psalm CII: "Lord, hear my prayer, and let my cry pass."
Psalm XXXII: "O happy are they that have forgiveness got."
Psalm XXXVIII: "O Lord, as I Thee have both prayed and pray."
Psalm VI: "O Lord, since in my mouth, Thy mighty name."
Psalm LI: "Rue on me, Lord, for Thy goodness and grace."
Quondam was I in my lady's gras.
Remembrance.
Renouncing of Hardly Escaped Love, A.
Renouncing of Love, A.
Resignation.
Resound my voice, ye woods that hear me plain.
Revocation, A.
Right true it is, and said full yore ago.
Rondeau: "Help me to seek, for I lost it there."
Rondeau: "What no, perdie [*or* perdy]! ye may be sure!"
Satire: "Mine own John Poynz."
Satire 3: To Sir Francis Brian.
Satires, *sels.*
Say Nay.
Since love is such that, as ye wot.
Since love will needs that I shall love.
Since so ye please to hear me plain.
Since ye delight to know.
Since You Will Needs.
Since you will needs that I shall sing.
So Unwarely Was Never No Man Caught.
Sometime I sigh, sometime I sing.
Songs and Lyrics.
Sonnet: "Divers doth use (as I have heard and know)."
Sonnet: "Each man me telleth I change most my devise."
Sonnet: "Farewell, Love, and all thy laws forever."
Sonnet: "I abide and abide and better abide."
Sonnet: "My love took scorn my service to retain."
Sonnet: "To rail or jest, ye know I use it not."
Sonnet: "Whoso list to hunt, I know where is an hind."
Sonnet: "You that in love find luck and abundaunce."
Speak Thou and Speed.
Spite hath no power to make me sad.
Steadfastness.
Such hap as I am happed in.
Such is the course that nature's kind hath wrought.
Such vain thought as wonted to mislead me.
Suffering in sorrow in hope to attain.
Sufficed not, madam, that you did tear.
Supplication, A.
Syghes ar my foode, drynke are my teares.
Tagus, Farewell.
Take heed betime lest ye be spied.
Tangled I Was in Love's Snare.
Tangled Was I in Love's Snare.
That Speaking or Proffering Brings Alway Speeding.
That time that mirth did steer my ship.
There Was Never Nothing More Me Pained.
They Flee from Me.
Tho' I can not your cruelty constrain.
Thou hast no faith of him that hath none.
Though I cannot your cruelty constrain.
Though this the port and I thy servant true.
Throughout the World.
To a Lady to Answer Directly with Yea or Nay.
To cause accord or to agree.
To His Heart.
To His Lady.
To His Lute.
To His Pen.
To John Poynz ("Mine own John Poynz, since ye delight to know").
To John Poynz ("My mother's maids when they do sew and spin").
To make an end of all this strife.
To seek each where, where man doth live.
To Sir Francis Brian [*or* Bryan].
To wet your eye withouten tear.
To wish and want and not obtain.
Treizaine.
Unstable Dream, According to the Place.
Varium et Mutabile.
Venomous thorns that are so sharp and keen.
Vixi Puellis Nuper Idoneus.
Wandering Gadling, The.
What death is worse than this.
What Does This Mean?
What needeth these threat'ning words and wasted wind?
What No, Perdy.
What Once I Was.
What rage is this? what furor [*or* furour] of what kind?
What Should I Say.
What Shulde I Saye.
What word is that that changeth not.
When first mine eyes did view and mark.
When that I call unto my mind.
Where shall I have at mine own will.
Who lyst his welthe and eas retayne.
Who So List to Hount.
Whoso list to hunt.
Will ye see what wonders love hath wrongt?
With Serving Still.
Within My Breast.
Wyatt Being in Prison, to Bryan.
Ye Know My Heart.
You That in Love Find Luck [and Abundance].
Your Looks So Often Cast.
Ys Yt Possyble.

Wycherley, William
Advice to a Young Friend on the Choice of His Library.
Drinking Song, A, against All Sorts of Disputes in Drinking; to One, Who Always Bawl'd to Have Reason Done Him, and Was Noisie, and Quarrelsom in His Cups.
Envious Critick, The.
He is not great who gives to others law.
Love in a Wood, *sel.*
Song, A: In the Name of a Lover, to His Mistress; Who Said, She Hated Him for His Grey Hairs, Which He Had at Thirty.
Song: "Spouse I do hate, A."
Spouse I Do Hate.
To a Good Physician.
To a Witty Man of Wealth and Quality; Who, after His Dismissal from Court, Said, He Might Justly Complain of It.
To His Mistress, Who Said She Hated Him for His Grey Hairs.
To Sir George Etheridge.
To the Duke of Buckingham, a Man of a Great Mind, Reduc'd to a Little Fortune, *sel.*
Upon the Most Useful Knowledge, Craft or Cunning, Which Is More Wisdom, as 'Tis Less Wit.
Wife I Do Hate, A.

Wylie, Elinor
Address to My Soul.
American in England, An.
As I Went Down by Havre de Grace.
Atavism.
August.
Beauty.

Wylie (continued)
Bells in the Rain.
Birthday Sonnet.
Castilian.
Child on the Curbstone, The.
Cold-blooded Creatures.
Confession of Faith.
Desolation Is a Delicate Thing.
Doomsday.
Eagle and the Mole, The.
Epitaph: "For this she starred her eyes with salt."
Escape.
Fair Annet's Song.
Falcon, The.
Farewell, Sweet Dust.
Full Moon.
Golden Bough.
Heroics.
House Sonnet.
Hughie at the Inn.
Hymn to Earth.
I Hereby Swear That to Uphold Your House.
Innocent Landscape.
Innocents, The.
King Honor's Eldest Son.
Knight Fallen on Evil Days, The.
Lament for Glasgerion.
Lavish Kindness.
Let No Charitable Hope.
Lion and the Lamb, The.
Little beauty that I was allowed, The.
Little Elegy.
Little Joke.
Lodging for the Night, A.
Love to Stephen.
Madman's Song.
Malediction upon Myself.
My honoured lord, forgive the unruly tongue.
Nameless Song.
Nebuchadnezzar.
O Virtuous Light.
On a Singing Girl.
One Person, *sels.*
Parting Gift.
Pebble, The.
Pegasus Lost.
Peregrine.
Peregrine's Sunday Song.
Peter and John.
Poor Old Cannon, The.
Pretty Words.
Prophecy.
Puritan Sonnet.
Puritan's Ballad, The.
Sanctuary.
Sea Lullaby.
Shepherd's Holiday.
Sonnet: "I hereby swear that to uphold your house."
Sonnet: "Let us leave talking of angelic hosts."
Sonnet: "My honoured lord, forgive the unruly tongue."
Sonnet: "When I perceive the sable of your hair."
Sonnet from " One Person."
Sonnets from "One Person."
Spring Pastoral.
Sunset on the Spire.
This Corruptible.
To a Book.
To Claudia Homonoea.
Tortoise in Eternity, The.
True Vine.
Unfinished Portrait.
Velvet Shoes.
Wild Peaches (I-IV).
Winter Sleep.

Wyn, Eifion
Son of the Mountain.
Wyn, Hedd
War.
Wyndham, Charles
Fair Thief, The.
Wynne, Annette
Airplane, The.
Book, Book.
Books Are Soldiers.
Cars Go Fast.
Chairs.
Christopher Columbus.
Columbus.
Elephant, The.
Excuse Us, Animals in the Zoo.
Fairy Shoes.
Happy Oxen in a Stall.
Harebells in June.
Hearts Were Made to Give Away.
House Cat, The.
I Heard It in the Valley.
I keep Three Wishes Ready.
I Wonder If the Lion Knows.
I'm Wishing the World Christmas.
Indian Children.
Leaves Do Not Mind at All, The.
Letter Is a Gypsy Elf, A.
Lions Running over the Green.
Little Folks in the Grass.
Little Maid of Far Japan.
Memorial Day.
My Book Holds Many Stories.
Once When You Were Walking.
Outside the Door.
Palos, Spain, 1492.
People buy a Lot of Things.
Pilgrims Came, The.
Ring around the World.
Song of the Snowflakes.
Teacher, The.
Telegraph, The.
Thanksgiving Day.
Tree Stands Very Straight and Still, The.
Wires Are So Still and High, The.
Wish Is Quite a Tiny Thing, A.

X

"Xariffa." *See* **Townsend, Mary Ashley**
Xavier, Sister Mary *See* **Partridge, Sybil F.**
Xenos Palaestes
Requirements: "Not too pallid, as if bleacht."

Y

Yaha
Quiet.
Yakamochi (Otomo no Yakamochi)
Blossoms.
Deer and Echo.
Dream encounters.
Echo.
Gazing at the Moon while Journeying Homewards.
In the spring garden.
On this night that is cold.
Pretext.
This Hill.
Vain Wish.
We were together.
When evening comes.
When I see the first.
Yako, St. J. Page
Year's Ending, The.
Yamanaka, Tiroux
Flesh, The.
Yang Kuei-fei
Dancing.
Yannai
And It Came to Pass at Midnight.
Yasuhide
Flowers of the Sea.
Yates, Edmund
All Saints'.
Yates, L. E.
Strange Talk.
"Yates, Peter"(William Long)
Smelling the End of Green July.
Star of Eternal Possibles and Joy.
Thought and the Poet.
Yauger, Fay McCormick
Planter's Charm.
Ybarra, Thomas Russell
Christian, A.
Christian Is a Man Who Feels, A.
Lay of Ancient Rome.
Limerick: "Mussolini's pet Marshal, Graziani."
Limerick: "There was a young fellow from Fife."
Little Swirl of Vers Libre, A.
Ode to Work in Springtime.
Prose and Poesy; a Rural Misadventure.
Yeatman, Jennette
Exile.
Yeatman, Robert Julian *and* **Walter Carruthers llar** *See* **Sellar, Walter Carruthers,** *and* **Robert Julian Yeatman**
Yeats, William Butler
Acre of Grass, An.
Adam's Curse.
Aedh Tells of the Rose in His Heart.
Aedh Wishes for the Cloths of Heaven.
After Long Silence.
Against Unworthy Praise.
All Souls' Night.
All Things Can Tempt Me.
Among School Children.
Ancestral Houses.
Another Song of a Fool.
Apologia Addressed to Ireland in the Coming Days.
Apparitions, The.
Appointment, An.
Arrow, The.
At Algeciras—Meditation upon Death.
At Galway Races.
At the Abbey Theatre.
Ballad of Father Gilligan, The.
Ballad of the Foxhunter, The.
Before the World Was Made.
Beggar to Beggar Cried.
Black Tower, The.
Blood and the Moon.
Bronze Head, A.
Brown Penny.
Byzantium.
Cap and Bells, The.
Cat and the Moon, The.
Certain Artists Bring Her Dolls and Drawings.
Chambermaid's Second Song, The.
Choice, The.
Chosen.
Church and State.
Circus Animals' Desertion, The.
Coat, A.
Cold Heaven, The.
Collar-Bone of a Hare, The.
Come Gather round Me, Parnellites.
Coming of Wisdom with Time, The.
Coole Park and Ballylee, 1931.
Coole Park, 1929.

Cradle Song, A: "Angels are stooping, The."
Crazed Girl, A.
Crazy Jane and Jack the Journeyman.
Crazy Jane and the Bishop.
Crazy Jane Grown Old Looks at the Dancers.
Crazy Jane on God.
Crazy Jane on the Day of Judgment.
Crazy Jane on the Mountain.
Crazy Jane Reproved.
Crazy Jane Talks with the Bishop.
Cuchulain Comforted.
Cuchulain's Fight with the Sea.
Curse of Cromwell, The.
Dancer at Cruachan and Cro-Patrick, The.
Dawn, The.
Death.
Death of Cuchulain [*or* Cuchullin], The.
Dedication to a Book of Stories Selected from the Irish Novelists, The.
Deep-Sworm Vow, A.
Deirdre, *sel.*
Dialogue of Self and Soul, A.
Dolls, The.
Down by the Salley Gardens.
Dream of Death, A.
Drinking Song, A.
Easter, 1916.
Ego Dominus Tuus.
End of Day, The.
Ephemera.
Everlasting Voices, The.
Faeries's Song.
Faery Song, A: "We who are old, old and gay."
Fairy Song.
Fallen Majesty.
Falling of the Leaves, The.
Fascination of What's Difficult, The.
Father Gilligan.
Fergus and the Druid.
Fiddler of Dooney, The.
Fisherman, The.
Folk of the Air, The.
Folly of Being Comforted, The.
Fool by the Roadside, The.
For Anne Gregory.
For His Own Epitaph.
For My Daughter.
Four Ages of Man, The.
Fragments.
Friends of His Youth, The.
Great Day, The.
Gyres, The.
Hanrahan and Cathleen the Daughter of Hoolihan, *sel.*
Happy Townland, The.
Hawk, The.
He Bids His Beloved Be at Peace.
He Gives His Beloved Certain Rhymes.
He Mourns for the Change That Has Come upon Him and His Beloved, and Longs for the End of the World.
He Remembers Forgotten Beauty.
He Thinks of His Past Greatness When a Part of the Constellations of Heaven.
He Thinks of Those Who Have Spoken Evil of His Beloved.
He Wishes for the Cloths of Heaven.
Heart of the Woman, The.
Her Courage.
Her Courtesy.
Her Friends Bring Her a Christmas Tree.
Her Praise.
Her Race.
Host of the Air, The.
Hosting of the Sidhe, The.
Hound Voice.
"I Am of Ireland."
I have walked and prayed for this young child an hour.
I See Phantoms of Hatred and of the Heart's Fullness and of the Coming Emptiness.
In Memory of Con and Eva Gore-Booth.
In Memory of Eva Gore-Booth and Con Markiewicz.
In Memory of Major Robert Gregory.
In the Seven Woods.
Indian Song, An.
Indian upon God, The.
Into the Twilight.
Irish Airman Foresees His Death, An.
Irish poets, learn your trade.
It Is Time That I Wrote My Will.
John Kinsella's Lament for Mrs. Mary Moore.
Lady's Third Song, The.
Lake Isle of Innisfree, The.
Lamentation of the Old Pensioner, The.
Land of Heart's Desire, The.
Lapis Lazuli.
Last Confession, A.
Leaders of the Crowd, The.
Leda and the Swan.
Let All Things Pass Away, *sel.*
Lines Written in Dejection.
Living man is blind and drinks his drop, A.
Long-legged Fly.
Lover Mourns for the Loss of Love, The.
Lover Tells of the Rose in His Heart, The.
Lullaby: "Beloved, may your sleep be sound."
Mad as the Mist and Snow.
Magi, The.
Man Who Dreamed of Faeryland, The.
Man Young and Old, A, *sel.*
Mask, The.
Meditations in Time of Civil War.
Men Improve with the Years.
Michael Robartes Bids His Beloved Be at Peace.
Michael Robartes Remembers Forgotten Beauty.
Model for the Laureate, A.
Mohini Chatterjee.
Moods, The.
Mother of God, The.
Municipal Gallery Revisited, The.
Must we part, Von Hügel, though much alike, for we.
My Descendants.
My House.
My Table.
Never Give All the Heart.
New Faces, The.
News for the Delphic Oracle.
Nineteen Hundred and Nineteen.
Nineteenth Century and After, The.
No Second Troy.
Old Memory.
Old Men Admiring Themselves in the Water, The.
Old Song Resung, An.
On a Picture of a Black Centaur by Edmund Dulac.
On a Political Prisoner.
On Being Asked for a War Poem.
On Hearing That the Students of Our New University Have Joined the Agitation against Immoral Literature.
On Woman.
Only Jealousy of Emer, The, *sel.*
Pardon, Old Fathers.
Parnell.
Parting.
Paudeen.
People, The.
Pilgrim, The.
Pity of Love, The.
Players Ask for a Blessing on the Psalteries and on Themselves, The.
Poet to His Beloved, A.
Politics.
Prayer for My Daughter, A.
Priest of Coloony, The.
Purgatory.
Ragged Wood, The.
Red Hanrahan's Song about Ireland.
Renowned Generations, The.
Responsibilities, *sel.*
Resurrection, The, *sel.*
Rivery field spread out below, A.
Road at My Door, The.
Rose of Peace, The.
Rose of the World, The.
Rose Tree, The.
Running to Paradise.
Sad Shepherd, The.
Sailing to Byzantium.
Salley Gardens, The.
Scholars, The.
Second Coming, The.
Seek out reality, leave things that seem.
September, 1913.
Shadowy Horses, The.
She Turns the Dolls' Faces to the Wall.
Sixteen Dead Men.
Solomon to Sheba.
Song: "I saw a staring virgin stand."
Song, A: I Thought No More Was Needed.
Song: "In pity for man's darkening thought."
Song: "Wind blows out of the gates of the day, The."
Song from a Play.
Song from "The Only Jealousy of Emer."
Song of a Fool.
Song of the Happy Shepherd, The.
Song of the Old Mother, The.
Song of Wandering Aengus, The.
Sorrow of Love, The.
Spur, The.
Stare's Nest by My Window, The.
Statesman's Holiday, The.
Statues, The.
Stolen Child, The.
Stream and Sun at Glendalough.
Swift's Epitaph.
Symbols.
That the Night Come.
Those Dancing Days Are Gone.
Those Images.
Three Bushes, The.
Three Hermits, The.
Three Movements.
Three Things.
To a Friend Whose Work Has Come to Nothing.
To a Poet, Who Would Have Me Praise Certain Bad Poets, Imitators of His and Mine.
To a Shade.
To a Squirrel at Kyle-na-no.
To a Young Beauty.
To an Isle in the Water.
To His Heart Bidding It Have No Fear.
To Ireland in the Coming Times.
To Some I Have Talked With by the Fire.
To the Rose upon the Rood of Time.
Tom O'Roughley.
Tom the Lunatic.
Too long a sacrifice.
Tower, The.
Two Songs from a Play.
Two Songs of a Fool.
Two Trees, The.
Under Ben Bulben.
Under the Moon.

Yeats (continued)
Under the Round Tower.
Upon a Dying Lady (I-VII).
Upon a House Shaken by the Land Agitation.
Vacillation.
Valley of the Black Pig, The.
Vision, A, *sel.*
Wanderings of Oisin, The.
We galloped over the glossy sea.
What Then?
What Was Lost.
Wheel, The.
When Helen Lived.
When You Are Old.
Where My Books Go.
White Birds, The.
Who Goes with Fergus?
Wild Old Wicked Man, The.
Wild Swans at Coole, The.
Witch, The.
Woman Homer Sung, A.
Youth and Age.

"Yehoash" (Solomon Bloomgarden [*or* Blumgarten])
Angelus.
At the Tomb of Rachel.
Harp of David, The.
Hunting.
Jephthah's Daughter.
Mystery.
Old Song, An.
Prayer, A: "Eternal God, our life is but."
Prophet, The.
Psalm: "Happy is the man whom Thou hast set apart."
Shadows.
Song, A: "Song of grass, A,/ A song of earth."
Song as Yet Unsung, A.
Strongest, The.
Terror.
Thanksgiving.
That Is All I Heard.
Tool of Fate, The.
Wanderer, The.
Withered Rose, A.
Yang-se-fu.

Yeiser, Vivian *See* **Laramore, Vivian Yeiser**

Yelland, Edna Holroyd
Damascus.

Yellen, Samuel
Cloisters, The.
Discourse on the Real.
Flower Arrangement.
Grisaille with a Spot of Red.
Personal.
Prognostic.
Time of Light, a Time of Shadow, A.
Wood of the Self-Destroyers, The.
Wooden Tiger, The.

Yerby, Frank
Calm after Storm.
Fishes and the Poet's Hands, The.
Weltschmerz.
Wisdom.
You Are a Part of Me.

Yevtushenko, Yevgeny
Against Borders.
Companion, The.
Envy.
Schoolmaster.

York, Esther Baldwin
Stranger at the Peace Table.

York, Eva Rose
I Shall Not Pass This Way Again.

Yosa Buson
Scampering over saucers.

Yosano, Akiko
Abandoned on the beach.
I saw a white bird once.
More rapid than hail.

Yoshiki *See* **Ono no Yoshiki**

Young, Al
Dance for Ma Rainey, A.
Dance for Militant Dilettantes, A.
Dancing All Alone.
Dancing on the Shore.
For Poets.
I Arrive in Madrid.
Moon-Watching by Lake Chapala.
Move Continuing, The.

Young, Andrew
At Amberley Wild Brooks.
Bee-Orchis, The.
Beech, The.
Bird, The.
Black Rock of Kiltearn, The.
Blind Man, The.
Chalk-Cliff, The.
Climbing in Glencoe.
Conversion.
Cuckoo.
Cuckoos.
Culbin Sands.
Daisies.
Dead Bird, A.
Dead Crab, The.
Dead Mole, A.
Eagle, The.
Echoing Cliff, The.
Elm Beetle, The.
Fairy Ring, The.
Fallen Tree, The.
Falls of Glomach, The.
Farmer's Gun, The.
Fear, The.
Field-Glasses.
Flesh-Scraper, The.
Flood, The.
Go Now, My Song.
Hard Frost.
Hymn: "Lord, by whose breath all souls and seeds are living."
Idleness.
In December.
Lane, The.
Last Snow.
Late Autumn.
March Hares.
Missel-Thrush, The.
Mist.
Nicodemus, *sel.*
Old Tree, The.
On Middleton Edge.
Passing the Graveyard.
Prehistoric Camp, A.
Prospect of Death, A.
Rat, The.
Reflections on the River.
Round Barrow, The.
Ruined Chapel, The.
Scarecrow, The.
Secret Wood, The.
Sheaf, The.
Shepherd's Hut, The.
Slow Race, The.
Snow Harvest.
Stars, The.
Stay, Spring.
Stockdoves, The.
Suilven.
Swans, The.
Walking in Beech Leaves.
Wiltshire Downs.
Windy Day, A.
Wood and Hill.

Young, Barbara
Being a Gypsy.
Being Gypsy.
Changeling.
Common Things, The.
I Hear It Said.
Little Stones of Arlington, The.
Road Fellows.
Sophisticate.
Town Child.
Wait's Carol: "Give ye good-den."

Young, Douglas
For a Wife in Jizzen.
Ice-Flumes Owregie Their Lades.
Last Lauch.
Winter Homily on the Calton Hill.

Young, Edith Lillian
Disappointment—His Appointment.
His Appointment.

Young, Edward (1683-1765)
Another writes because his father writ.
Characters of Women.
Complaint, The; or, Night Thoughts.
Criminality of War, The.
Day of Judgement, The.
Extempore to Voltaire Criticising Milton.
Happiness an Art.
Lament of the Damned in Hell, The.
Live ever here, Lorenzo?—shocking thought!
Love of Fame, the Universal Passion, *sels.*
Man.
Night ("Tired Nature's sweet restorer").
Night Thoughts, *sels.*
On nature's Alps I stand.
Procrastination ("Be wise to-day").
Satire I: "My verse is satire; Dorset, lend your ear."

Young, Edward (b. 1818)
Under the Violets.

Young, Edward Hilton, 1st Baron Kennet of The De
Boy Was Born at Bethlehem, A.
Christmas.

Young, Edwin
Have I Done My Best for Jesus?

Young, Eleanor G. R.
Man from Sangamon, at Gettysburg, The.

Young, Ella
Bed Time.
Greeting.
Holiday.
Invitation.
Rain.
Shape-Changer.
Unicorn, The.

Young, Emily May
World without Pain, A.

Young, Ethel Fanning
Remembering Calvary.

Young, Francis Brett
Atlantic Charter; 1942.
Bête Humaine.
Dhows, The.
February.
Five Degrees South.
Island, The, *sel.*
Prothalamion.
Song at Santa Cruz.

Young, George W.
Lips That Touch Liquor.

Young, Marguerite
Death by Rarity.
Noah's Ark.
Speculative Evening.
Whales, The.
White Rat, The.

Young, Roland
Ape, The.
Flea, The.
Goat, The.
Happy Bounding Flea, The.
Jungle Pest, The.
Miscegeneous Zebra, The.
Owl, The.

Zebra, The.
Young, Ruth Comfort Mitchell *See* **Mitchell, Ruth Comfort**
Young, Samuel Hall
Into the Sunset.
Let Me Die Working.
Young, Stanley
Epitaph for a Concord Boy.
Young, Virginia Brady
Teacher, The.
Young, William
Bells, The.
Bridal Pair, The.
Conscience-Keeper, The.
Flower-Seller, The.
Judith.
Losers, The.
Pawns, The.
Philomel to Corydon.
Victor, The.
Wishmakers' Town, *sels.*
Youngs, Mary Fanny
Edge of the World, The.
In the Cove.
Yozei, Emperor
Falling from the ridge.
Yuan Chen
Elegy, An: "O youngest, best-loved daughter of Hsieh."
Pitcher, The.
Yriarte, Tomás de *See* **Iriarte, Tomás de**
Yüan Chieh
Civilization.
Yüan Mei
By Chance I Walk.
Chopsticks.
In an Old Library.
Only Be Willing to Search for Poetry.
Standing at the Foot of the Steps at Night.
Yu Ch'ien
Honeymooners, The.
Yud, Nachum
Like the Eyes of Wolves.
Yuhara, Prince
Dialogue.
"What am I to do with my Sister?"
Yuke, Prince
With a rocking.
Yule, Sir Henry
Birkenhead, The, *sel.*
Not with the cheer of battle in the throat.

Z

Zabel, Morton Dauwen
Herakles Archer.
Homage to Mürren.
Nettle, the Flower, The.
Scene à Faire.
Storm at Nightfall, The.
Teufelsdröckh Minor.
Traitors, The.
Zangwill, Israel
At the Worst.
At the Zoo.
Death's Transfiguration.
Despair and Hope.
Dreams.
Evil is here? That's work for us to do.
Evolution.
In the City.
In the Morgue.
Inexhaustible.
Israel.
Jehovah.
"Might Is Right."
Moses and Jesus.
Seder-Night.
Sundered.
Tabernacle Thought, A.
Theodor Herzl.
To a Pretty Girl.
Vanitas Vanitatum.
Vision.
Why Do We Live?
Yom Kippur.
Zarathustra *See* **Zoroaster**
Zaturenska, Marya Alexandrovna (Mrs. Horace Gregory)
Castaways, The.
Chorale for Autumn.
Daisy, The.
Elegies over John Reed.
Elegy of the Kremlin Bells, The.
False Summer, The.
Flight of the Sparrows.
Girl Takes Her Place among the Mothers, The.
Girl's Song.
Head of Medusa.
Lightning for Atmosphere.
Lovers, The.
Old Tale, An.
Repeated in Thin Gold.
Song: "Life with her weary eyes."
Song of a Factory Girl.
Spinners at Willowsleigh.
Tempest, The.
Variations on a Theme by George Herbert.
Water and Shadow.
White Dress, The.
Woman at the Piano.
Zeb-un-Nissa, Princess
Lament: "Within my bosom stirs once more tonight."
Zech, Paul
Factory Street in Daylight.
Forest, The.
Houses Have Open Eyes.
Zeitlin, Israel *See* **Tiempo, César**
Zeldis, Chayyim
Holy Ones, the Young Ones, The.
Zerea Jacob, Emperor of Abyssinia
Hymn to Mary.
Salutation.
Zilles, Luke
Bunch of Wild Flowers.
Details.
Zinnes, Harriet
Cocktail Party, The.
Zinzendorf, Nikolaus Ludwig, Graf von
He Leads.
Lowly Bethlehem.
My Light! My Way!
O Bottomless Depths of God's Infinite Love.
Plea, A.
Zoroaster [*or* Zarathustra]
Divine Songs to Ahura Mazda.
Zorrilla y Moral, Jose
Toledo ("No more the jousts").
Zuckmayer, Carl
My Death.
Zuker, Anne
Waiting Mothers.
Zukofsky, Louis
A 11.
Chloride of Lime and Charcoal.
Green Leaf, The.
Guests, The.
Peri Poietikes.
Poem Beginning "The."
So That Even a Lover.
Song: "Old friends/ when I was young."
This Is after All Vacation.
You Who Were Made for This Music.
Zwall, Ruth Gibbs
Fragrance.
Zweig, Stefan
Chosen of God.
Flowering without End.
Jeremiah, *sels.*
Zwicker, Kenneth
Shantyboys' Song, The.

SUBJECT INDEX

Aachen, Germany
Aix-la-Chappelle, 1945. Bowers.
Abbey Asaroe, Ireland
Abbey Asaroe. Allingham.
Abbey Theatre, Dublin
Old Woman, An, Outside the Abbey Theatre. Strong.
Abel
Abel. Capetanakis.
Abelard, Peter
Eloisa's Prayer for Abelard. Pope.
Sic et Non. Read.
Aberdare, Wales
Mountain over Aberdare, The. Lewis.
Abishag
Abishag. Spire.
Abolitionists
Abolitionist, The. Conquest.
John Brown's Prayer. *Fr.* John Brown's Body. S. V. Benét.
Abraham
Abraham. Muir.
Abraham to kill him. Dickinson.
Abraham's Madness. Noll.
Absalom
Dispraise of Absalom, The. *Unknown.*
Absence
Absence. Arnold.
Absence. Hoskins.
Absence. Jago.
Absence. Mew.
Absence, The. Warner.
Absences. Larkin.
Being your slave, what should I do but tend. Sonnets, LVII. Shakespeare.
For Anne. Cohen.
Present in Absence. *Unknown.*
Acacia
Acacia Leaves, The. *Fr.* Scented Leaves from a Chinese Jar. Upward.
Wattle and Myrtle. Cuthbertson.
Whisperings in Wattle-Boughs. Gordon.
Young Acacia, The. Bialik.
Acadia
Evangeline. Smith.
In ev'ry thought, in ev'ry wish I own. *Fr.* Acadia. Howe.
Acadians
Evangeline. Longfellow.
Few days more they drifted, ever west, A. *Fr.* The Emigration of the Fairies. Duvar.
Accordion
Man with a Little Pleated Piano, A. Welles.
Achilles
Achilles. Myers.
Achilles and the King. Logan.
Achilles' Shield. *Fr.* The Iliad. Homer.
Before a Statue of Achilles. Santayana.
Epitaph on Achilles. *Unknown.*
Wrath of Achilles, The. *Fr.* The Iliad. Homer.
Aconite
Aconite, The. Graham.
Acorns
Acorn, The. *Unknown.*
Acorns. King.
Actaeon
Actaeon. Heppenstall.
Acteon. *Fr.* Metamorphoses. Ovid.
Acting and Actors
Actress, The. Parker.
Ballade of Dead Actors. Henley.
David Garrick. *Fr.* Retaliation. Goldsmith.
Mad Actor. Montague.
Thespians at Thermopylae, The. Cameron.
They All Want to Play Hamlet. Sandburg.
When Burbadge Played. Dobson.
Adam
Adam. Rilke.
Adam and Eve. Genesis, Bible, *O.T.*
Adam and Eve. Manger.
Adam and Eve. Shapiro.
Adam Lay Ibounden. *Unknown.*
Adam Posed. Countess of Winchilsea.
Adam—the First Kiss. Porter.
Age of Innocence. Hough.
Begetting of Cain, The. Plutzik.
Circle, A. Spencer.
Exile, The. De la Mare.
Imperial Adam. Hope.
Jealous Adam. Manger.
Lady's-Maid's Song, The. Hollander.
Lilith. Kennedy.
"O Felix Culpa!" *Unknown.*
Old Adam, The. W. R. Benét.
Recognition of Eve, The. *Fr.* Adam and Eve. Shapiro.
Reflection, A. Hood.
Sickness of Adam, The. *Fr.* Adam and Eve. Shapiro.
Temptation and Fall of Man, The. *Fr.* Genesis. *Unknown.*
229. Villa.
When Adam Day by Day. Housman.
Adamastor
Adamastor, whom Camoens and the sea. *Fr.* A Voyage to Africa. Wright.
Adams, Franklin Pierce ("F.P.A.")
Lines Written on November 15, 1933, by a Man Born November 15, 1881. Hamilton.
Adams, John Quincy
John Quincy Adams. S. V. Benét.
Addison, Joseph
Atticus. *Fr.* Epistle to Dr. Arbuthnot. Pope.
To the Earl of Warwick on the Death of Mr. Addison. Tickell.
Adlestrop, England
Adlestrop. Thomas.
Adolescence
Certain Age, A. McGinley.
For Karen. Hughes.
My Girl, My Stringbean, My Lovely Woman. Sexton.
Portrait of a Girl with a Comic Book. McGinley.
Waking. Anderson.
Adonis
Adonis. Doolittle.
Lament for Adonis. Bion.
Shepherd's Song of Venus and Adonis, The. Constable.
Venus and Adonis. Shakespeare.
Adur (river), England
Flood, The. Young.
Advent
Advent. Fletcher.
Advent. C. G. Rossetti.
Advent Meditation. Meynell.
Farewell! Advent. Ryman.
No Sudden Thing of Glory. Meynell.
Two Songs of Advent. Winters.
Advertising
Advertising Agency Song, The. *Unknown.*
It Pays to Advertise. *Unknown.*
Memorial to the Great Big Beautiful Self-sacrificing Advertisers. Ebright.
Nightmare Number Four. Bloch.
Sky-Writer. Starrett.
Aegean Sea
Aegean. Simpson.
Santorin. Flecker.
Aeneas
Aeneas at Washington. Tate.

Aeneas *(continued)*
Aeneid, The, *sels.* Virgil.
Dido. Campion.
Staye, staye Aeneas, for theyne owne sake staye. *Unknown.*
Aeneid, The (Vergil)
Concerning Virgil's Aeneids. Grimald.
Falling Asleep over the Aeneid. R. Lowell.
Aengus
Song of Wandering Aengus, The. Yeats.
Æolian Harps
Ode to an Æolus's Harp. Mason.
Aesop
Aesop. Lang.
Aesop at Play. Phaedrus.
Africa
Afar in the Desert. Pringle.
Africa. Alexander.
Africa. Diop.
Africa. McKay.
Africa. Naudé.
Africa Speaks. Dei-Anang.
African Dance. Hughes.
African Heaven. Parkes.
Africa's Plea. Dempster.
Bantu on a Bicycle. Ross.
Congo, The. Lindsay.
Continent That Lies within Us, The. Nicol.
Dawn in the Heart of Africa. Lumumba.
Deep Down the Blackman's Mind. Armattoe.
Distance. Delius.
Far Cry from Africa, A. Walcott.
Far from Africa. Danner.
Heritage. Cullen.
Invocation to the African Muse. *Fr.* The Flaming Terrapin. Campbell.
Is This Africa. Dempster.
Meaning of Africa, The. Nicol.
Memorial of Africa, A. Macdonald.
My Africa. Dei-Anang.
Scorpion, The. Plomer.
Song-Maker, The. Fairbridge.
Stages. Macnab.
Tribes, The. Fuller.
Volubilis, North Africa. Currey.
What Is Africa to Me? *Fr.* Heritage. Cullen.
Who Knows? Milner-Brown.
Young Africa's Resolve. Osadebay.
Book of South African Verse, A (BoSA). Guy Butler, ed.
Penguin Book of South African Verse, The (PeSA). Jack Cope and Uys Krige, eds.
Poems from Black Africa (PBA). Langston Hughes, ed.
Africa, South. *See* **South Africa, Republic of.**
Afternoon
Afternoon for a Small Boy. Noll.
Afternoon on a Hill. Millay.
City-Afternoon, A. Wyatt.
Post-Meridian. Garrison.
Afton (river), Scotland
Afton Water. Burns.
Flow Gently, Sweet Afton. Burns.
Afzal Khan
Rise of Shivaji, The. Ghose.
Agamemnon
Agamemnon's Tomb. S. Sitwell.
Agassiz, Louis
Farewell to Agassiz, A. Holmes.
Fiftieth Birthday of Agassiz, The. Longfellow.
Three Friends of Mine. Longfellow.
Age *See* **Middle Age; Old Age.**
Aghadoe, Ireland
Aghadoe. Todhunter.
Agincourt, Battle of
Agincourt. Drayton.
Before Agincourt. *Fr.* King Henry V. Shakespeare.
Carol of Agincourt, A. *Unknown.*
Agnosticism
Agnostic's Creed, The. Malone.
Agnosto Theo. Hardy.
Biography of an Agnostic. Ginsberg.
Harald, the Agnostic Ale-loving Old Shepherd Enemy of the Whisky-drinking Ploughmen and Harvesters, Walks over the Sabbath Hill to the Shearing. Brown.
Agricola, Johannes
Johannes Agricola in Meditation. R. Browning.
Agrigento, Italy
Agrigento. Ross.
Aguinaldo, Emilio
Aginualdo. Shadwell.
Aikman, William
On the Death of Mr. William Aikman the Painter. Thomson.
Ailsa Craig, Scotland
To Ailsa Rock. Keats.
Air
Air. Raine.
Day the Winds, The. Miles.
Oxygen. Swift.
Air Plants
Air Plant, The. Crane.
Air Raids
Air Raid across the Bay of Plymouth. Spender.
Among Those Killed in the Dawn Raid Was a Man Aged a Hundred. Thomas.
Bombardment. Lawrence.
Bombers. Day Lewis.
Bombing Casualties in Spain. Read.
Brother Fire. MacNeice.
Ceremony after a Fire Raid. Thomas.
Dead in Europe, The. R. Lowell.
Erige Cor Tuum ad Me in Caelum. Doolittle.
Fury of Aerial Bombardment, The. Eberhart.
In the Shelter. Day Lewis.
Losses. Jarrell.
On the Pilots Who Destroyed Germany in the Spring of 1945. Spender.
Raider, The. Rodgers.
Refusal to Mourn the Death, by Fire, of a Child in London, A. Thomas.
Still Falls the Rain. E. Sitwell.
Air Warfare
Death of the Ball Turret Gunner, The. Jarrell.
Fury of Aerial Bombardment, The. Eberhart.
Irish Airman Foresees His Death, An. Yeats.
Pilot from the Carrier, A. Updike.
Pilots, Man Your Planes. Jarrell.
Second Air Force. Jarrell.
Airline Stewardesses
Falling. Dickey.
Airplanes. *See* **Aviation and Aviators.**
Ajanta, India
Ajanta. Rukeyser.
Ajax (Telemonian Ajax)
Leaving Troy. Irwin.
Akhenaton (Amenhotep IV)
Akhnaton. Jones.
Alabama (ship)
Alabama, The. Bell.
Eagle and Vulture, The. Read.
Kearsarge and *Alabama. Unknown.*
Alabama (state)
Alabama. Field.
Alabama. Tutwiler.
Daybreak in Alabama. Hughes.
Alamo
Defense (*or* Defence) of the Alamo, The. Miller.
Lament for the Alamo. Guiterman.
Men of the Alamo, The. Roche.
Alaric I
Dirge of Alaric the Visigoth. Everett.
Alaska
Alaska. Miller.
Alaska. *Unknown.*
Cremation of Sam McGee, The. Service.
In the Yukon. Gustafson.
Shooting of Dan McGrew. Service.
Albatross
Albatross, The. Baudelaire.
Albatross, The. Biram.
Albatross. Burgess.
Albatross, The. Reeves.
Albatross. Stoddard.
Albert I, King of the Belgians
King of the Belgians. Smith.

Alcestis
Alcestis. Verry.
Alchemy and Alchemists
Alchemist, The, *sels.* Jonson.
Alcott, Louisa May
Louisa May Alcott. Moulton.
Alden, John, and Priscilla Alden
American History. Adams.
Ale
Back and Side Go Bare, Go Bare. *Fr.* Gammer Gurton's Needle. *At. to* Stevenson.
Bring Us in Good Ale. *Unknown.*
In Praise of Ale. Bonham.
Mannerly Margery Milk and Ale. Skelton.
Tunning of Elinour Rumming, The. Skelton.
Aleichem, Sholom
Epitaph: "Here lies a simple Jew." Aleichem.
Sholom Aleichem. Lieberman.
Alexander Jannaeus, King of Judah
Alexander Jannai. Cavafy.
Alexander the Great
Alexander the Great. *Unknown.*
Alexander's Feast; or, The Power of Music. Dryden.
How We Heard the Name. Dugan.
Alexandra, Queen of England
Welcome to Alexandra, A. Tennyson.
Alfred the Great
Alfred the Harper. Sterling.
Ballad of the White Horse, The. Chesterton.
Fact, and an Imagination, A. Wordsworth.
Alfonso X, King of Castile and Leon
Alphonso of Castile. Emerson.
Alhambra. *See* **Granada.**
Ali, Muhammed. *See* **Clay, Cassius.**
Aliens
Alien. Frazee-Bower.
Alien. MacLeish.
Alien, The. Murray.
America Greets an Alien. *Unknown.*
All Fools' Day. *See* **April Fools' Day.**
All Saints' Eve. *See* **Halloween.**
All-Souls' Day
All-Souls' Day. Sassoon.
Pray for the Dead. Eaton.
Souling Song, The. *Unknown.*
All Souls' Night
All Souls' Night. Shorter.
All Souls' Night. *Fr.* A Vision. Yeats.
On Kingston Bridge. Cortissoz.
Allen, Edward
In Ed. Allen. Weever.
To Edward Allen. Jonson.
Allen, Ethan
Green Mountain Boy. Smyth.
Alligators
Alligator, The. Ravenel.
Alligator on the Escalator. Merriam.
Almond Trees
Almond Blossom. Arnold.
Almond Blossom in Wartime. Spender.
Almond Blossoms. *Fr.* Three Pictures. Dalmon.
Pink Almond. Tynan.
When Almonds Bloom. Shinn.
Alnwick Castle, England
Alnwick Castle. Halleck.
Aloes
Aloe Plant, The. Harbaugh.
Alpheus
Alpheus and Arethusa. Daly.
Arethusa. Shelley.
Alphonsus Rodriguez, Saint
St. Alphonsus Rodriguez. Hopkins.
Alps
Alpine Flowers, The. Sigourney.
Mont Blanc. Shelley.
Alsace, France
First Snow in Alsace. Wilbur.
Altars
Altar, The. Herbert.
Altgeld, John Peter
Eagle That Is Forgotten, The. Lindsay.
Altolaguirre, Manuel
To a Spanish Poet. Spender.
Alumni
Blues for an Old Blue. Gibson.
Tenth Reunion. Steese.
Amagansett, New York
Amagansett Beach Revisited. Wheelock.
America (United States of). *See* **United States.**
American Revolution
Ancient Prophecy, An. Freneau.
Bonhomme Richard and *Serapis,* The. Freneau.
Bunker Hill. Calvert.
Carmen Bellicosum. McMaster.
Centenarian's Story, The. Whitman.
Chester. Billings.
Concord Hymn. Emerson.
Cornwallis's Surrender. *Unknown.*
Cruise of the *Fair American.* *Unknown.*
Daughter's Rebellion, The. Hopkinson.
Emily Geiger. *Unknown.*
Epitaph for a Concord Boy. Young.
Green Mountain Boys, The. Bryant.
Hospital Prison Ship, The. *Fr.* The British Prison Ship. Freneau.
Independence Bell—July 4, 1776. *Unknown.*
Lexington. *Fr.* The Psalm of the West. Lanier.
Lexington. Whittier.
Liberty-Pole, The. *Fr.* M'Fingal. Trumbull.
Little Black-eyed Rebel, The. Carleton.
Major André. *Unknown.*
Maryland Battalion, The. Palmer.
Minute-Men of North-Boro', The. Rice.
Modern Jonas, The. *Unknown.*
Molly Maguire at Monmouth. Collins.
Molly Pitcher. Richards.
Molly Pitcher. Sherwood.
Morgan Stanwood. Rich.
Mugford's Victory. Chadwick.
Nathan Hale. Finch.
New England's Chevy Chase. Hale.
New England's Dead. McLellan.
News from Yorktown. Smith.
Northern Soldier, The. Freneau.
Off from Boston. *Unknown.*
On Disbanding the Army. Humphreys.
On Independence. Sewell.
On the Departure of the British from Charleston. Freneau.
On the Eve of Bunker Hill. Scollard.
Paul Revere's Ride. *Fr.* Tales of a Wayside Inn. Longfellow.
Poem Containing Some Remarks on the Present War, A. *Unknown.*
Progress of Sir Jack Brag, The. *Unknown.*
Prophecy in Flame. Howard.
Riflemen's Song at Bennington. *Unknown.*
Rodney's Ride. Brooks.
Royal Adventurer, The. Freneau.
Running the Blockade. Perry.
Seventy-six. Bryant.
Storming of Stony Point, The. Guiterman.
Swamp Fox, The. Simms.
Ticonderoga. Wilson.
To the Memory of the Brave Americans. Freneau.
Town-Meeting, A. *Fr.* M'Fingal. Trumbull.
Trip to Cambridge, The. *Unknown.*
Wagoner of the Alleghanies, The. *sels.* Read.
War and Washington. *Fr.* Cato. Sewall.
Warren's Address at Bunker Hill. Pierpont.
What a Court Hath Old England. *Unknown.*
Yankee Doodle's Expedition to Rhode Island. *Unknown.*
Yankee Privateer, The. Hale.
Americans
American Laughter. Robinson.
Americans All. Irving.
Ave Caesar. Jeffers.
Blood Is Thicker than Water. Rice.
Blue Meridian, The. Toomer.
Boy-Man. Shapiro.
Coming American, The. Foss.
England and America in 1782. Tennyson.
I Am an American. Lieberman.
I Hear America Singing. Whitman.

Americans *(continued)*
I Like Americans. Boyd.
I, Too, Sing America. Hughes.
Men of America, Answering the Call. Borland.
New Englanders Are Maples. Coffin.
Over the Carnage Rose Prophetic a Voice. Whitman.
People, Yes, The, *sels.* Sandburg.
Peregrine White and Virginia Dare. R. *and* S. V. Benét.
"Scum o' the Earth." Schauffler.
To America. Austin.
To the Younger Old-Americans. Porter.
Two 'Mericana Men. Daly.
What Does It Mean to Be American? Montgomery.
Yanks. Foley.
Young American, The. Everett.
See also **United States.**
Amnesia
Amnesiac. Plath.
Amsterdam, Holland
Amsterdam. Jammes.
Amsterdam Letter. Garrigue.
Robinson Crusoe Returns to Amsterdam. *Fr.* Amsterdam. Jammes.
Ancestors and Ancestry
Ancestors. Graves.
Ancestors, The. Wright.
Ancestral Faces. Brew.
Ancestry. *Fr.* The Black Riders. Crane.
Children of Light. R. Lowell.
Forebears. Gibbon.
Forebears. Riddell.
Forefathers. Blunden.
Idea of Ancestory, The. Knight.
Lineage. Walker.
On the Photograph of a Man I Never Saw. Plutzik.
Anchises
Anchises. Salkeld.
Anchors
Anchor: "Oft I must strive with wind and wave." *Fr.* Riddles. *Unknown.*
Forging of the Anchor, The. Ferguson.
Andalusia, Spain
Andalusian Sereno, The. Saltus.
Little Town. Garcia Lorca.
Andersen, Hans Christian
Hans Christian Andersen. Gosse.
Hans Christian Andersen in Central Park. Sobiloff.
Anderson, Marian
For Marian Anderson. Bock.
André, John
André. Bates
André's Request to Washington. Willis.
Brave Paulding and the Spy. *Unknown.*
Andrea Doria (ship)
Last Words. Hollander.
Andrewes, Lancelot
Upon Bishop Andrewes His Picture before His Sermons. Crashaw.
Andromeda
Andromeda. Aldrich.
Andromeda. *Fr.* Pauline. R. Browning.
Andromeda, *sels.* Kingsley.
Andromeda. Roche.
Anemones
Anemones of Collioure, The. Unterecker.
To a Wind Flower. Cawein.
White Anemone, The. "Meredith."
Windflower, A. Carman.
Wind-Flower, The. Very.
Angels
Images of Angels. Page.
On a Fifteenth-Century Flemish Angel. Ray.
On Angels. Ross.
Tom's Angels. De la Mare.
Angelus
Angelus Domini. *Unknown.*
Anger
Anger. Creeley.
Anger in Its Time and Place. Lamb.
He That Is Slow to Anger. Bible, *O.T.*
Poison Tree, A. *Fr.* Songs of Experience. Blake.
Aminals
About Animals. Conkling.
Allie. Graves.
Animal Fair. *Unknown.*
Animal Kingdom. Clouts.
Animal Store, The. Field.
Animals, The. Jacobsen.
Animals, The. Muir.
Aminals. *Fr.* Song of Myself. Whitman.
Ariel. Campbell.
At the Zoo. Milne.
Auguries of Innocence. Blake.
Beasts. Wilbur.
Beasts, Birds and Fishes. O'Keefe.
Bells of Heaven, The. Hodgson.
Bestiary, A. *sels.* Rexroth.
Christmas Folk Song, A. Reese.
Circus-postered Barn, The. Coatsworth.
Color. Bennett.
Come into Animal Presence. Levertov.
Daydreamers. Davis.
Earthy Anecdote. Stevens.
Familiar Friends. Tippett.
Family, The. *Unknown.*
Farmyard Song, A. Hastings.
Feather or Fur. Becker.
Four Friends, The. Milne.
Friendly Beasts, The. *Unknown.*
Heaven of Animals, The. Dickey.
How to Tell the Wild Animals. Wells.
In the Wilderness. Graves.
It's Pleasant to Think. Coatsworth.
Jump or Jingle. Beyer.
Kindness to Animals. *Unknown.*
Kingly lyon, and the strong arm'd beare, The. Wood.
Little Things. Stephens.
Menagerie, The. Moody.
Native Inhabitant. Stewart.
Nature's Friend. Davies.
Over the Meadow. Wadsworth.
Parley of Beasts. "MacDiarmid."
Peaceable Kingdom, The. Bible, *O.T.*
Spangled Pandemonium, The. Brown.
Tame Animals I Have Known. Waterman.
Wild Beasts. Stein.
Out of the Ark (OA). Gwendolyn Reed, comp.
Under the Tent of the Sky (UTS). John E. Brewton, comp.
Ann, Cape, Massachusetts
Cape Ann: A View. Brinnan.
Landscapes. Eliot.
Anne, Queen of England
On Queen Anne's Death. *Unknown.*
Queen Anne. *Unknown.*
Anne of Denmark
His Petition to Queen Anne of Denmark (1618). Raleigh.
Annunciation of the Virgin. *See* **Mary, the Virgin.**
Antarctica
Traveller's Guide to Antarctica. Stoutenburg.
White, said Worsley, and glistening, the ridgy plain. *Fr.* Worsley Enchanted. Stewart.
Anteaters
Pangolin, The. Moore.
Antelopes
Antelope. Smith.
Antelopes, The. Baxter.
Last Antelope, The. Piper.
Anthony, Saint
Saint Antony. Thomas.
Temptation of Saint Anthony, The. Symons.
Anthony of Padua, Saint
Death-Bed Hymn of Saint Anthony of Padua. St. Anthony of Padua.
Prayer to Saint Anthony of Padua, A. Symons.
Antietam Campaign
Victor of Antietam, The. Melville.
Antigone
Antigone, *sels.* Sophocles.
For the Antigone. Hamori.
Antiques
Antique Shop. Carmer.

Antonioni, Michelangelo
In Praise of Antonioni. Holden.
Antony (Mark Antony)
Antony and Cleopatra. Heredia.
Antony and Cleopatra, *sels.* Shakespeare.
Antony to Cleopatra. Lytle.
Early in the Morning. Simpson.
Mark Antony. Cleveland.
Tact. Pascal.
Anthony, Saint. *See* **Anthony, Saint.**
Ants
Ant, The. Armour.
Ant, The. Herford.
Ant, The. Nash.
Ant and the Cricket, The. *Unknown.*
Ant Battle. Dresbach.
Ant Explorer, The. Dennis.
Ant Village, The. Edey *and* Grider.
Ants. Kreymborg.
Ants and Others. Stoutenburg.
Bee, the Ant, and the Sparrow, The. Cotton.
By an Ant-Heap. Heywood.
Departmental. Frost.
Apache Indians
Dance of the Maskers. *Unknown.*
Apelles
Apelles the Painter. Leonidas of Tarentum.
Apes
Ape, The. Young.
Aphrodite
Aphrodite Pandemos. *Unknown.*
Hymn to Aphrodite. *Fr.* Homeric Hymns. *Unknown.*
Immortal Aphrodite. Sappho.
Ode to Aphrodite. Sappho.
See also **Venus.**
Apia, Western Samoa
In Apia Bay. Roberts.
Apollinaire, Guillaume
For Guillaume Apollinaire. Meredith.
I Am Almost Asleep. Grier.
Apollo
Apollo. Chivers.
Apollo Alone Approves. Turbyfill.
Archaic Torso of Apollo. Rilke.
Before a Statue of Apollo. Tchernichovsky.
Callicles' Song. *Fr.* Empedocles on Etna. Arnold.
Hunting Song. *Fr.* Apollo and Daphne. Whitehead.
Hymn of Apollo. Shelley.
Many Are Called. Robinson.
Phoebus, Arise! Drummond of Hawthornden.
Phoebus with Admetus. Meredith.
Shepherd of King Admetus. The. J. R. Lowell.
Song: "Stay, Phoebus, stay!" Waller.
Song to Apollo. *Fr.* Midas. Lyly.
Sun-God, The. De Vere.
Apostles
Christus Mattaeum et Discipulos Alloquitor. Sherburne.
Conversion. *Fr.* Nicodemus. Young.
Peter and John. Wylie.
Last Supper, The. Williams.
Starlight like Intuition Pierced the Twelve. Schwartz.
Te Martyrum Candidatus. Johnson.
Appalachia
Appalachian Front. Weeks.
Appian Way
Appian Way, The. Johnson.
Apple Trees
Appile Tree, De. Harris.
Apple Blossom. Brown.
Apple Blossoms. Bergengren.
Apple Blossoms. Parker.
Apple Blossoms. Wing.
Apple Gathering, An. C. G. Rossetti.
Apple Harvest. Leuty.
Apple Season. F. Frost.
Apple Tree, The. Brown.
Apple-Tree, The. Campbell.
Apples in New Hampshire. Gilchrist.
Comfortable Apple Trees, The. Hallock.
Mine Host of the "Golden Apple." Westwood.
Planting of the Apple-Tree, The. Bryant.
With a Spray of Apple Blossoms. Learned.
Apples
After Apple-picking. Frost.
Apple, The. Sackville.
Apple Gathering, An. C. G. Rossetti.
Apple Season. F. Frost.
Apple Song. F. Frost.
Apples. Lee.
Apples. Mueller.
Apples in New Hampshire. Gilchrist.
Autumn Apples. Lee.
Cider Song. Weston.
Moonlit Apples. Drinkwater.
On Apples. Ross.
Sunday Morning Apples. H. Crane.
Unharvested. Frost.
Appleseed, Johnny. *See* **Chapman, John.**
Appomattox, Virginia
Surrender at Appomattox, The. Melville.
April
All in the April Morning. Tynan.
Alone in April. Cabell.
Altered look about the hills, An. Dickinson.
April. Auringer.
April. Belleau.
April. Garrison.
April. Loveman.
April. McFadden.
April. O'Donnell.
April. Robinson.
April. Shorter.
April. *Fr.* Shepheardes Calender. Spenser.
April. Sweeney.
April. Teasdale.
April. Tietjens.
April. Watson.
April Adoration, An. Roberts.
April—and Dying. Aldrich.
April and May. *Fr.* May-Day. Emerson.
April and May. Robinson.
April Day, An. Cotter.
April Earth, The. Eastman.
April Midnight. Symons.
April Morning, An. Carman.
April Mortality. Adams.
April of the Ages, The. Bolben.
April Rain. Blind.
April Rain. Loveman.
April Rain Song. Hughes.
April Rise. Lee.
April Weather. McDermott.
April Weather. Reese.
April Winds. Lewis.
April's Amazing Meaning. Dillon.
Awakening, The. Morgan.
Birds in April. Henley.
Blue Squills. Teasdale.
Cherry Tree. C. G. Rossetti.
Concert, The. McGinley.
Day before April, The. Davies.
Early April. Frost.
First Warm Days. Denby.
For City Spring. S. V. Benét.
Great Farm. Booth.
Heigh-ho, April! Farjeon.
Home Thoughts from Abroad. R. Browning.
How Long til April? Fields.
In April. Allen.
In April. Arnold.
In April. Wetherald.
In the April Rain. Anderson.
In the Month of April. *Unknown.*
In Two Months Now. Dillon.
Lady April. Le Gallienne.
Now the Noisy Winds Are Still. Dodge.
One April Day. Moreland.
Peepers. Cane.
Prayer in April. Hay.
Prologue to "The Canterbury Tales." Chaucer.
Rain in April. Hammond.
Renewal. Towne.

April *(continued)*
Shore Roads of April. Adams.
Sign of Spring, A. Rexford.
Song: "April, April." Watson.
Song: "O lovely April, rich and bright." Kahn.
Song from "April." McLeod.
Spring Song. Carman.
Street in April, A. Dudek.
Succession of the Four Sweet Months, The. Herrick.
Sweet Wild April. Stead.
Switch Cut in April, A. Dyment.
This Fevers Me. Eberhart.
West Wind, The. Masefield.
April Fools' Day
All Fools' Day. *Unknown.*
April Fool. Coatsworth.
April Fool. Hammond.
April Fools' Day. Pomeroy.
First of April, The. Hone.
First of April, The. Johnson.
Oh Did You Hear? Silverstein.
Aquariums
Aquarium. Wright.
At the Aquarium. Eastman.
Aquinas, Thomas
Thomas in the Fields. Moyles.
Arabia
Arabia. De la Mare.
Arabs
Arab Love Song. Thompson.
Arab Music. Enright.
Arab to His Favorite Steed, The. Norton.
Arabs. Kreymborg.
Bedouin Song. Taylor.
Arachne
Birth of Arachne, the Spider, The. Schevill.
Arbor Day
Arbor Day. Thomson.
Arbor Day Song. Heermans.
Arbor Day Tree, An. *Unknown.*
Child's Song in Spring. Nesbit.
City Trees. Dargan.
Cross and the Tree, The. Stidger.
Fir Forest. Fuller.
Heart of the Tree, The. Bunner.
On Entering a Forest. Lennen.
Plant a Tree. Larcom.
Prayer, A: "Teach me Father, how to go." Markham.
Temple of the Trees, The. Pellow.
They All Belong to Me. Cook.
Tree-Building. Cable.
Tree Feelings. Stetson.
Trees. Clark.
What Do We Plant? Abbey.
White Tree in Bloom, A. Moreland.
Woodman, Spare That Tree. Morris.
Arborvitae
Arbor Vitae. Patmore.
Arbutus
Pink, small and punctual. Dickinson.
To a Mayflower. Marshall.
Trailing Arbutus. Abbey.
Trailing Arbutus, The. Whittier.
Architects
On Sir John Vanbrugh, Architect. Evans.
Architecture
Greek Architecture. Melville.
Arctic
Arctic Vision. Harte.
Expedition North. Morgan.
Wolf Cry, The. Sarett.
Arcturus
Arcturus in Autumn. Teasdale.
Arden Forest, England
Thirteenth Song, The. *Fr.* Polyolbion. Drayton.
Ares. *See* **Mars.**
Arethusa
Alpheus and Arethusa. Daly.
Arethusa. Shelley.
Shelley's Arethusa Set to New Measures. Duncan.
Ariadne
Theseus and Ariadne. Mifflin.
Aristophanes
On Aristophanes. *Unknown.*
Arithmetic. *See* **Mathematics.**
Arizona
Arizona. Clifford.
Arizona. Hall.
Arizona. *Unknown.*
Arizona Boys and Girls, The. *Unknown.*
Arizona Poems, *sels.* Fletcher.
Arizona Village. Davieau.
New Mexico and Arizona. Canterbury.
Painted Hills of Arizona, The. Curran.
Ark
Ark, The. *Fr.* Paradise Lost. Milton.
One More River. *Unknown.*
Arkansas
Arkansas Traveler, The. *At. to* Faulkner.
State of Arkansas, The. *Unknown.*
Arlington National Cemetery
Arlington Cemetery Looking toward the Capitol. Palmer.
Little Stones of Arlington, The. Young.
Potomac, The. Shapiro.
Armada. *See* **Spanish Armada.**
Armadillos
Armadillo, The. Gordon.
Armagh, Ireland
Distant Prospect of the City of Armagh, A. *Fr.* Morna's Hill. Stuart.
Armenia
Turk in Armenia, The. Watson.
Armistice Day. *See* **Veterans' Day.**
Armstrong, John or Johnie (Scots, *fl.* 1530)
Johnie Armstrong. *Unknown.*
Armstrong, Louis ("Satchmo")
Lamda. Tolson.
Armstrong, William (Scots, *fl.* 1596)
Kinmont Willie. *Unknown.*
Arnold, Benedict
Arnold at Stillwater. English.
Arnold, the Vile Traitor. *Unknown.*
Epigram: "Quoth Satan to Arnold." *Unknown.*
Arnold, Matthew
Matthew Arnold. Auden.
Pax Paganica. Guiney.
Arnold, Thomas
Rugby Chapel. M. Arnold.
Aroostook War
Annie McConkus. Adams.
Arrows
Song of the Arrow, The. *Fr.* Gisli, the Chieftain. Crawford.
Art
Accident in Art. Hovey.
Age demanded an image, The. *Fr.* Hugh Selwyn Mauberley. Pound.
Ajanta. Rukeyser.
Andrea del Sarto. R. Browning.
Ars Victrix. Dobson.
Art. Gautier.
Art. Emerson.
Art. Melville.
Art. Noyes.
Art. Perry.
Art. *Unknown.*
Art and Life. Ridge.
Artist, The. Koch.
Birth of Arachne, the Spider, The. Schevill.
Chicago Picasso, The. Brooks.
Craftsman, The. Christian.
Cubism. Sobiloff.
Exercise in Aesthetics. Scott.
First Essay on the Art of the U. S. Welburn.
Gaspar Becerra. Longfellow.
I would not paint a picture. Dickinson.
Japanese Vase Wrought in Metal, A. Seiffert.
Joys of Art, The. Taylor.
Leaf-Makers, The. Stewart.
Let dainty wits cry on the sisters nine. *Fr.* Astrophel and Stella. Sidney.
Marble Statuette Harpist. Allen.

Musée des Beaux Arts. Auden.
Ode on a Grecian Urn. Keats.
On Seeing the Elgin Marbles. Keats.
Palace of Art, The. Tennyson.
Pavement Artist, The. Kirkup.
Ransom, The. Baudelaire.
Rock Paintings, Drakensberg. Ross.
Sarolla's women in their picture hats. *Fr.* Pictures of the Gone World. Ferlinghetti.
Technique. Eaton.
To the Stone-Cutters. Jeffers.
When I Buy Pictures. Moore.
Why I Am Not a Painter. O'Hara.
Woodcut. Wilson.
See also **Painting and Painters; Portraits; Sculpture and Sculptors; Statues.**

Artemis
Artemis. Deamer.
Artemis. Nerval.
Artemis Prologizes. R. Browning.
See also **Diana.**

Artevelde, Philip van
Philip van Artevelde, *sels.* Taylor.

Arthurian Legend
Brut, The, *sels.* Layamon.
But here at starting. *Fr.* Sir Launfal. Moultrie.
Cablegram. Kramer.
Defence of Guenevere, The. Morris.
Grave of Arthur, The. Chesterton.
Grave of King Arthur, The. Warton.
Hunting Song. *Fr.* King Arthur. Hovey.
Idylls of the King, *sels.* Tennyson.
King Arthur, *sels.* Dryden.
King Arthur and King Cornwall. *Unknown.*
King Arthur's Death. *Unknown.*
King Arthur's Dream. *Unknown.*
Lady of Shalott, The. Tennyson.
Lancelot. Bontemps.
Lancelot and Guinevere. Gould.
Marriage of Sir Gawain, The. *Unknown.*
Merlin and the Gleam. Tennyson.
Morte Arthure, *sels.* *Unknown.*
Morte d'Arthur. Tennyson.
Myth of Arthur, The. Chesterton.
Near Avalon. Morris.
On King Arthur's Round Table, at Winchester. Warton.
Round Table, The. Mannyng.
Sir Galahad. Tennyson.
Sir Gawain and the Green Knight. *Unknown.*
Sir Launcelot and Queen Guinevere. Tennyson.
Sir Launfal. Chester.
Vision of Sir Launfal. J. R. Lowell.
Ylen's Song. *Fr.* The Birth of Galahad. Hovey.

Ascanius
Iulus. Wallis.

Ascension Day
Ascension Day. Kaye-Smith.
Ascension-Day. Vaughan.
Ascention. Donne.
At the Ascension. Léon.
They Are All Gone. Vaughan.

Ash Trees
Rowan Tree, The. Nairne.
Timid Ash Tree, The. K. Millay.

Ash Wednesday
Ash Wednesday. Eliot.
Ash Wednesday. Marinoni.

Ashby, Turner
Ashby. Thompson.

Aspen Trees
Aspens. Thomas.
Spring Song of Aspens. Spencer.

Assassinations and Assassins
Abraham Lincoln: an Horation Ode. Stoddard.
Abraham Lincoln: Assassinated Good Friday, 1865. Stedman.
Assassination. Lee.
Buffalo. Coates.
Channel U.S.A.—Live. Stoutenburg.
Charles Guiteau. *Unknown.*
Down in Dallas. Kennedy.
Garfield's Murder. *Unknown.*
Great man, Abraham Lincoln, woke on morning, The. *Fr.* John Brown's Body. S. V. Benét.
J. F. K. Sister Mary Stanislaus.
Julius Caesar, *sels.* Shakespeare.
Lincoln Slain. Markham.
Lotus Eaters, The. Alexander.
Martyr, The. Melville.
November Twenty-sixth Nineteen Hundred and Sixty-three. Berry.
On the Murder of Martin Luther King. Rice.
Pardon. Howe.
Traction: November 22, 1963. Moss.
Vaticide. O'Higgins.

Asses. *See* **Donkeys.**

Assisi, Italy
Assisi. Moyes.

Assumption of the Virgin. *See* **Mary, the Virgin.**

Astarte
To Ashtaroth and Bel. Tchernichowsky.

Astrology
Astrologer's Song, An. Kipling.
Astrology. Marshall.
In Conjunction. Madge.
Moonpoison, mullock of sacrifice. *Fr.* The Ecliptic: Cancer, or, The Crab. Macleod.
Though dusty wits dare scorn astrology. *Fr.* Astrophel and Stella. Sidney.

Astronomers and Astronomy
Astronomer, The. Doherty.
Astronomers of Mont Blanc, The. Bowers.
Uranus. Clough.
When I Heard the Learned Astronomer. Whitman.

Atalanta
Atalanta in Calydon. Swinburne.

Atheism
Atheist. Harburg.
Atheist and the Acorn, The. Countess of Winchelsea.
Faith. Daley.
Old Atheist Pauses by the Sea, An. Kinsella.
Skeptic, The. Service.
There Is No God, As I Was Taught. Masefield.
"There Is No God," the Wicked Saith. *Fr.* Dipsychus. Clough.
Village Atheist, The. *Fr.* Spoon River Anthology. Masters.

Athens, Greece
Spring Wind, A. Spencer.

Athletes
Ageing Athlete, The. Weiss.
Athletes. Gibson.
Breed of Athletes, The. Euripides.
Of Kings and Things. Morrison.
Runner, The. Whitman.
To an Athlete Dying Young. Housman.

Atlanta, Georgia
Litany at Atlanta, A. DuBois.

Atlantic Cable
How Cyrus Laid the Cable. Saxe.

Atlantis
Atlantis. *Fr.* Priapus and the Pool. Aiken.
Atlantis. Bottomley.
Atlantis. Coblentz.
Atlantis. *Fr.* The Bridge. H. Crane.
Song at Santa Cruz. Young.

Atomic Bomb
Any Day Now. McCord.
Atomic Courtesy. Jacobson.
Back Again from Yucca Flats. Kelley.
Dirge for the New Sunrise. *Fr.* Three Poems of the Atomic Age. E. Sitwell.
Earth. Wheelock.
Hark, the herald angels sing. Dehn.
Hydrogen Dog and the Cobalt Cat, The. Winsor.
Primer of Consequences. Brasier.
Seventh Hell, The: Of Smoke, Where Fire-Raisers Try in Vain to Escape from a Shower of Hot Sand Falling from a Cloud. Rothenberg.
There Is Yet Time. Steece.
See also **Hiroshima; Nuclear War.**

Attics
Attic, The. Coulette.

Attucks, Crispus
Crispus Attucks. O'Reilly.
Auburn, Ireland
Deserted Village, The. Goldsmith.
Auctions
Auction Sale, The. Reed.
Auden, Wystan Hugh
Just a Smack at Auden. Empson.
Their Last Will and Testament. MacNeice.
To Auden on His Fiftieth. Eberhart.
To W. H. Auden on His Fiftieth Birthday. Howes.
Audubon, John James
John James Audubon. S. V. Benét.
Aughrim, Ireland
After Aughrim. Georgehegan.
After Aughrim. Lawless.
August
August. Binyon.
August. Fallon.
August. Ledwidge.
August. Lewis.
August. MacNeice.
August. Nicholson.
August. *Fr.* The Shepheardes Calendar. Spenser.
August. Swinburne.
August. Thaxter.
August. Winslow.
August. Wylie.
August Afternoon. Edey.
August Night. Roberts.
August Smiles. Coatsworth.
Cold August. Harrison.
Golden Month, The. Doyle.
In August. Howells.
Mid-August. Driscoll.
Month of Falling Stars. Higginson.
Tansy for August. Enslin.
Augustine, Saint
Petitions of Saint Augustine. *Unknown.*
Aurora Borealis
Sights and Sounds of the Night. Wilcox.
Auschwitz, Poland
Annotations of Auschwitz. Porter.
Austen, Jane
Anemones for Miss Austen. Bergonzi.
Jane's Marriage. Kipling.
Australia
Aboriginal Mother's Lament, An. Harpur.
Australia. Hope.
Australia. Rentoul.
Australia to England. *Fr.* Sonnets of the Empire. Strong.
Australian Federation. Gay.
Australian Symphony, An. Evans.
Ballade of the Southern Cross. *Fr.* Ballades in Blue China. Lang.
Birth of Australia, The. Russell.
Dominion of Australia, The. Stephens.
Dutch Seamen and New Holland, The. Reeves.
Midsummer Noon in the Australian Forest, A. Harpur.
September in Australia. Kendall.
Song of the Darling River. Lawson.
Temple by the Sea, The. Dutton.
Book of Australian and New Zealand Verse, A (BoAu). Walter Murdoch, ed.
Book of Australian Verse, A (BoAV). Judith Wright, Comp.
Modern Australian Poetry (MoAuPo). H. M. Green, comp.
New Land, New Language (NeLNL). Judith Wright, comp.
Poetry in Australia. Volume I: From the Ballads to Brennan (PoAu-1). T. I. Moore, comp.
Poetry in Australia. Volume II: Modern Australian Verse (PoAu-2). Douglas Stewart, comp.
Australians
Australian Girl, An. Castilla.
Boundary Rider, The. Heney.
Circling Hearths, The. Quinn.
Last Aboriginal, The. "Macleod."
Authors and Authorship
Author to Her Book, The. Bradstreet.
Boatman, The. Macpherson.
But "nameless somethings" and "unbounded spaces." *Fr.* A Veld Eclogue; the Pioneers. Campbell.
Canadian Authors Meet, The. Scott.
Devil's Advice to Story-Tellers, The. Graves.
Elephant and the Bookseller, The. Gay.
I Have Approached. Paton.
Lazy Writer, The. Taylor.
Literary Zodiac. Piddington.
Mrs. Brown and the Famous Author. King.
Novel, The. Levertov.
Obit on Parnassus. Fitzgerald.
On His Books. Belloc.
On Some South African Novelists. Campbell.
Poet at Seven, The. Rimbaud.
Squeal. Simpson.
There Is No Opera Like "Lohengrin." Wheelwright.
To a Writer of the Day. "Varley."
To an Author. Freneau.
Vital Statistics. Rella.
Writer to His Book, The. Campion.
Young Author, The. Johnson.
Automation
Epitaph: "Here he lies moulding." Mellichamp.
Four Quartz Crystal Clocks. Moore.
Valedictory to Standard Oil of Indiana, A. Wagoner.
Automobile Accidents
Another Kind of Burning. Fox.
Auto Wreck. Shapiro.
Big Crash Out West. Viereck.
Highway: Michigan. Roethke.
Automobiles
Auto Wreck. Shapiro.
Automobile, The. Mackaye.
Automobile Mechanics. Baruch.
Buick. Shaprio.
Driver's Prayer, A. *Unknown.*
Eight-Cylinder Man. Mastin.
Klaxon. Reaney.
Lather as You Go. Nash.
Merritt Parkway. Levertov.
Motor Cars. Bennett.
One, Two, Three. Albert.
Pedestrian's Plaint, The. Lucas.
Reason. Miles.
Song for a Blue Roadster. Field.
Southbound on the Freeway. Swenson.
This Dim and Ptolemaic Man. Bishop.
Tract for Autos, A. Guiterman.
Autumn
Abundance. Meyer.
Adios. Babcock.
Against the Cold. Bynner.
Alms in Autumn. Fyleman.
As imperceptibly as grief. Dickinson.
Autumn. Campbell.
Autumn. Carman.
Autumn. Carruth.
Autumn. Clare.
Autumn. Contoski.
Autumn. Curran.
Autumn. De la Mare.
Autumn. Hoatson.
Autumn. Hood.
Autumn. Hubbell.
Autumn. Hulme.
Autumn. Irwin.
Autumn. Knipe.
Autumn. Liliencron.
Autumn. Longfellow.
Autumn. Manager.
Autumn. *Fr.* Summer's Last Will and Testament. Nashe.
Autumn. Pushkin.
Autumn. Rice.
Autumn. Rilke.
Autumn. Roberts.
Autumn. Rodgers.
Autumn. Sassoon.
Autumn. Smith.
Autumn. Stephens.
Autumn. Tagore.
Autumn. *Fr.* The Seasons. Thomson.
Autumn. *Unknown.*
Autumn. Untermeyer.

Autumn. Watson.
Autumn. Winwar.
Autumn: a Dirge. Shelley.
Autumn again, the Leopardlike and burning. *Fr.* The Leaves of Europe. Sergeant.
Autumn along the Beaches. Wheelock.
Autumn; an Ode. Gullans.
Autumn Bird. Corning.
Autumn Breeze, An. Hayne.
Autumn, Crystal Eye. Ruddock.
Autumn, Dark Wanderer. Daryush.
Autumn Day. Rilke.
Autumn Daybreak. Millay.
Autumn Eve. Andriello.
Autumn Fancies. *Unknown.*
Autumn Fashions. Thomas.
Autumn Fields. Roberts.
Autumn Fires. Stevenson.
Autumn, Forsake These Hills. Hill.
Autumn Garden, An. Carman.
Autumn Haze. Munkittrick.
Autumn Healing. Ward.
Autumn Hour. Chapman.
Autumn Idleness. *Fr.* The House of Life. D. G. Rossetti.
Autumn in Carmel. Sterling.
Autumn in the Highlands. Clough.
Autumn in the West. Gallagher.
Autumn Is a Season. Cotter.
Autumn Leaves. Heyward.
Autumn Leaves. Hopkins.
Autumn Leaves. Sutphen.
Autumn Leaves. *Unknown.*
Autumn Memories. Savage-Armstrong.
Autumn Morning, An. *Unknown.*
Autumn Morning. White.
Autumn Morning at Cambridge. Cornford.
Autumn Movement. Sandburg.
Autumn Night. Scott.
Autumn on the Land. Thomas.
Autumn Refrain. Stevens.
Autumn Riddle, An. *Unknown.*
Autumn Road, An. Dresbach.
Autumn Rose-Tree, An. Earls.
Autumn Song. Long.
Autumn Song. Rose.
Autumn Song. D. G. Rossetti.
Autumn Song. Tieck.
Autumn Train. Shacklett.
Autumn Twilight. Régnier.
Autumn Wind, The. Clare.
Autumn Woods. Bryant.
Autumn Woods. Tippett.
Autumnal. Colony.
Autumnal, The. *Fr.* Elegies. Donne.
Autumnal. Dowson.
Autumnal Clouds. Fletcher.
Autumnal Consummation. Stevenson.
Autumnal Evening, An. "Macleod."
Autumnal Ode. De Vere.
Autumnal Spring Song. Miller.
Autumn's Fete. McGeorge.
Autumn's Mirth. Peck.
Autumn's Processional. Craik.
Autumnus. Sylvester.
Battle Autumn of 1862, The. Whittier.
Beech Leaves. Reeves.
Blue Smoke. F. Frost.
Bonny Harvest Moon, The. Barr of Craigielee.
Burning of the Leaves, The. Binyon.
Calvinist Autumnal. Harrod.
Chansons d'Automne. Verlaine.
Chant for Skippers. Gallagher.
Chorale for Autumn. Zaturenska.
Child's Thought of Harvest, A. "Coolidge."
City Autumn. March.
Clear after Rain. Tu Fu.
Colour. White.
Come, Little Leaves. Cooper.
Comes Fall. Nathan.
Counter-Serenade; She Invokes the Autumn Instant. Viereck.
Cranes, The. Po Chü-i.
Day in Autumn, A. Thomas.
Days like These. Egbert.
Death of the Flowers, The. Bryant.
Disillusion. Sister Mary Edwardine.
Down! Down! Farjeon.
End of Summer, The. Basho.
End of Summer. Kunitz.
Fall, The. Barnes.
Fall. Fisher.
Fall. Hölderlin.
Fall Days. Conger.
Fall in Corrales. Wilbur.
Fall, Leaves, Fall. E. Brontë.
Fall of the Leaf, The. Thoreau.
Fall of the Year. Ellison.
Falltime. Sandburg.
Farmer. Bailey.
Field of Autumn. Lee.
First Autumn, The. Schacht.
For Autumn. Farjeon.
Friends. Warner.
Glimpse in Autumn. Untermeyer.
God's World. Millay.
Golden Bough. Wylie.
Harvest Moon, The. Longfellow.
Hound, The. Deutsch.
How One Winter Came in the Lake Region. Campbell.
How the Leaves Came Down. "Coolidge."
Hurrahing in Harvest. Hopkins.
I Am the Autumn. Manger.
Immortal Autumn. MacLeish.
In an Autumn Wood. Percy.
In Autumn. Derwood.
In Coventry. Daly.
In the Elegy Season. Wilbur.
In the Fall o' Year. Jones.
Indian Summer. Draper.
Joys of the Road, The. Carman.
Lament in Autumn. Stewart.
Last Flower, The. Moore.
Last Walk in Autumn, The. Whittier.
Late Autumn. Allingham.
Late Autumn. Sullivan.
Late Autumn. Young.
Leaves Do Not Mind at All, The. Wynne.
Load. Hewitt.
Marigold. Nicholl.
Memory Green. MacLeish.
Merry Autumn Days. Dickens.
Mild Is the Parting Year. Landor.
Mist and All, The. Willson.
Mnemosyne. Stickney.
Morns are meeker than they were, The. Dickinson.
My Autumn Walk. Bryant.
My Wind Is Turned to Bitter North. Clough.
Naseby; Late Autumn. Dowling.
New York—Albany. Ferlinghetti.
Ninth Moon. Li Ho.
O Amber Day, amid the Autumn Gloom. Allison.
October. Frost.
October Maples, Portland. Wilbur.
October's Husbandry. Tusser.
Ode to Autumn. Keats.
Ode to the West Wind. Shelley.
On Lake Pend Oreille. Shelton.
Pastoral X: "Grapes are ripe, the frost is near, The." Hillyer.
Pirate Wind. Carr.
Pity of the Leaves, The. Robinson.
Poem in October. Thomas.
Real Property. Monro.
Red in Autumn. Gould.
Rich Days. Davies.
Ripe and Bearded Barley, The. *Unknown.*
Scene in a Garden. *Fr.* Paracelsus. R. Browning.
Seed-Time. Meredith.
Shape of Autumn, The. Russ.
Sigh. Mallarmé.
So This Is Autumn. Watt.
Some time now past in the autumnal tide. *Fr.* Contemplations. Bradstreet.
Something Told the Wild Geese. Field.

Autumn *(continued)*
Song: "Again rejoicing Nature sees." Burns.
Song: "Feathers of the willow, The." Dixon.
Song: "It Autumne was, and on our Hemispheare." Drummond of Hawthornden.
Song: "Spirit haunts the year's last hours, A." Tennyson.
Song: "Why fadest thou in death." Dixon.
Song of Autumn, A. Gordon.
Song of Autumn, A. Rodd.
Song of Early Autumn, A. Gilder.
Sonnet in Autumn. Petersen.
Spell before Winter, A. Nemerov.
Spring and Autumn. Linton.
Summer Is Gone. *Unknown.*
Tell Me Not Here. Housman.
Theme in Yellow. Sandburg.
Thief, The. Pawsey.
Threnody: "Red leaves fall upon the lake, The." Farrar.
'Tis the Last Rose of Summer. Moore.
To Autumn. Blake.
To Autumn. Keats.
Torch-Light in Autumn. Piatt.
Tropes of One Season. Eaton.
Vagabond Song, A. Carman.
Watching the Moon. McCord.
When the Frost Is on the Punkin. Riley.
Wind of Fall, A. Adams.
Words for the Raker of Leaves. Adams.
Auvergne, France
In the Caves of Auvergne. Turner.
Aviation and Aviators
Aeroplane. Green.
Aircraft, Landing. Thiele.
Airman Who Flew over Shakespeare's England, The. Plutzik.
Airman's Alphabet, The. *Fr.* Journal of an Airman. Auden.
Airplane, The. Bennett.
Airplane, The. Wynne.
Aviator, The. Blok.
Ceiling Unlimited. Rukeyser.
Chavez. Sweeney.
Cockpit in the Clouds. Dorrance.
Crash at Leithfield. Curnow.
Dead Aviator, The. Hackett.
Ego. Philip Booth.
Epitaph for an American Bomber. Bertram.
Europe. Ashbery.
First Flight. Coffin.
Flight, The. *Fr.* A Time to Dance. Day Lewis.
Flight to Australia. Day Lewis.
High Flight. Magee.
Icarus. Iremonger.
Irish Airman Foresees His Death, An. Yeats.
Jet Plane. Sullivan.
Landscape near an Aerodrome, The. Spender.
Looking Up at Airplanes, Always. Humphries.
Losses. Jarrell.
Night Plane. F. Frost.
Norfolk Memorials. Leavenworth.
Prayer for a Pilot. Roberts.
Riding in an Airplane. Baruch.
Silver Ships. Meigs.
Sparrows at the Airport, The. Ostroff.
Taking Off. Green.
Three Jet Planes. Swenson.
To Beachey, 1912. Sandburg.
To Poets and Airmen. Spender.
Trans Canada. Scott.
Up in the Air. Tippett.
Up Silver Stairsteps. Stuart.
See also **Air Warfare.**
Avignon, France
Orchard at Avignon, An. Robinson.
Avoca (river), Ireland
Meeting of the Waters, The. Moore.
Avon (ship, War of 1812)
Ocean-Fight, The. *Unknown.*
Avon River, Canada
To the Avon River above Stratford, Canada. Reaney.
Avon River, England
Ebb Tide, The. Southey.
Pastoral. Wright.
Upon Eckington Bridge, River Avon. Quiller-Couch.
Ayr, Scotland
When heavy, dark, continued, a'day rains. *Fr.* The Brigs of Ayr. Burns.
Azaleas
Azalea, The. *Fr.* The Unknown Eros. Patmore.
White Azaleas. Kimball.
Azrael
Azrael. Longfellow.
Azrael. Welsh.
Aztecs
Aztec City, The. Ware.

B

Baal
To Ashtaroth and Bel. Tchernichowsky.
Babies
Anniversary in September. Brown.
Baby. Eastman.
Baby. Frank.
Baby. Macdonald.
Baby, The. Taylor.
Baby Asleep after Pain, A. Lawrence.
Baby at Play. *Unknown.*
Baby's World. Tagore.
Bacchante to Her Babe, The. Tietjens.
Blessing for the Blessed, A. Alma-Tadema.
Blest the Infant Babe. *Fr.* The Prelude. Wordsworth.
Child Crying. Thwaite.
Cradle Song: "Sleep, sleep, beauty bright." Blake.
Cradle Song, A: "Sweet dreams form a shade." *Fr.* Songs of Innocence. Blake.
Cradle Song: "What is the little one thinking about?" *Fr.* Bitter-sweet. Holland.
Errantry. Fitzgerald.
Eskimo Baby, An. Diamond.
Etude Réaliste. Swinburne.
Five Days Old. Webb.
For a Child Expected. Ridler.
For My Son. Nims.
I Found God. Thacker.
In Go-Cart So Tiny. Greenaway.
Infant Joy. *Fr.* Songs of Innocence. Blake.
Infant Sorrow. *Fr.* Songs of Experience. Blake.
Johneen. "O'Neill."
Kadia the Young Mother Speaks. Sampter.
King of the Cradle, The. Ashby-Sterry.
Little. Aldis.
Little Brown Baby. Dunbar.
Little Papoose. Conkling.
Methinks 'Tis Pretty Sport. Bastard.
Modern Baby, The. Doane.
Mother's Soliloquy, A. Wright.
Mundus et Infans. Auden.
My Little Lover. Sauvage.
New Arrival, The. Cable.
New-born, The. Hoyt.
News of a Baby. Riddell.
No Baby in the House. Dolliver.
O sleep, my babe, hear not the rippling wave. *Fr.* Phantasmion. Coleridge.
Only a Baby Small. Barr.
Ringely, Ringely. Follen.
Six Weeks Old. Morley.
Slippery. Sandburg.
Sweetes' Li'l Feller. Stanton.
To a New-born Baby Girl. Conkling.
To a New-born Child. Monkhouse.
To Charlotte Pulteney. Philips.
To Rose. Teasdale.
Unknown Girl in the Maternity Ward. Sexton.
Where Did You Come From? Macdonald.
Wonder-Child, The. Le Gallienne.
Baboons
Baboon. *Unknown.*
Baboon 2. *Unknown.*
Big Baboon, The. Belloc.
Theology of Bongwi, the Baboon, The. Campbell.

Babylon
Babylon. L. Benét.
Babylon. Hodgson.
Babylon. Sassoon.
Bacchus
Bacchus. Emerson.
Bacchus. Sherman.
Bacchus's Opinion of Wine, and Other Beverages. *Fr.* Bacchus in Tuscany. Redi.
Bach, Johann Sebastian
All Those Hymnings up to God. Evans.
Bach Cantata, A. Stanley-Wrench.
Dream. Moore.
Four Friends. Ward.
Homage to J. S. Bach. Heath-Stubbs.
Meditating in silence after the last note. *Fr.* Considerations on Certain Music of J. S. Bach. Beaglehole.
To J. S. Bach. Thwaites.
Bachelors
Bachelor, The. Barnes.
Bachelor Hall. Field.
Bachelor's Dream, The. Hood.
Bachelor's Hall. Finley.
Bachelor's Mono-Rhyme, A. Mackay.
Batchelors Song, The. Flatman.
Song: "Love a woman! y're an Ass." Rochester.
Where the Single Men Go in Summer. Bourne.
Badagry, Nigeria
Safari West. Williams.
Badgers
Badger, The. Chalmers.
Badger. Clare.
Six Badgers, The. Graves.
Bagpipes
Bagpipe Man, The. Turner.
Bahamas
Bahamas. Oppen.
Balaam (Bible)
Balaam. Keble.
Balaclava, Crimea
Charge of the Light Brigade, The. Tennyson.
Balboa, Vasco Núñz de
Balboa. Perry.
Balder (Norse god of light)
Balder Dead, *sels.* Arnold.
Baldness
Baldness and the Swan. Scott.
Penalties of Baldness, The. Seaman.
Bale, John
To Doctor Bale. Googe.
Ball, John
He Loathed his bond, but could not stir. *Fr.* The Song of the Plow. Hewlett.
Sermon to the Rebels at Blackheath. Ball.
Ballads and Folk Songs
American Ballads and Folk Songs (ABF). John A. Lomax *and* Alan Lomax, eds.
American Songbag, The (AS). Carl Sandburg, comp.
Ballad Book, The (BaBo). MacEdward Leach, ed.
Ballads and Folk Songs of the Southwest (BFSS). Ethel *and* Chauncey O. Moore, comps.
Bundle of Ballads, A (BuBa). Ruth Manning-Sanders, comp.
Cowboy Songs and Other Frontier Ballads (CoSo). John A. Lomax *and* Alan Lomax, eds.
English and Scottish Popular Ballads (ESPB). Helen Child Sargent *and* George L. Kittredge, eds.
Our Singing Country (OuSiCo). John A. Lomax *and* Alan Lomax, eds.
Oxford Book of Ballads, The (OBB). Arthur Quiller-Couch, ed.
Oxford Book of Ballads, The (OxBB). James Kinsley, ed.
Oxford Book of Scottish Verse (OxBS). John MacQueen *and* Tom Scott, eds.
Saucy Sailor and Other Dramatized Ballads, The (SaSa). Alice M. G. White *and* Janet E. Tobitt, comps.
Songs of the Cattle Trail and Cow Camp (SCC). John A. Lomax, ed.
Songs of the Gold Rush, The (SGR). Richard A. Dwyer *and* Richard E. Lingenfelter, eds.
Treasury of American Song, A (TrAS). Olin Downes *and* Elie Siegmeister, comps.
See also **Sea Chanteys.**
Ballet
I cannot dance upon my toes. Dickinson.
Pediment: Ballet. Nicholl.
Song of the Ballet. Morton.
To Potapovitch. H. Crane.
Balliol College, Oxford
Masque of Balliol, The, *sels.* Beeching *and others.*
To the Balliol Men Still in Africa. Belloc.
Balloons
Balloon, The. Kuskin.
Balloon Man, The. Fyleman.
Balloon Man, The. Morton.
Balloon Man. North.
Les Ballons. Wilde.
Ballyshannon, Ireland
Adieu to Belashanny. Allingham.
Winding Banks of Erne, The. Allingham.
Baltic, Battle of
Battle of the Baltic, The. Campbell.
Baltimore, Ireland.
Sack of Baltimore, The. Davis.
Baltimore, Maryland
Battle of Baltimore, The. *Unknown.*
Incident. Cullen.
Streets of Baltimore. *Unknown.*
Through Baltimore. Taylor.
Balzac, Honore de
Balzac. Gottlieb.
Bamboo
Bamboo. Plomer.
Bananas
Banana. Bell.
Banana. Mitchell.
Bancroft, George
Decanter of Madeira, Aged 86, to George Bancroft, Aged 86. Mitchell.
Bandits
Bandit. Klein.
Bandit Peter Mancino's Death, The. *Unknown.*
Bandit's Grave, The. Pitt.
Bands
Band, The. John.
Basie Band, The. Cooper.
Colored Band, The. Dunbar.
Dance Band. Tessimond.
Park Concert. Michie.
Bangkok, Thailand
Bangkok. Scott.
Banjos
Banjo of the Past, The. Weeden.
Banjo Player, The. Johnson.
Song of the Banjo, The. Kipling.
Banking and Bankers
Bankers Are Just like Anybody Else, except Richer. Nash.
Banners. *See* **Flags.**
Bannockburn, Battle of.
Scots Wha Hae. Burns.
Baptism
At a Child's Baptism. Miller.
On the Baptized Ethiopian. Crashaw.
H. Baptisme ("As he that sees a dark and shadie grove"). Herbert.
Holy Baptism ("Since, Lord, to thee/ A narrow way and little gate"). Herbert.
Bar Kokba, Simon
Bar Kochba. Lazarus.
Barberries
Barberry-Bush, The. Very.
Barbers
Ballad of a Barber, A. Beardsley.
Barber, The. Browne.
Barber's, The. De la Mare.
Barber's Clippers. Baruch.
For the Barbers. Oppenheimer.
Haircut. Shapiro.
To My Hairdresser. St. Leger.
Village Barber, The. Lopez.
Bards
Good Tradition, The. *Unknown.*
On the Breaking-up of a School. O'Huiginn.
Were Not the Gael Fallen. O'Mulconry.

Bards *(continued)*
Who Will Buy a Poem? O'Heffernan.
Barebone, Praise-God
Praise-God Barebones. Cortissoz.
Barley
Barley-Mowers' Song, The. Howitt.
Like Barley Bending. Teasdale.
Barnacles
Barnacle, The. Herbert.
Barnacles. Lanier.
Barnegat Bay, New Jersey
Patrolling Barnegat. Whitman.
Barnes, William
Last Signal, The. Hardy.
Barns
Barn, The. Blunden.
Barn, The. Coatsworth.
Barn, The. Spender.
Barn in Winter, The. MacIntosh.
Hayloft, The. Stevenson.
Human Things. Nemerov.
Barnyard
Barnyard, The. Burnham.
In the Barnyard. Aldis.
Barons' War
Against the Baron's Enemies. *Unknown.*
Barrel Organs. *See* **Hurdy-Gurdies.**
Barry, Kevin
Kevin Barry. Ward.
Barton, Andrew
Sir Andrew Barton. *Unknown.*
Baseball
At the Ball Game. Williams.
Base Stealer, The. Francis.
Baseball Note. Adams.
Baseball's Sad Lexicon. Adams.
Casey at the Bat. Thayer.
Casey—Twenty Years After. *Unknown.*
Casey's Revenge. Wilson.
Cobb Would Have Caught It. Fitzgerald.
Decline and Fall of a Roman Umpire. Nash.
Double-Play, The. Wallace.
Dream of a Baseball Star. Corso.
Hits and Runs. Sandburg.
Line-up for Yesterday. Nash.
Origin of Baseball, The. Patchen.
Pitcher. Francis.
Polo Grounds. Humphries.
Slide, Kelly, Slide. Kelly.
Umpire, The. Bracker.
Umpire, The. Gibson.
Villanelle. Feld.
Where, O Where? Bracker.
Basie, Count
Basie Band, The. Cooper.
Basketball
Ex-Basketball Player. Updike.
Foul Shot. Hoey.
Jump Shooter, The. Trudell.
Poet Tries to Turn in His Jock, The. Hilton.
Bass, Sam
Sam Bass. *Unknown.*
Bath, England
At the Roman Baths, Bath. Lucie-Smith.
Farewell to Bath. Montagu.
New Bath Guide, The, *sels.* Anstey.
Baths and Bathing
Bath, The. Graham.
Bath, The. Oppenheimer.
Gloire de Dijon. Lawrence.
I Wonder What It Feels Like To Be Drowned. Graves.
In the Tub We Soak Our Skin. Horn.
Soap, the Oppressor. Johnson.
Voyage of Jimmy Poo, The. Emanuel.
Washing. Drinkwater.
Bats
Bat. *Fr.* Childhood. Clare.
Bat. Lawrence.
Bat, The. Nash.
Bat, The. Pitter.
Bat, The. Roethke.
Bats, The. Hillyer.
Bats. Jarrell.
Bats. Newsome.
Intruder, The. Kizer.
Outlaws. Graves.
"Twinkle, twinkle, little bat!" *Fr.* Alice's Adventures in Wonderland. "Lewis Carroll."
Baucis and Philemon
Baucis and Philemon. Ovid.
Baucis and Philemon. Swift.
Baudelaire, Charles
Ave atque Vale. Swinburne.
Baudelaire. Schwartz.
Bavaria
Lines on Leaving a Scene in Bavaria. Campbell.
Sonnet in a Pass of Bavaria. Trench.
Beaches
Afternoon: Amagansett Beach. Wheelock.
Skin Divers, The. Starbuck.
Bean, Roy
Roy Bean. *Unknown, at. to* Finger.
Bears
Adventures of Isabel. Nash.
Bear, The. Carpenter.
Bear, The. Frost.
Bear, The. Kinnell.
Bear Hunt, The. Widdemer.
Bear in the Hill, The. *Unknown.*
Bear on the Delhi Road, The. Birney.
Bears. Guiterman.
Brown Bear, The. Austin.
Furry Bear. Milne.
Grizzly. Harte.
Grizzly Bear. Austin.
Little Brown Bear. Wilkins.
Lost Silvertip. Reed.
Tails. Bennett.
Beatrice Portinari
Canzone: "Eyes that weep for pity of the heart, The." Dante.
Sonnet: Of Beatrice de Portinari on All Saints' Day. Dante.
Beaumont, Francis
Bards of Passion and of Mirth. Keats.
On Mr. Francis Beaumont (Then Newly Dead). Corbet.
To Francis Beaumont. Jonson.
Beaumont, Francis, and John Fletcher
Beaumont and Fletcher. *Fr.* Sonnets on English Dramatic Poets (1590-1650). Swinburne.
Beaumont, Sir George
Elegiac Stanzas. Wordsworth.
Beauregard, Pierre Gustave Toutant.
Beauregard. Warfield.
Beauty
Barter. Teasdale.
Beauté, La. Baudelaire.
Beauty. Binyon.
Beauty. Cowley.
Beauty. E-Yeh-Shure'.
Beauty. Hille.
Beauty. *Fr.* Tamburlaine the Great. Marlowe.
Beauty. Masefield.
Beauty. Rosenberg.
Beauty. Spingarn.
Beauty. Thomas.
Beauty. Wylie.
Beauty and Terror. Harford.
Beauty crowds me till I die. Dickinson.
Beauty Is Ever to the Lonely Mind. Nathan.
Beauty of the World. Wilmot.
Beauty, sweet love, is like the morning dew. *Fr.* To Delia. Daniel.
Beauty's Hands Are Cool. Baker.
Behold, O Aspasia! I Send You Verses. *Fr.* Pericles and Aspasia. Landor.
Body's Beauty. *Fr.* The House of Life. D. G. Rossetti.
Brittle Beauty. Surrey.
Changeful Beauty. Lang.
Color. Gibson.
Colours of Love, The. Devlin.
Craftsman, The. Christian.
Definition of Beauty, The. Herrick.
Description of Beauty, A. Marino.

Dim Face of Beauty. "Macleod."
Do Not, Oh Do Not Prize. *Unknown.*
Each and All. Emerson.
Earth's Common Things. Savage.
Euclid Alone Has Looked on Beauty Bare. Millay.
Exhortation to the Artists. Plutzik.
Frailty and Hurtfulness of Beauty, The. Surrey.
Gascoigne's Arraignment. Gascoigne.
Give Beauty All Her Right. Campion.
Gloire de Dijon. Lawrence.
Great Breath, The. "Æ."
He Remembers Forgotten Beauty. Yeats.
Hen and the Oriole, The. *Fr.* Archy and Mehitabel. Marquis.
Here Is the Place Where Loveliness Keeps House. Cawein.
Hymn to Intellectual Beauty. Shelley.
Hymne in Honour of Beautie, An. Spenser.
I died for beauty—but was scarce. Dickinson.
I Hear the Woodlands Calling. Cawein.
I Never See the Red Rose Crown the Year. Masefield.
Ideal Beauty. Herrera.
Immortal, The. Pickthall.
Independence Day. Smith.
Inner Man, The. Plato.
It was a beauty that I saw. *Fr.* The New Inn. Jonson.
Ladies, You See Time Flieth. *Unknown.*
Like Music. Wheelock.
Little Things. Johns.
Lonely Beauty. *Fr.* The Complaint of Rosamund. Daniel.
Lord, I have not time to pray. *Fr.* Impiety. Magaret.
Lord of the Far Horizons. Carman.
Loveliness. Nicholson.
Merciles Beaute. Chaucer.
Modern Beauty. Symons.
Ode on a Grecian Urn. Keats.
Ode to Beauty. Emerson.
Pied Beauty. Hopkins.
Prayer, A: "Each day I walk with wonder." Scollard.
Prayer: "Lord, make me sensitive to the sight." Marr.
Primer of Plato. Garrigue.
Rose of the World, The. Yeats.
Say Not That Beauty. Flower.
Scribe, The. De la Mare.
Snare, The. Davison.
Song, A: "It is not Beauty I demand." Darley.
Song for Beauty, A. Lal.
Sonnet to Heavenly Beauty, A. Du Bellay.
Soul's Beauty. *Fr.* The House of Life. D. G. Rossetti.
Spring Night. Teasdale.
Thing of Beauty, A [Is a Joy Forever]. *Fr.* Endymion. Keats.
This Is the Shape of the Leaf. *Fr.* Priapus and the Pool. Aiken.
To His Friend. Turberville.
'Twas at thatt hour of beauty when the setting sun. *Fr.* The Testament of Beauty. Bridges.
Unutterable Beauty, The. Studdert-Kennedy.
Vale. Plunkett.
Wayfarer, The. Pearse.
Wherever Beauty Has Been Quick in Clay. Masefield.
Who Pilots Ships. Hicky.
Who Walks with Beauty. Morton.

Beavers
Beaver Pond. Marriott.
Paddy the Beaver. Burgess.

Becerra, Gaspar
Gaspar Becerra. Longfellow.

Bedford, Countess of. *See* **Russell, Lucy, Countess of Bedford.**

Beds
Bed without a Woman, A. Souster.
For the Bed at Kelmscott. Morris.
My Bed. Mitchell.
Saturday Morning. Howard.

Beech Trees
Beech, The. Daeubler.
Beech, The. Young.
Beech Trees. Sister Mary Madeleva.
Beech Tree's Petition, The. Campbell.
To My Totem. Beeching.

Beecher, Henry Ward
Henry Ward Beecher. Phelps.
Limerick: "Reverend Henry Ward Beecher, The." *At. to* Holmes.

Beecher Island (Colo.), Battle of
Beecher Island. Chapman.

Beer
Beer. Arnold.
Beer. Calverley.
Beer. *Unknown.*
Glass of Beer, A. Stephens.
Hermit Hoar. Johnson.

Bees
Against Idleness and Mischief. Watts.
Arrival of the Bee Box, The. Plath.
Bee, The. Fandel.
Bee, The. Fitzgeffry.
Bee, The. Hawkins.
Bee, The. *Unknown.*
Bee, The. Watts.
Bee and the Lily, The. Westwood.
Bee-Master. Sackville-West.
Bee Sets Sail, A. Morse.
Bee Song. Sandburg.
Bee, the Ant, and the Sparrow, The. Cotton.
Beehive. Toomer.
Beekeeper. Matthews.
Bees. Chute.
Bees, The. Gibbon.
Bees, The. Ridge.
Bees. Sherman.
Bees before Winter. Moore.
Bees of Myddleton Manor, The. Probyn.
Bees' Song, The. De la Mare.
Browny Bee. Pawsey.
Bumble Bee. Brown.
Bumblebee. Wood.
Bumble-Bee and Clover. *Unknown.*
Bufferfly and the Bee, The. Bowles.
Charm: Against a Swarm of Bees. *Unknown.*
Flowers. Behn.
Fuscara or the Bee Errant. Cleveland.
Happy World, The. Rands.
Honey. Miller.
Honey Bee. McCoy.
Honey Bee, The. Marquis.
Honey-Bee. Perkins.
How Doth the Little Busy Bee. Watts.
Humble-Bee, The. Emerson.
Humble Bumble Bee, The. Lindsay.
I Would Like to Be—a Bee. Baruch.
Julius Caesar and the Honey-Bee. Turner.
Like trains of cars on tracks of plush. Dickinson.
Limerick: "There Was an Old Man in a Tree." Lear.
Merry Bee, A. Skipsey.
More Ancient Mariner, A. Carman.
Near Dusk. Auslander.
On a Honey Bee. Freneau.
Pedigree of honey, The. Dickinson.
Riddle: "As I went over Tipple Tyne." *Unknown.*
Song of the Bees. Gould.
Song of the Queen Bee. White.
Swarm of Bees in May, A. *Unknown.*
Tax-Gatherer, The. Tabb.
Telling the Bees. Lang.
Telling the Bees. Reese.
Telling the Bees. Whittier.
To a Bee. Southey.
Venerable Bee, The. Klein.
What Does the Bee Do? *Fr.* Sing-Song. C. G. Rossetti.
Where the Bee Sucks. *Fr.* The Tempest. Shakespeare.
Wild Bees. Baxter.
Wild Bees. Clare.

Beethoven, Ludwig van
Beethoven. Carpenter.
Beethoven Andante, A. Conkling.
Beethoven's Death Mask. Spender.
Eleusis and Beethoven. Press.
Four Friends. Ward.
Higgledy-piggledy/ Ludwig van Beethoven. Seaman.
On First Hearing Beethoven. Barker.
Wrath. Hollander.

Beetles
Beetle, The. King.
Beetle, The. Riley.

Beetles *(continued)*
Beetle Bemused. Lister.
Beetle in the Country Bathtub, The. Wheelock.
Beetle on the Shasta Daylight. Kaufman.
Riddle: "Wee man o' leather." *Unknown.*
World's End. Chettur.
Begging and Beggars
Beggar, The. Bruner.
Beggar, The. Doak.
Beggar. Flint.
Beggar. Parra.
Beggar Laddie, The. *Unknown.*
Beggar to Burgher. Fairburn.
Beggars. Carpenter.
Beggars. Davidson.
Beggars. Higginson.
Beggars, The. Widdemer.
Cante Hondo. Kay.
Cast Our Caps and Cares Away. *Fr.* Beggars' Bush. Fletcher.
Happy Beggarman, The. *Unknown.*
In Praise of a Beggar's Life. "A. W."
In Railway Halls, On Pavements. Spender.
Jolly Beggar, The. *At. to* James V, King of Scotland.
Jolly Beggar, The. *Unknown.*
Jolly Beggars, The. Burns.
Loving Mad Tom. *Unknown.*
Maunding Souldier, The; or, The Fruits of Warre Is Beggery. *Unknown.*
Monk Begging, Kyoto. Shiffert.
Old Cumberland Beggar, The. Wordsworth.
On a Fair Beggar. Ayres.
Song of the Beggars. Brome.
Street Beggar. Scruggs.
Three Beggars, The. De la Mare.
Tom o' Bedlam's Song. *Unknown.*
West London. Arnold.
Belgium
Homeland, The. Cammaerts.
Moon and the Night and the Men, The. Berryman.
Belgrade, Yugoslavia
Siege of Belgrade, The. *Unknown.*
Belief, Religious. *See* **Faith.**
Belisarius
Belisarius. Longfellow.
Bell, Alexander Graham
Alexander Graham Bell Did Not Invent the Telephone. Coffin.
Bellbirds
Bell-Birds. Kendall.
Bells
Ave Maria Bells. Stoddard.
Belfry, The. Binyon.
Bell, A. Scollard.
Bell Speech. Wilbur.
Bell Tower. Adams.
Bells, The. Fogazzaro.
Bells, The. Poe.
Bells. Scott.
Bells, The. *Unknown.*
Bells across the Snow. Havergal.
Bell's Dream. Weatherly.
Bells in the Country. Nathan.
Bells in the Rain. Wylie.
Bells of London, The. *Unknown.*
Bells of Shandon, The. Mahony.
Bells of Youth, The. "Macleod."
Bells, Ostend, The. Bowles.
Bredon Hill. Housman.
Broken Tower, The. H. Crane.
Carillon, The. Castro.
Catholic Bells, The. Williams.
Chanson of the Bells of Oseney. Rice.
Children's Bells, The. Farjeon.
Chimes. Meynell.
Christ Church Bells. Aldrich.
Christmas Bells. Longfellow.
Church Bell in the Night, The. *Unknown.*
Cracked Bell, The. Baudelaire.
Great Tom. Corbet.
Little Bell. Westwood.
London Bells. *Unknown.*
Merry Are the Bells. *Unknown.*
Minaret Bells, The. Thackeray.
Oxford Bells. Sister Maris Stella.
Passing Bell, The. Shirley.
Passing-Bell, The. *Unknown.*
Passing Bell at Stratford, The. Winter.
Theme. Spitteler.
Upon a Ring of Bells. Bunyan.
Victory Bells. Conkling.
Wantage Bells. Betjeman.
Belshazzar
Belshazzar had a letter. Dickinson.
Vision of Belshazzar, The. Byron.
Ben Bulben, Ireland
Under Ben Bulben. Yeats.
Benbow, Admiral John
Admiral Benbow. *Unknown.*
Death of Admiral Benbow, The. *Unknown.*
Bendemeer, Wales
By Bendemeer's Stream. *Fr.* Lalla Rookh. Moore.
Benet, Stephen Vincent
Love to Stephen. Wylie.
Bennington, Battle of
Battle of Bennington, The. Rodman.
Rifleman's Song at Bennington, The. *Unknown.*
Bentley, Edmund Clerihew
Edmund Clerihew Bentley. Smith.
Instead of blushing cherry hue. Laing.
Bentley, Richard
Stanzas to Mr. Bentley. Gray.
Beowulf
Beowulf. Wilbur.
Berengaria, Queen
Coeur de Lion to Berengaria. Tilton.
Bergman, Ingmar
Ingmar Bergman's Seventh Seal. Duncan.
Berkeley, George
Fountain, The. Davie.
Berkshire Hills, Massachusetts
Monument Mountain. Bryant.
Whole Duty of Berkshire Brooks, The. Conkling.
Berkshire Symphonic Festival
Tanglewood. Sweeney.
Bermuda
Battle of the Summer-Islands, The. Waller.
Bermuda Suite. Scott.
Bermudas. Marvell.
Bernadette, Saint
Canticle of Bernadette, The. *Unknown.*
Bertrand de Born
Near Perigord. Pound.
Beth Gêlert
Beth Gêlert. Spencer.
Bethlehem
At Bethlehem. Tabb.
Bethlehem. Canton.
Bethlehem. Farrington.
Bethlehem Road, The. Munson.
Bethlehem-Town. Field.
Birds of Bethlehem, The. Gilder.
How Far to Bethlehem? Miller.
Light of Bethlehem, The. Tabb.
Little Town, The. Scollard.
Little Town of Bethlehem. Brooks.
Once in Royal David's City. Alexander.
While to Bethlehem We Are Going. Sister Violante do Ceo.
Bethune, Mary McLeod
For Mary McLeod Bethune. Walker.
Beverly, Massachusetts
Hymn Written for the 200th Anniversary of the Old South Church, Beverly, Mass. Larcom.
Bialik, Hayyim Nahman
Harangue on the Death of Hayyim Nahman Bialik. Tiempo.
Bible
Anvil of God's Word, The. *Unknown.*
Apocrypha. Kennedy.
Believe the Bible. Simpson.
Bible, The, *sel.* Levi.
Bible, The. Stroud.
Bible, The. Traherne.
Bible, A. *Fr.* Riddle. *Unknown.*
Bible, The. *Fr.* Miriam. Whittier.

Bible is an antique volume, The. Dickinson.
Bit of the Book, A. Sangster.
Book, The. Garrison.
Book of Books, The. *Fr.* The Monastery. Scott.
Book Our Mothers Read, The. Whittier.
Divine Volume, The. *Fr.* The Monastery. Scott.
God's Treasure. "A. M. N."
H. Scriptures, The. Herbert.
H. Scriptures. Vaughan.
Holy Bible, Book Divine. Burton.
Incomparable Treasure, The. *Unknown.*
Inscription on the Flyleaf of a Bible. Abse.
Living Book, The. Bates.
Knowledge. *Unknown.*
My Bible and I. *Unknown.*
My Companion. Wesley.
My Mother's Bible. Morris.
My Old Bible. *Unknown.*
New Testament, The. Russell.
Of the Incomparable Treasure of the Scriptures. *Unknown.*
Old Testament, The. Russell.
Read the Bible Through. Wells.
Reading the Book. *Unknown.*
Spirit breathes upon the world, The. *Fr.* The Light and Glory of the World. Cowper.
Sublimity! Sublimity! I lay thee down. *Fr.* Line on a Re-reading of Parts of the Old Testament. Campbell.
Word of God, The. Gwynne.
Sourcebook of Poetry (SoP). Al Bryant, Comp.

Bicycles and Bicycling
Bicycalamity. Peters.
Different Bicycles. Baruch.
Going down Hill on a Bicycle. Beeching.
Gol-darned Wheel, The. *Unknown.*

Biddle, Nicholas
On the Death of Captain Nicholas Biddle. Freneau.

Big Bethel, Virginia
Bethel. Duganne.

Big Thompson Canyon, Colorado
Big Thompson Canon. Gower.

Billy the Kid (William H. Booney)
Billy the Kid. *Unknown.*

Bindweed
Bind-Weed. "Coolidge."
Bindweed, The. De la Mare.

Bingen, Germany
Bingen on the Rhine. Norton.

Bion
Lament for Bion, A. *At. to* Moschus.

Birch Trees
Absent Minded Birch Tree, The. K. Millay.
Birch-Tree at Loschwitz, The. Levy.
Birch Trees. Moreland.
Birches. Frost.
Little Birches. Newsome.
Young Birch, A. Frost.

Birds
After the Storm. Vaughan.
Afternoon in a Tree. Sister Maris Stella.
All These Birds. Wilbur.
Angler's Reveille, The. Van Dyke.
Answer to a Child's Question. Coleridge.
Any Bird. Orleans.
Ariel. Campbell.
". . . As When Emotion Too Far Exceeds Its Cause." Oden.
Asian Birds. Bridges.
At Common Dawn. Ellis.
Auspex. J. R. Lowell.
Autumn Birds. Clare.
Autumn Flitting, An. Cotterell.
Balcony with Birds, A. Moss.
Be like the Bird. Hugo.
Beasts, Birds and Fishes. O'Keeffe.
Bird, The. Allingham.
Bird, The. Hoffenstein.
Bird, The. Michaelson.
Bird, The. Tagore.
Bird, The. Sister Mary Thérèse.
Bird, The. Vaughan.
Bird, The. Countess of Winchilsea.
Bird at Dawn, The. Monro.
Bird came down the walk, A. Dickinson.
Bird from the West, A. Shorter.
Bird in a Cage, The. Bowles.
Bird in a Cage, The. *Unknown.*
Bird, Let Loose in Eastern Skies, The. Moore.
Bird Raptures. C. G. Rossetti.
Bird Song. Hay.
Bird Trades. *Unknown.*
Bird Was Singing, A. Dietmar von Aist.
Bird-Witted. Moore.
Birds, The, *sels.* Aristophanes.
Birds, The. Blake.
Birds, The. Dracontius.
Birds. Jeffers.
Birds. Miller.
Birds. "O'Neill."
Birds, The. Posner.
Birds, The. Squire.
Birds. Stoddard.
Birds All Singing. MacCaig.
Birds' Courting Song, The. *Unknown.*
Birds Go By, The. Neilson.
Birds in April. Henley.
Birds in Summer. Howitt.
Birds in the Fens. *Fr.* Polyolbion. Drayton.
Birds of America, The. Broughton.
Birds of Passage, The. Hemans.
Bird's Song at Morning. Dawson.
Blinded Bird, The. Hardy.
Broken Pinion, The. Butterworth.
Canticle to the Waterbirds, A. Brother Antoninus.
Cape Ann. *Fr.* Landscapes. Eliot.
Cat and the Bird, The. Solomon.
Cedar Waxwing. Matchett.
Chaste Arabian Bird, The. Rochester.
Children of the Wind. *Fr.* The People, Yes. Sandburg.
Choristers, The. Carman.
Chough. Warner.
Come Not Near. Osborn.
Crumbs to the Birds. Lamb.
Death of a Bird. Silkin.
Death of the Bird, The. Hope.
Do You Ask What the Birds Say? Coleridge.
Dream, The. *Fr.* The Book of the Duchesse. Chaucer.
Educated Love Bird, The. Newell.
Epitaph on Lady Ossory's Bullfinch. Walpole.
Fifteen Acres, The. Stephens.
Firetail's Nest, The. Clare.
Flying Fish, The. Gray.
Four Birds. *Unknown.*
Great Scarf of Birds, The. Updike.
Green Rain. Webb.
I Heard a Linnet Courting. Bridges.
In a Bird Sanctuary. Wilbur.
In Glencullen. Synge.
In Her Song She Is Alone. Swan.
Introduction: "Twas late in my long journey, when I had clomb to where." *Fr.* The Testament of Beauty. Bridges.
Invitation. Behn.
Joe. McCord.
Joy of the Morning. Markham.
Lady Lost. Ransom.
Lark's Song, The. *Fr.* Milton. Blake.
Listener's Guide to the Birds, A. White.
Little Bird, The. *Unknown.*
Little Beach Bird, The. Dana.
Little Birds. *Fr.* Sylvie and Bruno Concluded. "Carroll."
Little Birds. Sternberg.
Little Morning Music, A. Schwartz.
L'Oiseau Bleu. M. E. Coleridge.
Lord of the Isle, The. George.
Making of Birds. Tynan.
Many Birds. *Fr.* Auguries of Innocence. Blake.
Marché aux Oiseaux. Wilbur.
Minor Bird, A. Frost.
Mopoke. Lavater.
My Little Birds. *Unknown.*
Native Companions Dancing. Neilson.
Nesting Time. Stewart.
Never Again Would Birds' Song Be the Same. Frost.
Night Bird, The. Kingsley.

Birds *(continued)*
Night Walkers, The. Smithyman.
Nightingale and Flowers. *Fr.* Milton. Blake.
No shop does the bird use. Coatsworth.
O Bird, So Lovely. Golding.
Of the Child with the Bird at the Bush. Bunyan.
Old Man in the Park. Osborn.
On a Cold Day. Davies.
Once I Nearly Touched a Bird. Carr.
Orphan's Song, The. Dobell.
Our Native Birds. Dole.
Our Singing Strength. Frost.
Oven Bird, The. Frost.
Over Sir John's Hill. Thomas.
Over the multiple terrors of Mars. *Fr.* Kokaburra. Moore.
Overflow. Tabb.
Pack, Clouds, Away. *Fr.* The Rape of Lucrece. Heywood.
Paradox; the Birds. Shapiro.
Parlement of Foules, The, *sels.* Chaucer.
People Buy a Lot of Things. Wynne.
Popular Rhymes. Blake.
Pretty Wantons. *Unknown.*
Princely eagle, and the soaring hawke, The. Wood.
Proud Songsters. Hardy.
Puzzled Game-Birds, The. Hardy.
Redwing, The. P. Dickinson.
Rivals, The. Stephens.
Robert of Lincoln. Bryant.
Saint Francis' Sermon to the Birds. Longfellow.
Sea Bird, The. Douglas.
Sea Birds, The. Brock.
Sea-Change. Masefield.
Seed-Eaters, The. Francis.
Shag Rookery. Hart-Smith.
Shore Birds. Gale.
Silver Bird of Herndyke Mill, The. Blunden.
Sing Little Birds. Hastings.
Sing On, Blithe Bird! Motherwell.
Small Birds. Quennell.
Song-Bird. Vrepont.
Speak with the Sun. Campbell.
Spring: The Lover and the Birds. Allingham.
Tea-Tree and the Lyrebird, The. Robinson.
That Is All I Heard. "Yehoash."
To A. D. Henley.
To a Waterfowl. Bryant.
Tom's Sleeping Song. *Fr.* Jonathan Genry. Van Doren.
Trail of the Bird, The. Courthope.
Trico's Song. *Fr.* Alexander and Campaspe. Lyly.
Unknown Bird, The. Thomas.
Up from the Egg: the Confessions of a Nuthatch Avoider. Nash.
Warblers. Hartley.
Water Ouzel. Matchett.
Whistling Jack, The. Neilson.
Widow Bird, A. *Fr.* Charles the First. Shelley.
Wind and the Bird, The. *Unknown.*
Windhover, The. Hopkins.
Wings. Hugo.
Yellow Warblers. Bates.
You That Sing in the Blackthorn. Noyes.
Bird Songs (BiS). Gwendolyn Reed, comp.
See also ***names of birds (e.g.,*** **Canaries).**

Birds' Nests
Bird's Nest, A. Allen.
Bird's Nest, The. Drinkwater.
Bird's Nest, The. Turner.
Birds' Nest. *Fr.* Childhood. Clare.
Birds' Nests, The. *Unknown.*
Discovery, The. Snaith.
Emperor's Bird's-Nest, The. Longfellow.
Nest, The. Elliot.
Ruined Nest, The. *Unknown.*
Thrush's Nest, The. Clare.
Turtle-Dove's Nests, The. *Unknown.*
Two Nests, The. Carlin.
What Robin Told. Cooper.
Who Stole the Bird's Nest? Child.
Within the Bush. *Fr.* A Rose-Bud by my Early Walk. Burns.

Birds of Paradise
Bird of Paradise, The. L. Benét.
Bird of Paradise, The. Davies.
Birds of Paradise, The. Bishop.

Birmingham, England
Birmingham. MacNeice.

Birth
Arrivals and Departures. La Follette.
At Birth. Thwaite.
Birth. Raymond.
Birth, A. Rukeyser.
Birth of a Great Man. Graves.
Childbirth. Hughes.
For Nicholas, Born in September. Perry.
In My Infancy. Ross.
Labor Room. Benn.
Morning Song. Plath.
Nativity. Hayford.
Prayer before Birth. MacNeice.
Prime. Auden.

Birthdays
Another Birthday. Jonson.
Betsy Jane's Sixth Birthday. Noyes.
Birthday, A. Field.
Birthday, A. C. G. Rossetti.
Birthday Candle, A. Justice.
Birthday Child, The. Fyleman.
Birthday Gifts. Asquith.
Birthday Song, A. Gilder.
Birthdays. Chute.
Birthdays. Driver.
Birthdays. *Unknown.*
It's Somebody's Birthday. Norris.
My Birthday. Moore.
My Gift. *Fr.* A Christmas Carol. C. G. Rossetti.
Our Birthday. Edey.
Party, A. Richards.
Poem in October. Thomas.
Poem on His Birthday. Thomas.
Seven Times One. *Fr.* Songs of Seven. Ingelow.
Birthday Candles Burning Bright (BiCB). Sara and John E. Brewton, eds.

Bishops. *See* **Clergy.**

Bismarck, Otto von
Lines on the Death of Bismarck. Chapman.

Black Verse. *See* **Negro Verse.**

Blackberries
Blackberry, The. Nicholson.
Blackberry-picking. Heaney.
Blackberry Thicket, The. Stanford.
Blackberrying. Plath.

Blackbirds
Blackbird, The. Barnes.
Blackbird, The. Beeching.
Blackbird, The. Craik.
Blackbird, The. Henley.
Blackbird, The. F. Tennyson.
Blackbird, The. *Unknown.*
Blackbird, The. Wolfe.
Blackbird by Belfast Lough, The. *Unknown.*
Blackbird Singing, A. Thomas.
Blackbird Suddenly, A. Auslander.
Death of a Bird. Silkin.
O What If the Fowler. Dalmon.
One Blackbird. *Fr.* Strange Meetings. Monro.
Ruined Nest, The. *Unknown.*
There were two blackbirds sitting on a hill. Mother Goose.
Thirteen Ways of Looking at a Blackbird. Stevens.
To an Irish Blackbird. MacAlpine.
Vespers. Brown.

Blackheath, London
Sermon to the Rebels at Blackheath. Ball.

Blacks. *See* **Negroes.**

Blacksmiths
Blacksmith, The. *Unknown.*
Blacksmiths. *Unknown.*
Legend. Wright.
Smith's Song. Sigerson.
Village Blacksmith, The. Longfellow.

Blackwater (river), Ireland
Beside the Blackwater. O'Conor.

Crossing the Blackwater. Joyce.
Blake, William
And before hell mouth; dry plain. *Fr.* Canto XVI. Pound.
Blake. Fletcher.
Mad Blake. W. R. Benét.
To William Blake. Dargan.
William Blake. *Fr.* Five English Poets. D. G. Rossetti.
William Blake. Thomson.
William Blake Sees God. McFadden.
Wiser than the Children of Light. Gibbon.
Blanc, Mont, Switzerland. *See* **Mont Blanc.**
Blarney, Ireland
Groves of Blarney, The. Millikin.
Blasphemy
For All Blasphemers. S. V. Benét.
Blenheim, Battle of
Battle of Blenheim, The. Southey.
Blenheim. *Fr.* The Campaign. Addison.
Blenheim Park, England
On Blenheim. Swift.
On Blenheim House. Evans.
Blennerhasset Island, West Virginia
Blennerhasset's Island. *Fr.* The New Pastoral. Read.
Blindness
All but Blind. De la Mare.
At a Country Fair. Hardy.
Blind. Pearce.
Blind Boy, The. Cibber.
Blind but Happy. Crosby.
Blind Highland Boy, The. Wordsworth.
Blind Man. Hamburger.
Blind Man. Miller.
Blind Man at the Fair, The. Campbell.
Blind Man Lay beside the Way. *Unknown.*
Blind Man's Morning, The. Meynell.
Blind Man's Regret, The. *Unknown.*
Blinded Bird, The. Hardy.
Blinded Soldier to His Love, The. Noyes.
Blindness of Samson, The. *Fr.* Samson Agonistes. Milton.
Braille. *Unknown.*
Cease thy wishes gentle boy. *Unknown.*
In the Garden of the Lord. Keller.
Mock Medicine. *Unknown.*
On a Blind Girl. Baha Ad-din Zuhayr.
On His Blindness. Milton.
Samson Agonistes. Milton.
Smoker, The. Huff.
Solitude, A. Levertov.
To Mr. Cyriack Skinner upon His Blindness. Milton.
Unblinding, The. Lieberman.
When I Consider How My Light Is Spent. Milton.
Blizzards
Lost in a Blizzard. Monroe.
Snowstorm, The. Crouch.
Block, Adriaen
Adrian Block's Song. Hale.
Block Island
Palatine, The. Whittier.
Blondel de Nesle
Blondel. Urmy.
Bloodhounds
Bloodhound, The. Anthony.
Ol' Rattler. *Unknown.*
Bloomer, Amelia Jenks
Crinolines and Bloomers. *Unknown.*
Blue Jays
Blue Jay. Conkling.
Blue Jay. Francis.
Blue-Jay, The. Swett.
Blue on White. Coatsworth.
Blue Ridge Mountains
Blue Ridge, The. Monroe.
Bluebells
Bluebell, The. E. Brontë.
Bluebells. De la Mare.
Bluebells. P. Dickinson.
Bluebells. Enoch.
Bluebells. Ewing.
Bluebells. Markham.
Bluebells. Ropes.
Bluebells of Scotland, The. *Unknown.*
To a Bluebell. E. Brontë.
Bluebirds
Advice to a Blue-Bird. Bodenheim.
Blue Bird, The. M. E. Coleridge.
Bluebird. Conkling.
Blue-Bird, The. Melville.
Bluebird, The. Miller.
Blue-Bird, The. Wilson.
Early Bluebird, An. Thompson.
Last Word of a Bluebird, The. Frost.
L'Oiseau Bleu. M. E. Coleridge.
Sign of Spring, A. Rexford.
Bluenose (ship)
Spirit of the *Bluenose,* The. MacIntosh.
Blues (mood)
Blues. Marxey.
Blues. Mungin.
Blues. Prettyman.
Blues. Sanchez.
Blues for Sallie. Crouch.
Get up, Blues. Emanuel.
Hesitating Blues. Handy.
I Got the Blues. *Unknown.*
Blues (music)
Blues Today, The. Jackson.
Homage to the Empress of the Blues. Hayden.
Twang. Robinson.
Weary Blues, The. Hughes.
Boadicea
Boadicea. Cowper.
Boats
Boats. Bennett.
Boats at Night. Shanks.
Boats in a Fog. Jeffers.
Crescent Boat, The. *Fr.* Peter Bell. Wordsworth.
East River. Thomas.
Eton Boating Song. Cory.
Excursion, The. Tu Fu.
Freight Boats. Tippett.
Kayak, The. *Unknown.*
Little Steamboat. Williams.
Old Boat, The. Pratt.
Paper Boats. Tagore.
Riding in a Motor Boat. Baruch.
River Boats, The. Hicky.
Ship Burning and a Comet All in One Day, A. Eberhart.
Where Go the Boats. Stevenson.
Whistles. Field.
See also **Ships.**
Bobolinks
Bobolink, The, Hill.
Bobolinks, The. Cranch.
O'Lincoln Family, The. Flagg.
Robert of Lincoln. Bryant.
Bobwhites
Bob White. Cooper.
Boer War
Boer War, The. Plomer.
Drummer Hodge. Hardy.
Rank and File. Dobson.
Bogs
Bog-Lands, The. Byrne.
Bohemia
City Nights: In Bohemia. Symons.
My Bohemia. Rimbaud.
Bolívar, Simon
To Bolivar. Pombo.
Boll Weevils
Ballet [*or* Ballit] of de Boll Weevil, De. *Unknown.*
Bolton Priory, England
Rounding of Bolton Priory, The. Wordsworth.
Bombay, India
Bombay. Miles.
Bombay Arrival. Lee.
Bombers
Bomber, The. Vrepont.
Bombs and bombing. *See* **Air raids.**
Bones
Bone Thoughts on a Dry Day. Starbuck.
Bones of a French Lady in a Museum. Gillman.

Bonhomme Richard (ship)
Bonhomme Richard and *Serapis*, The. Freneau.
Paul Jones. *Unknown.*
Bonnie Dundee. *See* **Dundee, John Graham of Claverhouse, 1st Viscount.**
Bonnie Prince Charlie. *See* **Stuart, Charles Edward.**
Bonnivard, Francois de
Prisoner of Chillon, The. Byron.
Bononcini, Giovanni Battista
Epigram on Handel and Bononcini. Byrom.
Books
Advice to a Young Friend on the Choice of His Library. Wycherley.
Author to Her Book, The. Bradstreet.
Book, A. More.
Book, A. Reese.
Book, The. Vaughan.
Book Is an Enchanted Gate, A. Beer.
Books. Conkling.
Books. *Fr.* The Library. Crabbe.
Books. Farjeon.
Books. Keith.
Books. *Unknown.*
Books. Van Cleve.
Books Are Keys. Poulsson.
Bookworm, The. De la Mare.
Bookworms, The. Burns.
Burning of Books, The. Brecht.
Classic Waits for Me, A. White.
Dedication on the Gift of a Book to a Child. Belloc.
Dickens in Camp. Harte.
Envoy: "Go, little book, and wish to all." Stevenson.
Fire at Alexandria, The. Weiss.
First Geography. McKee.
First Reader. Leary.
First Reader (Fifth Reading). McKee.
Golden Spurs. Miner.
"Good from a Book." *Fr.* Aurora Leigh. E. B. Browning.
Half Your Book. Swift.
He ate and drank the precious words. Dickinson.
If someone asks you. Donian.
I've Got a New Book from My Grandfather Hyde. Jackson.
Land of Story Books, The. Stevenson.
Letter to Hitler, A. Laughlin.
My Books. Longfellow.
My Books I'd Fain Cast Off, I Cannot Read. Thoreau.
My Days among the Dead Are Past. Southey.
New Book, The. Turner.
O for a Booke. *Unknown.*
Of Books. *At. to* Florio.
Of the Book-Hunter. Lang.
Old Books Are Best. Chew.
Old Susan. De la Mare.
On Opening a New Book. Brown.
On the Detraction Which Followed upon My Writing Certain Treatises. Milton.
Precious—mouldering pleasure—'tis, A. Dickinson.
Reading in War Time. Muir.
Shut Not Your Doors. Whitman.
Sibrandus Schafnaburgensis. *Fr.* Garden Fancies. R. Browning.
Tables Turned, The. Wordsworth.
There is no frigate like a book. Dickinson.
To His Book. Martial.
To His Book. Walsh.
To His Books. Vaughan.
To My Book. Jonson.
To My Bookseller. Jonson.
To the Lady with a Book. *Unknown.*
To the Reader. *Unknown.*
Troubles of a Book, The. Riding.
Valediction, A; of the Booke. Donne.
"What Five Books Would You Pick to Be Marooned with on a Desert Island?" Leary.
Where My Books Go. Yeats.
Who Hath a Book. Nesbit.
Boone, Daniel
Daniel Boone. S. V. Benét.
Daniel Boone. Guiterman.
For the Grave of Daniel Boone. Stafford.
Booth, Edwin
Edwin Booth. Brown.
Sargent's Portrait of Edwin Booth at "The Players." Aldrich.
Booth, John Wilkes
Pardon. Howe.
Booth, William
General William Booth Enters into Heaven. Lindsay.
Borden, Lizzie
Lizzie Borden. *Unknown.*
Borgia, Lucrezia
On Seeing a Hair of Lucretia Borgia. Landor.
Born, Bertrand de. *See* **Bertrand de Born.**
Borneo
Naked in Borneo. Swenson.
Boston, Massachusetts
Ballad of the Boston Tea-Party, A. Holmes.
Boston. Emerson.
Boston. O'Reilly.
Boston. *Unknown.*
Boston Toast, A. Bossidy.
Calf-Path, The. Foss.
Church of the Revolution, The. Butterworth.
Communication to the City Fathers of Boston. Starbuck.
In the "Old South." Whittier.
New Order, The. McGinley.
Off from Boston. *Unknown.*
On a Fortification at Boston Begun by Women. Thompson.
Poem Containing Some Remarks on the Present War, A. *Unknown.*
Poems from a First Year in Boston. Starbuck.
Sunday Evening in the Common. Wheelock.
South End. Aiken.
Thanksgiving in Boston Harbor, The. Butterworth.
Whaddaya Do for Action in This Place? Starbuck.
Where the Rainbow Ends. R. Lowell.
Boston Evening Transcript (newspaper)
Boston Evening Transcript, The. Eliot.
Boston Massacre
Unhappy Boston. Revere.
Boston Tea Party
Ballad of the Boston Tea-Party, A. Holmes.
New Song, A. *Unknown.*
Botany Bay, Australia
Botany Bay. *Unknown.*
Bothwell, James Hepburn, 4th Earl of
Earl Bothwell. *Unknown.*
Bothwell, Scotland
Bothwell Bridge. *Unknown.*
Covenanter's Lament for Bothwell Brigg, The. Praed.
Bouncing Bet (plant)
Ragged Robin and Bouncing Bet. Reid.
Bourgeoisie
How Beastly the Bourgeois Is. Lawrence.
Bowdoin College
Morituri Salutamus. Longfellow.
Bowery, The, New York City
Bowery, The. Hoyt.
Bowles, William Lisle
To the Reverend W. L. Bowles. Coleridge.
William Lisle Bowles. *Fr.* English Bards and Scotch Reviewers. Byron.
Boxing and Boxers
Boxer. Clancy.
Boxer's Face, The. Lucilius.
Boxing Match, The. *Fr.* The Aeneid. Vergil.
Fancy, The. W. R. Benét.
Gallantly within the Ring. Reynolds.
Morrissey and the Russian Sailor. *Unknown.*
My Lord, What a Morning. Cuney.
Nonpareil's Grave, The. McMahon.
On Hurricane Jackson. Dugan.
World's Worst Boxer, The. Lucilius.
Boyhood. *See* **Childhood and Children; Youth.**
Boyne, Battle of The
Boyne Water, The. *Unknown.*
King William and King James. *Unknown.*
William of Orange; or, The Battle of Boyne. *Unknown.*
Boyne, Ireland
Boyne Walk, The. Higgins.
Father and Son. Higgins.
Boys. *See* **Childhood and Children; Youth.**

Bozzaris, Marco
Marco Bozzaris. Halleck.
Braddock, Edward
Braddock's Defeat. *Unknown.*
Braddock's Fate, with an Incitement to Revenge. Tilden.
Ned Braddock. Palmer.
Song of Braddock's Men, The. *Unknown.*
Bradstreet, Anne
Funeral Elogy, upon. . .Mrs. Anne Bradstreet, A. Norton.
Homage to Mistress Bradstreet. Berryman.
Upon Mrs. Anne Bradstreet Her Poems. Rogers.
Upon the Author; by a Known Friend. Woodbridge.
Brahe, Tycho
Old Astronomer to His Pupil, The. Williams.
Brahma
Brahma. Emerson.
Brahms, Johannes
Brahms, The. Morris.
Brahms Peruses the Score of "Siegfried." Fuller.
Braithwaite, William Stanley
To William Stanley Braithwaite. Johnson.
Brancusi, Constantin
Overheard at a Sculpture Show at a Museum. *Unknown.*
Braque, Georges
Braque. Joseph.
Brawne, Fanny
Lines Supposed to Have Been Addressed to Fanny Brawne. Keats.
To Fanny. Keats.
Bray, Ireland
Lough Bray. O'Grady.
Brazil
Brazil. Carvalho.
Bread
Bread. Burnshaw.
Bread. Keesing.
Bread. Klein.
Brébeuf, Jean de
Brébeuf and His Brethren, *sels.* Pratt.
Brendan, Saint
Burial of Saint Brendan, The. Colum.
Pattern of Saint Brendan. MacManus.
Saint Brandan. Arnold.
Brian Boru
Lamentation of Mac Liag for Kincora. *Unknown.*
Brides. *See* **Marriage.**
Bridger, James
Mountain Liars. Hafen.
Bridges, Robert
To R. B. Hopkins.
Bridges
Bridge, The. H. Crane.
Bridge. Damon.
Bridge, The. Köhler.
Bridge, The. Longfellow.
Bridge, The. Peterson.
Bridges. Bacmeister.
Covered Bridge, The. Cawein.
Covered Bridge. Coffin.
Oh, What Are You Waiting For. *Fr.* Sunday up the River. Thomson.
Old Bridge, The. Conkling.
River Bridge, The. Tippett.
Bridget, Saint
Feast of Saint Brigid of Kildare, The. *At. to* St. Brigid.
Giveaway, The. McGinley.
I Should Like to Have a Great Pool of Ale. *At. to* St. Bridget.
St. Brigid. McCarthy.
Bright, John
John Bright. Gummere.
Brighton, England
Winter Boats at Brighton. Ross.
Bristol, England
Last Verses. Chatterton.
Bristol, Rhode Island
Bombardment of Bristol, The. *Unknown.*
British Empire
At Gibraltar. Woodberry.
Ballade of the Southern Cross. *Fr.* Ballades in Blue China. Lang.
British Guiana
Over Guiana, Clouds. Seymour.
British Museum, London
At the British Museum. Aldington.
British Museum Reading Room, The. MacNeice.
Homage to the British Museum. Empson.
Brittany, France
In Brittany. Willard.
Broadway, New York City
Broadway's Canyon. Fletcher.
Rhyme about an Electrical Advertising Sign, A. Lindsay.
Brock, Sir Isaac
Come All You Bold Canadians. *Unknown.*
Brontë, Anne
On the Death of Anne Brontë. C. Brontë.
Brontë, Branwell
Wanderer from the Fold, The. E. Brontë.
Brontë, Charlotte
All overgrown by cunning moss. Dickinson.
Brontë, Emily
Emily Brontë. Day Lewis.
Grace. Patrick.
Brontë Sisters
Visit to Brontëland, A. Kirkup.
Bronx, New York City
Bronx. Drake.
Brooke, Rupert
Going, The. Gibson.
Rupert Brooke. Gibson.
Brooklyn, New York City
Allegorical Figure of Brooklyn, The. Towle.
Brooklyn Heights. Wain.
Crossing Brooklyn Ferry. Whitman.
Joralemon Street. Hubbell.
Meditation on the BMT. Blackburn.
To a Portrait of Whistler in the Brooklyn Art Museum. Cox.
Brooklyn (ship)
Brooklyn at Santiago, The. Rice.
Brooklyn Bridge
Bridge, The. H. Crane.
Brooklyn Bridge, The. Proctor.
Brooklyn Bridge. Roberts.
Brooklyn Bridge at Dawn. Le Gallienne.
Granite and Steel. Moore.
View of the Brooklyn Bridge, A. Meredith.
Brooks, Van Wyck
Dear Men and Women. Wheelock.
Brooks and Streams
Hushed with broad sunlight lies the hill. *Fr.* Beaver Brook. J. R. Lowell.
Brook, The. Lord.
Brook, The. Tennyson.
Brook, The. Thomas.
Brook in February, The. Roberts.
Brook in the City, A. Frost.
Brook in Winter, The. *Fr.* The Vision of Sir Launfal. J. R. Lowell.
Brook Song. Morse.
Brook Song, The. Riley.
Brookside, The. Milnes.
By the Bridge. Walker.
Creek, The. Ross.
Hurrying Brook, The. Blunden.
Hyla Brook. Frost.
Inversnaid. Hopkins.
Ladder, The. Baro.
Meadow Brook Runs Over, The. Corning.
Orara. Kendall.
Pretty brook was running at play, A. *Unknown.*
Rivulet, The. Larcom.
Runaway Brook. Follen.
That Is All I Heard. "Yehoash."
There Is a Little Unpretending Rill. Wordsworth.
Water, The! the Water! Motherwell.
West-running Brook. Frost.
What Is a Brook? Mitchell.
Whole Duty of Berkshire Brooks, The. Conkling.
Broom (plant)
Broom Flower, The. Howitt.
Brooms
Broom. Farrar.

Brotherhood
All Hail, the Pageant of the Years. Holmes.
Any Human to Another. Cullen.
Ballad of East and West, The. Kipling.
Brother, The. Nadson.
Brotherhood. Davis.
Brotherhood. Markham.
Brothers. Day.
Brothers of the Faith. Oxenham.
Calamity. Scott.
Creed, A. Markham.
Creed and Deed. Loveman.
Dance of Saul with the Prophets, The. Tchernichowsky.
Day Is Coming, The. Morris.
Fatherland, The. J. R. Lowell.
Fellow-Citizens. Heidenstam.
Fraternitas. Confucius.
Gentle Park, A. Herbert.
German Prisoners. Lee.
Goliath and David. Untermeyer.
He Is My Countryman. Slonimski.
I Believe. Tchernichowsky.
I Dream a World. Hughes.
I Sought My Soul. *Unknown.*
In Distrust of Merits. Moore.
In the City. Zangwill.
Indian Prayer. Strongwolf.
Interracial. Johnson.
It Is a Dream? Studdert-Kennedy.
Liberty for All. Garrison.
Like Water down a Slope. Schneour.
Little Black Boy, The. *Fr.* Songs of Innocence. Blake.
London Spring. Slonimski.
Love. Immanuel di Roma.
Love We as Brothers. *Fr.* Vision of Piers Plowman. Langland.
Lying in the Grass. Gosse.
Man unto His Fellow Man. *Fr.* On a Note of Triumph. Corwin.
Modern Saint, The. Burton.
New Jewish Hospital at Hamburg, The. Heine.
New Patriotism, A. Piety.
O sprawling city! worlds in a world! *Fr.* New York Skyscraper. Oppenheim.
Nihil Humani Alienum. Coan.
No East or West. Oxenham.
O Brother Man. Whittier.
Out of Our Shame. Rosten.
Prayer for Brotherhood, A. Hoyland.
Prayer for Brotherhood. Wilder.
Pronouns. Baker.
Something in Common. Church.
Speech to Those Who Say Comrade. MacLeish.
Street Scene—1946. Porter.
There shall come from out of this noise of strife and groaning. *Fr.* Brotherhood. Morris.
These Things Shall Be. Symonds.
This Moment Yearning and Thoughtful. Whitman.
Through the Varied Patterned Lace. Danner.
Thy Brother. Williams.
To Edom. Heine.
To Him That Was Crucified. Whitman.
To Life I Said Yes. Grade.
Tomorrow. Pedroso.
True Brotherhood. Wilcox.
Universal Republic, The. Hugo.
We Are Brethren A'. Nicoll.
We Bear the Strain of Earthly Care. Davis.
We Shall Overcome. *Unknown.*
What Doth the Lord Require of Thee. Cross.
When I See Another's Pain. Leib.
Where Is Thy Brother? *Unknown.*
Where the Rainbow Ends. Rive.
Who Is So Low. Harlow.
World State, The. Chesterton.

Brown, John
Battle of Charlestown, The. Brownell.
Brown of Ossawatomie. Whittier.
Glory Hallelujah! or, John Brown's Body. *Unknown.*
Harper's Ferry. Rodman.
How Old Brown Took Harper's Ferry. Stedman.
John Brown. Koopman.
John Brown. *Fr.* Booker Washington Trilogy. Lindsay.
John Brown. Proctor.
John Brown's Body, *sels.* S. V. Benét.
John Brown's Body. *Unknown.*
October 16: The Raid. Hughes.
Portent, The. Melville.

Browning, Elizabeth Barrett
E. B. B. Thomson.
On the Death of Mrs. Browning. Dobell.
Sisters, The. A. Lowell.

Browning, Robert
Browning at Asolo. Johnson.
Burial of Robert Browning, The. "Field."
Life-long, Poor Browning. Spencer.
On Hearing the News from Venice. Meredith.
On the Death of Robert Browning. Swinburne.
To Robert Browning. Landor.

Bruce, Robert
Bruce and the Spider. Barton.
Freedom. *Fr.* The Bruce. Barbour.
King Bruce and the Spider. Cook.
Scots Wha Hae. Burns.

Brueghel, Pieter
Breughel's Winter. De la Mare.
Dance, The. Williams.
Et Quid Amabo nisi Quod Aenigma Est. Sandy.
Hunters in the Snow: Brueghel. Langland.
Landscape with the Fall of Icarus. Williams.

Bruges, Belgium
Belfry of Bruges, The. Longfellow.

Brumell, George Bryan ("Beau")
Brumell at Calais. Glassco.

Brunanburh, Battle of
Battle of Brunanburh, The. *Unknown.*

Bruno, Giordano
For the Feast of Giordano Bruno. Swinburne.

Brut (legendary founder of Britain)
Albion's England, *sels.* Warner.
First Song, The. *Fr.* Polyolbion. Drayton.

Brutus (Marcus Junius Brutus)
Noblest Roman, The. *Fr.* Julius Caesar. Shakespeare.

Bryan, William Jennings
Bryan, Bryan, Bryan, Bryan. Lindsay.

Bryant, William Cullen
Bryant. *Fr.* A Fable for Critics. J. R. Lowell.
Bryant Dead. Hayne.
Bryant on His Seventieth Birthday. Whittier.

Buber, Martin
Martin Buber in the Pub. Harris.

Buckingham, George Villiers, 2d Duke of
Death of the Duke of Buckingham, The. *Fr.* Moral Essays. Pope.
Duke of Buckingham, The. *Fr.* Absalom and Achitophel. Dryden.
Epitaph on the Duke of Buckingham. Shirley.
George Villiers, Duke of Buckingham. *Fr.* Absalom and Achitophel. Dryden.

Buckland, William
Serio-Comic Elegy, A. Whately.

Buddha
Buddha. Holmes.
Buddha. Holz.
Buddha at Kamakura, The. Kipling.
Buddha in Glory. Rilke.
Gautama in the Deer Park at Benares. Patchen.
Proofs of Buddha's Existence. *Unknown.*

Buena Vista, Battle of
Angels of Buena Vista, The. Whittier.
Buena Vista. Pike.

Buffalo Bill (William Frederick Cody)
Buffalo Bill's Defunct. Cummings.

Buffaloes
Buffalo. Daniells.
Buffalo. Eglington.
Buffalo, The. Price.
Buffalo Dusk. Sandburg.
Buffalo Hunters, The. *Unknown.*
Buffalo Skinners, The. *Unknown.*
Flower-fed Buffaloes, The. Lindsay.
Ghosts of the Buffaloes, The. Lindsay.
Passing of the Buffalo, The. Garland.

We Put on the Buffalo. Coffin.
Bugles
Bugle Song. *Fr.* The Princess. Tennyson.
Call of the Bugles, The. Hovey.
No One Cares Less than I. Thomas.
Splendor Falls, The. *Fr.* The Princess. Tennyson.
Words for Army Bugle Calls. *Unknown.*
Bull Run, Battles of
Manassas. Warfield.
Our Left. Ticknor.
Run from Manassas Junction, The. *Unknown.*
Upon the Hill before Centreville. Boker.
Bullfights and Bullfighters
Juan Belmonte, Torero. Finkel.
Lament for Ignacio Sachez Mejias. García Lorca.
Matador. Eberhart.
Picador Bit, The. Noll.
Bulls
Bull, The. Hodgson.
Bull, The. Williams.
Hoosen Johnny. *Unknown.*
Bundling
New Bundling Song, A. *Unknown.*
Bunker Hill, Battle of
American Hero, The. Niles.
Ballad of Bunker Hill, The. Hale.
Bunker Hill. Calvert.
Eve of Bunker Hill, The. Scollard.
Grandmother's Story of Bunker Hill Battle. Holmes.
Lonely Bugle Grieves, The. *Fr.* Ode on the Celebration of the Battle of Bunker Hill. Mellen.
On the Eve of Bunker Hill. Scollard.
Sword of Bunker Hill, The. Wallace.
Then once more men's ears were full of "Yankee Doodle." *Fr.* The Poem of Bunker Hill. Brown.
Warren's Address at Bunker Hill. Pierpont.
Bunker Hill Monument
On Laying the Corner-Stone of the Bunker Hill Monument. Pierpont.
Bunyan, John
Of John Bunyans Life. James.
Bunyan, Paul
Paul Bunyan. Bourinot.
Buoys
Buoy-Bell, The. Turner.
Burbage, Richard
When Burbadge Played. Dobson.
Burghley or Burleigh, William Cecil, 1st Baron
Lord of Burleigh, The. Tennyson.
Burgos, Spain
Recollections of Burgos. Trench.
Burgoyne, John
Fate of John Burgoyne, The. *Unknown.*
Progress of Sir Jack Brag, The. *Unknown.*
Burke, Edmund
Retaliation. Goldsmith.
Burlesque
National Winter Garden. H. Crane.
Burma
Burma Hills. Gutteridge.
Mandalay. Kipling.
Burns, Robert
At the Grave of Burns, 1803. Wordsworth.
Bard's Epitaph, A. Burns.
Burns. Halleck.
Burns. Whittier.
On Visiting the Tomb of Burns. Keats.
Poet's Epitaph, A. Elliott.
Robert Burns. Alexander.
Burr, Aaron
Aaron Burr. S. V. Benét.
Aaron Burr's Wooing. Stedman.
Colonel B. Carrier.
To Aaron Burr, under Trial for High Treason. Morton.
Burr, Theodosia
Theodosia Burr. Terrell.
Theodosia Burr; the Wrecker's Story. Palmer.
Burros. *See* **Asses.**
Burroughs, John
To the Memory of John Burroughs. Parmenter.
Buses
B's the Bus. *Fr.* All around the Town. McGinley.
Bus Ride. *Fr.* Ferry Ride. Robinson.
Bushmen
By Momba Tracks. Quinn.
Man from Snowy River, The. Paterson.
Businessmen
Accountant in His Bath, The. Mitchell.
Any Man to His Secretary. Corke.
Business Men. Chen Tzu-ang.
Report, The. Swan.
Butler, Samuel
English Liberal. Taylor.
To the Setting Up of Mr. Butler's Monument in Westminster Abbey. Wesley.
Buttercups
Buttercup, A. *Unknown.*
Buttercups. Ginsberg.
Buttercups. Radford.
Buttercups. Thorley.
Buttercups and Daisies. Howitt.
On Some Buttercups. Sherman.
Butterflies
Butterflies. Chu Miao Tuan.
Butterflies. Davidson.
Butterflies. Davies.
Butterflies. Kageki.
Butterflies. Long.
Butterflies. Noyes.
Butterfly, The. Burr.
Butterfly. Conkling.
Butterfly, The. James.
Butterfly, The. Kikaku.
Butterfly, The. O'Keeffe.
Butterfly, The. Palmer.
Butterfly, The. Scollard.
Butterfly, The. Skipsey.
Butterfly. Smith.
Butterfly, The. *Fr.* Muiopotmos. Spenser.
Butterfly, The. Tabb.
Butterfly and the Bee, The. Bowles.
Butterfly and the Caterpillar, The. Lauren.
Butterfly's Ball, The. Roscoe.
Butterfly's First Flight, The. *Unknown.*
Caterpillar and the Butterfly, The. Moreno.
Envoi: "Fly, white butterflies, out to sea." Swinburne.
Example, The. Davies.
Flying Crooked. Graves.
From a Chinese Vase. Welles.
Genesis of Butterflies, The. Hugo.
Graceful Bastion, The. Williams.
Haiku: "Falling flower, The." Moritake.
Ode to a Butterfly. Higginson.
On Discovering a Butterfly. Nabokov.
Redbreast Chasing a Butterfly, The. Wordsworth.
To a Butterfly. Hastings.
To a Butterfly ("I've watched you"). Wordsworth.
To Butterfly. Percy.
Trap. Ammons.
Tuft of Flowers, The. Frost.
Was Worm. Swenson.
White Butterflies. Swinburne.
Buzzards
Buzzards, The. Armstrong.
Byrd, Richard Evelyn
Admiral Byrd. Nash.
Byrd, William
William Byrd. Keyes.
Byron, George Gordon Noel Byron, 6th Baron
Byron, *sel.* Miller.
Byron Recollected at Bologna. *Fr.* Italy. Rogers.
Byron the Voluptuary. Watson.
Damnation of Byron, The. Hope.
Memorial Verses. Arnold.
On the Proposal to Erect a Monument in England to Lord Byron. Lazarus.
On This Day I Complete My Thirty-sixth Year. Byron.
Sketch of Lord Byron's Life, *sel.* Moore.
Sonnet to Byron. Keats.
To Byron. Keats.

Byzantium
Byzantium. Yeats.
Sailing to Byzantium. Yeats.

C

Cabot, John
First Voyage of John Cabot, The. Bates.
Cabot, Richard
White-haired Man, The. Sarton.
Cactus
Cactus. Heywood.
Cade, Jack
How Jack Cade Traiterously Rebelling agaynst His Kyng... *Fr.* A Mirror for Magistrates. *At. to* Baldwin
Cadiz, Spain, Battle of (1596)
Winning of Cales, The. Deloney.
Cædmon
Cædmon Jones.
Cædmon Nicholson.
Caesar, Julius
Anthony's Oration. *Fr.* Julius Caesar. Shakespeare.
Brutus Explains Why He Murderd Caesar. *Fr.* Julius Caesar. Shakespeare.
Caesar. Valéry.
Caesar Remembers. Seymour.
Early in the Morning. Simpson.
Fragment: "As if stone Caesar shook." McCrae.
Rider at the Gate, The. Masefield.
Wars worse than civil on Thessalian plains. *Fr.* Pharsalia. Lucan.
Cain and Abel
Abel. Capetanakis.
Cainsmorning. Moraes.
Calais, France
Burgesses of Calais, The. Minot.
On Calais Sands. Lang.
Caliban
Caliban. *Fr.* The Tempest. Shakespeare.
Caliban upon Setebos. R. Browning.
California
California. Harris.
California. Sigourney.
California. *Unknown.*
Californians, The. Spencer.
Exile. Maynard.
Flying above California. Gunn.
He Spends Time in Southern California. Cott.
Orange County Plague: Scenes. Lieberman.
Our Beautiful West Coast Thing. Brautigan.
Report from California. Moyles.
Song of the Redwood-Tree. Whitman.
Yes, I have walked in California. *Fr.* The Golden Whales of California. Lindsay.
Caligula
Caligula. R. Lowell.
Calliope (goddess)
To Calliope. Graves.
Calliope (circus)
Calliope. *Unknown.*
Kallyope Yell, The. Lindsay.
Calvary. *See* **Crucifixion, The.**
Calves
Bull Calf, The. Layton.
New Baby Calf, The. Chase.
Our Little Calf. Aldis.
Young Calves, The. Coffin.
Calvin, John
Calvinist Autumnal. Harrod.
Calvinism
Holy Willie's Prayer. Burns.
Johannes Agricola in Meditation. R. Browning.
To the Rev. John M'Math. Burns.
Calypso (mythology)
Beaten Path, The. Winslow.
Camargue, France
Horses on the Camargue. Campbell.
Cambridge, England
Autumn Morning at Cambridge. Cornford.
Water Color of Grantchester Meadows. Plath.
Cambridge, Massachusetts
Cambridge Ladies, The. Cummings.
Cambridge University
Autumn Morning at Cambridge. Cornford.
Hic Vir, Hic Est. Calverley.
Inside of Kings College Chapel, Cambridge. *Fr.* Ecclesiastical Sketches. Wordsworth.
King's College Chapel. Causley.
St. John's, Cambridge. Longfellow.
Sunday Morning, King's Cambridge. Betjeman.
Written at Cambridge. Lamb.
Camden, William
To William Camden. Jonson.
Camellias
Camellia, The. Basho.
Camels
Camel, The. Gasztold.
Camel. Miller.
Camel, The. Nash.
Camel. Stallworthy.
Camel's Complaint, The. Carryl.
Camel's Nose, The. Sigourney.
Dromedary, The. Campbell.
Exile. Sheard.
Fruit of the Tree, The. Wagoner.
Legend of the First Cam-u-el, The. Guiterman.
Plaint of the Camel, The. Carryl.
Song of the Camels. Coatsworth.
Cameron, Donald
Lochiel's Warning. Campbell.
Camoes [*or* Camoens], Luís de
Camoens. Melville.
Camoens in the Hospital. Melville.
Luis de Camoes. Campbell.
Campagna di Roma, Italy
High Noon at Midsummer on the Campagna. "Macleod."
On the Campagna. Stoddard.
Campaigns, Political
Autumn. Roberts.
Bryan, Bryan, Bryan, Bryan. Lindsay.
What Mr. Robinson Thinks. J. R. Lowell.
Campanula
Bed of Campanula, A. "Crichton."
Campbell, Alexander
My Fathers Came from Kentucky. *Fr.* Alexander Campbell. Lindsay.
Campbell, Roy
In Memoriam: Roy Campbell. Currey.
Seven South African Poems. Wright.
Campbell, Thomas
Charade. Praed.
Camping
Bunyip and the Whistling Kettle, The. Manifold.
Camper's Night Song. *Fr.* Travels with a Donkey. Stevenson.
Camping Out. Empson.
Staying Alive. Wagoner.
Two Campers in Cloud Country. Plath.
Wanderers. Hebblethwaite.
Campion, Edmund
Edmund Campion. Sister Mary St. Virginia.
Martyrdom of Father Campion. Walpole.
Canada
Canada. Roberts.
Canada; Case History. Birney.
Canada to England. Pickthall.
Canadian Boat Song, A. Moore.
Canadian Boat Song. *Unknown.*
Canadian Hunter's Song. Moodie.
Carta Canadensis. Gustafson.
East Coast—Canada. Brewster.
Hymn for Canada, A. Watson.
Maple Leaf Forever, The. Muir.
O Canada. Routhier.
Poem on Canada, *sels.* Anderson.
Sonnet Series of French Canada, A, *sels.* Call.
You have asked me, "What am I? *Fr.* Between Two Furious Oceans. Diespecker.

Canadian Poetry in English (CaP). Bliss Carman, Lorne Pierce, *and* V. B. Rhodenizer, eds.
Modern Canadian Verse (MoCV). A. J. M. Smith, ed.
Oxford Book of Canadian Verse, The (OBCV). A. J. M. Smith, ed.
Penguin Book of Canadian Verse, The (PeCV). Ralph Gustafson, ed.
Twentieth Century Canadian Poetry (TwCaPo). Earle Birney, ed.
Canaries
Canary, The. Nash.
Canary, The. Turner.
To the Canary Bird. Very.
Canberra, Australia
Canberra in April. Rowland.
Cancer (disease)
Cancer Cells, The. Eberhart.
Death from Cancer. *Fr.* In Memory of Arthur Winslow. R. Lowell.
Candlemas
Candlemas. Blunt.
Candlemas. Brown.
Candlemas. *Unknown.*
Carol, for Candlemas Day. *Unknown.*
Ceremonies for Candlemas Day, The ("Kindle the Christmas brand"). Herrick.
Ceremonies for Candlemas Day, The. Jonson.
Ceremonies for Candlemass Eve ("Down with the rosemary and bays"). Herrick.
Ceremony for Candlemas Day, A ("Down with the rosemary and so"). Herrick.
Ground Hog Day. Pomeroy.
If Candlemas Day Be fair and bright. *Unknown.*
If Candlemas Day be dry and fair. *Unknown.*
Simeon's Light Remembered. Simons.
Candy
Candy Bar. Veitch.
Dakota: Five Times Six. Hansen.
Lollypops, The. Thomas.
Pennycandystore beyond the El. Ferlinghetti.
Canoes and Canoeing
Backwater Pond: The Canoeists. Merwin.
Canoe. Anderson.
Canoe, The. Crawford.
Canoe Song at Twilight. McCully.
Canoe Speaks, The, *sel.* Stevenson.
Lullaby: "Long canoe, The." Hillyer.
Paddling Song. *Unknown.*
Song My Paddle Sing, The. Johnson.
White Canoe, The. Sullivan.
Canonicus
Canonicus and Roger Williams. *Unknown.*
Canterbury, New Zealand
Canterbury. Dowling.
Canute, King
Canute the Great, *sel.* "Field."
Face, and an Imagination, A. Wordsworth.
King Canute. Thackeray.
Capistrano. *See* **San Juan Capistrano Mission, California.**
Capitalism
After They Have Tired of the Brilliance of Cities. Spender.
Deserted Village, The. Goldsmith.
Empire Builders. MacLeish.
Latest Decalogue, The. Clough.
Symphony, The. Lanier.
Capital (Washington, D.C.)
Smoke Rose Gold. Sandburg.
View of the Capitol from the Library of Congress. Bishop.
Caravaggio, Michelangelo Merisi da
In Santa Maria del Popolo. Gunn.
Carcassonne, France
At Carcassonne. Garrison.
Carcassonne. Nadaud.
Cardinals (birds)
Cardinal. Harrison.
Cardinal, The. *Fr.* Kentucky Mountain Farm. Warren.
Cardinal Bird, The. Gallagher.
Caribbean Sea
Caribbean, The. Ormsby.
Carlyle, Thomas
After Looking into Carlyle's Reminiscences. Swinburne.
As I was laying on the green. *Unknown.*
Carlyle and Emerson. Schuyler.
On the Deaths of Thomas Carlyle and George Eliot. Swinburne.
Thomas Carlyle. *Unknown.*
Carmarthenshire, Wales
Grongar Hill. Dyer.
Carmel, California
Autumn in Carmel. Sterling.
Carnations
White Carnation, The. Sangster.
Carolinas, The
Report from the Carolinas, *sel.* Bevington.
Carpe Diem
Before Sunset. Swinburne.
Begging Another Kiss. Jonson.
Blue Girls. Ransom.
Catullus to Lesbia. Reeves.
Come, My Celia, Let Us Prove. Jonson.
Come Shepherds, Come. Fletcher.
Come, You Pretty False-eyed Wanton. Campion.
Complaint. Bennett.
Corinna's Going A-Maying. Herrick.
Corinna in Vendome. Ronsard.
Cupid's Call. Shirley.
Enjoy Thy April Now. Daniel.
Fading Beauty. *Unknown.*
Fresh spring the herald of love's mighty king. *Fr.* Amoretti. Spenser.
Gather Ye Roses. Stevenson.
Go, Lovely Rose. Waller.
In a Prominent Bar in Secaucus. Kennedy.
Invitation to Youth. *Unknown.*
Laugh and Be Merry. Masefield.
Logical Song, A. *Unknown.*
Love in thy youth, fair maid; be wise. *Unknown.*
Love's Prime. *Fr.* The Old Couple. May.
My Sweetest Lesbia. Campion.
Now the Lusty Spring. Beaumont *and* Fletcher.
O Mistress Mine. *Fr.* Twelfth Night. Shakespeare.
Resolute Courtier, The. Shipman.
Rubáiyát of Omar Khayyám of Naishápúr, The. Omar Khayyám.
Sick Love. Graves.
Song: "Phillis, be gentler I advise." Rochester.
Song: "Pluck the fruit and taste the pleasure." *Fr.* Robert Second Duke of Normandy. Lodge.
Song: "Young Philander woo'd me long." *Unknown.*
Song for a Girl. Dryden.
Song, on Reading That the Cyclotron Has Produced Cosmic Rays, Blasted the Atom into Twenty-two Particles, Solved the Mystery of the Transmutation of Elements and Devil Knows What. Hoffenstein.
Then Lose in Time Thy Maidenhead. *Unknown.*
To His Coy Mistress. Marvell.
To Phyllis. Waller.
To the Virgins, to Make Much of Time. Herrick.
Vita Brevis. *Unknown.*
Vivamus, Mea Lesbia. Catullus.
Young Men Come Less Often, The—Isn't It So? Horace.
Youth Sings a Song of Rosebuds. Cullen.
Carpenters
Busy Carpenters. Tippett.
Carpenter, The. Dyment.
Carpenter. Lucas.
Carpenter's Plane, The. Kazin.
Carrickfergus, Northern Ireland
Carrickfergus. MacNeice.
"Carroll, Lewis"
In Memory of Lewis Carroll. *Unknown.*
Carrots
Poetry of a Root Crop. Kingsley.
Carrousels
Merry-go-round. Baruch.
Merry-go-round. Field.
Merry-go-round. Jenkins.
Merry-go-round, The. Noel.
Merry-go-round, The. Rilke.
Cars. *See* **Automobiles.**
Carson, Kit
Kit Carson. Guiterman.

Carson *(continued)*
Kit Carson's Last Smoke. "Vestal."
Kit Carson's Ride. Miller.
Carthusians
Carthusians. Dowson.
Cartier, Jacques
Jacques Cartier. McGee.
Cary, Sir Lucius
To the Immortall Memorie, and Friendship of That Noble Paire, Sir Lucius Cary, and Sir H. Morison. Jonson.
Casabianca, Louis
Casabianca. Bishop.
Casabianca. Hemans.
Casement, Roger David
On the Death of Roger Casement. Colum.
Cashel, Ireland
Rock of Cashel, The. De Vere.
Cassandra
Cassandra. Bogan.
Castiglione, Baldassare, Conte
Thomas Sackville in Commendation of the Work to the Reader. Sackville.
Castile, Spain
Castile. Unamuno.
Castle, Vernon
Vernon Castle. Monroe.
Castleconnell, Ireland
Castleconnell. De Vere.
Castlereagh, Robert Stewart, 2d Viscount
Dedication: "Bob Southey! You're a poet—Poet-laureate." *Fr.* Don Juan. Byron.
Epigrams on Castlereagh. Byron.
Castles
Castles and Distances. Wilbur.
Castro, Fidel
Ode to Fidel Castro. Field.
One Thousand Fearful Words for Fidel Castro. Ferlinghetti.
Casuarina Trees
Our Casuarina Tree. Dutt.
Catalpa Trees
Catalpa Tree. Colum.
Catalpa Tree. Waddington.
Cataracts. *See* **Waterfalls.**
Catbirds
My Catbird. Venable.
Caterpillars
Butterfly and the Caterpillar, The. Lauren.
Caterpillar, The. Graves.
Caterpillar, The. Noyes.
Caterpillar, The. *Fr.* Sing-Song. C. G. Rossetti.
Caterpillar and the Butterfly, The. Moreno.
Caterpillars. Freeman.
Caterpillar's Apology for Eating a Favorite Gladiolus, A. Dalmon.
Cocoon. McCord.
Fuzzy Wuzzy, Creepy Crawly. Vanada.
My Friend the Caterpillar. Russell.
Only My Opinion. Shannon.
Oubit, The. Kingsley.
Tickle Rhyme, The. Serraillier.
Tired Caterpillar, The. *Unknown.*
Catfish
Catfish. Farrar.
Catfish, The. Herford.
Catfish, The. Mathews.
Catherine of Alexandria, Saint
For a Marriage of St. Catherine. D. G. Rossetti.
Catherine of Siena, Saint
Laud of Saint Catherine, The. *Fr.* Siena. Swinburne.
To Saint Catherine. Constable.
Catholicism
Catholic Bells, The. Williams.
Catholic Faith, The. Digby.
Christ Brought Home. *Unknown.*
Hind and the Panther, The,*sels.* Dryden.
I hold as faith. *Unknown.*
Patient Church, The. Newman.
Popish Plot, The. *Fr.* Absalom and Achitophel. Dryden.
Religio Laici. Dryden.
To the Noblest and Best of Ladies, the Countess of Denbigh. Crashaw.
Anthology of Catholic Poets, An (ACP). Shane Leslie, ed.
Catholic Anthology, The (CAW). Thomas Walsh, ed.
Golden Book of Catholic Poetry, The (GoBC). Alfred Noyes, ed.
I Sing of a Maiden (ISi). Sister M. Thérèse, ed.
Joyce Kilmer's Anthology of Catholic Poets (JKCP). Joyce Kilmer, ed.
Poetry and Life (PoLi). F. J. Sheed, comp.
Cato the Younger
Cato, *sels.* Addison.
Cats
Ad-dressing of Cats, The. Eliot.
All the Cats. Greenaway.
Alley Cat, An. Turner.
Bad Kittens, The. Coatsworth.
Bird Fancier, The. Kirkup.
Black Cat. Dunetz.
Brothers. Edwards.
Calling in the Cats. Coatsworth.
Cat. Baruch.
Cat, The. Baudelaire.
Cat, The. Brennan.
Cat, The. *Fr.* Sad Memories. Calverley.
Cat, The. Herford.
Cat. Lewis.
Cat. Miller.
Cat, The. Roberts.
Cat. "Struther."
Cat, A. Thomas.
Cat, The. Whitney.
Cat and the Bird, The. Solomon.
Cat and the Moon, The. Yeats.
Cat and the Weather. Swenson.
Cat Ballerina Assoluta. Glen.
Cat Goddesses. Graves.
Cat in the Long Grass. Dixon.
Cat on Couch. Howes.
Cat on the Porch at Dusk. Harriman.
Cat to Her Kittens, A. Grove.
Catalog. Moore.
Cats, The. Baudelaire.
Cats. Farjeon.
Cats, The. Kees.
Cats. Tessimond.
Cats and Kings. Noyes.
Cat's Conscience, A. *Unknown.*
Cat's Meat. Monro.
Catts as other creatures doe, The. *Unknown.*
Colubriad, The. Cowper.
Country Cat. Coatsworth.
Cruel Clever Cat. Taylor.
Cursing of the Cat, The. *Fr.* Phyllyp Sparowe. Skelton.
Death of a Cat. Schevill.
Diamond Cut Diamond. Milne.
Dinah. Gale.
Divination by a Cat. Hecht.
Dog and the Cat, The. Hallock.
Domestic Cat, A. Denby.
Epitaph for a Cat. Bruner.
Esther's Tomcat. Hughes.
Fight. Jaszi.
Five Eyes. De la Mare.
Fourteen Ways of Touching the Peter. MacBeth.
Garden-Lion. Hayes.
Gardener's Cat, The. Chalmers.
Greater Cats, The. Sackville-West.
Growltiger's Last Stand. Eliot.
Gus, the Theatre Cat. Eliot.
Hearth. Bacon.
House Cat, The. Wynne.
I Like Little Pussy. Taylor.
In Honor of Taffy Topaz. Morley.
Kilkenny Cats, The. *Unknown.*
Kitten, The. Baillie.
Kitten, A. Farjeon.
Kitten, The. Nash.
Kitten and the Falling Leaves, The. Wordsworth.
Kittens, The. Hey.
Kitty. Prentiss.
Kitty: What She Thinks of Herself. Rands.
Last Words to a Dumb Friend. Hardy.

Lat Take a Cat. *Fr.* The Canterbury Tales: The Mauncip-le's Tale. Chaucer.
Long Time Ago. Prentiss.
Look, See the Cat. Price.
Love for a Hare. La Follette.
Macavity: The Mystery Cat. Eliot.
Matron-Cat's Song, The. Pitter.
Midwife Cat. Van Doren.
Milk for the Cat. Monro.
Monk and His Cat, The. *Unknown.*
Moon. Smith.
My Cat Jeoffry. *Fr.* Jubilate Agno. Smart.
Mysterious Cat, The. Lindsay.
Naming of Cats, The. Eliot.
Night. McKay.
O Cat of Carlish Kind. *Fr.* Phyllyp Sparowe. Skelton.
Ode on the Death of a Favorite Cat, Drowned in a Tub of Goldfishes. Gray.
Old Gumbie Cat, The. Eliot.
On a Night of Snow. Coatsworth.
Our Cat. Vaughn.
Owl and the Pussy-Cat, The. Lear.
Pangur Bán. *Unknown.*
Poem: "As the cat/ climbed over." Williams.
Prayer of the Cat, The. Gasztold.
Prize Cat, The. Pratt.
Pussy, Pussy, Do Not Mew. Peabody.
Pussy Sits beside the Fire. *Unknown.*
Retired Cat, The. Cowper.
Rum Tum Tugger, The. Eliot.
Run, Kitty, Run! Garthwaite.
Scholar and the Cat, The. *Unknown.*
Shadow. Delius.
She sights a bird—she chuckles. Dickinson.
Singing Cat, The. Smith.
Skimbleshanks, the Railway Cat. Eliot.
Song for a Child. Davis.
Song of Methitabel, The. *Fr.* Archy and Mehitabel. Marquis.
Song of the Jellicles, The. Eliot.
Sound in Cambridge, Mass., A. R. Whitman.
Sunday. Coatsworth.
The Cat. King.
There was a Presbyterian cat. *Unknown.*
Three Little Kittens. *Unknown.*
Tiger-Cat Tim. Chase.
To a Cat. Keats.
To My Cat. Watson.
Tomcat, The. Marquis.
Tortoiseshell Cat, The. Chalmers.
Tracks in the Snow. Coatsworth.
V Is for Victory, as You Can Plainly See. Hartley.
Vengence on Cats. *Fr.* Phyllyp Sparowe. Skelton.
What the Gray Cat Sings. Guiterman.
White Cat. Knister.
Who's that ringing at my doorbell? *Unknown.*
Witch Cat. Bennett.
Yellow Cat, The. Jennings.
Cat in Verse, The (CIV). Carolyn Wells *and* Luella D. Everett, comps.

Cattails
When We Went Gathering Cat-Tails. Field.

Cattle
Branding Iron Herd, The. Rigby.
Cattle. Banko.
Cattle. *Unknown.*
Cattle Round-Up, The. McLachlan.
Driving Cattle to Casas Buenas. Campbell.
Drover, A. Colum.
Eighteen-ninety. Shipp.
From the Gulf. Ogilvie.
Fulani Cattle. Clark.
Highland Cattle, *sel.* Craik.
Pastoral: "Farmhouse skyline, draped with trees, The." Creighton.
Riddle, A: "Four stiff-standers." *Unknown.*
Round-up, The. Howard.
Stampede, The. Brininstool.
Stampede, The. Coburn.
Trees and Cattle. Dickey.
Whoopee Ti Yi Yo, Git Along, Little Dogies. *Unknown.*
Wires. Larkin.
Woman of Llyn y Fan's Call to Her Cattle, The. *Unknown.*
Yoke of Steers, A. Heyward.
See also **Bulls; Calves; Cows; Oxen.**

Catullus
"Frater Ave Atque Vale." Tennyson.
On Catullus. Landor.

Caucasus
Caucasus, The. Pasternak.
Snow in the Caucasus. Gillespie.

Cauterets Valley, France
In the Valley of Cauteretz. Tennyson.

Cavalcanti, Guido
Sonnet: To Guido Cavalcanti. Dante.

Cavaliers
Cavalier Tunes. R. Browning.
Come drawer some wine or wele pull downe your signe. *Unknown.*
Melting of the Earl's Plate. Thornbury.
Old Cavalier, The. Doyle.
Young Windebank. Woods.

Cavalry
Cavalry Crossing a Ford. Whitman.

Cavell, Edith
Edith Cavell. Woodberry.

Caves
Caves, The. Roberts.

Cecilia, Saint
Saint Cecilia. Heath-Stubbs.
Song for St. Cecilia's Day. Auden.
Song for Saint Cecilia's Day, 1687. Dryden.
Verses to St. Cecilia. Wright.
Walking Home on St. Cecilia's Day. Porter.

Cedar Trees
Cedars of Lebanon, The. Lamartine.

Celandine
Lesson, A. Wordsworth.
To the Small Celandine. Wordsworth.

Celery
Celery. Nash.

Cellos
Cello, The. Gilder.

Celts
Celts, The. McGee.

Cemeteries
At the British War Cemetery, Bayeux. Causley.
Cemetery at Academy, California, The. Levine.
Cemetery by the Sea, The. Valéry.
Cemetery Is, The. McGaffin.
Churchyard of St. Mary Magdalene, Old Milton. Heath-Stubbs.
Elegy Written in a Country Churchyard. Gray.
God's-Acre. Longfellow.
Grave, The. Blair.
Graves at Inishbofin. Murphy.
Graves of a Household, The. Hemans.
Graves of Infants. Clare.
Graveyard, The. Bialik.
Graveyard. Coffin.
Hughley Steeple. *Fr.* Shropshire Lad. Housman.
In Clonmel Parish Churchyard. Piatt.
In the Churchyard at Cambridge. Longfellow.
Indian Burying Ground, The. Freneau.
Island Cemetery, The. Auden.
Jewish Cemetery at Newport, The. Longfellow.
Lines Written at the Grave of Alexander Dumas. Bennett.
Mountain Cemetery, The. Bowers.
Old Burying-Ground, The. Whittier.
Old Churchyard of Bonchurch, The. Marston.
Oldest Cemetery. Van Doren.
On the Road to Woodlawn. Roethke.
Papermill Graveyard. Belitt.
Part-Time Tenant. Meudt.
Prairie Graveyard. Marriott.
Quaker Graveyard, The. Mitchell.
Quaker Graveyard in Nantucket, The. R. Lowell.
Sleeping Village. Vinal.
Soul Longs to Return Whence It Came, The. Eberhart.
This quiet dust was gentlemen and ladies. Dickinson.
To the Holy Spirit. Winters.
See also **Graves.**

Censorship
Lass in Wonderland, A. Scott.
Centaurs
Ambuscade. McCrae.
Centaur, The. Roethke.
Centaurs, The. Stephens.
Centaurs and Lapithae. *Fr.* Battles of the Centaurs. S. Sitwell.
Centipedes
Centipede, The. Herbert.
Centipede, The. Nash.
Centipede, A. *Unknown.*
Centipede Was Happy Quite, A. Craster.
Puzzled Centipede, The. *Unknown.*
Central Park, New York City
Central Park. R. Lowell.
Central Park Tourney. Weston.
Ceres. *See* **Demeter.**
Cervantes Saavedra, Miguel de
To Miguel de Cervantes Saavadra. Munkitrick.
Ceylon
Ceylon. Fisher.
Cézanne, Paul
Cézanne. Kreymborg.
Oh, You Wholly Rectangular. Cole.
Chaffinches
Chaffinch's Nest at Sea, The. Cowper.
Chagall, Marc
Poem for Marc Chagall. Cohen.
Chagres River, Panama
Beyond the Chagres. Gilbert.
Chaleur Bay, Canada
Phantom Light of the Baie des Chaleurs, The. Eaton.
Chameleons
Chameleon. Delius.
Chameleon. Engle.
Chameleon, The. Herbert.
Chameleon, The. Merrick.
To a Chameleon. Moore.
Chamois
Glad Young Chamois, The. Johnson.
Chamonix, France
Chamonix. Hookham.
Champlain, Lake, Battle of
Battle of Lake Champlain, The. Freneau.
Chance. *See* **Fortune.**
Chancellorsville, Battle of
Keenan's Charge. Lathrop.
Change
Answering a Letter from a Younger Poet. Ghiselin.
Beautiful Changes, The. Wilbur.
Change. *Fr.* Caelica. Greville.
Change. Knister.
Disguises. Jennings.
Dreary Change, The. Scott.
Fair Annet's Song. Wylie.
Fault, The. Lucie-Smith.
Harvest Moon. Miles.
Locksley Hall Sixty Years After. Tennyson.
Matter of Life and Death, A, *sel.* Ridler.
Mutability. Shelley.
Mutability. *Fr.* Ecclesiastical Sonnets. Wordsworth.
New Sun, The. Wain.
Spring and Fall. Hopkins.
Two Cantos of Mutabilitie. *Fr.* The Faerie Queene. Spenser.
Van-Winkle. *Fr.* The Bridge. H. Crane.
Channing, William Henry
Channing. Alcott.
Ode: Inscribed to W. H. Channing. Emerson.
Chanteys. *See* **Sea Chanteys.**
Chanticleer. *See* **Cocks.**
Chapman, George
On First Looking into Chapman's Homer. Keats.
To George Chapman. Freeman.
Was it the proud full sail of his great verse? Sonnets, LXXXVI. Shakespeare.
Chapman, John (Johnny Appleseed)
Apple-Barrel of Johnny Appleseed, The. Lindsay.
Apple-Seed John. Child.
Ballad of Johnny Appleseed, A. Oleson.
In Praise of Johnny Appleseed. Lindsay.
Johnny Appleseed. R. *and* S. V. Benét.
Johnny Appleseed. Bourinot.
Johnny Appleseed, *sel.*. Lindsay.
Johnny Appleseed. Venable.
Chapultepec, Mexico
Chapultepec Park. Rukeyser.
Siege of Chapultepec, The. Lytle.
Charing Cross, London
As I Was Going by Charing Cross. *Unknown.*
Charing Cross. Roberts.
Chariot Racing
Chariot Race, The. *Fr.* Georgics. Vergil.
Charity
Ballad of Charity, The. Leland.
Charity. Lathrop.
Charity. *Unknown.*
Charity in Thought. Coleridge.
In Men Whom Men Condemn As Ill. *Fr.* Byron. Miller.
Charlemagne
Charlemangne. Longfellow.
Opening of the Tomb of Charlemagne, The. De Vere.
Charles, Ray
Bishop of Atlanta, The: Ray Charles. Bond.
Charles V, Emperor
Charles the Fifth and the Peasant. R. Lowell.
Charles I, King of England
As I was going by Charing Cross. *Unknown.*
Bright soule, instruct poore mortalls how to mourne. *Unknown.*
By the Statue of King Charles at Charing Cross. Johnson.
Cavalier Tunes. R. Browning.
Elegy upon the Most Incomparable King Charles the First, An, *sel.* King.
Epigram to King Charles for an Hundred Pounds He Sent Me in My Sickness, An. Jonson.
Execution of King Charles, The. Marvell.
Fall, The *Fr.* Il Pastor Fido. Fanshawe.
Here lyes Charles the first the great. *Unknown.*
King Charles upon the Scaffold. *Fr.* An Horatian Ode upon Cromwell's Return from Ireland. Marvell.
On the Death of Charles I. Graham.
Pastoral on the King's Death, The. Written in 1648. Brome.
To the King, Upon His Comming with His Army into the West. Herrick.
To the King, upon His Welcome to Hampton-Court. Herrick.
Charles II, King of England
Absalom and Achitophel, Pt. I. Dryden.
Astraea Redux. Dryden.
Epitaph on Charles II. Rochester.
Glee for King Charles. *Fr.* Woodstock. Scott.
Last Instructions to a Painter: Charles II. Marvell.
On the Lord Mayor and Court of Aldermen. Marvell.
To His Sacred Majesty, a Panegyrick on His Coronation, 1661, *sel.* Dryden.
To the King, upon His Majesty's Happy Return. Waller.
Vicar of Bray, The. *Unknown.*
Will Ye No Come Back Again? Nairne.
Charles II, King of Spain
Charles II of Spain to Approaching Death. Lee-Hamilton.
Charles XII, King of Sweden
Charles XII. *Fr.* The Vanity of Human Wishes. Johnson.
Charles River, Massachusetts
Some Refrains at the Charles River. Viereck.
Walk by the Charles, A. Rich.
Charleston, South Carolina
At Magnolia Cemetery. Timrod.
Battle of Charleston Harbor, The. Hayne.
Charleston. Gilder.
Charleston. Hayne.
Charleston. Timrod.
Charleston Garden, A. Bellamann.
Dusk. Heyward.
Song about Charleston, A. *Unknown.*
Charleton, Walter
To My Honored Friend, Dr. Charleton. Dryden.
Chartism
Alton Locke, *sels.* Kingsley.
Chartist Song. Cooper.
Old Chartist, The. Meredith.
Chartres, France
Chartres Cathedral. Babcock.
Chattahoochee River, Georgia
Song of the Chattahoochee. Lanier.

Chatterton, Thomas
Five English Poets: Thomas Chatterton. D. G. Rossetti.
Last Verses. Chatterton.
Sonnet to Chatterton. Keats.
Chancer, Geoffrey
Chaucer. Brawley.
Chaucer. Longfellow.
Chaucers Words to Adam, His Owne Scriveyn. Chaucer.
Description of Sir Geoffrey Chaucer, The. *Fr.* Greene's Vision. Greene.
For a Statue of Chaucer at Woodstock. Akenside.
Lament for Chaucer. *Fr.* De Regime Principum. Hoccleve.
"Lyf So Short, The." Stafford.
O reverend Chaucere, rose of rethoris all. *Fr.* The Golden Targe. Dunbar.
Sonnet: Written at the End of "The Floure and the Lefe." Keats.
To Chaucer. *Fr.* De Regimine Principum. Hoccleve.
Cheetahs
Cheetah. Eglington.
Cheops, Pharaoh of Egypt.
Cheops. Schevill.
Cherry Trees
Cherries. Weatherly.
Cherry Tree. Eastwick.
Crimson Cherry Tree, The. Treece.
Discouraged Cherry Tree, The. Millay.
Hokku: Wayside Cherry Tree, A. Basho.
Japanese Cherries. Brégy.
Legend of Cherries, A. Dalmon.
Loveliest of Trees, the Cherry Now. *Fr.* A Shropshire Lad. Housman.
Now is the Cherry in Blossom. Freeman.
Oh! fair to see. *Fr.* Sing-Song. C. G. Rossetti.
Three Cherry Trees, The. De la Mare.
Under the Boughs. Baro.
Wild Cherry Tree. Blunden.
Chesapeake (ship)
Chesapeake and the *Shannon,* The. *Unknown.*
Shannon and the *Chesapeake,* The. Bouvé.
Chesapeake Bay
Chesapeake. Kennedy.
Chess
Duel in the Park. Grenelle.
Game of Chess, The. Foster.
Song of Chess, The. *At. to* Ibn Ezra.
Chesterton, Gilbert Keith
G. K. Chesterton. Wolfe.
In Memory of G. K. Chesterton. De la Mare.
To G. K. Chesterton. Plunkett.
Chestnut Trees
Horse Chestnut Tree, The. Eberhart.
Chevy Chase, Battle of. *See* **Otterbourne Battle of.**
Chicago, Illinois
Chicago. Anderson.
Chicago. Harte.
Chicago. Kinnell.
Chicago. O'Reilly.
Chicago. Sandburg.
Chicago. Whittier.
Chicago Poem. Welch.
Dawn Patrol; Chicago. Durham.
I Am Thinking of Chicago and of What Survives. Lipsitz.
Tenement Room; Chicago. Davis.
To Chicago at Night. Meigs.
Tonight in Chicago. *Unknown.*
Chickadees
Chickadee. Conkling.
Chickadee, The. Emerson.
Chickadee. Walker.
Song of the Chickadee. *Unknown.*
Titmouse. De la Mare.
Chickamauga, Battle of
Bury Me Not on the Chickamauga. *Unknown.*
Memorials on the Slain at Chickamauga. Melville.
Chickens
Blue Ribbon at Amesbury, A. Frost.
Chickens, The. *Unknown.*
Five Little Chickens. *Unknown.*
Gettin' Born. Euwer.
Hen's Nest. Clare.
Poultries, The. Nash.
Child Labor
Chimney Sweeper, The. *Fr.* Songs of Experience. Blake.
Cry of the Children, The. E. B. Browning.
Factories, The. Widdemer.
Factory Children. Burton.
Golf Links, The. Cleghorn.
Little Children, The. Granich.
Childhood and Children
Address to a Child during a Boisterous Winter Evening. D. Wordsworth.
Adventures. Kramer.
Among School Children. Yeats.
Around the Child. Landor.
Baal-Shem Tov. Klein.
Baby Running Barefoot. Lawrence.
Barefoot Boy, The. Whittier.
Barren. "Rachel".
Bathers. Tiller.
Boy's Day. Henderson.
Boy's Summer Song, A. Dunbar.
Builder of Houses, The. Cooper.
Centaur, The. Swenson.
Certain Age, A. McGinley.
Characteristics of a Child Three Years Old. Wordsworth.
Chercheuses de poux, Les. Rimbaud.
Child, The. Sara Coleridge.
Child, A. Gilder.
Child, The. Hall.
Child. Sandburg.
Child and Poet. Swinburne.
Child and the World, The. Wiggin.
Child and the Year, The. Thaxter.
Child in the Garden, The. Van Dyke.
Child Looks Out, The. Livesay.
Child Next Door, The. Fyleman.
Child of a Day. Landor.
Child of To-Day, A. Buckham.
Child on Top of a Greenhouse. Roethke.
Childhood. Baggesen.
Childhood. Ginsberg.
Childhood. More.
Childhood. Muir.
Childhood. O'Gorman.
Childhood. Percikow.
Childhood. Read.
Childhood. Tabb.
Childhood. *Unknown.*
Childhood. Vaughan.
Childhood and School-Time. *Fr.* The Prelude. Wordsworth.
Childhood Church, The. Wilson.
Childhood Fled. Lamb.
Childless. Mac Conmidhe.
Children, The. Dickinson.
Children, The. Dyment.
Children. Longfellow.
Children, The. Stembridge.
Children. Swinburne.
Children, The. Urdang.
Children at Night. Morse.
Children Look at the Parents, The. Tessimond.
Children's Hour, The. Longfellow.
Children's Song. Ford.
Child's Laughter, A. Swinburne.
Child's Power of Wonder, The. Saha.
Chronicle of Meola Creek, The. Sinclair.
Civilizing the Child. Mueller.
Conjuror, The. Lucas.
Cradle Song, A: "Sleep, sleep, beauty bright." Blake.
Cry of the Children. E. B. Browning.
Daughter at Evening, The. Nathan.
David. Gibson.
Days Gone By, The. Riley.
Elementary School Class Room in a Slum, An. Spender.
Eleven. MacLeish.
Eyes of Wonder, The. Pegis.
Fern Hill. Thomas.
Fern House at Kew. Dehn.
First Song. Kinnell.
For a Child. Glover.
For a Child Expected. Ridler.

Childhood *(continued)*
For a Child Who Died. Hopkins.
For Vicki at Seven. Russell.
Four. Gibbs.
Gardener, The. Stevenson.
Going into Breeches. C. *and* M. Lamb.
Good and Bad Children. Stevenson.
Growing Up. Behn.
Growing Up. Milne.
Growing Up. Wallace.
Happy Child, The. Davies.
Hiding. Aldis.
Holy Thursday. *Fr.* Songs of Experience. Blake.
Holy Thursday. *Fr.* Songs of Innocence. Blake.
I Am Called Childhood. More.
I Remember, I Remember. Hood.
If I Could Only Live at the Pitch That Is near Madness. Eberhart.
Impetuous Resolve, An. Riley.
In the Children's Hospital. Tennyson.
Indoor Games near Newbury. Betjeman.
Invitation. Torrence.
Japanese Children. Kirkup.
Jemima. *Unknown.*
Jenny White and Johnny Black. Farjeon.
Jest 'fore Christmas. Field.
Jo Jo, My Child. *Unknown.*
John Plans. Pierce.
Land of Our Birth. *Fr.* Puck of Pook's Hill. Kipling.
Life-Lesson, A. Riley.
Lilliput Levee. Rands.
Little Boy Blue. Field.
Little Blue-Ribbons. Dobson.
Little Boy in the Morning, A. Ledwidge.
Little Chap Who Follows Me, The. *Unknown.*
Little Child, The. Paine.
Little Children, The. Granich.
Little Children. Howitt.
Little Orphant Annie. Riley.
Little Rebel, The. Ashby-Sterry.
Lives of Gulls and Children, The. Nemerov.
Lonely Child, The. Oppenheim.
Long Time a Child. H. Coleridge.
Lullaby: "O! hush thee, my darling, sleep soundly my son." *Unknown.*
Mein Kind, wir waren Kinder. Heine.
Middle-aged Child. Hogan.
Minnie and Mattie. C. G. Rossetti.
Monday's Child Is Fair of Face. *Unknown.*
Mountainy Childer, The. Shane.
My Child. Pierpont.
My Parents Kept Me from Children Who Were Rough. Spender.
My Plan. Chute.
Navajo Children, Canyon de Chelly, Arizona. Middleton.
Nikki-Roasa. Giovanni.
Nurse's Song. *Fr.* Songs of Innocence. Blake.
Oh Come, Little Children. McGinley.
Ode: Intimations of Immortality from Recollections of Early Childhood. Wordsworth.
Ode on a Distant Prospect of Eton College. Gray.
Ode on Miss Harriet Hanbury at Six Years Old, An. Williams.
Old Man, The. Herford.
Old Oaken Bucket, The. Woodworth.
On a Child Beginning to Talk. Bastard.
On a Dead Child. Bridges.
On Children. *Fr.* The Prophet. Gibran.
On the Mountain. Joseph.
One, Two, Three. Bunner.
Other Children. Wing.
Palm Leaves of Childhood. Adali-Mortti.
Parental Ode to My Son, Aged Three Years and Five Months, A. Hood.
Parental Recollections. M. Lamb.
Party. Carrier.
Party, The. Whittemore.
Peregrine White and Virginia Dare. R. *and* S. V. Benét.
Plans. Thompson.
Poem by the Clock Tower, Sumner. Baxter.
Poor Children, The. Hugo.
Puer Aeternus. Raine.
Reserved. De la Mare.
Retreat, The. Vaughan.
Review, The. Traherne.
Ring-a-Ring. Greenaway.
Rustic Childhood. Barnes.
Seein' Things. Field.
Sephestia's Song to Her Child. *Fr.* Menaphon. Greene.
Sick Child, A. Jarrell.
Six of Cups. Wakoski.
Snow Globe, The. Nemerov.
So Long Folks, Off to the War. Ostroff.
Song about Myself, A. Keats.
Song against Children. Kilmer.
Song at Summer's End. Fairburn.
Song in the Front Yard, A. Brooks.
Speak Gently. Bates.
Speak Roughly to Your Little Boy. *Fr.* Alice's Adventures in Wonderland. "Carroll."
Squatter's Children. Bishop.
Stern Parent, The. Graham.
System. Stevenson.
Tamerlane. Daley.
There Was a Boy. *Fr.* The Prelude. Wordsworth.
There Was a Child Went Forth. Whitman.
There Was a Little Girl. Longfellow.
These Children Singing. Cummings.
Third Duino Elegy, The. Rilke.
Three Children near Clonmel, The. Shanahan.
Three Years She Grew. Wordsworth.
Time of Light, a Time of Shadow, A. Yellen.
To a Child. Gardons.
To a Child. Montgomery.
To a Child. Morley.
To a Child of Quality. Prior.
To a Hurt Child. Litchfield.
To a Young Child. Scudder.
To His Saviour, a Child; a Present by a Child. Herrick.
Town Child. Young.
Toys, The. *Fr.* The Unknown Eros. Patmore.
Twenty Years Ago. *Unknown.*
Two Children. Guillén.
Two Deep Clear Eyes. De la Mare.
Under the Apple Boughs. Thomas.
Walk, The. Clark.
Warning to Children. Graves.
When a Feller's Itchin' to be Spanked. Dunbar.
When I Grow Up. Holland.
When I Grow Up. Wise.
When I Was a Little Girl. Milligan.
When I Was Six. Cross.
Whole Duty of Children, The. Stevenson.
Wise Child. Lucie-Smith.
Wishes for My Son. MacDonagh.
Sourcebook of Poetry (SoP). Al Bryant, comp.
See also **Babies; Youth.**
Children's Crusade
Children Band, The. De Vere.
Children's Verse
Beastly Boys and Ghastly Girls. (BBGG). William Cole, ed.
Bird Songs (BiS) Gwendolyn Reed, comp.
Book of Children's Literature, A (BoChLi). Lillian Hollowell, ed.
Boy's Book of Verse, The (BBV). Helen Dean Fish, comp.
Bridled with Rainbows (BrR). Sara Brewton *and* John E. Brewton, eds.
Come Hither (CH). Walter de la Mare, ed.
Days and Deeds (DD). Burton Egbert Stevenson *and* Elizabeth E. Stevenson, comps.
Faber Book of Children's Verse, The (FaBoCh). Janet Adam Smith, comp.
Flock of Words, A (FlW). David Mackay, ed.
Four and Twenty Blackbirds (FTB). Helen Dean Fish, ed.
Gaily We Parade (GaP). John E. Brewton, comp.
Girls Book of Verse, The (GBV). Mary Gould Davis, comp.
Golden Flute, The (GFA). Alice Hubbard *and* Adeline Babbitt, comps.
Golden Numbers (GN). Kate Doublas Wiggin *and* Nora Archibald Smith, eds.
Golden Treasury of Poetry, The (GoTP). Louis Untermeyer, comp.
Great Story Poems (GSP). Theodoric Jones, comp.

Magic Circle, The (MaC). Louis Untermeyer, ed.
More Silver Pennies (MoSiPe). Blanche Thompson, comp.
On City Streets (OCS). Nancy Larrick, comp.
One Thousand Poems for Children (OTPC). Roger Ingpen, ed. (1923); Elizabeth Hough Sechrist, ed. (1946).
Out of the Ark (OA). Gwendolyn Reed, Comp.
Oxford Nursery Rhyme Book, The (OxNR). Iona Opie *and* Peter Opie, comps.
Patriotic Poems America Loves (PAL). Jean Anne Vincent, comp.
Piping Down the Valleys Wild (PDV). Nancy Larrick, ed.
Pocketful of Rhymes, A (PoRh). Katherine Love, ed.
Poems for the Children's Hour (PCH). Josephine Bouton, comp.
Posy Ring, The (PRWS). Kate Douglas Wiggin *and* Nora Archibald Smith, eds.
Rainbow Gold (RG). Sara Teasdale, comp.
Rainbow in the Sky (RIS). Louis Untermeyer, ed.
Reading of Poetry, The (RePo). William D. Sheldon, Nellie Lyons, *and* Polly Rouault, eds.
Silver Pennies (SP). Blanche Jennings Thompson, comp.
Sing a Song of Seasons (SiSoSe). Sara *and* John E. Brewton, comps.
Sound of Poetry, The (SoPo). Mary C. Austin *and* Queenie B. Mills, eds.
Stars to Steer By (StaSt). Louis Untermeyer, ed.
Story and Verse for Children (StVeCh). Miriam Blanton Huber, ed.
Sugar and Spice (SAS). Mary Wilder Tileston, comp.
Sung under the Silver Umbrella (SUS). Association for Childhood Education.
Time for Poetry (TiPo). May Hill Arbuthnot, ed.
Treasury of Verse for Little Children, A (TVC). M. G. Edgar, ed.
Wind Has Wings The: Poems from Canada (WHW). Mary Alice Downie *and* Barbara Robertson, comps.
Young American's Treasury of English Poetry, A (YAT). Shirley E. Marshall, ed.

Chillingham, England
Chillingham. Coleridge.
Chillon Castle, Switzerland
Prisoner of Chillon, The. Byron.
Chimborazo, Ecuador
Romance. Turner.
Chimney Sweepers
Chimney Sweeper, The. *Fr.* Songs of Innocence. Blake.
Wmffre the Sweep. Humphries.
Chimpanzees
Chimpanzee, The. Herford.
China
At the Great Wall of China. Blunden.
Battle Hymn of the Chinese Republic. *Unknown.*
Ch'i Lai' (March of the Volunteers). Shih Ee.
Chinese Nightingale, The. Lindsay.
Digging for China. Wilbur.
Road to China, The. Miller.
South, The. Wang Chien.
Wall of China, The. Colum.
Chinaware
Ballade of Blue China. Lang.
Bone China. Lister.
On a Nankin Plate. Dobson.
To a Lady on Her Passion for Old China. Gay.
Chipeta (wife **of Ute chief Ouray)**
Chipeta. Field.
Chipeta's Ride. Taylor.
Chipmunks
Chipmunk, The. Brand.
Chipmunk. Welch.
Chipmunk's Song, The. Jarrell.
Little Charlie Chipmunk. LeCron.
Chisholm Trail
Old Chisholm Trail, The. *Unknown.*
Chopin, Frederic
Chopin in London. *Fr.* Study in a Minor Key. Hobsbaum.
Chopin Prelude. Norton.
Christ. *See* **Jesus Christ.**
Christ of the Andes
Christ of the Andes, The. Markham.
Christenings
Christening, The. De la Mare.
Christening-Day Wishes for My God-Child, Grace Lane Berkley II. Coffin.
For a Christening. Watkins.
Gifts. Harris.
It Really Happened. Henley.
To Patricia on Her Christening Day. Price.
When I Was Christened. McCord.
Christmas
Above the Stable. Duffy.
Adeste Fidelis. *Unknown.*
Adoration—A Carol. Clarkson.
Al the Meryere. *Unknown.*
Alchemy. Love.
All You That in This House Be Here. *Unknown.*
Ancient Carol, An. *Unknown.*
"And Lo, the Star!" Haley.
Ane Sang of the Birth of Christ, with the Tune of Baw Lula Low. Luther.
Angelic Chorus, The. Donahoe.
Angels, The. Drummond of Hawthornden.
Angels' Song, The. Sears.
Another Christmas. Baxter.
As I Sat on a Sunny Bank. *Unknown.*
As I Went Out on Christmas Day. *Unknown.*
As Joseph Was a-Walking. *Unknown.*
As with Gladness Men of Old. Dix.
At Christmas Time. Clapp.
At Christmastide. Simmons.
Awake! Glad Heart! Vaughan.
Babe of Bethlehem, The. Beer.
Babe of Bethlehem, The. Pallen.
Babushka. Thomas.
Ballad of the Unmiraculous Miracle. Miller.
Barn, The. Coatsworth.
Bed in My Heart, A. Luther.
Before Dawn. De la Mare.
Before the Paling of the Stars. C. G. Rossetti.
Beggar's Rhyme. *Unknown.*
Bells across the Snow. Havergal.
Bethlehem of Judea. *Unknown.*
Bethlehem-Town. Field.
Bethlehem's Babe. H. Frost.
Birth of Christ. Rilke.
Birthday of the Lord, The. Carr.
Brightest and Best of the Sons of the Morning. Heber.
Bundles. Farrar.
Burning Babe, The. Southwell.
Burning the Christmas Greens. Williams.
Can I Not Sing. *Unknown.*
Candle and Star. Coatsworth.
Carol, A: "Angels to the shepherds sang, The." Weatherly.
Carol; "When the herds were watching." Canton.
Carol, Bringing in the Boar's Head, A. *Unknown.*
Carol, Brothers, Carol. Muhlenberg.
Carol for Children, A. Nash.
Carol for Christmas Day, A. *Unknown.*
Carol for His Darling on Christmas Day. Stanford.
Carol Singers, The. Farjeon.
Carol Singers, The. Rhodes.
Catch by the Hearth, A. *Unknown.*
Cause for Wonder, A. *Unknown.*
Ceremonies for Christmas. Herrick.
Chanson Innocente ("Little tree"). Cummings.
Cherry-Tree Carol, The. *Unknown.*
Child Is Born, A. *Unknown.*
Childlike Heart. Catlin.
Child's Carol. Farjeon.
Child's Christmas Carol, A. Chaundler.
Child's Christmas Song, A. Daly.
Child's Song of Christmas, A. Pickthall.
Choir-Boys on Christmas Eve. Nicholl.
Christ Candle, The. Brown.
Christ Child, The. Portor.
Christ Climbed Down. Ferlinghetti.
Christmas. Avison.
Christmas. Betjeman.
Christmas. Bryant.
Christmas. Chute.
Christmas. Dodge.

Christmas *(continued)*
Christmas. Herbert.
Christmas. Parmenter.
Christmas. Timrod.
Christmas. *Unknown.*
Christmas. Young.
Christmas Amnesty. Pierce.
Christmas and Common Birth. Ridler.
Christmas and Ireland. Johnson.
Christmas Antiphon. Swinburne.
Christmas at Babbitt's. Tweedy.
Christmas at Freelands. Stephens.
Christmas at Sea. Stevenson.
Christmas Bells. Cooper.
Christmas Bells. Longfellow.
Christmas Candle, The. Brown.
Christmas Carols. *See* Christmas Carol *in* Title and First Line Index.
Christmas Chant. Shaw.
Christmas Child, The. *Unknown.*
Christmas Childhood, A. Kavanagh.
Christmas Cradlesong, A. Lope de Vega.
Christmas Dawn at Sea, A. Morgan.
Christmas Day. Sangster.
Christmas Day. *Fr.* Hymns and Spiritual Songs. Smart.
Christmas Day in the Workhouse. Sims.
Christmas Day Is Come. Wadding.
Christmas Dusk. Nesbit.
Christmas, 1898. Martin.
Christmas Eve. Cole.
Christmas Eve. Davidson.
Christmas Eve. Drinkwater.
Christmas Eve. Edey.
Christmas Eve. Field.
Christmas Eve. Parmenter.
Christmas Eve. Shapiro.
Christmas Eve. Wallace.
Christmas Eve—Another Ceremony. Herrick.
Christmas Eve—Another to the Maids. Herrick.
Christmas Eve Choral, A. Carman.
Christmas Eve in France. Fauset.
Christmas Eve; Market Square. Page.
Christmas Everywhere. Brooks.
Christmas Folk-Song, A. Reese.
Christmas Greeting. *Unknown.*
Christmas Holly, The. Cook.
Christmas Husbandly Fare. Tusser.
Christmas Hymn. Domett.
Christmas Hymn, A. Gilder.
Christmas in Provence. Sister Mary Madeleva.
Christmas in the Heart. *Unknown.*
Christmas in the North. Sangster.
Christmas in the Olden Time. *Fr.* Marmion. Scott.
Christmas in the Woods. F. Frost.
Christmas Is Remembering. Binns.
Christmas Landscape. Lee.
Christmas Legend, A. Sidgwick.
Christmas Lullaby, A. Symonds.
Christmas Lullaby. Troubetzkoy.
Christmas Morning. Miller.
Christmas Morning. Roberts.
Christmas Morning I. Freeman.
Christmas Night. Lochhead.
Christmas Night. MacCawell.
Christmas Night. Meynell.
Christmas Night in the Quarters. Russell.
Christmas Night of '62. McCabe.
Christmas 1942. Irvin.
Christmas, 1942. Nathan.
Christmas, 1930. Scruggs.
Christmas on Three Continents. Peter.
Christmas Party, A. Bailey.
Christmas Party, The. White.
Christmas Pastoral. Hillyer.
Christmas Prayer, A. Haley.
Christmas Prayer, A. Hines.
Christmas Prayer. Macdonald.
Christmas Prayer. Morse.
Christmas Rede. Barlow.
Christmas Silence, The. Deland.
Christmas Singing. Chandler.
Christmas Song. Brayton.
Christmas Song. Carman.
Christmas Song. Field.
Christmas Song. Long.
Christmas Sonnet, A. Robinson.
Christmas Star. Pasternak.
Christmas, the Year One, A.D. Hay.
Christmas Tree, The. De Savitzsky.
Christmas Tree, The. Day Lewis.
Christmas Tree. Fisher.
Christmas Tree, The. Freeman.
Christmas Tree, The. Shillito.
Christmas Tree in the Nursery, The. Gilder.
Christmas-Tree Song, A. Bennett.
Christmas Trees, The. Butts.
Christmas Wish, A. Fyleman.
Christ's Nativity. Vaughan.
Come Carol, Make Carol. Gould.
Come, Holy Babe! Bangham.
Come, Ride with Me to Toyland. Bennett.
Contrast. Duggan.
Cradle and Throne. *Unknown.*
Cradle Hymn. Luther.
Cradle Hymn. Watts.
Crossroads, The. Parmenter.
Dame, get up and bake your pies. *Unknown.*
David, Aged Four. *Unknown.*
Day before Christmas, The. Souster.
Day Dawn of the Heart. *Unknown.*
Dear Son, Leave Thy Weeping. *Unknown.*
Dogs of Bethlehem, The. Bates.
Earth and Sky. Farjeon.
Earth Listens. Bates.
Eclogue for Christmas, An. MacNeice.
Eddi's Service. Kipling.
Eighth Street West. Field.
End of the Play, The. *Fr.* Dr. Birch and His Young Friends. Thackeray.
Epic, The. Tennyson.
Eternal Christmas. Phelps.
Everywhere, Everywhere, Christmas Tonight. Brooks.
Falcon, The. *Unknown.*
Far Trumpets Blowing. Benson.
Festum Nativitatis. De Vere.
First Christmas, The. Luke, Bible, *N.T.*
First Christmas, The. Poulsson.
First Christmas Night of All. Turner.
First Nowell, The. *Unknown.*
For Christmas. Field.
For Christmas Day. Farjeon.
For Christmas Day. Kinwelmarsh.
For the Nativity. Heath-Stubbs.
Forgotten Star, The. Clark.
Friendly Beasts, The. *Unknown.*
From Bethlehem Blown. Leitch.
Gates and Doors. Kilmer.
Gift, The. Portor.
Glad Day. Robertson.
Glory of Christmas, The. Drake.
God Rest Ye, Merry Gentlemen. Craik.
God Rest You Merry, Gentlemen. *Unknown.*
God with Us. Turner.
Good King Wenceslaus. *Unknown.*
Good Tidings of Great Joy! Alexander.
Gracious Time, The. *Fr.* Hamlet. Shakespeare.
Happy Christmases, *sels.* O'Donnell.
Hark! The Herald Angels Sing. Wesley.
Hayll, Comly and Clene. *Unknown.*
"He Is Our Peace." Haley.
Heart Is Bethlehem, The. Hanson.
Here Have I Dwelt. *Unknown.*
Here We Come a-Caroling. *Unknown.*
His Name at the Top. *Unknown.*
Holly and the Ivy, The. *Unknown.*
Holy Night. Benson.
Holy Star, The. Bryant.
House of Christmas, The. Chesterton.
How Far Is It to Bethlehem? Chesterton.
Humble Pomp. Southwell.
Hymn for Christmas. Hemans.
Hymn for Christmas Day. Byrom.

Hymn for Christmas Day, A. Chatterton.
Hymne on the Nativitie of My Saviour, A. Jonson.
I Saw a Stable. M. E. Coleridge.
I Saw Three Ships. *Unknown.*
I Will Keep Christmas. Ropes.
If. Bailey.
I'm Wishing the Whole World Christmas. Wynne.
In Dulci Jubilo. *Unknown.*
In Freezing Winter Night. Southwell.
In Honour of Christmas. *Unknown.*
In Terra Nostra. Tarbat.
In the Bleak Midwinter. C. G. Rossetti.
In the Holy Nativity of Our Lord God. Crashaw.
In the Week When Christmas Comes. Farjeon.
Indignation Dinner, An. Corrothers.
Instead of Neat Inclosures. *Fr.* An Ode of the Birth of Our Saviour. Herrick.
It Came upon the Midnight Clear. Sears.
It Isn't Far to Bethlehem. Macdougall.
It was a night in winter. *Fr.* The Witnesses. Sansom.
It Was Not Strange. Hagg.
Jesous Ahatonhia. Middleton.
Jest 'fore Christmas. Field.
Journey of the Magi. Eliot.
Joy to the World. *Unknown.*
Karma. Robinson.
Kid Stuff. Horne.
Kolendy for Christmas. *Unknown.*
Know It Is Christmas. Snelling.
Laudate for Christmas. Prudentius.
Legend of the Christmas Rose, The. Davis.
Let Us Keep Christmas. Crowell.
Life. *Fr.* Christmas-Eve and Easter-Day. R. Browning.
Light Now Shineth, The. *Unknown.*
Light of Bethlehem, The. Tabb.
Little Christ Child. Fowler.
Little Christmas Tree, The. "Coolidge."
Little Fir Tree, The. Rose.
Little Gottlieb. Cary.
Little Ones, The. Davies.
Little Tree. Cummings.
Long, Long Ago. *Unknown.*
Lord of the World, The. Studdert-Kennedy.
Lordings, Listen to Our Lay. *Unknown.*
"Los Pastores." Agnew.
Lullaby of the Nativity, A. *Unknown.*
Maid-Servant at the Inn, The. Parker.
Man Exalted. *Unknown.*
Mangers. Davies.
Mary Tired. Pickthall.
Mary's Baby. O'Sheel.
Mary's Song. Farjeon.
Masters, in This Hall. Morris.
Meditation for Christmas, A. Image.
Merry Christmas. Michael.
Mrs. Santa Claus' Christmas Present. Morris.
More Sonnets at Christmas. Tate.
Mother's Tale, The. Farjeon.
My Gift. *Fr.* A Christmas Carol. C. G. Rossetti.
My Master. Lee.
Nativitie. Donne.
Nativitie of Christ, The. Southwell.
Nativity, The. H. Frost.
Nativity. Hayford.
Nativity, The. Root.
Nativity, The. *Unknown.*
Nativity Ode. St. Cosmas.
Nativity of Christ, The. Góngora.
Nativity of Our Lord and Savior Jesus Christ, The. *Fr.* Hymns and Spiritual Songs. Smart.
Nativity Song. Jacopone da Todi.
Neighbors of Bethlehem. *Unknown.*
New Prince, New Pomp. Southwell.
New Things and Old. Sister Mary Madeleva.
No Sweeter Thing. Love.
Noel. Belloc.
Noel. Burket.
Noël. Gilder.
Noel; Christmas Eve, 1913. Bridges.
Noel! Noel! Simmons.
Nor House nor Heart. Lennen.
Now Every Child. Farjeon.
Now Is the Time of Christmas. *Unknown.*
Now the Most High Is Born. Ryman.
Now Thrice Welcome, Christmas. *Unknown.*
Nowell, Nowell. Finch.
Nowell Sing We. *Unknown.*
O Come, All Ye Faithful. *Unknown.*
O Little Town of Bethlehem. Brooks.
O Years Unborn. Moreland.
Ode on the Birth of Our Saviour, An. Herrick.
Of a Rose, a Lovely Rose. *Unknown.*
Old Christmas. Howitt.
Old Christmas Greeting, An. *Unknown.*
Old Christmastide. Scott.
On Christmas Day. Paman.
On Christmas Eve. Pierce.
On Christmas Morn. *Unknown.*
On the Morning of Christ's Nativity. Milton.
On the Nativity of Christ. Dunbar.
On the Nativity of Christ Our Lord. Bennett.
Once In Royal David's City. Alexander.
Our Joyful Feast. Wither.
Outlanders, Whence Come Ye Last? Morris.
Ox and Donkey's Carol. Sister Maris Stella.
Oxen, The. Hardy.
Perfect Gift, The. Parker.
Perpetual Christmas. Field.
Pilgrimage. Lennen.
Poem for Christmas, A. Snodgrass.
Prayer: "Last night I crept across the snow." Farrar.
Prayer on Christmas Eve. Turner.
Psalm for Christmas Day. Pestell.
Riding of the Kings, The. Farjeon.
Romance of a Christmas Card, The. Wiggin.
Round and Round. Thompson.
Said the Innkeeper. Connolly.
Second Shepherds' Play, The. *Unknown.*
Shepheards, The. Vaughan.
Shepherd and the King, The. Farjeon.
Shepherd Speaks, The. Erskine.
Shepherd upon a Hill, The. *Unknown.*
Shepherds, The. Coleridge.
Shepherds, The. Portor.
Shepherds' Hymn, The. Crashaw.
Shepherd's Tale, The. Kirkup.
Silent Night. Mohr.
Silver Bells. Hendry.
Simple Sam. Jackson.
Since Christmas. McCreary.
Sing We Yule. *Unknown.*
Sleep, Holy Babe. Caswall.
Song: "Why do bells for Christmas ring?" Field.
Song of the Angels. Tate.
Song of the Wise Men. Pierce.
Sonnet for Christmas. Burns.
Sonnets at Christmas. Tate.
Special Starlight. Sandburg.
Star, The. Munson.
Star of the East. Field.
Star of the Nativity. Pasternak.
Stars of Cheer. Swan.
Stay, Christmas! Eastwick.
Swedish Angel. Scott.
Sweet Was the Song. *Unknown.*
Sword in a Cloud of Light, A. Rexroth.
Taking Down the Tree. Fisher.
Ten Little Christmas Trees. Bennett.
Terly Terlow. *Unknown.*
There's a Song in the Air! Holland.
This day our Savior Christ was born. *Unknown.*
Three Kings, The. Longfellow.
Through the Ages. Hope.
Tidings of Great Joy. St. Luke, Bible, *N.T.*
Time draws near the birth of Christ, The. *Fr.* In Memoriam, A. H. H. Tennyson.
Tis Christmas now, 'tis Christmas now. *Unknown.*
To Christ Our Lord. Kinnell.
To Jesus on His Birthday. Millay.
Today in Bethlehem Hear I. St. John of Damascus.
Trumpet for Yuletide. Sanker.
Tryste Noel. Guiney.

Christmas *(continued)*
Twelve Days of Christmas, The. *Unknown.*
Two Inscriptions for the Christmas Candle. Branch.
Under the Holly Bough. Mackay.
Unto Us a Son Is Given. Meynell.
Upon Christ His Birth. Suckling.
Upon Christmas Eve. Suckling.
Village Christmas. Widdemer.
Visit from St. Nicholas, A. Moore.
Wait's Carol: "Give ye good-den." Young.
Wassail Chorus at the Mermaid Tavern. Watts-Dunton.
We Have Seen His Star in the East. Haley.
What Can I Give Him? C. G. Rossetti.
What Child Is This? Dix.
What the Christmas Tree Thinks. Davies.
When Christ Was Born. Tabb.
When Christ Was Born of Mary Free. *Unknown.*
While Shepherds Watched Their Flocks by Night. Tate.
White Christmas. Rodgers.
Whole Year Christmas, The. Morgan.
Why Do the Bells of Christmas Ring? Field.
Widow Brown's Christmas. Trowbridge.
Words from an Old Spanish Carol. *Unknown.*
Yule Days, The. *Unknown.*
Yule Log, The. Hayne.
Yuletide. Furlong.
Yule-Tide Fires. *Unknown.*
Beautiful Poems on Jesus (BePJ). Basil Miller, comp.
Christmas Bells Are Ringing (ChBR). Sara Brewton *and* John E. Brewton, eds.
Christmas Book of Legends and Stories, The (ChrBoLe). Elva Sophronia Smith *and* Alice Isabel Hazeltine, eds.
Sourcebook of Poetry (SoP). Al Bryant, comp.
Story of Jesus in the World's Literature, The (StJW). Edward Wagenknecht, ed.
Yale Carol Book, The (YaCaBo). H. Frank Bozyan *and* Sidney Lovett, eds.
See also **Santa Claus; Magi; Twelfth Night.**
Chrysanthemums
Last Chrysanthemum, The. Hardy.
Shadows of Chrysanthemums. Scovell.
White chrysanthemum, The. Mitsune.
White Chrysanthemum, The. Ryota.
Church of England. *See* **England, Church of.**
Churches
At Church Next Sunday. *Unknown.*
Cathedral, The. J. R. Lowell.
Cathedral of Rheims, The. Rostand.
Cathedral of Rheims, The. Verhaeren.
Childhood Church, The. Wilson.
Church, The. Muir.
Church, The. Piper.
Church, The. Willard.
Church Going. Larkin.
Church of the Holy Innocents, Dunedin. "Hyde".
Church Today, The. Watson.
Church Universal, The. S. Longfellow.
Churches. *Unknown.*
Churches of Rome and of England, The. *Fr.* The Hind and the Panther. Dryden.
City Church, The. "E. H. K."
Country Church. Coffin.
Diary of a Church Mouse. Betjeman.
Great Churches. *Unknown.*
How Amiable Are Thy Tabernacles! Bryant.
How We Built a Church at Ashcroft. Leahy.
I Am a Little Church (No Great Cathedral). Cummings.
I Love Thy Kingdom, Lord. Dwight.
In Church. Barnes.
In Santa Maria del Popolo. Gunn.
Ladies' Aid, The. *Unknown.*
Little Brown Church in the Vale, The. Pitts.
Mightier Church, A. Carpenter.
Morwennae Statio. Hawker.
My Church ("My church has but one temple"). "E. O. G."
My Church ("On me nor Priest nor Presbyter nor Pope"). *Unknown.*
New England Church, A. Barrett.
Parish Church, The. Herrera y Reissig.
Prayer in a Country Church. Van Dusen.
Russian Cathedral. McKay.
St. Isaac's Church, Petrograd. McKay.
St. Saviour's, Aberdeen Park, Highbury, London, N. Betjeman.
Sunday Afternoon Service in St. Enodoc Church, Cornwall. Betjeman.
Sunday Morning, King's Cambridge. Betjeman.
When the Church Is No Longer Regarded. *Fr.* The Rock. Eliot.
Sourcebook of Poetry (SoP). Al Bryant, comp.
Churchill, Winston Leonard Spencer
Homage to Our Leaders. Symons.
"Spoken Word, The." Morley.
Cicadas
Cicada, The. Green.
Cicada, The. Ou-yang Hsiu.
Cicada. Stoutenburg.
Cicada. *Unknown.*
Cicada-Shell. Basho.
Cicadas, The. Huxley.
Cicadas. Wilbur.
Cicadas, The. Wright.
Cinderella
Cinderella. Pickard.
Cinderella's Song. Roberts.
Coach. Farjeon.
Cicero (Marcus Tullius Cicero)
Marcus Tullius Cicero's Death. Grimald.
On the Banishment of Cicero. Wharton.
Cid ***or*** **Cid Campeador**
Cid, The, *sels.* *Unknown.*
Cid's Rising, The. Hemans.
Cigarettes
Blind, I Speak to the Cigarette. De Longchamps.
Cinque Ports, England
Cinque Port, A. Davidson.
Cintra, Portugal
On Revisiting Cintra after the Death of Catarina. Camoes.
Circe
Circe. De Tabley.
Circe. Kreymborg.
Circe. MacNeice.
For the Wine of Circe; a Picture by Edward Burne-Jones. D. G. Rossetti.
Strayed Reveller, The. Arnold.
Circus
At the Circus. Aldis.
Big Tent under the Roof, The. Nash.
C Is for the Circus. *Fr.* All around the Town. McGinley.
Circus, The. Davis.
Circus, The. Kaplan.
Circus, The. Koch.
Circus, The. Roberts.
Circus Garland, A, *sels.* Field.
Circus Parade, The. Miller.
Circus Parade. Tippett.
Cirque d'Hiver. Bishop.
Our Circus. Randall.
Thirty-three Ring Circus, The. Logan.
When I Went to the Circus. Lawrence.
Cisterns
Secrets of Cisterns, The. McNail.
Cities
Across the Straits. Dobson.
Approach to a City. Williams.
Beleaguered Cities. Lucas.
Broadway's Canyon. Fletcher.
Cities and Science. McCord.
City. Hughes.
City Afternoon. Howes.
City Considered as a Tulip Tree, The. *Fr.* London Sonnets. Bode.
City-Life. Lawrence.
City Lights. Baker.
City Lights. Field.
City Streets and Country Roads. Farjeon.
Complacent Cliff-Dweller, The. Fishback.
Composed upon Westminster Bridge, September 3, 1802. Wordsworth.
Country Mouse, The. Cowley.
Dark City, The. Dyment.
Disclaimer of Prejudice. Siegel.
"Everything in the Air Is a Bird." Guest.

For, Lord, the Crowded Cities Be. Rilke.
From the Country to the City. Bishop.
Greatest City, The. Whitman.
Hymn of the City. Bryant.
I Went to the City. Patchen.
In the Cities. Lawrence.
Lion Named Passion, A. Hollander.
Master City, The. Orente.
Mr. Frost Goes South to Boston. Houghton.
More Foreign Cities. Tomlinson.
Native Son. Callaghan.
Our Largest and Smallest Cities. Rhodes.
Preludes. Eliot.
Purse-Seine, The. Jeffers.
Rudolph Is Tired of the City. Brooks.
Tall City. Pulsifer.
This Is the City. Johnson.
Unwilling Guest, The; an Urban Dialogue. Gregory.
Up at a Villa—Down in the City. R. Browning.
Urban History. Kallman.
Waving of the Corn, The. Lanier.
City in All Directions (CAD). Arnold Adoff, ed.
On City Streets (OCS). Nancy Larrick, comp.

Civil Rights. *See* **Social Protest.**

Civil War, American
Abraham's Daughter. Winner.
All Quiet along the Potomac. Beers.
Alphabet, The. *Unknown.*
Apocalypse. Realf.
Army Corps on the March, An. Whitman.
Army Correspondent's Last Ride. Townsend.
As Toilsome I Wander'd Virginia's Woods. Whitman.
At Fredericksburg (December 13, 1862). O'Reilly.
At Magnolia Cemetery. Timrod.
Barbara Frietchie. Whittier.
Battle-Hymn of the Republic. Howe.
Battle Autumn of 1862, The. Whittier.
Bay Fight, The. Brownell.
Beauregard. Warfield.
Bivouac on a Mountain Side. Whitman.
Black Regiment, The. Boker.
Blue and the Gray, The. Finch.
"Brigade Must Not Know, Sir, The." *Unknown.*
Brother Green. *Unknown.*
Brother Jonathan's Lament for Sister Caroline. Holmes.
By the Bivouac's Fitful Flame. Whitman.
Cavalry Crossing a Ford. Whitman.
Charleston. Timrod.
Civil War. Van Doren.
Come Up from the Fields, Father. Whitman.
Cruise of the *Monitor,* The. Boker.
Cumberland, The. Longfellow.
Dixie. Emmett.
Dupont's Round Fight. Melville.
Dying Soldier, The. *Unknown.*
Eagle and Vulture, The. Read.
Eagle's Song, The. Mansfield.
1861-1865. *Fr.* For Decoration Day. Hughes.
Ethnogenesis. Timrod.
Farragut. Meredith.
Fortitude of the North, The. Melville.
From Potomac to Merrimac. Hale.
Garfield's Ride at Chickamauga. Butterworth.
Grant at Appomattox. Claytor.
High Tide at Gettysburg, The. Thompson.
John Brown's Body, *sels.* S. V. Benét.
Joined the Blues. Rooney.
Jonathan to John. *Fr.* The Biglow Papers. J. R. Lowell.
Keenan's Charge. Lathrop.
Kentucky Belle. Woolson.
Last Fierce Charge, The. *Unknown.*
Lee in the Mountains. Davidson.
Lincoln. Schwartz.
Little Giffen. Ticknor.
Malvern Hill. Melville.
Manassas. Warfield.
March in the Ranks Hard-prest, and the Road Unknown, A. Whitman.
March into Virginia, The. Melville.
Memorial Wreath. Randall.
Memorials on the Slain at Chicakamauga. Melville.
Men of the North and West. Stoddard.
Misgivings. Melville.
Mosby at Hamilton. Cawein.
Mumford. Porter.
Nineteenth of April (1861), The. Larcom.
Ode: "Sleep sweetly in your humble graves." Timrod.
Ode Recited at the Harvard Commemoration, July 21, 1865. J. R. Lowell.
Ode to the Confederate Dead. Tate.
On the Slain Collegians. Melville.
On to Richmond. Thompson.
Our Country's Call. Bryant.
Picket-Guard, The. Beers.
Portent, The. Melville.
Rebel, The. Randolph.
Rebel Soldier, The. *Unknown.*
Reveillé, The. Harte.
River-Fight, The. Brownell.
Romance. Henley.
Run from Manassas Junction, The. *Unknown.*
Running the Batteries. Melville.
Shenandoah. Sandburg.
Sheridan's Ride. Read.
Shiloh; a Requiem. Melville.
Sight in Camp, A. Whitman.
Soldier from Missouri, A. *Unknown.*
Stonewall Jackson's Way. Palmer.
Sumter. Brownell.
Surrender at Appomattox, The. Melville.
Three Hundred Thousand More. Gibbons.
Through Baltimore. Taylor.
Uninscribed Monument on One of the Battle-Fields of the Wilderness, An. Melville.
Unknown Dead, The. Timrod.
Unsung Heroes, The. Dunbar.
Upon the Hill before Centreville. Boker.
Utilitarian View of the *Monitor's* Fight, A. Melville.
Varuna, The. Boker.
Vicksburg—a Ballad. Hayne.
Victor of Antietam, The. Melville.
Vigil Strange I Kept on the Field One Night. Whitman.
When Johnny Comes Marching Home. Gilmore.
When Sherman Marched Down to the Sea. Byers.
Whisperin' Bill. Bacheller.
With Corse at Allatoona. Byers.
Wound-Dresser, The. Whitman.
Year of Jubilo, The. Work.
Zagonyi. Boker.
Zollicoffer. Flash.

Civil War, Spanish
Ballad of the Spanish Civil Guard. García Lorca.
Banished, The. Serrano Plaja.
Battle Hymn of the Spanish Rebellion. MacKay.
Bombing Casualties in Spain. Read.
International Brigade Arrives at Madrid, The. "Neruda."
Look, the Soldiers! Ramos.
November 7th. "Neruda."
Port Bou. Spender.
Spain 1937. Auden.
To a Spanish Poet. Spender.
To the International Brigade. Alberti.
To the Veterans of the Abraham Lincoln Brigade. Taggard.
Two Armies. Spender.

Clams and Clamming
Clamming. Whittemore.
Covering the Subject. Armour.

Clare, John
At the Grave of John Clare. Causley.
Vain Dream for John Clare. Hutton.

Clare Island, Ireland
Clare Coast. Lawless.

Clark, William
Lewis and Clark. S. V. Benét.

Clarke, Charles Cowden
To Charles Cowden Clarke. Keats.

Clay, Cassius (Muhammed Ali)
Ali. Corbin.
Black Lady in an Afro Hairdo Cheers for Cassius. Holmes.

Clay, Henry
On the Defeat of Henry Clay. Lord.

Clemens, Samuel Langhorne. *See* **"Twain, Mark."**

Cleopatra
Antony and Cleopatra. Heredia.
Antony and Cleopatra, *sels.* Shakespeare.
Antony to Cleopatra. Lytle.
Cleopatra. Story.
Cleopatra. Swinburne.
Cleopatra and Antony. *Fr.* All for Love. Dryden.
Cleopatra Dying. Collier.
Dead Cleopatra Lies in a Crystal Casket.*Fr.* Discordants. Aiken.
Death of Cleopatra, The. *Fr.* Odes. Horace.
In Praise of a Gentlewoman. Gascoigne.
Mark Antony. John Cleveland.
Clergy
Aaron. Herbert.
Amorous Temper, An. *Fr.* The Progress of Dullness. Trumbull.
Ballad of Father Gilligan, The. Yeats.
Bishop Orders His Tomb at Saint Praxed's Church, The. R. Browning.
Clerical Oppressors. Whittier.
Collar, The. Herbert.
Colyn Cloute, *sels.* Skelton.
Confessional, The. *Unknown.*
Confessor, The. Belli.
Country Clergy, The. Thomas.
Curé's Progress. Dobson.
Epitaph on a Worth Clergyman. Franklin.
Father Mat. Kavanagh.
Good Parson, The. *Fr.* The Canterbury Tales: Prologue. Chaucer.
Heaven ("Heaven is closed, proclaims the preacher"). *Unknown.*
High Priest, The. *Unknown.*
I say the pulpit (in the sober use). *Fr.* The Task. Cowper.
In Church. Hardy.
Lay Preacher Ponders, The. Davies.
Minister, The. Johnson.
Near yonder copse, where once the garden smiled. *Fr.* The Deserted Village. Goldsmith.
Of Clergymen and Their Livings. Harington.
On Clergymen Preaching Politics. Byrom.
Parson, The. *Fr.* The Deserted Village. Goldsmith.
Parson of a country town was he, The. *Fr.* The Canterbury Tales: Prologue. Chaucer.
Pastor, The. Summers.
Prayer for a Priest. *Unknown.*
Preacher's Prayer, The. Macdonald.
Preachment for Preachers. *Fr.* The Ship of Fools. Brant.
Priest, A. Gale.
Priest and Pagan. Watson.
Priest of Christ, The. Ken.
Priest or Poet. Leslie.
Priesthood, The. Herbert.
Priesthood, The. Winters.
Priest's Lament, The. Benson.
Priest's Prayer, A. Bianchi.
Problem, The. Emerson.
Prosopopoia; or, Mother Hubberd's Tale. Spenser.
Rival Curates, The. Gilbert.
Sermon, The. Hughes.
Servants of the Great Adventure. Dearmer.
Smooth Divine, The. Dwight.
Soft Job. Summers.
Some Bird. *Unknown.*
To a Young Priest. Payne.
Tom Brainless as Student and Preacher. *Fr.* The Progress of Dulness. Trumbull.
True Preacher, The. *Fr.* The Task. Cowper.
Unfrocked Priest, The. Campbell.
Vicar, The. *Fr.* The Borough. Crabbe.
Vicar, The. *Fr.* Every-Day Characters. Praed.
Village Preacher, The. *Fr.* The Deserted Village. Goldsmith.
Would I describe a preacher, such as Paul. *Fr.* The Task. Cowper.
See also **Rabbis.**
Clerks
Dolor. Roethke.
Report, The. Swan.
Song from a Two-Desk Office. Buck.
Ticket Agent, The. Leamy.
To a Salesgirl, Weary of Artificial Holiday Trees. Wright.
Clevedon, England
Clevedon Church. Lang.
Cleveland, Barbara Villiers, Duchess of
Pindarick. *Unknown.*
Cleveland, Grover
Cleveland. Brown.
Grover Cleveland. Benton.
Cliff Dwellers
Cliff Dwelling, The. Monroe.
Homes of the Cliff Dwellers. Wood.
Clifton, England
Clifton Chapel. Newbolt.
Clinton, Sir Henry
On Sir Henry Clinton's Recall. *Unknown.*
Sir Henry Clinton's Invitation to the Refugees. Freneau.
Clive, Robert
Clive. Bentley.
Clocks
Big Clock, The. *Unknown.*
Clock, The. Jaszi.
Clock. Monro.
Clock Shop, The. Shirk.
Clock Tower, The. Thibaudeau.
Clocks. Ginsberg.
Clocks. Sandburg.
Clock's Song, The. Lathrop.
Cuckoo Clock, The. Farrar.
Eight-Day Clock, The. Cochrane.
Four Quartz Crystal Clocks. Moore.
Grandfather's Clock. Work.
Kitchen Clock, The. Cheney.
Old Clock on the Stairs, The. Longfellow.
Old Kitchen Clock, The. Hawkshaw.
Our Clock. Eakman.
Sad Tale of Mr. Mears, The. *Unknown.*
Song for a Little Cuckoo Clock. Coatsworth.
Sun-Dial, The. *Fr.* Melincourt. Peacock.
Ticking Clocks. Field.
Watch, The. Cornford.
Cloisters, The (New York City)
Cloisters, The. Yellen.
Clonmacnoise, Ireland
Dead at Clonmacnois, The. O'Gillan.
End of Clonmacnois, The. *Unknown.*
Clonmel, Ireland
In Clonmel Parish Churchyard. Piatt.
Clothing
Beau's Receipt for a Lady's Dress, The. *Unknown.*
Braid Claith. Fergusson.
Clothes. F. Frost.
Cold Fact. Emmons.
Crinolines and Bloomers. *Unknown.*
Delight in Disorder. Herrick.
First Aid. Hopegood.
Her Favorites. Hausgen.
Lady's Receipt for a Beau's Dress, The. *Unknown.*
My Love in Her Attire. *Unknown.*
New Vestments, The. Lear.
Nothing to Wear. Butler.
Simplex Munditiis. Jonson.
Think of Dress in Every Light. *Fr.* Achilles. Gay.
Underwear. Ferlinghetti.
Upon Julia's Clothes. Herrick.
"Vanity, Saith the Preacher." Peabody.
Clouds
Among the Millet. Lampman.
Cloud, The. Herford.
Cloud, The. Lanier.
Cloud, The. Shelley.
Cloud Country. Merrill.
Clouded Morning, The. Very.
Clouds. Aldis.
Cloud. Ault.
Clouds. Brooke.
Clouds. Chapman.
Clouds, The. Croswell.
Clouds. Hill.
Clouds. Jazzi.
Clouds. Reaney.
Clouds. Sherman.

Clouds. *Unknown.*
Clouds. Wing.
Clouds across the Canyon. Fletcher.
Clouds Have Left the Sky, The. Bridges.
Clouds That Are So Light, The. Thomas.
Evening Cloud, The. "North."
Loaves, The. Everson.
Low-anchored Cloud. Thoreau.
Night Clouds. A. Lowell.
Rain Clouds. Long.
Song of the Clouds. *Fr.* The Clouds. Aristophanes.
Summer Sky. Gordon.
Watching Clouds. Farrar.
When clouds appear like rocks and towers. *Unknown.*
Clough, Arthur Hugh
Thyrsis. Arnold.
To a Republican Friend, 1848. Arnold.
Clover
Clover, The. Deland.
Clover. Tabb.
Four-Leaf-Clover. Higginson.
Four-Leaf Clover, The. Shannon.
Song of Clover, A. Jackson.
Sweet Clover. Rice.
There is a flower that bees prefer. Dickinson.
Weed Month. *Fr.* The Land. Sackville-West.
Clowns
Clown, The. Aldis.
Clown, The. Bruner.
Clown, The. Hall.
Clown, The. Rose.
Clown's Baby, The. "Vandegrift."
Old-Time Circus Clown, The. Staunton.
Quoth John to Joan. *Unknown.*
Clyde, Firth of
Mother's Malison, The; or, Clyde's Waters. *Unknown.*
Coal Mining and Miners
Avondale Mine Disaster, The. *Unknown.*
Ballad of a Mine, A. R. Skelton.
Caliban in the Coal Mines. Untermeyer.
Cleator Moor. Nicholson.
Coal-Owner and the Pitman's Wife, The. *Unknown.*
Collier, The. Watkins.
Down in a Coal Mine. Geoghegan.
Hills above the Mine, The. Cowley.
Miners. Owen.
Plodder Seam, The. *Unknown.*
Poems from the Coalfields. Healy.
Cobbett, William
Elegy on William Cobbett. Elliott.
Cobequid Bay, Nova Scotia
By Cobequid Bay. Fraser.
Cobham, Edward
To Master Edward Cobham. Googe.
Cobblers. *See* **Shoemakers.**
Cobras
Lower Animals. Anderson.
To a Pet Cobra. Campbell.
Cobwebs
Cobweb. Welles.
Cobwebs. *Unknown.*
Cochiti, New Mexico
Dance for Rain, A. Bynner.
Cockaigne, land of
Cokaygne. *Unknown.*
Cockayne County. Robinson.
Cockatoos
Red Cockatoo, The. Po Chü-i.
Cockroaches
Ballad of the Under Side. Marquis.
Colloquy with Cockroach. Warren.
Him: the Roach. Bond.
Nursery Rhyme for the Tender-hearted. Morley.
To a Humble Bug. Van Voorhis.
Cocks
Battle between a Cock and a Capon, The. Heyrick.
Before the Barn Door Crowing. *Fr.* The Beggar's Opera. Gay.
Chanticleer. Farrar.
Chanticleer. Irvin.
Chanticleer. Thaxter.
Chanticleer. Tynan.
Cock, The. Farjeon.
Cock, The. Fyleman.
Cock. Ostroff.
Cock and Hens. Follen.
Cock Again, The. Kikaku.
Cock-Crow. Currey.
Epigrams on Priapus. *Unknown.*
I Have a Gentil Cok. *Unknown.*
Nun's Priest's Tale, The. *Fr.* The Canterbury Tales. Chaucer.
On a Cock at Rochester. Sedley.
Prayer of the Cock, The. Gasztold.
Roosters. Bishop.
To Be or Not to Be. *Unknown.*
What They Do. Farjeon.
Cocoa
In Praise of Cocoa, Cupid's Nightcap. Sharpless.
Coconuts
Coconut, The. "Ande."
Cody, William Frederick. *See* **Buffalo Bill.**
Cold
Bañlbufar, a Brazier, Relativity, Cloud Formations & the Kindness & Relentlessness of Time All Seen through a Window While Keeping the Feet Warm at the Same Time As. Blackburn.
Cold. Francis.
Cold. Parton.
Tramontana at Lerici. Tomlinson.
Twenty Below. Ford.
Cole, Thomas
To Cole, the Painter, Departing for Europe. Bryant.
Coleridge, Hartley
To H. C. Wordsworth.
Coleridge, Samuel Taylor
Bards, The. De la Mare.
Coleridge. De Vere.
Coleridge. Hellman.
Coleridge. Watts-Dunton.
Next comes the dull disciple of thy school. *Fr.* English Bards and Scotch Reviewers. Byron.
Epitaph: "Stop, Christian passer-by!—Stop, child of God." Coleridge.
Man from Porlock, The. Bevington.
On the Late S. T. Coleridge. Allston.
Person from Porlock, The. Graves.
Person from Porlock A. Thomas.
S. T. Coleridge Dismisses a Caller from Porlock. Meyer.
Samuel Taylor Coleridge. *Fr.* Five English Poets. D. G. Rossetti.
To Coleridge. Shelley.
To Coleridge in Sicily. *Fr.* The Prelude. Wordsworth.
To S.T.C. on His 179th Birthday, October 12th, 1951. Carpenter.
Colette (Sidonie Gabrielle Colette)
Cortege for Colette. Garrigue.
Coliseum. *See* **Colosseum.**
Colleges and Universities
Alma Mater, Forget Me. Cole.
Epigram: "No wonder that Oxford and Cambridge profound." *Unknown.*
Old College Song with Variant Lines to Suit. *Unknown.*
Schools. *Fr.* The Borough. Crabbe.
University. Shapiro.
Views of the Favorite Colleges. Brinnin.
Collies
Collies, The. Anthony.
Collins, Michael
Tomb of Michael Collins. Devlin.
Rememberance of Collins. Wordsworth.
Cologne, Germany
Cologne. Bate.
Cologne Cathedral. Shaw.
On My Joyful Departure from the City of Cologne. Coleridge.
Colonna, Vittoria
To Vittoria Colonna. Michelangelo.
Colorado (state)
Colorado. Dillenback.
Colorado Sand Storm, A. Field.
Land Where the Columbines Grow. Fynn.
Colorado (river)
Rivers of the West. "Sunset Joe."
Song of the Colorado, The. Hall.

Colors
Color. *Fr.* Sing-Song. C. G. Rossetti.
Dun-Color. Pitter.
Green and the Black, The. Bailey.
Red Nude, The. Etter.
What is Pink? *Fr.* Sing-Song. C. G. Rossetti.
Colosseum
Coliseum, The ("Arches on arches"). *Fr.* Childe Harold's Pilgrimage. Byron.
Coliseum, The ("Stars are forth, The"). *Fr.* Manfred; Dramatic Poem. Byron.
Coliseum, The. Poe.
Colosseum. Norse.
Coltrane, John
After the Rain. Crouch.
Homage to John Coltrane. Sinclair.
How Long Has Trane Been Gone? Cortez.
Jazz Coltrane Sings. Dancy.
Now/ poem and month. *Fr.* Treasury Holiday. Harmon.
Columba, Saint. *See* **Columcille, Saint.**
Columbines
Colombine. McCrae.
Columbus, Christopher
And of Columbus. Gregory.
Ave Maria. *Fr.* The Bridge. H. Crane.
Boy Columbus, The. *Unknown.*
Caravels of Columbus, The. Lieberman.
Christopher Columbus. Adams.
Christopher Columbus. R. *and* S. V. Benét.
Christopher Columbus. Wynne.
Columbian Ode. Dunbar.
Columbus. Clough.
Columbus. Coates.
Columbus. Going.
Columbus. Hale.
Columbus. Hutchison.
Columbus. Jackson.
Columbus, *sel.* J. R. Lowell.
Columbus. Miller.
Columbus. *Fr.* The West Indies. Montgomery.
Columbus. Sigourney.
Columbus. Wynne.
Columbus and the *Mayflower.* Milnes.
Columbus at the Convent. Trowbridge.
Columbus Day. Tennyson.
Columbus Dying. Proctor.
Columbus Goes West. Hart-Smith.
Columbus in Chains. Freneau.
Columbus Never Knew. Burket.
Columbus the World-Giver. Egan.
Columbus to Ferdinand. Freneau.
Dary-eyed Lad Columbus. Turner.
Discoverer, The. Field.
Discovery, The. Squire.
Great Discovery, The. Farjeon.
Final Struggle, The. *Fr.* The New World. Block.
Immortal Morn. Butterworth.
Light in the Darkness. Fisher.
Mysterious Biography. Sandburg.
Night Before America, The. Farber.
On a Portrait of Columbus. Woodberry.
Palos, Spain, 1492. Wynne.
Passage to India. Whitman.
Prayer of Columbus, The. Whitman.
Psalm of the West, *sels.* Lanier.
Space. Hart-Smith.
Thanksgiving for America, The. Butterworth.
There Was an Indian. Squire.
To Columbus. Fletcher.
Columcille, Saint
Cross of the Dumb, The. "MacLeod."
St. Columcille the Scribe. *At. to* Saint Columcille.
St. Columcille's Island Hermitage. *Unknown.*
Comic Strips
Farm Implements and Rutabagas in a Landscape. Ashbery.
Katzenjammer Kids, The. Reaney.
Comet
Comet. Fullerton.
Commencement Day
At Graduating Time. *Unknown.*
Commencement. Sangster.
Invocation: "Help me to make this working day." Miller.
Parody, A: "Farwell! A long farewell to all our school days!" Painton.
Ruth Goes By. Muth.
There Is No Dream. Sangster.
Communion. *See* **Eucharist.**
Communism
Dostoievsky to a Young Communist. Honan.
H——y P——tt. Unknown.
Comox, Vancouver Island, Canada
Lairdless Place, The. Archer.
Concentration Camps
Annotations of Auschwitz. Porter.
Bird, The. Simpson.
Camp in the Prussian Forest. Jarrell.
Cradle Song: "Sleep, my child, my little daughter." *Unknown.*
From Tomorrow On. *Unknown.*
Funeral, The. "M. J."
Genesis. Wein.
Gift, The. Ciardi.
Memento. Spender.
"More Light! More Light!" Hecht.
Shipment to Maidanek. Fogel.
Concord, Massachusetts
Concord. R. Lowell.
Concord Hymn. Emerson.
Condors
Condors. Colum.
Conemaugh (river), **Pennsylvania**
By the Conemaugh. Coates.
Conemaugh. Phelps.
Confederacy
At Magnolia Cemetery. Timrod.
Bonnie Blue Flag, The. Ketchum.
Conquered Banner, The. Ryan.
Lines on the Back of a Confederate Note. Jonas.
Ode: "Sleep sweetly in your humble graves." Timrod.
Ode to the Confederate Dead. Tate.
We Conquer or Die. Pierpont.
Confederate Cruisers
Eagle and Vulture, The. Read.
Congreve, William
To My Dear Friend Mr. Congreve. Dryden.
Connaught, Ireland
Vision of Connaught in the Thirteenth Century, A. Mangan.
Connecticut (state)
Connecticut Road Song. Branch.
State We Honor, The. Crosby.
Connolly, James
Connolly. MacGowan.
Conquistadors
Conquistador. Coatsworth.
Conquistador. McElhaney.
Conquistador, *sels.* MacLeish.
Conscientious Objectors. *See* **Pacifism and Pacifists.**
Conscience
Conscience, The. *Fr.* The Limeratomy. Euwer.
Conscience. Herbert.
Conscience. Thoreau.
Conservation. *See* **Ecology.**
Constable, John
Meditation on John Constable, A. Tomlinson.
Constantine I (Constantine the Great)
Constantine's Vision of the Cross. *Fr.* Elene. Cynewulf.
Constellation (ship)
Constellation and the *Insurgente,* The. *Unknown.*
Constitution (ship)
Constitution and *Guerrière,* The. *Unknown.*
Constitution's Last Fight, The. Roche.
Old Ironsides. Holmes.
Contentment
Ah, sweet content, where is thy mild abode? *Fr.* Parthenophil and Parthenophe. Barnes.
Art thou poor, yet hast thou golden slumbers? *Fr.* The Pleasant Comedy of Patient Grissell. Dekker *and others.*
Careless Content. Byrom.
Character of a Happy Life. Wotton.
Cheerfulness Taught by Reason. E. B. Browning.
Content. Campion.
Content. *Fr.* The Black Riders. Crane.

Content. Gale.
Content. *Fr.* Farewell to Folly. Greene.
Content. Vaughan.
Content. Vaux.
Content and Rich. Southwell.
Contented at Forty. Cleghorn.
Contented Mind, A. Sylvester.
Contented wi' Little. Burns.
Contentment. Calverley.
Contentment. Cowper.
Contentment. *Fr.* The Autocrat of the Breakfast Table. Holmes.
Contentment. Sadi.
Contentment. Schlipf.
Contentment: or, the Happy Workman's Song. Byrom.
Coridon's Song. Chalkhill.
Epigram: "Things that make the happpier life, are these, The." Martial.
Golden Mean, The. Surrey.
Happy Were He. Essex.
His Content in the Country. Herrick.
His Grange, or Private Wealth. Herrick.
Hymn to Contentment, A. Parnell.
Man of Life Upright, The. Campion.
Means to Attain a Happy Life Martial.
My Mind to Me a Kingdom Is. Dyer.
Oh, Sweet Content. Davies.
Ode on Solitude. Pope.
Of a Contented Mind. Vaux.
On Peace. Speed.
Prayer for Contentment. Poteat.
Quiet Life, The. Pope.
Quiet Life, The. Seneca.
Shepherd Boy's Song, The. *Fr.* The Pilgrim's Progress. Bunyan.
Some Murmur When Their Sky Is Clear. Trench.
Sweet Are the Thoughts That Savor of Content. *Fr.* Greene's Farewell to Folly. Greene.
They of the Meane Estate Are Happiest. *Unknown.*
To Licinius. *Fr.* Odes. Horace.
True as the church clock. *Fr.* The Cottager. Clare.
Vanity of Riches, The. *Fr.* Odes. Horace.

Convents
Convent Echoes. Moriarty.
Hawkesyard. Sister Mary Benvenuta.
Mountain Convent. L. Benét.

Conway, Wales
With a Rose from Conway Castle. Dorr.

Cook, Capt. James
Captain Cook. *Fr.* Ranolf and Amohia. Domett.
Five Visions of Captain Cook. Slessor.

Cooking and Cooks
Aunt Nerissa's Muffin. Irwin.
Ballad of Culinary Frustration. McGinley.
Mummy Slept Late and Daddy Fixed Breakfast. Ciardi.
Roundup Cook, The. Carr.
Ship's Cook, a Captive Sings, The. Hofmannsthal.
Some Cook. Ciardi.
This and That. Davis.

Coole, Ireland
Coole Park, 1929. Yeats.
Coole and Ballylee, 1931. Yeats.
Wild Swans at Coole, The. Yeats.

Cooper, James Fenimore
Cooper. *Fr.* A Fable for Critics. J. R. Lowell.

Cooper, Peter
Peter Cooper. Miller.

Copenhagen, Denmark
Non Sum Qualis Eram in Bona Urbe Nordica Illa. Hollander.

Copenhagen, Battle of
Battle of the Baltic, The. Campbell.

Córdoba, Spain
Cordova. Ibn Zaydun.
Quién Sabe? Mitchell.

Corinth, Greece
Siege of Corinth, The. Byron.

Cork, Ireland
Bells of Shandon, The. Mahony.

Cormac Mac Art
Burial of King Cormac, The. Ferguson.

Cormorants
Common Cormorant, The. *Unknown.*
Cormorants. Blight.

Corn
America Is Corn. Coffin.
Columbia's Emblem. Proctor.
Corn. Lanier.
Corn-grinding Song. *Unknown.*
Corn Must Be Sown. Carlyle.
Corn Song, The. *Fr.* The Huskers. Whittier.
Cornfield. Cox.
Cornfield, The. Roberts.
Cornfields. Howitt.
Korosta Katzina Song. *Unknown.*
Last Corn Shock, The. Dresbach.
Ploughman, The. Bottomley.
Story of the Corn. Fisher.
Waving of the Corn, The. Lanier.

Corncrakes
First Corncrake. Hewitt.
Landrail, The. De Vere.

"Cornwall, Barry" (Bryan Waller Proctor)
In Memory of "Barry Cornwall." Swinburne.

Cornwall, England
Ballad of a Mine, A. Skelton.
In Memoriam: A. C., R. J. O., K. S. Betjeman.
Seasons in North Cornwall, The. Causley.
Song of the Western Men, The. Hawker.

Cornwallis, Charles Cornwallis, 1st Marquess
Cornwallis's Surrender. *Unknown.*

Coromandel Coast, India
Coromandel Fishers, The. Naidu.
On the Coast of Coromandel. O. Sitwell.

Coronado, Francisco Vásquez de
Quivira. Guiterman.

Correggio (Antonio Allegri)
Correggio's Cupolas at Parma. De Vere.

Cortés, Hernán
With Cortez in Mexico. Campbell.

Coruña, La, Spain
Burial of Sir John Moore. Wolfe.

Cosmetics
Government Injunction Restraining Harlem Cosmetic Co. Miles.
Her Powder Box. Stead.
On a Painted Woman. Shelley.
Progress of Beauty, The. Swift.
To an Old Gentlewoman Who Painted Her Face. Turberville

Cotopaxi, Ecuador
Romance. Turner.

Cotton, Charles
Grasshopper, The. Lovelace.

Cotton, John
Upon the Tomb of the Most Reverend Mr. John Cotton. Woodbridge.

Cotton
Cotton Boll, The. Timrod.
Cotton Field Song. *Unknown.*
Cotton Song. Toomer.

Country Clubs
Country Club Sunday. McGinley.

Country Dances
Dance by the Roadside, The. Fröding.

Country Life
Baucis and Philemon. Swift.
Bright Abandon. Webb.
Burials. *Fr.* The Parish Register. Crabbe.
City Streets and Country Roads. Farjeon.
Come Spur Away. Randolph.
Coridon's Song. Chalkhill.
Country Life. *Fr.* Epodes. Horace.
Country Life, A: To His Brother, M. Tho. Herrick. Herrick.
Country Mouse, The. Cowley.
Country Pleasures. Martial.
Country Reverie. Coates.
Country Summer. Adams.
Country Towns. Slessor.
Country Tune. Riddell.
Deserted Village, The. Goldsmith.
Early Morning at Bargis. Hagedorn.
Elegy Written in a Country Churchyard. Gray.

Country *(continued)*
Epistle to Miss Blount. Pope.
Epode: "Happy the man whom bount'ous Gods allow." Horace.
Far from the Madding Crowd. Waterman.
Fire of Drift-Wood, The. Longfellow.
Francis Beaumont's Letter from the Country to Jonson. Jonson.
Georgics, *sels.* Vergil.
Grass and Milk. Gatto.
Happy is the Country Life. *Unknown.*
His Content in the Country. Herrick.
In Derision of a Country Life. *Fr.* The Italian Husband. Ravenscroft.
Jack and Joan. Campion.
Letter from the Country, A. Baker.
Merry Country Lad, The. *Fr.* The Passionate Shepherd. Breton.
Minnie and Mattie. *Fr.* Sing-Song. C. G. Rossetti.
Ode to Mr. Anthony Stafford to Hasten Him into the Country, An Randolph.
On Westwell Downs. Strode.
Our Village—by a Villager. Hood.
Pastoral: "Who can live in heart so glad." *Fr.* The Passionate Shepherd. Breton.
Pasture, The. Frost.
Philemon and Baucis. *Fr.* Metamorphoses. Ovid.
Poor, Poor Country, The. Neilson.
Praises of a Countrie Life, The. Jonson.
Returning to the Fields. T'ao Ch'ien.
Rudolph Is Tired of the City. Brooks.
Streams. Scollard.
To a Friend in the Country. Gogarty.
To My Honoured Kinsman John Dryden of Chesterton. Dryden.
To One Who Has Been Long in City Pent. Keats.
Tree-Top Road, The. Smith.
Up at a Villa—Down in the City. R. Browning.
Upon Himself. Herrick.
Village, The, *sels.* Crabbe.
Village, The. Gashe.
Village, The. Thomas.
We Who Were Born. Lewis.
Winter Evening, The. *Fr.* The Task. Cowper.
Courage
Abnormal Is Not Courage, The. Gilbert.
Battle Cry, A. Shippey.
Besieged. Schneour.
Captain Death. *Unknown.*
Courage. Brooke.
Courage. Earhart.
Courage. Frazee-Bower.
Courage. Gerhardt.
Courage. *Fr.* The Church Porch. Herbert.
Courage. Mason.
Courage, All. Markham.
Courage Has a Crimson Coat. Turner.
Courage to Live. Crowell.
Dare to Be True. *Fr.* The Church Porch. Herbert.
Inevitable, The. Bolton.
Invictus. Henley.
Leak in the Dike, The. Cary.
Losers. Sandburg.
Never Admit the Pain. Gilmore.
Prayer for Courage. Tagore.
Resolution and Independence. Wordsworth.
To fight aloud is very brave. Dickinson.
You Are the Brave. Patterson.
Coureurs de Bois
Coureurs de Bois. Le Pan.
Courtier, The (Castiglione)
Thomas Sackville in Commendation of the Work to the Reader. Sackville.
Courtiers
Of the Mean and Sure Estate. Wyatt.
Old and the New Courtier, The. *Unknown.*
Prosopopoia; or, Mother Hubberd's Tale. Spenser.
Up-Start Courtier. Rowlands.
Coventry, England
I Remember, I Remember. Larkin.
Cowboys
At a Cowboy Dance. Adams.
Closing of the Rodeo, The. Smith.
Country Tune. Riddell.
Cowboy, The. Antrobus.
Cowboy, The ("He wears a big hat"). *Unknown.*
Cowboy Boasting Chants. *Unknown.*
Cowboy Song. Causley.
Cowboy Song ("One night as I lay on the prairie"). *Unknown.*
Cowboy to Pitching Bronco. *Unknown.*
Cowboys' Christmas Ball, The. Chittenden.
Cowboy's Dream, The. Finger.
Cowboy's Dream, The. *Unknown.*
Cowboys' Gettin'-up Holler. *Unknown.*
Cowboy's Lament, The. *Unknown.*
Cowboy's Life, The. *At. to* Adams.
Cow-Boys's Song, The. Wells.
Dying Cowboy, The ("Oh bury me not on the lone prairie"). *Unknown.*
From the Ballad of Two-Gun Freddy. Brooks.
I Want to Be a Cowboy. *Unknown.*
O, Bury Me Not on the Lone Prairie. *Unknown.*
Old Chisholm Trail, The. *Unknown.*
Poor Lonesome Cowboy. *Unknown.*
Vaquero. Dorn.
Vaquero. Miller.
When the Work's All Done This Fall. *Unknown.*
Whoopee High Ogie. *Unknown.*
Whoopee Ti Yi Yo, Git Along Little Dogies. *Unknown.*
Zebra Dun. *Unknown.*
Cowboy Songs and Other Frontier Ballads (CoSo). John A. Lomax *and* Alan Lomax, eds. (1938).
Poems of the Old West: a Rocky Mountain Anthology (PoOW). Levette J. Davidson, ed.
Songs of the Cattle Trail and Cow Camp (SCC). John A. Lomax, ed.
See also **Stockmen.**
Cowley, Abraham
On Mr. Abraham Cowley, His Death and Burial amongst the Ancient Poets. Denham.
Cowpens, Battle of
Battle of the Cowpens, The. English.
Cowper, William
Cowper. Clare.
Cowper. Nicholson.
Cowper at Olney. Lynd.
Cowper's Grave. E. B. Browning.
Homage to William Cowper. Davie.
Cows
Buttercup Cow. Rendall.
Calling the Cows Home. *Fr.* The High Tide on the Coast of Lincolnshire, 1571. Ingelow.
Canadian Herd-boy, The. Moodie.
Colly, My Cow. Unknown.
Cow. Massingham.
Cow, The. Motherly.
Cow, The. O'Dowd.
Cow, The. Roethke.
Cow, The. Stevenson.
Cow, The. Taylor.
Cow at Sullington, A. Dalmon.
Cow Dance. Beaver.
Cow in Apple-Time, The. Frost.
Cow Time. Shannon.
Cows. Reeves.
Driving Home the Cows. Osgood.
Fable of the Speckled Cow. Opperman.
Fetching Cows. MacCaig.
Kerry Cow, The. Letts.
Lament for a Dead Cow. Slater.
Lily-Pool and the Cow, The. Brown.
Milk-white Moon, Put the Cows to Sleep. Sandburg.
Milking Kraal. Slater.
Milking Time. Roberts.
Moo! Hillyer.
Moo-Cow-Moo, The. Cooke.
Pleasant Cow, The. Hallock.
Purple Cow, The. Burgess.
Red Cow Is Dead, The. White.
See also **Cattle.**
Cowslips

With Rosy Hand. Landor.
Coyotes
Coyote and the Locust, The. *Unknown.*
Father Coyote. Sterling.
Prairie Wolves. Carr.
Crab Apple Tree
Crab Tree, The. Gogarty.
Crabbe, George Robinson.
Crabs and Crabbing
Crustaceans. Fuller.
Dead Crab, The. Young.
Old Chang, The Crab. *Unknown.*
Mother Crab and Her Family, The. Manyase.
Cracow, Poland
Waiting for Death. Gebirtig.
Cradle Songs. *See* **Cradle Song and Lullaby in Title and First Line Index.**
Crail, Scotland
Coves of Crail, The. "Macleod."
Crane, Hart
Fish Food. Wheelwright.
Hart Crane. Creeley.
Hart Crane. Symons.
Look, Hart, That Horse You Ride Is Wood. Viereck.
Words for Hart Crane. R. Lowell.
Cranes (birds)
Crane. Langland.
Crane Is My Neighbour, The. Neilson.
Cranes of Ibycus, The. Lazarus.
Dying Crane, The. Drayton.
Herald Crane, The. Garland.
I Hear the Crane. *Fr.* Du Bartas His Divine Weeks. Sylvester.
Pet Crane, A. *Unknown.*
Sandhill Crane, The. Austin.
Tanka: Cry of the Crane, The. Tsurayuki.
Whooping Crane, The. Miller.
Crashaw, Richard
On the Death of Mr. Crashaw. Cowley.
Crazy Horse (Indian Chief)
Wildwest. *Fr.* Frescoes for Mr. Rockefeller's City. MacLeish.
Creation
All Things Bright and Beautiful. Alexander.
Almighty Maker God. *Fr.* Sincere Praise. Watts.
Beginning and the End, The. *Fr.* The Elder Edda. *Unknown.*
Carmen Genesis. Thompson.
Chant Out of Doors, A. Wilkinson.
Creation. Bhushan.
Creation. Bierce.
Creation, The. Johnson.
Creation. Nicholl.
Creation. Noyes.
Father, thy hand. *Fr.* A Forest Hymn. Bryant.
First Day of the First Week, The. *Fr.* Du Bartas: His First Week or Birth of the World. Sylvester.
Genesis. Hill.
Genesis. Sullivan.
Glory of God in Creation, The. Moore.
God of the granite and the rose! *Fr.* Reconciliation. Doten.
God, through All and in You All. S. Longfellow.
Hymn of Creation. *Fr.* The Rigveda. *Unknown.*
Hymn of the World's Creator, The. Caedmon.
In the Beginning Was the Bird. Treece.
Morning Hymn of Adam. *Fr.* Paradise Lost. Milton.
Over All the Face of Earth Main Ocean Flowed. *Fr.* Paradise Lost. Milton.
Pastoral Hymn, A. Hall.
Pulley, The. Herbert.
Preface: "Infinity, when all things it beheld." *Fr.* God's Determinations. Taylor.
Room, The. Aiken.
Spacious Firmament on High, The. Addison.
Spell of Creation. Raine.
Thou Art, O God. Moore.
Tiger, The. *Fr.* Songs of Experience. Blake.
To God, the Architect. Kemp.
Walum Olum. *Unknown.*
What Is the World? *Fr.* To My Honor'd Friend Sir Robert Howard. Dryden.
Crécy, Battle of
Crecy. Palgrave.
Eve of Crecy, The. Morris.
Credo. *See* **Faith.**
Creede, Colorado
Creede. Warman.
Rise and Fall of Creede, The. Warman.
Cressida. *See* **Troilus and Cressida.**
Crete
Paranoia in Crete. Corso.
Tomb of Lt. John Learmonth, AIF, The. Manifold.
Crew Racing
Boat Race, The. *Fr.* The Aeneid. Vergil.
Crew Cut. McCord.
Eight Oars and a Coxswain. Guiterman.
Racing Eight, A. Cuthbertson.
Cricket (game)
At Lord's. Thompson.
Cricket Triolet, A. Kernahan.
How McDougal Topped the Score. Spencer.
Crickets
Ant and the Cricket, The. Unknown.
Chirrupy Cricket, The. Thomas.
Cricket, The. Barrows.
Cricket, The. Bourne.
Cricket. Scollard.
Cricket, The. Tu Fu.
Cricket, The. Tuckerman.
Crickets. McCord.
Crickets. Saroyan.
Crickets. Wing.
Crickets at Dawn. Speyer.
Cricket's Story, The. Nason.
Little Night Music, A. Stefanile.
O cricket from your cheery cry. Basho.
On the Grasshopper and Cricket. Keats.
Poems to a Brown Cricket. Wright.
Prayer of the Cricket, The. Gasztold.
Singing. Aldis.
Splinter. Sandburg.
Spring Cricket. Rodman.
Thinker, The. Delius.
To a Cricket. Bennett.
To an Obscure Poet Who Lives on My Hearth. Hildreth.
To the Grasshopper and the Cricket. Hunt.
Crime and Criminals
Beggar's Opera, The,*sels.* Gay.
Boston Burgler, The. *Unknown.*
Burgler of Babylon, The. Bishop.
Bushrangers, The. Harrington.
Capture of Edwin Alonzo Boyd, The. Miller.
Cole Younger. *Unknown.*
Death of Ben Hall, The. Ogilvie.
Dick Turpin and the Lawyer. *Unknown.*
Dupree. *Unknown.*
Execrators, The. Galler.
Hold-Up, The. Wagoner.
Jesse James. *Unknown.*
Morgan. Harrington.
Sam Bass. *Unknown.*
Shooting of John Dillinger Outside the Biograph Theater. Wagoner.
Wild Colonial Boy, The. *Unknown.*
Crimean War
Charge of the Light Brigade, The. Tennyson.
Song of the Camp, The. Taylor.
Criticism and Critics
Critic, A. Landor.
Criticaster, A. *Fr.* The Rosciad. Churchill.
Critics. Crabbe.
Critics, The. Durrell.
Critics, The. Spencer.
Critics. *Fr.* On Poetry; a Rhapsody. Swift.
Critics and Cooks. Martial.
English Bards and Scotch Reviewers, *sels.* Byron.
Envious Critick, The. Wycherley.
Essay on Criticism, An. Pope.
His Defense against the Idle Critic. Drayton.
Interpreters, The. Enright.
Lines for an Eminent Poet and Critic. P. Dickinson.
Lines to a Critic. Shelley.
Narcissus and Some Tadpoles. Daley.
Notes on a Certain Terribly Critical Piece. Whittemore.
Obituary. Brode.

Criticism *(continued)*
On Critics. Prior.
On First Looking in on Blodgett's Keats's "Chapman's Homer." Starbuck.
Pains, reading, study, are their just pretense. *Fr.* Epistle to Dr. Arbuthnot. Pope.
Pipling. Roethke.
Poets, The. Wevill.
Poet's Fate, The. Hood.
Reactionary Critic. Martial.
To a Captious Critic. Dunbar.
To a Steam Roller. Moore.
To Critics. Herrick.
To His Noble Friend, Mr. Richard Lovelace, upon His Poems. Marvell.
To Some Reviewers Who Have Wilfully Abused Certain True Poets. Palmer.
To the Learned Critic. Jonson.
Ultra-Germano-Criticasterism. Hunt.
Verbal Critics. *Fr.* Epistle to Dr. Arbuthnot. Pope.
Crivelli, Carlo
Detail from an Annunciation by Crivelli. Dobson.
Crockett, Samuel Rutherford
To S. R. Crockett. Stevenson.
Crocodiles
Amphibious Crocodile. Ransom.
Crocodile, A. *Fr.* The Last Man. Beddoes.
Crocodile, The. *Fr.* Alice in Wonderland. "Carroll."
Crocodile, The. *Unknown.*
Don't Ever Cross a Crocodile. Starbird.
How Doth the Little Crocodile. *Fr.* Alice's Adventures in Wonderland. "Carroll."
If You Should Meet a Crocodile. *Unknown.*
Lady and Crocodile. Burgess.
Lower Animals. Anderson.
Monkeys and the Crocodile, The. Richards.
Crocuses
Crocus, The. W. Crane.
Crocus. Day.
Crocus, The. Elliott.
Crocus, The. King.
Crocus. Kreymborg.
Crocus, The. Nicholson.
Crocus ("Warm sunshine came down"). *Unknown.*
Crocus. Walker.
Crocuses. Josa.
Crocuses. Platt.
Crocuses in the Grass. Gray.
Cromwell, Oliver
Cromwell and Henrietta Maria. *Fr.* Charles the First. Wills.
Cromwell, Our Chief of Men. Milton.
First Anniversary of the Government under His Royal Highness the Lord Protector. Marvell.
Heroic Stanzas, Consecrated to the Glorious Memory of His Highness, Oliver, Late Protector of This Commonwealth. Dryden.
Horatian Ode upon Cromwell's Return from Ireland, An. Marvell.
More Power to Cromwell. O'Rahilly.
Panegyrick to My Lord Protector, A. Waller.
Poem upon the Death of His Late Highness the Lord Protector, A. Marvell.
Protector, The. Wither.
To the Lord General Cromwell. Milton.
Cromwell, Thomas
Cromwell, I Did Not Think to Shed a Tear. *Fr.* King Henry VIII. Shakespeare.
Thomas Cromwell. *Unknown.*
Cross, The
A. B. C. of Devotion, An. *Unknown.*
Above the Hills of Time. Tiplady.
Ballad of Trees and the Master, A. Lanier.
Cross, The. Braden.
Cross, The. Calderón.
Cross, The. Gore-Booth.
Cross, The. Tobias.
Cross, The. Waite.
Cross and the Tree, The. Stidger.
Crucifix. Olson.
Crucifix, A. *Fr.* Amour. Verlaine.
Dream of the Rood, The. *Unknown.*
Golgotha's Cross. Kresensky.
Holy Cross, The. *Unknown.*
Hymn to the Cross, A. *Unknown.*
I Am the Cross. Stidger.
I Saw Death Slain. Capell.
Après-Midi d'un faune, L'. Mallarmé.
In Thine Own Heart. "Angelus Silesius."
Royal Way of the Holy Cross, The. Thomas à Kempis.
Sign of the Cross, The. Newman.
Symbol of Hope. Weist.
Thought, A. Sangster.
Two Crosses. Hedrick.
Waking Thought. Wilkinson.
Whatsoever/ The form of building or the creed professed. *Fr.* The Cathedral. J. R. Lowell.
Crows
Always with Us!—The Black Preacher. Melville.
Crow, The. Alexander.
Crow, The. Canton.
Crow, The. Clare.
Crow, The. Page.
Crow, The. Thoreau.
Crow. Van Doren.
Crow and Pie. *Unknown.*
Crow and the Fox, The. La Fontaine.
Crow Country. Slessor.
Crows, The. Bogan.
Crows. McCord.
Crows. Reese.
Crows, The. *Unknown.*
Crown in Spring. Clare.
Crows in the Garden. *Unknown.*
Flight. Johnston.
In Air. Clarke.
Night Crow. Roethke.
Old Crow, The. *Unknown.*
Over in the Meadow. *Unknown.*
Three Crows, The. *Unknown.*
To a Crow. Wilson.
To Be or Not to Be. *Unknown.*
Twa Corbies, The. *Unknown.*
Crucifixion
"And When He Had Scourged Jesus, He Delivered Him to Be Crucified." Rodgers.
At the Cross. *Unknown.*
Behold the Man! *Unknown.*
Calvary. Hallet.
Calvary. Howells.
Calvary. Orr.
Calvary. Robinson.
Calvary. Stopple.
Calvary. *Unknown.*
Calvary and Easter. "Coolidge."
Christ Crucified. Crashaw.
Christ Is Crucified Anew. Moreland.
Christ Tells of His Passion. *Fr.* Christ. Cynewulf.
Crucifix, The. Lamartine.
Crucifix. Olson.
Crucifix, The. Pushkin.
Crucifixion. Gore-Booth.
Crucifixion. Isbell.
Crucifixion, The. Lynch.
Crucifixion, The. Meynell.
Crucifixion. Pelfer.
Crucifixion. Scott.
Crucifixion, The. *Unknown.*
Crucifixion, The ("At the cry of the first bird"). *Unknown.*
Crucifixion, The ("They crucified my Lord"). *Unknown.*
Crucifixion and the Harrowing of Hell, The. *Fr.* The Vision of Piers Plowman. Langland.
Crucifixion to the World, by the Cross of Christ. Watts.
Crucifying. Donne.
Dream of the Rood, The. *Unknown.*
Early Lynching. Sandburg.
Earth Worshiped, The! Coblentz.
Ecce Homo. Gascoyne.
Gambler. Studdert-Kennedy.
Golgotha. Wheelock.
Good Friday. C. G. Rossetti.
He Gave Himself for Me. *Unknown.*
His Garments. Hagg.

Hours of the Passion, The. *Unknown.*
I Saw One Hanging. *Unknown.*
In Memory of Two Sons. Stellwagon.
In My Place. Archibald.
Indifference. Studdert-Kennedy.
It Is Finished. Wheelock.
It was a deliberate moment, and O. *Fr.* Resurrection—an Easter Sequence. Rodgers.
Jesus of Nazareth. Colwell.
Killing, The. Muir.
Last Day, The. Derosier.
Martyr, The. Flohr.
Ninth Hour, The. Hazard.
O My Harte Is Wo. *Unknown.*
Passion of Jesus, The. *Unknown.*
Pastoral: "Dove walks with sticky feet, The." Patchen.
Resurgam. Moreland.
Sacrifice, The. Herbert.
Scarred. *Unknown.*
Still Falls the Rain. E. Sitwell.
Sunset on Calvary. *Unknown.*
There Is a Man on the Cross. Cheney.
They Crucified My Lord. *Unknown.*
Thy Nail-pierced Hands. Bowsher.
Upon a Hill. Crouse.
Upon the Body of Our Blessed Lord, Naked and Bloody. Crashaw.
Upon the Ensignes of Christes Crucifyinge. Alabaster.
Veteran of Heaven, The. Thompson.
We May Not Know. Alexander.
We'll Never Know. Hoellein.
When I Survey the Wondrous Cross. Watts.
Yes, I Have Been to Calvary. Christiansen.
Yet Listen Now. Carmichael.

Crusades
Crusade. Belloc.
Crusade, The. Warton.
Crusaders. Waddell.
Crusaders' Song. *Unknown.*
God Wills It. Grady.
Jerusalem Delivered, *sels.* Tasso.
Lepanto. Chesterton.
Tomb of God before us, The. *Fr.* Crusader Chorus. Kingsley.
Victory in Hungary, The. *Fr.* The Squire of Alsatia. Shadwell.

Crystal Palace (London)
Crystal Palace, The. Davidson.
Mr. Molony's Account of the Crystal Palace. Thackeray.

Cuba
Apostrophe to the Island of Cuba. Percival.
Cuba. Rice.
Cuba. Stedman.
Cuba Libre. Miller.
Cuba to Columbia. Carleton.
Farewell to Cuba. Brooks.

Cuchulain (Irish legendary hero)
Cuchulain's Fight with the Sea. Yeats.
Death of Cuchulain. Cox.
Death of Cuchullin, The. Yeats.
Fand Yields Cuchulain to Emer. *Unknown.*

Cuckoos
Beware the Cuckoo. Moll.
Cuckoo! Belloc.
Cuckoo, The. Fyleman.
Cuckoo, The. Hopkins.
Cuckoo, The, Locker-Lampson.
Cuckoo, The. Thomas.
Cuckoo, The ("The cuckoo's a bonny bird"). *Unknown.*
Cuckoo, The ("In April/ Come he Will"). *Unknown.*
Cuckoo ("In former days my father and mother"). *Fr.* Riddles. *Unknown.*
Cuckoo, The ("O meeting is a pleasure"). *Unknown.*
Cuckoo, The ("Sumer is icumen in"). *Unknown.*
Cuckoo. Young.
Cuckoo in the Pear-Tree. Rands.
Cuckoo's Palace. Rands.
Cuckoo's Song, The. Josui.
Gowk, The. Soutar.
Late Winter. McAuley.
Merry cuckoo, messenger of spring, The. *Fr.* Amoretti. Spenser.
O cuckoo. *Fr.* Kokin Shu. *Unknown.*
Ode to the Cuckoo. Bruce.
Oocuck, The. Richardson.
Pallid Cuckoo. Campbell.
Sumer Is Icumen In. *Unknown.*
To the Cuckoo. Townsend.
To the Cuckoo. Wordsworth.
When Daisies Pied. *Fr.* Love's Labour's Lost. Shakespeare.

Cuernavaca, Mexico
View from the Gorge. Belitt.

Cullen, Countee
Countee Cullen. Maleska.

Culloden, Battle of
Lament for Culloden. Burns.
Lochiel's Warning. Campbell.
Old Scottish Cavalier, The. Aytoun.

Cumberland, Margaret Clifford, Countess of
To the Lady Margaret, Countess of Cumberland. Daniel.

Cumberland (ship)
Cumberland, The. Longfellow.
Cumberland, The. Melville.
Cumberland's Crew, The. *Unknown.*
How the *Cumberland* Went Down. Mitchell.
On Board the *Cumberland* (March 7, 1862). Boker.

Cupid
Ah Cupid, I Mistook Thee. Davison.
Alexander and Campaspe, *sels.* Lyly.
Beauties, Have Ye Seen. *Fr.* The Hue and Cry after Cupid. Jonson.
Cheat of Cupid, The; or, The Ungentle Guest. Herrick.
Children of Love. Monro.
Cupid. Blake.
Cupid. *Fr.* Arcadia. Sidney.
Cupid. *Unknown.*
Cupid Abroad Was Lated. *Fr.* Greene's Orpharion. Greene.
Cupid in a Bed of Roses. *Unknown.*
Cupid Mistaken. Prior.
Cupid Stung. Moore.
Cupid Ungodded. Shirley.
Cupid's Darts. *Unknown.*
Cupid's Indictment. *Fr.* Galathea. Lyly.
Damon and Cupid. Gay.
Dream of Venus, A. Bion.
Eros. Bridges.
Eros. Patmore.
His skin is brilliant with the nimble flood. *Fr.* Eros and Psyche. Apuleius.
I Dreamt I Saw Great Venus. Bion.
O Cupid! Monarch over Kings. *Fr.* Mother Bombie. Lyly.
O Gentle Love. *Fr.* The Arraignment of Paris. Peele.
Of His Cynthia. *Fr.* Caelica. Greville.
Plea to Eros. *Unknown.*
To Cupid. Davison.
To Cupid. Drayton.
Warning to Cupid. *Unknown.*
When I Was Fair and Young. Elizabeth I, Queen of England.
Wounded Cupid, The. Herrick.

Curfew
Curfew. Longfellow.
Curfew Must Not Ring To-Night. Thorpe.

Curlew
Curlew's Call, A. Barlow.

Curran, Sarah
She Is Far from the Land. Moore.

Cushing, William Barker
"Albemarle" Cushing. Roche.
At the Cannon's Mouth. Melville.

Custer, George Armstrong
Custer. Stedman.
Custer's Last Charge. Whittaker.
Custer's Last Fierce Charge. *Unknown.*
Death of Custer, The. Crawford.
Revenge of Rain-in-the-Face, The. Longfellow.

Cyclamen
Cyclamen, The. Bates.
Sicilian Cyclamens. Lawrence.
To a Cyclamen. Landor.

Cyclones
Cyclone at Sea, A. Hayne.
Sherman Cyclone, The. *Unknown.*

Cyclops
Cyclops, *sels.* Euripides.

Cyclops *(continued)*
Cyclops. *Fr.* Metamorphoses. Ovid.
Song of the Cyclops. *Fr.* London's Tempe. Dekker.
Cypress Trees
Cypress. Peter.

D

Dachshunds
Dachshund, The. Anthony.
Dachshunds. Smith.
Daedalus
Be Daedalus. Alba.
Daedalus. *Fr.* Metamorphoses. Ovid.
Daffodils
Daffodils. Ballantyne.
Daffodils. Harding.
Daffodils, The. Herrick.
Daffodils. Reese.
Daffodil's Return. Carman.
Daffodils. Kikurio.
Daffy-down-Dilly. Warner.
Divination by a Daffodil. Herrick.
Growing in the Vale. *Fr.* Sing-Song. C. G. Rossetti.
I Wandered Lonely as a Cloud. Wordsworth.
Lent Lily, The. *Fr.* A Shropshire Lad. Housman.
To Daffodils. Dobson.
To Daffodils. Herrick.
Dahlgren, Ulric
Ulric Dahlgren. Sherwood.
Dahlias
Dahlias. Colum.
Daisies
Buttercups and Daisies. Howitt.
Daisies, The. Carman.
Daisies, The. Greenaway.
Daisies. Sherman.
Daisies, The. Stephens.
Daisy, The. Burns.
Daisy, The. Montgomery.
Daisy, The. Rodd.
Daisy, The. Tennyson.
Daisy. Thompson.
Daisy. Williams.
Daisy's Song, A. Keats.
Field Daisy, The. Taylor.
I'd Choose to Be a Daisy. *Unknown.*
Of all the floures in the mede. *Fr.* The Legend of Good Women. Chaucer.
To a Daisy. Hartley.
To a Daisy. Meynell.
To a Mountain Daisy. Burns.
To Daisies. Thompson.
To Daisies, Not to Shut So Soon. Herrick.
To the Daisy ("Bright flower! whose home is everywhere"). Wordsworth.
To the Daisy ("In youth from rock to rock I went"). Wordsworth.
To the Daisy ("With little here to do or see"). Wordsworth.
Where innocent, bright-eyed daisies are. C. G. Rossetti.
Damascus, Syria
Gates of Damascus. Flecker.
Damien, Father
Father Damien. Tabb.
Damocles
Damocles. Graves.
Dams
Big Dam. Moses.
Bucyrus. Holmes.
Danaë
Danaë. Simonides.
Gold That Fell on Danaë, The. Colony.
Dancing and Dancers
African Dance. Hughes.
At a Cowboy Dance. Adams.
Ballroom Dancing Class. McGinley.
Bill Haller's Dance. Carr.
Cowboy's Ball, The. Knibbs.
Dance, The. Duncan.
Dance, The. Lehmann.
Dance, The. Roethke.
Dance. Weeden.
Dance, The. Williams.
Dance of the Abakweta. *Fr.* Far from Africa. Danner.
Dancer, The. Campbell.
Dancers with a Hop, The. Schevill.
Dancing. Yang Kuei-fei.
Dancing Girl, A. Osgood.
Fancy's Knell. Housman.
Female Dancer. Camp.
Fiddler of Dooney, The. Yeats.
Gratiana Dancing and Singing. Lovelace.
Javanese Dancers. Symons.
La Mélinte: Moulin Rouge. Symons.
Learning to Dance. Graham.
Life Is Motion. Stevens.
Little Dancers, The. Binyon.
May Day Dancing, The. Nemerov.
Minuet, The. Dodge.
My Cousin German Came from France. *Unknown.*
Negro Reel. *Unknown.*
Off the Ground. De la Mare.
Orchestra; or, A Poem of Dancing. Davies.
Reasons for Attendance. Larkin.
Reminiscences of a Dancing Man. Hardy.
Re-run. Scott.
Rumba. Tallet.
Seeing Her Dancing. Heath.
Tarantella. Belloc.
Upon His Mistress Dancing. Shirley.
Waltz, The. Byron.
Waltz in the Afternoon, A. Bentley.
War Dance, The. Carr.
When Dutchy Plays the Mouth Harp. Carr.
Untune the Sky (UnS). Helen Plotz, comp.
Dandelions
Casual Gold. Uschold.
Dandelion. Annan.
Dandelion. Brown.
Dandelion. Conkling.
Dandelion. Garabrant.
Dandelion. The. Lindsay.
Dandelion. The. Pyle.
Dandelion. The("O dandelion, yellow as gold"). *Unknown.*
Dandelion ("There was a pretty dandelion"). *Unknown.*
Dandelions. Albee.
Dandelions, The. Cone.
Dandelions. Nemerov.
Dandelions. S. Sitwell.
Dandelions, The. *Unknown.*
First Dandelion, The. Whitman.
Late Dandelions. Belitt.
Little Dandelion. Bostwick.
Little Dandelion, The. Weeden.
Lucky Thing, A. Aldis.
To the Dandelion. J. R. Lowell.
Young Dandelion, The. Craik.
Danes
King of Ulster, The. *Unknown.*
Murrough Defeats the Danes, 994. *Unknown.*
Daniel (Bible)
Daniel. Lindsay.
Daniel, Samuel
Ad Samuelem Danielem. Bastard.
Remembrance of Some English Poets, A. Barnfield.
To Samuel Daniel, Prince of English Poets. Davison.
D'Annunzio, Gabriele
To D'Annunzio: Lines from the Sea. Nichols.
Dante Alighieri
Dante. Bryant.
Dante("Tuscan, that wanderest"). Longfellow.
Dante. Michelangelo.
Dante at Verona. D. G. Rossetti.
Elegy: "Floods of tears well from my deepest heart, The." Immanuel di Roma.
Fiammetta. Boccaccio.
Inscription for Portrait of Dante. Boccaccio.
Man Called Dante, I Have Heard, A. King.
On a Bust of Dante. Parsons.

On the "Vita Nuova" of Dante. D. G. Rossetti.
Sonnet: To Dante Alighieri (He Commends the Work of Dante's Life). Quirino.
Sonnet: To Dante Alighieri (He Conceives of Some Compensation in Death). Cino da Pistoia.
Sonnet: To Dante Alighieri (He Interprets Dante Alighieri's Dream). Maiano.
Sonnet: To Dante Alighieri (He Interprets Dante's Dream). Cavalcanti.
Sonnet: To Dante Alighieri (He Interprets Dante's Dream). Cino da Pistoia.
Sonnet: To Dante Alighieri (He Mistrusts the Love of Lapo Giannl). Cavalcanti.
Sonnet: To Dante Alighieri (He Reports the Successful Issue of Lapo Gianni's Love). Cavalcanti.
Sonnet: To Dante Alighieri (He Writes to Dante, Defying Him). Cecco Angiolieri da Siena.
Sonnet: To Dante Alighieri (On the Last Sonnet of the "Vita Nuova"). Cecco Angiolieri da Siena.
Sonnets on the Divina Commedia. Longfellow.
Soul of Dante, The. Michelangelo.
To Dante. Alfieri.
To Dante. Cavalcanti.
Danube (river)
Danube River, The. Aïdé.
Daphne
Daphne. Carman.
Daphne. Galler.
Daphne. Rodman.
Hunting Song. *Fr.* Apollo and Daphne. Whitehead.
Story of Phoebus and Daphne Applied, The. Waller.
Dare, Virginia
Peregrine White and Virginia Dare. R. *and* S. V. Benét.
Darwin, Charles
Darwinity. Merivale.
Davenant, Sir William
To Sir William Davenant upon His Two First Books of Gondibert. Cowley.
Davenport, Abraham
Abraham Davenport. Whittier.
David (Bible)
Abishag. Spire.
David. Butler.
David. Davies.
Davideis, *sels.* Cowley.
Goliath and David. Untermeyer.
Harp of David, The. Cohen.
Harp of David, The. "Yehoash."
In Honour of St. David's Day. *Unknown.*
King David. S. V. Benét.
King David. Heine.
King Solomon and King David. *Unknown.*
Listen, David! Jacobsen.
Saul. R. Browning.
Song to David, A. Smart.
Davidson, John
In Memoriam; John Davidson. Macfie.
Davies, Sir John
Four for Sir John Davies. Roethke.
To Mr. John Davies. Harington.
Davies, William
I Am the Poet Davies, William. Davies.
Davis, Jefferson
Jefferson D. Cornwell.
Jefferson Davis. Bell.
Davis, Miles
Miles' Delight. Joans.
Davis, Thomas Osborne
Lament for Thomas Davis. Ferguson.
Davy, Sir Humphry
Sir Humphry Davy. *Fr.* Clerihews. Bentley.
Dawn
Alba. Walcott.
At Dawn. Hugo.
At Dawn. Symons.
Aubade. E. Sitwell.
Awake! Awake! *Fr.* Song of the Dawn. Ruskin.
Before Dawn. Chipp.
Before Dawn in the Woods. Wilkinson.
Break of Day. Clare.
Break of Day, The. Neilson.
Clearing at Dawn. Li Po.
Cock Crow. Thomas.
Dawn. Dunbar.
Dawn. Logan.
Dawn. Masefield.
Dawn. Sherman.
Dawn, The ("One morning I rose and looked upon the world"). *Unknown.*
Dawn ("Thou enemy of love, how slow you creep"). *Unknown.*
Dawn. Williams.
Dawn, The. Yeats.
Dawn amid Scotch Firs. "Macleod".
Dawn and Dark. Gale.
Dawn Has Yet to Ripple in. Cane.
Dawn in Inishtrahull. O'Sullivan.
Dawn of Day. *Fr.* The Shepherd's Pipe. Browne.
Dawn on Mid-Ocean. Wheelock.
Dawn on the Headland. Watson.
Dawn on the Lievre, The. Lampman.
Dawning of the Day, The. Mangan.
Dawning of the Day, The. *Unknown.*
Day came slow, till five o'clock, The. Dickinson.
Daybreak. Longfellow.
Daybreak. Shelley.
Early Dawn. Belloc.
Early News. Pratt.
Edge of Day, The. Lee.
Hark, Hark! the Lark. *Fr.* Cymbeline. Shakespeare.
Hymn before Sun-Rise, in the Vale of Chamouni. Coleridge.
Improvisation III. Silverman.
In the Naked Bed, in Plato's Cave. Schwartz.
Lark Now Leaves His Wat'ry Nest, The. Davenant.
Miracle of the Dawn, The. Cawein.
Morning Light Is Breaking, The. Smith.
Morning on the St. John's. Cooper.
Music of the Dawn. Harrison.
Night Is Near Gone, The. Montgomerie.
Perturbation at Dawn. Ibn Maatuk.
Phoebus, Arise! Drummond of Hawthordon.
Prayer at Dawn. Poteat.
Prelude: "Night was dark, though sometimes a faint star, The." *Fr.* The New Day. Gilder.
Salutation of the Dawn, The. *Unknown.*
Song of the Night at Day-Break. Meynell.
Spectre Is on the Move, The. Allana.
Summer Dawn. Morris.
Sunrise. Bennett.
Thy dawn, O Master of the world, thy dawn. *Fr.* Hassan. Flecker.
Very Early. Kuskin.
With the Dawn. Irwin.
See Also **Morning; Sunrise.**
Day
Break of Day. Donne.
Chanticleer. Austin.
Day and Night. Daley.
Day and Night. Dhingra.
Day and Night. Lindsay.
Days. Emerson.
Night and Day. Dodge.
Revolution. Housman.
Stoush o'Day, The. Dennis.
Daybreak. *See* **Dawn.**
Daydreams. *See* **Dreams.**
Deafness
Deaf. Higgs.
Deaf-and-Dumb School Delius.
Mutterings over the Crib of a Deaf Child. Wright.
Rhapsody of the Deaf Man. Corbière.
Dean, James
For James Dean. O'Hara.
Death
Absent, The. Muir.
Acceptance. Frost.
Adieu, Farewell Earth's Bliss! *Fr.* Summer's Last Will and Testament. Nashe.
After Death. Mason.
After Death. C. G. Rossetti.
After Death. Swinburne.
After Sunset. Conkling.
After the Burial. J. R. Lowell.
After Work. Oxenham.

Death *(continued)*
Afterwards. Hardy.
Against the Fear of Death. Dryden.
Algonkian Burial. Bailey.
All Men Are Free. Napier.
All the Hills and Vales Along. Sorley.
And Death Shall Have No Dominion. Thomas.
And the Earth Rebelled. Suhl.
And There Shall Be No More Death, *sels.* Gilbert.
And You as Well Must Die, Belovéd Dust. Millay.
Ante Mortem. Jeffers.
Apostrophe to Death. *Fr.* Carmen Paschale. Sedulius.
Archer, The. Smith.
Argumentum ad Hominem. Plutzik.
Asleep. Owen.
At Last. Whittier.
Aunt Mary. Ciardi.
Auto Wreck. Shapiro.
Autumnal. Humphries.
Away. Riley.
Away, Delights! *Fr.* The Captain. Fletcher.
Ballad: White Rose. S. Sitwell.
Ballad of Death, A. Swinburne.
Ballad of Past Meridian, A. Meredith.
Ballad of Sister Anne, The. O. Sitwell.
Ballad of the Outer Life. Hofmannsthal.
Beautiful Lie the Dead. Phillips.
Because I could not stop for Death. Dickinson.
Bells for John Whiteside's Daughter. Ransom.
Beside Lilia Dead. Sister Mary Catherine.
Beside the Bed. Mew.
Bird of Paradise, The. Davies.
Birth and Death. Swinburne.
Blind Date. Aiken.
Bourne, The. C. G. Rossetti.
Bridge of Sighs, The. Hood.
Buck in the Snow, The. Millay.
Buffalo Bill's. Cummings.
Bull, The. Hodgson.
Burn Out Burn Quick. Reisen.
Bustle in a house, The. Dickinson.
Canticle. Berry.
Cavalier. Bruce.
Child Dying, The. Muir.
Child Ill, A. Betjeman.
Children's Elegy. *Fr.* Eighth Elegy. Rukeyser.
Choricos. Aldington.
Chorus: "Alas, with what tormenting fire." *Fr.* Antonius. Garnier.
City Dead-House, The. Whitman.
City of the Dead, The. Burton.
Closing Prayer. Patrick.
Coastguardsman in the Fog, The. Schevill.
Cold Green Element, The. Layton.
Colloquy in Black Rock. R. Lowell.
Come Away, Come Away, Death. *Fr.* Twelfth Night. Shakespeare.
Come Away, Death. Pratt.
Comparison of Life and Death. *Unknown.*
Complaint on the Oblivion of the Dead. Laforgue.
Conqueror Worm, The. Poe.
Cool Tombs. Sandburg.
Coronach. *Fr.* The Lady of the Lake. Scott.
Corpses in the Wood. Toller.
Could I Believe. Milne.
Crossing the Bar. Tennyson.
Cry, A. Clarke.
Dance of Death, The. Dobson.
Dancing Partners. Child.
Dark Cat, The. Brown.
Dark Hotel. Dorn.
D'Avalos' Prayer. Masefield.
Dead, The ("Blow out, you bugles"). *Fr.* 1914. Brooke.
Dead, The ("These hearts were woven"). *Fr.* 1914. Brooke.
Dead, The. Williams.
Dead Boy. Ransom.
Dead Child, The. Dowson.
Dead Man's Dump. Rosenberg.
Death. Babcock.
Death. Bodenheim.
Death. E. Brontë.
Death. Cawein.
Death. Clare.
Death. Coates.
Death. Herbert.
Death. Hood.
Death, A. Jennings.
Death. Landor.
Death. Turner.
Death. Vaughan.
Death. Yeats.
Death and Birth. Swinburne.
Death Alone. "Neruda."
Death and Resurrection. Croly.
Death and the Maiden, *sel.* Oliver.
Death and the Maiden. *Unknown.*
Death, Be Not Proud. *Fr.* Holy Sonnets. Donne.
Death Fugue. Celan.
Death Great Smoothener. Swenson.
Death in Bed. *Unknown.*
Death in Hospital, A. Lehmann.
Death in Leamington. Betjeman.
Death Is a Blessed Thing. "Silesius."
Death is a dialogue. Dickinson.
Death Is but Death. Dyson.
Death is the supple suitor. Dickinson.
Death May Be Very Gentle. Gogarty.
Death of a Bird. Silkin.
Death of a Dove, The. Schevill.
Death of a Son. Silkin.
Death of an Old Man, The. Hamburger.
Death of Friends, The. Levi.
Death of the Ball Turret Gunner, The. Jarrell.
Death Snips Proud Men. Sandburg.
Death Song. Hawker.
Death Stands above Me. Landor.
Death the Great. Lasynys.
Death the Leveller. *Fr.* The Contention of Ajax and Ulysses. Shirley.
Death, Thou Hast Seized Me. Luzzatto.
Death Was a Woman. Russell.
Death—What Is It? Matthews.
Death-Bed. Rowse.
Death-Bed, The. Sassoon.
Deaths at Paragon, Indiana, The. Woods.
Death's Transfiguration. Zangwill.
Death's Warning to Beauty. *Unknown.*
Departed Friends. Vaughan.
Departure. *Fr.* The Unknown Eros. Patmore.
Devil's Dream. Fearing.
Dirge: "Never the nightingale." Crapsey.
Dirge: "Swallow leaves her nest, The." *Fr.* Death's Jest Book. Beddoes.
Dirge: "What longer need hath she of loveliness." Naidu.
Dirge in the Woods. Meredith.
Dirge without Music. Millay.
Discoverer, The. Stedman.
Disquisition on Death, *sel.* Fairburn.
Do Not Go Gentle into That Good Night. Thomas.
Dominus Illuminatio Mea. Blackmore.
Downe downe afflicted soule and paie thy due. *Unknown.*
Downgoing. Davidson.
Dream of a Decent Death. Borgese.
Dream of Gerontius, The. Cardinal Newman.
Dream of the World without Death, The. *Fr.* The Book of Orm. Buchanan.
Dying: An Introduction. Sissman.
Dying Californian, The. *Unknown.*
Dying Child, The. Clare.
Dying Christian to His Soul, The. Pope.
Dying Enthusiast, The. Mangan.
Dying Stockman, The. *Unknown.*
Early Death. H. Coleridge.
Early Death and Fame. Arnold.
East Coker. *Fr.* Four Quartets. Eliot.
Earth out of Earth. *Unknown.*
Elegy: "Fled is the swiftness of all the white-footed ones." Auslander.
Elegy: "My prime of youth is but a frost of cares." Tichbourne.
Elegy: "Tumult of death, dizziness hath seized me, The." Rimos of Majorca.
Elegy against a Latter Day. Smithyman.

Elegy for Jane. Roethke.
Elegy on Gordon Barber. Derwood.
Elegy over a Tomb. Herbert of Cherbury.
Emperor of Ice-Cream, The. Stevens.
Empty House. Spender.
End, The. Masefield.
End, The. Owen.
End of Man Is Death, The. Ibn Ezra.
Epilogue: "At the midnight in the silence of the sleep-time." *Fr.* Asolando. R. Browning.
Epistle to be Left in the Earth. MacLeish.
Epitaph: "Man who in his life trusts in this world, A." *Unknown.*
Epitaph: "This is the end of him, here he lies." Levy.
Epitaph. Caecil. Boulstr. Herbert of Cherbury.
Epitaph of Graunde Amoure, The. *Fr.* The Pastime of Pleasure. Hawes.
Epitaph on S.P., a Child of Q. El. Chapel, An. Jonson.
Escape. Graves.
"Ex Libris." Upson.
Executive's Death, The. Bly.
Exequy, The. King.
Exequy: To Peter Allt. Dobbs.
Exhortation to the Artists. Plutzik.
Exile from God. Wheelock.
Exit. Fletcher.
Exit. MacDonald.
Extended Invitation. Stuart.
Falstaff's Song. Stedman.
Fantasy in Purple. Hughes.
Farewell. Press.
Fear No More the Heat o' the Sun. *Fr.* Cymbeline. Shakespeare.
Fear of Death Confounds Me, The. Dunbar.
Fearful Death. *Unknown.*
Finale: Presto. Davison.
First Death in Nova Scotia. Bishop.
Five Minutes. Nicholson.
Flat One, A. Snodgrass.
For a Dead Lady. Robinson.
For E. McC. Pound.
For Johnny. Pudney.
For My Funeral. Housman.
For Sleep, or Death. Pitter.
Foreboding, The. Graves.
Forever. O'Reilly.
Fragment on Death. Villon.
Friends Beyond. Hardy.
Friends Departed. Vaughan.
French Polisher, The. Davies.
Frozen City, The. Nemerov.
Funeral. Bennett.
Funeral, The. Donne.
Funeral, The. "M. J".
Funeral Hymn. *Unknown.*
Futility. Owen.
Garden of Proserpine, The. Swinburne.
Gardner, The. Housman.
Gee I Like to Think of Dead. Cummings.
Geist's Grave. Arnold.
Ghostly Reaper. Vinal.
Gift of a Skull, The. Skelton.
Giorno dei Morti. Lawrence.
Go Down, Death. Johnson.
Golden Falcon. Coffin.
Good-bye My Fancy! Whitman.
Grave, The. Blair.
Grave, The. Jones.
Grave, A. Moore.
Grave, The. Winters.
Grave in Ukraine, A. Tchernichowsky.
Gravestones. Watkins.
Green and Red and Darkness. Scott.
Guitar Lament for a Mountain Boy. De Suze.
Hath any loved you well, down there. O'Shaughnessy.
Hence flattring hopes. Cease longing and give ore. *Unknown.*
Here Dead Lie We. Housman.
Here Lies a Lady. Ransom.
Hero Song. Duncan.
Hide-and-Seek. Francis.
His Lady's Death. Ronsard.
His Winding-Sheet. Herrick.
Hos Ego Versiculos. *Fr.* Argalus and Parthenia. Quarles.
Hour of Death, The. Hemans.
Hours, The. Bishop.
House of Falling Leaves, The. Braithwaite.
House of Night, The, *sels.* Freneau.
How Death Comes. *Unknown.*
How Great unto the Living Seem the Dead! Heavysege.
I Am the Reaper. Henley.
I Die Alive. Southwell.
I Die, Being Young. Gray.
I died for Beauty—but was scarce. Dickinson.
I felt a funeral in my brain. Dickinson.
I Have a Rendezvous with Death. Seeger.
I Have Got My Leave. *Fr.* Gitanjali. Tagore.
I heard a fly buzz when I died. Dickinson.
I never heard that one is dead. Dickinson.
I Stood with the Dead. Sassoon.
I Tell of Another Young Death. Tiempo.
I Wage Not Any Feud with Death. *Fr.* In Memoriam A. H. H. Tennyson.
Ignorance of Death. Empson.
Ilicet. Swinburne.
Illi Morituri. Webster.
Imagining How It Would Be to Be Dead. Eberhart.
Immortal is an ample word. Dickinson.
Improvisation on an Old Theme. Livesay.
In Battle. Stevens.
In the Deep Museum. Sexton.
In the Museum. Gardner.
In the subtraction of my yeares. *Unknown.*
In the Trench. Gellert.
In the Year's Morning. Ross.
In Time of Plague. *Fr.* Summer's Last Will and Testament. Nashe.
Invocation of Death. Raine.
Invocation to Death. Carnevali.
Irony. Untermeyer.
Is It Far to Go. Day Lewis.
It Is Not Death to Die. Bethune.
It was not death, for I stood up. Dickinson.
I've seen a dying eye. Dickinson.
Journey's End. Wolfe.
Juggling Jerry. Meredith.
Jugurtha. Longfellow.
Keys of Morning, The. De la Mare.
Lament: "Listen, children." Millay.
Lament for the Makaris. Dunbar.
Lament of a Man for His Son. *Unknown.*
Land o' the Leal. Nairne.
Landscape with Figures. Douglas.
Last Conqueror, The. *Fr.* Cupid and Death. Shirley.
Last Invocation, The. Whitman.
Last Journey, The. Leonidas.
Last Lines. E. Brontë.
Last Lines,*sels.* "Meredith."
Last night that she lived, The. Dickinson.
Last Plea. Untermeyer.
Leaf after Leaf. Landor.
L'Envoi: "Who findeth comfort in the stars and flowers." *Fr.* Death's Jest Book. Beddoes.
Let Me Go Down to Dust. Sarett.
Let Me Live Out My Years. Neihardt.
Let Me Not Die. Pierce.
Let's Talk of Graves. *Fr.* Richard II. Shakespeare.
Libel of Divorce, A. Gascoigne.
Life and Death. *Fr.* The Christians Reply to the Philosopher. Davenant.
Life and Death. Perry.
Life and Death. Scott.
Lights Out. Thomas.
Litany of the Rooms of the Dead. Werfel.
Little Boy Blue. Field.
Little Elegy. Kennedy.
Little Shroud, The. Landon.
Lone Prairie, The. *Unknown.*
Luke Havergal. Robinson.
Malefic Surgeon, The. Lansing.
Man Walking and Singing, A. Berry.
Man's Mortality. *Unknown.*
Margaritae Sorori. Henley.

Death *(continued)*
Meditation, A. Eberhart.
Memento for Mortality, A. *At. to* Basse.
Memorial Rain. MacLeish.
Midnight Lamentation. Monro.
Mirror of Mortality, A. Proctor.
Missing. Pudney.
Missing. Tabb.
Mrs. Southern's Enemy. O. Sitwell.
Mither's Lament, The. Smith.
Moriturus. Millay.
Mortality. Devaney.
Mortification. Herbert.
Mother Marie Therese. R. Lowell.
Mother's Lament for the Death of Her Son, A. Burns.
My Death. Smith.
My Death. Zuckmayer.
My life closed twice its close. Dickinson.
My Life Is Like the Summer Rose. Wilde.
My Sister. Plutzik.
My Sister's Sleep. D. G. Rossetti.
Nature. Longfellow.
Next of Kin. C. G. Rossetti.
Next, Please. Larkin.
Never More Will the Wind. *Fr.* Hymen. Doolittle.
Night-Piece on Death, A. Parnell.
No Death. Marston.
Non Dolet. Gogarty.
O Death, Rock Me Asleep. *Unknown.*
Oh Death Will Find Me. Brooke.
Oh, for the Time When I Shall Sleep. *Fr.* The Philosopher. E. Brontë.
Oh, Let Us Howl Some Heavy Note. *Fr.* The Duchess of Malfi. Webster.
O Mariners! Rutledge.
O Mors! Quam Amara Est Memoria Tua Homini Pacem Habenti in Substantiis Suis. Dowson.
Oh, Thou! Who Dry'st the Mourner's Tear. Moore.
Obituary. Untermeyer.
Ode on the Death of His Father. Manrique.
Ode to the Confederate Dead. Tate.
Of Death. *Fr.* Antonius. Garnier.
Of Death. Harding.
Of the Progresse of the Soule: The Second Anniversary. Donne.
Old man dozed, The. The hospital quietened. *Fr.* Sonnets for a Dying Man. Singer.
Omnia Somnia. Sylvester.
On a Dead Child. Bridges.
On a Dead Lady. Musset.
On a Dying Boy. Bell.
On an Infant Dying as Soon as Born. Lamb.
On Death. Keats.
On Death. Landor.
On Death. *Fr.* Measure for Measure. Shakespeare.
On My First Daughter. Jonson.
On My First Son. Jonson.
On the Acequia Madre. Corbin.
On the Brink of Death. Michelangelo.
On the Death of a Recluse. Darley.
On the Death of His Son. Cothi.
On the Eve of His Execution. Tichborne.
On the Tombs in Westminster Abbey. *At. to* Beaumont, *also to* Basse.
On the Verge. Winter.
One Who Watches. Sassoon.
Original Sin. Laing.
Out of the Cradle Endlessly Rocking. Whitman.
Over Sir John's Hill. Thomas.
Overtakelessness of those, The. Dickinson.
Overtures to Death. Day Lewis.
Pardon, The. Wilbur.
Parted Souls. Herbert of Cherbury.
Passer Mortuus Est. Millay.
Patchwork Quilt, The. Shorter.
Pause en Route. Kinsella.
Peaceful Death. Whitman.
People Has No Obituary, The. Clark.
Per Iter Tenebricosum. Gogarty.
Philosophic Flight, The. *At. to* Bruno.
Pietà. McAuley.
Plaint. Elliott.
Poem: "And when I pay death's duty." Blaser.
Poor Wayfaring Stranger. *Unknown.*
Postscript. Souster.
Prayer in the Prospect of Death, A. Burns.
Precipice, The. Tabb.
Presence, The. Graves.
Prospice. R. Browning.
Pure Death. Graves.
Quaker Graveyard in Nantucket, The. R. Lowell.
Quiet of the Dead, The. Webster.
Rain on a Grave. Hardy.
Reaper, The. Duncan.
Reapers, The. Watt.
Reconciliation. Day Lewis.
Refusal to Mourn the Death, by Fire, of a Child in London, A. Thomas.
Remembrance. E. Brontë.
Remorse after Death. Baudelaire.
Requiescat. Arnold.
Requiescat. Wilde.
Respice Finem. Proctor.
Resurgam. Burt.
Resurgam. Pickthall.
Rest. C. G. Rossetti.
Rich men, trust not in wealth. Nashe.
Rites for a Demagogue. Thwaite.
Rose, A. Fanshawe.
Rumination. Eberhart.
Safe in their alabaster chambers. Dickinson.
Sea of Death, The. Hood.
Sense of Death, The. Hoyt.
Serious and a Curious Night-Meditation, A. Traherne.
Sestina: "I die, no matter what I do I die." Eberhart.
Shadow, The. De la Mare.
Shapes of Death Haunt Life. Spender.
Ship, The. *Unknown.*
Ship of Death. Lawrence.
Should You Go First. Rowswell.
Show, The. Owen.
Silver swan, who living had no note, The. *Unknown.*
Simplify Me When I'm Dead. Douglas.
Sleep and His Brother Death. Hayne.
Sleepe O sleepe thou sacred dust. *Unknown.*
Sleepe, sleepe faire virgin, sleepe in peace. *Unknown.*
Sleeper, The. Poe.
Sleeping at Last. C. G. Rossetti.
Snow Globe, The. Nemerov.
So Might It Be. Galsworthy.
Soliloquy on Death. Fiawoo.
Solioquy 2. Aldington.
Some Late Lark Singing. Henley.
Some Time at Eve. Hardy.
Some, too fragile for winter winds. Dickinson.
Something Has Spoken to Me in the Night. Wolfe.
Song: "Spirit haunts the year's last hours, A." Tennyson.
Song: "Victorious men of Earth, no more." *Fr.* Cupid and Death. Shirley.
Song: "When I am dead, my dearest." C. G. Rossetti.
Song: "Why art thou slow, thou rest of trouble, Death." *Fr.* The Emperor of the East. Massinger.
Song from "Chartivel." Marie de France.
Song to Death. Escrivá.
Sonnet: "And you as well must die, belovèd dust." Millay.
Sonnet: Death Warnings. Quevedo y Villegas.
Sonnet I: "He came in silvern armor, trimmed with black." Bennett.
Sonnet: "How all men wrongly death to dignify." Smith.
Sonnet: "It is not death." Hood.
Sonnet: "Poor soul, the center of my sinful earth." Sonnets, CXLVI. Shakespeare.
Sonnet: You Were Born; Must Die. Spender.
Soul's Garment, The. Duchess of Newcastle.
Space in the Air, A. Silkin.
Speech of the Dead, The. Ridler.
Speed. Davies.
Spring and Death. Hopkins.
Stand Close Around. Landor.
Stirrup-Cup, The. Lanier.
Stop All the Clocks. Auden.
Strange Meeting. Owen.

Strangeness of Heart. Sassoon.
Strangers Are We All upon the Earth. Werfel.
Suffering. Ehrenstein.
Sunlight on the Garden, The. MacNeice.
Suppose in Perfect Reason. Griffin.
Surrender. Grimké.
Tarantula or the Dance of Death. Hecht.
Tenancy, The. Gilmore.
Terminus. Emerson.
Testament. Holmes.
Thanatopsis. Bryant.
That Death Is Not So Much to Be Feared as Daily Diseases Are. Turberville.
That Familiar Stranger. Stefanile.
That such have died enables us. Dickinson.
There Is No Death. McCreery.
There Is No Death. *Unknown.*
There Is No Reason Why Not to Look at Death. Sward.
Therefore, We Thank Thee, God. Grossman.
There's a certain slant of light. Dickinson.
They Are All Gone. Vaughan.
They closed her eyes. *Fr.* Rimas. Bécquer.
Things Dead. Schwob.
Think upon death, 'tis good to think of death. H. Coleridge.
This is my playes last scene, here heavens appoint. *Fr.* Holy Sonnets. Donne.
Though I Am Young. *Fr.* The Sad Shepherd. Jonson.
Thought. Whitman.
Thought in Two Moods, A. Hardy.
Thought of Death, A. Flatman.
Threnody: "Only quiet death." Cuney.
Threnody: "South-wind brings, The." Emerson.
'Tis not that dying hurts us so. Dickinson.
To a Child in Death. Mew.
To a Mistress Dying. Davenant.
To an Athlete Dying Young. Housman.
To Azrael. Baudelaire.
To Be or Not to Be. *Fr.* Hamlet. Shakespeare.
To Claudia Homonoea. Wylie.
To Daffodils. Herrick.
To Death. Bowles.
To Death. Herrick.
To Death. Countess of Winchilsea.
To Death, Castara Being Sicke. Habington.
To Giulia Grisi. Willis.
To His Mistress for Her True Picture. Herbert of Cherbury.
To know just how he suffered would be dear. Dickinson.
To think of time. . .to think through the retrospection. *Fr.* To Think of Time. Whitman.
Transmigration. Cudjoe.
Truth the Dead Know, The. Sexton.
Twa Corbies, The. *Unknown.*
'Twas just this time, last year, I died. Dickinson.
'Twas warm at first, like us. Dickinson.
Two Garden Scenes. Burgess.
Two Societies, The. Wheelock.
Two Sonnets. Sorley.
Ultima Ratio Regum. Spender.
Unillumined Verge, The. Bridges.
Unquiet Grave, The. *Unknown.*
Upon a Dead Man's Head. Skelton.
Upon the Image of Death. Southwell.
Vacillation. Yeats.
Valley of the Shadow. Galsworthy.
Vergissmeinnicht. Douglas.
Verses Written in a Lady's Sherlock "Upon Death." Earl of Chesterfield.
Vesta. Whittier.
Victorious Men of Earth. *Fr.* Cupid and Death. Shirley.
Vision, A. Hofmannsthal.
Vital Spark of Heavenly Flame. Pope.
Wake All the Dead. *Fr.* The Law against Lovers. Davenant.
Warning and Reply. E. Brontë.
We Are Alone. De Bary.
We Are Seven. Wordsworth.
Welcome Death. Escrivá.
What Has This Bugbear Death. *Fr.* De Rerum Natura. Lucretius.
What inn is this? Dickinson.
We Lay Us Down to Sleep. Moulton.
Welcome, Thou Safe Retreat. Habington.
What Am I Who Dare. Habington.
What Profit? Immanuel di Roma.
When Death Comes. *Unknown.*
When Death to Either Shall Come. Bridges.
When I Am Dead. Wilson.
When I Am Dead, My Dearest. C. G. Rossetti.
When I Have Fears That I May Cease to Be. Keats.
When I Have Gone Weird Ways. Neihardt.
When Lilacs Last in the Dooryard Bloom'd. Whitman.
When the Grass Shall Cover Me. Coolbrith.
When tongues will tax me in the public ear. *Fr.* A Wreath. Baylebridge.
When You See Millions of the Mouthless Dead. Sorley.
Where the Dead Men Lie. Boake.
Who's Most Afraid of Death? Thou. Cummings.
Why Fear to Die? *Fr.* Arcadia. Sidney.
Wills Dies in Solitude. *Fr.* Burke and Wills. Thiele.
Wind of Death, The. Wetherald.
Wisdom of Old Jelly Roll, The. Smith.
Within the city of my death. *Fr.* Divine Poems. Villa.
Written by the Authoress on Her Death Bed. Pilkington.
Years-End. Wilbur.
You Need Not Fear. Frieseke.
Sourcebook of Poetry (SoP). Al Bryant, comp.

Decatur, Stephen
How We Burned the *Philadelphia.* Eastman.

December
December. Fisher.
December. Irwin.
December. C. G. Rossetti.
December. Vanderbilt.
December Day, A. Teasdale.
December Stillness. Sassoon.
I Heard a Bird Sing. Herford.
Long Night Moon, The: December. F. Frost.
Stanzas: "In a drear-nighted December." Keats.

Declaration of Independence
Emancipation from British Dependence. Freneau.

Decoration Day. *See* **Memorial Day.**

Deer
Blacktail Deer. Sarett.
Buck in the Snow, The. Millay.
Deer. Austin.
Deer. Drinkwater.
Deer. *Fr.* A Bestiary. Rexroth.
Deer of Ireland, The. Colum.
Deer on the Mountain. Norton.
Doe at Evening, A. Lawrence.
Fallow Deer at the Lonely House, The. Hardy.
Fawn, The. Holden.
Fawn in the Snow, The. W. R. Benét.
Four Deer, The. Jones.
In the Falling Deer's Mouth. Levien.
Landscape, Deer Season. Howes.
Like as a huntsman. *Fr.* Amoretti. Spenser.
Milk White Doe, The. *Unknown.*
Nimble Stag, The. Knox.
Nymph Complaining for the Death of Her Fawn, The. Marvell.
Old Man Said, An. Colum.
Runnable Stag, A. Davidson.
Song for the Greenwood Fawn. Salomon.
Tame Stag, The. Gay.
Travelling through the Dark. Stafford.
White-footed Deer, The. Bryant.
Young Flash the Deer. Burgess.

Deerfield, Massachusetts
Sack of Deerfield, The. English.

Defoe, Daniel
Daniel Defoe. Landor.

Degas, Edgar
Museum Piece. Wilbur.

Deirdre
Deirdre, *sel.* Ferguson.
Deirdre. Stephens.
Deirdre, *sels.* Yeats.
Deirdre's Farwell to Alba. *Unknown.*
Deirdre's Lament for the Sons of Usnach. *Unknown.*
Foretelling of Cathbad the Druid at Deirdre's Birth, The. *Unknown.*

Deism
There Is No God, as I Was Taught. Masefield.

Deism *(continued)*
World-Soul, The. Emerson.
Dejection
Dejection; An Ode. Coleridge.
De la Mare, Walter
Mr. Walter de la Mare Makes the Little Ones Dizzy. Hoffenstein.
Delaware River
Across the Delaware. Carleton.
Delaware (state)
Our Delaware. Hynson.
Delft, Holland
At Delft. Tomlinson.
Delius, Frederick
Delius in the Cathedral. Parker.
Delphi, Oracle of
Oracle at Delphi. Bagg.
Oracle of Delphi, The. Naudé.
Demeter
Demeter and Persephone. Tennyson.
Democracy
Black Man Speaks, The. Hughes.
Democracy. *Fr.* Commemoration Ode. Monroe.
Demos. Robinson.
For You O Democracy. Whitman.
Young Democracy. O'Dowd.
Demosthenes
Demosthenes to the Radio Announcer. Ross.
Dempsey, Jack ("Nonpareil")
Nonpareil's Grave, The. McMahon.
Denmark
Ninth of April, The. Gelsted.
There Is a Charming Land. Oehlenschlager.
Dentists
Dentist, The. Fyleman.
Epitaph on a Dentist. *Unknown.*
Ode to a Dental Hygienist. Hooton.
Denver, Colorado
Camels Have Come, The. *Unknown.*
Carrier's Address. *Unknown.*
Curtain, The (Old Tabor Grand Opera House). Gower.
Doing Railroads for *The Rocky Mountain News.* Warman.
Grand Opening of the People's Theatre. Goldrick.
House in Denver. Ferril.
Descartes, René
Theological. Fadiman.
Deserts
Asian Desert. Wellesley.
Desert, The. Knibbs.
Desert Shipwreck. Jordan.
Deserts. Hanes.
In the Day's Work. Litchfield.
In the Desert. Corbin.
Scot in the Desert. Lee.
Toll of the Desert, The. Monroe.
Two Deserts, The. Patmore.
De Soto, Hernando
Distant Runners, The. Van Doren.
Fall of Maubila, The. English.
Despair
Another While. Rosenfeld.
Carrion Comfort. Hopkins.
Castaway, The. Cowper.
Circumstance. Shelley.
City of Dreadful Night, The. Thomson.
Dance of Despair, The. Bialik.
Darkling Thrush, The. Hardy.
Despair. Merwin.
Despair. Reed.
Despair. *Fr.* The Faerie Queene. Spenser.
Die My Shriek. Kushniroff.
Flow my teares fau from your springs. *Unknown.*
I Wake and Feel the Fell of Dark. Hopkins.
Knife, The. Kaplan.
Leaden Echo and the Golden Echo, The. Hopkins.
When They Have Lost. Day Lewis.
Wintertime nighs. *Fr.* In Tenebris. Hardy.
Destiny. *See* **Fate.**
Deutschland (ship)
Wreck of the *Deutschland,* The. Hopkins.
Devil. *See* **Satan.**
Devonshire, England
Dean-bourn, a Rude River in Devon, by Which Sometimes He Lived. Herrick.
Devon to Me. Galsworthy.
Devonshire Lane, A. Marriott.
Devonshire Rhyme, A. *Unknown.*
Devonshire Song, A. *Unknown.*
Discontents in Devon. Herrick.
Frolic Mariners of Devon, The. *Fr.* Britannia's Pastorals. Browne.
Dew
Dew. Williamson.
Dewdrop, A. Sherman.
Dewdrop, Wind and Sun. Skipsey.
Dewdrops, The. Mackay.
Diamond, A. Loveman.
Drop of Dew, A. Halkin.
Haiku: "World of dew, The." Issa.
On a Drop of Dew. Marvell.
Prayer for Dew. Ben Kalir.
Quick-falling Dew. Basho.
When the Dews Are Earliest Falling. Clough.
Dewey, George
Dewey and His Men. Rice.
Dewey at Manila. Johnson.
Dewey in Manila Bay. Risley.
Manila. Ware.
Diana (goddess)
Homage to Diana. Ralegh.
Hymn to Diana. Catullus.
Hymn to Diana. *Fr.* The Golden Age. Heywood.
Hymn to Diana. *Fr.* Cynthia's Revels. Jonson.
Orion Seeks the Goddess Diana. *Fr.* Landscape with the Giant Orion. S. Sitwell.
Praised Be Diana's Fair and Harmless Light. Ralegh.
Díaz del Castillo, Bernál
Bernál Díaz's Preface to His Book. *Fr.* Conquistador. MacLeish.
Dickens, Charles
Dickens. Swinburne.
Dickens in Camp. Harte.
Owed to Dickens, 1956. Burroway.
Dickinson, Emily
Altitudes. Wilbur.
"I Am in Danger—Sir." Rich.
Not to Forget Miss Dickinson. Schacht.
Sisters, The. A. Lowell.
To Emily Dickinson. H. Crane.
To Emily Dickinson. Winters.
Dictators
Litany for Dictatorships. S. V. Benét.
Dido
Beaten Path, The. Winslow.
But now the wounded queen, with heavy care. *Fr.* The Aeneid. Vergil.
Dido. Campion.
Dido among the Shades. *Fr.* The Aeneid. Vergil.
Dido to Aeneas. *Fr.* The Aeneid. Vergil.
Dido's Hunting. *Fr.* The Aeneid. Vergil.
Staye, staye Aeneas, for theyne owne sake staye. *Unknown.*
Dieppe, France
Road to Dieppe, The. Finley.
Dies Irae. *See* **Judgment Day.**
Dieting
I Can't Have a Martini, Dear, but You Take One. Nash.
Digby, Lady Venetia
Elegie Made by Mr. Aurelian Townshend in Remembrance of the Ladie Venetia Digby, An. Townsend.
Lady Venetia Digby, The. Jonson.
Picture of Her Mind, The. Jonson.
Dikes
Leak in the Dike, The. Cary.
Dillinger, John
Shooting of John Dillinger outside the Biograph Theater, July 22, 1934, The. Wagoner.
Dinas Vawr
War Song of Dinas Vawr, The. *Fr.* The Misfortune of Elphin. Peacock.
Dingoes
Trapped Dingo. Wright.

Dinosaurs
Dinosaur, The. Junge.
Dinosaur, The. Taylor.
Diocletian
Great Diocletian. *Fr.* The Garden. Cowley.
Diogenes
Diogenes. Eastman.
Tomb of Diogenes, The. *Unknown.*
Dionysius
Ambrosia of Dionysius and Semele, The. Graves.
Diplomacy and Diplomats
I Had a Duck-billed Platypus. Barrington.
On Reading the War Diary of a Defunct Ambassador. Sassoon.
Dirigibles
Dirigible, The. Bergengren.
Zeppelin, The. Bennett.
Disraeli, Benjamin
Old Pilot Tunnels under the English Channel, The. Schevill.
Ditmars, Raymond Lee
Lines to Dr. Ditmars. Robinson.
Dives (Bible)
Dives and Lazarus. *Unknown.*
Dives Asking a Drop. Crashaw.
On Dives. Crashaw.
Diving and Divers
Cold Logic. Hutchinson.
Diver, The. Mayo.
Diver, The. Ross.
Fantasia. Livesay.
High Diver. Francis.
Divorce
Betsey and I Are Out. Carleton.
For My Sister, Contemplating Divorce. Bell.
Dobson, Austin
On Receiving a Copy of Mr. Austin Dobson's "Old World Idylls." J. R. Lowell.
Doctors. *See* **Physicians.**
Dogs
Animal Store, The. Field.
At Breakfast. Mills.
At the Dog Show. Morley.
Bandog, The. De la Mare.
Beau's Reply. Cowper.
Beth Gêlert. Spencer.
Bishop Doane on His Dog. Doane.
Brave Rover. Beerbohm.
Come Hither, Little Puppy-Dog. *Unknown.*
Daley's Dorg Wattle. Goodge.
Dog. Ferlinghetti.
Dog, The. Herford.
Dog. Monro.
Dog. Smith.
Dog and the Water-Lily, The. Cowper.
Dog around the Block. White.
Dog at Night. Untermeyer.
Dog in a Car. McCord.
Dog trots freely in the streets, The. *Fr.* Oral Messages. Ferlinghetti.
Dog Who Ate a Pond Lily. Welles.
Dogs. Cornford.
Dogs and Weather. Welles.
Dog's Cold Nose, The. Guiterman.
Elegy on a Lap Dog, An. Gay.
Elegy on the Death of a Mad Dog. Goldsmith.
Epitaph to a Newfoundland Dog. Byron.
Extraordinary Dog, The. Turner.
Fashions in Dogs. White.
Feri's Dream. Cornford.
Flush or Faunus. E. B. Browning.
Geist's Grave. Arnold.
Gluskap's Hound. Roberts.
Hairy Dog, The. Asquith.
Harper, The. Campbell.
His friends he loved. His direst earthly foes. Watson.
Hound, The. Lanier.
Hounds, The. Freeman.
I Think I Know No Finer Things than Dogs. Brent.
Introduction to Dogs, An. Nash.
Island Dogs. Bell.
Joy Meets Boy. Coffin.
Little Black Dog, The. Reynolds.
Little Dog-Angel, A. Holland.
Little Dog under the Wagon, The. *Unknown.*
Little Dog's Day, The. Brooke.
Listening to Foxhounds. Dickey.
Little Lost Pup. Guiterman.
Little Puppy. *Unknown.*
Lone Dog. McLeod.
Lonely Dog, The. Bruner.
Lost Dog. Rodman.
Love Me, Love My Dog. Crawford.
Malemute Dog, A. O'Cotter.
Maltese Dog, A. Tymnes.
Morning Overture; Chorus of Dogs. Strachan.
My Airedale Dog. Mason.
My Dog. Bangs.
My Dog. Chute.
My Dog. Robinson.
My Dog Tray. Byrom.
My Dog Tray. Campbell.
My Last Terrier. Halsham.
Noctambule. Johnston.
Obituary. Parsons.
Old Blue. *Unknown.*
Old Dog, An. Duffin.
Old Hound. Mastin.
On a Puppy. Feng Chih.
On a Spaniel, Called Beau, Killing a Young Bird. Cowper.
Ordinary Dog, The. Turner.
Old Dog. Vaughn.
Pardon, The. Wilbur.
Poor Dog Tray. Campbell.
Prayer of the Dog, The. Gasztold.
Pup een da Snow, Da. Daly.
Puppy. Fisher.
Puppy and I. Milne.
Rest in Peace. Funk.
Road to Vagabondia, The. Burnet.
Roo. Oliver.
Scholar and His Dog, A. Marston.
Shepherd Dog of the Pyrenees, The. Murray.
Song of the Mischievous Dog, The. Thomas.
Sonnet: To Tarter, a Terrier Beauty. Beddoes.
Span of Life, The. Frost.
Stray Dog. Mish.
Stray Dog, near Ecully, Valley of the Rhône. Avison.
Sunning. Tippett.
Tim, an Irish Terrier. Letts.
To a Black Dog, Bereaved. Coatsworth.
To a Black Greyhound. Grenfell.
To a Dog. Branch.
To a Dog Injured in the Street. Williams.
To an English Setter. Walsh.
To My Auld Dog Dash. Barr of Craigielee.
To My Dog "Blanco." Holland.
To My Setter, Scout. Seldon.
To Our House-Dog Captain. Landor.
To Scott. Letts.
Train Dogs, The. Johnson.
Uncle Dog: The Poet at 9. Sward.
Vern. Brooks.
Woodman's Dog, The. Cowper.
Dolls
Doll Song. "Carroll."
Dolladine. Rands.
Dolls, The. Ciardi.
Doll's House, The. Barbauld.
Doll's Wooing, The. Field.
Dressing the Doll. Rands.
Lost Doll, The. *Fr.* The Water Babies. Kingsley.
Dolphins
Dolphin. Unterecker.
Dolphins, The. Maclaren.
Dolphins. Michaels.
Dolphins in Blue Water. A. Lowell.
Porpoise, The. Nash.
Don Juan
Don Juan Declaims. Flecker.
Don Juan in Hell. Baudelaire.
Haidee and Don Juan. *Fr.* Don Juan. Byron.
Don Quixote
Don Quixote. Betts.

Don *(continued)*
Don Quixote. Dobson.
Don Quixote. Ficke.
Donegal, Ireland
Springtime in Donegal. Stevenson.
Donkeys
Ass, The. Allan.
Brother Ass. Irvin.
Burro, The. Gibbons.
Burro with the Long Ears. *Unknown.*
Donkey, The. Chesterton.
Donkey, The. Kaikini.
Donkey, The. *Unknown.*
Donkey. Van Doren.
Lament for a Dead Burro. Penalosa.
Little Danny Donkey. Le Cron.
Me and Prunes. Sherwood.
Nicholas Nye. De la Mare.
Ol' Jinny Mine, The. Detrick.
Prayer to Go to Paradise with the Asses. Jammes.
Time Out. Montague.
Donne, John
Dr. Donne. Alling.
Elegie upon the Death of the Dean of Pauls, Dr. John Donne, An. Carew.
Elegy for Doctor Dunn. Herbert of Cherbury.
John Donne's Defiance. Hervey.
On Donne's Poetry. Coleridge.
On John Donne's Book of Poems. Marriott.
To John Donne ("Donne, the delight of Phoebus, and each Muse"). Jonson.
To John Donne ("Who shall doubt, Donne, where I a Poet bee"). Jonson.
Upon the Death of My Ever Desired Friend Doctor Donne Dean of Pauls. King.
Donnybrook Fair, Dublin, Ireland
Humours of Donnybrook Fair, The. O'Flaherty.
Humours of Donnybrook Fair, The. *Unknown.*
Dordrecht, Holland
Nightfall in Dordrecht. Field.
Douglas, Stephen Arnold
Lecompton's Black Brigade. Halpine.
Douglass, Frederick
Frederick Douglass. Dunbar.
Frederick Douglass. Hayden.
Dover, England
Dover Beach. Arnold.
Dover Cliff. Home.
Dover Cliffs. Bowles.
Dover Cliffs. *Fr.* King Lear. Shakespeare.
Doves
Dove, The. Barnes.
Dove and the Wren, The. *Unknown.*
Dove Apologizes to His God for Being Caught by a Cat, The. Eaton.
Doves. Guiney.
Doves, The. Tynan.
Dove's Loneliness, The. Darley.
Dove's Nest. Taylor.
Girl with Doves. Gray.
High in the afternoon the dove. *Fr.* Considerations of Norfolk Island. Smithyman.
I Had a Dove. Keats.
Literary Landscape with Dove and Poet. McGinley.
My Doves. E. B. Browning.
Old Sweet Dove of Wiveton, The. Smith.
Stockdove, The. Pitter.
Two doves upon the selfsame branch. C. G. Rossetti.
Voice of the Dove, The. Miller.
Dowson, Ernest
Ernest Dowson. Wheelock.
Dragonflies
Devil's Darning Needle. McCoy.
Dragon Flies. Turner.
Dragonfly, The. Chisoku.
Dragonfly. Davies.
Dragon-Fly, A. Farjeon.
Dragon-Fly, The. Landor.
Dragonfly, The. Rand.
Dragon-Fly, The. *Fr.* The Two Voices. Tennyson.
Hunter's Moon. Sandy.
Dragons
Dragon, The. *Fr.* The Faerie Queene. Spenser.
Gold-tinted Dragon, The. Kuskin.
O to Be a Dragon. Moore.
Serious Omission. Farrar.
Sir Eglamour, That Worthy Knight. *Fr.* The Melancholy Knight. Rowlands.
Tale of Custard the Dragon, The. Nash.
Drake, Sir Francis
Admiral's Ghost, The. Noyes.
Dragon of the Seas. Page.
Drake. Noyes.
Drake's Drum. Newbolt.
Epigram: On Sir Francis Drake. *Unknown.*
Epitaph on Drake. Beedome.
Farewell to Sir John Norris and Sir Francis Drake, A. Peele.
First American Sailors, The. Rice.
Of the Great and Famous Sir Francis Drake. Hayman.
On Sir Francis Drake. *Unknown.*
Upon Sir Francis Drake's Return from His Voyage about the World, and the Queen's Meeting Him. *Unknown.*
To the Noble Sir Francis Drake. Beedome.
Drake, Joseph Rodman
On the Death of Joseph Rodman Drake. Halleck.
Drayton, Michael
Ad Michaelem Drayton. Weever.
Funeral Elegy on the Death of His Very Good Friend, Mr. Michael Drayton. Cokayne.
Remebrance of Some English Poets, A. Barnfield.
To Master Michael Drayton. Lodge.
Dreaming and Dreams
Adventure. L. Benét.
All Is Well. Clough.
Awake, My Lute! Lewis.
Bad Dreams. R. Browning.
Cry of the Dreamer, The. O'Reilly.
Dark Chateau. De la Mare.
Dream, A. Blake.
Dream, The. Donne.
Dream, A. Poe.
Dream. Smith.
Dream-Land. Poe.
Dream Love. C. G. Rossetti.
Dream-Pedlary. Beddoes.
Dream the Great Dream. Coates.
Dream within a Dream, A. Poe.
Dreamers, The. Jephcott.
Dreamers of Dreams. Carruth.
Dreams. Alexander.
Dreams. Daley.
Dreams. Herrick.
Dreams. Hughes.
Dreams. Poe.
Dreams. Timrod.
Dreams within Dreams. "Macleod."
Epistle to John Hamilton Reynolds. Keats.
Eye of Humility, The. Smith.
First of All My Dreams, The. Cummings.
Forgotten Dreams. Davis.
Give Us Great Dreams. LeNart.
Harlequin of Dreams, The. Lanier.
He Whom a Dream Hath Possessed. O'Sheel.
Hold Fast Your Dreams. Driscoll.
If Only the Dreams Abide. Scollard.
Isle of Lost Dreams. "Macleod."
Ivory, Coral, Gold, The. Drummond of Hawthornden.
Kubla Khan. Coleridge.
Land of Nod, The. Stevenson.
Lines Written in Objection; or, The Limpopo Express. Hey.
New Dreams for Old. Rice.
Nightmare. Brennan.
Nightmare. Gardner.
Nightmare. Grenville.
Nightmare. Marx.
Ode: "We are the music-makers." O'Shaughnessy.
On Dreams. Brydges.
Orchard-Pit, The. D. G. Rossetti.
Pinch of Salt, A. Graves.
Plain Man's Dream, A. Keppel.
Poem: "We are such stuff as dreams are made of, and these." Hofmannsthal.

Prelude to an Evening. Ransom.
Reverie at Dawn. O'Rahilly.
Rhyme of the Dream-Maker Man, A. White.
Romance. Turner.
Say, Lovely Dream. Waller.
Scythe of Dreams, The. Brennan.
Shepherd's Dream, A. Breton.
Sleeping Saint, The. La Follette.
Snow Globe, The. Nemerov.
Soft, lovely, rose-like lips, conjoined with mine. *Fr.* Parthenophil and Parthenophe. Barnes.
Song: "Don't Tell Me What You Dreamt Last Night." Adams.
'Tis Sair to Dream. Gilfillan.
To Young Dreamers. Trent.
Trance, The. Spender.
True to a Dream. Petersen.
Wharf of Dreams, The. Markham.
What Was My Dream? O'Connor.
Yes, wonderful are dreams: and I have known. *Fr.* The Tower of the Dream. Harpur.
Youth Dreams, The. Rilke.

Dress. *See* **Clothing.**

Driftwood
Driftwood. Wilbur.
Fires of Driftwood. MacKay.

Drinking
Absinthe-Drinker, The. Symons.
Alcibiades to a Jealous Girl. Ficke.
Alcohol. MacNeice.
Anacreontic on Drinking. Cowley.
Bacchus on Beverages. Redi.
Back and Side Go Bare, Go Bare. *Fr.* Gammar Gurton's Needle. *At. to* William Stevenson.
Ballad of the Drinker in His Pub. Van Wyk Louw.
Bar, The. *Unknown.*
Bee quick my boyes drinke off your wine. *Unknown.*
Beer. Arnold.
Beer. Calverley.
Blood thirsty care goe packe. *Unknown.*
Brewer's Coachman, The. Taylor.
Captain Stratton's Fancy. Masefield.
Careless Gallant, The. Jordan.
Come, Thou Monarch. *Fr.* Anthony and Cleopatra. Shakespeare.
Company One Keeps, The. Dickson.
Cruiskeen Lawn, The. *Unknown.*
Cup, The. Oldham.
Drink Today, and Drown All Sorrow. *Fr.* The Bloody Brother. Fletcher, *and others.*
Drink with Something in It, A. Nash.
Drinker. Anderson.
Drinking. Cowley.
Drinking. Hsin Ch'i-chi.
Drinking Alone in the Moonlight. Li Po.
Drinking Bout, A, Liu Chia.
Drinking-Song, A. Carey.
Drinking Song. *Fr.* Gammer Gurton's Needle. *At. to* Stevenson *and* Still.
Drinking Song. *Unknown.*
Drinking Song, A, against All Sorts of Disputes in Drinking. Wycherley.
Drinking Song for Present-Day Gatherings. Bishop.
Drunkards, The. Lowry.
Empty Jar, The. Stenhouse.
Epicure, The ("Fill the bowl"). Cowley.
Epigram: "He is not drunk who, from the floor." Field.
Fill fill the bowele the lusty wyne will dye. *Unknown.*
Fill the Bowl, Butler! *Unknown.*
Five Reasons for Drinking, The. Aldrich.
Food and Drink. Untermeyer.
Friend Advises Me to Stop Drinking, A. Mei Yao Ch'en.
Glass of Beer, A. Stephens.
His Fare-well to Sack. Herrick.
If thou doest not love sacke. *Unknown.*
John Barleycorn. Burns.
Let the Toast Pass. Sheridan.
Lips That Touch Liquor. Young.
Lips That Touch Liquor Shall Never Touch Mine. Glazebrook.
Liquor and Longevity. *Unknown.*
Little Brown Jug. *Unknown.*
Little Vagabond, The. Blake.
Logical Vegetarian, The. Chesterton.
Lord Alcohol. Beddoes.
McSorley's Bar. Denney.
Miniver Cheevy. Robinson.
Mint Julep, The. Hoffman.
Mistaken Resolve, The. Martial.
Notes from an Ohio Tavern. Lyne.
Of Drunkenness. Turberville.
Old Keg of Rum, The. *Unknown.*
On Going to a Tavern. Wang Chi.
O'Tuomy's Drinking Song. O'Tuomy.
Pox on pelfe why should we love it. *Unknown.*
Price of a Drink. Pollard.
Quebec Liquor Commission Store. Klein.
Reasons for Drinking. Aldrich.
R-e-m-o-r-s-e. Ade.
Said the Whisky Flask. *Unknown.*
Sir John Barleycorn. *Unknown.*
Some love Marce and some love Venus. *Unknown.*
Song: "Let schoolmasters puzzle their brains." *Fr.* She Stoops to Conquer. Goldsmith.
Song: "Who tames the lion now?" Beddoes.
Stein Song, A. Hovey.
Stirrup-Cup, A. Ainslie.
Stirrup-Cup, The. Hay.
Stirrup Cup, The. Kilmer.
Stirrup-Cup, The. Lanier.
Stirrup Cup, The. Percy.
Swell Me a Bowl. *Fr.* The Poetaster. Jonson.
Temperate Drinking. Anacreon.
To His Cup Bearer. Catullus.
Two Drinking Songs. Alcaeus.
Upon Drinking in a Bowl. Earl of Rochester.
Villon's Straight Tip to All Cross Coves. Henley.
Wassell wassell wassell wassell. *Unknown.*
Welcome to Sack, The. Herrick.
Whisky, Drink Divine. O'Leary.
Whisky Song, A. *Unknown.*
Why, Liquor of Life? Carolan.
Willie Brewed a Peck o' Maut. Burns.
Wine and Water. Chesterton.
See also **Drunkards.**

Dromedaries. *see* **Camels.**

Drought
Drought. Laight.
Drought. Ogilvie.
Drouth. Austin.
Dry Time. Davis.
Dust Bowl. Davis.
Said Hanrahan. Hartigan.
Soliloquy. Laight.
Sky is a blue, coiled serpent, The. *Fr.* Drought. Slater.
Sun Drops Red, The. Miller.

Drowning
Drowned Sailor. Shaw.
Drowned Wife, The. Horan.
Drowning is not so pitiful. Dickinson.
Elegy on Gordon Barber. Derwood.
Full fathom five thy father lies. *Fr.* The Tempest. Shakespeare.
Ezra Shank. *Unknown.*
How the waters closed above him. Dickinson.
Lifeguard, The. Dickey.
Not Waving but Drowning. Smith.
On the Memory of Mr. Edward King, Drown'd in the Irish Seas. Cleveland.
Silly Willy. "R. L. B."
Water Island. Moss.

Drug Addiction
Addict, The. Rubin.
Addict, The. Sexton.
Cocteau's *Opium:* 1. Finkel.
Drug Addict, The. *Fr.* Three Prison Portraits. Waddington.
Honey, Take a Whiff on Me. *Unknown.*
Pudgy. Lima.
She Tasted Death. Giorno.
Solo for Bent Spoon. Finkel.
Success. Empson.
White Powder! Cruz.

Drug Stores
Drug Store. Shapiro.

Drug *(continued)*
Drug Store. Weaver.
Les Réalités. Guest.
Druids
Trepidation of the Druids. *Fr.* Ecclesiastical Sonnets. Wordsworth.
Drums
African Dance. Hughes.
Drum, The. Farrar.
Drum, The. Scott.
Piano and Drums. Okara.
Talking Drums, The. Kyei.
Drunkards
Anacreontick. Cotton.
But by this time Tongues 'gan to rest. *Fr.* Bacchanalia: or, A Description of a Drunken Club. Darby.
Closing Time. Michie.
Drunk in the Furnace, The. Merwin.
Drunkard, The. Levine.
Drunkard, The. Proverbs, Bible, *O.T.*
Drunkard to His Bottle, A. Le Fanu.
Drunkard's Doom, The. *Unknown.*
Drunken Man on Highgate Hill, A. Hasluck.
Face upon the Floor, The. D'Arcy.
Hemmed-in Males. Williams.
I'll Never Get Drunk Any More. *Unknown.*
Interview with Doctor Drink. Cunningham.
My Papa's Waltz. Roethke.
On an Imaginary Journey to the Continent. Porson.
Resentments Composed Because of the Clamor of Town Topers outside My Apartment. Knight.
Third Avenue in Sunlight. Hecht.
Two Hangovers. Wright.
Willie's and Nellie's Wish. Moore.
Drury, Sir William
Epitaph upon the Death of Sir William Drury, An. Rich.
Drury Lane Theatre, London
Prologue Spoken by Mr. Garrick at the Opening of the Theatre Royal, 1747. Johnson.
Dryden, John
Progress of Poesy, The. Gray.
Dublin, Ireland
Arrival: The Capital. O'Grady.
Back to Dublin. Ford.
Dublin. MacNeice.
Dublin Made Me. MacDonagh.
Magazine Fort, Phoenix Park, Dublin. Wilkins.
Dubois, William Edward Burghardt
Booker T. and W. E. B. Randall.
For William Edward Burghardt Dubois on His Eightieth Birthday. Latimer.
On the Death of William Edward Burghardt DuBois by African Moonlight and Forgotten Stars. Rivers.
Ducks
Blue Duck, The. Sarett.
Dame Duck's First Lecture on Education. Hawkshaw.
Duck, The. King.
Duck, The. Nash.
Duck-Chasing. Kinnell.
Duck in Central Park. Savage.
Ducks. Ault.
Ducks. Bly.
Ducks. Daniells.
Ducks. Harvey.
Ducks, The. Wilkins.
Ducks at Dawn. Tippett.
Duck's Ditty. *Fr.* The Wind in the Willows. Grahame.
Four Ducks on a Pond. Allingham.
Little Duck, The. Joso.
Nearing Winter. Saunders.
New Duckling, The. Noyes.
Prayer of the Little Ducks Who Went into the Ark, The. Gasztold.
Quack! De la Mare.
Regent's Park. Fyleman.
Sing-Song Rhyme. *Unknown.*
Sonnet: The Wild Duck's Nest. Wordsworth.
Trueblue Gentleman, A. Patchen.
Wilk Duck, The. Masefield.
Duddon River, England
River Duddon, The, *sels.* Wordsworth.
To the River Duddon. Nicholson.
Dulles, John Foster
Just Dropped In. Cole.
Dumas, Alexandre
Lines Written at the Grave of Alexandre Dumas. Bennett.
Dunbar, Paul Laurence
Dunbar. Spencer.
For Paul Laurence Dunbar. Cullen.
Paul Laurence Dunbar. Corrothers.
Duncan, Isadora
Photograph of Isadora Duncan, A. Hayden.
Sergey Yesenin Speaking Isadora Duncan. Knott.
Dundee, John Graham of Claverhouse, 1st Viscount (Bonnie Dundee)
Bonnie Dundee. *Fr.* The Doom of Devergoil. Scott.
Upon the Death of the Earl of Dundee. Dryden.
Dunedin, New Zealand
Dunedin in the Gloaming. Mackay.
Dunes
On the Dunes. Teasdale.
Sand Dunes and Sea. Moreland.
Dunkirk, France
Dunkirk. Nathan.
Dunkirk. Pratt.
Little Boats of Britain, The. Carsley.
Duns Scotus, John
Duns Scotus. Merton.
Duns Scotus's Oxford. Hopkins.
Dunwich, England
At Dunwich. Thwaite.
Dupree, Frank
Dupree. *Unknown.*
Duquesne, Fort
Fort Duquesne. Plimpton.
Dürer, Albrecht
On Dürer's "Melencolia." Watson.
Steeple-Jack, The. Moore.
Duse, Eleanora
Eleanora Duse of Magda. Binyon.
Dusk. *See* **Twilight.**
Dust
Dust. Russell.
In Praise of Dust. Field.
Praise of Dust, The. Chesterton.
Dutch Wars
Last Instructions to a Painter *sels.* Marvell.
Song: "To all you ladies now at land." Sackville.
Duty
Duty. Emerson.
Duty. Hooper.
Duty. Markham.
Duty—That's to Say Complying. Clough.
Kind of an Ode to Duty. Nash.
Ode to Duty. Wordsworth.
Reward of Service. *Fr.* A Drama of Exile. *At.* to E. B. Browning.
So nigh is grandeur to man. Cook.
Stopping by Woods on a Snowy Evening. Frost.
Voluntaries. Emerson.
Dyer, Sir William
Epitaph on the Monument of Sir William Dyer at Colmworth, 1641. Lady Dyer.

E

Eagles
Dalliance of the Eagles, The. Whitman.
Dead Eagle, The. Campbell.
Dying Eagle, The. Pratt.
Eagle, The. Tennyson.
Eagle, The. Young.
Eagle and the Mole, The. Wylie.
Eagle Plain. Francis.
Eagle's Nature, The. *Fr.* The Bestiary. *Unknown.*
Eagle's Song, The. Austin.
Painting of an Eagle, The. Tu Fu.
Salmon Drowns Eagle. Lowry.
Sea and the Eagle, The. Clouts.
White Eagle, The. McDonald.

Ears
Ears, The. *Fr.* The Limeratomy. Euwer.
On Wearing Ears. Harris.
Earth
Book of the World, The. Drummond of Hawthornden.
Earth. Bryant.
Earth, The. Emerson.
Earth, The. Mann.
Earth. Roscoe.
Earth, The. Very.
Earth. Wheelock.
Earth and Sky. Euripides.
Earth Breath, The. "Æ."
Earth in Spring, The. Halevi.
Earth Listens. Bates.
Eye, The. Jeffers.
False World, Thou Ly'st. *Fr.* Emblems. Quarles.
First Morning of the Second World, The. Schwartz.
Golden Elegy, The. Staff.
Hamatreya. Emerson.
Hymn of the Earth. Channing.
Hymn to Earth. Wylie.
Hymn to Earth the Mother of All. *Unknown.*
I Saw God Wash the World. Stidger.
In the Immense Cathedral. *Fr.* The Holy Earth. Wheelock.
Last Man, The. Campbell.
Mother Earth. Monroe.
Notable Description of the World, A. *At. to* Smith.
O Earth, Sufficing All Our Needs. Roberts.
O Earth, Turn. Johnston.
O Sweet Spontaneous Earth. Cummings.
Praise of Earth. E. B. Browning.
Salutation, The. Traherne.
To an Old Lady. Empson.
Wonder. Traherne.
Wonderful World, The. Rands.
Word, The. Realf.
World, The. Drummond of Hawthornden.
World, The. Herbert.
World, The. *Fr.* Symbolisms. Realf.
World, The. Vaughan.
World, The. *Unknown.*
World a Hunt. Drummond of Hawthornden.
World, The; a Ghazel. Mangan.
World in Making, The. Parker.
World Music. Bushnell.
Earthquakes
Earth Tremor in Lugano. Kirkup.
Earthquake. Kirkup.
East Wind
East Wind, The. Lodge.
Easter
African Easter. Nicol.
All Dressed Up for Easter. Fisher.
Alleluia! Alleluia! Let the Holy Anthem Rise. *Unknown.*
Assurance. Crowell.
Assurance. Munson.
At Easter Time. Richards.
Blessing and Honor. Bonar.
Calvary and Easter. "Coolidge."
Christ Has Risen. "Coolidge."
Cross and the Tomb, The. Flint.
Dawn. Crouse.
Day of Resurrection, The. St. John of Damascus.
Down a Sunny Easter Meadow. Turner.
Drizzling Easter Morning, A. Hardy.
Early, Early Easter Day. Fisher.
Easter. Coatsworth.
Easter. Conkling.
Easter. Davies.
Easter. Gilder.
Easter ("I got me flowers"). Herbert.
Easter ("Rise heart, thy Lord is risen"). Herbert.
Easter. Kilmer.
Easter. Oxenham.
Easter. Sabin.
Easter. Tynan.
Easter. *Unknown.*
Easter. Van Brakle.
Easter. Whitaker.
Easter Canticle, An: "In every trembling bud and bloom." Towne.
Easter Carol, An: "Flash forth, thou sun." C. G. Rossetti.
Easter Carol: "O Earth, throughout thy borders." Lovejoy.
Easter Carol, An: "Spring bursts to-day." C. G. Rossetti.
Easter Chorus: "Christ is arisen." *Fr.* Faust. Goethe.
Easter Communion. Hopkins.
Easter Day. Clough.
Easter Day. Crashaw.
Easter Day. Jasper Heywood.
Easter Day. C. G. Rossetti.
Easter-Day. Vaughan.
Easter Day; Naples, 1849. Clough.
Easter, Day of Christ Eternal. Moore.
Easter Eve, 1945. Rukeyser.
Easter Gloves. *Unknown.*
Easter Hymn. Housman.
Easter Hymn. St. John of Damascus.
Easter Hymn. Thwaites.
Easter Hymn. Vaughan.
Easter Hymn. Wesley.
Easter in the Woods. F. Frost.
Easter Joy. Price.
Easter Joy. Turner.
Easter Light. Munson.
Easter Message. Van Brakle.
Easter Monday. Barnes.
Easter Morn. *Fr.* Christ's Victory and Triumph. Fletcher.
Easter Morning. Brooks.
Easter Morning. Garrison.
Easter Music. Deland.
Easter Night. Meynell.
Easter, 1923. Neihardt.
Easter Poem. Prichard.
Easter Poem. Raine.
Easter Praise. Bennett.
Easter Prayer, An. Towne.
Easter Sacraments. Schauffler.
Easter Snowfall. Behn.
Easter Song. Alishan.
Easter Song. "Coolidge."
Easter Song. Lathbury.
Easter Song. Leslie.
Easter Thought. Cox.
Easter Week. Kingsley.
Easter Wings. Herbert.
Easter Zunday. Barnes.
Eastertide. *Fr.* The Sacred Seasons. Bode.
Follow Me. Longfellow.
For Easter. Havergal.
For Our Sakes. Wilde.
From Bethlehem to Calvary. Nicholson.
Good Friday in My Heart. M. E. Coleridge.
Harrowing of Hell, The. *Fr.* The Vision of Piers Plowman. Langland.
He Is Risen. Flint.
He Lives! He Lives to Bless! Stroud.
His Last Week. Lennen.
His Life Is Ours. Stroud.
Hymn of the Resurrection, A. Dunbar.
If a Man Die, Shall He Live Again? Moreland.
If Easter Be Not True. Barstow.
If Easter Eggs Would Hatch. Malloch.
Jesus Lives and So Shall I. Gellert.
Lacking my love, I go from place to place. *Fr.* Amoretti. Spenser.
Legend of the Easter Eggs, The. O'Brien.
Lent Lily, The. Housman.
Mary. Sangster.
Meeting the Easter Bunny. Bennett.
Most glorious Lord of life, that on this day. *Fr.* Amoretti. Spenser.
My Risen Lord. *Unknown.*
Nature's Easter Music. Larcom.
Not There. *Unknown.*
O Bells in the Steeple. Smith.
Of the Resurrection of Christ. Dunbar.
On Easter Day. Thaxter.
On Easter Morning. Rexford.
Poem for Easter. Lee.

Easter *(continued)*
Rest Remaineth. *Fr.* Christmas-Eve and Easter-Day. R. Browning.
Resurrection, The. Brooks.
Resurrection. Munson.
Resurrection Hymn. Weiss.
Sepulcher, The. Flint.
Seven Stanzas at Easter. Updike.
Softly through the Mellow Starlight. *Unknown.*
Some Things That Easter Brings. Parrish.
Song of Easter. Thaxter.
Sonnet at Easter. Nemerov.
That Nature Is a Heraclitean Fire and of the Comfort of the Resurrection. Hopkins.
They Saw and Believed. Hagg.
Third Day, The. Pierce.
This Easter Day. Nicholson.
To Pius X at Easter. Wildman.
Upon an Easter Morning. Farjeon.
What Does Easter Mean to You? Conrad.
Words for a Resurrection. Kennedy.
Sourcebook of Poetry (SoP). Al Bryant, comp.
Easter Island
Easter Island. Scott.
Eatherly, Claude R.
Song about Major Eatherly, A. Wain.
Eating. *See* **Food.**
Echo (nymph)
Narcissus. Campbell.
Sad Nymph, Gaho, followed to the shadie woods, The. *Unknown.*
Sweet Echo. *Fr.* Comus. Milton.
Echoes
Bugle Song, The. *Fr.* The Princess. Tennyson.
Echo. De la Mare.
Echo. Grey.
Echo. Moore.
Echo. Saxe.
Echo. *Fr.* Arcadia. Sidney.
Echo. *Unknown.*
Ecology
All the Smoke. Siegel.
Axe in the Wood, The. Dyment.
Baby Ten Months Old Looks at the Public Domain, A. Stafford.
Binsey Poplars. Hopkins.
Fate of the Elms, The. Francis.
Flower-Fed Buffaloes, The. Lindsay.
Habitat. Anderson.
Hermit, The. Silcock.
Indian at the Burial-Place of His Fathers, An. Bryant.
Invention of New Jersey. Anderson.
Little Things. Stephens.
Mouth of the Hudson, The. R. Lowell.
Mystic River. Ciardi.
Poisoned Lands. Montague.
Report on the Planet, Earth. Oppenheim.
Rural Dumpheap. Cane.
Science. Jeffers.
Sonic Boom. Updike.
Strip Mining Pit. Gillespie.
Swan Song. Ranchan.
War Against the Trees, The. Kunitz.
Windscale. Nicholson.
Woodman, Spare That Tree. Morris.
Eden, William
Rondeau Humbly Inscribed to the Right Hon. William Eden Minister Plenipotentiary of Commercial Affairs at the Court of Versailles. *At. to* Ellis.
Eden River, England
By the River Eden. Raine.
Edinburgh, Scotland
Auld Reikie. Fergusson.
Edinburgh. Guiterman.
Edinburgh. Noyes.
Written in Edinburgh. Hallam.
Edison, Thomas Alva
And Yet Fools Say. Holmes.
Edison. Jeffers.
Modern Columbus, A. Wilson.
Progress. Belfrage.
Education
Elementary School Classroom in a Slum, An. Spender.
Modern Ode to the Modern School. Erskine.
Pains of Education, The. Churchill..
Tables Turned, The. Wordsworth.
Trusty Learning A, B, C. Follen.
See also **Teaching and Teachers; Scholars and Scholarshhip.**
Edward I, King of England
Bard, The. Gray.
Death of King Edward I, The. *Unknown.*
Edward II, King of England
Mortimeriados, *sels.* Drayton.
Edward IV, King of England
King Edward the Fourth and a Tanner of Tamworth. *Unknown.*
On the Death of the Noble Prince King Edward the Fourth. Skelton.
Edward VII, King of England
Death of King Edward VII, The. *Unknown.*
Elegy on Albert Edward the Peacemaker. *Unknown.*
New Song on the Birth of the Prince of Wales, A. *Unknown.*
Edward the Confessor
Edward the Confessor. *Unknown.*
Edwards, Jonathan
Becalmed in old Back Bay's dead water sulk. *Fr.* Poems from a First Year in Boston. Starbuck.
Jonathan Edwards in Western Massachusetts. R. Lowell.
Mr. Edwards and the Spider. R. Lowell.
Theology of Jonathan Edwards, The. McGinley.
Edwards, Richard
Of Edwards of the Chapel. Googe.
Eels
Bucket of Sea-Serpents. Ant.
Eel, The. Nash.
Egerton, Thomas. *See* **Ellesmere, Thomas Egerton, Baron.**
Eggs
First Lesson. Willard.
Inefficacious Egg, The. Bishop.
Egrets
Egrets. Wright.
Two Egrets. Ciardi.
Egypt
De Rosis Hibernis. Gosse.
Egypt. Doolittle.
Egypt. Ghose.
Egypt's Might Is Tumbled Down. M. E. Coleridge.
Herodotus in Egypt. Lang.
Einstein, Albert
Einstein. MacLeish.
Gift to Be Simple, The. Moss.
Eisenhower, Dwight D.
Eisenhower's Visit to Franco, 1959. Wright.
Inauguration Day: January 1953. R. Lowell.
Tentative Description of a Dinner to Promote the Impeachment of President Eisenhower. Ferlinghetti.
El Greco. *See* **Greco, El (Domenicos Theotocopoulos).**
Elands
Seele in Raum. Jarrell.
Eleanor of Aquitaine
Queen Eleanor's Confession. *Unknown.*
Rose of the World, The. Masefield.
Elephants
Blind Men and the Elephant, The. Saxe.
Circus Elephant. Worth.
Cradle Song of the Elephants. Valle.
Death of an Elephant. Warr.
Dignity. Bhartrihari.
Elephant, The. Asquith.
Elephant, The. Belloc.
Elephant. Brettell.
Elephant, The. *Fr.* A Circus Garland. Field.
Elephant, An. Francis.
Elephant. McFadden.
Elephant! Scherman.
Elephant. *Unknown.*
Elephant I, The. *Unknown.*
Elephant, The. Wynne.
Elephant Is Slow to Mate, The. Lawrence.
Elephant, or the Force of Habit, The. Housman.
Elephants. Moore.
Elephants Are Different to Different People. Sandburg.
Elephant's Trunk. Wilkins.

Eletelephony. Richards.
Erin (Elephant). *Unknown.*
Holding Hands. Link.
Indian Elephant, The. Kaberry.
Melancthon. Moore.
Pete at the Zoo. Brooks.
To a Dead Elephant. Livingstone.
Elgar, Edward
Edward Elgar. Day Lewis.
Elgin Marbles
On Seeing the Elgin Marbles. Keats.
Elijah
Angel, The. Hayes.
"Eliot, George" (Mary Ann Evans Cross)
On the Deaths of Thomas Carlyle and George Eliot. Swinburne.
Eliot, Thomas Sterns
Chard Whitlow. Reed.
Expatriates, The. *Fr.* A Critical Fable. A. Lowell.
For T. S. E. Only. Plutzik.
Mr. Eliot's Day. Francis.
T. S. Eliot. Whitbread.
To T. S. Eliot on His Sixtieth Birthday. Auden.
Verses for the 60th Birthday of T. S. Eliot. Barker.
Elizabeth, Queen of Bohemia
On His Mistress, the Queen of Bohemia. Wotton.
Elizabeth I, Queen of England
Ad Reginam Elizabetham ("Live long, Elisa, that the wolf of Spain"). Bastard.
Ad Reginam Elizabetham ("Mother of England, and sweet nurse of all"). Bastard.
Author to Queen Elizabeth, in Praise of Her Reading, The. Harington.
Ballad to Queen Elizabeth, A. Dobson.
Dedication: "To that clear majesty which in the north." *Fr.* Nosce Teipsum. Davies.
Elizabeth. Saul.
Fair Oriana in the Morn. Milton.
Hard by a Crystal Fountain. *Unknown.*
Hymns of Astraea, *sels.* Davies.
Looking-Glass, The. Kipling.
Queen Elizabeth at Tilbury. Deloney.
Queen Elizabeth Tudor, as a Girl, on Trial for Heresy. *Unknown.*
Silent Lover, The. Ralegh.
Songe betwene the Quenes Majestie and Englande, A. Birche.
Sorrowful Verses Made on the Death of Our Most Sovereign Lady Queen Elizabeth My Gracious Mistress. Churchyard.
To My Most Gracious Dread Sovereign. *Fr.* Nosce Teipsum. Davies.
To Queen Elizabeth. Ralegh.
With Fragrant Flowers We Strew the Way. Watson.
Elizabeth, Queen Consort of Henry VII
Rueful Lamentation on the Death of Queen Elizabeth, A. More.
Elizabeth, Saint
Plain Chant of the Hill Country. Sister Mary David.
Ellesmere, Thomas Egerton, Baron
To Sir Thomas Egerton. Daniel.
To Thomas Lord Chancellor. Jonson.
Ellsworth, Elmer Ephraim
Colonel Ellsworth. Stoddard.
Ellsworth. *Unknown.*
Elm Trees
Connecticut Elm, The. Swan.
Dilemma of the Elm. Taggard.
Elm, The. Shepard.
Fate of Elms, The. Francis.
Elves *See* **Fairies.**
Ely, City of, England
Monks of Ely, The. *Unknown.*
Emancipation Proclamation (1863)
Fifty Years, 1863-1913. Johnson.
Laus Deo! Whittier.
No Slave beneath the Flag. Taylor.
Proclamation, The. Whittier.
Slav'ry Chain. *Unknown.*
Emerson, Ralph Waldo
Carlyle and Emerson. Schuyler.
Emerson. Alcott.
Emerson. Dodge.
Emerson. *Fr.* A Fable for Critics. J. R. Lowell.
Emerson: Last Days at Concord. Gregory.
Emmet, Robert
Bold Robert Emmet. Maguire.
Oh! Breathe Not His Name. Moore.
On the Speech of Robert Emmet. Southey.
She Is Far from the Land. Moore.
Empire State Building, New York City
Looking at the Empire State Building. Pomeroy.
Empson, William
Just a Fishing Smack at Empson. Barker.
Emus
Emus. Fullerton.
Enda, Saint
St. Enda. Lerner.
Endecott, John
John Endicott. Longfellow.
Endymion
Endimion and Phoebe, *sels.* Drayton.
Endymion, *sels.* Keats.
Endymion. Longfellow.
Oh, Sleep Forever in the Latmian Cave. Millay.
Song by Fairies. *Fr.* Endymion. Lyly.
Engineers
Engineers. Garthwaite.
England
Airman Who Flew over Shakespeare's England, The. Plutzik.
Albion's England, *sels.* Warner.
America. Dobell.
American in England, An. Wylie.
Ancient Music. Pound.
And Did Those Feet in Ancient Time. *Fr.* Milton. Blake.
August, 1914. Masefield.
Australia to England. *Fr.* Sonnets of the Empire. Strong.
Battle of Maldon, The. *Unknown.*
Channel Crossing. Barker.
Chant of Hate against England, A. Lissauer.
Coastwise Lights, The. Kipling.
Colonist in His Garden, A. Reeves.
Come to Britain; a Humble Contribution to the Movement. Herbert.
Composed by the Sea-Side, Near Calais. Wordsworth.
"De Gustibus." R. Browning.
Distant View of England from the Sea. Bowles.
Dying Patriot, The. Flecker.
Elegy in a Country Churchyard. Chesterton.
England. *Fr.* The Task. Cowper.
England. Day.
England. Massey.
England. Montgomery.
England. Moore.
England. Cardinal Newman.
England. *Unknown.*
England; an Ode. Swinburne.
England and America in 1782. Tennyson.
England and Switzerland, 1802. Wordsworth.
England, Arise! Carpenter.
England in 1819. Shelley.
England, My England. Henley.
England My Mother. Watson.
England! once Europs envye now her scorne. *Unknown.*
England! the time is come when thou shouldst wean. Wordsworth.
English Fog, The. *Fr.* The Fleece. Dyer.
English Garden, The, *sel.* Mason.
English Weather. *Fr.* The Fleece. Dyer.
Evening in England, An. Ledwidge.
Exile. Maynard.
Fair England. Cone.
Fears in Solitude. Coleridge.
For England. Burns.
Gates to England, The. Wilson.
Going towards Spain. Googe.
Green Fields of England! *Fr.* Songs in Absence. Clough.
Grongar Hill. Dyer.
Hands All Round. Tennyson.
Happy Is England. Keats.
Home Thoughts. Glover.
Home Thoughts from Abroad. R. Browning.
Home Thoughts, from the Sea. R. Browning.
Home Thoughts in Laventie. Tennant.

England *(continued)*
Home Truths from Abroad. *Unknown.*
Homes of England, The. Hemans.
How Sleep the Brave. De la Mare.
I Have Loved England. *Fr.* The White Cliffs. Miller.
I Traveled among Unknown Men. *Fr.* Lucy. Wordsworth.
I was five when we moved to England. *Fr.* For England in Grateful Appreciation. Vogt.
International Hymn. Huntington.
Island, The. Morley.
Jerusalem. Blake.
Landscape with Figures. Fairburn.
Last Buccaneer, The. Kingsley.
Letter from Italy, A. Addison.
Letty's Globe. Turner.
London, 1802. Wordsworth.
Look for Me on England. Mallalieu.
Look, Stranger, on This Island Now. Auden.
Love Thou Thy Land with Love Far-brought. Tennyson.
Mask of Anarchy, The. Shelley.
Merry Green Fields of England. *Unknown.*
Mother England. Thomas.
No! Hood.
O England, Country of My Heart's Desire. Lucas.
Oh, to be in England. R. Browning.
Ode Written in the Beginning of the Year 1746. Collins.
Of England and of Its Marvels. Uberti.
Old Vicarage, Grantchester, The. Brooke.
Old Chartist, The. Meredith.
On Wenlock Edge. Housman.
O'Reilly's Reply. Weber.
Pennines in April. Hughes.
Polyolbion, *sels.* Drayton.
Puck's Song. *Fr.* Puck of Pook's Hill. Kipling.
Ready, Ay, Ready. Merivale.
Return, The. Silkin.
Rolling English Road, The. Chesterton.
Ruins of a Great House. Walcott.
Rule, Britannia. Thomson.
Soldier, The. *Fr.* 1914. Brooke.
Song: "Old England is eaten by knaves." *Fr.* The Emigrant. McLachlan.
Song of the Bow, the. *Fr.* The White Company. Doyle.
Song to the Men of England. Shelley.
Sonnet: England in 1819. Shelley.
Sonnet: On a Distant View of England. Bowles.
South Country, The. Belloc.
Spring in England. Going.
Third of February, 1852, The. Tennyson.
This England. *Fr.* King Richard II. Shakespeare.
This Is England. Binyon.
This Landscape, These People. Ghose.
Thought of a Briton on the Subjugation of Switzerland. Wordsworth.
To a River in the South. Newbolt.
To England. Boker.
To England. Moore.
To the English Martyrs. Thompson.
Town Clerk's Views, The. Betjeman.
Truth's Complaint over England. Lodge.
Upon Eckington Bridge, River Avon. Quiller-Couch.
Whack Fol the Diddle. Kearney.
What Constitutes a State? *Fr.* An Ode in Imitation of Alcaeus. Jones.
You Ask Me, Why, though Ill at Ease. Tennyson.
England, Church of
Bristol and Clifton. Betjeman.
British Church, The. Herbert.
Churches of Rome and of England, The. *Fr.* The Hind and the Panther. Dryden.
Hippopotamus, The. Eliot.
I hold as faith. *Unknown.*
English, The
British, The. Tessimond.
British Journalist, The. Wolfe.
Britons and Guests. Thomas.
Dear Old Village, The. Betjeman.
Dunkirk. Nathan.
England and America in 1782. Tennyson.
England, Unprepared for War. *Fr.* An Ode to the Country Gentleman of England. Akenside.
England's Heart. Topper.
English Are Frosty, The. *Fr.* The White Cliffs. Miller.
Englishman, The. Cook.
For the Rain It Raineth Every Day. Graves.
Gloriana's England. *Fr.* Sonnets of the Empire. Strong.
It Is Not to Be Thought of. Wordsworth.
Mad Dogs and Englishmen. Coward.
Men of England. Campbell.
North Coast Recollections. Betjeman.
Private of the Buffs, A. Doyle.
Secret People, The. Chesterton.
To America. Austin.
Tragic Guilt. Rhys.
True-born Englishmen, The, *sels.* Defoe.
Vitaï Lampada. Newbolt.
Who Calls the English Cold? *Fr.* London Sonnets. Bode.
Why Should I Care for the Men of Thames? Blake.
World Is a Bundle of Hay, The. Byron.
English Channel
Channel Crossing. Barker.
Channel Passage, A. Brooke.
Outlanders, The. Glaze.
English Language. *See* **Language.**
Epicureans
Epicure, The. Cowley.
Epicurus
Garden of Epicurus, The. Meredith.
Epigram
Epigram: "What Is an Epigram? Coleridge.
Epiphany. *See* **Twelfth Night.**
Epping Forest, England
Epping Forest. *Fr.* November. Davidson.
Erceldoune, Thomas of. *See* Thomas the Rhymer.
Erie (Lake)
Autumn Squall—Lake Erie. Russo.
Great Lakes Suite, The. Reaney.
Erie, Lake, Battle of
Battle of Erie, The. *Unknown.*
James Bird. *Unknown.*
Perry's Victory. *Unknown.*
Perry's Victory on Lake Erie. Percival.
Erie Canal
Erie, The ("We were forty miles from Albany"). *Unknown.*
Erie Canal, The ("I've got a mule, her name is Sal"). Allen.
Erie Canal ("It was a long, long trip on the Erie"). *Unknown.*
Erie Canal Ballad, The. *Unknown.*
Trip on the Erie, A. *Unknown.*
Erne (river), Ireland
Winding Banks of Erne, The; or, The Emigrant's Adieu to Ballyshannon. Allingham.
Eros. *See* **Cupid.**
Erskine, John
Lament of the Master of Erskine. Scott.
Escalators
E is the Escalator. *Fr.* All Around the Town. McGinley.
Eskimo
Eskimo Baby, An. Diamond.
Eskimo Chant. *Unknown.*
For an Eskimo. Dalton.
Immoral Artic, The. Bishop.
Kayak, The. *Unknown.*
Manerathiak's Song. *Unknown.*
Wind Has Wings, The. *Unknown.*
Essex, Robert Devereux, 2d Earl of
Lementable New Ballad upon the Earls of Essex Death, A. *Unknown.*
Essex, England
Map of the Western Part of the County of Essex in England, A. Levertov.
Esther (Bible)
"I, if I perish, perish"—Esther spake. *Fr.* Monna Innominata. C. G. Rossetti.
Eternity
Face of the Waters, The. Fitzgerald.
Frozen City, The. Nemerov.
I Saw Eternity. Bogan.
Invite to Eternity, An. Clare.
Waters. Slessor.
World, The. Vaughan.
Ethiopia
Ode to Ethiopia. Dunbar.

On the Baptized Ethiopian. Crashaw.
Star of Ethiopia. Watkins.
Etiquette
Etiquette. Gilbert.
Little Gentleman, The. *Unknown.*
Politeness. Turner.
Visitor, The. Pyle.
Eton College
Founder's Day. Bridges.
Ode on a Distant Prospect of Eton College. Gray.
Etruscan Civilization
Etruscan Tombs. Robinson.
Etruscan Warrior's Head. Henze.
Eucharist
Bread of Life, The. Lathbury.
Canticle to the Christ in the Holy Eucharist, A. Antoninus.
Dressing. Vaughan.
Eucharist. Root.
H. Communion, The. Herbert.
O Salutaris Hostia. *Unknown.*
Of the Holy Eucharist. *Unknown.*
On the Sacrament. Rowe.
Receiving Communion. Miller.
Sacrament, The. Donne.
Sacrament. Harsen.
Sacrament of the Altar, The. *Unknown.*
"This Do in Remembrance of Me." *Unknown.*
To the Blessed Sacrament. Constable.
Euclid
Euclid. Lindsay.
Euclid Alone Has Looked on Beauty Bare. Millay.
Euripides
Euripides. *Unknown.*
Europa
Europa. Cory.
Europe
Channel Crossing. Barker.
Europe. Whitman.
Home Thoughts. Butler.
Of Commerce and Society. Hill.
To Cole, the Painter, Departing for Europe. Bryant.
To Walt Whitman in America. Swinburne.
Zone. Apollinaire.
Europeans
Some Europeans. *Unknown.*
Eurydice
Eurydice. Bourdillon.
Eurydice to Orpheus. R. Browning.
Orpheus' Dream. Muir.
Orpheus, O Orpheus, gently touch thy Lesbyan lyre. *Unknown.*
Thus sang Orpheus to his strings. *Unknown.*
Eurydice (ship)
Last of the *Eurydice,* The. Paton.
Loss of the *Eurydice,* The. Hopkins.
Eurynome (goddess)
Eurynome. MacPherson.
Eutaw Springs, South Carolina
Battle of Eutaw. Simms.
To the Memory of the Brave Americans. Freneau.
Eve
Adam and Eve. Bible, *O.T.*
Adam and Eve. Manger.
Adam and Eve. Shapiro.
Age of Innocence. Hough.
Begetting of Cain, The. Plutzik.
Circle, A. Spencer.
Eve. Gascoyne.
Eve. Hodgson.
Eve. C. G. Rossetti.
Eve in Reflection. Macpherson.
Eve's Lament. *Unknown.*
Imperial Adam. Hope.
Jealous Adam. Manger.
Lady's Maid's Song, The. Hollander.
Legend of the Dove, A. Sterling.
Reflection, A. Hood.
She. Wilbur.
229. Villa.
Evening
After Sunset. Conkling.
And Suddenly It's Evening. Quasimodo.
As Day Begins to Wane. Coleman.
Autumn Evening. Tyutchev.
Autumnal Evening, An. "Macleod."
Child's Evening Prayer, A. Coleridge.
Cricket sang, The. Dickinson.
Day Is Done, The. Longfellow.
Day's End. Binyon.
Descend, Fair Sun! *Fr.* The Masque of the Middle Temple and Lincoln's Inn. Chapman.
Description of a Summer's Eve. White.
End of the Day, The. Scott.
Evenen in the Village. Barnes.
Evening. Aldington.
Evening, An. Allingham.
Evening. Behn.
Evening. *Fr.* Don Juan. Byron.
Evening. Cotton.
Evening. Doolittle.
Evening, The. *Fr.* Trivia. Gay.
Evening. Matheson.
Evening. McCrae.
Evening. Sangster.
Evening. Sill.
Evening. Stephens.
Evening. Vriesland.
Evening. Wallace.
Evening, and Maidens. Barnes.
Evening Ebb. Jeffers.
Evening Falls, An. Stephens.
Evening in England, An. Ledwidge.
Evening in Paradise. *Fr.* Paradise Lost. Milton.
Evening in Tyringham Valley. Gilder.
Evening Landscape. Pol de Mont.
Evening on the Farm. Trowbridge.
Evening on the Harbor. Tunstall.
Evening; Ponte al Mare, Pisa. Shelley.
Evening Quatrains. Cotton.
Evening Song. Alexander.
Evening Song. Davis.
Evening Song. *Fr.* The Faithful Shepherdess. Fletcher.
Evening Song. Lanier.
Evening Songs. Cheney.
Evening Sun, The. E. Brontë.
Evening Walk, An, *sels.* Wordsworth.
Evening Wind, The. Bryant.
Evensong. Aiken.
Even-Song, An. Dobell.
Evensong. Schaumann.
Evensong. Stevenson.
Grace before Sleep. Teasdale.
Harmonie du soir. Baudelaire.
In the Cool of the Evening. Noyes.
It Is a Beauteous Evening, Calm and Free. Wordsworth.
Morning and Evening. Slonimski.
Mountain Evenings. Holme.
Nurse's Song. *Fr.* Songs of Experience. Blake.
O God whose daylight leadeth down. *Fr.* Evening Hymn. Macdonald.
Ode to Evening. Collins.
Ode to Evening. Warton.
On a Calm Summer's Night. Nicholson.
On a Midsummer Eve. Hardy.
On Eastnor Knoll. Masefield.
Post-Meridian. Garrison.
Prelude: "Winter evening settles down, The." *Fr.* Preludes. Eliot.
Progress of Evening. Landor.
Shadows of the Evening Hours. Procter.
Shoreham: Twilight Time. Palmer.
Small Song. F. Frost.
Softly Now the Light of Day. Doane.
Sonnet: "Evening, as slow thy placid shades descend." Bowles.
Summer Evening. De la Mare.
Summer Evening, A. Lampman.
Sunken Evening. Lee.
This Is My Rock. McCord.
Vespers. Mitchell.
Vespers. Shepard.
Western Waves of Ebbing Day, The. *Fr.* The Lady of the Lake. Scott.
When Even Cometh On. Tilley.

Evening *(continued)*
Winter Evening. *Fr.* The Task. Cowper.
Winter Evening. Lampman.
Winter Evening. Pushkin.
See also **Twilight; Sunset.**
Evening Primroses
Evening Primrose, The. Clare.
Evening Primrose, The. Langhorne.
Evening Primrose, The. Parker.
Evening Star
Evening Star. Barker.
Evening Star, The. Clare.
Evening Star. Poe.
Ode to the Evening Star. Akenside.
Star of the Evening. Sayles.
To the Evening Star. Blake.
To the Evening Star ("Gem of the crimson-colour'd Even"). Campbell.
To the Evening Star("Star that bringest home the bee"). Campbell.
See also **Venus (planet).**
Everest (mountain)
Victory. Miller.
Evers, Medgar
Medgar Evers. Brooks.
Evolution
By an Evolutionist. Tennyson.
Darwinism. Robinson.
Darwinity. Merivale.
Evolution. Smith.
Love Song to Eohippus. Viereck.
On Becoming Man. Lister.
Similar Cases. Gilman.
"This is the sorroful story." *Fr.* The Legends of Evil. Kipling.
"Time of Man, The." Webb.
Executions
Culprit, The. Housman.
Eight o'Clock. Housman.
Epitaph in Form of a Ballad, The, Which Villon Made for Himself and His Comrades Expecting To Be Hanged Along with Them. Villon.
Gallows, The. Thomas.
Hanging of Billy Budd, The. Wilson.
London Fete, A. Patmore.
"More Light! More Light!" Hecht.
On Moonlit Heath. Housman.
Summons to Execution. *Fr.* The Duchess of Malfi. Webster.
Tichborne's Elegy, Written in the Tower before His Execution. Tichborne.
Upon the Image of Death. Southwell.
What Birds Were There. Brother Antoninus.
See also **Hanging.**
Exile
Before Exile. Mack.
Canadian Boat Song, The. *Unknown.*
Canadian Exile, The. Gerin-Lajoie.
Castaways, The. Zaturenska.
Come to Me Dearest. Brennan.
Dublin. MacNeice.
Emigrant Song. "Ansky."
Exile. Heine.
Exile. Tu Fu.
Exile at Rest, The. Pierpont.
Exile in Nigeria. Mphahlele.
Exile of Erin, The. Campbell.
Exile Song. Rosenfeld.
Exiles. Hayne.
Exile's Devotion, The. McGee.
Exile's Letter. Li Po.
Exile's Song, The. Gilfillan.
In Exile. Baughan.
Lament of the Scotch-Irish Exile. Roche.
On His Exile to Iona. St. Columcille.
Sea Wind. Mallarmé.
Song of the Siberian Exiles, The. Nekrasov.
Travelogue for Exiles. Shapiro.
Wanderer, The. Field.
Existentialism
Existentialism. Frankenberg.
For the Existentialist. Palmer.
Exmoor, England
For Exmoor. Ingelow.
Exodus from Egypt
Exodus from Egypt, The. Ezekielos of Alexandria.
Flowering without End. *Fr.* Jeremiah. Zweig.
Go Down, Moses. *Unknown.*
Parting of the Red Sea, The. *Fr.* Exodus. *Unknown.*
Sound the Loud Timbrel. Moore.
Explorers and Exploring
Discoverer of the North Cape, The. Longfellow.
Explorer, The. Delius.
Explorer, The. Plomer.
Hakluyt Unpurchased. McDuffee.
Polar Quest, The. Burton.
Projection, A. Whittemore.
Sonnet: "There was an Indian, who had known no change." Squire.
Southward Sidonian Hanno. Allen.
Terra Australis. Stewart.
Ulysses. Tennyson.
Verses Supposed to Be Written by Alexander Selkirk. Cowper.
Extreme Unction
Extreme Unction. Dowson.
In Extremis. Chavez.
Eyes
Eye, The. Benedikt.
Her Eyes. Ransom.
On My Short-Sightedness. Chaya.
Upon Black Eyes, and Becoming Frowns. Howell.

F

Factories
Factory Windows Are Always Broken. Lindsay.
Fair American (ship)
Cruise of the *Fair American.* *Unknown.*
Fairfax, Thomas Fairfax, 3d Baron
Fairfax, Whose Name in Arms Through Europe Rings. Milton.
Fairies
About the Fairies. Ingelow.
Ann and the Fairy Song. *Fr.* A Child's Day. De la Mare.
Apple-Elf, The. Braine.
Arming of Pigwiggen, The. *Fr.* Nymphidia. Drayton.
Best Game the Fairies Play, The. Fyleman.
Bubbles. Shorey.
By the Moon We Sport and Play. *Fr.* The Mayde's Metamorphosis. *Unknown.*
Child and the Fairies, The. *Unknown.*
Come unto These Yellow Sands. *Fr.* The Tempest. Shakespeare.
Confession in Holy Week. Morley.
Could It Have Been a Shadow? Shannon.
Crab-Apple. Talbot.
Culprit Fay, The, *sel.* Drake.
Differences. Fyleman.
Door at the End of Our Garden, The. Weatherly.
Dream Fairy, The. *Fr.* Queen Mab. Hood.
Dream Song. Middleton.
Dusk in the Domain. Mackellar.
Elf and the Dormouse, The. Herford.
Elf Singing, The. Allingham.
Elfin Plane, The. Bennett.
Elfin Wife, The. "Falstaff."
Elves' Dance The. *Fr.* The Mayde's Metamorphosis. *Unknown.*
Emigration of the Fairies, The, *sel.* Duvar.
Enchanted Garden, The. Barrows.
Epilogue to "A Midsummer Night's Dream." Shakespeare.
Explanation of the Grasshopper, An. Lindsay.
Faerie Fair, The. Harrison.
Faëry Reaper, The. Buchanan.
Fairies, The. Allingham.
Fairies. Conkling.
Fairies. Fyleman.
Fairies, The. Herndon.
Fairies, The. Herrick.
Fairies, The. Morford.
Fairies. *Fr.* Kensington Garden. Tickell.

Fairies' Dance, The ("Dare you haunt our hallow'd green?"). *Unknown.*
Fairies' Farewell, The. Corbet.
Fairies Feast, The. Doughty.
Fairies Have Never a Penny to Spend, The. Fyleman.
Fairies in New Ross, The. *Unknown.*
Fairies' Lights. Wilkins.
Fairies of the Caldon-Low, The. Howitt.
Fairies' Recall. Hemans.
Fairies' Shopping, The. Deland.
Fairies' Song. Hunt.
Fairy Book, The. Brown.
Fairy Book, The. Gale.
Fairy Boy, The. Lover.
Fairy Bread. Stevenson.
Fairy Carpets. Payne.
Fairy Days. Thackeray.
Fairy Folk, The. Allingham.
Fairy Folk, The. Bird.
Fairy Frilly. Hoatson.
Fairy Frock, The. Morse.
Fairy Frolic. Rentoul.
Fairy Godmothers. Lee-Hamilton.
Fairy Harpers, The. Dollard.
Fairy Host, The. *Tr. by* Graves.
Fairy in Armor, A. Drake.
Fairy King, The. Allingham.
Fairy Lough, The. "O'Neill".
Fairy Maimounè, The. Moultrie.
Fairy Music. Fyleman.
Fairy Nurse, The. *Unknown.*
Fairy Queen, The ("Come, follow, follow me"). *Unknown.*
Fairy Ring, The. *Unknown.*
Fairy Shoes. Wynne.
Fairy Song, A. Dillingham.
Fairy Song. Hemans.
Fairy Song. Keats.
Fairy Song. Praed.
Fairy Tailor, The. Fyleman.
Fairy Tempter, The. Lover.
Fairy Thorn, The. Ferguson.
Fairy Thrall, The. Byron.
Fairy Umbrellas. Diamond.
Fairy Voyage, A. *Unknown.*
Fairy Went a-Marketing, A. Fyleman.
Fairy Wings. Howard.
Fairy-Land. Poe.
Fairy's Wander-Song. *Fr.* A Midsummer Night's Dream. Shakespeare.
Farewell to the Fairies. Corbet.
Five Little Fairies, The. Burnham.
Fountain of the Fairies, The. Southey.
Goblin, The. Fyleman.
Goblin Market. C. G. Rossetti.
Goblinade, A. Jaques.
Godmother. Morden.
Green Gnome, The. Buchanan.
Have You Watched the Fairies? Fyleman.
Host of the Air, The. Yeats.
How to Tell Goblins from Elves. Shannon.
How to Treat Elves. Bishop.
I Keep Three Wishes Ready. Wynne.
I'd Love to Be a Fairy's Child. Graves.
If You Never. Fowler.
In the Moonlight. O'Conor.
Kallundborg Church. Whittier.
La Belle Dame sans Merci. Keats.
Lake and a Fairy Boat, A. Hood.
Last Voyage of the Fairies, The. Adams.
Leprahaun. Joyce.
Leprecaun, or Fairy Shoemaker, The. Allingham.
Light-hearted Fairy, The. *Unknown.*
Little Elf, The. Bangs.
Little Men, The. Fearne.
Little Orphant Annie. Riley.
Mab. *Fr.* The Satyr. Jonson.
Man Who Hid His Own Front Door, The. MacKinstry.
Mickleham Way. Eastwick.
Midnight Performance, A. Wing.
Midsummer Magic. Eastwick.
Midsummer Night's Dream, A, *sels.* Shakespeare.
Mountain Sprite, The. Moore.
Now the Hungry Lion Roars. *Fr.* A Midsummer Night's Dream. Shakespeare.
Nymphidia; or, The Court of Fairy. Drayton.
Oh! Where Do Fairies Hide Their Heads. Bayly.
Of Certain Irish Fairies. Guiterman.
One of the Sidhe. Kennedy.
Others, The. "O'Sullivan."
Overheard on a Saltmarsh. Monro.
Palace of the Fairies, The. Drayton.
Plea of the Midsummer Fairies, The, *sels.* Hood.
Plumpuppets, The. Morley.
Queen Mab. Hood.
Queen Mab. *Fr.* The Satyr. Jonson.
Queen Mab. *Fr.* Romeo and Juliet. Shakespeare.
Queen of Elfland's Nourice, The. *Unknown.*
Return of the Fairy, The. Wolfe.
Robin Goodfellow. *Unknown.*
Sea Fairies. Mathias.
Sea Princess, The. Pyle.
Seven Ages of Elf-Hood, The. Field.
Shadow People, The. Ledwidge.
Shakespeare. *Fr.* The Plea of the Midsummer Fairies. Hood.
Sir Olaf. Herder.
Song: "Lake and a fairy boat, A." Hood.
Song by Fairies. *Fr.* Endymion. Lyly.
Song of the Elfin Miller. Cunningham.
Song of the Elfin Steersman. Hill.
Stocking Fairy. Welles.
Stolen Child, The. Yeats.
There was a little goblin. Herbertson.
Thomas the Rhymer. *Unknown.*
Three Beggars, The. De la Mare.
Tim, the Fairy. Livesay.
To Mother Fairie. Cary.
To the Leanan Sidhe. Boyd.
Tree Stands Very Straight and Still, The. Wynne.
Very Nearly. Scott-Hopper.
Vision. Fyleman.
Visitor, The. Field.
Water-Lilies. Hemans.
Water Sprite. Wandrei.
Wee Wee Man, The. *Unknown.*
When a Ring's around the Moon. Carr.
When I Was Six. Cross.
Where the Bee Sucks, There Suck I. *Fr.* The Tempest. Shakespeare.
White Horses. Howard.
Wind Blows Out of the Gates of Day, The. *Fr.* The Land of the Heart's Desire. Yeats.
Yesterday in Oxford Street. Fyleman.

Faith

After the Surprising Conversions. R. Lowell.
Apostasy. Aus of Kuraiza.
Argument, An—of the Passion of Christ. Merton.
As a Plane Tree by the Water. R. Lowell.
Belief. Miles.
Belief and Unbelief. Freneau.
Bishop Blougram's Apology. R. Browning.
Candle and Book. Walter.
Captains of the Years, The. MacDougall.
Credo. Jeffers.
Credo. Kreymborg.
Credo. "O'Sullivan."
Credo. Oxenham.
Credo. Robinson.
Credo. Symons.
Credo, A. Thackeray.
Creed, A. Masefield.
Creed. Spencer.
Creeds. Baker.
Disappointment. Young.
Dominus Illuminatio Mea. Blackmore.
Dover Beach. Arnold.
Dream is the thought in the ghost. *Fr.* A Faith on Trial. Meredith.
Dying Hymn. Cary.
Eclipse of Faith, The. Woolsey.
Epi-Strauss-ium. Clough.
Eternal Goodness, The. Whittier.
Evensong. Stevenson.

Faith *(continued)*
Faith. Cambridge.
Faith. Case.
Faith. Clark.
Faith. Daley.
Faith. Edwards.
Faith. Howells.
Faith. Isbell.
Faith. Maynard.
Faith. Meyer.
Faith. Moreland.
Faith. Oxenham.
Faith. Poteat.
Faith. Sangster.
Faith. Sill.
Faith. Tabb.
Faith. *Fr.* The Ancient Sage. Tennyson.
Faith. Wilcox.
Faith. Whittier.
Faith and Freedom. *Fr.* It is Not to Be Thought of. Wordsworth.
Faith and Science. Clark.
Faith and Sight. *Fr.* Not Knowing. King.
Faith, Hope and Love. *Unknown.*
Faith is a fine invention. Dickinson.
Faith of Christ's Freeman, The. Clark.
Faith of Our Fathers. Faber.
Faith Trembling. "Bridges."
Faith's Difficulty. Maynard.
Faith's Visita. Abbey.
Feathered Faith. *Unknown.*
Firm Belief. *Unknown.*
Foundation of Faith. Drinkwater.
God in Whom We Trust, The. *Unknown.*
Happy Change. Cowper.
Have Faith in God. Budzynski.
His Creed. Herrick.
Homeward Journey, The. Aaronson.
Hymn for Atonement Day. Halevi.
I Am the Way. Meynell.
I in Thee, and Thou in Me. Cranch.
I know not what shall befall me: God hangs a mist o'er my eyes. *Fr.* Not Knowing. Brainard.
I never saw a moor. Dickinson.
I Saw a Monk of Charlemaine. *Fr.* Jerusalem. Blake.
If This Were Faith. *Fr.* Songs of Travel. Stevenson.
Impercipient, The. Hardy.
Implicit Faith. *Fr.* May Carols. De Vere.
Joy and Peace in Believing. Cowper.
Last Lines. E. Brontë.
Last Man, The. Campbell.
Leaden Echo and the Golden Echo, The. Hopkins.
Light Shining Out of Darkness. Cowper.
Love Song, A. Halevi.
Man without Faith, The. Church.
Meditation on Communion with God. Halevi.
Milk-white Hind, immortal and unchanged, A. *Fr.* The Hind and the Panther. Dryden.
My Faith. Acharya.
My Faith. Knowles.
My Faith Looks Up to Thee. Palmer.
My Times Are in Thy Hand. Hall.
No Coward Soul Is Mine. E. Brontë.
Noble Voyage, The. Surrey.
Not Knowing. Brainard.
O World, Thou Choosest Not the Better Part. Santayana.
Oh Yet We Trust that Somehow Good. *Fr.* In Memoriam A. H. H. Tennyson.
Obedience. Macdonald.
Pastoral Hymn. Addison.
Poet's Simple Faith, The. Hugo.
Possession. *Unknown.*
Prayer for Faith, A. Michelangelo.
Prisoner, The. E. Brontë.
Readings, Forecasts, Personal Guidance. Fearing.
Religio Laici. Dryden.
Return, The. Rukeyser.
Riddle of the World, The. Whittier.
Rugby Chapel. Arnold.
Say Not the Struggle Nought Availeth. Clough.
Second Crucifixion, The. Le Gallienne.
Shema Yisrael. *Unknown.*
Silence. Towne.
Supposed Confessions of a Second-rate Sensitive Mind. Tennyson.
That There Are Powers above Us I Admit. Clough.
That's Faith. Leitner.
There In No Unbelief. Case.
Thy Way, Not Mine. Bonar.
Tide of Faith, The. *Fr.* A Minor Prophet. "Eliot."
To My Children. Strobel.
Trust. Kemble.
Trust. Reese.
Trust—a Song. Rexford.
Trust and Obedience. *Unknown.*
Trust Him. *Unknown.*
Voyagers. Van Dyke.
When Gathering Clouds. Grant.
Why Are Yee Afraid, O Yee of Little Faith? Crashaw.
Wit Wonders. *Unknown.*
Sourcebook of Poetry (SoP). Al Bryant, comp.

Falcons
Falcon, The. *Unknown.*
Gay Goss-Hawk, The. *Unknown.*
Golden Falcon. Coffin.
Hawking. *Fr.* Polyolbion. Drayton.
Lux, My Fair Falcon. Wyatt.
Old Falcon, The. Baldwin.
Windhover, The. Hopkins.

Fall. *See* **Autumn.**

Falmouth, England
Home. Henley.

Fame
Earth's Immortalities. R. Browning.
Fame. Cantus.
Fame. Tabb.
Fame Is a Food That Dead Men Eat. Dobson.
Fame is the one that does not stay. Dickinson.
I'm nobody! Who are you? Dickinson.
Inquisition upon Fame and Honour, An. Greville.
Making It, or Black Corruption. Green.
Not marble, nor the gilded monuments. Sonnets, LV. Shakespeare.
On Fame. Banks.
On Fame. Keats.
Perry Zoll. *Fr.* Spoon River Anthology. Masters.
Pillar of Fame, The. Herrick.
Stanzas Written on the Road between Florence and Pisa. Byron.
Substance, Shadow, and Spirit. T'ao Ch'ien.
To an Athlete Dying Young. Housman.
Two Sonnets On Fame. Keats.
Whilst thus my pen strives to eternize thee. *Fr.* Idea. Drayton.
You that do search for every purling spring. *Fr.* Astrophel and Stella. Sidney.

Family Life
Autobiographical. Klein.
Cotter's Saturday Night, The. Burns.
Family, The. Lydston.
Family. *Unknown.*
Family Court. Nash.
Family Meeting, The. Sprague.
Folded Flock, The. Meynell.
From a Childhood. Rilke.
Somerset Dam for Supper, The. Holmes.

Famine
Famine Year, The. Lady Wilde.

Fancy *See* **Imagination.**
Fire and Sleet and Candlelelight (FiSC). August Derleth, ed.

Farming and Farmers
Affinity. Thomas.
Anxious Farmer, The. Johnson.
Argument with a Millionaire, An. "Grayson."
Behold him, priests, and though he stink of sweat. *Fr.* The Steel Glass. Gascoigne.
Canadian Farmer. Bartole.
Code, The. Frost.
Country Summer. Adams.
Crafty Farmer, The. *Unknown.*
Cynddylan on a Tractor. Thomas.
Day at the Farm, A. "L. J."

Death of the Hired Man, The. Frost.
Defeated Farmer. Van Doren.
Digression from Husbandry to a Point or Two of Huswifery, A. Tusser.
Drinking Time. O'Sullivan.
Ecologues. Schmitz.
Evening at the Farm. Trowbridge.
Farewell to the Farm. Stevenson.
Farm, The. Taylor.
Farm Life. Stanton.
Farm near Norman's Lane, The. Finnin.
Farm Picture, A. Whitman.
Farm Wife. Mitchell.
Farmer. Bailey.
Farmer. Fallon.
Farmer, The. *Unknown.*
Farmer and the Farmer's Wife, The. Hiebert.
Farmer Comes to Town, The. *Unknown.*
Farmers. Mullins.
Farmer's Boy, The, *sels.* Bloomfield.
Farmer's Ingle, The. Fergusson.
Farmer's Round, The. *Unknown.*
Farming. *Fr.* Shi King. *Unknown.*
Fruit Rancher, The. Roberts.
Good Farmer, The. *Unknown.*
Happy Farmer, The. Tse Nan.
Happy Farmer, The. *Unknown.*
Hayfield, The. *Fr.* The Flowing Summer. Bruce.
Haying. Herbin.
Haymaking. Thomas.
Hill Farmer Speaks, The. Thomas.
Hillside Farmer, A. Farrar.
His Grange, or Private Wealth. Herrick.
Hock-Cart, or Harvest Home, The. Herrick.
How was November's melancholy endear'd to me. *Fr.* The Testament of Beauty. Bridges.
Hundreth good points of good husbandry, A. Tusser.
I Will Go with My Father a-Ploughing. Campbell.
July. Tusser.
Man with the Hoe; a Reply. Cheney.
Manor Farm, The. Thomas.
March. Tusser.
Milking Before Dawn. Dallas.
Mowers, The. Allingham.
Mowing, The. Roberts.
Muck Farmer, The. Thomas.
Northern Farmer: New Style. Tennyson.
Northern Farmer: Old Style. Tennyson.
October's Husbandry. Tusser.
Old Farmer Alone. Coffin.
On Our Farm. Antin.
Peter Simson's Farm. Dyson.
Planting Beans. T'ao Ch'ien.
Ploughing on Sunday. Stevens.
Plowman, The. Knister.
Praise of Husbandry, The. Tusser.
Putting in the Seed. Frost.
Ranchers. Lesemann.
Reaper, The. Allen.
Rival, The. Warner.
Seed. Bosman.
September. Tusser.
Sheep-washing, The. *Fr.* The Seasons: Summer. Thomson.
Sower, The. Figueroa.
Sower, The. Roberts.
Sower's Song, The. Carlyle.
Sowing. Thomas.
Strong Are Saying Nothing, The. Frost.
Summer Farm. MacCaig.
Times Have Altered, The. *Unknown.*
Young Man Who Wouldn't Plow Corn, The. *Unknown.*
See also **Fields and Pastures.**

Farragut, David Glasgow
Farragut. Meredith.
River Fight, The. Brownell.
Through Fire in Mobile Bay. *At. to* Farragut.

Fate
As I Gird On for Fighting. Housman.
At the Crossroads. Hovey.
Destiny. Arnold.
Dice Were Loaded, The. Gilmore.
Eros Turannos. Robinson.
Fate. Block.
Fate. Cooper.
Fate. Emerson.
Fate. Spalding.
Hap. Hardy.
Hymn to Chance. Putnam.
Inevitable, The. Bolton.
Lachesis. Raine.
Nemesis. Emerson.
To Leuconoë. Horace.
Wanderer, The. *Unknown.*
Winds of Fate, The. Wilcox.
See also **Fortune.**

Fathers
Abraham's Madness. Noll.
All My Pretty Ones. Sexton.
American Primitive. Smith.
Anecdote for Fathers. Wordsworth.
At My Father's Grave. "MacDiarmid."
Au Tombeau de Mon Pere. McCuaig.
Celebration, A. Sarton.
Daddy. Fyleman.
Daddy. Plath.
Dear Old Dad. Shaver.
Dedicatory. Gilmore.
Does Daddy Go? *Unknown.*
Early Morning Feed. Redgrove.
Elegy: "My father was born with a spade in his hand and traded it." Ciardi.
Elegy for My Father. Moss.
Elegy on My Father. Curnow.
Epitaph on My Father. Burns.
Father. F. Frost.
Father. Pack.
Father. Weston.
Father and Son. Higgins.
Father Does His Best, A. White.
Father Is Coming. Howitt.
Father Knows, The. "F. L. H."
Fathers and Sons. *Unknown.*
Father's Day (So He Says). *Unknown.*
Father's Place, A. Gray.
Father's Story. Roberts.
Father's Testament, A. Ibn Tibbon.
Figures of Authority. Watkins.
Forgetful Pa. Guest.
Gardener, The. Wheelock.
Guilty Father to His Daughter, A. Schevill.
Hallelujah; a Sestina. Francis.
Her Great Secret. Gillilan.
I Sit with My Dolls. *Unknown.*
If I could rise and see my father young. *Fr.* Art of the Sonnet. Orlovitz.
In the Year's Morning. Ross.
Kind of Dad I'd Buy. Evans.
Lament of a Man for His Son. *Unknown.*
Lines to His Son on Reaching Adolescence. Logan.
Lines to My Father. Daiken.
My Dad's Dinner Pail. Harrigan.
My Father Moved through Dooms of Love. Cummings.
My Father, My Son. Brinnan.
My Father's Child. "Sterne."
My Father's Voice in Prayer. Nottage.
My Papa's Waltz. Roethke.
My Son. Malloch.
On My First Son. Jonson.
On the Death of His Son. Glyn Cothi.
On the Seventh Anniversary of the Death of My Father. Pack.
Our Father. Mathew.
Poem for Fathers, A. Wilson.
Radio, The. Guest.
Russian Cradle Song, A. Nomberg.
Secret Heart, The. Coffin.
Shabby Old Dad. Campbell.
Sohrab and Rustum. Arnold.
Those Winter Sundays. Hayden.
To Any Daddy. *Unknown.*
To My Father. Baxter.
To My Father. Tree.
To My Son, Aged Three Years and Five Months. Hood.

Fathers *(continued)*
To the Reverend Shade of His Religious Father. Herrick.
Way to Know a Father, The. Coffin.
When Father Carves the Duck. Wright.
When Father Played Baseball. Guest.
When He Goes to Play with the Boys. Gillilan.
Wonderful Man, A. Fisher.
Fauns
Après-Midi d'un faune, L'. Mallarmé.
Faun, The. Pound.
Fauré, Gabriel
Fauré. Causley.
Faust
Dr. Faustus, *sels.* Marlowe.
Faust. Ashbery.
Faust, *sels.* Goethe.
Faustus. *Fr.* Horatio. Plutzik.
Progress of Faust, The. Shapiro.
Fawkes, Guy
Guy Fawkes Day. *Unknown.*
Fawn. *See* **Deer.**
Fear
Appointment in Doctor's Office. Miles.
Ballad of Sister Anne, The. O. Sitwell.
Fairy Tale, A. Mackenzie.
Fears in Solitude. Coleridge.
Lost Son, The. Roethke.
News, The. "Sec."
Ode to Fear. Collins.
Shape of Fear, The. Russell.
Song of the Little Hunter. *Fr.* The Second Jungle Book. Kipling.
Storm Fear. Frost.
Variation: Ode to Fear. Warren.
Woods Grow Darker, The. Drake.
February
At the Nadir. Kennedy.
Brook in February, The. Roberts.
February. *Fr.* The Shepherd's Calendar. Clare.
February. *Fr.* The Earthly Paradise. Morris.
February. Ratcliffe.
February. Sherman.
February. *Unknown.*
February. Whitney.
February. Young.
February, Tall and Trim. Gilmore.
February Twilight. Teasdale.
First Words before Spring. Untermeyer.
In February. Ropes.
In February. Simpson.
In February. Symonds.
In the Month of February. *Unknown.*
Late Winter. Savage.
March 1st. Spivak.
Mirror in February. Kinsella.
Poem in February. Thomas.
Snowdrop, The. Tennyson.
To February. Wetherald.
Way of Looking, A. Bevington.
When. Aldis.
Federal Constitutional Convention
Convention Song. *Unknown.*
Federal Convention. *Unknown.*
To the Federal Convention. Dwight.
Feet
Take Notice. Robin.
Fences
Fence Wire. Dickey.
Fencing
For E. McC. Pound.
Fernández de Córdoba, Francisco
Bernál Diaz' Preface to His Book. MacLeish.
Ferns
New Fern, A. "A."
Petrified Fern, The. Branch.
Ferry Boats
Back and Forth. Mitchell.
Ferry-Boats. Tippett.
Ferryman, The. C. G. Rossetti.
Letter Written on a Ferry Crossing Long Island Sound. Sexton.
Fiddles and Fiddlers
Fiddler of Dooney, The. Yeats.
Green Fiddler, The. Field.
Mountain Whippoorwill, The. S. V. Benét.
Paging Professor Gooseberry. Stem.
Seven Fiddlers, The. Evans.
'Tis I Go Fiddling, Fiddling. Hopper.
Field, Cyrus West
How Cyrus Laid the Cable. Saxe.
Field Athletics
After the Record Is Broken. Emanuel.
Challenge. Hazo.
Discobulus. Locher.
Pole Vault. Murano.
Fields, James T.
In Memory of James T. Fields. Whittier.
Fields and Pastures
Beanfield, The. Clare.
Cornfield, The. Roberts.
Deserted Pasture, The. Carman.
Fallow Field, The. Dorr.
Field-Path, The. Swain.
Fields Are Full, The. Shanks.
Green Cornfield, A. C. G. Rossetti.
Hayfield. Fisher.
In the Field. Davis.
In the Fields. Mew.
Meadow-Field, The. *Fr.* Pleasant Memories. Sangster.
Meadow Talk. Smith.
Meadows, The. Taylor.
Mountain Meadows. Keller.
Mower's Song, The. Marvell.
Out in the Fields with God. *At. to* Guiney *and to* E. B. Browning.
Over in the Meadow. "Wadsworth."
Pastoral: "If it were only still!" Millay.
Pasture, The. Frost.
Pasture, A. Knowles.
Poplar Field, The. Cowper.
Psalm of the Fruitful Field. Klein.
Return, The. Ostenso.
Simple Field That I Shall Buy, The. McNeal.
To Meadows. Herrick.
To One Who Has Been Long in City Pent. Keats.
When You Will Walk in the Field. Goldberg.
White Fields. Stephens.
See also **Farming and Farmers.**
Fiesole, Italy
Fiesolan Idyl. Landor.
Financiers
New Order of Chivalry, A. Peacock.
Finches
Epitaph on Lady Ossory's Bullfinch. Walpole.
Finches, The. Murray.
Finches, The. Shapcott.
Fink, Mike
Shooting of the Cup, The. *Fr.* The Song of Three Friends. Neihardt.
Finn mac Cumhail (Finn MacCool)
Death of Dermid, The. Ferguson.
Finnsburg, Battle of
Battle of Finnsburg, The. *Unknown.*
Fir Trees
Fir-Tree, The. Thomas.
Firwood. Clare.
Young Fir-Wood, A. D. G. Rossetti.
Fire
Adolphus Elfinstone. Burgess.
Arthur with a lighted taper. *Fr.* Science for the Young. Irwin.
Banking Coal. Toomer.
Barnfire during Church. Bly.
Brother Fire. MacNeice.
Execration upon Vulcan, An. Jonson.
Fire, The. Burford.
Fire, A. Field.
Fire and Ice. Frost.
Fire at Alexandria, The. Weiss.
Fire on the Hills. Jeffers.
Flames. Root.
Honesty at a Fire. Squire.
Looking West. Stafford.

Marriage of Heaven and Earth, The. Nemerov.
Movies in the Fire. Shacklett.
Smithfield Market Fire, The. Dallas.
Some Verses upon the Burning of Our House, July 10th, 1666. Bradstreet.
There's a Fire in the Forest. Ross.
Two Fires, The. Wright.
Upon the Burning of Our House. Bradstreet.

Fire Engines
Fire-Truck, A. Wilbur.

Fire of London (1666)
Fire of London, The. *Fr.* Annus Mirabilis. Dryden.
London Mourning in Ashes. *Unknown.*

Fireworks
Fireworks. Deutsch.
Fireworks. Reeves.

First World War. *See* **World War, First.**

Fireflies
Fireflies. Coplen.
Fireflies. Fisher.
Fireflies. Hall.
Fireflies, The. Tu Fu.
Fireflies in the Corn. Lawrence.
Fireflies in the Garden. Frost.
Firefly, The. Issa.
Firefly, The. Nash.
Firefly. Roberts.
Fire-Fly, The. Tabb.
Firefly, The. Taigi.
Firefly Lights His Lamp. *Unknown.*
Phosphorescence. Cane.

Fish
Alas, Alack! De la Mare.
Aquarium. Wright.
At the Aquarium. Eastman.
Average. Page.
Ballade: To a Fish of the Brooke. Wolcot.
Beast, Birds and Fishes. O'Keeffe.
Blow Fish. Congdon.
Description of a Strange (and Miraculous) Fish, A. Parker.
Eating Fish. Johnston.
Fish, The. Bishop.
Fish, The. Brooke.
Fish. Ross.
Fish. Smith.
Fish. Unterecker.
Fish, the Man, and the Spirit, The. Hunt.
Flying Fish, The. Cope.
Flying Fish. Fenollosa.
Flying Fish, The. Gray.
Flying Fish. Miller.
Flying Fish. Taylor.
Gar, The. Bell.
Heaven. Brooke.
King of waters, the sea shouldering whale, The. Wood.
Kinds of Shel-fish. Wood.
Leviathan. Gould.
Minnows. *Fr.* I Stood Tiptoe upon a Little Hill. Keats.
Movement of Fish, The. Dickey.
Parrot Fish, The. Merrill.
Pike, The. Blunden.
Pike. Hughes.
Pisces. Thomas.
Purse-Seine, The. Jeffers.
Sea School. Howes.
Sonnet of Fishes. Barker.
To a Fish. Hunt.
To the Immortal Memory of the Halibut on Which I Dined This Day. Cowper.
Where the Manatee Plays and the Manta Ray Flutters. Witt.

Fish Hawks
Fish-Hawk, The. Wheelock.

Fisher, John, Cardinal (Saint John Fisher)
Cardinal Fisher. Heywood.

Fishing and Fishermen
And Angling, Too. *Fr.* Don Juan. Byron.
Angler, The. Chalkhill.
Angler's Ballad, The. Cotton.
Angler's Invitation, The. Stoddart.
Angler's Reveille, The. *Fr.* The Toiling of Felix. Van Dyke.
Angler's Song, The. Basse.
Angler's Song, The. *Fr.* The Secrets of Angling. Dennys.
Angler's Wish, An. Van Dyke.
Angler's Wish, The. *Fr.* The Compleat Angler. Walton.
At the Fishhouses. Bishop.
Boston Come-All-Ye, The. *Unknown.*
Boy Fishing, The. Scovell.
Caller Herrin'. Nairne.
Careful Angler, The. Stevenson.
Cod-Fisher, The. Lincoln.
Coracle Fishers, The. *Fr.* The Banks of Wye. Bloomfield.
Coromandel Fishers, The. Naidu.
Crabbing. Levine.
De Piscatione. Bastard.
Drunken Fisherman, The. R. Lowell.
Feast of Saint Andrew the Apostle. *Fr.* The Sacred Seasons. Bode.
Fish, The. Bishop.
Fish, The. Gustafson.
Fish with the Deep Sea Smile, The. Brown.
Fisher, The. Renton.
Fisherman, The. Brown.
Fisherman, The. McCord.
Fisherman. S. Sitwell.
Fisherman, The. *Unknown.*
Fisherman, The. Yeats.
Fisherman's Chant, The. Burnand.
Fisherman's Hymn, The. Wilson.
Fisherman's Luck. Gibson.
Fisherman's Song, The. D'Urfey.
Fishermen. Emanuel.
Fishermen, The. Theocritus.
Fishermen, The. Whittier.
Fishers, The. Pitter.
Fisher's Life, The. *Unknown.*
Fishing. Wright.
Fishing. *Fr.* The Prelude. Wordsworth.
Fishing Pole, The. Davies.
Fishing Season. Vallis.
Fishing Song, A. Rands.
Fly-fishing. *Fr.* Rural Sports. Gay.
Fun with Fishing. Tietjens.
Gamblers, The. Delius.
Green Stream, A. Wang Wei.
How They Bite. *Unknown.*
Ike Walton's Prayer. Riley.
Instruction in the Art. Booth.
Last Chance, The. Lang.
Neither Hook nor Line. Bunyan.
Net Menders, The. Vrepont.
Off to the Fishing Ground. Montgomery.
Old Angler, The. De la Mare.
Old Fisherman, The. *Unknown.*
On the Coast near Sausalito. Hass.
Out Fishin'. Guest.
Pike, The. Bruce.
Purse-Seine, The. Jeffers.
Salmon-fishing. Jeffers.
Sea Scape with Parable. Eberhart.
Silver Herring Throbbed Thick in My Seine, The. Leslie.
Skipper-Hermit, The. Rich.
Sockeye Salmon. Hambleton.
Surface Fishing. Moses.
Three Fishers, The. Kingsley.
Two Fishers. *Unknown.*
We Fish. *Fr.* Mardi. Melville.
We'll Go to Sea No More. *Unknown.*
Words Are Never Enough. Bruce.

Fisk, James
Jim Fisk. *Unknown.*

Fitzgerald, Edward
To E. FitzGerald. Tennyson.

Fitzgerald, F. Scott
On Editing Scott Fitzgerald's Papers. Wilson.

Fitzgerald, Sir Maurice
Lamentation for the Death of Sir Maurice Fitzgerald, Knight of Kerry, A. Ferriter.

Fitzgeralds, The
Geraldines, The! the Geraldines!—'tis full a thousand years. *Fr.* The Geraldines. Davis.

Five Forks, Battle of
Army Correspondent's Last Ride. Townsend.

Flags, Confederacy
Bonnie Blue Flag, The. Ketcham.
Conquered Banner, The. Ryan.
Flags, Great Britain
Union Jack, The. Kirby.
Flags, United States
American Boy, The. *Unknown.*
American Flag, The. Drake.
Battle-Plane in France, A. Child.
Betsy's Battle Flag. Irving.
Boy, Bare Your Head. Turner.
Brother, Lift Your Flag with Mine. Bacon.
Call to the Colors, The. Guiterman.
Flag, The. Boker.
Flag, The. Flash.
Flag, The. Horton.
Flag, The. Larcom.
Flag, The. Roche.
Flag, The. Silverstein.
Flag Goes By, The. Bennett.
Flag of the *Constellation,* The. Read.
Flag of the Free. Field.
Flag Song. Ward.
Flag Speaks, The. Balch.
Flag We Fly, The. Fisher.
Flower of Liberty, The. Holmes.
God Bless the Flag. *Unknown.*
God Save the Flag. Holmes.
Good Morning, America! Kemp.
Hang Out the Flags. Tippett.
I Am the Flag. Jones.
I Am What You Make Me. Lane.
Lift up the banner of our Love. *Fr.* Raising of the Flag, The. Pallen.
Little Flags, The. Minot.
My Country Is the World. Whitaker.
My Country's Flag. Stafford.
Name of Old Glory, The. Riley.
New Banner, The. Trask.
Ode to the Flag. Crellin.
Old Flag, The. Bunner.
Old Flag. Parker.
Old Flag. Hamlet.
Old Flag. Sangster.
Old Flag Forever, The. Stanton.
Raising of the Flag, The. Pallen.
Service Flag, The. Herschell.
Song for Our Flag, A. Sangster.
Song for the Flag, A. McCarthy.
Song of Liberty. Garnett.
Stand by the Flag. Wilder.
Star-spangled Banner, The. Key.
To the Flag of Stars. Clark.
Toast to the Flag, A. Daly.
Under the Stars. Rice.
Unfurling of the Flag, The. Sears.
Your Flag and My Flag. Nesbit.
Flamingos
Flamingos, The. Rilke.
Turtle and Flamingo, The. Fields.
Flanders, Belgium
Another Reply to "In Flanders Fields." Galbreath.
How They Brought the Good News from Ghent to Aix. R. Browning.
In Flanders Fields. McCrae.
In Flanders Now. Jaques.
Into Battle. Grenfell.
Old House of Flanders, The. Ford.
Reply to "In Flanders Fields." Mitchell.
Flattery
Flattery. Swift.
Flax
Flax. Bunin.
Flax Flower, The. Howitt.
Fleas
Flea, The. Donne.
Flea, The. Young.
Flea and a fly in a flue, A. *Unknown.*
Fleas, The. De Morgan.
Partners. Castiello.
To a Flea in a Glass of Water. Greig.
Fleet Street, London
Song of Fleet Street, A. Werner.
Fletcher, John
Bards of Passion and of Mirth. Keats.
To Fletcher Reviv'd. Lovelace.
Upon Master Fletchers Incomparable Playes. Herrick.
Upon the Dramatick Poems of Mr. John Fletcher. Cartwright.
Fleur-de-lis. *See* **Iris.**
Flies
Blue-fly, The. Graves.
Calvus to a Fly. Turner.
Death to Us, A. Silkin.
Flea and a fly in a flue, A. *Unknown.*
Flies. Aldis.
Fly, The. *Fr.* Songs of Experience. Blake.
Fly, The. De la Mare.
Fly, The. Nash.
Fly, The. Shapiro.
Fly Caught in a Cobweb, A. Lovelace.
Fly in December. Wallace.
Luther to a Bluebottle Fly (1540). Lee-Hamilton.
Near Dusk. Auslander.
October Flies. Kessler.
On a Fly Drinking from His Cup. Oldys.
Spider and the Fly, The. Howitt.
Flodden Field, England
Flodden. *Fr.* Marmion. Scott.
Flodden Field. *Unknown.*
Flowers of the Forest. Elliot.
Lament for Flodden. Elliot.
Floods
Flood. Anderson.
Flood. Charles.
Flood, The. *Fr.* Metamorphoses. Ovid.
High Tide on the Coast of Lincolnshire, The. Ingelow.
No More the Slow Stream. McLaren.
To Flood Stage Again. Wright.
Florence, Italy
Above the Arno. Swenson.
Casa Guidi Windows, *sels.* E. B. Browning.
Daisies of Florence, The. Raine.
Florence. Landor.
Giotto's Tower. Longfellow.
Old Bridge at Florence, The. Longfellow.
Old Pictures in Florence. R. Browning.
San Marco Museum, Florence. Sister Maris Stella.
Santa Maria del Fiore. Clarke.
Florida
Florida. Bishop.
Florida Road Workers. Hughes.
Flowers
Alpine Flowers, The. Sigourney.
Behold, O Man. *Fr.* The Faerie Queene. Spenser.
Birth of the Flowers, The. Fenollosa.
Bloom. Kreymborg.
Blossom, The. Blake.
Blossom, The. Donne.
Bunch of Wild Flowers. Zilles.
Buttercups and Daisies. Howitt.
Chanted Calendar, A. *Fr.* Balder. Dobell.
Charm for Spring Flowers, A. Field.
Cheddar Pinks. Bridges.
Choir of Day, The. *Fr.* Milton. Blake.
City Child, The. Tennyson.
Contemplation upon Flowers, A. King.
Cut Flower, A. Shapiro.
Cycle. Hughes.
Death of the Flowers, The. Bryant.
Evening. Doolittle.
Faithless Flowers, The. Widdemer.
Fear of Flowers, The. Clare.
Field Flowers. Campbell.
Flower, The. Dodd.
Flower, The. Herbert.
Flower, The. Tennyson.
Flower Arrangement. Yellen.
Flower-Cart Man, The. Field.
Flower Chorus. *Unknown.*
Flower Factory. Evans.
Flower in the Crannied Wall. Tennyson.
Flower Market, The. Po Chü-i.

Flowers. Behn.
Flowers. Hood.
Flowers. Longfellow.
Flowers. Rimbaud.
Flowers, The. Stevenson.
Flowers, The. *Unknown.*
Flowers by the Sea. Williams.
Flowers in a Meadow, The. Cornford.
Flowers in the Valley. *Unknown.*
Flower's Name, The. *Fr.* Garden Fancies. R. Browning.
Flowers of Perdita, The. *Fr.* The Winter's Tale. Shakespeare.
Flowers of the Forest, The. Elliot.
For the doubling of flowers is the improvement of the gard'ner's talent. *Fr.* Jubilate Agno. Smart.
Funeral Home, The. Mezey.
How the Flowers Grow. "Setoun."
I Walked the Other Day. Vaughan.
Idle Flowers, The. Bridges.
Lark's Song, The. *Fr.* Milton. Blake.
Nosegay Always Sweet, for Lovers to Send for Tokens of Love at New Year's Tide or for Fairings, A. *At. to* Hunnis.
Path Flower. Dargan.
Picture of Little T. C. in a Prospect of Flowers. Marvell.
Poem: "Geranium, houseleek, laid in oblong beds." Gray.
Roadside flowers. Carman.
Scandal among the Flowers, A. Taylor.
Seek Flowers of Heaven. Southwell.
Some Flowers o' the Spring. *Fr.* The Winter's Tale. Shakespeare.
Song: "Primrose in the green forest, The." Delaney.
Song in Spring. Ginsberg.
Spring Flowers. *Fr.* The Seasons. Thomson.
Spring Flowers from Ireland. McCarthy.
Tapers. Gray.
Thirsty Flowers. Knipe.
Time to Go. "Coolidge."
'Tis But a Little Faded Flower. Howarth.
To a Blue Flower. Neilson.
To Blossoms. Herrick.
To Primroses Fill'd with Morning-Dew. Herrick.
Trees in the Garden, The. S. Crane.
Troll's Nosegay, The. Graves.
Valley of Pale Blue Flowers, The. "Macleod."
Violets, daffodils. Coatsworth.
Window Boxes. Farjeon.
Woman Looking At a Vase of Flowers. Stevens.
Wonga Vine. Wright.

Flutes
Amateur Flute, The. *Unknown.*
Flute of the Lonely, The. Lindsay.
Flute Players. Rabéarivelo.
Lament of the Flutes. Okigbo.
Musical Instrument, A. E. B. Browning.

Flycatchers
Flycatchers. Bridges.

Flying Dutchman (ship)
Flying Dutchman, The. Sullivan.
Flying Dutchman, The. *Unknown.*

Flying Saucers
Go Fly a Saucer. McCord.

Fog
Coastguardsman in the Fog, The. Schevill.
Coming of the Fog. Dyment.
English Fog, The. Dyer.
Fog. Binyon.
Fog, The. Coffin.
Fog, The. Davies.
Fog. Sandburg.
Fog-Horn. Clarke.
Fog-Horn. Merwin.
Haze. Thoreau.
Morning Mist, The. Southey.
New England Fog. Callaghan.
River-Fog. Kiyowara.
Sea Fog, The. Jackson.
Sounding Fog, The. Pulsifer.
Yellow fog that rubs its back upon the window-panes, The. *Fr.* The Love Song of J. Alfred Prufrock. Eliot.
See also **Haze; Mist.**

Folk Songs. *See* **Ballads and Folk Songs.**

Fontenoy, Battle of
Fontenoy. Davis.
Fontenoy, 1745. Lawless.

Food
Beautiful soup, so rich and green. *Fr.* Alice's Adventures in Wonderland. "Carroll."
Essay on Lunch. Gibson.
Food. Chute.
Food and Drink. Untermeyer.
Goody O'Grumpity. Brink.
Hasty-Pudding, The. Barlow.
Hot Cake. Shu Hsi.
Hymn to the Belly. Jonson.
Inviting a Friend to Supper. Jonson.
Life would be an easy matter. *Fr.* If We Didn't Have to Eat. Waterman.
Marble-Top. White.
Melton Mowbray Pork Pie, A. Le Gallienne.
My Other Chinee Cook. Stephens.
Nightmare of a Cook. Kallman.
Salad. Collins.
Salad, A. Smith.
Spectator ab Extra. Clough.
Table Richly Spread, A. *Fr.* Paradise Regained. Milton.
This Is Just To Say. Williams.
Thoughts of Loved Ones. Fishback.
To a Baked Fish. Wells.
To a Poor Old Woman. Williams.
We may live without poetry, music and art. *Fr.* Lucile. "Meredith."
When in Rome. Evans.

Fools
Fool's Prayer, The. Sill.
Fools, they are the only nation. *Fr.* Volpone. Jonson.
Plays. Landor.
Ship of Fools, The, *sels.* Brandt.

Football
Football. Mason.
In the Beginning Was the. Murchison.
Passer, The. Abbe.
Say Good-bye to Big Daddy. Jarrell.
Second Half. McCord.
Settling Some Old Football Scores. Bishop.
Under the Goal Posts. Guiterman.
See also **Soccer.**

Forbes, Edward
Epigram on the Death of Edward Forbes. Dobell.

Ford, Ford Madox
Ford Madox Ford. R. Lowell.
To Ford Madox Ford in Heaven. Williams.

Ford, John
Upon Ford's Two Tragedies, "Love Sacrifice" and "The Broken Heart." Crashaw.

Forest Fires
Forest Fire, The. Monroe.
Forest Fire. Romig.

Forest Rangers
Song of the Forest Ranger, The. Bashford.

Forests
Advice to a Forest. Bodenheim.
By Canoe through the Fir Forest. Dickey.
Copse, The. Wade.
Deep in the Woods. Shacklett.
Dirge in Woods. Meredith.
Dogwood, The. *Fr.* Dark Woods. Warren.
English Wood, An. Graves.
Font in the Forest, The. Adams.
Forest. Blackwell.
Forest Hymn. Bryant.
Forest Glade, The. Turner.
Forest Shapes. Wandrei.
Forest Song. Venable.
Green Inn, The. Garrison.
In Hardwood Groves. Frost.
In November. Lampman.
In the Redwood Forest. Pomeroy.
In the Wood of Finvarra. Symons.
In the Woods. Baker.
In the Woods. Scott.
Inscription for the Entrance to a Wood. Bryant.
Midsummer Noon in the Australian Forest, A. Harpur.

Forests *(continued)*
Nutting. Wordsworth.
O Sweet Woods. *Fr.* Arcadia. Sidney.
Passing of the Forest, The. Reeves.
Piney Woods. Cowley.
Plants Stand Silent Round Me, The. Jorgensen.
Solitary Woodsman, The. Roberts.
Solitude. Lampman.
Sylvan Ode. Chocano.
There's a Fire in the Forest. Ross.
Under the Greenwood Tree. *Fr.* As You Like It. Shakespeare.
Waldeinsamkeit. Emerson.
Walk, The. Ross.
Way through the Woods, The. Kipling.
Windsor-Forest. Pope.
Wood of Flowers, The. Stephens.
Wood Song, A. Hodgson.
Woodland. Sister Margaret Teresa.
Woodland Revel, A. Urmy.
Woodland Worship. Wetherald.
Woodlands, The. Barnes.
Woodnotes, I. Emerson.
Woods. Auden.
Woods and Kestrel. Bell.
Woods Are Still, The. "Field."
Woods in Winter. Longfellow.
Woods of Westermain, The. Meredith.
Forget-me-nots
Forget-me-not, The. *Unknown.*
Forsythia
Aspects of Some Forsythia Branches. Gustafson.
Fort Laramie Trail
Laramie Trail. Hanson.
Fortitude
Nevertheless. Moore.
Fortune
Casino. Auden.
Comming of Good Luck, The. Herrick.
Davy, the Dicer. *Fr.* Two Short Ballettes. More.
For Ever, Fortune, Wilt Thou Prove. Thomson.
Fortune ("The Lady Fortune is both friend and foe"). *Unknown.*
Fortune. Wyatt.
Fortune and Virtue. *Fr.* Old Fortunatus. Dekker.
Fortune's Treachery. Halevi.
Fortune's Wheel. De Tabley.
From a Hint in the Minor Poets. Wesley.
Hap. Hardy.
Hard Luck. Hughes.
Lewis, the Lost Lover. *Fr.* Two Short Ballettes. More.
Of Fortune. More.
Of Fortune's Power. Edwards.
Times Go by Turns. Southwell.
Thomas More to Them That Seek Fortune. More.
To Fortune. Herrick.
To Fortune. More.
Wert Thou But Blind, O Fortune, Then Perhaps. Landor.
Winters Morning Muse, A. Howell.
See also **Fate.**
Fortunetellers
Crepe de Chine. Williams.
Spaewife, The. Stevenson.
Forty-niners
Songs of the Gold Rush, The (SGR). Richard A. Dwyer *and* Richard E. Lingenfelter, eds.
Fotheringay, England
At Fotheringay. Southwell.
Fountains
Baroque Wall-Fountain in the Villa Sciarra, A. Wilbur.
Dried-up Fountain. Leighton.
Fountain, The. Davie.
Fountain, The. Fyleman.
Fountain. Jennings.
Fountain, The. J. R. Lowell.
Fountain, The. Mu'tamid, King of Seville.
Fountain, The. Teasdale.
Fountain, The. Wordsworth.
Fountains, The. Rodgers.
Inscription for a Fountain on a Heath. Coleridge.
To the Fountain of Bandusia. Horace.
Fourth of July
After the Fourth of July. Dawson.
American Independence. Street.
Centennial Meditation of Columbia, The. Lanier.
Chester. Billings.
Choice. Farrar.
Emancipation from British Dependence. Freneau.
Fireworks. Reeves.
Flower of Liberty, The. Holmes.
Fourth of July. Chute.
Fourth of July. Field.
Fourth of July, The. Pierpont.
Fourth of July Night. Aldis.
Fourth of July Ode. J. R. Lowell.
Fourth of July Song. Lenski.
Freedom, Our Queen. Holmes.
Grandfather Watt's Private Fourth. Bunner.
If I Had a Firecracker. Silverstein.
Independence Bell—July 4, 1776. *Unknown.*
Independence Day. Tyler.
Independence Day To-Day. Sangster.
I've Got a Rocket. *Unknown.*
Listen to the People: Independence Day, 1941, *sel.* S. V. Benét.
Nation's Birthday, The. Vandyne.
Ode: "O tenderly the haughty day." Emerson.
Ode for the Fourth of July, 1876, An. J. R. Lowell.
Ode to the Fourth of July. George.
Prayer on Fourth of July. Turner.
Fox, Charles James
Lines Composed at Grasmere. Wordsworth.
Nelson, Pitt, Fox. *Fr.* Marmion. Scott.
Foxes
Ballad of Red Fox, The. La Follette.
Ballad of the Fox. *Unknown.*
Crow and the Fox, The. La Fontaine.
False Fox, The. *Unknown.*
Four Little Foxes. Sarett.
Fox. Dyment.
Fox, The. Ford.
Fox, The. Hesketh.
Fox, The. Parry.
Fox, The. Salomon.
Fox, The. Scheuer.
Fox, The. Serraillier.
Fox, The. Tomlinson.
Fox, The *(ballad)*. *Unknown.*
Fox and the Grapes, The. La Fontaine.
Fox and the Grapes, The. Lauren.
Fox at the Point of Death, The. Gay.
Fox Awakes, The. *Fr.* Reynard the Fox. Masefield.
Fox Walked Out, The. *Unknown.*
Foxes among the Lambs. Moll.
From the Gallows Hill to the Tineton Copse. *Fr.* Reynard the Fox. Masefield.
Hunt, The. Kent.
Little White Fox. Rowbotham.
Night of Wind. F. Frost.
Owl and the Fox, The. *Unknown.*
Raven and the Fox, The. La Fontaine.
Sycophantic Fox and the Gullible Raven, The. Carryl.
Two Foxes, The. *Unknown.*
Foxgloves
Foxgloves. Hughes.
Foxgloves. Webb.
France, Anatole
Anatole France at Eighty. Oaks.
France
Four Sheets to the Wind and a One-Way Ticket to France, 1933. Rivers.
France. Napier.
France; an Ode. Coleridge.
In France. Cornford.
Liberté, Égalité, Fraternité. Converse.
O France When Thou Art Prone and Bound. Hugo.
O Star of France. Whitman.
Provincia Deserta. Pound.
Reflections on the Fall of France, June, 1940. Lewis.
Republic to Republic. Bynner.
Rioupéroux. Flecker.
Road to France, The. Henderson.
Spell of France, The. Blunden.

Third of February, 1852, The. Tennyson.
To France. Chaplin.
Zone. Apollinaire.
Francesca da Rimini
Ready she sat with one hand to turn o'er. *Fr.* The Story of Rimini. Hunt.
Francis Borgia, Saint
Saint Francis Borgia; or, A Refutation for Heredity. McGinley.
Francis of Assisi, Saint
Blessing of St. Francis, The. Sister Maura.
Little Litany to St. Francis, A. Murray.
Little Song in Assisi, A. Barker.
Old Man in the Park. Osborn.
Return. Hawling.
Saint Francis. Bishop.
Saint Francis. Pfingston.
Saint Francis and the Birds. Heaney.
Saint Francis and the Birds. McFadden.
St. Francis and the Cloud. Welch.
Saint Francis of Assisi. Ramsay.
St. Francis' Sermon to the Birds. Longfellow.
Vocation of St. Francis, The. Sister Mary Eleanore.
Francis I, King of France
Glove and the Lions, The. Hunt.
Franck, César
All Those Hymnings Up to God. Evans.
At the Symphony. Nathan.
César Franck. Auslander.
Four Friends. Ward.
Franco, Francisco
Eisenhower's Visit to Franco, 1959. Wright.
Franco-Prussian War
In Time of "The Breaking of Nations". Hardy.
Frankenstein
Bride of Frankenstein, The. Field.
Frankenstein. Colombo.
Franklin, Benjamin
Ben Franklin's Head (1728). Howe.
Benjamin Franklin, 1706-1790. R. *and* S. V. Benét.
On the Death of Benjamin Franklin. Freneau.
Franklin, Sir John
Ballad of Sir John Franklin, A. Boker.
Lady Franklin's Lament. *Unknown.*
Sir John Franklin; On the Cenotaph in Westminster Abbey. Tennyson.
Fraser (river), British Columbia
Trail to Lillooet, The. Johnson.
Fredericksburg, Virginia
In the Old Churchyard at Fredericksburg. Loring.
Fredericksburg, Battle of
At Fredericksburg. O'Reilly.
Crossing at Fredericksburg, The. Boker.
Fredericksburg. Aldrich.
Freedom
All Men Are Free! Napier.
Ante-Bellum Sermon, An. Dunbar.
Antiquity of Freedom, The. Bryant.
At the Zoo. Zangwill.
Boston Hymn. Emerson.
Country Justice, The. Langhorne.
Dame Liberty Reports from Travel. Pinkney.
1536-1936. Humphreys.
Flower of Liberty, The. Holmes.
France; an Ode. Coleridge.
Free Nation, A. Markham.
Freedom. *Fr.* The Bruce. Barbour.
Freedom. Barlow.
Freedom. J. R. Lowell.
Freedom. Mann.
Freedom. Reber.
Freedom. Tennyson.
Freedom, Our Queen. Holmes.
Harp That Once through Tara's Halls, The. Moore.
In After Days. Cameron.
Independence. Fullerton.
Independence. *Fr.* Ode to Independence. Smollett.
Independence. Thoreau.
Liberty. Hay.
Liberty for All. Garrison.
Liberty Song. J. Dickinson.
Liberty Tree. Paine.
London 1802. Wordsworth.
Loyalty Confin'd. L'Estrange.
Moral Warfare, The. Whittier.
My Political Faith. Cameron.
No Master. Davies.
Notes for My Son. Comfort.
Ode: "God save the Rights of Man!" Freneau.
Ode: "O tenderly the haughty day." Emerson.
Ode to Liberty. *Fr.* Goddwyn. Chatterton.
Ode to Liberty. Shelley.
Of Old Sat Freedom on the Heights. Tennyson.
Of True Liberty. Beaumont.
On the Detraction Which Followed upon My Writing Certain Treatises. Milton.
On the Subjugation of Switzerland. Wordsworth.
Our Cause. Linton.
Present Crisis, The. J. R. Lowell.
Pride. Miles.
Proem: "I love the old melodious lays." Whittier.
Republican Genius of Europe, The. Freneau.
Returning to the Fields. T'ao Yuan-ming.
Runagate Runagate. Hayden.
Shine, Republic. Jeffers.
Song, A: "Hark! 'tis Freedom that calls, come, patriots, awake!" *Unknown.*
Song of Freedom, A. Milligan.
Song of Liberty, A. Blake.
Song of the Settlers. West.
Sonnet to Liberty. Wilde.
Stanzas on Freedom. J. R. Lowell.
This Is for Freedom, My Son. Stewart.
To Althea, from Prison. Lovelace.
To Freedom. Barlow.
To Toussaint L'Ouverture. Wordsworth.
To Walt Whitman in America. Swinburne.
Torch of Liberty, The. Moore.
Unknown Citizen, The. Auden.
Wanderers. Hebblethwaite.
When a Man Hath No Freedom to Fight for at Home. Byron.
Why I Am a Liberal. R. Browning.
Winter Morning Walk, The. *Fr.* The Task. Cowper.
Poetry of Freedom, The (PoFr). William Rose Benét *and* Norman Cousins, eds.
Freemasonry
Lodge Room over Simpkins' Store, The. Greenleaf.
Frémont, John Charles
John Charles Frémont. Lummis.
On Recrossing the Rocky Mountains after Many Years. Frémont.
To John C. Frémont. Whittier.
French, The
Epistle III: "Pult'ney, methinks you blame my breach of word." Gay.
Letter to Wilbur Frohock, A. Hoffman.
French and Indian Wars
Captives' Hymn, The. Proctor.
French Revolution
Carmagnole, La. *Unknown.*
France; an Ode. Coleridge.
French Revolution, The. Blake.
French Revolution, The. Darwin.
French Revolution, The. *Fr.* The Prelude. Wordsworth.
Girondins, The. Dumas.
Ode: "God save the Rights of Man!" Freneau.
On the Anniversary of the Storming of the Bastille, at Paris, July 14th, 1789. Freneau.
Freud, Sigmund
In Memory of Sigmund Freud. Auden.
Return from the Freudian Islands, The. Hope.
Song: "Don't Tell Me What You Dreamt Last Night." Adams.
Friars
Friar Complains, A. *Unknown.*
Friar of Orders Gray, The. O'Keeffe.
Friars' Enormities. *Unknown.*
Friar's Hunting Song. Peacock.
Friends, Society of
First-Day Thoughts. Whittier.
Quaker Meeting-House. Leonard.
Quaker Widow, The. Taylor.
Quakeress Bride, The. Kinney.
Quaker's Meeting, The. Lover.

Friendship
After They Have Tired of the Brilliance of Cities. Spender.
Amantium Irae Amoris Redintegratio Est. Edwards.
Around the Corner. Towne.
Arrow and the Song, The. Longfellow.
Auld Lang Syne. Burns.
Best Treasure, The. Moment.
Burden, The. Pereira.
Comrades. Woodberry.
Confide in a Friend. *Unknown.*
Departed Friends. Vaughan.
Do They Whisper. Schwartz.
Fame and Friendship. Dobson.
Friend, A. Johnson.
Friend, A. Power.
Friend, A. Santob de Carrion.
Friend, A. *Unknown.*
Friend or Two, A. Nesbit.
Friend Who Just Stands By, The. Williams.
Friends and Enemies. *At. to* Ali Ben Abu Taleb.
Friends Old and New. Parry.
Friendship. *Fr.* The Testament of Beauty. Bridges.
Friendship. H. Coleridge.
Friendship. Craik.
Friendship. Emerson.
Friendship. *Unknown.*
Friendship. Wilcox.
Friendship Is Love without His Wings. Byron.
Gone. M. E. Coleridge.
Great Friend. Thoreau.
Hare and Many Friends, The. Gay.
House by the Side of the Road, The. Foss.
I Tell of Another Young Death. Tiempo.
If You Had a Friend. Lewis.
If You Have a Friend. *Unknown.*
In Memory of Major Robert Gregory. Yeats.
La Belle Confidente. Stanley.
Letter, The. Po Chü-i.
Letter to a Friend. Thompson.
Love and Friendship. E. Brontë.
My Comrade. Roche.
My Friends Are Little Lamps to Me. Whittemore.
New Friends and Old Friends. Parry.
O Tan-faced Prairie-Boy. Whitman.
Ode, An: "As it fell upon a day." Barnfield.
Of Friendship. Grimald.
Of Friendship. Harington.
Old Familiar Faces, The. Lamb.
Old Friendship. Tietjens.
On Friendship. Whitehead.
On Parting with Moses ibn Ezra. Halevi.
Only Way to Have a Friend, The. *Unknown.*
Plain Description of Perfect Friendship, A. *Unknown.*
Qua Cursum Ventus. Clough.
Quest, The. Coolidge.
Rejoicing at the arrival of Ch'en Hsiung. Po Chü-i.
Sincere Man, The. Walton.
Sonnet: To a Friend. H. Coleridge.
Speech to Those Who Say Comrade. MacLeish.
Starting from Paumanok. Whitman.
Stimulus of Friendship, The. *Unknown.*
Temple to Friendship. Moore.
That He Findeth Others as Fair, but Not So Faithful as His Friend. Turberville.
They Say That in the Unchanging Place. *Fr.* Dedicatory Ode. Belloc.
To a Friend. H. Coleridge.
To a Friend. Gullans.
To a Friend. A. Lowell.
To a Friend in the Wilderness, *sel.* Fairburn.
To My Friend. Campbell.
To the Immortal Memory and Friendship of That Noble Pair, Sir Lucius Cary and Sir H. Morison. Jonson.
To Thomas Moore. Byron.
True Friendship. *Fr.* The Panchatantra. *Unknown.*
Two Friends, The. Leland.
Under All Change. Johnson.
We Have Been Friends Together. Norton.
When to the sessions of sweet silent thought. Sonnets, XXX. Shakespeare.
Whirlpool, The. *Unknown.*
Why Art Thou Silent. Wordsworth.
With Rue My Heart Is Laden. Housman.
Without My Friends the Day Is Dark. Moses ibn Ezra.
Written in the Album of a Child. Wordsworth.
Sourcebook of Poetry (SoP). Al Bryant, comp.

Frietchie, Barbara
Barbara Frietchie. Whittier.

Frith, John
From William Tyndale to John Frith. Bowers.

Frithjof
Frithiof's Saga. Tegner.

Frogs
Brown Frog, The. Robinson.
Facing Up. Scully.
Frog, The. Belloc.
Frog, The. *Unknown.*
Frogs. Simpson.
Frogs' Singing-School, The. Carbell.
Grandfather Frog. Bechtel.
Moral Song. Farrar.
Peepers. Cane.
There Was a Frog Lived in a Well. *Unknown.*
Toad and the Frog, The. *Unknown.*
Wood Frog, The. Hay.

Frontiers
Geography of This Time. MacLeish.
Last Frontier, The. Fletcher.
Lay of the Last Frontier. Hersey.
Lullaby for Peregrine. Coffin.

Frontiersmen
Old Scout's Lament, The. Drannan.
Shooting of the Cup, The. *Fr.* The Song of Three Friends. Neihardt.
Stationed Scout, The. Sproull.
Texas Types—"The Bad Man." Chittenden.
Tough Cuss from Bitter Creek, A. Adams.

Fontainebleau, France
At Fontainebleau. Symons.

Frost, Robert
Frostbite. Aiken.
Letter to Robert Frost, A. Hillyer.
On Looking into Robert Frost in Kanji. Meredith.
Robert Frost. Untermeyer.
Three around the Old Gentleman. Berryman.

Frost
Apparently with no surprise. Dickinson.
Devonshire Rhyme, A. *Unknown.*
Fairy Artist, The. Garabrant.
First Frost. Curran.
Frost. Davies.
Frost. Fuller.
Frost, The. Gould.
Frost. Johnston.
Frost. Pratt.
Frost. Thomas.
Frost at Midnight. Coleridge.
Frost Pane, The. McCord.
Frost Spirit, The. Whittier.
Frosted Pane, The. Roberts.
Hard Frost. Young.
Hoar-Frost. A. Lowell.
Jack Frost. Davis.
Jack Frost. Pike.
Jack Frost. "Setoun."
Jack Frost in the Garden. Smeeton.
John Frost. Miller.
Little Jack Frost. *Unknown.*
Pageant, The. Whittier.
Sudden Frost. Wagoner.

Fruit
Fruit. Miller.

Fry, Elizabeth
Friendly Address, A. Hood.

Fuchsia
Fuchsia Hedges in Connacht. Colum.

Fuller, Margaret
Margaret Fuller. Alcott.
On the Death of M. d'Ossoli and His Wife, Margaret Fuller. Landor.

Fundisi (lake), Africa
Fundisi. Miller.

Fundy, Bay of
Arnold, Master of the *Scud.* Carman.
Funerals
After the Funeral. Thomas.
Attitudes. Eberhart.
Choirmaster's Burial, The. Hardy.
Dead of Winter. Towne.
Dirge for McPherson, A. Melville.
Está Muy Caliente. Bowering.
Funeral, The. De la Mare.
Funeral, The. Donne.
Funeral, The. Hall.
Italian Extravaganza. Corso.
Lovers, The. Aiken.
My Grandfather's Funeral. Applewhite.
My Grandmother's Funeral. Kessler.
Pauper's Funeral, The. *Fr.* The Village. Crabbe.
Sea-Ritual, The. *Fr.* Syren Songs. Darley.
They Closed Her Eyes. Bécquer.
Tract. Williams.
Fuseli, Henry
Only man that e'er I knew, The. Blake.

G

Gabriel, the Archangel
Crusader, The. Parker.
Gage, Thomas
Tom Gage's Proclamation. Flucker.
Galatea
Galatea Again. Taggard.
Pygmalion to Galatea. Graves.
Question, A. Livingston.
Galilee, Palestine
Galilee Shore. Ginsberg.
In Galilee. Butts.
Galileo
Galileo Galilei. Smith.
Galley Slaves
Galley-Slave, The. Kipling.
Press-Gang, The. *Unknown.*
Song of the Galley-Slaves. Kipling.
Galliéni, Joseph Simon
General Gallieni. Hillyer.
Galoshes
Galoshes. Bacmeister.
Galuppi, Baldassaro
Toccata of Galuppi's, A. R. Browning.
Galveston, Texas
Sailor's Song, A. Harris.
Galway, Ireland
Galway. MacNeice.
Galway. O'Neill.
Gambling
Casino. Auden.
Gambler, The. *Unknown.*
Gambler, The. Stone.
Gambler's Repentance, The. Gerald, Baron of Offaly.
Gamesters All. Heyward.
Midnight Raffle. Hughes.
Nickle Bet, A. Knight.
One Time Henry Dreamed the Number. Long.
Plain Language from Truthful James. Harte.
Games. *See* **Sports and Games.**
Gandhi, Mohandas Karamchand
Gandhi. Morgan.
In India. Shapiro.
Vaticide. O'Higgins.
Gannets
Long-billed Gannets. Emery.
García Lorca, Federico
Crime Took Place at Granada, The. Machado.
Federico. Guillén.
García Lorca. Dudek.
In Memory of Garcia Lorca. Grier.
In Memory of the Spanish Poet Federico García Lorca. Merton.
Garda, Lake, Italy.
There Is a Pool on Garda. Scollard.
Gardens
A B C's in Green. Speyer.
Benedictine Garden, A. Brown.
Charleston Garden, A. Bellamann.
Child's Song: "I have a garden of my own." Moore.
Colonist in His Garden, A. Reeves.
Eleven. MacLeish.
Flowers in a Garden. Smart.
Flower's Name, The. *Fr.* Garden Fancies. R. Browning.
For Jim, Easter Eve. Spencer.
Forsaken Garden, A. Swinburne.
Garden, The. Beaumont.
Garden A. Brown.
Garden, The. *Fr.* The Task. Cowper.
Garden, The. Giltinan.
Garden The. Grimald.
Garden, The. Marvell.
Garden, The. Masters.
Garden, The. Shirley.
Garden, The. Very.
Garden by Moonlight, The. A. Lowell.
Garden Fancies. R. Browning.
Garden Lyric, A. Locker-Lampson.
Garden of a London House, The. Jones.
Garden of Proserpine, The. Swinburne.
Garden Path, A. Justus.
Garden Prayer, A. Walsh.
Garden-Song. Cabell.
Garden Song, A. Dobson.
Garden Song, A. Moore.
Gardening. Stuart.
Gardens. *Unknown.*
Gardens Are All My Heart. Triem.
Grace for Gardens. Driscoll.
In a Garden. Swinburne.
In a Glorious Garden Grene. *Unknown.*
In a Lovely Garden Walking. Uhland.
In a Rose Garden. Bennett.
In a Southern Garden. Mackellar.
In Green Old Gardens. "Fane."
In the Garden. Crosby.
In the Garden. Flint.
Le Jardin. Wilde.
Little Dutch Garden, A. Durbin.
Little Garden, A. A. Lowell.
May Garden. Drinkwater.
Midways of a Walled Garden. *Fr.* Golden Wings. Morris.
Mower against Gardens, The. Marvell.
My Garden. Brown.
My Garden. Davies.
My Garden. Succorsa.
My Garden. Weatherly.
My Garden Is a Pleasant Place. Driscoll.
My Mother's Garden. Allen.
New Garden, The. Arkall.
Old-fashioned Garden, The. Hayes.
Old Garden, The. Eichendorff.
Old Gardens. Upson.
Old Quin Queeribus. Turner.
Once More Fields and Gardens. T'ao Yuan-ming.
Poet of Gardens, The. Henderson.
Public Gardens, The. R. Lowell.
Rented Garden, The. Noll.
Salt Garden, The. Nemerov.
Secrets of Our Garden, The. Holland.
Sensitive Plant, The. Shelley.
Spring Arithmetic. *Unknown.*
Sunken Garden, The. De la Mare.
Sunset Garden, The. Webb.
Tale from the Garden, A. Jones.
Their Lonely Betters. Auden.
Thy Garden. Mu'tamid, King of Seville.
To Mrs. Boteler. Chandler.
Trees in the Garden. Lawrence.
Unwatch'd, the garden bough. *Fr.* In Memoriam A. H. H. Tennyson.
Vision. Browne.
Way Over in the Blooming Garden. *Unknown.*
Who Loves a Garden. Jones.

Gardens *(continued)*
Widow's Weeds, A. De la Mare.
Garfield, James Abram
At the President's Grave. Gilder.
Bells at Midnight, The. Aldrich.
Charles Guiteau. *Unknown.*
Garfield's Murder. *Unknown.*
Garfield's Ride at Chickamauga. Butterworth.
Midnight—September 19, 1881. O'Reilly.
On the Death of President Garfield. Holmes.
President Garfield. Longfellow.
Garlic
Garlic. Richardson.
Garrick, David
David Garrick. *Fr.* Retaliation. Goldsmith.
Garrison, William Lloyd
Garrison. Alcott.
To William Lloyd Garrison. Whittier.
Gath (Biblical city)
Sonnet To Gath. Millay.
Gatineau (river), Quebec
Nicolas Gatineau. Bourinot.
Gauguin, Paul
Vor a Gauguin Picture zu Singen. Stein.
Gautier, Théophile
Funeral Toast. Mallarmé.
Sonnet: "This is the golden book of spirit and sense." Swinburne.
Gaza, Palestine
How Samson Bore Away the Gates of Gaza. Lindsay.
Gazelles
Gazelles, The. Moore.
Geese
Barnacle Geese. Higham.
Flight of the Geese, The. Roberts.
Flight of the Wild Geese. Channing.
Flight of Wild Geese, A. Stewart.
Geese in Autumn. *Unknown.*
Grey Goose, The. *Unknown.*
Night Flight. Whalley.
Panegyric on Geese, A. Mahony.
Some Geese. Herford.
Something Told the Wild Geese. Field.
Swan and the Goose, The. Aesop.
To a Goose. Southey.
Wild Geese. Chipp.
Wild Geese. Ise.
Wild Geese, The. Morse.
Wild Geese. Thaxter.
Wild Geese. Tynan.
Wild geese returning, The. Kunimoto.
Gehrig, Henry Louis (Lou)
To Lou Gehrig. Kieran.
Genêt, Edmond Charles Edouard
Ode: "God save the Rights of Man!" Freneau.
Geneva, Switzerland
Geneva. Reid.
Gentians
Bavarian Gentians. Lawrence.
Fringed Gentians. A. Lowell.
Gentian. E. Crane.
God made a little gentian. Dickinson.
To the Fringed Gentian. Bryant.
Geography and Geographers
Geographers. *Fr.* The Ship of Fools. Barclay.
Geography. *Fr.* Songs of Education. Chesterton.
Geography. Farjeon.
George, Saint
Carol of St. George, A. *Unknown.*
Saint George of England. Fox-Smith.
George III, King of England
Absolvers, The. *Fr.* A Vision of Judgement. Southey.
George the Third. Bentley.
George the Third. *Fr.* The Vision of Judgment. Byron.
Royal Tour, The. "Pindar."
George VI, King of England
Praises of King George VI. Ngani.
Georgia
Georgia. Loveman.
Georgia Dusk. Toomer.
Georgia Towns. Hicky.
Georgia Volunteer, A. Townsend.
Geraniums
Geranium, The. Roethke.
Red Geranium and Godly Mignonette. Lawrence.
Red Geraniums. Clark.
Germans
Ode to the Germans. Campbell.
Germany
German Fatherland, The. Arndt.
High Germany. Shanks.
On a German Tour. Porson.
To Germany. Sorley.
Weavers, The. Heine.
Germs
Germ, The. Nash.
Some Little Bug. Atwell.
Geronimo
Geronimo. McGaffey.
Gethsemane
Ballad of Trees and the Master, A. Lanier.
Christ's Prayer in Gethsemane. *Unknown.*
Garden of Gethsemane. Pasternak.
Garden of Olives, The. Rilke.
Gethsemane. Bontemps.
Gethsemane. Drose-Hülshoff.
Gethsemane. Leamy.
Gethsemane. Tappan.
Gethsemane. Wakeley.
Gethsemane. Wilcox.
Gethsemane Now. Hamilton.
Gettysburg, Pennsylvania
Night at Gettysburg. Seitz.
Gettysburg, Battle of
Battle of Gettysburg, The. *Fr.* John Brown's Body. S. V. Benét.
Battlefield, The. Mifflin.
Gettysburg. Roche.
Gettysburg. Stedman.
Gettysburg Ode, The. Taylor.
High Tide at Gettysburg, The. Thompson.
John Burns of Gettysburg. Harte.
Ghettos
Autobiographical. Klein.
Back to the Ghetto. Glatstein.
Dark People. Cumbo.
Ghetto. Johnson.
Rush City—the Hole. Redmond.
Ghost Towns
Ghost-Town Saloon: Winter. Brennan.
News of My Friends. Code.
Ghosts
Apparition, The. Donne.
Body and Spirit. Davies.
Companions. Widdemer.
Eidolon. Warren.
Ghost, The. De la Mare.
Ghost, The. R. Lowell.
Ghost. Grenville.
Ghost. Weaver.
Ghost, The. Wright.
Ghost That Jim Saw, The. Harte.
Ghost to Come. Widdemer.
Ghosts. Jennings.
Ghosts. Reid.
Ghost's Moonshine, The. Beddoes.
Ghosts of the Dead, The. Brigham.
Ghost's Promenade, The. Irwin.
Gone, The. Stuart.
Grandfathers's Ghost. Brennan.
Haunted House, The, *sel.* Hood.
Listeners, The. De la Mare.
Old Ghost, The. Beddoes.
Old Wife and the Ghost, The. Reeves.
Phantom. Coleridge.
Phantom-Wooer, The. Beddoes.
Phantoms. Ashe.
Phantoms. McGuire.
Phantoms All. Spofford.
Place-Ghost. Derleth.
Shadowed. Eaton.
Shepherd's Hut, The. Young.

Specter, The. Hardt.
Spooks. N. Crane.
Spring Voices. Stuart.
Suffolk Miracle, The. *Unknown.*
Superstitious Ghost, The. Guiterman.
Sweet William's Ghost. *Unknown.*
Tenant. Gray.
To a Persistent Phantom. Horne.
To a Shade. Yeats.
Unquiet Grave, The. *Unknown.*
Why He Was There. Robinson.
Wilderness Road. Keller.
Gioconda, La. *See* **Mona Lisa.**
Gibbon, Edward
Card of Invitation to Mr. Gibbon, at Brighthelmstone, A. Hayley.
Lausanne. Hardy.
Voltaire and Gibbon. *Fr.* Childe Harold's Pilgrimage. Byron.
Gibbs, Josiah Willard
It was much later in his life he rose. *Fr.* Gibbs. Rukeyser.
Gibraltar
At Gibraltar. Woodberry.
Gibraltar. Blunt.
Gibraltar. Trench.
Gilbert, Sir Humphrey
First American Sailors, The. Rice.
Sir Humphrey Gilbert. Longfellow.
Gin
White Chimes. Hamilton.
Giotto di Bondone
Giotto's Campanile. O'Hagan.
Giotto's Tower. Longfellow.
To Giotto. Trimpi.
Gipsies. *See* **Gypsies.**
Giraffes
Giraffe, The. Dearmer.
Giraffe, The. Gumilev.
Giraffe, The. Solomon.
Giraffe. *Unknown.*
Giraffe and Tree. Turner.
Giraffes. Brettell.
Giraffes, The. Fuller.
To a Giraffe. Moore.
To and on Other Intellectual Poets on Reading That the U.S.A.F. Had Sent a Team of Scientists to Africa. Guthrie.
Girls. *See* **Childhood and Children; Youth.**
Glassblowers
Glassblower, The. Johnson.
Glass Blower, The. Scully.
Globe Theatre
Sonnet upon the Pitiful Burning of the Globe Playhouse in London, A. *Unknown.*
Gloucester, Massachusetts
Evening in Gloucester Harbor. Sargent.
Gloucester Harbor. Ward.
Gloucester Moors. Moody.
Out from Gloucester. Trott.
Gloves
Ellinda's Glove. Lovelace.
Glove, The. Bond.
Glowworms
Dream, A. Blake.
Glow-Worm, The. Shanks.
Glow-Worms, The. Hawkshaw.
Mower to the Glow-Worms, The. Marvell.
Gluttony and Gluttons
Glutton, The. *Fr.* The Vision of Piers Plowman. Langland.
Greedy Jane. Taylor.
Griselda. Farjeon.
Little Thomas. Evans.
On Gut. Jonson.
Glyn, Elinor
Would you like to sin? *Unknown.*
Gnats
Gnat, The. Beaumont.
Gnat. Moore.
Riddle: Gnats. *Unknown.*
Gnus
G. Belloc.
Goats
All Goats. Coatsworth.
April. Winters.
Goat, The. *Unknown.*
Goat and the Three Red Shirts, The. *Unknown.*
Goat Paths, The. Stephens.
Goats. Wood.
Sad Goat, The. *Unknown.*
Smile of the Goat, The. Herford.
Goblins. *See* **Fairies.**
God
Adon 'Olam. *Unknown.*
All the Hosts of Heaven. Simeon ben Isaac ben Abun of Mainz.
Allah. Mahlmann.
Anvil, The—God's Word. Clifford.
"Are You There?" Gillilan.
At a Solemn Musick. Schwartz.
Author of Light. Campion.
Autumn. Rilke.
Ave Maria. *Fr.* The Bridge. H. Crane.
Belief in Plan of Thee. Whitman.
Best for Us, The. Burnett.
Bless Him. *Unknown.*
Brahma. Emerson.
Caliban upon Setebos. R. Browning.
Canticle of the Sun, The. St. Francis of Assisi.
Celestial Surgeon, The. Stevenson.
Child's Thought of God, A. E. B. Browning.
City, The. "Æ."
Conversion. Angermayer.
Crazy Jane on God. Yeats.
Dawning, The. Vaughan.
Delight in God Only. Quarles.
Divine Image, The. *Fr.* Songs of Innocence. Blake.
Divine Presence, The. *Fr.* May Carols. De Vere.
Divinity, The. Arnold.
Down in the Depth of Mine Iniquity. *Fr.* Caelica. Greville.
Each in His Own Tongue. Carruth.
Elements, The. Newman.
Essay on Deity. Olson.
Eternal Goodness, The. Whittier.
Eternal Jew, The. Cohen.
Even-Song. Herbert.
Excesses of God, The. Jeffers.
Exit God. Bradford.
Experience, The. *Fr.* Preparatory Meditations. Taylor.
Eyewitness. Hall.
Father, The. Savage-Armstrong.
First Autumn, The. Schacht.
For the Letter Which Signifies God. *Fr.* Jubilate Agno. Smart.
Glory of God in Creation, The. Moore.
God. Bradford.
God. Coblentz.
God. Tabb.
God Be in My Head. *Unknown.*
God Cares. "Farningham."
God Does Do Such Wonderful Things. Morgan.
God Doeth All Things Well. *Unknown.*
God Everywhere. Ibn Ezra.
God-forgotten. Hardy.
God Is at the Anvil. Sarett.
God Is at the Organ. Sandford.
God, Is, like, Scissors. Villa.
God Is Love. Bowring.
God Is There. Isenhour.
God Is with Me. Smith.
God Knows What He's About. *Unknown.*
God Makes a Path. Williams.
God of Galaxies, The. Van Doren.
God of love my shepperd is, The. *Unknown.*
God of Might, God of Right. *Unknown.*
God of Our Fathers. Roberts.
God of the Earth, the Sky, the Sea. S. Longfellow.
God Scatters Beauty. Landor.
God the Architect. Kemp.
God, the Artist. *At. to* Morgan.
God the Omniscient. Wallace.
God, Whom Shall I Compare to Thee? Halevi.
God with Us. *Fr.* Saul. R. Browning.
God's Grandeur. Hopkins.
God's Will Is Best. Curtis.
Hail, Thou great mysterious Being! *Fr.* God. McLachlen.

God *(continued)*
Higher Pantheism, The. Tennyson.
Highest Divinity. *Unknown.*
His Hand Shall Cover Us. Isaac ben Samuel of Dampière.
His Plan. *Unknown.*
His Sovereignty. Kalonymos ben Moses of Lucca.
Holy God, We Praise Thy Name. Walworth.
Holy of Holies. Chesterton.
Hound of Heaven, The. Thompson.
How Many Heavens. E. Sitwell.
Hymn of Joy. Van Dyke.
Hymn of the World's Creator. Caedmon.
Hymn of Unity. *Unknown.*
Hymn to God the Father, A. Donne.
Hymnos Ahymnos. Clough.
I Am the Reaper. Henley.
I Have Sought Thee Daily. Ibn Gabirol.
I have wandered. *Fr.* Cherubim. Heywood.
I See God. *Unknown.*
I Sing the Mighty Power of God. Watts.
If He Were Anywhere. Hemley.
Image of God, The. Aldana.
Imagery. Chattopadhyaya.
Immanence. Hovey.
In the castle of my soul. *Fr.* Postern Gate, The. Rauschenbusch.
Incarnatio Est Maximum Donum Dei. Alabaster.
Indian upon God, The. Yeats.
Instantaneous. Ayers.
Invocation, An: "To God, the everlasting, who abides." Symonds.
Kingdom of God, The. Rab.
Kingdom of God, The. Thompson.
Laus Deo. Dobell.
Laus Deo! Whittier.
Let Us with a Gladsome Mind. Milton.
Light Shining Out of Darkness. Cowper.
Little Gate to God, The. Rauschenbusch.
Livid lightnings flashed in the clouds, The. *Fr.* The Black Riders. S. Crane.
Living God, The. Ben Judah.
Living God, The. Ibn Ezra.
Loneliness. Essex.
Look, How Beautiful. Jeffers.
Lord Is King, The. *Unknown.*
Lord Is My Shepherd, The. Baker.
Lord of the World. *Unknown.*
Majesty and Mercy of God, The. Grant.
Man went before a strange God, A. *Fr.* The Black Riders. S. Crane.
Master Weaver, The. *Unknown.*
Meditation Six ("Am I thy gold? Or purse, Lord, for thy wealth.") *Fr.* Preparatory Meditations, First Series. Taylor.
Mighty Fortress Is Our God, A. Luther.
Mihi Adhaerere Deo Bonum Est. *Unknown.*
Moon is distant from the sea, The. Dickinson.
Morning Hours, The. *Unknown.*
My Absent God. Hemley.
My Father Knows. Tillett.
My God Has Spoken. Verlaine.
My God, How Wonderful Thou Art. Faber.
My Hiding Place. Bowsher.
Mystery, The. Hyde.
O God, Our Help in Ages Past. Watts.
O God, the Rock of Ages. Bickersteth.
O God to Thee I Yield. Brown.
Old Repair Man, The. Johnson.
On the Universality and Other Attributes of the God of Nature. Freneau.
Our Father. Swartz.
Our Rock. Key.
Paradox, The. Pereira.
"Pater Noster," The. *Unknown.*
Peace. Vaughan.
Pillar of the Could, The. Cardinal Newman.
Prayer: "In the bright bay of your morning, O God." Goll.
Prayer for Every Day. *Unknown.*
Prayer to the Father of Heaven, A. Skelton.
Preface: "Infinity, when all things it beheld." *Fr.* God's Determinations. Taylor.
Presence, The. Very.
Psalm: "I proclaim Thee great and wonderful." Mendes.
Revival, The. Vaughan.
Royal Crown, The, *sels.* Ibn Gabirol.
Salutation, The. Traherne.
Scribe, The. De la Mare.
Sculptor, The. *Unknown.*
Search for God, The. *Fr.* Hierarchie for the Blessed Angels. Heywood.
Secret, The. Cushman.
Security. Sandell.
Seeking God. Dowden.
Send Me. C. G. Rossetti.
Shadows, The. Macdonald.
Shape God Wears, The. Hay.
Sighs and Grones. Herbert.
Song of David, The. *Fr.* A Song to David. Smart.
Song of the Creatures, The. St. Francis of Assisi.
Song of the Wind and the Rain. Ibn Gabirol.
Sonnet XI: "Is God invisible? This very room." Greeff.
Sonnet: "My God, where is that ancient heat towards Thee." Herbert.
Spacious Firmament on High, The. Addison.
Sun. Moore.
Sun-Day Hymn. A. Holmes.
There Is No God. *Fr.* Dipsychus. Clough.
There Is Nothing False in Thee. Patchen.
There's a Wideness in God's Mercy. Faber.
Third Enemy Speaks. *Fr.* The Magnetic Mountain. Day Lewis.
This Is My Father's World. Babcock.
Those—dying then. Dickinson.
Thou Great God. *Unknown.*
Though Mine Eye Sleep Not. *Fr.* The Dead Sea Scrolls. *Unknown.*
Three Hymns, 1 ("Thou didst, O mighty God, exist"). Rowe.
To God. Herrick.
To God the Father. Constable.
To the Supreme Being. Michelangelo.
Transcendence. Hovey.
Veni Creator. Carman.
Vestigia. Carman.
Vision of God, The. *Fr.* Divina Commedia. Dante.
What Tomas Said in a Pub. Stephens.
With Thee. Pinkham.
Wherefore Hidest Thou Thy Face, and Holdest Me for Thy Enemie? *Fr.* Emblems. Quarles.
Whose Hand. *Unknown.*
You. Masefield.
Yours. Tagore.
Zebaoth. Lasker-Schüler.
Sourcebook of Poetry (SoP). Al Bryant, comp.

Godiva, Lady
Godiva. Tennyson.
Lady Godiva. Shanks.

Godolphin, Sidney, 1st Earl Godolphin
Sidney Godolphin. Scollard.

Godwin, William
Letter to Maria Gisborne. Shelley.

Goethals, George Washington
Goethals, the Prophet Engineer. MacKaye.

Goethe, Johann Wolfgang von
Memorial Verses. Arnold.
Sorrows of Werther, The. Thackeray.

Gogh, Vincent van
Farewell to Van Gogh. Tomlinson.
Starry Night, The. Sexton.
Visit to Van Gogh, A. Causley.

Gold
Arrowtown. Glover.
Gold. Hood.
Gold Seekers, The. Richardson.
Gold Seeker's Song, The. *Unknown.*
Song for the Pike's Peaker. *Unknown.*
Yellow Witch of Caribou, The. Robertson.

Gold Mining and Miners
Arawata Bill. Glover.
Ballad of Chicken Bill, The. Vaughn.
Broken-down Digger, The. *Unknown.*
Cleaning Up. Dyson.
Dow's Flat. Harte.

Gold-Seekers, The. Garland.
Golden Gullies of the Palmer, The. *Unknown.*
Hit at the Times, A. McGrew.
In the Gold Mines. Vilakazi.
In the Summer of Sixty. *Unknown.*
Klondike Miner, The. *Unknown.*
Little Johnny Mine, The. Detrick.
Look Out Below! Thatcher.
Marching Song of the California Gold Rush, The. *Unknown.*
Me and Prunes. Sherwood.
Mistress of the Matchless Mine. Robertson.
Ol' Jinny Mine, The. Detrick.
On the Gold Mines. Vilakazi.
Pike's Peakers, The. Greenleaf.
Slide at the Empire Mine, The. Wason.
Soliloquy of the Returned Gold Adventurer. *Unknown.*
Song: "We came to Tamichi in 1880." Judy *and* Hammond.
Spell of the Yukon, The. Service.
Songs of the Gold Rush, The (SGR). Richard A. Dwyer *and* Richard E. Lingenfelter, eds.

Goldenrod
Golden Rod, The. Sherman.

Goldfinches
Goldfinch, A. De la Mare.
Goldfinches. Keats.

Goldfish
Bowl of Goldfish, The: a Fable. Kirkup.
Goldfish, The. Brown.
Goldfish. Monro.
Goldfish. Nemerov.
Prayer of the Goldfish, The. Gasztold.

Golem
How They Made the Golem. Colombo.

Golf
Afforestation. Wodehouse.
Ball and the Club, The. Lindsay.
City of Golf, The. Murray.
Golfers. Layton.
Mullion. Herbert.
One Down. Armour.
Public Nuisance, A. Arkell.
Seaside Golf. Betjeman.

Golgotha. *See* **Crucifixion, The.**

Goliath
Apocryphal Soliloquies. Untermeyer.

Good Friday
Good Friday. Herbert.
Good Friday. Holme.
Good Friday. Jurica.
Good Friday. Kramer.
Good Friday. Reese.
Good Friday. C. G. Rossetti.
Good Friday. Savonarola.
Good Friday. Smith.
Good Friday. *Unknown.*
Good Friday Evening. C. G. Rossetti.
Good Friday in My Heart. Coleridge.
Good Friday Night. Moody.
Good Friday, 1613. Riding Westward. Donne.
Good Friday; the Third Nocturn. Abelard.
Madman's Song, The. *Fr.* Good Friday. Masefield.
Poem for Good Friday. Jones.
Praetorium Scene; Good Friday. Lennen.
Unkept Good Fridays. Hardy.
See also **Crucifixion, The.**

Good Hope, Cape of
Rounding the Cape. Campbell.

Gore-Booth, Eva
In Memory of Eva Gore-Booth and Con Markiewicz. Yeats.

Gorillas
Best Loved of Africa. Danner.

Gorse
Song of Winter, A. Pfeiffer.

Gospel Singers
And the Old Women Gathered. Evans.

Gosse, Sir Edmund
Fame Is a Food That Dead Men Eat. Dobson.

Gould, Benjamin Apthorp
Welcome to Dr. Benjamin Apthorp Gould, A. Holmes.

Govan, Saint
St. Govan. Prys-Jones.

Government
Builders of the State. Gilder.
God Give Us Men! Holland.

Goya y Lucientes, Francisco José de
Church of San Antonio de la Florida, The. Petrie.
Goya. Aiken.
In Goya's greatest scenes we seem to see. *Fr.* A Coney Island of the Mind. Ferlinghetti.

Grackles
Grackle, The. Nash.

Graduation. *See* **Commencement Day.**

Graffiti
Aphrodite Metropolis. Fearing.
Graffiti. Field.
Graffiti Poet. Willard.
Thesis, Antithesis, and Nostalgia. Dugan.
Wall, Cave, and Pillar Statements, after Asôka. Dugan.

Graham, James, 5th Earl of Montrose. *See* **Montrose, James Graham, 5th Earl of.**

Granada, Spain
Conquest of Granada, The, *sels.* Dryden.
Road to Granada, The. Ketchum.

Grand Lake, Colorado
Legend of Grand Lake, The. Westcott.

Grand Pré, Nova Scotia
Low Tide on Grand Pré. Carman.

Grandfathers
Epitaph on His Grandfather, An. Shipman.
Grandfather Watts's Private Fourth. Bunner.
Grandparents. R. Lowell.
I've Got a New Book from My Grandfather Hyde. Jackson.
Old Man Playing with Children. Ransom.
Under Your Voice, among Legends. Harris.

Grandmothers
Afternoon with Grandmother. Huff.
At My Grandmother's. Malouf.
Cupboard, The. De la Mare.
For My Grandmother. *Fr.* Four Epitaphs. Cullen.
Grandmamma's Birthday. Belloc.
Grandmother and Child. Dallas.
Grandmother and Grandson. Merwin.
Grandmother's Visit. Wise.
Grandparents. R. Lowell.
My Grandmother. Adams.
My Grandmother's Funeral. Kessler.
Sea Lavender. Bowman.
To My Grandmother. Locker-Lampson.

Granicus, Battle of (334 B.C.)
How We Heard the Name. Dugan.

Grant, Ulysses Simpson
Aged Stranger, The. Harte.
Death of Grant, The. Bierce.
In Memory of General Grant. Abbey.
Lee's Parole. Manville.
Ulysses S. Grant. Bliss.
Vanquished. Browne.

Grantchester, England
At Grantchester. Causley.
Old Vicarage, Grantchester, The. Brooke.

Grapes
American Vineyard. Cousens.
Catawba Wine. Longfellow.
Grapes. Sister Maris Stella.
Grapes. Pushkin.
Grapes. *Unknown.*
Grapes Making. Adams.

Grasmere, England
Two Long Vacations; Grasmere. Butler.

Grass
About the Grass. Weil.
Blade of Grass, A. Williams.
Blade of Grass Sings to the River, The. Goldberg.
Blades of Grass, The. *Fr.* The Black Riders. S. Crane.
Former Barn Lot. Van Doren.
Grass, The. Bowering.
Grass. Fraser.
Grass. Sandburg.
Grass. Webster.
Grass. *Fr.* Song of Myself. Whitman.
Grass Fingers. Grimké.
Grass on the Mountain, The. *Unknown.*

Grass *(continued)*
Grass so little has to do, The. Dickinson.
Long Feud. Untermeyer.
Shearing Grass. Redgrove.
Song the Grass Sings, A. Blanden.
Spring Grass. Sandburg.
Tribute to Grass. Ingalls.
Turn to the Grass. Mary Gilmore.
Voice of the Grass, The. Boyle.
Grasse, France
Grasse: the Olive Trees. Wilbur.
Grasshoppers
Explanation of the Grasshopper, An. Lindsay.
Grasshopper, The. *At. to* Anacreon.
Grasshopper, The. Lovelace.
Grasshopper, The. Wilbur.
Grasshopper Green. *Unknown.*
Grasshopper Hop-o-the Grasses. Hallock.
Grasshoppers, The. Aldis.
My What-is-it. Frost.
On the Grasshopper and Cricket. Keats.
R-P-O-P-H-E-S-S-A-G-R. Cummings.
To the Grasshopper and the Cricket. Hunt.
Graves, Robert
Poet with Sea Horse. Reid.
Graves
Ah, Are You Digging on My Grave? Hardy.
Ample make this bed. Dickinson.
Beach Burial. Slessor.
Black Angel, The. Coulette.
Brief Biography. George.
Call for the Robin Redbreast. *Fr.* The White Devil. Webster.
Country Graveyard. Etter.
Grave, The. Jones.
Graveyard, The. Cooper.
Hide-and-Seek. Graves.
In the Grave No Flower. Millay.
Invocation: "Let me be buried in the rain." Johnson.
Manhood End. Thwaite.
My Burial Place. Jeffers.
My Grave. Davis.
Poem: "The only response." Knott.
Sarcophagus Cover. Feldman.
Sibylla's Dirge. *Fr.* Death's Jest Book. Beddoes.
Simpson's Rest. Simpson.
Unknown Dead, The. Timrod.
Wanderer's Grave, The. Sage.
We do not play on graves. Dickinson.
Graveyards. *See* **Cemeteries.**
Gray, Thomas
Sketch of His Own Character. Gray.
To Mr. Gray. Garrick.
To Mr. Gray. *Fr.* Sonnets. Warton, the Younger.
Great Britain
America to Great Britain. Allston.
Britannia, *sels.* Thomson.
England and America in 1782. Tennyson.
I Vow to Thee, My Country. Spring-Rice.
Peace Hymn for England and America. Huntington.
To America. Austin.
See also **England.**
Great Lakes
Great Lakes Suite, The. Reaney.
Lake Boats, The. Masters.
Great Smoky Mountains
Evening in the Great Smokies. Heyward.
Greatness
Grey Company, The. Mackay.
I Think Continually of Those Who Were Truly Great. Spender.
On the Vanity of Earthly Greatness. Guiterman.
Song about Great Men, A. Hamburger.
Song of Greatness, A. *Unknown.*
Stop!—for thy tread is on an Empire's dust! *Fr.* Childe Harold's Pilgrimage. Byron.
Greco, El (Domenicos Theotocopoulos)
El Greco. Mayo.
El Greco. Trypanis.
El Greco: Espolio. Birney.
Greece
After Greece. Merrill.
Cleon. R. Browning.
Clime of the unforgotten brave! *Fr.* The Giaour. Byron.
Constitution of Athens, The. Solon.
First Day, The. Weiss.
Greece. *Fr.* Childe Harold's Pilgrimage. Byron.
Greek War Song. *Unknown.*
Hellas, *sels.* Shelley.
Invasion of Greece, The. Ingalls.
Isles of Greece, The. *Fr.* Don Juan. Byron.
Isles of Greece, The. Capetanakis.
Nemea. Durrell.
On This Day I Complete My Thirty-sixth Year. Byron.
Salute to Greece. "Dane."
Take It from Me. Hanson.
To a Greek Ship in the Port of Dublin. Stanford.
Greene, Nathanael
To the Memory of the Brave Americas. Freneau.
Greene, Robert
Due Commendation of the Quipping Autor, A. *Fr.* Four Letters and Certain Sonnets. Harvey.
His Admonition to Greene's Companions. *Fr.* Greene's Memorial. Harvey.
Greenfield Hill, Connecticut
Greenfield Hill, *sels.* Dwight.
Greenland
Greenland Whale Fishery, The. *Unknown.*
Greenland Winter, A. Diamond.
Gregory, Horace
Citation for Horace Gregory. Rukeyser.
Gregory, Robert
In Memory of Major Robert Gregory. Yeats.
Grenfell, Julian
Julian Grenfell. Baring.
Grenville, Sir Richard
First American Sailors, The. Rice.
Revenge, The. Tennyson.
Greyhounds
Englyn on a Yellow Greyhound, An. Barnes.
To a Black Greyhound. Grenfell.
Grief
After great pain, a formal feeling comes. Dickinson.
Alone. De la Mare.
Amphora, The. Sologub.
Angel of Patience, The. Whittier.
Another Weeping Woman. Stevens.
Because My Grief Seems Quiet and Apart. Nathan.
Break, Break, Break. Tennyson.
Brooding Grief. Lawrence.
But unto him came swift calamity. *Fr.* Sonnets. Tuckerman.
Carousel, The. Oden.
Chamber over the Gate, The. Longfellow.
Come Sorrow wrap me in thy sable cloake. *Unknown.*
Cypress Curtain of the Night Is Spread, The. Campion.
Desdichado, El. Nerval.
Dirge, A: "Rough wind, that moanest loud." Shelley.
Dirge: "Sorrow, lie still and wear." Beddoes.
Elegy: "Floods of tears well from my deepest heart, The." Immanuel di Roma.
Eyes that weep for pity of the heart, The. *Fr.* La Vita Nuova. Dante.
Farewell to the Court. Ralegh.
Flow my teares fau from your springs. *Unknown.*
Flow Not So Fast, Ye Fountains. *Unknown.*
Folded Power. Cromwell.
Forsaken. Schneour.
Fraternity. Aldrich.
From a Car-Window. Harding.
Ghost, The. De la Mare.
Grey Eye Weeping, A. O'Rahilly.
Grief. E. B. Browning.
Grief. Contoski.
Grief. Ehrenstein.
Grief. Lawrence.
Grief and God. Phillips.
Grief, find the words; for thou hast my brain. *Fr.* Astrophel and Stella. Sidney.
Grief is a mouse. Dickinson.
Grief Plucked Me Out of Sleep. King.
Has Sorrow Thy Young Days Shaded? Moore.
How most unworthy, echoing in mine ears. *Fr.* Sonnets. Tuckerman.
I, a Most Wretched Atlas. *Fr.* Homeward Bound. Heine.

I measure every grief I meet. Dickinson.
I rise, & greive. *Unknown.*
Il pleut doucement sur la ville. Verlaine.
In Sorrow. Hastings.
In sorrowes drown'd I wast my weary dayes. *Unknown.*
It's such a little thing to weep. Dickinson.
Lachrimae. *Unknown.*
Lamentations. Brody.
Let Us Break Down the Barriers. Thomas.
Lost Love. Graves.
Mad Song. Blake.
Maid's Lament, The. *Fr.* The Citation and Examination of William Shakespeare. Landor.
Meanwhile Achilles, plung'd. *Fr.* The Iliad. Homer.
Minstrel's Song. *Fr.* Aella. Chatterton.
Mourning. Marvell.
My Grief on the Sea. *Unknown.*
No Worst, There Is None. Hopkins.
Nurse No Long Grief. Gilmore.
Oh, Thou! Who Dry'st the Mourner's Tear. Moore.
Of My Dear Son, Gervase Beaumont. Beaumont.
On a Grave in Christ-Church, Hants. Adams.
On Another's Sorrow. *Fr.* Songs of Innocence. Blake.
On My First Son. Jonson.
On My Sorrowful Life. Ibn Ezra.
One still dark night, I sat alone and wrote. *Fr.* Sonnets. Tuckerman.
Pale inke, thou art not black enough of hew. *Unknown.*
Portrait, The ("This is her picture"). D. G. Rossetti.
Raven Days, The. Lanier.
Remembering Golden Bells. Po Chü-i.
Remembrance. E. Brontë.
Sad Shepherd, The. Yeats.
Safe dispair it is that raves. Dickinson.
Sephestia's Song to Her Child. *Fr.* Menaphon. Greene.
Shrubbery, The. Cowper.
Sleepless Night, A. O'Rahilly.
Slow, Slow, Fresh Fount. *Fr.* Cynthia's Revels. Jonson.
Song, The: "Have pity (Grief) I can not pay." *Fr.* The Rival Friends. Hausted.
Song: "Spirit haunts the year's last hours, A." Tennyson.
Song: "When I was young, I said to Sorrow." De Vere.
Song before Grief, A. Lathrop.
Sonnet: Grief. Chivers.
Sonnet: "In vain to me the smiling mornings shine." Gray.
Stanzas: "With tears thy grief thou dost bemoan." Ibn Gabirol.
Time and Grief. Bowles.
To Mary. Cowper.
Vesta. Whittier.
Victory in Defeat. Markham.
Weep You No More, Sad Fountains. *Unknown.*
Weepe O Mine Eyes. *Unknown.*
When Lilacs Last in the Dooryard Bloom'd. Whitman.
Widow's Lament in Springtime, The. Williams.
Wine and Grief. Ibn Gabirol.

Grimald, Nicholas
Epitaph of the Death of Nicholas Grimald, An. Googe.

Grindelwald, Switzerland
On a Grave at Grindelwald. Myers.

Grocers
Song against Grocers, The. Chesterton.

Grongar Hill, Wales
Grongar Hill. Dyer.

Grottoes
Inscription for a Grotto. Akenside.

Ground-Hog Day. *See* **Candlemas.**

Groundhogs
Groundhog, The. Eberhart.
Groundhog Day. Pomeroy.

Guadalupe, Spain
Guadalupe. Conkling.

Guelphs
To the Guelf Faction. San Geminiano.

Guérin, Maurice de
Maurice de Guérin. Egan.

Guernica, Spain
Oak of Guernica, The. Wordsworth.

Guernsey
In Guernsey. Swinburne.

Guerriere (ship)
Constitution and the *Guerriere,* The. *Unknown.*
On the Capture of the *Guerrière.* Freneau.

Guest, Edgar Albert
Edgar A. Guest Considers "The Good Old Woman Who Lived in a Shoe" and the Good Old Truths Simultaneously. Untermeyer.
Edgar Guest. Williams.

Guevara, Ernesto ("Che")
Che Guevara Is Dead. Schjeldahl.

Guided missiles
Guided Missiles Experimental Range. Conquest.

Guilt.
Crisis. Auden.
Fish in the Unruffled Lakes. Auden.
Guilty. Wilkinson.
I have sinned; I have betrayed the innocent blood. *Fr.* The Just Vengeance. Sayers.
Pursuit. Warren.
Rime of the Ancient Mariner, The. Coleridge.
To Pontius Washing His Hands. Crashaw.

Guitars
Guitarist Tunes Up, The. Cornford.
On My Old Ramkiekie. Leipoldt.

Guiteau, Charles J.
Charles Guiteau. *Unknown.*

Gulf Stream
Gulf Stream, The. Bellamann.
Gulf Stream. "Coolidge."
Song of the Gulf Stream. Ford.

Gull Lake, Canada
At Gull Lake: August, 1810. Scott.

Gulls
Afternoon: Amagansett Beach. Wheelock.
Alien. MacLeish.
Ballet of the Fifth Year, The. Schwartz.
Dialectics of Flight. Wheelock.
Gull. Jones.
Gull. Smith.
Gull. Stuart.
Gull Goes Up, A. Adams.
Gulls. Williams.
Gulls and Dreams. Stevenson.
Harbor, The. Sandburg.
Lines Addressed to a Seagull, Seen Off the Cliffs of Moher, in the County of Clare. Griffin.
Lives of Gulls and Children, The. Nemerov.
Pater Vester Pascit Illa. Hawker.
Sea-Birds. Allen.
Sea-Gull, The. Howitt.
Sea Gull, The. Jackson.
Sea-Gull, The. Nash.
Sea Gull, The. *Unknown.*
Sea gull curves his wings, The. Coatsworth.
Sea-Gulls. Holland.
Seagulls. Hubbell.
Sea Gulls. Pratt.
Seagulls. Updike.
Seagulls on the Serpentine. Noyes.
Sea-Mew, The. E. B. Browning.
Self Unsatisfied Runs Everywhere, The. Schwartz.
Signal, The. Florit.
To a Sea-Gull. Symons.
To a Seamew. Swinburne.
Visit from the Sea, The. Stevenson.
Winged Mariner. Howes.
Winter Gulls. Ross.

Gum Trees
Gnarled Riverina Gum-Tree, A. Moll.
Snow-Gum, The. Stewart.

Gunpowder Plot
Canto I: "Of Men, nay Beasts: worse, Monsters: worst of all." *Fr.* The Locusts, or Apollyonists. Fletcher.

Guns
Defensive Position. Manifold.
Description of a Gun. Wyatt.
Shooting, The. Pack.

Gustavus II (Gustavus Adolphus), King of Sweden
Battle Hymn. Altenburg.
In Answer of an Elegiacall Letter upon the Death of the King of Sweden. Carew.

Guthlac, Saint
Death of Saint Guthlac. *Fr.* Guthlac. Cynewulf.

Gwyn, Eleanor
Nell Gwynne's Looking-Glass. Blanchard.
Gypsies
Being a Gypsy. Young.
Gipsies. Clare.
Gipsies, The. "Scrace."
Gipsy Camp, The. Clare.
Gipsy Girl, The. Hodgson.
Gipsy Jane. Rands.
Gipsy Trail, The. Kipling.
Gipsy Vans. Kipling.
Gypsies. *Fr.* The Flight of the Duchess. R. Browning.
Gypsies. Field.
Gypsies on the March. Baudelaire.
Gypsies' Road, The. Shorter.
Gypsy, The. Farjeon.
Gypsy, The. Pound.
Gypsy, The. Thomas.
Gypsy Children. Field.
Gypsy Countess, The. *Unknown.*
Gypsy Girl, The. Alford.
Gypsy Heart, The. Pratt.
Gypsy Laddie, The. *Unknown.*
Gypsy Man. Hughes.
Gypsy's Window, The. Levertov.
Idlers, The. Blunden.
Meg Merrilies. Keats.
Mendicants, The. Carman.
Princess and the Gypsies, The. Cornford.
Scholar-Gypsy, The. Arnold.
Trip It, Gipsies. *Fr.* The Spanish Gipsy. Middleton *and* Rowley.
Where Do the Gipsies Come From? Bashford.
Wraggle Taggle Gipsies, The. *Unknown.*

H

Hafiz
To Hafiz. Aldrich.
Haggard, Henry Rider
To R. K. Stephen.
Haida Indians
Bear's Song, The. *Tr. by* Skinner.
Hair
Don't Pay. Saunders.
For Anne Gregory. Yeats.
Girl with Long Dark Hair. Gray.
Girl with the Afro, The. Bennett.
Hairdresser's Art, The. *Fr.* Epithalamium for Honorius and Maria. Claudian.
Lady in the Barbershop, The. Rudnik.
Maiden and Her Hair, A. Davies.
More Hair. Hoffenstein.
On the Ladies' Head-Dresses. Greenwood.
Song: This Tress. R. Browning.
To Amarantha, That She Would Dishevel Her Hair. Lovelace.
To Her Hair. Herbert of Cherbury.
To His Mistress Who Said She Hated Him for His Grey Hairs. Wycherley.
What changes here, O hair. *Fr.* Diana. Montemayor.
Haircuts
Barber's, The. De la Mare.
Haircut. Packard.
Haircut. Shapiro.
Haiti
Coming of Dusk upon a Village in Haiti, The. Rago.
Drums of Haiti. Christian.
Hale, Nathan
Nathan Hale. Finch.
Nathan Hale. Partridge.
Nathan Hale. *Unknown.*
Hallam, Arthur Henry
In Memoriam A. H. H. Tennyson.
Halley's Comet
Stella Flammarum. Campbell.
Halloween
All Hallow Eve. Wells.
Black and Gold. Turner.
Ghoulies and Ghosties. *Unknown.*
Hag, The. Herrick.
Hallowe'en. Behn.
Halloween. Benton.
Hallowe'en. Burns.
Hallowe'en. Coxe.
Hallowe'en. F. Frost.
Halloween. Lawson.
Hallowe'en. Mayne.
Hallowe'en. Medary.
Halloween. Pomeroy.
Hallowe'en. Sheard.
Hallowe'en. *Unknown.*
Hallowe'en. Wing.
Halloween Concert. Fisher.
Hallowe'en Indignation Meeting. Fishback.
Hallowe'en Memory, A. Morley.
If You've Never. Fowler.
Jack o'Lantern. Ayre.
Litany for Halloween. *Unknown.*
Mr. Macklin's Jack o'Lantern. McCord.
October Magic. Livingston.
On Halloween. Silverstein.
One Forgotten, The. Shorter.
Riddle: What Am I? Aldis.
Theme in Yellow. Sandburg.
This Is Halloween. Thompson.
What Night Would It Be? Ciardi.
Hamilton, New Zealand
Hamilton. Pitt.
Hampstead Heath, London
As we rush, as we rush in the Train. *Fr.* Sunday at Hampstead. Thompson.
Breath of Hampstead Heath. Thomas.
On Hampstead Heath. *Fr.* Thoroughfares. Gibson.
Sunday on Hampstead Heath. Woodcock.
Hampton Roads, Virginia
Cumberland, The. Longfellow.
Handel, George Frideric
Epigram on Handel and Bononcini. Byrom.
Listening to Handel's "Messiah." Rowse.
Hands
Hands, The. *Fr.* The Limeratomy. Euwer.
Hands. Law.
Hands. Untermeyer.
Love for a Hand. Shapiro.
Your Hands. Dowson.
Handwriting
Lesson in Handwriting, A. Reid.
Writing. Nemerov.
Hanging
Briton Who Shot at His King, A. Ross.
Death-Doomed. Carleton.
Hanging, The. MacDonald.
One Good Turn Deserves Another. *Unknown.*
Salvation of Texas Peters, The. Foley.
Tyburn and Westminster. Heywood.
See also **Executions *and* Lynching.**
Hanks, Nancy
Fire-Logs. Sandburg.
I Saw a Ghost. Boilleau.
Nancy Hanks. R. Benét.
Nancy Hanks. Monroe.
Nancy Hanks, Mother of Abraham Lincoln. Lindsay.
Reply to Nancy Hanks, A. Silberger.
Hannibal
When Hannibal Crossed the Alps. Farjeon.
Hanno
Southward Sidonian Hanno. Allen.
Hanukkah
Blessings for Chanukah. Sampter.
Dreidel Song. Rosenzweig.
For Hanukkah. Bialik.
Happiness
Character of a Happy Life. Wotton.
Happiness. Isenhour.
Happiness. Leonard.
Happiness Betrays Me. Hoyt.
Her Merriment. Davies.
Interlude. Duggan.
Joy. Delany.
Means to Attain Happy Life, The. Martial.

Of God we ask one favor. Dickinson.
Song of Happiness, A. Lee.
Song of Happiness, A. Rhys.
They of the Meane Estate Are Happiest. *Unknown.*
True Happiness. Talpalar.
Wish, The. *Fr.* The Mistress. Cowley.
Work of Happiness, The. Sarton.

Harbors and Ports
Cinque Port, A. Davidson.
Harbor, The. Letts.
Harbor, The. Sandburg.
Plymouth Harbor. Radford.
Waiwera. Smithyman.

Harding, Warren Gamaliel
Two Poems about President Harding. Wright.

Hardy, Thomas
Birthday Poem for Thomas Hardy. Day Lewis.
For Thomas Hardy. Cooper.
Thomas Hardy, Poet. Van Doren.
Thoughts of Thomas Hardy. Blunden.
To Thomas Hardy. Housman.

Harebells
Harebells in June. Wynne.

Hares
Ecclesiastes. Langland.
Epitaph on a Hare. Cowper.
Hare, The. De la Mare.
Hare and Many Friends, The. Gay.
Hares at Play. Clare.
March Hares. Young.
On Seeing a Wounded Hare Limp by Me. Burns.
See also **Rabbits.**

Harfleur, France, Battle of
Once More unto the Breach, Dear Friends, Once More. *Fr.* King Henry V. Shakespeare.

Harlem, New York City
Esthete in Harlem. Hughes.
Harlem. Brierre.
Harlem ("Here on the edge of hell.") Hughes
Harlem ("What happens to a dream deferred") Hughes.
Harlem Dancer, The. McKay.
Harlem Freeze Frame. Bethune.
Harlem in January. Fields.
Harlem Night Song. Hughes.
Harlem Shadows. McKay.
Harlem '67. Reed.
Harlem Sweeties. Hughes.
Keep on Pushing. Henderson.
Lady from Harlem, The. Cowley.
Lenox Avenue. Alexander.
Lenox Avenue Mural. Hughes.
Neon Diaspora. Henderson.
On the Block: Another Night Scratch. Wright.
Sketches of Harlem. Henderson.
Sonnet to a Negro in Harlem. Johnson.
Still Voice of Harlem, The. Rivers.
Train Runs Late to Harlem. Rivers.
Walking East on 125th Street (Spring 1959). Johnson.

Harlem Heights, Battle of
Haarlem Heights. Guiterman.

Harley, Robert, 1st Earl of Oxford and Earl Mortimer
To Robert Earl of Oxford and Earl Mortimer. Pope.

Harpers Ferry, West Virginia
Harpers Ferry. Rodman.
How Old Brown Took Harpers Ferry. Stedman.

Harps
Aeolian Harp. Allingham.
Aeolian Harp, An. "Field."
Bishop's Harp, The. Manning.
Dear Harp of My Country. Moore.
Harp That Once through Tara's Halls, The. Moore.
Harper, The. *Unknown.*
Minstrel Boy, The. Moore.

Harrison, William Henry
Death of Harrison, The. Willis.
Old Tippecanoe. *Unknown.*

Harvard University
Fair Harvard. Gilman.
Harvard. R. Lowell.
In and Out: Severance of Connections, 1946. Sissman.
To the University of Cambridge, in New-England. Wheatley.
Unicorns at Harvard. Farber.

Harvest
Antique Harvesters. Ransom.
At Harvest. Campbell.
At Husking Time. Johnson.
Child's Thought of Harvest, A. "Coolidge."
Cocooning, The. *Fr.* The Mirèio. Mistral.
Dead Harvest, A. Meynell.
Harvest. Bonar.
Harvest. Cortissoz.
Harvest. Gore-Booth.
Harvest. Hutchinson.
Harvest. Sandburg.
Harvest and Consecration. Jennings.
Harvest Dust. Welles.
Harvest Home. Alford.
Harvest Home. Guiterman.
Harvest-Home Song. Davidson.
Harvest Hymn. *Fr.* For an Autumnal Festival. Whittier.
Harvest Song. Dehmel.
Harvest Song. Georgakas.
Harvest Song. Holty.
Harvest Song, A. Markham.
Harvest Song. *Unknown.*
Harvest Time. Powers.
Hay Harvest. Chalmers.
Haying. Herbin.
Hock-Cart, or Harvest Home, The. Herrick.
Hurrahing in Harvest. Hopkins.
Huskers, The. Whittier.
Load. Hewitt.
Mowers, The. Benton.
Potato Harvest, The. Roberts.
Praise of Ceres. *Fr.* The Silver Age. Heywood.
Reaper, The. Allen.
Reapers, The. Toomer.
Reaping the Barley. Carrera Andrade.
Returning from Harvest. Watkins.
Ripe and Bearded Barley, The. *Unknown.*
Singing the Reapers Homeward Come. *Unknown.*
Solitary Reaper, The. Wordsworth.
Song: "Your hay it is mowed." *Fr.* King Arthur. Dryden.
Song of the Harvest. Washburn.
Story of the Corn. Fisher.
Toward Harvest. Morse.
Valley Harvest, The. Davis.
Winnowers, The. Bridges.

Harvey, Gabriel
To the Right Worshipful, My Singular Good Friend, M[aster] Gabriel Harvey, Doctor of the Laws. Spenser.

Harvey, William
Ode upon Dr. Harvey, *sel.* Cowley.

Hastings, Warren
Fifth Day. Fitzgerald.

Hate
Explanation. Tarver.
Hate. Antokolsky.
Hate. Stephens.
Hate-Song, A. Shelley.
Hatred. Bennett.
Law in the Country of the Cats. Hughes.
Love and Hate. *Unknown.*
My Hate. Bell.
Poison Tree, A. *Fr.* Song of Experience. Blake.
Song about Major Eatherly, A. Wain.
Song of Hate. Frances.
Tragedy. "Æ."
World I See, The. Evans.

Hats
Hat Bar. Weston.
Hattage. Herbert.

Hatteras, Cape
Cape Hatteras. *Fr.* The Bridge. H. Crane.

Havana, Cuba
Habana. Bond.
Havana Dreams; Havana. Hughes.

Hawaii
Honolulu and Back. Logan.
Our Native Land. Kalakaua, King of the Hawaiian Islands

Hawke of Towton, Edward Hawke, 1st Baron
Hawke. Newbolt.

Hawke *(continued)*
Hawke. *Fr.* Sonnets of the Empire. Strong.
Hawkins, Sir John
First American Sailors, The. Rice.
Hawks
Fish-Hawk, The. Wheelock.
Hawk, The. Clouts.
Hawk, The. Knister.
Hawk, The. Yeats.
Hawk in the Rain, The. Hughes.
Hawk Remembered. Phoenice.
Hawk Roosting. Hughes.
Hawks. Stephens.
Hurt Hawks. Jeffers.
Look Now, the Hawk. Parr.
Over Sir John's Hill. Thomas.
Sea-Hawk. Eberhart.
Shepherd and the Hawk, The. Hart-Smith.
To a Marsh Hawk in Spring. Thoreau.
To the Man-of-War-Bird. Whitman.
Wounded Hawk, The. Palmer.
Hawthorn
Hawthorn, The. *Unknown.*
Hawthorn Hedge, The Wright.
Hawthorn Tree, The. Cather.
I Bended unto Me. Brown.
Old Saul. Reese.
Hawthorne, Nathaniel
Hawthorne. Alcott.
Hawthorne. Longfellow.
Hawthorne. *Fr.* A Fable for Critics. Lowell.
Monody. Melville.
On Visiting the Graves of Hawthorne and Thoreau. Very.
Hayden Planetarium (New York City)
Ode to the Hayden Planetarium. Guiterman.
Haydn, Franz Joseph
Hayden—Military Symphony. Douglas.
Haydon, Benjamin Robert
Addressed to Haydon. Keats.
Hayley, William
To Hayley. Blake.
Haze. *See* **Fog.**
Heat
Heat. Doolittle.
Heat. Lampman.
Heat. Mackenzie.
Heather
Heather, The. Munro.
Heaven
At Last. Whittier.
Ballad of Heaven, A. Davidson.
Childless Woman in Heaven, The. Tynan.
Cold Heaven, The. Yeats.
Description of Elysium. Agee.
Dick Said. Untermeyer.
General William Booth Enters into Heaven. Lindsay.
God's Residence. Dickinson.
Going Home with Jesus. Isenhour.
Heaven. Brooke.
Heaven. Dolben.
Heaven. Herbert.
Heaven (Heaven is closed, proclaims the preacher"). *Unknown.*
Heaven ("Think of—/Stepping on shore"). *Unknown.*
Heaven has different signs to me. Dickinson.
Heaven Is Heaven. C. G. Rossetti.
Heaven Overarches. C. G. Rossetti.
Home at Last. Chesterton.
Homeland, The. Haweis.
I never saw a moor. Dickinson.
I went to heaven. Dickinson.
In Him. Flint.
Lady I Know, A. Cullen.
Let Us Go Down, the Long Dead Night Is Done. *Fr.* Towards the Source. Brennan.
Letter from Brooklyn, A. Walcott.
Life after Death. Pindar.
Life of the Blessed, The. León.
My Ain Countree. Demarest.
Nothing in Heaven Functions as It Ought. Kennedy.
O Happy Soul. Gladden.
One Centred System. *Fr.* The Columbiad. Barlow.
Paradiso, *sels.* *Fr.* Divina Commedia. Dante.
Peace. Vaughan.
Port of Many Ships. Masefield.
Promise. "Æ."
Promised Country, The. Strahan.
Prospect of Heaven Makes Death Easy, A. Watts.
Safely Home. *Unknown.*
Seek Flowers of Heaven. Southwell.
Sister Lou. Brown.
Song: "Before we shall again behold." Davenant.
Surprises. *Unknown.*
Theology. Dunbar.
There Is a Land. Watts.
To His Friend in Elysium. Du Bellay.
Two Homes. Nicholson.
We Are God's Chosen Few. Swift.
We'll Meet Again. Smith.
What is—"paradise." Dickinson.
Where is Heaven? *Fr.* Here and Now. Carman.
White Island, The; or, The Place of the Blest. Herrick.
World, The. Vaughan.
You cannot traffick in peace. *Fr.* The Uncelestial City. Wolfe.
Sourcebook of Poetry (SoP). Al Bryant, comp.
See also **Paradise.**
Hebe
Hebe. J. R. Lowell.
Hector
Hector. Iremonger.
Hector to Andromache. *Fr.* The Iliad. Homer.
Last Parting of Hector and Andromache, The. *Fr.* The Iliad. Homer.
Hedgehogs
Hedgehog, The. *Fr.* The Shepherd's Calender. Clare.
Hedgehog, The. King.
Hedgehog and His Coat, The. Fleming.
Heidelberg, Germany
Thinking of Hölderlin. Middleton.
Heimdall
Heimdall. Vinal.
Heine, Heinrich
Heine's Grave. Arnold.
Heinrich Heine. Lewisohn.
Helen of Troy
Helen. Doolittle.
Helen. *Fr.* Dr. Faustus. Marlowe.
Helen. Valentine.
Helen Grown Old. Lewis.
Helen of Troy. *Fr.* Troilus and Cressida. Shakespeare.
Helen—Old. MacKay.
Hélène (Helen, the Sad Queen). Valéry.
Mythmaking. Spivack.
Oenone. Tennyson.
Past Ruin'd Ilion Helen Lives. *Fr.* Ianthe. Landor.
To Helen. Poe.
To Helen. Schwartz.
Troy Town. D. G. Rossetti.
Was This the Face. *Fr.* Dr. Faustus. Marlowe.
White Queen. Fuller.

Heliotrope
Heliotrope. Peck.
Hell
Ballad of Hell, A. Davidson.
Good Man in Hell, The. Muir.
Inferno, *sels.* *Fr.* Divina Commedia. Dante.
Lament of an Idle Demon. Lister.
Nothing in Heaven Functions as It Ought. Kennedy.
Place of the Damned, The. *Fr.* Paradise Lost. Milton.
Satan's Speech. *Fr.* Paradise Lost. Milton.
Song about Major Eatherly, A. Wain.
Theology. Dunbar.
Hengist and Horsa
Hengest Cyning. Borges.
Ode to Hengist and Horsa. Jeffers.
Henry I, King of England
White Ship, The. D. G. Rossetti.
Henry II, King of England
Rose of the World, The. Masefield.
Henry V, King of England
Agincourt. Drayton.

Henry before Agincourt: October 25, 1415. Lydgate.
King Henry V, *sels.* Shakespeare.
Henry VIII, King of England
Ballade of the Scottyshe Kynge, A. Skelton.
Henry VIII. E. and H. Farjeon.
Portrait of Henry VIII, The. Surrey.
Henry IV, King of France
Ivry. Macaulay.
Henry the Navigator
Prince Henry the Navigator. Clouts.
"Henry, O." (William Sydney Porter)
Knight in Disguise, The. Lindsay.
Henry Frederick, Prince of Wales
Lamentation, A. Campion.
Hens
Clucking Hen, The. Hawkshaw.
Cock and Hens. Follen.
Complete Hen, The. Coatsworth.
Flock of Guinea Hens Seen from a Car, A. Welty.
Hen, The. Claudius.
Hen Overboard. Coffin.
Hens, The. Roberts.
Janet Walking. Ransom.
What They Do. Farjeon.
Henschel, Sir George
For the Eightieth Birthday of a Great Singer. Shanks.
Heraclitus
Heraclitus. Cory.
Herbert, George
George Herbert. Jones.
On George Herbert's "The Temple" Sent to a Gentlewoman. Crashaw.
Herbs
Lines with a Gift of Herbs. Lewis.
On His Mistress's Garden of Herbs. *Unknown.*
Hercules
Heracles. Winters.
Heresy and Heretics
Cold heritique. *Unknown.*
Hermit Thrushes. *See* **Thrushes.**
Hermits
Desire for Hermitage, The. *Unknown.*
Eremites, The. Graves.
Hermit, The. "Æ."
Hermit, The. Baxter.
Hermit, The. Hsu Pen.
Hermit, The. Moss.
Hermit, The. Silcock.
Hermitage, The. *Unknown.*
Hermit's Song, The. *Unknown.*
Seraphion. Baxter.
Hero and Leander
Hero and Leander. Marlowe.
On an Engraved Gem of Leander. Keats.
Shall I come, if I swim? wide are the waves, you see. Campion.
Sonnet: "Fair and lovely maid, look from the shore." *Fr.* To Delia. Daniel.
Subjectivity at Sestos. Hubbard.
Herod the Great
Ballad of Two Kings. Code.
Flight into Egypt, The. Southwell.
Innocents, The. Macpherson.
Innocent's Song. Causley.
St. Stephen and Herod. *Unknown.*
Herodotus
Herodotus in Egypt. Lang.
Heroes and Heroines
At the Cedars. Scott.
Ballad of Hell, A. Davidson.
Ballad of Heroes, A. Dobson.
Gee-up Dar, Mules. Piper.
He Fell among Thieves. Newbolt.
Hero, The. Bierce.
Hero, The. Nicoll.
Hero, The. Taylor.
Heroes, The. Simpson.
Heroism. Emerson.
Hervé Riel. R. Browning.
How Sleep the Brave. Collins.
I Think Continually of Those Who Were Truly Great. Spender.
John Maynard. Alger.
Litany of the Heroes, *sels.* Lindsay.
Little Griffen. Ticknor.
Man from the Crowd, The. Foss.
Of a Poet Patriot. MacDonagh.
Private of the Buffs, The. Doyle.
Red Thread of Honour, The. Doyle.
Revenge, The. Tennyson.
Sixteen Dead Men. Shorter.
Song for Heroes, A. Markham.
Speaking: The Hero. Pollak.
Strong Swimmer, The. W. R. Benét.
Upstream. Sandburg.
Young Hero, The. Tyrtaeus.
Herons
Ardan Mor. Ledwidge.
Blue Heron, The. Roberts.
Great Blue Heron, The. Kizer.
Heron. Booth.
Heron, The. Donaghy.
Heron, The. Hovell-Thurlow.
Heron, The. Roethke.
Heron, The. Vrepont.
Heron. Walker.
Heron, The. Watkins.
Heron in Swamp. Howard.
Herons, The. Ledwidge.
Herons. *Unknown.*
Herrick, Robert
To His Book's End. Herrick.
To the Author of Hesperides and Noble Numbers. Van Doren.
With a Copy of Herrick. Gosse.
Herring
Herring. *Fr.* A Bestiary. Rexroth.
Hervey, William
On the Death of Mr. William Hervey. Cowley.
Herzl, Theodor
Theodor Herzl. Zangwill.
Hesiod
Hesiod, 1908. Mair.
Hess, Dame Myra
Jesu, Joy of Man's Desiring. Fitzgerald.
Heywood, John
Ad Modernos Epigrammatistas. Heath.
Of Heywood. Heywood.
To Old John Heywood the Epigrammatist, Wheresoever. Davies of Hereford.
Heywood, Thomas
Thomas Heywood. Swinburne.
Hiawatha
Modern Hiawatha, The. *Fr.* The Song of Milkanwatha. Strong.
Song of Hiawatha, The, *sels.* Longfellow.
What I Think of Hiawatha. Morris.
Highlands of Scotland
Canadian Boat-Song. *Unknown.*
In the Highlands. Stevenson.
My Heart's in the Highlands. Burns.
Hills and Mountains
Afternoon on a Hill. Millay.
Alpine Spirit's Song. Beddoes.
Climbing in Glencoe. Young.
David. Birney.
Evening in the Great Smokies. Heyward.
Golgotha is a Mountain. Bontemps.
Grass on the Mountain, The. *Unknown.*
Having Climbed to the Topmost Peak of the Incense-Burner Mountain. Po Chü-i.
Hemlock Mountain. Cleghorn.
Hike, The. Weiss.
Hill, A. Hecht.
Hills, The. Braley.
Hills. Conkling.
Hills, The. Cornford.
Hills, The. Field.
Hills. Guiterman.
Hills and the Sea. Campbell.
Holy Hill, A "Æ."
Hymn before Sunrise, in the Vale of Chamouni. Coleridge.
I Stood Tiptoe upon a Little Hill. Keats.
In a Desert Town. Stevenson.
In the Highlands. Stevenson.

Hills *(continued)*
In the Mountains on a Summer Day. Li Po.
In the Selkirks. Scott.
Joy of the Hills, The. Markham.
Kinchinjunga. Rice.
Main Range. Picot.
Most-sacred Mountain, The. Tietjens.
Mountain, The, *sel.* Channing.
Mountain, The. Frost.
Mountain, The. Lermontov.
Mountain Air. Galsworthy.
Mountain Evenings. Holme.
Mountain Heart's-Ease, The. Harte.
Mountain in the Sky, The. Corning.
Mountain Lake, The. Church.
Mountain Song. Monroe.
Mountain to the Pine, The. Hawkes.
Mountain Wind, A. "Æ."
Mountaineer, The. Nathan.
Mountains. Clark.
Mountains, The. De la Mare.
Mountains, The. Gibson.
Mountains. Larcom.
Mountains Are a Lonely Folk, The. Garland.
Mountains grow unnoticed, The. Dickinson.
Old Man Mountain. Noyes.
On Bala Hill. Coleridge.
On Middleton Edge. Young.
Pause. Bethell.
Peaks, The. *Fr.* War Is Kind. S. Crane.
Praise of Engineers. Donohue.
Sleeping Giant, The. Hall.
Song to the Mountains. *Unknown.*
Sunset on the Cunimbla Valley, Blue Mountains. Sladen.
That Dark Other Mountain. Francis.
That Far Lone Mountain. Sister Mary Stephanie.
Three Hills, The. Squire.
To a Mountain. Kendall.
To My Mountain. Raine.
To Walk on Hills. Graves.
Who Knows a Mountain? Fuller.
Hindus
Indian upon God, The. Yeats.
Hippopotamuses
Dawn Hippo. Clouts.
Habits of the Hippopotamus. Guiterman.
Hippopotamothalamion. Wheelock.
Hippopotamus, The. Belloc.
Hippopotamus, The. Durston.
Hippopotamus, The. Herford.
Hippopotamus, The. Nash.
I Had a Hippopotamus. Barrington.
To a Blue Hippopotamus. Kay.
Hiroshige, Ando
Hiroshige. Perlberg.
Hiroshima, Japan
Dirge for the New Sunrise. *Fr.* Three Poems of the Atomic Age. E. Sitwell.
Ghosts, Fire, Water. Kirkup.
Hiroshima. Noss.
Hiroshima. Rockwell.
Hiroshima Crewman. Georgakas.
Hiroshima Lullaby, A. Langland.
Horse, The. Levine.
Kimono, The. Gordon.
No More Hiroshimas. Kirkup.
Shadow of Cain, The. E. Sitwell.
History and Historians
Ancient Historian. Wallace-Crabbe.
Human Greatness. Barclay.
Hitler, Adolf
Letter to Hitler, A. Laughlin.
Hobbes, Thomas
To Mr. Hobbes. Cowley.
Hobson, Richard Pearson
Hobson and His Men. Loveman.
Hoby, Sir Thomas
Thomas Sackville in Commendation of the Work to the Reader. Sackville.
Hogg, James
Extempore Effusion upon the Death of James Hogg. Wordsworth.
Hogue, La, Battle of
Hervé Riel. R. Browning.
Hohenlinden, Battle of
Battle of Hohenlinden, The. Campbell.
Hokusai, Katsushika
Camden Magpie. McCrae.
Great Wave, The: Hokusai. Finkel.
Holbein, Hans
Fancy Dress. Mackellar.
Hölderlin, Johann Christian Friedrich
Death of Hoelderlin, The. Oppenheimer.
Hölderlin. Schwartz.
Holiday, Billie (Eleanora Fagan McKay)
Blues and Bitterness. Bennett.
Day Lady Died, The. O'Hara.
Holidays
On This Day; an Anthology of Poetry and Prose for Every Day of the Year. (OTD). Phyllis Detz *and* Kermit M. Stover, eds.
Our Holidays in Poetry (OHIP). Mildred P. Harrington *and* Josephine H. Thomas, comps.
Pieces for Every Day the Schools Celebrate (PEDC). Norma H. Deming *and* Katharine I. Bemis, eds.
Poems for Red Letter Days (PoRL). Elizabeth Hough Sechrist, comp.
Poems for Seasons and Celebrations (PoSC). William Cole, ed.
Poems for the Great Days (PGD). Thomas Curtis Clark *and* Robert Earle Clark, comps.
See also **specific holidays.**
Holland. *See* **Netherlands.**
Holly
Aunt Mary. Hawker.
But Give Me Holly, Bold and Jolly. C. G. Rossetti.
Green Groweth the Holly. Henry VIII, King of England.
Holly, The. De la Mare.
Holly, The. King.
Holly against Ivy. *Unknown.*
Holly and Ivy ("Holly and ivy made a great party"). *Unknown.*
Holly and the Ivy, The ("The holly and the ivy,/ When they are both full grown"). *Unknown*
Holly fairies. Fisher.
Holly-Tree. Southey.
Nay, Ivy, Nay. *Unknown.*
Hollyhocks
Hollyhock, A. Sherman.
Hollyhocks, The. Betts.
Hollywood, California
Hollywood. Blanding.
Hollywood. Shapiro.
Holmes, Oliver Wendell (1809-94)
Holmes. *Fr.* A Fable for Critics. J. R. Lowell.
Oliver Wendell Holmes. Hayne.
To O. W. Holmes. Hayne.
Holy Family
Cherry-Tree Carol, The. *Unknown.*
Flight into Egypt. *Fr.* Cursor Mundi. *Unknown.*
Return from Egypt, The. Pope Leo XIII.
Holy Ghost
His Letanie, to the Holy Spirit. Herrick.
Person, or a Hymn on and to the Holy Ghost. Avison.
Holy Grail
Holy Grail, The. *Fr.* Idylls of the King. Tennyson.
Vision of Sir Launfal, The. J. R. Lowell.
Home
Altars Raised to God. Nicholson.
At Home, Alone with the Cat. De la Mare.
At Home, Alone with the Dog. Monro.
Autumn. *Fr.* Seasons of the Soul. Tate.
Better than Gold. Ryan.
Bless This House. Taylor.
Cup of Happiness, The. Thomas.
Dearest Spot on Earth, The. Wrighton.
Death of the Hired Man, The. Frost.
Dedication: "O thou whose gracious presence blest." Benson.
Deserted Home, A. Lysaght.
For a New Home. Marinoni.
God Bless Our Home. Freeman.
Good-bye. Emerson.
Hame, Hame, Hame. Cunningham.
Hearthstone. Monro.

Heart's Content. *Unknown.*
Heureux qui, comme Ulysse, a fait un beau voyage. *Fr.* Regrets. Du Bellay.
Home. Armes.
Home. *Fr.* The Death of the Hired Man. Frost.
Home. Greenwell.
Home. Guest.
Home. Harris.
Home. Hines.
Home. Nicholson.
Home. Sill.
Homecoming in Storm. Kenyon.
Home Fire, The. Johns.
Home from Abroad. Lee.
Home Is Where There Is One to Love Us. Swain.
Home No More Home to Me. Stevenson.
Home on the Range, A. *Unknown.*
Home Song. Longfellow.
Home, Sweet Home. Payne.
Homes of England, The. Hemans.
House, The. Treece.
House and Home. Beaumont.
House and Home. Hugo.
House Blessing. Guiterman.
House on the Hill, The. Robinson.
Hymn for a Household. Henderson.
I Am the Only Being. E. Brontë.
I saw green banks of daffodil. Tennant.
Little Bird, The. De la Mare.
Long Voyage, The. Cowley.
My Ain Fireside. Hamilton.
My Early Home. Clare.
My Little Lodge. *Unknown.*
My Mother's House. Tietjens.
O Happy Home. Spitta.
Old Folks at Home. Foster.
Old Home, The. Cawein.
Old Homes. Blunden.
Old Place, The. Baughan.
Old Woman of the Roads, An. Colum.
Our House. Thompson.
Pilgrim from the East, The. Kahn.
Poetry of Departures. Larkin.
Prayer for a Little Home, A. Bone.
Prayer for a New House. Nicholson.
Prayer for Our Home. Hoyland.
Prayer for the Home, *sel.* Guest.
Prayer for the Household, A. Stevenson.
Prayer for This House. Untermeyer.
Return of the Native, The. Matthews.
Returning Home. De Bellay.
Roofs. Kilmer.
Search. Marriott.
Shiny Little House, The. Hayes.
So Long as There Are Homes. Crowell.
So Long Had I Travelled. Gibson.
Sometimes a Little House Will Please. Coatsworth.
Song for a Little House. Morley.
Sun Rises Bright in France, The. Cunningham.
Sweetest Home, The. *Unknown.*
Thanksgiving for a Habitat. Auden.
Thanksgiving to God for His House, A. Herrick.
Traveller's Return, The. Southey.
True Riches. Martin.
Urn, The. Cowley.
What Makes a Home? *Unknown.*
When a Man Turns Homeward. Hicky.
Wish, The. Cowley.
Young and Old. *Fr.* The Water Babies. Kingsley.

Homer
After Reading Homer. Dolben.
By Deputy. Adcock.
Homer. Ehrenstein.
Iliad. Wolfe.
Life through Verse. Alpheus of Mitylene.
On First Looking into Chapman's Homer. Keats.
On Homer's Birthplace. Heywood.
School-Boy Reads His Iliad, The. Morton.
Seven Wealthy Towns. *Unknown.*
To a Friend. Arnold.
To Homer. Bulloch.
To Homer. Keats.
Tourist. Van Doren.

Homesickness
City Clerk, The. Ashe.
Homesick Blues. Hughes.

Homesteaders
Hurrah for Greer County. *Unknown.*
Little Old Sod Shanty. *Unknown.*

Honesty
Be True. Bonar.
Honest Man, An. *Fr.* An Essay on Man. Pope.

Honey
Brown Bear's Honey Song. Jackson.
Honey. Cane.
Honey. Miller.

Honeysuckle
Honeysuckle, The. D. G. Rossetti.
Spray of Honeysuckle, A. Bradley.
To the Herald Honeysuckle. Pfeiffer.
Wild Honeysuckle, The. Freneau.

Honor
Definitions. Keith.
Inquisition upon Fame and Honour, An. Greville.
Prison Sonnet. Blunt.
Vitaï Lampada. Newbolt.

Hood, Thomas
On The Hood. Landor.
Thomas Hood. Robinson.
Thomas Hood. Watson.
Stanzas to the Memory of Thomas Hood. Simmons.

Hooker, Joseph
Hooker's Across. Boker.

Hoopoes
Hoopoe. *Fr.* Nepenthe. Darley.

Hope
Against Hope. Cowley.
Answer for Hope. Crashaw.
Anticipation. E. Brontë.
Assassination, The. Hillyer.
At summer eve, when Heaven's ethereal bow. *Fr.* The Pleasures of Hope. Campbell.
"Bottle Should Be Plainly Labeled 'Poison'." Hay
Circumstance. Shelley.
Darkling Thrush, The. Hardy.
For Hope. Crashaw.
Hope. Carmichael.
Hope. *Fr.* The Mistress. Cowley.
Hope. Fanshawe.
Hope. *Fr.* The Captivity; an Oratorio. Goldsmith.
Hope. Howells.
Hope. Jarrell.
Hope. Mezquida.
Hope. Taylor.
Hope. Theognis.
Hope and Fear. Swinburne.
Hope is a subtle glutton. Dickinson.
Hope is the thing with feathers. Dickinson.
I dwell in possibility. Dickinson.
Leaden Echo and the Golden Echo, The. Hopkins.
M. Crashaws Answer for Hope. Crashaw.
Message of the March Wind, The. Morris.
New Every Morning. *Unknown.*
Pause of Thought, A. C. G. Rossetti.
Pleasure of Hope, The. *Fr.* An Essay on Man. Pope.
Prime. Auden.
Put Forth Thy Leaf, Thou Lofty Plane. Clough.
Say Not the Struggle Nought Availeth. Clough.
Song of Hope. Hardy.
Song of Hope. Lathbury.
What We, When Face to Face We See. Clough.

Hopkins, Gerard Manley
Breakfast with Gerard Manley Hopkins. Brode.
Poem for Gerard. Mayo
To Father Gerard Manley Hopkins, S.J. Barker.

Horace
After Horace. Godley.
Allusion to Horace, An. The Tenth Satire of the First Book. Rochester.
Horace. Sargent.
Horations, The. Auden.
Ode: Allusion to Horace. Akenside.

Horace *(continued)*
On First Looking into Loeb's Horace. Durrell.
Horatius
Horatius. *Fr.* Lays of Ancient Rome. Macaulay.
Horn, Cape
Coming around the Horn. *Unknown.*
Round Cape Horn. *Unknown.*
Rounding the Horn. *Fr.* Dauber. Masefield.
Horns (musical instruments)
Riddle #14: A Horn. *Unknown.*
Sound of the Horn, The. Vigny.
Horsa. *See* **Hengist and Horsa.**
Horse Chestnut Trees
Horse Chestnut Tree, The. Eberhart.
Horse Racing
At Galway Races. Yeats.
At Grass. Larkin.
Beautiful Horses, The. Hall.
Camptown Races, De. Foster.
Galway Races. *Unknown.*
How the Old Horse Won the Bet. Holmes.
How We Beat the Favourite. Gordon.
Morning Workout. Deutsch.
Morning Track, The. Parone.
Racing-Man, The. Herbert.
Tom Fool at Jamaica. Moore.
Horses
Arab's Farewell to His Steed. Norton.
At Amberley Wild Brooks. Young.
At Grass. Larkin.
Blessing, A [*or* The]. Wright.
Blood Horse, The. "Cornwall."
Broncho That Would Not Be Broken, The. Lindsay.
Colt, The. Knister.
Daniel Webster's Horses. Coatsworth.
Distant Runners, The. Van Doren.
Dream of Horses, A. Hughes.
Duchess. Bowes-Lyon.
Dusk of Horses, The. Dickey.
Flash; the Fireman's Story. Carleton.
Foal. Miller.
For Sale, a Horse. Taylor.
Gallop of Fire, A. Pitt.
Horse, The. Job, Bible, *O.T.*
Horse. Harrison.
Horse. Roberts.
Horse, The. Royde-Smith.
Horse, The. *Fr.* King Henry V. Shakespeare.
Horse, A. *Fr.* Venus and Adonis. Shakespeare.
Horse, The. Williams.
Horse Thief, The. W. R. Benét.
Horsemen, The. Baro.
Horses. Armour.
Horses, The. Hughes.
Horses, The. Muir.
Horses. Wellesley.
Horses and Men in Rain. Sandburg.
Horses Chawin' Hay. Garland.
Horses of Marini, The. Van Zyl.
Horses of the Sea, The. C. G. Rossetti.
Horses on the Camargue. Campbell.
Huckster's Horse, The. Strong.
Hunter Trials. Betjeman.
Kentucky Belle. Woolson.
Kentucky Thoroughbred, The. Riley.
Last Leap, The. Gordon.
Man from Snowy River, The. Paterson.
Mare, A. Barnes.
Mares of the Camargue, The. *Fr.* Mirèio. Mistral.
Milk-Cart Pony, The. Farjeon.
Milkman's Horse, The. *Unknown.*
Mongolian Horse, The. Tu Fu.
My Bonny Black Bess. *Unknown.*
My Horses. Jaszi.
My Little Pony. *Unknown.*
Nell. *Fr.* A Row of Stalls. Knister.
Noonday Sun. Jackson.
Old Brown Horse, The. Holmes.
Orchard. Stone.
Phar Lap in the Melbourne Museum. Porter.
Poor Old Horse. *Unknown.*
Prayer of the Old Horse, The. Gasztold.
Roan Stallion. Jeffers.
Runaway, The. Frost.
Say This of Horses. Moody.
Song of the Horse. *Unknown.*
Stable-Talk. Knister.
Steeds. Hiebert.
Stricken Colts, The. Peck.
There Was a Little Nobby Colt. *Unknown.*
Thoroughbred, The. Magaret.
To a Man on His Horse. Prince.
Tom Fool at Jamaica. Moore.
War God's Horse Song, The. *Unknown.*
What a Proud Dreamhorse. Cummings.
White Horses. Farjeon.
White Horses. Howard.
Wild Horse Jerry's Story. Howard.
Wild Horses. Sandburg.
Work Horses. Chase.
Hospital
Hospital. Funk.
Hospital, A. Noyes.
Hospital Observation. Symons.
Hospital Waiting-Room, The. Davies.
In Hospital. Henley.
In Hospital: Poona (II). Lewis.
In the Children's Hospital. Tennyson.
In the Hospital. Guiterman.
In the Hospital. Howland.
Notes for the Chart on 306. Nash.
Operation, The. Snodgrass.
Red Cross Nurses. Stewart.
Reflections in a Hospital. Eisenberg.
Viaticum. MacCarthy.
Hotels
Casey's Table d'Hote. Field.
Irish Hotel. Wevill.
Lament for Lost Lodgings. McGinley.
Hottentots
Midsummer Fantasy. Levy.
Housekeeping
Digression from Husbandry to a Point or Two of Huswifery, A. Tusser.
Housewife, The. Coblentz.
Hundreth good points of good husbandry, A. Tusser.
I Like Housecleaning. Thompson.
On a Tired Housewife. *Unknown.*
Houses
After Reading in a Letter Proposals for Building a Cottage. Clare.
Ancestral Dwellings, The. Van Dyke.
Bless This House. Taylor.
Breaking a line of pines, a wide white gate. *Fr.* Golden Wedding. Mulgan.
Consecration of the House. Fairbridge.
Deserted House, The. M. E. Coleridge.
Deserted House, The. Tennyson.
Destruction of Bulfinch's House, The. Sandy.
Directive. Frost.
Empty House, The. Howells.
House, The. Van Zyl.
House and Grounds, A. Hunt.
House and Home. Beaumont.
House and Home. Hugo.
House Blessing. Guiterman.
House in Wartime, A. Church.
House of the Eighties, A. Wilson.
House on the Hill, The. Robinson.
House That Was, The. Binyon.
House with Nobody in It, The. Kilmer.
I know some lonely houses off the road. Dickinson.
My House. Krows.
My House. McKay.
My House. Stevenson.
My House Has Windows. Mazquida.
My Little House. M. Byron.
New House, The. Thomas.
New Houses. Crowell.
O Blessed House, That Cheerfully Receiveth. Spitta.
O Thou Whose Gracious Presence Blest. Benson.
Old House, The. Barnes.

Old House, The. Woodberry.
Old Houses. D'Lettuso.
Old Houses. Romano.
Old Houses of Flanders, The. Ford.
Old Log House. Tippett.
On Gaulstown House. Swift.
Our House. Miller.
Out of the Old House, Nancy. Carleton.
Prayer for a New House. Untermeyer.
Ruin, The. Tomlinson.
Ruined Cabin, The. King.
Song for a Little House. Morley.
Suburbs, The. Derham.
Thanksgiving to God for His House, A. Herrick.
Treasure of the Haunted Rambler, The. Sladek.
To the Little House. Morley.
To the New Owner. Reynolds.
Two Houses, The. Hardy.
Vacant Farmhouse, The. De la Mare.
Your House. *Unknown.*
See also **Home**

Housman, Alfred Edward
A. E. Housman and a Few Friends. Wolfe.
To A. E. Housman. Bynner.

Howard, Sir Robert
To My Honor'd Friend Sir Robert Howard, on His Excellent Poems. Dryden.

Hudson, Henry
Henry Hudson's Quest. Stevenson.

Hudson River
Egyptian Passage, An. Weiss.
Hudson, The. Hellman.
Lordly Hudson, The. Goodman.
Mouth of the Hudson, The. R. Lowell.

Hughes, Langston
Langston. Evans.

Hugo, Victor
To Victor Hugo. Swinburne.

Huguenots
Huguenot, A. M. E. Coleridge.
Psalm, The. Bridges.

Hull, William
Hull's Surrender. *Unknown.*

Humility
Blades of Grass, The. Crane.
Fool's Prayer, The. Sill.
Happiest Heart, The. Cheney.
Humility. Herbert.
Humility. Herrick.
Humility. *Fr.* God's Two Dwellings. Washbourne.
Immanence. Underhill.
Magnanimous, The. Kay.
Shepherd Boy's Song, The. Bunyan.

Hummingbirds
Humming-Bird, The. Howitt.
Hummingbird, The. Kemp.
Humming-Bird. Lawrence.
Route of evanescence, A. Dickinson.
To a Humming Bird in a Garden. Murray.
Vision. Eberhart.
Within my garden rides a bird. Dickinson.

Humorous Verse
Anthology of Light Verse (ALV). Louis Kronenberger, ed.
Book of Humorous Verse, The (BOHV). Carolyn Wells, comp.
Century of Humorous Verse, 1850-1950, A (CenHV). Roger Lancelyn Green, ed.
Fireside Book of Humorous Poetry, The (FiBHP). William Cole, ed.
Innocent Merriment (InMe). Franklin P. Adams, comp.
Little Book of American Humorous Verse, A (LHV). T. A. Daly, ed.
Little Book of Limericks, The (LiBL). H. I. Brock, ed.
Little Book of Necessary Nonsense, A (LBN). Burges Johnson, ed.
Moon Is Shining Bright as Day, The (MoShBr). Ogden Nash, ed.
Nonsense Anthology, A (NA). Carolyn Wells, ed.
Oxford Book of Light Verse, The (OxBoli). W. H. Auden, comp.
Pith & Vinegar; an Anthology of Short Humorous Poetry (PV). William Cole, ed.
Shrieks at Midnight: Macabre Poems, Eerie and Humorous (ShM). Sara and John E. Brewton, eds.
Silver Treasury of Light Verse, The (SiTL). Oscar Williams, ed.
What Cheer (WhC). David McCord, ed.

Hundred Years War
Ballad of Banners (1944), The. Lehmann.

Hungary
Music of Hungary. Aldrich.

Hunger
Hug Your Hunger, Brother. Goodman.
Hunger. Binyon.
Hunger. Hall.
Hunger. Rimbaud.
Hunger. *Unknown.*
Late Rising. Prévert.
Little Cart, The. Ch'en Tzu-lung.
Long time ago, A. Tao Yuan-ming.
When I Think of the Hungry People. O-Shi-O.

Hunt, Leigh
Sonnet: Written on the Day That Mr. Leigh Hunt Left Prison. Keats.
To Leigh Hunt, Esq. Keats.
You are now/ In London that great sea. *Fr.* Letter to Maria Gisborne. Shelley.

Hunting and Hunters
All in Green Went My Love Riding. Cummings.
Badger. Clare.
Beagles. Rodgers.
Bear Hunt, The. Widdemer.
Brother Solon's Hunting Song. D'Urfey.
Canadian Hunter's Song. Moodie.
Castles and Distances. Wilbur.
Cazador (Hunter). García Lorca.
Charm for Going a-Hunting. Austin.
Chevy Chase. *Unknown.*
Fox-Hunters, The. Elliot.
From the Gallows Hill to the Tineton Corpse. *Fr.* Reynard the Fox. Masefield.
Haymakers, Rakers. *Fr.* The Sun's Darling. Dekker.
Horse & Rider. Robinson.
Hunt, The. Deutsch.
Hunt. La Follette.
Hunt, The. Kent.
Hunt, The. Spofford.
Hunt Is Up, The. Gray.
Hunt of Sliabh Truim, The, *sel.* *Unknown.*
Hunter, The. Nash.
Hunter, The. Turner.
Hunter of the Prairies, The. Bryant.
Hunters, The. Lindsay.
Hunters of Kentucky, The. Woodworth.
Hunter's Song, The. "Cornwall."
Hunting Song. *Fr.* Zapolya. Coleridge.
Hunting Song. *Fr.* Don Quixote in England. Fielding.
Hunting Song. Finkel.
Hunting Song. *Fr.* King Arthur. Hovey.
Hunting Song. Scott.
Hunting Song, The ("Come, come my hearts, a-hunting let us wend"). *Unknown.*
Hunting Song, A. *Fr.* Apollo and Daphne. Whitehead.
Huntsmen, The. De la Mare.
John Peel. Graves.
King's Hunt Is Up, The. Gray.
Like as a huntsman after weary chase. *Fr.* Amoretti. Spenser.
Mighty Hunter, The. Worley.
Mountain Lion. Lawrence.
Old Squire, The. Blunt.
Rainbow. Huff.
Revenge of the Hunted. Ford.
Reynard the Fox. *Unknown.*
Rock Painting. Cope.
Rousing Canoe Song, The Fraser.
Runnable Stag, A. Davidson.
See! from the brake the whirring pleasant springs. *Fr.* Windsor Forest. Pope.
September. *Fr.* Sonnets of the Months. San Geminiano.
Small Game. Levine.
Target Practice. Finkel.
Three Huntsmen, The. *Unknown.*
Three Jolly Hunters, The. Riley.
Three Jolly Huntsmen. *Unknown.*

Hunting *(continued)*
Wild Huntsmen, The. Hamerton.
Yolp, Yolp, Yolp, Yolp. *Unknown.*
Hurdy-Gurdies
Barrel Organ, The. Noyes.
Hurdy-Gurdy Man in Winter. Watkins.
Lines on Hearing the Organ. Calverley.
Organ Grinders' Garden, The. Merryman.
Huron, Lake
Great Lakes Suite, The. Reaney.
Hurricanes
Hurricane, The. Crane.
Hurricane, The. Freneau.
Hurricane, The. Matos.
Hurricane at Sea, A. Swenson.
Husbands. *See* **Marriage.**
Hutchinson, Anne
Anne Hutchinson's Exile. Hale.
Hyacinths
Admonition for Spring. MacKay.
Babiaantje, The. Prince.
Hyacinths to Feed Thy Soul. *Fr.* The Gulistan. Sadi.
Hyderabad, India
In the Bazaars of Hyderabad. Naidu.
Hyenas
Hyena ("My father came in the darkness"). *Unknown.*
Hyena ("The fire threatens"). *Unknown.*
Hyena's Song to Her Children. *Unknown.*
Hypocrisy
Address to the Unco Guid, or the Rigidly Righteous. Burns.
Confessional, The. *Unknown.*
Confessor, The. Belli.
Heaven ("Heaven is closed, proclaims the preacher"). *Unknown.*
Hypocrisy. Butler.
Hypocrite, The. Kalonymos ben Kalonymos.
In Westminster Abbey. Betjeman.
Mistake, The. *Unknown.*
Next to of Course God America I. Cummings.
Holy Willie's Prayer. Burns.

I

I.W.W. *See* **Industrial Workers of the World.**
Ibn Ezra, Abraham ben Meir
Rabbi Ben Ezra. R. Browning.
Ibn Ezra, Moses
On Parting with Moses ibn Ezra. Halevi.
Ibycus
Cranes of Ibycus, The. Lazarus.
Ibycus. Heath-Stubbs.
Icarus
Daedalus. *Fr.* Metamorphoses. Ovid.
Icarus. Bottrall.
Icarus. Iremonger.
Icarus. Koopman.
Icarus. Smithyman.
Icarus. *Unknown.*
Landscape with the Fall of Icarus. Williams.
Love Winged My Hopes. *Unknown.*
New Icarus, The. Miller.
Ice
Fire and Ice. Frost.
Ice. Aldis.
Ice. Roberts.
Ice-Floes, The. Pratt.
Ice Cream
Good Humor Man, The. McGinley.
Ice-Cream Man, The. Field.
Ice-Skating. *See* **Skating and Skates.**
Icebergs
Berg, The. Melville.
Iceberg, The. Merwin.
Iceberg, The. *Fr.* The *Titanic.* Pratt.
Iceberg, The. Roberts.
Icebergs. Foster.
Imaginary Iceberg, The. Bishop.
White, said Worsley, and glistening, the ridgy plain. *Fr.* Worsley Enchanted. Stewart.
Iceland
Iceland First Seen. Morris.
Iceland's Song. Thomsen.
Idaho
Here We Have Idaho. Powell.
On the Trail to Idaho. *Unknown.*
Idleness
Idler, The. Jennings.
Ode on Indolence. Keats.
Sluggard, The. Watts.
Tired Tim. De la Mare.
Iguanas
Iguanas. Atamian.
Illinois
Across Illinois. Stoltze.
El-a-noy. *Unknown.*
Illinois. Chamberlain.
Illness
Bout with Burning. Miller.
Dark Women. Hughes.
Far Cry after a Close Call, A. Howard.
Fever 103 degrees. Plath.
Flat One, A. Snodgrass.
Hymn of Praise, on a Recovery from Sickness, A. Colman.
Hymn to My God in a Night of My Late Sicknesse. Wotton.
In Praise of Music in Time of Pestilence. Hine.
Land of Counterpane, The. Stevenson.
Lion, Leopard, Lady. Le Pan.
Night Nurse Goes Her Round, The. Gray.
Passing Out. Levine.
Pastoral. *Fr.* In Hospital. Henley.
Sick Boy. Ridler.
To Mary. Cowper.
Utopian Journey, A. Jarrell.
Imagination
Attic, The. Coulette.
Blanket Street. Hogan.
Block City. Stevenson.
Falcon, The. Wylie.
Idols of Imagination. Eberhart.
Land of Counterpane, The. Stevenson.
Land of Story-Books, The. Stevenson.
Little Land, The. Stevenson.
Lunatic, the Lover, and the Poet, The. *Fr.* A Midsummer Night's Dream. Shakespeare.
Make Believe. Behn.
Mrs. Alfred Uruguay. Stevens.
Ode to Fancy. Warton.
On Imagination. Wheatley.
One Day When We Went Walking. Hobbs.
Pictures in the Fire. Strong.
Pleasures of Imagaination, The, *sels.* Akenside.
Power of Fancy, The. Freneau.
Realm of Fancy, The. Keats.
Secret Land, The. Graves.
Seein' Things. Field.
Ships of Yule, The. Carman.
Tell Me, Where Is Fancy Bred. *Fr.* The Merchant of Venice. Shakespeare.
Underwood. Moss.
Immigrants
Immigrants. Turner.
My Father. Dalven.
New Colossus, The. Lazarus.
"Scum o' the Earth." Schauffler.
Immortality
All, all for immortality. *Fr.* Song of the Universal. Whitman.
All That Was Mortal. Teasdale.
Because I could not stop for death. Dickinson.
Cato's Soliloquy. *Fr.* Cato. Addison.
Christus Triumphans. Pallen.
Cities and Thrones and Powers. *Fr.* Puck of Pook's Hill. Kipling.
Death, Be Not Proud. *Fr.* Holy Sonnets. Donne.
Demeter and Persephone. Tennyson.
He has outsoared the shadow of our night. *Fr.* Adonais. Shelley.
Human Life; on the Denial of Immortality. Coleridge.
I Lost the Love of Heaven. Clare.
If my bark sink. Dickinson.
Immortal. Teasdale.

Immortal Mind. Byron.
Immortal Spirit, The. Spender.
Immortality. "Æ."
Immortality. Arnold.
Immortality. Dana.
Immortality. Hardy.
Immortality. Horne.
Immortality. Jefferson.
Immortality. Minski.
Immortality. Mitchell.
Immortality. Myers.
Immortality. Reese.
Immortality. *Unknown.*
In After Time. Eberhart.
Invite to Eternity, An. Clare.
It is an honorable thought. Dickinson.
Man's Mortality. *Fr.* Microbiblion. Wastell.
My Sun Sets to Rise Again. *Fr.* At the Mermaid. R. Browning.
New Birth, The. Very.
Night Thoughts, *sels.* Young.
No Death. Marston.
Not to Die. Simonides.
O May I Join the Choir Invisible. "Eliot."
Ode: Intimations of Immortality from Recollections of Early Childhood. Wordsworth.
Of the Progresse of the Soule; the Second Anniversary. Donne.
Of the Soul of Men and the Immortality Thereof. *Fr.* Nosce Teipsum. Davies.
Of the Terrible Doubt of Appearances. Whitman.
One Immortality. Engels.
Pantheist's Song of Immortality, The. Naden.
Paradox, The. Pitter.
Past Ruin'd Ilion Helen Lives. *Fr.* Ianthe. Landor.
Question Whither, The. Meredith.
Recapitulation, The. Eberhart.
Resurrection and Immortality. Vaughan.
Sailing to Byzantium. Yeats.
Saon of Acanthus. Callimachus.
Song's Eternity. Clare.
Sonnet: "Not marble, nor the gilded monuments." *Fr.* Sonnets. Shakespeare.
Sudden Light. *Fr.* The House of Life. D. G. Rossetti.
There Is No Death. McCreery.
There In No Death. *Unknown.*
There is no Death. What seems so is transition. *Fr.* Resignation. Longfellow.
They Are All Gone into the World of Light. Vaughan.
Tithonus. Tennyson.
Tithonus. Thomas.
Village Atheist, The. *Fr.* Spoon River Anthology. Masters.
We thirst at first—'tis nature's act. Dickinson.
While Immortality Endures. Briggs.
White Island, The; or, Place of the Blest. Herrick.
Who Hath His Fancy Pleasèd. Sidney.

Imperialism
Scythians, The. Blok.
White Man's Burden, The. Kipling.

Inauguration Day
Inauguration Day. Gilder.

Independence Day. *See* **Fourth of July.**

India
Child, The. Massey.
Hot Weather in the Plains—India. Tipple.
In Hospital: Poona (II). Lewis.
In India. Shapiro.
India. Coates.
India the Magic. Jules-Bois.
Passage to India. Whitman.
Studies at Delhi. Lyall.
Third Continent, The. Erulkar.
This Landscape, These People. Ghose.

Indian Pipe (flower)
Indian Pipe and Moccasin Flower. Guiterman.

Indian Summer
Indian Summer. Campbell.
Indian Summer. Moodie.
Indian Summer. Tabb.
Indian Summer—Buffalo Summer. Scott.
Indian Summer Day on the Prairie, An. Lindsay.
These are the days when birds come back. Dickinson.
Vermont; Indian Summer. Booth.

Indiana
July in Indiana. Fitzgerald.
Midwest. Nims.
On the Banks of the Wabash, Far Away. Dresser.

Indians, American
Adulteries, murthers, robberies, thefts. Williams.
As Brothers Live Together. *Fr.* The Song of Hiawatha. Longfellow.
Blackfeet, Blood and Piegan Hunters. Welch.
Caughnawaga Beadwork Seller, The. Lighthall.
Christmas Comes to Moccasin Flat. Welch.
Copperfaces, The. *Fr.* The People, Yes. Sandburg.
Courteous Pagan Shall Condemn, The. *Fr.* A Key into the Language of America. Williams.
Dance for Rain, A. Bynner.
Feet of the Young Men, The. Kipling.
Flower-fed Buffaloes, The. Lindsay.
Gathering on the Plains, The. Butler.
Ghosts of the Buffaloes, The. Lindsay.
Half-Breed Girl, The. Scott.
Hiawatha. Sandy.
Hiawatha's Childhood. *Fr.* The Song of Hiawatha. Longfellow.
In My First Hard Springtime. Welch.
In the Oregon County. Stafford.
Indian Burying Ground, The. Freneau.
Indian Children. Wynne.
Indian Ghost Dance and War, The. Prather.
Indian Hunter, The. Cook.
Indian Names. Sigourney.
Indian Reservation: Caughnawaga. Klein.
Indian Sky. Kreymborg.
Indian Student, The. Freneau.
Indian Summer—Buffalo Summer. Scott.
Indians. Fandel.
Indians Come Down from Mixco, The. Asturias.
Lament of a Man for His Son. *Unknown.*
Last Reservation, The. Learned.
Little Papoose. Conkling.
Lullaby of the Iroquois. Johnson.
Missouri Traveller Writes Home, A, 1830. Bly.
Navajo Prayer. *Unknown.*
Once we were strong. *Fr.* Tecumseh. Mair.
Portrait of an Indian. Rashley.
Powwow. Snodgrass.
Pride, The. Newlove.
Red Men, The. Sangster.
Song of Greatness, A. *Unknown.*
Song of the Micmac, The. Howe.
Sonnet: "There was an Indian, who had known no change." Squire.
Speech of the Salish Chief. *Fr.* Damnation of Vancouver. Birney.
There Came an Ancient Huron. *Unknown.*
There Was an Indian. Squire.
To the Driving Cloud. Longfellow.
Ute Lover, The. Garland.
Vision of a Past Warrior. La Farge.
War Dance, The. Carr.
Watkwenies. Scott.
Western Trail, The. Carr.
White Man's Road, The. Chapman.
Winter Indian. Welch.
Wolf Song, the Rain. Welch.

Industrial Revolution
Deserted Village, The. Goldsmith.
Symphony, The. Lanier.

Industrial Workers of the World
There Is Power in a Union. *Unknown.*

Infants. *See* **Babies.**

Infidelity
Faithless. *Unknown.*
Faithless Shepherdess, The. *Unknown.*
Faithless Wife, The. García Lorca.
False Though She Be. Congreve.
Maid's Complaint, A. Campion.
Lover Showeth How He is Forsaken of Such as He Sometimes Enjoyed, The. Wyatt.
Non Sum Qualis Eram Bonae sub Regno Cynarae. Dowson.
Scrutiny, The. Lovelace.

Infidelity *(continued)*
Song: "Go and catch a falling star." Donne.
To His Forsaken Mistress. Aytoun.
To My Inconstant Mistress. Carew.
To the Inconstant Cynthia. Howard.
Woman's Constancy. Donne.
Inge, William Ralph
On Dean Inge. Wolfe.
Injustice
Agony of God, The. Harkness.
Charcoal-Seller, The. Po Chü-i.
How Can I Sing? *Unknown.*
I Sit and Look Out. Whitman.
Jericho Road, The. Poteat.
Litany at Alabama, A. Dubois.
Man's Inhumanity to Man. *Fr.* Man Was Made to Mourn. Burns.
When I Think of the Hungry People. O-Shi-O.
Inkwells
To a Post-Office Inkwell. Morley.
Innisfree, Ireland
Lake Isle of Innisfree, The. Yeats.
Innocents, Slaughter of the. *See* **Herod the Great.**
Inns. *See* **Hotels.**
Insanity. *See* **Madness.**
Insects
Ant Explorer, The. Dennis.
Divine Insect, The. Wheelock.
Hurt No Living Thing. *Fr.* Sing-Song. C. G. Rossetti.
Little Black Bug. Brown.
Near Dusk. Auslander.
Insurance
Epitaph: "Insured for every accident." Armour.
Insurgente (ship)
Constellation and the *Insurgente,* The. *Unknown.*
Intellect
Brain is wider than the sky, The. Dickinson.
Cleon. R. Browning.
Details. Zilles.
First Philosopher's Song. Huxley.
Freedom for the Mind. Garrison.
Heart and Mind. E. Sitwell.
Human Mind, The. Ai Shih-te.
Hymn to Intellectual Beauty. Shelley.
In a Hard Intellectual Light. Eberhart.
In This Strange House. Drewry.
Matthew met Richard when or where. *Fr.* Alma; or, The Progress of the Mind. Prior.
Mind. Wilbur.
Mind Is an Enchanting Thing, The. Moore.
My Mind to Me a Kingdom Is. Dyer.
Of a Contented Mind. Thomas, Lord Vaux.
Perishing Bird, The. Jones.
Riddles. Kirby.
Send Forth the High Falcon. Adams.
Thought. Emerson.
Thunderstorms. Davies.
Ye sons of men, with just regard attend. *Fr.* Solomon on the Vanity of the World. Prior.
International Brigade. *See* **Civil War, Spanish.**
Inventors
Edison. Jeffers.
Inventor's Wife, The. Corbett.
Modern Columbus, A. Wilson.
Wilbur Wright and Orville Wright. R. Benét *and* S. V. Benét.
Wheel, The. Sully-Prudhomme.
Investors and Investments
Investor's Soliloquy. Ward.
Iona, Scotland
Iona. Coxe.
Iona. Tennyson.
Iowa
Conspiracy in Iowa. Hathaway.
Iowa. Browne.
Prairie Summer. Etter.
Song of Iowa, The. Byers.
Iran. *See* **Persia.**
Ireland
After Death. Parnell.
Andromeda. Roche.
Back to Dublin. Ford.
Castle Hyde. Kenealy.
Christmas and Ireland. Johnson.
Colin Clout's Come Home Again. Spenser.
Corrib. An Emblem. Davie.
Corrymeela. "O'Neill."
County of Mayo, The. Lavelle.
Cradle Song of a Celtic Queen. Tobin.
Dark Rosaleen. *Unknown.*
Dear Harp of My Country. Moore.
Deer of Ireland, The. Colum.
Easter, 1916. Yeats.
Erin. Digby.
Fair Hills of Eiré, The. Colum.
Fair Hills of Eiré, O, The. Mac-Con-Mara.
Fair Hills of Ireland, The. *Unknown.*
Famine Year, The. Lady Wilde.
Farewell to Ireland. *At. to* St. Columcille.
First Invasion of Ireland, The. Montague.
Gods of the Dana, The. Drake.
Harbor, The. Letts.
Harp That Once through Tara's Halls, The. Moore.
I Am Ireland. Pearse.
"I Am of Ireland." Yeats.
Ich Am of Irlonde. *Unknown.*
In Ireland: By the Pool at the Third Rosses. Symons.
Inis Fal. *Unknown.*
Ireland. Gwynn.
Ireland. Johnson.
Ireland. W. S. Landor.
Ireland. Leamy.
Ireland. MacCarthy.
Ireland. Piatt.
Ireland. Shorter.
Ireland, Mother of Priests. Leslie.
Ireland Never Was Contented. Landor.
Ireland Weeping. Livingston.
Ireland with Emily. Betjeman.
Irish Dancer, The. *Unknown.*
Irish Rapparees, The. Duffy.
Island, The. Jennett.
Kathaleen Ny-Houlahan. *Unknown.*
Lady Day in Ireland. Carroll.
Let Erin Remember the Days of Old. Moore.
Little Black Rose, The. De Vere.
Little Waves of Breffny, The. Gore-Booth.
Minstrel Boy, The. Moore.
Municipal Gallery Revisited, The. Yeats.
My Land. Davis.
Neutrality. MacNeice.
On His Exile to Iona. St. Columcille.
On Not Hearing the Birds Sing in Ireland. Colum.
Poem Written in a Time of Trouble by an Irish Priest Who Had Taken Orders in France, A. *Unknown.*
Portrait with Background. Gogarty.
Red Hanrahan's Song about Ireland. Yeats.
Road of Ireland, A. O'Donnell.
Rose Tree, The. Yeats.
September 1913. Yeats.
Shan Van Vocht, The. *Unknown.*
Sixteen Dead Men. Shorter.
Soggarth Aroon. Banim.
Song of the Little Villages. Dollard.
Spenser's Ireland. Moore.
Spring Flowers from Ireland. McCarthy.
Sthreets of Home. McCarthy.
Sweet Innisfallen. Moore.
To God and Ireland True. O'Leary.
To the Dead of '98. Johnson.
Valediction. MacNeice.
"View of the Present State of Ireland, A." Blunden.
Vision of Connaught in the Thirteenth Century, A. Mangan.
Wearing' o' the Green. *Unknown.*
Whack Fol the Diddle. Kearney.
Winding Banks of Erne, The. Allingham.
Year of Sorrow, The: Ireland, 1849. De Vere.
Anthology of Irish Literature, An (AnIL). David H. Greene, ed.
Anthology of Irish Verse, An (AnIV). Padraic Colum, ed.
Irish Poets of the Nineteenth Century (IrPN). Geoffrey Taylor, ed.

Kings, Lords & Commons; an Anthology from the Irish (KiLC). Frank O'Connor, tr.
New Irish Poets (NeIP). Devin A. Garrity, ed.
1000 Years of Irish Poetry (OnYI). Kathleen Hoagland, ed.
Oxford Book of Irish Verse; XVIIth Century-XXth Century (OxBI). Donagh MacDonagh *and* Lennox Robinson, comps.

Iris (flower)
Beds of Fleur-de-Lys, The. Gilman.
Blue Flag, The. Donelly.
Iris. "Field."
Iris, The. Gasetsu.
Iris. *Unknown.*
Irises. Colum.
White Iris, A. Barrington.

Irish
Boys of Wexford, The. *Unknown.*
Civil Irish and Wild Irish. Mac an Bhaird.
Cremona. Doyle.
Downfall of the Gael. O'Gnive.
Fighting Race, The. Clarke.
Gods and Heroes of the Gael. Cox.
I'll Wear a Shamrock. Davies.
Irish, The. Carlin.
Irish. O'Brien.
Irish Grandmother. Edelman.
Lament of the Irish Emigrant. Sheridan.
Native Irishman, The. *Unknown.*
O Bruadair. Stephens.
On Behalf of Some Irishmen Not Followers of Tradition. "Æ."
Peaceable Race. Daly.
Slainthe! MacGill.
Written on the Sense of Isolation in Contempory Ireland. Greacen.

Ironsides (ship). *See* **Constitution.**

Irving, Washington
Irving. *Fr.* A Fable for Critics. J. R. Lowell.

Isaac
Abraham to kill him. Dickinson.

Isaiah
Isaiah of Souillac, The. Merwin.

Ischl, Austria
Inscription on a Shrine near Ischl. Elizabeth, Empress of Austria-Hungary.

Ishmael
Ishmael. Palmer.

Islands
Barred Island. Booth.
Enviable Isles, The. Melville.
If Once You Have Slept on an Island. Field.
Islands. Pomeroy.

Israel
But We Shall Bloom. Guri.
Canaan. Spark.
Israeli Navy, The. Bell.
Pictures at an Exhibition. Rosenbaum.

Israelov, Khasan
Sestina for Khasan Israelov. *Fr.* Wildtrack. Wain.

Italians
Boy from Rome, Da. Daly.
Cigarette for the Bambino. Ewart.
Modern Romans, The. Johnson.

Italy
Ah Me, Do You Remember Still. Robinson.
Daisy, The. Tennyson.
"De Gustibus." R. Browning.
Englishman in Italy, The. R. Browning.
Farewell to Italy. Landor.
Forza D'Agro. Denby.
Hotel Paradiso e Commerciale. Brinnin.
In Ampezzo. Stickney.
Italia, Io Ti Saluto! C. G. Rossetti.
Italian Rhapsody. Johnson.
Italy. *Fr.* Beppo. Byron.
Italy. Filicaja.
Italy, *sels.* Rogers.
Letter from Italy, A. Addison.
Lines Written among the Euganean Hills. Shelley.
Non Dolet. Swinburne.
Nona Domenica Garnaro sits in the sun. *Fr.* Fragments from Italy. Ciardi.
On an Italian Hillside. Weber.
Political Chaos In Italy. Dante.
Song of the Standard, The. Swinburne.
Street Melody, A. Cooper.
Super Flumina Babylonis. Swinburne.
Sweet are the rosy memoires. *Fr.* A Night in Italy. "Meredith."
To Italy. Guidiccioni.
To Italy. Leopardi.
Walls and Arches, The. Leopardi.

Ives, Charles
This is Charles Ives. *Fr.* Ives. Rukeyser.

Ivry-La-Bataille, France
Ivry. Macaulay.

Ivy
Holly against Ivy. *Unknown.*
Holly and Ivy ("Holly and ivy made a great party"). *Unknown.*
Holly and the Ivy, The ("The holly and the ivy/ When they are both full grown"). *Unknown.*
In Praise of Ivy. *Unknown.*
Ivy. Sherman.
Ivy Green, The. *Fr.* The Pickwick Papers. Dickens.
Nay, Ivy, Nay. *Unknown.*
To the Ivy. Clare.

J

Jack-in-the-pulpit (plant)
Jack-in-the-Pulpit. Bennett.
Jack-in-the-Pulpit. Eastwick.
Jack-in-the-Pulpit. Holland.

Jackson, Andrew
Andrew Jackson. S. V. Benét.
Andrew Jackson. Keller.
Jackson at New Orleans. Rice.
Oration, An, Entitled "Old, Old, Old, Old Andrew Jackson." Lindsay.

Jackson, Helen Hunt.
Helen Hunt Jackson. Coolbrith.

Jackson, Thomas Jonathan (Stonewall Jackson)
Brigade Must Not Know, Sir, The. *Unknown.*
Dying Words of Stonewall Jackson, The. Lanier.
Stonewall Jackson. Flash.
Stonewall Jackson. Melville.
Stonewall Jackson's Way. Palmer.
Under the Shade of the Trees. Preston.

Jacob
Jacob. Clough.
Jacob and the Angel. Brother Antoninus.
Wrestling Jacob. Wesley.

Jacobites
Jacobite on Tower Hill, The. Thornbury.
Jacobite's Exile, 1746, A. Swinburne.
Jacobite's Farewell, A. Swinburne.
Old Scottish Cavalier, The. Aytoun.

Jacopone da Todi
Austerity of Poetry. Arnold.

Jaguars
Jaguar, The. Hughes.
Second Glance at a Jaguar. Hughes.

Jamaica, British West Indies
Slave, The. Horne.

James I, King of England
Gratulatory Elegy of the Peaceable Entry of King James, A. Harington.
To His Late Majesty, Concerning the True Form of English Poetry. Beaumont.
To King James. Jonson.

James II, King of England
King James II. *Fr.* The Hind and the Panther. Dryden.

James I, King of Scotland
King's Tragedy, The. D. G. Rossetti.

James IV, King of Scotland
Ballade of the Scottyshe Kynge, A. Skelton.

James V, King of Scotland
Childhood of James V, The. *Fr.* The Complaynt of Schir David Lindesay. Lindsay.

James, Henry
At the Grave of Henry James. Auden.
Henry James. Stevenson.

James *(continued)*
Jacobean. Fadiman.
James, Jesse
Death of Jesse James, The. *Unknown.*
Jesse James. W. R. Benét.
Jesse James ("It was on a Wednesday night, the moon was shining bright"). *Unknown.*
Jesse James ("Jesse James was a man, and he had a robber band"). *Unknown.*
Jesse James ("Jesse James was a man who killed many a man"). *Unknown.*
James, Reuben
Reuben James. Roche.
Jamestown, Virginia
Burning of Jamestown, The. English.
Ode to Jamestown. Paulding.
January
January. Applewhite.
January. Kees.
January. Lambdin.
January. Larcom.
January. "Lewis."
January. *Fr.* The Vision of Sir Launfal. J. R. Lowell.
January. Sherman.
January. Updike.
January. Williams.
January Is Here. Fawcett.
January Morning, A. Lampman.
January Snow. Fisher.
On the Wind of January. *Fr.* A Year's Windfalls. C. G. Rossetti.
Song of January. Kennedy.
Janus
Janus. Mason.
Japan
Japan. Hecht.
Japan That Sank under the Sea. Sato.
Japanesque. Herford.
Sakunami. Kirkup.
Walk in Kyoto, A. Birney.
Japanese, The
Impression Japonais. Wilde.
Japanese, the. Nash.
Jasmine
White Jessamine, The. Tabb.
Yellow Jessamine. Woolson.
Jason
Jason. Moraes.
Jazz
Jazz. Brown.
Jazz Fantasia. Sandburg.
Jazz of This Hotel, The. Lindsay.
Jazzonia. Hughes.
Two Jazz Poems. Hines.
Jealousy
Answer to Chloe Jealous. Prior.
I Can't Think What He Sees in Her. Herbert.
Jealosie. Donne.
Jealous Lovers, The. Hall.
Jealous Man, A. Graves.
Jealous Man, A. *Unknown.*
Jealousy. M. E. Coleridge.
Jealousy. *Fr.* The Siege of Rhodes. Davenant.
Jealousy. Countess of Winchilsea.
Tale for Husbands, A. Sidney.
Upon a Wife That Dyed Mad with Jealousie. Herrick.
Jeanne d'Arc. *See* **Joan of Arc.**
Jeffers, Robinson
In Memory of Robinson Jeffers. Barker.
Jefferson, Thomas
Air Tunnel, Monticello. Noll.
Ballad of the Common Man. Kreymborg.
Brave New World. MacLeish.
Death of Jefferson, The. Butterworth.
Jefferson and Liberty. *Unknown.*
Thomas Jefferson. S. V. Benét.
Jeffreys of Wem, George Jeffreys, 1st Baron
Lord Chancellours Villanies Discovered, The; or His Rise and Fall in the Four Last Years. *Unknown.*
Sir T. J.'s Speech to His Wife and Children. *Unknown.*
Jephthah
Jephthah's Daughter. Tennyson.
Jeremiah
Jeremiah. Bynner.
Prophet Jeremiah and the Personification of Israel, The. *At. to* Ben Kalir.
Jerez de la Frontera, Spain
Ballad of the Spanish Civil Guard. García Lorca.
Jerome, Saint
Leonardo da Vinci's. Moore.
Thunderer, The. McGinley.
Jerusalem
By the Rivers of Babylon. Psalms, Bible, *O.T.*
By the Waters of Babylon. *Fr.* Hebrew Melodies. Heine.
Holy City. Weatherley.
If I Forget Thee. Litvinoff.
In the Old City. Fichman.
Jerusalem. Drummond of Hawthornden.
Jerusalem Delivered, *sels.* Tasso.
Jerusalem Delivered. Untermeyer.
Jerusalem, My Happy Home. *Unknown.*
Jerusalem the Dismembered. *Fr.* Jerusalem. Greenberg.
Jerusalem, the Golden. *Fr.* De Contemptu Mundi. Bernard of Cluny.
Longing for Jerusalem. Halevi.
New Jerusalem, The. *Unknown.*
Prayer for Redemption. *Unknown.*
Prisoner's Song of Jerusalem, A. *Unknown.*
Wandering Jew Comes to the Wall, The. *Fr.* The Wall of Weeping. Fleg.
Jesuits
Canto I: "Of Men nay Beasts: worse, Monsters: worst of all." *Fr.* The Locusts, or Apollyonists. Fletcher.
Prologue: "For who can longer hold?" *Fr.* Satires upon the Jesuits. Oldham.
Jesus Christ
Advent. Brother Antoninus.
After the Agony in the Garden. Hine.
Agonie, The. Herbert.
Ah My Dere. *Unknown.*
Al the Meryere. *Unknown.*
All in the Morning. *Unknown.*
Amid the Din of Earthly Strife. Hawkes.
And Did Those Feet in Ancient Time. *Fr.* Milton. Blake.
Approaches. Macdonald.
Argument, An—of the Passion of Christ. Merton.
At least—to pray—is left—is left. Dickinson.
Attraction. *Unknown.*
Ave Verum Corpus Natum. *Unknown.*
Bag, The. Herbert.
Ballad of the Golden Bowl. Hay.
Ballad of the Goodly Fere. Pound.
Ballad of Trees and the Master, A. Lanier.
Ballade of Illegal Ornaments. Belloc.
Barnfloor and Winepress. Hopkins.
Beautiful Gift, The. Crowell.
Because He Was Tempted. *Unknown.*
Better Part, The. Arnold.
Birthplace. Pearson.
Bitter Withy, The. *Unknown.*
Blessing and Honor. Bonar.
Brothers of the Faith. Oxenham.
Burning Babe, The. Southwell.
By Him. Jonson.
Calvary. Robinson.
Cantica: Our Lord Christ. St. Francis of Assisi.
Carpenter, The. Studdert-Kennedy.
Carpenter of Galilee, The. Smith.
Charitas Nimia; or, The Dear Bargain. Crashaw.
Cherry-Tree Carol, The. *Unknown.*
Child. Sandburg.
Child Jesus to Mary the Rose, The. Lydgate.
Child My Choice, A. Southwell.
Child's Prayer, A. Thompson.
Christ, *sels.* Cynewulf.
Christ. Holmes.
Christ, The. Oxenham.
Christ and His Mother at the Cross. Jacopone da Todi.
Christ and the Little Ones. Gill.
Christ and the Mourners. Conway.
Christ and the Pagan. Tabb.

Christ-Child, The. St. Gregory of Narek.
Christ-Child, The. Lee.
Christ Complains to Sinners. *Unknown.*
Christ Crucified. Crashaw.
Christ for Everything. Belsham.
Christ in the Clay-Pit. Clemo.
Christ in the Universe. Meynell.
Christ Is Coming. Macomber.
Christ of Common Folks, The. Liddell.
Christ of the Andes. Coates.
Christ of the Andes, The. Markham.
Christ Quiets the Tempest. *Fr.* Carmen Paschale. Sedulius.
Christ the Comrade. Colum.
Christ Walking on the Water. Rogers.
Christ with me, Christ before me, Christ behind me. *Fr.* St. Patrick. Garlick.
Christmas Carol, A: "Thys endernyght." *Unknown.*
Christmas Folk-Song, A. Reese.
Christ's Bloody Sweat. Southwell.
Christ's Nativity. Vaughan.
Christs Returne out of Egypt. Southwell.
Christ's Tear Breaks My Heart. *Unknown.*
Christ's Victory and Triumph, *sels.* Fletcher.
Church's One Foundation, The. Stone.
Come to Your Heaven, You Heavenly Choirs! Southwell.
Coming Child, The. Crashaw.
Coming of Christ, The. *Unknown.*
Companionship. Babcock.
Comrade Jesus. Cleghorn.
Cradle and the Cross, The. Reitz.
Crow and the Crane, The. *Unknown.*
Dawning, The. Herbert.
Devout Prayer of the Passion, A. *Unknown.*
Discerning the Lord's Body. Montgomery.
Do We Not Hear Thy Footfall? Carmichael.
Dream of the Rood, The. *Unknown.*
Earliest Christian Hymn. Clement of Alexandria.
Ecce Homo. Gascoyne.
Ecce Homunclus. Mason.
El Greco: Espolio. Birney.
Eve of Christmas, The. Kirkup.
Evening Thought, An. Hammon.
Evil Days. Pasternak.
Eye-Witness. Torrence.
Fairest Lord Jesus. *Unknown.*
Falcon, The. *Unknown.*
Father to the Man. Knight.
Feet of Judas, The. McClellan.
Go to Dark Gethsemane. Montgomery.
Good Shepherd, The. Lope de Vega.
Good Shepherd with the Kid, The. Arnold.
Guest, The. *Unknown.*
Hayll, Comly and Clene. *Unknown.*
He. Kunitz.
He Is a Path. *Fr.* Christ's Victory and Triumph. Fletcher.
He Knows the Way. *Unknown.*
He Made Us Free. Egan.
He Never Will Forget. "M. G. H."
He Was Not Willing. Meyer.
Head That Once Was Crowned with Thorns, The. Kelly.
Him Evermore I Behold. Longfellow.
His Are the Thousand Sparkling Rills. Alexander.
His Hands. Moreland.
Holy Eclogue, The. Sister Francisca Josefa del Castillo.
Holy Name of Jesus, The. Crashaw.
Holy Well, The. *Unknown.*
Hora Christi. Brown.
Hound of Heaven, The. Thompson.
Hymn of Labor. Van Dyke.
Hymn of the Incarnation, A. *Unknown.*
Hymn to the Holy Cross. Fortunatus.
I Heard Christ Sing. "MacDiarmid."
I Heard Immanuel Singing. Lindsay.
I know that my Redeemer lives & I. *Unknown.*
I Met the Master. *Unknown.*
I See His Blood upon the Rose. Plunkett.
I Turn to Jesus. Smith.
I Wonder as I Wander. *Unknown.*
If Christ Were Here To-Night. Sangster.
If He Should Come. Lorraine.
In Galilee. Mackay.
In-Group. Kearns.
In the Heart of Jesus. O'Daly.
In the Name of Jesus Christ. Cranston.
In the Wilderness. Graves.
Inasmuch! Brooks.
Insight. Kearns.
It Was for Me. Gray.
Jesu. Herbert.
Jesu Dulcis. St. Bernard of Clairvaux.
Jesu, Dulcis Memoria. *Unknown.*
Jesukin. *At. to* St. Ita.
Jesus. Parker.
Jesus. Pimentel Coronel.
Jesus. *Unknown.*
Jesus and His Mother. Gunn.
Jesus Bids Man Remember. *Unknown.*
Jesus Contrasts Man and Himself. *Unknown.*
Jesus, My Sweet Lover. *Unknown.*
Jesus of the Scars. Shillito.
Jesus Reassures His Mother. *Unknown.*
Jesus Reproaches His People. *Unknown.*
Jesus the Carpenter. Liddell.
Jesus, the Carpenter. Sheldon.
Jesus, Thou Joy of Loving Hearts. St. Bernard of Clairvaux.
Jesus! thy Crucifix. Dickinson.
Jesus to Those Who Pass By. *Unknown.*
Journey to Golgotha, The. Rao.
Killing, The. Muir.
La Corona. Donne.
Lachrymae. Gascoyne.
Last Words of Don Henriquez, The. Schneour.
Let Mine Eyes See Thee. St. Theresa of Avila.
Life of the Blessed, The. Luis de León.
Light in the Temple, The. W. R. Benét.
Little Family, The. *Unknown.*
Little Jesus. Thompson.
Live Christ. Oxenham.
Lord, The. Gabriel y Galán.
Love Unknown. Crossman.
Love Unlike Love. *Unknown.*
Lovely was the death. *Fr.* Religious Musings. Coleridge.
Lulla, My Sweet Little Baby. *Unknown.*
Man Christ, The. Lindsey.
Marigold, The. Wither.
Mary's Baby. O'Sheel.
May the Sweet Name of Jesus. *Unknown.*
Messias. Merton.
Middle-Time, The. Fowler.
Mighty Fortress Is Our God, A. Luther.
Moses and Jesus. Zangwill.
Mother and Her Son on the Cross, The. *Unknown.*
Most glorious Lord of life, that on this day. *Fr.* Amoretti. Spenser.
Mount of Olives. Vaughan.
My Dancing Day. *Unknown.*
My Friend. Buster.
My Master Was So Very Poor. Lee.
My Risen Lord. *Unknown.*
Name of Jesus, The. Newton.
New Heaven, New Warre. Southwell.
New Prince New Pomp. Southwell.
Night, The ("Through that pure Virgin-shrine"). Vaughan.
Night Song for a Child. Williams.
O Master, Let Me Walk with Thee. Gladden.
O Master-Workman of the Race. Stocking.
O Son of God, Afflicted. *Unknown.*
O Young and Fearless Prophet. Harlow.
Of the Resurrection of Christ. Dunbar.
On the Infancy of Our Saviour. Quarles.
On the Miracle of Loaves. Crashaw.
On the Nativity of Christ. Dunbar.
On the Safe Side. Lord Dunsany.
On the Swag. Mason.
One in Christ. Van Dyke.
Our Christ. Farrington.
Our Lord and Our Lady. Belloc.
Our Master. Whittier.
Out of Bounds. Tabb.
Pair of Wings, A. Hawes.
Palm-Sunday Hymn, A. Herebert.
Poet Lived in Galilee, A. Bynner.

Jesus *(continued)*
Preparatory Meditations, *sels.* Taylor.
Protagonist, The. Hopegood.
Quia Amore Langueo. *Unknown.*
Rabboni! Master! Mother Loyola.
Redemption. Herbert.
Rime of the Road, A. O'Donnell.
Rosa Mystica. *Unknown.*
Sacrifice, The. Herbert.
St. Patrick's Breastplate. *At. to* St. Patrick.
Sapphics upon the Passion of Christ. *Unknown.*
Savior must have been, The. Dickinson.
Search, The. J. R. Lowell.
Search, The. Vaughan.
Second Crucifixion, The. Le Gallienne.
Sheep and Lambs. Tynan.
Shine Out, Fair Sun, with All Your Heat. *Fr.* The Masque of the Twelve Months. *Unknown.*
Signum Cui Contradicetur. Sister Mary Angelita.
Simon the Cyrenian Speaks. Cullen.
Son, The. Herbert.
Son, The. Muir.
Son of God, The. O'Donnell.
Song of a Heathen, The. Gilder.
Song of Love for Jesus, A. Rolle.
Sonnet: "And I Have Seen Again the Marvelous Child." Verlaine.
Starlight Like Intuition Pierced the Twelve. Schwartz.
Still Falls the Rain. E. Sitwell.
Subversive. W. R. Benét.
Sunset on Calvary. *Unknown.*
Terly Terlow. *Unknown.*
That Holy Thing. Macdonald.
There Is a Floure Sprung of a Tree. *Unknown.*
This Blessed Christ of Calvary. *Unknown.*
Thou Who Taught the Thronging People. Minde.
To Christ Crucified. *Unknown.*
To Holy Jesus. Princess Phillipa.
To Jesus on His Birthday. Millay.
To Jesus on the Cross. Tejada.
To Our Blessed Lord upon the Choice of His Sepulchre. Crashaw.
To the Sun. *Fr.* Mithraic Emblems. Campbell.
To the Young Man Jesus. Dalton.
Transfiguration, The. Hayes.
Upon the Bleeding Crucifix. Crashaw.
Upon the Body of Our Blessed Lord, Naked and Bloody. Crashaw.
Upon the Savior's Tomb. Crashaw.
Veni, Coronaberis. *Unknown.*
Veni, Domine Jesu! Rawes.
Vexilla Regis. Fortunatus.
Virgin's Song, The. *Unknown.*
Virile Christ, A. Boundy.
Vision of Jesus, The. *Fr.* The Vision of Piers Plowman. Langland.
Voice of Christmas, The. Kemp.
Wake oh my Soule awake & raise. *Unknown.*
We Bear the Strain of Earthly Care. Davis.
We Would See Jesus. *Unknown.*
When Love of us called Him to see. Crashaw.
When Will He Come? *Unknown.*
Windhover, The. Hopkins.
Woefully Arrayed. Skelton.
Wondrous Son of God. Goertz.
Words of Jesus, The. W. R. Benét.
Yet if His Majesty, our sovereign Lord. *Unknown.*
Beautiful Poems on Jesus (BePJ). Basil Miller, comp.
Christ in Poetry (ChIP). Thomas Curtis Clark *and* Hazel Davis Clark, eds.
Sourcebook of Poetry (SoP). Al Bryant, comp.
Story of Jesus in the World's Literature, The (StJW). Edward Wagenknecht, ed.
Jewel, John, Bishop of Salisbury
Epitaph upon the Death of the Right Reverent Father in God J. Jewel, An. Bourman.
Jews
Alphabet, The. Shapiro.
Ark, The. Feldman.
Autobiographical. Klein.
Banner of the Jew, The. Lazarus.
Breaking of the Day, The. Davison.
Debate with the Rabbi. Nemerov.
Design for Mediaeval Tapestry. Klein.
Epilogue of the Wandering Jew, The. Newbury.
Exile Song. Rosenfeld.
For All That Ever Has Been Ours. Landau.
Genius, The. Cohen.
Hebrews. Oppenheim.
Heirloom. Klein.
In re Solomon Warshawer. Klein.
Jew, The. Rosenberg.
Jew. Shapiro.
Jew to Jesus, The. Frank.
Jew Wrecked in the German Cell, The. Auden.
Jewish Conscript, The. Frank.
Jewish Lullaby. Untermeyer.
Jewish Main Street. Layton.
Jews, The. Herbert.
Jews, The. Vaughan.
Jews at Haifa. Jarrell.
Judaism. Cardinal Newman.
Lay of the Levite, The. Aytoun.
Mathmid, The. Bialik.
Moses and Jesus. Zangwill.
Note in Lieu of a Suicide. Finkel.
Old Jew, The. Bodenheim.
On the Russian Persecution of the Jews. Swinburne.
151st Psalm, The. Shapiro.
One of the Jews (50 A.D.). Cavafy.
Permanent Delegate, The. Suhl.
Portrait. Plutzik.
Scene of a Summer Morning. Feldman.
Sound the Loud Timbrel. Moore.
Still Small Voice, The. Klein.
Summa contra Gentiles. Leary.
To Philip Levine, on the Day of Atonement. Mezey.
To Russia. Miller.
Victim, The. Greenberg.
Wandering Jew, The. Mezey.
Wandering Jew, The. Robinson.
Weeping and Singing. Tiempo.
World's Justice, The. Lazarus.
Wrack. Feldman.
Treasury of Jewish Poetry, A (TrJP). Nathan Ausubel *and* Marynn Ausubel, eds.
Jezebel
Song for the Clatter-Bones. Higgins.
Joan of Arc
Farewell, ye mountains, and ye much-loved paths. *Fr.* The Maid of Orleans, *play.* Schiller.
Good Joan, The. Reese.
Joan of Arc. McCrae.
Joan of Arc to the Tribunal. Frisch.
Maid, The. Brégy.
Maid, The. Roberts.
Maid of Arc, The. Bottomley.
Maid of Orleans, The, *poem.* Schiller.
One Day at Rouen. Sister Mary Bernetta.
Saint, The. *Fr.* Requiem. Wolfe.
Saint Jeanne. Garrison.
Scot to Jeanne d'Arc, A. Lang.
Job (Bible)
God's Thanks to Job. *Fr.* A Masque of Reason. Frost.
Job. Coleridge.
Job. Sewell.
Job. Thomas.
Jogues, Saint Isaac
Knowest Thou Isaac Jogues? Grey.
Johannesburg, Republic of South Africa
Johannesburg. Plomer.
Each time I return to Johannesburg it is summer. *Fr.* Seven South African Poems. Wright.
John, Saint
Peter and John. Wylie.
Song to John, Christ's Friend, A. *Unknown.*
John, King of England
King John and the Abbot of Canterbury. *Unknown.*
John Henry (folk hero)
John Henry ("John Henry told his old captain"). *Unknown.*
John Henry ("When John Henry was about three days old"). *Unknown.*

Old John Henry. Riley.
John of Austria
Lepanto. Chesterton.
John the Baptist, Saint
For the Baptist. Drummond of Hawthornden.
John the Baptist. Simpson.
Saint John. Coatsworth.
St. John Baptist. O'Shaughnessy.
Saint John the Baptist. Drummond of Hawthornden.
Johnson, Andrew
Mr. Johnson's Policy of Reconstruction. Halpine.
Johnson, Jack (John Arthur Johnson)
My Lord, What a Morning. Cuney.
Johnson, Lionel
In Memory of Major Robert Gregory. Yeats.
Johnson, Samuel
Epitaph on Dr. Johnson. Jenyns.
Epitaph on Johnson. Cowper.
Postscript to "Retaliation," A. Dobson.
Johnston, Albert Sidney
Albert Sidney Johnston. Sherwood.
Albert Sidney Johnston. Ticknor.
Johnstown Flood
Man Who Rode to Conemaugh. Bowen.
Jonah
Father Mapple's Hymn. *Fr.* Moby Dick. Melville.
Jonah. Huxley.
Jonah. Jarrell.
Jonah. *Fr.* Patience. *Unknown.*
Jonah and the Whale. Meynell.
Noah an' Jonah an' Cap'n John Smith. Marquis.
Song of Jonah in the Whale's Belly, The. *Fr.* The Harmony of the Church. Drayton.
Jones, Casey (John Luther Jones)
Casey Jones. *Unknown.*
Jones, John Paul
Battle of the *Bonhomme Richard* and the *Serapis.* *Fr.* Song of Myself. Whitman.
Bonhomme Richard and *Serapis,* The. Freneau.
John Paul Jones. Gilder.
John Paul Jones. *Fr.* Song of Myself. Whitman.
Paul Jones ("An American frigate from Baltimore came"). *Unknown.*
Paul Jones ("A song unto Liberty's brave buccaneer". *Unknown.*
Paul Jones—a New Song. *Unknown.*
Paul Jones' Victory. *Unknown.*
Yankee Man-of-War, The. *Unknown.*
Jones, LeRoi
Sermonette. Reed.
Jonson, Ben
Ad Jo. Marston et Ben. Jonson. Weever.
Ben Jonson. *Fr.* Sonnets on English Dramatic Poets. Swinburne.
Eclogue to Mr. Johnson, An. Randolph.
Elegy on Ben. Jonson, An. Cleveland.
Epistle Answering to One That Asked to Be Sealed of the Tribe of Ben, An. Jonson.
Gratulatory to Mr. Ben Johnson for His Adopting of Him to Be His Son, A. Randolph.
His Prayer to Ben Jonson. Herrick.
Humble Petition of Poor Ben to the Best of Monarchs, Masters, Men, King Charles, The. Jonson.
Master Francis Beaumont's Letter to Ben Jonson. Beaumont.
Ode for Ben Jonson, An. Herrick.
Ode to Himselfe ("Come leave the loathed stage"). Jonson.
Ode to Himselfe, An ("Where do'st thou carelesse lie"). Jonson.
On Ben Jonson. Cleyton.
On Ben Jonson. Godolphin.
Prologue Spoken by Mr. Garrick at the Opening of the Theatre in Drury Lane, 1747. Johnson.
Scorne then their censure. *Fr.* To the Memory of Ben Johnson. Mayne.
To Ben. Jonson. Carew.
To His Friend Ben. Johnson, of His Horace Made English. Herbert of Cherbury.
To My Dead Friend Ben: Johnson. King.
Upon Ben Jonson. Herrick.
Upon Ben Jonson. Waller.
Upon the Works of Ben Jonson, *sel.* Oldham.
Joseph (Bible, *O.T.*)
Joseph and His Brethren. Wells.
Joseph, Saint
Father, The. Ballard.
Joseph's Suspicion. Rilke.
Man of the House, The. Tynan.
To St. Joseph. O'Donnell.
Vigil of Joseph, The. Barker.
Jowett, Benjamin
I am the great Professor Jowett. *Unknown.*
Judas Iscariot
Betrayal. Cholmondeley.
Descent for the Lost. Child.
Entrance into Heaven. Hay.
Judas. Bradford.
Judas. Corning.
Judas. *Unknown.*
Judas Iscariot. *Fr.* The Ballad of Judas Iscariot. Buchanan.
Judas Iscariot. Cullen.
Judas Iscariot. Martin.
Judas Iscariot. Mason.
Judas Iscariot. Spender.
Judas Sells His Lord. *Unknown.*
Sacrifice, The. Barrax.
Saint Judas. Wright.
Simon and Judas. Porter.
Wife of Judas Iscariot, The. Rice.
Jude, Saint
St. Simon and St. Jude's Day. Alexander.
Upon the Feast of St. Simon and St. Jude. Johnson.
Judgment Day
Apocalypse. Pierce.
Day of Doom. Wigglesworth.
Day of Judgement, The. Watts.
Day of Judgment, The. Buchanan.
Day of Judgment, The. Swift.
Dies Irae. Duff.
Dies Irae. Hagerup.
Dies Irae. Thomas of Celano.
Eternal Justice, The. Aldrich.
Fifteen Days of Judgement, The. Evans.
Human Race Comes to Be Judged, The. *Fr.* Christ. Cynewulf.
Judgement. Herbert.
Judgment Day. Howells.
Judgment Day. Oxenham.
Last Judgment, The. *Fr.* Christ. Cynewulf.
Lyke-Wake Dirge, A. *Unknown.*
Poet's Resurrection. *Fr.* To the Pious Memory of the Accomplished Young Lady, Mrs. Anne Killigrew. Dryden.
Remember the Day of Judgment. *Unknown.*
Rise and Shine. Lattimore.
Vision of Judgment, The. Byron.
Judith (Apocrypha)
Judith of Bethulia. Ransom.
Jugglers
Juggler. Wilbur.
Juggling Jerry. Meredith.
Juke Boxes
King Juke. Fearing.
July
July. Clare.
July. Swett.
July. Tatyanicheva.
July. *At. to* Whittier.
July Dawn, A, *sel.* O'Donnell.
July Meadow. Driscoll.
Labor of Fields. Coatsworth.
Succession of the Four Sweet Months, The. Herrick.
That's July. Butts.
June
Adlestrop. Thomas.
Dawning of the Day, The. Mangan.
Full early in the morning. *Unknown.*
In June. Perry.
June. Bryant.
June. Davies.
June. Fisher.
June. Hopper.
June. Ledwidge.
June. *Fr.* The Vision of Sir Launfal. J. R. Lowell.

June *(continued)*
June. MacDonald.
June. Malloch.
June. Morris.
June. Pawsey.
June. Rand.
June. Reaney.
June. Stewart.
June Bracken and Heather. Tennyson.
June Morning. McCrae.
June Night. Hall.
June Rapture. Morgan.
June Thunder. MacNeice.
Knee-Deep in June. Riley.
Night in June, A. Scott.
Night in June, A. *Fr.* The Sun Has Long Been Set. Wordsworth.
May and June. *Fr.* Under the Willows. J. R. Lowell.
Poem in June. Acorn.
Spring Lilt, A. *Unknown.*
Stay, June, Stay! C. G. Rossetti.
Succession of the Four Sweet Months, The. Herrick.
That's June. Butts.
To a June Breeze. Bunner.
What Is So Rare as a Day in June. *Fr.* The Vision of Sir Launfal. J. R. Lowell.
Jungfrau (mountain)
Jungfrau's Cry, The. Brooke.
Jungles
Jungle. Haring.
Juniper
Sing a Song of Juniper. Francis.
Justice
Carl Hamblin. *Fr.* Spoon River Anthology. Masters.
For Justice. Trotter.

K

Kafka, Franz
To Franz Kafka. Muir.
Kalamazoo, Michigan
Kalamazoo. Lindsay.
Kambara, Ariake
To Ariake Kambara. Rosten.
Kane, Elisha Kent
Kane. O'Brien.
Kangaroos
Are You a Marsupial? Becker.
I Saw the Beauty Go. Gilmore.
Kangaroo, The. Coatsworth.
Kangaroo. Lawrence.
Kangaroo, The. *Unknown.*
Kangaroo by Nightfall. Macainsh.
Native-born. Langley.
Pockets. Bennett.
Sing-Song of Old Man Kangaroo, The. Kipling.
Tails. Bennett.
Kansas
Crossing Kansas by Train. Justice.
Home on the Range, A. Lomax.
Kansas. Lindsay.
Kansas Emigrants, The. Whittier.
Kant, Immanuel
Third Wonder, The. Markham.
Kashmir, India
Light of the Haram, The. *Fr.* Lalla Rookh. Moore.
Katharine of Aragon, Queen of England
Ballad for Katharine of Aragon, A. Causley.
Katmandu, Nepal
Here in Katmandu. Justice.
Katydids
Katy-did. McCoy.
To a Caty-did. Freneau.
To an Insect. Holmes.
Katzenjammer Kids
Katzenjammer Kids, The. Reaney.
Kayaks
Kayak, The. *Unknown.*
Kearny, Philip
Kearny at Seven Pines. Stedman.
Kearsarge (ship)
Eagle and Vulture, The. Read.
Kearsarge. Mitchell.
Kearsarge, The. Roche.
Kearsarge and *Alabama.* *Unknown.*
Keats, John
Adonais. Shelley.
After a Lecture on Keats. Holmes.
Association Copy. Kurth.
At Lulworth Cove a Century Back. Hardy.
Death of Keats, The. Watkins.
For John Keats, Apostle of Beauty. *Fr.* Four Epitaphs. Cullen.
For Keats and the Florentine Night. Kennedy.
Grave of Keats, The. Wilde.
John Keats. *Fr.* Five English Poets. D. G. Rossetti.
Keats. Longfellow.
Keats. *Fr.* Ode to England. Lord.
Keats. Reese.
Keats. Tabb.
Keats at Teignmouth. Causley.
October XXIX, 1795 (Keats' Birthday). Braithwaite.
On Keats. Shelley.
On the Sale by Auction of Keats's Love-Letters. Wilde.
Popularity. R. Browning.
Rome. Hardy.
To John Keats. Hunt.
To John Keats, Poet. At Springtime. Cullen.
To Keats. Reynolds.
To the Spirit of Keats. J. R. Lowell.
Who Kill'd John Keats? Byron.
Keller, Helen
Helen Keller. Stedman.
Kemble, John Mitchell
To J. M. K. Tennyson.
Kempe, Margery
Poem of Margery Kempe, A. Nemerov.
Kempenfelt, Richard
On the Loss of the *Royal George.* Cowper.
Kennedy, John Fitzgerald
Channel U.S.A.—Live. Stoutenburg.
Down in Dallas. Kennedy.
Elegy for J. F. K. Auden.
J. F. K. O'Neill.
J. F. K. Sister M. Stanislaus.
John Fitzgerald Kennedy. Masefield.
November 26, 1963 Berry.
Thanksgiving, 1963. Kazan.
Traction: November 22, 1963. Moss.
Kensington Gardens, London
Dead Harvest, A. Meynell.
Kensington Garden, *sels.* Tickell.
Lines Written in Kensington Gardens. Arnold.
Kent, England
Memory of Kent, The. Blunden.
Kentucky
Kentucky Philosophy. Robertson.
My Old Kentucky Home. Foster.
Kerguelen (islands), Indian Ocean
Beyond Kerguelen. Kendall.
Kew Gardens, London
Barrel Organ, The. Noyes.
Kidd, William
Captain Kidd. S. V. Benét.
Captain Kidd. *Unknown.*
Kilcash, Ireland
Kilcash. *Unknown.*
Kilimanjaro (mountain)
Kilimandjaro. Taylor.
Killarney, Ireland
Killarney. Falconer.
Killarney. *Fr.* Fand. Larminie.
Killdeers
Nesting Ground, The. Wagoner.
Killigrew, Anne
To the Pious Memory of the Accomplished Young Lady, Mrs. Anne Killigrew. Dryden.
Kilmallock, Ireland
Kilmallock. De Vere.

Kilmer, Joyce
Joyce Kilmer. Burr.
Kilpatrick, Hugh Judson
Riding with Kilpatrick. Scollard.
Kimberley, Republic of South Africa
Outside Kimberley. Brettell.
King, Edward
Lycidas. Milton.
On the Memory of Mr. Edward King, Drown'd in the Irish Seas. Cleveland.
King, Martin Luther, Jr.
Assassination. Lee.
Epitaph to a Man. Reedburg.
Funeral of Martin Luther King, Jr., The. Giovanni.
Lotus Eaters, The. Alexander.
Martin Luther King Jr. Brooks.
On the Murder of Martin Luther King. Rice.
What Good Are Words? Smith.
White Weekend. Troupe.
King, William, Archbishop of Dublin
Excellent New Song upon His Grace Our Good Lord Archbishop of Dublin, An. Swift.
King Philip's War
Lamentable Ballad of the Bloody Brook. Hale.
Kingcups
Kingcups. Farjeon.
Kingfishers
Kingfisher, The. Davies.
Kingfisher, The. Kelly.
Kingfisher, The. *Fr.* Upon Appleton House. Marvell.
Kings
Cloth of Gold. Scott.
Of the Death of Kings. *Fr.* Richard II. Shakespeare.
There Lived a King. Gilbert.
King's Mountain, Battle of
Battle of King's Mountain, The. *Unknown.*
Kipling, Rudyard
Ballad, A: "As I was walkin' the jungle round, a-killin' of tigers an' time." Carryl.
Rhyme of the Kipperling, The. Seaman.
To R. K. Stephen.
Kit-Kat Club
Epigram on the Toasts of the Kit-Kat Club, Anno 1716. Pope.
Kites
How the Little Kite Learned to Fly. *Unknown.*
Kite, The. Behn.
Kite, The. Fang Che Chai.
Kite. McCord.
Kite, The. MacEwen.
Kite. Summers.
Kite, A. *Unknown.*
Kite, The. Villa.
Kite Days. Sawyer.
Kite Is a Victim, A. Cohen.
Kite Tales. Waldo.
My Kite. Brown.
Klee, Paul
Paul Klee. Haines.
Klondike
Klondike, The. Robinson.
Klondike Miner, The. *Unknown.*
Knife-Grinders
Sparkles from the Wheel. Whitman.
Knighthood and Knights
False Knight upon the Road, The. *Unknown.*
Flowers in the Valley. *Unknown.*
Having this day my horse, my hand, my lance. *Fr.* Astrophel and Stella. Sidney.
Knight Stained from Battle, The. Herebert.
New Order of Chivalry, A. Peacock.
Old Knight, The. *Fr.* Polyhymnia. Peele.
Riddling Knight, The. *Unknown.*
True Knight, The. *Fr.* The Pastime of Pleasure. Hawes.
Knoxville, Tennessee
Knoxville, Tennessee. Giovanni.
Kollwitz, Kaethe
Death Swoops. Pitchford.
Korea
Korea. Buckley.
Korea Bound, 1952. Childress.
Ode for the American Dead in Korea. McGrath.
On a Certain Engagement South of Seoul. Carruth.
Kosciusko, Thaddeus
Kosciusko. Coleridge.
To Kosciusko. Keats.
Kossuth, Louis
Kossuth. J. R. Lowell.
Kraken
Kraken, The. Tennyson.
Ku Klux Klan
Ku Kluck Klan. Gellert.
Ku-Klux Cawein.
Kubelik, Jan
Jan Kubelik. Sandburg.
Kuan Yin (Chinese goddess of mercy)
Bronze Statuette of Kwan-yin, A. Stork.

L

La Crosse, Wisconsin
La Crosse at Ninety Miles an Hour. Eberhart.
Labor and Laborers
Artisan, The. Brown.
Blessing of Toil. Kiser.
Burying Ground by the Ties. MacLeish.
Carpenter's Plane, The. Kazin.
Case for the Miners, The. Sassoon.
Child of the Romans. Sandburg.
Clinker, The. *Unknown.*
Day and the Work, The. Markham.
Dedication: "I would the gift I offer here." *Fr.* Songs of Labor. Whittier.
Diggers' Song, The. Winstanley.
Dignity of Labor, The. Bersohn.
Do Thy Day's Work. *Unknown.*
Dream of Apricots, A. Schevill.
Equipment. Dunbar.
Factories, The. Widdemer.
Felix Randal. Hopkins.
Florida Road Workers. Hughes.
Forgotten Man, The. Markham.
Glory to Them. Scruggs.
God and the Strong Ones. Widdemer.
Golf Links, The. Cleghorn.
Good Day's Work, A. Replansky.
Gospel of Labor, The. Van Dyke.
Hand of Labor. Townsend.
Harvest Song, A. Markham.
How Doth the Little Busy Bee. Watts.
Hymn of Labor. Van Dyke.
I Hear America Singing. Whitman.
I Was a Labourer. *Fr.* Cycle; Seven War Poems. Jennett.
Ice Handler. Sandburg.
Labor. F. S. Osgood.
Labor ("We have fed you all"). *Unknown.*
Labor and Capital. Howells.
Labor Day. Pomeroy.
Laborer, The. Dehmel.
Laborer, The. Heredia.
Labourer, A. Thomas.
Lay of the Laborer. Hood.
Life-Mosaic. Havergal.
Living among the Toilers. Percikow.
Man with the Hoe, The. Markham.
Morning Work. Lawrence.
O Son of Man, Thou Madest Known. Littlefield.
Old Flagman, The. Sandburg.
On Work. *Fr.* The Prophet. Gibran.
Pittsburgh. Oppenheim.
Prayer, A: "Let me work and be glad." Garrison.
Psalm of Those Who Go Forth before Daylight. Sandburg.
Quiet Work. Arnold.
Reflections in an Iron Works. "MacDiarmid."
Reveille. Ridge.
Riveter, The. Sangster.
Rivets. Olds.
Serf, The. Campbell.
Six o'Clock. Stickney.
Song of a Factory Girl. Zaturensky.
Song of Christian Workingmen. Clark.

Labor *(continued)*
Song of Labor, The. Lowater.
Song of Street Labor, A. Lord.
Song of the Builders. Murton.
Song of the Lower Classes, The. Jones.
Song of the Shirt, The. Hood.
Song of the Wage-Slave, The. Jones.
Song of Work, A. Blake.
Song to a Negro Wash-Woman. Hughes.
Song to the Men of England. Shelley.
Stevedores, The. *Fr.* Down the Mississippi. Fletcher.
Street Scene—1946. Porter.
Structural Iron Workers. Black.
Testament. Sister M. Thérèse.
There you sit. Silverstein.
They Who Tread the Path of Labor. Van Dyke.
Thinker, The. Braley.
Time-Clock, The. Towne.
Tired Worker, The. McKay.
To Iron-Founders and Others. Bottomley.
To Labor. Gilman.
Toads. Larkin.
Toil. *Unknown.*
Toil Away. Chapman.
Toiler, The. Markham.
Tom's Garland. Hopkins.
Too Old to Work. Glazer.
True Aristocrat, The. Stewart.
Two Tramps in Mud Time. Frost.
Village Blacksmith, The. Longfellow.
Voice of Toil, The. Morris.
Washer-Woman, The. Bohanan.
We Are the Burden-Bearers! Stidger.
When Smoke Stood Up from Ludlow. Housman.
Work. Block.
Work. Cox.
Work. Lawrence.
Work. J. R. Lowell.
Work. Pushkin.
Work. Thompson.
Work. *Fr.* The Three Best Things. Van Dyke.
Work; a Song of Triumph. Morgan.
Work without Hope. Coleridge.
Workers, The. Woodson.
Working Class. Warr.
Workman. *Unknown.*
World Is Waiting for You, The. Calkins.
World of Work, as a Poet Would Like It to Be, The. Lawrence.
Sourcebook of Poetry (SoP). Al Bryant, comp.
Labor Unions. *See* **Unions, Labor.**
Laburnum
Laburnum. Wolfe.
Ladybirds
Clock-a-clay. Clare.
Lady-Bird. Bowles.
Ladybird, ladybird. Mother Goose.
Lady Bug. McCoy.
To the Lady-Bird. *Unknown.*
La Fayette, Marie Joseph, Marquis de
La Fayette. Coleridge.
La Fayette. Madison.
Lakes and Ponds
Forest Lake, A. Turner.
Lake, The. Coxe.
Lake, The. Hughes.
Lake, The: To——. Poe.
Lakes. Auden.
Lakeshore. Scott.
Little Lough, The. Hewitt.
Pond, The. Nemerov.
Pond, The. Taylor.
Pool, The. Corbin.
Rock Pool, The. Hobsbaum.
Shaded Pool, The. Gale.
Sonnet: Composed by the Side of Grasmere Lake. Wordsworth.
Spring Pools. Frost.
To Leven Water. Smollett.
To the Lakes. Campbell.
Unnamed Lake, The. Scott.
Winter Lakes, The. Campbell.
Winter Pond. Belitt.
Young Argonauts. Wingfield.
Lalemant, Gabriel
Martyrdom of Brébeuf and Lalemant, 16 March 1649, The. *Fr.* Brébeuf and His Brethren. Pratt.
Père Lalemant. Pickthall.
Lamartine, Alphonse Marie Louis de
Copse, The. Wade.
Lamb, Charles
Charles Lamb. Beatty.
This Lime-Tree Bower My Prison. Coleridge.
Written after the Death of Charles Lamb. Wordsworth.
Lamb, Mary
To the Sister of Elia. Landor.
Lambs
All in the April Morning. Tynan.
For a Lamb. Eberhart.
I Held a Lamb. Worthington.
Lamb, The. *Fr.* Songs of Innocence. Blake.
Lamb, The. Greenaway.
Lamb, The. *Unknown.*
Lamb. Wolfe.
Lambs in the Meadow. Alma-Tadema.
Little Lamb Went Straying, A. Midland.
Little Young Lambs, The. Chalmers.
Mary and Her Lamb. Hale.
On the Grassy Banks. *Fr.* Sing-Song. C. G. Rossetti.
Pallid Cuckoo. Campbell.
Pet Lamb, The. Wordsworth.
Sheep and Lambs. Tynan.
Young Lambs. Clare.
Lamplighters
Lamplighter, The. Stevenson.
Light the Lamps Up, Lamplighter. Farjeon.
Lampman, Archibald
Bereavement of the Fields. Campbell.
Lancelot du Lac
Lancelot and Elaine. *Fr.* Idylls of the King. Tennyson.
Landlords
Ballad of the Landlord. Hughes.
Landor, Walter Savage
In Memory of Walter Savage Landor. Swinburne.
Landor. Albee.
Landor. Japp.
Landrails. *See* **Corncrakes.**
Lang, Andrew
Ballade of Andrew Lang. MacColl.
To Andrew Lang. Stevenson.
Language
At a Vacation Exercise. Milton.
Bonne Entente. Scott.
Conversational Reformer, The. Graham.
Cool Web, The. Graves.
Dirty Word, The. Shapiro.
English A. Ciardi.
English Language, The. Story.
Hearing Russian Spoken. Davie.
Hints on Pronunciation for Foreigners. "T. S. W."
Language has not the power to speak what love indites. Clare.
Latin Tongue, The. Daly.
Letter to a Teacher of English. Hillyer.
Many a phrase has the English language. Dickinson.
Naughty Preposition, The. Bishop.
On the Manner of Addressing Clouds. Stevens.
Our Mother Tongue. Milnes.
Permanently. Koch.
Pretty Words. Wylie.
Primer Lesson. Sandburg.
Rhyme for a Phonetician. Cornford.
To a Thesaurus. Adams.
To the Peoples of Earth. Sun-Ra.
Tree of Silence, The. Miller.
Upon Dr. Davies' British Grammar. Howell.
Varitalk. Holbrook.
Very like a Whale. Nash.
Word. Spender.
Words. Harpur.
Words. *Unknown.*
Lanier, Sidney
At Lanier's Grave. Tabb.
Lanterns
Street Lanterns. M. E. Coleridge.

Laocoon
Laocoon. Hall.
Lao-tze
Lao-tzu. Po Chü-i.
Lapraik, John
Epistle to John Lapraik, an Old Scottish Bard. Burns.
La Prairie, Battle of
Battle of La Prairie, The. Lighthall.
Lapwings
O Lapwing. Blake.
Larch Trees
Larch Trees. Faber.
Larch Wood Secrets. Eastwick.
Song of the Wulfshaw Larches. Rhys.
Larks
Address to a Lark Singing in Winter. *Fr.* Address to a Lark. Clare.
Caged Skylark, The. Hopkins.
Desert Lark, The. Marais.
Ecstatic, The. Day Lewis.
First Skylark of Spring, The. Watson.
For Saturday. *Fr.* Hymns for the Amusement of Children. Smart.
Green Cornfield, A. C. G. Rossetti.
Hark! Hark! the Lark. *Fr.* Cymbeline. Shakespeare.
Lark. Miles.
Lark, The. Reese.
Lark, The. *Unknown.*
Lark and the Nightingale, The. H. Coleridge.
Lark and the Rook, The. *Unknown.*
Lark Ascending, The. Meredith.
Lark in the Morning, The. *Unknown.*
Lark Now Leaves His Wat'ry Nest, The. Davenant.
Larks. Tynan.
Lark's Grave, The. Westwood.
Lark's Nest, A. Smart.
Lark's Song, The. *Fr.* Milton. Blake.
Late Lark, A. Henley.
Little Red Lark, The. Graves.
Over Salève. Clarke.
Sea and the Skylark, The. Hopkins.
Shelley's Skylark. Hardy.
Sir Lark and King Sun. *Fr.* Adela Cathcart. Macdonald.
Skylark, The. Hogg.
Skylark, The. C. G. Rossetti.
Skylark, The. Tennyson.
Skylark's Nest, The. Long.
Super-Lark, The. Long.
To a Lark in War-Time. Werfel.
To a Skylark. Shelley.
To a Skylark ("Ethereal minstrel!"). Wordsworth.
To a Sky-Lark ("Up with me!"). Wordsworth.
Upon the Lark and the Fowler. Bunyan.
Violinist, A. Bourdillon.
Waking of the Lark, The. Mackay.
Word with a Skylark, A. Piatt.
Larkspur
Blue Larkspur. Sister Mariella.
Larkspur. Haines.
Last Supper
Last Supper, The. Rilke.
Last Supper, The. Williams.
Latimer, Hugh
Latimer and Ridley. Wordsworth.
Latimer's Light. *Unknown.*
Latin
Latin. *Unknown.*
Laughter
American Laughter. Robinson
Early Supper. Howes.
Laughing Song. *Fr.* Songs of Innocence. Blake.
Laughter. Crawford.
Laughter. Waddington.
Technique of Laughter, The. Kessler.
To Laughter, to Leering. Eberhart.
Why Did I Laugh. Keats.
Laundry and Laundering
Bendix. Updike.
In an Iridescent Time. Stone.
Love Calls Us to the Things of This World. Wilbur.
Old Ellen Sullivan. Welles.
Song to a Negro Wash-Woman. Hughes.
Washing. Jarrell.
Laurels
Laurels and Immortelles. *Unknown.*
To Laurels. Herrick.
Laurentian Mountains, Canada
Laurentian Shield. Scott.
Lavender
Lavender Bush, The. Fleming.
Lavender's Blue. *Unknown.*
Lavender's for Ladies. Chalmers.
Lawes, Henry
To Mr. H. Lawes on His Airs. Milton.
To M. Henry Lawes, the Excellent Composer, of His Lyrics. Herrick.
To Mr. Henry Lawes, Who Had Then Newly Set a Song of Mine, in the Year 1635. Waller.
Lawrence, Edward
To Mr. Lawrence. Milton.
Lawrence, Thomas Edward
Out of the East the plane spun. *Fr.* Lawrence; the Last Crusade. Rodman.
Lawrence, Kansas
Defense of Lawrence, The. Realf.
Lawrence Justinian, Saint
San Lorenzo Giustiniani's Mother. Meynell.
Lawyers and Law
Briefless Barrister, The. Saxe.
Law like Love. Auden.
Laws of God, the Laws of Man, The. Housman.
Lawyers Know Too Much, The. Sandburg.
Legal Fiction. Empson.
Manhattan Epitaphs: Lawyer. Kreymborg.
Net of Law, The. Roche.
Statute. Miles.
Lazarus
Another sate near him. *Fr.* The Vision of Lazarus. Johnson.
Convert, The. Chesterton.
Dives and Lazarus. *Unknown.*
Epistle, An, Containing the Strange Medical Experience of Karshish, the Arab Physician. R. Browning.
Raising of the Dead, The. Dobson.
Lazarus, Emma
Homecoming of Emma Lazarus, The. Kinnell.
Leadership
God, Give Us Men! Holland.
Leader, A. "Æ."
Masters. Amis.
League of Nations
League of Nations, The. Siegrist.
Leander. *See* **Hero and Leander.**
Lear, King
King Lear, *sels.* Shakespeare.
Lear. Hood.
Now of the conqueror this isle had Brutain unto name. *Fr.* Albion's England. Warner.
On Sitting Down to Read "King Lear" Once Again. Keats.
Lear, Edward
Edward Lear. Auden.
How Pleasant to Know Mr. Lear. Lear.
Self-Portrait of the Laureate of Nonsense. Lear.
Learning
After Passing the Examination. Po Chü-i.
Father's Testament, A. Ibn Tibbon.
Learning. Fullerton.
Little Learning Is a Dangerous Thing, A. *Fr.* Essay on Criticism. Pope.
Musophilus. Daniel.
On the Prospect of Planting Arts and Learning in America. Berkeley.
To a Boy. *Unknown.*
To Young Imaginaries in Knowledge. *Fr.* Seven Penitential Psalms. Petrarch.
Leaves
Beech Leaves. Reeves.
Blue Smoke. F. Frost.
Burning of the Leaves, The. Binyon.
City of Falling Leaves, The. A. Lowell.
College of Surgeons, The. Stephens.
Color. Cane.
Come, Little Leaves. Cooper.

Leaves *(continued)*
Dead Metaphors. Holbrook.
Fallen Leaves. Munro.
Gathering Leaves. Frost.
Golden Bough. Wylie.
How the Leaves Came Down. "Coolidge."
In the College of Surgeons. Stephens.
Last Leaf, The. Behn.
Leaf Mirrors. Applewhite.
Leaf-Treader, A. Frost.
Leaves. Davies.
Leaves. Teasdale.
Leaves. Tynan.
Leaves, The. *Unknown.*
Leaves. Westrup.
Leaves at My Window. Piatt.
Leaves Do Not Mind at All, The. Wynne.
Leaves Drink, The. Wilkins.
Looking Up at Leaves. Howes.
Maple Leaves. Aldrich.
Maple Leaves. Shiko.
Master and the Leaves, The. Hardy.
New York—Albany. Ferlinghetti.
Red o'er the forest glows the setting sun. *Fr.* November. Keble.
So This Is Autumn. Watt.
Sonnet: Leaves. Barnes.
To an Autumn Leaf. Mathews.
Windfall. Scott.
Leda
Leda and the Swan. Gogarty.
Leda and the Swan. Yeats.
Ledwidge, Francis
In Memoriam: Francis Ledwidge. O'Conor.
Lee, Robert Edward
Lee in the Mountains. Davidson.
Lee to the Rear. Thompson.
Lee's Parole. Manville.
Robert E. Lee. *Fr.* John Brown's Body. S. V. Benét.
Robert E. Lee. Howe.
Sword of Robert Lee, The. Ryan.
Legree, Simon
Simon Legree—a Negro Sermon. Lindsay.
Legs
Poem in Which My Legs Are Accepted. Fraser.
Leicester, Robert Dudley, Earl of
Epitaph on the Earl of Leicester. Ralegh.
Leif Ericsson
Saga of Leif the Lucky. Lalen.
Story of Vinland, The. *Fr.* Psalm of the West. Lanier.
Leiden, Holland
Word of God to Leyden Came, The. Rankin.
Leigh, Augusta
Stanzas to Augusta. Byron.
Leinster, Ireland
In Leinster. Guiney.
Leman, Lake, Switzerland
Sonnet to Lake Leman. Byron.
Leisure
Leisure. Davies.
Lemmings
Lemmings, The. Masefield.
Lemonade
Lemonade Stand. Thompson.
Lenin, Vladimir Ilyich
So I came down the steps. *Fr.* Lenin. Wellesley.
Skeleton of the Future, The. "MacDiarmid."
Lent
Easter. Whitaker.
Lent. Rodgers.
Stanzas for Lent. Howell.
To Keep a True Lent. Herrick.
To Search Our Souls. Lanning.
Two Old Lenten Rhymes. *Unknown.*
Leon, Luis de
After Reading Saint Teresa, Luis de Leon, and Ramon Lull. Lee.
Leonardo da Vinci
Leonardo da Vinci's. Moore.
There Lived a Lady in Milan. W. R. Benét.
Leonidas
Leonidas. Croly.
Leopards
Snow-Leopard, The. Jarrell.
Leopold III, King of the Belgians
Moon and the Night and the Men, The. Berryman.
Leopold, Duke of Albany
Death of Prince Leopold, The. McGonagall.
Lepanto, Battle of
Lepanto. Chesterton.
Lepers
Leper, The. Swinburne.
Leper, The. Willis.
Lesbos (island), Greece
Night in Lesbos, A. Horton.
L'Estrange, Sir Roger
Loyalty Confin'd. L'Estrange.
Letters
Aunt Maud. *Unknown.*
Going to him! Happy Letter! Dickinson.
How to Write a Letter. Turner.
Letters, The. Tennyson.
Letters Found near a Suicide. Horne.
Missive, The. Gosse.
My letters! all dead paper, mute and white! *Fr.* Sonnets from the Portuguese. E. B. Browning.
Night Mail. Auden.
Pillar-Box, The. Wolker.
Postman's Bell Is Answered Everywhere, The. Gregory.
Way I read a letter's this, The. Dickinson.
Leven (river), Scotland
Ode to Leven Water. Smollett.
Levett, Robert
On the Death of Mr. Robert Levet. Johnson.
Lewis, Meriwether
Lewis and Clark. S. V. Benét.
On the Discoveries of Captain Lewis. Barlow.
Lexington, Battle of
Lexington. Holmes.
Lexington. *Fr.* The Psalm of the West. Lanier.
Lexington. Whittier.
New England's Chevy Chase. Hale.
Song for Lexington, A. Weeks.
Liberalism and Liberals
"Liberalissimo." Bibbs.
Lost Leader, The. R. Browning.
Pride and Prejudice. Smith.
Why I Am a Liberal. R. Browning.
Liberia
Do. *Fr.* Libretto for the Republic of Liberia. Tolson.
Liberty. See Freedom.
Liberty, Statue of
Bartholdi Statue, The. Whittier.
Fairest of Freedom's Daughters. Rankin.
Inscription for the Statue of Liberty. Lazarus.
Liberty Enlightening the World. Van Dyke.
New Colossus, The. Lazarus.
Statue of Liberty, The. Crooke.
To the Goddess of Liberty. Sterling.
Libraries
Advice to a Young Friend on the Choice of His Library. Wycherley.
British Museum Reading Room, The. MacNeice.
Fire at Alexandria, The. Weiss.
In an Old Library. Yuan Mei.
Library, The, *sels.* Crabbe.
Library, The. Huff.
Library, The. Sherman.
Precious—mouldering pleasure—'tis, A. Dickinson.
Public Library. Stevenson.
Lice
Immortals, The. Rosenberg.
Louse Crept Out of My Lady's Shift, A. Bottomley.
To a Louse. Burns.
Lidice, Czechoslovakia
Lady of Lidice. Chavez.
Liège, Belgium
Between Namur and Liège. Wordsworth.
Lies and Lying
Against Mustolphus His Lying. Davies of Hereford.
Liar, The. *Unknown.*

Lie, The. Nemerov.
Lie, The. Ralegh.
Lies have short wings. He lies that so sing. Davies of Hereford.
Lying. Moore.
Matilda. Belloc.
Unfortunate Coincidence. Parker.
Word of Encouragement, A. Pope.
Lièvre River, Quebec
Dawn on the Lièvre, The. Lampman.
Morning on the Lièvre. Lampman.
Life
All the World's a Stage. *Fr.* As You Like It. Shakespeare.
Alumnus Football. Rice.
Anniversary. Wain.
Any Man's Advice to His Son. Fearing.
Anyone Lived in a Pretty How Town. Cummings.
Ballad of the Outer Life. Hofmannsthal.
Bankrupt. Sayres.
Behind me—dips eternity. Dickinson.
Comparison of Life and Death. *Unknown.*
Dying Enthusiast, The. Mangan.
For an Autograph. J. R. Lowell.
For Life I Had Never Cared Greatly. Hardy.
Glad World. Fitzgerald.
House of Life, The. Tynan.
Human Life. Arnold.
Human Life, *sels.* Rogers.
I Am a Parcel of Vain Strivings Tied. Thoreau.
I Ponder on Life. Ehrmann.
In My End Is My Beginning. Dobson.
It's in Your Face. *Unknown.*
Life. Bacon.
Life. Barbauld.
Life. Bonar.
Life. C. Brontë.
Life. Brown.
Life. "Cornwall."
Life. Crabbe.
Life. Dunbar.
Life. Herbert.
Life. Sill.
Life, a Question. Robinson.
Life and Death. Perry.
Life and Death. Scott.
Life is a Poet's fable. *Unknown.*
Life Is Struggle. Clough.
Life's a Funny Proposition After All. Cohan.
Life's Chequer-Board. Oxenham.
Life's Lessons. *Unknown.*
Living. Howells.
Long Hill, The. Teasdale.
Madrigal: "This life, which seems so fair." Drummond of Hawthornden.
May It Be. Pasternak.
Meditation, A. Eberhart.
My Life has stood a loaded gun. Dickinson.
Nature and Life. Meredith.
Nothing to do but work. *Fr.* The Sun of Life. King.
Of Human Life. King.
Of Life. Lang.
Our share of night to bear. Dickinson.
Psalm of Life, A. Longfellow.
Quickness. Vaughan.
Rainy Day, The. Longfellow.
Sic Vita. Braithwaite.
Sic Vita. King.
Song of Life, A. Werfel.
Sonnet: "You were born; must die." Spender.
Story of Life, The. Saxe.
Sunday Morning. Stevens.
This Life Is All Chequer'd with Pleasures and Woes. Moore.
'Tis not that dying hurts us so. Dickinson.
To K. de M. Henley.
Tomorrow and Tomorrow and Tomorrow. *Fr.* Macbeth. Shakespeare.
Triumph of Life, The. Shelley.
Various the Roads of Life. Landor.
Voyage, The. Baudelaire.
Voyage of Life, The. *Fr.* Christ. Cynewulf.
Voyage to Cythera, A. Baudelaire.
We cannot retrace our steps. *Fr.* The Mother of Us All. Stein.
We hurry on, nor passing note. Dolben.
We live, while we see the sun. *Fr.* Life Is a Dream. Calderón de la Barca.
What Is Our Life? Ralegh.
When I Consider Life. *Fr.* Aureng-Zebe. Dryden.
Whist. Ware.
Willing Suspension, A. Holmes.
Sourcebook of Poetry (SoP). Al Bryant, comp.
Liffey (river), Ireland
To the Liffey with the Swans. Gogarty.
Light
Hymn to Light. Cowley.
Light. Hagedorn.
Light at Equinox. Adams.
Song-Offering, A. Tagore.
Lighthouses
Epitaph for a Lighthouse-keeper's Horse. Morton.
Flannan Isle. Gibson.
I'd Like to Be a Lighthouse. Field.
Lighthouse, The. Scott.
Lighthouse, The. Wilson.
Skerryvore ("For love of lovely words"). Stevenson.
Skerryvore: The Parallel ("Here all is sunny"). Stevenson.
Lightning
At Great Torrington, Devon. *Unknown.*
Dance-Song of the Lightning. *Unknown.*
Miramichi Lightning. Bailey.
Young Mystic, The. Untermeyer.
Lilacs
Lilac. Flint.
Lilac, The. Wolfe.
Lilacs. Conkling.
Lilacs. A. Lowell.
With Lilacs. Crandall.
Lilies
How Lillies Came White. Herrick.
Lilies. Colum.
Lilies. Marquis.
Lilies. Shiko.
Lilly in a Christal, The. Herrick.
Lily, The. Williams.
Lily Flower. Brownstein.
Little White Lily. Macdonald.
Mariposa Lily, The. Coolbrith.
On a Bed of Guernsey Lilies. Smart.
On Easter Day. Thaxter.
Orange Lilies. Reaney.
Rock-Lily. Robinson.
Song of the Lilies, The. Wheelock.
Tiger-Lilies. Aldrich.
Tiger Lily. McCord.
Lilies of the Valley
Lilies of the Valley. Walker.
Lily of the Valley, The. Beddoes.
White coral bells upon a slender stalk. *Unknown.*
Lilith
Body's Beauty. *Fr.* The House of Life. D. G. Rossetti.
Eden Bower. D. G. Rossetti.
Limbo
Limbo. Coleridge.
Limerick, Ireland
Here I've got you, Philip Desmond, standing in the market-place. *Fr.* Limerick Town. O'Donnell.
Limericks
Little Book of Limericks, The (LiBL). H. I. Brock, ed.
Lincoln, Abraham
Abraham Lincoln. Ames.
Abraham Lincoln. Auslander.
Abraham Lincoln. S. V. Benét.
Abraham Lincoln. Benton.
Abraham Lincoln. Brownell.
Abraham Lincoln. Bryant.
Abraham Lincoln. Cole.
Abraham Lincoln. Meigs.
Abraham Lincoln. Miller.
Abraham Lincoln. Stedman.
Abraham Lincoln ("Not as when some great captain falls"). Stoddard.
Abraham Lincoln ("This man whose homely face"). Stoddard.
Abraham Lincoln. Taylor.
Abraham Lincoln. Whitaker.

Lincoln *(continued)*
Abraham Lincoln, the Master. Clark.
Abraham Lincoln Walks at Midnight. Lindsay.
Anne Rutledge. *Fr.* Spoon River Anthology. Masters.
At the Lincoln Memorial. Brooks.
Ballad of the Lincoln Penny. Kreymborg.
Cenotaph of Lincoln, The. McKay.
Death of Lincoln, The. Bryant.
Farmer Remembers Lincoln, A. Bynner.
February Twelfth. Hepburn.
For February Twelfth. Gessner.
Glory of Lincoln, The. Clark.
Hand of Lincoln, The. Stedman.
His Living Monument. Irving.
House in Springfield. Burket.
How Shall We Honor Lincoln? Clark.
Hush'd Be the Camps Today. Whitman.
If Lincoln Should Return. Bruner.
In Hardin County, 1809. Thompson.
Kentucky Birthday; February 12, 1815. F. Frost.
Lincoln. *Fr.* Our Heroic Times. Boker.
Lincoln. Cheney.
Lincoln. Clark.
Lincoln. Ditmars.
Lincoln. Dunbar.
Lincoln. Fletcher.
Lincoln. Hardy.
Lincoln. Hill.
Lincoln. Howe.
Lincoln. Mitchell.
Lincoln. Riley.
Lincoln. Robinson.
Lincoln. Schwartz.
Lincoln. Stafford.
Lincoln. Thompson.
Lincoln. Trowbridge.
Lincoln. Turner.
Lincoln. Tyrrell.
Lincoln. *Unknown.*
Lincoln?/ He was a mystery in smoke and flags. *Fr.* The People, Yes. Sandburg.
Lincoln and Liberty. Simpson.
Lincoln and the Poets. Betts.
Lincoln at Gettysburg. *Fr.* The Gettysburg Ode. Taylor.
Lincoln Calls for Volunteers. *Fr.* John Brown's Body. S. V. Benét.
Lincoln Child, The. Oppenheim.
Lincoln, Come Back. Clark.
Lincoln Memorial. Wiley.
Lincoln Portrait. Copland.
Lincoln Statue, The. Collins.
Lincoln, the Man of the People. Markham.
Lincoln Triumphant. Markham.
Lincoln's Birthday. Bangs.
Long Shadow of Lincoln, The. Sandburg.
Man of Men, A. Van Noppen.
Man of Peace, The. Carman.
Martyr, The. Melville.
Master, The. Robinson.
Nancy Hanks. R. Benét.
O Captain! My Captain! Whitman.
Ode Recited at the Harvard Commemoration, July 21, 1865. J. R. Lowell.
Old Abe Lincoln. *Unknown.*
On a Bust of Lincoln. Scollard.
On a Picture of Lincoln. Cheney.
On the Life-Mask of Abraham Lincoln. Gilder.
Parricide. Howe.
Prairie. Llewellyn.
President Lincoln's Grave. Mason.
Prophecy, A. *Fr.* Lincoln's Grave. Thompson.
Remembering Lincoln. Mundorf.
Snarlers, The. Guiterman.
Soliloquy of Lincoln before Manassas. *Fr.* John Brown's Body. S. V. Benét.
Soul of Lincoln, The. Piety.
Star of Sangamon, The. Allen.
They Will Look for a Few Words. Turner.
This Dust Was Once the Man. *Fr.* Memories of President Lincoln. Whitman.
"Thou Shouldst Be Living at This Hour." West.
Three Hundred Thousand More. Gibbons.
To Abraham Lincoln. Piatt.
To Borglum's Seated Statue of Abraham Lincoln. Jordan.
Tolling. Larcom.
Tribute, A. *Unknown.*
Warning for Abraham Lincoln, A. Fombano Pachano.
Washington and Lincoln. Stafford.
When Lilacs Last in the Dooryard Bloom'd. Whitman.
Would I Might Rouse the Lincoln in Your All. *Fr.* Litany of the Heroes. Lindsay.
Young Lincoln. Markham.
Your Glory, Lincoln. Goodman.

Lincoln Cathedral, England
At Lincoln. Adams.

Lincolnshire, England
High Tide on the Coast of Lincolnshire, The. Ingelow.
Lincolnshire Remembered. Cornford.

Lindbergh, Charles
Lindbergh. Michaelis.
Lindbergh. Morgan.
Lyric Deed, The. Neihardt.

Lindsay, Vachel
Supper with Lindsay. Roethke.

Linnets
Green Linnet, The. Wordsworth.
Grey Linnet, The. McCarroll.
I Heard a Linnet Courting. Bridges.
Linnet, The. De la Mare.
Linnet in a Gilded Cage, A. C. G. Rossetti.
Sir Walter Raleigh to a Caged Linnet. Lee-Hamilton.
To a Linnet in a Cage. Ledwidge.
Young Linnets, The. Hawkshaw.

Lions
Incident with Lions. Hay.
Lion, A. Francis.
Lion, The. Howitt.
Lion, The. Lindsay.
Lion. Miller.
Lion, The. Nash.
Lion. *Fr.* A Bestiary. Rexroth.
Lion. Swenson.
Lion, The. Turner.
Lion. *Unknown.*
Lion and the Mouse, The. Taylor.
Lion at Noon, The. Hugo.
Lion Grown Old, The. La Fontaine.
Lion-House, The. Wheelock.
Lion's Cub, The. Thompson.
Lion's Nature, The. *Fr.* The Bestiary. *Unknown.*
Lions Running over the Green. Wynne.
Lion's Skeleton, The. Turner.
Plains, The. Fuller.
Why Nobody Pets the Lion at the Zoo. Ciardi.

Li Po
Li Po. Alexander.
Li Po. Gilbert.
On the Subject of Waves. Grier.

Lippi, Fra Filippo
Fra Lippo Lippi. R. Browning.

Lipscomb, Eugene ("Big Daddy")
Say Good-bye to Big Daddy. Jarrell.

Little Bighorn, Battle of
Death of Custer, The. Crawford.
Down the Little Big Horn. Brooks.
Little Big Horn. McGaffey.
Miles Keogh's Horse. Hay.
Revenge of Rain-in-the-Face, The. Longfellow.

Little Rock, Arkansas
Chicago *Defender* Sends a Man to Little Rock, Fall, 1957, The. Brooks.

Live-oak Trees
I Saw in Louisiana a Live-Oak Growing. Whitman.

Liverpool, England
Dawn at Liverpool. *Fr.* Sonnets of the Empire. Strong.

Livingstone, David
David Livingstone. *Unknown.*

Lizard Head, England
To Lizard Head. Laube.

Lizards
Americans Are Afraid of Lizards. Shapiro.
Lizard, The. Brown.

Lower Animals. Anderson.
On a Bougainvillea Vine in Haiti. Howes.
Llamas
In Praise of Llamas. Guiterman.
Lama, The. Nash.
Llama, The. Belloc.
Snap Judgement on the Llama, A. Bennett.
Lobsters
Lobster, The. *Unknown.*
Lobsters in the Window. Snodgrass.
Locomotives
To a Locomotive in Winter. Whitman.
Locusts
Coyote and the Locust, The. *Unknown.*
Four Things. Proverbs, Bible, *O.T.*
Locust Hunt, The. Murray.
Lodge, Thomas
Barnabe Rich, Gentleman Soldier, in Praise of the Author. Rich.
Lodore, England
Cataract of Lodore, The. Southey.
Logan, John Alexander
Logan at Peach Tree Creek. Garland.
London, England
After London. Pellow.
Annus Mirabilis, *sels.* Dryden.
At Piccadilly Circus. Pinto.
Ballad of the Londoner. Flecker.
Barrel-Organ, The. Noyes.
Bells of London, The. *Unknown.*
City Show, The. Farjeon.
Composed upon Westminster Bridge, September 3, 1802. Wordsworth.
Description of a City Shower, A. Swift.
Description of a View. Empson.
Description of London, A. Banks.
East London. Arnold.
Epilogue to a Human Drama. Spender.
Farewell to London in the Year 1715, A. Pope.
Fleet Street. Adams.
Fleet Street. Leslie.
Going Up to London. Turner.
Hay's Wharf. Church.
His Return to London. Herrick.
Important Statement. Kavanagh.
Impression de Nuit; London. Douglas.
In Honour of the City of London. Dunbar.
In Regent's Park. Ridler.
In the Mile End Road. Levy.
London. Betjeman.
London. *Fr.* Songs of Experience. Blake.
London. Davidson.
London. Flint.
London. Ghose.
London. Johnson.
London. Rhys.
London. Wilson.
London Beautiful. Le Gallienne.
London Bridge. Weatherly.
London Despair. Cornford.
London, 1802. Wordsworth.
London Feast. Rhys.
London Is a Fine Town. *Unknown.*
London Lickpenny. *Unknown.*
London Nightfall. Fletcher.
London Sad London. *Unknown.*
London Snow. Bridges.
London Sonnets, *sels.* Bode.
London Town. Johnson.
London Town. Masefield.
London under Bombardment. Briggs.
London Voluntaries. Henley.
New London, The. *Fr.* Annus Mirabilis. Dryden.
North London. Ross.
November Blue. Meynell.
Oh, Blank Confusion. *Fr.* The Prelude. Wordsworth.
Of London Bridge, and the Stupendous Sight, and Structure Thereof. Howell.
On the Lord Mayor and Court of Alderman. Marvell.
Parliament Hill. Bashford.
Piccadilly. Burke.
Primrose Hill. Custance.
Quo Ruis ab Demens? London's Progress. Freeman.
Rotten Row. Locker-Lampson.
Satire on London, A. Surrey.
Simplicity's Song. Wilson.
Slaves to London. Motteux.
Song: "Closes and courts and lanes." Davidson.
Streets of Loredo, The. MacNeice.
To the City of London. Dunbar.
Trivia; or, The Art of Walking the Streets of London, *sels.* Gay.
Troynovant. *Fr.* Entertainment to James. Dekker.
West London. Arnold.
Which is the way to London Town. *Unknown.*
Ye Flags of Piccadilly. Clough.
Yesterday in Oxford Street. Fyleman.
Loneliness
Alone. Sassoon.
Bereft. Frost.
Buried Life, The. Arnold.
Desert Places. Frost.
Desolate. Dobell.
Dove's Loneliness, The. Darley.
I Explain. *Fr.* War Is Kind. S. Crane.
Loneliness. Essex.
Loneliness. *Fr.* The Hill Wife. Frost.
Loneliness. Hashin.
Loneliness. Werfel.
Lonely. Modisane.
Lonely. Spire.
Lonely Child, The. Briggs.
Lonely Road. Abrahams.
Mnemosyne. Stickney.
Mr. Flood's Party. Robinson.
Search. Souster.
To Marguerite. *Fr.* Switzerland. Arnold.
Long, Crawford Williamson
Crawford Long and William Morton. R. Benét *and* S. V. Benét.
Long, Huey
Road, The. Plutzik.
Longfellow, Henry Wadsworth
H. W. L. Nichol.
Henry Wadsworth Longfellow. Dobson.
Longfellow. Betts.
Longfellow. Riley.
Poe and Longfellow. *Fr.* A Fable for Critics. J. R. Lowell.
Longleat House
Stanzas on a Visit to Longleat House in Wiltshire, October 1953. Barker.
Lookout Mountain, Battle of
Battle in the Clouds, The. Howells.
Battle of Lookout Mountain, The. Boker.
Loons
Loon, The. Rand.
Loon, The. Sarett.
Loon, The. Street.
Loons, The. Lampman.
Lord's Supper. *See* **Eucharist.**
Lorelei
Lorelei, The. Heine.
Lorenzo di Credi
Italian Chest, An. Seiffert.
Lot (Bible)
Lot Later. Nemerov.
Lotus
Egyptian Lotus, The. Eaton.
He Is like the Lotus. *Fr.* Book of the Dead. *Unknown.*
Lotos-Eaters, The. Tennyson.
Lotus-Flower, The. Heine.
Lotus Leaves. Mitsukuni.
Louis XV, King of France
Louis XV. Sterling.
Louis, Madame (daughter of Louis XV of France)
Aux Carmélites. Tynan.
Louisiana
African in Louisiana. Kyei.
In Louisiana. Paine.
Song of Louisiana. Stopher.
Louisburg, Nova Scotia
Louisburg. *Unknown.*
On the Late Successful Expedition against Louisbourg. Hopkinson.

Louse. *See* **Lice.**
Love
Book of Love Poems, A (BoLP). William Cole, ed.
Come Live with Me; Five Centuries of Romantic Poetry (CLWM). Charles Norman, ed.
English Love Poems (EnLoPo). John Betjeman *and* Geoffrey Taylor, eds.
Erotic Poetry (ErPo). William Cole, ed.
Little Treasury of Love Poems, A (LiTL). John Holmes, ed.
Love (LO). Walter de la Mare, ed.
Love's Enchantment (LoEn). Helen Ferris, comp.
Men and Women: the Poetry of Love (MeWo). Louis Untermeyer, ed.
Modern Love Poems (MoLP). D. J. Klemer, ed.
Sourcebook of Poetry (SoP). Al Bryant, comp.
Uninhibited Treasury of Erotic Poetry (UnTe). Louis Untermeyer, ed.
Lovelace, Richard
To His Noble Friend Mr. Richard Lovelace. Marvell.
Lowell, James Russell
James Russell Lowell. Holmes.
James Russell Lowell. Whittier.
Lowell. *Fr.* A Fable for Critics. J. R. Lowell.
Lucifer. *See* **Satan.**
Lucknow, India
Defence of Lucknow, The. Tennyson.
Pipes at Lucknow, The. Whittier.
Lucretius
Lucretius. Tennyson.
Luddites
Framework-Knitters Lamentation, The. *Unknown.*
Framework-Knitters Petition, The. Briggs.
Ode to the Framers of the Frame Bill, An. Byron.
Song for the Luddites. Byron.
Luke, Saint
Saint Luke the Painter. *Fr.* The House of Life. D. G. Rossetti.
Lull, Ramon
After Reading Saint Teresa, Luis de Leon and Ramon Lull. Lee.
Lullabies. *See* **Cradle Song *and* Lullaby *in* Title and First Line Index.**
Lumbering and Lumbermen
Buffalo Skinners, The. *Unknown.*
Jack Haggerty. McGinnis.
Jam on Gerry's Rock, The. *Unknown.*
James Whaland. *Unknown.*
Jim the Splitter. Kendall.
Logs, The. Roberts.
Lumbermen, The. Whittier.
On Meesh-e-gan. *Unknown.*
Paul's Wife. Frost.
Saws Were Shrieking, The. Ross.
When the Drive Goes Down. Malloch.
Shantymen and Shantyboys (ShS). William Main Doerflinger, comp.
Lundy's Lane, Battle of
Battle of Bridgewater, The. *Unknown.*
Lupin
Lupin. Wolfe.
Lusitania (ship)
S. S. Lusitania. Arnold.
White Ships and the Red. Kilmer.
Lust
Away with Silks. Herrick.
Battle between a Cock and a Capon, The. Heyrick.
Dirty Thoughts. Contoski.
Expense of spirit in a waste of shame, The. Sonnets, CXXIX. Shakespeare.
Invitation. Jarrett.
Late-Flowering Lust. Betjeman.
Nymphs and Satyrs. Ewart.
Snake, The. Corke.
Toast, A ("Here's to you and here's to me"). *Unknown.*
Lutes
Blame Not My Lute. Wyatt.
Lover Complaineth the Unkindness of His Love, The. Wyatt.
Lute, The. Rilke.
O Softly Singing Lute. Pilkington.
On a Lute Found in a Sarcophagus. Gosse.
Sonnet: "My lute, be as thou wast when thou didst grow." Drummond of Hawthornden.
Luxury
Persian Fopperies. Horace.
Vanity of Riches, The. Horace.
Lyautey, Louis Hubert Gonzalve
Marshal Lyautey. Currey.
Lynching
Between the World and Me. Wright.
Bird and the Tree, The. Torrence.
Black Boy. Rosten.
Brothers. Johnson.
Haunted Oak, The. Dunbar.
I Saw Them Lynch. Freeman.
Litany at Atlanta, A. DuBois.
Lynched Negro. Bodenheim.
Lynching, The. McKay.
Lynching Bee, The. Leonard.
Man Hunt, The. Cawein.
Nice Day for a Lynching. Patchen.
On the Photograph of a Lynching. Stafford.
Plaint. Ford.
So Quietly. Hill.
Swimmers, The. Tate.
Lynn, Massachusetts
Bells of Lynn, The. Longfellow.
Lynx
Lesser Lynx, The. Rieu.
Lynx. Ford.
Wailing Lynx. Sarett.
Lyon, Nathaniel
Death of Lyon. Peterson.
Lyonesse
Chapel in Lyoness, The. Morris.
Sunk Lyonesse. De la Mare.
When I Set Out for Lyonnesse. Hardy.
Lyre
Listen to the Lyre! Darley.
Solitary Lyre, The. Darley.
Supplication, A. Cowley.
Lyrebirds
Lyre-Bird, The. Robinson.
Lyrebirds. Wright.
Tea-Tree and the Lyrebird, The. Robinson.

M

Macaulay, Thomas Babington
Macaulay. Landor.
MacCarthy, Denis Florence
Florence MacCarthy's Farewell to His English Love. De Vere.
McClellan, George Brinton
How McClellan Took Manassas. *Unknown.*
Victor of Antietam, The. Melville.
Macdonough, Thomas
Blue Hen's Chickens, The. Guiterman.
Thomas MacDonagh. Ledwidge.
Macedonian (ship)
United States and *Macedonian*, The ("Banner of Freedom high floated unfurled"). *Unknown.*
United States and *Macedonian*, The ("How flows each patriot bosom that boasts a Yankee heart"). *Unknown.*
McHenry, Fort
Fort McHenry. *Unknown.*
Star-spangled Banner, The. Key.
Machines
Concrete Mixers. Hubbell.
Crane, The. Tomlinson.
Egg and the Machine, The. Frost.
Horatian Variation. Bacon.
Machine Hand, A. Ashe.
Machines. Hicky.
Ode to Machines. Ginsberg.
Portrait of a Machine. Untermeyer.
Power. *Fr.* The Bridge. H. Crane.
Secret of the Machines, The. Kipling.
Steam Shovel. Malam.
Steam Shovel, The. Tietjens.
Steam Threshing-Machine, The. Tennyson-Turner.
Time for Building, A. Livingston.
Trial Run, A. Frost.

Turbine, The. Monroe.
Work. Lawrence.
McKay, Claude
To Claude McKay. Virtue.
McKenzie, Sir John
Burial of Sir John McKenzie, The. Mackay.
McKinley, William
Buffalo. Coates.
Faithful unto Death. Titherington.
McKinley. *Unknown.*
MacLeish, Archibald
Omelet of A. MacLeish, The. Wilson.
"Macleod, Fiona" (William Sharp)
To William Sharp. Scollard.
McLuhan, Marshall
Taste of Space, The. Smith.
MacNeice, Louis
Their Last Will and Testament. MacNeice.
McPherson, James Birdseye
Dirge for McPherson, A. Melville.
MacSwiney, Terence James
Terence MacSwiney. "Æ."
Madness
Brain, within it's groove, The. Dickinson.
Counting the Mad. Justice.
Darkened Mind, The. J. R. Lowell.
Division. Ratti.
Flee on Your Donkey. Sexton.
Hatters, The. McDonald.
Heard in a Violent Ward. Roethke.
I Am. Clare.
Letter from a State Hospital. Mundorf.
Lines Written during a Period of Insanity. Cowper.
Mad Maid's Whim. Stow.
Madhouse. Hernton.
Madman, The. Pretorius.
Madman, The. Urdang.
Madman's Song. Wylie.
Maniac, The. Russell.
Maud. Tennyson.
Mental Cases. Owen.
Much madness is divinest sense. Dickinson.
On a Painting by Patient B of the Independence State Hospital for the Insane. Justice.
Poem: "It must be true." Knott.
Ringing the Bells. Sexton.
Scene in a Madhouse. De Vere.
Song of the Mad Prince, The. De la Mare.
Sonnet Found in a Deserted Madhouse. *Unknown.*
To One in Bedlam. Dowson.
Tom o' Bedlam's Song. *Unknown.*
Walking in the Blue. R. Lowell.
You, Doctor Martin. Sexton.
Madrid, Spain
Segovia and Madrid. Cooks.
Madroñ
Madroñ. Harte.
Maecenas
To Maecenas. *Fr.* Odes. Horace.
Magellan, Ferdinand
Magellan. Curnow.
Magi
Caravans. Petterson.
Christmas Carol: "Kings they came from out the south, The." Teasdale.
Different Way, A. Hagg.
Epiphany. Heber.
Gift, The. Williams.
Hymne for the Epiphanie, A. Sung as by the Three Kings. Crashaw.
Journey of the Magi. Eliot.
Kings from the East, The. Heine.
Kings of the East, The. Bates.
Magi. Clark.
Magi, The. Yeats.
Magi, The. *Fr.* On the Morning of Christ's Nativity. Milton.
Magi Visit Herod, The. Sedulius.
Mystic Magi, The. Hawker.
Poem for Epiphany. Nicholson.
Riding of the Kings, The. Farjeon.
Song of the Wise Men. Pierce.
Take Frankincense, O God. *Fr.* Holy Transportations. Fitzgeffry.
Three Kings, The. Longfellow.
Three Kings of Cologne, The. Field.
Three Wise Kings. Brooks.
Three Wise Men, The. Finley.
Wise Men Seeking Jesus. East.
Magic
Fairy Story. Todd.
Sorcerer, The. Smith.
Story of the Alchemist, The. Williams.
Poems of Magic and Spells (PoMS). William Cole, ed.
Magna Carta
Barons Bold, The. Fox.
Magna Charta. *Unknown.*
Reeds of Runnymede, The. Kipling.
Magnets
Fable of the Magnet and the Churn, The. Gilbert.
Magnet is Mistaken, The. Ginsberg.
Of Natural Forces. Chesley.
Magnolia Trees
Magnolia Tree, The. Witheford.
Magnolia Tree in Summer. S. Sitwell.
To a Magnolia Flower in the Garden of the Armenian Convent at Venice. Mitchell.
Magpies
Camden Magpie. McCrae.
Magpie Singing His Delight, The. Campbell.
Magpie's Nest. C. *and* M. Lamb.
Magpie's Song, The. Williamson.
Maguire, Hugh, Lord of Fermanagh.
O'Hussey's Ode to the Maguire. *At. to.* O'Hussey.
Maguire, Molly
Molly Maguire at Monmouth. Collins.
Maia
Fragment of an Ode to Maia. Keats.
Mailmen
Mailman and Das Ewig Weibliche, The. Schevill.
Postman, The. Richards.
Maimonides, Moses
Duel with Verses over a Great Man, *sels.* *Unknown.*
Maine (state)
Lovely Rivers and Lakes of Maine, The. Wallis.
Maine. Booth.
Maine Trail, A. McGiffert.
State of Maine Song. Snow.
Maine (ship)
Battle Song. Wilson.
Half-Mast. Mifflin.
Martyrs of the *Maine*, The. Hughes.
Men of the *Maine*, The. Scollard.
Spirit of the *Maine*, The. Jenks.
Malachy, Saint
St. Malachy. Merton.
Malachi (Bible)
Malachi. Marlatt.
Malaga, Battle of
Famous Fight at Malago, The; or The Englishmen's Victory over the Spaniards. *Unknown.*
Malcolm X (Malcolm Little)
Aardvark. Fields.
At That Moment. Patterson.
Brother Malcolm: Waste Limit. Major.
For Brother Malcolm. Spriggs.
For Malcolm X. Walker.
I Remember. Jackson.
It Was a Funky Deal. Knight.
Malcolm. Cumbo.
Malcolm. Sanchez.
Malcolm. Smith.
Malcolm X. Brooks.
Malcolm X. Hite.
Malcolm X—an Autobiography. Neal.
My Ace of Spades. Joans.
Poem for Black Hearts, A. Jones.
That Old Time Religion. Jackmon.
Maldon (England), Battle of
Battle of Maldon, The. *Unknown.*
Man
Afterthought. Richardson.

Man *(continued)*
All the Flowers of the Spring. *Fr.* The Devil's Law Case. Webster.
All the World's a Stage. *Fr.* As You Like It. Shakespeare.
As Concerning Man. Radcliffe.
Autonomous. Van Doren.
Average Man, The. *Fr.* The Vision of Piers Plowman. Langland.
Before the Beginning of Years. *Fr.* Atalanta in Calydon. Swinburne.
Cant. Davies.
Cantata for Two Lovers. H. Sandburg.
Collective Portrait, The. Finch.
Contemplations. Bradstreet.
Dialogue between the Soul and Body, A. Marvell.
Divine Image, The. *Fr.* Songs of Innocence. Blake.
Divine Ship Sales the Divine Sea for You, The. Whitman.
Elements, The. Cardinal Newman.
Enough of Humble Arguments. *Fr.* The Prelude. Wordsworth.
Essay on Man, An. Pope.
Faces. Whitman.
First Chorus, The. *Fr.* The Glass of Government. Gascoigne.
Fish, the Man, and the Spirit, The. Hunt.
For A' That and A' That. Burns.
For metaphors of man we search the skies. Watson.
From dust I rise. *Fr.* The Salutation. Traherne.
Here lies, and none to mourn him but the sea. *Fr.* Epitaph for the Race of Man. Millay.
Human Races, The. Lister.
Human Seasons, The. Keats.
Human Soul Speaks, The. *Fr.* The Vision of Piers Plowman. Langland.
Humn to Earth. Wylie.
I Sing the Body Electric. Whitman.
If. Kipling.
In Harmony with Nature. Arnold.
Inquisitors, The. Jeffers.
Invocation: "O world watched over by the cold moon and the mindless stars." Drewry.
It Is Not Growing like a Tree. *Fr.* A Pindaric Ode. Jonson.
Knowing the heart of man is set to be. *Fr.* To the Lady Margaret, Countess of Cumberland. Daniel.
Last Man, The. Campbell.
Like as the Damask Rose You See. *Unknown.*
Like Flowers We Spring. *Unknown.*
Man. *Fr.* Aurora Leigh. E. B. Browning.
Man. Cook.
Man. *Fr.* Nosce Teipsum. Davies.
Man. Greenberg.
Man. Herbert.
Man ("What a piece of work is a man!"). *Fr.* Hamlet. Shakespeare.
Man. Vaughan.
Man. Wolfe.
Man against the Sky, The. Robinson.
Man and Nature. Weeks.
Man in the Bowler Hat, The. Tessimond.
Man, Man, Man. *Unknown.*
Man Meeting Himself. *Fr.* The Leaves of Europe. Sergeant.
Man Said to the Universe, A. *Fr.* War Is Kind. S. Crane.
Man Was Made to Mourn; a Dirge. Burns.
Man's a Bubble. Dodsley.
Man's a Man for A' That. Burns.
Man's Mortality. *Unknown.*
Man's Need. Ross.
Man's roots are not in earth; while trees and flowers. *Fr.* Man's Roots. Currey.
Measure of a Man. *Unknown.*
Measuring a Man. *Unknown.*
Meditatio. Pound.
Men. MacLeish.
Men. Parker.
Men. Reid.
Men of Old, The. Milnes.
Monkey. Miles.
New Being, The. Patchen.
On Man. Landor.
On the Life of Man. Ralegh.
One's-Self I Sing. Whitman.
Original Sin. Jeffers.
Our birth is but a sleep and a forgetting. *Fr.* Ode: Intimatious of Immortality from Recollections of Early Childhood. Wordsworth.
Pity This Busy Monster, Manunkind. Cummings.
Poem: "And this digester, this digester of food." *Fr.* Time in the Rock. Aiken.
Salutation, The. Traherne.
Sans Equity and sans Poise. *Fr.* The Classic Anthology: Yung Wind. Confucius.
Satire against Mankind, A. Rochester.
Sic Vita. King.
Sirens, The, *sels.* Binyon.
Small Comment. Sanchez.
So, Man? Derwood.
Sonnet: "Blast of wind, a momentary breath, A." *Fr.* A Divine Century of Spiritual Sonnets. Barnes.
Stand, Stately Tavie. *Unknown.*
Truant, The. Pratt.
Up from the Bed of the River. *Fr.* The Creation. Johnson.
Vanity. Herbert.
Weak Is the Will of Man, His Judgment Blind. Wordsworth.
Words Made of Water. Singer.
Years That Go to Make Me Man, The. Brennan.

Manassas, Battles of. *See* **Bull Run, Battles of.**

Manchester, England
Murphy in Manchester. Montague.

Manchouli, Manchuria
Manchouli. Empson.

Mandeville, Sir John
Part of Mandevil's Travels. Empson.

Mangan, James Clarence
Nameless One, The. Mangan.

Manhasset, New York
Limerick: "Then the pair followed Pa to Manhasset." *Unknown.*
Manhattan. *See* New York (city).

Manila, Philippine Islands
Battle of Manila, The. Hovey.
Captive Ships at Manila, The. Paul.
Manila. Ware.
Manila Bay. Hale.

Manning, Henry Edward
Cardinal Manning. De Vere.
To the Dead Cardinal of Westminster. Thompson.

Mansfield, Katherine
Horse in a Field. De la Mare.

Mansfield, Mount, Vermont
Sunrise on Mansfield Mountain. Brown.

Mantis
Chance, The. Holmes.
Don't Sit under the Apple Tree with Anyone Else but Me. Pack.
Mantis. Heywood.
Mantis Friend, The. McHugh.
Praying-Mantis, The. Dalton.
Praying Mantis, The. Nash.
Praying Mantis. Stefanile.
Praying Mantis Visits a Penthouse, The. Williams.

Maple Syrup
Maple Feast. F. Frost.
Sap Bucket Song. Stoddard.
Sugaring, The. Klein.

Maple Trees
Dusk in the Sugar Woods. Malam.
Five-fingered Maple, The. Brown.
Sleepy Maple Trees, The. Hammond.

Maps
Map, The. Bishop.
Map, The. Oden.
Map, The. Strand.
Mapmaker on His Art, The. Nemerov.
Mappemounde. Birney.
Maps. Thompson.
Mermaids. *Fr.* The Atlas. Slessor.
Old Maps. Tietjens.
Private Letter to Brazil, A. Oden.
Quilt. Updike.

Marais du Cygne (river), Kansas
Le Marais du Cygne. Whittier.

Marathon, Battle of
Persian Version, The. Graves.

Marble
Island Quarry. H. Crane.
Marc Antony. *See* **Antony.**
March
Change in the Year, A. *Fr.* To My Sister. Wordsworth.
Counting-out Rhyme for March. F. Frost.
Dear March, come in. Dickinson.
Earliest Spring. Howells.
Flower Chorus. Emerson.
In March. Martin.
March. Bryant.
March. Clare.
March. Coatsworth.
March. H. Crane.
March. Guiterman.
March. Hammond.
March. Hopper.
March. Housman.
March. Larcom.
March. Loveman.
March. *Fr.* The Earthly Paradise. Morris.
March. Webb.
March brings the lamb. *Unknown.*
March Evening. Strong.
March Thoughts from England. Woods.
March Weather. Swan.
March Wind, The. *Unknown.*
March Wind. Uschold.
March Wind. Wing.
March Winds, The. Houghton.
March Winds. Lloyd.
Merry Month of March, The. Wordsworth.
One March Day. *Unknown.*
Passing of March, The. Wilson.
Song in March. Simms.
'Tis March. Nelson.
Twilight in Middle March, A. Ledwidge.
Wild March. Woolson.
Written in March. Wordsworth.
Margaret, Saint
To Saint Margaret. Constable.
Margaret Tudor (Queen of Scotland)
To the Princess Margaret Tudor. Dunbar.
Margate, England
Misadventures at Margate. "Ingoldsby."
Maria Christina, Queen of Spain
Christina. R. Browning.
Marib, Yemen
High Place at Marib, The. Code.
Marie-Antoinette, Queen of France
On the Toilet Table of Queen Marie-Antoinette. Nichols.
Marigolds
Marigold. Garnett.
Marigold, The. *Fr.* Scented Leaves from a Chinese Jar. Upward.
Marigold, The. Wither.
Marigold So Likes the Lovely Sunne, The. Watson.
Marigolds. Driscoll.
Marigolds. Graves.
New Ballade of the Marigold, A. Forrest.
Marin, John
Marin. Booth.
Marines. *See* **United States Marine Corps.**
Marion, Francis
Song of Marion's Men. Bryant.
Swamp Fox, The. Simms.
Mark Antony. *See* **Antony.**
Markiewicz, Constance Georgine, Countess
In Memory of Eva Gore-Booth and Con Markiewicz. Yeats.
Marlborough, John Churchill, 1st Duke of
Death of Marlborough, The. Thornbury.
Satirical Elegy on the Death of a Late Famous General, A. Swift.
Marlowe, Christopher
Christopher Marlowe. *Fr.* To Henry Reynolds, of Poets and Poesy. Drayton.
Christopher Marlowe. *Fr.* Sonnets on English Dramatic Poets. Swinburne.
Marlowe. Bayldon.
Marrakesh, Morocco
Marrakech. Currey.
Marquette, Jacques
Marquette on the Shores of the Mississippi. Rooney.
Marriage
Adversaries. Johnson.
After Our Wedding Day. Heine.
Against Women either Good or Bad. Norton.
Anniversary. Thomas.
Any Wife or Husband. Haynes.
Any Wife to Any Husband. R. Browning.
Arise, get up, my dear love, rise, make haste, begone thee! *Unknown.*
Bachelor's Song, The. Flatman.
Ballad of the Despairing Husband. Creeley.
Ballad upon a Wedding, A. Suckling.
Before and After Marriage. Campbell.
Bridge Instead of a Wall, A. *Unknown.*
But That Is Another Story. Justice.
Careful Husband, The. *Unknown.*
Conformers, The. Hardy.
Contention, A, betwixt a Wife, a Widow, and a Maid. Davies.
Counsel upon Marriage. Chaucer.
Curate's Kindness, The. Hardy.
Disappointed Wife, The. Wright.
Downe too farre usurping day. *Unknown.*
Dying Wife to Her Husband, A. Ibn Ezra.
Epigram: "How many drag the marriage chain." Tyler.
Epitaph upon a Young Married Couple Dead and Buried Together, An. Crashaw.
Eurynome. Macpherson.
Family Life. Laing.
Farmer's Bride, The. Mew.
Fisherman Husband. Chamberlain.
For a Second Marriage. Merrill.
Fortitude. Reinmar von Zweter.
Good & Bad Wives. *Unknown.*
Hail Matrimony, made of love. *Fr.* An Island in the Moon. Blake.
Hector to Andromache. *Fr.* The Iliad. Homer.
Holy Matrimony. Keble.
Honeymoon. Albert.
Husband and Wife. Guiterman.
Huswifery. Taylor.
Hymen hath together tyed. *Unknown.*
Hymeneall Dialogue, An. Carew.
I Am Your Wife. *Unknown.*
I'm Married. Torgersen.
Investment, The. Frost.
It really must. *Fr.* Is 5. Cummings.
Jack and Joan. Campion.
Jealous Wife, The. Scannell.
Jeane's Wedden Day in Mornen. Barnes.
Les Sylphides. MacNeice.
Letter. Bergman.
Love and Marriage. Mathew.
Love in a Life. R. Browning.
Love's Matrimony. Duke of Newcastle.
Lucky Marriage, The. Blackburn.
Marriage. Clarke.
Marriage. Corso.
Marriage. Gibson.
Marriage. Hall.
Marriage. Van Doren.
Marriage, The. Winters.
Marriage and the Care o't. Lochore.
Marriage of Two. Day Lewis.
Marriage Ring, A. Crabbe.
Marriage: To K. Hall.
Mehitabel Tries Marriage. *Fr.* Archys Life of Mehitabel. Marquis.
Men Marry What They Need. I Marry You. Ciardi.
Midnight Court, The. Merriman.
Minion Wife, A. *Fr.* Ralph Roister Doister. Udall.
Modern Love. Meredith.
Most like an Arch This Marriage. Ciardi.
My Wife. Stevenson.
New Ring, The. Shapiro.
New Wine, Old Bottles. Newbury.
Newly-wedded, The. Praed.
Newlyweds, The. Criswell.
No Love, to Love of Man and Wife. Eedes.
Now you're married you must obey. *Unknown.*

Marriage *(continued)*
Nun's Priest's Tale, The. *Fr.* The Canterbury Tales. Chaucer.
Nuptiall Song, or Epithalmie, A. Herrick.
O, the Marriage! Davis.
Old Cloak, The. *Unknown.*
On Marriage. Crashaw.
On Marriage. Flatman.
On the Marriage of a Virgin. Thomas.
One Wife for One Man. Aig-Imoukuede.
Ou Phrontis. Causley.
Our Happy Home. *Unknown.*
Peggy's Wedding. Brown.
Poem in Prose. MacLeish.
Prayer for a Marriage, A. Davies.
Progress of Marriage, The. Swift.
Sanctum, The. Daly.
Sandgate Girl's Lamentation, The. *Unknown.*
Song for a Marriage. Miller.
Thinker, The. Williams.
Three Seamstresses, The. Peretz.
'Tis the White Plum Tree. Neilson.
To a Lady on Her Marriage. Bell.
To a Mate. Robinson.
To His Wife on the Sixteenth Anniversary of Her Wedding-day, with a Ring. Bishop.
To My Dear and Loving Husband. Bradstreet.
"To Speak of Woe That Is in Marriage." R. Lowell.
To the Last Wedding Guest. Gregory.
Together. Lewisohn.
Unthrift. *Fr.* The Angel in the House. Patmore.
Upon the Death of Sir Albertus Morton's Wife. Wotton.
Washing the Dishes. Morley.
Wedded Love. *Fr.* Paradise Lost. Milton.
Wedding Procession. Emanuel.
Wedding Signs. *Unknown.*
Wedlock. Greenberg.
Why Should a Foolish Marriage Vow. *Fr.* Marriage-a-la-Mode. Dryden.
Wife, A. Brome.
Wife, The. Creeley.
Wife of Bath's Prologue, The. *Fr.* The Canterbury Tales. Chaucer.
Wife of Bath's Tale, The. *Fr.* The Canterbury Tales. Chaucer.
Winchester Wedding, The. D'Urfey.
Young Bride's Dream, The. Coghill.
Young Wife, A. Lawrence.
High Wedlock Then Be Honored (HW). Virginia Tufte, ed.
See also **Wedding Songs.**
Mars (god)
Ares. Ehrenstein.
Song of Momus to Mars, The. *Fr.* The Secular Masque. Dryden.
To Mars. *Unknown.*
Mars
Light of Stars, The. Longfellow.
Marshes
Flood-Time on the Marshes. Stein.
In Romney Marsh. Davidson.
Marsh, The. Snodgrass.
Marsh Song—At Sunset. Lanier.
Marshes of Glynn, The. Lanier.
Marston, John
Ad Jo. Marston & Ben. Jonson. Weever.
John Marston. *Fr.* Sonnets on English Dramatic Poets. Swinburne.
Marsyas
Marsyas. Roberts.
Martha's Vineyard, Massachusetts
Making Port. McKay.
Martí, José
On a Monument to Martí. Roberts.
Martial
De Poeta Martiali. Bastard.
Martin, Saint
St. Martin and the Beggar. Gunn.
Martins Ferry, Ohio
Autumn Begins in Martins Ferry, Ohio. Wright.
Martyrs
City of Slaughter, The. Bialik.
Da Silva Gives the Cue. Blumenthal.
Elegy: "I die for Your holy word without regret." Gomez.
Here Followeth the Songe of the Death of Mr. Thewlis. *Unknown.*
Last Words of Don Henriquez, The. Schneour.
Martrdom. Learsi.
Martyrdom of Bishop Farrar, The. Hughes.
Martyrdom of Father Campion. Walpole.
Martyr's Death, A. Menahem ben Jacob.
Martyr's Hymn, The. Luther.
Martyr's Mass, A. Barrett.
Martyr's Memorial. Guiney.
On the Late Massacre in Piedmont. Milton.
Sebastian. Baro.
Song of Four Priests Who Suffered Death at Lancaster, A. *Unknown.*
These Things I Do Remember. Solomon Ephraim ben Aaron of Lenczicz.
Through the straight pass of suffering. Dickinson.
Thy Faithful Sons. Eleazar.
To the English Martyrs. Thompson.
True Martyr, The. Wade.
Marvell, Andrew
Poet of Gardens. Henderson.
Mary, The Virgin
Against Women's Fashions. Lydgate.
Ah, My Dere. *Unknown.*
Ah (You Say), This Is Holy Wisdom. Doolittle.
Aishah Shechinah. Hawker.
Annunciation, The. Conway.
Annunciation. *Fr.* La Corona. Donne.
Annunciation, The. Merwin.
Annunciation, The. Muir.
Annunciation, The. Procter.
Annunciation, The. *Unknown.*
Annunciation Night. Conway.
Annunciation to All Women. Foote.
As Dew in Aprille. *Unknown.*
Assumption, The. Beaumont.
At the Assumption. Luis de León.
Ave. D. G. Rossetti.
Ave Maria. Charasson.
Ave Maria. Rooney.
"Ave Maria Gratia Plena." Wilde.
Ave, Maris Stella. *Unknown.*
Ave Regina. *Unknown.*
Ave Sanctissima. *Unknown.*
Ballad of Our Lady. Dunbar.
Ballade of Illegal Ornaments. Belloc.
Ballade to Our Lady of Czestochowa. Belloc.
Bee, The. Hawkins.
Birth of Mary. Rilke.
Black Madonna, The. Rice.
Blessed Virgin Compared to the Air We Breathe, The. Hopkins.
Cantiga. Vicente.
Carol: Five Joys of the Virgin, The. *Unknown.*
Cherry-Tree Carol, The. *Unknown.*
Death of Our Ladie, The. Southwell.
Dei Genitrix. De Vere.
Devout Man Prays to His Relations, The. Herebert.
Epithalamium. Crashaw.
Evening Prayer, An. *Unknown.*
Expectation, The. *Fr.* Our Lady's Expectation. Faber.
Five Joys of Mary, The. *Unknown.*
Flemish Madonna, A. Stork.
For "Our Lady of the Rocks." D. G. Rossetti.
Fourth Station. *Fr.* The Stations of the Cross. Donaghy.
Gaelic Litany to Our Lady, The. *Unknown.*
Ghyrlond of the Blessed Virgin Marie, The. Jonson.
Grandeurs of Mary, The. Faber.
Her Nativity. Southwell.
His Mother's Service to Our Lady. Villon.
Hymn to Mary, A. Dunbar.
Hymn to Mary, A. *Unknown.*
Hymn to the Virgin, A. *Unknown.*
I Sing of a Maiden. *Unknown.*
In Praise of Mary. *Unknown.*
Jesus and His Mother. Gunn.
Jesus Comforts His Mother. *Unknown.*
Jesus Reassures His Mother. *Unknown.*
L'Annunciazione. O'Gorman.
Latin Hymn to the Virgin. Praed.
Little Hymn to Mary, A. *Unknown.*

Lulla, la lulla, lulla lullaby./ My sweet little baby. *Unknown.*
Lullaby: "Upon my lap my sovereign sits." Verstegan.
Lullay My Liking. *Unknown.*
Madonna Remembers. Sister Mary Edwardine.
Madonna, to Her Sleeping Child. Lope de Vega.
Maiden Ring-adorned, A. Cynewulf.
Maria Immaculata. Pallen.
Maris Stella. Drane.
Mary. Downing.
Mary. Knight.
Mary. Trumbull.
Mary at the Cross. McGee.
Mary Complains to Other Mothers. *Unknown.*
Mary Immaculate. Donnelly.
Mary Is with Child. *Unknown.*
Mary Pondered All These Things. Poteat.
Mary, Queen of Heaven. *Unknown.*
Mary Tired. Pickthall.
Mary, Virgin and Mother. Seton.
Mary Weeps for Her Child. *Unknown.*
Mary's Girlhood. *Fr.* Sonnets for Pictures. D. G. Rossetti.
Mater Christi. *Fr.* May Carols. De Vere.
Mater Dolorosa. Fitzpatrick.
Mater Misericordiae. Sister St. Miriam of the Temple.
May Magnificat, The. Hopkins.
Mother and Child. Eastwick.
Mother and Her Son on the Cross, The. *Unknown.*
Mother Most Powerful. Dominici.
Mother, White as Lily Flower. *Unknown.*
Name of Mary. O'Reilly.
New Song of Mary, A. *Unknown.*
O Mooder Mayde. *Fr.* The Canterbury Tales: The Prioress's Tale. Chaucer.
Of a Rose, a Lovely Rose. *Unknown.*
On the Assumption. Crashaw.
On the Blessed Virgin's Bashfulness. Crashaw.
On the Feast of the Assumption. Downing.
On the Glorious Assumption of Our Blessed Lady. Crashaw.
On the Infancy of Our Saviour. Quarles.
Our Lady. Bridges.
Our Lady. M. E. Coleridge.
Our Lady in the Middle Ages. Faber.
Our Lady's Assumption. Sister Agnes.
Our Lady's Death. Hill.
Our Lady's Lullaby. Verstegan.
Our Lady's Song. *Unknown.*
Our Lord and Our Lady. Belloc.
Penitent Hopes in Mary, The. *Unknown.*
Pieta. Butler.
Prayer to the Virgin. *Unknown.*
Prayer to the Virgin of Chartres. Adams.
Prologue, A: "Thou Speaker of all wisdom in a Word." Patmore.
Quaerit Jesum Suum Maria. Crashaw.
Quia Amore Langueo. *Unknown.*
Quickening, The. S. W. Tuttle.
Regina Coeli. Patmore.
Regina Coeli. *Unknown.*
Return of Eve, The. Chesterton.
Rosa Mystica. Hopkins.
St. Bernard's Prayer to the Virgin Mary. *Fr.* Divina Commedia: Paradiso. Dante.
Sonetto XXXV: To Guido Orlando. Cavalcanti.
Song to Mary, A. *At. to* William of Shoreham.
Song to the Virgin, A. *Unknown.*
Sonnet for the Madonna of the Cherries. Wavell.
Spinner, The. O'Donnell.
Stabat Mater Dolorosa. *At. to* Jacopone Da Todi.
Stabat Mater Speciosa. *At. to* Jacopone Da Todi.
Star of the Sea. *Fr.* The Ship of Fools. Barclay.
Sweet Was the Song. *Unknown.*
Thirteenth Station, The. Giltinan.
To Mary, Mother of Christ. Harsen.
To Our Blessed Lady. Constable.
To Our Lady. Henryson.
To the Virgin. Lydgate.
To the Virgin Mary. *Fr.* Sonnets to Laura. Petrarch.
Two Carols to Our Lady. *Unknown.*
Veni, Coronaberis. *Unknown.*
Venite Adoremus. Cannon.
Vigil of the Immaculate Conception. Egan.
Virgin, The. Wordsworth.
Virgin Mary, The. Bowers.
Virgin Mary's Conception, The. Southwell.
Virgin's Song, The. *Unknown.*
Visitation, The. Jennings.
Visitation, The. Southwell.
Vow to Heavenly Venus, A. Du Bellay.
Wayside Virgin, The. Mitchell.
Well of Pity, The. *Fr.* An A.B.C. Chaucer.
When Mary thro' the Garden Went. M. E. Coleridge.
I Sing of a Maiden (ISi). Sister M. Thérèse, ed.

Mary I, Queen of England
Christ Brought Home. *Unknown.*
Marigold, The. Forrest.

Mary Magdalen
And She Washed His Feet with Her Tears, and Wiped Them with Hairs of Her Head. Sherburne.
At Glastonbury. Kingsley.
Conversion of the Magdalene, The, *sel.* Malon de Chaide.
For the Magdalene. Drummond of Hawthornden.
Lent. Rogers.
Magdalen. Kingsley.
Magdalen. Randall.
Magdalen, The. Sherburne.
Magdalene. Pasternak.
Marie Magdalene. Herbert.
Marie Magdalens Complaint at Christs Death. Southwell.
Mary Knew. Munson.
Mary Magdalene. Burton.
Mary Magdalene. Speyer.
Mary Magdalene at the Door of Simon the Pharisee. D. G. Rossetti.
"Multum Dilexit." H. Coleridge.
To Mary Magdalen. Argensola.
To St. Mary Magdalen. Constable.
To St. Mary Magdalen. Hill.
Weeper, The. Crashaw.
Woman. Barrett.

Mary Queen of Scots.
Adieux à Marie Stuart. Swinburne.
Alas! Poor Queen. Angus.
At Fotheringay. Southwell.
Mary, Queen of Scots. Bell.
Mary Queen of Scots. Burns.
Mary Queen of Scots. Turner.
Tragic Mary Queen of Scots, The. "Field."

Maryland
Maryland Battalion, The. Palmer.
Maryland Resolves. *Unknown.*
My Maryland. Randall.

Massachusetts
Massachusetts to Virginia. Whittier.

Masts
Choosing a Mast. Campbell.

Mathematics
Arithmetic. Sandburg.
Equation, An. Plutzik.
Of the Mathematician. Mathews.
Seven Times One. Ingelow.
Statistician, The. Stork.
Imagination's Other Place (ImOP). Helen Plotz, comp.

Mather, Cotton
Ben Franklin's Head (1728). Howe.
Cotton Mather. S. V. Benét.

Matisse, Henri
Picasso and Matisse. Francis.

Matlock Bath, England
Matlock Bath. Betjeman.

Matterhorn
High Brow. Fitch.
Zermatt: To the Matterhorn. Hardy.

Matthew, Saint
Christus Matthaeum et Discipulos Alloquitur. Sherburne.

Matthews, Brander
In Vain Today. Dobson.

Maximilian, Emperor of Mexico
Manet: The Execution of Emperor Maximilian. Snodgrass.

Maxwell, John, 9th Baron Maxwell
Lord Maxwell's Last Goodnight. *Unknown.*

May

May *(continued)*
A-Maying, a-Playing. *Fr.* Summer's Last Will and Testament. Nashe.
Apple Blossoms. Larcom.
April and May. *Fr.* May-Day. Emerson.
April and May. Robinson.
Archer, The. Scollard.
Corinna's Going a-Maying. Herrick.
Eidolon. Warren.
Fairy Music. Ledwidge.
Flute of May, The. Woodbourne.
For Good Luck. Ewing.
Gardener, The. Perkins.
Gladness of the May, The. Wordsworth.
Glycine's Song. *Fr.* Zapolya. Coleridge.
Here We Come a-Piping. *Unknown.*
In May. Davies.
In May. *Unknown.*
In Obitum M.S., X Maii, 1614. Browne.
In Praise of May. *Unknown.*
In this merry morn of May. *Unknown.*
Jewish May, The. Rosenfeld.
Judgment of the May, The. Dixon.
Love in May. Passerat.
Lusty May. *Unknown.*
M. Edwards' May. Edwards.
May. Barnes.
May. Bird.
May. Cornwell.
May. Macdonald.
May. Neilson.
May. Percival.
May. C. G. Rossetti.
May. *Fr.* The Faerie Queene. Spenser.
May. *Unknown.*
May Basket, The. Goodale.
May Basket, A. West.
May Carol ("In vain thy altars do they heap"). De Vere.
May-Day. Hill.
May Day. Teasdale.
May Day. *Unknown.*
May-Day at Sea. Finerty.
May Day Carol. *Unknown.*
May Day Garland, The. Blunden.
May-Day on Magdalen Tower. Warren.
May Is Building Her House. Le Gallienne.
May Magnificat, The. Hopkins.
May Morning. Barrows.
May Morning. Milton.
May Morning. Thaxter.
May Mornings. Eastwick.
May Queen, The. Tennyson.
May Song, A. "Fane."
May Sun Sheds an Amber Light, The. Bryant.
Maytime. *Fr.* The Shoemaker's Holiday. Dekker.
May-Time. Gant.
May-Time. *Unknown.*
Month of May, The. *Fr.* The Knight of the Burning Pestle. Beaumont *and* Fletcher.
Nightingale, The. *Fr.* The Passionate Pilgrim. Barnfield.
Oh, the Month of May! *Fr.* The Shoemaker's Holiday. Dekker.
Ode in May. Watson.
Old May Song ("All in this pleasant evening"). *Unknown.*
On a Bank as I Sat a-Fishing. *Fr.* A Description of the Spring. Wotton.
On Mayday we dance. *Unknown.*
Open, sweet flowers, your eyes. *Fr.* May. O'Donnell.
Poem in May. Hewitt.
Queen of Seasons, The. Cardinal Newman.
Resurgam. Burt.
Rhyme for Remembrance of May. Burton.
Sing All Ye Joyful. Tolkien.
Song: "Drink and be merry, merry, merry boys." *Fr.* New England Canaan. Morton.
Song: "Now is the month of maying." *Unknown.*
Song for May Day, A. Adler.
Song on May Morning. Milton.
Succession of the Four Sweet Months, The. Herrick.
Summer Is Nigh. *Unknown.*
There is but one May in the year. *Fr.* Sing-Song. C. G Rossetti.
This month of May, one pleasant eventide. *Unknown.*
Why It Was Cold in May. Eliot.
Wonderful Country. Waddington.
Young May Moon, The. Moore.

Mayflower. *See* **Arbutus.**

Mayflower (ship)
Columbus and the *Mayflower.* Milnes.
Mayflower, The. Ellsworth.
Mayflower. O'Reilly.

Mayo, Ireland
County Mayo, The. Raftery.
County of Mayo, The. *At. to* Flavell.
Summer Is Coming, The. Guinness.

Mazeppa
Mazeppa. Byron.

Mazzini, Giuseppe
Lines on the Monument Erected to Mazzini at Genoa. Swinburne.

Meadow Larks
Meadow Lark, The. Garland.
Meadow Lark. Walker.

Meadows. *See* **Fields and Pastures.**

Meadowsweet
Meadowsweet. Allingham.

Meath, Ireland
Boyne Walk, The. Higgins.
Father and Son. Higgins.

Mecklenburg Declaration of Independence
Mecklenburg Declaration, The. Elam.

Medea
Jason and Medea. *Fr.* Confessio Amantis. Gower.

Medici, Ferdinand de'
Statue and the Bust, The. R. Browning.

Medici, Lorenzo de'
Statue of Lorenzo de' Medici, The. Nesmith.

Mediterranean Sea
Mare Mediterraneum. Nichol.
Mediterranean, The. Tate.
"Of Thee the Northman." Santayana.

Medusa
Medusa. Bogan.

Meigs, Fort, Ohio
Old Fort Meigs. *Unknown.*

Melampus
Melampus. Meredith.

Melancholy
Dejection. Bridges.
Dejection; an Ode. Coleridge.
Il Penseroso. Milton.
Melancholy. *Fr.* The Nice Valour. Fletcher.
Melancholy. Thomas.
Ode on Melancholy. Keats.

Meleager
Meleager. *Fr.* Metamorphoses. Ovid.

Melbourne, Australia
Towers at Evening, The. *Fr.* Melbourne and Memory. Wilmot.

Melton Mowbray, England
Melton Mowbray Pork-Pie, A. Le Gallienne.

Melville, Herman
At Melville's Tomb. H. Crane.
Herman Melville. Auden.
Letter for Melville 1951. Olson.

Memling, Hans
Memling's Virgin with Apple. Naudé.

Memorial Day
Aftermath. McCulloch.
America's Answer. Lillard.
Ballad of Heroes, A. Dobson.
Bitter Question. Macdougall.
Bivouac of the Dead, The. O'Hara.
Blue and the Gray, The. Finch.
Comrade, Remember. Kresensky.
Criminality of War, The. Young.
Crosses. Hicks.
Dead, The. *Fr.* 1914. Brooke.
Debt, The. Garrison.
Decoration Day. Howe.
Decoration Day. Longfellow.

Decoration Day Prayer. Bemis.
For Decoration Day. Hughes.
For Our Dead. Scollard.
For Those Who Died. Clark.
From Beyond. Trent.
High Flight. Magee.
How Shall We Honor Them? Markham.
How Sleep the Brave. Collins.
Hymn to the Victorious Dead. Hagedorn.
I Have a Son. Pottle.
If These Endure. Lorraine.
In Memoriam. Jackson.
In the Name of Our Sons. Gould.
It Is Not Too Late. Trent.
Knot of Blue and Gray, A. *Unknown.*
Lament of the Voiceless, The. Everett.
Little Flags, The. Minot.
March, The. Squire.
May Thirtieth. *Unknown.*
Memorial. Goodman.
Memorial Day. Brooks.
Memorial Day. Dunning.
Memorial Day. Garrison.
Memorial Day. Guiney.
Memorial Day. Kilmer.
Memorial Day. Lent.
Memorial Day. Warman.
Memorial Day. Wiley.
Memorial Day. Wilson.
Memorial Day. Wynne.
Memorial Day, 1889. Kiser.
Memorials on the Slain at Chickamauga. Melville.
Monument for the Soldiers, A. Riley.
Mother before a Soldier's Monument, A. Rockett.
New Banner, The. Trask.
New Memorial Day, The. Paine.
No More the Thunder of Cannon. Dorr.
Ode for Decoration Day. Peterson.
Ode for Decoration Day. Timrod.
Ode to the Confederate Dead. Tate.
On a World War Battlefield. Clark.
Parade, The. Badley.
Remembering Day. Saunders.
Requiem for a Dead Warrior. McInnis.
Soldier-Dead. Emery.
Soldier, Rest! *Fr.* The Lady of the Lake. Scott.
Song for Decoration Day. Bacon.
Song for Heroes, A. Markham.
Song for Memorial Day. Scollard.
Their Victory Won. Coates.
There Will Be Peace. Pettengill.
Thus Speak the Slain. Holliday.
Toward a True Peace, A. *Fr.* Ten Years After. Trent *and* Cheyney.
Tribute to Our Soldiers. Kennedy.
Veterans, The. McCarthy.
We Shall Remember Them. White.
We Who Are Dead. Benjamin.
We Whom the Dead Have Not Forgiven. Field.

Memory
Among the Beautiful Pictures. Cary.
Ballade Catalogue of Lovely Things, A. Le Gallienne.
Coin, The. Teasdale.
Empty Jar, The. Stenhouse.
Essay on Memory. Fitzgerald.
Four Ducks on a Pond. Allingham.
I Remember, I Remember. Hood.
Inscription on a Grot. *Fr.* The Pleasures of Memory. Rogers.
Light of Other Days, The. Moore.
Memories. Whittier.
Memory. Aldrich.
Memory. Erskine, Earl of Rosslyn.
Memory. Hoyt.
Memory, A. Knowles.
Memory. Landor.
Memory. Lincoln.
Memory. Rimbaud.
Memory. D. G. Rossetti.
Memory. Stagnelius.
Memory, A. Strong.
Memory as Memorial in the Last. Marshall.
Memory of Earth, A. "Æ."
Memory of the Dead, The. Ingram.
Moment He Remembers, The. Van Doren.
Most Quietly at Times. Flaischlen.
Ode to Memory. Shenstone.
Oft in the Stilly Night. Moore.
Old Familiar Faces, The. Lamb.
Old Man's Carousal, The. Paulding.
Remember. C. G. Rossetti.
Remembrance. E. Brontë.
Remembrance. Slonimski.
Remembrances. Clare.
Song: "Memory, hither come." Blake.
Song of My Heart, A. Bridges.
To Memory. M. E. Coleridge.
Tune, A. Symons.
What Need Have I for Memory? Johnson.
When to the sessions of sweet silent thought. Sonnets, XXX. Shakespeare.

Memphis, Tennessee
At Memphis Station. Jensen.
Beale Street, Memphis. Snyder.
Memphis Blues. Brown.

Men. *See* **Man.**

Menageries. *See* **Zoos.**

Menalaus
Menalaus. Day.

Menkure, Pharaoh of Egypt
Mycerinus. Arnold.

Mephistopheles. *See* **Satan.**

Mercy
Ode to Mercy. Collins.
Quality of mercy is not strain'd, The. *Fr.* The Merchant of Venice. Shakespeare.
Song for an Allegorical Play. Ciardi.

Meredith, George
George Meredith. Hardy.

Merlin
Merlin. Emerson.
Merlin. Muir.
Merlin and the Gleam. Tennyson.
Merlin Enthralled. Wilbur.

Mermaid Tavern
Lines on the Mermaid Tavern. Keats.
Seven Wise Men. *Fr.* Tales of the Mermaid Tavern. Noyes.
Wassail Chorus at the Mermaid Tavern. Watts-Dunton.

Mermaids and Mermen
Ballad of the Mermaid. Leland.
Clark Colven. *Unknown.*
Elegy on a Dead Mermaid Washed Ashore at Plymouth Rock. Hillyer.
Enchanted Island, The. Conolly.
Figure-Head, The. Garstin.
Fisherman's Blunder off New Bedford, Massachusetts. Ewing.
Forsaken Merman, The. Arnold.
Great Silkie of Sule Skerry, The. *Unknown.*
Little John Bottlejohn. Richards.
Mermaid, The. Smith.
Mermaid, The. Tennyson.
Mermaid, The. *Unknown.*
Mermaiden, A. Hennell.
Mermaidens, The. Heine.
Mermaidens, The. Richards.
Mermaiden's Vesper Hymn, The. *Fr.* Syren Songs. Darley.
Mermaids. *Fr.* The Atlas. Slessor.
Mermaids, The. *Fr.* The Faerie Queene. Spenser.
Mermaids and Mermen. *Fr.* The Pirate. Scott.
Merman, The. Tennyson.
Moon-Child, The. "Macleod."
My Cabinets Are Oyster-Shells. Duchess of Newcastle.
Neckan, The. Arnold.
Old Angler, The. De la Mare.
Rowing, I reach'd a rock—the sea was low. *Fr.* A Vision of the Mermaids. Hopkins.
Sam. De la Mare.
Santorin. Flecker.
Sea-Maiden, The. De Forest.
Sea-Maids' Music, The. Myers.
Song of the Mermaids. Darley.

Merrimac (ship)
Men of the *Merrimac*, The. Scollard.

Merrimac *(continued)*
Sinking of the *Merrimac*. Larcom.
Turtle, The. *Unknown.*
Merritt Parkway, Connecticut
Merritt Parkway. Levertov.
Sleet Storm on the Merritt Parkway. Bly.
Merry-go-rounds. *See* **Carrousels.**
Messiah
Ballad of the Days of the Messiah. Klein.
Hush, Hush. Leib.
O Hark to the Herald. Ben Kalir.
When the Days Shall Grow Long. Bialik.
Methuselah
Methuselah. *Fr.* The Devil and the Angel. Dobson.
Mexican War
Angels of Buena Vista, The. Whittier.
Battle of the King's Mill. English.
Biglow Papers, The, 1st Series, *sels.* J. R. Lowell.
Bivouac of the Dead, The. O'Hara.
Buena Vista. Pike.
Crisis, The. Whittier.
Monterey. Hoffman.
Santa Anna; or, The Plains of Mexico. *Unknown.*
Siege of Chapultepec, The. Lytle.
Mexicans
Una Anciana Mexicana. Corbin.
Mexico
Bernal Diaz' Preface. *Fr.* Conquistador. MacLeish.
Dawn on the Wall-Head There. *Fr.* Conquistador. MacLeish.
Epitaph to the Liberty of America. Fernández de Lizardi.
Hex on the Mexican X, A. McCord.
In Mexico. Stein.
Indians Come Down from Mixco, The. Asturias.
Irapuato. Birney.
Mexican Market Woman. Hughes.
Mexican Serenade. Guiterman.
Ode to the Fatherland. Flores.
Small Soldiers with Drum in Large Landscape. *Fr.* Mexico Is a Foreign Country. Warren.
Mexico, Gulf of
Gulf of Mexico. Reyes.
Meynell, Alice
On Looking at a Copy of Alice Meynell's Poems, Given Me, Years Ago, by a Friend. A. Lowell.
Mezeray, Françis Eudes de
Written in the Beginning of Mezeray's History of France. Prior.
Mice
Change of Heart, A. Hobbs.
City Mouse and the Garden Mouse, The. *Fr.* Sing-Song. C. G. Rossetti.
Diary of a Church Mouse. Betjeman.
Field-Mouse, The. Blyton.
Field Mouse, The. "Macleod."
Four III. Cummings.
Funeral Oration for a Mouse. Dugan.
House of the Mouse, The. Mitchell.
I was lying still in a field one day. Gay.
Lion and the Mouse, The. Taylor.
Madame Mouse Trots. E. Sitwell.
Martial Mouse, A. Butler.
Meadow Mouse, The. Roethke.
Mice. Fyleman.
Missing. Milne.
Mouse, The. Coatsworth.
Mouse. Conkling.
Mouse, The. McCrae.
Mouse, The. Wakley.
Mouse, a Cat, and an Irish Bull, A. Tabb.
Mouse and the Cake, The. Cook.
Mouse in the Wainscot, The. Serraillier.
Mouse That Gnawed the Oak-Tree Down, The. Lindsay.
Mouse's Nest. Clare.
Prayer of the Mouse, The. Gasztold.
Satin Mice Creaking Last Summer's Grass, The. Coffin.
To a Mouse. Burns.
Wood-Mouse, The. Howitt.
Young Mouse, The. Taylor.
Michael, the Archangel
Michael the Archangel. Tynan.
Michael the Archangel. Williams.
Michaelmas
Michaelmas. Nicholson.
Michelangelo Buonarroti
Medici Tombs, The. Ross.
Old Age of Michelangelo, The. Prince.
Michigan
Michigan, My Michigan! Lyster.
Michigan, Lake
Cook County. MacLeish.
Great Lakes Suite, The. Reaney.
Mickleham, England
Mirage at Mickleham. Meynell.
Microbes
Lines Written on the Antiquity of Microbes. Gillilan.
Midas
King Midas. Moss.
King Midas. *Fr.* Metamorphoses. Ovid.
Ungrateful Garden, The. Kizer.
Middle Age
Advice to Colonel Valentine. Graves.
April Inventory. Snodgrass.
Autumnal, The. Donne.
End of Summer. Kunitz.
Journey Toward Evening. McGinley.
Lady's Complaint, The. Heath-Stubbs.
Loved One, The. Hansen.
Middle-Age. Jones.
Middle Age. Lehmann.
Middle Age. R. Lowell.
Middle-aged, The. Rich.
Next Day. Jarrell.
Rondel for Middle Age. Nicholl.
Mignonette
Pitcher of Mignonette, A. Bunner.
Red Geranium and Godly Mignonette. Lawrence.
Milam, Ben
Valor of Ben Milam, The. Scollard.
Milk and Milking
Milk. Schuyler.
Milker, The. Duggan.
Milking Time. Roberts.
Milkmaid. Lee.
When the Cows Come Home. C. G. Rossetti.
Milkmen
Milkman, The. Krows.
Milkweed
Silkweed. Savage.
To the Milkweed. Mifflin.
Two Voices in a Meadow. Wilbur.
Milky Way
Milky Way, The. *Fr.* Scented Leaves from a Chinese Jar. Upward.
Mill, John Stuart
J. S. Mill. Bentley.
Millet, Jean Françis
Angelus, The. Coates.
Mills and Millers
Lesson of the Water-Mill, The. *Fr.* The Man o' Airlie. Doudney.
Miller That Made His Will. *Unknown.*
Water Mill, The. Hawkshaw.
Milton, John
Afternoon in Artillery Walk, An; Mary Milton Loquitur. Bacon.
Epigram on Milton. Dryden.
How Could You Know? Redman.
Johannes Milton, Senex. Bridges.
Lines Printed under the Engraved Portrait of Milton. Dryden.
London, 1802, ("Milton! Thou shouldst be living at this hour"). Wordsworth.
Milton, *sels.* Blake.
Milton. Longfellow.
Milton. Mifflin.
Milton. Tennyson.
Milton. Wilde.
Milton by Firelight. Snyder.
Milton: On the Busts of Milton, in Youth and Age. Bowles.
Milton's Prayer. Howell.
On His Blindness. Milton.
On Milton's Paradise Lost. Marvell.
On Seeing a Lock of Milton's Hair. Keats.

Progress of Poesy, The. Gray.
Rhapsody to Milton. Davies.
Shakespeare and Milton. Landor.
To the Ghost of John Milton. Sandburg.

Milton, Katherine
Katherine Milton: Died MDCLVIII. Milton.

Mind. *See* **Intellect.**

Minerals
Mineral Collection. Evans.
Mining and Miners
Cornish Miner, The. Gries.
Drilling Missed Holes. Cameron.
Miner, The. King.
Miner, The. Bodenheim.
Miner's Protégée, The. *Unknown.*
Miner's Song, The. Winter.
Mother Wept. Skipsey.
Song of the Leadville Mine Boss. Cameron.
Worked-out Mine, The. Dyson.
See also **Coal Mining and Miners; Gold Mining and Miners.**

Ministers. *See* **Clergy.**

Minnesota
Minnesota! Rickard *and* Upson.

Minot, Laurence
Song of Laurence Minot. Minot.

Minstrels
Deor's Lament. *Unknown.*
Minstrel, The. Goethe.
Minstrel Boy, The. Moore.
Minstrel's Song. *Fr.* Aella. Chatterton.
Widsith, the Minstrel. *Fr.* Widsith. *Unknown.*

Miracles
Higher Calling, The. Czamanske.
How Miracles Abound. Scollard.
Miracle, The. De la Mare.
Miracle, A. "Klingle."
Miracle, The. *Fr.* Carmen Paschale. Sedulius.
Miracle for Breakfast, A. Bishop.
Miracles. Bontemps.
Miracles. Helton.
Miracles. Whitman.

Mirages
Mirage. Blackmur.
Yon Far Country. Housman.

Mirrors
Hand-Mirror, A. Whitman.
Lady Who Offers Her Looking-Glass to Venus, The. Prior.
Mirror. Plath.
Mirror. Updike.
Nell Gwynne's Looking Glass. Blanchard.

Misanthropy
Complete Misanthropist, The. Bishop.
Satyr against Mankind, A. Rochester.
Wishes of an Elderly Man. Raleigh.

Missionaries
India became his jasmined youth, Goa. *Fr.* The Man of Grace. Macnab.
Missionaries, The. McIntyre.
Sourcebook of Poetry (SoP). Al Bryant, comp.

Mississippi (state)
Way Down South in Mississippi. Barnes.

Mississippi River
Down the Mississippi. Fletcher.
Marquette on the Shores of the Mississippi. Rooney.
River, The. *Fr.* The Bridge. Crane.
River, The. Lorentz.

Missouri (state)
Missouri Rhapsody. Daugherty.

Missouri River
Foreclosure. Brown.
Missouri Traveller Writes Home, A, 1830. Bly.
Others May Praise What They Like. Whitman.
Shenandoah. *Unknown.*

Mist
Haze. *Fr.* A Week on the Concord and Merrimack Rivers. Thoreau.
Mist, The. Miller.
Mist. *Fr.* A Week on the Concord and Merrimack River. Thoreau.
Mist, The. *Unknown.*
Mist. Young.
Mist and All, The. Willson.
Night Mists. Hayne.
See also **Fog.**

Mistletoe
Mistletoe Bough, The. Bayly.
Mistletoe Sprites. Russell.
Under the Mistletoe. Cullen.

Mithra
Song to Mithras, A. Kipling.

Mithridates the Great
Mithridates. Emerson.

Mnemosyne
Memory. Landor.

Mobile Bay, Battle of
Bay Fight, The. Brownell.
Craven. Newbolt.
Farragut. Meredith.
Through Fire in Mobile Bay. *Unknown.*

Mockingbirds
Lament of a Mocking-Bird. Kemble.
Listen to the Mocking-Bird. Winner.
Look at Six Eggs. *Fr.* Prairie. Sandburg.
Mocking-Bird, The. Hayne.
Mocking Bird, The. Hovey.
Mockingbird, The. Jarrell.
Mocking Bird, The. Lanier.
Mocking Bird and the Donkey, The. Rosas.
Moonlight Song of the Mocking-Bird. Hayne.
To the Mocking-Bird. Pike.
To the Mocking-Bird. Wilde.

Mohave Desert
In the Mohave. Orr.

Moles
All but Blind. De la Mare.
Dead Mole, A. Young.
Eagle and the Mole, The. Wylie.
Gardener and the Mole, The. Landor.
Mole, The. Clare.
Mole, The. Daniells.
Mole, The. King.
Mole, The. Matchett.
Mole, The. Mayo.
Mole. Smith.
Mole Catcher. Blunden.
Moles. Stafford.
To a Mole. Darcy.
Unfortunate Mole, The. Kennedy.

Mona Lisa
La Gioconda, by Leonardo Da Vinci, in the Louvre. "Field."
Mona Lisa. Dowden.
Mona Lisa. Pater.

Monadnock, Mount, New Hampshire
Monadnock through the Trees. Robinson.

Monasteries
Decayed Monastery, A. Dermody.
In the Monastery. O'Conor.
Trappist Abbey, The: Matins. Merton.
Semblables, The. Williams.

Money
American Change. Ginsberg.
As I Sat at the Café, I Said to Myself. *Fr.* Dipsychus. Clough.
Avarice. Herbert.
Away with this cash. *Unknown.*
Basic. Durem.
Behaviour of Money. Spencer.
Dialogue. Nemerov.
Fatigue. Belloc.
Hardship of Accounting, The. Frost.
Hero in the Land of Dough, A. Clairmont.
How the Money Rolls In. *Unknown.*
I sing not of Angelica the fair. *Fr.* Lady Pecunia; or, The Praise of Money. Barnfield.
Impact of a Dollar upon the Heart, The. Crane.
Investor's Soliloquy. Ward.
Letrilla; the Lord of Dollars. Quevedo y Villegas.
Money. Armour.
Money. Contoski.
Money. Davies.
Money. Pontalais.
Money. *Unknown.*
Money and a Friend. *Unknown.*

Money *(continued)*
Money Is What Matters. *Unknown.*
My masters, I thank you, it's time to pack home. *Fr.* Jack of Newbury. Deloney.
Of Money. Googe.
On Melting down the Plate; or, The Piss-Pot's Farewell, 1697. *Unknown.*
Penny Problem. Farrar.
Quatrains for a Bank Cashier. DeWitt.
Render unto Caesar. Humphries.
Rule of Money, The. *Unknown.*
Song to His Purse for the King, A. Chaucer.
Spectator ab Extra. Clough.
Wilt Thou Lend Me Thy Mare? *Unknown.*
Ye tradeful merchants, that with weary toil. *Fr.* Amoretti. Spenser.
Your Money and Mine. *Unknown.*
Mongoose
Mongoos, The. Herford.
Monitor (ship)
Cruise of the *Monitor,* The. Boker.
Utilitarian View of the *Monitor's* Fight, A. Melville.
Monkeys
Monkey, The. Campbell.
Monkey, The. Howitt.
Monkey, The. Khodasevich.
Monkey. Miles.
Monkey. Smith.
Monkey and the Cat, The. La Fontaine.
Monkeys. *Fr.* With Walker in Nicaragua. Miller.
Monkeys, The. Thompson.
Monkeys and the Crocodile, The. Richards.
Monkey's Glue, The. Goldsmith.
So Many Monkeys. Edey *and* Grider.
Sonnet on a Monkey, A. Fleming.
Tails. Bennett.
Three Monkeys. *Unknown.*
Three Wise Monkeys, The. Davis.
Monks
Carthusians. Dowson.
Elegy for the Monastery Barn. Merton.
Monasteries. Webb.
Monk and His Pet Cat, The. *Unknown.*
Monk in the Kitchen, The. Branch.
Monk of Casal-Maggiore, The. Longfellow.
Monks. Cardinal Newman.
Monks at Ards, The. Maybin.
Monks of Bangor's March, The. Scott.
Monks of Ely, The. *Unknown.*
Palmer, The. Scott.
Pangur Ban. *Unknown.*
Practical Program for Monks. Merton.
San Lorenzo Giustiniani's Mother. Meynell.
Soliloquy of the Spanish Cloister. R. Browning.
Stanzas from the Grande Chartreuse. Arnold.
Monmouth, James Scott, Duke of
Dutchess of Monmouth's Lamentation for the Loss of Her Duke, The. *Unknown.*
England's Darling; or, Great Britain's Joy and Hope on That Noble Prince James, Duke of Monmouth. *Unknown.*
Monmouth, Battle of
Battle of Monmouth, The. English.
Battle of Monmouth, The. "R. H."
Molly Maguire at Monmouth. Collins.
Molly Pitcher. Richards.
Monroe, James
James Monroe. R. Benét *and* S. V. Benét.
Mont Blanc
Hymn before Sunrise, in the Vale of Chamouni. Coleridge.
Mont Blanc. Shelley.
Montana
In Montana. McCormick.
Montana. Cohan.
Montana Eclogue. Stafford.
Montana, Nothing like Boston. Welch.
Montenegro
Montenegro. Tennyson.
Monterrey, Mexico
Monterey. Hoffman.
Montgomery, Richard
Montgomery at Quebec. Scollard.
Months
Days of the Month, The. Mother Goose.
Garden Year, The. Sara Coleridge.
Marjorie's Almanac. Aldrich.
Months, The. Sara Coleridge.
Months, The. C. G. Rossetti.
Months, The. Sheridan.
Odes of the Months, *sel.* Aneirin.
Of the Months. San Geminiano.
Succession of the Four Sweet Months, The. Herrick.
Thirty Days Hath September. *Unknown.*
Monticello, Virginia
Air Tunnel, Monticello. Noll.
Montreal, Canada
Bonne Entente. Scott.
Cartier at St. Malo. *Fr.* A View of Montreal. Webb.
Montreal. Klein.
Montreal. Lighthall.
O God! O Montreal! Butler.
Montrose, James Graham, 5th Earl of
Execution of Montrose, The. Aytoun.
Verses Composed on the Eve of His Execution. Graham.
Montserrat (monastery), Spain
Monserrat. Collin.
Moon
Above the Dock. Hulme.
African Moonrise. Campbell.
Arctic Moon, The. *Fr.* The Yukon. Miller.
At a Lunar Eclipse. Hardy.
Auctioneer. Sandburg.
Aware. Lawrence.
Bonny Harvest Moon, The. Barr.
Cat and the Moon, The. Yeats.
Chase, The. Davies.
Clair de Lune. Symons.
Clair de Lune. Verlaine.
Crescent Moon. Basho.
Crescent Moon. Roberts.
Cruel Moon, The. Graves.
Diana. Ralegh.
Early Moon. Sandburg.
Encounter. Hughes.
Fields Are Spread, The. Coatsworth.
Fragment: To the Moon. Shelley.
Full Moon. De la Mare.
Full Moon. *Fr.* Down the Mississippi. Fletcher.
Full Moon. Hayden.
Full Moon. Kinnell.
Full Moon. Wylie.
Full Moon; Santa Barbara. Teasdale.
Gathering Sticks on Sunday. Nicholson.
Golden Bird, The. Ingamells.
Harvest Moon, The. Longfellow.
Harvest Moon. Ryota.
Horseman, The. De la Mare.
Hymn to the Moon. *Fr.* Homeric Hymns. *Unknown.*
I Have Cared for You, Moon. Conkling.
In Dispraise of the Moon. M. E. Coleridge.
In the Moonlight. Hardy.
In the Moonlight. O'Conor.
In the Moonlight. Patchen.
In the Moonlight. Wright.
In the Night of the Full Moon. Busse.
Is the Moon Tired? *Fr.* Sing-Song. C. G. Rossetti.
It Was the Lovely Moon. Freeman.
July Dawn. Bogan.
La Fruite de la Lune. *Fr.* Impressions. Wilde.
Lady Moon. Milnes.
Languishing Moon, The. Sidney.
Little Day Moon. Miller.
Look Down Fair Moon. Whitman.
Lunae Custodiens. Carter.
Man in the Moon, The. *Unknown.*
May Moon. Driver.
Match with the Moon, A. D. G. Rossetti.
Milk-white Moon, Put the Cows to Sleep. Sandburg.
Mr. Moon. Carman.
Mockery. Riggs.
Moon, The. Azumamaro.
Moon, The. Bhasa.
Moon, The. Davies.

Moon, The. Follen.
Moon, The. Herford.
Moon, The. Kotomichi.
Moon. Rowe.
Moon, The ("And like a dying lady"). Shelley.
Moon, The ("Art thou pale for weariness"). Shelley.
Moon, The. Södergran.
Moon and Fog. Derleth.
Moon behind High Tranquil Leaves, The. Nichols.
Moon-Children. Lewis.
Moon Compasses. Frost.
Moon Fishing. Mueller.
Moon in September, The. Ghose.
Moon in the Water, The. Ryota.
Moon is distant from the sea, The. Dickinson.
Moon It Shines, The. *Unknown.*
Moon-Madness. Starbuck.
Moon Magic. Hanes.
Moon of Brooklyn, The. N. Crane.
Moon Rider. W. R. Benét.
Moon Shadow. Bowering.
Moon Ship, The. *Unknown.*
Moon, So Round and Yellow. Barr.
Moon Song. Conkling.
Moon was but a chin of gold, The. Dickinson.
Moonbeam. Conkling.
Moonlight. De la Mare.
Moonlight. Moxon.
Moonlight. Tahureau.
Moonlight. *Unknown.*
Moonlight in Italy. Kinney.
Moonlight on Lake Sydenham. MacDonald.
Moonrise. Doolittle.
Moonrise. Evans.
Moonrise. Hopkins.
Moonrise. Lawrence.
Moonrise. Sherman.
Moonrise in the Rockies. Bradley.
Moons. Haines.
Moon's Orchestra, The. *Fr.* Down the Mississippi. Fletcher.
Moon's the North Wind's Cooky, The. Lindsay.
Moontan. Strand.
My Wish. Strong.
New Moon, The. Blunden.
New Moon, The. Bryant.
New Moon. Lawrence.
New Moon in January. Hughes.
Nocturne, A: "Moon has gone to her rest, The." Blunt.
O for a Moon to Light Me Home. De la Mare.
O Lady Moon. C. G. Rossetti.
Ocean to Cynthia, The. Ralegh.
Ode to the Moon. Hood.
On Aesthetics, More or Less. Dufault.
On the Eclipse of the Moon of October 1865. Tennyson-Turner.
On the Telescopic Moon. Drennan.
Pale Cold Moon, The. Renton.
Phases of the Moon. *Fr.* One Word More. R. Browning.
Poetic Thought. *Unknown.*
Possum and the Moon, The. Campbell.
Praised Be Diana's Fair and Harmless Light. Ralegh.
Prayer by Moonlight. Swartz.
Prayer to the Young Moon. *Unknown.*
Re-Birth. *Unknown.*
Riddle #29: The Moon and the Sun. *Unknown.*
Rising of the Moon, The, A.D. 1798. Casey.
River Moons. Sandburg.
Satyrs and the Moon, The. Gorman.
Shiny. Reeves.
Silver. De la Mare.
Silver Road, The. Hendry.
Sing a Song of Moonlight. Eastwick.
Song of the Moon, A. McKay.
Sonnet: "O bitter moon, O cold and bitter moon." Wood.
Sonnet of the Moon, A. Best.
Summer Moonlight. Strong.
Thoughts on the Sight of the Moon. Knight.
To the Afternoon Moon, at Sea. Rice.
To the Moon. Darley.
To the Moon. Hardy.
To the Moon. Ronsard.
To the Moon. Shelley.
To the Moon. Smith.
To the Moon. Wordsworth.
Tonight the Pacifist Moon. Alexander.
Turn of the Moon. Graves.
Under the Harvest Moon. Sandburg.
Under the Moon. Yeats.
Wandering Moon, The. Reeves.
Waning Moon, The. Shelley.
Watching the Moon. McCord.
Welcome to the Moon. *Unknown.*
White in the moon the long road lies. *Fr.* A Shropshire Lad. Housman.
White Window, The. Stephens.
Wind and the Moon, The. Macdonald.
With how sad steps, O Moon, thou climb'st the skies. *Fr.* Astrophel and Stella. Sidney.
Young May Moon, The. Moore.

Moonflower
To the Moonflower. Betts.

Moore, Sir John
Burial of Sir John Moore after Corunna, The. Wolfe.

Moore, Marianne
Invitation to Miss Marianne Moore. Bishop.

Moore, Thomas
On Thomas Moore's Poems. *Unknown.*
To Thomas Moore ("My boat is on the shore"). Byron.
Will you come to the bower I have shaded for you? *Fr.* A Reply to Lines by Thomas Moore. Landor.

Moors
Barren Moors, The. Channing.
Gloucester Moors. Moody.
Moor, The. Thomas.
On Westwall Downes. Strode.
Owre the Muir amang the Heather. Glover.

More, Sir Thomas (Saint Thomas More)
Ballad of St. Thomas, A. Brady.
Case of Thomas More, The. Sister Mary St. Virginia.

Moreau, Gustave
From Sappho's Death: Three Pictures by Gustave Moreau. Moore.

Morgan, Sir Henry
Morgan. Stedman.

Morgan, John Hunt
Kentucky Belle. Woolson.

Morison, Sir Henry
To the Immortall Memorie, and Friendship of That Noble Paire, Sir Lucius Cary, and Sir H. Morison. Jonson.

Mormons
Early This Spring We'll Leave Nauvoo. Fife.

Morning
Aubade: Lake Erie. Merton.
Awake, Mine Eyes. *Unknown.*
Bird's Song at Morning. Dawson.
Call of the Morning, The. Darley.
Cock-Crow Song. *Unknown.*
Cock-crowing. Vaughan.
Composed upon Westminster Bridge. Wordsworth.
Description of the Morning, A. Swift.
Early Morn. Davies.
Early Morning, The. Belloc.
Early Morning at Bargis. Hagedorn.
Early Morning in a Glade. Dresbach.
Early Morning Meadow Song. Dalmon.
Early Rising. Saxe.
Field of Light, A. Roethke.
Full many a glorious morning have I seen. Sonnets, XXXIII. Shakespeare.
Good Morning. Baillie.
Hail, Fair Morning. *Fr.* The Life of St. Cellach of Killala. *Unknown.*
Haze. Buson.
Herald. Miles.
Hymn to the Morning, An. Leapor.
I Stood Tiptoe upon a Little Hill. Keats.
Impression du Matin. Wilde.
In the Morning. Loftus.
Is It Morning? Is It the Little Morning? Schwartz.
January Morning, A. Lampman.
June Morning. McCrae.
Joy of the Morning. Markham.

Morning *(continued)*
Keys of Morning, The. De la Mare.
Lark Now Leaves His Wat'ry Nest, The. Davenant.
Matins. Levertov.
Mattens. Herbert.
Morgenlied. Symonds.
Morn. Jackson.
Morning. Blake.
Morning. Conkling.
Morning. Gallagher.
Morning, The. *Fr.* Trivia. Gay.
Morning. Golden.
Morning. Harrison.
Morning. Keble.
Morning. McCrae.
Morning. Savage.
Morning. Taylor.
Morning. Teasdale.
Morning. Very.
Morning. Waddington.
Morning and Evening. Slonimski.
Morning at the Beach. Farrar.
Morning at the Window. Eliot.
Morning Clouds. Miller.
Morning comes to the consciousness, The. *Fr.* Preludes. Eliot.
Morning Hymn. Alexander.
Morning Hymn. St. Gregory the Great.
Morning Hymn. Ken.
Morning Hymn. Wesley.
Morning in the North-West. Stringer.
Morning Light. Newsome.
Morning Light for One with Too Much Luck, The. Schwartz.
Morning Mist, The. Southey.
'Morning, Morning. Mathew.
Morning Song. Baker.
Morning Song, A. Farjeon.
Morning Song. Fet.
Morning Song of Senlin. *Fr.* Senlin, a Biography. Aiken.
Morning Sun. MacNeice.
Morning-Watch, The. Vaughan.
Mornin's Mornin', The. Brennan.
No Time for Poetry. Fields.
Ode to Morning. Mason.
One Morning When the Rain-Birds Call. Roberts.
Pack, Clouds, Away. *Fr.* The Rape of Lucrece. Heywood.
Parting at Morning. R. Browning.
Poem About Morning. Meredith.
Prayer for Dreadful Morning. Root.
Rainy Morning. North.
Reveille. Housman.
Sister, Awake! *Unknown.*
Small Song. F. Frost.
Softly, Drowsily. De la Mare.
Summer Morning. Clare.
Summer Morning, A. Field.
Sung on a Sunny Morning. Untermeyer.
Time to Rise. Stevenson.
To Morning. Blake.
Tropical Morning at Sea, A. Sill.
Turning. Finch.
Upon Westminster Bridge. Wordsworth.
Very Early. Kuskin.
Waking Time. Eastwick.
Will there really be a morning? Dickinson.
Yonder See the Morning Blink. Housman.
See also **Dawn; Sunrise.**

Morning-Glories
Morning-Glory, The. Coates.
Morning-Glory, The. M. S. Lowell.

Morocco
Morocco. Currey.

Morris, William
Rondel: "Behold the works of William Morris." *Unknown.*
William Morris. Davies.

Morton, Sir Albertus
Tears at the Grave of Sir Albertus Morton. Wotton.

Morton, Jelly Roll (Ferdinand La Menthe)
Wisdom of Old Jelly Roll, The. Smith.
Morton, William Thomas Green
Crawford Long and William Morton. R. Benét *and* S. V. Benét.

Mosby, John Singleton
Mosby at Hamilton. Cawein.

Moses
Angels Came a-Mustering, The. *Unknown.*
Burial of Moses. Alexander.
Death of Moses, The. *Unknown.*
Go Down, Moses. *Unknown.*
Moses and Jesus. Zangwill.
Murder of Moses, The. Shapiro.
When Moses came down from the mountain and the cloud. *Fr.* The Eleventh Commandment. Holmes.

Mosquitoes
Mosquito, The. Lawrence.
Mosquito. Updike.
To a Mosquito. Bryant.

Mother
Are All the Children In? *Unknown.*
At My Mother's Knee. *Unknown.*
Autumn. Untermeyer.
Beautiful Hands. Gates.
Between the Porch and the Altar. R. Lowell.
Boy's Mother, A. Riley.
C. L. M. Masefield.
Certain True Woords Spoken Concerning One Benet Corbett after Her Death. Corbett.
Childless Woman in Heaven, The. Tynan.
Cradle Song: "Sleep, my child, my little daughter." *Unknown.*
Dear Old Mothers. Ross.
Definition. Crowell.
Division of Parts, The. Sexton.
Echo of a Song, The. Foley.
English Mother, An. Johnson.
Epitaph on My Dear and Ever Honoured Mother, An. Bradstreet.
First Aid. Hopegood.
For Mother on Father's Day. Tate.
For You, Mother. Conkling.
Funeral Song upon the Decease of Annes, His Mother, A. Grimald.
Gift, The. *Unknown.*
God's Ideal Mother. Pinkham.
God's Mothers. Malloch.
Greatest Battle That Ever Was Fought. Miller.
Hand That Rocks the Cradle Is the Hand That Rules the World, The. Wallace.
Her Hands. *Fr.* Songs for My Mother. Branch.
Her Little Boy. *Unknown.*
Her Words. *Fr.* Songs for My Mother. Branch.
Hide of My Mother, The. Dorn.
How she grew old happened in fine-darned places. *Fr.* The People. "Hyde."
How's My Boy? Dobell.
I Must Not Tease My Mother. Sigourney.
Identity. Sister Mary Helen.
Irish Mother in the Penal Days, The. Banim.
Jean Richepin's Song. Trench.
Keine Lazarovitch. Layton.
Like Mother, like Son. Grafflin.
Little Girl That Mother Used to Be. Turner.
Little Mother. "M. P. D."
Lonesome. Dunbar.
Lord Christ, My Darling Is So Dear. Hansen-Bay.
Love's Tribute. Sturgeon.
Mary at the Cross. McGee.
Mary Complains to Other Mothers. *Unknown.*
Ma's Tools. *Unknown.*
Mater Amabilis. Lazarus.
Maternity. Meynell.
Message, A. Reed.
Mother, The. Arnold.
Mother, The. Campbell.
Mother, The. Sara Coleridge.
Mother. Cooper.
Mother. Ehrmann.
Mother. Sister M. Eulalia.
Mother. Fyleman.
Mother, The. Gardons.
Mother. Helburn.
Mother. Kelleher.
Mother. Lovejoy.
Mother, The. Palmer.

Mother, The. Ryan.
Mother. Sinclair.
Mother. Taylor.
Mother ("Each day to her a miracle"). *Unknown.*
Mother, The ("From out the South the genial breezes sigh"). *Unknown.*
Mother ("Whenever I look in her kind eyes"). *Unknown.*
Mother. Waxman.
Mother—a Portrait. Fuller.
Mother and Son. Tate.
Mother, Home, Heaven. Brown.
Mother in gladness, Mother in sorrow. Wedgefarth.
Mother in the House, The. Hagedorn.
Mother Is a Sun, A. Bennett.
Mother Love. Alford.
Mother o' Mine. *Fr.* The Light That Failed. Kipling.
Mother of a Daughter. Johnson.
Mother of Men. Hooker.
Mother of Men. Southwold.
Mother of the House. Proverbs, Bible, *O.T.*
Mother Thought, A. Guest.
Mother to Her Infant, The. Miller.
Mother to Son. Hughes.
Mother Understands, A. Studdert-Kennedy.
Mother Who Died Too, The. Thomas.
Motherhood. Bacon.
Motherhood. Chworowsky.
Motherhood. Lee.
Motherhood. Stidger.
Motherhood. Swenson.
Mothers. Sabin.
Mothers. *Unknown.*
Mothers—and Others. Wells.
Mother's Birthday, A. Van Dyke.
Mothers, Daughters. Kaufman.
Mother's Day. Muth.
Mother's Hands. Wedgefarth.
Mother's Hymn, The. Bryant.
Mother's Lament for the Death of Her Son, A. Burns.
Mother's Love. Clapp.
Mother's Love. Montgomery.
Mother's Love ("Her love is like an island"). *Unknown.*
Mother's Name, A. *Unknown.*
Mothers of Men. Burr.
Mothers of Men, The. Miller.
Mothers of the Earth, The. Crowell.
Mothers of the West, The. Gallagher.
Mother's Prayer, A. Coon.
Mother's Prayer, A. Sangster.
Mother's Prayer, The. Shorter.
Mother's Reward, A. Lathrop.
Mother's Sacrifice, The. Sigourney.
Mother's Song, The. Cloud.
Mother's Song ("My Heart is like a fountain true"). *Unknown.*
My Altar. Styles.
My Beige Mom. Spriggs.
My Mother. Burr.
My Mother. Creelman.
My Mother. Ledwidge.
My Mother. Nolan.
My Mother. Taylor.
My Mother. *Unknown.*
My Mother. Wilson.
My mother and your mother. *Unknown.*
My Mother's Garden. Allen.
My Mother's House. Tietjens.
My Mother's Love. *Unknown.*
My Mother's Prayer. O'Kane.
My Trundle Bed. Baker.
My Trust. Whittier.
Name of Mother, The. Fetter.
Nancy Hanks, Mother of Abraham Lincoln. Lindsay.
Night and Morning. Aldis.
Nobody Knows—but Mother. *Unknown.*
Now That Can Never Be Done. Sister Maris Stella.
O Mothers of the Human Race. Whitaker.
Oedipus at San Francisco. Finkel.
Old Arm-Chair, The. Cook.
Old Face, An. Miller.
Old Mother, The. *Unknown.*
Old Mothers. Ross.
On the Receipt of My Mother's Picture Out of Norfolk. Cowper.
One Who Struggles, The. Toller.
Only One Mother. Cooper.
Our Mother. Cooper.
Our Mother. *Unknown.*
Our Mothers. *Unknown.*
Our Mother's Tunes. Farjeon.
Over the Hill to the Poor-House. Carleton.
Piano. Lawrence.
Plácido's Sonnet to His Mother. Plácido.
Queen of the World. *Unknown.*
Reading Mother, The. Gillilan.
Recollection. Govan.
Remembrance. Bruner.
Rock Me to Sleep, Mother. Allen.
Shrine, The. Dolben.
Sick Child, The. Stevenson.
Somebody's Mother. Brine.
Song of the Old Mother, The. Yeats.
Songs for My Mother. Branch.
Sonnet to My Mother. Barker.
Soul of a Mother, The. Sangster.
Starred Mother, The. Whitaker.
To a Polish Mother. Michiewicz.
To C. L. M. Masefield.
To His Mother. Heine.
To Mother. Fessenden.
To Mother—in Heaven. Weaver.
To My First Love, My Mother. C. G. Rossetti.
To My Mother. Barker.
To My Mother. Brock.
To My Mother. Ginsberg.
To My Mother. Heine.
To My Mother. Henley.
To My Mother. Moore.
To My Mother. Poe.
To the Anxious Mother. Malangatana.
To the Mothers. Toller.
To Whom Shall They Go? *Unknown.*
Waiting Mothers. Zuker.
Watcher, The. Widdemer.
What Is Home without a Mother? Winner.
What Rules the World. Wallace.
When a Girl Looks Down. Smith.
When Mother Reads Aloud. *Unknown.*
When Mother Scrubs. *Unknown.*
Which Loved Her Best? "Allison."
White Carnation, The. Sangster.
Wondrous Motherhood. *Unknown.*
You Mean My Mother. *Unknown.*
Sourcebook of Poetry (SoP). Al Bryant, comp.

Mothers-in-law
His Mother-in-Law. Parke.

Moths
Green Moth. Welles.
Lying Awake. Snodgrass.
Moth, The. De la Mare.
Moth Miller. Fisher.
Moth-Song. Cortissoz.
Moth-Terror. De Casseres.
Moths, The. Matchett.
Near Dark. Auslander.
Night Moths, The. Markham.
Riddle: Book-Moth. *Unknown.*
To a Moth. Thomas.
To a Moth that Drinketh of the Ripe October. Pfeiffer.
Where More Is Meant. Morley.

Motion Pictures
Day with the Foreign Legion, A. Whittemore.
Essay in Defense of the Movies. Gibson.
Horror Movie. Moss.
Ingmar Bergman's Seventh Seal. Duncan.
Movie-Going. Hollander.
Movies, The. Frank.
Movies for the Home. Moss.
Song of the Movie Mexican, A. Robinson.
Triple Feature. Levertov.

Motley, John Lothrop
In Memory of John Lothrop Motley. Bryant.

Motorcycles and Motorcycling
Lordly and Isolate Satyrs, The. Olson.
Motorcycle. Pray.
On the Move. Gunn.
Poems of My Lambretta. Goodman.
305 Honda. Fowler.
Unsettled Motorcyclist's Vision of His Death, The. Gunn.
Mount Vernon, Virginia
Inscription at Mount Vernon. *Unknown.*
Mount Vernon, the Home of Washington. Day.
Mountain Climbing
Climbers. Birney.
David. Birney.
De Gustibus. Hankin.
Mountain Climber, The. Pozzi.
On a Grave at Grindelwald. Myers.
On Scafell Pike. Walker.
On the Heights. Foote.
Spring Mountain Climb. Eberhart.
Mountain Lion
Mountain Lion. Lawrence.
Mountains. *See* **Hills and Mountains.**
Mouse. *See* **Mice.**
Movies. *See* **Motion Pictures.**
Moving Day
Leaving Ithaca. Snodgrass.
Moving Day. Hartman.
Mowing and Mowers
Damon the Mower. Marvell.
Lawn and Light. *Fr.* Steps from the Stream. Applewhite.
Lawn-Mower. Baruch.
Lost. Brand.
Mower, The. *Unknown.*
Mower to the Glowworms. Marvell.
Mowers, The. Allingham.
Mowers, The. Benton.
Mower's Song. Marvell.
Mowing. Frost.
Mowing, The. Roberts.
Old Field Mowed, An. Meredith.
Scythe Song. Lang.
Mozart, Wolfgang Amadeus
Corner Knot, The. Graves.
Four Friends. Ward.
Mozart. Baring.
Mozart. Higham.
Mozart. Mayhall.
Mozart at Zell-am-See. Watkins.
Mozart, 1935. Stevens.
Mozart's Grave. Mowrer.
Mozart's "Linz" Symphony. Stanley-Wrench.
Mud
Colloquy in Black Rock. R. Lowell.
Mud. Boyden.
Muhammed Ali. *See* **Clay, Cassius.**
Mulberry Trees
Banjo Boomer. Stevens.
Mules
Cincirinella Had a Mule. *Unknown.*
Ever Since. Coatsworth.
Old Balaam. *Unknown.*
Mummies
Dead Cleopatra Lies in a Crystal Casket. Aiken.
In the Egyptian Museum. Lewis.
In the Museum. Gardner.
Mumps
Mumps. Roberts.
Munch, Edvard
Munch's Scream. Hall.
Munster, Ireland
Cashel of Munster. *Unknown.*
Murder and Murderers
At the Executed Murderer's Grave. Wright.
Ballad of Charlotte Dymond, The. Causley.
Murder of William Remington, The. Nemerov.
Murder Trial, The. Adams.
Murdered Girl Is Found on a Bridge. Hayman.
Murderer, The. Petrie.
Tom Dooley. *Unknown.*
Wexford Girl, The. *Unknown.*
Murfreesboro, Battle of
Battle of Murfreesboro, The. Cornwallis.
Muses
Invocation to the Muse. Hughes.
Muse, The. Davies.
My Muse and I, Ere Youth and Spirits Fled. Colman.
To the Contemporary Muse. Bowers.
To the Muses. Blake.
You muses nurses of delight. *Unknown.*
Museums
Antwerp: Musée des Beaux-Arts. Ross.
Bone Thoughts on a Dry Day. Starbuck.
Elegy in a Museum. Griffin.
Homage to the British Museum. Empson.
In a Museum. Deutsch.
In a Museum. Wilson.
In the Egyptian Museum. Lewis.
Meditations in a Museum Cloister. Sister Maryanna.
Municipal Gallery Revisited, The. Yeats.
Museum Piece. Wilbur.
Museums. MacNeice.
Poem for Museum Goers, A. Wieners.
San Marco Museum, Florence. Sister Maris Stella.
War Museum in Nagasaki, The. Higham.
Mushrooms
Morels. Smith.
Mushroom is the elf of plants, The. Dickinson.
Mushrooms. Plath.
Music
Abt Vogler. R. Browning.
After a Dolmetsch Concert. Upson.
After Music. Peabody.
Alexander's Feast; or, The Power of Music. Dryden.
Anthem for St. Cecilia's Day. Auden.
Asia. *Fr.* Prometheus Unbound. Shelley.
At a Solemn Music. Milton.
At the Symphony. Nathan.
Ballad of Heaven, A. Davidson.
Barrel-Organ, The. Noyes.
Beethoven Andante, A. Conkling.
Boy Playing an Organ. Sweeney.
Calyx of the Oboe Breaks, The. Aiken.
Choral Symphony Conductor. Coates.
Church-Music. Herbert.
Commendation of Music, The. Strode.
Composer, The. Auden.
Concert-Interpretation. Sassoon.
Constant One, The. Dillon.
Envoy: "Go, songs, for ended is our brief, sweet play." Thompson.
Epitaph upon the Celebrated Claudy Philips, Musician Who Died Very Poor, An. Johnson.
Fascinating chill that music leaves, The. Dickinson.
Fiddler Jones. *Fr.* Spoon River Anthology. Masters.
Fiddler of Dooney, The. Yeats.
Four Friends. Ward.
Harper, The. *Unknown.*
Harper of Chao, The. Po Chü-i.
Haunting Fingers. Hardy.
How oft, when thou, my music, music play'st. Sonnets, CXXVIII. Shakespeare.
In Commendation of Music. Strode.
In Gusts of Music. Sister Davida.
In Praise of Music in Time of Pestilence. Hine.
Instruments, The. Smart.
Italian Music in Dakota. Whitman.
Italian Opera. Miller.
Jazz Fantasia. Sandburg.
Jesu, Joy of Man's Desiring. Fitzgerald.
L'Envoi: "Now in a thought, now in a shadowed word." Robinson.
Lines on Hearing the Organ. Calverley.
Lost Chord, A. Procter.
Love. Tieck.
Man with a Little Pleated Piano, A. Welles.
Military Harpist, The. Pitter.
Music. Aiken.
Music, The. Baudelaire.
Music. Chesterton.
Music. Conkling.
Music. Corbin.

Music. De la Mare.
Music. Du Maurier.
Music. Emerson.
Music. Farjeon.
Music. A. Lowell.
Music. Phillips.
Music. Ryan.
Music. Thomas.
Music and Memory. Albee.
Music at Twilight. Sterling.
Music I Heard with You. *Fr.* Discordants. Aiken.
Music in Camp. Thompson.
Music in the Night. Spofford.
Music Magic. Leamy.
Music of Hungary. Aldrich.
Music, When Soft Voices Die. Shelley.
Musician. Bogan.
Musick in time. *Unknown.*
Musicks Duell. Crashaw.
Musick's Empire. Marvell.
Night Concert. Earle.
O Black and Unknown Bards. Johnson.
Ode for Music on St. Cecilia's Day. Pope.
On Christmas Day. Paman.
On Hearing a Symphony of Beethoven. Millay.
On Music. Landor.
Orpheus with His Lute. *Fr.* King Henry VIII. *At. to* Fletcher *and to* Shakespeare.
Passions, The; an Ode for Music. Collins.
Peter Quince at the Clavier. Stevens.
Piano, The. Verlaine.
Piano after War. Brooks.
Piano Recital. Deutsch.
Piper, The. Field.
Piper's Progress, The. "Prout."
Rubinstein Staccato Etude, The. Dett.
Soft Musick. Herrick.
Softly through my spirit flow. Heine.
Song for St. Cecilia's Day, A. Dryden.
Song of Shadows, The. De la Mare.
Song of the Banjo, The. Kipling.
Song, to the Gods, Is Sweetest Sacrifice. Fields.
Song's Eternity. Clare.
Splendour Falls, The. *Fr.* The Princess. Tennyson.
Stanzas for Music ("There be none of Beauty's daughters"). Byron.
Symphony, The. Lanier.
Tanglewood. Sweeney.
Thus sang Orpheus to his strings. *Unknown.*
To a Lad Who Would Wed Himself with Music. Doro.
To a Scarlatti Passepied. Hillyer.
To His Friend Master R. L., in Praise of Music and Poetry. Barnfield.
To Melody. Allen.
To Music. Seymour.
To Music, to Becalm His Fever. Herrick.
To Sheila Playing Haydn. Lynd.
To Song. Jones.
To the One of Fictive Music. Stevens.
Toccata of Galuppi's, A. R. Browning.
Variations for Two Pianos. Justice.
Verses to St. Cecilia. Wright.
Violinist, The. Lampman.
Voice, The. Arnold.
Vow. Updike.
What Kind of Music? Reeves.
When de Saints Go Ma'chin' Home. Brown.
What We Listened for in Music. Burr.
With a Guitar; to Jane. Shelley.
You muses nurses of delights. *Unknown.*
Music and Sweet Poetry (MuSP). John Bishop, comp.
Untune the Sky (UnS). Helen Plotz, comp.

Musselburgh, Scotland
Musselburgh Field. *Unknown.*

Musset, Alfred de
Alfred de Musset. *Unknown.*
Byway in Biography. Hare.

Mycenae, Greece
Mycenae. Alphaeus.

Myrtle
Amid the Myrtles. Halevi.
To My Mirtle. Blake.

Mysticism
Mystic, The. Rice.
Mystic's Prayer, The. "Macleod."
Song of the Mystic. Ryan.

Mythology
He Inspects His Armory. Plutzik.
Hellenics, The, *sels.* Landor.
Myths. Butler.

N

Nabara (ship)
Nabara, The. Day Lewis.

Nagasaki, Japan
Song about Major Eatherly, A. Wain.

Namaqualand, Africa
Namaqualand after Rain. Plomer.

Names
American Names. S. V. Benét.
Baby's Name, The. Jenks.
Boys' Names. Farjeon.
Choosing a Name. Lamb.
Christening, The. Milne.
Gentle Name. Robinson.
Girls' Names. Farjeon.
Maiden Name. Larkin.
Mima. De la Mare.
My Name and I. Graves.
Naming the Baby. Richstone.
Sampler, The. Field.
Very Names of Things, The. Bridges.

Namur, Belgium
Between Namur and Liège. Wordsworth.
English Ballad, on the Taking of Namur by the King of Great Britain, 1695, An. Prior.

Nantucket, Massachusetts
Alarmed Skipper, The. Fields.
Nantucket Whalers. Henderson.
Quaker Graveyard in Nantucket, The. R. Lowell.
That Nantucket Limerick, and What Followed. *Unknown.*
With a Nantucket Shell. Webb.

Naples, Italy
City of Beggars, The. Hayes.
Een Napoli. Daly.
Naples Again. Freeman.
Ode to Naples. Shelley.
To Naples. Mallalieu.
Written in Naples. Emerson.

Napoleon I
Advice to a Raven in Russia, December, 1812. Barlow.
Boney. *Unknown.*
Bonny Bunch of Roses, The. *Unknown.*
Buonaparte. Tennyson.
Feelings of a Republican on the Fall of Bonaparte. Shelley.
Fifth of May, The—Napoleon. *Fr.* Ode. Manzoni.
Funeral of Napoleon I. Hagarty.
Hop-o-My Thumb. *Fr.* Ballads on Napoleon. *Unknown.*
I Grieved for Buonaparté. Wordsworth.
Incident of the French Camp. R. Browning.
Lines Written on Hearing the News of the Death of Napoleon. Shelley.
March to Moscow, The. Southey.
Napoleon. De la Mare.
Napoleon and the British Sailor. Campbell.
October, 1803 ("When, looking on the present face of things"). Wordsworth.
Ode to Napoleon Bonaparte, *sels.* Byron.
Return of Napoleon from St. Helena, The. Sigourney.
St. Helena Lullaby, A. Kipling.
Thought of a Briton on the Subjugation of Switzerland. Wordsworth.

Napoleonic Wars
By Moscow Self-devoted to a Blaze. Wordsworth.
Here Pause: The Poet Claims at Least This Praise. Wordsworth.
Incident of the French Camp, An. R. Browning.
November, 1806. Wordsworth.

Narcissus (mythology)
Farewell to Narcissus. Horah.
Narcissus. Campbell.
Narcissus. Gullans.
Narcissus. Petersen.
Narcissus. Valéry.
Sad nymph, Gaho, followed to the shadie woods, The. *Unknown.*
Narcissus (flower)
Narcissus. Cowper.
Narcotics. *See* **Drug Addiction.**
Naseby, New Zealand
Naseby; Late Autumn. Dowling.
Naseby, Battle of
Battle of Naseby, The. Macaulay.
Nash, Ogden
Ogden Nash Gets All the Cash. McCord.
Nash, Richard (Beau Nash)
On Beau Nash's Picture, Which Once Stood between the Busts of Newton and Pope. Brereton.
Nasturtiums
Big Nasturtiums, The. Hale.
Lines to a Nasturtium. Spencer.
Nasturtiums, The. *Unknown.*
Nativity, The. *See* **Christmas.**
Nature
Alastor. Shelley.
All That's Past. De la Mare.
All the Scenes of Nature Quicken. Smart.
And Do They So? Vaughan.
Art and Nature. Medrano.
Beyond the End. Levertov.
Bonac. Wheeloek.
Book of the World, The. Drummond of Hawthornden.
Chant Out of Doors, A. Wilkinson.
Comparison and Complaint, The. Watts.
Composed While Under Arrest. Lermontov.
Contemplations. Bradstreet.
Correspondences. Baudelaire.
Cosmic Fabric, The. Polonsky.
Dry Loaf. Stevens.
Enthusiast, The; or, The Lover of Nature. Warton.
Eternity of Nature. Clare.
Expostulation and Reply. Wordsworth.
Father, thy hand. *Fr.* A Forest Hymn. Bryant.
Fern Hill. Thomas.
Field of Light, A. Roethke.
For I have lov'd the rural walk through lanes. *Fr.* The Task. Cowper.
Forest of Arden, The. *Fr.* Polyolbion: The Thirteenth Song. Drayton.
Fragment: "There is a river clear and fair." Fanshawe.
Gentian weaves her fringes, The. Dickinson.
Give Me the Splendid Silent Sun. Whitman.
Gladness of Nature, The. Bryant.
Glory of Nature, The. Tennyson.
God, through All and in You All. S. Longfellow.
God's Grandeur. Hopkins.
God's World. Millay.
Green Inn, The. Garrison.
Green Symphony Fletcher.
Handiwork of God, The. *Unknown.*
Hard Weather. Meredith.
How was November's melancholy endear'd to me. *Fr.* The Testament of Beauty. Bridges.
Hymn on the Seasons, A. *Fr.* The Seasons. Thomson.
I taste a liquor never brewed. Dickinson.
In Ampezzo. Stickney.
In Harmony with Nature. Arnold.
Inward Morning, The. Thoreau.
Landscapes. Untermeyer.
Lessons of Nature, The. Drummond of Hawthornden.
Lines Composed a Few Miles above Tintern Abbey. Wordsworth.
Maid's Thought, The. Jeffers.
Man and Nature. Weeks.
Man in Harmony with Nature. Very.
Manuscripts of God, The. Longfellow.
Morning Hymn of Adam. *Fr.* Paradise Lost. Milton.
Morning Watch, The. Vaughan.
Musketaquid. Emerson.
My Books I'd Fain Cast Off, I Cannot Read. Thoreau.
My Heart Leaps Up When I Behold. Wordsworth.
Natura Naturata. Denham.
Natural Magic. "Æ."
Nature ("The rounded world"). Emerson.
Nature ("A subtle choice of countless rings"). Emerson.
Nature ("Winters know"). Emerson.
Nature. Herbert.
Nature. Longfellow.
Nature. Stone.
Nature. Thoreau.
Nature. Vigny.
Nature and Life. Meredith.
Nature Be Damned. Wilkinson.
Nature Note. Guiterman.
Nature one hour appears a thing unsexed. *Fr.* Contemplation. Thompson.
Nature, the Artist. Knowles.
Nature the False Goddess. Roche.
Nature's Creed. *Unknown.*
Nature's Key-Notes. Irwin.
Nature's Questioning. Hardy.
Nature's Travail. *Unknown.*
On the Religion of Nature. Freneau.
On the Uniformity and Perfection of Nature. Freneau.
On the Universality and Other Attributes of the God of Nature. Freneau.
Out-of-Doors. Whitaker.
Out of the Vast. Bamberger.
Pastoral Hymn, A. Hall.
Pied Beauty. Hopkins.
Pleasant Sounds. Clare.
Poem on His Birthday. Thomas.
Poets Love Nature. Clare.
Prayer, A: "O Earth, O dewy mother, breathe on us." Lampman.
Prayer, A: "Tend me my birds, and bring again." Gale.
Prelude: "Along the roadside, like the flowers of gold." *Fr.* Among the Hills. Whittier.
Quiet Work. Arnold.
Reason for Not Writing Orthodox Nature Poetry. Wain.
Revival, The. Vaughan.
River has not any care, The. *Fr.* Contemplation. Thompson.
Sailing Homeward. Chan Fang-sheng.
Shrubbery, The. Cowper.
Sky is low, the clouds are mean, The. Dickinson.
Song: "Again rejoicing nature sees." Burns.
Song of Nature. Emerson.
Song Tournement: New Style. Untermeyer.
Spring, The. *Fr.* The Mistress. Cowley.
Stanzas: "Nature doth have her dawn each day." Thoreau.
Starting from Paumanok. Whitman.
Sweetness of Nature, The. *Unknown.*
Tables Turned, The. Wordsworth.
Thanatopsis. Bryant.
That Nature Is a Heraclitean Fire and of the Comfort of the Resurrection. Hopkins.
This Is My Father's World. Babcock.
This is my letter to the world. Dickinson.
Thou Art, O God. Moore.
To God, the Architect. Kemp.
To Mother Nature. Knowles.
To Nature. Coleridge.
To Nature. Hölderlin.
'Twere Long to Tell. *Fr.* The Prelude. Wordsworth.
Vantage Point, The. Frost.
Voice of Nature, The. Bridges.
Voice That Beautifies the Land, The. *Unknown.*
Wabanaki Song. *Unknown.*
Waldeinsamkeit. Emerson.
Walking. Traherne.
While I Was Yet a Boy. Hölderlin.
Why, Lord. Van Doren.
Wind in the Pine. Sarett.
Wish of Manchin of Liath, The. *Unknown.*
Within the Circuit of This Plodding Life. Thoreau.
World, The. *Fr.* Symbolisms. Realf.
Written in Early Spring. Wordsworth.
Book of Nature Poems, A (BoNaP). William Cole, comp.
Wind Is Round, The (WIRo). Sara Hannum *and* John Terry Chase, comps.

Nautilus (shell)
Chambered Nautilus, The. *Fr.* The Autocrat of the Breakfast Table. Holmes.
To the Nautilus. H. Coleridge.
Navaho Indians
Dawn Boy's Song. *Unknown.*
Hunting-Song. *Unknown.*
Navajo, The. Coatsworth.
Navajo Prayer. *Unknown.*
Song of the Navajo. Pike.
Navarino, Battle of
Battle of Navarino, The. *Unknown.*
Glorious Victory of Navarino, The! *Unknown.*
Navy, France
Hervé Riel. R. Browning.
Navy, Great Britain
Battle of the Baltic, The. Campbell.
Captain Death. *Unknown.*
Captain Stood on the Carronade, The. *Fr.* Snarleyyow; or, The Dog Fiend. Marryat.
Essay on the Fleet Riding in the Downes, An. "J. D."
Famous Fight at Malago, The; or The Englishmen's Victory over the Spaniards. *Unknown.*
Fighting *Téméraire, The.* Newbolt.
Hawke. Newbolt.
Joyful New Ballad, A. Deloney.
Kilmeny. Noyes.
Loss of the Birkenhead, The. Doyle.
On the Loss of the *Royal George.* Cowper.
Revenge, The [a Ballad of the Fleet]. Tennyson.
Sailing at Dawn. Newbolt.
To the King of His Navy. Waller.
Ye Mariners of England. Campbell.
Navy, Holland
Famous Sea-Fight, A. Looke.
Navy, Spain
Famous Sea-Fight, A. Looke.
Navy, United States
Bay Fight, The. Brownell.
Blood Is Thicker than Water. Rice.
Constitution and the *Guerrière*, The. *Unknown.*
Cumberland, The. Longfellow.
Farragut. Meredith.
Fleet at Santiago, The. Russell.
How We Burned the *Philadelphia.* Eastman.
Men behind the Guns, The. Rooney.
Old Ironsides. Holmes.
River Fight, The. Brownell.
Running the Batteries. Melville.
Strong Swimmer, The. W. R. Benét.
When the Great Gray Ships Come In. Carryl.
Yankee Privateer, The. Hale.
Nazis
Ad. Fearing.
Years Later. Lerner.
Nebraska
My Nebraska. Diers.
Nebraska. Swan.
Nebuchadnezzar
Warm Babies. Preston.
Negro Spirituals
Negro Spirituals. R. *and* S. V. Benét.
Negro Spirituals. Trott.
Books of American Negro Spirituals, The (BoAN). James Weldon Johnson, ed.
Negro Verse
American Negro Poetry (AmNP). Arna Bontemps, ed.
Black American Literature: Poetry (BALP). Darwin T. Turner, ed.
Black Fire (BF). LeRoi Jones *and* Larry Neal, eds.
Black Out Loud: An Anthology of Modern Poems by Black Americans (BOLo). Arnold Adoff, ed.
Black Poetry: A Supplement to Anthologies Which Exclude Black Poets (BP). Dudley Randall, ed.
Book of American Negro Poetry, The (BANP). James Weldon Johnson, ed.
Book of American Negro Spirituals, The (BoAN). James Weldon Johnson, ed.
Caroling Dusk (CDC). Countee Cullen, ed.
Golden Slippers (GoSl). Arna Bontemps, comp.
I Am the Darker Brother (IDB). Arnold Adoff, ed.
Kaleidoscope (Kal). Robert Hayden, ed.
New Black Poetry, The (NBP). Clarence Major, ed.
New Negro Poets: USA (NNP). Langston Hughes, ed.
Poems from Black Africa (PBA). Langston Hughes, ed.
Poetry of the Negro, The, 1746-1949 (PoNe). Langston Hughes *and* Arna Wendell Bontemps, eds.
3000 Years of Black Poetry (TTY). Alan Lomax *and* Raoul Abdul, eds.
Today's Negro Voices (TNV). Beatrice M. Murphy, ed.
We Speak as Liberators: Young Black Poets (WSL). Orde Coombs, ed.
Negroes
Ancestry. Donaghy.
An What Shall You Say? Cotter.
Ante-Bellum Sermon, An. Dunbar.
As I Grew Older. Hughes.
Astraea at the Capitol. Whittier.
August Saturday Night on the Negro Street. Shapiro.
Award. Durem.
Ballad of the Landlord. Hughes.
Beautiful Negress, The. Pitter.
Black Boy. Rosten.
Black Magdalens. Cullen.
Black Man Speaks, The. Hughes.
Black Marble. O'Shaughnessy.
Black Regiment, The. Boker.
Black Tambourine. H. Crane.
Colored Band, The. Dunbar.
Congo, The. Lindsay.
Crispus Attucks. O'Reilly.
Cross. Hughes.
Ethiopia Saluting the Colors. Whitman.
For a Lady I Know. Cullen.
For de Lawd. Clifton.
For My People. Walker.
Gee-up Dar, Mules. Piper.
George Robinson; Blues. Rukeyser.
Good Times. Clifton.
Hard to Be a Nigger. *Unknown.*
I, Too, Sing America. Hughes.
If We Must Die. McKay.
Incident. Cullen.
Learned Negro, The. *Unknown.*
Lift Every Voice and Sing. Johnson.
Litany of the Dark People, The. Cullen.
Little Black Boy, The. *Fr.* Songs of Innocence. Blake.
Negro Speaks of Rivers, The. Hughes.
Negro Spirituals. R. *and* S. V. Benét.
Notes for a Speech. Jones.
Ode in Time of Hesitation, An. Moody.
Old Thad Stevens. Porter.
Outcast. McKay.
Plaint. Ford.
Poem: "Little brown boy." Johnson.
Poem for 8th Graders. Sanchez.
Strong Men. Brown.
Tired. Johnson.
To a Gentleman in Love with a Negro Woman. Davies.
To Sir Toby. Freneau.
Trumpet Player. Hughes.
Two-an-Six. McKay.
Unsung Heroes, The. Dunbar.
Neighbors
Near Neighbors. Swift.
Neighbors, The. Garrison.
Neighbors. Guiterman.
Neighbors. Payne.
Neighbors. Spencer.
Neighbors. Wing.
New Neighbor, The. Fyleman.
Portrait by a Neighbor. Millay.
This and That. Davis.
Welcome. Waldo.
Neilson, Adelaide
Adelaide Neilson. Winter.
Lilian Adelaide Neilson. Scott.
Nelson, Horatio Nelson, Viscount
Admiral's Ghost, The. Noyes.
Ballad of the Good Lord Nelson, A. Durrell.
Battle of the Baltic, The. Campbell.
Character of the Happy Warrior. Wordsworth.

Nelson *(continued)*
Death of Nelson, The. *Unknown.*
1805. Graves.
Nelson. *Fr.* Sonnets of the Empire. Strong.
Nelson and Pitt. *Fr.* Marmion.
Nelson at Palermo. Ross.
New Song Composed on the Death of Lord Nelson, A. *Unknown.*
Night of Trafalgar, The. *Fr.* The Dynasts. Hardy.
Neptune (god)
Court of Neptune, The. Hughes.
Homeric Hymn to Neptune. *Unknown.*
Hymn in Praise of Neptune, A. Campion.
Next unto Him Was Neptune Pictured. *Fr.* The Faerie Queene. Spenser.
Neri, Filippo de'. *See* **Philip Neri, Saint.**
Nero
Ave! Nero Imperator. Osborne.
Nerval, Gérard de
In a Warm Chicken House. Wright.
Netherlands
Character of Holland, The. Marvell.
Dutch Picture, A. Longfellow.
Dutch Seacoast. *Fr.* The Atlas. Slessor.
Holland. Provost.
Leak in the Dike, The. Cary.
Little Toy Land of the Dutch, The. *Unknown.*
Lowlands o' Holland, The. *Unknown.*
Such Is Holland. Genestet.
Netley Abbey, Southampton, England
Sonnet: Netley Abbey. Bowles.
Nettles
Nettle, the Flower, The. Zabel.
Tall Nettles. Thomas.
With Seed the Sowers Scatter. Housman.
Nevada
Home Means Nevada. Raffetto.
Nevada. Gurney.
Neville, Alexander
To Alexander Neville. Googe.
New England
Citizens in the Round. Coffin.
Having New England Fathers. Holmes.
Hundred Collars, A. Frost.
Late Comer. Hastings.
Lilacs. A. Lowell.
New England. Percival.
New England. Prentice.
New England. Robinson.
New England Fog. Callaghan.
New England Is New England Is New England. Green.
New England's Annoyances. *Unknown.*
New England's Chevy-Chase. Hale.
New England's Crisis. Tompson.
Praise of New England. Chubb.
Stone Crop, The. Coffin.
New Guinea
New Guinea. McAuley.
New Guinea Lament. McAuley.
New Hampshire
Apples in New Hampshire. Gilchrist.
New Hampshire. *Fr.* Landscapes. Eliot.
New Hampshire. Frost.
New Hampshire. Hall.
New Hampshire Boy, A. Bishop.
Old New Hampshire. Holmes.
Spring in New Hampshire. McKay.
New Haven, Connecticut
On the Democracy of Yale. Jones.
New Jersey
Invention of New Jersey, The. Anderson.
Jersey Marsh, The. Galler.
Legend. Weaver.
Ode to New Jersey. Carr.
New Mexico
New Mexico. Boyden.
New Mexico and Arizona. Canterbury.
O, Fair New Mexico. Garrett.
On the Great Plateau. Wyatt.
Railroad Cars Are Coming, The. *Unknown.*
New Orleans, Louisiana
Girod Street Cemetery; New Orleans. Morris.
New Orleans. Carruth.
New Orleans. Ridge.
New Orleans Balcony, A. Haight.
Vieux Carré. Roberts.
Zulu King, The; New Orleans. Copeland.
New Orleans, Battle of
Battle of New Orleans, The. English.
Jackson at New Orleans. Rice.
Surrender of New Orleans, The. Manville.
To the Defenders of New Orleans. Drake.
New South Wales, Australia
Lichtenberg. Kipling.
New Year
Address to the New Year. Craik.
Another New Year. Michael.
Another Year. Smith.
Another Year. O'Hagan.
Another Year Is Dawning. Havergal.
At Dawn of the Year. "Klingle."
At the New Year. Patchen.
At the Portal. Havergal.
At Yearsend. Wilbur.
Bells of New Year. Field.
Cheerful Welcome, A. *Unknown.*
Dawning o' the Year, The. Blake.
Death of the Old Year. Tennyson.
Diary. Fuller.
Dying Year, The. Hill.
End of the Year, The. Su T'ung-po.
Facing the New Year. Pearse.
Facing the New Year. *Unknown.*
Farewell and Hail! Clark.
Farewell to the Old Year. Farjeon.
For the New Year. Markham.
For the New Year. Nicholson.
Gates of the Year, The. Hull.
Happy New Year! Happy New Year! *Unknown.*
Here We Come a-Caroling. *Unknown.*
Here We Come a-Wassailing. *Unknown.*
Higher Good, The. Parker.
Hymn for the Eve of the New Year. Gerondi.
I Buried the Year. Luff.
In Trust. Dodge.
Invocation for the New Year. Armstrong.
January 1. Pomeroy.
Last Day of the Year, The. Smart.
Message of the Bells, The. Clark.
Message of the New Year, The. *Unknown.*
Midnight Mass for the Dying Year. Longfellow.
New Leaf, A. Wheeler.
New Year, The. Cooke.
New Year, The. Cooper.
New Year, The. Cotton.
New Year, The. Craik.
New Year, A. Davies.
New Year, The. Gard.
New Year, The. Homer-Dixon.
New Year, The. Powers.
New Year, A. Sangster.
New Year, A. Shorter.
New Year, The. Templeton.
New Year, The ("I am the little New Year, ho, ho!"). *Unknown.*
New Year, The ("Oh! I'm the New Year,/ Come, look at my wares"). *Unknown.*
New Year ("Over the threshold a gallant newcomer"). *Unknown.*
New Year, The ("With gladness hail the dawning year"). *Unknown.*
New Year. Wearing.
New Year Carol, A: "Here we bring new water." *Unknown.*
Near Year Ditty. C. G. Rossetti.
New Year Idyl, A, *sel.* Field.
New Year Is a Banner, The. Sangster.
New year forth looking out of Janus' gate. *Fr.* Amoretti. Spenser.
New-Year Prayer. Kramer.
New Year Song. Miller.
New Year Wish, A. Havergal.

New Year Wishes. Sarton.
New yeares, expect new gifts: Sister, your harpe. Jonson.
New Years and Old. Jackson.
New Year's Day. Crashaw.
New Year's Day. Field.
New Year's Day. R. Lowell.
New Year's Day. *Unknown.*
New Year's Eve. Bartleson.
New Year's Eve. Berryman.
New Year's Eve, *sel.* Davidson.
New Year's Eve. Hardy.
New Year's Eve—Midnight. Macdonald.
New Year's Eve, 1938. Nims.
New Year's Poem. Avison.
New Year's Promise, A. *Unknown.*
New Year's Thoughts. Gray.
New Year's Wish, A. "J. H. S."
New Year's Wishes. Havergal.
News! News! Farjeon.
Old Father Annum. Jackson.
Old Year, The. Clare.
Old Year, The. Urmy.
Old Year's Prayer, The. Irving.
On New Year's Day. *Unknown.*
On the Threshold. Baldwin.
Parable, A. Kress.
Peter Stuyvesant's New Year's Call. Stedman.
Prayer: "Bless Thou this year, O Lord!" Clark.
Prayer for the New Year, A. Armitage.
Reconsecration. Gould.
Resolutions?—New and Old. Rolfe.
Ring, Joyful Bells! Fuller.
Ring Out Wild Bells. *Fr.* In Memoriam A. H. H. Tennyson.
Secular Masque, The. Dryden.
Song for December Thirty-first. F. Frost.
Song for New Year's Eve, A. Bryant.
Sonnet: "Comes the New Year; wailing the north winds blow." *Fr.* Thysia. Luce.
Thought for a New Year. Burket.
To the New Yeere. Drayton.
Up the Hill, down the Hill. Farjeon.
Upon New Year's Eve. Quiller-Couch.
Vow for New Year's, A. Davies.
Wassail Song, The. *Unknown.*
Way to a Happy New Year, A. Beattie.
Welcome to the New Year. Farjeon.
When the Year Grows Old. Millay.
Wish for the New Year, A. Brooks.
Years-End. Wilbur.
Sourcebook of Poetry (SoP). Al Bryant, comp.

New York (state)
Praise of New Netherland, The. Steendam.

New York (city)
...& Forty-second Street. MacLeish.
Avenue Bearing the Initial of Christ into the New World, The. Kinnell.
B Negative. Kennedy.
Bleat of Protest. Weston.
Bottled; New York. Johnson.
Bowery, The. Hoyt.
Broadway's Canyon. Fletcher.
City Birds. Johnson.
City of Orgies. Whitman.
Complaint of New Amsterdam, The. Steendam.
Crossing Brooklyn Ferry. Whitman.
Day in the City, A. Sissman.
Early Dutch. Palen.
Empire City. Georgakas.
Ferry Ride.*sel.* Robinson.
Give Me the Splendid Silent Sun. Whitman.
Good Green Bus. Field.
Greenwich Village Saturday Night. Feldman.
I'd rather listen to a flute. Hoffenstein.
Letter to New York. Bishop.
Lights of New York, The. Teasdale.
Manhattan. Beer.
Manhattan. Lawless.
Manhattan. Towne.
Manhattan Menagerie. Cherwinski.
Mannahatta ("I was asking for something specific"). Whitman.
Metropolitan Nightmare. S. V. Benét.
My City. Johnson.
N. Y. Pound.
New York. "Æ."
New York. Guiterman.
New York City. Abbe.
New York City. Bodenheim.
New York in August. Davie.
New York Skyscraper, A, *sel.* Oppenheim.
Owed to New York. Newton.
Peter Stuyvesant's New Year's Call. Stedman.
Proud New York. Reed.
School Days in New Amsterdam. Guiterman.
Sidewalks of New York, The. Blake.
Speakers, Columbus Circle. Souster.
Steps. O'Hara.
Storm on Fifth Avenue. Sassoon.
To New York. Sédar-Senghor.
To the Greatest City in the World. Humphries.
Tropics in New York, The; New York. McKay.
Tunnel, The. H. Crane.
West Forties, The: Morning, Noon, and Night. Sissman.
When Dawn Comes to the City; New York. McKay.

New Yorker, The (magazine)
Talk of the Town, The. Fisher.

New Zealand
Colonist in His Garden, A. Reeves.
In Town. Wright.
It was a wondrous realm beguiled. *Fr.* Ranolf and Amohia. Domett.
Long Harbour, The. Bethell.
New Zealand Regret, A. Montgomery.
October in New Zealand. Mackay.
Anthology of New Zealand Verse, An (AnNZ). Robert Chapman *and* Jonathan Bennett, eds.
Book of Australian and New Zealand Verse, A (BoAn). Walter Murdock, ed.

Newark, New Jersey
Newark, for Now (68). Rodgers.

Newfoundland
Gazeteer of Newfoundland. Harrington.
Newfoundland. Pratt.

Newgate Prison (London)
Friendly Address, A. Hood.

Newman, John Henry, Cardinal
Newman. Shuster.

Newport, Rhode Island
Jewish Cemetery at Newport, The. Longfellow.
Letter from Newport, A. Myers.
Newport Street, E. Goldring.

Newspapers
Boston Evening Transcript, The. Eliot.
Carrier's Address. *Unknown.*
Daily Globe, The. Nemerov.
Doing Railroads for *The Rocky Mountain News.* Warman.
Fleet Street. Leslie.
Headline History. Plomer.
Herald. Miles.
Newspaper, The, *sels.* Crabbe.
Newspaper, A. *Fr.* War Is Kind. S. Crane.
Pious Editor's Creed, The. *Fr.* Biglow Papers. J. R. Lowell.
Press, The. *Unknown.*
Sunday Edition. Keith.
To a Dead Journalist. Williams.

Newsreels
Newsreel. Day Lewis.

Newton, Sir Isaac
Epitaph Intended for Sir Isaac Newton. Pope.
Merry Old Souls. Bishop.
Newton. *Fr.* The Prelude. Wordsworth.
Newton to Einstein. Chappell.
On Mr. Nash's Picture. Brereton.
Poem Sacred to the Memory of Sir Isaac Newton, A. Thomson.

Niagara Falls
At the Leap of the Waters. Garesché.
Fall of Niagara, The. Brainard.
Niagara. Garesché.
Niagara. Sigourney.

Nibelungen Legends
First Lay of Gudrun, The. *Fr.* The Elder Edda. *Unknown.*
Norns Watering Yggdrasill, The. Scott.

Nicaragua
With Walker in Nicaragua, *sels.* Miller.
Night
Acquainted with the Night. Frost.
Allah's Tent. Colton.
At Night. Cornford.
At Night. Meynell.
At Night. Montgomery.
At Night. Payne.
At Night in the Wood. Hayes.
At Nightfall. Towne.
Be Not Afraid. Nathan.
Beautiful Night, A. *Fr.* Fragments Intended for the Dramas. Beddoes.
Black pitchy night, companion of my woe. *Fr.* Idea's Mirrour. Drayton.
Breath of Night, The. Jarrell.
By the Fire. Coatsworth.
Check. Stephens.
City, The: Midnight. Dawe.
Coming of Night, The. Wade.
Curfew. Longfellow.
Dark Stag, The. Crawford.
Darkness. Bacon.
Day and Night. Daley.
Day and Night. Dhingra.
Day and Night. Lindsay.
Day Is Done, The. Longfellow.
Day's-End. Newbolt.
Defence of Night, The. Michelangelo.
Domination of Black. Stevens.
Draw On, Sweet Night. *Unknown.*
Drowzy night hir wings has spred, The. *Unknown.*
End of the Day, The. Creeley.
Evening in Paradise. *Fr.* Paradise Lost. Milton.
Four Glimpses of Night. Davis.
Full Heart, The. Nichols.
God's Dark. Martin.
Going to Sleep in the Country. Moss.
Good Night. Pierce.
How sweet the moonlight sleeps upon this bank! *Fr.* The Merchant of Venice. Shakespeare.
Hymn to Night. Cane.
Hymn to Night, A. Michelson.
Hymn to Night. *Fr.* The Rigveda. *Unknown.*
Hymn to the Night. Longfellow.
In the Azure Night. Galindez.
In the Night. Jennings.
In the Night. J. Stephens.
In the Night. *Unknown.*
In the Still, Star-lit Night. Stoddard.
In the Wide Awe and Wisdom of the Night. Roberts.
Knowing What Time It Is at Night. Nicholl.
Light the Lamps Up, Lamplighter. Farjeon.
Lines for a Night Driver. Dufault.
Looking Down on Mesopotamia. Bethell.
Lux in Tenebris. Tynan.
Midnight. Dryden.
Midnight. Lampman.
Midnight. *Fr.* Blurt, Master Constable. Middleton.
Midnight. Roberts.
Midnight. Sackville.
Midnight. Vaughan.
Midnight Prayer. Bialik.
Moment Musicale. Carman.
Music of the Night. Neal.
Natura in Urbe. White.
Night. Baring-Gould.
Night, The. Belloc.
Night. Bialik.
Night. *Fr.* Songs of Innocence. Blake.
Night. Bullwinkle.
Night. *Fr.* The Shadow of Night. Chapman.
Night. H. Coleridge.
Night. Hayes.
Night. Heavysege.
Night. Hesse.
Night. Hubbell.
Night. Ibn Gabirol.
Night. Jami.
Night. Jeffers.
Night, The. Leuty.
Night. McKay.
Night. Montgomery.
Night, *sels.* Oppenheim.
Night, *sel.* Péguy.
Night. Regnier.
Night. Rolleston.
Night. *Fr.* Thalaba the Destroyer. Southey.
Night. Sutu.
Night. Symons.
Night. Teasdale.
Night, The. Vaughan.
Night and Day. Dodge.
Night and the Pines. Scott.
Night Cometh. Dyer.
Night Enchantment. Muth.
Night for Adventures. Starbuck.
Night Hymns on Lake Nipigon. Scott.
Night in a Village, A. Nikitin.
Night in Camp. Bashford.
Night in Italy, A, *sel.* "Meredith."
Night in June, A. Scott.
Night Is Darkening, The. E. Brontë.
Night Is Near Gone, The. Montgomerie.
Night Magic. Burr.
Night of Spring. Westwood.
Night on the Downland. Masefield.
Night on the Prairie. Sage.
Night-Piece, A. Wordsworth.
Night-Ride, The. Slessor.
Night Serene, The. León.
Night Things Are Soft and Loud. Gay.
Night Watch, A. *Fr.* The Passionate Pilgrim. *Unknown.*
Night Will Never Stay, The. Farjeon.
Night-Wind. Lloyd.
Nightfall. Kalidasa.
Nightfall. Trueba.
Nightfall. Tyutchev.
Nightfall in Dordrecht. Field.
Night's Mardi Gras. Wheeler.
Nights Remember, The. Vinal.
No Moon, No Star. Deutsch.
Nocturnal Reverie, A. Countess of Winchilsea.
Nocturnal Sketch, A. Hood.
Nocturne: "Keen winds of cloud and vaporous drifts." Garnett.
Nocturne: "Red flame flowers bloom and die, The." Garstin.
Nocturne: "Softly blow lightly." Hayes.
Nocturne: "This cool night is strange." Bennett.
Now through Night's Caressing Grip. Auden.
Now while the Night her sable veil hath spread. Drummond of Hawthornden.
Now Winter Nights Enlarge. Campion.
Nox Benigna. Reeves.
Nox Nocti Indicat Scientiam. Habington.
Old Adam, The. W. R. Benét.
Orange Tree by Night. *Fr.* The Red-gold Rain. S. Sitwell.
Out in the Dark. Thomas.
Poem: "Night is beautiful, The." Hughes.
Questions at Night. Untermeyer.
Quiet Street, The. McDonald.
Revolution. Housman.
River Night. F. Frost.
Sacred Night. Michelangelo.
Samarian Nights. Fichman.
Serenade: "Stars of the summer night." *Fr.* The Spanish Student. Longfellow.
Shadow of Night, The. Patmore.
Shadow of the Night, A. Aldrich.
Song: "Night is an ancient sorceress, The." Frug.
Song to Night. Coatsworth.
Sound of Night, The. Kumin.
Star That Bids the Shepherd Fold, The. *Fr.* Comus. Milton.
Starlit Night, The. Hopkins.
Starry Night, The. Sexton.
Stoush o' Day, The. Dennis.
Summer Moonlight. Strong.
Summer Night, A. Arnold.
There Are Sweet Flowers. Landor.
There Is Shrill Music in High Winds at Night. Stuart.
Tiptoe Night. Drinkwater.
To Night. Beddoes.

To Night. Shelley.
To Night. *Unknown.*
To Night. White.
To Night, the Mother of Sleep and Death. Symonds.
Tom o' Bedlam's Song. *Unknown.*
Train in the Night, The. Riddell.
'Twas Night. *Unknown.*
Upon a Gloomy Night. *Fr.* The Dark Night of the Soul. St. John of the Cross.
Venetian Night, A. Hofmannsthal.
Wakeful Night. Droste-Hülshoff.
Walking at Night. Hare.
Watchman, What of the Night? Swinburne.
Wet Windy Night on a Pavement. Tessimond.
When night has been announced as theme, will it not cause surprise. *Fr.* Megalometropolitan Carnival. Gascoyne.
Winter Night, A, *sel.* Burns.
Winter Night. Fitzgerald.
Winter Night. Millay.
Winter Nightfall. Squire.
Winter Nights. Campion.
See also **Evening.**

Night-blooming Cereus
Night-blooming Cereus, The. Monroe.

Nightingale, Florence
Santa Filomena. Longfellow.

Nightingales
Bianca among the Nightingales. E. B. Browning.
Canadian Rossignol, The. Thomson.
Fields Abroad with Spangled Flowers, The. *Unknown.*
Hast Thou Heard the Nightingale? Gilder.
If it were not for the voice. Nakatsukasa.
Itylus. Swinburne.
Lark and the Nightingale, The. H. Coleridge.
Music's Duel. Crashaw.
Nightingale, The. Barnfield.
Nightingale, The. Belloc.
Nightingale, The. Brathwaite.
Nightingale, The. Coleridge.
Nightingale, The. Griffin.
Nightingale, The. Moxon.
Nightingale, The. Petrarch.
Nightingale, The. Sidney.
Nightingale, The. Symonds.
Nightingale, The. Tynan.
Nightingale, The ("The little pretty nightingale"). *Unknown.*
Nightingale, The. Wordsworth.
Nightingale and the Glow-Worm, The. Cowper.
Nightingale and the Lark, The. Whitney.
Nightingale near the House, The. Monro.
Nightingale Weather. Lang.
Nightingales. Bridges.
Nightingales. Conkling.
Nightingale's Nest, The. Clare.
O nightingale of woodland gay. *Unknown.*
O Nightingale, That on Yon Bloomy Spray. Milton.
Ode, An: "As it fell upon a day." Barnfield.
Ode to a Nightingale. Keats.
Ode to the Evening Star. Akenside.
On a Nightingale in April. "Macleod."
On the Death of a Nightingale. Ranoldph.
Owl and the Nightingale, The. *At. to* Guildford.
Philomela. Arnold.
Philomela. Ransom.
Secret of the Nightingale, The. Noel.
Singing Lesson, The. Ingelow.
To a Nightingale. Drummond of Hawthornden.
To the Nightingale. Ayres.
To the Nightingale. Cowper.
To the Nightingale. Milton.
To the Nightingale. Countess of Winchilsea.
Vision of the Lamentation of Beulah, A. *Fr.* Milton. Blake.
Whenas the nightingale chanted her vespers. Cleveland.
Where is the nightingale. *Fr.* Songs from Cyprus. Doolittle.

Nijinsky, Vaslav
For Nijinsky's Tomb. Cornford.
Homage to Vaslav Nijinsky. Kirkup.
Nijinsky. Ferne.

Nijmegen, Netherlands
Road to Nijmegen, The. Birney.

Nile (river)
Nile, The. Coatsworth.
Nile, The. Hunt.
To the Nile. Keats.
To the Nile. Shelley.

Nineveh, Assyria
Burden of Nineveh, The. D. G. Rossetti.

Nipigon Lake, Canada
Night Hymns on Lake Nipigon. Scott.

Noah
Ballad of the Flood. Muir.
History of the Flood, The. Heath-Stubbs.
Missing Like, The. Herford.
Noah. *Fr.* Flaming Terrapin. Campbell.
Noah. Daniells.
Noah. Hagedorn.
Noah an' Jonah an' Cap'n John Smith. Marquis.
Noah and the Rabbit. Chesterman.
Noah's Carpenters. *Unknown.*
Noah's Flood. *Fr.* Genesis. *Unknown.*
Noah's Song. Jones.
Wine and Water. Chesterton.

Nonconformists
Matlock Bath. Betjeman.

Nonsense Verse. *See* **Humorous Verse.**

Noon
Midsummer Noon in the Australian Forest, A. Harpur.
Noon. Clare.
Noon Is on the Cattle-Track, The. Ingamells.
Noontide. Keble.

Nordau, Max
Poem for Max Nordeau, A. Robinson.

Norfolk, England
Norfolk. Betjeman.

Normandy
In Normandy. Lucas.

Norris, Sir John
Farewell to Sir John Norris and Sir Francis Drake, A. Peele.

Norris Dam, Tennessee
Norris Dam. Rodman.

North, Christopher
To Christopher North. Tennyson.

North, Frederick, Earl of Guilford and Baron North
Lord North's Recantation. *Unknown.*

North Cape, Norway
Discoverer of the North Cape, The. Longfellow.

North Carolina
Old North State, The. Gaston.

North Dakota
North Dakota Hymn. Foley.

North Pole
90 North. Jarrell.

North Wind
Blow, Northern Wind. *Unknown.*
Exile in Nigeria. Mphahlele.
Northwind. Baro.
North Wind, The. Gradon.
North Wind, The. Reis.
North Wind Came Up Yesternight, The. Bridges.
"North Wind, North Wind—Oh, whither so fast?" *Unknown.*
Snow-Storm, The. Emerson.

Northboro, Massachusetts
Minute-Men of North-Boro', The. Rice.

Northern Lights. *See* **Aurora Borealis.**

Norumbega
Norembega. Whittier.

Norway
Man with the Broken Fingers, The. Sandburg.

Noses
Smell. Williams.

Notre Dame Cathedral
On the Parapet of Notre Dame. *Fr.* Quatrains. Quirk.
Smiling Demon of Notre Dame, A. Jewett.

November
Dream of November, A. Gosse.
Fields of November, The. Van Doren.
Hearth Song. J. Johnson.
In November. Aldrich.
In November. Lampman.
In November. Scott.
Mist and All, The. Willson.

November *(continued)*
My November Guest. Frost.
No! Hood.
November. Binyon.
November. Bridges.
November. Bryant.
November. Clare.
November. Cleaveland.
November. Coatsworth.
November. *Fr.* Sonnets on the Seasons. H. Coleridge.
November. A. Fisher.
November. M. L. Fisher.
November. Hughes.
November. Keble.
November. Malloch.
November. Morris.
November. Rose.
November. C. G. Rossetti.
November. Stoddard.
November. Verhaeren.
November Afternoons. Sister Mary Madeleva.
November Blue. Meynell.
November Evening. *Fr.* The Cotter's Saturday Night. Burns.
November Eves. Flecker.
November Garden. Driscoll.
November Morning. Blunden.
November Morning. Stein.
November Night. Crapsey.
November Rain. Uschold.
November Surf. Jeffers.
November Through a Giant Copper Beech. Honig.
November Wears a Paisley Shawl. Morris.
Out of November: Speaking for One. McCord.
Sonnet: November. H. Coleridge.
Weather Vanes. F. Frost.
Nubia, Africa
Nubia. Taylor.
Nuclear War
Advice to a Prophet. Wilbur.
Desert, The. Dyment.
Earth. Wheelock.
Survivors, The. Hine.
Your Attention Please. Porter.
Nudists
L'Ile du Levant; The Nudist Colony. Howes.
Nuns
Ballad of a Nun, A. Davidson.
Effigy of a Nun. Teasdale.
Fixture, A. Swenson.
For the Sisters of the Hôtel Dieu. Klein.
Heaven-Haven. Hopkins.
Hymn of the Moravian Nuns of Bethlehem. Longfellow.
Maid of Honour, The. Massinger.
Mother Marie Therese. R. Lowell.
Notre Dames des Champs. Synge.
Nun, The. Moore.
Nun, The. Symons.
Nuns at Eve. Brinnin.
Nuns fret not at their convent's narrow room. Wordsworth.
Nuns in the Wind. Rukeyser.
Nuns of the Perpetual Adoration. Dowson.
Old Nuns. Hayes.
On a Nun. Vittorelli.
Soeur Marie Emilie. Houselander.
Street Scene. Mezey.
To a Cloistress. Tassis.
To a Severe Nun. Merton.
Vestal, The. *Fr.* Eloise to Abeland. Pope.
Wreck of the *Deutschland*, The. Hopkins.
Nuremberg, Germany
Nuremberg. Longfellow.
Nurses
Night Nurse Goes Her Round, The. Gray.
Nurse's Prayer, A. Wheeler.
Nurse's Song. *Fr.* Songs of Experience. Blake.
Santa Filomena. Longfellow.
Staff-Nurse: New Style. *Fr.* In Hospital. Henley.
Staff-Nurse: Old Style. *Fr.* In Hospital. Henley.
To Be a Nurse. Lawrence.
Nymphs
Après-Midi d'un faune, L'. Mallarmé.
I flung me round him. *Fr.* Water-Nymph and the Boy. Noel.
Nymph and a Swain, A. *Fr.* Love for Love. Congreve.
Nymph Complaining for the Death of Her Fawn, The. Marvell.
Ode to a Water Nymph. Mason.
Oenone. Tennyson.
Overheard on a Saltmarsh. Monro.
Sabrina. *Fr.* Comus. Milton.
Sea-Nymph's Parting, The. *Fr.* Gebir. Landor.
There are the fair-limbed nymphs o' the woods. *Fr.* The Nymphs. Hunt.

O

Oak Trees
Bearded Oaks. Warren.
Brave Old Oak, The. Chorley.
Eliot's Oak. Longfellow.
Fate of the Oak, The. "Cornwall."
Girt Woak Tree That's in the Dell, The. Barnes.
Great Oak. Chapple.
Oak. Child.
Oak, The. Dryden.
Oak, The. Elliott.
Oak, The. Hill.
Oak, The. Morris.
Oak, The. Tennyson.
Oak and Olive. Flecker.
Oak Leaves. Coatsworth.
Scrub Oak. Root.
Spring Oak. Kinnell.
To an Oak Tree. *Fr.* Waverley. Scott.
Voice in the Wild Oak, The. Kendall.
Yardley Oak. Cowper.
Oates, Titus
Ballad upon the Popish Plot, A. Gadbury.
Panegyrick upon Oates, A. Duke.
Oban, Scotland
End of the Season on a Stormy Day—Oban. Smith.
Oberammergau, Germany
Oberammergau. Speyer.
Obesity
Fatness. Ansen.
Oblivion
To Everlasting Oblivion. *Fr.* The Scourge of Villany. Marston.
Observatories
Greenwich Observatory. Keyes.
Ocean. *See* **Sea.**
O'Conaire, Padraic
Padraic O'Conaire—Gaelic Storyteller. Higgins.
O'Connell, Daniel
Dead Tribune, The. MacCarthy.
O'Connor, Rory
Grave of Rury, The. Rolleston.
October
Birthday. Untermeyer.
Bowl of October, A. Bevington.
Boys in October. Layton.
Especially When the October Wind. Thomas.
Fall. Fisher.
Harvest Home. Guiterman.
In October. Carman.
In the Month of Green Fire. Himmell.
Late October. Carleton.
Late October. Teasdale.
Mallee in October. Hudson.
October. Aldrich.
October. T. A. Daly.
October. Frost.
October. Fyleman.
October. Gibbon.
October. Kavanagh.
October. Levertov.
October. McMahan.
October. *Fr.* The Earthly Paradise. Morris.
October. Radford.
October. *Fr.* The Shepheardes Calender. Spenser.
October. Thomas.
October. Trask.

October. Updike.
October. Very.
October. Whitman.
October in New Zealand. Mackay.
October in Tennessee. Malone.
October Journey. Walker.
October Morning. Piatt.
October Night. Dean.
October of the Angels. Daly.
October Winds. Randall.
October's Bright Blue Weather. Jackson.
October's Husbandry. Tusser.
October's Party. Cooper.
October's Song. Farjeon.
Old October. Constable.
Poem in October. Thomas.
Vagabond Song, A. Carman.
Woodbines in October. Bates.

Octopuses
Octopus. A. C. Hilton.
Octopus, The. Nash.
Parkinson and the Octopus. Farber.

Odin
Descent of Odin, The. Gray.

O'Donnell, Hugh Roe
Aodh Ruadh O Domhnaill. McGreery.

Odysseus. *See* **Ulysses.**

Odyssey
Odyssey, The. Lang.

Oedipus
Oedipus. Blackburn.
Oedipus. Muir.

O'Hara, Frank
On the Anniversary of the Death of Frank O'Hara. Torregian.
On the Death of Frank O'Hara. Torregian.
Red River. Mac Adams.

Ohio (state)
Founders of Ohio, The. Venable.

Ojibwa Indians
Ojibwa War Songs. *Unknown.*

Okefenokee Swamp, Georgia and Florida
Legend of Lake Okeefinokee. Richards.
Okefenokee Swamp. Hicky.

Oklahoma
Oklahoma. Camden.

Old Age
Academic. Roethke.
Acre of Grass, An. Yeats.
Adios. Babcock.
After a Line by John Peale Bishop. Justice.
After Seeing "Lear." Syrkin.
Age. Cowley.
Age. Garnett.
Age. Landor.
Age. More.
Age. Winter.
Age in Prospect. Jeffers.
Aged, Aged Man, The. *Fr.* Through the Looking-Glass. "Carroll."
Aged Lover Renounceth Love, the. Vaux.
Aged Ninety Years. Snow.
Almost Ninety. Whitman.
Ancient Sage, The. Tennyson.
Ancient to Ancients, An. Hardy.
As I Grow Old. *Unknown.*
As We Grow Older. Wells.
At Eighty-three. Landels.
At the Doors. "Der Nistor."
Autumn. Wolfe.
Bedtime Story. Mezey.
Behind the Looking Glass. Beard.
Birthday. Emans.
Changed. Calverley.
Chough, The. Reaney.
Come, Captain Age. Cleghorn.
Comfort. Widdemer.
Complaint of the Fair Armoress. Villon.
Corner, The. De la Mare.
Convent Garden Market. *Fr.* London Sonnets. Bode.
Crabbed Age and Youth. *Fr.* The Passionate Pilgrim. Shakespeare.
Curate's Kindness, The. Hardy.
Danny Murphy. Stephens.
Days of My Youth. Tucker.
Descending. Iremonger.
Do Not Go Gentle into That Good Night. Thomas.
Double Ritual. Rainer.
Dregs. Dowson.
Ever On. *Unknown.*
Faded Face, The. Hardy.
Father William. *Fr.* Alice's Adventures in Wonderland. "Carroll."
Fawn's Foster Mother. Jeffers.
Flight of Youth. Stoddard.
Former Beauties. *Fr.* At Casterbridge Fair. Hardy.
Forty Years Ago. *Unknown.*
Frailty of Beauty, The. "J. C."
Frost-Morning. Alexander.
Garadh. Colum.
Gascoigne's Lullaby. Gascoigne.
Gerontion. Eliot.
Goodness of Age. *Unknown.*
Great-Grandmother, The. Graves.
Green Leaves All Turn Yellow, The. Kenney.
Growing Gray. Dobson.
Growing Old. Arnold.
Growing Old. Henderson.
Growning Old. Learned.
Growing Old. *Unknown.*
Growing Old. Wells.
Healing. Reisen.
His Age. Herrick.
His Golden Locks Time Hath to Silver Turn'd. *Fr.* Polyhymnia. Peele.
How Old Are You? *At. to* Tuck *and* Fritsch.
I Look into My Glass. Hardy.
If I Should Die Before I Wake. Mezey.
If You Never. Fowler.
I'm Here. *Fr.* Meditations of an Old Woman. Roethke.
Infirmity. Roethke.
Isaac and Archibald. Robinson.
It Is Too Late! *Fr.* Morituri Salutamus. Longfellow.
John Anderson, My Jo. Burns.
Just as I used to say. *Fr.* Pictures of the Gone World. Ferlinghetti.
Laid in My Quiet Bed. Surrey.
Lamentation of the Old Pensioner. Yeats.
Last Leaf, The. Holmes.
Late Leaves. Landor.
Leaden Echo and the Golden Echo, The. Hopkins.
Leitrim Woman, A. Donaghy.
Let Me Grow Lovely. Baker.
Letter. Bergman.
Letter from a Girl to Her Own Old Age, A. Meynell.
Life's Last Scene. *Fr.* The Vanity of Human Wishes. Johnson.
Light and Dark. Howes.
Lines for an Old Man. Eliot.
Litany for Old Age, A. Harsen.
Little Old Lady in Lavender Silk, The. Parker.
Lonely, The. "Æ."
Long Hill, The. Teasdale.
Long Time a Child. H. Coleridge.
Love Is like the Wild Rose-Briar. E. Brontë.
Man's Going Hence. *Fr.* Human Life. Rogers.
Meditations of an Old Woman. Roethke.
Mr. Flood's Party. Robunson.
My Birthday. Moore.
Night Is Falling, The. Mangan.
Night Thoughts in Age. Wheelock.
Nod. De la Mare.
Ode on Advancing Age. Dixon.
Of His Lady's Old Age. Ronsard.
Of the Last Verses in the Book. Waller.
Oisin. *Unknown.*
Old. Hoyt.
Old, The. Noel.
Old Age. Bodenheim.
Old Age. *Fr.* Arcadia. Sidney.
Old Age. *Fr.* Oedipus at Colonus. Sophocles.
Old Age Home, The. Holmes.
Old Age Pensioner, The. Campbell.

Old *(continued)*
Old and Young. Bourdillon.
Old Are Sleepy, The. Davis.
Old Black Men. Johnson.
Old Crabbed Men. Reeves.
Old Familiar Faces, The. Lamb.
Old Habitant, An. Call.
Old I Am. Bosman.
Old Knight, The. *Fr.* Polyhymnia. Peele.
Old Lady, The. Wolfe.
Old Man. Jennings.
Old Man, An. Wordsworth.
Old Man Dreams, The. Holmes.
Old Man's Comforts and How He Gained Them, The. Southey.
Old Man's Winter Night, An. Frost.
Old Man's Wish, The. W. Pope.
Old Men, The. De la Mare.
Old Men, The. Javitz.
Old Men. Keesing.
Old Men. Nash.
Old Men, The. Rhys.
Old Men Admiring Themselves in the Water. Yeats.
Old Men and Young Men. Holmes.
Old Men Are Facts. Smith.
Old Men on the Blue. Ferril.
Old men, white-haired, beside the ancestral graves. Basho.
Old Mr. Tatterlock. Cheyne.
Old Peasant in the Billiard Saloon, The. Menai.
Old Seawoman. LeClaire.
Old Song Reversed, An. Stoddard.
Old Woman, The. Bunker.
Old Woman, The. Campbell.
Old Woman. Smith.
Old Woman Laments in Springtime, An. E. Sitwell.
Old Woman of the Roads, An. Colum.
Old Woman Sitting in the Sun. Inman.
Old Woman with Flowers, An. Lee.
Old Woman's Lamentations, An. Villon.
Old Women. Deutsch.
Old Women, The. Symons.
Omnia Somnia. Watson.
On a Valetudinarian. Ibn al-Rumi.
On an Old Woman. Lucillius.
On Being Sixty. Po Chü-i
On Falling Asleep to Birdsong. Meredith.
On Growing Old. Masefield.
On Growing Old. Rayaprol.
On Having Grown Old. Noll.
On Living Too Long. Landor.
One White Hair, The. Landor.
Out of November: Speaking for One. McCord.
Over the Hill to the Poor-House. Carleton.
Pause for Breath, A. Hughes.
Peekaboo, I Almost See You. Nash.
Philosopher, The. Teasdale.
Piazza Piece. Ransom.
Pigeon-Feeders in Battery Park, The. Altrocchi.
Pity of the Leaves, The. Robinson.
Points of View. A. Lowell.
Poor Relation, The. Robinson.
Portrait of a Very Old Man. Carsley.
Portrait of an Old Woman. Ficke.
Prayer: "Lord God of the oak and the elm." Villiers.
Prologue: "Poet's age is sad, The: for why?" *Fr.* Asolando. R. Browning.
Promise of Peace. Jeffers.
Provide, Provide. Frost.
Rabbi Ben Ezra. R. Browning.
Retirement. *Unknown.*
Retrospect. Crouch.
Sad Song about Greenwich Village, A. Park.
Sailing to Byzantium. Yeats.
Silver Threads among the Gold. Rexford.
Simon Lee. Wordsworth.
Sing Me a Song. Stevenson.
Sixty-eighth Birthday. J. R. Lowell.
Small Celandine, The. Wordsworth.
Song from a Country Fair. Adams.
Song of Reaching Seventy. Wheelock.
Song of the Old Mother, The. Yeats.
Span of Life, The. Frost.
Superseded, The. Hardy.
Terminus. Emerson.
Thanks in Old Age. Whitman.
That time of year thou may'st in me behold. Sonnets, LXXIII. Shakespeare.
Thesis and Antithesis. Clough.
Though You Are Young. Campion.
Threescore and Ten. Stoddard.
To Age. Landor.
To an Old Lady. Empson.
To My Ninth Decade. Landor.
To Old Age. Whitman.
To One Being Old. Mitchell.
To Waken an Old Lady. Williams.
Too Late. Ludlow.
Too Old to Work. Glazer.
Tower, The. Yeats.
'Twas Just before the Hay Was Mown. Swain.
Twenty Golden Years Ago. Mangan.
Upon His Picture. Randolph.
Uselessness. Wilcox.
We Are Never Old. *Fr.* The World-Soul. Emerson.
Welcome Eild. *Unknown.*
When forty winters shall besiege thy brow. Sonnets, II. Shakespeare.
When I Am Old. Mason.
When I See Old Men. Souster.
When They Grow Old. Ralph.
When You Are Old. Henley.
When You Are Old. Yeats.
Whisperer, The. Bullen.
Whom the Gods Love, Bruner.
Woman of Beare, The. *Unknown.*
Wrinkles ("When Helen first saw wrinkles in her face.") Landor.
Years, The. Wheelock.
Young and Old. *Fr.* The Water Babies. Kingsley.
Young Woman. Nemerov.
Youth and Age. Arnold.
Youth and Age. Byron.
Youth and Age. Campion.
Youth and Age. Coleridge.
Youth and Age. Mimnermus.
Youth and Age. Palmer.
Youth and Age. Scott.
Youth and Age on Beaulieu River, Hants. Betjeman.

Old South Meetinghouse, Boston
Church of the Revolution, The. Butterworth.
In the "Old South." Whittier.

Oldham, John
To the Memory of Mr. Oldham. Dryden.

O'Leary, Arthur
Lament for Art O'Leary. *Unknown.*

Olive Trees
Olive Tree, The. Baring-Gould.
Olive Trees. Colum.
Olive Trees. Spencer.

Omar Khayyám
In a Copy of Omar Khayyám. J. R. Lowell.
Toast to Omar Khayyám. Watts.

O'More, Rory
Dirge of Rory O'More. De Vere.

O'Neill, Owen Roe
Lament for the Death of Owen Roe O'Neill. Davis.

O'Neill, Shane
Shane O'Neill. MacManus.

Onions
Onions. *Fr.* Verses for Fruitwomen. Swift.

Ontario, Lake
Great Lakes Suite, The. Reaney.

Opal
Opal. Miles.

Opera
After the Opera. Lawrence.
Benefit Night at the Opera, A. Bell.
Carmen. Levy.
Dunce's Opera. *Fr.* The Dunciad. Pope.
Grand Opera. Reeves.
Ill Met by Zenith. Nash.
Performance of "Boris Godunov," A. Conquest.
Verdi at Eighty. Bell.

Ophelia
Ballad of Another Ophelia. Lawrence.
Ophelia. Rimbaud.
Ophelia. Watkins.
Opossums
Opossum. Smith.
Possum and the Moon, The. Campbell.
Opportunity
Opportunity. Cawein.
Opportunity. Ingalls.
Opportunity. Machiavelli.
Opportunity. Malone.
Opportunity. Markham.
Opportunity. Sill.
Optimism
Difference, The. *Unknown.*
Optimist, The. *Unknown.*
Optimist and Pessimist. *At. to* Wilson.
Oranges
Orange, The. Lamb.
Orange Tree, The. Neilson.
Orange Tree by Day. *Fr.* The Red-gold Rain. S. Sitwell.
Orange Tree by Night. *Fr.* The Red-gold Rain. S. Sitwell.
Orchards
Among the Orchards. Lampman.
Apple Howling Songs ("Here's to thee, old apple tree"). *Unknown.*
Crowns, The. Freeman.
In an Old Orchard. Dufault.
In the Orchard. Ibsen.
In the Orchard. Stuart.
Little Green Orchard, The. De la Mare.
Lost Orchard, The. Masters.
Of an Orchard. Tynan.
Orchard. Doolittle.
Orchard by the Shore, The; a Pastoral. Sweetman.
Overheard in an Orchard. Cheney.
Orchids
Orchids. Roethke.
Sun Orchids. Stewart.
Oregon (state)
Exodus for Oregon. Miller.
Oregon State Song. Buchanan.
Oregon Winter. McGahey.
Oregon (ship)
Battle-Song of the Oregon. Rice.
Race of the *Oregon*, The. Meehan.
Rush of the *Oregon*, The. Guiterman.
Oregon Trail
Oregon Trail, The. W. R. Benét.
Oregon Trail, 1851. Marshall.
Oregon Trail, The; 1843. Guiterman.
Organ-grinders. *See* **Hurdy-gurdies.**
Organists
Organist, The. Stevens.
Organist, The. *Unknown.*
Organist in Heaven, The. Brown.
Over His Keys. *Fr.* The Vision of Sir Launfal. J. R. Lowell.
Orient (ship)
Brave Old Ship, *The Orient*, The. R. Lowell.
Original Sin
Adam Lay Ibounden. *Unknown.*
Alas! that ever that speche was spoken. *Fr.* Eva's Lament. *Unknown.*
Corruption. Vaughan.
Original Sin; a Short Story. Warren.
Orioles
Hearing the Early Oriole. Po Chü-i.
Oriole. Fawcett.
Oriole. Walker.
Orioles. Langland.
Song the Oriole Sings, The. Howells.
To an Oriole. Fawcett.
To hear an oriole sing. Dickinson.
Orion (mythology)
Orion Seeks the Goddess Diana. *Fr.* Landscape with the Giant Orion. S. Sitwell.
Orion (constellation)
Orion. Turner.
Oriskany, Battle of
Battle of Oriskany. Helmer.
Orkney Islands, Scotland
In Orknay. Fowler.
Ormonde, Elizabeth Preston Butler, Countess of
To the Excellent Pattern of Beauty and Virtue, Lady Elizabeth, Countess of Ormond. Shirley.
Orphans
Elf Child, The. Riley.
Little Orphant Annie. Riley.
Nobody's Child. Case.
Orphan, The, *sels.* Otway.
Orphan, The. *Unknown.*
Orphan Born. Burdette.
Orphan Boy's Tale, The. Opie.
Orphans. Rhody.
Orpheus
Eurydice to Orpheus. R. Browning.
Greater Music, The. Weiss.
Orpheus. Snodgrass.
Orpheus. Winters.
Orpheus and Eurydice. R. Browning.
Orpheus, O Orpheus, gently touch thy Lesbyan lyre. *Unknown.*
Orpheus with His Lute. *Fr.* King Henry VIII. *At. to* Shakespeare *and to* Fletcher.
Sonnets to Orpheus, *sels.* Rilke.
Thus sang Orpheus to his strings. *Unknown.*
Osgood, Frances S.
Simple Duty, A. Poe.
Ossian
Spoke my heart in the dearth of the night. *Fr.* Ossian. O'Donnell.
Ostend, Belgium
Sonnet: At Ostend, July 22, 1787. Bowles.
Ostriches
Ostrich Is a Silly Bird, The. Freeman.
O'Sullivan Beare, Donall
Dirge of O'Sullivan Bear. Callanan.
Otago, New Zealand
There's Nae Place like Otago Yet. Barr of Craigielee.
Othello
Cataclysm. Brettell.
Ottawa (city), Canada
Ottawa. Scott.
Ottawa (river), **Canada**
Deep Dark River. Roberts.
Otter (river), Devon, England
Sonnet: To the River Otter. Coleridge.
Otterburn, Battle of
Battle of Otterbourne, The. *Unknown.*
Chevy Chase. *Unknown.*
Otters
Otter, An. Hughes.
Otters. Colum.
Ouray, Colorado
Lines on Mountain Villages. "Sunset Joe."
Ouse (river), England
Reflections on the River. Young.
Outdoor Life
Song of the Open Road. Nash.
Song of the Open Road, A. *Unknown.*
Song of the Open Road. Whitman.
Toil of the Trail, The. Garland.
When in the Woods I Wander All Alone. Hovell-Thurlow.
Outlaws. *See* **Crime and Criminals.**
Ovenbirds
Oven Bird, The. Frost.
Overland Trail
Dust of the Overland Trail, The. Adams.
Ovid (Publius Ovidius Naso)
Notes to the Life of Ovid. Hamori.
Ovid on the Dacian Coast. Thompson.
Owain Gwynedd, Prince of North Wales
Triumphs of Owen, The. Gwalchmai.
Owls
Aziola, The. Shelley.
Bird of Night, The. Jarrell.
Bonny, Bonny Owl, The. *Fr.* Kenilworth. Scott.
Eyes. Davies.
Great Brown Owl, The. Hawkshaw.
Hunter, The. Wallis.
Outlaws. Graves.
Owl. Brathwaite.

Owls *(continued)*
Owl. Corso.
Owl. Dufault.
Owl, The. Smith.
Owl, The. Tennyson.
Owl, The. Thomas.
Owl, The. *Unknown.*
Owl, The. Young.
Owl and the Fox, The. *Unknown.*
Owl and the Nightingale, The. *At. to* Guildford.
Owl and the Pussy-Cat, The. Lear.
Owl-Critic, The. Fields.
Screech Owl, The. *Unknown.*
Song: Owl, The. Tennyson.
Sweet Suffolk Owl. *Unknown.*
There Was an Old Owl. *Unknown.*
Town Owl. Lee.
We rode out with the pealing day before us. *Fr.* Wind and an Eagle Owl. Brettell.
White Owl, The. *Fr.* Love in a Valley. Meredith.
Winter. *Fr.* Love's Labour's Lost. Shakespeare.
Wise Old Owl, A. Richards.
Oxen
Arctic Ox, The. Moore.
Bullocks, The. Comfort.
Crossing the Plains. Miller.
Draught-Ox, The. Addaeus.
I Have Twelve Oxen. *Unknown.*
Ox, The. Carducci.
Ox, The. Webster.
Ox-Tamer, The. Whitman.
Oxen, The. Hardy.
Partners. Castiello.
Teams, The. Lawson.
Twelve Oxen. *Unknown.*
Oxford, England
Above the High. Grigson.
Alma Mater. Quiller-Couch.
Christ Church Meadows, Oxford. Hall.
Duns Scotus's Oxford. Hopkins.
Epilogue Spoken at Oxford by Mrs. Marshall. Dryden.
Letter, A. Quiller-Couch.
Methought I met a Lady yester even. *Fr.* A Vision of Oxford. Alexander.
On Oxford. Keats.
Oxford. Aldridge.
Oxford. Johnson.
Oxford. *Fr.* Sonnets of the Empire. Strong.
Oxford Bells. Sister Maris Stella.
Oxford Idyll, An. Brown.
Oxford Is a Stage. Nolan.
Oxford Nights. Johnson.
Prologue to the University of Oxford. Dryden.
Sonnet: To Oxford. Russell.
Spires of Oxford, The. Latts.
To Oxford. *Fr.* Low Sunday and Monday. Hopkins.
To the University of Oxford, 1674. Dryden.
Verses on Sir Joshua Reynolds's Painted Window at New-College, Oxford. Warton.
Views of the Oxford Colleges. Leary.
Oysters
Oyster, The. Nash.
Oysters. Swift.
Precious Pearl, The. Wilson.

P

Pacific Ocean
By the Pacific. Bashford.
By the Pacific Ocean. Miller.
Eye, The. Jeffers.
On the Edge of the Pacific. Maynard.
Once by the Pacific. Frost.
Pacific Door. Birney.
Slow Pacific Swell, The. Winters.
Pacifism and Pacifists
Arms and the Boy. Owen.
Arsenal at Springfield, The. Longfellow.
Breakthrough. Sinclair.
Conscientious Objector, The. Shapiro.
Dooley Is a Traitor. Michie.
I Sing of Olaf. Cummings.
In the one-two domestic goose one-two one-two step. *Fr.* New Wings for Icarus. Beissel.
Pacifist, The. Belloc.
Put Up Again Thy Sword into Its Place. Eden.
Thinking about the Unthinkable. Gibson.
Ultimate Atrocity, The. Sassoon.
We Pass. Murphy.
Wisdom of the Abbot Macarius I. Beecher.
Paganini, Niccolò
Paganini. Middleton.
Paget, Violet ("Vernon Lee")
To Vernon Lee. Levy.
Paige, Leroy ("Satchel")
To Satch. Allen.
Pain
After great pain a formal feeling comes. Dickinson.
For All in Pain. Carmichael.
I dreaded that first robin, so. Dickinson.
If my vain soul needs blows and bitter losses. *Fr.* The Christian's New-Year Prayer. Wilcox.
Never Admit the Pain. Gilmore.
90 North. Jarrell.
No Pleasure without Some Pain. Vaux.
Pain. Robinson.
Pain has an element of blank. Dickinson.
Place of Pain in the Universe, The. Hecht.
Prayer for Pain. Neihardt.
Process. O'Donnell.
Security. O'Donnell.
Sympathizers, The. Miles.
To My New Mistress. Bowie.
Paine, Thomas
On Mr. Paine's "Rights of Man." Freneau.
Painting and Painters
Abstract Painter. Kennedy.
Andrea del Sarto. R. Browning.
Anonymous Drawing. Justice.
Bather in a Painting, A. Greene.
Cardinal's Dog, The. Glassco.
Dance, The. Williams.
Detail from an Annunciation by Crivelli. Dobson.
Elegiac Stanzas. Wordsworth.
Episode, An. Symonds.
Face, A. R. Browning.
For a Venetian Pastoral. D. G. Rossetti.
For "The Wine of Circe." D. G. Rossetti.
"Found." D. G. Rossetti.
Fra Lippo Lippi. R. Browning.
Gallery, The. Marvell.
Great Wave, The: Hokusai. Finkel.
History of the World as Pictures, The. Sullivan.
I Paint What I See. White.
In Santa Maria del Popolo. Gunn.
Large Bad Picture. Bishop.
Laughing Hyena, by Hokusai, The. Enright.
Limitations of Human Art. *Fr.* Three Fragments. Collins.
Meditation on John Constable, A. Tomlinson.
Monet: "Les Nymphéas." Snodgrass.
Musée des Beaux Arts. Auden.
Museum Piece. Wilbur.
Nocturne, The. Bode.
Old Paintings on Italian Walls. Raine.
Old Pictures in Florence. R. Browning.
On a Fifteenth-Century Flemish Angel. Ray.
On an Unsuccessful Attempt to Draw Lord Boyle's Picture. Rowe.
On the Picture of the Three Fates in the Palazzo Pitti, at Florence. Hallam.
Painted Head. Ransom.
Painter in New England, A. Stork.
Paul Veronese: Three Sonnets. Ferguson.
Pictor Ignotus. R. Browning.
Poet to a Painter, A. De Vere.
Politics of Rich Painters, The. Jones.
Portrait of a Cree. "Hale."
Quatrains: "Brushes and paint are all I have." Bennett.
Raphael's San Sisto Madonna. Miles.
Requiem for an Abstract Artist. Kessler.

Romney, The. Monroe.
Sargent's Portrait of Edwin Booth at "The Players." Aldrich.
Sonnet for a Picture. Swinburne.
Starry Night, The. Sexton.
Story of Soutine, A. Schevill.
Sunday Morning Apples. H. Crane.
Three Paintings by Arthur Dove. Johnson.
Unpraised Picture, An. Burton.
Vuillard: "The Mother and Sister of the Artist." Snodgrass.
Why I Am Not a Painter. O'Hara.
Winter Landscape. Berryman.
Palestine
Judean Hills Are Holy. Stidger.
Palestine. Whittier.
See also **Israel; Zion.**
Palm Sunday
Donkey, The. Chesterton.
For Palm Sunday. Milman.
Palm Sunday. Moment.
Palm-Sunday. Vaughan.
Palm Sunday and Monday. Poteat.
Palm Sunday Hymn. "Klingle."
Riding through Jerusalem. Campbell.
Triumphant Entry, The. Vaughan.
Palm Trees
Palm House, Botanic Gardens. Hetherington.
Palm-Tree, The. Abd-ar-Rahman, I.
Palm-Tree and the Pine, The. Milnes.
Royal Palm. H. Crane.
Song of the Palm. Robinson.
Palomar, Mount
Two Mountains Men Have Climbed. Starkweather.
Palos, Spain
Palos, Spain, 1492. Wynne.
Pan (god)
Dead Pan, The. E. B. Browning.
Great God Pan, The. E. B. Browning.
God of Sheep, The. *Fr.* The Faithful Shepherdess. Fletcher.
Hymn of Pan. Shelley.
Hymn to Pan. *Fr.* Endymion. Keats.
Musical Instrument, A. E. B. Browning.
Pan. Emerson.
Pan and Syrinx. Rogers.
Pan and the Cherries. Fort.
Pan in Wall Street. Stedman.
Pan-Pipes. Chalmers.
Pan with Us. Frost.
Pan's Syrinx was a girl indeed. *Fr.* Midas. Lyly.
Villanelle of the Living Pan. Roberts.
Panama
Panama. Jones.
Panama. Roche.
Panama Canal
Goethals, the Prophet Engineer. McKaye.
Song of Panama, A. Runyon.
Panderers
Upon Mr. Bennet, Procurer Extraordinary. Radcliffe.
Pangolins. *See* **Anteaters.**
Pansies
Pansy. Newsome.
Pansy and the Prayer-Book, The. Betham-Edwards.
Yellow Pansy, A. Cone.
Panthers
Black Panther, The. Wheelock.
Panther, The. Nash.
Panther, The. Rilke.
Paphos, Cyprus
Paphos. Durrell.
Parachutes
Parachute. Snaith.
Parades
Parade, The. Badley.
Parade, A. Rose.
Triumphal March. *Fr.* Coriolan. Eliot.
Two Hundred Girls in Tights and Halters. Hoffman.
Paradise
Paradise. Blanden.
Paradise. Faber.
Paradise. C. G. Rossetti.
Paradise Lost, *sels.* Milton.
Paradise Regained, sels. Milton.
Paradisi Gloria. Parsons.
Tiare Tahiti. Brooke.
See also **Heaven.**
Parakeets
Bird with the Coppery, Keen Claws, The. Stevens.
Paranoia
Tunnel, The. Strand.
Parenthood
Adam. Hecht.
Andre. Brooks.
Any Father to Any Son. Money-Coutts.
Becoming a Dad. Guest.
Culprit, The. Housman.
Dad's Greatest Job. *Unknown.*
Daedalus. Read.
Eight Months Old. Strobel.
Father, The. Finkel.
For a Child Expected. Ridler.
For My Newborn Son. Smith.
Fruit of the Flower. Cullen.
Heart's Needle. Snodgrass.
Homecoming. Kramer.
If I Had a Boy. *Unknown.*
If We Could Only Be! Shippey.
Joyful Prophecy. Miller.
Letter to My Daughter. Finkel.
Little Chap Who Follows Me, The. *Unknown.*
Little Girl, My Stringbean, My Lovely Woman. Sexton.
Little Son. Johnson.
Name, The. Creeley.
Nativity. *Fr.* The Blossom of the Branches. Gilbert.
On My First Daughter. Jonson.
On My First Son. Jonson.
On the Birth of a Child. Untermeyer.
On the Birth of His Son. Su T'ung-po.
Parental Ode to My Son, Aged Three Years and Five Months, A. Hood.
Parental Recollections. Lamb.
Parenthood. Farrar.
Personal History; for My Son. Todd.
Poems for My Daughter. Gregory.
Poet's Welcome to His Illegitimate Child, The. Burns.
Prayer for My Daughter, A. Yeats.
Separate Parties. Stuart.
Service Supreme. *Unknown.*
Song: "If a daughter you have, she's the plague of your life." *Fr.* The Duenna. Sheridan.
To a New Daughter-in-Law. *Unknown.*
To His Son. Ralegh.
To His Son, Vincent Corbet. Corbet.
To My Daughter Betty, the Gift of God. Kettle.
To My Firstborn. Durward.
To My Son. Griffin.
Toys, The. Patmore.
Two Parents, The. "MacDiarmid."
Two Sons. Buchanan.
Upon Wedlock and Death of Children. Taylor.
Which Shall It Be? Beers.
Wishes for My Son. MacDonagh.
See also **Fathers; Mother.**
Paret, Benny ("Kid")
Memory of Boxer Benny (Kid) Paret, The. Lima.
Paris, France
A Fauxbourg. *Fr.* Paris in 1815. Croly.
Four Sheets to the Wind and a One-Way Ticket to France. Rivers.
Impression de Paris. Wilde.
In Paris. MacDonagh.
Paris. Symons.
Paris Nocturne, A. "Macleod."
Paris; the Seine at Night. Divine.
Paris; This April Sunset Completely Utters. Cummings.
Public Holiday; Paris. Horner.
Spring in the Student's Quarter. Murger.
Unromantic Song. Brode.
Zone. Apollinaire.
Parker, Charlie
Requiem for "Bird" Parker. Corso.
Yardbird's Skull. Dodson.
Parker, Sir Peter
New War Song by Sir Peter Parker A. *Unknown.*

Parker *(continued)*
Parkman, Francis
Francis Parkman. Kroll.
Parks
Central Park Tourney. Weston.
City Park, A. Brody.
False Summer, The. Zaturenska.
From the Duck-Pond to the Carousel. Rukeyser.
Park is green and quiet, The. Reznikoff.
Public Garden The. R. Lowell.
Sunday in the Park. *Fr.* Paterson. Williams.
Water Picture. Swenson.
Parliament (Great Britain)
Cavalier Tunes. R. Browning.
Free Parliament Litany, A. *Unknown.*
On the New Forcers of Conscience under the Long Parliament. Milton.
Ye Parliament of England. *Unknown.*
Parnell, Charles Stewart
Come Gather Round Me, Parnellites. Yeats.
Parnell. Johnson.
Parnell. Yeats.
Parnell's Memory. Kettle.
Parodies
Parodies: An Anthology from Chaucer to Beerbohm—and After (Par). Dwight Macdonald, ed.
See also the special parody sections in:
Anthology of Light Verse, An (ALV). Louis Kronenberger, ed.
Book of Humorous Verse, The (BOHV). Carolyn Wells, comp.
Fireside Book of Humorous Poetry (FiBHP). William Cole, ed.
Home Book of Verse, The (HBV). Burton Egbert Stevenson, ed.
Innocent Merriment (InMe). Franklin P. Adams, comp.
What Cheer (WhC). David McCord, ed.
Parrots
Deprecating Parrots. May.
Parrot, The. Campbell.
Parrot, The. Flecker.
Parrot, The. Gibson.
Parrot. Smith.
Parrots, The. Gibson.
Parrot's Sololoquy. *Fr.* Speak, Parrot. Skelton.
Pretty Polly. Root.
"Psittachus Eois Imitatrix Ales ab Indis." S. Sitwell.
Sailor to His Parrot, The. Davies.
Song of the Parrot. Coatsworth.
Parsnips
Parsnip, The. Nash.
Pasadena, California
On a View of Pasadena from the Hills. Winters.
Passage West, Ireland
Attractions of a Fashionable Irish Watering-Place, The. Mahony.
Passionflowers
Passion Flower, The. Blanden.
Passion-Flower, The. Fuller.
Passover
Angel, The. Hayes.
Mother in Egypt, A. Pickthall.
Passover Eve. Kruger.
Passover in the Holy Family, The. D. G. Rossetti.
Pesach Has Come to the Ghetto Again. Heller.
Still Small Voice, The. Klein.
Pasternak, Boris
In Memory of Boris Pasternak. Levertov.
Letter to Pasternak. Pomeroy.
Pastors. *See* **Clergy.**
Pastures. *See* **Fields and Pastures.**
Pater, Walter
Gemlike Flame, The. Lister.
Paterson, New Jersey
Paterson, *sels.* Williams.
Patience
Patient Griselda. *Fr.* The Canterbury Tales: The Clerk's Tale. Chaucer.
St. Teresa's Book-Mark. St. Theresa of Avila.
Sonnet: "Patience, hard thing! the hard thing but to pray." Hopkins.
Patrick, Saint
At Saint Patrick's Purgatory. *At. to* O'Dala.
Bard's Chant. *Fr.* Saint Patrick for Ireland. Shirley.
Birth of Saint Patrick, The. Lover.
Breastplate of St. Patrick, The. *At. to* St. Patrick.
Dawn Song—St. Patrick's Day. Storey.
I'll Wear a Shamrock. Davies.
Praise of Fionn, The. *Unknown.*
Prayer to St. Patrick. Ninine.
Saint Patrick. Bennett.
Saint Patrick. Markham.
St. Patrick Was a Gentleman. Bennett.
Saint Patrick's Day. Hammond.
Saint Patrick's Treasure. Carroll.
Wearin' of the Green, The. *Unknown.*
Wearing of the Green. Fisher.
Patriotic Songs, American
Adams and Liberty. Paine.
America. Smith.
America for Me. Van Dyke.
America the Beautiful. Bates.
Battle Cry of Freedom, The. Root.
Battle Hymn of the Republic. Howe.
Columbia. Dwight.
Columbia, the Gem of the Ocean. Shaw.
Hail, Columbia! Hopkinson.
Liberty Song, The. J. Dickinson.
Marching through Georgia. Work.
National Song ("America, my own!"). Venable.
O Beautiful, My Country. Hosmer.
Ode: "God save the Rights of Man!" Freneau.
Ode on Science. Sumner.
Song for Our Flag, A. Sangster.
Star-spangled Banner, The. Key.
Tenting on the Old Camp Ground. Kittredge.
Three Hundred Thousand More. Gibbons.
Yankee Doodle. *Unknown.*
Yorktown Centennial Lyric. Hayne.
I Hear America Singing (IHA). Ruth Barnes, ed.
Patriotic Anthology, The (PaA). Introduced by Carl Van Doren.
Patriotic Poems America Loves (PAL). Jean Anne Vincent, comp.
Poems of American Patriotism (PAP). Brander Matthews, ed.
See also **Patriotic Songs, Confederate.**
Patriotic Songs, Chinese
Battle Hymn of the Chinese Revolution. *Unknown.*
Ch'i Lai' (March of the Volunteers). Shih Ee.
Patriotic Songs, Confederate
Bonnie Blue Flag, The ("Come, Brother! rally for the right"). Ketchum.
Dixie ("I wish I was in de land ob cotton"). Emmett.
Dixie ("Southrons, hear your country call you!"). Pike.
My Maryland. Randall.
Patriotic Songs, Danish
King Christian. Evald.
Patriotic Songs, English
God Save the King. *Unknown.*
Ready, Ay, Ready. Merivale.
Rule Britannia. *Fr.* Alfred, a Masque. Thomson.
Song: "There is no land like England". *Fr.* The Foresters. Tennyson.
Patriotic Songs, Finnish
National Anthem. Runeberg.
Patriotic Songs, French
Ç ira! *Unknown.*
Marseillaise, The. De Lisle.
Patriotic Songs, German
Watch on the Rhine. Schneckenburger.
Patriotic Songs, Greek
Greek War-Song. *Unknown.*
Patriotic Songs, Hungarian
National Song. Petöfi.
Patriotic Songs, Icelandic
Iceland's Song. Thomsen.
Patriotic Songs, Italian
Garibaldi Hymn, The. Mercantini.
Patriotic Songs, Norwegian.
Fatherland Song. Björnson.
Patriotic Songs, Polish
Polish National Hymn. Felsinki.
Patriotic Songs, Russian
Hymn of the Soviet Union. Mihalkov *and* El-Registan.

Patriotic Songs, Swedish
Swedish National Hymn. Strandberg.
Patriotic Songs, Welsh
Men of Harlech. *Unknown.*
Patriotism
Ad Patriam. Scollard.
Barbara Frietchie. Whittier.
Border March. *Fr.* The Monastery. Scott.
Breathes There the Man with Soul So Dead. *Fr.* The Lay of the Last Minstrel. Scott.
Bruce to His Men at Bannockburn. Burns.
Call of the Bugles, The. Hovoy.
Celebrations. Clarke.
Children's Song, The. Kipling.
Dear Harp of My Country. Moore.
Dulce et Decorum Est. Owen.
Fatherland, The. J. R. Lowell.
Flag Goes By, The. Bennett.
I am an American. Lieberman.
I Hear America Singing. Whitman.
In Westminster Abbey. Betjeman.
Kid Has Gone to the Colors, The. Herschell.
My Native Land. *Fr.* The Lay of the Last Minstrel. Scott.
Nationality. Gilmore.
Oh, Breathe Not His Name! Moore.
Our Country's Call. Bryant.
Patriot, The. R. Browning.
Patriotism. "Coolidge."
Petition, A. Vernède.
Pro Patria Mori. Moore.
Sail on, O Ship of State! *Fr.* The Building of the Ship. Longfellow.
Scots Wha Hae. Burns.
Soldier, The. *Fr.* 1914. Brooke.
There Is a Land. Montgomery.
To Those Who Reproved the Author for Too Sanguine Patriotism. Woodberry.
Yesterday. Anderson.
Young Hero, The. Tyrtaeus.
Patriotic Anthology, The (PaA). Introduced by Carl Van Doren.
Patriotic Poems America Loves (PAL). Jean Anne Vincent, comp.
Poems of American Patriotism (PAP). Brander Matthews, ed.
Poetry of Freedom, The (PoFr.). William Rose Benet *and* Norman Cousins, eds.
Sourcebook of Poetry (SoP). Al Bryant, comp.
Patrons.
Miserly Patron, A. *Unknown.*
Patroness. Barrax.
Paul, Saint
Paul. Marlatt.
Paul. Oxenham.
Saint Paul, *sels.* Myers.
To St. Peter and St. Paul. Constable.
Pavlova, Anna
Elegy on the Death of Mme Anna Pavlova, *sel.* Meyerstein.
Pawlet, Lady Jane, Marchioness of Winton
Elegie on the Lady Jane Pawlet, Marchion: of Winton, An. Jonson.
Pawnshops
Pawnbroker, The. Kumin.
Pawnshop Window. Grenville.
Peace
And They Shall Beat Their Swords into Plowshares. Micah, Bible, *O.T.*
As Brothers Live Together. *Fr.* The Song of Hiawatha. Longfellow.
Bells of Peace, The. Fisher.
Bucolic. Merwin.
Bugle Song of Peace. Clark.
Child of Peace, The. Lagerlöf.
Christ of the Andes, The. Markham.
Christian Soldier, The. Studdert-Kennedy.
Dear Lord and Father of Mankind. *Fr.* The Brewing of Soma. Whittier.
Disarmament. Whittier.
Even during War. *Fr.* Letter to the Front. Rukeyser.
Evening Star, The. Carmichael.
Flag of Peace, The. Gilman.
Gospel of Peace, The. Roche.
He Shall Speak Peace. Clark.
He Shall Speak Peace unto the Nations. Walters.
He Walks at Peace. *Fr.* Tao Teh King. *Unknown.*
History of Peace, A. Graves.
Hope's Forecast. Fuller.
Hush, All Ye Sounds of War. Draper.
Hymnal: "Bringer of sun, arrower of evening, star-begetter and moon-riser." Vinal.
In Distrust of Merits. Moore.
In the End of Days. Isaiah, Bible, *O.T.*
In the Way of Peace. Watt.
Let Us Have Peace. Turner.
Man unto His Fellow Man. *Fr.* On a Note of Triumph. Corwin.
Message of Peace, The. Howe.
Message of Peace, A. O'Reilly.
More than Flowers We Have Brought. Turner.
New Mars, The. Coates.
New Victory, The. Widdemer.
O Brother Man. Whittier.
Ode to Peace. *Unknown.*
Peace. Bhartrihari.
Peace. *Fr.* 1914. Brooke.
Peace. Cary.
Peace. Clare.
Peace. De la Mare.
Peace. Edman.
Peace. Greenberg.
Peace. Herbert.
Peace. Hopkins.
Peace. Markham.
Peace. Oxenham.
Peace. Pulsifer.
Peace. Sangster.
Peace. Scollard.
Peace. Vaughan.
Peace. Warren.
Peace. Whitney.
Peace and Rest. Davies.
Peace, like a Lamb. Clark.
Peace Must Come as a Troubadour. Drennan.
Peace on Earth. Bacchylides.
Peace on Earth. Cole.
Peace on Earth. S. Longfellow.
Peace on Earth. Sears.
Peace Triumphant. Rice.
Peace Universal. Thorne.
Peace Was My Earliest Love. Millay.
Per Pacem ad Lucem. Procter.
Prayer to Peace. *Fr.* Cresophontes. Euripides.
Prepare. Bynner.
Prince of Peace, The. Fosdick.
Reconciliation. Wheelock.
Reign of Peace, The. Starck.
Reign of Peace, The. Thornton.
Rose of Peace, The. Yeats.
Scythians, The. Blok.
Shalom Aleichem. *Unknown.*
To Men Unborn. Hamilton.
When the Cannon Booms No More. Carruth.
When the Great Grey Ships Come In. Carryl.
When War Shall Be No More. *Fr.* The Arsenal at Springfield. Longfellow.
Where the Rainbow Ends. R. Lowell.
Why. Freeman.
Winds of God, The. Scollard.
You cannot traffick in peace. *Fr.* The Uncelestial City. Wolfe.
See also **Veterans' Day.**
Peach Trees
Peach, The. Brown.
Peach, The. Lamb.
Peach Tree, The. E. Sitwell.
Peach Tree in the Garden of an Empty House. Press.
Peach Tree with Fruit. Colum.
Peacock, Margaret Love
Margaret Love Peacock for Her Tombstone, 1826. Peacock.
Peacock, Thomas Love
You are now/ In London, that great sea. *Fr.* Letter to Maria Gisborne. Shelley.
Peacocks
Peacock and Nightingale. Finch.

Peacocks *(continued)*
Peacock of Java, The. Smith.
Peacocks. Roberts.
White Peacock, The. "Macleod."
Pear Trees
Pear Tree. Doolittle.
Study of Two Pears. Stevens.
Peas
I Eat My Peas with Honey. *Unknown.*
Peas. *Unknown.*
Peasants
Death of a Peasant. Thomas.
Forebears. Gibbons.
French Peasants. Gibbon.
Peasant. Kreymborg.
Peasant. Merwin.
Peasant, A. Thomas.
Peasant and the Sheep, The. Kriloff.
Peasants, The. Lewis.
Plougher, The. Colum.
Peddling and Peddlers
Connecticut Peddler, The. *Unknown.*
Peddler's Caravan, The. Rands.
Pedlar, The. *Fr.* The Winter's Tale. Shakespeare.
Pedler, The. Mew.
Peele Castle, England
Elegiac Stanzas. Wordsworth.
Peewees. *See* **Pewees.**
Pegasus
Pegasus. Day Lewis.
Pegasus. Kavanagh.
Pelicans
Frigate Pelican, The. Moore.
Pelican, The. Thaun.
Pelicans My Father Sees, The. Sister Maris Stella.
Reason for the Pelican, The. Ciardi.
Pembroke, Mary Sidney Herbert, Countess of
On the Countess Dowager of Pembroke. Browne.
To the Right Honorable, the Lady Mary, Countess of Pembroke. *Fr.* Delia. Daniel.
Pembroke, William, Earl of
To William Earle of Pembroke. Jonson.
Penelope (mythology)
Penelope. Thurman.
World as Meditation, The. Stevens.
Penguins
My Penguin Playmate. Cooke.
On the Death of an Emperor Penguin in Regent's Park, London. Wright.
Penguin, A. Herford.
Penguin on the Beach. Miller.
Seven themes from the Zoo, No. 2. Bennett.
View from Here, The. Stafford.
Pennsylvania
Ode to the Inhabitants of Pennsylvania. *Unknown.*
Pennsylvania. Bucher.
William Penn/ Was the most level-headed of men. Smith.
Pennsylvania Station, New York City
Pennsylvania Station. Hughes.
Penshurst, England
At Penshurst. Waller.
To Penshurst. Jonson.
Pentagon (building)
Pentagon Exorcism. Ginsberg.
Pentagonia. Bates.
Pentecost
Call to Pentecost, A. Tyler.
Hymn for Pentecost. Mangan.
Pentecost. Coats.
Pentecost. Kirkup.
Peonies
Red Peony, The. Buson.
Pepper Trees
Pepper Tree, The. Sister M. Madeleva.
Scenes from the Life of the Peppertrees. Levertov.
Pequot Indians
Assault on the Fortress, The. Dwight.
Perry, Oliver Hazard
On the Death of Commodore Oliver H. Perry. Brainard.
Perry's Victory. *Unknown.*
Perry's Victory on Lake Erie. Percival.
Persephone
Demeter and Persephone. Tennyson.
Garden of Proserpina, The. *Fr.* The Faerie Queene. Spenser.
Garden of Proserpine, The. Swinburne.
Goddess, The. Gunn.
Hark, All You Ladies That Do Sleep! Campion.
Hymn to Proserpine. Swinburne.
Kore. Creeley.
Proserpine at Enna. Bottrall.
Perseus
Perseus. MacNeice.
Peru
Of History More like Myth. Garrigue.
Perugia, Italy
Perugia. Burr.
Pessimism
Difference, The, *Unknown.*
For a Pessimist. Cullen.
Optimist and Pessimist. *At. to* Wilson.
Pessimist, The. *Unknown.*
Violent Storm. Strand.
Peter, Saint
Domine, Quo Vadis? *Unknown.*
Focus of That Face, The. Poteat.
In the Servants' Quarters. Hardy.
Look, The. E. B. Browning.
Meaning of the Look, The. E. B. Browning.
Peter. Marlatt.
Peter and John. Wylie.
St. Peter. Duggan.
St. Peter at the Gate. Smiley.
Simon and Judas. Porter.
To St. Peter and St. Paul. Constable.
Upon This Rock. Duff.
Peterloo Massacre
Song to the Men of England. Shelley.
Sonnet: England in 1819. Shelley.
Petrarch
Petrarch. Carducci.
Praise of Petrarch and of Laura, His Lady, A. *Unknown.*
With Petrarch's Sonnets. Landor.
Petrels
Stormy Petrel, The. "Cornwall."
To see the petrel cropping in the farmyard. *Fr.* Sonnets for a Dying Man. Singer.
Petrillo, James Caesar
Petrillo, *parody.* "Gilbertulus."
Petronius
To Petronius Arbiter. Gogarty.
Pewees
Pewee, The. Trowbridge.
Peewits on the Hills. Stuart.
Two Pewits. Thomas.
Phaeton
Phaeton. Mandel.
Pheasants
Cock-Pheasant. Lee.
Pheasant, The. Coffin.
Pheasant. Ghose.
Pheasant. Keyes.
Pheasant, The. Pope.
Philadelphia, Pennsylvania
Independence Square, Christmas 1783. Guiterman.
Philadelphia (ship)
How We Burned the *Philadelphia.* Eastman.
Philip, King (American Indian Chief)
King Philip's Last Stand. Scollard.
Philip Neri, Saint
St. Philip in Himself. Cardinal Newman.
Philiphaugh, Battle of
Battle of Philiphaugh, The. *Unknown.*
Philippine Islands
My Last Though. Rizal.
On a Soldier Fallen in the Philippines. Moody.
Phillips, Wendell
Wendell Phillips. Alcott.
Wendell Phillips, *sel.* O'Reilly.
Philodendron
Woolworth Philodendron, The. Sandy.
Philosophy and Philosophers
Business Men. Chen Tzu-ang.

Coronet for His Mistress Philosophy, A, *els.* Chapman.
Homage to the Philosopher. Deutsch.
In Defense of Metaphysics. Tomlinson.
On the Death of a Metaphysician. Santayana.
Philosopher and Her Father, The. Brooks.
Story of Two Gentlemen and the Gardener, The. Logue.
To an Old Philosopher in Rome. Stevens.
To the Royal Society. Cowley.
Phoebes
I was a phoebe—nothing more. Dickinson.
To a Phoebe Bird. Bynner.
Phoebus Apollo. *See* **Apollo.**
Phoenix
I Saw a Phoenix in the Wood Alone. *Fr.* The Visions of Petrarch. Spenser.
News of the Phoenix. Smith.
Phoenix, The. Benson.
Phoenix, The. Cunningham.
Phoenix, The. *Fr.* Nepenthe. Darley.
Phoenix, The. Nash.
Phoenix, The. Oliver.
Phoenix, The. Sassoon.
Phoenix, The. Selig.
Phoenix, The. Spencer.
Phoenix, The, *sels.* *Unknown.*
Phoenix Self-born, The. *Fr.* Metamorphoses. Ovid.
Photographs
Glance at the Album, A. Burr.
Lines on a Young Lady's Photograph Album. Larkin.
Our Photographs. Locker-Lampson.
Photograph. Galvin.
Physicians
And Can the Physician Make Sick Men Well. *Unknown.*
Correct Compassion, A. Kirkup.
Crawford Long and William Morton. R. *and* S. V. Benét.
Dispensary, The. Garth.
Epistle, An, Containing the Strange Medical Experience of Karshish, the Arab Physician. R. Browning.
New Physician, The. Chalmers.
On Dr. Crank's Victory over the Gout. Davies.
Surgeons must be very careful. Dickinson.
That Holy Thing. *Fr.* Paul Faber, Surgeon. Macdonald.
To a Good Physician. Wycherley.
Pianos
Key-Board, The. Watson.
Piano. Lawrence.
Piano Recital. Deutsch.
To a Child at the Piano. Reid.
Picasso, Pablo
Father, The. Lattimore.
Picasso and Matisse. Francis.
Picasso's "Portrait de Femme." Feldman.
What Pablo Picasso Did in "Les Demoiselles d'Avignon." Colombo.
Pickpockets
Of Pick-Pockets. *Fr.* Trivia. Gay.
Picnics
Archaeological Picnic, The. Betjeman.
Let's Have a Picnic Out-of-Doors. Davies.
Picnic, The. Aldis.
Picnic, A. Fisher.
Picnic. Lofting.
Picnic, The. Roberts.
Picnic Day. Field.
Song of Bread and Honey, A. Le Gallienne.
Pico Della Mirandola, Giovanni
Pico Della Mirandola. Mason.
Picts
Pict Song, A. Kipling.
Piedmont, Italy
On the Late Massacre in Piedmont. Milton.
Piero della Francesca
Nativity. Sarton.
Piero della Francesca. Ridler.
Pigeons
Country Rhyme. *Unknown.*
Homing Pigeons. Walker.
Mrs. Peck-Pigeon. Farjeon.
Park Pigeons. Cane.
Pigeon, The. Church.
Pigeon English. Hay.
Pigeons, The. Burnham.
Pigeons. Reid.
Pigeons Just Awake. Conkling.
Trinity Place. McGinley.
Wood-Pigeons. Masefield.
Pigs
Animals Are Passing from Our Lives. Levine.
Boar, The. Kelly.
Feed. Knister.
If I Were a Pig. Fleming.
Little Piggy. Hood.
Melancholy Pig, The. *Fr.* Sylvie and Bruno. "Carroll."
Pig, The. Nash.
Pig, The. Southey.
Pig-Tale, The. *Fr.* Sylvie and Bruno Concluded. "Carroll."
Poor Man's Pig, The. Blunden.
Silver Sty, The. *Unknown.*
Unknown Color, The. Cullen.
View of a Pig. Hughes.
Pike, Zebulon Montgomery
Death of General Pike, The. Osborn.
Pike
Pike, The. Bruce.
Pike. Hughes.
Pike's Peak
Gold Seeker's Song, The. *Unknown.*
Hit at the Times, A. McGrew.
In the Summer of Sixty. *Unknown.*
Pikes Peak. *Unknown.*
Pike's Peakers, The. Greenleaf.
Soliloquy of the Returned Gold Adventurer. *Unknown.*
Song for the Pike's Peaker. *Unknown.*
To Pikes Peak. Hills.
Ute Pass. Whitney.
Pilate. *See* **Pontius Pilate.**
Pilgrim Fathers
Atlantic Charter: 1942. *Fr.* The Island. Young.
Boston Hymn. Emerson.
Children of Light. R. Lowell.
Courtship of Miles Standish, The. Longfellow.
First Proclamation of Miles Standish, The. Preston.
If I Were a Pilgrim Child. Bennett.
Indian's Welcome to the Pilgrim Fathers, The. Sigourney.
Landing of the Pilgrim Fathers in New England. Hemans.
Pilgrim Fathers, The. Bacon.
Pilgrim Fathers, The. O'Reilly.
Pilgrim Fathers, The. Pierpont.
Pilgrim Fathers, The. Wordsworth.
Pilgrim Song. Coates.
Pilgrims Came, The. Wynne.
Song of the Pilgrims. Upham.
Twenty-second of February, The. Bryant.
Uppon the First Sight of New England. Tilliam.
Word of God to Leyden Came, The. Rankin.
Pilgrims and Pilgrimages
As You Came from the Holy Land. *Unknown.*
At Saint Patrick's Purgatory. *At. to* O'Dala.
Palmer, The. *Fr.* The Vision of Piers Plowman. Langland.
Passionate Man's Pilgrimage, The. Ralegh.
Pilgrim, The. *Fr.* The Pilgrim's Progress. Bunyan.
Pilgrim, The. Downing.
Pilgrim, The. "Foxton."
Pilgrim and the Herdboy, The. Buchanan.
Pilgrim at Rome, The. *Unknown.*
Pilgrim Song, The. *Fr.* The Pilgrim's Progress. Bunyan.
Pilgrim Way, The. Oxenham.
Pilgrimage, The. Herbert.
Prologue to "The Canterbury Tales." Chaucer.
Quiet Pilgrim, The. Thomas.
Pindar
Honeybee, The. Bevington.
Praise of Pindar, The. Cowley.
Pine Trees
Aspects of the Pines. Hayne.
Choosing a Mast. Campbell.
Christmas Tree, The. Freeman.
Family Trees. Malloch.
Fichtenbaum steht einsam, Ein. Heine.
Foxtail Pine. Snyder.
Hill Pines Were Sighing, The. Bridges.
Murmuring of Pine Trees, The. Ryokwan.

Pine *(continued)*
O pine-tree standing. Hakutsu.
Palm-Tree and the Pine, The. Milnes.
Pine, The. Webster.
Pine at Timber-Line, The. Monroe.
Pine Bough, The. Aldridge.
Pine Gum. Ross.
Pine-Tree Buoy, A. Morris.
Pine Tree for Diana, The. *Fr.* Odes. Horace.
Pine Trees and the Sky: Evening. Brooke.
Pine Woods, The. Hanmer.
Pines, The. Lippmann.
Pines. Scruggs.
Pines, The. Spofford.
Pines and the Sea, The. Cranch.
Snowing of the Pines, The. Higginson.
Solitary Pine. Prince Ichihara.
This Pine-Tree. Morrow.
Voices of Pine Trees, The. Rengetsu.
Whispering Pine Tree, The. Van Rensselaer.
Pinkham, Lydia
Lydia Pinkham. *Unknown.*
Pioneers
American History. Moses.
American Laughter. Robinson.
Axe, The. Crawford.
Ballad of William Sycamore, The. S. V. Benét.
Camp within the West, The. Quinn.
Cleary Pioneer, A. Crewe.
Early Days, The. Dowling.
Emigrant's Child, The. Sproull.
Emigrants, The: Introductory Stanzas. Pringle.
Exodus for Oregon. Miller.
Farther. Piatt.
Final Soliloquy, The. *Fr.* Burke and Wills. Thiele.
Founders of Ohio, The. Venable.
Home Winner, The. Lindberg.
Indiana. *Fr.* The Bridge. H. Crane.
Kansas Emigrants, The. Whittier.
Man from Snowy River, The. Paterson.
Missouri Rhapsody. Daugherty.
Mothers of the West, The. Gallagher.
Mountain in the Sky, The. Corning.
My Father Loved the Jumping-off Place. Coffin.
New England's Annoyances. *Unknown.*
New Mexico and Arizona. Canterbury.
Old Log House. Tippett.
On the Emigration to America and Peopling the Western Country. Freneau.
Oregon Trail, The. W. R. Benét.
Oregon Trail, 1851. Marshall.
Pathfinders, The. Palmer.
Pioneer, The. Field.
Pioneer, The. Guiterman.
Pioneer Mother, The. Fuller.
Pioneer Woman. Crawford.
Pioneer Woman, The—In the North Country. Tietjens.
Pioneers. Clark.
Pioneers. Garland.
Pioneers. Jose.
Pioneers. Ophel.
Pioneers. *Unknown.*
Pioneers! O Pioneers. Whitman.
Pioneers, The; or, Twenty Years After. Plomer.
Prairie Schooner, The. Piper.
Roaring Days, The. Lawson.
Root Hog or Die. Small.
Settler, The. Macnab.
Settler, The. Street.
Settler in the olden times went forth, A. *Fr.* The Creek of the Four Graves. Harpur.
Silhouette in Sepia. Carr.
Teams, The. Lawson.
Trail Breakers. Daugherty.
Two Hundred Years Ago. Drummond.
Voortrekker, The. Kipling.
Westward Ho! Miller.
Whalin' Up the Lachlan. Esson.
Wheel Ruts. Daugherty.
Where the Dead Men Lie. Boake.
Where the Pelican Builds. Foott.
Wilderness Theme. Mudie.
Woman in the Wagon, The. Robertson.
Women of the West, The. Evans.
Pirates and Piracy
Ballad of John Silver, A. Masefield.
Ballad of O'Bruadir, The. Higgins.
Captain Kidd. *Unknown.*
Captain Ward and the *Rainbow.* *Unknown.*
Derelict. Allison.
Downfall of Piracy, The. Franklin.
Dutch Picture, A. Longfellow.
Flying Cloud, The. *Unknown.*
Henry Martyn. *Unknown.*
Last Buccaneer, The. Kingsley.
Last Buccaneer, The. Macaulay.
Morgan. Stedman.
Pirate Don Durk of Dowdee, The. Merryman.
Pirate Story. Stevenson.
Pirate Treasure. Brown.
Pirates. Coatsworth.
Pirates. Noyes.
Pirates' Fight, The. *Fr.* The Legend of Ghost Lagoon. Schull.
Reformed Pirate, The. Roberts.
Sack of Baltimore, The. Davis.
Sack of Old Panama, The. Burnet.
Salcombe Seaman's Flaunt to the Proud Pirate, The. *Unknown.*
Sir Andrew Barton. *Unknown.*
Spanish Waters. Masefield.
Tarry Buccaneer, The. Masefield.
To the Roving Pirate. Turberville.
Pisa, Italy
Evening: Ponte al Mare, Pisa. Shelley.
Pitcher, Molly
Molly Pitcher. Richards.
Molly Pitcher. Sherwood.
Pitt, William
Nelson, Pitt, Fox. *Fr.* Marmion. Scott.
Pittsburgh, Pennsylvania
Fort Duquesne. Plimpton.
Pittsburgh. Bynner.
Pittsburgh. Oppenheim.
Pity
Forebearance. Cowper.
God's Pity. Driscoll.
Ode to Pity. Collins.
Pity of Love, The. Yeats.
Pitying Heart, The. Goldsmith.
There Are Four Doors Which Open on the Skies. Nathan.
Pius X, Pope
To Pius X at Easter. Wildman.
Pius XII, Pope
Eugenio Pacelli. Neilson.
Place Names
American Names. S. V. Benét.
American Traveller, The. "Kerr."
Indian Names. Sigourney.
Localities. Sandburg.
Maiden of Passamaquoddy, The. De Mille.
Names from the War. Catton.
Rivers of the West. "Sunset Joe."
Plague
Adieu, Farewell, Earth's Bliss. *Fr.* Summer's Last Will and Testament. Nashe.
Tarantula or the Dance of Death. Hecht.
Plains
Call of the Plains. MacDiarmid.
Crossing the Plains. Miller.
Great Grey Plain, The. Lawson.
On the Plains. *Fr.* Intaglios. Brooks.
Summer on the Great American Desert. Sage.
Plane Trees
London Plane-Tree, A. Levy.
Plane-Tree. Flint.
Planets
Undiscovered Planet, The. Nicholson.
Plants
Plant Poems. Field.
See also **Flowers, Trees, *etc.***
Plato
Plato, a Musician. Leontius.
Plato to Theon. Freneau.

Spirit of Plato. *Unknown.*

Plattsburgh, Battle of
Battle of Plattsburgh, The. *Unknown.*
Battle of Plattsburgh Bay, The. Scollard.

Platypuses
I Had a Duck-billed Platypus. Barrington.
Platypus, The. Herford.

Pleiades
Pleiades, The. Coatsworth.

Plowing and Plowmen
Harry Ploughman. Hopkins.
I Will Go with My Father a-Ploughing. Campbell.
Ploughboy, The. Clare.
Plougher, The. Colum.
Ploughing on Sunday. Stevens.
Ploughman, The. Baker.
Ploughman, The. Thomas.
Ploughman at the Plough. Golding.
Plow: "My beak is bent downward, I burrow below." *Fr.* Riddles. *Unknown.*
Plowing; a Memory. Garland.
Plowman, The. Knister.
Plowman of Today, The. Garland.
Plowman's Song. Knister.
Plowmen. Frost.
Seed. Bosman.
Sod-Breaker, The. Stringer.
Song: "We, who are men, how shall we know?" Thomas.
Useful Plough, The. *Unknown.*
When Smoke Stood Up from Ludlow. Housman.
See also **Farming and Farmers.**

Plum Trees
Fall of the Plum Blossoms, The. Ranko.
Old Scent of the Plum Tree. Ietaka.
Plum Blossoms. Basho.
Plum Tree, The. Reaney.
Plum Tree by the House, The. Gogarty.
Plum Trees. Ranko.
'Tis the White Plum Tree. Neilson.

Plutarch
Plutarch. Agathias.

Pluto (planet)
Undiscovered Planet, The. Nicholson.

Plymouth, England
For an Age of Plastics. Plymouth. Davie.
Plymouth Harbor. Radford.

Plymouth Rock
Plymouth Rock. Driver.

Po Chü-i
As I Step over a Puddle at the End of Winter, I Think of an Ancient Chinese Governor. Wright.

Poaching and Poachers
Lincolnshire Poacher, The. *Unknown.*

Pocahontas
Last Meeting of Pocahontas and the Great Captain, The. Preston.
Marriage of Pocahontas, The. Webster.
Pocahontas. Thackeray.

Poe, Edgar Allan
Edgar Allan Poe. Barlow.
Edgar Allan Poe. Lanier.
Poe and Longfellow. *Fr.* A Fable for Critics. J. R. Lowell.
Poe's Cottage at Fordham. Boner.
Sonnets from the Series Relating to Edgar Allan Poe, *sels.* S. H. Whitman.
Streets of Baltimore. *Unknown.*

Poetry and Poets
Abbreviated Interviews with a Few Disgruntled Literary Celebrities. Whittemore.
Achievement. Beer.
Adam's Curse. Yeats.
Advice to the Grub-Street Verse-Writers. Swift.
Against the Dispraisers of Poetry. Barnfield.
Albatross, The. Baudelaire.
All Things Can Tempt Me. Yeats.
Alli Veri Figlioli delle Muse. *Fr.* Zepheria. *Unknown.*
Alma; or, The Progress of the Mind, *sel.* Prior.
American Poetry. Simpson.
Apologia. Gascoyne.
Apologia Pro Vita Sua. Coleridge.
Apparition of His Mistress Calling Him to Elysium, The. Herrick.
Argument of His Book, The. Herrick.
Aristotelian Elegy, A. Bogle.
Ars Poetica. MacLeish.
Ars Poetica. Vriesland.
Art of Poetry, The. Horace.
Art of Poetry, An. McAuley.
Art poétique. Verlaine.
As other men, so I myself do muse. *Fr.* Idea. Drayton.
As You Say; an Anti-Poem. Shapiro.
At the Top of My Voice. Mayakovsky.
Atlantis. Bottomley.
Austerity of Poetry. Arnold.
Awaking of the Poetic Faculty, The. Boker.
Bantams in Pine-Woods. Stevens.
Bards, The. De la Mare.
Bards, The. Graves.
Bards of Passion and of Mirth. Keats.
Bards We Quote, The. Taylor.
Birth of the Poet, The. Prettyman.
Birth of Tragedy, The. Layton.
Black Art. Jones.
Black Narrator, The. Alhamisi.
Black Poetry Day, A. Johnson.
Blind Steersmen. Parkes.
Bookshop Idyl, A. Amis.
Brief History. Briggs.
British Leftist Poetry, 1930-40. "MacDiarmid."
Broken Tower, The. H. Crane.
But I Am Growing Old and Indolent. Jeffers.
Canadian Authors Meet, The. Scott.
Caution to Poets, A. Arnold.
Certain American Poets. Shepard.
Changeless. Meynell.
Child and Poet. Swinburne.
Circus Animals' Desertion, The. Yeats.
Classical Criticism. Richardson.
Cliques and Critics. Sa'ib of Isfahan.
Coat, A. Yeats.
Coffee-House Lecture, A. Mezey.
Comparison of the Sonnet and the Epigram. Harington.
Confession, The. Wen Yi-tuo.
Confidential. Scott.
Constantly risking absurdity. *Fr.* A Coney Island of the Mind. Ferlinghetti.
Correspondences. Baudelaire.
Crepuscular. Howard.
Crowned Poet, A. Aldrich.
Crystal, The. Lanier.
Day Is Done, The. Longfellow.
Dead Poet, The. Douglas.
Dearest Poets, The. Hunt.
Dedication: "Bob Southey! You're a poet—Poet laureate." *Fr.* Don Juan. Byron.
Dedication: "I would the gift I offer here." *Fr.* Songs of Labor. Whittier.
Dedication, A: "Life of my learning, fire of all my Art." M. E. Coleridge.
Dedication, A: "They are rhymes rudely strung with intent less." Gordon.
Didactic Poem, The. Garnett.
Dissuasive against Poetry, A. *Fr.* A Satyr. Oldham.
Distant Drum, The. Hernton.
Drawing-Room Ballad, A. Traill.
Earth. Wheelock.
East Coker. *Fr.* Four Quartets. Eliot.
Eating Poetry. Strand.
Eclogue to Mr. Johnson, An. Randolph.
Editor's Private Cocktail Party, The. Williams.
Egoist, The. Wickham.
Elegy for Minor Poets. MacNeice.
Embryo. Townsend.
Enamored Architect of Airy Rhyme. Aldrich.
English Bards and Scotch Reviewers. Byron.
Envoy: "If homely virtues draw from me a tune." Johnson.
Epic. Kavanagh.
Epic, The. Tennyson.
Epigram: "Yes, every Poet is a Fool." Prior.
Epilogue: "Poets, like disputants, when reasons fail." *Fr.* All for Love. Dryden.

Poetry *(continued)*
Epilogue: "Pretty task, A; and so I told the fool." *Fr.* Aureng-Zebe. Dryden.
Epistemology of Poetry. Conquest.
Epistle to Dr. Arbuthnot. Pope.
Epistle to James Smith. Burns.
Essay on Criticism, An, *sels.* Pope.
Evening of Russian Poetry, An. Nabokov.
Experience. Harford.
Explanatory Epistle, An. Banks.
Fable: Poet and His Patron, The. Moore.
Fable for Critics, A. J. R. Lowell.
False Poets and True. Hood.
Fishes and the Poet's Hands, The. Yerby.
Fit of Rime against Rime, A. Jonson.
For Black Poets Who Think of Suicide. Knight.
For My Contemporaries. Cunningham.
For Some Poets. Jackson.
Forerunners, The. Herbert.
Fourth Egloge of Alexander Barclay, The. Barclay.
Fresh Air. Koch.
Fresh Start, The. Wickham.
Frightened Ploughman, The. Clare.
Further Instructions. Pound.
Gift of Song, The. Horace.
Great Men Have Been Among Us. Wordsworth.
Had I the Choice. Whitman.
Hands. Finkel.
Hear the Voice of the Bard. *Fr.* Songs of Experience. Blake.
His Muse Speakes to Him. Habington.
His Poetry His Pillar. Herrick.
His Prayer for Absolution. Herrick.
Historic Moment, An. Harris.
Honor Done to Poets of Old and Modern Poets, The. Heywood.
House. R. Browning.
How It Strikes a Contemporary. R. Browning.
How Many Bards Gild the Lapses of Time! Keats.
How many paltry, foolish, painted things. *Fr.* Idea. Drayton.
Hugh Selwyn Mauberley. Pound.
I Am Raftery. Raftery.
I Am 25. Corso.
I Broke the Spell That Held Me Long. Bryant.
I Cannot Forget with What Fervid Devotion. Bryant.
I Carried with Me Poems. Dusenbery.
I Like to Quote. Follansbee.
I Never Drank of Aganippe Well. *Fr.* Astrophel and Stella. Sidney.
I Sing an Old Song. Williams.
I Think Continually of Those Who Were Truly Great. Spender.
If All the Pens That Ever Poets Held. *Fr.* Tamburlaine the Great. Marlowe.
Image, The. Fuller.
Image-Maker, The. Gogarty.
Immortality of Verse, The. Pope.
Impression. Gosse.
In a Poem. Frost.
In Defense of Black Poets. Rivers.
In Memory of W. B. Yeats. Auden.
In My Craft or Sullen Art. Thomas.
In My Old Verses. Guérin.
In New York I got drunk, to tell the truth. *Fr.* A Trip to Four or Five Towns. Logan.
Ingrateful Beauty Threatened. Carew.
Invocation. Raine.
Invocation: "American muse, whose strong and diverse heart." *Fr.* John Brown's Body. S. V. Benét.
Invocation to the Muse. Hughes.
Invocation to the Social Muse. MacLeish.
January 1940. Fuller.
Jester's Plea, The. Locker-Lampson.
Jocosa Lyra. Dobson.
Jordan ("When first my lines of heavenly joys made mention"). Herbert.
Jordan ("Who says that ficitons only and false hair"). Herbert.
Jugurtha. Longfellow.
Lake Isle, The. Pound.
Lament for a Poor Poet. Connolly.
Lament for the Poets: 1916. Ledwidge.
Last Mathematician. Edelstein.
Late Tutorial. Buckley.
Lately Our Poets. Landor.
Laureate, The. Aytoun.
Laureate, The. Graves.
Lecture Note: Elizabethan Period. Grigson.
Lens. Wilkinson.
Let Them Alone. Jeffers.
Letter to a Young Poet. Barker.
Life of the Poet, The. Dow.
Like as the waves make towards the pebbled shore. Sonnets, LX. Shakespeare.
Line of an American Poet, The. Whittemore.
Lines on the Mermaid Tavern. Keats.
Literary Landscape with Dove and Poet. McGinley.
London Poets. Levy.
Lost Language, The. Feldman.
Love-sicke Poet, The. *Fr.* Satires. Hall.
Lyric Barber. Romano.
Madly Singing in the Mountains. P Chü-i.
Makers, The. McDonald.
Man with the Rake, The. *Fr.* Translations from the Chinese. Morley.
Masters of the Heart Touched the Unknown, The. Schwartz.
Memo from the Desk of X. Justice.
Mens Creatrix. Kunitz.
Merlin. Emerson.
Metre Columbian, The. *Unknown.*
Metrical Feet. Coleridge.
Mighty mother, and her son, who brings, The. *Fr.* The Dunciad. Pope.
Mirror, The. Hess.
Mirror for Poets, A. Gunn.
Miss Snooks, Poetess. Smith.
Mr. Pollington Remembers a Poet. Plutzik.
Mrs. Arbuthnot. Smith.
Musophilus. Daniel.
My Desk. Wolfe.
My Study. Hayne.
Mystical Poets. Nervo.
Namby-Pamby. Carey.
Negro Poets. Johnson.
New Poet, A. Canton.
New Technique. Armour.
No Uneasy Refuge. Salkeld.
Not marble nor the gilded monuments. Sonnets, LV. Shakespeare.
Not mine own fears, nor the prophetic soul. Sonnets, CVII. Shakespeare.
Nothing Is Easy! Pity Then. Stephens.
Oh for a Poet—for a Beacon Bright. Robinson.
O you chorus of indolent reviewers. Tennyson.
Ode, An: "Awake fair Muse for I intend." Browne.
Ode, An: Secundum Artem. Cowper.
Ode: "We are the music-makers." O'Shaughnessy.
Ode on Lyric Poetry. Marriott.
Ode on the Poetical Character. Collins.
Ode on the Poets. Keats.
Ode to Apollo. Keats.
Ode to Himself, An. Jonson.
Of English Verse. Waller.
Of Modern Poetry. Stevens.
Old Bard Speaks, The. Maxwell.
Old-fashioned Poet, An. Murray.
On a Dead Poet. Osgood.
On a Magazine Sonnet. Loines.
On a Miscellany of Poems. Gay.
On a Spider. Littleton.
On a Young Poetess's Grave. Buchanan.
On First Looking into Chapman's Homer. Keats.
On His "Sonnets of the Wingless Hours." Lee-Hamilton.
On No Work of Words. Thomas.
On Poetry; a Rhapsody. Swift.
On Reading A Poet's First Book. Bunner.
On the Future of Poetry. Dobson.
On the Make-up of a Poet. Sieber.
On the Oxford Book of Victorian Verse. "MacDiarmid."
On the Praise of Poetry. Cowley.
On the Sonnet. Keats.
On the Use of New and Old Words in Poetry. Seward.
Onan. Leary.
One day I wrote her name upon the strand. Amoretti, LXXV. Spenser.

One Poet Visits Another. Davies.
One-Talent Man. Pearson.
Only Be Willing to Search for Poetry. Yuan Mei.
Origin of Didactic Poetry, The. J. R. Lowell.
Orpheus in the Underworld. Gascoyne.
Orson of the Muse, An. Meredith.
Our Poets' Breed. Montoto y Rautenstrauch.
Past Ruin'd Ilion Helen Lives. Landor.
Pastoral Poesy. Clare.
Peasant Poet, The. Clare.
Pegasus. Day Lewis.
Peri Poietikes. Zukofsky.
Perpetuam Mobile. E. Sitwell.
Persistency of Poetry. Arnold.
Person from Porlock, The. Graves.
Person from Porlock, A. Thomas.
Petit, the Poet. *Fr.* Spoon River Anthology. Masters.
Pinch of Salt. Graves.
Piping down the Valleys Wild. *Fr.* Songs of Innocence. Blake.
Plea. Duggan.
Plea to Boys and Girls, A. Graves.
Poem: "If the drink that satisfied." Mason.
Poem: "Supremest fictions grow with fungus speed." Boyars.
Poem I Should Like to Write, The. Windes.
Poems. Conkling.
Poems Come Easier, The. Mathew.
Poems of Our Climate, The. Stevens.
Poet, The. Benton.
Poet, The. Bosman.
Poet, The. E. B. Browning.
Poet, The. Bryant.
Poet, The. Crowell.
Poet, The. Davies.
Poet, The. Emerson.
Poet, The. Grannis.
Poet, A. Hardy.
Poet, The. Keats.
Poet, The. Leitch.
Poet, The. Long.
Poet, The. A. Lowell.
Poet, The. Markham.
Poet, The. Mathews.
Poet, The. Morgan.
Poet, The. Noguchi.
Poet, The. O'Brien.
Poet, The. O'Dowd.
Poet, The. Pope.
Poet, The. Rooney.
Poet. Shapiro.
Poet, The. Tennyson.
Poet. Viereck.
Poet, The. *Fr.* By Blue Ontario's Shore. Whitman.
Poet and His Book, The. Millay.
Poet and His Patron, The. *Fr.* Fables for the Ladies. Moore.
Poet and His Song, The. Dunbar.
Poet and Lark. "Bridges."
Poet and the Child, The. Howells.
Poet and the Rose, The. *Fr.* Fables. Gay.
Poet at Fifty, The. Lerner.
Poet at Night-Fall, The. Wescott.
Poet at the Breakfast Table, The, *sels.* Holmes.
Poet Confides, The. Coleman.
Poet Describes His Love, The. Nathan.
Poet, A;—He Hath Put His Heart to School. Wordsworth.
Poet-Hearts. Eichendorff.
Poet in the City, The. Liddell.
Poet in the Desert, The, *sels.* Wood.
Poet in Winter. Lucie-Smith.
Poet Lived in Galilee, A. Bynner.
Poet of Earth. Thayer.
Poet of Gardens, The. Henderson.
Poet of One Mood, A. Meynell.
Poet on the Island, The. Murphy.
Poet Prays, The. Crowell.
Poet Songs. Baker.
Poet Speaks from the Visitors' Gallery, A. MacLeish.
Poet Tells about Nature, The. Moore.
Poet Thinks, A. Lui Chi.
Poet to His Father, A. Fisher.
Poet to His Love, The. Bodenheim.
Poet to the Birds, The. Meynell.
Poeta Fit, Non Nascitur. "Carroll."
Poeta Nascitur. Ashe.
Poetic Land, The. Roscoe.
Poetic Pains. Cowper.
Poetical Economy. Graham.
Poetics. R. Browning.
Poetics against the Angel of Death. Webb.
Poetry. Foote.
Poetry. Heath.
Poetry. Markham.
Poetry. Moore.
Poetry. Soutar.
Poetry and Learning. *Fr.* The Epistle Dedicatory to Chapman's Translation of the Iliad. Chapman.
Poetry and Philosophy. *Fr.* An Eclogue to Mr. Johnson. Randolph.
Poetry and Science. Turner.
Poetry and Thoughts on Same. Adams.
Poetry for Supper. Thomas.
Poetry Is a Destructive Force. Stevens.
Poetry Is Death Cast Out. Clouts.
Poetry Is Happiness. Gardiner.
Poets. Flexner.
Poets, The. Hunt.
Poets, The. Middleton.
Poets and Linnets. Hood.
Poet's Bread. Sister Mary Philip.
Poet's Dream, The. *Fr.* Prometheus Unbound. Shelley.
Poet's Fate, The. Hood.
Poet's Harvesting. O'Malley.
Poets in Africa. Campbell.
Poets in Time of War. Warr.
Poet's Lot, The. Holmes.
Poets Love Nature. Clare.
Poets light but lamps, The. Dickinson.
Poet's Mind, The. Tennyson.
Poets of Hell, The. Shapiro.
Poet's Prayer. Love.
Poet's Prayer, A. Phillips.
Poet's Progress, A. Hamburger.
Poet's Protest. Hedges.
Poet's Secret, The. Stoddard.
Poet's Simple Faith, The. Hugo.
Poet's Song, The. Tennyson.
Poet's Thought, A. "Cornwall."
Poets to Come. Whitman.
Poet's Voice, The. Blake.
Poet's Wish, A; an Ode. Ramsay.
Poietes Apoietes. Coleridge.
Pomegranates. Valéry.
Portrait of a Poet. *Fr.* Jack Kelso. Masters.
Post-Obits and the Poets. Martial.
Poverty and Poetry. Tickell.
Prayer for All Poets at This Time. Edman.
Prayer for Song. Noble.
Prefatory Sonnet. Kendall.
Printer to the Reader, The. *Unknown.*
Proem: "I love the old melodious lays." Whittier.
Progress of Poesy, The. Arnold.
Progress of Poesy, The. Gray.
Progress of Poetry, The. Swift.
Prologue, The: "Famous poets with the muses nine, The." *Fr.* Certain Eclogues. Barclay.
Prologue: "Our author, by experience, finds it true." *Fr.* Aureng-Zebe. Dryden.
Prologue, The: "To sing of wars, of captains, and of kings." *Fr.* The Four Elements, the Four Humours, the Four Ages, and the Four Seasons. Bradstreet.
Prologue: "What flocks of critics hover here to-day." *Fr.* All for Love. Dryden.
Prologue to "Love Triumphant." Dryden.
Prologue to "Secret-Love; or, The Maiden Queen." Dryden.
Pure Poet, The. Fuller.
Quidditie, The. Herbert.
Reader Writes, The. C. Crane.
Reaper, The. Duncan.
Reason for Not Writing Orthodox Nature Poetry. Wain.
Remembrance of Some English Poets, A. Barnfield.
Reply to a Lady Editor. Roethke.
Reproach to Dead Poets. MacLeish.
Rhymes. Segal.

Poetry *(continued)*
Rhymester, A. Coleridge.
Road to the Bow, The. Corrothers.
Roundel, The: "Roundel is wrought as a ring or a starbright sphere, A." Swinburne.
Sacred Poetry. "North".
Sacrifice to Apollo, The. Drayton.
Salutation the Second. Pound.
Satire: "Satire, my friend ('twixt me and you)." Geddes.
Scorn Not the Sonnet. Wordsworth.
Scribe, The. De la Mare.
Scribe's Prayer, The. Guiterman.
Scribe's Prayer, The. Service.
Seaweed. Longfellow.
Self-Criticism in February. Jeffers.
Self Unsatisfied Runs Everywhere, The. Schwartz.
Serving No Haughty Muse. Wordsworth.
Session of the Poets, A. Suckling.
Seven-year-old Poet. Rimbaud.
Shall I take thee, the Poet said. Dickinson.
Shepherds, The. Van Slyke.
Single Sonnet. Bogan.
Sisters, The. A. Lowell.
Six Lines Unheard. Hovanessian.
Six Poets in Search of a Lawyer. Hall.
Sleep and Poetry. Keats.
So is it with me as with that Muse. Sonnets, XXI. Shakespeare.
So That's Who I Remind Me Of. Nash.
Song Maker, The. Fairbridge.
Song Tournement: New Style. Untermeyer.
Sonnet: "Oh for a poet—for a beacon bright." Robinson.
Sonnet, The: "Sonnet is a fruit which long hath slept, The." Symonds.
Sonnet: "Sweet poets of the gentle antique line." Reynolds.
Sonnet, The: "What is a sonnet? 'Tis the pearly shell." Gilder.
Sonnet, The ("A sonnet is a moment's monument"). *Fr.* The House of Life. D. G. Rossetti.
Sonnet on the Sonnet. Keats.
Sonnet upon Sonnets, A. Burns.
Sonneteering Made Easy. Botsford.
Sonnet's Voice, The. Watts-Dunton.
Sound and Sense. *Fr.* An Essay on Criticism. Pope.
Sovereign Poet, The. Watson.
Speaking of Poetry. Bishop.
Spirit of Poetry, The. Longfellow.
Stillness of the Poem, The. Loewinsohn.
Strike among the Poets, A. *Unknown.*
Succession, The. Mace.
Survey of Literature. Ransom.
Ten Definitions of Poetry. Sandburg.
Terence, This Is Stupid Stuff. Housman.
Test, The. Emerson.
Theory of Poetry. MacLeish.
There Is a Time. Osborn.
There is no frigate like a book. Dickinson.
There's No Lust Like to Poetry. *Unknown.*
These Are the Live. Fearing.
These Poems I Have So Loved. Speyer.
This is my letter to the world. Dickinson.
This was a poet—it is that. Dickinson.
Thought and the Poet. Yates.
Thought-Fox, The. Hughes.
Thought in Time, A. Hillyer.
Three Corners of Reality, The. Bell.
Threnody for a Poet. Carman.
Time and the Garden. Winters.
To a Boy-Poet of the Decadence. Seaman.
To a Poet. Sister Mary Angelita.
To a Poet a Thousand Years Hence. Flecker.
To a Poet, Who Would Have Me Praise Certain Bad Poets, Imitators of His and Mine. Yeats.
To a Town Poet. Reese.
To a Young Poet. Meacham.
To a Young Poet. Millay.
To American Poets. Knott.
To an Author. Freneau.
To an Old Lady Asleep at a Poetry Reading. Kirkup.
To Critics. Herrick.
To Detraction I Present My Poesy. *Fr.* The Scourge of Villainy. Marston.
To Haydon. Keats.
To His Friend Master R. L., in Praise of Music and Poetry. Barnfield.
To His Late Majesty, Concerning the True Forme of English Poetry. Beaumont.
To His Muse. Herrick.
To His Pen. Wyatt.
To His Reader. Daniel.
To Hold in a Poem. Smith.
To Live Merrily, and to Trust to Good Verses. Herrick.
To Mary Unwin. Cowper.
To Music Bent Is My Retired Mind. Campion.
To My Book. Jonson.
To My Friends. Levi.
To My Most Dearly Loved Friend Henry Reynolds, Esquire, of Poets and Poesy. Drayton.
To My Readers. Holmes.
To Nysus. Sedley.
To Poets. Darley.
To Poets. Sorley.
To R. B. Hopkins.
To Stella. Swift.
To the Five Members of the Honourable House of Commons. Denham.
To the Muses. Blake.
To the Nightingale. Countess of Winchilsea.
To the Poets of India. Scott.
To the Spirit of Poetry. Marston.
To the Stone-Cutters. Jeffers.
To Verse Let Kings Give Place. Ovid.
To Wordsworth. Landor.
Transcendentalism; a Poem in Twelve Books. R. Browning.
True and False Singing. *Unknown.*
Truth, The. Joans.
Two Poets, The. Meynell.
Unutterable Beauty, The. Studdert-Kennedy.
Us Poets. Adams.
Velvet Sonneteers, The. MacInnes.
Verse: "What should we know." Gogarty.
Verses Placed over the Door at the Entrance into the Apollo Room at the Devil Tavern. Jonson.
Verses versus Verses. Bell.
Verses Why Burnt. Landor.
Versions of Love. Fuller.
Very Minor Poet Speaks, A. Valle.
Villanelle. Henley.
Villanelle of the Poet's Road. Dowson.
Visiting Poet. Nims.
Voice in the Crowd. Joans.
Volunteer's Reply to the Poet, The. *Fr.* Talking Bronco. Campbell.
Wapentake. Longfellow.
War Poet. Keyes.
Was it the proud full sail of his great verse. Sonnets, LXXXVI. Shakespeare.
We Poets Speak. *Fr.* Sister Songs. Thompson.
Weltschmerz. Yerby.
"Wen Gott Betrügt, Ist Wohl Betrogen." Clough.
What Poetry Is for Me. Scott.
What the Sonnet Is. Lee-Hamilton.
When He Would Have His Verses Read. Herrick.
When I Have Fears That I May Cease to Be. Keats.
When in the chronicle of wasted time. Sonnets, CVI. Shakespeare.
Where's the Poet. Keats.
Who Does Not Love True Poetry. Hall.
Who Translates a Poet Badly. Prada.
Who will believe my verse in time to come. Sonnets, XVII. Shakespeare.
Whoever You Are Holding Me Now in Hand. Whitman.
Whole Duty of a Poem, The. Guiterman.
Why I Am Not a Painter. O'Hara.
Why is my verse so barren of new pride. Sonnets, LXXVI. Shakespeare.
Why My Poems Died. Bhartrihari.
Wild Strawberries. Graves.
Will of Writing, The. Schevill.
Wiser than the Children of Light. Gibbon.
With some pot-fury, ravished from their wit. *Fr.* Virgidemiarum. Hall.
Words. Parry-Williams.

Words. Thomas.
Words in Time. MacLeish.
Words may well want, both ink and paper fail. *Fr.* Sonnets of the Christian Passions. Lok.
Written in a Volume of Shakespeare. Hood.
Yet Do I Marvel. Cullen.
Marvelous Light, The (ML). Helen Plotz, ed.
Poems on Poetry (PP). Robert Wallace *and* James G. Taaffe, eds.
See also ***names of individual poets.***

Poison Ivy
Poison Ivy! Gallagher.

Poland
On the Victory of Poland and Her Allies over the Sultan Osman, 1621. Sarbiewski.
Song of the Mound. Pol.
Stabat Mater. Wittlin.
To a Polish Mother. Mickiewicz.

Poles, The
All. Slonimski.

Policemen
Bobby Blue. Drinkwater.
Corner. Pomeroy.
I'm the Police Cop Man, I Am. Morrison.
London Bobby, The. Guiterman.
My Policeman. Fyleman.
P's the Proud Policeman. *Fr.* All Around the Town. McGinley.
Poem to a Nigger Cop. Hamilton.
Policeman's Lot, A. *Fr.* The Pirates of Penzance. Gilbert.

Politics and Politicians
Bryan, Bryan, Bryan, Bryan. Lindsay.
Candidate's Creed, The. *Fr.* The Biglow Papers. J. R. Lowell.
Dead Statesman, A. *Fr.* Epitaphs of the War. Kipling.
Eisenhower's Visit to Franco, 1959. Wright.
Election, The. Pack.
Election Day (Newark, New Jersey). Jones.
Election Reflection. Jones.
Epitaph on the Politician. Belloc.
God Give Us Men! Holland.
On a Politician. Belloc.
Political Meeting. Klein.
Politician Is an Arse Upon, A. Cummings.
Politics. Tennyson.
Said ("President Johnson to"). Starbuck.
Similes for Two Political Characters of 1819. Shelley.
Snapshot: Politician. Garrett.
Time's Changes. *Fr.* The Art of Politicks. Bramston.
Tom Dunstan; or, The Politician. Buchanan.
Town Meeting, The. Trumbull.
What Mr. Robinson Thinks. *Fr.* The Biglow Papers. J. R. Lowell.
What the Moon Saw. Lindsay.

Pollock, Jackson
Requiem for an Abstract Artist. Kessler.

Pollution. *See* **Ecology.**

Polo, Marco
Marco Polo. Day.

Polo
Polo Match. Sunday, 2 P.M. Miles.

Polonius
Polonius. De la Mare.

Pomegranates
Pomergranate, The. Dudek.
Pomegranates. Campbell.

Pompadour, Marquise de
On a Fan That Belonged to the Marquise de Pompadour. Dobson.
Pompadour, The. Thornbury.

Pompeii, Italy
New Excavations. Speyer.

Ponce de León, Juan
Ponce de Leon. Thomas.

Ponds. *See* **Lakes and Ponds.**

Pontius Pilate
Pilate Remembers. *Fr.* Pontius Pilate. Landels.
To Pontius Washing His Hands. Crashaw.

Pony Express
Pony Express, The. Thompson.

Pool (game)
Recreation. Priestly.
Rotation. Bond.

Poorhouses
Christmas Day in the Workhouse. Sims.
Curate's Kindness, The. Hardy.
Over the Hill to the Poor-House. Carleton.

Popcorn
Pop Corn Song, A. Turner.

Pope, Alexander
Alexander Pope at Stanton Harcourt. *Fr.* Sour Land. Keyes.
Epistle to Mr. Pope, An. Lyttelton.
Johnson on Pope. Ferry.
Mr. Pope. Tate.
Mr. Pope's Welcome from Greece. Gay.
On Mr. Nash's Picture. Brereton.
On the Edition of Mr. Pope's Works with a Commentary and Notes. Edwards.
Pope at Twickenham. Kent.
'Tis not so much, these men more forms survey. *Fr.* Essay on the Genius of Pope. Lloyd.
To Mr. Pope. Harte.
When None Shall Rail. Lewis.
Written at Mr. Pope's House at Twickenham. Lyttelton.

Poplar Trees
Binsey Poplars (Felled 1879). Hopkins.
Black Poplar-Boughs. Freeman.
Fallen Poplar, The. Webb.
In France. Cornford.
Poplar, The. Aldington.
Poplar. Benn.
Poplar-Field, The. Cowper.
Poplar Tree. Colum.
Poplars. Conkling.
Poplars, The. Garrison.
Poplars. Leuty.
Poplars. Reed.
Poplars, The. Trotter.
Poplar's Shadow, The. Swenson.
Song of Poplars. Huxley.

Popocatapetl (volcano), Mexico
Romance. Turner.

Poppies
Italian Poppies. Spingarn.
November Poppies. Corke.
Poppies. Ropes.
Poppies. *Unknown.*
Poppies in the Garden, The. Wolfe.
Poppies in the Wheat. Jackson.
Poppy, The. Taylor.
Poppy, The. Thompson.
Poppy Grows upon the Shore, A. Bridges.
Valley of White Poppies, The. "Macleod."

Porcupines
Porcupine, The. Nash.

Porpoises
Off Spectacle Island. Eberhart.
Porpoise, The. Nash.

Portia (Shakespeare)
Portia. Wilde.

Portland, Maine
My Lost Youth. Longfellow.

Portraits
Dorothy Q. Holmes.
Faded Pictures. Moody.
Likeness, A. R. Browning.
Portrait of a Florentine Lady, The. Reese.
Portrait of a Lady in the Exhibition of the Royal Academy. *Fr.* Every-Day Characters. Praed.
Three Portraits of Prince Charles. Lang.
To a Portrait. Symons.
To a Portrait of Whistler in the Brooklyn Art Museum. Cox.

Ports. *See* **Harbors and Ports.**

Poseidon. *See* **Neptune.**

Potatoes
Potato. Wilbur.
Potatoes. Lucas.
Potatoes' Dance, The. Lindsay.
Spraying the Potatoes. Kavanagh.
To a Sinister Potato. Viereck.

Potomac (river)
By the Potomac. Aldrich.
Picket-Guard, The. Beers.

Potomac *(continued)*
Potomac, The. Shapiro.
Pound, Ezra
After the Release of Ezra Pound. Abse.
Asylum. Clark.
Ezry. MacLeish.
Homage to Ezra Pound. Highet.
Visits to St. Elizabeths. Bishop.
Poverty
All Things Be Dear but Poor Mens Labour; or, The Sad Complaint of Poor People. *Unknown.*
Challenge, The. Longfellow.
Charcoal-Seller, The. Po Chü-i.
Children of the Poor. Hugo.
Cloister. O'Donnell.
Come Live with Me and Be My Love. Day Lewis.
Contentment in Poverty. Issa.
Country Justice, The. Langhorne.
Down on My Luck. Fairburn.
Dry Loaf. Stevens.
Elementary School Class Room in a Slum, An. Spender.
Epistle to Dylan Thomas. Barker.
Face of Poverty. Smith.
Franciscan Dream, A. Dinnis.
Furnished Lives. Silkin.
Holy Thursday. *Fr.* Songs of Experience. Blake.
Hunger. Davies.
Hymn to Poverty, A. Moore.
If Lincoln Should Return. Bruner.
In the Pauper's Turnip-Field. Melville.
In the Workhouse: Christmas Day. Sims.
Is There for Honest Poverty? Burns.
Lady Poverty, The. Meynell.
Lady Poverty, The. Underhill.
London Lickpenny. *Unknown.*
Lousy Peter. O. Sitwell.
Map of Mock-Begger Hall, The. *Unknown.*
Masses. Sandburg.
Monotone. Kreymborg.
On a Fair Beggar. Ayres.
On Lydia Distracted. Ayres.
Over the Hill to the Poor-House. Carleton.
Parley with His Empty Purse, A. Randolph.
Pauper's Drive, The. Noel.
People's Petition, The. Call.
Poor, The. Strahan.
Poor, The. Verhaeren.
Poor, The. Williams.
Poor Children. Hugo.
Poor Girl's Meditation, The. *Unknown.*
Poor Man, The. Carlin.
Poor Man's Daily Bread, The. McCarthy.
Poor Old Man, The. Squire.
Poverty. Simic.
Poverty. Theognis.
Poverty and Poetry. Tickell.
Poverty in London. *Fr.* London. Johnson.
Poverty Not All Loss. *Fr.* The Vision of Piers Plowman. Langland.
Prayer for the Poor. *Fr.* The Vision of Piers Plowman. Langland.
Proletaria. O'Dowd.
Said the Innkeeper. Connolly.
Slum Dwelling, A. *Fr.* The Borough. Crabbe.
Sonnet: He Jests concerning His Poverty. Sant' Angelo.
Sufferings of the Poor, The. *Fr.* The Vision of Piers Plowman. Langland.
Symphony, The. Lanier.
Third Wonder, The. Markham.
Thirty Bob a Week. Davidson.
Through Streets Where Crooked Wicklow Flows. Gregory.
Timothy Winters. Causley.
Village life, and every care that reigns, The. *Fr.* The Village. Crabbe.
Voice of the Poor, The. Lady Wilde.
We Live in a Rickety House. McLachlan.
Wench in the Street, The. *Unknown.*
What shall I give my children? who are poor. *Fr.* The Children of the Poor. Brooks.
Winter Offering. Savage.
Prague, Czechoslovakia
Beleaguered City, The. Longfellow.
Prairie Dogs
Prairie-Dog Town. Austin.
Prairie Schooner
Prairie Schooner, The. Piper.
Prairies
Across Illinois. Stoltze.
In the Days When the Cattle Ran. Garland.
Kit Carson's Ride. Miller.
My Prairies. Garland.
Nebraska. Swan.
Night on the Prairie. Sage.
Night on the Prairies. Whitman.
Prairie. Bates.
Prairie. Sandburg.
Prairie Birth. Coates.
Prairie-Grass Dividing, The. Whitman.
Prairie Graveyard. Marriott.
Prairie Ride, A. Moody.
Prairie Sunset, A. Whitman.
Prairie Water Colour, A. Scott.
Prairie Wind. Scott.
Prairies, The. Bryant.
Song of the Golden Sea. Blewett.
Songs of the Plains (I-IV). Dresbach.
To make a prairie it takes a clover and one bee. Dickinson.
Wind of the Prairie. Howes.
Praxiteles
Praxiteles and Phryne. Story.
Prayer
Cell, The. Hamilton.
Do I Really Pray? Burton.
Forme of Prayer, A. Quarles.
Hour of Prayer, The. Elliott.
I Dare Not Pray to Thee. Baring.
John Wesley's Grace before Meals. Wesley.
Larger Prayer, The. Cheney.
More Prayer. *Unknown.*
Pray! Arnold.
Pray! Wells.
Pray, Christian, Pray! *Unknown.*
Pray On! *Unknown.*
Prayer: "Be not afraid to pray—to pray is right." H. Coleridge.
Prayer: "Prayer must be grounded on the Word." *Unknown.*
Prayer: "Prayer, the church's banquet, angel's age." Herbert.
Prayer Moves the Hand That Moves the World. Wallace.
Prayer of an Unknown Confederate Soldier. *Unknown.*
Private Devotions. Brown.
Proof. Fuller.
Qui Laborat, Orat. Clough.
Right Use of Prayer, The. De Vere.
Saying a Prayer. Bennett.
Secret Place, The. Pollard.
Secret Place of Prayer, The. Adams.
Somebody Prayed. *Unknown.*
Sonnet: "Lord, what a change within us one short hour." Trench.
Sweet Hour of Prayer. Walford.
Taste of Prayer, The. Seager.
Thy Will Be Done. Flint.
Two Went Up to the Temple to Pray. Crashaw.
Universal Prayer, The. Pope.
What Is Prayer? Montgomery.
Whirring Wheels. Oxenham.
Who Prayed? *Unknown.*
Sourcebook of Poetry (SoP). Al Bryant, comp.
Praying Mantis. *See* **Mantis.**
Preachers. *See* **Clergy.**
Precedent
Calf-Path, The. Foss.
Precedents. Newman.
Predestination
Johannes Agricola in Meditation. R. Browning.
Prejudice. *See* **Racial Prejudice.**
Pretzels
Pretzel Man, The. Field.
Pride
Godolphin Horne. Belloc.
It is time that I wrote my will. *Fr.* The Tower. Yeats.
On a Proud Fellow. *Unknown.*

Poem of Margery Kempe, A. Nemerov.
Pointless Pride of Man, The. *Unknown.*
Pride. Miles.
Pride Is Out. *Unknown.*
Primer Lesson. Sandburg.
Priests. *See* **Clergy.**
Primitive Man
Double Ballade of Primitive Man. Tylor *and* Lang.
Primroses
Evening Primrose. Clare.
Primrose, The. Donne.
Primroses. Austin.
To a Primrose. Clare.
To an Early Primrose. White.
To Primroses Fill'd with Morning-Dew. Herrick.
Princeton, Battle of
Trenton and Princeton. *Unknown.*
Printing and Printers
Printer's Error. Wodehouse.
Prior, Matthew
For My Own Monument. Prior.
Prisons and Prisoners
American Twilights, 1957. Wright.
Ballad of Reading Gaol, The. Wilde.
Captivity. Rogers.
Certain Mercies. Graves.
Chesspieces. Campbell.
Convict of Clonmel, The. *Unknown.*
Elegy Wrote in the Tower, 1554. Harington.
Epistle in Form of a Ballad to His Friends. Villon.
Five Peas on a Barrelhead. Sarett.
Gorse, The. Gibson.
Imprisoned Revolutionist, The. Damadian.
In Prison. Morris.
In the Dock. De la Mare.
In the Prison Pen. Melville.
London, Hast Thou Accused Me. Surrey.
Loyalty Confin'd. L'Estrange.
Memories of West Street and Lepke. R. Lowell.
Message to Siberia. Pushkin.
My Body in the Walls Captived. Ralegh.
Now That I Am Clean Again. S. V. Benét.
Old Prison, The. Wright.
On a Political Prisoner. Yeats.
Prison. *Unknown.*
Prison House, The. Paton.
Prison Song. Richard Coeur de Lion.
Prison Sonnet. Blunt.
Prisoned in Windsor, He Recounteth His Pleasure There Passed. Surrey.
Prisoner, The. E. Brontë.
Prisoner, The. Plomer.
Prisoner, The. Po Chü-i.
Prisoner for Life, A. *Unknown.*
Prisoner Freed, A. Dutton.
Prisoner of Chillon, The. Byron.
Prisoner's Song. Gregory.
Prisoner's Song of Jerusalem, A. *Unknown.*
Seven Long Years in State Prison. *Unknown.*
Song of the Old Man in Chains. Lunacharsky.
Sonnet on Chillon. Byron.
Southern Road. Brown.
To Althea, from Prison. Lovelace.
Tramp, Tramp, Tramp. Root.
Walker, The. Giovannitti.
Wind at Your Door, The. Fitzgerald.
Written in Prison. Clare.
Written on the Walls of His Dungeon. Luis de León.
Prisoners of War
For an Ex-Far East Prisoner of War. Causley.
German Prisoners. Lee.
Hospital Prison Ship, The. *Fr.* The British Prison Ship. Freneau.
Officers' Prison Camp Seen from a Troop-Train, An. Jarrell.
Prisoner of War. Lutz.
Prisoners. Jarrell.
Progress
Thoughts on Progress. Daiches.
Prometheus
Prometheus. Byron.
Prometheus. Gibson.
Prometheus. Goethe.
Prometheus. Longfellow.
Prometheus Bound. Aeschylus.
Prometheus Unbound. Sister Miriam.
Prometheus Unbound. Shelley.
Prometheus, with Wings. Ondaatje.
Propertius, Sextus
Ghost, The. R. Lowell.
Homage to Sextus Propertius, *sels.* Pound.
Proserpina *or* **Proserpine.** *See* **Persephone.**
Prospectors. *See* **Gold Mining and Miners.**
Prostitution and Prostitutes
Bridge of Sighs, The. Hood.
Comrades in Arms: Conversation Piece. *Unknown.*
Crow-Marble Whores of Paris, The. Schevill.
In Response to a Rumor That the Oldest Whorehouse in Wheeling, West Virginia Has Been Condemned. Wright.
Jenny. D. G. Rossetti.
Ruined Maid, The. Hardy.
Scarlet Woman, The. Johnson.
She Was Poor, but She Was Honest. *Unknown.*
Village-Born Beauty. *Unknown.*
Whore. Fowler.
Protest, Social
Alabama Centennial. Madgett.
America. Ginsberg.
Factory Windows Are Always Broken. Lindsay.
Feeding the Lions. Jordan.
It Is Time. Joans.
Man with the Hoe, The. Markham.
Old Chartist, The. Meredith.
On a Recent Protest against Social Conditions. Posner.
Reflections in a Slum. "MacDiarmid."
Song to the Men of England. Shelley.
Thirty Bob a Week. Davidson.
Those Being Eaten by America. Bly.
Trinity Place. McGinley.
We Shall Overcome. *Unknown.*
Why I Rebel. Sye.
Poems of Protest Old and New (PPON). Arnold Kenseth, *ed.*
We Speak As Liberators: Young Black Poets (WSL). Orde Coombs, *ed.*
Writing on the Wall, The (WOW). Walter Lowenfels, *ed.*
Proust, Marcel
Hymn to Proust. Ewart.
Marcel Proust. Smith.
Provence, France
At a Country Dance in Provence. Monro.
Cocooning, The. *Fr.* Mirèio. Mistral.
Provincetown, Massachusetts
Provincetown, *sels.* Dudek.
Psyche
Eros and Psyche. Apuleius.
Ode to Psyche. Keats.
Psychoanalysis
Ballade to My Psychoanalyst. Lillington.
Psychoanalysis. Gavin.
Puck
Death of Puck, The. Lee-Hamilton.
To Puck. Thomas.
Puerto Ricans
Man I Thought You Was Talking Another Language That Day. Cruz.
Puerto Rican Side-Street. Dudek.
Pumpkins
Mr. Macklin's Jack o'Lantern. McCord.
Pumpkin, The. Graves.
Pumpkin, The. Whittier.
Theme in Yellow. Sandburg.
Puppets
Marionettes, The. De la Mare.
Puppet Play, The. Colum.
Puppet Player, The. Grimké.
Puppets. Symons.
Purcell, Henry
Henry Purcell. Hopkins.
On the Death of Mr. Purcell. Dryden.
Purgatory
Purgatorio, *sels.* Fr. Divina Commedia. Dante.
Puritans and Puritanism
Cavalier Tunes. R. Browning.

Puritans *(continued)*
Come drawer some wine or wele pull downe your signe. *Unknown.*
Grasshopper, The. Lovelace.
Hudibras, *sels.* Butler.
On Those That Deserve It. Quarles.
Religio Laici. Dryden.
Say puritan ist come to passe. *Unknown.*
Zealous Puritan, The. *Unknown.*
Pussy Willows
Little Gray Pussy. *Unknown.*
Pussy Willow. Brown.
Pussy Willows. Bennett.
Pussy-Willows. Fisher.
Pussy-Willows. Guiterman.
Pussy Willows. Plummer.
Pussy Willows. *Unknown.*
Willow Cats, The. Widdemer.
Putnam, Israel
Death and General Putnam. Guiterman.
Pygmalion
Pygmalion. Johnson.
Pygmalion. Scott.
Pygmalion to Galatea. Graves.
Pygmies
Ogres and Pygmies. Graves.
Pym, John
Pyms Anarchy. *At. to* Jordan.
Pyramids
Pelters of Pyramids. Horne.
Pyramis; or, The House of Ascent. Hope.
Pythons
Python, The. Belloc.
Python. Conkling.

Q

Quaker Ladies (flower)
Quaker Ladies. Cortissoz.
Quakers. *See* **Friends, Society of.**
Quantrill, William Clarke
Quantrell. *Unknown.*
Quebec, Canada
At Quebec. Blewett.
Quḗbec May. Birney.
Queen Anne's Lace
Queen Anne's Lace. Newton.
Queenstown, Battle of
Battle of Queenstown, The. Banker.
Quivira
Quivira. Guiterman.

R

Rabbis
Bratzlav Rabbi to His Scribe, The. Glatstein.
Debate with the Rabbi. Nemerov.
Legend of Rabbi Ben Levi, The. *Fr.* Tales of a Wayside Inn. Longfellow.
Rabbi Yom-Tob of Mayence Petitions His God. Klein.
Rabbi Yussel Luksh of Chelm. Glatstein.
Two Rabbins, The. Whittier.
Rabbits
Four Things. Proverbs, Bible, *O.T.*
Love for a Hare. La Follette.
Noah and the Rabbit. Chesterman.
Perfect Life, The. Carrera Andrade.
Rabbit, The. Davies.
Rabbit, The. Durston.
Rabbit, The. King.
Rabbit, The. Lewisohn.
Rabbit, The. Roberts.
Rabbit. Robinson.
Rabbit, The. *Unknown.*
Rabbit Cry. Lucie-Smith.
Rabbits. Baruch.
Rabbits, The. *Unknown.*
Snare, The. Stephens.
Song of the Rabbits outside the Tavern. Coatsworth.
Story in the Snow, A. Crouch.
To a Jack Rabbit. Barker.
Tracks. Farrar.
White Season. F. Frost.
See also **Hares.**
Raccoons
Diary of a Raccoon. Bennett.
Raccoon on the Road. Brennan.
Raccoons. Fisher.
Racoon. Rexroth.
Race, Cape, Newfoundland
Way of Cape Race, The. Pratt.
Rachel (Bible)
Rachel. Gilbert.
Racial Prejudice
Alarm Clock, The. Evans.
Auditions. Saunders.
Baby Villon. Levine.
Birmingham Sunday (September 15, 1963). Hughes.
Circled by a Horsefly. Quigless.
Circles. Sandburg.
Cross. Hughes.
Defeat. Bynner.
Differences. Tarver.
Family Goldschmitt, The. Coulette.
For a Lady I Know. Cullen.
For Denise McNair. Inez.
In re Solomon Warshawer. Klein.
Incident. Cullen.
Jitterbugging in the Streets. Hernton.
Little White Schoolhouse Blues. Lennon.
Merry-Go-Round. Hughes.
Permanent Delegate, The. Suhl.
Recapitulations. Shapiro.
Salute. Pitcher.
Status Quo. Dismond.
Telephone Conversation. Soyinka.
Ther's Somethin'. Small.
Ultimate Equality. Durem.
Way It Is, The. Goncalves.
Well, old spy/ looks like I. *Fr.* Award. Durem.
White Houses. McKay.
You Know, Joe. Durem.
You've Got To Be Taught. Hammerstein.
Racing. *See* **Horse Racing.**
Rackham, Arthur
Inscription for Arthur Rackham's Rip Van Winkle. Flecker.
Radcliffe, James, 3d Earl of Derwentwater
Lord Derwentwater. *Unknown.*
Radio
Broadcast, The. Simons.
Elegy for Helen Trent. Leary.
In Memory of Radio. Jones.
Microphone, The. Van Winkle.
My Radio. Van Winkle.
Next Voice You Hear, The. McDonnell.
Radio, The. Guest.
Radio. Tessimond.
Radio Under the Bed, The. Whittemore.
Sonnet on Turning a Radio Dial. Scruggs.
Ragged Robin (plant)
Ragged Robin and Bouncing Bet. Reid.
Ragwort
Ragwort, The. Clare.
Railroad Trains. *See* **Trains.**
Railroads
Burying Ground by the Ties. *Fr.* Frescoes for Mr. Rockefeller's City. MacLeish.
Casey Jones. *Unknown.*
Crossing. Booth.
Conductor Bradley. Whittier.
D.L. and W.'s Phoebe Snow, The. *Unknown.*
Dr. Fell and Points West. Nash.
Finnigan to Flannigan. Gillilan.
Georgie Allen. *Unknown.*
Great Central Railway, Sheffield Victoria to Banbury. Betjeman.
Guild's Signal. Harte.

I've Been Workin' on the Railroad. *Unknown.*
Joseph Mica. *Unknown.*
Pacific Railway, The. Ballard.
Paddy Works on the Railway. *Unknown.*
Rail-road crossing. *Unknown.*
Railway Junction, The. De la Mare.
Railway Tunnel, The. Scott-Hopper.
Terminal. Shapiro.
There's Many a Man Killed on the Railroad. *Unknown.*
What's the Railroad to Me? Thoreau.
Wreck of Number Nine, The. *Unknown.*
Wreck of the Old 97, The. *Unknown.*

Rain
All Night I Heard. Moffatt.
And Then It Rained. Van Doren.
April Puddle. Bennett.
April Rain. Loveman.
April Rain Song. Hughes.
April Showers. Stephens.
At Dieppe: Rain on the Down. Symons.
Autumn Rain. Fisher.
Autumn Rain. Lawrence.
Before the Rain. Aldrich.
Before the Rain. Rives.
City Rain. Field.
Conversation with Rain. Gunn.
Cycle, The. Roethke.
Dark and Falling Summer, The. Schwartz.
Dark gray clouds, The. Belting.
Deluge. Clare.
Description of a City Shower, A. Swift.
Down the Rain Falls. Coatsworth.
Fallen Rain. Dixon.
First Night of Fall and Falling Rain, The. Schwartz.
Footwear. Justus.
Green Rain. Webb.
How Gray the Rain. Coatsworth.
I Saw God Wash the World. Stidger.
Il pleut doucement sur la ville. Verlaine.
In Time of Silver Rain. Hughes.
Invocation to Rain in Summer. Bennett.
It Is Raining. Mitchell.
It Rains. Thomas.
June Thunder. MacNeice.
Latter Rain, The. Very.
Like the Touch of Rain. Thomas.
Lime Avenue, The. S. Sitwell.
Little Pagan Rain Song. Shaw.
Little Rain. Roberts.
Little Rain, The. Tu Fu.
Little Rain Men. Hussey.
Little Raindrops. Hawkshaw.
London Rain. MacNeice.
Memorial Rain. MacLeish.
Mists and Rain. Baudelaire.
Monsoon. Wevill.
Moods of Rain. Scannell.
Night of Rain. Kenyon.
Ode on Contemplating Clapham Junction. *Fr.* Herman Moon's Hourbook. Middleton.
Ode to Rain. *Unknown.*
Old Man Rain. Cawein.
Ombres Chinoises. Deutsch.
Others. Behn.
Prayer for Rain. Palmer.
Rain. Alling.
Rain. Benediktsson.
Rain. Coxe.
Rain, The. Creeley.
Rain, The. Davies.
Rain. *Fr.* The Boy with a Cart. Fry.
Rain. Henley.
Rain, The. Herbert.
Rain. Kirby.
Rain. Levy.
Rain. "O'Sullivan."
Rain. Parmenter.
Rain. Riley.
Rain. Shaw.
Rain. Stevenson.
Rain. Stoutenberg.
Rain. Taylor.
Rain. Tu Fu.
Rain, The ("Open the window"). *Unknown.*
Rain, The ("The rain came down"). *Unknown.*
Rain. Williams.
Rain. Wing.
Rain. Young.
Rain and the Rainbow, The. Fredericks.
Rain at Night. Homan.
Rain at Night. Hoyt.
Rain at Night, The. Tu Fu.
Rain at Wildwood. Swenson.
Rain in April. Hammond.
Rain in Summer. Longfellow.
Rain in the City. Field.
Rain in the Night. Burr.
Rain in the Southwest. Kelley.
Rain Music. Cotter.
Rain on a Grave. Hardy.
Rain on Castle Island. Hakushu.
Rain on South-East England. Davie.
Rain on the Down. Symons.
Rain on the Roof. Kinney.
Rain, Rain. Akins.
Rain, Rain! *Unknown.*
Rain, Rain, Go Away. *Unknown.*
Rain Riders. Scollard.
Rain Sizes. Ciardi.
Rain Song. Garrigue.
Rain Song, The. Rogers.
Rain-Talk. White.
Raindrops. *Unknown.*
Rains of Spring, The. Lady Ise.
Rainy Day, A. Lincoln.
Rainy Day, The. Tagore.
Rainy Day Song. Storey.
Rainy Summer, The. Meynell.
Redhaw Rain. Sandburg.
Reprieve. Cormack.
Rhyme of Rain. Holmes.
Shower, The. Vaughan.
Signs of Rain. Jenner.
Smoky Smirr o' Rain, The. Hay.
Song of the Rain. McCrae.
Song of the Rain-Chant. *Unknown.*
Sower, The. Figueroa.
Spring Rain. Behn.
Spring Rain. Chute.
Sudden Shower. Clare.
Summer Rain. Coatsworth.
Summer Rain. Lee.
Summer Rain. Merriam.
Summer Rain. Read.
Summer Rain, The. Thoreau.
Sun and Rain. C. G. Rossetti.
Sun-Shower, The. Amabile.
Sunshine after a Shower. *Fr.* On the Approch of Summer. Warton.
There Will Come Soft Rains. Teasdale.
Thunder Pools. Coffin.
Tumult Ends, The. Robinson.
Turn of the Moon. Graves.
Umbrella Brigade, The. Richards.
Umbrellas. Bennett.
Very Lovely. Fyleman.
Way Through, The. Levertov.
Wet Thursday. Kees.
What Could Be Lovelier than to Hear. Coatsworth.
What to Do. Wise.
Who Is Tapping at My Window. Deming.
Who Likes the Rain? Bates.
Who Loves the Rain. Shaw.
Wind and the Rain, The. Frost.
Winter Rain. C. G. Rossetti.
Woodyards in Rain. Marriott.

Rain-in-the-Face (Indian chief)
On the Big Horn. Whittier.
Revenge of Rain-in-the-Face, The. Longfellow.

Rainbirds
Rain-Crow, The. Cawein.

Rainbows
Boats sail on the rivers. *Fr.* Sing-Song. C. G. Rossetti.
Lord of the World, The. Studdert-Kennedy.
Moon Rainbow, A. R. Browning.
My Heart Leaps Up. Wordsworth.
Rainbow, The. Genesis, Bible, *O.T.*
Rainbow, The. Colby.
Rainbow, The. Davies.
Rainbow, The. De la Mare.
Rainbow, The. Keble.
Rainbow, The. Lawrence.
Rainbow, The. McCord.
Rainbow, The. *Fr.* The Angel in the House. Patmore.
Rainbow Fairies, The. Hadley.
Rainbow at night. *Unknown.*
Rainbows. Willson.
To the Rainbow. Campbell.
Raine, Kathleen
For K. R. on Her Sixtieth Birthday. Wilbur.
Rainey, Gertrude (Ma)
Dance for Ma Rainey, A. Young.
Rainier, Mount
Mount Rainier. Bashford.
Ralegh, Sir Walter
Call on Sir Walter Raleigh, A. Piatt.
Conclusion, The. Ralegh.
Elegy, An: "I will not weep, for 'twere as great a sin." King.
Epitaph: On Sir Walter Rawleigh at His Execution. *Unknown.*
First American Sailors, The. Rice.
Lady Ralegh's Lament. R. Lowell.
Silent Lover, The. Ralegh.
Sir Walter Raleigh. *Fr.* In the American Grain. Williams.
Sir Walter Raleigh to a Caged Linnet. Lee-Hamilton.
Sir Walter Rauleigh His Lamentation. *Unknown.*
'Tis pleasant, stretched on grassy lawn. *Fr.* Elizabethan Days. Irwin.
Rameau, Jean Philippe
On an Air of Rameau. Symons.
Ranching and Ranchers. *See* **Farming and Farmers.**
Randolph, John
Randolph of Roanoke. Whittier.
Rats
Jerboa, The. Moore.
Pied Piper of Hamelin, The. R. Browning.
Rat, The. Davies.
Rat, The. Young.
Rat Riddles. Sandburg.
Rats, The. Trakl.
"Trade" Rat. Wallis.
Wanted. Silverstein.
Rattlesnakes
Rattlesnake, The. Carr.
Rattlesnake, The. Purdy.
Rattlesnake, The. *Unknown.*
Ravenglass, England
Ravenglass Railway Station, Cumberland. Nicholson.
Ravens
Advice to a Raven in Russia, December, 1812. Barlow.
Raven. Coleridge.
Raven, The. Poe.
Raven, The. Rich.
Raven, The. Robinson.
Raven and the Fox, The. La Fontaine.
Sycophantic Fox and the Gullible Raven, The. Carryl.
Three Ravens, The. *Unknown.*
Twa Corbies, The. *Unknown.*
Reading
Old Susan. De la Mare.
On a Boy's First Reading of "King Henry V." Mitchell.
On Reading. Aldrich.
Passionate Reader to His Poet, The. Le Gallienne.
Reading the Brothers Grimm to Jenny. Mueller.
To the Reader. Jonson.
When the Mississippi Flowed in Indiana. Lindsay.
Reason
Credibility. Ciardi.
Mock on, Mock on, Voltaire, Rousseau. Blake.
Reason. Hodgson.
Reason. Miles.
Reason and Imagination. *Fr.* Milton. Blake.
Reason, in faith thou art well served, that still. *Fr.* Astrophel and Stella. Sidney.
Reason, the Use of It in Divine Matters. Cowley.
See also **Intellect.**
Reconstruction, United States
Mr. Johnson's Policy of Reconstruction. Halpine.
Old Thad Stevens. Porter.
To the Thirty-ninth Congress. Whittier.
Red Cross
Army of the Red Cross, The. Trask.
Compensation. Mitchell.
Great Cross of Mercy, The. Garrison.
If Ever Time Shall Come. Brown.
League of Love in Action, The. Markham.
Medical Corps, The. Barry.
Red Cross, The. Jacques.
Red Cross, The. Van Dyke.
Red Cross Christmas Seal, The. Garrison.
Red Cross Nurse, The. Thomas.
Red Cross Nurses, The. Masson.
Red Cross Spirit Speaks, The. Finley.
Soldier of the Silences, The. Herschell.
Somebody's Boy. Bates.
Three Crosses, The. Cooke.
Under the Red Cross. Hickox.
Your Cross and My Cross. Cox.
Red Jacket (Indian Chief)
Red Jacket. Halleck.
Red Sea
Parting of the Red Sea, The. *Fr.* Exodus. *Unknown.*
Redbirds. *See* **Cardinal.**
Redwings
Redwing, The. P. Dickinson.
Redwood Trees. *See* **Sequoia Trees.**
Reed, John
Elegies over John Reed. Zaturenska.
Reed, Walter
Walter Reed. R. *and* S. V. Benét.
Refugees
Algerian Refugee Camp, Aïn-Khemouda. Ross.
Banished, The. Serrano Plaja.
One Race, One Flag. Fairburn.
Refugee. Witherspoon.
Refugee Blues. Auden.
Refugee in America. Hughes.
Refugee in New England. F. Frost.
Refugees. Conkling.
Refugees, The. Jarrell.
Refugees. MacNeice.
Refugees, The. Read.
Reindeer
Rigorists. Moore.
Religion
After Lorca. Creeley.
Ballade of the Heresiarchs. Belloc.
Bangkok. Scott.
Black Church on Sunday. Mosley.
Garden of Love, The. *Fr.* Songs of Experience. Blake.
Hind and the Panther, The, *sels.* Dryden.
Kind pity chokes my spleen; brave scorn forbids. Satires, III. Donne.
Love Lifted Me. Leary.
New Sinai, The. Clough.
Religio Laici. Dryden.
Religion. Vaughan.
Religion. Vauquelin de la Fresnaye.
Sir Hudibras's Religion. *Fr.* Hudibras. Butler.
Sunday Morning. Stevens.
There was a Presbyterian cat. *Unknown.*
Religious Verse
Anthology of Catholic Poets, An (ACP). Shane Leslie, ed.
Best Loved Religious Poems, The (BLRP). James Gilchrist Lawson, comp.
Book of Comfort, A (BoC). Elizabeth Goudge, ed.
Catholic Anthology, The (CAW). Thomas Walsh, ed.
Earth Is the Lord's, The (EaLo). Helen Plotz, comp.
Favorite Christian Poems (FaChP). Donald T. Kauffman, ed.
Golden Book of Catholic Poetry, The (GoBC). Alfred Noyes, ed.
Joyce Kilmer's Anthology of Catholic Poets (JKCP). Joyce Kilmer, ed.

Masterpieces of Religious Verse (MaRV). James Dalton Morrison, Ed.
Meditative Poem, the (MeP). Louis L. Martz, ed.
Modern Religious Poems (MoRP). Jacob Trapp, ed.
Oxford Book of Christian Verse, The (OxBoCh). Lord David Cecil, ed.
Poems of Doubt and Belief (PoDB). Tom F. Driver *and* Robert Pack, eds.
Sourcebook of Poetry (SoP). Al Bryant, comp.
Speaker's Treasury of 400 Quotable Poems, The (STF). Croft M. Pentz, comp.
Treasury of Jewish Poetry, A (TrJP). Wathan Ausubel *and* Marynn Ausubel, eds.
Treasury of Poems for Worship and Devotion, A (TrPWD). Charles L. Wallis, ed.
Treasury of Religious Verse, The (TRV). Donald T. Kauffman, comp.
World's Great Religious Poetry, The (WGRP). Caroline Miles Hill, ed.

Renaissance
Exodus from a Renaissance Gallery. Acton.
Renaissance. Avrett.
Renaissance. Davies.

Reptiles
Prayer for Reptiles. Hubbell.

Restaurants
La Carte. Richardson.
R is for the Restaurant. McGinley.

Resurrection, The. *See* **Easter.**

Revenge (ship)
Revenge, The. Tennyson.

Revenge
King Lear Pledges Revenge. *Fr.* King Lear. Shakespeare.

Revere, Paul
Paul Revers's Ride. *Fr.* Tales of a Wayside Inn. Longfellow.

Revolution
Come Here, My Friends. Hall.
For the Truth. Spriggs.
"It is Time for Action." Bennett.
Making of a Militant. Bey.
My Poem. Giovanni.
Poem: "Black Revolution is passing you by." Giovanni.
Revolution!! Thomas.
Semi-Revolution, A. Frost.
Song of Fire, The. Snellings.
Total Revolution, A. Williams.
See also **American Revolution; French Revolution; Russian Revolution.**

Revolution of 1848
At the Sunrise in 1848. D.G. Rossetti.

Revolutionary War, American. *See* **American Revolution.**

Reynolds, Henry
To My Most Dearly-loved Friend, Henry Reynolds, Esquire, of Poets and Poesy. Drayton.

Reynolds, Sir Joshua
Sir Joshua Reynolds. Blake.
Sir Joshua Reynolds. *Fr.* Retaliation. Goldsmith.
Verses on Sir Joshua Reynold's Painted Window at New-College, Oxford. Warton.

Rheims Cathedral
Cathedral of Rheims, The. Rostand.
Cathedral of Rheims, The. Verhaeren.

Rhinoceros
Rhinoceros. Belloc.
Rhinoceros, The. Nash.

Rhode Island
Rhode Island. Brown.

Rhodes, Cecil John
At the Grave of Cecil Rhodes. Jackson.
Burial, The. Kipling.
Resurgat. Cripps.

Rhodora
Rhodora, The. Emerson.

Rhys, Ernest
Autobiography, An. Rhys.

Richard I, King of England (Richard Coeur de Lion)
Coeur de Lion to Berengaria. Tilton.
Crusade, The. Warton.
Prison Song. Richard Coeur de Lion.

Richard II, King of England
Richard II as Captive. *Fr.* The Civil Wars. Daniel.

Richard III, King of England
Tudor Rose, The. *Fr.* The Ship of Fools. Brant.

Richard, Earl of Cornwall
Song of Lewes, The. *Unknown.*

Richardson, Dorothy M.
Lower Criticism, The. Hollander.

Richardson, Samuel
To the Author of *Clarissa.* Edwards.

Riches. *See* **Wealth.**

Richmond, Virginia
Fall of Richmond, The. Melville.

Ridley, Nicholas
Latimer and Ridley. Wordsworth.

Rienzi, Cola di
Rienzi to the Romans. *Fr.* Rienzi. Mitford.

Rifles
Naming of Parts. *Fr.* Lessons of the War. Reed.
Springfield Calibre Fifty, The. Hanson.

Riley, James Whitcomb
To James Whitcomb Riley. Kipling.

Rilke, Rainer Maria
Rilke. Webb.
Straining. Spivack.

Rimbaud, Arthur
Aeterna Poetae Memoria. MacLeish.
Response to Rimbauld's Later Manner. Moore.
Rimbaud. Auden.
Rimbaud and Verlaine, precious pair of poets. *Fr.* Preludes for Mennon. Aiken.
Rimbaud in Africa. Rickword.
To Rimbaud in Hell. Cardarelli.

Riots
Black Cop's Communion, A. Kemp.
New Dance, A. Anderson.
"Oh Shit a Riot." Balagon.
On Riots. Leslie.
Riot. Brooks.

Rivera, Diego
I Paint What I See. White.

Rivers
Blade of Grass Sings to the River, The. Goldberg.
Call of the River Nun, The. Okara.
Elegy: "Clear and gentle stream." Bridges.
Green River. Bryant.
Growing River, The. Bennett.
Musing by a River. Browne.
Negro Speaks of Rivers, The. Hughes.
Repose of Rivers. H. Crane.
River, The. Davie.
River, The. Emerson.
River Afram. Opoku.
River Cherwell, The. Bowles.
River Glideth in a Secret Tongue, The Ostroff.
River God, The. *Fr.* The Faithful Shepherdess. Fletcher.
River God's Song. Ridler.
River Is a Piece of Sky, The. Ciardi.
Rivers. Storer.
Rivers Arise; a Fragment. Milton.
Rivers of the West. "Sunset Joe."
Rivers Remember, The. Turner.
Rivers Unknown to Song. Meynell.
Sailing upon the River. *Fr.* The Borough. Crabbe.
Thus the Mayne Glideth. *Fr.* Paracelsus. R. Browning.
Tide River, The. Kingsley.
To a River in the South. Newbolt.
To the Nile. Shelley.
To the River Otter. Coleridge.
Two Rivers. Emerson.
Two Streams, The. Holmes.
Way to the Sea, The. Lerner.
Where Runs the River. Bourdillon.

Rivière du Loup, Quebec
Off Rivière du Loup. Scott.

Roads
Autostrada, The. Johnson.
Best Road of All, The. Towne.
Creek-Road, The. Cawein.
Joys of the Road, The. Carman.
King's Highway, The. McGroarty.
Little Road, The. Turner.
Merritt Parkway. Levertov.

Roads *(continued)*
Mountain Road, The. Derham.
My Road. Opdyke.
Old Coach Road, The. Field.
Old Road, The. Very.
On the Expressway. Dana.
Path, The. Thomas.
Post-Roads. *Fr.* The Atlas. Slessor.
Road, The. Fletcher.
Road, The. Johnson.
Road, The. Ogarev.
Road, The. Sassoon.
Road Not Taken, The. Frost.
Road Song. Untermeyer.
Road to Town, The. Sarson.
Roads. Dallas.
Roads. Field.
Roads Go Ever Ever On. Tolkien.
Roadways. Masefield.
Rolling English Road, The. Chesterton.
Roman Road, The. Taylor.
Song of the Open Road. Whitman.
Tewkesbury Road. Masefield.
Threnody: "There's a grass-grown road." Harding.
Tree-Top Road, The. Smith.
Turn of the Road, The. Coe.
Turn of the Road, The. Davis.
Walking Road, The. Hughes.
Way through the Woods, The. Kipling.
You Are on U.S. 40 Headed West. White.
Roanoke Island, North Carolina
Mystery of Cro-a-tàn, The. Preston.
Robbers. *See* **Crime and Criminals.**
Robert I *or* **Robert the Bruce, King of Scotland.** *See* **Bruce, Robert.**
Robert I, Duke of Normandy
Legend of Robert, Duke of Normandy, The, *sel.* Drayton.
Robin Goodfellow
Robin Goodfellow. *Unknown.*
Robin Hood
Birth of Robin Hood, The. *Unknown.*
Bold Peddler and Robin Hood, The. *Unknown.*
Death of Robert, Earl of Hungingdon, *sel.* Munday *and* Chettle.
Death of Robin Hood, The. W. R. Benét.
Death of Robin Hood, The. Field.
Death of Robin Hood, The. *Unknown.*
Gest of Robyn Hood, A. *Unknown.*
How Robin Hood Rescued the Widow's Sons. *Unknown.*
In Sherwood lived stout Robin Hood. *Unknown.*
Jolly Pinder of Wakefield, The. *Unknown.*
Little John a Begging. *Unknown.*
Noble Fisherman, The; or, Robin Hood's Preferment. *Unknown.*
Robin Hood. Keats.
Robin Hood and Allen-a-Dale. *Unknown.*
Robin Hood and Guy of Gisborne. *Unknown.*
Robin Hood and Little John. *Unknown.*
Robin Hood and Maid Marian. *Unknown.*
Robin Hood and Queen Katherine. *Unknown.*
Robin Hood and the Beggar, I ("Come light and listen, you gentlemen all"). *Unknown.*
Robin Hood and the Beggar, II ("Lyth and listen, gentlemen"). Unknown.
Robin Hood and the Bishop. *Unknown.*
Robin Hood and the Bishop of Hereford. *Unknown.*
Robin Hood and the Butcher. *Unknown.*
Robin Hood and the Curtal Friar. *Unknown.*
Robin Hood and the Golden Arrow. *Unknown.*
Robin Hood and the Monk. *Unknown.*
Robin Hood and the Pedlars. *Unknown.*
Robin Hood and the Potter. *Unknown.*
Robin Hood and the Prince of Aragon. *Unknown.*
Robin Hood and the Ranger. *Unknown.*
Robin Hood and the Scotchman. *Unknown.*
Robin Hood and the Shepherd. *Unknown.*
Robin Hood and the Tanner. Unknown.
Robin Hood and the Tinker. *Unknown.*
Robin Hood and the Two Priests. *Unknown.*
Robin Hood and the Valiant Knight. *Unknown.*
Robin Hood and the Widow's Three Sons. *Unknown.*
Robin Hood Newly Revived. *Unknown.*
Robin Hood Rescuing the Widow's Three Sons. *Unknown.*
Robin Hood Rescuing Three Squires. *Unknown.*
Robin Hood Rescuing Will Stutly. *Unknown.*
Robin Hood's Birth, Breeding, Valor, and Marriage. *Unknown.*
Robin Hood's Chase. *Unknown.*
Robin Hood's Death. *Unknown.*
Robin Hood's Delight. *Unknown.*
Robin Hood's End. *Unknown.*
Robin Hood's Golden Prize. *Unknown.*
Robin Hood's Progress to Nottingham. *Unknown.*
Song of Sherwood, A. Noyes.
True Tale of Robin Hood, A. *Unknown.*
Robins
Autumn Robin, The. Clare.
Birds. "O'Neill."
Cat and the Bird, The. Canning.
Come Here Little Robin. *Unknown.*
Come Hither, Sweet Robin. *Unknown.*
Death and Burial of Cock Robbin, The. *Unknown.*
Epitaph on a Robin Redbreast, An. Rogers.
First Robin, The. Leveridge.
Gay Robin Is Seen No More. Bridges.
Golden-Robin's Nest, The. Chadwick.
Little Robin Redbreast came to visit me. *Unknown.*
Lost—Three Little Robins. *Unknown.*
Red Robin, The. Clare.
Redbreast Chasing a Butterfly, The. Wordsworth.
Robin, The. Alma-Tadema.
Robin, The. Bent.
Robin, A. De la Mare.
Robin. Payne.
Robin, The. *Unknown.*
Robin, The. Very.
Robin and Man. Gordon.
Robin and the Cows, the. Howells.
Robin and the Wren, The. *Unknown.*
Robin is a Gabriel, The. Dickinson.
Robin is the one, The. Dickinson.
Robin Redbreast. Allingham.
Robin Redbreast. Doane.
Robin Red Breast. Weeden.
Robin Redbreasts, The. Hawkshaw.
Robin to His Mate, The. Carter.
Robin's Come. Caldwell.
Robin's Egg, The. Dalton.
Robin's Epitaph, A. Rogers.
Robin's Secret. Bates.
Robin's Song. Bennett.
Robin's Song. King.
Secret, The. *Unknown.*
Sir Robin. Larcom.
Song of the Robin, The. Bergquist.
Tampa Robins. Lanier.
Three Things to Remember. Blake.
To a Robin. Daly.
To Robin Red-Breast. Herrick.
To the Redbreast. Bampfylde.
What Robin Told. Cooper.
When the snow is on the ground. *Unknown.*
Why the Robin's Breast Was Red. Randall.
Wrens and Robins. *Fr.* Sing-Song. C. G. Rossetti.
Robinson Crusoe
Crusoe. McLaren.
Robinson Crusoe Returns to Amsterdam. *Fr.* Amsterdam. Jammes.
Robinson Crusoe's Story. Carryl.
Robots
Man from the Top of the Mind, The. Wagoner.
Rocks. *See* **Stones and Rocks.**
Rocky Mountains
David. Birney.
Lines on Mountain Villages. "Sunset Joe."
On Recrossing the Rocky Mountains after Many Years. Frémont.
Rodney, Caesar
Rodney's Ride. Brooks.
Rodney, George Brydges, Rodney 1st Baron
Rodney's Glory. O'Sullivan.
Roentgen, Wilhelm Conrad
Walk in Würzburg, A. Plomer.

Rockefeller Center, New York City
I Paint What I See. White.
Roethke, Theodore
On the Death of Theodore Roethke. Witherup.
Roethke. Healy.
Roller-coasters
Flight of the Roller-Coaster. Souster.
Rolvaag, Ole Edvart
No Gull's Wings. Engle.
Roman Catholic Church. *See* **Catholicism.**
Rome
Against the Court of Rome. Petrarch.
Amours de Voyage. Clough.
Appian Way, The. Johnson.
Boy from Rome, Da. Daly.
For the New Railway Station in Rome. Wilbur.
Oh Rome! My Country! *Fr.* Childe Harold's Pilgrimage. Byron.
Roma. Rutilius.
Roma Aeterna. Crapsey.
Roma Mater Sempaeterna. O'Sheel.
Rome. Du Bellay.
Rome. Hardy.
Rome. Menendez y Pelayo.
Rome Remember. Keyes.
Ruins of Rome. Du Bellay.
Ruins of Rome. Dyer.
Trastevere. Denby.
Villa Sciarra; Rome. Curtis.
Wars worse then civil on Thessalian plains. *Fr.* Pharsalia. Lucan.
Romeo and Juliet
Play, The. *Fr.* The Sentimental Bloke. Dennis.
Romney Marsh, England
In Romney Marsh. Davidson.
Romulus and Remus
Romulus and Remus. Kipling.
Ronsard, Pierre de
Ronsard. deFord.
Roosevelt, Franklin Delano
At Warm Springs. W. R. Benét.
Danish Wit. Hollander.
Homage to Our Leaders. Symons.
When Death Came April Twelve 1945. Sandburg.
Roosevelt, Theodore
Close Up the Ranks. Van Zile.
Great-Heart. Kipling.
Man, A. Scollard.
Our Colonel. Guiterman.
Pilgrimage. Parmenter.
Pilot and Prophet. Towne.
Prophet, The. Clark.
Roosevelt. Davis.
Roosevelt. Fandel.
Roosevelt. Thomas.
Sagamore. Robinson.
Star, The; Dedicated to Theodore Roosevelt, Following His Death, January 6, 1919. Smith.
Theodore Roosevelt. Cole.
To Theodore Roosevelt. Darío.
Valiant for Truth. Robinson.
With the Tide. Wharton.
Roosters. *See* **Cocks.**
Rope
Ropewalk, The. Longfellow.
Rosamond (Fair Rosamond)
Complaint of Rosamond, The. Daniel.
Rosemary
Rosemary Spray, The. Góngora.
Roses
Ah me, if I grew sweet to man. Field.
Autumn Rose-Tree, An. Earls.
Ballad: White Rose. S. Sitwell.
Bowl of Roses, A. Henley.
Branch of the Sweet and Early Rose. Drennan.
Briar-Rose. *Unknown.*
Bunch of Roses, A. Tabb.
Cliff Rose, The. Fewster.
Dramas of the Rose. Schevill.
Fable XLV: Poet and the Rose, The. Gay.
Fancy from Fontenelle, A. Dobson.
Florist Rose, The. Graves.
Gold-of-Ophir Roses. Dennen.
Green and Red and Darkness. Scott.
How Roses Came Red. Herrick.
I Never See the Red Rose Crown the Year. Masefield.
I'll Tell you whence the Rose did first grow red. Strode.
Landscape as Metal and Flowers. Scott.
Legend of the Christmas Rose, The. Davis.
Little Rose Is Dust, My Dear, The. Conkling.
Little Rose Tree, The. Field.
Moss-Rose, The. Newbolt.
O, how much more doth beauty beauteous seem. Sonnets, LIV. Shakespeare.
On a Rosebud Sent to Her Lover. *Unknown.*
Overnight, a Rose. Giltinan.
Poor Withered Rose. Bridges.
Ramblers, The. Linton.
Rosarie, The. Herrick.
Rose, A. Bates.
Rose, The. *Fr.* Visions. Browne.
Rose, A. Fanshawe.
Rose, The. Goethe.
Rose, The. Hammond.
Rose, The. Howell.
Rose, The. Lovelace.
Rose, The. Ronsard.
Rose. Swinburne.
Rose. Thompson.
Rose and Root. Piatt.
Rose and the Thorn, The. Hayne.
Rose and the Wind, The. Marston.
Rose Family, The. Frost.
Rose Is a Royal Lady, The. Blanden.
Rose Song, The. Vincente.
Roses. "Eliot."
Roses. Ronsard.
Roses. Stanley.
Roses Are Beauty, but I Never See. Masefield.
Roses in December. Studdert-Kennedy.
Roses on the Breakfast Table. Lawrence.
Roses Only. Moore.
Sick Rose, The. *Fr.* Songs of Experience. Blake.
Song: "When the Rose came I loved the Rose." O'Shaughnessy.
Sweet is the rose, but grows upon a brere. *Fr.* Amoretti. Spenser.
Sweet Violets, Love's Paradise. *Unknown.*
There's Nothing like the Rose. C. G. Rossetti.
'Tis the Last Rose of Summer. Moore.
To a Rose. Sherman.
To a Rose. Tabb.
To a Wild Rose Found in October. Clarke.
To a Withered Rose. Bangs.
To Roses in the Bosom of Castara. *Fr.* Castara. Habington.
To the Rose. *Fr.* Hymns of Astrea. Davies.
To the Rose; Song. Herrick.
To the Rose upon the Rood of Time. Yeats.
Violet and the Rose, The. Skipsey.
Violet and the Rose, The. Webster.
White Rose, A. O'Reilly.
White Roses. Fabbri.
White Roses. Rhys.
Wild Rose. Allingham.
Wild Roses. Fawcett.
Wild Roses. Newsome.
Ross, Betsy
Betsy's Battle Flag. Irving.
Rossetti, Christina Georgina
To Christina Rossetti. Greenwell.
To Christina Rossetti. Watson.
Rossetti, Dante Gabriel
At the Grave of Dante Gabriel Rossetti. Bell.
Voice of D. G. R., The. Gosse.
Rousseau, Jean Jacques
Mock On, Mock On, Voltaire, Rousseau. Blake.
Royal George (ship)
On the Loss of the *Royal George.* Cowper.
Royal Society
To the Royal Society. Cowley.
Rubinstein, Anton Grigoryevich
Rubinstein Staccato Etude, The. Dett.

Rugby
Rugby League Game. Kirkup.
Russell, Lucy, Countess of Bedford
On Lucy Countess of Bedford. Jonson.
To Lucy, Countess of Bedford, with Mr. Donne's Satires. Jonson.
To the Countesse of Bedford on New-Yeares Day. Donne.
To the Excellent and Most Accomplish'd Lady, Lucy, Countess of Bedford. *Fr.* Mortimeriados. Drayton.
To the Lady Lucy, Countess of Bedford. Daniel.
Russia
Advice to a Raven in Russia, December, 1812. Barlow.
At the Top of My Voice. Mayakovsky.
Capitals Are Rocked, The. Nekrasov.
Hymn, A: "Lord, give them freedom who are weak." Nekrasov.
Land of Masters. Lermentov.
My Country. Lermontov.
November 7th. "Neruda."
On Reading a Soviet Novel. Fuller.
Russia. Blok.
Russia. Dole.
Russia. Napier.
Sestina for Khasan Israelov. *Fr.* Wildtrack. Wain.
Song to the Soviet Union. Crespo.
To Russia. Miller.
Russian Revolution
All Is Sold. "Akhmatova."
Revolution, The. Shkulev.
Sons of Our Sons, The. Ehrenburg.
Twelve, The. Blok.
Russians
Old Peasant Woman at the Monastery of Zagorsk. Schevill.
Rostov. Fraser.
We Grow Out of Iron. Gastev.
Ruth (Biblical)
Immigrant, The. Kendon.
Rutledge, Ann
Anne Rutledge. *Fr.* Spoon River Anthology. Masters.
Rydal Water, England
Sunrise on Rydal Water. Drinkwater.

S

Sabbath
Come, O Friend, to Greet the Bride. Heine.
How Sweet Thy Precious Gift of Rest. Menahem ben Makhir of Ratisbon.
Keep Ye Holy Sabbath Rest. *Unknown.*
Light and Rejoicing to Israel. *Unknown.*
Outgoing Sabbath. *Unknown.*
Princess Sabbath. Heine.
Queen Sabbath. Bialik.
Sabbath, The. Grahame.
Sabbath, My Love. Halevi.
Sabbath of Rest, A. Luria.
Some keep the sabbath going to church. Dickinson.
Summer Sabbath. Sampter.
Thou Beautiful Sabbath. *Unknown.*
Welcome, Queen Sabbath. Schneour.
See also **Sunday.**
Sacajawea
Sa-Ca-Ga-We-A. Proctor.
Sacco-Vanzetti Case
Justice Denied in Massachusetts. Millay.
Sacco Writes to His Son. Lewis.
Sagamore Hill, Oyster Bay, Long Island
Sagamore. Robinson.
Sagittarius (constellation)
Sagittarius or the Archer. MacLeod.
Sahara Desert
Desert Travellers, The. Lerner.
Sailing and Sailors
Alarmed Skipper, The. Fields.
At Sea. Rogers.
Ave Sanctissima. *Unknown.*
Beach Burial. Slessor.
Becalmed. Blight.
Birlinn Chlann-Raghnaill. MacDonald.
Bloody Bill. Ross.
Boatman's Hymn. *At. to* Magrath.
Chief Petty Officer. Causley.
Child and the Mariner, The. Davies.
Clipper Captain. Barker.
Coasters, The. Day.
Coming around the Horn. *Unknown.*
Drowned Mariner, The. Smith.
Drowned Seaman, The. Goldring.
Dutch Seamen and New Holland, The. Reeves.
Epitaph for a Sailor Buried Ashore. Roberts.
Falmouth. Henley.
Fiddler's Green. Roberts.
First American Sailors, The. Rice.
Flying Cloud, The. *Unknown.*
Forging of the Anchor, The. Ferguson.
Forty Singing Seamen. Noyes.
Frankie's Trade. Kipling.
Good Play, A. Stevenson.
Hakluyt Unpurchased. McDuffee.
Harp Song of the Dane Women. Kipling.
Homeward Bound. Allingham.
Homeward Bound. Rogers.
"How's My Boy?" Dobell.
In the Trades. Smith.
It's cold, says Crean at the tiller. *Fr.* Worsley Enchanted. Stewart.
Jack Was Every Inch a Sailor. *Unknown.*
Jovial Marriner, The; or, The Sea-Man's Renown. Playford.
Landfall in Unknown Seas. Curnow.
Life on the Ocean Wave, A. Sargent.
Long Trail, The. Kipling.
Lords of the Main. Stansbury.
Mariners. Morton.
Mariners, The. Woods.
Mariner's Dream, The. Dimond.
Mariners' Song. *Fr.* Death's Jest Book. Beddoes.
Mariner's Song, The. Davies.
Men behind the Guns. Rooney.
Messmates. Newbolt.
Nanny's Sailor Lad. Allingham.
Norse Sailor's Joy. Thorley.
Ode for a Master Mariner Ashore. Guiney.
Off Rivière du Loup. Scott.
Offshore. Booth.
Old Grey Squirrel. Noyes.
Old Quartermaster, The. Grant.
Old Song Re-sung, An. Masefield.
Over Bright Summer Seas. Hillyer.
Pageant of Seamen, The. Byron.
Peg-Leg's Fiddle. Adams.
Pier. Scully.
Quaker Graveyard in Nantucket, The. R. Lowell.
Rambling Sailor, The. Mew.
Rime of the Ancient Mariner, The. Coleridge.
Rounding the Horn. *Fr.* Dauber. Masefield.
Sail, A. Lermontov.
Sailboat, Your Secret. Francis.
Sailing at Dawn. Newbolt.
Sailing beyond Seas. Ingelow.
Sailing, Sailing. Burr.
Sailing to an Island. Murphy.
Sailor, The. Allingham.
Sailor. Hughes.
Sailor, The. MacDonald.
Sailor. Page.
Sailor, The. Warner.
Sailors, The. Woestijne.
Sailor's Consolation, The. Pitt.
Sailors for My Money. Parker.
Sailor's Wife, A. Bernhardt.
Sailor's Wife, The. Mickel.
Salcombe Seaman's Flaunt to the Proud Pirate, The. *Unknown.*
Say That He Loved Old Ships. Hicky.
Sea-Fever. Masefield.
Sea Gypsy, The. Hovey.
Sea Song, A. Cunningham.
Sea Urge. *Unknown.*
Seafarer, The. *Unknown.*
Seumas Beg. Stephens.
Shipman, The. *Fr.* The Canterbury Tales. Chaucer.
Silence of God, The. O. Sitwell.

Son of the Sea, A. Carman.
Song: "To all you ladies now at land." Sackville.
Song for All Seas, All Ships. Whitman.
Storm at Sea. Davenant.
Southerly. Brady.
Spring Sailing. Leonidas.
Symphony in Gray Major. Darío.
Tacking Ship off Shore. Mitchell.
Vacationer. Gibson.
Voyage, The. Tennyson.
Wet Sheet and a Flowing Sea, A. Cunningham.
What the Red-haired Bo'sun Said. Souter.
Where Lies the Land? Clough.
Who Pilots Ships. Hicky.
Windlass Song. Allingham.
Yankee Privateer, The. Hale.
Yankee Thunders. *Unknown.*
Ye Mariners of England. Campbell.
Eternal Sea, The; an Anthology of Sea Poetry (EtS). W. M. Williamson, ed.
See also **Sea Chanteys.**

St. Agnes Eve
Eve of St. Agnes, The. Keats.
St. Agnes' Eve. Tennyson.

Saint Bartholomew's Eve
For St. Bartholomew's Eve. Cowley.

St. Clair, Arthur
Sainclare's Defeat. *Unknown.*

Saint Croix, (island), Virgin Islands
Beauties of Santa Cruz, The. Freneau.

Saint John, New Brunswick
Saint John, The. Clarke.
Ships of Saint John, The. Carman.

Saint Keyne's Well, Cornwall
Well of St Keyne, The. Southey.

Saint Leger, Barry
Saint Leger. Scollard.

St. Louis, Missouri
Sunset; St. Louis. Teasdale.

St. Michael's Mount, England
St. Michael's Mount. Davidson.

Saint Peter, Lake, Quebec
Wreck of the *Julie Plante*, The. Drummond.

Saint Valentine's Day. *See* **Valentine's Day.**

Sainte Anne des Monts, Quebec
Bells of Ste. Anne des Monts, The. Cox.

Saints
Any Saint. Thompson.
Nameless Saints, The. Hale.
Saints. Garrett.
Why Do I Use My Paper, Ink, and Pen. *Unknown.*

Salamanders
Salamander. Rukeyser.

Salamis, Battle of
Salamis. *Fr.* Persians. Aeschylus.

Salem, Massachusetts
Salem. R. Lowell.
Salem. Stedman.
Salems of Oppression. Keith.
Ship Comes In, A. Jenkins.

Salerno, Italy
Above Salerno. Murray.

Salmon
Salmon Drowns Eagle. Lowry.
Sockeye Salmon. Hambleton.

Salt
Salt. Francis.

Salt Lake City, Utah
Salt Lake City. Carruth.

Salvation Army
General William Booth Enters into Heaven. Lindsay.
We'll Roll the Golden Chariot Along. *Unknown.*

Samarkand
Golden Journey to Samarkand, The. Flecker.

Samson (Bible)
How Samson Bore Away the Gates of Gaza. Lindsay.
Samson. Scott.
Samson Agonistes. Milton.

Samuel (Bible)
What now? Thou look'st surprised. *Fr.* Saul. Heavysege.

San Blas, Mexico
Bells of San Blas, The. Longfellow.

San Francisco, California
Book Buying in the Tenderloin. Hass.
City: San Francisco. Hughes.
Great Chinese Dragon, The. Ferlinghetti.
Resurge San Francisco. Miller.
Returned to Frisco, 1946. Snodgrass.
San Francisco. Cheney.
San Francisco. Miller.
San Francisco. Roberts.
Scenic. Updike.
Seal Rocks: San Francisco. Conquest.
To San Francisco. Alexander.
Trip: San Francisco. Hughes.

San Gabriel, Mission of, California
Bells of San Gabriel, The. Stoddard.

San Jacinto, Battle of
Fight at San Jacinto, The. Palmer.

San Juan Capistrano Mission, California
San Juan Capistrano. Cooper.
Swallows, the/ returned at dawn today. Giorno.

San Miguel, Mexico
Streets of San Miguel, The. Wilson.

Sancho Panza
Sancho. Collin.

Sand, George
George Sand. Parker.

Sand
Culbin Sands. Young.
Sand-between-the-Toes. Milne.
White Sand and Grey Sand. *Unknown.*

Sandpipers
Sandpiper. Bishop.
Sandpiper, The. Bynner.
Sandpiper, The. Thaxter.
Sandpipers. Egerton.
Sandpipers. Sandburg.
Summer's Early End at Hudson Bay. Carruth.

Sandy Hook, New Jersey
Sandy Hook. Houghton.

Sandys, George
To My Honoured Friend Mr. George Sandys. King.
To My Worthy Friend Master Geo. Sandys. Carew.

Santa Barbara, California
Santa Barbara. Browne.
Santa Barbara Beach. Torrence.

Santa Claus
Boy Who Laughed at Santa Claus, The. Nash.
Conversation between Mr. and Mrs. Santa Claus. Bennett.
Death of Santa Claus, The. Starrett.
Kris Kringle. Scollard.
Kriss Kringle. Aldrich.
Mrs. Santa Claus' Christmas Present. Morris.
Old Santa Is an Active Man. Lenski.
Real Santa Claus, A. Sherman.
Santa Claus. *Unknown.*
Santa Claus and the Mouse. Poulsson.
Visit from St. Nicholas, A. Moore.
When Santa Claus Comes. *Unknown.*

Santa Fe, New Mexico
Spring Morning—Santa Fé. Riggs.

Santa Fé Trail
Effortlessly Democratic Santa Fe Trail. Baird.
Old Santa Fé Trail, The. Burton.

Santayana, George
For George Santayana. R. Lowell.
Upon the Death of George Santayana. Hecht.

Santiago de Cuba
Charge at Santiago, The. Hayne.
Deeds of Valor at Santiago. Scollard.
Santiago. Janvier.
Spain's Last Armada. Rice.

Santos, Brazil
Arrival at Santos. Bishop.

Sappho
Sapphics. Swinburne.
Sappho. Catullus.
Sappho. Cope.
Sappho Rehung. Smith.
Sappho's Tomb. Stringer.

Sappho *(continued)*
Sisters, The. A. Lowell.
Saracens
War Song of the Saracens. *Fr.* Hassan. Flecker.
Sarajevo, Yugoslavia
Sarajevo. Durrell.
Saratoga, New York
Field of the Grounded Arms, The. Halleck.
Sardanapulus
Sardanapulus. Surrey.
Sarsfield, Patrick, Earl of Lucan
Ballad of Sarsfield, A De Vere.
Farewell, O Patrick Sarsfield. *Unknown.*
Sarto, Andrea del
Andrea del Sarto. R. Browning.
Sassafras
Sassafras. Peck.
Witchwood. Justus.
Satan
Address to the Deil. Burns.
Dark Angel, The. Johnson.
Devil, The. *Unknown.*
Devil and the Angel, The, *sels.* Dobson.
Devil's Walk on Earth, The. Southey.
Epilogue: "Truly, my Satan, thou art but a dunce." *Fr.* The Gates of Paradise. Blake.
Fall of Satan, The. *Fr.* The Flaming Terrapin. Campbell.
Fallen Angels. *Fr.* Paradise Lost. Milton.
Faust, *sels.* Goethe.
Fulness of Time, The. Stephens.
Litany to Satan. Baudelaire.
Lucifer. Anderson.
Lucifer. Cameron.
Lucifer. Lawrence.
Lucifer in Starlight. Meredith.
Lucifer in the Train. Rich.
Man's Amazement. *Unknown.*
Sir, I commend you to the spirit. *Fr.* Divine Poems. Villa.
Top Hat and Tales. Beers.
Whale, The. *Fr.* Physiologus. *Unknown.*
When Satan Fell. Lawrence.
Satellites
Little Satellite. Krows.
Satie, Erik
Three Organ Rituals for Erik Satie. Kelly.
Satire
I first adventure with foolhardy might. *Fr.* Virgidemiarum. Hall.
Satire: "Satire, my friend ('twixt me and you)." Geddes.
Satire should be like the porcupine, The. *Fr.* Virgidemiarum. Hall.
Satiric Verse
Absalom and Achitophel, Pt. I. Dryden.
Absalom and Achitophel, Pt. II, *sels.* Tate *and* Dryden.
Absolute and Abitofhell. Knox.
Adam and God. Wilkinson.
All Men Are Free! Napier.
American Primitive. Smith.
Anatomy of Humor, The. Bishop.
Anno 1829. Heine.
Anthologistics. Guiterman.
Antichrist, or the Reunion of Christendom; an Ode. Chesterton.
Art for Art's Sake. *Fr.* The Cradle Will Rock. Blitzstein.
Ataraxia. Taylor.
Awake! Walther von der Vogelweide.
Baylon and Sion. Camoes.
Bagpipe Music. MacNeice.
Baker's Duzzen uv Wize Sawz, A. Sill.
Ballad of the Good Lord Nelson, A. Durrell.
Ballade of Suicide, A. Chesterton.
Ballade of Unfortunate Mammals. Parker.
Bankers Are Just Like Anybody Else, except Richer. Nash.
Base Details. Sassoon.
Battle of Blenheim, The. Southey.
Beasts' Confession, The. Swift.
Beau, The. *Unknown.*
Beau's Receipt for a Lady's Dress, The. *Unknown.*
Beautiful Young Nymph Going to Bed, A. Swift.
Bells of Heaven, The. Hodgson.
Beppo. Byron.
Bewick Finzer. Robinson.
Blind Men and the Elephant, The. Saxe.
Book of How, The. Moore.
Boom! Nemerov.
Boy and the Schoolmaster, The. La Fontaine.
Brass Spittoons. Hughes.
Britannia Rules of Orthography. "Firth."
Bunthorne's Song. *Fr.* Patience. Gilbert.
But hark! What hubbub now is this that comes. *Fr.* The Temple of Infamy. Harpur.
Cambridge Ladies, The. Cummings.
Canadian Authors Meet, The. Scott.
Canopus. Taylor.
Captain Carpenter. Ransom.
Carol with Variations. McGinley.
Charcoal-Seller, The. Po Chü-i.
Child of the Romans. Sandburg.
Clean Curtains. Sandburg.
Clever Tom Clinch Going to Be Hanged. Swift.
Cockerel, the Cat, and the Young Mouse, The. La Fontaine.
Coda. Parker.
Cologne. Coleridge.
Come Live with Me and Be My Love. Day Lewis.
Companions. Calverley.
Congress, 1878. Montagne.
Contentment. *Fr.* The Autocrat of the Breakfast Table. Holmes.
Conundrum of the Workshops, The. Kipling.
Country Club Sunday. McGinley.
Country Justice, The. Langhorne.
Country Mouse, The. Cowley.
Crocodile, The. *Fr.* Alice's Adventures in Wonderland. "Carroll."
Crossroads. Silva.
Cultural Notes. Fearing.
Dawn. Baudelaire.
Debutantrum. W. R. Benét.
Departed Friend, The. Novo.
Dirge: "1-2-3 was the number he played but today the number came 3-2-1." Fearing.
Discovery. Freneau.
Does It Matter? Sassoon.
Don'ts. Lawrence.
Drugstore. Weaver.
Duke of Plaza-Toro, The. *Fr.* The Gondoliers. Gilbert.
During Lambing Season. Rhys.
Elegy on a Lap Dog, An. Gay.
Enfant perdu. Heine.
England and America. Stephen.
English Bards and Scotch Reviewers, *sels.* Byron.
Epistle III: "Pult'ney, methinks you blame my breach of word." Gay.
Epistle to Dr. Arbuthnot, An. Pope.
Epistle to Miss Blount. Pope.
Epitaph, An: "Interred ebeneath this marble stone." Prior.
Etiquette. Gilbert.
Evening Primrose, The. Parker.
Exit God. Bradford.
Experience. Parker.
Fable: "Mountain and the squirrel, The." Emerson.
Family Fool, The. *Fr.* The Yeoman of the Guard. Gilbert.
Farmhands' Refrain. Lewis.
Fighting Words. Parker.
Flower Market, The. Po Chü-i.
For One Who Would Not Be Buried in Westminster Abbey. Pope.
For whiles I mark this weak and wretched world. *Fr.* The Steel Glass. Gascoigne.
"Forever." Calverley.
Frescoes for Mr. Rockefeller's City. MacLeish.
Friar Lubin. Marot.
Friend of Humanity and the Knife Grinder, The. Canning *and* Frere.
Furniture of a Woman's Mind, The. Swift.
Godolphin Horne. Belloc.
Golf Links, The. Cleghorn.
Good and Bad Luck. Hay.
Good Rich Man, The. Chesterton.
Gray Squirrel, The. Wolfe.
Heaven. Brooke.
Here Lies a Lady. Ranson.

Higher Pantheism in a Nutshell, The. Swinburne.
Homage. Fearing.
Horace Paraphrased. Watts.
Horrors of Civil War, The. Horace.
House of Lords, The. *Fr.* Iolanthe. Gilbert.
How Beastly the Bourgeois Is. Lawrence.
How to Raise a Son. Martial.
Hudibras, *sels.* Butler.
Hybris, Nemesis, One, Two, Three. Ostriker.
I Paint What I See. White.
I Wonder What Became of Rand, McNally. Levy.
In Church. Hardy.
In Ciprium. Davies.
In Gerontem. Davies.
In Hardin County, 1809. Thompson.
In Haywodum. Davies.
In Rufum. Davies.
In Severum. Davies.
In the Great Metropolis. Clough.
In Titum. Davies.
In Westminster Abbey. Betjeman.
Indignation. Hugo.
Italy. Filicaja.
Japanese, The. Nash.
Joe Greene. Moore.
Journey to Exeter, A. Gay.
Kings of the Rainy Country, The. Baudelaire.
Ko-Ko's Song. *Fr.* The Mikado. Gilbert.
Lady's Dressing Room, The. Swift.
Latest Decalogue, The. Clough.
Letter to Hitler, A. Laughlin.
Lie, The. Ralegh.
Little Billee. Thackeray.
London. *Fr.* Songs of Experience. Blake.
London. Johnson.
London Is a Fine Town. *Unknown.*
Lovers, The. Aiken.
MacFlecknoe; or, A Satire upon the True-Blue Protestant Poet, T. S. Dryden.
Male and Female Created He Them. Huxley.
Man in the Bowler Hat, The. Tessimond.
Man of Culture, A. Tessimond.
Memorial Rain. MacLeish.
Memorial to the Great Big Beautiful Self-sacrificing Advertisers. Ebright.
Message to Siberia. Pushkin.
Mews Flat Mona. Plomer.
Miniver Cheevy. Robinson.
Miniver Cheevy, Jr., *parody.* Parry.
Mrs. Brown and the Famous Author. King.
Mrs. Frances Harris's Petition. Swift.
Modern Major-General, The. *Fr.* The Pirates of Penzance. Gilbert.
Mouse That Gnawed the Oak-Tree Down, The. Lindsay.
Museums. MacNeice.
My Country 'Tis of Thee. Bierce.
Nephelidia. Swinburne.
Next to of Course God. Cummings.
Nightmare Number Four. Bloch.
Nobody Loses All the Time. Cummings.
Now You're Content. Spire.
Oh Come, Little Children. McGinley.
Obit on Parnassus. Fitzgerald.
Ode Inscribed to W. H. Channing. Emerson.
Of Tabacco. Davies.
Of the Characters of Women. *Fr.* Moral Essays. Pope.
Of the Mean and Sure Estate. Wyatt.
Of the Use of Riches. *Fr.* Moral Essays. Pope.
Old Grimes. Greene.
On an Old Woman. Lucilius.
On Charles II. Rochester.
On Some South African Novelists. Campbell.
On the Bad Government of Toledo. Manrique.
On the Birth of His Son. Su T'ung-po.
Ozymandias. Shelley.
Pamphlet. Marín.
Parley of Beasts. "MacDiarmid."
Passion of M'Phail, The, *sels.* Gregory.
People, The. Campenella.
Petit Testament, Le. Villon.
Pity This Busy Monster, Manunkind. Cummings.
Plato Told. Cummings.
Playboy of the Demi-World, The, 1938. Plomer.
Poem for Mother's Day. Fishback.
Poem, or Beauty Hurts Mr. Vinal. Cummings.
Poems in Praise of Practically Nothing, *sels.* Hoffenstein.
Political Chaos in Italy. Dante.
Poor, The. Verhaeren.
Portrait. Fearing.
Post-Impressionism. Taylor.
Progress. Hoffenstein.
Progress of Beauty, The. Swift.
Progress of Dullness, The, *sels.* Trumbull.
Progress of Marriage, The. Swift.
Progress of Poetry, The. Swift.
Rape of the Lock, The. Pope.
Razor Seller, The. "Pindar."
Reasonable Affliction, A. Prior.
Recitation and Song. *Fr.* Patience. Gilbert.
Refugee Blues. Auden.
Relations. Tassoni.
Restricted. Merriam.
Résumé. Parker.
Rich Man, The. Adams.
Richard Cory. Robinson.
Rooster, The. Orlovitz.
Russia. Blok.
SOS. Fearing.
Sabbath-Day Chace. Freneau.
Sail, A. Lermontov.
Salesman Is an It That Stinks Excuse, A. Cummings.
Satire against Manking, A. Rochester.
Satire on Paying Calls. Ch'eng Hsiao.
Satires, *sels.* Donne.
Satires, *sels.* Horace.
Satires, *sels.* Persius.
Satires, *sels.* Juvenal.
Satires of Circumstance, *sels.* Hardy.
Satirical Elegy on the Death of a Late Famous General, A. Swift.
Satyr Address'd to a Friend That Is About to Leave the University, and Come Abroad in the World, A, *sel.* Oldham.
Satyrical Elegy on the Death of a Late Famous General, 1722, A. Swift.
Scarlet Woman, The. Johnson.
Scourge of Villany, The, The, *sels.* Marston.
Season 'Tis, My Lovely Lambs, The. Cummings.
Ship of Fools, The, *sels.* Brandt.
Short Song of Congratulation, A. Johnson.
Siege of Ismail, The. *Fr.* Don Juan. Byron.
Sir Christopher Wren. Bentley.
Sir Joseph's Song. *Fr.* H.M.S. Pinafore. Gilbert.
Skialetheia, *sels.* Guilpin.
Soldier Boy, The. Runeberg.
Some Beautiful Letters. Parker.
Song to the Men of England. Shelley.
Sorrows of Werther. Thackeray.
Spider and the Fly, The, *sel.* Heywood.
Strong Hand, A. Hill.
Stupidity Street. Hodgson.
Syracusan Women, The. *Fr.* Idylls. Theocritus.
Thalia. Aldrich.
There Lived a King. *Fr.* The Gondoliers. Gilbert.
Thought, A. Lermontov.
Thrushes. Wolfe.
To a Fat Lady Seen from the Train. Cornford.
To a Louse. Burns.
To a Plagiarist. Ibn Ezra.
To an Ungentle Critic. Graves.
To Italy. Leopardi.
To Master Everard Digby. Lodge.
To Theodore Roosevelt. Darío.
Tourist Time. Scott.
Town-Meeting, A. *Fr.* M'Fingal. Trumbull.
Tract. Williams.
Travel Bureau, The. Mitchell.
Treason. Harington.
Tropic Siesta. López.
Trumpets of the Mind, The. Hugo.
Two Confessions. *Fr.* The Vision of Piers Plowman. Langland.
Tunnyng of Elynour Rummyng, The, *sels.* Skelton.

Satiric *(continued)*
Under Which Lyre. Auden.
Unknown Citizen, The. Auden.
Upon a Dead Man's Head. Skelton.
Valentine for a Lady, A. Lucilius.
Vanity of Human Wishes, The. Johnson.
Verses on the Death of Dr. Swift. Swift.
Victory Dance, A. Noyes.
Virgidemiarum, *sels.* Hall.
Virtuous Fox and the Self-righteous Cat, The. Cunningham.
Vision of Judgment, The. Byron.
Waifs and Strays. Rimbaud.
War Is Kind. S. Crane.
Warning for Abraham Lincoln, A. Fombona Pachano.
Wayzgoose, The, *sel.* Campbell.
We Have Been Here Before. Bishop.
Were I a King. Vere.
What Mr. Robinson Thinks. *Fr.* The Biglow Papers. J. R. Lowell.
When a Man Hath No Freedom to Fight for at Home. Byron.
Where the Cedars. Glatstein.
White Christmas. Rodgers.
Wicked Treasonable Libel, A. Swift.
Wine and Water. *Fr.* The Flying Inn. Chesterton.
With Freedom's Seed. Pushkin.
Woman. Fu Hsüan.
World State, The. Chesterton.
Your Excellency. Giusti.
Zeuxis, the painter, strove in vain. *Fr.* The Romance of the Rose. Jean de Meun.
Book of Humorous Verse, The (BOHV). Carolyn Wells, comp.
Innocent Merriment; an Anthology of Light Verse (InMe). Franklin P. Adams, comp.
Pith and Vinegar (PV). William Cole, ed.
Silver Treasury of Light Verse, The (SiTL). Oscar Williams, ed.
See also **Parodies.**

Satsuma Peninsula, Japan
Sunrise in the Hills of Satsuma. Fenollosa.

Saturday Review, The (magazine)
Saturday Review, The. Cole.

Satyrs
Crackling Twig, The. Stephens.
Satyr, The. Stephens.
Satyrs and the Moon, The. Gorman.

Saul (Bible)
Dance of Saul with the Prophets, The. Tchernichowsky.
In guilty night & his in false disguise. *Unknown.*
Saul. Alterman.
Saul. R. Browning.
Saul, *sels.* Heavysege.
Saul. Sterling.
Song of Saul before His Last Battle. Byron.

Savannah, Georgia
About Savannah. *Unknown.*
Savannah. Burroughs.

Savile, Henry
To Sir Henrie Savile. Jonson.

Scarecrows
Lonely Scarecrow, The. Kirkup.

Scarlatti, Alessandro
Sonata by Scarlatti, A. Heath-Stubbs.

Schoenberg, Arnold
Ode to Arnold Schoenberg. Tomlinson.

Scholars and Scholarship
Andrew M'Crie. Murray.
Clerk of Oxenford, The. *Fr.* The Canterbury Tales. Chaucer.
Clerk Ther Was of Caunterbrigge Also, A. Skeat.
End of April, The. Murray.
For My Students, Returning to College. Williams.
Grammarian's Funeral, A. R. Browning.
"If, Jerusalem, I Ever Should Forget Thee." Heine.
In the Lecture Room. *Fr.* Cressida. Baxter.
Letter to a Teacher of English. Hillyer.
My Days among the Dead are Past. Southey.
Ode on the Despoilers of Learning in an American University (1947), An. Winters.
On Taking a Bachelor's Degree. Smart.
Poor Scholar, The. Ibn Chasdai.
Poor Scholar of the Forties, A. Colum.
Scholar, The. Southey.
Scholar and His Dog, A. Marston.
Scholar and the Cat, The. *Unknown.*
Scholar Complains, The. *Unknown.*
Scholar-Gypsy, The. Arnold.
Scholar in the Narrow Street, The. Tso Ssu.
Scholars, The. Yeats.
Scholar's Life, The. *Fr.* The Vanity of Human Wishes. Johnson.
Schools. *Fr.* The Borough. Crabbe.
Sons of Our Sons, The. Ehrenburg.
Talmud Student, The. Bialik.
To a Friend, on Her Examination for the Doctorate in English. Cunningham.
Treasure, A. Whittemore.
See also **Teaching and Teachers; Students.**

School
After School: Room Three. Stafford.
At School-Close. Whittier.
At This Farewell. Wordsworth.
Big Brother. Roberts.
Classroom in October. Lieberman.
Collegiate Angels, The. Alberti.
Country School. Curnow.
Departed Friend, The. Novo.
Education. Miles.
Elementary School Class Room in a Slum, An. Spender.
Exercise Book. Dehn.
Farm Boy after Summer. Francis.
First Departure. F. Frost.
Getting Back. Thompson.
Goodbye to Regal. Huws.
In a Girls' School. Morton.
In School-Days. Whittier.
Monday morning back to school. McCord.
Ode on a Distant Prospect of Clapham Academy. Hood.
Old Brown Schoolhouse, The. *Unknown.*
Patrick Goes to School. Aspinwall.
School and Schoolfellows. Praed.
School Begins. Price.
School-Bell. Farjeon.
School Is Out. F. Frost.
Schoolboy, The. *Fr.* Songs of Experience. Blake.
School Boy Reads His Iliad, The. Morton.
Schoolboys in Winter. Clare.
Schoolmistress, The. Shenstone.
Schoolroom on a Wet Afternoon. Scannell.
Schools. *Fr.* The Borough. Crabbe.
School's Out. Davies.
Sing-Song Rhyme. *Unknown.*
Tom Brainless at College. *Fr.* The Progress of Dulness. Trumbull.
Under All This Slate. Hayford.
See also **Colleges and Universities.**

Schoolmasters. *See* **Teaching and Teachers.**

Schubert, Franz
Schubert's Ninth Symphony. Stanley-Wrench.

Schwartz, Delmore
To Delmore Schwartz. R. Lowell.

Science
Coy nature (which remain'd, though aged grown). *Fr.* Ode Upon Dr. Harvey. Cowley.
Dr. Sigmund Freud Discovers the Sea Shell. MacLeish.
Epitaph: "Nature and Nature's laws lay hid in night." Pope.
Hymn to Science. Akenside.
In an Age of Science. Clark.
Laboratory Poem. Merrill.
Letter to Alex Comfort. Abse.
Man of Science Speaks, The. Monroe.
New Sinai, The. Clough.
Old Astronomer to His Pupil, The. Williams.
Patient Scientists, The. Woods.
Revelation. Keesing.
Sonnet to Science. *Fr.* Al Aaraaf. Poe.
To My Honoured Friend Dr. Charleton. Dryden.
V. B. Nimble, V. B. Quick. Updike.
Imagination's Other Place (ImOP). Helen Plotz, comp.

Science Fiction
Science Fiction. Amis.
Holding Your Eight Hands (HYE). Lucie-Smith, ed.

Scorpions
Scorpion, The. Plomer.

Scotland
Bagpipe Music. MacNeice.
Before Bannockburn. Burns.
Bluebells of Scotland, The. *Unknown.*
Complaint of the Common Weill of Scotland. Lindsay.
Cotter's Saturday Night, The. Burns.
Deirdre's Farewell to Alba. *Unknown.*
In City Streets. Smith.
Meditation of a Patriot. Fraser.
My Heart's in the Highlands. Burns.
Ode on the Popular Superstitions of the Highlands of Scotland, An. Collins.
On Scotland. Cleveland.
Patriot, The. *Fr.* The Lay of the Last Minstrel. Scott.
Scotland. Gray.
Scots Wha Hae. Burns.
Tears of Scotland, The. Smollett.
Golden Treasury of Scottish Poetry, The (GoTS). Hugh MacDiarmid, ed.
Oxford Book of Scottish Verse, The (OxBS). John MacQueen *and* Tom Scott, comps.
Scots, The
Gathering, The. *Fr.* Towards the Last Spike. Pratt.
Scott, Sir Walter
On Scott's Poem "The Field of Waterloo." Erskine.
Scott, Winfield
Hero of Bridgewater. Jones.
Scott and the Veteran. Taylor.
Scottish Border
Lock the Door, Lariston. Hogg.
Scottsboro Case
Communication to Nancy Cunard, A. Boyle.
They Are Ours. Magil.
Trial, The. Rukeyser.
Scribes
Scribe, The. *Unknown.*
Sculpture and Sculptors
Archaic Torso of Apollo. Rilke.
Arundel Tomb, An. Larkin.
Carrara. Murray.
Carver and the Rock Are One, The. Brigham.
Crack, The. Goldman.
Medici Tombs, The. Ross.
On a Bas-Relief. Trimpi.
On Seeing the Elgin Marbles. Keats.
Prisoner, The—Galleria dell' Academia. Stark.
Proem, A: "When in my walks I meet some ruddy lad." Ward.
Sculptors, The. Purdy.
Statue, The. Fuller.
Statuette: Late Minoan. Day Lewis.
Venus of Bolsover Castle, The. S. Sitwell.
Sea
Absences. Larkin.
Amoris Exsul: In the Bay. Symons.
At Melville's Tomb. H. Crane.
At Sainte-Marguerite. Stickney.
At Sea. Rogers.
At the Seaside. Stevenson.
At the Slackening of the Tide. Wright.
Bathymeter. Hart-Smith.
Beautiful Proud Sea. Teasdale.
Break, Break, Break. Tennyson.
Breeze is sharp, the sky is hard and blue, The. *Fr.* Sonnets. Tuckerman.
By the Sea. Dixon.
By the Sea. Hollander.
By the Sea. C. G. Rossetti.
Calm, The. Donne.
Cemetery by the Sea, The. Valéry.
Chime of the Sea. D. G. Rossetti.
Christmas at Sea. Stevenson.
Cold Divinities, The. Wright.
Coming Homeward Out of Spain. Googe.
Coral Grove, The. Percival.
Coral Reef, The. Lieberman.
Crab. Blight.
Dancing Sea, The. *Fr.* Orchestra. Davies.
Dover Beach. Arnold.
Drama. Hart-Smith.
East Anglian Bathe. Betjeman.
Evening by the Sea. Swinburne.
Eye, The. Jeffers.
Face, The. Muir.
Face of the Waters, The. Fitzgerald.
Father's Testament, A. Ibn Tibbon.
Five Visions of Captain Cook. Slessor.
Forgotten Objects on a Beach. Excell.
Grave, A. Moore.
Gravedigger, The. Carman.
Grim and Gloomy. Reeves.
He Who Loves the Ocean. Leitch.
Her Heards Be Thousand Fishes. *Fr.* Colin Clout's Come Home Again. Spenser.
Hills and the Sea. Campbell.
Horses of the Sea, The. C. G. Rossetti.
I started early, took my dog. Dickinson.
I will go back to the great sweet mother. *Fr.* The Triumph of Time. Swinburne.
Iphione. Irwin.
Kraken, The. Tennyson.
La Mer. Wilde.
Last Chantey, The. Kipling.
Leave-taking, A. Broome.
Lighthouse Keeper's Offspring, The. Broughton.
Main-Deep, The. Stephens.
Man Whom the Sea Kept Awake, The. Bly.
Moon is distant from the sea, The. Dickinson.
Neither Out Far nor in Deep. Frost.
Northern Seas. Howitt.
November Surf. Jeffers.
Ocean, The ("Roll on, thou deep and dark blue Ocean—roll!"). *Fr.* Childe Harold's Pilgrimage. Byron.
Ocean. Jeffers.
Ocean, The. Moschus.
Ocean. Stoutenburg.
Ocean Burial, The. Chapin.
Ocean Spills, The. Hoffenstein.
Ocean to Cynthia, The. Ralegh.
Ocean Wood, The. De Tabley.
Ode: "I am the spirit of the morning sea." Gilder.
Ode to the Sea. Baker.
Off Saguenay. Bailey.
On the Sea. Keats.
Once by the Pacific. Frost.
Open Sea, The. Mackellar.
Open Sea, The. Meredith.
Oread. Doolittle.
Out of the Cradle Endlessly Rocking. Whitman.
Patrolling Barnegat. Whitman.
Pebbles. Melville.
Pines and the Sea, The. Cranch.
Plague of Dead Sharks. Dugan.
Purse, The—Seine. Blackburn.
Quaker Graveyard in Nantucket, The. R. Lowell.
Rime of the Ancient Mariner, The. Coleridge.
Salt Garden, The. Nemerov.
Sea, The. "Cornwall."
Sea, The. H. Crane.
Sea, The. Frankenberg.
Sea, The. Gorter.
Sea, The. Lawrence.
Sea, The. Stoddard.
Sea, The. *Fr.* The Triumph of Time. Swinburne.
Sea, The. *Unknown.*
Sea and Shore. Koopman.
Sea and the Eagle, The. Clouts.
Sea and the Hills, The. Kipling.
Sea and the Skylark, The. Hopkins.
Sea Born. Vinal.
Sea Call. Widdemer.
Sea-Change. Masefield.
Sea-Change. Taggard.
Sea-Chronicles. Ingamells.
Sea Dirge. Archias of Byzantium.
Sea Dirge, A. "Carroll."
Sea Eats the Land at Home, The. Awoonor.
Sea Fever. Masefield.
Sea Gods. Doolittle.
Sea-Grief. O'Reilly.
Sea Gypsy, The. Hovey.
Sea Irony. Heaton.
Sea Island Miscellany, *sels.* Blackmur.

Sea *(continued)*
Sea-Limits, The. D. G. Rossetti.
Sea Longing. Vinal.
Sea Lullaby. Wylie.
Sea Pieces. Fitzgerald.
Sea retains such images, The. *Fr.* Europe. Dudek.
Sea Ritual, The. Darley.
Sea Song. *Fr.* Death's Jest Book. Beddoes.
Sea Song. Holland.
Sea-Song. McLeod.
Sea-Song from the Shore, A. Riley.
Sea Sonnet. Lay.
Sea Surface Full of Clouds. Stevens.
Sea, the sea, The. Alberti.
Sea Urge. *Unknown.*
Sea-Way. Cortissoz.
Sea-Wind. Mallarmé.
Seafarer, The. *Unknown.*
Sea's Spell, The. Spalding.
Seascape. Auden.
Seascape. Spender.
Sea-Shore. Emerson.
Seaward. Thaxter.
Seaweed. Longfellow.
Secret of the Sea, The. Longfellow.
Shell, The. Stephens.
Silences. Pratt.
Ship and the Sea, The. Baughan.
Shore Scene. Logan.
Sketch. Sandburg.
Slow Pacific Swell, The. Winters.
Son of the Sea, A. Carman.
Song for All Seas, All Ships. Whitman.
Song from the Ship. *Fr.* Death's Jest Book. Beddoes.
Song of the Sea. Burton.
Song of the Sea. *Unknown.*
Song of the Wave, A. Lodge.
Sonnet on the Sea. Keats.
Sound of the Sea, The. Longfellow.
Southerly. Brady.
Stone-Age Sea, The. Hoyt.
Storm, The. Donne.
Storm at Sea, A. *Unknown.*
This Air That Blows In from the Sea. Coatsworth.
Tide Rises, the Tide Falls, The. Longfellow.
To Sea! To Sea! *Fr.* Death's Jest Book. Beddoes.
Told by Seafarers. Kinnell.
Training. Demetrio.
Twilight at Sea. Welby.
Two Old Men Look at the Sea. Hervey.
Upon the Shore. Bridges.
Uses of Ocean. Seaman.
View of the Sea, A. Mabuchi.
Visiting Sea, The. Meynell.
Wanderer's Song, A. Masefield.
Wave. Guest.
Waves. Emerson.
Waves Gleam in the Sunshine, The. *Fr.* Songs to Seraphine. Heine.
Waves on the Sea-Shore, The. Hawkshaw.
Wet Sheet and a Flowing Sea, A. Cunningham.
Who Pilots Ships. Hicky.
Winter Views Serene. *Fr.* The Borough. Crabbe.
Wonders of the Deep, The. Parmentier.
World below the Brine, The. Whitman.
Would I Might Go Far over Sea. O'Shaughnessy.
Young Sea. Sandburg.
Zennor. Ridler.
Eternal Sea, The (ETS). W. M. Williamson, ed.
Sea Chanteys
American Sea Songs and Chanteys (AmSS). Frank Shay, ed.
Shantymen and Shantyboys (ShS). William Main Doerflinger, comp.
Song of American Sailormen (SoAmSa). Joanna C. Colcord, ed.
Sea Gulls. *See* **Gulls.**
Sea Serpents
Sea Serpant, The. Irwin.
Sea Shells. *See* **Shells.**
Sea Voyages. *See* **Voyages.**
Seals
Dancing Seal, The. Gibson.
Dead Seal. Purdy.
Hymn to the Seal. Smith.
Ice-Floes, The. Pratt.
Off Spectacle Island. Eberhart.
Performing Seal, The. Field.
Seal. Smith.
Seal Lullaby. Kipling.
Seals, The. Aldis.
Seals in Penobscot Bay, The. Hoffman.
Seasons
Against Seasons. Mezey.
Four Seasons. Bennett.
Four Seasons of the Year, The. Bradstreet.
Frost at Midnight. Coleridge.
Human Seasons, The. Keats.
Hymn on the Seasons, A. *Fr.* The Seasons. Thomson.
Is Life Worth Living? Austin.
Love Song, A. Hawley.
Pencil and Paint. Farjeon.
Procession, The. Widdemer.
Seasons, The. Cheney.
Seasons, The. Humphries.
Seasons, The, *sels.* Kalidasa.
Seasons, The. Roberts.
Seasons. C. G. Rossetti.
Seasons of the Soul. Tate.
Sing a Song of Seasons! Stevenson.
Solace. Delany.
Song for the Seasons, A. "Cornwall."
Song of the Four Seasons, A. Dobson.
Song of the Seasons. Lofton.
Song of the Seasons, A. Monkhouse.
Sonnet: "Quickly and pleasantly the seasons blow." Hillyer.
Summer sunshine,/ Autumn gold. Lathbury.
Three Seasons. C. G. Rossetti.
Wheel, The. Yeats.
While Immortality Endures. Briggs.
Winter Will Follow. Dixon.
Year, The. Patmore.
Sing a Song of Seasons (SiSoSe). Sara Brewton *and* John E. Brewton, comps.
Year Around, The (YeAr). Alice I. Hazeltine *and* Elva S. Smith, eds.
Second World War. *See* **World War, Second.**
Secretaries
Secretary. Hughes.
Sedition
Medal, The; a Satire against Sedition. Dryden.
Seed
Baby Seed Song. Nesbit.
In the Heart of a Seed. Brown.
Seed Leaves. Wilbur.
Seed Shop, The. Stuart.
Seeds. De la Mare.
Seeds. Stuart.
Seeds. Webster.
Sowing Seeds. Cornwall.
To a Maple Seed. Mifflin.
Segovia, Spain
Segovia and Madrid. Cooke.
Selkirk, Alexander
Verses Supposed to Be Written by Alexander Selkirk. Cowper.
Selkirk Mountains, British Columbia
In the Selkirks. Scott.
Semele
Ambrosia of Dionysius and Semele, The. Graves.
Semmerwater (lake), England
Ballad of Semmerwater, The. Sir William Watson.
Senancour, Etienne Pivert de
Stanzas in Memory of the Author of "Obermann." Arnold.
Seneca
Picture of Seneca Dying in a Bath. Prior.
Seneca. Merton.
Seneca Lake, New York
To Seneca Lake. Percival.
Sennacherib, King of Assyria
Destruction of Sennacherib, The. Byron.
Separation
After the Supper and Talk. Whitman.

By Return Mail. Aldridge.
Division, The. Hardy.
Farewell, A. Fairburn.
Farewell, A. Patmore.
Forsaken. Schneour.
In Exile. Baughan.
Journey Onwards. Moore.
Letter to Her Husband, Absent upon Public Employment, A. Bradstreet.
Meeting, The. Rukeyser.
On Parting with Moses ibn Ezra. Halevi.
Parting. "Æ."
Parting, The. *Fr.* Cressida. Baxter.
Parting, The. Drayton.
Parting. Halevi.
Parting. Massey.
Parting. Roscoe.
Parting after a Quarrel. Tietjens.
Parting Gift. Wylie.
Remembrance. E. Brontë.
Separation, A. Cory.
Separation. Merwin.
Strange. Burnshaw.
Sundered. Zangwill.
V-Letter. Shapiro.
When We Two Parted. Byron.

September
Another September. Kinsella.
In a September Night. Home.
In September. Hammond.
In September. Ledwidge.
Man's Bread, A. Peabody.
Remember September. Justus.
Rondel for September. Baker.
September. Arnold.
September. Fallis.
September. Jackson.
September. Lampman.
September. Reed.
September Afternoon. Carpenter.
September in Australia. Kendall.
September in the Park. Snodgrass.
Tell Me Not Here, It Needs Not Saying. Housman.
To the Month of September. *Fr.* Hymns of Astraea. Davies.

Sequoia Trees
Redwoods, The. Simpson.
Summit Redwood, The. Jeffers.
Washington Sequoia, The, *sel.* Shinn.

Serfs. *See* **Slavery.**

Servants
Familiar Faces, Long Departed. Hillyer.

Service (plant)
Life of Service, The. Davie.

Settle, Elkanah
Og and Doeg. *Fr.* Absalom and Achitophel. Dryden.

Seurat, Georges
Seurat. Schevill.

Severn (river), England
Playmates, The. Watson.
Severn, The. *Fr.* The Baron's War. Drayton.

Seville, Spain
Seville. Walters.

Sewall, Samuel
Samuel Sewall. Hecht.

Sewing
Crewel. Willard.
Instruction. Hall.
My Needle Says. Hall.
Needle, The. Woodworth.
Needle Travel. Patton.
Pocket Handkerchief to Hem, A. *Fr.* Sing-Song. C. G. Rossetti.
Three Seamstresses, The. Peretz.

Seymour, Edward, Duke of Somerset
On Edward Seymour, Duke of Somerset. *Unknown.*

Seymour, Jane
Death of Queen Jane, The. *Unknown.*

Shadows
Calculation, The. Wagoner.
Child and the Shadow, The. Jennings.
Could It Have Been a Shadow? Shannon.
Countershadow, The. Booth.
I Heard a Noise and Wished for a Sight. *Unknown.*
Lecture upon the Shadow, A. Donne.
My Shadow. Stevenson.
My Swinging Shadow. Coplen.
Shadow. Bruce.
Shadow. De la Mare.
Shadow, The. Stoddard.
Shadow Dance. Eastwick.
Shadow to Shadow. Allen.
Shadows, The. Duncan.
Shadows in the Water. Traherne.

Sadrach, Meshach and Abed-nego. *See* **Three Holy Children.**

Shadwell, Thomas
MacFlecknoe; or, A Satire upon the True-Blue Protestant Poet, T. S. Dryden.
Og and Doeg. *Fr.* Absalom and Achitophel. Dryden.

Shaftesbury, Anthony Ashley Cooper, 1st Earl of
Achitophel. *Fr.* Absalom and Achitophel. Dryden.
Ballad upon the Popish Plot, A. Gadbury.
Dutchess of Monmouth's Lamentation for the Loss of Her Duke, The. *Unknown.*

Shakers (religious group)
Meditation by Mascoma Lake. Babcock.

Shakespeare, William
Ad Gulielmum Shakespeare. Weever.
At Stratford-on-Avon. Bell.
Before Rereading Shakespeare's Sonnets. Moore.
Ben Jonson Entertains a Man from Stratford. Robinson.
Breath of Avon, The. Watts-Dunton.
By Deputy. Adcock.
Charms of Nature, The. Warton.
Elegy on Shakespeare. Basse.
Epitaph on the Admirable Dramatic Poet, William Shakespeare, An. Milton.
For My Shakespeare Class. Adrian.
Guilielmus Rex. Aldrich.
Mary Shakespeare. Jackson.
On Mr. Wm. Shakespeare. Basse.
On Shakespeare. Milton.
On Sitting Down to Read "King Lear" Once Again. Keats.
On the Portrait of Shakespeare Prefixed to the First Folio Edition, 1623. Jonson.
On the Site of a Mulberry-Tree; Planted by Wm. Shakespeare; Felled by the Rev. F. Gastrell. D. G. Rossetti.
Pete the Parrot and Shakespeare. Marquis.
Progress of Poesy, The. Gray.
Prologue Spoken by Mr. Garrick at the Opening of the Theatre in Drury Lane, 1747. Johnson.
Remembrance of Some English Poets, A. Barnfield.
Schoolroom: 158. Warren.
Shakespeare. Arnold.
Shakespeare. Blood.
Shakespeare. Lee.
Shakespeare. Longfellow.
Shakespeare. Sterling.
Shakespeare. Watson.
Shakespeare; an Epistle to Mr. Garrick. Lloyd.
Shakespeare and Milton. Landor.
Shakespeare Dead. Holland.
Shakespeare, Possibly, in California. Whittemore.
Shakespeare's Mourners. Tabb.
Sonnet to Shakespeare. Holland.
Spirit of Shakespeare, The. Meredith.
To an Artist, to Take Heart. Bogan.
To Master W. Shakespeare. Freeman.
To Our English Terence, Mr. Will. Shakespeare. Davies of Hereford.
To Shakespeare. H. Coleridge.
To Shakespeare. H. Crane.
To Shakespeare. Day.
To Shakespeare. Edwards.
To Shakespeare. Kemble.
To the Memory of Master W. Shakespeare. "I. M."
To the Memory of My Beloved Master William Shakespeare. Jonson.
To the Memory of the Deceased Author Master W. Shakespeare. Digges.
To the Reader. Jonson.
Two Argosies. Bruce.

Shakespeare *(continued)*
Upon the Lines and Life of the Famous Scenic Poet, Master William Shakespeare. Holland.
When I Read Shakespeare. Lawrence.
William Shakespeare. *Fr.* Sonnets on English Dramatic Poets. Swinburne.
William Shakespeare to Mrs. Anne, Regular Servant to the Rev. Mr. Precentor of York. Gray.
Shamrocks
Green Little Shamrock of Ireland, The. Cherry.
Shamrock, The. *Unknown.*
Shannon (ship)
Chesapeake and *Shannon.* *Unknown.*
Shannon and the *Chesapeake,* The. Bouvé.
Shapiro, Karl
V-Letter to Karl Shapiro in Australia. Rodman.
Sharecroppers
Down on Roberts' Farm. Reeves.
Sharks
Birth of a Shark, The. Wevill.
Maldive Shark, The. Melville.
Rhyme of the Chivalrous Shark, The. Irwin.
Shark, The. Pratt.
Sharks, The. Levertov.
Shark's Parlor, The. Dickey.
Sharp, William. *See* **"Macleod, Fiona."**
Shaw, George Bernard
Heartbreak House. P. Dickinson.
Shaw, Robert Gould
My Hero; to Robert Gould Shaw. Brawley.
Ode, An: On the Unveiling of the Shaw Memorial on Boston Common. Aldrich.
Ode in Time of Hesitation, An. Moody.
Robert Gould Shaw. Dunbar.
Shays's Rebellion
Radical Song of 1786, A. Honeywood.
Sheep
Ariel. Campbell.
Black Sheep. Burton.
Child's Pet, A. Davies.
Derby Ram, The. *Unknown.*
Eighteen-ninety. Shipp.
Happy Sheep, The. Thorley.
Homecoming of the Sheep, The. Ledwidge.
Look at Sheep. Thomas.
Rocky Mountain Sheep, The. Austin.
Shearing. Wright.
Sheep. Davies.
Sheep. Hoffenstein.
Sheep, The. "O'Sullivan."
Sheep. Porter.
Sheep, The. Taylor.
Sheep and Lambs. Tynan.
Sheep in Winter. Clare.
Sheep-washing, The. *Fr.* The Seasons. Thomson.
Sheepherders
Tom Farley. Thiele.
Sheep-Herder, The. Clark.
Sheepherder, The. Sarett.
Sheep Herders. Lesemann.
Shepherd, The. Gilmore.
See also **Shepherds and Shepherdesses.**
Sheepshearing
Click Go the Shears, Boys. *Unknown.*
Flash Jack from Gundagai. *Unknown.*
Shearer's Song, The. *Unknown.*
Sheffield, John, Duke of Buckingham and Normanby
My Lord All-Pride. Rochester.
Shelley, Mary Wollstonecraft
To Mary. Shelley.
Shelley, Percy Bysshe
Cor Cordium. Swinburne.
Fishes and the Poet's Hands, The. Yerby.
General Public, The. S. V. Benét.
Lines Written in a Blank Leaf of the Prometheus Unbound. Beddoes.
Man Whom Men Deplore, A. Kreymborg.
Memorabilia. R. Browning.
Percy Bysshe Shelley. *Fr.* Five English Poets. D. G. Rossetti.
Percy Shelley. Bishop.
Rome. Hardy.
Shelley. Japp.
Shelley's Centenary. Watson.
Shelley's Skylark. Hardy.
To Percy Shelley. Hunt.
To Shelley. Tabb.
Wiser than the Children of Light. Gibbon.
Shells
Broken Shell. Scott.
Chambered Nautilus, The. *Fr.* The Autocrat of the Breakfast Table. Holmes.
Child with Shell. Everson.
Enduring Music, The. Vinal.
Frutta di Mare. Scott.
I have the shells now in a leather box. Jennings.
Lonely Shell, The. Perry.
Mantelpiece of Shells, A. Todd.
Palace. Johnson.
Sea Shell. Hardy.
Sea Shell. A. Lowell.
Sea-Shell Murmurs. Lee-Hamilton.
Sea Shells. Scollard.
Shell, The. Stephens.
Shell, The. *Fr.* Maud. Tennyson.
Shells. Raine.
Shells. Wordsworth.
Shell's Song, The. Keats.
Wanderer, The. Field.
With a Nantucket Shell. Webb.
Wonder Shell, The. Holender.
Shenandoah River
Shenandoah. *Unknown.*
Shenandoah Valley, Virginia
Portent, The. Melville.
Shenandoah. Sandburg.
Shepherds and Shepherdesses
Blow, shepherds, blow your pipes with gladsome glee resounding. *Unknown.*
Colin Clout's Come Home Again, *sels.* Spenser.
Damon and Cupid. Gay.
Eclogues, *sels.* Vergil.
Egloga Secunda: "My beasts, go feed upon the plain." Googe.
Eighth Eclogue, The. *Fr.* The Shepherd's Garland. Drayton.
Fourth Egloge of Alexander Barclay, The. Barclay.
Friday; or, The Dirge. *Fr.* The Shepherd's Week. Gay.
Gentle Shepherd, The, *sels.* Ramsay.
Green Shepherd, The. Simpson.
Herd Boy, The. Long.
Herdsman, The. *Fr.* The Idylls. Theocritus.
Little Shepherd's Song, The. Percy.
Long, Long Ago. *Unknown.*
Michael. Wordsworth.
Moonlight. . .Scattered Clouds. *Fr.* The Farmer's Boy. Bloomfield.
Nod. De la Mare.
Nymph's Reply to the Shepherd, The. Ralegh.
Passionate Shepherd to His Love, The. Marlowe.
Pastoral. *Fr.* The Passionate Shepherd. Breton.
Phillida's Love-Call to Her Corydon, and His Replying. *Unknown.*
Phoebe on Latmus. *Fr.* Endimion and Phoebe. Drayton.
Saturday; or, The Flights. *Fr.* The Shepherd's Week. Gay.
Second Shepherds' Play, The. *Unknown.*
Sheepheards Daffadill, The. Drayton.
Shepheardes Calender, The, *sels.* Spenser.
Shepheards, The. Vaughan.
Shepherd, The. *Fr.* Songs of Innocence. Blake.
Shepherd. Blunden.
Shepherd, The. *Fr.* The Prelude. Wordsworth.
Shepherd and the Hawk, The. Hart-Smith.
Shepherd Boy, The. O'Brien.
Shepherd Boys, The. Saboly.
Shepherd of Meriador, The. Childe.
Shepherd Speaks, The. Erskine.
Shepherdess, The. Meynell.
Shepherds, The. Portor.
Shepherd's Dream, A. Breton.
Shepherd's Gift, A. Anyte.
Shepherd's Holiday. Wylie.
Shepherd's Hut, The. Young.
Shepherd's Lament, The. Goethe.

Shepherd's Wife's Song, The. *Fr.* Greene's Mourning Garment. Greene.
Son of the Mountain. Wyn.
Song: "One day the god of fond desire." Thomson.
Southwestern Night. Chavez.
Terly Terlow. *Unknown.*
Thistledown. Reese.
Thursday; or, The Spell. *Fr.* The Shepherd's Week. Gay.
Thus, Thus Begin. *Fr.* Pan's Anniversary. Jonson.
To the Most Excellent and Learned Shepherd, Colin Clout. *Fr.* Chloris. Smith.
Unknown Shepherd's Complaint, The. Barnfield.
What Pleasure Have Great Princes. *Unknown.*
Ye goatherd gods, that love the grassy mountains. *Fr.* Arcadia. Sidney.
Young Shepherd Bathing His Feet. Clarke.
See also **Sheepherders.**

Sheridan, Philip Henry
Sheridan at Cedar Creek. Melville.
Sheridan's Ride. Read.

Sheridan, Thomas
Mary the Cook-Maid's Letter to Dr. Sheridan. Swift.

Sherman, William Tecumseh
Marching through Georgia. Work.
Sherman. Gilder.
Sherman's in Savannah. Holmes.
Sherman's March to the Sea. Byers.
Song of Sherman's Army, The. Halpine.

Shiloh, Battle of
Shiloh. Melville.

Ships
Aboard at a Ship's Helm. Whitman.
After the Sea-Ship. Whitman.
As the proud horse, with costly trappings gay. *Fr.* The Shipwreck. Falconer.
Big Steamers. Kipling.
Building of the Ship, The. Longfellow.
By the Deep Nine. Pearce.
Cargoes. Masefield.
Choosing a Mast. Campbell.
Clinker, The. *Unknown.*
Clipper Ships and Captains. S. V. Benét.
Dismantled Ship, The. Whitman.
Famous Fight at Malago, The; or The Englishmen's Victory over the Spaniards. *Unknown.*
Forging of the Anchor, The. Ferguson.
Freighter. Ruddick.
Garden of Ships, The. Stewart.
George Aloe and the *Sweepstake*, The. *Unknown.*
Golden Vanity, The. *Unknown.*
High Barbaree. *Unknown.*
Joyfull New Ballad, A. Deloney.
Kilmeny. Noyes.
Lament for the Great Yachts. P. Dickinson.
Leave Her, Johnny. *Unknown.*
Leave-taking, A. Broome.
Liner She's a Lady, The. Kipling.
Lover Compareth His State to a Ship in Perilous Storm Tossed on the Sea, The. Wyatt.
Lustily, lustily, lustily let us sail forth. *Fr.* Common Conditions. *Unknown.*
Marooned. Field.
Merchantmen, The. Davidson.
My Brigantine. *Fr.* The Water Witch. Cooper.
My Ship. Leamy.
Nautical Ballad, A. Carryl.
Nocturne of the Wharves. Bontemps.
North Ship, The. Larkin.
O Gentle Ships. Meleager.
O Ship, Ship, Ship. *Fr.* Songs in Absence. Clough.
Old Ironsides. Holmes.
Old Ships, The. Flecker.
Old Ships. Ginsberg.
Old Ships. Morton.
Passer-by, A. Bridges.
"S.S.R., Lost at Sea."—The Times. Gustafson.
She Is Far from the Land. Hood.
Ship, The. Mackay.
Ship, The. Mifflin.
Ship, The. Squire.
Ship and Her Makers, The. Masefield.
Ship and the Sea, The. Baughan.
Ship Bottom. Lattimore.
Ship Comes In, A. Jenkins.
Ship near Shoals. Wickham.
Ship of Rio, The. De la Mare.
Ship Sails Up to Bideford, A. Asquith.
Ship That Never Returned, The. *Unknown.*
Ship That Sails, The. *Unknown.*
Ships, The. Bell.
Ships. Masefield.
Ships. Turner.
Ships at Sea. Gray.
Ship's Bell. Dresbach.
Ships in Harbour. Morton.
Ships of Yule, The. Carman.
Silver Ships. Meigs.
Sir Andrew Barton. *Unknown.*
Song for All Seas, All Ships. Whitman.
South Street. Falkenbury.
Stone Fleet, The. Melville.
Tacking Ship off Shore. Mitchell.
Tanker. Middleton.
Wanderer, The. Masefield.
Where Lies the Land? Clough.
Where Lies the Land to Which Yon Ship Must Go? Wordsworth.
With Ships the Sea Was Sprinkled Far and Nigh. Wordsworth.
Wooden Ships. Morton.
Would you hear of an old-time sea-fight? *Fr.* Song of Myself. Whitman.
Eternal Sea, The; an Anthology of Sea Poetry (EtS). W. M. Williamson, ed.
See also **Boats; Yachts.**

Shipwrecks
Aeolian Harp, The. Melville.
Alec Yeaton's Son. Aldrich.
Berg, The. Melville.
Brave Old Ship, the *Orient,* The. R. T. S. Lowell.
Convergence of the Twain, The. Hardy.
Dream of Wrecks, A. *Fr.* Richard III. Shakespeare.
Fisherman Husband. Chamberlain.
Full Fathom Five. *Fr.* The Tempest. Shakespeare.
In Memory of the Circus Ship *Euzkera*, Wrecked in the Caribbean Sea, 1 September 1948. Gibson.
In Wintry Midnight, o'er a Stormy Main. Petrarch.
Inchcape Rock, The. Southey.
Inscription by the Sea, An. *Unknown.*
Last Words. Hollander.
Loss of the *Birkenhead*, The. Doyle.
Loss of the *Cedar Grove*, The. *Unknown.*
Loss of the *Eurydice*, The. Hopkins.
Mary Ross, The. Baughan.
On the Loss of the *Royal George.* Cowper.
Portland Going Out, The. Merwin.
Sea Story, A. Hickey.
Second Mate, The. O'Brien.
Shipwreck, The. *Fr.* Don Juan. Byron.
Shipwreck, The, *sels.* Falconer.
Silent Tower of Bottreaux, The. Hawker.
Sir Patrick Spens. *Unknown.*
Skipper Ireson's Ride. Whittier.
Three Bells, The. Whittier.
Titanic, The. *Unknown.*
Trouble at Sea. Prys.
White Ship, The. D. G. Rossetti.
Wreck, The. Ruskin.
Wreck of the *Deutschland*, The. Hopkins.
Wreck of the *Hesperus*, The. Longfellow.
Wreck of the *Julie Plante*, The. Drummond.
Yarn of the *Loch Achray*, The. Masefield.
Yarn of the *Nancy Bell*, The. Gilbert.

Shirley, James
James Shirley. *Fr.* Sonnets on English Dramatic Poets. Swinburne.

Shiva. *See* **Siva.**

Shivaji
Rise of Shivaji, The. Ghose.

Shoemakers
Amends to the Tailors and Soutars. Dunbar.
Cobbler. Bacon.
Cobbler, The. Chaffee.

Shoemakers *(continued)*
Cobbler, The. *Unknown.*
Cobbler in Willow Street, The. O'Neil.
Shoemaker, The. *Unknown.*
Shoemakers, The. *Fr.* Songs of Labor. Whittier.
Shoemaker's Booth, The. Hershon.
Shoemaker's Holiday, The, *sels.* Dekker.
Shoes
Choosing Shoes. Wolfe.
Footwear. Justus.
I Have Lost My Shoes. Suasnavar.
It's fun to go out and buy new shoes to wear. Hoberman.
My Mistress's Boots. Locker-Lampson.
My Shoes. Simic.
New Shoes. Watts.
Sale. Miles.
Shoes. Robinson.
To a Pair of Egyptian Slippers. Arnold.
Shooting gallery
Travelogue in a Shooting-Gallery. Fearing.
Shopping and Shops
Counters. Coatsworth.
Emma's Store. Aldis.
Enigma in Altman's. McGinley.
General Store. Field.
Junk Shop, The. Coulette.
Market, The. *Fr.* Mountains & Rivers. Snyder.
Miss Thompson Goes Shopping. Armstrong.
Pushcart Row. Field.
Saturday Shopping. Edelman.
Shop Windows. Fyleman.
Street Window. Sandburg.
Victoria Markets Recollected in Tranquillity, The. Wilmot.
Shore, Jane
How Shore's Wife, Edward the Fourth's Concubine, Was by King Richard Despoiled of All Her Goods. *Fr.* A Mirror for Magistrates. Churchyard.
Shoreham-by-Sea, England
Shoreham: Twilight Time. Palmer.
Shrews
Masked Shrew, The. Gardner.
Shrew, The. Nash.
Shrimps
Shrimp, The. Browne.
Sibelius, Jean Julius Christian
Baldness and the Swan. Scott.
For the 90th Birthday of Sibelius. Kirkup.
Program Note on Sibelius. Babcock.
Siberia
Message to Siberia. Pushkin.
Siberia. Mangan.
Song of the Siberian Exiles, The. Nekrasov.
Sibyl
Sibyl, The. LaBombard.
Sicily
Bare Almond Trees. Lawrence.
Siciliana; the Landings at Gela. Koehler.
Sickness. *See* **Illness.**
Sidney, Sir Philip
Elegy on the Death of Sidney. Dyer.
Epitaph on Sir Philip Sidney. *At. to* Greville.
Epitaph on Sir Philip Sidney. Herbert of Cherbury.
Epitaph on Sir Philip Sidney, An. James I, King of England.
Epitaph upon the Death of Sir Philip Sidney, Knight, Lord-Governor of Vlissing, An. Barnfield.
Epitaph upon the Right Honorable Sir Philip Sidney, Knight, Lord Governor of Flushing, An. *At. to* Ralegh.
Funerall Song, A: "(Come to me, grief for ever.") *Unknown.*
Of Sir Philip Sidney. Beaumont.
On Sir Philip Sidney. *Fr.* An Elegy, or Friend's Passion for His Astrophil. Royden.
On the Death of Sir Philip Sidney. Constable.
Shepheards boy, The (best knowen by that name). *Fr.* Colin Clout's Come Home Again. Spenser.
Sir Philip Sidney. Farjeon.
To Sir Philip Sidney's Soul. Constable.
Siegfried
Battle-Flag of Sigurd, The. Greenwell.
Siena, Italy
Siena. Swinburne.
Sierra Nevada
Ascent to the Sierras. Jeffers.
Dead in the Sierras. Miller.
Signorelli, Luca
Episode, An. Symonds.
Silence
After the Dazzle of Day. Whitman.
Burke and Wills. Barratt.
Faint Music. De la Mare.
Golden Silences. C. G. Rossetti.
Invocation of Silence. Flecknoe.
Pastourelle. Hayes.
Precept of Silence, The. Johnson.
Q Is for the Quietness. McGinley.
Rest and Silence. Trakl.
Silence. Barnett.
Silence. Hageman.
Silence. Hood.
Silence, The. MacLeish.
Silence. Masters.
Silence. Moore.
Silence. T. S. Moore.
Silence. Morse.
Silence. Spalding.
Silence. Towne.
Silence. Welles.
Silence, The. Wickham.
Silences. Pratt.
Silentium. Tyutchev.
Sonnet—Silence. Poe.
Stillness, The. Basho.
Sweet Silence after Bells. Brennan.
There Must Be Silence. Tansey.
This Is the Shape of the Leaf. Aiken.
To Silence. Beddoes.
To Silence. Moore.
Triad. Crapsey.
Valley of Silence, The. "Macleod."
Witnesses. Hemley.
Silkworms
Psyche. Very.
Silkworms. Elliott.
Silkworms, The. Stewart.
Simaetha
Beaten Path, The. Winslow.
Simeon (Bible)
Light in the Temple, The. W. R. Benét.
Song for Simeon, A. Eliot.
Simhath Torah
Hand, The. Feldman.
Simchas Torah. Rosenfeld.
Simhat Torah. Gordon.
This Feast of the Law. *Unknown.*
Similes
New Song of New Similes, A. Gay.
Simon, Saint
Men Follow Simon. Kresensky.
St. Simon and St. Jude's Day. Alexander.
Upon the Feast of St. Simon and St. Jude. Johnson.
Simon of Cyrene
Simon of Cyrene. Harkness.
Simon the Cyrenian Speaks. Baker.
Simon the Cyrenian Speaks. Cullen.
Simplicity
Ode to Simplicity. Collins.
To Simplicity. Coleridge.
Simplon Pass, Switzerland
Simplon Pass, The. Wordsworth.
Sin
Christ Complains to Sinners. *Unknown.*
I Stood upon a High Place. *Fr.* The Black Riders. S. Crane.
Sin and Its Cure. *Unknown.*
Sinne. Herbert.
Sinner, The. Herbert.
Sinnes Heavie Loade. Southwell.
Sin's Round. Herbert.
String of Death, The. Scott.
Vision of Sin, The. Tennyson.
Singing and singers
At a Solemn Musick. Milton.
Celia Singing. Carew.

Everyone Sang. Sassoon.
I Hear America Singing. Whitman.
M., Singing. Bogan.
O Black and Unknown Bards. Johnson.
Of Ballad-Singers. *Fr.* Trivia. Gay.
Of Corinna's Singing. Campion.
Quartette, The. De la Mare.
Schmaltztenor. Branch.
Singer, The. Stedman.
Singer Asleep, A. Hardy.
Singing. Stevenson.
Singing-Time. Fyleman.
Solitary Reaper, The. Wordsworth.
Song about Singing, A. Aldrich.
Swans Sing. Coleridge.
To a Lady Playing and Singing in the Morning. Hardy.
To a Lady Who Did Sing Excellently. Herbert of Cherbury.
To Constantia Singing. Shelley.
When Malindy Sings. Dunbar.
Why Should I Wander Sadly. Süsskind von Trimberg.
Untune the Sky (UnS). Helen Plotz, comp.

Sioux Indians
Remember the Promise, Dakotah. Carr.
Sioux, The. Field.
Sioux Indians. *Unknown.*

Sirens (mythology)
Sirens, The. Manifold.

Sisyphus (mythology)
Sisyphus. Miles.

Sitars
Sitar Player, The. Cooper.

Sitwell, Edith
Thin Facade for Edith Sitwell, A. Brinnin.

Siva
Shiva. Jeffers.

Skating and Skates
Black Water and Bright Air. Carrier.
Elfin Skates. Lee-Hamilton.
Fast. Tagliabue.
Ice-Skaters. Olson.
On the Frozen Lake. *Fr.* The Prelude. Wordsworth.
River Skater. Welles.
Roller Skates. Farrar.
Skaters, The. Fletcher.
Skaters, The. Williams.
Skater's Waltz, A. Burr.
Skating. Asquith.
Skating. Kipling.
Skating Song. Morley.
To Kate, Skating Better than Her Date. Daiches.

Skelton, John
John Skelton. Graves.

Skiing
Ski Train. Anderson.
Skier. Francis.
Skiers, The. Frisch.
Skiing Song. Lewis.
Song of the Ski, The. MacDonald.
T-Bar. Page.

Skunks
Skunk, The. Baruch.
Skunk, The. Coffin.
Skunk, The. Noyes.
Tale of the Skunk and Poor Jez, The. Becker.
Wood-Weasel, The. Moore.

Sky
God Said: Let There Be Sky. Donohue.
Heaven Tree. Robinson.
Night Sky, The. Roberts.
Sky, The. Stoddard.
Sky Is Up above the Roof, The. Verlaine.
Sky's unresting cloudland, that with varying play, The. *Fr.* The Testament of Beauty. Bridges.
Spacious Firmament on High, The. Addison.
Unending Sky, The. Masefield.
Winter Heavens. Meredith.

Skylarks. *See* **Larks.**

Skyscrapers
Elegy on an Empty Skyscraper. Fletcher.
Of Man and Nature. Mungin.
On Watching the Construction of a Skyscraper. Raffel.
Skyscraper. Sandburg.
Skyscraper Is a City's House. Lambert.
Skyscrapers. Field.
Tall City. Pulsifer.
Towers at Evening, The. *Fr.* Melbourne and Memory. Wilmot.

Skywriting
Sky-Writer. Starrett.

Slander
To Detraction I Present My Poesy. *Fr.* The Scourge of Villainy. Marston.
To the Detracted. Andrewes.

Slaughter of the Innocents. *See* **Herod the Great.**

Slavery
African Chief, The. Bryant.
Boston Hymn. Emerson.
Bwagamoyo. Bethune.
Clerical Oppressors. Whittier.
Curse for a Nation, A. E. B. Browning.
Death of Slavery, The. Bryant.
Enslaved. McKay.
Farewell, The: "Gone, gone—sold and gone." Whittier.
For Righteousness' Sake. Whittier.
Fugitive Slaves, The. Very.
Independence. Faleti.
Massachusetts to Virginia. Whittier.
Middle Passage. Hayden.
Mother Dark. Pereira.
Old Cabin, The. Dunbar.
On Liberty and Slavery. Horton.
Present Crisis, The. J. R. Lowell.
Runagate Runagate. Hayden.
Runaway Slave at Pilgrim's Point, The. E. B. Browning.
Safari West. Williams.
Serf, The. Campbell.
Slave, the. Horne.
Slave, The. Oppenheim.
Slave Auction, The. Harper.
Slave Chase, The. *Unknown.*
Slave in the Dismal Swamp, The. Longfellow.
Slave Quarters. Dickey.
Slaver, The. *Fr.* John Brown's Body. S. V. Benét.
Slaves. J. R. Lowell.
Slave's Dream, The. Longfellow.
Runaway Slave, The. *Fr.* Song of Myself. Whitman.
Song of Slaves in the Desert. Whittier.
Song of the Galley-Slaves. Kipling.
Song of the Son. Toomer.
Stanzas on Freedom. J. R. Lowell.
Suffer, Poor Negro. Diop.
Sympathy. Dunbar.
Those Who Lost Everything. Diop.
To Sir Toby. Freneau.
Two Poems Concerning the Slave Trade. Southey.
Witnesses, The. Longfellow.
Wounded Person, The. *Fr.* Song of Myself. Whitman.

Sleds
Little Red Sled, The. Bush.
Sledding Song, A. Schlichter.

Sleep
And on My Eyes Dark Sleep by Night. "Field."
Before Sleep. Prudentius.
Care-Charmer Sleep. *Fr.* To Delia. Daniel.
Care-charming Sleep. *Fr.* The Tragedy of Valentinian. Fletcher.
Come, Heavy Sleep. *Unknown.*
Come, Sleep. *Fr.* The Woman-Hater. Beaumont *and* Fletcher.
Come, Sleep, O Sleep, The Certain Knot of Peace. *Fr.* Astrophel and Stella. Sidney.
Cradle Song, A: "Sleep, Sleep, Beauty bright." Blake.
Cypress Curtain of the Night, The. Campion.
Disillusionment of Ten o'Clock. Stevens.
Down to Sleep. Jackson.
Evening Watch, The. Vaughan.
Falling Asleep. Sassoon.
Final Hunger, The. Miller.
For Sleep, or Death. Pitter.
For Sleep When Overtired. Cleghorn.
Golden Slumbers Kiss Your Eyes. *Fr.* The Pleasant Comedy of Patient Grisell. Dekker, *and others.*

Sleep *(continued)*
Good Night. Hood.
Good-Night, A. Quarles.
Grania. *Unknown.*
Hymn to the Night. "Novalis."
In Sleep. Burton.
Insomnia. Tabb.
Invitation to Sleep. C. G. Rossetti.
Land of Nod, The. Stevenson.
Lights Out. Thomas.
Lines for a Drawing of Our Lady of the Night. Thompson.
Lonely Are the Fields of Sleep. Baldwin.
Lotos-Eaters, The. Tennyson.
Lullaby: "Beloved, may your sleep be sound." Yeats.
Lullaby: "Sleep, Mouseling, Sleep." Coatsworth.
Matthew, Mark, Luke and John. *Unknown.*
Nap. Van Doren.
Nocturne: "Sleep that like the couched dove." Griffin.
Now through Night's Caressing Grip. Auden.
O Sleep. Norton.
Oh, Sleep, Fond Fancy. *Unknown.*
Ode to Sleep. Smollett.
Old Lizette on Sleep. Lee.
On a Quiet Conscience. Charles I, King of England.
Pains of Sleep, The. Coleridge.
Rock-a-by Lady, The. Field.
Sacrament of Sleep, The. Oxenham.
Siesta, The. *Unknown.*
Sleep. Aldrich.
Sleep. Brown.
Sleep, The. E. B. Browning.
Sleep. McAuley.
Sleep. "Macleod."
Sleep. Martin.
Sleep. Péguy.
Sleep. Tooker.
Sleep. Viau.
Sleep and His Brother Death. Hayne.
Sleep and Poetry. Keats.
Sleep Is a Reconciling. *Unknown.*
Sleep, My Child. Aleichem.
Sleep Sweet. Gates.
Sleep the Mother. Kiper.
Sleep, this is the time for sleep. *Unknown.*
Sleep Will Come Singly. Oliver.
Sleeper, The. Clouts.
Sleeper, The. De la Mare.
Sleeper, The. "Hume."
Sleeper, The. Scollard.
Sleeper of the Valley, The. Rimbaud.
Sleepers. Miller.
Sleeping on Her Couch. Leigh.
Slumber Song: "Sleep; and my song shall build about your bed." Sassoon.
Soliloquy on Sleep. *Fr.* King Henry IV, Pt. II. Shakespeare.
Somnus. Denham.
Song: "Sleep, O Sleep." Gay.
Song: "While Morpheus thus doth gently lay." Killigrew.
Sonnet: "Sleep, Silence' Child, sweet father of soft rest." Drummond of Hawthornden.
Spell of Sleep. Raine.
Sweet and Low. *Fr.* The Princess. Tennyson.
To Sleep. Casa.
To Sleep. Fleming.
To Sleep. Keats.
To Sleep. Kochanowski.
To Sleep. Landor.
To Sleep. MacKaye.
To Sleep. Osgood.
To Sleep. Smith.
To Sleep ("Flock of sheep that leisurely pass by, A"). Wordsworth.
To Sleep ("Fond words have oft been spoken to thee, Sleep"). Wordsworth.
To Sleep ("O gentle Sleep! do they belong to thee"). Wordsworth.
We are not wholly blest who use the earth. *Fr.* Dreamland. Mair.
Weep You No More, Sad Fountains. *Unknown.*
With the Dawn. Irwin.

Sleet
Sleet Storm. Tippett.
Sleighs
Blue Sleigh. Scott.
Sleigh Bells at Night. Coatsworth.
Sleighride. Anderson.
Sloth
Ant, The. Johnson.
Sluggard, The. Watts.
Tenth Muse. R. Lowell.
Sloths
Sloth, The. Roethke.
Slough, England
Slough. Betjeman.
Slugs
Slug in Woods. Birney.
Slums
Elementary School Class Room in a Slum, An. Spender.
Reflections in a Slum. "MacDiarmid."
Smart, Christopher
History, A. Williams.
Smells
Sense of Smell, The. MacNeice.
Smell on the Landing, The. Porter.
Smells. Morley.
Smells. Worth.
Smells (Junior). Morley.
Smiles
Growing Smiles. *Unknown.*
Little Things. *Unknown.*
Mask, The. E. B. Browning.
Only a Smile. *Unknown.*
Simile for Her Smile, A. Wilbur.
Smile, The. *Fr.* The Limeratomy. Euwer.
Smiles. Schjeldahl.
They might not need me; but they might. Dickinson.
Two Smiles. Herford.
Smith, Bessie
Blues for Bessie. O'Higgins.
Ode to the Smiths. Thomas.
Smith, Horace
Letter to Maria Gisborne. Shelley.
Smith, John
John Smith's Approach to Jamestown. Hope.
Last Meeting of Pocahontas and the Great Captain, The. Preston.
Noah an' Jonah an' Cap'n John Smith. Marquis.
Smoke
Smoke. Thoreau.
Smoke Animals. Bennett.
Smoke in Winter. Thoreau.
Trails of Smoke. Bennett.
Smugglers
Smuggler, The. *Unknown.*
Snails
Considering the Snail. Gunn.
Housekeeper, The. Bourne.
Little Snail. Conkling.
Lucky Snail, The. Welles.
Odyssey of a Snail, The. Garcia Lorca.
Poor Snail, The. Westrup.
Snail, The. Bourne.
Snail, The. Conkling.
Snail, The. Cowper.
Snail. Drinkwater.
Snail. Eybers.
Snail. Hughes.
Snail, The. Lamb.
Snail. McCord.
Snail. McCoy.
Snail, The. Reeves.
Snail, The ("Little snail"). *Unknown.*
Snail, The ("The snail he lives"). *Unknown.*
Snail's Dream, The. Herford.
Snakes and Snails. Hallock.
Snayl, The. Lovelace.
To a Snail. Moore.
Upon the Snail. Bunyan.
Snakes
Black Snake, The. Hubbell.
Colubriad, The. Cowper.

Crotalus. Harte.
Death of the Snake, The. Plomer.
Five Serpents. Burgess.
Goodbye to Serpents. Dickey.
In a Garden. Babcock.
Massasauga, The. Garland.
Narrow fellow in the grass, A. Dickinson.
Prologue: Moments in a Glade. Stephens.
Rattlesnake, The. Carr.
Serpent's Nature, The. *Fr.* The Bestiary. *Unknown.*
Silent Snake, The. *Unknown.*
Snake, The. Kyoshi.
Snake. Lawrence.
Snake, The. Mackenzie.
Snake, The. Moore.
Snake. Roethke.
Snake Charmer, The. Sheppard.
Snake Story. Johnstone.
Snake Trying, The. Ross.
Snakecharmer. Plath.
Snakes and Snails. Hallock.
Spring Serpent, A. Winters.
To the Snake. Levertov.
Viper, The. Pitter.
Water Snake. Jacobson.

Snapdragons
Lucky Thing, A. Aldis.
Snapdragon. Cardinal Newman.

Sneezes
Sneezing. Hunt.

Snipes
To the Snipe. Clare.

Snow
April Snow, The. Very.
Beautiful Snow, The. Watson.
Brindabella. Stewart.
Cynthia in the Snow. Brooks.
Dafydd Ap Gwilym Resents the Winter. Humphries.
Devonshire Rhyme, A. *Unknown.*
Digging It Out. Hollander.
Dust of Snow. Frost.
Easter Snowfall. Behn.
Effect of Snow, The. Finch.
Falling of the Snow, The. Souster.
Falling Snow. A. Lowell.
Falling Snow. *Unknown.*
Fire in the Snow, The. Watkins.
First Snow. Allen.
First Snow. Eastwick.
First Snow In Alsace. Wilbur.
First Snowfall. Carducci.
First Snow-Fall, The. J. R. Lowell.
First Winter's Day. Aldis.
Flowers of Snow. Tsurayuki.
For Snow. Farjeon.
Hillside Thaw, A. Frost.
I come more softly than a bird. *Fr.* Rhyming Riddles. Austin.
In the Ravine. Ross.
It sifts from leaden sieves. Dickinson.
January. Coatsworth.
Late Snow. Issa.
London Snow. Bridges.
New Forms. Redgrove.
New Snow. Rowles.
On a Gentlewoman Walking in the Snow. Strode.
On a Snowy Day. Aldis.
Onset, The. Frost.
Outside the Door. Wynne.
Patch of Old Snow, A. Frost.
Presence of Snow. Cane.
Riddle: "White bird floats down through the air, A." *Unknown.*
Slushy snow splashes and sploshes, The. Hoberman.
Snow. Aldis.
Snow. Allen.
Snow. Cawein.
Snow. Coatsworth.
Snow, The. Dyment.
Snow, The. Elliott.
Snow, The. Gibson.
Snow, The. Hall.
Snow. Lampman.
Snow, The. Miller.
Snow. Rodgers.
Snow. Stone.
Snow. Taylor.
Snow. Thomas.
Snow. *Unknown.*
Snow. Wilkins.
Snow Anthology. Bourinot.
Snow by Morning. Swenson.
Snow Fell with a Will. Gillman.
Snow in October. Nelson.
Snow In Spring. Eastwick.
Snow in the City. Field.
Snow in the Suburbs. Hardy.
Snow in Town. Mark.
Snow Man, The. Stevens.
Snowman. *Unknown.*
Snow-Shower, The. Bryant.
Snow toward Evening. Cane.
Snow-bound; a Winter Idyl. Whittier.
Snowfall. Carducci.
Snowfall, The. Justice.
Snow Fall, The. MacLeish.
Snowfall: Four Variations. Amabile.
Snow-flake Song. Conkling.
Snowflakes. Arthur.
Snowflakes. Behrend.
Snowflakes. Chute.
Snowflakes ("Little white feathers"). Dodge.
Snowflakes ("Whenever a snowflake leaves the sky"). Dodge.
Snow-Flakes. Longfellow.
Snowstorm. Clare.
Snowstorm, The. Emerson.
Snow Storm. Sister Mary Madeleva.
Snowstorm, The. Scott.
Snow Storm, The. Wetherald.
Soft Snow. Blake.
Song of White Snow, A. Ts'en Ts'an.
Stopping by Woods on a Snowy Evening. Frost.
Stories of Snow. Page.
There Blooms No Bud in May. De la Mare.
To a Snowflake. Thompson.
Under the Snow. Collyer.
Velvet Shoes. Wylie.
Waiting. Behn.
Walker of the Snow, The. Shanley.
Weaver of Snow, The. "Macleod."
White Fields. Stephens.
Why Does It Snow? Richards.
Winter. Joso.
Winter Noon. Teasdale.
Winter Hymn, A—to the Snow. Jones.

Snowbirds
Snow-Bird, The. Butterworth.
Snow-Bird, The. Sherman.
Snow-Bird's Song, The. Woodworth.
Southern Snow-Bird, The. Hayne.

Snowdon, Wales
Conclusion: "It was a close, warm, breezeless summer night." *Fr.* The Prelude. Wordsworth.

Snowdrops
Snowdrop. De Bary.
Snowdrop, A. Spofford.
Snowdrop. Story.
Snowdrop. Tennyson.
Snowdrops. Alma-Tadema.
Snowdrops. Robertson.
Snowdrops. Vivian.

Snowshoeing
Snowshoeing Song. Weir.

Soccer
Dangers of Foot-ball, The. *Fr.* Trivia. Gay.
Football Field: Evening. McKellar.
Football Song. Scott.
Heaps on Heaps. *Fr.* A Match at Football. Concanen.
Man from Inversnaid, The. Murray.

Social Protest. *See* **Protest, Social.**

Socialism
Day Is Coming, The. Morris.
Day of Days, The. Morris.
Death Song, A. Morris.

Socialism *(continued)*
Down among the Dead Men. Morris.
Emigrant Song. "Ansky."
Man with the Hoe, The. Markham.
No Master. Morris.
Voice of Toil, The. Morris.
Why I Voted the Socialist Ticket. Lindsay.
Society for the Prevention of Cruelty to Animals
S.P.C.A. Sermon. Hemsley.
Socrates
Reply of Socrates, The. Thomas.
Socrates Prays a Day and a Night. O'Neil.
Sodom
Ballad of the Trial of Sodom. Watkins.
Sodom. Grade.
This Place Rumord to Have Been Sodom. Duncan.
Soldiers
A Terre. Owen.
Air Sentry, The. Barrington.
All Day It Has Rained. Lewis.
All That Is Left. Basho.
All the Hills and Vales Along. Sorley.
American Soldier's Hymn, The. *Unknown.*
America's Welcome Home. Van Dyke.
Anthem for Doomed Youth. Owen.
Apologia pro Poemate Meo. Owen.
Apples and Water. Graves.
Aristocrats. Douglas.
Arms and the Boy. Owen.
Army Corps on the March, An. Whitman.
As Toilsome I Wander'd Virginia's Woods. Whitman.
"Atkins." Meredith.
Ballad: "O what is that sound which so thrills the ear." Auden.
Barrack Yard, The. Palmer.
Battery Moving Up to a New Position from Rest Camp: Dawn. Nichols.
Base Details. Sassoon.
Before Action. Gellert.
Bivouac of the Dead, The. O'Hara.
Bivouac on a Mountain Side. Whitman.
Boots. Kipling.
Bridge-Guard in the Karroo. Kipling.
British Grenadiers, The. *Unknown.*
By the Bivouac's Fitful Flame. Whitman.
Caisson Song, The. Gruber.
Call to the Guard by a Drum, A. Radcliffe.
Cavalier's Song, The. Motherwell.
Cavalry Crossing a Ford. Whitman.
Connaught Rangers, The. Letts.
Conscript, The. Gibson.
Conversion. Angermayer.
Cry for a Dead Soldier. Inman.
Danny Deever. Kipling.
Dead Soldier. Guillén.
Death of the Ball Turret Gunner, The. Jarrell.
Death of the Soldier, The. Stevens.
Deserter, The. Housman.
Dirge: For One Who Fell in Battle. Parsons.
Dirge for Two Veterans. Whitman.
Disabled. Owen.
Dreamers. Sassoon.
Drill, The. Brown.
Dry Loaf. Stevens.
Duke of Plaza-Toro, The. *Fr.* The Gondoliers. Gilbert.
Dulce et Decorum Est. Owen.
Elegy for a Dead Soldier. Shapiro.
Elegy for an Unknown Soldier. Baxter.
Epicedium. Miller.
Epitaph on an Army of Mercenaries. Housman.
Exposure. Owen.
Fable of the War, A. Nemerov.
Faithless Nelly Gray. Hood.
Fallen, The. Scott.
Farewell, adieu, that court-like life! *Fr.* Horestes. Pickering.
Fighting South of the Castle. *Unknown.*
Five Souls. Ewer.
Foot Soldiers. Tabb.
For Soldiers. Gifford.
For the Blinded Soldiers. Dobson.
For the Fallen. Binyon.
Forced Recruit, The. E. B. Browning.
Foxhole for the Night, A. Quinn.
General, The. Sassoon.
Great Love. Owen.
Gunga Din. Kipling.
Happy Warrior, The. Read.
Hialmar. Campbell.
Homecoming of the Sheep, The. Ledwidge.
How Can Man Die Better. Tyrtaeus.
I Stood with the Dead. Sassoon.
In a London Terminus. Lehmann.
In an Age of Fops and Toys. *Fr.* Voluntaries. Emerson.
In the Trench. Gellert.
Incident of the French Camp. R. Browning.
Insensibility. Owen.
Into Battle. Grenfell.
Jester in the Trench, The. Gellert.
Jewish Conscript, The. Frank.
Jimmy's Enlisted; or The Recruited Collier. *Unknown.*
Johnny, I Hardly Knew Ye. *Unknown.*
Just behind the Battle, Mother. *Unknown.*
Kid Has Gone to the Colors, The. Herschell.
Kid in Upper 4, The. Metcalf.
Kilroy. Viereck.
Lancashire Lads. *Unknown.*
Lancer. Housman.
Leg, The. Shapiro.
Lessons of the War. Reed.
Let the youth hardened by a sharp soldier's life. Horace.
Little Giffen. Ticknor.
Lofty Lane. Gerard.
Lost in France. Rhys.
Lullaby, A: "For wars his life and half a world away." Jarrell.
Man He Killed, The. Hardy.
Maunding Souldier, The; or, The Fruits of Warre Is Beggery. *Unknown.*
Memorial Rain. MacLeish.
Men in Green. Campbell.
Men Who March Away. Hardy.
Misfit, The—1939-1945. Day Lewis.
Monument for the Soldiers, A. Riley.
More than Flowers We Have Brought. Turner.
Negro Soldiers, The. Jamison.
1918-1941. Fitzgerald.
Nostalgia. Shapiro.
Ode for the American Dead in Korea. McGrath.
Ode to the Confederate Dead. Tate.
Ode Written in the Beginning of the Year 1746. Collins.
Old Sergeant, The, *sel.* Willson.
Old Soldier. Colum.
Old Soldiers. Garstin.
Old Soldier of the Queens, An. *Unknown.*
Old Timers. Sandburg.
Oldest Soldier, The. Graves.
On a Soldier Fallen in the Philippines. Moody.
On a Very Young, Very Dead Soldier. Gillman.
On the Photograph of a Corps Commander. Melville.
One of the Regiment. Le Pan.
Our Modest Doughboys. Andrews.
Over the Heather the Wet Wind Blows. Auden.
Peace to the Slumberers. Moore.
Picket-Guard, The. Beers.
Pipes o' Gordon's Men. Glasgow.
Poem of the Conscripted Warrior. "Nogar."
Portrait in the Guards, A. Whistler.
Praise of Our Soldiers, The. Churchyard.
Prayer: "Thy blessing on the boys—for time has come." Guri.
Prayer of a Soldier in France. Kilmer.
Prelude: Troops, The. Sassoon.
Private Blair of the Regulars. Scollard.
Private of the Buffs, The. Doyle.
Rank and File. Dobson.
Rear-Guard, The. Sassoon.
Rebel Soldier, The. *Unknown.*
Recruit, The. Chambers.
Recruiting Drive. Causley.
Returned Soldier. Moll.
Returned Volunteer to His Rifle, The. Melville.
Scott and the Veteran. Taylor.
Sentry, The. Lewis.
Sergeant-Major Money. Graves.
"Service Man, The." Kipling.

Shillin' a Day. Kipling.
Sight in Camp in the Daybreak Gray and Dim, A. Whitman.
Soldier, The. *Fr.* 1914. Brooke.
Soldier, A. Frost.
Soldier, The. Krige.
Soldier, A. Suckling.
Soldier from the Wars Returning. Housman.
Soldier, Rest! *Fr.* The Lady of the Lake. Scott.
Soldier: Twentieth Century. Rosenberg.
Soldier, What Did You See? Blanding.
Soldiers. Bodenheim.
Soldiers, The. Ungaretti.
Soldiers Bathing. Prince.
Soldier's Dream, The. Campbell.
Soldier's Farewell to Manchester, The. *Unknown.*
Soldier's Friend, The. Canning.
Soldier's Grave, A. Albee.
Soldier's Grave, The. Muir.
Soldier's Prayer, A. Freeman.
Soldier's Song. Campbell.
Soldier's Song. Hume.
Soldier's Song, The. *Unknown.*
Soldier's Wife, The. Southey.
Soldier's Wife to Her Husband, A. Liu Chi.
Somebody's Darling. Lacoste.
Song for the Heroes. Comfort.
Song of the Camp, The. Taylor.
Souldier Going to the Field, The. Davenant.
Souldiers Farewel to His Love, The. *Unknown.*
Spring Offensive. Owen.
Strange Meeting. Owen.
Such Is the Death the Soldier Dies. Wilson.
Ten Days Leave. Snodgrass.
These fought in any case. *Fr.* Hugh Selwyn Mauberley. Pound.
These Men. Gellert.
Thus spoke to my Lady the knight full of care. *Fr.* A Soldier and a Scholar. Swift.
To a Comrade in Arms. Lewis.
Tomb of Lt. John Learmonth, A.I.F., The. Manifold.
Tommies in the Train. Lawrence.
Tommy. Kipling.
Trooper Temple Pulvermacher. Branford.
Troops, The. Sassoon.
Two Armies. Spender.
Ultima Ratio Regum. Spender.
Valley of the Shadow. Galsworthy.
Vergissmeinnicht. Douglas.
Victory March. Joseph.
Volunteer, The. Asquith.
Volunteer's Reply to the Poet, The. *Fr.* Talking Bronco. Campbell.
Warrior to His Dead Bride, The. Procter.
Warrior's Prayer, A. Dunbar.
We'll All Feel Gay. Scott.
Which Side Am I Supposed to Be On? Auden.
Whisperin' Bill. Bacheller.
Widow at Windsor, The. Kipling.
Working Party, A. Sassoon.
Wound-Dresser, The. Whitman.
Youth in Arms. Monro.
See Also **War.**

Solitude
Alastor; or, The Spirit of Solitude. Shelley.
Alone and ever weary with dark care. *Fr.* Sonnets to Laura: To Laura in Life. Petrarch.
Beata Solitudo. Dowson.
Charcoal-Burner, The. Gosse.
Deviator, The. Warr.
Hymn on Solitude. Thomson.
Love and Solitude. Clare.
O Solitude! If I Must with Thee Dwell. Keats.
Ode on Solitude. Pope.
Of Solitude. Cowley.
On Looking into Henry Moore. Livesay.
Peace. Bhartrihari.
Quarry Pool, The. Levertov.
Quiet. Pickthall.
Room, The. Day Lewis.
Solitude. *Fr.* Retirement. Beattie.
Solitude. Clare.
Solitude. De la Mare.
Solitude. Deutsch.
Solitude. Lampman.
Solitude. Mollineux.
Solitude. Peterson.
Solitude. Rilke.
Solitude. Savage.
Solitude. Traherne.
Solitude. Wilcox.
Solitudes. Wheelock.
There is a solitude of space. Dickinson.
Thrice Happy He. Drummond of Hawthornden.
To Solitude. Keats.
Valley Wind, The. Lu Yün.
Wants. Larkin.

Solomon
King Solomon and King David. *Unknown.*
Solomon. Hagedorn.
Solomon. Heine.
Solomon, *sels.* *Unknown.*
Solomon and the Bees. Saxe.
Solomon on the Vanity of the World, *sels.* Prior.
Solomon to Sheba. Yeats.

Solway Firth, Scotland and England
Solway Sands. Craigmyle.

Somerset, Robert Carr, Earl of
Upon the Sudden Restraint of the Earl of Sommerset, Falling from Favour. Wotton.

Sophocles
On the Tomb of Sophocles. Simmias of Thebes.
To a Friend. Arnold.
Wind, Gentle Evergreen. *Unknown.*

Sonnets
On the Sonnet. Keats.
Scorn Not the Sonnet. Wordsworth.
Sonnet, A. *Fr.* The House of Life. D. G. Rossetti.

Sordello
That autumn eve was stilled. *Fr.* Sordello. R. Browning.

Sorel, Canada
Old Nick in Sorel. O'Grady.

Sorrow
Sorrow. De Vere.
Sorrow. Eden.
Sorrow. Eva.
Sorrow. Lawrence.
Sorrow. Phillips.
Sorrow. Trask.
Sorrow. *Unknown.*
Sorrow Is the Only Faithful One. Dodson.
Sorrow seldom killeth any. Davison.
See also **Grief.**

Sousa, John Philip
Sousa. Dorn.

South, The
Legacy: My South. Randall.
My South. West.
Southern Mansion. Bontemps.
Southern Ships and Settlers. R. *and* S. V. Benét.
Southerner, The. Shapiro.
Stricken South to the North, The. Hayne.
When the Mint Is in the Liquor. Ousley.

South Africa, Republic of
And this is now their home. *Fr.* A Reminiscence of 1820. Dugmore.
Attend my fable if your ears be clean. *Fr.* The Wayzgoose. Campbell.
Autumn Song. Brettell.
Camp Fire. Bromley.
Coming, The. Delius.
Hark! heard ye the signals of triumph afar? *Fr.* The Caffer Commando. Pringle.
Namaqualand after Rain. Plomer.
North, south, east, west, the settlers scatter wide. *Fr.* The Landing of the British Settlers of 1820. Wilmot.
On Some South African Novelists. Campbell.
On the Back Veld. Garstin.
Poets in Africa. Campbell.
Seven South African Poems. David Wright.
To the Veld. Cripps.
Book of South African Verse, A (BoSA). Guy Butler, ed.

South *(continued)*
Penguin Book of South African Verse. The (PeSA). Jack Cope *and* Uys Krige, eds.
South America
To Theodore Roosevelt. Darío.
South Carolina
Brother Jonathan's Lament for Sister Caroline. Holmes.
Carolina. Timrod.
Carolina Spring Song. Allen.
South Carolina to the States of the North. Hayne.
South Carolina (ship)
South Carolina, The. *Unknown.*
South Dakota
Hail! South Dakota. Hammitt.
South Pole
Southerly. Brady.
South Wind
South Wind, The. Bridges.
South-Wind. Lathrop.
South Wind. Sassoon.
Southern Cross (constellation)
Southern Cross. Melville.
Southey, Robert
Dedication: "Bob Southey! You're a poet—Poet-laureate." *Fr.* Don Juan. Byron.
Epitaph on Robert Southey. Moore.
On the Death of Southey. Landor.
Southey and Wordsworth. *Fr.* Don Juan. Byron.
Vision of Judgment, The. Byron.
Soutine, Chaim
Story of Soutine, A. Schevill.
Space (outer space)
Among the Stars. *Fr.* Peter Bell. Wordsworth.
Autosonic Door. Thompson.
Expanding Universe, The. Nicholson.
Jodrell Bank. P. Dickinson.
Space. Hogan.
Space Travel. Krows.
Tea in a Space-Ship. Kirkup.
Undiscovered Planet, The. Nicholson.
Spain
Coming Homeward out of Spain. Googe.
Evening. Turner.
In Spain. Lawless.
Song from Old Spain, A. Corbin.
Spain 1937. Auden.
Spanish Alleluja. Galvin.
To Spain—a Last Word. Thomas.
Spanish-American War
Battle Cry. Venable.
Battle Song. Wilson.
Brooklyn at Santiago, The. Rice.
Hobson and His Men. Loveman.
McIlrath of Malate. Rooney.
Martyrs of the *Maine*, The. Hughes.
"Mene, Mene, Tekel, Upharsin." Cawein.
Ode in Time of Hesitation, An. Moody.
Off Manilly. Cooke.
On a Soldier Fallen in the Philippines. Moody.
Rush of the *Oregon*, The. Guiterman.
Santiago. Janvier.
Spain's Last Armada. Rice.
To the Dead of '98. Johnson.
Wheeler at Santiago. Gordon.
Wheeler's Brigade at Santiago. Rice.
When the Great Grey Ships Come In. Carryl.
Spanish Armada
Armada, The. Macaulay.
Ballad to Queen Elizabeth, A. Dobson.
Defeat of the Armada, The. *Unknown.*
Drake. Noyes.
Spanish Civil War. *See* **Civil War, Spanish.**
Spanish Main
Song of the Spanish Main, The. Bennett.
Spanish Needle (flower)
Spanish Needle, The. McKay.
Sparrows
Bee, the Ant, and the Sparrow, The. Cotton.
Bonny, bonny bird I had, A. *Fr.* The Northern Lass. Brome.
Child and the Sparrow, The. Westwood.
City Sparrow. Kreymborg.
Dead Sparrow, The. Cartwright.
Dead Sparrow, The. Catullus.
Did You Ever Hear an English Sparrow Sing? Johnston.
First Song-Sparrow, The. *Unknown.*
Flight of the Sparrows. Zaturenska.
House and Shutter. Turco.
Let Ye Then my Birds Alone. *Fr.* Summer Evening. Clare.
Of All the Birds That I Do Know. Gascoigne.
Praise of Philip Sparrow, The. Gascoigne.
Sparrows among Dry Leaves. Williams.
Sparrow's Song, The. *Unknown.*
Song Sparrow, The. Van Dyke.
Sparrows at the Airport, The. Ostroff.
To a Hedge-Sparrow. *Unknown.*
To a Sparrow. Ledwidge.
To Sparrows Fighting. Davies.
White-Throat Sings, A. Eaton.
Spender, Stephen
To Stephen Spender. Corsellis.
Spenser, Edmund
In Obitum Ed. Spenser Poetae Prestaniss. Weever.
Of Spenser's Fairy Queen. Freeman.
Remembrance of Some English Poets, A. Barnfield.
To Spenser. Keats.
To Spenser. Reynolds.
Vision upon This Conceipt of the Faerie Queene, A. Ralegh.
Sphinx
Le Repos en Egypte; the Sphinx. Repplier.
Sphinx, The. Brownell.
Sphinx, The. Emerson.
Sphinx, The. Wilde.
Sphinx Speaks, The. Saltus.
Spicewood
Spicewood. Reese.
Spiders
Arachne. Cooke.
Arachne. Empson.
Arachnida, Female. Humphreys.
Huntress, The. Johnston.
Image, The. Fuller.
Little City. Horan.
Mr. Edwards and the Spider. R. Lowell.
Mrs. Spider. Livingston.
Noiseless Patient Spider, A. Whitman.
Of a Spider. Thorley.
On a Spider. Littleton.
Orb Weaver, The. Francis.
Parson's Pleasure. Higgs.
Spider, The. Coffin.
Spider. Colum.
Spider, The. Herbert.
Spider. Jones.
Spider, The. McCord.
Spider and His Wife, The. Taylor.
Spider and the Fly, The. Heywood.
Spider and the Fly, The. Howitt.
Spider as an artist, The. Dickinson.
Spider Web, The. Hausgen.
Spider Webs. Tippett.
Spider's Web, The. Cole.
Tarantula, The. Whittemore.
To the Spider. Russell.
Upon a Spider Catching a Fly. Taylor.
Vowel Englyn to the Spider. *Unknown.*
Voyage. Donaghy.
Wedding, The. Aiken.
Spinners
Spinners at Willowsleigh. Zaturenska.
Spinning. Jackson.
Spinning in April. Peabody.
Spinning Song, A. O'Donnell.
Spinning-Wheel. Kitahara.
Spinning Wheel, The. Klein.
Spinning Woman, The. Leonidas of Tarentum.
Spohr, Ludwig
Violinist, The. Lampman.
Spring
Abishag. Fichman.
Admonition for Spring. MacKay.
After Winter. Bailey.
Air in Spring, The. Dowling.

All the Flowers of the Spring. *Fr.* The Devil's Law Case. Webster.
Alons au bois le may cueillir. Orléans.
American Spring Song. Anderson.
Another Spring. C. G. Rossetti.
Apple Orchard in the Spring, An. Martin.
April, 1885. Bridges.
A-Roving. Daley.
As It Fell upon a Day. Barnfield.
Aspects of Spring in Greater Boston. Starbuck.
At the Edge of the Bay. Chubb.
At Winter's End. Sister Mary Madeleva.
Australian Spring. McCrae.
Autumnal Spring Song. Miller.
Awakening of Spring, The. Ku Shih.
Barrel-Organ, The. Noyes.
Barren Spring. *Fr.* The House of Life. D. G. Rossetti.
Before Spring. Ropes.
Bells of Youth, The. "Macleod."
Blossom Themes. Sandburg.
Budding Spring. Lindsay.
Call of the Spring, The. Noyes.
Catch for Spring, A. Nichols.
Chanson Innocent. Cummings.
Chanted Calendar, A. *Fr.* Balder. Dobell.
Child's Song in Spring. Nesbit.
Cold Spring, A. Bishop.
Come, Love, Let's Walk. *Unknown.*
Coming. Larkin.
Coming of Spring, The. Perry.
Coming of Spring, The. *Unknown.*
Composed in Spring. Burns.
Corinna's Going A-Maying. Herrick.
Darling! Because My Blood Can Sing. Cummings.
Day before April, The. Davies.
Day in Spring, A. "Falstaff."
Days Too Short. Davies.
Description of the Spring, Wherein Each Thing Renews Save Only the Lover. Surrey.
Dress of Spring, The. Justus.
Eager Spring. Bottomley.
Earliest Spring. Howells.
Early Spring. Keyes.
Early Spring. Tennyson.
Earth in Spring, The. Halevi.
Echoing Green, The. *Fr.* Songs of Innocence. Blake.
Edict. Vinal.
Epistle for Spring. Larsson.
First Spring Day, The. C. G. Rossetti.
First Spring Morning, The. Bridges.
First Words before Spring. Untermeyer.
Flower Chorus. *Unknown.*
Four Ducks on a Pond. Allingham.
Four Sweet Months, The. Herrick.
Fresh spring, the herald of love's mighty king. *Fr.* Amoretti. Spenser.
Glad Earth. Forbes.
Golden spring redeems the withered year, The. Hillyer.
Green Lady, The. Cole.
Green Song. Booth.
Harbingers. Basho.
Hello! Garnett.
Here We Come a-Piping. *Unknown.*
Holy Spring. Thomas.
Home Thoughts from Abroad. R. Browning.
Home Truths from Abroad. *Unknown.*
Hope and Faith. Peretz.
Now Each Thing Save the Lover in Spring Reviveth to Pleasure. Surrey.
I dreaded that first robin, so. Dickinson.
If Ice. Ross.
If it were not for the voice. Nakatsukasa.
In a Spring Still Not Written Of. Wallace.
In Earliest Spring. Howells.
In Early Spring. Aldridge.
In Early Spring. Meynell.
In Hellbrunn. Trakl.
In Just-Spring. Cummings.
In Spring in Warm Weather. Aldis.
In the Spring. Meleager.
In the Spring. *Fr.* Locksley Hall. Tennyson.
In Two Months Now. Dillon.
It Might as Well Be Spring. Hammerstein.
It Is in Winter That We Dream of Spring. Wilson.
It Is Spring and All Is Well. Wood.
It Was a Lover and His Lass. *Fr.* As You Like It. Shakespeare.
Jonathan Bing Dances for Spring. Brown.
Joy. *Fr.* Humanitad. Wilde.
Just a Mile Beyond. Fisher.
Kerchoo! Fishback.
Kite Days. Sawyer.
Land, The, *sels.* Sackville-West.
Lawyer's Invocation to Spring, The. Brownell.
Lenten Is Come. *Unknown.*
Letter to His Friend Isaac, A. Halevi.
Light exists in spring, A. Dickinson.
Lines Written in Early Spring. Wordsworth.
Little madness in the spring, A. Dickinson.
Little Song of Spring, A. Austin.
Loveliest of Trees. Housman.
Love's Emblems. *Fr.* The Tragedy of Valentinian. Fletcher.
Lumber of Spring. Ridler.
Magic Piper, The. Marsh.
May Day. *Fr.* The Dark Cup. Teasdale.
May 10th. Kumin.
Miracle. Bailey.
My Lady Spring. *Unknown.*
New feet within my garden go. Dickinson.
Night of Spring. Westwood.
Northern Spring, A. Baro.
Now That the Winter's Gone. Carew.
O Heart of Spring. Neilson.
O Spring, Come Prettily In. Strodtmann.
O Sweet Spontaneous. Cummings.
Ode on the Spring. Gray.
Of Red in Spring. McCord.
On a Banck as I Sate a Fishing. Wotton.
On the Mountain. Neidhart von Reuental.
One Morning When the Rain-Birds Call. Roberts.
Open Secret, An. *Unknown.*
Our Singing Strength. Frost.
Out of Tune. Henley.
Outside. Chesterman.
Over the Wintry Threshold. Carman.
Page's Road Song, A. Percy.
Pale Sun, The. Clare.
Pastoral. *Fr.* In Hospital. Henley.
Peaceful Western Wind, The. Campion.
Poem on Spring, The. Guiterman.
Prairie Spring. Fallis.
Prayer for This Day. Flanner.
Prayer in Spring, A. Frost.
Prelude for Spring. Livesay.
Prologue to "The Canterbury Tales." Chaucer.
Promise. Lacey.
Put Forth Thy Leaf, Thou Lofty Plane. Clough.
Rains of Spring, The. Lady Ise.
Returning Spring. Eichendorff.
Revival, The. Vaughan.
Russian Spring Song with Minaiev, A. Walsh.
Screw Spring. Hoffman.
Secret, The. Moreland.
Shadow, The. Williams.
Sleep of Spring, The. Clare.
Slow Spring. Tynan.
Slumber in Spring. Gould.
Smells. Worth.
Song: "Light of spring, the." Miller.
Song: "Spring lights her candles everywhere." Shove.
Song in Spring. Ginsberg.
Song of Waking, A. Bates.
Sonnet: "Oh spring that hides the wrinkled earth in green." Boker.
Sonnet: "Sweet Spring, thou turn'st with all thy goodly train." Drummond of Hawthornden.
Sonnet Written at the Close of Spring. Smith.
Soon with the Lilac Fades Another Spring. MacDonogh.
Spring. Allingham.
Spring, The. Barnes.
Spring. Behn.
Spring. *Fr.* Songs of Innocence. Blake.

Spring *(continued)*
Spring. *Fr.* The Four Seasons of the Year. Bradstreet.
Spring. Carpenter.
Spring, The. Chang Chung-sur.
Spring. Chute.
Spring. Cornish.
Spring, The. *Fr.* The Mistress. Cowley.
Spring. *Fr.* The Tragedy of Valentinian. Fletcher.
Spring. Giltinan.
Spring. Guarini.
Spring. Hopkins.
Spring. Irwin.
Spring. Kuskin.
Spring. Larkin.
Spring. Loveman.
Spring. Maddock.
Spring. Millay.
Spring ("The year has changed his mantle cold"). Orléans.
Spring, The. Pound.
Spring. Rodgers.
Spring. C. G. Rossetti.
Spring. E. Sitwell.
Spring. *Fr.* St. Philip and St. James. Smart.
Spring. Southey.
Spring. Spire.
Spring. Stanley.
Spring. *Fr.* In Memoriam A. H. H. Tennyson.
Spring. Thaxter.
Spring. *Fr.* The Seasons. Thomson.
Spring. Timrod.
Spring ("When from her winter-prison"). *Unknown.*
Spring Air. Derwood.
Spring and All. Williams.
Spring and Autumn. Linton.
Spring and Death. Hopkins.
Spring and Fall: To a Young Child. Hopkins.
Spring Bereaved ("That zephyr..."). Drummond of Hawthornden.
Spring Comes to Our Garden. Sister Mary Immaculata.
Spring Doggerel. Coghill.
Spring Ecstasy. Reese.
Spring Equinox, The. Ridler.
Spring, etc. Whittemore.
Spring Families. F. Frost.
Spring Goeth All in White. Bridges.
Spring Has Come. *Unknown.*
Spring in England. Going.
Spring in Hiding. F. Frost.
Spring in My Hut. Sodo.
Spring in New Hampshire. McKay.
Spring in New Zealand. Church.
Spring in the Student's Quarter. Murger.
Spring Is a Looping-free Time. Robbins.
Spring Is at Work with Beginnings of Things. Rose.
Spring Is Coming. Howitt.
Spring Is in the Making. Duffy.
Spring Is Late, The. Moulton.
Spring Is like a Perhaps Hand. Cummings.
Spring Journey, A. Palmer.
Spring Landscape. La Follette.
Spring Lilt, A. *Unknown.*
Spring Market. Driscoll.
Spring Morning. Cornford.
Spring Morning. Lawrence.
Spring Nocturne. Liessin.
Spring Oak. Kinnell.
Spring of the Year, The. Cunningham.
Spring on the Ochils. Robertson.
Spring Pools. Frost.
Spring Quiet. C. G. Rossetti.
Spring Returns, The. Moore.
Spring Song. Carman.
Spring Song. Conkling.
Spring Song. De Vere.
Spring Song. *Fr.* The Spanish Gypsy. "Eliot."
Spring Song. Griffith.
Spring Song. Hesse.
Spring Song, A. Howitt.
Spring Song. Nahum.
Spring Song. O'Brien.
Spring Song. Swinburne.
Spring Song, A ("Old Mother Earth woke up from her sleep."). *Unknown.*
Spring Song ("Spring, beautiful spring"). *Unknown.*
Spring Song ("Spring is come to town with love"). *Unknown.*
Spring Song in the City. Buchanan.
Spring Song of Aspens. Spencer.
Spring Song of the Birds. *Fr.* The Kingis Quair. James I, King of Scotland.
Spring: The Lover and the Birds. Allingham.
Spring, the Sweet Spring. *Fr.* Summer's Last Will and Testament. Nashe.
Spring, the Travelling Man. Letts.
Spring Voices. MacNeice.
Spring Walk, The. Miller.
Spring Will Come, The. Lowry.
Spring Wind. Turner.
Spring Work at the Farm. Wakley.
Spring's Arrival. *Unknown.*
Spring's Delights. Sterry.
Spring's Immortality. Bell.
Springtime. Kreymborg.
Springtime in Cookham Dean. Roberts.
Stay, Spring. Young.
Sudden Spring. Coulby.
Sweet o' the Year, The. Meredith.
Sweet Spring Is Your. Cummings.
Talking in Their Sleep. Thomas.
Tardy Spring. Meredith.
There breaks upon my sight. *Fr.* The Gully. Wilmot.
To Spring. Blake.
To Spring, *sel.* O'Donnell.
To Spring. Roscoe.
To the Spring. *Fr.* Hymns of Astraea. Davies.
To the Spring Sun. Laughton.
To-day I saw a butterfly. Hooley.
Trico's Song. *Fr.* Alexander and Campaspe. Lyly.
Turn o' the Year. Tynan.
Twist-Rime on Spring. Guiterman.
Two Sewing. Hall.
Vernal Equinox. A. Lowell.
Vernal Sentiment. Roethke.
Vision of Spring in Winter, A. Swinburne.
Vision of the Lamentation of Beulah, A. *Fr.* Milton. Blake.
Voice of Spring, The. Hemans.
Waking of Spring, The. Custance.
Waking Up ("Pretty little crocus. . ."). *Unknown.*
Walk in Spring, A. Lart.
Was There Another Spring? Whitney.
Welcome to Spring. Thompson.
When Daffodils Begin to Peer. *Fr.* The Winter's Tale. Shakespeare.
When Daisies Pied and Violets Blue. *Fr.* Love's Labour's Lost. Shakespeare.
When faces called flowers float out of the ground. Cummings.
When Green Buds Hang. Housman.
When Spring Comes Back to England. Noyes.
When the Hounds of Spring Are on Winter's Traces. *Fr.* Atalanta in Calydon. Swinburne.
White Fury of the Spring, The. Reese.
Who Calls? Clarke.
Winter and Spring. *Unknown.*
Winter is Past, The. Bible, *O.T.*
Winter Spring. Wilbur.
Winter to Spring. Horace.
Wise Johnny. Fallis.
Wistful Days, The. Johnson.
Wonder and a Thousand Springs. Percy.
Woodland Choir, The. *Fr.* The Seasons: Spring. Thomson.
Written in Early Spring. Wordsworth.
Year, The. Patmore.
Year's at the Spring, The. *Fr.* Pippa Passes. R. Browning.
Year's Awakening, The. Hardy.
Young Lambs. Clare.

Springbok, Thailand
Springbok. *Unknown.*

Springfield, Illinois
Abraham Lincoln Walks at Midnight. Lindsay.
House in Springfield. Burket.
On the Building of Springfield. Lindsay.
Springfield of the Far Future, The. Lindsay.

Springfield, Massachusetts
Arsenal at Springfield, The. Longfellow.
Springs
Enchanted Spring, The. Darley.
Love's Limit. *Unknown.*
Spruce Trees
Proud Little Spruce Fir. Kirby.
Squash (sport)
After a Game of Squash. Albert.
Civilities. Whitbread.
Game Resumed. Lattimore.
Squirrels
Fable: "Mountain and the squirrel, The." Emerson.
Five little squirrels. *Unknown.*
Fred. McCord.
Gray Squirrel, The. Wolfe.
Grey Squirrels, The. Howitt.
Joe. McCord.
Mr. Squirrel. Julian.
My Little Neighbor. Mason.
Of All the Idiots That Abound. Hoffenstein.
On a Squirrel Crossing the Road in Autumn, in New England. Eberhart.
Questions for a Flying Squirrel to Answer. Field.
Sacrifice of a Red Squirrel. Langland.
Squirrel, The. Barton.
Squirrel, The. Cowper.
Squirrel, The. Howitt.
Squirrel, The. Nash.
Squirrel. Tippett.
Squirrel, The. *Unknown.*
Squirrel and the Wind, The. *Unknown.*
Squirrel in the Rain. F. Frost.
Story of the Baby Squirrel, The. Aldis.
To a Squirrel at Kyle-Na-No. Yeats.
Stagecoaches
Baldy Green. *Unknown.*
Stairs
Halfway Down. Milne.
On the Staircase. Farjeon.
Stairs. Herford.
Stalin, Joseph
Homage to Our Leaders. Symons.
Stalingrad, USSR
"Spoken Word, The." Morley.
Standard Oil of Indiana
Valedictory to Standard Oil of Indiana, A. Wagoner.
Standish, Miles
Courtship of Miles Standish, The. Longfellow.
Stanley, Arthur Penrhyn
Westminster Abbey. Arnold.
Stanley, Sir Henry Morton
Stanley Meets Mutesa. Rubadiri.
Starfish
Starfish, The. Coffin.
Starfish. Welles.
Stonefish and Starfish. Blight.
Stark, John
Marching Song of Stark's Men, The. Hale.
Starlings
Dead Starling, The. Catullus.
Starling, The. Heath-Stubbs.
Starling's Spring Rondel, A. Cousins.
Stars
After the Dazzle of Day. Whitman.
Aldebaran at Dusk. Sterling.
And Each Man's Leave. Robinson.
Baby Toes. Sandburg.
Beauty of the Stars, The. Ibn Ezra.
Bright Star! Would I Were Steadfast as Thou Art. Keats.
Canopus. Taylor.
Choose Something like a Star. Frost.
Comfort of the Stars, The. Burton.
Constellation, The. Vaughan.
Daisies. Sherman.
Daisies. Young.
Es stehen unbeweglich. Heine.
Escape at Bedtime. Stevenson.
Evening Star. Sappho.
Fallen Star, The. Darley.
Falling Star, The. Teasdale.
Great Bear, The. Hollander.
Hymn to the North Star. Bryant.
I see the golden hunter go. *Fr.* Songs of the Sea-Children. Carman.
If stars dropped out of heaven. *Fr.* Sing-Song. C. G. Rossetti.
In the Field. Wilbur.
Light of Stars, The. Furness.
Light of Stars, The. Longfellow.
Like as a ship that through the ocean wide. *Fr.* Amoretti. Spenser.
Meditation under Stars. Meredith.
Morning and Evening Star. Plato.
My Star. R. Browning.
Noctiflora. Leseman.
Nox Nocti Indicat Scientiam. Habington.
O Ye Sweet Heavens. Parsons.
On the Beach at Night. Whitman.
Pleiades. Barnard.
Pleiades, The. Coatsworth.
Pole Star. MacLeish.
Silver Sheep. Payne.
So in the empty sky the stars appear. Masefield.
Softly through the Mellow Starlight. *Unknown.*
Song: "There's one great bunch of stars in heaven." Marzials.
Star, The. Conkling.
Star, The. Herbert.
Star, The. Redpath.
Star, The. Weaving.
Star Drill. Moore.
Star in the West, The. Cook.
Star Morals. Nietzsche.
Star Sirius, The. Meredith.
Star Sirius and the Pole Star dwell afar. *Fr.* Later Life. C. G. Rossetti.
Star Song. Johnson.
Star-Splitter, The. Frost.
Star-Talk. Graves.
Star Thought. Shaw.
Star-gaze Poem. Lyne.
Starlight. Chadwick.
Starlight. Cook.
Starlight. Meredith.
Starlight Night, The. Hopkins.
Starlighter, The. Guiterman.
Starry Night, The. Sexton.
Stars. Bacmeister.
Stars, The. "Cornwall."
Stars, The. Dafydd ap Gwilym.
Stars, The. Davies.
Stars, The. Dodge.
Stars. Frost.
Stars. Hancock.
Stars. Hughes.
Stars. Teasdale.
Stars. *Unknown.*
Stars, The. Young.
Stars Are Glittering in the Frosty Sky, The. Heavysege.
Stars Begin to Fall. *Unknown.*
Stars, I Have Seen Them Fall. Housman.
Stars of the superior class. *Fr.* The Stars. Smart.
Stars Sang in God's Garden, The. Plunkett.
Stars Stand Up in the Air, The. *Unknown.*
Starscape, A. Bellenden.
Summer Stars. Sandburg.
Suns in a skein, the uncut stones of night. *Fr.* Mythological Sonnets. Fuller.
To the Evening Star. Blake.
To the Evening Star. Campbell.
Twilight at Sea. Welby.
Twinkle, Twinkle, Little Star. Taylor.
Until We Built a Cabin. Fisher.
When I Heard the Learn'd Astronomer. Whitman.
Winter Galaxy, The. Heavysege.
You Black Bright Stars. *Unknown.*
Statue of Liberty. *See* **Liberty, Statue of.**
Statues
Carver and the Rock Are One, The. Brigham.
Frozen, Hero, The. Vance.
Hans Christian Andersen in Central Park. Sobiloff.
O God! O Montreal! Butler.
Prisoner, The—Galleria dell' Academia. Stark.

Statues *(continued)*
Queen Victoria. Wolfe.
Rider Victory, The. Muir.
Spanish Lions, The. McGinley.
Statue at Charing Cross, The. Marvell.
Statue in the Stocks-Market, The. Marvell.
Statues. Raine.
Steel
Prayers of Steel. Sandburg.
Smoke and Steel, *sel.* Sandburg.
Steel. Saylor.
Steel Mills after Midnight. Ray.
Steeples
Steeple-Jack, The. Moore.
Steers. *See* **Oxen.**
Stenographers
Stenographers, The. Page.
Stephen, Saint
St. Stephen and Herod. *Unknown.*
St. Stephen's Word. Heppenstall.
Stepinac, Aloysius.
To Archbishop Stepinac. Sister Mary Eulalia.
Stevedores
Stevedore. Collins.
Stevens, Thaddeus
Old Thad Stevens. Porter.
Stevens, Wallace
To Wallace Stevens. Berrigan.
Stevenson, Robert Louis
Apparition. *Fr.* In Hospital. Henley.
R. L. S. Housman.
Robert Louis Stevenson. Reese.
Saint R. L. S. Cleghorn.
Seamark, A. Carman.
Stevenson's Birthday. Miller.
To Robert Louis Stevenson. Henley.
Stock Market
Investor's Soliloquy. Ward.
Stockmen
Andy's Gone with Cattle. Lawson.
Ballad of the Drover. Lawson.
Dying Stockman, The. *Unknown.*
Harry Pearce. Campbell.
Man from Snowy River, The. Paterson.
My Mate Bill. Gibson.
Sick Stockrider, The. Gordon.
See also **Cowboys.**
Stoicism
Old Stoic, The. E. Brontë.
Stoic, The. Durrell.
Stonecutters
To the Stone-Cutters. Jeffers.
Stonefish
Stonefish and Starfish. Blight.
Stonehenge, England
Sonnet IV: Written at Stonehenge. *Fr.* Sonnets. Warton.
To My Honour'd Friend, Dr. Charleton. Dryden.
Stones and Rocks
Cutting Edge, The. Levine.
How happy is the little stone. Dickinson.
Rocks Partly Held in Mist. Gregor.
Runes. Jarrett.
Sandstone. Marriott.
Stone, The. Blackburn.
Stone. Simic.
This is My Rock. McCord.
To Ailsa Rock. Keats.
Two Voices in a Meadow. Wilbur.
Stonington Battle of
Battle of Stonington on the Seaboard of Connecticut, The. Freneau.
Stony Point, New York
Storming of Stony Point, The. Guiterman.
Storks
Stork in Jerez. Lee.
Village Stork, The. Taylor.
Stormcocks. *See* **Woodpeckers.**
Storms
After the Storm. Bartlett.
Arnold, Master of the *Scud.* Carman.
Awful tempest mashed the air, An. Dickinson.
Ballad of the Strange and Wonderful Storm of Hail, A. *Unknown.*
Ballad of the Tempest. Fields.
Before the Squall. Symons.
Before the Storm. Dehmel.
Blossoms and Storm. Sadaiye.
City-Storm. Monro.
Darkling Summer, Ominous Dusk, Rumerous Rain. Schwartz.
December Storm. Hay.
Electrical Storm. Bishop.
Equinox, The. *Fr.* Seaweed. Longfellow.
Golden Hour, The. *Fr.* Lalla Rookh. Moore.
Hatteras Calling. Aiken.
Haying before Storm. Rukeyser.
High o'er the Poop the Audacious Seas Aspire. Falconer.
June Thunder. MacNeice.
Little Exercise. Bishop.
Low Barometer. Bridges.
Misgivings. Melville.
Night Storm. Simms.
Now Is the Air Made of Chiming Balls. Eberhart.
Ode on a Storm. *Unknown.*
On a Sea-Storm nigh the Coast. Steere.
One A.M. Kennedy.
Patrolling Barnegat. Whitman.
Presage of Storme. *Fr.* Eugenia. Chapman.
Rainy Day, The. Tagore.
Reefing Topsails. Mitchell.
Snow-Storm, The. Emerson.
Song of the Tempest, The. *Fr.* The Pirate. Scott.
Song of the Wild Storm-Waves, The. Sinnett.
Spring Thunder. Van Doren.
Stanzas Occasioned by the Ruins of a Country Inn Unroofed and Blown Down by the Storm. Freneau.
Storm, The. Alcaeus.
Storm, The. Chora.
Storm, The. "Christopher."
Storm, The. Donne.
Storm, The. Heine.
Storm, The. Jennings.
Storm, The. Patmore.
Storm, The. Shanks.
Storm, A. *Fr.* Riddles. *Unknown.*
Storm, The. R. *and* L. Untermeyer.
Storm. Wright.
Storm at Sea. Davenant.
Storm at Sea, A. *Unknown.*
Storm Cone, The. Kipling.
Storm Fear. Frost.
Storm from the East, A. Whittemore.
Storm in Childhood, A. Jones.
Storm in the Distance, A. Hayne.
Storm Is Over, The. Bridges.
Storm on Fifth Avenue. Sassoon.
Storm Song. Taylor.
Summer Storm, A. Whitehead.
Summer Storm (circa 1916), and God's Grace. Warren.
Tempest, The. Smith.
Tempest, The. Zaturenska.
That Is All I Heard. "Yehoash."
Thunder Shower. Conkling.
Thunder-Shower, The. Wheelock.
Thunderstorm, A. Lampman.
Tornado. Stafford.
Viking Terror, The. *Unknown.*
Winter Storm at Sea, The. *Fr.* The Borough. Crabbe.
Wind began to rock the grass, The. Dickinson.
See also **Blizzards.**
Story Poems
Best Loved Story Poems (BeLS). Walter E. Thwing, ed.
Dark Tower, The; Nineteenth Century Narrative Poems (DTo). Dairine Coffey, comp.
Great Story-Poems (GSP). Theodoric Jones, comp.
Love's Enchantment; Story Poems and Ballads (LoEn). Helen Ferris, comp.
Magic Circle; Stories and People in Poetry (MaC). Louis Untermeyer, ed.
Modern Ballads and Story Poems (MoBS). Charles Causley, ed.
100 More Story Poems (OnMSP). Elinor Parker, comp.
One Hundred Story Poems (OnSP). Elinor Parker, comp.

Parlour Poetry; a Casquet of Gems (PaPo). Michael R. Turner, ed.
Story and Verse for Children (StVeCh). Miriam Blanton Huber, ed.
Story Poems, New and Old (StPo). William Cole, ed.
Stowe, Harriet Beecher
Harriet Beecher Stowe. Dunbar.
Stradivari, Antonio
Working with God. *Fr.* Stradivarius. "Eliot."
Strasbourg, France
O Strassburg. *Unknown.*
Stravinsky, Igor
Concert-Interpretation. Sassoon.
Stravinsky. Cooper.
Strawberries
Millions of Strawberries. Taggard.
Netted Strawberries. Bottomley.
Strawberries in November. Neilson.
Strawberry Jam. Justus.
With Strawberries. Henley.
Streams. *See* **Brooks and Streams.**
Streets
Quiet Street, The. McDonald.
Street, The. Baro.
Strikes and Strikers
Bread and Roses. Oppenheim.
Late Snow & Lumber Strike of the Summer of Fifty-four, The. Snyder.
Wanderer, The. Williams.
What Shall We Do for the Striking Seamen? *Unknown.*
Struwwelpeter
Fräulein Reads Instructive Rhymes. Kumin.
Slovenly Peter. Hoffmann.
Stuart, Charles Edward, the Young Pretender
Bonnie Prince Charlie. Hogg.
Charlie Is My Darling. Nairne.
Moy Castle. *Unknown.*
O'er the Water to Charlie. Burns.
Old Scottish Cavalier, The. Aytoun.
Three Portraits of Prince Charles. Lang.
Wae's Me for Prince Charlie. Glen.
Wha'll Be King but Charlie. Nairne.
Stuart, James Ewell Brown (Jeb)
Obsequies of Stuart. Thompson.
Stuart, James Francis Edward, the Old Pretender
New Song Entitled the Warming Pan, A. *Unknown.*
Stubbs, George
On Looking at Stubbs's Anatomy of the Horse. Lucie-Smith.
Students
After Passing the Examination. Po Chü-i.
Bound Together. Schechter.
Elementary School Class Room in a Slum, An. Spender.
Student, The. Moore.
Student, The. *Unknown.*
Trouble Is, The, *sel.* Resendez.
See also **Education; Scholars and Scholarship; School.**
Sturminster Newton, England
On Sturminster Foot-Bridge. Hardy.
Stuttering
Praise to the Stutterer. Katz.
Stutterer. Dugan.
Stuyvesant, Peter
Epitaph for Peter Stuyvesant. Selyns.
Peter Stuyvesant. R. Benét *and* S. V. Benét.
Peter Stuyvesant's New Year's Call. Stedman.
Submarines
Mare Liberum. Van Dyke.
Suburbs
Do It Yrself. Eigner.
In the Suburbs. Simpson.
Northern Suburb, A. Davidson.
Suburban Homecoming. Ciardi.
Subways
Graffiti. Field.
Husbands and Wives. Hershenson.
In a Station of the Metro. Pound.
In the Tube. Aldington.
On a Subway Express. Firkins.
Riding the "A". Swenson.
Subway, The. Rivers.
Subway, The. Tate.
Subway Builders. Lee.
Subway Rush Hour. Hughes.
Tunnel, The. *Fr.* The Bridge. H. Crane.
Underground, The. Boas.
Walk about the Subway Station. Reznikoff.
Success
Don't Give Up. *Unknown.*
Kindly Unhitch That Star, Buddy. Nash.
Measure of Success. *Unknown.*
Success is counted sweetest. Dickinson.
Villanelle: "Woods we're lost in aren't real, The." Kerr.
Suckling, Sir John
Brief Lines in Not So Brief. Nash.
Suffrage
Ballot, The. Pierpont.
Protest against the Ballot. Wordsworth.
Suicide
Abandoned, The. Symons.
After the Surprising Conversions. R. Lowell.
Anniversary of Antonia Pozzi's Death by Suicide. Serini.
Bridge of Sighs, The. Hood.
Dispute over Suicide, A. *Unknown.*
Empedocles on Etna. Arnold.
Felo de Se. Hughes.
Justice Is Reason Enough. Wakoski.
Letters Found near a Suicide. Horne.
Mill, The. Robinson.
Of One Self-Slain. Towne.
On the Suicide of a Friend. Whittemore.
Ordinary People on Sunday. Veitch.
Résumé. Parker.
Richard Cory. Robinson.
Song for a Suicide. Hughes.
Suicide. *Fr.* In Hospital. Henley.
Suicide. MacNeice.
Suicide in Trenches. Sassoon.
Suicide off Egg Rock. Plath.
To Be or Not to Be. *Fr.* Hamlet. Shakespeare.
Two Voices, The. Tennyson.
Woman Takes Life with Own Hand. *Fr.* Variations on *The Aeneid.* Morgan.
Summer
Alike. Aldis.
As imperceptibly as grief. Dickinson.
Bed in Summer. Stevenson.
Belonging to Summer. Shacklett.
Body of Summer, The. "Elytis."
Boy's Summer Song, A. Dunbar.
Comfort of the Fields. Lampman.
Coolness in Summer. Ryusui.
Country Summer. Adams.
Credences of Summer. Stevens.
Darkling Summer, Ominous Dusk, Rumerous Rain. Schwartz.
Description of a Summer's Eve. White.
Dirge for Summer, A. Evans.
Drop fell on the apple tree, A. Dickinson.
Ear Is Not Deaf. Dayton.
Early Summer Thought. Post.
End of Summer, The. Millay.
End of Summer. Untermeyer.
End-of-Summer Poem. Bennett.
Exeunt. Wilbur.
Fair Summer Droops. *Fr.* Summer's Last Will and Testament. Nashe.
Farewell to Summer. Arnold.
Farm Boy after Summer. Francis.
Flowers of Middle Summer. *Fr.* The Winter's Tale. Shakespeare.
Haymakers, Rakers. *Fr.* The Sun's Darling. Dekker.
Heat. Lampman.
Heaven Is Heaven. C. G. Rossetti.
Hock-Cart, or Harvest Home, The. Herrick.
In Fields of Summer. Kinnell.
In Summer. Towne.
In the Elegy Season. Wilbur.
Invocation to Rain in Summer. Bennett.
Joy of Life. Mitford.
Landscape, A. Cunningham.
Lanes in Summer. Hemphrey.
Level of Abstraction, A. Conquest.
Long Summer. Lee.

Summer *(continued)*
Midsummer. Allingham.
Midsummer. Hesse.
Midsummer. Russell.
Midsummer. Scully.
Midsummer. Trowbridge.
Midsummer. Wilcox.
Midsummer Holiday, A, *sels.* Swinburne.
Midsummer Madness. *Unknown.*
Midsummer Night. Gould.
Midsummer Noon in the Australian Forest, A. Harpur.
Midsummer Pause. Lape.
Midsummer Song, A. Gilder.
Night Enchantment. Muth.
Now Welcome, Somer. *Fr.* The Parlement of Foules. Chaucer.
On a Midsummer Eve. Hardy.
On the Approach of Summer, *sel.* Warton.
On the Unusual Cold and Rainie Weather in the Summer, 1648. Heath.
Qui Bien Aime à Tard Oublie. Chaucer.
Rainy Summer, The. Meynell.
Rainy Summer. Pitter.
School Is Out. F. Frost.
Secret. Doolittle.
Song: "In summer when the rose-bushes." E. Sitwell.
Song: "O spirit of the Summertime!" Allingham.
Song of Summer. Dunbar.
Song of Summer Days. Foley.
Soote Season, The. Surrey.
Succession of the Four Sweet Months, The. Herrick.
Sumer Is Icumen In. *Unknown.*
Summer. Clare.
Summer. Davidson.
Summer. Page.
Summer. *Fr.* Pastorals. Pope.
Summer. C. G. Rossetti.
Summer. *Fr.* The Seasons. Thomson.
Summer Afternoon. Dowling.
Summer Afternoon. Souster.
Summer and Winter. Fraser.
Summer and Winter. Shelley.
Summer Comes. Agnew.
Summer Comes. Petrarch.
Summer Commentary, A. Winters.
Summer Dawn. Morris.
Summer Day, A. Beeching.
Summer Day, A. Harrison.
Summer Day. Hume.
Summer Days. Call.
Summer Days. Daniells.
Summer Days. C. G. Rossetti.
Summer Days Are Come Again, The. S. Longfellow.
Summer Evening. Clare.
Summer Evening. De la Mare.
Summer Evening, A. Lampman.
Summer Has Come. *Unknown.*
Summer has two beginnings. Dickinson.
Summer Idyll. Barker.
Summer Images. Clare.
Summer in England 1914. Meynell.
Summer Is Coming, The. Guinness.
Summer Is Gone. *Unknown.*
Summer Longings. MacCarthy.
Summer Lullaby, A. Bumstead.
Summer Magic. Hill.
Summer Matures. Johnson.
Summer Moods. Clare.
Summer Morning. Clare.
Summer Music. Sarton.
Summer Night, A. "Æ."
Summer Night. Ranko.
Summer Night, A. Stoddard.
Summer Noon at Sea, A. Sargent.
Summer Pool, The. Buchanan.
Summer Rain. Lee.
Summer Sabbath. Sampter.
Summer Sanctuary, A. Ingham.
Summer Song. Nesbit.
Summer Stars. Sandburg.
Summer Storm, A. Douglas.
Summer Twilight, A. Turner.
Summer Wind. Bryant.
Summer Wish. Farrar.
Tell All the World. Kemp.
That Summer. Treece.
These are the days when birds come back. Dickinson.
Thistledown. Reese.
Throstle, The. Tennyson.
Time of Roses. Hood.
To Summer. Blake.
Touring. Morton.
Vacation Song. Millay.
Walk in Late Summer, A. Roethke.
Welcome, Summer. *Fr.* The Parlement of Foules. Chaucer.
What Could Be Lovelier than to Hear. Coatsworth.
When Summer's End Is Nighing. Housman.
Wet Summer. Ward.

Sumter, Fort, South Carolina
Battle of Mooris' Island, The. *Unknown.*
Fight at Sumter, The. *Unknown.*
On Fort Sumter. *Unknown.*
Sumter. Brownell.
Sumter. Stedman.
Sumter; a Ballad of 1861. *Unknown.*
Sumter's Band. Simmons.
Twilight on Sumter. Stoddard.

Sun
Canticle of the Sun. St. Francis of Assisi.
Cockerel Sun. Dobson.
Druids' Hymn to the Sun. *Fr.* The Dawn in Britain. Doughty.
Energy of Light, The. Hay.
Forecast. Miles.
Full many a glorious morning have I seen. Sonnets, XXXIII. Shakespeare.
Give Me the Splendid Silent Sun. Whitman.
Glory, Glory to the Sun. Alford.
Hint from Voiture. Shenstone.
Hymn to Light. Cowley.
Hymn to the Sun. Ikhnaton.
Hymn to the Sun. Percy.
I'll tell you how the sun rose. Dickinson.
In Praise of the Sun. "A. W."
Indian Summer Day on the Prairie, An. Lindsay.
Johnny Appleseed's Hymn to the Sun. Lindsay.
Last Man, The. Campbell.
Light Is Sweet, The. Ecclesiastes, Bible, *O.T.*
Marigold So Likes the Lovely Sunne, The. Watson.
On a cleere morne as Phoebus run his race. *Unknown.*
On Mt. Iron. Brasch.
Riddle: "On yonder hill there is a red deer." *Unknown.*
Riddle: The Moon and the Sun. *Unknown.*
September Sun, 1947. Gascoyne.
Shine Out, Fair Sun. *Unknown.*
Some say the sun is a golden earring. Belting.
Sun, The. Davis.
Sun, The. Drinkwater.
Sun, The. Miller.
Sun! Moore.
Sun. Rowe.
Sun, The. Sexton.
Sun, The. *Fr.* Ode to the Setting Sun. Thompson.
Sun and Rain. C. G. Rossetti.
Sun God, The. De Vere.
Sun Rising, The. Donne.
Sunning. Tippett.
Sun's Travels, The. Stevenson.
There's Nothing like the Sun. Thomas.
To the Sun. Bachmann.
To the Sun. *Fr.* Mithraic Emblems. Campbell.
To the Sun. Gezelle.
True Account of Talking to the Sun at Fire Island, A. O'Hara.
Welcome to the Sun. *Fr.* The Aeneid. Vergil.

Sunday
Attending Church. *Unknown.*
First-Day Thoughts. Whittier.
May Sunday, A. Irwin.
Not on Sunday Night. *Unknown.*
O Day of Rest and Gladness. Wordsworth.
People on Sunday. Denby.
Q Is for the Quietness. McGinley.
Some keep the Sabbath going to church. Dickinson.

Son-Dayes. Vaughan.
Sunday. Coatsworth.
Sunday, A. De la Mare.
Sunday. Herbert.
Sunday Bells. Allingham.
Sunday Evenings. Hollander.
Sunday Morning. MacNeice.
Sunday Morning. Stevens.
Sun-Days. Vaughan.
See also **Sabbath.**

Sunderland, Charles Spencer, Earl of
Ode Inscribed to the Earl of Sunderland at Windsor, An. Tickell.

Sundew
Sundew, The. Swinburne.

Sundials
On a Sundial. Belloc.
On the Needle of a Sundial. Quarles.

Sunflowers
Ah! Sunflower. *Fr.* Songs of Experience. Blake.
Sunflower, The. Montale.
Sunflower, The. Quennell.
Sunflower. Updike.
Sunflower Sutra. Ginsberg.
Sunflower to the Sun, The. Stebbins.
Sunflowers. Scollard.
Sunflowers, The. Stewart.

Sunrise
Ant Sun, The. *Fr.* Herman Moon's Hourbook. Middleton.
Day came slow, till five o'clock, the. Dickinson.
Deirdre's Song at Sunrise. Sister Maura.
Design for a Stream-lined Sunrise. Sister Mary Madeleva.
Fingernail Sunrise. Watkins.
I'll tell you how the sun rose. Dickinson.
Reveille. Housman.
Sing a Song of Sunshine. Eastwick.
Sun Rising, The. Donne.
Sunrise. *Fr.* Hymns of the Marshes. Lanier.
Sunrise. Reese.
Sunrise. Wood.
Sunrise at Sea. Atherstone.
Sunrise at Sea. Sargent.
Sunrise at Sea. *Fr.* Tristram of Lyonesse. Swinburne.
Sunrise Trumpets. Auslander.
See also **Dawn; Morning.**

Sunset
Acceptance. Frost.
After Sunset. Allingham.
Afterglow. Borges.
Allie. Graves.
Any Sunset. Untermeyer.
At Set of Sun. Townsend.
At Sunset. Ledoux.
Datur Hora Quieti. *Fr.* The Doom of Devorgoil. Scott.
Fire in the Heavens. Brennan.
Looking Down on Mesopotamia. Bethell.
Ode to the Setting Sun. Thompson.
Of the Going Down of the Sun. Bunyan.
Prairie Sunset, A. Whitman.
Setting Sun, The. Horton.
Sundown. Adams.
Sunset. Bashford.
Sunset. Bayldon.
Sunset. Bailik.
Sunset, A. Coleridge.
Sunset, A. Hugo.
Sunset, A. Loveman.
Sunset. Muir.
Sunset at Les Eboulements, A. Lampman.
Sunset over the Aegean. *Fr.* The Corsair. Byron.
Sunset Wings. D. G. Rossetti.
This—is the land—the sunset washes. Dickinson.
'Twas at thatt hour of beauty when the setting sun. *Fr.* Testament of Beauty. Bridges.
Village before Sunset. Cornford.
Winter Sunset. Laforgue.
Whole gulfs of red and fleets of red. Dickinson.
See also **Evening; Twilight.**

Superb (ship)
Old *Superb*, The. Newbolt.

Superior, Lake
Great Lakes Suite, The. Reaney.
Lake Superior. Goodrich.
Memory of Lake Superior. Dillon.

Supernatural
Fire and Sleet and Candlelight (FiSC). August Derleth, ed.
Shrieks at Midnight; Macabre Poems, Eerie and Humorous (ShM). Sara Brewton *and* John E. Brewton, eds.

Surgeons. *See* **Physicians.**

Surrey, Henry Howard, Earl of
Henry Howard, Earl of Surrey, to the Lady Geraldine. *Fr.* England's Heroical Epistles. Drayton.
Verse in Praise of Lord Henry Howard, Earl of Surrey. Turberville.

Surrey, England
Pot-Pourri from a Surrey Garden. Betjeman.

Susanna (Bible)
Peter Quince at the Clavier. Stevens.
Susanna Fair, Sometime of Love Requested. *Unknown.*
Susannah and the Elders. *Unknown.*

Sussex, England
South Country, The. Belloc.
Southdown Summer. "Sagittarius."
Sussex. Kipling.

Sutter, John
John Sutter. Winters.

Swallows
Barn Swallow. Bell.
Barn-Swallow, The. Sargent.
Children's Song, The. *Unknown.*
Chimney Swallows. Powers.
Departure of the Swallow, The. Howitt.
First Swallow, The. Smith.
Homing Swallows. McKay.
Itylus. Swinburne.
O Master Masons. Toller.
O My Swallows! Toller.
Swallow, The. Aird.
Swallow, The. Cowley.
Swallow, The. Gasztold.
Swallow, The. *Fr.* Sing-Song. C. G. Rossetti.
Swallow, The. Stanley.
Swallow Flight. Teasdale.
Swallow Song. Pickthall.
Swallow Tails. Robinson.
Swallows, The. Arnold.
Swallows, The. P. Dickinson.
Swallows, The; an Elegy. Jago.
Swallow's Flight, The. Levy.
Swallow's Nest, The. Arnold.
Swallows over the Camp. Krige.
To a Swallow Building under Our Eaves. Carlyle.

Swan Lake (ballet)
Swan, The. Spender.

Swans
Black Swan, The. Jarrell.
Dark World, A. Scovell.
Dying Swan, The. Moore.
Dying Swan, The. Tennyson.
Dying Swan, The. *Unknown.*
Goe bidd the swan in silence dye. *Unknown.*
Gray Swan, The. Cary.
Icebound Swans, The. *Unknown.*
Love of Swans, The. Mann.
Riddle, A: "Clothes make no sound when I tread ground." *Unknown.*
Romance of the Swan's Nest, The. E. B. Browning.
Silver Swan, The. *Unknown.*
Sitting Pretty. Fishback.
Swan, The. Baudelaire.
Swan, The. Fletcher.
Swan, The. Flint.
Swan, The. Gosse.
Swan. Lowbury.
Swan, The. Macpherson.
Swan, The. Mallarmé.
Swan, The. Rodgers.
Swan, A. *Fr.* Riddles. *Unknown.*
Swan and the Goose, The. Aesop.
Swan Bathing, The. Pitter.
Swan Boat, A. Utter.

Swans *(continued)*
Swan, The—Vain Pleasures. Horton.
Swans. Durrell.
Swans, The. Dyment.
Swans, The. E. Sitwell.
Swans, The. Young.
Swans at Night, *sel.* Gilmore.
Swan's Nest, The. Griffin.
To the Liffey with the Swans. Gogarty.
Transfigured Swan. Untermeyer.
Two Swans, The. Hood.
Watch of a Swan, The. Piatt.
Wild Swan. *Fr.* Riddles. *Unknown.*
Wild Swans. Millay.
Wild Swans at Coole, The. Yeats.
With that I saw two swannes of goodly hewe. *Fr.* Prothalamion. Spenser.
Swansea, Wales
Swansea Bay. Prichard.
Sweden
Carriage from Sweden, A. Moore.
Hymn: "O God, Who guid'st the fate of nations." Wennerberg.
March for Youth, A. Ossian-Nilsson.
Swedish National Hymn. Strandberg.
Sweet Peas
Sweet Peas. Keats.
Sweetbrier
O brier scents, on yon wet wing. Meredith.
Swift, Jonathan
Life and Genuine Character of Dean Swift, The. Swift.
On Seeing Swift in Laracor. MacNamara.
Swift's Epitaph. Yeats.
To Dr. Swift on His Birthday. Johnson.
Tryst in Brobdingnag. Rich.
Two women loved him, shapes of Heaven. *Fr.* Swift. Irwin.
Verses on the Death of Dr. Swift. Swift.
With a Copy of Swift's Works. *Fr.* Epigrams. Cunningham.
Swimming and Swimmers
Bathers. Tiller.
Bathing Song. Ridler.
Black Water and Bright Air. Carrier.
Come On In. *Unknown.*
Diver, The. Herbin.
400-Meter Freestyle. Kumin.
Idea of a Swimmer. Bloch.
Lakeshore. Scott.
Lesson, The. Krows.
Lone Bather. Klein.
Merrill's Brook. Scott.
Mother, May I Go Out to Swim? *Unknown.*
Of Swimming in Lakes and Rivers. Brecht.
Old Swimmer, The. Morley.
Our Silly Little Sister. Aldis.
Swim off the Rocks, A. Moss.
Swimmer. Francis.
Swimmer, The. Layton.
Swimmer, The. Noel.
Swimmer, The. Ransom.
Swimmer of Nemi, The. "Macleod."
Swimmers. Untermeyer.
Swimming. Scollard.
Yes, by Golly. *Unknown.*
Swinburne, Algernon Charles
Singer Asleep, A. Hardy.
Swings
Swing, The. Stevenson.
Swing Song, A. Allingham.
Swinging Song, A. Howitt.
Swiss, the
Swiss Peasant, The. Wordsworth.
Swithin, St.
St. Swithin. Henderson.
Switzerland
Arnold von Winkelreid. Montgomery.
Switzerland. *Fr.* William Tell. Knowles.
Thought of a Briton on the Subjugation of Switzerland. Wordsworth.
Sycamores. *See* **Plane Trees.**
Sydney, Australia
To Sydney. Mack.
Synge, John Millington
In Memory of Major Robert Gregory. Yeats.
Synge's Grave. Letts.
Syracuse, Sicily
Syracuse. Coatsworth.

T

Tabor, Elizabeth McCourt
Mistress of the Matchless Mine. Robertson.
Tabor, Horace Austin Warner
Ballad of Chicken Bill, The. Vaughn.
Tabor Grand Opera House (Denver, Colo.)
Curtain, The. Gower.
Tadoussac, Canada
Tadoussac. Bancroft.
Tadpoles
Boy and Tadpoles. Untermeyer.
Fatlipped, You Formless. Spivack.
Tadpole, The. Gould.
Tagus River, Spain and Portugal
Tagus, farewell, that westward with thy streams. Wyatt.
Tahiti
Tiare Tahiti. Brooke.
Vor a Gauguin Picture zu Singen. Stein.
Tai, China
Most-sacred Mountain, The. Tietjens.
Tailors
Amends to the Tailors and Soutars. Dunbar.
Flying Tailor, The. Hogg.
Tailor, The. "Ansky."
Tailor, The. De la Mare.
Tailor, The. Leftwich.
Taliesin
Prophecy of Taliesin, The. Taliesin.
Taliesin, *sels.* Hovey.
Taliessin's Return to Logres. Williams.
Talmud, The
Talmud, The. Frug.
Talmud Student, The. Bialik.
Tamalpais, Mount, California
As I Came down Mount Tamalpais. Urmy.
Tamerlane
Tamburlaine the Great, *sels.* Marlowe.
Tamerlane. Poe.
Tammuz
Death of Tammuz, The. Tchernichowsky.
Tampico, Mexico
Tampico. Conkling.
Tanagers
Scarlet Tanager, The. Benton.
Scarlet Tanager, The. Mason.
Tanglewood, Massachusetts. *See* **Berkshire Symphonic Festival.**
Tannhäuser
Tannhäuser. Payne.
Taos, New Mexico
House in Taos, A. Hughes.
Tapestry
Beyond the Tapestries. Farber.
Tapestry Weavers, The. Chester.
Unicorn and the Lady, The. Garrigue.
Tara, Ireland
Harp That Once through Tara's Halls, The. Moore.
Tara. *Fr.* Dinnshenchas. *Unknown.*
Tara Is Grass. *Unknown.*
Tasmania
Van Dieman's Land. *Unknown.*
Tattoos
"Blackie, the Electric Rembrandt." Gunn.
Taxes
Ballad on the Taxes, A. Ward.
Taxis
After Anacreon. Welch.
Taxis. Field.
Taylor, Bayard
Bayard Taylor. Longfellow.
Bayard Taylor. Whittier.

Taylor, Zachary
Zachary Taylor. R. Benét *and* S. V. Benét.
Tea
Poets at Tea, The. Pain.
Sassafras Tea. Newsome.
Tea Flowers. Rito.
Teaching and Teachers
Absent-Minded Professor. Nemerov.
Air Mail, Special. Sister Mary Philip.
America Was Schoolmasters. Coffin.
Education. Guiterman.
Examiner. Scott.
First Day of Teaching. Overstreet.
Flycatchers. Bridges.
For My Shakespeare Class. Adrian.
For WGF Who Was Told He Didn't Publish Enough To Be Promoted To Associate Professor. Lipsitz.
Freshmen. Spacks.
Golgotha. Kennedy.
Jolly Old Pedagogue, The. Arnold.
Late Tutorial. Buckley.
No teacher I of boys or smaller fry. Ramsay.
Oh, what harper could worthily harp it. *Fr.* The Schoolmaster Abroad with His Son. Calverley.
Old Brown Schoolhouse, The. *Unknown.*
On Returning to Teach. Bell.
Pedagogical Principles. Amoss.
Prayer of a Beginning Teacher. Dunnam.
Prayer of a Teacher. Littlewort.
Professor of Medieval Balladry. Sister Mary Maura.
Purist, The. Nash.
Scholars, The. Yeats.
Schoolmaster, The. *Fr.* Snow-bound. Whittier.
Schoolmaster. Yevtushenko.
Schoolmistress, The. Shenstone.
Snowy Day in School, A. Lawrence.
Teacher, The. Hill.
Teachers, The. Pilcher.
Teacher's Dream, The. Venable.
Teacher's Prayer, The. "Mistral."
Village Schoolmaster, The. *Fr.* The Deserted Village. Goldsmith.
"When the Students Resisted, a Minor Clash Ensued." Knight.
Tears
Eyes and Tears. Marvell.
Flow Not So Fast. *Unknown.*
Hymn, A: "Drop, drop, slow tears." Fletcher.
Lachrymae. Gascoyne.
My Lady's Tears. *Unknown.*
Saint Mary Magdalene; or, The Weeper. Crashaw.
Sonnet: "Three sortes of teares doe from myne eies distraine." Alabaster.
Tear, The. Byron.
Teare, The. Crashaw.
Tears. *Unknown.*
Tears, Flow No More. Herbert of Cherbury.
Tears, Idle Tears. *Fr.* The Princess. Tennyson.
Valediction, A: Of Weeping. Donne.
Weeper, The. Crashaw.
Tecumseh (Indian chief)
Fall of Tecumseh, The. *Unknown.*
Tecumseh, *sels.* Mair.
Tecumseh and the Eagles. Carman.
Teignmouth, England
Teignmouth. Keats.
Telegrams
Telegram. Wise.
Telegraph
On the Completion of the Pacific Telegraph. Very.
Telephone Poles
Telephone Poles. Updike.
Under a Telephone Pole. Sandburg.
Telephones
Dial Tone, The. Nemerov.
Eletelephony. Richards.
Think of Eight Numbers. Silverstein.
Television
Mousemeal. Nemerov.
News. Rutsula.
So let the month end: the new fiscal year. *Fr.* Treasury Holiday. Harmon.
Watching Television. Bly.
Winning of the TV West, The. Alexander.
Tell, William
Archer, The. Scollard.
Temeraire (ship)
Temeraire, The. Melville.
Temperance
Face upon the Floor, The. D'Arcy.
Temperance ("Wine taken with excess"). *Unknown.*
Temperance, or the Cheap Physician. Crashaw.
Teneriffe, Canary Islands
Atlantid islands, phantom-fair. *Fr.* Teneriffe. Myers.
Tennessee
October in Tennessee. Malone.
Tennessee. Boyle.
Tennessee. *Fr.* Intaglios. Brooks.
When It's Iris Time in Tennessee. Waid.
Tennessee Valley Authority
T. V. A., The. *Unknown.*
Tennis
At the Tennis Clinic. Martin.
Ballade of Lawn Tennis, A. Adams.
Dark Eyes at Forest Hills. Martin.
Miraculously, through prayer to Saint Anthony. *Fr.* Adulescentia. Fitzgerald.
Near the Base Line. Albert.
Old Tennis Player. Brooks.
Olympic Girl, The. Betjeman.
Prothalamion. Kumin.
Snapshot for Miss Bricka Who Lost in the Semi-final Round of the Pennsylvania Lawn Tennis Tournament at Haverford, July, 1960, A. Wallace.
Tennis. Avison.
Tennis in San Juan. Denney.
Tennyson, Alfred Tennyson, 1st Baron
Alfred, Lord Tennyson. Whittemore.
I Entreat You, Alfred Tennyson. Landor.
Lacrimae Musarum. Watson.
Tennyson. Aldrich.
Tennyson. Coates.
Tennyson. Huxley.
Wapentake. Longfellow.
Teresa, Saint. *See* **Theresa, Saint.**
Termites
Termite, The. Nash.
Termites. Bell.
Termites, The. Hillyer.
Terns
Arctic Tern in a Museum. Newsome.
Common Terns. P. Dickinson.
Texas
All Girls Drill Team, The. Bell.
Cowboy's Lament, The. *Unknown.*
Disheartened Ranger, The. *Unknown.*
Homage to Texas. Graves.
Lasca. Desprez.
Little Boys of Texas. Coffin.
Mississippi Girls. *Unknown.*
Mustang Gray, The. *Unknown.*
Song of Texas. Hosmer.
Texas. Daugherty.
Texas. A. Lowell.
Texas. Whittier.
Texas, Our Texas. Wright.
Texas Rangers, The. *Unknown.*
Texas Trains and Trails. Austin.
Texas Types—"The Bad Man." Chittenden.
We Love the Name of Texas. *Unknown.*
Wisconsin Soldier Boy, The. *Unknown.*
Thalia (mythology)
Thalia. Aldrich.
Thames (river), England
Bab-Lock-Hythe. Binyon.
Lover to the Thames of London to Favour His Lady Passing Thereon, The. Turberville.
Song of the River Thames, A. *Fr.* Albion and Albanius. Dryden.
Thames, The. Hutchinson.
Thames from Cooper's Hill, The. *Fr.* Cooper's Hill. Denham.
There Is a Hill beside the Silver Thames. Bridges.

Thanksgiving
Another Grace for a Child. Herrick.
Are We Thankful? *Unknown.*
Be Thankful. Bullock.
Child's Grace, A. Burns.
For Beauty, We Thank Thee. Oxenham.
Give Thanks. Tupper.
God, You Have Been Too Good to Me. Stork.
Grace. De la Mare.
Grace. Emerson.
Grace, A. Tiplady.
Grace and Thanksgiving. Gould.
Grace at Evening. Guest.
Grace at Evening. Poteat.
Grace before Sleep. Teasdale.
How Are Thy Servants Blest. Addison.
Hymn: "For Summer's bloom and Autumn's blight." *Fr.* Bittersweet. Holland.
Hymn: "Lord, by whose breath all souls and seeds are living." Young.
Hymn of Thanksgiving. *Unknown.*
I Have a Roof. Jackson.
I Thank You God for Most This Amazing. Cummings.
In Every Thing Give Thanks. *Unknown.*
In Thankfull Remembrance for My Dear Husband's Safe Arrivall Sept. 3, 1662. Bradstreet.
Let Us Give Thanks. Farningham.
Little Te Deum of the Commonplace, A, *sels.* Oxenham.
Morning Thanksgiving. Drinkwater.
Not Alone for Mighty Empire. Merrill.
Now Thank We All Our God. Rinkart.
One Thousandth Psalm, The. Hale.
Our Prayer. Herbert.
Our Prayer of Thanks. Sandburg.
People's Thanksgiving, The. Merrill.
Poet's Grace, A. Burns.
Prayer before Meat. Harsen.
Prayer for Thanksgiving, A. Auslander.
Song of Thanks, A. Jones.
Song of Thanksgiving. Moreland.
Sunset. Carmichael.
Thank-You, A. Canton.
Thank you for the world so sweet. Leatham.
Thankful Heart. Davis.
Thankfulness. Procter.
Thanks. Gale.
Thanks Be to God. Alford.
Thanks in Old Age. Whitman.
Thanks to God. Hultman.
Thanksgiving, A. Bangs.
Thanksgiving. Barr.
Thanksgiving. Best.
Thanksgiving. Coates.
Thanksgiving. Driscoll.
Thsnksgiving, The. Herbert.
Thanksgiving. Howells.
Thanksgiving. Ketchum.
Thanksgiving, A. Larcom.
Thanksgiving. Morgan.
Thanksgiving, A. Cardinal Newman.
Thanksgiving. Nichols.
Thanksgiving. Osborne.
Thanksgiving. Oxenham.
Thanksgiving. Shepard.
Thanksgiving, A. Taylor.
Thanksgiving. Towne.
Thanksgiving. Wilder.
Thanksgiving Day. Bridges.
Thanksgiving for Thanksgiving. Wells.
Thanksgiving for the Earth. Goudge.
Thanksgiving Hymn. *Unknown.*
Thanksgiving Rosary, A. Markham.
Thanksgiving Song. Scollard.
Thanksgiving to God for His House, A. Herrick.
Things I Miss, The. Higginson.
To the Spirit Great and Good. Hunt.
We Plow the Fields. Claudius.
We Thank Thee. *Unknown.*
We Thank Thee, Lord. Oxenham.
Whether we mutter a thank you or not. *Unknown.*
Youth's Thankfulness. Kramer.
Sourcebook of Poetry (SoP). Al Bryant, comp.

Thanksgiving Day
Every Day Thanksgiving Day. Spofford.
Feast Day, The. McDonall.
First Thanksgiving Day, The. Brotherton.
First Thanksgiving Day, The. Preston.
First Thanksgiving of All. Turner.
For an Autumn Festival. Whittier.
Forever on Thanksgiving Day. Nesbit.
Giving Thanks. *Unknown.*
Good Thanksgiving, A. Robinson.
Gratitude. Sangster.
Harvest Hymn. *Fr.* For an Autumnal Festival. Whittier.
Hymn of Thanksgiving, A. Nesbit.
Hymn Written for the 200th Anniversary of the Old South Church, Beverly, Mass. Larcom.
If I Were a Pilgrim Child. Bennett.
Pumpkin, The. Whittier.
Thanksgiving. Brotherton.
Thanksgiving, A. Larcom.
Thanksgiving. Münsterberg.
Thanksgiving. Sangster.
Thanksgiving. Simpson.
Thanksgiving Day. Child.
Thanksgiving Day. Montague.
Thanksgiving Day. Wynne.
Thanksgiving Fable, A. Herford.
Thanksgiving in Boston Harbor, The. Butterworth.
Thanksgiving Magic. Bennett.
Thanksgiving Night. Nesbit.
Thanksgiving Time. *Unknown.*
Thanksgiving Wishes. Guiterman.
Thanksgiving. Piety.
Turkey Time. *Unknown.*
We Thank Thee ("For glowing autumn's brimming yield"). Clark.
We Thank Thee ("Not for our lands, our wide-flung prairie wealth"). Clark.
We Thank Thee. Renwick.
Sourcebook of Poetry (SoP). Al Bryant, comp.

Theater
At the Theater. Field.
"Ej Blot til Lyst." Payne.
Grand Opening of the People's Theatre. Goldrick.
Ode to Himself. Jonson.
Prologue Spoken by Mr. Garrick at the Opening of the Theater Royal, 1747. Johnson.
Theatre, The. Smith.
With some pot-fury, ravished from their wit. *Fr.* Virgidemiarum. Hall.

Theocritus
Ballade to Theocritus, in Winter. Lang.
For a Copy of Theocritus. Dobson.
Theocritus. Fields.
Theocritus. Gosse.
Theocritus. Langhorne.
Theocritus. Wilde.
Written on a Fly-Leaf of Theocritus. Thompson.

Theology
Theology. Kilmer.

Thera (island), Greece
Santorin. Flecker.

Theresa, Saint, of Avila
After Reading Saint Teresa, Luis de Leon and Ramon Lull. Lee.
Apologie for the Precedent Hymnes on Teresa, An. Crashaw.
Conversation in Avila. McGinley.
Flaming Heart, The. Crashaw.
Hymn to the Name and Honor of the Admirable Saint Teresa, A. Crashaw.
Teresa of Avila. Jennings.

Thermopylae, Battle of
Thermopylae. Simonides.
Thermopylae. Thwaites.
Variations on Simonides. Ely.

Theseus
Labyrinth, The. Muir.
Theseus and Ariadne. Mifflin.

Thirty Years War
Ode, upon Occasion of His Majesties Proclamation in the Year 1630, An. *Fr.* Il Pastor Fido. Fanshawe.

Thistles
Roadside thistle, eager, The. Basho.
Thistledown. Monro.
Thomas, Dylan
Contempt for Dylan Thomas, A. Watson.
Dylan Thomas. Spender.
Thousandth Poem for Dylan Thomas, A. Ciardi.
When a Warlock Dies. Gardner.
Thomas, Edward
To E. T. Frost.
To Edward Thomas. Lewis.
Thomas, George Henry
Thomas at Chickamauga. Sherwood.
Thomas à Becket, Saint
Becket's Diadem. *Unknown.*
Murder of Saint Thomas of Kent, The. *Unknown.*
Thomas à Kempis
Paraphrase on Thomas à Kempis. Pope.
Thomas à Kempis. Bowker.
Thomas à Kempis. Reese.
Thomas Aquinas, Saint
Master-Welder, The. Taylor.
Saint Thomas Aquinas. Jones.
St. Thomas Aquinas. Miller.
Thomas the Rhymer (Thomas of Erceldoune)
Thomas the Rhymer. *Unknown.*
Thompson, Francis
On the Death of Francis Thompson. Noyes.
Quiet Singer, The. Towne.
Thomson, James (1700-1748)
Ode on the Death of Mr. Thomson. Collins.
Thomson, Tom.
Tom Thomson. Bourinot.
Thoreau, Henry David
Alimentary. Fadiman.
On Visiting the Graves of Hawthorne and Thoreau. Very.
Savages, The. Miles.
Thoreau. A. B. Alcott.
Thoreau's Flute. L. M. Alcott.
Thousand Islands, New York and Ontario
Thousand Islands, The. *Fr.* The St. Lawrence and the Saguenay. Sangster.
Three Holy Children (Shadrach, Meshach, Abed-nego)
Warm Babies. Preston.
Three Kings. *See* **Magi.**
Thrushes
Blow Softly, Thrush. Taylor.
Brown Thrush, The. Larcom.
Come In. Frost.
Darkling Thrush, The. Hardy.
Might these be thrushes climbing through almost. Cummings.
My Thrush. Collins.
Northern Water Thrushes. Jones.
On a Thrush Singing in Autumn. Morris.
Overflow. Tabb.
Singer, The. Dowden.
Song of the Thrush, The. Daly.
Throstle, The. Tennyson.
Thrush, The. L. Benét.
Thrush, The. Corsellis.
Thrush, The. Duffy.
Thrush Sings, A. Henley.
Thrushes. Hughes.
Thrushes. Wolfe.
Thrush's Nest, The. Clare.
Thrush's Song, The. *Unknown.*
To a Thrush. Daly.
What the Thrush Said. Keats.
What the Thrush Says. Scott-Hopper.
Where the Wood-Thrush Calls. Hughan.
Thunder
Song of the Thunder. *Unknown.*
Thunder over Earth. Colony.
Thyme
Wild Thyme. Sambrook.
Tibet
Pilgrims of Thibet, The. Rice.
Tichborne, Chidiock
Elegy: "My prime of youth is but a frost of cares." Tichborne.
Ticonderoga, Battle of
On the Defeat at Ticonderoga or Carilong. *Unknown.*
Surprise at Ticonderoga, The. Stansbury.
Ticonderoga. Wilson.
Tides
High Tide on the Coast of Lincolnshire. Ingelow.
Tide Rises, the Tide Falls, The. Longfellow.
Tide Will Win, The. Leonard.
Tides, The. Tapper.
Tides. Williams.
Tigers
Here She Is. Miller.
India. Turner.
Tiger, The. *Fr.* Songs of Experience. Blake.
Tigress, The. Pitter.
Young Lady of Niger, The. *Unknown.*
Tilghman, Tench
Ride of Tench Tilghman, The. Scollard.
Till (river), England
Two Rivers. *Unknown.*
Timagami Lake, Canada
Temagami. Lampman.
Timber Line
At Timber Line. Mayer.
Timber Line Trees. Holme.
Time
Alas, How Soon the Hours. Landor.
All That's Bright Must Fade. Moore.
All That's Past. De la Mare.
And Lightly, like the Flowers. Ronsard.
As I Walked Out One Evening. Auden.
August. MacNeice.
Burnt Norton. *Fr.* Four Quartets. Eliot.
Chronometer, The. Sullivan.
Cities and Thrones and Powers. *Fr.* Puck of Pook's Hill. Kipling.
Clock, The. Baudelaire.
Coach of Time, The. Pushkin.
Cold Fall. Eberhart.
Conclusion, The. Ralegh.
Day, The. Spencer.
Days. Emerson.
Description of Time and the Year, A. Tusser.
Devouring Time, blunt thou the lion's paws. Sonnets, XIX. Shakespeare.
Dialogue betwixt Time and a Pilgrim, A. Townsend.
Earthly Illusion. Leighton.
End of the Year, The. Su T'ung-po.
Enemy, The. Baudelaire.
Father Father Son and Son. Swan.
Father Time. Ault.
Four Quartz Crystal Clocks. Moore.
Gone in the Wind. Mangan.
Harvest to Seduce, A. Cane.
How Many Seconds in a Minute? C. G. Rossetti.
I Could Give All to Time. Frost.
If you were coming in the fall. Dickinson.
In a Prominent Bar in Secaucus One Day. Kennedy.
In Railway Halls, on Pavements. Spender.
Influence of Time on Grief. Bowles.
Into a little close of mine I went. Lorenzo de' Medici.
Isle of Long Ago, The. Taylor.
Jade Flower Palace. Tu Fu.
Ladies, You See Time Flieth. *Unknown.*
Last Leaf, The. Holmes.
Like as the waves make towards the pebbled shore. Sonnets, LC. Shakespeare.
Meditation on Time. Sister Mary Athanasius.
Minute, The. Shapiro.
Moment, The. Raine.
Moods, The. Yeats.
Mount, The. Adams.
Mouse Whose Name Is Time, The. Francis.
Nature, That Washed Her Hands in Milk. Ralegh.
Next, Please. Larkin.
Noise That Time Makes, The. Moore.
North Infinity Street. Aiken.
O Heavy Step of Slow Monotony. Toller.
Old Gardener Time. Field.
On Time. Milton.
One by One. Hall.

Time *(continued)*
Our Bias. Auden.
Palinode. Gogarty.
Paradox of Time, The. Dobson.
Petition to Time, A. "Cornwall."
Plays. Landor.
Plutus, Cupid and Time. *Fr.* Fables. Gay.
Power of Time, The. Swift.
Porper Sonnet, How Time Consumeth All Earthly Things, A. *Unknown.*
Quod Tegit Omnia. Winters.
River of Life, The. Campbell.
Roses. Ronsard.
Sands of Time, The. Howard.
Since brass, nor stone, nor earth, nor boundless sea. Sonnets, LXV. Shakespeare.
So, So. Clerke.
Song Set by John Farmer. *Unknown.*
Sun-Dial, The. *Fr.* Melincourt. Peacock.
Take time while time doth last. *Unknown.*
There Isn't Time. Farjeon.
They say that "time assuages." Dickinson.
Thought Suggested by the New Year, A. Campbell.
Thy Beauty Fades. Very.
Time. Bharthrihari.
Time. Collier.
Time. Curnow.
Time. Graves.
Time. Herbert.
Time. Hodgson.
Time. Mayne.
Time. Shelley.
Time. Schiller.
Time. Scollard.
Time. Scott.
Time. Wilkinson.
Time and Death. Whitworth.
Time and Eternity. Bunyan.
Time and Grief. Bowles.
Time and Tide. Lamarre.
Time, cruel Time, come and subdue that brow. *Fr.* To Delia. Daniel.
Time Eating. Douglas.
Time Has Come, the Clock Says Time Has Come, The. *Fr.* Preludes for Memnon. Aiken.
Time Lags Abed. Cresswell.
Time Passes. Lister.
Time, Real and Imaginary. Coleridge.
Time stands still, with gazing on her face! *Unknown.*
Time, the Faithless. Iremonger.
Time to Die. Dendridge.
Time wasteth years, and months, and days, and hours. *Fr.* Hecatompathia. Watson.
Time, You Old Gypsy Man. Hodgson.
Timers. Arnstein.
Time's Bright Sand. Finch.
Time's Revenge. Learned.
Time's Revenges. R. Browning.
To His Coy Mistress. Marvell.
To His Watch, When He Could Not Sleep. Herbert of Cherbury.
To Leuconöe. *Fr.* Odes. Horace.
To the Virgins, to Make Much of Time. Herrick.
To Think of Time. Whitman.
Trumpet, The. Ehrenburg.
What if a Day or a Month or a Year. Campion.
What Time of Day? *Unknown.*
When I consider every thing that grows. Sonnets, XV. Shakespeare.
When I do count the clock that tells the time. Sonnets, XII. Shakespeare.
When I have seen by Time's fell hand defaced. Sonnets, LXIV. Shakespeare.
Who Was It, Tell Me. Heine.
Words in Time. MacLeish.
Time (magazine)
Sub-average *Time* Reader, The. Wittenberg.
Time like an Ever-rolling Stream. Wodehouse.
Times Square, New York City
City Birds. Johnson.
Tintoretto (Jacopo Robusti)
La Creazione degli Animali. Brinnin.
Lament for Tintoretta *Fr.* Three Fragments. Collins.
Tippecanoe, Battle of
Battle of Tippecanoe, The. *Unknown.*
Tipperary, Ireland
Ah, Sweet Is Tipperary. McCarthy.
Tipperary. Kelly.
Tipperary Recruiting Song. *Unknown.*
Tiresias
Tiresias. Garrett.
Titanic (ship)
Convergence of the Twain, The. Hardy.
Titanic, The, *sels.* Pratt.
Titanic, The. *Unknown.*
Titian (Tiziano Vecellio)
From Titian's "Bacchanal" in the Prado at Madrid. Moore.
Titmice. *See* **Chickadees.**
Titus (Roman emperor)
Titus and Berenice. Heath-Stubbs.
Toads
At the Garden Gate. McCord.
Death of a Toad, The. Wilbur.
Friend in the Garden, A. Ewing.
Hoppity Toads. Fisher.
Little Horned Toad. *Unknown.*
Our Mr. Toad. McCord.
Proud Toad, The. Hallock.
Song of Mr. Toad, The. *Fr.* The wind in the Willows. Grahame.
Song of the Toad, The. Burroughs.
Spring Song. Finkel.
Toad, The. Corbière.
Toad, The. Kent.
Toad and the Frog, The. *Unknown.*
Tree Toad, The. Shannon.
Warty Bliggens, the Toad. Marquis.
Tobacco
Farewell to Tobacco, A. Lamb.
Humor of Tobacco and the Rest, The. Parrot.
Man Has No Smokestack. *Unknown.*
O Metaphysical Tobacco. *Unknown.*
Ode to Tobacco. Calverley.
On Tobacco. Pestel.
Pernicious Weed. Cowper.
Pipe of Tobacco, A, *sels.* Browne.
Pipe of Tobacco, The. *At. to* Usher.
Religious Use of Taking Tobacco, A. *At. to* Wisdome.
Said the Whisky Flask. *Unknown.*
Tocacco. Hemminger.
Tobacco, Tobacco. *Unknown.*
Tobacco's a musician. *Fr.* Technogamia. Holyday.
Toledo, Spain
High Bridge above the Tagus River at Toledo, The. Williams.
Toledo. Restrapo.
Toledo. Zorilla.
Toledo, July 1936. Campbell.
Toller, Ernst
In Memory of Ernst Toller. Auden.
Tolstoy, Leo
Reading Tolstoy. Peter.
Tolstoy Seeks the Peasant Rhythm. Schevill.
Tomi, Rumania
Winter at Tomi. Ovid.
Tone, Theobald Wolfe
Tone's Grave. Davis.
Tonson, Jacob
Jacob Tonson, His Publisher. Dryden.
Toothache
Charm against the Toothache, A. Heath-Stubbs.
Meditation upon the Toothache, A. Lerner.
Toothbrushes
My Six Toothbrushes. McGinley.
Torah, The
Angels Came a-Mustering, The. *Unknown.*
Simhat Torah. Gordon.
Talmud Student, The. Bialik.
This Feast of the Law. *Unknown.*
Tornadoes
Tornado. Stafford.

Tortoises
Baby Tortoise. Lawrence.
Legend of the Tortoise, The. Tennant.
Meditations of a Tortoise Dozing under a Rosetree near a Beehive. Rieu.
Night Thought of a Tortoise Suffering from Insomnia on a Lawn. Rieu.
On Amaryllis, a Tortoyse. Pickthall.
Soliloquy of a Tortoise on Revisiting the Lettuce Beds. Rieu.
To My Tortoise Araykn (Ananke). Lee-Hamilton.
To My Tortoise Chronos. Lee-Hamilton.
Tortoise, The. Asquith.
Tortoise Family Connections. Lawrence.
Tortoise Gallantry. Lawrence.
Tortoise in Eternity, The. Wylie.
Tortoise Shell. Lawrence.
Tourists
Arrival at Santos. Bishop.
Conducted Tour. Swan.
Tourist and the Town, The. Rich.
Tourist Time. Scott.
Tourists. Moss.
Who Wants to Travel All Over Europe and See Nothing but a Lot of American Tourists? I Do. Nash.
Toussaint L'Ouverture, Françis Dominique
To Toussaint L'Ouverture. Wordsworth.
Toussaint L'Ouverture. Robinson.
Toyokuni Utagawa
Ballade of a Toyokuni Color-Print. Henley.
Toys
Block City. Stevenson.
Cirque d'Hiver. Bishop.
Duel, The. Field.
Dumb Soldier, The. Stevenson.
Land of Counterpane, The. Stevenson.
Little Boy Blue. Field.
Lost Doll, The. *Fr.* The Water Babies. Kingsley.
Toys, The. Patmore.
What the Toys Are Thinking. Wolfe.
Track Athletics
From the Greek Anthology. Crinagoras.
Mighty Runner, A. Robinson.
Notes on a Track Meet. McCord.
Runner. Auden.
Runner, The. Whitman.
Sluggard, The. Lucilius.
Sprinters, The. Murchison.
To James. Horne.
Tractors
New Farm Tractor. Sandburg.
Tractor. Hart-Smith.
Trafalgar, Battle of
Night of Trafalgar, the. *Fr.* The Dynasts. Hardy.
Trafalgar. Palgrave.
Trafalgar Square, London
Sunken Evening in Trafalgar Square. Lee.
Trafalgar Square. Fyleman.
Traherne, Thomas
Of Thomas Traherne and the Pebble Outside. Clouts.
Trailing Arbutus. *See* **Arbutus.**
Trains
As We Rush, as We Rush in the Train. *Fr.* Sunday at Hampstead. Thompson.
Beautiful Train, The. Empson.
Box-Car Letters. Baker.
City Nights: In the Train. Symons.
Engine. Tippett.
Engineer, The. Milne.
Express, The. Spender.
Express Trains. Black.
Freight Train, The. Bennett.
From a Railway Carriage. Stevenson.
From the Train. Wilson.
I like to see it lap the miles. Dickinson.
In the Train. Bax.
Iron Horse, The. Newman.
Landscape as Metal and Flowers. Scott.
Limited. Sandburg.
Modern Dragon, A. Bennett.
Morning Express. Sassoon.
Night Express. Black.
Night Express, The. Monkhouse.
Night Journey. Roethke.
Night Mail. Auden.
Night-Ride, The. Slessor.
Night Train. Francis.
Night Train. Stoutenburg.
Orient Express, The. Jarrell.
Passenger Train. Chase.
Praises of the Train. Segooa.
Railroad Cars Are Coming, The. *Unknown.*
Rhyme of the Rail. Saxe.
Shunting. Dowling.
Song of a Train. Davidson.
Song of the Train. McCord.
To a Locomotive in Winter. Whitman.
Train, The. M. E. Coleridge.
Train, The. *Unknown.*
Train in the Night, The. Riddell.
Train Will Fight to the Pass, The. Pitter.
Train Window. Finch.
Trains. Tippett.
Trains at Night. F. Frost.
Travel. Millay.
Travelling Backwards. Baro.
View. Miles.
Wabash Cannonball, The. *Unknown.*
Ways of Trains, The. Coatsworth.
Tramps. *See* **Vagabonds.**
Transcendentalism
Transcendentalism; a Poem in Twelve Books. R. Browning.
Translations and Translators
On First Looking into Chapman's Homer. Keats.
On First Looking into Loeb's Horace. Durrell.
To His Friend Ben. Johnson, of His Horace Made English. Herbert of Cherbury.
To the Translator of Lucan. Ralegh.
Who Translates a Poet Badly. Prada.
Transvaal, South Africa
Lichtenberg. Kipling.
Trash
Junk. Wilbur.
Traubel, Helen
I Like to Sing Also. Updike.
Travel
Advice against Travel. Mangan.
Flight, The. *Fr.* A Time to Dance. Day Lewis.
Home Leave. Howes.
Journey, The. Winters.
Lonely Traveller, The. Brew.
Missouri Traveller Writes Home, A, 1830. Bly.
Movies for the Home. Moss.
On the Move. Gunn.
Over 2000 Illustrations and a Complete Concordance. Bishop.
Plain Fare. Hine.
Sailing Homeward. Chan Fang-sheng.
St. Gervais. Roberts.
Song about Myself. Keats.
Song of the Open Road. Whitman.
Song of the Road, A. Stevenson.
Starting from Paumanok. Whitman.
There Are So Many Ways of Going Places. Thompson.
To a Poet Who Has Never Travelled. Causley.
To Sir Henry Goodyere. Donne.
Travel. Millay.
Travel. Stevenson.
Travel Bureau, The. Mitchell.
Travel Song. Hofmannsthal.
Traveller, The. Auden.
Traveller's Curse After Misdirection. Graves.
Traveller's Tale, A. Plomer.
Travelling. Gradon.
Two Travelers. Day Lewis.
Treason
Of Treason. Harington.
Tree Toads
Tree-Toad. Conkling.
Tree-Toad, The. Johns.
Tree Toad, The. Shannon.
Trees
A B C's in Green. Speyer.
Autumn Fashions. Thomas.

Trees *(continued)*
Autumnal Spring Song. Miller.
Axe in the Wood, The. Dyment.
Ballad of Trees and the Master, A. Lanier.
Bare Almond-Trees. Lawrence.
Be Different to Trees. Davies.
Bedtime. Coatsworth.
Brooms. Aldis.
Bushfeller, The. Duggan.
Child's Song in Spring. Nesbit.
City Tree, The. Crawford.
City Trees. Millay.
City Trees. Scruggs.
Coming of the Trees, The. Guiterman.
Cocoa-Tree, The. Stoddard.
Comfort of the Trees, The. Gilder.
Cross and the Tree, The. Stidger.
Cut It Down. M. E. Coleridge.
Detail. Bethell.
Double Tree, The. Scott.
Every Time I Climb a Tree. McCord.
Fallen Tree, The. Young.
For the Slender Beech and the Sapling Oak. *Fr.* Maid Marian. Peacock.
Forest Song. Venable.
Fur trees—upon a solitary acre. Dickinson.
Good Company. Baker.
Green Councillors. Corning.
Heart of the Tree, The. Bunner.
Heresy for a Classroom. Humphries.
Hill-Side Tree. Bodenheim.
House of the Trees, The. Wetherald.
I Planted Little Trees To-Day. Carrington.
I Saw in Louisiana a Live-Oak Growing. Whitman.
In a Wood. *Fr.* The Woodlanders. Hardy.
Jungle Trees, The. Wilson.
Leafless Tree, A. Thompson.
Legends for Trees, *sels.* Ketchum.
Motto for a Tree-planting. Gilder.
Mountain Tree, The. Connell.
Note on Local Flora. Empson.
O Brother Tree. Michelson.
Old Tree, The. Young.
Paradigm. Deutsch.
Plant a Tree. Larcom.
Planting a Tree. Turner.
Planting Trees. Friedlaender.
Proud Trees, The. Kerr.
Reflection. Allonby.
Roots. Ginsberg.
Salute to Trees, A. Van Dyke.
Sapling. Johnson.
Song: "For the tender beech and the sapling oak." Peacock.
Song of the Forest Trees. *Unknown.*
Song of the Trees. Colborne-Veel.
Song of the Wood, The. Weatherly.
Song to a Tree. Markham.
Sound of the Trees, The. Frost.
Strange Tree. Roberts.
Tall Trees. Kramer.
Tapestry Trees. Morris.
This Way Only. Harford.
Three Green Trees. Morgan.
Three Trees. Crandall.
Timber Line Trees. Holme.
To the Wayfarer. *Unknown.*
Tree, The. Björnson.
Tree, The. Ehrenburg.
Tree, The. Kreymborg.
Tree, A. C. G. Rossetti.
Tree, The. Very.
Tree, The. Wilson.
Tree, The. Countess of Winchilsea.
Tree and Sky. Sassoon.
Tree at Dusk, A. Welles.
Tree at My Window. Frost.
Tree Birthdays. Davies.
Tree Design, A. Bontemps.
Tree Feelings. Gilman.
Tree in the Desert, The. Hebbel.
Tree on the Hill. *Unknown.*
Tree-planting. Smith.
Tree Planting. *Unknown.*
Tree Shadows. *Unknown.*
Tree Stands Very Straight and Still, The. Wynne.
Trees. Behn.
Trees. Carman.
Trees. Clark.
Trees, The. Cole.
Trees. Sara Coleridge.
Trees. De la Mare.
Trees. Hughes.
Trees. Kilmer.
Trees, The. Larcom.
Trees, The. Morley.
Trees. Nemerov.
Trees, The. Rich.
Trees. *Fr.* The Faerie Queene. Spenser.
Trees. Trench.
Trees and Cattle. Dickey.
Trees Are Down, The. Mew.
Trees both in hills and plaines, in plenty be. Wood.
Trees in the Garden. Lawrence.
Trees That Shade a House. Worth.
Trees, Who are Distant. Warr.
Very Tree. Kunitz.
War against the Trees, The. Kunitz.
What Do We Plant? Abbey.
Wild Trees, The. Lee.
Winter Branches. Widdemer.
Winter Night. Hutchison.
Winter Trees, The. Dyment.
Winter Trees. Williams.
Wood Music. King.
Woodman, Spare That Tree. Morris.
Yes! I have seen the ancient oak. *Fr.* The Brereton Omen. Hemans.
See also ***names of trees (e.g.,*** **Oak Trees).**
Trelawny, Edward John
Trelawny Lies by Shelley. O'Donnell.
Trelawny, Sir Jonathan
Song of the Western Men, The. Hawker.
Trent (river), England
Sirena. *Fr.* The Shepherd's Sirena. Drayton.
Trenton, Battle of
Battle of Trenton, The. *Unknown.*
Trenton and Princeton. *Unknown.*
Trinity, the
To the Holy Trinity. Jonson.
Trinitas. Whittier.
Trinity, The. *Unknown.*
Tristan da Cunha (islands)
Tristan de Cunha. Campbell.
Tristram
Tristram and Iseult. Arnold.
Tristram of Lyonnesse, *sels.* Swinburne.
Tristram's End. Binyon.
Troilus and Cressida
Comparison of His Love with the Faithful and Painful Love of Troilus to Cressid, A. *Unknown.*
Cressid's Complaint. Whetstone.
Testament of Cresseid, The. Henryson.
Troilus and Cressida. De Vere.
Troilus and Cressida, *sels.* Dryden.
Troilus and Cressida, *sels.* Shakespeare.
Troilus and Criseyde, *sels.* Chaucer.
Trojan War
Illiad, The, *sels.* Homer.
Leaving Troy. Irwin.
Prayer of Calcas, The. *Fr.* Troelus a Chresyd. *Unknown.*
Troy. Muir.
Why They Waged War. Bishop.
Trolls
Troll's Nosegay, The. Graves.
Tropics
Tropical Town. Selva.
Tropics, The. Sladen.
Trossachs, The, Scotland
Trossachs, The. Wordsworth.
Trout
Heritage. Sullivan.
Sacrifice of a Rainbow Trout. Langland.

Sanctuary, The. Nemerov.
Trout, The. Hine.
Trout, The. Montague.
Troy
Ilion, Ilion. Tennyson.
Menelaus and Helen. Brooke.
Palladium. Arnold.
Troy. *Fr.* Trojan Women. Euripides.
Troy. Flower.
Troy. Muir.
Troy. *Fr.* A Mirror for Magistrates. Sackville.
Trucks
Country Trucks. Shannon.
Grumbling Truck, The. Bennett.
Song of the Truck. Frankel.
Trucker, A. Gunn.
Trucks. Tippett.
Trumpets
Lewis Has a Trumpet. Kuskin.
Truth, Sojourner (Isabella Van Wagener).
Oriflamme. Fauset.
Truth
Be True. Bonar.
Blind Men and the Elephant, The. Saxe.
Cassandra. Jeffers.
Coming of Wisdom with Time, The. Yeats.
Faustus. *Fr.* Horatio. Plutzik.
Goddess, The. Levertov.
I died for beauty. Dickinson.
Invocation: "Truth, be more precious to me than the eyes." Eastman.
Lie, The. Ralegh.
Magna Est Veritas. Patmore.
Ostler, The. *Fr.* Horatio. Plutzik.
Revenge. Nugent.
Simple Faith. *Fr.* Truth. Cowper.
1643 "Veritas" 1878. *Fr.* Two Sonnets: Harvard. Holmes.
Standing on Tiptoe. Cameron.
Tell all the truth but tell it slant. Dickinson.
Truth. "Æ."
Truth, The. Joans.
Truth, The. Lampman.
Truth. Lloyd.
Truth. Masefield.
Truth. North.
Truth Crushed to Earth. *Fr.* The Battlefield. Bryant.
Truth Is Quite Messy, The. Harris.
Truth Never Dies. *Unknown.*
"Truth," said a traveller. *Fr.* The Black Riders. Crane.
Ultima Veritas. Gladden.
Wayfarer, The. *Fr.* War Is Kind. S. Crane.
"With Whom Is No Variableness, neither Shadow of Turning." Clough.
Winter Lightning, The. Nemerov.
Truxton, Thomas
Truxton's Victory. *Unknown.*
Tu Fu
For Tu Fu. Feng Chih.
Tuberose
Tuberose. Block.
Tubman, Harriet
Harriet Tubman. Walker.
Tuileries, Paris
Le Jardin des Tuileries. Wilde.
Tulip Trees
Tulip Tree. S. Sitwell.
Tulips
Sleepy Tulips, The. Walker.
Stately Lady, The. Sandstrom.
Tulip. Smith.
Tulips. Colum.
Tulips. Plath.
Tulips and Addresses. Field.
Turberville, George
Epitaph in Commendation of George Turberville, a Learned Gentleman, An. Harington.
Turkeys
Black November Turkey, A. Wilbur.
Melancholy Lay, A. Fleming.
November's Come. Lincoln.
Table-Birds. Mackenzie.
Three Turkeys. Fleming.
Turkey, The. Nash.
Turkeys Observed. Heaney.
Turner, Nat
Ballad of Nat Turner, The. Hayden.
Remembering Nat Turner. Brown.
Turnips
Mr. Finney's Turnip. *Unknown.*
Turpin, Richard (Dick Turpin)
Dick Turpin and the Lawyer. *Unknown.*
My Bonny Black Bess. *Unknown.*
Turtle Doves
Phoenix and the Turtle, The. Shakespeare.
Turtle-Dove's Nest, The. *Unknown.*
Turtles
Covering the Subject. Armour.
Little Turtle, The. Lindsay.
Mud Turtle, The. Nemerov.
Mud Turtles. Hallock.
Turtle, The. Nash.
Turtle, The. Schevill.
Turtle and Flamingo, The. Fields.
Tuscany, Italy
Festival in Tuscany. Stead.
In Tuscany. Mackay.
Somewhere in Tuscany. Holbrook.
Tuskegee Institute
Tuskegee. Hill.
Tussaud, Madame
At Madame Tussaud's in Victorian Years. Hardy.
"Twain, Mark" (Samuel Langhorne Clemens)
Mark Twain; a Pipe Dream. Herford.
Tweed (river), Scotland and England
Twilight on Tweed. Lang.
Two Rivers. *Unknown.*
Twelfth Night
Ballad of the Epiphany. Dalmon.
Epiphany. Heber.
In the Glorious Epiphanie of Our Lord God. Crashaw.
Old Christmas Morning. Helton.
Poem for Epiphany. Nicholson.
Twelfth Night. Bishop.
Twelfth Night. Booth.
Twelfth Night. Lee.
Twelfth Night Carol. *Unknown.*
Twelve Days of Christmas, The. *Unknown.*
Twickenham, England
Twickenham Ferry. Marzials.
Twicknam Garden. Donne.
Written at Mr. Pope's House at Twickenham. Lyttelton.
Twilight
Approach of Evening. Croly.
As Soon as Ever Twilight Comes. De la Mare.
At Twilight. Van Rensselaer.
Beauty Is Most at Twilight's Close. Lagerkvist.
Broadway: Twilight. Prideaux.
Children's Hour, The. Longfellow.
Close of Day, The. Curtwright.
Dusk. Grimkè.
Dusk. Heyward.
Dusk. Lopez-Penha.
Dusk. MacLeish.
Dusk of Horses, The. Dickey.
Dusk Song. Moore.
Georgia Dusk. Toomer.
In the Gloaming. Bayles.
In the Twilight, *sels.* O'Donnell.
June Twilight. Masefield.
Near Dusk. Auslander.
Song of Twilight, A. *Unknown.*
Summer Twilight, A. Turner.
Sundown. Adams.
Twilight. Ch'en Yün.
Twilight. Custance.
Twilight. Heavysege.
Twilight. Heine.
Twilight. Lawrence.
Twilight. Longfellow.
Twilight. McCormick.
Twilight. Pagaza.
Twilight. Robinson.

Twilight *(continued)*
Twilight. Tyutchev.
Twilight at Sea. Welby.
Twilight at the Heights. Miller.
Twilight Calm. C. G. Rossetti.
Twilight in Middle March, A. Ledwidge.
Twilight on Tweed. Lang.
Twilight Song. *Fr.* De Roberval; a Drama. Hunter-Duvar.
Twilight Song. Robinson.
Winter Twilight, A. Bates.
Winter Twilight. Elliot.
Written in Very Early Youth. Wordsworth.
See also **Evening; Sunset**
Twins
Being Twins. Jackson.
Betwixt and Between. Lofting.
Dick and Will. Roberts.
Grace Ananne. Borie.
Twins, The. Aldis.
Twins. Graves.
Twins, The. Jackson.
Twins, The. Leigh.
Twins, The. Roberts.
Twins, The. Shapiro.
Tyburn Gallows, London
Tyburn and Westminster. Heywood.
Tyndale, William
From William Tyndale to John Frith. Bowers.
Tyranny
Antiquity of Freedom, The. Bryant.
England in 1819. Shelley.
Song to the Men of England. Shelley.
Tyrconnel, Richard Talbot, Duke and Earl of
Lilli Burlero. Wharton.
Tyringham, Massachusetts
Evening in Tyringham Valley. Gilder.
999U

U

Uccello, Paolo
Rout of San Romano, The. White.
Uccello. Corso.
Ulysses
Canto I: "And then went down to the ship." Pound.
Haunted Odysseus; the Last Testament. Gregory.
Homecoming, The. Baxter.
Odysseus Dying. Wingfield.
Odyssey, The, *sels.* Homer.
Odyssey, The. Lang.
Old Ships, The. Flecker.
Return, The. Muir.
Strayed Reveller, The. Arnold.
Ulysses. Graves.
Ulysses. Tennyson.
Ulysses and the Siren. Daniel.
Ulysses in Autumn. Auslander.
Ulysses Pondering. Plumly.
Ulysses Returns. Montgomery.
World as Meditation, The. Stevens.
Umbrellas
Elf and the Dormouse, The. Herford.
Umbrellas. Bennett.
Underhill, John
John Underhill. Whittier.
Unemployment
Hymn of the Unemployed. Tiplady.
Laid Off. Webb.
Prayer of an Unemployed Man. Ackerly.
Prayer of the Unemployed. *Unknown.*
Unemployed, The. Roberts.
Unicorns
Inhuman Henry; or, Cruelty to Fabulous Animals. Housman.
Strangers, The. Brown.
Unicorn, The. *Fr.* Nepenthe. Darley.
Unicorn, The. Pitter.
Unicorn, The. Young.
Unicorn and the Lady, The. Garrigue.
Unicorns at Harvard. Farber.
Virgin and Unicorn. Heath-Stubbs.
Union of Soviet Socialist Republics. *See* **Russia.**
Unions, Labor
My Master and I. *Unknown.*
There Is Power in a Union. *Unknown.*
Which Side Are You On? Reese.
United States
Ad Patriam. Scollard.
America. Babcock.
America. *Fr.* The Torch-Bearers. Bates.
America. Coates.
America. Dobell.
America. Dumas.
America. Ginsberg.
America. Hamilton.
America. Kreymborg.
America. McKay.
America. Smith.
America. *Fr.* National Ode. Taylor.
America First. Oldham.
America for Me. Van Dyke.
America Greets an Alien. *Unknown.*
America Is Corn. Coffin.
America Is Great Because. *At. to* De Tocqueville.
America my country, can the mind. *Fr.* Journals. Emerson.
America the Beautiful. Bates.
America to Great Britain. Allston.
America Was Promises, *sels.* MacLeish.
America Was Schoolmasters. Coffin.
American Feuillage. Whitman.
American Freedom, The. Biller.
American Letter. MacLeish.
American Names. S. V. Benét.
America's Answer. Lilliard.
America's Prosperity. Van Dyke.
Ancestral Dwellings, The. Van Dyke.
Approaching America. Squire.
Axe Has Cut the Forest Down, The. Coatsworth.
Background with Revolutionaries. MacLeish.
Brown River, Smile. Toomer.
Building of the Ship, The. Longfellow.
By Blue Ontario's Shore, *sels.* Whitman.
Centennial Hymn. Pierpont.
Columbia. Dwight.
Columbia, the Gem of the Ocean. Shaw.
Coming Back to America. Dickey.
Eagle's Song, The. Mansfield.
Empire Builders. MacLeish.
England and America in 1782. Tennyson.
For thou art founded in the eternal fact. *Fr.* My Country. Woodberry.
Free America. *At. to* Warren.
From Paumanok Starting I Fly like a Bird. Whitman.
Gift Outright, The. Frost.
God Bless America. Berlin.
History of the U.S., The. Stoner.
Howl. Ginsberg.
Hymn of the New World. MacKaye.
I Hear America Singing. Whitman.
I, Too. Hughes.
In the States. Stevenson.
International Hymn. Huntington.
Invocation: "American muse, whose strong and diverse heart." *Fr.* John Brown's Body. S. V. Benét.
It Is Time. Joans.
Land of Destiny. Parmenter.
Land of the Free. Hosking.
Land of the Free. MacLeish.
Land Where Hate Should Die, The. McCarthy.
Last Whiskey Cup, The. Engle.
Let America Be America Again. Hughes.
Localities. Sandburg.
Long, Too Long America. Whitman.
Map of My Country. Holmes.
Men. MacLeish.
Millions Are Learning How. Agee.
My America. Clark.
My America. La Grone.
My Country. Woodberry.
My Country, Right! Clark.
My Country 'Tis of Thee. Smith.
My Land. Davis.
National Hymn Roberts

New Colossus, The. Lazarus.
Next to of Course God. Cummings.
O Beautiful, My Country. Hosmer.
Oh Mother of a Mighty Race. Bryant.
Observe the Whole of It. Wolfe.
Ode Inscribed to W. H. Channing. Emerson.
Ode Recited at the Harvard Commemoration. J. R. Lowell.
On an Invitation to the United States. Hardy.
On the Emigration to America. Freneau.
On the Prospect of Planting Arts and Learning in America. Berkeley.
One Country. Stanton.
Our Country. Howe.
Our Country. Strong.
Our Country's Call. Bryant.
Our First Century. Woodberry.
Our Nation Forever. Bruce.
Over the Carnage Rose Prophetic a Voice. Whitman.
Peace Hymn of the Republic. Van Dyke.
People's Prayer, The. Wells.
Plain-Chant for America. Chapin.
Prairie-Grass Dividing, The. Whitman.
Prairies, The. Bryant.
Prospect of the Future Glory of America. Trumbull.
Quilt. Updike.
Refugee in America. Hughes.
Rooster, The. Orlovitz.
Santa-Fé Trail, The. Lindsay.
Shine, Perishing Republic. Jeffers.
Ship of State, The. *Fr.* The Building of the Ship. Longfellow.
Sleep, My Child. Aleichem.
Song for the States, A. Whitman.
Song of the Universal, *sels.* Whitman.
Star-spangled Banner, The. Key.
Star Spangled Ode. McGinley.
Starting from Paumanok. Whitman.
Sweet Land. Maguire.
There Is a Land. Montgomery.
This Is America. Clark.
To America. Austin.
To America. Garnett.
To Cole, the Painter, Departing for Europe. Bryant.
To My Countrymen. Johnson.
To the States. Whitman.
To the United States of America. Bridges.
To the Western World. Simpson.
Toast to Our Native Land, A. Bridges ("Droch").
Thou Mother with Thy Equal Brood. Whitman.
Travelling America. "Struther."
USA. Engle.
Under the Stars. Rice.
Union and Liberty. Holmes.
United States. Keble.
Watch, America. Nathan.
America Forever New (AmFN). Sara *and* John E. Brewton, comps.
My Country (MC). Burton Egbert Stevenson, ed.
Patriotic Anthology, The, (PaA). Introduced by Carl Van Doren.
Poems of American History (PAH). Burton Egbert Stevenson, ed.
Poems of American Patriotism (PAP). Brander Matthews, ed.
This Land is Mine (ThLM). Al Hine, ed.

United States (ship)
United States and *Macedonian*, The ("The Banner of Freedom high floated unfurled"). *Unknown.*
United States and *Macedonian*, The ("How glows each patriot bosom that boasts a Yankee heart"). *Unknown.*

United States Air Force
U. S. Air Force, The. Crawford.

United States Marine Corps
Marines' Hymn, The. *Unknown.*

Unknown Soldier
Epitaph for the Unknown Soldier. Kohn.
Passing of the Unknown Soldier, The. Owens.
Unknown, The. Laughlin.
Unknown Soldier. Dunn.
Unknown Soldier, The. Rhinow.
Unknown Soldier, The. Rose.

Universities. *See* **Colleges and Universities.**

Untermeyer, Louis
Mr. U Will Not Be Missed. Cummings.

Unwin, Mary
To Mary Unwin. Cowper.
To the Same. Cowper.

Upson, Arthur
Ave atque Vale. Jones.

Urania (mythology)
Urania. Arnold.
Urania. De Vere.
Urania. Pitter.

Uriel
Uriel. Emerson.

Ursa Major
Great Bear, The. Hollander.
Ursa Major. Kirkup.

Usk, England
Landscapes. Eliot.

Usury
Canto XLV: "With Usura." Pound.
Ditty of the Pen Inveighing against Usury and False Dealing, A. Hall.

Utah
Utah, We Love Thee. Stephens.

Ute Indians
Chipeta. Field.
Chipeta's Ride. Taylor.
Legend of Grand Lake, The. Westcott.
Red Ghosts Chant, The. Spencer.

Utrillo, Maurice
Utrillo's World. Glassco.

V

Vacation
Far from the Madding Crowd. Waterman.
Movies for the Home. Moss.
School Is Out. F. Frost.
Thy Blessing, Lord, on All Vacation Days! Haley.
Vacation Time. Bennett.
Vacation Time. Sangster.

Vagabonds
African Tramp, The. Haresnape.
Big Rock Candy Mountain, The. *Unknown.*
Hunchback in the Park, The. Thomas.
In Praise of a Beggar's Life. "A. W."
Mendicants, The. Carman.
Needle Travel. Patton.
November. Hughes.
On the Road. Roberts.
Road to Vagabondia, The. Burnet.
Sestina of the Tramp-Royal. Kipling.
Things of the Spirit. Mason.
To a Vagabond. Woodrow.
Tramp. Hughes.
Vagabond, The. Stevenson.
Vagabond House. Blanding.
Vagabonds, The. Johnson.
Vagabonds, The. Trowbridge.
Vagrant, The. Slender.

Valentine's Day
Ditty, A: "My true-love hath my heart, and I have his." Sidney.
Epithalamion, An: "Haile Bishop Valentine, whose day this is." Donne.
Good Bishop Valentine. Farjeon.
Hearts Were Made to Give Away. Wynne.
Mary's eyes are blue as azure. Silverstein.
My Valentine. Parsons.
Romance. Stevenson.
St. Valentine. Moore.
St. Valentine's Day. *Fr.* The Love Sonnets of Proteus. Blunt.
Saint Valentine's Day. Patmore.
St. Valentine's Way. Farjeon.
Special Delivery. Winton.
Sure Sign, A. Turner.
To Clarastella on St. Valentines Day Morning. Heath.
To His Valentine. Drayton.
To St. Valentine. Hartswick.
To-morrow Is Saint Valentine's Day. *Fr.* Hamlet. Shakespeare.
Valentine, A. Betham-Edwards.
Valentine. Blanden.
Valentine, A. Field.

Valentine's *(continued)*
Valentine, A. Hammond.
Valentine, A. Richards.
Valentine. Silverstein.
Valentine. "C. W. T."
Valentine Promise. *Unknown.*
Valentine to a Little Girl. Cardinal Newman.
Valentine Verses. Page.
Valentine's Day. Fisher.
Valentine's Message, The. Hill.
Valentines to My Mother, *sels.* C. G. Rossetti.
When You Send a Valentine. Hill.
Valkyries
Fatal Sisters, The. Gray.
Song of the Valkyries, The. *Unknown.*
Valparaiso, Battle of
Battle of Valparaiso, The. *Unknown.*
Vampires
Vampire. Kerr.
Vampire Bride. Stefanile.
Van Diemen's Land. *See* **Tasmania.**
Van Gogh, Vincent. *See* **Gogh, Vincent van.**
Vanbrugh, Sir John
Epitaph on Sir John Vanbrugh. Evans.
Vanbrug's House. Swift.
Vancouver, British Columbia
Lairdless Place, The. Archer.
Vancouver Lights. Birney.
Vane, Sir Henry
To Sir Henry Vane the Younger. Milton.
Vanity
Song of Emptiness to Fill Up the Empty Pages Following. Wigglesworth.
To Vanity. Turner.
Vanity. Graves.
Vanity. Herbert.
Vanity of All Worldly Things, The. Bradstreet.
Vanity of Existence, The. Freneau.
Varuna (ship)
Varuna, The. Boker.
Vases
Japanese Vase Wrought in Metal, A. Seiffert.
V-a-s-e, The. Roche.
Vaudeville
Vaudeville Dancer. Wheelock.
Vaughan, Henry
At the Grave of Henry Vaughan. Sassoon.
To Henry Vaughan. Smith.
Veeries
Veery, The. Van Dyke.
Verry-Thrush, The. Taylor.
Vegetables
Vegetables. Farjeon.
Vegetables. Field.
Vegetarians
Flying Bum, The: 1944. Plomer.
Logical Vegetarian, The. Chesterton.
Veils
Veil, The. De la Mare.
Velázquez, Diego Rodríquez de Silva y
Castilian. Wylie.
Veld
Nocturne: "Red flame flowers bloom and die." Garstin.
Veld Ecloque, A; the Pioneers, *sel.* Campbell.
Venice, Italy
At Venice. Clough.
Doves of Venice, The. Hutton.
For "A Venetian Pastorial" by Giorgione. D. G. Rossetti.
From a Venetian Sequence. Naudé.
Grand Canal. Ross.
Lines Written among the Euganean Hills. Shelley.
Music in Venice. Simpson.
Musing on Venice and the thought of thee. Symonds.
Notes Made in the Piazza San Marco. Swenson.
Ode on Venice. Byron.
On the Extinction of the Venetian Republic. Wordsworth.
Toccata of Galuppi's, A. R. Browning.
Venetian Night, A. Hofmannsthal.
Venetian Scene. Ridler.
Venetian Serenade, The. Milnes.
Venice. Longfellow.
Venice. Symonds.
Water-Colour of Venice, A. Durrell.
Venus (goddess)
Address to Venus. *Fr.* De Rerum Natura *and fr.* The Faerie Queene. Lucretius, *tr. by* Spenser.
Birth of Venus, The. *Unknown.*
Darling of God and Men, beneath the gliding stars. *Fr.* De Rerum Natura. Lucretius.
Death of Venus, The. Creeley.
Invocation. Watson.
Invocation to the Goddess, An. Wright.
Laus Veneris. Swinburne.
Queen of Paphos, Erycine, The. *Unknown.*
Shepherd's Song of Venus and Adonis, The. Constable.
Song of Venus. *Fr.* King Arthur. Dryden.
To Venus. Horace.
Venus. D. G. Rossetti.
Venus Accoutered as Mars. *Unknown.*
Venus and Adonis. *Fr.* Britannia's Pastorals. Browne.
Venus and Adonis. Shakespeare.
See also **Aphrodite.**
Venus (planet)
Hesperus. Clare.
Morning Star, The. E. Brontë.
Ode to the Evening Star. Akenside.
See also **Evening Star.**
Venus Fly Trap
Readymade. Perreault.
Veracruz, Mexico
Veracruz. Hayden.
Verchères, Marie Madeleine Jarret de
Madeleine Verchères. Drummond.
Verdi, Giuseppe
Verdi at Eighty. Bell.
Vergil
Thinking of a Master. Church.
To the Ship in which Vergil Sailed to Athens. Horace.
To Virgil. Tennyson.
Virgil's Tomb. Rogers.
Verlaine, Paul
Prelude: "Rimbaud and Verlaine, precious pair of poets." *Fr.* Preludes for Memnon. Aiken.
Vermeer, Jan
Lacemaker, The (Vermeer). Marx.
Vermont
Hail, Vermont! Perry.
Vermont. Cleghorn.
Vermont; Indian Summer. Booth.
Verona, Italy
Map of Verona, A. Reed.
Veronese, Paolo
Paul Veronese: Three Sonnets. Ferguson.
Versailles, France
No Swan So Fine. Moore.
Versailles. Brooke.
Versailles. Rich.
Veterans' Day (Armistice Day)
"And There Was a Great Calm." Hardy.
Apparitions. Clark.
Architects of Dream. Trent.
Armistice. Going.
Armistice. Lehmer.
Armistice. Sangster.
Armistice Day. Montgomery.
Armistice Day. Trent.
Armistice Day Vow. Gould.
Armistice Night. Wheeler.
At the Cenotaph. Sassoon.
Blow, Bugle! Clark.
Brotherhood. Markham.
Challenge. Clark.
Day, The. Bynner.
Dedication: "'They shall not die in vain,' we said." Gustafson.
Design for Peace. Bangs.
"Disabled"—Armistice Day. Parmenter.
Dreamers Cry Their Dream, The. Trent.
Everyone Sang. Sassoon.
For the Fallen. Binyon.
Goal and the Way, The. Oxenham.
Golden Day, The. Peach.
Great Powers Conference. Pierce.

Hymn of Hate, The. Miller.
Lessons. Weber.
Let Dreamers Wake. Lorraine.
Let Us Declare. Morgan.
Litany for Peace. Clark.
Make Way! Comfort.
Memorial Rain. MacLeish.
Message of Peace, The. Howe.
New City, The. Wilkinson.
New Song, The. Field.
Next Time. Simmons.
No Armistice in Love's War. Cheyney.
November Eleventh. Burton.
Peace. Pulsifer.
Peace. Warren.
Peace Call, The. Hampton.
Peace Triumphant. Rice.
Peace Universal. Thorne.
Prepare. Bynner.
Preparedness. Paxton.
Reign of Peace, The. Thornton.
Requiem. Clark.
Song for Tomorrow. Trent.
This Is the Last. Waterhouse.
Today Is Armistice, A Holiday. Schwartz.
Tournament of Man, The. Crosby.
True Freedom. Mackay.
Valley of Decision, The. Oxenham.
Victory Bells. Conkling.
Victory Parade. Hoffman.
Waste of War, The. Stidger.
We Who Build Visions. Coblentz.
When the Cannon Booms (No More). Carruth.
Which Sword? Pierce.
Wild Weather. Bates.
Without Regret. Lorraine.
World Planners. Steece.

Viareggio, Italy
Off Viareggio. Pitchford.

Vicksburg Campaign
Before Vicksburg. Boker.
Running the Batteries. Melville.
Vicksburg (a Ballad). Hayne.

Victoria, Queen of England
Mr. Barney Maguire's Account of the Coronation. *Fr.* The Ingoldsby Legends. "Ingoldsby."
Old Pilot Tunnels under the English Channel, The. Schevill.
Queen Victoria. *Unknown.*
To the Queen ("Revered, beloved—O you that hold"). Tennyson.
Widow at Windsor, The. Kipling.

Victoria Falls, Africa
Victoria Falls, The. Plomer.

Vietnam
Condemnation. Thich Nhat Hanh.
Gods in Vietnam. Redmond.
It Is Not Enough. Henderson.
Junglegrave. Anderson.
Musical Vietnam. Allen.
Non Poem about Vietnam, A. Rodgers.
Nuremburg, U.S.A. Knott.
Story of White Man Leading Viet Cong Patrol, The. Torgersen.
Vietnam #4. Major.
War Poem. West.
What Were They Like? Levertov.
Wichita Vortex Sutra, *sel.* Ginsberg.

Vigilantes
Lay of the Vigilantes, The. *Unknown.*
Vigilantes, The. Ashmun.

Vikings
Battle of Maldon, The. *Unknown.*
Discoverer of the North Cape, The. Longfellow.
Heritage, The. Reed.
O'er the Wild Gannet's Bath. Darley.
Skeleton in Armor, The. Longfellow.
Viking, The. Stokes.
Viking Terror, The. *Unknown.*
Vikings, The. *Unknown.*

Villiers de l'Isle-Adam, Philippe Auguste Mathias, Comte de
Villiers de l'Isle-Adam. Huxley.

Villon, François
Ballad of François Villon, A. Swinburne.
Dispute of the Heart and Body of François Villon, The. Villon.
Would I Be Shrived? Villon.

Vilna, Lithuania
Like Groping Fingers. Sutzkever.
Secret Town, The, *sel.* Sutzkever.
We Survive! Glick.

Vinland
Story of Vinland, The. *Fr.* Psalm of the West. Lanier.

Violets
Bay Violets. Sister Maris Stella.
Calling the Violet. Larcom.
How Violets Came Blue. Herrick.
I Spoke to the Violet. Neilson.
On a Faded Violet. Shelley.
Sonnet: "I had no thought of violets of late." Nelson.
Sweet Violets, Love's Paradise. *Unknown.*
To a Wood-Violet. Tabb.
To Violets. Herrick.
Violet, The. Story.
Violet, The. Taylor.
Violet and the Rose, The. Skipsey.
Violet and the Rose, The. Webster.
Violets, The. *Fr.* War Is Kind. Crane.
Violets. Moultrie.
Violets. Ropes.
Violets. *Unknown.*
White Violet. Osborne.
White Violets. Low.
Yellow Violets, The. Bryant.

Violins
Fiddler, The. Hardy.
Neighbor, The. Rilke.
Old Violin, The. Egan.
Stradivarius to an Unfinished Violin (1710). Lee-Hamilton.
Violin, The. Andrade.
Violin, The. Gilder.
Violin's Complaint, The. Thayer.

Violoncellos. *See* **Cellos.**

Virgil. *See* **Vergil.**

Virgin Mary. *See* **Mary, the Virgin.**

Virginia
As Toilsom I Wander'd Virginia's Woods. Whitman.
Carry Me Back to Old Virginny. Bland.
Life-long, Poor Browning. Spencer.
Massachusetts to Virginia. Whittier.
Newes from Virginia. Rich.
To the Virginian Voyage. Drayton.
Virginia. *Fr.* Landscapes. Eliot.
Virginia. Lindsay.
Virginia Britannia. Moore.
Virginia Capta. Preston.
Virginiana. Johnston.
Virginians Are Coming Again, The. Lindsay.
Virginians of the Valley, The. Ticknor.

Virginity
Alas How Long. *Unknown.*
How Can I Keep My Maidenhead. Burns.
Sonnet: "Virgins terrify too many men." Scott.
Then Lose in Time Thy Maidenhead. *Unknown.*
To the Virgins to Make Much of Time. Herrick.
To Virgins. Herrick.
Too Literal Pupil, The. Martial.
Tormenting Virgin. *Unknown.*
True Maid, A. Prior.
Virgin Declares Her Beauties, A. Barberini.
Whistle Daughter Whistle. *Unknown.*

Vishnu
Gita Govinda, The. Jayadeva.

Vivaldi, Antonio
Vivaldi. Schwartz.

Vodka
Vodka. Ciardi.

Vogler, Georg Joseph
Abt Vogler. R. Browning.

Voltaire
Mock On, Mock On, Voltaire, Rousseau. Blake.
Voltaire and Gibbon. *Fr.* Childe Harold's Pilgrimage. Byron.
Voltaire at Ferney. Auden.

Voortrekkers
Voortrekker, The. Kipling.
Voters and Voting
Ballot, The. Pierpont.
Poor Voter on Election Day, The. Whittier.
Voyages
Arrival and Departure. Eglington.
Coming Homeward out of Spain. Googe.
Dedication: "With favoring winds, o'er sunlit seas." *Fr.* Ultima Thule. Longfellow.
It Should Be Easy. Van Doren.
Ode to the Virginian Voyage. Drayton.
Passage to India. Whitman.
Pilgrims, The Delius.
Que Cursum Ventus. Clough.
Ulysses. Tennyson.
Voyage, The. Baudelaire.
Voyage, The. Tennyson.
Voyage to Cythera, A. Baudelaire.
Voyages. H. Crane.
Where Lies the Land to Which the Ship Would Go? Clough.
Would I Might Go Far Over Sea. O'Shaughnessy.
Vowels
Genesis of Vowels. Broughton.
Vulcan
Achilles' Shield. *Fr.* The Iliad. Homer.
Execration upon Vulcan, An. Jonson.
Song in Making of the Arrows, The. *Fr.* Sapho and Phao. Lyly.
Vulpius, Melchior
Melchior Vulpius. Moore.
Vultures
Black Vulture, The. Sterling.
Still, Citizen Sparrow. Wilbur.
Vulture, The. Hoh.

W

Wabash River
On the Banks of the Wabash, Far Away. Dresser.
Wagner, Richard
Death of Richard Wagner, The. Swinburne.
Wagner. Baring.
Wagtails
Little Trotty Wagtail. Clare.
Waiters
Epitaph on a Waiter. McCord.
To a Junior Waiter. Herbert.
Walden Pond
Walden in July. Junkins.
Waldenses
Hymn of the Waldenses. Bryant.
On the Late Massacre in Piedmont. Milton.
Wales
Bard, The. Gray.
Days that have been. Davies.
Dysynni Valley, The. Holmes.
Fall of Llywelyn, The Last Welsh Prince, The. Beddyn Fardd.
For My Ancestors. Humphries.
Gwalia Deserta, *sel.* Davies.
In Hospital: Poona (I). Lewis.
In the Valley of the Elwy. Hopkins.
I'r hen Iaith a'i Chanedon. Dowding.
Liberty. Hughes.
On the Welsh Marches. Stone.
Peace in the Welsh Hills. Watkins.
Wales. Nicholson.
Wales Visitation. Ginsberg.
We Who Were Born. Lewis.
Welsh History. Thomas.
Welsh Landscape. Thomas.
Welsh Sea, The. Flecker.
Welsh Testament, A. Thomas.
Presenting Welsh Poetry (PrWP). Gwyn Williams, ed.
Waley, Arthur
Homage to Arthur Waley. Fuller.
Homage to Arthur Waley. Kees.
Walker, William
With Walker in Nicaragua, *sel.* Miller.
Wall Street, New York City
Pan in Wall Street. Stedman.
Wallace, Sir William
Gude Wallace. *Unknown.*
Scotland's Tribute to Wallace. MacFarlan.
Wallace, The, *sels.* Henry the Minstrel.
Wallflowers
Black Wall-Flower, The. Kemble.
Wall-Flower, The. Landor.
Wall-Flower, The. Wergeland.
Walls
Divisibility. Plutzik.
Mending Wall. Frost.
Old Grey Wall, The. Carman.
Stone Walls. Lippmann.
Wall, The. Phelps.
Wall, The. Schneider.
Walls. Cavafy.
Walls. Francis.
Walnuts
Raking Walnuts in the Rain. Shannon.
Riddle: "I am within as white as snow." *Unknown.*
Walnut. Carrera Andrade.
Walpole, Robert, 1st Earl of Oxford
Letter to Sir Robert Walpole, A. Fielding.
To the Right Honourable Robert Walpole, Esq. Philips.
Walruses
Smile of the Walrus, The. Herford.
Walsingham, England
As You Came from the Holy land. *Unknown.*
Lament for Our Lady's Shrine at Walsingham. *Unknown.*
Lament for the Priory of Walsingham, A, *sel.* *Unknown.*
Walton, Izaak
Ike Walton's Prayer. Riley.
Izaak Walton to River and Brook. Lee-Hamilton.
To My Dear and Most Worthy Friend, Mr. Isaac Walton. Cotton.
Wanderer (ship)
Wanderer, The. Masefield.
Wanderlust
Down on My Luck. Fairburn.
Early One Morning. Thomas.
Far-away. Sigerson.
Feet of the Young Men, The. Kipling.
I Want to Go Wandering. Lindsay.
Long Trail, The. Kipling.
Over the Hills and Far Away. Henley.
Sea Gypsy, The. Hovey.
Song: "Something calls and whispers, along the city street." *Fr.* The Way of Perfect Love. King.
Song of the Open Road. Whitman.
Vagabond, The. Stevenson.
Visions. Leamy.
Wakeful in the Township. Riddell.
Wander-Lovers, The. Hovey.
Wanderer, The, *sels.* Brennan.
Wanderers, The. Symons.
Wander-Thirst. Gould.
Wang Wei
Note to Wang Wei. Berryman.
War
A Terre. Owen.
Absolution. Sassoon.
Ad. Fearing.
Aftermath. Sassoon.
Against the Age. Simpson.
Air Raid Across the Bay of Plymouth. Spender.
Airman's Prayer, A. Brodie.
All, All of a Piece Throughout. *Fr.* The Secular Masque. Dryden.
All Quiet along the Potomac. Beers.
All That Is Left. Basho.
Alliteration; or, The Siege of Belgrade. *Unknown.*
Angels at Hamburg, The. Jarrell.
Anthem for Doomed Youth. Owen.
Apologia pro Poemate Meo. Owen.
Apparitions. Clark.
Ares. Ehrenstein.
Arms and the Boy. Owen.

Arsenal at Springfield, The. Longfellow.
Asking for It. Sassoon.
At the British War Cemetery, Bayeux. Causley.
At the Cenotaph. "MacDiarmid."
Awakened War God, The. Widdemer.
Barrage. Aldington.
Battle. Ch'ü Yüan.
Battle, The. Simpson.
Battle of Blenheim, The. Southey.
Battle of Brunanburh, The. *Unknown.*
Battle of the Summer Islands, The. Waller.
Battle Song. Elliott.
Battlefield, The. Bryant.
Bayonet Charge. Hughes.
Beach Burial. Slessor.
Beat! Beat! Drums! Whitman.
Before Action. Gellert.
Before Bannockburn. Burns.
Before Sedan. Dobson.
Between Two Prisoners. Dickey.
Bloody Sire, The. Jeffers.
Brave Old World. Lambert.
Break of Day in the Trenches. Rosenberg.
But We Shall Bloom. Guri.
Carol with Variations. McGinley.
Channel Firing. Hardy.
Charge of the Light Brigade, The. Tennyson.
Charing Cross. Roberts.
Christmas Eve under Hooker's Statue. R. Lowell.
Chronicler, The. Bergman.
Combat, The. Stanley.
Come Up From the Fields Father. Whitman.
Consolation in War. Mumford.
Corporal Stare. Graves.
Counter-Attack. Sassoon.
Criminality of War, The. Young.
Crucifix, The. Read.
Cry to Arms, A. Timrod.
Daughters of War. Rosenberg.
David's Lament. Second Samuel, Bible, *O.T.*
Dead Man's Dump. Rosenberg.
Death of the Ball Turret Gunner, The. Jarrell.
Destruction of Sennacherib, The. Byron.
Disabled. Owen.
"Disabled"—Armistice Day. Parmenter.
Does It Matter? Sassoon.
Drum, The. Scott.
Dry Loaf. Stevens.
Dug-out, The. Sassoon.
Dulce et Decorum Est. Owen.
Elegy for a Dead Soldier. Shapiro.
Elegy on Gordon Barber. Derwood.
Eleventh Hour, The. Morris.
End of a War, The. Read.
Epitaph for an American Bomber. Bertram.
Epitaph on an Army of Mercenaries. Housman.
Escape. Graves.
Evening Meal in the Twentieth Century. Holmes.
Execution of Cornelius Vane, The. Read.
Exposure. Owen.
Extras. Burton.
Fable of the War, A. Nemerov.
Fife Tune. Manifold.
Fighting South of the Castle. *Unknown.*
Five Souls. Ewer.
Flight to Australia. Day Lewis.
For the Fallen. Binyon.
Foxhole for the Night, A. Quinn.
From Many a Mangled Truth a War Is Won. Dyment.
Fruits of War, The. Gascoigne.
Fury of Aerial Bombardment, The. Eberhart.
Futility. Owen.
Galway. MacNeice.
General, The. Sassoon.
Glories of Our Blood and State, The. *Fr.* The Contention of Ajax and Ulysses. Shirley.
Glory of Women, The. Sassoon.
God of us who kill our kind! *Fr.* A Prayer of the Peoples. MacKaye.
Greater Love. Owen.
Griefs for Dead Soldiers. Hughes.
Guerrilla Camp. Wilson.
Gunner, The. Webb.
Hialmar. Campbell.
Hohenlinden. Campbell.
Holy Innocents, The. Lowell.
Home in War-Time. Dobell.
Horses, The. Muir.
Housemates. Shepard.
How Is the Gold Become Dim. Jeremiah, Bible, *O.T.*
How the Women Will Stop War. *Fr.* Lysistrata. Aristophanes.
I have been,/ Three separate times, in war. *Fr.* What Is Truth? Manning.
I Hear an Army Charging upon the Land. Joyce.
I Sing of Olaf. Cummings.
In Distrust of Merits. Moore.
In the Trench. Gellert.
In Time of "The Breaking of Nations." Hardy.
In Time of War. Auden.
Insensibility. Owen.
Invocation: "There is no balm on earth." Thomas.
Iron-Wind Dances. *Fr.* Thunderdrums. Sarett.
It's a Queen Time. Graves.
I've Heard Them Lilting at Loom and Belting. Day Lewis.
Jewish Conscript, The. Frank.
Jumbled in the Common Box. Auden.
Karl. Spear.
King of Ulster, The. *Unknown.*
Korea. Buckley.
Lament: "We who are left, how shall we look again." Gibson.
Legion, The. Graves.
Lessons of the War. Reed.
Let War's Tempests Cease. Longfellow.
Little Cart, The. Ch'en Tzu-lung.
Long War, The. Lee.
Losses. Jarrell.
Man He Killed, The. Hardy.
Man-made World, A. Spender.
March, The. Squire.
Marching. Rosenberg.
Men in Green. Campbell.
Mental Cases. Owen.
Metal Checks, The. Driscoll.
Mine Sweepers. Kipling.
Mud. Church.
Munich Elegy No. 1. Barker.
Murrough Defeats the Danes, 994. *Unknown.*
My Company. Read.
Nationality. Gilmore.
Nature in War-Time. Palmer.
New Mars, The. Coates.
Next Time. Simmons.
Next War, The. Graves.
Next War, The. Owen.
Night Patrol. Ross.
No Man Knows War. Rolfe.
Northern Legion, A. Read.
Not to Keep. Frost.
Nuns in the Wind. Rukeyser.
On a Certain Engagement South of Seoul. Carruth.
On Being Asked for a War Poem. Yeats.
On Limited Warfare. *Unknown.*
On the Danger of War. Meredith.
On the Eve of New Wars. Untermeyer.
On the Eve of War. Dandridge.
On the idle hill of summer. Housman.
On the March. Aldington.
On War. Kilgore.
One Morning the World Woke Up. Williams.
Our Orders. Howe.
Out of Our Shame. Rosten.
Pact, The. Noyes.
Peaceful Shepherd, The. Frost.
Perhaps a Prayer. Schevill.
Permanence of the Young Men, The. Soutar.
Prayer during Battle. Hagedorn.
Prayer for Light. Coblentz.
Prayer for the Age. Broomell.
Prayer from 1936, A. Sassoon.
Prelude: Troops, The. Sassoon.
Prospect. Clark.

War *(continued)*
Protest in the Sixth Year of Ch'ien Fu, A. Ts'ao Sung.
Reapers, The. Watt.
Rear-Guard, The. Sassoon.
Rearmament. Jeffers.
Rebel, The. Belloc.
Recalling War. Graves.
Refugees, The. Read.
Return, The. Bishop.
Return. *Unknown.*
Revelation. Soutar.
Rondeau in Wartime. Bertram.
Rumors. Arkell.
Scapegoats. Breed.
Scyros. Shapiro.
Scythians, The. Blok.
Security. Glover.
Send-off, The. Owen.
September 1, 1939. Auden.
Sestina; Altaforte. Pound.
Show, The. Owen.
Sick Nought, The. Jarrell.
Silent Slain, The. MacLeish.
Silent Testimony. Parmenter.
Since our hair was plaited and we became man and wife. Su Wu.
Slant of Sun on Dull Brown Walls, A. *Fr.* War Is Kind. Crane.
Small Soldiers with Drum in Large Landscape. *Fr.* Mexico Is a Foreign Country. Warren.
Soldier, What Did You See? Blanding.
Song for the New Year. Auden.
Song of Carroll's Sword, The. *At. to* MacMore.
Song of the Borderguard, The. Duncan.
Song of the Dying Gunner. Causley.
Songbooks of the War. Sassoon.
Sons of Our Sons, The. Ehrenburg.
Spires of Oxford, The. Letts.
Spring Offensive. Owen.
Story of White Man Leading Viet Cong Patrol, The. Torgersen.
Strange Meeting. Owen.
Sunset Horn. O'Higgins.
Survivors. Ross.
Take Your Gun. Bronowski.
"Tan Ta Ra, Cries Mars. . ." Wagoner.
There Are Children in the Dusk. Warr.
There was crimson clash of war. *Fr.* The Black Riders. S. Crane.
There Will Come Soft Rains. Teasdale.
These Men. Gellert.
This Is War. Le Gallienne.
Trail All Your Pikes, Dispirit Every Drum. Countess of Winchilsea.
To God: From the Warring Nations. Wilmot.
To the Mothers. Toller.
Tomb of Lt. John Learmonth, A.I.F., The. Manifold.
Too-late Born, The. MacLeish.
Triumphal March. Eliot.
Two Armies. Spender.
Two Sides of War. Rice.
Ultima Ratio Regum. Spender.
Ultimate Atrocity, The. Sassoon.
Under the Frontier Post. Wang Chang-ling.
Unpardonable Sin, The. Lindsay.
Vale from Carthage. Viereck.
Valley of the Black Pig, The. Yeats.
Vampire, The. Aiken.
Victory. Duggan.
Villages Demolis. Read.
Vision of War, A. *Fr.* Induction to "The Mirror for Magistrates." Sackville.
Voices of Heroes. Gregory.
Volunteer's Reply to the Poet, The. *Fr.* Talking Bronco. Campbell.
War. Fullerton.
War. Hall.
War. Ish-Kishor.
War. Langland.
War! Lawson.
War. McLean.
War. Root.
War. Stringer.
War. Wyn.
War Comes. Schneour.
War Films, The. Newbolt.
War in Chang-An City. Wang Tsan.
War Is Kind, *sels.* S. Crane.
War Song. Davidson.
War Song. *Unknown.*
War-Song of Dinas Vawr, The. *Fr.* The Misfortunes of Elphin. Peacock.
War Song to Englishmen, A. *Fr.* King Edward the Third. Blake.
War Story. Starbuck.
War Suite. Harrison.
Wars worse then civil on Thessalian Plains. *Fr.* Pharsalia. Lucan.
Ways of War. Johnson.
We were glad together in gladsome meads. *Fr.* The Rhyme of Joyous Garde. Gordon.
We Who Are about to Die. Fey.
We Who Are Left. Whalley.
Well Pleaseth Me the Sweet Time of Easter. Bertrand de Born.
What the Orderly Dog Saw. Ford.
Which Side Am I Supposed to Be On? Auden.
While We Slept. Wolff.
White Horse, The. Tu Fu.
Women at the Corners Stand, The. Golding.
World Wars. *Unknown.*
Wound-Dresser, The. Whitman.
Y.M.C.A. Writing Room. Fuller.
Youth. Bates.
Youth in Arms. Monro.
War and the Poet (WaaP). Richard Eberhart *and* Selden Rodman, eds.
War Poets, The (WaP). Oscar Williams, ed.
See also **Soldiers; World War, First; World War, Second.**

War of 1812
Battle of Baltimore, The. *Unknown.*
Battle of Bridgewater, The. *Unknown.*
Blue Hen's Chickens, The. Guiterman.
Bower of Peace, The. *Fr.* Ode Written during the War with America, 1814. Southey.
Come All You Bold Canadians. *Unknown.*
Halifax Station. *Unknown.*
Jackson at New Orleans. Rice.
Ocean-Fight, The. *Unknown.*
On the British Invasion. Freneau.
Perry's Victory. *Unknown.*
Perry's Victory—a Song. *Unknown.*
Perry's Victory on Lake Erie. Percival.
Reid at Fayal. Palmer.
To the Defenders of New Orleans. Drake.
United States and *Macedonian,* The ("The Banner of Freedom high floated unfurled"). *Unknown.*
United States and *Macedonian,* The ("How glows each patriot bosom that boasts a Yankee heart"). *Unknown.*
Yankee Thunders. *Unknown.*
Ye Parliament of England. *Unknown.*

Warblers
Maryland Yellow-Throat, The. Van Dyke.
Warblers. Hartley.

Ward, John
Captain Ward and the *Rainbow.* *Unknown.*

Ward, William George
Valedictory. Tennyson.

Warner, William
Ad Gulielmum Warner. Weever.

Warren, Joseph
Death of Warren, The. Sargent.
Warren's Address to the American Soldiers. Pierpont.

Warsaw, Poland
Pesach Has Come to the Ghetto Again. Heller.

Warton, Thomas, the Younger
Lines Written in Ridicule of Certain Poems Published in 1777. Johnson.

Washington, Booker Taliaferro
Alabama Earth. Hughes.
Booker T. and W. E. B. Randall.
Booker Washington Trilogy, The, *sels.* Lindsay.

Washington, George
André's Request to Washington. Willis.
At Mount Vernon. Clark.
At the Tomb of Washington. Scollard.

Boy Washington, The. Thompson.
Cincinnatus of the West, The. *Fr.* Ode to Napoleon Buonaparte. Byron.
Crown Our Washington. Butterworth.
Ever Since. Coatsworth.
Footnote to History. Coatsworth.
George Washington. R. Benét *and* S. V. Benét.
George Washington ("Only a baby, fair"). *At. to* Cook.
George Washington. Ingham.
George Washington. Miller.
George Washington. Silverstein.
George Washington. Tippett.
George Washington. *Unknown.*
George Washington Absent from His Country. Wakoski.
His Excellency General Washington. Wheatley.
His Task—and Ours. Gould.
Inscription at Mount Vernon. *Unknown.*
Leetla Giorgio Washeenton. Daly.
Man, A. Scollard.
Mount Vernon, the Home of Washington. Day.
Name of Washington, The. Field.
Name of Washington, The. Lathrop.
Occasioned by General Washington's Arrival in Philadelphia, on His Way to His Residence in Virginia. Freneau.
Ode for Washington's Birthday. Holmes.
Our Washington. Durbin.
Picture People. Bennett.
Rivers Remember, The. Turner.
Snarlers, The. Guiterman.
Stanzas: "No tongue can tell, no pen describe." Freneau.
Star in the West, The. Cook.
Tribute to Washington. *Unknown.*
Twenty-second of February, The. Bryant.
Under the Old Elm, *sels.* J. R. Lowell.
Vow of Washington, The. Whittier.
War and Washington. *Fr.* Cato. Sewall.
Washington. *Fr.* Ode to Napoleon Buonaparte. Byron.
Washington. Goodman.
Washington. Meyrich.
Washington. *Fr.* Commemoration Ode. Monroe.
Washington. O'Crowley.
Washington. Prentice.
Washington. Roche.
Washington. Schauffler.
Washington. Turner.
Washington. Williams.
Washington. Wingate.
Washington and Lincoln. Stafford.
Washington, man of mystery. *Unknown.*
Washington's Birthday. Burdick.
Washington's Birthday. Sangster.
Washington's Last Birthday. Noyes.
Washington's Statue. Tuckerman.
Washington's Tomb. Lawrence.
Young Washington. Guiterman.

Washington (state)
Washington's Song. Meany.

Washington, D.C.
Aeneas at Washington. Tate.
City of Monuments. Rukeyser.
D. C. Shapiro.
Effigy. McElhaney.
View of the Capitol from the Library of Congress. Bishop.
Washington Cathedral. Shapiro.

Washington Monument
Washington Monument, The. Wiley.
Washington Monument by Night. Sandburg.
Washington's Monument. *Unknown.*

Washington Square, New York City
Villanelle of Washington Square. Roberts.

Wasp (ship, War of 1812)
Ocean-Fight, The. *Unknown.*
Wasp's Frolic, The. *Unknown.*

Wasps
New Hampshire, February. Eberhart.
Queen Wasp, A. De la Mare.
Upon a Wasp Chilled with Cold. Taylor.
Wasp, The. Hine.
Wasp, The. "Macleod."
Wasps' Nest, The. MacBeth.

Wastwater, England
Written on the Banks of Wastwater during a Calm. "North."

Water
Bucyrus. Holmes.
Glass Town, The. Reid.
Like Water down a Slope. Schneour.
Reflections on Water. Pitchford.
Shadows in the Water. Traherne.
Song of the Artesian Water. Paterson.
Water. Conkling.
Water, *sel.* Raine.
Water. Sexton.
Water-Images. Osborn.
Water Noises. Roberts.
Water Song. Ibn Gabirol.
Well, The. Levertov.
Wine and Water. Chesterton.

Water Lilies
Cherwell Waterlily, The. Faber.
Clote, The. Barnes.
Dog and the Water-Lily. Cowper
To Paint a Water Lily. Hughes.
Water-Lilies. Hemans.
Water-Lilies. Teasdale.
Waterlily, The. Tabb.

Water Ouzels
Water-Ousel, The. Webb.
Water Ouzel. Matchett.
Water Ouzel, The. Monroe.

Waterfalls
By the Waterfall. Adler.
Cataract of Lodore, The. Southey.
Fragment: "Cataract, whirling to the precipice, The." Clare.
Leaping Falls. Kinnell.
Waterfall, The. Sherman.
Waterfall, The. Vaughan.
Waterfall. Welsh.
Waterfall and the Eglantine, The. Wordsworth.

Waterford, Ireland
My Blessing Be on Waterford. Letts.

Waterfowl
To a Waterfowl. Bryant.

Waterloo, Battle of
Drummer Boy of Waterloo, The. *Unknown.*
Field of Waterloo, The. *Fr.* The Dynasts. Hardy.
Waterloo. *Fr.* Childe Harold's Pilgrimage. Byron.
Waterloo. De Vere.

Watts, Isaac
For the Bicentenary of Isaac Watts. Nicholson.

Watts, Los Angeles, California.
Watts. Kaufman.
Watts. Rivers.
Yesterday's Child. Reedburg.

Waugh, Evelyn
Elegy: E. W. Sissman.

Waves
Hungry Waves, The. Aldis.
Sea Bird to the Wave, The. Colum.
Waves. Miller.

Wayne, Anthony
Anthony Wayne. Guiterman.
Wayne at Stony Point. Scollard.

Wealth
Of the Use of Riches. *Fr.* Moral Essays. Pope.
Rich fools there be whose base and filthy heart. *Fr.* Astrophel and Stella. Sidney.
Rich Man, The. Adams.
Very Rich Man, The. Parker.
Wealth. *Fr.* The Gulistan. Sadi.

Weasels
Weasel, The. *Unknown.*

Weather
As to the Weather. *Unknown.*
August Weather. Tynan.
Final Thoughts on the Weather in England during 1953. Daiches.
Hard Weather. Meredith.
Hot Weather. Aldis.
Hydrographic Report. F. Frost.
I love snow and all the forms. Shelley.
Oh, to Be in England Now the Weather's There! *Unknown.*

Weather *(continued)*
Self and the Weather, The. Whittemore.
Song on the Way, The. *Unknown.*
Sun and Wind. Farjeon.
Weather. Bethell.
Weather. Conkling.
Weather Rule, A. *Unknown.*
Weather Signs. *Unknown.*
Weathers. Hardy.
What the Weather Does. Hendry.
Weavers
Weaver, The. Burleigh.
Weaver, The ("I sat at my loom in silence"). *Unknown.*
Weavers. Heine.
Weaver's Song, The. *Fr.* Jack of Newbury. *Unknown.*
Webern, Anton
For the Death of Anton Webern Particularly. Tarn.
Webster, Daniel
At Marshfield. *Fr.* Webster, an Ode. Wilkinson.
Birthday of Daniel Webster. Holmes.
Daniel Webster's Horses. Coatsworth.
Ichabod. Whittier.
Voice of Webster, The. *sel.* Johnson.
Webster, John
John Webster. *Fr.* Sonnets on Engish Dramatic Poets. Swinburne.
Whispers of Immortality. Eliot.
Wedding Songs
At the Wedding March. Hopkins.
Epithalamion, An. Donne.
Epithalamion. Spenser.
Epithalamion Made at Lincolnes Inne. Donne.
Epithalamion Teratus. *Fr.* Hero and Leander. Chapman.
Marriage Song. Halevi.
Nuptiall Song, or Epithalamie, on Sir Clipseby Crew and His Lady, A. Herrick.
Prothalamion. Spenser.
Rejoice, O Bridegroom! *Unknown.*
Wedding-Hymn. Lanier.
Wedding Morn. Lawrence.
Wedding Night, The. Secundus.
High Wedlock Then Be Honored (HW). Virginia Tufte, ed.
Weddings. *See* **Marriage.**
Weil, Simone
For Simone Weil. Sister M. Thérèse.
Wellington, Arthur Wellesley, 1st Duke of
He Said That He Was Not Our Brother. Banim.
Ode on the Death of the Duke of Wellington. Tennyson.
Warden of the Cinque Ports, The. Longfellow.
Wellington. *Fr.* Don Juan. Byron.
Wellington. Disraeli.
Welsh, The
Tragic Guilt. Rhys.
Variation on a Theme by Dylan Thomas. Bode.
Welsh Testament, A. Thomas.
Welshmen of Tirawley, The. Ferguson.
Wenceslaus, Saint
Good King Wenceslaus. *Unknown.*
Werewolves
Were-Wolf. Hawthorne.
Were-Wolves, The. Campbell.
Werfel, Franz
Shooting of Werfel, The. Watkins.
Wesley, Charles
Wesley in Heaven. Brown.
Wesley, John
John Wesley's Rule. Wesley.
Wessex, England
Wessex Guidebook. MacNeice.
Wessex Heights. Hardy.
West, Benjamin
To Benjamin West. Allston.
West, Richard
Sonnet on the Death of Richard West. Gray.
West (United States)
Étude Géographique. King.
Hymn of the West. Stedman.
Long Road West, The. Knibbs.
Man of the Open West, The. Monroe.
Others May Praise What They Like. Whitman.
Out Where the West Begins. Chapman.
Prairie Schooner, The. Dale.
Redhaw Rain. Sandburg.
Ruin of Bobtail Bend, The. Adams.
Slabs of the Sunburnt West, *sel.* Sandburg.
Spanish Johnny. Cather.
Westering. Kane.
Western Wagons. S. V. Benét.
Westward Ho! Miller.
Wounded wilderness of Morris Graves, The. *Fr.* A Coney Island of the Mind. Ferlinghetti.
Poems of the Old West (PoOW). Levette J. Davidson, ed.
West Indies
West Indies, The, *sels.* James Montgomery.
West Point, New York
Benny Havens, Oh! O'Brien.
West Virginia
West Virginia Hills, The. King *and* Engle.
West Wind
Ode to the West Wind. Shelley.
Spring Wind. Turner.
To the Western Wind. Halevi.
To the Western Wind. Herrick.
West Wind, The. Masefield.
Westminster Abbey
In Westminster Abbey. Betjeman.
On First Entering Westminster Abbey. Guiney.
On the Tombs in Westminster Abbey. *At. to* Beaumont, *also to* Basse.
Tennyson. Huxley.
Whales and Whaling
And God Created the Great Whales. *Fr.* Paradise Lost. Milton.
Before the Storm. Hanson.
Bill the Whaler. Lawson.
Brand Fire New Whaling Song Right from the Pacific Ocean. *Unknown.*
Cachalot, The, *sel.* Pratt.
Coast of Peru, The. *Unknown.*
Famous Tay Whale, The. McGonagall.
Father Mapple's Hymn. *Fr.* Moby Dick. Melville.
Greenland Whale Fishery, The. *Unknown.*
Harpooning, The. Walker.
Jonah and the Whale. Meynell.
Leviathan. Merwin.
Leviathan; a Poem in Four Movements. Pitchford.
Nantucket Whalers. Henderson.
Quaker Graveyard in Nantucket, The. R. Lowell.
Song of the Hatteras Whale, A. *Unknown.*
There She Blows! *Unknown.*
Triumph of the Whale, The. Lamb.
Waterwitch, The. *Unknown.*
Whale. W. R. Benét.
Whale, The. Buson.
Whale, The. Darwin.
Whale, The. *Fr.* The Progress of the Soul. Donne.
Whale, The ("Now I will fashion the tale of a fish"). *Fr.* Physiologus. *Unknown.*
Whale, The ("'Tis a hundred years"). *Unknown.*
Whale and Jonah, The. Meynell.
Whale and the *Essex,* The. Sullivan.
Whale, His Bulwark, The. Walcott.
Whale's Nature, The. *Fr.* The Bestiary. *Unknown.*
Whales Weep Not! Lawrence.
Wharves
Bight, The. Bishop.
Jake's Wharf. Booth.
Old Wharves, The. Field.
Wheat
Bread the Holy. Coatsworth.
Sheaves, The. Robinson.
Spirit of the Wheat, The. Valentine.
Wind-swept Wheat, The. "Bridges."
Wheatley, Phillis
Address to Miss Phillis Wheatley, An. Hammon.
Wheeler, Joseph
Wheeler at Santiago. Gordon.
Wheeler's Brigade at Santiago. Rice.
Whigs (English political party)
Absalom and Achitophel, Pt. I. Dryden.
Whippoorwills
Mountain Whippoorwill, The. S. V. Benét.

Whippoorwill. Moreland.
Whisky
Raftery's Dialogue with the Whiskey. Fallon.
Rye Whisky. *Unknown.*
Whisky Johnny. *Unknown.*
Whistler, James Abbott McNeill
To a Portrait of Whistler in the Brooklyn Art Museum. Cox.
To James McNeill Whistler. Henley.
Whitby, England
Old Parish Church, Whitby, The. Rawnsley.
White, Peregrine
Peregrine White and Virginia Dare. R. *and* S. V. Benét.
White, William Allen
To William Allen White. Ferber.
Whitman, Marcus
Whitman's Ride for Oregon. Butterworth.
Whitman, Walt
Cape Hatteras. *Fr.* The Bridge. H. Crane.
Fast Ball. Williams.
Grand republic's Poet is, The. Denby.
Imitation of Walt Whitman. "Judy."
Letters to Walt Whitman. Johnson.
Memories of Whitman and Lincoln. Oppenheim.
Old Walt. Hughes.
Pact, A. Pound.
Sincere Flattery. Stephen.
Somebody Called Walt Whitman. *Fr.* The New World. Bynner.
Song of Myself. Whitman.
Supermarket in California, A. Ginsberg.
To Walt Whitman. MacInnes.
To Walt Whitman in America. Swinburne.
Walt Whitman. Honig.
Walt Whitman. Morris.
Walt Whitman. Robinson.
Walt Whitman. Williams.
Walt Whitman at Bear Mountain. Simpson.
Whittier, John Greenleaf
Autograph, An. Whittier.
John Greenleaf Whittier. Cary.
John Greenleaf Whittier. Grant.
Mr. Whittier. Scott.
My Triumph. Whittier.
Three Silences of Molinos, The. Longfellow.
To John Greenleaf Whittier. Ward.
To Whittier. J. R. Lowell.
White Magic; an Ode. Braithwaite.
Whittier. *Fr.* A Fable for Critics. J. R. Lowell.
Whittier. Sangster.
Widecombe Fair
Widdicombe Fair. *Unknown.*
Widows and Widowers
Consider These Greek Widows of America. Georgakas.
Racer's Widow, The. Glück.
Reasons for and against Marrying Widows. Selyns.
Widow in Wintertime. Kizer.
Widow's Lament in Springtime, The. Williams.
Wilberforce, William
To William Wilberforce, Esq. Cowper.
Wilde, Oscar
Arrest of Oscar Wilde at the Cadogan Hotel, The. Betjeman.
Dead Poet, The. Douglas.
Oscar Wilde. *At. to* Swinburne.
Wildebeests
Wildebeest, The. Daly.
William II, Emperor of Germany
Kaiser & Co. Rose.
William I, King of England. *See* **William the Conqueror.**
William III, King of England (William of Orange)
King William and King James. *Unknown.*
New Song of an Orange, A. *Unknown.*
William of Orange; or, The Battle of Boyne. *Unknown.*
William IV, King of England
Royal Adventurer, The. Freneau.
William P. Frye (ship)
William P. Frye, The. Foster.
William the Conqueror
William I—1066. Farjeon.
Williams, Roger
Canonicus and Roger Williams. *Unknown.*
Roger Williams. Butterworth.
Williams, Theodore Samuel (Ted)
Dream of a Baseball Star. Corso.
Williams, William Carlos
Doctor Bill Williams. Walsh.
Letter to William Carlos Williams, A. Rexroth.
Out of Your Hands. Weiss.
To William Carlos Williams. Kinnell.
Willow Trees
Green Willow, The. *Unknown.*
To the Willow-Tree. Herrick.
Weeping Willow. Aldridge.
Willow, The. Tu Fu.
Willow Bend and Weep. Johnson.
Willow Poem. Williams.
Willow-Tree, The. Thackeray.
Willows, The. Eaton.
Willows. Langland.
Willows in the Snow. Tsuru.
Word of Willow, The. Drake.
Wills (testamentary)
Woman's Will. Saxe.
Wilson, Woodrow
Woodrow Wilson. Barker.
Woodrow Wilson. Gillies.
Woodrow Wilson. Johnson.
Winchester, Jane Savage, Marchioness of
Epitaph on the Marchioness of Winchester, An. Milton.
Winchester, Virginia
Sheridan's Ride. Read.
Winchester Cathedral, England
Winchester. Johnson.
Wind
Aeolus. Humphries.
Another Ode to the North-East Wind. *Unknown.*
Autumn Storm, The. Basho.
Autumnal Equinox on Mediterranean Beach. Warren.
Beggar Wind, The. Austin.
Big Wind. Roethke.
Blow, Blow, Thou Winter Wind. *Fr.* As You Like It. Shakespeare.
Blow, Northern Wind. *Unknown.*
Cook County. MacLeish.
Description of the Properties of Winds at All Times of the Year, A. Tusser.
Evening Wind, The. Bryant.
Four Winds, The. Leslie.
Four Winds, The. Luders.
Four Winds, The. Sherman.
Four Winds. Teasdale.
Gentle Wind, A. Fu Hsuan.
Happy Wind. Davies.
Hearing the Wind at Night. Swenson.
High Wind at the Battery. Pomeroy.
I Saw the Wind Today. Colum.
Immobile Wind, The. Winters.
Little Wind. Greenaway.
Lubber Breeze. Moore.
March Winds, The. Houghton.
Mid-Country Blow. Roethke.
Mistral. Howes.
Moon's the North Wind's Cooky, The. Lindsay.
My Lady Wind. *Unknown.*
Nautical Extravaganza, A. Irwin.
Night Wind, The. Field.
Now Close the Windows. Frost.
O look how the loops and baloons of bloom. *Fr.* Stormy Day. Rodgers.
O Wind of the Mountain! Westwood.
O wind, why do you never rest. *Fr.* Sing-Song. C. G. Rossetti.
Ode to the West Wind. Shelley.
On a Windy Day. Gay.
On Wenlock Edge the wood's in trouble. *Fr.* A Shropshire Lad. Housman.
Pirate Wind. Carr.
Prairie Wind. Scott.
Prayer to the Wind, A. Carew.
Song: "Bring from the craggy haunts of birch and pine." Todhunter.
Song of the Four Winds, The. *Fr.* The Misfortunes of Elphin. Peacock.
Song to the Wind, A. Taliesin.

Wind *(continued)*
South Wind. Sassoon.
South Wind laid his moccasins aside, The. *Fr.* Malcolm's Katie. Crawford.
Storm, The. Chora.
Street-Walker in March. Albert.
Strong Wind, A. Clarke.
Summer Wind. Bryant.
Summer Winds. Darley.
That Wind. E. Brontë.
There came a wind like a bugle. Dickinson.
Three Winds, The. Lee.
To the Thawing Wind. Frost.
To the Winds. Ayres.
To the Winter Wind. Fletcher.
Unknown Wind, The. "Macleod."
West Wind, The. Masefield.
What the Winds Bring. Stedman.
Which Way Does the Wind Blow? Aikin.
Whichever Way the Wind Doth Blow. Mason.
Who Has Seen the Wind? *Fr.* Sing-Song. C. G. Rossetti.
Wild Winds. Butts.
Wind, The. Farjeon.
Wind. Feeney.
Wind. Fisher.
Wind, The. Ginsberg.
Wind. Hughes.
Wind, The. Landon.
Wind, The. Miller.
Wind, The. Morris.
Wind, The. Rendall.
Wind, The. Stephens.
Wind, The. Stevenson.
Wind. *Fr.* Riddles. *Unknown.*
Wind and the Bird, The. *Unknown.*
Wind and the Moon, The. Macdonald.
Wind and Wave. Stoddard.
Wind and Window-Flower. Frost.
Wind at Penistone, The. Davie.
Wind Force. Mayer.
Wind has such a rainy sound, The. *Fr.* Sing-Song. C. G. Rossetti.
Wind in a Frolic, The. Howitt.
Wind in the Dusk. Monro.
Wind in the Elms, The. Miller.
Wind in the Grass. Van Doren.
Wind in the Pines, The. Cawein.
Wind Is a Cat. Fuller.
Wind Is Blind, The. Meynell.
Wind Is Round, The. Moss.
Wind on the Hills, The. Shorter.
Wind Our Enemy, The, *sel.* Marriott.
Wind Song. Sandburg.
Wind-Song. *Unknown.*
Wind tapped like a tired man, The. Dickinson.
Wind took up the northern things, The. Dickinson.
Wind Weather. Brasier.
Wind-Wolves. Sargent.
Winds, The. Cawein.
Winds, The. "Eglinton."
Winds, The. Swinburne.
Winds, The. Tusser.
Winds, The. Williams.
Winds a-Blowing. Justus.
Wind's Head, The. Sweeney.
Wind's Song, The. "Setoun."
Wind's Way, The. Conkling.
Wind's Way, The. Le Gallienne.
Wind's Work. Moore.
Windy Day, A. Young.
Windy Morning. Behn.
Windy Nights. Stevenson.
Winter Night. Butts.
See also **East Wind; North Wind; South Wind; West Wind.**
Windhovers. *See* **Falcons.**
Windmills
Windmill, The. De Tabley.
Windmill. Farrar.
Windmill, The. Johnson.
Windmill, The. Longfellow.
Windmill, The. Lucas.
Windmill on the Cape. Sieller.
Windmills, The. Fletcher.
Windsor, Wallace Warfield, Duchess of
Hark the herald angels sing. *Unknown.*
Windsor Castle, England
Prisoned in Windsor, He Recounteth His Pleasure There Passed. Surrey.
Windsor Forest, England
Lines Written in Windsor Forest. Pope.
Windsor Forest. Pope.
Wine
Bacchus. Emerson.
Bacchus in Tuscany, *sels.* Redi.
Bottle of Chianti, The. Souster.
Bubbling Wine. Zakariya.
Catawba Wine. Longfellow.
England's Triumph; or, The Subjects' Joy. *Unknown.*
Excellency of Wine, The. Orrery.
Five Arabic Verses in Praise of Wine. *Unknown.*
His Farewell to Sack. Herrick.
If thou doest not love sacke. *Unknown.*
In a Wine Cellar. Daley.
Love and Wine. Shadwell.
Man in the Moon Drinks Clarret, The. *Unknown.*
Red Wine. Richardson.
Song and Wine. Bacchylides.
Spirit of Wine, The. Henley.
To His Cup-Bearer. Catullus.
Under Leafy Bowers. Al-Harizi.
Welcome to Sack, The. Herrick.
Wine. Carlin.
Wine. Dakiki.
Wine. Lebensohn.
Wine and Dew. Stoddard.
Wine and Water. Chesterton.
Wine-Songs. Ibn Ezra.
Would you be a man in fashion? *Unknown.*
Winkelried, Arnold von
Arnold von Winkelried. Montgomery.
Winnipeg, Canada
Farewell to Winnipeg. Daniells.
Winnipeg at Christmas. Fyleman.
Winnipesaukee, Lake, New Hampshire
Lake Winnipesaukee. Driver.
Winslow, John Ancrum
Eagle and Vulture, The. Read.
Winter
Ancient Music. Pound.
At the Winter Solstice. Hoffman.
Autumn Hath All the Summer's Fruitful Treasure. *Fr.* Summer's Last Will and Testament. Nashe.
Before Sunrise in Winter. Sill.
Before Winter. McCreary.
Blow, Blow, Thou Winter Wind. *Fr.* As You Like It. Shakespeare.
Brilliancies of Winter, The. Peacock.
Brook in Winter, The. *Fr.* The Vision of Sir Launfal. J. R. Lowell.
Cold winter now is in the wood. Coatsworth.
Colonial Set. Bailey.
Coming, The. Delius.
Crumbs. De la Mare.
Dead of Winter. Towne.
Elegy, An: "In early winter before the first snow." Scovell.
Emmonsail's Heath in Winter. Clare.
Frost at Night. *Fr.* The Seasons. James Thomson.
Frost Fancy, A. Le Gallienne.
Frost-Morning. Alexander.
Glee for Winter, A. Domett.
Greenland Winter, A. Diamond.
How One Winter Came in the Lake Region. Campbell.
Human Things. Nemerov.
I singularly moved. Patmore.
Ice. Roberts.
In Defense of Felons. Mezey.
In the Barn-Yard's Southerly Corner. Roberts.
In the Wood. Mathias.
In Winter. Wallace.
It Is in Winter That We Dream of Spring. Wilson.
Jack Frost. "Setoun."
Jingle Bells. Pierpont.

Just a Mile Beyond. Fisher.
Kernel, The. Kendon.
Lalique. Porter.
Last Night of Winter, The. Welles.
Late Winter. Hall.
Meditation in Winter. Dunbar.
Meditation in Winter. Mann.
Meeting in Winter. Morris.
Midnight. Lampman.
Midwinter. Trowbridge.
Midwinter Thaw. Pratt.
Million Little Diamonds, A. Butts.
New Year's Days. Standish.
Night Is Freezing Fast, The. Housman.
No Possum, No Sop, No Taters. Stevens.
Now Comes the Blast of Winter. *Unknown.*
Now the Winter's Come to Stay. *Unknown.*
Now Winter Nights Enlarge. Campion.
Ode to Winter. Campbell.
Old Man's Winter Night, An. Frost.
Old Nurse Winter. Untermeyer.
Old Winter. Noel.
Out of My Study Window. Whittemore.
Outside. Chesterman.
Pacific Winter. Flanner.
Prelude: "Winter evening settles down, The." *Fr.* Preludes. Eliot.
Prelude: "Winter for a moment takes the mind; the snow." *Fr.* Preludes for Memnon. Aiken.
Remembering the Winter. Bennett.
Schoolboys in Winter. Clare.
Shine Out, Fair Sun. *Unknown.*
Signs of Winter. Clare.
Snow Man, The. Stevens.
Snow-bound. Whittier.
Somehow You Know When It Arrives. Livingston.
Something Told the Wild Geese. Field.
Song: "Lovely hill-torrents are." Turner.
Song in a Winter Night. Noll.
Song of Winter, A. Pfeiffer.
Song of Winter, A. *Unknown.*
Sonnet: "Winter deepening, the hay all in, The." Wilbur.
Spate in Winter Midnight. MacCaig.
Spring and Winter. *Fr.* Love's Labour's Lost. Shakespeare.
Stanzas: "In a drear-nighted December." Keats.
Still Day, A. Cherwinski.
Stopping by Woods on a Snowy Evening. Frost.
Storm, The. *Fr.* Snow-bound. Whittier.
Summer and Winter. Fraser.
Summer and Winter. Shelley.
Summer Is Gone. *Unknown.*
Talking in Their Sleep. Thomas.
Thaw. Thomas.
There's a certain slant of light. Dickinson.
There's Snow on the Fields. *Fr.* Sing-Song. C. G. Rossetti.
Thin ice/ Free advice. McCord.
Three Trees at Solstice. Finnin.
To Hampstead. Hunt.
To Winter. Blake.
Triolet on a Dark Day. Fishback.
Turning. Finch.
Up in the Morning Early. Burns.
Visit, The. Mezey.
Walk on a Winter Day. Allen.
What Is Winter? Blunden.
When biting Boreas. *Fr.* A Winter Night. Burns.
When Icicles Hang by the Wall. *Fr.* Love's Labour's Lost. Shakespeare.
Where It Is Winter. O'Neil.
Whirl-Blast. Wordsworth.
White Fields. Stephens.
Widow Bird Sate Mourning for Her Love, A. *Fr.* Charles the First. Shelley.
Winter. Blyton.
Winter. Campion.
Winter. Clare.
Winter. *Fr.* The Task. Cowper.
Winter. De la Mare.
Winter. Douglas.
Winter. Hughes.
Winter. Hurnard.
Winter. Jaszi.
Winter. Joso.
Winter. Landor.
Winter. Livesay.
Winter. Mair.
Winter. *Fr.* Pastorals. Pope.
Winter. C. G. Rossetti.
Winter. *Fr.* Induction to "The Mirror for Magistrates." Sackville.
Winter. *Fr.* Love's Labour's Lost. Shakespeare.
Winter. Southey.
Winter. *Fr.* Faerie Queene. Spenser.
Winter. Stevenson.
Winter. Synge.
Winter. Tennyson.
Winter. *Fr.* The Seasons. Thomson.
Winter ("Keen is the wind"). *Fr.* The Black Book of Carmarthen. *Unknown.*
Winter ("Old Winter is a sturdy one"). *Unknown.*
Winter; a Dirge. Burns.
Winter among the Days. Holden.
Winter: An Ode. Johnson.
Winter and Spring. *Unknown.*
Winter at Tomi. Ovid.
Winter Circus. Fisher.
Winter Days. Abbey.
Winter deepening, the hay all in, The. Wilbur.
Winter Evening, The. *Fr.* The Task. Cowper.
Winter Evening. Lampman.
Winter Evening. Pushkin.
Winter Feast. F. Frost.
Winter for a Moment Takes the Mind. *Fr.* Preludes for Memnon. Aiken.
Winter Galaxy, The. Heavysege.
Winter Garden. Gascoyne.
Winter Has Come. *Unknown.*
Winter Hymn, A—to the Snow. Jones.
Winter in Dunbarton. R. Lowell.
Winter in Durnover Field. Hardy.
Winter in East Anglia. Blunden.
Winter in Lower Canada. *Fr.* The Emigrant. O'Grady.
Winter in the Fens. Clare.
Winter in the Wood. Eastwick.
Winter Is Coming. Carmichael.
Winter Is Icumen In. Smith.
Winter Joys. Gradon.
Winter Lakes, The. Campbell.
Winter Landscape. Berryman.
Winter Life and Scenery. Irwin.
Winter Lightning, The. Nemerov.
Winter Memories. Thoreau.
Winter Morning. Smith.
Winter Night, A. Barnes.
Winter Night. Butts.
Winter Night. Fairburn.
Winter Night. Fitzgerald.
Winter Night. Millay.
Winter Night. Pasternak.
Winter Night, The. *Fr.* Snow-bound. Whittier.
Winter-Night Song. Ford.
Winter Nightfall. Bridges.
Winter Nightfall. Squire.
Winter Nights. Campion.
Winter Noon. Teasdale.
Winter Piece, A. Bryant.
Winter-Piece, A. Philips.
Winter Portrait. Southey.
Winter Remembered. Ransom.
Winter Rune. Coatsworth.
Winter Shore, The. Wade.
Winter Sketch. Bourinot.
Winter Sleep. Thomas.
Winter Sleep. Wylie.
Winter Song, A. Bennett.
Winter Song. Daiches.
Winter Song. *Fr.* The Land. Sackville-West.
Winter Song. *Unknown.*
Winter Spring. Wilbur.
Winter Storm at Sea, The. *Fr.* The Borough. Crabbe.
Winter Storms, The. Davenant.
Winter Streams. Carmen.

Winter *(continued)*
Winter the Huntsman. O. Sitwell.
Winter Treats. Shacklett.
Winter Westerlies. Devaney.
Winter with the Gulf Stream. Hopkins.
Winter's Cold. Rodgers.
Winter's Come, The. Clare.
Winter's Spring, The. Clare.
Winter's Tale, A. Thomas.
Winter's Troops. *Fr.* Winter. Cotton.
Winter-Time. Stevenson.
Wintry Day. *Unknown.*
Wisdom in Winter. *Fr.* The Black Book of Carmarthen. *Unknown.*
With witchlike branches, barren, bleak, and drear. *Fr.* Winter Noon in the Woods. Irwin.
Wizard Frost. Sherman.
Woods in Winter. Longfellow.
Words of Finn, The. *Unknown.*
Year's End. Wilbur.
You Could Say. Mezey.
Book of the Winter, A (BoW). Edith Sitwell, comp.

Winters, Yvor
Letter to Yvor Winters, A. Rexroth.
To Yvor Winters, 1955. Gunn.

Winthrop, Theodore
Dirge: For One Who Fell in Battle. Parsons.

Wisdom
For This Is Wisdom. *Fr.* The Teak Forest. "Hope."
Gone in the Wind. Mangan.
House of Wisdom, The. Proverbs, Bible, *O.T.*
O World. *Fr.* Sonnets. Santayana.
Wisdom. *Fr.* The Task. Cowper.
Wisdom. Ford.
Wisdom. Middleton.
Wisdom of Solomon, The, *sels.* Bible, Apocrypha.

Wise Men. *See* **Magi.**

Wishes
I Keep Three Wishes Ready. Wynne.
My Wishes. Healy.
Rathers. Austin.
Sometimes Wish, A. Shacklett.
Spring Wish. Farrar.
Wish, A. Arnold.
Wish, The. Cowley.
Wish, A. Garland.
Wish, A. *Fr.* The Gypsies Metamorphosed. Jonson.
Wish, A. Sherman.
Wish, The. Stanley.
Wish Is Quite a Tiny Thing, A. Wynne.
Wishes. Ault.
Wishing. Allingham.

Wit
Ode: Of Wit. Cowley.

Witchcraft
Alison Gross. *Unknown.*
Country Witch, A. Barnes.
Fatal Sisters, The. Gray.
Hag, The. Herrick.
Herbs and Simples. Keller.
In guilty night & hid in false disguise. *Unknown.*
Little Creature, The. De la Mare.
Mistress Hale of Beverly. Larcom.
Molly Means. Walker.
Mother Maudlin the Witch. *Fr.* The Sad Shepherd. Jonson.
Pauper Witch of Grafton, The. Frost.
Ride-by-Nights, The. De la Mare.
Riverman, The. Bishop.
Salem Witch, A. Clarke.
Spell, A. *Fr.* Oedipus. Dryden.
Tailor, The. Beddoes.
Tam o' Shanter. Burns.
Twist Ye, Twine Ye! Even So. *Fr.* Guy Mannering. Scott.
White Witch, The. Johnson.
Witch, A. Barnes.
Witch, The. M. E. Coleridge.
Witch, The. Douglas.
Witch, The. McNail.
Witch, The. Southey.
Witch, The. Tynan.
Witch-Mother, The. Swinburne.
Witch of Coös, The. Frost.
Witch of East Seventy-Second Street, The. Bishop.
Witch of Willowby Wood, The. Bennett.
Witches, The. Drake.
Witches. Hughes.
Witches, The. *Unknown.*
Witches' Charm. *Fr.* Macbeth. Shakespeare.
Witches' Ride, The. Kuskin.
Witches' Song. Coatsworth.
Witching Hour. Farber.
Witch's Ballad, The. Scott.
Witch's Charm, A. *Fr.* The Masque of Queens. Jonson.

Wives. *See* **Marriage.**

Wolfe, Charles
In Clonmel Parish Churchyard. Piatt.

Wolfe, James
Brave Wolfe. *Unknown.*
Death of Wolfe, The. *Unknown.*

Wolsey, Thomas, Cardinal
Cardinal Wolsey's Farewell. *Fr.* King Henry VIII. Shakespeare.
Colyn Cloute, *sels.* Skelton.
How Thomas Wolsey Did Arise unto Great Authority and Government. . . *Fr.* A Mirror for Magistrates. Churchyard.
Speak, Parrot, *sels.* Skelton.

Wolves
Day of the Wolf. Wilson.
Story for a Child, A. Taylor.
Wolf, The. Durston.
Wolf Cry, The. Sarett.
Wolves, The. Roberts.
Wolves, The. Tate.

Wombats
Wombat, The. Nash.

Women
Against Blame of Women. Gerald, Earl of Desmond.
Against Them Who Lay Unchastity to the Sex of Women. Habington.
Against Women. *Unknown.*
Against Women. *Fr.* The Satires. Juvenal.
And There Was Mary Magdalene and the Other Mary, Sitting Over against the Sepulchre. Rodgers.
As Joe Gould says. Cummings.
Ballad Warning Men to Beware of Deceitful Women, A, *sel.* Lydgate.
Ballade of the Women of Paris. Villon.
Beatitudes for a Housewife. Oesch.
C. L. M. Masefield.
Cantata for Two Lovers. H. Sandburg.
Changes. "Meredith."
Choice, The. Pomfret.
Colours of Love, The. Devlin.
Creatrix. Wickham.
Dawn of Womanhood. Monro.
December: Of Aphrodite. Merwin.
Divine Office of the Kitchen, The. Hallack.
Dream of Fair Women, A. Amis.
Duplicity of Women, The. Lydgate.
Evening Out, The. Nash.
Farm Wife. Mitchell.
For Our Women. Neal.
Former Beauties. *Fr.* At Casterbridge Fair. Hardy.
Free Woman, The. Garrison.
Furniture of a Woman's Mind, The. Swift.
Garment of Good Ladies, The. Henryson.
Gert Swasey. Scott.
Hand That Rocks the Cradle Is the Hand That Rules the World, The. Wallace.
Hares on the Mountain. *Unknown.*
Heart of a Woman, The. Johnson.
Here's to the Maiden. *Fr.* The School for Scandal. Sheridan.
Home Winner, The. Lindberg.
How the Women Will Stop War. Aristophanes.
I Am as Light as Any Roe. *Unknown.*
I Never Even Suggested It. Nash.
I Sing the Body Electric. Whitman.
If Women Could Be Fair. Vere.
Impossible to Trust Women. *Unknown.*
In Defense of Their Inconstancy. Jonson.
In her first passion woman loves her lover. *Fr.* Don Juan. Byron.

Indifferent, The. Beaumont.
Korean Woman Seated by a Wall, A. Meredith.
Ladies, The. Kipling.
Legend of Good Women, *sels.* Chaucer.
Legend of Viable Women, A. Eberhart.
Let the Toast Pass. *Fr.* The School for Scandal. Sheridan.
Lonely Woman, The. Forrest.
Lords of Creation, The. *Unknown.*
Lost and Given Over. Brady.
Lovely Woman, A. Davies.
Man, Man, Man. *Unknown.*
Man's Woman, A. Davies.
Mrs. Frances Harris's Petition. Swift.
Mrs. Severin. Scott.
Mistresses. *Unknown.*
Modern Woman to Her Lover, The. Widdemer.
Mountain Woman, The. Heyward.
No Fault in Women. Herrick.
No Thyng Ys to Man So Dere. Mannyng.
Oh, Please Don't Get Up! Nash.
Oh, what is longer than the way? *Unknown.*
Of the Characters of Women. *Fr.* Moral Essays. Pope.
Of Women. Edwards.
Of Women. *Fr.* The Thousand and One Nights. *Unknown.*
Of Women No More Evil. *Unknown.*
Old Woman, The. Campbell.
Old Women, The. Symons.
On Woman. Yeats.
Personal Poem. Smithyman.
Peter Parasol. Stevens.
Pioneer Woman. Crawford.
Plaint of the Wife. *Unknown.*
Portrait d'une Femme. Pound.
Praise of Women. Mannyng.
Praise of Women. Palladas.
Prayer for My Daughter, A. Yeats.
Red-haired Man's Wife, The. Stephens.
Renunciation, A. Vere.
Shack, The. Miller.
She. Wilbur.
She Walked Unaware. MacDonogh.
She Was a Phantom of Delight. Wordsworth.
Sisters. "Hyde."
Sisters, The. A. Lowell.
Song: That Women Are but Men's Shadows. Jonson.
Song: "When lovely woman stoops to folly." *Fr.* The Vicar of Wakefield. Goldsmith.
Song: "Woman's face is full of wiles, A." Gifford.
Song of Songs, The. Heine.
Sun Was Slumbering in the West, The. Hood.
That Reminds Me. Nash.
These Women All. Heath.
Thought, A. Stephen.
This Poem for Black Women. Lockett.
Three American Women and a German Bayonet. Scott.
To a Lady. Pope.
To a Pretty Girl. Zangwill.
To a Woman. Glover.
To Daphne and Virginia. Williams.
To onpreise womene it were a shame. *Unknown.*
To the Eternal Feminine. Corbière.
To the New Women. Davidson.
Tribute, The. *Fr.* The Angel in the House. Patmore.
Triolet: "All women born are so perverse." Bridges.
Trust in Women. *Unknown.*
Tunnynge of Elynour Rummynge, The. Skelton.
Two Strange Worlds. Pereira.
Two Wives, The. Howells.
Unseen Spirits. Willis.
Upon Some Women. Herrick.
Upon the Loss of His Mistresses. Herrick.
Villon's Straight Tip to All Cross Coves. Henley.
Virtuous Wife, The. Trimberg.
Virtuous Woman, The. Proverbs, Bible, *O.T.*
Washer-Woman, The. Bohanan.
What One May and May Not Call a Woman. *Unknown.*
What Women Are Not. *Unknown.*
When Lovely Woman. Cary.
When my gloomy hour comes on me. *Fr.* Woman. McLachlan.
Wife Speaks, The. Stanley.
Wise Woman, The. Untermeyer.
Woman. Barrett.
Woman. Ellis.
Woman. Fu Hsüan.
Woman. Kalidasa.
Woman. Layton.
Woman. Malangatana.
Woman. O'Hagan.
Woman, A. Thayer.
Woman. *Fr.* Shi King. *Unknown.*
Woman. *Unknown.*
Woman and Her Dead Husband, A. Lawrence.
Woman I Am, The. Allen.
Woman in Sunshine, The. Stevens.
Woman in the Wagon, The. Robertson.
Woman Is a Branchy Tree, A. Stephens.
Woman of Three Cows, The. *Unknown.*
Woman of Words, A. Hall.
Woman Passes the Door, A. O'Neil.
Woman Waits for Me, A. Whitman.
Woman Who Understands, The. Appleton.
Woman with the Serpent's Tongue, The. Watson.
Woman's Arms. Anacreon.
Woman's Constancy. Donne.
Woman's Execution, A. King.
Woman's looks, A/ Are barbed hooks. *Unknown.*
Woman's Pride, A. Whitney.
Woman's Question, A. Procter.
Woman's Shortcomings, A. E. B. Browning.
Woman's Song, A. Lee.
Woman's Thought, A. Gilder.
Woman's Will. Saxe.
Woman's Will. *Unknown.*
Women. Bogan.
Women. Cartwright.
Women. Heath.
Women Are Worthy. *Unknown.*
Women at the Corners Stand, The. Golding.
Women Folk, The. Hogg.
Women Toilers, The. Evans.
Women Will Soon Knit Again, The. Burlingame.
Young Acacia, The. Bialik.
Young Woman. Nemerov.

Women's Liberation
Affinity, The. Wickham.
Belly Dancer. Wakoski.
Crinolines and Bloomers. *Unknown.*
Dedication of the Cook. Wickham.
Evening in the Suburbs. Barnett.
Fighting Words. Parker.
Friend Cato. Wickham.
He and She. Ware.
In Your Arrogance. Lawner.
It's No Good. Lawrence.
Lady's-Maid Song, The. Hollander.
Let No Charitable Hope. Wylie.
Lover, The; a Ballad. Montagu.
Man Within, The. Ewing.
Meditation at Kew. Wickham.
Mutes, The. Levertov.
Old Feminist, The. McGinley.
Poem to the Man on My Fire Escape. Wakoski.
Seeing-Eye Dog, A. Sharp.
Sonnet: "I being born a woman and distressed." Millay.
To Kate Skating Better Than Her Date. Daiches.
Women Speak Out in Defense of Themselves. Aristophanes.

Wood
Old Boards. Bly.
Wood-Pile, The. Frost.

Woodbine
Woodbines in October. Bates.

Woodchucks
Clover for Breakfast. F. Frost.
Drumlin Woodchuck, A. Frost.
Jolly Woodchuck, The. Edey *and* Grider.

Woodpeckers
Hewel, or Woodpecker, The. *Fr.* Upon Appleton House. Marvell.
Legend of the Northland, A. Cary.
Stormcock in Elder. Pitter.
Who's There? F. Frost.

Woodpeckers *(continued)*
Woodpecker, The. Church.
Woodpecker, The. Roberts.
Woodpecker, The. Sambrook.
Woodpecker, The. Tabb.
Woods. *See* **Forests.**
Wool
Wool Trade, The. *Fr.* The Fleece. Dyer.
Woolf, Virginia
Water-Images. Osborn.
Words. *See* **Language.**
Wordsworth, Catherine
To Catherine Wordsworth 1808-1812. Wordsworth.
Wordsworth, Christopher
On "Who Wrote Icon Basilike" By Dr. Christopher Wordsworth, Master of Trinity. Kennedy.
Wordsworth, William
Bards, The. De la Mare.
Bells for William Wordsworth. Moraes.
Epilogue: "There's something in a stupid ass." Byron.
He Lived amidst th' Untrodden Ways. H. Coleridge.
Lost Leader, The. R. Browning.
Memorial Verses. Arnold.
Next comes the dull disciple of the school. *Fr.* English Bards and Scotch Reviewers. Byron.
On Wordsworth. H. Coleridge.
On Wordsworth. *Unknown.*
Resolution of Dependence. Barker.
Some of Wordsworth. Landor.
Sonnet on Wordsworth, A. Stephen.
Southey and Wordsworth. *Fr.* Don Juan. Byron.
To William Wordsworth. Coleridge.
To Wordsworth. Clare.
To Wordsworth. H. Coleridge.
To Wordsworth. Landor.
To Wordsworth. Shelley.
William Wordsworth. Keyes.
William Wordsworth. Palgrave.
With Wordsworth at Rydal. Fields.
Wordsworth. *Fr.* Ode to England. Lord.
Wordsworth and the Woman. Whittemore.
Wordsworth's Grave. Watson.
Youth of Nature, The. Arnold.
Work. *See* **Labor and Laborers.**
World. *See* **Earth.**
World War, First
A. E. F. Sandburg.
Aftermath. Sassoon.
"And There Was a Great Calm." Hardy.
Anxious Dead, The. McCrae.
Anzac Cove. Gellert.
Apologia pro Poemate Meo. Owen.
Armistice. Going.
Armistice Day. Montgomery.
At the Front. Erskine.
Attack. Sassoon.
August, 1914. Masefield.
Break of Day in the Trenches. Rosenberg.
Corpses in the Wood. Toller.
Counter-Attack. Sassoon.
Dead, The. *Fr.* 1914. Brooke.
Dead Man's Dump. Rosenberg.
Dulce et Decorum Est. Owen.
Exposure. Owen.
Farmer Remembers the Somme, The. Palmer.
First Division Marches, The. Rice.
General Galliéni. Hillyer.
Hell-Gate of Soissons, The. Kaufman.
I Sing of Olaf Glad and Big. Cummings.
In Flanders Fields. McCrae.
In Flanders Now. Jaques.
In Memoriam: Easter 1915. Thomas.
It Shall Not Be Again! Clark.
It's jolly/ odd what pops into. Cummings.
Lines for an Interment. MacLeish.
March, The. Squire.
Mare Liberum. Van Dyke.
Memorial Day. Brooks.
Memorial Rain. MacLeish.
Mesopotamia. Kipling.
Ode in Memory of the American Volunteers Fallen for France. Seeger.
Our Dead, Overseas. Markham.
Private, A. Thomas.
Recalling War. Graves.
Republic to Republic. Bynner.
Road to France, The. Henderson.
Rouge Bouquet. Kilmer.
Sentry, The. Owen.
Smoke-blue Plains, The. Clark.
Song-Books of the War. Sassoon.
Sonnets Written in the Fall of 1914. Woodberry.
Spring Offensive. Owen.
Strange Meeting. Owen.
There's About Two Million Fellows. Cook.
These Fought. *Fr.* Hugh Selwyn Mauberley. Pound.
These Men. Gellert.
To a Conscript of 1940. Read.
To a Young Leader of the First World War. George.
To America, on Her First Sons Fallen in the Great War. Walker.
Unscarred Fighter Remembers France, The. Alling.
White Ships and the Red. Kilmer.
William P. Frye, The. Foster.
World War I. *Unknown.*
Ypres. Guerney.
Men Who March Away: Poems of the First World War (MMA). I. M. Parsons, ed.
World War, Second
Ballad of Banners (1944), The. Lehmann.
Battle. Jeffers.
Beach Burial. Slessor.
Before Invasion, 1940. Betjeman.
Bird, The. Simpson.
Black-out. Jeffers.
Breaking. Allan.
Carentan O Carentan. Simpson.
Carol with Variations. McGinley.
Chez-Nous. Austin.
Children's Crusade 1939. Brecht.
Christmas 1942. Irvin.
Commandos Embarking. Whalley.
D-Dawn. McGarvey.
Dead in Europe, The. R. Lowell.
Death of an Aircraft. Causley.
Death of the Ball Turret Gunner, The. Jarrell.
Drunken Gunners. Joseph.
Dunkirk. Nathan.
Eighth Air Force. Jarrell.
El Alamein Revisited. Macnab.
For Lover Man, and All the Other Young Men Who Failed to Return from World War II. Williams.
Four Men of God. Guest.
Fourth Act. Jeffers.
From Dover to Dunkirk. *Fr.* Dunkirk. Pratt.
Full Moon: New Guinea. Shapiro.
Homecoming. Shapiro.
In Distrust of Merits. Moore.
In Westminster Abbey. Betjeman.
Incident on a Front Not Far from Castel di Sangro. Brown.
Kilroy. Viereck.
Landscape with Figures. Douglas.
Little Boats of Britain, The. Carsley.
Long Roads. Matusovsky.
Losses. Jarrell.
Lunch on Omaha Beach. Noll.
Man unto His Fellow Man. *Fr.* On a Note of Triumph. Corwin.
May—June, 1940. Jeffers.
Memorial to the Great Big Beautiful Self-sacrificing Advertisers. Ebright.
Moon and the Night and the Men, The. Berryman.
Neutrality. MacNeice.
New Moses, The. Joseph.
Ninth of April, The. Gelsted.
Norfolk Memorials. Leavenworth.
Notes for a Movie Script. Holman.
Ode to Our Young Pro-Consuls of the Air. Tate.
On the Pilots Who Destroyed Germany in the Spring of 1945. Spender.
Palermo, Mother's Day, 1943. Belvin.

Pearl Harbor. Frolicher.
Poland, October. *Fr.* Nineteen Thirty-Nine. Brasch.
Psalm of the Singing Grave. Janta.
Reflections of the Fall of France, June, 1940. Lewis.
Remembering That Island. McGrath.
Road to Nijmegen. Birney.
Scyros. Shapiro.
Second Air Force. Jarrell.
September 1, 1939. Auden.
Siciliana; the Landings at Gela. Koehler.
Silent Generation, The. Simpson.
Snow in Europe. Gascoyne.
"Spoken Word, The." Morley.
Spring, 1942. Fuller.
Spring Offensive, 1941. Biggs.
Streets of Laredo, The. MacNeice.
Sunday: New Guinea. Shapiro.
There Is Yet Time. Steece.
To a Conscript of 1940. Read.
U. S. Sailor with the Japanese Skull. Scott.
V-J Day. Ciardi.
V-Letter. Shapiro.
War. Langland.
Wartime Dawn, A. Gascoyne.
Whatever doubt the eye might have imposed. *Fr.* Behind the Log. Pratt.
World War II. *Unknown.*
Written in a Time of Crisis. S. V. Benét.

World's Fair, 1939
Flushing Meadows, 1939. Hoffman.

Worms
Bookworms, The. Burns.
Fishing Song, A. Rands.
Our little kinsmen after rain. Dickinson.
Wee Little Worm, A. Riley.
Worm, The. Bergengren.
Worm, The. Souster.
Worms and the Wind. Sandburg.

Wormwood
Tall Ambrosia. Thoreau.

Worship
For them, O God who only worship. *Fr.* Worship. Lord.
Joy of Church Fellowship Rightly Attended, The. *Fr.* God's Determinations. Taylor.
One Thing I Have Desired. Carmichael.
Worship. Emerson.
Worship. MacFie.
Sourcebook of Poetry (SoP). Al Bryant, comp.

Worth, Charles Frederick
Crinolines and Bloomers. *Unknown.*

Wotton, Sir Henry
Ad Henricum Wottonum ("Wotton the country and the country swain"). Bastard.
Letter to Sir H. Wotton at His Going Ambassador to Venice. Donne.

Wren, Sir Christopher
Said Sir Christopher Wren. *Unknown.*
Sir Christopher Wren. *Fr.* Clerihews. Bentley.

Wrens
Bird's Nest, A. Allen.
Country Rhyme. *Unknown.*
Dove and the Wren, The. *Unknown.*
Jenny Wren. Davies.
Jenny Wren. De la Mare.
Little Brown Wren, The. Scollard.
Little Lady Wren. Robinson.
Netted Strawberries. Bottomley.
No Communication. Van Doren.
Robin and the Wren, The. *Unknown.*
'Twas once upon a time, when Jenny Wren was young. Mother Goose.
Wrens, The. Burke.
Wrens and Robins. *Fr.* Sing-Song. C. G. Rossetti.
Wrens of the Lake. *Unknown.*

Wrestling and Wrestlers
Wrestlers. *Fr.* Polyolbion. Drayton.
Wrestling Match, The. Warren.

Wright, Orville, and Wilbur Wright
Wilbur Wright and Orville Wright. R. Benét and S. V. Benét.

Writing. *See* **Handwriting.**

Würzburg, Germany
Walk in Würtzburg, A. Plomer.

Wyatt, Sir Thomas
Another Tribute to Wyatt. Surrey.
Death of Wyatt, The. Surrey.
In Praise of Wyatt's Psalms. Surrey.
On the Death of Sir Thomas Wyatt. Surrey.

Wye (river), Wales and England
Lines Composed a Few Miles above Tintern Abbey, on Revisiting the Banks of the Wye during a Tour, July 13, 1798. Wordsworth.
Meandering Wye. *Fr.* The Banks of Wye. Bloomfield.
Playmates, The. Watson.

Wyoming
Wyoming. Winter.

Wyoming Massacre
Wyoming Massacre, The. Terry.

Wyre Forest, England
As through the Wild Green Hills of Wyre. Housman.

X

X-Rays
Rontgen Photograph. Eybers.

Xenophanes
Xenophanes. Emerson.

Y

Yachts
Lament for the Great Yachts. P. Dickinson.
Yachts, The. Williams.
Yachts on the Nile. Spencer.

Yaks
Mad Yak, The. Corso.
Yak, The. Belloc.
Yak, The. N. Crane.
Yak, The. *Fr.* Child's Natural History. Herford.
Yak, The. Roethke.
Yak, The. Sheard.
Yak. Smith.

Yale University
On the Democracy of Yale. Jones.
To the Memory of Yale College. Putnam.

Yarrow or Yarrow Water, Scotland
Braes of Yarrow, The. Hamilton of Bangour.
Braes of Yarrow, The. Logan.
Yarrow Revisited. Wordsworth.
Yarrow Unvisited. Wordsworth.
Yarrow Visited. Wordsworth.

Yeats, John Butler
John Butler Yeats. Foster.

Yeats, William Butler
Bring Home the Poet. MacDonough.
Death of Yeats, The. Barker.
For His Own Epitaph. *Fr.* Under Ben Bulben. Yeats.
In Memory of W. B. Yeats. Auden.
Ode: On the Death of W. B. Yeats. Smith.
Reading Yeats I Do Not Think. Ferlinghetti.
To W. B. Yeats Who Says That His Castle of Ballylee Is His Monument. Gogarty.
William Yeats in Limbo. Keyes.
Winter Mask. Tate.
Yeats in Dublin, *sel.* Watkins.

Yesenin, Sergey
Sergey Yesenin Speaking Isadora Duncan. Knott.

Yew Trees
Old Warder of These Buried Bones. *Fr.* In Memoriam A. H. H. Tennyson.
Old Yew, Which Graspest at the Stones. *Fr.* In Memoriam A. H. H. Tennyson.
Yew-Trees. Wordsworth.

Yom Kippur
Kol Nidra. *Fr.* The Day of Atonement. Leiser.
Yom Kippur. Zangwill.

Yorkshire, England
Visit to Brontëland, A. Kirkup.
Yorkshire Moors, The. Summers.
Young, Brigham
Brigham Young. *Unknown.*
Young, Lester
Lester Young. Joans.
Younger, Cole
Cole Younger. *Unknown.*
Youth
Alas for Youth. Firdausi.
Apology for Youth. Sister Mary Madeleva.
At Majority. Rich.
At the Doors. "Der Nistor."
Ball Poem, The. Berryman.
Ballade of Lost Objects. McGinley.
Ballade of Youth and Age. Henley.
Barefoot Boy, The. Whittier.
Birches. Frost.
Blessing on Little Boys. Guiterman.
Boy. Allingham.
Boy, The. Field.
Boy. Welles.
Boy and a Pup, A. Guiterman.
Boy and His Top, The. Frere.
Boy and Tadpoles. Untermeyer.
Boy's Prayer, A. Beeching.
Boy's Song, A. Hogg.
Cherries. Schneour.
Chestnut Casts His Flambeaux, The. Housman.
Country Tune. Riddell.
Crabbed Age and Youth. *Fr.* The Passionate Pilgrim. Shakespeare.
Days of Our Youth. *Unknown.*
Deceptrices, The. Williams.
Dedication to the Generation Knocking at the Door. Davidson.
Departed Friend, The. Novo.
English Schoolboy, The. *Fr.* The Play of the Weather. Heywood.
Extremes. Riley.
Fair Seed-Time Had My Soul. *Fr.* The Prelude. Wordsworth.
Fern Hill. Thomas.
Flight of Youth, The. Stoddard.
Flood Tide. S. V. Benét.
Funeral of Youth, The: Threnody. Brooke.
Furniture. Harris.
Generous Years, The. Spender.
Girl, A. Deutsch.
Girl Athletes. Long.
Girl of All Periods, The. Patmore.
Girl of Pompeii, A. Martin.
Girl of the Red Mouth. MacDermott.
Girl's Mood, A. Reese.
Has Sorrow Thy Young Days Shaded? Moore.
Horse Chestnut Tree, The. Eberhart.
How No Age Is Content. Surrey.
I Remember. Glover.
I Saw from the Beach. Moore.
In a Spring Still Not Written Of. Wallace.
In an Age of Fops and Toys. *Fr.* Voluntaries. Emerson.
Intimations of Sublimity. *Fr.* The Prelude. Wordsworth.
Invitation to Youth. *Unknown.*
Invocation to Youth. Binyon.
It Was My June. Duke.
Just Sixteen. Hsü Chien.
Lads in Their Hundreds, The. Housman.
Laid in My Quiet Bed. Surrey.
Lightly like Music Running. Garrigue.
Lines on a Young Lady's Photograph Album. Larkin.
Little Girl, A. Angoff.
Lost Shipmate, The. Roberts.
Lusty Juventus, *sel.* Wever.
Maidenhood. Longfellow.
My Lost Youth. Longfellow.
O Boys! O Boys! Gogarty.
O Tan-faced Prairie-Boy. Whitman.
O Youth Whose Hope Is High. Bridges.
O Youth with Blossoms Laden. Peach.
Old and Young. Bourdillon.
Old Man's Comforts and How He Gained Them, The. Southey.
Old Swimmin'-Hole, The. Riley.
On His Having Arrived at the Age of Twenty-three. Milton.
On the Instability of Youth. Vaux.
Orange Tree, The. Neilson.
Points of View. A. Lowell.
Rejoyce whyle in thy youth thou art. *Unknown.*
Retreat, The. Vaughan.
Rules for the Road. Markham.
Schoolboy, The. *Fr.* Songs of Experience. Blake.
Schoolgirls Hastening. Neilson.
Seein' Things. Field.
Short Song of Congratulation, A. Johnson.
Since Youth Is All for Gladness. Dresbach.
Song about Myself, A. Keats.
Stanzas for Music ("There's not a joy"). Byron.
There Was a Boy. *Fr.* The Prelude. Wordsworth.
These Are the Young. Lindsay.
Thesis and Antithesis. Clough.
Thieves. Adams.
Though You Are Young. Campion.
To Youth. Landor.
Torn Hat, The. Willis.
Two Boys, The. Lamb.
"What You See Is Me." Gibbs.
When I Was Fair and Young. Elizabeth, Queen of England.
When I Was One-and-twenty. Housman.
Wisdom. Hicky.
Wisdom Cometh with the Years. Cullen.
Wonder. Traherne.
Young and Old. *Fr.* The Water Babies. Kingsley.
Young Boy, A. North.
Young Ones, Flip Side, The. Emanuel.
Youth. Bates.
Youth. Clark.
Youth. Cloud.
Youth. Cornford.
Youth. Helburn.
Youth. Hughes.
Youth. Johnson.
Youth. Jones.
Youth. Lodge.
Youth. Rittenhouse.
Youth. Salkeld.
Youth. *Unknown.*
Youth and Age. Arnold.
Youth and Age. Coleridge.
Youth and Age. Mimnermus.
Youth and Age. Palmer.
Youth and Age. Scott.
Youth and Age on Beaulieu River, Hants. Betjeman.
Youth and Beauty. Townsend.
Youth and Calm. Arnold.
Youth and Death. Root.
Youth and Maidenhood. Williams.
Youth Dreams, The. Rilke.
Youth Sings a Song of Rosebuds. Cullen.
Youth's Agitations. Arnold.
Youth's the Season. *Fr.* The Beggar's Opera. Gay.
Yucatan, Mexico
Hunter, The. Turner.
Yukon Territory
Law of the Yukon, The. Service.
Men of the High North. Service.
Spell of the Yukon,The. Service.
Yuma, Arizona
Yuma. Phelps.

Z

Zacchaeus
On Zacheus. Quarles.
Zambia
Leader, The. Livesay.
Zante (island), **Greece**
Sonnet to Zante. Poe.
Zebras
Zebra. "Dinesen."
Zebra. Smith.
Zebra. *Unknown*
Zebra Stallion. *Unknown*

Zebras, The. Campbell.
Zechariah
Zechariah. Marlatt.
Zeppelin. *See* **Dirigibles.**
Zeus
Europa. Plomer.
Hymn to Zeus. Cleanthes.
Leda and the Swan. Yeats.
Zion
By the Waters of Babylon. *Fr.* Hebrew Melodies. Heine.
Hatikvah—a Song of Hope. Imber.
Kadia the Young Mother Speaks. Sampter.
Last Words of Don Henriquez, The. Schneour.
Light and Rejoicing to Israel. *Unknown.*
My Heart Is in the East. Halevi.
Ode to Zion. Halevi.
Prayer for Redemption. *Unknown.*
Promised Land, The. Sampter.
Road, The. Schneour.
Song: "There stands a lonely pine-tree." Heine.
Theodor Herzl. Zangwill.
Through These Pale Cold Days. Rosenberg.
To the Western Wind. Halevi.
To Zion. Halevi.
Zionist Marching Song. Imber.
Zola, Émile
Zola. Robinson.
Zoos
At the Zoo. Milne.
Au Jardin des Plantes. Wain.
Excuse Us, Animals in the Zoo. Wynne.
Jaguar, The. Hughes.
Menagerie, The. Moody.
Van Amburgh's Menagerie. *Unknown.*
Woman at the Washington Zoo, The. Jarrell.
Zoo, The. Pasternak.
Zoo, The. Wolfe.
Zoo in the City, The. Allen.
Zoo Manners. Mathias.
Zulus
Death of a Zulu, The. Plomer.
Fallen Zulu Commander, The. Van Den Heever.
Lalela Zulu. *Unknown.*
Zulu Girl, The. Campbell.
Zürich, Switzerland
Bahnhofstrasse. Dyment.
Reflections on the Fall of France, June, 1940. Lewis.